THE OFFICIAL® 2004 PRICE GUIDE TO BASEBALL CARDS

DR. JAMES BECKETT

TWENTY-FOURTH EDITION

House of Collectibles
New York

House of Collectibles and colophon
are trademarks of Random House, Inc.

Published by:
House of Collectibles
Random House Reference
New York, New York

Distributed by Random House Reference,
an imprint of Random House, Inc.,
New York, and simultaneously in Canada by
Random House of Canada Limited, Toronto.

www.houseofcollectibles.com

Manufactured in the United States of America

ISSN: 1062-7138

ISBN: 0-375-72055-3

10 9 8 7 6 5 4 3 2 1

Twenty-fourth Edition: April 2004

Table of Contents

About the Author 7
How to Use This Book 7
How to Collect 8
- Obtaining Cards 8
- Preserving Your Cards 9
- Collecting vs. Investing 9

Terminology 10
Glossary/Legend 11
Understanding Card Values 15
- Determining Value 15
- Regional Variation 15
- Set Prices 16
- Scarce Series 16

Grading Your Cards 17
- Centering 17
- Corner Wear 17
- Creases 17
- Alterations 18
- Categorization of Defects 18

Condition Guide 18
- Grades 18

Selling Your Cards 19
Interesting Notes 20
History of Baseball Cards 20
- Increasing Popularity 22
- Intensified Competition 25
- Sharing the Pie 25

Additional Reading 33
Advertising 33
Prices in This Guide 34
Acknowledgements 34, 610

2003 Bazooka 35
2000 Black Diamond Rookie 36
1948 Bowman 37
1949 Bowman 37
1950 Bowman 38
1951 Bowman 39
1952 Bowman 40
1953 Bowman Color 42
1954 Bowman 42
1955 Bowman 43
1989 Bowman 45
1990 Bowman 47
1991 Bowman 49
1992 Bowman 52
1993 Bowman 55
1994 Bowman 58
1995 Bowman 60
1996 Bowman 62
1997 Bowman 64
1998 Bowman 66
1999 Bowman 67
2000 Bowman 69
2000 Bowman Draft Picks 71
2001 Bowman 72
2001 Bowman Draft Picks 73
2002 Bowman 74
2002 Bowman Draft 76
2003 Bowman 76
2003 Bowman Draft 78
1997 Bowman Chrome 79
1998 Bowman Chrome 80
1999 Bowman Chrome 82
2000 Bowman Chrome 83
2000 Bowman Chrome Draft Picks 85
2001 Bowman Chrome 86
2002 Bowman Chrome 87
2002 Bowman Chrome Draft 89
2003 Bowman Chrome 90
2003 Bowman Chrome Draft 91
2001 Bowman Heritage 92
2002 Bowman Heritage 94
1994 Bowman's Best 96
1995 Bowman's Best 97
1996 Bowman's Best 98
1997 Bowman's Best 98
1998 Bowman's Best 99
1999 Bowman's Best 100
2000 Bowman's Best 101
2001 Bowman's Best 102
2002 Bowman's Best 103
2003 Bowman's Best 104
1987 Classic Update Yellow 104
1989 Classic Travel Orange 104
1989 Classic Travel Purple 105
1994 Collector's Choice 105
1981 Donruss 108
1982 Donruss 111
1983 Donruss 114
1984 Donruss 117
1985 Donruss 120
1986 Donruss 123
1986 Donruss Rookies 125
1987 Donruss 126
1987 Donruss Rookies 128
1987 Donruss Opening Day 129
1989 Donruss 130
1989 Donruss Rookies 133
1989 Donruss Baseball's Best 133
1990 Donruss 134
2001 Donruss 138
2001 Donruss Rookies 139
2002 Donruss 139

2002 Donruss Rookies 140
2003 Donruss 141
2004 Donruss 143
2001 Donruss Baseball's Best Bronze ..144
2001 Donruss Class of 2001 146
2001 Donruss Classics 147
2002 Donruss Classics 148
2003 Donruss Classics 149
2002 Donruss Diamond Kings 150
2003 Donruss Diamond Kings 150
2001 Donruss Elite 151
2002 Donruss Elite 152
2003 Donruss Elite 154
1998 Donruss Signature 155
2001 Donruss Signature 155
2003 Donruss Signature 156
2003 Donruss Team Heroes 157
2003 Timeless Treasures 159
2001 eTopps 160
2002 eTopps 160
2003 eTopps 161
2001 E-X 161
2002 E-X 162
2003 E-X 162
1999 Finest 163
2000 Finest 164
2001 Finest 166
2002 Finest 166
2003 Finest 167
1994 Flair 167
2002 Flair 169
2003 Flair 170
2003 Flair Greats 170
1963 Fleer 171
1981 Fleer 171
1982 Fleer 175
1983 Fleer 178
1984 Fleer 180
1984 Fleer Update 183
1985 Fleer 184
1986 Fleer 187
1986 Fleer Update 189
1987 Fleer 190
1987 Fleer Update 193
1988 Fleer 193
1988 Fleer Update 196
1989 Fleer 197
1990 Fleer 201
1992 Fleer Update 204
1994 Fleer Update 204
2002 Fleer 205
2002 Fleer Authentix 207
2003 Fleer Authentix 208
2001 Fleer Authority 209
2003 Fleer Avant 210
2002 Fleer Box Score 210
2003 Fleer Box Score 211
2003 Fleer Double Header 213
2002 Fleer Fall Classics 214
2003 Fleer Fall Classics 214
2001 Fleer Focus 215
2002 Fleer Focus JE 216
2003 Fleer Focus JE 217
2001 Fleer Futures 218
2001 Fleer Game Time 219
2001 Fleer Genuine 220
2002 Fleer Genuine 220
2003 Fleer Genuine 221
2002 Fleer Greats of the Game 222
2003 Fleer Hardball 222
2002 Fleer Hot Prospects 223
2003 Fleer Hot Prospects 224
2001 Fleer Legacy 224
1999 Fleer Mystique 225
2003 Fleer Mystique 226
2001 Fleer Platinum 226
2002 Fleer Platinum 229
2003 Fleer Patchworks 230
2003 Fleer Platinum 231
2001 Fleer Premium 232
2001 Fleer Showcase 233
2002 Fleer Showcase 234
2003 Fleer Showcase 235
2003 Fleer Splendid Splinters 235
1998 Fleer Tradition Update 236
1999 Fleer Tradition Update 236
2000 Fleer Tradition Glossy 237
2000 Fleer Tradition Update 237
2001 Fleer Tradition 238
2002 Fleer Tradition 241
2002 Fleer Tradition Update 243
2003 Fleer Tradition 244
2003 Fleer Tradition Update 246
2001 Fleer Triple Crown 248
1949 Leaf 250
1990 Leaf 250
2002 Leaf 252
2003 Leaf 253
2001 Leaf Certified Materials 255
2002 Leaf Certified 255
2003 Leaf Certified Materials 256
2001 Leaf Limited 257
2003 Leaf Limited 259
1998 Leaf Rookies and Stars 260
2001 Leaf Rookies and Stars 261
2002 Leaf Rookies and Stars 263
2003 MLB Showdown Pennant Run 265
2003 MLB Showdown Trading Deadline 265

2003 MLB Showdown 266
2000 Pacific Omega 267
1993 Pinnacle 269
2001 Playoff Absolute Memorabilia 271
2002 Playoff Absolute Memorabilia 272
2003 Playoff Absolute Memorabilia 273
2002 Playoff Piece of The Game 274
2003 Playoff Piece of the Game 274
2003 Playoff Portraits 275
2003 Playoff Prestige 276
2004 Playoff Prime Cuts 277
1988 Score Rookie/Traded 277
1989 Score Rookie/Traded 278
1990 Score 278
1991 Score 281
1993 Score 285
1994 Score Rookie/Traded 288
1993 Select 289
1993 SP 291
1994 SP 292
2000 SP Authentic 293
2001 SP Authentic 294
2002 SP Authentic 295
2003 SP Authentic 296
2001 SP Game Bat Milestone 297
2001 SP Game-Used Edition 297
2002 SP Legendary Cuts 298
2003 SP Legendary Cuts 298
1986 Sportflics Rookies 299
1994 Sportflics Rookie/Traded 299
1996 SPx 300
1999 SPx 300
2000 SPx 301
2001 SPx 301
2002 SPx 302
2003 SPx 304
1992 Stadium Club Dome 305
1993 Stadium Club Murphy 305
1994 Stadium Club Draft Picks 306
2001 Stadium Club 307
2002 Stadium Club 308
2003 Stadium Club 308
2001 Sweet Spot 312
2001 Studio 309
2002 Studio 310
2003 Studio 311
2001 Sweet Spot 312
2002 Sweet Spot 313
2003 Sweet Spot 313
2002 Sweet Spot Classics 314
2003 Sweet Spot Classics 315
1952 Topps 316
1953 Topps 318
1954 Topps 319
1955 Topps 320
1956 Topps 321
1957 Topps 323
1958 Topps 325
1959 Topps 327
1960 Topps 330
1961 Topps 332
1962 Topps 335
1963 Topps 339
1964 Topps 342
1965 Topps 345
1966 Topps 347
1967 Topps 350
1968 Topps 354
1969 Topps 356
1970 Topps 360
1971 Topps 363
1972 Topps 367
1973 Topps 370
1974 Topps 374
1975 Topps 377
1976 Topps 381
1977 Topps 384
1978 Topps 387
1979 Topps 390
1980 Topps 393
1981 Topps 397
1981 Topps Traded 400
1982 Topps 400
1982 Topps Traded 404
1983 Topps 405
1983 Topps Traded 408
1984 Topps 409
1984 Topps Traded 412
1985 Topps 413
1986 Topps 416
1986 Topps Traded 419
1987 Topps 420
1987 Topps Traded 423
1988 Topps 424
1988 Topps Traded 427
1989 Topps 428
1989 Topps Traded 431
1990 Topps 432
1990 Topps Debut '89 435
1991 Topps 436
1991 Topps Traded 440
1992 Topps 440
1992 Topps Traded 444
1993 Topps 444
1993 Topps Traded 448
1994 Topps 449
1994 Topps Traded 452
1995 Topps 453
1995 Topps Traded 456

1996 Topps 456
1997 Topps 459
1998 Topps 461
1999 Topps 463
1999 Topps Traded 466
2000 Topps 466
2000 Topps Traded 469
2001 Topps 470
2001 Topps Traded 473
2002 Topps 474
2002 Topps Traded 478
2003 Topps 479
2003 Topps Traded 482
2004 Topps 483
2003 Topps 205 485
2002 Topps 206 486
2003 Topps All-Time Fan Favorites 488
1999 Topps Chrome 489
1999 Topps Chrome Traded 491
2000 Topps Chrome Traded 492
2001 Topps Chrome 492
2001 Topps Chrome Traded 495
2002 Topps Chrome 497
2002 Topps Chrome Traded 499
2003 Topps Chrome 500
2003 Topps Chrome Traded 502
1999 Topps Gallery 503
2001 Topps Gallery 504
2002 Topps Gallery 505
2003 Topps Gallery 506
2003 Topps Gallery HOF 507
1999 Topps Gold Label Class 1 507
2002 Topps Gold Label 508
2001 Topps Heritage 509
2002 Topps Heritage 511
2003 Topps Heritage 513
2003 Topps Opening Day 514
2002 Topps Pristine 515
2003 Topps Pristine 516
2001 Topps Reserve 517
2002 Topps Reserve 518
2003 Topps Retired Signature 518
1997 Topps Stars 519
1999 Topps Stars 519
2001 Topps Stars 520
2002 Topps Total 521
2003 Topps Total 525
2001 Topps Tribute 529
2002 Topps Tribute 529
2003 Topps Tribute Contemporary 530
2003 Topps Tribute Perennial All-Star ..530
2003 Topps Tribute World Series 531
2002 UD Authentics 531
2003 UD Authentics 532
2003 UD Patch Collection 533
2001 UD Reserve 534
1991 Ultra Update 535
2001 Ultra 535
2002 Ultra 536
2003 Ultra 538
2004 Ultra 539
1989 Upper Deck 540
1990 Upper Deck 543
1991 Upper Deck 547
1991 Upper Deck Final Edition 551
1993 Upper Deck 551
1994 Upper Deck 555
1995 Upper Deck 557
1999 Upper Deck 559
2001 Upper Deck 561
2002 Upper Deck 563
2003 Upper Deck 566
2004 Upper Deck 569
2002 Upper Deck 40-Man 570
2003 Upper Deck 40-Man 575
2003 Upper Deck Classic Portraits 579
2002 Upper Deck Diamond Connection 580
2001 Upper Deck Evolution 582
2003 Upper Deck First Pitch 583
2003 Upper Deck Game Face 584
2001 Upper Deck Gold Glove 585
2003 Upper Deck Honor Roll 586
2001 Upper Deck MVP 586
2002 Upper Deck MVP 588
2003 Upper Deck MVP 589
2001 Upper Deck Ovation 590
2002 Upper Deck Ovation 591
2003 Upper Deck Play Ball 592
2000 Upper Deck Pros and Prospects ..592
2001 Upper Deck Pros and Prospects ..593
2001 Upper Deck Prospect Premieres ..594
2002 Upper Deck Prospect Premieres ..594
2003 Upper Deck Prospect Premieres ..595
2003 Upper Deck Standing O 595
2001 Ultimate Collection 596
2002 Ultimate Collection 596
1999 Upper Deck Ultimate Victory 597
2000 Upper Deck Ultimate Victory 598
2001 Upper Deck Victory 598
2003 Upper Deck Victory 601
2001 Upper Deck Vintage 602
2002 Upper Deck Vintage 605
2003 Upper Deck Vintage 607
2003 Upper Deck Yankees Signature 609
Acknowledgements 610

About the Author

Jim Beckett, the leading authority on sports card values in the United States, maintains a wide range of activities in the world of sports. He possesses one of the finest collections of sports cards and autographs in the world, has made numerous appearances on radio and television, and has been frequently cited in many national publications. He was awarded the first "Special Achievement Award" for Contributions to the Hobby by the National Sports Collectors Convention in 1980, the "Jock Jaspersen Award" for Hobby Dedication in 1983, and the "Buck Barker, Spirit of the Hobby" award in 1991.

Dr. Beckett is the author of *Beckett Baseball Card Price Guide, The Official Price Guide to Baseball Cards, Price Guide to Baseball Collectibles, The Sport Americana Baseball Memorabilia and Autograph Price Guide, Beckett Almanac of Baseball Cards and Collectibles, Beckett Football Card Price Guide, The Official Price Guide to Football Cards, Beckett Hockey Card Price Guide, The Official Price Guide to Hockey Cards, Beckett Basketball Card Price Guide, The Official Price Guide to Basketball Cards, The Beckett Baseball Card Alphabetical Checklist, The Beckett Basketball Card Alphabetical Checklist,* and *The Beckett Football Card Alphabetical Checklist*. In addition, he is the founder, publisher, and editor of *Beckett Baseball Card Monthly, Beckett Basketball Monthly, Beckett Football Card Monthly, Beckett Hockey Collector, Beckett Sports Collectibles,* and *Beckett Racing and Motorsports Marketplace.*

Jim Beckett received his Ph.D. in Statistics from Southern Methodist University in 1975. Prior to starting Beckett Publications in 1984, Dr. Beckett served as an Associate Professor of Statistics at Bowling Green State University and as a vice president of a consulting firm in Dallas, Texas.

How to Use This Book

Isn't it great? Every year this book gets better with all the new sets coming out. But even more exciting is that every year there are more options in collecting the cards we love so much. This edition has been enhanced and expanded from the previous edition. The cards you collect — who appears on them, what they look like, where they are from, and (most important to most of you) what their current values are — are enumerated within. Many of the features contained in the other *Beckett Price Guides* have been incorporated into this volume since condition grading, terminology, and many other aspects of collecting are common to the card hobby in general. We hope you find the book both interesting and useful in your collecting pursuits.

The Beckett Guide has been successful where other attempts have failed because it is complete, current, and valid. This price guide contains not just one, but three prices by condition for all the baseball cards listed. The prices were added to the card lists just prior to printing and reflect not the author's opinions or desires but the going retail prices for each card, based on the marketplace (sports memorabilia conventions and shows, sports card shops, hobby papers, current mail-order catalogs, local club meetings, auction results, and other firsthand reportings of actually realized prices).

What is the best price guide available on the market today? Of course, card sellers prefer the price guide with the highest prices, while card buyers naturally prefer the one with the lowest prices. Accuracy, however, is the true test. Use the price guide trusted by more collectors and dealers than all the others combined. Look for the Beckett® name. I won't put my name on anything I won't stake my reputation on. Not the lowest and not the highest — but the most accurate, with integrity.

To facilitate your use of this book, read the complete introductory section on the following pages before going to the pricing pages. Every collectible field has its own terminology; we've tried to capture most of these terms and definitions in our glossary. Please read carefully the section on grading and the condition of your cards, as you cannot determine which price column is appropriate for a given card without first knowing its condition.

Welcome to the world of baseball cards.

How to Collect

Each collection is personal and reflects the individuality of its owner. There are no set rules on how to collect cards. Since card collecting is a hobby or leisure pastime, what you collect, how much you collect, and how much time and money you spend collecting are entirely up to you. The funds you have available for collecting and your own personal taste should determine how you collect. Information and ideas presented here are intended to help you get the most enjoyment from this hobby.

It is impossible to collect every card ever produced. Therefore, beginners as well as intermediate and advanced collectors usually specialize in some way. One of the reasons this hobby is popular is that individual collectors can define and tailor their collecting methods to match their own tastes. To give you some idea of the various approaches to collecting, we will list some of the more popular areas of specialization.

Many collectors select complete sets from particular years. For example, they may concentrate on assembling complete sets from all the years since their birth or since they became avid sports fans. They may try to collect a card for every player during that specified period of time.

Many others wish to acquire only certain players. Usually such players are the superstars of the sport, but occasionally collectors will specialize in all the cards of players who attended a particular college or came from a certain town. Some collectors are interested in only the first cards or Rookie Cards of certain players. A handy guide for collectors interested in pursuing the hobby this way is *The Sport Americana Baseball Card Alphabetical Checklist.*

Another fun way to collect cards is by team. Most fans have a favorite team, and it is natural for that loyalty to be translated into a desire for cards of the players on that favorite team. For most of the recent years, team sets (all the cards from a given team for that year) are readily available at a reasonable price. The Sport *Americana Team Baseball Card Checklist* will open up this field to the collector.

Obtaining Cards

Several avenues are open to card collectors. Cards still can be purchased in the traditional way: by the pack at the local candy, grocery, drug, or major discount store.

But there are also thousands of card shops across the country that specialize in selling cards individually or by the pack, box, or set. Another alternative are the thousands of card shows held each month around the country, which feature anywhere from 8 to 800 tables of sports cards and memorabilia for sale.

For many years, it has been possible to purchase complete sets of baseball cards through mail-order advertisers found in traditional sports media publications, such as the *Sporting News, Baseball Digest*, and, *Street & Smith* yearbooks. These sets also are advertised in the card collecting periodicals. Many collectors will begin by subscribing to at least one of the hobby periodicals, all with good up-to-date information. In fact, subscription offers can be found in the advertising section of this book.

Most serious card collectors obtain old (and new) cards from one or more of several main sources: (1) trading or buying from other collectors or dealers; (2) responding to sale or auction ads in the hobby publications; (3) buying at a local hobby store; (4) attending sports collectibles shows or conventions; and (5) purchasing cards over the Internet.

We advise that you try all five methods since each has its own distinct advantages: (1) trading is a great way to make new friends; (2) hobby periodicals help you keep up with what´s going on in the hobby (including when and where the conventions are happening); (3) stores provide the opportunity to enjoy personalized service and consider a great diversity of material in a relaxed sports-oriented atmosphere; (4) shows allow you to choose from multiple dealers and thousands of cards under one roof in a competitive situation; and (5) the Internet allows one to purchase cards in a convenient manner from almost anywhere in the world.

Preserving Your Cards

Cards are fragile. They must be handled properly in order to retain their value. Careless handling can easily result in creased or bent cards. It is, however, not recommended that tweezers or tongs be used to pick up your cards since such utensils might mar or indent card surfaces and thus reduce those cards´ conditions and values.

In general, your cards should be handled directly as little as possible. This is sometimes easier to say than to do.

Although there are still many who use custom boxes, storage trays, or even shoe boxes, plastic sheets are the preferred method of many collectors for storing cards.

A collection stored in plastic pages in a three-ring album allows you to view your collection at any time without the need to touch the card itself. Cards can also be kept in single holders (of various types and thicknesses) designed for the enjoyment of each card individually.

For a large collection, some collectors may use a combination of the above methods. When purchasing plastic sheets for your cards, be sure that you find the pocket size that fits the cards snugly. Don´t put your 1951 Bowman in a sheet designed to fit 1981 Topps.

Most hobby and collectibles shops and virtually all collectors´ conventions will have these plastic pages available in quantity for the various sizes offered, or you can purchase them directly from the advertisers in this book.

Also, remember that pocket size isn´t the only factor to consider when looking for plastic sheets. Other factors such as safety, economy, appearance, availability, or personal preference also may influence which types of sheets a collector may want to buy.

Damp, sunny, and/or hot conditions — no, this is not a weather forecast — are three elements to avoid in extremes if you are interested in preserving your collection. Too much (or too little) humidity can cause the gradual deterioration of a card. Direct, bright sun (or fluorescent light) over time will bleach out the color of a card. Extreme heat accelerates the decomposition of the card. On the other hand, many cards have lasted more than 75 years without much scientific intervention. So be cautious, even if the above factors typically present a problem only when present in the extreme. It never hurts to be prudent.

Collecting vs. Investing

Collecting individual players and collecting complete sets are both popular vehicles for investment and speculation.

Most investors and speculators stock up on complete sets or on quantities of players they think have good investment potential.

There is obviously no guarantee in this book, or anywhere else for that matter, that cards will outperform the stock market or other investment alternatives in the future. After all, baseball cards do not pay quarterly dividends and cards cannot be sold at their "current values" as easily as stocks or bonds.

Nevertheless, investors have noticed a favorable long-term trend in the past performance of baseball and other sports collectibles, and certain cards and sets have outperformed just about any other investment in some years.

Many hobbyists maintain that the best investment is and always will be the building of a collection, which traditionally has held up better than outright speculation.

Some of the obvious questions are: Which cards? When to buy? When to sell? The best investment you can make is in your own education.

The more you know about your collection and the hobby, the more informed the decisions you will be able to make. We´re not selling investment tips. We´re selling information about the current value of baseball cards. It´s up to you to use that information to your best advantage.

Terminology

Each hobby has its own language to describe its area of interest. The nomenclature traditionally used for trading cards is derived from the American Card Catalog, published in 1960 by Nostalgia Press. That catalog, written by Jefferson Burdick (who is called the "Father of Card Collecting" for his pioneering work), uses letter and number designations for each separate set of cards. The letter used in the ACC designation refers to the generic type of card. While both sport and nonsport issues are classified in the ACC, we shall confine ourselves to the sport issues. The following list defines the letters and their meanings as used by the American Card Catalog.

(none) or N - 19th Century U.S. Tobacco.
B - Blankets.
D - Bakery Inserts Including Bread.
E - Early Candy and Gum.
F - Food Inserts.
H - Advertising.
M - Periodicals.
PC - Postcards.
R - Candy and Gum since 1930.
T - Tobacco.

Following the letter prefix and an optional hyphen are one-, two-, or three-digit numbers, R(-)999. These typically represent the company or entity issuing the cards. In several cases, the ACC number is extended by an additional hyphen and another one- or two-digit numerical suffix. For example, the 1957 Topps regular-series baseball card issue carries an ACC designation of R414-11. The "R" indicates a Candy or Gum card produced since 1930. The "414" is the ACC designation for Topps Chewing Gum baseball card issues, and the "11" is the ACC designation for the 1957 regular issue (Topps´ eleventh baseball set). Like other traditional methods of identification, this system provides order to the process of cataloging cards; however, most serious collectors learn the ACC designation of the popular sets by repetition and familiarity, rather than by attempting to "figure out" what they might or should be. From 1948 forward, collectors and dealers commonly refer to all sets by their year, maker, type of issue, and any other distinguishing characteristic. For example, such a characteristic could be an unusual issue or one of several regular issues put out by a specific maker in a single year. Regional issues are usually referred to by year, maker, and sometimes by title or theme of the set.

Glossary/Legend

Our glossary defines terms used in the card collecting hobby and in this book. Many of these terms are also common to other types of sports memorabilia collecting. Some terms may have several meanings depending on use and context.

ACETATE—A transparent plastic.

AS—All-Star card. A card portraying an All-Star Player of the previous year that says "All-Star" on its face.

ATG—All-Time Great card.

ATL—All-Time Leaders card.

AU(TO)—Autographed card.

AW—Award Winner.

BB—Building Blocks.

BC—Bonus card.

BF—Bright Futures.

BL—Blue letters.

BNR—Banner Season.

BOX CARD—Card issued on a box (e.g., 1987 Topps Box Bottoms).

BRICK—A group of 50 or more cards having common characteristics that is intended to be bought, sold, or traded as a unit.

CABINETS—Popular and highly valuable photographs on thick card stock produced in the 19th and early 20th century.

CC—Curtain Call.

CG—Cornerstones of the Game.

CHECKLIST—A list of the cards contained in a particular set. The list is always in numerical order if the cards are numbered. Some unnumbered sets are artificially numbered in alphabetical order, by team and alphabetically within the team, or by uniform number for convenience.

CL—Checklist card. A card that lists in order the cards and players in the set or series. Older checklist cards in Mint condition that have not been marked are very desirable and command premiums.

CP—Changing Places.

CO—Coach.

COMM—Commissioner.

COMMON CARD—The typical card of any set; it has no premium value accruing from subject matter, numerical scarcity, popular demand, or anomaly.

CONVENTION—A gathering of dealers and collectors at a single location for the purpose of buying, selling, and trading sports memorabilia items. Conventions are open to the public and sometimes feature autograph guests, door prizes, contests, seminars, etc. They are frequently referred to simply as "shows."

COOP—Cooperstown.

COR—Corrected card.

CT—Cooperstown.

CY—Cy Young Award.

DD—Decade of Dominance.

DEALER—A person who engages in buying, selling, and trading sports collectibles or supplies. A dealer may also be a collector, but as a dealer, his main goal is to earn a profit.

DIE-CUT—A card with part of its stock partially cut, allowing one or more parts to be folded or removed. After removal or appropriate folding, the remaining part of the card can frequently be made to stand up.

DK—Diamond King.

DL—Division Leaders.

DP—Double Print (a card that was printed in double the quantity compared to the other cards in the same series) or a Draft Pick card.

DT—Dream Team.

DUFEX—A method of card manufacturing technology patented by Pinnacle Brands, Inc. It involves a refractive quality to a card with a foil coating.

ERA—Earned Run Average.

ERR—Error card. A card with erroneous information, spelling, or depiction on either side of the card. Most errors are not corrected by the producing card company.

FC—Fan Club.

FDP—First or First-Round Draft Pick.

FF—Future Foundation.

FOIL—Foil embossed stamp on card.

FOLD—Foldout.

FP—Franchise Player.

Fran—Franchise.

FS—Father/son card.

FS—Future Star.

FUN—Fun cards.

FY—First Year.

GL—Green letters.

GLOSS—A card with luster; a shiny finish as in a card with UV coating.

HG—Heroes of the Game.

HIGH NUMBER—The cards in the last series of numbers in a year in which such higher-numbered cards were printed or distributed in significantly lesser amounts than the lower-numbered cards. The high-number designation refers to a scarcity of the high-numbered cards. Not all years have high numbers in terms of this definition.

HL—Highlight card.

HOF—Hall of Fame, or a card that portrays a Hall of Famer (HOFer).

HOLOGRAM—A three-dimensional photographic image.

HH—Hometown Heroes.

HOR—Horizontal pose on card as opposed to the standard vertical orientation found on most cards.

IA—In Action card.

IF—Infielder.

INSERT—A card of a different type or any other sports collectible (typically a poster or sticker) contained and sold in the same package along with a card or cards of a major set. An insert card is either unnumbered or not numbered in the same sequence as the major set. Sometimes the inserts are randomly distributed and are not found in every pack.

INTERACTIVE—A concept that involves collector participation.

IRT—International Road Trip.

ISSUE—Synonymous with set, but usually used in conjunction with a manufaturer, e.g., a Topps issue.

JSY—means Jersey.

KM—K-Men.

LHP—Left-handed pitcher.

LL—League Leaders or large letters on card.

LUM—Lumberjack.

MAJOR SET—A set produced by a national manufacturer of cards containing a large number of cards. Usually 100 or more different cards constitute a major set.

MB—Master Blasters.

MEM—Memorial card. For example, the 1990 Donruss and Topps Bart Giamatti cards.

METALLIC—A glossy design method that enhances card features.

MG—Manager.

MI—Maximum Impact.

MINI—A small card; for example, a 1975 Topps card of identical design but smaller dimensions than the regular Topps issue of 1975.

ML—Major League.

MM—Memorable Moments.

MULTI-PLAYER CARD—A single card depicting two or more players (but not a team card).

MVP—Most Valuable Player.

NAU—No autograph on card.

NG—Next Game.

NH—No-Hitter.

NNOF—No name on front.

NOF—Name on front.

NOTCHING—The grooving of the card, usually caused by fingernails, rubber bands, or bumping card edges against other objects.

NT—Now and Then.

NV—Novato.

OF—Outfield or Outfielder.

OLY—Olympics Card.

P—Pitcher or Pitching pose.

P1—First Printing.
P2—Second Printing.
P3—Third Printing.
PACKS—A means by which cards are issued in terms of pack type (wax, cello, foil, rack, etc.) and channel of distribution (hobby, retail, etc.).
PARALLEL— A card that is similar in design to its counterpart from a basic set but offers a distinguishing quality.
PF—Profiles.
PG—Postseason Glory.
PLASTIC SHEET—A clear, plastic page that is punched for insertion into a binder (with standard three-ring spacing) containing pockets for displaying cards. Many different styles of sheets exist with pockets of varying sizes to hold the many differing card formats. Also called a display sheet or storage sheet.
PP—Power Passion.
PLATINUM—A metallic element used in the process of creating a glossy card.
PR—Printed name on back.
PREMIUM—A card, sometimes on photographic stock, that is purchased or obtained in conjunction with, or redemption for, another card or product. The premium is not packaged in the same unit as the primary item.
PRES—President.
PRISMATIC/PRISM—A glossy or bright design that refracts or disperses light.
PS—Pace Setters.
PT—Power Tools.
PUZZLE CARD—A card whose back contains a part of a picture which, when joined correctly with other puzzle cards, forms the completed picture.
PUZZLE PIECE—A die-cut piece designed to interlock with similar pieces (e.g., early 1980s Donruss).
PVC—Polyvinyl chloride, a substance used to make many of the popular card display protective sheets. Non-PVC sheets are considered preferable for long-term storage of cards by many.
RARE—A card or series of cards of very limited availability. Unfortunately, "rare" is a subjective term frequently used indiscriminately to hype value. "Rare" cards are harder to obtain than "scarce" cards.
RB—Record Breaker.
RC—Rookie Card.
REDEMPTION—A program established by multiple card manufacturers that allows collectors to mail in a special card (usually a random insert) in return for special cards, sets, or other prizes not available through conventional channels.
REFRACTORS—A card that features a design element that enhances (distorts) its color/appearance through deflecting light.
REV NEG—Reversed or flopped photo side of the card. This is a major type of error card, but only some are corrected.
RHP—Right-handed pitcher.
RHW—Rookie Home Whites.
RIF—Rifleman.
RPM—Rookie Premiere Materials.
RR—Rated Rookie.
ROO—Rookie.
ROY—Rookie of the Year.
RP—Relief pitcher.
RTC—Rookie True Colors.
SA—Super Action card.
SASE—Self-Addressed, Stamped Envelope.

SB—Scrapbook.

SB—Stolen Bases.

SCARCE—A card or series of cards of limited availability. This subjective term is sometimes used indiscriminately to hype value. "Scarce" cards are not as difficult to obtain as "rare" cards.

SCR—Script name on back.

SD—San Diego Padres.

SEMI-HIGH—A card from the next-to-last series of a sequentially issued set. It has more value than an average card and generally less value than a high number. A card is not called a semi-high unless the next-to-last series in which it exists has an additional premium attached to it.

SERIES—The entire set of cards issued by a particular producer in a particular year; e.g., the 1971 Topps series. Also, within a particular set, series can refer to a group of (consecutively numbered) cards printed at the same time, e.g., the first series of the 1957 Topps issue (#1 through #88).

SET—One each of the entire run of cards of the same type produced by a particular manufacturer during a single year. In other words, if you have a complete set of 1976 Topps then you have every card from #1 up to and including #660; i.e., all the different cards that were produced.

SF—Starflics.

SH—Season Highlight.

SHEEN—Brightness or luster emitted by card.

SKIP-NUMBERED—A set that has many unissued card numbers between the lowest number in the set and the highest number in the set, e.g., the 1948 Leaf baseball set contains 98 cards skip-numbered from #1 to #168. A major set in which a few numbers were not printed is not considered to be skip-numbered.

SP—Single or Short Print (a card that was printed in lesser quantity compared to the other cards in the same series; see also DP and TP).

SPECIAL CARD—A card that portrays something other than a single player or team, for example, a card that portrays the previous year´s statistical leaders or the results from the previous year´s World Series.

SS—Shortstop.

STANDARD SIZE—Most modern sports cards measure 2—1/2 by 3-1/2 inches. Exceptions are noted in card descriptions throughout this book.

STAR CARD—A card that portrays a player of some repute, usually determined by his ability; but sometimes referring to sheer popularity.

STOCK—The cardboard or paper on which the card is printed.

SUPERIMPOSED—To be affixed on top of something; i.e., a player photo over a solid background.

SUPERSTAR CARD—A card that portrays a superstar, e.g., a Hall of Famer or player with strong Hall of Fame potential.

TC—Team Checklist.

TEAM CARD—A card that depicts an entire team.

THREE-DIMENSIONAL (3D)—A visual image that provides an illusion of depth and perspective.

TOPICAL—A subset or group of cards that have a common theme (e.g., MVP award winners).

TP—Triple Print (a card that was printed in triple the quantity compared to the other cards in the same series).

TR—Trade reference on card.

TRANSPARENT—Clear, see-through.

UDCA—Upper Deck Classic Alumni.

UER—Uncorrected Error.

UMP—Umpire.

USA—Team USA.
UV—Ultraviolet, a glossy coating used in producing cards.
VAR—Variation card. One of two or more cards from the same series with the same number (or player with identical pose if the series is unnumbered) differing from one another by some aspect, the different feature stemming from the printing or stock of the card. This can be caused when the manufacturer of the cards notices an error in one or more of the cards, makes the changes, and then resumes the print run. In this case there will be two versions or variations of the same card. Sometimes one of the variations is relatively scarce.
VERT—Vertical pose on card.
WAS—Washington National League (1974 Topps).
WC—What´s the Call?
WL—White letters on front.
WS—World Series card.
YL—Yellow letters on front.
YT—Yellow team name on front.
*****—to denote multi-sport sets.

Understanding Card Values

Determining Value

Why are some cards more valuable than others? Obviously, the economic laws of supply and demand are applicable to card collecting just as they are to any other field where a commodity is bought, sold, or traded in a free, unregulated market.

Supply (the number of cards available on the market) is less than the total number of cards originally produced since attrition diminishes that original quantity. Each year a percentage of cards is typically thrown away, destroyed, or otherwise lost to collectors. This percentage is much, much smaller today than it was in the past because more and more people have become increasingly aware of the value of their cards.

For those who collect only Mint condition cards, the supply of older cards can be quite small indeed. Until recently, collectors were not so conscious of the need to preserve the condition of their cards. For this reason, it is difficult to know exactly how many 1953 Topps are currently available, Mint or otherwise. It is generally accepted that there are fewer 1953 Topps available than 1963, 1973, or 1983 Topps cards. If demand were equal for each of these sets, the law of supply and demand would increase the price for the least available sets. Demand, however, is never equal for all sets, so price correlations can be complicated. The demand for a card is influenced by many factors. These include: (1) the age of the card; (2) the number of cards printed; (3) the player(s) portrayed on the card; (4) the attractiveness and popularity of the set; and (5) the physical condition of the card.

In general, (1) the older the card, (2) the fewer the number of the cards printed, (3) the more famous, popular, and talented the player, (4) the more attractive and popular the set, and (5) the better the condition of the card, the higher the value of the card will be. There are exceptions to all but one of these factors: the condition of the card. Given two cards similar in all respects except condition, the one in the best condition will always be valued higher.

While those guidelines help to establish the value of a card, the countless exceptions and peculiarities make any simple, direct mathematical formula to determine card values impossible.

Regional Variation

Since the market varies from region to region, card prices of local players may be higher. This is known as a regional premium. How significant the premium is — and if there is any premium at all — depends on the local popularity of the team and the player.

The largest regional premiums usually do not apply to superstars, who often are so well known nationwide that the prices of their key cards are too high for local dealers to realize a premium.

Lesser stars often command the strongest premiums. Their popularity is concentrated in their home region, creating local demand that greatly exceeds overall demand.

Regional premiums can apply to popular retired players and sometimes can be found in the areas where the players grew up or starred in college.

A regional discount is the converse of a regional premium. Regional discounts occur when a player has been so popular in his region for so long that local collectors and dealers have accumulated quantities of his key cards. The abundant supply may make the cards available in that area at the lowest prices anywhere.

Set Prices

A somewhat paradoxical situation exists in the price of a complete set versus the combined cost of the individual cards in the set. In nearly every case, the sum of the prices for the individual cards is higher than the cost for the complete set. This is prevalent especially in the cards of the last few years. The reasons for this apparent anomaly stem from the habits of collectors and from the carrying costs to dealers. Today, each card in a set normally is produced in the same quantity as all other cards in its set.

Many collectors pick up only stars, superstars, and particular teams. As a result, the dealer is left with a shortage of certain player cards and an abundance of others. He therefore incurs an expense in simply "carrying" these less desirable cards in stock. On the other hand, if he sells a complete set, he gets rid of large numbers of cards at one time. For this reason, he generally is willing to receive less money for a complete set. By doing this, he recovers all of his costs and also makes a profit.

The disparity between the price of the complete set and the sum of the individual cards also has been influenced by the fact that some of the major manufacturers now are pre-collating card sets. Since "pulling" individual cards from the sets involves a specific type of labor (and cost), the singles or star card market is not affected significantly by pre-collation.

Set prices also do not include rare card varieties, unless specifically stated. Of course, the prices for sets do include one example of each type for the given set, but this is the least expensive variety.

Scarce Series

Scarce series occur because cards issued before 1974 were made available to the public each year in several series of finite numbers of cards, rather than all cards of the set being available for purchase at one time. At some point during the year, usually toward the end of the baseball season, interest in current year baseball cards waned. Consequently, the manufacturers produced smaller numbers of these later-series cards.

Nearly all nationwide issues from post–World War II manufacturers (1948 to 1973) exhibit these series variations. In the past, Topps, for example, may have issued series consisting of many different numbers of cards, including 55, 66, 80, 88, and others. Recently, Topps has settled on what is now its standard sheet size of 132 cards, six of which constitute its 792-card set.

While the number of cards within a given series is usually the same as the number of cards on one printed sheet, this is not always the case. For example, Bowman used 36 cards on its standard printed sheets, but in 1948 substituted 12 cards during later print runs of that year's baseball cards. Twelve of the cards from the initial sheet of 36 cards were removed and replaced by 12 different cards, giving, in effect, a first series of 36 cards and a second series of 12 new cards. This replacement produced a scarcity of 24 cards — the 12 cards removed from the original sheet and the 12 new cards added to the sheet. A full sheet of 1948 Bowman cards (second printing) shows that card numbers 37 through 48 have replaced 12 of the cards on the first printing sheet.

The Topps Company also has created scarcities and/or excesses of certain cards in many of its sets. Topps, however, has most frequently gone the other direction by double printing some of the cards. Double printing causes an abundance of cards of the players who are on the same sheet more than one time. During the years from 1978 to 1981, Topps double printed 66 cards out of their large 726-card set. The Topps practice of double printing cards in earlier years is the most logical explanation for the known scarcities of particular cards in some of these Topps sets.

From 1988 through 1990, Donruss short printed and double printed certain cards in its major sets. Ostensibly this was because of its addition of bonus team MVP cards in its regular-issue wax packs.

We are always looking for information or photographs of printing sheets of cards for research. Each year, we try to update the hobby's knowledge of distribution anomalies. Please let us know at the address in this book if you have firsthand knowledge that would be helpful in this pursuit.

Grading Your Cards

Each hobby has its own grading terminology — stamps, coins, comic books, record collecting, etc. Collectors of sports cards are no exception. The one invariable criterion for determining the value of a card is its condition: The better the condition of the card, the more valuable it is. Condition grading, however, is subjective. Individual card dealers and collectors differ in the strictness of their grading, but the stated condition of a card should be determined without regard to whether it is being bought or sold.

No allowance is made for age. A 1952 card is judged by the same standards as a 1992 card. But there are specific sets and cards that are condition-sensitive (marked with "!" in the Price Guide) because of their border color, consistently poor centering, etc. Such cards and sets sometimes command premiums above the listed percentages in Mint condition.

Centering

Current centering terminology uses numbers representing the percentage of border on either side of the main design. Obviously, centering is diminished in importance for borderless cards such as Stadium Club.

Slightly Off-Center (60/40): A slightly off-center card is one that, upon close inspection, is found to have one border bigger than the opposite border. This degree once was offensive only to purists, but now some hobbyists try to avoid cards that are anything other than perfectly centered.

Off-Center (70/30): An off-center card has one border that is noticeably more than twice as wide as the opposite border.

Badly Off-Center (80/20 or worse): A badly off-center card has virtually no border on one side of the card.

Miscut: A miscut card actually shows part of the adjacent card in its larger border and consequently a corresponding amount of its card is cut off.

Corner Wear

Corner wear is the most scrutinized grading criteria in the hobby. These are the major categories of corner wear:

Corner with a slight touch of wear: The corner still is sharp, but there is a slight touch of wear showing. On a dark-bordered card, this shows as a dot of white.

Fuzzy corner: The corner still comes to a point, but the point has just begun to fray. A slightly "dinged" corner is considered the same as a fuzzy corner.

Slightly rounded corner: The fraying of the corner has increased to where there is only a hint of a point. Mild layering may be evident. A "dinged" corner is considered the same as a slightly rounded corner.

Rounded corner: The point is completely gone. Some layering is noticeable.

Badly rounded corner: The corner is completely round and rough. Severe layering is evident.

Creases

A third common defect is the crease. The degree of creasing in a card is difficult to show in a drawing or picture. On giving the specific condition of an expensive card for sale, the seller should note any creases additionally. Creases can be categorized as to severity according to the following scale:

Light Crease: A light crease is a crease that is barely noticeable upon close inspection. In fact, when cards are in plastic sheets or holders, a light crease may not be seen (until the card is taken out of the holder). A light crease on the front is much more serious than a light crease on the card back only.

Medium Crease: A medium crease is noticeable when held and studied at arm´s length by the naked eye, but does not overly detract from the appearance of the card. It is an obvious crease, but not one that breaks the picture surface of the card.

Heavy Crease: A heavy crease is one that has torn or broken through the card´s picture surface; i.e., puts a tear in the photo surface.

Alterations

Deceptive Trimming: This occurs when someone alters the card in order (1) to shave off edge wear, (2) to improve the sharpness of the corners, or (3) to improve centering — obviously their objective is to falsely increase the perceived value of the card to an unsuspecting buyer. The shrinkage usually is evident only if the trimmed card is compared to an adjacent full-size card or if the trimmed card is itself measured.

Obvious Trimming: Obvious trimming is noticeable and unfortunate. It is usually performed by noncollectors who give no thought to the present or future value of their cards.

Deceptively Retouched Borders: This occurs when the borders (especially on those cards with dark borders) are touched up on the edges and corners with magic marker or crayons of appropriate color in order to make the card appear Mint.

Categorization of Defects—Miscellaneous Flaws

The following are common minor flaws that, depending on severity, lower a card´s condition by one to four grades and often render it no better than Excellent-Mint: bubbles (lumps in surface), gum and wax stains, diamond cutting (slanted borders), notching, off-centered backs, paper wrinkles, scratched-off cartoons or puzzles on back, rubber band marks, scratches, surface impressions, and warping.

The following are common serious flaws that, depending on severity, lower a card´s condition at least four grades and often render it no better than Good: chemical or sun fading, erasure marks, mildew, miscutting (severe off-centering), holes, bleached or retouched borders, tape marks, tears, trimming, water or coffee stains, and writing.

Condition Guide

Grades

Mint (Mt)—A card with no flaws or wear. The card has four perfect corners, 60/40 or better centering from top to bottom and from left to right, original gloss, smooth edges, and original color borders. A Mint card does not have print spots or color or focus imperfections.

Near Mint-Mint (NrMt-Mt)—A card with one minor flaw. Any one of the following would lower a Mint card to Near Mint-Mint: one corner with a slight touch of wear, barely noticeable print spots, or color or focus imperfections. The card must have

60/40 or better centering in both directions, original gloss, smooth edges, and original color borders.

Near Mint (NrMt)—A card with one minor flaw. Any one of the following would lower a Mint card to Near Mint: one fuzzy corner or two to four corners with slight touches of wear, 70/30 to 60/40 centering, slightly rough edges, minor print spots, color or focus imperfections. The card must have original gloss and original color borders.

Excellent-Mint (ExMt)—A card with two or three fuzzy, but not rounded, corners and centering no worse than 80/20. The card may have no more than two of the following: slightly rough edges, very slightly discolored borders, minor print spots, color or focus imperfections. The card must have original gloss.

Excellent (Ex)—A card with four fuzzy but definitely not rounded corners and centering no worse than 80/20. The card may have a small amount of original gloss lost, rough edges, slightly discolored borders, and minor print spots or color or focus imperfections.

Very Good (Vg)—A card that has been handled but not abused: slightly rounded corners with slight layering, slight notching on edges, a significant amount of gloss lost from the surface (but no scuffing) and moderate discoloration of borders. The card may have a few light creases.

Good (G), Fair (F), Poor (P)—A well-worn, mishandled, or abused card: badly rounded and layered corners, scuffing, most or all original gloss missing, seriously discolored borders, moderate or heavy creases, and one or more serious flaws. The grade of Good, Fair, or Poor depends on the severity of wear and flaws. Good, Fair, and Poor cards generally are used only as fillers.

The most widely used grades are defined above. Obviously, many cards will not perfectly fit one of the definitions.

Therefore, categories between the major grades known as in-between grades are used, such as Good to Very Good (G-Vg), Very Good to Excellent (VgEx), and Excellent-Mint to Near Mint (ExMt-NrMt). Such grades indicate a card with all qualities of the lower category but with at least a few qualities of the higher category.

Beckett Baseball Card Price Guide lists each card and set in two grades, with the middle grade valued at about 40%–45% of the top grade.

The value of cards that fall between the listed columns can also be calculated using a percentage of the top grade. For example, a card that falls between the top and middle grades (Ex, ExMt, or NrMt in most cases) will generally be valued at anywhere from 50% to 90% of the top grade.

Similarly, a card that falls between the middle and bottom grades (G-Vg, Vg, or VgEx in most cases) will generally be valued at anywhere from 20%–40% of the top grade.

There are also cases where cards are in better condition than the top grade or worse than the bottom grade. Cards that grade worse than the lowest grade are generally valued at 5%–10% of the top grade.

When a card exceeds the top grade by one — such as NrMt-Mt when the top grade is NrMt, or Mint when the top grade is NrMt-Mt — a premium of up to 50% is possible, with 10%–20% the usual norm.

When a card exceeds the top grade by two — such as Mint when the top grade is NrMt, or NrMt-Mt when the top grade is ExMt — a premium of 25%–50% is the usual norm. But certain condition-sensitive cards or sets, particularly those from the pre-war era, can bring premiums of up to 100% or even more.

Unopened packs, boxes, and factory-collated sets are considered Mint in their unknown (and presumed perfect) state. Once opened, however, each card can be graded (and valued) in its own right by taking into account any defects that may be present in spite of the fact that the card has never been handled.

Selling Your Cards

Just about every collector sells cards or will sell cards eventually. Someday you may be interested in selling your duplicates or maybe even your whole collection. You may sell to other collectors, friends, or dealers. You may even sell cards you purchased from a certain dealer back to that same dealer. In any event, it helps to know some of the mechanics of the typical transaction between buyer and seller.

Dealers will buy cards in order to resell them to other collectors who are interested in the cards. Dealers will always pay a higher percentage for items that (in their opinion) can be resold quickly, and a much lower percentage for those items that are perceived as having low demand and hence are slow moving. In either case, dealers must buy at a price that allows for the expense of doing business and a margin for profit.

If you have cards for sale, the best advice we can give is that you get several offers for your cards — either from card shops or at a card show — and take the best offer, all things considered. Note, the "best" offer may not be the one for the highest amount. And remember, if a dealer really wants your cards, he won´t let you get away without making his best competitive offer. Another alternative is to place your cards in an auction as one or several lots.

Many people think nothing of going into a department store and paying $15 for an item of clothing for which the store paid $5. But if you were selling your $15 card to a dealer and he offered you $5 for it, you might consider his markup unreasonable. To complete the analogy: Most department stores (and card dealers) that consistently pay $10 for $15 items eventually go out of business. An exception is when the dealer has lined up a willing buyer for the item(s) you are attempting to sell, or if the cards are so hot that it´s likely he´ll have to hold the cards for just a short period of time.

In those cases, an offer of up to 75% of book value still will allow the dealer to make a reasonable profit considering the short time he will need to hold the merchandise. In general, however, most cards and collections will bring offers in the range of 25%–50% of retail price. Also consider that most material from the last 5 to 10 years is plentiful. If that´s what you´re selling, don´t be surprised if your best offer is well below that range.

Interesting Notes

The first card numerically of an issue is the single card most likely to obtain excessive wear.

Consequently, you typically will find the price on the #1 card (in NrMt or Mint condition) somewhat higher than might otherwise be the case.

Similarly, but to a lesser extent (because normally the less important, reverse side of the card is the one exposed), the last card numerically in an issue also is prone to abnormal wear. This extra wear and tear occurs because the first and last cards are exposed to the elements (human element included) more than any of the other cards. They are generally end cards in any brick formations and are subject to rubber bandings, stackings on wet surfaces, and like activities.

Sports cards have no intrinsic value. The value of a card, like the value of other collectibles, can be determined only by you and your enjoyment in viewing and possessing these cardboard treasures.

Remember, the buyer ultimately determines the price of each baseball card. You are the determining price factor because you have the ability to say "No" to the price of any card by not exchanging your hard-earned money for a given issue. When the cost of a trading card exceeds the enjoyment you will receive from it, your answer should be "No." We assess and report the prices. You set them!

We are always interested in receiving the price input of collectors and dealers. We happily credit major contributors.

We welcome your opinions, since your contributions assist us in ensuring a better guide each year.

If you would like to join our survey list for the next editions of this book and others authored by Dr. Beckett, please send your name and address to Dr. James Beckett, 15850 Dallas Parkway, Dallas, TX 75248.

History of Baseball Cards

Today´s version of the baseball card, with its colorful and oftentimes high-tech front and back, is a far cry from its earliest predecessors. The issue remains cloudy as to which was the very first baseball card ever produced, but the institution of base-

Centering

Well-centered

Slightly Off-centered

Off-centered

Badly Off-centered

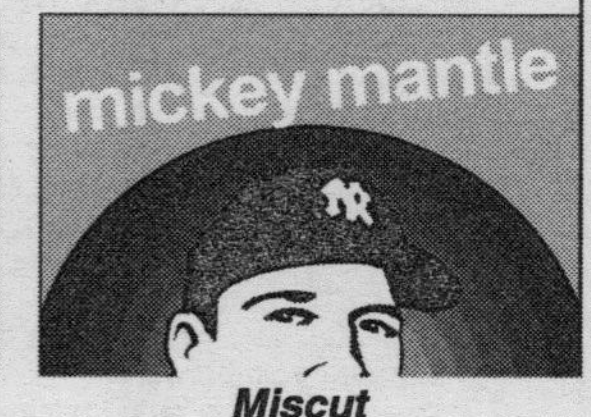

Miscut

ball cards dates from the latter half of the 19th century, more than 100 years ago. Early issues, generally printed on heavy cardboard, were of poor quality, with photographs, drawings, and printing far short of today´s standards.

Goodwin & Co., of New York, makers of Gypsy Queen, Old Judge, and other cigarette brands, is considered by many to be the first issuer of baseball and other sports cards. Its issues, predominantly sized 1-1/2 by 2-1/2 inches, generally consisted of photographs of baseball players, boxers, wrestlers, and other subjects mounted on stiff cardboard. More than 2,000 different photos of baseball players alone have been identified. These "Old Judges," a collective name commonly used for the Goodwin & Co. cards, were issued from 1886 to 1890 and are treasured parts of many collections today.

Among the other cigarette companies that issued baseball cards still attracting attention today are Allen & Ginter, D. Buchner & Co. (Gold Coin Chewing Tobacco), and P. H. Mayo & Brother. Cards from the first two companies bear colored line drawings, while the Mayos are sepia photographs on black cardboard. In addition to the small-size cards from this era, several tobacco companies issued cabinet-size baseball cards. These "cabinets" were considerably larger than the small cards, usually about 4-1/4 by 6-1/2 inches, and were printed on heavy stock. Goodwin & Co.´s Old Judge cabinets and the National Tobacco Works´ "Newsboy" baseball photos are two that remain popular today.

By 1895, the American Tobacco Company began to dominate its competition. They discontinued baseball card inserts in their cigarette packages (actually slide boxes in those days). The lack of competition in the cigarette market had made these inserts unnecessary. This marked the end of the first era of baseball cards. At the dawn of the 20th century, few baseball cards were being issued. But once again, it was the cigarette companies, particularly, the American Tobacco Company, followed to a lesser extent by the candy and gum makers that revived the practice of including baseball cards with their products. The bulk of these cards, identified in the American Card Catalog (designated hereafter as ACC) as T or E cards for 20th century "Tobacco" or "Early Candy and Gum" issues, respectively, were released from 1909 to 1915.

This romantic and popular era of baseball card collecting produced many desirable items. The most outstanding is the fabled T-206 Honus Wagner card. Other perennial favorites among collectors are the T-206 Eddie Plank card, and the T-206 Magee error card. The former was once the second most valuable card and only recently relinquished that position to a more distinctive and aesthetically pleasing Napoleon Lajoie card from the 1933–34 Goudey Gum series. The latter misspells the player´s name as "Magie"; the most famous and most valuable blooper card.

The ingenuity and distinctiveness of this era has yet to be surpassed. Highlights include:

- The T-202 Hassan triple-folders, one of the best looking and the most distinctive cards ever issued;
- The durable T-201 Mecca double-folders, one of the first sets with players´ records on the reverse;
- The T-3 Turkey Reds, the hobby´s most popular cabinet card;
- The E-145 Cracker Jacks, the only major set containing Federal League player cards; and
- The T-204 Ramlys, with their distinctive black-and-white oval photos and ornate gold borders.

These are but a few of the varieties issued during this period.

Increasing Popularity

While the American Tobacco Company dominated the field, several other tobacco companies, as well as clothing manufacturers, newspapers and periodicals, game makers, and companies whose identities remain anonymous, also issued cards during this period. In fact, the Collins-McCarthy Candy Company, makers of Zeenuts Pacific Coast League baseball cards, issued cards yearly from 1911 to 1938. Its record for continuous annual card production has been exceeded only by the Topps Chewing Gum Company. The era of the tobacco card issues closed with the onset of World War I, with the exception of the Red Man chewing tobacco sets produced from

Corner Wear

The partial cards here have been photographed at 300%. This was done in order to magnify each card's corner wear to such a degree that differences could be shown on a printed page.

The 1962 Topps Mickey Mantle card definitely has a rounded corner. Some may say that this card is badly rounded, but that is a judgment call.

The 1962 Topps Hank Aaron card has a slightly rounded corner. Note that there is definite corner wear evident by the fraying and that the corner no longer sports a sharp point.

The 1962 Topps Gil Hodges card has corner wear; it is slightly better than the Aaron card above. Nevertheless, some collectors might classify this Hodges corner as slightly rounded.

The 1962 Topps Manager's Dream card showing Mantle and Mays has slight corner wear. This is not a fuzzy corner as very slight wear is noticeable on the card's photo surface.

The 1962 Topps Don Mossi card has very slight corner wear such that it might be called a fuzzy corner. A close look at the original card shows the corner is not perfect, but almost. However, note that corner wear is somewhat academic on this card. As you can plainly see, the heavy crease going across his name breaks through the photo surface.

1952 to 1955.

The next flurry of card issues broke out in the roaring and prosperous 1920s, the era of the E card. The caramel companies (National Caramel, American Caramel, York Caramel) were the leading distributors of these E cards. In addition, the strip card, a continuous strip with several cards divided by dotted lines or other sectioning features, flourished during this time. While the E cards and the strip cards generally are considered less imaginative than the T cards or the recent candy and gum issues, they still are pursued by many advanced collectors.

Another significant event of the 1920s was the introduction of the arcade card. Taking its designation from its issuer, the Exhibit Supply Company of Chicago, it is usually known as the "Exhibit" card. Once a trademark of the penny arcades, amusement parks, and county fairs across the country, Exhibit machines dispensed nearly postcard-size photos on thick stock for one penny. These picture cards bore likenesses of a favorite cowboy, actor, actress, or baseball player. Exhibit Supply and its associated companies produced baseball cards during a longer time span, although discontinuous, than any other manufacturer. Its first cards appeared in 1921, while its last issue was in 1966. In 1979, the Exhibit Supply Company was bought and somewhat revived by a collector/dealer who has since reprinted Exhibit photos of the past.

If the T card period, from 1909 to 1915, can be designated the "Golden Age" of baseball card collecting, then perhaps the "Silver Age" commenced with the introduction of the Big League Gum series of 239 cards in 1933 (a 240th card was added in 1934). These are the forerunners of today´s baseball gum cards, and the Goudey Gum Company of Boston is responsible for their success. This era spanned the period from the Depression days of 1933 to America´s formal involvement in World War II in 1941.

Goudey´s attractive designs, with full-color line drawings on thick card stock, greatly influenced other cards being issued at that time. As a result, the most attractive and popular vintage cards in history were produced in this "Silver Age." The 1933 Goudey Big League Gum series also owes its popularity to the more than 40 Hall of Fame players in the set. These include four cards of Babe Ruth and two of Lou Gehrig. Goudey´s reign continued in 1934, when it issued a 96-card set in color, together with the single remaining card from the 1933 series, #106, the Napoleon Lajoie card.

In addition to Goudey, several other bubblegum manufacturers issued baseball cards during this era. DeLong Gum Company issued an extremely attractive set in 1933. National Chicle Company´s 192-card "Batter-Up" series of 1934—36 became the largest die-cut set in card history. In addition, that company offered the popular "Diamond Stars" series during the same period. Other popular sets included the "Tattoo Orbit" set of 60 color cards issued in 1933 and Gum Products´ 75-card "Double Play" set, featuring sepia depictions of two players per card.

In 1939, Gum Inc., which later became Bowman Gum, replaced Goudey Gum as the leading baseball card producer. In 1939 and the following year, it issued two important sets of black-and-white cards. In 1939, its "Play Ball America" set consisted of 162 cards. The larger, 240-card "Play Ball" set of 1940 still is considered by many to be the most attractive black-and-white cards ever produced. That firm introduced its only color set in 1941, consisting of 72 cards titled "Play Ball Sports Hall of Fame." Many of these were colored repeats of poses from the black-and-white 1940 series.

In addition to regular gum cards, many manufacturers distributed premium issues during the 1930s. These premiums were printed on paper or photographic stock, rather than card stock. They were much larger than the regular cards and were sold for a penny across the counter with gum (which was packaged separately from the premium). They often were redeemed at the store or through the mail in exchange for the wrappers of previously purchased gum cards, like proof-of-purchase box-top premiums today. The gum premiums are scarcer than the card issues of the 1930s and in most cases no manufacturer´s name is present.

World War II brought an end to this popular era of card collecting when paper and rubber shortages curtailed the production of bubblegum baseball cards. They were resurrected again in 1948 by the Bowman Gum Company (the direct descendent of Gum Inc.). This marked the beginning of the modern era of card collecting.

In 1948, Bowman Gum issued a 48-card set in black and white consisting of one card and one slab of gum in every 1-cent pack. That same year, the Leaf Gum Company also issued a set of cards. Although rather poor in quality, these cards were issued in color. A squabble over the rights to use players' pictures developed between Bowman and Leaf. Eventually Leaf dropped out of the card market, but not before it had left a lasting heritage to the hobby by issuing some of the rarest cards now in existence. Leaf's baseball card series of 1948—49 contained 98 cards, skip numbered to #168 (not all numbers were printed). Of these 98 cards, 49 are relatively plentiful; the other 49, however, are rare and quite valuable.

Bowman continued its production of cards in 1949 with a color series of 240 cards. Because there are many scarce "high numbers," this series remains the most difficult Bowman regular issue to complete. Although the set was printed in color and commands great interest due to its scarcity, it is considered aesthetically inferior to the Goudey and National Chicle issues of the 1930s. In addition to the regular issue of 1949, Bowman also produced a set of 36 Pacific Coast League players. Although this was not a regular issue, it still is prized by collectors. In fact, it has become the most valuable Bowman series.

In 1950 (representing Bowman's one-year monopoly of the baseball card market), the company began a string of top-quality cards that continued until its demise in 1955. The 1950 series was itself something of an oddity because the low numbers, rather than the traditional high numbers, were the more difficult cards to obtain.

The year 1951 marked the beginning of the most competitive and perhaps the highest quality period of baseball card production. In that year, Topps Chewing Gum Company of Brooklyn entered the market. Topps' 1951 series consisted of two sets of 52 cards each, one set with red backs and the other with blue backs. In addition, Topps also issued 31 insert cards, three of which remain the rarest Topps cards ("Current All-Stars" Konstanty, Roberts, and Stanky). The 1951 Topps cards were unattractive and paled in comparison to the 1951 Bowman issues. They were successful, however, and Topps has continued to produce cards ever since.

Intensified Competition

Topps issued a larger and more attractive card set in 1952. This larger size became standard for the next five years. (Bowman followed with larger-size baseball cards in 1953.) This 1952 Topps set has become, like the 1933 Goudey series and the T-206 white border series, the classic set of its era. The 407-card set is a collector's dream of scarcities, rarities, errors, and variations. It also contains the first Topps issues of Mickey Mantle and Willie Mays.

As with Bowman and Leaf in the late 1940s, competition over player rights arose. Ensuing court battles occurred between Topps and Bowman. The market split due to stiff competition, and in January 1956, Topps bought out Bowman. (Topps, using the Bowman name, resurrected Bowman as a label in 1989.) Topps remained essentially unchallenged as the primary producer of baseball cards through 1980. So, the story of major baseball card sets from 1956 through 1980 is by and large the story of Topps' issues. Notable exceptions include the small sets produced by Fleer Gum in 1959, 1960, 1961, and 1963, and the Kellogg's Cereal and Hostess Cakes baseball cards issued to promote their products.

A court decision in 1980 paved the way for two other large gum companies to enter (or reenter, in Fleer's case) the baseball card arena. Fleer, which had last made photo cards in 1963, and the Donruss Company (then a division of General Mills) secured rights to produce baseball cards of current players, thus breaking Topps' monopoly. Each company issued major card sets in 1981 with bubblegum products.

Then a higher court decision in that year overturned the lower court ruling against Topps. It appeared that Topps had regained its sole position as a producer of baseball cards. Undaunted by the revocation ruling, Fleer and Donruss continued to issue cards in 1982 but without bubblegum or any other edible product. Fleer issued its current player baseball cards with "team logo stickers," while Donruss issued its cards with a piece of a baseball jigsaw puzzle.

Sharing the Pie

Since 1981, these three major baseball card producers all have thrived, sharing relatively equal recognition. Each has steadily increased its involvement in terms of numbers of issues per year. To the delight of collectors, their competition has generated novel, and in some cases exceptional, issues of current Major League Baseball players. Collectors also eagerly accepted the debut efforts of Score (1988) and Upper Deck (1989). These five companies were about to embark on a wild ride through the 1990s.

Upper Deck's successful entry into the market turned out to be very important. The company's card stock, photography, packaging, and marketing gave baseball cards a new standard for quality and began the "premium card" trend that continues today. The second premium baseball card set to be issued was the 1990 Leaf set, named for and issued by the parent company of Donruss. To gauge the significance of the premium card trend, one need only note that two of the most valuable post-1986 regular-issue cards in the hobby are the 1989 Upper Deck Ken Griffey Jr. and 1990 Leaf Frank Thomas Rookie Cards.

The impressive debut of Leaf in 1990 was followed by Studio, Ultra, and Stadium Club in 1991. Of those, Stadium Club with its dramatic borderless photo, uncoated card fronts made the biggest impact. In 1992, Bowman and Pinnacle joined the premium fray. In 1992, Donruss and Fleer abandoned the traditional 50-cent pack market and instead produced premium sets comparable to (and presumably designed to compete against) Upper Deck's set. Those moves, combined with the almost instantaneous spread of premium cards to the other major team sports cards, serve as strong indicators that premium cards were here to stay. Bowman had been a lower-level product from 1989 to 1991.

In 1993, Fleer, Topps, and Upper Deck produced the first "super premium" cards with Flair, Finest, and SP, respectively. The success of all three products was an indication the baseball card market was headed toward even higher price levels, and that turned out to be the case in 1994 with the introduction of Bowman's Best (a Topps hybrid of prospect-oriented Bowman and the superpremium Finest) and Leaf Limited. Other 1994 debuts included Upper Deck's entry-level Collector's Choice and Pinnacle's hobby-only Select.

Overall, inserts continued to dominate the hobby scene. Specifically, the parallel chase cards introduced in 1992 with Topps Gold became the latest major hobby trend. Topps Gold was followed by 1993 Finest Refractors (at the time the scarcest insert ever produced and still a landmark set) and the one-per-box Stadium Club First Day Issue.

Of course, the biggest on-field news of 1994 was the owner-provoked players' strike that halted the season prematurely. While the baseball card hobby suffered noticeably from the strike, there was no catastrophic market crash as some had feared. However, the strike drastically slowed down a market that was both strong and growing and contributed to a serious hobby contraction that continues to this day.

By 1995, parallel insert sets were commonplace and had taken on a new complexion: the most popular ones were those that had announced (or at least suspected) print runs of 500 or less, such as Finest Refractors and Select Artist's Proofs.

This trend continued in 1996, with several parallel inserts that were printed in quantities of 250 or less, such as Finest Gold Refractors, Fleer Circa Rave, Studio Silver Press Proofs, and three of the six Select Certified parallels. It could be argued that the high price tags on these extremely limited parallel cards (many exceeded the $1,000 plateau) were driving many single-player collectors to frustration, and even completely out of the hobby. At the same time, average pack prices soared while average number of cards per pack dropped, making the baseball card hobby increasingly expensive.

On the positive side, two trends from 1996 clearly brought in new collectors: Topps' Mickey Mantle retrospective inserts in both series of Topps and Stadium Club and Leaf's Signature Series, which included one certified autograph per pack. Although the Mantle craze following his passing seemed to be a short-term phenomenon, the inclusion of autographs in packs seemed to have more long-term significance.

In 1997 the print runs in selected sets got even lower. Both Fleer/SkyBox and

Pinnacle brands issued cards of which only one exists.

The growth in popularity of autographs also continued. Many products had autographed cards in their packs. A very positive trend was a return to basics. Many collectors bought Rookie Cards, as they understood that concept, and worked on finishing sets.

There was also an increase in international players collecting. Hideo Nomo was incredibly popular in Japan while Chan Ho Park was in demand in Korea. This bodes well for an international growth in the hobby.

Clearly, 1998 was a year of rebirth and growth for the hobby. The big boost came from the home run chase being conducted by Mark McGwire and Sammy Sosa, as well as the continued brilliance of stalwarts like Ken Griffey Jr. and Roger Clemens. The baseball card hobby received a great deal of positive publicity from the renewed interest in the game.

Rookie Cards of the key players of 1998 made significant gains in value as the hobby once again turned to Rookie Cards as the collectible of choice. Also, cards professionally graded by companies such as PSA and SGC were becoming more heavily traded in both older and newer material.

In addition, the Internet and various services such as eBay contributed to the strong growth in collecting interest over the year.

There were downsides in 1998, though. Pinnacle Brands folded, leaving a legacy of innovation and promotions not seen by other companies. In addition, there still was the problem of collectors being frustrated by the extremely short printed cards of their favorite players, making set completion almost impossible.

During 1998, Pacific received a full baseball license and added many innovations to the card market. Their 1998 OnLine set is the most comprehensive set issued in the last five years and many veteran collectors applauded Pacific´s continuing attempts to get as many players as possible into their sets.

In the last couple of years, card companies have been printing specific subsets (usually young players or Rookie Cards) in shorter supply than the regular cards. This is not in every set, but in many sets produced since 1998.

In 1999, many of the trends of the last couple of years continued to gain strength. Buying, selling, and trading cards over the Internet became a dominant factor in the secondary market. Beckett Publications began its own Marketplace, offering the collectors a chance to search across inventory from many of the finest dealers nationwide in one comprehensive on-line database; eBay continued to flourish, while many other parties began to reap the benefits of the burgeoning online auction market. The Barry Halper collection was auctioned off; bringing many museum quality items to the market and giving the older memorabilia market a significant boost as many treasures were made available to collectors.

Also, the boom in Internet trading created a perfect fit for professionally graded cards, as buyers and sellers traded cards sight unseen with the confidence established by a third-party grader.

From a field of almost a dozen contenders, three companies emerged in 1999 to dominate the field of professional grading, BGS (Beckett Grading Services), PSA (Professional Sports Authenticator), and SGC (Sportscard Guaranty L.L.C.). In 1999 these companies made dramatic expansions in on-site grading and submissions at card shows throughout the nation. In response to the widespread acceptance of graded cards, the line of monthly Beckett Price Guides each added a separate section within the price guide area for professionally graded cards.

Similar to 1998, four licensed manufacturers (Fleer/SkyBox, Pacific, Topps, and Upper Deck) produced slightly more than fifty different products for 1999.

Perhaps the biggest hit of the 1999 card season was created by Topps. Card #220 within the basic issue first series 1999 Topps brand featured Home Run King Mark McGwire in 70 variations, one for each homer he slugged in 1998, and many collectors went after the whole set. Continuing a legacy as strong as the Yankees, the basic Topps issue was one of the most popular sets released in 1999.

Closely trailing the Topps McGwire promotion was Upper Deck´s dynamic A Piece of History bat card promotion. The card that kicked off the frenzy was the Babe Ruth A Piece of History distributed in 1999 Upper Deck series 1 packs. Upper Deck actually purchased a cracked game-used Babe Ruth bat for $24,000 and proceeded to cut it up into approximately 350-400 chips of wood to create the now famous Ruth bat card. The card instantly created polar opposites of opinion among hobbyists. Traditional collectors howled at the sacrilegious act of destroying such a historic piece of memorabilia while more open-minded collectors jumped at the opportunity to chase such an important card. The Ruth card was followed up by the cross-brand "500 Club" bat card promotion, whereby UD produced bat cards from every major league ballplayer who hit 500 or more home runs in their career (except for Mark McGwire, who hit his 500th in the midst of the 1999 season and promptly stated that he did not support Upper Deck´s promotion).

More memorabilia cards than ever were offered to collectors in 1999 as Fleer/SkyBox kicked up their efforts to match the standards set by Upper Deck in previous years. Batting gloves, hats, and shoes joined the typical bats and jerseys as pieces of game-used equipment to be featured on trading cards. Sets like E-X Century Authen-Kicks and Fleer Mystique Feel the Game typified the new offerings.

Topps only dabbled with memorabilia cards in 1999, but continued to offer some of the hottest autographed inserts, highlighted by the Topps Stars Rookie Reprint Autographs and the Topps Nolan Ryan Autographs.

Pacific made a clear decision to steer free of memorabilia and autograph inserts, instead focusing on offering collectors a wide selection of beautifully designed insert and parallel cards. Those themes worked beautifully with their established presence for making comprehensive sets, providing collectors with the necessary challenge to pursue regional stars and a favorite team in addition to the typical superstars.

An astounding total of 264 players made their first appearance on a major league licensed trading card in 1999. What may go down as the deepest class of Rookie Cards of all time features a cornucopia of talented youngsters led by Rick Ankiel, Josh Beckett, Pat Burrell, Josh Hamilton, Eric Munson, Corey Patterson, and Alfonso Soriano.

As in years past, Topps continued to provide collectors with a fistful of Rookie Cards within their Bowman, Bowman Chrome, and Bowman´s Best brands. In a trend established in 1998 by Fleer when they released their Fleer Update set (fueled largely by a J. D. Drew Rookie Card), hobbyists enjoyed a bevy of late-season sets chock full of RC´s. Fleer/SkyBox made an all-out effort by stuffing more than 100 Rookie Cards into their 1999 Fleer Update set. Topps produced their first boxed Traded set since 1994. Each 1999 Topps Traded set contained 1 of 75 different cards autographed by a rookie prospect. Considering how much wider the selection of Rookie Cards became in 1999, it´s amazing to see that so few of these RC´s were serial numbered. When one looks at the success established with serial numbered Rookie Cards in the basketball and football card markets with brands like SP Authentic and SPx Finite, one can only scratch his head when realizing that Fleer Mystique was the only brand to offer baseball collectors serial numbered RC´s. Thus, it´s not surprising to see that despite having 25 different Rookie Cards issued in 1999, Pat Burrell´s Fleer Mystique RC (#´d of 2,999) had been established as his "best" RC by year´s end.

Youngsters weren´t the only players in the limelight in 1999 as retired stars and Hall of Famers were featured on more cards than any other year in the 1990s. Upper Deck´s Century Legends brand, featuring the top 50 active and top 50 retired players of the decade as chosen by the Sporting News was a runaway hit.

Perhaps the most popular insert set of the year, outpacing all of the dazzling high-dollar memorabilia cards, was Topps Gallery Heritage. Utilizing the design and painting style of artist Gerry Dvorak from the classic 1953 Topps set, these modern masterpieces proved that insert cards can still be a hot commodity in the secondary market, albeit assuming they´re well conceived and well made, an unfortunate rarity these days.

The spate of basic issue sets with short-printed subsets continued across many brands in 1999. In reaction to many frustrated dealers and collectors struggling to complete these sets, Fleer/SkyBox created dual versions of each prospect card for the 1999 SkyBox Premium set, an action shot was short-printed and a posed shot was seeded at the same rate as other basic issue cards. The idea was well received by collectors but enjoyed a surprisingly short-lived period of active trading in the secondary market.

The year 2000 was marked by several major developments that would continue shaping the future of our hobby. First off, Pacific decided to forfeit their baseball card license on January 1st, 2000, in an effort to more sharply focus their production expenditures into football and hockey.

In a separate development, Wizards of the Coast (primarily known for their non-sport gaming cards) was granted a license to produce baseball trading cards and debuted their MLB Showdown brand. The cards proved to be quite successful in that they were collected as a set by veteran collectors and played as a game by children (and some adults) both inside and outside of the typical collecting community.

By year´s end, Fleer fazed out their SkyBox and Flair brand names in an effort to take full advantage of the historic significance and brand recognition of their flagship Fleer sets issued sporadically during the late 1950s—1970s and consistently from 1981 to the present.

Almost sixty brands of MLB-licensed cards, issued by five manufacturers, were produced in 2000. In addition, Just Minors and Team Best produced a variety of attractive minor league products. Most shop owners continued to generate their income primarily through the sales of packs and boxes of new product, and, as in years past, they had to make careful decisions as to what to keep in stock for customers and what to pass up in fear of a low sell through.

Vintage (or retro-themed) sets dominated the market highlighted by Fleer Greats of the Game, Upper Deck Yankees Legends, and the run of 3,000 hit club and Joe DiMaggio game-used cards issued by Fleer and Upper Deck. In 2001, Topps Heritage (mimicking the style of the classic ´52 Topps cards), Upper Deck Vintage (in an homage to ´63 Topps baseball), and the return of Topps Archives (after a six-year hiatus) added fuel to the fire.

Using the vintage-theme to tap into a base of wealthy consumers, Upper Deck rolled out their line of Master Collection products (which debuted in basketball a year prior with a Michael Jordan set). Both the Yankees Master Collection and Brooklyn Dodgers Master Collection sets carried initial SRP´s of $4,000 or more, marking the most expensive "factory set" of all-time. Each of these sets was serial numbered (500 Yankees and 250 Dodgers), came in a stylish wood box and contained an assortment of game-used and autograph cards from legends of days gone by.

Game-used memorabilia cards became more abundant in all products to the point where a few early 2001 releases (2001 Pacific Private Stock and 2001 SP Game Bat Edition both carrying SRP´s in the $15—$20 range) included them at a rate of one per pack. Both products enjoyed a dynamic sell through and proved to be very popular in the secondary market. The result, however, on the secondary market values of game-used memorabilia cards has been dramatic. An Alex Rodriguez or Ken Griffey Jr. game bat or game jersey card that sold for $200+ in 1999 could be had for as little as $25—$50 in early 2001.

Patch cards (a swatch of jersey that contains part of a multi-colored patch) really caught on by year´s end as the market formalized premium values on these cards. Upper Deck was the first to create separate "super-premium" jersey Patch inserts within 2000 Upper Deck 1 and 2000 Upper Deck Game Jersey Edition (aka series 2). Pacific followed suit with their Game Gear patch subset within the invincible brand.

By early 2001, Major League Baseball Properties had gotten involved with the trading card autograph and memorabilia programs. From 2001 on, all MLB-licensed trading cards produced by the manufacturers that involved an autograph or game-used memorabilia item had to have the procurement of the item witnessed by a representative of Andersen Consulting, a firm hired by MLB to oversee this historic program. Never before had consumers been provided such an effort by the league and manufacturers to be offered autographed or game-used memorabilia trading cards of such authentic provenance.

Short-printed subset cards, a trend started in 1999, continued to be a common element in most basic sets. The trend, however, evolved to the point where these short prints were now being serial numbered, autographed by the player, or incorporating an element of game-used material onto the card. The result was higher values on the key singles, but lower odds of actually finding a good RC in a pack. By year´s end, a general sentiment of frustration over not being able to pull good Rookie Cards from a box was beginning to be heard more and more often from collectors.

Rookie Cards incorporating game-used material debuted at year's end in 2000 Black Diamond Rookie Edition. Also, Rookie Cards signed by the player, introduced within the basketball and football card markets in 1999 (with Upper Deck's SPx brand), made their baseball debut in 2000 SPx. Serial-numbered Rookie Cards grew in total usage, but shrank in print run numbers as production figures reached an all-time low of 999 copies for a basic issue RC within the 2000 Pacific Omega set.

Year-end boxed sets, a trend brought back from a four-year hiatus by Fleer in 1998 with their Fleer Update set, continued to expand as Topps issued their Bowman Draft Picks and Bowman Chrome Draft Picks sets to cap the now single-series accompanying standard Bowman and Bowman Chrome products.

Fleer broke new ground by blending a 1980s "old-school" concept with some postmodern angles in their 2000 Fleer Glossy boxed set. Harkening back to the run of Glossy parallel factory sets produced from 1987 to 1989, the 2000 Fleer Glossy set included a parallel version of the complete 400-card basic 2000 Fleer set. In addition, 50 new cards (card #'s 401—450, each serial numbered to 1,000 copies) featuring a selection of prospects and rookies were created. Each Glossy factory set contained 5 of the 50 new cards, making it a real challenge to complete the Glossy set.

In a first of its kind for the baseball market, Upper Deck issued a product in December 2000 called Rookie Update that incorporated new cards for three separate popular brands (SP Authentic, SPx, and UD Pros and Prospects) into each pack of cards.

Upper Deck came to terms with Major League Baseball for a license to produce cards featuring members of past and present Team USA squads (bringing back a run of cards last seen in 1993 Topps Traded). That allowed Upper Deck the opportunity to radically expand their production of "true" Rookie Cards in year-end 2000 products, adding a spate of cards featuring heroes from the Olympics in Sydney, Australia, like Ben Sheets. Not surprisingly, the number of prospects making their Rookie Card debut in 2000 sets jumped from about 280 players in 1999 to slightly more than 350 players in 2000.

The influence of sports card dealers and collectors from the Far East (and most noticeably Japan) continued to grow in 2000 as stateside buying approached frenzied levels over scarce Hideo Nomo and Kazuhiro Sasaki cards. A much-traveled starter these days, Nomo's first-ever certified autograph card (issued within the Fleer Mystique Fresh Ink insert set) was the hottest card in the hobby for two months (initially trading for as much as $600—$800).

Not all trends were met with success this year. In particular, low-end products geared towards the youth audience (like 2000 Impact by Fleer) were roundly ignored. The hobby still faces a tough road ahead to keep new waves of collectors involved from generation to generation. Part of the Catch-22 with creating affordable brands catered to youths is that the same customers are most interested in the high-end, expensive material.

Also, Upper Deck's PowerDeck product faced an indifferent audience for a second year in a row, as collectors and even general sports enthusiasts outside the hobby failed to get excited over the CD-ROM cards. More success was met by UD's e-Card insert program, whereby collectors who pulled an e-Card from a pack of UD cards had to go to UD's Website and check the serial number printed on the card to see whether it could evolve into an autograph, game jersey, or game jersey autograph exchange.

The Internet continued to have profound ramifications on shaping the destiny of sports card collecting. By 2000, nearly every dealer (and hard-core collector) was buying or selling cards to some degree in on-line auctions. Auction sales had become so prolific that they were now having a strong effect on the secondary market sales levels of trading cards in arenas entirely outside of cyberspace, like shops, shows, and mail order.

The eBay site continued to dominate the on-line auction action, introducing what appears to be a popular "Buy It Now" option to their already established auction format. The Pit.com opened in mid-year with their concept of buying and selling a portfolio of professionally graded sports cards through their Web site. The concept is based almost exactly upon the methodology used for buying and selling stocks through a brokerage house, with daily ebbs and flows in posted buy and sell prices on your inventory.

Beckett.com made radical improvements to their Marketplace search engines and expanded their inventory of sports cards to the point where they were providing both a wider and a deeper selection of trading cards than any site on the Internet. In addition, a company-wide effort to provide daily news content on their site (coupled with a weekly newsletter sent to over 400,000 collectors) began at year's end, and the hobby has reaped the benefits ever since.

As the 2001 season approached, hobbyists waited with bated breath for seven-time Japanese batting champ Ichiro Suzuki to make his debut in the Seattle Mariner's outfield. And what a stunning debut it was. Ichiro led the league in hitting, led the Mariners to their best record ever, and walked off with the A.L. Rookie of the Year and Most Valuable Player awards. Upper Deck obtained the exclusive rights to produce his autograph cards and they hit a grand slam in midsummer by releasing his SPx Rookie Card, featuring a game jersey swatch and a cut signature autograph. In a year studded with notable cards this one was likely the most memorable.

In the National League, 37-year-old San Francisco Giants superstar Barry Bonds captivated the nation by bashing a jaw-dropping 73 home runs, shattering Mark McGwire's 1998 single-season home run record.

Cardinals' rookie Albert Pujols emerged out of the low minor leagues to become an instant hobby superstar and walk away with N.L. Rookie of the Year honors.

The year 2001 was a tumultuous one for sports cards. Topps started the year off with a bang by celebrating their 50th anniversary producing baseball cards. Pacific forfeited its license to make baseball cards after an eight-year run to focus on football and hockey cards. Playoff, a company based out of Grand Prairie, Texas, that had earned its stripes producing football cards in the late 1990s, purchased the rights to the much-hallowed Donruss corporate name and became a formal MLB licensee in the spring of 2001. Their entrance into the baseball card market heralded the return of benchmark brands like Donruss, Donruss Signature, and Leaf.

Competition was fiercer than ever amongst the four primary licensees (Donruss-Playoff, Fleer, Topps, and Upper Deck) as they cranked out almost 80 different products over the course of 2001.

Of all these, likely the most historically important product, Upper Deck Prospect Premieres, was widely overlooked upon release. In a bold move, Upper Deck created a set of 102 prospects, none of which had played a day in the majors. Each player was pictured, however, in the major league uniforms of their parent ballclubs and signed to individual contracts. Because no active major leaguers were featured, Upper Deck did not have to include licensing rights from the MLB Players Association, though they did get licensing from Major League Properties. The industry had never seen a major release featuring active ballplayers marketed to the mainstream audience that lacked licensing from the MLBPA. Because of its lack of historical predecessors and a mixed reception from collectors, the cards were tagged by Beckett Baseball Card Monthly as XRC's (or Extended Rookie Cards), a term that had not been used since 1989.

UD's Prospect Premieres was the first major effort by a manufacturer to level the playing field between Topps and everyone else in that Topps has exclusive rights from the MLBPA to include minor leaguers in their basic brands.

Rookie Cards continued to fascinate collectors, especially in a year with talents like Ichiro and Albert Pujols. The number of players featured on Rookie Cards in 2001 ballooned to an almost absurd figure of 505.

Exchange cards became more prevalent than ever, as manufacturers expanded their use from autograph cards that didn't get returned in time for pack out to slots within basic sets left open in brands released early in the year to fill in with late-season rookie call-ups.

Certified autograph cards remained a huge player in how brands were structured, but the quality of the players suffered greatly as autograph fees continued to spiral out of control. Signatures from superstars like Barry Bonds and Derek Jeter were now being featured on cards with miniscule print runs of 25 or 50 copies while unknown (and often aging and talentless) prospects signed their serial-numbered Rookies Cards by the hundred count.

More serial-numbered Rookie Cards were produced than ever before, but the quantities produced kept sinking lower and lower as companies tried to create secondary market value by simply limiting supply, a dangerous move to say the least. Donruss-Playoff produced the scarcest Rookie Cards of the year, a handful of Game Base cards (including Ichiro) each serial #'d to a scant 100 copies, within their Leaf Limited set.

After a six-month delay, Topps released their much awaited e-Topps program, a product sold entirely on their Web site whereby trading is conducted in a similar fashion to the buying and selling of stocks, in September.

Several products incorporated non-card memorabilia such as signed caps, bobbing head dolls, and signed baseballs with mixed results.

Memorabilia cards continued their slide into mediocrity as the number of cards featuring various bits and pieces of balls, bases, bats, jerseys, pants, shoes, seats, and whatever else could be dreamt up continued to be offered to consumers, who found the cards less appealing with each passing month. To battle consumer apathy, companies often started to offer combination memorabilia cards featuring notable teammates or several pieces of equipment from a notable star.

Retro-themed cards continued to grow in popularity, and some of the innovations seen in these sets were remarkable. Of particular note was Upper Deck's SP Legendary Cuts Autographs set, featuring 84 deceased players. The set required UD to purchase more than 3,300 autograph cuts, which were then incorporated into a windowpane card design. The result was the first certified autograph cards for legends like Roger Maris, Satchell Paige, and Jackie Robinson. Also, Topps Tribute released at year's end and carrying a hefty $40 per pack suggested retail was widely hailed as one of the most beautiful retro-themed cards ever designed, with their crystal-board fronts encasing full-color, razor-sharp photos.

Pack prices continued to escalate, but surprisingly, the public did not balk as long as they delivered value. The most notable high-end product to hit the market in 2001 was Upper Deck Ultimate Collection with a suggested retail of $100 per pack.

September 11th, 2001, is a day that will go down as one of the most devastating in the history of the United States of America. The game of baseball and the hobby of collecting sports cards were rightfully cast aside as the nation mourned the tragic loss of lives in New York, Pennsylvania, and Washington, D.C. America's economy tumbled as airline traveling ground to a near halt and threats of anthrax crippled the mail system. An economy threatening to slip into recession at the beginning of the year dove headlong into it. The sports card market, along with many other industries, felt the hit for several months. Slowly, Americans looked to move past the grief and the sports card industry, steeped in American nostalgia, provided an ideal retreat for many.

The Arizona Diamondbacks beat the New York Yankees in one of the finest World Series ever played, a much-needed diversion for a grief-stricken nation and a calling card for the dramatic power and glory of our National Pastime.

Last year was a relatively quiet one for baseball cards. Dodger's rookie pitcher Kazuhisa Ishii got off to a blazing first half start and his cards carried many releases through to the All-Star break. Ishii stumbled badly in the second half and no notable rookies were in place to pick up market interest. Cubs hurler Mark Prior created a stir, and his 2001 Rookie Cards were red hot at mid-season. For the second straight season, Barry Bonds was the most dominant star in our sport. His early cards continued to outpace all others in volume trading and professional grading submissions.

The number of players featured on Rookie Cards (or Extended Rookie Cards) reached an all-time high of 524 in 2002 as the manufacturers continued to push the envelope toward more immediate coverage of the current year draft. Though few collectors took notice at the time of release, Upper Deck's incorporation of collegiate Team USA athletes into several year-end brands may take hold and grow into a more prominent position in our industry for collegiate ballplayers. The results of these trends, however, are cards that feature a lot of talented youngsters whom most collectors, unfortunately, have never heard of and won't see in a major league uniform for several years.

To make up for the void in excitement generated by rookies and prospects, the manufacturers made some interesting innovations in product distribution and brand development. In general, base sets got noticeably bigger (including Upper Deck's 1,182 card 40-Man brand and Topps 990-card Topps Total brand). In addition, brands like Topps 206, Leaf Rookies and Stars, and Fleer Fall Classics started to incorporate variations of the base cards directly into the basic issue set (different images, switched out teams, etc.).

One of the bigger surprise hits of the year was the aforementioned Topps 206 brand, which borrowed design elements and set composition from the legendary T-206 tobacco set. Other brands continued to successfully mine from cards and eras long since passed.

Donruss continued to push the creative envelope by incorporating 8½" by 11" framed signature pieces directly into boxes of their Playoff Absolute brand. After a four-year hiatus, Fleer brought back their eponymous "Fleer" name brand with a 540-card set. Donruss introduced their wildly successful Diamond Kings brand, of which featured a 150-card painted set. Fleer's Box Score brand was also a popular debut utilizing a unique box-inside-a-box distribution concept. Popular brands like SP Legendary Cuts, Leaf Certified, Topps Heritage, and Topps Tribute all received warm welcomes for their follow-ups to their successes achieved the prior year.

The 2003 season brought us again a growing number of set with price points ranging from $1.29 to $150. There were also many new heroes during the 2003 season as players such as Josh Beckett, Miguel Cabrera, and Dontrelle Willis of the World Champion Florida Marlins were very strong sellers.

Hideki Matsui, who was the most anticipated rookie for the 2003 season, had a very fine year for the American League Champion Yankees but did not draw the same interest from collectors as Ichiro Suzuki did during the 2001 season.

As we enter 2004, the nation is still struggling to dig out of recession and the sport of baseball is still working towards regaining its place as the National Pastime. For the fourth straight season, the top prospect to have a significant impact on the industry hails from Japan. This year it's legendary player Kazuo Matsui, who was perhaps the best shortstop ever in the Japanese leagues.

Despite the struggles the sport of baseball had to endure in 2003, the baseball card market has stepped back to the forefront of the card-collecting hobby, outpacing football, basketball, hockey, golf, and motor sports in volume dollars. As the hobby of collecting baseball cards moves towards the 21st century, we face a market that is blessed with bold creativity and superlative quality and also challenged with the need to reach new consumers both in mass retail and in cyberspace to continue its growth.

Additional Reading

Each year Beckett Publications produces comprehensive annual price guides for several sports: *Beckett Baseball Card Price Guide, Beckett Basketball Card Price Guide, Beckett Football Card Price Guide, Beckett Hockey Card Price Guide, Beckett Racing Price Guide,* and a line of *Beckett Alphabetical Checklists Books* have been released as well. The aim of these annual guides is to provide information and accurate pricing on a wide array of sports cards, ranging from main issues by the major card manufacturers to various regional, promotional, and food issues. Alphabetical checklist books are published to assist the collector in identifying all the cards of any particular player. The seasoned collector will find these tools valuable sources of information that will enable him to pursue his hobby interests.

In addition, abridged editions of the *Beckett Price Guides* have been published for each of these major sports as part of the House of Collectibles series: *The Official Price Guide to Baseball Cards, The Official Price Guide to Football Cards,* and *The Official Price Guide to Basketball Cards*. Published in a convenient mass-market paperback format, these price guides provide information and accurate pricing on all the main issues by the major card manufacturers.

Advertising

Within this price guide you will find advertisements for sports memorabilia material, mail-order, and retail sports collectibles establishments. All advertisements were accepted in good faith based on the reputation of the advertiser; however, neither the author, the publisher, the distributors, nor the other advertisers in this price guide accept any responsibility for any particular advertiser not complying with the terms of his or her ad.

Readers also should be aware that prices in advertisements are subject to change over the annual period before a new edition of this volume is issued each spring. When replying to an advertisement late in the baseball year, the reader should take this into account and contact the dealer by phone or in writing for up-to-date price information. Should you come into contact with any of the advertisers in this guide as a result of their advertisement herein, please mention this source as your contact.

Prices in this Guide

Prices found in this guide reflect current retail rates just prior to the printing of this book. They do not reflect the FOR SALE prices of the author, the publisher, the distributors, the advertisers, or any card dealers associated with this guide. No one is obligated in any way to buy, sell, or trade his or her cards based on these prices. The price listings were compiled by the author from actual buy/sell transactions at sports conventions, sports card shops, buy/sell advertisements in the hobby papers, for sale prices from dealer catalogs and price lists, and discussions with leading hobbyists in the United States and Canada. All prices are in U.S. dollars.

Acknowledgments

A great deal of diligence, hard work, and dedicated effort went into this year's volume. However, the high standards to which we hold ourselves could not have been met without the expert input and generous amount of time contributed by many people. Our sincere thanks are extended to each and every one of you.

A complete list of these invaluable contributors appears after the **Price Guide** section.

Work in Progress

Because we intend the *Almanac* to be the most comprehensive price guide book available, we occasionally include sets with incomplete checklists and/or information. In these cases we have exhausted our resources in an attempt to fill in the missing data but have been unsuccessful. This is where you can help. We always appreciate assistance from our readers to make sure the next edition of this book is even more accurate and more complete. Write to Dr. James Beckett, 15850 Dallas Parkway, Dallas, Texas 75248.

2003 Bazooka

	Nm-Mt	Ex-Mt
COMP.SET w/LOGO's (330)	80.00	24.00
COMPLETE SET (310)	60.00	18.00
COMP.SET w/o JOE's (280)	50.00	15.00
COMMON CARD (1-280)	.40	.12
COMMON ROOKIE	.40	.12
COMMON LOGO	.40	.12
❑ 1 Luis Castillo	.40	.12
❑ 2 Randy Winn	.40	.12
❑ 3 Orlando Hudson	.40	.12
❑ 3A Orlando Hudson Logo	.40	.12
❑ 4 Fernando Vina	.40	.12
❑ 5 Pat Burrell	.40	.12
❑ 6 Brad Wilkerson	.40	.12
❑ 7 Bazooka Joe	.40	.12
❑ 7AN Bazooka Joe Angels	.40	.12
❑ 7AS Bazooka Joe A's	.40	.12
❑ 7AT Bazooka Joe Astros	.40	.12
❑ 7BL Bazooka Joe Blue Jays	.40	.12
❑ 7BR Bazooka Joe Braves	.40	.12
❑ 7BW Bazooka Joe Brewers	.40	.12
❑ 7CA Bazooka Joe Cardinals	.40	.12
❑ 7CU Bazooka Joe Cubs	.40	.12
❑ 7DE Bazooka Joe Devil Rays	.40	.12
❑ 7DI Bazooka Joe Diamondbacks	.40	.12
❑ 7DO Bazooka Joe Dodgers	.40	.12
❑ 7EX Bazooka Joe Expos	.40	.12
❑ 7GI Bazooka Joe Giants	.40	.12
❑ 7IN Bazooka Joe Indians	.40	.12
❑ 7MA Bazooka Joe Mariners	.40	.12
❑ 7ME Bazooka Joe Mets	.40	.12
❑ 7MR Bazooka Joe Marlins	.40	.12
❑ 7OR Bazooka Joe Orioles	.40	.12
❑ 7PA Bazooka Joe Padres	.40	.12
❑ 7PH Bazooka Joe Phillies	.40	.12
❑ 7PI Bazooka Joe Pirates	.40	.12
❑ 7RA Bazooka Joe Rangers	.40	.12
❑ 7RC Bazooka Joe Rockies	.40	.12
❑ 7RD Bazooka Joe Reds	.40	.12
❑ 7RS Bazooka Joe Red Sox	.40	.12
❑ 7RY Bazooka Joe Royals	.40	.12
❑ 7TI Bazooka Joe Tigers	.40	.12
❑ 7TW Bazooka Joe Twins	.40	.12
❑ 7WS Bazooka Joe White Sox	.40	.12
❑ 7YA Bazooka Joe Yankees	.40	.12
❑ 8 Javy Lopez	.40	.12
❑ 9 Juan Pierre	.40	.12
❑ 10 Hideo Nomo	1.00	.30
❑ 11 Barry Larkin	1.00	.30
❑ 12 Alfonso Soriano	1.00	.30
❑ 12A Alfonso Soriano Logo	1.00	.30
❑ 13 Rodrigo Lopez	.40	.12
❑ 14 Mark Ellis	.40	.12
❑ 15 Tim Salmon	.60	.18
❑ 16 Garret Anderson	.40	.12
❑ 16A Garret Anderson Logo	.40	.12
❑ 17 Aaron Boone	.40	.12
❑ 18 Jason Kendall	.40	.12
❑ 19 Hee Seop Choi	.40	.12
❑ 20 Jorge Posada	.60	.18
❑ 21 Sammy Sosa	1.50	.45
❑ 22 Mark Prior	2.00	.60
❑ 22A Mark Prior Logo	2.00	.60
❑ 23 Mark Teixeira	.60	.18
❑ 24 Manny Ramirez	.40	.12
❑ 25 Jim Thome	1.00	.30
❑ 26 A.J. Pierzynski	.40	.12
❑ 27 Scott Rolen	.60	.18
❑ 28 Austin Kearns	.60	.18
❑ 29 Bret Boone	.40	.12
❑ 30 Ken Griffey Jr.	1.50	.45
❑ 31 Greg Maddux	2.00	.60
❑ 32 Derek Lowe	.40	.12
❑ 33 David Wells	.40	.12
❑ 34 A.J. Burnett	.40	.12
❑ 35 Randall Simon	.40	.12
❑ 36 Nick Johnson	.40	.12
❑ 37 Junior Spivey	.40	.12
❑ 38 Eric Gagne	.60	.18
❑ 39 Darin Erstad	.40	.12
❑ 40 Marty Cordova	.40	.12
❑ 41 Brett Myers	.40	.12
❑ 42 Mo Vaughn	.40	.12
❑ 43 Randy Wolf	.40	.12
❑ 44 Vicente Padilla	.40	.12
❑ 45 Elmer Dessens	.40	.12
❑ 46 Jason Simontacchi	.40	.12
❑ 47 John Mabry	.40	.12
❑ 48 Torii Hunter	.40	.12
❑ 48A Torii Hunter Logo	.40	.12
❑ 49 Lyle Overbay	.40	.12
❑ 50 Kirk Saarloos	.40	.12
❑ 51 Bernie Williams	.60	.18
❑ 52 Wade Miller	.40	.12
❑ 53 Bobby Abreu	.40	.12
❑ 54 Wilson Betemit	.40	.12
❑ 55 Edwin Almonte	.40	.12
❑ 56 Jarrod Washburn	.40	.12
❑ 57 Drew Henson	.40	.12
❑ 58 Tony Batista	.40	.12
❑ 59 Juan Rivera	.40	.12
❑ 60 Larry Walker	.60	.18
❑ 61 Brandon Phillips	.40	.12
❑ 62 Franklyn German	.40	.12
❑ 63 Victor Martinez	.40	.12
❑ 63A Victor Martinez Logo	.40	.12
❑ 64 Moises Alou	.40	.12
❑ 65 Nomar Garciaparra	2.00	.60
❑ 66 Willie Harris	.40	.12
❑ 67 Sean Casey	.40	.12
❑ 68 Omar Vizquel	.40	.12
❑ 69 Robert Fick	.40	.12
❑ 70 Curt Schilling	.60	.18
❑ 70A Curt Schilling Logo	.60	.18
❑ 71 Adam Kennedy	.40	.12
❑ 72 Scott Hairston	.40	.12
❑ 73 Jimmy Journell	.40	.12
❑ 74 Rafael Furcal	.40	.12
❑ 75 Barry Zito	1.00	.30
❑ 76 Ed Rogers	.40	.12
❑ 77 Cliff Floyd	.40	.12
❑ 78 Matt Clement	.40	.12
❑ 79 Mike Lowell	.40	.12
❑ 80 Randy Johnson	1.00	.30
❑ 81 Craig Biggio	.60	.18
❑ 82 Carlos Beltran	.40	.12
❑ 83 Paul Lo Duca	.40	.12
❑ 84 Jose Vidro	.40	.12
❑ 85 Gary Sheffield	.40	.12
❑ 86 Jacque Jones	.40	.12
❑ 87 Corey Hart	.40	.12
❑ 88 Roberto Alomar	1.00	.30
❑ 89 Robin Ventura	.40	.12
❑ 90 Pedro Martinez	1.00	.30
❑ 91 Scott Hatteberg	.40	.12
❑ 92 Marlon Byrd	.40	.12
❑ 93 Pokey Reese	.40	.12
❑ 94 Sean Burroughs	.40	.12
❑ 95 Magglio Ordonez	.40	.12
❑ 96 Mariano Rivera	.60	.18
❑ 97 John Olerud	.40	.12
❑ 98 Edgar Renteria	.40	.12
❑ 99 Ben Grieve	.40	.12
❑ 100 Barry Bonds	2.50	.75
❑ 100A Barry Bonds Logo	2.50	.75
❑ 101 Ivan Rodriguez	1.00	.30
❑ 102 Josh Phelps	.40	.12
❑ 103 Nobuaki Yoshida RC	.50	.15
❑ 103A Nobuaki Yoshida Logo	.50	.15
❑ 104 Roy Halladay	.40	.12
❑ 105 Mark Buehrle	.40	.12
❑ 106 Chan Ho Park	.40	.12
❑ 107 Joe Kennedy	.40	.12
❑ 108 Shin-Soo Choo	.40	.12
❑ 108A Shin-Soo Choo Logo	.40	.12
❑ 109 Ryan Jensen	.40	.12
❑ 110 Todd Helton	.60	.18
❑ 111 Chris Duncan RC	.50	.15
❑ 112 Taggert Bozied	.60	.18
❑ 113 Sean Burnett	.40	.12
❑ 114 Mike Lieberthal	.40	.12
❑ 115 Josh Beckett	.60	.18
❑ 116 Andy Pettitte	.60	.18
❑ 117 Jose Reyes	.60	.18
❑ 117A Jose Reyes Logo	.60	.18
❑ 118 Bartolo Colon	.40	.12
❑ 119 Justin Morneau	.40	.12
❑ 120 Lance Berkman	.40	.12
❑ 121 Mike Wodnicki RC	.50	.15
❑ 122 Craig Brazell RC	1.25	.35
❑ 122A Craig Brazell Logo	1.25	.35
❑ 123 Troy Glaus	.60	.18
❑ 124 John Smoltz	.60	.18
❑ 125 Mike Sweeney	.40	.12
❑ 126 Jay Gibbons	.40	.12
❑ 127 Kerry Wood	1.00	.30
❑ 128 Ellis Burks	.40	.12
❑ 129 Carlos Pena	.40	.12
❑ 130 Shawn Green	.40	.12
❑ 131 Jason Stokes	1.00	.30
❑ 131A Jason Stokes Logo	1.00	.30
❑ 132 Raul Ibanez	.40	.12
❑ 133 Francisco Rodriguez	.40	.12
❑ 133A Francisco Rodriguez Logo	.40	.12
❑ 134 Adrian Beltre	.40	.12
❑ 135 Richie Sexson	.40	.12
❑ 136 Paul Byrd	.40	.12
❑ 137 Bobby Kielty	.40	.12
❑ 138 Dewon Brazelton	.40	.12
❑ 139 Jeremy Griffiths RC	.75	.23
❑ 140 Vladimir Guerrero	1.00	.30
❑ 140A Vladimir Guerrero Logo	1.00	.30
❑ 141 Jake Peavy	.40	.12
❑ 142 Bryan Bullington RC	2.50	.75
❑ 143 Orlando Cabrera	.40	.12
❑ 144 Scott Erickson	.40	.12
❑ 145 Doug Mientkiewicz	.40	.12
❑ 146 Derrek Lee	.40	.12
❑ 147 Daryl Clark RC	.75	.23
❑ 148 Trevor Hoffman	.40	.12
❑ 149 Gabe Gross	.40	.12
❑ 150 Roger Clemens	2.00	.60
❑ 151 Khalil Greene	.60	.18
❑ 151A Khalil Greene Logo	.60	.18
❑ 152 Cory Doyne RC	.50	.15
❑ 153 Brandon Roberson RC	.50	.15
❑ 154 Josh Fogg	.40	.12
❑ 155 Eric Chavez	.40	.12
❑ 156 Kris Benson	.40	.12
❑ 157 Billy Koch	.40	.12
❑ 158 Jermaine Dye	.40	.12
❑ 159 Kip Bouknight RC	.75	.23
❑ 160 Brian Giles	.40	.12
❑ 161 Justin Huber	.40	.12
❑ 162 Mike Restovich	.40	.12
❑ 163 Brandon Webb RC	3.00	.90
❑ 164 Odalis Perez	.40	.12
❑ 165 Phil Nevin	.40	.12
❑ 166 Dontrelle Willis	1.50	.45
❑ 167 Aaron Heilman	.40	.12
❑ 168 Dustin Moseley RC	.75	.23
❑ 169 Rylan Reed RC	.50	.15
❑ 170 Miguel Tejada	.40	.12
❑ 171 Nic Jackson	.40	.12
❑ 172 Anthony Webster RC	.75	.23
❑ 173 Jorge Julio	.40	.12
❑ 174 Kevin Millwood	.40	.12
❑ 175 Brian Jordan	.40	.12
❑ 176 Terry Tiffee RC	.75	.23
❑ 177 Dallas McPherson	.40	.12
❑ 178 Freddy Garcia	.40	.12
❑ 179 Jaime Moyer	.40	.12
❑ 180 Rafael Palmeiro	.60	.18
❑ 181 Mike O'Keefe RC	.50	.15
❑ 182 Kevin Youkilis RC	2.50	.75
❑ 183 Kip Wells	.40	.12
❑ 184 Joe Mauer	1.00	.30

❑ 185 Edgar Martinez .60 .18
❑ 186 Jamie Bubela RC .50 .15
❑ 187 Jose Hernandez .40 .12
❑ 188 Josh Hamilton .40 .12
❑ 189 Matt Diaz RC 1.25 .35
❑ 190 Chipper Jones 1.00 .30
❑ 191 Kevin Mench .40 .12
❑ 192 Joey Gomes RC .75 .23
❑ 193 Shannon Stewart .40 .12
❑ 194 David Eckstein .40 .12
❑ 195 Mike Piazza 1.50 .45
❑ 196 Damian Moss .40 .12
❑ 197 Mike Fontenot .40 .12
❑ 198 Shea Hillenbrand .40 .12
❑ 199 Evel Bastida-Martinez RC .50 .15
❑ 200 Jason Giambi 1.00 .30
❑ 201 Aron Weston RC .50 .15
❑ 202 Frank Thomas 1.00 .30
❑ 203 Carlos Lee .40 .12
❑ 204 C.C. Sabathia .40 .12
❑ 205 Jim Edmonds .40 .12
❑ 206 Jemel Spearman RC .50 .15
❑ 207 Jason Jennings .40 .12
❑ 208 Jeremy Bonderman RC 2.00 .60
❑ 209 Preston Wilson .40 .12
❑ 210 Eric Hinske .40 .12
❑ 210A Eric Hinske Logo .40 .12
❑ 211 Will Smith .40 .12
❑ 212 Matthew Hagen RC 1.25 .35
❑ 213 Joe Randa .40 .12
❑ 214 James Loney .40 .12
❑ 215 Carlos Delgado .40 .12
❑ 216 Chris Kroski RC .50 .15
❑ 217 Cristian Guzman .40 .12
❑ 218 Tomo Ohka .40 .12
❑ 219 Al Leiter .40 .12
❑ 220 Adam Dunn .60 .18
❑ 221 Raul Mondesi .40 .12
❑ 222 Donald Hood RC .75 .23
❑ 223 Mark Mulder .40 .12
❑ 224 Mike Williams .40 .12
❑ 225 Ryan Klesko .40 .12
❑ 226 Rich Aurilia .40 .12
❑ 227 Chris Snelling .40 .12
❑ 228 Gary Schneidmiller RC .50 .15
❑ 229 Ichiro Suzuki 2.00 .60
❑ 229A Ichiro Suzuki Logo 2.00 .60
❑ 230 Luis Gonzalez .40 .12
❑ 231 Rocco Baldelli 2.00 .60
❑ 232 Callix Crabbe RC .75 .23
❑ 233 Adrian Gonzalez .40 .12
❑ 234 Corey Koskie .40 .12
❑ 235 Tom Glavine 1.00 .30
❑ 236 Kevin Beavers RC .50 .15
❑ 237 Frank Catalanotto .40 .12
❑ 238 Kevin Cash .40 .12
❑ 239 Nick Trzesniak RC .50 .15
❑ 240 Paul Konerko .40 .12
❑ 241 Jose Cruz Jr. .40 .12
❑ 242 Hank Blalock .60 .18
❑ 243 J.D. Drew .40 .12
❑ 244 Kazuhiro Sasaki .40 .12
❑ 245 Jeff Bagwell .60 .18
❑ 246 Jason Schmidt .40 .12
❑ 247 Xavier Nady .40 .12
❑ 248 Aramis Ramirez .40 .12
❑ 249 Jimmy Rollins .40 .12
❑ 250 Alex Rodriguez 2.00 .60
❑ 250A Alex Rodriguez Logo 2.00 .60
❑ 251 Terrence Long .40 .12
❑ 252 Derek Jeter 2.50 .75
❑ 253 Edgardo Alfonzo .40 .12
❑ 254 Toby Hall .40 .12
❑ 255 Kazuhisa Ishii .40 .12
❑ 256 Brad Nelson .40 .12
❑ 257 Kevin Brown .40 .12
❑ 258 Roy Oswalt .40 .12
❑ 259 Mike Cameron .40 .12
❑ 260 Juan Gonzalez 1.00 .30
❑ 261 Dmitri Young .40 .12
❑ 262 Jose Jimenez .40 .12
❑ 263 Wily Mo Pena .40 .12
❑ 264 Joe Borchard .40 .12
❑ 265 Mike Mussina 1.00 .30
❑ 266 Fred McGriff .60 .18
❑ 267 Johnny Damon .40 .12
❑ 268 Joel Pineiro .40 .12
❑ 269 Andruw Jones .60 .18
❑ 270 Tim Hudson .40 .12
❑ 271 Chad Tracy .40 .12
❑ 272 Brad Fullmer .40 .12
❑ 273 Boof Bonser .40 .12
❑ 274 Clint Nageotte .40 .12
❑ 275 Jeff Kent .40 .12
❑ 276 Tino Martinez .60 .18
❑ 277 Matt Morris .40 .12
❑ 278 Jonny Gomes .40 .12
❑ 279 Benito Santiago .40 .12
❑ 280 Albert Pujols 2.00 .60
❑ 280A Albert Pujols Logo 2.00 .60

2000 Black Diamond Rookie Edition

	Nm-Mt	Ex-Mt
COMP.SET w/o SP's (90)	25.00	7.50
COMMON CARD (1-90)	.40	.12
COMMON GEMS (91-120)	5.00	1.50
COMMON JSY. (121-136)	8.00	2.40
COMMON USA (137-154)	8.00	2.40

❑ 1 Troy Glaus .60 .18
❑ 2 Mo Vaughn .40 .12
❑ 3 Darin Erstad .40 .12
❑ 4 Jason Giambi 1.00 .30
❑ 5 Tim Hudson .60 .18
❑ 6 Ben Grieve .40 .12
❑ 7 Eric Chavez .40 .12
❑ 8 Tony Batista .40 .12
❑ 9 Carlos Delgado .40 .12
❑ 10 David Wells .40 .12
❑ 11 Greg Vaughn .40 .12
❑ 12 Fred McGriff .60 .18
❑ 13 Manny Ramirez .40 .12
❑ 14 Roberto Alomar 1.00 .30
❑ 15 Jim Thome 1.00 .30
❑ 16 Alex Rodriguez 2.00 .60
❑ 17 Edgar Martinez .60 .18
❑ 18 John Olerud .40 .12
❑ 19 Albert Belle .40 .12
❑ 20 Mike Mussina 1.00 .30
❑ 21 Cal Ripken 3.00 .90
❑ 22 Ivan Rodriguez 1.00 .30
❑ 23 Rafael Palmeiro .60 .18
❑ 24 Pedro Martinez 1.00 .30
❑ 25 Nomar Garciaparra 2.00 .60
❑ 26 Carl Everett .40 .12
❑ 27 Jermaine Dye .40 .12
❑ 28 Mike Sweeney .40 .12
❑ 29 Juan Gonzalez 1.00 .30
❑ 30 Bobby Higginson .40 .12
❑ 31 Dean Palmer .40 .12
❑ 32 Jacque Jones .40 .12
❑ 33 Eric Milton .40 .12
❑ 34 Matt Lawton .40 .12
❑ 35 Magglio Ordonez .40 .12
❑ 36 Paul Konerko .40 .12
❑ 37 Frank Thomas 1.00 .30
❑ 38 Ray Durham .40 .12
❑ 39 Roger Clemens 2.00 .60
❑ 40 Derek Jeter 2.50 .75
❑ 41 Bernie Williams .60 .18
❑ 42 Jose Canseco 1.00 .30
❑ 43 Craig Biggio .60 .18
❑ 44 Richard Hidalgo .40 .12
❑ 45 Jeff Bagwell .60 .18
❑ 46 Greg Maddux 2.00 .60
❑ 47 Chipper Jones 1.00 .30
❑ 48 Rafael Furcal .40 .12
❑ 49 Andruw Jones .60 .18
❑ 50 Geoff Jenkins .40 .12
❑ 51 Jeromy Burnitz .40 .12
❑ 52 Mark McGwire 2.50 .75
❑ 53 Rick Ankiel .40 .12
❑ 54 Jim Edmonds .40 .12
❑ 55 Kerry Wood 1.00 .30
❑ 56 Sammy Sosa 1.50 .45
❑ 57 Matt Williams .40 .12
❑ 58 Randy Johnson 1.00 .30
❑ 59 Steve Finley .40 .12
❑ 60 Curt Schilling .60 .18
❑ 61 Kevin Brown .40 .12
❑ 62 Gary Sheffield .40 .12
❑ 63 Shawn Green .40 .12
❑ 64 Jose Vidro .40 .12
❑ 65 Vladimir Guerrero 1.00 .30
❑ 66 Jeff Kent .40 .12
❑ 67 Barry Bonds 2.50 .75
❑ 68 Ryan Dempster .40 .12
❑ 69 Cliff Floyd .40 .12
❑ 70 Preston Wilson .40 .12
❑ 71 Mike Piazza 1.50 .45
❑ 72 Al Leiter .40 .12
❑ 73 Edgardo Alfonzo .40 .12
❑ 74 Derek Bell .40 .12
❑ 75 Ryan Klesko .40 .12
❑ 76 Tony Gwynn 1.25 .35
❑ 77 Bob Abreu .40 .12
❑ 78 Pat Burrell .60 .18
❑ 79 Scott Rolen .60 .18
❑ 80 Mike Lieberthal .40 .12
❑ 81 Jason Kendall .40 .12
❑ 82 Brian Giles .40 .12
❑ 83 Ken Griffey Jr. 1.50 .45
❑ 84 Pokey Reese .40 .12
❑ 85 Dmitri Young .40 .12
❑ 86 Sean Casey .40 .12
❑ 87 Jeff Cirillo .40 .12
❑ 88 Todd Helton .60 .18
❑ 89 Jeffrey Hammonds .40 .12
❑ 90 Larry Walker .60 .18
❑ 91 Barry Zito RC 20.00 6.00
❑ 92 Keith Ginter RC 5.00 1.50
❑ 93 Dane Sardinha RC 5.00 1.50
❑ 94 Kenny Kelly RC 5.00 1.50
❑ 95 Ryan Kohlmeier RC 5.00 1.50
❑ 96 Leo Estrella RC 5.00 1.50
❑ 97 Danys Baez RC 8.00 2.40
❑ 98 Paul Rigdon RC 5.00 1.50
❑ 99 Mike Lamb RC 5.00 1.50
❑ 100 Aaron McNeal RC 5.00 1.50
❑ 101 Juan Pierre RC 10.00 3.00
❑ 102 Rico Washington RC 5.00 1.50
❑ 103 Luis Matos RC 10.00 3.00
❑ 104 Adam Bernero RC 5.00 1.50
❑ 105 Wascar Serrano RC 5.00 1.50
❑ 106 Chris Richard RC 5.00 1.50
❑ 107 Justin Miller RC 5.00 1.50
❑ 108 Julio Zuleta RC 5.00 1.50
❑ 109 Alex Cabrera RC 5.00 1.50
❑ 110 G.Stechschulte RC 5.00 1.50
❑ 111 Tony Mota RC 5.00 1.50
❑ 112 Tomo Ohka RC 5.00 1.50
❑ 113 Geraldo Guzman RC 5.00 1.50
❑ 114 Scott Downs RC 5.00 1.50
❑ 115 Timo Perez RC 5.00 1.50
❑ 116 Chad Durbin RC 5.00 1.50
❑ 117 Sun-Woo Kim RC 5.00 1.50
❑ 118 Tomas De la Rosa RC 5.00 1.50
❑ 119 Javier Cardona RC 5.00 1.50
❑ 120 Kazuhiro Sasaki RC 8.00 2.40
❑ 121 Brad Cresse JSY RC 8.00 2.40
❑ 122 M.Wheatland JSY RC 8.00 2.40
❑ 123 Joe Torres JSY RC 8.00 2.40
❑ 124 Dave Krynzel JSY RC 8.00 2.40
❑ 125 Ben Diggins JSY RC 8.00 2.40
❑ 126 Sean Burnett JSY RC 15.00 4.50
❑ 127 D.Espinosa JSY RC 8.00 2.40
❑ 128 Scott Heard JSY RC 8.00 2.40

Card	NM	Ex
129 Daylan Holt JSY RC	8.00	2.40
130 Koyie Hill JSY RC	10.00	3.00
131 Mark Buehrle JSY RC	15.00	4.50
132 Xavier Nady JSY RC	15.00	4.50
133 Mike Tonis JSY RC	10.00	3.00
134 Matt Ginter JSY RC	8.00	2.40
135 L.Barcelo JSY RC	8.00	2.40
136 Cory Vance JSY RC	8.00	2.40
137 Sean Burroughs USA	10.00	3.00
138 Todd Williams USA	8.00	2.40
139 B.Wilkerson USA RC	10.00	3.00
140 Ben Sheets USA RC	15.00	4.50
141 K.Ainsworth USA RC	10.00	3.00
142 Anthony Sanders USA	8.00	2.40
143 R.Franklin USA RC	8.00	2.40
144 S.Heams USA RC	8.00	2.40
145 Roy Oswalt USA RC	20.00	6.00
146 Jon Rauch USA RC	8.00	2.40
147 B.Abernathy USA RC	8.00	2.40
148 Ernie Young USA	8.00	2.40
149 Chris George USA	8.00	2.40
150 Gookie Dawkins USA	8.00	2.40
151 Adam Everett USA	8.00	2.40
152 John Cotton USA RC	8.00	2.40
153 Pat Borders USA	8.00	2.40
154 D.Mientkiewicz USA	8.00	2.40

1948 Bowman

	NM	Ex
COMPLETE SET (48)	3600.00	1800.00
COMMON CARD (1-36)	20.00	10.00
COMMON CARD (37-48)	30.00	15.00
WRAPPER (5-CENT)	700.00	350.00
WRAPPER (1-CENT)	-	
1 Bob Elliott RC	125.00	19.00
2 Ewell Blackwell RC	60.00	30.00
3 Ralph Kiner RC	150.00	75.00
4 Johnny Mize	125.00	60.00
5 Bob Feller	250.00	125.00
6 Yogi Berra RC	450.00	220.00
7 Pete Reiser SP	120.00	60.00
8 Phil Rizzuto SP	350.00	180.00
9 Walker Cooper RC	20.00	10.00
10 Buddy Rosar	20.00	10.00
11 Johnny Lindell	25.00	12.50
12 Johnny Sain RC	80.00	40.00
13 Willard Marshall SP	40.00	20.00
14 Allie Reynolds RC	60.00	30.00
15 Eddie Joost	20.00	10.00
16 Jack Lohrke SP	40.00	20.00
17 Enos Slaughter	100.00	50.00
18 Warren Spahn RC	300.00	150.00
19 Tommy Henrich	60.00	30.00
20 Buddy Kerr SP	40.00	20.00
21 Ferris Fain RC	40.00	20.00
22 Floyd Bevens SP RC	50.00	25.00
23 Larry Jansen RC	25.00	12.50
24 Dutch Leonard SP	40.00	20.00
25 Barney McCosky	20.00	10.00
26 Frank Shea SP RC	50.00	25.00
27 Sid Gordon RC	25.00	12.50
28 Emil Verban SP	40.00	20.00
29 Joe Page SP RC	75.00	38.00
30 W.Lockman SP RC	50.00	25.00
31 Bill McCahan	20.00	10.00
32 Bill Rigney RC	20.00	10.00
33 Bill Johnson	25.00	12.50
34 Sheldon Jones SP	40.00	20.00
35 Snuffy Stirnweiss RC	40.00	20.00
36 Stan Musial RC	800.00	400.00
37 Clint Hartung RC	30.00	15.00
38 Red Schoendienst RC	200.00	100.00
39 Augie Galan	30.00	15.00
40 Marty Marion RC	80.00	40.00
41 Rex Barney RC	60.00	30.00
42 Ray Poat	30.00	15.00
43 Bruce Edwards	40.00	20.00
44 Johnny Wyrostek	30.00	15.00
45 Hank Sauer RC	60.00	30.00
46 Herman Wehmeier	30.00	15.00
47 Bobby Thomson RC	100.00	50.00
48 Dave Koslo RC	80.00	19.50

1949 Bowman

	NM	Ex
COMP. MASTER SET (252)	16000.00	8000.00
COMPLETE SET (240)	15000.00	7500.00
COMMON CARD (1-144)	15.00	7.50
COMMON (145-240)	50.00	25.00
WRAPPER (1-CENT,Rd,Wh,Bl)		
WRAP.(5-CENT,GREEN)	250.00	125.00
WRAP.(5-CENT,BLUE)	200.00	100.00
1 Vern Bickford RC	125.00	25.00
2 Whitey Lockman	40.00	20.00
3 Bob Porterfield	15.00	7.50
4A Jerry Priddy NNOF	15.00	7.50
4B Jerry Priddy NOF	50.00	25.00
5 Hank Sauer	40.00	20.00
6 Phil Cavarretta	40.00	20.00
7 Joe Dobson	15.00	7.50
8 Murry Dickson	15.00	7.50
9 Ferris Fain	40.00	20.00
10 Ted Gray	15.00	7.50
11 Lou Boudreau	75.00	38.00
12 Cass Michaels	15.00	7.50
13 Bob Chesnes	15.00	7.50
14 Curt Simmons RC	40.00	20.00
15 Ned Garver	15.00	7.50
16 Al Kozar	15.00	7.50
17 Earl Torgeson	15.00	7.50
18 Bobby Thomson	40.00	20.00
19 Bobby Brown RC	60.00	30.00
20 Gene Hermanski	15.00	7.50
21 Frank Baumholtz	25.00	12.50
22 Peanuts Lowrey	15.00	7.50
23 Bobby Doerr	75.00	38.00
24 Stan Musial	500.00	250.00
25 Carl Scheib	15.00	7.50
26 George Kell RC	75.00	38.00
27 Bob Feller	200.00	100.00
28 Don Kolloway	15.00	7.50
29 Ralph Kiner	125.00	60.00
30 Andy Seminick	40.00	20.00
31 Dick Kokos	15.00	7.50
32 Eddie Yost RC	60.00	30.00
33 Warren Spahn	200.00	100.00
34 Dave Koslo	15.00	7.50
35 Vic Raschi RC	60.00	30.00
36 Pee Wee Reese	200.00	100.00
37 Johnny Wyrostek	15.00	7.50
38 Emil Verban	15.00	7.50
39 Billy Goodman	25.00	12.50
40 Red Munger	15.00	7.50
41 Lou Brissie	15.00	7.50
42 Hoot Evers	15.00	7.50
43 Dale Mitchell RC	40.00	20.00
44 Dave Philley	15.00	7.50
45 Wally Westlake	15.00	7.50
46 Robin Roberts RC	250.00	125.00
47 Johnny Sain	60.00	30.00
48 Willard Marshall	15.00	7.50
49 Frank Shea	25.00	12.50
50 Jackie Robinson RC	1000.00	500.00
51 Herman Wehmeier	15.00	7.50
52 Johnny Schmitz	15.00	7.50
53 Jack Kramer	15.00	7.50
54 Marty Marion	60.00	30.00
55 Eddie Joost	15.00	7.50
56 Pat Mullin	15.00	7.50
57 Gene Bearden	40.00	20.00
58 Bob Elliott	40.00	20.00
59 Jack Lohrke	15.00	7.50
60 Yogi Berra	300.00	150.00
61 Rex Barney	40.00	20.00
62 Grady Hatton	15.00	7.50
63 Andy Pafko	40.00	20.00
64 Dom DiMaggio	60.00	30.00
65 Enos Slaughter	75.00	38.00
66 Elmer Valo	15.00	7.50
67 Alvin Dark RC	40.00	20.00
68 Sheldon Jones	15.00	7.50
69 Tommy Henrich	40.00	20.00
70 Carl Furillo RC	125.00	60.00
71 Vern Stephens	15.00	7.50
72 Tommy Holmes	40.00	20.00
73 Billy Cox RC	40.00	20.00
74 Tom McBride	15.00	7.50
75 Eddie Mayo	15.00	7.50
76 Bill Nicholson RC	25.00	12.50
77 Ernie Bonham	15.00	7.50
78A Sam Zoldak NNOF	15.00	7.50
78B Sam Zoldak NOF	50.00	25.00
79 Ron Northey	15.00	7.50
80 Bill McCahan	15.00	7.50
81 Virgil Stallcup	15.00	7.50
82 Joe Page	60.00	30.00
83A Bob Scheffing NNOF	15.00	7.50
83B Bob Scheffing NOF	50.00	25.00
84 Roy Campanella RC	700.00	350.00
85A Johnny Mize NNOF	100.00	50.00
85B Johnny Mize NOF	150.00	75.00
86 Johnny Pesky	60.00	30.00
87 Randy Gumpert	15.00	7.50
88A Bill Salkeld NNOF	15.00	7.50
88B Bill Salkeld NOF	50.00	25.00
89 Mizell Platt	15.00	7.50
90 Gil Coan	15.00	7.50
91 Dick Wakefield	15.00	7.50
92 Willie Jones	40.00	20.00
93 Ed Stevens	15.00	7.50
94 Mickey Vernon RC	40.00	20.00
95 Howie Pollet RC	15.00	7.50
96 Taft Wright	15.00	7.50
97 Danny Litwhiler	15.00	7.50
98A Phil Rizzuto NNOF	200.00	100.00
98B Phil Rizzuto NOF	250.00	125.00
99 Frank Gustine	15.00	7.50
100 Gil Hodges RC	250.00	125.00
101 Sid Gordon	15.00	7.50
102 Stan Spence	15.00	7.50
103 Joe Tipton	15.00	7.50
104 Eddie Stanky RC	40.00	20.00
105 Bill Kennedy	15.00	7.50
106 Jake Early	15.00	7.50
107 Eddie Lake	15.00	7.50
108 Ken Heintzelman	15.00	7.50
109A Ed Fitzgerald SCR	15.00	7.50
109B Ed Fitzgerald PR	60.00	30.00
110 Early Wynn RC	150.00	75.00
111 Red Schoendienst	100.00	50.00
112 Sam Chapman	40.00	20.00
113 Ray LaManno	15.00	7.50
114 Allie Reynolds	60.00	30.00
115 Dutch Leonard	15.00	7.50
116 Joe Hatton	15.00	7.50
117 Walker Cooper	15.00	7.50
118 Sam Mele	15.00	7.50
119 Floyd Baker	15.00	7.50
120 Cliff Fannin	15.00	7.50
121 Mark Christman	15.00	7.50
122 George Vico	15.00	7.50
123 Johnny Blatnick	15.00	7.50
124A D.Murtaugh SCR RC	50.00	25.00
124B D.Murtaugh PR RC	70.00	35.00
125 Ken Keltner	25.00	12.50

	NM	Ex
❑ 126A Al Brazle SCR	15.00	7.50
❑ 126B Al Brazle PR	60.00	30.00
❑ 127A Hank Majeski SCR	15.00	7.50
❑ 127B Hank Majeski PR	60.00	30.00
❑ 128 Johnny VanderMeer	60.00	30.00
❑ 129 Bill Johnson	40.00	20.00
❑ 130 Harry Walker	15.00	7.50
❑ 131 Paul Lehner	15.00	7.50
❑ 132A Al Evans SCR	15.00	7.50
❑ 132B Al Evans PR	60.00	30.00
❑ 133 Aaron Robinson	15.00	7.50
❑ 134 Hank Borowy	15.00	7.50
❑ 135 Stan Rojek	15.00	7.50
❑ 136 Hank Edwards	15.00	7.50
❑ 137 Ted Wilks	15.00	7.50
❑ 138 Buddy Rosar	15.00	7.50
❑ 139 Hank Arft	15.00	7.50
❑ 140 Ray Scarborough	15.00	7.50
❑ 141 Tony Lupien	15.00	7.50
❑ 142 Eddie Waitkus RC	40.00	20.00
❑ 143A B.Dillinger RC SCR	25.00	12.50
❑ 143B Bob Dillinger RC PR	60.00	30.00
❑ 144 Mickey Haefner	15.00	7.50
❑ 145 Sylvester Donnelly	50.00	25.00
❑ 146 Mike McCormick	50.00	25.00
❑ 147 Bert Singleton	50.00	25.00
❑ 148 Bob Swift	50.00	25.00
❑ 149 Roy Partee	50.00	25.00
❑ 150 Allie Clark	50.00	25.00
❑ 151 Mickey Harris	50.00	25.00
❑ 152 Clarence Maddern	50.00	25.00
❑ 153 Phil Masi	50.00	25.00
❑ 154 Clint Hartung	60.00	30.00
❑ 155 Mickey Guerra	50.00	25.00
❑ 156 Al Zarilla	50.00	25.00
❑ 157 Walt Masterson	50.00	25.00
❑ 158 Harry Brecheen	60.00	30.00
❑ 159 Glen Moulder	50.00	25.00
❑ 160 Jim Blackburn	50.00	25.00
❑ 161 Jocko Thompson	50.00	25.00
❑ 162 Preacher Roe RC	125.00	60.00
❑ 163 Clyde McCullough	50.00	25.00
❑ 164 Vic Wertz RC	75.00	38.00
❑ 165 Snuffy Stirnweiss	75.00	38.00
❑ 166 Mike Tresh	50.00	25.00
❑ 167 Babe Martin	50.00	25.00
❑ 168 Doyle Lade	50.00	25.00
❑ 169 Jeff Heath	60.00	30.00
❑ 170 Bill Rigney	60.00	30.00
❑ 171 Dick Fowler	50.00	25.00
❑ 172 Eddie Pellagrini	50.00	25.00
❑ 173 Eddie Stewart	50.00	25.00
❑ 174 Terry Moore RC	75.00	38.00
❑ 175 Luke Appling	125.00	60.00
❑ 176 Ken Raffensberger	50.00	25.00
❑ 177 Stan Lopata	60.00	30.00
❑ 178 Tom Brown	60.00	30.00
❑ 179 Hugh Casey	75.00	38.00
❑ 180 Connie Berry	50.00	25.00
❑ 181 Gus Niarhos	50.00	25.00
❑ 182 Hal Peck	50.00	25.00
❑ 183 Lou Stringer	50.00	25.00
❑ 184 Bob Chipman	50.00	25.00
❑ 185 Pete Reiser	75.00	38.00
❑ 186 Buddy Kerr	50.00	25.00
❑ 187 Phil Marchildon	50.00	25.00
❑ 188 Karl Drews	50.00	25.00
❑ 189 Earl Wooten	50.00	25.00
❑ 190 Jim Hearn	50.00	25.00
❑ 191 Joe Haynes	50.00	25.00
❑ 192 Harry Gumbert	50.00	25.00
❑ 193 Ken Trinkle	50.00	25.00
❑ 194 Ralph Branca RC	100.00	50.00
❑ 195 Eddie Bockman	50.00	25.00
❑ 196 Fred Hutchinson	60.00	30.00
❑ 197 Johnny Lindell	60.00	30.00
❑ 198 Steve Gromek	50.00	25.00
❑ 199 Tex Hughson	50.00	25.00
❑ 200 Jess Dobernic	50.00	25.00
❑ 201 Sibby Sisti	50.00	25.00
❑ 202 Larry Jansen	60.00	30.00
❑ 203 Barney McCosky	50.00	25.00
❑ 204 Bob Savage	50.00	25.00
❑ 205 Dick Sisler	60.00	30.00
❑ 206 Bruce Edwards	50.00	25.00
❑ 207 Johnny Hopp	50.00	25.00
❑ 208 Dizzy Trout	60.00	30.00
❑ 209 Charlie Keller	75.00	38.00
❑ 210 Joe Gordon	75.00	38.00
❑ 211 Boo Ferriss	50.00	25.00
❑ 212 Ralph Hamner	50.00	25.00
❑ 213 Red Barrett	50.00	25.00
❑ 214 Richie Ashburn RC	600.00	300.00
❑ 215 Kirby Higbe	50.00	25.00
❑ 216 Schoolboy Rowe	60.00	30.00
❑ 217 Marino Pieretti	50.00	25.00
❑ 218 Dick Kryhoski	50.00	25.00
❑ 219 Virgil Fire Trucks	60.00	30.00
❑ 220 Johnny McCarthy	50.00	25.00
NY Giants Cap but listed as Sioux City MG		
❑ 221 Bob Muncrief	50.00	25.00
❑ 222 Alex Kellner	50.00	25.00
❑ 223 Bobby Hofman	50.00	25.00
❑ 224 Satchell Paige RC	1200.00	600.00
❑ 225 Jerry Coleman RC	75.00	38.00
❑ 226 Duke Snider RC	1000.00	500.00
❑ 227 Fritz Ostermueller	50.00	25.00
❑ 228 Jackie Mayo	50.00	25.00
❑ 229 Ed Lopat RC	125.00	60.00
❑ 230 Augie Galan	60.00	30.00
❑ 231 Earl Johnson	50.00	25.00
❑ 232 George McQuinn	60.00	30.00
❑ 233 Larry Doby RC	200.00	100.00
❑ 234 Rip Sewell	50.00	25.00
❑ 235 Jim Russell	50.00	25.00
❑ 236 Fred Sanford	50.00	25.00
❑ 237 Monte Kennedy	50.00	25.00
❑ 238 Bob Lemon RC	200.00	100.00
❑ 239 Frank McCormick	50.00	25.00
❑ 240 Babe Young UER	100.00	25.00
(Photo actually Bobby Young)		

1950 Bowman

	NM	Ex
COMPLETE SET (252)	8500.00	4200.00
COMMON CARD (1-72)	50.00	25.00
COMMON CARD (73-252)	15.00	7.50
WRAPPER (1-cent)	250.00	125.00
WRAPPER (5-cent)	250.00	125.00

	NM	Ex
❑ 1 Mel Parnell RC	150.00	30.00
❑ 2 Vern Stephens	60.00	30.00
❑ 3 Dom DiMaggio	80.00	40.00
❑ 4 Gus Zernial RC	60.00	30.00
❑ 5 Bob Kuzava	50.00	25.00
❑ 6 Bob Feller	300.00	150.00
❑ 7 Jim Hegan	60.00	30.00
❑ 8 George Kell	80.00	40.00
❑ 9 Vic Wertz	60.00	30.00
❑ 10 Tommy Henrich	80.00	40.00
❑ 11 Phil Rizzuto	250.00	125.00
❑ 12 Joe Page	80.00	40.00
❑ 13 Ferris Fain	60.00	30.00
❑ 14 Alex Kellner	50.00	25.00
❑ 15 Al Kozar	50.00	25.00
❑ 16 Roy Sievers RC	80.00	40.00
❑ 17 Sid Hudson	50.00	25.00
❑ 18 Eddie Robinson	50.00	25.00
❑ 19 Warren Spahn	300.00	150.00
❑ 20 Bob Elliott	60.00	30.00
❑ 21 Pee Wee Reese	300.00	150.00
❑ 22 Jackie Robinson	1000.00	500.00
❑ 23 Don Newcombe RC	150.00	75.00
❑ 24 Johnny Schmitz	50.00	25.00
❑ 25 Hank Sauer	60.00	30.00
❑ 26 Grady Hatton	50.00	25.00
❑ 27 Herman Wehmeier	50.00	25.00
❑ 28 Bobby Thomson	80.00	40.00
❑ 29 Eddie Stanky	60.00	30.00
❑ 30 Eddie Waitkus	60.00	30.00
❑ 31 Del Ennis	80.00	40.00
❑ 32 Robin Roberts	150.00	75.00
❑ 33 Ralph Kiner	100.00	50.00
❑ 34 Murry Dickson	50.00	25.00
❑ 35 Enos Slaughter	100.00	50.00
❑ 36 Eddie Kazak	60.00	30.00
❑ 37 Luke Appling	80.00	40.00
❑ 38 Bill Wight	50.00	25.00
❑ 39 Larry Doby	100.00	50.00
❑ 40 Bob Lemon	80.00	40.00
❑ 41 Hoot Evers	50.00	25.00
❑ 42 Art Houtteman	50.00	25.00
❑ 43 Bobby Doerr	80.00	40.00
❑ 44 Joe Dobson	50.00	25.00
❑ 45 Al Zarilla	50.00	25.00
❑ 46 Yogi Berra	375.00	190.00
❑ 47 Jerry Coleman	80.00	40.00
❑ 48 Lou Brissie	50.00	25.00
❑ 49 Elmer Valo	50.00	25.00
❑ 50 Dick Kokos	50.00	25.00
❑ 51 Ned Garver	60.00	30.00
❑ 52 Sam Mele	50.00	25.00
❑ 53 Clyde Vollmer	50.00	25.00
❑ 54 Gil Coan	50.00	25.00
❑ 55 Buddy Kerr	50.00	25.00
❑ 56 Del Crandall RC	60.00	30.00
❑ 57 Vern Bickford	50.00	25.00
❑ 58 Carl Furillo	80.00	40.00
❑ 59 Ralph Branca	80.00	40.00
❑ 60 Andy Pafko	60.00	30.00
❑ 61 Bob Rush	50.00	25.00
❑ 62 Ted Kluszewski	125.00	60.00
❑ 63 Ewell Blackwell	60.00	30.00
❑ 64 Alvin Dark	60.00	30.00
❑ 65 Dave Koslo	50.00	25.00
❑ 66 Larry Jansen	60.00	30.00
❑ 67 Willie Jones	60.00	30.00
❑ 68 Curt Simmons	60.00	30.00
❑ 69 Wally Westlake	50.00	25.00
❑ 70 Bob Chesnes	50.00	25.00
❑ 71 Red Schoendienst	80.00	40.00
❑ 72 Howie Pollet	50.00	25.00
❑ 73 Willard Marshall	15.00	7.50
❑ 74 Johnny Antonelli RC	60.00	30.00
❑ 75 Roy Campanella	275.00	140.00
❑ 76 Rex Barney	40.00	20.00
❑ 77 Duke Snider	275.00	140.00
❑ 78 Mickey Owen	25.00	12.50
❑ 79 Johnny VanderMeer	40.00	20.00
❑ 80 Howard Fox	15.00	7.50
❑ 81 Ron Northey	15.00	7.50
❑ 82 Whitey Lockman	25.00	12.50
❑ 83 Sheldon Jones	15.00	7.50
❑ 84 Richie Ashburn	100.00	50.00
❑ 85 Ken Heintzelman	15.00	7.50
❑ 86 Stan Rojek	15.00	7.50
❑ 87 Bill Werle	15.00	7.50
❑ 88 Marty Marion	40.00	20.00
❑ 89 Red Munger	15.00	7.50
❑ 90 Harry Brecheen	40.00	20.00
❑ 91 Cass Michaels	15.00	7.50
❑ 92 Hank Majeski	15.00	7.50
❑ 93 Gene Bearden	40.00	20.00
❑ 94 Lou Boudreau	60.00	30.00
❑ 95 Aaron Robinson	15.00	7.50
❑ 96 Virgil Trucks	25.00	12.50
❑ 97 Maurice McDermott RC	15.00	7.50
❑ 98 Ted Williams	1000.00	500.00
❑ 99 Billy Goodman	25.00	12.50
❑ 100 Vic Raschi	60.00	30.00
❑ 101 Bobby Brown	60.00	30.00
❑ 102 Billy Johnson	25.00	12.50
❑ 103 Eddie Joost	15.00	7.50
❑ 104 Sam Chapman	15.00	7.50
❑ 105 Bob Dillinger	15.00	7.50
❑ 106 Cliff Fannin	15.00	7.50
❑ 107 Sam Dente	15.00	7.50
❑ 108 Ray Scarborough	15.00	7.50
❑ 109 Sid Gordon	15.00	7.50

	Player	NM	Ex
❑ 110	Tommy Holmes	25.00	12.50
❑ 111	Walker Cooper	15.00	7.50
❑ 112	Gil Hodges	125.00	60.00
❑ 113	Gene Hermanski	15.00	7.50
❑ 114	Wayne Terwilliger RC	15.00	7.50
❑ 115	Roy Smalley	15.00	7.50
❑ 116	Virgil Stallcup	15.00	7.50
❑ 117	Bill Rigney	15.00	7.50
❑ 118	Clint Hartung	15.00	7.50
❑ 119	Dick Sisler	25.00	12.50
❑ 120	John Thompson	15.00	7.50
❑ 121	Andy Seminick	25.00	12.50
❑ 122	Johnny Hopp	25.00	12.50
❑ 123	Dino Restelli	15.00	7.50
❑ 124	Clyde McCullough	15.00	7.50
❑ 125	Del Rice	15.00	7.50
❑ 126	Al Brazle	15.00	7.50
❑ 127	Dave Philley	15.00	7.50
❑ 128	Phil Masi	15.00	7.50
❑ 129	Joe Gordon	25.00	12.50
❑ 130	Dale Mitchell	25.00	12.50
❑ 131	Steve Gromek	15.00	7.50
❑ 132	Mickey Vernon	25.00	12.50
❑ 133	Don Kolloway	15.00	7.50
❑ 134	Paul Trout	15.00	7.50
❑ 135	Pat Mullin	15.00	7.50
❑ 136	Warren Rosar	15.00	7.50
❑ 137	Johnny Pesky	25.00	12.50
❑ 138	Allie Reynolds	60.00	30.00
❑ 139	Johnny Mize	80.00	40.00
❑ 140	Pete Suder	15.00	7.50
❑ 141	Joe Coleman	25.00	12.50
❑ 142	Sherman Lollar RC	40.00	20.00
❑ 143	Eddie Stewart	15.00	7.50
❑ 144	Al Evans	15.00	7.50
❑ 145	Jack Graham	15.00	7.50
❑ 146	Floyd Baker	15.00	7.50
❑ 147	Mike Garcia RC	40.00	20.00
❑ 148	Early Wynn	80.00	40.00
❑ 149	Bob Swift	15.00	7.50
❑ 150	George Vico	15.00	7.50
❑ 151	Fred Hutchinson	25.00	12.50
❑ 152	Ellis Kinder RC	15.00	7.50
❑ 153	Walt Masterson	15.00	7.50
❑ 154	Gus Niarhos	15.00	7.50
❑ 155	Frank Shea	25.00	12.50
❑ 156	Fred Sanford	25.00	12.50
❑ 157	Mike Guerra	15.00	7.50
❑ 158	Paul Lehner	15.00	7.50
❑ 159	Joe Tipton	15.00	7.50
❑ 160	Mickey Harris	15.00	7.50
❑ 161	Sherry Robertson	15.00	7.50
❑ 162	Eddie Yost	25.00	12.50
❑ 163	Earl Torgeson	15.00	7.50
❑ 164	Sibby Sisti	15.00	7.50
❑ 165	Bruce Edwards	15.00	7.50
❑ 166	Joe Hatton	15.00	7.50
❑ 167	Preacher Roe	60.00	30.00
❑ 168	Bob Scheffing	15.00	7.50
❑ 169	Hank Edwards	15.00	7.50
❑ 170	Dutch Leonard	15.00	7.50
❑ 171	Harry Gumbert	15.00	7.50
❑ 172	Peanuts Lowrey	15.00	7.50
❑ 173	Lloyd Merriman	15.00	7.50
❑ 174	Hank Thompson RC	40.00	20.00
❑ 175	Monte Kennedy	15.00	7.50
❑ 176	Sylvester Donnelly	15.00	7.50
❑ 177	Hank Borowy	15.00	7.50
❑ 178	Ed Fitzgerald	15.00	7.50
❑ 179	Chuck Diering	15.00	7.50
❑ 180	Harry Walker	25.00	12.50
❑ 181	Marino Pieretti	15.00	7.50
❑ 182	Sam Zoldak	15.00	7.50
❑ 183	Mickey Haefner	15.00	7.50
❑ 184	Randy Gumpert	15.00	7.50
❑ 185	Howie Judson	15.00	7.50
❑ 186	Ken Keltner	25.00	12.50
❑ 187	Lou Stringer	15.00	7.50
❑ 188	Earl Johnson	15.00	7.50
❑ 189	Owen Friend	15.00	7.50
❑ 190	Ken Wood	15.00	7.50
❑ 191	Dick Starr	15.00	7.50
❑ 192	Bob Chipman	15.00	7.50
❑ 193	Pete Reiser	40.00	20.00
❑ 194	Billy Cox	60.00	30.00
❑ 195	Phil Cavarretta	40.00	20.00
❑ 196	Doyle Lade	15.00	7.50
❑ 197	Johnny Wyrostek	15.00	7.50
❑ 198	Danny Litwhiler	15.00	7.50
❑ 199	Jack Kramer	15.00	7.50
❑ 200	Kirby Higbe	25.00	12.50
❑ 201	Pete Castiglione	15.00	7.50
❑ 202	Cliff Chambers	15.00	7.50
❑ 203	Danny Murtaugh	25.00	12.50
❑ 204	Granny Hamner RC	40.00	20.00
❑ 205	Mike Goliat	15.00	7.50
❑ 206	Stan Lopata	25.00	12.50
❑ 207	Max Lanier	15.00	7.50
❑ 208	Jim Hearn	15.00	7.50
❑ 209	Johnny Lindell	15.00	7.50
❑ 210	Ted Gray	15.00	7.50
❑ 211	Charlie Keller	40.00	20.00
❑ 212	Jerry Priddy	15.00	7.50
❑ 213	Carl Scheib	15.00	7.50
❑ 214	Dick Fowler	15.00	7.50
❑ 215	Ed Lopat	60.00	30.00
❑ 216	Bob Porterfield	25.00	12.50
❑ 217	Casey Stengel MG	125.00	60.00
❑ 218	Cliff Mapes RC	25.00	12.50
❑ 219	Hank Bauer RC	100.00	50.00
❑ 220	Leo Durocher MG	60.00	30.00
❑ 221	Don Mueller RC	40.00	20.00
❑ 222	Bobby Morgan	15.00	7.50
❑ 223	Jim Russell	15.00	7.50
❑ 224	Jack Banta	15.00	7.50
❑ 225	Eddie Sawyer MG	25.00	12.50
❑ 226	Jim Konstanty RC	60.00	30.00
❑ 227	Bob Miller	25.00	12.50
❑ 228	Bill Nicholson	25.00	12.50
❑ 229	Frank Frisch MG	60.00	30.00
❑ 230	Bill Serena	15.00	7.50
❑ 231	Preston Ward	15.00	7.50
❑ 232	Al Rosen RC	60.00	30.00
❑ 233	Allie Clark	15.00	7.50
❑ 234	Bobby Shantz RC	60.00	30.00
❑ 235	Harold Gilbert	15.00	7.50
❑ 236	Bob Cain	15.00	7.50
❑ 237	Bill Salkeld	15.00	7.50
❑ 238	Nippy Jones	15.00	7.50
❑ 239	Bill Howerton	15.00	7.50
❑ 240	Eddie Lake	15.00	7.50
❑ 241	Neil Berry	15.00	7.50
❑ 242	Dick Kryhoski	15.00	7.50
❑ 243	Johnny Groth	15.00	7.50
❑ 244	Dale Coogan	15.00	7.50
❑ 245	Al Papai	15.00	7.50
❑ 246	Walt Dropo RC	40.00	20.00
❑ 247	Irv Noren RC	25.00	12.50
❑ 248	Sam Jethroe RC	60.00	30.00
❑ 249	Snuffy Stirnweiss	25.00	12.50
❑ 250	Ray Coleman	15.00	7.50
❑ 251	Les Moss	15.00	7.50
❑ 252	Billy DeMars RC	60.00	16.50

1951 Bowman

	NM	Ex
COMPLETE SET (324)	20000.00	10000.00
COMMON CARD (1-252)	18.00	9.00
COMMON (253-324)	50.00	25.00
WRAPPER (1-cent)	200.00	100.00
WRAPPER (5-cent)	250.00	125.00

	Player	NM	Ex
❑ 1	Whitey Ford RC	1400.00	350.00
❑ 2	Yogi Berra	400.00	200.00
❑ 3	Robin Roberts	75.00	38.00
❑ 4	Del Ennis	25.00	12.50
❑ 5	Dale Mitchell	25.00	12.50
❑ 6	Don Newcombe	60.00	30.00
❑ 7	Gil Hodges	125.00	60.00
❑ 8	Paul Lehner	18.00	9.00
❑ 9	Sam Chapman	18.00	9.00
❑ 10	Red Schoendienst	60.00	30.00
❑ 11	Red Munger	18.00	9.00
❑ 12	Hank Majeski	18.00	9.00
❑ 13	Eddie Stanky	25.00	12.50
❑ 14	Alvin Dark	40.00	20.00
❑ 15	Johnny Pesky	25.00	12.50
❑ 16	Maurice McDermott	18.00	9.00
❑ 17	Pete Castiglione	18.00	9.00
❑ 18	Gil Coan	18.00	9.00
❑ 19	Sid Gordon	18.00	9.00
❑ 20	Del Crandall UER (Misspelled Crandell on card)	25.00	12.50
❑ 21	Snuffy Stirnweiss wearing St.L.Browns hat	25.00	12.50
❑ 22	Hank Sauer	25.00	12.50
❑ 23	Hoot Evers	18.00	9.00
❑ 24	Ewell Blackwell	40.00	20.00
❑ 25	Vic Raschi	60.00	30.00
❑ 26	Phil Rizzuto	125.00	60.00
❑ 27	Jim Konstanty	25.00	12.50
❑ 28	Eddie Waitkus	18.00	9.00
❑ 29	Allie Clark	18.00	9.00
❑ 30	Bob Feller	125.00	60.00
❑ 31	Roy Campanella	250.00	125.00
❑ 32	Duke Snider	250.00	125.00
❑ 33	Bob Hooper	18.00	9.00
❑ 34	Marty Marion	40.00	20.00
❑ 35	Al Zarilla	18.00	9.00
❑ 36	Joe Dobson	18.00	9.00
❑ 37	Whitey Lockman	40.00	20.00
❑ 38	Al Evans	18.00	9.00
❑ 39	Ray Scarborough	18.00	9.00
❑ 40	Gus Bell RC	60.00	30.00
❑ 41	Eddie Yost	25.00	12.50
❑ 42	Vern Bickford	18.00	9.00
❑ 43	Billy DeMars	18.00	9.00
❑ 44	Roy Smalley	18.00	9.00
❑ 45	Art Houtteman	18.00	9.00
❑ 46	George Kell 1941 UER	60.00	30.00
❑ 47	Grady Hatton	18.00	9.00
❑ 48	Ken Raffensberger	18.00	9.00
❑ 49	Jerry Coleman	25.00	12.50
❑ 50	Johnny Mize	75.00	38.00
❑ 51	Andy Seminick	18.00	9.00
❑ 52	Dick Sisler	40.00	20.00
❑ 53	Bob Lemon	60.00	30.00
❑ 54	Ray Boone RC	40.00	20.00
❑ 55	Gene Hermanski	18.00	9.00
❑ 56	Ralph Branca	60.00	30.00
❑ 57	Alex Kellner	18.00	9.00
❑ 58	Enos Slaughter	60.00	30.00
❑ 59	Randy Gumpert	18.00	9.00
❑ 60	Chico Carrasquel RC	60.00	30.00
❑ 61	Jim Hearn	25.00	12.50
❑ 62	Lou Boudreau	60.00	30.00
❑ 63	Bob Dillinger	18.00	9.00
❑ 64	Bill Werle	18.00	9.00
❑ 65	Mickey Vernon	40.00	20.00
❑ 66	Bob Elliott	25.00	12.50
❑ 67	Roy Sievers	25.00	12.50
❑ 68	Dick Kokos	18.00	9.00
❑ 69	Johnny Schmitz	18.00	9.00
❑ 70	Ron Northey	18.00	9.00
❑ 71	Jerry Priddy	18.00	9.00
❑ 72	Lloyd Merriman	18.00	9.00
❑ 73	Tommy Byrne	18.00	9.00
❑ 74	Billy Johnson	25.00	12.50
❑ 75	Russ Meyer RC	25.00	12.50
❑ 76	Stan Lopata	25.00	12.50
❑ 77	Mike Goliat	18.00	9.00
❑ 78	Early Wynn	60.00	30.00
❑ 79	Jim Hegan	25.00	12.50
❑ 80	Pee Wee Reese	150.00	75.00
❑ 81	Carl Furillo	60.00	30.00
❑ 82	Joe Tipton	18.00	9.00
❑ 83	Carl Scheib	18.00	9.00
❑ 84	Barney McCosky	18.00	9.00

	No.	Player	NM	Ex
❑	85	Eddie Kazak	18.00	9.00
❑	86	Harry Brecheen	25.00	12.50
❑	87	Floyd Baker	18.00	9.00
❑	88	Eddie Robinson	18.00	9.00
❑	89	Hank Thompson	25.00	12.50
❑	90	Dave Koslo	18.00	9.00
❑	91	Clyde Vollmer	18.00	9.00
❑	92	Vern Stephens	25.00	12.50
❑	93	Danny O'Connell	18.00	9.00
❑	94	Clyde McCullough	18.00	9.00
❑	95	Sherry Robertson	18.00	9.00
❑	96	Sandy Consuegra	18.00	9.00
❑	97	Bob Kuzava	18.00	9.00
❑	98	Willard Marshall	18.00	9.00
❑	99	Earl Torgeson	18.00	9.00
❑	100	Sherm Lollar	25.00	12.50
❑	101	Owen Friend	18.00	9.00
❑	102	Dutch Leonard	18.00	9.00
❑	103	Andy Pafko	40.00	20.00
❑	104	Virgil Trucks	25.00	12.50
❑	105	Don Kolloway	18.00	9.00
❑	106	Pat Mullin	18.00	9.00
❑	107	Johnny Wyrostek	18.00	9.00
❑	108	Virgil Stallcup	18.00	9.00
❑	109	Allie Reynolds	60.00	30.00
❑	110	Bobby Brown	40.00	20.00
❑	111	Curt Simmons	25.00	12.50
❑	112	Willie Jones	18.00	9.00
❑	113	Bill Nicholson	18.00	9.00
❑	114	Sam Zoldak	18.00	9.00
		Pictured in Indians uniform		
❑	115	Steve Gromek	18.00	9.00
❑	116	Bruce Edwards	18.00	9.00
❑	117	Eddie Miksis	18.00	9.00
❑	118	Preacher Roe	60.00	30.00
❑	119	Eddie Joost	18.00	9.00
❑	120	Joe Coleman	25.00	12.50
❑	121	Jerry Staley	18.00	9.00
❑	122	Joe Garagiola RC	100.00	50.00
❑	123	Howie Judson	18.00	9.00
❑	124	Gus Niarhos	18.00	9.00
❑	125	Bill Rigney	25.00	12.50
❑	126	Bobby Thomson	60.00	30.00
❑	127	Sal Maglie RC	60.00	30.00
❑	128	Ellis Kinder	18.00	9.00
❑	129	Matt Batts	18.00	9.00
❑	130	Tom Saffell	18.00	9.00
❑	131	Cliff Chambers	18.00	9.00
❑	132	Cass Michaels	18.00	9.00
❑	133	Sam Dente	18.00	9.00
❑	134	Warren Spahn	125.00	60.00
❑	135	Walker Cooper	18.00	9.00
❑	136	Ray Coleman	18.00	9.00
❑	137	Dick Starr	18.00	9.00
❑	138	Phil Cavarretta	25.00	12.50
❑	139	Doyle Lade	18.00	9.00
❑	140	Eddie Lake	18.00	9.00
❑	141	Fred Hutchinson	25.00	12.50
❑	142	Aaron Robinson	18.00	9.00
❑	143	Ted Kluszewski	80.00	40.00
❑	144	Herman Wehmeier	18.00	9.00
❑	145	Fred Sanford	25.00	12.50
❑	146	Johnny Hopp	25.00	12.50
❑	147	Ken Heintzelman	18.00	9.00
❑	148	Granny Hamner	18.00	9.00
❑	149	Bubba Church	18.00	9.00
❑	150	Mike Garcia	25.00	12.50
❑	151	Larry Doby	60.00	30.00
❑	152	Cal Abrams	18.00	9.00
❑	153	Rex Barney	25.00	12.50
❑	154	Pete Suder	18.00	9.00
❑	155	Lou Brissie	18.00	9.00
❑	156	Del Rice	18.00	9.00
❑	157	Al Brazle	18.00	9.00
❑	158	Chuck Diering	18.00	9.00
❑	159	Eddie Stewart	18.00	9.00
❑	160	Phil Masi	18.00	9.00
❑	161	Wes Westrum RC	18.00	9.00
❑	162	Larry Jansen	25.00	12.50
❑	163	Monte Kennedy	18.00	9.00
❑	164	Bill Wight	18.00	9.00
❑	165	Ted Williams UER	800.00	400.00
		Wrong birthdate		
❑	166	Stan Rojek	18.00	9.00
		Pictured in Pirates uniform		
❑	167	Murry Dickson	18.00	9.00
❑	168	Sam Mele	18.00	9.00
❑	169	Sid Hudson	18.00	9.00
❑	170	Sibby Sisti	18.00	9.00
❑	171	Buddy Kerr	18.00	9.00
❑	172	Ned Garver	18.00	9.00
❑	173	Hank Arft	18.00	9.00
❑	174	Mickey Owen	25.00	12.50
❑	175	Wayne Terwilliger	18.00	9.00
❑	176	Vic Wertz	40.00	20.00
❑	177	Charlie Keller	25.00	12.50
❑	178	Ted Gray	18.00	9.00
❑	179	Danny Litwhiler	18.00	9.00
❑	180	Howie Fox	18.00	9.00
❑	181	Casey Stengel MG	75.00	38.00
❑	182	Tom Ferrick	18.00	9.00
❑	183	Hank Bauer	60.00	30.00
❑	184	Eddie Sawyer MG	40.00	20.00
❑	185	Jimmy Bloodworth	18.00	9.00
❑	186	Richie Ashburn	100.00	50.00
❑	187	Al Rosen	40.00	20.00
❑	188	Bobby Avila RC	25.00	12.50
❑	189	Erv Palica	18.00	9.00
❑	190	Joe Hatten	18.00	9.00
❑	191	Billy Hitchcock	18.00	9.00
❑	192	Hank Wyse	18.00	9.00
❑	193	Ted Wilks	18.00	9.00
❑	194	Peanuts Lowrey	18.00	9.00
❑	195	Paul Richards MG	25.00	12.50
		(Caricature)		
❑	196	Billy Pierce RC	60.00	30.00
❑	197	Bob Cain	18.00	9.00
❑	198	Monte Irvin RC	100.00	50.00
❑	199	Sheldon Jones	18.00	9.00
❑	200	Jack Kramer	18.00	9.00
		Pictured in NY Giants uniform		
❑	201	Steve O'Neill MG	18.00	9.00
❑	202	Mike Guerra	18.00	9.00
❑	203	Vernon Law RC	60.00	30.00
❑	204	Vic Lombardi	18.00	9.00
❑	205	Mickey Grasso	18.00	9.00
❑	206	Conrado Marrero	18.00	9.00
❑	207	Billy Southworth MG	18.00	9.00
❑	208	Blix Donnelly	18.00	9.00
❑	209	Ken Wood	18.00	9.00
❑	210	Les Moss	18.00	9.00
		Pictured in St.L.Browns uniform		
❑	211	Hal Jeffcoat	18.00	9.00
❑	212	Bob Rush	18.00	9.00
❑	213	Neil Berry	18.00	9.00
❑	214	Bob Swift	18.00	9.00
❑	215	Ken Peterson	18.00	9.00
❑	216	Connie Ryan	18.00	9.00
❑	217	Joe Page	25.00	12.50
❑	218	Ed Lopat	60.00	30.00
❑	219	Gene Woodling RC	60.00	30.00
❑	220	Bob Miller	18.00	9.00
❑	221	Dick Whitman	18.00	9.00
❑	222	Thurman Tucker	18.00	9.00
❑	223	Johnny VanderMeer	40.00	20.00
❑	224	Billy Cox	25.00	12.50
❑	225	Dan Bankhead	40.00	20.00
❑	226	Jimmy Dykes MG	18.00	9.00
❑	227	Bobby Shantz UER	25.00	12.50
		Sic, Schantz		
❑	228	Cloyd Boyer	25.00	12.50
❑	229	Bill Howerton	18.00	9.00
		Pictured in St.L.Cardinals uniform		
❑	230	Max Lanier	18.00	9.00
❑	231	Luis Aloma	18.00	9.00
❑	232	Nelson Fox RC	250.00	125.00
❑	233	Leo Durocher MG	60.00	30.00
❑	234	Clint Hartung	25.00	12.50
❑	235	Jack Lohrke	18.00	9.00
❑	236	Warren Rosar	18.00	9.00
❑	237	Billy Goodman	25.00	12.50
❑	238	Pete Reiser	40.00	20.00
❑	239	Bill MacDonald	18.00	9.00
❑	240	Joe Haynes	18.00	9.00
❑	241	Irv Noren	25.00	12.50
❑	242	Sam Jethroe	25.00	12.50
❑	243	Johnny Antonelli	25.00	12.50
❑	244	Cliff Fannin	18.00	9.00
❑	245	John Berardino RC	60.00	30.00
❑	246	Bill Serena	18.00	9.00
❑	247	Bob Ramazzotti	18.00	9.00
❑	248	Johnny Klippstein	18.00	9.00
❑	249	Johnny Groth	18.00	9.00
❑	250	Hank Borowy	18.00	9.00
❑	251	Willard Ramsdell	18.00	9.00
❑	252	Dixie Howell	18.00	9.00
❑	253	Mickey Mantle RC	8500.00	4200.00
❑	254	Jackie Jensen RC	100.00	50.00
❑	255	Milo Candini	50.00	25.00
❑	256	Ken Sylvestri	50.00	25.00
❑	257	Birdie Tebbetts RC	60.00	30.00
❑	258	Luke Easter RC	60.00	30.00
❑	259	Chuck Dressen MG	60.00	30.00
❑	260	Carl Erskine RC	100.00	50.00
❑	261	Wally Moses	60.00	30.00
❑	262	Gus Zernial	60.00	30.00
❑	263	Howie Pollet	60.00	30.00
		Pictured in Cardinals uniform		
❑	264	Don Richmond	50.00	25.00
❑	265	Steve Bilko	50.00	25.00
❑	266	Harry Dorish	50.00	25.00
❑	267	Ken Holcombe	50.00	25.00
❑	268	Don Mueller	60.00	30.00
❑	269	Ray Noble	50.00	25.00
❑	270	Willard Nixon	50.00	25.00
❑	271	Tommy Wright	50.00	25.00
❑	272	Billy Meyer MG	50.00	25.00
❑	273	Danny Murtaugh	60.00	30.00
❑	274	George Metkovich	50.00	25.00
❑	275	Bucky Harris MG	80.00	40.00
❑	276	Frank Quinn	50.00	25.00
❑	277	Roy Hartsfield	50.00	25.00
❑	278	Norman Roy	50.00	25.00
❑	279	Jim Delsing	50.00	25.00
❑	280	Frank Overmire	50.00	25.00
		Pictured in Browns uniform		
❑	281	Al Widmar	50.00	25.00
❑	282	Frank Frisch MG	100.00	50.00
❑	283	Walt Dubiel	50.00	25.00
❑	284	Gene Bearden	60.00	30.00
❑	285	Johnny Lipon	50.00	25.00
❑	286	Bob Usher	50.00	25.00
❑	287	Jim Blackburn	50.00	25.00
❑	288	Bobby Adams	50.00	25.00
❑	289	Cliff Mapes	60.00	30.00
❑	290	Bill Dickey CO	100.00	50.00
❑	291	Tommy Henrich CO	80.00	40.00
❑	292	Eddie Pellegrini	50.00	25.00
❑	293	Ken Johnson	50.00	25.00
❑	294	Jocko Thompson	50.00	25.00
❑	295	Al Lopez MG	125.00	60.00
❑	296	Bob Kennedy	60.00	30.00
❑	297	Dave Philley	50.00	25.00
❑	298	Joe Astroth	50.00	25.00
❑	299	Clyde King	50.00	25.00
❑	300	Hal Rice	50.00	25.00
❑	301	Tommy Glaviano	50.00	25.00
❑	302	Jim Busby	50.00	25.00
❑	303	Marv Rotblatt	50.00	25.00
❑	304	Al Gettell	50.00	25.00
❑	305	Willie Mays RC	3000.00	1500.00
❑	306	Jim Piersall RC	125.00	60.00
❑	307	Walt Masterson	50.00	25.00
❑	308	Ted Beard	50.00	25.00
❑	309	Mel Queen	50.00	25.00
❑	310	Erv Dusak	50.00	25.00
❑	311	Mickey Harris	50.00	25.00
❑	312	Gene Mauch RC	60.00	30.00
❑	313	Ray Mueller	50.00	25.00
❑	314	Johnny Sain	80.00	40.00
❑	315	Zack Taylor MG	50.00	25.00
❑	316	Duane Pillette	50.00	25.00
❑	317	Smoky Burgess RC	80.00	40.00
❑	318	Warren Hacker	50.00	25.00
❑	319	Red Rolfe MG	60.00	30.00
❑	320	Hal White	50.00	25.00
❑	321	Earl Johnson	50.00	25.00
❑	322	Luke Sewell MG	60.00	30.00
❑	323	Joe Adcock RC	80.00	40.00
❑	324	Johnny Pramesa RC	125.00	38.00

1952 Bowman

	NM	Ex
COMPLETE SET (252)	8500.00	4200.00
COMMON CARD (1-216)	15.00	6.75
COMMON (217-252)	60.00	30.00
WRAPPER (1-cent)	200.00	100.00

WRAPPER (5-cent)	100.00	50.00
❑ 1 Yogi Berra	600.00	190.00
❑ 2 Bobby Thomson	40.00	20.00
❑ 3 Fred Hutchinson	25.00	12.50
❑ 4 Robin Roberts	60.00	30.00
❑ 5 Minnie Minoso RC	125.00	60.00
❑ 6 Virgil Stallcup	15.00	7.50
❑ 7 Mike Garcia	25.00	12.50
❑ 8 Pee Wee Reese	150.00	75.00
❑ 9 Vern Stephens	25.00	12.50
❑ 10 Bob Hooper	15.00	7.50
❑ 11 Ralph Kiner	60.00	30.00
❑ 12 Max Surkont	15.00	7.50
❑ 13 Cliff Mapes	15.00	7.50
❑ 14 Cliff Chambers	15.00	7.50
❑ 15 Sam Mele	15.00	7.50
❑ 16 Turk Lown	15.00	7.50
❑ 17 Ed Lopat	40.00	20.00
❑ 18 Don Mueller	25.00	12.50
❑ 19 Bob Cain	15.00	7.50
❑ 20 Willie Jones	15.00	7.50
❑ 21 Nellie Fox	100.00	50.00
❑ 22 Willard Ramsdell	15.00	7.50
❑ 23 Bob Lemon	60.00	30.00
❑ 24 Carl Furillo	40.00	20.00
❑ 25 Mickey McDermott	15.00	7.50
❑ 26 Eddie Joost	15.00	7.50
❑ 27 Joe Garagiola	40.00	20.00
❑ 28 Roy Hartsfield	15.00	7.50
❑ 29 Ned Garver	15.00	7.50
❑ 30 Red Schoendienst	60.00	30.00
❑ 31 Eddie Yost	25.00	12.50
❑ 32 Eddie Miksis	15.00	7.50
❑ 33 Gil McDougald RC	80.00	40.00
❑ 34 Alvin Dark	25.00	12.50
❑ 35 Granny Hamner	15.00	7.50
❑ 36 Cass Michaels	15.00	7.50
❑ 37 Vic Raschi	25.00	12.50
❑ 38 Whitey Lockman	25.00	12.50
❑ 39 Vic Wertz	25.00	12.50
❑ 40 Bubba Church	15.00	7.50
❑ 41 Chico Carrasquel	25.00	12.50
❑ 42 Johnny Wyrostek	15.00	7.50
❑ 43 Bob Feller	150.00	75.00
❑ 44 Roy Campanella	250.00	125.00
❑ 45 Johnny Pesky	25.00	12.50
❑ 46 Carl Scheib	15.00	7.50
❑ 47 Pete Castiglione	15.00	7.50
❑ 48 Vern Bickford	15.00	7.50
❑ 49 Jim Hearn	15.00	7.50
❑ 50 Jerry Staley	15.00	7.50
❑ 51 Gil Coan	15.00	7.50
❑ 52 Phil Rizzuto	150.00	75.00
❑ 53 Richie Ashburn	100.00	50.00
❑ 54 Billy Pierce	25.00	12.50
❑ 55 Ken Raffensberger	15.00	7.50
❑ 56 Clyde King	25.00	12.50
❑ 57 Clyde Vollmer	15.00	7.50
❑ 58 Hank Majeski	15.00	7.50
❑ 59 Murry Dickson	15.00	7.50
❑ 60 Sid Gordon	15.00	7.50
❑ 61 Tommy Byrne	15.00	7.50
❑ 62 Joe Presko	15.00	7.50
❑ 63 Irv Noren	15.00	7.50
❑ 64 Roy Smalley	15.00	7.50
❑ 65 Hank Bauer	40.00	20.00
❑ 66 Sal Maglie	25.00	12.50
❑ 67 Johnny Groth	15.00	7.50
❑ 68 Jim Busby	15.00	7.50
❑ 69 Joe Adcock	25.00	12.50
❑ 70 Carl Erskine	40.00	20.00
❑ 71 Vernon Law	25.00	12.50
❑ 72 Earl Torgeson	15.00	7.50
❑ 73 Jerry Coleman	25.00	12.50
❑ 74 Wes Westrum	25.00	12.50
❑ 75 George Kell	60.00	30.00
❑ 76 Del Ennis	25.00	12.50
❑ 77 Eddie Robinson	15.00	7.50
❑ 78 Lloyd Merriman	15.00	7.50
❑ 79 Lou Brissie	15.00	7.50
❑ 80 Gil Hodges	90.00	45.00
❑ 81 Billy Goodman	25.00	12.50
❑ 82 Gus Zernial	25.00	12.50
❑ 83 Howie Pollet	15.00	7.50
❑ 84 Sam Jethroe	25.00	12.50
❑ 85 Marty Marion CO	25.00	12.50
❑ 86 Cal Abrams	15.00	7.50
❑ 87 Mickey Vernon	25.00	12.50
❑ 88 Bruce Edwards	15.00	7.50
❑ 89 Billy Hitchcock	15.00	7.50
❑ 90 Larry Jansen	25.00	12.50
❑ 91 Don Kolloway	15.00	7.50
❑ 92 Eddie Waitkus	25.00	12.50
❑ 93 Paul Richards MG	25.00	12.50
❑ 94 Luke Sewell MG	25.00	12.50
❑ 95 Luke Easter	25.00	12.50
❑ 96 Ralph Branca	25.00	12.50
❑ 97 Willard Marshall	15.00	7.50
❑ 98 Jimmy Dykes MG	25.00	12.50
❑ 99 Clyde McCullough	15.00	7.50
❑ 100 Sibby Sisti	15.00	7.50
❑ 101 Mickey Mantle	2000.00	1000.00
❑ 102 Peanuts Lowrey	15.00	7.50
❑ 103 Joe Haynes	15.00	7.50
❑ 104 Hal Jeffcoat	15.00	7.50
❑ 105 Bobby Brown	25.00	12.50
❑ 106 Randy Gumpert	15.00	7.50
❑ 107 Del Rice	15.00	7.50
❑ 108 George Metkovich	15.00	7.50
❑ 109 Tom Morgan	15.00	7.50
❑ 110 Max Lanier	15.00	7.50
❑ 111 Hoot Evers	15.00	7.50
❑ 112 Smoky Burgess	25.00	12.50
❑ 113 Al Zarilla	15.00	7.50
❑ 114 Frank Hiller	15.00	7.50
❑ 115 Larry Doby	60.00	30.00
❑ 116 Duke Snider	200.00	100.00
❑ 117 Bill Wight	15.00	7.50
❑ 118 Ray Murray	15.00	7.50
❑ 119 Bill Howerton	15.00	7.50
❑ 120 Chet Nichols	15.00	7.50
❑ 121 Al Corwin	15.00	7.50
❑ 122 Billy Johnson	15.00	7.50
❑ 123 Sid Hudson	15.00	7.50
❑ 124 Birdie Tebbetts	15.00	7.50
❑ 125 Howie Fox	15.00	7.50
❑ 126 Phil Cavarretta	25.00	12.50
❑ 127 Dick Sisler	15.00	7.50
❑ 128 Don Newcombe	60.00	30.00
❑ 129 Gus Niarhos	15.00	7.50
❑ 130 Allie Clark	15.00	7.50
❑ 131 Bob Swift	15.00	7.50
❑ 132 Dave Cole	15.00	7.50
❑ 133 Dick Kryhoski	15.00	7.50
❑ 134 Al Brazle	15.00	7.50
❑ 135 Mickey Harris	15.00	7.50
❑ 136 Gene Hermanski	15.00	7.50
❑ 137 Stan Rojek	15.00	7.50
❑ 138 Ted Wilks	15.00	7.50
❑ 139 Jerry Priddy	15.00	7.50
❑ 140 Ray Scarborough	15.00	7.50
❑ 141 Hank Edwards	15.00	7.50
❑ 142 Early Wynn	60.00	30.00
❑ 143 Sandy Consuegra	15.00	7.50
❑ 144 Joe Hatton	15.00	7.50
❑ 145 Johnny Mize	60.00	30.00
❑ 146 Leo Durocher MG	60.00	30.00
❑ 147 Marlin Stuart	15.00	7.50
❑ 148 Ken Heintzelman	15.00	7.50
❑ 149 Howie Judson	15.00	7.50
❑ 150 Herman Wehmeier	15.00	7.50
❑ 151 Al Rosen	25.00	12.50
❑ 152 Billy Cox	15.00	7.50
❑ 153 Fred Hatfield	15.00	7.50
❑ 154 Ferris Fain	25.00	12.50
❑ 155 Billy Meyer MG	15.00	7.50
❑ 156 Warren Spahn	125.00	60.00
❑ 157 Jim Delsing	15.00	7.50
❑ 158 Bucky Harris MG	40.00	20.00
❑ 159 Dutch Leonard	15.00	7.50
❑ 160 Eddie Stanky	25.00	12.50
❑ 161 Jackie Jensen	40.00	20.00
❑ 162 Monte Irvin	60.00	30.00
❑ 163 Johnny Lipon	15.00	7.50
❑ 164 Connie Ryan	15.00	7.50
❑ 165 Saul Rogovin	15.00	7.50
❑ 166 Bobby Adams	15.00	7.50
❑ 167 Bobby Avila	25.00	12.50
❑ 168 Preacher Roe	25.00	12.50
❑ 169 Walt Dropo	25.00	12.50
❑ 170 Joe Astroth	15.00	7.50
❑ 171 Mel Queen	15.00	7.50
❑ 172 Ebba St.Claire	15.00	7.50
❑ 173 Gene Bearden	15.00	7.50
❑ 174 Mickey Grasso	15.00	7.50
❑ 175 Randy Jackson	15.00	7.50
❑ 176 Harry Brecheen	25.00	12.50
❑ 177 Gene Woodling	25.00	12.50
❑ 178 Dave Williams RC	25.00	12.50
❑ 179 Pete Suder	15.00	7.50
❑ 180 Ed Fitzgerald	15.00	7.50
❑ 181 Joe Collins RC	25.00	12.50
❑ 182 Dave Koslo	15.00	7.50
❑ 183 Pat Mullin	15.00	7.50
❑ 184 Curt Simmons	25.00	12.50
❑ 185 Eddie Stewart	15.00	7.50
❑ 186 Frank Smith	15.00	7.50
❑ 187 Jim Hegan	25.00	12.50
❑ 188 Chuck Dressen MG	25.00	12.50
❑ 189 Jimmy Piersall	25.00	12.50
❑ 190 Dick Fowler	15.00	7.50
❑ 191 Bob Friend RC	40.00	20.00
❑ 192 John Cusick	15.00	7.50
❑ 193 Bobby Young	15.00	7.50
❑ 194 Bob Porterfield	15.00	7.50
❑ 195 Frank Baumholtz	15.00	7.50
❑ 196 Stan Musial	600.00	300.00
❑ 197 Charlie Silvera RC	15.00	7.50
❑ 198 Chuck Diering	15.00	7.50
❑ 199 Ted Gray	15.00	7.50
❑ 200 Ken Silvestri	15.00	7.50
❑ 201 Ray Coleman	15.00	7.50
❑ 202 Harry Perkowski	15.00	7.50
❑ 203 Steve Gromek	15.00	7.50
❑ 204 Andy Pafko	25.00	12.50
❑ 205 Walt Masterson	15.00	7.50
❑ 206 Elmer Valo	15.00	7.50
❑ 207 George Strickland	15.00	7.50
❑ 208 Walker Cooper	15.00	7.50
❑ 209 Dick Littlefield	15.00	7.50
❑ 210 Archie Wilson	15.00	7.50
❑ 211 Paul Minner	15.00	7.50
❑ 212 Solly Hemus RC	15.00	7.50
❑ 213 Monte Kennedy	15.00	7.50
❑ 214 Ray Boone	15.00	7.50
❑ 215 Sheldon Jones	15.00	7.50
❑ 216 Matt Batts	15.00	7.50
❑ 217 Casey Stengel MG	150.00	75.00
❑ 218 Willie Mays	1200.00	600.00
❑ 219 Neil Berry	60.00	30.00
❑ 220 Russ Meyer	60.00	30.00
❑ 221 Lou Kretlow	60.00	30.00
❑ 222 Dixie Howell	60.00	30.00
❑ 223 Harry Simpson	60.00	30.00
❑ 224 Johnny Schmitz	60.00	30.00
❑ 225 Del Wilber	60.00	30.00
❑ 226 Alex Kellner	60.00	30.00
❑ 227 Clyde Sukeforth CO	60.00	30.00
❑ 228 Bob Chipman	60.00	30.00
❑ 229 Hank Arft	60.00	30.00
❑ 230 Frank Shea	60.00	30.00
❑ 231 Dee Fondy	60.00	30.00
❑ 232 Enos Slaughter	90.00	45.00
❑ 233 Bob Kuzava	60.00	30.00
❑ 234 Fred Fitzsimmons CO	70.00	35.00
❑ 235 Steve Souchock	60.00	30.00
❑ 236 Tommy Brown	60.00	30.00
❑ 237 Sherm Lollar	70.00	35.00
❑ 238 Roy McMillan RC	70.00	35.00

	NM	Ex
❑ 239 Dale Mitchell	70.00	35.00
❑ 240 Billy Loes RC	70.00	35.00
❑ 241 Mel Parnell	70.00	35.00
❑ 242 Everett Kell	60.00	30.00
❑ 243 Red Munger	60.00	30.00
❑ 244 Lew Burdette RC	80.00	40.00
❑ 245 George Schmees	60.00	30.00
❑ 246 Jerry Snyder	60.00	30.00
❑ 247 Johnny Pramesa	60.00	30.00
❑ 248 Bill Werle Full name in signature	60.00	30.00
❑ 248A Bill Werle Signature on front has no W	60.00	30.00
❑ 249 Hank Thompson	70.00	35.00
❑ 250 Ike Delock	60.00	30.00
❑ 251 Jack Lohrke	60.00	30.00
❑ 252 Frank Crosetti CO	110.00	28.00

1953 Bowman Color

	NM	Ex
COMPLETE SET (160)	16000.00	8000.00
COMMON CARD (1-112)	40.00	20.00
COMMON (113-128)	80.00	40.00
COMMON (129-160)	75.00	38.00
WRAPPER (1-cent)	400.00	200.00
WRAPPER (5-CENT)	300.00	150.00

	NM	Ex
❑ 1 Dave Williams	175.00	35.00
❑ 2 Vic Wertz	50.00	25.00
❑ 3 Sam Jethroe	50.00	25.00
❑ 4 Art Houtteman	40.00	20.00
❑ 5 Sid Gordon	40.00	20.00
❑ 6 Joe Ginsberg	40.00	20.00
❑ 7 Harry Chiti	40.00	20.00
❑ 8 Al Rosen	50.00	25.00
❑ 9 Phil Rizzuto	225.00	110.00
❑ 10 Richie Ashburn	150.00	75.00
❑ 11 Bobby Shantz	50.00	25.00
❑ 12 Carl Erskine	60.00	30.00
❑ 13 Gus Zernial	50.00	25.00
❑ 14 Billy Loes	50.00	25.00
❑ 15 Jim Busby	40.00	20.00
❑ 16 Bob Friend	50.00	25.00
❑ 17 Gerry Staley	40.00	20.00
❑ 18 Nellie Fox	150.00	75.00
❑ 19 Alvin Dark	50.00	25.00
❑ 20 Don Lenhardt	40.00	20.00
❑ 21 Joe Garagiola	60.00	30.00
❑ 22 Bob Porterfield	40.00	20.00
❑ 23 Herman Wehmeier	40.00	20.00
❑ 24 Jackie Jensen	60.00	30.00
❑ 25 Hoot Evers	40.00	20.00
❑ 26 Roy McMillan	50.00	25.00
❑ 27 Vic Raschi	60.00	30.00
❑ 28 Smoky Burgess	50.00	25.00
❑ 29 Bobby Avila	50.00	25.00
❑ 30 Phil Cavarretta	50.00	25.00
❑ 31 Jimmy Dykes MG	50.00	25.00
❑ 32 Stan Musial	700.00	350.00
❑ 33 Pee Wee Reese	800.00	400.00
❑ 34 Gil Coan	40.00	20.00
❑ 35 Maurice McDermott	40.00	20.00
❑ 36 Minnie Minoso	80.00	40.00
❑ 37 Jim Wilson	40.00	20.00
❑ 38 Harry Byrd	40.00	20.00
❑ 39 Paul Richards MG	50.00	25.00
❑ 40 Larry Doby	100.00	50.00
❑ 41 Sammy White	40.00	20.00
❑ 42 Tommy Brown	40.00	20.00
❑ 43 Mike Garcia	50.00	25.00
❑ 44 Yogi Berra Hank Bauer Mickey Mantle	700.00	350.00
❑ 45 Walt Dropo	50.00	25.00
❑ 46 Roy Campanella	350.00	180.00
❑ 47 Ned Garver	40.00	20.00
❑ 48 Hank Sauer	50.00	25.00
❑ 49 Eddie Stanky MG	50.00	25.00
❑ 50 Lou Kretlow	40.00	20.00
❑ 51 Monte Irvin	80.00	40.00
❑ 52 Marty Marion MG	50.00	25.00
❑ 53 Del Rice	40.00	20.00
❑ 54 Chico Carrasquel	40.00	20.00
❑ 55 Leo Durocher MG	80.00	40.00
❑ 56 Bob Cain	40.00	20.00
❑ 57 Lou Boudreau MG	80.00	40.00
❑ 58 Willard Marshall	40.00	20.00
❑ 59 Mickey Mantle	2000.00	1000.00
❑ 60 Granny Hamner	40.00	20.00
❑ 61 George Kell	80.00	40.00
❑ 62 Ted Kluszewski	100.00	50.00
❑ 63 Gil McDougald	80.00	40.00
❑ 64 Curt Simmons	50.00	25.00
❑ 65 Robin Roberts	110.00	55.00
❑ 66 Mel Parnell	50.00	25.00
❑ 67 Mel Clark	40.00	20.00
❑ 68 Allie Reynolds	60.00	30.00
❑ 69 Charlie Grimm MG	50.00	25.00
❑ 70 Clint Courtney	40.00	20.00
❑ 71 Paul Minner	40.00	20.00
❑ 72 Ted Gray	40.00	20.00
❑ 73 Billy Pierce	50.00	25.00
❑ 74 Don Mueller	50.00	25.00
❑ 75 Saul Rogovin	40.00	20.00
❑ 76 Jim Hearn	40.00	20.00
❑ 77 Mickey Grasso	40.00	20.00
❑ 78 Carl Furillo	60.00	30.00
❑ 79 Ray Boone	50.00	25.00
❑ 80 Ralph Kiner	100.00	40.00
❑ 81 Enos Slaughter	100.00	40.00
❑ 82 Joe Astroth	40.00	20.00
❑ 83 Jack Daniels	40.00	20.00
❑ 84 Hank Bauer	60.00	30.00
❑ 85 Solly Hemus	40.00	20.00
❑ 86 Harry Simpson	40.00	20.00
❑ 87 Harry Perkowski	40.00	20.00
❑ 88 Joe Dobson	40.00	20.00
❑ 89 Sandy Consuegra	40.00	20.00
❑ 90 Joe Nuxhall	50.00	25.00
❑ 91 Steve Souchock	40.00	20.00
❑ 92 Gil Hodges	200.00	100.00
❑ 93 Phil Rizzuto and Billy Martin	275.00	140.00
❑ 94 Bob Addis	40.00	20.00
❑ 95 Wally Moses CO	50.00	25.00
❑ 96 Sal Maglie	50.00	25.00
❑ 97 Eddie Mathews	300.00	150.00
❑ 98 Hector Rodriguez	40.00	20.00
❑ 99 Warren Spahn	350.00	180.00
❑ 100 Bill Wight	40.00	20.00
❑ 101 Red Schoendienst	80.00	40.00
❑ 102 Jim Hegan	50.00	25.00
❑ 103 Del Ennis	50.00	25.00
❑ 104 Luke Easter	50.00	25.00
❑ 105 Eddie Joost	40.00	20.00
❑ 106 Ken Raffensberger	40.00	20.00
❑ 107 Alex Kellner	40.00	20.00
❑ 108 Bobby Adams	40.00	20.00
❑ 109 Ken Wood	40.00	20.00
❑ 110 Bob Rush	40.00	20.00
❑ 111 Jim Dyck	40.00	20.00
❑ 112 Toby Atwell	40.00	20.00
❑ 113 Karl Drews	80.00	40.00
❑ 114 Bob Feller	500.00	250.00
❑ 115 Cloyd Boyer	80.00	40.00
❑ 116 Eddie Yost	100.00	50.00
❑ 117 Duke Snider	600.00	300.00
❑ 118 Billy Martin	400.00	200.00
❑ 119 Dale Mitchell	100.00	50.00
❑ 120 Marlin Stuart	80.00	40.00
❑ 121 Yogi Berra	800.00	400.00
❑ 122 Bill Serena	80.00	40.00
❑ 123 Johnny Lipon	80.00	40.00
❑ 124 Charlie Dressen MG	100.00	50.00
❑ 125 Fred Hatfield	80.00	40.00
❑ 126 Al Corwin	80.00	40.00
❑ 127 Dick Kryhoski	80.00	40.00
❑ 128 Whitey Lockman	100.00	50.00
❑ 129 Russ Meyer	75.00	38.00
❑ 130 Cass Michaels	75.00	38.00
❑ 131 Connie Ryan	75.00	38.00
❑ 132 Fred Hutchinson	90.00	45.00
❑ 133 Willie Jones	75.00	38.00
❑ 134 Johnny Pesky	90.00	45.00
❑ 135 Bobby Morgan	75.00	38.00
❑ 136 Jim Brideweser	75.00	38.00
❑ 137 Sam Dente	75.00	38.00
❑ 138 Bubba Church	75.00	38.00
❑ 139 Pete Runnels	90.00	45.00
❑ 140 Al Brazle	75.00	38.00
❑ 141 Frank Shea	75.00	38.00
❑ 142 Larry Miggins	75.00	38.00
❑ 143 Al Lopez MG	110.00	55.00
❑ 144 Warren Hacker	75.00	38.00
❑ 145 George Shuba	90.00	45.00
❑ 146 Early Wynn	200.00	100.00
❑ 147 Clem Koshorek	75.00	38.00
❑ 148 Billy Goodman	90.00	45.00
❑ 149 Al Corwin	75.00	38.00
❑ 150 Carl Scheib	75.00	38.00
❑ 151 Joe Adcock	110.00	55.00
❑ 152 Clyde Vollmer	75.00	38.00
❑ 153 Whitey Ford	700.00	350.00
❑ 154 Turk Lown	75.00	38.00
❑ 155 Allie Clark	75.00	38.00
❑ 156 Max Surkont	75.00	38.00
❑ 157 Sherm Lollar	90.00	45.00
❑ 158 Howard Fox	75.00	38.00
❑ 159 Mickey Vernon UER (Photo actually Floyd Baker)	90.00	45.00
❑ 160 Cal Abrams	250.00	85.00

1954 Bowman

	NM	Ex
COMPLETE SET (224)	4000.00	2000.00
WRAP.(1-CENT, DATED)	150.00	75.00
WRAP.(1-CENT, UNDATED)	200.00	100.00
WRAP.(5-CENT, DATED)	150.00	75.00
WRAP.(5-CENT, UNDATED)	60.00	30.00

	NM	Ex
❑ 1 Phil Rizzuto	160.00	47.50
❑ 2 Jackie Jensen	30.00	15.00
❑ 3 Marion Fricano	12.00	6.00
❑ 4 Bob Hooper	12.00	6.00
❑ 5 Billy Hunter	12.00	6.00
❑ 6 Nellie Fox	75.00	38.00
❑ 7 Walt Dropo	20.00	10.00
❑ 8 Jim Busby	12.00	6.00
❑ 9 Dave Williams	12.00	6.00
❑ 10 Carl Erskine	20.00	10.00
❑ 11 Sid Gordon	12.00	6.00
❑ 12 Roy McMillan	20.00	10.00
❑ 13 Paul Minner	12.00	6.00
❑ 14 Jerry Staley	12.00	6.00
❑ 15 Richie Ashburn	75.00	38.00
❑ 16 Jim Wilson	12.00	6.00
❑ 17 Tom Gorman	12.00	6.00
❑ 18 Hoot Evers	12.00	6.00
❑ 19 Bobby Shantz	20.00	10.00

Card	NM	Ex
❑ 20 Art Houtteman	12.00	6.00
❑ 21 Vic Wertz	20.00	10.00
❑ 22 Sam Mele	12.00	6.00
❑ 23 Harvey Kuenn RC	30.00	15.00
❑ 24 Bob Porterfield	12.00	6.00
❑ 25 Wes Westrum	20.00	10.00
❑ 26 Billy Cox	20.00	10.00
❑ 27 Dick Cole	12.00	6.00
❑ 28 Jim Greengrass	12.00	6.00
❑ 29 Johnny Klippstein	12.00	6.00
❑ 30 Del Rice	12.00	6.00
❑ 31 Smoky Burgess	20.00	10.00
❑ 32 Del Crandall	20.00	10.00
❑ 33A Vic Raschi (No mention of trade on back)	20.00	10.00
❑ 33B Vic Raschi (Traded to St.Louis)	30.00	15.00
❑ 34 Sammy White	12.00	6.00
❑ 35 Eddie Joost	12.00	6.00
❑ 36 George Strickland	12.00	6.00
❑ 37 Dick Kokos	12.00	6.00
❑ 38 Minnie Minoso	30.00	15.00
❑ 39 Ned Garver	12.00	6.00
❑ 40 Gil Coan	12.00	6.00
❑ 41 Alvin Dark	20.00	10.00
❑ 42 Billy Loes	20.00	10.00
❑ 43 Bob Friend	20.00	10.00
❑ 44 Harry Perkowski	12.00	6.00
❑ 45 Ralph Kiner	50.00	25.00
❑ 46 Rip Repulski	12.00	6.00
❑ 47 Granny Hamner	12.00	6.00
❑ 48 Jack Dittmer	12.00	6.00
❑ 49 Harry Byrd	12.00	6.00
❑ 50 George Kell	50.00	25.00
❑ 51 Alex Kellner	12.00	6.00
❑ 52 Joe Ginsberg	12.00	6.00
❑ 53 Don Lenhardt	12.00	6.00
❑ 54 Chico Carrasquel	12.00	6.00
❑ 55 Jim Delsing	12.00	6.00
❑ 56 Maurice McDermott	12.00	6.00
❑ 57 Hoyt Wilhelm	50.00	25.00
❑ 58 Pee Wee Reese	75.00	38.00
❑ 59 Bob Schultz	12.00	6.00
❑ 60 Fred Baczewski	12.00	6.00
❑ 61 Eddie Miksis	12.00	6.00
❑ 62 Enos Slaughter	50.00	25.00
❑ 63 Earl Torgeson	12.00	6.00
❑ 64 Eddie Mathews	75.00	38.00
❑ 65 Mickey Mantle	1200.00	600.00
❑ 66A Ted Williams	3000.00	1500.00
❑ 66B Jimmy Piersall	75.00	38.00
❑ 67 Carl Scheib	12.00	6.00
❑ 68 Bobby Avila	20.00	10.00
❑ 69 Clint Courtney	12.00	6.00
❑ 70 Willard Marshall	12.00	6.00
❑ 71 Ted Gray	12.00	6.00
❑ 72 Eddie Yost	20.00	10.00
❑ 73 Don Mueller	20.00	10.00
❑ 74 Jim Gilliam	30.00	15.00
❑ 75 Max Surkont	12.00	6.00
❑ 76 Joe Nuxhall	20.00	10.00
❑ 77 Bob Rush	12.00	6.00
❑ 78 Sal Yvars	12.00	6.00
❑ 79 Curt Simmons	20.00	10.00
❑ 80 Johnny Logan	12.00	6.00
❑ 81 Jerry Coleman	20.00	10.00
❑ 82 Billy Goodman	20.00	10.00
❑ 83 Ray Murray	12.00	6.00
❑ 84 Larry Doby	50.00	25.00
❑ 85 Jim Dyck	12.00	6.00
❑ 86 Harry Dorish	12.00	6.00
❑ 87 Don Lund	12.00	6.00
❑ 88 Tom Umphlett	12.00	6.00
❑ 89 Willie Mays	400.00	200.00
❑ 90 Roy Campanella	150.00	75.00
❑ 91 Cal Abrams	12.00	6.00
❑ 92 Ken Raffensberger	12.00	6.00
❑ 93 Bill Serena	12.00	6.00
❑ 94 Solly Hemus	12.00	6.00
❑ 95 Robin Roberts	50.00	25.00
❑ 96 Joe Adcock	20.00	10.00
❑ 97 Gil McDougald	20.00	10.00
❑ 98 Ellis Kinder	12.00	6.00
❑ 99 Pete Suder	12.00	6.00
❑ 100 Mike Garcia	20.00	10.00
❑ 101 Don Larsen RC	75.00	38.00
❑ 102 Billy Pierce	20.00	10.00
❑ 103 Steve Souchock	12.00	6.00
❑ 104 Frank Shea	12.00	6.00
❑ 105 Sal Maglie	20.00	10.00
❑ 106 Clem Labine	20.00	10.00
❑ 107 Paul LaPalme	12.00	6.00
❑ 108 Bobby Adams	12.00	6.00
❑ 109 Roy Smalley	12.00	6.00
❑ 110 Red Schoendienst	50.00	25.00
❑ 111 Murry Dickson	12.00	6.00
❑ 112 Andy Pafko	20.00	10.00
❑ 113 Allie Reynolds	20.00	10.00
❑ 114 Willard Nixon	12.00	6.00
❑ 115 Don Bollweg	12.00	6.00
❑ 116 Luke Easter	20.00	10.00
❑ 117 Dick Kryhoski	12.00	6.00
❑ 118 Bob Boyd	12.00	6.00
❑ 119 Fred Hatfield	12.00	6.00
❑ 120 Mel Hoderlein	12.00	6.00
❑ 121 Ray Katt	12.00	6.00
❑ 122 Carl Furillo	30.00	15.00
❑ 123 Toby Atwell	12.00	6.00
❑ 124 Gus Bell	20.00	10.00
❑ 125 Warren Hacker	12.00	6.00
❑ 126 Cliff Chambers	12.00	6.00
❑ 127 Del Ennis	20.00	10.00
❑ 128 Ebba St.Claire	12.00	6.00
❑ 129 Hank Bauer	30.00	15.00
❑ 130 Milt Bolling	12.00	6.00
❑ 131 Joe Astroth	12.00	6.00
❑ 132 Bob Feller	75.00	38.00
❑ 133 Duane Pillette	12.00	6.00
❑ 134 Luis Aloma	12.00	6.00
❑ 135 Johnny Pesky	20.00	10.00
❑ 136 Clyde Vollmer	12.00	6.00
❑ 137 Al Corwin	12.00	6.00
❑ 138 Gil Hodges	75.00	38.00
❑ 139 Preston Ward	12.00	6.00
❑ 140 Saul Rogovin	12.00	6.00
❑ 141 Joe Garagiola	30.00	15.00
❑ 142 Al Brazle	12.00	6.00
❑ 143 Willie Jones	12.00	6.00
❑ 144 Ernie Johnson RC	30.00	15.00
❑ 145 Billy Martin	75.00	38.00
❑ 146 Dick Gernert	12.00	6.00
❑ 147 Joe DeMaestri	12.00	6.00
❑ 148 Dale Mitchell	20.00	10.00
❑ 149 Bob Young	12.00	6.00
❑ 150 Cass Michaels	12.00	6.00
❑ 151 Pat Mullin	12.00	6.00
❑ 152 Mickey Vernon	20.00	10.00
❑ 153 Whitey Lockman	20.00	10.00
❑ 154 Don Newcombe	30.00	15.00
❑ 155 Frank Thomas RC	20.00	10.00
❑ 156 Rocky Bridges	12.00	6.00
❑ 157 Turk Lown	12.00	6.00
❑ 158 Stu Miller	20.00	10.00
❑ 159 Johnny Lindell	12.00	6.00
❑ 160 Danny O'Connell	12.00	6.00
❑ 161 Yogi Berra	175.00	90.00
❑ 162 Ted Lepcio	12.00	6.00
❑ 163A Dave Philley (No mention of trade on back)	20.00	10.00
❑ 163B Dave Philley (Traded to Cleveland)	30.00	15.00
❑ 164 Early Wynn	50.00	25.00
❑ 165 Johnny Groth	12.00	6.00
❑ 166 Sandy Consuegra	12.00	6.00
❑ 167 Billy Hoeft	12.00	6.00
❑ 168 Ed Fitzgerald	12.00	6.00
❑ 169 Larry Jansen	20.00	10.00
❑ 170 Duke Snider	150.00	75.00
❑ 171 Carlos Bernier	12.00	6.00
❑ 172 Andy Seminick	12.00	6.00
❑ 173 Dee Fondy	12.00	6.00
❑ 174 Pete Castiglione	12.00	6.00
❑ 175 Mel Clark	12.00	6.00
❑ 176 Vern Bickford	12.00	6.00
❑ 177 Whitey Ford	100.00	50.00
❑ 178 Del Wilber	12.00	6.00
❑ 179 Morrie Martin	12.00	6.00
❑ 180 Joe Tipton	12.00	6.00
❑ 181 Les Moss	12.00	6.00
❑ 182 Sherm Lollar	20.00	10.00
❑ 183 Matt Batts	12.00	6.00
❑ 184 Mickey Grasso	12.00	6.00
❑ 185 Daryl Spencer	12.00	6.00
❑ 186 Russ Meyer	12.00	6.00
❑ 187 Vern Law	20.00	10.00
❑ 188 Frank Smith	12.00	6.00
❑ 189 Randy Jackson	12.00	6.00
❑ 190 Joe Presko	12.00	6.00
❑ 191 Karl Drews	12.00	6.00
❑ 192 Lou Burdette	20.00	10.00
❑ 193 Eddie Robinson	12.00	6.00
❑ 194 Sid Hudson	12.00	6.00
❑ 195 Bob Cain	12.00	6.00
❑ 196 Bob Lemon	50.00	25.00
❑ 197 Lou Kretlow	12.00	6.00
❑ 198 Virgil Trucks	12.00	6.00
❑ 199 Steve Gromek	12.00	6.00
❑ 200 Conrado Marrero	12.00	6.00
❑ 201 Bobby Thomson	30.00	15.00
❑ 202 George Shuba	20.00	10.00
❑ 203 Vic Janowicz	20.00	10.00
❑ 204 Jack Collum	12.00	6.00
❑ 205 Hal Jeffcoat	12.00	6.00
❑ 206 Steve Bilko	12.00	6.00
❑ 207 Stan Lopata	12.00	6.00
❑ 208 Johnny Antonelli	20.00	10.00
❑ 209 Gene Woodling	12.00	6.00
❑ 210 Jimmy Piersall	30.00	15.00
❑ 211 Al Robertson	12.00	6.00
❑ 212 Owen Friend	12.00	6.00
❑ 213 Dick Littlefield	12.00	6.00
❑ 214 Ferris Fain	20.00	10.00
❑ 215 Johnny Bucha	12.00	6.00
❑ 216 Jerry Snyder	12.00	6.00
❑ 217 Hank Thompson	20.00	10.00
❑ 218 Preacher Roe	20.00	10.00
❑ 219 Hal Rice	12.00	6.00
❑ 220 Hobie Landrith	12.00	6.00
❑ 221 Frank Baumholtz	12.00	6.00
❑ 222 Memo Luna	12.00	6.00
❑ 223 Steve Ridzik	12.00	6.00
❑ 224 Bill Bruton	50.00	12.50

1955 Bowman

	NM	Ex
COMPLETE SET (320)	5000.00	2500.00
COMMON CARD (1-96)	12.00	6.00
COMMON CARD (97-224)	10.00	5.00
COMMON (225-320)	15.00	7.50
COMMON UMP. 225-320	30.00	15.00
WRAPPER (1-CENT)	60.00	30.00
WRAPPER (5-CENT)	60.00	30.00

Card	NM	Ex
❑ 1 Hoyt Wilhelm	100.00	22.00
❑ 2 Alvin Dark	15.00	7.50
❑ 3 Joe Coleman	15.00	7.50
❑ 4 Eddie Waitkus	15.00	7.50
❑ 5 Jim Robertson	12.00	6.00
❑ 6 Pete Suder	12.00	6.00
❑ 7 Gene Baker	12.00	6.00
❑ 8 Warren Hacker	12.00	6.00
❑ 9 Gil McDougald	20.00	10.00
❑ 10 Phil Rizzuto	100.00	50.00
❑ 11 Bill Bruton	15.00	7.50
❑ 12 Andy Pafko	15.00	7.50
❑ 13 Clyde Vollmer	12.00	6.00

❑ 14 Gus Keriazakos 12.00 6.00
❑ 15 Frank Sullivan 12.00 6.00
❑ 16 Jimmy Piersall 20.00 10.00
❑ 17 Del Ennis 15.00 7.50
❑ 18 Stan Lopata 12.00 6.00
❑ 19 Bobby Avila 15.00 7.50
❑ 20 Al Smith 15.00 7.50
❑ 21 Don Hoak 12.00 6.00
❑ 22 Roy Campanella 125.00 60.00
❑ 23 Al Kaline 150.00 75.00
❑ 24 Al Aber 12.00 6.00
❑ 25 Minnie Minoso 30.00 15.00
❑ 26 Virgil Trucks 15.00 7.50
❑ 27 Preston Ward 12.00 6.00
❑ 28 Dick Cole 12.00 6.00
❑ 29 Red Schoendienst 30.00 15.00
❑ 30 Bill Sarni 12.00 6.00
❑ 31 Johnny Temple RC 15.00 7.50
❑ 32 Wally Post 15.00 7.50
❑ 33 Nellie Fox 50.00 25.00
❑ 34 Clint Courtney 12.00 6.00
❑ 35 Bill Tuttle 12.00 6.00
❑ 36 Wayne Belardi 12.00 6.00
❑ 37 Pee Wee Reese 75.00 38.00
❑ 38 Early Wynn 30.00 15.00
❑ 39 Bob Darnell 15.00 7.50
❑ 40 Vic Wertz 15.00 7.50
❑ 41 Mel Clark 12.00 6.00
❑ 42 Bob Greenwood 12.00 6.00
❑ 43 Bob Buhl 15.00 7.50
❑ 44 Danny O'Connell 12.00 6.00
❑ 45 Tom Umphlett 12.00 6.00
❑ 46 Mickey Vernon 15.00 7.50
❑ 47 Sammy White 12.00 6.00
❑ 48A Milt Bolling ERR 20.00 10.00
(Name on back is Frank Bolling)
❑ 48B Milt Bolling COR 20.00 10.00
❑ 49 Jim Greengrass 12.00 6.00
❑ 50 Hobie Landrith 12.00 6.00
❑ 51 Elvin Tappe 12.00 6.00
❑ 52 Hal Rice 12.00 6.00
❑ 53 Alex Kellner 12.00 6.00
❑ 54 Don Bollweg 12.00 6.00
❑ 55 Cal Abrams 12.00 6.00
❑ 56 Billy Cox 15.00 7.50
❑ 57 Bob Friend 15.00 7.50
❑ 58 Frank Thomas 15.00 7.50
❑ 59 Whitey Ford 100.00 50.00
❑ 60 Enos Slaughter 30.00 15.00
❑ 61 Paul LaPalme 12.00 6.00
❑ 62 Royce Lint 12.00 6.00
❑ 63 Irv Noren 15.00 7.50
❑ 64 Curt Simmons 15.00 7.50
❑ 65 Don Zimmer RC 20.00 10.00
❑ 66 George Shuba 20.00 10.00
❑ 67 Don Larsen 20.00 10.00
❑ 68 Elston Howard RC 75.00 38.00
❑ 69 Billy Hunter 12.00 6.00
❑ 70 Lou Burdette 20.00 10.00
❑ 71 Dave Jolly 12.00 6.00
❑ 72 Chet Nichols 12.00 6.00
❑ 73 Eddie Yost 15.00 7.50
❑ 74 Jerry Snyder 12.00 6.00
❑ 75 Brooks Lawrence RC 12.00 6.00
❑ 76 Tom Poholsky 12.00 6.00
❑ 77 Jim McDonald 12.00 6.00
❑ 78 Gil Coan 12.00 6.00
❑ 79 Willie Miranda 12.00 6.00
❑ 80 Lou Limmer 12.00 6.00
❑ 81 Bobby Morgan 12.00 6.00
❑ 82 Lee Walls 12.00 6.00
❑ 83 Max Surkont 12.00 6.00
❑ 84 George Freese 12.00 6.00
❑ 85 Cass Michaels 12.00 6.00
❑ 86 Ted Gray 12.00 6.00
❑ 87 Randy Jackson 12.00 6.00
❑ 88 Steve Bilko 12.00 6.00
❑ 89 Lou Boudreau MG 30.00 15.00
❑ 90 Art Ditmar 12.00 6.00
❑ 91 Dick Marlowe 12.00 6.00
❑ 92 George Zuverink 12.00 6.00
❑ 93 Andy Seminick 12.00 6.00
❑ 94 Hank Thompson 15.00 7.50
❑ 95 Sal Maglie 15.00 7.50
❑ 96 Ray Narleski RC 12.00 6.00
❑ 97 Johnny Podres 30.00 15.00
❑ 98 Jim Gilliam 20.00 10.00
❑ 99 Jerry Coleman 15.00 7.50
❑ 100 Tom Morgan 10.00 5.00
❑ 101A Don Johnson ERR 20.00 10.00
(Photo actually Ernie Johnson)
❑ 101B Don Johnson COR 20.00 10.00
❑ 102 Bobby Thomson 15.00 7.50
❑ 103 Eddie Mathews 60.00 30.00
❑ 104 Bob Porterfield 10.00 5.00
❑ 105 Johnny Schmitz 10.00 5.00
❑ 106 Del Rice 10.00 5.00
❑ 107 Solly Hemus 10.00 5.00
❑ 108 Lou Kretlow 10.00 5.00
❑ 109 Vern Stephens 15.00 7.50
❑ 110 Bob Miller 10.00 5.00
❑ 111 Steve Ridzik 10.00 5.00
❑ 112 Granny Hamner 10.00 5.00
❑ 113 Bob Hall 10.00 5.00
❑ 114 Vic Janowicz 15.00 7.50
❑ 115 Roger Bowman 10.00 5.00
❑ 116 Sandy Consuegra 10.00 5.00
❑ 117 Johnny Groth 10.00 5.00
❑ 118 Bobby Adams 10.00 5.00
❑ 119 Joe Astroth 10.00 5.00
❑ 120 Ed Burtschy 10.00 5.00
❑ 121 Rufus Crawford 10.00 5.00
❑ 122 Al Corwin 10.00 5.00
❑ 123 Marv Grissom 10.00 5.00
❑ 124 Johnny Antonelli 15.00 7.50
❑ 125 Paul Giel 15.00 7.50
❑ 126 Billy Goodman 15.00 7.50
❑ 127 Hank Majeski 10.00 5.00
❑ 128 Mike Garcia 15.00 7.50
❑ 129 Hal Naragon 10.00 5.00
❑ 130 Richie Ashburn 50.00 25.00
❑ 131 Willard Marshall 10.00 5.00
❑ 132A Harvey Kueen ERR 50.00 25.00
(Sic, Kuenn)
❑ 132B Harvey Kuenn COR 30.00 15.00
❑ 133 Charles King 10.00 5.00
❑ 134 Bob Feller 70.00 35.00
❑ 135 Lloyd Merriman 10.00 5.00
❑ 136 Rocky Bridges 10.00 5.00
❑ 137 Bob Talbot 10.00 5.00
❑ 138 Davey Williams 15.00 7.50
❑ 139 Shantz Brothers 15.00 7.50
Wilmer Shantz
Bobby Shantz
❑ 140 Bobby Shantz 15.00 7.50
❑ 141 Wes Westrum 15.00 7.50
❑ 142 Rudy Regalado 10.00 5.00
❑ 143 Don Newcombe 30.00 15.00
❑ 144 Art Houtteman 10.00 5.00
❑ 145 Bob Nieman 10.00 5.00
❑ 146 Don Liddle 10.00 5.00
❑ 147 Sam Mele 10.00 5.00
❑ 148 Bob Chakales 10.00 5.00
❑ 149 Cloyd Boyer 10.00 5.00
❑ 150 Billy Klaus 10.00 5.00
❑ 151 Jim Brideweser 10.00 5.00
❑ 152 Johnny Klippstein 10.00 5.00
❑ 153 Eddie Robinson 10.00 5.00
❑ 154 Frank Lary RC 15.00 7.50
❑ 155 Gerry Staley 10.00 5.00
❑ 156 Jim Hughes 15.00 7.50
❑ 157A Ernie Johnson ERR 20.00 10.00
(Photo actually Don Johnson)
❑ 157B Ernie Johnson COR 20.00 10.00
❑ 158 Gil Hodges 50.00 25.00
❑ 159 Harry Byrd 10.00 5.00
❑ 160 Bill Skowron 20.00 10.00
❑ 161 Matt Batts 10.00 5.00
❑ 162 Charlie Maxwell 10.00 5.00
❑ 163 Sid Gordon 15.00 7.50
❑ 164 Toby Atwell 10.00 5.00
❑ 165 Maurice McDermott 10.00 5.00
❑ 166 Jim Busby 10.00 5.00
❑ 167 Bob Grim RC 20.00 10.00
❑ 168 Yogi Berra 100.00 50.00
❑ 169 Carl Furillo 30.00 15.00
❑ 170 Carl Erskine 20.00 10.00
❑ 171 Robin Roberts 50.00 25.00
❑ 172 Willie Jones 10.00 5.00
❑ 173 Chico Carrasquel 10.00 5.00
❑ 174 Sherm Lollar 15.00 7.50
❑ 175 Wilmer Shantz 10.00 5.00
❑ 176 Joe DeMaestri 10.00 5.00
❑ 177 Willard Nixon 10.00 5.00
❑ 178 Tom Brewer 10.00 5.00
❑ 179 Hank Aaron 225.00 110.00
❑ 180 Johnny Logan 15.00 7.50
❑ 181 Eddie Miksis 10.00 5.00
❑ 182 Bob Rush 10.00 5.00
❑ 183 Ray Katt 10.00 5.00
❑ 184 Willie Mays 225.00 110.00
❑ 185 Vic Raschi 10.00 5.00
❑ 186 Alex Grammas 10.00 5.00
❑ 187 Fred Hatfield 10.00 5.00
❑ 188 Ned Garver 10.00 5.00
❑ 189 Jack Collum 10.00 5.00
❑ 190 Fred Baczewski 10.00 5.00
❑ 191 Bob Lemon 30.00 15.00
❑ 192 George Strickland 10.00 5.00
❑ 193 Howie Judson 10.00 5.00
❑ 194 Joe Nuxhall 15.00 7.50
❑ 195A Erv Palica 15.00 7.50
(Without trade)
❑ 195B Erv Palica 40.00 20.00
(With trade)
❑ 196 Russ Meyer 15.00 7.50
❑ 197 Ralph Kiner 30.00 15.00
❑ 198 Dave Pope 10.00 5.00
❑ 199 Vern Law 15.00 7.50
❑ 200 Dick Littlefield 10.00 5.00
❑ 201 Allie Reynolds 20.00 10.00
❑ 202 Mickey Mantle UER 800.00 400.00
Birthdate listed as 10/30/31
Should be 10/20/31
❑ 203 Steve Gromek 10.00 5.00
❑ 204A Frank Bolling ERR 20.00 10.00
(Name on back is Milt Bolling)
❑ 204B Frank Bolling COR 20.00 10.00
❑ 205 Rip Repulski 10.00 5.00
❑ 206 Ralph Beard 10.00 5.00
❑ 207 Frank Shea 10.00 5.00
❑ 208 Ed Fitzgerald 10.00 5.00
❑ 209 Smoky Burgess 15.00 7.50
❑ 210 Earl Torgeson 10.00 5.00
❑ 211 Sonny Dixon 10.00 5.00
❑ 212 Jack Dittmer 10.00 5.00
❑ 213 George Kell 30.00 15.00
❑ 214 Billy Pierce 15.00 7.50
❑ 215 Bob Kuzava 10.00 5.00
❑ 216 Preacher Roe 20.00 10.00
❑ 217 Del Crandall 15.00 7.50
❑ 218 Joe Adcock 15.00 7.50
❑ 219 Whitey Lockman 15.00 7.50
❑ 220 Jim Hearn 10.00 5.00
❑ 221 Hector Brown 10.00 5.00
❑ 222 Russ Kemmerer 10.00 5.00
❑ 223 Hal Jeffcoat 10.00 5.00
❑ 224 Dee Fondy 10.00 5.00
❑ 225 Paul Richards MG 15.00 7.50
❑ 226 Bill McKinley UMP RC 30.00 15.00
❑ 227 Frank Baumholtz 15.00 7.50
❑ 228 John Phillips 15.00 7.50
❑ 229 Jim Brosnan RC 20.00 10.00
❑ 230 Al Brazle 15.00 7.50
❑ 231 Jim Konstanty 20.00 10.00
❑ 232 Birdie Tebbetts MG 20.00 10.00
❑ 233 Bill Serena 15.00 7.50
❑ 234 Dick Bartell CO 20.00 10.00
❑ 235 Joe Paparella UMP RC 30.00 15.00
❑ 236 Murry Dickson 15.00 7.50
❑ 237 Johnny Wyrostek 15.00 7.50
❑ 238 Eddie Stanky MG 20.00 10.00
❑ 239 Edwin Rommel UMP 40.00 20.00
❑ 240 Billy Loes 20.00 10.00
❑ 241 Johnny Pesky CO 20.00 10.00
❑ 242 Ernie Banks 350.00 180.00
❑ 243 Gus Bell 20.00 10.00
❑ 244 Duane Pillette 15.00 7.50
❑ 245 Bill Miller 15.00 7.50
❑ 246 Hank Bauer 30.00 15.00
❑ 247 Dutch Leonard CO 15.00 7.50
❑ 248 Harry Dorish 15.00 7.50
❑ 249 Billy Gardner RC 20.00 10.00
❑ 250 Larry Napp UMP RC 30.00 15.00

❑ 251 Stan Jok	15.00	7.50
❑ 252 Roy Smalley	15.00	7.50
❑ 253 Jim Wilson	15.00	7.50
❑ 254 Bennett Flowers	15.00	7.50
❑ 255 Pete Runnels	20.00	10.00
❑ 256 Owen Friend	15.00	7.50
❑ 257 Tom Alston	15.00	7.50
❑ 258 John Stevens UMP RC	30.00	15.00
❑ 259 Don Mossi RC	30.00	15.00
❑ 260 Edwin Hurley UMP RC	30.00	15.00
❑ 261 Walt Moryn	20.00	10.00
❑ 262 Jim Lemon	15.00	7.50
❑ 263 Eddie Joost	15.00	7.50
❑ 264 Bill Henry	15.00	7.50
❑ 265 Albert Barlick UMP RC	75.00	38.00
❑ 266 Mike Fornieles	15.00	7.50
❑ 267 Jim Honochick UMP RC	75.00	38.00
❑ 268 Roy Lee Hawes	15.00	7.50
❑ 269 Joe Amalfitano RC	20.00	10.00
❑ 270 Chico Fernandez	20.00	10.00
❑ 271 Bob Hooper	15.00	7.50
❑ 272 John Flaherty UMP RC	30.00	15.00
❑ 273 Bubba Church	15.00	7.50
❑ 274 Jim Delsing	15.00	7.50
❑ 275 William Grieve UMP RC	30.00	15.00
❑ 276 Ike Delock	15.00	7.50
❑ 277 Ed Runge UMP RC	30.00	15.00
❑ 278 Charlie Neal RC	40.00	20.00
❑ 279 Hank Soar UMP RC	40.00	20.00
❑ 280 Clyde McCullough	15.00	7.50
❑ 281 Charles Berry UMP	40.00	20.00
❑ 282 Phil Cavarretta	20.00	10.00
❑ 283 Nestor Chylak UMP RC	75.00	38.00
❑ 284 Bill Jackowski UMP RC	30.00	15.00
❑ 285 Walt Dropo	20.00	10.00
❑ 286 Frank Secory UMP RC	30.00	15.00
❑ 287 Ron Mrozinski	15.00	7.50
❑ 288 Dick Smith	15.00	7.50
❑ 289 Arthur Gore UMP RC	30.00	15.00
❑ 290 Hershell Freeman	15.00	7.50
❑ 291 Frank Dascoli UMP RC	30.00	15.00
❑ 292 Marv Blaylock	15.00	7.50
❑ 293 Thomas Gorman UMP RC	40.00	20.00
❑ 294 Wally Moses CO	15.00	7.50
❑ 295 Lee Ballanfant UMP RC	30.00	15.00
❑ 296 Bill Virdon RC	30.00	15.00
❑ 297 Dusty Boggess UMP RC	30.00	15.00
❑ 298 Charlie Grimm MG	20.00	10.00
❑ 299 Lon Warneke UMP	40.00	20.00
❑ 300 Tommy Byrne	20.00	10.00
❑ 301 William Engeln UMP RC	30.00	15.00
❑ 302 Frank Malzone RC	30.00	15.00
❑ 303 Jocko Conlan UMP	75.00	38.00
❑ 304 Harry Chiti	15.00	7.50
❑ 305 Frank Umont UMP RC	30.00	15.00
❑ 306 Bob Cerv	20.00	10.00
❑ 307 Babe Pinelli UMP	40.00	20.00
❑ 308 Al Lopez MG	50.00	25.00
❑ 309 Hal Dixon UMP RC	30.00	15.00
❑ 310 Ken Lehman	15.00	7.50
❑ 311 Lawrence Goetz UMP RC	30.00	15.00
❑ 312 Bill Wight	15.00	7.50
❑ 313 Augie Donatelli UMP RC	50.00	25.00
❑ 314 Dale Mitchell	20.00	10.00
❑ 315 Cal Hubbard UMP RC	75.00	38.00
❑ 316 Marion Fricano	15.00	7.50
❑ 317 W. Summers UMP	20.00	10.00
❑ 318 Sid Hudson	15.00	7.50
❑ 319 Al Schroll	15.00	7.50
❑ 320 George Susce RC	50.00	10.00

1989 Bowman

	Nm-Mt	Ex-Mt
COMPLETE SET (484)	25.00	10.00
COMP.FACT.SET (484)	25.00	10.00

❑ 1 Oswald Peraza	.05	.02
❑ 2 Brian Holton	.05	.02
❑ 3 Jose Bautista RC	.10	.04
❑ 4 Pete Harnisch RC	.25	.10
❑ 5 Dave Schmidt	.05	.02
❑ 6 Gregg Olson RC	.25	.10
❑ 7 Jeff Ballard	.05	.02
❑ 8 Bob Melvin	.05	.02
❑ 9 Cal Ripken	.75	.30

❑ 10 Randy Milligan	.05	.02
❑ 11 Juan Bell RC	.10	.04
❑ 12 Billy Ripken	.05	.02
❑ 13 Jim Traber	.05	.02
❑ 14 Pete Stanicek	.05	.02
❑ 15 Steve Finley RC	.50	.20
❑ 16 Larry Sheets	.05	.02
❑ 17 Phil Bradley	.05	.02
❑ 18 Brady Anderson RC	.50	.20
❑ 19 Lee Smith	.10	.04
❑ 20 Tom Fischer	.05	.02
❑ 21 Mike Boddicker	.05	.02
❑ 22 Rob Murphy	.05	.02
❑ 23 Wes Gardner	.05	.02
❑ 24 John Dopson	.05	.02
❑ 25 Bob Stanley	.05	.02
❑ 26 Roger Clemens	.50	.20
❑ 27 Rich Gedman	.05	.02
❑ 28 Marty Barrett	.05	.02
❑ 29 Luis Rivera	.05	.02
❑ 30 Jody Reed	.05	.02
❑ 31 Nick Esasky	.05	.02
❑ 32 Wade Boggs	.15	.06
❑ 33 Jim Rice	.10	.04
❑ 34 Mike Greenwell	.05	.02
❑ 35 Dwight Evans	.10	.04
❑ 36 Ellis Burks	.15	.06
❑ 37 Chuck Finley	.10	.04
❑ 38 Kirk McCaskill	.05	.02
❑ 39 Jim Abbott RC*	.50	.20
❑ 40 Bryan Harvey RC *	.25	.10
❑ 41 Bert Blyleven	.10	.04
❑ 42 Mike Witt	.05	.02
❑ 43 Bob McClure	.05	.02
❑ 44 Bill Schroeder	.05	.02
❑ 45 Lance Parrish	.05	.02
❑ 46 Dick Schofield	.05	.02
❑ 47 Wally Joyner	.10	.04
❑ 48 Jack Howell	.05	.02
❑ 49 Johnny Ray	.05	.02
❑ 50 Chili Davis	.10	.04
❑ 51 Tony Armas	.05	.02
❑ 52 Claudell Washington	.05	.02
❑ 53 Brian Downing	.05	.02
❑ 54 Devon White	.10	.04
❑ 55 Bobby Thigpen	.05	.02
❑ 56 Bill Long	.05	.02
❑ 57 Jerry Reuss	.05	.02
❑ 58 Shawn Hillegas	.05	.02
❑ 59 Melido Perez	.05	.02
❑ 60 Jeff Bittiger	.05	.02
❑ 61 Jack McDowell	.10	.04
❑ 62 Carlton Fisk	.15	.06
❑ 63 Steve Lyons	.05	.02
❑ 64 Ozzie Guillen	.05	.02
❑ 65 Robin Ventura RC	.75	.30
❑ 66 Fred Manrique	.05	.02
❑ 67 Dan Pasqua	.05	.02
❑ 68 Ivan Calderon	.05	.02
❑ 69 Ron Kittle	.05	.02
❑ 70 Daryl Boston	.05	.02
❑ 71 Dave Gallagher	.05	.02
❑ 72 Harold Baines	.10	.04
❑ 73 Charles Nagy RC	.25	.10
❑ 74 John Farrell	.05	.02
❑ 75 Kevin Wickander	.05	.02
❑ 76 Greg Swindell	.05	.02
❑ 77 Mike Walker	.05	.02
❑ 78 Doug Jones	.05	.02
❑ 79 Rich Yett	.05	.02
❑ 80 Tom Candiotti	.05	.02
❑ 81 Jesse Orosco	.05	.02
❑ 82 Bud Black	.05	.02
❑ 83 Andy Allanson	.05	.02
❑ 84 Pete O'Brien	.05	.02
❑ 85 Jerry Browne	.05	.02
❑ 86 Brook Jacoby	.05	.02
❑ 87 Mark Lewis RC	.10	.04
❑ 88 Luis Aguayo	.05	.02
❑ 89 Cory Snyder	.05	.02
❑ 90 Oddibe McDowell	.05	.02
❑ 91 Joe Carter	.15	.06
❑ 92 Frank Tanana	.05	.02
❑ 93 Jack Morris	.10	.04
❑ 94 Doyle Alexander	.05	.02
❑ 95 Steve Searcy	.05	.02
❑ 96 Randy Bockus	.05	.02
❑ 97 Jeff M. Robinson	.05	.02
❑ 98 Mike Henneman	.05	.02
❑ 99 Paul Gibson	.05	.02
❑ 100 Frank Williams	.05	.02
❑ 101 Matt Nokes	.05	.02
❑ 102 Rico Brogna RC UER (Misspelled Ricco on card back)	.40	.16
❑ 103 Lou Whitaker	.10	.04
❑ 104 Al Pedrique	.05	.02
❑ 105 Alan Trammell	.15	.06
❑ 106 Chris Brown	.05	.02
❑ 107 Pat Sheridan	.05	.02
❑ 108 Chet Lemon	.05	.02
❑ 109 Keith Moreland	.05	.02
❑ 110 Mel Stottlemyre Jr.	.05	.02
❑ 111 Bret Saberhagen	.10	.04
❑ 112 Floyd Bannister	.05	.02
❑ 113 Jeff Montgomery	.10	.04
❑ 114 Steve Farr	.05	.02
❑ 115 Tom Gordon UER RC (Front shows autograph of Don Gordon)	.25	.10
❑ 116 Charlie Leibrandt	.05	.02
❑ 117 Mark Gubicza	.05	.02
❑ 118 Mike Macfarlane RC	.25	.10
❑ 119 Bob Boone	.10	.04
❑ 120 Kurt Stillwell	.05	.02
❑ 121 George Brett	.60	.24
❑ 122 Frank White	.10	.04
❑ 123 Kevin Seitzer	.05	.02
❑ 124 Willie Wilson	.05	.02
❑ 125 Pat Tabler	.05	.02
❑ 126 Bo Jackson	.25	.10
❑ 127 Hugh Walker RC	.10	.04
❑ 128 Danny Tartabull	.05	.02
❑ 129 Teddy Higuera	.05	.02
❑ 130 Don August	.05	.02
❑ 131 Juan Nieves	.05	.02
❑ 132 Mike Birkbeck	.05	.02
❑ 133 Dan Plesac	.05	.02
❑ 134 Chris Bosio	.05	.02
❑ 135 Bill Wegman	.05	.02
❑ 136 Chuck Crim	.05	.02
❑ 137 B.J. Surhoff	.10	.04
❑ 138 Joey Meyer	.05	.02
❑ 139 Dale Sveum	.05	.02
❑ 140 Paul Molitor	.15	.06
❑ 141 Jim Gantner	.05	.02
❑ 142 Gary Sheffield RC	1.50	.60
❑ 143 Greg Brock	.05	.02
❑ 144 Robin Yount	.25	.10
❑ 145 Glenn Braggs	.05	.02
❑ 146 Rob Deer	.05	.02
❑ 147 Fred Toliver	.05	.02
❑ 148 Jeff Reardon	.10	.04
❑ 149 Allan Anderson	.05	.02
❑ 150 Frank Viola	.05	.02
❑ 151 Shane Rawley	.05	.02
❑ 152 Juan Berenguer	.05	.02
❑ 153 Johnny Ard	.05	.02
❑ 154 Tim Laudner	.05	.02
❑ 155 Brian Harper	.05	.02
❑ 156 Al Newman	.05	.02
❑ 157 Kent Hrbek	.10	.04
❑ 158 Gary Gaetti	.10	.04
❑ 159 Wally Backman	.05	.02

❑ 160 Gene Larkin .05 .02
❑ 161 Greg Gagne .05 .02
❑ 162 Kirby Puckett .25 .10
❑ 163 Dan Gladden .05 .02
❑ 164 Randy Bush .05 .02
❑ 165 Dave LaPoint .05 .02
❑ 166 Andy Hawkins .05 .02
❑ 167 Dave Righetti .05 .02
❑ 168 Lance McCullers .05 .02
❑ 169 Jimmy Jones .05 .02
❑ 170 Al Leiter .25 .10
❑ 171 John Candelaria .05 .02
❑ 172 Don Slaught .05 .02
❑ 173 Jamie Quirk .05 .02
❑ 174 Rafael Santana .05 .02
❑ 175 Mike Pagliarulo .05 .02
❑ 176 Don Mattingly .60 .24
❑ 177 Ken Phelps .05 .02
❑ 178 Steve Sax .05 .02
❑ 179 Dave Winfield .15 .06
❑ 180 Stan Jefferson .05 .02
❑ 181 Rickey Henderson .40 .16
❑ 182 Bob Brower .05 .02
❑ 183 Roberto Kelly .10 .04
❑ 184 Curt Young .05 .02
❑ 185 Gene Nelson .05 .02
❑ 186 Bob Welch .05 .02
❑ 187 Rick Honeycutt .05 .02
❑ 188 Dave Stewart .10 .04
❑ 189 Mike Moore .05 .02
❑ 190 Dennis Eckersley .10 .04
❑ 191 Eric Plunk .05 .02
❑ 192 Storm Davis .05 .02
❑ 193 Terry Steinbach .10 .04
❑ 194 Ron Hassey .05 .02
❑ 195 Stan Royer RC .10 .04
❑ 196 Walt Weiss .05 .02
❑ 197 Mark McGwire 1.00 .40
❑ 198 Carney Lansford .10 .04
❑ 199 Glenn Hubbard .05 .02
❑ 200 Dave Henderson .05 .02
❑ 201 Jose Canseco .25 .10
❑ 202 Dave Parker .10 .04
❑ 203 Scott Bankhead .05 .02
❑ 204 Tom Niedenfuer .05 .02
❑ 205 Mark Langston .05 .02
❑ 206 Erik Hanson RC .25 .10
❑ 207 Mike Jackson .05 .02
❑ 208 Dave Valle .05 .02
❑ 209 Scott Bradley .05 .02
❑ 210 Harold Reynolds .10 .04
❑ 211 Tino Martinez RC .75 .30
❑ 212 Rich Renteria .05 .02
❑ 213 Rey Quinones .05 .02
❑ 214 Jim Presley .05 .02
❑ 215 Alvin Davis .05 .02
❑ 216 Edgar Martinez .15 .06
❑ 217 Darnell Coles .05 .02
❑ 218 Jeffrey Leonard .05 .02
❑ 219 Jay Buhner .10 .04
❑ 220 Ken Griffey Jr. RC 8.00 3.20
❑ 221 Drew Hall .05 .02
❑ 222 Bobby Witt .05 .02
❑ 223 Jamie Moyer .10 .04
❑ 224 Charlie Hough .10 .04
❑ 225 Nolan Ryan 1.00 .40
❑ 226 Jeff Russell .05 .02
❑ 227 Jim Sundberg .05 .02
❑ 228 Julio Franco .05 .02
❑ 229 Buddy Bell .10 .04
❑ 230 Scott Fletcher .05 .02
❑ 231 Jeff Kunkel .05 .02
❑ 232 Steve Buechele .05 .02
❑ 233 Monty Fariss .05 .02
❑ 234 Rick Leach .05 .02
❑ 235 Ruben Sierra .05 .02
❑ 236 Cecil Espy .05 .02
❑ 237 Rafael Palmeiro .25 .10
❑ 238 Pete Incaviglia .05 .02
❑ 239 Dave Stieb .05 .02
❑ 240 Jeff Musselman .05 .02
❑ 241 Mike Flanagan .05 .02
❑ 242 Todd Stottlemyre .15 .06
❑ 243 Jimmy Key .10 .04
❑ 244 Tony Castillo RC .10 .04
❑ 245 Alex Sanchez .05 .02
❑ 246 Tom Henke .05 .02
❑ 247 John Cerutti .05 .02
❑ 248 Ernie Whitt .05 .02
❑ 249 Bob Brenly .05 .02
❑ 250 Rance Mulliniks .05 .02
❑ 251 Kelly Gruber .05 .02
❑ 252 Ed Sprague RC .25 .10
❑ 253 Fred McGriff .25 .10
❑ 254 Tony Fernandez .05 .02
❑ 255 Tom Lawless .05 .02
❑ 256 George Bell .05 .02
❑ 257 Jesse Barfield .05 .02
❑ 258 Roberto Alomar .25 .10
Sandy Alomar
❑ 259 Ken Griffey Jr. 1.00 .40
Ken Griffey Sr.
❑ 260 Cal Ripken Jr. .25 .10
Cal Ripken Sr.
❑ 261 Mel Stottlemyre Jr. .05 .02
Mel Stottlemyre Sr.
❑ 262 Zane Smith .05 .02
❑ 263 Charlie Puleo .05 .02
❑ 264 Derek Lilliquist RC .10 .04
❑ 265 Paul Assenmacher .05 .02
❑ 266 John Smoltz RC 1.00 .40
❑ 267 Tom Glavine .25 .10
❑ 268 Steve Avery RC .25 .10
❑ 269 Pete Smith .05 .02
❑ 270 Jody Davis .05 .02
❑ 271 Bruce Benedict .05 .02
❑ 272 Andres Thomas .05 .02
❑ 273 Gerald Perry .05 .02
❑ 274 Ron Gant .10 .04
❑ 275 Darrell Evans .10 .04
❑ 276 Dale Murphy .25 .10
❑ 277 Dion James .05 .02
❑ 278 Lonnie Smith .05 .02
❑ 279 Geronimo Berroa .05 .02
❑ 280 Steve Wilson RC .10 .04
❑ 281 Rick Sutcliffe .10 .04
❑ 282 Kevin Coffman .05 .02
❑ 283 Mitch Williams .05 .02
❑ 284 Greg Maddux .60 .24
❑ 285 Paul Kilgus .05 .02
❑ 286 Mike Harkey RC .10 .04
❑ 287 Lloyd McClendon .05 .02
❑ 288 Damon Berryhill .05 .02
❑ 289 Ty Griffin .05 .02
❑ 290 Ryne Sandberg .40 .16
❑ 291 Mark Grace .25 .10
❑ 292 Curt Wilkerson .05 .02
❑ 293 Vance Law .05 .02
❑ 294 Shawon Dunston .05 .02
❑ 295 Jerome Walton .25 .10
❑ 296 Mitch Webster .05 .02
❑ 297 Dwight Smith RC .10 .04
❑ 298 Andre Dawson .10 .04
❑ 299 Jeff Sellers .05 .02
❑ 300 Jose Rijo .05 .02
❑ 301 John Franco .10 .04
❑ 302 Rick Mahler .05 .02
❑ 303 Ron Robinson .05 .02
❑ 304 Danny Jackson .05 .02
❑ 305 Rob Dibble RC * .50 .20
❑ 306 Tom Browning .05 .02
❑ 307 Bo Diaz .05 .02
❑ 308 Manny Trillo .05 .02
❑ 309 Chris Sabo RC * .40 .16
❑ 310 Ron Oester .05 .02
❑ 311 Barry Larkin .25 .10
❑ 312 Todd Benzinger .05 .02
❑ 313 Paul O'Neill .15 .06
❑ 314 Kal Daniels .05 .02
❑ 315 Joel Youngblood .05 .02
❑ 316 Eric Davis .10 .04
❑ 317 Dave Smith .05 .02
❑ 318 Mark Portugal .05 .02
❑ 319 Brian Meyer .05 .02
❑ 320 Jim Deshaies .05 .02
❑ 321 Juan Agosto .05 .02
❑ 322 Mike Scott .05 .02
❑ 323 Rick Rhoden .05 .02
❑ 324 Jim Clancy .05 .02
❑ 325 Larry Andersen .05 .02
❑ 326 Alex Trevino .05 .02
❑ 327 Alan Ashby .05 .02
❑ 328 Craig Reynolds .05 .02
❑ 329 Bill Doran .05 .02
❑ 330 Rafael Ramirez .05 .02
❑ 331 Glenn Davis .05 .02
❑ 332 Willie Ansley RC .10 .04
❑ 333 Gerald Young .05 .02
❑ 334 Cameron Drew .05 .02
❑ 335 Jay Howell .05 .02
❑ 336 Tim Belcher .05 .02
❑ 337 Fernando Valenzuela .10 .04
❑ 338 Ricky Horton .05 .02
❑ 339 Tim Leary .05 .02
❑ 340 Bill Bene .05 .02
❑ 341 Orel Hershiser .10 .04
❑ 342 Mike Scioscia .05 .02
❑ 343 Rick Dempsey .05 .02
❑ 344 Willie Randolph .10 .04
❑ 345 Alfredo Griffin .05 .02
❑ 346 Eddie Murray .25 .10
❑ 347 Mickey Hatcher .05 .02
❑ 348 Mike Sharperson .05 .02
❑ 349 John Shelby .05 .02
❑ 350 Mike Marshall .05 .02
❑ 351 Kirk Gibson .10 .04
❑ 352 Mike Davis .05 .02
❑ 353 Bryn Smith .05 .02
❑ 354 Pascual Perez .05 .02
❑ 355 Kevin Gross .05 .02
❑ 356 Andy McGaffigan .05 .02
❑ 357 Brian Holman RC * .10 .04
❑ 358 Dave Wainhouse RC .10 .04
❑ 359 Dennis Martinez .10 .04
❑ 360 Tim Burke .05 .02
❑ 361 Nelson Santovenia .05 .02
❑ 362 Tim Wallach .05 .02
❑ 363 Spike Owen .05 .02
❑ 364 Rex Hudler .05 .02
❑ 365 Andres Galarraga .10 .04
❑ 366 Otis Nixon .05 .02
❑ 367 Hubie Brooks .05 .02
❑ 368 Mike Aldrete .05 .02
❑ 369 Tim Raines .10 .04
❑ 370 Dave Martinez .05 .02
❑ 371 Bob Ojeda .05 .02
❑ 372 Ron Darling .05 .02
❑ 373 Wally Whitehurst RC .10 .04
❑ 374 Randy Myers .10 .04
❑ 375 David Cone .10 .04
❑ 376 Dwight Gooden .15 .06
❑ 377 Sid Fernandez .05 .02
❑ 378 Dave Proctor .05 .02
❑ 379 Gary Carter .15 .06
❑ 380 Keith Miller .05 .02
❑ 381 Gregg Jefferies .10 .04
❑ 382 Tim Teufel .05 .02
❑ 383 Kevin Elster .05 .02
❑ 384 Dave Magadan .05 .02
❑ 385 Keith Hernandez .15 .06
❑ 386 Mookie Wilson .10 .04
❑ 387 Darryl Strawberry .15 .06
❑ 388 Kevin McReynolds .05 .02
❑ 389 Mark Carreon .05 .02
❑ 390 Jeff Parrett .05 .02
❑ 391 Mike Maddux .05 .02
❑ 392 Don Carman .05 .02
❑ 393 Bruce Ruffin .05 .02
❑ 394 Ken Howell .05 .02
❑ 395 Steve Bedrosian .05 .02
❑ 396 Floyd Youmans .05 .02
❑ 397 Larry McWilliams .05 .02
❑ 398 Pat Combs RC * .10 .04
❑ 399 Steve Lake .05 .02
❑ 400 Dickie Thon .05 .02
❑ 401 Ricky Jordan RC * .25 .10
❑ 402 Mike Schmidt .50 .20
❑ 403 Tom Herr .05 .02
❑ 404 Chris James .05 .02
❑ 405 Juan Samuel .05 .02
❑ 406 Von Hayes .05 .02
❑ 407 Ron Jones .05 .02
❑ 408 Curt Ford .05 .02
❑ 409 Bob Walk .05 .02
❑ 410 Jeff D. Robinson .05 .02
❑ 411 Jim Gott .05 .02
❑ 412 Scott Medvin .05 .02
❑ 413 John Smiley .05 .02

❑ 414	Bob Kipper	.05	.02
❑ 415	Brian Fisher	.05	.02
❑ 416	Doug Drabek	.05	.02
❑ 417	Mike LaValliere	.05	.02
❑ 418	Ken Oberkfell	.05	.02
❑ 419	Sid Bream	.05	.02
❑ 420	Austin Manahan	.05	.02
❑ 421	Jose Lind	.05	.02
❑ 422	Bobby Bonilla	.10	.04
❑ 423	Glenn Wilson	.05	.02
❑ 424	Andy Van Slyke	.10	.04
❑ 425	Gary Redus	.05	.02
❑ 426	Barry Bonds	1.25	.50
❑ 427	Don Heinkel	.05	.02
❑ 428	Ken Dayley	.05	.02
❑ 429	Todd Worrell	.05	.02
❑ 430	Brad DuVall	.05	.02
❑ 431	Jose DeLeon	.05	.02
❑ 432	Joe Magrane	.05	.02
❑ 433	John Ericks	.05	.02
❑ 434	Frank DiPino	.05	.02
❑ 435	Tony Pena	.05	.02
❑ 436	Ozzie Smith	.25	.10
❑ 437	Terry Pendleton	.10	.04
❑ 438	Jose Oquendo	.05	.02
❑ 439	Tim Jones	.05	.02
❑ 440	Pedro Guerrero	.05	.02
❑ 441	Milt Thompson	.05	.02
❑ 442	Willie McGee	.10	.04
❑ 443	Vince Coleman	.05	.02
❑ 444	Tom Brunansky	.05	.02
❑ 445	Walt Terrell	.05	.02
❑ 446	Eric Show	.05	.02
❑ 447	Mark Davis	.05	.02
❑ 448	Andy Benes RC	.40	.16
❑ 449	Ed Whitson	.05	.02
❑ 450	Dennis Rasmussen	.05	.02
❑ 451	Bruce Hurst	.05	.02
❑ 452	Pat Clements	.05	.02
❑ 453	Benito Santiago	.10	.04
❑ 454	Sandy Alomar Jr. RC	.40	.16
❑ 455	Garry Templeton	.05	.02
❑ 456	Jack Clark	.05	.02
❑ 457	Tim Flannery	.05	.02
❑ 458	Roberto Alomar	.30	.12
❑ 459	Carmelo Martinez	.05	.02
❑ 460	John Kruk	.10	.04
❑ 461	Tony Gwynn	.30	.12
❑ 462	Jerald Clark RC	.10	.04
❑ 463	Don Robinson	.05	.02
❑ 464	Craig Lefferts	.05	.02
❑ 465	Kelly Downs	.05	.02
❑ 466	Rick Reuschel	.05	.02
❑ 467	Scott Garrelts	.05	.02
❑ 468	Wil Tejada	.05	.02
❑ 469	Kirt Manwaring	.05	.02
❑ 470	Terry Kennedy	.05	.02
❑ 471	Jose Uribe	.05	.02
❑ 472	Royce Clayton RC	.40	.16
❑ 473	Robby Thompson	.05	.02
❑ 474	Kevin Mitchell	.10	.04
❑ 475	Ernie Riles	.05	.02
❑ 476	Will Clark	.25	.10
❑ 477	Donell Nixon	.05	.02
❑ 478	Candy Maldonado	.05	.02
❑ 479	Tracy Jones	.05	.02
❑ 480	Brett Butler	.10	.04
❑ 481	Checklist 1-121	.05	.02
❑ 482	Checklist 122-242	.05	.02
❑ 483	Checklist 243-363	.05	.02
❑ 484	Checklist 364-484	.05	.02

1990 Bowman

	Nm-Mt	Ex-Mt
COMPLETE SET (528)	25.00	7.50
COMP.FACT.SET (528)	25.00	7.50

❑ 1	Tommy Greene RC	.10	.03
❑ 2	Tom Glavine	.25	.07
❑ 3	Andy Nezelek	.05	.02
❑ 4	Mike Stanton RC	.25	.07
❑ 5	Rick Luecken	.05	.02
❑ 6	Kent Mercker RC	.25	.07
❑ 7	Derek Lilliquist	.05	.02
❑ 8	Charlie Leibrandt	.05	.02

❑ 9	Steve Avery	.05	.02
❑ 10	John Smoltz	.25	.07
❑ 11	Mark Lemke	.05	.02
❑ 12	Lonnie Smith	.05	.02
❑ 13	Oddibe McDowell	.05	.02
❑ 14	Tyler Houston RC	.25	.07
❑ 15	Jeff Blauser	.05	.02
❑ 16	Ernie Whitt	.05	.02
❑ 17	Alexis Infante	.05	.02
❑ 18	Jim Presley	.05	.02
❑ 19	Dale Murphy	.25	.07
❑ 20	Nick Esasky	.05	.02
❑ 21	Rick Sutcliffe	.10	.03
❑ 22	Mike Bielecki	.05	.02
❑ 23	Steve Wilson	.05	.02
❑ 24	Kevin Blankenship	.05	.02
❑ 25	Mitch Williams	.05	.02
❑ 26	Dean Wilkins	.05	.02
❑ 27	Greg Maddux	.50	.15
❑ 28	Mike Harkey	.05	.02
❑ 29	Mark Grace	.25	.07
❑ 30	Ryne Sandberg	.40	.12
❑ 31	Greg Smith	.05	.02
❑ 32	Dwight Smith	.05	.02
❑ 33	Damon Berryhill	.05	.02
❑ 34	E.Cunningham UER RC (Errant * by the word "in")	.10	.03
❑ 35	Jerome Walton	.05	.02
❑ 36	Lloyd McClendon	.05	.02
❑ 37	Ty Griffin	.05	.02
❑ 38	Shawon Dunston	.05	.02
❑ 39	Andre Dawson	.10	.03
❑ 40	Luis Salazar	.05	.02
❑ 41	Tim Layana	.05	.02
❑ 42	Rob Dibble	.10	.03
❑ 43	Tom Browning	.05	.02
❑ 44	Danny Jackson	.05	.02
❑ 45	Jose Rijo	.05	.02
❑ 46	Scott Scudder	.05	.02
❑ 47	Randy Myers UER (Career ERA .274, should be 2.74)	.10	.03
❑ 48	Brian Lane RC	.10	.03
❑ 49	Paul O'Neill	.15	.04
❑ 50	Barry Larkin	.25	.07
❑ 51	Reggie Jefferson RC	.25	.07
❑ 52	Jeff Branson RC**	.10	.03
❑ 53	Chris Sabo	.05	.02
❑ 54	Joe Oliver	.05	.02
❑ 55	Todd Benzinger	.05	.02
❑ 56	Rolando Roomes	.05	.02
❑ 57	Hal Morris	.05	.02
❑ 58	Eric Davis	.10	.03
❑ 59	Scott Bryant	.05	.02
❑ 60	Ken Griffey Sr.	.10	.03
❑ 61	Darryl Kile RC	1.00	.30
❑ 62	Dave Smith	.05	.02
❑ 63	Mark Portugal	.05	.02
❑ 64	Jeff Juden RC	.10	.03
❑ 65	Bill Gullickson	.05	.02
❑ 66	Danny Darwin	.05	.02
❑ 67	Larry Andersen	.05	.02
❑ 68	Jose Cano	.05	.02
❑ 69	Dan Schatzeder	.05	.02
❑ 70	Jim Deshaies	.05	.02
❑ 71	Mike Scott	.05	.02
❑ 72	Gerald Young	.05	.02
❑ 73	Ken Caminiti	.10	.03
❑ 74	Ken Oberkfell	.05	.02
❑ 75	Dave Rohde	.05	.02
❑ 76	Bill Doran	.05	.02
❑ 77	Andujar Cedeno RC	.10	.03
❑ 78	Craig Biggio	.15	.04
❑ 79	Karl Rhodes RC	.25	.07
❑ 80	Glenn Davis	.05	.02
❑ 81	Eric Anthony RC	.10	.03
❑ 82	John Wetteland	.25	.07
❑ 83	Jay Howell	.05	.02
❑ 84	Orel Hershiser	.10	.03
❑ 85	Tim Belcher	.05	.02
❑ 86	Kiki Jones	.05	.02
❑ 87	Mike Hartley	.05	.02
❑ 88	Ramon Martinez	.05	.02
❑ 89	Mike Scioscia	.05	.02
❑ 90	Willie Randolph	.10	.03
❑ 91	Juan Samuel	.05	.02
❑ 92	Jose Offerman RC	.25	.07
❑ 93	Dave Hansen RC	.25	.07
❑ 94	Jeff Hamilton	.05	.02
❑ 95	Alfredo Griffin	.05	.02
❑ 96	Tom Goodwin RC	.25	.07
❑ 97	Kirk Gibson	.10	.03
❑ 98	Jose Vizcaino RC	.25	.07
❑ 99	Kal Daniels	.05	.02
❑ 100	Hubie Brooks	.05	.02
❑ 101	Eddie Murray	.25	.07
❑ 102	Dennis Boyd	.05	.02
❑ 103	Tim Burke	.05	.02
❑ 104	Bill Sampen	.05	.02
❑ 105	Brett Gideon	.05	.02
❑ 106	Mark Gardner RC	.10	.03
❑ 107	Howard Farmer	.05	.02
❑ 108	Mel Rojas RC	.10	.03
❑ 109	Kevin Gross	.05	.02
❑ 110	Dave Schmidt	.05	.02
❑ 111	Dennis Martinez	.10	.03
❑ 112	Jerry Goff	.05	.02
❑ 113	Andres Galarraga	.10	.03
❑ 114	Tim Wallach	.05	.02
❑ 115	Marquis Grissom RC	.25	.07
❑ 116	Spike Owen	.05	.02
❑ 117	Larry Walker RC	1.50	.45
❑ 118	Tim Raines	.10	.03
❑ 119	Delino DeShields RC	.25	.07
❑ 120	Tom Foley	.05	.02
❑ 121	Dave Martinez	.05	.02
❑ 122	Frank Viola UER (Career ERA .384 should be 3.84)	.05	.02
❑ 123	Julio Valera RC	.05	.02
❑ 124	Alejandro Pena	.05	.02
❑ 125	David Cone	.10	.03
❑ 126	Dwight Gooden	.15	.04
❑ 127	Kevin D. Brown	.05	.02
❑ 128	John Franco	.10	.03
❑ 129	Terry Bross	.05	.02
❑ 130	Blaine Beatty	.05	.02
❑ 131	Sid Fernandez	.05	.02
❑ 132	Mike Marshall	.05	.02
❑ 133	Howard Johnson	.05	.02
❑ 134	Jaime Roseboro	.05	.02
❑ 135	Alan Zinter RC	.10	.03
❑ 136	Keith Miller	.05	.02
❑ 137	Kevin Elster	.05	.02
❑ 138	Kevin McReynolds	.05	.02
❑ 139	Barry Lyons	.05	.02
❑ 140	Gregg Jefferies	.10	.03
❑ 141	Darryl Strawberry	.15	.04
❑ 142	Todd Hundley RC	.25	.07
❑ 143	Scott Service	.05	.02
❑ 144	Chuck Malone	.05	.02
❑ 145	Steve Ontiveros	.05	.02
❑ 146	Roger McDowell	.05	.02
❑ 147	Ken Howell	.05	.02
❑ 148	Pat Combs	.05	.02
❑ 149	Jeff Parrett	.05	.02
❑ 150	Chuck McElroy RC	.10	.03
❑ 151	Jason Grimsley RC	.10	.03
❑ 152	Len Dykstra	.10	.03
❑ 153	M.Morandini RC	.25	.07
❑ 154	John Kruk	.10	.03
❑ 155	Dickie Thon	.05	.02
❑ 156	Ricky Jordan	.05	.02

❑ 157 Jeff Jackson RC .10 .03
❑ 158 Darren Daulton .10 .03
❑ 159 Tom Herr .05 .02
❑ 160 Von Hayes .05 .02
❑ 161 Dave Hollins RC .25 .07
❑ 162 Carmelo Martinez .05 .02
❑ 163 Bob Walk .05 .02
❑ 164 Doug Drabek .05 .02
❑ 165 Walt Terrell .05 .02
❑ 166 Bill Landrum .05 .02
❑ 167 Scott Ruskin .05 .02
❑ 168 Bob Patterson .05 .02
❑ 169 Bobby Bonilla .10 .03
❑ 170 Jose Lind .05 .02
❑ 171 Andy Van Slyke .10 .03
❑ 172 Mike LaValliere .05 .02
❑ 173 Willie Greene RC .10 .03
❑ 174 Jay Bell .10 .03
❑ 175 Sid Bream .05 .02
❑ 176 Tom Prince .05 .02
❑ 177 Wally Backman .05 .02
❑ 178 Moises Alou RC .50 .15
❑ 179 Steve Carter .05 .02
❑ 180 Gary Redus .05 .02
❑ 181 Barry Bonds .60 .18
❑ 182 Don Slaught UER .05 .02
(Card back shows
headings for a pitcher)
❑ 183 Joe Magrane .05 .02
❑ 184 Bryn Smith .05 .02
❑ 185 Todd Worrell .05 .02
❑ 186 Jose DeLeon .05 .02
❑ 187 Frank DiPino .05 .02
❑ 188 John Tudor .05 .02
❑ 189 Howard Hilton .05 .02
❑ 190 John Ericks .05 .02
❑ 191 Ken Dayley .05 .02
❑ 192 Ray Lankford RC .25 .07
❑ 193 Todd Zeile .10 .03
❑ 194 Willie McGee .10 .03
❑ 195 Ozzie Smith .25 .07
❑ 196 Milt Thompson .05 .02
❑ 197 Terry Pendleton .10 .03
❑ 198 Vince Coleman .05 .02
❑ 199 Paul Coleman RC .10 .03
❑ 200 Jose Oquendo .05 .02
❑ 201 Pedro Guerrero .05 .02
❑ 202 Tom Brunansky .05 .02
❑ 203 Roger Smithberg .05 .02
❑ 204 Eddie Whitson .05 .02
❑ 205 Dennis Rasmussen .05 .02
❑ 206 Craig Lefferts .05 .02
❑ 207 Andy Benes .10 .03
❑ 208 Bruce Hurst .05 .02
❑ 209 Eric Show .05 .02
❑ 210 Rafael Valdez .05 .02
❑ 211 Joey Cora .10 .03
❑ 212 Thomas Howard .05 .02
❑ 213 Rob Nelson .05 .02
❑ 214 Jack Clark .10 .03
❑ 215 Garry Templeton .05 .02
❑ 216 Fred Lynn .05 .02
❑ 217 Tony Gwynn .30 .09
❑ 218 Benito Santiago .10 .03
❑ 219 Mike Pagliarulo .05 .02
❑ 220 Joe Carter .10 .03
❑ 221 Roberto Alomar .25 .07
❑ 222 Bip Roberts .05 .02
❑ 223 Rick Reuschel .05 .02
❑ 224 Russ Swan .05 .02
❑ 225 Eric Gunderson .05 .02
❑ 226 Steve Bedrosian .05 .02
❑ 227 Mike Remlinger .05 .02
❑ 228 Scott Garrelts .05 .02
❑ 229 Ernie Camacho .05 .02
❑ 230 Andres Santana RC .10 .03
❑ 231 Will Clark .25 .07
❑ 232 Kevin Mitchell .05 .02
❑ 233 Robby Thompson .05 .02
❑ 234 Bill Bathe .05 .02
❑ 235 Tony Perezchica .05 .02
❑ 236 Gary Carter .15 .04
❑ 237 Brett Butler .10 .03
❑ 238 Matt Williams .10 .03
❑ 239 Earnie Riles .05 .02
❑ 240 Kevin Bass .05 .02
❑ 241 Terry Kennedy .05 .02
❑ 242 Steve Hosey RC .10 .03
❑ 243 Ben McDonald RC .25 .07
❑ 244 Jeff Ballard .05 .02
❑ 245 Joe Price .05 .02
❑ 246 Curt Schilling 1.00 .30
❑ 247 Pete Harnisch .05 .02
❑ 248 Mark Williamson .05 .02
❑ 249 Gregg Olson .10 .03
❑ 250 Chris Myers .05 .02
❑ 251 David Segui RC ERR .25 .07
(Missing vital stats
at top of card back
under name)
❑ 251B David Segui COR RC .25 .07
❑ 252 Joe Orsulak .05 .02
❑ 253 Craig Worthington .05 .02
❑ 254 Mickey Tettleton .05 .02
❑ 255 Cal Ripken .75 .23
❑ 256 Bill Ripken .05 .02
❑ 257 Randy Milligan .05 .02
❑ 258 Brady Anderson .10 .03
❑ 259 Chris Hoiles RC UER .25 .07
Baltimore is spelled Balitmore
❑ 260 Mike Devereaux .05 .02
❑ 261 Phil Bradley .05 .02
❑ 262 Leo Gomez RC .10 .03
❑ 263 Lee Smith .10 .03
❑ 264 Mike Rochford .05 .02
❑ 265 Jeff Reardon .10 .03
❑ 266 Wes Gardner .05 .02
❑ 267 Mike Boddicker .05 .02
❑ 268 Roger Clemens .50 .15
❑ 269 Rob Murphy .05 .02
❑ 270 Mickey Pina .05 .02
❑ 271 Tony Pena .05 .02
❑ 272 Jody Reed .05 .02
❑ 273 Kevin Romine .05 .02
❑ 274 Mike Greenwell .05 .02
❑ 275 Maurice Vaughn RC 1.00 .30
❑ 276 Danny Heep .05 .02
❑ 277 Scott Cooper RC .10 .03
❑ 278 Greg Blosser RC .10 .03
❑ 279 Dwight Evans UER .10 .03
(* by "1990 Team
Breakdown")
❑ 280 Ellis Burks .15 .04
❑ 281 Wade Boggs .15 .04
❑ 282 Marty Barrett .05 .02
❑ 283 Kirk McCaskill .05 .02
❑ 284 Mark Langston .05 .02
❑ 285 Bert Blyleven .10 .03
❑ 286 Mike Fetters RC .25 .07
❑ 287 Kyle Abbott .05 .02
❑ 288 Jim Abbott .25 .07
❑ 289 Chuck Finley .10 .03
❑ 290 Gary DiSarcina RC .25 .07
❑ 291 Dick Schofield .05 .02
❑ 292 Devon White .05 .02
❑ 293 Bobby Rose .05 .02
❑ 294 Brian Downing .05 .02
❑ 295 Lance Parrish .05 .02
❑ 296 Jack Howell .05 .02
❑ 297 Claudell Washington .05 .02
❑ 298 John Orton RC .10 .03
❑ 299 Wally Joyner .10 .03
❑ 300 Lee Stevens .10 .03
❑ 301 Chili Davis .10 .03
❑ 302 Johnny Ray .05 .02
❑ 303 Greg Hibbard RC .10 .03
❑ 304 Eric King .05 .02
❑ 305 Jack McDowell .05 .02
❑ 306 Bobby Thigpen .05 .02
❑ 307 Adam Peterson .05 .02
❑ 308 Scott Radinsky RC .25 .07
❑ 309 Wayne Edwards .05 .02
❑ 310 Melido Perez .05 .02
❑ 311 Robin Ventura .25 .07
❑ 312 Sammy Sosa RC 10.00 3.00
❑ 313 Dan Pasqua .05 .02
❑ 314 Carlton Fisk .15 .04
❑ 315 Ozzie Guillen .05 .02
❑ 316 Ivan Calderon .05 .02
❑ 317 Daryl Boston .05 .02
❑ 318 Craig Grebeck RC .25 .07
❑ 319 Scott Fletcher .05 .02
❑ 320 Frank Thomas RC 2.00 .60
❑ 321 Steve Lyons .05 .02
❑ 322 Carlos Martinez .05 .02
❑ 323 Joe Skalski .05 .02
❑ 324 Tom Candiotti .05 .02
❑ 325 Greg Swindell .05 .02
❑ 326 Steve Olin RC .25 .07
❑ 327 Kevin Wickander .05 .02
❑ 328 Doug Jones .05 .02
❑ 329 Jeff Shaw .05 .02
❑ 330 Kevin Bearse .05 .02
❑ 331 Dion James .05 .02
❑ 332 Jerry Browne .05 .02
❑ 333 Joey Belle .25 .07
❑ 334 Felix Fermin .05 .02
❑ 335 Candy Maldonado .05 .02
❑ 336 Cory Snyder .05 .02
❑ 337 Sandy Alomar Jr. .10 .03
❑ 338 Mark Lewis .05 .02
❑ 339 Carlos Baerga RC .25 .07
❑ 340 Chris James .05 .02
❑ 341 Brook Jacoby .05 .02
❑ 342 Keith Hernandez .15 .04
❑ 343 Frank Tanana .05 .02
❑ 344 Scott Aldred .05 .02
❑ 345 Mike Henneman .05 .02
❑ 346 Steve Wapnick .05 .02
❑ 347 Greg Gohr RC .10 .03
❑ 348 Eric Stone .05 .02
❑ 349 Brian DuBois .05 .02
❑ 350 Kevin Ritz .05 .02
❑ 351 Rico Brogna .25 .07
❑ 352 Mike Heath .05 .02
❑ 353 Alan Trammell .15 .04
❑ 354 Chet Lemon .05 .02
❑ 355 Dave Bergman .05 .02
❑ 356 Lou Whitaker .10 .03
❑ 357 Cecil Fielder UER .10 .03
* by 1990 Team Breakdown
❑ 358 Milt Cuyler RC .10 .03
❑ 359 Tony Phillips .05 .02
❑ 360 Travis Fryman RC .50 .15
❑ 361 Ed Romero .05 .02
❑ 362 Lloyd Moseby .05 .02
❑ 363 Mark Gubicza .05 .02
❑ 364 Bret Saberhagen .10 .03
❑ 365 Tom Gordon .10 .03
❑ 366 Steve Farr .05 .02
❑ 367 Kevin Appier .25 .07
❑ 368 Storm Davis .05 .02
❑ 369 Mark Davis .05 .02
❑ 370 Jeff Montgomery .10 .03
❑ 371 Frank White .10 .03
❑ 372 Brent Mayne RC .25 .07
❑ 373 Bob Boone .10 .03
❑ 374 Jim Eisenreich .05 .02
❑ 375 Danny Tartabull .05 .02
❑ 376 Kurt Stillwell .05 .02
❑ 377 Bill Pecota .05 .02
❑ 378 Bo Jackson .25 .07
❑ 379 Bob Hamelin RC .25 .07
❑ 380 Kevin Seitzer .05 .02
❑ 381 Rey Palacios .05 .02
❑ 382 George Brett .60 .18
❑ 383 Gerald Perry .05 .02
❑ 384 Teddy Higuera .05 .02
❑ 385 Tom Filer .05 .02
❑ 386 Dan Plesac .05 .02
❑ 387 Cal Eldred RC .25 .07
❑ 388 Jaime Navarro .05 .02
❑ 389 Chris Bosio .05 .02
❑ 390 Randy Veres .05 .02
❑ 391 Gary Sheffield .25 .07
❑ 392 George Canale .05 .02
❑ 393 B.J. Surhoff .10 .03
❑ 394 Tim McIntosh .05 .02
❑ 395 Greg Brock .05 .02
❑ 396 Greg Vaughn .10 .03
❑ 397 Darryl Hamilton .05 .02
❑ 398 Dave Parker .10 .03
❑ 399 Paul Molitor .15 .04
❑ 400 Jim Gantner .05 .02
❑ 401 Rob Deer .05 .02
❑ 402 Billy Spiers .05 .02
❑ 403 Glenn Braggs .05 .02
❑ 404 Robin Yount .25 .07

❑ 405	Rick Aguilera	.10	.03
❑ 406	Johnny Ard	.05	.02
❑ 407	Kevin Tapani RC	.25	.07
❑ 408	Park Pittman	.05	.02
❑ 409	Allan Anderson	.05	.02
❑ 410	Juan Berenguer	.05	.02
❑ 411	Willie Banks RC	.10	.03
❑ 412	Rich Yett	.05	.02
❑ 413	Dave West	.05	.02
❑ 414	Greg Gagne	.05	.02
❑ 415	Chuck Knoblauch RC	.50	.15
❑ 416	Randy Bush	.05	.02
❑ 417	Gary Gaetti	.10	.03
❑ 418	Kent Hrbek	.10	.03
❑ 419	Al Newman	.05	.02
❑ 420	Danny Gladden	.05	.02
❑ 421	Paul Sorrento RC	.25	.07
❑ 422	Derek Parks RC	.10	.03
❑ 423	Scott Leius RC	.10	.03
❑ 424	Kirby Puckett	.25	.07
❑ 425	Willie Smith	.05	.02
❑ 426	Dave Righetti	.05	.02
❑ 427	Jeff D. Robinson	.05	.02
❑ 428	Alan Mills RC	.10	.03
❑ 429	Tim Leary	.05	.02
❑ 430	Pascual Perez	.05	.02
❑ 431	Alvaro Espinoza	.05	.02
❑ 432	Dave Winfield	.15	.04
❑ 433	Jesse Barfield	.05	.02
❑ 434	Randy Velarde	.05	.02
❑ 435	Rick Cerone	.05	.02
❑ 436	Steve Balboni	.05	.02
❑ 437	Mel Hall	.05	.02
❑ 438	Bob Geren	.05	.02
❑ 439	Bernie Williams RC	1.50	.45
❑ 440	Kevin Maas RC	.25	.07
❑ 441	Mike Blowers RC	.10	.03
❑ 442	Steve Sax	.05	.02
❑ 443	Don Mattingly	.60	.18
❑ 444	Roberto Kelly	.05	.02
❑ 445	Mike Moore	.05	.02
❑ 446	Reggie Harris RC	.10	.03
❑ 447	Scott Sanderson	.05	.02
❑ 448	Dave Otto	.05	.02
❑ 449	Dave Stewart	.10	.03
❑ 450	Rick Honeycutt	.05	.02
❑ 451	Dennis Eckersley	.10	.03
❑ 452	Carney Lansford	.10	.03
❑ 453	Scott Hemond RC	.10	.03
❑ 454	Mark McGwire	.60	.18
❑ 455	Felix Jose	.05	.02
❑ 456	Terry Steinbach	.05	.02
❑ 457	Rickey Henderson	.40	.12
❑ 458	Dave Henderson	.05	.02
❑ 459	Mike Gallego	.05	.02
❑ 460	Jose Canseco	.25	.07
❑ 461	Walt Weiss	.05	.02
❑ 462	Ken Phelps	.05	.02
❑ 463	Darren Lewis RC	.10	.03
❑ 464	Ron Hassey	.05	.02
❑ 465	Roger Salkeld RC	.10	.03
❑ 466	Scott Bankhead	.05	.02
❑ 467	Keith Comstock	.05	.02
❑ 468	Randy Johnson	.40	.12
❑ 469	Erik Hanson	.05	.02
❑ 470	Mike Schooler	.05	.02
❑ 471	Gary Eave	.05	.02
❑ 472	Jeffrey Leonard	.05	.02
❑ 473	Dave Valle	.05	.02
❑ 474	Omar Vizquel	.25	.07
❑ 475	Pete O'Brien	.05	.02
❑ 476	Henry Cotto	.05	.02
❑ 477	Jay Buhner	.10	.03
❑ 478	Harold Reynolds	.10	.03
❑ 479	Alvin Davis	.05	.02
❑ 480	Darnell Coles	.05	.02
❑ 481	Ken Griffey Jr.	.75	.23
❑ 482	Greg Briley	.05	.02
❑ 483	Scott Bradley	.05	.02
❑ 484	Tino Martinez	.25	.07
❑ 485	Jeff Russell	.05	.02
❑ 486	Nolan Ryan	1.00	.30
❑ 487	Robb Nen RC	1.00	.30
❑ 488	Kevin Brown	.10	.03
❑ 489	Brian Bohanon RC	.10	.03
❑ 490	Ruben Sierra	.05	.02
❑ 491	Pete Incaviglia	.05	.02
❑ 492	Juan Gonzalez RC	2.00	.60
❑ 493	Steve Buechele	.05	.02
❑ 494	Scott Coolbaugh	.05	.02
❑ 495	Geno Petralli	.05	.02
❑ 496	Rafael Palmeiro	.15	.04
❑ 497	Julio Franco	.05	.02
❑ 498	Gary Pettis	.05	.02
❑ 499	Donald Harris	.05	.02
❑ 500	Monty Fariss	.05	.02
❑ 501	Harold Baines	.10	.03
❑ 502	Cecil Espy	.05	.02
❑ 503	Jack Daugherty	.05	.02
❑ 504	Willie Blair RC	.10	.03
❑ 505	Dave Stieb	.10	.03
❑ 506	Tom Henke	.05	.02
❑ 507	John Cerutti	.05	.02
❑ 508	Paul Kilgus	.05	.02
❑ 509	Jimmy Key	.10	.03
❑ 510	John Olerud RC	1.00	.30
❑ 511	Ed Sprague	.10	.03
❑ 512	Manuel Lee	.05	.02
❑ 513	Fred McGriff	.25	.07
❑ 514	Glenallen Hill	.05	.02
❑ 515	George Bell	.05	.02
❑ 516	Mookie Wilson	.10	.03
❑ 517	Luis Sojo RC	.25	.07
❑ 518	Nelson Liriano	.05	.02
❑ 519	Kelly Gruber	.05	.02
❑ 520	Greg Myers	.05	.02
❑ 521	Pat Borders	.05	.02
❑ 522	Junior Felix	.05	.02
❑ 523	Eddie Zosky RC	.10	.03
❑ 524	Tony Fernandez	.05	.02
❑ 525	Checklist 1-132 UER (No copyright mark on the back)	.05	.02
❑ 526	Checklist 133-264	.05	.02
❑ 527	Checklist 265-396	.05	.02
❑ 528	Checklist 397-528	.05	.02

1991 Bowman

		Nm-Mt	Ex-Mt
COMPLETE SET (704)		40.00	12.00
COMP.FACT.SET (704)		40.00	12.00
❑ 1	Rod Carew I	.15	.04
❑ 2	Rod Carew II	.15	.04
❑ 3	Rod Carew III	.15	.04
❑ 4	Rod Carew IV	.15	.04
❑ 5	Rod Carew V	.15	.04
❑ 6	Willie Fraser	.05	.02
❑ 7	John Olerud	.10	.03
❑ 8	William Suero	.05	.02
❑ 9	Roberto Alomar	.25	.07
❑ 10	Todd Stottlemyre	.05	.02
❑ 11	Joe Carter	.10	.03
❑ 12	Steve Karsay RC	.50	.15
❑ 13	Mark Whiten	.05	.02
❑ 14	Pat Borders	.05	.02
❑ 15	Mike Timlin RC	.50	.15
❑ 16	Tom Henke	.05	.02
❑ 17	Eddie Zosky	.05	.02
❑ 18	Kelly Gruber	.05	.02
❑ 19	Jimmy Key	.10	.03
❑ 20	Jerry Schunk	.05	.02
❑ 21	Manuel Lee	.05	.02
❑ 22	Dave Stieb	.05	.02
❑ 23	Pat Hentgen RC	.50	.15
❑ 24	Glenallen Hill	.05	.02
❑ 25	Rene Gonzales	.05	.02
❑ 26	Ed Sprague	.05	.02
❑ 27	Ken Dayley	.05	.02
❑ 28	Pat Tabler	.05	.02
❑ 29	Denis Boucher RC	.15	.04
❑ 30	Devon White	.05	.02
❑ 31	Dante Bichette	.10	.03
❑ 32	Paul Molitor	.15	.04
❑ 33	Greg Vaughn	.10	.03
❑ 34	Dan Plesac	.05	.02
❑ 35	Chris George RC	.15	.04
❑ 36	Tim McIntosh	.05	.02
❑ 37	Franklin Stubbs	.05	.02
❑ 38	Bo Dodson RC	.15	.04
❑ 39	Ron Robinson	.05	.02
❑ 40	Ed Nunez	.05	.02
❑ 41	Greg Brock	.05	.02
❑ 42	Jaime Navarro	.05	.02
❑ 43	Chris Bosio	.05	.02
❑ 44	B.J. Surhoff	.10	.03
❑ 45	Chris Johnson	.05	.02
❑ 46	Willie Randolph	.10	.03
❑ 47	Narciso Elvira	.05	.02
❑ 48	Jim Gantner	.05	.02
❑ 49	Kevin Brown	.05	.02
❑ 50	Julio Machado	.05	.02
❑ 51	Chuck Crim	.05	.02
❑ 52	Gary Sheffield	.10	.03
❑ 53	Angel Miranda RC	.15	.04
❑ 54	Ted Higuera	.05	.02
❑ 55	Robin Yount	.25	.07
❑ 56	Cal Eldred	.05	.02
❑ 57	Sandy Alomar Jr.	.05	.02
❑ 58	Greg Swindell	.05	.02
❑ 59	Brook Jacoby	.05	.02
❑ 60	Efrain Valdez	.05	.02
❑ 61	Ever Magallanes	.05	.02
❑ 62	Tom Candiotti	.05	.02
❑ 63	Eric King	.05	.02
❑ 64	Alex Cole	.05	.02
❑ 65	Charles Nagy	.05	.02
❑ 66	Mitch Webster	.05	.02
❑ 67	Chris James	.05	.02
❑ 68	Jim Thome RC	4.00	1.20
❑ 69	Carlos Baerga	.05	.02
❑ 70	Mark Lewis	.05	.02
❑ 71	Jerry Browne	.05	.02
❑ 72	Jesse Orosco	.05	.02
❑ 73	Mike Huff	.05	.02
❑ 74	Jose Escobar	.05	.02
❑ 75	Jeff Manto	.05	.02
❑ 76	Turner Ward RC	.15	.04
❑ 77	Doug Jones	.05	.02
❑ 78	Bruce Egloff	.05	.02
❑ 79	Tim Costo RC	.15	.04
❑ 80	Beau Allred	.05	.02
❑ 81	Albert Belle	.10	.03
❑ 82	John Farrell	.05	.02
❑ 83	Glenn Davis	.05	.02
❑ 84	Joe Orsulak	.05	.02
❑ 85	Mark Williamson	.05	.02
❑ 86	Ben McDonald	.05	.02
❑ 87	Billy Ripken	.05	.02
❑ 88	Leo Gomez UER (Baltimore is spelled Baltimore)	.05	.02
❑ 89	Bob Melvin	.05	.02
❑ 90	Jeff M. Robinson	.05	.02
❑ 91	Jose Mesa	.05	.02
❑ 92	Gregg Olson	.05	.02
❑ 93	Mike Devereaux	.05	.02
❑ 94	Luis Mercedes RC	.15	.04
❑ 95	Arthur Rhodes RC	.50	.15
❑ 96	Juan Bell	.05	.02
❑ 97	Mike Mussina RC	3.00	.90
❑ 98	Jeff Ballard	.05	.02
❑ 99	Chris Hoiles	.05	.02
❑ 100	Brady Anderson	.10	.03
❑ 101	Bob Milacki	.05	.02
❑ 102	David Segui	.05	.02
❑ 103	Dwight Evans	.10	.03
❑ 104	Cal Ripken	.75	.23
❑ 105	Mike Linskey	.05	.02
❑ 106	Jeff Tackett RC	.15	.04

☐ 107 Jeff Reardon .10 .03
☐ 108 Dana Kiecker .05 .02
☐ 109 Ellis Burks .10 .03
☐ 110 Dave Owen .05 .02
☐ 111 Danny Darwin .05 .02
☐ 112 Mo Vaughn .10 .03
☐ 113 Jeff McNeely RC .15 .04
☐ 114 Tom Bolton .05 .02
☐ 115 Greg Blosser .05 .02
☐ 116 Mike Greenwell .05 .02
☐ 117 Phil Plantier RC .15 .04
☐ 118 Roger Clemens .50 .15
☐ 119 John Marzano .05 .02
☐ 120 Jody Reed .05 .02
☐ 121 Scott Taylor RC .15 .04
☐ 122 Jack Clark .10 .03
☐ 123 Derek Livernois .05 .02
☐ 124 Tony Pena .05 .02
☐ 125 Tom Brunansky .05 .02
☐ 126 Carlos Quintana .05 .02
☐ 127 Tim Naehring .05 .02
☐ 128 Matt Young .05 .02
☐ 129 Wade Boggs .15 .04
☐ 130 Kevin Morton .05 .02
☐ 131 Pete Incaviglia .05 .02
☐ 132 Rob Deer .05 .02
☐ 133 Bill Gullickson .05 .02
☐ 134 Rico Brogna .05 .02
☐ 135 Lloyd Moseby .05 .02
☐ 136 Cecil Fielder .10 .03
☐ 137 Tony Phillips .05 .02
☐ 138 Mark Leiter RC .15 .04
☐ 139 John Cerutti .05 .02
☐ 140 Mickey Tettleton .05 .02
☐ 141 Milt Cuyler .05 .02
☐ 142 Greg Gohr .05 .02
☐ 143 Tony Bernazard .05 .02
☐ 144 Dan Gakeler .05 .02
☐ 145 Travis Fryman .10 .03
☐ 146 Dan Petry .05 .02
☐ 147 Scott Aldred .05 .02
☐ 148 John DeSilva .05 .02
☐ 149 Rusty Meacham RC .15 .04
☐ 150 Lou Whitaker .10 .03
☐ 151 Dave Haas .05 .02
☐ 152 Luis de los Santos .05 .02
☐ 153 Ivan Cruz .05 .02
☐ 154 Alan Trammell .15 .04
☐ 155 Pat Kelly RC .05 .02
☐ 156 Carl Everett RC 1.00 .30
☐ 157 Greg Cadaret .05 .02
☐ 158 Kevin Maas .05 .02
☐ 159 Jeff Johnson .05 .02
☐ 160 Willie Smith .05 .02
☐ 161 Gerald Williams RC .50 .15
☐ 162 Mike Humphreys RC .15 .04
☐ 163 Alvaro Espinoza .05 .02
☐ 164 Matt Nokes .05 .02
☐ 165 Wade Taylor .05 .02
☐ 166 Roberto Kelly .05 .02
☐ 167 John Habyan .05 .02
☐ 168 Steve Farr .05 .02
☐ 169 Jesse Barfield .05 .02
☐ 170 Steve Sax .05 .02
☐ 171 Jim Leyritz .05 .02
☐ 172 Robert Eenhoorn RC .15 .04
☐ 173 Bernie Williams .25 .07
☐ 174 Scott Lusader .05 .02
☐ 175 Torey Lovullo .05 .02
☐ 176 Chuck Cary .05 .02
☐ 177 Scott Sanderson .05 .02
☐ 178 Don Mattingly .60 .18
☐ 179 Mel Hall .05 .02
☐ 180 Juan Gonzalez .25 .07
☐ 181 Hensley Meulens .05 .02
☐ 182 Jose Offerman .05 .02
☐ 183 Jeff Bagwell RC 2.00 .60
☐ 184 Jeff Conine RC 1.00 .30
☐ 185 Henry Rodriguez RC .50 .15
☐ 186 Jimmie Reese CO .10 .03
☐ 187 Kyle Abbott .05 .02
☐ 188 Lance Parrish .10 .03
☐ 189 Rafael Montalvo .05 .02
☐ 190 Floyd Bannister .05 .02
☐ 191 Dick Schofield .05 .02
☐ 192 Scott Lewis .05 .02
☐ 193 Jeff D. Robinson .05 .02
☐ 194 Kent Anderson .05 .02
☐ 195 Wally Joyner .10 .03
☐ 196 Chuck Finley .10 .03
☐ 197 Luis Sojo .05 .02
☐ 198 Jeff Richardson .05 .02
☐ 199 Dave Parker .10 .03
☐ 200 Jim Abbott .25 .07
☐ 201 Junior Felix .05 .02
☐ 202 Mark Langston .05 .02
☐ 203 Tim Salmon RC 2.00 .60
☐ 204 Cliff Young .05 .02
☐ 205 Scott Bailes .05 .02
☐ 206 Bobby Rose .05 .02
☐ 207 Gary Gaetti .10 .03
☐ 208 Ruben Amaro RC .15 .04
☐ 209 Luis Polonia .05 .02
☐ 210 Dave Winfield .15 .04
☐ 211 Bryan Harvey .05 .02
☐ 212 Mike Moore .05 .02
☐ 213 Rickey Henderson .40 .12
☐ 214 Steve Chitren .05 .02
☐ 215 Bob Welch .05 .02
☐ 216 Terry Steinbach .05 .02
☐ 217 Earnest Riles .05 .02
☐ 218 Todd Van Poppel RC .50 .15
☐ 219 Mike Gallego .05 .02
☐ 220 Curt Young .05 .02
☐ 221 Todd Burns .05 .02
☐ 222 Vance Law .05 .02
☐ 223 Eric Show .05 .02
☐ 224 Don Peters .05 .02
☐ 225 Dave Stewart .10 .03
☐ 226 Dave Henderson .05 .02
☐ 227 Jose Canseco .25 .07
☐ 228 Walt Weiss .05 .02
☐ 229 Dann Howitt .05 .02
☐ 230 Willie Wilson .05 .02
☐ 231 Harold Baines .10 .03
☐ 232 Scott Hemond .05 .02
☐ 233 Joe Slusarski .05 .02
☐ 234 Mark McGwire .60 .18
☐ 235 K.Dressendorfer RC .15 .04
☐ 236 Craig Paquette RC .50 .15
☐ 237 Dennis Eckersley .10 .03
☐ 238 Dana Allison .05 .02
☐ 239 Scott Bradley .05 .02
☐ 240 Brian Holman .05 .02
☐ 241 Mike Schooler .05 .02
☐ 242 Rich DeLucia .05 .02
☐ 243 Edgar Martinez .15 .04
☐ 244 Henry Cotto .05 .02
☐ 245 Omar Vizquel .10 .03
☐ 246 Ken Griffey Jr. .50 .15
(See also 255)
☐ 247 Jay Buhner .10 .03
☐ 248 Bill Krueger .05 .02
☐ 249 Dave Fleming RC .15 .04
☐ 250 Patrick Lennon .05 .02
☐ 251 Dave Valle .05 .02
☐ 252 Harold Reynolds .10 .03
☐ 253 Randy Johnson .30 .09
☐ 254 Scott Bankhead .05 .02
☐ 255 Ken Griffey Sr. UER .05 .02
(Card number is 246)
☐ 256 Greg Briley .05 .02
☐ 257 Tino Martinez .15 .04
☐ 258 Alvin Davis .05 .02
☐ 259 Pete O'Brien .05 .02
☐ 260 Erik Hanson .05 .02
☐ 261 Bret Boone RC 3.00 .90
☐ 262 Roger Salkeld .05 .02
☐ 263 Dave Burba RC .50 .15
☐ 264 Kerry Woodson RC .15 .04
☐ 265 Julio Franco .10 .03
☐ 266 Dan Peltier RC .15 .04
☐ 267 Jeff Russell .05 .02
☐ 268 Steve Buechele .05 .02
☐ 269 Donald Harris .05 .02
☐ 270 Robb Nen .15 .04
☐ 271 Rich Gossage .10 .03
☐ 272 Ivan Rodriguez RC 2.50 .75
☐ 273 Jeff Huson .05 .02
☐ 274 Kevin Brown .10 .03
☐ 275 Dan Smith RC .15 .04
☐ 276 Gary Pettis .05 .02
☐ 277 Jack Daugherty .05 .02
☐ 278 Mike Jeffcoat .05 .02
☐ 279 Brad Arnsberg .05 .02
☐ 280 Nolan Ryan 1.00 .30
☐ 281 Eric McCray .05 .02
☐ 282 Scott Chiamparino .05 .02
☐ 283 Ruben Sierra .05 .02
☐ 284 Geno Petralli .05 .02
☐ 285 Monty Fariss .05 .02
☐ 286 Rafael Palmeiro .15 .04
☐ 287 Bobby Witt .05 .02
☐ 288 Dean Palmer UER .10 .03
Photo is Dan Peltier
☐ 289 Tony Scruggs .05 .02
☐ 290 Kenny Rogers .10 .03
☐ 291 Bret Saberhagen .10 .03
☐ 292 Brian McRae RC .50 .15
☐ 293 Storm Davis .05 .02
☐ 294 Danny Tartabull .05 .02
☐ 295 David Howard .05 .02
☐ 296 Mike Boddicker .05 .02
☐ 297 Joel Johnston RC .15 .04
☐ 298 Tim Spehr .05 .02
☐ 299 Hector Wagner .05 .02
☐ 300 George Brett .60 .18
☐ 301 Mike Macfarlane .05 .02
☐ 302 Kirk Gibson .10 .03
☐ 303 Harvey Pulliam RC .15 .04
☐ 304 Jim Eisenreich .05 .02
☐ 305 Kevin Seitzer .05 .02
☐ 306 Mark Davis .05 .02
☐ 307 Kurt Stillwell .05 .02
☐ 308 Jeff Montgomery .05 .02
☐ 309 Kevin Appier .10 .03
☐ 310 Bob Hamelin .05 .02
☐ 311 Tom Gordon .05 .02
☐ 312 Kerwin Moore RC .15 .04
☐ 313 Hugh Walker .05 .02
☐ 314 Terry Shumpert .05 .02
☐ 315 Warren Cromartie .05 .02
☐ 316 Gary Thurman .05 .02
☐ 317 Steve Bedrosian .05 .02
☐ 318 Danny Gladden .05 .02
☐ 319 Jack Morris .10 .03
☐ 320 Kirby Puckett .25 .07
☐ 321 Kent Hrbek .10 .03
☐ 322 Kevin Tapani .05 .02
☐ 323 Denny Neagle RC .50 .15
☐ 324 Rich Garces RC .15 .04
☐ 325 Larry Casian .05 .02
☐ 326 Shane Mack .05 .02
☐ 327 Allan Anderson .05 .02
☐ 328 Junior Ortiz .05 .02
☐ 329 Paul Abbott RC .50 .15
☐ 330 Chuck Knoblauch .10 .03
☐ 331 Chili Davis .10 .03
☐ 332 Todd Ritchie RC .50 .15
☐ 333 Brian Harper .05 .02
☐ 334 Rick Aguilera .10 .03
☐ 335 Scott Erickson .05 .02
☐ 336 Pedro Munoz RC .15 .04
☐ 337 Scott Leius .05 .02
☐ 338 Greg Gagne .05 .02
☐ 339 Mike Pagliarulo .05 .02
☐ 340 Terry Leach .05 .02
☐ 341 Willie Banks .05 .02
☐ 342 Bobby Thigpen .05 .02
☐ 343 R.Hernandez RC .50 .15
☐ 344 Melido Perez .05 .02
☐ 345 Carlton Fisk .15 .04
☐ 346 Norberto Martin .05 .02
☐ 347 Johnny Ruffin RC .15 .04
☐ 348 Jeff Carter .05 .02
☐ 349 Lance Johnson .05 .02
☐ 350 Sammy Sosa .50 .15
☐ 351 Alex Fernandez .05 .02
☐ 352 Jack McDowell .05 .02
☐ 353 Bob Wickman RC .15 .04
☐ 354 Wilson Alvarez .05 .02
☐ 355 Charlie Hough .10 .03
☐ 356 Ozzie Guillen .05 .02
☐ 357 Cory Snyder .05 .02
☐ 358 Robin Ventura .10 .03
☐ 359 Scott Fletcher .05 .02
☐ 360 Cesar Bernhardt .05 .02
☐ 361 Dan Pasqua .05 .02

❑ 362 Tim Raines .10 .03
❑ 363 Brian Drahman .05 .02
❑ 364 Wayne Edwards .05 .02
❑ 365 Scott Radinsky .05 .02
❑ 366 Frank Thomas .25 .07
❑ 367 Cecil Fielder SLUG .05 .02
❑ 368 Julio Franco SLUG .05 .02
❑ 369 Kelly Gruber SLUG .05 .02
❑ 370 Alan Trammell SLUG .10 .03
❑ 371 R.Henderson SLUG .25 .07
❑ 372 Jose Canseco SLUG .10 .03
❑ 373 Ellis Burks SLUG .05 .02
❑ 374 Lance Parrish SLUG .05 .02
❑ 375 Dave Parker SLUG .05 .02
❑ 376 Eddie Murray SLUG .15 .04
❑ 377 Ryne Sandberg SLUG .25 .07
❑ 378 Matt Williams SLUG .05 .02
❑ 379 Barry Larkin SLUG .10 .03
❑ 380 Barry Bonds SLUG .30 .09
❑ 381 Bobby Bonilla SLUG .05 .02
❑ 382 D.Strawberry SLUG .10 .03
❑ 383 Benny Santiago SLUG .05 .02
❑ 384 Don Robinson SLUG .05 .02
❑ 385 Paul Coleman .05 .02
❑ 386 Milt Thompson .05 .02
❑ 387 Lee Smith .10 .03
❑ 388 Ray Lankford .05 .02
❑ 389 Tom Pagnozzi .05 .02
❑ 390 Ken Hill .05 .02
❑ 391 Jamie Moyer .10 .03
❑ 392 Greg Carmona .05 .02
❑ 393 John Ericks .05 .02
❑ 394 Bob Tewksbury .05 .02
❑ 395 Jose Oquendo .05 .02
❑ 396 Rheal Cormier RC .15 .04
❑ 397 Mike Milchin .05 .02
❑ 398 Ozzie Smith .25 .07
❑ 399 Aaron Holbert RC .15 .04
❑ 400 Jose DeLeon .05 .02
❑ 401 Felix Jose .05 .02
❑ 402 Juan Agosto .05 .02
❑ 403 Pedro Guerrero .10 .03
❑ 404 Todd Zeile .05 .02
❑ 405 Gerald Perry .05 .02
❑ 406 D.Osborne UER RC .15 .04
Card number is 410
❑ 407 Bryn Smith .05 .02
❑ 408 Bernard Gilkey .05 .02
❑ 409 Rex Hudler .05 .02
❑ 410 Bobby Thomson .25 .07
Ralph Branca
Shot Heard Round the World
See also 406
❑ 411 Lance Dickson RC .15 .04
❑ 412 Danny Jackson .05 .02
❑ 413 Jerome Walton .05 .02
❑ 414 Sean Cheetham .05 .02
❑ 415 Joe Girardi .05 .02
❑ 416 Ryne Sandberg .40 .12
❑ 417 Mike Harkey .05 .02
❑ 418 George Bell .05 .02
❑ 419 Rick Wilkins RC .15 .04
❑ 420 Earl Cunningham .05 .02
❑ 421 H.Slocumb RC .15 .04
❑ 422 Mike Bielecki .05 .02
❑ 423 Jessie Hollins RC .15 .04
❑ 424 Shawon Dunston .05 .02
❑ 425 Dave Smith .05 .02
❑ 426 Greg Maddux .50 .15
❑ 427 Jose Vizcaino .05 .02
❑ 428 Luis Salazar .05 .02
❑ 429 Andre Dawson .10 .03
❑ 430 Rick Sutcliffe .10 .03
❑ 431 Paul Assenmacher .05 .02
❑ 432 Erik Pappas .05 .02
❑ 433 Mark Grace .25 .07
❑ 434 Dennis Martinez .10 .03
❑ 435 Marquis Grissom .05 .02
❑ 436 Wil Cordero RC .50 .15
❑ 437 Tim Wallach .05 .02
❑ 438 Brian Barnes .05 .02
❑ 439 Barry Jones .05 .02
❑ 440 Ivan Calderon .05 .02
❑ 441 Stan Spencer .05 .02
❑ 442 Larry Walker .25 .07
❑ 443 Chris Haney RC .15 .04
❑ 444 Hector Rivera .05 .02
❑ 445 Delino DeShields .10 .03
❑ 446 Andres Galarraga .10 .03
❑ 447 Gilberto Reyes .05 .02
❑ 448 Willie Greene .05 .02
❑ 449 Greg Colbrunn RC .50 .15
❑ 450 Rondell White RC .75 .23
❑ 451 Steve Frey .05 .02
❑ 452 Shane Andrews RC .15 .04
❑ 453 Mike Fitzgerald .05 .02
❑ 454 Spike Owen .05 .02
❑ 455 Dave Martinez .05 .02
❑ 456 Dennis Boyd .05 .02
❑ 457 Eric Bullock .05 .02
❑ 458 Reid Cornelius RC .15 .04
❑ 459 Chris Nabholz .05 .02
❑ 460 David Cone .10 .03
❑ 461 Hubie Brooks .05 .02
❑ 462 Sid Fernandez .05 .02
❑ 463 Doug Simons .05 .02
❑ 464 Howard Johnson .05 .02
❑ 465 Chris Donnels .05 .02
❑ 466 Anthony Young RC .15 .04
❑ 467 Todd Hundley .05 .02
❑ 468 Rick Cerone .05 .02
❑ 469 Kevin Elster .05 .02
❑ 470 Wally Whitehurst .05 .02
❑ 471 Vince Coleman .05 .02
❑ 472 Dwight Gooden .15 .04
❑ 473 Charlie O'Brien .05 .02
❑ 474 Jeromy Burnitz RC .75 .23
❑ 475 John Franco .10 .03
❑ 476 Daryl Boston .05 .02
❑ 477 Frank Viola .10 .03
❑ 478 D.J. Dozier .05 .02
❑ 479 Kevin McReynolds .05 .02
❑ 480 Tom Herr .05 .02
❑ 481 Gregg Jefferies .05 .02
❑ 482 Pete Schourek RC .15 .04
❑ 483 Ron Darling .05 .02
❑ 484 Dave Magadan .05 .02
❑ 485 Andy Ashby RC .50 .15
❑ 486 Dale Murphy .25 .07
❑ 487 Von Hayes .05 .02
❑ 488 Kim Batiste RC .15 .04
❑ 489 Tony Longmire RC .15 .04
❑ 490 Wally Backman .05 .02
❑ 491 Jeff Jackson .05 .02
❑ 492 Mickey Morandini .05 .02
❑ 493 Darrel Akerfelds .05 .02
❑ 494 Ricky Jordan .05 .02
❑ 495 Randy Ready .05 .02
❑ 496 Darrin Fletcher .05 .02
❑ 497 Chuck Malone .05 .02
❑ 498 Pat Combs .05 .02
❑ 499 Dickie Thon .05 .02
❑ 500 Roger McDowell .05 .02
❑ 501 Len Dykstra .10 .03
❑ 502 Joe Boever .05 .02
❑ 503 John Kruk .10 .03
❑ 504 Terry Mulholland .05 .02
❑ 505 Wes Chamberlain RC .15 .04
❑ 506 Mike Lieberthal RC .75 .23
❑ 507 Darren Daulton .10 .03
❑ 508 Charlie Hayes .05 .02
❑ 509 John Smiley .05 .02
❑ 510 Gary Varsho .05 .02
❑ 511 Curt Wilkerson .05 .02
❑ 512 Orlando Merced RC .15 .04
❑ 513 Barry Bonds .60 .18
❑ 514 Mike LaValliere .05 .02
❑ 515 Doug Drabek .05 .02
❑ 516 Gary Redus .05 .02
❑ 517 W.Pennyfeather RC .15 .04
❑ 518 Randy Tomlin RC .05 .02
❑ 519 Mike Zimmerman RC .15 .04
❑ 520 Jeff King .05 .02
❑ 521 Kurt Miller RC .15 .04
❑ 522 Jay Bell .10 .03
❑ 523 Bill Landrum .05 .02
❑ 524 Zane Smith .05 .02
❑ 525 Bobby Bonilla .10 .03
❑ 526 Bob Walk .05 .02
❑ 527 Austin Manahan .05 .02
❑ 528 Joe Ausanio .05 .02
❑ 529 Andy Van Slyke .10 .03
❑ 530 Jose Lind .05 .02
❑ 531 Carlos Garcia RC .15 .04
❑ 532 Don Slaught .05 .02
❑ 533 Gen.Colin Powell .50 .15
❑ 534 Frank Bolick RC .15 .04
❑ 535 Gary Scott .05 .02
❑ 536 Nikco Riesgo .05 .02
❑ 537 Reggie Sanders RC .75 .23
❑ 538 Tim Howard RC .15 .04
❑ 539 Ryan Bowen RC .15 .04
❑ 540 Eric Anthony .05 .02
❑ 541 Jim Deshaies .05 .02
❑ 542 Tom Nevers RC .15 .04
❑ 543 Ken Caminiti .10 .03
❑ 544 Karl Rhodes .05 .02
❑ 545 Xavier Hernandez .05 .02
❑ 546 Mike Scott .05 .02
❑ 547 Jeff Juden .05 .02
❑ 548 Darryl Kile .10 .03
❑ 549 Willie Ansley .05 .02
❑ 550 Luis Gonzalez RC 1.50 .45
❑ 551 Mike Simms .05 .02
❑ 552 Mark Portugal .05 .02
❑ 553 Jimmy Jones .05 .02
❑ 554 Jim Clancy .05 .02
❑ 555 Pete Harnisch .05 .02
❑ 556 Craig Biggio .15 .04
❑ 557 Eric Yelding .05 .02
❑ 558 Dave Rohde .05 .02
❑ 559 Casey Candaele .05 .02
❑ 560 Curt Schilling .15 .04
❑ 561 Steve Finley .10 .03
❑ 562 Javier Ortiz .05 .02
❑ 563 Andujar Cedeno .05 .02
❑ 564 Rafael Ramirez .05 .02
❑ 565 Kenny Lofton RC 1.00 .30
❑ 566 Steve Avery .05 .02
❑ 567 Lonnie Smith .05 .02
❑ 568 Kent Mercker .05 .02
❑ 569 Chipper Jones RC 4.00 1.20
❑ 570 Terry Pendleton .10 .03
❑ 571 Otis Nixon .05 .02
❑ 572 Juan Berenguer .05 .02
❑ 573 Charlie Leibrandt .05 .02
❑ 574 David Justice .10 .03
❑ 575 Keith Mitchell RC .15 .04
❑ 576 Tom Glavine .25 .07
❑ 577 Greg Olson .05 .02
❑ 578 Rafael Belliard .05 .02
❑ 579 Ben Rivera RC .15 .04
❑ 580 John Smoltz .15 .04
❑ 581 Tyler Houston .05 .02
❑ 582 Mark Wohlers RC .50 .15
❑ 583 Ron Gant .10 .03
❑ 584 Ramon Caraballo RC .15 .04
❑ 585 Sid Bream .05 .02
❑ 586 Jeff Treadway .05 .02
❑ 587 Javy Lopez RC 3.00 .90
❑ 588 Deion Sanders .10 .03
❑ 589 Mike Heath .05 .02
❑ 590 Ryan Klesko RC 1.00 .30
❑ 591 Bob Ojeda .05 .02
❑ 592 Alfredo Griffin .05 .02
❑ 593 Raul Mondesi RC 1.00 .30
❑ 594 Greg Smith .05 .02
❑ 595 Orel Hershiser .10 .03
❑ 596 Juan Samuel .05 .02
❑ 597 Brett Butler .10 .03
❑ 598 Gary Carter .15 .04
❑ 599 Stan Javier .05 .02
❑ 600 Kal Daniels .05 .02
❑ 601 Jamie McAndrew RC .15 .04
❑ 602 Mike Sharperson .05 .02
❑ 603 Jay Howell .05 .02
❑ 604 Eric Karros RC 1.00 .30
❑ 605 Tim Belcher .05 .02
❑ 606 Dan Opperman .05 .02
❑ 607 Lenny Harris .05 .02
❑ 608 Tom Goodwin .05 .02
❑ 609 Darryl Strawberry .15 .04
❑ 610 Ramon Martinez .05 .02
❑ 611 Kevin Gross .05 .02
❑ 612 Zakary Shinall .05 .02
❑ 613 Mike Scioscia .05 .02
❑ 614 Eddie Murray .25 .07
❑ 615 Ronnie Walden RC .15 .04

❑ 616 Will Clark .25 .07
❑ 617 Adam Hyzdu RC .50 .15
❑ 618 Matt Williams .10 .03
❑ 619 Don Robinson .05 .02
❑ 620 Jeff Brantley .05 .02
❑ 621 Greg Litton .05 .02
❑ 622 Steve Decker .05 .02
❑ 623 Robby Thompson .05 .02
❑ 624 Mark Leonard .05 .02
❑ 625 Kevin Bass .05 .02
❑ 626 Scott Garrelts .05 .02
❑ 627 Jose Uribe .05 .02
❑ 628 Eric Gunderson .05 .02
❑ 629 Steve Hosey .05 .02
❑ 630 Trevor Wilson .05 .02
❑ 631 Terry Kennedy .05 .02
❑ 632 Dave Righetti .10 .03
❑ 633 Kelly Downs .05 .02
❑ 634 Johnny Ard .05 .02
❑ 635 E.Christopherson RC .15 .04
❑ 636 Kevin Mitchell .05 .02
❑ 637 John Burkett .05 .02
❑ 638 Kevin Rogers RC .15 .04
❑ 639 Bud Black .05 .02
❑ 640 Willie McGee .10 .03
❑ 641 Royce Clayton .05 .02
❑ 642 Tony Fernandez .05 .02
❑ 643 Ricky Bones RC .15 .04
❑ 644 Thomas Howard .05 .02
❑ 645 Dave Staton RC .15 .04
❑ 646 Jim Presley .05 .02
❑ 647 Tony Gwynn .30 .09
❑ 648 Marty Barrett .05 .02
❑ 649 Scott Coolbaugh .05 .02
❑ 650 Craig Lefferts .05 .02
❑ 651 Eddie Whitson .05 .02
❑ 652 Oscar Azocar .05 .02
❑ 653 Wes Gardner .05 .02
❑ 654 Bip Roberts .05 .02
❑ 655 Robbie Beckett RC .15 .04
❑ 656 Benito Santiago .10 .03
❑ 657 Greg W.Harris .05 .02
❑ 658 Jerald Clark .05 .02
❑ 659 Fred McGriff .15 .04
❑ 660 Larry Andersen .05 .02
❑ 661 Bruce Hurst .05 .02
❑ 662 Steve Martin UER RC .15 .04
Card said he pitched at Waterloo
He's an outfielder
❑ 663 Rafael Valdez .05 .02
❑ 664 Paul Faries .05 .02
❑ 665 Andy Benes .05 .02
❑ 666 Randy Myers .05 .02
❑ 667 Rob Dibble .10 .03
❑ 668 Glenn Sutko .05 .02
❑ 669 Glenn Braggs .05 .02
❑ 670 Billy Hatcher .05 .02
❑ 671 Joe Oliver .05 .02
❑ 672 Freddie Benavides RC .15 .04
❑ 673 Barry Larkin .25 .07
❑ 674 Chris Sabo .05 .02
❑ 675 Mariano Duncan .05 .02
❑ 676 Chris Jones RC .05 .02
❑ 677 Gino Minutelli .05 .02
❑ 678 Reggie Jefferson .05 .02
❑ 679 Jack Armstrong .05 .02
❑ 680 Chris Hammond .05 .02
❑ 681 Jose Rijo .05 .02
❑ 682 Bill Doran .05 .02
❑ 683 Terry Lee .05 .02
❑ 684 Tom Browning .05 .02
❑ 685 Paul O'Neill .15 .04
❑ 686 Eric Davis .10 .03
❑ 687 Dan Wilson RC .50 .15
❑ 688 Ted Power .05 .02
❑ 689 Tim Layana .05 .02
❑ 690 Norm Charlton .05 .02
❑ 691 Hal Morris .05 .02
❑ 692 Rickey Henderson .25 .07
❑ 693 Sam Militello RC .15 .04
❑ 694 Matt Mieske RC .15 .04
❑ 695 Paul Russo RC .15 .04
❑ 696 Domingo Mota MVP .05 .02
❑ 697 Todd Guggiana RC .15 .04
❑ 698 Marc Newfield RC .15 .04
❑ 699 Checklist 1-122 .05 .02
❑ 700 Checklist 123-244 .05 .02
❑ 701 Checklist 245-366 .05 .02
❑ 702 Checklist 367-471 .05 .02
❑ 703 Checklist 472-593 .05 .02
❑ 704 Checklist 594-704 .05 .02

1992 Bowman

	Nm-Mt	Ex-Mt
COMPLETE SET (705)	180.00	55.00

❑ 1 Ivan Rodriguez 1.25 .35
❑ 2 Kirk McCaskill .50 .15
❑ 3 Scott Livingstone .50 .15
❑ 4 Salomon Torres RC .50 .15
❑ 5 Carlos Hernandez .50 .15
❑ 6 Dave Hollins .50 .15
❑ 7 Scott Fletcher .50 .15
❑ 8 Jorge Fabregas RC 1.00 .30
❑ 9 Andujar Cedeno .50 .15
❑ 10 Howard Johnson .50 .15
❑ 11 Trevor Hoffman RC 5.00 1.50
❑ 12 Roberto Kelly .50 .15
❑ 13 Gregg Jefferies .50 .15
❑ 14 Marquis Grissom .50 .15
❑ 15 Mike Ignasiak .50 .15
❑ 16 Jack Morris .50 .15
❑ 17 William Pennyfeather .50 .15
❑ 18 Todd Stottlemyre .50 .15
❑ 19 Chito Martinez .50 .15
❑ 20 Roberto Alomar 1.25 .35
❑ 21 Sam Militello .50 .15
❑ 22 Hector Fajardo RC .50 .15
❑ 23 Paul Quantrill RC .50 .15
❑ 24 Chuck Knoblauch .50 .15
❑ 25 Reggie Jefferson .50 .15
❑ 26 Jeremy McGarity RC .50 .15
❑ 27 Jerome Walton .50 .15
❑ 28 Chipper Jones 8.00 2.40
❑ 29 Brian Barber RC .50 .15
❑ 30 Ron Darling .50 .15
❑ 31 Roberto Petagine RC 1.00 .30
❑ 32 Chuck Finley .50 .15
❑ 33 Edgar Martinez .75 .23
❑ 34 Napoleon Robinson .50 .15
❑ 35 Andy Van Slyke .50 .15
❑ 36 Bobby Thigpen .50 .15
❑ 37 Travis Fryman .50 .15
❑ 38 Eric Christopherson .50 .15
❑ 39 Terry Mulholland .50 .15
❑ 40 Darryl Strawberry .75 .23
❑ 41 Manny Alexander RC .50 .15
❑ 42 Tracy Sanders RC .50 .15
❑ 43 Pete Incaviglia .50 .15
❑ 44 Kim Batiste .50 .15
❑ 45 Frank Rodriguez .50 .15
❑ 46 Greg Swindell .50 .15
❑ 47 Delino DeShields .50 .15
❑ 48 John Ericks .50 .15
❑ 49 Franklin Stubbs .50 .15
❑ 50 Tony Gwynn 1.50 .45
❑ 51 Clifton Garrett RC .50 .15
❑ 52 Mike Gardella .50 .15
❑ 53 Scott Erickson .50 .15
❑ 54 Gary Caraballo RC .50 .15
❑ 55 Jose Oliva RC .50 .15
❑ 56 Brook Fordyce .50 .15
❑ 57 Mark Whiten .50 .15
❑ 58 Joe Slusarski .50 .15
❑ 59 J.R. Phillips RC 1.00 .30
❑ 60 Barry Bonds 3.00 .90
❑ 61 Bob Milacki .50 .15
❑ 62 Keith Mitchell .50 .15
❑ 63 Angel Miranda .50 .15
❑ 64 Raul Mondesi 5.00 1.50
❑ 65 Brian Koelling RC .50 .15
❑ 66 Brian McRae .50 .15
❑ 67 John Patterson RC .50 .15
❑ 68 John Wetteland .50 .15
❑ 69 Wilson Alvarez .50 .15
❑ 70 Wade Boggs .75 .23
❑ 71 Darryl Ratliff RC .50 .15
❑ 72 Jeff Jackson .50 .15
❑ 73 Jeremy Hernandez RC .50 .15
❑ 74 Darryl Hamilton .50 .15
❑ 75 Rafael Belliard .50 .15
❑ 76 Rick Trlicek RC .50 .15
❑ 77 Felipe Crespo RC .50 .15
❑ 78 Carney Lansford .50 .15
❑ 79 Ryan Long RC .50 .15
❑ 80 Kirby Puckett 1.25 .35
❑ 81 Earl Cunningham .50 .15
❑ 82 Pedro Martinez 15.00 4.50
❑ 83 Scott Hatteberg RC 1.00 .30
❑ 84 Juan Gonzalez UER 1.25 .35
(65 doubles vs. Tigers)
❑ 85 Robert Nutting RC .50 .15
❑ 86 Pokey Reese RC 1.00 .30
❑ 87 Dave Silvestri .50 .15
❑ 88 Scott Ruffcorn RC .50 .15
❑ 89 Rick Aguilera .50 .15
❑ 90 Cecil Fielder .50 .15
❑ 91 Kirk Dressendorfer .50 .15
❑ 92 Jerry DiPoto RC .50 .15
❑ 93 Mike Felder .50 .15
❑ 94 Craig Paquette .50 .15
❑ 95 Elvin Paulino RC .50 .15
❑ 96 Donovan Osborne .50 .15
❑ 97 Hubie Brooks .50 .15
❑ 98 Derek Lowe RC 5.00 1.50
❑ 99 David Zancanaro .50 .15
❑ 100 Ken Griffey Jr. 2.00 .60
❑ 101 Todd Hundley .50 .15
❑ 102 Mike Trombley RC .50 .15
❑ 103 Ricky Gutierrez RC 1.00 .30
❑ 104 Braulio Castillo .50 .15
❑ 105 Craig Lefferts .50 .15
❑ 106 Rick Sutcliffe .50 .15
❑ 107 Dean Palmer .50 .15
❑ 108 Henry Rodriguez .50 .15
❑ 109 Mark Clark RC 1.00 .30
❑ 110 Kenny Lofton .75 .23
❑ 111 Mark Carreon .50 .15
❑ 112 J.T. Bruett .50 .15
❑ 113 Gerald Williams .50 .15
❑ 114 Frank Thomas 1.25 .35
❑ 115 Kevin Reimer .50 .15
❑ 116 Sammy Sosa 2.00 .60
❑ 117 Mickey Tettleton .50 .15
❑ 118 Reggie Sanders .50 .15
❑ 119 Trevor Wilson .50 .15
❑ 120 Cliff Brantley .50 .15
❑ 121 Spike Owen .50 .15
❑ 122 Jeff Montgomery .50 .15
❑ 123 Alex Sutherland .50 .15
❑ 124 Brien Taylor RC 1.00 .30
❑ 125 Brian Williams RC .50 .15
❑ 126 Kevin Seitzer .50 .15
❑ 127 Carlos Delgado RC 25.00 7.50
❑ 128 Gary Scott .50 .15
❑ 129 Scott Cooper .50 .15
❑ 130 Domingo Jean RC .50 .15
❑ 131 Pat Mahomes RC 1.00 .30
❑ 132 Mike Boddicker .50 .15
❑ 133 Roberto Hernandez .50 .15
❑ 134 Dave Valle .50 .15
❑ 135 Kurt Stillwell .50 .15
❑ 136 Brad Pennington RC .50 .15
❑ 137 Jermaine Swinton RC .50 .15
❑ 138 Ryan Hawblitzel RC .50 .15
❑ 139 Tito Navarro RC .50 .15
❑ 140 Sandy Alomar Jr. .50 .15
❑ 141 Todd Benzinger .50 .15
❑ 142 Danny Jackson .50 .15

❏ 143 Melvin Nieves RC .50 .15
❏ 144 Jim Campanis .50 .15
❏ 145 Luis Gonzalez .75 .23
❏ 146 D.Dooreweerd RC .50 .15
❏ 147 Charlie Hayes .50 .15
❏ 148 Greg Maddux 2.50 .75
❏ 149 Brian Harper .50 .15
❏ 150 Brent Miller RC .50 .15
❏ 151 Shawn Estes RC 1.00 .30
❏ 152 Mike Williams RC 1.00 .30
❏ 153 Charlie Hough .50 .15
❏ 154 Randy Myers .50 .15
❏ 155 Kevin Young RC 1.00 .30
❏ 156 Rick Wilkins .50 .15
❏ 157 Terry Shumpert .50 .15
❏ 158 Steve Karsay .50 .15
❏ 159 Gary DiSarcina .50 .15
❏ 160 Deion Sanders .50 .15
❏ 161 Tom Browning .50 .15
❏ 162 Dickie Thon .50 .15
❏ 163 Luis Mercedes .50 .15
❏ 164 Riccardo Ingram .50 .15
❏ 165 Tavo Alvarez RC .50 .15
❏ 166 Rickey Henderson 2.00 .60
❏ 167 Jaime Navarro .50 .15
❏ 168 Billy Ashley RC .50 .15
❏ 169 Phil Dauphin RC .50 .15
❏ 170 Ivan Cruz .50 .15
❏ 171 Harold Baines .50 .15
❏ 172 Bryan Harvey .50 .15
❏ 173 Alex Cole .50 .15
❏ 174 Curtis Shaw RC .50 .15
❏ 175 Matt Williams .50 .15
❏ 176 Felix Jose .50 .15
❏ 177 Sam Horn .50 .15
❏ 178 Randy Johnson 1.25 .35
❏ 179 Ivan Calderon .50 .15
❏ 180 Steve Avery .50 .15
❏ 181 William Suero .50 .15
❏ 182 Bill Swift .50 .15
❏ 183 Howard Battle RC .50 .15
❏ 184 Ruben Amaro .50 .15
❏ 185 Jim Abbott 1.25 .35
❏ 186 Mike Fitzgerald .50 .15
❏ 187 Bruce Hurst .50 .15
❏ 188 Jeff Juden .50 .15
❏ 189 Jeromy Burnitz 1.25 .35
❏ 190 Dave Burba .50 .15
❏ 191 Kevin Brown .50 .15
❏ 192 Patrick Lennon .50 .15
❏ 193 Jeff McNeely .50 .15
❏ 194 Wil Cordero .50 .15
❏ 195 Chili Davis .50 .15
❏ 196 Milt Cuyler .50 .15
❏ 197 Von Hayes .50 .15
❏ 198 Todd Revenig RC .50 .15
❏ 199 Joel Johnston .50 .15
❏ 200 Jeff Bagwell 1.25 .35
❏ 201 Alex Fernandez .50 .15
❏ 202 Todd Jones RC 1.00 .30
❏ 203 Charles Nagy .50 .15
❏ 204 Tim Raines .50 .15
❏ 205 Kevin Maas .50 .15
❏ 206 Julio Franco .50 .15
❏ 207 Randy Velarde .50 .15
❏ 208 Lance Johnson .50 .15
❏ 209 Scott Leius .50 .15
❏ 210 Derek Lee .50 .15
❏ 211 Joe Sondrini RC .50 .15
❏ 212 Royce Clayton .50 .15
❏ 213 Chris George .50 .15
❏ 214 Gary Sheffield .50 .15
❏ 215 Mark Gubicza .50 .15
❏ 216 Mike Moore .50 .15
❏ 217 Rick Huisman RC .50 .15
❏ 218 Jeff Russell .50 .15
❏ 219 D.J. Dozier .50 .15
❏ 220 Dave Martinez .50 .15
❏ 221 Alan Newman RC .50 .15
❏ 222 Nolan Ryan 4.00 1.20
❏ 223 Teddy Higuera .50 .15
❏ 224 Damon Buford RC .50 .15
❏ 225 Ruben Sierra .50 .15
❏ 226 Tom Nevers .50 .15
❏ 227 Tommy Greene .50 .15
❏ 228 Nigel Wilson RC 1.00 .30
❏ 229 John DeSilva .50 .15
❏ 230 Bobby Witt .50 .15
❏ 231 Greg Cadaret .50 .15
❏ 232 John Vander Wal RC 1.00 .30
❏ 233 Jack Clark .50 .15
❏ 234 Bill Doran .50 .15
❏ 235 Bobby Bonilla .50 .15
❏ 236 Steve Olin .50 .15
❏ 237 Derek Bell .50 .15
❏ 238 David Cone .50 .15
❏ 239 Victor Cole .50 .15
❏ 240 Rod Bolton RC .50 .15
❏ 241 Tom Pagnozzi .50 .15
❏ 242 Rob Dibble .50 .15
❏ 243 Michael Carter RC .50 .15
❏ 244 Don Peters .50 .15
❏ 245 Mike LaValliere .50 .15
❏ 246 Joe Perona RC .50 .15
❏ 247 Mitch Williams .50 .15
❏ 248 Jay Buhner .50 .15
❏ 249 Andy Benes .50 .15
❏ 250 Alex Ochoa RC 1.00 .30
❏ 251 Greg Blosser .50 .15
❏ 252 Jack Armstrong .50 .15
❏ 253 Juan Samuel .50 .15
❏ 254 Terry Pendleton .50 .15
❏ 255 Ramon Martinez .50 .15
❏ 256 Rico Brogna .50 .15
❏ 257 John Smiley .50 .15
❏ 258 Carl Everett .75 .23
❏ 259 Tim Salmon 1.25 .35
❏ 260 Will Clark 1.25 .35
❏ 261 Ugueth Urbina RC 1.00 .30
❏ 262 Jason Wood RC .50 .15
❏ 263 Dave Magadan .50 .15
❏ 264 Dante Bichette .50 .15
❏ 265 Jose DeLeon .50 .15
❏ 266 Mike Neill RC 1.00 .30
❏ 267 Paul O'Neill .75 .23
❏ 268 Anthony Young .50 .15
❏ 269 Greg W. Harris .50 .15
❏ 270 Todd Van Poppel .50 .15
❏ 271 Pedro Castellano RC .50 .15
❏ 272 Tony Phillips .50 .15
❏ 273 Mike Gallego .50 .15
❏ 274 Steve Cooke RC .50 .15
❏ 275 Robin Ventura .50 .15
❏ 276 Kevin Mitchell .50 .15
❏ 277 Doug Linton RC .50 .15
❏ 278 Robert Eenhoorn .50 .15
❏ 279 Gabe White RC .50 .15
❏ 280 Dave Stewart .50 .15
❏ 281 Mo Sanford .50 .15
❏ 282 Greg Perschke .50 .15
❏ 283 Kevin Flora RC .50 .15
❏ 284 Jeff Williams RC 1.00 .30
❏ 285 Keith Miller .50 .15
❏ 286 Andy Ashby .50 .15
❏ 287 Doug Dascenzo .50 .15
❏ 288 Eric Karros .50 .15
❏ 289 Glenn Murray RC .50 .15
❏ 290 Troy Percival RC 3.00 .90
❏ 291 Orlando Merced .50 .15
❏ 292 Peter Hoy .50 .15
❏ 293 Tony Fernandez .50 .15
❏ 294 Juan Guzman .50 .15
❏ 295 Jesse Barfield .50 .15
❏ 296 Sid Fernandez .50 .15
❏ 297 Scott Cepicky .50 .15
❏ 298 Garret Anderson RC 10.00 3.00
❏ 299 Cal Eldred .50 .15
❏ 300 Ryne Sandberg 2.50 .75
❏ 301 Jim Gantner .50 .15
❏ 302 Mariano Rivera RC 12.00 3.60
❏ 303 Ron Lockett RC .50 .15
❏ 304 Jose Offerman .50 .15
❏ 305 Dennis Martinez .50 .15
❏ 306 Luis Ortiz RC .50 .15
❏ 307 David Howard .50 .15
❏ 308 Russ Springer RC 1.00 .30
❏ 309 Chris Howard .50 .15
❏ 310 Kyle Abbott .50 .15
❏ 311 Aaron Sele RC 2.00 .60
❏ 312 David Justice .50 .15
❏ 313 Pete O'Brien .50 .15
❏ 314 Greg Hansell RC .50 .15
❏ 315 Dave Winfield .75 .23
❏ 316 Lance Dickson .50 .15
❏ 317 Eric King .50 .15
❏ 318 Vaughn Eshelman RC .50 .15
❏ 319 Tim Belcher .50 .15
❏ 320 Andres Galarraga .50 .15
❏ 321 Scott Bullett RC .50 .15
❏ 322 Doug Strange .50 .15
❏ 323 Jerald Clark .50 .15
❏ 324 Dave Righetti .50 .15
❏ 325 Greg Hibbard .50 .15
❏ 326 Eric Hillman RC .50 .15
❏ 327 Shane Reynolds RC 1.00 .30
❏ 328 Chris Hammond .50 .15
❏ 329 Albert Belle .50 .15
❏ 330 Rich Becker RC .50 .15
❏ 331 Eddie Williams RC .50 .15
❏ 332 Donald Harris .50 .15
❏ 333 Dave Smith .50 .15
❏ 334 Steve Fireovid .50 .15
❏ 335 Steve Buechele .50 .15
❏ 336 Mike Schooler .50 .15
❏ 337 Kevin McReynolds .50 .15
❏ 338 Hensley Meulens .50 .15
❏ 339 Benji Gil RC 1.00 .30
❏ 340 Don Mattingly 3.00 .90
❏ 341 Alvin Davis .50 .15
❏ 342 Alan Mills .50 .15
❏ 343 Kelly Downs .50 .15
❏ 344 Leo Gomez .50 .15
❏ 345 Tarrik Brock RC .50 .15
❏ 346 Ryan Turner RC .50 .15
❏ 347 John Smoltz .75 .23
❏ 348 Bill Sampen .50 .15
❏ 349 Paul Byrd RC 1.00 .30
❏ 350 Mike Bordick .50 .15
❏ 351 Jose Lind .50 .15
❏ 352 David Wells .50 .15
❏ 353 Barry Larkin 1.25 .35
❏ 354 Bruce Ruffin .50 .15
❏ 355 Luis Rivera .50 .15
❏ 356 Sid Bream .50 .15
❏ 357 Julian Vasquez RC .50 .15
❏ 358 Jason Bere RC 1.00 .30
❏ 359 Ben McDonald .50 .15
❏ 360 Scott Stahoviak RC .50 .15
❏ 361 Kirt Manwaring .50 .15
❏ 362 Jeff Johnson .50 .15
❏ 363 Rob Deer .50 .15
❏ 364 Tony Pena .50 .15
❏ 365 Melido Perez .50 .15
❏ 366 Clay Parker .50 .15
❏ 367 Dale Sveum .50 .15
❏ 368 Mike Scioscia .50 .15
❏ 369 Roger Salkeld .50 .15
❏ 370 Mike Stanley .50 .15
❏ 371 Jack McDowell .50 .15
❏ 372 Tim Wallach .50 .15
❏ 373 Billy Ripken .50 .15
❏ 374 Mike Christopher .50 .15
❏ 375 Paul Molitor .75 .23
❏ 376 Dave Stieb .50 .15
❏ 377 Pedro Guerrero .50 .15
❏ 378 Russ Swan .50 .15
❏ 379 Bob Ojeda .50 .15
❏ 380 Donn Pall .50 .15
❏ 381 Eddie Zosky .50 .15
❏ 382 Darnell Coles .50 .15
❏ 383 Tom Smith RC .50 .15
❏ 384 Mark McGwire 3.00 .90
❏ 385 Gary Carter .75 .23
❏ 386 Rich Amaral RC .50 .15
❏ 387 Alan Embree RC .50 .15
❏ 388 Jonathan Hurst RC .50 .15
❏ 389 Bobby Jones RC 1.00 .30
❏ 390 Rico Rossy .50 .15
❏ 391 Dan Smith .50 .15
❏ 392 Terry Steinbach .50 .15
❏ 393 Jon Farrell RC .50 .15
❏ 394 Dave Anderson .50 .15
❏ 395 Benny Santiago .50 .15
❏ 396 Mark Wohlers .50 .15
❏ 397 Mo Vaughn .50 .15
❏ 398 Randy Kramer .50 .15
❏ 399 John Jaha RC 1.00 .30
❏ 400 Cal Ripken 4.00 1.20

	No.	Player		
❑	401	Ryan Bowen	.50	.15
❑	402	Tim McIntosh	.50	.15
❑	403	Bernard Gilkey	.50	.15
❑	404	Junior Felix	.50	.15
❑	405	Cris Colon RC	.50	.15
❑	406	Marc Newfield	.50	.15
❑	407	Bernie Williams	.75	.23
❑	408	Jay Howell	.50	.15
❑	409	Zane Smith	.50	.15
❑	410	Jeff Shaw	.50	.15
❑	411	Kerry Woodson	.50	.15
❑	412	Wes Chamberlain	.50	.15
❑	413	Dave Mlicki RC	1.00	.30
❑	414	Benny Distefano	.50	.15
❑	415	Kevin Rogers	.50	.15
❑	416	Tim Naehring	.50	.15
❑	417	Clemente Nunez RC	.50	.15
❑	418	Luis Sojo	.50	.15
❑	419	Kevin Ritz	.50	.15
❑	420	Omar Olivares	.50	.15
❑	421	Manuel Lee	.50	.15
❑	422	Julio Valera	.50	.15
❑	423	Omar Vizquel	.50	.15
❑	424	Darren Burton RC	.50	.15
❑	425	Mel Hall	.50	.15
❑	426	Dennis Powell	.50	.15
❑	427	Lee Stevens	.50	.15
❑	428	Glenn Davis	.50	.15
❑	429	Willie Greene	.50	.15
❑	430	Kevin Wickander	.50	.15
❑	431	Dennis Eckersley	.50	.15
❑	432	Joe Orsulak	.50	.15
❑	433	Eddie Murray	1.25	.35
❑	434	Matt Stairs RC	1.00	.30
❑	435	Wally Joyner	.50	.15
❑	436	Rondell White	1.25	.35
❑	437	Rob Maurer	.50	.15
❑	438	Joe Redfield	.50	.15
❑	439	Mark Lewis	.50	.15
❑	440	Darren Daulton	.50	.15
❑	441	Mike Henneman	.50	.15
❑	442	John Cangelosi	.50	.15
❑	443	Vince Moore RC	.50	.15
❑	444	John Wehner	.50	.15
❑	445	Kent Hrbek	.50	.15
❑	446	Mark McLemore	.50	.15
❑	447	Bill Wegman	.50	.15
❑	448	Robby Thompson	.50	.15
❑	449	Mark Anthony RC	.50	.15
❑	450	Archi Cianfrocco RC	.50	.15
❑	451	Johnny Ruffin	.50	.15
❑	452	Javy Lopez	2.50	.75
❑	453	Greg Gohr	.50	.15
❑	454	Tim Scott	.50	.15
❑	455	Stan Belinda	.50	.15
❑	456	Darrin Jackson	.50	.15
❑	457	Chris Gardner	.50	.15
❑	458	Esteban Beltre	.50	.15
❑	459	Phil Plantier	.50	.15
❑	460	Jim Thome	8.00	2.40
❑	461	Mike Piazza RC	40.00	12.00
❑	462	Matt Sinatro	.50	.15
❑	463	Scott Servais	.50	.15
❑	464	Brian Jordan RC	3.00	.90
❑	465	Doug Drabek	.50	.15
❑	466	Carl Willis	.50	.15
❑	467	Bret Barberie	.50	.15
❑	468	Hal Morris	.50	.15
❑	469	Steve Sax	.50	.15
❑	470	Jerry Willard	.50	.15
❑	471	Dan Wilson	.50	.15
❑	472	Chris Hoiles	.50	.15
❑	473	Rheal Cormier	.50	.15
❑	474	John Morris	.50	.15
❑	475	Jeff Reardon	.50	.15
❑	476	Mark Leiter	.50	.15
❑	477	Tom Gordon	.50	.15
❑	478	Kent Bottenfield RC	1.00	.30
❑	479	Gene Larkin	.50	.15
❑	480	Dwight Gooden	.75	.23
❑	481	B.J. Surhoff	.50	.15
❑	482	Andy Stankiewicz	.50	.15
❑	483	Tino Martinez	.75	.23
❑	484	Craig Biggio	.75	.23
❑	485	Denny Neagle	.50	.15
❑	486	Rusty Meacham	.50	.15
❑	487	Kal Daniels	.50	.15
❑	488	Dave Henderson	.50	.15
❑	489	Tim Costo	.50	.15
❑	490	Doug Davis	.50	.15
❑	491	Frank Viola	.50	.15
❑	492	Cory Snyder	.50	.15
❑	493	Chris Martin	.50	.15
❑	494	Dion James	.50	.15
❑	495	Randy Tomlin	.50	.15
❑	496	Greg Vaughn	.50	.15
❑	497	Dennis Cook	.50	.15
❑	498	Rosario Rodriguez	.50	.15
❑	499	Dave Staton	.50	.15
❑	500	George Brett	3.00	.90
❑	501	Brian Barnes	.50	.15
❑	502	Butch Henry RC	.50	.15
❑	503	Harold Reynolds	.50	.15
❑	504	David Nied RC	1.00	.30
❑	505	Lee Smith	.50	.15
❑	506	Steve Chitren	.50	.15
❑	507	Ken Hill	.50	.15
❑	508	Robbie Beckett	.50	.15
❑	509	Troy Afenir	.50	.15
❑	510	Kelly Gruber	.50	.15
❑	511	Bret Boone	1.25	.35
❑	512	Jeff Branson	.50	.15
❑	513	Mike Jackson	.50	.15
❑	514	Pete Harnisch	.50	.15
❑	515	Chad Kreuter	.50	.15
❑	516	Joe Vitko RC	.50	.15
❑	517	Orel Hershiser	.50	.15
❑	518	John Doherty RC	.50	.15
❑	519	Jay Bell	.50	.15
❑	520	Mark Langston	.50	.15
❑	521	Dann Howitt	.50	.15
❑	522	Bobby Reed RC	.50	.15
❑	523	Bobby Munoz RC	.50	.15
❑	524	Todd Ritchie	.50	.15
❑	525	Bip Roberts	.50	.15
❑	526	Pat Listach RC	1.00	.30
❑	527	Scott Brosius RC	3.00	.90
❑	528	John Roper RC	.50	.15
❑	529	Phil Hiatt RC	.50	.15
❑	530	Denny Walling	.50	.15
❑	531	Carlos Baerga	.50	.15
❑	532	Manny Ramirez RC	25.00	7.50
❑	533	Pat Clements UER	.50	.15
		(Mistakenly numbered 553)		
❑	534	Ron Gant	.50	.15
❑	535	Pat Kelly	.50	.15
❑	536	Bill Spiers	.50	.15
❑	537	Darren Reed	.50	.15
❑	538	Ken Caminiti	.50	.15
❑	539	Butch Huskey RC	.50	.15
❑	540	Matt Nokes	.50	.15
❑	541	John Kruk	.50	.15
❑	542	John Jaha FOIL	.50	.15
❑	543	Justin Thompson RC	.50	.15
❑	544	Steve Hosey	.50	.15
❑	545	Joe Kmak	.50	.15
❑	546	John Franco	.50	.15
❑	547	Devon White	.50	.15
❑	548	E.Hansen FOIL RC	.50	.15
❑	549	Ryan Klesko	1.25	.35
❑	550	Danny Tartabull	.50	.15
❑	551	Frank Thomas FOIL	1.25	.35
❑	552	Kevin Tapani	.50	.15
❑	553	Willie Banks	.50	.15
		(See also 533)		
❑	554	B.J. Wallace RC FOIL	.50	.15
❑	555	Orlando Miller RC	.50	.15
❑	556	Mark Smith RC	.50	.15
❑	557	Tim Wallach FOIL	.50	.15
❑	558	Bill Gullickson	.50	.15
❑	559	Derek Bell FOIL	.50	.15
❑	560	Joe Randa FOIL RC	1.00	.30
❑	561	Frank Seminara RC	.50	.15
❑	562	Mark Gardner	.50	.15
❑	563	Rick Greene RC FOIL	.50	.15
❑	564	Gary Gaetti	.50	.15
❑	565	Ozzie Guillen	.50	.15
❑	566	Charles Nagy FOIL	.50	.15
❑	567	Mike Milchin	.50	.15
❑	568	Ben Shelton RC	.50	.15
❑	569	Chris Roberts FOIL	.50	.15
❑	570	Ellis Burks	.50	.15
❑	571	Scott Scudder	.50	.15
❑	572	Jim Abbott FOIL	1.25	.35
❑	573	Joe Carter	.50	.15
❑	574	Steve Finley	.50	.15
❑	575	Jim Olander FOIL	.50	.15
❑	576	Carlos Garcia	.50	.15
❑	577	Gregg Olson	.50	.15
❑	578	Greg Swindell FOIL	.50	.15
❑	579	Matt Williams FOIL	.50	.15
❑	580	Mark Grace	1.25	.35
❑	581	Howard House FOIL RC	.50	.15
❑	582	Luis Polonia	.50	.15
❑	583	Erik Hanson	.50	.15
❑	584	Salomon Torres FOIL	.50	.15
❑	585	Carlton Fisk	.75	.23
❑	586	Bret Saberhagen	.50	.15
❑	587	C.McConnell FOIL RC	.50	.15
❑	588	Jimmy Key	.50	.15
❑	589	Mike Macfarlane	.50	.15
❑	590	Barry Bonds FOIL	3.00	.90
❑	591	Jamie McAndrew	.50	.15
❑	592	Shane Mack	.50	.15
❑	593	Kerwin Moore	.50	.15
❑	594	Joe Oliver	.50	.15
❑	595	Chris Sabo	.50	.15
❑	596	Alex Gonzalez RC	2.00	.60
❑	597	Brett Butler	.50	.15
❑	598	Mark Hutton RC	.50	.15
❑	599	Andy Benes FOIL	.50	.15
❑	600	Jose Canseco	1.25	.35
❑	601	Darryl Kile	.50	.15
❑	602	Matt Stairs FOIL	.50	.15
❑	603	R.Butler RC FOIL	.50	.15
❑	604	Willie McGee	.50	.15
❑	605	Jack McDowell FOIL	.50	.15
❑	606	Tom Candiotti	.50	.15
❑	607	Ed Martel RC	.50	.15
❑	608	Matt Mieske FOIL	.50	.15
❑	609	Darrin Fletcher	.50	.15
❑	610	Rafael Palmeiro	.75	.23
❑	611	Bill Swift FOIL	.50	.15
❑	612	Mike Mussina	1.25	.35
❑	613	Vince Coleman	.50	.15
❑	614	Scott Cepicky COR	.50	.15
❑	614A	S.Cepicky FOIL UER	.50	.15
		Bats: LEFLT		
❑	615	Mike Greenwell	.50	.15
❑	616	Kevin McGehee RC	.50	.15
❑	617	J.Hammonds FOIL	.50	.15
❑	618	Scott Taylor	.50	.15
❑	619	Dave Otto	.50	.15
❑	620	Mark McGwire FOIL	3.00	.90
❑	621	Kevin Tatar RC	.50	.15
❑	622	Steve Farr	.50	.15
❑	623	Ryan Klesko FOIL	.50	.15
❑	624	Dave Fleming	.50	.15
❑	625	Andre Dawson	.50	.15
❑	626	Tino Martinez FOIL	.75	.23
❑	627	Chad Curtis RC	1.00	.30
❑	628	Mickey Morandini	.50	.15
❑	629	Gregg Olson FOIL	.50	.15
❑	630	Lou Whitaker	.50	.15
❑	631	Arthur Rhodes	.50	.15
❑	632	Brandon Wilson RC	.50	.15
❑	633	Lance Jennings RC	.50	.15
❑	634	Allen Watson RC	.50	.15
❑	635	Len Dykstra	.50	.15
❑	636	Joe Girardi	.50	.15
❑	637	K.Hernandez RC FOIL	.50	.15
❑	638	Mike Hampton RC	3.00	.90
❑	639	Al Osuna	.50	.15
❑	640	Kevin Appier	.50	.15
❑	641	Rick Helling FOIL	.50	.15
❑	642	Jody Reed	.50	.15
❑	643	Ray Lankford	.50	.15
❑	644	John Olerud	.50	.15
❑	645	Paul Molitor FOIL	.75	.23
❑	646	Pat Borders	.50	.15
❑	647	Mike Morgan	.50	.15
❑	648	Larry Walker	.75	.23
❑	649	P.Castellano FOIL	.50	.15
❑	650	Fred McGriff	.75	.23
❑	651	Walt Weiss	.50	.15
❑	652	C.Murray RC FOIL	1.00	.30
❑	653	Dave Nilsson	.50	.15
❑	654	Greg Pirkl RC	.50	.15

❑ 655	Robin Ventura FOIL	.50	.15
❑ 656	Mark Portugal	.50	.15
❑ 657	Roger McDowell	.50	.15
❑ 658	Rick Hirtensteiner FOIL RC	.50	.15
❑ 659	Glenallen Hill	.50	.15
❑ 660	Greg Gagne	.50	.15
❑ 661	Charles Johnson FOIL	.75	.23
❑ 662	Brian Hunter	.50	.15
❑ 663	Mark Lemke	.50	.15
❑ 664	Tim Belcher FOIL	.50	.15
❑ 665	Rich DeLucia	.50	.15
❑ 666	Bob Walk	.50	.15
❑ 667	Joe Carter FOIL	.50	.15
❑ 668	Jose Guzman	.50	.15
❑ 669	Otis Nixon	.50	.15
❑ 670	Phil Nevin FOIL	.75	.23
❑ 671	Eric Davis	.50	.15
❑ 672	Damion Easley RC	1.00	.30
❑ 673	Will Clark FOIL	1.25	.35
❑ 674	Mark Kieter RC	.50	.15
❑ 675	Ozzie Smith	1.25	.35
❑ 676	Manny Ramirez FOIL	5.00	1.50
❑ 677	Gregg Olson	.50	.15
❑ 678	Cliff Floyd RC	5.00	1.50
❑ 679	Duane Singleton RC	.50	.15
❑ 680	Jose Rijo	.50	.15
❑ 681	Willie Randolph	.50	.15
❑ 682	M.Tucker FOIL RC	1.00	.30
❑ 683	Darren Lewis	.50	.15
❑ 684	Dale Murphy	1.25	.35
❑ 685	Mike Pagliarulo	.50	.15
❑ 686	Paul Miller RC	.50	.15
❑ 687	Mike Robertson RC	.50	.15
❑ 688	Mike Devereaux	.50	.15
❑ 689	Pedro Astacio RC	1.00	.30
❑ 690	Alan Trammell	.75	.23
❑ 691	Roger Clemens	2.50	.75
❑ 692	Bud Black	.50	.15
❑ 693	Turk Wendell RC	1.00	.30
❑ 694	Barry Larkin FOIL	1.25	.35
❑ 695	Todd Zeile	.50	.15
❑ 696	Pat Hentgen	.50	.15
❑ 697	Eddie Taubensee RC	1.00	.30
❑ 698	G.Velasquez RC	.50	.15
❑ 699	Tom Glavine	1.25	.35
❑ 700	Robin Yount	1.25	.35
❑ 701	Checklist 1-141	.50	.15
❑ 702	Checklist 142-282	.50	.15
❑ 703	Checklist 283-423	.50	.15
❑ 704	Checklist 424-564	.50	.15
❑ 705	Checklist 565-705	.50	.15

1993 Bowman

		Nm-Mt	Ex-Mt
COMPLETE SET (708)		50.00	15.00
❑ 1	Glenn Davis	.15	.04
❑ 2	Hector Roa RC	.25	.07
❑ 3	Ken Ryan RC	.25	.07
❑ 4	Derek Wallace RC	.25	.07
❑ 5	Jorge Fabregas	.15	.04
❑ 6	Joe Oliver	.15	.04
❑ 7	Brandon Wilson	.15	.04
❑ 8	Mark Thompson RC	.25	.07
❑ 9	Tracy Sanders	.15	.04
❑ 10	Rich Renteria	.15	.04
❑ 11	Lou Whitaker	.30	.09
❑ 12	Brian L. Hunter RC	.50	.15
❑ 13	Joe Vitiello	.15	.04
❑ 14	Eric Karros	.30	.09
❑ 15	Joe Kmak	.15	.04
❑ 16	Tavo Alvarez	.15	.04
❑ 17	Steve Dunn RC	.25	.07
❑ 18	Tony Fernandez	.15	.04
❑ 19	Melido Perez	.15	.04
❑ 20	Mike Lieberthal	.30	.09
❑ 21	Terry Steinbach	.15	.04
❑ 22	Stan Belinda	.15	.04
❑ 23	Jay Buhner	.30	.09
❑ 24	Allen Watson	.15	.04
❑ 25	Daryl Henderson RC	.25	.07
❑ 26	Ray McDavid RC	.25	.07
❑ 27	Shawn Green	1.00	.30
❑ 28	Bud Black	.15	.04
❑ 29	Sherman Obando RC	.25	.07
❑ 30	Mike Hostetler RC	.25	.07
❑ 31	Nate Minchey RC	.25	.07
❑ 32	Randy Myers	.15	.04
❑ 33	Brian Grebeck	.15	.04
❑ 34	John Roper	.15	.04
❑ 35	Larry Thomas	.15	.04
❑ 36	Alex Cole	.15	.04
❑ 37	Tom Kramer RC	.25	.07
❑ 38	Matt Whisenant RC	.25	.07
❑ 39	Chris Gomez RC	.50	.15
❑ 40	Luis Gonzalez	.30	.09
❑ 41	Kevin Appier	.30	.09
❑ 42	Omar Daal RC	.50	.15
❑ 43	Duane Singleton	.15	.04
❑ 44	Bill Risley	.15	.04
❑ 45	Pat Meares RC	.50	.15
❑ 46	Butch Huskey	.15	.04
❑ 47	Bobby Munoz	.15	.04
❑ 48	Juan Bell	.15	.04
❑ 49	Scott Lydy RC	.25	.07
❑ 50	Dennis Moeller	.15	.04
❑ 51	Marc Newfield	.15	.04
❑ 52	Tripp Cromer RC	.25	.07
❑ 53	Kurt Miller	.15	.04
❑ 54	Jim Pena	.15	.04
❑ 55	Juan Guzman	.15	.04
❑ 56	Matt Williams	.30	.09
❑ 57	Harold Reynolds	.30	.09
❑ 58	Donnie Elliott RC	.25	.07
❑ 59	Jon Shave RC	.25	.07
❑ 60	Kevin Roberson RC	.25	.07
❑ 61	Hilly Hathaway RC	.25	.07
❑ 62	Jose Rijo	.15	.04
❑ 63	Kerry Taylor RC	.15	.04
❑ 64	Ryan Hawblitzel	.15	.04
❑ 65	Glenallen Hill	.15	.04
❑ 66	Ramon Martinez RC	.25	.07
❑ 67	Travis Fryman	.30	.09
❑ 68	Tom Nevers	.15	.04
❑ 69	Phil Hiatt	.15	.04
❑ 70	Tim Wallach	.15	.04
❑ 71	B.J. Surhoff	.30	.09
❑ 72	Rondell White	.30	.09
❑ 73	Denny Hocking RC	.50	.15
❑ 74	Mike Oquist RC	.25	.07
❑ 75	Paul O'Neill	.50	.15
❑ 76	Willie Banks	.15	.04
❑ 77	Bob Welch	.15	.04
❑ 78	Jose Sandoval RC	.25	.07
❑ 79	Bill Haselman	.15	.04
❑ 80	Rheal Cormier	.15	.04
❑ 81	Dean Palmer	.30	.09
❑ 82	Pat Gomez RC	.25	.07
❑ 83	Steve Karsay	.15	.04
❑ 84	Carl Hanselman RC	.25	.07
❑ 85	T.R. Lewis RC	.25	.07
❑ 86	Chipper Jones	.75	.23
❑ 87	Scott Hatteberg	.15	.04
❑ 88	Greg Hibbard	.15	.04
❑ 89	Lance Painter RC	.25	.07
❑ 90	Chad Mottola RC	.50	.15
❑ 91	Jason Bere	.15	.04
❑ 92	Dante Bichette	.30	.09
❑ 93	Sandy Alomar Jr.	.15	.04
❑ 94	Carl Everett	.30	.09
❑ 95	Danny Bautista RC	1.00	.30
❑ 96	Steve Finley	.30	.09
❑ 97	David Cone	.30	.09
❑ 98	Todd Hollandsworth	.15	.04
❑ 99	Matt Mieske	.15	.04
❑ 100	Larry Walker	.50	.15
❑ 101	Shane Mack	.15	.04
❑ 102	Aaron Ledesma RC	.25	.07
❑ 103	Andy Pettitte RC	8.00	1.50
❑ 104	Kevin Stocker	.15	.04
❑ 105	Mike Mohler RC	.25	.07
❑ 106	Tony Menendez	.15	.04
❑ 107	Derek Lowe	.30	.09
❑ 108	Basil Shabazz	.15	.04
❑ 109	Dan Smith	.15	.04
❑ 110	Scott Sanders RC	.50	.15
❑ 111	Todd Stottlemyre	.15	.04
❑ 112	Benji Simonton RC	.25	.07
❑ 113	Rick Sutcliffe	.30	.09
❑ 114	Lee Heath RC	.25	.07
❑ 115	Jeff Russell	.15	.04
❑ 116	Dave Stevens RC	.25	.07
❑ 117	Mark Holzemer RC	.25	.07
❑ 118	Tim Belcher	.15	.04
❑ 119	Bobby Thigpen	.15	.04
❑ 120	Roger Bailey RC	.25	.07
❑ 121	Tony Mitchell RC	.25	.07
❑ 122	Junior Felix	.15	.04
❑ 123	Rich Robertson RC	.25	.07
❑ 124	Andy Cook RC	.25	.07
❑ 125	Brian Bevil RC	.25	.07
❑ 126	Darryl Strawberry	.50	.15
❑ 127	Cal Eldred	.15	.04
❑ 128	Cliff Floyd	.50	.15
❑ 129	Alan Newman	.15	.04
❑ 130	Howard Johnson	.15	.04
❑ 131	Jim Abbott	.75	.23
❑ 132	Chad McConnell	.15	.04
❑ 133	Miguel Jimenez RC	.25	.07
❑ 134	Brett Backlund RC	.25	.07
❑ 135	John Cummings RC	.25	.07
❑ 136	Brian Barber	.15	.04
❑ 137	Rafael Palmeiro	.50	.15
❑ 138	Tim Worrell RC	.25	.07
❑ 139	Jose Pett RC	.25	.07
❑ 140	Barry Bonds	2.00	.60
❑ 141	Damon Buford	.15	.04
❑ 142	Jeff Blauser	.15	.04
❑ 143	Frankie Rodriguez	.15	.04
❑ 144	Mike Morgan	.15	.04
❑ 145	Gary DiSarcina	.15	.04
❑ 146	Pokey Reese	.15	.04
❑ 147	Johnny Ruffin	.15	.04
❑ 148	David Nied	.15	.04
❑ 149	Charles Nagy	.15	.04
❑ 150	Mike Myers RC	.25	.07
❑ 151	Kenny Carlyle RC	.25	.07
❑ 152	Eric Anthony	.15	.04
❑ 153	Jose Lind	.15	.04
❑ 154	Pedro Martinez	1.50	.45
❑ 155	Mark Kiefer	.15	.04
❑ 156	Tim Laker RC	.25	.07
❑ 157	Pat Mahomes	.15	.04
❑ 158	Bobby Bonilla	.30	.09
❑ 159	Domingo Jean	.15	.04
❑ 160	Darren Daulton	.30	.09
❑ 161	Mark McGwire	2.00	.60
❑ 162	Jason Kendall RC	1.50	.45
❑ 163	Desi Relaford	.15	.04
❑ 164	Ozzie Canseco	.15	.04
❑ 165	Rick Helling	.15	.04
❑ 166	Steve Pegues RC	.25	.07
❑ 167	Paul Molitor	.50	.15
❑ 168	Larry Carter RC	.15	.04
❑ 169	Arthur Rhodes	.15	.04
❑ 170	Damon Hollins RC	.50	.15
❑ 171	Frank Viola	.30	.09
❑ 172	Steve Trachsel RC	.50	.15
❑ 173	J.T. Snow RC	1.50	.45
❑ 174	Keith Gordon RC	.25	.07
❑ 175	Carlton Fisk	.50	.15
❑ 176	Jason Bates RC	.25	.07
❑ 177	Mike Crosby RC	.25	.07
❑ 178	Benny Santiago	.30	.09
❑ 179	Mike Moore	.15	.04
❑ 180	Jeff Juden	.15	.04
❑ 181	Darren Burton	.15	.04
❑ 182	Todd Williams RC	.50	.15
❑ 183	John Jaha	.15	.04

❑ 184 Mike Lansing RC .50 .15
❑ 185 Pedro Grifol RC .25 .07
❑ 186 Vince Coleman .15 .04
❑ 187 Pat Kelly .15 .04
❑ 188 Clemente Alvarez RC .25 .07
❑ 189 Ron Darling .15 .04
❑ 190 Orlando Merced .15 .04
❑ 191 Chris Bosio .15 .04
❑ 192 Steve Dixon RC .25 .07
❑ 193 Doug Dascenzo .15 .04
❑ 194 Ray Holbert RC .25 .07
❑ 195 Howard Battle .15 .04
❑ 196 Willie McGee .30 .09
❑ 197 John O'Donoghue RC .25 .07
❑ 198 Steve Avery .15 .04
❑ 199 Greg Blosser .15 .04
❑ 200 Ryne Sandberg 1.25 .35
❑ 201 Joe Grahe .15 .04
❑ 202 Dan Wilson .30 .09
❑ 203 Domingo Martinez RC .25 .07
❑ 204 Andres Galarraga .30 .09
❑ 205 Jamie Taylor RC .25 .07
❑ 206 Darrell Whitmore RC .25 .07
❑ 207 Ben Blomdahl RC .25 .07
❑ 208 Doug Drabek .15 .04
❑ 209 Keith Miller .15 .04
❑ 210 Billy Ashley .15 .04
❑ 211 Mike Farrell RC .25 .07
❑ 212 John Wetteland .30 .09
❑ 213 Randy Tomlin .15 .04
❑ 214 Sid Fernandez .15 .04
❑ 215 Quilvio Veras RC .50 .15
❑ 216 Dave Hollins .15 .04
❑ 217 Mike Neill .15 .04
❑ 218 Andy Van Slyke .30 .09
❑ 219 Bret Boone .50 .15
❑ 220 Tom Pagnozzi .15 .04
❑ 221 Mike Welch RC .25 .07
❑ 222 Frank Seminara .15 .04
❑ 223 Ron Villone .15 .04
❑ 224 D.J. Thielen RC .25 .07
❑ 225 Cal Ripken 2.50 .75
❑ 226 Pedro Borbon Jr. RC .25 .07
❑ 227 Carlos Quintana .15 .04
❑ 228 Tommy Shields .15 .04
❑ 229 Tim Salmon .50 .15
❑ 230 John Smiley .15 .04
❑ 231 Ellis Burks .30 .09
❑ 232 Pedro Castellano .15 .04
❑ 233 Paul Byrd .15 .04
❑ 234 Bryan Harvey .15 .04
❑ 235 Scott Livingstone .15 .04
❑ 236 James Mouton RC .25 .07
❑ 237 Joe Randa .30 .09
❑ 238 Pedro Astacio .15 .04
❑ 239 Darryl Hamilton .15 .04
❑ 240 Joey Eischen RC .25 .07
❑ 241 Edgar Herrera RC .25 .07
❑ 242 Dwight Gooden .50 .15
❑ 243 Sam Militello .15 .04
❑ 244 Ron Blazier RC .25 .07
❑ 245 Ruben Sierra .15 .04
❑ 246 Al Martin .15 .04
❑ 247 Mike Felder .15 .04
❑ 248 Bob Tewksbury .15 .04
❑ 249 Craig Lefferts .15 .04
❑ 250 Luis Lopez RC .25 .07
❑ 251 Devon White .15 .04
❑ 252 Will Clark .75 .23
❑ 253 Mark Smith .15 .04
❑ 254 Terry Pendleton .30 .09
❑ 255 Aaron Sele .15 .04
❑ 256 Jose Viera RC .25 .07
❑ 257 Damion Easley .15 .04
❑ 258 Rod Lofton RC .25 .07
❑ 259 Chris Snopek RC .25 .07
❑ 260 Q.McCracken RC .50 .15
❑ 261 Mike Matthews RC .25 .07
❑ 262 Hector Carrasco RC .25 .07
❑ 263 Rick Greene .15 .04
❑ 264 Chris Holt RC .50 .15
❑ 265 George Brett 2.00 .60
❑ 266 Rick Gorecki RC .25 .07
❑ 267 Francisco Gamez RC .25 .07
❑ 268 Marquis Grissom .15 .04
❑ 269 Kevin Tapani UER .15 .04
(Misspelled Tapan on card front)
❑ 270 Ryan Thompson .15 .04
❑ 271 Gerald Williams .15 .04
❑ 272 Paul Fletcher RC .25 .07
❑ 273 Lance Blankenship .15 .04
❑ 274 Marty Neff RC .25 .07
❑ 275 Shawn Estes .15 .04
❑ 276 Rene Arocha RC .50 .15
❑ 277 Scott Eyre RC .25 .07
❑ 278 Phil Plantier .15 .04
❑ 279 Paul Spoljaric RC .25 .07
❑ 280 Chris Gambs .15 .04
❑ 281 Harold Baines .30 .09
❑ 282 Jose Oliva .15 .04
❑ 283 Matt Whiteside RC .25 .07
❑ 284 Brant Brown RC .50 .15
❑ 285 Russ Springer .15 .04
❑ 286 Chris Sabo .15 .04
❑ 287 Ozzie Guillen .15 .04
❑ 288 Marcus Moore RC .25 .07
❑ 289 Chad Ogea .15 .04
❑ 290 Walt Weiss .15 .04
❑ 291 Brian Edmondson .15 .04
❑ 292 Jimmy Gonzalez .15 .04
❑ 293 Danny Miceli RC .50 .15
❑ 294 Jose Offerman .15 .04
❑ 295 Greg Vaughn .30 .09
❑ 296 Frank Bolick .15 .04
❑ 297 Mike Maksudian RC .25 .07
❑ 298 John Franco .30 .09
❑ 299 Danny Tartabull .15 .04
❑ 300 Len Dykstra .30 .09
❑ 301 Bobby Witt .15 .04
❑ 302 Trey Beamon RC .25 .07
❑ 303 Tino Martinez .50 .15
❑ 304 Aaron Holbert .15 .04
❑ 305 Juan Gonzalez .75 .23
❑ 306 Billy Hall RC .25 .07
❑ 307 Duane Ward .15 .04
❑ 308 Rod Beck .15 .04
❑ 309 Jose Mercedes RC .25 .07
❑ 310 Otis Nixon .15 .04
❑ 311 Gettys Glaze RC .25 .07
❑ 312 Candy Maldonado .15 .04
❑ 313 Chad Curtis .15 .04
❑ 314 Tim Costo .15 .04
❑ 315 Mike Robertson .15 .04
❑ 316 Nigel Wilson .15 .04
❑ 317 Greg McMichael RC .50 .15
❑ 318 Scott Pose RC .25 .07
❑ 319 Ivan Cruz .15 .04
❑ 320 Greg Swindell .15 .04
❑ 321 Kevin McReynolds .15 .04
❑ 322 Tom Candiotti .15 .04
❑ 323 Rob Wishnevski RC .25 .07
❑ 324 Ken Hill .15 .04
❑ 325 Kirby Puckett .75 .23
❑ 326 Tim Bogar RC .25 .07
❑ 327 Mariano Rivera 1.00 .30
❑ 328 Mitch Williams .15 .04
❑ 329 Craig Paquette .15 .04
❑ 330 Jay Bell .30 .09
❑ 331 Jose Martinez RC .25 .07
❑ 332 Rob Deer .15 .04
❑ 333 Brook Fordyce .15 .04
❑ 334 Matt Nokes .15 .04
❑ 335 Derek Lee .15 .04
❑ 336 Paul Ellis RC .25 .07
❑ 337 Desi Wilson RC .25 .07
❑ 338 Roberto Alomar .75 .23
❑ 339 Jim Tatum FOIL RC .25 .07
❑ 340 J.T. Snow FOIL .75 .23
❑ 341 Tim Salmon FOIL .50 .15
❑ 342 Russ Davis FOIL RC .50 .15
❑ 343 Javy Lopez FOIL .50 .15
❑ 344 Troy O'Leary FOIL RC .50 .15
❑ 345 M.Cordova FOIL RC 1.00 .30
❑ 346 Bubba Smith RC FOIL .25 .07
❑ 347 Chipper Jones FOIL .75 .23
❑ 348 Jessie Hollins FOIL .15 .04
❑ 349 Willie Greene FOIL .15 .04
❑ 350 Mark Thompson FOIL .15 .04
❑ 351 Nigel Wilson FOIL .15 .04
❑ 352 Todd Jones FOIL .15 .04
❑ 353 Raul Mondesi FOIL .30 .09
❑ 354 Cliff Floyd FOIL .50 .15
❑ 355 Bobby Jones FOIL .30 .09
❑ 356 Kevin Stocker FOIL .15 .04
❑ 357 M.Cummings FOIL .15 .04
❑ 358 Allen Watson FOIL .15 .04
❑ 359 Ray McDavid FOIL .15 .04
❑ 360 Steve Hosey FOIL .15 .04
❑ 361 B.Pennington FOIL .15 .04
❑ 362 F.Rodriguez FOIL .15 .04
❑ 363 Troy Percival FOIL .50 .15
❑ 364 Jason Bere FOIL .15 .04
❑ 365 Manny Ramirez FOIL .75 .23
❑ 366 J.Thompson FOIL .15 .04
❑ 367 Joe Vitiello FOIL .15 .04
❑ 368 Tyrone Hill FOIL .15 .04
❑ 369 David McCarty FOIL .15 .04
❑ 370 Brien Taylor FOIL .15 .04
❑ 371 T.Van Poppel FOIL .15 .04
❑ 372 Marc Newfield FOIL .15 .04
❑ 373 T.Lowery RC FOIL .50 .15
❑ 374 Alex Gonzalez FOIL .15 .04
❑ 375 Ken Griffey Jr. 1.25 .35
❑ 376 Donovan Osborne .15 .04
❑ 377 Ritchie Moody RC .25 .07
❑ 378 Shane Andrews .15 .04
❑ 379 Carlos Delgado .75 .23
❑ 380 Bill Swift .15 .04
❑ 381 Leo Gomez .15 .04
❑ 382 Ron Gant .30 .09
❑ 383 Scott Fletcher .15 .04
❑ 384 Matt Walbeck RC .50 .15
❑ 385 Chuck Finley .30 .09
❑ 386 Kevin Mitchell .15 .04
❑ 387 Wilson Alvarez UER .15 .04
(Misspelled Alverez on card front)
❑ 388 John Burke RC .25 .07
❑ 389 Alan Embree .15 .04
❑ 390 Trevor Hoffman .30 .09
❑ 391 Alan Trammell .50 .15
❑ 392 Todd Jones .15 .04
❑ 393 Felix Jose .15 .04
❑ 394 Orel Hershiser .30 .09
❑ 395 Pat Listach .15 .04
❑ 396 Gabe White .15 .04
❑ 397 Dan Serafini RC .25 .07
❑ 398 Todd Hundley .15 .04
❑ 399 Wade Boggs .50 .15
❑ 400 Tyler Green .15 .04
❑ 401 Mike Bordick .15 .04
❑ 402 Scott Bullett .15 .04
❑ 403 LaGrande Russell RC .25 .07
❑ 404 Ray Lankford .15 .04
❑ 405 Nolan Ryan 3.00 .90
❑ 406 Robbie Beckett .15 .04
❑ 407 Brent Bowers RC .25 .07
❑ 408 Adell Davenport RC .25 .07
❑ 409 Brady Anderson .30 .09
❑ 410 Tom Glavine .75 .23
❑ 411 Doug Hecker RC .25 .07
❑ 412 Jose Guzman .15 .04
❑ 413 Luis Polonia .15 .04
❑ 414 Brian Williams .15 .04
❑ 415 Bo Jackson .75 .23
❑ 416 Eric Young .15 .04
❑ 417 Kenny Lofton .30 .09
❑ 418 Orestes Destrade .15 .04
❑ 419 Tony Phillips .15 .04
❑ 420 Jeff Bagwell .50 .15
❑ 421 Mark Gardner .15 .04
❑ 422 Brett Butler .30 .09
❑ 423 Graeme Lloyd RC .50 .15
❑ 424 Delino DeShields .15 .04
❑ 425 Scott Erickson .15 .04
❑ 426 Jeff Kent .75 .23
❑ 427 Jimmy Key .30 .09
❑ 428 Mickey Morandini .15 .04
❑ 429 Marcos Armas RC .25 .07
❑ 430 Don Slaught .15 .04
❑ 431 Randy Johnson .75 .23
❑ 432 Omar Olivares .15 .04
❑ 433 Charlie Leibrandt .15 .04
❑ 434 Kurt Stillwell .15 .04
❑ 435 Scott Brow RC .25 .07
❑ 436 Robby Thompson .15 .04
❑ 437 Ben McDonald .15 .04

❑ 438 Deion Sanders .30 .09
❑ 439 Tony Pena .15 .04
❑ 440 Mark Grace .75 .23
❑ 441 Eduardo Perez .15 .04
❑ 442 Tim Pugh RC .25 .07
❑ 443 Scott Ruffcorn .15 .04
❑ 444 Jay Gainer RC .25 .07
❑ 445 Albert Belle .30 .09
❑ 446 Bret Barberie .15 .04
❑ 447 Justin Mashore .15 .04
❑ 448 Pete Harnisch .15 .04
❑ 449 Greg Gagne .15 .04
❑ 450 Eric Davis .30 .09
❑ 451 Dave Mlicki .15 .04
❑ 452 Moises Alou .30 .09
❑ 453 Rick Aguilera .15 .04
❑ 454 Eddie Murray .75 .23
❑ 455 Bob Wickman .15 .04
❑ 456 Wes Chamberlain .15 .04
❑ 457 Brent Gates .15 .04
❑ 458 Paul Wagner .15 .04
❑ 459 Mike Hampton .30 .09
❑ 460 Ozzie Smith .75 .23
❑ 461 Tom Henke .15 .04
❑ 462 Ricky Gutierrez .15 .04
❑ 463 Jack Morris .30 .09
❑ 464 Joel Chimelis .15 .04
❑ 465 Gregg Olson .15 .04
❑ 466 Javy Lopez .50 .15
❑ 467 Scott Cooper .15 .04
❑ 468 Willie Wilson .15 .04
❑ 469 Mark Langston .15 .04
❑ 470 Barry Larkin .75 .23
❑ 471 Rod Bolton .15 .04
❑ 472 Freddie Benavides .15 .04
❑ 473 Ken Ramos RC .25 .07
❑ 474 Chuck Carr .15 .04
❑ 475 Cecil Fielder .30 .09
❑ 476 Eddie Taubensee .15 .04
❑ 477 Chris Eddy RC .25 .07
❑ 478 Greg Hansell .15 .04
❑ 479 Kevin Reimer .15 .04
❑ 480 Dennis Martinez .30 .09
❑ 481 Chuck Knoblauch .30 .09
❑ 482 Mike Draper .15 .04
❑ 483 Spike Owen .15 .04
❑ 484 Terry Mulholland .15 .04
❑ 485 Dennis Eckersley .30 .09
❑ 486 Blas Minor .15 .04
❑ 487 Dave Fleming .15 .04
❑ 488 Dan Cholowsky .15 .04
❑ 489 Ivan Rodriguez .75 .23
❑ 490 Gary Sheffield .30 .09
❑ 491 Ed Sprague .15 .04
❑ 492 Steve Hosey .15 .04
❑ 493 Jimmy Haynes RC .50 .15
❑ 494 John Smoltz .50 .15
❑ 495 Andre Dawson .30 .09
❑ 496 Rey Sanchez .15 .04
❑ 497 Ty Van Burkleo .15 .04
❑ 498 Bobby Ayala RC .25 .07
❑ 499 Tim Raines .30 .09
❑ 500 Charlie Hayes .15 .04
❑ 501 Paul Sorrento .15 .04
❑ 502 Richie Lewis RC .25 .07
❑ 503 Jason Pfaff RC .25 .07
❑ 504 Ken Caminiti .30 .09
❑ 505 Mike Macfarlane .15 .04
❑ 506 Jody Reed .15 .04
❑ 507 Bobby Hughes RC .25 .07
❑ 508 Wil Cordero .15 .04
❑ 509 George Tsamis RC .25 .07
❑ 510 Bret Saberhagen .30 .09
❑ 511 Derek Jeter RC 25.00 7.50
❑ 512 Gene Schall .15 .04
❑ 513 Curtis Shaw .15 .04
❑ 514 Steve Cooke .15 .04
❑ 515 Edgar Martinez .50 .15
❑ 516 Mike Milchin .15 .04
❑ 517 Billy Ripken .15 .04
❑ 518 Andy Benes .15 .04
❑ 519 Juan de la Rosa RC .25 .07
❑ 520 John Burkett .15 .04
❑ 521 Alex Ochoa .15 .04
❑ 522 Tony Tarasco RC .50 .15
❑ 523 Luis Ortiz .15 .04
❑ 524 Rick Wilkins .15 .04
❑ 525 Chris Turner RC .25 .07
❑ 526 Rob Dibble .30 .09
❑ 527 Jack McDowell .15 .04
❑ 528 Daryl Boston .15 .04
❑ 529 Bill Wertz RC .25 .07
❑ 530 Charlie Hough .30 .09
❑ 531 Sean Bergman .15 .04
❑ 532 Doug Jones .15 .04
❑ 533 Jeff Montgomery .15 .04
❑ 534 Roger Cedeno RC .50 .15
❑ 535 Robin Yount .75 .23
❑ 536 Mo Vaughn .30 .09
❑ 537 Brian Harper .15 .04
❑ 538 Juan Castillo RC .15 .04
❑ 539 Steve Farr .15 .04
❑ 540 John Kruk .30 .09
❑ 541 Troy Neel .15 .04
❑ 542 Danny Clyburn RC .25 .07
❑ 543 Jim Converse RC .25 .07
❑ 544 Gregg Jefferies .15 .04
❑ 545 Jose Canseco .75 .23
❑ 546 Julio Bruno RC .25 .07
❑ 547 Rob Butler .15 .04
❑ 548 Royce Clayton .15 .04
❑ 549 Chris Hoiles .15 .04
❑ 550 Greg Maddux 1.50 .45
❑ 551 Joe Ciccarella RC .25 .07
❑ 552 Ozzie Timmons .15 .04
❑ 553 Chili Davis .30 .09
❑ 554 Brian Koelling .15 .04
❑ 555 Frank Thomas .75 .23
❑ 556 Vinny Castilla .30 .09
❑ 557 Reggie Jefferson .15 .04
❑ 558 Rob Natal .15 .04
❑ 559 Mike Henneman .15 .04
❑ 560 Craig Biggio .50 .15
❑ 561 Billy Brewer .15 .04
❑ 562 Dan Melendez .15 .04
❑ 563 Kenny Felder RC .25 .07
❑ 564 Miguel Batista RC 1.00 .30
❑ 565 Dave Winfield .50 .15
❑ 566 Al Shirley .15 .04
❑ 567 Robert Eenhoorn .15 .04
❑ 568 Mike Williams .15 .04
❑ 569 Tanyon Sturtze RC .50 .15
❑ 570 Tim Wakefield .30 .09
❑ 571 Greg Pirkl .15 .04
❑ 572 Sean Lowe RC .25 .07
❑ 573 Terry Burrows RC .25 .07
❑ 574 Kevin Higgins .15 .04
❑ 575 Joe Carter .30 .09
❑ 576 Kevin Rogers .15 .04
❑ 577 Manny Alexander .15 .04
❑ 578 David Justice .30 .09
❑ 579 Brian Conroy RC .25 .07
❑ 580 Jessie Hollins .15 .04
❑ 581 Ron Watson RC .25 .07
❑ 582 Bip Roberts .15 .04
❑ 583 Tom Urbani RC .25 .07
❑ 584 Jason Hutchins RC .25 .07
❑ 585 Carlos Baerga .15 .04
❑ 586 Jeff Mutis .15 .04
❑ 587 Justin Thompson .15 .04
❑ 588 Orlando Miller .15 .04
❑ 589 Brian McRae .15 .04
❑ 590 Ramon Martinez .15 .04
❑ 591 Dave Nilsson .15 .04
❑ 592 Jose Vidro RC 4.00 1.20
❑ 593 Rich Becker .15 .04
❑ 594 Preston Wilson RC 3.00 .90
❑ 595 Don Mattingly 2.00 .60
❑ 596 Tony Longmire .15 .04
❑ 597 Kevin Seitzer .15 .04
❑ 598 Midre Cummings RC .25 .07
❑ 599 Omar Vizquel .30 .09
❑ 600 Lee Smith .30 .09
❑ 601 David Hulse RC .25 .07
❑ 602 Darrell Sherman RC .25 .07
❑ 603 Alex Gonzalez .15 .04
❑ 604 Geronimo Pena .15 .04
❑ 605 Mike Devereaux .15 .04
❑ 606 S.Hitchcock RC .50 .15
❑ 607 Mike Greenwell .15 .04
❑ 608 Steve Buechele .15 .04
❑ 609 Troy Percival .50 .15
❑ 610 Roberto Kelly .15 .04
❑ 611 James Baldwin RC .50 .15
❑ 612 Jerald Clark .15 .04
❑ 613 Albie Lopez RC .50 .15
❑ 614 Dave Magadan .15 .04
❑ 615 Mickey Tettleton .15 .04
❑ 616 Sean Runyan RC .25 .07
❑ 617 Bob Hamelin .15 .04
❑ 618 Raul Mondesi .30 .09
❑ 619 Tyrone Hill .15 .04
❑ 620 Darrin Fletcher .15 .04
❑ 621 Mike Trombley .15 .04
❑ 622 Jeromy Burnitz .30 .09
❑ 623 Bernie Williams .50 .15
❑ 624 Mike Farmer RC .25 .07
❑ 625 Rickey Henderson 1.25 .35
❑ 626 Carlos Garcia .15 .04
❑ 627 Jeff Darwin RC .25 .07
❑ 628 Todd Zeile .15 .04
❑ 629 Benji Gil .15 .04
❑ 630 Tony Gwynn 1.00 .30
❑ 631 Aaron Small RC .25 .07
❑ 632 Joe Rosselli RC .25 .07
❑ 633 Mike Mussina .75 .23
❑ 634 Ryan Klesko .30 .09
❑ 635 Roger Clemens 1.50 .45
❑ 636 Sammy Sosa 1.25 .35
❑ 637 Orlando Palmeiro RC .25 .07
❑ 638 Willie Greene .15 .04
❑ 639 George Bell .15 .04
❑ 640 Garvin Alston RC .25 .07
❑ 641 Pete Janicki RC .25 .07
❑ 642 Chris Sheff RC .25 .07
❑ 643 Felipe Lira RC .25 .07
❑ 644 Roberto Petagine .15 .04
❑ 645 Wally Joyner .30 .09
❑ 646 Mike Piazza 2.00 .60
❑ 647 Jaime Navarro .15 .04
❑ 648 Jeff Hartsock .15 .04
❑ 649 David McCarty .15 .04
❑ 650 Bobby Jones .30 .09
❑ 651 Mark Hutton .15 .04
❑ 652 Kyle Abbott .15 .04
❑ 653 Steve Cox RC .50 .15
❑ 654 Jeff King .15 .04
❑ 655 Norm Charlton .15 .04
❑ 656 Mike Gulan RC .25 .07
❑ 657 Julio Franco .30 .09
❑ 658 C.Cairncross RC .25 .07
❑ 659 John Olerud .30 .09
❑ 660 Salomon Torres .15 .04
❑ 661 Brad Pennington .15 .04
❑ 662 Melvin Nieves .15 .04
❑ 663 Ivan Calderon .15 .04
❑ 664 Turk Wendell .15 .04
❑ 665 Chris Pritchett .15 .04
❑ 666 Reggie Sanders .30 .09
❑ 667 Robin Ventura .30 .09
❑ 668 Joe Girardi .15 .04
❑ 669 Manny Ramirez .75 .23
❑ 670 Jeff Conine .30 .09
❑ 671 Greg Gohr .15 .04
❑ 672 Andujar Cedeno .15 .04
❑ 673 Les Norman RC .25 .07
❑ 674 Mike James RC .25 .07
❑ 675 Marshall Boze RC .25 .07
❑ 676 B.J. Wallace .15 .04
❑ 677 Kent Hrbek .30 .09
❑ 678 Jack Voigt RC .25 .07
❑ 679 Brien Taylor .15 .04
❑ 680 Curt Schilling .50 .15
❑ 681 Todd Van Poppel .15 .04
❑ 682 Kevin Young .30 .09
❑ 683 Tommy Adams .15 .04
❑ 684 Bernard Gilkey .15 .04
❑ 685 Kevin Brown .30 .09
❑ 686 Fred McGriff .50 .15
❑ 687 Pat Borders .15 .04
❑ 688 Kirt Manwaring .15 .04
❑ 689 Sid Bream .15 .04
❑ 690 John Valentin .15 .04
❑ 691 Steve Olsen RC .25 .07
❑ 692 Roberto Mejia RC .25 .07
❑ 693 Carlos Delgado FOIL .75 .23
❑ 694 S.Gibralter FOIL RC .25 .07
❑ 695 Gary Mota FOIL RC .25 .07

❑ 696 Jose Malave FOIL RC .25 .07
❑ 697 Larry Sutton FOIL RC .25 .07
❑ 698 Dan Frye FOIL RC .25 .07
❑ 699 Tim Clark FOIL RC .25 .07
❑ 700 Brian Rupp FOIL RC .25 .07
❑ 701 Felipe Alou FOIL .30 .09
Moises Alou
❑ 702 Barry Bonds FOIL .75 .23
Bobby Bonds
❑ 703 Ken Griffey Sr. FOIL .75 .23
Ken Griffey Jr.
❑ 704 Brian McRae FOIL .15 .04
Hal McRae
❑ 705 Checklist 1 .15 .04
❑ 706 Checklist 2 .15 .04
❑ 707 Checklist 3 .15 .04
❑ 708 Checklist 4 .15 .04

1994 Bowman

	Nm-Mt	Ex-Mt
COMPLETE SET (682)	60.00	18.00

❑ 1 Joe Carter .40 .12
❑ 2 Marcus Moore .25 .07
❑ 3 Doug Creek RC .50 .15
❑ 4 Pedro Martinez 1.00 .30
❑ 5 Ken Griffey Jr. 1.50 .45
❑ 6 Greg Swindell .25 .07
❑ 7 J.J. Johnson .25 .07
❑ 8 Homer Bush RC 1.00 .30
❑ 9 Arquimedez Pozo RC .50 .15
❑ 10 Bryan Harvey .25 .07
❑ 11 J.T. Snow .40 .12
❑ 12 Alan Benes RC 1.00 .30
❑ 13 Chad Kreuter .25 .07
❑ 14 Eric Karros .40 .12
❑ 15 Frank Thomas 1.00 .30
❑ 16 Bret Saberhagen .40 .12
❑ 17 Terrell Lowery .25 .07
❑ 18 Rod Bolton .25 .07
❑ 19 Harold Baines .40 .12
❑ 20 Matt Walbeck .25 .07
❑ 21 Tom Glavine 1.00 .30
❑ 22 Todd Jones .25 .07
❑ 23 Alberto Castillo RC .50 .15
❑ 24 Ruben Sierra .25 .07
❑ 25 Don Mattingly 2.50 .75
❑ 26 Mike Morgan .25 .07
❑ 27 Jim Musselwhite RC .50 .15
❑ 28 Matt Brunson RC .50 .15
❑ 29 A.Meinershagen RC .50 .15
❑ 30 Joe Girardi .25 .07
❑ 31 Shane Halter .25 .07
❑ 32 Jose Paniagua RC 1.00 .30
❑ 33 Paul Perkins RC .50 .15
❑ 34 John Hudek RC .50 .15
❑ 35 Frank Viola .40 .12
❑ 36 David Lamb RC .50 .15
❑ 37 Marshall Boze .25 .07
❑ 38 Jorge Posada RC 8.00 2.40
❑ 39 Brian Anderson RC 1.00 .30
❑ 40 Mark Whiten .25 .07
❑ 41 Sean Bergman .25 .07
❑ 42 Jose Parra RC .50 .15
❑ 43 Mike Robertson .25 .07
❑ 44 Pete Walker RC .50 .15
❑ 45 Juan Gonzalez 1.00 .30
❑ 46 Cleveland Ladell RC .50 .15
❑ 47 Mark Smith .25 .07
❑ 48 Kevin Jarvis UER .50 .15
(team listed as Yankees on back)
❑ 49 Amaury Telemaco RC .50 .15
❑ 50 Andy Van Slyke .40 .12
❑ 51 Rikkert Faneyte RC .50 .15
❑ 52 Curtis Shaw .25 .07
❑ 53 Matt Drews RC .50 .15
❑ 54 Wilson Alvarez .25 .07
❑ 55 Manny Ramirez .60 .18
❑ 56 Bobby Munoz .25 .07
❑ 57 Ed Sprague .25 .07
❑ 58 Jamey Wright RC 1.00 .30
❑ 59 Jeff Montgomery .25 .07
❑ 60 Kirk Rueter .40 .12
❑ 61 Edgar Martinez .60 .18
❑ 62 Luis Gonzalez .40 .12
❑ 63 Tim Vanegmond RC .50 .15
❑ 64 Bip Roberts .25 .07
❑ 65 John Jaha .25 .07
❑ 66 Chuck Carr .25 .07
❑ 67 Chuck Finley .40 .12
❑ 68 Aaron Holbert .25 .07
❑ 69 Cecil Fielder .40 .12
❑ 70 Tom Engle RC .50 .15
❑ 71 Ron Karkovice .25 .07
❑ 72 Joe Orsulak .25 .07
❑ 73 Duff Brumley RC .50 .15
❑ 74 Craig Clayton RC .50 .15
❑ 75 Cal Ripken 3.00 .90
❑ 76 Brad Fulmer RC 2.50 .75
❑ 77 Tony Tarasco .25 .07
❑ 78 Terry Farrar RC .50 .15
❑ 79 Matt Williams .40 .12
❑ 80 Rickey Henderson 1.50 .45
❑ 81 Terry Mulholland .25 .07
❑ 82 Sammy Sosa 1.50 .45
❑ 83 Paul Sorrento .25 .07
❑ 84 Pete Incaviglia .25 .07
❑ 85 Darren Hall RC .50 .15
❑ 86 Scott Klingenbeck .25 .07
❑ 87 Dario Perez RC .50 .15
❑ 88 Ugueth Urbina .25 .07
❑ 89 Dave Vanhof RC .50 .15
❑ 90 Domingo Jean .25 .07
❑ 91 Otis Nixon .25 .07
❑ 92 Andres Berumen .25 .07
❑ 93 Jose Valentin .25 .07
❑ 94 Edgar Renteria RC 6.00 1.80
❑ 95 Chris Turner .25 .07
❑ 96 Ray Lankford .25 .07
❑ 97 Danny Bautista .25 .07
❑ 98 Chan Ho Park RC 2.50 .75
❑ 99 Glenn DiSarcina RC .50 .15
❑ 100 Butch Huskey .25 .07
❑ 101 Ivan Rodriguez 1.00 .30
❑ 102 Johnny Ruffin .25 .07
❑ 103 Alex Ochoa .25 .07
❑ 104 Torii Hunter RC 12.00 3.60
❑ 105 Ryan Klesko .40 .12
❑ 106 Jay Bell .40 .12
❑ 107 Kurt Peltzer RC .50 .15
❑ 108 Miguel Jimenez .25 .07
❑ 109 Russ Davis .25 .07
❑ 110 Derek Wallace .25 .07
❑ 111 Keith Lockhart RC 1.00 .30
❑ 112 Mike Lieberthal .40 .12
❑ 113 Dave Stewart .40 .12
❑ 114 Tom Schmidt .25 .07
❑ 115 Brian McRae .25 .07
❑ 116 Moises Alou .40 .12
❑ 117 Dave Fleming .25 .07
❑ 118 Jeff Bagwell .60 .18
❑ 119 Luis Ortiz .25 .07
❑ 120 Tony Gwynn 1.25 .35
❑ 121 Jaime Navarro .25 .07
❑ 122 Benito Santiago .40 .12
❑ 123 Darrell Whitmore .25 .07
❑ 124 John Mabry RC 1.00 .30
❑ 125 Mickey Tettleton .25 .07
❑ 126 Tom Candiotti .25 .07
❑ 127 Tim Raines .40 .12
❑ 128 Bobby Bonilla .40 .12
❑ 129 John Dettmer .25 .07
❑ 130 Hector Carrasco .25 .07
❑ 131 Chris Hoiles .25 .07
❑ 132 Rick Aguilera .25 .07
❑ 133 David Justice .40 .12
❑ 134 Esteban Loaiza RC 8.00 2.40
❑ 135 Barry Bonds 2.50 .75
❑ 136 Bob Welch .25 .07
❑ 137 Mike Stanley .25 .07
❑ 138 Roberto Hernandez .25 .07
❑ 139 Sandy Alomar Jr. .25 .07
❑ 140 Darren Daulton .40 .12
❑ 141 Angel Martinez RC .50 .15
❑ 142 Howard Johnson .25 .07
❑ 143 Bob Hamelin UER .25 .07
(name and card number colors don't match)
❑ 144 J.J. Thobe RC .50 .15
❑ 145 Roger Salkeld .25 .07
❑ 146 Orlando Miller .25 .07
❑ 147 Dmitri Young .40 .12
❑ 148 Tim Hyers RC .50 .15
❑ 149 Mark Loretta RC 1.50 .45
❑ 150 Chris Hammond .25 .07
❑ 151 Joel Moore RC .50 .15
❑ 152 Todd Zeile .25 .07
❑ 153 Wil Cordero .25 .07
❑ 154 Chris Smith .25 .07
❑ 155 James Baldwin .25 .07
❑ 156 Edgardo Alfonzo RC 2.50 .75
❑ 157 Kym Ashworth RC .50 .15
❑ 158 Paul Bako RC .50 .15
❑ 159 Rick Krivda RC .50 .15
❑ 160 Pat Mahomes .25 .07
❑ 161 Damon Hollins .40 .12
❑ 162 Felix Martinez RC .50 .15
❑ 163 Jason Myers RC .50 .15
❑ 164 Izzy Molina RC .50 .15
❑ 165 Brien Taylor .25 .07
❑ 166 Kevin Orie RC .50 .15
❑ 167 Casey Whitten RC .50 .15
❑ 168 Tony Longmire .25 .07
❑ 169 John Olerud .40 .12
❑ 170 Mark Thompson .25 .07
❑ 171 Jorge Fabregas .25 .07
❑ 172 John Wetteland .40 .12
❑ 173 Dan Wilson .25 .07
❑ 174 Doug Drabek .25 .07
❑ 175 Jeff McNeely .25 .07
❑ 176 Melvin Nieves .25 .07
❑ 177 Doug Glanville RC 1.00 .30
❑ 178 Javier De La Hoya RC .50 .15
❑ 179 Chad Curtis .25 .07
❑ 180 Brian Barber .25 .07
❑ 181 Mike Henneman .25 .07
❑ 182 Jose Offerman .25 .07
❑ 183 Robert Ellis RC .50 .15
❑ 184 John Franco .40 .12
❑ 185 Benji Gil .25 .07
❑ 186 Hal Morris .25 .07
❑ 187 Chris Sabo .25 .07
❑ 188 Blaise Ilsley RC .50 .15
❑ 189 Steve Avery .25 .07
❑ 190 Rick White RC .50 .15
❑ 191 Rod Beck .25 .07
❑ 192 Mark McGwire UER 2.50 .75
(No card number on back)
❑ 193 Jim Abbott 1.00 .30
❑ 194 Randy Myers .25 .07
❑ 195 Kenny Lofton .40 .12
❑ 196 Mariano Duncan .25 .07
❑ 197 Lee Daniels RC .50 .15
❑ 198 Armando Reynoso .25 .07
❑ 199 Joe Randa .40 .12
❑ 200 Cliff Floyd .40 .12
❑ 201 Tim Harkrider RC .50 .15
❑ 202 Kevin Gallaher RC .50 .15
❑ 203 Scott Cooper .25 .07
❑ 204 Phil Stidham RC .50 .15
❑ 205 Jeff D'Amico RC 1.00 .30
❑ 206 Matt Whisenant .25 .07
❑ 207 De Shawn Warren .25 .07
❑ 208 Rene Arocha .25 .07
❑ 209 Tony Clark RC 1.00 .30
❑ 210 Jason Jacome RC .50 .15
❑ 211 Scott Christman RC .50 .15
❑ 212 Bill Pulsipher .40 .12
❑ 213 Dean Palmer .40 .12

	No.	Player	Price 1	Price 2
❑	214	Chad Mottola	.25	.07
❑	215	Manny Alexander	.25	.07
❑	216	Rich Becker	.25	.07
❑	217	Andre King RC	.50	.15
❑	218	Carlos Garcia	.25	.07
❑	219	Ron Pezzoni RC	.50	.15
❑	220	Steve Karsay	.25	.07
❑	221	Jose Musset RC	.50	.15
❑	222	Karl Rhodes	.25	.07
❑	223	Frank Cimorelli RC	.50	.15
❑	224	Kevin Jordan RC	.50	.15
❑	225	Duane Ward	.25	.07
❑	226	John Burke	.25	.07
❑	227	Mike Macfarlane	.25	.07
❑	228	Mike Lansing	.25	.07
❑	229	Chuck Knoblauch	.40	.12
❑	230	Ken Caminiti	.40	.12
❑	231	Gar Finnvold RC	.50	.15
❑	232	Derrek Lee RC	2.50	.75
❑	233	Brady Anderson	.40	.12
❑	234	Vic Darensbourg RC	.50	.15
❑	235	Mark Langston	.25	.07
❑	236	T.J. Mathews RC	.50	.15
❑	237	Lou Whitaker	.40	.12
❑	238	Roger Cedeno	.25	.07
❑	239	Alex Fernandez	.25	.07
❑	240	Ryan Thompson	.25	.07
❑	241	Kerry Lacy RC	.50	.15
❑	242	Reggie Sanders	.40	.12
❑	243	Brad Pennington	.25	.07
❑	244	Bryan Eversgerd RC	.50	.15
❑	245	Greg Maddux	2.00	.60
❑	246	Jason Kendall	.40	.12
❑	247	J.R. Phillips	.25	.07
❑	248	Bobby Witt	.25	.07
❑	249	Paul O'Neill	.60	.18
❑	250	Ryne Sandberg	1.50	.45
❑	251	Charles Nagy	.25	.07
❑	252	Kevin Stocker	.25	.07
❑	253	Shawn Green	1.00	.30
❑	254	Charlie Hayes	.25	.07
❑	255	Donnie Elliott	.25	.07
❑	256	Rob Fitzpatrick RC	.50	.15
❑	257	Tim Davis	.25	.07
❑	258	James Mouton	.25	.07
❑	259	Mike Greenwell	.25	.07
❑	260	Ray McDavid	.25	.07
❑	261	Mike Kelly	.25	.07
❑	262	Andy Larkin RC	.50	.15
❑	263	Marquis Riley UER (No card number on back)	.25	.07
❑	264	Bob Tewksbury	.25	.07
❑	265	Brian Edmondson	.25	.07
❑	266	Eduardo Lantigua RC	.50	.15
❑	267	Brandon Wilson	.25	.07
❑	268	Mike Welch	.25	.07
❑	269	Tom Henke	.25	.07
❑	270	Pokey Reese	.25	.07
❑	271	Greg Zaun RC	1.00	.30
❑	272	Todd Ritchie	.25	.07
❑	273	Javier Lopez	.40	.12
❑	274	Kevin Young	.25	.07
❑	275	Kirt Manwaring	.25	.07
❑	276	Bill Taylor RC	.50	.15
❑	277	Robert Eenhoorn	.25	.07
❑	278	Jessie Hollins	.25	.07
❑	279	Julian Tavarez RC	1.00	.30
❑	280	Gene Schall	.25	.07
❑	281	Paul Molitor	.60	.18
❑	282	Neifi Perez RC	1.00	.30
❑	283	Greg Gagne	.25	.07
❑	284	Marquis Grissom	.25	.07
❑	285	Randy Johnson	1.00	.30
❑	286	Pete Harnisch	.25	.07
❑	287	Joel Bennett RC	.50	.15
❑	288	Derek Bell	.25	.07
❑	289	Darryl Hamilton	.25	.07
❑	290	Gary Sheffield	.40	.12
❑	291	Eduardo Perez	.25	.07
❑	292	Basil Shabazz	.25	.07
❑	293	Eric Davis	.40	.12
❑	294	Pedro Astacio	.25	.07
❑	295	Robin Ventura	.40	.12
❑	296	Jeff Kent	.40	.12
❑	297	Rick Helling	.25	.07
❑	298	Joe Oliver	.25	.07
❑	299	Lee Smith	.40	.12
❑	300	Dave Winfield	.60	.18
❑	301	Deion Sanders	.40	.12
❑	302	R.Manzanillo RC	.50	.15
❑	303	Mark Portugal	.25	.07
❑	304	Brent Gates	.25	.07
❑	305	Wade Boggs	.60	.18
❑	306	Rick Wilkins	.25	.07
❑	307	Carlos Baerga	.25	.07
❑	308	Curt Schilling	.60	.18
❑	309	Shannon Stewart	1.00	.30
❑	310	Darren Holmes	.25	.07
❑	311	Robert Toth RC	.50	.15
❑	312	Gabe White	.25	.07
❑	313	Mac Suzuki RC	1.00	.30
❑	314	Alvin Morman RC	.50	.15
❑	315	Mo Vaughn	.40	.12
❑	316	Bryce Florie RC	.50	.15
❑	317	Gabby Martinez RC	.50	.15
❑	318	Carl Everett	.40	.12
❑	319	Kerwin Moore	.25	.07
❑	320	Tom Pagnozzi	.25	.07
❑	321	Chris Gomez	.25	.07
❑	322	Todd Williams	.25	.07
❑	323	Pat Hentgen	.25	.07
❑	324	Kirk Presley RC	.50	.15
❑	325	Kevin Brown	.40	.12
❑	326	J.Isringhausen RC	1.50	.45
❑	327	Rick Forney RC	.50	.15
❑	328	Carlos Pulido RC	.50	.15
❑	329	Terrell Wade RC	.50	.15
❑	330	Al Martin	.25	.07
❑	331	Dan Carlson RC	.50	.15
❑	332	Mark Acre RC	.50	.15
❑	333	Sterling Hitchcock	.25	.07
❑	334	Jon Ratliff RC	.50	.15
❑	335	Alex Ramirez RC	.50	.15
❑	336	Phil Geisler RC	.25	.07
❑	337	E.Zambrano FOIL RC	.50	.15
❑	338	Jim Thome FOIL	1.00	.30
❑	339	James Mouton FOIL	.25	.07
❑	340	Cliff Floyd FOIL	.40	.12
❑	341	Carlos Delgado FOIL	.60	.18
❑	342	R.Petagine FOIL	.25	.07
❑	343	Tim Clark FOIL	.25	.07
❑	344	Bubba Smith FOIL	.25	.07
❑	345	Randy Curtis FOIL RC	.50	.15
❑	346	Joe Biasucci FOIL RC	.50	.15
❑	347	D.J. Boston FOIL RC	.50	.15
❑	348	R.Rivera FOIL RC	.50	.15
❑	349	Bryan Link FOIL RC	.50	.15
❑	350	Mike Bell FOIL RC	.50	.15
❑	351	M.Watson FOIL RC	.50	.15
❑	352	Jason Myers FOIL	.25	.07
❑	353	Chipper Jones FOIL	1.00	.30
❑	354	B.Kieschnick FOIL	.25	.07
❑	355	Pokey Reese FOIL	.25	.07
❑	356	John Burke FOIL	.25	.07
❑	357	Kurt Miller FOIL	.25	.07
❑	358	Orlando Miller FOIL	.25	.07
❑	359	T.Hollandsworth FOIL	.25	.07
❑	360	Rondell White FOIL	.40	.12
❑	361	Bill Pulsipher FOIL	.40	.12
❑	362	Tyler Green FOIL	.25	.07
❑	363	M.Cummings FOIL	.25	.07
❑	364	Brian Barber FOIL	.25	.07
❑	365	Melvin Nieves FOIL	.25	.07
❑	366	Salomon Torres FOIL	.25	.07
❑	367	Alex Ochoa FOIL	.25	.07
❑	368	F.Rodriguez FOIL	.25	.07
❑	369	Brian Anderson FOIL	.40	.12
❑	370	James Baldwin FOIL	.25	.07
❑	371	Manny Ramirez FOIL	.60	.18
❑	372	J.Thompson FOIL	.25	.07
❑	373	Johnny Damon FOIL	1.00	.30
❑	374	Jeff D'Amico FOIL	1.00	.30
❑	375	Rich Becker FOIL	.25	.07
❑	376	Derek Jeter FOIL	3.00	.90
❑	377	Steve Karsay FOIL	.25	.07
❑	378	Mac Suzuki FOIL	.40	.12
❑	379	Benji Gil FOIL	.25	.07
❑	380	Alex Gonzalez FOIL	.25	.07
❑	381	Jason Bere FOIL	.25	.07
❑	382	Brett Butler FOIL	.40	.12
❑	383	Jeff Conine FOIL	.40	.12
❑	384	Darren Daulton FOIL	.40	.12
❑	385	Jeff Kent FOIL	.40	.12
❑	386	Don Mattingly FOIL	2.50	.75
❑	387	Mike Piazza FOIL	2.00	.60
❑	388	Ryne Sandberg FOIL	1.50	.45
❑	389	Rich Amaral	.25	.07
❑	390	Craig Biggio	.60	.18
❑	391	Jeff Suppan RC	1.00	.30
❑	392	Andy Benes	.25	.07
❑	393	Cal Eldred	.25	.07
❑	394	Jeff Conine	.40	.12
❑	395	Tim Salmon	.60	.18
❑	396	Ray Suplee RC	.50	.15
❑	397	Tony Phillips	.25	.07
❑	398	Ramon Martinez	.25	.07
❑	399	Julio Franco	.40	.12
❑	400	Dwight Gooden	.60	.18
❑	401	Kevin Lomon RC	.50	.15
❑	402	Jose Rijo	.25	.07
❑	403	Mike Devereaux	.25	.07
❑	404	Mike Zolecki RC	.50	.15
❑	405	Fred McGriff	.60	.18
❑	406	Danny Clyburn	.25	.07
❑	407	Robby Thompson	.25	.07
❑	408	Terry Steinbach	.25	.07
❑	409	Luis Polonia	.25	.07
❑	410	Mark Grace	1.00	.30
❑	411	Albert Belle	.40	.12
❑	412	John Kruk	.40	.12
❑	413	Scott Spiezio RC	2.50	.75
❑	414	Ellis Burks UER (Name spelled Elkis on front)	.40	.12
❑	415	Joe Vitiello	.25	.07
❑	416	Tim Costo	.25	.07
❑	417	Marc Newfield	.25	.07
❑	418	Oscar Henriquez RC	.50	.15
❑	419	Matt Perisho RC	.50	.15
❑	420	Julio Bruno	.25	.07
❑	421	Kenny Felder	.25	.07
❑	422	Tyler Green	.25	.07
❑	423	Jim Edmonds	.60	.18
❑	424	Ozzie Smith	1.00	.30
❑	425	Rick Greene	.25	.07
❑	426	Todd Hollandsworth	.25	.07
❑	427	Eddie Pearson RC	.50	.15
❑	428	Quilvio Veras	.25	.07
❑	429	Kenny Rogers	.40	.12
❑	430	Willie Greene	.25	.07
❑	431	Vaughn Eshelman	.25	.07
❑	432	Pat Meares	.25	.07
❑	433	Jermaine Dye RC	2.50	.75
❑	434	Steve Cooke	.25	.07
❑	435	Bill Swift	.25	.07
❑	436	Fausto Cruz RC	.50	.15
❑	437	Mark Hutton	.25	.07
❑	438	B.Kieschnick RC	1.00	.30
❑	439	Yorkis Perez	.25	.07
❑	440	Len Dykstra	.40	.12
❑	441	Pat Borders	.25	.07
❑	442	Doug Walls RC	.50	.15
❑	443	Wally Joyner	.40	.12
❑	444	Ken Hill	.25	.07
❑	445	Eric Anthony	.25	.07
❑	446	Mitch Williams	.25	.07
❑	447	Cory Bailey RC	.50	.15
❑	448	Dave Staton	.25	.07
❑	449	Greg Vaughn	.40	.12
❑	450	Dave Magadan	.25	.07
❑	451	Chili Davis	.40	.12
❑	452	Gerald Santos RC	.50	.15
❑	453	Joe Perona	.25	.07
❑	454	Delino DeShields	.25	.07
❑	455	Jack McDowell	.25	.07
❑	456	Todd Hundley	.25	.07
❑	457	Ritchie Moody	.25	.07
❑	458	Bret Boone	.40	.12
❑	459	Ben McDonald	.25	.07
❑	460	Kirby Puckett	1.00	.30
❑	461	Gregg Olson	.25	.07
❑	462	Rich Aude RC	.50	.15
❑	463	John Burkett	.25	.07
❑	464	Troy Neel	.25	.07
❑	465	Jimmy Key	.40	.12
❑	466	Ozzie Timmons	.25	.07
❑	467	Eddie Murray	1.00	.30
❑	468	Mark Tranberg RC	.50	.15
❑	469	Alex Gonzalez	.25	.07

No.	Player	Nm-Mt	Ex-Mt
470	David Nied	.25	.07
471	Barry Larkin	1.00	.30
472	Brian Looney RC	.50	.15
473	Shawn Estes	.25	.07
474	A.J. Sager RC	.50	.15
475	Roger Clemens	2.00	.60
476	Vince Moore	.25	.07
477	Scott Karl RC	.50	.15
478	Kurt Miller	.25	.07
479	Garret Anderson	1.00	.30
480	Allen Watson	.25	.07
481	Jose Lima RC	1.50	.45
482	Rick Gorecki	.25	.07
483	Jimmy Hurst RC	.50	.15
484	Preston Wilson	.60	.18
485	Will Clark	1.00	.30
486	Mike Ferry RC	.50	.15
487	Curtis Goodwin RC	.50	.15
488	Mike Myers	.25	.07
489	Chipper Jones	1.00	.30
490	Jeff King	.25	.07
491	W.VanLandingham RC	.50	.15
492	Carlos Reyes RC	.50	.15
493	Andy Pettitte	1.00	.30
494	Brant Brown	.25	.07
495	Daron Kirkreit	.25	.07
496	Ricky Bottalico RC	1.00	.30
497	Devon White	.25	.07
498	Jason Johnson RC	.50	.15
499	Vince Coleman	.25	.07
500	Larry Walker	.60	.18
501	Bobby Ayala	.25	.07
502	Steve Finley	.40	.12
503	Scott Fletcher	.25	.07
504	Brad Ausmus	.25	.07
505	Scott Talanoa RC	.50	.15
506	Orestes Destrade	.25	.07
507	Gary DiSarcina	.25	.07
508	Willie Smith RC	.50	.15
509	Alan Trammell	.60	.18
510	Mike Piazza	2.00	.60
511	Ozzie Guillen	.25	.07
512	Jeromy Burnitz	.40	.12
513	Darren Oliver RC	1.00	.30
514	Kevin Mitchell	.25	.07
515	Rafael Palmeiro	.60	.18
516	David McCarty	.25	.07
517	Jeff Blauser	.25	.07
518	Trey Beamon	.25	.07
519	Royce Clayton	.25	.07
520	Dennis Eckersley	.40	.12
521	Bernie Williams	.60	.18
522	Steve Buechele	.25	.07
523	Dennis Martinez	.40	.12
524	Dave Hollins	.25	.07
525	Joey Hamilton	.25	.07
526	Andres Galarraga	.40	.12
527	Jeff Granger	.25	.07
528	Joey Eischen	.25	.07
529	Desi Relaford	.25	.07
530	Roberto Petagine	.25	.07
531	Andre Dawson	.40	.12
532	Ray Holbert	.25	.07
533	Duane Singleton	.25	.07
534	Kurt Abbott RC	1.00	.30
535	Bo Jackson	1.00	.30
536	Gregg Jefferies	.25	.07
537	David Mysel	.25	.07
538	Raul Mondesi	.40	.12
539	Chris Snopek	.25	.07
540	Brook Fordyce	.25	.07
541	Ron Frazier RC	.50	.15
542	Brian Koelling	.25	.07
543	Jimmy Haynes	.25	.07
544	Marty Cordova	.25	.07
545	Jason Green RC	.50	.15
546	Orlando Merced	.25	.07
547	Lou Pote RC	.50	.15
548	Todd Van Poppel	.25	.07
549	Pat Kelly	.25	.07
550	Turk Wendell	.25	.07
551	Herbert Perry RC	1.00	.30
552	Ryan Karp RC	.50	.15
553	Juan Guzman	.25	.07
554	Bryan Rekar RC	.50	.15
555	Kevin Appier	.40	.12
556	Chris Schwab RC	.50	.15
557	Jay Buhner	.40	.12
558	Andujar Cedeno	.25	.07
559	Ryan McGuire RC	.50	.15
560	Ricky Gutierrez	.25	.07
561	Keith Kimsey RC	.50	.15
562	Tim Clark	.25	.07
563	Damion Easley	.25	.07
564	Clint Davis RC	.50	.15
565	Mike Moore	.25	.07
566	Orel Hershiser	.40	.12
567	Jason Bere	.25	.07
568	Kevin McReynolds	.25	.07
569	Leland Macon RC	.50	.15
570	John Courtright RC	.50	.15
571	Sid Fernandez	.25	.07
572	Chad Roper	.25	.07
573	Terry Pendleton	.40	.12
574	Danny Miceli	.25	.07
575	Joe Rosselli	.25	.07
576	Mike Bordick	.25	.07
577	Danny Tartabull	.25	.07
578	Jose Guzman	.25	.07
579	Omar Vizquel	.40	.12
580	Tommy Greene	.25	.07
581	Paul Spoljaric	.25	.07
582	Walt Weiss	.25	.07
583	Oscar Jimenez RC	.50	.15
584	Rod Henderson	.25	.07
585	Derek Lowe	.40	.12
586	Richard Hidalgo RC	2.50	.75
587	Shayne Bennett RC	.50	.15
588	Tim Belk RC	.50	.15
589	Matt Mieske	.25	.07
590	Nigel Wilson	.25	.07
591	Jeff Knox RC	.50	.15
592	Bernard Gilkey	.25	.07
593	David Cone	.40	.12
594	Paul LoDuca RC	8.00	2.40
595	Scott Ruffcorn	.25	.07
596	Chris Roberts	.25	.07
597	Oscar Munoz RC	.50	.15
598	Scott Sullivan RC	.50	.15
599	Matt Jarvis RC	.50	.15
600	Jose Canseco	1.00	.30
601	Tony Graffanino RC	1.00	.30
602	Don Slaught	.25	.07
603	Brett King RC	.50	.15
604	Jose Herrera RC	.50	.15
605	Melido Perez	.25	.07
606	Mike Hubbard RC	.50	.15
607	Chad Ogea	.25	.07
608	Wayne Gomes RC	1.00	.30
609	Roberto Alomar	1.00	.30
610	Angel Echevarria RC	.50	.15
611	Jose Lind	.25	.07
612	Darrin Fletcher	.25	.07
613	Chris Bosio	.25	.07
614	Darryl Kile	.40	.12
615	Frankie Rodriguez	.25	.07
616	Phil Plantier	.25	.07
617	Pat Listach	.25	.07
618	Charlie Hough	.40	.12
619	Ryan Hancock RC	.50	.15
620	Darrel Deak RC	.50	.15
621	Travis Fryman	.40	.12
622	Brett Butler	.40	.12
623	Lance Johnson	.25	.07
624	Pete Smith	.25	.07
625	James Hurst RC	.50	.15
626	Roberto Kelly	.25	.07
627	Mike Mussina	1.00	.30
628	Kevin Tapani	.25	.07
629	John Smoltz	.60	.18
630	Midre Cummings	.25	.07
631	Salomon Torres	.25	.07
632	Willie Adams	.25	.07
633	Derek Jeter	3.00	.90
634	Steve Trachsel	.25	.07
635	Albie Lopez	.25	.07
636	Jason Moler	.25	.07
637	Carlos Delgado	.60	.18
638	Roberto Mejia	.25	.07
639	Darren Burton	.25	.07
640	B.J. Wallace	.25	.07
641	Brad Clontz RC	.50	.15
642	Billy Wagner RC	2.50	.75
643	Aaron Sele	.25	.07
644	Cameron Cairncross	.25	.07
645	Brian Harper	.25	.07
646	Marc Valdes UER (No card number on back)	.25	.07
647	Mark Ratekin	.25	.07
648	Terry Bradshaw RC	.50	.15
649	Justin Thompson	.25	.07
650	Mike Busch RC	.50	.15
651	Joe Hall RC	.50	.15
652	Bobby Jones	.25	.07
653	Kelly Stinnett RC	1.00	.30
654	Rod Steph RC	.50	.15
655	Jay Powell RC	1.00	.30
656	K.Garagozzo RC UER No card number on back	.50	.15
657	Todd Dunn	.25	.07
658	Charles Peterson RC	.50	.15
659	Darren Lewis	.25	.07
660	John Wasdin RC	.50	.15
661	Tate Seefried RC	.50	.15
662	Hector Trinidad RC	.50	.15
663	John Carter RC	.25	.07
664	Larry Mitchell	.25	.07
665	David Catlett RC	.50	.15
666	Dante Bichette	.40	.12
667	Felix Jose	.25	.07
668	Rondell White	.40	.12
669	Tino Martinez	.60	.18
670	Brian L. Hunter	.25	.07
671	Jose Malave	.25	.07
672	Archi Cianfrocco	.25	.07
673	Mike Matheny RC	1.00	.30
674	Bret Barberie	.25	.07
675	Andrew Lorraine RC	.50	.15
676	Brian Jordan	.40	.12
677	Tim Belcher	.25	.07
678	Antonio Osuna RC	.50	.15
679	Checklist	.25	.07
680	Checklist	.25	.07
681	Checklist	.25	.07
682	Checklist	.25	.07

1995 Bowman

	Nm-Mt	Ex-Mt
COMPLETE SET (439)	200.00	60.00

No.	Player	Nm-Mt	Ex-Mt
1	Billy Wagner	.50	.15
2	Chris Widger	.25	.07
3	Brent Bowers	.25	.07
4	Bob Abreu RC	6.00	1.80
5	Lou Collier RC	1.00	.30
6	Juan Acevedo RC	.50	.15
7	Jason Kelley RC	.50	.15
8	Brian Sackinsky	.25	.07
9	Scott Christman	.25	.07
10	Damon Hollins	.25	.07
11	Willis Otanez RC	.50	.15
12	Jason Ryan RC	.50	.15
13	Jason Giambi	1.25	.35
14	Andy Taulbee RC	.50	.15
15	Mark Thompson	.25	.07
16	Hugo Pivaral RC	.50	.15
17	Brien Taylor	.25	.07
18	Antonio Osuna	.25	.07
19	Edgardo Alfonzo	.50	.15

❑ 20 Carl Everett .50 .15
❑ 21 Matt Drews .25 .07
❑ 22 Bartolo Colon RC 6.00 1.80
❑ 23 Andruw Jones RC 25.00 7.50
❑ 24 Robert Person RC 1.00 .30
❑ 25 Derrek Lee .50 .15
❑ 26 John Ambrose RC .50 .15
❑ 27 Eric Knowles RC .50 .15
❑ 28 Chris Roberts .25 .07
❑ 29 Don Wengert .25 .07
❑ 30 Marcus Jensen RC 1.00 .30
❑ 31 Brian Barber .25 .07
❑ 32 Kevin Brown C .50 .15
❑ 33 Benji Gil .25 .07
❑ 34 Mike Hubbard .25 .07
❑ 35 Bart Evans RC .50 .15
❑ 36 Enrique Wilson RC .50 .15
❑ 37 Brian Buchanan RC 1.00 .30
❑ 38 Ken Ray RC .50 .15
❑ 39 Micah Franklin RC .50 .15
❑ 40 Ricky Otero RC .50 .15
❑ 41 Jason Kendall .50 .15
❑ 42 Jimmy Hurst .25 .07
❑ 43 Jerry Wolak RC .50 .15
❑ 44 Jayson Peterson RC .50 .15
❑ 45 Allen Battle RC .50 .15
❑ 46 Scott Stahoviak .25 .07
❑ 47 Steve Schrenk RC .50 .15
❑ 48 Travis Miller RC .50 .15
❑ 49 Eddie Rios RC .50 .15
❑ 50 Mike Hampton .50 .15
❑ 51 Chad Frontera RC .50 .15
❑ 52 Tom Evans .25 .07
❑ 53 C.J. Nitkowski .25 .07
❑ 54 Clay Caruthers RC .50 .15
❑ 55 Shannon Stewart .50 .15
❑ 56 Jorge Posada 1.25 .35
❑ 57 Aaron Holbert .25 .07
❑ 58 Harry Berrios RC .50 .15
❑ 59 Steve Rodriguez .25 .07
❑ 60 Shane Andrews .25 .07
❑ 61 Will Cunnane RC .50 .15
❑ 62 Richard Hidalgo .50 .15
❑ 63 Bill Selby RC .50 .15
❑ 64 Jay Cranford RC .50 .15
❑ 65 Jeff Suppan .25 .07
❑ 66 Curtis Goodwin .25 .07
❑ 67 John Thomson RC 1.00 .30
❑ 68 Justin Thompson .25 .07
❑ 69 Troy Percival .50 .15
❑ 70 Matt Wagner RC .50 .15
❑ 71 Terry Bradshaw .25 .07
❑ 72 Greg Hansell .25 .07
❑ 73 John Burke .25 .07
❑ 74 Jeff D'Amico .25 .07
❑ 75 Ernie Young .25 .07
❑ 76 Jason Bates .25 .07
❑ 77 Chris Stynes .25 .07
❑ 78 Cade Gaspar RC .50 .15
❑ 79 Melvin Nieves .25 .07
❑ 80 Rick Gorecki .25 .07
❑ 81 Felix Rodriguez RC 1.00 .30
❑ 82 Ryan Hancock .25 .07
❑ 83 Chris Carpenter RC 1.00 .30
❑ 84 Ray McDavid .25 .07
❑ 85 Chris Wimmer .25 .07
❑ 86 Doug Glanville .25 .07
❑ 87 DeShawn Warren .25 .07
❑ 88 Damian Moss RC 3.00 .90
❑ 89 Rafael Orellano RC .50 .15
❑ 90 Vladimir Guerrero RC 50.00 15.00
❑ 91 Raul Casanova RC .50 .15
❑ 92 Karim Garcia RC 3.00 .90
❑ 93 Bryce Florie .25 .07
❑ 94 Kevin Orie .25 .07
❑ 95 Ryan Nye RC .50 .15
❑ 96 Matt Sachse RC .50 .15
❑ 97 Ivan Arteaga RC .50 .15
❑ 98 Glenn Murray .25 .07
❑ 99 Stacy Hollins RC .50 .15
❑ 100 Jim Pittsley .25 .07
❑ 101 Craig Mattson RC .50 .15
❑ 102 Neifi Perez .25 .07
❑ 103 Keith Williams .25 .07
❑ 104 Roger Cedeno .25 .07
❑ 105 Tony Terry RC .50 .15
❑ 106 Jose Malave .25 .07
❑ 107 Joe Rosselli .25 .07
❑ 108 Kevin Jordan .25 .07
❑ 109 Sid Roberson RC .50 .15
❑ 110 Alan Embree .25 .07
❑ 111 Terrell Wade .25 .07
❑ 112 Bob Wolcott .25 .07
❑ 113 Carlos Perez RC 1.00 .30
❑ 114 Mike Bovee RC .50 .15
❑ 115 Tommy Davis RC .50 .15
❑ 116 Jeremey Kendall RC .50 .15
❑ 117 Rich Aude .25 .07
❑ 118 Rick Huisman .25 .07
❑ 119 Tim Belk .25 .07
❑ 120 Edgar Renteria .75 .23
❑ 121 Calvin Maduro RC .50 .15
❑ 122 Jerry Martin RC .50 .15
❑ 123 Ramon Fermin RC .50 .15
❑ 124 Kimera Bartee RC .50 .15
❑ 125 Mark Farris .25 .07
❑ 126 Frank Rodriguez .25 .07
❑ 127 Bobby Higginson RC 3.00 .90
❑ 128 Bret Wagner .25 .07
❑ 129 Edwin Diaz RC .50 .15
❑ 130 Jimmy Haynes .25 .07
❑ 131 Chris Weinke RC 5.00 1.50
❑ 132 Damian Jackson RC 1.00 .30
❑ 133 Felix Martinez .25 .07
❑ 134 Edwin Hurtado RC .50 .15
❑ 135 Matt Raleigh RC .50 .15
❑ 136 Paul Wilson .25 .07
❑ 137 Ron Villone .25 .07
❑ 138 E.Stuckenschneider RC .50 .15
❑ 139 Tate Seefried .25 .07
❑ 140 Rey Ordonez RC 2.00 .60
❑ 141 Eddie Pearson .25 .07
❑ 142 Kevin Gallaher .25 .07
❑ 143 Torii Hunter .75 .23
❑ 144 Daron Kirkreit .25 .07
❑ 145 Craig Wilson .25 .07
❑ 146 Ugueth Urbina .25 .07
❑ 147 Chris Snopek .25 .07
❑ 148 Kym Ashworth .25 .07
❑ 149 Wayne Gomes .25 .07
❑ 150 Mark Loretta .25 .07
❑ 151 Ramon Morel RC .50 .15
❑ 152 Trot Nixon .50 .15
❑ 153 Desi Relaford .25 .07
❑ 154 Scott Sullivan .25 .07
❑ 155 Marc Barcelo .25 .07
❑ 156 Willie Adams .25 .07
❑ 157 Derrick Gibson RC .50 .15
❑ 158 Brian Meadows RC .50 .15
❑ 159 Julian Tavarez .25 .07
❑ 160 Bryan Rekar .25 .07
❑ 161 Steve Gibralter .25 .07
❑ 162 Esteban Loaiza .75 .23
❑ 163 John Wasdin .25 .07
❑ 164 Kirk Presley .25 .07
❑ 165 Mariano Rivera .75 .23
❑ 166 Andy Larkin .25 .07
❑ 167 Sean Whiteside RC .50 .15
❑ 168 Matt Apana RC .50 .15
❑ 169 Shawn Senior RC .50 .15
❑ 170 Scott Gentile .25 .07
❑ 171 Quilvio Veras .25 .07
❑ 172 Eli Marrero RC 1.50 .45
❑ 173 Mendy Lopez RC .50 .15
❑ 174 Homer Bush .25 .07
❑ 175 Brian Stephenson RC .50 .15
❑ 176 Jon Nunnally .25 .07
❑ 177 Jose Herrera .25 .07
❑ 178 Corey Avrard RC .50 .15
❑ 179 David Bell .25 .07
❑ 180 Jason Isringhausen .50 .15
❑ 181 Jamey Wright .25 .07
❑ 182 Lonell Roberts RC .25 .07
❑ 183 Marty Cordova .25 .07
❑ 184 Amaury Telemaco .25 .07
❑ 185 John Mabry .25 .07
❑ 186 Andrew Vessel RC .50 .15
❑ 187 Jim Cole RC .50 .15
❑ 188 Marquis Riley .25 .07
❑ 189 Todd Dunn .25 .07
❑ 190 John Carter .25 .07
❑ 191 Donnie Sadler RC 1.00 .30
❑ 192 Mike Bell .25 .07
❑ 193 Chris Cumberland RC .50 .15
❑ 194 Jason Schmidt 1.50 .45
❑ 195 Matt Brunson .25 .07
❑ 196 James Baldwin .25 .07
❑ 197 Bill Simas RC .50 .15
❑ 198 Gus Gandarillas .25 .07
❑ 199 Mac Suzuki .25 .07
❑ 200 Rick Holifield RC .50 .15
❑ 201 Fernando Lunar RC .50 .15
❑ 202 Kevin Jarvis .25 .07
❑ 203 Everett Stull .25 .07
❑ 204 Steve Wojciechowski .25 .07
❑ 205 Shawn Estes .25 .07
❑ 206 Jermaine Dye .50 .15
❑ 207 Marc Kroon .25 .07
❑ 208 Peter Munro RC 1.00 .30
❑ 209 Pat Watkins .25 .07
❑ 210 Matt Smith .25 .07
❑ 211 Joe Vitiello .25 .07
❑ 212 Gerald Witasick Jr. .25 .07
❑ 213 Freddy A. Garcia RC .50 .15
❑ 214 Glenn Dishman RC .50 .15
❑ 215 Jay Canizaro RC .50 .15
❑ 216 Angel Martinez .25 .07
❑ 217 Yamil Benitez RC .50 .15
❑ 218 Fausto Macey RC .50 .15
❑ 219 Eric Owens .25 .07
❑ 220 Checklist .25 .07
❑ 221 D.Hosey FOIL RC .50 .15
❑ 222 B.Woodall FOIL RC .50 .15
❑ 223 Billy Ashley FOIL .25 .07
❑ 224 M.Grudzielanek FOIL RC 2.00 .60
❑ 225 M.Johnson FOIL RC 1.00 .30
❑ 226 Tim Unroe FOIL RC .50 .15
❑ 227 Todd Greene FOIL .25 .07
❑ 228 Larry Sutton FOIL .25 .07
❑ 229 Derek Jeter FOIL 4.00 1.20
❑ 230 Sal Fasano FOIL RC .50 .15
❑ 231 Ruben Rivera FOIL .25 .07
❑ 232 Chris Truby FOIL RC 1.00 .30
❑ 233 John Donati FOIL .25 .07
❑ 234 D.Conner FOIL RC .50 .15
❑ 235 Sergio Nunez FOIL RC .50 .15
❑ 236 Ray Brown FOIL RC .50 .15
❑ 237 Juan Melo FOIL RC .50 .15
❑ 238 Hideo Nomo FOIL RC 5.00 1.50
❑ 239 Jamie Bluma RC FOIL .50 .15
❑ 240 Jay Payton FOIL RC 2.00 .60
❑ 241 Paul Konerko FOIL 1.00 .30
❑ 242 Scott Elarton FOIL RC 1.00 .30
❑ 243 Jeff Abbott FOIL RC 1.00 .30
❑ 244 Jim Brower FOIL RC .50 .15
❑ 245 Geoff Blum FOIL RC 1.00 .30
❑ 246 Aaron Boone FOIL RC 10.00 3.00
❑ 247 J.R. Phillips FOIL .25 .07
❑ 248 Alex Ochoa FOIL .25 .07
❑ 249 N.Garciaparra FOIL 10.00 3.00
❑ 250 Garret Anderson FOIL .50 .15
❑ 251 Ray Durham FOIL .50 .15
❑ 252 Paul Shuey FOIL .25 .07
❑ 253 Tony Clark FOIL .25 .07
❑ 254 Johnny Damon FOIL .75 .23
❑ 255 Duane Singleton FOIL .25 .07
❑ 256 LaTroy Hawkins FOIL .25 .07
❑ 257 Andy Pettitte FOIL .75 .23
❑ 258 Ben Grieve FOIL .50 .15
❑ 259 Marc Newfield FOIL .25 .07
❑ 260 Terrell Lowery FOIL .25 .07
❑ 261 Shawn Green FOIL .50 .15
❑ 262 Chipper Jones FOIL 1.25 .35
❑ 263 B.Kieschnick FOIL .25 .07
❑ 264 Pokey Reese FOIL .25 .07
❑ 265 Doug Million FOIL .25 .07
❑ 266 Marc Valdes FOIL .25 .07
❑ 267 Brian L.Hunter FOIL .25 .07
❑ 268 T.Hollandsworth FOIL .25 .07
❑ 269 Rod Henderson FOIL .25 .07
❑ 270 Bill Pulsipher FOIL .25 .07
❑ 271 Scott Rolen FOIL RC 15.00 4.50
❑ 272 Trey Beamon FOIL .25 .07
❑ 273 Alan Benes FOIL .25 .07
❑ 274 D.Hermanson FOIL .25 .07
❑ 275 Ricky Bottalico .25 .07
❑ 276 Albert Belle .50 .15
❑ 277 Deion Sanders .50 .15

	No.	Player	Nm-Mt	Ex-Mt
❑	278	Matt Williams	.50	.15
❑	279	Jeff Bagwell	.75	.23
❑	280	Kirby Puckett	1.25	.35
❑	281	Dave Hollins	.25	.07
❑	282	Don Mattingly	3.00	.90
❑	283	Joey Hamilton	.25	.07
❑	284	Bobby Bonilla	.50	.15
❑	285	Moises Alou	.50	.15
❑	286	Tom Glavine	1.25	.35
❑	287	Brett Butler	.50	.15
❑	288	Chris Hoiles	.25	.07
❑	289	Kenny Rogers	.50	.15
❑	290	Larry Walker	.75	.23
❑	291	Tim Raines	.50	.15
❑	292	Kevin Appier	.50	.15
❑	293	Roger Clemens	2.50	.75
❑	294	Chuck Carr	.25	.07
❑	295	Randy Myers	.25	.07
❑	296	Dave Nilsson	.25	.07
❑	297	Joe Carter	.50	.15
❑	298	Chuck Finley	.50	.15
❑	299	Ray Lankford	.25	.07
❑	300	Roberto Kelly	.25	.07
❑	301	Jon Lieber	.25	.07
❑	302	Travis Fryman	.50	.15
❑	303	Mark McGwire	3.00	.90
❑	304	Tony Gwynn	1.50	.45
❑	305	Kenny Lofton	.50	.15
❑	306	Mark Whiten	.25	.07
❑	307	Doug Drabek	.25	.07
❑	308	Terry Steinbach	.25	.07
❑	309	Ryan Klesko	.50	.15
❑	310	Mike Piazza	2.00	.60
❑	311	Ben McDonald	.25	.07
❑	312	Reggie Sanders	.50	.15
❑	313	Alex Fernandez	.25	.07
❑	314	Aaron Sele	.25	.07
❑	315	Gregg Jefferies	.25	.07
❑	316	Rickey Henderson	2.00	.60
❑	317	Brian Anderson	.25	.07
❑	318	Jose Valentin	.25	.07
❑	319	Rod Beck	.25	.07
❑	320	Marquis Grissom	.25	.07
❑	321	Ken Griffey Jr.	2.00	.60
❑	322	Bret Saberhagen	.50	.15
❑	323	Juan Gonzalez	1.25	.35
❑	324	Paul Molitor	.75	.23
❑	325	Gary Sheffield	.50	.15
❑	326	Darren Daulton	.50	.15
❑	327	Bill Swift	.25	.07
❑	328	Brian McRae	.25	.07
❑	329	Robin Ventura	.50	.15
❑	330	Lee Smith	.50	.15
❑	331	Fred McGriff	.75	.23
❑	332	Delino DeShields	.25	.07
❑	333	Edgar Martinez	.75	.23
❑	334	Mike Mussina	1.25	.35
❑	335	Orlando Merced	.25	.07
❑	336	Carlos Baerga	.25	.07
❑	337	Wil Cordero	.25	.07
❑	338	Tom Pagnozzi	.25	.07
❑	339	Pat Hentgen	.25	.07
❑	340	Chad Curtis	.25	.07
❑	341	Darren Lewis	.25	.07
❑	342	Jeff Kent	.50	.15
❑	343	Bip Roberts	.25	.07
❑	344	Ivan Rodriguez	1.25	.35
❑	345	Jeff Montgomery	.25	.07
❑	346	Hal Morris	.25	.07
❑	347	Danny Tartabull	.25	.07
❑	348	Raul Mondesi	.50	.15
❑	349	Ken Hill	.25	.07
❑	350	Pedro Martinez	1.25	.35
❑	351	Frank Thomas	1.25	.35
❑	352	Manny Ramirez	.50	.15
❑	353	Tim Salmon	.75	.23
❑	354	W. VanLandingham	.25	.07
❑	355	Andres Galarraga	.50	.15
❑	356	Paul O'Neill	.75	.23
❑	357	Brady Anderson	.50	.15
❑	358	Ramon Martinez	.25	.07
❑	359	John Olerud	.50	.15
❑	360	Ruben Sierra	.25	.07
❑	361	Cal Eldred	.25	.07
❑	362	Jay Buhner	.50	.15
❑	363	Jay Bell	.50	.15
❑	364	Wally Joyner	.50	.15
❑	365	Chuck Knoblauch	.50	.15
❑	366	Len Dykstra	.50	.15
❑	367	John Wetteland	.50	.15
❑	368	Roberto Alomar	1.25	.35
❑	369	Craig Biggio	.75	.23
❑	370	Ozzie Smith	1.25	.35
❑	371	Terry Pendleton	.50	.15
❑	372	Sammy Sosa	2.00	.60
❑	373	Carlos Garcia	.25	.07
❑	374	Jose Rijo	.25	.07
❑	375	Chris Gomez	.25	.07
❑	376	Barry Bonds	3.00	.90
❑	377	Steve Avery	.25	.07
❑	378	Rick Wilkins	.25	.07
❑	379	Pete Harnisch	.25	.07
❑	380	Dean Palmer	.50	.15
❑	381	Bob Hamelin	.25	.07
❑	382	Jason Bere	.25	.07
❑	383	Jimmy Key	.50	.15
❑	384	Dante Bichette	.50	.15
❑	385	Rafael Palmeiro	.75	.23
❑	386	David Justice	.50	.15
❑	387	Chili Davis	.50	.15
❑	388	Mike Greenwell	.25	.07
❑	389	Todd Zeile	.25	.07
❑	390	Jeff Conine	.50	.15
❑	391	Rick Aguilera	.25	.07
❑	392	Eddie Murray	1.25	.35
❑	393	Mike Stanley	.25	.07
❑	394	Cliff Floyd UER (numbered 294)	.50	.15
❑	395	Randy Johnson	1.25	.35
❑	396	David Nied	.25	.07
❑	397	Devon White	.50	.15
❑	398	Royce Clayton	.25	.07
❑	399	Andy Benes	.25	.07
❑	400	John Hudek	.25	.07
❑	401	Bobby Jones	.25	.07
❑	402	Eric Karros	.50	.15
❑	403	Will Clark	1.25	.35
❑	404	Mark Langston	.25	.07
❑	405	Kevin Brown	.50	.15
❑	406	Greg Maddux	2.50	.75
❑	407	David Cone	.50	.15
❑	408	Wade Boggs	.75	.23
❑	409	Steve Trachsel	.25	.07
❑	410	Greg Vaughn	.50	.15
❑	411	Mo Vaughn	.50	.15
❑	412	Wilson Alvarez	.25	.07
❑	413	Cal Ripken	4.00	1.20
❑	414	Rico Brogna	.25	.07
❑	415	Barry Larkin	1.25	.35
❑	416	Cecil Fielder	.50	.15
❑	417	Jose Canseco	1.25	.35
❑	418	Jack McDowell	.25	.07
❑	419	Mike Lieberthal	.50	.15
❑	420	Andrew Lorraine	.25	.07
❑	421	Rich Becker	.25	.07
❑	422	Tony Phillips	.25	.07
❑	423	Scott Ruffcorn	.25	.07
❑	424	Jeff Granger	.25	.07
❑	425	Greg Pirkl	.25	.07
❑	426	Dennis Eckersley	.50	.15
❑	427	Jose Lima	.25	.07
❑	428	Russ Davis	.25	.07
❑	429	Armando Benitez	.50	.15
❑	430	Alex Gonzalez	.25	.07
❑	431	Carlos Delgado	.50	.15
❑	432	Chan Ho Park	.50	.15
❑	433	Mickey Tettleton	.25	.07
❑	434	Dave Winfield	.75	.23
❑	435	John Burkett	.25	.07
❑	436	Orlando Miller	.25	.07
❑	437	Rondell White	.50	.15
❑	438	Jose Oliva	.25	.07
❑	439	Checklist	.25	.07

1996 Bowman

	No.	Player	Nm-Mt	Ex-Mt
		COMPLETE SET (385)	60.00	18.00
❑	1	Cal Ripken	2.50	.75
❑	2	Ray Durham	.30	.09
❑	3	Ivan Rodriguez	.75	.23

	No.	Player	Nm-Mt	Ex-Mt
❑	4	Fred McGriff	.50	.15
❑	5	Hideo Nomo	.75	.23
❑	6	Troy Percival	.30	.09
❑	7	Moises Alou	.30	.09
❑	8	Mike Stanley	.30	.09
❑	9	Jay Buhner	.30	.09
❑	10	Shawn Green	.30	.09
❑	11	Ryan Klesko	.30	.09
❑	12	Andres Galarraga	.30	.09
❑	13	Dean Palmer	.30	.09
❑	14	Jeff Conine	.30	.09
❑	15	Brian L.Hunter	.30	.09
❑	16	J.T. Snow	.30	.09
❑	17	Larry Walker	.50	.15
❑	18	Barry Larkin	.75	.23
❑	19	Alex Gonzalez	.30	.09
❑	20	Edgar Martinez	.50	.15
❑	21	Mo Vaughn	.30	.09
❑	22	Mark McGwire	2.00	.60
❑	23	Jose Canseco	.75	.23
❑	24	Jack McDowell	.30	.09
❑	25	Dante Bichette	.30	.09
❑	26	Wade Boggs	.50	.15
❑	27	Mike Piazza	1.25	.35
❑	28	Ray Lankford	.30	.09
❑	29	Craig Biggio	.50	.15
❑	30	Rafael Palmeiro	.50	.15
❑	31	Ron Gant	.30	.09
❑	32	Javy Lopez	.30	.09
❑	33	Brian Jordan	.30	.09
❑	34	Paul O'Neill	.50	.15
❑	35	Mark Grace	.75	.23
❑	36	Matt Williams	.30	.09
❑	37	Pedro Martinez	.75	.23
❑	38	Rickey Henderson	1.25	.35
❑	39	Bobby Bonilla	.30	.09
❑	40	Todd Hollandsworth	.30	.09
❑	41	Jim Thome	.75	.23
❑	42	Gary Sheffield	.75	.23
❑	43	Tim Salmon	.50	.15
❑	44	Gregg Jefferies	.30	.09
❑	45	Roberto Alomar	.75	.23
❑	46	Carlos Baerga	.30	.09
❑	47	Mark Grudzielanek	.30	.09
❑	48	Randy Johnson	.75	.23
❑	49	Tino Martinez	.50	.15
❑	50	Robin Ventura	.30	.09
❑	51	Ryne Sandberg	1.25	.35
❑	52	Jay Bell	.30	.09
❑	53	Jason Schmidt	.30	.09
❑	54	Frank Thomas	.75	.23
❑	55	Kenny Lofton	.30	.09
❑	56	Ariel Prieto	.30	.09
❑	57	David Cone	.30	.09
❑	58	Reggie Sanders	.30	.09
❑	59	Michael Tucker	.30	.09
❑	60	Vinny Castilla	.30	.09
❑	61	Len Dykstra	.30	.09
❑	62	Todd Hundley	.30	.09
❑	63	Brian McRae	.30	.09
❑	64	Dennis Eckersley	.30	.09
❑	65	Rondell White	.30	.09
❑	66	Eric Karros	.30	.09
❑	67	Greg Maddux	1.50	.45
❑	68	Kevin Appier	.30	.09
❑	69	Eddie Murray	.75	.23
❑	70	John Olerud	.30	.09
❑	71	Tony Gwynn	1.00	.30

❑ 72 David Justice .30 .09
❑ 73 Ken Caminiti .30 .09
❑ 74 Terry Steinbach .30 .09
❑ 75 Alan Benes .30 .09
❑ 76 Chipper Jones .75 .23
❑ 77 Jeff Bagwell .50 .15
❑ 78 Barry Bonds 2.00 .60
❑ 79 Ken Griffey Jr. 1.50 .45
❑ 80 Roger Cedeno .30 .09
❑ 81 Joe Carter .30 .09
❑ 82 Henry Rodriguez .30 .09
❑ 83 Jason Isringhausen .30 .09
❑ 84 Chuck Knoblauch .30 .09
❑ 85 Manny Ramirez .30 .09
❑ 86 Tom Glavine .75 .23
❑ 87 Jeffrey Hammonds .30 .09
❑ 88 Paul Molitor .50 .15
❑ 89 Roger Clemens 1.50 .45
❑ 90 Greg Vaughn .30 .09
❑ 91 Marty Cordova .30 .09
❑ 92 Albert Belle .30 .09
❑ 93 Mike Mussina .75 .23
❑ 94 Garret Anderson .30 .09
❑ 95 Juan Gonzalez .75 .23
❑ 96 John Valentin .30 .09
❑ 97 Jason Giambi .75 .23
❑ 98 Kirby Puckett .75 .23
❑ 99 Jim Edmonds .30 .09
❑ 100 Cecil Fielder .30 .09
❑ 101 Mike Aldrete .30 .09
❑ 102 Marquis Grissom .30 .09
❑ 103 Derek Bell .30 .09
❑ 104 Raul Mondesi .30 .09
❑ 105 Sammy Sosa 1.25 .35
❑ 106 Travis Fryman .30 .09
❑ 107 Rico Brogna .30 .09
❑ 108 Will Clark .75 .23
❑ 109 Bernie Williams .50 .15
❑ 110 Brady Anderson .30 .09
❑ 111 Torii Hunter .30 .09
❑ 112 Derek Jeter 2.00 .60
❑ 113 Mike Kusiewicz RC .50 .15
❑ 114 Scott Rolen .75 .23
❑ 115 Ramon Castro .30 .09
❑ 116 Jose Guillen RC 3.00 .90
❑ 117 Wade Walker RC .50 .15
❑ 118 Shawn Senior .30 .09
❑ 119 Onan Masaoka RC .75 .23
❑ 120 Marlon Anderson RC 1.50 .45
❑ 121 Katsuhiro Maeda RC .75 .23
❑ 122 G.Stephenson RC .75 .23
❑ 123 Butch Huskey .30 .09
❑ 124 D'Angelo Jimenez RC 1.50 .45
❑ 125 Tony Mounce RC .50 .15
❑ 126 Jay Canizaro .30 .09
❑ 127 Juan Melo .30 .09
❑ 128 Steve Gibralter .30 .09
❑ 129 Freddy Garcia .30 .09
❑ 130 Julio Santana UER .30 .09
Card has him born in 1993
❑ 131 Richard Hidalgo .30 .09
❑ 132 Jermaine Dye .30 .09
❑ 133 Willie Adams .30 .09
❑ 134 Everett Stull .30 .09
❑ 135 Ramon Morel .30 .09
❑ 136 Chan Ho Park .30 .09
❑ 137 Jamey Wright .30 .09
❑ 138 Luis R.Garcia RC .50 .15
❑ 139 Dan Serafini .30 .09
❑ 140 Ryan Dempster RC 1.00 .30
❑ 141 Tate Seefried .30 .09
❑ 142 Jimmy Hurst .30 .09
❑ 143 Travis Miller .30 .09
❑ 144 Curtis Goodwin .30 .09
❑ 145 Rocky Coppinger RC .50 .15
❑ 146 Enrique Wilson .30 .09
❑ 147 Jaime Bluma .30 .09
❑ 148 Andrew Vessel .30 .09
❑ 149 Damian Moss .30 .09
❑ 150 Shawn Gallagher RC .50 .15
❑ 151 Pat Watkins .30 .09
❑ 152 Jose Paniagua .30 .09
❑ 153 Danny Graves .30 .09
❑ 154 Bryon Gainey RC .50 .15
❑ 155 Steve Soderstrom .30 .09
❑ 156 Cliff Brumbaugh RC .50 .15
❑ 157 Eugene Kingsale RC .75 .23
❑ 158 Lou Collier .30 .09
❑ 159 Todd Walker .50 .15
❑ 160 Kris Detmers RC .50 .15
❑ 161 Josh Booty RC .75 .23
❑ 162 Greg Whiteman RC .50 .15
❑ 163 Damian Jackson .30 .09
❑ 164 Tony Clark .30 .09
❑ 165 Jeff D'Amico .30 .09
❑ 166 Johnny Damon .30 .09
❑ 167 Rafael Orellano .30 .09
❑ 168 Ruben Rivera .30 .09
❑ 169 Alex Ochoa .30 .09
❑ 170 Jay Powell .30 .09
❑ 171 Tom Evans .30 .09
❑ 172 Ron Villone .30 .09
❑ 173 Shawn Estes .30 .09
❑ 174 John Wasdin .30 .09
❑ 175 Bill Simas .30 .09
❑ 176 Kevin Brown .30 .09
❑ 177 Shannon Stewart .30 .09
❑ 178 Todd Greene .30 .09
❑ 179 Bob Wolcott .30 .09
❑ 180 Chris Snopek .30 .09
❑ 181 Nomar Garciaparra 2.00 .60
❑ 182 Cameron Smith RC .50 .15
❑ 183 Matt Drews .30 .09
❑ 184 Jimmy Haynes .30 .09
❑ 185 Chris Carpenter .30 .09
❑ 186 Desi Relaford .30 .09
❑ 187 Ben Grieve .30 .09
❑ 188 Mike Bell .30 .09
❑ 189 Luis Castillo RC 3.00 .90
❑ 190 Ugueth Urbina .30 .09
❑ 191 Paul Wilson .30 .09
❑ 192 Andruw Jones 1.25 .35
❑ 193 Wayne Gomes .30 .09
❑ 194 Craig Counsell RC 2.00 .60
❑ 195 Jim Cole .30 .09
❑ 196 Brooks Kieschnick .30 .09
❑ 197 Trey Beamon .30 .09
❑ 198 Marino Santana RC .50 .15
❑ 199 Bob Abreu .30 .09
❑ 200 Pokey Reese .30 .09
❑ 201 Dante Powell .30 .09
❑ 202 George Arias .30 .09
❑ 203 Jorge Velandia RC .50 .15
❑ 204 George Lombard RC .75 .23
❑ 205 Byron Browne RC .50 .15
❑ 206 John Frascatore .30 .09
❑ 207 Terry Adams .30 .09
❑ 208 Wilson Delgado RC .50 .15
❑ 209 Billy McMillon .30 .09
❑ 210 Jeff Abbott .30 .09
❑ 211 Trot Nixon .30 .09
❑ 212 Amaury Telemaco .30 .09
❑ 213 Scott Sullivan .30 .09
❑ 214 Justin Thompson .30 .09
❑ 215 Decomba Conner .30 .09
❑ 216 Ryan McGuire .30 .09
❑ 217 Matt Luke .30 .09
❑ 218 Doug Million .30 .09
❑ 219 Jason Dickson RC .50 .15
❑ 220 Ramon Hernandez RC 1.50 .45
❑ 221 Mark Bellhorn RC 2.00 .60
❑ 222 Eric Ludwick RC .50 .15
❑ 223 Luke Wilcox RC .50 .15
❑ 224 Marty Malloy RC .50 .15
❑ 225 Gary Coffee RC .50 .15
❑ 226 Wendell Magee RC .50 .15
❑ 227 Brett Tomko RC .75 .23
❑ 228 Derek Lowe .30 .09
❑ 229 Jose Rosado RC .50 .15
❑ 230 Steve Bourgeois RC .50 .15
❑ 231 Neil Weber RC .50 .15
❑ 232 Jeff Ware .30 .09
❑ 233 Edwin Diaz .30 .09
❑ 234 Greg Norton .30 .09
❑ 235 Aaron Boone .30 .09
❑ 236 Jeff Suppan .30 .09
❑ 237 Bret Wagner .30 .09
❑ 238 Elieser Marrero .30 .09
❑ 239 Will Cunnane .30 .09
❑ 240 Brian Barkley RC .50 .15
❑ 241 Jay Payton .30 .09
❑ 242 Marcus Jensen .30 .09
❑ 243 Ryan Nye .30 .09
❑ 244 Chad Mottola .30 .09
❑ 245 Scott McClain RC .50 .15
❑ 246 Jessie Ibarra RC .50 .15
❑ 247 Mike Darr RC .75 .23
❑ 248 Bobby Estalella RC .75 .23
❑ 249 Michael Barrett .30 .09
❑ 250 Jamie Lopiccolo RC .50 .15
❑ 251 Shane Spencer RC 2.00 .60
❑ 252 Ben Petrick RC .75 .23
❑ 253 Jason Bell RC .50 .15
❑ 254 Arnold Gooch RC .50 .15
❑ 255 T.J. Mathews .30 .09
❑ 256 Jason Ryan .30 .09
❑ 257 Pat Cline RC .50 .15
❑ 258 Rafael Carmona RC .50 .15
❑ 259 Carl Pavano RC 1.00 .30
❑ 260 Ben Davis .30 .09
❑ 261 Matt Lawton RC .75 .23
❑ 262 Kevin Sefcik RC .50 .15
❑ 263 Chris Fussell RC .50 .15
❑ 264 Mike Cameron RC 3.00 .90
❑ 265 Marty Janzen RC .50 .15
❑ 266 Livan Hernandez RC 1.00 .30
❑ 267 Raul Ibanez RC 2.00 .60
❑ 268 Juan Encarnacion .30 .09
❑ 269 David Yocum RC .50 .15
❑ 270 Jonathan Johnson RC .50 .15
❑ 271 Reggie Taylor .30 .09
❑ 272 Danny Buxbaum RC .50 .15
❑ 273 Jacob Cruz .30 .09
❑ 274 Bobby Morris RC .50 .15
❑ 275 Andy Fox RC .50 .15
❑ 276 Greg Keagle .30 .09
❑ 277 Charles Peterson .30 .09
❑ 278 Derrek Lee .30 .09
❑ 279 Bryant Nelson RC .50 .15
❑ 280 Antone Williamson .30 .09
❑ 281 Scott Elarton .30 .09
❑ 282 Shad Williams RC .50 .15
❑ 283 Rich Hunter RC .50 .15
❑ 284 Chris Sheff .30 .09
❑ 285 Derrick Gibson .30 .09
❑ 286 Felix Rodriguez .30 .09
❑ 287 Brian Banks RC .50 .15
❑ 288 Jason McDonald .30 .09
❑ 289 Glendon Rusch RC .75 .23
❑ 290 Gary Rath .30 .09
❑ 291 Peter Munro .30 .09
❑ 292 Tom Fordham .30 .09
❑ 293 Jason Kendall .30 .09
❑ 294 Russ Johnson .30 .09
❑ 295 Joe Long .30 .09
❑ 296 Robert Smith RC .75 .23
❑ 297 Jarrod Washburn RC 2.00 .60
❑ 298 Dave Coggin RC .50 .15
❑ 299 Jeff Yoder RC .50 .15
❑ 300 Jed Hansen RC .50 .15
❑ 301 Matt Morris RC 4.00 1.20
❑ 302 Josh Bishop RC .50 .15
❑ 303 Dustin Hermanson .30 .09
❑ 304 Mike Gulan .30 .09
❑ 305 Felipe Crespo .30 .09
❑ 306 Quinton McCracken .30 .09
❑ 307 Jim Bonnici RC .50 .15
❑ 308 Sal Fasano .30 .09
❑ 309 Gabe Alvarez RC .50 .15
❑ 310 Heath Murray RC .50 .15
❑ 311 Javier Valentin RC .50 .15
❑ 312 Bartolo Colon .30 .09
❑ 313 Olmedo Saenz .30 .09
❑ 314 Norm Hutchins RC .50 .15
❑ 315 Chris Holt .30 .09
❑ 316 David Doster RC .50 .15
❑ 317 Robert Person .30 .09
❑ 318 Donne Wall RC .50 .15
❑ 319 Adam Riggs RC .50 .15
❑ 320 Homer Bush .30 .09
❑ 321 Brad Rigby RC .50 .15
❑ 322 Lou Merloni RC .75 .23
❑ 323 Neifi Perez .30 .09
❑ 324 Chris Cumberland .30 .09
❑ 325 Alvie Shepherd RC .50 .15
❑ 326 Jarrod Patterson RC .50 .15
❑ 327 Ray Ricken RC .50 .15
❑ 328 Danny Klassen RC .50 .15

❑ 329 David Miller RC .50 .15
❑ 330 Chad Alexander RC .50 .15
❑ 331 Matt Beaumont .30 .09
❑ 332 Damon Hollins .30 .09
❑ 333 Todd Dunn .30 .09
❑ 334 Mike Sweeney RC 5.00 1.50
❑ 335 Richie Sexson .50 .15
❑ 336 Billy Wagner .30 .09
❑ 337 Ron Wright RC .50 .15
❑ 338 Paul Konerko .30 .09
❑ 339 Tommy Phelps RC .50 .15
❑ 340 Karim Garcia .30 .09
❑ 341 Mike Grace RC .50 .15
❑ 342 Russell Branyan RC .75 .23
❑ 343 Randy Winn RC 1.50 .45
❑ 344 A.J. Pierzynski RC 4.00 1.20
❑ 345 Mike Busby RC .50 .15
❑ 346 Matt Beech RC .50 .15
❑ 347 Jose Cepeda RC .50 .15
❑ 348 Brian Stephenson .30 .09
❑ 349 Rey Ordonez .30 .09
❑ 350 Rich Aurilia RC 2.50 .75
❑ 351 Edgard Velazquez RC .50 .15
❑ 352 Raul Casanova .30 .09
❑ 353 Carlos Guillen RC 1.50 .45
❑ 354 Bruce Aven RC .50 .15
❑ 355 Ryan Jones RC .50 .15
❑ 356 Derek Aucoin RC .50 .15
❑ 357 Brian Rose RC .50 .15
❑ 358 Richard Almanzar RC .50 .15
❑ 359 Fletcher Bates RC .50 .15
❑ 360 Russ Ortiz RC 3.00 .90
❑ 361 Wilton Guerrero RC .75 .23
❑ 362 Geoff Jenkins RC 2.50 .75
❑ 363 Pete Janicki .30 .09
❑ 364 Yamil Benitez .30 .09
❑ 365 Aaron Holbert .30 .09
❑ 366 Tim Belk .30 .09
❑ 367 Terrell Wade .30 .09
❑ 368 Terrence Long .30 .09
❑ 369 Brad Fullmer .30 .09
❑ 370 Matt Wagner .30 .09
❑ 371 Craig Wilson RC .50 .15
❑ 372 Mark Loretta .30 .09
❑ 373 Eric Owens .30 .09
❑ 374 Vladimir Guerrero 1.50 .45
❑ 375 Tommy Davis .30 .09
❑ 376 Donnie Sadler .30 .09
❑ 377 Edgar Renteria .30 .09
❑ 378 Todd Helton 1.50 .45
❑ 379 Ralph Milliard RC .50 .15
❑ 380 Darin Blood RC .50 .15
❑ 381 Shayne Bennett .30 .09
❑ 382 Mark Redman .30 .09
❑ 383 Felix Martinez .30 .09
❑ 384 Sean Watkins RC .50 .15
❑ 385 Oscar Henriquez .30 .09
❑ M20 Mickey Mantle 5.00 1.50
1952 Bowman Reprint
❑ NNO Checklists .30 .09

1997 Bowman

	Nm-Mt	Ex-Mt
COMPLETE SET (441)	60.00	18.00
COMP. SERIES 1 (221)	30.00	9.00
COMP. SERIES 2 (220)	30.00	9.00

❑ 1 Derek Jeter 2.00 .60
❑ 2 Edgar Renteria .30 .09
❑ 3 Chipper Jones .75 .23
❑ 4 Hideo Nomo .75 .23
❑ 5 Tim Salmon .50 .15
❑ 6 Jason Giambi .75 .23
❑ 7 Robin Ventura .30 .09
❑ 8 Tony Clark .30 .09
❑ 9 Barry Larkin .75 .23
❑ 10 Paul Molitor .50 .15
❑ 11 Bernard Gilkey .30 .09
❑ 12 Jack McDowell .30 .09
❑ 13 Andy Benes .30 .09
❑ 14 Ryan Klesko .30 .09
❑ 15 Mark McGwire 2.00 .60
❑ 16 Ken Griffey Jr. 1.25 .35
❑ 17 Robb Nen .30 .09
❑ 18 Cal Ripken 2.50 .75
❑ 19 John Valentin .30 .09
❑ 20 Ricky Bottalico .30 .09
❑ 21 Mike Lansing .30 .09
❑ 22 Ryne Sandberg 1.25 .35
❑ 23 Carlos Delgado .30 .09
❑ 24 Craig Biggio .50 .15
❑ 25 Eric Karros .30 .09
❑ 26 Kevin Appier .30 .09
❑ 27 Mariano Rivera .50 .15
❑ 28 Vinny Castilla .30 .09
❑ 29 Juan Gonzalez .75 .23
❑ 30 Al Martin .30 .09
❑ 31 Jeff Cirillo .30 .09
❑ 32 Eddie Murray .75 .23
❑ 33 Ray Lankford .30 .09
❑ 34 Manny Ramirez .30 .09
❑ 35 Roberto Alomar .75 .23
❑ 36 Will Clark .75 .23
❑ 37 Chuck Knoblauch .30 .09
❑ 38 Harold Baines .30 .09
❑ 39 Trevor Hoffman .30 .09
❑ 40 Edgar Martinez .50 .15
❑ 41 Geronimo Berroa .30 .09
❑ 42 Rey Ordonez .30 .09
❑ 43 Mike Stanley .30 .09
❑ 44 Mike Mussina .75 .23
❑ 45 Kevin Brown .30 .09
❑ 46 Dennis Eckersley .30 .09
❑ 47 Henry Rodriguez .30 .09
❑ 48 Tino Martinez .50 .15
❑ 49 Eric Young .30 .09
❑ 50 Bret Boone .30 .09
❑ 51 Raul Mondesi .30 .09
❑ 52 Sammy Sosa 1.25 .35
❑ 53 John Smoltz .50 .15
❑ 54 Billy Wagner .30 .09
❑ 55 Jeff D'Amico .30 .09
❑ 56 Ken Caminiti .30 .09
❑ 57 Jason Kendall .30 .09
❑ 58 Wade Boggs .50 .15
❑ 59 Andres Galarraga .30 .09
❑ 60 Jeff Brantley .30 .09
❑ 61 Mel Rojas .30 .09
❑ 62 Brian L. Hunter .30 .09
❑ 63 Bobby Bonilla .30 .09
❑ 64 Roger Clemens 1.50 .45
❑ 65 Jeff Kent .30 .09
❑ 66 Matt Williams .30 .09
❑ 67 Albert Belle .30 .09
❑ 68 Jeff King .30 .09
❑ 69 John Wetteland .30 .09
❑ 70 Deion Sanders .30 .09
❑ 71 Bubba Trammell RC .50 .15
❑ 72 Felix Heredia RC .50 .15
❑ 73 Billy Koch RC .75 .23
❑ 74 Sidney Ponson RC 1.25 .35
❑ 75 Ricky Ledee RC .50 .15
❑ 76 Brett Tomko .30 .09
❑ 77 Braden Looper RC .50 .15
❑ 78 Damian Jackson .30 .09
❑ 79 Jason Dickson .30 .09
❑ 80 Chad Green RC .50 .15
❑ 81 R.A. Dickey RC .50 .15
❑ 82 Jeff Liefer .30 .09
❑ 83 Matt Wagner .30 .09
❑ 84 Richard Hidalgo .30 .09
❑ 85 Adam Riggs .30 .09
❑ 86 Robert Smith .30 .09
❑ 87 Chad Hermansen RC .50 .15
❑ 88 Felix Martinez .30 .09
❑ 89 J.J. Johnson .30 .09
❑ 90 Todd Dunwoody .30 .09
❑ 91 Katsuhiro Maeda .30 .09
❑ 92 Darin Erstad .30 .09
❑ 93 Elieser Marrero .30 .09
❑ 94 Bartolo Colon .30 .09
❑ 95 Chris Fussell .30 .09
❑ 96 Ugueth Urbina .30 .09
❑ 97 Josh Paul RC .50 .15
❑ 98 Jaime Bluma .30 .09
❑ 99 Seth Greisinger RC .50 .15
❑ 100 Jose Cruz Jr. RC 2.00 .60
❑ 101 Todd Dunn .30 .09
❑ 102 Joe Young RC .50 .15
❑ 103 Jonathan Johnson .30 .09
❑ 104 Justin Towle RC .50 .15
❑ 105 Brian Rose .30 .09
❑ 106 Jose Guillen .30 .09
❑ 107 Andruw Jones .50 .15
❑ 108 Mark Kotsay RC .50 .15
❑ 109 Wilton Guerrero .30 .09
❑ 110 Jacob Cruz .30 .09
❑ 111 Mike Sweeney .30 .09
❑ 112 Julio Mosquera .30 .09
❑ 113 Matt Morris .30 .09
❑ 114 Wendell Magee .30 .09
❑ 115 John Thomson .30 .09
❑ 116 Javier Valentin .30 .09
❑ 117 Tom Fordham .30 .09
❑ 118 Ruben Rivera .30 .09
❑ 119 Mike Drumright RC .50 .15
❑ 120 Chris Holt .30 .09
❑ 121 Sean Maloney .30 .09
❑ 122 Michael Barrett .30 .09
❑ 123 Tony Saunders RC .50 .15
❑ 124 Kevin Brown C .30 .09
❑ 125 Richard Almanzar .30 .09
❑ 126 Mark Redman .30 .09
❑ 127 Anthony Sanders RC .50 .15
❑ 128 Jeff Abbott .30 .09
❑ 129 Eugene Kingsale .30 .09
❑ 130 Paul Konerko .30 .09
❑ 131 Randall Simon RC .75 .23
❑ 132 Andy Larkin .30 .09
❑ 133 Rafael Medina .30 .09
❑ 134 Mendy Lopez .30 .09
❑ 135 Freddy Adrian Garcia .30 .09
❑ 136 Karim Garcia .30 .09
❑ 137 Larry Rodriguez RC .50 .15
❑ 138 Carlos Guillen .30 .09
❑ 139 Aaron Boone .30 .09
❑ 140 Donnie Sadler .30 .09
❑ 141 Brooks Kieschnick .30 .09
❑ 142 Scott Spiezio .30 .09
❑ 143 Everett Stull .30 .09
❑ 144 Enrique Wilson .30 .09
❑ 145 Milton Bradley RC 3.00 .90
❑ 146 Kevin Orie .30 .09
❑ 147 Derek Wallace .30 .09
❑ 148 Russ Johnson .30 .09
❑ 149 Joe Lagarde RC .50 .15
❑ 150 Luis Castillo .30 .09
❑ 151 Jay Payton .30 .09
❑ 152 Joe Long .30 .09
❑ 153 Livan Hernandez .30 .09
❑ 154 Vladimir Nunez RC .50 .15
❑ 155 Pokey Reese UER .30 .09
Card actually numbered 156
❑ 156 George Arias .30 .09
❑ 157 Homer Bush .30 .09
❑ 158 Chris Carpenter UER .30 .09
Card numbered 159
❑ 159 Eric Milton RC .75 .23
❑ 160 Richie Sexson .30 .09
❑ 161 Carl Pavano .30 .09
❑ 162 Chris Gissell RC .50 .15
❑ 163 Mac Suzuki .30 .09
❑ 164 Pat Cline .30 .09
❑ 165 Ron Wright .30 .09
❑ 166 Dante Powell .30 .09
❑ 167 Mark Bellhorn .30 .09
❑ 168 George Lombard .30 .09
❑ 169 Pee Wee Lopez RC .50 .15
❑ 170 Paul Wilder RC .50 .15

❑ 171 Brad Fullmer .30 .09
❑ 172 Willie Martinez RC .50 .15
❑ 173 Dario Veras RC .50 .15
❑ 174 Dave Coggin .30 .09
❑ 175 Kris Benson RC .75 .23
❑ 176 Torii Hunter .30 .09
❑ 177 D.T. Cromer .30 .09
❑ 178 Nelson Figueroa RC .50 .15
❑ 179 Hiram Bocachica RC .50 .15
❑ 180 Shane Monahan .30 .09
❑ 181 Jimmy Anderson RC .50 .15
❑ 182 Juan Melo .30 .09
❑ 183 Pablo Ortega RC .50 .15
❑ 184 Calvin Pickering RC .50 .15
❑ 185 Reggie Taylor .30 .09
❑ 186 Jeff Farnsworth RC .50 .15
❑ 187 Terrence Long .30 .09
❑ 188 Geoff Jenkins .30 .09
❑ 189 Steve Rain RC .50 .15
❑ 190 Nerio Rodriguez RC .50 .15
❑ 191 Derrick Gibson .30 .09
❑ 192 Darin Blood .30 .09
❑ 193 Ben Davis .30 .09
❑ 194 Adrian Beltre RC 2.00 .60
❑ 195 Damian Sapp RC UER .50 .15
❑ 196 Kerry Wood RC 8.00 2.40
❑ 197 Nate Rolison RC .50 .15
❑ 198 Fernando Tatis RC .50 .15
❑ 199 Brad Penny RC 2.00 .60
❑ 200 Jake Westbrook RC .50 .15
❑ 201 Edwin Diaz .30 .09
❑ 202 Joe Fontenot RC .50 .15
❑ 203 Matt Halloran RC .50 .15
❑ 204 Blake Stein RC .50 .15
❑ 205 Onan Masaoka .30 .09
❑ 206 Ben Petrick .30 .09
❑ 207 Matt Clement RC 1.25 .35
❑ 208 Todd Greene .30 .09
❑ 209 Ray Ricken .30 .09
❑ 210 Eric Chavez RC 4.00 1.20
❑ 211 Edgard Velazquez .30 .09
❑ 212 Bruce Chen RC .50 .15
❑ 213 Danny Patterson .30 .09
❑ 214 Jeff Yoder .30 .09
❑ 215 Luis Ordaz RC .50 .15
❑ 216 Chris Widger .30 .09
❑ 217 Jason Brester .30 .09
❑ 218 Carlton Loewer .30 .09
❑ 219 Chris Reitsma RC .50 .15
❑ 220 Neifi Perez .30 .09
❑ 221 Hideki Irabu RC .50 .15
❑ 222 Ellis Burks .30 .09
❑ 223 Pedro Martinez .75 .23
❑ 224 Kenny Lofton .30 .09
❑ 225 Randy Johnson .75 .23
❑ 226 Terry Steinbach .30 .09
❑ 227 Bernie Williams .50 .15
❑ 228 Dean Palmer .30 .09
❑ 229 Alan Benes .30 .09
❑ 230 Marquis Grissom .30 .09
❑ 231 Gary Sheffield .30 .09
❑ 232 Curt Schilling .50 .15
❑ 233 Reggie Sanders .30 .09
❑ 234 Bobby Higginson .30 .09
❑ 235 Moises Alou .30 .09
❑ 236 Tom Glavine .75 .23
❑ 237 Mark Grace .75 .23
❑ 238 Ramon Martinez .30 .09
❑ 239 Rafael Palmeiro .50 .15
❑ 240 John Olerud .30 .09
❑ 241 Dante Bichette .30 .09
❑ 242 Greg Vaughn .30 .09
❑ 243 Jeff Bagwell .50 .15
❑ 244 Barry Bonds 2.00 .60
❑ 245 Pat Hentgen .30 .09
❑ 246 Jim Thome .75 .23
❑ 247 J.Allensworth .30 .09
❑ 248 Andy Pettitte .50 .15
❑ 249 Jay Bell .30 .09
❑ 250 John Jaha .30 .09
❑ 251 Jim Edmonds .30 .09
❑ 252 Ron Gant .30 .09
❑ 253 David Cone .30 .09
❑ 254 Jose Canseco .75 .23
❑ 255 Jay Buhner .30 .09
❑ 256 Greg Maddux 1.50 .45
❑ 257 Brian McRae .30 .09
❑ 258 Lance Johnson .30 .09
❑ 259 Travis Fryman .30 .09
❑ 260 Paul O'Neill .50 .15
❑ 261 Ivan Rodriguez .75 .23
❑ 262 Gregg Jefferies .30 .09
❑ 263 Fred McGriff .50 .15
❑ 264 Derek Bell .30 .09
❑ 265 Jeff Conine .30 .09
❑ 266 Mike Piazza 1.25 .35
❑ 267 Mark Grudzielanek .30 .09
❑ 268 Brady Anderson .30 .09
❑ 269 Marty Cordova .30 .09
❑ 270 Ray Durham .30 .09
❑ 271 Joe Carter .30 .09
❑ 272 Brian Jordan .30 .09
❑ 273 David Justice .30 .09
❑ 274 Tony Gwynn 1.00 .30
❑ 275 Larry Walker .50 .15
❑ 276 Cecil Fielder .30 .09
❑ 277 Mo Vaughn .30 .09
❑ 278 Alex Fernandez .30 .09
❑ 279 Michael Tucker .30 .09
❑ 280 Jose Valentin .30 .09
❑ 281 Sandy Alomar Jr. .30 .09
❑ 282 Todd Hollandsworth .30 .09
❑ 283 Rico Brogna .30 .09
❑ 284 Rusty Greer .30 .09
❑ 285 Roberto Hernandez .30 .09
❑ 286 Hal Morris .30 .09
❑ 287 Johnny Damon .30 .09
❑ 288 Todd Hundley .30 .09
❑ 289 Rondell White .30 .09
❑ 290 Frank Thomas .75 .23
❑ 291 Don Denbow RC .50 .15
❑ 292 Derrek Lee .30 .09
❑ 293 Todd Walker .30 .09
❑ 294 Scott Rolen .50 .15
❑ 295 Wes Helms .30 .09
❑ 296 Bob Abreu .30 .09
❑ 297 John Patterson RC .75 .23
❑ 298 Alex Gonzalez RC 1.25 .35
❑ 299 Grant Roberts RC .50 .15
❑ 300 Jeff Suppan .30 .09
❑ 301 Luke Wilcox .30 .09
❑ 302 Marlon Anderson .30 .09
❑ 303 Ray Brown .30 .09
❑ 304 Mike Caruso RC .50 .15
❑ 305 Sam Marsonek RC .50 .15
❑ 306 Brady Raggio RC .50 .15
❑ 307 Kevin McGlinchy RC .50 .15
❑ 308 Roy Halladay RC 4.00 1.20
❑ 309 Jeremi Gonzalez RC .50 .15
❑ 310 Aramis Ramirez RC 2.50 .75
❑ 311 Dee Brown RC .50 .15
❑ 312 Justin Thompson .30 .09
❑ 313 Jay Tessmer RC .50 .15
❑ 314 Mike Johnson RC .50 .15
❑ 315 Danny Clyburn .30 .09
❑ 316 Bruce Aven .30 .09
❑ 317 Keith Foulke RC .50 .15
❑ 318 Jimmy Osting RC .50 .15
❑ 319 Val.De Los Santos RC .50 .15
❑ 320 Shannon Stewart .30 .09
❑ 321 Willie Adams .30 .09
❑ 322 Larry Barnes RC .50 .15
❑ 323 Mark Johnson RC .50 .15
❑ 324 Chris Stowers RC .50 .15
❑ 325 Brandon Reed .30 .09
❑ 326 Randy Winn .30 .09
❑ 327 Steve Chavez RC .50 .15
❑ 328 Nomar Garciaparra 1.50 .45
❑ 329 Jacque Jones RC 1.50 .45
❑ 330 Chris Clemons .30 .09
❑ 331 Todd Helton .75 .23
❑ 332 Ryan Brannan RC .50 .15
❑ 333 Alex Sanchez RC .50 .15
❑ 334 Arnold Gooch .30 .09
❑ 335 Russell Branyan .30 .09
❑ 336 Daryle Ward .50 .15
❑ 337 John LeRoy RC .50 .15
❑ 338 Steve Cox .30 .09
❑ 339 Kevin Witt .30 .09
❑ 340 Norm Hutchins .30 .09
❑ 341 Gabby Martinez .30 .09
❑ 342 Kris Detmers .30 .09
❑ 343 Mike Villano RC .50 .15
❑ 344 Preston Wilson .30 .09
❑ 345 James Manias RC .50 .15
❑ 346 Deivi Cruz RC .50 .15
❑ 347 Donzell McDonald RC .50 .15
❑ 348 Rod Myers RC .50 .15
❑ 349 Shawn Chacon RC 2.50 .75
❑ 350 Elvin Hernandez RC .50 .15
❑ 351 Orlando Cabrera RC .75 .23
❑ 352 Brian Banks .30 .09
❑ 353 Robbie Bell .50 .15
❑ 354 Brad Rigby .30 .09
❑ 355 Scott Elarton .30 .09
❑ 356 Kevin Sweeney RC .50 .15
❑ 357 Steve Soderstrom .30 .09
❑ 358 Ryan Nye .30 .09
❑ 360 Donny Leon RC .75 .23
❑ 361 Garrett Neubart RC .50 .15
❑ 362 Abraham Nunez RC .50 .15
❑ 363 Adam Eaton RC .50 .15
❑ 364 Octavio Dotel RC .50 .15
❑ 365 Dean Crow RC .50 .15
❑ 366 Jason Baker RC .50 .15
❑ 367 Sean Casey .50 .15
❑ 368 Joe Lawrence RC .50 .15
❑ 369 Adam Johnson RC .50 .15
❑ 370 S.Schoeneweis RC .50 .15
❑ 371 Gerald Witasick Jr. .30 .09
❑ 372 Ronnie Belliard RC .50 .15
❑ 373 Russ Ortiz .30 .09
❑ 374 Robert Stratton RC .75 .23
❑ 375 Bobby Estalella .30 .09
❑ 376 Corey Lee RC .50 .15
❑ 377 Carlos Beltran .50 .15
❑ 378 Mike Cameron .30 .09
❑ 379 Scott Randall RC .50 .15
❑ 380 Corey Erickson RC .50 .15
❑ 381 Jay Canizaro .30 .09
❑ 382 Kerry Robinson RC .50 .15
❑ 383 Todd Noel RC .50 .15
❑ 384 A.J. Zapp RC .50 .15
❑ 385 Jarrod Washburn .30 .09
❑ 386 Ben Grieve .30 .09
❑ 387 Javier Vazquez RC 4.00 .90
❑ 388 Tony Graffanino .30 .09
❑ 389 Travis Lee RC .75 .23
❑ 390 DaRond Stovall .30 .09
❑ 391 Dennis Reyes RC .50 .15
❑ 392 Danny Buxbaum .30 .09
❑ 393 Marc Lewis RC .50 .15
❑ 394 Kelvim Escobar RC .50 .15
❑ 395 Danny Klassen .30 .09
❑ 396 Ken Cloude RC .50 .15
❑ 397 Gabe Alvarez .30 .09
❑ 398 Jaret Wright RC .50 .15
❑ 399 Raul Casanova .30 .09
❑ 400 Clayton Bruner RC .50 .15
❑ 401 Jason Marquis RC .50 .15
❑ 402 Marc Kroon .30 .09
❑ 403 Jamey Wright .30 .09
❑ 404 Matt Snyder RC .50 .15
❑ 405 Josh Garrett RC .50 .15
❑ 406 Juan Encarnacion .30 .09
❑ 407 Heath Murray .30 .09
❑ 408 Brett Herbison RC .50 .15
❑ 409 Brent Butler RC .50 .15
❑ 410 Danny Peoples RC .50 .15
❑ 411 Miguel Tejada RC 5.00 1.50
❑ 412 Damian Moss .30 .09
❑ 413 Jim Pittsley .30 .09
❑ 414 Dmitri Young .30 .09
❑ 415 Glendon Rusch .30 .09
❑ 416 Vladimir Guerrero .75 .23
❑ 417 Cole Liniak RC .50 .15
❑ 418 R.Hernandez UER .30 .09
Card back says 1st Bowman card is 1997, he had a 1996 Bowman
❑ 419 Cliff Politte RC .50 .15
❑ 420 Mel Rosario RC .50 .15
❑ 421 Jorge Carrion RC .50 .15
❑ 422 John Barnes RC .50 .15
❑ 423 Chris Stowe RC .50 .15
❑ 424 Vernon Wells RC 4.00 1.20
❑ 425 Brett Caradonna RC .50 .15
❑ 426 Scott Hodges RC .50 .15
❑ 427 Jon Garland RC .75 .23

❑ 428 Nathan Haynes RC .50 .15
❑ 429 Geoff Goetz RC .50 .15
❑ 430 Adam Kennedy RC 1.25 .35
❑ 431 T.J. Tucker RC .50 .15
❑ 432 Aaron Akin RC .50 .15
❑ 433 Jayson Werth RC .50 .15
❑ 434 Glenn Davis RC .50 .15
❑ 435 Mark Mangum RC .50 .15
❑ 436 Troy Cameron RC .50 .15
❑ 437 J.J. Davis RC .50 .15
❑ 438 Lance Berkman RC 5.00 1.50
❑ 439 Jason Standridge RC .50 .15
❑ 440 Jason Dellaero RC .50 .15
❑ 441 Hideki Irabu .50 .15

1998 Bowman

	Nm-Mt	Ex-Mt
COMPLETE SET (441)	60.00	18.00
COMP. SERIES 1 (221)	30.00	9.00
COMP. SERIES 2 (220)	30.00	9.00

❑ 1 Nomar Garciaparra 1.50 .45
❑ 2 Scott Rolen .50 .15
❑ 3 Andy Pettitte .50 .15
❑ 4 Ivan Rodriguez .75 .23
❑ 5 Mark McGwire 2.00 .60
❑ 6 Jason Dickson .30 .09
❑ 7 Jose Cruz Jr. .30 .09
❑ 8 Jeff Kent .30 .09
❑ 9 Mike Mussina .75 .23
❑ 10 Jason Kendall .30 .09
❑ 11 Brett Tomko .30 .09
❑ 12 Jeff King .30 .09
❑ 13 Brad Radke .30 .09
❑ 14 Robin Ventura .30 .09
❑ 15 Jeff Bagwell .50 .15
❑ 16 Greg Maddux 1.50 .45
❑ 17 John Jaha .30 .09
❑ 18 Mike Piazza 1.25 .35
❑ 19 Edgar Martinez .50 .15
❑ 20 David Justice .30 .09
❑ 21 Todd Hundley .30 .09
❑ 22 Tony Gwynn 1.00 .30
❑ 23 Larry Walker .50 .15
❑ 24 Bernie Williams .50 .15
❑ 25 Edgar Renteria .30 .09
❑ 26 Rafael Palmeiro .50 .15
❑ 27 Tim Salmon .50 .15
❑ 28 Matt Morris .30 .09
❑ 29 Shawn Estes .30 .09
❑ 30 Vladimir Guerrero .75 .23
❑ 31 Fernando Tatis .30 .09
❑ 32 Justin Thompson .30 .09
❑ 33 Ken Griffey Jr. 1.25 .35
❑ 34 Edgardo Alfonzo .30 .09
❑ 35 Mo Vaughn .30 .09
❑ 36 Marty Cordova .30 .09
❑ 37 Craig Biggio .50 .15
❑ 38 Roger Clemens 1.50 .45
❑ 39 Mark Grace .75 .23
❑ 40 Ken Caminiti .30 .09
❑ 41 Tony Womack .30 .09
❑ 42 Albert Belle .30 .09
❑ 43 Tino Martinez .50 .15
❑ 44 Sandy Alomar Jr. .30 .09
❑ 45 Jeff Cirillo .30 .09
❑ 46 Jason Giambi .75 .23
❑ 47 Darin Erstad .30 .09
❑ 48 Livan Hernandez .30 .09
❑ 49 Mark Grudzielanek .30 .09
❑ 50 Sammy Sosa 1.25 .35
❑ 51 Curt Schilling .50 .15
❑ 52 Brian Hunter .30 .09
❑ 53 Neifi Perez .30 .09
❑ 54 Todd Walker .30 .09
❑ 55 Jose Guillen .30 .09
❑ 56 Jim Thome .75 .23
❑ 57 Tom Glavine .75 .23
❑ 58 Todd Greene .30 .09
❑ 59 Rondell White .30 .09
❑ 60 Roberto Alomar .75 .23
❑ 61 Tony Clark .30 .09
❑ 62 Vinny Castilla .30 .09
❑ 63 Barry Larkin .75 .23
❑ 64 Hideki Irabu .30 .09
❑ 65 Johnny Damon .30 .09
❑ 66 Juan Gonzalez .75 .23
❑ 67 John Olerud .30 .09
❑ 68 Gary Sheffield .30 .09
❑ 69 Raul Mondesi .30 .09
❑ 70 Chipper Jones .75 .23
❑ 71 David Ortiz .30 .09
❑ 72 Warren Morris RC .30 .09
❑ 73 Alex Gonzalez .30 .09
❑ 74 Nick Bierbrodt .30 .09
❑ 75 Roy Halladay .50 .15
❑ 76 Danny Buxbaum .30 .09
❑ 77 Adam Kennedy .30 .09
❑ 78 Jared Sandberg .30 .09
❑ 79 Michael Barrett .30 .09
❑ 80 Gil Meche 1.50 .45
❑ 81 Jayson Werth .30 .09
❑ 82 Abraham Nunez .30 .09
❑ 83 Ben Petrick .30 .09
❑ 84 Brett Caradonna .30 .09
❑ 85 Mike Lowell RC 2.50 .75
❑ 86 Clayton Bruner .30 .09
❑ 87 John Curtice RC .50 .15
❑ 88 Bobby Estalella .30 .09
❑ 89 Juan Melo .30 .09
❑ 90 Arnold Gooch .30 .09
❑ 91 Kevin Millwood RC 2.00 .60
❑ 92 Richie Sexson .30 .09
❑ 93 Orlando Cabrera .30 .09
❑ 94 Pat Cline .30 .09
❑ 95 Anthony Sanders .30 .09
❑ 96 Russ Johnson .30 .09
❑ 97 Ben Grieve .30 .09
❑ 98 Kevin McGlinchy .30 .09
❑ 99 Paul Wilder .30 .09
❑ 100 Russ Ortiz .30 .09
❑ 101 Ryan Jackson RC .30 .09
❑ 102 Heath Murray .30 .09
❑ 103 Brian Rose .30 .09
❑ 104 R.Radmanovich RC .30 .09
❑ 105 Ricky Ledee .30 .09
❑ 106 Jeff Wallace RC .30 .09
❑ 107 Ryan Minor RC .30 .09
❑ 108 Dennis Reyes .30 .09
❑ 109 James Manias .30 .09
❑ 110 Chris Carpenter .30 .09
❑ 111 Daryle Ward .30 .09
❑ 112 Vernon Wells .50 .15
❑ 113 Chad Green .30 .09
❑ 114 Mike Stoner RC .30 .09
❑ 115 Brad Fullmer .30 .09
❑ 116 Adam Eaton .30 .09
❑ 117 Jeff Liefer .30 .09
❑ 118 Corey Koskie RC 1.50 .45
❑ 119 Todd Helton .50 .15
❑ 120 Jaime Jones RC .30 .09
❑ 121 Mel Rosario .30 .09
❑ 122 Geoff Goetz .30 .09
❑ 123 Adrian Beltre .30 .09
❑ 124 Jason Dellaero .30 .09
❑ 125 Gabe Kapler RC .75 .23
❑ 126 Scott Schoeneweis .30 .09
❑ 127 Ryan Brannan .30 .09
❑ 128 Aaron Akin .30 .09
❑ 129 Ryan Anderson RC .50 .15
❑ 130 Brad Penny .30 .09
❑ 131 Bruce Chen .30 .09
❑ 132 Eli Marrero .30 .09
❑ 133 Eric Chavez .50 .15
❑ 134 Troy Glaus RC 5.00 1.50
❑ 135 Troy Cameron .30 .09
❑ 136 Brian Sikorski RC .30 .09
❑ 137 Mike Kinkade RC .30 .09
❑ 138 Braden Looper .30 .09
❑ 139 Mark Mangum .30 .09
❑ 140 Danny Peoples .30 .09
❑ 141 J.J. Davis .30 .09
❑ 142 Ben Davis .30 .09
❑ 143 Jacque Jones .30 .09
❑ 144 Derrick Gibson .30 .09
❑ 145 Bronson Arroyo .30 .09
❑ 146 L.De Los Santos RC UER .30 .09
has hitting stat line instead of pitching
❑ 147 Jeff Abbott .30 .09
❑ 148 Mike Cuddyer RC 1.50 .45
❑ 149 Jason Romano .30 .09
❑ 150 Shane Monahan .30 .09
❑ 151 Ntema Ndungidi RC .30 .09
❑ 152 Alex Sanchez .30 .09
❑ 153 Jack Cust RC .50 .15
❑ 154 Brent Butler .30 .09
❑ 155 Ramon Hernandez .30 .09
❑ 156 Norm Hutchins .30 .09
❑ 157 Jason Marquis .30 .09
❑ 158 Jacob Cruz .30 .09
❑ 159 Rob Burger RC .30 .09
❑ 160 Dave Coggin .30 .09
❑ 161 Preston Wilson .30 .09
❑ 162 Jason Fitzgerald RC .30 .09
❑ 163 Dan Serafini .30 .09
❑ 164 Peter Munro .30 .09
❑ 165 Trot Nixon .30 .09
❑ 166 Homer Bush .30 .09
❑ 167 Dermal Brown .30 .09
❑ 168 Chad Hermansen .30 .09
❑ 169 Julio Moreno RC .30 .09
❑ 170 John Roskos RC .30 .09
❑ 171 Grant Roberts .30 .09
❑ 172 Ken Cloude .30 .09
❑ 173 Jason Brester .30 .09
❑ 174 Jason Conti .30 .09
❑ 175 Jon Garland .30 .09
❑ 176 Robbie Bell .30 .09
❑ 177 Nathan Haynes .30 .09
❑ 178 Ramon Ortiz RC 1.25 .35
❑ 179 Shannon Stewart .30 .09
❑ 180 Pablo Ortega .30 .09
❑ 181 Jimmy Rollins RC 1.50 .45
❑ 182 Sean Casey .30 .09
❑ 183 Ted Lilly RC .75 .23
❑ 184 Chris Enochs RC .30 .09
❑ 185 M.Ordonez RC UER 3.00 .90
Front photo is Mario Valdez
❑ 186 Mike Drumright .30 .09
❑ 187 Aaron Boone .30 .09
❑ 188 Matt Clement .30 .09
❑ 189 Todd Dunwoody .30 .09
❑ 190 Larry Rodriguez .30 .09
❑ 191 Todd Noel .30 .09
❑ 192 Geoff Jenkins .30 .09
❑ 193 George Lombard .30 .09
❑ 194 Lance Berkman .50 .15
❑ 195 Marcus McCain .30 .09
❑ 196 Ryan McGuire .30 .09
❑ 197 Jhensy Sandoval .30 .09
❑ 198 Corey Lee .30 .09
❑ 199 Mario Valdez .30 .09
❑ 200 Robert Fick RC 1.50 .45
❑ 201 Donnie Sadler .30 .09
❑ 202 Marc Kroon .30 .09
❑ 203 David Miller .30 .09
❑ 204 Jarrod Washburn .30 .09
❑ 205 Miguel Tejada .50 .15
❑ 206 Raul Ibanez .30 .09
❑ 207 John Patterson .30 .09
❑ 208 Calvin Pickering .30 .09
❑ 209 Felix Martinez .30 .09
❑ 210 Mark Redman .30 .09
❑ 211 Scott Elarton .30 .09
❑ 212 Jose Amado RC .30 .09
❑ 213 Kerry Wood .75 .23
❑ 214 Dante Powell .30 .09
❑ 215 Aramis Ramirez .30 .09
❑ 216 A.J. Hinch .30 .09

❑ 217 Dustin Carr RC .30 .09
❑ 218 Mark Kotsay .30 .09
❑ 219 Jason Standridge .30 .09
❑ 220 Luis Ordaz .30 .09
❑ 221 O.Hernandez RC 1.50 .45
❑ 222 Cal Ripken 2.50 .75
❑ 223 Paul Molitor .50 .15
❑ 224 Derek Jeter 2.00 .60
❑ 225 Barry Bonds 2.00 .60
❑ 226 Jim Edmonds .30 .09
❑ 227 John Smoltz .50 .15
❑ 228 Eric Karros .30 .09
❑ 229 Ray Lankford .30 .09
❑ 230 Rey Ordonez .30 .09
❑ 231 Kenny Lofton .30 .09
❑ 232 Alex Rodriguez 1.50 .45
❑ 233 Dante Bichette .30 .09
❑ 234 Pedro Martinez .75 .23
❑ 235 Carlos Delgado .30 .09
❑ 236 Rod Beck .30 .09
❑ 237 Matt Williams .30 .09
❑ 238 Charles Johnson .30 .09
❑ 239 Rico Brogna .30 .09
❑ 240 Frank Thomas .75 .23
❑ 241 Paul O'Neill .50 .15
❑ 242 Jaret Wright .30 .09
❑ 243 Brant Brown .30 .09
❑ 244 Ryan Klesko .30 .09
❑ 245 Chuck Finley .30 .09
❑ 246 Derek Bell .30 .09
❑ 247 Delino DeShields .30 .09
❑ 248 Chan Ho Park .30 .09
❑ 249 Wade Boggs .50 .15
❑ 250 Jay Buhner .30 .09
❑ 251 Butch Huskey .30 .09
❑ 252 Steve Finley .30 .09
❑ 253 Will Clark .75 .23
❑ 254 John Valentin .30 .09
❑ 255 Bobby Higginson .30 .09
❑ 256 Darryl Strawberry .50 .15
❑ 257 Randy Johnson .75 .23
❑ 258 Al Martin .30 .09
❑ 259 Travis Fryman .30 .09
❑ 260 Fred McGriff .50 .15
❑ 261 Jose Valentin .30 .09
❑ 262 Andruw Jones .50 .15
❑ 263 Kenny Rogers .30 .09
❑ 264 Moises Alou .30 .09
❑ 265 Denny Neagle .30 .09
❑ 266 Ugueth Urbina .30 .09
❑ 267 Derrek Lee .30 .09
❑ 268 Ellis Burks .30 .09
❑ 269 Mariano Rivera .50 .15
❑ 270 Dean Palmer .30 .09
❑ 271 Eddie Taubensee .30 .09
❑ 272 Brady Anderson .30 .09
❑ 273 Brian Giles .30 .09
❑ 274 Quinton McCracken .30 .09
❑ 275 Henry Rodriguez .30 .09
❑ 276 Andres Galarraga .30 .09
❑ 277 Jose Canseco .75 .23
❑ 278 David Segui .30 .09
❑ 279 Bret Saberhagen .30 .09
❑ 280 Kevin Brown .50 .15
❑ 281 Chuck Knoblauch .30 .09
❑ 282 Jeromy Burnitz .30 .09
❑ 283 Jay Bell .30 .09
❑ 284 Manny Ramirez .30 .09
❑ 285 Rick Helling .30 .09
❑ 286 Francisco Cordova .30 .09
❑ 287 Bob Abreu .30 .09
❑ 288 J.T. Snow .30 .09
❑ 289 Hideo Nomo .75 .23
❑ 290 Brian Jordan .30 .09
❑ 291 Javy Lopez .30 .09
❑ 292 Travis Lee .30 .09
❑ 293 Russell Branyan .30 .09
❑ 294 Paul Konerko .30 .09
❑ 295 Masato Yoshii RC .75 .23
❑ 296 Kris Benson .30 .09
❑ 297 Juan Encarnacion .30 .09
❑ 298 Eric Milton .30 .09
❑ 299 Mike Caruso .30 .09
❑ 300 R.Aramboles RC .50 .15
❑ 301 Bobby Smith .30 .09
❑ 302 Billy Koch .30 .09
❑ 303 Richard Hidalgo .30 .09
❑ 304 Justin Baughman RC .30 .09
❑ 305 Chris Gissell .30 .09
❑ 306 Donnie Bridges RC .50 .15
❑ 307 Nelson Lara RC .30 .09
❑ 308 Randy Wolf RC 1.25 .35
❑ 309 Jason LaRue RC .50 .15
❑ 310 Jason Gooding RC .30 .09
❑ 311 Edgard Clemente .30 .09
❑ 312 Andrew Vessel .30 .09
❑ 313 Chris Reitsma .30 .09
❑ 314 Jesus Sanchez RC .30 .09
❑ 315 Buddy Carlyle RC .30 .09
❑ 316 Randy Winn .30 .09
❑ 317 Luis Rivera RC .30 .09
❑ 318 Marcus Thames RC .50 .15
❑ 319 A.J. Pierzynski .30 .09
❑ 320 Scott Randall .30 .09
❑ 321 Damian Sapp .30 .09
❑ 322 Ed Yarnall RC .30 .09
❑ 323 Luke Allen RC .50 .15
❑ 324 J.D. Smart .30 .09
❑ 325 Willie Martinez .30 .09
❑ 326 Alex Ramirez .30 .09
❑ 327 Eric DuBose RC .30 .09
❑ 328 Kevin Witt .30 .09
❑ 329 Dan McKinley RC .30 .09
❑ 330 Cliff Politte .30 .09
❑ 331 Vladimir Nunez .30 .09
❑ 332 John Halama RC .50 .15
❑ 333 Nerio Rodriguez .30 .09
❑ 334 Desi Relaford .30 .09
❑ 335 Robinson Checo .30 .09
❑ 336 John Nicholson .50 .15
❑ 337 Tom LaRosa RC .30 .09
❑ 338 Kevin Nicholson RC .30 .09
❑ 339 Javier Vazquez .50 .09
❑ 340 A.J. Zapp .30 .09
❑ 341 Tom Evans .30 .09
❑ 342 Kerry Robinson .30 .09
❑ 343 Gabe Gonzalez RC .30 .09
❑ 344 Ralph Milliard .30 .09
❑ 345 Enrique Wilson .30 .09
❑ 346 Elvin Hernandez .30 .09
❑ 347 Mike Lincoln RC .30 .09
❑ 348 Cesar King RC .30 .09
❑ 349 Cristian Guzman RC 1.50 .45
❑ 350 Donzell McDonald .30 .09
❑ 351 Jim Parque RC .50 .15
❑ 352 Mike Saipe RC .30 .09
❑ 353 Carlos Febles RC .50 .15
❑ 354 Dernell Stenson RC .50 .15
❑ 355 Mark Osborne RC .30 .09
❑ 356 Odalis Perez RC .75 .23
❑ 357 Jason Dewey RC .30 .09
❑ 358 Joe Fontenot .30 .09
❑ 359 Jason Grilli RC .30 .09
❑ 360 Kevin Haverbusch RC .30 .09
❑ 361 Jay Yennaco RC .30 .09
❑ 362 Brian Buchanan .30 .09
❑ 363 John Barnes .30 .09
❑ 364 Chris Fussell .30 .09
❑ 365 Kevin Gibbs RC .30 .09
❑ 366 Joe Lawrence .30 .09
❑ 367 DaRond Stovall .30 .09
❑ 368 Brian Fuentes RC .30 .09
❑ 369 Jimmy Anderson .30 .09
❑ 370 Lariel Gonzalez RC .30 .09
❑ 371 Scott Williamson RC .50 .15
❑ 372 Milton Bradley .30 .09
❑ 373 Jason Halper RC .30 .09
❑ 374 Brent Billingsley RC .30 .09
❑ 375 Joe DePastino RC .30 .09
❑ 376 Jake Westbrook .30 .09
❑ 377 Octavio Dotel .30 .09
❑ 378 Jason Williams RC .30 .09
❑ 379 Julio Ramirez RC .30 .09
❑ 380 Seth Greisinger .30 .09
❑ 381 Mike Judd RC .30 .09
❑ 382 Ben Ford RC .30 .09
❑ 383 Tom Bennett RC .30 .09
❑ 384 Adam Butler RC .30 .09
❑ 385 Wade Miller RC 1.50 .45
❑ 386 Kyle Peterson RC .30 .09
❑ 387 Tommy Peterman RC .30 .09
❑ 388 Onan Masaoka .30 .09
❑ 389 Jason Rakers RC .30 .09
❑ 390 Rafael Medina .30 .09
❑ 391 Luis Lopez RC .30 .09
❑ 392 Jeff Yoder .30 .09
❑ 393 Vance Wilson RC .30 .09
❑ 394 F.Seguignol RC .30 .09
❑ 395 Ron Wright .30 .09
❑ 396 Ruben Mateo RC .50 .15
❑ 397 Steve Lomasney RC .50 .15
❑ 398 Damian Jackson .30 .09
❑ 399 Mike Jerzembeck RC .30 .09
❑ 400 Luis Rivas RC 1.25 .35
❑ 401 Kevin Burford RC .30 .09
❑ 402 Glenn Davis .30 .09
❑ 403 Robert Luce RC .30 .09
❑ 404 Cole Liniak .30 .09
❑ 405 Matt LeCroy RC .50 .15
❑ 406 Jeremy Giambi RC .50 .15
❑ 407 Shawn Chacon .30 .09
❑ 408 Dewayne Wise RC .30 .09
❑ 409 Steve Woodard .30 .09
❑ 410 F.Cordero RC .50 .15
❑ 411 Damon Minor RC .50 .15
❑ 412 Lou Collier .30 .09
❑ 413 Justin Towle .30 .09
❑ 414 Juan LeBron .30 .09
❑ 415 Michael Coleman .30 .09
❑ 416 Felix Rodriguez .30 .09
❑ 417 Paul Ah Yat RC .30 .09
❑ 418 Kevin Barker RC .30 .09
❑ 419 Brian Meadows .30 .09
❑ 420 Darnell McDonald RC .50 .15
❑ 421 Matt Kinney RC .50 .15
❑ 422 Mike Vavrek RC .30 .09
❑ 423 Courtney Duncan RC .30 .09
❑ 424 Kevin Millar RC 1.50 .45
❑ 425 Ruben Rivera .30 .09
❑ 426 Steve Shoemaker RC .30 .09
❑ 427 Dan Reichert RC .50 .15
❑ 428 Carlos Lee RC 1.50 .45
❑ 429 Rod Barajas .30 .09
❑ 430 Pablo Ozuna RC .50 .15
❑ 431 Todd Belitz RC .30 .09
❑ 432 Sidney Ponson .30 .09
❑ 433 Steve Carver RC .30 .09
❑ 434 Esteban Yan RC .50 .15
❑ 435 Cedrick Bowers .30 .09
❑ 436 Marlon Anderson .30 .09
❑ 437 Carl Pavano .30 .09
❑ 438 Jae Weong Seo RC .75 .23
❑ 439 Jose Taveras RC .30 .09
❑ 440 Matt Anderson RC .50 .15
❑ 441 Darron Ingram RC .30 .09
❑ NNO S.Hasegawa '91 BBM 10.00 3.00
❑ NNO H.Irabu '91 BBM 10.00 3.00
❑ NNO H.Nomo '91 BBM 25.00 7.50

1999 Bowman

	Nm-Mt	Ex-Mt
COMPLETE SET (440)	100.00	30.00
COMP. SERIES 1 (220)	40.00	12.00
COMP. SERIES 2 (220)	60.00	18.00

❑ 1 Ben Grieve .30 .09
❑ 2 Kerry Wood .75 .23
❑ 3 Ruben Rivera .30 .09
❑ 4 Sandy Alomar Jr. .30 .09

	Card	Nr. Mt	Ex-Mt
❑	5 Cal Ripken	2.50	.75
❑	6 Mark McGwire	2.00	.60
❑	7 Vladimir Guerrero	.75	.23
❑	8 Moises Alou	.30	.09
❑	9 Jim Edmonds	.30	.09
❑	10 Greg Maddux	1.50	.45
❑	11 Gary Sheffield	.30	.09
❑	12 John Valentin	.30	.09
❑	13 Chuck Knoblauch	.30	.09
❑	14 Tony Clark	.30	.09
❑	15 Rusty Greer	.30	.09
❑	16 Al Leiter	.30	.09
❑	17 Travis Lee	.30	.09
❑	18 Jose Cruz Jr.	.30	.09
❑	19 Pedro Martinez	.75	.23
❑	20 Paul O'Neill	.50	.15
❑	21 Todd Walker	.30	.09
❑	22 Vinny Castilla	.30	.09
❑	23 Barry Larkin	.75	.23
❑	24 Curt Schilling	.50	.15
❑	25 Jason Kendall	.30	.09
❑	26 Scott Erickson	.30	.09
❑	27 Andres Galarraga	.30	.09
❑	28 Jeff Shaw	.30	.09
❑	29 John Olerud	.30	.09
❑	30 Orlando Hernandez	.30	.09
❑	31 Larry Walker	.50	.15
❑	32 Andruw Jones	.50	.15
❑	33 Jeff Cirillo	.30	.09
❑	34 Barry Bonds	2.00	.60
❑	35 Manny Ramirez	.30	.09
❑	36 Mark Kotsay	.30	.09
❑	37 Ivan Rodriguez	.75	.23
❑	38 Jeff King	.30	.09
❑	39 Brian Hunter	.30	.09
❑	40 Ray Durham	.30	.09
❑	41 Bernie Williams	.50	.15
❑	42 Darin Erstad	.30	.09
❑	43 Chipper Jones	.75	.23
❑	44 Pat Hentgen	.30	.09
❑	45 Eric Young	.30	.09
❑	46 Jaret Wright	.30	.09
❑	47 Juan Guzman	.30	.09
❑	48 Jorge Posada	.50	.15
❑	49 Bobby Higginson	.30	.09
❑	50 Jose Guillen	.30	.09
❑	51 Trevor Hoffman	.30	.09
❑	52 Ken Griffey Jr.	1.25	.35
❑	53 David Justice	.30	.09
❑	54 Matt Williams	.30	.09
❑	55 Eric Karros	.30	.09
❑	56 Derek Bell	.30	.09
❑	57 Ray Lankford	.30	.09
❑	58 Mariano Rivera	.50	.15
❑	59 Brett Tomko	.30	.09
❑	60 Mike Mussina	.75	.23
❑	61 Kenny Lofton	.30	.09
❑	62 Chuck Finley	.30	.09
❑	63 Alex Gonzalez	.30	.09
❑	64 Mark Grace	.75	.23
❑	65 Raul Mondesi	.30	.09
❑	66 David Cone	.30	.09
❑	67 Brad Fullmer	.30	.09
❑	68 Andy Benes	.30	.09
❑	69 John Smoltz	.50	.15
❑	70 Shane Reynolds	.30	.09
❑	71 Bruce Chen	.30	.09
❑	72 Adam Kennedy	.30	.09
❑	73 Jack Cust	.30	.09
❑	74 Matt Clement	.30	.09
❑	75 Derrick Gibson	.30	.09
❑	76 Darnell McDonald	.30	.09
❑	77 Adam Everett RC	.50	.15
❑	78 Ricardo Aramboles	.30	.09
❑	79 Mark Quinn RC	.50	.15
❑	80 Jason Rakers	.30	.09
❑	81 Seth Etherton RC	.50	.15
❑	82 Jeff Urban RC	.50	.15
❑	83 Manny Aybar	.30	.09
❑	84 Mike Nannini RC	.50	.15
❑	85 Onan Masaoka	.30	.09
❑	86 Rod Barajas	.30	.09
❑	87 Mike Frank	.30	.09
❑	88 Scott Randall	.30	.09
❑	89 Justin Bowles RC	.40	.12
❑	90 Chris Haas	.30	.09
❑	91 Arturo McDowell RC	.50	.15
❑	92 Matt Belisle RC	.50	.60
❑	93 Scott Elarton	.30	.09
❑	94 Vernon Wells	.30	.09
❑	95 Pat Cline	.30	.09
❑	96 Ryan Anderson	.30	.09
❑	97 Kevin Barker	.30	.09
❑	98 Ruben Mateo	.30	.09
❑	99 Robert Fick	.30	.09
❑	100 Corey Koskie	.30	.09
❑	101 Ricky Ledee	.30	.09
❑	102 Rick Elder RC	.50	.15
❑	103 Jack Cressend RC	.40	.12
❑	104 Joe Lawrence	.30	.09
❑	105 Mike Lincoln	.30	.09
❑	106 Kit Pellow RC	.40	.12
❑	107 Matt Burch RC	.50	.15
❑	108 Cole Liniak	.30	.09
❑	109 Jason Dewey	.30	.09
❑	110 Cesar King	.30	.09
❑	111 Julio Ramirez	.30	.09
❑	112 Jake Westbrook	.30	.09
❑	113 Eric Valent RC	.50	.15
❑	114 Roosevelt Brown RC	.50	.15
❑	115 Choo Freeman RC	.50	.15
❑	116 Juan Melo	.30	.09
❑	117 Jason Grilli	.30	.09
❑	118 Jared Sandberg	.30	.09
❑	119 Glenn Davis	.30	.09
❑	120 David Riske RC	.40	.12
❑	121 Jacque Jones	.30	.09
❑	122 Corey Lee	.30	.09
❑	123 Michael Barrett	.30	.09
❑	124 Lariel Gonzalez	.30	.09
❑	125 Mitch Meluskey	.30	.09
❑	126 Freddy Adrian Garcia	.30	.09
❑	127 Tony Torcato RC	.50	.15
❑	128 Jeff Liefer	.30	.09
❑	129 Ntema Ndungidi	.30	.09
❑	130 Andy Brown RC	.50	.15
❑	131 Ryan Mills RC	.50	.15
❑	132 Andy Abad RC	.40	.12
❑	133 Carlos Febles	.30	.09
❑	134 Jason Tyner RC	.50	.15
❑	135 Mark Osborne	.30	.09
❑	136 Phil Norton RC	.40	.12
❑	137 Nathan Haynes	.30	.09
❑	138 Roy Halladay	.30	.09
❑	139 Juan Encarnacion	.30	.09
❑	140 Brad Penny	.30	.09
❑	141 Grant Roberts	.30	.09
❑	142 Aramis Ramirez	.30	.09
❑	143 Cristian Guzman	.30	.09
❑	144 Mamon Tucker RC	.50	.15
❑	145 Ryan Bradley	.30	.09
❑	146 Brian Simmons	.30	.09
❑	147 Dan Reichert	.30	.09
❑	148 Russ Branyan	.30	.09
❑	149 Victor Valencia RC	.30	.09
❑	150 Scott Schoeneweis	.30	.09
❑	151 Sean Spencer RC	.40	.12
❑	152 Odalis Perez	.30	.09
❑	153 Joe Fontenot	.30	.09
❑	154 Milton Bradley	.30	1.30
❑	155 Josh McKinley RC	.50	.15
❑	156 Terrence Long	.30	.09
❑	157 Danny Klassen	.30	.09
❑	158 Paul Hoover RC	.50	.15
❑	159 Ron Belliard	.30	.09
❑	160 Armando Rios	.30	.09
❑	161 Ramon Hernandez	.30	.09
❑	162 Jason Conti	.30	.09
❑	163 Chad Hermansen	.30	.09
❑	164 Jason Standridge	.30	.09
❑	165 Jason Dellaero	.30	.09
❑	166 John Curtice	.30	.09
❑	167 Clayton Andrews RC	.50	.15
❑	168 Jeremy Giambi	.30	.09
❑	169 Alex Ramirez	.30	.09
❑	170 Gabe Molina RC	.40	.12
❑	171 M.Encarnacion RC	.40	.12
❑	172 Mike Zywica RC	.40	.12
❑	173 Chip Ambres RC	.50	.15
❑	174 Trot Nixon	.30	.09
❑	175 Pat Burrell RC	5.00	1.50
❑	176 Jeff Yoder	.30	.09
❑	177 Chris Jones RC	.50	.15
❑	178 Kevin Witt	.30	.09
❑	179 Keith Luuloa RC	.40	.12
❑	180 Billy Koch	.30	.09
❑	181 Damaso Marte RC	.40	.12
❑	182 Ryan Glynn RC	.40	.12
❑	183 Calvin Pickering	.30	.09
❑	184 Michael Cuddyer	.30	.09
❑	185 Nick Johnson RC	2.50	.75
❑	186 D.Mientkiewicz RC	1.50	.45
❑	187 Nate Cornejo RC	.75	.23
❑	188 Octavio Dotel	.30	.09
❑	189 Wes Helms	.30	.09
❑	190 Nelson Lara	.30	.09
❑	191 Chuck Abbott RC	.40	.12
❑	192 Tony Armas Jr.	.30	.09
❑	193 Gil Meche	.30	.09
❑	194 Ben Petrick	.30	.09
❑	195 Chris George RC	.75	.23
❑	196 Scott Hunter RC	.40	.12
❑	197 Ryan Brannan	.30	.09
❑	198 Amaury Garcia RC	.50	.15
❑	199 Chris Gissell	.30	.09
❑	200 Austin Kearns RC	8.00	2.40
❑	201 Alex Gonzalez	.30	.09
❑	202 Wade Miller	.30	.09
❑	203 Scott Williamson	.30	.09
❑	204 Chris Enochs	.30	.09
❑	205 Fernando Seguignol	.30	.09
❑	206 Marlon Anderson	.30	.09
❑	207 Todd Sears RC	.50	.15
❑	208 Nate Bump RC	.40	.12
❑	209 J.M. Gold RC	.50	.15
❑	210 Matt LeCroy	.30	.09
❑	211 Alex Hernandez	.30	.09
❑	212 Luis Rivera	.30	.09
❑	213 Troy Cameron	.30	.09
❑	214 Alex Escobar RC	.50	.15
❑	215 Jason LaRue	.30	.09
❑	216 Kyle Peterson	.30	.09
❑	217 Brent Butler	.30	.09
❑	218 Dernell Stenson	.30	.09
❑	219 Adrian Beltre	.30	.09
❑	220 Daryle Ward	.30	.09
❑	221 Jim Thome	.75	.23
❑	222 Cliff Floyd	.30	.09
❑	223 Rickey Henderson	1.25	.35
❑	224 Garret Anderson	.30	.09
❑	225 Ken Caminiti	.30	.09
❑	226 Bret Boone	.30	.09
❑	227 Jeromy Burnitz	.30	.09
❑	228 Steve Finley	.30	.09
❑	229 Miguel Tejada	.30	.09
❑	230 Greg Vaughn	.30	.09
❑	231 Jose Offerman	.30	.09
❑	232 Andy Ashby	.30	.09
❑	233 Albert Belle	.30	.09
❑	234 Fernando Tatis	.30	.09
❑	235 Todd Helton	.50	.15
❑	236 Sean Casey	.30	.09
❑	237 Brian Giles	.30	.09
❑	238 Andy Pettitte	.50	.15
❑	239 Fred McGriff	.50	.15
❑	240 Roberto Alomar	.75	.23
❑	241 Edgar Martinez	.50	.15
❑	242 Lee Stevens	.30	.09
❑	243 Shawn Green	.30	.09
❑	244 Ryan Klesko	.30	.09
❑	245 Sammy Sosa	1.25	.35
❑	246 Todd Hundley	.30	.09
❑	247 Shannon Stewart	.30	.09
❑	248 Randy Johnson	.75	.23
❑	249 Rondell White	.30	.09
❑	250 Mike Piazza	1.25	.35
❑	251 Craig Biggio	.50	.15
❑	252 David Wells	.30	.09
❑	253 Brian Jordan	.30	.09
❑	254 Edgar Renteria	.30	.09
❑	255 Bartolo Colon	.30	.09
❑	256 Frank Thomas	.75	.23
❑	257 Will Clark	.75	.23
❑	258 Dean Palmer	.30	.09
❑	259 Dmitri Young	.30	.09
❑	260 Scott Rolen	.50	.15
❑	261 Jeff Kent	.30	.09
❑	262 Dante Bichette	.30	.09

Card	Nm-Mt	Ex-Mt
❑ 263 Nomar Garciaparra	1.50	.45
❑ 264 Tony Gwynn	1.00	.30
❑ 265 Alex Rodriguez	1.50	.45
❑ 266 Jose Canseco	.75	.23
❑ 267 Jason Giambi	.75	.23
❑ 268 Jeff Bagwell	.50	.15
❑ 269 Carlos Delgado	.30	.09
❑ 270 Tom Glavine	.75	.23
❑ 271 Eric Davis	.30	.09
❑ 272 Edgardo Alfonzo	.30	.09
❑ 273 Tim Salmon	.50	.15
❑ 274 Johnny Damon	.30	.09
❑ 275 Rafael Palmeiro	.50	.15
❑ 276 Denny Neagle	.30	.09
❑ 277 Neifi Perez	.30	.09
❑ 278 Roger Clemens	1.50	.45
❑ 279 Brant Brown	.30	.09
❑ 280 Kevin Brown	.50	.15
❑ 281 Jay Bell	.30	.09
❑ 282 Jay Buhner	.30	.09
❑ 283 Matt Lawton	.30	.09
❑ 284 Robin Ventura	.30	.09
❑ 285 Juan Gonzalez	.75	.23
❑ 286 Mo Vaughn	.30	.09
❑ 287 Kevin Millwood	.30	.09
❑ 288 Tino Martinez	.50	.15
❑ 289 Justin Thompson	.30	.09
❑ 290 Derek Jeter	2.00	.60
❑ 291 Ben Davis	.30	.09
❑ 292 Mike Lowell	.30	.09
❑ 293 Calvin Murray	.30	.09
❑ 294 Micah Bowie RC	.40	.12
❑ 295 Lance Berkman	.30	.09
❑ 296 Jason Marquis	.30	.09
❑ 297 Chad Green	.30	.09
❑ 298 Dee Brown	.30	.09
❑ 299 Jerry Hairston Jr.	.30	.09
❑ 300 Gabe Kapler	.30	.09
❑ 301 Brent Stentz RC	.50	.15
❑ 302 Scott Mullen RC	.40	.12
❑ 303 Brandon Reed	.30	.09
❑ 304 Shea Hillenbrand RC	2.50	.75
❑ 305 J.D. Closser RC	.50	.15
❑ 306 Gary Matthews Jr.	.30	.09
❑ 307 Toby Hall RC	.75	.23
❑ 308 Jason Phillips RC	.40	.12
❑ 309 Jose Macias RC	.40	.12
❑ 310 Jung Bong RC	.50	.15
❑ 311 Ramon Soler RC	.50	.15
❑ 312 Kelly Dransfeldt RC	.40	.12
❑ 313 Carl. E. Hernandez RC	.50	.15
❑ 314 Kevin Haverbusch	.30	.09
❑ 315 Aaron Myette RC	.50	.15
❑ 316 Chad Harville RC	.40	.12
❑ 317 Kyle Farnsworth RC	1.25	.35
❑ 318 Gookie Dawkins RC	.50	.15
❑ 319 Willie Martinez	.30	.09
❑ 320 Carlos Lee	.30	.09
❑ 321 Carlos Pena RC	1.25	.35
❑ 322 Peter Bergeron RC	.50	.15
❑ 323 A.J. Burnett RC	.75	.23
❑ 324 Bucky Jacobsen RC	.50	.15
❑ 325 Mo Bruce RC	.40	.12
❑ 326 Reggie Taylor	.30	.09
❑ 327 Jackie Rexrode	.30	.09
❑ 328 Alvin Morrow RC	.40	.12
❑ 329 Carlos Beltran	.30	.09
❑ 330 Eric Chavez	.30	.09
❑ 331 John Patterson	.30	.09
❑ 332 Jayson Werth	.30	.09
❑ 333 Richie Sexson	.30	.09
❑ 334 Randy Wolf	.30	.09
❑ 335 Eli Marrero	.30	.09
❑ 336 Paul LoDuca	.30	.09
❑ 337 J.D Smart	.30	.09
❑ 338 Ryan Minor	.30	.09
❑ 339 Kris Benson	.30	.09
❑ 340 George Lombard	.30	.09
❑ 341 Troy Glaus	.50	.15
❑ 342 Eddie Yarnall	.30	.09
❑ 343 Kip Wells RC	.75	.23
❑ 344 C.C. Sabathia RC	1.25	.35
❑ 345 Sean Burroughs RC	4.00	1.20
❑ 346 Felipe Lopez RC	.50	.15
❑ 347 Ryan Rupe RC	.50	.15
❑ 348 Orber Moreno RC	.40	.12
❑ 349 Rafael Roque RC	.40	.12
❑ 350 Alfonso Soriano RC	12.00	3.60
❑ 351 Pablo Ozuna	.30	.09
❑ 352 Corey Patterson RC	5.00	1.50
❑ 353 Braden Looper	.30	.09
❑ 354 Robbie Bell	.30	.09
❑ 355 Mark Mulder RC	5.00	1.50
❑ 356 Angel Pena	.30	.09
❑ 357 Kevin McGlinchy	.30	.09
❑ 358 M.Restovich RC	1.50	.45
❑ 359 Eric DuBose	.30	.09
❑ 360 Geoff Jenkins	.30	.09
❑ 361 Mark Harriger RC	.40	.12
❑ 362 Junior Herndon RC	.50	.15
❑ 363 Tim Raines Jr. RC	.50	.15
❑ 364 Rafael Furcal RC	2.50	.75
❑ 365 Marcus Giles RC	3.00	.90
❑ 366 Ted Lilly	.30	.09
❑ 367 Jorge Toca RC	.50	.15
❑ 368 David Kelton RC	1.25	.35
❑ 369 Adam Dunn RC	8.00	2.40
❑ 370 Guillermo Mota RC	.40	.12
❑ 371 Brett Laxton RC	.40	.12
❑ 372 Travis Harper RC	.50	.15
❑ 373 Tom Davey RC	.40	.12
❑ 374 Darren Blakely RC	.40	.12
❑ 375 Tim Hudson RC	5.00	1.50
❑ 376 Jason Romano	.30	.09
❑ 377 Dan Reichert	.30	.09
❑ 378 Julio Lugo RC	.50	.15
❑ 379 Jose Garcia RC	.40	.12
❑ 380 Erubiel Durazo RC	2.00	.60
❑ 381 Jose Jimenez	.30	.09
❑ 382 Chris Fussell	.30	.09
❑ 383 Steve Lomasney	.30	.09
❑ 384 Juan Pena RC	.50	.15
❑ 385 Allen Levrault RC	.50	.15
❑ 386 Juan Rivera RC	1.50	.45
❑ 387 Steve Colyer RC	.50	.15
❑ 388 Joe Nathan RC	.40	.12
❑ 389 Ron Walker RC	.40	.12
❑ 390 Nick Bierbrodt	.30	.09
❑ 391 Luke Prokopec RC	.50	.15
❑ 392 Dave Roberts RC	.75	.23
❑ 393 Mike Darr	.30	.09
❑ 394 Abraham Nunez RC	.50	.15
❑ 395 G.Chiaramonte RC	.40	.12
❑ 396 J.Van Buren RC	.50	.15
❑ 397 Mike Kusiewicz	.30	.09
❑ 398 Matt Wise RC	.40	.12
❑ 399 Joe McEwing RC	.50	.15
❑ 400 Matt Holliday RC	.50	.15
❑ 401 Willi Mo Pena RC	2.50	.75
❑ 402 Ruben Quevedo RC	.50	.15
❑ 403 Rob Ryan RC	.40	.12
❑ 404 Freddy Garcia RC	2.00	.60
❑ 405 Kevin Eberwein RC	.50	.15
❑ 406 Jesus Colome RC	.40	.12
❑ 407 Chris Singleton	.30	.09
❑ 408 Bubba Crosby RC	.75	.23
❑ 409 Jesus Cordero RC	.50	.15
❑ 410 Donny Leon	.30	.09
❑ 411 G.Tomlinson RC	.50	.15
❑ 412 Jeff Winchester RC	.50	.15
❑ 413 Adam Piatt RC	.50	.15
❑ 414 Robert Stratton	.30	.09
❑ 415 T.J. Tucker	.30	.09
❑ 416 Ryan Langerhans RC	.50	.15
❑ 417 A.Shumaker RC	.40	.12
❑ 418 Matt Miller RC	.40	.12
❑ 419 Doug Clark RC	.40	.12
❑ 420 Kory DeHaan RC	.40	.12
❑ 421 David Eckstein RC	1.25	.35
❑ 422 Brian Cooper RC	.40	.12
❑ 423 Brady Clark RC	.40	.12
❑ 424 Chris Magruder RC	.50	.15
❑ 425 Bobby Seay RC	.50	.15
❑ 426 Aubrey Huff RC	3.00	.90
❑ 427 Mike Jerzembeck	.30	.09
❑ 428 Matt Blank RC	.50	.15
❑ 429 Benny Agbayani RC	.50	.15
❑ 430 Kevin Beirne RC	.50	.15
❑ 431 Josh Hamilton RC	2.00	.60
❑ 432 Josh Girdley RC	.50	.15
❑ 433 Kyle Snyder RC	.50	.15
❑ 434 Mike Paradis RC	.50	.15
❑ 435 Jason Jennings RC	.75	.23
❑ 436 David Walling RC	.50	.15
❑ 437 Omar Ortiz RC	.50	.15
❑ 438 Jay Gehrke RC	.50	.15
❑ 439 Casey Burns RC	.50	.15
❑ 440 Carl Crawford RC	2.50	.75

2000 Bowman

	Nm-Mt	Ex-Mt
COMPLETE SET (440)	80.00	24.00
❑ 1 Vladimir Guerrero	.75	.23
❑ 2 Chipper Jones	.75	.23
❑ 3 Todd Walker	.30	.09
❑ 4 Barry Larkin	.75	.23
❑ 5 Bernie Williams	.50	.15
❑ 6 Todd Helton	.50	.15
❑ 7 Jermaine Dye	.30	.09
❑ 8 Brian Giles	.30	.09
❑ 9 Freddy Garcia	.30	.09
❑ 10 Greg Vaughn	.30	.09
❑ 11 Alex Gonzalez	.30	.09
❑ 12 Luis Gonzalez	.30	.09
❑ 13 Ron Belliard	.30	.09
❑ 14 Ben Grieve	.30	.09
❑ 15 Carlos Delgado	.30	.09
❑ 16 Brian Jordan	.30	.09
❑ 17 Fernando Tatis	.30	.09
❑ 18 Ryan Rupe	.30	.09
❑ 19 Miguel Tejada	.30	.09
❑ 20 Mark Grace	.75	.23
❑ 21 Kenny Lofton	.30	.09
❑ 22 Eric Karros	.30	.09
❑ 23 Cliff Floyd	.30	.09
❑ 24 John Halama	.30	.09
❑ 25 Cristian Guzman	.30	.09
❑ 26 Scott Williamson	.30	.09
❑ 27 Mike Lieberthal	.30	.09
❑ 28 Tim Hudson	.50	.15
❑ 29 Warren Morris	.30	.09
❑ 30 Pedro Martinez	.75	.23
❑ 31 John Smoltz	.50	.15
❑ 32 Ray Durham	.30	.09
❑ 33 Chad Allen	.30	.09
❑ 34 Tony Clark	.30	.09
❑ 35 Tino Martinez	.50	.15
❑ 36 J.T. Snow	.30	.09
❑ 37 Kevin Brown	.30	.09
❑ 38 Bartolo Colon	.30	.09
❑ 39 Rey Ordonez	.30	.09
❑ 40 Jeff Bagwell	.50	.15
❑ 41 Ivan Rodriguez	.75	.23
❑ 42 Eric Chavez	.30	.09
❑ 43 Eric Milton	.30	.09
❑ 44 Jose Canseco	.75	.23
❑ 45 Shawn Green	.30	.09
❑ 46 Rich Aurilia	.30	.09
❑ 47 Roberto Alomar	.75	.23
❑ 48 Brian Daubach	.30	.09
❑ 49 Magglio Ordonez	.30	.09
❑ 50 Derek Jeter	2.00	.60
❑ 51 Kris Benson	.30	.09
❑ 52 Albert Belle	.30	.09
❑ 53 Rondell White	.30	.09
❑ 54 Justin Thompson	.30	.09
❑ 55 Nomar Garciaparra	1.50	.45
❑ 56 Chuck Finley	.30	.09

	No.	Player		
❑	57	Omar Vizquel	.30	.09
❑	58	Luis Castillo	.30	.09
❑	59	Richard Hidalgo	.30	.09
❑	60	Barry Bonds	2.00	.60
❑	61	Craig Biggio	.50	.15
❑	62	Doug Glanville	.30	.09
❑	63	Gabe Kapler	.30	.09
❑	64	Johnny Damon	.30	.09
❑	65	Pokey Reese	.30	.09
❑	66	Andy Pettitte	.50	.15
❑	67	B.J. Surhoff	.30	.09
❑	68	Richie Sexson	.30	.09
❑	69	Javy Lopez	.30	.09
❑	70	Raul Mondesi	.30	.09
❑	71	Darin Erstad	.30	.09
❑	72	Kevin Millwood	.30	.09
❑	73	Ricky Ledee	.30	.09
❑	74	John Olerud	.30	.09
❑	75	Sean Casey	.30	.09
❑	76	Carlos Febles	.30	.09
❑	77	Paul O'Neill	.50	.15
❑	78	Bob Abreu	.30	.09
❑	79	Neifi Perez	.30	.09
❑	80	Tony Gwynn	1.00	.30
❑	81	Russ Ortiz	.30	.09
❑	82	Matt Williams	.30	.09
❑	83	Chris Carpenter	.30	.09
❑	84	Roger Cedeno	.30	.09
❑	85	Tim Salmon	.50	.15
❑	86	Billy Koch	.30	.09
❑	87	Jeromy Burnitz	.30	.09
❑	88	Edgardo Alfonzo	.30	.09
❑	89	Jay Bell	.30	.09
❑	90	Manny Ramirez	.30	.09
❑	91	Frank Thomas	.75	.23
❑	92	Mike Mussina	.75	.23
❑	93	J.D. Drew	.30	.09
❑	94	Adrian Beltre	.30	.09
❑	95	Alex Rodriguez	1.50	.45
❑	96	Larry Walker	.50	.15
❑	97	Juan Encarnacion	.30	.09
❑	98	Mike Sweeney	.30	.09
❑	99	Rusty Greer	.30	.09
❑	100	Randy Johnson	.75	.23
❑	101	Jose Vidro	.30	.09
❑	102	Preston Wilson	.30	.09
❑	103	Greg Maddux	1.50	.45
❑	104	Jason Giambi	.75	.23
❑	105	Cal Ripken	2.50	.75
❑	106	Carlos Beltran	.30	.09
❑	107	Vinny Castilla	.30	.09
❑	108	Mariano Rivera	.50	.15
❑	109	Mo Vaughn	.30	.09
❑	110	Rafael Palmeiro	.50	.15
❑	111	Shannon Stewart	.30	.09
❑	112	Mike Hampton	.30	.09
❑	113	Joe Nathan	.30	.09
❑	114	Ben Davis	.30	.09
❑	115	Andruw Jones	.50	.15
❑	116	Robin Ventura	.30	.09
❑	117	Damion Easley	.30	.09
❑	118	Jeff Cirillo	.30	.09
❑	119	Kerry Wood	.75	.23
❑	120	Scott Rolen	.50	.15
❑	121	Sammy Sosa	1.25	.35
❑	122	Ken Griffey Jr.	1.25	.35
❑	123	Shane Reynolds	.30	.09
❑	124	Troy Glaus	.50	.15
❑	125	Tom Glavine	.75	.23
❑	126	Michael Barrett	.30	.09
❑	127	Al Leiter	.30	.09
❑	128	Jason Kendall	.30	.09
❑	129	Roger Clemens	1.50	.45
❑	130	Juan Gonzalez	.75	.23
❑	131	Corey Koskie	.30	.09
❑	132	Curt Schilling	.50	.15
❑	133	Mike Piazza	1.25	.35
❑	134	Gary Sheffield	.30	.09
❑	135	Jim Thome	.75	.23
❑	136	Orlando Hernandez	.30	.09
❑	137	Ray Lankford	.30	.09
❑	138	Geoff Jenkins	.30	.09
❑	139	Jose Lima	.30	.09
❑	140	Mark McGwire	2.00	.60
❑	141	Adam Piatt	.30	.09
❑	142	Pat Manning RC	.50	.15
❑	143	Marcos Castillo RC	.50	.15
❑	144	Lesli Brea RC	.50	.15
❑	145	Humberto Cota RC	.50	.15
❑	146	Ben Petrick	.30	.09
❑	147	Kip Wells	.30	.09
❑	148	Wily Pena	.30	.09
❑	149	Chris Wakeland RC	.30	.09
❑	150	Brad Baker RC	.50	.15
❑	151	Robbie Morrison RC	.30	.09
❑	152	Reggie Taylor	.30	.09
❑	153	Matt Ginter RC	.50	.15
❑	154	Peter Bergeron	.30	.09
❑	155	Roosevelt Brown	.30	.09
❑	156	Matt Cepicky RC	.50	.15
❑	157	Ramon Castro	.30	.09
❑	158	Brad Baisley RC	.50	.15
❑	159	Jeff Goldbach RC	.50	.15
❑	160	Mitch Meluskey	.30	.09
❑	161	Chad Harville	.30	.09
❑	162	Brian Cooper	.30	.09
❑	163	Marcus Giles	.30	.09
❑	164	Jim Morris	2.00	.60
❑	165	Geoff Goetz	.30	.09
❑	166	Bobby Bradley RC	.50	.15
❑	167	Rob Bell	.30	.09
❑	168	Joe Crede	.30	.09
❑	169	Michael Restovich	.30	.09
❑	170	Quincy Foster RC	.30	.09
❑	171	Enrique Cruz RC	.50	.15
❑	172	Mark Quinn	.30	.09
❑	173	Nick Johnson	.30	.09
❑	174	Jeff Liefer	.30	.09
❑	175	Kevin Mench RC	.75	.23
❑	176	Steve Lomasney	.30	.09
❑	177	Jayson Werth	.30	.09
❑	178	Tim Drew	.30	.09
❑	179	Chip Ambres	.30	.09
❑	180	Ryan Anderson	.30	.09
❑	181	Matt Blank	.30	.09
❑	182	G.Chiaramonte	.30	.09
❑	183	Corey Myers RC	.50	.15
❑	184	Jeff Yoder	.30	.09
❑	185	Craig Dingman RC	.30	.09
❑	186	Jon Hamilton RC	.30	.09
❑	187	Toby Hall	.30	.09
❑	188	Russell Branyan	.30	.09
❑	189	Brian Falkenborg RC	.50	.15
❑	190	Aaron Harang RC	.50	.15
❑	191	Juan Pena	.30	.09
❑	192	Travis Thompson RC	.30	.09
❑	193	Alfonso Soriano	1.25	.35
❑	194	Alejandro Diaz RC	.50	.15
❑	195	Carlos Pena	.30	.09
❑	196	Kevin Nicholson	.30	.09
❑	197	Mo Bruce	.30	.09
❑	198	C.C. Sabathia	.30	.09
❑	199	Carl Crawford	.30	.09
❑	200	Rafael Furcal	.30	.09
❑	201	Andrew Beinbrink RC	.30	.09
❑	202	Jimmy Osting	.30	.09
❑	203	Aaron McNeal RC	.50	.15
❑	204	Brett Laxton	.30	.09
❑	205	Chris George	.30	.09
❑	206	Felipe Lopez	.30	.09
❑	207	Ben Sheets RC	1.50	.45
❑	208	Mike Meyers RC	.50	.15
❑	209	Jason Conti	.30	.09
❑	210	Milton Bradley	.30	.09
❑	211	Chris Mears RC	.50	.15
❑	212	Carlos Hernandez RC	.75	.23
❑	213	Jason Romano	.30	.09
❑	214	Geofrey Tomlinson	.30	.09
❑	215	Jimmy Rollins	.30	.09
❑	216	Pablo Ozuna	.30	.09
❑	217	Steve Cox	.30	.09
❑	218	Terrence Long	.30	.09
❑	219	Jeff DaVanon RC	.50	.15
❑	220	Rick Ankiel	.30	.09
❑	221	Jason Standridge	.30	.09
❑	222	Tony Armas Jr.	.30	.09
❑	223	Jason Tyner	.30	.09
❑	224	Ramon Ortiz	.30	.09
❑	225	Daryle Ward	.30	.09
❑	226	Enger Veras RC	.50	.15
❑	227	Chris Jones	.30	.09
❑	228	Eric Cammack RC	.30	.09
❑	229	Ruben Mateo	.30	.09
❑	230	Ken Harvey RC	1.50	.45
❑	231	Jake Westbrook	.30	.09
❑	232	Rob Purvis RC	.30	.09
❑	233	Choo Freeman	.30	.09
❑	234	Aramis Ramirez	.30	.09
❑	235	A.J. Burnett	.30	.09
❑	236	Kevin Barker	.30	.09
❑	237	Chance Caple RC	.50	.15
❑	238	Jarrod Washburn	.30	.09
❑	239	Lance Berkman	.30	.09
❑	240	Michael Wenner RC	.30	.09
❑	241	Alex Sanchez	.30	.09
❑	242	Pat Daneker	.30	.09
❑	243	Grant Roberts	.30	.09
❑	244	Mark Ellis RC	.75	.23
❑	245	Donny Leon	.30	.09
❑	246	David Eckstein	.30	.09
❑	247	Dicky Gonzalez RC	.50	.15
❑	248	John Patterson	.30	.09
❑	249	Chad Green	.30	.09
❑	250	Scot Shields RC	.30	.09
❑	251	Troy Cameron	.30	.09
❑	252	Jose Molina	.30	.09
❑	253	Rob Pugmire RC	.50	.15
❑	254	Rick Elder	.30	.09
❑	255	Sean Burroughs	.50	.15
❑	256	Josh Kalinowski RC	.30	.09
❑	257	Matt LeCroy	.30	.09
❑	258	Alex Graman RC	.30	.09
❑	259	Tomo Ohka RC	.50	.15
❑	260	Brady Clark	.30	.09
❑	261	Rico Washington RC	.50	.15
❑	262	Gary Matthews Jr.	.30	.09
❑	263	Matt Wise	.30	.09
❑	264	Keith Reed RC	.50	.15
❑	265	Santiago Ramirez RC	.30	.09
❑	266	Ben Broussard RC	.50	.15
❑	267	Ryan Langerhans	.30	.09
❑	268	Juan Rivera	.30	.09
❑	269	Shawn Gallagher	.30	.09
❑	270	Jorge Toca	.30	.09
❑	271	Brad Lidge	.30	.09
❑	272	Leoncio Estrella RC	.30	.09
❑	273	Ruben Quevedo	.30	.09
❑	274	Jack Cust	.30	.09
❑	275	T.J. Tucker	.30	.09
❑	276	Mike Colangelo	.30	.09
❑	277	Brian Schneider	.30	.09
❑	278	Calvin Murray	.30	.09
❑	279	Josh Girdley	.30	.09
❑	280	Mike Paradis	.30	.09
❑	281	Chad Hermansen	.30	.09
❑	282	Ty Howington RC	.50	.15
❑	283	Aaron Myette	.30	.09
❑	284	D'Angelo Jimenez	.30	.09
❑	285	Dernell Stenson	.30	.09
❑	286	Jerry Hairston Jr.	.30	.09
❑	287	Gary Majewski RC	.50	.15
❑	288	Derrin Ebert	.30	.09
❑	289	Steve Fish RC	.30	.09
❑	290	Carlos E. Hernandez	.30	.09
❑	291	Allen Levrault	.30	.09
❑	292	Sean McNally RC	.30	.09
❑	293	Randey Dorame RC	.50	.15
❑	294	Wes Anderson RC	.50	.15
❑	295	B.J. Ryan	.30	.09
❑	296	Alan Webb RC	.50	.15
❑	297	Brandon Inge RC	.50	.15
❑	298	David Walling	.30	.09
❑	299	Sun Woo Kim RC	.50	.15
❑	300	Pat Burrell	.50	.15
❑	301	Rick Guttormson RC	.30	.09
❑	302	Gil Meche	.30	.09
❑	303	Carlos Zambrano RC	2.50	.75
❑	304	Eric Byrnes UER RC Bo Porter pictured	1.50	.45
❑	305	Robb Quinlan RC	.50	.15
❑	306	Jackie Rexrode	.30	.09
❑	307	Nate Bump	.30	.09
❑	308	Sean DePaula RC	.30	.09
❑	309	Matt Riley	.30	.09
❑	310	Ryan Minor	.30	.09
❑	311	J.J. Davis	.30	.09
❑	312	Randy Wolf	.30	.09
❑	313	Jason Jennings	.30	.09

	Card	Nm-Mt	Ex-Mt
❑	314 Scott Seabol RC	.30	.09
❑	315 Doug Davis	.30	.09
❑	316 Todd Moser RC	.30	.09
❑	317 Rob Ryan	.30	.09
❑	318 Bubba Crosby	.30	.09
❑	319 Ryan Knox RC	.75	.23
❑	320 Mario Encarnacion	.30	.09
❑	321 F.Rodriguez RC	2.50	.75
❑	322 Michael Cuddyer	.30	.09
❑	323 Ed Yarnall	.30	.09
❑	324 Cesar Saba RC	.50	.15
❑	325 Gookie Dawkins	.30	.09
❑	326 Alex Escobar	.30	.09
❑	327 Julio Zuleta RC	.50	.15
❑	328 Josh Hamilton	.30	.09
❑	329 Nick Neugebauer RC	.50	.15
❑	330 Matt Belisle	.30	.09
❑	331 Kurt Ainsworth RC	.75	.23
❑	332 Tim Raines Jr.	.30	.09
❑	333 Eric Munson	.30	.09
❑	334 Donzell McDonald	.30	.09
❑	335 Larry Bigbie RC	.75	.23
❑	336 Matt Watson RC	.50	.15
❑	337 Aubrey Huff	.30	.09
❑	338 Julio Ramirez	.30	.09
❑	339 Jason Grabowski RC	.50	.15
❑	340 Jon Garland	.30	.09
❑	341 Austin Kearns	.75	.23
❑	342 Josh Pressley RC	.50	.15
❑	343 Miguel Olivo RC	.50	.15
❑	344 Julio Lugo	.30	.09
❑	345 Roberto Vaz	.30	.09
❑	346 Ramon Soler	.30	.09
❑	347 Brandon Phillips RC	1.50	.45
❑	348 Vince Faison RC	.50	.15
❑	349 Mike Venafro	.30	.09
❑	350 Rick Asadoorian RC	.50	.15
❑	351 B.J. Garbe RC	.50	.15
❑	352 Dan Reichert	.30	.09
❑	353 Jason Stumm RC	.50	.15
❑	354 Ruben Salazar RC	.50	.15
❑	355 Francisco Cordero	.30	.09
❑	356 Juan Guzman RC	.50	.15
❑	357 Mike Bacsik RC	.30	.09
❑	358 Jared Sandberg	.30	.09
❑	359 Rod Barajas	.30	.09
❑	360 Junior Brignac RC	.50	.15
❑	361 J.M. Gold	.30	.09
❑	362 Octavio Dotel	.30	.09
❑	363 David Kelton	.30	.09
❑	364 Scott Morgan	.30	.09
❑	365 Wascar Serrano RC	.50	.15
❑	366 Wilton Veras	.30	.09
❑	367 Eugene Kingsale	.30	.09
❑	368 Ted Lilly	.30	.09
❑	369 George Lombard	.30	.09
❑	370 Chris Haas	.30	.09
❑	371 Wilton Pena RC	.30	.09
❑	372 Vernon Wells	.30	.09
❑	373 Jason Royer RC	.50	.15
❑	374 Jeff Heaverlo RC	.50	.15
❑	375 Calvin Pickering	.30	.09
❑	376 Mike Lamb RC	.50	.15
❑	377 Kyle Snyder	.30	.09
❑	378 Javier Cardona RC	.30	.09
❑	379 Aaron Rowand RC	.50	.15
❑	380 Dee Brown	.30	.09
❑	381 Brett Myers RC	3.00	.90
❑	382 Abraham Nunez	.30	.09
❑	383 Eric Valent	.30	.09
❑	384 Jody Gerut RC	3.00	.90
❑	385 Adam Dunn	.75	.23
❑	386 Jay Gehrke	.30	.09
❑	387 Omar Ortiz	.30	.09
❑	388 Darnell McDonald	.30	.09
❑	389 Tony Schrager RC	.30	.09
❑	390 J.D. Closser	.30	.09
❑	391 Ben Christensen RC	.50	.15
❑	392 Adam Kennedy	.30	.09
❑	393 Nick Green RC	.30	.09
❑	394 Ramon Hernandez	.30	.09
❑	395 Roy Oswalt RC	5.00	1.50
❑	396 Andy Tracy RC	.30	.09
❑	397 Eric Gagne	.75	.23
❑	398 Michael Tejera RC	.30	.09
❑	399 Adam Everett	.30	.09
❑	400 Corey Patterson	.50	.15
❑	401 Gary Knotts RC	.30	.09
❑	402 Ryan Christianson RC	.50	.15
❑	403 Eric Ireland RC	.30	.09
❑	404 Andrew Good RC	.50	.15
❑	405 Brad Penny	.30	.09
❑	406 Jason LaRue	.30	.09
❑	407 Kit Pellow	.30	.09
❑	408 Kevin Beirne	.30	.09
❑	409 Kelly Dransfeldt	.30	.09
❑	410 Jason Grilli	.30	.09
❑	411 Scott Downs RC	.30	.09
❑	412 Jesus Colome	.30	.09
❑	413 John Sneed RC	.30	.09
❑	414 Tony McKnight	.30	.09
❑	415 Luis Rivera	.30	.09
❑	416 Adam Eaton	.30	.09
❑	417 Mike MacDougal RC	.75	.23
❑	418 Mike Nannini	.30	.09
❑	419 Barry Zito RC	6.00	1.80
❑	420 DeWayne Wise	.30	.09
❑	421 Jason Dellaero	.30	.09
❑	422 Chad Moeller	.30	.09
❑	423 Jason Marquis	.30	.09
❑	424 Tim Redding RC	1.25	.35
❑	425 Mark Mulder	.50	.15
❑	426 Josh Paul	.30	.09
❑	427 Chris Enochs	.30	.09
❑	428 W.Rodriguez RC	.50	.15
❑	429 Kevin Witt	.30	.09
❑	430 Scott Sobkowiak RC	.30	.09
❑	431 McKay Christensen	.30	.09
❑	432 Jung Bong	.30	.09
❑	433 Keith Evans RC	.30	.09
❑	434 Garry Maddox Jr. RC	.30	.09
❑	435 Ramon Santiago RC	.50	.15
❑	436 Alex Cora	.30	.09
❑	437 Carlos Lee	.30	.09
❑	438 Jason Repko RC	.50	.15
❑	439 Matt Burch	.30	.09
❑	440 Shawn Sonnier RC	.30	.09

2000 Bowman Draft Picks

		Nm-Mt	Ex-Mt
	COMP.FACT.SET (111)	40.00	12.00
	COMPLETE SET (110)	30.00	9.00
❑	1 Pat Burrell	.50	.15
❑	2 Rafael Furcal	.30	.09
❑	3 Grant Roberts	.30	.09
❑	4 Barry Zito	2.00	.60
❑	5 Julio Zuleta	.30	.09
❑	6 Mark Mulder	.50	.15
❑	7 Rob Bell	.30	.09
❑	8 Adam Piatt	.30	.09
❑	9 Mike Lamb	.30	.09
❑	10 Pablo Ozuna	.30	.09
❑	11 Jason Tyner	.30	.09
❑	12 Jason Marquis	.30	.09
❑	13 Eric Munson	.30	.09
❑	14 Seth Etherton	.30	.09
❑	15 Milton Bradley	.30	.09
❑	16 Nick Green	.30	.09
❑	17 Chin-Feng Chen RC	1.00	.30
❑	18 Matt Boone RC	.40	.12
❑	19 Kevin Gregg RC	.40	.12
❑	20 Eddy Garabito RC	.40	.12
❑	21 Aaron Capista RC	.40	.12
❑	22 Esteban German RC	.40	.12
❑	23 Derek Thompson RC	.40	.12
❑	24 Phil Merrell RC	.30	.09
❑	25 Brian O'Connor RC	.30	.09
❑	26 Yamid Haad	.30	.09
❑	27 Hector Mercado RC	.30	.09
❑	28 Jason Woolf RC	.30	.09
❑	29 Eddy Furniss RC	.30	.09
❑	30 Cha Sueng Baek RC	.40	.12
❑	31 Colby Lewis RC	.50	.15
❑	32 Pasqual Coco RC	.30	.09
❑	33 Jorge Cantu RC	.40	.12
❑	34 Erasmo Ramirez RC	.30	.09
❑	35 Bobby Kielty RC	.50	.15
❑	36 Joaquin Benoit RC	.40	.12
❑	37 Brian Esposito RC	.40	.12
❑	38 Michael Wenner	.30	.09
❑	39 Juan Rincon RC	.40	.12
❑	40 Yorvit Torrealba RC	.40	.12
❑	41 Chad Durham RC	.40	.12
❑	42 Jim Mann RC	.30	.09
❑	43 Shane Loux RC	.40	.12
❑	44 Luis Rivas	.30	.09
❑	45 Ken Chenard RC	.40	.12
❑	46 Mike Lockwood RC	.30	.09
❑	47 Yovanny Lara RC	.30	.09
❑	48 Bubba Carpenter RC	.30	.09
❑	49 Ryan Dittfurth RC	.40	.12
❑	50 John Stephens RC	.40	.12
❑	51 Pedro Feliz RC	.40	.12
❑	52 Kenny Kelly RC	.40	.12
❑	53 Neil Jenkins RC	.40	.12
❑	54 Mike Glendenning RC	.30	.09
❑	55 Bo Porter	.30	.09
❑	56 Eric Byrnes	1.00	.30
❑	57 Tony Alvarez RC	.40	.12
❑	58 Kazuhiro Sasaki RC	1.00	.30
❑	59 Chad Durbin RC	.30	.09
❑	60 Mike Bynum RC	.40	.12
❑	61 Travis Wilson RC	.30	.09
❑	62 Jose Leon RC	.30	.09
❑	63 Ryan Vogelsong RC	.40	.12
❑	64 Geraldo Guzman RC	.30	.09
❑	65 Craig Anderson RC	.40	.12
❑	66 Carlos Silva RC	.40	.12
❑	67 Brad Thomas RC	.30	.09
❑	68 Chin-Hui Tsao RC	1.50	.45
❑	69 Mark Buehrle RC	1.25	.35
❑	70 Juan Salas RC	.40	.12
❑	71 Denny Abreu RC	.40	.12
❑	72 Keith McDonald RC	.30	.09
❑	73 Chris Richard RC	.40	.12
❑	74 Tomas De la Rosa RC	.30	.09
❑	75 Vicente Padilla RC	.75	.23
❑	76 Justin Brunette RC	.30	.09
❑	77 Scott Linebrink RC	.30	.09
❑	78 Jeff Sparks RC	.30	.09
❑	79 Tike Redman RC	.40	.12
❑	80 John Lackey RC	.50	.15
❑	81 Joe Strong RC	.30	.09
❑	82 Brian Tollberg RC	.30	.09
❑	83 Steve Sisco RC	.30	.09
❑	84 Chris Clapinski RC	.30	.09
❑	85 Augie Ojeda RC	.30	.09
❑	86 Adrian Gonzalez RC	1.50	.45
❑	87 Mike Stodolka RC	.40	.12
❑	88 Adam Johnson RC	.40	.12
❑	89 Matt Wheatland RC	.30	.09
❑	90 Corey Smith RC	.50	.15
❑	91 Rocco Baldelli RC	10.00	3.00
❑	92 Keith Bucktrot RC	.40	.12
❑	93 Adam Wainwright RC	1.25	.35
❑	94 Blaine Boyer RC	.40	.12
❑	95 Aaron Herr RC	.40	.12
❑	96 Scott Thorman RC	.50	.15
❑	97 Bryan Digby RC	.40	.12
❑	98 Josh Shortslef RC	.40	.12
❑	99 Sean Smith RC	.40	.12
❑	100 Alex Cruz RC	.40	.12
❑	101 Marc Love RC	.40	.12
❑	102 Kevin Lee RC	.40	.12
❑	103 Victor Ramos RC	.40	.12
❑	104 Jason Kaanoi RC	.30	.09
❑	105 Luis Escobar RC	.40	.12

❑ 106 Tripper Johnson RC	.50	.15
❑ 107 Phil Dumatrait RC	.40	.12
❑ 108 Bryan Edwards RC	.40	.12
❑ 109 Grady Sizemore RC	8.00	2.40
❑ 110 Thomas Mitchell RC	.40	.12

2001 Bowman

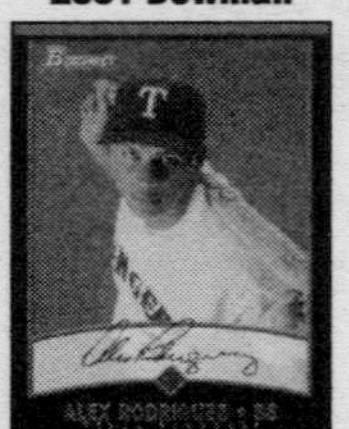

	Nm-Mt	Ex-Mt
COMPLETE SET (440)	100.00	30.00
COMMON CARD (1-440)	.30	.09
❑ 1 Jason Giambi	.75	.23
❑ 2 Rafael Furcal	.30	.09
❑ 3 Rick Ankiel	.30	.09
❑ 4 Freddy Garcia	.30	.09
❑ 5 Magglio Ordonez	.30	.09
❑ 6 Bernie Williams	.50	.15
❑ 7 Kenny Lofton	.30	.09
❑ 8 Al Leiter	.30	.09
❑ 9 Albert Belle	.30	.09
❑ 10 Craig Biggio	.50	.15
❑ 11 Mark Mulder	.30	.09
❑ 12 Carlos Delgado	.30	.09
❑ 13 Darin Erstad	.30	.09
❑ 14 Richie Sexson	.30	.09
❑ 15 Randy Johnson	.75	.23
❑ 16 Greg Maddux	1.50	.45
❑ 17 Cliff Floyd	.30	.09
❑ 18 Mark Buehrle	.30	.09
❑ 19 Chris Singleton	.30	.09
❑ 20 Orlando Hernandez	.30	.09
❑ 21 Javier Vazquez	.30	.09
❑ 22 Jeff Kent	.30	.09
❑ 23 Jim Thome	.75	.23
❑ 24 John Olerud	.30	.09
❑ 25 Jason Kendall	.30	.09
❑ 26 Scott Rolen	.50	.15
❑ 27 Tony Gwynn	1.00	.30
❑ 28 Edgardo Alfonzo	.30	.09
❑ 29 Pokey Reese	.30	.09
❑ 30 Todd Helton	.50	.15
❑ 31 Mark Quinn	.30	.09
❑ 32 Dan Tosca RC	.50	.15
❑ 33 Dean Palmer	.30	.09
❑ 34 Jacque Jones	.30	.09
❑ 35 Ray Durham	.30	.09
❑ 36 Rafael Palmeiro	.50	.15
❑ 37 Carl Everett	.30	.09
❑ 38 Ryan Dempster	.30	.09
❑ 39 Randy Wolf	.30	.09
❑ 40 Vladimir Guerrero	.75	.23
❑ 41 Livan Hernandez	.30	.09
❑ 42 Mo Vaughn	.30	.09
❑ 43 Shannon Stewart	.30	.09
❑ 44 Preston Wilson	.30	.09
❑ 45 Jose Vidro	.30	.09
❑ 46 Fred McGriff	.50	.15
❑ 47 Kevin Brown	.30	.09
❑ 48 Peter Bergeron	.30	.09
❑ 49 Miguel Tejada	.30	.09
❑ 50 Chipper Jones	.75	.23
❑ 51 Edgar Martinez	.50	.15
❑ 52 Tony Batista	.30	.09
❑ 53 Jorge Posada	.50	.15
❑ 54 Ricky Ledee	.30	.09
❑ 55 Sammy Sosa	1.25	.35
❑ 56 Steve Cox	.30	.09
❑ 57 Tony Armas Jr.	.30	.09
❑ 58 Gary Sheffield	.30	.09
❑ 59 Bartolo Colon	.30	.09
❑ 60 Pat Burrell	.30	.09
❑ 61 Jay Payton	.30	.09
❑ 62 Sean Casey	.30	.09
❑ 63 Larry Walker	.50	.15
❑ 64 Mike Mussina	.75	.23
❑ 65 Nomar Garciaparra	1.50	.45
❑ 66 Darren Dreifort	.30	.09
❑ 67 Richard Hidalgo	.30	.09
❑ 68 Troy Glaus	.50	.15
❑ 69 Ben Grieve	.30	.09
❑ 70 Jim Edmonds	.30	.09
❑ 71 Raul Mondesi	.30	.09
❑ 72 Andruw Jones	.50	.15
❑ 73 Luis Castillo	.30	.09
❑ 74 Mike Sweeney	.30	.09
❑ 75 Derek Jeter	2.00	.60
❑ 76 Ruben Mateo	.30	.09
❑ 77 Carlos Lee	.30	.09
❑ 78 Cristian Guzman	.30	.09
❑ 79 Mike Hampton	.30	.09
❑ 80 J.D. Drew	.30	.09
❑ 81 Matt Lawton	.30	.09
❑ 82 Moises Alou	.30	.09
❑ 83 Terrence Long	.30	.09
❑ 84 Geoff Jenkins	.30	.09
❑ 85 Manny Ramirez	.30	.09
❑ 86 Johnny Damon	.30	.09
❑ 87 Barry Larkin	.75	.23
❑ 88 Pedro Martinez	.75	.23
❑ 89 Juan Gonzalez	.75	.23
❑ 90 Roger Clemens	1.50	.45
❑ 91 Carlos Beltran	.30	.09
❑ 92 Brad Radke	.30	.09
❑ 93 Orlando Cabrera	.30	.09
❑ 94 Roberto Alomar	.75	.23
❑ 95 Barry Bonds	2.00	.60
❑ 96 Tim Hudson	.30	.09
❑ 97 Tom Glavine	.75	.23
❑ 98 Jeromy Burnitz	.30	.09
❑ 99 Adrian Beltre	.30	.09
❑ 100 Mike Piazza	1.25	.35
❑ 101 Kerry Wood	.75	.23
❑ 102 Steve Finley	.30	.09
❑ 103 Alex Cora	.30	.09
❑ 104 Bob Abreu	.30	.09
❑ 105 Neifi Perez	.30	.09
❑ 106 Mark Redman	.30	.09
❑ 107 Paul Konerko	.30	.09
❑ 108 Jermaine Dye	.30	.09
❑ 109 Brian Giles	.30	.09
❑ 110 Ivan Rodriguez	.75	.23
❑ 111 Vinny Castilla	.30	.09
❑ 112 Adam Kennedy	.30	.09
❑ 113 Eric Chavez	.30	.09
❑ 114 Billy Koch	.30	.09
❑ 115 Shawn Green	.30	.09
❑ 116 Matt Williams	.30	.09
❑ 117 Greg Vaughn	.30	.09
❑ 118 Gabe Kapler	.30	.09
❑ 119 Jeff Cirillo	.30	.09
❑ 120 Frank Thomas	.75	.23
❑ 121 David Justice	.30	.09
❑ 122 Cal Ripken	2.50	.75
❑ 123 Rich Aurilia	.30	.09
❑ 124 Curt Schilling	.50	.15
❑ 125 Barry Zito	.75	.23
❑ 126 Brian Jordan	.30	.09
❑ 127 Chan Ho Park	.30	.09
❑ 128 J.T. Snow	.30	.09
❑ 129 Kazuhiro Sasaki	.30	.09
❑ 130 Alex Rodriguez	1.50	.45
❑ 131 Mariano Rivera	.50	.15
❑ 132 Eric Milton	.30	.09
❑ 133 Andy Pettitte	.50	.15
❑ 134 Scott Elarton	.30	.09
❑ 135 Ken Griffey Jr.	1.25	.35
❑ 136 Bengie Molina	.30	.09
❑ 137 Jeff Bagwell	.50	.15
❑ 138 Kevin Millwood	.30	.09
❑ 139 Tino Martinez	.50	.15
❑ 140 Mark McGwire	2.00	.60
❑ 141 Larry Barnes	.30	.09
❑ 142 John Buck RC	.75	.23
❑ 143 Freddie Bynum RC	.50	.15
❑ 144 Abraham Nunez	.30	.09
❑ 145 Felix Diaz RC	.50	.15
❑ 146 Horacio Estrada	.30	.09
❑ 147 Ben Diggins	.30	.09
❑ 148 Tsuyoshi Shinjo RC	1.50	.45
❑ 149 Rocco Baldelli	2.00	.60
❑ 150 Rod Barajas	.30	.09
❑ 151 Luis Terrero	.30	.09
❑ 152 Milton Bradley	.30	.09
❑ 153 Kurt Ainsworth	.30	.09
❑ 154 Russell Branyan	.30	.09
❑ 155 Ryan Anderson	.30	.09
❑ 156 Mitch Jones RC	.50	.15
❑ 157 Chip Ambres	.30	.09
❑ 158 Steve Bennett RC	.50	.15
❑ 159 Ivanon Coffie	.30	.09
❑ 160 Sean Burroughs	.30	.09
❑ 161 Keith Bucktrot	.30	.09
❑ 162 Tony Alvarez	.30	.09
❑ 163 Joaquin Benoit	.30	.09
❑ 164 Rick Asadoorian	.30	.09
❑ 165 Ben Broussard	.30	.09
❑ 166 Ryan Madson RC	.50	.15
❑ 167 Dee Brown	.30	.09
❑ 168 Sergio Contreras RC	.50	.15
❑ 169 John Barnes	.30	.09
❑ 170 Ben Washburn RC	.50	.15
❑ 171 Erick Almonte RC	.50	.15
❑ 172 Shawn Fagan RC	.50	.15
❑ 173 Gary Johnson RC	.50	.15
❑ 174 Brady Clark	.30	.09
❑ 175 Grant Roberts	.30	.09
❑ 176 Tony Torcato	.30	.09
❑ 177 Ramon Castro	.30	.09
❑ 178 Esteban German	.30	.09
❑ 179 Joe Hamer RC	.50	.15
❑ 180 Nick Neugebauer	.30	.09
❑ 181 Dernell Stenson	.30	.09
❑ 182 Yhency Brazoban RC	.50	.15
❑ 183 Aaron Myette	.30	.09
❑ 184 Juan Sosa	.30	.09
❑ 185 Brandon Inge	.30	.09
❑ 186 Domingo Guante RC	.50	.15
❑ 187 Adrian Brown	.30	.09
❑ 188 Deivi Mendez RC	.50	.15
❑ 189 Luis Matos	.30	.09
❑ 190 Pedro Liriano RC	.50	.15
❑ 191 Donnie Bridges	.30	.09
❑ 192 Alex Cintron	.30	.09
❑ 193 Jace Brewer	.30	.09
❑ 194 Ron Davenport RC	.50	.15
❑ 195 Jason Belcher RC	.50	.15
❑ 196 Adrian Hernandez RC	.30	.09
❑ 197 Bobby Kielty	.30	.09
❑ 198 Reggie Griggs RC	.50	.15
❑ 199 R. Abercrombie RC	.50	.15
❑ 200 Troy Farnsworth RC	.50	.15
❑ 201 Matt Belisle	.30	.09
❑ 202 Miguel Villilo RC	.50	.15
❑ 203 Adam Everett	.30	.09
❑ 204 John Lackey	.30	.09
❑ 205 Pasqual Coco	.30	.09
❑ 206 Adam Wainwright	.30	.09
❑ 207 Matt White RC	.50	.15
❑ 208 Chin-Feng Chen	.30	.09
❑ 209 Jeff Andra RC	.50	.15
❑ 210 Willie Bloomquist	.30	.09
❑ 211 Wes Anderson	.30	.09
❑ 212 Enrique Cruz	.30	.09
❑ 213 Jerry Hairston Jr.	.30	.09
❑ 214 Mike Bynum	.30	.09
❑ 215 Brian Hitchcox RC	.50	.15
❑ 216 Ryan Christianson	.30	.09
❑ 217 J.J. Davis	.30	.09
❑ 218 Jovanny Cedeno	.30	.09
❑ 219 Elvin Nina	.30	.09
❑ 220 Alex Graman	.30	.09
❑ 221 Arturo McDowell	.30	.09
❑ 222 Deivis Santos RC	.50	.15
❑ 223 Jody Gerut	.30	.09
❑ 224 Sun Woo Kim	.30	.09
❑ 225 Jimmy Rollins	.30	.09
❑ 226 Ntema Ndungidi	.30	.09
❑ 227 Ruben Salazar	.30	.09
❑ 228 Josh Girdley	.30	.09

❑ 229 Carl Crawford .30 .09
❑ 230 Luis Montanez RC .50 .15
❑ 231 Ramon Carvajal RC .50 .15
❑ 232 Matt Riley .30 .09
❑ 233 Ben Davis .30 .09
❑ 234 Jason Grabowski .30 .09
❑ 235 Chris George .30 .09
❑ 236 Hank Blalock RC 6.00 1.80
❑ 237 Roy Oswalt .50 .15
❑ 238 Eric Reynolds RC .50 .15
❑ 239 Brian Cole .30 .09
❑ 240 Denny Bautista RC 2.00 .60
❑ 241 Hector Garcia RC .50 .15
❑ 242 Joe Thurston RC 1.25 .35
❑ 243 Brad Cresse .30 .09
❑ 244 Corey Patterson .30 .09
❑ 245 Brett Evert RC .50 .15
❑ 246 Elpidio Guzman RC .50 .15
❑ 247 Vernon Wells .30 .09
❑ 248 Roberto Miniel RC .50 .15
❑ 249 Brian Bass RC .50 .15
❑ 250 Mark Burnett RC .50 .15
❑ 251 Juan Silvestre .30 .09
❑ 252 Pablo Ozuna .30 .09
❑ 253 Jayson Werth .30 .09
❑ 254 Russ Jacobson .30 .09
❑ 255 Chad Hermansen .30 .09
❑ 256 Travis Hafner RC 1.25 .35
❑ 257 Brad Baker .30 .09
❑ 258 Gookie Dawkins .30 .09
❑ 259 Michael Cuddyer .30 .09
❑ 260 Mark Buehrle .30 .09
❑ 261 Ricardo Aramboles .30 .09
❑ 262 Esix Snead RC .50 .15
❑ 263 Wilson Betemit RC .50 .15
❑ 264 Albert Pujols RC 30.00 9.00
❑ 265 Joe Lawrence .30 .09
❑ 266 Ramon Ortiz .30 .09
❑ 267 Ben Sheets .30 .09
❑ 268 Luke Lockwood RC .50 .15
❑ 269 Toby Hall .30 .09
❑ 270 Jack Cust .30 .09
❑ 271 Pedro Feliz UER .30 .09
No facsimile signature on card
❑ 272 Noel Devarez RC .50 .15
❑ 273 Josh Beckett .50 .15
❑ 274 Alex Escobar .30 .09
❑ 275 Doug Gredvig RC .50 .15
❑ 276 Marcus Giles .30 .09
❑ 277 Jon Rauch .30 .09
❑ 278 Brian Schmitt RC .50 .15
❑ 279 Seung Song RC 1.25 .35
❑ 280 Kevin Mench .30 .09
❑ 281 Adam Eaton .30 .09
❑ 282 Shawn Sonnier .30 .09
❑ 283 Andy Van Hekken RC .50 .15
❑ 284 Aaron Rowand .30 .09
❑ 285 Tony Blanco RC .50 .15
❑ 286 Ryan Kohlmeier .30 .09
❑ 287 C.C. Sabathia .30 .09
❑ 288 Bubba Crosby .30 .09
❑ 289 Josh Hamilton .30 .09
❑ 290 Dee Haynes RC .75 .23
❑ 291 Jason Marquis .30 .09
❑ 292 Julio Zuleta .30 .09
❑ 293 Carlos Hernandez .30 .09
❑ 294 Matt Lecroy .30 .09
❑ 295 Andy Beal RC .50 .15
❑ 296 Carlos Pena .30 .09
❑ 297 Reggie Taylor .30 .09
❑ 298 Bob Keppel RC .50 .15
❑ 299 Miguel Cabrera UER 2.50 .75
Photo is Manuel Esquivia
❑ 300 Ryan Franklin .30 .09
❑ 301 Brandon Phillips .30 .09
❑ 302 Victor Hall RC .50 .15
❑ 303 Tony Pena Jr. .30 .09
❑ 304 Jim Journell RC .50 .15
❑ 305 Cristian Guerrero .30 .09
❑ 306 Miguel Olivo .30 .09
❑ 307 Jin Ho Cho .30 .09
❑ 308 Choo Freeman .30 .09
❑ 309 Danny Borrell RC .50 .15
❑ 310 Doug Mientkiewicz .30 .09
❑ 311 Aaron Herr .30 .09
❑ 312 Keith Ginter .30 .09
❑ 313 Felipe Lopez .30 .09
❑ 314 Jeff Goldbach .30 .09
❑ 315 Travis Harper .30 .09
❑ 316 Paul LoDuca .30 .09
❑ 317 Joe Torres .30 .09
❑ 318 Eric Byrnes .30 .09
❑ 319 George Lombard .30 .09
❑ 320 Dave Krynzel .30 .09
❑ 321 Ben Christensen .30 .09
❑ 322 Aubrey Huff .30 .09
❑ 323 Lyle Overbay .30 .09
❑ 324 Sean McGowan .30 .09
❑ 325 Jeff Heaverlo .30 .09
❑ 326 Timo Perez .30 .09
❑ 327 Octavio Martinez RC .50 .15
❑ 328 Vince Faison .30 .09
❑ 329 David Parrish RC .50 .15
❑ 330 Bobby Bradley .30 .09
❑ 331 Jason Miller RC .50 .15
❑ 332 Corey Spencer RC .50 .15
❑ 333 Craig House .30 .09
❑ 334 Maxim St. Pierre RC .50 .15
❑ 335 Adam Johnson .30 .09
❑ 336 Joe Crede .30 .09
❑ 337 Greg Nash RC .50 .15
❑ 338 Chad Durbin .30 .09
❑ 339 Pat Magness RC .50 .15
❑ 340 Matt Wheatland .30 .09
❑ 341 Julio Lugo .30 .09
❑ 342 Grady Sizemore .75 .23
❑ 343 Adrian Gonzalez .30 .09
❑ 344 Tim Raines Jr. .30 .09
❑ 345 Ranier Olmedo RC .50 .15
❑ 346 Phil Dumatrait .30 .09
❑ 347 Brandon Mims RC .50 .15
❑ 348 Jason Jennings .30 .09
❑ 349 Phil Wilson RC .50 .15
❑ 350 Jason Hart .30 .09
❑ 351 Cesar Izturis .30 .09
❑ 352 Matt Butler RC .50 .15
❑ 353 David Kelton .30 .09
❑ 354 Luke Prokopec .30 .09
❑ 355 Corey Smith .30 .09
❑ 356 Joel Pineiro 1.25 .35
❑ 357 Ken Chenard .30 .09
❑ 358 Keith Reed .30 .09
❑ 359 David Walling .30 .09
❑ 360 Alexis Gomez RC .50 .15
❑ 361 Justin Morneau RC 4.00 1.20
❑ 362 Josh Fogg RC .50 .15
❑ 363 J.R. House .30 .09
❑ 364 Andy Tracy .30 .09
❑ 365 Kenny Kelly .30 .09
❑ 366 Aaron McNeal .30 .09
❑ 367 Nick Johnson .30 .09
❑ 368 Brian Esposito .30 .09
❑ 369 Charles Frazier RC .50 .15
❑ 370 Scott Heard .30 .09
❑ 371 Pat Strange .30 .09
❑ 372 Mike Meyers .30 .09
❑ 373 Ryan Ludwick RC .50 .15
❑ 374 Brad Wilkerson .30 .09
❑ 375 Allen Levrault .30 .09
❑ 376 Seth McClung RC .50 .15
❑ 377 Joe Nathan .30 .09
❑ 378 Rafael Soriano RC 1.50 .45
❑ 379 Chris Richard .30 .09
❑ 380 Jared Sandberg .30 .09
❑ 381 Tike Redman .30 .09
❑ 382 Adam Dunn UER .50 .15
Card lists him as a pitcher
❑ 383 Jared Abruzzo RC .50 .15
❑ 384 Jason Richardson RC .50 .15
❑ 385 Matt Holliday .30 .09
❑ 386 Darwin Cubillan RC .50 .15
❑ 387 Mike Nannini .30 .09
❑ 388 Blake Williams RC .50 .15
❑ 389 V. Pascucci RC .50 .15
❑ 390 Jon Garland .30 .09
❑ 391 Josh Pressley .30 .09
❑ 392 Jose Ortiz .30 .09
❑ 393 Ryan Hannaman RC .50 .15
❑ 394 Steve Smyth RC .50 .15
❑ 395 John Patterson .30 .09
❑ 396 Chad Petty RC .50 .15
❑ 397 Jake Peavy RC 2.00 .60
UER last name misspelled Peavey
❑ 398 Onix Mercado RC .50 .15
❑ 399 Jason Romano .30 .09
❑ 400 Luis Torres RC .50 .15
❑ 401 Casey Fossum RC .50 .15
❑ 402 Eduardo Figueroa RC .50 .15
❑ 403 Bryan Barnowski RC .50 .15
❑ 404 Tim Redding .30 .09
❑ 405 Jason Standridge .30 .09
❑ 406 Marvin Seale RC .50 .15
❑ 407 Todd Moser .30 .09
❑ 408 Alex Gordon .30 .09
❑ 409 Steve Smitherman RC 2.00 .60
❑ 410 Ben Petrick .30 .09
❑ 411 Eric Munson .30 .09
❑ 412 Luis Rivas .30 .09
❑ 413 Matt Ginter .30 .09
❑ 414 Alfonso Soriano .75 .23
❑ 415 Rafael Boitel RC .50 .15
❑ 416 Dany Morban RC .50 .15
❑ 417 Justin Woodrow RC .50 .15
❑ 418 Wilfredo Rodriguez .30 .09
❑ 419 Derrick Van Dusen RC .50 .15
❑ 420 Josh Spoerl RC .50 .15
❑ 421 Juan Pierre .30 .09
❑ 422 J.C. Romero .30 .09
❑ 423 Ed Rogers RC .50 .15
❑ 424 Tomo Ohka .30 .09
❑ 425 Ben Hendrickson RC .50 .15
❑ 426 Carlos Zambrano .30 .09
❑ 427 Brett Myers .30 .09
❑ 428 Scott Seabol .30 .09
❑ 429 Thomas Mitchell .30 .09
❑ 430 Jose Reyes RC 6.00 1.80
❑ 431 Kip Wells .30 .09
❑ 432 Donzell McDonald .30 .09
❑ 433 Adam Pettyjohn RC .50 .15
❑ 434 Austin Kearns .50 .15
❑ 435 Rico Washington .30 .09
❑ 436 Doug Nickle RC .50 .15
❑ 437 Steve Lomasney .30 .09
❑ 438 Jason Jones RC .50 .15
❑ 439 Bobby Seay .30 .09
❑ 440 Justin Wayne RC .75 .23
❑ ROYR Kazuhiro Sasaki 40.00 12.00
Rafael Furcal ROY Jsy
❑ NNO Sean Burroughs Ball/80 50.00 15.00

2001 Bowman Draft Picks

	Nm-Mt	Ex-Mt
COMP.FACT.SET (112)	40.00	12.00
COMPLETE SET (110)	25.00	7.50

❑ BDP1 Alfredo Amezaga RC .60 .18
❑ BDP2 Andrew Good .30 .09
❑ BDP3 Kelly Johnson RC .40 .12
❑ BDP4 Larry Bigbie .30 .09
❑ BDP5 Matt Thompson RC .40 .12
❑ BDP6 Wilton Chavez RC .40 .12
❑ BDP7 Joe Borchard RC 1.50 .45
❑ BDP8 David Espinosa .30 .09
❑ BDP9 Zach Day RC .60 .18
❑ BDP10 Brad Hawpe RC 4.00 1.20
❑ BDP11 Nate Cornejo .30 .09
❑ BDP12 Matt Cooper RC .40 .12
❑ BDP13 Brad Lidge .30 .09

❑ BDP14 Angel Berroa RC 2.00 .60
❑ BDP15 L. Matthews RC .40 .12
❑ BDP16 Jose Garcia .30 .09
❑ BDP17 Grant Balfour RC .30 .09
❑ BDP18 Ron Chiavacci RC .30 .09
❑ BDP19 Jae Seo .30 .09
❑ BDP20 Juan Rivera .30 .09
❑ BDP21 D'Angelo Jimenez .30 .09
❑ BDP22 Juan A.Pena RC .40 .12
❑ BDP23 Marlon Byrd RC 2.50 .75
❑ BDP24 Sean Burnett .30 .09
❑ BDP25 Josh Pearce RC .40 .12
❑ BDP26 B. Duckworth RC .40 .12
❑ BDP27 Jack Taschner RC .40 .12
❑ BDP28 Marcus Thames .30 .09
❑ BDP29 Brent Abernathy .30 .09
❑ BDP30 David Elder RC .40 .12
❑ BDP31 Scott Cassidy RC .40 .12
❑ BDP32 D. Tankersley RC .40 .12
❑ BDP33 Denny Stark .30 .09
❑ BDP34 Dave Williams RC .40 .12
❑ BDP35 Boof Bonser RC .60 .18
❑ BDP36 Kris Foster RC .30 .09
❑ BDP37 Luis Garcia RC .40 .12
❑ BDP38 Shawn Chacon .30 .09
❑ BDP39 Mike Rivera RC .40 .12
❑ BDP40 Will Smith RC .40 .12
❑ BDP41 M. Ensberg RC 1.25 .35
❑ BDP42 Ken Harvey .30 .09
❑ BDP43 R. Rodriguez RC .40 .12
❑ BDP44 Jose Mieses RC .40 .12
❑ BDP45 Luis Maza RC .40 .12
❑ BDP46 Julio Perez RC .40 .12
❑ BDP47 Dustan Mohr RC .40 .12
❑ BDP48 Randy Flores RC .30 .09
❑ BDP49 Covelli Crisp RC 1.00 .30
❑ BDP50 Kevin Reese RC .40 .12
❑ BDP51 Brad Thomas UER .30 .09
Card back is BDP71 Alex Herrera
❑ BDP52 Xavier Nady .30 .09
❑ BDP53 Ryan Vogelsong .30 .09
❑ BDP54 Carlos Silva .30 .09
❑ BDP55 Dan Wright .30 .09
❑ BDP56 Brent Butler .30 .09
❑ BDP57 Brandon Knight RC .30 .09
❑ BDP58 Brian Reith RC .40 .12
❑ BDP59 M. Valenzuela RC .40 .12
❑ BDP60 Bobby Hill RC 1.00 .30
❑ BDP61 Rich Rundles RC .40 .12
❑ BDP62 Rick Elder .30 .09
❑ BDP63 J.D. Closser .30 .09
❑ BDP64 Scot Shields .30 .09
❑ BDP65 Miguel Olivo .30 .09
❑ BDP66 Stubby Clapp RC .30 .09
❑ BDP67 J. Williams RC 3.00 .90
❑ BDP68 Jason Lane RC .60 .18
❑ BDP69 Chase Utley RC 4.00 1.20
❑ BDP70 Erik Bedard RC .40 .12
❑ BDP71 A. Herrera UER RC .30 .09
Card back is BDP51 Brad Thomas
❑ BDP72 Juan Cruz RC .40 .12
❑ BDP73 Billy Martin RC .40 .12
❑ BDP74 Ronnie Merrill RC .40 .12
❑ BDP75 Jason Kinchen RC .40 .12
❑ BDP76 Wilkin Ruan RC .40 .12
❑ BDP77 Cody Ransom RC .30 .09
❑ BDP78 Bud Smith RC .40 .12
❑ BDP79 Wily Mo Pena .30 .09
❑ BDP80 Jeff Nettles RC .40 .12
❑ BDP81 Jamal Strong RC .40 .12
❑ BDP82 Bill Ortega RC .40 .12
❑ BDP83 Mike Bell .30 .09
❑ BDP84 Ichiro Suzuki RC 8.00 2.40
❑ BDP85 F. Rodney RC .40 .12
❑ BDP86 Chris Smith RC .40 .12
❑ BDP87 J.VanBenschoten RC 1.50 .45
❑ BDP88 Bobby Crosby RC 3.00 .90
❑ BDP89 Kenny Baugh RC .40 .12
❑ BDP90 Jake Gautreau RC .40 .12
❑ BDP91 Gabe Gross RC .60 .18
❑ BDP92 Kris Honel RC 1.25 .35
❑ BDP93 Dan Denham RC .40 .12
❑ BDP94 Aaron Heilman RC 1.00 .30
❑ BDP95 Irvin Guzman RC 1.50 .45
❑ BDP96 Mike Jones RC .40 .12
❑ BDP97 J. Griffin RC .60 .18
❑ BDP98 Macay McBride RC .40 .12
❑ BDP99 J. Rheinecker RC .40 .12
❑ BDP100 B. Sardinha RC .60 .18
❑ BDP101 J. Weintraub RC .40 .12
❑ BDP102 J.D. Martin RC .40 .12
❑ BDP103 Jayson Nix RC 1.00 .30
❑ BDP104 Noah Lowry RC .40 .12
❑ BDP105 Richard Lewis RC .40 .12
❑ BDP106 B. Hennessey RC .40 .12
❑ BDP107 Jeff Mathis RC 2.00 .60
❑ BDP108 Jon Skaggs RC .40 .12
❑ BDP109 Justin Pope RC .40 .12
❑ BDP110 Josh Burrus RC .40 .12

2002 Bowman

	Nm-Mt	Ex-Mt
COMPLETE SET (440)	80.00	24.00
COMMON CARD (1-110)	.30	.09
COMMON CARD (111-440)	.30	.09

❑ 1 Adam Dunn .50 .15
❑ 2 Derek Jeter 2.00 .60
❑ 3 Alex Rodriguez 1.50 .45
❑ 4 Miguel Tejada .30 .09
❑ 5 Nomar Garciaparra 1.50 .45
❑ 6 Toby Hall .30 .09
❑ 7 Brandon Duckworth .30 .09
❑ 8 Paul LoDuca .30 .09
❑ 9 Brian Giles .30 .09
❑ 10 C.C. Sabathia .30 .09
❑ 11 Curt Schilling .50 .15
❑ 12 Tsuyoshi Shinjo .30 .09
❑ 13 Ramon Hernandez .30 .09
❑ 14 Jose Cruz Jr. .30 .09
❑ 15 Albert Pujols 1.50 .45
❑ 16 Joe Mays .30 .09
❑ 17 Javy Lopez .30 .09
❑ 18 J.T. Snow .30 .09
❑ 19 David Segui .30 .09
❑ 20 Jorge Posada .50 .15
❑ 21 Doug Mientkiewicz .30 .09
❑ 22 Jerry Hairston Jr. .30 .09
❑ 23 Bernie Williams .50 .15
❑ 24 Mike Sweeney .30 .09
❑ 25 Jason Giambi .75 .23
❑ 26 Ryan Dempster .30 .09
❑ 27 Ryan Klesko .30 .09
❑ 28 Mark Quinn .30 .09
❑ 29 Jeff Kent .30 .09
❑ 30 Eric Chavez .30 .09
❑ 31 Adrian Beltre .30 .09
❑ 32 Andruw Jones .50 .15
❑ 33 Alfonso Soriano .75 .23
❑ 34 Aramis Ramirez .30 .09
❑ 35 Greg Maddux 1.50 .45
❑ 36 Andy Pettitte .50 .15
❑ 37 Bartolo Colon .30 .09
❑ 38 Ben Sheets .30 .09
❑ 39 Bobby Higginson .30 .09
❑ 40 Ivan Rodriguez .75 .23
❑ 41 Brad Penny .30 .09
❑ 42 Carlos Lee .30 .09
❑ 43 Damion Easley .30 .09
❑ 44 Preston Wilson .30 .09
❑ 45 Jeff Bagwell .50 .15
❑ 46 Eric Milton .30 .09
❑ 47 Rafael Palmeiro .50 .15
❑ 48 Gary Sheffield .30 .09
❑ 49 J.D. Drew .30 .09
❑ 50 Jim Thome .75 .23
❑ 51 Ichiro Suzuki 1.50 .45
❑ 52 Bud Smith .30 .09
❑ 53 Chan Ho Park .30 .09
❑ 54 D'Angelo Jimenez .30 .09
❑ 55 Ken Griffey Jr. 1.25 .35
❑ 56 Wade Miller .30 .09
❑ 57 Vladimir Guerrero .75 .23
❑ 58 Troy Glaus .50 .15
❑ 59 Shawn Green .30 .09
❑ 60 Kerry Wood .75 .23
❑ 61 Jack Wilson .30 .09
❑ 62 Kevin Brown .30 .09
❑ 63 Marcus Giles .30 .09
❑ 64 Pat Burrell .30 .09
❑ 65 Larry Walker .50 .15
❑ 66 Sammy Sosa 1.25 .35
❑ 67 Raul Mondesi .30 .09
❑ 68 Tim Hudson .30 .09
❑ 69 Lance Berkman .30 .09
❑ 70 Mike Mussina .75 .23
❑ 71 Barry Zito .75 .23
❑ 72 Jimmy Rollins .30 .09
❑ 73 Barry Bonds 2.00 .60
❑ 74 Craig Biggio .50 .15
❑ 75 Todd Helton .50 .15
❑ 76 Roger Clemens 1.50 .45
❑ 77 Frank Catalanotto .30 .09
❑ 78 Josh Towers .30 .09
❑ 79 Roy Oswalt .30 .09
❑ 80 Chipper Jones .75 .23
❑ 81 Cristian Guzman .30 .09
❑ 82 Darin Erstad .30 .09
❑ 83 Freddy Garcia .30 .09
❑ 84 Jason Tyner .30 .09
❑ 85 Carlos Delgado .30 .09
❑ 86 Jon Lieber .30 .09
❑ 87 Juan Pierre .30 .09
❑ 88 Matt Morris .30 .09
❑ 89 Phil Nevin .30 .09
❑ 90 Jim Edmonds .30 .09
❑ 91 Magglio Ordonez .30 .09
❑ 92 Mike Hampton .30 .09
❑ 93 Rafael Furcal .30 .09
❑ 94 Richie Sexson .30 .09
❑ 95 Luis Gonzalez .30 .09
❑ 96 Scott Rolen .50 .15
❑ 97 Tim Redding .30 .09
❑ 98 Moises Alou .30 .09
❑ 99 Jose Vidro .30 .09
❑ 100 Mike Piazza 1.25 .35
❑ 101 Pedro Martinez UER .75 .23
Career strikeout total incorrect
❑ 102 Geoff Jenkins .30 .09
❑ 103 Johnny Damon .30 .09
❑ 104 Mike Cameron .30 .09
❑ 105 Randy Johnson .75 .23
❑ 106 David Eckstein .30 .09
❑ 107 Javier Vazquez .30 .09
❑ 108 Mark Mulder .30 .09
❑ 109 Robert Fick .30 .09
❑ 110 Roberto Alomar .75 .23
❑ 111 Wilson Betemit .30 .09
❑ 112 Chris Tritle RC .50 .15
❑ 113 Ed Rogers .30 .09
❑ 114 Juan Pena .30 .09
❑ 115 Josh Beckett .75 .23
❑ 116 Juan Cruz .30 .09
❑ 117 Noochie Varner RC 1.25 .35
❑ 118 Taylor Buchholz RC .50 .15
❑ 119 Mike Rivera .30 .09
❑ 120 Hank Blalock 1.25 .35
❑ 121 Hansel Izquierdo RC .50 .15
❑ 122 Orlando Hudson .30 .09
❑ 123 Bill Hall .30 .09
❑ 124 Jose Reyes 1.25 .35
❑ 125 Juan Rivera .50 .15
❑ 126 Eric Valent .30 .09
❑ 127 Scotty Layfield RC .50 .15
❑ 128 Austin Kearns .75 .23
❑ 129 Nic Jackson RC .75 .23
❑ 130 Chris Baker RC .50 .15
❑ 131 Chad Qualls RC .50 .15
❑ 132 Marcus Thames .30 .09

❑ 133 Nathan Haynes .30 .09
❑ 134 Brett Evert .30 .09
❑ 135 Joe Borchard .50 .15
❑ 136 Ryan Christianson .30 .09
❑ 137 Josh Hamilton .50 .15
❑ 138 Corey Patterson .50 .15
❑ 139 Travis Wilson .30 .09
❑ 140 Alex Escobar .30 .09
❑ 141 Alexis Gomez .30 .09
❑ 142 Nick Johnson .50 .15
❑ 143 Kenny Kelly .30 .09
❑ 144 Marlon Byrd .50 .15
❑ 145 Kory DeHaan .30 .09
❑ 146 Matt Belisle .30 .09
❑ 147 Carlos Hernandez .30 .09
❑ 148 Sean Burroughs .50 .15
❑ 149 Angel Berroa .50 .15
❑ 150 Aubrey Huff .50 .15
❑ 151 Travis Hafner .30 .09
❑ 152 Brandon Berger .30 .09
❑ 153 David Krynzel .30 .09
❑ 154 Ruben Salazar .30 .09
❑ 155 J.R. House .30 .09
❑ 156 Juan Silvestre .30 .09
❑ 157 Dewon Brazelton .30 .09
❑ 158 Jayson Werth .30 .09
❑ 159 Larry Barnes .30 .09
❑ 160 Elvis Pena .30 .09
❑ 161 Ruben Gotay RC .75 .23
❑ 162 Tommy Marx RC .50 .15
❑ 163 John Suomi RC .50 .15
❑ 164 Javier Colina .30 .09
❑ 165 Greg Sain RC .50 .15
❑ 166 Robert Cosby RC .50 .15
❑ 167 Angel Pagan RC .50 .15
❑ 168 Ralph Santana RC .50 .15
❑ 169 Joe Orloski RC .50 .15
❑ 170 Shayne Wright RC .50 .15
❑ 171 Jay Caligiuri RC .50 .15
❑ 172 Greg Montalbano RC .75 .23
❑ 173 Rich Harden RC 6.00 1.80
❑ 174 Rich Thompson RC .50 .15
❑ 175 Fred Bastardo RC .50 .15
❑ 176 Alejandro Giron RC .50 .15
❑ 177 Jesus Medrano RC .50 .15
❑ 178 Kevin Deaton RC .50 .15
❑ 179 Mike Rosamond RC .50 .15
❑ 180 Jon Guzman RC .50 .15
❑ 181 Gerard Oakes RC .50 .15
❑ 182 Francisco Liriano RC .75 .23
❑ 183 Matt Allegra RC .75 .23
❑ 184 Mike Snyder RC .50 .15
❑ 185 James Shanks RC .50 .15
❑ 186 Anderson Hernandez RC .75 .23
❑ 187 Dan Trumble RC .50 .15
❑ 188 Luis DePaula RC .50 .15
❑ 189 Randall Shelley RC .75 .23
❑ 190 Richard Lane RC .50 .15
❑ 191 Antwon Rollins RC .75 .23
❑ 192 Ryan Bukvich RC .75 .23
❑ 193 Derrick Lewis .30 .09
❑ 194 Eric Miller RC .50 .15
❑ 195 Justin Schuda RC .50 .15
❑ 196 Brian West RC .50 .15
❑ 197 Adam Roller RC .50 .15
❑ 198 Neal Frendling RC .50 .15
❑ 199 Jeremy Hill RC .50 .15
❑ 200 James Barrett RC .75 .23
❑ 201 Brett Kay RC .50 .15
❑ 202 Ryan Mottl RC .75 .23
❑ 203 Brad Nelson RC 2.00 .60
❑ 204 Juan M. Gonzalez RC .50 .15
❑ 205 Curtis Legendre RC .50 .15
❑ 206 Ronald Acuna RC .50 .15
❑ 207 Chris Flinn RC .50 .15
❑ 208 Nick Alvarez RC .50 .15
❑ 209 Jason Ellison RC .50 .15
❑ 210 Blake McGinley RC .50 .15
❑ 211 Dan Phillips RC .50 .15
❑ 212 Demetrius Heath RC .50 .15
❑ 213 Eric Bruntlett RC .50 .15
❑ 214 Joe Jiannetti RC .50 .15
❑ 215 Mike Hill RC .50 .15
❑ 216 Ricardo Cordova RC .50 .15
❑ 217 Mark Hamilton RC .50 .15
❑ 218 David Mattox RC .50 .15
❑ 219 Jose Morban RC .75 .23
❑ 220 Scott Wiggins RC .50 .15
❑ 221 Steve Green .30 .09
❑ 222 Brian Rogers .30 .09
❑ 223 Chin-Hui Tsao .50 .15
❑ 224 Kenny Baugh .30 .09
❑ 225 Nate Teut .30 .09
❑ 226 Josh Wilson RC .75 .23
❑ 227 Christian Parker .30 .09
❑ 228 Tim Raines Jr. .30 .09
❑ 229 Anastacio Martinez RC .50 .15
❑ 230 Richard Lewis .30 .09
❑ 231 Tim Kalita RC .50 .15
❑ 232 Edwin Almonte RC .50 .15
❑ 233 Hee-Seop Choi .75 .23
❑ 234 Ty Howington .30 .09
❑ 235 Victor Alvarez RC .50 .15
❑ 236 Morgan Ensberg .50 .15
❑ 237 Jeff Austin RC .50 .15
❑ 238 Luis Terrero .30 .09
❑ 239 Adam Wainwright .50 .15
❑ 240 Clint Weibl RC .50 .15
❑ 241 Eric Cyr .30 .09
❑ 242 Marlyn Tisdale RC .50 .15
❑ 243 John VanBenschoten .75 .23
❑ 244 Ryan Raburn RC .50 .15
❑ 245 Miguel Cabrera 2.00 .60
❑ 246 Jung Bong .30 .09
❑ 247 Raul Chavez RC .50 .15
❑ 248 Erik Bedard .30 .09
❑ 249 Chris Snelling RC 1.50 .45
❑ 250 Joe Rogers RC .50 .15
❑ 251 Nate Field RC .50 .15
❑ 252 Matt Herges RC .50 .15
❑ 253 Matt Childers RC .50 .15
❑ 254 Erick Almonte .30 .09
❑ 255 Nick Neugebauer .30 .09
❑ 256 Ron Calloway RC .50 .15
❑ 257 Seung Song .30 .09
❑ 258 Brandon Phillips .30 .09
❑ 259 Cole Barthel RC .75 .23
❑ 260 Jason Lane .30 .09
❑ 261 Jae Seo .30 .09
❑ 262 Randy Flores .30 .09
❑ 263 Scott Chiasson .30 .09
❑ 264 Chase Utley .75 .23
❑ 265 Tony Alvarez .30 .09
❑ 266 Ben Howard RC .50 .15
❑ 267 Nelson Castro RC .50 .15
❑ 268 Mark Lukasiewicz RC .30 .09
❑ 269 Eric Glaser RC .50 .15
❑ 270 Rob Henkel RC .50 .15
❑ 271 Jose Valverde RC .75 .23
❑ 272 Ricardo Rodriguez .30 .09
❑ 273 Chris Smith .30 .09
❑ 274 Mark Prior 3.00 .90
❑ 275 Miguel Olivo .30 .09
❑ 276 Ben Broussard .30 .09
❑ 277 Zach Sorensen .30 .09
❑ 278 Brian Mallette RC .50 .15
❑ 279 Brad Wilkerson .30 .09
❑ 280 Carl Crawford .50 .15
❑ 281 Chone Figgins RC .50 .15
❑ 282 Jimmy Alvarez RC .50 .15
❑ 283 Gavin Floyd RC 3.00 .90
❑ 284 Josh Bonifay RC .75 .23
❑ 285 Garrett Guzman RC .50 .15
❑ 286 Blake Williams .30 .09
❑ 287 Matt Holliday .30 .09
❑ 288 Ryan Madson .30 .09
❑ 289 Luis Torres .30 .09
❑ 290 Jeff Verplancke RC .50 .15
❑ 291 Nate Espy RC .50 .15
❑ 292 Jeff Lincoln RC .50 .15
❑ 293 Ryan Snare RC .75 .23
❑ 294 Jose Ortiz .30 .09
❑ 295 Eric Munson .30 .09
❑ 296 Denny Bautista .50 .15
❑ 297 Willy Aybar .30 .09
❑ 298 Kelly Johnson .30 .09
❑ 299 Justin Morneau .75 .23
❑ 300 Derrick Van Dusen .30 .09
❑ 301 Chad Petty .50 .15
❑ 302 Mike Restovich .50 .15
❑ 303 Shawn Fagan .30 .09
❑ 304 Yurendell DeCaster RC .75 .23
❑ 305 Justin Wayne .30 .09
❑ 306 Mike Peeples RC .50 .15
❑ 307 Joel Guzman .50 .15
❑ 308 Ryan Vogelsong .30 .09
❑ 309 Jorge Padilla RC .75 .23
❑ 310 Grady Sizemore .75 .23
❑ 311 Joe Jester RC .50 .15
❑ 312 Jim Journell .30 .09
❑ 313 Bobby Seay .30 .09
❑ 314 Ryan Church RC 1.25 .35
❑ 315 Grant Balfour .30 .09
❑ 316 Mitch Jones .30 .09
❑ 317 Travis Foley RC .75 .23
❑ 318 Bobby Crosby 1.25 .35
❑ 319 Adrian Gonzalez .50 .15
❑ 320 Ronnie Merrill .30 .09
❑ 321 Joel Pineiro .50 .15
❑ 322 John-Ford Griffin .30 .09
❑ 323 Brian Forystek RC .50 .15
❑ 324 Sean Douglass .30 .09
❑ 325 Manny Delcarmen RC .75 .23
❑ 326 Donnie Bridges .30 .09
❑ 327 Jim Kavourias RC .50 .15
❑ 328 Gabe Gross .30 .09
❑ 329 Jon Rauch .30 .09
❑ 330 Bill Ortega .30 .09
❑ 331 Joey Hammond RC .50 .15
❑ 332 Ramon Moreta RC .50 .15
❑ 333 Ron Davenport .30 .09
❑ 334 Brett Myers .50 .15
❑ 335 Carlos Pena .30 .09
❑ 336 Ezequiel Astacio RC .50 .15
❑ 337 Edwin Yan RC .50 .15
❑ 338 Josh Girdley .30 .09
❑ 339 Shaun Boyd .30 .09
❑ 340 Juan Rincon .30 .09
❑ 341 Chris Duffy RC .50 .15
❑ 342 Jason Kinchen .30 .09
❑ 343 Brad Thomas .30 .09
❑ 344 David Kelton .30 .09
❑ 345 Rafael Soriano .50 .15
❑ 346 Colin Young RC .50 .15
❑ 347 Eric Byrnes .30 .09
❑ 348 Chris Narveson RC .75 .23
❑ 349 John Rheinecker .30 .09
❑ 350 Mike Wilson RC .50 .15
❑ 351 Justin Sherrod RC .75 .23
❑ 352 Deivi Mendez .30 .09
❑ 353 Wily Mo Pena .50 .15
❑ 354 Brett Roneberg RC .50 .15
❑ 355 Trey Lunsford RC .50 .15
❑ 356 Jimmy Gobble RC 2.50 .75
❑ 357 Brent Butler .30 .09
❑ 358 Aaron Heilman .30 .09
❑ 359 Wilkin Ruan .30 .09
❑ 360 Brian Wolfe RC .50 .15
❑ 361 Cody Ransom .30 .09
❑ 362 Koyie Hill .30 .09
❑ 363 Scott Cassidy .30 .09
❑ 364 Tony Fontana RC .50 .15
❑ 365 Mark Teixeira 1.25 .35
❑ 366 Doug Sessions RC .50 .15
❑ 367 Victor Hall .30 .09
❑ 368 Josh Cisneros RC .50 .15
❑ 369 Kevin Mench .30 .09
❑ 370 Tike Redman .30 .09
❑ 371 Jeff Heaverlo .30 .09
❑ 372 Carlos Brackley RC .50 .15
❑ 373 Brad Hawpe 1.50 .45
❑ 374 Jesus Colome .30 .09
❑ 375 David Espinosa .30 .09
❑ 376 Jesse Foppert RC 3.00 .90
❑ 377 Ross Peeples RC .75 .23
❑ 378 Alex Requena RC .75 .23
❑ 379 Joe Mauer RC 8.00 2.40
❑ 380 Carlos Silva .30 .09
❑ 381 David Wright RC 2.50 .75
❑ 382 Craig Kuzmic RC .50 .15
❑ 383 Pete Zamora RC .50 .15
❑ 384 Matt Parker RC .50 .15
❑ 385 Keith Ginter .30 .09
❑ 386 Gary Cates Jr. .50 .15
❑ 387 Justin Reid RC .50 .15
❑ 388 Jake Mauer RC .50 .15
❑ 389 Dennis Tankersley .30 .09
❑ 390 Josh Barfield RC 3.00 .90

Card	Nm-Mt	Ex-Mt
❑ 391 Luis Maza	.30	.09
❑ 392 Henry Pichardo RC	.50	.15
❑ 393 Michael Floyd RC	.50	.15
❑ 394 Clint Nageotte RC	1.50	.45
❑ 395 Raymond Cabrera RC	.50	.15
❑ 396 Mauricio Lara RC	.50	.15
❑ 397 Alejandro Cadena RC	.50	.15
❑ 398 Jonny Gomes RC	1.50	.45
❑ 399 Jason Bulger RC	.50	.15
❑ 400 Bobby Jenks RC	2.00	.60
❑ 401 David Gil RC	.50	.15
❑ 402 Joel Crump RC	.50	.15
❑ 403 Kazuhisa Ishii RC	2.00	.60
❑ 404 So Taguchi RC	2.00	.60
❑ 405 Ryan Doumit RC	.75	.23
❑ 406 Macay McBride	.30	.09
❑ 407 Brandon Claussen	1.25	.35
❑ 408 Chin-Feng Chen	.50	.15
❑ 409 Josh Phelps	.50	.15
❑ 410 Freddie Money RC	.75	.23
❑ 411 Cliff Bartosh RC	.50	.15
❑ 412 Josh Pearce	.30	.09
❑ 413 Lyle Overbay	.30	.09
❑ 414 Ryan Anderson	.30	.09
❑ 415 Terrance Hill RC	.50	.15
❑ 416 John Rodriguez RC	.50	.15
❑ 417 Richard Stahl	.30	.09
❑ 418 Brian Specht	.30	.09
❑ 419 Chris Latham RC	.50	.15
❑ 420 Carlos Cabrera RC	.50	.15
❑ 421 Jose Bautista RC	1.25	.35
❑ 422 Kevin Frederick RC	.50	.15
❑ 423 Jerome Williams	1.25	.35
❑ 424 Napoleon Calzado RC	.50	.15
❑ 425 Benito Baez	.30	.09
❑ 426 Xavier Nady	.50	.15
❑ 427 Jason Botts RC	.50	.15
❑ 428 Steve Bechler RC	.50	.15
❑ 429 Reed Johnson RC	.75	.23
❑ 430 Mark Outlaw RC	.50	.15
❑ 431 Billy Sylvester	.30	.09
❑ 432 Luke Lockwood	.30	.09
❑ 433 Jake Peavy	.50	.15
❑ 434 Alfredo Amezaga	.30	.09
❑ 435 Aaron Cook RC	.75	.23
❑ 436 Josh Shaffer RC	.50	.15
❑ 437 Dan Wright	.30	.09
❑ 438 Ryan Gripp RC	.50	.15
❑ 439 Alex Herrera	.30	.09
❑ 440 Jason Bay RC	1.50	.45

2002 Bowman Draft

	Nm-Mt	Ex-Mt
COMPLETE SET (165)	40.00	12.00
❑ BDP1 Clint Everts RC	1.25	.35
❑ BDP2 Fred Lewis RC	.75	.23
❑ BDP3 Jon Broxton RC	.50	.15
❑ BDP4 Jason Anderson RC	.50	.15
❑ BDP5 Mike Eusebio RC	.50	.15
❑ BDP6 Zack Greinke RC	5.00	1.50
❑ BDP7 Joe Blanton RC	4.00	1.20
❑ BDP8 Sergio Santos RC	2.50	.75
❑ BDP9 Jason Cooper RC	1.00	.30
❑ BDP10 Delwyn Young RC	1.50	.45
❑ BDP11 Jeremy Hermida RC	1.50	.45
❑ BDP12 Dan Ortmeier RC	1.00	.30
❑ BDP13 Kevin Jepsen RC	1.00	.30
❑ BDP14 Russ Adams RC	1.00	.30
❑ BDP15 Mike Nixon RC	.50	.15
❑ BDP16 Nick Swisher RC	2.00	.60
❑ BDP17 Cole Hamels RC	5.00	1.50
❑ BDP18 Brian Dopirak RC	2.00	.60
❑ BDP19 James Loney RC	2.50	.75
❑ BDP20 Denard Span RC	1.00	.30
❑ BDP21 Billy Petrick RC	.50	.15
❑ BDP22 Jared Doyle RC	.50	.15
❑ BDP23 Jeff Francoeur RC	5.00	1.50
❑ BDP24 Nick Bourgeois RC	.50	.15
❑ BDP25 Matt Cain RC	1.50	.45
❑ BDP26 John McCurdy RC	.50	.15
❑ BDP27 Mark Kiger RC	.50	.15
❑ BDP28 Bill Murphy RC	.75	.23
❑ BDP29 Matt Craig RC	.75	.23
❑ BDP30 Mike Megrew RC	.50	.15
❑ BDP31 Ben Crockett RC	.50	.15
❑ BDP32 Luke Hagerty RC	1.00	.30
❑ BDP33 Matt Whitney RC	1.00	.30
❑ BDP34 Dan Meyer RC	1.00	.30
❑ BDP35 Jeremy Brown RC	1.25	.35
❑ BDP36 Doug Johnson RC	.50	.15
❑ BDP37 Steve Obenchain RC	.50	.15
❑ BDP38 Matt Clanton RC	.75	.23
❑ BDP39 Mark Teahen RC	.50	.15
❑ BDP40 Tom Carrow RC	.50	.15
❑ BDP41 Micah Schilling RC	1.00	.30
❑ BDP42 Blair Johnson RC	.75	.23
❑ BDP43 Jason Pridie RC	1.50	.45
❑ BDP44 Joey Votto RC	.75	.23
❑ BDP45 Taber Lee RC	.50	.15
❑ BDP46 Adam Peterson RC	.50	.15
❑ BDP47 Adam Donachie RC	.75	.23
❑ BDP48 Josh Murray RC	.75	.23
❑ BDP49 Brent Clevlen RC	1.25	.35
❑ BDP50 Chad Pleiness RC	.75	.23
❑ BDP51 Zach Hammes RC	.75	.23
❑ BDP52 Chris Snyder RC	1.00	.30
❑ BDP53 Chris Smith RC	.50	.15
❑ BDP54 Justin Maureau RC	.50	.15
❑ BDP55 David Bush RC	2.00	.60
❑ BDP56 Tim Gilhooly RC	.50	.15
❑ BDP57 Blair Barbier RC	.50	.15
❑ BDP58 Zach Segovia RC	1.00	.30
❑ BDP59 Jeremy Reed RC	6.00	1.80
❑ BDP60 Matt Pender RC	.50	.15
❑ BDP61 Eric Thomas RC	.50	.15
❑ BDP62 Justin Jones RC	1.50	.45
❑ BDP63 Brian Slocum RC	.75	.23
❑ BDP64 Larry Broadway RC	2.00	.60
❑ BDP65 Bo Flowers RC	.50	.15
❑ BDP66 Scott White RC	1.00	.30
❑ BDP67 Steve Stanley RC	.50	.15
❑ BDP68 Alex Merricks RC	.50	.15
❑ BDP69 Josh Womack RC	.75	.23
❑ BDP70 Dave Jensen RC	.50	.15
❑ BDP71 Curtis Granderson RC	1.25	.35
❑ BDP72 Pat Osborn RC	1.00	.30
❑ BDP73 Nic Carter RC	.50	.15
❑ BDP74 Mitch Talbot RC	.50	.15
❑ BDP75 Don Murphy RC	.50	.15
❑ BDP76 Val Majewski RC	1.00	.30
❑ BDP77 Javy Rodriguez RC	.50	.15
❑ BDP78 Fernando Pacheco RC	.75	.23
❑ BDP79 Steve Russell RC	.50	.15
❑ BDP80 Jon Slack RC	.50	.15
❑ BDP81 John Baker RC	.50	.15
❑ BDP82 Aaron Coonrod RC	.50	.15
❑ BDP83 Josh Johnson RC	.75	.23
❑ BDP84 Jake Blalock RC	2.50	.75
❑ BDP85 Alex Hart RC	1.25	.35
❑ BDP86 Wes Bankston RC	2.50	.75
❑ BDP87 Josh Rupe RC	.75	.23
❑ BDP88 Dan Cevette RC	1.00	.30
❑ BDP89 Kiel Fisher RC	.75	.23
❑ BDP90 Alan Rick RC	.50	.15
❑ BDP91 Charlie Morton RC	.75	.23
❑ BDP92 Chad Spann RC	1.25	.35
❑ BDP93 Kyle Boyer RC	.75	.23
❑ BDP94 Bob Malek RC	.50	.15
❑ BDP95 Ryan Rodriguez RC	.50	.15
❑ BDP96 Jordan Renz RC	.50	.15
❑ BDP97 Randy Frye RC	.50	.15
❑ BDP98 Rich Hill RC	.50	.15
❑ BDP99 B.J. Upton RC	6.00	1.80
❑ BDP100 Dan Christensen RC	1.00	.30
❑ BDP101 Casey Kotchman RC	3.00	.90
❑ BDP102 Eric Good RC	.40	.12
❑ BDP103 Mike Fontenot RC	1.00	.30
❑ BDP104 John Webb RC	.50	.15
❑ BDP105 Jason Dubois RC	2.00	.60
❑ BDP106 Ryan Kibler RC	.50	.15
❑ BDP107 John Peralta RC	.75	.23
❑ BDP108 Kirk Saarloos RC	1.00	.30
❑ BDP109 Rhett Parrott RC	.50	.15
❑ BDP110 Jason Grove RC	.50	.15
❑ BDP111 Colt Griffin RC	1.25	.35
❑ BDP112 Dallas McPherson RC	2.50	.75
❑ BDP113 Oliver Perez RC	1.25	.35
❑ BDP114 Marshall McDougall RC	.50	.15
❑ BDP115 Mike Wood RC	.75	.23
❑ BDP116 Scott Hairston RC	2.00	.60
❑ BDP117 Jason Simontacchi RC	.75	.23
❑ BDP118 Taggert Bozied RC	2.00	.60
❑ BDP119 Shelley Duncan RC	.50	.15
❑ BDP120 Dontrelle Willis RC	8.00	2.40
❑ BDP121 Sean Burnett	.30	.09
❑ BDP122 Aaron Cook	.50	.15
❑ BDP123 Brett Evert	.30	.09
❑ BDP124 Jimmy Journell	.30	.09
❑ BDP125 Brett Myers	.30	.09
❑ BDP126 Brad Baker	.30	.09
❑ BDP127 Billy Traber RC	1.00	.30
❑ BDP128 Adam Wainwright	.30	.09
❑ BDP129 Jason Young RC	.75	.23
❑ BDP130 John Buck	.30	.09
❑ BDP131 Kevin Cash RC	.50	.15
❑ BDP132 Jason Stokes RC	5.00	1.50
❑ BDP133 Drew Henson	.30	.09
❑ BDP134 Chad Tracy RC	2.00	.60
❑ BDP135 Orlando Hudson	.30	.09
❑ BDP136 Brandon Phillips	.30	.09
❑ BDP137 Joe Borchard	.30	.09
❑ BDP138 Marlon Byrd	.30	.09
❑ BDP139 Carl Crawford	.30	.09
❑ BDP140 Michael Restovich	.30	.09
❑ BDP141 Corey Hart RC	2.00	.60
❑ BDP142 Edwin Almonte	.30	.09
❑ BDP143 Francis Beltran RC	.50	.15
❑ BDP144 Jorge De La Rosa RC	.50	.15
❑ BDP145 Gerardo Garcia RC	.50	.15
❑ BDP146 Franklyn German RC	.50	.15
❑ BDP147 Francisco Liriano	.50	.15
❑ BDP148 Francisco Rodriguez	.30	.09
❑ BDP149 Ricardo Rodriguez	.30	.09
❑ BDP150 Seung Song	.30	.09
❑ BDP151 John Stephens	.30	.09
❑ BDP152 Justin Huber RC	1.25	.35
❑ BDP153 Victor Martinez	.30	.09
❑ BDP154 Hee Seop Choi	.50	.15
❑ BDP155 Justin Morneau	.50	.15
❑ BDP156 Miguel Cabrera	2.00	.60
❑ BDP157 Victor Diaz RC	2.00	.60
❑ BDP158 Jose Reyes	.75	.23
❑ BDP159 Omar Infante	.30	.09
❑ BDP160 Angel Berroa	.30	.09
❑ BDP161 Tony Alvarez	.30	.09
❑ BDP162 Shin Soo Choo RC	2.00	.60
❑ BDP163 Wily Mo Pena	.30	.09
❑ BDP164 Andres Torres	.30	.09
❑ BDP165 Jose Lopez RC	2.50	.75

2003 Bowman

	Nm-Mt	Ex-Mt
COMPLETE SET (330)	80.00	24.00
COMMON CARD (1-155)	.30	.09
COMMON CARD (156-330)	.30	.09
❑ 1 Garret Anderson	.30	.09
❑ 2 Derek Jeter	2.00	.60
❑ 3 Gary Sheffield	.30	.09
❑ 4 Matt Morris	.30	.09
❑ 5 Derek Lowe	.30	.09
❑ 6 Andy Van Hekken	.30	.09
❑ 7 Sammy Sosa	1.25	.35
❑ 8 Ken Griffey Jr.	1.25	.35
❑ 9 Omar Vizquel	.30	.09
❑ 10 Jorge Posada	.50	.15
❑ 11 Lance Berkman	.30	.09

❑ 12 Mike Sweeney .30 .09
❑ 13 Adrian Beltre .30 .09
❑ 14 Richie Sexson .30 .09
❑ 15 A.J. Pierzynski .30 .09
❑ 16 Bartolo Colon .30 .09
❑ 17 Mike Mussina .75 .23
❑ 18 Paul Byrd .30 .09
❑ 19 Bobby Abreu .30 .09
❑ 20 Miguel Tejada .30 .09
❑ 21 Aramis Ramirez .30 .09
❑ 22 Edgardo Alfonzo .30 .09
❑ 23 Edgar Martinez .50 .15
❑ 24 Albert Pujols 1.50 .45
❑ 25 Carl Crawford .30 .09
❑ 26 Eric Hinske .30 .09
❑ 27 Tim Salmon .50 .15
❑ 28 Luis Gonzalez .30 .09
❑ 29 Jay Gibbons .30 .09
❑ 30 John Smoltz .50 .15
❑ 31 Tim Wakefield .30 .09
❑ 32 Mark Prior 1.50 .45
❑ 33 Magglio Ordonez .30 .09
❑ 34 Adam Dunn .50 .15
❑ 35 Larry Walker .50 .15
❑ 36 Luis Castillo .30 .09
❑ 37 Wade Miller .30 .09
❑ 38 Carlos Beltran .30 .09
❑ 39 Odalis Perez .30 .09
❑ 40 Alex Sanchez .30 .09
❑ 41 Torii Hunter .30 .09
❑ 42 Cliff Floyd .30 .09
❑ 43 Andy Pettitte .50 .15
❑ 44 Francisco Rodriguez .30 .09
❑ 45 Eric Chavez .30 .09
❑ 46 Kevin Millwood .30 .09
❑ 47 Dennis Tankersley .30 .09
❑ 48 Hideo Nomo .75 .23
❑ 49 Freddy Garcia .30 .09
❑ 50 Randy Johnson .75 .23
❑ 51 Aubrey Huff .30 .09
❑ 52 Carlos Delgado .30 .09
❑ 53 Troy Glaus .50 .15
❑ 54 Junior Spivey .30 .09
❑ 55 Mike Hampton .30 .09
❑ 56 Sidney Ponson .30 .09
❑ 57 Aaron Boone .30 .09
❑ 58 Kerry Wood .75 .23
❑ 59 Runelvys Hernandez .30 .09
❑ 60 Nomar Garciaparra 1.50 .45
❑ 61 Todd Helton .50 .15
❑ 62 Mike Lowell .30 .09
❑ 63 Roy Oswalt .30 .09
❑ 64 Raul Ibanez .30 .09
❑ 65 Brian Jordan .30 .09
❑ 66 Geoff Jenkins .30 .09
❑ 67 Jermaine Dye .30 .09
❑ 68 Tom Glavine .75 .23
❑ 69 Bernie Williams .50 .15
❑ 70 Vladimir Guerrero .75 .23
❑ 71 Mark Mulder .30 .09
❑ 72 Jimmy Rollins .30 .09
❑ 73 Oliver Perez .30 .09
❑ 74 Rich Aurilia .30 .09
❑ 75 Joel Pineiro .30 .09
❑ 76 J.D. Drew .30 .09
❑ 77 Ivan Rodriguez .75 .23
❑ 78 Josh Phelps .30 .09
❑ 79 Darin Erstad .30 .09
❑ 80 Curt Schilling .50 .15
❑ 81 Paul Lo Duca .30 .09
❑ 82 Marty Cordova .30 .09
❑ 83 Manny Ramirez .30 .09
❑ 84 Bobby Hill .30 .09
❑ 85 Paul Konerko .30 .09
❑ 86 Austin Kearns .50 .15
❑ 87 Jason Jennings .30 .09
❑ 88 Brad Penny .30 .09
❑ 89 Jeff Bagwell .50 .15
❑ 90 Shawn Green .30 .09
❑ 91 Jason Schmidt .30 .09
❑ 92 Doug Mientkiewicz .30 .09
❑ 93 Jose Vidro .30 .09
❑ 94 Bret Boone .30 .09
❑ 95 Jason Giambi .75 .23
❑ 96 Barry Zito .75 .23
❑ 97 Roy Halladay .30 .09
❑ 98 Pat Burrell .30 .09
❑ 99 Sean Burroughs .30 .09
❑ 100 Barry Bonds 2.00 .60
❑ 101 Kazuhiro Sasaki .30 .09
❑ 102 Fernando Vina .30 .09
❑ 103 Chan Ho Park .30 .09
❑ 104 Andruw Jones .50 .15
❑ 105 Adam Kennedy .30 .09
❑ 106 Shea Hillenbrand .30 .09
❑ 107 Greg Maddux 1.50 .45
❑ 108 Jim Edmonds .30 .09
❑ 109 Pedro Martinez .75 .23
❑ 110 Moises Alou .30 .09
❑ 111 Jeff Weaver .30 .09
❑ 112 C.C. Sabathia .30 .09
❑ 113 Robert Fick .30 .09
❑ 114 A.J. Burnett .30 .09
❑ 115 Jeff Kent .30 .09
❑ 116 Kevin Brown .30 .09
❑ 117 Rafael Furcal .30 .09
❑ 118 Cristian Guzman .30 .09
❑ 119 Brad Wilkerson .30 .09
❑ 120 Mike Piazza 1.25 .35
❑ 121 Alfonso Soriano .75 .23
❑ 122 Mark Ellis .30 .09
❑ 123 Vicente Padilla .30 .09
❑ 124 Eric Gagne .50 .15
❑ 125 Ryan Klesko .30 .09
❑ 126 Ichiro Suzuki 1.50 .45
❑ 127 Tony Batista .30 .09
❑ 128 Roberto Alomar .75 .23
❑ 129 Alex Rodriguez 1.50 .45
❑ 130 Jim Thome .75 .23
❑ 131 Jarrod Washburn .30 .09
❑ 132 Orlando Hudson .30 .09
❑ 133 Chipper Jones .75 .23
❑ 134 Rodrigo Lopez .30 .09
❑ 135 Johnny Damon .30 .09
❑ 136 Matt Clement .30 .09
❑ 137 Frank Thomas .75 .23
❑ 138 Ellis Burks .30 .09
❑ 139 Carlos Pena .30 .09
❑ 140 Josh Beckett .50 .15
❑ 141 Joe Randa .30 .09
❑ 142 Brian Giles .30 .09
❑ 143 Kazuhisa Ishii .30 .09
❑ 144 Corey Koskie .30 .09
❑ 145 Orlando Cabrera .30 .09
❑ 146 Mark Buehrle .30 .09
❑ 147 Roger Clemens 1.50 .45
❑ 148 Tim Hudson .30 .09
❑ 149 Randy Wolf UER .30 .09
resume says AL leaders; he pitches in NL
❑ 150 Josh Fogg .30 .09
❑ 151 Phil Nevin .30 .09
❑ 152 John Olerud .30 .09
❑ 153 Scott Rolen .50 .15
❑ 154 Joe Kennedy .30 .09
❑ 155 Rafael Palmeiro .50 .15
❑ 156 Chad Hutchinson .30 .09
❑ 157 Quincy Carter XRC .75 .23
❑ 158 Hee Seop Choi .30 .09
❑ 159 Joe Borchard .30 .09
❑ 160 Brandon Phillips .30 .09
❑ 161 Wily Mo Pena .30 .09
❑ 162 Victor Martinez .30 .09
❑ 163 Jason Stokes .75 .23
❑ 164 Ken Harvey .30 .09
❑ 165 Juan Rivera .30 .09
❑ 166 Jose Contreras RC 2.50 .75
❑ 167 Dan Haren RC 1.50 .45
❑ 168 Michel Hernandez RC .50 .15
❑ 169 Eider Torres RC .50 .15
❑ 170 Chris De La Cruz RC .50 .15
❑ 171 Ramon Nivar-Martinez RC 1.50 .45
❑ 172 Mike Adams RC .50 .15
❑ 173 Justin Arneson RC .50 .15
❑ 174 Jamie Athas RC .50 .15
❑ 175 Dwaine Bacon RC .50 .15
❑ 176 Clint Barmes RC .75 .23
❑ 177 B.J. Barns RC .50 .15
❑ 178 Tyler Johnson RC .50 .15
❑ 179 Bobby Basham RC 1.25 .35
❑ 180 T.J. Bohn RC .50 .15
❑ 181 J.D. Durbin RC 1.25 .35
❑ 182 Brandon Bowe RC .50 .15
❑ 183 Craig Brazell RC 1.25 .35
❑ 184 Dusty Brown RC .50 .15
❑ 185 Brian Bruney RC .75 .23
❑ 186 Greg Bruso RC .50 .15
❑ 187 Jaime Bubela RC .50 .15
❑ 188 Bryan Bullington RC 2.50 .75
❑ 189 Brian Burgamy RC .50 .15
❑ 190 Eny Cabreja RC .50 .15
❑ 191 Daniel Cabrera RC .50 .15
❑ 192 Ryan Cameron RC .50 .15
❑ 193 Lance Caracciolí RC .50 .15
❑ 194 David Cash RC .50 .15
❑ 195 Bernie Castro RC .50 .15
❑ 196 Ismael Castro RC .75 .23
❑ 197 Daryl Clark RC .75 .23
❑ 198 Jeff Clark RC .50 .15
❑ 199 Chris Colton RC .50 .15
❑ 200 Dexter Cooper RC .50 .15
❑ 201 Callix Crabbe RC .75 .23
❑ 202 Chien-Ming Wang RC 2.50 .75
❑ 203 Eric Crozier RC .75 .23
❑ 204 Nook Logan RC .50 .15
❑ 205 David DeJesus RC 1.25 .35
❑ 206 Matt DeMarco RC .50 .15
❑ 207 Chris Duncan RC .50 .15
❑ 208 Eric Eckenstahler .30 .09
❑ 209 Willie Eyre RC .50 .15
❑ 210 Evel Bastida-Martinez RC .50 .15
❑ 211 Chris Fallon RC .50 .15
❑ 212 Mike Flannery RC .50 .15
❑ 213 Mike O'Keefe RC .50 .15
❑ 214 Ben Francisco RC 1.25 .35
❑ 215 Kason Gabbard RC .50 .15
❑ 216 Mike Gallo RC .50 .15
❑ 217 Jairo Garcia RC .50 .15
❑ 218 Angel Garcia RC .75 .23
❑ 219 Michael Garciaparra RC 1.50 .45
❑ 220 Joey Gomes RC .75 .23
❑ 221 Dusty Gomon RC 1.25 .35
❑ 222 Bryan Grace RC .50 .15
❑ 223 Tyson Graham RC .50 .15
❑ 224 Henry Guerrero RC .50 .15
❑ 225 Franklin Gutierrez RC 3.00 .75
❑ 226 Carlos Guzman RC .75 .23
❑ 227 Matthew Hagen RC 1.25 .35
❑ 228 Josh Hall RC .75 .23
❑ 229 Rob Hammock RC 1.25 .35
❑ 230 Brendan Harris RC 1.25 .35
❑ 231 Gary Harris RC .50 .15
❑ 232 Clay Hensley RC .50 .15
❑ 233 Michael Hinckley RC 1.25 .35
❑ 234 Luis Hodge RC .50 .15
❑ 235 Donnie Hood RC .75 .23
❑ 236 Travis Ishikawa RC .75 .23
❑ 237 Edwin Jackson RC 4.00 1.20
❑ 238 Ardley Jansen RC .75 .23
❑ 239 Ferenc Jongejan RC .50 .15
❑ 240 Matt Kata RC 1.50 .45
❑ 241 Kazuhiro Takeoka RC .50 .15
❑ 242 Beau Kemp RC .50 .15
❑ 243 Il Kim RC .50 .15
❑ 244 Brennan King RC .50 .15
❑ 245 Chris Kroski RC .50 .15
❑ 246 Jason Kubel RC 1.25 .35
❑ 247 Pete LaForest RC .75 .23
❑ 248 Wil Ledezma RC .50 .15
❑ 249 Jeremy Bonderman RC 2.00 .60

❑ 250 Gonzalo Lopez RC .50 .15
❑ 251 Brian Luderer RC .50 .15
❑ 252 Ruddy Lugo RC .50 .15
❑ 253 Wayne Lydon RC .75 .23
❑ 254 Mark Malaska RC .50 .15
❑ 255 Andy Marte RC 3.00 .90
❑ 256 Tyler Martin RC .50 .15
❑ 257 Branden Florence RC .50 .15
❑ 258 Aneudis Mateo RC .50 .15
❑ 259 Derell McCall RC .50 .15
❑ 260 Brian McCann RC 1.25 .35
❑ 261 Mike McNutt RC .50 .15
❑ 262 Jacabo Meque RC .50 .15
❑ 263 Derek Michaelis RC .75 .23
❑ 264 Aaron Miles RC .50 .15
❑ 265 Jose Morales RC .50 .15
❑ 266 Dustin Moseley RC .75 .23
❑ 267 Adrian Myers RC .50 .15
❑ 268 Dan Neil RC .50 .15
❑ 269 Jon Nelson RC .75 .23
❑ 270 Mike Neu RC .50 .15
❑ 271 Leigh Neuage RC .50 .15
❑ 272 Wes O'Brien RC .50 .15
❑ 273 Trent Oeltjen RC .75 .23
❑ 274 Tim Olson RC 1.25 .35
❑ 275 David Pahucki RC .50 .15
❑ 276 Nathan Panther RC 1.25 .35
❑ 277 Arnie Munoz RC .50 .15
❑ 278 Dave Pember RC .50 .15
❑ 279 Jason Perry RC 1.50 .45
❑ 280 Matthew Peterson RC .50 .15
❑ 281 Ryan Shealy RC 1.25 .35
❑ 282 Jorge Piedra RC .75 .23
❑ 283 Simon Pond RC .75 .23
❑ 284 Aaron Rakers RC .50 .15
❑ 285 Hanley Ramirez RC 2.50 .75
❑ 286 Manuel Ramirez RC 1.25 .35
❑ 287 Kevin Randel RC .50 .15
❑ 288 Darrell Rasner RC .50 .15
❑ 289 Prentice Redman RC .50 .15
❑ 290 Eric Reed RC 1.25 .35
❑ 291 Wilton Reynolds RC .75 .23
❑ 292 Eric Riggs RC .75 .23
❑ 293 Carlos Rijo RC .50 .15
❑ 294 Rajai Davis RC .75 .23
❑ 295 Aron Weston RC .50 .15
❑ 296 Arturo Rivas RC .50 .15
❑ 297 Kyle Roat RC .50 .15
❑ 298 Bubba Nelson RC 1.50 .45
❑ 299 Levi Robinson RC .50 .15
❑ 300 Ray Sadler RC .50 .15
❑ 301 Gary Schneidmiller RC .50 .15
❑ 302 Jon Schuerholz RC .50 .15
❑ 303 Corey Shafer RC .75 .23
❑ 304 Brian Shackelford RC .50 .15
❑ 305 Bill Simon RC .50 .15
❑ 306 Haj Turay RC .75 .23
❑ 307 Sean Smith RC .75 .23
❑ 308 Ryan Spataro RC .50 .15
❑ 309 Jemel Spearman RC .50 .15
❑ 310 Keith Stamler RC .50 .15
❑ 311 Luke Steidlmayer RC .50 .15
❑ 312 Adam Stern RC .50 .15
❑ 313 Jay Sitzman RC .50 .15
❑ 314 Thomari Story-Harden RC .75 .23
❑ 315 Terry Tiffee RC .75 .23
❑ 316 Nick Trzesniak RC .50 .15
❑ 317 Denny Tussen RC .50 .15
❑ 318 Scott Tyler RC .75 .23
❑ 319 Shane Victorino RC .50 .15
❑ 320 Doug Waechter RC 1.25 .35
❑ 321 Brandon Watson RC .50 .15
❑ 322 Todd Wellemeyer RC .75 .23
❑ 323 Eli Whiteside RC .50 .15
❑ 324 Josh Willingham RC 2.00 .60
❑ 325 Travis Wong RC .75 .23
❑ 326 Brian Wright RC .50 .15
❑ 327 Kevin Youkilis RC 2.50 .75
❑ 328 Andy Sisco RC 2.00 .60
❑ 329 Dustin Yount RC 1.25 .35
❑ 330 Andrew Dominique RC .50 .15
❑ NNO Eric Hinske Bat 15.00 4.50
Jason Jennings Jsy
ROY Relic

2003 Bowman Draft

	MINT	NRMT
COMPLETE SET (165)	40.00	18.00

❑ 1 Dontrelle Willis 1.00 .45
❑ 2 Freddy Sanchez .30 .14
❑ 3 Miguel Cabrera 1.00 .45
❑ 4 Ryan Ludwick .30 .14
❑ 5 Ty Wigginton .30 .14
❑ 6 Mark Teixeira .50 .23
❑ 7 Trey Hodges .30 .14
❑ 8 Laynce Nix .75 .35
❑ 9 Antonio Perez .30 .14
❑ 10 Jody Gerut .30 .14
❑ 11 Jae Weong Seo .30 .14
❑ 12 Erick Almonte .30 .14
❑ 13 Lyle Overbay .30 .14
❑ 14 Billy Traber .30 .14
❑ 15 Andres Torres .30 .14
❑ 16 Jose Valverde .30 .14
❑ 17 Aaron Heilman .30 .14
❑ 18 Brandon Larson .30 .14
❑ 19 Jung Bong .30 .14
❑ 20 Jesse Foppert .30 .14
❑ 21 Angel Berroa .30 .14
❑ 22 Jeff DaVanon .30 .14
❑ 23 Kurt Ainsworth .30 .14
❑ 24 Brandon Claussen .30 .14
❑ 25 Xavier Nady .30 .14
❑ 26 Travis Hafner .30 .14
❑ 27 Jerome Williams .30 .14
❑ 28 Jose Reyes .50 .23
❑ 29 Sergio Mitre RC .50 .23
❑ 30 Bo Hart RC 2.00 .90
❑ 31 Adam Miller RC 1.00 .45
❑ 32 Brian Finch RC .50 .23
❑ 33 Taylor Mattingly RC 3.00 1.35
❑ 34 Daric Barton RC 2.00 .90
❑ 35 Chris Ray RC .75 .35
❑ 36 Jarrod Saltalamacchia RC 1.00 .45
❑ 37 Dennis Dove RC .50 .23
❑ 38 James Houser RC .75 .35
❑ 39 Clint King RC 1.00 .45
❑ 40 Lou Palmisano RC 2.50 1.10
❑ 41 Dan Moore RC .50 .23
❑ 42 Craig Stansberry RC 1.00 .45
❑ 43 Jo Jo Reyes RC 1.00 .45
❑ 44 Jake Stevens RC .75 .35
❑ 45 Tom Gorzelanny RC .50 .23
❑ 46 Brian Marshall RC .50 .23
❑ 47 Scott Beerer RC .50 .23
❑ 48 Javi Herrera RC .75 .35
❑ 49 Steve LeRud RC 1.00 .45
❑ 50 Josh Banks RC 1.25 .55
❑ 51 Jon Papelbon RC .50 .23
❑ 52 Juan Valdes RC .75 .35
❑ 53 Beau Vaughan RC .75 .35
❑ 54 Matt Chico RC .75 .35
❑ 55 Todd Jennings RC .75 .35
❑ 56 Anthony Gwynn RC 2.00 .90
❑ 57 Matt Harrison RC .75 .35
❑ 58 Aaron Marsden RC .75 .35
❑ 59 Casey Abrams RC .50 .23
❑ 60 Cory Stuart RC .50 .23
❑ 61 Mike Wagner RC .50 .23
❑ 62 Jordan Pratt RC .75 .35
❑ 63 Andre Randolph RC .50 .23
❑ 64 Blake Balkcom RC 1.00 .45
❑ 65 Josh Muecke RC .50 .23
❑ 66 Jamie D'Antona RC 2.00 .90
❑ 67 Cole Seifrig RC 2.00 .90
❑ 68 Josh Anderson RC .75 .35
❑ 69 Matt Lorenzo RC .75 .35
❑ 70 Nate Spears RC 1.00 .45
❑ 71 Chris Goodman RC .50 .23
❑ 72 Brian McFall RC 1.00 .45
❑ 73 Billy Hogan RC 1.00 .45
❑ 74 Jamie Romak RC 1.00 .45
❑ 75 Jeff Cook RC .75 .35
❑ 76 Brooks McNiven RC .50 .23
❑ 77 Xavier Paul RC 3.00 1.35
❑ 78 Bob Zimmermann RC .50 .23
❑ 79 Mickey Hall RC .75 .35
❑ 80 Shaun Marcum RC .50 .23
❑ 81 Matt Nachreiner RC .75 .35
❑ 82 Chris Kinsey RC .50 .23
❑ 83 Jonathan Fulton RC .75 .35
❑ 84 Edgardo Baez RC 1.00 .45
❑ 85 Robert Valido RC 3.00 1.35
❑ 86 Kenny Lewis RC .75 .35
❑ 87 Trent Peterson RC .50 .23
❑ 88 Johnny Woodard RC .75 .35
❑ 89 Wes Littleton RC 1.00 .45
❑ 90 Sean Rodriguez RC 1.00 .45
❑ 91 Kyle Pearson RC .50 .23
❑ 92 Josh Rainwater RC .75 .35
❑ 93 Travis Schlichting RC .75 .35
❑ 94 Tim Battle RC .75 .35
❑ 95 Aaron Hill RC 1.25 .55
❑ 96 Bob McCrory RC .50 .23
❑ 97 Rick Guarno RC .75 .35
❑ 98 Brandon Yarbrough RC .50 .23
❑ 99 Peter Stonard RC .50 .23
❑ 100 Darin Downs RC 1.00 .45
❑ 101 Matt Bruback RC .50 .23
❑ 102 Danny Garcia RC .50 .23
❑ 103 Cory Stewart RC .50 .23
❑ 104 Ferdin Tejeda RC .50 .23
❑ 105 Kade Johnson RC .50 .23
❑ 106 Andrew Brown RC .50 .23
❑ 107 Aquilino Lopez RC .50 .23
❑ 108 Stephen Randolph RC .50 .23
❑ 109 Dave Matranga RC .50 .23
❑ 110 Dustin McGowan RC 1.00 .45
❑ 111 Juan Camacho RC .50 .23
❑ 112 Cliff Lee .30 .14
❑ 113 Jeff Duncan RC .75 .35
❑ 114 C.J. Wilson .30 .14
❑ 115 Brandon Roberson RC .50 .23
❑ 116 David Corrente RC .50 .23
❑ 117 Kevin Beavers RC .50 .23
❑ 118 Anthony Webster RC .75 .35
❑ 119 Oscar Villarreal RC .50 .23
❑ 120 Hong-Chih Kuo RC 1.00 .45
❑ 121 Josh Barfield .30 .14
❑ 122 Denny Bautista .30 .14
❑ 123 Chris Burke RC .75 .35
❑ 124 Robinson Cano RC .75 .35
❑ 125 Jose Castillo .30 .14
❑ 126 Neal Cotts .30 .14
❑ 127 Jorge De La Rosa .30 .14
❑ 128 J.D. Durbin 1.00 .45
❑ 129 Edwin Encarnacion .30 .14
❑ 130 Gavin Floyd .30 .14
❑ 131 Alexis Gomez .30 .14
❑ 132 Edgar Gonzalez RC .50 .23
❑ 133 Khalil Greene .50 .23
❑ 134 Zack Greinke .75 .35
❑ 135 Franklin Gutierrez 1.00 .45
❑ 136 Rich Harden .75 .35
❑ 137 J.J. Hardy RC 2.00 .90
❑ 138 Ryan Howard RC 1.25 .55
❑ 139 Justin Huber .30 .14
❑ 140 David Kelton .30 .14
❑ 141 Dave Krynzel .30 .14
❑ 142 Pete LaForest .60 .25
❑ 143 Adam LaRoche .30 .14
❑ 144 Preston Larrison RC .50 .23
❑ 145 John Maine RC 2.50 1.10
❑ 146 Andy Marte 1.25 .55
❑ 147 Jeff Mathis .30 .14
❑ 148 Joe Mauer .75 .35
❑ 149 Clint Nageotte .30 .14

❑ 150 Chris Narveson	.30	.14
❑ 151 Ramon Nivar	1.00	.45
❑ 152 Felix Pie RC	4.00	1.80
❑ 153 Guillermo Quiroz RC	1.25	.55
❑ 154 Rene Reyes	.30	.14
❑ 155 Royce Ring	.30	.14
❑ 156 Alexis Rios	1.00	.45
❑ 157 Grady Sizemore	.30	.14
❑ 158 Stephen Smitherman	.30	.14
❑ 159 Seung Song	.30	.14
❑ 160 Scott Thorman	.30	.14
❑ 161 Chad Tracy	.30	.14
❑ 162 Chin-Hui Tsao	.30	.14
❑ 163 John VanBenschoten	.30	.14
❑ 164 Kevin Youkilis	1.00	.45
❑ 165 Chien-Ming Wang	1.00	.45

1997 Bowman Chrome

	Nm-Mt	Ex-Mt
COMPLETE SET (300)	180.00	55.00
❑ 1 Derek Jeter	3.00	.90
❑ 2 Chipper Jones	1.25	.35
❑ 3 Hideo Nomo	1.25	.35
❑ 4 Tim Salmon	.75	.23
❑ 5 Robin Ventura	.50	.15
❑ 6 Tony Clark	.50	.15
❑ 7 Barry Larkin	1.25	.35
❑ 8 Paul Molitor	.75	.23
❑ 9 Andy Benes	.50	.15
❑ 10 Ryan Klesko	.50	.15
❑ 11 Mark McGwire	3.00	.90
❑ 12 Ken Griffey Jr.	2.00	.60
❑ 13 Robb Nen	.50	.15
❑ 14 Cal Ripken	4.00	1.20
❑ 15 John Valentin	.50	.15
❑ 16 Ricky Bottalico	.50	.15
❑ 17 Mike Lansing	.50	.15
❑ 18 Ryne Sandberg	2.00	.60
❑ 19 Carlos Delgado	.50	.15
❑ 20 Craig Biggio	.75	.23
❑ 21 Eric Karros	.50	.15
❑ 22 Kevin Appier	.50	.15
❑ 23 Mariano Rivera	.75	.23
❑ 24 Vinny Castilla	.50	.15
❑ 25 Juan Gonzalez	1.25	.35
❑ 26 Al Martin	.50	.15
❑ 27 Jeff Cirillo	.50	.15
❑ 28 Ray Lankford	.50	.15
❑ 29 Manny Ramirez	.50	.15
❑ 30 Roberto Alomar	1.25	.35
❑ 31 Will Clark	1.25	.35
❑ 32 Chuck Knoblauch	.50	.15
❑ 33 Harold Baines	.50	.15
❑ 34 Edgar Martinez	.75	.23
❑ 35 Mike Mussina	1.25	.35
❑ 36 Kevin Brown	.50	.15
❑ 37 Dennis Eckersley	.50	.15
❑ 38 Tino Martinez	.75	.23
❑ 39 Raul Mondesi	.50	.15
❑ 40 Sammy Sosa	2.00	.60
❑ 41 John Smoltz	.75	.23
❑ 42 Billy Wagner	.50	.15
❑ 43 Ken Caminiti	.50	.15
❑ 44 Wade Boggs	.75	.23
❑ 45 Andres Galarraga	.50	.15
❑ 46 Roger Clemens	2.50	.75
❑ 47 Matt Williams	.50	.15
❑ 48 Albert Belle	.50	.15
❑ 49 Jeff King	.50	.15
❑ 50 John Wetteland	.50	.15
❑ 51 Deion Sanders	.50	.15
❑ 52 Ellis Burks	.50	.15
❑ 53 Pedro Martinez	1.25	.35
❑ 54 Kenny Lofton	.50	.15
❑ 55 Randy Johnson	1.25	.35
❑ 56 Bernie Williams	.75	.23
❑ 57 Marquis Grissom	.50	.15
❑ 58 Gary Sheffield	.50	.15
❑ 59 Curt Schilling	.75	.23
❑ 60 Reggie Sanders	.50	.15
❑ 61 Bobby Higginson	.50	.15
❑ 62 Moises Alou	.50	.15
❑ 63 Tom Glavine	1.25	.35
❑ 64 Mark Grace	1.25	.35
❑ 65 Rafael Palmeiro	.75	.23
❑ 66 John Olerud	.50	.15
❑ 67 Dante Bichette	.50	.15
❑ 68 Jeff Bagwell	.75	.23
❑ 69 Barry Bonds	3.00	.90
❑ 70 Pat Hentgen	.50	.15
❑ 71 Jim Thome	1.25	.35
❑ 72 Andy Pettitte	.75	.23
❑ 73 Jay Bell	.50	.15
❑ 74 Jim Edmonds	.50	.15
❑ 75 Ron Gant	.50	.15
❑ 76 David Cone	.50	.15
❑ 77 Jose Canseco	1.25	.35
❑ 78 Jay Buhner	.50	.15
❑ 79 Greg Maddux	2.50	.75
❑ 80 Lance Johnson	.50	.15
❑ 81 Travis Fryman	.50	.15
❑ 82 Paul O'Neill	.75	.23
❑ 83 Ivan Rodriguez	1.25	.35
❑ 84 Fred McGriff	.75	.23
❑ 85 Mike Piazza	2.00	.60
❑ 86 Brady Anderson	.50	.15
❑ 87 Marty Cordova	.50	.15
❑ 88 Joe Carter	.50	.15
❑ 89 Brian Jordan	.50	.15
❑ 90 David Justice	.50	.15
❑ 91 Tony Gwynn	1.50	.45
❑ 92 Larry Walker	.75	.23
❑ 93 Mo Vaughn	.50	.15
❑ 94 Sandy Alomar Jr.	.50	.15
❑ 95 Rusty Greer	.50	.15
❑ 96 Roberto Hernandez	.50	.15
❑ 97 Hal Morris	.50	.15
❑ 98 Todd Hundley	.50	.15
❑ 99 Rondell White	.50	.15
❑ 100 Frank Thomas	1.25	.35
❑ 101 Bubba Trammell RC	1.50	.45
❑ 102 Sidney Ponson RC	4.00	1.20
❑ 103 Ricky Ledee RC	1.50	.45
❑ 104 Brett Tomko	.50	.15
❑ 105 Braden Looper RC	1.00	.30
❑ 106 Jason Dickson	.50	.15
❑ 107 Chad Green RC	1.00	.30
❑ 108 R.A. Dickey RC	1.00	.30
❑ 109 Jeff Liefer	.50	.15
❑ 110 Richard Hidalgo	.50	.15
❑ 111 Chad Hermansen RC	1.50	.45
❑ 112 Felix Martinez	.50	.15
❑ 113 J.J. Johnson	.50	.15
❑ 114 Todd Dunwoody	.50	.15
❑ 115 Katsuhiro Maeda	.50	.15
❑ 116 Darin Erstad	.50	.15
❑ 117 Elieser Marrero	.50	.15
❑ 118 Bartolo Colon	.50	.15
❑ 119 Ugueth Urbina	.50	.15
❑ 120 Jaime Bluma	.50	.15
❑ 121 Seth Greisinger RC	1.50	.45
❑ 122 Jose Cruz Jr. RC	8.00	2.40
❑ 123 Todd Dunn	.50	.15
❑ 124 Justin Towle RC	1.00	.30
❑ 125 Brian Rose	.50	.15
❑ 126 Jose Guillen	.50	.15
❑ 127 Andruw Jones	.75	.23
❑ 128 Mark Kotsay RC	1.50	.45
❑ 129 Wilton Guerrero	.50	.15
❑ 130 Jacob Cruz	.50	.15
❑ 131 Mike Sweeney	.50	.15
❑ 132 Matt Morris	.50	.15
❑ 133 John Thomson	.50	.15
❑ 134 Javier Valentin	.50	.15
❑ 135 Mike Drumright RC	1.00	.30
❑ 136 Michael Barrett	.50	.15
❑ 137 Tony Saunders RC	1.00	.30
❑ 138 Kevin Brown	.50	.15
❑ 139 Anthony Sanders RC	1.00	.30
❑ 140 Jeff Abbott	.50	.15
❑ 141 Eugene Kingsale	.50	.15
❑ 142 Paul Konerko	.50	.15
❑ 143 Randall Simon RC	2.50	.75
❑ 144 Freddy Adrian Garcia	.50	.15
❑ 145 Karim Garcia	.50	.15
❑ 146 Carlos Guillen	.50	.15
❑ 147 Aaron Boone	.50	.15
❑ 148 Donnie Sadler	.50	.15
❑ 149 Brooks Kieschnick	.50	.15
❑ 150 Scott Spiezio	.50	.15
❑ 151 Kevin Orie	.50	.15
❑ 152 Russ Johnson	.50	.15
❑ 153 Livan Hernandez	.50	.15
❑ 154 Vladimir Nunez RC	1.00	.30
❑ 155 Pokey Reese	.50	.15
❑ 156 Chris Carpenter	.50	.15
❑ 157 Eric Milton RC	2.50	.75
❑ 158 Richie Sexson	.50	.15
❑ 159 Carl Pavano	.50	.15
❑ 160 Pat Cline	.50	.15
❑ 161 Ron Wright	.50	.15
❑ 162 Dante Powell	.50	.15
❑ 163 Mark Bellhorn	.50	.15
❑ 164 George Lombard	.50	.15
❑ 165 Paul Wilder RC	1.00	.30
❑ 166 Brad Fullmer	.50	.15
❑ 167 Kris Benson RC	2.50	.75
❑ 168 Torii Hunter	.50	.15
❑ 169 D.T. Cromer RC	1.00	.30
❑ 170 Nelson Figueroa RC	1.50	.45
❑ 171 Hiram Bocachica RC	1.50	.45
❑ 172 Shane Monahan	.50	.15
❑ 173 Juan Melo	.50	.15
❑ 174 Calvin Pickering RC	1.50	.45
❑ 175 Reggie Taylor	.50	.15
❑ 176 Geoff Jenkins	.50	.15
❑ 177 Steve Rain RC	1.00	.30
❑ 178 Nerio Rodriguez RC	1.00	.30
❑ 179 Derrick Gibson	.50	.15
❑ 180 Darin Blood	.50	.15
❑ 181 Ben Davis	.50	.15
❑ 182 Adrian Beltre RC	8.00	2.40
❑ 183 Kerry Wood RC	25.00	7.50
❑ 184 Nate Rolison RC	1.00	.30
❑ 185 Fernando Tatis RC	1.50	.45
❑ 186 Jake Westbrook RC	1.50	.45
❑ 187 Edwin Diaz	.50	.15
❑ 188 Joe Fontenot RC	1.00	.30
❑ 189 Matt Halloran RC	1.00	.30
❑ 190 Matt Clement RC	4.00	1.20
❑ 191 Todd Greene	.50	.15
❑ 192 Eric Chavez RC	15.00	4.50
❑ 193 Edgard Velazquez	.50	.15
❑ 194 Bruce Chen RC	1.50	.45
❑ 195 Jason Brester	.50	.15
❑ 196 Chris Reitsma RC	1.50	.45
❑ 197 Neifi Perez	.50	.15
❑ 198 Hideki Irabu RC	1.50	.45
❑ 199 Don Denbow RC	1.00	.30
❑ 200 Derrek Lee	.50	.15
❑ 201 Todd Walker	.50	.15
❑ 202 Scott Rolen	.75	.23
❑ 203 Wes Helms	.50	.15
❑ 204 Bob Abreu	.50	.15
❑ 205 John Patterson RC	2.50	.75
❑ 206 Alex Gonzalez RC	4.00	1.20
❑ 207 Grant Roberts RC	1.50	.45
❑ 208 Jeff Suppan	.50	.15
❑ 209 Luke Wilcox	.50	.15
❑ 210 Marlon Anderson	.50	.15
❑ 211 Mike Caruso RC	1.00	.30
❑ 212 Roy Halladay RC	15.00	4.50
❑ 213 Jeremi Gonzalez RC	1.00	.30
❑ 214 Aramis Ramirez RC	10.00	3.00
❑ 215 Dee Brown RC	1.50	.45
❑ 216 Justin Thompson	.50	.15
❑ 217 Danny Clyburn	.50	.15
❑ 218 Bruce Aven	.50	.15

❑ 219 Keith Foulke RC	1.50	.45
❑ 220 Shannon Stewart	.50	.15
❑ 221 Larry Barnes RC	1.00	.30
❑ 222 Mark Johnson RC	1.00	.30
❑ 223 Randy Winn	.50	.15
❑ 224 Nomar Garciaparra	2.50	.75
❑ 225 Jacque Jones RC	6.00	1.80
❑ 226 Chris Clemons	.50	.15
❑ 227 Todd Helton	1.25	.35
❑ 228 Ryan Brannan RC	1.00	.30
❑ 229 Alex Sanchez RC	1.50	.45
❑ 230 Russell Branyan	.50	.15
❑ 231 Daryle Ward	1.00	.30
❑ 232 Kevin Witt	.50	.15
❑ 233 Gabby Martinez	.50	.15
❑ 234 Preston Wilson	.50	.15
❑ 235 Donzell McDonald RC	1.00	.30
❑ 236 Orlando Cabrera RC	2.50	.75
❑ 237 Brian Banks	.50	.15
❑ 238 Robbie Bell	1.00	.30
❑ 239 Brad Rigby	.50	.15
❑ 240 Scott Elarton	.50	.15
❑ 241 Donny Leon RC	1.50	.45
❑ 242 Abraham Nunez RC	1.00	.30
❑ 243 Adam Eaton RC	1.50	.45
❑ 244 Octavio Dotel RC	1.50	.45
❑ 245 Sean Casey	1.50	.45
❑ 246 Joe Lawrence RC	1.50	.45
❑ 247 Adam Johnson RC	1.00	.30
❑ 248 Ronnie Belliard RC	1.00	.30
❑ 249 Bobby Estalella	.50	.15
❑ 250 Corey Lee RC	1.00	.30
❑ 251 Mike Cameron	.50	.15
❑ 252 Kerry Robinson RC	1.00	.30
❑ 253 A.J. Zapp RC	1.50	.45
❑ 254 Jarrod Washburn	.50	.15
❑ 255 Ben Grieve	.50	.15
❑ 256 Javier Vazquez RC	15.00	3.60
❑ 257 Travis Lee RC	2.50	.75
❑ 258 Dennis Reyes RC	1.00	.30
❑ 259 Danny Buxbaum	.50	.15
❑ 260 Kelvim Escobar RC	1.50	.45
❑ 261 Danny Klassen	.50	.15
❑ 262 Ken Cloude RC	1.50	.45
❑ 263 Gabe Alvarez	.50	.15
❑ 264 Clayton Bruner RC	1.00	.30
❑ 265 Jason Marquis RC	1.50	.45
❑ 266 Jamey Wright	.50	.15
❑ 267 Matt Snyder RC	1.00	.30
❑ 268 Josh Garrett RC	1.00	.30
❑ 269 Juan Encarnacion	.50	.15
❑ 270 Heath Murray	.50	.15
❑ 271 Brent Butler RC	1.50	.45
❑ 272 Danny Peoples RC	1.00	.30
❑ 273 Miguel Tejada RC	20.00	6.00
❑ 274 Jim Pittsley	.50	.15
❑ 275 Dmitri Young	.50	.15
❑ 276 Vladimir Guerrero	1.25	.35
❑ 277 Cole Liniak RC	1.00	.30
❑ 278 Ramon Hernandez	.50	.15
❑ 279 Cliff Politte RC	1.00	.30
❑ 280 Mel Rosario RC	1.00	.30
❑ 281 Jorge Carrion RC	1.00	.30
❑ 282 John Barnes RC	1.00	.30
❑ 283 Chris Stowe RC	1.00	.30
❑ 284 Vernon Wells RC	15.00	4.50
❑ 285 Brett Caradonna RC	1.00	.30
❑ 286 Scott Hodges RC	1.50	.45
❑ 287 Jon Garland RC	2.50	.75
❑ 288 Nathan Haynes RC	1.50	.45
❑ 289 Geoff Goetz RC	1.00	.30
❑ 290 Adam Kennedy RC	4.00	1.20
❑ 291 T.J. Tucker RC	1.00	.30
❑ 292 Aaron Akin RC	1.00	.30
❑ 293 Jayson Werth RC	1.50	.45
❑ 294 Glenn Davis RC	1.00	.30
❑ 295 Mark Mangum RC	1.00	.30
❑ 296 Troy Cameron RC	1.50	.45
❑ 297 J.J. Davis RC	1.50	.45
❑ 298 Lance Berkman RC	20.00	6.00
❑ 299 Jason Standridge RC	1.50	.45
❑ 300 Jason Dellaero RC	1.00	.30

1998 Bowman Chrome

	Nm-Mt	Ex-Mt
COMPLETE SET (441)	160.00	47.50
COMP. SERIES 1 (221)	80.00	24.00
COMP. SERIES 2 (220)	80.00	24.00

❑ 1 Nomar Garciaparra	2.50	.75
❑ 2 Scott Rolen	.75	.23
❑ 3 Andy Pettitte	.75	.23
❑ 4 Ivan Rodriguez	1.25	.35
❑ 5 Mark McGwire	3.00	.90
❑ 6 Jason Dickson	.50	.15
❑ 7 Jose Cruz Jr.	.50	.15
❑ 8 Jeff Kent	.50	.15
❑ 9 Mike Mussina	1.25	.35
❑ 10 Jason Kendall	.50	.15
❑ 11 Brett Tomko	.50	.15
❑ 12 Jeff King	.50	.15
❑ 13 Brad Radke	.50	.15
❑ 14 Robin Ventura	.50	.15
❑ 15 Jeff Bagwell	.75	.23
❑ 16 Greg Maddux	2.50	.75
❑ 17 John Jaha	.50	.15
❑ 18 Mike Piazza	2.00	.60
❑ 19 Edgar Martinez	.75	.23
❑ 20 David Justice	.50	.15
❑ 21 Todd Hundley	.50	.15
❑ 22 Tony Gwynn	1.50	.45
❑ 23 Larry Walker	.75	.23
❑ 24 Bernie Williams	.75	.23
❑ 25 Edgar Renteria	.50	.15
❑ 26 Rafael Palmeiro	.75	.23
❑ 27 Tim Salmon	.75	.23
❑ 28 Matt Morris	.50	.15
❑ 29 Shawn Estes	.50	.15
❑ 30 Vladimir Guerrero	1.25	.35
❑ 31 Fernando Tatis	.50	.15
❑ 32 Justin Thompson	.50	.15
❑ 33 Ken Griffey Jr.	2.00	.60
❑ 34 Edgardo Alfonzo	.50	.15
❑ 35 Mo Vaughn	.50	.15
❑ 36 Marty Cordova	.50	.15
❑ 37 Craig Biggio	.75	.23
❑ 38 Roger Clemens	2.50	.75
❑ 39 Mark Grace	1.25	.35
❑ 40 Ken Caminiti	.50	.15
❑ 41 Tony Womack	.50	.15
❑ 42 Albert Belle	.50	.15
❑ 43 Tino Martinez	.75	.23
❑ 44 Sandy Alomar Jr.	.50	.15
❑ 45 Jeff Cirillo	.50	.15
❑ 46 Jason Giambi	1.25	.35
❑ 47 Darin Erstad	.50	.15
❑ 48 Livan Hernandez	.50	.15
❑ 49 Mark Grudzielanek	.50	.15
❑ 50 Sammy Sosa	2.00	.60
❑ 51 Curt Schilling	.75	.23
❑ 52 Brian Hunter	.50	.15
❑ 53 Neifi Perez	.50	.15
❑ 54 Todd Walker	.50	.15
❑ 55 Jose Guillen	.50	.15
❑ 56 Jim Thome	1.25	.35
❑ 57 Tom Glavine	1.25	.35
❑ 58 Todd Greene	.50	.15
❑ 59 Rondell White	.50	.15
❑ 60 Roberto Alomar	1.25	.35
❑ 61 Tony Clark	.50	.15
❑ 62 Vinny Castilla	.50	.15
❑ 63 Barry Larkin	1.25	.35
❑ 64 Hideki Irabu	.50	.15
❑ 65 Johnny Damon	.50	.15
❑ 66 Juan Gonzalez	1.25	.35
❑ 67 John Olerud	.50	.15
❑ 68 Gary Sheffield	.50	.15
❑ 69 Raul Mondesi	.50	.15
❑ 70 Chipper Jones	1.25	.35
❑ 71 David Ortiz	2.50	.75
❑ 72 Warren Morris RC	1.00	.30
❑ 73 Alex Gonzalez	.50	.15
❑ 74 Nick Bierbrodt	.50	.15
❑ 75 Roy Halladay	.75	.23
❑ 76 Danny Buxbaum	.50	.15
❑ 77 Adam Kennedy	.50	.15
❑ 78 Jared Sandberg	.50	.15
❑ 79 Michael Barrett	.50	.15
❑ 80 Gil Meche	5.00	1.50
❑ 81 Jayson Werth	.50	.15
❑ 82 Abraham Nunez	.50	.15
❑ 83 Ben Petrick	.50	.15
❑ 84 Brett Caradonna	.50	.15
❑ 85 Mike Lowell RC	8.00	2.40
❑ 86 Clay Bruner	.50	.15
❑ 87 John Curtice RC	1.50	.45
❑ 88 Bobby Estalella	.50	.15
❑ 89 Juan Melo	.50	.15
❑ 90 Arnold Gooch	.50	.15
❑ 91 Kevin Millwood RC	6.00	1.80
❑ 92 Richie Sexson	.50	.15
❑ 93 Orlando Cabrera	.50	.15
❑ 94 Pat Cline	.50	.15
❑ 95 Anthony Sanders	.50	.15
❑ 96 Russ Johnson	.50	.15
❑ 97 Ben Grieve	.50	.15
❑ 98 Kevin McGlinchy	.50	.15
❑ 99 Paul Wilder	.50	.15
❑ 100 Russ Ortiz	.50	.15
❑ 101 Ryan Jackson RC	1.00	.30
❑ 102 Heath Murray	.50	.15
❑ 103 Brian Rose	.50	.15
❑ 104 R.Radmanovich RC	1.00	.30
❑ 105 Ricky Ledee	.50	.15
❑ 106 Jeff Wallace RC	1.00	.30
❑ 107 Ryan Minor RC	1.00	.30
❑ 108 Dennis Reyes	.50	.15
❑ 109 James Manias	.50	.15
❑ 110 Chris Carpenter	.50	.15
❑ 111 Daryle Ward	.50	.15
❑ 112 Vernon Wells	.75	.23
❑ 113 Chad Green	.50	.15
❑ 114 Mike Stoner RC	1.00	.30
❑ 115 Brad Fullmer	.50	.15
❑ 116 Adam Eaton	.50	.15
❑ 117 Jeff Liefer	.50	.15
❑ 118 Corey Koskie RC	5.00	1.50
❑ 119 Todd Helton	.75	.23
❑ 120 Jaime Jones RC	1.00	.30
❑ 121 Mel Rosario	.50	.15
❑ 122 Geoff Goetz	.50	.15
❑ 123 Adrian Beltre	.50	.15
❑ 124 Jason Dellaero	.50	.15
❑ 125 Gabe Kapler RC	2.50	.75
❑ 126 Scott Schoeneweis	.50	.15
❑ 127 Ryan Brannan	.50	.15
❑ 128 Aaron Akin	.50	.15
❑ 129 Ryan Anderson RC	1.50	.45
❑ 130 Brad Penny	.50	.15
❑ 131 Bruce Chen	.50	.15
❑ 132 Eli Marrero	.50	.15
❑ 133 Eric Chavez	.75	.23
❑ 134 Troy Glaus RC	15.00	4.50
❑ 135 Troy Cameron	.50	.15
❑ 136 Brian Sikorski RC	1.00	.30
❑ 137 Mike Kinkade RC	1.00	.30
❑ 138 Braden Looper	.50	.15
❑ 139 Mark Mangum	.50	.15
❑ 140 Danny Peoples	.50	.15
❑ 141 J.J. Davis	.50	.15
❑ 142 Ben Davis	.50	.15
❑ 143 Jacque Jones	.50	.15
❑ 144 Derrick Gibson	.50	.15
❑ 145 Bronson Arroyo	1.00	.30
❑ 146 L.De Los Santos RC	1.00	.30
❑ 147 Jeff Abbott	.50	.15

	No.	Player		
❑	148	Mike Cuddyer RC	5.00	1.50
❑	149	Jason Romano	.50	.15
❑	150	Shane Monahan	.50	.15
❑	151	Ntema Ndungidi RC	1.00	.30
❑	152	Alex Sanchez	.50	.15
❑	153	Jack Cust RC	1.50	.45
❑	154	Brent Butler	.50	.15
❑	155	Ramon Hernandez	.50	.15
❑	156	Norm Hutchins	.50	.15
❑	157	Jason Marquis	.50	.15
❑	158	Jacob Cruz	.50	.15
❑	159	Rob Burger RC	1.00	.30
❑	160	Dave Coggin	.50	.15
❑	161	Preston Wilson	.50	.15
❑	162	Jason Fitzgerald RC	1.00	.30
❑	163	Dan Serafini	.50	.15
❑	164	Pete Munro	.50	.15
❑	165	Trot Nixon	.50	.15
❑	166	Homer Bush	.50	.15
❑	167	Dermal Brown	.50	.15
❑	168	Chad Hermansen	.50	.15
❑	169	Julio Moreno RC	1.00	.30
❑	170	John Roskos RC	1.00	.30
❑	171	Grant Roberts	.50	.15
❑	172	Ken Cloude	.50	.15
❑	173	Jason Brester	.50	.15
❑	174	Jason Conti	.50	.15
❑	175	Jon Garland	.50	.15
❑	176	Robbie Bell	.50	.15
❑	177	Nathan Haynes	.50	.15
❑	178	Ramon Ortiz RC	4.00	1.20
❑	179	Shannon Stewart	.50	.15
❑	180	Pablo Ortega	.50	.15
❑	181	Jimmy Rollins RC	5.00	1.50
❑	182	Sean Casey	.50	.15
❑	183	Ted Lilly RC	2.50	.75
❑	184	Chris Enochs RC	1.00	.30
❑	185	M.Ordonez RC UER	10.00	3.00
		Front photo is Mario Valdez		
❑	186	Mike Drumright	.50	.15
❑	187	Aaron Boone	.50	.15
❑	188	Matt Clement	.50	.15
❑	189	Todd Dunwoody	.50	.15
❑	190	Larry Rodriguez	.50	.15
❑	191	Todd Noel	.50	.15
❑	192	Geoff Jenkins	.50	.15
❑	193	George Lombard	.50	.15
❑	194	Lance Berkman	.75	.23
❑	195	Marcus McCain	.50	.15
❑	196	Ryan McGuire	.50	.15
❑	197	Jhensy Sandoval	.50	.15
❑	198	Corey Lee	.50	.15
❑	199	Mario Valdez	.50	.15
❑	200	Robert Fick RC	5.00	1.50
❑	201	Donnie Sadler	.50	.15
❑	202	Marc Kroon	.50	.15
❑	203	David Miller	.50	.15
❑	204	Jarrod Washburn	.50	.15
❑	205	Miguel Tejada	.75	.23
❑	206	Raul Ibanez	.50	.15
❑	207	John Patterson	.50	.15
❑	208	Calvin Pickering	.50	.15
❑	209	Felix Martinez	.50	.15
❑	210	Mark Redman	.50	.15
❑	211	Scott Elarton	.50	.15
❑	212	Jose Amado RC	1.00	.30
❑	213	Kerry Wood	1.25	.35
❑	214	Dante Powell	.50	.15
❑	215	Aramis Ramirez	.50	.15
❑	216	A.J. Hinch	.50	.15
❑	217	Dustin Carr RC	1.00	.30
❑	218	Mark Kotsay	.50	.15
❑	219	Jason Standridge	.50	.15
❑	220	Luis Ordaz	.50	.15
❑	221	O.Hernandez RC	5.00	1.50
❑	222	Cal Ripken	4.00	1.20
❑	223	Paul Molitor	.75	.23
❑	224	Derek Jeter	3.00	.90
❑	225	Barry Bonds	3.00	.90
❑	226	Jim Edmonds	.50	.15
❑	227	John Smoltz	.75	.23
❑	228	Eric Karros	.50	.15
❑	229	Ray Lankford	.50	.15
❑	230	Rey Ordonez	.50	.15
❑	231	Kenny Lofton	.50	.15
❑	232	Alex Rodriguez	2.50	.75
❑	233	Dante Bichette	.50	.15
❑	234	Pedro Martinez	1.25	.35
❑	235	Carlos Delgado	.50	.15
❑	236	Rod Beck	.50	.15
❑	237	Matt Williams	.50	.15
❑	238	Charles Johnson	.50	.15
❑	239	Rico Brogna	.50	.15
❑	240	Frank Thomas	1.25	.35
❑	241	Paul O'Neill	.75	.23
❑	242	Jaret Wright	.50	.15
❑	243	Brant Brown	.50	.15
❑	244	Ryan Klesko	.50	.15
❑	245	Chuck Finley	.50	.15
❑	246	Derek Bell	.50	.15
❑	247	Delino DeShields	.50	.15
❑	248	Chan Ho Park	.50	.15
❑	249	Wade Boggs	.75	.23
❑	250	Jay Buhner	.50	.15
❑	251	Butch Huskey	.50	.15
❑	252	Steve Finley	.50	.15
❑	253	Will Clark	1.25	.35
❑	254	John Valentin	.50	.15
❑	255	Bobby Higginson	.50	.15
❑	256	Darryl Strawberry	.75	.23
❑	257	Randy Johnson	1.25	.35
❑	258	Al Martin	.50	.15
❑	259	Travis Fryman	.50	.15
❑	260	Fred McGriff	.75	.23
❑	261	Jose Valentin	.50	.15
❑	262	Andruw Jones	.75	.23
❑	263	Kenny Rogers	.50	.15
❑	264	Moises Alou	.50	.15
❑	265	Denny Neagle	.50	.15
❑	266	Ugueth Urbina	.50	.15
❑	267	Derrek Lee	.50	.15
❑	268	Ellis Burks	.50	.15
❑	269	Mariano Rivera	.75	.23
❑	270	Dean Palmer	.50	.15
❑	271	Eddie Taubensee	.50	.15
❑	272	Brady Anderson	.50	.15
❑	273	Brian Giles	.50	.15
❑	274	Quinton McCracken	.50	.15
❑	275	Henry Rodriguez	.50	.15
❑	276	Andres Galarraga	.50	.15
❑	277	Jose Canseco	1.25	.35
❑	278	David Segui	.50	.15
❑	279	Bret Saberhagen	.50	.15
❑	280	Kevin Brown	.75	.23
❑	281	Chuck Knoblauch	.50	.15
❑	282	Jeromy Burnitz	.50	.15
❑	283	Jay Bell	.50	.15
❑	284	Manny Ramirez	.50	.15
❑	285	Rick Helling	.50	.15
❑	286	Francisco Cordova	.50	.15
❑	287	Bob Abreu	.50	.15
❑	288	J.T. Snow	.50	.15
❑	289	Hideo Nomo	1.25	.35
❑	290	Brian Jordan	.50	.15
❑	291	Javy Lopez	.50	.15
❑	292	Travis Lee	.50	.15
❑	293	Russell Branyan	.50	.15
❑	294	Paul Konerko	.50	.15
❑	295	Masato Yoshii RC	2.50	.75
❑	296	Kris Benson	.50	.15
❑	297	Juan Encarnacion	.50	.15
❑	298	Eric Milton	.50	.15
❑	299	Mike Caruso	.50	.15
❑	300	R. Aramboles RC	1.50	.45
❑	301	Bobby Smith	.50	.15
❑	302	Billy Koch	.50	.15
❑	303	Richard Hidalgo	.50	.15
❑	304	Justin Baughman RC	1.00	.30
❑	305	Chris Gissell	.50	.15
❑	306	Donnie Bridges RC	1.50	.45
❑	307	Nelson Lara RC	1.00	.30
❑	308	Randy Wolf RC	4.00	1.20
❑	309	Jason LaRue RC	1.50	.45
❑	310	Jason Gooding RC	1.00	.30
❑	311	Edgard Clemente	.50	.15
❑	312	Andrew Vessel	.50	.15
❑	313	Chris Reitsma	.50	.15
❑	314	Jesus Sanchez RC	1.00	.30
❑	315	Buddy Carlyle RC	1.00	.30
❑	316	Randy Winn	.50	.15
❑	317	Luis Rivera RC	1.00	.30
❑	318	Marcus Thames RC	1.50	.45
❑	319	A.J. Pierzynski	.50	.15
❑	320	Scott Randall	.50	.15
❑	321	Damian Sapp	.50	.15
❑	322	Ed Yarnall RC	1.00	.30
❑	323	Luke Allen RC	1.50	.45
❑	324	J.D. Smart	.50	.15
❑	325	Willie Martinez	.50	.15
❑	326	Alex Ramirez	.50	.15
❑	327	Eric DuBose RC	1.00	.30
❑	328	Kevin Witt	.50	.15
❑	329	Dan McKinley RC	1.00	.30
❑	330	Cliff Politte	.50	.15
❑	331	Vladimir Nunez	.50	.15
❑	332	John Halama RC	1.50	.45
❑	333	Nerio Rodriguez	.50	.15
❑	334	Desi Relaford	.50	.15
❑	335	Robinson Checo	.50	.15
❑	336	John Nicholson	.75	.23
❑	337	Tom LaRosa RC	1.00	.30
❑	338	Kevin Nicholson RC	1.00	.30
❑	339	Javier Vazquez	.75	.15
❑	340	A.J. Zapp	.50	.15
❑	341	Tom Evans	.50	.15
❑	342	Kerry Robinson	.50	.15
❑	343	Gabe Gonzalez RC	1.00	.30
❑	344	Ralph Milliard	.50	.15
❑	345	Enrique Wilson	.50	.15
❑	346	Elvin Hernandez	.50	.15
❑	347	Mike Lincoln RC	1.00	.30
❑	348	Cesar King RC	1.00	.30
❑	349	Cristian Guzman RC	5.00	1.50
❑	350	Donzell McDonald	.50	.15
❑	351	Jim Parque RC	1.50	.45
❑	352	Mike Saipe RC	1.00	.30
❑	353	Carlos Febles RC	1.50	.45
❑	354	Dernell Stenson RC	1.50	.45
❑	355	Mark Osborne RC	1.00	.30
❑	356	Odalis Perez RC	2.50	.75
❑	357	Jason Dewey RC	1.00	.30
❑	358	Joe Fontenot	.50	.15
❑	359	Jason Grilli RC	1.00	.30
❑	360	Kevin Haverbusch RC	1.00	.30
❑	361	Jay Yennaco RC	1.00	.30
❑	362	Brian Buchanan	.50	.15
❑	363	John Barnes	.50	.15
❑	364	Chris Fussell	.50	.15
❑	365	Kevin Gibbs RC	1.00	.30
❑	366	Joe Lawrence	.50	.15
❑	367	DaRond Stovall	.50	.15
❑	368	Brian Fuentes RC	1.00	.30
❑	369	Jimmy Anderson	.50	.15
❑	370	Lariel Gonzalez RC	1.00	.30
❑	371	Scott Williamson RC	1.50	.45
❑	372	Milton Bradley	.50	.15
❑	373	Jason Halper RC	1.00	.30
❑	374	Brent Billingsley RC	1.00	.30
❑	375	Joe DePastino RC	1.00	.30
❑	376	Jake Westbrook	.50	.15
❑	377	Octavio Dotel	.50	.15
❑	378	Jason Williams RC	1.00	.30
❑	379	Julio Ramirez RC	1.00	.30
❑	380	Seth Greisinger	.50	.15
❑	381	Mike Judd RC	1.00	.30
❑	382	Ben Ford RC	1.00	.30
❑	383	Tom Bennett RC	1.00	.30
❑	384	Adam Butler RC	1.00	.30
❑	385	Wade Miller RC	5.00	1.50
❑	386	Kyle Peterson RC	1.00	.30
❑	387	Tommy Peterman RC	1.00	.30
❑	388	Onan Masaoka	.50	.15
❑	389	Jason Rakers RC	1.00	.30
❑	390	Rafael Medina	.50	.15
❑	391	Luis Lopez RC	1.00	.30
❑	392	Jeff Yoder	.50	.15
❑	393	Vance Wilson RC	1.00	.30
❑	394	F. Seguignol RC	1.00	.30
❑	395	Ron Wright	.50	.15
❑	396	Ruben Mateo RC	1.50	.45
❑	397	Steve Lomasney RC	1.50	.45
❑	398	Damian Jackson	.50	.15
❑	399	Mike Jerzembeck RC	1.00	.30
❑	400	Luis Rivas RC	4.00	1.20
❑	401	Kevin Burford RC	1.00	.30
❑	402	Glenn Davis	.50	.15
❑	403	Robert Luce RC	1.00	.30
❑	404	Cole Liniak	.50	.15

❑ 405	Matt LeCroy RC	1.50	.45
❑ 406	Jeremy Giambi RC	1.50	.45
❑ 407	Shawn Chacon	.50	.15
❑ 408	Dewayne Wise RC	1.00	.30
❑ 409	Steve Woodard	.50	.15
❑ 410	F.Cordero RC	1.50	.45
❑ 411	Damon Minor RC	1.50	.45
❑ 412	Lou Collier	.50	.15
❑ 413	Justin Towle	.50	.15
❑ 414	Juan LeBron	.50	.15
❑ 415	Michael Coleman	.50	.15
❑ 416	Felix Rodriguez	.50	.15
❑ 417	Paul Ah Yat RC	1.00	.30
❑ 418	Kevin Barker RC	1.00	.30
❑ 419	Brian Meadows	.50	.15
❑ 420	Darnell McDonald RC	1.50	.45
❑ 421	Matt Kinney RC	1.50	.45
❑ 422	Mike Vavrek RC	1.00	.30
❑ 423	Courtney Duncan RC	1.00	.30
❑ 424	Kevin Millar RC	5.00	1.50
❑ 425	Ruben Rivera	.50	.15
❑ 426	Steve Shoemaker RC	1.00	.30
❑ 427	Dan Reichert RC	1.50	.45
❑ 428	Carlos Lee RC	5.00	1.50
❑ 429	Rod Barajas	1.00	.30
❑ 430	Pablo Ozuna RC	1.50	.45
❑ 431	Todd Belitz RC	1.00	.30
❑ 432	Sidney Ponson	.50	.15
❑ 433	Steve Carver RC	1.00	.30
❑ 434	Esteban Yan RC	1.50	.45
❑ 435	Cedrick Bowers	.50	.15
❑ 436	Marlon Anderson	.50	.15
❑ 437	Carl Pavano	.50	.15
❑ 438	Jae Weong Seo RC	2.50	.75
❑ 439	Jose Taveras RC	1.00	.30
❑ 440	Matt Anderson RC	1.50	.45
❑ 441	Darron Ingram RC	1.00	.30

1999 Bowman Chrome

	Nm-Mt	Ex-Mt
COMPLETE SET (440)	300.00	90.00
COMP. SERIES 1 (220)	100.00	30.00
COMP. SERIES 2 (220)	200.00	60.00

❑ 1	Ben Grieve	.50	.15
❑ 2	Kerry Wood	1.25	.35
❑ 3	Ruben Rivera	.50	.15
❑ 4	Sandy Alomar Jr.	.50	.15
❑ 5	Cal Ripken	4.00	1.20
❑ 6	Mark McGwire	3.00	.90
❑ 7	Vladimir Guerrero	1.25	.35
❑ 8	Moises Alou	.50	.15
❑ 9	Jim Edmonds	.50	.15
❑ 10	Greg Maddux	2.50	.75
❑ 11	Gary Sheffield	.50	.15
❑ 12	John Valentin	.50	.15
❑ 13	Chuck Knoblauch	.50	.15
❑ 14	Tony Clark	.50	.15
❑ 15	Rusty Greer	.50	.15
❑ 16	Al Leiter	.50	.15
❑ 17	Travis Lee	.50	.15
❑ 18	Jose Cruz Jr.	.50	.15
❑ 19	Pedro Martinez	1.25	.35
❑ 20	Paul O'Neill	.75	.23
❑ 21	Todd Walker	.50	.15
❑ 22	Vinny Castilla	.50	.15
❑ 23	Barry Larkin	1.25	.35
❑ 24	Curt Schilling	.75	.23
❑ 25	Jason Kendall	.50	.15
❑ 26	Scott Erickson	.50	.15
❑ 27	Andres Galarraga	.50	.15
❑ 28	Jeff Shaw	.50	.15
❑ 29	John Olerud	.50	.15
❑ 30	Orlando Hernandez	.50	.15
❑ 31	Larry Walker	.75	.23
❑ 32	Andruw Jones	.75	.23
❑ 33	Jeff Cirillo	.50	.15
❑ 34	Barry Bonds	3.00	.90
❑ 35	Manny Ramirez	.50	.15
❑ 36	Mark Kotsay	.50	.15
❑ 37	Ivan Rodriguez	1.25	.35
❑ 38	Jeff King	.50	.15
❑ 39	Brian Hunter	.50	.15
❑ 40	Ray Durham	.50	.15
❑ 41	Bernie Williams	.75	.23
❑ 42	Darin Erstad	.50	.15
❑ 43	Chipper Jones	1.25	.35
❑ 44	Pat Hentgen	.50	.15
❑ 45	Eric Young	.50	.15
❑ 46	Jaret Wright	.50	.15
❑ 47	Juan Guzman	.50	.15
❑ 48	Jorge Posada	.75	.23
❑ 49	Bobby Higginson	.50	.15
❑ 50	Jose Guillen	.50	.15
❑ 51	Trevor Hoffman	.50	.15
❑ 52	Ken Griffey Jr.	2.00	.60
❑ 53	David Justice	.50	.15
❑ 54	Matt Williams	.50	.15
❑ 55	Eric Karros	.50	.15
❑ 56	Derek Bell	.50	.15
❑ 57	Ray Lankford	.50	.15
❑ 58	Mariano Rivera	.75	.23
❑ 59	Brett Tomko	.50	.15
❑ 60	Mike Mussina	1.25	.35
❑ 61	Kenny Lofton	.50	.15
❑ 62	Chuck Finley	.50	.15
❑ 63	Alex Gonzalez	.50	.15
❑ 64	Mark Grace	1.25	.35
❑ 65	Raul Mondesi	.50	.15
❑ 66	David Cone	.50	.15
❑ 67	Brad Fullmer	.50	.15
❑ 68	Andy Benes	.50	.15
❑ 69	John Smoltz	.75	.23
❑ 70	Shane Reynolds	.50	.15
❑ 71	Bruce Chen	.50	.15
❑ 72	Adam Kennedy	.50	.15
❑ 73	Jack Cust	.50	.15
❑ 74	Matt Clement	.50	.15
❑ 75	Derrick Gibson	.50	.15
❑ 76	Darnell McDonald	.50	.15
❑ 77	Adam Everett RC	1.50	.45
❑ 78	Ricardo Aramboles	.50	.15
❑ 79	Mark Quinn RC	1.50	.45
❑ 80	Jason Rakers	.50	.15
❑ 81	Seth Etherton RC	1.50	.45
❑ 82	Jeff Urban RC	1.00	.30
❑ 83	Manny Aybar	.50	.15
❑ 84	Mike Nannini RC	1.50	.45
❑ 85	Onan Masaoka	.50	.15
❑ 86	Rod Barajas	.50	.15
❑ 87	Mike Frank	.50	.15
❑ 88	Scott Randall	.50	.15
❑ 89	Justin Bowles RC	1.00	.30
❑ 90	Chris Haas	.50	.15
❑ 91	Arturo McDowell RC	1.50	.45
❑ 92	Matt Belisle RC	1.50	.45
❑ 93	Scott Elarton	.50	.15
❑ 94	Vernon Wells	.50	.15
❑ 95	Pat Cline	.50	.15
❑ 96	Ryan Anderson	.50	.15
❑ 97	Kevin Barker	.50	.15
❑ 98	Ruben Mateo	.50	.15
❑ 99	Robert Fick	.50	.15
❑ 100	Corey Koskie	.50	.15
❑ 101	Ricky Ledee	.50	.15
❑ 102	Rick Elder RC	1.50	.45
❑ 103	Jack Cressend RC	1.00	.30
❑ 104	Joe Lawrence	.50	.15
❑ 105	Mike Lincoln	.50	.15
❑ 106	Kit Pellow RC	1.00	.30
❑ 107	Matt Burch RC	1.00	.30
❑ 108	Cole Liniak	.50	.15
❑ 109	Jason Dewey	.50	.15
❑ 110	Cesar King	.50	.15
❑ 111	Julio Ramirez	.50	.15
❑ 112	Jake Westbrook	.50	.15
❑ 113	Eric Valent RC	1.50	.45
❑ 114	Roosevelt Brown RC	1.50	.45
❑ 115	Choo Freeman RC	1.50	.45
❑ 116	Juan Melo	.50	.15
❑ 117	Jason Grilli	.50	.15
❑ 118	Jared Sandberg	.50	.15
❑ 119	Glenn Davis	.50	.15
❑ 120	David Riske RC	1.00	.30
❑ 121	Jacque Jones	.50	.15
❑ 122	Corey Lee	.50	.15
❑ 123	Michael Barrett	.50	.15
❑ 124	Lariel Gonzalez	.50	.15
❑ 125	Mitch Meluskey	.50	.15
❑ 126	Freddy Adrian Garcia	.50	.15
❑ 127	Tony Torcato RC	1.50	.45
❑ 128	Jeff Liefer	.50	.15
❑ 129	Ntema Ndungidi	.50	.15
❑ 130	Andy Brown RC	1.50	.45
❑ 131	Ryan Mills RC	1.50	.45
❑ 132	Andy Abad RC	1.00	.30
❑ 133	Carlos Febles	.50	.15
❑ 134	Jason Tyner RC	1.50	.45
❑ 135	Mark Osborne	.50	.15
❑ 136	Phil Norton RC	1.00	.30
❑ 137	Nathan Haynes	.50	.15
❑ 138	Roy Halladay	.50	.15
❑ 139	Juan Encarnacion	.50	.15
❑ 140	Brad Penny	.50	.15
❑ 141	Grant Roberts	.50	.15
❑ 142	Aramis Ramirez	.50	.15
❑ 143	Cristian Guzman	.50	.15
❑ 144	Mamon Tucker RC	1.50	.45
❑ 145	Ryan Bradley	.50	.15
❑ 146	Brian Simmons	.50	.15
❑ 147	Dan Reichert	.50	.15
❑ 148	Russell Branyan	.50	.15
❑ 149	Victor Valencia RC	1.00	.30
❑ 150	Scott Schoeneweis	.50	.15
❑ 151	Sean Spencer RC	1.00	.30
❑ 152	Odalis Perez	.50	.15
❑ 153	Joe Fontenot	.50	.15
❑ 154	Milton Bradley	.50	.15
❑ 155	Josh McKinley RC	1.50	.45
❑ 156	Terrence Long	.50	.15
❑ 157	Danny Klassen	.50	.15
❑ 158	Paul Hoover RC	1.00	.30
❑ 159	Ron Belliard	.50	.15
❑ 160	Armando Rios	.50	.15
❑ 161	Ramon Hernandez	.50	.15
❑ 162	Jason Conti	.50	.15
❑ 163	Chad Hermansen	.50	.15
❑ 164	Jason Standridge	.50	.15
❑ 165	Jason Dellaero	.50	.15
❑ 166	John Curtice	.50	.15
❑ 167	Clayton Andrews RC	1.50	.45
❑ 168	Jeremy Giambi	.50	.15
❑ 169	Alex Ramirez	.50	.15
❑ 170	Gabe Molina RC	1.00	.30
❑ 171	M.Encarnacion RC	1.00	.30
❑ 172	Mike Zywica RC	1.00	.30
❑ 173	Chip Ambres RC	1.50	.45
❑ 174	Trot Nixon	.50	.15
❑ 175	Pat Burrell RC	15.00	4.50
❑ 176	Jeff Yoder	.50	.15
❑ 177	Chris Jones RC	1.50	.45
❑ 178	Kevin Witt	.50	.15
❑ 179	Keith Luuloa RC	1.00	.30
❑ 180	Billy Koch	.50	.15
❑ 181	Damaso Marte RC	1.00	.30
❑ 182	Ryan Glynn RC	1.00	.30
❑ 183	Calvin Pickering	.50	.15
❑ 184	Michael Cuddyer	.50	.15
❑ 185	Nick Johnson RC	8.00	2.40
❑ 186	D.Mientkiewicz RC	5.00	1.50
❑ 187	Nate Cornejo RC	2.50	.75
❑ 188	Octavio Dotel	.50	.15
❑ 189	Wes Helms	.50	.15
❑ 190	Nelson Lara	.50	.15
❑ 191	Chuck Abbott RC	1.00	.30
❑ 192	Tony Armas Jr.	.50	.15
❑ 193	Gil Meche	.50	.15
❑ 194	Ben Petrick	.50	.15
❑ 195	Chris George RC	1.50	.45

No.	Player	Nm-Mt	Ex-Mt
196	Scott Hunter RC	1.00	.30
197	Ryan Brannan	.50	.15
198	Amaury Garcia RC	1.00	.30
199	Chris Gissell	.50	.15
200	Austin Kearns RC	25.00	7.50
201	Alex Gonzalez	.50	.15
202	Wade Miller	.50	.15
203	Scott Williamson	.50	.15
204	Chris Enochs	.50	.15
205	Fernando Seguignol	.50	.15
206	Marlon Anderson	.50	.15
207	Todd Sears RC	1.50	.45
208	Nate Bump RC	1.00	.30
209	J.M. Gold RC	1.50	.45
210	Matt LeCroy	.50	.15
211	Alex Hernandez	.50	.15
212	Luis Rivera	.50	.15
213	Troy Cameron	.50	.15
214	Alex Escobar RC	1.50	.45
215	Jason LaRue	.50	.15
216	Kyle Peterson	.50	.15
217	Brent Butler	.50	.15
218	Dernell Stenson	.50	.15
219	Adrian Beltre	.50	.15
220	Daryle Ward	.50	.15
221	Jim Thome	1.25	.35
222	Cliff Floyd	.50	.15
223	Rickey Henderson	2.00	.60
224	Garret Anderson	.50	.15
225	Ken Caminiti	.50	.15
226	Bret Boone	.50	.15
227	Jeromy Burnitz	.50	.15
228	Steve Finley	.50	.15
229	Miguel Tejada	.50	.15
230	Greg Vaughn	.50	.15
231	Jose Offerman	.50	.15
232	Andy Ashby	.50	.15
233	Albert Belle	.50	.15
234	Fernando Tatis	.50	.15
235	Todd Helton	.75	.23
236	Sean Casey	.50	.15
237	Brian Giles	.50	.15
238	Andy Pettitte	.75	.23
239	Fred McGriff	.75	.23
240	Roberto Alomar	1.25	.35
241	Edgar Martinez	.75	.23
242	Lee Stevens	.50	.15
243	Shawn Green	.50	.15
244	Ryan Klesko	.50	.15
245	Sammy Sosa	2.00	.60
246	Todd Hundley	.50	.15
247	Shannon Stewart	.50	.15
248	Randy Johnson	1.25	.35
249	Rondell White	.50	.15
250	Mike Piazza	2.00	.60
251	Craig Biggio	.75	.23
252	David Wells	.50	.15
253	Brian Jordan	.50	.15
254	Edgar Renteria	.50	.15
255	Bartolo Colon	.50	.15
256	Frank Thomas	1.25	.35
257	Will Clark	1.25	.35
258	Dean Palmer	.50	.15
259	Dmitri Young	.50	.15
260	Scott Rolen	.75	.23
261	Jeff Kent	.50	.15
262	Dante Bichette	.50	.15
263	Nomar Garciaparra	2.50	.75
264	Tony Gwynn	1.50	.45
265	Alex Rodriguez	2.50	.75
266	Jose Canseco	1.25	.35
267	Jason Giambi	1.25	.35
268	Jeff Bagwell	.75	.23
269	Carlos Delgado	.50	.15
270	Tom Glavine	1.25	.35
271	Eric Davis	.50	.15
272	Edgardo Alfonzo	.50	.15
273	Tim Salmon	.75	.23
274	Johnny Damon	.50	.15
275	Rafael Palmeiro	.75	.23
276	Denny Neagle	.50	.15
277	Neifi Perez	.50	.15
278	Roger Clemens	2.50	.75
279	Brant Brown	.50	.15
280	Kevin Brown	.75	.23
281	Jay Bell	.50	.15
282	Jay Buhner	.50	.15
283	Matt Lawton	.50	.15
284	Robin Ventura	.50	.15
285	Juan Gonzalez	1.25	.35
286	Mo Vaughn	.50	.15
287	Kevin Millwood	.50	.15
288	Tino Martinez	.75	.23
289	Justin Thompson	.50	.15
290	Derek Jeter	3.00	.90
291	Ben Davis	.50	.15
292	Mike Lowell	.50	.15
293	Calvin Murray	.50	.15
294	Micah Bowie RC	1.00	.30
295	Lance Berkman	.50	.15
296	Jason Marquis	.50	.15
297	Chad Green	.50	.15
298	Dee Brown	.50	.15
299	Jerry Hairston Jr.	.50	.15
300	Gabe Kapler	.50	.15
301	Brent Stentz RC	1.00	.30
302	Scott Mullen RC	1.00	.30
303	Brandon Reed	.50	.15
304	Shea Hillenbrand RC	8.00	2.40
305	J.D. Closser RC	1.50	.45
306	Gary Matthews Jr.	.50	.15
307	Toby Hall RC	2.50	.75
308	Jason Phillips RC	1.00	.30
309	Jose Macias RC	1.00	.30
310	Jung Bong RC	1.50	.45
311	Ramon Soler RC	1.50	.45
312	Kelly Dransfeldt RC	1.00	.30
313	Carlos E. Hernandez RC	1.50	.45
314	Kevin Haverbusch	.50	.15
315	Aaron Myette RC	1.50	.45
316	Chad Harville RC	1.00	.30
317	Kyle Farnsworth RC	4.00	1.20
318	Gookie Dawkins RC	1.50	.45
319	Willie Martinez	.50	.15
320	Carlos Lee	.50	.15
321	Carlos Pena RC	4.00	1.20
322	Peter Bergeron RC	1.50	.45
323	A.J. Burnett RC	2.50	.75
324	Bucky Jacobsen RC	1.50	.45
325	Mo Bruce RC	1.00	.30
326	Reggie Taylor	.50	.15
327	Jackie Rexrode	.50	.15
328	Alvin Morrow RC	1.00	.30
329	Carlos Beltran	.50	.15
330	Eric Chavez	.50	.15
331	John Patterson	.50	.15
332	Jayson Werth	.50	.15
333	Richie Sexson	.50	.15
334	Randy Wolf	.50	.15
335	Eli Marrero	.50	.15
336	Paul LoDuca	.50	.15
337	J.D Smart	.50	.15
338	Ryan Minor	.50	.15
339	Kris Benson	.50	.15
340	George Lombard	.50	.15
341	Troy Glaus	.75	.23
342	Eddie Yarnall	.50	.15
343	Kip Wells RC	2.50	.75
344	C.C. Sabathia RC	4.00	1.20
345	Sean Burroughs RC	12.00	3.60
346	Felipe Lopez RC	1.50	.45
347	Ryan Rupe RC	1.50	.45
348	Orber Moreno RC	1.00	.30
349	Rafael Roque RC	1.00	.30
350	Alfonso Soriano RC	50.00	15.00
351	Pablo Ozuna	.50	.15
352	Corey Patterson RC	15.00	4.50
353	Braden Looper	.50	.15
354	Robbie Bell	.50	.15
355	Mark Mulder RC	15.00	4.50
356	Angel Pena	.50	.15
357	Kevin McGlinchy	.50	.15
358	M.Restovich RC	5.00	1.50
359	Eric DuBose	.50	.15
360	Geoff Jenkins	.50	.15
361	Mark Harriger RC	1.00	.30
362	Junior Herndon RC	1.50	.45
363	Tim Raines Jr. RC	1.50	.45
364	Rafael Furcal RC	8.00	2.40
365	Marcus Giles RC	8.00	2.40
366	Ted Lilly	.50	.15
367	Jorge Toca RC	1.50	.45
368	David Kelton RC	4.00	1.20
369	Adam Dunn RC	25.00	7.50
370	Guillermo Mota RC	1.00	.30
371	Brett Laxton RC	1.00	.30
372	Travis Harper RC	1.00	.30
373	Tom Davey RC	1.00	.30
374	Darren Blakely RC	1.00	.30
375	Tim Hudson RC	15.00	4.50
376	Jason Romano	.50	.15
377	Dan Reichert	.50	.15
378	Julio Lugo RC	1.50	.45
379	Jose Garcia RC	1.00	.30
380	Erubiel Durazo RC	6.00	1.80
381	Jose Jimenez	.50	.15
382	Chris Fussell	.50	.15
383	Steve Lomasney	.50	.15
384	Juan Pena RC	1.00	.30
385	Allen Levrault RC	1.50	.45
386	Juan Rivera RC	5.00	1.50
387	Steve Colyer RC	1.50	.45
388	Joe Nathan RC	1.00	.30
389	Ron Walker RC	1.00	.30
390	Nick Bierbrodt	.50	.15
391	Luke Prokopec RC	1.50	.45
392	Dave Roberts RC	2.50	.75
393	Mike Darr	.50	.15
394	Abraham Nunez RC	1.50	.45
395	G.Chiaramonte RC	1.00	.30
396	J.Van Buren RC	1.50	.45
397	Mike Kusiewicz	.50	.15
398	Matt Wise RC	1.00	.30
399	Joe McEwing RC	1.50	.45
400	Matt Holliday RC	1.50	.45
401	Willi Mo Pena RC	8.00	2.40
402	Ruben Quevedo RC	1.50	.45
403	Rob Ryan RC	1.00	.30
404	Freddy Garcia RC	6.00	1.80
405	Kevin Eberwein RC	1.50	.45
406	Jesus Colome RC	1.00	.30
407	Chris Singleton	.50	.15
408	Bubba Crosby RC	2.50	.75
409	Jesus Cordero RC	1.50	.45
410	Donny Leon	.50	.15
411	G.Tomlinson RC	1.00	.30
412	Jeff Winchester RC	1.50	.45
413	Adam Piatt RC	1.50	.45
414	Robert Stratton	.50	.15
415	T.J. Tucker	.50	.15
416	Ryan Langerhans RC	1.50	.45
417	A.Shumaker RC	1.00	.30
418	Matt Miller RC	1.00	.30
419	Doug Clark RC	1.00	.30
420	Kory DeHaan RC	1.00	.30
421	David Eckstein RC	4.00	1.20
422	Brian Cooper RC	1.00	.30
423	Brady Clark RC	1.00	.30
424	Chris Magruder RC	1.00	.30
425	Bobby Seay RC	1.50	.45
426	Aubrey Huff RC	8.00	2.40
427	Mike Jerzembeck	.50	.15
428	Matt Blank RC	1.00	.30
429	Benny Agbayani RC	1.50	.45
430	Kevin Beirne RC	1.50	.45
431	Josh Hamilton RC	6.00	1.80
432	Josh Girdley RC	1.50	.45
433	Kyle Snyder RC	1.50	.45
434	Mike Paradis RC	1.50	.45
435	Jason Jennings RC	2.50	.75
436	David Walling RC	1.50	.45
437	Omar Ortiz RC	1.00	.30
438	Jay Gehrke RC	1.50	.45
439	Casey Burns RC	1.00	.30
440	Carl Crawford RC	8.00	2.40

2000 Bowman Chrome

	Nm-Mt	Ex-Mt
COMPLETE SET (440)	120.00	36.00
1 Vladimir Guerrero	1.25	.35
2 Chipper Jones	1.25	.35
3 Todd Walker	.50	.15
4 Barry Larkin	1.25	.35
5 Bernie Williams	.75	.23
6 Todd Helton	.75	.23
7 Jermaine Dye	.50	.15

❑ 8 Brian Giles .50 .15
❑ 9 Freddy Garcia .50 .15
❑ 10 Greg Vaughn .50 .15
❑ 11 Alex Gonzalez .50 .15
❑ 12 Luis Gonzalez .50 .15
❑ 13 Ron Belliard .50 .15
❑ 14 Ben Grieve .50 .15
❑ 15 Carlos Delgado .50 .15
❑ 16 Brian Jordan .50 .15
❑ 17 Fernando Tatis .50 .15
❑ 18 Ryan Rupe .50 .15
❑ 19 Miguel Tejada .50 .15
❑ 20 Mark Grace 1.25 .35
❑ 21 Kenny Lofton .50 .15
❑ 22 Eric Karros .50 .15
❑ 23 Cliff Floyd .50 .15
❑ 24 John Halama .50 .15
❑ 25 Cristian Guzman .50 .15
❑ 26 Scott Williamson .50 .15
❑ 27 Mike Lieberthal .50 .15
❑ 28 Tim Hudson .75 .23
❑ 29 Warren Morris .50 .15
❑ 30 Pedro Martinez 1.25 .35
❑ 31 John Smoltz .75 .23
❑ 32 Ray Durham .50 .15
❑ 33 Chad Allen .50 .15
❑ 34 Tony Clark .50 .15
❑ 35 Tino Martinez .75 .23
❑ 36 J.T. Snow .50 .15
❑ 37 Kevin Brown .75 .23
❑ 38 Bartolo Colon .50 .15
❑ 39 Rey Ordonez .50 .15
❑ 40 Jeff Bagwell .75 .23
❑ 41 Ivan Rodriguez 1.25 .35
❑ 42 Eric Chavez .50 .15
❑ 43 Eric Milton .50 .15
❑ 44 Jose Canseco 1.25 .35
❑ 45 Shawn Green .50 .15
❑ 46 Rich Aurilia .50 .15
❑ 47 Roberto Alomar 1.25 .35
❑ 48 Brian Daubach .50 .15
❑ 49 Magglio Ordonez .50 .15
❑ 50 Derek Jeter 3.00 .90
❑ 51 Kris Benson .50 .15
❑ 52 Albert Belle .50 .15
❑ 53 Rondell White .50 .15
❑ 54 Justin Thompson .50 .15
❑ 55 Nomar Garciaparra 2.50 .75
❑ 56 Chuck Finley .50 .15
❑ 57 Omar Vizquel .50 .15
❑ 58 Luis Castillo .50 .15
❑ 59 Richard Hidalgo .50 .15
❑ 60 Barry Bonds 3.00 .90
❑ 61 Craig Biggio .75 .23
❑ 62 Doug Glanville .50 .15
❑ 63 Gabe Kapler .50 .15
❑ 64 Johnny Damon .50 .15
❑ 65 Pokey Reese .50 .15
❑ 66 Andy Pettitte .75 .23
❑ 67 B.J. Surhoff .50 .15
❑ 68 Richie Sexson .50 .15
❑ 69 Javy Lopez .50 .15
❑ 70 Raul Mondesi .50 .15
❑ 71 Darin Erstad .50 .15
❑ 72 Kevin Millwood .50 .15
❑ 73 Ricky Ledee .50 .15
❑ 74 John Olerud .50 .15
❑ 75 Sean Casey .50 .15
❑ 76 Carlos Febles .50 .15
❑ 77 Paul O'Neill .75 .23
❑ 78 Bob Abreu .50 .15
❑ 79 Neifi Perez .50 .15
❑ 80 Tony Gwynn 1.50 .45
❑ 81 Russ Ortiz .50 .15
❑ 82 Matt Williams .50 .15
❑ 83 Chris Carpenter .50 .15
❑ 84 Roger Cedeno .50 .15
❑ 85 Tim Salmon .75 .23
❑ 86 Billy Koch .50 .15
❑ 87 Jeromy Burnitz .50 .15
❑ 88 Edgardo Alfonzo .50 .15
❑ 89 Jay Bell .50 .15
❑ 90 Manny Ramirez .50 .15
❑ 91 Frank Thomas 1.25 .35
❑ 92 Mike Mussina 1.25 .35
❑ 93 J.D. Drew .50 .15
❑ 94 Adrian Beltre .50 .15
❑ 95 Alex Rodriguez 2.50 .75
❑ 96 Larry Walker .75 .23
❑ 97 Juan Encarnacion .50 .15
❑ 98 Mike Sweeney .50 .15
❑ 99 Rusty Greer .50 .15
❑ 100 Randy Johnson 1.25 .35
❑ 101 Jose Vidro .50 .15
❑ 102 Preston Wilson .50 .15
❑ 103 Greg Maddux 2.50 .75
❑ 104 Jason Giambi 1.25 .35
❑ 105 Cal Ripken 4.00 1.20
❑ 106 Carlos Beltran .50 .15
❑ 107 Vinny Castilla .50 .15
❑ 108 Mariano Rivera .75 .23
❑ 109 Mo Vaughn .50 .15
❑ 110 Rafael Palmeiro .75 .23
❑ 111 Shannon Stewart .50 .15
❑ 112 Mike Hampton .50 .15
❑ 113 Joe Nathan .50 .15
❑ 114 Ben Davis .50 .15
❑ 115 Andruw Jones .75 .23
❑ 116 Robin Ventura .50 .15
❑ 117 Damion Easley .50 .15
❑ 118 Jeff Cirillo .50 .15
❑ 119 Kerry Wood 1.25 .35
❑ 120 Scott Rolen .75 .23
❑ 121 Sammy Sosa 2.00 .60
❑ 122 Ken Griffey Jr. 2.00 .60
❑ 123 Shane Reynolds .50 .15
❑ 124 Troy Glaus .75 .23
❑ 125 Tom Glavine 1.25 .35
❑ 126 Michael Barrett .50 .15
❑ 127 Al Leiter .50 .15
❑ 128 Jason Kendall .50 .15
❑ 129 Roger Clemens 2.50 .75
❑ 130 Juan Gonzalez 1.25 .35
❑ 131 Corey Koskie .50 .15
❑ 132 Curt Schilling .75 .23
❑ 133 Mike Piazza 2.00 .60
❑ 134 Gary Sheffield .50 .15
❑ 135 Jim Thome 1.25 .35
❑ 136 Orlando Hernandez .50 .15
❑ 137 Ray Lankford .50 .15
❑ 138 Geoff Jenkins .50 .15
❑ 139 Jose Lima .50 .15
❑ 140 Mark McGwire 3.00 .90
❑ 141 Adam Piatt .50 .15
❑ 142 Pat Manning RC 1.50 .45
❑ 143 Marcos Castillo RC 1.50 .45
❑ 144 Lesli Brea RC 1.50 .45
❑ 145 Humberto Cota RC 1.50 .45
❑ 146 Ben Petrick .50 .15
❑ 147 Kip Wells .50 .15
❑ 148 Wily Pena .50 .15
❑ 149 Chris Wakeland RC 1.00 .30
❑ 150 Brad Baker RC 1.50 .45
❑ 151 Robbie Morrison RC 1.00 .30
❑ 152 Reggie Taylor .50 .15
❑ 153 Matt Ginter RC 1.50 .45
❑ 154 Peter Bergeron .50 .15
❑ 155 Roosevelt Brown .50 .15
❑ 156 Matt Cepicky RC 1.50 .45
❑ 157 Ramon Castro .50 .15
❑ 158 Brad Baisley RC 1.50 .45
❑ 159 Jason Hart RC 1.50 .45
❑ 160 Mitch Meluskey .50 .15
❑ 161 Chad Harville .50 .15
❑ 162 Brian Cooper .50 .15
❑ 163 Marcus Giles .50 .15
❑ 164 Jim Morris 6.00 1.80
❑ 165 Geoff Goetz .50 .15
❑ 166 Bobby Bradley RC 1.50 .45
❑ 167 Rob Bell .50 .15
❑ 168 Joe Crede .50 .15
❑ 169 Michael Restovich .50 .15
❑ 170 Quincy Foster RC 1.00 .30
❑ 171 Enrique Cruz RC 1.50 .45
❑ 172 Mark Quinn .50 .15
❑ 173 Nick Johnson .50 .15
❑ 174 Jeff Liefer .50 .15
❑ 175 Kevin Mench RC 2.50 .75
❑ 176 Steve Lomasney .50 .15
❑ 177 Jayson Werth .50 .15
❑ 178 Tim Drew .50 .15
❑ 179 Chip Ambres .50 .15
❑ 180 Ryan Anderson .50 .15
❑ 181 Matt Blank .50 .15
❑ 182 G. Chiaramonte .50 .15
❑ 183 Corey Myers RC 1.50 .45
❑ 184 Jeff Yoder .50 .15
❑ 185 Craig Dingman RC 1.00 .30
❑ 186 Jon Hamilton RC 1.00 .30
❑ 187 Toby Hall .50 .15
❑ 188 Russell Branyan .50 .15
❑ 189 Brian Falkenborg RC 1.50 .45
❑ 190 Aaron Harang RC 1.50 .45
❑ 191 Juan Pena .50 .15
❑ 192 Chin-Hui Tsao RC 8.00 2.40
❑ 193 Alfonso Soriano 2.00 .60
❑ 194 Alejandro Diaz RC 1.50 .45
❑ 195 Carlos Pena .50 .15
❑ 196 Kevin Nicholson .50 .15
❑ 197 Mo Bruce .50 .15
❑ 198 C.C. Sabathia .50 .15
❑ 199 Carl Crawford .50 .15
❑ 200 Rafael Furcal .50 .15
❑ 201 Andrew Beinbrink RC 1.00 .30
❑ 202 Jimmy Osting .50 .15
❑ 203 Aaron McNeal RC 1.50 .45
❑ 204 Brett Laxton .50 .15
❑ 205 Chris George .50 .15
❑ 206 Felipe Lopez .50 .15
❑ 207 Ben Sheets RC 5.00 1.50
❑ 208 Mike Meyers RC 1.50 .45
❑ 209 Jason Conti .50 .15
❑ 210 Milton Bradley .50 .15
❑ 211 Chris Mears RC 1.50 .45
❑ 212 Carlos Hernandez RC 1.50 .45
❑ 213 Jason Romano .50 .15
❑ 214 Geofrey Tomlinson .50 .15
❑ 215 Jimmy Rollins .50 .15
❑ 216 Pablo Ozuna .50 .15
❑ 217 Steve Cox .50 .15
❑ 218 Terrence Long .50 .15
❑ 219 Jeff DaVanon RC 1.50 .45
❑ 220 Rick Ankiel .50 .15
❑ 221 Jason Standridge .50 .15
❑ 222 Tony Armas Jr. .50 .15
❑ 223 Jason Tyner .50 .15
❑ 224 Ramon Ortiz .50 .15
❑ 225 Daryle Ward .50 .15
❑ 226 Enger Veras RC 1.50 .45
❑ 227 Chris Jones .50 .15
❑ 228 Eric Cammack RC 1.00 .30
❑ 229 Ruben Mateo .50 .15
❑ 230 Ken Harvey RC 5.00 1.50
❑ 231 Jake Westbrook .50 .15
❑ 232 Rob Purvis RC 1.00 .30
❑ 233 Choo Freeman .50 .15
❑ 234 Aramis Ramirez .50 .15
❑ 235 A.J. Burnett .50 .15
❑ 236 Kevin Barker .50 .15
❑ 237 Chance Caple RC 1.50 .45
❑ 238 Jarrod Washburn .50 .15
❑ 239 Lance Berkman .50 .15
❑ 240 Michael Wenner RC 1.00 .30
❑ 241 Alex Sanchez .50 .15
❑ 242 Pat Daneker .50 .15
❑ 243 Grant Roberts .50 .15
❑ 244 Mark Ellis RC 2.50 .75
❑ 245 Donny Leon .50 .15
❑ 246 David Eckstein .50 .15
❑ 247 Dicky Gonzalez RC 1.50 .45

Card	Nm-Mt	Ex-Mt
❑ 248 John Patterson	.50	.15
❑ 249 Chad Green	.50	.15
❑ 250 Scot Shields RC	1.00	.30
❑ 251 Troy Cameron	.50	.15
❑ 252 Jose Molina	.50	.15
❑ 253 Rob Pugmire RC	1.50	.45
❑ 254 Rick Elder	.50	.15
❑ 255 Sean Burroughs	.75	.23
❑ 256 Josh Kalinowski RC	1.00	.30
❑ 257 Matt LeCroy	.50	.15
❑ 258 Alex Graman RC	1.00	.30
❑ 259 Juan Silvestre RC	1.50	.45
❑ 260 Brady Clark	.50	.15
❑ 261 Rico Washington RC	1.50	.45
❑ 262 Gary Matthews Jr.	.50	.15
❑ 263 Matt Wise	.50	.15
❑ 264 Keith Reed RC	1.50	.45
❑ 265 Santiago Ramirez RC	1.00	.30
❑ 266 Ben Broussard RC	1.50	.45
❑ 267 Ryan Langerhans	.50	.15
❑ 268 Juan Rivera	.50	.15
❑ 269 Shawn Gallagher	.50	.15
❑ 270 Jorge Toca	.50	.15
❑ 271 Brad Lidge	.50	.15
❑ 272 Leoncio Estrella RC	1.00	.30
❑ 273 Ruben Quevedo	.50	.15
❑ 274 Jack Cust	.50	.15
❑ 275 T.J. Tucker	.50	.15
❑ 276 Mike Colangelo	.50	.15
❑ 277 Brian Schneider	.50	.15
❑ 278 Calvin Murray	.50	.15
❑ 279 Josh Girdley	.50	.15
❑ 280 Mike Paradis	.50	.15
❑ 281 Chad Hermansen	.50	.15
❑ 282 Ty Howington RC	1.50	.45
❑ 283 Aaron Myette	.50	.15
❑ 284 D'Angelo Jimenez	.50	.15
❑ 285 Dernell Stenson	.50	.15
❑ 286 Jerry Hairston Jr.	.50	.15
❑ 287 Gary Majewski RC	1.50	.45
❑ 288 Derrin Ebert	.50	.15
❑ 289 Steve Fish RC	1.00	.30
❑ 290 Carlos E. Hernandez	.50	.15
❑ 291 Allen Levrault	.50	.15
❑ 292 Sean McNally RC	1.00	.30
❑ 293 Randey Dorame RC	1.50	.45
❑ 294 Wes Anderson RC	1.50	.45
❑ 295 B.J. Ryan	.50	.15
❑ 296 Alan Webb RC	1.50	.45
❑ 297 Brandon Inge RC	1.50	.45
❑ 298 David Walling	.50	.15
❑ 299 Sun Woo Kim RC	1.50	.45
❑ 300 Pat Burrell	.75	.23
❑ 301 Rick Guttormson RC	1.00	.30
❑ 302 Gil Meche	.50	.15
❑ 303 Carlos Zambrano RC	8.00	2.40
❑ 304 Eric Byrnes UER RC Bo Porter pictured	5.00	1.50
❑ 305 Robb Quinlan RC	1.50	.45
❑ 306 Jackie Rexrode	.50	.15
❑ 307 Nate Bump	.50	.15
❑ 308 Sean DePaula RC	1.00	.30
❑ 309 Matt Riley	.50	.15
❑ 310 Ryan Minor	.50	.15
❑ 311 J.J. Davis	.50	.15
❑ 312 Randy Wolf	.50	.15
❑ 313 Jason Jennings	.50	.15
❑ 314 Scott Seabol RC	1.00	.30
❑ 315 Doug Davis	.50	.15
❑ 316 Todd Moser RC	1.00	.30
❑ 317 Rob Ryan	.50	.15
❑ 318 Bubba Crosby	.50	.15
❑ 319 Lyle Overbay RC	2.50	.75
❑ 320 Mario Encarnacion	.50	.15
❑ 321 F.Rodriguez RC	8.00	2.40
❑ 322 Michael Cuddyer	.50	.15
❑ 323 Ed Yarnall	.50	.15
❑ 324 Cesar Saba RC	1.50	.45
❑ 325 Gookie Dawkins	.50	.15
❑ 326 Alex Escobar	.50	.15
❑ 327 Julio Zuleta RC	1.50	.45
❑ 328 Josh Hamilton	.50	.15
❑ 329 Carlos Urquiola RC	1.50	.45
❑ 330 Matt Belisle	.50	.15
❑ 331 Kurt Ainsworth RC	2.50	.75
❑ 332 Tim Raines Jr.	.50	.15
❑ 333 Eric Munson	.50	.15
❑ 334 Donzell McDonald	.50	.15
❑ 335 Larry Bigbie RC	2.50	.75
❑ 336 Matt Watson RC	1.50	.45
❑ 337 Aubrey Huff	.50	.15
❑ 338 Julio Ramirez	.50	.15
❑ 339 Jason Grabowski RC	1.50	.45
❑ 340 Jon Garland	.50	.15
❑ 341 Austin Kearns	1.25	.35
❑ 342 Josh Pressley RC	1.50	.45
❑ 343 Miguel Olivo RC	1.50	.45
❑ 344 Julio Lugo	.50	.15
❑ 345 Roberto Vaz	.50	.15
❑ 346 Ramon Soler	.50	.15
❑ 347 Brandon Phillips RC	5.00	1.50
❑ 348 Vince Faison RC	1.50	.45
❑ 349 Mike Venafro	.50	.15
❑ 350 Rick Asadoorian RC	1.50	.45
❑ 351 B.J. Garbe RC	1.50	.45
❑ 352 Dan Reichert	.50	.15
❑ 353 Jason Stumm RC	1.50	.45
❑ 354 Ruben Salazar RC	1.50	.45
❑ 355 Francisco Cordero	.50	.15
❑ 356 Juan Guzman RC	1.50	.45
❑ 357 Mike Bacsik RC	1.00	.30
❑ 358 Jared Sandberg	.50	.15
❑ 359 Rod Barajas	.50	.15
❑ 360 Junior Brignac RC	1.50	.45
❑ 361 J.M. Gold	.50	.15
❑ 362 Octavio Dotel	.50	.15
❑ 363 David Kelton	.50	.15
❑ 364 Scott Morgan	.50	.15
❑ 365 Wascar Serrano RC	1.50	.45
❑ 366 Wilton Veras	.50	.15
❑ 367 Eugene Kingsale	.50	.15
❑ 368 Ted Lilly	.50	.15
❑ 369 George Lombard	.50	.15
❑ 370 Chris Haas	.50	.15
❑ 371 Wilton Pena RC	1.00	.30
❑ 372 Vernon Wells	.50	.15
❑ 373 Keith Ginter RC	1.00	.30
❑ 374 Jeff Heaverlo RC	1.50	.45
❑ 375 Calvin Pickering	.50	.15
❑ 376 Mike Lamb RC	1.50	.45
❑ 377 Kyle Snyder	.50	.15
❑ 378 Javier Cardona RC	1.00	.30
❑ 379 Aaron Rowand RC	1.50	.45
❑ 380 Dee Brown	.50	.15
❑ 381 Brett Myers RC	10.00	3.00
❑ 382 Abraham Nunez	.50	.15
❑ 383 Eric Valent	.50	.15
❑ 384 Jody Gerut RC	10.00	3.00
❑ 385 Adam Dunn	1.25	.35
❑ 386 Jay Gehrke	.50	.15
❑ 387 Omar Ortiz	.50	.15
❑ 388 Darnell McDonald	.50	.15
❑ 389 Tony Schrager RC	1.00	.30
❑ 390 J.D. Closser	.50	.15
❑ 391 Ben Christensen RC	1.50	.45
❑ 392 Adam Kennedy	.50	.15
❑ 393 Nick Green RC	1.00	.30
❑ 394 Ramon Hernandez	.50	.15
❑ 395 Roy Oswalt RC	15.00	4.50
❑ 396 Andy Tracy RC	1.00	.30
❑ 397 Eric Gagne	1.25	.35
❑ 398 Michael Tejera RC	1.00	.30
❑ 399 Adam Everett	.50	.15
❑ 400 Corey Patterson	.75	.23
❑ 401 Gary Knotts RC	1.00	.30
❑ 402 Ryan Christianson RC	1.50	.45
❑ 403 Eric Ireland RC	1.00	.30
❑ 404 Andrew Good RC	1.50	.45
❑ 405 Brad Penny	.50	.15
❑ 406 Jason LaRue	.50	.15
❑ 407 Kit Pellow	.50	.15
❑ 408 Kevin Beirne	.50	.15
❑ 409 Kelly Dransfeldt	.50	.15
❑ 410 Jason Grilli	.50	.15
❑ 411 Scott Downs RC	1.00	.30
❑ 412 Jesus Colome	.50	.15
❑ 413 John Sneed RC	1.00	.30
❑ 414 Tony McKnight	.50	.15
❑ 415 Luis Rivera	.50	.15
❑ 416 Adam Eaton	.50	.15
❑ 417 Mike MacDougal RC	2.50	.75
❑ 418 Mike Nannini	.50	.15
❑ 419 Barry Zito RC	20.00	6.00
❑ 420 DeWayne Wise	.50	.15
❑ 421 Jason Dellaero	.50	.15
❑ 422 Chad Moeller	.50	.15
❑ 423 Jason Marquis	.50	.15
❑ 424 Tim Redding RC	4.00	1.20
❑ 425 Mark Mulder	.75	.23
❑ 426 Josh Paul	.50	.15
❑ 427 Chris Enochs	.50	.15
❑ 428 W.Rodriguez RC	1.50	.45
❑ 429 Kevin Witt	.50	.15
❑ 430 Scott Sobkowiak RC	1.00	.30
❑ 431 McKay Christensen	.50	.15
❑ 432 Jung Bong	.50	.15
❑ 433 Keith Evans RC	1.00	.30
❑ 434 Garry Maddox Jr. RC	1.00	.30
❑ 435 Ramon Santiago RC	1.50	.45
❑ 436 Alex Cora	.50	.15
❑ 437 Carlos Lee	.50	.15
❑ 438 Jason Repko RC	1.50	.45
❑ 439 Matt Burch	.50	.15
❑ 440 Shawn Sonnier RC	1.00	.30

2000 Bowman Chrome Draft Picks

	Nm-Mt	Ex-Mt
COMP.FACT.SET (110)	60.00	18.00
❑ 1 Pat Burrell	.75	.23
❑ 2 Rafael Furcal	.50	.15
❑ 3 Grant Roberts	.50	.15
❑ 4 Barry Zito	8.00	2.40
❑ 5 Julio Zuleta	1.00	.30
❑ 6 Mark Mulder	.75	.23
❑ 7 Rob Bell	.50	.15
❑ 8 Adam Piatt	.50	.15
❑ 9 Mike Lamb	.50	.15
❑ 10 Pablo Ozuna	.50	.15
❑ 11 Jason Tyner	.50	.15
❑ 12 Jason Marquis	.50	.15
❑ 13 Eric Munson	.50	.15
❑ 14 Seth Etherton	.50	.15
❑ 15 Milton Bradley	.50	.15
❑ 16 Nick Green	.50	.15
❑ 17 Chin-Feng Chen RC	3.00	.90
❑ 18 Matt Boone RC	1.00	.30
❑ 19 Kevin Gregg RC	1.00	.30
❑ 20 Eddy Garabito RC	1.00	.30
❑ 21 Aaron Capista RC	1.00	.30
❑ 22 Esteban German RC	1.00	.30
❑ 23 Derek Thompson RC	1.00	.30
❑ 24 Phil Merrell RC	.50	.15
❑ 25 Brian O'Connor RC	.50	.15
❑ 26 Yamid Haad	.50	.15
❑ 27 Hector Mercado RC	.50	.15
❑ 28 Jason Woolf RC	.50	.15
❑ 29 Eddy Furniss RC	.50	.15
❑ 30 Cha Sueng Baek RC	1.00	.30
❑ 31 Colby Lewis RC	1.50	.45
❑ 32 Pasqual Coco RC	.50	.15
❑ 33 Jorge Cantu RC	1.00	.30
❑ 34 Erasmo Ramirez RC	.50	.15
❑ 35 Bobby Kielty RC	1.50	.45
❑ 36 Joaquin Benoit RC	1.00	.30
❑ 37 Brian Esposito RC	1.00	.30
❑ 38 Michael Wenner	.50	.15
❑ 39 Juan Rincon RC	1.00	.30

❑ 40 Yorvit Torrealba RC	1.00	.30
❑ 41 Chad Durham RC	1.00	.30
❑ 42 Jim Mann RC	.50	.15
❑ 43 Shane Loux RC	1.00	.30
❑ 44 Luis Rivas	.50	.15
❑ 45 Ken Chenard RC	1.00	.30
❑ 46 Mike Lockwood RC	.50	.15
❑ 47 Yovanny Lara RC	.50	.15
❑ 48 Bubba Carpenter RC	.50	.15
❑ 49 Ryan Dittfurth RC	1.00	.30
❑ 50 John Stephens RC	1.00	.30
❑ 51 Pedro Feliz RC	1.00	.30
❑ 52 Kenny Kelly RC	1.00	.30
❑ 53 Neil Jenkins RC	1.00	.30
❑ 54 Mike Glendenning RC	.50	.15
❑ 55 Bo Porter	.50	.15
❑ 56 Eric Byrnes	2.00	.60
❑ 57 Tony Alvarez RC	1.00	.30
❑ 58 Kazuhiro Sasaki RC	3.00	.90
❑ 59 Chad Durbin RC	.50	.15
❑ 60 Mike Bynum RC	1.00	.30
❑ 61 Travis Wilson RC	.50	.15
❑ 62 Jose Leon RC	.50	.15
❑ 63 Ryan Vogelsong RC	1.00	.30
❑ 64 Geraldo Guzman RC	.50	.15
❑ 65 Craig Anderson RC	1.00	.30
❑ 66 Carlos Silva RC	1.00	.30
❑ 67 Brad Thomas RC	.50	.15
❑ 68 Chin-Hui Tsao	3.00	.90
❑ 69 Mark Buehrle RC	4.00	1.20
❑ 70 Juan Salas RC	1.00	.30
❑ 71 Denny Abreu RC	1.00	.30
❑ 72 Keith McDonald RC	.50	.15
❑ 73 Chris Richard RC	1.00	.30
❑ 74 Tomas De la Rosa RC	.50	.15
❑ 75 Vicente Padilla RC	2.50	.75
❑ 76 Justin Brunette RC	.50	.15
❑ 77 Scott Linebrink RC	.50	.15
❑ 78 Jeff Sparks RC	.50	.15
❑ 79 Tike Redman RC	1.00	.30
❑ 80 John Lackey RC	1.50	.45
❑ 81 Joe Strong RC	.50	.15
❑ 82 Brian Tollberg RC	.50	.15
❑ 83 Steve Sisco RC	.50	.15
❑ 84 Chris Clapinski RC	.50	.15
❑ 85 Augie Ojeda RC	.50	.15
❑ 86 Adrian Gonzalez RC	5.00	1.50
❑ 87 Mike Stodolka RC	1.00	.30
❑ 88 Adam Johnson RC	1.00	.30
❑ 89 Matt Wheatland RC	.50	.15
❑ 90 Corey Smith RC	1.50	.45
❑ 91 Rocco Baldelli RC	30.00	9.00
❑ 92 Keith Bucktrot RC	1.00	.30
❑ 93 Adam Wainwright RC	4.00	1.20
❑ 94 Blaine Boyer RC	1.00	.30
❑ 95 Aaron Herr RC	1.00	.30
❑ 96 Scott Thorman RC	1.50	.45
❑ 97 Bryan Digby RC	1.00	.30
❑ 98 Josh Shortslef RC	1.00	.30
❑ 99 Sean Smith RC	1.00	.30
❑ 100 Alex Cruz RC	1.00	.30
❑ 101 Marc Love RC	1.00	.30
❑ 102 Kevin Lee RC	1.00	.30
❑ 103 Timo Perez RC	1.00	.30
❑ 104 Alex Cabrera RC	1.00	.30
❑ 105 Shane Hearns RC	.50	.15
❑ 106 Tripper Johnson RC	1.50	.45
❑ 107 Brent Abernathy RC	1.00	.30
❑ 108 John Cotton RC	.50	.15
❑ 109 Brad Wilkerson RC	1.50	.45
❑ 110 Jon Rauch RC	1.00	.30

2001 Bowman Chrome

	Nm-Mt	Ex-Mt
COMP.SET w/o SP's (220)	50.00	15.00
COMMON (1-110/201-310)	.50	.15
COMMON (111-200/311-330)	5.00	1.50
COMMON (331-350)	25.00	7.50

❑ 1 Jason Giambi	1.25	.35
❑ 2 Rafael Furcal	.50	.15
❑ 3 Bernie Williams	.75	.23
❑ 4 Kenny Lofton	.50	.15
❑ 5 Al Leiter	.50	.15
❑ 6 Albert Belle	.50	.15

❑ 7 Craig Biggio	.75	.23
❑ 8 Mark Mulder	.50	.15
❑ 9 Carlos Delgado	.50	.15
❑ 10 Darin Erstad	.50	.15
❑ 11 Richie Sexson	.50	.15
❑ 12 Randy Johnson	1.25	.35
❑ 13 Greg Maddux	2.50	.75
❑ 14 Orlando Hernandez	.50	.15
❑ 15 Javier Vazquez	.50	.15
❑ 16 Jeff Kent	.50	.15
❑ 17 Jim Thome	1.25	.35
❑ 18 John Olerud	.50	.15
❑ 19 Jason Kendall	.50	.15
❑ 20 Scott Rolen	.75	.23
❑ 21 Tony Gwynn	1.50	.45
❑ 22 Edgardo Alfonzo	.50	.15
❑ 23 Pokey Reese	.50	.15
❑ 24 Todd Helton	.75	.23
❑ 25 Mark Quinn	.50	.15
❑ 26 Dean Palmer	.50	.15
❑ 27 Ray Durham	.50	.15
❑ 28 Rafael Palmeiro	.75	.23
❑ 29 Carl Everett	.50	.15
❑ 30 Vladimir Guerrero	1.25	.35
❑ 31 Livan Hernandez	.50	.15
❑ 32 Preston Wilson	.50	.15
❑ 33 Jose Vidro	.50	.15
❑ 34 Fred McGriff	.75	.23
❑ 35 Kevin Brown	.50	.15
❑ 36 Miguel Tejada	.50	.15
❑ 37 Chipper Jones	1.25	.35
❑ 38 Edgar Martinez	.75	.23
❑ 39 Tony Batista	.50	.15
❑ 40 Jorge Posada	.75	.23
❑ 41 Sammy Sosa	2.00	.60
❑ 42 Gary Sheffield	.50	.15
❑ 43 Bartolo Colon	.50	.15
❑ 44 Pat Burrell	.50	.15
❑ 45 Jay Payton	.50	.15
❑ 46 Mike Mussina	1.25	.35
❑ 47 Nomar Garciaparra	2.50	.75
❑ 48 Darren Dreifort	.50	.15
❑ 49 Richard Hidalgo	.50	.15
❑ 50 Troy Glaus	.75	.23
❑ 51 Ben Grieve	.50	.15
❑ 52 Jim Edmonds	.50	.15
❑ 53 Raul Mondesi	.50	.15
❑ 54 Andruw Jones	.75	.23
❑ 55 Mike Sweeney	.50	.15
❑ 56 Derek Jeter	3.00	.90
❑ 57 Ruben Mateo	.50	.15
❑ 58 Cristian Guzman	.50	.15
❑ 59 Mike Hampton	.50	.15
❑ 60 J.D. Drew	.50	.15
❑ 61 Matt Lawton	.50	.15
❑ 62 Moises Alou	.50	.15
❑ 63 Terrence Long	.50	.15
❑ 64 Geoff Jenkins	.50	.15
❑ 65 Manny Ramirez	.50	.15
❑ 66 Johnny Damon	.50	.15
❑ 67 Pedro Martinez	1.25	.35
❑ 68 Juan Gonzalez	1.25	.35
❑ 69 Roger Clemens	2.50	.75
❑ 70 Carlos Beltran	.50	.15
❑ 71 Roberto Alomar	1.25	.35
❑ 72 Barry Bonds	3.00	.90
❑ 73 Tim Hudson	.50	.15
❑ 74 Tom Glavine	1.25	.35
❑ 75 Jeromy Burnitz	.50	.15
❑ 76 Adrian Beltre	.50	.15
❑ 77 Mike Piazza	2.00	.60
❑ 78 Kerry Wood	1.25	.35
❑ 79 Steve Finley	.50	.15
❑ 80 Bob Abreu	.50	.15
❑ 81 Neifi Perez	.50	.15
❑ 82 Mark Redman	.50	.15
❑ 83 Paul Konerko	.50	.15
❑ 84 Jermaine Dye	.50	.15
❑ 85 Brian Giles	.50	.15
❑ 86 Ivan Rodriguez	1.25	.35
❑ 87 Adam Kennedy	.50	.15
❑ 88 Eric Chavez	.50	.15
❑ 89 Billy Koch	.50	.15
❑ 90 Shawn Green	.50	.15
❑ 91 Matt Williams	.50	.15
❑ 92 Greg Vaughn	.50	.15
❑ 93 Jeff Cirillo	.50	.15
❑ 94 Frank Thomas	1.25	.35
❑ 95 David Justice	.50	.15
❑ 96 Cal Ripken	4.00	1.20
❑ 97 Curt Schilling	.75	.23
❑ 98 Barry Zito	1.25	.35
❑ 99 Brian Jordan	.50	.15
❑ 100 Chan Ho Park	.50	.15
❑ 101 J.T. Snow	.50	.15
❑ 102 Kazuhiro Sasaki	.50	.15
❑ 103 Alex Rodriguez	2.50	.75
❑ 104 Mariano Rivera	.75	.23
❑ 105 Eric Milton	.50	.15
❑ 106 Andy Pettitte	.75	.23
❑ 107 Ken Griffey Jr.	2.00	.60
❑ 108 Bengie Molina	.50	.15
❑ 109 Jeff Bagwell	.75	.23
❑ 110 Mark McGwire	3.00	.90
❑ 111 Dan Tosca RC	8.00	2.40
❑ 112 Sergio Contreras RC	8.00	2.40
❑ 113 Mitch Jones RC	8.00	2.40
❑ 114 Ramon Carvajal RC	8.00	2.40
❑ 115 Ryan Madson RC	8.00	2.40
❑ 116 Hank Blalock RC	60.00	18.00
❑ 117 Ben Washburn RC	8.00	2.40
❑ 118 Erick Almonte RC	8.00	2.40
❑ 119 Shawn Fagan RC	8.00	2.40
❑ 120 Gary Johnson RC	8.00	2.40
❑ 121 Brett Evert RC	8.00	2.40
❑ 122 Joe Hamer RC	8.00	2.40
❑ 123 Yhency Brazoban RC	8.00	2.40
❑ 124 Domingo Guante RC	8.00	2.40
❑ 125 Deivi Mendez RC	8.00	2.40
❑ 126 Adrian Hernandez RC	8.00	2.40
❑ 127 R. Abercrombie RC	8.00	2.40
❑ 128 Steve Bennett RC	5.00	1.50
❑ 129 Matt White RC	8.00	2.40
❑ 130 Brian Hitchcox RC	5.00	1.50
❑ 131 Deivis Santos RC	8.00	2.40
❑ 132 Luis Montanez RC	8.00	2.40
❑ 133 Eric Reynolds RC	5.00	1.50
❑ 134 Denny Bautista RC	20.00	6.00
❑ 135 Hector Garcia RC	8.00	2.40
❑ 136 Joe Thurston RC	12.00	3.60
❑ 137 Tsuyoshi Shinjo RC	15.00	4.50
❑ 138 Elpidio Guzman RC	8.00	2.40
❑ 139 Brian Bass RC	8.00	2.40
❑ 140 Mark Burnett RC	8.00	2.40
❑ 141 Russ Jacobson UER Last name misspelled Jacobsen on front	5.00	1.50
❑ 142 Travis Hafner RC	12.00	3.60
❑ 143 Wilson Betemit RC	8.00	2.40
❑ 144 Luke Lockwood RC	8.00	2.40
❑ 145 Noel Devarez RC	8.00	2.40
❑ 146 Doug Gredvig RC	8.00	2.40
❑ 147 Seung Song RC	12.00	3.60
❑ 148 Andy Van Hekken RC	8.00	2.40
❑ 149 Ryan Kohlmeier	5.00	1.50
❑ 150 Dee Haynes RC	8.00	2.40
❑ 151 Jim Journell RC	8.00	2.40
❑ 152 Chad Petty RC	8.00	2.40
❑ 153 Danny Borrell RC	8.00	2.40
❑ 154 Dave Krynzel	5.00	1.50
❑ 155 Octavio Martinez RC	8.00	2.40
❑ 156 David Parrish RC	8.00	2.40
❑ 157 Jason Miller RC	8.00	2.40
❑ 158 Corey Spencer RC	5.00	1.50

	Card	Nm-Mt	Ex-Mt
❑	159 Maxim St. Pierre RC	8.00	2.40
❑	160 Pat Magness RC	8.00	2.40
❑	161 Ranier Olmedo RC	8.00	2.40
❑	162 Brandon Mims RC	8.00	2.40
❑	163 Phil Wilson RC	8.00	2.40
❑	164 Jose Reyes RC	70.00	21.00
❑	165 Matt Butler RC	8.00	2.40
❑	166 Joel Pineiro	15.00	4.50
❑	167 Ken Chenard	5.00	1.50
❑	168 Alexis Gomez RC	8.00	2.40
❑	169 Justin Morneau RC	40.00	12.00
❑	170 Josh Fogg RC	8.00	2.40
❑	171 Charles Frazier RC	8.00	2.40
❑	172 Ryan Ludwick RC	8.00	2.40
❑	173 Seth McClung RC	8.00	2.40
❑	174 Justin Wayne RC	8.00	2.40
❑	175 Rafael Soriano RC	15.00	4.50
❑	176 Jared Abruzzo RC	8.00	2.40
❑	177 Jason Richardson RC	8.00	2.40
❑	178 Darwin Cubillan RC	5.00	1.50
❑	179 Blake Williams RC	8.00	2.40
❑	180 V. Pascucci RC	8.00	2.40
❑	181 Ryan Hannaman RC	8.00	2.40
❑	182 Steve Smyth RC	8.00	2.40
❑	183 Jake Peavy RC	20.00	6.00
❑	184 Onix Mercado RC	8.00	2.40
❑	185 Luis Torres RC	8.00	2.40
❑	186 Casey Fossum RC	8.00	2.40
❑	187 Eduardo Figueroa RC	8.00	2.40
❑	188 Bryan Barnowski RC	8.00	2.40
❑	189 Jason Standridge	5.00	1.50
❑	190 Marvin Seale RC	8.00	2.40
❑	191 Steve Smitherman RC	20.00	6.00
❑	192 Rafael Boitel RC	8.00	2.40
❑	193 Dany Morban RC	8.00	2.40
❑	194 Justin Woodrow RC	8.00	2.40
❑	195 Ed Rogers RC	8.00	2.40
❑	196 Ben Hendrickson RC	8.00	2.40
❑	197 Thomas Mitchell	5.00	1.50
❑	198 Adam Pettyjohn RC	8.00	2.40
❑	199 Doug Nickle RC	5.00	1.50
❑	200 Jason Jones RC	8.00	2.40
❑	201 Larry Barnes	.50	.15
❑	202 Ben Diggins	.50	.15
❑	203 Dee Brown	.50	.15
❑	204 Rocco Baldelli	4.00	1.20
❑	205 Luis Terrero	.50	.15
❑	206 Milton Bradley	.50	.15
❑	207 Kurt Ainsworth	.50	.15
❑	208 Sean Burroughs	.50	.15
❑	209 Rick Asadoorian	.50	.15
❑	210 Ramon Castro	.50	.15
❑	211 Nick Neugebauer	.50	.15
❑	212 Aaron Myette	.50	.15
❑	213 Luis Matos	.50	.15
❑	214 Donnie Bridges	.50	.15
❑	215 Alex Cintron	.50	.15
❑	216 Bobby Kielty	.50	.15
❑	217 Matt Belisle	.50	.15
❑	218 Adam Everett	.50	.15
❑	219 John Lackey	.50	.15
❑	220 Adam Wainwright	.50	.15
❑	221 Jerry Hairston Jr.	.50	.15
❑	222 Mike Bynum	.50	.15
❑	223 Ryan Christianson	.50	.15
❑	224 J.J. Davis	.50	.15
❑	225 Alex Graman	.50	.15
❑	226 Abraham Nunez	.50	.15
❑	227 Sun Woo Kim	.50	.15
❑	228 Jimmy Rollins	.50	.15
❑	229 Ruben Salazar	.50	.15
❑	230 Josh Girdley	.50	.15
❑	231 Carl Crawford	.50	.15
❑	232 Ben Davis	.50	.15
❑	233 Jason Grabowski	.50	.15
❑	234 Chris George	.50	.15
❑	235 Roy Oswalt	.75	.23
❑	236 Brian Cole	.50	.15
❑	237 Corey Patterson	.50	.15
❑	238 Vernon Wells	.50	.15
❑	239 Brad Baker	.50	.15
❑	240 Gookie Dawkins	.50	.15
❑	241 Michael Cuddyer	.50	.15
❑	242 Ricardo Aramboles	.50	.15
❑	243 Ben Sheets	.50	.15
❑	244 Toby Hall	.50	.15
❑	245 Jack Cust	.50	.15
❑	246 Pedro Feliz	.50	.15
❑	247 Josh Beckett	.75	.23
❑	248 Alex Escobar	.50	.15
❑	249 Marcus Giles	.50	.15
❑	250 Jon Rauch	.50	.15
❑	251 Kevin Mench	.50	.15
❑	252 Shawn Sonnier	.50	.15
❑	253 Aaron Rowand	.50	.15
❑	254 C.C. Sabathia	.50	.15
❑	255 Bubba Crosby	.50	.15
❑	256 Josh Hamilton	.50	.15
❑	257 Carlos Hernandez	.50	.15
❑	258 Carlos Pena	.50	.15
❑	259 Miguel Cabrera	5.00	1.50
❑	260 Brandon Phillips	.50	.15
❑	261 Tony Pena Jr.	.50	.15
❑	262 Cristian Guerrero	.50	.15
❑	263 Jin Ho Cho	.50	.15
❑	264 Aaron Herr	.50	.15
❑	265 Keith Ginter	.50	.15
❑	266 Felipe Lopez	.50	.15
❑	267 Travis Harper	.50	.15
❑	268 Joe Torres	.50	.15
❑	269 Eric Byrnes	.50	.15
❑	270 Ben Christensen	.50	.15
❑	271 Aubrey Huff	.50	.15
❑	272 Lyle Overbay	.50	.15
❑	273 Vince Faison	.50	.15
❑	274 Bobby Bradley	.50	.15
❑	275 Joe Crede	.50	.15
❑	276 Matt Wheatland	.50	.15
❑	277 Grady Sizemore	1.25	.35
❑	278 Adrian Gonzalez	.50	.15
❑	279 Tim Raines Jr.	.50	.15
❑	280 Phil Dumatrait	.50	.15
❑	281 Jason Hart	.50	.15
❑	282 David Kelton	.50	.15
❑	283 David Walling	.50	.15
❑	284 J.R. House	.50	.15
❑	285 Kenny Kelly	.50	.15
❑	286 Aaron McNeal	.50	.15
❑	287 Nick Johnson	.50	.15
❑	288 Scott Heard	.50	.15
❑	289 Brad Wilkerson	.50	.15
❑	290 Allen Levrault	.50	.15
❑	291 Chris Richard	.50	.15
❑	292 Jared Sandberg	.50	.15
❑	293 Tike Redman	.50	.15
❑	294 Adam Dunn	.75	.23
❑	295 Josh Pressley	.50	.15
❑	296 Jose Ortiz	.50	.15
❑	297 Jason Romano	.50	.15
❑	298 Tim Redding	.50	.15
❑	299 Alex Gordon	.50	.15
❑	300 Ben Petrick	.50	.15
❑	301 Eric Munson	.50	.15
❑	302 Luis Rivas	.50	.15
❑	303 Matt Ginter	.50	.15
❑	304 Alfonso Soriano	1.25	.35
❑	305 Wilfredo Rodriguez	.50	.15
❑	306 Brett Myers	.50	.15
❑	307 Scott Seabol	.50	.15
❑	308 Tony Alvarez	.50	.15
❑	309 Donzell McDonald	.50	.15
❑	310 Austin Kearns	.75	.23
❑	311 Will Ohman RC	8.00	2.40
❑	312 Ryan Soules RC	5.00	1.50
❑	313 Cody Ross RC	8.00	2.40
❑	314 Bill Whitecotton RC	8.00	2.40
❑	315 Mike Burns RC	8.00	2.40
❑	316 Manuel Acosta RC	8.00	2.40
❑	317 Lance Niekro RC	8.00	2.40
❑	318 Travis Thompson RC	8.00	2.40
❑	319 Zach Sorensen RC	8.00	2.40
❑	320 Austin Evans RC	5.00	1.50
❑	321 Brad Stiles RC	8.00	2.40
❑	322 Joe Kennedy RC	8.00	2.40
❑	323 Luke Martin RC	8.00	2.40
❑	324 Juan Diaz RC	8.00	2.40
❑	325 Pat Hallmark RC	5.00	1.50
❑	326 Christian Parker RC	5.00	1.50
❑	327 Ronny Corona RC	8.00	2.40
❑	328 Jermaine Clark RC	5.00	1.50
❑	329 Scott Dunn RC	8.00	2.40
❑	330 Scott Chiasson RC	8.00	2.40
❑	331 Greg Nash AU RC	25.00	7.50
❑	332 Brad Cresse AU	25.00	7.50
❑	333 John Buck AU RC	40.00	12.00
❑	334 Freddie Bynum AU RC	25.00	7.50
❑	335 Felix Diaz AU RC	25.00	7.50
❑	336 Jason Belcher AU RC	25.00	7.50
❑	337 T.Farnsworth AU RC	25.00	7.50
❑	338 Roberto Miniel AU RC	25.00	7.50
❑	339 Esix Snead AU RC	25.00	7.50
❑	340 Albert Pujols AU RC	700.00	210.00
❑	341 Jeff Andra AU RC	25.00	7.50
❑	342 Victor Hall AU RC	25.00	7.50
❑	343 Pedro Liriano AU RC	25.00	7.50
❑	344 Andy Beal AU RC	25.00	7.50
❑	345 Bob Keppel AU RC	25.00	7.50
❑	346 Brian Schmitt AU RC	25.00	7.50
❑	347 Ron Davenport AU RC	120.00	36.00
❑	348 Tony Blanco AU RC	25.00	7.50
❑	349 Reggie Griggs AU RC	25.00	7.50
❑	350 D. Van Dusen AU RC	25.00	7.50
❑	351A I. Suzuki English RC	60.00	18.00
❑	351B I. Suzuki Japan RC	60.00	18.00

2002 Bowman Chrome

	Nm-Mt	Ex-Mt
COMP.RED SET (110)	40.00	12.00
COMP.BLUE w/o SP's (110)	40.00	12.00
COMMON RED (1-110)	.50	.15
COMMON BLUE (111-383)	.75	.23
COMMON AU (324B/384-405)	10.00	3.00
324B/384-405 GROUP A AUTO ODDS 1:28	-	
403-404 GROUP B AUTO ODDS 1:1290	-	
324B/384-405 OVERALL AUTO ODDS 1:27	-	

	Card	Nm-Mt	Ex-Mt
❑	1 Adam Dunn	.75	.23
❑	2 Derek Jeter	3.00	.90
❑	3 Alex Rodriguez	2.50	.75
❑	4 Miguel Tejada	.50	.15
❑	5 Nomar Garciaparra	2.50	.75
❑	6 Toby Hall	.50	.15
❑	7 Brandon Duckworth	.50	.15
❑	8 Paul LoDuca	.50	.15
❑	9 Brian Giles	.50	.15
❑	10 C.C. Sabathia	.50	.15
❑	11 Curt Schilling	.75	.23
❑	12 Tsuyoshi Shinjo	.50	.15
❑	13 Ramon Hernandez	.50	.15
❑	14 Jose Cruz Jr.	.50	.15
❑	15 Albert Pujols	2.50	.75
❑	16 Joe Mays	.50	.15
❑	17 Javy Lopez	.50	.15
❑	18 J.T. Snow	.50	.15
❑	19 David Segui	.50	.15
❑	20 Jorge Posada	.75	.23
❑	21 Doug Mientkiewicz	.50	.15
❑	22 Jerry Hairston Jr.	.50	.15
❑	23 Bernie Williams	.75	.23
❑	24 Mike Sweeney	.50	.15
❑	25 Jason Giambi	1.25	.35
❑	26 Ryan Dempster	.50	.15
❑	27 Ryan Klesko	.50	.15
❑	28 Mark Quinn	.50	.15
❑	29 Jeff Kent	.50	.15
❑	30 Eric Chavez	.50	.15
❑	31 Adrian Beltre	.50	.15
❑	32 Andruw Jones	.75	.23
❑	33 Alfonso Soriano	1.25	.35
❑	34 Aramis Ramirez	.50	.15

	No.	Player		
❑	35	Greg Maddux	2.50	.75
❑	36	Andy Pettitte	.75	.23
❑	37	Bartolo Colon	.50	.15
❑	38	Ben Sheets	.50	.15
❑	39	Bobby Higginson	.50	.15
❑	40	Ivan Rodriguez	1.25	.35
❑	41	Brad Penny	.50	.15
❑	42	Carlos Lee	.50	.15
❑	43	Damion Easley	.50	.15
❑	44	Preston Wilson	.50	.15
❑	45	Jeff Bagwell	.75	.23
❑	46	Eric Milton	.50	.15
❑	47	Rafael Palmeiro	.75	.23
❑	48	Gary Sheffield	.50	.15
❑	49	J.D. Drew	.50	.15
❑	50	Jim Thome	1.25	.35
❑	51	Ichiro Suzuki	2.50	.75
❑	52	Bud Smith	.50	.15
❑	53	Chan Ho Park	.50	.15
❑	54	D'Angelo Jimenez	.50	.15
❑	55	Ken Griffey Jr.	2.00	.60
❑	56	Wade Miller	.50	.15
❑	57	Vladimir Guerrero	1.25	.35
❑	58	Troy Glaus	.75	.23
❑	59	Shawn Green	.50	.15
❑	60	Kerry Wood	1.25	.35
❑	61	Jack Wilson	.50	.15
❑	62	Kevin Brown	.50	.15
❑	63	Marcus Giles	.50	.15
❑	64	Pat Burrell	.50	.15
❑	65	Larry Walker	.75	.23
❑	66	Sammy Sosa	2.00	.60
❑	67	Raul Mondesi	.50	.15
❑	68	Tim Hudson	.50	.15
❑	69	Lance Berkman	.50	.15
❑	70	Mike Mussina	1.25	.35
❑	71	Barry Zito	1.25	.35
❑	72	Jimmy Rollins	.50	.15
❑	73	Barry Bonds	3.00	.90
❑	74	Craig Biggio	.75	.23
❑	75	Todd Helton	.75	.23
❑	76	Roger Clemens	2.50	.75
❑	77	Frank Catalanotto	.50	.15
❑	78	Josh Towers	.50	.15
❑	79	Roy Oswalt	.50	.15
❑	80	Chipper Jones	1.25	.35
❑	81	Cristian Guzman	.50	.15
❑	82	Darin Erstad	.50	.15
❑	83	Freddy Garcia	.50	.15
❑	84	Jason Tyner	.50	.15
❑	85	Carlos Delgado	.50	.15
❑	86	Jon Lieber	.50	.15
❑	87	Juan Pierre	.50	.15
❑	88	Matt Morris	.50	.15
❑	89	Phil Nevin	.50	.15
❑	90	Jim Edmonds	.50	.15
❑	91	Maggio Ordonez	.50	.15
❑	92	Mike Hampton	.50	.15
❑	93	Rafael Furcal	.50	.15
❑	94	Richie Sexson	.50	.15
❑	95	Luis Gonzalez	.50	.15
❑	96	Scott Rolen	.75	.23
❑	97	Tim Redding	.50	.15
❑	98	Moises Alou	.50	.15
❑	99	Jose Vidro	.50	.15
❑	100	Mike Piazza	2.00	.60
❑	101	Pedro Martinez	1.25	.35
❑	102	Geoff Jenkins	.50	.15
❑	103	Johnny Damon	.50	.15
❑	104	Mike Cameron	.50	.15
❑	105	Randy Johnson	1.25	.35
❑	106	David Eckstein	.50	.15
❑	107	Javier Vazquez	.50	.15
❑	108	Mark Mulder	.50	.15
❑	109	Robert Fick	.50	.15
❑	110	Roberto Alomar	1.25	.35
❑	111	Wilson Betemit	.75	.23
❑	112	Chris Tritle SP RC	5.00	1.50
❑	113	Ed Rogers	.75	.23
❑	114	Juan Pena	.75	.23
❑	115	Josh Beckett	2.00	.60
❑	116	Juan Cruz	.75	.23
❑	117	Noochie Varner SP RC	10.00	3.00
❑	118	Blake Williams	.75	.23
❑	119	Mike Rivera	.75	.23
❑	120	Hank Blalock	3.00	.90
❑	121	Hansel Izquierdo SP RC	5.00	1.50
❑	122	Orlando Hudson	.75	.23
❑	123	Bill Hall SP	5.00	1.50
❑	124	Jose Reyes	3.00	.90
❑	125	Juan Rivera	1.25	.35
❑	126	Eric Valent	.75	.23
❑	127	Scotty Layfield SP RC	5.00	1.50
❑	128	Austin Kearns	2.00	.60
❑	129	Nic Jackson SP RC	8.00	2.40
❑	130	Scott Chiasson	.75	.23
❑	131	Chad Qualls SP RC	5.00	1.50
❑	132	Marcus Thames	.75	.23
❑	133	Nathan Haynes	.75	.23
❑	134	Joe Borchard	1.25	.35
❑	135	Josh Hamilton	1.25	.35
❑	136	Corey Patterson	1.25	.35
❑	137	Travis Wilson	.75	.23
❑	138	Alex Escobar	.75	.23
❑	139	Alexis Gomez	.75	.23
❑	140	Nick Johnson	1.25	.35
❑	141	Marlon Byrd	1.25	.35
❑	142	Kory DeHaan	.75	.23
❑	143	Carlos Hernandez	.75	.23
❑	144	Sean Burroughs	1.25	.35
❑	145	Angel Berroa	1.25	.35
❑	146	Aubrey Huff	1.25	.35
❑	147	Travis Hafner	.75	.23
❑	148	Brandon Berger	.75	.23
❑	149	J.R. House	.75	.23
❑	150	Dewon Brazelton	.75	.23
❑	151	Jayson Werth	.75	.23
❑	152	Larry Barnes	.75	.23
❑	153	Ruben Gotay SP RC	8.00	2.40
❑	154	Tommy Marx SP RC	5.00	1.50
❑	155	John Suomi SP RC	5.00	1.50
❑	156	Javier Colina SP	5.00	1.50
❑	157	Greg Sain SP RC	5.00	1.50
❑	158	Robert Cosby SP RC	5.00	1.50
❑	159	Angel Pagan SP RC	5.00	1.50
❑	160	Ralph Santana RC	1.25	.35
❑	161	Joe Orloski RC	1.25	.35
❑	162	Shayne Wright SP RC	5.00	1.50
❑	163	Jay Caligiuri SP RC	5.00	1.50
❑	164	Greg Montalbano SP RC	8.00	2.40
❑	165	Rich Harden SP RC	30.00	9.00
❑	166	Rich Thompson SP RC	5.00	1.50
❑	167	Fred Bastardo SP RC	5.00	1.50
❑	168	Alejandro Giron SP RC	5.00	1.50
❑	169	Jesus Medrano SP RC	5.00	1.50
❑	170	Kevin Deaton SP RC	5.00	1.50
❑	171	Mike Rosamond RC	1.25	.35
❑	172	Jon Guzman SP RC	5.00	1.50
❑	173	Gerard Oakes SP RC	5.00	1.50
❑	174	Francisco Liriano SP RC	8.00	2.40
❑	175	Matt Allegra SP RC	8.00	2.40
❑	176	Mike Snyder SP RC	5.00	1.50
❑	177	James Shanks SP RC	5.00	1.50
❑	178	Anderson Hernandez SP RC	8.00	2.40
❑	179	Dan Trumble SP RC	5.00	1.50
❑	180	Luis DePaula SP RC	5.00	1.50
❑	181	Randall Shelley SP RC	8.00	2.40
❑	182	Richard Lane SP RC	5.00	1.50
❑	183	Antwon Rollins SP RC	8.00	2.40
❑	184	Ryan Bukvich SP RC	8.00	2.40
❑	185	Derrick Lewis SP	5.00	1.50
❑	186	Eric Miller SP RC	5.00	1.50
❑	187	Justin Schuda SP RC	5.00	1.50
❑	188	Brian West SP RC	5.00	1.50
❑	189	Brad Wilkerson	.75	.23
❑	190	Neal Frendling SP RC	5.00	1.50
❑	191	Jeremy Hill SP RC	5.00	1.50
❑	192	James Barrett SP RC	8.00	2.40
❑	193	Brett Kay SP RC	5.00	1.50
❑	194	Ryan Mottl SP RC	8.00	2.40
❑	195	Brad Nelson SP RC	15.00	4.50
❑	196	Juan M. Gonzalez SP RC	5.00	1.50
❑	197	Curtis Legendre SP RC	5.00	1.50
❑	198	Ronald Acuna SP RC	5.00	1.50
❑	199	Chris Flinn SP RC	5.00	1.50
❑	200	Nick Alvarez SP RC	5.00	1.50
❑	201	Jason Ellison SP RC	5.00	1.50
❑	202	Blake McGinley SP RC	5.00	1.50
❑	203	Dan Phillips SP RC	5.00	1.50
❑	204	Demetrius Heath SP RC	5.00	1.50
❑	205	Eric Bruntlett SP RC	5.00	1.50
❑	206	Joe Jiannetti SP RC	5.00	1.50
❑	207	Mike Hill SP RC	5.00	1.50
❑	208	Ricardo Cordova SP RC	5.00	1.50
❑	209	Mark Hamilton SP RC	5.00	1.50
❑	210	David Mattox SP RC	5.00	1.50
❑	211	Jose Morban SP RC	8.00	2.40
❑	212	Scott Wiggins SP RC	5.00	1.50
❑	213	Steve Green	.75	.23
❑	214	Brian Rogers SP	5.00	1.50
❑	215	Kenny Baugh	.75	.23
❑	216	Anastacio Martinez SP RC	5.00	1.50
❑	217	Richard Lewis	.75	.23
❑	218	Tim Kalita SP RC	5.00	1.50
❑	219	Edwin Almonte SP RC	5.00	1.50
❑	220	Hee Seop Choi	2.00	.60
❑	221	Ty Howington	.75	.23
❑	222	Victor Alvarez SP RC	5.00	1.50
❑	223	Morgan Ensberg	1.25	.35
❑	224	Jeff Austin SP RC	5.00	1.50
❑	225	Clint Weibl SP RC	5.00	1.50
❑	226	Eric Cyr	.75	.23
❑	227	Marlyn Tisdale SP RC	5.00	1.50
❑	228	John VanBenschoten	2.00	.60
❑	229	David Krynzel	.75	.23
❑	230	Raul Chavez SP RC	5.00	1.50
❑	231	Brett Evert	.75	.23
❑	232	Joe Rogers SP RC	5.00	1.50
❑	233	Adam Wainwright	1.25	.35
❑	234	Matt Herges RC	.75	.23
❑	235	Matt Childers SP RC	5.00	1.50
❑	236	Nick Neugebauer	.75	.23
❑	237	Carl Crawford	1.25	.35
❑	238	Seung Song	.75	.23
❑	239	Randy Flores	.75	.23
❑	240	Jason Lane	.75	.23
❑	241	Chase Utley	2.00	.60
❑	242	Ben Howard SP RC	5.00	1.50
❑	243	Eric Glaser SP RC	5.00	1.50
❑	244	Josh Wilson RC	2.00	.60
❑	245	Jose Valverde SP RC	8.00	2.40
❑	246	Chris Smith	.75	.23
❑	247	Mark Prior	10.00	3.00
❑	248	Brian Mallette SP RC	5.00	1.50
❑	249	Chone Figgins SP RC	5.00	1.50
❑	250	Jimmy Alvarez SP RC	5.00	1.50
❑	251	Luis Terrero	.75	.23
❑	252	Josh Bonifay SP RC	8.00	2.40
❑	253	Garrett Guzman SP RC	5.00	1.50
❑	254	Jeff Verplancke SP RC	5.00	1.50
❑	255	Nate Espy SP RC	5.00	1.50
❑	256	Jeff Lincoln SP RC	5.00	1.50
❑	257	Ryan Snare SP RC	8.00	2.40
❑	258	Jose Ortiz	.75	.23
❑	259	Denny Bautista	1.25	.35
❑	260	Willy Aybar	.75	.23
❑	261	Kelly Johnson	.75	.23
❑	262	Shawn Fagan	.75	.23
❑	263	Yurendell DeCaster SP RC	8.00	2.40
❑	264	Mike Peeples SP RC	5.00	1.50
❑	265	Joel Guzman	1.25	.35
❑	266	Ryan Vogelsong	.75	.23
❑	267	Jorge Padilla SP RC	8.00	2.40
❑	268	Joe Jester SP RC	5.00	1.50
❑	269	Ryan Church SP RC	10.00	3.00
❑	270	Mitch Jones	.75	.23
❑	271	Travis Foley SP RC	8.00	2.40
❑	272	Bobby Crosby	5.00	1.50
❑	273	Adrian Gonzalez	1.25	.35
❑	274	Ronnie Merrill	.75	.23
❑	275	Joel Pineiro	1.25	.35
❑	276	John-Ford Griffin	.75	.23
❑	277	Brian Forystek SP RC	5.00	1.50
❑	278	Sean Douglass	.75	.23
❑	279	Manny Delcarmen SP RC	8.00	2.40
❑	280	Jim Kavourias SP RC	5.00	1.50
❑	281	Gabe Gross	.75	.23
❑	282	Bill Ortega	.75	.23
❑	283	Joey Hammond SP RC	5.00	1.50
❑	284	Brett Myers	1.25	.35
❑	285	Carlos Pena	.75	.23
❑	286	Ezequiel Astacio SP RC	5.00	1.50
❑	287	Edwin Yan SP RC	5.00	1.50
❑	288	Chris Duffy SP RC	5.00	1.50
❑	289	Jason Kinchen	.75	.23
❑	290	Rafael Soriano	1.25	.35
❑	291	Colin Young RC	5.00	1.50
❑	292	Eric Byrnes	.75	.23

Card	Nm-Mt	Ex-Mt
❑ 293 Chris Narveson SP RC	8.00	2.40
❑ 294 John Rheinecker	.75	.23
❑ 295 Mike Wilson SP RC	5.00	1.50
❑ 296 Justin Sherrod SP RC	8.00	2.40
❑ 297 Deivi Mendez	.75	.23
❑ 298 Wily Mo Pena	1.25	.35
❑ 299 Brett Roneberg SP RC	5.00	1.50
❑ 300 Trey Lunsford SP RC	5.00	1.50
❑ 301 Christian Parker	.75	.23
❑ 302 Brent Butler	.75	.23
❑ 303 Aaron Heilman	.75	.23
❑ 304 Wilkin Ruan	.75	.23
❑ 305 Kenny Kelly	.75	.23
❑ 306 Cody Ransom	.75	.23
❑ 307 Koyie Hill SP	5.00	1.50
❑ 308 Tony Fontana SP RC	5.00	1.50
❑ 309 Mark Teixeira	3.00	.90
❑ 310 Doug Sessions SP RC	5.00	1.50
❑ 311 Josh Cisneros SP RC	5.00	1.50
❑ 312 Carlos Brackley SP RC	5.00	1.50
❑ 313 Tim Raines Jr.	.75	.23
❑ 314 Ross Peeples SP RC	8.00	2.40
❑ 315 Alex Requena SP RC	8.00	2.40
❑ 316 Chin-Hui Tsao	1.25	.35
❑ 317 Tony Alvarez	.75	.23
❑ 318 Craig Kuzmic SP RC	5.00	1.50
❑ 319 Pete Zamora SP RC	5.00	1.50
❑ 320 Matt Parker SP RC	5.00	1.50
❑ 321 Keith Ginter	.75	.23
❑ 322 Gary Cates Jr. SP RC	5.00	1.50
❑ 323 Matt Belisle	.75	.23
❑ 324A Ben Broussard	.75	.23
❑ 324B Ja.Mauer AU A RC EXCH UER	10.00	3.00
Card was mistakenly numbered as 324		
❑ 325 Dennis Tankersley	.75	.23
❑ 326 Juan Silvestre	.75	.23
❑ 327 Henry Pichardo SP RC	5.00	1.50
❑ 328 Michael Floyd SP RC	5.00	1.50
❑ 329 Clint Nageotte SP RC	12.00	3.60
❑ 330 Raymond Cabrera SP RC	5.00	1.50
❑ 331 Mauricio Lara SP RC	5.00	1.50
❑ 332 Alejandro Cadena SP RC	5.00	1.50
❑ 333 Jonny Gomes SP RC	12.00	3.60
❑ 334 Jason Bulger SP RC	5.00	1.50
❑ 335 Nate Teut	.75	.23
❑ 336 David Gil SP RC	5.00	1.50
❑ 337 Joel Crump SP RC	5.00	1.50
❑ 338 Brandon Phillips	.75	.23
❑ 339 Macay McBride	.75	.23
❑ 340 Brandon Claussen	5.00	1.50
❑ 341 Josh Phelps	1.25	.35
❑ 342 Freddie Money SP RC	5.00	1.50
❑ 343 Cliff Bartosh SP RC	5.00	1.50
❑ 344 Terrance Hill SP RC	5.00	1.50
❑ 345 John Rodriguez SP RC	5.00	1.50
❑ 346 Chris Latham SP RC	5.00	1.50
❑ 347 Carlos Cabrera SP RC	5.00	1.50
❑ 348 Jose Bautista SP RC	10.00	3.00
❑ 349 Kevin Frederick SP RC	5.00	1.50
❑ 350 Jerome Williams	3.00	.90
❑ 351 Napoleon Calzado SP RC	5.00	1.50
❑ 352 Benito Baez SP	5.00	1.50
❑ 353 Xavier Nady	1.25	.35
❑ 354 Jason Botts SP RC	5.00	1.50
❑ 355 Steve Bechler SP RC	5.00	1.50
❑ 356 Reed Johnson SP RC	8.00	2.40
❑ 357 Mark Outlaw SP RC	5.00	1.50
❑ 358 Jake Peavy	1.25	.35
❑ 359 Josh Shaffer SP RC	5.00	1.50
❑ 360 Dan Wright SP	5.00	1.50
❑ 361 Ryan Gripp SP RC	5.00	1.50
❑ 362 Nelson Castro SP RC	5.00	1.50
❑ 363 Jason Bay SP RC	12.00	3.60
❑ 364 Franklyn German SP RC	5.00	1.50
❑ 365 Corwin Malone SP RC	8.00	2.40
❑ 366 Kelly Ramos SP RC	5.00	1.50
❑ 367 John Ennis SP RC	5.00	1.50
❑ 368 George Perez SP	5.00	1.50
❑ 369 Rene Reyes SP RC	5.00	1.50
❑ 370 Rolando Viera SP RC	5.00	1.50
❑ 371 Earl Snyder SP RC	5.00	1.50
❑ 372 Kyle Kane SP RC	5.00	1.50
❑ 373 Mario Ramos SP RC	8.00	2.40
❑ 374 Tyler Yates SP RC	5.00	1.50
❑ 375 Jason Young SP RC	8.00	2.40
❑ 376 Chris Bootcheck SP RC	10.00	3.00
❑ 377 Jesus Cota SP RC	10.00	3.00
❑ 378 Corky Miller SP	5.00	1.50
❑ 379 Matt Erickson SP RC	5.00	1.50
❑ 380 Justin Huber SP RC	15.00	4.50
❑ 381 Felix Escalona SP RC	5.00	1.50
❑ 382 Kevin Cash SP RC	5.00	1.50
❑ 383 J.J. Putz SP RC	5.00	1.50
❑ 384 Chris Snelling AU A RC	25.00	7.50
❑ 385 David Wright AU A RC	30.00	9.00
❑ 386 Brian Wolfe AU A RC	10.00	3.00
❑ 387 Justin Reid AU A RC	10.00	3.00
❑ 389 Ryan Raburn AU A RC	10.00	3.00
❑ 390 Josh Barfield AU A RC	40.00	12.00
❑ 391 Joe Mauer AU A RC	100.00	36.00
❑ 392 Bobby Jenks AU A RC	25.00	7.50
❑ 393 Rob Henkel AU A RC	10.00	3.00
❑ 394 Jimmy Gobble AU A RC	30.00	9.00
❑ 395 Jesse Foppert AU A RC	40.00	12.00
❑ 396 Gavin Floyd AU A RC	40.00	12.00
❑ 397 Nate Field AU A RC	10.00	3.00
❑ 398 Ryan Doumit AU A RC	15.00	4.50
❑ 399 Ron Calloway AU A RC	10.00	3.00
❑ 400 Taylor Buchholz AU A RC	10.00	3.00
❑ 401 Adam Roller AU A RC	10.00	3.00
❑ 402 Cole Barthel AU A RC	15.00	4.50
❑ 403 Kazuhisa Ishii SP RC	10.00	3.00
❑ 403 Kazuhisa Ishii AU B	80.00	24.00
❑ 404 So Taguchi SP RC	8.00	2.40
❑ 404 So Taguchi AU B	50.00	15.00
❑ 405 Chris Baker AU A RC	10.00	3.00

2002 Bowman Chrome Draft

	Nm-Mt	Ex-Mt
COMPLETE SET (175)	300.00	90.00
COMP.SET w/o AU's (165)	160.00	47.50
COMMON CARD (1-165)	.40	.12
COMMON CARD (166-175)	15.00	4.50

Card	Nm-Mt	Ex-Mt
❑ 1 Clint Everts RC	3.00	.90
❑ 2 Fred Lewis RC	1.50	.45
❑ 3 Jon Broxton RC	1.00	.30
❑ 4 Jason Anderson RC	1.00	.30
❑ 5 Mike Eusebio RC	1.00	.30
❑ 6 Zack Greinke RC	12.00	3.60
❑ 7 Joe Blanton RC	8.00	2.40
❑ 8 Sergio Santos RC	6.00	1.80
❑ 9 Jason Cooper RC	2.50	.75
❑ 10 Delwyn Young RC	4.00	1.20
❑ 11 Jeremy Hermida RC	4.00	1.20
❑ 12 Dan Ortmeier RC	2.50	.75
❑ 13 Kevin Jepsen RC	2.50	.75
❑ 14 Russ Adams RC	2.50	.75
❑ 15 Mike Nixon RC	1.00	.30
❑ 16 Nick Swisher RC	5.00	1.50
❑ 17 Cole Hamels RC	15.00	4.50
❑ 18 Brian Dopirak RC	5.00	1.50
❑ 19 James Loney RC	6.00	1.80
❑ 20 Denard Span RC	2.50	.75
❑ 21 Billy Petrick RC	1.00	.30
❑ 22 Jared Doyle RC	1.00	.30
❑ 23 Jeff Francoeur RC	15.00	4.50
❑ 24 Nick Bourgeois RC	1.00	.30
❑ 25 Matt Cain RC	4.00	1.20
❑ 26 John McCurdy RC	1.00	.30
❑ 27 Mark Kiger RC	1.00	.30
❑ 28 Bill Murphy RC	1.50	.45
❑ 29 Matt Craig RC	1.50	.45
❑ 30 Mike Megrew RC	1.00	.30
❑ 31 Ben Crockett RC	1.00	.30
❑ 32 Luke Hagerty RC	2.50	.75
❑ 33 Matt Whitney RC	2.50	.75
❑ 34 Dan Meyer RC	2.50	.75
❑ 35 Jeremy Brown RC	3.00	.90
❑ 36 Doug Johnson RC	1.00	.30
❑ 37 Steve Obenchain RC	1.00	.30
❑ 38 Matt Clanton RC	1.50	.45
❑ 39 Mark Teahen RC	1.00	.30
❑ 40 Tom Carrow RC	1.00	.30
❑ 41 Micah Schilling RC	2.50	.75
❑ 42 Blair Johnson RC	1.50	.45
❑ 43 Jason Pridie RC	4.00	1.20
❑ 44 Joey Votto RC	1.50	.45
❑ 45 Taber Lee RC	1.00	.30
❑ 46 Adam Peterson RC	1.00	.30
❑ 47 Adam Donachie RC	1.50	.45
❑ 48 Josh Murray RC	1.50	.45
❑ 49 Brent Clevlen RC	3.00	.90
❑ 50 Chad Pleiness RC	1.50	.45
❑ 51 Zach Hammes RC	1.50	.45
❑ 52 Chris Snyder RC	2.50	.75
❑ 53 Chris Smith RC	1.00	.30
❑ 54 Justin Maureau RC	1.00	.30
❑ 55 David Bush RC	5.00	1.50
❑ 56 Tim Gilhooly RC	1.00	.30
❑ 57 Blair Barbier RC	1.00	.30
❑ 58 Zach Segovia RC	2.50	.75
❑ 59 Jeremy Reed RC	15.00	6.00
❑ 60 Matt Pender RC	1.00	.30
❑ 61 Eric Thomas RC	1.00	.30
❑ 62 Justin Jones RC	4.00	1.20
❑ 63 Brian Slocum RC	1.50	.45
❑ 64 Larry Broadway RC	5.00	1.50
❑ 65 Bo Flowers RC	1.00	.30
❑ 66 Scott White RC	2.50	.75
❑ 67 Steve Stanley RC	1.00	.30
❑ 68 Alex Merricks RC	1.00	.30
❑ 69 Josh Womack RC	1.50	.45
❑ 70 Dave Jensen RC	1.00	.30
❑ 71 Curtis Granderson RC	3.00	.90
❑ 72 Pat Osborn RC	2.50	.75
❑ 73 Nic Carter RC	1.00	.30
❑ 74 Mitch Talbot RC	1.00	.30
❑ 75 Don Murphy RC	1.00	.30
❑ 76 Val Majewski RC	2.50	.75
❑ 77 Javy Rodriguez RC	1.00	.30
❑ 78 Fernando Pacheco RC	1.50	.45
❑ 79 Steve Russell RC	1.00	.30
❑ 80 Jon Slack RC	1.00	.30
❑ 81 John Baker RC	1.00	.30
❑ 82 Aaron Coonrod RC	1.00	.30
❑ 83 Josh Johnson RC	1.50	.45
❑ 84 Jake Blalock RC	6.00	1.80
❑ 85 Alex Hart RC	3.00	.90
❑ 86 Wes Bankston RC	6.00	1.80
❑ 87 Josh Rupe RC	1.50	.45
❑ 88 Dan Cevette RC	2.50	.75
❑ 89 Kiel Fisher RC	1.50	.45
❑ 90 Alan Rick RC	1.00	.30
❑ 91 Charlie Morton RC	1.50	.45
❑ 92 Chad Spann RC	3.00	.90
❑ 93 Kyle Boyer RC	1.50	.45
❑ 94 Bob Malek RC	1.00	.30
❑ 95 Ryan Rodriguez RC	1.00	.30
❑ 96 Jordan Renz RC	1.00	.30
❑ 97 Randy Frye RC	1.00	.30
❑ 98 Rich Hill RC	1.00	.30
❑ 99 B.J. Upton RC	15.00	4.50
❑ 100 Dan Christensen RC	2.50	.75
❑ 101 Casey Kotchman RC	8.00	2.40
❑ 102 Eric Good RC	1.00	.30
❑ 103 Mike Fontenot RC	2.50	.75
❑ 104 John Webb RC	1.00	.30
❑ 105 Jason Dubois RC	5.00	1.50
❑ 106 Ryan Kibler RC	1.00	.30
❑ 107 John Peralta RC	1.50	.45
❑ 108 Kirk Saarloos RC	2.50	.75
❑ 109 Rhett Parrott RC	1.00	.30
❑ 110 Jason Grove RC	1.00	.30
❑ 111 Colt Griffin RC	3.00	.90
❑ 112 Dallas McPherson RC	6.00	1.80
❑ 113 Oliver Perez RC	3.00	.90
❑ 114 Marshall McDougall RC	1.00	.30

Card	MINT	NRMT
❑ 115 Mike Wood RC	1.50	.45
❑ 116 Scott Hairston RC	5.00	1.50
❑ 117 Jason Simontacchi RC	1.50	.45
❑ 118 Taggert Bozied RC	5.00	1.50
❑ 119 Shelley Duncan RC	1.00	.30
❑ 120 Dontrelle Willis RC	20.00	6.00
❑ 121 Sean Burnett	.60	.18
❑ 122 Aaron Cook	1.00	.30
❑ 123 Brett Evert	.40	.12
❑ 124 Jimmy Journell	.40	.12
❑ 125 Brett Myers	.60	.18
❑ 126 Brad Baker	.40	.12
❑ 127 Billy Traber RC	3.00	.90
❑ 128 Adam Wainwright	.60	.18
❑ 129 Jason Young	1.50	.45
❑ 130 John Buck	.40	.12
❑ 131 Kevin Cash	1.00	.30
❑ 132 Jason Stokes RC	15.00	4.50
❑ 133 Drew Henson	.60	.18
❑ 134 Chad Tracy RC	5.00	1.50
❑ 135 Orlando Hudson	.40	.12
❑ 136 Brandon Phillips	.40	.12
❑ 137 Joe Borchard	.60	.18
❑ 138 Marlon Byrd	.60	.18
❑ 139 Carl Crawford	.60	.18
❑ 140 Michael Restovich	.60	.18
❑ 141 Corey Hart RC	5.00	1.50
❑ 142 Edwin Almonte	.60	.18
❑ 143 Francis Beltran RC	1.00	.30
❑ 144 Jorge De La Rosa RC	1.00	.30
❑ 145 Gerardo Garcia RC	1.00	.30
❑ 146 Franklyn German RC	1.00	.30
❑ 147 Francisco Liriano	.60	.18
❑ 148 Francisco Rodriguez	.60	.18
❑ 149 Ricardo Rodriguez	.40	.12
❑ 150 Seung Song	.40	.12
❑ 151 John Stephens	.40	.12
❑ 152 Justin Huber RC	3.00	.90
❑ 153 Victor Martinez	.60	.18
❑ 154 Hee Seop Choi	1.00	.30
❑ 155 Justin Morneau	1.00	.30
❑ 156 Miguel Cabrera	3.00	.90
❑ 157 Victor Diaz RC	5.00	1.50
❑ 158 Jose Reyes	1.50	.45
❑ 159 Omar Infante	.40	.12
❑ 160 Angel Berroa	.60	.18
❑ 161 Tony Alvarez	.40	.12
❑ 162 Shin Soo Choo RC	5.00	1.50
❑ 163 Wily Mo Pena	.60	.18
❑ 164 Andres Torres	.40	.12
❑ 165 Jose Lopez RC	6.00	1.80
❑ 166 Scott Moore AU RC	20.00	6.00
❑ 167 Chris Gruler AU RC	15.00	4.50
❑ 168 Joe Saunders AU RC	15.00	4.50
❑ 169 Jeff Francis AU RC	15.00	4.50
❑ 170 Royce Ring AU RC	15.00	4.50
❑ 171 Greg Miller AU RC	40.00	12.00
❑ 172 Brandon Weeden AU RC	15.00	4.50
❑ 173 Drew Meyer AU RC	15.00	4.50
❑ 174 Khalil Greene AU RC	50.00	15.00
❑ 175 Mark Schramek AU RC	20.00	6.00

2003 Bowman Chrome

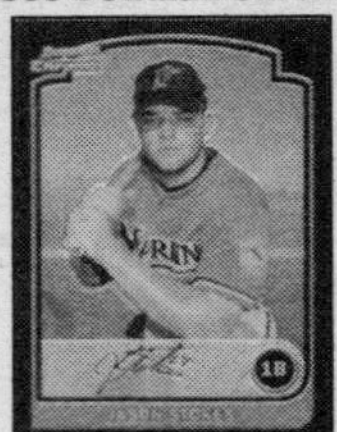

	MINT	NRMT
COMPLETE SET (351)	600.00	275.00
COMP.SET w/o AU's (331)	250.00	110.00
COMMON CARD (1-165)	.50	.23
COMMON CARD (166-330)	.50	.23
COMMON RC (156-330)	1.00	.45
COMP.SET w/o AU'S INCLUDES 351 MAYS		-
MAYS AU IS NOT PART OF 351-CARD SET		-
❑ 1 Garret Anderson	.50	.23
❑ 2 Derek Jeter	3.00	1.35
❑ 3 Gary Sheffield	.50	.23
❑ 4 Matt Morris	.50	.23
❑ 5 Derek Lowe	.50	.23
❑ 6 Andy Van Hekken	.50	.23
❑ 7 Sammy Sosa	2.00	.90
❑ 8 Ken Griffey Jr.	2.00	.90
❑ 9 Omar Vizquel	.50	.23
❑ 10 Jorge Posada	.75	.35
❑ 11 Lance Berkman	.50	.23
❑ 12 Mike Sweeney	.50	.23
❑ 13 Adrian Beltre	.50	.23
❑ 14 Richie Sexson	.50	.23
❑ 15 A.J. Pierzynski	.50	.23
❑ 16 Bartolo Colon	.50	.23
❑ 17 Mike Mussina	1.25	.55
❑ 18 Paul Byrd	.50	.23
❑ 19 Bobby Abreu	.50	.23
❑ 20 Miguel Tejada	.50	.23
❑ 21 Aramis Ramirez	.50	.23
❑ 22 Edgardo Alfonzo	.50	.23
❑ 23 Edgar Martinez	.75	.35
❑ 24 Albert Pujols	2.50	1.10
❑ 25 Carl Crawford	.50	.23
❑ 26 Eric Hinske	.50	.23
❑ 27 Tim Salmon	.75	.35
❑ 28 Luis Gonzalez	.50	.23
❑ 29 Jay Gibbons	.50	.23
❑ 30 John Smoltz	.50	.23
❑ 31 Tim Wakefield	.50	.23
❑ 32 Mark Prior	2.50	1.10
❑ 33 Magglio Ordonez	.50	.23
❑ 34 Adam Dunn	.75	.35
❑ 35 Larry Walker	.75	.35
❑ 36 Luis Castillo	.50	.23
❑ 37 Wade Miller	.50	.23
❑ 38 Carlos Beltran	.50	.23
❑ 39 Odalis Perez	.50	.23
❑ 40 Alex Sanchez	.50	.23
❑ 41 Torii Hunter	.50	.23
❑ 42 Cliff Floyd	.50	.23
❑ 43 Andy Pettitte	.75	.35
❑ 44 Francisco Rodriguez	.50	.23
❑ 45 Eric Chavez	.50	.23
❑ 46 Kevin Millwood	.50	.23
❑ 47 Dennis Tankersley	.50	.23
❑ 48 Hideo Nomo	1.25	.55
❑ 49 Freddy Garcia	.50	.23
❑ 50 Randy Johnson	1.25	.55
❑ 51 Aubrey Huff	.50	.23
❑ 52 Carlos Delgado	.50	.23
❑ 53 Troy Glaus	.75	.35
❑ 54 Junior Spivey	.50	.23
❑ 55 Mike Hampton	.50	.23
❑ 56 Sidney Ponson	.50	.23
❑ 57 Aaron Boone	.50	.23
❑ 58 Kerry Wood	1.25	.55
❑ 59 Willie Harris	.50	.23
❑ 60 Nomar Garciaparra	2.50	1.10
❑ 61 Todd Helton	.75	.35
❑ 62 Mike Lowell	.50	.23
❑ 63 Roy Oswalt	.50	.23
❑ 64 Raul Ibanez	.50	.23
❑ 65 Brian Jordan	.50	.23
❑ 66 Geoff Jenkins	.50	.23
❑ 67 Jermaine Dye	.50	.23
❑ 68 Tom Glavine	1.25	.55
❑ 69 Bernie Williams	.75	.35
❑ 70 Vladimir Guerrero	1.25	.55
❑ 71 Mark Mulder	.50	.23
❑ 72 Jimmy Rollins	.50	.23
❑ 73 Oliver Perez	.50	.23
❑ 74 Rich Aurilia	.50	.23
❑ 75 Joel Pineiro	.50	.23
❑ 76 J.D. Drew	.50	.23
❑ 77 Ivan Rodriguez	1.25	.55
❑ 78 Josh Phelps	.50	.23
❑ 79 Darin Erstad	.50	.23
❑ 80 Curt Schilling	.75	.35
❑ 81 Paul Lo Duca	.50	.23
❑ 82 Marty Cordova	.50	.23
❑ 83 Manny Ramirez	.50	.23
❑ 84 Bobby Hill	.50	.23
❑ 85 Paul Konerko	.50	.23
❑ 86 Austin Kearns	.75	.35
❑ 87 Jason Jennings	.50	.23
❑ 88 Brad Penny	.50	.23
❑ 89 Jeff Bagwell	.75	.35
❑ 90 Shawn Green	.50	.23
❑ 91 Jason Schmidt	.50	.23
❑ 92 Doug Mientkiewicz	.50	.23
❑ 93 Jose Vidro	.50	.23
❑ 94 Bret Boone	.50	.23
❑ 95 Jason Giambi	1.25	.55
❑ 96 Barry Zito	1.25	.55
❑ 97 Roy Halladay	.50	.23
❑ 98 Pat Burrell	.50	.23
❑ 99 Sean Burroughs	.50	.23
❑ 100 Barry Bonds	3.00	1.35
❑ 101 Kazuhiro Sasaki	.50	.23
❑ 102 Fernando Vina	.50	.23
❑ 103 Chan Ho Park	.50	.23
❑ 104 Andruw Jones	.75	.35
❑ 105 Adam Kennedy	.50	.23
❑ 106 Shea Hillenbrand	.50	.23
❑ 107 Greg Maddux	2.50	1.10
❑ 108 Jim Edmonds	.50	.23
❑ 109 Pedro Martinez	1.25	.55
❑ 110 Moises Alou	.50	.23
❑ 111 Jeff Weaver	.50	.23
❑ 112 C.C. Sabathia	.50	.23
❑ 113 Robert Fick	.50	.23
❑ 114 A.J. Burnett	.50	.23
❑ 115 Jeff Kent	.50	.23
❑ 116 Kevin Brown	.50	.23
❑ 117 Rafael Furcal	.50	.23
❑ 118 Cristian Guzman	.50	.23
❑ 119 Brad Wilkerson	.50	.23
❑ 120 Mike Piazza	2.00	.90
❑ 121 Alfonso Soriano	1.25	.55
❑ 122 Mark Ellis	.50	.23
❑ 123 Vicente Padilla	.50	.23
❑ 124 Eric Gagne	.75	.35
❑ 125 Ryan Klesko	.50	.23
❑ 126 Ichiro Suzuki	2.50	1.10
❑ 127 Tony Batista	.50	.23
❑ 128 Roberto Alomar	1.25	.55
❑ 129 Alex Rodriguez	2.50	1.10
❑ 130 Jim Thome	1.25	.55
❑ 131 Jarrod Washburn	.50	.23
❑ 132 Orlando Hudson	.50	.23
❑ 133 Chipper Jones	1.25	.55
❑ 134 Rodrigo Lopez	.50	.23
❑ 135 Johnny Damon	.50	.23
❑ 136 Matt Clement	.50	.23
❑ 137 Frank Thomas	1.25	.55
❑ 138 Ellis Burks	.50	.23
❑ 139 Carlos Pena	.50	.23
❑ 140 Josh Beckett	.75	.35
❑ 141 Joe Randa	.50	.23
❑ 142 Brian Giles	.50	.23
❑ 143 Kazuhisa Ishii	.50	.23
❑ 144 Corey Koskie	.50	.23
❑ 145 Orlando Cabrera	.50	.23
❑ 146 Mark Buehrle	.50	.23
❑ 147 Roger Clemens	2.50	1.10
❑ 148 Tim Hudson	.50	.23
❑ 149 Randy Wolf	.50	.23
❑ 150 Josh Fogg	.50	.23
❑ 151 Phil Nevin	.50	.23
❑ 152 John Olerud	.50	.23
❑ 153 Scott Rolen	.75	.35
❑ 154 Joe Kennedy	.50	.23
❑ 155 Rafael Palmeiro	.75	.35
❑ 156 Chad Hutchinson	.50	.23
❑ 157 Quincy Carter XRC	2.00	.90
❑ 158 Hee Seop Choi	.50	.23
❑ 159 Joe Borchard	.50	.23
❑ 160 Brandon Phillips	.50	.23
❑ 161 Wily Mo Pena	.50	.23
❑ 162 Victor Martinez	.50	.23
❑ 163 Jason Stokes	1.25	.55
❑ 164 Ken Harvey	.50	.23
❑ 165 Juan Rivera	.50	.23
❑ 166 Joe Valentine RC	1.50	.70
❑ 167 Dan Haren RC	4.00	1.80
❑ 168 Michel Hernandez RC	1.50	.70

❑ 169 Eider Torres RC 1.50 .70
❑ 170 Chris De La Cruz RC 1.50 .70
❑ 171 Ramon Nivar-Martinez RC 4.00 1.80
❑ 172 Mike Adams RC 1.50 .70
❑ 173 Justin Arneson RC 1.50 .70
❑ 174 Jamie Athas RC 1.50 .70
❑ 175 Dwaine Bacon RC 1.50 .70
❑ 176 Clint Barmes RC 2.00 .90
❑ 177 B.J. Barns RC 1.50 .70
❑ 178 Tyler Johnson RC 1.50 .70
❑ 179 Brandon Webb RC 10.00 4.50
❑ 180 T.J. Bohn RC 1.50 .70
❑ 181 Ozzie Chavez RC 1.50 .70
❑ 182 Brandon Bowe RC 1.50 .70
❑ 183 Craig Brazell RC 3.00 1.35
❑ 184 Dusty Brown RC 1.50 .70
❑ 185 Brian Bruney RC 2.00 .90
❑ 186 Greg Bruso RC 1.50 .70
❑ 187 Jaime Bubela RC 1.50 .70
❑ 188 Matt Diaz RC 3.00 1.35
❑ 189 Brian Burgamy RC 1.50 .70
❑ 190 Eny Cabreja RC 1.50 .70
❑ 191 Daniel Cabrera RC 1.50 .70
❑ 192 Ryan Cameron RC 1.50 .70
❑ 193 Lance Caraccioli RC 1.50 .70
❑ 194 David Cash RC 1.50 .70
❑ 195 Bernie Castro RC 1.50 .70
❑ 196 Ismael Castro RC 2.00 .90
❑ 197 Cory Doyne RC 1.50 .70
❑ 198 Jeff Clark RC 1.50 .70
❑ 199 Chris Colton RC 1.50 .70
❑ 200 Dexter Cooper RC 1.50 .70
❑ 201 Callix Crabbe RC 2.00 .90
❑ 202 Chien-Ming Wang RC 6.00 2.70
❑ 203 Eric Crozier RC 2.00 .90
❑ 204 Nook Logan RC 1.50 .70
❑ 205 David DeJesus RC 3.00 1.35
❑ 206 Matt DeMarco RC 1.50 .70
❑ 207 Chris Duncan RC 1.50 .70
❑ 208 Eric Eckenstahler .50 .23
❑ 209 Willie Eyre RC 1.50 .70
❑ 210 Evel Bastida-Martinez RC 1.50 .70
❑ 211 Chris Fallon RC 1.50 .70
❑ 212 Mike Flannery RC 1.50 .70
❑ 213 Mike O'Keefe RC 1.50 .70
❑ 214 Lew Ford RC 2.00 .90
❑ 215 Kason Gabbard RC 1.50 .70
❑ 216 Mike Gallo RC 1.50 .70
❑ 217 Jairo Garcia RC 1.50 .70
❑ 218 Angel Garcia RC 2.00 .90
❑ 219 Michael Garciaparra RC 3.00 1.35
❑ 220 Jeremy Griffiths RC 2.00 .90
❑ 221 Dusty Gomon RC 3.00 1.35
❑ 222 Bryan Grace RC 1.50 .70
❑ 223 Tyson Graham RC 1.50 .70
❑ 224 Henry Guerrero RC 1.50 .70
❑ 225 Franklin Gutierrez RC 10.00 4.50
❑ 226 Carlos Guzman RC 2.00 .90
❑ 227 Matthew Hagen RC 3.00 1.35
❑ 228 Josh Hall RC 2.00 .90
❑ 229 Rob Hammock RC 3.00 1.35
❑ 230 Brendan Harris RC 3.00 1.35
❑ 231 Gary Harris RC 1.50 .70
❑ 232 Clay Hensley RC 1.50 .70
❑ 233 Michael Hinckley RC 3.00 1.35
❑ 234 Luis Hodge RC 1.50 .70
❑ 235 Donnie Hood RC 2.00 .90
❑ 236 Matt Hensley RC 1.50 .70
❑ 237 Edwin Jackson RC 10.00 4.50
❑ 238 Ardley Jansen RC 2.00 .90
❑ 239 Ferenc Jongejan RC 1.50 .70
❑ 240 Matt Kata RC 4.00 1.80
❑ 241 Kazuhiro Takeoka RC 1.50 .70
❑ 242 Charlie Manning RC 1.50 .70
❑ 243 Il Kim RC 1.50 .70
❑ 244 Brennan King RC 1.50 .70
❑ 245 Chris Kroski RC 1.50 .70
❑ 246 David Martinez RC 1.50 .70
❑ 247 Pete LaForest RC 2.00 .90
❑ 248 Wil Ledezma RC 1.50 .70
❑ 249 Jeremy Bonderman RC 5.00 2.20
❑ 250 Gonzalo Lopez RC 1.50 .70
❑ 251 Brian Luderer RC 1.50 .70
❑ 252 Ruddy Lugo RC 1.50 .70
❑ 253 Wayne Lydon RC 2.00 .90
❑ 254 Mark Malaska RC 1.50 .70
❑ 255 Andy Marte RC 10.00 4.50
❑ 256 Tyler Martin RC 1.50 .70
❑ 257 Branden Florence RC 1.50 .70
❑ 258 Aneudis Mateo RC 1.50 .70
❑ 259 Derell McCall RC 1.50 .70
❑ 260 Elizardo Ramirez RC 5.00 2.20
❑ 261 Mike McNutt RC 1.50 .70
❑ 262 Jacobo Meque RC 1.50 .70
❑ 263 Derek Michaelis RC 2.00 .90
❑ 264 Aaron Miles RC 1.50 .70
❑ 265 Jose Morales RC 1.50 .70
❑ 266 Dustin Moseley RC 2.00 .90
❑ 267 Adrian Myers RC 1.50 .70
❑ 268 Dan Neil RC 1.50 .70
❑ 269 Jon Nelson RC 2.00 .90
❑ 270 Mike Neu RC 1.50 .70
❑ 271 Leigh Neuage RC 1.50 .70
❑ 272 Wes O'Brien RC 1.50 .70
❑ 273 Trent Oeltjen RC 2.00 .90
❑ 274 Tim Olson RC 3.00 1.35
❑ 275 David Pahucki RC 1.50 .70
❑ 276 Nathan Panther RC 3.00 1.35
❑ 277 Arnie Munoz RC 1.50 .70
❑ 278 Dave Pember RC 1.50 .70
❑ 279 Jason Perry RC 3.00 1.35
❑ 280 Matthew Peterson RC 1.50 .70
❑ 281 Greg Aquino RC 1.50 .70
❑ 282 Jorge Piedra RC 2.00 .90
❑ 283 Simon Pond RC 2.00 .90
❑ 284 Aaron Rakers RC 1.50 .70
❑ 285 Felix Sanchez RC 1.50 .70
❑ 286 Manuel Ramirez RC 3.00 1.35
❑ 287 Kevin Randel RC 1.50 .70
❑ 288 Kelly Shoppach RC 5.00 2.20
❑ 289 Prentice Redman RC 1.50 .70
❑ 290 Eric Reed RC 3.00 1.35
❑ 291 Wilton Reynolds RC 2.00 .90
❑ 292 Eric Riggs RC 2.00 .90
❑ 293 Carlos Rijo RC 1.50 .70
❑ 294 Tyler Adamczyk RC 1.50 .70
❑ 295 Jon-Mark Sprowl RC 3.00 1.35
❑ 296 Arturo Rivas RC 1.50 .70
❑ 297 Kyle Roat RC 1.50 .70
❑ 298 Bubba Nelson RC 4.00 1.80
❑ 299 Levi Robinson RC 1.50 .70
❑ 300 Ray Sadler RC 1.50 .70
❑ 301 Rylan Reed RC 1.50 .70
❑ 302 Jon Schuerholz RC 1.50 .70
❑ 303 Nobuaki Yoshida RC 1.50 .70
❑ 304 Brian Shackelford RC 1.50 .70
❑ 305 Bill Simon RC 1.50 .70
❑ 306 Haj Turay RC 2.00 .90
❑ 307 Sean Smith RC 2.00 .90
❑ 308 Ryan Spataro RC 1.50 .70
❑ 309 Jemel Spearman RC 1.50 .70
❑ 310 Keith Stamler RC 1.50 .70
❑ 311 Luke Steidlmayer RC 1.50 .70
❑ 312 Adam Stern RC 1.50 .70
❑ 313 Jay Sitzman RC 1.50 .70
❑ 314 Mike Wodnicki RC 1.50 .70
❑ 315 Terry Tiffee RC 2.00 .90
❑ 316 Nick Trzesniak RC 1.50 .70
❑ 317 Denny Tussen RC 1.50 .70
❑ 318 Scott Tyler RC 2.00 .90
❑ 319 Shane Victorino RC 1.50 .70
❑ 320 Doug Waechter RC 3.00 1.35
❑ 321 Brandon Watson RC 1.50 .70
❑ 322 Todd Wellemeyer RC 2.00 .90
❑ 323 Eli Whiteside RC 1.50 .70
❑ 324 Josh Willingham RC 5.00 2.20
❑ 325 Travis Wong RC 2.00 .90
❑ 326 Brian Wright RC 1.50 .70
❑ 327 Felix Pie RC 15.00 6.75
❑ 328 Andy Sisco RC 5.00 2.20
❑ 329 Dustin Yount RC 3.00 1.35
❑ 330 Andrew Dominique RC 1.50 .70
❑ 331 Brian McCann AU A RC 20.00 9.00
❑ 332 Jose Contreras AU B RC 200.00 90.00
❑ 333 Corey Shafer AU A RC 20.00 9.00
❑ 334 Hanley Ramirez AU A RC 40.00 18.00
❑ 335 Ryan Shealy AU A RC 20.00 9.00
❑ 336 Kevin Youkilis AU A RC 40.00 18.00
❑ 337 Jason Kubel AU A RC 20.00 9.00
❑ 338 Aron Weston AU A RC 15.00 6.75
❑ 338B Rajai Davis AU A ERR - -
❑ 339 J.D. Durbin AU A RC 20.00 9.00
❑ 340 Gary Schneidmiller AU A RC 15.00 6.75
❑ 341 Travis Ishikawa AU A RC 20.00 9.00
❑ 342 Ben Francisco AU A RC 20.00 9.00
❑ 343 Bobby Basham AU A RC 20.00 9.00
❑ 344 Joey Gomes AU A RC 20.00 9.00
❑ 345 Beau Kemp AU A RC 15.00 6.75
❑ 346 T.Story-Harden AU A RC 20.00 9.00
❑ 347 Daryl Clark AU A RC 20.00 9.00
❑ 348 B.Bullington AU A RC EXCH 40.00 18.00
❑ 349 Rajai Davis AU A RC 20.00 9.00
❑ 350 Darrell Rasner AU A RC 15.00 6.75
❑ 351 Willie Mays 2.00 .90
❑ 351AU Willie Mays AU 250.00 110.00

2003 Bowman Chrome Draft

	MINT	NRMT
COMP.SET w/o AU's (165)	120.00	55.00
COMMON CARD (1-165)	.40	.18
1-165 TWO PER BOWMAN DRAFT PACK		-
COMMON CARD (166-176)	20.00	9.00
166-176 STATED ODDS 1:41	-	
168- ARE ALL PARTIAL LIVE/EXCH DIST.		-
168-176 EXCH.DEADLINE 11/30/05		-

❑ 1 Dontrelle Willis 2.00 .90
❑ 2 Freddy Sanchez .40 .18
❑ 3 Miguel Cabrera 2.00 .90
❑ 4 Ryan Ludwick .40 .18
❑ 5 Ty Wigginton .60 .25
❑ 6 Mark Teixeira 1.00 .45
❑ 7 Trey Hodges .40 .18
❑ 8 Laynce Nix 1.50 .70
❑ 9 Antonio Perez .40 .18
❑ 10 Jody Gerut .60 .25
❑ 11 Jae Weong Seo .40 .18
❑ 12 Erick Almonte .40 .18
❑ 13 Lyle Overbay .40 .18
❑ 14 Billy Traber .40 .18
❑ 15 Andres Torres .40 .18
❑ 16 Jose Valverde .40 .18
❑ 17 Aaron Heilman .40 .18
❑ 18 Brandon Larson .40 .18
❑ 19 Jung Bong .40 .18
❑ 20 Jesse Foppert .60 .25
❑ 21 Angel Berroa .60 .25
❑ 22 Jeff DaVanon .40 .18
❑ 23 Kurt Ainsworth .40 .18
❑ 24 Brandon Claussen .60 .25
❑ 25 Xavier Nady .60 .25
❑ 26 Travis Hafner .40 .18
❑ 27 Jerome Williams .60 .25
❑ 28 Jose Reyes 1.00 .45
❑ 29 Sergio Mitre RC 1.00 .45
❑ 30 Bo Hart RC 5.00 2.20
❑ 31 Adam Miller RC 2.50 1.10
❑ 32 Brian Finch RC 1.00 .45
❑ 33 Taylor Mattingly RC 8.00 3.60
❑ 34 Daric Barton RC 5.00 2.20
❑ 35 Chris Ray RC 1.50 .70
❑ 36 Jarrod Saltalamacchia RC 2.50 1.10
❑ 37 Dennis Dove RC 1.00 .45
❑ 38 James Houser RC 1.50 .70
❑ 39 Clint King RC 2.50 1.10
❑ 40 Lou Palmisano RC 6.00 2.70
❑ 41 Dan Moore RC 1.00 .45
❑ 42 Craig Stansberry RC 2.50 1.10
❑ 43 Jo Jo Reyes RC 2.50 1.10

❑ 44 Jake Stevens RC 1.50 .70
❑ 45 Tom Gorzelanny RC 1.00 .45
❑ 46 Brian Marshall RC 1.00 .45
❑ 47 Scott Beerer RC 1.00 .45
❑ 48 Javi Herrera RC 1.50 .70
❑ 49 Steve LeRud RC 2.50 1.10
❑ 50 Josh Banks RC 3.00 1.35
❑ 51 Jon Papelbon RC 1.00 .45
❑ 52 Juan Valdes RC 1.50 .70
❑ 53 Beau Vaughan RC 1.50 .70
❑ 54 Matt Chico RC 1.50 .70
❑ 55 Todd Jennings RC 1.50 .70
❑ 56 Anthony Gwynn RC 5.00 2.20
❑ 57 Matt Harrison RC 1.50 .70
❑ 58 Aaron Marsden RC 1.50 .70
❑ 59 Casey Abrams RC 1.00 .45
❑ 60 Cory Stuart RC 1.00 .45
❑ 61 Mike Wagner RC 1.00 .45
❑ 62 Jordan Pratt RC 1.50 .70
❑ 63 Andre Randolph RC 1.00 .45
❑ 64 Blake Balkcom RC 2.50 1.10
❑ 65 Josh Muecke RC 1.00 .45
❑ 66 Jamie D'Antona RC 5.00 2.20
❑ 67 Cole Seifrig RC 5.00 2.20
❑ 68 Josh Anderson RC 1.50 .70
❑ 69 Matt Lorenzo RC 1.50 .70
❑ 70 Nate Spears RC 2.50 1.10
❑ 71 Chris Goodman RC 1.00 .45
❑ 72 Brian McFall RC 2.50 1.10
❑ 73 Billy Hogan RC 2.50 1.10
❑ 74 Jamie Romak RC 2.50 1.10
❑ 75 Jeff Cook RC 1.50 .70
❑ 76 Brooks McNiven RC 1.00 .45
❑ 77 Xavier Paul RC 8.00 3.60
❑ 78 Bob Zimmerman RC 1.00 .45
❑ 79 Mickey Hall RC 1.50 .70
❑ 80 Shaun Marcum RC 1.00 .45
❑ 81 Matt Nachreiner RC 1.50 .70
❑ 82 Chris Kinsey RC 1.00 .45
❑ 83 Jonathan Fulton RC 1.50 .70
❑ 84 Edgardo Baez RC 2.50 1.10
❑ 85 Robert Valido RC 8.00 3.60
❑ 86 Kenny Lewis RC 1.50 .70
❑ 87 Trent Peterson RC 1.00 .45
❑ 88 Johnny Woodard RC 1.50 .70
❑ 89 Wes Littleton RC 2.50 1.10
❑ 90 Sean Rodriguez RC 2.50 1.10
❑ 91 Kyle Pearson RC 1.00 .45
❑ 92 Josh Rainwater RC 1.50 .70
❑ 93 Travis Schlichting RC 1.50 .70
❑ 94 Tim Battle RC 1.50 .70
❑ 95 Aaron Hill RC 3.00 1.35
❑ 96 Bob McCrory RC 1.00 .45
❑ 97 Rick Guarno RC 1.50 .70
❑ 98 Brandon Yarbrough RC 1.00 .45
❑ 99 Peter Stonard RC 1.00 .45
❑ 100 Darin Downs RC 2.50 1.10
❑ 101 Matt Bruback RC 1.00 .45
❑ 102 Danny Garcia RC 1.00 .45
❑ 103 Cory Stewart RC 1.00 .45
❑ 104 Ferdin Tejeda RC 1.00 .45
❑ 105 Kade Johnson RC 1.00 .45
❑ 106 Andrew Brown RC 1.00 .45
❑ 107 Aquilino Lopez RC 1.00 .45
❑ 108 Stephen Randolph RC 1.00 .45
❑ 109 Dave Matranga RC 1.00 .45
❑ 110 Dustin McGowan RC 2.50 1.10
❑ 111 Juan Camacho RC 1.00 .45
❑ 112 Cliff Lee .40 .18
❑ 113 Jeff Duncan RC 1.50 .70
❑ 114 C.J. Wilson .40 .18
❑ 115 Brandon Roberson RC 1.00 .45
❑ 116 David Corrente RC 1.00 .45
❑ 117 Kevin Beavers RC 1.00 .45
❑ 118 Anthony Webster RC 1.50 .70
❑ 119 Oscar Villarreal RC 1.00 .45
❑ 120 Hong-Chih Kuo RC 2.50 1.10
❑ 121 Josh Barfield .60 .25
❑ 122 Denny Bautista .40 .18
❑ 123 Chris Burke RC 1.50 .70
❑ 124 Robinson Cano RC 1.50 .70
❑ 125 Jose Castillo .60 .25
❑ 126 Neal Cotts .40 .18
❑ 127 Jorge De La Rosa .40 .18
❑ 128 J.D. Durbin 1.50 .70
❑ 129 Edwin Encarnacion .40 .18
❑ 130 Gavin Floyd .60 .25
❑ 131 Alexis Gomez .40 .18
❑ 132 Edgar Gonzalez RC 1.00 .45
❑ 133 Khalil Greene 1.00 .45
❑ 134 Zack Greinke 1.50 .70
❑ 135 Franklin Gutierrez 2.50 1.10
❑ 136 Rich Harden 1.50 .70
❑ 137 J.J. Hardy RC 5.00 2.20
❑ 138 Ryan Howard RC 3.00 1.35
❑ 139 Justin Huber .60 .25
❑ 140 David Kelton .40 .18
❑ 141 Dave Krynzel .40 .18
❑ 142 Pete LaForest 1.00 .45
❑ 143 Adam LaRoche .60 .25
❑ 144 Preston Larrison RC 1.00 .45
❑ 145 John Maine RC 6.00 2.70
❑ 146 Andy Marte 3.00 1.35
❑ 147 Jeff Mathis .60 .25
❑ 148 Joe Mauer 1.50 .70
❑ 149 Clint Nageotte .60 .25
❑ 150 Chris Narveson .40 .18
❑ 151 Ramon Nivar 1.50 .70
❑ 152 Felix Pie 5.00 2.20
❑ 153 Guillermo Quiroz RC 3.00 1.35
❑ 154 Rene Reyes .40 .18
❑ 155 Royce Ring .40 .18
❑ 156 Alexis Rios 5.00 2.20
❑ 157 Grady Sizemore .60 .25
❑ 158 Stephen Smitherman .40 .18
❑ 159 Seung Song .40 .18
❑ 160 Scott Thorman .40 .18
❑ 161 Chad Tracy .60 .25
❑ 162 Chin-Hui Tsao .60 .25
❑ 163 John VanBenschoten .60 .25
❑ 164 Kevin Youkilis 2.50 1.10
❑ 165 Chien-Ming Wang 2.50 1.10
❑ 166 Chris Lubanski AU RC 25.00 11.00
❑ 167 Ryan Harvey AU RC 50.00 22.00
❑ 168 Matt Murton AU RC 20.00 9.00
❑ 169 Jay Sborz AU RC 20.00 9.00
❑ 170 Brandon Wood AU RC 25.00 11.00
❑ 171 Nick Markakis AU RC 25.00 11.00
❑ 172 Rickie Weeks AU RC 60.00 27.00
❑ 173 Eric Duncan AU RC 30.00 13.50
❑ 174 Chad Billingsley AU RC 20.00 9.00
❑ 175 Ryan Wagner AU RC 25.00 11.00
❑ 176 Delmon Young AU RC 70.00 32.00

2001 Bowman Heritage

	Nm-Mt	Ex-Mt
COMPLETE SET (440)	250.00	75.00
COMP.SET w/o SP's (330)	50.00	15.00
COMMON CARD (1-330)	.40	.12
COMMON RC (1-330)	.50	.15
COMMON (331-440)	2.00	.60

❑ 1 Chipper Jones 1.00 .30
❑ 2 Pete Harnisch .40 .12
❑ 3 Brian Giles .75 .23
❑ 4 J.T. Snow .75 .23
❑ 5 Bartolo Colon .75 .23
❑ 6 Jorge Posada .60 .18
❑ 7 Shawn Green .75 .23
❑ 8 Derek Jeter 2.50 .75
❑ 9 Benito Santiago .75 .23
❑ 10 Ramon Hernandez .40 .12
❑ 11 Bernie Williams .60 .18
❑ 12 Greg Maddux 2.00 .60
❑ 13 Barry Bonds 2.50 .75
❑ 14 Roger Clemens 2.00 .60
❑ 15 Miguel Tejada .75 .23
❑ 16 Pedro Feliz .40 .12
❑ 17 Jim Edmonds .75 .23
❑ 18 Tom Glavine 1.00 .30
❑ 19 David Justice .75 .23
❑ 20 Rich Aurilia .75 .23
❑ 21 Jason Giambi 1.00 .30
❑ 22 Orlando Hernandez .75 .23
❑ 23 Shawn Estes .40 .12
❑ 24 Nelson Figueroa .40 .12
❑ 25 Terrence Long .75 .23
❑ 26 Mike Mussina 1.00 .30
❑ 27 Eric Davis .75 .23
❑ 28 Jimmy Rollins .75 .23
❑ 29 Andy Pettitte .60 .18
❑ 30 Shawon Dunston .40 .12
❑ 31 Tim Hudson .75 .23
❑ 32 Jeff Kent .75 .23
❑ 33 Scott Brosius .75 .23
❑ 34 Livan Hernandez .40 .12
❑ 35 Alfonso Soriano 1.00 .30
❑ 36 Mark McGwire 2.50 .75
❑ 37 Russ Ortiz .75 .23
❑ 38 Fernando Vina .75 .23
❑ 39 Ken Griffey Jr. 1.50 .45
❑ 40 Edgar Renteria .75 .23
❑ 41 Kevin Brown .75 .23
❑ 42 Robb Nen .75 .23
❑ 43 Paul LoDuca .75 .23
❑ 44 Bobby Abreu .75 .23
❑ 45 Adam Dunn .60 .18
❑ 46 Osvaldo Fernandez .40 .12
❑ 47 Marvin Benard .40 .12
❑ 48 Mark Gardner .40 .12
❑ 49 Alex Rodriguez 2.00 .60
❑ 50 Preston Wilson .75 .23
❑ 51 Roberto Alomar 1.00 .30
❑ 52 Ben Davis .40 .12
❑ 53 Derek Bell .40 .12
❑ 54 Ken Caminiti .75 .23
❑ 55 Barry Zito 1.00 .30
❑ 56 Scott Rolen .60 .18
❑ 57 Geoff Jenkins .75 .23
❑ 58 Mike Cameron .75 .23
❑ 59 Ben Grieve .40 .12
❑ 60 Chuck Knoblauch .75 .23
❑ 61 Matt Lawton .40 .12
❑ 62 Chan Ho Park .75 .23
❑ 63 Lance Berkman .75 .23
❑ 64 Carlos Beltran .75 .23
❑ 65 Dean Palmer .75 .23
❑ 66 Alex Gonzalez .40 .12
❑ 67 Larry Walker .60 .18
❑ 68 Magglio Ordonez .75 .23
❑ 69 Ellis Burks .75 .23
❑ 70 Mark Mulder .75 .23
❑ 71 Randy Johnson 1.00 .30
❑ 72 John Smoltz .60 .18
❑ 73 Jerry Hairston Jr. .40 .12
❑ 74 Pedro Martinez 1.00 .30
❑ 75 Fred McGriff .60 .18
❑ 76 Sean Casey .75 .23
❑ 77 C.C. Sabathia .75 .23
❑ 78 Todd Helton .60 .18
❑ 79 Brad Penny .40 .12
❑ 80 Mike Sweeney .75 .23
❑ 81 Billy Wagner .75 .23
❑ 82 Mark Buehrle .75 .23
❑ 83 Cristian Guzman .75 .23
❑ 84 Jose Vidro .75 .23
❑ 85 Pat Burrell .75 .23
❑ 86 Jermaine Dye .75 .23
❑ 87 Brandon Inge .40 .12
❑ 88 David Wells .75 .23
❑ 89 Mike Piazza 1.50 .45
❑ 90 Jose Cabrera .40 .12
❑ 91 Cliff Floyd .75 .23
❑ 92 Matt Morris .75 .23
❑ 93 Raul Mondesi .75 .23
❑ 94 Joe Kennedy RC .50 .15
❑ 95 Jack Wilson RC .50 .15
❑ 96 Andruw Jones .60 .18
❑ 97 Mariano Rivera .60 .18

❑ 98 Mike Hampton .75 .23
❑ 99 Roger Cedeno .40 .12
❑ 100 Jose Cruz .75 .23
❑ 101 Mike Lowell .75 .23
❑ 102 Pedro Astacio .40 .12
❑ 103 Joe Mays .40 .12
❑ 104 John Franco .75 .23
❑ 105 Tim Redding .40 .12
❑ 106 Sandy Alomar Jr. .40 .12
❑ 107 Bret Boone .75 .23
❑ 108 Josh Towers RC .50 .15
❑ 109 Matt Stairs .40 .12
❑ 110 Chris Truby .40 .12
❑ 111 Jeff Suppan .40 .12
❑ 112 J.C. Romero .40 .12
❑ 113 Felipe Lopez .40 .12
❑ 114 Ben Sheets .75 .23
❑ 115 Frank Thomas 1.00 .30
❑ 116 A.J. Burnett .40 .12
❑ 117 Tony Clark .40 .12
❑ 118 Mac Suzuki .40 .12
❑ 119 Brad Radke .75 .23
❑ 120 Jeff Shaw .40 .12
❑ 121 Nick Neugebauer .40 .12
❑ 122 Kenny Lofton .75 .23
❑ 123 Jacque Jones .75 .23
❑ 124 Brent Mayne .40 .12
❑ 125 Carlos Hernandez .40 .12
❑ 126 Shane Spencer .40 .12
❑ 127 John Lackey .40 .12
❑ 128 Sterling Hitchcock .40 .12
❑ 129 Darren Dreifort .40 .12
❑ 130 Rusty Greer .75 .23
❑ 131 Michael Cuddyer .75 .23
❑ 132 Tyler Houston .40 .12
❑ 133 Chin-Feng Chen .75 .23
❑ 134 Ken Harvey .40 .12
❑ 135 Marquis Grissom .40 .12
❑ 136 Russell Branyan .40 .12
❑ 137 Eric Karros .75 .23
❑ 138 Josh Beckett .60 .18
❑ 139 Todd Zeile .75 .23
❑ 140 Corey Koskie .75 .23
❑ 141 Steve Sparks .40 .12
❑ 142 Bobby Seay .40 .12
❑ 143 Tim Raines Jr. .40 .12
❑ 144 Julio Zuleta .40 .12
❑ 145 Jose Lima .40 .12
❑ 146 Dante Bichette .75 .23
❑ 147 Randy Keisler .40 .12
❑ 148 Brent Butler .40 .12
❑ 149 Antonio Alfonseca .40 .12
❑ 150 Bryan Rekar .40 .12
❑ 151 Jeffrey Hammonds .40 .12
❑ 152 Larry Bigbie .40 .12
❑ 153 Blake Stein .40 .12
❑ 154 Robin Ventura .75 .23
❑ 155 Rondell White .75 .23
❑ 156 Juan Silvestre .40 .12
❑ 157 Marcus Thames .40 .12
❑ 158 Sidney Ponson .40 .12
❑ 159 Juan A. Pena RC .50 .15
❑ 160 C.J. Nitkowski .40 .12
❑ 161 Adam Everett .40 .12
❑ 162 Eric Munson .40 .12
❑ 163 Jason Isringhausen .75 .23
❑ 164 Brad Fullmer .75 .23
❑ 165 Miguel Olivo .40 .12
❑ 166 Fernando Tatis .40 .12
❑ 167 Freddy Garcia .75 .23
❑ 168 Tom Goodwin .40 .12
❑ 169 Armando Benitez .75 .23
❑ 170 Paul Konerko .75 .23
❑ 171 Jeff Cirillo .75 .23
❑ 172 Shane Reynolds .40 .12
❑ 173 Kevin Tapani .40 .12
❑ 174 Joe Crede .40 .12
❑ 175 Omar Infante RC 1.50 .45
❑ 176 Jake Peavy RC 2.00 .60
❑ 177 Corey Patterson .75 .23
❑ 178 Mike Penney RC .50 .15
❑ 179 Jeromy Burnitz .75 .23
❑ 180 David Segui .40 .12
❑ 181 Marcus Giles .75 .23
❑ 182 Paul O'Neill .60 .18
❑ 183 John Olerud .75 .23
❑ 184 Andy Benes .40 .12
❑ 185 Brad Cresse .40 .12
❑ 186 Ricky Ledee .40 .12
❑ 187 Allen Levrault UER .40 .12
Last name misspelled Leverault
❑ 188 Royce Clayton .40 .12
❑ 189 Kelly Johnson RC .50 .15
❑ 190 Quilvio Veras .40 .12
❑ 191 Mike Williams .40 .12
❑ 192 Jason Lane RC .75 .23
❑ 193 Rick Helling .40 .12
❑ 194 Tim Wakefield .75 .23
❑ 195 James Baldwin .40 .12
❑ 196 Cody Ransom RC .50 .15
❑ 197 Bobby Kielty .40 .12
❑ 198 Bobby Jones .40 .12
❑ 199 Steve Cox .40 .12
❑ 200 Jamal Strong RC .50 .15
❑ 201 Steve Lomasney .40 .12
❑ 202 Brian Cardwell RC .50 .15
❑ 203 Mike Matheny .40 .12
❑ 204 Jeff Randazzo RC .50 .15
❑ 205 Aubrey Huff .75 .23
❑ 206 Chuck Finley .75 .23
❑ 207 Denny Bautista RC 2.00 .60
❑ 208 Terry Mulholland .40 .12
❑ 209 Rey Ordonez .40 .12
❑ 210 Keith Surkont RC .50 .15
❑ 211 Orlando Cabrera .40 .12
❑ 212 Juan Encarnacion .40 .12
❑ 213 Dustin Hermanson .40 .12
❑ 214 Luis Rivas .40 .12
❑ 215 Mark Quinn .40 .12
❑ 216 Randy Velarde .40 .12
❑ 217 Billy Koch .40 .12
❑ 218 Ryan Rupe .40 .12
❑ 219 Keith Ginter .40 .12
❑ 220 Woody Williams .40 .12
❑ 221 Ryan Franklin .40 .12
❑ 222 Aaron Myette .40 .12
❑ 223 Joe Borchard RC 2.00 .60
❑ 224 Nate Cornejo .40 .12
❑ 225 Julian Tavarez .40 .12
❑ 226 Kevin Millwood .75 .23
❑ 227 Travis Hafner RC 1.25 .35
❑ 228 Charles Nagy .40 .12
❑ 229 Mike Lieberthal .75 .23
❑ 230 Jeff Nelson .40 .12
❑ 231 Ryan Dempster .40 .12
❑ 232 Andres Galarraga .75 .23
❑ 233 Chad Durbin .40 .12
❑ 234 Timo Perez .40 .12
❑ 235 Troy O'Leary .40 .12
❑ 236 Kevin Young .40 .12
❑ 237 Gabe Kapler .40 .12
❑ 238 Juan Cruz RC .50 .15
❑ 239 Masato Yoshii .40 .12
❑ 240 Aramis Ramirez .75 .23
❑ 241 Matt Cooper RC .50 .15
❑ 242 Randy Flores RC .50 .15
❑ 243 Rafael Furcal .75 .23
❑ 244 David Eckstein .40 .12
❑ 245 Matt Clement .40 .12
❑ 246 Craig Biggio .60 .18
❑ 247 Rick Reed .40 .12
❑ 248 Jose Macias .40 .12
❑ 249 Alex Escobar .40 .12
❑ 250 Roberto Hernandez .40 .12
❑ 251 Andy Ashby .40 .12
❑ 252 Tony Armas Jr. .40 .12
❑ 253 Jamie Moyer .75 .23
❑ 254 Jason Tyner .40 .12
❑ 255 Charles Kegley RC .50 .15
❑ 256 Jeff Conine .75 .23
❑ 257 Francisco Cordova .40 .12
❑ 258 Ted Lilly .40 .12
❑ 259 Joe Randa .40 .12
❑ 260 Jeff D'Amico .40 .12
❑ 261 Albie Lopez .40 .12
❑ 262 Kevin Appier .75 .23
❑ 263 Richard Hidalgo .75 .23
❑ 264 Omar Daal .40 .12
❑ 265 Ricky Gutierrez .40 .12
❑ 266 John Rocker .40 .12
❑ 267 Ray Lankford .40 .12
❑ 268 Beau Hale RC .50 .15
❑ 269 Tony Blanco RC .50 .15
❑ 270 Derrek Lee UER .75 .23
First name misspelled Derrick
❑ 271 Jamey Wright .40 .12
❑ 272 Alex Gordon .40 .12
❑ 273 Jeff Weaver .40 .12
❑ 274 Jaret Wright .40 .12
❑ 275 Jose Hernandez .40 .12
❑ 276 Bruce Chen .40 .12
❑ 277 Todd Hollandsworth .40 .12
❑ 278 Wade Miller .75 .23
❑ 279 Luke Prokopec .40 .12
❑ 280 Rafael Soriano RC 1.50 .45
❑ 281 Damion Easley .40 .12
❑ 282 Darren Oliver .40 .12
❑ 283 B. Duckworth RC .50 .15
❑ 284 Aaron Herr .40 .12
❑ 285 Ray Durham .75 .23
❑ 286 Wilmy Caceras RC .50 .15
❑ 287 Ugueth Urbina .40 .12
❑ 288 Scott Seabol .40 .12
❑ 289 Lance Niekro RC .50 .15
❑ 290 Trot Nixon .75 .23
❑ 291 Adam Kennedy .40 .12
❑ 292 Brian Schmitt RC .50 .15
❑ 293 Grant Roberts .40 .12
❑ 294 Benny Agbayani .40 .12
❑ 295 Travis Lee .40 .12
❑ 296 Erick Almonte RC .50 .15
❑ 297 Jim Thome 1.00 .30
❑ 298 Eric Young .40 .12
❑ 299 Dan Denham RC .50 .15
❑ 300 Boof Bonser RC .75 .23
❑ 301 Denny Neagle .40 .12
❑ 302 Kenny Rogers .75 .23
❑ 303 J.D. Closser .40 .12
❑ 304 Chase Utley RC 2.50 .75
❑ 305 Rey Sanchez .40 .12
❑ 306 Sean McGowan .40 .12
❑ 307 Justin Pope RC .50 .15
❑ 308 Torii Hunter .75 .23
❑ 309 B.J. Surhoff .75 .23
❑ 310 Aaron Heilman RC 1.25 .35
❑ 311 Gabe Gross RC .75 .23
❑ 312 Lee Stevens .40 .12
❑ 313 Todd Hundley .40 .12
❑ 314 Macay McBride RC .50 .15
❑ 315 Edgar Martinez .60 .18
❑ 316 Omar Vizquel .75 .23
❑ 317 Reggie Sanders .75 .23
❑ 318 John-Ford Griffin RC .75 .23
❑ 319 Tim Salmon UER .60 .18
Photo is Troy Glaus
❑ 320 Pokey Reese .40 .12
❑ 321 Jay Payton .40 .12
❑ 322 Doug Glanville .40 .12
❑ 323 Greg Vaughn .75 .23
❑ 324 Ruben Sierra .40 .12
❑ 325 Kip Wells .40 .12
❑ 326 Carl Everett .75 .23
❑ 327 Garret Anderson .75 .23
❑ 328 Jay Bell .75 .23
❑ 329 Barry Larkin 1.00 .30
❑ 330 Jeff Mathis RC 2.50 .75
❑ 331 Adrian Gonzalez SP 2.00 .60
❑ 332 Juan Rivera SP 2.00 .60
❑ 333 Tony Alvarez SP 2.00 .60
❑ 334 Xavier Nady SP 2.00 .60
❑ 335 Josh Hamilton SP 2.00 .60
❑ 336 Will Smith SP RC 2.00 .60
❑ 337 Israel Alcantara SP 2.00 .60
❑ 338 Chris George SP 2.00 .60
❑ 339 Sean Burroughs SP 2.00 .60
❑ 340 Jack Cust SP 2.00 .60
❑ 341 Henry Mateo SP RC 2.00 .60
❑ 342 Carlos Pena SP 2.00 .60
❑ 343 J.R. House SP 2.00 .60
❑ 344 Carlos Silva SP 2.00 .60
❑ 345 Mike Rivera SP RC 2.00 .60
❑ 346 Adam Johnson SP 2.00 .60
❑ 347 Scott Heard SP 2.00 .60
❑ 348 Alex Cintron SP 2.00 .60
❑ 349 Miguel Cabrera SP 10.00 3.00
❑ 350 Nick Johnson SP 2.00 .60
❑ 351 Albert Pujols SP RC 40.00 12.00
❑ 352 Ichiro Suzuki SP RC 25.00 7.50

Card	Nm-Mt	Ex-Mt
❑ 353 Carlos Delgado SP	2.00	.60
❑ 354 Troy Glaus SP	3.00	.90
❑ 355 Sammy Sosa SP	5.00	1.50
❑ 356 Ivan Rodriguez SP	3.00	.90
❑ 357 Vladimir Guerrero SP	3.00	.90
❑ 358 Manny Ramirez SP	2.00	.60
❑ 359 Luis Gonzalez SP	2.00	.60
❑ 360 Roy Oswalt SP	3.00	.90
❑ 361 Moises Alou SP	2.00	.60
❑ 362 Juan Gonzalez SP	3.00	.90
❑ 363 Tony Gwynn SP	4.00	1.20
❑ 364 Hideo Nomo SP	3.00	.90
❑ 365 T. Shinjo SP RC	4.00	1.20
❑ 366 Kazuhiro Sasaki SP	2.00	.60
❑ 367 Cal Ripken SP	10.00	3.00
❑ 368 Rafael Palmeiro SP	3.00	.90
❑ 369 J.D. Drew SP	2.00	.60
❑ 370 Doug Mientkiewicz SP	2.00	.60
❑ 371 Jeff Bagwell SP	3.00	.90
❑ 372 Darin Erstad SP	2.00	.60
❑ 373 Tom Gordon SP	2.00	.60
❑ 374 Ben Petrick SP	2.00	.60
❑ 375 Eric Milton SP	2.00	.60
❑ 376 N. Garciaparra SP	6.00	1.80
❑ 377 Julio Lugo SP	2.00	.60
❑ 378 Tino Martinez SP	3.00	.90
❑ 379 Javier Vazquez SP	2.00	.60
❑ 380 Jeremy Giambi SP	2.00	.60
❑ 381 Marty Cordova SP	2.00	.60
❑ 382 Adrian Beltre SP	2.00	.60
❑ 383 John Burkett SP	2.00	.60
❑ 384 Aaron Boone SP	2.00	.60
❑ 385 Eric Chavez SP	2.00	.60
❑ 386 Curt Schilling SP	3.00	.90
❑ 387 Cory Lidle UER	2.00	.60
First name misspelled Corey		
❑ 388 Jason Schmidt SP	2.00	.60
❑ 389 Johnny Damon SP	2.00	.60
❑ 390 Steve Finley SP	2.00	.60
❑ 391 Edgardo Alfonzo SP	2.00	.60
❑ 392 Jose Valentin SP	2.00	.60
❑ 393 Jose Canseco SP	3.00	.90
❑ 394 Ryan Klesko SP	2.00	.60
❑ 395 David Cone SP	2.00	.60
❑ 396 Jason Kendall UER	2.00	.60
Last name misspelled Kendell		
❑ 397 Placido Polanco SP	2.00	.60
❑ 398 Glendon Rusch SP	2.00	.60
❑ 399 Aaron Sele SP	2.00	.60
❑ 400 D'Angelo Jimenez SP	2.00	.60
❑ 401 Mark Grace SP	3.00	.90
❑ 402 Al Leiter SP	2.00	.60
❑ 403 Brian Jordan SP	2.00	.60
❑ 404 Phil Nevin SP	2.00	.60
❑ 405 Brent Abernathy SP	2.00	.60
❑ 406 Kerry Wood SP	3.00	.90
❑ 407 Alex Gonzalez SP	2.00	.60
❑ 408 Robert Fick SP	2.00	.60
❑ 409 Dmitri Young UER	2.00	.60
First name misspelled Dimitri		
❑ 410 Wes Helms SP	2.00	.60
❑ 411 Trevor Hoffman SP	2.00	.60
❑ 412 Rickey Henderson SP	5.00	1.50
❑ 413 Bobby Higginson SP	2.00	.60
❑ 414 Gary Sheffield SP	2.00	.60
❑ 415 Darryl Kile SP	2.00	.60
❑ 416 Richie Sexson SP	2.00	.60
❑ 417 F. Menechino SP RC	2.00	.60
❑ 418 Javy Lopez SP	2.00	.60
❑ 419 Carlos Lee SP	2.00	.60
❑ 420 Jon Lieber SP	2.00	.60
❑ 421 Hank Blalock SP RC	15.00	4.50
❑ 422 Marlon Byrd SP RC	8.00	2.40
❑ 423 Jason Kinchen SP RC	2.00	.60
❑ 424 M. Ensberg SP RC	4.00	1.20
❑ 425 Greg Nash SP RC	2.00	.60
❑ 426 D. Tankersley SP RC	2.00	.60
❑ 427 Nate Murphy SP RC	2.00	.60
❑ 428 Chris Smith SP RC	2.00	.60
❑ 429 Jake Gautreau SP RC	2.00	.60
❑ 430 J. VanBenschoten SP RC	5.00	1.50
❑ 431 T.Thompson SP RC	2.00	.60
❑ 432 O.Hudson SP RC	2.00	.60
❑ 433 J.Williams SP RC	10.00	3.00
❑ 434 Kevin Reese SP RC	2.00	.60
❑ 435 Ed Rogers SP RC	2.00	.60
❑ 436 Ryan Jamison SP RC	2.00	.60
❑ 437 A. Pettyjohn SP RC	2.00	.60
❑ 438 Hee Seop Choi SP RC	10.00	3.00
❑ 439 J. Morneau SP RC	10.00	3.00
❑ 440 Mitch Jones SP RC	2.00	.60

2002 Bowman Heritage

	Nm-Mt	Ex-Mt
COMP.SET w/o SP's (324)	50.00	15.00
COMMON CARD (1-439)	.40	.12
COMMON SP	2.00	.60

Card	Nm-Mt	Ex-Mt
❑ 1 Brent Abernathy	.40	.12
❑ 2 Jermaine Dye	.40	.12
❑ 3 James Shanks RC	.50	.15
❑ 4 Chris Flinn RC	.50	.15
❑ 5 Mike Peeples SP RC	2.00	.60
❑ 6 Gary Sheffield	.40	.12
❑ 7 Livan Hernandez SP	2.00	.60
❑ 8 Jeff Austin RC	.50	.15
❑ 9 Jeremy Giambi	.40	.12
❑ 10 Adam Roller RC	.50	.15
❑ 11 Sandy Alomar Jr. SP	2.00	.60
❑ 12 Matt Williams SP	2.00	.60
❑ 13 Hee Seop Choi	.60	.18
❑ 14 Jose Offerman	.40	.12
❑ 15 Robin Ventura	.40	.12
❑ 16 Craig Biggio	.60	.18
❑ 17 David Wells	.40	.12
❑ 18 Rob Henkel RC	.50	.15
❑ 19 Edgar Martinez	.60	.18
❑ 20 Matt Morris SP	2.00	.60
❑ 21 Jose Valentin	.40	.12
❑ 22 Barry Bonds	2.50	.75
❑ 23 Justin Schuda RC	.50	.15
❑ 24 Josh Phelps	.40	.12
❑ 25 John Rodriguez RC	.50	.15
❑ 26 Angel Pagan RC	.50	.15
❑ 27 Aramis Ramirez	.40	.12
❑ 28 Jack Wilson	.40	.12
❑ 29 Roger Clemens	2.00	.60
❑ 30 Kazuhisa Ishii RC	2.00	.60
❑ 31 Carlos Beltran	.40	.12
❑ 32 Drew Henson SP	2.00	.60
❑ 33 Kevin Young SP	2.00	.60
❑ 34 Juan Cruz SP	2.00	.60
❑ 35 Curtis Legendre RC	.50	.15
❑ 36 Jose Morban RC	.75	.23
❑ 37 Ricardo Cordova SP RC	2.00	.60
❑ 38 Adam Everett	.40	.12
❑ 39 Mark Prior	4.00	1.20
❑ 40 Jose Bautista RC	1.25	.35
❑ 41 Travis Foley RC	.75	.23
❑ 42 Kerry Wood	1.00	.30
❑ 43 B.J. Surhoff	.40	.12
❑ 44 Moises Alou	.40	.12
❑ 45 Joey Hammond	.40	.12
❑ 46 Eric Bruntlett RC	.50	.15
❑ 47 Carlos Guillen	.40	.12
❑ 48 Joe Crede	.40	.12
❑ 49 Dan Phillips RC	.50	.15
❑ 50 Jason LaRue	.40	.12
❑ 51 Javy Lopez	.40	.12
❑ 52 Larry Bigbie SP	2.00	.60
❑ 53 Chris Baker RC	.50	.15
❑ 54 Marty Cordova	.40	.12
❑ 55 C.C. Sabathia	.40	.12
❑ 56 Mike Piazza	1.50	.45
❑ 57 Brian Giles	.40	.12
❑ 58 Mike Bordick SP	2.00	.60
❑ 59 Tyler Houston SP	2.00	.60
❑ 60 Gabe Kapler	.40	.12
❑ 61 Ben Broussard	.40	.12
❑ 62 Steve Finley SP	2.00	.60
❑ 63 Koyie Hill	.40	.12
❑ 64 Jeff D'Amico	.40	.12
❑ 65 Edwin Almonte RC	.50	.15
❑ 66 Pedro Martinez	1.00	.30
❑ 66B Nomar Garciaparra 66	2.00	.60
❑ 67 Travis Fryman SP	2.00	.60
❑ 68 Brady Clark SP	2.00	.60
❑ 69 Reed Johnson SP RC	3.00	.90
❑ 70 Mark Grace SP	5.00	1.50
❑ 71 Tony Batista SP	2.00	.60
❑ 72 Roy Oswalt	.40	.12
❑ 73 Pat Burrell SP	2.00	.60
❑ 74 Dennis Tankersley	.40	.12
❑ 75 Ramon Ortiz	.40	.12
❑ 76 Neal Frendling SP RC	2.00	.60
❑ 77 Omar Vizquel SP	2.00	.60
❑ 78 Hideo Nomo	1.00	.30
❑ 79 Orlando Hernandez SP	2.00	.60
❑ 80 Andy Pettitte	.60	.18
❑ 81 Cole Barthel RC	.50	.15
❑ 82 Bret Boone	.40	.12
❑ 83 Alfonso Soriano	1.00	.30
❑ 84 Brandon Duckworth	.40	.12
❑ 85 Ben Grieve	.40	.12
❑ 86 Mike Rosamond SP RC	2.00	.60
❑ 87 Luke Prokopec	.40	.12
❑ 88 Chone Figgins RC	.50	.15
❑ 89 Rick Ankiel SP	2.00	.60
❑ 90 David Eckstein	.40	.12
❑ 91 Corey Koskie	.40	.12
❑ 92 David Justice	.40	.12
❑ 93 Jimmy Alvarez RC	.50	.15
❑ 94 Jason Schmidt	.40	.12
❑ 95 Reggie Sanders	.40	.12
❑ 96 Victor Alvarez RC	.50	.15
❑ 97 Brett Roneberg RC	.50	.15
❑ 98 D'Angelo Jimenez	.40	.12
❑ 99 Hank Blalock	1.00	.30
❑ 100 Juan Rivera	.40	.12
❑ 101 Mark Buehrle SP	2.00	.60
❑ 102 Juan Uribe	.40	.12
❑ 103 Royce Clayton SP	2.00	.60
❑ 104 Brett Kay RC	.50	.15
❑ 105 John Olerud	.40	.12
❑ 106 Richie Sexson	.40	.12
❑ 107 Chipper Jones	1.00	.30
❑ 108 Adam Dunn	.60	.18
❑ 109 Tim Salmon SP	3.00	.90
❑ 110 Eric Karros	.40	.12
❑ 111 Jose Vidro	.40	.12
❑ 112 Jerry Hairston Jr.	.40	.12
❑ 113 Anastacio Martinez RC	.50	.15
❑ 114 Robert Fick SP	2.00	.60
❑ 115 Randy Johnson	1.00	.30
❑ 116 Trot Nixon SP	2.00	.60
❑ 117 Nick Bierbrodt SP	2.00	.60
❑ 118 Jim Edmonds	.40	.12
❑ 119 Rafael Palmeiro	.60	.18
❑ 120 Jose Macias	.40	.12
❑ 121 Josh Beckett	.60	.18
❑ 122 Sean Douglass	.40	.12
❑ 123 Jeff Kent	.40	.12
❑ 124 Tim Redding	.40	.12
❑ 125 Xavier Nady	.40	.12
❑ 126 Carl Everett	.40	.12
❑ 127 Joe Randa	.40	.12
❑ 128 Luke Hudson SP	2.00	.60
❑ 129 Eric Miller RC	.50	.15
❑ 130 Melvin Mora	.40	.12
❑ 131 Adrian Gonzalez	.40	.12
❑ 132 Larry Walker SP	3.00	.90
❑ 133 Nic Jackson SP RC	3.00	.90
❑ 134 Mike Lowell SP	2.00	.60
❑ 135 Jim Thome	1.00	.30
❑ 136 Eric Milton	.40	.12
❑ 137 Rich Thompson SP RC	2.00	.60
❑ 138 Placido Polanco SP	2.00	.60
❑ 139 Juan Pierre	.40	.12
❑ 140 David Segui	.40	.12

❑ 141 Chuck Finley .40 .12
❑ 142 Felipe Lopez .40 .12
❑ 143 Toby Hall .40 .12
❑ 144 Fred Bastardo RC .50 .15
❑ 145 Troy Glaus .60 .18
❑ 146 Todd Helton .60 .18
❑ 147 Ruben Gotay SP RC 3.00 .90
❑ 148 Darin Erstad .40 .12
❑ 149 Ryan Gripp SP RC 2.00 .60
❑ 150 Orlando Cabrera .40 .12
❑ 151 Jason Young RC .75 .23
❑ 152 Sterling Hitchcock SP 2.00 .60
❑ 153 Miguel Tejada .40 .12
❑ 154 Al Leiter .40 .12
❑ 155 Taylor Buchholz RC .50 .15
❑ 156 Juan M. Gonzalez RC .50 .15
❑ 157 Damion Easley .40 .12
❑ 158 Jimmy Gobble RC 2.50 .75
❑ 159 Dennis Ulacia SP RC 2.00 .60
❑ 160 Shane Reynolds SP 2.00 .60
❑ 161 Javier Colina .40 .12
❑ 162 Frank Thomas 1.00 .30
❑ 163 Chuck Knoblauch .40 .12
❑ 164 Sean Burroughs .40 .12
❑ 165 Greg Maddux 2.00 .60
❑ 166 Jason Ellison RC .50 .15
❑ 167 Tony Womack .40 .12
❑ 168 Randall Shelley SP RC 3.00 .90
❑ 169 Jason Marquis .40 .12
❑ 170 Brian Jordan .40 .12
❑ 171 Vicente Padilla .40 .12
❑ 172 Barry Zito 1.00 .30
❑ 173 Matt Allegra SP RC 3.00 .90
❑ 174 Ralph Santana SP RC 2.00 .60
❑ 175 Carlos Lee .40 .12
❑ 176 Richard Hidalgo SP 2.00 .60
❑ 177 Kevin Deaton RC .50 .15
❑ 178 Juan Encarnacion .40 .12
❑ 179 Mark Quinn .40 .12
❑ 180 Rafael Furcal .40 .12
❑ 181 Garret Anderson .40 .12
❑ 182 David Wright RC 2.50 .75
❑ 183 Jose Reyes 1.00 .30
❑ 184 Mario Ramos SP RC 3.00 .90
❑ 185 J.D. Drew .40 .12
❑ 186 Juan Gonzalez 1.00 .30
❑ 187 Nick Neugebauer .40 .12
❑ 188 Alejandro Giron RC .50 .15
❑ 189 John Burkett .40 .12
❑ 190 Ben Sheets .40 .12
❑ 191 Vinny Castilla SP 2.00 .60
❑ 192 Cory Lidle .40 .12
❑ 193 Fernando Vina .40 .12
❑ 194 Russell Branyan SP 2.00 .60
❑ 195 Ben Davis .40 .12
❑ 196 Angel Berroa .40 .12
❑ 197 Alex Gonzalez .40 .12
❑ 198 Jared Sandberg .40 .12
❑ 199 Travis Lee SP 2.00 .60
❑ 200 Luis DePaula SP 2.00 .60
❑ 201 Ramon Hernandez SP 2.00 .60
❑ 202 Brandon Inge .40 .12
❑ 203 Aubrey Huff .40 .12
❑ 204 Mike Rivera .40 .12
❑ 205 Brad Nelson RC 2.00 .60
❑ 206 Colt Griffin SP RC 6.00 1.80
❑ 207 Joel Pineiro .40 .12
❑ 208 Adam Pettyjohn .40 .12
❑ 209 Mark Redman .40 .12
❑ 210 Roberto Alomar SP 5.00 1.50
❑ 211 Denny Neagle .40 .12
❑ 212 Adam Kennedy .40 .12
❑ 213 Jason Arnold SP RC 6.00 1.80
❑ 214 Jamie Moyer .40 .12
❑ 215 Aaron Boone .40 .12
❑ 216 Doug Glanville .40 .12
❑ 217 Nick Johnson SP 2.00 .60
❑ 218 Mike Cameron SP 2.00 .60
❑ 219 Tim Wakefield SP 2.00 .60
❑ 220 Todd Stottlemyre SP 2.00 .60
❑ 221 Mo Vaughn SP 2.00 .60
❑ 222 Vladimir Guerrero 1.00 .30
❑ 223 Bill Ortega .40 .12
❑ 224 Kevin Brown .40 .12
❑ 225 Peter Bergeron SP 2.00 .60
❑ 226 Shannon Stewart SP 2.00 .60
❑ 227 Eric Chavez .40 .12
❑ 228 Clint Weibl RC .50 .15
❑ 229 Todd Hollandsworth SP 2.00 .60
❑ 230 Jeff Bagwell .60 .18
❑ 231 Chad Qualls RC .50 .15
❑ 232 Ben Howard RC .50 .15
❑ 233 Rondell White SP 2.00 .60
❑ 234 Fred McGriff .60 .18
❑ 235 Steve Cox SP 2.00 .60
❑ 236 Chris Tritle RC .50 .15
❑ 237 Eric Valent .40 .12
❑ 238 Joe Mauer RC 8.00 2.40
❑ 239 Shawn Green .40 .12
❑ 240 Jimmy Rollins .40 .12
❑ 241 Edgar Renteria .40 .12
❑ 242 Edwin Yan RC .50 .15
❑ 243 Noochie Varner RC 1.25 .35
❑ 244 Kris Benson SP 2.00 .60
❑ 245 Mike Hampton .40 .12
❑ 246 So Taguchi RC .75 .23
❑ 247 Sammy Sosa 1.50 .45
❑ 248 Terrence Long .40 .12
❑ 249 Jason Bay RC 1.50 .45
❑ 250 Kevin Millar SP 2.00 .60
❑ 251 Albert Pujols 2.00 .60
❑ 252 Chris Latham RC .50 .15
❑ 253 Eric Byrnes .40 .12
❑ 254 Napoleon Calzado SP RC 2.00 .60
❑ 255 Bobby Higginson .40 .12
❑ 256 Ben Molina .40 .12
❑ 257 Torii Hunter SP 2.00 .60
❑ 258 Jason Giambi 1.00 .30
❑ 259 Bartolo Colon .40 .12
❑ 260 Benito Baez .40 .12
❑ 261 Ichiro Suzuki 2.00 .60
❑ 262 Mike Sweeney .40 .12
❑ 263 Brian West RC .50 .15
❑ 264 Brad Penny .40 .12
❑ 265 Kevin Millwood SP 2.00 .60
❑ 266 Orlando Hudson .40 .12
❑ 267 Doug Mientkiewicz .40 .12
❑ 268 Luis Gonzalez SP 2.00 .60
❑ 269 Jay Caligiuri RC .50 .15
❑ 270 Nate Cornejo SP 2.00 .60
❑ 271 Lee Stevens .40 .12
❑ 272 Eric Hinske .40 .12
❑ 273 Antwon Rollins RC .75 .23
❑ 274 Bobby Jenks RC 2.00 .60
❑ 275 Joe Mays .40 .12
❑ 276 Josh Shaffer RC .50 .15
❑ 277 Jonny Gomes RC 1.50 .45
❑ 278 Bernie Williams .60 .18
❑ 279 Ed Rogers .40 .12
❑ 280 Carlos Delgado .40 .12
❑ 281 Raul Mondesi SP 2.00 .60
❑ 282 Jose Ortiz .40 .12
❑ 283 Cesar Izturis .40 .12
❑ 284 Ryan Dempster SP 2.00 .60
❑ 285 Brian Daubach .40 .12
❑ 286 Hansel Izquierdo RC .50 .15
❑ 287 Mike Lieberthal SP 2.00 .60
❑ 288 Marcus Thames .40 .12
❑ 289 Nomar Garciaparra 2.00 .60
❑ 290 Brad Fullmer .40 .12
❑ 291 Tino Martinez .60 .18
❑ 292 James Barrett RC .75 .23
❑ 293 Jacque Jones .40 .12
❑ 294 Nick Alvarez SP RC 2.00 .60
❑ 295 Jason Grove SP RC 2.00 .60
❑ 296 Mike Wilson SP RC 2.00 .60
❑ 297 J.T. Snow .40 .12
❑ 298 Cliff Floyd .40 .12
❑ 299 Todd Hundley SP 2.00 .60
❑ 300 Tony Clark SP 2.00 .60
❑ 301 Demetrius Heath RC .50 .15
❑ 302 Morgan Ensberg .40 .12
❑ 303 Cristian Guzman .40 .12
❑ 304 Frank Catalanotto .40 .12
❑ 305 Jeff Weaver .40 .12
❑ 306 Tim Hudson .40 .12
❑ 307 Scott Wiggins SP RC 2.00 .60
❑ 308 Shea Hillenbrand SP 2.00 .60
❑ 309 Todd Walker SP 2.00 .60
❑ 310 Tsuyoshi Shinjo .40 .12
❑ 311 Adrian Beltre .40 .12
❑ 312 Craig Kuzmic RC .50 .15
❑ 313 Paul Konerko .40 .12
❑ 314 Scott Hairston RC 2.50 .75
❑ 315 Chan Ho Park .40 .12
❑ 316 Jorge Posada .60 .18
❑ 317 Chris Snelling RC 1.50 .45
❑ 318 Keith Foulke .40 .12
❑ 319 John Smoltz .60 .18
❑ 320 Ryan Church SP RC 5.00 1.50
❑ 321 Mike Mussina 1.00 .30
❑ 322 Tony Armas Jr. SP 2.00 .60
❑ 323 Craig Counsell .40 .12
❑ 324 Marcus Giles .40 .12
❑ 325 Greg Vaughn .40 .12
❑ 326 Curt Schilling .60 .18
❑ 327 Jeromy Burnitz .40 .12
❑ 328 Eric Byrnes .40 .12
❑ 329 Johnny Damon .40 .12
❑ 330 Michael Floyd SP RC 2.00 .60
❑ 331 Edgardo Alfonzo .40 .12
❑ 332 Jeremy Hill RC .50 .15
❑ 333 Josh Bonifay RC .75 .23
❑ 334 Byung-Hyun Kim .40 .12
❑ 335 Keith Ginter .40 .12
❑ 336 Ronald Acuna SP RC 2.00 .60
❑ 337 Mike Hill SP RC 2.00 .60
❑ 338 Sean Casey .40 .12
❑ 339 Matt Anderson SP 2.00 .60
❑ 340 Dan Wright .40 .12
❑ 341 Ben Petrick .40 .12
❑ 342 Mike Sirotka SP 2.00 .60
❑ 343 Alex Rodriguez 2.00 .60
❑ 344 Einar Diaz .40 .12
❑ 345 Derek Jeter 2.50 .75
❑ 346 Jeff Conine .40 .12
❑ 347 Ray Durham SP 2.00 .60
❑ 348 Wilson Betemit SP 2.00 .60
❑ 349 Jeffrey Hammonds .40 .12
❑ 350 Dan Trumble RC .50 .15
❑ 351 Phil Nevin SP 2.00 .60
❑ 352 A.J. Burnett .40 .12
❑ 353 Bill Mueller .40 .12
❑ 354 Charles Nagy .40 .12
❑ 355 Rusty Greer SP 2.00 .60
❑ 356 Jason Botts RC .50 .15
❑ 357 Magglio Ordonez .40 .12
❑ 358 Kevin Appier .40 .12
❑ 359 Brad Radke .40 .12
❑ 360 Chris George .40 .12
❑ 361 Chris Piersoll RC .50 .15
❑ 362 Ivan Rodriguez 1.00 .30
❑ 363 Jim Kavourias RC .50 .15
❑ 364 Rick Helling SP 2.00 .60
❑ 365 Dean Palmer .40 .12
❑ 366 Rich Aurilia SP 2.00 .60
❑ 367 Ryan Vogelsong .40 .12
❑ 368 Matt Lawton .40 .12
❑ 369 Wade Miller .40 .12
❑ 370 Dustin Hermanson .40 .12
❑ 371 Craig Wilson .40 .12
❑ 372 Todd Zeile SP 2.00 .60
❑ 373 Jon Guzman RC .50 .15
❑ 374 Ellis Burks .40 .12
❑ 375 Robert Cosby SP RC 2.00 .60
❑ 376 Jason Kendall .40 .12
❑ 377 Scott Rolen SP 3.00 .90
❑ 378 Andruw Jones .60 .18
❑ 379 Greg Sain RC .50 .15
❑ 380 Paul LoDuca .40 .12
❑ 381 Scotty Layfield RC .50 .15
❑ 382 Tomo Ohka .40 .12
❑ 383 Garrett Guzman RC .50 .15
❑ 384 Jack Cust SP 2.00 .60
❑ 385 Shayne Wright RC .50 .15
❑ 386 Derrek Lee .40 .12
❑ 387 Jesus Medrano RC .50 .15
❑ 388 Javier Vazquez .40 .12
❑ 389 Preston Wilson SP 2.00 .60
❑ 390 Gavin Floyd RC 3.00 .90
❑ 391 Sidney Ponson SP 2.00 .60
❑ 392 Jose Hernandez .40 .12
❑ 393 Scott Erickson SP 2.00 .60
❑ 394 Jose Valverde RC .75 .23
❑ 395 Mark Hamilton SP RC 2.00 .60
❑ 396 Brad Cresse .40 .12
❑ 397 Danny Bautista .40 .12
❑ 398 Ray Lankford SP 2.00 .60

	Card	Nm-Mt	Ex-Mt
❑ 399	Miguel Batista SP	2.00	.60
❑ 400	Brent Butler	.40	.12
❑ 401	Manny Delcarmen SP RC	3.00	.90
❑ 402	Kyle Farnsworth SP	2.00	.60
❑ 403	Freddy Garcia	.40	.12
❑ 404	Joe Jiannetti RC	.50	.15
❑ 405	Josh Barfield RC	3.00	.90
❑ 406	Corey Patterson	.40	.12
❑ 407	Josh Towers	.40	.12
❑ 408	Carlos Pena	.40	.12
❑ 409	Jeff Cirillo	.40	.12
❑ 410	Jon Lieber	.40	.12
❑ 411	Woody Williams SP	2.00	.60
❑ 412	Richard Lane SP RC	2.00	.60
❑ 413	Alex Gonzalez	.40	.12
❑ 414	Wilkin Ruan	.40	.12
❑ 415	Geoff Jenkins	.40	.12
❑ 416	Carlos Hernandez	.40	.12
❑ 417	Matt Clement SP	2.00	.60
❑ 418	Jose Cruz Jr.	.40	.12
❑ 419	Jake Mauer RC	.50	.15
❑ 420	Matt Childers RC	.50	.15
❑ 421	Tom Glavine SP	5.00	1.50
❑ 422	Ken Griffey Jr.	1.50	.45
❑ 423	Anderson Hernandez RC	.75	.23
❑ 424	John Suomi RC	.50	.15
❑ 425	Doug Sessions RC	.50	.15
❑ 426	Jaret Wright	.40	.12
❑ 427	Rolando Viera SP RC	2.00	.60
❑ 428	Aaron Sele	.40	.12
❑ 429	Dmitri Young	.40	.12
❑ 430	Ryan Klesko	.40	.12
❑ 431	Kevin Tapani SP	2.00	.60
❑ 432	Joe Kennedy	.40	.12
❑ 433	Austin Kearns	.60	.18
❑ 434	Roger Cedeno SP	2.00	.60
❑ 435	Lance Berkman	.40	.12
❑ 436	Frank Menechino	.40	.12
❑ 437	Brett Myers	.40	.12
❑ 438	Bob Abreu	.40	.12
❑ 439	Shawn Estes SP	2.00	.60

1994 Bowman's Best

		Nm-Mt	Ex-Mt
COMPLETE SET (200)		40.00	12.00
❑ B1	Chipper Jones	1.25	.35
❑ B2	Derek Jeter	4.00	1.20
❑ B3	Bill Pulsipher	.50	.15
❑ B4	James Baldwin	.25	.07
❑ B5	Brooks Kieschnick RC	1.00	.30
❑ B6	Justin Thompson	.25	.07
❑ B7	Midre Cummings	.25	.07
❑ B8	Joey Hamilton	.25	.07
❑ B9	Pokey Reese	.25	.07
❑ B10	Brian Barber	.25	.07
❑ B11	John Burke	.25	.07
❑ B12	DeShawn Warren	.25	.07
❑ B13	Edgardo Alfonzo RC	2.50	.75
❑ B14	Eddie Pearson RC	.50	.15
❑ B15	Jimmy Haynes	.25	.07
❑ B16	Danny Bautista	.25	.07
❑ B17	Roger Cedeno	.25	.07
❑ B18	Jon Lieber	.25	.07
❑ B19	Billy Wagner RC	2.50	.75
❑ B20	Tate Seefried RC	.50	.15
❑ B21	Chad Mottola	.25	.07
❑ B22	Jose Malave	.25	.07
❑ B23	Terrell Wade RC	.50	.15
❑ B24	Shane Andrews	.25	.07
❑ B25	Chan Ho Park RC	2.50	.75
❑ B26	Kirk Presley RC	.50	.15
❑ B27	Robbie Beckett	.25	.07
❑ B28	Orlando Miller	.25	.07
❑ B29	Jorge Posada RC	8.00	2.40
❑ B30	Frankie Rodriguez	.25	.07
❑ B31	Brian L. Hunter	.25	.07
❑ B32	Billy Ashley	.25	.07
❑ B33	Rondell White	.50	.15
❑ B34	John Roper	.25	.07
❑ B35	Marc Valdes	.25	.07
❑ B36	Scott Ruffcorn	.25	.07
❑ B37	Rod Henderson	.25	.07
❑ B38	Curtis Goodwin RC	.50	.15
❑ B39	Russ Davis	.25	.07
❑ B40	Rick Gorecki	.25	.07
❑ B41	Johnny Damon	1.25	.35
❑ B42	Roberto Petagine	.25	.07
❑ B43	Chris Snopek	.25	.07
❑ B44	Mark Acre RC	.50	.15
❑ B45	Todd Hollandsworth	.25	.07
❑ B46	Shawn Green	1.25	.35
❑ B47	John Carter RC	.50	.15
❑ B48	Jim Pittsley RC	.50	.15
❑ B49	John Wasdin RC	.50	.15
❑ B50	D.J. Boston RC	.50	.15
❑ B51	Tim Clark	.25	.07
❑ B52	Alex Ochoa	.25	.07
❑ B53	Chad Roper	.25	.07
❑ B54	Mike Kelly	.25	.07
❑ B55	Brad Fullmer RC	2.50	.75
❑ B56	Carl Everett	.50	.15
❑ B57	Tim Belk RC	.50	.15
❑ B58	Jimmy Hurst RC	.50	.15
❑ B59	Mac Suzuki RC	1.00	.30
❑ B60	Mike Moore	.25	.07
❑ B61	Alan Benes RC	.50	.15
❑ B62	Tony Clark RC	1.00	.30
❑ B63	Edgar Renteria RC	6.00	1.80
❑ B64	Trey Beamon	.25	.07
❑ B65	LaTroy Hawkins RC	1.00	.30
❑ B66	Wayne Gomes RC	1.00	.30
❑ B67	Ray McDavid	.25	.07
❑ B68	John Dettmer	.25	.07
❑ B69	Willie Greene	.25	.07
❑ B70	Dave Stevens	.25	.07
❑ B71	Kevin Orie RC	.25	.07
❑ B72	Chad Ogea	.25	.07
❑ B73	Ben Van Ryn RC	.50	.15
❑ B74	Kym Ashworth RC	.50	.15
❑ B75	Dmitri Young	.50	.15
❑ B76	Herbert Perry RC	1.00	.30
❑ B77	Joey Eischen	.25	.07
❑ B78	Arquimedez Pozo RC	.50	.15
❑ B79	Ugueth Urbina	.25	.07
❑ B80	Keith Williams RC	.50	.15
❑ B81	John Frascatore RC	.50	.15
❑ B82	Garey Ingram RC	.50	.15
❑ B83	Aaron Small	.25	.07
❑ B84	Olmedo Saenz RC	.50	.15
❑ B85	Jesus Tavarez RC	.50	.15
❑ B86	Jose Silva RC	1.00	.30
❑ B87	Jay Witasick RC	.50	.15
❑ B88	Jay Maldonado RC	.50	.15
❑ B89	Keith Heberling RC	.50	.15
❑ B90	Rusty Greer RC	1.50	.45
❑ R1	Paul Molitor	.75	.23
❑ R2	Eddie Murray	1.25	.35
❑ R3	Ozzie Smith	1.25	.35
❑ R4	Rickey Henderson	2.00	.60
❑ R5	Lee Smith	.50	.15
❑ R6	Dave Winfield	.75	.23
❑ R7	Roberto Alomar	1.25	.35
❑ R8	Matt Williams	.50	.15
❑ R9	Mark Grace	1.25	.35
❑ R10	Lance Johnson	.25	.07
❑ R11	Darren Daulton	.50	.15
❑ R12	Tom Glavine	1.25	.35
❑ R13	Gary Sheffield	.50	.15
❑ R14	Rod Beck	.25	.07
❑ R15	Fred McGriff	.75	.23
❑ R16	Joe Carter	.50	.15
❑ R17	Dante Bichette	.50	.15
❑ R18	Danny Tartabull	.25	.07
❑ R19	Juan Gonzalez	1.25	.35
❑ R20	Steve Avery	.25	.07
❑ R21	John Wetteland	.50	.15
❑ R22	Ben McDonald	.25	.07
❑ R23	Jack McDowell	.25	.07
❑ R24	Jose Canseco	1.25	.35
❑ R25	Tim Salmon	.75	.23
❑ R26	Wilson Alvarez	.25	.07
❑ R27	Gregg Jefferies	.25	.07
❑ R28	John Burkett	.25	.07
❑ R29	Greg Vaughn	.50	.15
❑ R30	Robin Ventura	.50	.15
❑ R31	Paul O'Neill	.75	.23
❑ R32	Cecil Fielder	.50	.15
❑ R33	Kevin Mitchell	.25	.07
❑ R34	Jeff Conine	.50	.15
❑ R35	Carlos Baerga	.25	.07
❑ R36	Greg Maddux	2.50	.75
❑ R37	Roger Clemens	2.50	.75
❑ R38	Deion Sanders	.50	.15
❑ R39	Delino DeShields	.25	.07
❑ R40	Ken Griffey Jr.	2.00	.60
❑ R41	Albert Belle	.50	.15
❑ R42	Wade Boggs	.75	.23
❑ R43	Andres Galarraga	.50	.15
❑ R44	Aaron Sele	.25	.07
❑ R45	Don Mattingly	3.00	.90
❑ R46	David Cone	.50	.15
❑ R47	Len Dykstra	.50	.15
❑ R48	Brett Butler	.50	.15
❑ R49	Bill Swift	.25	.07
❑ R50	Bobby Bonilla	.50	.15
❑ R51	Rafael Palmeiro	.75	.23
❑ R52	Moises Alou	.50	.15
❑ R53	Jeff Bagwell	.75	.23
❑ R54	Mike Mussina	1.25	.35
❑ R55	Frank Thomas	1.25	.35
❑ R56	Jose Rijo	.25	.07
❑ R57	Ruben Sierra	.25	.07
❑ R58	Randy Myers	.25	.07
❑ R59	Barry Bonds	3.00	.90
❑ R60	Jimmy Key	.50	.15
❑ R61	Travis Fryman	.50	.15
❑ R62	John Olerud	.50	.15
❑ R63	David Justice	.50	.15
❑ R64	Ray Lankford	.25	.07
❑ R65	Bob Tewksbury	.25	.07
❑ R66	Chuck Carr	.25	.07
❑ R67	Jay Buhner	.50	.15
❑ R68	Kenny Lofton	.50	.15
❑ R69	Marquis Grissom	.25	.07
❑ R70	Sammy Sosa	2.00	.60
❑ R71	Cal Ripken	4.00	1.20
❑ R72	Ellis Burks	.50	.15
❑ R73	Jeff Montgomery	.25	.07
❑ R74	Julio Franco	.50	.15
❑ R75	Kirby Puckett	1.25	.35
❑ R76	Larry Walker	.75	.23
❑ R77	Andy Van Slyke	.50	.15
❑ R78	Tony Gwynn	1.50	.45
❑ R79	Will Clark	1.25	.35
❑ R80	Mo Vaughn	.50	.15
❑ R81	Mike Piazza	2.50	.75
❑ R82	James Mouton	.25	.07
❑ R83	Carlos Delgado	.75	.23
❑ R84	Ryan Klesko	.50	.15
❑ R85	Javier Lopez	.50	.15
❑ R86	Raul Mondesi	.50	.15
❑ R87	Cliff Floyd	.50	.15
❑ R88	Manny Ramirez	.75	.23
❑ R89	Hector Carrasco	.25	.07
❑ R90	Jeff Granger	.25	.07
❑ X91	Frank Thomas Dmitri Young	.75	.23
❑ X92	Fred McGriff Brooks Kieschnick	.50	.15
❑ X93	Matt Williams Shane Andrews	.25	.07
❑ X94	Cal Ripken Kevin Orie	2.00	.60
❑ X95	Barry Larkin Derek Jeter	2.00	.60
❑ X96	Ken Griffey Jr. Johnny Damon	1.00	.30
❑ X97	Barry Bonds	1.50	.45

Rondell White
❑ X98 Albert Belle .50 .15
Jimmy Hurst
❑ X99 Raul Mondesi .50 .15
Ruben Rivera RC
❑ X100 Roger Clemens 1.25 .35
Scott Ruffcorn
❑ X101 Greg Maddux 1.25 .35
John Wasdin
❑ X102 Tim Salmon .75 .23
Chad Mottola
❑ X103 Carlos Baerga .25 .07
Arquimedez Pozo
❑ X104 Mike Piazza 1.25 .35
Bobby Hughes
❑ X105 Carlos Delgado .75 .23
Melvin Nieves
❑ X106 Javier Lopez 2.50 .75
Jorge Posada
❑ X107 Manny Ramirez .75 .23
Jose Malave
❑ X108 Travis Fryman .75 .23
Chipper Jones
❑ X109 Steve Avery .25 .07
Bill Pulsipher
❑ X110 John Olerud 1.25 .35
Shawn Green

1995 Bowman's Best

	Nm-Mt	Ex-Mt
COMPLETE SET (195)	250.00	75.00
COMMON CARD (B1-R90)	.50	.15
COMMON CARD (X1-X15)	.50	.15

❑ B1 Derek Jeter 3.00 .90
❑ B2 Vladimir Guerrero RC 80.00 24.00
❑ B3 Bob Abreu RC 10.00 3.00
❑ B4 Chan Ho Park .50 .15
❑ B5 Paul Wilson .50 .15
❑ B6 Chad Ogea .50 .15
❑ B7 Andruw Jones RC 50.00 15.00
❑ B8 Brian Barber .50 .15
❑ B9 Andy Larkin .50 .15
❑ B10 Richie Sexson RC 15.00 4.50
❑ B11 Everett Stull .50 .15
❑ B12 Brooks Kieschnick .50 .15
❑ B13 Matt Murray .50 .15
❑ B14 John Wasdin .50 .15
❑ B15 Shannon Stewart .50 .15
❑ B16 Luis Ortiz .50 .15
❑ B17 Marc Kroon .50 .15
❑ B18 Todd Greene .50 .15
❑ B19 Juan Acevedo RC 1.00 .30
❑ B20 Tony Clark .50 .15
❑ B21 Jermaine Dye .50 .15
❑ B22 Derrek Lee .50 .15
❑ B23 Pat Watkins .50 .15
❑ B24 Pokey Reese .50 .15
❑ B25 Ben Grieve .50 .15
❑ B26 Julio Santana RC .50 .15
❑ B27 Felix Rodriguez RC 2.00 .60
❑ B28 Paul Konerko 2.00 .60
❑ B29 Nomar Garciaparra 10.00 3.00
❑ B30 Pat Ahearne .50 .15
❑ B31 Jason Schmidt 1.50 .45
❑ B32 Billy Wagner .50 .15
❑ B33 Rey Ordonez RC 3.00 .90
❑ B34 Curtis Goodwin .50 .15
❑ B35 Sergio Nunez RC 1.00 .30
❑ B36 Tim Belk .50 .15
❑ B37 Scott Elarton RC 2.00 .60
❑ B38 Jason Isringhausen .50 .15
❑ B39 Trot Nixon .50 .15
❑ B40 Sid Roberson RC 1.00 .30
❑ B41 Ron Villone .50 .15
❑ B42 Ruben Rivera .50 .15
❑ B43 Rick Huisman .50 .15
❑ B44 Todd Hollandsworth .50 .15
❑ B45 Johnny Damon .75 .23
❑ B46 Garret Anderson .50 .15
❑ B47 Jeff D'Amico .50 .15
❑ B48 Dustin Hermanson .50 .15
❑ B49 Juan Encarnacion RC 5.00 1.50
❑ B50 Andy Pettitte .75 .23
❑ B51 Chris Stynes .50 .15
❑ B52 Troy Percival .50 .15
❑ B53 LaTroy Hawkins .50 .15
❑ B54 Roger Cedeno .50 .15
❑ B55 Alan Benes .50 .15
❑ B56 Karim Garcia RC 5.00 1.50
❑ B57 Andrew Lorraine .50 .15
❑ B58 Gary Rath RC 1.00 .30
❑ B59 Bret Wagner .50 .15
❑ B60 Jeff Suppan .50 .15
❑ B61 Bill Pulsipher .50 .15
❑ B62 Jay Payton RC 3.00 .90
❑ B63 Alex Ochoa .50 .15
❑ B64 Ugueth Urbina .50 .15
❑ B65 Armando Benitez .50 .15
❑ B66 George Arias .50 .15
❑ B67 Raul Casanova RC 1.00 .30
❑ B68 Matt Drews .50 .15
❑ B69 Jimmy Haynes .50 .15
❑ B70 Jimmy Hurst .50 .15
❑ B71 C.J. Nitkowski .50 .15
❑ B72 Tommy Davis RC 1.00 .30
❑ B73 Bartolo Colon RC 10.00 3.00
❑ B74 Chris Carpenter RC 2.00 .60
❑ B75 Trey Beamon .50 .15
❑ B76 Bryan Rekar .50 .15
❑ B77 James Baldwin .50 .15
❑ B78 Marc Valdes .50 .15
❑ B79 Tom Fordham RC 1.00 .30
❑ B80 Marc Newfield .50 .15
❑ B81 Angel Martinez .50 .15
❑ B82 Brian L. Hunter .50 .15
❑ B83 Jose Herrera .50 .15
❑ B84 Glenn Dishman RC 1.00 .30
❑ B85 Jacob Cruz RC 2.00 .60
❑ B86 Paul Shuey .50 .15
❑ B87 Scott Rolen RC 25.00 7.50
❑ B88 Doug Million .50 .15
❑ B89 Desi Relaford .50 .15
❑ B90 Michael Tucker .50 .15
❑ R1 Randy Johnson 1.25 .35
❑ R2 Joe Carter .50 .15
❑ R3 Chili Davis .50 .15
❑ R4 Moises Alou .50 .15
❑ R5 Gary Sheffield .50 .15
❑ R6 Kevin Appier .50 .15
❑ R7 Denny Neagle .50 .15
❑ R8 Ruben Sierra .50 .15
❑ R9 Darren Daulton .50 .15
❑ R10 Cal Ripken 4.00 1.20
❑ R11 Bobby Bonilla .50 .15
❑ R12 Manny Ramirez .50 .15
❑ R13 Barry Bonds 3.00 .90
❑ R14 Eric Karros .50 .15
❑ R15 Greg Maddux 2.50 .75
❑ R16 Jeff Bagwell .75 .23
❑ R17 Paul Molitor .75 .23
❑ R18 Ray Lankford .50 .15
❑ R19 Mark Grace 1.25 .35
❑ R20 Kenny Lofton .50 .15
❑ R21 Tony Gwynn 1.50 .45
❑ R22 Will Clark 1.25 .35
❑ R23 Roger Clemens 2.50 .75
❑ R24 Dante Bichette .50 .15
❑ R25 Barry Larkin 1.25 .35
❑ R26 Wade Boggs .75 .23
❑ R27 Kirby Puckett 1.25 .35
❑ R28 Cecil Fielder .50 .15
❑ R29 Jose Canseco 1.25 .35
❑ R30 Juan Gonzalez 1.25 .35
❑ R31 David Cone .50 .15
❑ R32 Craig Biggio .75 .23
❑ R33 Tim Salmon .75 .23
❑ R34 David Justice .50 .15
❑ R35 Sammy Sosa 2.00 .60
❑ R36 Mike Piazza 2.00 .60
❑ R37 Carlos Baerga .50 .15
❑ R38 Jeff Conine .50 .15
❑ R39 Rafael Palmeiro .75 .23
❑ R40 Bret Saberhagen .50 .15
❑ R41 Len Dykstra .50 .15
❑ R42 Mo Vaughn .50 .15
❑ R43 Wally Joyner .50 .15
❑ R44 Chuck Knoblauch .50 .15
❑ R45 Robin Ventura .50 .15
❑ R46 Don Mattingly 3.00 .90
❑ R47 Dave Hollins .50 .15
❑ R48 Andy Benes .50 .15
❑ R49 Ken Griffey Jr. 2.00 .60
❑ R50 Albert Belle .50 .15
❑ R51 Matt Williams .50 .15
❑ R52 Rondell White .50 .15
❑ R53 Raul Mondesi .50 .15
❑ R54 Brian Jordan .50 .15
❑ R55 Greg Vaughn .50 .15
❑ R56 Fred McGriff .75 .23
❑ R57 Roberto Alomar 1.25 .35
❑ R58 Dennis Eckersley .50 .15
❑ R59 Lee Smith .50 .15
❑ R60 Eddie Murray 1.25 .35
❑ R61 Kenny Rogers .50 .15
❑ R62 Ron Gant .50 .15
❑ R63 Larry Walker .75 .23
❑ R64 Chad Curtis .50 .15
❑ R65 Frank Thomas 1.25 .35
❑ R66 Paul O'Neill .75 .23
❑ R67 Kevin Seitzer .50 .15
❑ R68 Marquis Grissom .50 .15
❑ R69 Mark McGwire 4.00 1.20
❑ R70 Travis Fryman .50 .15
❑ R71 Andres Galarraga .50 .15
❑ R72 Carlos Perez RC 2.00 .60
❑ R73 Tyler Green .50 .15
❑ R74 Marty Cordova .50 .15
❑ R75 Shawn Green .50 .15
❑ R76 Vaughn Eshelman .50 .15
❑ R77 John Mabry .50 .15
❑ R78 Jason Bates .50 .15
❑ R79 Jon Nunnally .50 .15
❑ R80 Ray Durham .50 .15
❑ R81 Edgardo Alfonzo .50 .15
❑ R82 Esteban Loaiza .75 .23
❑ R83 Hideo Nomo RC 12.00 3.60
❑ R84 Orlando Miller .50 .15
❑ R85 Alex Gonzalez .50 .15
❑ R86 M.Grudzielanek RC 3.00 .90
❑ R87 Julian Tavarez .50 .15
❑ R88 Benji Gil .50 .15
❑ R89 Quilvio Veras .50 .15
❑ R90 Ricky Bottalico .50 .15
❑ X1 Ben Davis RC 1.50 .45
Ivan Rodriguez
❑ X2 Mark Redman RC 2.50 .75
Manny Ramirez
❑ X3 Reggie Taylor RC .75 .23
Deion Sanders
❑ X4 Ryan Jaroncyk RC .50 .15
Shawn Green
❑ X5 Juan LeBron RC 1.50 .45
Juan Gonzalez UER
Card pictures Carlos Beltran instead of Juan LeBron.
❑ X6 Tony McKnight RC .50 .15
Craig Biggio
❑ X7 Michael Barrett RC 2.50 .75
Travis Fryman
❑ X8 Corey Jenkins RC .50 .15
Mo Vaughn
❑ X9 Ruben Rivera 1.25 .35
Frank Thomas
❑ X10 Curtis Goodwin .50 .15
Kenny Lofton
❑ X11 Brian L. Hunter .75 .23
Tony Gwynn
❑ X12 Todd Greene 1.25 .35

		Nm-Mt	Ex-Mt
	Ken Griffey Jr.		
❑ X13	Karim Garcia	1.25	.35
	Matt Williams		
❑ X14	Billy Wagner	.75	.23
	Randy Johnson		
❑ X15	Pat Watkins	.75	.23
	Jeff Bagwell		

1996 Bowman's Best

		Nm-Mt	Ex-Mt
COMPLETE SET (180)		40.00	12.00
❑ 1	Hideo Nomo	1.00	.30
❑ 2	Edgar Martinez	.60	.18
❑ 3	Cal Ripken	3.00	.90
❑ 4	Wade Boggs	.60	.18
❑ 5	Cecil Fielder	.40	.12
❑ 6	Albert Belle	.40	.12
❑ 7	Chipper Jones	1.00	.30
❑ 8	Ryne Sandberg	1.50	.45
❑ 9	Tim Salmon	.60	.18
❑ 10	Barry Bonds	2.50	.75
❑ 11	Ken Caminiti	.40	.12
❑ 12	Ron Gant	.40	.12
❑ 13	Frank Thomas	1.00	.30
❑ 14	Dante Bichette	.40	.12
❑ 15	Jason Kendall	.40	.12
❑ 16	Mo Vaughn	.40	.12
❑ 17	Rey Ordonez	.40	.12
❑ 18	Henry Rodriguez	.40	.12
❑ 19	Ryan Klesko	.40	.12
❑ 20	Jeff Bagwell	.60	.18
❑ 21	Randy Johnson	1.00	.30
❑ 22	Jim Edmonds	.40	.12
❑ 23	Kenny Lofton	.40	.12
❑ 24	Andy Pettitte	.60	.18
❑ 25	Brady Anderson	.40	.12
❑ 26	Mike Piazza	1.50	.45
❑ 27	Greg Vaughn	.40	.12
❑ 28	Joe Carter	.40	.12
❑ 29	Jason Giambi	1.00	.30
❑ 30	Ivan Rodriguez	1.00	.30
❑ 31	Jeff Conine	.40	.12
❑ 32	Rafael Palmeiro	.60	.18
❑ 33	Roger Clemens	2.00	.60
❑ 34	Chuck Knoblauch	.40	.12
❑ 35	Reggie Sanders	.40	.12
❑ 36	Andres Galarraga	.40	.12
❑ 37	Paul O'Neill	.60	.18
❑ 38	Tony Gwynn	1.25	.35
❑ 39	Paul Wilson	.40	.12
❑ 40	Garret Anderson	.40	.12
❑ 41	David Justice	.40	.12
❑ 42	Eddie Murray	1.00	.30
❑ 43	Mike Grace RC	.50	.15
❑ 44	Marty Cordova	.40	.12
❑ 45	Kevin Appier	.40	.12
❑ 46	Raul Mondesi	.40	.12
❑ 47	Jim Thome	1.00	.30
❑ 48	Sammy Sosa	1.50	.45
❑ 49	Craig Biggio	.60	.18
❑ 50	Marquis Grissom	.40	.12
❑ 51	Alan Benes	.40	.12
❑ 52	Manny Ramirez	.40	.12
❑ 53	Gary Sheffield	.40	.12
❑ 54	Mike Mussina	1.00	.30
❑ 55	Robin Ventura	.40	.12
❑ 56	Johnny Damon	.40	.12
❑ 57	Jose Canseco	1.00	.30
❑ 58	Juan Gonzalez	1.00	.30
❑ 59	Tino Martinez	.60	.18
❑ 60	Brian Hunter	.40	.12
❑ 61	Fred McGriff	.60	.18
❑ 62	Jay Buhner	.40	.12
❑ 63	Carlos Delgado	.40	.12
❑ 64	Moises Alou	.40	.12
❑ 65	Roberto Alomar	1.00	.30
❑ 66	Barry Larkin	1.00	.30
❑ 67	Vinny Castilla	.40	.12
❑ 68	Ray Durham	.40	.12
❑ 69	Travis Fryman	.40	.12
❑ 70	Jason Isringhausen	.40	.12
❑ 71	Ken Griffey Jr.	1.50	.45
❑ 72	John Smoltz	.60	.18
❑ 73	Matt Williams	.40	.12
❑ 74	Chan Ho Park	.40	.12
❑ 75	Mark McGwire	3.00	.90
❑ 76	Jeffrey Hammonds	.40	.12
❑ 77	Will Clark	1.00	.30
❑ 78	Kirby Puckett	1.00	.30
❑ 79	Derek Jeter	2.50	.75
❑ 80	Derek Bell	.40	.12
❑ 81	Eric Karros	.40	.12
❑ 82	Len Dykstra	.40	.12
❑ 83	Larry Walker	.60	.18
❑ 84	Mark Grudzielanek	.40	.12
❑ 85	Greg Maddux	2.00	.60
❑ 86	Carlos Baerga	.40	.12
❑ 87	Paul Molitor	.60	.18
❑ 88	John Valentin	.40	.12
❑ 89	Mark Grace	1.00	.30
❑ 90	Ray Lankford	.40	.12
❑ 91	Andruw Jones	1.50	.45
❑ 92	Nomar Garciaparra	2.50	.75
❑ 93	Alex Ochoa	.40	.12
❑ 94	Derrick Gibson	.40	.12
❑ 95	Jeff D'Amico	.40	.12
❑ 96	Ruben Rivera	.40	.12
❑ 97	Vladimir Guerrero	2.00	.60
❑ 98	Pokey Reese	.40	.12
❑ 99	Richard Hidalgo	.40	.12
❑ 100	Bartolo Colon	.40	.12
❑ 101	Karim Garcia	.40	.12
❑ 102	Ben Davis	.40	.12
❑ 103	Jay Powell	.40	.12
❑ 104	Chris Snopek	.40	.12
❑ 105	Glendon Rusch RC	.75	.23
❑ 106	Enrique Wilson	.40	.12
❑ 107	A.Alfonseca RC	.75	.23
❑ 108	Wilton Guerrero RC	.75	.23
❑ 109	Jose Guillen RC	4.00	1.20
❑ 110	Miguel Mejia RC	.50	.15
❑ 111	Jay Payton	.40	.12
❑ 112	Scott Elarton	.40	.12
❑ 113	Brooks Kieschnick	.40	.12
❑ 114	Dustin Hermanson	.40	.12
❑ 115	Roger Cedeno	.40	.12
❑ 116	Matt Wagner	.40	.12
❑ 117	Lee Daniels	.40	.12
❑ 118	Ben Grieve	.40	.12
❑ 119	Ugueth Urbina	.40	.12
❑ 120	Danny Graves	.40	.12
❑ 121	Dan Donato RC	.50	.15
❑ 122	Matt Ruebel RC	.50	.15
❑ 123	Mark Sievert RC	.50	.15
❑ 124	Chris Stynes	.40	.12
❑ 125	Jeff Abbott	.40	.12
❑ 126	Rocky Coppinger RC	.50	.15
❑ 127	Jermaine Dye	.40	.12
❑ 128	Todd Greene	.40	.12
❑ 129	Chris Carpenter	.40	.12
❑ 130	Edgar Renteria	.40	.12
❑ 131	Matt Drews	.40	.12
❑ 132	Edgard Velazquez RC	.50	.15
❑ 133	Casey Whitten	.40	.12
❑ 134	Ryan Jones RC	.50	.15
❑ 135	Todd Walker	.60	.18
❑ 136	Geoff Jenkins RC	4.00	1.20
❑ 137	Matt Morris RC	5.00	1.50
❑ 138	Richie Sexson	.60	.18
❑ 139	Todd Dunwoody RC	.50	.15
❑ 140	Gabe Alvarez RC	.50	.15
❑ 141	J.J. Johnson	.40	.12
❑ 142	Shannon Stewart	.40	.12
❑ 143	Brad Fullmer	.40	.12
❑ 144	Julio Santana	.40	.12
❑ 145	Scott Rolen	1.25	.35
❑ 146	Amaury Telemaco	.40	.12
❑ 147	Trey Beamon	.40	.12
❑ 148	Billy Wagner	.40	.12
❑ 149	Todd Hollandsworth	.40	.12
❑ 150	Doug Million	.40	.12
❑ 151	Javier Valentin RC	.50	.15
❑ 152	Wes Helms RC	1.25	.35
❑ 153	Jeff Suppan	.40	.12
❑ 154	Luis Castillo RC	4.00	1.20
❑ 155	Bob Abreu	.40	.12
❑ 156	Paul Konerko	.40	.12
❑ 157	Jamey Wright	.40	.12
❑ 158	Eddie Pearson	.40	.12
❑ 159	Jimmy Haynes	.40	.12
❑ 160	Derrek Lee	.40	.12
❑ 161	Damian Moss	.40	.12
❑ 162	Carlos Guillen RC	2.00	.60
❑ 163	Chris Fussell RC	.50	.15
❑ 164	Mike Sweeney RC	6.00	1.80
❑ 165	Donnie Sadler	.40	.12
❑ 166	Desi Relaford	.40	.12
❑ 167	Steve Gibralter	.40	.12
❑ 168	Neifi Perez	.40	.12
❑ 169	Antone Williamson	.40	.12
❑ 170	Marty Janzen RC	.50	.15
❑ 171	Todd Helton	2.00	.60
❑ 172	Raul Ibanez RC	2.50	.75
❑ 173	Bill Selby	.40	.12
❑ 174	Shane Monahan RC	.50	.15
❑ 175	Robin Jennings	.40	.12
❑ 176	Bobby Chouinard	.40	.12
❑ 177	Einar Diaz	.40	.12
❑ 178	Jason Thompson	.40	.12
❑ 179	Rafael Medina RC	.50	.15
❑ 180	Kevin Orie	.40	.12
❑ NNO	Mickey Mantle	10.00	3.00
	1952 Bowman Atomic Ref.		
❑ NNO	Mickey Mantle	5.00	1.50
	1952 Bowman Refractor		
❑ NNO	Mickey Mantle	2.50	.75
	1952 Bowman Chrome		

1997 Bowman's Best

		Nm-Mt	Ex-Mt
COMPLETE SET (200)		40.00	12.00
❑ 1	Ken Griffey Jr.	1.50	.45
❑ 2	Cecil Fielder	.40	.12
❑ 3	Albert Belle	.40	.12
❑ 4	Todd Hundley	.40	.12
❑ 5	Mike Piazza	1.50	.45
❑ 6	Matt Williams	.40	.12
❑ 7	Mo Vaughn	.40	.12
❑ 8	Ryne Sandberg	1.50	.45
❑ 9	Chipper Jones	1.00	.30
❑ 10	Edgar Martinez	.60	.18
❑ 11	Kenny Lofton	.40	.12
❑ 12	Ron Gant	.40	.12
❑ 13	Moises Alou	.40	.12
❑ 14	Pat Hentgen	.40	.12
❑ 15	Steve Finley	.40	.12
❑ 16	Mark Grace	1.00	.30
❑ 17	Jay Buhner	.40	.12

❑ 18	Jeff Conine	.40	.12
❑ 19	Jim Edmonds	.40	.12
❑ 20	Todd Hollandsworth	.40	.12
❑ 21	Andy Pettitte	.60	.18
❑ 22	Jim Thome	1.00	.30
❑ 23	Eric Young	.40	.12
❑ 24	Ray Lankford	.40	.12
❑ 25	Marquis Grissom	.40	.12
❑ 26	Tony Clark	.40	.12
❑ 27	Jermaine Allensworth	.40	.12
❑ 28	Ellis Burks	.40	.12
❑ 29	Tony Gwynn	1.25	.35
❑ 30	Barry Larkin	1.00	.30
❑ 31	John Olerud	.40	.12
❑ 32	Mariano Rivera	.60	.18
❑ 33	Paul Molitor	.60	.18
❑ 34	Ken Caminiti	.40	.12
❑ 35	Gary Sheffield	.40	.12
❑ 36	Al Martin	.40	.12
❑ 37	John Valentin	.40	.12
❑ 38	Frank Thomas	1.00	.30
❑ 39	John Jaha	.40	.12
❑ 40	Greg Maddux	2.00	.60
❑ 41	Alex Fernandez	.40	.12
❑ 42	Dean Palmer	.40	.12
❑ 43	Bernie Williams	.60	.18
❑ 44	Deion Sanders	.40	.12
❑ 45	Mark McGwire	3.00	.90
❑ 46	Brian Jordan	.40	.12
❑ 47	Bernard Gilkey	.40	.12
❑ 48	Will Clark	1.00	.30
❑ 49	Kevin Appier	.40	.12
❑ 50	Tom Glavine	1.00	.30
❑ 51	Chuck Knoblauch	.40	.12
❑ 52	Rondell White	.40	.12
❑ 53	Greg Vaughn	.40	.12
❑ 54	Mike Mussina	1.00	.30
❑ 55	Brian McRae	.40	.12
❑ 56	Chili Davis	.40	.12
❑ 57	Wade Boggs	.60	.18
❑ 58	Jeff Bagwell	.60	.18
❑ 59	Roberto Alomar	1.00	.30
❑ 60	Dennis Eckersley	.40	.12
❑ 61	Ryan Klesko	.40	.12
❑ 62	Manny Ramirez	.40	.12
❑ 63	John Wetteland	.40	.12
❑ 64	Cal Ripken	3.00	.90
❑ 65	Edgar Renteria	.40	.12
❑ 66	Tino Martinez	.60	.18
❑ 67	Larry Walker	.60	.18
❑ 68	Gregg Jefferies	.40	.12
❑ 69	Lance Johnson	.40	.12
❑ 70	Carlos Delgado	.40	.12
❑ 71	Craig Biggio	.60	.18
❑ 72	Jose Canseco	1.00	.30
❑ 73	Barry Bonds	2.50	.75
❑ 74	Juan Gonzalez	1.00	.30
❑ 75	Eric Karros	.40	.12
❑ 76	Reggie Sanders	.40	.12
❑ 77	Robin Ventura	.40	.12
❑ 78	Hideo Nomo	1.00	.30
❑ 79	David Justice	.40	.12
❑ 80	Vinny Castilla	.40	.12
❑ 81	Travis Fryman	.40	.12
❑ 82	Derek Jeter	2.50	.75
❑ 83	Sammy Sosa	1.50	.45
❑ 84	Ivan Rodriguez	1.00	.30
❑ 85	Rafael Palmeiro	.60	.18
❑ 86	Roger Clemens	2.00	.60
❑ 87	Jason Giambi	1.00	.30
❑ 88	Andres Galarraga	.40	.12
❑ 89	Jermaine Dye	.40	.12
❑ 90	Joe Carter	.40	.12
❑ 91	Brady Anderson	.40	.12
❑ 92	Derek Bell	.40	.12
❑ 93	Randy Johnson	1.00	.30
❑ 94	Fred McGriff	.60	.18
❑ 95	John Smoltz	.60	.18
❑ 96	Harold Baines	.40	.12
❑ 97	Raul Mondesi	.40	.12
❑ 98	Tim Salmon	.60	.18
❑ 99	Carlos Baerga	.40	.12
❑ 100	Dante Bichette	.40	.12
❑ 101	Vladimir Guerrero	1.00	.30
❑ 102	Richard Hidalgo	.40	.12
❑ 103	Paul Konerko	.40	.12
❑ 104	Alex Gonzalez RC	1.00	.30
❑ 105	Jason Dickson	.40	.12
❑ 106	Jose Rosado	.40	.12
❑ 107	Todd Walker	.40	.12
❑ 108	Seth Greisinger RC	.50	.15
❑ 109	Todd Helton	1.00	.30
❑ 110	Ben Davis	.40	.12
❑ 111	Bartolo Colon	.40	.12
❑ 112	Elieser Marrero	.40	.12
❑ 113	Jeff D'Amico	.40	.12
❑ 114	Miguel Tejada RC	5.00	1.50
❑ 115	Darin Erstad	.40	.12
❑ 116	Kris Benson RC	.75	.23
❑ 117	Adrian Beltre RC	2.00	.60
❑ 118	Neifi Perez	.40	.12
❑ 119	Pokey Reese	.40	.12
❑ 120	Carl Pavano	.40	.12
❑ 121	Juan Melo	.40	.12
❑ 122	Kevin McGlinchy RC	.40	.12
❑ 123	Pat Cline	.40	.12
❑ 124	Felix Heredia RC	.40	.12
❑ 125	Aaron Boone	.40	.12
❑ 126	Glendon Rusch	.40	.12
❑ 127	Mike Cameron	.40	.12
❑ 128	Justin Thompson	.40	.12
❑ 129	Chad Hermansen RC	.50	.15
❑ 130	Sidney Ponson RC	1.00	.30
❑ 131	Willie Martinez RC	.40	.12
❑ 132	Paul Wilder RC	.40	.12
❑ 133	Geoff Jenkins	.40	.12
❑ 134	Roy Halladay RC	4.00	1.20
❑ 135	Carlos Guillen	.40	.12
❑ 136	Tony Batista	.40	.12
❑ 137	Todd Greene	.40	.12
❑ 138	Luis Castillo	.40	.12
❑ 139	Jimmy Anderson RC	.40	.12
❑ 140	Edgard Velazquez	.40	.12
❑ 141	Chris Snopek	.40	.12
❑ 142	Ruben Rivera	.40	.12
❑ 143	Javier Valentin	.40	.12
❑ 144	Brian Rose	.40	.12
❑ 145	Fernando Tatis RC	.50	.15
❑ 146	Dean Crow RC	.40	.12
❑ 147	Karim Garcia	.40	.12
❑ 148	Dante Powell	.40	.12
❑ 149	Hideki Irabu RC	.50	.15
❑ 150	Matt Morris	.40	.12
❑ 151	Wes Helms	.40	.12
❑ 152	Russ Johnson	.40	.12
❑ 153	Jarrod Washburn	.40	.12
❑ 154	Kerry Wood RC	8.00	2.40
❑ 155	Joe Fontenot RC	.40	.12
❑ 156	Eugene Kingsale	.40	.12
❑ 157	Terrence Long	.40	.12
❑ 158	Calvin Maduro	.40	.12
❑ 159	Jeff Suppan	.40	.12
❑ 160	DaRond Stovall	.40	.12
❑ 161	Mark Redman	.40	.12
❑ 162	Ken Cloude RC	.50	.15
❑ 163	Bobby Estalella	.40	.12
❑ 164	Abraham Nunez RC	.40	.12
❑ 165	Derrick Gibson	.40	.12
❑ 166	Mike Drumright RC	.40	.12
❑ 167	Katsuhiro Maeda	.40	.12
❑ 168	Jeff Liefer	.40	.12
❑ 169	Ben Grieve	.40	.12
❑ 170	Bob Abreu	.40	.12
❑ 171	Shannon Stewart	.40	.12
❑ 172	Braden Looper RC	.40	.12
❑ 173	Brant Brown	.40	.12
❑ 174	Marlon Anderson	.40	.12
❑ 175	Brad Fullmer	.40	.12
❑ 176	Carlos Beltran	.60	.18
❑ 177	Nomar Garciaparra	2.00	.60
❑ 178	Derrek Lee	.40	.12
❑ 179	Val.De Los Santos RC	.40	.12
❑ 180	Dmitri Young	.40	.12
❑ 181	Jamey Wright	.40	.12
❑ 182	Hiram Bocachica RC	.50	.15
❑ 183	Wilton Guerrero	.40	.12
❑ 184	Chris Carpenter	.40	.12
❑ 185	Scott Spiezio	.40	.12
❑ 186	Andruw Jones	.60	.18
❑ 187	Travis Lee RC	.75	.23
❑ 188	Jose Cruz Jr. RC	2.00	.60
❑ 189	Jose Guillen	.40	.12
❑ 190	Jeff Abbott	.40	.12
❑ 191	Ricky Ledee RC	.50	.15
❑ 192	Mike Sweeney	.40	.12
❑ 193	Donnie Sadler	.40	.12
❑ 194	Scott Rolen	.60	.18
❑ 195	Kevin Orie	.40	.12
❑ 196	Jason Conti RC	.40	.12
❑ 197	Mark Kotsay RC	.50	.15
❑ 198	Eric Milton RC	.75	.23
❑ 199	Russell Branyan	.40	.12
❑ 200	Alex Sanchez RC	.50	.15

1998 Bowman's Best

		Nm-Mt	Ex-Mt
COMPLETE SET (200)		40.00	12.00
❑ 1	Mark McGwire	2.50	.75
❑ 2	Jeromy Burnitz	.40	.12
❑ 3	Barry Bonds	2.50	.75
❑ 4	Dante Bichette	.40	.12
❑ 5	Chipper Jones	1.00	.30
❑ 6	Frank Thomas	1.00	.30
❑ 7	Kevin Brown	.60	.18
❑ 8	Juan Gonzalez	1.00	.30
❑ 9	Jay Buhner	.40	.12
❑ 10	Chuck Knoblauch	.40	.12
❑ 11	Cal Ripken	3.00	.90
❑ 12	Matt Williams	.40	.12
❑ 13	Jim Edmonds	.40	.12
❑ 14	Manny Ramirez	.40	.12
❑ 15	Tony Clark	.40	.12
❑ 16	Mo Vaughn	.40	.12
❑ 17	Bernie Williams	.60	.18
❑ 18	Scott Rolen	.60	.18
❑ 19	Gary Sheffield	.40	.12
❑ 20	Albert Belle	.40	.12
❑ 21	Mike Piazza	1.50	.45
❑ 22	John Olerud	.40	.12
❑ 23	Tony Gwynn	1.25	.35
❑ 24	Jay Bell	.40	.12
❑ 25	Jose Cruz Jr.	.40	.12
❑ 26	Justin Thompson	.40	.12
❑ 27	Ken Griffey Jr.	1.50	.45
❑ 28	Sandy Alomar Jr.	.40	.12
❑ 29	Mark Grudzielanek	.40	.12
❑ 30	Mark Grace	1.00	.30
❑ 31	Ron Gant	.40	.12
❑ 32	Javy Lopez	.40	.12
❑ 33	Jeff Bagwell	.60	.18
❑ 34	Fred McGriff	.60	.18
❑ 35	Rafael Palmeiro	.60	.18
❑ 36	Vinny Castilla	.40	.12
❑ 37	Andy Benes	.40	.12
❑ 38	Pedro Martinez	1.00	.30
❑ 39	Andy Pettitte	.60	.18
❑ 40	Marty Cordova	.40	.12
❑ 41	Rusty Greer	.40	.12
❑ 42	Kevin Orie	.40	.12
❑ 43	Chan Ho Park	.40	.12
❑ 44	Ryan Klesko	.40	.12
❑ 45	Alex Rodriguez	2.00	.60
❑ 46	Travis Fryman	.40	.12
❑ 47	Jeff King	.40	.12
❑ 48	Roger Clemens	2.00	.60
❑ 49	Darin Erstad	.40	.12
❑ 50	Brady Anderson	.40	.12
❑ 51	Jason Kendall	.40	.12

	No.	Player	Nm-Mt	Ex-Mt
❑	52	John Valentin	.40	.12
❑	53	Ellis Burks	.40	.12
❑	54	Brian Hunter	.40	.12
❑	55	Paul O'Neill	.60	.18
❑	56	Ken Caminiti	.40	.12
❑	57	David Justice	.40	.12
❑	58	Eric Karros	.40	.12
❑	59	Pat Hentgen	.40	.12
❑	60	Greg Maddux	2.00	.60
❑	61	Craig Biggio	.60	.18
❑	62	Edgar Martinez	.60	.18
❑	63	Mike Mussina	1.00	.30
❑	64	Larry Walker	.60	.18
❑	65	Tino Martinez	.60	.18
❑	66	Jim Thome	1.00	.30
❑	67	Tom Glavine	1.00	.30
❑	68	Raul Mondesi	.40	.12
❑	69	Marquis Grissom	.40	.12
❑	70	Randy Johnson	1.00	.30
❑	71	Steve Finley	.40	.12
❑	72	Jose Guillen	.40	.12
❑	73	Nomar Garciaparra	2.00	.60
❑	74	Wade Boggs	.60	.18
❑	75	Bobby Higginson	.40	.12
❑	76	Robin Ventura	.40	.12
❑	77	Derek Jeter	2.50	.75
❑	78	Andruw Jones	.60	.18
❑	79	Ray Lankford	.40	.12
❑	80	Vladimir Guerrero	1.00	.30
❑	81	Kenny Lofton	.40	.12
❑	82	Ivan Rodriguez	1.00	.30
❑	83	Neifi Perez	.40	.12
❑	84	John Smoltz	.60	.18
❑	85	Tim Salmon	.60	.18
❑	86	Carlos Delgado	.40	.12
❑	87	Sammy Sosa	1.50	.45
❑	88	Jaret Wright	.40	.12
❑	89	Roberto Alomar	1.00	.30
❑	90	Paul Molitor	.60	.18
❑	91	Dean Palmer	.40	.12
❑	92	Barry Larkin	1.00	.30
❑	93	Jason Giambi	1.00	.30
❑	94	Curt Schilling	.60	.18
❑	95	Eric Young	.40	.12
❑	96	Denny Neagle	.40	.12
❑	97	Moises Alou	.40	.12
❑	98	Livan Hernandez	.40	.12
❑	99	Todd Hundley	.40	.12
❑	100	Andres Galarraga	.40	.12
❑	101	Travis Lee	.40	.12
❑	102	Lance Berkman	.60	.18
❑	103	Orlando Cabrera	.40	.12
❑	104	Mike Lowell RC	3.00	.90
❑	105	Ben Grieve	.40	.12
❑	106	Jae Weong Seo RC	1.00	.30
❑	107	Richie Sexson	.40	.12
❑	108	Eli Marrero	.40	.12
❑	109	Aramis Ramirez	.40	.12
❑	110	Paul Konerko	.40	.12
❑	111	Carl Pavano	.40	.12
❑	112	Brad Fullmer	.40	.12
❑	113	Matt Clement	.40	.12
❑	114	Donzell McDonald	.40	.12
❑	115	Todd Helton	.60	.18
❑	116	Mike Caruso	.40	.12
❑	117	Donnie Sadler	.40	.12
❑	118	Bruce Chen	.40	.12
❑	119	Jarrod Washburn	.40	.12
❑	120	Adrian Beltre	.40	.12
❑	121	Ryan Jackson RC	.40	.12
❑	122	Kevin Millar RC	2.00	.60
❑	123	Corey Koskie RC	2.00	.60
❑	124	Dermal Brown	.40	.12
❑	125	Kerry Wood	1.00	.30
❑	126	Juan Melo	.40	.12
❑	127	Ramon Hernandez	.40	.12
❑	128	Roy Halladay	.60	.18
❑	129	Ron Wright	.40	.12
❑	130	Darnell McDonald RC	.60	.18
❑	131	Odalis Perez RC	1.00	.30
❑	132	Alex Cora RC	.60	.18
❑	133	Justin Towle	.40	.12
❑	134	Juan Encarnacion	.40	.12
❑	135	Brian Rose	.40	.12
❑	136	Russell Branyan	.40	.12
❑	137	Cesar King RC	.40	.12
❑	138	Ruben Rivera	.40	.12
❑	139	Ricky Ledee	.40	.12
❑	140	Vernon Wells	.60	.18
❑	141	Luis Rivas RC	1.50	.45
❑	142	Brent Butler	.40	.12
❑	143	Karim Garcia	.40	.12
❑	144	George Lombard	.40	.12
❑	145	Masato Yoshii RC	1.00	.30
❑	146	Braden Looper	.40	.12
❑	147	Alex Sanchez	.40	.12
❑	148	Kris Benson	.40	.12
❑	149	Mark Kotsay	.40	.12
❑	150	Richard Hidalgo	.40	.12
❑	151	Scott Elarton	.40	.12
❑	152	Ryan Minor RC	.40	.12
❑	153	Troy Glaus RC	5.00	1.50
❑	154	Carlos Lee RC	2.00	.60
❑	155	Michael Coleman	.40	.12
❑	156	Jason Grilli RC	.40	.12
❑	157	Julio Ramirez RC	.40	.12
❑	158	Randy Wolf RC	1.50	.45
❑	159	Ryan Brannan	.40	.12
❑	160	Edgard Clemente	.40	.12
❑	161	Miguel Tejada	.60	.18
❑	162	Chad Hermansen	.40	.12
❑	163	Ryan Anderson RC	.60	.18
❑	164	Ben Petrick	.40	.12
❑	165	Alex Gonzalez	.40	.12
❑	166	Ben Davis	.40	.12
❑	167	John Patterson	.40	.12
❑	168	Cliff Politte	.40	.12
❑	169	Randall Simon	.40	.12
❑	170	Javier Vazquez	.60	.12
❑	171	Kevin Witt	.40	.12
❑	172	Geoff Jenkins	.40	.12
❑	173	David Ortiz	.40	.12
❑	174	Derrick Gibson	.40	.12
❑	175	Abraham Nunez	.40	.12
❑	176	A.J. Hinch	.40	.12
❑	177	Ruben Mateo RC	.60	.18
❑	178	Magglio Ordonez RC	3.00	.90
❑	179	Todd Dunwoody	.40	.12
❑	180	Daryle Ward	.40	.12
❑	181	Mike Kinkade RC	.40	.12
❑	182	Willie Martinez	.40	.12
❑	183	O.Hernandez RC	2.00	.60
❑	184	Eric Milton	.40	.12
❑	185	Eric Chavez	.60	.18
❑	186	Damian Jackson	.40	.12
❑	187	Jim Parque RC	.60	.18
❑	188	Dan Reichert RC	.60	.18
❑	189	Mike Drumright	.40	.12
❑	190	Todd Walker	.40	.12
❑	191	Shane Monahan	.40	.12
❑	192	Derrek Lee	.40	.12
❑	193	Jeremy Giambi RC	.60	.18
❑	194	Dan McKinley RC	.40	.12
❑	195	Tony Armas Jr. RC	.60	.18
❑	196	Matt Anderson RC	.60	.18
❑	197	Jim Chamblee RC	.40	.12
❑	198	F.Cordero RC	.60	.18
❑	199	Calvin Pickering	.40	.12
❑	200	Reggie Taylor	.40	.12

1999 Bowman's Best

	Nm-Mt	Ex-Mt
COMPLETE SET (200)	50.00	15.00
COMP.SET w/o SP's (150)	25.00	7.50
COMMON CARD (1-150)	.40	.12
COMMON (151-200)	.50	.15

	No.	Player	Nm-Mt	Ex-Mt
❑	1	Chipper Jones	1.00	.30
❑	2	Brian Jordan	.40	.12
❑	3	David Justice	.40	.12
❑	4	Jason Kendall	.40	.12
❑	5	Mo Vaughn	.40	.12
❑	6	Jim Edmonds	.40	.12
❑	7	Wade Boggs	.60	.18
❑	8	Jeromy Burnitz	.40	.12
❑	9	Todd Hundley	.40	.12
❑	10	Rondell White	.40	.12
❑	11	Cliff Floyd	.40	.12
❑	12	Sean Casey	.40	.12
❑	13	Bernie Williams	.60	.18
❑	14	Dante Bichette	.40	.12
❑	15	Greg Vaughn	.40	.12
❑	16	Andres Galarraga	.40	.12
❑	17	Ray Durham	.40	.12
❑	18	Jim Thome	1.00	.30
❑	19	Gary Sheffield	.40	.12
❑	20	Frank Thomas	1.00	.30
❑	21	Orlando Hernandez	.40	.12
❑	22	Ivan Rodriguez	1.00	.30
❑	23	Jose Cruz Jr.	.40	.12
❑	24	Jason Giambi	1.00	.30
❑	25	Craig Biggio	.60	.18
❑	26	Kerry Wood	1.00	.30
❑	27	Manny Ramirez	.40	.12
❑	28	Curt Schilling	.60	.18
❑	29	Mike Mussina	1.00	.30
❑	30	Tim Salmon	.60	.18
❑	31	Mike Piazza	1.50	.45
❑	32	Roberto Alomar	1.00	.30
❑	33	Larry Walker	.60	.18
❑	34	Barry Larkin	1.00	.30
❑	35	Nomar Garciaparra	2.00	.60
❑	36	Paul O'Neill	.60	.18
❑	37	Todd Walker	.40	.12
❑	38	Eric Karros	.40	.12
❑	39	Brad Fullmer	.40	.12
❑	40	John Olerud	.40	.12
❑	41	Todd Helton	.60	.18
❑	42	Raul Mondesi	.40	.12
❑	43	Jose Canseco	1.00	.30
❑	44	Matt Williams	.40	.12
❑	45	Ray Lankford	.40	.12
❑	46	Carlos Delgado	.40	.12
❑	47	Darin Erstad	.40	.12
❑	48	Vladimir Guerrero	1.00	.30
❑	49	Robin Ventura	.40	.12
❑	50	Alex Rodriguez	2.00	.60
❑	51	Vinny Castilla	.40	.12
❑	52	Tony Clark	.40	.12
❑	53	Pedro Martinez	1.00	.30
❑	54	Rafael Palmeiro	.60	.18
❑	55	Scott Rolen	.60	.18
❑	56	Tino Martinez	.60	.18
❑	57	Tony Gwynn	1.25	.35
❑	58	Barry Bonds	2.50	.75
❑	59	Kenny Lofton	.40	.12
❑	60	Javy Lopez	.40	.12
❑	61	Mark Grace	1.00	.30
❑	62	Travis Lee	.40	.12
❑	63	Kevin Brown	.60	.18
❑	64	Al Leiter	.40	.12
❑	65	Albert Belle	.40	.12
❑	66	Sammy Sosa	1.50	.45
❑	67	Greg Maddux	2.00	.60
❑	68	Mark Kotsay	.40	.12
❑	69	Dmitri Young	.40	.12
❑	70	Mark McGwire	2.50	.75
❑	71	Juan Gonzalez	1.00	.30
❑	72	Andruw Jones	.60	.18
❑	73	Derek Jeter	2.50	.75
❑	74	Randy Johnson	1.00	.30
❑	75	Cal Ripken	3.00	.90
❑	76	Shawn Green	.40	.12
❑	77	Moises Alou	.40	.12
❑	78	Tom Glavine	1.00	.30
❑	79	Sandy Alomar Jr.	.40	.12
❑	80	Ken Griffey Jr.	1.50	.45
❑	81	Ryan Klesko	.40	.12
❑	82	Jeff Bagwell	.60	.18

Card	Nm-Mt	Ex-Mt
❑ 83 Ben Grieve	.40	.12
❑ 84 John Smoltz	.60	.18
❑ 85 Roger Clemens	2.00	.60
❑ 86 Ken Griffey Jr. BP	1.00	.30
❑ 87 Roger Clemens BP	1.00	.30
❑ 88 Derek Jeter BP	1.25	.35
❑ 89 Nomar Garciaparra BP	1.00	.30
❑ 90 Mark McGwire BP	1.25	.35
❑ 91 Sammy Sosa BP	1.00	.30
❑ 92 Alex Rodriguez BP	1.00	.30
❑ 93 Greg Maddux BP	1.00	.30
❑ 94 Vladimir Guerrero BP	.60	.18
❑ 95 Chipper Jones BP	.60	.18
❑ 96 Kerry Wood BP	.60	.18
❑ 97 Ben Grieve BP	.40	.12
❑ 98 Tony Gwynn BP	.60	.18
❑ 99 Juan Gonzalez BP	.60	.18
❑ 100 Mike Piazza BP	.75	.23
❑ 101 Eric Chavez	.40	.12
❑ 102 Billy Koch	.40	.12
❑ 103 Dernell Stenson	.40	.12
❑ 104 Marlon Anderson	.40	.12
❑ 105 Ron Belliard	.40	.12
❑ 106 Bruce Chen	.40	.12
❑ 107 Carlos Beltran	.40	.12
❑ 108 Chad Hermansen	.40	.12
❑ 109 Ryan Anderson	.40	.12
❑ 110 Michael Barrett	.40	.12
❑ 111 Matt Clement	.40	.12
❑ 112 Ben Davis	.40	.12
❑ 113 Calvin Pickering	.40	.12
❑ 114 Brad Penny	.40	.12
❑ 115 Paul Konerko	.40	.12
❑ 116 Alex Gonzalez	.40	.12
❑ 117 George Lombard	.40	.12
❑ 118 John Patterson	.40	.12
❑ 119 Rob Bell	.40	.12
❑ 120 Ruben Mateo	.40	.12
❑ 121 Troy Glaus	.60	.18
❑ 122 Ryan Bradley	.40	.12
❑ 123 Carlos Lee	.40	.12
❑ 124 Gabe Kapler	.40	.12
❑ 125 Ramon Hernandez	.40	.12
❑ 126 Carlos Febles	.40	.12
❑ 127 Mitch Meluskey	.40	.12
❑ 128 Michael Cuddyer	.40	.12
❑ 129 Pablo Ozuna	.40	.12
❑ 130 Jayson Werth	.40	.12
❑ 131 Ricky Ledee	.40	.12
❑ 132 Jeremy Giambi	.40	.12
❑ 133 Danny Klassen	.40	.12
❑ 134 Mark DeRosa	.40	.12
❑ 135 Randy Wolf	.40	.12
❑ 136 Roy Halladay	.40	.12
❑ 137 Derrick Gibson	.40	.12
❑ 138 Ben Petrick	.40	.12
❑ 139 Warren Morris	.40	.12
❑ 140 Lance Berkman	.40	.12
❑ 141 Russell Branyan	.40	.12
❑ 142 Adrian Beltre	.40	.12
❑ 143 Juan Encarnacion	.40	.12
❑ 144 Fernando Seguignol	.40	.12
❑ 145 Corey Koskie	.40	.12
❑ 146 Preston Wilson	.40	.12
❑ 147 Homer Bush	.40	.12
❑ 148 Daryle Ward	.40	.12
❑ 149 Joe McEwing RC	.50	.15
❑ 150 Peter Bergeron RC	.50	.15
❑ 151 Pat Burrell RC	5.00	1.50
❑ 152 Choo Freeman RC	.50	.15
❑ 153 Matt Belisle RC	.50	.15
❑ 154 Carlos Pena RC	1.25	.35
❑ 155 A.J. Burnett RC	.75	.23
❑ 156 D.Mientkiewicz RC	1.50	.45
❑ 157 Sean Burroughs RC	4.00	1.20
❑ 158 Mike Zywica RC	.50	.15
❑ 159 Corey Patterson RC	5.00	1.50
❑ 160 Austin Kearns RC	8.00	2.40
❑ 161 Chip Ambres RC	.50	.15
❑ 162 Kelly Dransfeldt RC	.50	.15
❑ 163 Mike Nannini RC	.50	.15
❑ 164 Mark Mulder RC	5.00	1.50
❑ 165 Jason Tyner RC	.50	.15
❑ 166 Bobby Seay RC	.50	.15
❑ 167 Alex Escobar RC	.50	.15
❑ 168 Nick Johnson RC	2.50	.75
❑ 169 Alfonso Soriano RC	15.00	4.50
❑ 170 Clayton Andrews RC	.50	.15
❑ 171 C.C. Sabathia RC	1.25	.35
❑ 172 Matt Holliday RC	.50	.15
❑ 173 Brad Lidge RC	.50	.15
❑ 174 Kit Pellow RC	.50	.15
❑ 175 J.M. Gold RC	.50	.15
❑ 176 Roosevelt Brown RC	.50	.15
❑ 177 Eric Valent RC	.50	.15
❑ 178 Adam Everett RC	.50	.15
❑ 179 Jorge Toca RC	.50	.15
❑ 180 Matt Roney RC	.50	.15
❑ 181 Andy Brown RC	.50	.15
❑ 182 Phil Norton RC	.50	.15
❑ 183 Mickey Lopez RC	.50	.15
❑ 184 Chris George RC	.50	.15
❑ 185 Arturo McDowell RC	.50	.15
❑ 186 Jose Fernandez RC	.50	.15
❑ 187 Seth Etherton RC	.50	.15
❑ 188 Josh McKinley RC	.50	.15
❑ 189 Nate Cornejo RC	.75	.23
❑ 190 G.Chiaramonte RC	.50	.15
❑ 191 Mamon Tucker RC	.50	.15
❑ 192 Ryan Mills RC	.50	.15
❑ 193 Chad Moeller RC	.50	.15
❑ 194 Tony Torcato RC	.50	.15
❑ 195 Jeff Winchester RC	.50	.15
❑ 196 Rick Elder RC	.50	.15
❑ 197 Matt Burch RC	.50	.15
❑ 198 Jeff Urban RC	.50	.15
❑ 199 Chris Jones RC	.50	.15
❑ 200 Masao Kida RC	.50	.15

2000 Bowman's Best

	Nm-Mt	Ex-Mt
COMP.SET w/o RC's (150)	50.00	15.00
COMMON CARD (1-150)	.40	.12
COMMON (151-200)	5.00	1.50

Card	Nm-Mt	Ex-Mt
❑ 1 Nomar Garciaparra	2.00	.60
❑ 2 Chipper Jones	1.00	.30
❑ 3 Tony Clark	.40	.12
❑ 4 Bernie Williams	.60	.18
❑ 5 Barry Bonds	2.50	.75
❑ 6 Jermaine Dye	.40	.12
❑ 7 John Olerud	.40	.12
❑ 8 Mike Hampton	.40	.12
❑ 9 Cal Ripken	3.00	.90
❑ 10 Jeff Bagwell	.60	.18
❑ 11 Troy Glaus	.60	.18
❑ 12 J.D. Drew	.40	.12
❑ 13 Jeromy Burnitz	.40	.12
❑ 14 Carlos Delgado	.40	.12
❑ 15 Shawn Green	.40	.12
❑ 16 Kevin Millwood	.40	.12
❑ 17 Rondell White	.40	.12
❑ 18 Scott Rolen	.60	.18
❑ 19 Jeff Cirillo	.40	.12
❑ 20 Barry Larkin	1.00	.30
❑ 21 Brian Giles	.40	.12
❑ 22 Roger Clemens	2.00	.60
❑ 23 Manny Ramirez	.40	.12
❑ 24 Alex Gonzalez	.40	.12
❑ 25 Mark Grace	1.00	.30
❑ 26 Fernando Tatis	.40	.12
❑ 27 Randy Johnson	1.00	.30
❑ 28 Roger Cedeno	.40	.12
❑ 29 Brian Jordan	.40	.12
❑ 30 Kevin Brown	.40	.12
❑ 31 Greg Vaughn	.40	.12
❑ 32 Roberto Alomar	1.00	.30
❑ 33 Larry Walker	.60	.18
❑ 34 Rafael Palmeiro	.60	.18
❑ 35 Curt Schilling	.60	.18
❑ 36 Orlando Hernandez	.40	.12
❑ 37 Todd Walker	.40	.12
❑ 38 Juan Gonzalez	1.00	.30
❑ 39 Sean Casey	.40	.12
❑ 40 Tony Gwynn	1.25	.35
❑ 41 Albert Belle	.40	.12
❑ 42 Gary Sheffield	.40	.12
❑ 43 Michael Barrett	.40	.12
❑ 44 Preston Wilson	.40	.12
❑ 45 Jim Thome	1.00	.30
❑ 46 Shannon Stewart	.40	.12
❑ 47 Mo Vaughn	.40	.12
❑ 48 Ben Grieve	.40	.12
❑ 49 Adrian Beltre	.40	.12
❑ 50 Sammy Sosa	1.50	.45
❑ 51 Bob Abreu	.40	.12
❑ 52 Edgardo Alfonzo	.40	.12
❑ 53 Carlos Febles	.40	.12
❑ 54 Frank Thomas	1.00	.30
❑ 55 Alex Rodriguez	2.00	.60
❑ 56 Cliff Floyd	.40	.12
❑ 57 Jose Canseco	1.00	.30
❑ 58 Erubiel Durazo	.40	.12
❑ 59 Tim Hudson	.60	.18
❑ 60 Craig Biggio	.60	.18
❑ 61 Eric Karros	.40	.12
❑ 62 Mike Mussina	1.00	.30
❑ 63 Robin Ventura	.40	.12
❑ 64 Carlos Beltran	.40	.12
❑ 65 Pedro Martinez	1.00	.30
❑ 66 Gabe Kapler	.40	.12
❑ 67 Jason Kendall	.40	.12
❑ 68 Derek Jeter	2.50	.75
❑ 69 Magglio Ordonez	.40	.12
❑ 70 Mike Piazza	1.50	.45
❑ 71 Mike Lieberthal	.40	.12
❑ 72 Andres Galarraga	.40	.12
❑ 73 Raul Mondesi	.40	.12
❑ 74 Eric Chavez	.40	.12
❑ 75 Greg Maddux	2.00	.60
❑ 76 Matt Williams	.40	.12
❑ 77 Kris Benson	.40	.12
❑ 78 Ivan Rodriguez	1.00	.30
❑ 79 Pokey Reese	.40	.12
❑ 80 Vladimir Guerrero	1.00	.30
❑ 81 Mark McGwire	2.50	.75
❑ 82 Vinny Castilla	.40	.12
❑ 83 Todd Helton	.60	.18
❑ 84 Andruw Jones	.60	.18
❑ 85 Ken Griffey Jr.	1.50	.45
❑ 86 Mark McGwire BP	1.25	.35
❑ 87 Derek Jeter BP	1.25	.35
❑ 88 Chipper Jones BP	.60	.18
❑ 89 Nomar Garciaparra BP	1.00	.30
❑ 90 Sammy Sosa BP	1.00	.30
❑ 91 Cal Ripken BP	1.50	.45
❑ 92 Juan Gonzalez BP	.60	.18
❑ 93 Alex Rodriguez BP	1.00	.30
❑ 94 Barry Bonds BP	1.25	.35
❑ 95 Sean Casey BP	.40	.12
❑ 96 Vladimir Guerrero BP	.60	.18
❑ 97 Mike Piazza BP	1.00	.30
❑ 98 Shawn Green BP	.40	.12
❑ 99 Jeff Bagwell BP	.40	.12
❑ 100 Ken Griffey Jr. BP	1.00	.30
❑ 101 Rick Ankiel	.40	.12
❑ 102 John Patterson	.40	.12
❑ 103 David Walling	.40	.12
❑ 104 Michael Restovich	.40	.12
❑ 105 A.J. Burnett	.40	.12
❑ 106 Pablo Ozuna	.40	.12
❑ 107 Chad Hermansen	.40	.12
❑ 108 Choo Freeman	.40	.12
❑ 109 Mark Quinn	.40	.12
❑ 110 Corey Patterson	.60	.18
❑ 111 Ramon Ortiz	.40	.12
❑ 112 Vernon Wells	.40	.12
❑ 113 Milton Bradley	.40	.12
❑ 114 Gookie Dawkins	.40	.12
❑ 115 Sean Burroughs	.60	.18

	Nm-Mt	Ex-Mt
❑ 116 Wily Mo Pena	.40	.12
❑ 117 Dee Brown	.40	.12
❑ 118 C.C. Sabathia	.40	.12
❑ 119 Adam Kennedy	.40	.12
❑ 120 Octavio Dotel	.40	.12
❑ 121 Kip Wells	.40	.12
❑ 122 Ben Petrick	.40	.12
❑ 123 Mark Mulder	.60	.18
❑ 124 Jason Standridge	.40	.12
❑ 125 Adam Piatt	.40	.12
❑ 126 Steve Lomasney	.40	.12
❑ 127 Jayson Werth	.40	.12
❑ 128 Alex Escobar	.40	.12
❑ 129 Ryan Anderson	.40	.12
❑ 130 Adam Dunn	1.00	.30
❑ 131 Ted Lilly	.40	.12
❑ 132 Brad Penny	.40	.12
❑ 133 Daryle Ward	.40	.12
❑ 134 Eric Munson	.40	.12
❑ 135 Nick Johnson	.40	.12
❑ 136 Jason Jennings	.40	.12
❑ 137 Tim Raines Jr.	.40	.12
❑ 138 Ruben Mateo	.40	.12
❑ 139 Jack Cust	.40	.12
❑ 140 Rafael Furcal	.40	.12
❑ 141 Eric Gagne	1.00	.30
❑ 142 Tony Armas Jr.	.40	.12
❑ 143 Mike Paradis	.40	.12
❑ 144 Peter Bergeron	.40	.12
❑ 145 Alfonso Soriano	1.50	.45
❑ 146 Josh Hamilton	.40	.12
❑ 147 Michael Cuddyer	.40	.12
❑ 148 Jay Gehrke	.40	.12
❑ 149 Josh Girdley	.40	.12
❑ 150 Pat Burrell	.60	.18
❑ 151 Brett Myers RC	25.00	7.50
❑ 152 Scott Seabol RC	5.00	1.50
❑ 153 Keith Reed RC	5.00	1.50
❑ 154 F.Rodriguez RC	20.00	6.00
❑ 155 Barry Zito RC	40.00	12.00
❑ 156 Pat Manning RC	5.00	1.50
❑ 157 Ben Christensen RC	5.00	1.50
❑ 158 Corey Myers RC	5.00	1.50
❑ 159 Wascar Serrano RC	5.00	1.50
❑ 160 Wes Anderson RC	5.00	1.50
❑ 161 Andy Tracy RC	5.00	1.50
❑ 162 Cesar Saba RC	5.00	1.50
❑ 163 Mike Lamb RC	5.00	1.50
❑ 164 Bobby Bradley RC	5.00	1.50
❑ 165 Vince Faison RC	5.00	1.50
❑ 166 Ty Howington RC	5.00	1.50
❑ 167 Ken Harvey RC UER	12.00	3.60
Card has pitching stats on the back		
❑ 168 Josh Kalinowski RC	5.00	1.50
❑ 169 Ruben Salazar RC	5.00	1.50
❑ 170 Aaron Rowand RC	5.00	1.50
❑ 171 Ramon Santiago RC	5.00	1.50
❑ 172 Scott Sobkowiak RC	5.00	1.50
❑ 173 Lyle Overbay RC	8.00	2.40
❑ 174 Rico Washington RC	5.00	1.50
❑ 175 Rick Asadoorian RC	5.00	1.50
❑ 176 Matt Ginter RC	5.00	1.50
❑ 177 Jason Stumm RC	5.00	1.50
❑ 178 B.J. Garbe RC	5.00	1.50
❑ 179 Mike MacDougal RC	8.00	2.40
❑ 180 Ryan Christianson RC	5.00	1.50
❑ 181 Kurt Ainsworth RC	8.00	2.40
❑ 182 Brad Baisley RC	5.00	1.50
❑ 183 Ben Broussard RC	5.00	1.50
❑ 184 Aaron McNeal RC	5.00	1.50
❑ 185 John Sneed RC	5.00	1.50
❑ 186 Junior Brignac RC	5.00	1.50
❑ 187 Chance Caple RC	5.00	1.50
❑ 188 Scott Downs RC	5.00	1.50
❑ 189 Matt Cepicky RC	5.00	1.50
❑ 190 Chin-Feng Chen RC	30.00	9.00
❑ 191 Johan Santana RC	25.00	7.50
❑ 192 Brad Baker RC	5.00	1.50
❑ 193 Jason Repko RC	5.00	1.50
❑ 194 Craig Dingman RC	5.00	1.50
❑ 195 Chris Wakeland RC	5.00	1.50
❑ 196 Rogelio Arias RC	5.00	1.50
❑ 197 Luis Matos RC	15.00	4.50
❑ 198 Rob Ramsay	5.00	1.50
❑ 199 Willie Bloomquist RC	25.00	7.50
❑ 200 Tony Pena Jr. RC	5.00	1.50

2001 Bowman's Best

	Nm-Mt	Ex-Mt
COMP.SET w/o SP's (150)	60.00	18.00
COMMON CARD (1-150)	.40	.12
COMMON (151-200)	8.00	2.40
❑ 1 Vladimir Guerrero	1.00	.30
❑ 2 Miguel Tejada	.40	.12
❑ 3 Geoff Jenkins	.40	.12
❑ 4 Jeff Bagwell	.60	.18
❑ 5 Todd Helton	.60	.18
❑ 6 Ken Griffey Jr.	1.50	.45
❑ 7 Nomar Garciaparra	2.00	.60
❑ 8 Chipper Jones	1.00	.30
❑ 9 Darin Erstad	.40	.12
❑ 10 Frank Thomas	1.00	.30
❑ 11 Jim Thome	1.00	.30
❑ 12 Preston Wilson	.40	.12
❑ 13 Kevin Brown	.40	.12
❑ 14 Derek Jeter	2.50	.75
❑ 15 Scott Rolen	.60	.18
❑ 16 Ryan Klesko	.40	.12
❑ 17 Jeff Kent	.40	.12
❑ 18 Raul Mondesi	.40	.12
❑ 19 Greg Vaughn	.40	.12
❑ 20 Bernie Williams	.60	.18
❑ 21 Mike Piazza	1.50	.45
❑ 22 Richard Hidalgo	.40	.12
❑ 23 Dean Palmer	.40	.12
❑ 24 Roberto Alomar	1.00	.30
❑ 25 Sammy Sosa	1.50	.45
❑ 26 Randy Johnson	1.00	.30
❑ 27 Manny Ramirez	.40	.12
❑ 28 Roger Clemens	2.00	.60
❑ 29 Terrence Long	.40	.12
❑ 30 Jason Kendall	.40	.12
❑ 31 Richie Sexson	.40	.12
❑ 32 David Wells	.40	.12
❑ 33 Andruw Jones	.60	.18
❑ 34 Pokey Reese	.40	.12
❑ 35 Juan Gonzalez	1.00	.30
❑ 36 Carlos Beltran	.40	.12
❑ 37 Shawn Green	.40	.12
❑ 38 Mariano Rivera	.60	.18
❑ 39 John Olerud	.40	.12
❑ 40 Jim Edmonds	.40	.12
❑ 41 Andres Galarraga	.40	.12
❑ 42 Carlos Delgado	.40	.12
❑ 43 Kris Benson	.40	.12
❑ 44 Andy Pettitte	.60	.18
❑ 45 Jeff Cirillo	.40	.12
❑ 46 Magglio Ordonez	.40	.12
❑ 47 Tom Glavine	1.00	.30
❑ 48 Garret Anderson	.40	.12
❑ 49 Cal Ripken	3.00	.90
❑ 50 Pedro Martinez	1.00	.30
❑ 51 Barry Bonds	2.50	.75
❑ 52 Alex Rodriguez	2.00	.60
❑ 53 Ben Grieve	.40	.12
❑ 54 Edgar Martinez	.60	.18
❑ 55 Jason Giambi	1.00	.30
❑ 56 Jeromy Burnitz	.40	.12
❑ 57 Mike Mussina	1.00	.30
❑ 58 Moises Alou	.40	.12
❑ 59 Sean Casey	.40	.12
❑ 60 Greg Maddux	2.00	.60
❑ 61 Tim Hudson	.40	.12
❑ 62 Mark McGwire	2.50	.75
❑ 63 Rafael Palmeiro	.60	.18
❑ 64 Tony Batista	.40	.12
❑ 65 Kazuhiro Sasaki	.40	.12
❑ 66 Jorge Posada	.60	.18
❑ 67 Johnny Damon	.40	.12
❑ 68 Brian Giles	.40	.12
❑ 69 Jose Vidro	.40	.12
❑ 70 Jermaine Dye	.40	.12
❑ 71 Craig Biggio	.60	.18
❑ 72 Larry Walker	.60	.18
❑ 73 Eric Chavez	.40	.12
❑ 74 David Segui	.40	.12
❑ 75 Tim Salmon	.60	.18
❑ 76 Javy Lopez	.40	.12
❑ 77 Paul Konerko	.40	.12
❑ 78 Barry Larkin	1.00	.30
❑ 79 Mike Hampton	.40	.12
❑ 80 Bobby Higginson	.40	.12
❑ 81 Mark Mulder	.40	.12
❑ 82 Pat Burrell	.40	.12
❑ 83 Kerry Wood	1.00	.30
❑ 84 J.T. Snow	.40	.12
❑ 85 Ivan Rodriguez	1.00	.30
❑ 86 Edgardo Alfonzo	.40	.12
❑ 87 Orlando Hernandez	.40	.12
❑ 88 Gary Sheffield	.40	.12
❑ 89 Mike Sweeney	.40	.12
❑ 90 Carlos Lee	.40	.12
❑ 91 Rafael Furcal	.40	.12
❑ 92 Troy Glaus	.60	.18
❑ 93 Bartolo Colon	.40	.12
❑ 94 Cliff Floyd	.40	.12
❑ 95 Barry Zito	1.00	.30
❑ 96 J.D. Drew	.40	.12
❑ 97 Eric Karros	.40	.12
❑ 98 Jose Valentin	.40	.12
❑ 99 Ellis Burks	.40	.12
❑ 100 David Justice	.40	.12
❑ 101 Larry Barnes	.40	.12
❑ 102 Rod Barajas	.40	.12
❑ 103 Tony Pena Jr.	.40	.12
❑ 104 Jerry Hairston Jr.	.40	.12
❑ 105 Keith Ginter	.40	.12
❑ 106 Corey Patterson	.40	.12
❑ 107 Aaron Rowand	.40	.12
❑ 108 Miguel Olivo	.40	.12
❑ 109 Gookie Dawkins	.40	.12
❑ 110 C.C. Sabathia	.40	.12
❑ 111 Ben Petrick	.40	.12
❑ 112 Eric Munson	.40	.12
❑ 113 Ramon Castro	.40	.12
❑ 114 Alex Escobar	.40	.12
❑ 115 Josh Hamilton	.40	.12
❑ 116 Jason Marquis	.40	.12
❑ 117 Ben Davis	.40	.12
❑ 118 Alex Cintron	.40	.12
❑ 119 Julio Zuleta	.40	.12
❑ 120 Ben Broussard	.40	.12
❑ 121 Adam Everett	.40	.12
❑ 122 Ramon Carvajal RC	.40	.12
❑ 123 Felipe Lopez	.40	.12
❑ 124 Alfonso Soriano	1.00	.30
❑ 125 Jayson Werth	.40	.12
❑ 126 Donzell McDonald	.40	.12
❑ 127 Jason Hart	.40	.12
❑ 128 Joe Crede	.40	.12
❑ 129 Sean Burroughs	.40	.12
❑ 130 Jack Cust	.40	.12
❑ 131 Corey Smith	.40	.12
❑ 132 Adrian Gonzalez	.40	.12
❑ 133 J.R. House	.40	.12
❑ 134 Steve Lomasney	.40	.12
❑ 135 Tim Raines Jr.	.40	.12
❑ 136 Tony Alvarez	.40	.12
❑ 137 Doug Mientkiewicz	.40	.12
❑ 138 Rocco Baldelli	3.00	.90
❑ 139 Jason Romano	.40	.12
❑ 140 Vernon Wells	.40	.12
❑ 141 Mike Bynum	.40	.12
❑ 142 Xavier Nady	.40	.12
❑ 143 Brad Wilkerson	.40	.12
❑ 144 Ben Diggins	.40	.12
❑ 145 Aubrey Huff	.40	.12
❑ 146 Eric Byrnes	.40	.12
❑ 147 Alex Gordon	.40	.12

❑ 148 Roy Oswalt .60 .18
❑ 149 Brian Esposito .40 .12
❑ 150 Scott Seabol .40 .12
❑ 151 Erick Almonte RC 8.00 2.40
❑ 152 Gary Johnson RC 8.00 2.40
❑ 153 Pedro Liriano RC 8.00 2.40
❑ 154 Matt White RC 8.00 2.40
❑ 155 Luis Montanez RC 8.00 2.40
❑ 156 Brad Cresse 8.00 2.40
❑ 157 Wilson Betemit RC 8.00 2.40
❑ 158 Octavio Martinez RC 8.00 2.40
❑ 159 Adam Pettyjohn RC 8.00 2.40
❑ 160 Corey Spencer RC 8.00 2.40
❑ 161 Mark Burnett RC 8.00 2.40
❑ 162 Ichiro Suzuki RC 40.00 12.00
❑ 163 Alexis Gomez RC 8.00 2.40
❑ 164 Greg Nash RC 8.00 2.40
❑ 165 Roberto Miniel RC 8.00 2.40
❑ 166 Justin Morneau RC 25.00 7.50
❑ 167 Ben Washburn RC 8.00 2.40
❑ 168 Bob Keppel RC 8.00 2.40
❑ 169 Deivi Mendez RC 8.00 2.40
❑ 170 Tsuyoshi Shinjo RC 12.00 3.60
❑ 171 Jared Abruzzo RC 8.00 2.40
❑ 172 Derrick Van Dusen RC 8.00 2.40
❑ 173 Hee Seop Choi RC 25.00 7.50
❑ 174 Albert Pujols RC 80.00 24.00
❑ 175 Travis Hafner RC 10.00 3.00
❑ 176 Ron Davenport RC 8.00 2.40
❑ 177 Luis Torres RC 8.00 2.40
❑ 178 Jake Peavy RC 15.00 4.50
❑ 179 Elvis Corporan RC 8.00 2.40
❑ 180 Dave Krynzel 8.00 2.40
❑ 181 Tony Blanco RC 8.00 2.40
❑ 182 Elpidio Guzman RC 8.00 2.40
❑ 183 Matt Butler RC 8.00 2.40
❑ 184 Joe Thurston RC 10.00 3.00
❑ 185 Andy Beal RC 8.00 2.40
❑ 186 Kevin Nulton RC 8.00 2.40
❑ 187 Sneideer Santos RC 8.00 2.40
❑ 188 Joe Dillon RC 8.00 2.40
❑ 189 Jeremy Blevins RC 8.00 2.40
❑ 190 Chris Amador RC 8.00 2.40
❑ 191 Mark Hendrickson RC 8.00 2.40
❑ 192 Willy Aybar RC 15.00 4.50
❑ 193 Antoine Cameron RC 8.00 2.40
❑ 194 J.J. Johnson RC 8.00 2.40
❑ 195 Ryan Ketchner RC 20.00 6.00
❑ 196 Bjorn Ivy RC 8.00 2.40
❑ 197 Josh Kroeger RC 20.00 6.00
❑ 198 Ty Wigginton RC 20.00 6.00
❑ 199 Stubby Clapp RC 8.00 2.40
❑ 200 Jerrod Riggan RC 8.00 2.40

2002 Bowman's Best

	Nm-Mt	Ex-Mt
COMP.SET w/o SP's (90)	100.00	30.00
COMMON CARD (1-90)	.75	.23
COMMON AUTO A (91-180)	8.00	2.40
AUTO GROUP A ODDS 1:3		
COMMON AUTO B (91-180)	10.00	3.00
AUTO GROUP B ODDS 1:19		
COMMON BAT (91-180)	5.00	1.50
91-180 BAT STATED ODDS 1:5	-	
181 ISHII BAT EXCHANGE ODDS 1:131		-

❑ 1 Josh Beckett 1.25 .35
❑ 2 Derek Jeter 5.00 1.50
❑ 3 Alex Rodriguez 4.00 1.20
❑ 4 Miguel Tejada .75 .23
❑ 5 Nomar Garciaparra 4.00 1.20
❑ 6 Aramis Ramirez .75 .23
❑ 7 Jeremy Giambi .75 .23
❑ 8 Bernie Williams 1.25 .35
❑ 9 Juan Pierre .75 .23
❑ 10 Chipper Jones 2.00 .60
❑ 11 Jimmy Rollins .75 .23
❑ 12 Alfonso Soriano 2.00 .60
❑ 13 Mark Prior 4.00 1.20
❑ 14 Paul Konerko .75 .23
❑ 15 Tim Hudson .75 .23
❑ 16 Doug Mientkiewicz .75 .23
❑ 17 Todd Helton 1.25 .35
❑ 18 Moises Alou .75 .23
❑ 19 Juan Gonzalez 2.00 .60
❑ 20 Jorge Posada 1.25 .35
❑ 21 Jeff Kent .75 .23
❑ 22 Roger Clemens 4.00 1.20
❑ 23 Phil Nevin .75 .23
❑ 24 Brian Giles .75 .23
❑ 25 Carlos Delgado .75 .23
❑ 26 Jason Giambi 2.00 .60
❑ 27 Vladimir Guerrero 2.00 .60
❑ 28 Cliff Floyd .75 .23
❑ 29 Shea Hillenbrand .75 .23
❑ 30 Ken Griffey Jr. 3.00 .90
❑ 31 Mike Piazza 3.00 .90
❑ 32 Carlos Pena .75 .23
❑ 33 Larry Walker 1.25 .35
❑ 34 Magglio Ordonez .75 .23
❑ 35 Mike Mussina 2.00 .60
❑ 36 Andruw Jones 1.25 .35
❑ 37 Nick Johnson .75 .23
❑ 38 Curt Schilling 1.25 .35
❑ 39 Eric Chavez .75 .23
❑ 40 Bartolo Colon .75 .23
❑ 41 Eric Hinske .75 .23
❑ 42 Sean Burroughs .75 .23
❑ 43 Randy Johnson 2.00 .60
❑ 44 Adam Dunn 1.25 .35
❑ 45 Pedro Martinez 2.00 .60
❑ 46 Garret Anderson .75 .23
❑ 47 Jim Thome 2.00 .60
❑ 48 Gary Sheffield .75 .23
❑ 49 Tsuyoshi Shinjo .75 .23
❑ 50 Albert Pujols 4.00 1.20
❑ 51 Ichiro Suzuki 4.00 1.20
❑ 52 C.C. Sabathia .75 .23
❑ 53 Bobby Abreu .75 .23
❑ 54 Ivan Rodriguez 2.00 .60
❑ 55 J.D. Drew .75 .23
❑ 56 Jacque Jones .75 .23
❑ 57 Jason Kendall .75 .23
❑ 58 Javier Vazquez .75 .23
❑ 59 Jeff Bagwell 1.25 .35
❑ 60 Greg Maddux 4.00 1.20
❑ 61 Jim Edmonds .75 .23
❑ 62 Hank Blalock 2.00 .60
❑ 63 Jose Vidro .75 .23
❑ 64 Kevin Brown .75 .23
❑ 65 Mark Teixeira 2.00 .60
❑ 66 Sammy Sosa 3.00 .90
❑ 67 Lance Berkman .75 .23
❑ 68 Mark Mulder .75 .23
❑ 69 Marty Cordova .75 .23
❑ 70 Frank Thomas 2.00 .60
❑ 71 Mike Cameron .75 .23
❑ 72 Mike Sweeney .75 .23
❑ 73 Barry Bonds 5.00 1.50
❑ 74 Troy Glaus 1.25 .35
❑ 75 Barry Zito 2.00 .60
❑ 76 Pat Burrell .75 .23
❑ 77 Paul LoDuca .75 .23
❑ 78 Rafael Palmeiro 1.25 .35
❑ 79 Austin Kearns 1.25 .35
❑ 80 Darin Erstad .75 .23
❑ 81 Richie Sexson .75 .23
❑ 82 Roberto Alomar 2.00 .60
❑ 83 Roy Oswalt .75 .23
❑ 84 Ryan Klesko .75 .23
❑ 85 Luis Gonzalez .75 .23
❑ 86 Scott Rolen 1.25 .35
❑ 87 Shannon Stewart .75 .23
❑ 88 Shawn Green .75 .23
❑ 89 Toby Hall .75 .23
❑ 90 Bret Boone .75 .23
❑ 91 Casey Kotchman Bat RC 20.00 6.00
❑ 92 Jose Valverde AU A RC 10.00 3.00
❑ 93 Cole Barthel Bat RC 5.00 1.50
❑ 94 Brad Nelson AU A RC 15.00 4.50
❑ 95 Mauricio Lara AU A RC 8.00 2.40
❑ 96 Ryan Gripp Bat RC 5.00 1.50
❑ 97 Brian West AU A RC 8.00 2.40
❑ 98 Chris Piersoll AU B RC 10.00 3.00
❑ 99 Ryan Church AU B RC 15.00 4.50
❑ 100 Javier Colina AU A 8.00 2.40
❑ 101 Juan M. Gonzalez AU A RC 8.00 2.40
❑ 102 Benito Baez AU A 8.00 2.40
❑ 103 Mike Hill Bat RC 5.00 1.50
❑ 104 Jason Grove AU B RC 10.00 3.00
❑ 105 Koyie Hill AU B 10.00 3.00
❑ 106 Mark Outlaw AU A RC 8.00 2.40
❑ 107 Jason Bay Bat RC 8.00 2.40
❑ 108 Jorge Padilla AU A RC 10.00 3.00
❑ 109 Pete Zamora AU A RC 8.00 2.40
❑ 110 Joe Mauer AU A RC 70.00 21.00
❑ 111 Franklyn German AU A RC 8.00 2.40
❑ 112 Chris Flinn AU A RC 8.00 2.40
❑ 113 David Wright Bat RC 12.00 3.60
❑ 114 Anastacio Martinez AU A RC 8.00 2.40
❑ 115 Nic Jackson Bat RC 8.00 2.40
❑ 116 Rene Reyes AU A RC 8.00 2.40
❑ 117 Colin Young AU A RC 8.00 2.40
❑ 118 Joe Orloski AU A RC 8.00 2.40
❑ 119 Mike Wilson AU A RC 8.00 2.40
❑ 120 Rich Thompson AU A RC 8.00 2.40
❑ 121 Jake Mauer AU B RC 10.00 3.00
❑ 122 Mario Ramos AU A RC 8.00 2.40
❑ 123 Doug Sessions AU B RC 10.00 3.00
❑ 124 Doug Devore Bat RC 5.00 1.50
❑ 125 Travis Foley AU A RC 10.00 3.00
❑ 126 Chris Baker AU A RC 8.00 2.40
❑ 127 Michael Floyd AU A RC 8.00 2.40
❑ 128 Josh Barfield Bat RC 15.00 4.50
❑ 129 Jose Bautista Bat RC 8.00 2.40
❑ 130 Gavin Floyd AU A RC 25.00 7.50
❑ 131 Jason Botts Bat RC 5.00 1.50
❑ 132 Clint Nageotte AU A RC 12.00 3.60
❑ 133 Jesus Cota AU B RC 15.00 4.50
❑ 134 Ron Calloway Bat RC 5.00 1.50
❑ 135 Kevin Cash Bat RC 5.00 1.50
❑ 136 Jonny Gomes AU B RC 20.00 6.00
❑ 137 Dennis Ulacia AU A RC 8.00 2.40
❑ 138 Ryan Snare AU A RC 10.00 3.00
❑ 139 Kevin Deaton AU A RC 8.00 2.40
❑ 140 Bobby Jenks AU B RC 25.00 7.50
❑ 141 Casey Kotchman AU A RC 30.00 9.00
❑ 142 Adam Walker AU A RC 8.00 2.40
❑ 143 Mike Gonzalez AU A RC 8.00 2.40
❑ 144 Ruben Gotay Bat RC 8.00 2.40
❑ 145 Jason Grove Bat RC 5.00 1.50
❑ 146 Freddy Sanchez AU B RC 15.00 4.50
❑ 147 Jason Arnold AU B RC 20.00 6.00
❑ 148 Scott Hairston AU A RC 20.00 6.00
❑ 149 Jason St. Clair AU B RC 10.00 3.00
❑ 150 Chris Tritle Bat RC 5.00 1.50
❑ 151 Edwin Yan Bat RC 5.00 1.50
❑ 152 Freddy Sanchez Bat RC 8.00 2.40
❑ 153 Greg Sain Bat RC 5.00 1.50
❑ 154 Yurendell De Caster Bat RC 8.00 2.40
❑ 155 Noochie Varner Bat RC 8.00 2.40
❑ 156 Nelson Castro AU B RC 10.00 3.00
❑ 157 Randall Shelley Bat RC 8.00 2.40
❑ 158 Reed Johnson Bat RC 8.00 2.40
❑ 159 Ryan Raburn AU A RC 8.00 2.40
❑ 160 Jose Morban Bat RC 8.00 2.40
❑ 161 Justin Schuda AU A RC 8.00 2.40
❑ 162 Henry Pichardo AU A RC 8.00 2.40
❑ 163 Josh Bard AU A RC 8.00 2.40
❑ 164 Josh Bonifay AU A RC 10.00 3.00
❑ 165 Brandon League AU B RC 15.00 4.50
❑ 166 Julio DePaula AU A RC 15.00 4.50
❑ 167 Todd Linden AU B RC 40.00 12.00
❑ 168 Francisco Liriano AU A RC 10.00 3.00
❑ 169 Chris Snelling AU A RC 12.00 3.60
❑ 170 Blake McGinley AU A RC 8.00 2.40
❑ 171 Cody McKay AU A RC 8.00 2.40
❑ 172 Jason Stanford AU A RC 8.00 2.40
❑ 173 Lenny Dinardo AU A RC 8.00 2.40
❑ 174 Greg Montalbano AU A RC 8.00 2.40

❑ 175 Earl Snyder AU A RC...... 8.00 2.40
❑ 176 Justin Huber AU A RC.. 12.00 3.60
❑ 177 Chris Narveson AU A RC 8.00 2.40
❑ 178 Jon Switzer AU A RC.... 10.00 3.00
❑ 179 Ronald Acuna AU A RC.. 8.00 2.40
❑ 180 Chris Duffy Bat RC 5.00 1.50
❑ 181 Kazuhisa Ishii Bat RC .. 10.00 3.00

2003 Bowman's Best

	MINT	NRMT
COMP.SET w/o SP's (50).........	40.00	18.00
COMMON CARD	.60	.25
COMMON AUTO	8.00	3.60
COMMON BAT............................	4.00	1.80

❑ AB Andrew Brown FY AU RC 8.00 3.60
❑ AK Austin Kearns .... 1.00 .45
❑ AM Aneudis Mateo FY AU RC 8.00 3.60
❑ AP Albert Pujols.................... 3.00 1.35
❑ AR Alex Rodriguez 3.00 1.35
❑ AS Alfonso Soriano .... 1.50 .70
❑ AW Aron Weston FY AU RC.. 8.00 3.60
❑ BB Bryan Bullington FY AU RC 20.00 9.00
❑ BC Bernie Castro FY RC........ 1.00 .45
❑ BFL Branden Florence FY AU RC 8.00 3.60
❑ BFR Ben Francisco FY AU RC 10.00 4.50
❑ BH Brendan Harris FY AU RC 10.00 4.50
❑ BJH Bo Hart FY RC 3.00 1.35
❑ BK Beau Kemp FY AU RC...... 8.00 3.60
❑ BLB Barry Bonds 4.00 1.80
❑ BM Brian McCann FY AU RC 10.00 4.50
❑ BSG Brian Giles .... .60 .25
❑ BWB Bobby Basham FY AU RC 10.00 4.50
❑ BZ Barry Zito .... 1.50 .70
❑ CAD Carlos Duran FY AU RC 8.00 3.60
❑ CDC Chris De La Cruz FY AU RC 8.00 3.60
❑ CJ Chipper Jones.................. 1.50 .70
❑ CJW C.J. Wilson FY AU........ 8.00 3.60
❑ CM Charlie Manning FY AU RC 8.00 3.60
❑ CMS Curt Schilling .... 1.00 .45
❑ CS Cory Stewart FY AU RC .. 8.00 3.60
❑ CSS Corey Shafer FY AU RC 10.00 4.50
❑ CW Chien-Ming Wang FY RC 4.00 1.80
❑ CWA Chien-Ming Wang FY AU 40.00 18.00
❑ DAM Dustin Moseley FY AU RC 10.00 4.50
❑ DC David Cash FY AU RC 8.00 3.60
❑ DH Dan Haren FY AU RC 12.00 5.50
❑ DJ Derek Jeter 4.00 1.80
❑ DM David Martinez FY AU RC 8.00 3.60
❑ DMM Dustin McGowan FY AU RC 10.00 4.50
❑ DR Darrell Rasner FY AU RC 8.00 3.60
❑ DW Doug Waechter FY AU RC 10.00 4.50
❑ DY Dustin Yount FY RC .... 1.50 .70
❑ ERA Elizardo Ramirez FY AU RC 15.00 6.75
❑ ERI Eric Riggs FY AU RC 10.00 4.50
❑ ET Eider Torres FY AU RC 8.00 3.60
❑ FP Felix Pie FY AU RC 50.00 22.00
❑ FS Felix Sanchez FY AU RC .. 8.00 3.60
❑ FT Ferdin Tejeda FY AU RC .. 8.00 3.60
❑ GA Greg Aquino FY AU RC .. 8.00 3.60
❑ GB Gregor Blanco FY AU RC 8.00 3.60
❑ GJA Garret Anderson .... .60 .25
❑ GM Greg Maddux.................. 3.00 1.35
❑ GS Gary Schneidmiller FY AU RC 8.00 3.60
❑ HR Hanley Ramirez FY AU RC 20.00 9.00
❑ HRB Hanley Ramirez FY Bat 10.00 4.50
❑ HT Haj Turay FY RC .... 1.50 .70
❑ IS Ichiro Suzuki 3.00 1.35
❑ JB Jeremy Bonderman FY RC 2.50 1.10
❑ JC Jose Contreras FY RC...... 3.00 1.35
❑ JDD J.D. Durbin FY AU RC 10.00 4.50
❑ JFK Jeff Kent .... .60 .25
❑ JG Joey Gomes FY AU RC .. 10.00 4.50
❑ JGB Joey Gomes FY Bat........ 5.00 2.20
❑ JGG Jason Giambi .... 1.50 .70
❑ JK Jason Kubel FY AU RC .. 10.00 4.50
❑ JKB Jason Kubel FY Bat........ 5.00 2.20
❑ JLB Jaime Bubela FY AU RC 8.00 3.60
❑ JM Jose Morales FY AU RC.. 8.00 3.60
❑ JMS Jon-Mark Sprowl FY RC 1.50 .70
❑ JRG Jeremy Griffiths FY AU RC 10.00 4.50
❑ JT Jim Thome .... 1.50 .70
❑ JV Joe Valentine FY AU RC .. 8.00 3.60
❑ JW Josh Willingham FY AU RC 20.00 6.75
❑ KG Ken Griffey Jr.................. 2.50 1.10
❑ KJ Kade Johnson FY AU RC.. 8.00 3.60
❑ KS Kelly Shoppach FY AU RC 15.00 6.75
❑ KSB Kelly Shoppach FY Bat .. 8.00 3.60
❑ KY Kevin Youkilis FY AU RC 20.00 9.00
❑ KYE Kevin Youkilis FY Bat .. 10.00 4.50
❑ LB Lance Berkman .... .60 .25
❑ LF Lew Ford FY AU RC 10.00 4.50
❑ LFJ Lew Ford FY Bat 5.00 2.20
❑ LW Larry Walker.................... 1.00 .45
❑ MB Matt Bruback FY RC ...... 1.00 .45
❑ MD Matt Diaz FY RC .... 1.50 .70
❑ MDA Matt Diaz FY AU 10.00 4.50
❑ MDH Matt Hensley FY AU RC 8.00 3.60
❑ MDM Mark Malaska FY AU RC 8.00 3.60
❑ MH Michel Hernandez FY AU RC 8.00 3.60
❑ MHI Michael Hinckley FY AU RC 10.00 4.50
❑ MJP Mike Piazza 2.50 1.10
❑ MK Matt Kata FY AU RC...... 12.00 5.50
❑ MNH Matt Hagen FY AU RC 10.00 4.50
❑ MO Mike O'Keefe FY RC ...... 1.00 .45
❑ MOR Magglio Ordonez........... .60 .25
❑ MP Mark Prior 3.00 1.35
❑ MR Manny Ramirez .... .60 .25
❑ MS Mike Sweeney .... .60 .25
❑ MT Miguel Tejada .... .60 .25
❑ NG Nomar Garciaparra.......... 3.00 1.35
❑ NL Nook Logan FY AU RC 8.00 3.60
❑ OC Ozzie Chavez FY AU RC .. 8.00 3.60
❑ PB Pat Burrell........................ .60 .25
❑ PL Pete LaForest FY AU RC 10.00 4.50
❑ PM Pedro Martinez .... 1.50 .70
❑ PR Prentice Redman FY AU RC 8.00 3.60
❑ RC Ryan Cameron FY AU RC 8.00 3.60
❑ RD Rajai Davis FY AU RC.... 10.00 4.50
❑ RDL Rajai Davis FY Bat 5.00 2.20
❑ RH Ryan Howard FY AU RC 12.00 5.50
❑ RHJ Ryan Howard FY Bat...... 6.00 2.70
❑ RJ Randy Johnson .... 1.50 .70
❑ RM Ramon Nivar-Martinez FY RC 2.00 .90
❑ RS Ryan Shealy FY AU RC .. 10.00 4.50
❑ RSB Ryan Shealy FY Bat 5.00 2.20
❑ RWH Robbie Hammock FY AU RC 10.00 4.50
❑ SG Shawn Green .... .60 .25
❑ SS Sammy Sosa.................... 2.50 1.10
❑ ST Scott Tyler FY AU RC 10.00 4.50
❑ SV Shane Victorino FY RC .... 1.00 .45
❑ TA Tyler Adamczyk FY AU RC 8.00 3.60
❑ TH Todd Helton .... 1.00 .45
❑ TI Travis Ishikawa FY AU RC 10.00 4.50
❑ TJ Tyler Johnson FY AU RC.. 8.00 3.60
❑ TJB T.J. Bohn FY RC .... 1.00 .45
❑ TKH Torii Hunter .... .60 .25
❑ TO Tim Olson FY AU RC 10.00 4.50
❑ TS T.Story-Harden FY AU RC 10.00 4.50
❑ TSB T.Story-Harden FY Bat .. 5.00 2.20
❑ TT Terry Tiffee FY RC .... 1.50 .70
❑ VG Vladimir Guerrero............ 1.50 .70
❑ WE Willie Eyre FY AU RC...... 8.00 3.60
❑ WL Wil Ledezma FY AU RC .. 8.00 3.60
❑ WRC Roger Clemens 3.00 1.35
❑ NNO Bryan Bullington 25.00 11.00
Opened Box AU
❑ NNO Bryan Bullington .... -
Sealed Box AU

1987 Classic Update Yellow

	Nm-Mt	Ex-Mt
COMP.FACT.SET (50)	25.00	10.00

❑ 101 Mike Schmidt .... 1.00 .40
❑ 102 Eric Davis .... .25 .10
❑ 103 Pete Rose .... 1.25 .50
❑ 104 Don Mattingly .... 1.25 .50
❑ 105 Wade Boggs .... .25 .10
❑ 106 Dale Murphy .... .40 .16
❑ 107 Glenn Davis....................... .10 .04
❑ 108 Wally Joyner .... .40 .16
❑ 109 Bo Jackson .... 1.00 .40
❑ 110 Cory Snyder .... .10 .04
❑ 111 Jim Lindeman .... .15 .06
❑ 112 Kirby Puckett...................... .40 .16
❑ 113 Barry Bonds 15.00 6.00
❑ 114 Roger Clemens .... 1.00 .40
❑ 115 Oddibe McDowell .... .10 .04
❑ 116 Bret Saberhagen .... .15 .06
❑ 117 Joe Magrane .... .10 .04
❑ 118 Scott Fletcher .... .10 .04
❑ 119 Mark McLemore .... .15 .06
❑ 120 Joe Niekro.......................... .15 .06
Who Me
❑ 121 Mark McGwire............. 10.00 4.00
❑ 122 Darryl Strawberry .... .25 .10
❑ 123 Mike Scott.......................... .10 .04
❑ 124 Andre Dawson .... .15 .06
❑ 125 Jose Canseco .... .60 .24
❑ 126 Kevin McReynolds .... .10 .04
❑ 127 Joe Carter .... 2.00 .80
❑ 128 Casey Candaele.................. .10 .04
❑ 129 Matt Nokes .... .40 .16
❑ 130 Kal Daniels .... .10 .04
❑ 131 Pete Incaviglia.................... .40 .16
❑ 132 Benito Santiago.................. .60 .24
❑ 133 Barry Larkin.................... 2.00 .80
❑ 134 Gary Pettis.......................... .10 .04
❑ 135 B.J. Surhoff........................ .60 .24
❑ 136 Juan Nieves........................ .10 .04
❑ 137 Jim Deshaies...................... .10 .04
❑ 138 Pete O'Brien .... .10 .04
❑ 139 Kevin Seitzer .... .40 .16
❑ 140 Devon White .... .60 .24
❑ 141 Rob Deer .... .10 .04
❑ 142 Kurt Stillwell .... .10 .04
❑ 143 Edwin Correa...................... .10 .04
❑ 144 Dion James......................... .10 .04
❑ 145 Danny Tartabull................... .10 .04
❑ 146 Jerry Browne....................... .15 .06
❑ 147 Ted Higuera........................ .10 .04
❑ 148 Jack Clark .... .10 .04
❑ 149 Ruben Sierra .... .60 .24
❑ 150 Mark McGwire and .... 1.00 .40
Eric Davis

1989 Classic Travel Orange

	Nm-Mt	Ex-Mt
COMP.FACT.SET (50)	15.00	6.00

❑ 101 Gary Sheffield .... 1.50 .60
❑ 102 Wade Boggs .... .15 .06

❑ 103 Jose Canseco .25 .10
❑ 104 Mark McGwire 1.00 .40
❑ 105 Orel Hershiser .10 .04
❑ 106 Don Mattingly .60 .24
❑ 107 Dwight Gooden .15 .06
❑ 108 Darryl Strawberry .15 .06
❑ 109 Eric Davis .10 .04
❑ 110 H.Meulens UER .05 .02
Listed on card as
Bam Bam Muelens
❑ 111 Andy Van Slyke .10 .04
❑ 112 Al Leiter .10 .04
❑ 113 Matt Nokes .05 .02
❑ 114 Mike Krukow .05 .02
❑ 115 Tony Fernandez .05 .02
❑ 116 Fred McGriff .25 .10
❑ 117 Barry Bonds 1.25 .50
❑ 118 Gerald Perry .05 .02
❑ 119 Roger Clemens .50 .20
❑ 120 Kirk Gibson .10 .04
❑ 121 Greg Maddux .60 .24
❑ 122 Bo Jackson .25 .10
❑ 123 Danny Jackson .05 .02
❑ 124 Dale Murphy .25 .10
❑ 125 David Cone .10 .04
❑ 126 Tom Browning .05 .02
❑ 127 Roberto Alomar .25 .10
❑ 128 Alan Trammell .15 .06
❑ 129 Ricky Jordan UER .05 .02
(Misspelled Jordon
on card back)
❑ 130 Ramon Martinez .25 .10
❑ 131 Ken Griffey Jr. 8.00 3.20
❑ 132 Gregg Olson .25 .10
❑ 133 Carlos Quintana .05 .02
❑ 134 Dave West .05 .02
❑ 135 Cameron Drew .05 .02
❑ 136 Teddy Higuera .05 .02
❑ 137 Sil Campusano .05 .02
❑ 138 Mark Gubicza .05 .02
❑ 139 Mike Boddicker .05 .02
❑ 140 Paul Gibson .05 .02
❑ 141 Jose Rijo .05 .02
❑ 142 John Costello .05 .02
❑ 143 Cecil Espy .05 .02
❑ 144 Frank Viola .05 .02
❑ 145 Erik Hanson .05 .02
❑ 146 Juan Samuel .05 .02
❑ 147 Harold Reynolds .10 .04
❑ 148 Joe Magrane .05 .02
❑ 149 Mike Greenwell .05 .02
❑ 150 Darryl Strawberry .10 .04
and Will Clark

1989 Classic Travel Purple

	Nm-Mt	Ex-Mt
COMP.FACT.SET (50)	12.00	4.80

❑ 151 Jim Abbott .40 .16
❑ 152 Ellis Burks .15 .06
❑ 153 Mike Schmidt .50 .20
❑ 154 Gregg Jefferies .10 .04
❑ 155 Mark Grace .25 .10
❑ 156 Jerome Walton .15 .06
❑ 157 Bo Jackson .25 .10
❑ 158 Jack Clark .05 .02
❑ 159 Tom Glavine .25 .10
❑ 160 Eddie Murray .25 .10
❑ 161 John Dopson .05 .02
❑ 162 Ruben Sierra .05 .02
❑ 163 Rafael Palmeiro .25 .10
❑ 164 Nolan Ryan 1.00 .40
❑ 165 Barry Larkin .25 .10
❑ 166 Tommy Herr .05 .02
❑ 167 Roberto Kelly .10 .04
❑ 168 Glenn Davis .05 .02
❑ 169 Glenn Braggs .05 .02
❑ 170 Juan Bell .05 .02
❑ 171 Todd Burns .05 .02
❑ 172 Derek Lilliquist .05 .02
❑ 173 Orel Hershiser .10 .04
❑ 174 John Smoltz .75 .30
❑ 175 Ozzie Guillen and .05 .02
Ellis Burks
❑ 176 Kirby Puckett .25 .10
❑ 177 Robin Ventura .75 .30
❑ 178 Allan Anderson .05 .02
❑ 179 Steve Sax .05 .02
❑ 180 Will Clark .25 .10
❑ 181 Mike Devereaux .05 .02
❑ 182 Tom Gordon .25 .10
❑ 183 Rob Murphy .05 .02
❑ 184 Pete O'Brien .05 .02
❑ 185 Cris Carpenter .05 .02
❑ 186 Tom Brunansky .05 .02
❑ 187 Bob Boone .10 .04
❑ 188 Lou Whitaker .10 .04
❑ 189 Dwight Gooden .15 .06
❑ 190 Mark McGwire 1.00 .40
❑ 191 John Smiley .05 .02
❑ 192 Tommy Gregg .05 .02
❑ 193 Ken Griffey Jr. 8.00 3.20
❑ 194 Bruce Hurst .05 .02
❑ 195 Greg Swindell .05 .02
❑ 196 Nelson Liriano .05 .02
❑ 197 Randy Myers .10 .04
❑ 198 Kevin Mitchell .10 .04
❑ 199 Dante Bichette .25 .10
❑ 200 Deion Sanders .50 .20

1994 Collector's Choice

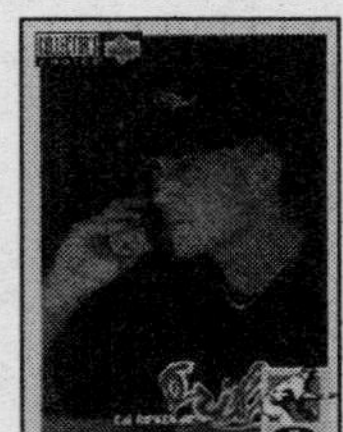

	Nm-Mt	Ex-Mt
COMPLETE SET (670)	25.00	7.50
COMP.FACT.SET (675)	30.00	9.00
COMP. SERIES 1 (320)	10.00	3.00
COMP. SERIES 2 (350)	15.00	4.50

❑ 1 Rich Becker .10 .03
❑ 2 Greg Blosser .10 .03
❑ 3 Midre Cummings .10 .03
❑ 4 Carlos Delgado .30 .09
❑ 5 Steve Dreyer RC .10 .03
❑ 6 Carl Everett .20 .06
❑ 7 Cliff Floyd .20 .06
❑ 8 Alex Gonzalez .10 .03
❑ 9 Shawn Green .50 .15
❑ 10 Butch Huskey .10 .03
❑ 11 Mark Hutton .10 .03
❑ 12 Miguel Jimenez .10 .03
❑ 13 Steve Karsay .10 .03
❑ 14 Marc Newfield .10 .03
❑ 15 Luis Ortiz .10 .03
❑ 16 Manny Ramirez .30 .09
❑ 17 Johnny Ruffin .10 .03
❑ 18 Scott Stahoviak .10 .03
❑ 19 Salomon Torres .10 .03
❑ 20 Gabe White .10 .03
❑ 21 Brian Anderson RC .25 .07
❑ 22 Wayne Gomes RC .10 .03
❑ 23 Jeff Granger .10 .03
❑ 24 Steve Soderstrom RC .10 .03
❑ 25 Trot Nixon RC .50 .15
❑ 26 Kirk Presley RC .10 .03
❑ 27 Matt Brunson RC .10 .03
❑ 28 Brooks Kieschnick RC .25 .07
❑ 29 Billy Wagner RC .50 .15
❑ 30 Matt Drews RC .10 .03
❑ 31 Kurt Abbott RC .25 .07
❑ 32 Luis Alicea .10 .03
❑ 33 Roberto Alomar .50 .15
❑ 34 Sandy Alomar Jr. .10 .03
❑ 35 Moises Alou .20 .06
❑ 36 Wilson Alvarez .10 .03
❑ 37 Rich Amaral .10 .03
❑ 38 Eric Anthony .10 .03
❑ 39 Luis Aquino .10 .03
❑ 40 Jack Armstrong .10 .03
❑ 41 Rene Arocha .10 .03
❑ 42 Rich Aude RC .10 .03
❑ 43 Brad Ausmus .10 .03
❑ 44 Steve Avery .10 .03
❑ 45 Bob Ayrault .10 .03
❑ 46 Willie Banks .10 .03
❑ 47 Bret Barberie .10 .03
❑ 48 Kim Batiste .10 .03
❑ 49 Rod Beck .10 .03
❑ 50 Jason Bere .10 .03
❑ 51 Sean Berry .10 .03
❑ 52 Dante Bichette .20 .06
❑ 53 Jeff Blauser .10 .03
❑ 54 Mike Blowers .10 .03
❑ 55 Tim Bogar .10 .03
❑ 56 Tom Bolton .10 .03
❑ 57 Ricky Bones .10 .03
❑ 58 Bobby Bonilla .20 .06
❑ 59 Bret Boone .20 .06
❑ 60 Pat Borders .10 .03
❑ 61 Mike Bordick .10 .03
❑ 62 Daryl Boston .10 .03
❑ 63 Ryan Bowen .10 .03
❑ 64 Jeff Branson .10 .03
❑ 65 George Brett 1.25 .35
❑ 66 Steve Buechele .10 .03
❑ 67 Dave Burba .10 .03
❑ 68 John Burkett .10 .03
❑ 69 Jeromy Burnitz .20 .06
❑ 70 Brett Butler .20 .06
❑ 71 Rob Butler .10 .03
❑ 72 Ken Caminiti .20 .06
❑ 73 Cris Carpenter .10 .03
❑ 74 Vinny Castilla .20 .06
❑ 75 Andujar Cedeno .10 .03
❑ 76 Wes Chamberlain .10 .03
❑ 77 Archi Cianfrocco .10 .03
❑ 78 Dave Clark .10 .03
❑ 79 Jerald Clark .10 .03
❑ 80 Royce Clayton .10 .03
❑ 81 David Cone .20 .06
❑ 82 Jeff Conine .20 .06
❑ 83 Steve Cooke .10 .03
❑ 84 Scott Cooper .10 .03
❑ 85 Joey Cora .10 .03
❑ 86 Tim Costo .10 .03

❑ 87 Chad Curtis .10 .03
❑ 88 Ron Darling .10 .03
❑ 89 Danny Darwin .10 .03
❑ 90 Rob Deer .10 .03
❑ 91 Jim Deshaies .10 .03
❑ 92 Delino DeShields .10 .03
❑ 93 Rob Dibble .20 .06
❑ 94 Gary DiSarcina .10 .03
❑ 95 Doug Drabek .10 .03
❑ 96 Scott Erickson .10 .03
❑ 97 Rikkert Faneyte RC .10 .03
❑ 98 Jeff Fassero .10 .03
❑ 99 Alex Fernandez .10 .03
❑ 100 Cecil Fielder .20 .06
❑ 101 Dave Fleming .10 .03
❑ 102 Darrin Fletcher .10 .03
❑ 103 Scott Fletcher .10 .03
❑ 104 Mike Gallego .10 .03
❑ 105 Carlos Garcia .10 .03
❑ 106 Jeff Gardner .10 .03
❑ 107 Brent Gates .10 .03
❑ 108 Benji Gil .10 .03
❑ 109 Bernard Gilkey .10 .03
❑ 110 Chris Gomez .10 .03
❑ 111 Luis Gonzalez .20 .06
❑ 112 Tom Gordon .10 .03
❑ 113 Jim Gott .10 .03
❑ 114 Mark Grace .50 .15
❑ 115 Tommy Greene .10 .03
❑ 116 Willie Greene .10 .03
❑ 117 Ken Griffey Jr. .75 .23
❑ 118 Bill Gullickson .10 .03
❑ 119 Ricky Gutierrez .10 .03
❑ 120 Juan Guzman .10 .03
❑ 121 Chris Gwynn .10 .03
❑ 122 Tony Gwynn .60 .18
❑ 123 Jeffrey Hammonds .10 .03
❑ 124 Erik Hanson .10 .03
❑ 125 Gene Harris .10 .03
❑ 126 Greg W. Harris .10 .03
❑ 127 Bryan Harvey .10 .03
❑ 128 Billy Hatcher .10 .03
❑ 129 Hilly Hathaway .10 .03
❑ 130 Charlie Hayes .10 .03
❑ 131 Rickey Henderson .75 .23
❑ 132 Mike Henneman .10 .03
❑ 133 Pat Hentgen .10 .03
❑ 134 Roberto Hernandez .10 .03
❑ 135 Orel Hershiser .20 .06
❑ 136 Phil Hiatt .10 .03
❑ 137 Glenallen Hill .10 .03
❑ 138 Ken Hill .10 .03
❑ 139 Eric Hillman .10 .03
❑ 140 Chris Hoiles .10 .03
❑ 141 Dave Hollins .10 .03
❑ 142 David Hulse .10 .03
❑ 143 Todd Hundley .10 .03
❑ 144 Pete Incaviglia .10 .03
❑ 145 Danny Jackson .10 .03
❑ 146 John Jaha .10 .03
❑ 147 Domingo Jean .10 .03
❑ 148 Gregg Jefferies .10 .03
❑ 149 Reggie Jefferson .10 .03
❑ 150 Lance Johnson .10 .03
❑ 151 Bobby Jones .10 .03
❑ 152 Chipper Jones .50 .15
❑ 153 Todd Jones .10 .03
❑ 154 Brian Jordan .20 .06
❑ 155 Wally Joyner .20 .06
❑ 156 David Justice .20 .06
❑ 157 Ron Karkovice .10 .03
❑ 158 Eric Karros .20 .06
❑ 159 Jeff Kent .20 .06
❑ 160 Jimmy Key .20 .06
❑ 161 Mark Kiefer .10 .03
❑ 162 Darryl Kile .20 .06
❑ 163 Jeff King .10 .03
❑ 164 Wayne Kirby .10 .03
❑ 165 Ryan Klesko .20 .06
❑ 166 Chuck Knoblauch .20 .06
❑ 167 Chad Kreuter .10 .03
❑ 168 John Kruk .20 .06
❑ 169 Mark Langston .10 .03
❑ 170 Mike Lansing .10 .03
❑ 171 Barry Larkin .50 .15
❑ 172 Manuel Lee .10 .03
❑ 173 Phil Leftwich RC .10 .03
❑ 174 Darren Lewis .10 .03
❑ 175 Derek Lilliquist .10 .03
❑ 176 Jose Lind .10 .03
❑ 177 Albie Lopez .10 .03
❑ 178 Javier Lopez .20 .06
❑ 179 Torey Lovullo .10 .03
❑ 180 Scott Lydy .10 .03
❑ 181 Mike Macfarlane .10 .03
❑ 182 Shane Mack .10 .03
❑ 183 Greg Maddux 1.00 .30
❑ 184 Dave Magadan .10 .03
❑ 185 Joe Magrane .10 .03
❑ 186 Kirk Manwaring .10 .03
❑ 187 Al Martin .10 .03
❑ 188 Pedro A. Martinez RC .10 .03
❑ 189 Pedro Martinez .50 .15
❑ 190 Ramon Martinez .10 .03
❑ 191 Tino Martinez .30 .09
❑ 192 Don Mattingly 1.25 .35
❑ 193 Derrick May .10 .03
❑ 194 David McCarty .10 .03
❑ 195 Ben McDonald .10 .03
❑ 196 Roger McDowell .10 .03
❑ 197 Fred McGriff UER .30 .09
(Stats on back have 73 stolen bases for 1989; should be 7)
❑ 198 Mark McLemore .10 .03
❑ 199 Greg McMichael .10 .03
❑ 200 Jeff McNeely .10 .03
❑ 201 Brian McRae .10 .03
❑ 202 Pat Meares .10 .03
❑ 203 Roberto Mejia .10 .03
❑ 204 Orlando Merced .10 .03
❑ 205 Jose Mesa .10 .03
❑ 206 Blas Minor .10 .03
❑ 207 Angel Miranda .10 .03
❑ 208 Paul Molitor .30 .09
❑ 209 Raul Mondesi .20 .06
❑ 210 Jeff Montgomery .10 .03
❑ 211 Mickey Morandini .10 .03
❑ 212 Mike Morgan .10 .03
❑ 213 Jamie Moyer .20 .06
❑ 214 Bobby Munoz .10 .03
❑ 215 Troy Neel .10 .03
❑ 216 Dave Nilsson .10 .03
❑ 217 John O'Donoghue .10 .03
❑ 218 Paul O'Neill .30 .09
❑ 219 Jose Offerman .10 .03
❑ 220 Joe Oliver .10 .03
❑ 221 Greg Olson .10 .03
❑ 222 Donovan Osborne .10 .03
❑ 223 Jayhawk Owens .10 .03
❑ 224 Mike Pagliarulo .10 .03
❑ 225 Craig Paquette .10 .03
❑ 226 Roger Pavlik .10 .03
❑ 227 Brad Pennington .10 .03
❑ 228 Eduardo Perez .10 .03
❑ 229 Mike Perez .10 .03
❑ 230 Tony Phillips .10 .03
❑ 231 Hipolito Pichardo .10 .03
❑ 232 Phil Plantier .10 .03
❑ 233 Curtis Pride RC .25 .07
❑ 234 Tim Pugh .10 .03
❑ 235 Scott Radinsky .10 .03
❑ 236 Pat Rapp .10 .03
❑ 237 Kevin Reimer .10 .03
❑ 238 Armando Reynoso .10 .03
❑ 239 Jose Rijo .10 .03
❑ 240 Cal Ripken 1.50 .45
❑ 241 Kevin Roberson .10 .03
❑ 242 Kenny Rogers .20 .06
❑ 243 Kevin Rogers .10 .03
❑ 244 Mel Rojas .10 .03
❑ 245 John Roper .10 .03
❑ 246 Kirk Rueter .20 .06
❑ 247 Scott Ruffcorn .10 .03
❑ 248 Ken Ryan .10 .03
❑ 249 Nolan Ryan 2.00 .60
❑ 250 Bret Saberhagen .20 .06
❑ 251 Tim Salmon .30 .09
❑ 252 Reggie Sanders .20 .06
❑ 253 Curt Schilling .30 .09
❑ 254 David Segui .10 .03
❑ 255 Aaron Sele .10 .03
❑ 256 Scott Servais .10 .03
❑ 257 Gary Sheffield .20 .06
❑ 258 Ruben Sierra .10 .03
❑ 259 Don Slaught .10 .03
❑ 260 Lee Smith .20 .06
❑ 261 Cory Snyder .10 .03
❑ 262 Paul Sorrento .10 .03
❑ 263 Sammy Sosa .75 .23
❑ 264 Bill Spiers .10 .03
❑ 265 Mike Stanley .10 .03
❑ 266 Dave Staton .10 .03
❑ 267 Terry Steinbach .10 .03
❑ 268 Kevin Stocker .10 .03
❑ 269 Todd Stottlemyre .10 .03
❑ 270 Doug Strange .10 .03
❑ 271 Bill Swift .10 .03
❑ 272 Kevin Tapani .10 .03
❑ 273 Tony Tarasco .10 .03
❑ 274 Julian Tavarez RC .10 .03
❑ 275 Mickey Tettleton .10 .03
❑ 276 Ryan Thompson .10 .03
❑ 277 Chris Turner .10 .03
❑ 278 John Valentin .10 .03
❑ 279 Todd Van Poppel .10 .03
❑ 280 Andy Van Slyke .20 .06
❑ 281 Mo Vaughn .20 .06
❑ 282 Robin Ventura .20 .06
❑ 283 Frank Viola .20 .06
❑ 284 Jose Vizcaino .10 .03
❑ 285 Omar Vizquel .20 .06
❑ 286 Larry Walker .30 .09
❑ 287 Duane Ward .10 .03
❑ 288 Allen Watson .10 .03
❑ 289 Bill Wegman .10 .03
❑ 290 Turk Wendell .10 .03
❑ 291 Lou Whitaker .20 .06
❑ 292 Devon White .10 .03
❑ 293 Rondell White .20 .06
❑ 294 Mark Whiten .10 .03
❑ 295 Darrel Whitmore .10 .03
❑ 296 Bob Wickman .10 .03
❑ 297 Rick Wilkins .10 .03
❑ 298 Bernie Williams .30 .09
❑ 299 Matt Williams .20 .06
❑ 300 Woody Williams .20 .06
❑ 301 Nigel Wilson .10 .03
❑ 302 Dave Winfield .30 .09
❑ 303 Anthony Young .10 .03
❑ 304 Eric Young .10 .03
❑ 305 Todd Zeile .10 .03
❑ 306 Jack McDowell TP .10 .03
John Burkett
Tom Glavine
❑ 307 Randy Johnson TP .30 .09
❑ 308 Randy Myers TP .10 .03
❑ 309 Jack McDowell TP .10 .03
❑ 310 Mike Piazza TP .50 .15
❑ 311 Barry Bonds TP .60 .18
❑ 312 Andres Galarraga TP .10 .03
❑ 313 Juan Gonzalez TP .60 .18
Barry Bonds
❑ 314 Albert Belle TP .20 .06
❑ 315 Kenny Lofton TP .10 .03
❑ 316 Barry Bonds CL .60 .18
❑ 317 Ken Griffey Jr. CL .50 .15
❑ 318 Mike Piazza CL .50 .15
❑ 319 Kirby Puckett CL .30 .09
❑ 320 Nolan Ryan CL .50 .15
❑ 321 Roberto Alomar CL .20 .06
❑ 322 Roger Clemens CL .50 .15
❑ 323 Juan Gonzalez CL .30 .09
❑ 324 Ken Griffey Jr. CL .50 .15
❑ 325 David Justice CL .10 .03
❑ 326 John Kruk CL .10 .03
❑ 327 Frank Thomas CL .20 .06
❑ 328 Tim Salmon TC .20 .06
❑ 329 Jeff Bagwell TC .20 .06
❑ 330 Mark McGwire TC .60 .18
❑ 331 Roberto Alomar TC .20 .06
❑ 332 David Justice TC .10 .03
❑ 333 Pat Listach TC .10 .03
❑ 334 Ozzie Smith TC .30 .09
❑ 335 Ryne Sandberg TC .50 .15
❑ 336 Mike Piazza TC .50 .15
❑ 337 Cliff Floyd TC .10 .03
❑ 338 Barry Bonds TC .60 .18

❑ 339 Albert Belle TC .20 .06
❑ 340 Ken Griffey Jr. TC .50 .15
❑ 341 Gary Sheffield TC .10 .03
❑ 342 Dwight Gooden TC .20 .06
❑ 343 Cal Ripken TC .75 .23
❑ 344 Tony Gwynn TC .30 .09
❑ 345 Lenny Dykstra TC .10 .03
❑ 346 Andy Van Slyke TC .10 .03
❑ 347 Juan Gonzalez TC .30 .09
❑ 348 Roger Clemens TC .50 .15
❑ 349 Barry Larkin TC .20 .06
❑ 350 Andres Galarraga TC .10 .03
❑ 351 Kevin Appier TC .10 .03
❑ 352 Cecil Fielder TC .10 .03
❑ 353 Kirby Puckett TC .30 .09
❑ 354 Frank Thomas TC .30 .09
❑ 355 Don Mattingly TC .60 .18
❑ 356 Bo Jackson .50 .15
❑ 357 Randy Johnson .50 .15
❑ 358 Darren Daulton .20 .06
❑ 359 Charlie Hough .20 .06
❑ 360 Andres Galarraga .20 .06
❑ 361 Mike Felder .10 .03
❑ 362 Chris Hammond .10 .03
❑ 363 Shawon Dunston .10 .03
❑ 364 Junior Felix .10 .03
❑ 365 Ray Lankford .10 .03
❑ 366 Darryl Strawberry .30 .09
❑ 367 Dave Magadan .10 .03
❑ 368 Gregg Olson .10 .03
❑ 369 Lenny Dykstra .20 .06
❑ 370 Darrin Jackson .10 .03
❑ 371 Dave Stewart .20 .06
❑ 372 Terry Pendleton .20 .06
❑ 373 Arthur Rhodes .10 .03
❑ 374 Benito Santiago .20 .06
❑ 375 Travis Fryman .20 .06
❑ 376 Scott Brosius .20 .06
❑ 377 Stan Belinda .10 .03
❑ 378 Derek Parks .10 .03
❑ 379 Kevin Seitzer .10 .03
❑ 380 Wade Boggs .30 .09
❑ 381 Wally Whitehurst .10 .03
❑ 382 Scott Leius .10 .03
❑ 383 Danny Tartabull .10 .03
❑ 384 Harold Reynolds .20 .06
❑ 385 Tim Raines .20 .06
❑ 386 Darryl Hamilton .10 .03
❑ 387 Felix Fermin .10 .03
❑ 388 Jim Eisenreich .10 .03
❑ 389 Kurt Abbott .20 .06
❑ 390 Kevin Appier .20 .06
❑ 391 Chris Bosio .10 .03
❑ 392 Randy Tomlin .10 .03
❑ 393 Bob Hamelin .10 .03
❑ 394 Kevin Gross .10 .03
❑ 395 Wil Cordero .10 .03
❑ 396 Joe Girardi .10 .03
❑ 397 Orestes Destrade .10 .03
❑ 398 Chris Haney .10 .03
❑ 399 Xavier Hernandez .10 .03
❑ 400 Mike Piazza 1.00 .30
❑ 401 Alex Arias .10 .03
❑ 402 Tom Candiotti .10 .03
❑ 403 Kirk Gibson .20 .06
❑ 404 Chuck Carr .10 .03
❑ 405 Brady Anderson .20 .06
❑ 406 Greg Gagne .10 .03
❑ 407 Bruce Ruffin .10 .03
❑ 408 Scott Hemond .10 .03
❑ 409 Keith Miller .10 .03
❑ 410 John Wetteland .20 .06
❑ 411 Eric Anthony .10 .03
❑ 412 Andre Dawson .20 .06
❑ 413 Doug Henry .10 .03
❑ 414 John Franco .20 .06
❑ 415 Julio Franco .20 .06
❑ 416 Dave Hansen .10 .03
❑ 417 Mike Harkey .10 .03
❑ 418 Jack Armstrong .10 .03
❑ 419 Joe Orsulak .10 .03
❑ 420 John Smoltz .30 .09
❑ 421 Scott Livingstone .10 .03
❑ 422 Darren Holmes .10 .03
❑ 423 Ed Sprague .10 .03
❑ 424 Jay Buhner .20 .06
❑ 425 Kirby Puckett .50 .15
❑ 426 Phil Clark .10 .03
❑ 427 Anthony Young .10 .03
❑ 428 Reggie Jefferson .10 .03
❑ 429 Mariano Duncan .10 .03
❑ 430 Tom Glavine .50 .15
❑ 431 Dave Henderson .10 .03
❑ 432 Melido Perez .10 .03
❑ 433 Paul Wagner .10 .03
❑ 434 Tim Worrell .10 .03
❑ 435 Ozzie Guillen .10 .03
❑ 436 Mike Butcher .10 .03
❑ 437 Jim Deshaies .10 .03
❑ 438 Kevin Young .10 .03
❑ 439 Tom Browning .10 .03
❑ 440 Mike Greenwell .10 .03
❑ 441 Mike Stanton .10 .03
❑ 442 John Doherty .10 .03
❑ 443 John Dopson .10 .03
❑ 444 Carlos Baerga .10 .03
❑ 445 Jack McDowell .10 .03
❑ 446 Kent Mercker .10 .03
❑ 447 Ricky Jordan .10 .03
❑ 448 Jerry Browne .10 .03
❑ 449 Fernando Vina .30 .09
❑ 450 Jim Abbott .50 .15
❑ 451 Teddy Higuera .10 .03
❑ 452 Tim Naehring .10 .03
❑ 453 Jim Leyritz .10 .03
❑ 454 Frank Castillo .10 .03
❑ 455 Joe Carter .20 .06
❑ 456 Craig Biggio .30 .09
❑ 457 Geronimo Pena .10 .03
❑ 458 Alejandro Pena .10 .03
❑ 459 Mike Moore .10 .03
❑ 460 Randy Myers .10 .03
❑ 461 Greg Myers .10 .03
❑ 462 Greg Hibbard .10 .03
❑ 463 Jose Guzman .10 .03
❑ 464 Tom Pagnozzi .10 .03
❑ 465 Marquis Grissom .10 .03
❑ 466 Tim Wallach .10 .03
❑ 467 Joe Grahe .10 .03
❑ 468 Bob Tewksbury .10 .03
❑ 469 B.J. Surhoff .20 .06
❑ 470 Kevin Mitchell .10 .03
❑ 471 Bobby Witt .10 .03
❑ 472 Milt Thompson .10 .03
❑ 473 John Smiley .10 .03
❑ 474 Alan Trammell .30 .09
❑ 475 Mike Mussina .50 .15
❑ 476 Rick Aguilera .10 .03
❑ 477 Jose Valentin .10 .03
❑ 478 Harold Baines .20 .06
❑ 479 Bip Roberts .10 .03
❑ 480 Edgar Martinez .30 .09
❑ 481 Rheal Cormier .10 .03
❑ 482 Hal Morris .10 .03
❑ 483 Pat Kelly .10 .03
❑ 484 Roberto Kelly .10 .03
❑ 485 Chris Sabo .10 .03
❑ 486 Kent Hrbek .20 .06
❑ 487 Scott Kamieniecki .10 .03
❑ 488 Walt Weiss .10 .03
❑ 489 Karl Rhodes .10 .03
❑ 490 Derek Bell .10 .03
❑ 491 Chili Davis .20 .06
❑ 492 Brian Harper .10 .03
❑ 493 Felix Jose .10 .03
❑ 494 Trevor Hoffman .20 .06
❑ 495 Dennis Eckersley .20 .06
❑ 496 Pedro Astacio .10 .03
❑ 497 Jay Bell .20 .06
❑ 498 Randy Velarde .10 .03
❑ 499 David Wells .20 .06
❑ 500 Frank Thomas .50 .15
❑ 501 Mark Lemke .10 .03
❑ 502 Mike Devereaux .10 .03
❑ 503 Chuck McElroy .10 .03
❑ 504 Luis Polonia .10 .03
❑ 505 Damion Easley .10 .03
❑ 506 Greg A. Harris .10 .03
❑ 507 Chris James .10 .03
❑ 508 Terry Mulholland .10 .03
❑ 509 Pete Smith .10 .03
❑ 510 Rickey Henderson .75 .23
❑ 511 Sid Fernandez .10 .03
❑ 512 Al Leiter .20 .06
❑ 513 Doug Jones .10 .03
❑ 514 Steve Farr .10 .03
❑ 515 Chuck Finley .20 .06
❑ 516 Bobby Thigpen .10 .03
❑ 517 Jim Edmonds .30 .09
❑ 518 Graeme Lloyd .10 .03
❑ 519 Dwight Gooden .30 .09
❑ 520 Pat Listach .10 .03
❑ 521 Kevin Bass .10 .03
❑ 522 Willie Banks .10 .03
❑ 523 Steve Finley .20 .06
❑ 524 Delino DeShields .10 .03
❑ 525 Mark McGwire 1.25 .35
❑ 526 Greg Swindell .10 .03
❑ 527 Chris Nabholz .10 .03
❑ 528 Scott Sanders .10 .03
❑ 529 David Segui .10 .03
❑ 530 Howard Johnson .10 .03
❑ 531 Jaime Navarro .10 .03
❑ 532 Jose Vizcaino .10 .03
❑ 533 Mark Lewis .10 .03
❑ 534 Pete Harnisch .10 .03
❑ 535 Robby Thompson .10 .03
❑ 536 Marcus Moore .10 .03
❑ 537 Kevin Brown .20 .06
❑ 538 Mark Clark .10 .03
❑ 539 Sterling Hitchcock .10 .03
❑ 540 Will Clark .50 .15
❑ 541 Denis Boucher .10 .03
❑ 542 Jack Morris .20 .06
❑ 543 Pedro Munoz .10 .03
❑ 544 Bret Boone .20 .06
❑ 545 Ozzie Smith .50 .15
❑ 546 Dennis Martinez .20 .06
❑ 547 Dan Wilson .10 .03
❑ 548 Rick Sutcliffe .20 .06
❑ 549 Kevin McReynolds .10 .03
❑ 550 Roger Clemens 1.00 .30
❑ 551 Todd Benzinger .10 .03
❑ 552 Bill Haselman .10 .03
❑ 553 Bobby Munoz .10 .03
❑ 554 Ellis Burks .20 .06
❑ 555 Ryne Sandberg .75 .23
❑ 556 Lee Smith .20 .06
❑ 557 Danny Bautista .10 .03
❑ 558 Rey Sanchez .10 .03
❑ 559 Norm Charlton .10 .03
❑ 560 Jose Canseco .50 .15
❑ 561 Tim Belcher .10 .03
❑ 562 Denny Neagle .20 .06
❑ 563 Eric Davis .20 .06
❑ 564 Jody Reed .10 .03
❑ 565 Kenny Lofton .20 .06
❑ 566 Gary Gaetti .20 .06
❑ 567 Todd Worrell .10 .03
❑ 568 Mark Portugal .10 .03
❑ 569 Dick Schofield .10 .03
❑ 570 Andy Benes .10 .03
❑ 571 Zane Smith .10 .03
❑ 572 Bobby Ayala .10 .03
❑ 573 Chip Hale .10 .03
❑ 574 Bob Welch .10 .03
❑ 575 Deion Sanders .20 .06
❑ 576 David Nied .10 .03
❑ 577 Pat Mahomes .10 .03
❑ 578 Charles Nagy .10 .03
❑ 579 Otis Nixon .10 .03
❑ 580 Dean Palmer .20 .06
❑ 581 Roberto Petagine .10 .03
❑ 582 Dwight Smith .10 .03
❑ 583 Jeff Russell .10 .03
❑ 584 Mark Dewey .10 .03
❑ 585 Greg Vaughn .20 .06
❑ 586 Brian Hunter .10 .03
❑ 587 Willie McGee .20 .06
❑ 588 Pedro Martinez .50 .15
❑ 589 Roger Salkeld .10 .03
❑ 590 Jeff Bagwell .30 .09
❑ 591 Spike Owen .10 .03
❑ 592 Jeff Reardon .20 .06
❑ 593 Erik Pappas .10 .03
❑ 594 Brian Williams .10 .03
❑ 595 Eddie Murray .50 .15
❑ 596 Henry Rodriguez .10 .03

❑ 597	Erik Hanson	.10	.03
❑ 598	Stan Javier	.10	.03
❑ 599	Mitch Williams	.10	.03
❑ 600	John Olerud	.20	.06
❑ 601	Vince Coleman	.10	.03
❑ 602	Damon Berryhill	.10	.03
❑ 603	Tom Brunansky	.10	.03
❑ 604	Robb Nen	.20	.06
❑ 605	Rafael Palmeiro	.30	.09
❑ 606	Cal Eldred	.10	.03
❑ 607	Jeff Brantley	.10	.03
❑ 608	Alan Mills	.10	.03
❑ 609	Jeff Nelson	.10	.03
❑ 610	Barry Bonds	1.25	.35
❑ 611	Carlos Pulido RC	.10	.03
❑ 612	Tim Hyers RC	.10	.03
❑ 613	Steve Howe	.10	.03
❑ 614	Brian Turang RC	.10	.03
❑ 615	Leo Gomez	.10	.03
❑ 616	Jesse Orosco	.10	.03
❑ 617	Dan Pasqua	.10	.03
❑ 618	Marvin Freeman	.10	.03
❑ 619	Tony Fernandez	.10	.03
❑ 620	Albert Belle	.20	.06
❑ 621	Eddie Taubensee	.10	.03
❑ 622	Mike Jackson	.10	.03
❑ 623	Jose Bautista	.10	.03
❑ 624	Jim Thome	.50	.15
❑ 625	Ivan Rodriguez	.50	.15
❑ 626	Ben Rivera	.10	.03
❑ 627	Dave Valle	.10	.03
❑ 628	Tom Henke	.10	.03
❑ 629	Omar Vizquel	.20	.06
❑ 630	Juan Gonzalez	.50	.15
❑ 631	Roberto Alomar UP	.20	.06
❑ 632	Barry Bonds UP	.60	.18
❑ 633	Juan Gonzalez UP	.30	.09
❑ 634	Ken Griffey Jr. UP	.50	.15
❑ 635	Michael Jordan UP	1.50	.45
❑ 636	David Justice UP	.10	.03
❑ 637	Mike Piazza UP	.50	.15
❑ 638	Kirby Puckett UP	.30	.09
❑ 639	Tim Salmon UP	.20	.06
❑ 640	Frank Thomas UP	.30	.09
❑ 641	Alan Benes FF RC	.10	.03
❑ 642	Johnny Damon FF	.50	.15
❑ 643	Brad Fullmer FF RC	.50	.15
❑ 644	Derek Jeter FF	1.50	.45
❑ 645	Derrek Lee FF RC	.50	.15
❑ 646	Alex Ochoa	.10	.03
❑ 647	Alex Rodriguez FF RC	10.00	3.00
❑ 648	Jose Silva FF RC	.10	.03
❑ 649	Terrell Wade FF RC	.10	.03
❑ 650	Preston Wilson FF	.30	.09
❑ 651	Shane Andrews	.10	.03
❑ 652	James Baldwin	.10	.03
❑ 653	Ricky Bottalico RC	.25	.07
❑ 654	Tavo Alvarez	.10	.03
❑ 655	Donnie Elliott	.10	.03
❑ 656	Joey Eischen	.10	.03
❑ 657	Jason Giambi	.50	.15
❑ 658	Todd Hollandsworth	.10	.03
❑ 659	Brian L. Hunter	.10	.03
❑ 660	Charles Johnson	.20	.06
❑ 661	Michael Jordan RC	3.00	.90
❑ 662	Jeff Juden	.10	.03
❑ 663	Mike Kelly	.10	.03
❑ 664	James Mouton	.10	.03
❑ 665	Ray Holbert	.10	.03
❑ 666	Pokey Reese	.10	.03
❑ 667	Ruben Santana RC	.10	.03
❑ 668	Paul Spoljaric	.10	.03
❑ 669	Luis Lopez	.10	.03
❑ 670	Matt Walbeck	.10	.03
❑ P50	Ken Griffey Jr. Promo	1.00	.30

1981 Donruss

		Nm-Mt	Ex-Mt
COMPLETE SET (605)		40.00	16.00
❑ 1	Ozzie Smith	3.00	1.20
❑ 2	Rollie Fingers	.25	.10
❑ 3	Rick Wise	.10	.04
❑ 4	Gene Richards	.10	.04
❑ 5	Alan Trammell	.50	.20
❑ 6	Tom Brookens	.10	.04
❑ 7A	Duffy Dyer P1	.25	.10
	1980 batting average has decimal point		
❑ 7B	Duffy Dyer P2	.10	.04
	1980 batting average has no decimal point		
❑ 8	Mark Fidrych	1.00	.40
❑ 9	Dave Rozema	.10	.04
❑ 10	Ricky Peters	.10	.04
❑ 11	Mike Schmidt	2.50	1.00
❑ 12	Willie Stargell	.50	.20
❑ 13	Tim Foli	.10	.04
❑ 14	Manny Sanguillen	.25	.10
❑ 15	Grant Jackson	.10	.04
❑ 16	Eddie Solomon	.10	.04
❑ 17	Omar Moreno	.10	.04
❑ 18	Joe Morgan	.50	.20
❑ 19	Rafael Landestoy	.10	.04
❑ 20	Bruce Bochy	.10	.04
❑ 21	Joe Sambito	.10	.04
❑ 22	Manny Trillo	.10	.04
❑ 23A	Dave Smith RC P1	.25	.10
	Line box around stats is not complete		
❑ 23B	Dave Smith RC P2	.25	.10
	Box totally encloses stats at top		
❑ 24	Terry Puhl	.10	.04
❑ 25	Bump Wills	.10	.04
❑ 26A	John Ellis P1 ERR	.50	.20
	Danny Walton photo on front		
❑ 26B	John Ellis P2 COR	.25	.10
❑ 27	Jim Kern	.10	.04
❑ 28	Richie Zisk	.10	.04
❑ 29	John Mayberry	.10	.04
❑ 30	Bob Davis	.10	.04
❑ 31	Jackson Todd	.10	.04
❑ 32	Alvis Woods	.10	.04
❑ 33	Steve Carlton	.50	.20
❑ 34	Lee Mazzilli	.10	.04
❑ 35	John Stearns	.10	.04
❑ 36	Roy Lee Jackson	.10	.04
❑ 37	Mike Scott	.25	.10
❑ 38	Lamar Johnson	.10	.04
❑ 39	Kevin Bell	.10	.04
❑ 40	Ed Farmer	.10	.04
❑ 41	Ross Baumgarten	.10	.04
❑ 42	Leo Sutherland	.10	.04
❑ 43	Dan Meyer	.10	.04
❑ 44	Ron Reed	.10	.04
❑ 45	Mario Mendoza	.10	.04
❑ 46	Rick Honeycutt	.10	.04
❑ 47	Glenn Abbott	.10	.04
❑ 48	Leon Roberts	.10	.04
❑ 49	Rod Carew	.50	.20
❑ 50	Bert Campaneris	.25	.10
❑ 51A	T.Donahue P1 ERR	.25	.10
	Name on front misspelled Donahue		
❑ 51B	Tom Donohue P2 COR	.10	.04
❑ 52	Dave Frost	.10	.04
❑ 53	Ed Halicki	.10	.04
❑ 54	Dan Ford	.10	.04
❑ 55	Garry Maddox	.10	.04
❑ 56A	Steve Garvey P1	.25	.10
	Surpassed 25 HR		
❑ 56B	Steve Garvey P2	.25	.10
	Surpassed 21 HR		
❑ 57	Bill Russell	.25	.10
❑ 58	Don Sutton	1.00	.40
❑ 59	Reggie Smith	.25	.10
❑ 60	Rick Monday	.25	.10
❑ 61	Ray Knight	.25	.10
❑ 62	Johnny Bench	1.00	.40
❑ 63	Mario Soto	.10	.04
❑ 64	Doug Bair	.10	.04
❑ 65	George Foster	.25	.10
❑ 66	Jeff Burroughs	.10	.04
❑ 67	Keith Hernandez	.50	.20
❑ 68	Tom Herr	.25	.10
❑ 69	Bob Forsch	.10	.04
❑ 70	John Fulgham	.10	.04
❑ 71A	Bobby Bonds P1 ERR	1.00	.40
	986 lifetime HR		
❑ 71B	Bobby Bonds P2 COR	.50	.20
	326 lifetime HR		
❑ 72A	Rennie Stennett P1	.25	.10
	Breaking broke leg		
❑ 72B	Rennie Stennett P2	.10	.04
	Word "broke" deleted		
❑ 73	Joe Strain	.10	.04
❑ 74	Ed Whitson	.10	.04
❑ 75	Tom Griffin	.10	.04
❑ 76	Billy North	.10	.04
❑ 77	Gene Garber	.10	.04
❑ 78	Mike Hargrove	.25	.10
❑ 79	Dave Rosello	.10	.04
❑ 80	Ron Hassey	.10	.04
❑ 81	Sid Monge	.10	.04
❑ 82A	J.Charboneau RC P1	1.00	.40
	'78 highlights For some reason		
❑ 82B	J.Charboneau RC P2	1.00	.40
	Phrase "For some reason" deleted		
❑ 83	Cecil Cooper	.25	.10
❑ 84	Sal Bando	.25	.10
❑ 85	Moose Haas	.10	.04
❑ 86	Mike Caldwell	.10	.04
❑ 87A	Larry Hisle P1	.25	.10
	'77 highlights line ends with "28 RBI"		
❑ 87B	Larry Hisle P2	.10	.04
	Correct line "28 HR"		
❑ 88	Luis Gomez	.10	.04
❑ 89	Larry Parrish	.10	.04
❑ 90	Gary Carter	.50	.20
❑ 91	Bill Gullickson RC	.50	.20
❑ 92	Fred Norman	.10	.04
❑ 93	Tommy Hutton	.10	.04
❑ 94	Carl Yastrzemski	1.00	.40
❑ 95	Glenn Hoffman	.10	.04
❑ 96	Dennis Eckersley	.50	.20
❑ 97A	Tom Burgmeier P1	.25	.10
	ERR Throws: Right		
❑ 97B	Tom Burgmeier P2	.10	.04
	COR Throws: Left		
❑ 98	Win Remmerswaal	.10	.04
❑ 99	Bob Horner	.25	.10
❑ 100	George Brett	3.00	1.20
❑ 101	Dave Chalk	.10	.04
❑ 102	Dennis Leonard	.10	.04
❑ 103	Renie Martin	.10	.04
❑ 104	Amos Otis	.25	.10
❑ 105	Graig Nettles	.25	.10
❑ 106	Eric Soderholm	.10	.04
❑ 107	Tommy John	.50	.20
❑ 108	Tom Underwood	.10	.04
❑ 109	Lou Piniella	.25	.10
❑ 110	Mickey Klutts	.10	.04
❑ 111	Bobby Murcer	.25	.10
❑ 112	Eddie Murray	1.50	.60
❑ 113	Rick Dempsey	.25	.10
❑ 114	Scott McGregor	.10	.04
❑ 115	Ken Singleton	.25	.10
❑ 116	Gary Roenicke	.10	.04
❑ 117	Dave Revering	.10	.04
❑ 118	Mike Norris	.10	.04
❑ 119	Rickey Henderson	6.00	2.40
❑ 120	Mike Heath	.10	.04
❑ 121	Dave Cash	.10	.04
❑ 122	Randy Jones	.10	.04
❑ 123	Eric Rasmussen	.10	.04

❑ 124 Jerry Mumphrey .10 .04
❑ 125 Richie Hebner .10 .04
❑ 126 Mark Wagner .10 .04
❑ 127 Jack Morris 1.00 .40
❑ 128 Dan Petry .10 .04
❑ 129 Bruce Robbins .10 .04
❑ 130 Champ Summers .10 .04
❑ 131 Pete Rose P1 3.00 1.20
Last line ends with
see card 251
❑ 131B Pete Rose P2 2.00 .80
Last line corrected
see card 371
❑ 132 Willie Stargell .50 .20
❑ 133 Ed Ott .10 .04
❑ 134 Jim Bibby .10 .04
❑ 135 Bert Blyleven .50 .20
❑ 136 Dave Parker .25 .10
❑ 137 Bill Robinson .25 .10
❑ 138 Enos Cabell .10 .04
❑ 139 Dave Bergman .10 .04
❑ 140 J.R. Richard .25 .10
❑ 141 Ken Forsch .10 .04
❑ 142 Larry Bowa UER .25 .10
Shortshop on front
❑ 143 Frank LaCorte UER .10 .04
Photo actually Randy Niemann
❑ 144 Denny Walling .10 .04
❑ 145 Buddy Bell .25 .10
❑ 146 Ferguson Jenkins .25 .10
❑ 147 Danny Darwin .25 .10
❑ 148 John Grubb .10 .04
❑ 149 Alfredo Griffin .10 .04
❑ 150 Jerry Garvin .10 .04
❑ 151 Paul Mirabella .10 .04
❑ 152 Rick Bosetti .10 .04
❑ 153 Dick Ruthven .10 .04
❑ 154 Frank Taveras .10 .04
❑ 155 Craig Swan .10 .04
❑ 156 Jeff Reardon RC 1.00 .40
❑ 157 Steve Henderson .10 .04
❑ 158 Jim Morrison .10 .04
❑ 159 Glenn Borgmann .10 .04
❑ 160 LaMarr Hoyt RC .25 .10
❑ 161 Rich Wortham .10 .04
❑ 162 Thad Bosley .10 .04
❑ 163 Julio Cruz .10 .04
❑ 164A Del Unser P1 .25 .10
No "3B" heading
❑ 164B Del Unser P2 .10 .04
Batting record on back
corrected "3B"
❑ 165 Jim Anderson .10 .04
❑ 166 Jim Beattie .10 .04
❑ 167 Shane Rawley .10 .04
❑ 168 Joe Simpson .10 .04
❑ 169 Rod Carew .50 .20
❑ 170 Fred Patek .10 .04
❑ 171 Frank Tanana .25 .10
❑ 172 Alfredo Martinez .10 .04
❑ 173 Chris Knapp .10 .04
❑ 174 Joe Rudi .25 .10
❑ 175 Greg Luzinski .25 .10
❑ 176 Steve Garvey .25 .10
❑ 177 Joe Ferguson .10 .04
❑ 178 Bob Welch .25 .10
❑ 179 Dusty Baker .50 .20
❑ 180 Rudy Law .10 .04
❑ 181 Dave Concepcion .25 .10
❑ 182 Johnny Bench 1.00 .40
❑ 183 Mike LaCoss .10 .04
❑ 184 Ken Griffey .50 .20
❑ 185 Dave Collins .10 .04
❑ 186 Brian Asselstine .10 .04
❑ 187 Garry Templeton .10 .04
❑ 188 Mike Phillips .10 .04
❑ 189 Pete Vuckovich .25 .10
❑ 190 John Urrea .10 .04
❑ 191 Tony Scott .10 .04
❑ 192 Darrell Evans .25 .10
❑ 193 Milt May .10 .04
❑ 194 Bob Knepper .10 .04
❑ 195 Randy Moffitt .10 .04
❑ 196 Larry Herndon .10 .04
❑ 197 Rick Camp .10 .04
❑ 198 Andre Thornton .25 .10
❑ 199 Tom Veryzer .10 .04
❑ 200 Gary Alexander .10 .04
❑ 201 Rick Waits .10 .04
❑ 202 Rick Manning .10 .04
❑ 203 Paul Molitor 2.00 .80
❑ 204 Jim Gantner .25 .10
❑ 205 Paul Mitchell .10 .04
❑ 206 Reggie Cleveland .10 .04
❑ 207 Sixto Lezcano .10 .04
❑ 208 Bruce Benedict .10 .04
❑ 209 Rodney Scott .10 .04
❑ 210 John Tamargo .10 .04
❑ 211 Bill Lee .25 .10
❑ 212 Andre Dawson UER .50 .20
Middle name Fernando
should be Nolan
❑ 213 Rowland Office .10 .04
❑ 214 Carl Yastrzemski 1.00 .40
❑ 215 Jerry Remy .10 .04
❑ 216 Mike Torrez .10 .04
❑ 217 Skip Lockwood .10 .04
❑ 218 Fred Lynn .25 .10
❑ 219 Chris Chambliss .25 .10
❑ 220 Willie Aikens .10 .04
❑ 221 John Wathan .10 .04
❑ 222 Dan Quisenberry .25 .10
❑ 223 Willie Wilson .25 .10
❑ 224 Clint Hurdle .10 .04
❑ 225 Bob Watson .25 .10
❑ 226 Jim Spencer .10 .04
❑ 227 Ron Guidry .25 .10
❑ 228 Reggie Jackson .50 .20
❑ 229 Oscar Gamble .10 .04
❑ 230 Jeff Cox .10 .04
❑ 231 Luis Tiant .25 .10
❑ 232 Rich Dauer .10 .04
❑ 233 Dan Graham .10 .04
❑ 234 Mike Flanagan .25 .10
❑ 235 John Lowenstein .10 .04
❑ 236 Benny Ayala .10 .04
❑ 237 Wayne Gross .10 .04
❑ 238 Rick Langford .10 .04
❑ 239 Tony Armas .25 .10
❑ 240A Bob Lacey P1 ERR .50 .20
Name misspelled Lacy
❑ 240B Bob Lacey P2 COR .10 .04
❑ 241 Gene Tenace .25 .10
❑ 242 Bob Shirley .10 .04
❑ 243 Gary Lucas .10 .04
❑ 244 Jerry Turner .10 .04
❑ 245 John Wockenfuss .10 .04
❑ 246 Stan Papi .10 .04
❑ 247 Milt Wilcox .10 .04
❑ 248 Dan Schatzeder .10 .04
❑ 249 Steve Kemp .10 .04
❑ 250 Jim Lentine .10 .04
❑ 251 Pete Rose 3.00 1.20
❑ 252 Bill Madlock .25 .10
❑ 253 Dale Berra .10 .04
❑ 254 Kent Tekulve .25 .10
❑ 255 Enrique Romo .10 .04
❑ 256 Mike Easler .10 .04
❑ 257 Chuck Tanner MG .25 .10
❑ 258 Art Howe .25 .10
❑ 259 Alan Ashby .10 .04
❑ 260 Nolan Ryan 5.00 2.00
❑ 261A Vern Ruhle P1 ERR .50 .20
Ken Forsch photo on front
❑ 261B Vern Ruhle P2 COR .25 .10
❑ 262 Bob Boone .25 .10
❑ 263 Cesar Cedeno .25 .10
❑ 264 Jeff Leonard .25 .10
❑ 265 Pat Putnam .10 .04
❑ 266 Jon Matlack .10 .04
❑ 267 Dave Rajsich .10 .04
❑ 268 Billy Sample .10 .04
❑ 269 Damaso Garcia .10 .04
❑ 270 Tom Buskey .10 .04
❑ 271 Joey McLaughlin .10 .04
❑ 272 Barry Bonnell .10 .04
❑ 273 Tug McGraw .25 .10
❑ 274 Mike Jorgensen .10 .04
❑ 275 Pat Zachry .10 .04
❑ 276 Neil Allen .10 .04
❑ 277 Joel Youngblood .10 .04
❑ 278 Greg Pryor .10 .04
❑ 279 Britt Burns .10 .04
❑ 280 Rich Dotson .10 .04
❑ 281 Chet Lemon .10 .04
❑ 282 Rusty Kuntz .10 .04
❑ 283 Ted Cox .10 .04
❑ 284 Sparky Lyle .25 .10
❑ 285 Larry Cox .10 .04
❑ 286 Floyd Bannister .10 .04
❑ 287 Byron McLaughlin .10 .04
❑ 288 Rodney Craig .10 .04
❑ 289 Bobby Grich .25 .10
❑ 290 Dickie Thon .25 .10
❑ 291 Mark Clear .10 .04
❑ 292 Dave Lemanczyk .10 .04
❑ 293 Jason Thompson .10 .04
❑ 294 Rick Miller .10 .04
❑ 295 Lonnie Smith .25 .10
❑ 296 Ron Cey .25 .10
❑ 297 Steve Yeager .10 .04
❑ 298 Bobby Castillo .10 .04
❑ 299 Manny Mota .25 .10
❑ 300 Jay Johnstone .25 .10
❑ 301 Dan Driessen .10 .04
❑ 302 Joe Nolan .10 .04
❑ 303 Paul Householder .10 .04
❑ 304 Harry Spilman .10 .04
❑ 305 Cesar Geronimo .10 .04
❑ 306A G.Mathews P1 ERR .50 .20
Name misspelled
❑ 306B G.Matthews P2 .25 .10
COR
❑ 307 Ken Reitz .10 .04
❑ 308 Ted Simmons .25 .10
❑ 309 John Littlefield .10 .04
❑ 310 George Frazier .10 .04
❑ 311 Dane Iorg .10 .04
❑ 312 Mike Ivie .10 .04
❑ 313 Dennis Littlejohn .10 .04
❑ 314 Gary Lavelle .10 .04
❑ 315 Jack Clark .25 .10
❑ 316 Jim Wohlford .10 .04
❑ 317 Rick Matula .10 .04
❑ 318 Toby Harrah .25 .10
❑ 319A D.Kuiper P1 ERR .25 .10
Name misspelled
❑ 319B D.Kuiper P2 COR .10 .04
❑ 320 Len Barker .10 .04
❑ 321 Victor Cruz .10 .04
❑ 322 Dell Alston .10 .04
❑ 323 Robin Yount 1.00 .40
❑ 324 Charlie Moore .10 .04
❑ 325 Lary Sorensen .10 .04
❑ 326A Gorman Thomas P1 .50 .20
2nd line on back:
"30 HR mark 4th"
❑ 326B Gorman Thomas P2 .25 .10
30 HR mark 3rd
❑ 327 Bob Rodgers MG .10 .04
❑ 328 Phil Niekro .25 .10
❑ 329 Chris Speier .10 .04
❑ 330A Steve Rodgers P1 .25 .10
ERR Name misspelled
❑ 330B S.Rogers P2 COR .10 .04
❑ 331 Woodie Fryman .10 .04
❑ 332 Warren Cromartie .10 .04
❑ 333 Jerry White .10 .04
❑ 334 Tony Perez .50 .20
❑ 335 Carlton Fisk .50 .20
❑ 336 Dick Drago .10 .04
❑ 337 Steve Renko .10 .04
❑ 338 Jim Rice .25 .10
❑ 339 Jerry Royster .10 .04
❑ 340 Frank White .25 .10
❑ 341 Jamie Quirk .10 .04
❑ 342A P.Spittorff P1 ERR .25 .10
Name misspelled
❑ 342B Paul Splittorff .10 .04
P2 COR
❑ 343 Marty Pattin .10 .04
❑ 344 Pete LaCock .10 .04
❑ 345 Willie Randolph .25 .10
❑ 346 Rick Cerone .10 .04
❑ 347 Rich Gossage .50 .20
❑ 348 Reggie Jackson .50 .20
❑ 349 Ruppert Jones .10 .04
❑ 350 Dave McKay .10 .04

❑ 351	Yogi Berra CO	.50	.20
❑ 352	Doug DeCinces	.25	.10
❑ 353	Jim Palmer	.25	.10
❑ 354	Tippy Martinez	.10	.04
❑ 355	Al Bumbry	.25	.10
❑ 356	Earl Weaver MG	1.00	.40
❑ 357A	Bob Picciolo P1 ERR	.25	.10
	Name misspelled		
❑ 357B	R.Picciolo P2 COR	.10	.04
❑ 358	Matt Keough	.10	.04
❑ 359	Dwayne Murphy	.10	.04
❑ 360	Brian Kingman	.10	.04
❑ 361	Bill Fahey	.10	.04
❑ 362	Steve Mura	.10	.04
❑ 363	Dennis Kinney	.10	.04
❑ 364	Dave Winfield	1.00	.40
❑ 365	Lou Whitaker	1.00	.40
❑ 366	Lance Parrish	.25	.10
❑ 367	Tim Corcoran	.10	.04
❑ 368	Pat Underwood	.10	.04
❑ 369	Al Cowens	.10	.04
❑ 370	Sparky Anderson MG	.25	.10
❑ 371	Pete Rose	3.00	1.20
❑ 372	Phil Garner	.25	.10
❑ 373	Steve Nicosia	.10	.04
❑ 374	John Candelaria	.25	.10
❑ 375	Don Robinson	.10	.04
❑ 376	Lee Lacy	.10	.04
❑ 377	John Milner	.10	.04
❑ 378	Craig Reynolds	.10	.04
❑ 379A	Luis Pujols P1 ERR	.25	.10
	Name misspelled Pujois		
❑ 379B	Luis Pujols P2 COR	.10	.04
❑ 380	Joe Niekro	.25	.10
❑ 381	Joaquin Andujar	.25	.10
❑ 382	Keith Moreland	.25	.10
❑ 383	Jose Cruz	.25	.10
❑ 384	Bill Virdon MG	.10	.04
❑ 385	Jim Sundberg	.25	.10
❑ 386	Doc Medich	.10	.04
❑ 387	Al Oliver	.25	.10
❑ 388	Jim Norris	.10	.04
❑ 389	Bob Bailor	.10	.04
❑ 390	Ernie Whitt	.10	.04
❑ 391	Otto Velez	.10	.04
❑ 392	Roy Howell	.10	.04
❑ 393	Bob Walk RC	.25	.10
❑ 394	Doug Flynn	.10	.04
❑ 395	Pete Falcone	.10	.04
❑ 396	Tom Hausman	.10	.04
❑ 397	Elliott Maddox	.10	.04
❑ 398	Mike Squires	.10	.04
❑ 399	Marvis Foley	.10	.04
❑ 400	Steve Trout	.10	.04
❑ 401	Wayne Nordhagen	.10	.04
❑ 402	Tony LaRussa MG	.25	.10
❑ 403	Bruce Bochte	.10	.04
❑ 404	Bake McBride	.10	.04
❑ 405	Jerry Narron	.10	.04
❑ 406	Rob Dressler	.10	.04
❑ 407	Dave Heaverlo	.10	.04
❑ 408	Tom Paciorek	.25	.10
❑ 409	Carney Lansford	.25	.10
❑ 410	Brian Downing	.25	.10
❑ 411	Don Aase	.10	.04
❑ 412	Jim Barr	.10	.04
❑ 413	Don Baylor	.50	.20
❑ 414	Jim Fregosi MG	.10	.04
❑ 415	Dallas Green MG	.10	.04
❑ 416	Dave Lopes	.25	.10
❑ 417	Jerry Reuss	.25	.10
❑ 418	Rick Sutcliffe	.25	.10
❑ 419	Derrel Thomas	.10	.04
❑ 420	Tom Lasorda MG	1.00	.40
❑ 421	Charlie Leibrandt RC	.50	.20
❑ 422	Tom Seaver	1.00	.40
❑ 423	Ron Oester	.10	.04
❑ 424	Junior Kennedy	.10	.04
❑ 425	Tom Seaver	1.00	.40
❑ 426	Bobby Cox MG	.25	.10
❑ 427	Leon Durham	.25	.10
❑ 428	Terry Kennedy	.10	.04
❑ 429	Silvio Martinez	.10	.04
❑ 430	George Hendrick	.10	.04
❑ 431	Red Schoendienst MG	.50	.20
❑ 432	Johnnie LeMaster	.10	.04
❑ 433	Vida Blue	.25	.10
❑ 434	John Montefusco	.10	.04
❑ 435	Terry Whitfield	.10	.04
❑ 436	Dave Bristol MG	.10	.04
❑ 437	Dale Murphy	1.00	.40
❑ 438	Jerry Dybzinski	.10	.04
❑ 439	Jorge Orta	.10	.04
❑ 440	Wayne Garland	.10	.04
❑ 441	Miguel Dilone	.10	.04
❑ 442	Dave Garcia MG	.10	.04
❑ 443	Don Money	.10	.04
❑ 444A	B.Martinez P1 ERR	.25	.10
	Reverse negative		
❑ 444B	Buck Martinez	.10	.04
	P2 COR		
❑ 445	Jerry Augustine	.10	.04
❑ 446	Ben Oglivie	.25	.10
❑ 447	Jim Slaton	.10	.04
❑ 448	Doyle Alexander	.10	.04
❑ 449	Tony Bernazard	.10	.04
❑ 450	Scott Sanderson	.10	.04
❑ 451	David Palmer	.10	.04
❑ 452	Stan Bahnsen	.10	.04
❑ 453	Dick Williams MG	.10	.04
❑ 454	Rick Burleson	.10	.04
❑ 455	Gary Allenson	.10	.04
❑ 456	Bob Stanley	.10	.04
❑ 457A	J. Tudor RC P1 ERR	.25	.10
	Lifetime W-L 9.7		
❑ 457B	J.Tudor RC P2 COR	.25	.10
	Lifetime W-L 9-7		
❑ 458	Dwight Evans	.50	.20
❑ 459	Glenn Hubbard	.10	.04
❑ 460	U.L. Washington	.10	.04
❑ 461	Larry Gura	.10	.04
❑ 462	Rich Gale	.10	.04
❑ 463	Hal McRae	.25	.10
❑ 464	Jim Frey MG	.10	.04
❑ 465	Bucky Dent	.25	.10
❑ 466	Dennis Werth	.10	.04
❑ 467	Ron Davis	.10	.04
❑ 468	Reggie Jackson UER	.50	.20
	32 HR in 1970		
	should be 23		
❑ 469	Bobby Brown	.10	.04
❑ 470	Mike Davis	.10	.04
❑ 471	Gaylord Perry	.25	.10
❑ 472	Mark Belanger	.25	.10
❑ 473	Jim Palmer	.25	.10
❑ 474	Sammy Stewart	.10	.04
❑ 475	Tim Stoddard	.10	.04
❑ 476	Steve Stone	.25	.10
❑ 477	Jeff Newman	.10	.04
❑ 478	Steve McCatty	.10	.04
❑ 479	Billy Martin MG	.50	.20
❑ 480	Mitchell Page	.10	.04
❑ 481	Steve Carlton CY	.25	.10
❑ 482	Bill Buckner	.25	.10
❑ 483A	I.DeJesus P1 ERR	.25	.10
	Lifetime hits 702		
❑ 483B	I.DeJesus P2 COR	.10	.04
	Lifetime hits 642		
❑ 484	Cliff Johnson	.10	.04
❑ 485	Lenny Randle	.10	.04
❑ 486	Larry Milbourne	.10	.04
❑ 487	Roy Smalley	.10	.04
❑ 488	John Castino	.10	.04
❑ 489	Ron Jackson	.10	.04
❑ 490A	Dave Roberts P1	.25	.10
	Career Highlights		
	Showed pop in		
❑ 490B	Dave Roberts P2	.10	.04
	Declared himself		
❑ 491	George Brett MVP	1.50	.60
❑ 492	Mike Cubbage	.10	.04
❑ 493	Rob Wilfong	.10	.04
❑ 494	Danny Goodwin	.10	.04
❑ 495	Jose Morales	.10	.04
❑ 496	Mickey Rivers	.25	.10
❑ 497	Mike Edwards	.10	.04
❑ 498	Mike Sadek	.10	.04
❑ 499	Lenn Sakata	.10	.04
❑ 500	Gene Michael MG	.10	.04
❑ 501	Dave Roberts	.10	.04
❑ 502	Steve Dillard	.10	.04
❑ 503	Jim Essian	.10	.04
❑ 504	Rance Mulliniks	.10	.04
❑ 505	Darrell Porter	.10	.04
❑ 506	Joe Torre MG	.25	.10
❑ 507	Terry Crowley	.10	.04
❑ 508	Bill Travers	.10	.04
❑ 509	Nelson Norman	.10	.04
❑ 510	Bob McClure	.10	.04
❑ 511	Steve Howe	.25	.10
❑ 512	Dave Rader	.10	.04
❑ 513	Mick Kelleher	.10	.04
❑ 514	Kiko Garcia	.10	.04
❑ 515	Larry Biittner	.10	.04
❑ 516A	Willie Norwood P1	.25	.10
	Career Highlights		
	Spent most of		
❑ 516B	Willie Norwood P2	.10	.04
	Traded to Seattle		
❑ 517	Bo Diaz	.10	.04
❑ 518	Juan Beniquez	.10	.04
❑ 519	Scot Thompson	.10	.04
❑ 520	Jim Tracy RC	.10	.04
❑ 521	Carlos Lezcano	.10	.04
❑ 522	Joe Amalfitano MG	.10	.04
❑ 523	Preston Hanna	.10	.04
❑ 524A	Ray Burris P1	.25	.10
	Career Highlights		
	Went on ...		
❑ 524B	Ray Burris P2	.10	.04
	Drafted by ...		
❑ 525	Broderick Perkins	.10	.04
❑ 526	Mickey Hatcher	.25	.10
❑ 527	John Goryl MG	.10	.04
❑ 528	Dick Davis	.10	.04
❑ 529	Butch Wynegar	.10	.04
❑ 530	Sal Butera	.10	.04
❑ 531	Jerry Koosman	.25	.10
❑ 532A	Geoff Zahn P1	.25	.10
	(Career Highlights		
	Was 2nd in		
❑ 532B	Geoff Zahn P2	.10	.04
	Signed a 3 year		
❑ 533	Dennis Martinez	.50	.20
❑ 534	Gary Thomasson	.10	.04
❑ 535	Steve Macko	.10	.04
❑ 536	Jim Kaat	.25	.10
❑ 537	George Brett	2.00	.80
	Rod Carew		
❑ 538	Tim Raines RC	2.00	.80
❑ 539	Keith Smith	.10	.04
❑ 540	Ken Macha	.10	.04
❑ 541	Burt Hooton	.10	.04
❑ 542	Butch Hobson	.10	.04
❑ 543	Bill Stein	.10	.04
❑ 544	Dave Stapleton	.10	.04
❑ 545	Bob Pate	.10	.04
❑ 546	Doug Corbett	.10	.04
❑ 547	Darrell Jackson	.10	.04
❑ 548	Pete Redfern	.10	.04
❑ 549	Roger Erickson	.10	.04
❑ 550	Al Hrabosky	.10	.04
❑ 551	Dick Tidrow	.10	.04
❑ 552	Dave Ford	.10	.04
❑ 553	Dave Kingman	.50	.20
❑ 554A	Mike Vail P1	.25	.10
	Career Highlights		
	After two		
❑ 554B	Mike Vail P2	.10	.04
	Traded to		
❑ 555A	Jerry Martin P1	.25	.10
	Career Highlights		
	Overcame a		
❑ 555B	Jerry Martin P2	.10	.04
	Traded to		
❑ 556A	Jesus Figueroa P1	.25	.10
	Career Highlights		
	Had an		
❑ 556B	Jesus Figueroa P2	.10	.04
	Traded to		
❑ 557	Don Stanhouse	.10	.04
❑ 558	Barry Foote	.10	.04
❑ 559	Tim Blackwell	.10	.04
❑ 560	Bruce Sutter	.25	.10
❑ 561	Rick Reuschel	.25	.10
❑ 562	Lynn McGlothen	.10	.04
❑ 563A	Bob Owchinko P1	.25	.10
	Career Highlights		

Traded to
❑ 563B Bob Owchinko P2 .... .10 .04
Involved in a
❑ 564 John Verhoeven .... .10 .04
❑ 565 Ken Landreaux .... .10 .04
❑ 566A Glen Adams P1 ERR ...... .25 .10
Name misspelled
❑ 566B G. Adams P2 COR.......... .10 .04
❑ 567 Hosken Powell .... .10 .04
❑ 568 Dick Noles........................ .10 .04
❑ 569 Danny Ainge RC .... 2.00 .80
❑ 570 Bobby Mattick MG .... .10 .04
❑ 571 Joe Lefebvre .... .10 .04
❑ 572 Bobby Clark .... .10 .04
❑ 573 Dennis Lamp...................... .10 .04
❑ 574 Randy Lerch .... .10 .04
❑ 575 Mookie Wilson RC .... .50 .20
❑ 576 Ron LeFlore........................ .25 .10
❑ 577 Jim Dwyer........................... .10 .04
❑ 578 Bill Castro .... .10 .04
❑ 579 Greg Minton .... .10 .04
❑ 580 Mark Littell .... .10 .04
❑ 581 Andy Hassler...................... .10 .04
❑ 582 Dave Stieb.......................... .25 .10
❑ 583 Ken Oberkfell...................... .10 .04
❑ 584 Larry Bradford .... .10 .04
❑ 585 Fred Stanley .... .10 .04
❑ 586 Bill Caudill .... .10 .04
❑ 587 Doug Capilla .... .10 .04
❑ 588 George Riley .... .10 .04
❑ 589 Willie Hernandez .... .25 .10
❑ 590 Mike Schmidt MVP 2.50 1.00
❑ 591 Steve Stone CY .... .10 .04
❑ 592 Rick Sofield........................ .10 .04
❑ 593 Bombo Rivera .... .10 .04
❑ 594 Gary Ward .... .10 .04
❑ 595A Dave Edwards P1 .... .25 .10
Career Highlights
Sidelined the
❑ 595B Dave Edwards P2 .... .10 .04
Traded to
❑ 596 Mike Proly........................... .10 .04
❑ 597 Tommy Boggs.................... .10 .04
❑ 598 Greg Gross .... .10 .04
❑ 599 Elias Sosa .... .10 .04
❑ 600 Pat Kelly .... .10 .04
❑ 601A Checklist 1-120 P1 .... .25 .10
ERR Unnumbered
51 Donahue
❑ 601B Checklist 1-120 P2 .... .50 .20
COR Unnumbered
51 Donohue
❑ 602 Checklist 121-240........... .25 .10
Unnumbered
❑ 603A CL 241-360 P1 .... .25 .10
ERR Unnumbered
306 Mathews
❑ 603B CL 241-360 P2.............. .25 .10
COR Unnumbered
306 Matthews
❑ 604A CL 361-480 P1 .... .25 .10
ERR Unnumbered
379 Pujois
❑ 604B CL 361-480 P2 .... .25 .10
COR Unnumbered
379 Pujols
❑ 605A CL 481-600 P1 .... .25 .10
ERR Unnumbered
566 Glen Adams
❑ 605B CL 481-600 P2.............. .25 .10
COR Unnumbered
566 Glenn Adams

1982 Donruss

	Nm-Mt	Ex-Mt
COMPLETE SET (660)	60.00	24.00
COMP.FACT.SET (660)	60.00	24.00
COMP.RUTH PUZZLE	10.00	4.00

❑ 1 Pete Rose DK 2.50 1.00
❑ 2 Gary Carter DK .... .20 .08
❑ 3 Steve Garvey DK .... .20 .08
❑ 4 Vida Blue DK........................ .10 .04
❑ 5 Alan Trammell DK................ .10 .04
COR

❑ 5A Alan Trammel DK ERR ...... .40 .16
(Name misspelled)
❑ 6 Len Barker DK...................... .10 .04
❑ 7 Dwight Evans DK.................. .40 .16
❑ 8 Rod Carew DK....................... .40 .16
❑ 9 George Hendrick DK .... .20 .08
❑ 10 Phil Niekro DK .... .20 .08
❑ 11 Richie Zisk DK..................... .10 .04
❑ 12 Dave Parker DK.................... .20 .08
❑ 13 Nolan Ryan DK 4.00 1.60
❑ 14 Ivan DeJesus DK.................. .10 .04
❑ 15 George Brett DK .... .75 .30
❑ 16 Tom Seaver DK.................... .75 .30
❑ 17 Dave Kingman DK .... .20 .08
❑ 18 Dave Winfield DK .... .20 .08
❑ 19 Mike Norris DK..................... .10 .04
❑ 20 Carlton Fisk DK.................... .40 .16
❑ 21 Ozzie Smith DK .... 1.50 .60
❑ 22 Roy Smalley DK .... .20 .08
❑ 23 Buddy Bell DK...................... .20 .08
❑ 24 Ken Singleton DK .... .10 .04
❑ 25 John Mayberry DK .... .10 .04
❑ 26 Gorman Thomas DK .... .20 .08
❑ 27 Earl Weaver MG .... .40 .16
❑ 28 Rollie Fingers .... .20 .08
❑ 29 Sparky Anderson MG .... .20 .08
❑ 30 Dennis Eckersley................. .40 .16
❑ 31 Dave Winfield .... .40 .16
❑ 32 Burt Hooton.......................... .10 .04
❑ 33 Rick Waits............................. .10 .04
❑ 34 George Brett 2.50 1.00
❑ 35 Steve McCatty...................... .10 .04
❑ 36 Steve Rogers........................ .10 .04
❑ 37 Bill Stein .... .10 .04
❑ 38 Steve Renko .... .10 .04
❑ 39 Mike Squires......................... .10 .04
❑ 40 George Hendrick .... .10 .04
❑ 41 Bob Knepper .... .10 .04
❑ 42 Steve Carlton........................ .40 .16
❑ 43 Larry Biittner .... .10 .04
❑ 44 Chris Welsh .... .10 .04
❑ 45 Steve Nicosia .... .10 .04
❑ 46 Jack Clark .... .20 .08
❑ 47 Chris Chambliss .... .20 .08
❑ 48 Ivan DeJesus........................ .10 .04
❑ 49 Lee Mazzilli .... .10 .04
❑ 50 Julio Cruz .... .10 .04
❑ 51 Pete Redfern .... .10 .04
❑ 52 Dave Stieb............................ .20 .08
❑ 53 Doug Corbett........................ .10 .04
❑ 54 Jorge Bell RC .... .75 .30
❑ 55 Joe Simpson .... .10 .04
❑ 56 Rusty Staub.......................... .20 .08
❑ 57 Hector Cruz .... .10 .04
❑ 58 Claudell Washington .... .10 .04
❑ 59 Enrique Romo .... .10 .04
❑ 60 Gary Lavelle .... .10 .04
❑ 61 Tim Flannery......................... .10 .04
❑ 62 Joe Nolan.............................. .10 .04
❑ 63 Larry Bowa .... .20 .08
❑ 64 Sixto Lezcano .... .10 .04
❑ 65 Joe Sambito .... .10 .04
❑ 66 Bruce Kison.......................... .10 .04
❑ 67 Wayne Nordhagen............... .10 .04
❑ 68 Woodie Fryman.................... .10 .04
❑ 69 Billy Sample .... .10 .04
❑ 70 Amos Otis .... .20 .08
❑ 71 Matt Keough .... .10 .04
❑ 72 Toby Harrah .... .20 .08
❑ 73 Dave Righetti RC .... .75 .30
❑ 74 Carl Yastrzemski .... .75 .30
❑ 75 Bob Welch............................ .20 .08
❑ 76 Alan Trammell COR............ .40 .16
❑ 76A Alan Trammel ERR .... .40 .16
(Name misspelled)
❑ 77 Rick Dempsey .... .20 .08
❑ 78 Paul Molitor .... 1.00 .40
❑ 79 Dennis Martinez .... .40 .16
❑ 80 Jim Slaton............................ .10 .04
❑ 81 Champ Summers .... .10 .04
❑ 82 Carney Lansford .... .20 .08
❑ 83 Barry Foote .... .10 .04
❑ 84 Steve Garvey .... .20 .08
❑ 85 Rick Manning .... .10 .04
❑ 86 John Wathan........................ .10 .04
❑ 87 Brian Kingman .... .10 .04
❑ 88 Andre Dawson UER............ .20 .08
(Middle name Fernando
should be Nolan)
❑ 89 Jim Kern .... .10 .04
❑ 90 Bobby Grich .... .20 .08
❑ 91 Bob Forsch .... .10 .04
❑ 92 Art Howe .... .20 .08
❑ 93 Marty Bystrom..................... .10 .04
❑ 94 Ozzie Smith .... 1.50 .60
❑ 95 Dave Parker......................... .20 .08
❑ 96 Doyle Alexander .... .10 .04
❑ 97 Al Hrabosky......................... .10 .04
❑ 98 Frank Taveras .... .10 .04
❑ 99 Tim Blackwell .... .10 .04
❑ 100 Floyd Bannister .... .10 .04
❑ 101 Alfredo Griffin .... .10 .04
❑ 102 Dave Engle .... .10 .04
❑ 103 Mario Soto .... .10 .04
❑ 104 Ross Baumgarten .... .10 .04
❑ 105 Ken Singleton .... .20 .08
❑ 106 Ted Simmons .... .20 .08
❑ 107 Jack Morris......................... .20 .08
❑ 108 Bob Watson........................ .20 .08
❑ 109 Dwight Evans .... .40 .16
❑ 110 Tom Lasorda MG .... .40 .16
❑ 111 Bert Blyleven...................... .40 .16
❑ 112 Dan Quisenberry................ .20 .08
❑ 113 Rickey Henderson 2.50 1.00
❑ 114 Gary Carter .... .40 .16
❑ 115 Brian Downing .... .10 .04
❑ 116 Al Oliver .... .20 .08
❑ 117 LaMarr Hoyt .... .10 .04
❑ 118 Cesar Cedeno .... .20 .08
❑ 119 Keith Moreland .... .10 .04
❑ 120 Bob Shirley......................... .10 .04
❑ 121 Terry Kennedy.................... .10 .04
❑ 122 Frank Pastore .... .10 .04
❑ 123 Gene Garber....................... .10 .04
❑ 124 Tony Pena........................... .20 .08
❑ 125 Allen Ripley......................... .10 .04
❑ 126 Randy Martz....................... .10 .04
❑ 127 Richie Zisk .... .10 .04
❑ 128 Mike Scott........................... .20 .08
❑ 129 Lloyd Moseby .... .10 .04
❑ 130 Rob Wilfong .... .10 .04
❑ 131 Tim Stoddard .... .10 .04
❑ 132 Gorman Thomas .... .20 .08
❑ 133 Dan Petry .... .10 .04
❑ 134 Bob Stanley........................ .10 .04
❑ 135 Lou Piniella......................... .20 .08
❑ 136 Pedro Guerrero .... .20 .08
❑ 137 Len Barker .... .10 .04
❑ 138 Rich Gale............................ .10 .04
❑ 139 Wayne Gross...................... .10 .04
❑ 140 Tim Wallach RC .... .40 .16
❑ 141 Gene Mauch MG .... .10 .04
❑ 142 Doc Medich......................... .10 .04
❑ 143 Tony Bernazard .... .10 .04
❑ 144 Bill Virdon MG .... .10 .04
❑ 145 John Littlefield .... .10 .04
❑ 146 Dave Bergman.................... .10 .04
❑ 147 Dick Davis........................... .10 .04
❑ 148 Tom Seaver .... .75 .30
❑ 149 Matt Sinatro .... .10 .04
❑ 150 Chuck Tanner MG .... .10 .04
❑ 151 Leon Durham .... .10 .04
❑ 152 Gene Tenace .... .20 .08
❑ 153 Al Bumbry........................... .10 .04

❑ 154 Mark Brouhard .10 .04
❑ 155 Rick Peters .10 .04
❑ 156 Jerry Remy .10 .04
❑ 157 Rick Reuschel .20 .08
❑ 158 Steve Howe .10 .04
❑ 159 Alan Bannister .10 .04
❑ 160 U.L. Washington .10 .04
❑ 161 Rick Langford .10 .04
❑ 162 Bill Gullickson .10 .04
❑ 163 Mark Wagner .10 .04
❑ 164 Geoff Zahn .10 .04
❑ 165 Ron LeFlore .20 .08
❑ 166 Dane Iorg .10 .04
❑ 167 Joe Niekro .20 .08
❑ 168 Pete Rose 2.50 1.00
❑ 169 Dave Collins .10 .04
❑ 170 Rick Wise .10 .04
❑ 171 Jim Bibby .10 .04
❑ 172 Larry Herndon .10 .04
❑ 173 Bob Horner .20 .08
❑ 174 Steve Dillard .10 .04
❑ 175 Mookie Wilson .20 .08
❑ 176 Dan Meyer .10 .04
❑ 177 Fernando Arroyo .10 .04
❑ 178 Jackson Todd .10 .04
❑ 179 Darrell Jackson .10 .04
❑ 180 Alvis Woods .10 .04
❑ 181 Jim Anderson .10 .04
❑ 182 Dave Kingman .20 .08
❑ 183 Steve Henderson .10 .04
❑ 184 Brian Asselstine .10 .04
❑ 185 Rod Scurry .10 .04
❑ 186 Fred Breining .10 .04
❑ 187 Danny Boone .10 .04
❑ 188 Junior Kennedy .10 .04
❑ 189 Sparky Lyle .20 .08
❑ 190 Whitey Herzog MG .20 .08
❑ 191 Dave Smith .10 .04
❑ 192 Ed Ott .10 .04
❑ 193 Greg Luzinski .20 .08
❑ 194 Bill Lee .20 .08
❑ 195 Don Zimmer MG .10 .04
❑ 196 Hal McRae .20 .08
❑ 197 Mike Norris .10 .04
❑ 198 Duane Kuiper .10 .04
❑ 199 Rick Cerone .10 .04
❑ 200 Jim Rice .20 .08
❑ 201 Steve Yeager .10 .04
❑ 202 Tom Brookens .10 .04
❑ 203 Jose Morales .10 .04
❑ 204 Roy Howell .10 .04
❑ 205 Tippy Martinez .10 .04
❑ 206 Moose Haas .10 .04
❑ 207 Al Cowens .10 .04
❑ 208 Dave Stapleton .10 .04
❑ 209 Bucky Dent .20 .08
❑ 210 Ron Cey .20 .08
❑ 211 Jorge Orta .10 .04
❑ 212 Jamie Quirk .10 .04
❑ 213 Jeff Jones .10 .04
❑ 214 Tim Raines .75 .30
❑ 215 Jon Matlack .10 .04
❑ 216 Rod Carew .40 .16
❑ 217 Jim Kaat .20 .08
❑ 218 Joe Pittman .10 .04
❑ 219 Larry Christenson .10 .04
❑ 220 Juan Bonilla RC .10 .04
❑ 221 Mike Easler .10 .04
❑ 222 Vida Blue .20 .08
❑ 223 Rick Camp .10 .04
❑ 224 Mike Jorgensen .10 .04
❑ 225 Jody Davis .10 .04
❑ 226 Mike Parrott .10 .04
❑ 227 Jim Clancy .10 .04
❑ 228 Hosken Powell .10 .04
❑ 229 Tom Hume .10 .04
❑ 230 Britt Burns .10 .04
❑ 231 Jim Palmer .20 .08
❑ 232 Bob Rodgers MG .10 .04
❑ 233 Milt Wilcox .10 .04
❑ 234 Dave Revering .10 .04
❑ 235 Mike Torrez .10 .04
❑ 236 Robert Castillo .10 .04
❑ 237 Von Hayes .20 .08
❑ 238 Renie Martin .10 .04
❑ 239 Dwayne Murphy .10 .04
❑ 240 Rodney Scott .10 .04
❑ 241 Fred Patek .10 .04
❑ 242 Mickey Rivers .10 .04
❑ 243 Steve Trout .10 .04
❑ 244 Jose Cruz .20 .08
❑ 245 Manny Trillo .10 .04
❑ 246 Lary Sorensen .10 .04
❑ 247 Dave Edwards .10 .04
❑ 248 Dan Driessen .10 .04
❑ 249 Tommy Boggs .10 .04
❑ 250 Dale Berra .10 .04
❑ 251 Ed Whitson .10 .04
❑ 252 Lee Smith RC 2.00 .80
❑ 253 Tom Paciorek .20 .08
❑ 254 Pat Zachry .10 .04
❑ 255 Luis Leal .10 .04
❑ 256 John Castino .10 .04
❑ 257 Rich Dauer .10 .04
❑ 258 Cecil Cooper .20 .08
❑ 259 Dave Rozema .10 .04
❑ 260 John Tudor .10 .04
❑ 261 Jerry Mumphrey .10 .04
❑ 262 Jay Johnstone .20 .08
❑ 263 Bo Diaz .10 .04
❑ 264 Dennis Leonard .10 .04
❑ 265 Jim Spencer .10 .04
❑ 266 John Milner .10 .04
❑ 267 Don Aase .10 .04
❑ 268 Jim Sundberg .10 .04
❑ 269 Lamar Johnson .10 .04
❑ 270 Frank LaCorte .10 .04
❑ 271 Barry Evans .10 .04
❑ 272 Enos Cabell .10 .04
❑ 273 Del Unser .10 .04
❑ 274 George Foster .20 .08
❑ 275 Brett Butler RC 1.00 .40
❑ 276 Lee Lacy .10 .04
❑ 277 Ken Reitz .10 .04
❑ 278 Keith Hernandez .40 .16
❑ 279 Doug DeCinces .20 .08
❑ 280 Charlie Moore .10 .04
❑ 281 Lance Parrish .40 .16
❑ 282 Ralph Houk MG .20 .08
❑ 283 Rich Gossage .40 .16
❑ 284 Jerry Reuss .20 .08
❑ 285 Mike Stanton .10 .04
❑ 286 Frank White .20 .08
❑ 287 Bob Owchinko .10 .04
❑ 288 Scott Sanderson .10 .04
❑ 289 Bump Wills .10 .04
❑ 290 Dave Frost .10 .04
❑ 291 Chet Lemon .10 .04
❑ 292 Tito Landrum .10 .04
❑ 293 Vern Ruhle .10 .04
❑ 294 Mike Schmidt 2.00 .80
❑ 295 Sam Mejias .10 .04
❑ 296 Gary Lucas .10 .04
❑ 297 John Candelaria .10 .04
❑ 298 Jerry Martin .10 .04
❑ 299 Dale Murphy .75 .30
❑ 300 Mike Lum .10 .04
❑ 301 Tom Hausman .10 .04
❑ 302 Glenn Abbott .10 .04
❑ 303 Roger Erickson .10 .04
❑ 304 Otto Velez .10 .04
❑ 305 Danny Goodwin .10 .04
❑ 306 John Mayberry .10 .04
❑ 307 Lenny Randle .10 .04
❑ 308 Bob Bailor .10 .04
❑ 309 Jerry Morales .10 .04
❑ 310 Rufino Linares .10 .04
❑ 311 Kent Tekulve .20 .08
❑ 312 Joe Morgan .40 .16
❑ 313 John Urrea .10 .04
❑ 314 Paul Householder .10 .04
❑ 315 Garry Maddox .10 .04
❑ 316 Mike Ramsey .10 .04
❑ 317 Alan Ashby .10 .04
❑ 318 Bob Clark .10 .04
❑ 319 Tony LaRussa MG .20 .08
❑ 320 Charlie Lea .10 .04
❑ 321 Danny Darwin .10 .04
❑ 322 Cesar Geronimo .10 .04
❑ 323 Tom Underwood .10 .04
❑ 324 Andre Thornton .10 .04
❑ 325 Rudy May .10 .04
❑ 326 Frank Tanana .20 .08
❑ 327 Dave Lopes .20 .08
❑ 328 Richie Hebner .20 .08
❑ 329 Mike Flanagan .20 .08
❑ 330 Mike Caldwell .10 .04
❑ 331 Scott McGregor .10 .04
❑ 332 Jerry Augustine .10 .04
❑ 333 Stan Papi .10 .04
❑ 334 Rick Miller .10 .04
❑ 335 Graig Nettles .20 .08
❑ 336 Dusty Baker .40 .16
❑ 337 Dave Garcia MG .10 .04
❑ 338 Larry Gura .10 .04
❑ 339 Cliff Johnson .10 .04
❑ 340 Warren Cromartie .10 .04
❑ 341 Steve Comer .10 .04
❑ 342 Rick Burleson .10 .04
❑ 343 John Martin RC .10 .04
❑ 344 Craig Reynolds .10 .04
❑ 345 Mike Proly .10 .04
❑ 346 Ruppert Jones .10 .04
❑ 347 Omar Moreno .10 .04
❑ 348 Greg Minton .10 .04
❑ 349 Rick Mahler .10 .04
❑ 350 Alex Trevino .10 .04
❑ 351 Mike Krukow .10 .04
❑ 352A Shane Rawley ERR .40 .16
(Photo actually Jim Anderson)
❑ 352B Shane Rawley COR .10 .04
❑ 353 Garth Iorg .10 .04
❑ 354 Pete Mackanin .10 .04
❑ 355 Paul Moskau .10 .04
❑ 356 Richard Dotson .10 .04
❑ 357 Steve Stone .20 .08
❑ 358 Larry Hisle .10 .04
❑ 359 Aurelio Lopez .10 .04
❑ 360 Oscar Gamble .10 .04
❑ 361 Tom Burgmeier .10 .04
❑ 362 Terry Forster .10 .04
❑ 363 Joe Charboneau .20 .08
❑ 364 Ken Brett .10 .04
❑ 365 Tony Armas .10 .04
❑ 366 Chris Speier .10 .04
❑ 367 Fred Lynn .20 .08
❑ 368 Buddy Bell .20 .08
❑ 369 Jim Essian .10 .04
❑ 370 Terry Puhl .10 .04
❑ 371 Greg Gross .10 .04
❑ 372 Bruce Sutter .20 .08
❑ 373 Joe Lefebvre .10 .04
❑ 374 Ray Knight .20 .08
❑ 375 Bruce Benedict .10 .04
❑ 376 Tim Foli .10 .04
❑ 377 Al Holland .10 .04
❑ 378 Ken Kravec .10 .04
❑ 379 Jeff Burroughs .10 .04
❑ 380 Pete Falcone .10 .04
❑ 381 Ernie Whitt .10 .04
❑ 382 Brad Havens .10 .04
❑ 383 Terry Crowley .10 .04
❑ 384 Don Money .10 .04
❑ 385 Dan Schatzeder .10 .04
❑ 386 Gary Allenson .10 .04
❑ 387 Yogi Berra CO .40 .16
❑ 388 Ken Landreaux .10 .04
❑ 389 Mike Hargrove .20 .08
❑ 390 Darryl Motley .10 .04
❑ 391 Dave McKay .10 .04
❑ 392 Stan Bahnsen .10 .04
❑ 393 Ken Forsch .10 .04
❑ 394 Mario Mendoza .10 .04
❑ 395 Jim Morrison .10 .04
❑ 396 Mike Ivie .10 .04
❑ 397 Broderick Perkins .10 .04
❑ 398 Darrell Evans .20 .08
❑ 399 Ron Reed .10 .04
❑ 400 Johnny Bench .75 .30
❑ 401 Steve Bedrosian RC .20 .08
❑ 402 Bill Robinson .10 .04
❑ 403 Bill Buckner .20 .08
❑ 404 Ken Oberkfell .10 .04
❑ 405 Cal Ripken RC 40.00 16.00
❑ 406 Jim Gantner .20 .08
❑ 407 Kirk Gibson .75 .30
❑ 408 Tony Perez .40 .16

❑ 409 Tommy John UER .40 .16
(Text says 52-56 as Yankee, should be 52-26)
❑ 410 Dave Stewart RC 1.00 .40
❑ 411 Dan Spillner .10 .04
❑ 412 Willie Aikens .10 .04
❑ 413 Mike Heath .10 .04
❑ 414 Ray Burris .10 .04
❑ 415 Leon Roberts .10 .04
❑ 416 Mike Witt .20 .08
❑ 417 Bob Molinaro .10 .04
❑ 418 Steve Braun .10 .04
❑ 419 Nolan Ryan UER 4.00 1.60
(Nisnumbering of Nolan's no-hitters on card back)
❑ 420 Tug McGraw .20 .08
❑ 421 Dave Concepcion .20 .08
❑ 422A Juan Eichelberger .40 .16
ERR (Photo actually Gary Lucas)
❑ 422B Juan Eichelberger .10 .04
COR
❑ 423 Rick Rhoden .10 .04
❑ 424 Frank Robinson MG .40 .16
❑ 425 Eddie Miller .10 .04
❑ 426 Bill Caudill .10 .04
❑ 427 Doug Flynn .10 .04
❑ 428 Larry Andersen UER .10 .04
(Misspelled Anderson on card front)
❑ 429 Al Williams .10 .04
❑ 430 Jerry Garvin .10 .04
❑ 431 Glenn Adams .10 .04
❑ 432 Barry Bonnell .10 .04
❑ 433 Jerry Narron .10 .04
❑ 434 John Stearns .10 .04
❑ 435 Mike Tyson .10 .04
❑ 436 Glenn Hubbard .10 .04
❑ 437 Eddie Solomon .10 .04
❑ 438 Jeff Leonard .10 .04
❑ 439 Randy Bass RC .10 .04
❑ 440 Mike LaCoss .10 .04
❑ 441 Gary Matthews .20 .08
❑ 442 Mark Littell .10 .04
❑ 443 Don Sutton .75 .30
❑ 444 John Harris .10 .04
❑ 445 Vada Pinson CO .20 .08
❑ 446 Elias Sosa .10 .04
❑ 447 Charlie Hough .20 .08
❑ 448 Willie Wilson .20 .08
❑ 449 Fred Stanley .10 .04
❑ 450 Tom Veryzer .10 .04
❑ 451 Ron Davis .10 .04
❑ 452 Mark Clear .10 .04
❑ 453 Bill Russell .10 .04
❑ 454 Lou Whitaker .75 .30
❑ 455 Dan Graham .10 .04
❑ 456 Reggie Cleveland .10 .04
❑ 457 Sammy Stewart .10 .04
❑ 458 Pete Vuckovich .10 .04
❑ 459 John Wockenfuss .10 .04
❑ 460 Glenn Hoffman .10 .04
❑ 461 Willie Randolph .20 .08
❑ 462 Fernando Valenzuela .75 .30
❑ 463 Ron Hassey .10 .04
❑ 464 Paul Splittorff .10 .04
❑ 465 Rob Picciolo .10 .04
❑ 466 Larry Parrish .10 .04
❑ 467 Johnny Grubb .10 .04
❑ 468 Dan Ford .10 .04
❑ 469 Silvio Martinez .10 .04
❑ 470 Kiko Garcia .10 .04
❑ 471 Bob Boone .20 .08
❑ 472 Luis Salazar .10 .04
❑ 473 Randy Niemann .10 .04
❑ 474 Tom Griffin .10 .04
❑ 475 Phil Niekro .20 .08
❑ 476 Hubie Brooks .20 .08
❑ 477 Dick Tidrow .10 .04
❑ 478 Jim Beattie .10 .04
❑ 479 Damaso Garcia .10 .04
❑ 480 Mickey Hatcher .10 .04
❑ 481 Joe Price .10 .04
❑ 482 Ed Farmer .10 .04
❑ 483 Eddie Murray .75 .30
❑ 484 Ben Oglivie .20 .08
❑ 485 Kevin Saucier .10 .04
❑ 486 Bobby Murcer .20 .08
❑ 487 Bill Campbell .10 .04
❑ 488 Reggie Smith .20 .08
❑ 489 Wayne Garland .10 .04
❑ 490 Jim Wright .10 .04
❑ 491 Billy Martin MG .20 .08
❑ 492 Jim Fanning MG .10 .04
❑ 493 Don Baylor .40 .16
❑ 494 Rick Honeycutt .10 .04
❑ 495 Carlton Fisk .40 .16
❑ 496 Denny Walling .10 .04
❑ 497 Bake McBride .10 .04
❑ 498 Darrell Porter .20 .08
❑ 499 Gene Richards .10 .04
❑ 500 Ron Oester .10 .04
❑ 501 Ken Dayley .10 .04
❑ 502 Jason Thompson .10 .04
❑ 503 Milt May .10 .04
❑ 504 Doug Bird .10 .04
❑ 505 Bruce Bochte .10 .04
❑ 506 Neil Allen .10 .04
❑ 507 Joey McLaughlin .10 .04
❑ 508 Butch Wynegar .10 .04
❑ 509 Gary Roenicke .10 .04
❑ 510 Robin Yount .75 .30
❑ 511 Dave Tobik .10 .04
❑ 512 Rich Gedman .20 .08
❑ 513 Gene Nelson .10 .04
❑ 514 Rick Monday .10 .04
❑ 515 Miguel Dilone .10 .04
❑ 516 Clint Hurdle .10 .04
❑ 517 Jeff Newman .10 .04
❑ 518 Grant Jackson .10 .04
❑ 519 Andy Hassler .10 .04
❑ 520 Pat Putnam .10 .04
❑ 521 Greg Pryor .10 .04
❑ 522 Tony Scott .10 .04
❑ 523 Steve Mura .10 .04
❑ 524 Johnnie LeMaster .10 .04
❑ 525 Dick Ruthven .10 .04
❑ 526 John McNamara MG .10 .04
❑ 527 Larry McWilliams .10 .04
❑ 528 Johnny Ray .20 .08
❑ 529 Pat Tabler .20 .08
❑ 530 Tom Herr .20 .08
❑ 531A SD Chicken RC .75 .30
ERR (Without TM)
❑ 531B San Diego Chicken .75 .30
COR (With TM)
❑ 532 Sal Butera .10 .04
❑ 533 Mike Griffin .10 .04
❑ 534 Kelvin Moore .10 .04
❑ 535 Reggie Jackson .40 .16
❑ 536 Ed Romero .10 .04
❑ 537 Derrel Thomas .10 .04
❑ 538 Mike O'Berry .10 .04
❑ 539 Jack O'Connor .10 .04
❑ 540 Bob Ojeda RC .40 .16
❑ 541 Roy Lee Jackson .10 .04
❑ 542 Lynn Jones .10 .04
❑ 543 Gaylord Perry .20 .08
❑ 544A Phil Garner ERR .40 .16
(Reverse negative)
❑ 544B Phil Garner COR .20 .08
❑ 545 Garry Templeton .10 .04
❑ 546 Rafael Ramirez .10 .04
❑ 547 Jeff Reardon .40 .16
❑ 548 Ron Guidry .20 .08
❑ 549 Tim Laudner .10 .04
❑ 550 John Henry Johnson .10 .04
❑ 551 Chris Bando .10 .04
❑ 552 Bobby Brown .10 .04
❑ 553 Larry Bradford .10 .04
❑ 554 Scott Fletcher RC .20 .08
❑ 555 Jerry Royster .10 .04
❑ 556 Shooty Babitt UER .10 .04
(Spelled Babbitt on front)
❑ 557 Kent Hrbek RC 1.00 .40
❑ 558 Yankee Winners .20 .08
Ron Guidry
Tommy John
❑ 559 Mark Bomback .10 .04
❑ 560 Julio Valdez .10 .04
❑ 561 Buck Martinez .10 .04
❑ 562 Mike A. Marshall .20 .08
❑ 563 Rennie Stennett .10 .04
❑ 564 Steve Crawford .10 .04
❑ 565 Bob Babcock .10 .04
❑ 566 Johnny Podres CO .20 .08
❑ 567 Paul Serna .10 .04
❑ 568 Harold Baines .75 .30
❑ 569 Dave LaRoche .10 .04
❑ 570 Lee May .20 .08
❑ 571 Gary Ward .10 .04
❑ 572 John Denny .10 .04
❑ 573 Roy Smalley .10 .04
❑ 574 Bob Brenly RC .40 .16
❑ 575 Bronx Bombers .20 .08
Reggie Jackson
Dave Winfield
❑ 576 Luis Pujols .10 .04
❑ 577 Butch Hobson .10 .04
❑ 578 Harvey Kuenn MG .20 .08
❑ 579 Cal Ripken Sr. CO .20 .08
❑ 580 Juan Berenguer .10 .04
❑ 581 Benny Ayala .10 .04
❑ 582 Vance Law .10 .04
❑ 583 Rick Leach .10 .04
❑ 584 George Frazier .10 .04
❑ 585 Phillies Finest 1.50 .60
Pete Rose
Mike Schmidt
❑ 586 Joe Rudi .10 .04
❑ 587 Juan Beniquez .10 .04
❑ 588 Luis DeLeon .10 .04
❑ 589 Craig Swan .10 .04
❑ 590 Dave Chalk .10 .04
❑ 591 Billy Gardner MG .10 .04
❑ 592 Sal Bando .20 .08
❑ 593 Bert Campaneris .20 .08
❑ 594 Steve Kemp .10 .04
❑ 595A Randy Lerch ERR .40 .16
(Braves)
❑ 595B Randy Lerch COR .10 .04
(Brewers)
❑ 596 Bryan Clark RC .10 .04
❑ 597 Dave Ford .10 .04
❑ 598 Mike Scioscia .20 .08
❑ 599 John Lowenstein .10 .04
❑ 600 Rene Lachemann MG .10 .04
❑ 601 Mick Kelleher .10 .04
❑ 602 Ron Jackson .10 .04
❑ 603 Jerry Koosman .20 .08
❑ 604 Dave Goltz .10 .04
❑ 605 Ellis Valentine .10 .04
❑ 606 Lonnie Smith .20 .08
❑ 607 Joaquin Andujar .20 .08
❑ 608 Garry Hancock .10 .04
❑ 609 Jerry Turner .10 .04
❑ 610 Bob Bonner .10 .04
❑ 611 Jim Dwyer .10 .04
❑ 612 Terry Bulling .10 .04
❑ 613 Joel Youngblood .10 .04
❑ 614 Larry Milbourne .10 .04
❑ 615 Gene Roof UER .10 .04
(Name on front is Phil Roof)
❑ 616 Keith Drumwright .10 .04
❑ 617 Dave Rosello .10 .04
❑ 618 Rickey Keeton .10 .04
❑ 619 Dennis Lamp .10 .04
❑ 620 Sid Monge .10 .04
❑ 621 Jerry White .10 .04
❑ 622 Luis Aguayo .10 .04
❑ 623 Jamie Easterly .10 .04
❑ 624 Steve Sax RC .75 .30
❑ 625 Dave Roberts .10 .04
❑ 626 Rick Bosetti .10 .04
❑ 627 Terry Francona .40 .16
❑ 628 Pride of Reds .75 .30
Tom Seaver
Johnny Bench
❑ 629 Paul Mirabella .10 .04
❑ 630 Rance Mulliniks .10 .04
❑ 631 Kevin Hickey RC .10 .04
❑ 632 Reid Nichols .10 .04
❑ 633 Dave Geisel .10 .04
❑ 634 Ken Griffey .20 .08

Card	Nm-Mt	Ex-Mt
❑ 635 Bob Lemon MG	.75	.30
❑ 636 Orlando Sanchez	.10	.04
❑ 637 Bill Almon	.10	.04
❑ 638 Danny Ainge	1.00	.40
❑ 639 Willie Stargell	.40	.16
❑ 640 Bob Sykes	.10	.04
❑ 641 Ed Lynch	.10	.04
❑ 642 John Ellis	.10	.04
❑ 643 Ferguson Jenkins	.20	.08
❑ 644 Lenn Sakata	.10	.04
❑ 645 Julio Gonzalez	.10	.04
❑ 646 Jesse Orosco	.10	.04
❑ 647 Jerry Dybzinski	.10	.04
❑ 648 Tommy Davis CO	.20	.08
❑ 649 Ron Gardenhire RC	.10	.04
❑ 650 Felipe Alou CO	.20	.08
❑ 651 Harvey Haddix CO	.20	.08
❑ 652 Willie Upshaw	.10	.04
❑ 653 Bill Madlock	.20	.08
❑ 654A DK Checklist 1-26 ERR (Unnumbered) (With Trammel)	.75	.30
❑ 654B DK Checklist 1-26 COR (Unnumbered) (With Trammell)	.20	.08
❑ 655 Checklist 27-130 (Unnumbered)	.20	.08
❑ 656 Checklist 131-234 (Unnumbered)	.20	.08
❑ 657 Checklist 235-338 (Unnumbered)	.20	.08
❑ 658 Checklist 339-442 (Unnumbered)	.20	.08
❑ 659 Checklist 443-544 (Unnumbered)	.20	.08
❑ 660 Checklist 545-653 (Unnumbered)	.20	.08

1983 Donruss

	Nm-Mt	Ex-Mt
COMPLETE SET (660)	60.00	24.00
COMP.FACT.SET (660)	80.00	32.00
COMP.COBB PUZZLE	5.00	2.00

Card	Nm-Mt	Ex-Mt
❑ 1 Fernando Valenzuela DK	.40	.16
❑ 2 Rollie Fingers DK	.20	.08
❑ 3 Reggie Jackson DK	.40	.16
❑ 4 Jim Palmer DK	.20	.08
❑ 5 Jack Morris DK	.10	.04
❑ 6 George Foster DK	.20	.08
❑ 7 Jim Sundberg DK	.10	.04
❑ 8 Willie Stargell DK	.20	.08
❑ 9 Dave Stieb DK	.20	.08
❑ 10 Joe Niekro DK	.20	.08
❑ 11 Rickey Henderson DK	1.50	.60
❑ 12 Dale Murphy DK	.75	.30
❑ 13 Toby Harrah DK	.10	.04
❑ 14 Bill Buckner DK	.10	.04
❑ 15 Willie Wilson DK	.10	.04
❑ 16 Steve Carlton DK	.40	.16
❑ 17 Ron Guidry DK	.20	.08
❑ 18 Steve Rogers DK	.10	.04
❑ 19 Kent Hrbek DK	.20	.08
❑ 20 Keith Hernandez DK	.40	.16
❑ 21 Floyd Bannister DK	.10	.04
❑ 22 Johnny Bench DK	.75	.30
❑ 23 Britt Burns DK	.10	.04
❑ 24 Joe Morgan DK	.40	.16
❑ 25 Carl Yastrzemski DK	.40	.16
❑ 26 Terry Kennedy DK	.10	.04
❑ 27 Gary Roenicke	.10	.04
❑ 28 Dwight Bernard	.10	.04
❑ 29 Pat Underwood	.10	.04
❑ 30 Gary Allenson	.10	.04
❑ 31 Ron Guidry	.20	.08
❑ 32 Burt Hooton	.10	.04
❑ 33 Chris Bando	.10	.04
❑ 34 Vida Blue	.20	.08
❑ 35 Rickey Henderson	1.50	.60
❑ 36 Ray Burris	.10	.04
❑ 37 John Butcher	.10	.04
❑ 38 Don Aase	.10	.04
❑ 39 Jerry Koosman	.20	.08
❑ 40 Bruce Sutter	.20	.08
❑ 41 Jose Cruz	.20	.08
❑ 42 Pete Rose	2.50	1.00
❑ 43 Cesar Cedeno	.20	.08
❑ 44 Floyd Chiffer	.10	.04
❑ 45 Larry McWilliams	.10	.04
❑ 46 Alan Fowlkes	.10	.04
❑ 47 Dale Murphy	.75	.30
❑ 48 Doug Bird	.10	.04
❑ 49 Hubie Brooks	.20	.08
❑ 50 Floyd Bannister	.10	.04
❑ 51 Jack O'Connor	.10	.04
❑ 52 Steve Senteney	.10	.04
❑ 53 Gary Gaetti RC	.75	.30
❑ 54 Damaso Garcia	.10	.04
❑ 55 Gene Nelson	.10	.04
❑ 56 Mookie Wilson	.20	.08
❑ 57 Allen Ripley	.10	.04
❑ 58 Bob Horner	.10	.04
❑ 59 Tony Pena	.10	.04
❑ 60 Gary Lavelle	.10	.04
❑ 61 Tim Lollar	.10	.04
❑ 62 Frank Pastore	.10	.04
❑ 63 Garry Maddox	.10	.04
❑ 64 Bob Forsch	.10	.04
❑ 65 Harry Spilman	.10	.04
❑ 66 Geoff Zahn	.10	.04
❑ 67 Salome Barojas	.10	.04
❑ 68 David Palmer	.10	.04
❑ 69 Charlie Hough	.20	.08
❑ 70 Dan Quisenberry	.20	.08
❑ 71 Tony Armas	.10	.04
❑ 72 Rick Sutcliffe	.20	.08
❑ 73 Steve Balboni	.10	.04
❑ 74 Jerry Remy	.10	.04
❑ 75 Mike Scioscia	.20	.08
❑ 76 John Wockenfuss	.10	.04
❑ 77 Jim Palmer	.20	.08
❑ 78 Rollie Fingers	.20	.08
❑ 79 Joe Nolan	.10	.04
❑ 80 Pete Vuckovich	.10	.04
❑ 81 Rick Leach	.10	.04
❑ 82 Rick Miller	.10	.04
❑ 83 Graig Nettles	.20	.08
❑ 84 Ron Cey	.20	.08
❑ 85 Miguel Dilone	.10	.04
❑ 86 John Wathan	.10	.04
❑ 87 Kelvin Moore	.10	.04
❑ 88A Byrn Smith ERR (Sic, Bryn)	.20	.08
❑ 88B Bryn Smith COR	.40	.16
❑ 89 Dave Hostetler	.10	.04
❑ 90 Rod Carew	.40	.16
❑ 91 Lonnie Smith	.10	.04
❑ 92 Bob Knepper	.10	.04
❑ 93 Marty Bystrom	.10	.04
❑ 94 Chris Welsh	.10	.04
❑ 95 Jason Thompson	.10	.04
❑ 96 Tom O'Malley	.10	.04
❑ 97 Phil Niekro	.20	.08
❑ 98 Neil Allen	.10	.04
❑ 99 Bill Buckner	.20	.08
❑ 100 Ed VandeBerg	.10	.04
❑ 101 Jim Clancy	.10	.04
❑ 102 Robert Castillo	.10	.04
❑ 103 Bruce Berenyi	.10	.04
❑ 104 Carlton Fisk	.40	.16
❑ 105 Mike Flanagan	.20	.08
❑ 106 Cecil Cooper	.20	.08
❑ 107 Jack Morris	.20	.08
❑ 108 Mike Morgan	.10	.04
❑ 109 Luis Aponte	.10	.04
❑ 110 Pedro Guerrero	.20	.08
❑ 111 Len Barker	.10	.04
❑ 112 Willie Wilson	.20	.08
❑ 113 Dave Beard	.10	.04
❑ 114 Mike Gates	.10	.04
❑ 115 Reggie Jackson	.40	.16
❑ 116 George Wright RC	.10	.04
❑ 117 Vance Law	.10	.04
❑ 118 Nolan Ryan	4.00	1.60
❑ 119 Mike Krukow	.10	.04
❑ 120 Ozzie Smith	1.25	.50
❑ 121 Broderick Perkins	.10	.04
❑ 122 Tom Seaver	.75	.30
❑ 123 Chris Chambliss	.20	.08
❑ 124 Chuck Tanner MG	.10	.04
❑ 125 Johnnie LeMaster	.10	.04
❑ 126 Mel Hall RC	.20	.08
❑ 127 Bruce Bochte	.10	.04
❑ 128 Charlie Puleo	.10	.04
❑ 129 Luis Leal	.10	.04
❑ 130 John Pacella	.10	.04
❑ 131 Glenn Gulliver	.10	.04
❑ 132 Don Money	.10	.04
❑ 133 Dave Rozema	.10	.04
❑ 134 Bruce Hurst	.10	.04
❑ 135 Rudy May	.10	.04
❑ 136 Tom Lasorda MG	.40	.16
❑ 137 Dan Spillner UER (Photo actually Ed Whitson)	.10	.04
❑ 138 Jerry Martin	.10	.04
❑ 139 Mike Norris	.10	.04
❑ 140 Al Oliver	.20	.08
❑ 141 Daryl Sconiers	.10	.04
❑ 142 Lamar Johnson	.10	.04
❑ 143 Harold Baines	.75	.30
❑ 144 Alan Ashby	.10	.04
❑ 145 Garry Templeton	.10	.04
❑ 146 Al Holland	.10	.04
❑ 147 Bo Diaz	.10	.04
❑ 148 Dave Concepcion	.20	.08
❑ 149 Rick Camp	.10	.04
❑ 150 Jim Morrison	.10	.04
❑ 151 Randy Martz	.10	.04
❑ 152 Keith Hernandez	.40	.16
❑ 153 John Lowenstein	.10	.04
❑ 154 Mike Caldwell	.10	.04
❑ 155 Milt Wilcox	.10	.04
❑ 156 Rich Gedman	.10	.04
❑ 157 Rich Gossage	.40	.16
❑ 158 Jerry Reuss	.20	.08
❑ 159 Ron Hassey	.10	.04
❑ 160 Larry Gura	.10	.04
❑ 161 Dwayne Murphy	.10	.04
❑ 162 Woodie Fryman	.10	.04
❑ 163 Steve Comer	.10	.04
❑ 164 Ken Forsch	.10	.04
❑ 165 Dennis Lamp	.10	.04
❑ 166 David Green RC	.10	.04
❑ 167 Terry Puhl	.10	.04
❑ 168 Mike Schmidt (Wearing 37 rather than 20)	2.00	.80
❑ 169 Eddie Milner	.10	.04
❑ 170 John Curtis	.10	.04
❑ 171 Don Robinson	.10	.04
❑ 172 Rich Gale	.10	.04
❑ 173 Steve Bedrosian	.20	.08
❑ 174 Willie Hernandez	.20	.08
❑ 175 Ron Gardenhire	.10	.04
❑ 176 Jim Beattie	.10	.04
❑ 177 Tim Laudner	.10	.04
❑ 178 Buck Martinez	.10	.04
❑ 179 Kent Hrbek	.20	.08
❑ 180 Alfredo Griffin	.10	.04
❑ 181 Larry Andersen	.10	.04
❑ 182 Pete Falcone	.10	.04
❑ 183 Jody Davis	.10	.04
❑ 184 Glenn Hubbard	.10	.04
❑ 185 Dale Berra	.10	.04
❑ 186 Greg Minton	.10	.04
❑ 187 Gary Lucas	.10	.04
❑ 188 Dave Van Gorder	.10	.04
❑ 189 Bob Dernier	.10	.04

	Card	Price	Price
❑ 190	Willie McGee RC	1.50	.60
❑ 191	Dickie Thon	.10	.04
❑ 192	Bob Boone	.20	.08
❑ 193	Britt Burns	.10	.04
❑ 194	Jeff Reardon	.20	.08
❑ 195	Jon Matlack	.10	.04
❑ 196	Don Slaught RC	.40	.16
❑ 197	Fred Stanley	.10	.04
❑ 198	Rick Manning	.10	.04
❑ 199	Dave Righetti	.20	.08
❑ 200	Dave Stapleton	.10	.04
❑ 201	Steve Yeager	.10	.04
❑ 202	Enos Cabell	.10	.04
❑ 203	Sammy Stewart	.10	.04
❑ 204	Moose Haas	.10	.04
❑ 205	Lenn Sakata	.10	.04
❑ 206	Charlie Moore	.10	.04
❑ 207	Alan Trammell	.40	.16
❑ 208	Jim Rice	.20	.08
❑ 209	Roy Smalley	.10	.04
❑ 210	Bill Russell	.10	.04
❑ 211	Andre Thornton	.10	.04
❑ 212	Willie Aikens	.10	.04
❑ 213	Dave McKay	.10	.04
❑ 214	Tim Blackwell	.10	.04
❑ 215	Buddy Bell	.20	.08
❑ 216	Doug DeCinces	.20	.08
❑ 217	Tom Herr	.20	.08
❑ 218	Frank LaCorte	.10	.04
❑ 219	Steve Carlton	.40	.16
❑ 220	Terry Kennedy	.10	.04
❑ 221	Mike Easler	.10	.04
❑ 222	Jack Clark	.20	.08
❑ 223	Gene Garber	.10	.04
❑ 224	Scott Holman	.10	.04
❑ 225	Mike Proly	.10	.04
❑ 226	Terry Bulling	.10	.04
❑ 227	Jerry Garvin	.10	.04
❑ 228	Ron Davis	.10	.04
❑ 229	Tom Hume	.10	.04
❑ 230	Marc Hill	.10	.04
❑ 231	Dennis Martinez	.20	.08
❑ 232	Jim Gantner	.10	.04
❑ 233	Larry Pashnick	.10	.04
❑ 234	Dave Collins	.10	.04
❑ 235	Tom Burgmeier	.10	.04
❑ 236	Ken Landreaux	.10	.04
❑ 237	John Denny	.10	.04
❑ 238	Hal McRae	.20	.08
❑ 239	Matt Keough	.10	.04
❑ 240	Doug Flynn	.10	.04
❑ 241	Fred Lynn	.20	.08
❑ 242	Billy Sample	.10	.04
❑ 243	Tom Paciorek	.20	.08
❑ 244	Joe Sambito	.10	.04
❑ 245	Sid Monge	.10	.04
❑ 246	Ken Oberkfell	.10	.04
❑ 247	Joe Pittman UER (Photo actually Juan Eichelberger)	.10	.04
❑ 248	Mario Soto	.10	.04
❑ 249	Claudell Washington	.10	.04
❑ 250	Rick Rhoden	.10	.04
❑ 251	Darrell Evans	.20	.08
❑ 252	Steve Henderson	.10	.04
❑ 253	Manny Castillo	.10	.04
❑ 254	Craig Swan	.10	.04
❑ 255	Joey McLaughlin	.10	.04
❑ 256	Pete Redfern	.10	.04
❑ 257	Ken Singleton	.10	.04
❑ 258	Robin Yount	.75	.30
❑ 259	Elias Sosa	.10	.04
❑ 260	Bob Ojeda	.10	.04
❑ 261	Bobby Murcer	.20	.08
❑ 262	Candy Maldonado RC	.20	.08
❑ 263	Rick Waits	.10	.04
❑ 264	Greg Pryor	.10	.04
❑ 265	Bob Owchinko	.10	.04
❑ 266	Chris Speier	.10	.04
❑ 267	Bruce Kison	.10	.04
❑ 268	Mark Wagner	.10	.04
❑ 269	Steve Kemp	.10	.04
❑ 270	Phil Garner	.20	.08
❑ 271	Gene Richards	.10	.04
❑ 272	Renie Martin	.10	.04
❑ 273	Dave Roberts	.10	.04
❑ 274	Dan Driessen	.10	.04
❑ 275	Rufino Linares	.10	.04
❑ 276	Lee Lacy	.10	.04
❑ 277	Ryne Sandberg RC	10.00	4.00
❑ 278	Darrell Porter	.10	.04
❑ 279	Cal Ripken	6.00	2.40
❑ 280	Jamie Easterly	.10	.04
❑ 281	Bill Fahey	.10	.04
❑ 282	Glenn Hoffman	.10	.04
❑ 283	Willie Randolph	.20	.08
❑ 284	Fernando Valenzuela	.40	.16
❑ 285	Alan Bannister	.10	.04
❑ 286	Paul Splittorff	.10	.04
❑ 287	Joe Rudi	.10	.04
❑ 288	Bill Gullickson	.10	.04
❑ 289	Danny Darwin	.10	.04
❑ 290	Andy Hassler	.10	.04
❑ 291	Ernesto Escarrega	.10	.04
❑ 292	Steve Mura	.10	.04
❑ 293	Tony Scott	.10	.04
❑ 294	Manny Trillo	.10	.04
❑ 295	Greg Harris	.10	.04
❑ 296	Luis DeLeon	.10	.04
❑ 297	Kent Tekulve	.20	.08
❑ 298	Atlee Hammaker	.10	.04
❑ 299	Bruce Benedict	.10	.04
❑ 300	Fergie Jenkins	.20	.08
❑ 301	Dave Kingman	.40	.16
❑ 302	Bill Caudill	.10	.04
❑ 303	John Castino	.10	.04
❑ 304	Ernie Whitt	.10	.04
❑ 305	Randy Johnson	.10	.04
❑ 306	Garth Iorg	.10	.04
❑ 307	Gaylord Perry	.20	.08
❑ 308	Ed Lynch	.10	.04
❑ 309	Keith Moreland	.10	.04
❑ 310	Rafael Ramirez	.10	.04
❑ 311	Bill Madlock	.20	.08
❑ 312	Milt May	.10	.04
❑ 313	John Montefusco	.10	.04
❑ 314	Wayne Krenchicki	.10	.04
❑ 315	George Vukovich	.10	.04
❑ 316	Joaquin Andujar	.10	.04
❑ 317	Craig Reynolds	.10	.04
❑ 318	Rick Burleson	.10	.04
❑ 319	Richard Dotson	.10	.04
❑ 320	Steve Rogers	.10	.04
❑ 321	Dave Schmidt	.10	.04
❑ 322	Bud Black RC	.20	.08
❑ 323	Jeff Burroughs	.10	.04
❑ 324	Von Hayes	.20	.08
❑ 325	Butch Wynegar	.10	.04
❑ 326	Carl Yastrzemski	.75	.30
❑ 327	Ron Roenicke	.10	.04
❑ 328	Howard Johnson RC	.75	.30
❑ 329	Rick Dempsey UER (Posing as a left-handed batter)	.20	.08
❑ 330A	Jim Slaton (Bio printed black on white)	.10	.04
❑ 330B	Jim Slaton (Bio printed black on yellow)	.20	.08
❑ 331	Benny Ayala	.10	.04
❑ 332	Ted Simmons	.20	.08
❑ 333	Lou Whitaker	.40	.16
❑ 334	Chuck Rainey	.10	.04
❑ 335	Lou Piniella	.20	.08
❑ 336	Steve Sax	.20	.08
❑ 337	Toby Harrah	.10	.04
❑ 338	George Brett	2.50	1.00
❑ 339	Dave Lopes	.20	.08
❑ 340	Gary Carter	.40	.16
❑ 341	John Grubb	.10	.04
❑ 342	Tim Foli	.10	.04
❑ 343	Jim Kaat	.20	.08
❑ 344	Mike LaCoss	.10	.04
❑ 345	Larry Christenson	.10	.04
❑ 346	Juan Bonilla	.10	.04
❑ 347	Omar Moreno	.10	.04
❑ 348	Chili Davis	.75	.30
❑ 349	Tommy Boggs	.10	.04
❑ 350	Rusty Staub	.20	.08
❑ 351	Bump Wills	.10	.04
❑ 352	Rick Sweet	.10	.04
❑ 353	Jim Gott RC	.10	.04
❑ 354	Terry Felton	.10	.04
❑ 355	Jim Kern	.10	.04
❑ 356	Bill Almon UER (Expos/Mets in 1983, not Padres/Mets)	.10	.04
❑ 357	Tippy Martinez	.10	.04
❑ 358	Roy Howell	.10	.04
❑ 359	Dan Petry	.10	.04
❑ 360	Jerry Mumphrey	.10	.04
❑ 361	Mark Clear	.10	.04
❑ 362	Mike Marshall	.10	.04
❑ 363	Lary Sorensen	.10	.04
❑ 364	Amos Otis	.20	.08
❑ 365	Rick Langford	.10	.04
❑ 366	Brad Mills	.10	.04
❑ 367	Brian Downing	.10	.04
❑ 368	Mike Richardt	.10	.04
❑ 369	Aurelio Rodriguez	.10	.04
❑ 370	Dave Smith	.10	.04
❑ 371	Tug McGraw	.20	.08
❑ 372	Doug Bair	.10	.04
❑ 373	Ruppert Jones	.10	.04
❑ 374	Alex Trevino	.10	.04
❑ 375	Ken Dayley	.10	.04
❑ 376	Rod Scurry	.10	.04
❑ 377	Bob Brenly	.10	.04
❑ 378	Scot Thompson	.10	.04
❑ 379	Julio Cruz	.10	.04
❑ 380	John Stearns	.10	.04
❑ 381	Dale Murray	.10	.04
❑ 382	Frank Viola RC	.75	.30
❑ 383	Al Bumbry	.10	.04
❑ 384	Ben Oglivie	.10	.04
❑ 385	Dave Tobik	.10	.04
❑ 386	Bob Stanley	.10	.04
❑ 387	Andre Robertson	.10	.04
❑ 388	Jorge Orta	.10	.04
❑ 389	Ed Whitson	.10	.04
❑ 390	Don Hood	.10	.04
❑ 391	Tom Underwood	.10	.04
❑ 392	Tim Wallach	.20	.08
❑ 393	Steve Renko	.10	.04
❑ 394	Mickey Rivers	.10	.04
❑ 395	Greg Luzinski	.20	.08
❑ 396	Art Howe	.20	.08
❑ 397	Alan Wiggins	.10	.04
❑ 398	Jim Barr	.10	.04
❑ 399	Ivan DeJesus	.10	.04
❑ 400	Tom Lawless	.10	.04
❑ 401	Bob Walk	.10	.04
❑ 402	Jimmy Smith	.10	.04
❑ 403	Lee Smith	.75	.30
❑ 404	George Hendrick	.10	.04
❑ 405	Eddie Murray	.75	.30
❑ 406	Marshall Edwards	.10	.04
❑ 407	Lance Parrish	.20	.08
❑ 408	Carney Lansford	.20	.08
❑ 409	Dave Winfield	.40	.16
❑ 410	Bob Welch	.20	.08
❑ 411	Larry Milbourne	.10	.04
❑ 412	Dennis Leonard	.10	.04
❑ 413	Dan Meyer	.10	.04
❑ 414	Charlie Lea	.10	.04
❑ 415	Rick Honeycutt	.10	.04
❑ 416	Mike Witt	.10	.04
❑ 417	Steve Trout	.10	.04
❑ 418	Glenn Brummer	.10	.04
❑ 419	Denny Walling	.10	.04
❑ 420	Gary Matthews	.20	.08
❑ 421	Charlie Leibrandt UER (Liebrandt on front of card)	.10	.04
❑ 422	J.Eichelberger UER Photo actually Joe Pittman	.10	.04
❑ 423	Cecilio Guante UER (Listed as Matt on card)	.10	.04
❑ 424	Bill Laskey	.10	.04
❑ 425	Jerry Royster	.10	.04
❑ 426	Dickie Noles	.10	.04
❑ 427	George Foster	.20	.08
❑ 428	Mike Moore RC	.20	.08
❑ 429	Gary Ward	.10	.04
❑ 430	Barry Bonnell	.10	.04

	No.	Player		
❑	431	Ron Washington	.10	.04
❑	432	Rance Mulliniks	.10	.04
❑	433	Mike Stanton	.10	.04
❑	434	Jesse Orosco	.10	.04
❑	435	Larry Bowa	.20	.08
❑	436	Biff Pocoroba	.10	.04
❑	437	Johnny Ray	.10	.04
❑	438	Joe Morgan	.40	.16
❑	439	Eric Show	.10	.04
❑	440	Larry Biittner	.10	.04
❑	441	Greg Gross	.10	.04
❑	442	Gene Tenace	.20	.08
❑	443	Danny Heep	.10	.04
❑	444	Bobby Clark	.10	.04
❑	445	Kevin Hickey	.10	.04
❑	446	Scott Sanderson	.10	.04
❑	447	Frank Tanana	.20	.08
❑	448	Cesar Geronimo	.10	.04
❑	449	Jimmy Sexton	.10	.04
❑	450	Mike Hargrove	.20	.08
❑	451	Doyle Alexander	.10	.04
❑	452	Dwight Evans	.20	.08
❑	453	Terry Forster	.10	.04
❑	454	Tom Brookens	.10	.04
❑	455	Rich Dauer	.10	.04
❑	456	Rob Picciolo	.10	.04
❑	457	Terry Crowley	.10	.04
❑	458	Ned Yost	.10	.04
❑	459	Kirk Gibson	.75	.30
❑	460	Reid Nichols	.10	.04
❑	461	Oscar Gamble	.10	.04
❑	462	Dusty Baker	.20	.08
❑	463	Jack Perconte	.10	.04
❑	464	Frank White	.20	.08
❑	465	Mickey Klutts	.10	.04
❑	466	Warren Cromartie	.10	.04
❑	467	Larry Parrish	.10	.04
❑	468	Bobby Grich	.20	.08
❑	469	Dane Iorg	.10	.04
❑	470	Joe Niekro	.20	.08
❑	471	Ed Farmer	.10	.04
❑	472	Tim Flannery	.10	.04
❑	473	Dave Parker	.20	.08
❑	474	Jeff Leonard	.10	.04
❑	475	Al Hrabosky	.10	.04
❑	476	Ron Hodges	.10	.04
❑	477	Leon Durham	.10	.04
❑	478	Jim Essian	.10	.04
❑	479	Roy Lee Jackson	.10	.04
❑	480	Brad Havens	.10	.04
❑	481	Joe Price	.10	.04
❑	482	Tony Bernazard	.10	.04
❑	483	Scott McGregor	.10	.04
❑	484	Paul Molitor	1.00	.40
❑	485	Mike Ivie	.10	.04
❑	486	Ken Griffey	.20	.08
❑	487	Dennis Eckersley	.40	.16
❑	488	Steve Garvey	.20	.08
❑	489	Mike Fischlin	.10	.04
❑	490	U.L. Washington	.10	.04
❑	491	Steve McCatty	.10	.04
❑	492	Roy Johnson	.10	.04
❑	493	Don Baylor	.40	.16
❑	494	Bobby Johnson	.10	.04
❑	495	Mike Squires	.10	.04
❑	496	Bert Roberge	.10	.04
❑	497	Dick Ruthven	.10	.04
❑	498	Tito Landrum	.10	.04
❑	499	Sixto Lezcano	.10	.04
❑	500	Johnny Bench	.75	.30
❑	501	Larry Whisenton	.10	.04
❑	502	Manny Sarmiento	.10	.04
❑	503	Fred Breining	.10	.04
❑	504	Bill Campbell	.10	.04
❑	505	Todd Cruz	.10	.04
❑	506	Bob Bailor	.10	.04
❑	507	Dave Stieb	.20	.08
❑	508	Al Williams	.10	.04
❑	509	Dan Ford	.10	.04
❑	510	Gorman Thomas	.10	.04
❑	511	Chet Lemon	.10	.04
❑	512	Mike Torrez	.10	.04
❑	513	Shane Rawley	.10	.04
❑	514	Mark Belanger	.10	.04
❑	515	Rodney Craig	.10	.04
❑	516	Onix Concepcion	.10	.04
❑	517	Mike Heath	.10	.04
❑	518	Andre Dawson UER (Middle name Fernando, should be Nolan)	.20	.08
❑	519	Luis Sanchez	.10	.04
❑	520	Terry Bogener	.10	.04
❑	521	Rudy Law	.10	.04
❑	522	Ray Knight	.20	.08
❑	523	Joe Lefebvre	.10	.04
❑	524	Jim Wohlford	.10	.04
❑	525	Julio Franco RC	1.00	.40
❑	526	Ron Oester	.10	.04
❑	527	Rick Mahler	.10	.04
❑	528	Steve Nicosia	.10	.04
❑	529	Junior Kennedy	.10	.04
❑	530A	Whitey Herzog MG (Bio printed black on white)	.20	.08
❑	530B	Whitey Herzog MG (Bio printed black on yellow)	.20	.08
❑	531A	Don Sutton (Blue border on photo)	.75	.30
❑	531B	Don Sutton (Green border on photo)	.75	.30
❑	532	Mark Brouhard	.10	.04
❑	533A	S.Anderson MG Bio printed black on white	.20	.08
❑	533B	S.Anderson MG Bio printed black on yellow	.20	.08
❑	534	Roger LaFrancois	.10	.04
❑	535	George Frazier	.10	.04
❑	536	Tom Niedenfuer	.10	.04
❑	537	Ed Glynn	.10	.04
❑	538	Lee May	.20	.08
❑	539	Bob Kearney	.10	.04
❑	540	Tim Raines	.75	.30
❑	541	Paul Mirabella	.10	.04
❑	542	Luis Tiant	.20	.08
❑	543	Ron LeFlore	.10	.04
❑	544	Dave LaPoint	.10	.04
❑	545	Randy Moffitt	.10	.04
❑	546	Luis Aguayo	.10	.04
❑	547	Brad Lesley	.20	.08
❑	548	Luis Salazar	.10	.04
❑	549	John Candelaria	.10	.04
❑	550	Dave Bergman	.10	.04
❑	551	Bob Watson	.20	.08
❑	552	Pat Tabler	.10	.04
❑	553	Brent Gaff	.10	.04
❑	554	Al Cowens	.10	.04
❑	555	Tom Brunansky	.20	.08
❑	556	Lloyd Moseby	.10	.04
❑	557A	Pascual Perez ERR (Twins in glove)	2.00	.80
❑	557B	Pascual Perez COR (Braves in glove)	.20	.08
❑	558	Willie Upshaw	.10	.04
❑	559	Richie Zisk	.10	.04
❑	560	Pat Zachry	.10	.04
❑	561	Jay Johnstone	.20	.08
❑	562	Carlos Diaz RC	.10	.04
❑	563	John Tudor	.10	.04
❑	564	Frank Robinson MG	.40	.16
❑	565	Dave Edwards	.10	.04
❑	566	Paul Householder	.10	.04
❑	567	Ron Reed	.10	.04
❑	568	Mike Ramsey	.10	.04
❑	569	Kiko Garcia	.10	.04
❑	570	Tommy John	.40	.16
❑	571	Tony LaRussa MG	.20	.08
❑	572	Joel Youngblood	.10	.04
❑	573	Wayne Tolleson	.10	.04
❑	574	Keith Creel	.10	.04
❑	575	Billy Martin MG	.20	.08
❑	576	Jerry Dybzinski	.10	.04
❑	577	Rick Cerone	.10	.04
❑	578	Tony Perez	.40	.16
❑	579	Greg Brock	.10	.04
❑	580	Glenn Wilson	.10	.04
❑	581	Tim Stoddard	.10	.04
❑	582	Bob McClure	.10	.04
❑	583	Jim Dwyer	.10	.04
❑	584	Ed Romero	.10	.04
❑	585	Larry Herndon	.10	.04
❑	586	Wade Boggs RC	8.00	3.20
❑	587	Jay Howell	.10	.04
❑	588	Dave Stewart	.20	.08
❑	589	Bert Blyleven	.40	.16
❑	590	Dick Howser MG	.10	.04
❑	591	Wayne Gross	.10	.04
❑	592	Terry Francona	.10	.04
❑	593	Don Werner	.10	.04
❑	594	Bill Stein	.10	.04
❑	595	Jesse Barfield	.20	.08
❑	596	Bob Molinaro	.10	.04
❑	597	Mike Vail	.10	.04
❑	598	Tony Gwynn RC	15.00	6.00
❑	599	Gary Rajsich	.10	.04
❑	600	Jerry Ujdur	.10	.04
❑	601	Cliff Johnson	.10	.04
❑	602	Jerry White	.10	.04
❑	603	Bryan Clark	.10	.04
❑	604	Joe Ferguson	.10	.04
❑	605	Guy Sularz	.10	.04
❑	606A	Ozzie Virgil (Green border on photo)	.20	.08
❑	606B	Ozzie Virgil (Orange border on photo)	.20	.08
❑	607	Terry Harper	.10	.04
❑	608	Harvey Kuenn MG	.10	.04
❑	609	Jim Sundberg	.20	.08
❑	610	Willie Stargell	.40	.16
❑	611	Reggie Smith	.20	.08
❑	612	Rob Wilfong	.10	.04
❑	613	The Niekro Brothers Joe Niekro Phil Niekro	.20	.08
❑	614	Lee Elia MG	.10	.04
❑	615	Mickey Hatcher	.10	.04
❑	616	Jerry Hairston	.10	.04
❑	617	John Martin	.10	.04
❑	618	Wally Backman	.10	.04
❑	619	Storm Davis RC	.10	.04
❑	620	Alan Knicely	.10	.04
❑	621	John Stuper	.10	.04
❑	622	Matt Sinatro	.10	.04
❑	623	Geno Petralli	.40	.16
❑	624	Duane Walker	.10	.04
❑	625	Dick Williams MG	.10	.04
❑	626	Pat Corrales MG	.10	.04
❑	627	Vern Ruhle	.10	.04
❑	628	Joe Torre MG	.20	.08
❑	629	Anthony Johnson	.10	.04
❑	630	Steve Howe	.10	.04
❑	631	Gary Woods	.10	.04
❑	632	LaMarr Hoyt	.20	.08
❑	633	Steve Swisher	.10	.04
❑	634	Terry Leach	.10	.04
❑	635	Jeff Newman	.10	.04
❑	636	Brett Butler	.75	.30
❑	637	Gary Gray	.10	.04
❑	638	Lee Mazzilli	.10	.04
❑	639A	Ron Jackson ERR (A's in glove)	20.00	8.00
❑	639B	Ron Jackson COR (Angels in glove, red border on photo)	.10	.04
❑	639C	Ron Jackson COR (Angels in glove, green border on photo)	.75	.30
❑	640	Juan Beniquez	.10	.04
❑	641	Dave Rucker	.10	.04
❑	642	Luis Pujols	.10	.04
❑	643	Rick Monday	.10	.04
❑	644	Hosken Powell	.10	.04
❑	645	The Chicken	.75	.30
❑	646	Dave Engle	.10	.04
❑	647	Dick Davis	.10	.04
❑	648	Frank Robinson Vida Blue Joe Morgan	.40	.16
❑	649	Al Chambers	.10	.04
❑	650	Jesus Vega	.10	.04

- ❑ 651 Jeff Jones .10 .04
- ❑ 652 Marvis Foley .10 .04
- ❑ 653 Ty Cobb Puzzle Card .75 .30
- ❑ 654A Dick Perez/Diamond .75 .30
  King Checklist 1-26
  (Unnumbered) ERR
  (Word "checklist"
  omitted from back)
- ❑ 654B Dick Perez/Diamond .75 .30
  King Checklist 1-26
  (Unnumbered) COR
  (Word "checklist"
  is on back)
- ❑ 655 Checklist 27-130 .10 .04
  (Unnumbered)
- ❑ 656 Checklist 131-234 .10 .04
  (Unnumbered)
- ❑ 657 Checklist 235-338 .10 .04
  (Unnumbered)
- ❑ 658 Checklist 339-442 .10 .04
  (Unnumbered)
- ❑ 659 Checklist 443-544 .10 .04
  (Unnumbered)
- ❑ 660 Checklist 545-653 .10 .04
  (Unnumbered)

1984 Donruss

	Nm-Mt	Ex-Mt
COMPLETE SET (660)	120.00	47.50
COMP.FACT.SET (658)	150.00	60.00
COMP.SNIDER PUZZLE	5.00	2.00

- ❑ 1 Robin Yount DK COR 2.00 .80
- ❑ 1A Robin Yount DK ERR 3.00 1.20
- ❑ 2 Dave Concepcion DK 1.50 .60
  COR
- ❑ 2A Dave Concepcion DK .75 .30
  ERR (Perez Steel)
- ❑ 3 Dwayne Murphy DK .75 .30
  COR
- ❑ 3A Dwayne Murphy DK .25 .10
  ERR (Perez Steel)
- ❑ 4 John Castino DK COR .75 .30
- ❑ 4A John Castino DK ERR .25 .10
  (Perez Steel)
- ❑ 5 Leon Durham DK COR .75 .30
- ❑ 5A Leon Durham DK ERR .25 .10
  (Perez Steel)
- ❑ 6 Rusty Staub DK COR 1.50 .60
- ❑ 6A Rusty Staub DK ERR .75 .30
  (Perez Steel)
- ❑ 7 Jack Clark DK COR .75 .30
- ❑ 7A Jack Clark DK ERR .75 .30
  (Perez Steel)
- ❑ 8 Dave Dravecky DK .75 .30
  COR
- ❑ 8A Dave Dravecky DK .75 .30
  ERR (Perez Steel)
- ❑ 9 Al Oliver DK COR 1.50 .60
- ❑ 9A Al Oliver DK ERR .75 .30
  (Perez Steel)
- ❑ 10 Dave Righetti DK .75 .30
  COR
- ❑ 10A Dave Righetti DK .75 .30
  ERR (Perez Steel)
- ❑ 11 Hal McRae DK COR 1.50 .60
- ❑ 11A Hal McRae DK ERR .75 .30
  (Perez Steel)
- ❑ 12 Ray Knight DK COR .75 .30
- ❑ 12A Ray Knight DK ERR .75 .30
  (Perez Steel)
- ❑ 13 Bruce Sutter DK COR 1.50 .60
- ❑ 13A Bruce Sutter DK ERR .75 .30
  (Perez Steel)
- ❑ 14 Bob Horner DK COR .75 .30
- ❑ 14A Bob Horner DK ERR .75 .30
  (Perez Steel)
- ❑ 15 Lance Parrish DK 1.50 .60
  COR
- ❑ 15A Lance Parrish DK .75 .30
  ERR (Perez Steel)
- ❑ 16 Matt Young DK COR .75 .30
- ❑ 16A Matt Young DK ERR .25 .10
  (Perez Steel)
- ❑ 17 Fred Lynn DK COR .75 .30
- ❑ 17A Fred Lynn DK ERR .25 .10
  (Perez Steel)
  (A's logo on back
- ❑ 18 Ron Kittle DK COR .75 .30
- ❑ 18A Ron Kittle DK ERR .25 .10
  (Perez Steel)
- ❑ 19 Jim Clancy DK COR .75 .30
- ❑ 19A Jim Clancy DK ERR .25 .10
  (Perez Steel)
- ❑ 20 Bill Madlock DK COR 1.50 .60
- ❑ 20A Bill Madlock DK ERR .75 .30
  (Perez Steel)
- ❑ 21 Larry Parrish DK .75 .30
  COR
- ❑ 21A Larry Parrish DK .25 .10
  ERR (Perez Steel)
- ❑ 22 Eddie Murray DK COR 3.00 1.20
- ❑ 22A Eddie Murray DK ERR 3.00 1.20
- ❑ 23 Mike Schmidt DK COR 5.00 2.00
- ❑ 23A M.Schmidt DK ERR 5.00 2.00
- ❑ 24 Pedro Guerrero DK .75 .30
  COR
- ❑ 24A Pedro Guerrero DK .75 .30
  ERR (Perez Steel)
- ❑ 25 Andre Thornton DK .75 .30
  COR
- ❑ 25A Andre Thornton DK .75 .30
  ERR (Perez Steel)
- ❑ 26 Wade Boggs DK COR 3.00 1.20
- ❑ 26A Wade Boggs DK ERR 2.50 1.00
- ❑ 27 Joel Skinner RR RC .25 .10
- ❑ 28 Tommy Dunbar RR RC .25 .10
- ❑ 29A M.Stenhouse RC RR .25 .10
  ERR No number on back
- ❑ 29B Mike Stenhouse RR 3.00 1.20
  COR Numbered on back
- ❑ 30A R.Darling RC RR ERR .75 .30
  No number on back
- ❑ 30B Ron Darling RR COR 3.00 1.20
  (Numbered on back)
- ❑ 31 Dion James RR RC .25 .10
- ❑ 32 Tony Fernandez RR RC 3.00 1.20
- ❑ 33 Angel Salazar RR RC .25 .10
- ❑ 34 K. McReynolds RR RC 1.50 .60
- ❑ 35 Dick Schofield RR RC .75 .30
- ❑ 36 Brad Komminsk RR RC .25 .10
- ❑ 37 Tim Teufel RR RC .25 .10
- ❑ 38 Doug Frobel RR RC .25 .10
- ❑ 39 Greg Gagne RR RC .75 .30
- ❑ 40 Mike Fuentes RR RC .25 .10
- ❑ 41 Joe Carter RR RC 10.00 4.00
- ❑ 42 Mike Brown RC RR .25 .10
  (Angels OF)
- ❑ 43 Mike Jeffcoat RR RC .25 .10
- ❑ 44 Sid Fernandez RR RC 1.50 .60
- ❑ 45 Brian Dayett RR RC .25 .10
- ❑ 46 Chris Smith RR RC .25 .10
- ❑ 47 Eddie Murray 3.00 1.20
- ❑ 48 Robin Yount 3.00 1.20
- ❑ 49 Lance Parrish 1.50 .60
- ❑ 50 Jim Rice .75 .30
- ❑ 51 Dave Winfield 1.50 .60
- ❑ 52 Fernando Valenzuela .75 .30
- ❑ 53 George Brett 10.00 4.00
- ❑ 54 Rickey Henderson 6.00 2.40
- ❑ 55 Gary Carter 1.50 .60
- ❑ 56 Buddy Bell .75 .30
- ❑ 57 Reggie Jackson 1.50 .60
- ❑ 58 Harold Baines 3.00 1.20
- ❑ 59 Ozzie Smith 4.00 1.60
- ❑ 60 Nolan Ryan UER 15.00 6.00
  (Text on back refers to 1972 as
  the year he struck out 383;
  the year was 1973)
- ❑ 61 Pete Rose 10.00 4.00
- ❑ 62 Ron Oester .25 .10
- ❑ 63 Steve Garvey .75 .30
- ❑ 64 Jason Thompson .25 .10
- ❑ 65 Jack Clark .75 .30
- ❑ 66 Dale Murphy 3.00 1.20
- ❑ 67 Leon Durham .25 .10
- ❑ 68 Darryl Strawberry RC 5.00 2.00
- ❑ 69 Richie Zisk .25 .10
- ❑ 70 Kent Hrbek .75 .30
- ❑ 71 Dave Stieb .25 .10
- ❑ 72 Ken Schrom .25 .10
- ❑ 73 George Bell .75 .30
- ❑ 74 John Moses .25 .10
- ❑ 75 Ed Lynch .25 .10
- ❑ 76 Chuck Rainey .25 .10
- ❑ 77 Biff Pocoroba .25 .10
- ❑ 78 Cecilio Guante .25 .10
- ❑ 79 Jim Barr .25 .10
- ❑ 80 Kurt Bevacqua .25 .10
- ❑ 81 Tom Foley .25 .10
- ❑ 82 Joe Lefebvre .25 .10
- ❑ 83 Andy Van Slyke RC 3.00 1.20
- ❑ 84 Bob Lillis MG .25 .10
- ❑ 85 Ricky Adams .25 .10
- ❑ 86 Jerry Hairston .25 .10
- ❑ 87 Bob James .25 .10
- ❑ 88 Joe Altobelli MG .25 .10
- ❑ 89 Ed Romero .25 .10
- ❑ 90 John Grubb .25 .10
- ❑ 91 John Henry Johnson .25 .10
- ❑ 92 Juan Espino .25 .10
- ❑ 93 Candy Maldonado .25 .10
- ❑ 94 Andre Thornton .25 .10
- ❑ 95 Onix Concepcion .25 .10
- ❑ 96 Donnie Hill UER .25 .10
  (Listed as P,
  should be 2B)
- ❑ 97 Andre Dawson UER .75 .30
  (Wrong middle name,
  should be Nolan)
- ❑ 98 Frank Tanana .75 .30
- ❑ 99 Curtis Wilkerson .25 .10
- ❑ 100 Larry Gura .25 .10
- ❑ 101 Dwayne Murphy .25 .10
- ❑ 102 Tom Brennan .25 .10
- ❑ 103 Dave Righetti .75 .30
- ❑ 104 Steve Sax .75 .30
- ❑ 105 Dan Petry .75 .30
- ❑ 106 Cal Ripken 20.00 8.00
- ❑ 107 Paul Molitor UER 1.50 .60
  ('83 stats should
  say .270 BA, 608 AB,
  and 164 hits)
- ❑ 108 Fred Lynn .75 .30
- ❑ 109 Neil Allen .25 .10
- ❑ 110 Joe Niekro .75 .30
- ❑ 111 Steve Carlton 1.50 .60
- ❑ 112 Terry Kennedy .25 .10
- ❑ 113 Bill Madlock .75 .30
- ❑ 114 Chili Davis 1.50 .60
- ❑ 115 Jim Gantner .25 .10
- ❑ 116 Tom Seaver 3.00 1.20
- ❑ 117 Bill Buckner .75 .30
- ❑ 118 Bill Caudill .25 .10
- ❑ 119 Jim Clancy .25 .10
- ❑ 120 John Castino .25 .10
- ❑ 121 Dave Concepcion .75 .30
- ❑ 122 Greg Luzinski .75 .30
- ❑ 123 Mike Boddicker .25 .10
- ❑ 124 Pete Ladd .25 .10
- ❑ 125 Juan Berenguer .25 .10
- ❑ 126 John Montefusco .25 .10
- ❑ 127 Ed Jurak .25 .10
- ❑ 128 Tom Niedenfuer .25 .10
- ❑ 129 Bert Blyleven .75 .30
- ❑ 130 Bud Black .25 .10
- ❑ 131 Gorman Heimueller .25 .10
- ❑ 132 Dan Schatzeder .25 .10
- ❑ 133 Ron Jackson .25 .10

	No.	Player	Nrmt-Mt	Exc
❑	134	Tom Henke RC	1.50	.60
❑	135	Kevin Hickey	.25	.10
❑	136	Mike Scott	.75	.30
❑	137	Bo Diaz	.25	.10
❑	138	Glenn Brummer	.25	.10
❑	139	Sid Monge	.25	.10
❑	140	Rich Gale	.25	.10
❑	141	Brett Butler	1.50	.60
❑	142	Brian Harper RC	.75	.30
❑	143	John Rabb	.25	.10
❑	144	Gary Woods	.25	.10
❑	145	Pat Putnam	.25	.10
❑	146	Jim Acker	.25	.10
❑	147	Mickey Hatcher	.25	.10
❑	148	Todd Cruz	.25	.10
❑	149	Tom Tellmann	.25	.10
❑	150	John Wockenfuss	.25	.10
❑	151	Wade Boggs UER	8.00	3.20
		1983 runs 10; should be 100		
❑	152	Don Baylor	1.50	.60
❑	153	Bob Welch	.25	.10
❑	154	Alan Bannister	.25	.10
❑	155	Willie Aikens	.25	.10
❑	156	Jeff Burroughs	.25	.10
❑	157	Bryan Little	.25	.10
❑	158	Bob Boone	.75	.30
❑	159	Dave Hostetler	.25	.10
❑	160	Jerry Dybzinski	.25	.10
❑	161	Mike Madden	.25	.10
❑	162	Luis DeLeon	.25	.10
❑	163	Willie Hernandez	.75	.30
❑	164	Frank Pastore	.25	.10
❑	165	Rick Camp	.25	.10
❑	166	Lee Mazzilli	.25	.10
❑	167	Scot Thompson	.25	.10
❑	168	Bob Forsch	.25	.10
❑	169	Mike Flanagan	.25	.10
❑	170	Rick Manning	.25	.10
❑	171	Chet Lemon	.25	.10
❑	172	Jerry Remy	.25	.10
❑	173	Ron Guidry	.75	.30
❑	174	Pedro Guerrero	.75	.30
❑	175	Willie Wilson	.25	.10
❑	176	Carney Lansford	.75	.30
❑	177	Al Oliver	.75	.30
❑	178	Jim Sundberg	.75	.30
❑	179	Bobby Grich	.75	.30
❑	180	Rich Dotson	.25	.10
❑	181	Joaquin Andujar	.25	.10
❑	182	Jose Cruz	.75	.30
❑	183	Mike Schmidt	8.00	3.20
❑	184	Gary Redus RC*	.25	.10
❑	185	Garry Templeton	.25	.10
❑	186	Tony Pena	.25	.10
❑	187	Greg Minton	.25	.10
❑	188	Phil Niekro	.75	.30
❑	189	Ferguson Jenkins	.75	.30
❑	190	Mookie Wilson	.75	.30
❑	191	Jim Beattie	.25	.10
❑	192	Gary Ward	.25	.10
❑	193	Jesse Barfield	.75	.30
❑	194	Pete Filson	.25	.10
❑	195	Roy Lee Jackson	.25	.10
❑	196	Rick Sweet	.25	.10
❑	197	Jesse Orosco	.25	.10
❑	198	Steve Lake	.25	.10
❑	199	Ken Dayley	.25	.10
❑	200	Manny Sarmiento	.25	.10
❑	201	Mark Davis	.25	.10
❑	202	Tim Flannery	.25	.10
❑	203	Bill Scherrer	.25	.10
❑	204	Al Holland	.25	.10
❑	205	Dave Von Ohlen	.25	.10
❑	206	Mike LaCoss	.25	.10
❑	207	Juan Beniquez	.25	.10
❑	208	Juan Agosto	.25	.10
❑	209	Bobby Ramos	.25	.10
❑	210	Al Bumbry	.25	.10
❑	211	Mark Brouhard	.25	.10
❑	212	Howard Bailey	.25	.10
❑	213	Bruce Hurst	.25	.10
❑	214	Bob Shirley	.25	.10
❑	215	Pat Zachry	.25	.10
❑	216	Julio Franco	1.50	.60
❑	217	Mike Armstrong	.25	.10
❑	218	Dave Beard	.25	.10
❑	219	Steve Rogers	.25	.10
❑	220	John Butcher	.25	.10
❑	221	Mike Smithson	.25	.10
❑	222	Frank White	.75	.30
❑	223	Mike Heath	.25	.10
❑	224	Chris Bando	.25	.10
❑	225	Roy Smalley	.25	.10
❑	226	Dusty Baker	.75	.30
❑	227	Lou Whitaker	3.00	1.20
❑	228	John Lowenstein	.25	.10
❑	229	Ben Oglivie	.25	.10
❑	230	Doug DeCinces	.25	.10
❑	231	Lonnie Smith	.25	.10
❑	232	Ray Knight	.75	.30
❑	233	Gary Matthews	.75	.30
❑	234	Juan Bonilla	.25	.10
❑	235	Rod Scurry	.25	.10
❑	236	Atlee Hammaker	.25	.10
❑	237	Mike Caldwell	.25	.10
❑	238	Keith Hernandez	1.50	.60
❑	239	Larry Bowa	.75	.30
❑	240	Tony Bernazard	.25	.10
❑	241	Damaso Garcia	.25	.10
❑	242	Tom Brunansky	.75	.30
❑	243	Dan Driessen	.25	.10
❑	244	Ron Kittle	.25	.10
❑	245	Tim Stoddard	.25	.10
❑	246	Bob L. Gibson RC	.25	.10
		(Brewers Pitcher)		
❑	247	Marty Castillo	.25	.10
❑	248	D.Mattingly RC UER	40.00	16.00
		traniing on back		
❑	249	Jeff Newman	.25	.10
❑	250	Alejandro Pena RC*	.75	.30
❑	251	Toby Harrah	.75	.30
❑	252	Cesar Geronimo	.25	.10
❑	253	Tom Underwood	.25	.10
❑	254	Doug Flynn	.25	.10
❑	255	Andy Hassler	.25	.10
❑	256	Odell Jones	.25	.10
❑	257	Rudy Law	.25	.10
❑	258	Harry Spilman	.25	.10
❑	259	Marty Bystrom	.25	.10
❑	260	Dave Rucker	.25	.10
❑	261	Ruppert Jones	.25	.10
❑	262	Jeff R. Jones	.25	.10
		(Reds OF)		
❑	263	Gerald Perry	.75	.30
❑	264	Gene Tenace	.75	.30
❑	265	Brad Wellman	.25	.10
❑	266	Dickie Noles	.25	.10
❑	267	Jamie Allen	.25	.10
❑	268	Jim Gott	.25	.10
❑	269	Ron Davis	.25	.10
❑	270	Benny Ayala	.25	.10
❑	271	Ned Yost	.25	.10
❑	272	Dave Rozema	.25	.10
❑	273	Dave Stapleton	.25	.10
❑	274	Lou Piniella	.75	.30
❑	275	Jose Morales	.25	.10
❑	276	Broderick Perkins	.25	.10
❑	277	Butch Davis RC	.25	.10
❑	278	Tony Phillips RC	3.00	1.20
❑	279	Jeff Reardon	.75	.30
❑	280	Ken Forsch	.25	.10
❑	281	Pete O'Brien RC*	.75	.30
❑	282	Tom Paciorek	.75	.30
❑	283	Frank LaCorte	.25	.10
❑	284	Tim Lollar	.25	.10
❑	285	Greg Gross	.25	.10
❑	286	Alex Trevino	.25	.10
❑	287	Gene Garber	.25	.10
❑	288	Dave Parker	.75	.30
❑	289	Lee Smith	3.00	1.20
❑	290	Dave LaPoint	.25	.10
❑	291	John Shelby	.25	.10
❑	292	Charlie Moore	.25	.10
❑	293	Alan Trammell	1.50	.60
❑	294	Tony Armas	.25	.10
❑	295	Shane Rawley	.25	.10
❑	296	Greg Brock	.25	.10
❑	297	Hal McRae	.75	.30
❑	298	Mike Davis	.25	.10
❑	299	Tim Raines	1.50	.60
❑	300	Bucky Dent	.75	.30
❑	301	Tommy John	1.50	.60
❑	302	Carlton Fisk	1.50	.60
❑	303	Darrell Porter	.25	.10
❑	304	Dickie Thon	.25	.10
❑	305	Garry Maddox	.25	.10
❑	306	Cesar Cedeno	.75	.30
❑	307	Gary Lucas	.25	.10
❑	308	Johnny Ray	.25	.10
❑	309	Andy McGaffigan	.25	.10
❑	310	Claudell Washington	.25	.10
❑	311	Ryne Sandberg	12.00	4.80
❑	312	George Foster	.75	.30
❑	313	Spike Owen RC	.75	.30
❑	314	Gary Gaetti	1.50	.60
❑	315	Willie Upshaw	.25	.10
❑	316	Al Williams	.25	.10
❑	317	Jorge Orta	.25	.10
❑	318	Orlando Mercado	.25	.10
❑	319	Junior Ortiz	.25	.10
❑	320	Mike Proly	.25	.10
❑	321	Randy Johnson UER	.25	.10
		('72-'82 stats are from Twins' Randy Johnson, '83 stats are from Braves' Randy Johnson)		
❑	322	Jim Morrison	.25	.10
❑	323	Max Venable	.25	.10
❑	324	Tony Gwynn	12.00	4.80
❑	325	Duane Walker	.25	.10
❑	326	Ozzie Virgil	.25	.10
❑	327	Jeff Lahti	.25	.10
❑	328	Bill Dawley	.25	.10
❑	329	Rob Wilfong	.25	.10
❑	330	Marc Hill	.25	.10
❑	331	Ray Burris	.25	.10
❑	332	Allan Ramirez	.25	.10
❑	333	Chuck Porter	.25	.10
❑	334	Wayne Krenchicki	.25	.10
❑	335	Gary Allenson	.25	.10
❑	336	Bobby Meacham	.25	.10
❑	337	Joe Beckwith	.25	.10
❑	338	Rick Sutcliffe	.75	.30
❑	339	Mark Huismann	.25	.10
❑	340	Tim Conroy	.25	.10
❑	341	Scott Sanderson	.25	.10
❑	342	Larry Biittner	.25	.10
❑	343	Dave Stewart	.75	.30
❑	344	Darryl Motley	.25	.10
❑	345	Chris Codiroli	.25	.10
❑	346	Rich Behenna	.25	.10
❑	347	Andre Robertson	.25	.10
❑	348	Mike Marshall	.25	.10
❑	349	Larry Herndon	.75	.30
❑	350	Rich Dauer	.25	.10
❑	351	Cecil Cooper	.75	.30
❑	352	Rod Carew	1.50	.60
❑	353	Willie McGee	1.50	.60
❑	354	Phil Garner	.75	.30
❑	355	Joe Morgan	1.50	.60
❑	356	Luis Salazar	.25	.10
❑	357	John Candelaria	.25	.10
❑	358	Bill Laskey	.25	.10
❑	359	Bob McClure	.25	.10
❑	360	Dave Kingman	1.50	.60
❑	361	Ron Cey	.75	.30
❑	362	Matt Young	.25	.10
❑	363	Lloyd Moseby	.25	.10
❑	364	Frank Viola	1.50	.60
❑	365	Eddie Milner	.25	.10
❑	366	Floyd Bannister	.25	.10
❑	367	Dan Ford	.25	.10
❑	368	Moose Haas	.25	.10
❑	369	Doug Bair	.25	.10
❑	370	Ray Fontenot	.25	.10
❑	371	Luis Aponte	.25	.10
❑	372	Jack Fimple	.25	.10
❑	373	Neal Heaton	.25	.10
❑	374	Greg Pryor	.25	.10
❑	375	Wayne Gross	.25	.10
❑	376	Charlie Lea	.25	.10
❑	377	Steve Lubratich	.25	.10
❑	378	Jon Matlack	.25	.10
❑	379	Julio Cruz	.25	.10
❑	380	John Mizerock	.25	.10
❑	381	Kevin Gross RC	.25	.10
❑	382	Mike Ramsey	.25	.10
❑	383	Doug Gwosdz	.25	.10

❑ 384 Kelly Paris .25 .10
❑ 385 Pete Falcone .25 .10
❑ 386 Milt May .25 .10
❑ 387 Fred Breining .25 .10
❑ 388 Craig Lefferts RC .25 .10
❑ 389 Steve Henderson .25 .10
❑ 390 Randy Moffitt .25 .10
❑ 391 Ron Washington .25 .10
❑ 392 Gary Roenicke .25 .10
❑ 393 Tom Candiotti RC 3.00 1.20
❑ 394 Larry Pashnick .25 .10
❑ 395 Dwight Evans .75 .30
❑ 396 Rich Gossage 1.50 .60
❑ 397 Derrel Thomas .25 .10
❑ 398 Juan Eichelberger .25 .10
❑ 399 Leon Roberts .25 .10
❑ 400 Dave Lopes .75 .30
❑ 401 Bill Gullickson .25 .10
❑ 402 Geoff Zahn .25 .10
❑ 403 Billy Sample .25 .10
❑ 404 Mike Squires .25 .10
❑ 405 Craig Reynolds .25 .10
❑ 406 Eric Show .25 .10
❑ 407 John Denny .25 .10
❑ 408 Dann Bilardello .25 .10
❑ 409 Bruce Benedict .25 .10
❑ 410 Kent Tekulve .75 .30
❑ 411 Mel Hall .75 .30
❑ 412 John Stuper .25 .10
❑ 413 Rick Dempsey .25 .10
❑ 414 Don Sutton 3.00 1.20
❑ 415 Jack Morris 3.00 1.20
❑ 416 John Tudor .25 .10
❑ 417 Willie Randolph .75 .30
❑ 418 Jerry Reuss .25 .10
❑ 419 Don Slaught .75 .30
❑ 420 Steve McCatty .25 .10
❑ 421 Tim Wallach .75 .30
❑ 422 Larry Parrish .25 .10
❑ 423 Brian Downing .25 .10
❑ 424 Britt Burns .25 .10
❑ 425 David Green .25 .10
❑ 426 Jerry Mumphrey .25 .10
❑ 427 Ivan DeJesus .25 .10
❑ 428 Mario Soto .25 .10
❑ 429 Gene Richards .25 .10
❑ 430 Dale Berra .25 .10
❑ 431 Darrell Evans .75 .30
❑ 432 Glenn Hubbard .25 .10
❑ 433 Jody Davis .25 .10
❑ 434 Danny Heep .25 .10
❑ 435 Ed Nunez RC .25 .10
❑ 436 Bobby Castillo .25 .10
❑ 437 Ernie Whitt .25 .10
❑ 438 Scott Ullger .25 .10
❑ 439 Doyle Alexander .25 .10
❑ 440 Domingo Ramos .25 .10
❑ 441 Craig Swan .25 .10
❑ 442 Warren Brusstar .25 .10
❑ 443 Len Barker .25 .10
❑ 444 Mike Easler .25 .10
❑ 445 Renie Martin .25 .10
❑ 446 D.Rasmussen RC .25 .10
❑ 447 Ted Power .25 .10
❑ 448 Charles Hudson .25 .10
❑ 449 Danny Cox RC .25 .10
❑ 450 Kevin Bass .25 .10
❑ 451 Daryl Sconiers .25 .10
❑ 452 Scott Fletcher .25 .10
❑ 453 Bryn Smith .25 .10
❑ 454 Jim Dwyer .25 .10
❑ 455 Rob Picciolo .25 .10
❑ 456 Enos Cabell .25 .10
❑ 457 Dennis Boyd .75 .30
❑ 458 Butch Wynegar .25 .10
❑ 459 Burt Hooton .25 .10
❑ 460 Ron Hassey .25 .10
❑ 461 Danny Jackson RC 1.50 .60
❑ 462 Bob Kearney .25 .10
❑ 463 Terry Francona .25 .10
❑ 464 Wayne Tolleson .25 .10
❑ 465 Mickey Rivers .25 .10
❑ 466 John Wathan .25 .10
❑ 467 Bill Almon .25 .10
❑ 468 George Vukovich .25 .10
❑ 469 Steve Kemp .25 .10
❑ 470 Ken Landreaux .25 .10
❑ 471 Milt Wilcox .25 .10
❑ 472 Tippy Martinez .25 .10
❑ 473 Ted Simmons .75 .30
❑ 474 Tim Foli .25 .10
❑ 475 George Hendrick .25 .10
❑ 476 Terry Puhl .25 .10
❑ 477 Von Hayes .25 .10
❑ 478 Bobby Brown .25 .10
❑ 479 Lee Lacy .25 .10
❑ 480 Joel Youngblood .25 .10
❑ 481 Jim Slaton .25 .10
❑ 482 Mike Fitzgerald .25 .10
❑ 483 Keith Moreland .25 .10
❑ 484 Ron Roenicke .25 .10
❑ 485 Luis Leal .25 .10
❑ 486 Bryan Oelkers .25 .10
❑ 487 Bruce Berenyi .25 .10
❑ 488 LaMarr Hoyt .25 .10
❑ 489 Joe Nolan .25 .10
❑ 490 Marshall Edwards .25 .10
❑ 491 Mike Laga .75 .30
❑ 492 Rick Cerone .25 .10
❑ 493 Rick Miller UER .25 .10
(Listed as Mike
on card front)
❑ 494 Rick Honeycutt .25 .10
❑ 495 Mike Hargrove .75 .30
❑ 496 Joe Simpson .25 .10
❑ 497 Keith Atherton .25 .10
❑ 498 Chris Welsh .25 .10
❑ 499 Bruce Kison .25 .10
❑ 500 Bobby Johnson .25 .10
❑ 501 Jerry Koosman .75 .30
❑ 502 Frank DiPino .25 .10
❑ 503 Tony Perez 1.50 .60
❑ 504 Ken Oberkfell .25 .10
❑ 505 Mark Thurmond .25 .10
❑ 506 Joe Price .25 .10
❑ 507 Pascual Perez .25 .10
❑ 508 Marvell Wynne .25 .10
❑ 509 Mike Krukow .25 .10
❑ 510 Dick Ruthven .25 .10
❑ 511 Al Cowens .25 .10
❑ 512 Cliff Johnson .25 .10
❑ 513 Randy Bush .25 .10
❑ 514 Sammy Stewart .25 .10
❑ 515 Bill Schroeder .25 .10
❑ 516 Aurelio Lopez .75 .30
❑ 517 Mike G. Brown RC .25 .10
❑ 518 Graig Nettles .75 .30
❑ 519 Dave Sax .25 .10
❑ 520 Jerry Willard .25 .10
❑ 521 Paul Splittorff .25 .10
❑ 522 Tom Burgmeier .25 .10
❑ 523 Chris Speier .25 .10
❑ 524 Bobby Clark .25 .10
❑ 525 George Wright .25 .10
❑ 526 Dennis Lamp .25 .10
❑ 527 Tony Scott .25 .10
❑ 528 Ed Whitson .25 .10
❑ 529 Ron Reed .25 .10
❑ 530 Charlie Puleo .25 .10
❑ 531 Jerry Royster .25 .10
❑ 532 Don Robinson .25 .10
❑ 533 Steve Trout .25 .10
❑ 534 Bruce Sutter .75 .30
❑ 535 Bob Horner .25 .10
❑ 536 Pat Tabler .25 .10
❑ 537 Chris Chambliss .75 .30
❑ 538 Bob Ojeda .25 .10
❑ 539 Alan Ashby .25 .10
❑ 540 Jay Johnstone .75 .30
❑ 541 Bob Dernier .25 .10
❑ 542 Brook Jacoby .75 .30
❑ 543 U.L. Washington .25 .10
❑ 544 Danny Darwin .25 .10
❑ 545 Kiko Garcia .25 .10
❑ 546 Vance Law UER .25 .10
(Listed as P
on card front)
❑ 547 Tug McGraw .75 .30
❑ 548 Dave Smith .25 .10
❑ 549 Len Matuszek .25 .10
❑ 550 Tom Hume .25 .10
❑ 551 Dave Dravecky .75 .30
❑ 552 Rick Rhoden .25 .10
❑ 553 Duane Kuiper .25 .10
❑ 554 Rusty Staub .75 .30
❑ 555 Bill Campbell .25 .10
❑ 556 Mike Torrez .25 .10
❑ 557 Dave Henderson .75 .30
❑ 558 Len Whitehouse .25 .10
❑ 559 Barry Bonnell .25 .10
❑ 560 Rick Lysander .25 .10
❑ 561 Garth Iorg .25 .10
❑ 562 Bryan Clark .25 .10
❑ 563 Brian Giles .25 .10
❑ 564 Vern Ruhle .25 .10
❑ 565 Steve Bedrosian .25 .10
❑ 566 Larry McWilliams .25 .10
❑ 567 Jeff Leonard UER .25 .10
(Listed as P
on card front)
❑ 568 Alan Wiggins .25 .10
❑ 569 Jeff Russell RC .75 .30
❑ 570 Salome Barojas .25 .10
❑ 571 Dane Iorg .25 .10
❑ 572 Bob Knepper .25 .10
❑ 573 Gary Lavelle .25 .10
❑ 574 Gorman Thomas .25 .10
❑ 575 Manny Trillo .25 .10
❑ 576 Jim Palmer .75 .30
❑ 577 Dale Murray .25 .10
❑ 578 Tom Brookens .75 .30
❑ 579 Rich Gedman .25 .10
❑ 580 Bill Doran RC* .75 .30
❑ 581 Steve Yeager .25 .10
❑ 582 Dan Spillner .25 .10
❑ 583 Dan Quisenberry .25 .10
❑ 584 Rance Mulliniks .25 .10
❑ 585 Storm Davis .25 .10
❑ 586 Dave Schmidt .25 .10
❑ 587 Bill Russell .25 .10
❑ 588 Pat Sheridan .25 .10
❑ 589 Rafael Ramirez .25 .10
UER (A's on front)
❑ 590 Bud Anderson .25 .10
❑ 591 George Frazier .25 .10
❑ 592 Lee Tunnell .25 .10
❑ 593 Kirk Gibson 3.00 1.20
❑ 594 Scott McGregor .25 .10
❑ 595 Bob Bailor .25 .10
❑ 596 Tom Herr .75 .30
❑ 597 Luis Sanchez .25 .10
❑ 598 Dave Engle .25 .10
❑ 599 Craig McMurtry .25 .10
❑ 600 Carlos Diaz .25 .10
❑ 601 Tom O'Malley .25 .10
❑ 602 Nick Esasky .25 .10
❑ 603 Ron Hodges .25 .10
❑ 604 Ed VandeBerg .25 .10
❑ 605 Alfredo Griffin .25 .10
❑ 606 Glenn Hoffman .25 .10
❑ 607 Hubie Brooks .25 .10
❑ 608 Richard Barnes UER .25 .10
(Photo actually
Neal Heaton)
❑ 609 Greg Walker .75 .30
❑ 610 Ken Singleton .25 .10
❑ 611 Mark Clear .25 .10
❑ 612 Buck Martinez .25 .10
❑ 613 Ken Griffey .75 .30
❑ 614 Reid Nichols .25 .10
❑ 615 Doug Sisk .25 .10
❑ 616 Bob Brenly .25 .10
❑ 617 Joey McLaughlin .25 .10
❑ 618 Glenn Wilson .75 .30
❑ 619 Bob Stoddard .25 .10
❑ 620 Lenn Sakata UER .25 .10
(Listed as Len
on card front)
❑ 621 Mike Young RC .25 .10
❑ 622 John Stefero .25 .10
❑ 623 Carmelo Martinez .25 .10
❑ 624 Dave Bergman .25 .10
❑ 625 Runnin' Reds UER 3.00 1.20
(Sic, Redbirds)
David Green
Willie McGee
Lonnie Smith
Ozzie Smith

❑ 626 Rudy May .25 .10
❑ 627 Matt Keough .25 .10
❑ 628 Jose DeLeon RC .25 .10
❑ 629 Jim Essian .25 .10
❑ 630 Darnell Coles RC .25 .10
❑ 631 Mike Warren .25 .10
❑ 632 Del Crandall MG .25 .10
❑ 633 Dennis Martinez .75 .30
❑ 634 Mike Moore .75 .30
❑ 635 Lary Sorensen .25 .10
❑ 636 Ricky Nelson .25 .10
❑ 637 Omar Moreno .25 .10
❑ 638 Charlie Hough .75 .30
❑ 639 Dennis Eckersley 1.50 .60
❑ 640 Walt Terrell .25 .10
❑ 641 Denny Walling .25 .10
❑ 642 Dave Anderson RC .25 .10
❑ 643 Jose Oquendo RC .75 .30
❑ 644 Bob Stanley .25 .10
❑ 645 Dave Geisel .25 .10
❑ 646 Scott Garrelts .25 .10
❑ 647 Gary Pettis .25 .10
❑ 648 Duke Snider 1.50 .60
Puzzle Card
❑ 649 Johnnie LeMaster .25 .10
❑ 650 Dave Collins .25 .10
❑ 651 The Chicken 1.50 .60
❑ 652 DK Checklist 1-26 .75 .30
(Unnumbered)
❑ 653 Checklist 27-130 .25 .10
(Unnumbered)
❑ 654 Checklist 131-234 .25 .10
(Unnumbered)
❑ 655 Checklist 235-338 .25 .10
(Unnumbered)
❑ 656 Checklist 339-442 .25 .10
(Unnumbered)
❑ 657 Checklist 443-546 .25 .10
(Unnumbered)
❑ 658 Checklist 547-651 .25 .10
(Unnumbered)
❑ A Living Legends A 2.50 1.00
Gaylord Perry
Rollie Fingers
❑ B Living Legends B 5.00 2.00
Carl Yastrzemski
Johnny Bench

1985 Donruss

	Nm-Mt	Ex-Mt
COMPLETE SET (660)	60.00	24.00
COMP.FACT.SET (660)	80.00	32.00
COMP.GEHRIG PUZZLE	4.00	1.60

❑ 1 Ryne Sandberg DK 1.25 .50
❑ 2 Doug DeCinces DK .15 .06
❑ 3 Richard Dotson DK .15 .06
❑ 4 Bert Blyleven DK .15 .06
❑ 5 Lou Whitaker DK .40 .16
❑ 6 Dan Quisenberry DK .40 .16
❑ 7 Don Mattingly DK 2.50 1.00
❑ 8 Carney Lansford DK .15 .06
❑ 9 Frank Tanana DK .15 .06
❑ 10 Willie Upshaw DK .15 .06
❑ 11 C.Washington DK .15 .06
❑ 12 Mike Marshall DK .15 .06
❑ 13 Joaquin Andujar DK .15 .06
❑ 14 Cal Ripken DK 2.50 1.00
❑ 15 Jim Rice DK .40 .16
❑ 16 Don Sutton DK .40 .16
❑ 17 Frank Viola DK .15 .06
❑ 18 Alvin Davis DK .15 .06
❑ 19 Mario Soto DK .15 .06
❑ 20 Jose Cruz DK .15 .06
❑ 21 Charlie Lea DK .15 .06
❑ 22 Jesse Orosco DK .15 .06
❑ 23 Juan Samuel DK .15 .06
❑ 24 Tony Pena DK .15 .06
❑ 25 Tony Gwynn DK 1.25 .50
❑ 26 Bob Brenly DK .15 .06
❑ 27 Danny Tartabull RR RC 1.25 .50
❑ 28 Mike Bielecki RR .15 .06
❑ 29 Steve Lyons RR RC .40 .16
❑ 30 Jeff Reed RR .15 .06
❑ 31 Tony Brewer RR .15 .06
❑ 32 John Morris RR RC .15 .06
❑ 33 Daryl Boston RR RC .15 .06
❑ 34 Al Pulido RR .15 .06
❑ 35 Steve Kiefer RR .15 .06
❑ 36 Larry Sheets RR .15 .06
❑ 37 Scott Bradley RR .15 .06
❑ 38 Calvin Schiraldi RR .15 .06
❑ 39 S.Dunston RR RC .75 .30
❑ 40 Charlie Mitchell RR .15 .06
❑ 41 Billy Hatcher RR RC .75 .30
❑ 42 Russ Stephans RR .15 .06
❑ 43 Alejandro Sanchez RR .15 .06
❑ 44 Steve Jeltz RR .15 .06
❑ 45 Jim Traber RR .15 .06
❑ 46 Doug Loman RR .15 .06
❑ 47 Eddie Murray 1.25 .50
❑ 48 Robin Yount 1.25 .50
❑ 49 Lance Parrish .40 .16
❑ 50 Jim Rice .40 .16
❑ 51 Dave Winfield .75 .30
❑ 52 Fernando Valenzuela .40 .16
❑ 53 George Brett 4.00 1.60
❑ 54 Dave Kingman .40 .16
❑ 55 Gary Carter .75 .30
❑ 56 Buddy Bell .40 .16
❑ 57 Reggie Jackson .75 .30
❑ 58 Harold Baines .40 .16
❑ 59 Ozzie Smith 1.25 .50
❑ 60 Nolan Ryan UER 6.00 2.40
(Set strikeout record
in 1973, not 1972)
❑ 61 Mike Schmidt 3.00 1.20
❑ 62 Dave Parker .40 .16
❑ 63 Tony Gwynn 2.50 1.00
❑ 64 Tony Pena .15 .06
❑ 65 Jack Clark .40 .16
❑ 66 Dale Murphy 1.25 .50
❑ 67 Ryne Sandberg 2.50 1.00
❑ 68 Keith Hernandez .75 .30
❑ 69 Alvin Davis RC* .40 .16
❑ 70 Kent Hrbek .40 .16
❑ 71 Willie Upshaw .15 .06
❑ 72 Dave Engle .15 .06
❑ 73 Alfredo Griffin .15 .06
❑ 74A Jack Perconte .15 .06
(Career Highlights
takes four lines)
❑ 74B Jack Perconte .15 .06
(Career Highlights
takes three lines)
❑ 75 Jesse Orosco .15 .06
❑ 76 Jody Davis .15 .06
❑ 77 Bob Horner .15 .06
❑ 78 Larry McWilliams .15 .06
❑ 79 Joel Youngblood .15 .06
❑ 80 Alan Wiggins .15 .06
❑ 81 Ron Oester .15 .06
❑ 82 Ozzie Virgil .15 .06
❑ 83 Ricky Horton .15 .06
❑ 84 Bill Doran .15 .06
❑ 85 Rod Carew .75 .30
❑ 86 LaMarr Hoyt .15 .06
❑ 87 Tim Wallach .40 .16
❑ 88 Mike Flanagan .15 .06
❑ 89 Jim Sundberg .15 .06
❑ 90 Chet Lemon .15 .06
❑ 91 Bob Stanley .15 .06
❑ 92 Willie Randolph .40 .16
❑ 93 Bill Russell .15 .06
❑ 94 Julio Franco .75 .30
❑ 95 Dan Quisenberry .40 .16
❑ 96 Bill Caudill .15 .06
❑ 97 Bill Gullickson .15 .06
❑ 98 Danny Darwin .15 .06
❑ 99 Curtis Wilkerson .15 .06
❑ 100 Bud Black .15 .06
❑ 101 Tony Phillips .15 .06
❑ 102 Tony Bernazard .15 .06
❑ 103 Jay Howell .15 .06
❑ 104 Burt Hooton .15 .06
❑ 105 Milt Wilcox .15 .06
❑ 106 Rich Dauer .15 .06
❑ 107 Don Sutton 1.25 .50
❑ 108 Mike Witt .15 .06
❑ 109 Bruce Sutter .40 .16
❑ 110 Enos Cabell .15 .06
❑ 111 John Denny .15 .06
❑ 112 Dave Dravecky .40 .16
❑ 113 Marvell Wynne .15 .06
❑ 114 Johnnie LeMaster .15 .06
❑ 115 Chuck Porter .15 .06
❑ 116 John Gibbons .15 .06
❑ 117 Keith Moreland .15 .06
❑ 118 Darnell Coles .15 .06
❑ 119 Dennis Lamp .15 .06
❑ 120 Ron Davis .15 .06
❑ 121 Nick Esasky .15 .06
❑ 122 Vance Law .15 .06
❑ 123 Gary Roenicke .15 .06
❑ 124 Bill Schroeder .15 .06
❑ 125 Dave Rozema .15 .06
❑ 126 Bobby Meacham .15 .06
❑ 127 Marty Barrett .15 .06
❑ 128 R.J. Reynolds .15 .06
❑ 129 Ernie Camacho UER .15 .06
(Photo actually
Rich Thompson)
❑ 130 Jorge Orta .15 .06
❑ 131 Lary Sorensen .15 .06
❑ 132 Terry Francona .15 .06
❑ 133 Fred Lynn .40 .16
❑ 134 Bob Jones .15 .06
❑ 135 Jerry Hairston .15 .06
❑ 136 Kevin Bass .15 .06
❑ 137 Garry Maddox .15 .06
❑ 138 Dave LaPoint .15 .06
❑ 139 Kevin McReynolds .40 .16
❑ 140 Wayne Krenchicki .15 .06
❑ 141 Rafael Ramirez .15 .06
❑ 142 Rod Scurry .15 .06
❑ 143 Greg Minton .15 .06
❑ 144 Tim Stoddard .15 .06
❑ 145 Steve Henderson .15 .06
❑ 146 George Bell .40 .16
❑ 147 Dave Meier .15 .06
❑ 148 Sammy Stewart .15 .06
❑ 149 Mark Brouhard .15 .06
❑ 150 Larry Herndon .15 .06
❑ 151 Oil Can Boyd .15 .06
❑ 152 Brian Dayett .15 .06
❑ 153 Tom Niedenfuer .15 .06
❑ 154 Brook Jacoby .15 .06
❑ 155 Onix Concepcion .15 .06
❑ 156 Tim Conroy .15 .06
❑ 157 Joe Hesketh .15 .06
❑ 158 Brian Downing .15 .06
❑ 159 Tommy Dunbar .15 .06
❑ 160 Marc Hill .15 .06
❑ 161 Phil Garner .40 .16
❑ 162 Jerry Davis .15 .06
❑ 163 Bill Campbell .15 .06
❑ 164 John Franco RC 1.25 .50
❑ 165 Len Barker .15 .06
❑ 166 Benny Distefano .15 .06
❑ 167 George Frazier .15 .06
❑ 168 Tito Landrum .15 .06
❑ 169 Cal Ripken 5.00 2.00
❑ 170 Cecil Cooper .40 .16
❑ 171 Alan Trammell .75 .30
❑ 172 Wade Boggs 1.50 .60
❑ 173 Don Baylor .40 .16
❑ 174 Pedro Guerrero .40 .16
❑ 175 Frank White .40 .16
❑ 176 Rickey Henderson 2.50 1.00
❑ 177 Charlie Lea .15 .06

	Card	Player	Price 1	Price 2
❑	178	Pete O'Brien	.15	.06
❑	179	Doug DeCinces	.15	.06
❑	180	Ron Kittle	.15	.06
❑	181	George Hendrick	.15	.06
❑	182	Joe Niekro	.15	.06
❑	183	Juan Samuel	.15	.06
❑	184	Mario Soto	.15	.06
❑	185	Rich Gossage	.40	.16
❑	186	Johnny Ray	.15	.06
❑	187	Bob Brenly	.15	.06
❑	188	Craig McMurtry	.15	.06
❑	189	Leon Durham	.15	.06
❑	190	Dwight Gooden RC	2.00	.80
❑	191	Barry Bonnell	.15	.06
❑	192	Tim Teufel	.15	.06
❑	193	Dave Stieb	.40	.16
❑	194	Mickey Hatcher	.15	.06
❑	195	Jesse Barfield	.15	.06
❑	196	Al Cowens	.15	.06
❑	197	Hubie Brooks	.15	.06
❑	198	Steve Trout	.15	.06
❑	199	Glenn Hubbard	.15	.06
❑	200	Bill Madlock	.40	.16
❑	201	Jeff D. Robinson	.15	.06
❑	202	Eric Show	.15	.06
❑	203	Dave Concepcion	.40	.16
❑	204	Ivan DeJesus	.15	.06
❑	205	Neil Allen	.15	.06
❑	206	Jerry Mumphrey	.15	.06
❑	207	Mike C. Brown	.15	.06
❑	208	Carlton Fisk	.75	.30
❑	209	Bryn Smith	.15	.06
❑	210	Tippy Martinez	.15	.06
❑	211	Dion James	.15	.06
❑	212	Willie Hernandez	.15	.06
❑	213	Mike Easler	.15	.06
❑	214	Ron Guidry	.40	.16
❑	215	Rick Honeycutt	.15	.06
❑	216	Brett Butler	.40	.16
❑	217	Larry Gura	.15	.06
❑	218	Ray Burris	.15	.06
❑	219	Steve Rogers	.15	.06
❑	220	Frank Tanana UER (Bats Left listed twice on card back)	.15	.06
❑	221	Ned Yost	.15	.06
❑	222	B.Saberhagen RC UER 18 career IP on back	1.25	.50
❑	223	Mike Davis	.15	.06
❑	224	Bert Blyleven	.40	.16
❑	225	Steve Kemp	.15	.06
❑	226	Jerry Reuss	.15	.06
❑	227	Darrell Evans UER (80 homers in 1980)	.40	.16
❑	228	Wayne Gross	.15	.06
❑	229	Jim Gantner	.15	.06
❑	230	Bob Boone	.40	.16
❑	231	Lonnie Smith	.15	.06
❑	232	Frank DiPino	.15	.06
❑	233	Jerry Koosman	.40	.16
❑	234	Graig Nettles	.40	.16
❑	235	John Tudor	.15	.06
❑	236	John Rabb	.15	.06
❑	237	Rick Manning	.15	.06
❑	238	Mike Fitzgerald	.15	.06
❑	239	Gary Matthews	.15	.06
❑	240	Jim Presley	.40	.16
❑	241	Dave Collins	.15	.06
❑	242	Gary Gaetti	.40	.16
❑	243	Dann Bilardello	.15	.06
❑	244	Rudy Law	.15	.06
❑	245	John Lowenstein	.15	.06
❑	246	Tom Tellmann	.15	.06
❑	247	Howard Johnson	.40	.16
❑	248	Ray Fontenot	.15	.06
❑	249	Tony Armas	.15	.06
❑	250	Candy Maldonado	.15	.06
❑	251	Mike Jeffcoat	.15	.06
❑	252	Dane Iorg	.15	.06
❑	253	Bruce Bochte	.15	.06
❑	254	Pete Rose Expos	4.00	1.60
❑	255	Don Aase	.15	.06
❑	256	George Wright	.15	.06
❑	257	Britt Burns	.15	.06
❑	258	Mike Scott	.15	.06
❑	259	Len Matuszek	.15	.06
❑	260	Dave Rucker	.15	.06
❑	261	Craig Lefferts	.15	.06
❑	262	Jay Tibbs	.15	.06
❑	263	Bruce Benedict	.15	.06
❑	264	Don Robinson	.15	.06
❑	265	Gary Lavelle	.15	.06
❑	266	Scott Sanderson	.15	.06
❑	267	Matt Young	.15	.06
❑	268	Ernie Whitt	.15	.06
❑	269	Houston Jimenez	.15	.06
❑	270	Ken Dixon	.15	.06
❑	271	Pete Ladd	.15	.06
❑	272	Juan Berenguer	.15	.06
❑	273	Roger Clemens RC	30.00	12.00
❑	274	Rick Cerone	.15	.06
❑	275	Dave Anderson	.15	.06
❑	276	George Vukovich	.15	.06
❑	277	Greg Pryor	.15	.06
❑	278	Mike Warren	.15	.06
❑	279	Bob James	.15	.06
❑	280	Bobby Grich	.40	.16
❑	281	Mike Mason RC	.15	.06
❑	282	Ron Reed	.15	.06
❑	283	Alan Ashby	.15	.06
❑	284	Mark Thurmond	.15	.06
❑	285	Joe Lefebvre	.15	.06
❑	286	Ted Power	.15	.06
❑	287	Chris Chambliss	.40	.16
❑	288	Lee Tunnell	.15	.06
❑	289	Rich Bordi	.15	.06
❑	290	Glenn Brummer	.15	.06
❑	291	Mike Boddicker	.15	.06
❑	292	Rollie Fingers	.40	.16
❑	293	Lou Whitaker	.75	.30
❑	294	Dwight Evans	.40	.16
❑	295	Don Mattingly	5.00	2.00
❑	296	Mike Marshall	.15	.06
❑	297	Willie Wilson	.15	.06
❑	298	Mike Heath	.15	.06
❑	299	Tim Raines	.40	.16
❑	300	Larry Parrish	.15	.06
❑	301	Geoff Zahn	.15	.06
❑	302	Rich Dotson	.15	.06
❑	303	David Green	.15	.06
❑	304	Jose Cruz	.40	.16
❑	305	Steve Carlton	.75	.30
❑	306	Gary Redus	.15	.06
❑	307	Steve Garvey	.40	.16
❑	308	Jose DeLeon	.15	.06
❑	309	Randy Lerch	.15	.06
❑	310	Claudell Washington	.15	.06
❑	311	Lee Smith	.75	.30
❑	312	Darryl Strawberry	1.25	.50
❑	313	Jim Beattie	.15	.06
❑	314	John Butcher	.15	.06
❑	315	Damaso Garcia	.15	.06
❑	316	Mike Smithson	.15	.06
❑	317	Luis Leal	.15	.06
❑	318	Ken Phelps	.15	.06
❑	319	Wally Backman	.15	.06
❑	320	Ron Cey	.40	.16
❑	321	Brad Komminsk	.15	.06
❑	322	Jason Thompson	.15	.06
❑	323	Frank Williams	.15	.06
❑	324	Tim Lollar	.15	.06
❑	325	Eric Davis RC	2.00	.80
❑	326	Von Hayes	.15	.06
❑	327	Andy Van Slyke	.75	.30
❑	328	Craig Reynolds	.15	.06
❑	329	Dick Schofield	.15	.06
❑	330	Scott Fletcher	.15	.06
❑	331	Jeff Reardon	.40	.16
❑	332	Rick Dempsey	.15	.06
❑	333	Ben Oglivie	.15	.06
❑	334	Dan Petry	.15	.06
❑	335	Jackie Gutierrez	.15	.06
❑	336	Dave Righetti	.40	.16
❑	337	Alejandro Pena	.15	.06
❑	338	Mel Hall	.15	.06
❑	339	Pat Sheridan	.15	.06
❑	340	Keith Atherton	.15	.06
❑	341	David Palmer	.15	.06
❑	342	Gary Ward	.15	.06
❑	343	Dave Stewart	.40	.16
❑	344	Mark Gubicza RC*	.40	.16
❑	345	Carney Lansford	.40	.16
❑	346	Jerry Willard	.15	.06
❑	347	Ken Griffey	.40	.16
❑	348	Franklin Stubbs	.15	.06
❑	349	Aurelio Lopez	.15	.06
❑	350	Al Bumbry	.15	.06
❑	351	Charlie Moore	.15	.06
❑	352	Luis Sanchez	.15	.06
❑	353	Darrell Porter	.15	.06
❑	354	Bill Dawley	.15	.06
❑	355	Charles Hudson	.15	.06
❑	356	Garry Templeton	.15	.06
❑	357	Cecilio Guante	.15	.06
❑	358	Jeff Leonard	.15	.06
❑	359	Paul Molitor	.75	.30
❑	360	Ron Gardenhire	.15	.06
❑	361	Larry Bowa	.40	.16
❑	362	Bob Kearney	.15	.06
❑	363	Garth Iorg	.15	.06
❑	364	Tom Brunansky	.40	.16
❑	365	Brad Gulden	.15	.06
❑	366	Greg Walker	.15	.06
❑	367	Mike Young	.15	.06
❑	368	Rick Waits	.15	.06
❑	369	Doug Bair	.15	.06
❑	370	Bob Shirley	.15	.06
❑	371	Bob Ojeda	.15	.06
❑	372	Bob Welch	.15	.06
❑	373	Neal Heaton	.15	.06
❑	374	Danny Jackson UER (Photo actually Frank Wills)	.15	.06
❑	375	Donnie Hill	.15	.06
❑	376	Mike Stenhouse	.15	.06
❑	377	Bruce Kison	.15	.06
❑	378	Wayne Tolleson	.15	.06
❑	379	Floyd Bannister	.15	.06
❑	380	Vern Ruhle	.15	.06
❑	381	Tim Corcoran	.15	.06
❑	382	Kurt Kepshire	.15	.06
❑	383	Bobby Brown	.15	.06
❑	384	Dave Van Gorder	.15	.06
❑	385	Rick Mahler	.15	.06
❑	386	Lee Mazzilli	.15	.06
❑	387	Bill Laskey	.15	.06
❑	388	Thad Bosley	.15	.06
❑	389	Al Chambers	.15	.06
❑	390	Tony Fernandez	.40	.16
❑	391	Ron Washington	.15	.06
❑	392	Bill Swaggerty	.15	.06
❑	393	Bob L. Gibson	.15	.06
❑	394	Marty Castillo	.15	.06
❑	395	Steve Crawford	.15	.06
❑	396	Clay Christiansen	.15	.06
❑	397	Bob Bailor	.15	.06
❑	398	Mike Hargrove	.40	.16
❑	399	Charlie Leibrandt	.15	.06
❑	400	Tom Burgmeier	.15	.06
❑	401	Razor Shines	.15	.06
❑	402	Rob Wilfong	.15	.06
❑	403	Tom Henke	.40	.16
❑	404	Al Jones	.15	.06
❑	405	Mike LaCoss	.15	.06
❑	406	Luis DeLeon	.15	.06
❑	407	Greg Gross	.15	.06
❑	408	Tom Hume	.15	.06
❑	409	Rick Camp	.15	.06
❑	410	Milt May	.15	.06
❑	411	Henry Cotto RC	.15	.06
❑	412	David Von Ohlen	.15	.06
❑	413	Scott McGregor	.15	.06
❑	414	Ted Simmons	.40	.16
❑	415	Jack Morris	.40	.16
❑	416	Bill Buckner	.40	.16
❑	417	Butch Wynegar	.15	.06
❑	418	Steve Sax	.15	.06
❑	419	Steve Balboni	.15	.06
❑	420	Dwayne Murphy	.15	.06
❑	421	Andre Dawson	.40	.16
❑	422	Charlie Hough	.40	.16
❑	423	Tommy John	.75	.30
❑	424A	Tom Seaver ERR (Photo actually Floyd Bannister)	1.25	.50
❑	424B	Tom Seaver COR	10.00	4.00
❑	425	Tom Herr	.40	.16
❑	426	Terry Puhl	.15	.06

❑ 427 Al Holland .15 .06
❑ 428 Eddie Milner .15 .06
❑ 429 Terry Kennedy .15 .06
❑ 430 John Candelaria .15 .06
❑ 431 Manny Trillo .15 .06
❑ 432 Ken Oberkfell .15 .06
❑ 433 Rick Sutcliffe .40 .16
❑ 434 Ron Darling .40 .16
❑ 435 Spike Owen .15 .06
❑ 436 Frank Viola .40 .16
❑ 437 Lloyd Moseby .15 .06
❑ 438 Kirby Puckett RC 12.00 4.80
❑ 439 Jim Clancy .15 .06
❑ 440 Mike Moore .15 .06
❑ 441 Doug Sisk .15 .06
❑ 442 Dennis Eckersley .75 .30
❑ 443 Gerald Perry .15 .06
❑ 444 Dale Berra .15 .06
❑ 445 Dusty Baker .40 .16
❑ 446 Ed Whitson .15 .06
❑ 447 Cesar Cedeno .40 .16
❑ 448 Rick Schu .15 .06
❑ 449 Joaquin Andujar .15 .06
❑ 450 Mark Bailey .15 .06
❑ 451 Ron Romanick .15 .06
❑ 452 Julio Cruz .15 .06
❑ 453 Miguel Dilone .15 .06
❑ 454 Storm Davis .15 .06
❑ 455 Jaime Cocanower .15 .06
❑ 456 Barbaro Garbey .15 .06
❑ 457 Rich Gedman .15 .06
❑ 458 Phil Niekro .40 .16
❑ 459 Mike Scioscia .15 .06
❑ 460 Pat Tabler .15 .06
❑ 461 Darryl Motley .15 .06
❑ 462 Chris Codiroli .15 .06
❑ 463 Doug Flynn .15 .06
❑ 464 Billy Sample .15 .06
❑ 465 Mickey Rivers .15 .06
❑ 466 John Wathan .15 .06
❑ 467 Bill Krueger .15 .06
❑ 468 Andre Thornton .15 .06
❑ 469 Rex Hudler .15 .06
❑ 470 Sid Bream RC .40 .16
❑ 471 Kirk Gibson .40 .16
❑ 472 John Shelby .15 .06
❑ 473 Moose Haas .15 .06
❑ 474 Doug Corbett .15 .06
❑ 475 Willie McGee .40 .16
❑ 476 Bob Knepper .15 .06
❑ 477 Kevin Gross .15 .06
❑ 478 Carmelo Martinez .15 .06
❑ 479 Kent Tekulve .15 .06
❑ 480 Chili Davis .40 .16
❑ 481 Bobby Clark .15 .06
❑ 482 Mookie Wilson .40 .16
❑ 483 Dave Owen .15 .06
❑ 484 Ed Nunez .15 .06
❑ 485 Rance Mulliniks .15 .06
❑ 486 Ken Schrom .15 .06
❑ 487 Jeff Russell .15 .06
❑ 488 Tom Paciorek .40 .16
❑ 489 Dan Ford .15 .06
❑ 490 Mike Caldwell .15 .06
❑ 491 Scottie Earl .15 .06
❑ 492 Jose Rijo RC .75 .30
❑ 493 Bruce Hurst .15 .06
❑ 494 Ken Landreaux .15 .06
❑ 495 Mike Fischlin .15 .06
❑ 496 Don Slaught .15 .06
❑ 497 Steve McCatty .15 .06
❑ 498 Gary Lucas .15 .06
❑ 499 Gary Pettis .15 .06
❑ 500 Marvis Foley .15 .06
❑ 501 Mike Squires .15 .06
❑ 502 Jim Pankovits .15 .06
❑ 503 Luis Aguayo .15 .06
❑ 504 Ralph Citarella .15 .06
❑ 505 Bruce Bochy .15 .06
❑ 506 Bob Owchinko .15 .06
❑ 507 Pascual Perez .15 .06
❑ 508 Lee Lacy .15 .06
❑ 509 Atlee Hammaker .15 .06
❑ 510 Bob Dernier .15 .06
❑ 511 Ed VandeBerg .15 .06
❑ 512 Cliff Johnson .15 .06
❑ 513 Len Whitehouse .15 .06
❑ 514 Dennis Martinez .40 .16
❑ 515 Ed Romero .15 .06
❑ 516 Rusty Kuntz .15 .06
❑ 517 Rick Miller .15 .06
❑ 518 Dennis Rasmussen .15 .06
❑ 519 Steve Yeager .15 .06
❑ 520 Chris Bando .15 .06
❑ 521 U.L. Washington .15 .06
❑ 522 Curt Young .15 .06
❑ 523 Angel Salazar .15 .06
❑ 524 Curt Kaufman .15 .06
❑ 525 Odell Jones .15 .06
❑ 526 Juan Agosto .15 .06
❑ 527 Denny Walling .15 .06
❑ 528 Andy Hawkins .15 .06
❑ 529 Sixto Lezcano .15 .06
❑ 530 Skeeter Barnes RC .15 .06
❑ 531 Randy Johnson .15 .06
❑ 532 Jim Morrison .15 .06
❑ 533 Warren Brusstar .15 .06
❑ 534A J.Pendleton RC ERR 1.25 .50
Wrong first name
❑ 534B T.Pendleton RC COR 1.25 .50
❑ 535 Vic Rodriguez .15 .06
❑ 536 Bob McClure .15 .06
❑ 537 Dave Bergman .15 .06
❑ 538 Mark Clear .15 .06
❑ 539 Mike Pagliarulo .15 .06
❑ 540 Terry Whitfield .15 .06
❑ 541 Joe Beckwith .15 .06
❑ 542 Jeff Burroughs .15 .06
❑ 543 Dan Schatzeder .15 .06
❑ 544 Donnie Scott .15 .06
❑ 545 Jim Slaton .15 .06
❑ 546 Greg Luzinski .40 .16
❑ 547 Mark Salas .15 .06
❑ 548 Dave Smith .15 .06
❑ 549 John Wockenfuss .15 .06
❑ 550 Frank Pastore .15 .06
❑ 551 Tim Flannery .15 .06
❑ 552 Rick Rhoden .15 .06
❑ 553 Mark Davis .15 .06
❑ 554 Jeff Dedmon .15 .06
❑ 555 Gary Woods .15 .06
❑ 556 Danny Heep .15 .06
❑ 557 Mark Langston RC .75 .30
❑ 558 Darrell Brown .15 .06
❑ 559 Jimmy Key RC 1.25 .50
❑ 560 Rick Lysander .15 .06
❑ 561 Doyle Alexander .15 .06
❑ 562 Mike Stanton .15 .06
❑ 563 Sid Fernandez .40 .16
❑ 564 Richie Hebner .15 .06
❑ 565 Alex Trevino .15 .06
❑ 566 Brian Harper .15 .06
❑ 567 Dan Gladden RC .40 .16
❑ 568 Luis Salazar .15 .06
❑ 569 Tom Foley .15 .06
❑ 570 Larry Andersen .15 .06
❑ 571 Danny Cox .15 .06
❑ 572 Joe Sambito .15 .06
❑ 573 Juan Beniquez .15 .06
❑ 574 Joel Skinner .15 .06
❑ 575 Randy St.Claire .15 .06
❑ 576 Floyd Rayford .15 .06
❑ 577 Roy Howell .15 .06
❑ 578 John Grubb .15 .06
❑ 579 Ed Jurak .15 .06
❑ 580 John Montefusco .15 .06
❑ 581 Orel Hershiser RC 2.00 .80
❑ 582 Tom Waddell .15 .06
❑ 583 Mark Huismann .15 .06
❑ 584 Joe Morgan .75 .30
❑ 585 Jim Wohlford .15 .06
❑ 586 Dave Schmidt .15 .06
❑ 587 Jeff Kunkel .15 .06
❑ 588 Hal McRae .40 .16
❑ 589 Bill Almon .15 .06
❑ 590 Carmelo Castillo .15 .06
❑ 591 Omar Moreno .15 .06
❑ 592 Ken Howell .15 .06
❑ 593 Tom Brookens .15 .06
❑ 594 Joe Nolan .15 .06
❑ 595 Willie Lozado .15 .06
❑ 596 Tom Nieto .15 .06
❑ 597 Walt Terrell .15 .06
❑ 598 Al Oliver .40 .16
❑ 599 Shane Rawley .15 .06
❑ 600 Denny Gonzalez .15 .06
❑ 601 Mark Grant .15 .06
❑ 602 Mike Armstrong .15 .06
❑ 603 George Foster .40 .16
❑ 604 Dave Lopes .40 .16
❑ 605 Salome Barojas .15 .06
❑ 606 Roy Lee Jackson .15 .06
❑ 607 Pete Filson .15 .06
❑ 608 Duane Walker .15 .06
❑ 609 Glenn Wilson .15 .06
❑ 610 Rafael Santana .15 .06
❑ 611 Roy Smith .15 .06
❑ 612 Ruppert Jones .15 .06
❑ 613 Joe Cowley .15 .06
❑ 614 Al Nipper UER .15 .06
(Photo actually
Mike Brown)
❑ 615 Gene Nelson .15 .06
❑ 616 Joe Carter 1.25 .50
❑ 617 Ray Knight .15 .06
❑ 618 Chuck Rainey .15 .06
❑ 619 Dan Driessen .15 .06
❑ 620 Daryl Sconiers .15 .06
❑ 621 Bill Stein .15 .06
❑ 622 Roy Smalley .15 .06
❑ 623 Ed Lynch .15 .06
❑ 624 Jeff Stone .15 .06
❑ 625 Bruce Berenyi .15 .06
❑ 626 Kelvin Chapman .15 .06
❑ 627 Joe Price .15 .06
❑ 628 Steve Bedrosian .15 .06
❑ 629 Vic Mata .15 .06
❑ 630 Mike Krukow .15 .06
❑ 631 Phil Bradley .40 .16
❑ 632 Jim Gott .15 .06
❑ 633 Randy Bush .15 .06
❑ 634 Tom Browning RC .40 .16
❑ 635 Lou Gehrig 1.25 .50
Puzzle Card
❑ 636 Reid Nichols .15 .06
❑ 637 Dan Pasqua RC .40 .16
❑ 638 German Rivera .15 .06
❑ 639 Don Schulze .15 .06
❑ 640A Mike Jones .15 .06
(Career Highlights,
takes five lines)
❑ 640B Mike Jones .15 .06
(Career Highlights,
takes four lines)
❑ 641 Pete Rose 4.00 1.60
❑ 642 Wade Rowdon .15 .06
❑ 643 Jerry Narron .15 .06
❑ 644 Darrell Miller .15 .06
❑ 645 Tim Hulett RC .15 .06
❑ 646 Andy McGaffigan .15 .06
❑ 647 Kurt Bevacqua .15 .06
❑ 648 John Russell .15 .06
❑ 649 Ron Robinson .15 .06
❑ 650 Donnie Moore .15 .06
❑ 651A Two for the Title 2.00 .80
Dave Winfield
Don Mattingly
(Yellow letters)
❑ 651B Two for the Title 5.00 2.00
Dave Winfield
Don Mattingly
(White letters)
❑ 652 Tim Laudner .15 .06
❑ 653 Steve Farr RC .40 .16
❑ 654 DK Checklist 1-26 .15 .06
(Unnumbered)
❑ 655 Checklist 27-130 .15 .06
(Unnumbered)
❑ 656 Checklist 131-234 .15 .06
(Unnumbered)
❑ 657 Checklist 235-338 .15 .06
(Unnumbered)
❑ 658 Checklist 339-442 .15 .06
(Unnumbered)
❑ 659 Checklist 443-546 .15 .06
(Unnumbered)
❑ 660 Checklist 547-653 .15 .06
(Unnumbered)

1986 Donruss

	Nm-Mt	Ex-Mt
COMPLETE SET (660)	50.00	20.00
COMP.FACT.SET (660)	50.00	20.00
COMP.AARON PUZZLE	2.00	.80
❑ 1 Kirk Gibson DK	.25	.10
❑ 2 Rich Gossage DK	.25	.10
❑ 3 Willie McGee DK	.25	.10
❑ 4 George Bell DK	.15	.06
❑ 5 Tony Armas DK	.15	.06
❑ 6 Chili Davis DK	.50	.20
❑ 7 Cecil Cooper DK	.15	.06
❑ 8 Mike Boddicker DK	.15	.06
❑ 9 Dave Lopes DK	.25	.10
❑ 10 Bill Doran DK	.15	.06
❑ 11 Bret Saberhagen DK	.25	.10
❑ 12 Brett Butler DK	.15	.06
❑ 13 Harold Baines DK	.50	.20
❑ 14 Mike Davis DK	.15	.06
❑ 15 Tony Perez DK	.25	.10
❑ 16 Willie Randolph DK	.15	.06
❑ 17 Bob Boone DK	.15	.06
❑ 18 Orel Hershiser DK	.25	.10
❑ 19 Johnny Ray DK	.15	.06
❑ 20 Gary Ward DK	.15	.06
❑ 21 Rick Mahler DK	.15	.06
❑ 22 Phil Bradley DK	.15	.06
❑ 23 Jerry Koosman DK	.25	.10
❑ 24 Tom Brunansky DK	.15	.06
❑ 25 Andre Dawson DK	.15	.06
❑ 26 Dwight Gooden DK	.75	.30
❑ 27 Kal Daniels RR	.50	.20
❑ 28 Fred McGriff RR RC	10.00	4.00
❑ 29 Cory Snyder RR	.15	.06
❑ 30 Jose Guzman RR RC	.15	.06
❑ 31 Ty Gainey RC	.15	.06
❑ 32 Johnny Abrego RC	.15	.06
❑ 33A A.Galarraga RC RR	4.00	1.60
No accent		
❑ 33B A.Galarraga RC RR	4.00	1.60
Accent over e		
❑ 34 Dave Shipanoff RC	.15	.06
❑ 35 M.McLemore RR RC	1.00	.40
❑ 36 Marty Clary RC	.15	.06
❑ 37 Paul O'Neill RR RC	5.00	2.00
❑ 38 Danny Tartabull RR	.25	.10
❑ 39 Jose Canseco RR RC	10.00	4.00
❑ 40 Juan Nieves RC	.15	.06
❑ 41 Lance McCullers RC	.15	.06
❑ 42 Rick Surhoff RC	.15	.06
❑ 43 Todd Worrell RR RC	.50	.20
❑ 44 Bob Kipper RC	.15	.06
❑ 45 John Habyan RR RC	.15	.06
❑ 46 Mike Woodard RC	.15	.06
❑ 47 Mike Boddicker	.15	.06
❑ 48 Robin Yount	.75	.30
❑ 49 Lou Whitaker	.25	.10
❑ 50 Oil Can Boyd	.15	.06
❑ 51 Rickey Henderson	1.50	.60
❑ 52 Mike Marshall	.15	.06
❑ 53 George Brett	2.50	1.00
❑ 54 Dave Kingman	.25	.10
❑ 55 Hubie Brooks	.15	.06
❑ 56 Oddibe McDowell	.15	.06
❑ 57 Doug DeCinces	.15	.06
❑ 58 Britt Burns	.15	.06
❑ 59 Ozzie Smith	.75	.30
❑ 60 Jose Cruz	.25	.10
❑ 61 Mike Schmidt	2.00	.80
❑ 62 Pete Rose	2.50	1.00
❑ 63 Steve Garvey	.25	.10
❑ 64 Tony Pena	.15	.06
❑ 65 Chili Davis	.50	.20
❑ 66 Dale Murphy	.75	.30
❑ 67 Ryne Sandberg	1.50	.60
❑ 68 Gary Carter	.50	.20
❑ 69 Alvin Davis	.15	.06
❑ 70 Kent Hrbek	.25	.10
❑ 71 George Bell	.25	.10
❑ 72 Kirby Puckett	2.00	.80
❑ 73 Lloyd Moseby	.15	.06
❑ 74 Bob Kearney	.15	.06
❑ 75 Dwight Gooden	.75	.30
❑ 76 Gary Matthews	.15	.06
❑ 77 Rick Mahler	.15	.06
❑ 78 Benny Distefano	.15	.06
❑ 79 Jeff Leonard	.15	.06
❑ 80 Kevin McReynolds	.25	.10
❑ 81 Ron Oester	.15	.06
❑ 82 John Russell	.15	.06
❑ 83 Tommy Herr	.15	.06
❑ 84 Jerry Mumphrey	.15	.06
❑ 85 Ron Romanick	.15	.06
❑ 86 Daryl Boston	.15	.06
❑ 87 Andre Dawson	.25	.10
❑ 88 Eddie Murray	.75	.30
❑ 89 Dion James	.15	.06
❑ 90 Chet Lemon	.15	.06
❑ 91 Bob Stanley	.15	.06
❑ 92 Willie Randolph	.25	.10
❑ 93 Mike Scioscia	.15	.06
❑ 94 Tom Waddell	.15	.06
❑ 95 Danny Jackson	.15	.06
❑ 96 Mike Davis	.15	.06
❑ 97 Mike Fitzgerald	.15	.06
❑ 98 Gary Ward	.15	.06
❑ 99 Pete O'Brien	.15	.06
❑ 100 Bret Saberhagen	.25	.10
❑ 101 Alfredo Griffin	.15	.06
❑ 102 Brett Butler	.25	.10
❑ 103 Ron Guidry	.25	.10
❑ 104 Jerry Reuss	.15	.06
❑ 105 Jack Morris	.25	.10
❑ 106 Rick Dempsey	.15	.06
❑ 107 Ray Burris	.15	.06
❑ 108 Brian Downing	.15	.06
❑ 109 Willie McGee	.25	.10
❑ 110 Bill Doran	.15	.06
❑ 111 Kent Tekulve	.15	.06
❑ 112 Tony Gwynn	1.25	.50
❑ 113 Marvell Wynne	.15	.06
❑ 114 David Green	.15	.06
❑ 115 Jim Gantner	.15	.06
❑ 116 George Foster	.25	.10
❑ 117 Steve Trout	.15	.06
❑ 118 Mark Langston	.15	.06
❑ 119 Tony Fernandez	.15	.06
❑ 120 John Butcher	.15	.06
❑ 121 Ron Robinson	.15	.06
❑ 122 Dan Spillner	.15	.06
❑ 123 Mike Young	.15	.06
❑ 124 Paul Molitor	.50	.20
❑ 125 Kirk Gibson	.25	.10
❑ 126 Ken Griffey	.25	.10
❑ 127 Tony Armas	.15	.06
❑ 128 Mariano Duncan RC*	.50	.20
❑ 129 Pat Tabler	.15	.06
❑ 130 Frank White	.25	.10
❑ 131 Carney Lansford	.25	.10
❑ 132 Vance Law	.15	.06
❑ 133 Dick Schofield	.15	.06
❑ 134 Wayne Tolleson	.15	.06
❑ 135 Greg Walker	.15	.06
❑ 136 Denny Walling	.15	.06
❑ 137 Ozzie Virgil	.15	.06
❑ 138 Ricky Horton	.15	.06
❑ 139 LaMarr Hoyt	.15	.06
❑ 140 Wayne Krenchicki	.15	.06
❑ 141 Glenn Hubbard	.15	.06
❑ 142 Cecilio Guante	.15	.06
❑ 143 Mike Krukow	.15	.06
❑ 144 Lee Smith	.50	.20
❑ 145 Edwin Nunez	.15	.06
❑ 146 Dave Stieb	.15	.06
❑ 147 Mike Smithson	.15	.06
❑ 148 Ken Dixon	.15	.06
❑ 149 Danny Darwin	.15	.06
❑ 150 Chris Pittaro	.15	.06
❑ 151 Bill Buckner	.25	.10
❑ 152 Mike Pagliarulo	.15	.06
❑ 153 Bill Russell	.15	.06
❑ 154 Brook Jacoby	.15	.06
❑ 155 Pat Sheridan	.15	.06
❑ 156 Mike Gallego RC	.15	.06
❑ 157 Jim Wohlford	.15	.06
❑ 158 Gary Pettis	.15	.06
❑ 159 Toby Harrah	.15	.06
❑ 160 Richard Dotson	.15	.06
❑ 161 Bob Knepper	.15	.06
❑ 162 Dave Dravecky	.25	.10
❑ 163 Greg Gross	.15	.06
❑ 164 Eric Davis	.50	.20
❑ 165 Gerald Perry	.15	.06
❑ 166 Rick Rhoden	.15	.06
❑ 167 Keith Moreland	.15	.06
❑ 168 Jack Clark	.25	.10
❑ 169 Storm Davis	.15	.06
❑ 170 Cecil Cooper	.25	.10
❑ 171 Alan Trammell	.50	.20
❑ 172 Roger Clemens	4.00	1.60
❑ 173 Don Mattingly	2.50	1.00
❑ 174 Pedro Guerrero	.25	.10
❑ 175 Willie Wilson	.15	.06
❑ 176 Dwayne Murphy	.15	.06
❑ 177 Tim Raines	.25	.10
❑ 178 Larry Parrish	.15	.06
❑ 179 Mike Witt	.15	.06
❑ 180 Harold Baines	.50	.20
❑ 181 V.Coleman RC* UER	1.00	.40
BA 2.67 on back		
❑ 182 Jeff Heathcock	.15	.06
❑ 183 Steve Carlton	.50	.20
❑ 184 Mario Soto	.15	.06
❑ 185 Rich Gossage	.25	.10
❑ 186 Johnny Ray	.15	.06
❑ 187 Dan Gladden	.15	.06
❑ 188 Bob Horner	.15	.06
❑ 189 Rick Sutcliffe	.25	.10
❑ 190 Keith Hernandez	.50	.20
❑ 191 Phil Bradley	.15	.06
❑ 192 Tom Brunansky	.15	.06
❑ 193 Jesse Barfield	.15	.06
❑ 194 Frank Viola	.25	.10
❑ 195 Willie Upshaw	.15	.06
❑ 196 Jim Beattie	.15	.06
❑ 197 Darryl Strawberry	.50	.20
❑ 198 Ron Cey	.25	.10
❑ 199 Steve Bedrosian	.15	.06
❑ 200 Steve Kemp	.15	.06
❑ 201 Manny Trillo	.15	.06
❑ 202 Garry Templeton	.15	.06
❑ 203 Dave Parker	.25	.10
❑ 204 John Denny	.15	.06
❑ 205 Terry Pendleton	.25	.10
❑ 206 Terry Puhl	.15	.06
❑ 207 Bobby Grich	.25	.10
❑ 208 Ozzie Guillen RC*	.50	.20
❑ 209 Jeff Reardon	.15	.06
❑ 210 Cal Ripken	3.00	1.20
❑ 211 Bill Schroeder	.15	.06
❑ 212 Dan Petry	.15	.06
❑ 213 Jim Rice	.25	.10
❑ 214 Dave Righetti	.15	.06
❑ 215 Fernando Valenzuela	.25	.10
❑ 216 Julio Franco	.25	.10
❑ 217 Darryl Motley	.15	.06
❑ 218 Dave Collins	.15	.06
❑ 219 Tim Wallach	.15	.06
❑ 220 George Wright	.15	.06
❑ 221 Tommy Dunbar	.15	.06
❑ 222 Steve Balboni	.15	.06
❑ 223 Jay Howell	.15	.06
❑ 224 Joe Carter	.75	.30
❑ 225 Ed Whitson	.15	.06
❑ 226 Orel Hershiser	.50	.20
❑ 227 Willie Hernandez	.15	.06
❑ 228 Lee Lacy	.15	.06
❑ 229 Rollie Fingers	.25	.10

Card	Player	Price 1	Price 2
❑ 230	Bob Boone	.25	.10
❑ 231	Joaquin Andujar	.15	.06
❑ 232	Craig Reynolds	.15	.06
❑ 233	Shane Rawley	.15	.06
❑ 234	Eric Show	.15	.06
❑ 235	Jose DeLeon	.15	.06
❑ 236	Jose Uribe	.15	.06
❑ 237	Moose Haas	.15	.06
❑ 238	Wally Backman	.15	.06
❑ 239	Dennis Eckersley	.50	.20
❑ 240	Mike Moore	.15	.06
❑ 241	Damaso Garcia	.15	.06
❑ 242	Tim Teufel	.15	.06
❑ 243	Dave Concepcion	.25	.10
❑ 244	Floyd Bannister	.15	.06
❑ 245	Fred Lynn	.25	.10
❑ 246	Charlie Moore	.15	.06
❑ 247	Walt Terrell	.15	.06
❑ 248	Dave Winfield	.50	.20
❑ 249	Dwight Evans	.25	.10
❑ 250	Dennis Powell	.15	.06
❑ 251	Andre Thornton	.15	.06
❑ 252	Onix Concepcion	.15	.06
❑ 253	Mike Heath	.15	.06
❑ 254A	David Palmer ERR (Position 2B)	.15	.06
❑ 254B	David Palmer COR (Position P)	.75	.30
❑ 255	Donnie Moore	.15	.06
❑ 256	Curtis Wilkerson	.15	.06
❑ 257	Julio Cruz	.15	.06
❑ 258	Nolan Ryan	4.00	1.60
❑ 259	Jeff Stone	.15	.06
❑ 260	John Tudor	.15	.06
❑ 261	Mark Thurmond	.15	.06
❑ 262	Jay Tibbs	.15	.06
❑ 263	Rafael Ramirez	.15	.06
❑ 264	Larry McWilliams	.15	.06
❑ 265	Mark Davis	.15	.06
❑ 266	Bob Dernier	.15	.06
❑ 267	Matt Young	.15	.06
❑ 268	Jim Clancy	.15	.06
❑ 269	Mickey Hatcher	.15	.06
❑ 270	Sammy Stewart	.15	.06
❑ 271	Bob L. Gibson	.15	.06
❑ 272	Nelson Simmons	.15	.06
❑ 273	Rich Gedman	.15	.06
❑ 274	Butch Wynegar	.15	.06
❑ 275	Ken Howell	.15	.06
❑ 276	Mel Hall	.15	.06
❑ 277	Jim Sundberg	.15	.06
❑ 278	Chris Codiroli	.15	.06
❑ 279	Herm Winningham	.15	.06
❑ 280	Rod Carew	.50	.20
❑ 281	Don Slaught	.15	.06
❑ 282	Scott Fletcher	.15	.06
❑ 283	Bill Dawley	.15	.06
❑ 284	Andy Hawkins	.15	.06
❑ 285	Glenn Wilson	.15	.06
❑ 286	Nick Esasky	.15	.06
❑ 287	Claudell Washington	.15	.06
❑ 288	Lee Mazzilli	.15	.06
❑ 289	Jody Davis	.15	.06
❑ 290	Darrell Porter	.25	.10
❑ 291	Scott McGregor	.15	.06
❑ 292	Ted Simmons	.25	.10
❑ 293	Aurelio Lopez	.15	.06
❑ 294	Marty Barrett	.15	.06
❑ 295	Dale Berra	.15	.06
❑ 296	Greg Brock	.15	.06
❑ 297	Charlie Leibrandt	.15	.06
❑ 298	Bill Krueger	.15	.06
❑ 299	Bryn Smith	.15	.06
❑ 300	Burt Hooton	.15	.06
❑ 301	Stu Cliburn	.15	.06
❑ 302	Luis Salazar	.15	.06
❑ 303	Ken Dayley	.15	.06
❑ 304	Frank DiPino	.15	.06
❑ 305	Von Hayes	.15	.06
❑ 306	Gary Redus	.15	.06
❑ 307	Craig Lefferts	.15	.06
❑ 308	Sammy Khalifa	.15	.06
❑ 309	Scott Garrelts	.15	.06
❑ 310	Rick Cerone	.15	.06
❑ 311	Shawon Dunston	.25	.10
❑ 312	Howard Johnson	.25	.10
❑ 313	Jim Presley	.15	.06
❑ 314	Gary Gaetti	.25	.10
❑ 315	Luis Leal	.15	.06
❑ 316	Mark Salas	.15	.06
❑ 317	Bill Caudill	.15	.06
❑ 318	Dave Henderson	.15	.06
❑ 319	Rafael Santana	.15	.06
❑ 320	Leon Durham	.15	.06
❑ 321	Bruce Sutter	.25	.10
❑ 322	Jason Thompson	.15	.06
❑ 323	Bob Brenly	.15	.06
❑ 324	Carmelo Martinez	.15	.06
❑ 325	Eddie Milner	.15	.06
❑ 326	Juan Samuel	.15	.06
❑ 327	Tom Nieto	.15	.06
❑ 328	Dave Smith	.15	.06
❑ 329	Urbano Lugo	.15	.06
❑ 330	Joel Skinner	.15	.06
❑ 331	Bill Gullickson	.15	.06
❑ 332	Floyd Rayford	.15	.06
❑ 333	Ben Oglivie	.15	.06
❑ 334	Lance Parrish	.25	.10
❑ 335	Jackie Gutierrez	.15	.06
❑ 336	Dennis Rasmussen	.15	.06
❑ 337	Terry Whitfield	.15	.06
❑ 338	Neal Heaton	.15	.06
❑ 339	Jorge Orta	.15	.06
❑ 340	Donnie Hill	.15	.06
❑ 341	Joe Hesketh	.15	.06
❑ 342	Charlie Hough	.25	.10
❑ 343	Dave Rozema	.15	.06
❑ 344	Greg Pryor	.15	.06
❑ 345	Mickey Tettleton RC	.50	.20
❑ 346	George Vukovich	.15	.06
❑ 347	Don Baylor	.50	.20
❑ 348	Carlos Diaz	.15	.06
❑ 349	Barbaro Garbey	.15	.06
❑ 350	Larry Sheets	.15	.06
❑ 351	Ted Higuera RC*	.50	.20
❑ 352	Juan Beniquez	.15	.06
❑ 353	Bob Forsch	.15	.06
❑ 354	Mark Bailey	.15	.06
❑ 355	Larry Andersen	.15	.06
❑ 356	Terry Kennedy	.15	.06
❑ 357	Don Robinson	.15	.06
❑ 358	Jim Gott	.15	.06
❑ 359	Earnie Riles	.15	.06
❑ 360	John Christensen	.15	.06
❑ 361	Ray Fontenot	.15	.06
❑ 362	Spike Owen	.15	.06
❑ 363	Jim Acker	.15	.06
❑ 364	Ron Davis	.15	.06
❑ 365	Tom Hume	.15	.06
❑ 366	Carlton Fisk	.50	.20
❑ 367	Nate Snell	.15	.06
❑ 368	Rick Manning	.15	.06
❑ 369	Darrell Evans	.25	.10
❑ 370	Ron Hassey	.15	.06
❑ 371	Wade Boggs	.50	.20
❑ 372	Rick Honeycutt	.15	.06
❑ 373	Chris Bando	.15	.06
❑ 374	Bud Black	.15	.06
❑ 375	Steve Henderson	.15	.06
❑ 376	Charlie Lea	.15	.06
❑ 377	Reggie Jackson	.50	.20
❑ 378	Dave Schmidt	.15	.06
❑ 379	Bob James	.15	.06
❑ 380	Glenn Davis	.25	.10
❑ 381	Tim Corcoran	.15	.06
❑ 382	Danny Cox	.15	.06
❑ 383	Tim Flannery	.15	.06
❑ 384	Tom Browning	.15	.06
❑ 385	Rick Camp	.15	.06
❑ 386	Jim Morrison	.15	.06
❑ 387	Dave LaPoint	.15	.06
❑ 388	Dave Lopes	.25	.10
❑ 389	Al Cowens	.15	.06
❑ 390	Doyle Alexander	.15	.06
❑ 391	Tim Laudner	.15	.06
❑ 392	Don Aase	.15	.06
❑ 393	Jaime Cocanower	.15	.06
❑ 394	Randy O'Neal	.15	.06
❑ 395	Mike Easler	.15	.06
❑ 396	Scott Bradley	.15	.06
❑ 397	Tom Niedenfuer	.15	.06
❑ 398	Jerry Willard	.15	.06
❑ 399	Lonnie Smith	.15	.06
❑ 400	Bruce Bochte	.15	.06
❑ 401	Terry Francona	.15	.06
❑ 402	Jim Slaton	.15	.06
❑ 403	Bill Stein	.15	.06
❑ 404	Tim Hulett	.15	.06
❑ 405	Alan Ashby	.15	.06
❑ 406	Tim Stoddard	.15	.06
❑ 407	Garry Maddox	.15	.06
❑ 408	Ted Power	.15	.06
❑ 409	Len Barker	.15	.06
❑ 410	Denny Gonzalez	.15	.06
❑ 411	George Frazier	.15	.06
❑ 412	Andy Van Slyke	.25	.10
❑ 413	Jim Dwyer	.15	.06
❑ 414	Paul Householder	.15	.06
❑ 415	Alejandro Sanchez	.15	.06
❑ 416	Steve Crawford	.15	.06
❑ 417	Dan Pasqua	.15	.06
❑ 418	Enos Cabell	.15	.06
❑ 419	Mike Jones	.15	.06
❑ 420	Steve Kiefer	.15	.06
❑ 421	Tim Burke	.15	.06
❑ 422	Mike Mason	.15	.06
❑ 423	Ruppert Jones	.15	.06
❑ 424	Jerry Hairston	.15	.06
❑ 425	Tito Landrum	.15	.06
❑ 426	Jeff Calhoun	.15	.06
❑ 427	Don Carman	.15	.06
❑ 428	Tony Perez	.50	.20
❑ 429	Jerry Davis	.15	.06
❑ 430	Bob Walk	.15	.06
❑ 431	Brad Wellman	.15	.06
❑ 432	Terry Forster	.15	.06
❑ 433	Billy Hatcher	.15	.06
❑ 434	Clint Hurdle	.15	.06
❑ 435	Ivan Calderon RC*	.50	.20
❑ 436	Pete Filson	.15	.06
❑ 437	Tom Henke	.25	.10
❑ 438	Dave Engle	.15	.06
❑ 439	Tom Filer	.15	.06
❑ 440	Gorman Thomas	.15	.06
❑ 441	Rick Aguilera RC	.50	.20
❑ 442	Scott Sanderson	.15	.06
❑ 443	Jeff Dedmon	.15	.06
❑ 444	Joe Orsulak RC*	.15	.06
❑ 445	Atlee Hammaker	.15	.06
❑ 446	Jerry Royster	.15	.06
❑ 447	Buddy Bell	.25	.10
❑ 448	Dave Rucker	.15	.06
❑ 449	Ivan DeJesus	.15	.06
❑ 450	Jim Pankovits	.15	.06
❑ 451	Jerry Narron	.15	.06
❑ 452	Bryan Little	.15	.06
❑ 453	Gary Lucas	.15	.06
❑ 454	Dennis Martinez	.25	.10
❑ 455	Ed Romero	.15	.06
❑ 456	Bob Melvin	.15	.06
❑ 457	Glenn Hoffman	.15	.06
❑ 458	Bob Shirley	.15	.06
❑ 459	Bob Welch	.15	.06
❑ 460	Carmen Castillo	.15	.06
❑ 461	Dave Leeper	.15	.06
❑ 462	Tim Birtsas	.15	.06
❑ 463	Randy St.Claire	.15	.06
❑ 464	Chris Welsh	.15	.06
❑ 465	Greg Harris	.15	.06
❑ 466	Lynn Jones	.15	.06
❑ 467	Dusty Baker	.25	.10
❑ 468	Roy Smith	.15	.06
❑ 469	Andre Robertson	.15	.06
❑ 470	Ken Landreaux	.15	.06
❑ 471	Dave Bergman	.15	.06
❑ 472	Gary Roenicke	.15	.06
❑ 473	Pete Vuckovich	.15	.06
❑ 474	Kirk McCaskill RC	.25	.10
❑ 475	Jeff Lahti	.15	.06
❑ 476	Mike Scott	.15	.06
❑ 477	Darren Daulton RC	1.50	.60
❑ 478	Graig Nettles	.25	.10
❑ 479	Bill Almon	.15	.06
❑ 480	Greg Minton	.15	.06
❑ 481	Randy Ready	.15	.06
❑ 482	Len Dykstra RC	1.50	.60
❑ 483	Thad Bosley	.15	.06
❑ 484	Harold Reynolds RC	1.50	.60

❑	485	Al Oliver	.25	.10
❑	486	Roy Smalley	.15	.06
❑	487	John Franco	.75	.30
❑	488	Juan Agosto	.15	.06
❑	489	Al Pardo	.15	.06
❑	490	Bill Wegman RC	.15	.06
❑	491	Frank Tanana	.15	.06
❑	492	Brian Fisher RC	.15	.06
❑	493	Mark Clear	.15	.06
❑	494	Len Matuszek	.15	.06
❑	495	Ramon Romero	.15	.06
❑	496	John Wathan	.15	.06
❑	497	Rob Picciolo	.15	.06
❑	498	U.L. Washington	.15	.06
❑	499	John Candelaria	.15	.06
❑	500	Duane Walker	.15	.06
❑	501	Gene Nelson	.15	.06
❑	502	John Mizerock	.15	.06
❑	503	Luis Aguayo	.15	.06
❑	504	Kurt Kepshire	.15	.06
❑	505	Ed Wojna	.15	.06
❑	506	Joe Price	.15	.06
❑	507	Milt Thompson RC	.15	.06
❑	508	Junior Ortiz	.15	.06
❑	509	Vida Blue	.25	.10
❑	510	Steve Engel	.15	.06
❑	511	Karl Best	.15	.06
❑	512	Cecil Fielder RC	1.50	.60
❑	513	Frank Eufemia	.15	.06
❑	514	Tippy Martinez	.15	.06
❑	515	Billy Joe Robidoux	.15	.06
❑	516	Bill Scherrer	.15	.06
❑	517	Bruce Hurst	.15	.06
❑	518	Rich Bordi	.15	.06
❑	519	Steve Yeager	.15	.06
❑	520	Tony Bernazard	.15	.06
❑	521	Hal McRae	.25	.10
❑	522	Jose Rijo	.15	.06
❑	523	Mitch Webster	.15	.06
❑	524	Jack Howell	.15	.06
❑	525	Alan Bannister	.15	.06
❑	526	Ron Kittle	.15	.06
❑	527	Phil Garner	.25	.10
❑	528	Kurt Bevacqua	.15	.06
❑	529	Kevin Gross	.15	.06
❑	530	Bo Diaz	.15	.06
❑	531	Ken Oberkfell	.15	.06
❑	532	Rick Reuschel	.15	.06
❑	533	Ron Meridith	.15	.06
❑	534	Steve Braun	.15	.06
❑	535	Wayne Gross	.15	.06
❑	536	Ray Searage	.15	.06
❑	537	Tom Brookens	.15	.06
❑	538	Al Nipper	.15	.06
❑	539	Billy Sample	.15	.06
❑	540	Steve Sax	.15	.06
❑	541	Dan Quisenberry	.15	.06
❑	542	Tony Phillips	.15	.06
❑	543	Floyd Youmans	.15	.06
❑	544	Steve Buechele RC	.50	.20
❑	545	Craig Gerber	.15	.06
❑	546	Joe DeSa	.15	.06
❑	547	Brian Harper	.15	.06
❑	548	Kevin Bass	.15	.06
❑	549	Tom Foley	.15	.06
❑	550	Dave Van Gorder	.15	.06
❑	551	Bruce Bochy	.15	.06
❑	552	R.J. Reynolds	.15	.06
❑	553	Chris Brown	.15	.06
❑	554	Bruce Benedict	.15	.06
❑	555	Warren Brusstar	.15	.06
❑	556	Danny Heep	.15	.06
❑	557	Darnell Coles	.15	.06
❑	558	Greg Gagne	.15	.06
❑	559	Ernie Whitt	.15	.06
❑	560	Ron Washington	.15	.06
❑	561	Jimmy Key	.75	.30
❑	562	Billy Swift	.15	.06
❑	563	Ron Darling	.15	.06
❑	564	Dick Ruthven	.15	.06
❑	565	Zane Smith	.15	.06
❑	566	Sid Bream	.15	.06
❑	567A	J.Youngblood ERR Position P	.15	.06
❑	567B	J.Youngblood COR Position IF	.75	.30
❑	568	Mario Ramirez	.15	.06
❑	569	Tom Runnells	.15	.06
❑	570	Rick Schu	.15	.06
❑	571	Bill Campbell	.15	.06
❑	572	Dickie Thon	.15	.06
❑	573	Al Holland	.15	.06
❑	574	Reid Nichols	.15	.06
❑	575	Bert Roberge	.15	.06
❑	576	Mike Flanagan	.15	.06
❑	577	Tim Leary	.15	.06
❑	578	Mike Laga	.15	.06
❑	579	Steve Lyons	.15	.06
❑	580	Phil Niekro	.25	.10
❑	581	Gilberto Reyes	.15	.06
❑	582	Jamie Easterly	.15	.06
❑	583	Mark Gubicza	.15	.06
❑	584	Stan Javier RC	.50	.20
❑	585	Bill Laskey	.15	.06
❑	586	Jeff Russell	.15	.06
❑	587	Dickie Noles	.15	.06
❑	588	Steve Farr	.15	.06
❑	589	Steve Ontiveros RC	.15	.06
❑	590	Mike Hargrove	.25	.10
❑	591	Marty Bystrom	.15	.06
❑	592	Franklin Stubbs	.15	.06
❑	593	Larry Herndon	.15	.06
❑	594	Bill Swaggerty	.15	.06
❑	595	Carlos Ponce	.15	.06
❑	596	Pat Perry	.15	.06
❑	597	Ray Knight	.25	.10
❑	598	Steve Lombardozzi	.15	.06
❑	599	Brad Havens	.15	.06
❑	600	Pat Clements	.15	.06
❑	601	Joe Niekro	.15	.06
❑	602	Hank Aaron Puzzle Card	.75	.30
❑	603	Dwayne Henry	.15	.06
❑	604	Mookie Wilson	.25	.10
❑	605	Buddy Biancalana	.15	.06
❑	606	Rance Mulliniks	.15	.06
❑	607	Alan Wiggins	.15	.06
❑	608	Joe Cowley	.15	.06
❑	609	Tom Seaver (Green borders on name)	.75	.30
❑	609B	Tom Seaver (Yellow borders on name)	2.00	.80
❑	610	Neil Allen	.15	.06
❑	611	Don Sutton	.75	.30
❑	612	Fred Toliver	.15	.06
❑	613	Jay Baller	.15	.06
❑	614	Marc Sullivan	.15	.06
❑	615	John Grubb	.15	.06
❑	616	Bruce Kison	.15	.06
❑	617	Bill Madlock	.15	.06
❑	618	Chris Chambliss	.25	.10
❑	619	Dave Stewart	.25	.10
❑	620	Tim Lollar	.15	.06
❑	621	Gary Lavelle	.15	.06
❑	622	Charles Hudson	.15	.06
❑	623	Joel Davis	.15	.06
❑	624	Joe Johnson	.15	.06
❑	625	Sid Fernandez	.25	.10
❑	626	Dennis Lamp	.15	.06
❑	627	Terry Harper	.15	.06
❑	628	Jack Lazorko	.15	.06
❑	629	Roger McDowell RC*	.50	.20
❑	630	Mark Funderburk	.15	.06
❑	631	Ed Lynch	.15	.06
❑	632	Rudy Law	.15	.06
❑	633	Roger Mason RC	.15	.06
❑	634	Mike Felder RC	.15	.06
❑	635	Ken Schrom	.15	.06
❑	636	Bob Ojeda	.15	.06
❑	637	Ed VandeBerg	.15	.06
❑	638	Bobby Meacham	.15	.06
❑	639	Cliff Johnson	.15	.06
❑	640	Garth Iorg	.15	.06
❑	641	Dan Driessen	.15	.06
❑	642	Mike Brown OF	.15	.06
❑	643	John Shelby	.15	.06
❑	644	Pete Rose (Ty-Breaking)	.75	.30
❑	645	The Knuckle Brothers Phil Niekro Joe Niekro	.25	.10
❑	646	Jesse Orosco	.15	.06
❑	647	Billy Beane RC	1.00	.40
❑	648	Cesar Cedeno	.25	.10
❑	649	Bert Blyleven	.25	.10
❑	650	Max Venable	.15	.06
❑	651	Fleet Feet Vince Coleman Willie McGee	.15	.06
❑	652	Calvin Schiraldi	.15	.06
❑	653	King of Kings (Pete Rose)	.75	.30
❑	654	Dia. Kings CL 1-26 Unnumbered	.15	.06
❑	655A	CL 1: 27-130 (Unnumbered) (45 Beane ERR)	.15	.06
❑	655B	CL 1: 27-130 (Unnumbered) (45 Habyan COR)	.15	.06
❑	656	CL 2: 131-234 (Unnumbered)	.15	.06
❑	657	CL 3: 235-338 (Unnumbered)	.15	.06
❑	658	CL 4: 339-442 (Unnumbered)	.15	.06
❑	659	CL 5: 443-546 (Unnumbered)	.15	.06
❑	660	CL 6: 547-653 (Unnumbered)	.15	.06

1986 Donruss Rookies

			Nm-Mt	Ex-Mt
		COMP.FACT.SET (56)	50.00	20.00
❑	1	Wally Joyner XRC	1.00	.40
❑	2	Tracy Jones	.15	.06
❑	3	Allan Anderson	.15	.06
❑	4	Ed Correa	.15	.06
❑	5	Reggie Williams	.15	.06
❑	6	Charlie Kerfeld	.15	.06
❑	7	Andres Galarraga	1.50	.60
❑	8	Bob Tewksbury XRC	.50	.20
❑	9	Al Newman	.15	.06
❑	10	Andres Thomas	.15	.06
❑	11	Barry Bonds XRC	40.00	16.00
❑	12	Juan Nieves	.15	.06
❑	13	Mark Eichhorn	.15	.06
❑	14	Dan Plesac XRC	.50	.20
❑	15	Cory Snyder	.15	.06
❑	16	Kelly Gruber	.15	.06
❑	17	Kevin Mitchell XRC	1.00	.40
❑	18	Steve Lombardozzi	.15	.06
❑	19	Mitch Williams XRC	.50	.20
❑	20	John Cerutti	.15	.06
❑	21	Todd Worrell	1.00	.40
❑	22	Jose Canseco	1.50	.60
❑	23	Pete Incaviglia XRC	.50	.20
❑	24	Jose Guzman	.15	.06
❑	25	Scott Bailes	.15	.06
❑	26	Greg Mathews	.15	.06
❑	27	Eric King	.15	.06
❑	28	Paul Assenmacher	.15	.06
❑	29	Jeff Sellers	.15	.06
❑	30	Bobby Bonilla XRC	1.00	.40
❑	31	Doug Drabek XRC	1.00	.40
❑	32	Will Clark UER	2.00	.80

Card	Nm-Mt	Ex-Mt
(Listed as throwing right, should be left) XRC		
❑ 33 Bip Roberts XRC	.50	.20
❑ 34 Jim Deshaies XRC	.50	.20
❑ 35 Mike LaValliere XRC	.50	.20
❑ 36 Scott Bankhead	.15	.06
❑ 37 Dale Sveum	.15	.06
❑ 38 Bo Jackson XRC	2.00	.80
❑ 39 Robby Thompson XRC	.50	.20
❑ 40 Eric Plunk	.15	.06
❑ 41 Bill Bathe	.15	.06
❑ 42 John Kruk XRC	1.50	.60
❑ 43 Andy Allanson	.15	.06
❑ 44 Mark Portugal XRC	.50	.20
❑ 45 Danny Tartabull	.25	.10
❑ 46 Bob Kipper	.15	.06
❑ 47 Gene Walter	.15	.06
❑ 48 Rey Quinones UER (Misspelled Quinonez)	.15	.06
❑ 49 Bobby Witt XRC	.50	.20
❑ 50 Bill Mooneyham	.15	.06
❑ 51 John Cangelosi	.15	.06
❑ 52 Ruben Sierra XRC	1.50	.60
❑ 53 Rob Woodward	.15	.06
❑ 54 Ed Hearn	.15	.06
❑ 55 Joel McKeon	.15	.06
❑ 56 Checklist 1-56	.15	.06

1987 Donruss

	Nm-Mt	Ex-Mt
COMPLETE SET (660)	40.00	16.00
COMP.FACT.SET (660)	50.00	20.00
COMP.CLEMENTE PUZZLE	1.50	.60

Card	Nm-Mt	Ex-Mt
❑ 1 Wally Joyner DK	.40	.16
❑ 2 Roger Clemens DK	.40	.16
❑ 3 Dale Murphy DK	.40	.16
❑ 4 Darryl Strawberry DK	.25	.10
❑ 5 Ozzie Smith DK	.25	.10
❑ 6 Jose Canseco DK	.50	.20
❑ 7 Charlie Hough DK	.10	.04
❑ 8 Brook Jacoby DK	.10	.04
❑ 9 Fred Lynn DK	.15	.06
❑ 10 Rick Rhoden DK	.10	.04
❑ 11 Chris Brown DK	.10	.04
❑ 12 Von Hayes DK	.10	.04
❑ 13 Jack Morris DK	.15	.06
❑ 14A Kevin McReynolds DK ERR (Yellow strip missing on back)	.40	.16
❑ 14B Kevin McReynolds DK COR	.10	.04
❑ 15 George Brett DK	.40	.16
❑ 16 Ted Higuera DK	.10	.04
❑ 17 Hubie Brooks DK	.10	.04
❑ 18 Mike Scott DK	.10	.04
❑ 19 Kirby Puckett DK	.25	.10
❑ 20 Dave Winfield DK	.15	.06
❑ 21 Lloyd Moseby DK	.10	.04
❑ 22A Eric Davis DK ERR (Yellow strip missing on back)	.40	.16
❑ 22B Eric Davis DK COR	.15	.06
❑ 23 Jim Presley DK	.10	.04
❑ 24 Keith Moreland DK	.10	.04
❑ 25A Greg Walker DK ERR (Yellow strip missing on back)	.40	.16
❑ 25B Greg Walker DK COR	.10	.04
❑ 26 Steve Sax DK	.10	.04
❑ 27 DK Checklist 1-26	.10	.04
❑ 28 B.J. Surhoff RR RC	.60	.24
❑ 29 Randy Myers RR RC	.60	.24
❑ 30 Ken Gerhart RC	.15	.06
❑ 31 Benito Santiago	1.00	.40
❑ 32 Greg Swindell RR RC	.40	.16
❑ 33 Mike Birkbeck RC	.15	.06
❑ 34 Terry Steinbach RR RC	.40	.16
❑ 35 Bo Jackson RR RC	1.50	.60
❑ 36 Greg Maddux UER RC middle name misspelled "Allen"	10.00	4.00
❑ 37 Jim Lindeman RC	.15	.06
❑ 38 Devon White RR RC	.60	.24
❑ 39 Eric Bell RC	.15	.06
❑ 40 Willie Fraser RC	.15	.06
❑ 41 Jerry Browne RR RC	.15	.06
❑ 42 Chris James RR RC*	.15	.06
❑ 43 Rafael Palmeiro RR RC	5.00	2.00
❑ 44 Pat Dodson RC	.15	.06
❑ 45 Duane Ward RR RC*	.40	.16
❑ 46 Mark McGwire RR	8.00	3.20
❑ 47 Bruce Fields UER RC (Photo actually Darnell Coles)	.15	.06
❑ 48 Eddie Murray	.40	.16
❑ 49 Ted Higuera	.10	.04
❑ 50 Kirk Gibson	.15	.06
❑ 51 Oil Can Boyd	.10	.04
❑ 52 Don Mattingly	1.25	.50
❑ 53 Pedro Guerrero	.10	.04
❑ 54 George Brett	1.25	.50
❑ 55 Jose Rijo	.10	.04
❑ 56 Tim Raines	.15	.06
❑ 57 Ed Correa	.10	.04
❑ 58 Mike Witt	.10	.04
❑ 59 Greg Walker	.10	.04
❑ 60 Ozzie Smith	.40	.16
❑ 61 Glenn Davis	.10	.04
❑ 62 Glenn Wilson	.10	.04
❑ 63 Tom Browning	.10	.04
❑ 64 Tony Gwynn	.60	.24
❑ 65 R.J. Reynolds	.10	.04
❑ 66 Will Clark RC	1.50	.60
❑ 67 Ozzie Virgil	.10	.04
❑ 68 Rick Sutcliffe	.15	.06
❑ 69 Gary Carter	.25	.10
❑ 70 Mike Moore	.10	.04
❑ 71 Bert Blyleven	.15	.06
❑ 72 Tony Fernandez	.10	.04
❑ 73 Kent Hrbek	.15	.06
❑ 74 Lloyd Moseby	.10	.04
❑ 75 Alvin Davis	.10	.04
❑ 76 Keith Hernandez	.25	.10
❑ 77 Ryne Sandberg	.75	.30
❑ 78 Dale Murphy	.40	.16
❑ 79 Sid Bream	.10	.04
❑ 80 Chris Brown	.10	.04
❑ 81 Steve Garvey	.15	.06
❑ 82 Mario Soto	.10	.04
❑ 83 Shane Rawley	.10	.04
❑ 84 Willie McGee	.15	.06
❑ 85 Jose Cruz	.15	.06
❑ 86 Brian Downing	.10	.04
❑ 87 Ozzie Guillen	.10	.04
❑ 88 Hubie Brooks	.10	.04
❑ 89 Cal Ripken	1.50	.60
❑ 90 Juan Nieves	.10	.04
❑ 91 Lance Parrish	.15	.06
❑ 92 Jim Rice	.15	.06
❑ 93 Ron Guidry	.15	.06
❑ 94 Fernando Valenzuela	.15	.06
❑ 95 Andy Allanson	.10	.04
❑ 96 Willie Wilson	.15	.06
❑ 97 Jose Canseco	1.00	.40
❑ 98 Jeff Reardon	.15	.06
❑ 99 Bobby Witt RC	.40	.16
❑ 100 Checklist 28-133	.10	.04
❑ 101 Jose Guzman	.10	.04
❑ 102 Steve Balboni	.10	.04
❑ 103 Tony Phillips	.10	.04
❑ 104 Brook Jacoby	.10	.04
❑ 105 Dave Winfield	.25	.10
❑ 106 Orel Hershiser	.15	.06
❑ 107 Lou Whitaker	.15	.06
❑ 108 Fred Lynn	.15	.06
❑ 109 Bill Wegman	.10	.04
❑ 110 Donnie Moore	.10	.04
❑ 111 Jack Clark	.15	.06
❑ 112 Bob Knepper	.10	.04
❑ 113 Von Hayes	.10	.04
❑ 114 Bip Roberts RC*	.40	.16
❑ 115 Tony Pena	.10	.04
❑ 116 Scott Garrelts	.10	.04
❑ 117 Paul Molitor	.25	.10
❑ 118 Darryl Strawberry	.25	.10
❑ 119 Shawon Dunston	.10	.04
❑ 120 Jim Presley	.10	.04
❑ 121 Jesse Barfield	.10	.04
❑ 122 Gary Gaetti	.15	.06
❑ 123 Kurt Stillwell	.10	.04
❑ 124 Joel Davis	.10	.04
❑ 125 Mike Boddicker	.10	.04
❑ 126 Robin Yount	.40	.16
❑ 127 Alan Trammell	.25	.10
❑ 128 Dave Righetti	.10	.04
❑ 129 Dwight Evans	.15	.06
❑ 130 Mike Scioscia	.10	.04
❑ 131 Julio Franco	.10	.04
❑ 132 Bret Saberhagen	.15	.06
❑ 133 Mike Davis	.10	.04
❑ 134 Joe Hesketh	.10	.04
❑ 135 Wally Joyner RC	.60	.24
❑ 136 Don Slaught	.10	.04
❑ 137 Daryl Boston	.10	.04
❑ 138 Nolan Ryan	2.00	.80
❑ 139 Mike Schmidt	1.00	.40
❑ 140 Tommy Herr	.10	.04
❑ 141 Garry Templeton	.10	.04
❑ 142 Kal Daniels	.10	.04
❑ 143 Billy Sample	.10	.04
❑ 144 Johnny Ray	.10	.04
❑ 145 Rob Thompson RC*	.40	.16
❑ 146 Bob Dernier	.10	.04
❑ 147 Danny Tartabull	.10	.04
❑ 148 Ernie Whitt	.10	.04
❑ 149 Kirby Puckett	.40	.16
❑ 150 Mike Young	.10	.04
❑ 151 Ernest Riles	.10	.04
❑ 152 Frank Tanana	.10	.04
❑ 153 Rich Gedman	.10	.04
❑ 154 Willie Randolph	.15	.06
❑ 155 Bill Madlock	.15	.06
❑ 156 Joe Carter	.40	.16
❑ 157 Danny Jackson	.10	.04
❑ 158 Carney Lansford	.15	.06
❑ 159 Bryn Smith	.10	.04
❑ 160 Gary Pettis	.10	.04
❑ 161 Oddibe McDowell	.10	.04
❑ 162 John Cangelosi	.10	.04
❑ 163 Mike Scott	.10	.04
❑ 164 Eric Show	.10	.04
❑ 165 Juan Samuel	.10	.04
❑ 166 Nick Esasky	.10	.04
❑ 167 Zane Smith	.10	.04
❑ 168 Mike C. Brown OF	.10	.04
❑ 169 Keith Moreland	.10	.04
❑ 170 John Tudor	.10	.04
❑ 171 Ken Dixon	.10	.04
❑ 172 Jim Gantner	.10	.04
❑ 173 Jack Morris	.15	.06
❑ 174 Bruce Hurst	.10	.04
❑ 175 Dennis Rasmussen	.10	.04
❑ 176 Mike Marshall	.10	.04
❑ 177 Dan Quisenberry	.10	.04
❑ 178 Eric Plunk	.10	.04
❑ 179 Tim Wallach	.10	.04
❑ 180 Steve Buechele	.10	.04
❑ 181 Don Sutton	.40	.16
❑ 182 Dave Schmidt	.10	.04
❑ 183 Terry Pendleton	.15	.06
❑ 184 Jim Deshaies RC *	.15	.06
❑ 185 Steve Bedrosian	.10	.04
❑ 186 Pete Rose	1.25	.50
❑ 187 Dave Dravecky	.15	.06
❑ 188 Rick Reuschel	.10	.04
❑ 189 Dan Gladden	.10	.04
❑ 190 Rick Mahler	.10	.04
❑ 191 Thad Bosley	.10	.04
❑ 192 Ron Darling	.10	.04

❑ 193 Matt Young .10 .04
❑ 194 Tom Brunansky .10 .04
❑ 195 Dave Stieb .10 .04
❑ 196 Frank Viola .10 .04
❑ 197 Tom Henke .10 .04
❑ 198 Karl Best .10 .04
❑ 199 Dwight Gooden .25 .10
❑ 200 Checklist 134-239 .10 .04
❑ 201 Steve Trout .10 .04
❑ 202 Rafael Ramirez .10 .04
❑ 203 Bob Walk .10 .04
❑ 204 Roger Mason .10 .04
❑ 205 Terry Kennedy .10 .04
❑ 206 Ron Oester .10 .04
❑ 207 John Russell .10 .04
❑ 208 Greg Mathews .10 .04
❑ 209 Charlie Kerfeld .10 .04
❑ 210 Reggie Jackson .25 .10
❑ 211 Floyd Bannister .10 .04
❑ 212 Vance Law .10 .04
❑ 213 Rich Bordi .10 .04
❑ 214 Dan Plesac .10 .04
❑ 215 Dave Collins .10 .04
❑ 216 Bob Stanley .10 .04
❑ 217 Joe Niekro .10 .04
❑ 218 Tom Niedenfuer .10 .04
❑ 219 Brett Butler .15 .06
❑ 220 Charlie Leibrandt .10 .04
❑ 221 Steve Ontiveros .10 .04
❑ 222 Tim Burke .10 .04
❑ 223 Curtis Wilkerson .10 .04
❑ 224 Pete Incaviglia RC * .40 .16
❑ 225 Lonnie Smith .10 .04
❑ 226 Chris Codiroli .10 .04
❑ 227 Scott Bailes .10 .04
❑ 228 Rickey Henderson .75 .30
❑ 229 Ken Howell .10 .04
❑ 230 Darnell Coles .10 .04
❑ 231 Don Aase .10 .04
❑ 232 Tim Leary .10 .04
❑ 233 Bob Boone .15 .06
❑ 234 Ricky Horton .10 .04
❑ 235 Mark Bailey .10 .04
❑ 236 Kevin Gross .10 .04
❑ 237 Lance McCullers .10 .04
❑ 238 Cecilio Guante .10 .04
❑ 239 Bob Melvin .10 .04
❑ 240 Billy Joe Robidoux .10 .04
❑ 241 Roger McDowell .10 .04
❑ 242 Leon Durham .10 .04
❑ 243 Ed Nunez .10 .04
❑ 244 Jimmy Key .15 .06
❑ 245 Mike Smithson .10 .04
❑ 246 Bo Diaz .10 .04
❑ 247 Carlton Fisk .25 .10
❑ 248 Larry Sheets .10 .04
❑ 249 Juan Castillo RC .15 .06
❑ 250 Eric King .10 .04
❑ 251 Doug Drabek RC .40 .16
❑ 252 Wade Boggs .25 .10
❑ 253 Mariano Duncan .10 .04
❑ 254 Pat Tabler .10 .04
❑ 255 Frank White .15 .06
❑ 256 Alfredo Griffin .10 .04
❑ 257 Floyd Youmans .10 .04
❑ 258 Rob Wilfong .10 .04
❑ 259 Pete O'Brien .10 .04
❑ 260 Tim Hulett .10 .04
❑ 261 Dickie Thon .10 .04
❑ 262 Darren Daulton .25 .10
❑ 263 Vince Coleman .10 .04
❑ 264 Andy Hawkins .10 .04
❑ 265 Eric Davis .25 .10
❑ 266 Andres Thomas .10 .04
❑ 267 Mike Diaz .10 .04
❑ 268 Chili Davis .25 .10
❑ 269 Jody Davis .10 .04
❑ 270 Phil Bradley .10 .04
❑ 271 George Bell .10 .04
❑ 272 Keith Atherton .10 .04
❑ 273 Storm Davis .10 .04
❑ 274 Rob Deer .10 .04
❑ 275 Walt Terrell .10 .04
❑ 276 Roger Clemens 1.00 .40
❑ 277 Mike Easler .10 .04
❑ 278 Steve Sax .10 .04
❑ 279 Andre Thornton .10 .04
❑ 280 Jim Sundberg .10 .04
❑ 281 Bill Bathe .10 .04
❑ 282 Jay Tibbs .10 .04
❑ 283 Dick Schofield .10 .04
❑ 284 Mike Mason .10 .04
❑ 285 Jerry Hairston .10 .04
❑ 286 Bill Doran .10 .04
❑ 287 Tim Flannery .10 .04
❑ 288 Gary Redus .10 .04
❑ 289 John Franco .15 .06
❑ 290 Paul Assenmacher .25 .10
❑ 291 Joe Orsulak .10 .04
❑ 292 Lee Smith .25 .10
❑ 293 Mike Laga .10 .04
❑ 294 Rick Dempsey .15 .06
❑ 295 Mike Felder .10 .04
❑ 296 Tom Brookens .10 .04
❑ 297 Al Nipper .10 .04
❑ 298 Mike Pagliarulo .10 .04
❑ 299 Franklin Stubbs .10 .04
❑ 300 Checklist 240-345 .10 .04
❑ 301 Steve Farr .10 .04
❑ 302 Bill Mooneyham .10 .04
❑ 303 Andres Galarraga .25 .10
❑ 304 Scott Fletcher .10 .04
❑ 305 Jack Howell .10 .04
❑ 306 Russ Morman .10 .04
❑ 307 Todd Worrell .15 .06
❑ 308 Dave Smith .10 .04
❑ 309 Jeff Stone .10 .04
❑ 310 Ron Robinson .10 .04
❑ 311 Bruce Bochy .10 .04
❑ 312 Jim Winn .10 .04
❑ 313 Mark Davis .10 .04
❑ 314 Jeff Dedmon .10 .04
❑ 315 Jamie Moyer RC 1.00 .40
❑ 316 Wally Backman .10 .04
❑ 317 Ken Phelps .10 .04
❑ 318 Steve Lombardozzi .10 .04
❑ 319 Rance Mulliniks .10 .04
❑ 320 Tim Laudner .10 .04
❑ 321 Mark Eichhorn .10 .04
❑ 322 Lee Guetterman .10 .04
❑ 323 Sid Fernandez .10 .04
❑ 324 Jerry Mumphrey .10 .04
❑ 325 David Palmer .10 .04
❑ 326 Bill Almon .10 .04
❑ 327 Candy Maldonado .10 .04
❑ 328 John Kruk RC .60 .24
❑ 329 John Denny .10 .04
❑ 330 Milt Thompson .10 .04
❑ 331 Mike LaValliere RC * .40 .16
❑ 332 Alan Ashby .10 .04
❑ 333 Doug Corbett .10 .04
❑ 334 Ron Karkovice RC .40 .16
❑ 335 Mitch Webster .10 .04
❑ 336 Lee Lacy .10 .04
❑ 337 Glenn Braggs RC .15 .06
❑ 338 Dwight Lowry .10 .04
❑ 339 Don Baylor .15 .06
❑ 340 Brian Fisher .10 .04
❑ 341 Reggie Williams .10 .04
❑ 342 Tom Candiotti .10 .04
❑ 343 Rudy Law .10 .04
❑ 344 Curt Young .10 .04
❑ 345 Mike Fitzgerald .10 .04
❑ 346 Ruben Sierra RC .60 .24
❑ 347 Mitch Williams RC * .40 .16
❑ 348 Jorge Orta .10 .04
❑ 349 Mickey Tettleton .10 .04
❑ 350 Ernie Camacho .10 .04
❑ 351 Ron Kittle .10 .04
❑ 352 Ken Landreaux .10 .04
❑ 353 Chet Lemon .10 .04
❑ 354 John Shelby .10 .04
❑ 355 Mark Clear .10 .04
❑ 356 Doug DeCinces .10 .04
❑ 357 Ken Dayley .10 .04
❑ 358 Phil Garner .10 .04
❑ 359 Steve Jeltz .10 .04
❑ 360 Ed Whitson .10 .04
❑ 361 Barry Bonds RC 15.00 6.00
❑ 362 Vida Blue .15 .06
❑ 363 Cecil Cooper .15 .06
❑ 364 Bob Ojeda .10 .04
❑ 365 Dennis Eckersley .25 .10
❑ 366 Mike Morgan .10 .04
❑ 367 Willie Upshaw .10 .04
❑ 368 Allan Anderson .10 .04
❑ 369 Bill Gullickson .10 .04
❑ 370 Bobby Thigpen RC .40 .16
❑ 371 Juan Beniquez .10 .04
❑ 372 Charlie Moore .10 .04
❑ 373 Dan Petry .10 .04
❑ 374 Rod Scurry .10 .04
❑ 375 Tom Seaver .40 .16
❑ 376 Ed VandeBerg .10 .04
❑ 377 Tony Bernazard .10 .04
❑ 378 Greg Pryor .10 .04
❑ 379 Dwayne Murphy .10 .04
❑ 380 Andy McGaffigan .10 .04
❑ 381 Kirk McCaskill .10 .04
❑ 382 Greg Harris .10 .04
❑ 383 Rich Dotson .10 .04
❑ 384 Craig Reynolds .10 .04
❑ 385 Greg Gross .10 .04
❑ 386 Tito Landrum .10 .04
❑ 387 Craig Lefferts .10 .04
❑ 388 Dave Parker .15 .06
❑ 389 Bob Horner .10 .04
❑ 390 Pat Clements .10 .04
❑ 391 Jeff Leonard .10 .04
❑ 392 Chris Speier .10 .04
❑ 393 John Moses .10 .04
❑ 394 Garth Iorg .10 .04
❑ 395 Greg Gagne .10 .04
❑ 396 Nate Snell .10 .04
❑ 397 Bryan Clutterbuck .10 .04
❑ 398 Darrell Evans .15 .06
❑ 399 Steve Crawford .10 .04
❑ 400 Checklist 346-451 .10 .04
❑ 401 Phil Lombardi .10 .04
❑ 402 Rick Honeycutt .10 .04
❑ 403 Ken Schrom .10 .04
❑ 404 Bud Black .10 .04
❑ 405 Donnie Hill .10 .04
❑ 406 Wayne Krenchicki .10 .04
❑ 407 Chuck Finley RC .60 .24
❑ 408 Toby Harrah .10 .04
❑ 409 Steve Lyons .10 .04
❑ 410 Kevin Bass .10 .04
❑ 411 Marvell Wynne .10 .04
❑ 412 Ron Roenicke .10 .04
❑ 413 Tracy Jones .10 .04
❑ 414 Gene Garber .10 .04
❑ 415 Mike Bielecki .10 .04
❑ 416 Frank DiPino .10 .04
❑ 417 Andy Van Slyke .15 .06
❑ 418 Jim Dwyer .10 .04
❑ 419 Ben Oglivie .10 .04
❑ 420 Dave Bergman .10 .04
❑ 421 Joe Sambito .10 .04
❑ 422 Bob Tewksbury RC * .40 .16
❑ 423 Len Matuszek .10 .04
❑ 424 Mike Kingery RC .15 .06
❑ 425 Dave Kingman .15 .06
❑ 426 Al Newman .10 .04
❑ 427 Gary Ward .10 .04
❑ 428 Ruppert Jones .10 .04
❑ 429 Harold Baines .15 .06
❑ 430 Pat Perry .10 .04
❑ 431 Terry Puhl .10 .04
❑ 432 Don Carman .10 .04
❑ 433 Eddie Milner .10 .04
❑ 434 LaMarr Hoyt .10 .04
❑ 435 Rick Rhoden .10 .04
❑ 436 Jose Uribe .10 .04
❑ 437 Ken Oberkfell .10 .04
❑ 438 Ron Davis .10 .04
❑ 439 Jesse Orosco .10 .04
❑ 440 Scott Bradley .10 .04
❑ 441 Randy Bush .10 .04
❑ 442 John Cerutti .10 .04
❑ 443 Roy Smalley .10 .04
❑ 444 Kelly Gruber .10 .04
❑ 445 Bob Kearney .10 .04
❑ 446 Ed Hearn .10 .04
❑ 447 Scott Sanderson .10 .04
❑ 448 Bruce Benedict .10 .04
❑ 449 Junior Ortiz .10 .04
❑ 450 Mike Aldrete .10 .04

❑ 451 Kevin McReynolds .10 .04
❑ 452 Rob Murphy .10 .04
❑ 453 Kent Tekulve .10 .04
❑ 454 Curt Ford .10 .04
❑ 455 Dave Lopes .15 .06
❑ 456 Bob Grich .15 .06
❑ 457 Jose DeLeon .10 .04
❑ 458 Andre Dawson .15 .06
❑ 459 Mike Flanagan .10 .04
❑ 460 Joey Meyer .10 .04
❑ 461 Chuck Cary .10 .04
❑ 462 Bill Buckner .15 .06
❑ 463 Bob Shirley .10 .04
❑ 464 Jeff Hamilton .10 .04
❑ 465 Phil Niekro .15 .06
❑ 466 Mark Gubicza .10 .04
❑ 467 Jerry Willard .10 .04
❑ 468 Bob Sebra .10 .04
❑ 469 Larry Parrish .10 .04
❑ 470 Charlie Hough .15 .06
❑ 471 Hal McRae .15 .06
❑ 472 Dave Leiper .10 .04
❑ 473 Mel Hall .10 .04
❑ 474 Dan Pasqua .10 .04
❑ 475 Bob Welch .10 .04
❑ 476 Johnny Grubb .10 .04
❑ 477 Jim Traber .10 .04
❑ 478 Chris Bosio RC .40 .16
❑ 479 Mark McLemore .15 .06
❑ 480 John Morris .10 .04
❑ 481 Billy Hatcher .10 .04
❑ 482 Dan Schatzeder .10 .04
❑ 483 Rich Gossage .15 .06
❑ 484 Jim Morrison .10 .04
❑ 485 Bob Brenly .10 .04
❑ 486 Bill Schroeder .10 .04
❑ 487 Mookie Wilson .15 .06
❑ 488 Dave Martinez RC .40 .16
❑ 489 Harold Reynolds .15 .06
❑ 490 Jeff Hearron .10 .04
❑ 491 Mickey Hatcher .10 .04
❑ 492 Barry Larkin RC 2.00 .80
❑ 493 Bob James .10 .04
❑ 494 John Habyan .10 .04
❑ 495 Jim Adduci .10 .04
❑ 496 Mike Heath .10 .04
❑ 497 Tim Stoddard .10 .04
❑ 498 Tony Armas .10 .04
❑ 499 Dennis Powell .10 .04
❑ 500 Checklist 452-557 .10 .04
❑ 501 Chris Bando .10 .04
❑ 502 David Cone RC 1.00 .40
❑ 503 Jay Howell .10 .04
❑ 504 Tom Foley .10 .04
❑ 505 Ray Chadwick .10 .04
❑ 506 Mike Loynd .10 .04
❑ 507 Neil Allen .10 .04
❑ 508 Danny Darwin .10 .04
❑ 509 Rick Schu .10 .04
❑ 510 Jose Oquendo .10 .04
❑ 511 Gene Walter .10 .04
❑ 512 Terry McGriff .10 .04
❑ 513 Ken Griffey .15 .06
❑ 514 Benny Distefano .10 .04
❑ 515 Terry Mulholland RC .40 .16
❑ 516 Ed Lynch .10 .04
❑ 517 Bill Swift .10 .04
❑ 518 Manny Lee .10 .04
❑ 519 Andre David .10 .04
❑ 520 Scott McGregor .10 .04
❑ 521 Rick Manning .10 .04
❑ 522 Willie Hernandez .10 .04
❑ 523 Marty Barrett .10 .04
❑ 524 Wayne Tolleson .10 .04
❑ 525 Jose Gonzalez RC .15 .06
❑ 526 Cory Snyder .10 .04
❑ 527 Buddy Biancalana .10 .04
❑ 528 Moose Haas .10 .04
❑ 529 Wilfredo Tejada .10 .04
❑ 530 Stu Cliburn .10 .04
❑ 531 Dale Mohorcic .10 .04
❑ 532 Ron Hassey .10 .04
❑ 533 Ty Gainey .10 .04
❑ 534 Jerry Royster .10 .04
❑ 535 Mike Maddux .10 .04
❑ 536 Ted Power .10 .04
❑ 537 Ted Simmons .15 .06
❑ 538 Rafael Belliard RC .40 .16
❑ 539 Chico Walker .10 .04
❑ 540 Bob Forsch .10 .04
❑ 541 John Stefero .10 .04
❑ 542 Dale Sveum .10 .04
❑ 543 Mark Thurmond .10 .04
❑ 544 Jeff Sellers .10 .04
❑ 545 Joel Skinner .10 .04
❑ 546 Alex Trevino .10 .04
❑ 547 Randy Kutcher .10 .04
❑ 548 Joaquin Andujar .10 .04
❑ 549 Casey Candaele .10 .04
❑ 550 Jeff Russell .10 .04
❑ 551 John Candelaria .10 .04
❑ 552 Joe Cowley .10 .04
❑ 553 Danny Cox .10 .04
❑ 554 Denny Walling .10 .04
❑ 555 Bruce Ruffin RC .15 .06
❑ 556 Buddy Bell .15 .06
❑ 557 Jimmy Jones RC .15 .06
❑ 558 Bobby Bonilla RC .60 .24
❑ 559 Jeff D. Robinson .10 .04
❑ 560 Ed Olwine .10 .04
❑ 561 Glenallen Hill RC .40 .16
❑ 562 Lee Mazzilli .10 .04
❑ 563 Mike G. Brown P .10 .04
❑ 564 George Frazier .10 .04
❑ 565 Mike Sharperson RC .15 .06
❑ 566 Mark Portugal RC * .15 .06
❑ 567 Rick Leach .10 .04
❑ 568 Mark Langston .10 .04
❑ 569 Rafael Santana .10 .04
❑ 570 Manny Trillo .10 .04
❑ 571 Cliff Speck .10 .04
❑ 572 Bob Kipper .10 .04
❑ 573 Kelly Downs RC .15 .06
❑ 574 Randy Asadoor .10 .04
❑ 575 Dave Magadan RC .40 .16
❑ 576 Marvin Freeman RC .15 .06
❑ 577 Jeff Lahti .10 .04
❑ 578 Jeff Calhoun .10 .04
❑ 579 Gus Polidor .10 .04
❑ 580 Gene Nelson .10 .04
❑ 581 Tim Teufel .10 .04
❑ 582 Odell Jones .10 .04
❑ 583 Mark Ryal .10 .04
❑ 584 Randy O'Neal .10 .04
❑ 585 Mike Greenwell RC .40 .16
❑ 586 Ray Knight .10 .04
❑ 587 Ralph Bryant .10 .04
❑ 588 Carmen Castillo .10 .04
❑ 589 Ed Wojna .10 .04
❑ 590 Stan Javier .10 .04
❑ 591 Jeff Musselman .10 .04
❑ 592 Mike Stanley RC .40 .16
❑ 593 Darrell Porter .10 .04
❑ 594 Drew Hall .10 .04
❑ 595 Rob Nelson .10 .04
❑ 596 Bryan Oelkers .10 .04
❑ 597 Scott Nielsen .10 .04
❑ 598 Brian Holton .10 .04
❑ 599 Kevin Mitchell RC * .60 .24
❑ 600 Checklist 558-660 .10 .04
❑ 601 Jackie Gutierrez .10 .04
❑ 602 Barry Jones .10 .04
❑ 603 Jerry Narron .10 .04
❑ 604 Steve Lake .10 .04
❑ 605 Jim Pankovits .10 .04
❑ 606 Ed Romero .10 .04
❑ 607 Dave LaPoint .10 .04
❑ 608 Don Robinson .10 .04
❑ 609 Mike Krukow .10 .04
❑ 610 Dave Valle RC ** .15 .06
❑ 611 Len Dykstra .25 .10
❑ 612 R.Clemente PUZ .50 .20
❑ 613 Mike Trujillo .10 .04
❑ 614 Damaso Garcia .10 .04
❑ 615 Neal Heaton .10 .04
❑ 616 Juan Berenguer .10 .04
❑ 617 Steve Carlton .25 .10
❑ 618 Gary Lucas .10 .04
❑ 619 Geno Petralli .10 .04
❑ 620 Rick Aguilera .15 .06
❑ 621 Fred McGriff .75 .30
❑ 622 Dave Henderson .10 .04
❑ 623 Dave Clark RC .15 .06
❑ 624 Angel Salazar .10 .04
❑ 625 Randy Hunt .10 .04
❑ 626 John Gibbons .10 .04
❑ 627 Kevin Brown RC 2.50 .80
❑ 628 Bill Dawley .10 .04
❑ 629 Aurelio Lopez .10 .04
❑ 630 Charles Hudson .10 .04
❑ 631 Ray Soff .10 .04
❑ 632 Ray Hayward .10 .04
❑ 633 Spike Owen .10 .04
❑ 634 Glenn Hubbard .10 .04
❑ 635 Kevin Elster RC .40 .16
❑ 636 Mike LaCoss .10 .04
❑ 637 Dwayne Henry .10 .04
❑ 638 Rey Quinones .10 .04
❑ 639 Jim Clancy .10 .04
❑ 640 Larry Andersen .10 .04
❑ 641 Calvin Schiraldi .10 .04
❑ 642 Stan Jefferson .10 .04
❑ 643 Marc Sullivan .10 .04
❑ 644 Mark Grant .10 .04
❑ 645 Cliff Johnson .10 .04
❑ 646 Howard Johnson .10 .04
❑ 647 Dave Sax .10 .04
❑ 648 Dave Stewart .15 .06
❑ 649 Danny Heep .10 .04
❑ 650 Joe Johnson .10 .04
❑ 651 Bob Brower .10 .04
❑ 652 Rob Woodward .10 .04
❑ 653 John Mizerock .10 .04
❑ 654 Tim Pyznarski .10 .04
❑ 655 Luis Aquino .10 .04
❑ 656 Mickey Brantley .10 .04
❑ 657 Doyle Alexander .10 .04
❑ 658 Sammy Stewart .10 .04
❑ 659 Jim Acker .10 .04
❑ 660 Pete Ladd .10 .04

1987 Donruss Rookies

	Nm-Mt	Ex-Mt
COMP.FACT.SET (56)	20.00	8.00

❑ 1 Mark McGwire 8.00 3.20
❑ 2 Eric Bell .15 .06
❑ 3 Mark Williamson .10 .04
❑ 4 Mike Greenwell .40 .16
❑ 5 Ellis Burks XRC .60 .24
❑ 6 DeWayne Buice .10 .04
❑ 7 Mark McLemore .25 .10
❑ 8 Devon White .60 .24
❑ 9 Willie Fraser .15 .06
❑ 10 Les Lancaster .10 .04
❑ 11 Ken Williams XRC .10 .04
❑ 12 Matt Nokes XRC .40 .16
❑ 13 Jeff M. Robinson .10 .04
❑ 14 Bo Jackson 1.00 .40
❑ 15 Kevin Seitzer XRC .40 .16
❑ 16 Billy Ripken XRC .40 .16
❑ 17 B.J. Surhoff .60 .24
❑ 18 Chuck Crim .10 .04
❑ 19 Mike Birkbeck .15 .06
❑ 20 Chris Bosio .40 .16
❑ 21 Les Straker .10 .04
❑ 22 Mark Davidson .10 .04
❑ 23 Gene Larkin XRC .40 .16
❑ 24 Ken Gerhart .10 .04

	Nm-Mt	Ex-Mt
❑ 25 Luis Polonia XRC	.15	.06
❑ 26 Terry Steinbach	.40	.16
❑ 27 Mickey Brantley	.10	.04
❑ 28 Mike Stanley	.40	.16
❑ 29 Jerry Browne	.15	.06
❑ 30 Todd Benzinger XRC	.40	.16
❑ 31 Fred McGriff	1.50	.60
❑ 32 Mike Henneman XRC	.40	.16
❑ 33 Casey Candaele	.10	.04
❑ 34 Dave Magadan	.40	.16
❑ 35 David Cone	1.00	.40
❑ 36 Mike Jackson XRC	.40	.16
❑ 37 John Mitchell XRC	.15	.06
❑ 38 Mike Dunne	.10	.04
❑ 39 John Smiley XRC	.40	.16
❑ 40 Joe Magrane XRC	.15	.06
❑ 41 Jim Lindeman	.15	.06
❑ 42 Shane Mack	.10	.04
❑ 43 Stan Jefferson	.10	.04
❑ 44 Benito Santiago	.50	.20
❑ 45 Matt Williams XRC	2.50	1.00
❑ 46 Dave Meads	.10	.04
❑ 47 Rafael Palmeiro	5.00	2.00
❑ 48 Bill Long	.10	.04
❑ 49 Bob Brower	.10	.04
❑ 50 James Steels	.10	.04
❑ 51 Paul Noce	.10	.04
❑ 52 Greg Maddux	8.00	3.20
❑ 53 Jeff Musselman	.10	.04
❑ 54 Brian Holton	.10	.04
❑ 55 Chuck Jackson	.10	.04
❑ 56 Checklist 1-56	.10	.04

1987 Donruss Opening Day

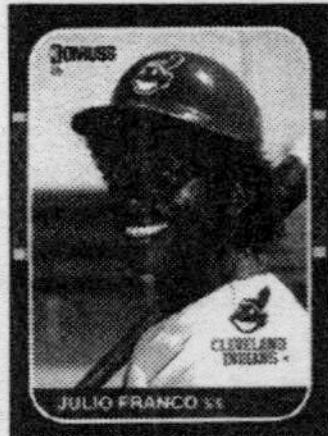

	Nm-Mt	Ex-Mt
COMP.FACT. SET (272)	50.00	20.00
❑ 1 Doug DeCinces	.10	.04
❑ 2 Mike Witt	.10	.04
❑ 3 George Hendrick	.10	.04
❑ 4 Dick Schofield	.10	.04
❑ 5 Devon White	.60	.24
❑ 6 Butch Wynegar	.10	.04
❑ 7 Wally Joyner	.40	.16
❑ 8 Mark McLemore	.15	.06
❑ 9 Brian Downing	.10	.04
❑ 10 Gary Pettis	.10	.04
❑ 11 Bill Doran	.10	.04
❑ 12 Phil Garner	.15	.06
❑ 13 Jose Cruz	.15	.06
❑ 14 Kevin Bass	.10	.04
❑ 15 Mike Scott	.10	.04
❑ 16 Glenn Davis	.10	.04
❑ 17 Alan Ashby	.10	.04
❑ 18 Billy Hatcher	.10	.04
❑ 19 Craig Reynolds	.10	.04
❑ 20 Carney Lansford	.15	.06
❑ 21 Mike Davis	.10	.04
❑ 22 Reggie Jackson	.25	.10
❑ 23 Mickey Tettleton	.10	.04
❑ 24 Jose Canseco	1.00	.40
❑ 25 Rob Nelson	.10	.04
❑ 26 Tony Phillips	.10	.04
❑ 27 Dwayne Murphy	.10	.04
❑ 28 Alfredo Griffin	.10	.04
❑ 29 Curt Young	.10	.04
❑ 30 Willie Upshaw	.10	.04
❑ 31 Mike Sharperson	.15	.06
❑ 32 Rance Mulliniks	.10	.04
❑ 33 Ernie Whitt	.10	.04
❑ 34 Jesse Barfield	.10	.04
❑ 35 Tony Fernandez	.10	.04
❑ 36 Lloyd Moseby	.10	.04
❑ 37 Jimmy Key	.15	.06
❑ 38 Fred McGriff	.75	.30
❑ 39 George Bell	.10	.04
❑ 40 Dale Murphy	.40	.16
❑ 41 Rick Mahler	.10	.04
❑ 42 Ken Griffey	.15	.06
❑ 43 Andres Thomas	.10	.04
❑ 44 Dion James	.10	.04
❑ 45 Ozzie Virgil	.10	.04
❑ 46 Ken Oberkfell	.10	.04
❑ 47 Gary Roenicke	.10	.04
❑ 48 Glenn Hubbard	.10	.04
❑ 49 Bill Schroeder	.10	.04
❑ 50 Greg Brock	.10	.04
❑ 51 Billy Joe Robidoux	.10	.04
❑ 52 Glenn Braggs	.15	.06
❑ 53 Jim Gantner	.10	.04
❑ 54 Paul Molitor	.25	.10
❑ 55 Dale Sveum	.10	.04
❑ 56 Ted Higuera	.10	.04
❑ 57 Rob Deer	.10	.04
❑ 58 Robin Yount	.40	.16
❑ 59 Jim Lindeman	.15	.06
❑ 60 Vince Coleman	.10	.04
❑ 61 Tommy Herr	.10	.04
❑ 62 Terry Pendleton	.15	.06
❑ 63 John Tudor	.10	.04
❑ 64 Tony Pena	.10	.04
❑ 65 Ozzie Smith	.40	.16
❑ 66 Tito Landrum	.10	.04
❑ 67 Jack Clark	.15	.06
❑ 68 Bob Dernier	.10	.04
❑ 69 Rick Sutcliffe	.15	.06
❑ 70 Andre Dawson	.15	.06
❑ 71 Keith Moreland	.10	.04
❑ 72 Jody Davis	.10	.04
❑ 73 Brian Dayett	.10	.04
❑ 74 Leon Durham	.10	.04
❑ 75 Ryne Sandberg	.75	.30
❑ 76 Shawon Dunston	.10	.04
❑ 77 Mike Marshall	.10	.04
❑ 78 Bill Madlock	.15	.06
❑ 79 Orel Hershiser	.15	.06
❑ 80 Mike Ramsey	.10	.04
❑ 81 Ken Landreaux	.10	.04
❑ 82 Mike Scioscia	.10	.04
❑ 83 Franklin Stubbs	.10	.04
❑ 84 Mariano Duncan	.10	.04
❑ 85 Steve Sax	.10	.04
❑ 86 Mitch Webster	.10	.04
❑ 87 Reid Nichols	.10	.04
❑ 88 Tim Wallach	.10	.04
❑ 89 Floyd Youmans	.10	.04
❑ 90 Andres Galarraga	.25	.10
❑ 91 Hubie Brooks	.10	.04
❑ 92 Jeff Reed	.10	.04
❑ 93 Alonzo Powell	.10	.04
❑ 94 Vance Law	.10	.04
❑ 95 Bob Brenly	.10	.04
❑ 96 Will Clark	1.00	.40
❑ 97 Chili Davis	.25	.10
❑ 98 Mike Krukow	.10	.04
❑ 99 Jose Uribe	.10	.04
❑ 100 Chris Brown	.10	.04
❑ 101 Robby Thompson	.40	.16
❑ 102 Candy Maldonado	.10	.04
❑ 103 Jeff Leonard	.10	.04
❑ 104 Tom Candiotti	.10	.04
❑ 105 Chris Bando	.10	.04
❑ 106 Cory Snyder	.10	.04
❑ 107 Pat Tabler	.10	.04
❑ 108 Andre Thornton	.10	.04
❑ 109 Joe Carter	.40	.16
❑ 110 Tony Bernazard	.10	.04
❑ 111 Julio Franco	.15	.06
❑ 112 Brook Jacoby	.10	.04
❑ 113 Brett Butler	.15	.06
❑ 114 Donell Nixon	.10	.04
❑ 115 Alvin Davis	.10	.04
❑ 116 Mark Langston	.10	.04
❑ 117 Harold Reynolds	.15	.06
❑ 118 Ken Phelps	.10	.04
❑ 119 Mike Kingery	.15	.06
❑ 120 Dave Valle	.15	.06
❑ 121 Rey Quinones	.10	.04
❑ 122 Phil Bradley	.10	.04
❑ 123 Jim Presley	.10	.04
❑ 124 Keith Hernandez	.25	.10
❑ 125 Kevin McReynolds	.10	.04
❑ 126 Rafael Santana	.10	.04
❑ 127 Bob Ojeda	.10	.04
❑ 128 Darryl Strawberry	.25	.10
❑ 129 Mookie Wilson	.15	.06
❑ 130 Gary Carter	.25	.10
❑ 131 Tim Teufel	.10	.04
❑ 132 Howard Johnson	.10	.04
❑ 133 Cal Ripken	1.50	.60
❑ 134 Rick Burleson	.10	.04
❑ 135 Fred Lynn	.15	.06
❑ 136 Eddie Murray	.40	.16
❑ 137 Ray Knight	.10	.04
❑ 138 Alan Wiggins	.10	.04
❑ 139 John Shelby	.10	.04
❑ 140 Mike Boddicker	.10	.04
❑ 141 Ken Gerhart	.10	.04
❑ 142 Terry Kennedy	.10	.04
❑ 143 Steve Garvey	.15	.06
❑ 144 Marvell Wynne	.10	.04
❑ 145 Kevin Mitchell	.25	.10
❑ 146 Tony Gwynn	.60	.24
❑ 147 Joey Cora	.25	.10
❑ 148 Benito Santiago	.25	.10
❑ 149 Eric Show	.10	.04
❑ 150 Garry Templeton	.10	.04
❑ 151 Carmelo Martinez	.10	.04
❑ 152 Von Hayes	.10	.04
❑ 153 Lance Parrish	.15	.06
❑ 154 Milt Thompson	.10	.04
❑ 155 Mike Easler	.10	.04
❑ 156 Juan Samuel	.10	.04
❑ 157 Steve Jeltz	.10	.04
❑ 158 Glenn Wilson	.10	.04
❑ 159 Shane Rawley	.10	.04
❑ 160 Mike Schmidt	1.00	.40
❑ 161 Andy Van Slyke	.15	.06
❑ 162 Johnny Ray	.10	.04
❑ 163A Barry Bonds ERR (Photo actually Johnny Ray wearing a black shirt)	300.00	120.00
❑ 163B Barry Bonds COR	20.00	8.00
❑ 164 Junior Ortiz	.10	.04
❑ 165 Rafael Belliard	.40	.16
❑ 166 Bob Patterson	.10	.04
❑ 167 Bobby Bonilla	.40	.16
❑ 168 Sid Bream	.10	.04
❑ 169 Jim Morrison	.10	.04
❑ 170 Jerry Browne	.15	.06
❑ 171 Scott Fletcher	.10	.04
❑ 172 Ruben Sierra	.60	.24
❑ 173 Larry Parrish	.10	.04
❑ 174 Pete O'Brien	.10	.04
❑ 175 Pete Incaviglia	.40	.16
❑ 176 Don Slaught	.10	.04
❑ 177 Oddibe McDowell	.10	.04
❑ 178 Charlie Hough	.15	.06
❑ 179 Steve Buechele	.10	.04
❑ 180 Bob Stanley	.10	.04
❑ 181 Wade Boggs	.25	.10
❑ 182 Jim Rice	.15	.06
❑ 183 Bill Buckner	.15	.06
❑ 184 Dwight Evans	.15	.06
❑ 185 Spike Owen	.10	.04
❑ 186 Don Baylor	.15	.06
❑ 187 Marc Sullivan	.10	.04
❑ 188 Marty Barrett	.10	.04
❑ 189 Dave Henderson	.10	.04
❑ 190 Bo Diaz	.10	.04
❑ 191 Barry Larkin	2.00	.80
❑ 192 Kal Daniels	.10	.04
❑ 193 Terry Francona	.15	.06
❑ 194 Tom Browning	.10	.04
❑ 195 Ron Oester	.10	.04
❑ 196 Buddy Bell	.15	.06
❑ 197 Eric Davis	.25	.10

❑ 198 Dave Parker .15 .06
❑ 199 Steve Balboni .10 .04
❑ 200 Danny Tartabull .10 .04
❑ 201 Ed Hearn .10 .04
❑ 202 Buddy Biancalana .10 .04
❑ 203 Danny Jackson .10 .04
❑ 204 Frank White .15 .06
❑ 205 Bo Jackson 1.00 .40
❑ 206 George Brett 1.25 .50
❑ 207 Kevin Seitzer .40 .16
❑ 208 Willie Wilson .15 .06
❑ 209 Orlando Mercado .10 .04
❑ 210 Darrell Evans .15 .06
❑ 211 Larry Herndon .10 .04
❑ 212 Jack Morris .15 .06
❑ 213 Chet Lemon .10 .04
❑ 214 Mike Heath .10 .04
❑ 215 Darnell Coles .10 .04
❑ 216 Alan Trammell .25 .10
❑ 217 Terry Harper .10 .04
❑ 218 Lou Whitaker .15 .06
❑ 219 Gary Gaetti .15 .06
❑ 220 Tom Nieto .10 .04
❑ 221 Kirby Puckett .40 .16
❑ 222 Tom Brunansky .10 .04
❑ 223 Greg Gagne .10 .04
❑ 224 Dan Gladden .10 .04
❑ 225 Mark Davidson .10 .04
❑ 226 Bert Blyleven .15 .06
❑ 227 Steve Lombardozzi .10 .04
❑ 228 Kent Hrbek .15 .06
❑ 229 Gary Redus .10 .04
❑ 230 Ivan Calderon .10 .04
❑ 231 Tim Hulett .10 .04
❑ 232 Carlton Fisk .25 .10
❑ 233 Greg Walker .10 .04
❑ 234 Ron Karkovice .40 .16
❑ 235 Ozzie Guillen .10 .04
❑ 236 Harold Baines .25 .10
❑ 237 Donnie Hill .10 .04
❑ 238 Rich Dotson .10 .04
❑ 239 Mike Pagliarulo .10 .04
❑ 240 Joel Skinner .10 .04
❑ 241 Don Mattingly 1.25 .50
❑ 242 Gary Ward .10 .04
❑ 243 Dave Winfield .25 .10
❑ 244 Dan Pasqua .10 .04
❑ 245 Wayne Tolleson .10 .04
❑ 246 Willie Randolph .15 .06
❑ 247 Dennis Rasmussen .10 .04
❑ 248 Rickey Henderson .75 .30
❑ 249 Angels Logo .05 .02
❑ 250 Astros Logo .05 .02
❑ 251 A's Logo .05 .02
❑ 252 Blue Jays Logo .05 .02
❑ 253 Braves Logo .05 .02
❑ 254 Brewers Logo .05 .02
❑ 255 Cardinals Logo .05 .02
❑ 256 Dodgers Logo .05 .02
❑ 257 Expos Logo .05 .02
❑ 258 Giants Logo .05 .02
❑ 259 Indians Logo .05 .02
❑ 260 Mariners Logo .05 .02
❑ 261 Orioles Logo .05 .02
❑ 262 Padres Logo .05 .02
❑ 263 Phillies Logo .05 .02
❑ 264 Pirates Logo .05 .02
❑ 265 Rangers Logo .05 .02
❑ 266 Red Sox Logo .05 .02
❑ 267 Reds Logo .05 .02
❑ 268 Royals Logo .05 .02
❑ 269 Tigers Logo .05 .02
❑ 270 Twins Logo .05 .02
❑ 271 Chicago Logos .05 .02
❑ 272 New York Logos .05 .02

1989 Donruss

	Nm-Mt	Ex-Mt
COMPLETE SET (660)	20.00	8.00
COMP.FACT.SET (672)	30.00	12.00
COMP.SPAHN PUZZLE	1.00	.40

❑ 1 Mike Greenwell DK .05 .02
❑ 2 Bobby Bonilla DK DP .10 .04
❑ 3 Pete Incaviglia DK .05 .02

❑ 4 Chris Sabo DK DP .05 .02
❑ 5 Robin Yount DK .10 .04
❑ 6 Tony Gwynn DK DP .15 .06
❑ 7 Carlton Fisk DK UER .15 .06
(OF on back)
❑ 8 Cory Snyder DK .05 .02
❑ 9 David Cone DK UER .05 .02
("hurdlers")
❑ 10 Kevin Seitzer DK .05 .02
❑ 11 Rick Reuschel DK .05 .02
❑ 12 Johnny Ray DK .05 .02
❑ 13 Dave Schmidt DK .05 .02
❑ 14 Andres Galarraga DK .10 .04
❑ 15 Kirk Gibson DK .05 .02
❑ 16 Fred McGriff DK .10 .04
❑ 17 Mark Grace DK .10 .04
❑ 18 Jeff M. Robinson DK .05 .02
❑ 19 Vince Coleman DK DP .05 .02
❑ 20 Dave Henderson DK .05 .02
❑ 21 Harold Reynolds DK .10 .04
❑ 22 Gerald Perry DK .05 .02
❑ 23 Frank Viola DK .05 .02
❑ 24 Steve Bedrosian DK .05 .02
❑ 25 Glenn Davis DK .05 .02
❑ 26 Don Mattingly DK UER .30 .12
(Doesn't mention Don's previous DK in 1985)
❑ 27 DK Checklist 1-26 DP .05 .02
❑ 28 S.Alomar Jr. RR RC .40 .16
❑ 29 Steve Searcy RR .05 .02
❑ 30 Cameron Drew RR .05 .02
❑ 31 Gary Sheffield RR RC 1.50 .60
❑ 32 Erik Hanson RR RC .25 .10
❑ 33 Ken Griffey Jr. RR RC 8.00 3.20
❑ 34 Greg W. Harris RR RC .10 .04
❑ 35 Gregg Jefferies RR .10 .04
❑ 36 Luis Medina RR .05 .02
❑ 37 Carlos Quintana RR RC .10 .04
❑ 38 Felix Jose RR RC .10 .04
❑ 39 Cris Carpenter RR RC* .10 .04
❑ 40 Ron Jones RR .05 .02
❑ 41 Dave West RR RC .10 .04
❑ 42 R.Johnson RC RR UER 3.00 1.20
Card says born in 1964 he was born in 1963
❑ 43 Mike Harkey RR RC .10 .04
❑ 44 P.Harnisch RR DP RC .25 .10
❑ 45 Tom Gordon RR DP RC .25 .10
❑ 46 Gregg Olson RC RR DP .25 .10
❑ 47 Alex Sanchez RR DP .05 .02
❑ 48 Ruben Sierra .05 .02
❑ 49 Rafael Palmeiro .25 .10
❑ 50 Ron Gant .10 .04
❑ 51 Cal Ripken .75 .30
❑ 52 Wally Joyner .10 .04
❑ 53 Gary Carter .15 .06
❑ 54 Andy Van Slyke .10 .04
❑ 55 Robin Yount .25 .10
❑ 56 Pete Incaviglia .05 .02
❑ 57 Greg Brock .05 .02
❑ 58 Melido Perez .05 .02
❑ 59 Craig Lefferts .05 .02
❑ 60 Gary Pettis .05 .02
❑ 61 Danny Tartabull .05 .02
❑ 62 Guillermo Hernandez .05 .02
❑ 63 Ozzie Smith .25 .10
❑ 64 Gary Gaetti .10 .04
❑ 65 Mark Davis .05 .02
❑ 66 Lee Smith .10 .04
❑ 67 Dennis Eckersley .10 .04
❑ 68 Wade Boggs .15 .06
❑ 69 Mike Scott .05 .02
❑ 70 Fred McGriff .25 .10
❑ 71 Tom Browning .05 .02
❑ 72 Claudell Washington .05 .02
❑ 73 Mel Hall .05 .02
❑ 74 Don Mattingly .60 .24
❑ 75 Steve Bedrosian .05 .02
❑ 76 Juan Samuel .05 .02
❑ 77 Mike Scioscia .05 .02
❑ 78 Dave Righetti .05 .02
❑ 79 Alfredo Griffin .05 .02
❑ 80 Eric Davis UER .10 .04
(165 games in 1988, should be 135)
❑ 81 Juan Berenguer .05 .02
❑ 82 Todd Worrell .05 .02
❑ 83 Joe Carter .15 .06
❑ 84 Steve Sax .05 .02
❑ 85 Frank White .10 .04
❑ 86 John Kruk .10 .04
❑ 87 Rance Mulliniks .05 .02
❑ 88 Alan Ashby .05 .02
❑ 89 Charlie Leibrandt .05 .02
❑ 90 Frank Tanana .05 .02
❑ 91 Jose Canseco .25 .10
❑ 92 Barry Bonds 1.25 .50
❑ 93 Harold Reynolds .10 .04
❑ 94 Mark McLemore .05 .02
❑ 95 Mark McGwire 1.00 .40
❑ 96 Eddie Murray .25 .10
❑ 97 Tim Raines .10 .04
❑ 98 Robby Thompson .05 .02
❑ 99 Kevin McReynolds .05 .02
❑ 100 Checklist 28-137 .05 .02
❑ 101 Carlton Fisk .15 .06
❑ 102 Dave Martinez .05 .02
❑ 103 Glenn Braggs .05 .02
❑ 104 Dale Murphy .25 .10
❑ 105 Ryne Sandberg .40 .16
❑ 106 Dennis Martinez .10 .04
❑ 107 Pete O'Brien .05 .02
❑ 108 Dick Schofield .05 .02
❑ 109 Henry Cotto .05 .02
❑ 110 Mike Marshall .05 .02
❑ 111 Keith Moreland .05 .02
❑ 112 Tom Brunansky .05 .02
❑ 113 Kelly Gruber UER .05 .02
(Wrong birthdate)
❑ 114 Brook Jacoby .05 .02
❑ 115 Keith Brown .05 .02
❑ 116 Matt Nokes .05 .02
❑ 117 Keith Hernandez .15 .06
❑ 118 Bob Forsch .05 .02
❑ 119 Bert Blyleven UER .10 .04
(... 3000 strikeouts in 1987, should be 1986)
❑ 120 Willie Wilson .05 .02
❑ 121 Tommy Gregg .05 .02
❑ 122 Jim Rice .10 .04
❑ 123 Bob Knepper .05 .02
❑ 124 Danny Jackson .05 .02
❑ 125 Eric Plunk .05 .02
❑ 126 Brian Fisher .05 .02
❑ 127 Mike Pagliarulo .05 .02
❑ 128 Tony Gwynn .30 .12
❑ 129 Lance McCullers .05 .02
❑ 130 Andres Galarraga .10 .04
❑ 131 Jose Uribe .05 .02
❑ 132 Kirk Gibson UER .10 .04
(Wrong birthdate)
❑ 133 David Palmer .05 .02
❑ 134 R.J. Reynolds .05 .02
❑ 135 Greg Walker .05 .02
❑ 136 Kirk McCaskill UER .05 .02
(Wrong birthdate)
❑ 137 Shawon Dunston .05 .02
❑ 138 Andy Allanson .05 .02
❑ 139 Rob Murphy .05 .02
❑ 140 Mike Aldrete .05 .02
❑ 141 Terry Kennedy .05 .02
❑ 142 Scott Fletcher .05 .02
❑ 143 Steve Balboni .05 .02
❑ 144 Bret Saberhagen .10 .04

	No.	Player		
❑	145	Ozzie Virgil	.05	.02
❑	146	Dale Sveum	.05	.02
❑	147	Darryl Strawberry	.15	.06
❑	148	Harold Baines	.10	.04
❑	149	George Bell	.05	.02
❑	150	Dave Parker	.10	.04
❑	151	Bobby Bonilla	.10	.04
❑	152	Mookie Wilson	.10	.04
❑	153	Ted Power	.05	.02
❑	154	Nolan Ryan	1.00	.40
❑	155	Jeff Reardon	.10	.04
❑	156	Tim Wallach	.05	.02
❑	157	Jamie Moyer	.10	.04
❑	158	Rich Gossage	.10	.04
❑	159	Dave Winfield	.15	.06
❑	160	Von Hayes	.05	.02
❑	161	Willie McGee	.10	.04
❑	162	Rich Gedman	.05	.02
❑	163	Tony Pena	.05	.02
❑	164	Mike Morgan	.05	.02
❑	165	Charlie Hough	.10	.04
❑	166	Mike Stanley	.05	.02
❑	167	Andre Dawson	.10	.04
❑	168	Joe Boever	.05	.02
❑	169	Pete Stanicek	.05	.02
❑	170	Bob Boone	.10	.04
❑	171	Ron Darling	.05	.02
❑	172	Bob Walk	.05	.02
❑	173	Rob Deer	.05	.02
❑	174	Steve Buechele	.05	.02
❑	175	Ted Higuera	.05	.02
❑	176	Ozzie Guillen	.05	.02
❑	177	Candy Maldonado	.05	.02
❑	178	Doyle Alexander	.05	.02
❑	179	Mark Gubicza	.05	.02
❑	180	Alan Trammell	.15	.06
❑	181	Vince Coleman	.05	.02
❑	182	Kirby Puckett	.25	.10
❑	183	Chris Brown	.05	.02
❑	184	Marty Barrett	.05	.02
❑	185	Stan Javier	.05	.02
❑	186	Mike Greenwell	.05	.02
❑	187	Billy Hatcher	.05	.02
❑	188	Jimmy Key	.10	.04
❑	189	Nick Esasky	.05	.02
❑	190	Don Slaught	.05	.02
❑	191	Cory Snyder	.05	.02
❑	192	John Candelaria	.05	.02
❑	193	Mike Schmidt	.50	.20
❑	194	Kevin Gross	.05	.02
❑	195	John Tudor	.05	.02
❑	196	Neil Allen	.05	.02
❑	197	Orel Hershiser	.10	.04
❑	198	Kal Daniels	.05	.02
❑	199	Kent Hrbek	.10	.04
❑	200	Checklist 138-247	.05	.02
❑	201	Joe Magrane	.05	.02
❑	202	Scott Bailes	.05	.02
❑	203	Tim Belcher	.05	.02
❑	204	George Brett	.60	.24
❑	205	Benito Santiago	.10	.04
❑	206	Tony Fernandez	.05	.02
❑	207	Gerald Young	.05	.02
❑	208	Bo Jackson	.25	.10
❑	209	Chet Lemon	.05	.02
❑	210	Storm Davis	.05	.02
❑	211	Doug Drabek	.05	.02
❑	212	Mickey Brantley UER (Photo actually Nelson Simmons)	.05	.02
❑	213	Devon White	.10	.04
❑	214	Dave Stewart	.10	.04
❑	215	Dave Schmidt	.05	.02
❑	216	Bryn Smith	.05	.02
❑	217	Brett Butler	.10	.04
❑	218	Bob Ojeda	.05	.02
❑	219	Steve Rosenberg	.05	.02
❑	220	Hubie Brooks	.05	.02
❑	221	B.J. Surhoff	.10	.04
❑	222	Rick Mahler	.05	.02
❑	223	Rick Sutcliffe	.10	.04
❑	224	Neal Heaton	.05	.02
❑	225	Mitch Williams	.05	.02
❑	226	Chuck Finley	.10	.04
❑	227	Mark Langston	.05	.02
❑	228	Jesse Orosco	.05	.02
❑	229	Ed Whitson	.05	.02
❑	230	Terry Pendleton	.10	.04
❑	231	Lloyd Moseby	.05	.02
❑	232	Greg Swindell	.05	.02
❑	233	John Franco	.10	.04
❑	234	Jack Morris	.10	.04
❑	235	Howard Johnson	.05	.02
❑	236	Glenn Davis	.05	.02
❑	237	Frank Viola	.05	.02
❑	238	Kevin Seitzer	.05	.02
❑	239	Gerald Perry	.05	.02
❑	240	Dwight Evans	.10	.04
❑	241	Jim Deshaies	.05	.02
❑	242	Bo Diaz	.05	.02
❑	243	Carney Lansford	.10	.04
❑	244	Mike LaValliere	.05	.02
❑	245	Rickey Henderson	.40	.16
❑	246	Roberto Alomar	.30	.12
❑	247	Jimmy Jones	.05	.02
❑	248	Pascual Perez	.05	.02
❑	249	Will Clark	.25	.10
❑	250	Fernando Valenzuela	.10	.04
❑	251	Shane Rawley	.05	.02
❑	252	Sid Bream	.05	.02
❑	253	Steve Lyons	.05	.02
❑	254	Brian Downing	.05	.02
❑	255	Mark Grace	.25	.10
❑	256	Tom Candiotti	.05	.02
❑	257	Barry Larkin	.25	.10
❑	258	Mike Krukow	.05	.02
❑	259	Billy Ripken	.05	.02
❑	260	Cecilio Guante	.05	.02
❑	261	Scott Bradley	.05	.02
❑	262	Floyd Bannister	.05	.02
❑	263	Pete Smith	.05	.02
❑	264	Jim Gantner UER (Wrong birthdate)	.05	.02
❑	265	Roger McDowell	.05	.02
❑	266	Bobby Thigpen	.05	.02
❑	267	Jim Clancy	.05	.02
❑	268	Terry Steinbach	.10	.04
❑	269	Mike Dunne	.05	.02
❑	270	Dwight Gooden	.15	.06
❑	271	Mike Heath	.05	.02
❑	272	Dave Smith	.05	.02
❑	273	Keith Atherton	.05	.02
❑	274	Tim Burke	.05	.02
❑	275	Damon Berryhill	.05	.02
❑	276	Vance Law	.05	.02
❑	277	Rich Dotson	.05	.02
❑	278	Lance Parrish	.05	.02
❑	279	Denny Walling	.05	.02
❑	280	Roger Clemens	.50	.20
❑	281	Greg Mathews	.05	.02
❑	282	Tom Niedenfuer	.05	.02
❑	283	Paul Kilgus	.05	.02
❑	284	Jose Guzman	.05	.02
❑	285	Calvin Schiraldi	.05	.02
❑	286	Charlie Puleo UER (Career ERA 4.24, should be 4.23)	.05	.02
❑	287	Joe Orsulak	.05	.02
❑	288	Jack Howell	.05	.02
❑	289	Kevin Elster	.05	.02
❑	290	Jose Lind	.05	.02
❑	291	Paul Molitor	.15	.06
❑	292	Cecil Espy	.05	.02
❑	293	Bill Wegman	.05	.02
❑	294	Dan Pasqua	.05	.02
❑	295	Scott Garrelts UER (Wrong birthdate)	.05	.02
❑	296	Walt Terrell	.05	.02
❑	297	Ed Hearn	.05	.02
❑	298	Lou Whitaker	.10	.04
❑	299	Ken Dayley	.05	.02
❑	300	Checklist 248-357	.05	.02
❑	301	Tommy Herr	.05	.02
❑	302	Mike Brumley	.05	.02
❑	303	Ellis Burks	.15	.06
❑	304	Curt Young UER (Wrong birthdate)	.05	.02
❑	305	Jody Reed	.05	.02
❑	306	Bill Doran	.05	.02
❑	307	David Wells	.10	.04
❑	308	Ron Robinson	.05	.02
❑	309	Rafael Santana	.05	.02
❑	310	Julio Franco	.05	.02
❑	311	Jack Clark	.05	.02
❑	312	Chris James	.05	.02
❑	313	Milt Thompson	.05	.02
❑	314	John Shelby	.05	.02
❑	315	Al Leiter	.25	.10
❑	316	Mike Davis	.05	.02
❑	317	Chris Sabo RC *	.40	.16
❑	318	Greg Gagne	.05	.02
❑	319	Jose Oquendo	.05	.02
❑	320	John Farrell	.05	.02
❑	321	Franklin Stubbs	.05	.02
❑	322	Kurt Stillwell	.05	.02
❑	323	Shawn Abner	.05	.02
❑	324	Mike Flanagan	.05	.02
❑	325	Kevin Bass	.05	.02
❑	326	Pat Tabler	.05	.02
❑	327	Mike Henneman	.05	.02
❑	328	Rick Honeycutt	.05	.02
❑	329	John Smiley	.05	.02
❑	330	Rey Quinones	.05	.02
❑	331	Johnny Ray	.05	.02
❑	332	Bob Welch	.05	.02
❑	333	Larry Sheets	.05	.02
❑	334	Jeff Parrett	.05	.02
❑	335	Rick Reuschel UER (For Don Robinson, should be Jeff)	.05	.02
❑	336	Randy Myers	.10	.04
❑	337	Ken Williams	.05	.02
❑	338	Andy McGaffigan	.05	.02
❑	339	Joey Meyer	.05	.02
❑	340	Dion James	.05	.02
❑	341	Les Lancaster	.05	.02
❑	342	Tom Foley	.05	.02
❑	343	Geno Petralli	.05	.02
❑	344	Dan Petry	.05	.02
❑	345	Alvin Davis	.05	.02
❑	346	Mickey Hatcher	.05	.02
❑	347	Marvell Wynne	.05	.02
❑	348	Danny Cox	.05	.02
❑	349	Dave Stieb	.05	.02
❑	350	Jay Bell	.15	.06
❑	351	Jeff Treadway	.05	.02
❑	352	Luis Salazar	.05	.02
❑	353	Len Dykstra	.10	.04
❑	354	Juan Agosto	.05	.02
❑	355	Gene Larkin	.05	.02
❑	356	Steve Farr	.05	.02
❑	357	Paul Assenmacher	.05	.02
❑	358	Todd Benzinger	.05	.02
❑	359	Larry Andersen	.05	.02
❑	360	Paul O'Neill	.15	.06
❑	361	Ron Hassey	.05	.02
❑	362	Jim Gott	.05	.02
❑	363	Ken Phelps	.05	.02
❑	364	Tim Flannery	.05	.02
❑	365	Randy Ready	.05	.02
❑	366	Nelson Santovenia	.05	.02
❑	367	Kelly Downs	.05	.02
❑	368	Danny Heep	.05	.02
❑	369	Phil Bradley	.05	.02
❑	370	Jeff D. Robinson	.05	.02
❑	371	Ivan Calderon	.05	.02
❑	372	Mike Witt	.05	.02
❑	373	Greg Maddux	.60	.24
❑	374	Carmen Castillo	.05	.02
❑	375	Jose Rijo	.05	.02
❑	376	Joe Price	.05	.02
❑	377	Rene Gonzales	.05	.02
❑	378	Oddibe McDowell	.05	.02
❑	379	Jim Presley	.05	.02
❑	380	Brad Wellman	.05	.02
❑	381	Tom Glavine	.25	.10
❑	382	Dan Plesac	.05	.02
❑	383	Wally Backman	.05	.02
❑	384	Dave Gallagher	.05	.02
❑	385	Tom Henke	.05	.02
❑	386	Luis Polonia	.05	.02
❑	387	Junior Ortiz	.05	.02
❑	388	David Cone	.10	.04
❑	389	Dave Bergman	.05	.02
❑	390	Danny Darwin	.05	.02
❑	391	Dan Gladden	.05	.02
❑	392	John Dopson	.05	.02
❑	393	Frank DiPino	.05	.02

❑ 394 Al Nipper	.05	.02
❑ 395 Willie Randolph	.10	.04
❑ 396 Don Carman	.05	.02
❑ 397 Scott Terry	.05	.02
❑ 398 Rick Cerone	.05	.02
❑ 399 Tom Pagnozzi	.05	.02
❑ 400 Checklist 358-467	.05	.02
❑ 401 Mickey Tettleton	.05	.02
❑ 402 Curtis Wilkerson	.05	.02
❑ 403 Jeff Russell	.05	.02
❑ 404 Pat Perry	.05	.02
❑ 405 Jose Alvarez RC	.05	.02
❑ 406 Rick Schu	.05	.02
❑ 407 Sherman Corbett	.05	.02
❑ 408 Dave Magadan	.05	.02
❑ 409 Bob Kipper	.05	.02
❑ 410 Don August	.05	.02
❑ 411 Bob Brower	.05	.02
❑ 412 Chris Bosio	.05	.02
❑ 413 Jerry Reuss	.05	.02
❑ 414 Atlee Hammaker	.05	.02
❑ 415 Jim Walewander	.05	.02
❑ 416 Mike Macfarlane RC *	.25	.10
❑ 417 Pat Sheridan	.05	.02
❑ 418 Pedro Guerrero	.05	.02
❑ 419 Allan Anderson	.05	.02
❑ 420 Mark Parent	.05	.02
❑ 421 Bob Stanley	.05	.02
❑ 422 Mike Gallego	.05	.02
❑ 423 Bruce Hurst	.05	.02
❑ 424 Dave Meads	.05	.02
❑ 425 Jesse Barfield	.05	.02
❑ 426 Rob Dibble RC *	.50	.20
❑ 427 Joel Skinner	.05	.02
❑ 428 Ron Kittle	.05	.02
❑ 429 Rick Rhoden	.05	.02
❑ 430 Bob Dernier	.05	.02
❑ 431 Steve Jeltz	.05	.02
❑ 432 Rick Dempsey	.05	.02
❑ 433 Roberto Kelly	.10	.04
❑ 434 Dave Anderson	.05	.02
❑ 435 Herm Winningham	.05	.02
❑ 436 Al Newman	.05	.02
❑ 437 Jose DeLeon	.05	.02
❑ 438 Doug Jones	.05	.02
❑ 439 Brian Holton	.05	.02
❑ 440 Jeff Montgomery	.10	.04
❑ 441 Dickie Thon	.05	.02
❑ 442 Cecil Fielder	.10	.04
❑ 443 John Fishel	.05	.02
❑ 444 Jerry Don Gleaton	.05	.02
❑ 445 Paul Gibson	.05	.02
❑ 446 Walt Weiss	.05	.02
❑ 447 Glenn Wilson	.05	.02
❑ 448 Mike Moore	.05	.02
❑ 449 Chili Davis	.10	.04
❑ 450 Dave Henderson	.05	.02
❑ 451 Jose Bautista RC	.10	.04
❑ 452 Rex Hudler	.05	.02
❑ 453 Bob Brenly	.05	.02
❑ 454 Mackey Sasser	.05	.02
❑ 455 Daryl Boston	.05	.02
❑ 456 Mike R. Fitzgerald	.05	.02
❑ 457 Jeffrey Leonard	.05	.02
❑ 458 Bruce Sutter	.05	.02
❑ 459 Mitch Webster	.05	.02
❑ 460 Joe Hesketh	.05	.02
❑ 461 Bobby Witt	.05	.02
❑ 462 Stu Cliburn	.05	.02
❑ 463 Scott Bankhead	.05	.02
❑ 464 Ramon Martinez RC	.25	.10
❑ 465 Dave Leiper	.05	.02
❑ 466 Luis Alicea RC *	.25	.10
❑ 467 John Cerutti	.05	.02
❑ 468 Ron Washington	.05	.02
❑ 469 Jeff Reed	.05	.02
❑ 470 Jeff M. Robinson	.05	.02
❑ 471 Sid Fernandez	.05	.02
❑ 472 Terry Puhl	.05	.02
❑ 473 Charlie Lea	.05	.02
❑ 474 Israel Sanchez	.05	.02
❑ 475 Bruce Benedict	.05	.02
❑ 476 Oil Can Boyd	.05	.02
❑ 477 Craig Reynolds	.05	.02
❑ 478 Frank Williams	.05	.02
❑ 479 Greg Cadaret	.05	.02
❑ 480 Randy Kramer	.05	.02
❑ 481 Dave Eiland	.05	.02
❑ 482 Eric Show	.05	.02
❑ 483 Garry Templeton	.05	.02
❑ 484 Wallace Johnson	.05	.02
❑ 485 Kevin Mitchell	.10	.04
❑ 486 Tim Crews	.05	.02
❑ 487 Mike Maddux	.05	.02
❑ 488 Dave LaPoint	.05	.02
❑ 489 Fred Manrique	.05	.02
❑ 490 Greg Minton	.05	.02
❑ 491 Doug Dascenzo UER	.05	.02
(Photo actually Damon Berryhill)		
❑ 492 Willie Upshaw	.05	.02
❑ 493 Jack Armstrong RC *	.25	.10
❑ 494 Kirt Manwaring	.05	.02
❑ 495 Jeff Ballard	.05	.02
❑ 496 Jeff Kunkel	.05	.02
❑ 497 Mike Campbell	.05	.02
❑ 498 Gary Thurman	.05	.02
❑ 499 Zane Smith	.05	.02
❑ 500 Checklist 468-577 DP	.05	.02
❑ 501 Mike Birkbeck	.05	.02
❑ 502 Terry Leach	.05	.02
❑ 503 Shawn Hillegas	.05	.02
❑ 504 Manny Lee	.05	.02
❑ 505 Doug Jennings	.05	.02
❑ 506 Ken Oberkfell	.05	.02
❑ 507 Tim Teufel	.05	.02
❑ 508 Tom Brookens	.05	.02
❑ 509 Rafael Ramirez	.05	.02
❑ 510 Fred Toliver	.05	.02
❑ 511 Brian Holman RC *	.10	.04
❑ 512 Mike Bielecki	.05	.02
❑ 513 Jeff Pico	.05	.02
❑ 514 Charles Hudson	.05	.02
❑ 515 Bruce Ruffin	.05	.02
❑ 516 L.McWilliams UER	.05	.02
New Richland, should be North Richland		
❑ 517 Jeff Sellers	.05	.02
❑ 518 John Costello	.05	.02
❑ 519 Brady Anderson RC	.50	.20
❑ 520 Craig McMurtry	.05	.02
❑ 521 Ray Hayward DP	.05	.02
❑ 522 Drew Hall DP	.05	.02
❑ 523 Mark Lemke DP RC	.40	.16
❑ 524 Oswald Peraza DP	.05	.02
❑ 525 Bryan Harvey DP RC *	.25	.10
❑ 526 Rick Aguilera DP	.10	.04
❑ 527 Tom Prince DP	.05	.02
❑ 528 Mark Clear DP	.05	.02
❑ 529 Jerry Browne DP	.05	.02
❑ 530 Juan Castillo DP	.05	.02
❑ 531 Jack McDowell DP	.10	.04
❑ 532 Chris Speier DP	.05	.02
❑ 533 Darrell Evans DP	.10	.04
❑ 534 Luis Aquino DP	.05	.02
❑ 535 Eric King DP	.05	.02
❑ 536 Ken Hill DP RC	.25	.10
❑ 537 Randy Bush DP	.05	.02
❑ 538 Shane Mack DP	.05	.02
❑ 539 Tom Bolton DP	.05	.02
❑ 540 Gene Nelson DP	.05	.02
❑ 541 Wes Gardner DP	.05	.02
❑ 542 Ken Caminiti DP	.10	.04
❑ 543 Duane Ward DP	.05	.02
❑ 544 Norm Charlton DP RC	.25	.10
❑ 545 Hal Morris DP RC	.25	.10
❑ 546 Rich Yett DP	.05	.02
❑ 547 H.Meulens DP RC	.10	.04
❑ 548 Greg A. Harris DP	.05	.02
❑ 549 Darren Daulton DP	.10	.04
(Posing as right-handed hitter)		
❑ 550 Jeff Hamilton DP	.05	.02
❑ 551 Luis Aguayo DP	.05	.02
❑ 552 Tim Leary DP	.05	.02
(Resembles M.Marshall)		
❑ 553 Ron Oester DP	.05	.02
❑ 554 S.Lombardozzi DP	.05	.02
❑ 555 Tim Jones DP	.05	.02
❑ 556 Bud Black DP	.05	.02
❑ 557 Alejandro Pena DP	.05	.02
❑ 558 Jose DeJesus DP	.05	.02
❑ 559 D.Rasmussen DP	.05	.02
❑ 560 Pat Borders DP RC*	.25	.10
❑ 561 Craig Biggio DP RC	.75	.30
❑ 562 Luis DeLosSantos DP	.05	.02
❑ 563 Fred Lynn DP	.05	.02
❑ 564 Todd Burns DP	.05	.02
❑ 565 Felix Fermin DP	.05	.02
❑ 566 Darnell Coles DP	.05	.02
❑ 567 Willie Fraser DP	.05	.02
❑ 568 Glenn Hubbard DP	.05	.02
❑ 569 Craig Worthington DP	.05	.02
❑ 570 Johnny Paredes DP	.05	.02
❑ 571 Don Robinson DP	.05	.02
❑ 572 Barry Lyons DP	.05	.02
❑ 573 Bill Long DP	.05	.02
❑ 574 Tracy Jones DP	.05	.02
❑ 575 Juan Nieves DP	.05	.02
❑ 576 Andres Thomas DP	.05	.02
❑ 577 Rolando Roomes DP	.05	.02
❑ 578 Luis Rivera UER DP	.05	.02
(Wrong birthdate)		
❑ 579 Chad Kreuter DP RC	.25	.10
❑ 580 Tony Armas DP	.05	.02
❑ 581 Jay Buhner	.10	.04
❑ 582 Ricky Horton DP	.05	.02
❑ 583 Andy Hawkins DP	.05	.02
❑ 584 Sil Campusano	.05	.02
❑ 585 Dave Clark	.05	.02
❑ 586 Van Snider DP	.05	.02
❑ 587 Todd Frohwirth DP	.05	.02
❑ 588 W.Spahn DP PUZ	.15	.06
❑ 589 William Brennan	.05	.02
❑ 590 German Gonzalez	.05	.02
❑ 591 Ernie Whitt DP	.05	.02
❑ 592 Jeff Blauser	.10	.04
❑ 593 Spike Owen DP	.05	.02
❑ 594 Matt Williams	.25	.10
❑ 595 Lloyd McClendon DP	.05	.02
❑ 596 Steve Ontiveros	.05	.02
❑ 597 Scott Medvin	.05	.02
❑ 598 Hipolito Pena DP	.05	.02
❑ 599 Jerald Clark DP RC	.10	.04
❑ 600A CL 578-660 DP	.05	.02
635 Kurt Schilling		
❑ 600B CL 578-660 DP	.05	.02
635 Curt Schilling; MVP's not listed on checklist card		
❑ 600C CL 578-660 DP	.05	.02
635 Curt Schilling; MVP's listed following 660		
❑ 601 Carmelo Martinez DP	.05	.02
❑ 602 Mike LaCoss	.05	.02
❑ 603 Mike Devereaux	.05	.02
❑ 604 Alex Madrid DP	.05	.02
❑ 605 Gary Redus DP	.05	.02
❑ 606 Lance Johnson	.10	.04
❑ 607 Terry Clark DP	.05	.02
❑ 608 Manny Trillo DP	.05	.02
❑ 609 Scott Jordan RC	.25	.10
❑ 610 Jay Howell DP	.05	.02
❑ 611 Francisco Melendez	.05	.02
❑ 612 Mike Boddicker	.05	.02
❑ 613 Kevin Brown DP	.25	.10
❑ 614 Dave Valle	.05	.02
❑ 615 Tim Laudner DP	.05	.02
❑ 616 Andy Nezelek UER	.05	.02
(Wrong birthdate)		
❑ 617 Chuck Crim	.05	.02
❑ 618 Jack Savage DP	.05	.02
❑ 619 Adam Peterson	.05	.02
❑ 620 Todd Stottlemyre	.15	.06
❑ 621 Lance Blankenship RC	.10	.04
❑ 622 Miguel Garcia DP	.05	.02
❑ 623 Keith A. Miller DP	.05	.02
❑ 624 Ricky Jordan DP RC*	.25	.10
❑ 625 Ernest Riles DP	.05	.02
❑ 626 John Moses DP	.05	.02
❑ 627 Nelson Liriano DP	.05	.02
❑ 628 Mike Smithson DP	.05	.02
❑ 629 Scott Sanderson	.05	.02
❑ 630 Dale Mohorcic	.05	.02
❑ 631 Marvin Freeman DP	.05	.02
❑ 632 Mike Young DP	.05	.02
❑ 633 Dennis Lamp	.05	.02

Card	Nm-Mt	Ex-Mt
❑ 634 Dante Bichette DP RC	.40	.16
❑ 635 Curt Schilling DP RC	2.50	1.00
❑ 636 Scott May DP	.05	.02
❑ 637 Mike Schooler	.05	.02
❑ 638 Rick Leach	.05	.02
❑ 639 Tom Lampkin UER (Throws Left, should be Throws Right)	.05	.02
❑ 640 Brian Meyer	.05	.02
❑ 641 Brian Harper	.05	.02
❑ 642 John Smoltz RC	1.00	.40
❑ 643 Jose Canseco (40/40 Club)	.10	.04
❑ 644 Bill Schroeder	.05	.02
❑ 645 Edgar Martinez	.15	.06
❑ 646 Dennis Cook RC	.25	.10
❑ 647 Barry Jones	.05	.02
❑ 648 Orel Hershiser (59 and Counting)	.10	.04
❑ 649 Rod Nichols	.05	.02
❑ 650 Jody Davis	.05	.02
❑ 651 Bob Milacki	.05	.02
❑ 652 Mike Jackson	.05	.02
❑ 653 Derek Lilliquist RC	.10	.04
❑ 654 Paul Mirabella	.05	.02
❑ 655 Mike Diaz	.05	.02
❑ 656 Jeff Musselman	.05	.02
❑ 657 Jerry Reed	.05	.02
❑ 658 Kevin Blankenship	.05	.02
❑ 659 Wayne Tolleson	.05	.02
❑ 660 Eric Hetzel	.05	.02
❑ BC Jose Canseco Blister Pack	2.00	.80

1989 Donruss Rookies

	Nm-Mt	Ex-Mt
COMP.FACT.SET (56)	15.00	6.00
❑ 1 Gary Sheffield	1.50	.60
❑ 2 Gregg Jefferies	.10	.04
❑ 3 Ken Griffey Jr.	8.00	3.20
❑ 4 Tom Gordon	.25	.10
❑ 5 Billy Spiers RC	.25	.10
❑ 6 Deion Sanders RC	.50	.20
❑ 7 Donn Pall	.05	.02
❑ 8 Steve Carter	.05	.02
❑ 9 Francisco Oliveras	.05	.02
❑ 10 Steve Wilson RC	.10	.04
❑ 11 Bob Geren	.05	.02
❑ 12 Tony Castillo RC	.10	.04
❑ 13 Kenny Rogers RC	.50	.20
❑ 14 Carlos Martinez RC	.10	.04
❑ 15 Edgar Martinez	.15	.06
❑ 16 Jim Abbott RC	.50	.20
❑ 17 Torey Lovullo RC	.10	.04
❑ 18 Mark Carreon	.05	.02
❑ 19 Geronimo Berroa	.05	.02
❑ 20 Luis Medina	.05	.02
❑ 21 Sandy Alomar Jr.	.15	.06
❑ 22 Bob Milacki	.05	.02
❑ 23 Joe Girardi RC	.40	.16
❑ 24 German Gonzalez	.05	.02
❑ 25 Craig Worthington	.05	.02
❑ 26 Jerome Walton	.25	.10
❑ 27 Gary Wayne	.05	.02
❑ 28 Tim Jones	.05	.02
❑ 29 Dante Bichette	.15	.06
❑ 30 Alexis Infante	.05	.02
❑ 31 Ken Hill	.25	.10
❑ 32 Dwight Smith RC	.25	.10
❑ 33 Luis de los Santos	.05	.02
❑ 34 Eric Yelding	.05	.02
❑ 35 Gregg Olson	.25	.10
❑ 36 Phil Stephenson	.05	.02
❑ 37 Ken Patterson	.05	.02
❑ 38 Rick Wrona	.05	.02
❑ 39 Mike Brumley	.05	.02
❑ 40 Cris Carpenter	.05	.02
❑ 41 Jeff Brantley RC	.25	.10
❑ 42 Ron Jones	.05	.02
❑ 43 Randy Johnson	3.00	1.20
❑ 44 Kevin Brown	.25	.10
❑ 45 Ramon Martinez	.10	.04
❑ 46 Greg W.Harris	.05	.02
❑ 47 Steve Finley RC	.50	.20
❑ 48 Randy Kramer	.05	.02
❑ 49 Erik Hanson	.10	.04
❑ 50 Matt Merullo	.05	.02
❑ 51 Mike Devereaux	.05	.02
❑ 52 Clay Parker	.05	.02
❑ 53 Omar Vizquel RC	.50	.20
❑ 54 Derek Lilliquist	.05	.02
❑ 55 Junior Felix RC	.10	.04
❑ 56 Checklist 1-56	.05	.02

1989 Donruss Baseball's Best

	Nm-Mt	Ex-Mt
COMP.FACT.SET (336)	100.00	40.00
❑ 1 Don Mattingly	1.50	.60
❑ 2 Tom Glavine	.60	.24
❑ 3 Bert Blyleven	.25	.10
❑ 4 Andre Dawson	.25	.10
❑ 5 Pete O'Brien	.15	.06
❑ 6 Eric Davis	.25	.10
❑ 7 George Brett	1.50	.60
❑ 8 Glenn Davis	.15	.06
❑ 9 Ellis Burks	.40	.16
❑ 10 Kirk Gibson	.25	.10
❑ 11 Carlton Fisk	.40	.16
❑ 12 Andres Galarraga	.25	.10
❑ 13 Alan Trammell	.40	.16
❑ 14 Dwight Gooden	.40	.16
❑ 15 Paul Molitor	.40	.16
❑ 16 Roger McDowell	.15	.06
❑ 17 Doug Drabek	.15	.06
❑ 18 Kent Hrbek	.25	.10
❑ 19 Vince Coleman	.15	.06
❑ 20 Steve Sax	.15	.06
❑ 21 Roberto Alomar	.75	.30
❑ 22 Carney Lansford	.25	.10
❑ 23 Will Clark	.60	.24
❑ 24 Alvin Davis	.15	.06
❑ 25 Bobby Thigpen	.15	.06
❑ 26 Ryne Sandberg	1.00	.40
❑ 27 Devon White	.25	.10
❑ 28 Mike Greenwell	.15	.06
❑ 29 Dale Murphy	.60	.24
❑ 30 Jeff Ballard	.15	.06
❑ 31 Kelly Gruber	.15	.06
❑ 32 Julio Franco	.15	.06
❑ 33 Bobby Bonilla	.25	.10
❑ 34 Tim Wallach	.15	.06

Card	Nm-Mt	Ex-Mt
❑ 35 Lou Whitaker	.25	.10
❑ 36 Jay Howell	.15	.06
❑ 37 Greg Maddux	1.50	.60
❑ 38 Bill Doran	.15	.06
❑ 39 Danny Tartabull	.15	.06
❑ 40 Darryl Strawberry	.40	.16
❑ 41 Ron Darling	.15	.06
❑ 42 Tony Gwynn	.75	.30
❑ 43 Mark McGwire	2.50	1.00
❑ 44 Ozzie Smith	.60	.24
❑ 45 Andy Van Slyke	.25	.10
❑ 46 Juan Berenguer	.15	.06
❑ 47 Von Hayes	.15	.06
❑ 48 Tony Fernandez	.15	.06
❑ 49 Eric Plunk	.15	.06
❑ 50 Ernest Riles	.15	.06
❑ 51 Harold Reynolds	.25	.10
❑ 52 Andy Hawkins	.15	.06
❑ 53 Robin Yount	.60	.24
❑ 54 Danny Jackson	.15	.06
❑ 55 Nolan Ryan	2.50	1.00
❑ 56 Joe Carter	.40	.16
❑ 57 Jose Canseco	.60	.24
❑ 58 Jody Davis	.15	.06
❑ 59 Lance Parrish	.15	.06
❑ 60 Mitch Williams	.15	.06
❑ 61 Brook Jacoby	.15	.06
❑ 62 Tom Browning	.15	.06
❑ 63 Kurt Stillwell	.15	.06
❑ 64 Rafael Ramirez	.15	.06
❑ 65 Roger Clemens	1.25	.50
❑ 66 Mike Scioscia	.15	.06
❑ 67 Dave Gallagher	.15	.06
❑ 68 Mark Langston	.15	.06
❑ 69 Chet Lemon	.15	.06
❑ 70 Kevin McReynolds	.15	.06
❑ 71 Rob Deer	.15	.06
❑ 72 Tommy Herr	.15	.06
❑ 73 Barry Bonds	3.00	1.20
❑ 74 Frank Viola	.15	.06
❑ 75 Pedro Guerrero	.15	.06
❑ 76 Dave Righetti UER (ML total of 7 wins incorrect)	.15	.06
❑ 77 Bruce Hurst	.15	.06
❑ 78 Rickey Henderson	1.00	.40
❑ 79 Robby Thompson	.15	.06
❑ 80 Randy Johnson	8.00	3.20
❑ 81 Harold Baines	.25	.10
❑ 82 Calvin Schiraldi	.15	.06
❑ 83 Kirk McCaskill	.15	.06
❑ 84 Lee Smith	.25	.10
❑ 85 John Smoltz	2.00	.80
❑ 86 Mickey Tettleton	.15	.06
❑ 87 Jimmy Key	.25	.10
❑ 88 Rafael Palmeiro	.60	.24
❑ 89 Sid Bream	.15	.06
❑ 90 Dennis Martinez	.25	.10
❑ 91 Frank Tanana	.15	.06
❑ 92 Eddie Murray	.60	.24
❑ 93 Shawon Dunston	.15	.06
❑ 94 Mike Scott	.15	.06
❑ 95 Bret Saberhagen	.25	.10
❑ 96 David Cone	.25	.10
❑ 97 Kevin Elster	.15	.06
❑ 98 Jack Clark	.15	.06
❑ 99 Dave Stewart	.25	.10
❑ 100 Jose Oquendo	.15	.06
❑ 101 Jose Lind	.15	.06
❑ 102 Gary Gaetti	.25	.10
❑ 103 Ricky Jordan	.50	.20
❑ 104 Fred McGriff	.60	.24
❑ 105 Don Slaught	.15	.06
❑ 106 Jose Uribe	.15	.06
❑ 107 Jeffrey Leonard	.15	.06
❑ 108 Lee Guetterman	.15	.06
❑ 109 Chris Bosio	.15	.06
❑ 110 Barry Larkin	.60	.24
❑ 111 Ruben Sierra	.15	.06
❑ 112 Greg Swindell	.15	.06
❑ 113 Gary Sheffield	3.00	1.20
❑ 114 Lonnie Smith	.15	.06
❑ 115 Chili Davis	.25	.10
❑ 116 Damon Berryhill	.15	.06
❑ 117 Tom Candiotti	.15	.06
❑ 118 Kal Daniels	.15	.06

❑ 119 Mark Gubicza .15 .06
❑ 120 Jim Deshaies .15 .06
❑ 121 Dwight Evans .25 .10
❑ 122 Mike Morgan .15 .06
❑ 123 Dan Pasqua .15 .06
❑ 124 Bryn Smith .15 .06
❑ 125 Doyle Alexander .15 .06
❑ 126 Howard Johnson .15 .06
❑ 127 Chuck Crim .15 .06
❑ 128 Darren Daulton .25 .10
❑ 129 Jeff Robinson .15 .06
❑ 130 Kirby Puckett .60 .24
❑ 131 Joe Magrane .15 .06
❑ 132 Jesse Barfield .15 .06
❑ 133 Mark Davis UER .15 .06
(Photo actually
Dave Leiper)
❑ 134 Dennis Eckersley .25 .10
❑ 135 Mike Krukow .15 .06
❑ 136 Jay Buhner .25 .10
❑ 137 Ozzie Guillen .15 .06
❑ 138 Rick Sutcliffe .25 .10
❑ 139 Wally Joyner .25 .10
❑ 140 Wade Boggs .40 .16
❑ 141 Jeff Treadway .15 .06
❑ 142 Cal Ripken 2.00 .80
❑ 143 Dave Stieb .15 .06
❑ 144 Pete Incaviglia .15 .06
❑ 145 Bob Walk .15 .06
❑ 146 Nelson Santovenia .15 .06
❑ 147 Mike Heath .15 .06
❑ 148 Willie Randolph .25 .10
❑ 149 Paul Kilgus .15 .06
❑ 150 Billy Hatcher .15 .06
❑ 151 Steve Farr .15 .06
❑ 152 Gregg Jefferies .25 .10
❑ 153 Randy Myers .25 .10
❑ 154 Garry Templeton .15 .06
❑ 155 Walt Weiss .15 .06
❑ 156 Terry Pendleton .25 .10
❑ 157 John Smiley .15 .06
❑ 158 Greg Gagne .15 .06
❑ 159 Len Dykstra .25 .10
❑ 160 Nelson Liriano .15 .06
❑ 161 Alvaro Espinoza .15 .06
❑ 162 Rick Reuschel .15 .06
❑ 163 Omar Vizquel UER 1.00 .40
Photo actually
Darnell Coles
❑ 164 Clay Parker .15 .06
❑ 165 Dan Plesac .15 .06
❑ 166 John Franco .25 .10
❑ 167 Scott Fletcher .15 .06
❑ 168 Cory Snyder .15 .06
❑ 169 Bo Jackson .60 .24
❑ 170 Tommy Gregg .15 .06
❑ 171 Jim Abbott 1.00 .40
❑ 172 Jerome Walton .50 .20
❑ 173 Doug Jones .15 .06
❑ 174 Todd Benzinger .15 .06
❑ 175 Frank White .25 .10
❑ 176 Craig Biggio 2.00 .80
❑ 177 John Dopson .15 .06
❑ 178 Alfredo Griffin .15 .06
❑ 179 Melido Perez .15 .06
❑ 180 Tim Burke .15 .06
❑ 181 Matt Nokes .15 .06
❑ 182 Gary Carter .40 .16
❑ 183 Ted Higuera .15 .06
❑ 184 Ken Howell .15 .06
❑ 185 Rey Quinones .15 .06
❑ 186 Wally Backman .15 .06
❑ 187 Tom Brunansky .15 .06
❑ 188 Steve Balboni .15 .06
❑ 189 Marvell Wynne .15 .06
❑ 190 Dave Henderson .15 .06
❑ 191 Don Robinson .15 .06
❑ 192 Ken Griffey Jr. 20.00 8.00
❑ 193 Ivan Calderon .15 .06
❑ 194 Mike Bielecki .15 .06
❑ 195 Johnny Ray .15 .06
❑ 196 Rob Murphy .15 .06
❑ 197 Andres Thomas .15 .06
❑ 198 Phil Bradley .15 .06
❑ 199 Junior Felix .25 .10
❑ 200 Jeff Russell .15 .06
❑ 201 Mike LaValliere .15 .06
❑ 202 Kevin Gross .15 .06
❑ 203 Keith Moreland .15 .06
❑ 204 Mike Marshall .15 .06
❑ 205 Dwight Smith .50 .20
❑ 206 Jim Clancy .15 .06
❑ 207 Kevin Seitzer .15 .06
❑ 208 Keith Hernandez .40 .16
❑ 209 Bob Ojeda .15 .06
❑ 210 Ed Whitson .15 .06
❑ 211 Tony Phillips .15 .06
❑ 212 Milt Thompson .15 .06
❑ 213 Randy Kramer .15 .06
❑ 214 Randy Bush .15 .06
❑ 215 Randy Ready .15 .06
❑ 216 Duane Ward .15 .06
❑ 217 Jimmy Jones .15 .06
❑ 218 Scott Garrelts .15 .06
❑ 219 Scott Bankhead .15 .06
❑ 220 Lance McCullers .15 .06
❑ 221 B.J. Surhoff .25 .10
❑ 222 Chris Sabo .75 .30
❑ 223 Steve Buechele .15 .06
❑ 224 Joel Skinner .15 .06
❑ 225 Orel Hershiser .25 .10
❑ 226 Derek Lilliquist .25 .10
❑ 227 Claudell Washington .15 .06
❑ 228 Lloyd McClendon .15 .06
❑ 229 Felix Fermin .15 .06
❑ 230 Paul O'Neill .40 .16
❑ 231 Charlie Leibrandt .15 .06
❑ 232 Dave Smith .15 .06
❑ 233 Bob Stanley .15 .06
❑ 234 Tim Belcher .15 .06
❑ 235 Eric King .15 .06
❑ 236 Spike Owen .15 .06
❑ 237 Mike Henneman .15 .06
❑ 238 Juan Samuel .15 .06
❑ 239 Greg Brock .15 .06
❑ 240 John Kruk .25 .10
❑ 241 Glenn Wilson .15 .06
❑ 242 Jeff Reardon .25 .10
❑ 243 Todd Worrell .15 .06
❑ 244 Dave LaPoint .15 .06
❑ 245 Walt Terrell .15 .06
❑ 246 Mike Moore .15 .06
❑ 247 Kelly Downs .15 .06
❑ 248 Dave Valle .15 .06
❑ 249 Ron Kittle .15 .06
❑ 250 Steve Wilson .25 .10
❑ 251 Dick Schofield .15 .06
❑ 252 Marty Barrett .15 .06
❑ 253 Dion James .15 .06
❑ 254 Bob Milacki .15 .06
❑ 255 Ernie Whitt .15 .06
❑ 256 Kevin Brown .60 .24
❑ 257 R.J. Reynolds .15 .06
❑ 258 Tim Raines .25 .10
❑ 259 Frank Williams .15 .06
❑ 260 Jose Gonzalez .15 .06
❑ 261 Mitch Webster .15 .06
❑ 262 Ken Caminiti .25 .10
❑ 263 Bob Boone .25 .10
❑ 264 Dave Magadan .15 .06
❑ 265 Rick Aguilera .25 .10
❑ 266 Chris James .15 .06
❑ 267 Bob Welch .15 .06
❑ 268 Ken Dayley .15 .06
❑ 269 Junior Ortiz .15 .06
❑ 270 Allan Anderson .15 .06
❑ 271 Steve Jeltz .15 .06
❑ 272 George Bell .15 .06
❑ 273 Roberto Kelly .25 .10
❑ 274 Brett Butler .25 .10
❑ 275 Mike Schooler .25 .10
❑ 276 Ken Phelps .15 .06
❑ 277 Glenn Braggs .15 .06
❑ 278 Jose Rijo .15 .06
❑ 279 Bobby Witt .15 .06
❑ 280 Jerry Browne .15 .06
❑ 281 Kevin Mitchell .25 .10
❑ 282 Craig Worthington .15 .06
❑ 283 Greg Minton .15 .06
❑ 284 Nick Esasky .15 .06
❑ 285 John Farrell .15 .06
❑ 286 Rick Mahler .15 .06
❑ 287 Tom Gordon .50 .20
❑ 288 Gerald Young .15 .06
❑ 289 Jody Reed .15 .06
❑ 290 Jeff Hamilton .15 .06
❑ 291 Gerald Perry .15 .06
❑ 292 Hubie Brooks .15 .06
❑ 293 Bo Diaz .15 .06
❑ 294 Terry Puhl .15 .06
❑ 295 Jim Gantner .15 .06
❑ 296 Jeff Parrett .15 .06
❑ 297 Mike Boddicker .15 .06
❑ 298 Dan Gladden .15 .06
❑ 299 Tony Pena .15 .06
❑ 300 Checklist Card .15 .06
❑ 301 Tom Henke .15 .06
❑ 302 Pascual Perez .15 .06
❑ 303 Steve Bedrosian .15 .06
❑ 304 Ken Hill .50 .20
❑ 305 Jerry Reuss .15 .06
❑ 306 Jim Eisenreich .15 .06
❑ 307 Jack Howell .15 .06
❑ 308 Rick Cerone .15 .06
❑ 309 Tim Leary .15 .06
❑ 310 Joe Orsulak .15 .06
❑ 311 Jim Dwyer .15 .06
❑ 312 Geno Petralli .15 .06
❑ 313 Rick Honeycutt .15 .06
❑ 314 Tom Foley .15 .06
❑ 315 Kenny Rogers 1.00 .40
❑ 316 Mike Flanagan .15 .06
❑ 317 Bryan Harvey .15 .06
❑ 318 Billy Ripken .15 .06
❑ 319 Jeff Montgomery .25 .10
❑ 320 Erik Hanson .50 .20
❑ 321 Brian Downing .15 .06
❑ 322 Gregg Olson .50 .20
❑ 323 Terry Steinbach .25 .10
❑ 324 Sammy Sosa 40.00 16.00
❑ 325 Gene Harris .15 .06
❑ 326 Mike Devereaux .15 .06
❑ 327 Dennis Cook .50 .20
❑ 328 David Wells .25 .10
❑ 329 Checklist Card .15 .06
❑ 330 Kirt Manwaring .15 .06
❑ 331 Jim Presley .15 .06
❑ 332 Checklist Card .15 .06
❑ 333 Chuck Finley .25 .10
❑ 334 Rob Dibble 1.00 .40
❑ 335 Cecil Espy .15 .06
❑ 336 Dave Parker .25 .10

1990 Donruss

	Nm-Mt	Ex-Mt
COMPLETE SET (716)	15.00	4.50
COMP.FACT.SET (728)	15.00	4.50
COMP.YAZ PUZZLE	1.00	.30

❑ 1 Bo Jackson DK .15 .04
❑ 2 Steve Sax DK .05 .02
❑ 3A Ruben Sierra DK ERR .05 .02
(No small line on top
border on card back)
❑ 3B Ruben Sierra DK COR .05 .02
❑ 4 Ken Griffey Jr. DK .40 .12
❑ 5 Mickey Tettleton DK .05 .02
❑ 6 Dave Stewart DK .05 .02
❑ 7 Jim Deshaies DK DP .05 .02

❑ 8 John Smoltz DK .25 .07
❑ 9 Mike Bielecki DK .05 .02
❑ 10A Brian Downing DK .25 .07
ERR (Reverse negative on card front)
❑ 10B Brian Downing DK .05 .02
COR
❑ 11 Kevin Mitchell DK .05 .02
❑ 12 Kelly Gruber DK .05 .02
❑ 13 Joe Magrane DK .05 .02
❑ 14 John Franco DK .05 .02
❑ 15 Ozzie Guillen DK .05 .02
❑ 16 Lou Whitaker DK .05 .02
❑ 17 John Smiley DK .05 .02
❑ 18 Howard Johnson DK .05 .02
❑ 19 Willie Randolph DK .10 .03
❑ 20 Chris Bosio DK .05 .02
❑ 21 Tommy Herr DK DP .05 .02
❑ 22 Dan Gladden DK .05 .02
❑ 23 Ellis Burks DK .10 .03
❑ 24 Pete O'Brien DK .05 .02
❑ 25 Bryn Smith DK .05 .02
❑ 26 Ed Whitson DK DP .05 .02
❑ 27 DK Checklist 1-27 DP .05 .02
(Comments on Perez-Steele on back)
❑ 28 Robin Ventura RR .25 .07
❑ 29 Todd Zeile RR .10 .03
❑ 30 Sandy Alomar Jr. .10 .03
❑ 31 Kent Mercker RR RC .25 .07
❑ 32 B.McDonald RC UER .25 .07
Middle name Benard not Benjamin
❑ 33A J.Gonzalez RC ERR 2.00 .60
Reverse negative
❑ 33B J.Gonzalez COR RC 1.50 .45
❑ 34 Eric Anthony RR RC .10 .03
❑ 35 Mike Fetters RR RC .25 .07
❑ 36 Marquis Grissom RC .25 .07
❑ 37 Greg Vaughn RR .10 .03
❑ 38 Brian DuBois RC .10 .03
❑ 39 Steve Avery RR UER .05 .02
(Born in MI, not NJ)
❑ 40 Mark Gardner RR RC .10 .03
❑ 41 Andy Benes .10 .03
❑ 42 D.DeShields RR RC .25 .07
❑ 43 Scott Coolbaugh RC .10 .03
❑ 44 Pat Combs DP .05 .02
❑ 45 Alex Sanchez DP .05 .02
❑ 46 Kelly Mann DP RC .10 .03
❑ 47 Julio Machado DP RC .10 .03
❑ 48 Pete Incaviglia .05 .02
❑ 49 Shawon Dunston .05 .02
❑ 50 Jeff Treadway .05 .02
❑ 51 Jeff Ballard .05 .02
❑ 52 Claudell Washington .05 .02
❑ 53 Juan Samuel .05 .02
❑ 54 John Smiley .05 .02
❑ 55 Rob Deer .05 .02
❑ 56 Geno Petralli .05 .02
❑ 57 Chris Bosio .05 .02
❑ 58 Carlton Fisk .15 .04
❑ 59 Kirt Manwaring .05 .02
❑ 60 Chet Lemon .05 .02
❑ 61 Bo Jackson .25 .07
❑ 62 Doyle Alexander .05 .02
❑ 63 Pedro Guerrero .05 .02
❑ 64 Allan Anderson .05 .02
❑ 65 Greg W. Harris .05 .02
❑ 66 Mike Greenwell .05 .02
❑ 67 Walt Weiss .05 .02
❑ 68 Wade Boggs .15 .04
❑ 69 Jim Clancy .05 .02
❑ 70 Junior Felix .05 .02
❑ 71 Barry Larkin .25 .07
❑ 72 Dave LaPoint .05 .02
❑ 73 Joel Skinner .05 .02
❑ 74 Jesse Barfield .05 .02
❑ 75 Tommy Herr .05 .02
❑ 76 Ricky Jordan .05 .02
❑ 77 Eddie Murray .25 .07
❑ 78 Steve Sax .05 .02
❑ 79 Tim Belcher .05 .02
❑ 80 Danny Jackson .05 .02
❑ 81 Kent Hrbek .10 .03
❑ 82 Milt Thompson .05 .02
❑ 83 Brook Jacoby .05 .02
❑ 84 Mike Marshall .05 .02
❑ 85 Kevin Seitzer .05 .02
❑ 86 Tony Gwynn .30 .09
❑ 87 Dave Stieb .10 .03
❑ 88 Dave Smith .05 .02
❑ 89 Bret Saberhagen .10 .03
❑ 90 Alan Trammell .15 .04
❑ 91 Tony Phillips .05 .02
❑ 92 Doug Drabek .05 .02
❑ 93 Jeffrey Leonard .05 .02
❑ 94 Wally Joyner .10 .03
❑ 95 Carney Lansford .10 .03
❑ 96 Cal Ripken .75 .23
❑ 97 Andres Galarraga .10 .03
❑ 98 Kevin Mitchell .05 .02
❑ 99 Howard Johnson .05 .02
❑ 100A Checklist 28-129 .05 .02
❑ 100B Checklist 28-125 .05 .02
❑ 101 Melido Perez .05 .02
❑ 102 Spike Owen .05 .02
❑ 103 Paul Molitor .15 .04
❑ 104 Geronimo Berroa .05 .02
❑ 105 Ryne Sandberg .40 .12
❑ 106 Bryn Smith .05 .02
❑ 107 Steve Buechele .05 .02
❑ 108 Jim Abbott .25 .07
❑ 109 Alvin Davis .05 .02
❑ 110 Lee Smith .10 .03
❑ 111 Roberto Alomar .25 .07
❑ 112 Rick Reuschel .05 .02
❑ 113A Kelly Gruber ERR .05 .02
(Born 2/22)
❑ 113B Kelly Gruber COR .05 .02
(Born 2/26; corrected in factory sets)
❑ 114 Joe Carter .10 .03
❑ 115 Jose Rijo .05 .02
❑ 116 Greg Minton .05 .02
❑ 117 Bob Ojeda .05 .02
❑ 118 Glenn Davis .05 .02
❑ 119 Jeff Reardon .10 .03
❑ 120 Kurt Stillwell .05 .02
❑ 121 John Smoltz .25 .07
❑ 122 Dwight Evans .10 .03
❑ 123 Eric Yelding .05 .02
❑ 124 John Franco .10 .03
❑ 125 Jose Canseco .25 .07
❑ 126 Barry Bonds .60 .18
❑ 127 Lee Guetterman .05 .02
❑ 128 Jack Clark .10 .03
❑ 129 Dave Valle .05 .02
❑ 130 Hubie Brooks .05 .02
❑ 131 Ernest Riles .05 .02
❑ 132 Mike Morgan .05 .02
❑ 133 Steve Jeltz .05 .02
❑ 134 Jeff D. Robinson .05 .02
❑ 135 Ozzie Guillen .05 .02
❑ 136 Chili Davis .10 .03
❑ 137 Mitch Webster .05 .02
❑ 138 Jerry Browne .05 .02
❑ 139 Bo Diaz .05 .02
❑ 140 Robby Thompson .05 .02
❑ 141 Craig Worthington .05 .02
❑ 142 Julio Franco .05 .02
❑ 143 Brian Holman .05 .02
❑ 144 George Brett .60 .18
❑ 145 Tom Glavine .25 .07
❑ 146 Robin Yount .25 .07
❑ 147 Gary Carter .15 .04
❑ 148 Ron Kittle .05 .02
❑ 149 Tony Fernandez .05 .02
❑ 150 Dave Stewart .10 .03
❑ 151 Gary Gaetti .10 .03
❑ 152 Kevin Elster .05 .02
❑ 153 Gerald Perry .05 .02
❑ 154 Jesse Orosco .05 .02
❑ 155 Wally Backman .05 .02
❑ 156 Dennis Martinez .10 .03
❑ 157 Rick Sutcliffe .10 .03
❑ 158 Greg Maddux .50 .15
❑ 159 Andy Hawkins .05 .02
❑ 160 John Kruk .10 .03
❑ 161 Jose Oquendo .05 .02
❑ 162 John Dopson .05 .02
❑ 163 Joe Magrane .05 .02
❑ 164 Bill Ripken .05 .02
❑ 165 Fred Manrique .05 .02
❑ 166 Nolan Ryan UER 1.00 .30
(Did not lead NL in K's in '89 as he was in AL in '89)
❑ 167 Damon Berryhill .05 .02
❑ 168 Dale Murphy .25 .07
❑ 169 Mickey Tettleton .05 .02
❑ 170A Kirk McCaskill ERR .05 .02
(Born 4/19)
❑ 170B Kirk McCaskill COR .05 .02
(Born 4/9; corrected in factory sets)
❑ 171 Dwight Gooden .15 .04
❑ 172 Jose Lind .05 .02
❑ 173 B.J. Surhoff .10 .03
❑ 174 Ruben Sierra .05 .02
❑ 175 Dan Plesac .05 .02
❑ 176 Dan Pasqua .05 .02
❑ 177 Kelly Downs .05 .02
❑ 178 Matt Nokes .05 .02
❑ 179 Luis Aquino .05 .02
❑ 180 Frank Tanana .05 .02
❑ 181 Tony Pena .05 .02
❑ 182 Dan Gladden .05 .02
❑ 183 Bruce Hurst .05 .02
❑ 184 Roger Clemens .50 .15
❑ 185 Mark McGwire .60 .18
❑ 186 Rob Murphy .05 .02
❑ 187 Jim Deshaies .05 .02
❑ 188 Fred McGriff .25 .07
❑ 189 Rob Dibble .10 .03
❑ 190 Don Mattingly .60 .18
❑ 191 Felix Fermin .05 .02
❑ 192 Roberto Kelly .05 .02
❑ 193 Dennis Cook .05 .02
❑ 194 Darren Daulton .10 .03
❑ 195 Alfredo Griffin .05 .02
❑ 196 Eric Plunk .05 .02
❑ 197 Orel Hershiser .10 .03
❑ 198 Paul O'Neill .15 .04
❑ 199 Randy Bush .05 .02
❑ 200A Checklist 130-231 .05 .02
❑ 200B Checklist 126-223 .05 .02
❑ 201 Ozzie Smith .25 .07
❑ 202 Pete O'Brien .05 .02
❑ 203 Jay Howell .05 .02
❑ 204 Mark Gubicza .05 .02
❑ 205 Ed Whitson .05 .02
❑ 206 George Bell .05 .02
❑ 207 Mike Scott .05 .02
❑ 208 Charlie Leibrandt .05 .02
❑ 209 Mike Heath .05 .02
❑ 210 Dennis Eckersley .10 .03
❑ 211 Mike LaValliere .05 .02
❑ 212 Darnell Coles .05 .02
❑ 213 Lance Parrish .05 .02
❑ 214 Mike Moore .05 .02
❑ 215 Steve Finley .10 .03
❑ 216 Tim Raines .10 .03
❑ 217A Scott Garrelts ERR .05 .02
(Born 10/20)
❑ 217B Scott Garrelts COR .05 .02
(Born 10/30; corrected in factory sets)
❑ 218 Kevin McReynolds .05 .02
❑ 219 Dave Gallagher .05 .02
❑ 220 Tim Wallach .05 .02
❑ 221 Chuck Crim .05 .02
❑ 222 Lonnie Smith .05 .02
❑ 223 Andre Dawson .10 .03
❑ 224 Nelson Santovenia .05 .02
❑ 225 Rafael Palmeiro .15 .04
❑ 226 Devon White .05 .02
❑ 227 Harold Reynolds .10 .03
❑ 228 Ellis Burks .15 .04
❑ 229 Mark Parent .05 .02
❑ 230 Will Clark .25 .07
❑ 231 Jimmy Key .10 .03
❑ 232 John Farrell .05 .02
❑ 233 Eric Davis .10 .03
❑ 234 Johnny Ray .05 .02
❑ 235 Darryl Strawberry .15 .04
❑ 236 Bill Doran .05 .02
❑ 237 Greg Gagne .05 .02

❑ 238	Jim Eisenreich	.05	.02
❑ 239	Tommy Gregg	.05	.02
❑ 240	Marty Barrett	.05	.02
❑ 241	Rafael Ramirez	.05	.02
❑ 242	Chris Sabo	.05	.02
❑ 243	Dave Henderson	.05	.02
❑ 244	Andy Van Slyke	.10	.03
❑ 245	Alvaro Espinoza	.05	.02
❑ 246	Garry Templeton	.05	.02
❑ 247	Gene Harris	.05	.02
❑ 248	Kevin Gross	.05	.02
❑ 249	Brett Butler	.10	.03
❑ 250	Willie Randolph	.10	.03
❑ 251	Roger McDowell	.05	.02
❑ 252	Rafael Belliard	.05	.02
❑ 253	Steve Rosenberg	.05	.02
❑ 254	Jack Howell	.05	.02
❑ 255	Marvell Wynne	.05	.02
❑ 256	Tom Candiotti	.05	.02
❑ 257	Todd Benzinger	.05	.02
❑ 258	Don Robinson	.05	.02
❑ 259	Phil Bradley	.05	.02
❑ 260	Cecil Espy	.05	.02
❑ 261	Scott Bankhead	.05	.02
❑ 262	Frank White	.10	.03
❑ 263	Andres Thomas	.05	.02
❑ 264	Glenn Braggs	.05	.02
❑ 265	David Cone	.10	.03
❑ 266	Bobby Thigpen	.05	.02
❑ 267	Nelson Liriano	.05	.02
❑ 268	Terry Steinbach	.05	.02
❑ 269	Kirby Puckett UER (Back doesn't consider Joe Torre's .363 in '71)	.25	.07
❑ 270	Gregg Jefferies	.10	.03
❑ 271	Jeff Blauser	.05	.02
❑ 272	Cory Snyder	.05	.02
❑ 273	Roy Smith	.05	.02
❑ 274	Tom Foley	.05	.02
❑ 275	Mitch Williams	.05	.02
❑ 276	Paul Kilgus	.05	.02
❑ 277	Don Slaught	.05	.02
❑ 278	Von Hayes	.05	.02
❑ 279	Vince Coleman	.05	.02
❑ 280	Mike Boddicker	.05	.02
❑ 281	Ken Dayley	.05	.02
❑ 282	Mike Devereaux	.05	.02
❑ 283	Kenny Rogers	.10	.03
❑ 284	Jeff Russell	.05	.02
❑ 285	Jerome Walton	.05	.02
❑ 286	Derek Lilliquist	.05	.02
❑ 287	Joe Orsulak	.05	.02
❑ 288	Dick Schofield	.05	.02
❑ 289	Ron Darling	.05	.02
❑ 290	Bobby Bonilla	.10	.03
❑ 291	Jim Gantner	.05	.02
❑ 292	Bobby Witt	.05	.02
❑ 293	Greg Brock	.05	.02
❑ 294	Ivan Calderon	.05	.02
❑ 295	Steve Bedrosian	.05	.02
❑ 296	Mike Henneman	.05	.02
❑ 297	Tom Gordon	.10	.03
❑ 298	Lou Whitaker	.10	.03
❑ 299	Terry Pendleton	.10	.03
❑ 300A	Checklist 232-333	.05	.02
❑ 300B	Checklist 224-321	.05	.02
❑ 301	Juan Berenguer	.05	.02
❑ 302	Mark Davis	.05	.02
❑ 303	Nick Esasky	.05	.02
❑ 304	Rickey Henderson	.40	.12
❑ 305	Rick Cerone	.05	.02
❑ 306	Craig Biggio	.15	.04
❑ 307	Duane Ward	.05	.02
❑ 308	Tom Browning	.05	.02
❑ 309	Walt Terrell	.05	.02
❑ 310	Greg Swindell	.05	.02
❑ 311	Dave Righetti	.05	.02
❑ 312	Mike Maddux	.05	.02
❑ 313	Len Dykstra	.10	.03
❑ 314	Jose Gonzalez	.05	.02
❑ 315	Steve Balboni	.05	.02
❑ 316	Mike Scioscia	.05	.02
❑ 317	Ron Oester	.05	.02
❑ 318	Gary Wayne	.05	.02
❑ 319	Todd Worrell	.05	.02
❑ 320	Doug Jones	.05	.02
❑ 321	Jeff Hamilton	.05	.02
❑ 322	Danny Tartabull	.05	.02
❑ 323	Chris James	.05	.02
❑ 324	Mike Flanagan	.05	.02
❑ 325	Gerald Young	.05	.02
❑ 326	Bob Boone	.10	.03
❑ 327	Frank Williams	.05	.02
❑ 328	Dave Parker	.10	.03
❑ 329	Sid Bream	.05	.02
❑ 330	Mike Schooler	.05	.02
❑ 331	Bert Blyleven	.10	.03
❑ 332	Bob Welch	.05	.02
❑ 333	Bob Milacki	.05	.02
❑ 334	Tim Burke	.05	.02
❑ 335	Jose Uribe	.05	.02
❑ 336	Randy Myers	.10	.03
❑ 337	Eric King	.05	.02
❑ 338	Mark Langston	.05	.02
❑ 339	Teddy Higuera	.05	.02
❑ 340	Oddibe McDowell	.05	.02
❑ 341	Lloyd McClendon	.05	.02
❑ 342	Pascual Perez	.05	.02
❑ 343	Kevin Brown UER (Signed is misspelled as signeed on back)	.10	.03
❑ 344	Chuck Finley	.10	.03
❑ 345	Erik Hanson	.05	.02
❑ 346	Rich Gedman	.05	.02
❑ 347	Bip Roberts	.05	.02
❑ 348	Matt Williams	.10	.03
❑ 349	Tom Henke	.05	.02
❑ 350	Brad Komminsk	.05	.02
❑ 351	Jeff Reed	.05	.02
❑ 352	Brian Downing	.05	.02
❑ 353	Frank Viola	.05	.02
❑ 354	Terry Puhl	.05	.02
❑ 355	Brian Harper	.05	.02
❑ 356	Steve Farr	.05	.02
❑ 357	Joe Boever	.05	.02
❑ 358	Danny Heep	.05	.02
❑ 359	Larry Andersen	.05	.02
❑ 360	Rolando Roomes	.05	.02
❑ 361	Mike Gallego	.05	.02
❑ 362	Bob Kipper	.05	.02
❑ 363	Clay Parker	.05	.02
❑ 364	Mike Pagliarulo	.05	.02
❑ 365	Ken Griffey Jr. UER (Signed through 1990, should be 1991)	.75	.23
❑ 366	Rex Hudler	.05	.02
❑ 367	Pat Sheridan	.05	.02
❑ 368	Kirk Gibson	.10	.03
❑ 369	Jeff Parrett	.05	.02
❑ 370	Bob Walk	.05	.02
❑ 371	Ken Patterson	.05	.02
❑ 372	Bryan Harvey	.05	.02
❑ 373	Mike Bielecki	.05	.02
❑ 374	Tom Magrann	.05	.02
❑ 375	Rick Mahler	.05	.02
❑ 376	Craig Lefferts	.05	.02
❑ 377	Gregg Olson	.10	.03
❑ 378	Jamie Moyer	.10	.03
❑ 379	Randy Johnson	.40	.12
❑ 380	Jeff Montgomery	.10	.03
❑ 381	Marty Clary	.05	.02
❑ 382	Bill Spiers	.05	.02
❑ 383	Dave Magadan	.05	.02
❑ 384	Greg Hibbard RC	.10	.03
❑ 385	Ernie Whitt	.05	.02
❑ 386	Rick Honeycutt	.05	.02
❑ 387	Dave West	.05	.02
❑ 388	Keith Hernandez	.15	.04
❑ 389	Jose Alvarez	.05	.02
❑ 390	Joey Belle	.25	.07
❑ 391	Rick Aguilera	.10	.03
❑ 392	Mike Fitzgerald	.05	.02
❑ 393	Dwight Smith	.05	.02
❑ 394	Steve Wilson	.05	.02
❑ 395	Bob Geren	.05	.02
❑ 396	Randy Ready	.05	.02
❑ 397	Ken Hill	.10	.03
❑ 398	Jody Reed	.05	.02
❑ 399	Tom Brunansky	.05	.02
❑ 400A	Checklist 334-435	.05	.02
❑ 400B	Checklist 322-419	.05	.02
❑ 401	Rene Gonzales	.05	.02
❑ 402	Harold Baines	.10	.03
❑ 403	Cecilio Guante	.05	.02
❑ 404	Joe Girardi	.15	.04
❑ 405A	Sergio Valdez ERR (Card front shows black line crossing S in Sergio)	.05	.02
❑ 405B	Sergio Valdez COR	.05	.02
❑ 406	Mark Williamson	.05	.02
❑ 407	Glenn Hoffman	.05	.02
❑ 408	Jeff Innis	.05	.02
❑ 409	Randy Kramer	.05	.02
❑ 410	Charlie O'Brien	.05	.02
❑ 411	Charlie Hough	.10	.03
❑ 412	Gus Polidor	.05	.02
❑ 413	Ron Karkovice	.05	.02
❑ 414	Trevor Wilson	.05	.02
❑ 415	Kevin Ritz	.05	.02
❑ 416	Gary Thurman	.05	.02
❑ 417	Jeff M. Robinson	.05	.02
❑ 418	Scott Terry	.05	.02
❑ 419	Tim Laudner	.05	.02
❑ 420	Dennis Rasmussen	.05	.02
❑ 421	Luis Rivera	.05	.02
❑ 422	Jim Corsi	.05	.02
❑ 423	Dennis Lamp	.05	.02
❑ 424	Ken Caminiti	.10	.03
❑ 425	David Wells	.10	.03
❑ 426	Norm Charlton	.05	.02
❑ 427	Deion Sanders	.25	.07
❑ 428	Dion James	.05	.02
❑ 429	Chuck Cary	.05	.02
❑ 430	Ken Howell	.05	.02
❑ 431	Steve Lake	.05	.02
❑ 432	Kal Daniels	.05	.02
❑ 433	Lance McCullers	.05	.02
❑ 434	Lenny Harris	.05	.02
❑ 435	Scott Scudder	.05	.02
❑ 436	Gene Larkin	.05	.02
❑ 437	Dan Quisenberry	.05	.02
❑ 438	Steve Olin RC	.25	.07
❑ 439	Mickey Hatcher	.05	.02
❑ 440	Willie Wilson	.05	.02
❑ 441	Mark Grant	.05	.02
❑ 442	Mookie Wilson	.10	.03
❑ 443	Alex Trevino	.05	.02
❑ 444	Pat Tabler	.05	.02
❑ 445	Dave Bergman	.05	.02
❑ 446	Todd Burns	.05	.02
❑ 447	R.J. Reynolds	.05	.02
❑ 448	Jay Buhner	.10	.03
❑ 449	Lee Stevens	.10	.03
❑ 450	Ron Hassey	.05	.02
❑ 451	Bob Melvin	.05	.02
❑ 452	Dave Martinez	.05	.02
❑ 453	Greg Litton	.05	.02
❑ 454	Mark Carreon	.05	.02
❑ 455	Scott Fletcher	.05	.02
❑ 456	Otis Nixon	.05	.02
❑ 457	Tony Fossas	.05	.02
❑ 458	John Russell	.05	.02
❑ 459	Paul Assenmacher	.05	.02
❑ 460	Zane Smith	.05	.02
❑ 461	Jack Daugherty	.05	.02
❑ 462	Rich Monteleone	.05	.02
❑ 463	Greg Briley	.05	.02
❑ 464	Mike Smithson	.05	.02
❑ 465	Benito Santiago	.10	.03
❑ 466	Jeff Brantley	.05	.02
❑ 467	Jose Nunez	.05	.02
❑ 468	Scott Bailes	.05	.02
❑ 469	Ken Griffey Sr.	.10	.03
❑ 470	Bob McClure	.05	.02
❑ 471	Mackey Sasser	.05	.02
❑ 472	Glenn Wilson	.05	.02
❑ 473	Kevin Tapani RC	.25	.07
❑ 474	Bill Buckner	.05	.02
❑ 475	Ron Gant	.10	.03
❑ 476	Kevin Romine	.05	.02
❑ 477	Juan Agosto	.05	.02
❑ 478	Herm Winningham	.05	.02
❑ 479	Storm Davis	.05	.02
❑ 480	Jeff King	.05	.02
❑ 481	Kevin Mmahat	.05	.02
❑ 482	Carmelo Martinez	.05	.02
❑ 483	Omar Vizquel	.25	.07

❑ 484 Jim Dwyer .05 .02
❑ 485 Bob Knepper .05 .02
❑ 486 Dave Anderson .05 .02
❑ 487 Ron Jones .05 .02
❑ 488 Jay Bell .10 .03
❑ 489 Sammy Sosa RC 8.00 2.40
❑ 490 Kent Anderson .05 .02
❑ 491 Domingo Ramos .05 .02
❑ 492 Dave Clark .05 .02
❑ 493 Tim Birtsas .05 .02
❑ 494 Ken Oberkfell .05 .02
❑ 495 Larry Sheets .05 .02
❑ 496 Jeff Kunkel .05 .02
❑ 497 Jim Presley .05 .02
❑ 498 Mike Macfarlane .05 .02
❑ 499 Pete Smith .05 .02
❑ 500A Checklist 436-537 DP .05 .02
❑ 500B Checklist 420-517 .05 .02
❑ 501 Gary Sheffield .25 .07
❑ 502 Terry Bross .05 .02
❑ 503 Jerry Kutzler .05 .02
❑ 504 Lloyd Moseby .05 .02
❑ 505 Curt Young .05 .02
❑ 506 Al Newman .05 .02
❑ 507 Keith Miller .05 .02
❑ 508 Mike Stanton RC .25 .07
❑ 509 Rich Yett .05 .02
❑ 510 Tim Drummond .05 .02
❑ 511 Joe Hesketh .05 .02
❑ 512 Rick Wrona .05 .02
❑ 513 Luis Salazar .05 .02
❑ 514 Hal Morris .05 .02
❑ 515 Terry Mulholland .05 .02
❑ 516 John Morris .05 .02
❑ 517 Carlos Quintana .05 .02
❑ 518 Frank DiPino .05 .02
❑ 519 Randy Milligan .05 .02
❑ 520 Chad Kreuter .05 .02
❑ 521 Mike Jeffcoat .05 .02
❑ 522 Mike Harkey .05 .02
❑ 523A Andy Nezelek ERR .05 .02
(Wrong birth year)
❑ 523B Andy Nezelek COR .25 .07
(Finally corrected
in factory sets)
❑ 524 Dave Schmidt .05 .02
❑ 525 Tony Armas .05 .02
❑ 526 Barry Lyons .05 .02
❑ 527 Rick Reed RC .25 .07
❑ 528 Jerry Reuss .05 .02
❑ 529 Dean Palmer RC .25 .07
❑ 530 Jeff Peterek .05 .02
❑ 531 Carlos Martinez .05 .02
❑ 532 Atlee Hammaker .05 .02
❑ 533 Mike Brumley .05 .02
❑ 534 Terry Leach .05 .02
❑ 535 Doug Strange .05 .02
❑ 536 Jose DeLeon .05 .02
❑ 537 Shane Rawley .05 .02
❑ 538 Joey Cora .10 .03
❑ 539 Eric Hetzel .05 .02
❑ 540 Gene Nelson .05 .02
❑ 541 Wes Gardner .05 .02
❑ 542 Mark Portugal .05 .02
❑ 543 Al Leiter .25 .07
❑ 544 Jack Armstrong .05 .02
❑ 545 Greg Cadaret .05 .02
❑ 546 Rod Nichols .05 .02
❑ 547 Luis Polonia .05 .02
❑ 548 Charlie Hayes .05 .02
❑ 549 Dickie Thon .05 .02
❑ 550 Tim Crews .05 .02
❑ 551 Dave Winfield .15 .04
❑ 552 Mike Davis .05 .02
❑ 553 Ron Robinson .05 .02
❑ 554 Carmen Castillo .05 .02
❑ 555 John Costello .05 .02
❑ 556 Bud Black .05 .02
❑ 557 Rick Dempsey .05 .02
❑ 558 Jim Acker .05 .02
❑ 559 Eric Show .05 .02
❑ 560 Pat Borders .05 .02
❑ 561 Danny Darwin .05 .02
❑ 562 Rick Luecken .05 .02
❑ 563 Edwin Nunez .05 .02
❑ 564 Felix Jose .05 .02
❑ 565 John Cangelosi .05 .02
❑ 566 Bill Swift .05 .02
❑ 567 Bill Schroeder .05 .02
❑ 568 Stan Javier .05 .02
❑ 569 Jim Traber .05 .02
❑ 570 Wallace Johnson .05 .02
❑ 571 Donell Nixon .05 .02
❑ 572 Sid Fernandez .05 .02
❑ 573 Lance Johnson .05 .02
❑ 574 Andy McGaffigan .05 .02
❑ 575 Mark Knudson .05 .02
❑ 576 Tommy Greene RC .10 .03
❑ 577 Mark Grace .25 .07
❑ 578 Larry Walker RC 1.00 .30
❑ 579 Mike Stanley .05 .02
❑ 580 Mike Witt DP .05 .02
❑ 581 Scott Bradley .05 .02
❑ 582 Greg A. Harris .05 .02
❑ 583A Kevin Hickey ERR .25 .07
❑ 583B Kevin Hickey COR .05 .02
❑ 584 Lee Mazzilli .05 .02
❑ 585 Jeff Pico .05 .02
❑ 586 Joe Oliver .05 .02
❑ 587 Willie Fraser DP .05 .02
❑ 588 Carl Yastrzemski .25 .07
Puzzle Card DP
❑ 589 Kevin Bass DP .05 .02
❑ 590 John Moses DP .05 .02
❑ 591 Tom Pagnozzi DP .05 .02
❑ 592 Tony Castillo DP .05 .02
❑ 593 Jerald Clark DP .05 .02
❑ 594 Dan Schatzeder .05 .02
❑ 595 Luis Quinones DP .05 .02
❑ 596 Pete Harnisch DP .05 .02
❑ 597 Gary Redus .05 .02
❑ 598 Mel Hall .05 .02
❑ 599 Rick Schu .05 .02
❑ 600A Checklist 538-639 .05 .02
❑ 600B Checklist 518-617 .05 .02
❑ 601 Mike Kingery DP .05 .02
❑ 602 Terry Kennedy DP .05 .02
❑ 603 Mike Sharperson DP .05 .02
❑ 604 Don Carman DP .05 .02
❑ 605 Jim Gott .05 .02
❑ 606 Donn Pall DP .05 .02
❑ 607 Rance Mulliniks .05 .02
❑ 608 Curt Wilkerson DP .05 .02
❑ 609 Mike Felder DP .05 .02
❑ 610 G.Hernandez DP .05 .02
❑ 611 Candy Maldonado DP .05 .02
❑ 612 Mark Thurmond DP .05 .02
❑ 613 Rick Leach DP .05 .02
❑ 614 Jerry Reed DP .05 .02
❑ 615 Franklin Stubbs .05 .02
❑ 616 Billy Hatcher DP .05 .02
❑ 617 Don August DP .05 .02
❑ 618 Tim Teufel .05 .02
❑ 619 Shawn Hillegas DP .05 .02
❑ 620 Manny Lee .05 .02
❑ 621 Gary Ward DP .05 .02
❑ 622 Mark Guthrie DP .05 .02
❑ 623 Jeff Musselman DP .05 .02
❑ 624 Mark Lemke DP .05 .02
❑ 625 Fernando Valenzuela .10 .03
❑ 626 Paul Sorrento DP RC .25 .07
❑ 627 Glenallen Hill DP .05 .02
❑ 628 Les Lancaster DP .05 .02
❑ 629 Vance Law DP .05 .02
❑ 630 Randy Velarde DP .05 .02
❑ 631 Todd Frohwirth DP .05 .02
❑ 632 Willie McGee .10 .03
❑ 633 Dennis Boyd DP .05 .02
❑ 634 Cris Carpenter DP .05 .02
❑ 635 Brian Holton .05 .02
❑ 636 Tracy Jones DP .05 .02
❑ 637A Terry Steinbach AS .05 .02
(Recent Major
League Performance)
❑ 637B Terry Steinbach AS .05 .02
(All-Star Game
Performance)
❑ 638 Brady Anderson .10 .03
❑ 639A Jack Morris ERR .10 .03
(Card front shows
black line crossing
J in Jack)
❑ 639B Jack Morris COR .10 .03
❑ 640 Jaime Navarro .05 .02
❑ 641 Darrin Jackson .05 .02
❑ 642 Mike Dyer .05 .02
❑ 643 Mike Schmidt .50 .15
❑ 644 Henry Cotto .05 .02
❑ 645 John Cerutti .05 .02
❑ 646 Francisco Cabrera .05 .02
❑ 647 Scott Sanderson .05 .02
❑ 648 Brian Meyer .05 .02
❑ 649 Ray Searage .05 .02
❑ 650A Bo Jackson AS .25 .07
(Recent Major
League Performance)
❑ 650B Bo Jackson AS .25 .07
(All-Star Game
Performance)
❑ 651 Steve Lyons .05 .02
❑ 652 Mike LaCoss .05 .02
❑ 653 Ted Power .05 .02
❑ 654A Howard Johnson AS .05 .02
(Recent Major
League Performance)
❑ 654B Howard Johnson AS .05 .02
(All-Star Game
Performance)
❑ 655 Mauro Gozzo .05 .02
❑ 656 Mike Blowers RC .10 .03
❑ 657 Paul Gibson .05 .02
❑ 658 Neal Heaton .05 .02
❑ 659 Nolan Ryan 5000K .40 .12
COR (Still an error as
Ryan did not lead AL
in K's in '75)
❑ 659A Nolan Ryan 5000K 1.50 .45
(665 King of
Kings back) ERR
❑ 660A Harold Baines AS .75 .23
(Black line through
star on front;
Recent Major
League Performance)
❑ 660B Harold Baines AS 1.00 .30
(Black line through
star on front;
All-Star Game
Performance)
❑ 660C Harold Baines AS .25 .07
(Black line behind
star on front;
Recent Major
League Performance)
❑ 660D Harold Baines AS .05 .02
(Black line behind
star on front;
All-Star Game
Performance)
❑ 661 Gary Pettis .05 .02
❑ 662 Clint Zavaras .05 .02
❑ 663A Rick Reuschel AS .05 .02
(Recent Major
League Performance)
❑ 663B Rick Reuschel AS .05 .02
(All-Star Game
Performance)
❑ 664 Alejandro Pena .05 .02
❑ 665 N.Ryan KING COR .40 .12
❑ 665A Nolan Ryan KING 1.50 .45
(659 5000 K
back) ERR
❑ 665C N.Ryan KING ERR .75 .23
No number on back
in factory sets
❑ 666 Ricky Horton .05 .02
❑ 667 Curt Schilling 1.00 .30
❑ 668 Bill Landrum .05 .02
❑ 669 Todd Stottlemyre .10 .03
❑ 670 Tim Leary .05 .02
❑ 671 John Wetteland .25 .07
❑ 672 Calvin Schiraldi .05 .02
❑ 673A Ruben Sierra AS .05 .02
(Recent Major
League Performance)
❑ 673B Ruben Sierra AS .05 .02
(All-Star Game
Performance)

❑ 674A Pedro Guerrero AS .05 .02 (Recent Major League Performance)
❑ 674B Pedro Guerrero AS .05 .02 (All-Star Game Performance)
❑ 675 Ken Phelps .05 .02
❑ 676A Cal Ripken AS .40 .12 (All-Star Game Performance)
❑ 676B Cal Ripken AS .75 .23 (Recent Major League Performance)
❑ 677 Denny Walling .05 .02
❑ 678 Goose Gossage .10 .03
❑ 679 Gary Mielke .05 .02
❑ 680 Bill Bathe .05 .02
❑ 681 Tom Lawless .05 .02
❑ 682 Xavier Hernandez RC .05 .02
❑ 683A Kirby Puckett AS .15 .04 (Recent Major League Performance)
❑ 683B Kirby Puckett AS .15 .04 (All-Star Game Performance)
❑ 684 Mariano Duncan .05 .02
❑ 685 Ramon Martinez .05 .02
❑ 686 Tim Jones .05 .02
❑ 687 Tom Filer .05 .02
❑ 688 Steve Lombardozzi .05 .02
❑ 689 Bernie Williams RC 1.00 .30
❑ 690 Chip Hale .05 .02
❑ 691 Beau Allred .05 .02
❑ 692A Ryne Sandberg AS .25 .07 (Recent Major League Performance)
❑ 692B Ryne Sandberg AS .25 .07 (All-Star Game Performance)
❑ 693 Jeff Huson RC .10 .03
❑ 694 Curt Ford .05 .02
❑ 695A Eric Davis AS .05 .02 (Recent Major League Performance)
❑ 695B Eric Davis AS .05 .02 (All-Star Game Performance)
❑ 696 Scott Lusader .05 .02
❑ 697A Mark McGwire AS .30 .09 (Recent Major League Performance)
❑ 697B Mark McGwire AS .30 .09 (All-Star Game Performance)
❑ 698 Steve Cummings .05 .02
❑ 699 George Canale .05 .02
❑ 700A Checklist 640-715 .25 .07 and BC1-BC26
❑ 700B Checklist 640-716 .10 .03 and BC1-BC26
❑ 700C Checklist 618-716 .05 .02
❑ 701A Julio Franco AS .05 .02 (Recent Major League Performance)
❑ 701B Julio Franco AS .05 .02 (All-Star Game Performance)
❑ 702 Dave Johnson (P) .05 .02
❑ 703A Dave Stewart AS .05 .02 (Recent Major League Performance)
❑ 703B Dave Stewart AS .05 .02 (All-Star Game Performance)
❑ 704 Dave Justice RC .50 .15
❑ 705 Tony Gwynn AS .15 .04 (All-Star Game Performance)
❑ 705A Tony Gwynn AS .15 .04 (Recent Major League Performance)
❑ 706 Greg Myers .05 .02
❑ 707A Will Clark AS .25 .07 (Recent Major League Performance)
❑ 707B Will Clark AS .25 .07 (All-Star Game Performance)
❑ 708A Benito Santiago AS .05 .02 (Recent Major League Performance)
❑ 708B Benito Santiago AS .05 .02 (All-Star Game Performance)
❑ 709 Larry McWilliams .05 .02
❑ 710A Ozzie Smith AS .15 .04 (Recent Major League Performance)
❑ 710B Ozzie Smith AS .15 .04 (All-Star Game Performance)
❑ 711 John Olerud RC .50 .15
❑ 712A Wade Boggs AS .10 .03 (Recent Major League Performance)
❑ 712B Wade Boggs AS .10 .03 (All-Star Game Performance)
❑ 713 Gary Eave .05 .02
❑ 714 Bob Tewksbury .05 .02
❑ 715A Kevin Mitchell AS .05 .02 (Recent Major League Performance)
❑ 715B Kevin Mitchell AS .05 .02 (All-Star Game Performance)
❑ 716 B.Giamatti RC COMM .25 .07 In Memoriam

2001 Donruss

	Nm-Mt	Ex-Mt
COMP.SET w/o SP's (150)	25.00	7.50
COMMON CARD (1-150)	.30	.09
COMMON (151-200)	8.00	2.40
COMMON (201-220)	3.00	.90

❑ 1 Alex Rodriguez 1.50 .45
❑ 2 Barry Bonds 2.00 .60
❑ 3 Cal Ripken 2.50 .75
❑ 4 Chipper Jones .75 .23
❑ 5 Derek Jeter 2.00 .60
❑ 6 Troy Glaus .50 .15
❑ 7 Frank Thomas .75 .23
❑ 8 Greg Maddux 1.50 .45
❑ 9 Ivan Rodriguez .75 .23
❑ 10 Jeff Bagwell .50 .15
❑ 11 Jose Canseco .75 .23
❑ 12 Todd Helton .50 .15
❑ 13 Ken Griffey Jr. 1.25 .35
❑ 14 Manny Ramirez .30 .09
❑ 15 Mark McGwire 2.00 .60
❑ 16 Mike Piazza 1.25 .35
❑ 17 Nomar Garciaparra 1.50 .45
❑ 18 Pedro Martinez .75 .23
❑ 19 Randy Johnson .75 .23
❑ 20 Rick Ankiel .30 .09
❑ 21 Rickey Henderson 1.25 .35
❑ 22 Roger Clemens 1.50 .45
❑ 23 Sammy Sosa 1.25 .35
❑ 24 Tony Gwynn 1.00 .30
❑ 25 Vladimir Guerrero .75 .23
❑ 26 Eric Davis .30 .09
❑ 27 Roberto Alomar .30 .09
❑ 28 Mark Mulder .30 .09
❑ 29 Pat Burrell .30 .09
❑ 30 Harold Baines .30 .09
❑ 31 Carlos Delgado .30 .09
❑ 32 J.D. Drew .30 .09
❑ 33 Jim Edmonds .30 .09
❑ 34 Darin Erstad .30 .09
❑ 35 Jason Giambi .75 .23
❑ 36 Tom Glavine .75 .23
❑ 37 Juan Gonzalez .75 .23
❑ 38 Mark Grace .75 .23
❑ 39 Shawn Green .30 .09
❑ 40 Tim Hudson .30 .09
❑ 41 Andruw Jones .50 .15
❑ 42 David Justice .30 .09
❑ 43 Jeff Kent .30 .09
❑ 44 Barry Larkin .75 .23
❑ 45 Pokey Reese .30 .09
❑ 46 Mike Mussina .75 .23
❑ 47 Hideo Nomo .75 .23
❑ 48 Rafael Palmeiro .50 .15
❑ 49 Adam Piatt .30 .09
❑ 50 Scott Rolen .50 .15
❑ 51 Gary Sheffield .30 .09
❑ 52 Bernie Williams .50 .15
❑ 53 Bob Abreu .30 .09
❑ 54 Edgardo Alfonzo .30 .09
❑ 55 Jermaine Clark RC .50 .15
❑ 56 Albert Belle .30 .09
❑ 57 Craig Biggio .50 .15
❑ 58 Andres Galarraga .30 .09
❑ 59 Edgar Martinez .50 .15
❑ 60 Fred McGriff .50 .15
❑ 61 Magglio Ordonez .30 .09
❑ 62 Jim Thome .75 .23
❑ 63 Matt Williams .30 .09
❑ 64 Kerry Wood .75 .23
❑ 65 Moises Alou .30 .09
❑ 66 Brady Anderson .30 .09
❑ 67 Garret Anderson .30 .09
❑ 68 Tony Armas Jr. .30 .09
❑ 69 Tony Batista .30 .09
❑ 70 Jose Cruz Jr. .30 .09
❑ 71 Carlos Beltran .30 .09
❑ 72 Adrian Beltre .30 .09
❑ 73 Kris Benson .30 .09
❑ 74 Lance Berkman .30 .09
❑ 75 Kevin Brown .30 .09
❑ 76 Jay Buhner .30 .09
❑ 77 Jeromy Burnitz .30 .09
❑ 78 Ken Caminiti .30 .09
❑ 79 Sean Casey .30 .09
❑ 80 Luis Castillo .30 .09
❑ 81 Eric Chavez .30 .09
❑ 82 Jeff Cirillo .30 .09
❑ 83 Bartolo Colon .30 .09
❑ 84 David Cone .30 .09
❑ 85 Freddy Garcia .30 .09
❑ 86 Johnny Damon .30 .09
❑ 87 Ray Durham .30 .09
❑ 88 Jermaine Dye .30 .09
❑ 89 Juan Encarnacion .30 .09
❑ 90 Terrence Long .30 .09
❑ 91 Carl Everett .30 .09
❑ 92 Steve Finley .30 .09
❑ 93 Cliff Floyd .30 .09
❑ 94 Brad Fullmer .30 .09
❑ 95 Brian Giles .30 .09
❑ 96 Luis Gonzalez .30 .09
❑ 97 Rusty Greer .30 .09
❑ 98 Jeffrey Hammonds .30 .09
❑ 99 Mike Hampton .30 .09
❑ 100 Orlando Hernandez .30 .09
❑ 101 Richard Hidalgo .30 .09
❑ 102 Geoff Jenkins .30 .09
❑ 103 Jacque Jones .30 .09
❑ 104 Brian Jordan .30 .09
❑ 105 Gabe Kapler .30 .09
❑ 106 Eric Karros .30 .09
❑ 107 Jason Kendall .30 .09
❑ 108 Adam Kennedy .30 .09
❑ 109 Byung-Hyun Kim .30 .09
❑ 110 Ryan Klesko .30 .09
❑ 111 Chuck Knoblauch .30 .09
❑ 112 Paul Konerko .30 .09
❑ 113 Carlos Lee .30 .09

❑ 114 Kenny Lofton .30 .09
❑ 115 Javy Lopez .30 .09
❑ 116 Tino Martinez .50 .15
❑ 117 Ruben Mateo .30 .09
❑ 118 Kevin Millwood .30 .09
❑ 119 Ben Molina .30 .09
❑ 120 Raul Mondesi .30 .09
❑ 121 Trot Nixon .30 .09
❑ 122 John Olerud .30 .09
❑ 123 Paul O'Neill .50 .15
❑ 124 Chan Ho Park .30 .09
❑ 125 Andy Pettitte .50 .15
❑ 126 Jorge Posada .50 .15
❑ 127 Mark Quinn .30 .09
❑ 128 Aramis Ramirez .30 .09
❑ 129 Mariano Rivera .50 .15
❑ 130 Tim Salmon .50 .15
❑ 131 Curt Schilling .50 .15
❑ 132 Richie Sexson .30 .09
❑ 133 John Smoltz .50 .15
❑ 134 J.T. Snow .30 .09
❑ 135 Jay Payton .30 .09
❑ 136 Shannon Stewart .30 .09
❑ 137 B.J. Surhoff .30 .09
❑ 138 Mike Sweeney .30 .09
❑ 139 Fernando Tatis .30 .09
❑ 140 Miguel Tejada .30 .09
❑ 141 Jason Varitek .30 .09
❑ 142 Greg Vaughn .30 .09
❑ 143 Mo Vaughn .30 .09
❑ 144 Robin Ventura UER .30 .09
Listed as playing for Yankees last 2 years
Also Bat and Throw information is wrong
❑ 145 Jose Vidro .30 .09
❑ 146 Omar Vizquel .30 .09
❑ 147 Larry Walker .50 .15
❑ 148 David Wells .30 .09
❑ 149 Rondell White .30 .09
❑ 150 Preston Wilson .30 .09
❑ 151 Brent Abernathy RR 8.00 2.40
❑ 152 Cory Aldridge RR RC 8.00 2.40
❑ 153 Gene Altman RR RC 8.00 2.40
❑ 154 Josh Beckett RR 10.00 3.00
❑ 155 W. Betemit RR RC 8.00 2.40
❑ 156 A.Pujols RR/500 RC 200.00 60.00
❑ 157 Joe Crede RR 8.00 2.40
❑ 158 Jack Cust RR 8.00 2.40
❑ 159 Ben Sheets RR/500 100.00 30.00
❑ 160 Alex Escobar RR 8.00 2.40
❑ 161 A. Hernandez RR RC 8.00 2.40
❑ 162 Pedro Feliz RR 8.00 2.40
❑ 163 Nate Frese RR RC 8.00 2.40
❑ 164 Carlos Garcia RR RC 8.00 2.40
❑ 165 Marcus Giles RR 8.00 2.40
❑ 166 Alexis Gomez RR RC 8.00 2.40
❑ 167 Jason Hart RR 8.00 2.40
❑ 168 Eric Hinske RR RC 10.00 3.00
❑ 169 Cesar Izturis RR 8.00 2.40
❑ 170 Nick Johnson RR 8.00 2.40
❑ 171 Mike Young RR 8.00 2.40
❑ 172 B. Lawrence RR RC 8.00 2.40
❑ 173 Steve Lomasney RR 8.00 2.40
❑ 174 Nick Maness RR 8.00 2.40
❑ 175 Jose Mieses RR RC 8.00 2.40
❑ 176 Greg Miller RR RC 8.00 2.40
❑ 177 Eric Munson RR 8.00 2.40
❑ 178 Xavier Nady RR 8.00 2.40
❑ 179 Blaine Neal RR RC 8.00 2.40
❑ 180 Abraham Nunez RR 8.00 2.40
❑ 181 Jose Ortiz RR 8.00 2.40
❑ 182 Jeremy Owens RR RC 8.00 2.40
❑ 183 Pablo Ozuna RR 8.00 2.40
❑ 184 Corey Patterson RR 8.00 2.40
❑ 185 Carlos Pena RR 8.00 2.40
❑ 186 Wily Mo Pena RR 8.00 2.40
❑ 187 Timo Perez RR 8.00 2.40
❑ 188 A. Pettyjohn RR RC 8.00 2.40
❑ 189 Luis Rivas RR 8.00 2.40
❑ 190 J. Melian RR RC 8.00 2.40
❑ 191 Wilken Ruan RR RC 8.00 2.40
❑ 192 D. Sanchez RR RC 8.00 2.40
❑ 193 Alfonso Soriano RR 10.00 3.00
❑ 194 Rafael Soriano RR RC 12.00 3.60
❑ 195 Ichiro Suzuki RR RC 60.00 18.00
❑ 196 Billy Sylvester RR RC 8.00 2.40
❑ 197 Juan Uribe RR RC 8.00 2.40
❑ 198 Eric Valent RR 8.00 2.40
❑ 199 C.Valderrama RR RC 8.00 2.40
❑ 200 Matt White RR RC 8.00 2.40
❑ 201 Alex Rodriguez FC 8.00 2.40
❑ 202 Barry Bonds FC 10.00 3.00
❑ 203 Cal Ripken FC 12.00 3.60
❑ 204 Chipper Jones FC 4.00 1.20
❑ 205 Derek Jeter FC 10.00 3.00
❑ 206 Troy Glaus FC 3.00 .90
❑ 207 Frank Thomas FC 4.00 1.20
❑ 208 Greg Maddux FC 8.00 2.40
❑ 209 Ivan Rodriguez FC 4.00 1.20
❑ 210 Jeff Bagwell FC 3.00 .90
❑ 211 Todd Helton FC 3.00 .90
❑ 212 Ken Griffey Jr. FC 6.00 1.80
❑ 213 Manny Ramirez FC 3.00 .90
❑ 214 Mark McGwire FC 10.00 3.00
❑ 215 Mike Piazza FC 6.00 1.80
❑ 216 Pedro Martinez FC 4.00 1.20
❑ 217 Sammy Sosa FC 6.00 1.80
❑ 218 Tony Gwynn FC 5.00 1.50
❑ 219 Vladimir Guerrero FC 4.00 1.20
❑ 220 Nomar Garciaparra FC 8.00 2.40
❑ NNO BB Best Coupon 2.00 .60
❑ NNO The Rookies Coupon .50 .15

2001 Donruss Rookies

	Nm-Mt	Ex-Mt
COMP.FACT.SET (106)	50.00	15.00
COMP.SET w/o SP's (105)	40.00	12.00

❑ R1 Adam Dunn .75 .23
❑ R2 Ryan Drese RC .40 .12
❑ R3 Bud Smith RC .40 .12
❑ R4 Tsuyoshi Shinjo RC 1.50 .45
❑ R5 Roy Oswalt .75 .23
❑ R6 Wilmy Caceres RC .40 .12
❑ R7 Willie Harris RC .40 .12
❑ R8 Andres Torres RC .40 .12
❑ R9 Brandon Knight RC .40 .12
❑ R10 Horacio Ramirez RC 1.25 .35
❑ R11 Benito Baez RC .40 .12
❑ R12 Jeremy Affeldt RC .40 .12
❑ R13 Ryan Jensen RC .40 .12
❑ R14 Casey Fossum RC .40 .12
❑ R15 Ramon Vazquez RC .40 .12
❑ R16 Dustan Mohr RC .40 .12
❑ R17 Saul Rivera RC .40 .12
❑ R18 Zach Day RC .75 .23
❑ R19 Erik Hiljus RC .40 .12
❑ R20 Cesar Crespo RC .40 .12
❑ R21 Wilson Guzman RC .40 .12
❑ R22 Travis Hafner RC 1.25 .35
❑ R23 Grant Balfour RC .40 .12
❑ R24 Johnny Estrada RC .75 .23
❑ R25 Morgan Ensberg RC 1.50 .45
❑ R26 Jack Wilson RC .40 .12
❑ R27 Aubrey Huff .40 .12
❑ R28 Endy Chavez RC .40 .12
❑ R29 Delvin James RC .40 .12
❑ R30 Michael Cuddyer .40 .12
❑ R31 Jason Michaels RC .40 .12
❑ R32 Martin Vargas RC .40 .12
❑ R33 Donaldo Mendez RC .40 .12
❑ R34 Jorge Julio RC .40 .12
❑ R35 T.Spooneybarger RC .40 .12
❑ R36 Kurt Ainsworth .40 .12
❑ R37 Josh Fogg RC .40 .12
❑ R38 Brian Reith RC .40 .12
❑ R39 Rick Bauer RC .40 .12
❑ R40 Tim Redding .40 .12
❑ R41 Erick Almonte RC .40 .12
❑ R42 Juan A.Pena RC .40 .12
❑ R43 Ken Harvey .40 .12
❑ R44 David Brous RC .40 .12
❑ R45 Kevin Olsen RC .40 .12
❑ R46 Henry Mateo RC .40 .12
❑ R47 Nick Neugebauer .40 .12
❑ R48 Mike Penney RC .40 .12
❑ R49 Jay Gibbons RC 1.50 .45
❑ R50 Tim Christman RC .40 .12
❑ R51 B.Duckworth RC .40 .12
❑ R52 Brett Jodie RC .40 .12
❑ R53 Christian Parker RC .40 .12
❑ R54 Carlos Hernandez .40 .12
❑ R55 Brandon Larson RC .40 .12
❑ R56 Nick Punto RC .40 .12
❑ R57 Elpidio Guzman RC .40 .12
❑ R58 Joe Beimel RC .40 .12
❑ R59 Junior Spivey RC 1.25 .35
❑ R60 Will Ohman RC .40 .12
❑ R61 Brandon Lyon RC .40 .12
❑ R62 Stubby Clapp RC .40 .12
❑ R63 J.Duchscherer RC .40 .12
❑ R64 Jimmy Rollins .40 .12
❑ R65 David Williams RC .40 .12
❑ R66 Craig Monroe RC .40 .12
❑ R67 Jose Acevedo RC .40 .12
❑ R68 Jason Jennings .40 .12
❑ R69 Josh Phelps .40 .12
❑ R70 Brian Roberts RC .40 .12
❑ R71 Claudio Vargas RC .40 .12
❑ R72 Adam Johnson .40 .12
❑ R73 Bart Miadich RC .40 .12
❑ R74 Juan Rivera .40 .12
❑ R75 Brad Voyles RC .40 .12
❑ R76 Nate Cornejo .40 .12
❑ R77 Juan Moreno RC .40 .12
❑ R78 Brian Rogers RC .40 .12
❑ R79 R.Rodriguez RC .40 .12
❑ R80 Geronimo Gil RC .40 .12
❑ R81 Joe Kennedy RC .40 .12
❑ R82 Kevin Joseph RC .40 .12
❑ R83 Josue Perez RC .40 .12
❑ R84 Victor Zambrano RC .40 .12
❑ R85 Josh Towers RC .40 .12
❑ R86 Mike Rivera RC .40 .12
❑ R87 Mark Prior RC 15.00 4.50
❑ R88 Juan Cruz RC .40 .12
❑ R89 Dewon Brazelton RC .40 .12
❑ R90 Angel Berroa RC 2.50 .75
❑ R91 Mark Teixeira RC 6.00 1.80
❑ R92 Cody Ransom RC .40 .12
❑ R93 Angel Santos RC .40 .12
❑ R94 Corky Miller RC .40 .12
❑ R95 Brandon Berger RC .40 .12
❑ R96 Corey Patterson UPD .40 .12
❑ R97 A. Pujols UPD UER 25.00 7.50
Homers and RBI Stats wrong
❑ R98 Josh Beckett UPD .75 .23
❑ R99 C.C. Sabathia UPD .40 .12
❑ R100 A. Soriano UPD 1.25 .35
❑ R101 Ben Sheets UPD .40 .12
❑ R102 Rafael Soriano UPD 1.50 .45
❑ R103 Wilson Betemit UPD .40 .12
❑ R104 Ichiro Suzuki UPD 10.00 3.00
❑ R105 Jose Ortiz UPD .40 .12

2002 Donruss

	Nm-Mt	Ex-Mt
COMPLETE SET (220)	200.00	60.00
COMP.SET w/o SP'S (150)	25.00	7.50
COMMON CARD (1-150)	.30	.09
COMMON CARD (151-200)	3.00	.90
COMMON CARD (201-220)	2.00	.60

❑ 1 Alex Rodriguez 1.50 .45
❑ 2 Barry Bonds 2.00 .60
❑ 3 Derek Jeter 2.00 .60
❑ 4 Robert Fick .30 .09

Card	Nm-Mt	Ex-Mt
❑ 5 Juan Pierre	.30	.09
❑ 6 Torii Hunter	.30	.09
❑ 7 Todd Helton	.50	.15
❑ 8 Cal Ripken	2.50	.75
❑ 9 Manny Ramirez	.30	.09
❑ 10 Johnny Damon	.30	.09
❑ 11 Mike Piazza	1.25	.35
❑ 12 Nomar Garciaparra	1.50	.45
❑ 13 Pedro Martinez	.75	.23
❑ 14 Brian Giles	.30	.09
❑ 15 Albert Pujols	1.50	.45
❑ 16 Roger Clemens	1.50	.45
❑ 17 Sammy Sosa	1.25	.35
❑ 18 Vladimir Guerrero	.75	.23
❑ 19 Tony Gwynn	1.00	.30
❑ 20 Pat Burrell	.30	.09
❑ 21 Carlos Delgado	.30	.09
❑ 22 Tino Martinez	.50	.15
❑ 23 Jim Edmonds	.30	.09
❑ 24 Jason Giambi	.75	.23
❑ 25 Tom Glavine	.75	.23
❑ 26 Mark Grace	.75	.23
❑ 27 Tony Armas Jr.	.30	.09
❑ 28 Andruw Jones	.50	.15
❑ 29 Ben Sheets	.30	.09
❑ 30 Jeff Kent	.30	.09
❑ 31 Barry Larkin	.75	.23
❑ 32 Joe Mays	.30	.09
❑ 33 Mike Mussina	.75	.23
❑ 34 Hideo Nomo	.75	.23
❑ 35 Rafael Palmeiro	.50	.15
❑ 36 Scott Brosius	.30	.09
❑ 37 Scott Rolen	.50	.15
❑ 38 Gary Sheffield	.30	.09
❑ 39 Bernie Williams	.50	.15
❑ 40 Bob Abreu	.30	.09
❑ 41 Edgardo Alfonzo	.30	.09
❑ 42 C.C. Sabathia	.30	.09
❑ 43 Jeremy Giambi	.30	.09
❑ 44 Craig Biggio	.50	.15
❑ 45 Andres Galarraga	.30	.09
❑ 46 Edgar Martinez	.50	.15
❑ 47 Fred McGriff	.50	.15
❑ 48 Magglio Ordonez	.30	.09
❑ 49 Jim Thome	.75	.23
❑ 50 Matt Williams	.30	.09
❑ 51 Kerry Wood	.75	.23
❑ 52 Moises Alou	.30	.09
❑ 53 Brady Anderson	.30	.09
❑ 54 Garret Anderson	.30	.09
❑ 55 Juan Gonzalez	.75	.23
❑ 56 Bret Boone	.30	.09
❑ 57 Jose Cruz Jr.	.30	.09
❑ 58 Carlos Beltran	.30	.09
❑ 59 Adrian Beltre	.30	.09
❑ 60 Joe Kennedy	.30	.09
❑ 61 Lance Berkman	.30	.09
❑ 62 Kevin Brown	.30	.09
❑ 63 Tim Hudson	.30	.09
❑ 64 Jeromy Burnitz	.30	.09
❑ 65 Jarrod Washburn	.30	.09
❑ 66 Sean Casey	.30	.09
❑ 67 Eric Chavez	.30	.09
❑ 68 Bartolo Colon	.30	.09
❑ 69 Freddy Garcia	.30	.09
❑ 70 Jermaine Dye	.30	.09
❑ 71 Terrence Long	.30	.09
❑ 72 Cliff Floyd	.30	.09
❑ 73 Luis Gonzalez	.30	.09
❑ 74 Ichiro Suzuki	1.50	.45
❑ 75 Mike Hampton	.30	.09
❑ 76 Richard Hidalgo	.30	.09
❑ 77 Geoff Jenkins	.30	.09
❑ 78 Gabe Kapler	.30	.09
❑ 79 Ken Griffey Jr.	1.25	.35
❑ 80 Jason Kendall	.30	.09
❑ 81 Josh Towers	.30	.09
❑ 82 Ryan Klesko	.30	.09
❑ 83 Paul Konerko	.30	.09
❑ 84 Carlos Lee	.30	.09
❑ 85 Kenny Lofton	.30	.09
❑ 86 Josh Beckett	.50	.15
❑ 87 Raul Mondesi	.30	.09
❑ 88 Trot Nixon	.30	.09
❑ 89 John Olerud	.30	.09
❑ 90 Paul O'Neill	.50	.15
❑ 91 Chan Ho Park	.30	.09
❑ 92 Andy Pettitte	.50	.15
❑ 93 Jorge Posada	.50	.15
❑ 94 Mark Quinn	.30	.09
❑ 95 Aramis Ramirez	.30	.09
❑ 96 Curt Schilling	.50	.15
❑ 97 Richie Sexson	.30	.09
❑ 98 John Smoltz	.50	.15
❑ 99 Wilson Betemit	.30	.09
❑ 100 Shannon Stewart	.30	.09
❑ 101 Alfonso Soriano	.75	.23
❑ 102 Mike Sweeney	.30	.09
❑ 103 Miguel Tejada	.30	.09
❑ 104 Greg Vaughn	.30	.09
❑ 105 Robin Ventura	.30	.09
❑ 106 Jose Vidro	.30	.09
❑ 107 Larry Walker	.50	.15
❑ 108 Preston Wilson	.30	.09
❑ 109 Corey Patterson	.30	.09
❑ 110 Mark Mulder	.30	.09
❑ 111 Tony Clark	.30	.09
❑ 112 Roy Oswalt	.30	.09
❑ 113 Jimmy Rollins	.30	.09
❑ 114 Kazuhiro Sasaki	.30	.09
❑ 115 Barry Zito	.75	.23
❑ 116 Javier Vazquez	.30	.09
❑ 117 Mike Cameron	.30	.09
❑ 118 Phil Nevin	.30	.09
❑ 119 Bud Smith	.30	.09
❑ 120 Cristian Guzman	.30	.09
❑ 121 Al Leiter	.30	.09
❑ 122 Brad Radke	.30	.09
❑ 123 Bobby Higginson	.30	.09
❑ 124 Robert Person	.30	.09
❑ 125 Adam Dunn	.50	.15
❑ 126 Ben Grieve	.30	.09
❑ 127 Rafael Furcal	.30	.09
❑ 128 Jay Gibbons	.30	.09
❑ 129 Paul LoDuca	.30	.09
❑ 130 Wade Miller	.30	.09
❑ 131 Tsuyoshi Shinjo	.30	.09
❑ 132 Eric Milton	.30	.09
❑ 133 Rickey Henderson	1.25	.35
❑ 134 Roberto Alomar	.75	.23
❑ 135 Darin Erstad	.30	.09
❑ 136 J.D. Drew	.30	.09
❑ 137 Shawn Green	.30	.09
❑ 138 Randy Johnson	.75	.23
❑ 139 Austin Kearns	.50	.15
❑ 140 Jose Canseco	.75	.23
❑ 141 Jeff Bagwell	.50	.15
❑ 142 Greg Maddux	1.50	.45
❑ 143 Mark Buehrle	.30	.09
❑ 144 Ivan Rodriguez	.75	.23
❑ 145 Frank Thomas	.75	.23
❑ 146 Rich Aurilia	.30	.09
❑ 147 Troy Glaus	.50	.15
❑ 148 Ryan Dempster	.30	.09
❑ 149 Chipper Jones	.75	.23
❑ 150 Matt Morris	.30	.09
❑ 151 Marlon Byrd RR	3.00	.90
❑ 152 Ben Howard RR RC	3.00	.90
❑ 153 Brandon Backe RR RC	3.00	.90
❑ 154 Jorge De La Rosa RR RC	3.00	.90
❑ 155 Corky Miller RR	3.00	.90
❑ 156 Dennis Tankersley RR	3.00	.90
❑ 157 Kyle Kane RR RC	3.00	.90
❑ 158 Justin Duchscherer RR	3.00	.90
❑ 159 Brian Mallette RR RC	3.00	.90
❑ 160 Chris Baker RR RC	3.00	.90
❑ 161 Jason Lane RR	3.00	.90
❑ 162 Hee Seop Choi RR	3.00	.90
❑ 163 Juan Cruz RR	3.00	.90
❑ 164 Rodrigo Rosario RR RC	3.00	.90
❑ 165 Matt Guerrier RR	3.00	.90
❑ 166 Anderson Machado RR RC	3.00	.90
❑ 167 Geronimo Gil RR	3.00	.90
❑ 168 Dewon Brazelton RR	3.00	.90
❑ 169 Mark Prior RR	15.00	4.50
❑ 170 Bill Hall RR	3.00	.90
❑ 171 Jorge Padilla RR RC	3.00	.90
❑ 172 Jose Cueto RR	3.00	.90
❑ 173 Allan Simpson RR RC	3.00	.90
❑ 174 Doug Devore RR RC	3.00	.90
❑ 175 Josh Pearce RR	3.00	.90
❑ 176 Angel Berroa RR	3.00	.90
❑ 177 Steve Bechler RR RC	3.00	.90
❑ 178 Antonio Perez RR	3.00	.90
❑ 179 Mark Teixeira RR	5.00	1.50
❑ 180 Erick Almonte RR	3.00	.90
❑ 181 Orlando Hudson RR	3.00	.90
❑ 182 Michael Rivera RR	3.00	.90
❑ 183 Raul Chavez RR RC	3.00	.90
❑ 184 Juan Pena RR	3.00	.90
❑ 185 Travis Hughes RR RC	3.00	.90
❑ 186 Ryan Ludwick RR	3.00	.90
❑ 187 Ed Rogers RR	3.00	.90
❑ 188 Andy Pratt RR RC	3.00	.90
❑ 189 Nick Neugebauer RR	3.00	.90
❑ 190 Tom Shearn RR RC	3.00	.90
❑ 191 Eric Cyr RR	3.00	.90
❑ 192 Victor Martinez RR	3.00	.90
❑ 193 Brandon Berger RR	3.00	.90
❑ 194 Erik Bedard RR	3.00	.90
❑ 195 Fernando Rodney RR	3.00	.90
❑ 196 Joe Thurston RR	3.00	.90
❑ 197 John Buck RR	3.00	.90
❑ 198 Jeff Deardorff RR	3.00	.90
❑ 199 Ryan Jamison RR	3.00	.90
❑ 200 Alfredo Amezaga RR	3.00	.90
❑ 201 Luis Gonzalez FC	2.00	.60
❑ 202 Roger Clemens FC	5.00	1.50
❑ 203 Barry Zito FC	2.50	.75
❑ 204 Bud Smith FC	2.00	.60
❑ 205 Magglio Ordonez FC	2.00	.60
❑ 206 Kerry Wood FC	2.50	.75
❑ 207 Freddy Garcia FC	2.00	.60
❑ 208 Adam Dunn FC	2.00	.60
❑ 209 Curt Schilling FC	2.00	.60
❑ 210 Lance Berkman FC	2.00	.60
❑ 211 Rafael Palmeiro FC	2.00	.60
❑ 212 Ichiro Suzuki FC	5.00	1.50
❑ 213 Bob Abreu FC	2.00	.60
❑ 214 Mark Mulder FC	2.00	.60
❑ 215 Roy Oswalt FC	2.00	.60
❑ 216 Mike Sweeney FC	2.00	.60
❑ 217 Paul LoDuca FC	2.00	.60
❑ 218 Aramis Ramirez FC	2.00	.60
❑ 219 Randy Johnson FC	2.50	.75
❑ 220 Albert Pujols FC	5.00	1.50

2002 Donruss Rookies

	Nm-Mt	Ex-Mt
COMPLETE SET (110)	40.00	12.00

❑ 1 Kazuhisa Ishii RC 1.50 .45
❑ 2 P.J. Bevis RC .40 .12
❑ 3 Jason Simontacchi RC .60 .18
❑ 4 John Lackey .25 .07
❑ 5 Travis Driskill RC .40 .12
❑ 6 Carl Sadler RC .40 .12
❑ 7 Tim Kalita RC .40 .12
❑ 8 Nelson Castro RC .40 .12
❑ 9 Francis Beltran RC .40 .12
❑ 10 So Taguchi RC .60 .18
❑ 11 Ryan Bukvich RC .60 .18
❑ 12 Brian Fitzgerald RC .40 .12
❑ 13 Kevin Frederick RC .40 .12
❑ 14 Chone Figgins RC .40 .12
❑ 15 Marlon Byrd .40 .12
❑ 16 Ron Calloway RC .40 .12
❑ 17 Jason Lane .25 .07
❑ 18 Satoru Komiyama RC .40 .12
❑ 19 John Ennis RC .40 .12
❑ 20 Juan Brito RC .40 .12
❑ 21 Gustavo Chacin RC .40 .12
❑ 22 Josh Bard RC .40 .12
❑ 23 Brett Myers .40 .12
❑ 24 Mike Smith RC .40 .12
❑ 25 Eric Hinske .25 .07
❑ 26 Jake Peavy .40 .12
❑ 27 Todd Donovan RC .40 .12
❑ 28 Luis Ugueto RC .40 .12
❑ 29 Corey Thurman RC .40 .12
❑ 30 Takahito Nomura RC .40 .12
❑ 31 Andy Shibilo RC .40 .12
❑ 32 Mike Crudale RC .40 .12
❑ 33 Earl Snyder RC .40 .12
❑ 34 Brian Tallet RC .60 .18
❑ 35 Miguel Asencio RC .40 .12
❑ 36 Felix Escalona RC .40 .12
❑ 37 Drew Henson .40 .12
❑ 38 Steve Kent RC .40 .12
❑ 39 Rene Reyes RC .40 .12
❑ 40 Edwin Almonte RC .40 .12
❑ 41 Chris Snelling RC 1.25 .35
❑ 42 Franklyn German RC .40 .12
❑ 43 Jeriome Robertson RC .60 .18
❑ 44 Colin Young RC .40 .12
❑ 45 Jeremy Lambert RC .40 .12
❑ 46 Kirk Saarloos RC 1.00 .30
❑ 47 Matt Childers RC .40 .12
❑ 48 Justin Wayne .25 .07
❑ 49 Jose Valverde RC .60 .18
❑ 50 Wily Mo Pena .40 .12
❑ 51 Victor Alvarez RC .40 .12
❑ 52 Julius Matos RC .40 .12
❑ 53 Aaron Cook RC .60 .18
❑ 54 Jeff Austin RC .40 .12
❑ 55 Adrian Burnside RC .40 .12
❑ 56 Brandon Puffer RC .40 .12
❑ 57 Jeremy Hill RC .40 .12
❑ 58 Jaime Cerda RC .40 .12
❑ 59 Aaron Guiel RC .60 .18
❑ 60 Ron Chiavacci .25 .07
❑ 61 Kevin Cash RC .40 .12
❑ 62 Elio Serrano RC .40 .12
❑ 63 Julio Mateo RC .40 .12
❑ 64 Cam Esslinger RC .40 .12
❑ 65 Ken Huckaby RC .40 .12
❑ 66 Will Nieves RC .40 .12
❑ 67 Luis Martinez RC .60 .18
❑ 68 Scotty Layfield RC .40 .12
❑ 69 Jeremy Guthrie RC 1.50 .45
❑ 70 Hansel Izquierdo RC .40 .12
❑ 71 Shane Nance RC .40 .12
❑ 72 Jeff Baker RC 2.50 .75
❑ 73 Cliff Bartosh RC .40 .12
❑ 74 Mitch Wylie RC .40 .12
❑ 75 Oliver Perez RC 1.25 .35
❑ 76 Matt Thornton RC .40 .12
❑ 77 John Foster RC .40 .12
❑ 78 Joe Borchard .40 .12
❑ 79 Eric Junge RC .40 .12
❑ 80 Jorge Sosa RC .40 .12
❑ 81 Runelvys Hernandez RC 1.00 .30
❑ 82 Kevin Mench .25 .07
❑ 83 Ben Kozlowski RC .40 .12
❑ 84 Trey Hodges RC .60 .18
❑ 85 Reed Johnson RC .60 .18
❑ 86 Eric Eckenstahler RC .40 .12
❑ 87 Franklin Nunez RC .40 .12
❑ 88 Victor Martinez .40 .12
❑ 89 Kevin Gryboski RC .40 .12
❑ 90 Jason Jennings .25 .07
❑ 91 Jim Rushford RC .40 .12
❑ 92 Jeremy Ward RC .40 .12
❑ 93 Adam Walker RC .40 .12
❑ 94 Freddy Sanchez RC 1.00 .30
❑ 95 Wilson Valdez RC .40 .12
❑ 96 Lee Gardner RC .40 .12
❑ 97 Eric Good RC .40 .12
❑ 98 Hank Blalock .75 .23
❑ 99 Mark Corey RC .40 .12
❑ 100 Jason Davis RC 1.00 .30
❑ 101 Mike Gonzalez RC .40 .12
❑ 102 David Ross RC .40 .12
❑ 103 Tyler Yates RC .40 .12
❑ 104 Cliff Lee RC 1.00 .30
❑ 105 Mike Moriarty RC .40 .12
❑ 106 Josh Hancock RC .40 .12
❑ 107 Jason Beverlin RC .40 .12
❑ 108 Clay Condrey RC .40 .12
❑ 109 Shawn Sedlacek RC .40 .12
❑ 110 Sean Burroughs .40 .12

2003 Donruss

	Nm-Mt	Ex-Mt
COMPLETE SET (400)	50.00	15.00
COMMON CARD (71-400)	.30	.09
COMMON CARD (1-20)	.50	.15
COMMON CARD (21-70)	.50	.15

❑ 1 Vladimir Guerrero DK .75 .23
❑ 2 Derek Jeter DK 2.00 .60
❑ 3 Adam Dunn DK .50 .15
❑ 4 Greg Maddux DK 1.50 .45
❑ 5 Lance Berkman DK .50 .15
❑ 6 Ichiro Suzuki DK 1.50 .45
❑ 7 Mike Piazza DK 1.25 .35
❑ 8 Alex Rodriguez DK 1.50 .45
❑ 9 Tom Glavine DK .75 .23
❑ 10 Randy Johnson DK .75 .23
❑ 11 Nomar Garciaparra DK 1.50 .45
❑ 12 Jason Giambi DK .75 .23
❑ 13 Sammy Sosa DK 1.25 .35
❑ 14 Barry Zito DK .50 .15
❑ 15 Chipper Jones DK .75 .23
❑ 16 Magglio Ordonez DK .50 .15
❑ 17 Larry Walker DK .50 .15
❑ 18 Alfonso Soriano DK .75 .23
❑ 19 Curt Schilling DK .50 .15
❑ 20 Barry Bonds DK 2.00 .60
❑ 21 Joe Borchard RR .50 .15
❑ 22 Chris Snelling RR .50 .15
❑ 23 Brian Tallet RR .50 .15
❑ 24 Cliff Lee RR .50 .15
❑ 25 Freddy Sanchez RR .50 .15
❑ 26 Chone Figgans RR .50 .15
❑ 27 Kevin Cash RR .50 .15
❑ 28 Josh Bard RR .50 .15
❑ 29 Jeriome Robertson RR .50 .15
❑ 30 Jeremy Hill RR .50 .15
❑ 31 Shane Nance RR .50 .15
❑ 32 Jake Peavy RR .50 .15
❑ 33 Trey Hodges RR .50 .15
❑ 34 Eric Eckenstahler RR .50 .15
❑ 35 Jim Rushford RR .50 .15
❑ 36 Oliver Perez RR .50 .15
❑ 37 Kirk Saarloos RR .50 .15
❑ 38 Hank Blalock RR .75 .23
❑ 39 Francisco Rodriguez RR .50 .15
❑ 40 Runelvys Hernandez RR .50 .15
❑ 41 Aaron Cook RR .50 .15
❑ 42 Josh Hancock RR .50 .15
❑ 43 P.J. Bevis RR .50 .15
❑ 44 Jon Adkins RR .50 .15
❑ 45 Tim Kalita RR .50 .15
❑ 46 Nelson Castro RR .50 .15
❑ 47 Colin Young RR .50 .15
❑ 48 Adrian Burnside RR .50 .15
❑ 49 Luis Martinez RR .50 .15
❑ 50 Pete Zamora RR .50 .15
❑ 51 Todd Donovan RR .50 .15
❑ 52 Jeremy Ward RR .50 .15
❑ 53 Wilson Valdez RR .50 .15
❑ 54 Eric Good RR .50 .15
❑ 55 Jeff Baker RR .50 .15
❑ 56 Mitch Wylie RR .50 .15
❑ 57 Ron Calloway RR .50 .15
❑ 58 Jose Valverde RR .50 .15
❑ 59 Jason Davis RR .50 .15
❑ 60 Scotty Layfield RR .50 .15
❑ 61 Matt Thornton RR .50 .15
❑ 62 Adam Walker RR .50 .15
❑ 63 Gustavo Chacin RR .50 .15
❑ 64 Ron Chiavacci RR .50 .15
❑ 65 Wiki Nieves RR .50 .15
❑ 66 Cliff Bartosh RR .50 .15
❑ 67 Mike Gonzalez RR .50 .15
❑ 68 Justin Wayne RR .50 .15
❑ 69 Eric Junge RR .50 .15
❑ 70 Ben Kozlowski RR .50 .15
❑ 71 Darin Erstad .30 .09
❑ 72 Garret Anderson .30 .09
❑ 73 Troy Glaus .50 .15
❑ 74 David Eckstein .30 .09
❑ 75 Adam Kennedy .30 .09
❑ 76 Kevin Appier .30 .09
❑ 77 Jarrod Washburn .30 .09
❑ 78 Scott Spiezio .30 .09
❑ 79 Tim Salmon .50 .15
❑ 80 Ramon Ortiz .30 .09
❑ 81 Bengie Molina .30 .09
❑ 82 Brad Fullmer .30 .09
❑ 83 Troy Percival .30 .09
❑ 84 David Segui .30 .09
❑ 85 Jay Gibbons .30 .09
❑ 86 Tony Batista .30 .09
❑ 87 Scott Erickson .30 .09
❑ 88 Jeff Conine .30 .09
❑ 89 Melvin Mora .30 .09
❑ 90 Buddy Groom .30 .09
❑ 91 Rodrigo Lopez .30 .09
❑ 92 Marty Cordova .30 .09
❑ 93 Geronimo Gil .30 .09
❑ 94 Kenny Lofton .30 .09
❑ 95 Shea Hillenbrand .30 .09
❑ 96 Manny Ramirez .30 .09
❑ 97 Pedro Martinez .75 .23
❑ 98 Nomar Garciaparra 1.50 .45
❑ 99 Rickey Henderson 1.25 .35
❑ 100 Johnny Damon .30 .09
❑ 101 Trot Nixon .30 .09
❑ 102 Derek Lowe .30 .09
❑ 103 Hee Seop Choi .30 .09
❑ 104 Mark Teixeira .50 .15
❑ 105 Tim Wakefield .30 .09
❑ 106 Jason Varitek .30 .09
❑ 107 Frank Thomas .75 .23
❑ 108 Joe Crede .30 .09
❑ 109 Magglio Ordonez .30 .09
❑ 110 Ray Durham .30 .09
❑ 111 Mark Buehrle .30 .09
❑ 112 Paul Konerko .30 .09
❑ 113 Jose Valentin .30 .09
❑ 114 Carlos Lee .30 .09
❑ 115 Royce Clayton .30 .09
❑ 116 C.C. Sabathia .30 .09
❑ 117 Ellis Burks .30 .09
❑ 118 Omar Vizquel .30 .09
❑ 119 Jim Thome .75 .23
❑ 120 Matt Lawton .30 .09
❑ 121 Travis Fryman .30 .09

❑ 122 Earl Snyder .30 .09
❑ 123 Ricky Gutierrez .30 .09
❑ 124 Einar Diaz .30 .09
❑ 125 Danys Baez .30 .09
❑ 126 Robert Fick .30 .09
❑ 127 Bobby Higginson .30 .09
❑ 128 Steve Sparks .30 .09
❑ 129 Mike Rivera .30 .09
❑ 130 Wendell Magee .30 .09
❑ 131 Randall Simon .30 .09
❑ 132 Carlos Pena .30 .09
❑ 133 Mark Redman .30 .09
❑ 134 Juan Acevedo .30 .09
❑ 135 Mike Sweeney .30 .09
❑ 136 Aaron Guiel .30 .09
❑ 137 Carlos Beltran .30 .09
❑ 138 Joe Randa .30 .09
❑ 139 Paul Byrd .30 .09
❑ 140 Shawn Sedlacek .30 .09
❑ 141 Raul Ibanez .30 .09
❑ 142 Michael Tucker .30 .09
❑ 143 Torii Hunter .30 .09
❑ 144 Jacque Jones .30 .09
❑ 145 David Ortiz .30 .09
❑ 146 Corey Koskie .30 .09
❑ 147 Brad Radke .30 .09
❑ 148 Doug Mientkiewicz .30 .09
❑ 149 A.J. Pierzynski .30 .09
❑ 150 Dustan Mohr .30 .09
❑ 151 Michael Cuddyer .30 .09
❑ 152 Eddie Guardado .30 .09
❑ 153 Cristian Guzman .30 .09
❑ 154 Derek Jeter 2.00 .60
❑ 155 Bernie Williams .50 .15
❑ 156 Roger Clemens 1.50 .45
❑ 157 Mike Mussina .75 .23
❑ 158 Jorge Posada .50 .15
❑ 159 Alfonso Soriano .75 .23
❑ 160 Jason Giambi .75 .23
❑ 161 Robin Ventura .30 .09
❑ 162 Andy Pettitte .50 .15
❑ 163 David Wells .30 .09
❑ 164 Nick Johnson .30 .09
❑ 165 Jeff Weaver .30 .09
❑ 166 Raul Mondesi .30 .09
❑ 167 Rondell White .30 .09
❑ 168 Tim Hudson .30 .09
❑ 169 Barry Zito .50 .15
❑ 170 Mark Mulder .30 .09
❑ 171 Miguel Tejada .30 .09
❑ 172 Eric Chavez .30 .09
❑ 173 Billy Koch .30 .09
❑ 174 Jermaine Dye .30 .09
❑ 175 Scott Hatteberg .30 .09
❑ 176 Terrence Long .30 .09
❑ 177 David Justice .30 .09
❑ 178 Ramon Hernandez .30 .09
❑ 179 Ted Lilly .30 .09
❑ 180 Ichiro Suzuki 1.50 .45
❑ 181 Edgar Martinez .50 .15
❑ 182 Mike Cameron .30 .09
❑ 183 John Olerud .30 .09
❑ 184 Bret Boone .30 .09
❑ 185 Dan Wilson .30 .09
❑ 186 Freddy Garcia .30 .09
❑ 187 Jamie Moyer .30 .09
❑ 188 Carlos Guillen .30 .09
❑ 189 Ruben Sierra .30 .09
❑ 190 Kazuhiro Sasaki .30 .09
❑ 191 Mark McLemore .30 .09
❑ 192 John Halama .30 .09
❑ 193 Joel Pineiro .30 .09
❑ 194 Jeff Cirillo .30 .09
❑ 195 Rafael Soriano .30 .09
❑ 196 Ben Grieve .30 .09
❑ 197 Aubrey Huff .30 .09
❑ 198 Steve Cox .30 .09
❑ 199 Toby Hall .30 .09
❑ 200 Randy Winn .30 .09
❑ 201 Brent Abernathy .30 .09
❑ 202 Chris Gomez .30 .09
❑ 203 John Flaherty .30 .09
❑ 204 Paul Wilson .30 .09
❑ 205 Chan Ho Park .30 .09
❑ 206 Alex Rodriguez 1.50 .45
❑ 207 Juan Gonzalez .75 .23
❑ 208 Rafael Palmeiro .50 .15
❑ 209 Ivan Rodriguez .75 .23
❑ 210 Rusty Greer .30 .09
❑ 211 Kenny Rogers .30 .09
❑ 212 Ismael Valdes .30 .09
❑ 213 Frank Catalanotto .30 .09
❑ 214 Hank Blalock .50 .15
❑ 215 Michael Young .30 .09
❑ 216 Kevin Mench .30 .09
❑ 217 Herbert Perry .30 .09
❑ 218 Gabe Kapler .30 .09
❑ 219 Carlos Delgado .30 .09
❑ 220 Shannon Stewart .30 .09
❑ 221 Eric Hinske .30 .09
❑ 222 Roy Halladay .30 .09
❑ 223 Felipe Lopez .30 .09
❑ 224 Vernon Wells .30 .09
❑ 225 Josh Phelps .30 .09
❑ 226 Jose Cruz .30 .09
❑ 227 Curt Schilling .50 .15
❑ 228 Randy Johnson .75 .23
❑ 229 Luis Gonzalez .30 .09
❑ 230 Mark Grace .75 .23
❑ 231 Junior Spivey .30 .09
❑ 232 Tony Womack .30 .09
❑ 233 Matt Williams .30 .09
❑ 234 Steve Finley .30 .09
❑ 235 Byung-Hyun Kim .30 .09
❑ 236 Craig Counsell .30 .09
❑ 237 Greg Maddux 1.50 .45
❑ 238 Tom Glavine .75 .23
❑ 239 John Smoltz .50 .15
❑ 240 Chipper Jones .75 .23
❑ 241 Gary Sheffield .30 .09
❑ 242 Andruw Jones .50 .15
❑ 243 Vinny Castilla .30 .09
❑ 244 Damian Moss .30 .09
❑ 245 Rafael Furcal .30 .09
❑ 246 Javy Lopez .30 .09
❑ 247 Kevin Millwood .30 .09
❑ 248 Kerry Wood .75 .23
❑ 249 Fred McGriff .50 .15
❑ 250 Sammy Sosa 1.25 .35
❑ 251 Alex Gonzalez .30 .09
❑ 252 Corey Patterson .30 .09
❑ 253 Moises Alou .30 .09
❑ 254 Juan Cruz .30 .09
❑ 255 Jon Lieber .30 .09
❑ 256 Matt Clement .30 .09
❑ 257 Mark Prior 1.50 .45
❑ 258 Ken Griffey Jr. 1.25 .35
❑ 259 Barry Larkin .75 .23
❑ 260 Adam Dunn .50 .15
❑ 261 Sean Casey .30 .09
❑ 262 Jose Rijo .30 .09
❑ 263 Elmer Dessens .30 .09
❑ 264 Austin Kearns .50 .15
❑ 265 Corky Miller .30 .09
❑ 266 Todd Walker .30 .09
❑ 267 Chris Reitsma .30 .09
❑ 268 Ryan Dempster .30 .09
❑ 269 Aaron Boone .30 .09
❑ 270 Danny Graves .30 .09
❑ 271 Brandon Larson .30 .09
❑ 272 Larry Walker .50 .15
❑ 273 Todd Helton .50 .15
❑ 274 Juan Uribe .30 .09
❑ 275 Juan Pierre .30 .09
❑ 276 Mike Hampton .30 .09
❑ 277 Todd Zeile .30 .09
❑ 278 Todd Hollandsworth .30 .09
❑ 279 Jason Jennings .30 .09
❑ 280 Josh Beckett .50 .15
❑ 281 Mike Lowell .30 .09
❑ 282 Derrek Lee .30 .09
❑ 283 A.J. Burnett .30 .09
❑ 284 Luis Castillo .30 .09
❑ 285 Tim Raines .30 .09
❑ 286 Preston Wilson .30 .09
❑ 287 Juan Encarnacion .30 .09
❑ 288 Charles Johnson .30 .09
❑ 289 Jeff Bagwell .50 .15
❑ 290 Craig Biggio .50 .15
❑ 291 Lance Berkman .30 .09
❑ 292 Daryle Ward .30 .09
❑ 293 Roy Oswalt .30 .09
❑ 294 Richard Hidalgo .30 .09
❑ 295 Octavio Dotel .30 .09
❑ 296 Wade Miller .30 .09
❑ 297 Julio Lugo .30 .09
❑ 298 Billy Wagner .30 .09
❑ 299 Shawn Green .30 .09
❑ 300 Adrian Beltre .30 .09
❑ 301 Paul Lo Duca .30 .09
❑ 302 Eric Karros .30 .09
❑ 303 Kevin Brown .30 .09
❑ 304 Hideo Nomo .75 .23
❑ 305 Odalis Perez .30 .09
❑ 306 Eric Gagne .50 .15
❑ 307 Brian Jordan .30 .09
❑ 308 Cesar Izturis .30 .09
❑ 309 Mark Grudzielanek .30 .09
❑ 310 Kazuhisa Ishii .30 .09
❑ 311 Geoff Jenkins .30 .09
❑ 312 Richie Sexson .30 .09
❑ 313 Jose Hernandez .30 .09
❑ 314 Ben Sheets .30 .09
❑ 315 Ruben Quevedo .30 .09
❑ 316 Jeffrey Hammonds .30 .09
❑ 317 Alex Sanchez .30 .09
❑ 318 Eric Young .30 .09
❑ 319 Takahito Nomura .30 .09
❑ 320 Vladimir Guerrero .75 .23
❑ 321 Jose Vidro .30 .09
❑ 322 Orlando Cabrera .30 .09
❑ 323 Michael Barrett .30 .09
❑ 324 Javier Vazquez .30 .09
❑ 325 Tony Armas Jr. .30 .09
❑ 326 Andres Galarraga .30 .09
❑ 327 Tomo Ohka .30 .09
❑ 328 Bartolo Colon .30 .09
❑ 329 Fernando Tatis .30 .09
❑ 330 Brad Wilkerson .30 .09
❑ 331 Masato Yoshii .30 .09
❑ 332 Mike Piazza 1.25 .35
❑ 333 Jeromy Burnitz .30 .09
❑ 334 Roberto Alomar .75 .23
❑ 335 Mo Vaughn .30 .09
❑ 336 Al Leiter .30 .09
❑ 337 Pedro Astacio .30 .09
❑ 338 Edgardo Alfonzo .30 .09
❑ 339 Armando Benitez .30 .09
❑ 340 Timo Perez .30 .09
❑ 341 Jay Payton .30 .09
❑ 342 Roger Cedeno .30 .09
❑ 343 Rey Ordonez .30 .09
❑ 344 Steve Trachsel .30 .09
❑ 345 Satoru Komiyama .30 .09
❑ 346 Scott Rolen .50 .15
❑ 347 Pat Burrell .30 .09
❑ 348 Bobby Abreu .30 .09
❑ 349 Mike Lieberthal .30 .09
❑ 350 Brandon Duckworth .30 .09
❑ 351 Jimmy Rollins .30 .09
❑ 352 Marlon Anderson .30 .09
❑ 353 Travis Lee .30 .09
❑ 354 Vicente Padilla .30 .09
❑ 355 Randy Wolf .30 .09
❑ 356 Jason Kendall .30 .09
❑ 357 Brian Giles .30 .09
❑ 358 Aramis Ramirez .30 .09
❑ 359 Pokey Reese .30 .09
❑ 360 Kip Wells .30 .09
❑ 361 Josh Fogg .30 .09
❑ 362 Mike Williams .30 .09
❑ 363 Jack Wilson .30 .09
❑ 364 Craig Wilson .30 .09
❑ 365 Kevin Young .30 .09
❑ 366 Ryan Klesko .30 .09
❑ 367 Phil Nevin .30 .09
❑ 368 Brian Lawrence .30 .09
❑ 369 Mark Kotsay .30 .09
❑ 370 Brett Tomko .30 .09
❑ 371 Trevor Hoffman .30 .09
❑ 372 Deivi Cruz .30 .09
❑ 373 Bubba Trammell .30 .09
❑ 374 Sean Burroughs .30 .09
❑ 375 Barry Bonds 2.00 .60
❑ 376 Jeff Kent .30 .09
❑ 377 Rich Aurilia .30 .09
❑ 378 Tsuyoshi Shinjo .30 .09
❑ 379 Benito Santiago .30 .09

		MINT	NRMT
❑ 380	Kirk Rueter	.30	.09
❑ 381	Livan Hernandez	.30	.09
❑ 382	Russ Ortiz	.30	.09
❑ 383	David Bell	.30	.09
❑ 384	Jason Schmidt	.30	.09
❑ 385	Reggie Sanders	.30	.09
❑ 386	J.T. Snow	.30	.09
❑ 387	Robb Nen	.30	.09
❑ 388	Ryan Jensen	.30	.09
❑ 389	Jim Edmonds	.30	.09
❑ 390	J.D. Drew	.30	.09
❑ 391	Albert Pujols	1.50	.45
❑ 392	Fernando Vina	.30	.09
❑ 393	Tino Martinez	.50	.15
❑ 394	Edgar Renteria	.30	.09
❑ 395	Matt Morris	.30	.09
❑ 396	Woody Williams	.30	.09
❑ 397	Jason Isringhausen	.30	.09
❑ 398	Placido Polanco	.30	.09
❑ 399	Eli Marrero	.30	.09
❑ 400	Jason Simontacchi	.30	.09

2004 Donruss

	MINT	NRMT
COMPLETE SET (400)	150.00	70.00
COMP.SET w/o SP's (300)	25.00	11.00
COMMON CARD (71-370)	.30	.14
COMMON CARD (1-25/371-400)	1.00	.45
COMMON CARD (26-70)	3.00	1.35

		MINT	NRMT
❑ 1	Derek Jeter DK	4.00	1.80
❑ 2	Greg Maddux DK	3.00	1.35
❑ 3	Albert Pujols DK	3.00	1.35
❑ 4	Ichiro Suzuki DK	3.00	1.35
❑ 5	Alex Rodriguez DK	3.00	1.35
❑ 6	Roger Clemens DK	3.00	1.35
❑ 7	Andruw Jones DK	1.00	.45
❑ 8	Barry Bonds DK	4.00	1.80
❑ 9	Jeff Bagwell DK	1.00	.45
❑ 10	Randy Johnson DK	1.50	.70
❑ 11	Scott Rolen DK	1.00	.45
❑ 12	Lance Berkman DK	1.00	.45
❑ 13	Barry Zito DK	1.50	.70
❑ 14	Manny Ramirez DK	1.00	.45
❑ 15	Carlos Delgado DK	1.00	.45
❑ 16	Alfonso Soriano DK	1.50	.70
❑ 17	Todd Helton DK	1.00	.45
❑ 18	Mike Mussina DK	1.50	.70
❑ 19	Austin Kearns DK	1.00	.45
❑ 20	Nomar Garciaparra DK	3.00	1.35
❑ 21	Chipper Jones DK	1.50	.70
❑ 22	Mark Prior DK	3.00	1.35
❑ 23	Jim Thome DK	1.50	.70
❑ 24	Vladimir Guerrero DK	1.50	.70
❑ 25	Pedro Martinez DK	1.50	.70
❑ 26	Sergio Mitre RR	3.00	1.35
❑ 27	Adam Loewen RR	3.00	1.35
❑ 28	Alfredo Gonzalez RR	3.00	1.35
❑ 29	Miguel Ojeda RR	3.00	1.35
❑ 30	Rosman Garcia RR	3.00	1.35
❑ 31	Arnie Munoz RR	3.00	1.35
❑ 32	Andrew Brown RR	3.00	1.35
❑ 33	Josh Hall RR	3.00	1.35
❑ 34	Josh Stewart RR	3.00	1.35
❑ 35	Clint Barmes RR	3.00	1.35
❑ 36	Brandon Webb RR	3.00	1.35
❑ 37	Chien-Ming Wang RR	3.00	1.35
❑ 38	Edgar Gonzalez RR	3.00	1.35
❑ 39	Alejandro Machado RR	3.00	1.35
❑ 40	Jeremy Griffiths RR	3.00	1.35
❑ 41	Craig Brazell RR	3.00	1.35
❑ 42	Daniel Cabrera RR	3.00	1.35
❑ 43	Fernando Cabrera RR	3.00	1.35
❑ 44	Termel Sledge RR	3.00	1.35
❑ 45	Rob Hammock RR	3.00	1.35
❑ 46	Francisco Rosario RR	3.00	1.35
❑ 47	Francisco Cruceta RR	3.00	1.35
❑ 48	Rett Johnson RR	3.00	1.35
❑ 49	Guillermo Quiroz RR	3.00	1.35
❑ 50	Hong-Chih Kuo RR	3.00	1.35
❑ 51	Ian Ferguson RR	3.00	1.35
❑ 52	Tim Olson RR	3.00	1.35
❑ 53	Todd Wellemeyer RR	3.00	1.35
❑ 54	Rich Fischer RR	3.00	1.35
❑ 55	Phil Seibel RR	3.00	1.35
❑ 56	Joe Valentine RR	3.00	1.35
❑ 57	Matt Kata RR	3.00	1.35
❑ 58	Michael Hessman RR	3.00	1.35
❑ 59	Michel Hernandez RR	3.00	1.35
❑ 60	Doug Waechter RR	3.00	1.35
❑ 61	Prentice Redman RR	3.00	1.35
❑ 62	Nook Logan RR	3.00	1.35
❑ 63	Oscar Villarreal RR	3.00	1.35
❑ 64	Pete LaForest RR	3.00	1.35
❑ 65	Matt Bruback RR	3.00	1.35
❑ 66	Dan Haren RR	3.00	1.35
❑ 67	Greg Aquino RR	3.00	1.35
❑ 68	Lew Ford RR	3.00	1.35
❑ 69	Jeff Duncan RR	3.00	1.35
❑ 70	Ryan Wagner RR	3.00	1.35
❑ 71	Bengie Molina	.30	.14
❑ 72	Brad Fullmer	.30	.14
❑ 73	Darin Erstad	.30	.14
❑ 74	David Eckstein	.30	.14
❑ 75	Garret Anderson	.30	.14
❑ 76	Jarrod Washburn	.30	.14
❑ 77	Kevin Appier	.30	.14
❑ 78	Scott Spiezio	.30	.14
❑ 79	Tim Salmon	.50	.23
❑ 80	Troy Glaus	.50	.23
❑ 81	Troy Percival	.30	.14
❑ 82	Jason Johnson	.30	.14
❑ 83	Jay Gibbons	.30	.14
❑ 84	Melvin Mora	.30	.14
❑ 85	Sidney Ponson	.30	.14
❑ 86	Tony Batista	.30	.14
❑ 87	Bill Mueller	.30	.14
❑ 88	Byung-Hyun Kim	.30	.14
❑ 89	David Ortiz	.30	.14
❑ 90	Derek Lowe	.30	.14
❑ 91	Johnny Damon	.30	.14
❑ 92	Casey Fossum	.30	.14
❑ 93	Manny Ramirez	.30	.14
❑ 94	Nomar Garciaparra	1.50	.70
❑ 95	Pedro Martinez	.75	.35
❑ 96	Todd Walker	.30	.14
❑ 97	Trot Nixon	.30	.14
❑ 98	Bartolo Colon	.30	.14
❑ 99	Carlos Lee	.30	.14
❑ 100	D'Angelo Jimenez	.30	.14
❑ 101	Esteban Loaiza	.30	.14
❑ 102	Frank Thomas	.75	.35
❑ 103	Joe Crede	.30	.14
❑ 104	Jose Valentin	.30	.14
❑ 105	Magglio Ordonez	.30	.14
❑ 106	Mark Buehrle	.30	.14
❑ 107	Paul Konerko	.30	.14
❑ 108	Brandon Phillips	.30	.14
❑ 109	C.C Sabathia	.30	.14
❑ 110	Ellis Burks	.30	.14
❑ 111	Jeremy Guthrie	.30	.14
❑ 112	Josh Bard	.30	.14
❑ 113	Matt Lawton	.30	.14
❑ 114	Milton Bradley	.30	.14
❑ 115	Omar Vizquel	.30	.14
❑ 116	Travis Hafner	.30	.14
❑ 117	Bobby Higginson	.30	.14
❑ 118	Carlos Pena	.30	.14
❑ 119	Dmitri Young	.30	.14
❑ 120	Eric Munson	.30	.14
❑ 121	Jeremy Bonderman	.30	.14
❑ 122	Nate Cornejo	.30	.14
❑ 123	Omar Infante	.30	.14
❑ 124	Ramon Santiago	.30	.14
❑ 125	Angel Berroa	.30	.14
❑ 126	Carlos Beltran	.30	.14
❑ 127	Desi Relaford	.30	.14
❑ 128	Jeremy Affeldt	.30	.14
❑ 129	Joe Randa	.30	.14
❑ 130	Ken Harvey	.30	.14
❑ 131	Mike MacDougal	.30	.14
❑ 132	Michael Tucker	.30	.14
❑ 133	Mike Sweeney	.30	.14
❑ 134	Raul Ibanez	.30	.14
❑ 135	Runelvys Hernandez	.30	.14
❑ 136	A.J. Pierzynski	.30	.14
❑ 137	Brad Radke	.30	.14
❑ 138	Corey Koskie	.30	.14
❑ 139	Cristian Guzman	.30	.14
❑ 140	Doug Mientkiewicz	.30	.14
❑ 141	Dustan Mohr	.30	.14
❑ 142	Jacque Jones	.30	.14
❑ 143	Kenny Rogers	.30	.14
❑ 144	Bobby Kielty	.30	.14
❑ 145	Kyle Lohse	.30	.14
❑ 146	Luis Rivas	.30	.14
❑ 147	Torii Hunter	.30	.14
❑ 148	Alfonso Soriano	.75	.35
❑ 149	Andy Pettitte	.50	.23
❑ 150	Bernie Williams	.50	.23
❑ 151	David Wells	.30	.14
❑ 152	Derek Jeter	2.00	.90
❑ 153	Hideki Matsui	1.50	.70
❑ 154	Jason Giambi	.75	.35
❑ 155	Jorge Posada	.50	.23
❑ 156	Jose Contreras	.30	.14
❑ 157	Mike Mussina	.75	.35
❑ 158	Nick Johnson	.30	.14
❑ 159	Robin Ventura	.30	.14
❑ 160	Roger Clemens	1.50	.70
❑ 161	Barry Zito	.75	.35
❑ 162	Chris Singleton	.30	.14
❑ 163	Eric Byrnes	.30	.14
❑ 164	Eric Chavez	.30	.14
❑ 165	Erubiel Durazo	.30	.14
❑ 166	Keith Foulke	.30	.14
❑ 167	Mark Ellis	.30	.14
❑ 168	Miguel Tejada	.30	.14
❑ 169	Mark Mulder	.30	.14
❑ 170	Ramon Hernandez	.30	.14
❑ 171	Ted Lilly	.30	.14
❑ 172	Terrence Long	.30	.14
❑ 173	Tim Hudson	.30	.14
❑ 174	Bret Boone	.30	.14
❑ 175	Carlos Guillen	.30	.14
❑ 176	Dan Wilson	.30	.14
❑ 177	Edgar Martinez	.50	.23
❑ 178	Freddy Garcia	.30	.14
❑ 179	Gil Meche	.30	.14
❑ 180	Ichiro Suzuki	1.50	.70
❑ 181	Jamie Moyer	.30	.14
❑ 182	Joel Pineiro	.30	.14
❑ 183	John Olerud	.30	.14
❑ 184	Mike Cameron	.30	.14
❑ 185	Randy Winn	.30	.14
❑ 186	Ryan Franklin	.30	.14
❑ 187	Kazuhiro Sasaki	.30	.14
❑ 188	Aubrey Huff	.30	.14
❑ 189	Carl Crawford	.30	.14
❑ 190	Joe Kennedy	.30	.14
❑ 191	Marlon Anderson	.30	.14
❑ 192	Rey Ordonez	.30	.14
❑ 193	Rocco Baldelli	1.25	.55
❑ 194	Toby Hall	.30	.14
❑ 195	Travis Lee	.30	.14
❑ 196	Alex Rodriguez	1.50	.70
❑ 197	Carl Everett	.30	.14
❑ 198	Chan Ho Park	.30	.14
❑ 199	Einar Diaz	.30	.14
❑ 200	Hank Blalock	.50	.23
❑ 201	Ismael Valdes	.30	.14
❑ 202	Juan Gonzalez	.75	.35
❑ 203	Mark Teixeira	.50	.23
❑ 204	Mike Young	.30	.14
❑ 205	Rafael Palmeiro	.50	.23
❑ 206	Carlos Delgado	.30	.14
❑ 207	Kelvim Escobar	.30	.14
❑ 208	Eric Hinske	.30	.14
❑ 209	Frank Catalanotto	.30	.14

❑ 210	Josh Phelps	.30	.14
❑ 211	Orlando Hudson	.30	.14
❑ 212	Roy Halladay	.30	.14
❑ 213	Shannon Stewart	.30	.14
❑ 214	Vernon Wells	.30	.14
❑ 215	Carlos Baerga	.30	.14
❑ 216	Curt Schilling	.50	.23
❑ 217	Junior Spivey	.30	.14
❑ 218	Luis Gonzalez	.30	.14
❑ 219	Lyle Overbay	.30	.14
❑ 220	Mark Grace	.75	.35
❑ 221	Matt Williams	.30	.14
❑ 222	Randy Johnson	.75	.35
❑ 223	Shea Hillenbrand	.30	.14
❑ 224	Steve Finley	.30	.14
❑ 225	Andruw Jones	.50	.23
❑ 226	Chipper Jones	.75	.35
❑ 227	Gary Sheffield	.30	.14
❑ 228	Greg Maddux	1.50	.70
❑ 229	Javy Lopez	.30	.14
❑ 230	John Smoltz	.50	.23
❑ 231	Marcus Giles	.30	.14
❑ 232	Mike Hampton	.30	.14
❑ 233	Rafael Furcal	.30	.14
❑ 234	Robert Fick	.30	.14
❑ 235	Russ Ortiz	.30	.14
❑ 236	Alex Gonzalez	.30	.14
❑ 237	Carlos Zambrano	.30	.14
❑ 238	Corey Patterson	.30	.14
❑ 239	Hee Seop Choi	.30	.14
❑ 240	Kerry Wood	.75	.35
❑ 241	Mark Bellhorn	.30	.14
❑ 242	Mark Prior	1.50	.70
❑ 243	Moises Alou	.30	.14
❑ 244	Sammy Sosa	1.25	.55
❑ 245	Aaron Boone	.30	.14
❑ 246	Adam Dunn	.50	.23
❑ 247	Austin Kearns	.50	.23
❑ 248	Barry Larkin	.75	.35
❑ 249	Felipe Lopez	.30	.14
❑ 250	Jose Guillen	.30	.14
❑ 251	Ken Griffey Jr.	1.25	.55
❑ 252	Jason LaRue	.30	.14
❑ 253	Scott Williamson	.30	.14
❑ 254	Sean Casey	.30	.14
❑ 255	Shawn Chacon	.30	.14
❑ 256	Chris Stynes	.30	.14
❑ 257	Jason Jennings	.30	.14
❑ 258	Jay Payton	.30	.14
❑ 259	Jose Hernandez	.30	.14
❑ 260	Larry Walker	.50	.23
❑ 261	Preston Wilson	.30	.14
❑ 262	Ronnie Belliard	.30	.14
❑ 263	Todd Helton	.50	.23
❑ 264	A.J. Burnett	.30	.14
❑ 265	Alex Gonzalez	.30	.14
❑ 266	Brad Penny	.30	.14
❑ 267	Derrek Lee	.30	.14
❑ 268	Ivan Rodriguez	.75	.35
❑ 269	Josh Beckett	.50	.23
❑ 270	Juan Encarnacion	.30	.14
❑ 271	Juan Pierre	.30	.14
❑ 272	Luis Castillo	.30	.14
❑ 273	Mike Lowell	.30	.14
❑ 274	Todd Hollandsworth	.30	.14
❑ 275	Billy Wagner	.30	.14
❑ 276	Brad Ausmus	.30	.14
❑ 277	Craig Biggio	.50	.23
❑ 278	Jeff Bagwell	.50	.23
❑ 279	Jeff Kent	.30	.14
❑ 280	Lance Berkman	.30	.14
❑ 281	Richard Hidalgo	.30	.14
❑ 282	Roy Oswalt	.30	.14
❑ 283	Wade Miller	.30	.14
❑ 284	Adrian Beltre	.30	.14
❑ 285	Brian Jordan	.30	.14
❑ 286	Cesar Izturis	.30	.14
❑ 287	Dave Roberts	.30	.14
❑ 288	Eric Gagne	.50	.23
❑ 289	Fred McGriff	.50	.23
❑ 290	Hideo Nomo	.75	.35
❑ 291	Kazuhisa Ishii	.30	.14
❑ 292	Kevin Brown	.30	.14
❑ 293	Paul Lo Duca	.30	.14
❑ 294	Shawn Green	.30	.14
❑ 295	Ben Sheets	.30	.14
❑ 296	Geoff Jenkins	.30	.14
❑ 297	Rey Sanchez	.30	.14
❑ 298	Richie Sexson	.30	.14
❑ 299	Wes Helms	.30	.14
❑ 300	Brad Wilkerson	.30	.14
❑ 301	Claudio Vargas	.30	.14
❑ 302	Endy Chavez	.30	.14
❑ 303	Fernando Tatis	.30	.14
❑ 304	Javier Vazquez	.30	.14
❑ 305	Jose Vidro	.30	.14
❑ 306	Michael Barrett	.30	.14
❑ 307	Orlando Cabrera	.30	.14
❑ 308	Tony Armas Jr.	.30	.14
❑ 309	Vladimir Guerrero	.75	.35
❑ 310	Zach Day	.30	.14
❑ 311	Al Leiter	.30	.14
❑ 312	Cliff Floyd	.30	.14
❑ 313	Jae Weong Seo	.30	.14
❑ 314	Jeromy Burnitz	.30	.14
❑ 315	Mike Piazza	1.25	.55
❑ 316	Mo Vaughn	.30	.14
❑ 317	Roberto Alomar	.75	.35
❑ 318	Roger Cedeno	.30	.14
❑ 319	Tom Glavine	.75	.35
❑ 320	Jose Reyes	.50	.23
❑ 321	Bobby Abreu	.30	.14
❑ 322	Brett Myers	.30	.14
❑ 323	David Bell	.30	.14
❑ 324	Jim Thome	.75	.35
❑ 325	Jimmy Rollins	.30	.14
❑ 326	Kevin Millwood	.30	.14
❑ 327	Marlon Byrd	.30	.14
❑ 328	Mike Lieberthal	.30	.14
❑ 329	Pat Burrell	.30	.14
❑ 330	Randy Wolf	.30	.14
❑ 331	Aramis Ramirez	.30	.14
❑ 332	Brian Giles	.30	.14
❑ 333	Jason Kendall	.30	.14
❑ 334	Kenny Lofton	.30	.14
❑ 335	Kip Wells	.30	.14
❑ 336	Kris Benson	.30	.14
❑ 337	Randall Simon	.30	.14
❑ 338	Reggie Sanders	.30	.14
❑ 339	Albert Pujols	1.50	.70
❑ 340	Edgar Renteria	.30	.14
❑ 341	Fernando Vina	.30	.14
❑ 342	J.D. Drew	.30	.14
❑ 343	Jim Edmonds	.30	.14
❑ 344	Matt Morris	.30	.14
❑ 345	Mike Matheny	.30	.14
❑ 346	Scott Rolen	.50	.23
❑ 347	Tino Martinez	.50	.23
❑ 348	Woody Williams	.30	.14
❑ 349	Brian Lawrence	.30	.14
❑ 350	Mark Kotsay	.30	.14
❑ 351	Mark Loretta	.30	.14
❑ 352	Ramon Vazquez	.30	.14
❑ 353	Rondell White	.30	.14
❑ 354	Ryan Klesko	.30	.14
❑ 355	Sean Burroughs	.30	.14
❑ 356	Trevor Hoffman	.30	.14
❑ 357	Xavier Nady	.30	.14
❑ 358	Andres Galarraga	.30	.14
❑ 359	Barry Bonds	2.00	.90
❑ 360	Benito Santiago	.30	.14
❑ 361	Deivi Cruz	.30	.14
❑ 362	Edgardo Alfonzo	.30	.14
❑ 363	J.T. Snow	.30	.14
❑ 364	Jason Schmidt	.30	.14
❑ 365	Kirk Rueter	.30	.14
❑ 366	Kurt Ainsworth	.30	.14
❑ 367	Marquis Grissom	.30	.14
❑ 368	Ray Durham	.30	.14
❑ 369	Rich Aurilia	.30	.14
❑ 370	Tim Worrell	.30	.14
❑ 371	Troy Glaus TC	1.00	.45
❑ 372	Melvin Mora TC	1.00	.45
❑ 373	Nomar Garciaparra TC	3.00	1.35
❑ 374	Magglio Ordonez TC	1.00	.45
❑ 375	Omar Vizquel TC	1.00	.45
❑ 376	Dmitri Young TC	1.00	.45
❑ 377	Mike Sweeney TC	1.00	.45
❑ 378	Torii Hunter TC	1.00	.45
❑ 379	Derek Jeter TC	4.00	1.80
❑ 380	Barry Zito TC	1.50	.70
❑ 381	Ichiro Suzuki TC	3.00	1.35
❑ 382	Rocco Baldelli TC	2.50	1.10
❑ 383	Alex Rodriguez TC	3.00	1.35
❑ 384	Carlos Delgado TC	1.00	.45
❑ 385	Randy Johnson TC	1.50	.70
❑ 386	Greg Maddux TC	3.00	1.35
❑ 387	Sammy Sosa TC	2.50	1.10
❑ 388	Ken Griffey Jr. TC	2.50	1.10
❑ 389	Todd Helton TC	1.00	.45
❑ 390	Ivan Rodriguez TC	1.50	.70
❑ 391	Jeff Bagwell TC	1.00	.45
❑ 392	Hideo Nomo TC	1.50	.70
❑ 393	Richie Sexson TC	1.00	.45
❑ 394	Vladimir Guerrero TC	1.50	.70
❑ 395	Mike Piazza TC	2.50	1.10
❑ 396	Jim Thome TC	1.50	.70
❑ 397	Jason Kendall TC	1.00	.45
❑ 398	Albert Pujols TC	3.00	1.35
❑ 399	Ryan Klesko TC	1.00	.45
❑ 400	Barry Bonds TC	4.00	1.80

2001 Donruss Baseball's Best Bronze

	Nm-Mt	Ex-Mt
COMP.FACT.SET (330)	200.00	60.00
*STARS 1-150: 2X TO 5X BASIC CARDS		-
*ROOKIES 151-200: .2X TO .5X BASIC		-
*FAN CLUB 201-220: .5X TO 1.2X BASIC		-

2003 Donruss Champions

	Nm-Mt	Ex-Mt
COMPLETE SET (309)	50.00	15.00

❑ 1	Adam Kennedy	.30	.09
❑ 2	Alfredo Amezaga	.30	.09
❑ 3	Chone Figgins	.30	.09
❑ 4	Darin Erstad	.50	.15
❑ 5	David Eckstein	.30	.09
❑ 6	Garret Anderson	.50	.15
❑ 7	Jarrod Washburn	.50	.15
❑ 8	Nolan Ryan Angels	4.00	1.20
❑ 9	Tim Salmon	.75	.23
❑ 10	Troy Glaus	.75	.23
❑ 11	Troy Percival	.50	.15
❑ 12	Curt Schilling	.75	.23
❑ 13	Junior Spivey	.30	.09
❑ 14	Luis Gonzalez	.50	.15
❑ 15	Mark Grace	1.25	.35

❑ 16 Randy Johnson 1.25 .35
❑ 17 Steve Finley .50 .15
❑ 18 Andruw Jones .75 .23
❑ 19 Chipper Jones 1.25 .35
❑ 20 Dale Murphy 1.25 .35
❑ 21 Gary Sheffield .50 .15
❑ 22 Greg Maddux 2.50 .75
❑ 23 John Smoltz .75 .23
❑ 24 Andy Pratt .30 .09
❑ 25 Adam LaRoche .50 .15
❑ 26 Trey Hodges .30 .09
❑ 27 Warren Spahn .75 .23
❑ 28 Cal Ripken 4.00 1.20
❑ 29 Ed Rogers .30 .09
❑ 30 Brian Roberts .30 .09
❑ 31 Geronimo Gil .30 .09
❑ 32 Jay Gibbons .50 .15
❑ 33 Josh Towers .30 .09
❑ 34 Casey Fossum .30 .09
❑ 35 Cliff Floyd .50 .15
❑ 36 Derek Lowe .50 .15
❑ 37 Fred Lynn .50 .15
❑ 38 Freddy Sanchez .50 .15
❑ 39 Manny Ramirez .50 .15
❑ 40 Nomar Garciaparra 2.50 .75
❑ 41 Pedro Martinez 1.25 .35
❑ 42 Rickey Henderson 2.00 .60
❑ 43 Shea Hillenbrand .50 .15
❑ 44 Trot Nixon .50 .15
❑ 45 Bobby Hill .30 .09
❑ 46 Corey Patterson .50 .15
❑ 47 Fred McGriff .75 .23
❑ 48 Hee Seop Choi .50 .15
❑ 49 Juan Cruz .30 .09
❑ 50 Kerry Wood 1.25 .35
❑ 51 Mark Prior 2.50 .75
❑ 52 Moises Alou .50 .15
❑ 53 Nic Jackson .30 .09
❑ 54 Ryne Sandberg 2.50 .75
❑ 55 Sammy Sosa 2.00 .60
❑ 56 Carlos Lee .50 .15
❑ 57 Corwin Malone .30 .09
❑ 58 Frank Thomas 1.25 .35
❑ 59 Joe Borchard .50 .15
❑ 60 Joe Crede .30 .09
❑ 61 Magglio Ordonez .50 .15
❑ 62 Mark Buehrle .50 .15
❑ 63 Paul Konerko .50 .15
❑ 64 Tim Hummel .30 .09
❑ 65 Jon Adkins .30 .09
❑ 66 Adam Dunn .75 .23
❑ 67 Austin Kearns .75 .23
❑ 68 Barry Larkin 1.25 .35
❑ 69 Jose Acevedo .30 .09
❑ 70 Corky Miller .30 .09
❑ 71 Eric Davis .50 .15
❑ 72 Ken Griffey Jr. 2.00 .60
❑ 73 Sean Casey .50 .15
❑ 74 Wily Mo Pena .50 .15
❑ 75 Bob Feller .75 .23
❑ 76 Brian Tallet .30 .09
❑ 77 C.C. Sabathia .50 .15
❑ 78 Cliff Lee .50 .15
❑ 79 Earl Snyder .30 .09
❑ 80 Ellis Burks .50 .15
❑ 81 Jeremy Guthrie .50 .15
❑ 82 Travis Hafner .30 .09
❑ 83 Luis Garcia .30 .09
❑ 84 Omar Vizquel .50 .15
❑ 85 Ricardo Rodriguez .30 .09
❑ 86 Ryan Church .50 .15
❑ 87 Victor Martinez .50 .15
❑ 88 Brandon Phillips .30 .09
❑ 89 Jack Cust .30 .09
❑ 90 Jason Jennings .30 .09
❑ 91 Jeff Baker .50 .15
❑ 92 Garrett Atkins .50 .15
❑ 93 Juan Uribe .30 .09
❑ 94 Larry Walker .75 .23
❑ 95 Rene Reyes .30 .09
❑ 96 Todd Helton .75 .23
❑ 97 Alan Trammell .50 .15
❑ 98 Fernando Rodney .30 .09
❑ 99 Carlos Pena .30 .09
❑ 100 Jack Morris .50 .15
❑ 101 Bobby Higginson .50 .15
❑ 102 Mike Maroth .30 .09
❑ 103 Robert Fick .50 .15
❑ 104 Jesus Medrano .30 .09
❑ 105 Josh Beckett .75 .23
❑ 106 Luis Castillo .50 .15
❑ 107 Mike Lowell .50 .15
❑ 108 Juan Pierre .50 .15
❑ 109 Josh Wilson .30 .09
❑ 110 Tim Redding .30 .09
❑ 111 Carlos Hernandez .30 .09
❑ 112 Craig Biggio .75 .23
❑ 113 Henri Stanley .30 .09
❑ 114 Jason Lane .30 .09
❑ 115 Jeff Bagwell .75 .23
❑ 116 John Buck .30 .09
❑ 117 Kirk Saarloos .50 .15
❑ 118 Lance Berkman .50 .15
❑ 119 Nolan Ryan Astros 4.00 1.20
❑ 120 Richard Hidalgo .50 .15
❑ 121 Rodrigo Rosario .30 .09
❑ 122 Roy Oswalt .50 .15
❑ 123 Tommy Whiteman .30 .09
❑ 124 Wade Miller .50 .15
❑ 125 Alexis Gomez .30 .09
❑ 126 Angel Berroa .50 .15
❑ 127 Brandon Berger .30 .09
❑ 128 Carlos Beltran .50 .15
❑ 129 George Brett 3.00 .90
❑ 130 Jimmy Gobble .50 .15
❑ 131 Dee Brown .30 .09
❑ 132 Mike Sweeney .50 .15
❑ 133 Raul Ibanez .50 .15
❑ 134 Runelvys Hernandez .50 .15
❑ 135 Adrian Beltre .50 .15
❑ 136 Brian Jordan .50 .15
❑ 137 Cesar Izturis .30 .09
❑ 138 Victor Alvarez .30 .09
❑ 139 Hideo Nomo 1.25 .35
❑ 140 Joe Thurston .30 .09
❑ 141 Kazuhisa Ishii .50 .15
❑ 142 Kevin Brown .50 .15
❑ 143 Odalis Perez .30 .09
❑ 144 Paul Lo Duca .50 .15
❑ 145 Shawn Green .50 .15
❑ 146 Ben Sheets .50 .15
❑ 147 Bill Hall .30 .09
❑ 148 Nick Neugebauer .30 .09
❑ 149 Richie Sexson .50 .15
❑ 150 Robin Yount 1.25 .35
❑ 151 Shane Nance .30 .09
❑ 152 Takahito Nomura .30 .09
❑ 153 A.J. Pierzynski .50 .15
❑ 154 Joe Mays .30 .09
❑ 155 Kirby Puckett 1.25 .35
❑ 156 Adam Johnson .30 .09
❑ 157 Rob Bowen .30 .09
❑ 158 Torii Hunter .50 .15
❑ 159 Andres Galarraga .50 .15
❑ 160 Endy Chavez .30 .09
❑ 161 Javier Vazquez .50 .15
❑ 162 Jose Vidro .50 .15
❑ 163 Vladimir Guerrero 1.25 .35
❑ 164 Dwight Gooden .75 .23
❑ 165 Mike Piazza 2.00 .60
❑ 166 Roberto Alomar 1.25 .35
❑ 167 Tom Glavine 1.25 .35
❑ 168 Alfonso Soriano 1.25 .35
❑ 169 Bernie Williams .75 .23
❑ 170 Brandon Claussen .50 .15
❑ 171 Derek Jeter 3.00 .90
❑ 172 Don Mattingly 3.00 .90
❑ 173 Drew Henson .50 .15
❑ 174 Jason Giambi 1.25 .35
❑ 175 Joe Torre MG .75 .23
❑ 176 Jorge Posada .75 .23
❑ 177 Mike Mussina 1.25 .35
❑ 178 Nick Johnson .50 .15
❑ 179 Roger Clemens 2.50 .75
❑ 180 Whitey Ford .75 .23
❑ 181 Adam Morrissey .50 .15
❑ 182 Barry Zito 1.25 .35
❑ 183 David Justice .50 .15
❑ 184 Eric Chavez .50 .15
❑ 185 Jermaine Dye .50 .15
❑ 186 Mark Mulder .50 .15
❑ 187 Miguel Tejada .50 .15
❑ 188 Reggie Jackson .75 .23
❑ 189 Terrence Long .50 .15
❑ 190 Tim Hudson .50 .15
❑ 191 Anderson Machado .30 .09
❑ 192 Bobby Abreu .50 .15
❑ 193 Brandon Duckworth .30 .09
❑ 194 Jim Thome 1.25 .35
❑ 195 Eric Junge .30 .09
❑ 196 Jeremy Giambi .30 .09
❑ 197 Johnny Estrada .30 .09
❑ 198 Jorge Padilla .30 .09
❑ 199 Marlon Byrd .50 .15
❑ 200 Mike Schmidt 2.50 .75
❑ 201 Pat Burrell .50 .15
❑ 202 Steve Carlton .75 .23
❑ 203 Aramis Ramirez .50 .15
❑ 204 Brian Giles .50 .15
❑ 205 Carlos Rivera .30 .09
❑ 206 Craig Wilson .30 .09
❑ 207 Dave Williams .30 .09
❑ 208 Jack Wilson .30 .09
❑ 209 Jose Castillo .50 .15
❑ 210 Kip Wells .30 .09
❑ 211 Roberto Clemente 3.00 .90
❑ 212 Walter Young .30 .09
❑ 213 Ben Howard .30 .09
❑ 214 Brian Lawrence .30 .09
❑ 215 Cliff Bartosh .30 .09
❑ 216 Dennis Tankersley .30 .09
❑ 217 Oliver Perez .50 .15
❑ 218 Phil Nevin .50 .15
❑ 219 Ryan Klesko .50 .15
❑ 220 Sean Burroughs .50 .15
❑ 221 Tony Gwynn 1.50 .45
❑ 222 Xavier Nady .50 .15
❑ 223 Mike Rivera .30 .09
❑ 224 Barry Bonds 3.00 .90
❑ 225 Benito Santiago .50 .15
❑ 226 Jason Schmidt .50 .15
❑ 227 Jeff Kent .50 .15
❑ 228 Kenny Lofton .50 .15
❑ 229 Rich Aurilia .50 .15
❑ 230 Robb Nen .50 .15
❑ 231 Tsuyoshi Shinjo .50 .15
❑ 232 Bret Boone .50 .15
❑ 233 Chris Snelling .50 .15
❑ 234 Edgar Martinez .75 .23
❑ 235 Freddy Garcia .50 .15
❑ 236 Ichiro Suzuki 2.50 .75
❑ 237 John Olerud .50 .15
❑ 238 Kazuhiro Sasaki .50 .15
❑ 239 Mike Cameron .50 .15
❑ 240 Rafael Soriano .30 .09
❑ 241 Albert Pujols 2.50 .75
❑ 242 J.D. Drew .50 .15
❑ 243 Jim Edmonds .50 .15
❑ 244 Ozzie Smith 1.25 .35
❑ 245 Scott Rolen .75 .23
❑ 246 So Taguchi .50 .15
❑ 247 Stan Musial 2.00 .60
❑ 248 Antonio Perez .30 .09
❑ 249 Aubrey Huff .50 .15
❑ 250 Dewon Brazelton .30 .09
❑ 251 Delvin James .30 .09
❑ 252 Joe Kennedy .30 .09
❑ 253 Toby Hall .30 .09
❑ 254 Alex Rodriguez 2.50 .75
❑ 255 Ben Kozlowski .30 .09
❑ 256 Gerald Laird .30 .09
❑ 257 Hank Blalock .75 .23
❑ 258 Ivan Rodriguez 1.25 .35
❑ 259 Juan Gonzalez 1.25 .35
❑ 260 Kevin Mench .30 .09
❑ 261 Mario Ramos .30 .09
❑ 262 Mark Teixeira .75 .23
❑ 263 Nolan Ryan Rangers 4.00 1.20
❑ 264 Rafael Palmeiro .75 .23
❑ 265 Alexis Rios .50 .15
❑ 266 Carlos Delgado .50 .15
❑ 267 Eric Hinske .30 .09
❑ 268 Josh Phelps .50 .15
❑ 269 Kevin Cash .30 .09
❑ 270 Orlando Hudson .30 .09
❑ 271 Roy Halladay .50 .15
❑ 272 Shannon Stewart .50 .15
❑ 273 Vernon Wells .50 .15

Card	Nm-Mt	Ex-Mt
❑ 274 Vinny Chulk	.30	.09
❑ 275 Jason Anderson	.30	.09
❑ 276 Craig Brazell RC	1.50	.45
❑ 277 Terrmel Sledge RC	1.00	.30
❑ 278 Ryan Cameron RC	.60	.18
❑ 279 Clint Barmes RC	1.00	.30
❑ 280 Jhonny Peralta RC	.60	.18
❑ 281 Todd Wellemeyer RC	1.00	.30
❑ 282 John Leicester RC	.60	.18
❑ 283 Brandon Webb RC	4.00	1.20
❑ 284 Tim Olson RC	1.50	.45
❑ 285 Matt Kata RC	2.00	.60
❑ 286 Rob Hammock RC	1.50	.45
❑ 287 Pete LaForest RC	1.00	.30
❑ 288 Nook Logan RC	.60	.18
❑ 289 Prentice Redman RC	.60	.18
❑ 290 Joe Valentine RC	.60	.18
❑ 291 Jose Contreras RC	3.00	.90
❑ 292 Josh Stewart RC	.60	.18
❑ 293 Mike Nicolas RC	.60	.18
❑ 294 Marshall McDougall	.30	.09
❑ 295 Travis Chapman	.30	.09
❑ 296 Jose Morban	.30	.09
❑ 297 Michael Hessman RC	.60	.18
❑ 298 Buddy Hernandez RC	.60	.18
❑ 299 Shane Victorino RC	.60	.18
❑ 300 Jason Dubois	.50	.15
❑ 301 Hideki Matsui RC	8.00	2.40
❑ 302 Ryan Wagner RC	-	
❑ 303 Adam Loewen RC	-	
❑ 304 Chien-Ming Wang RC	-	
❑ 305 Hong-Chih Kuo RC	-	
❑ 306 Delmon Young RC	-	
❑ 307 Dan Haren RC	-	
❑ 308 Rickie Weeks RC	-	
❑ 309 Ramon Nivar RC	-	

2001 Donruss Class of 2001

	Nm-Mt	Ex-Mt
COMP.SET w/o SP's (100)	25.00	7.50
COMMON CARD (1-100)	.40	.12
COMMON (101-200)	5.00	1.50
COMMON (201-300)	10.00	3.00
❑ 1 Alex Rodriguez	2.00	.60
❑ 2 Barry Bonds	2.50	.75
❑ 3 Vladimir Guerrero	1.00	.30
❑ 4 Jim Edmonds	.40	.12
❑ 5 Derek Jeter	2.50	.75
❑ 6 Jose Canseco	1.00	.30
❑ 7 Rafael Furcal	.40	.12
❑ 8 Cal Ripken	3.00	.90
❑ 9 Brad Radke	.40	.12
❑ 10 Miguel Tejada	.40	.12
❑ 11 Pat Burrell	.40	.12
❑ 12 Ken Griffey Jr.	1.50	.45
❑ 13 Cliff Floyd	.40	.12
❑ 14 Luis Gonzalez	.40	.12
❑ 15 Frank Thomas	1.00	.30
❑ 16 Mike Sweeney	.40	.12
❑ 17 Paul LoDuca	.40	.12
❑ 18 Lance Berkman	.40	.12
❑ 19 Tony Gwynn	1.25	.35
❑ 20 Chipper Jones	1.00	.30
❑ 21 Eric Chavez	.40	.12
❑ 22 Kerry Wood	1.00	.30
❑ 23 Jorge Posada	.60	.18
❑ 24 J.D. Drew	.40	.12
❑ 25 Garret Anderson	.40	.12
❑ 26 Mike Piazza	1.50	.45
❑ 27 Kenny Lofton	.40	.12
❑ 28 Mike Mussina	1.00	.30
❑ 29 Paul Konerko	.40	.12
❑ 30 Bernie Williams	.60	.18
❑ 31 Eric Milton	.40	.12
❑ 32 Shawn Green	.40	.12
❑ 33 Paul O'Neill	.60	.18
❑ 34 Juan Gonzalez	1.00	.30
❑ 35 Andres Galarraga	.40	.12
❑ 36 Gary Sheffield	.40	.12
❑ 37 Ben Grieve	.40	.12
❑ 38 Scott Rolen	.60	.18
❑ 39 Mark Grace	1.00	.30
❑ 40 Hideo Nomo	1.00	.30
❑ 41 Barry Zito	1.00	.30
❑ 42 Edgar Martinez	.60	.18
❑ 43 Jarrod Washburn	.40	.12
❑ 44 Greg Maddux	2.00	.60
❑ 45 Mark Buehrle	.40	.12
❑ 46 Larry Walker	.60	.18
❑ 47 Trot Nixon	.40	.12
❑ 48 Nomar Garciaparra	2.00	.60
❑ 49 Robert Fick	.40	.12
❑ 50 Sean Casey	.40	.12
❑ 51 Joe Mays	.40	.12
❑ 52 Roger Clemens	2.00	.60
❑ 53 Chan Ho Park	.40	.12
❑ 54 Carlos Delgado	.40	.12
❑ 55 Phil Nevin	.40	.12
❑ 56 Jason Giambi	1.00	.30
❑ 57 Raul Mondesi	.40	.12
❑ 58 Roberto Alomar	1.00	.30
❑ 59 Ryan Klesko	.40	.12
❑ 60 Andruw Jones	.60	.18
❑ 61 Gabe Kapler	.40	.12
❑ 62 Darin Erstad	.40	.12
❑ 63 Cristian Guzman	.40	.12
❑ 64 Kazuhiro Sasaki	.40	.12
❑ 65 Doug Mientkiewicz	.40	.12
❑ 66 Sammy Sosa	1.50	.45
❑ 67 Mike Hampton	.40	.12
❑ 68 Rickey Henderson	1.50	.45
❑ 69 Mark Mulder	.40	.12
❑ 70 Mark McGwire	2.50	.75
❑ 71 Freddy Garcia	.40	.12
❑ 72 Ivan Rodriguez	1.00	.30
❑ 73 Terrence Long	.40	.12
❑ 74 Jeff Bagwell	.60	.18
❑ 75 Moises Alou	.40	.12
❑ 76 Todd Helton	.60	.18
❑ 77 Preston Wilson	.40	.12
❑ 78 Pedro Martinez	1.00	.30
❑ 79 Bobby Abreu	.40	.12
❑ 80 Manny Ramirez	.40	.12
❑ 81 Jose Vidro	.40	.12
❑ 82 Randy Johnson	1.00	.30
❑ 83 Richie Sexson	.40	.12
❑ 84 Troy Glaus	.60	.18
❑ 85 Kevin Brown	.40	.12
❑ 86 Carlos Lee	.40	.12
❑ 87 Adrian Beltre	.40	.12
❑ 88 Brian Giles	.40	.12
❑ 89 Jermaine Dye	.40	.12
❑ 90 Craig Biggio	.60	.18
❑ 91 Richard Hidalgo	.40	.12
❑ 92 Magglio Ordonez	.40	.12
❑ 93 Aramis Ramirez	.40	.12
❑ 94 Jeff Kent	.40	.12
❑ 95 Curt Schilling	.60	.18
❑ 96 Tim Hudson	.40	.12
❑ 97 Fred McGriff	.60	.18
❑ 98 Barry Larkin	1.00	.30
❑ 99 Jim Thome	1.00	.30
❑ 100 Tom Glavine	1.00	.30
❑ 101 S.Douglass/1875 RC	5.00	1.50
❑ 102 R.MacKowiak/1875 RC	5.00	1.50
❑ 103 J.Fikac/1875 RC	5.00	1.50
❑ 104 Henry Mateo/1875 RC	5.00	1.50
❑ 105 G. Gil/1875 RC	5.00	1.50
❑ 106 R. Vazquez/1875 RC	5.00	1.50
❑ 107 P. Santana/1875 RC	5.00	1.50
❑ 108 Ryan Jensen/1875 RC	5.00	1.50
❑ 109 Paul Phillips/1625 RC	5.00	1.50
❑ 110 Saul Rivera/1875 RC	5.00	1.50
❑ 111 Larry Bigbie/1875	5.00	1.50
❑ 112 Josh Phelps/1875	5.00	1.50
❑ 113 Justin Kaye/1875 RC	5.00	1.50
❑ 114 Kris Keller/1625 RC	5.00	1.50
❑ 115 Adam Bernero/1625	5.00	1.50
❑ 116 V.Zambrano/1875 RC	5.00	1.50
❑ 117 Felipe Lopez/1875	5.00	1.50
❑ 118 B.Roberts/1875 RC	5.00	1.50
❑ 119 Kurt Ainsworth/1875	5.00	1.50
❑ 120 G.Perez/1625 RC	5.00	1.50
❑ 121 W.Guzman/1875 RC	5.00	1.50
❑ 122 D.Lewis/1875 RC	5.00	1.50
❑ 123 Nate Teut/1625 RC	5.00	1.50
❑ 124 M. Vargas/1625 RC	5.00	1.50
❑ 125 Brandon Inge/1875	5.00	1.50
❑ 126 T. Phelps/1875 RC	5.00	1.50
❑ 127 Les Walrond/1625 RC	5.00	1.50
❑ 128 J. Atchley/1875 RC	5.00	1.50
❑ 129 S. Clapp/1875 RC	5.00	1.50
❑ 130 Bret Prinz/1875 RC	5.00	1.50
❑ 131 Bert Snow/1875 RC	5.00	1.50
❑ 132 Joe Crede/1625	5.00	1.50
❑ 133 Nick Punto/1875 RC	5.00	1.50
❑ 134 C. Hernandez/1875	5.00	1.50
❑ 135 Ken Vining/1875 RC	5.00	1.50
❑ 136 Luis Pineda/1875 RC	5.00	1.50
❑ 137 W. Abreu/1625 RC	5.00	1.50
❑ 138 Matt Ginter/1625	5.00	1.50
❑ 139 Jason Smith/1875 RC	5.00	1.50
❑ 140 Gene Altman/1625 RC	5.00	1.50
❑ 141 B. Rogers/1875 RC	5.00	1.50
❑ 142 M.Cuddyer/1625	5.00	1.50
❑ 143 Mike Penney/1625 RC	5.00	1.50
❑ 144 S.Podsednik/1875 RC	20.00	6.00
❑ 145 Esix Snead/1625 RC	5.00	1.50
❑ 146 S.Watkins/1875 RC	5.00	1.50
❑ 147 O.Woodards/1625 RC	5.00	1.50
❑ 148 J.Deardorff/1775 RC	5.00	1.50
❑ 149 Eric Cyr/1875 RC	5.00	1.50
❑ 150 Blaine Neal/1625 RC	5.00	1.50
❑ 151 Ben Sheets/1875	5.00	1.50
❑ 152 S.Stewart/1875 RC	5.00	1.50
❑ 153 M.Koplove/1875 RC	5.00	1.50
❑ 154 Kyle Lohse/1875 RC	8.00	2.40
❑ 155 F. Rodney/1875 RC	5.00	1.50
❑ 156 Aubrey Huff/1625	5.00	1.50
❑ 157 Pablo Ozuna/1625	5.00	1.50
❑ 158 Bill Ortega/1625 RC	5.00	1.50
❑ 159 Toby Hall/1875	5.00	1.50
❑ 160 Kevin Olsen/1625 RC	5.00	1.50
❑ 161 Will Ohman/1625 RC	5.00	1.50
❑ 162 Nate Cornejo/1875	5.00	1.50
❑ 163 Jack Cust/1625	5.00	1.50
❑ 164 Juan Rivera/1875	5.00	1.50
❑ 165 J. Riggan/1875 RC	5.00	1.50
❑ 166 D.Mohr/1875 RC	5.00	1.50
❑ 167 Doug Nickle/1875 RC	5.00	1.50
❑ 168 C.Monroe/1625 RC	5.00	1.50
❑ 169 Jason Jennings/1625	5.00	1.50
❑ 170 Bart Miadich/1875 RC	5.00	1.50
❑ 171 Luis Rivas/1625	5.00	1.50
❑ 172 T. Christman/1875 RC	5.00	1.50
❑ 173 L. Hudson/1625 RC	5.00	1.50
❑ 174 Brett Jodie/1875 RC	5.00	1.50
❑ 175 Jorge Julio/1875 RC	5.00	1.50
❑ 176 David Espinosa/1625	5.00	1.50
❑ 177 Mike Maroth/1625 RC	5.00	1.50
❑ 178 Keith Ginter/1625	5.00	1.50
❑ 179 J. Moreno/1875 RC	5.00	1.50
❑ 180 B. Knight/1875 RC	5.00	1.50
❑ 181 Steve Lomasney/1625	5.00	1.50
❑ 182 J. Grabow/1625 RC	5.00	1.50
❑ 183 Steve Green/1875 RC	5.00	1.50
❑ 185 Bob File/1875 RC	5.00	1.50
❑ 186 Brent Abernathy/1625	5.00	1.50
❑ 187 M.Ensberg/1875 RC	10.00	3.00
❑ 188 Wily Mo Pena/1625	5.00	1.50
❑ 189 Ken Harvey/1875	5.00	1.50
❑ 190 Josh Pearce/1875 RC	5.00	1.50
❑ 191 Cesar Izturis/1625	5.00	1.50
❑ 192 Eric Hinske/1625 RC	8.00	2.40
❑ 193 Joe Beimel/1875 RC	5.00	1.50
❑ 194 Timo Perez/1775	5.00	1.50
❑ 195 Troy Mattes/1875 RC	5.00	1.50

		Nm-Mt	Ex-Mt
196	Eric Valent/1625	5.00	1.50
197	Ed Rogers/1875 RC	5.00	1.50
198	G.Balfour/1875 RC	5.00	1.50
199	Benito Baez/1875 RC	5.00	1.50
200	Vernon Wells/1875	5.00	1.50
201	J.Kennedy PH/525 RC	10.00	3.00
202	W.Betemit PH/525 RC	10.00	3.00
203	C.Parker PH/525 RC	10.00	3.00
204	J.Gibbons PH/525 RC	15.00	4.50
205	C.Garcia PH/425 RC	10.00	3.00
206	J.Wilson PH/525 RC	10.00	3.00
207	J.Estrada PH/425 RC	15.00	4.50
208	W.Ruan PH/425 RC	10.00	3.00
209	B.Duckworth PH/525 RC	10.00	3.00
210	W.Harris PH/625 RC	10.00	3.00
211	M.Byrd PH/525 RC	25.00	7.50
212	C.C. Sabathia PH/600	10.00	3.00
213	D.Tankersley PH/525 RC	10.00	3.00
214	B.Larson PH/425 RC	10.00	3.00
215	A.Gomez PH/425 RC	10.00	3.00
216	Bill Hall PH/525 RC	10.00	3.00
217	A.Perez PH/525 RC	10.00	3.00
218	J.Affeldt PH/425 RC	10.00	3.00
219	J.Spivey PH/625 RC	15.00	4.50
220	C.Fossum PH/425 RC	10.00	3.00
221	B.Lyon PH/625 RC	10.00	3.00
222	A.Santos PH/625 RC	10.00	3.00
223	L.Davis PH/625 RC	10.00	3.00
224	Zach Day PH/425 RC	15.00	4.50
225	D.Williams PH/425 RC	10.00	3.00
226	C.Crespo PH/625 RC	10.00	3.00
227	J.Acevedo PH/425 RC	10.00	3.00
228	T.Hafner PH/625 RC	15.00	4.50
229	O.Hudson PH/525 RC	15.00	4.50
230	J.Mieses PH/425 RC	10.00	3.00
231	R.Rodriguez PH/425 RC	10.00	3.00
232	A.Soriano PH/525	15.00	4.50
233	Jason Hart PH/525	10.00	3.00
234	E.Chavez PH/425 RC	10.00	3.00
235	D.James PH/525 RC	10.00	3.00
236	R.Drese PH/625 RC	10.00	3.00
237	J.Owens PH/425 RC	10.00	3.00
238	B.Voyles PH/425 RC	10.00	3.00
239	Nate Frese PH/425 RC	10.00	3.00
240	Josh Beckett PH/600	15.00	4.50
241	Roy Oswalt PH/525	15.00	4.50
242	J.Uribe PH/475 RC	10.00	3.00
243	C.Aldridge PH/425 RC	10.00	3.00
244	Adam Dunn PH/525	15.00	4.50
245	Bud Smith PH/425 RC	10.00	3.00
246	A.Hernandez PH/525 RC	10.00	3.00
247	M.Guerrier PH/625 RC	10.00	3.00
248	J.Rollins PH/625	10.00	3.00
249	W.Caceres PH/425 RC	10.00	3.00
250	J.Michaels PH/425 RC	10.00	3.00
251	I.Suzuki PH/625 RC	50.00	15.00
252	John Buck PH/525 RC	15.00	4.50
252	Adam Johnson PH/625	10.00	3.00
253	A.Torres PH/525 RC	10.00	3.00
254	A.Amezaga PH/625 RC	15.00	4.50
255	C.Miller PH/525 RC	10.00	3.00
256	R.Soriano PH/425 RC	15.00	4.50
257	D.Mendez PH/425 RC	10.00	3.00
258	V.Martinez PH/625 RC	25.00	7.50
259	C.Patterson PH/525	10.00	3.00
260	H.Ramirez PH/425 RC	15.00	4.50
261	E.Guzman PH/425 RC	10.00	3.00
262	Juan Diaz PH/425 RC	10.00	3.00
263	M.Rivera PH/625 RC	10.00	3.00
264	B.Lawrence PH/425 RC	10.00	3.00
265	J.Perez PH/425 RC	10.00	3.00
266	J.Nunez PH/425 RC	10.00	3.00
267	E.Bedard PH/625 RC	10.00	3.00
268	A.Pujols PH/525 RC	80.00	24.00
269	D.Sanchez PH/425 RC	10.00	3.00
270	C.Ransom PH/625 RC	10.00	3.00
271	G.Miller PH/425 RC	10.00	3.00
272	A.Pettyjohn PH/425 RC	10.00	3.00
273	T.Shinjo PH/625 RC	15.00	4.50
274	C.Vargas PH/425 RC	10.00	3.00
275	J.Duchscherer PH/625 RC	10.00	3.00
276	Tim Spooneybarger PH/625 RC	10.00	3.00
277	R.Bauer PH/625 RC	10.00	3.00
278	Josh Fogg PH/625 RC	10.00	3.00
279	B.Reith PH/425 RC	10.00	3.00
280	S.MacRae PH/625 RC	10.00	3.00
281	R.Ludwick PH/625 RC	10.00	3.00
282	E.Almonte PH/625 RC	10.00	3.00
283	J.Towers PH/625 RC	10.00	3.00
284	J. A.Pena PH/625 RC	10.00	3.00
285	D. Brous PH/425 RC	10.00	3.00
286	Erik Hiljus PH/625 RC	10.00	3.00
287	N.Neugebauer PH/525	10.00	3.00
288	J.Melian PH/625 RC	10.00	3.00
289	B.Sylvester PH/425 RC	10.00	3.00
290	Carlos Valderrama PH/425 RC	10.00	3.00
291	J.Cueto PH/625 RC	10.00	3.00
292	M.White PH/425 RC	10.00	3.00
293	N.Maness PH/425 RC	10.00	3.00
294	J.Lane PH/625 RC	15.00	4.50
295	B.Berger PH/625 RC	10.00	3.00
296	A.Berroa PH/525 RC	20.00	6.00
297	Juan Cruz PH/525 RC	10.00	3.00
298	D.Brazelton PH/525 RC	10.00	3.00
299	M.Prior PH/525 RC	60.00	18.00
300	M.Teixeira PH/525 RC	40.00	12.00

2001 Donruss Classics

	Nm-Mt	Ex-Mt
COMP.SET w/o SP's (100)	25.00	7.50
COMMON CARD (1-100)	.75	.23
COMMON (101-150)	10.00	3.00
COMMON (151-200)	4.00	1.20

		Nm-Mt	Ex-Mt
1	Alex Rodriguez	4.00	1.20
2	Barry Bonds	5.00	1.50
3	Cal Ripken	6.00	1.80
4	Chipper Jones	2.00	.60
5	Derek Jeter	5.00	1.50
6	Troy Glaus	1.25	.35
7	Frank Thomas	2.00	.60
8	Greg Maddux	4.00	1.20
9	Ivan Rodriguez	2.00	.60
10	Jeff Bagwell	1.25	.35
11	Cliff Floyd	.75	.23
12	Todd Helton	1.25	.35
13	Ken Griffey Jr.	3.00	.90
14	Manny Ramirez	.75	.23
15	Mark McGwire	5.00	1.50
16	Mike Piazza	3.00	.90
17	Nomar Garciaparra	4.00	1.20
18	Pedro Martinez	2.00	.60
19	Randy Johnson	2.00	.60
20	Rick Ankiel	.75	.23
21	Rickey Henderson	3.00	.90
22	Roger Clemens	4.00	1.20
23	Sammy Sosa	3.00	.90
24	Tony Gwynn	2.50	.75
25	Vladimir Guerrero	2.00	.60
26	Kazuhiro Sasaki	.75	.23
27	Roberto Alomar	2.00	.60
28	Barry Zito	2.00	.60
29	Pat Burrell	.75	.23
30	Harold Baines	.75	.23
31	Carlos Delgado	.75	.23
32	J.D. Drew	.75	.23
33	Jim Edmonds	.75	.23
34	Darin Erstad	.75	.23
35	Jason Giambi	2.00	.60
36	Tom Glavine	2.00	.60
37	Juan Gonzalez	2.00	.60
38	Mark Grace	2.00	.60
39	Shawn Green	.75	.23
40	Tim Hudson	.75	.23
41	Andruw Jones	1.25	.35
42	Jeff Kent	.75	.23
43	Barry Larkin	2.00	.60
44	Rafael Furcal	.75	.23
45	Mike Mussina	2.00	.60
46	Hideo Nomo	2.00	.60
47	Rafael Palmeiro	1.25	.35
48	Scott Rolen	1.25	.35
49	Gary Sheffield	.75	.23
50	Bernie Williams	1.25	.35
51	Bob Abreu	.75	.23
52	Edgardo Alfonzo	.75	.23
53	Edgar Martinez	1.25	.35
54	Magglio Ordonez	.75	.23
55	Kerry Wood	2.00	.60
56	Adrian Beltre	.75	.23
57	Lance Berkman	.75	.23
58	Kevin Brown	.75	.23
59	Sean Casey	.75	.23
60	Eric Chavez	.75	.23
61	Bartolo Colon	.75	.23
62	Johnny Damon	.75	.23
63	Jermaine Dye	.75	.23
64	Juan Encarnacion	.75	.23
65	Carl Everett	.75	.23
66	Brian Giles	.75	.23
67	Mike Hampton	.75	.23
68	Richard Hidalgo	.75	.23
69	Geoff Jenkins	.75	.23
70	Jacque Jones	.75	.23
71	Jason Kendall	.75	.23
72	Ryan Klesko	.75	.23
73	Chan Ho Park	.75	.23
74	Richie Sexson	.75	.23
75	Mike Sweeney	.75	.23
76	Fernando Tatis	.75	.23
77	Miguel Tejada	.75	.23
78	Jose Vidro	.75	.23
79	Larry Walker	1.25	.35
80	Preston Wilson	.75	.23
81	Craig Biggio	1.25	.35
82	Fred McGriff	1.25	.35
83	Jim Thome	2.00	.60
84	Garret Anderson	.75	.23
85	Russell Branyan	.75	.23
86	Tony Batista	.75	.23
87	Terrence Long	.75	.23
88	Brad Fullmer	.75	.23
89	Rusty Greer	.75	.23
90	Orlando Hernandez	.75	.23
91	Gabe Kapler	.75	.23
92	Paul Konerko	.75	.23
93	Carlos Lee	.75	.23
94	Kenny Lofton	.75	.23
95	Raul Mondesi	.75	.23
96	Jorge Posada	1.25	.35
97	Tim Salmon	1.25	.35
98	Greg Vaughn	.75	.23
99	Mo Vaughn	.75	.23
100	Omar Vizquel	.75	.23
101	Aubrey Huff SP	10.00	3.00
102	Jimmy Rollins SP	10.00	3.00
103	Cory Aldridge SP RC	10.00	3.00
104	Wilmy Caceres SP RC	10.00	3.00
105	Josh Beckett SP	15.00	4.50
106	Wilson Betemit SP RC	10.00	3.00
107	Timo Perez SP	10.00	3.00
108	Albert Pujols SP RC	80.00	24.00
109	Bud Smith SP RC	10.00	3.00
110	Jack Wilson SP RC	10.00	3.00
111	Alex Escobar SP	10.00	3.00
112	J. Estrada SP RC	15.00	4.50
113	Pedro Feliz SP	10.00	3.00
114	Nate Frese SP RC	10.00	3.00
115	Carlos Garcia SP RC	10.00	3.00
116	Brandon Larson SP RC	10.00	3.00
117	Alexis Gomez SP RC	10.00	3.00
118	Jason Hart SP	10.00	3.00
119	Adam Dunn SP	15.00	4.50
120	Marcus Giles SP	10.00	3.00
121	C. Parker SP RC	10.00	3.00
122	J.Melian SP RC	10.00	3.00
123	Endy Chavez SP RC	10.00	3.00

No.	Player	Nm-Mt	Ex-Mt
❑ 124	A.Hernandez SP RC	10.00	3.00
❑ 125	Joe Kennedy SP RC	10.00	3.00
❑ 126	Jose Mieses SP RC	10.00	3.00
❑ 127	C.C. Sabathia SP	10.00	3.00
❑ 128	Eric Munson SP	10.00	3.00
❑ 129	Xavier Nady SP	10.00	3.00
❑ 130	H. Ramirez SP RC	15.00	4.50
❑ 131	Abraham Nunez SP	10.00	3.00
❑ 132	Jose Ortiz SP	10.00	3.00
❑ 133	Jeremy Owens SP RC	10.00	3.00
❑ 134	Claudio Vargas SP RC	10.00	3.00
❑ 135	Corey Patterson SP	10.00	3.00
❑ 136	Andres Torres SP RC	10.00	3.00
❑ 137	Ben Sheets SP	10.00	3.00
❑ 138	Joe Crede SP	10.00	3.00
❑ 139	A.Pettyjohn SP RC	10.00	3.00
❑ 140	E.Guzman SP RC	10.00	3.00
❑ 141	Jay Gibbons SP RC	15.00	4.50
❑ 142	Wilkin Ruan SP RC	10.00	3.00
❑ 143	Tsuyoshi Shinjo SP RC	15.00	4.50
❑ 144	Alfonso Soriano SP	15.00	4.50
❑ 145	Nick Johnson SP	10.00	3.00
❑ 146	Ichiro Suzuki SP RC	60.00	18.00
❑ 147	Juan Uribe SP RC	10.00	3.00
❑ 148	Jack Cust SP	10.00	3.00
❑ 149	C.Valderrama SP RC	10.00	3.00
❑ 150	Matt White SP RC	10.00	3.00
❑ 151	Hank Aaron LGD	15.00	4.50
❑ 152	Ernie Banks LGD	6.00	1.80
❑ 153	Johnny Bench LGD	6.00	1.80
❑ 154	George Brett LGD	15.00	4.50
❑ 155	Lou Brock LGD	6.00	1.80
❑ 156	Rod Carew LGD	6.00	1.80
❑ 157	Steve Carlton LGD	6.00	1.80
❑ 158	Bob Feller LGD	6.00	1.80
❑ 159	Bob Gibson LGD	6.00	1.80
❑ 160	Reggie Jackson LGD	6.00	1.80
❑ 161	Al Kaline LGD	6.00	1.80
❑ 162	Sandy Koufax LGD SP	-	-
❑ 163	Don Mattingly LGD	15.00	4.50
❑ 164	Willie Mays LGD	12.00	3.60
❑ 165	Willie McCovey LGD	4.00	1.20
❑ 166	Joe Morgan LGD	4.00	1.20
❑ 167	Stan Musial LGD	10.00	3.00
❑ 168	Jim Palmer LGD	4.00	1.20
❑ 169	Brooks Robinson LGD	6.00	1.80
❑ 170	Frank Robinson LGD	6.00	1.80
❑ 171	Nolan Ryan LGD	20.00	6.00
❑ 172	Mike Schmidt LGD	12.00	3.60
❑ 173	Tom Seaver LGD	6.00	1.80
❑ 174	Warren Spahn LGD	6.00	1.80
❑ 175	Robin Yount LGD	6.00	1.80
❑ 176	Wade Boggs LGD	6.00	1.80
❑ 177	Ty Cobb LGD	10.00	3.00
❑ 178	Lou Gehrig LGD	12.00	3.60
❑ 179	Luis Aparicio LGD	4.00	1.20
❑ 180	Babe Ruth LGD	20.00	6.00
❑ 181	Ryne Sandberg LGD	12.00	3.60
❑ 182	Yogi Berra LGD	6.00	1.80
❑ 183	R.Clemente LGD	15.00	4.50
❑ 184	Eddie Murray LGD	6.00	1.80
❑ 185	Robin Roberts LGD SP	-	-
❑ 186	Duke Snider LGD	6.00	1.80
❑ 187	Orlando Cepeda LGD	4.00	1.20
❑ 188	Billy Williams LGD	4.00	1.20
❑ 189	Juan Marichal LGD	4.00	1.20
❑ 190	Harmon Killebrew LGD	6.00	1.80
❑ 191	Kirby Puckett LGD	6.00	1.80
❑ 192	Carlton Fisk LGD	6.00	1.80
❑ 193	Dave Winfield LGD	6.00	1.80
❑ 194	Whitey Ford LGD	6.00	1.80
❑ 195	Paul Molitor LGD	6.00	1.80
❑ 196	Tony Perez LGD	4.00	1.20
❑ 197	Ozzie Smith LGD	6.00	1.80
❑ 198	Ralph Kiner LGD	6.00	1.80
❑ 199	Fergie Jenkins LGD	4.00	1.20
❑ 200	Phil Rizzuto LGD	6.00	1.80

2002 Donruss Classics

	Nm-Mt	Ex-Mt
COMP.SET w/o SP's (100)	25.00	7.50
COMMON CARD (1-100)	.75	.23
COMMON (101-150/201-225)	5.00	1.50
COMMON CARD (151-200)	4.00	1.20

No.	Player	Nm-Mt	Ex-Mt
❑ 1	Alex Rodriguez	4.00	1.20
❑ 2	Barry Bonds	5.00	1.50
❑ 3	C.C. Sabathia	.75	.23
❑ 4	Chipper Jones	2.00	.60
❑ 5	Derek Jeter	5.00	1.50
❑ 6	Troy Glaus	1.25	.35
❑ 7	Frank Thomas	2.00	.60
❑ 8	Greg Maddux	4.00	1.20
❑ 9	Ivan Rodriguez	2.00	.60
❑ 10	Jeff Bagwell	1.25	.35
❑ 11	Mark Buehrle	.75	.23
❑ 12	Todd Helton	1.25	.35
❑ 13	Ken Griffey Jr.	3.00	.90
❑ 14	Manny Ramirez	.75	.23
❑ 15	Brad Penny	.75	.23
❑ 16	Mike Piazza	3.00	.90
❑ 17	Nomar Garciaparra	4.00	1.20
❑ 18	Pedro Martinez	2.00	.60
❑ 19	Randy Johnson	2.00	.60
❑ 20	Bud Smith	.75	.23
❑ 21	Rickey Henderson	3.00	.90
❑ 22	Roger Clemens	4.00	1.20
❑ 23	Sammy Sosa	3.00	.90
❑ 24	Brandon Duckworth	.75	.23
❑ 25	Vladimir Guerrero	2.00	.60
❑ 26	Kazuhiro Sasaki	.75	.23
❑ 27	Roberto Alomar	2.00	.60
❑ 28	Barry Zito	2.00	.60
❑ 29	Rich Aurilia	.75	.23
❑ 30	Ben Sheets	.75	.23
❑ 31	Carlos Delgado	.75	.23
❑ 32	J.D. Drew	.75	.23
❑ 33	Jermaine Dye	.75	.23
❑ 34	Darin Erstad	.75	.23
❑ 35	Jason Giambi	2.00	.60
❑ 36	Tom Glavine	2.00	.60
❑ 37	Juan Gonzalez	2.00	.60
❑ 38	Luis Gonzalez	.75	.23
❑ 39	Shawn Green	.75	.23
❑ 40	Tim Hudson	.75	.23
❑ 41	Andruw Jones	1.25	.35
❑ 42	Shannon Stewart	.75	.23
❑ 43	Barry Larkin	2.00	.60
❑ 44	Wade Miller	.75	.23
❑ 45	Mike Mussina	2.00	.60
❑ 46	Hideo Nomo	2.00	.60
❑ 47	Rafael Palmeiro	1.25	.35
❑ 48	Scott Rolen	1.25	.35
❑ 49	Gary Sheffield	.75	.23
❑ 50	Bernie Williams	1.25	.35
❑ 51	Bob Abreu	.75	.23
❑ 52	Javier Vazquez	.75	.23
❑ 53	Edgar Martinez	1.25	.35
❑ 54	Magglio Ordonez	.75	.23
❑ 55	Kerry Wood	2.00	.60
❑ 56	Adrian Beltre	.75	.23
❑ 57	Lance Berkman	.75	.23
❑ 58	Kevin Brown	.75	.23
❑ 59	Sean Casey	.75	.23
❑ 60	Eric Chavez	.75	.23
❑ 61	Robert Person	.75	.23
❑ 62	Jeremy Giambi	.75	.23
❑ 63	Freddy Garcia	.75	.23
❑ 64	Alfonso Soriano	2.00	.60
❑ 65	Doug Davis	.75	.23
❑ 66	Brian Giles	.75	.23
❑ 67	Moises Alou	.75	.23
❑ 68	Richard Hidalgo	.75	.23
❑ 69	Paul LoDuca	.75	.23
❑ 70	Aramis Ramirez	.75	.23
❑ 71	Andres Galarraga	.75	.23
❑ 72	Ryan Klesko	.75	.23
❑ 73	Chan Ho Park	.75	.23
❑ 74	Richie Sexson	.75	.23
❑ 75	Mike Sweeney	.75	.23
❑ 76	Aubrey Huff	.75	.23
❑ 77	Miguel Tejada	.75	.23
❑ 78	Jose Vidro	.75	.23
❑ 79	Larry Walker	1.25	.35
❑ 80	Roy Oswalt	.75	.23
❑ 81	Craig Biggio	1.25	.35
❑ 82	Juan Pierre	.75	.23
❑ 83	Jim Thome	2.00	.60
❑ 84	Josh Towers	.75	.23
❑ 85	Alex Escobar	.75	.23
❑ 86	Cliff Floyd	.75	.23
❑ 87	Terrence Long	.75	.23
❑ 88	Curt Schilling	1.25	.35
❑ 89	Carlos Beltran	.75	.23
❑ 90	Albert Pujols	4.00	1.20
❑ 91	Gabe Kapler	.75	.23
❑ 92	Mark Mulder	.75	.23
❑ 93	Carlos Lee	.75	.23
❑ 94	Robert Fick	.75	.23
❑ 95	Raul Mondesi	.75	.23
❑ 96	Ichiro Suzuki	4.00	1.20
❑ 97	Adam Dunn	1.25	.35
❑ 98	Corey Patterson	.75	.23
❑ 99	Tsuyoshi Shinjo	.75	.23
❑ 100	Joe Mays	.75	.23
❑ 101	Juan Cruz ROO	5.00	1.50
❑ 102	Marlon Byrd ROO	5.00	1.50
❑ 103	Luis Garcia ROO	5.00	1.50
❑ 104	Jorge Padilla ROO RC	8.00	2.40
❑ 105	Dennis Tankersley ROO	5.00	1.50
❑ 106	Josh Pearce ROO	5.00	1.50
❑ 107	Ramon Vazquez ROO	5.00	1.50
❑ 108	Chris Baker ROO RC	5.00	1.50
❑ 109	Eric Cyr ROO	5.00	1.50
❑ 110	Reed Johnson ROO RC	8.00	2.40
❑ 111	Ryan Jamison ROO	5.00	1.50
❑ 112	Antonio Perez ROO	5.00	1.50
❑ 113	Satoru Komiyama ROO RC	5.00	1.50
❑ 114	Austin Kearns ROO	8.00	2.40
❑ 115	Juan Pena ROO	5.00	1.50
❑ 116	Orlando Hudson ROO	5.00	1.50
❑ 117	Kazuhisa Ishii ROO RC	10.00	3.00
❑ 118	Erik Bedard ROO	5.00	1.50
❑ 119	Luis Ugueto ROO RC	5.00	1.50
❑ 120	Ben Howard ROO RC	5.00	1.50
❑ 121	Morgan Ensberg ROO	5.00	1.50
❑ 122	Doug Devore ROO RC	5.00	1.50
❑ 123	Josh Phelps ROO	5.00	1.50
❑ 124	Angel Berroa ROO	5.00	1.50
❑ 125	Ed Rogers ROO	5.00	1.50
❑ 126	Takahito Nomura ROO RC	5.00	1.50
❑ 127	John Ennis ROO RC	5.00	1.50
❑ 128	Bill Hall ROO	5.00	1.50
❑ 129	Dewon Brazelton ROO	5.00	1.50
❑ 130	Hank Blalock ROO	8.00	2.40
❑ 131	So Taguchi ROO RC	8.00	2.40
❑ 132	Jorge De La Rosa ROO RC	5.00	1.50
❑ 133	Matt Thornton ROO RC	5.00	1.50
❑ 134	Brandon Backe ROO RC	5.00	1.50
❑ 135	Jeff Deardorff ROO	5.00	1.50
❑ 136	Steve Smyth ROO	5.00	1.50
❑ 137	Anderson Machado ROO RC	8.00	2.40
❑ 138	John Buck ROO	5.00	1.50
❑ 139	Mark Prior ROO	15.00	4.50
❑ 140	Sean Burroughs ROO	5.00	1.50
❑ 141	Alex Herrera ROO	5.00	1.50
❑ 142	Francis Beltran ROO RC	5.00	1.50
❑ 143	Jason Romano ROO	5.00	1.50
❑ 144	Michael Cuddyer ROO	5.00	1.50
❑ 145	Steve Bechler ROO RC	5.00	1.50
❑ 146	Alfredo Amezaga ROO	5.00	1.50
❑ 147	Ryan Ludwick ROO	5.00	1.50
❑ 148	Martin Vargas ROO	5.00	1.50
❑ 149	Allan Simpson ROO RC	5.00	1.50
❑ 150	Mark Teixeira ROO	8.00	2.40
❑ 151	Dale Murphy LGD	6.00	1.80
❑ 152	Ernie Banks LGD	6.00	1.80
❑ 153	Johnny Bench LGD	6.00	1.80
❑ 154	George Brett LGD	15.00	4.50

Card	Nm-Mt	Ex-Mt
❑ 155 Lou Brock LGD	6.00	1.80
❑ 156 Rod Carew LGD	6.00	1.80
❑ 157 Steve Carlton LGD	6.00	1.80
❑ 158 Joe Torre LGD	6.00	1.80
❑ 159 Dennis Eckersley LGD	4.00	1.20
❑ 160 Reggie Jackson LGD	6.00	1.80
❑ 161 Al Kaline LGD	6.00	1.80
❑ 162 Dave Parker LGD	4.00	1.20
❑ 163 Don Mattingly LGD	15.00	4.50
❑ 164 Tony Gwynn LGD	8.00	2.40
❑ 165 Willie McCovey LGD	4.00	1.20
❑ 166 Joe Morgan LGD	4.00	1.20
❑ 167 Stan Musial LGD	10.00	3.00
❑ 168 Jim Palmer LGD	4.00	1.20
❑ 169 Brooks Robinson LGD	6.00	1.80
❑ 170 Bo Jackson LGD	6.00	1.80
❑ 171 Nolan Ryan LGD	20.00	6.00
❑ 172 Mike Schmidt LGD	12.00	3.60
❑ 173 Tom Seaver LGD	8.00	2.40
❑ 174 Cal Ripken LGD	20.00	6.00
❑ 175 Robin Yount LGD	6.00	1.80
❑ 176 Wade Boggs LGD	6.00	1.80
❑ 177 Gary Carter LGD	6.00	1.80
❑ 178 Ron Santo LGD	6.00	1.80
❑ 179 Luis Aparicio LGD	4.00	1.20
❑ 180 Bobby Doerr LGD	6.00	1.80
❑ 181 Ryne Sandberg LGD	12.00	3.60
❑ 182 Yogi Berra LGD	6.00	1.80
❑ 183 Will Clark LGD	6.00	1.80
❑ 184 Eddie Murray LGD	6.00	1.80
❑ 185 Andre Dawson LGD	4.00	1.20
❑ 186 Duke Snider LGD	6.00	1.80
❑ 187 Orlando Cepeda LGD	4.00	1.20
❑ 188 Billy Williams LGD	4.00	1.20
❑ 189 Juan Marichal LGD	4.00	1.20
❑ 190 Harmon Killebrew LGD	6.00	1.80
❑ 191 Kirby Puckett LGD	6.00	1.80
❑ 192 Carlton Fisk LGD	6.00	1.80
❑ 193 Dave Winfield LGD	6.00	1.80
❑ 194 Alan Trammell LGD	6.00	1.80
❑ 195 Paul Molitor LGD	6.00	1.80
❑ 196 Tony Perez LGD	4.00	1.20
❑ 197 Ozzie Smith LGD	6.00	1.80
❑ 198 Ralph Kiner LGD	4.00	1.20
❑ 199 Fergie Jenkins LGD	4.00	1.20
❑ 200 Phil Rizzuto LGD	6.00	1.80
❑ 201 Oliver Perez ROO RC	8.00	2.40
❑ 202 Aaron Cook ROO RC	8.00	2.40
❑ 203 Eric Junge ROO RC	5.00	1.50
❑ 204 Freddy Sanchez ROO RC	8.00	2.40
❑ 205 Cliff Lee ROO RC	8.00	2.40
❑ 206 Runelvys Hernandez ROO RC	8.00	2.40
❑ 207 Chone Figgins ROO RC	5.00	1.50
❑ 208 Rodrigo Rosario ROO RC	5.00	1.50
❑ 209 Kevin Cash ROO RC	5.00	1.50
❑ 210 Josh Bard ROO RC	5.00	1.50
❑ 211 Felix Escalona ROO RC	5.00	1.50
❑ 212 Jeriome Robertson ROO RC	8.00	2.40
❑ 213 Jason Simontacchi ROO RC	8.00	2.40
❑ 214 Shane Nance ROO RC	5.00	1.50
❑ 215 Ben Kozlowski ROO RC	5.00	1.50
❑ 216 Brian Tallet ROO RC	8.00	2.40
❑ 217 Earl Snyder ROO RC	5.00	1.50
❑ 218 Andy Pratt ROO RC	5.00	1.50
❑ 219 Trey Hodges ROO RC	8.00	2.40
❑ 220 Kirk Saarloos ROO RC	8.00	2.40
❑ 221 Rene Reyes ROO RC	5.00	1.50
❑ 222 Joe Borchard ROO	5.00	1.50
❑ 223 Wilson Valdez ROO RC	5.00	1.50
❑ 224 Miguel Asencio ROO RC	5.00	1.50
❑ 225 Chris Snelling ROO RC	8.00	2.40

2003 Donruss Classics

	Nm-Mt	Ex-Mt
COMP.SET w/o SP's (100)	25.00	7.50
COMMON CARD (1-100)	.75	.23
COMMON CARD (101-150)	4.00	1.20
COMMON CARD (151-200)	5.00	1.50
❑ 1 Troy Glaus	1.25	.35
❑ 2 Barry Bonds	5.00	1.50
❑ 3 Miguel Tejada	.75	.23
❑ 4 Randy Johnson	2.00	.60
❑ 5 Eric Hinske	.75	.23
❑ 6 Barry Zito	2.00	.60

Card	Nm-Mt	Ex-Mt
❑ 7 Jason Jennings	.75	.23
❑ 8 Derek Jeter	5.00	1.50
❑ 9 Vladimir Guerrero	2.00	.60
❑ 10 Corey Patterson	.75	.23
❑ 11 Manny Ramirez	.75	.23
❑ 12 Edgar Martinez	1.25	.35
❑ 13 Roy Oswalt	.75	.23
❑ 14 Andruw Jones	1.25	.35
❑ 15 Alex Rodriguez	4.00	1.20
❑ 16 Mark Mulder	.75	.23
❑ 17 Kazuhisa Ishii	.75	.23
❑ 18 Gary Sheffield	.75	.23
❑ 19 Jay Gibbons	.75	.23
❑ 20 Roberto Alomar	2.00	.60
❑ 21 A.J. Pierzynski	.75	.23
❑ 22 Eric Chavez	.75	.23
❑ 23 Roger Clemens	4.00	1.20
❑ 24 C.C. Sabathia	.75	.23
❑ 25 Jose Vidro	.75	.23
❑ 26 Shannon Stewart	.75	.23
❑ 27 Mark Teixeira	1.25	.35
❑ 28 Joe Thurston	.75	.23
❑ 29 Josh Beckett	1.25	.35
❑ 30 Jeff Bagwell	1.25	.35
❑ 31 Geronimo Gil	.75	.23
❑ 32 Curt Schilling	1.25	.35
❑ 33 Frank Thomas	2.00	.60
❑ 34 Lance Berkman	.75	.23
❑ 35 Adam Dunn	1.25	.35
❑ 36 Christian Parker	.75	.23
❑ 37 Jim Thome	2.00	.60
❑ 38 Shawn Green	.75	.23
❑ 39 Drew Henson	.75	.23
❑ 40 Chipper Jones	2.00	.60
❑ 41 Kevin Mench	.75	.23
❑ 42 Hideo Nomo	2.00	.60
❑ 43 Andres Galarraga	.75	.23
❑ 44 Doug Davis	.75	.23
❑ 45 Mark Prior	4.00	1.20
❑ 46 Sean Casey	.75	.23
❑ 47 Magglio Ordonez	.75	.23
❑ 48 Tom Glavine	2.00	.60
❑ 49 Marlon Byrd	.75	.23
❑ 50 Albert Pujols	4.00	1.20
❑ 51 Mark Buehrle	.75	.23
❑ 52 Aramis Ramirez	.75	.23
❑ 53 Pat Burrell	.75	.23
❑ 54 Craig Biggio	1.25	.35
❑ 55 Alfonso Soriano	2.00	.60
❑ 56 Kerry Wood	2.00	.60
❑ 57 Wade Miller	.75	.23
❑ 58 Hank Blalock	1.25	.35
❑ 59 Cliff Floyd	.75	.23
❑ 60 Jason Giambi	2.00	.60
❑ 61 Carlos Beltran	.75	.23
❑ 62 Brian Roberts	.75	.23
❑ 63 Paul Lo Duca	.75	.23
❑ 64 Tim Redding	.75	.23
❑ 65 Sammy Sosa	3.00	.90
❑ 66 Joe Borchard	.75	.23
❑ 67 Ryan Klesko	.75	.23
❑ 68 Richie Sexson	.75	.23
❑ 69 Carlos Lee	.75	.23
❑ 70 Rickey Henderson	3.00	.90
❑ 71 Brian Tallet	.75	.23
❑ 72 Luis Gonzalez	.75	.23
❑ 73 Satoru Komiyama	.75	.23
❑ 74 Tim Hudson	.75	.23
❑ 75 Ken Griffey Jr.	3.00	.90
❑ 76 Adam Johnson	.75	.23
❑ 77 Bobby Abreu	.75	.23
❑ 78 Adrian Beltre	.75	.23
❑ 79 Rafael Palmeiro	1.25	.35
❑ 80 Ichiro Suzuki	4.00	1.20
❑ 81 Kenny Lofton	.75	.23
❑ 82 Brian Giles	.75	.23
❑ 83 Barry Larkin	2.00	.60
❑ 84 Robert Fick	.75	.23
❑ 85 Ben Sheets	.75	.23
❑ 86 Scott Rolen	1.25	.35
❑ 87 Nomar Garciaparra	4.00	1.20
❑ 88 Brandon Phillips	.75	.23
❑ 89 Ben Kozlowski	.75	.23
❑ 90 Bernie Williams	1.25	.35
❑ 91 Pedro Martinez	2.00	.60
❑ 92 Todd Helton	1.25	.35
❑ 93 Jermaine Dye	.75	.23
❑ 94 Carlos Delgado	.75	.23
❑ 95 Mike Piazza	3.00	.90
❑ 96 Junior Spivey	.75	.23
❑ 97 Torii Hunter	.75	.23
❑ 98 Mike Sweeney	.75	.23
❑ 99 Ivan Rodriguez	2.00	.60
❑ 100 Greg Maddux	4.00	1.20
❑ 101 Ernie Banks LGD	6.00	1.80
❑ 102 Steve Garvey LGD	4.00	1.20
❑ 103 George Brett LGD	15.00	4.50
❑ 104 Lou Brock LGD	6.00	1.80
❑ 105 Hoyt Wilhelm LGD	4.00	1.20
❑ 106 Steve Carlton LGD	6.00	1.80
❑ 107 Joe Torre LGD	6.00	1.80
❑ 108 Dennis Eckersley LGD	4.00	1.20
❑ 109 Reggie Jackson LGD	6.00	1.80
❑ 110 Al Kaline LGD	6.00	1.80
❑ 111 Harold Reynolds LGD	4.00	1.20
❑ 112 Don Mattingly LGD	15.00	4.50
❑ 113 Tony Gwynn LGD	8.00	2.40
❑ 114 Willie McCovey LGD	4.00	1.20
❑ 115 Joe Morgan LGD	4.00	1.20
❑ 116 Stan Musial LGD	10.00	3.00
❑ 117 Jim Palmer LGD	4.00	1.20
❑ 118 Brooks Robinson LGD	6.00	1.80
❑ 119 Don Sutton LGD	4.00	1.20
❑ 120 Nolan Ryan LGD	20.00	6.00
❑ 121 Mike Schmidt LGD	12.00	3.60
❑ 122 Tom Seaver LGD	6.00	1.80
❑ 123 Cal Ripken LGD	20.00	6.00
❑ 124 Robin Yount LGD	6.00	1.80
❑ 125 Bob Feller LGD	6.00	1.80
❑ 126 Joe Carter LGD	4.00	1.20
❑ 127 Jack Morris LGD	4.00	1.20
❑ 128 Luis Aparicio LGD	4.00	1.20
❑ 129 Bobby Doerr LGD	4.00	1.20
❑ 130 Dave Parker LGD	4.00	1.20
❑ 131 Yogi Berra LGD	6.00	1.80
❑ 132 Will Clark LGD	6.00	1.80
❑ 133 Fred Lynn LGD	4.00	1.20
❑ 134 Andre Dawson LGD	4.00	1.20
❑ 135 Duke Snider LGD	6.00	1.80
❑ 136 Orlando Cepeda LGD	4.00	1.20
❑ 137 Billy Williams LGD	4.00	1.20
❑ 138 Dale Murphy LGD	6.00	1.80
❑ 139 Harmon Killebrew LGD	6.00	1.80
❑ 140 Kirby Puckett LGD	6.00	1.80
❑ 141 Carlton Fisk LGD	6.00	1.80
❑ 142 Eric Davis LGD	4.00	1.20
❑ 143 Alan Trammell LGD	6.00	1.80
❑ 144 Paul Molitor LGD	6.00	1.80
❑ 145 Jose Canseco LGD	6.00	1.80
❑ 146 Ozzie Smith LGD	6.00	1.80
❑ 147 Ralph Kiner LGD	4.00	1.20
❑ 148 Dwight Gooden LGD	6.00	1.80
❑ 149 Phil Rizzuto LGD	6.00	1.80
❑ 150 Lenny Dykstra LGD	4.00	1.20
❑ 151 Adam LaRoche ROO	5.00	1.50
❑ 152 Tim Hummel ROO	5.00	1.50
❑ 153 Matt Kata ROO RC	8.00	2.40
❑ 154 Jeff Baker ROO	5.00	1.50
❑ 155 Josh Stewart ROO RC	5.00	1.50
❑ 156 Marshall McDougall ROO	5.00	1.50
❑ 157 Jhonny Peralta ROO RC	5.00	1.50
❑ 158 Mike Nicolas ROO RC	5.00	1.50
❑ 159 Jeremy Guthrie ROO	5.00	1.50
❑ 160 Craig Brazell ROO RC	8.00	2.40

Card	Nm-Mt	Ex-Mt
❑ 161 Joe Valentine ROO RC	5.00	1.50
❑ 162 Buddy Hernandez ROO RC	5.00	1.50
❑ 163 Freddy Sanchez ROO	5.00	1.50
❑ 164 Shane Victorino ROO RC	5.00	1.50
❑ 165 Corwin Malone ROO	5.00	1.50
❑ 166 Jason Dubois ROO	5.00	1.50
❑ 167 Josh Wilson ROO	5.00	1.50
❑ 168 Tim Olson ROO RC	8.00	2.40
❑ 169 Cliff Bartosh ROO	5.00	1.50
❑ 170 Michael Hessman ROO RC	5.00	1.50
❑ 171 Ryan Church ROO	5.00	1.50
❑ 172 Garrett Atkins ROO	5.00	1.50
❑ 173 Jose Morban ROO	5.00	1.50
❑ 174 Ryan Cameron ROO RC	5.00	1.50
❑ 175 Todd Wellemeyer ROO RC	8.00	2.40
❑ 176 Travis Chapman ROO	5.00	1.50
❑ 177 Jason Anderson ROO	5.00	1.50
❑ 178 Adam Morrissey ROO	5.00	1.50
❑ 179 Jose Contreras ROO RC	10.00	3.00
❑ 180 Nic Jackson ROO	5.00	1.50
❑ 181 Rob Hammock ROO RC	8.00	2.40
❑ 182 Carlos Rivera ROO	5.00	1.50
❑ 183 Vinny Chulk ROO	5.00	1.50
❑ 184 Pete LaForest ROO RC	8.00	2.40
❑ 185 Jon Leicester ROO RC	5.00	1.50
❑ 186 Terrmel Sledge ROO RC	8.00	2.40
❑ 187 Jose Castillo ROO	5.00	1.50
❑ 188 Gerald Laird ROO	5.00	1.50
❑ 189 Nook Logan ROO RC	5.00	1.50
❑ 190 Clint Barmes ROO RC	8.00	2.40
❑ 191 Jesus Medrano ROO	5.00	1.50
❑ 192 Henri Stanley ROO	5.00	1.50
❑ 193 Hideki Matsui ROO RC	20.00	6.00
❑ 194 Walter Young ROO	5.00	1.50
❑ 195 Jon Adkins ROO	5.00	1.50
❑ 196 Tommy Whiteman ROO	5.00	1.50
❑ 197 Rob Bowen ROO	5.00	1.50
❑ 198 Brandon Webb ROO RC	12.00	3.60
❑ 199 Prentice Redman ROO RC	5.00	1.50
❑ 200 Jimmy Gobble ROO	5.00	1.50
❑ 201 Jeremy Bonderman ROO RC		-
❑ 202 Adam Loewen ROO RC	-	
❑ 203 Chien-Ming Wang ROO RC	-	
❑ 204 Hong-Chih Kuo ROO RC	-	
❑ 205 Ryan Wagner ROO RC	-	
❑ 206 Dan Haren ROO RC	-	
❑ 207 Dontrelle Willis ROO	-	
❑ 208 Rickie Weeks ROO RC	-	
❑ 209 Ramon Nivar ROO RC	-	
❑ 210 Chad Gaudin ROO RC	-	
❑ 211 Delmon Young ROO RC	-	

2002 Donruss Diamond Kings

	Nm-Mt	Ex-Mt
COMP.LOW SET (150)	200.00	60.00
COMP.LOW w/o SP's (100)	50.00	15.00
COMP.UPDATE SET (10)	50.00	15.00
COMMON CARD (1-100)	.50	.15
COMMON PROSPECT (101-150)	4.00	1.20
COMMON RETIRED (101-150)	4.00	1.20
COMMON CARD (151-160)	5.00	1.50

Card	Nm-Mt	Ex-Mt
❑ 1 Vladimir Guerrero	1.25	.35
❑ 2 Adam Dunn	.75	.23
❑ 3 Tsuyoshi Shinjo	.50	.15
❑ 4 Adrian Beltre	.50	.15
❑ 5 Troy Glaus	.75	.23
❑ 6 Albert Pujols	2.50	.75
❑ 7 Trot Nixon	.50	.15
❑ 8 Alex Rodriguez	2.50	.75
❑ 9 Tom Glavine	1.25	.35
❑ 10 Alfonso Soriano	1.25	.35
❑ 11 Todd Helton	.75	.23
❑ 12 Joe Torre	1.25	.35
❑ 13 Tim Hudson	.50	.15
❑ 14 Andruw Jones	.75	.23
❑ 15 Shawn Green	.50	.15
❑ 16 Aramis Ramirez	.50	.15
❑ 17 Shannon Stewart	.50	.15
❑ 18 Barry Bonds	3.00	.90
❑ 19 Sean Casey	.50	.15
❑ 20 Barry Larkin	1.25	.35
❑ 21 Scott Rolen	.75	.23
❑ 22 Barry Zito	1.25	.35
❑ 23 Sammy Sosa	2.00	.60
❑ 24 Bartolo Colon	.50	.15
❑ 25 Ryan Klesko	.50	.15
❑ 26 Ben Grieve	.50	.15
❑ 27 Roy Oswalt	.50	.15
❑ 28 Kazuhiro Sasaki	.50	.15
❑ 29 Roger Clemens	2.50	.75
❑ 30 Bernie Williams	.75	.23
❑ 31 Roberto Alomar	1.25	.35
❑ 32 Bobby Abreu	.50	.15
❑ 33 Robert Fick	.50	.15
❑ 34 Bret Boone	.50	.15
❑ 35 Rickey Henderson	2.00	.60
❑ 36 Brian Giles	.50	.15
❑ 37 Richie Sexson	.50	.15
❑ 38 Bud Smith	.50	.15
❑ 39 Richard Hidalgo	.50	.15
❑ 40 C. C. Sabathia	.50	.15
❑ 41 Rich Aurilia	.50	.15
❑ 42 Carlos Beltran	.50	.15
❑ 43 Raul Mondesi	.50	.15
❑ 44 Carlos Delgado	.50	.15
❑ 45 Randy Johnson	1.25	.35
❑ 46 Chan Ho Park	.50	.15
❑ 47 Rafael Palmeiro	.75	.23
❑ 48 Chipper Jones	1.25	.35
❑ 49 Phil Nevin	.50	.15
❑ 50 Cliff Floyd	.50	.15
❑ 51 Pedro Martinez	1.25	.35
❑ 52 Craig Biggio	.75	.23
❑ 53 Paul LoDuca	.50	.15
❑ 54 Cristian Guzman	.50	.15
❑ 55 Pat Burrell	.50	.15
❑ 56 Curt Schilling	.75	.23
❑ 57 Orlando Cabrera	.50	.15
❑ 58 Darin Erstad	.50	.15
❑ 59 Omar Vizquel	.50	.15
❑ 60 Derek Jeter	3.00	.90
❑ 61 Nomar Garciaparra	2.50	.75
❑ 62 Edgar Martinez	.75	.23
❑ 63 Moises Alou	.50	.15
❑ 64 Eric Chavez	.50	.15
❑ 65 Mike Sweeney	.50	.15
❑ 66 Frank Thomas	1.25	.35
❑ 67 Mike Piazza	2.00	.60
❑ 68 Gary Sheffield	.50	.15
❑ 69 Mike Mussina	1.25	.35
❑ 70 Greg Maddux	2.50	.75
❑ 71 Juan Gonzalez	1.25	.35
❑ 72 Hideo Nomo	1.25	.35
❑ 73 Miguel Tejada	.50	.15
❑ 74 Ichiro Suzuki	2.50	.75
❑ 75 Matt Morris	.50	.15
❑ 76 Ivan Rodriguez	1.25	.35
❑ 77 Mark Mulder	.50	.15
❑ 78 J.D. Drew	.50	.15
❑ 79 Mark Grace	1.25	.35
❑ 80 Jason Giambi	1.25	.35
❑ 81 Mark Buehrle	.50	.15
❑ 82 Jose Vidro	.50	.15
❑ 83 Manny Ramirez	.50	.15
❑ 84 Jeff Bagwell	.75	.23
❑ 85 Magglio Ordonez	.50	.15
❑ 86 Ken Griffey Jr.	2.00	.60
❑ 87 Luis Gonzalez	.50	.15
❑ 88 Jim Edmonds	.50	.15
❑ 89 Larry Walker	.75	.23
❑ 90 Jim Thome	1.25	.35
❑ 91 Lance Berkman	.50	.15
❑ 92 Jorge Posada	.75	.23
❑ 93 Kevin Brown	.50	.15
❑ 94 Joe Mays	.50	.15
❑ 95 Kerry Wood	1.25	.35
❑ 96 Mark Ellis	.50	.15
❑ 97 Austin Kearns	.75	.23
❑ 98 Jorge De La Rosa RC	.50	.15
❑ 99 Brandon Berger	.50	.15
❑ 100 Ryan Ludwick	.50	.15
❑ 101 Marlon Byrd SP	4.00	1.20
❑ 102 Brandon Backe SP RC	4.00	1.20
❑ 103 Juan Cruz SP	4.00	1.20
❑ 104 Anderson Machado SP RC	4.00	1.20
❑ 105 So Taguchi SP RC	4.00	1.20
❑ 106 Dewon Brazelton SP	4.00	1.20
❑ 107 Josh Beckett SP	4.00	1.20
❑ 108 John Buck SP	4.00	1.20
❑ 109 Jorge Padilla SP RC	4.00	1.20
❑ 110 Hee Seop Choi SP	4.00	1.20
❑ 111 Angel Berroa SP	4.00	1.20
❑ 112 Mark Teixeira SP	5.00	1.50
❑ 113 Victor Martinez SP	4.00	1.20
❑ 114 Kazuhisa Ishii SP RC	6.00	1.80
❑ 115 Dennis Tankersley SP	4.00	1.20
❑ 116 Wilson Valdez SP RC	4.00	1.20
❑ 117 Antonio Perez SP	4.00	1.20
❑ 118 Ed Rogers SP	4.00	1.20
❑ 119 Wilson Betemit SP	4.00	1.20
❑ 120 Mike Rivera SP	4.00	1.20
❑ 121 Mark Prior SP	10.00	3.00
❑ 122 Roberto Clemente SP	10.00	3.00
❑ 123 Roberto Clemente SP	10.00	3.00
❑ 124 Roberto Clemente SP	10.00	3.00
❑ 125 Roberto Clemente SP	10.00	3.00
❑ 126 Roberto Clemente SP	10.00	3.00
❑ 127 Babe Ruth SP	15.00	4.50
❑ 128 Ted Williams SP	10.00	3.00
❑ 129 Andre Dawson SP	4.00	1.20
❑ 130 Eddie Murray SP	5.00	1.50
❑ 131 Juan Marichal SP	4.00	1.20
❑ 132 Kirby Puckett SP	5.00	1.50
❑ 133 Alan Trammell SP	4.00	1.20
❑ 134 Bobby Doerr SP	4.00	1.20
❑ 135 Carlton Fisk SP	4.00	1.20
❑ 136 Eddie Mathews SP	5.00	1.50
❑ 137 Mike Schmidt SP	10.00	3.00
❑ 138 Catfish Hunter SP	4.00	1.20
❑ 139 Nolan Ryan SP	15.00	4.50
❑ 140 George Brett SP	12.00	3.60
❑ 141 Gary Carter SP	4.00	1.20
❑ 142 Paul Molitor SP	4.00	1.20
❑ 143 Lou Gehrig SP	8.00	2.40
❑ 144 Ryne Sandberg SP	8.00	2.40
❑ 145 Tony Gwynn SP	6.00	1.80
❑ 146 Ron Santo SP	4.00	1.20
❑ 147 Cal Ripken SP	15.00	4.50
❑ 148 Al Kaline SP	5.00	1.50
❑ 149 Bo Jackson SP	5.00	1.50
❑ 150 Don Mattingly SP	12.00	3.60
❑ 151 Chris Snelling RC	6.00	1.80
❑ 152 Satoru Komiyama RC	5.00	1.50
❑ 153 Oliver Perez RC	6.00	1.80
❑ 154 Kirk Saarloos RC	6.00	1.80
❑ 155 Rene Reyes RC	5.00	1.50
❑ 156 Runelvys Hernandez RC	6.00	1.80
❑ 157 Rodrigo Rosario RC	5.00	1.50
❑ 158 Jason Simontacchi RC	6.00	1.80
❑ 159 Miguel Asencio RC	5.00	1.50
❑ 160 Aaron Cook RC	6.00	1.80

2003 Donruss Diamond Kings

	Nm-Mt	Ex-Mt
COMPLETE SET (201)	150.00	45.00
COMP.SET w/o SP's (150)	50.00	15.00
COMMON CARD (1-150)	.50	.15
COMMON CARD (151-158)	2.00	.60
COMMON CARD (159-175)	4.00	1.20

Card	Nm-Mt	Ex-Mt
❑ 1 Darin Erstad	.50	.15
❑ 2 Garret Anderson	.50	.15
❑ 3 Troy Glaus	.75	.23
❑ 4 David Eckstein	.50	.15

❑ 5 Jarrod Washburn .50 .15
❑ 6 Adam Kennedy .50 .15
❑ 7 Jay Gibbons .50 .15
❑ 8 Tony Batista .50 .15
❑ 9 Melvin Mora .50 .15
❑ 10 Rodrigo Lopez .50 .15
❑ 11 Manny Ramirez .50 .15
❑ 12 Pedro Martinez 1.25 .35
❑ 13 Nomar Garciaparra 2.50 .75
❑ 14 Rickey Henderson 2.00 .60
❑ 15 Johnny Damon .50 .15
❑ 16 Derek Lowe .50 .15
❑ 17 Cliff Floyd .50 .15
❑ 18 Frank Thomas 1.25 .35
❑ 19 Magglio Ordonez .50 .15
❑ 20 Paul Konerko .50 .15
❑ 21 Mark Buehrle .50 .15
❑ 22 C.C. Sabathia .50 .15
❑ 23 Omar Vizquel .50 .15
❑ 24 Jim Thome 1.25 .35
❑ 25 Ellis Burks .50 .15
❑ 26 Robert Fick .50 .15
❑ 27 Bobby Higginson .50 .15
❑ 28 Randall Simon .50 .15
❑ 29 Carlos Pena .50 .15
❑ 30 Carlos Beltran .50 .15
❑ 31 Paul Byrd .50 .15
❑ 32 Raul Ibanez .50 .15
❑ 33 Mike Sweeney .50 .15
❑ 34 Torii Hunter .50 .15
❑ 35 Corey Koskie .50 .15
❑ 36 A.J. Pierzynski .50 .15
❑ 37 Cristian Guzman .50 .15
❑ 38 Jacque Jones .50 .15
❑ 39 Derek Jeter 3.00 .90
❑ 40 Bernie Williams .75 .23
❑ 41 Roger Clemens 2.50 .75
❑ 42 Mike Mussina 1.25 .35
❑ 43 Jorge Posada .75 .23
❑ 44 Alfonso Soriano 1.25 .35
❑ 45 Jason Giambi 1.25 .35
❑ 46 Robin Ventura .50 .15
❑ 47 David Wells .50 .15
❑ 48 Tim Hudson .50 .15
❑ 49 Barry Zito 1.25 .35
❑ 50 Mark Mulder .50 .15
❑ 51 Miguel Tejada .50 .15
❑ 52 Eric Chavez .50 .15
❑ 53 Jermaine Dye .50 .15
❑ 54 Ichiro Suzuki 2.50 .75
❑ 55 Edgar Martinez .75 .23
❑ 56 John Olerud .50 .15
❑ 57 Dan Wilson .50 .15
❑ 58 Joel Pineiro .50 .15
❑ 59 Kazuhiro Sasaki .50 .15
❑ 60 Freddy Garcia .50 .15
❑ 61 Aubrey Huff .50 .15
❑ 62 Steve Cox .50 .15
❑ 63 Randy Winn .50 .15
❑ 64 Alex Rodriguez 2.50 .75
❑ 65 Juan Gonzalez 1.25 .35
❑ 66 Rafael Palmeiro .75 .23
❑ 67 Ivan Rodriguez 1.25 .35
❑ 68 Kenny Rogers .50 .15
❑ 69 Carlos Delgado .50 .15
❑ 70 Eric Hinske .50 .15
❑ 71 Roy Halladay .50 .15
❑ 72 Vernon Wells .50 .15
❑ 73 Shannon Stewart .50 .15
❑ 74 Curt Schilling .75 .23
❑ 75 Randy Johnson 1.25 .35
❑ 76 Luis Gonzalez .50 .15
❑ 77 Mark Grace 1.25 .35
❑ 78 Junior Spivey .50 .15
❑ 79 Greg Maddux 2.50 .75
❑ 80 Tom Glavine 1.25 .35
❑ 81 John Smoltz .75 .23
❑ 82 Chipper Jones 1.25 .35
❑ 83 Gary Sheffield .50 .15
❑ 84 Andruw Jones .75 .23
❑ 85 Kerry Wood 1.25 .35
❑ 86 Fred McGriff .75 .23
❑ 87 Sammy Sosa 2.00 .60
❑ 88 Mark Prior 2.50 .75
❑ 89 Ken Griffey Jr. 2.00 .60
❑ 90 Barry Larkin 1.25 .35
❑ 91 Adam Dunn .75 .23
❑ 92 Sean Casey .50 .15
❑ 93 Austin Kearns .75 .23
❑ 94 Aaron Boone .50 .15
❑ 95 Larry Walker .75 .23
❑ 96 Todd Helton .75 .23
❑ 97 Jason Jennings .50 .15
❑ 98 Jay Payton .50 .15
❑ 99 Josh Beckett .75 .23
❑ 100 Mike Lowell .50 .15
❑ 101 A.J. Burnett .50 .15
❑ 102 Jeff Bagwell .75 .23
❑ 103 Craig Biggio .75 .23
❑ 104 Lance Berkman .50 .15
❑ 105 Roy Oswalt .50 .15
❑ 106 Wade Miller .50 .15
❑ 107 Shawn Green .50 .15
❑ 108 Adrian Beltre .50 .15
❑ 109 Hideo Nomo 1.25 .35
❑ 110 Kazuhisa Ishii .50 .15
❑ 111 Odalis Perez .50 .15
❑ 112 Paul Lo Duca .50 .15
❑ 113 Ben Sheets .50 .15
❑ 114 Richie Sexson .50 .15
❑ 115 Jose Hernandez .50 .15
❑ 116 Vladimir Guerrero 1.25 .35
❑ 117 Jose Vidro .50 .15
❑ 118 Tomo Ohka .50 .15
❑ 119 Andres Galarraga .50 .15
❑ 120 Bartolo Colon .50 .15
❑ 121 Mike Piazza 2.00 .60
❑ 122 Roberto Alomar 1.25 .35
❑ 123 Mo Vaughn .50 .15
❑ 124 Al Leiter .50 .15
❑ 125 Edgardo Alfonzo .50 .15
❑ 126 Pat Burrell .50 .15
❑ 127 Bobby Abreu .50 .15
❑ 128 Mike Lieberthal .50 .15
❑ 129 Vicente Padilla .50 .15
❑ 130 Marlon Byrd .50 .15
❑ 131 Jason Kendall .50 .15
❑ 132 Brian Giles .50 .15
❑ 133 Aramis Ramirez .50 .15
❑ 134 Kip Wells .50 .15
❑ 135 Ryan Klesko .50 .15
❑ 136 Phil Nevin .50 .15
❑ 137 Brian Lawrence .50 .15
❑ 138 Sean Burroughs .50 .15
❑ 139 Mark Kotsay .50 .15
❑ 140 Barry Bonds 3.00 .90
❑ 141 Jeff Kent .50 .15
❑ 142 Benito Santiago .50 .15
❑ 143 Kirk Rueter .50 .15
❑ 144 Jason Schmidt .50 .15
❑ 145 Jim Edmonds .50 .15
❑ 146 J.D. Drew .50 .15
❑ 147 Albert Pujols 2.50 .75
❑ 148 Tino Martinez .75 .23
❑ 149 Matt Morris .50 .15
❑ 150 Scott Rolen .75 .23
❑ 151 Joe Borchard ROO 2.00 .60
❑ 152 Cliff Lee ROO 2.00 .60
❑ 153 Brian Tallet ROO 2.00 .60
❑ 154 Freddy Sanchez ROO 2.00 .60
❑ 155 Chone Figgins ROO 2.00 .60
❑ 156 Kevin Cash ROO 2.00 .60
❑ 157 Justin Wayne ROO 2.00 .60
❑ 158 Ben Kozlowski ROO 2.00 .60
❑ 159 Babe Ruth RET 10.00 3.00
❑ 160 Jackie Robinson RET 6.00 1.80
❑ 161 Ozzie Smith RET 5.00 1.50
❑ 162 Lou Gehrig RET 8.00 2.40
❑ 163 Stan Musial RET 6.00 1.80
❑ 164 Mike Schmidt RET 10.00 3.00
❑ 165 Carlton Fisk RET 5.00 1.50
❑ 166 George Brett RET 12.00 3.60
❑ 167 Dale Murphy RET 8.00 2.40
❑ 168 Cal Ripken RET 12.00 3.60
❑ 169 Tony Gwynn RET 5.00 1.50
❑ 170 Don Mattingly RET 10.00 3.00
❑ 171 Jack Morris RET 4.00 1.20
❑ 172 Ty Cobb RET 5.00 1.50
❑ 173 Nolan Ryan RET 12.00 3.60
❑ 174 Ryne Sandberg RET 8.00 2.40
❑ 175 Thurman Munson RET 6.00 1.80
❑ 176 Jose Contreras ROO RC 10.00 3.00
❑ 177 Hideki Matsui ROO RC -
❑ 178 Jeremy Bonderman ROO RC -
❑ 179 Brandon Webb ROO RC -
❑ 180 Adam Loewen ROO RC -
❑ 181 Chien-Ming Wang ROO RC -
❑ 182 Hong-Chih Kuo ROO RC -
❑ 183 Clint Barmes ROO RC -
❑ 184 Guillermo Quiroz ROO RC -
❑ 185 Edgar Gonzalez ROO RC -
❑ 186 Todd Wellemeyer ROO RC -
❑ 187 Dan Haren ROO RC -
❑ 188 Dustin McGowan ROO RC -
❑ 189 Preston Larrison ROO RC -
❑ 190 Does Not Exist -
❑ 191 Kevin Youkilis ROO RC -
❑ 192 Bubba Nelson ROO RC -
❑ 193 Chris Burke ROO RC -
❑ 194 J.D. Durbin ROO RC -
❑ 195 Ryan Howard ROO RC -
❑ 196 Jason Kubel ROO RC -
❑ 197 Brendan Harris ROO RC -
❑ 198 Brian Bruney ROO RC -
❑ 199 Ramon Nivar ROO RC -
❑ 200 Rickie Weeks ROO RC -
❑ 201 Delmon Young ROO RC -

2001 Donruss Elite

	Nm-Mt	Ex-Mt
COMP.SET w/o SP's (150)	40.00	12.00
COMMON CARD (1-150)	.50	.15
COMMON (151-200)	10.00	3.00
COMMON CARD (201-250)	10.00	3.00

❑ 1 Alex Rodriguez 2.50 .75
❑ 2 Barry Bonds 3.00 .90
❑ 3 Cal Ripken 4.00 1.20
❑ 4 Chipper Jones 1.25 .35
❑ 5 Derek Jeter 3.00 .90
❑ 6 Troy Glaus .75 .23
❑ 7 Frank Thomas 1.25 .35
❑ 8 Greg Maddux 2.50 .75
❑ 9 Ivan Rodriguez 1.25 .35
❑ 10 Jeff Bagwell .75 .23
❑ 11 Jose Canseco 1.25 .35
❑ 12 Todd Helton .75 .23
❑ 13 Ken Griffey Jr. 2.00 .60
❑ 14 Manny Ramirez .50 .15
❑ 15 Mark McGwire 3.00 .90
❑ 16 Mike Piazza 2.00 .60

- ❑ 17 Nomar Garciaparra 2.50 .75
- ❑ 18 Pedro Martinez 1.25 .35
- ❑ 19 Randy Johnson 1.25 .35
- ❑ 20 Rick Ankiel .50 .15
- ❑ 21 Rickey Henderson 2.00 .60
- ❑ 22 Roger Clemens 2.50 .75
- ❑ 23 Sammy Sosa 2.00 .60
- ❑ 24 Tony Gwynn 1.50 .45
- ❑ 25 Vladimir Guerrero 1.25 .35
- ❑ 26 Eric Davis .50 .15
- ❑ 27 Roberto Alomar 1.25 .35
- ❑ 28 Mark Mulder .50 .15
- ❑ 29 Pat Burrell .50 .15
- ❑ 30 Harold Baines .50 .15
- ❑ 31 Carlos Delgado .50 .15
- ❑ 32 J.D. Drew .50 .15
- ❑ 33 Jim Edmonds .50 .15
- ❑ 34 Darin Erstad .50 .15
- ❑ 35 Jason Giambi 1.25 .35
- ❑ 36 Tom Glavine 1.25 .35
- ❑ 37 Juan Gonzalez 1.25 .35
- ❑ 38 Mark Grace 1.25 .35
- ❑ 39 Shawn Green .50 .15
- ❑ 40 Tim Hudson .50 .15
- ❑ 41 Andruw Jones .75 .23
- ❑ 42 David Justice .50 .15
- ❑ 43 Jeff Kent .50 .15
- ❑ 44 Barry Larkin 1.25 .35
- ❑ 45 Pokey Reese .50 .15
- ❑ 46 Mike Mussina 1.25 .35
- ❑ 47 Hideo Nomo 1.25 .35
- ❑ 48 Rafael Palmeiro .75 .23
- ❑ 49 Adam Piatt .50 .15
- ❑ 50 Scott Rolen .75 .23
- ❑ 51 Gary Sheffield .50 .15
- ❑ 52 Bernie Williams .75 .23
- ❑ 53 Bob Abreu .50 .15
- ❑ 54 Edgardo Alfonzo .50 .15
- ❑ 55 Jermaine Clark RC .75 .23
- ❑ 56 Albert Belle .50 .15
- ❑ 57 Craig Biggio .75 .23
- ❑ 58 Andres Galarraga .50 .15
- ❑ 59 Edgar Martinez .75 .23
- ❑ 60 Fred McGriff .75 .23
- ❑ 61 Magglio Ordonez .50 .15
- ❑ 62 Jim Thome 1.25 .35
- ❑ 63 Matt Williams .50 .15
- ❑ 64 Kerry Wood 1.25 .35
- ❑ 65 Moises Alou .50 .15
- ❑ 66 Brady Anderson .50 .15
- ❑ 67 Garret Anderson .50 .15
- ❑ 68 Tony Armas Jr. .50 .15
- ❑ 69 Tony Batista .50 .15
- ❑ 70 Jose Cruz Jr. .50 .15
- ❑ 71 Carlos Beltran .50 .15
- ❑ 72 Adrian Beltre .50 .15
- ❑ 73 Kris Benson .50 .15
- ❑ 74 Lance Berkman .50 .15
- ❑ 75 Kevin Brown .50 .15
- ❑ 76 Jay Buhner .50 .15
- ❑ 77 Jeromy Burnitz .50 .15
- ❑ 78 Ken Caminiti .50 .15
- ❑ 79 Sean Casey .50 .15
- ❑ 80 Luis Castillo .50 .15
- ❑ 81 Eric Chavez .50 .15
- ❑ 82 Jeff Cirillo .50 .15
- ❑ 83 Bartolo Colon .50 .15
- ❑ 84 David Cone .50 .15
- ❑ 85 Freddy Garcia .50 .15
- ❑ 86 Johnny Damon .50 .15
- ❑ 87 Ray Durham .50 .15
- ❑ 88 Jermaine Dye .50 .15
- ❑ 89 Juan Encarnacion .50 .15
- ❑ 90 Terrence Long .50 .15
- ❑ 91 Carl Everett .50 .15
- ❑ 92 Steve Finley .50 .15
- ❑ 93 Cliff Floyd .50 .15
- ❑ 94 Brad Fullmer .50 .15
- ❑ 95 Brian Giles .50 .15
- ❑ 96 Luis Gonzalez .50 .15
- ❑ 97 Rusty Greer .50 .15
- ❑ 98 Jeffrey Hammonds .50 .15
- ❑ 99 Mike Hampton .50 .15
- ❑ 100 Orlando Hernandez .50 .15
- ❑ 101 Richard Hidalgo .50 .15
- ❑ 102 Geoff Jenkins .50 .15
- ❑ 103 Jacque Jones .50 .15
- ❑ 104 Brian Jordan .50 .15
- ❑ 105 Gabe Kapler .50 .15
- ❑ 106 Eric Karros .50 .15
- ❑ 107 Jason Kendall .50 .15
- ❑ 108 Adam Kennedy .50 .15
- ❑ 109 Byung-Hyun Kim .50 .15
- ❑ 110 Ryan Klesko .50 .15
- ❑ 111 Chuck Knoblauch .50 .15
- ❑ 112 Paul Konerko .50 .15
- ❑ 113 Carlos Lee .50 .15
- ❑ 114 Kenny Lofton .50 .15
- ❑ 115 Javy Lopez .50 .15
- ❑ 116 Tino Martinez .75 .23
- ❑ 117 Ruben Mateo .50 .15
- ❑ 118 Kevin Millwood .50 .15
- ❑ 119 Ben Molina .50 .15
- ❑ 120 Raul Mondesi .50 .15
- ❑ 121 Trot Nixon .50 .15
- ❑ 122 John Olerud .50 .15
- ❑ 123 Paul O'Neill .75 .23
- ❑ 124 Chan Ho Park .50 .15
- ❑ 125 Andy Pettitte .75 .23
- ❑ 126 Jorge Posada .75 .23
- ❑ 127 Mark Quinn .50 .15
- ❑ 128 Aramis Ramirez .50 .15
- ❑ 129 Mariano Rivera .75 .23
- ❑ 130 Tim Salmon .75 .23
- ❑ 131 Curt Schilling .75 .23
- ❑ 132 Richie Sexson .50 .15
- ❑ 133 John Smoltz .75 .23
- ❑ 134 J.T. Snow .50 .15
- ❑ 135 Jay Payton .50 .15
- ❑ 136 Shannon Stewart .50 .15
- ❑ 137 B.J. Surhoff .50 .15
- ❑ 138 Mike Sweeney .50 .15
- ❑ 139 Fernando Tatis .50 .15
- ❑ 140 Miguel Tejada .50 .15
- ❑ 141 Jason Varitek .50 .15
- ❑ 142 Greg Vaughn .50 .15
- ❑ 143 Mo Vaughn .50 .15
- ❑ 144 Robin Ventura UER .50 .15
  Listed as playing for Yankees last 2 years,
  Also Bat and Throw information is wrong
- ❑ 145 Jose Vidro .50 .15
- ❑ 146 Omar Vizquel .50 .15
- ❑ 147 Larry Walker .75 .23
- ❑ 148 David Wells .50 .15
- ❑ 149 Rondell White .50 .15
- ❑ 150 Preston Wilson .50 .15
- ❑ 151 Brent Abernathy SP 10.00 3.00
- ❑ 152 Cory Aldridge SP RC 10.00 3.00
- ❑ 153 Gene Altman SP RC 10.00 3.00
- ❑ 154 Josh Beckett SP 15.00 4.50
- ❑ 155 Wilson Betemit SP RC 10.00 3.00
- ❑ 156 Albert Pujols SP RC 200.00 60.00
- ❑ 157 Joe Crede SP 10.00 3.00
- ❑ 158 Jack Cust SP 10.00 3.00
- ❑ 159 Ben Sheets SP 10.00 3.00
- ❑ 160 Alex Escobar SP 10.00 3.00
- ❑ 161 A. Hernandez SP RC 10.00 3.00
- ❑ 162 Pedro Feliz SP 10.00 3.00
- ❑ 163 Nate Frese SP RC 10.00 3.00
- ❑ 164 Carlos Garcia SP RC 10.00 3.00
- ❑ 165 Marcus Giles SP 10.00 3.00
- ❑ 166 Alexis Gomez SP RC 10.00 3.00
- ❑ 167 Jason Hart SP 10.00 3.00
- ❑ 168 Aubrey Huff SP 10.00 3.00
- ❑ 169 Cesar Izturis SP 10.00 3.00
- ❑ 170 Nick Johnson SP 10.00 3.00
- ❑ 171 Jack Wilson SP RC 10.00 3.00
- ❑ 172 B.Lawrence SP RC 10.00 3.00
- ❑ 173 C. Parker SP RC 10.00 3.00
- ❑ 174 Nick Maness SP RC 10.00 3.00
- ❑ 175 Jose Mieses SP RC 10.00 3.00
- ❑ 176 Greg Miller SP RC 10.00 3.00
- ❑ 177 Eric Munson SP 10.00 3.00
- ❑ 178 Xavier Nady SP 10.00 3.00
- ❑ 179 Blaine Neal SP RC 10.00 3.00
- ❑ 180 Abraham Nunez SP 10.00 3.00
- ❑ 181 Jose Ortiz SP 10.00 3.00
- ❑ 182 Jeremy Owens SP RC 10.00 3.00
- ❑ 183 Jay Gibbons SP RC 15.00 4.50
- ❑ 184 Corey Patterson SP 10.00 3.00
- ❑ 185 Carlos Pena SP 10.00 3.00
- ❑ 186 C.C. Sabathia SP 10.00 3.00
- ❑ 187 Timo Perez SP 10.00 3.00
- ❑ 188 A. Pettyjohn SP RC 10.00 3.00
- ❑ 189 D. Mendez SP RC 10.00 3.00
- ❑ 190 J. Melian SP RC 10.00 3.00
- ❑ 191 Wilkin Ruan SP RC 10.00 3.00
- ❑ 192 D. Sanchez SP RC 10.00 3.00
- ❑ 193 Alfonso Soriano SP 15.00 4.50
- ❑ 194 Rafael Soriano SP RC 15.00 4.50
- ❑ 195 Ichiro Suzuki SP RC 100.00 30.00
- ❑ 196 Billy Sylvester SP RC 10.00 3.00
- ❑ 197 Juan Uribe SP RC 10.00 3.00
- ❑ 198 T. Shinjo SP RC 15.00 4.50
- ❑ 199 C. Valderrama SP RC 10.00 3.00
- ❑ 200 Matt White SP RC 10.00 3.00
- ❑ 201 Adam Dunn/468 15.00 4.50
- ❑ 202 Joe Kennedy/465 XRC 10.00 3.00
- ❑ 203 Mike Rivera/427 XRC 10.00 3.00
- ❑ 204 Erick Almonte/401 XRC 10.00 3.00
- ❑ 205 Bran Duckworth EXCH 10.00 3.00
- ❑ 206 Victor Martinez/410 XRC 50.00 15.00
- ❑ 207 Rick Bauer/390 XRC 10.00 3.00
- ❑ 208 Jeff Deardorff/396 XRC 10.00 3.00
- ❑ 209 Antonio Perez/448 XRC 10.00 3.00
- ❑ 210 Bill Hall/404 XRC 10.00 3.00
- ❑ 211 D. Tankersley EXCH 10.00 3.00
- ❑ 212 Jeremy Affeldt/386 XRC 10.00 3.00
- ❑ 213 Junior Spivey/377 XRC 25.00 7.50
- ❑ 214 Casey Fossum/393 XRC 10.00 3.00
- ❑ 215 Brandon Lyon/402 XRC 10.00 3.00
- ❑ 216 Angel Santos/408 XRC 10.00 3.00
- ❑ 217 Cody Ransom/404 XRC 10.00 3.00
- ❑ 218 Jason Lane/424 XRC 15.00 4.50
- ❑ 219 David Williams/408 XRC 10.00 3.00
- ❑ 220 Alex Herrera/405 XRC 10.00 3.00
- ❑ 221 Ryan Drese/378 XRC 10.00 3.00
- ❑ 222 Travis Hafner/419 XRC 25.00 7.50
- ❑ 223 Bud Smith/468 XRC 10.00 3.00
- ❑ 224 Johnny Estrada/415 XRC 15.00 4.50
- ❑ 225 R. Rodriguez EXCH 10.00 3.00
- ❑ 226 Brandon Berger/428 XRC 10.00 3.00
- ❑ 227 Claudio Vargas/395 XRC 10.00 3.00
- ❑ 228 Luis Garcia/438 XRC 10.00 3.00
- ❑ 229 Marlon Byrd/452 XRC 50.00 15.00
- ❑ 230 Hee Seop Choi/479 XRC 60.00 18.00
- ❑ 231 Corky Miller/431 XRC 10.00 3.00
- ❑ 232 J. Duchscherer EXCH 10.00 3.00
- ❑ 233 T. Spooneybarger EXCH 10.00 3.00
- ❑ 234 Roy Oswalt/427 15.00 4.50
- ❑ 235 Willie Harris/418 XRC 10.00 3.00
- ❑ 236 Josh Towers/437 XRC 10.00 3.00
- ❑ 237 Juan A.Pena/400 XRC 10.00 3.00
- ❑ 238 A. Amezaga EXCH 15.00 4.50
- ❑ 239 Geronimo Gil/396 XRC 10.00 3.00
- ❑ 240 Juan Cruz/489 XRC 10.00 3.00
- ❑ 241 Ed Rogers/429 XRC 10.00 3.00
- ❑ 242 Joe Thurston/420 XRC 25.00 7.50
- ❑ 243 O.Hudson EXCH 15.00 4.50
- ❑ 244 John Buck/416 XRC 15.00 4.50
- ❑ 245 Martin Vargas/400 XRC 10.00 3.00
- ❑ 246 David Brous/399 XRC 10.00 3.00
- ❑ 247 D. Brazelton EXCH 10.00 3.00
- ❑ 248 Mark Prior/556 XRC 200.00 60.00
- ❑ 249 Angel Berroa/420 XRC 40.00 12.00
- ❑ 250 Mark Teixeira/543 XRC 100.00 30.00

2002 Donruss Elite

	Nm-Mt	Ex-Mt
COMP.LO SET w/o SP's (100)	20.00	6.00
COMMON CARD (1-100)	.40	.12
COMMON CARD (101-150)	4.00	1.20
COMMON CARD (151-200)	5.00	1.50
COMMON CARD (201-275)	8.00	2.40

- ❑ 1 Vladimir Guerrero 1.00 .30
- ❑ 2 Bernie Williams .60 .18
- ❑ 3 Ichiro Suzuki 2.00 .60
- ❑ 4 Roger Clemens 2.00 .60
- ❑ 5 Greg Maddux 2.00 .60
- ❑ 6 Fred McGriff .60 .18
- ❑ 7 Jermaine Dye .40 .12
- ❑ 8 Ken Griffey Jr. 1.50 .45
- ❑ 9 Todd Helton .60 .18
- ❑ 10 Torii Hunter .40 .12

❑	11 Pat Burrell	.40	.12
❑	12 Chipper Jones	1.00	.30
❑	13 Ivan Rodriguez	1.00	.30
❑	14 Roy Oswalt	.40	.12
❑	15 Shannon Stewart	.40	.12
❑	16 Magglio Ordonez	.40	.12
❑	17 Lance Berkman	.40	.12
❑	18 Mark Mulder	.40	.12
❑	19 Al Leiter	.40	.12
❑	20 Sammy Sosa	1.50	.45
❑	21 Scott Rolen	.60	.18
❑	22 Aramis Ramirez	.40	.12
❑	23 Alfonso Soriano	1.00	.30
❑	24 Phil Nevin	.40	.12
❑	25 Barry Bonds	2.50	.75
❑	26 Joe Mays	.40	.12
❑	27 Jeff Kent	.40	.12
❑	28 Mark Quinn	.40	.12
❑	29 Adrian Beltre	.40	.12
❑	30 Freddy Garcia	.40	.12
❑	31 Pedro Martinez	1.00	.30
❑	32 Darryl Kile	.40	.12
❑	33 Mike Cameron	.40	.12
❑	34 Frank Catalanotto	.40	.12
❑	35 Jose Vidro	.40	.12
❑	36 Jim Thome	1.00	.30
❑	37 Javy Lopez	.40	.12
❑	38 Paul Konerko	.40	.12
❑	39 Jeff Bagwell	.60	.18
❑	40 Curt Schilling	.60	.18
❑	41 Miguel Tejada	.40	.12
❑	42 Jim Edmonds	.40	.12
❑	43 Ellis Burks	.40	.12
❑	44 Mark Grace	1.00	.30
❑	45 Robb Nen	.40	.12
❑	46 Jeff Conine	.40	.12
❑	47 Derek Jeter	2.50	.75
❑	48 Mike Lowell	.40	.12
❑	49 Javier Vazquez	.40	.12
❑	50 Manny Ramirez	.40	.12
❑	51 Bartolo Colon	.40	.12
❑	52 Carlos Beltran	.40	.12
❑	53 Tim Hudson	.40	.12
❑	54 Rafael Palmeiro	.60	.18
❑	55 Jimmy Rollins	.40	.12
❑	56 Andruw Jones	.60	.18
❑	57 Orlando Cabrera	.40	.12
❑	58 Dean Palmer	.40	.12
❑	59 Bret Boone	.40	.12
❑	60 Carlos Febles	.40	.12
❑	61 Ben Grieve	.40	.12
❑	62 Richie Sexson	.40	.12
❑	63 Alex Rodriguez	2.00	.60
❑	64 Juan Pierre	.40	.12
❑	65 Bobby Higginson	.40	.12
❑	66 Barry Zito	1.00	.30
❑	67 Raul Mondesi	.40	.12
❑	68 Albert Pujols	2.00	.60
❑	69 Omar Vizquel	.40	.12
❑	70 Bobby Abreu	.40	.12
❑	71 Corey Koskie	.40	.12
❑	72 Tom Glavine	1.00	.30
❑	73 Paul LoDuca	.40	.12
❑	74 Terrence Long	.40	.12
❑	75 Matt Morris	.40	.12
❑	76 Andy Pettitte	.60	.18
❑	77 Rich Aurilia	.40	.12
❑	78 Todd Walker	.40	.12
❑	79 John Olerud UER Career Header stats are those for a pitcher	.40	.12
❑	80 Mike Sweeney	.40	.12
❑	81 Ray Durham	.40	.12
❑	82 Fernando Vina	.40	.12
❑	83 Nomar Garciaparra	2.00	.60
❑	84 Mariano Rivera	.60	.18
❑	85 Mike Piazza	1.50	.45
❑	86 Mark Buehrle	.40	.12
❑	87 Adam Dunn	.60	.18
❑	88 Luis Gonzalez	.40	.12
❑	89 Richard Hidalgo	.40	.12
❑	90 Brad Radke	.40	.12
❑	91 Russ Ortiz	.40	.12
❑	92 Brian Giles	.40	.12
❑	93 Billy Wagner	.40	.12
❑	94 Cliff Floyd	.40	.12
❑	95 Eric Milton	.40	.12
❑	96 Bud Smith	.40	.12
❑	97 Wade Miller	.40	.12
❑	98 Jon Lieber	.40	.12
❑	99 Derrek Lee	.40	.12
❑	100 Jose Cruz Jr.	.40	.12
❑	101 Dmitri Young STAR	4.00	1.20
❑	102 Mo Vaughn STAR	4.00	1.20
❑	103 Tino Martinez STAR	5.00	1.50
❑	104 Larry Walker STAR	5.00	1.50
❑	105 Chuck Knoblauch STAR	4.00	1.20
❑	106 Troy Glaus STAR	5.00	1.50
❑	107 Jason Giambi STAR	8.00	2.40
❑	108 Travis Fryman STAR	4.00	1.20
❑	109 Josh Beckett STAR	5.00	1.50
❑	110 Edgar Martinez STAR	5.00	1.50
❑	111 Tim Salmon STAR	5.00	1.50
❑	112 C.C. Sabathia STAR	4.00	1.20
❑	113 Randy Johnson STAR	8.00	2.40
❑	114 Juan Gonzalez STAR	8.00	2.40
❑	115 Carlos Delgado STAR	4.00	1.20
❑	116 Hideo Nomo STAR	8.00	2.40
❑	117 Kerry Wood STAR	8.00	2.40
❑	118 Brian Jordan STAR	4.00	1.20
❑	119 Carlos Pena STAR	4.00	1.20
❑	120 Roger Cedeno STAR	4.00	1.20
❑	121 Chan Ho Park STAR	4.00	1.20
❑	122 Rafael Furcal STAR	4.00	1.20
❑	123 Frank Thomas STAR	8.00	2.40
❑	124 Mike Mussina STAR	8.00	2.40
❑	125 Rickey Henderson STAR	12.00	3.60
❑	126 Sean Casey STAR	4.00	1.20
❑	127 Barry Larkin STAR	8.00	2.40
❑	128 Kazuhiro Sasaki STAR	4.00	1.20
❑	129 Moises Alou STAR	4.00	1.20
❑	130 Jeff Cirillo STAR	4.00	1.20
❑	131 Jason Kendall STAR	4.00	1.20
❑	132 Gary Sheffield STAR	4.00	1.20
❑	133 Ryan Klesko STAR	4.00	1.20
❑	134 Kevin Brown STAR	4.00	1.20
❑	135 Darin Erstad STAR	4.00	1.20
❑	136 Roberto Alomar STAR	8.00	2.40
❑	137 Brad Fullmer STAR	4.00	1.20
❑	138 Eric Chavez STAR	4.00	1.20
❑	139 Ben Sheets STAR	4.00	1.20
❑	140 Trot Nixon STAR	4.00	1.20
❑	141 Garret Anderson STAR	4.00	1.20
❑	142 Shawn Green STAR	4.00	1.20
❑	143 Troy Percival STAR	4.00	1.20
❑	144 Craig Biggio STAR	5.00	1.50
❑	145 Jorge Posada STAR	5.00	1.50
❑	146 J.D. Drew STAR	4.00	1.20
❑	147 Johnny Damon STAR	4.00	1.20
❑	148 Jeromy Burnitz STAR	4.00	1.20
❑	149 Robin Ventura STAR	4.00	1.20
❑	150 Aaron Sele STAR	4.00	1.20
❑	151 Cam Esslinger ROO RC	5.00	1.50
❑	152 Ben Howard ROO RC	5.00	1.50
❑	153 Brandon Backe ROO RC	5.00	1.50
❑	154 Jorge De La Rosa ROO RC	5.00	1.50
❑	155 Austin Kearns ROO	8.00	2.40
❑	156 Carlos Zambrano ROO	5.00	1.50
❑	157 Kyle Kane ROO RC	5.00	1.50
❑	158 So Taguchi ROO RC	8.00	2.40
❑	159 Brian Mallette ROO RC	5.00	1.50
❑	160 Brett Jodie ROO	5.00	1.50
❑	161 Elio Serrano ROO RC	5.00	1.50
❑	162 Joe Thurston ROO	5.00	1.50
❑	163 Kevin Olsen ROO	5.00	1.50
❑	164 Rodrigo Rosario ROO RC	5.00	1.50
❑	165 Matt Guerrier ROO	5.00	1.50
❑	166 Anderson Machado ROO RC	8.00	2.40
❑	167 Bert Snow ROO	5.00	1.50
❑	168 Franklyn German ROO RC	5.00	1.50
❑	169 Brandon Claussen ROO	8.00	2.40
❑	170 Jason Romano ROO	5.00	1.50
❑	171 Jorge Padilla ROO RC	8.00	2.40
❑	172 Jose Cueto ROO	5.00	1.50
❑	173 Allan Simpson ROO RC	5.00	1.50
❑	174 Doug Devore ROO RC	5.00	1.50
❑	175 Justin Duchscherer ROO	5.00	1.50
❑	176 Josh Pearce ROO	5.00	1.50
❑	177 Steve Bechler ROO RC	5.00	1.50
❑	178 Josh Phelps ROO	5.00	1.50
❑	179 Juan Diaz ROO	5.00	1.50
❑	180 Victor Alvarez ROO RC	5.00	1.50
❑	181 Ramon Vazquez ROO	5.00	1.50
❑	182 Mike Rivera ROO	5.00	1.50
❑	183 Kazuhisa Ishii ROO RC	10.00	3.00
❑	184 Henry Mateo ROO	5.00	1.50
❑	185 Travis Hughes ROO RC	8.00	2.40
❑	186 Zach Day ROO	5.00	1.50
❑	187 Brad Voyles ROO	5.00	1.50
❑	188 Sean Douglass ROO	5.00	1.50
❑	189 Nick Neugebauer ROO	5.00	1.50
❑	190 Tom Shearn ROO RC	5.00	1.50
❑	191 Eric Cyr ROO	5.00	1.50
❑	192 Adam Johnson ROO	5.00	1.50
❑	193 Michael Cuddyer ROO	5.00	1.50
❑	194 Erik Bedard ROO	5.00	1.50
❑	195 Mark Ellis ROO	5.00	1.50
❑	196 Carlos Hernandez ROO	5.00	1.50
❑	197 Deivis Santos ROO	5.00	1.50
❑	198 Morgan Ensberg ROO	5.00	1.50
❑	199 Ryan Jamison ROO	5.00	1.50
❑	200 Cody Ransom ROO	5.00	1.50
❑	201 Chris Snelling ROO RC	15.00	4.50
❑	202 Satoru Komiyama ROO RC	8.00	2.40
❑	203 Jason Simontacchi ROO RC	10.00	3.00
❑	204 Tim Kalita ROO RC	8.00	2.40
❑	205 Runelvys Hernandez ROO RC	20.00	6.00
❑	206 Kirk Saarloos ROO RC	15.00	4.50
❑	207 Aaron Cook ROO RC	10.00	3.00
❑	208 Luis Ugueto ROO RC	8.00	2.40
❑	209 Gustavo Chacin ROO RC	8.00	2.40
❑	210 Francis Beltran ROO RC	8.00	2.40
❑	211 Takahito Nomura ROO RC	8.00	2.40
❑	212 Oliver Perez ROO RC	15.00	4.50
❑	213 Miguel Asencio ROO RC	8.00	2.40
❑	214 Rene Reyes ROO RC	8.00	2.40
❑	215 Jeff Baker ROO RC	30.00	9.00
❑	216 Jon Adkins ROO RC	8.00	2.40
❑	217 Carlos Rivera ROO RC	15.00	4.50
❑	218 Corey Thurman ROO RC	8.00	2.40
❑	219 Earl Snyder ROO RC	8.00	2.40
❑	220 Felix Escalona ROO RC	8.00	2.40
❑	221 Jeremy Guthrie ROO RC	20.00	6.00
❑	222 Josh Hancock ROO RC	8.00	2.40
❑	223 Ben Kozlowski ROO RC	8.00	2.40
❑	224 Eric Good ROO RC	8.00	2.40
❑	225 Eric Junge ROO RC	8.00	2.40
❑	226 Andy Pratt ROO RC	8.00	2.40
❑	227 Matt Thornton ROO RC	8.00	2.40
❑	228 Jorge Sosa ROO RC	8.00	2.40
❑	229 Mike Smith ROO RC	8.00	2.40
❑	230 Mitch Wylie ROO RC	8.00	2.40
❑	231 John Ennis ROO RC	8.00	2.40
❑	232 Reed Johnson ROO RC	10.00	3.00
❑	233 Joe Borchard ROO	8.00	2.40
❑	234 Ron Calloway ROO RC	8.00	2.40
❑	235 Brian Tallet ROO RC	10.00	3.00
❑	236 Chris Baker ROO RC	8.00	2.40
❑	237 Cliff Lee ROO RC	15.00	4.50
❑	238 Matt Childers ROO RC	8.00	2.40
❑	239 Freddy Sanchez ROO RC	15.00	4.50
❑	240 Chone Figgins ROO RC	8.00	2.40
❑	241 Kevin Cash ROO RC	8.00	2.40
❑	242 Josh Bard ROO RC	8.00	2.40
❑	243 Jeriome Robertson ROO RC	10.00	3.00
❑	244 Jeremy Hill ROO RC	8.00	2.40
❑	245 Shane Nance ROO RC	8.00	2.40
❑	246 Wes Obermueller ROO RC	8.00	2.40
❑	247 Trey Hodges ROO RC	10.00	3.00
❑	248 Eric Eckenstahler ROO RC	8.00	2.40

❑ 249	Jim Rushford ROO RC	8.00	2.40
❑ 250	Jose Castillo ROO RC	30.00	9.00
❑ 251	Garrett Atkins ROO RC	15.00	4.50
❑ 252	Alexis Rios ROO RC	60.00	18.00
❑ 253	Ryan Church ROO RC	15.00	4.50
❑ 254	Jimmy Gobble ROO RC	20.00	6.00
❑ 255	Corwin Malone ROO RC	10.00	3.00
❑ 256	Does Not Exist	-	
❑ 257	Nic Jackson ROO RC	10.00	3.00
❑ 258	Tommy Whiteman ROO RC	15.00	4.50
❑ 259	Mario Ramos ROO RC	8.00	2.40
❑ 260	Rob Bowen ROO RC	8.00	2.40
❑ 261	Josh Wilson ROO RC	10.00	3.00
❑ 262	Tim Hummel ROO RC	8.00	2.40
❑ 263	Does Not Exist	-	
❑ 264	Gerald Laird ROO RC	15.00	4.50
❑ 265	Vinny Chulk ROO RC	8.00	2.40
❑ 266	Jesus Medrano ROO RC	8.00	2.40
❑ 267	Does Not Exist	-	
❑ 268	Does Not Exist	-	
❑ 269	Does Not Exist	-	
❑ 270	Does Not Exist	-	
❑ 271	Does Not Exist	-	
❑ 272	Adam LaRoche ROO RC	30.00	9.00
❑ 273	Adam Morrissey ROO RC	10.00	3.00
❑ 274	Henri Stanley ROO RC	10.00	3.00
❑ 275	Walter Young ROO RC	15.00	4.50

2003 Donruss Elite

	Nm-Mt	Ex-Mt
COMP.SET w/o SP's (180)	20.00	6.00
COMMON CARD (1-180)	.40	.12
COMMON CARD (181-200)	8.00	2.40

❑ 1	Darin Erstad	.40	.12
❑ 2	David Eckstein	.40	.12
❑ 3	Garret Anderson	.40	.12
❑ 4	Jarrod Washburn	.40	.12
❑ 5	Tim Salmon	.60	.18
❑ 6	Troy Glaus	.60	.18
❑ 7	Marty Cordova	.40	.12
❑ 8	Melvin Mora	.40	.12
❑ 9	Rodrigo Lopez	.40	.12
❑ 10	Tony Batista	.40	.12
❑ 11	Derek Lowe	.40	.12
❑ 12	Johnny Damon	.40	.12
❑ 13	Manny Ramirez	.40	.12
❑ 14	Nomar Garciaparra	2.00	.60
❑ 15	Pedro Martinez	1.00	.30
❑ 16	Shea Hillenbrand	.40	.12
❑ 17	Carlos Lee	.40	.12
❑ 18	Joe Crede	.40	.12
❑ 19	Frank Thomas	1.00	.30
❑ 20	Magglio Ordonez	.40	.12
❑ 21	Mark Buehrle	.40	.12
❑ 22	Paul Konerko	.40	.12
❑ 23	C.C. Sabathia	.40	.12
❑ 24	Ellis Burks	.40	.12
❑ 25	Omar Vizquel	.40	.12
❑ 26	Brian Tallet	.40	.12
❑ 27	Bobby Higginson	.40	.12
❑ 28	Carlos Pena	.40	.12
❑ 29	Mark Redman	.40	.12
❑ 30	Steve Sparks	.40	.12
❑ 31	Carlos Beltran	.40	.12
❑ 32	Joe Randa	.40	.12
❑ 33	Mike Sweeney	.40	.12
❑ 34	Raul Ibanez	.40	.12
❑ 35	Runelvys Hernandez	.40	.12
❑ 36	Brad Radke	.40	.12
❑ 37	Corey Koskie	.40	.12
❑ 38	Cristian Guzman	.40	.12
❑ 39	David Ortiz	.40	.12
❑ 40	Doug Mientkiewicz	.40	.12
❑ 41	Jacque Jones	.40	.12
❑ 42	Torii Hunter	.40	.12
❑ 43	Alfonso Soriano	1.00	.30
❑ 44	Andy Pettitte	.60	.18
❑ 45	Bernie Williams	.60	.18
❑ 46	David Wells	.40	.12
❑ 47	Derek Jeter	2.50	.75
❑ 48	Jason Giambi	1.00	.30
❑ 49	Jeff Weaver	.40	.12
❑ 50	Jorge Posada	.60	.18
❑ 51	Mike Mussina	1.00	.30
❑ 52	Roger Clemens	2.00	.60
❑ 53	Barry Zito	1.00	.30
❑ 54	Eric Chavez	.40	.12
❑ 55	Jermaine Dye	.40	.12
❑ 56	Mark Mulder	.40	.12
❑ 57	Miguel Tejada	.40	.12
❑ 58	Tim Hudson	.40	.12
❑ 59	Bret Boone	.40	.12
❑ 60	Chris Snelling	.40	.12
❑ 61	Edgar Martinez	.60	.18
❑ 62	Freddy Garcia	.40	.12
❑ 63	Ichiro Suzuki	2.00	.60
❑ 64	Jamie Moyer	.40	.12
❑ 65	John Olerud	.40	.12
❑ 66	Kazuhiro Sasaki	.40	.12
❑ 67	Aubrey Huff	.40	.12
❑ 68	Joe Kennedy	.40	.12
❑ 69	Paul Wilson	.40	.12
❑ 70	Alex Rodriguez	2.00	.60
❑ 71	Chan Ho Park	.40	.12
❑ 72	Hank Blalock	.60	.18
❑ 73	Juan Gonzalez	1.00	.30
❑ 74	Kevin Mench	.40	.12
❑ 75	Rafael Palmeiro	.60	.18
❑ 76	Carlos Delgado	.40	.12
❑ 77	Eric Hinske	.40	.12
❑ 78	Josh Phelps	.40	.12
❑ 79	Roy Halladay	.40	.12
❑ 80	Shannon Stewart	.40	.12
❑ 81	Vernon Wells	.40	.12
❑ 82	Curt Schilling	.60	.18
❑ 83	Junior Spivey	.40	.12
❑ 84	Luis Gonzalez	.40	.12
❑ 85	Mark Grace	1.00	.30
❑ 86	Randy Johnson	1.00	.30
❑ 87	Steve Finley	.40	.12
❑ 88	Andruw Jones	.60	.18
❑ 89	Chipper Jones	1.00	.30
❑ 90	Gary Sheffield	.40	.12
❑ 91	Greg Maddux	2.00	.60
❑ 92	John Smoltz	.60	.18
❑ 93	Corey Patterson	.40	.12
❑ 94	Kerry Wood	1.00	.30
❑ 95	Mark Prior	2.00	.60
❑ 96	Moises Alou	.40	.12
❑ 97	Sammy Sosa	1.50	.45
❑ 98	Adam Dunn	.60	.18
❑ 99	Austin Kearns	.60	.18
❑ 100	Barry Larkin	1.00	.30
❑ 101	Ken Griffey Jr.	1.50	.45
❑ 102	Sean Casey	.40	.12
❑ 103	Jason Jennings	.40	.12
❑ 104	Jay Payton	.40	.12
❑ 105	Larry Walker	.60	.18
❑ 106	Todd Helton	.60	.18
❑ 107	A.J. Burnett	.40	.12
❑ 108	Josh Beckett	.60	.18
❑ 109	Juan Encarnacion	.40	.12
❑ 110	Mike Lowell	.40	.12
❑ 111	Craig Biggio	.60	.18
❑ 112	Daryle Ward	.40	.12
❑ 113	Jeff Bagwell	.60	.18
❑ 114	Lance Berkman	.40	.12
❑ 115	Roy Oswalt	.40	.12
❑ 116	Jason Lane	.40	.12
❑ 117	Adrian Beltre	.40	.12
❑ 118	Hideo Nomo	1.00	.30
❑ 119	Kazuhisa Ishii	.40	.12
❑ 120	Kevin Brown	.40	.12
❑ 121	Odalis Perez	.40	.12
❑ 122	Paul Lo Duca	.40	.12
❑ 123	Shawn Green	.40	.12
❑ 124	Ben Sheets	.40	.12
❑ 125	Jeffrey Hammonds	.40	.12
❑ 126	Jose Hernandez	.40	.12
❑ 127	Richie Sexson	.40	.12
❑ 128	Bartolo Colon	.40	.12
❑ 129	Brad Wilkerson	.40	.12
❑ 130	Javier Vazquez	.40	.12
❑ 131	Jose Vidro	.40	.12
❑ 132	Michael Barrett	.40	.12
❑ 133	Vladimir Guerrero	1.00	.30
❑ 134	Al Leiter	.40	.12
❑ 135	Mike Piazza	1.50	.45
❑ 136	Mo Vaughn	.40	.12
❑ 137	Pedro Astacio	.40	.12
❑ 138	Roberto Alomar	1.00	.30
❑ 139	Pat Burrell	.40	.12
❑ 140	Vicente Padilla	.40	.12
❑ 141	Jimmy Rollins	.40	.12
❑ 142	Bobby Abreu	.40	.12
❑ 143	Marlon Byrd	.40	.12
❑ 144	Brian Giles	.40	.12
❑ 145	Jason Kendall	.40	.12
❑ 146	Aramis Ramirez	.40	.12
❑ 147	Josh Fogg	.40	.12
❑ 148	Ryan Klesko	.40	.12
❑ 149	Phil Nevin	.40	.12
❑ 150	Sean Burroughs	.40	.12
❑ 151	Mark Kotsay	.40	.12
❑ 152	Barry Bonds	2.50	.75
❑ 153	Damian Moss	.40	.12
❑ 154	Jason Schmidt	.40	.12
❑ 155	Benito Santiago	.40	.12
❑ 156	Rich Aurilia	.40	.12
❑ 157	Scott Rolen	.60	.18
❑ 158	J.D. Drew	.40	.12
❑ 159	Jim Edmonds	.40	.12
❑ 160	Matt Morris	.40	.12
❑ 161	Tino Martinez	.60	.18
❑ 162	Albert Pujols	2.00	.60
❑ 163	Russ Ortiz	.40	.12
❑ 164	Rey Ordonez	.40	.12
❑ 165	Paul Byrd	.40	.12
❑ 166	Kenny Lofton	.40	.12
❑ 167	Kenny Rogers	.40	.12
❑ 168	Rickey Henderson	1.50	.45
❑ 169	Fred McGriff	.60	.18
❑ 170	Charles Johnson	.40	.12
❑ 171	Mike Hampton	.40	.12
❑ 172	Jim Thome	1.00	.30
❑ 173	Travis Hafner	.40	.12
❑ 174	Ivan Rodriguez	1.00	.30
❑ 175	Ray Durham	.40	.12
❑ 176	Jeremy Giambi	.40	.12
❑ 177	Jeff Kent	.40	.12
❑ 178	Cliff Floyd	.40	.12
❑ 179	Kevin Millwood	.40	.12
❑ 180	Tom Glavine	1.00	.30
❑ 181	Hideki Matsui ROO RC	20.00	6.00
❑ 182	Jose Contreras ROO RC	10.00	3.00
❑ 183	Termel Sledge ROO RC	10.00	3.00
❑ 184	Lew Ford ROO RC	10.00	3.00
❑ 185	Jhonny Peralta ROO RC	8.00	2.40
❑ 186	Alexis Rios ROO	8.00	2.40
❑ 187	Jeff Baker ROO	8.00	2.40
❑ 188	Jeremy Guthrie ROO	8.00	2.40
❑ 189	Jose Castillo ROO	8.00	2.40
❑ 190	Garrett Atkins ROO	8.00	2.40
❑ 191	Jeremy Bonderman ROO RC	10.00	3.00
❑ 192	Adam LaRoche ROO	8.00	2.40
❑ 193	Vinny Chulk ROO	8.00	2.40
❑ 194	Walter Young ROO	8.00	2.40
❑ 195	Jimmy Gobble ROO	8.00	2.40
❑ 196	Prentice Redman ROO RC	8.00	2.40
❑ 197	Jason Anderson ROO	8.00	2.40
❑ 198	Nic Jackson ROO	8.00	2.40
❑ 199	Travis Chapman ROO	8.00	2.40
❑ 200	Shane Victorino ROO RC	8.00	2.40

1998 Donruss Signature

	Nm-Mt	Ex-Mt
COMPLETE SET (140)	80.00	24.00
❏ 1 David Justice	.50	.15
❏ 2 Derek Jeter	3.00	.90
❏ 3 Nomar Garciaparra	2.50	.75
❏ 4 Ryan Klesko	.50	.15
❏ 5 Jeff Bagwell	.75	.23
❏ 6 Dante Bichette	.50	.15
❏ 7 Ivan Rodriguez	1.25	.35
❏ 8 Albert Belle	.50	.15
❏ 9 Cal Ripken	4.00	1.20
❏ 10 Craig Biggio	.75	.23
❏ 11 Barry Larkin	1.25	.35
❏ 12 Jose Guillen	.50	.15
❏ 13 Will Clark	1.25	.35
❏ 14 J.T. Snow	.50	.15
❏ 15 Chuck Knoblauch	.50	.15
❏ 16 Todd Walker	.50	.15
❏ 17 Scott Rolen	.75	.23
❏ 18 Rickey Henderson	2.00	.60
❏ 19 Juan Gonzalez	1.25	.35
❏ 20 Justin Thompson	.50	.15
❏ 21 Roger Clemens	2.50	.75
❏ 22 Ray Lankford	.50	.15
❏ 23 Jose Cruz Jr.	.50	.15
❏ 24 Ken Griffey Jr.	2.00	.60
❏ 25 Andruw Jones	.75	.23
❏ 26 Darin Erstad	.50	.15
❏ 27 Jim Thome	1.25	.35
❏ 28 Wade Boggs	.75	.23
❏ 29 Ken Caminiti	.50	.15
❏ 30 Todd Hundley	.50	.15
❏ 31 Mike Piazza	2.00	.60
❏ 32 Sammy Sosa	2.00	.60
❏ 33 Larry Walker	.75	.23
❏ 34 Matt Williams	.50	.15
❏ 35 Frank Thomas	1.25	.35
❏ 36 Gary Sheffield	.50	.15
❏ 37 Alex Rodriguez	2.50	.75
❏ 38 Hideo Nomo	1.25	.35
❏ 39 Kenny Lofton	.50	.15
❏ 40 John Smoltz	.75	.23
❏ 41 Mo Vaughn	.50	.15
❏ 42 Edgar Martinez	.75	.23
❏ 43 Paul Molitor	.75	.23
❏ 44 Rafael Palmeiro	.75	.23
❏ 45 Barry Bonds	3.00	.90
❏ 46 Vladimir Guerrero	1.25	.35
❏ 47 Carlos Delgado	.50	.15
❏ 48 Bobby Higginson	.50	.15
❏ 49 Greg Maddux	2.50	.75
❏ 50 Jim Edmonds	.50	.15
❏ 51 Randy Johnson	1.25	.35
❏ 52 Mark McGwire	3.00	.90
❏ 53 Rondell White	.50	.15
❏ 54 Raul Mondesi	.50	.15
❏ 55 Manny Ramirez	.50	.15
❏ 56 Pedro Martinez	1.25	.35
❏ 57 Tim Salmon	.75	.23
❏ 58 Moises Alou	.50	.15
❏ 59 Fred McGriff	.75	.23
❏ 60 Garret Anderson	.50	.15
❏ 61 Sandy Alomar Jr.	.50	.15
❏ 62 Chan Ho Park	.50	.15
❏ 63 Mark Kotsay	.50	.15
❏ 64 Mike Mussina	1.25	.35
❏ 65 Tom Glavine	1.25	.35
❏ 66 Tony Clark	.50	.15
❏ 67 Mark Grace	1.25	.35
❏ 68 Tony Gwynn	1.50	.45
❏ 69 Tino Martinez	.75	.23
❏ 70 Kevin Brown	.75	.23
❏ 71 Todd Greene	.50	.15
❏ 72 Andy Pettitte	.75	.23
❏ 73 Livan Hernandez	.50	.15
❏ 74 Curt Schilling	.75	.23
❏ 75 Andres Galarraga	.50	.15
❏ 76 Rusty Greer	.50	.15
❏ 77 Jay Buhner	.50	.15
❏ 78 Bobby Bonilla	.50	.15
❏ 79 Chipper Jones	1.25	.35
❏ 80 Eric Young	.50	.15
❏ 81 Jason Giambi	1.25	.35
❏ 82 Javy Lopez	.50	.15
❏ 83 Roberto Alomar	1.25	.35
❏ 84 Bernie Williams	.75	.23
❏ 85 A.J. Hinch	.50	.15
❏ 86 Kerry Wood	1.25	.35
❏ 87 Juan Encarnacion	.50	.15
❏ 88 Brad Fullmer	.50	.15
❏ 89 Ben Grieve	.50	.15
❏ 90 Magglio Ordonez RC	10.00	3.00
❏ 91 Todd Helton	.75	.23
❏ 92 Richard Hidalgo	.50	.15
❏ 93 Paul Konerko	.50	.15
❏ 94 Aramis Ramirez	.50	.15
❏ 95 Ricky Ledee	.50	.15
❏ 96 Derrek Lee	.50	.15
❏ 97 Travis Lee	.50	.15
❏ 98 Matt Anderson RC	.75	.23
❏ 99 Jaret Wright	.50	.15
❏ 100 David Ortiz	.50	.15
❏ 101 Carl Pavano	.50	.15
❏ 102 O.Hernandez RC	2.50	.75
❏ 103 Fernando Tatis	.50	.15
❏ 104 Miguel Tejada	.75	.23
❏ 105 Rolando Arrojo RC	.75	.23
❏ 106 Kevin Millwood RC	4.00	1.20
❏ 107 Ken Griffey Jr. CL	1.25	.35
❏ 108 Frank Thomas CL	.75	.23
❏ 109 Cal Ripken CL	2.00	.60
❏ 110 Greg Maddux CL	1.25	.35
❏ 111 John Olerud	.50	.15
❏ 112 David Cone	.50	.15
❏ 113 Vinny Castilla	.50	.15
❏ 114 Jason Kendall	.50	.15
❏ 115 Brian Jordan	.50	.15
❏ 116 Hideki Irabu	.50	.15
❏ 117 Bartolo Colon	.50	.15
❏ 118 Greg Vaughn	.50	.15
❏ 119 David Segui	.50	.15
❏ 120 Bruce Chen	.50	.15
❏ 121 Julio Ramirez RC	.50	.15
❏ 122 Troy Glaus RC	12.00	3.60
❏ 123 Jeremy Giambi RC	.75	.23
❏ 124 Ryan Minor RC	.50	.15
❏ 125 Richie Sexson	.50	.15
❏ 126 Dermal Brown	.50	.15
❏ 127 Adrian Beltre	.50	.15
❏ 128 Eric Chavez	.75	.23
❏ 129 J.D. Drew RC	8.00	2.40
❏ 130 Gabe Kapler RC	1.25	.35
❏ 131 Masato Yoshii RC	1.25	.35
❏ 132 Mike Lowell RC	5.00	1.50
❏ 133 Jim Parque RC	.75	.23
❏ 134 Roy Halladay	.75	.23
❏ 135 Carlos Lee RC	2.50	.75
❏ 136 Jin Ho Cho RC	.75	.23
❏ 137 Michael Barrett	.50	.15
❏ 138 F.Seguignol RC	.75	.23
❏ 139 Odalis Perez RC UER Back pictures John Rocker	1.25	.35
❏ 140 Mark McGwire CL	1.50	.45

2001 Donruss Signature

	Nm-Mt	Ex-Mt
COMP.SET w/o SP'S (110)	50.00	15.00
COMMON CARD (1-110)	1.00	.30
COMMON (111-165)	15.00	4.50
COMMON (166-311)	8.00	2.40

	Nm-Mt	Ex-Mt
❏ 1 Alex Rodriguez	5.00	1.50
❏ 2 Barry Bonds	6.00	1.80
❏ 3 Cal Ripken	8.00	2.40
❏ 4 Chipper Jones	2.50	.75
❏ 5 Derek Jeter	6.00	1.80
❏ 6 Troy Glaus	1.50	.45
❏ 7 Frank Thomas	2.50	.75
❏ 8 Greg Maddux	5.00	1.50
❏ 9 Ivan Rodriguez	2.50	.75
❏ 10 Jeff Bagwell	1.50	.45
❏ 11 John Olerud	1.00	.30
❏ 12 Todd Helton	1.50	.45
❏ 13 Ken Griffey Jr.	4.00	1.20
❏ 14 Manny Ramirez	1.00	.30
❏ 15 Mark McGwire	6.00	1.80
❏ 16 Mike Piazza	4.00	1.20
❏ 17 Nomar Garciaparra	5.00	1.50
❏ 18 Moises Alou	1.00	.30
❏ 19 Aramis Ramirez	1.00	.30
❏ 20 Curt Schilling	1.50	.45
❏ 21 Pat Burrell	1.00	.30
❏ 22 Doug Mientkiewicz	1.00	.30
❏ 23 Carlos Delgado	1.00	.30
❏ 24 J.D. Drew	1.00	.30
❏ 25 Cliff Floyd	1.00	.30
❏ 26 Freddy Garcia	1.00	.30
❏ 27 Roberto Alomar	2.50	.75
❏ 28 Barry Zito	2.50	.75
❏ 29 Juan Encarnacion	1.00	.30
❏ 30 Paul Konerko	1.00	.30
❏ 31 Mark Mulder	1.00	.30
❏ 32 Andy Pettitte	1.50	.45
❏ 33 Jim Edmonds	1.00	.30
❏ 34 Darin Erstad	1.00	.30
❏ 35 Jason Giambi	2.50	.75
❏ 36 Tom Glavine	2.50	.75
❏ 37 Juan Gonzalez	2.50	.75
❏ 38 Fred McGriff	1.50	.45
❏ 39 Shawn Green	1.00	.30
❏ 40 Tim Hudson	1.00	.30
❏ 41 Andruw Jones	1.50	.45
❏ 42 Jeff Kent	1.00	.30
❏ 43 Barry Larkin	2.50	.75
❏ 44 Brad Radke	1.00	.30
❏ 45 Mike Mussina	2.50	.75
❏ 46 Hideo Nomo	2.50	.75
❏ 47 Rafael Palmeiro	1.50	.45
❏ 48 Scott Rolen	1.50	.45
❏ 49 Gary Sheffield	1.00	.30
❏ 50 Bernie Williams	1.50	.45
❏ 51 Bob Abreu	1.00	.30
❏ 52 Edgardo Alfonzo	1.00	.30
❏ 53 Edgar Martinez	1.50	.45
❏ 54 Magglio Ordonez	1.00	.30
❏ 55 Kerry Wood	2.50	.75
❏ 56 Adrian Beltre	1.00	.30
❏ 57 Lance Berkman	1.00	.30
❏ 58 Kevin Brown	2.50	.75
❏ 59 Sean Casey	1.00	.30
❏ 60 Eric Chavez	1.00	.30
❏ 61 Bartolo Colon	1.00	.30
❏ 62 Sammy Sosa	4.00	1.20
❏ 63 Jermaine Dye	1.00	.30
❏ 64 Tony Gwynn	3.00	.90
❏ 65 Carl Everett	1.00	.30
❏ 66 Brian Giles	1.00	.30
❏ 67 Mike Hampton	1.00	.30
❏ 68 Richard Hidalgo	1.00	.30

❑ 69 Geoff Jenkins 1.00 .30
❑ 70 Tony Clark 1.00 .30
❑ 71 Roger Clemens 5.00 1.50
❑ 72 Ryan Klesko 1.00 .30
❑ 73 Chan Ho Park 1.00 .30
❑ 74 Richie Sexson 1.00 .30
❑ 75 Mike Sweeney 1.00 .30
❑ 76 Kazuhiro Sasaki 1.00 .30
❑ 77 Miguel Tejada 1.00 .30
❑ 78 Jose Vidro 1.00 .30
❑ 79 Larry Walker 1.50 .45
❑ 80 Preston Wilson 1.00 .30
❑ 81 Craig Biggio 1.50 .45
❑ 82 Andres Galarraga 1.00 .30
❑ 83 Jim Thome 2.50 .75
❑ 84 Vladimir Guerrero 2.50 .75
❑ 85 Rafael Furcal 1.00 .30
❑ 86 Cristian Guzman 1.00 .30
❑ 87 Terrence Long 1.00 .30
❑ 88 Bret Boone 1.00 .30
❑ 89 Wade Miller 1.00 .30
❑ 90 Eric Milton 1.00 .30
❑ 91 Gabe Kapler 1.00 .30
❑ 92 Johnny Damon 1.00 .30
❑ 93 Carlos Lee 1.00 .30
❑ 94 Kenny Lofton 1.00 .30
❑ 95 Raul Mondesi 1.00 .30
❑ 96 Jorge Posada 1.50 .45
❑ 97 Mark Grace 2.50 .75
❑ 98 Robert Fick 1.00 .30
❑ 99 Joe Mays 1.00 .30
❑ 100 Aaron Sele 1.00 .30
❑ 101 Ben Grieve 1.00 .30
❑ 102 Luis Gonzalez 1.00 .30
❑ 103 Ray Durham 1.00 .30
❑ 104 Mark Quinn 1.00 .30
❑ 105 Jose Canseco 2.50 .75
❑ 106 David Justice 1.00 .30
❑ 107 Pedro Martinez 2.50 .75
❑ 108 Randy Johnson 2.50 .75
❑ 109 Phil Nevin 1.00 .30
❑ 110 Rickey Henderson 4.00 1.20
❑ 111 Alex Escobar AU 15.00 4.50
❑ 112 J.Estrada AU RC 25.00 7.50
❑ 113 Pedro Feliz AU 15.00 4.50
❑ 114 Nate Frese AU RC 15.00 4.50
❑ 115 R. Rodriguez AU RC 15.00 4.50
❑ 116 B.Larson AU RC 15.00 4.50
❑ 117 Alexis Gomez AU RC 15.00 4.50
❑ 118 Jason Hart AU 15.00 4.50
❑ 119 C.C. Sabathia AU 15.00 4.50
❑ 120 Endy Chavez AU RC 15.00 4.50
❑ 121 C.Parker AU RC 15.00 4.50
❑ 122 Jackson Melian RC 8.00 2.40
❑ 123 Joe Kennedy AU RC 15.00 4.50
❑ 124 A.Hernandez AU RC 15.00 4.50
❑ 125 Cesar Izturis AU 15.00 4.50
❑ 126 Jose Mieses AU RC 15.00 4.50
❑ 127 Roy Oswalt AU 25.00 7.50
❑ 128 Eric Munson AU 15.00 4.50
❑ 129 Xavier Nady AU 15.00 4.50
❑ 130 H.Ramirez AU RC 25.00 7.50
❑ 131 Abraham Nunez AU 15.00 4.50
❑ 132 Jose Ortiz AU 15.00 4.50
❑ 133 Jeremy Owens AU RC 15.00 4.50
❑ 134 Claudio Vargas AU RC 15.00 4.50
❑ 135 Corey Patterson AU 25.00 7.50
❑ 136 Carlos Pena 8.00 2.40
❑ 137 Bud Smith AU RC 15.00 4.50
❑ 138 Adam Dunn AU 40.00 12.00
❑ 139 A.Pettyjohn AU RC 15.00 4.50
❑ 140 E.Guzman AU RC 15.00 4.50
❑ 141 Jay Gibbons AU RC 25.00 7.50
❑ 142 Wilkin Ruan AU RC 15.00 4.50
❑ 143 Tsuyoshi Shinjo RC 12.00 3.60
❑ 144 Alfonso Soriano AU 60.00 18.00
❑ 145 Marcus Giles AU 15.00 4.50
❑ 146 Ichiro Suzuki RC 80.00 24.00
❑ 147 Juan Uribe AU RC 15.00 4.50
❑ 148 David Williams AU RC 15.00 4.50
❑ 149 C. Valderrama AU RC 15.00 4.50
❑ 150 Matt White AU RC 15.00 4.50
❑ 151 Albert Pujols AU RC 400.00 120.00
❑ 152 D.Mendez AU RC 15.00 4.50
❑ 153 Cory Aldridge AU RC 15.00 4.50
❑ 154 B. Duckworth AU RC 15.00 4.50
❑ 155 Josh Beckett AU 40.00 12.00
❑ 156 W.Betemit AU RC 15.00 4.50
❑ 157 Ben Sheets AU 15.00 4.50
❑ 158 Andres Torres AU RC 15.00 4.50
❑ 159 Aubrey Huff AU 15.00 4.50
❑ 160 Jack Wilson AU RC 15.00 4.50
❑ 161 Rafael Soriano AU RC 40.00 12.00
❑ 162 Nick Johnson AU 15.00 4.50
❑ 163 Carlos Garcia AU RC 15.00 4.50
❑ 164 Josh Towers AU RC 15.00 4.50
❑ 165 J.Michaels AU RC 15.00 4.50
❑ 166 Ryan Drese RC 8.00 2.40
❑ 167 Dewon Brazelton RC 8.00 2.40
❑ 168 Kevin Olsen RC 8.00 2.40
❑ 169 Benito Baez RC 8.00 2.40
❑ 170 Mark Prior RC 80.00 24.00
❑ 171 Wilmy Caceres RC 8.00 2.40
❑ 172 Mark Teixeira RC 40.00 12.00
❑ 173 Willie Harris RC 8.00 2.40
❑ 174 Mike Koplove RC 8.00 2.40
❑ 175 Brandon Knight RC 8.00 2.40
❑ 176 John Grabow RC 8.00 2.40
❑ 177 Jeremy Affeldt RC 8.00 2.40
❑ 178 Brandon Inge 8.00 2.40
❑ 179 Casey Fossum RC 8.00 2.40
❑ 180 Scott Stewart RC 8.00 2.40
❑ 181 Luke Hudson RC 8.00 2.40
❑ 182 Ken Vining RC 8.00 2.40
❑ 183 Toby Hall 8.00 2.40
❑ 184 Eric Knott RC 8.00 2.40
❑ 185 Kris Foster RC 8.00 2.40
❑ 186 David Brous RC 8.00 2.40
❑ 187 Roy Smith RC 8.00 2.40
❑ 188 Grant Balfour RC 8.00 2.40
❑ 189 Jeremy Fikac RC 8.00 2.40
❑ 190 Morgan Ensberg RC 12.00 3.60
❑ 191 Ryan Freel RC 8.00 2.40
❑ 192 Ryan Jensen RC 8.00 2.40
❑ 193 Lance Davis RC 8.00 2.40
❑ 194 Delvin James RC 8.00 2.40
❑ 195 Timo Perez 8.00 2.40
❑ 196 Michael Cuddyer 8.00 2.40
❑ 197 Bob File RC 8.00 2.40
❑ 198 Martin Vargas RC 8.00 2.40
❑ 199 Kris Keller RC 8.00 2.40
❑ 200 T.Spooneybarger RC 8.00 2.40
❑ 201 Adam Everett 8.00 2.40
❑ 202 Josh Fogg RC 8.00 2.40
❑ 203 Kip Wells 8.00 2.40
❑ 204 Rick Bauer RC 8.00 2.40
❑ 205 Brent Abernathy 8.00 2.40
❑ 206 Erick Almonte RC 8.00 2.40
❑ 207 Pedro Santana RC 8.00 2.40
❑ 208 Ken Harvey 8.00 2.40
❑ 209 Jerrod Riggan RC 8.00 2.40
❑ 210 Nick Punto RC 8.00 2.40
❑ 211 Steve Green RC 8.00 2.40
❑ 212 Nick Neugebauer 8.00 2.40
❑ 213 Chris George 8.00 2.40
❑ 214 Mike Penney RC 8.00 2.40
❑ 215 Bret Prinz RC 8.00 2.40
❑ 216 Tim Christman RC 8.00 2.40
❑ 217 Sean Douglass RC 8.00 2.40
❑ 218 Brett Jodie RC 8.00 2.40
❑ 219 Juan Diaz RC 8.00 2.40
❑ 220 Carlos Hernandez 8.00 2.40
❑ 221 Alex Cintron 8.00 2.40
❑ 222 Juan Cruz RC 8.00 2.40
❑ 223 Larry Bigbie 8.00 2.40
❑ 224 Junior Spivey RC 10.00 3.00
❑ 225 Luis Rivas 8.00 2.40
❑ 226 Brandon Lyon RC 8.00 2.40
❑ 227 Tony Cogan RC 8.00 2.40
❑ 228 J.Duchscherer RC 8.00 2.40
❑ 229 Tike Redman 8.00 2.40
❑ 230 Jimmy Rollins 8.00 2.40
❑ 231 Scott Podsednik RC 40.00 12.00
❑ 232 Jose Acevedo RC 8.00 2.40
❑ 233 Luis Pineda RC 8.00 2.40
❑ 234 Josh Phelps 8.00 2.40
❑ 235 Paul Phillips RC 8.00 2.40
❑ 236 Brian Roberts RC 8.00 2.40
❑ 237 O.Woodards RC 8.00 2.40
❑ 238 Bart Miadich RC 8.00 2.40
❑ 239 Les Walrond RC 8.00 2.40
❑ 240 Brad Voyles RC 8.00 2.40
❑ 241 Joe Crede 8.00 2.40
❑ 242 Juan Moreno RC 8.00 2.40
❑ 243 Matt Ginter 8.00 2.40
❑ 244 Brian Rogers RC 8.00 2.40
❑ 245 Pablo Ozuna 8.00 2.40
❑ 246 Geronimo Gil RC 8.00 2.40
❑ 247 Mike Maroth RC 8.00 2.40
❑ 248 Josue Perez RC 8.00 2.40
❑ 249 Dee Brown 8.00 2.40
❑ 250 Victor Zambrano RC 8.00 2.40
❑ 251 Nick Maness RC 8.00 2.40
❑ 252 Kyle Lohse RC 10.00 3.00
❑ 253 Greg Miller RC 8.00 2.40
❑ 254 Henry Mateo RC 8.00 2.40
❑ 255 Duaner Sanchez RC 8.00 2.40
❑ 256 Rob MacKowiak RC 8.00 2.40
❑ 257 Steve Lomasney 8.00 2.40
❑ 258 Angel Santos RC 8.00 2.40
❑ 259 Winston Abreu RC 8.00 2.40
❑ 260 Brandon Berger RC 8.00 2.40
❑ 261 Tomas De La Rosa 8.00 2.40
❑ 262 Ramon Vazquez RC 8.00 2.40
❑ 263 Mickey Callaway RC 8.00 2.40
❑ 264 Corky Miller RC 8.00 2.40
❑ 265 Keith Ginter 8.00 2.40
❑ 266 Cody Ransom RC 8.00 2.40
❑ 267 Doug Nickle RC 8.00 2.40
❑ 268 Derrick Lewis RC 8.00 2.40
❑ 269 Eric Hinske RC 10.00 3.00
❑ 270 Travis Phelps RC 8.00 2.40
❑ 271 Eric Valent 8.00 2.40
❑ 272 Michael Rivera RC 8.00 2.40
❑ 273 Esix Snead RC 8.00 2.40
❑ 274 Troy Mattes RC 8.00 2.40
❑ 275 Jermaine Clark RC 8.00 2.40
❑ 276 Nate Cornejo 8.00 2.40
❑ 277 George Perez RC 8.00 2.40
❑ 278 Juan Rivera 8.00 2.40
❑ 279 Justin Atchley RC 8.00 2.40
❑ 280 Adam Johnson 8.00 2.40
❑ 281 Gene Altman RC 8.00 2.40
❑ 282 Jason Jennings 8.00 2.40
❑ 283 Scott MacRae RC 8.00 2.40
❑ 284 Craig Monroe RC 8.00 2.40
❑ 285 Bert Snow RC 8.00 2.40
❑ 286 Stubby Clapp RC 8.00 2.40
❑ 287 Jack Cust 8.00 2.40
❑ 288 Will Ohman RC 8.00 2.40
❑ 289 Wily Mo Pena 8.00 2.40
❑ 290 Joe Beimel RC 8.00 2.40
❑ 291 Jason Karnuth RC 8.00 2.40
❑ 292 Bill Ortega RC 8.00 2.40
❑ 293 Nate Teut RC 8.00 2.40
❑ 294 Erik Hiljus RC 8.00 2.40
❑ 295 Jason Smith RC 8.00 2.40
❑ 296 Juan A.Pena RC 8.00 2.40
❑ 297 David Espinosa 8.00 2.40
❑ 298 Tim Redding 8.00 2.40
❑ 299 Brian Lawrence RC 8.00 2.40
❑ 300 Brian Reith RC 8.00 2.40
❑ 301 Chad Durbin 8.00 2.40
❑ 302 Kurt Ainsworth 8.00 2.40
❑ 303 Blaine Neal RC 8.00 2.40
❑ 304 Jorge Julio RC 8.00 2.40
❑ 305 Adam Bernero 8.00 2.40
❑ 306 Travis Hafner RC 10.00 3.00
❑ 307 Dustan Mohr RC 8.00 2.40
❑ 308 Cesar Crespo RC 8.00 2.40
❑ 309 Billy Sylvester RC 8.00 2.40
❑ 310 Zach Day RC 10.00 3.00
❑ 311 Angel Berroa RC 15.00 4.50

2003 Donruss Signature

	MINT	NRMT
COMMON CARD (1-100)	1.00	.45
COMMON CARD (101-150)	1.00	.45

❑ 1 Garret Anderson 1.00 .45
❑ 2 Tim Salmon 1.50 .70
❑ 3 Troy Glaus 1.50 .70
❑ 4 Curt Schilling 1.50 .70
❑ 5 Luis Gonzalez 1.00 .45
❑ 6 Mark Grace 2.50 1.10
❑ 7 Matt Williams 1.00 .45
❑ 8 Randy Johnson 2.50 1.10

❑ 9 Andruw Jones 1.50 .70
❑ 10 Chipper Jones 2.50 1.10
❑ 11 Gary Sheffield 1.00 .45
❑ 12 Greg Maddux 5.00 2.20
❑ 13 Johnny Damon 1.00 .45
❑ 14 Manny Ramirez 1.00 .45
❑ 15 Nomar Garciaparra 5.00 2.20
❑ 16 Pedro Martinez 2.50 1.10
❑ 17 Corey Patterson 1.00 .45
❑ 18 Kerry Wood 2.50 1.10
❑ 19 Mark Prior 5.00 2.20
❑ 20 Sammy Sosa 4.00 1.80
❑ 21 Bartolo Colon 1.00 .45
❑ 22 Frank Thomas 2.50 1.10
❑ 23 Magglio Ordonez 1.00 .45
❑ 24 Paul Konerko 1.00 .45
❑ 25 Adam Dunn 1.50 .70
❑ 26 Austin Kearns 1.50 .70
❑ 27 Barry Larkin 2.50 1.10
❑ 28 Ken Griffey Jr. 4.00 1.80
❑ 29 C.C. Sabathia 1.00 .45
❑ 30 Omar Vizquel 1.00 .45
❑ 31 Larry Walker 1.50 .70
❑ 32 Todd Helton 1.50 .70
❑ 33 Ivan Rodriguez 2.50 1.10
❑ 34 Josh Beckett 1.50 .70
❑ 35 Craig Biggio 1.50 .70
❑ 36 Jeff Bagwell 1.50 .70
❑ 37 Jeff Kent 1.00 .45
❑ 38 Lance Berkman 1.00 .45
❑ 39 Richard Hidalgo 1.00 .45
❑ 40 Roy Oswalt 1.00 .45
❑ 41 Carlos Beltran 1.00 .45
❑ 42 Mike Sweeney 1.00 .45
❑ 43 Runelvys Hernandez 1.00 .45
❑ 44 Hideo Nomo 2.50 1.10
❑ 45 Kazuhisa Ishii 1.00 .45
❑ 46 Paul Lo Duca 1.00 .45
❑ 47 Shawn Green 1.00 .45
❑ 48 Ben Sheets 1.00 .45
❑ 49 Richie Sexson 1.00 .45
❑ 50 A.J. Pierzynski 1.00 .45
❑ 51 Torii Hunter 1.00 .45
❑ 52 Javier Vazquez 1.00 .45
❑ 53 Jose Vidro 1.00 .45
❑ 54 Vladimir Guerrero 2.50 1.10
❑ 55 Cliff Floyd 1.00 .45
❑ 56 David Cone 1.00 .45
❑ 57 Mike Piazza 4.00 1.80
❑ 58 Roberto Alomar 2.50 1.10
❑ 59 Tom Glavine 2.50 1.10
❑ 60 Alfonso Soriano 2.50 1.10
❑ 61 Derek Jeter 6.00 2.70
❑ 62 Drew Henson 1.00 .45
❑ 63 Jason Giambi 2.50 1.10
❑ 64 Mike Mussina 2.50 1.10
❑ 65 Nick Johnson 1.00 .45
❑ 66 Roger Clemens 5.00 2.20
❑ 67 Barry Zito 2.50 1.10
❑ 68 Eric Chavez 1.00 .45
❑ 69 Mark Mulder 1.00 .45
❑ 70 Miguel Tejada 1.00 .45
❑ 71 Tim Hudson 1.00 .45
❑ 72 Bobby Abreu 1.00 .45
❑ 73 Jim Thome 2.50 1.10
❑ 74 Kevin Millwood 1.00 .45
❑ 75 Pat Burrell 1.00 .45
❑ 76 Brian Giles 1.00 .45
❑ 77 Jason Kendall 1.00 .45
❑ 78 Kenny Lofton 1.00 .45
❑ 79 Phil Nevin 1.00 .45
❑ 80 Ryan Klesko 1.00 .45
❑ 81 Andres Galarraga 1.00 .45
❑ 82 Barry Bonds 6.00 2.70
❑ 83 Rich Aurilia 1.00 .45
❑ 84 Edgar Martinez 1.50 .70
❑ 85 Freddy Garcia 1.00 .45
❑ 86 Ichiro Suzuki 5.00 2.20
❑ 87 Albert Pujols 5.00 2.20
❑ 88 Jim Edmonds 1.00 .45
❑ 89 Scott Rolen 1.50 .70
❑ 90 So Taguchi 1.00 .45
❑ 91 Rocco Baldelli 5.00 2.20
❑ 92 Alex Rodriguez 5.00 2.20
❑ 93 Hank Blalock 1.50 .70
❑ 94 Juan Gonzalez 2.50 1.10
❑ 95 Mark Teixeira 1.50 .70
❑ 96 Rafael Palmeiro 1.50 .70
❑ 97 Carlos Delgado 1.00 .45
❑ 98 Eric Hinske 1.00 .45
❑ 99 Roy Halladay 1.00 .45
❑ 100 Vernon Wells 1.00 .45
❑ 101 Hideki Matsui ROO RC 12.00 5.50
❑ 102 Jose Contreras ROO RC 5.00 2.20
❑ 103 Jeremy Bonderman ROO RC 5.00 2.20
❑ 104 Bernie Castro ROO RC 1.00 .45
❑ 105 Alfredo Gonzalez ROO RC 1.00 .45
❑ 106 Arnie Munoz ROO RC 1.00 .45
❑ 107 Andrew Brown ROO RC 1.00 .45
❑ 108 Josh Hall ROO RC 1.50 .70
❑ 109 Josh Stewart ROO RC 1.00 .45
❑ 110 Clint Barmes ROO RC 1.50 .70
❑ 111 Brandon Webb ROO RC 6.00 2.70
❑ 112 Chien-Ming Wang ROO RC 5.00 2.20
❑ 113 Edgar Gonzalez ROO RC 1.00 .45
❑ 114 Alejandro Machado ROO RC 1.00 .45
❑ 115 Jeremy Griffiths ROO RC 1.50 .70
❑ 116 Craig Brazell ROO RC 2.50 1.10
❑ 117 Shane Bazzell ROO RC 1.00 .45
❑ 118 Fernando Cabrera ROO RC 1.50 .70
❑ 119 Terrmel Sledge ROO RC 1.50 .70
❑ 120 Rob Hammock ROO RC 2.50 1.10
❑ 121 Francisco Rosario ROO RC 1.00 .45
❑ 122 Francisco Cruceta ROO RC 1.00 .45
❑ 123 Rett Johnson ROO RC 1.50 .70
❑ 124 Guillermo Quiroz ROO RC 3.00 1.35
❑ 125 Hong-Chih Kuo ROO RC 2.50 1.10
❑ 126 Ian Ferguson ROO RC 1.00 .45
❑ 127 Tim Olson ROO RC 2.50 1.10
❑ 128 Todd Wellemeyer ROO RC 1.50 .70
❑ 129 Rich Fischer ROO RC 1.00 .45
❑ 130 Phil Seibel ROO RC 1.00 .45
❑ 131 Joe Valentine ROO RC 1.00 .45
❑ 132 Matt Kata ROO RC 3.00 1.35
❑ 133 Michael Hessman ROO RC 1.00 .45
❑ 134 Michel Hernandez ROO RC 1.00 .45
❑ 135 Doug Waechter ROO RC 2.50 1.10
❑ 136 Prentice Redman ROO RC 1.00 .45
❑ 137 Nook Logan ROO RC 1.00 .45
❑ 138 Oscar Villarreal ROO RC 1.00 .45
❑ 139 Pete LaForest ROO RC 1.50 .70
❑ 140 Matt Bruback ROO RC 1.00 .45
❑ 141 Dontrelle Willis ROO 5.00 2.20
❑ 142 Greg Aquino ROO RC 1.00 .45
❑ 143 Lew Ford ROO RC 1.50 .70
❑ 144 Jeff Duncan ROO RC 1.50 .70
❑ 145 Dan Haren ROO RC 3.00 1.35
❑ 146 Miguel Ojeda ROO RC 1.00 .45
❑ 147 Rosman Garcia ROO RC 1.00 .45
❑ 148 Felix Sanchez ROO RC 1.00 .45
❑ 149 Jon Leicester ROO RC 1.00 .45
❑ 150 Roger Deago ROO RC 1.00 .45

2003 Donruss Team Heroes

	Nm-Mt	Ex-Mt
COMPLETE SET (548)	80.00	24.00

❑ 1 Adam Kennedy .30 .09
❑ 2 Steve Green .30 .09
❑ 3 Rod Carew Angels .75 .23
❑ 4 Alfredo Amezaga .30 .09

❑ 5 Reggie Jackson Angels .75 .23
❑ 6 Jarrod Washburn .30 .09
❑ 7 Nolan Ryan Angels 4.00 1.20
❑ 8 Tim Salmon .50 .15
❑ 9 Garret Anderson .30 .09
❑ 10 Darin Erstad .30 .09
❑ 11 Elpidio Guzman .30 .09
❑ 12 David Eckstein .30 .09
❑ 13 Troy Percival .30 .09
❑ 14 Troy Glaus .50 .15
❑ 15 Doug Devore .30 .09
❑ 16 Tony Womack .30 .09
❑ 17 Matt Williams .30 .09
❑ 18 Junior Spivey .30 .09
❑ 19 Mark Grace .75 .23
❑ 20 Curt Schilling .50 .15
❑ 21 Erubiel Durazo .30 .09
❑ 22 Craig Counsell .30 .09
❑ 23 Byung-Hyun Kim .30 .09
❑ 24 Randy Johnson D'backs .75 .23
❑ 25 Luis Gonzalez .30 .09
❑ 26 John Smoltz .50 .15
❑ 27 Tim Spooneybarger .30 .09
❑ 28 Dale Murphy 1.25 .35
❑ 29 Warren Spahn .75 .23
❑ 30 Jason Marquis .30 .09
❑ 31 Kevin Millwood .30 .09
❑ 32 Javy Lopez .30 .09
❑ 33 Vinny Castilla .30 .09
❑ 34 Julio Franco .30 .09
❑ 35 Trey Hodges .30 .09
❑ 36 Chipper Jones .75 .23
❑ 37 Gary Sheffield .30 .09
❑ 38 Billy Sylvester .30 .09
❑ 39 Tom Glavine .75 .23
❑ 40 Rafael Furcal .30 .09
❑ 41 Cory Aldridge .30 .09
❑ 42 Greg Maddux Braves 1.50 .45
❑ 43 John Ennis .30 .09
❑ 44 Wes Helms .30 .09
❑ 45 Horacio Ramirez .30 .09
❑ 46 Derrick Lewis .30 .09
❑ 47 Marcus Giles .30 .09
❑ 48 Eddie Mathews 1.25 .35
❑ 49 Wilson Betemit .30 .09
❑ 50 Andruw Jones .50 .15
❑ 51 Josh Towers .30 .09
❑ 52 Ed Rogers .30 .09
❑ 53 Kris Foster .30 .09
❑ 54 Brooks Robinson 1.25 .35
❑ 55 Cal Ripken 4.00 1.20
❑ 56 Brian Roberts .30 .09
❑ 57 Luis Rivera .30 .09
❑ 58 Rodrigo Lopez .30 .09
❑ 59 Geronimo Gil .30 .09
❑ 60 Erik Bedard .30 .09
❑ 61 Jim Palmer .50 .15
❑ 62 Jay Gibbons .30 .09
❑ 63 Travis Driskill .30 .09
❑ 64 Larry Bigbie .30 .09
❑ 65 Eddie Murray 1.25 .35
❑ 66 Hoyt Wilhelm .50 .15
❑ 67 Bobby Doerr .50 .15
❑ 68 Pedro Martinez .75 .23
❑ 69 Roger Clemens Red Sox 1.50 .45
❑ 70 Nomar Garciaparra 1.50 .45
❑ 71 Trot Nixon .30 .09
❑ 72 Dennis Eckersley Red Sox .50 .15

❑ 73 John Burkett .30 .09
❑ 74 Tim Wakefield .30 .09
❑ 75 Wade Boggs Red Sox .75 .23
❑ 76 Cliff Floyd .30 .09
❑ 77 Casey Fossum .30 .09
❑ 78 Johnny Damon .30 .09
❑ 79 Fred Lynn .50 .15
❑ 80 Rickey Henderson Red Sox 1.25 .35
❑ 81 Juan Diaz .30 .09
❑ 82 Manny Ramirez .30 .09
❑ 83 Carlton Fisk Red Sox .75 .23
❑ 84 Jorge De La Rosa .30 .09
❑ 85 Shea Hillenbrand .30 .09
❑ 86 Derek Lowe .30 .09
❑ 87 Jason Varitek .30 .09
❑ 88 Carlos Baerga .30 .09
❑ 89 Freddy Sanchez .30 .09
❑ 90 Ugueth Urbina .30 .09
❑ 91 Rey Sanchez .30 .09
❑ 92 Josh Hancock .30 .09
❑ 93 Tony Clark .30 .09
❑ 94 Dustin Hermanson .30 .09
❑ 95 Ryne Sandberg 2.50 .75
❑ 96 Fred McGriff .50 .15
❑ 97 Alex Gonzalez .30 .09
❑ 98 Mark Bellhorn .30 .09
❑ 99 Fergie Jenkins .50 .15
❑ 100 Jon Lieber .30 .09
❑ 101 Francis Beltran .30 .09
❑ 102 Greg Maddux Cubs 1.50 .45
❑ 103 Nate Frese .30 .09
❑ 104 Andre Dawson Cubs .75 .23
❑ 105 Carlos Zambrano .30 .09
❑ 106 Steve Smyth .30 .09
❑ 107 Ernie Banks 1.25 .35
❑ 108 Will Ohman .30 .09
❑ 109 Kerry Wood .75 .23
❑ 110 Bobby Hill .30 .09
❑ 111 Moises Alou .30 .09
❑ 112 Hee Seop Choi .30 .09
❑ 113 Corey Patterson .30 .09
❑ 114 Sammy Sosa 1.25 .35
❑ 115 Mark Prior 1.50 .45
❑ 116 Juan Cruz .30 .09
❑ 117 Ron Santo .75 .23
❑ 118 Billy Williams .50 .15
❑ 119 Antonio Alfonseca .30 .09
❑ 120 Matt Clement .30 .09
❑ 121 Carlton Fisk White Sox .75 .23
❑ 122 Joe Crede .30 .09
❑ 123 Magglio Ordonez .30 .09
❑ 124 Frank Thomas .75 .23
❑ 125 Joe Borchard .30 .09
❑ 126 Royce Clayton .30 .09
❑ 127 Luis Aparicio .50 .15
❑ 128 Willie Harris .30 .09
❑ 129 Kyle Kane .30 .09
❑ 130 Paul Konerko .30 .09
❑ 131 Matt Ginter .30 .09
❑ 132 Carlos Lee .30 .09
❑ 133 Mark Buehrle .30 .09
❑ 134 Adam Dunn .50 .15
❑ 135 Eric Davis .50 .15
❑ 136 Johnny Bench 1.25 .35
❑ 137 Joe Morgan .50 .15
❑ 138 Austin Kearns .50 .15
❑ 139 Barry Larkin .75 .23
❑ 140 Ken Griffey Jr. Reds 1.25 .35
❑ 141 Luis Pineda .30 .09
❑ 142 Corky Miller .30 .09
❑ 143 Brandon Larson .30 .09
❑ 144 Wily Mo Pena .30 .09
❑ 145 Lance Davis .30 .09
❑ 146 Tom Seaver Reds 1.25 .35
❑ 147 Luke Hudson .30 .09
❑ 148 Sean Casey .30 .09
❑ 149 Tony Perez .50 .15
❑ 150 Todd Walker .30 .09
❑ 151 Aaron Boone .30 .09
❑ 152 Jose Rijo .30 .09
❑ 153 Ryan Dempster .30 .09
❑ 154 Danny Graves .30 .09
❑ 155 Matt Lawton .30 .09
❑ 156 Cliff Lee .30 .09
❑ 157 Ryan Drese .30 .09
❑ 158 Danys Baez .30 .09
❑ 159 Einar Diaz .30 .09
❑ 160 Milton Bradley .30 .09
❑ 161 Earl Snyder .30 .09
❑ 162 Ellis Burks .30 .09
❑ 163 Lou Boudreau .50 .15
❑ 164 Bob Feller .75 .23
❑ 165 Ricardo Rodriguez .30 .09
❑ 166 Victor Martinez .30 .09
❑ 167 Alex Herrera .30 .09
❑ 168 Omar Vizquel .30 .09
❑ 169 David Elder .30 .09
❑ 170 C.C. Sabathia .30 .09
❑ 171 Alex Escobar .30 .09
❑ 172 Brian Tallet .30 .09
❑ 173 Jim Thome .75 .23
❑ 174 Rene Reyes .30 .09
❑ 175 Juan Uribe .30 .09
❑ 176 Jason Romano .30 .09
❑ 177 Juan Pierre .30 .09
❑ 178 Jason Jennings .30 .09
❑ 179 Jose Ortiz .30 .09
❑ 180 Larry Walker .50 .15
❑ 181 Cam Esslinger .30 .09
❑ 182 Todd Helton .50 .15
❑ 183 Aaron Cook .30 .09
❑ 184 Jack Cust .30 .09
❑ 185 Jack Morris Tigers .50 .15
❑ 186 Mike Rivera .30 .09
❑ 187 Bobby Higginson .30 .09
❑ 188 Fernando Rodney .30 .09
❑ 189 Al Kaline 1.25 .35
❑ 190 Carlos Pena .30 .09
❑ 191 Alan Trammell .75 .23
❑ 192 Mike Maroth .30 .09
❑ 193 Adam Pettyjohn .30 .09
❑ 194 David Espinosa .30 .09
❑ 195 Adam Bernero .30 .09
❑ 196 Franklyn German .30 .09
❑ 197 Robert Fick .30 .09
❑ 198 Andres Torres .30 .09
❑ 199 Luis Castillo .30 .09
❑ 200 Preston Wilson .30 .09
❑ 201 Pablo Ozuna .30 .09
❑ 202 Brad Penny .30 .09
❑ 203 Josh Beckett .50 .15
❑ 204 Charles Johnson .30 .09
❑ 205 Wilson Valdez .30 .09
❑ 206 A.J. Burnett .30 .09
❑ 207 Abraham Nunez .30 .09
❑ 208 Mike Lowell .30 .09
❑ 209 Jose Cueto .30 .09
❑ 210 Jeriome Robertson .30 .09
❑ 211 Jeff Bagwell .50 .15
❑ 212 Kirk Saarloos .30 .09
❑ 213 Craig Biggio .50 .15
❑ 214 Rodrigo Rosario .30 .09
❑ 215 Roy Oswalt .30 .09
❑ 216 John Buck .30 .09
❑ 217 Tim Redding .30 .09
❑ 218 Morgan Ensberg .30 .09
❑ 219 Richard Hidalgo .30 .09
❑ 220 Wade Miller .30 .09
❑ 221 Lance Berkman .30 .09
❑ 222 Raul Chavez .30 .09
❑ 223 Carlos Hernandez .30 .09
❑ 224 Greg Miller .30 .09
❑ 225 Tom Shearn .30 .09
❑ 226 Jason Lane .30 .09
❑ 227 Nolan Ryan Astros 4.00 1.20
❑ 228 Billy Wagner .30 .09
❑ 229 Octavio Dotel .30 .09
❑ 230 Shane Reynolds .30 .09
❑ 231 Julio Lugo .30 .09
❑ 232 Daryle Ward .30 .09
❑ 233 Mike Sweeney .30 .09
❑ 234 Angel Berroa .30 .09
❑ 235 George Brett 3.00 .90
❑ 236 Brad Voyles .30 .09
❑ 237 Brandon Berger .30 .09
❑ 238 Chad Durbin .30 .09
❑ 239 Alexis Gomez .30 .09
❑ 240 Jeremy Affeldt .30 .09
❑ 241 Bo Jackson 1.25 .35
❑ 242 Dee Brown .30 .09
❑ 243 Tony Cogan .30 .09
❑ 244 Carlos Beltran .30 .09
❑ 245 Joe Randa .30 .09
❑ 246 Pee Wee Reese .75 .23
❑ 247 Andy Ashby .30 .09
❑ 248 Cesar Izturis .30 .09
❑ 249 Duke Snider .75 .23
❑ 250 Mark Grudzielanek .30 .09
❑ 251 Chin-Feng Chen .30 .09
❑ 252 Brian Jordan .30 .09
❑ 253 Steve Garvey .50 .15
❑ 254 Odalis Perez .30 .09
❑ 255 Hideo Nomo .75 .23
❑ 256 Kevin Brown .30 .09
❑ 257 Eric Karros .30 .09
❑ 258 Joe Thurston .30 .09
❑ 259 Carlos Garcia .30 .09
❑ 260 Shawn Green .30 .09
❑ 261 Paul Lo Duca .30 .09
❑ 262 Kazuhisa Ishii .30 .09
❑ 263 Victor Alvarez .30 .09
❑ 264 Eric Gagne .50 .15
❑ 265 Don Sutton .50 .15
❑ 266 Orel Hershiser .50 .15
❑ 267 Dave Roberts .30 .09
❑ 268 Adrian Beltre .30 .09
❑ 269 Don Drysdale 1.25 .35
❑ 270 Jackie Robinson 2.00 .60
❑ 271 Tyler Houston .30 .09
❑ 272 Omar Daal .30 .09
❑ 273 Marquis Grissom .30 .09
❑ 274 Paul Quantrill .30 .09
❑ 275 Paul Molitor .75 .23
❑ 276 Jose Hernandez .30 .09
❑ 277 Takahito Nomura .30 .09
❑ 278 Nick Neugebauer .30 .09
❑ 279 Jose Mieses .30 .09
❑ 280 Richie Sexson .30 .09
❑ 281 Matt Childers .30 .09
❑ 282 Bill Hall .30 .09
❑ 283 Ben Sheets .30 .09
❑ 284 Brian Mallette .30 .09
❑ 285 Geoff Jenkins .30 .09
❑ 286 Robin Yount 1.25 .35
❑ 287 Jeff Deardorff .30 .09
❑ 288 Luis Rivas .30 .09
❑ 289 Harmon Killebrew 1.25 .35
❑ 290 Michael Cuddyer .30 .09
❑ 291 Torii Hunter .30 .09
❑ 292 Kevin Frederick .30 .09
❑ 293 Adam Johnson .30 .09
❑ 294 Jack Morris Twins .50 .15
❑ 295 Rod Carew Twins .75 .23
❑ 296 Kirby Puckett 1.25 .35
❑ 297 Joe Mays .30 .09
❑ 298 Jacque Jones .30 .09
❑ 299 Cristian Guzman .30 .09
❑ 300 Kyle Lohse .30 .09
❑ 301 Eric Milton .30 .09
❑ 302 Brad Radke .30 .09
❑ 303 Doug Mientkiewicz .30 .09
❑ 304 Corey Koskie .30 .09
❑ 305 Jose Vidro .30 .09
❑ 306 Claudio Vargas .30 .09
❑ 307 Gary Carter Expos .75 .23
❑ 308 Andre Dawson Expos .75 .23
❑ 309 Henry Mateo .30 .09
❑ 310 Andres Galarraga .30 .09
❑ 311 Zach Day .30 .09
❑ 312 Bartolo Colon .30 .09
❑ 313 Endy Chavez .30 .09
❑ 314 Javier Vazquez .30 .09
❑ 315 Michael Barrett .30 .09
❑ 316 Vladimir Guerrero .75 .23
❑ 317 Orlando Cabrera .30 .09
❑ 318 Al Leiter .30 .09
❑ 319 Timo Perez .30 .09
❑ 320 Rey Ordonez .30 .09
❑ 321 Gary Carter .75 .23
❑ 322 Armando Benitez .30 .09
❑ 323 Dwight Gooden .75 .23
❑ 324 Pedro Astacio .30 .09
❑ 325 Roberto Alomar .75 .23
❑ 326 Edgardo Alfonzo .30 .09
❑ 327 Nolan Ryan Mets 4.00 1.20
❑ 328 Mo Vaughn .30 .09
❑ 329 Ryan Jamison .30 .09
❑ 330 Satoru Komiyama .30 .09

Card	Nm-Mt	Ex-Mt
❑ 331 Mike Piazza	1.25	.35
❑ 332 Tom Seaver Mets	1.25	.35
❑ 333 Jorge Posada	.50	.15
❑ 334 Derek Jeter	2.00	.60
❑ 335 Babe Ruth	3.00	.90
❑ 336 Lou Gehrig	2.50	.75
❑ 337 Andy Pettitte	.50	.15
❑ 338 Mariano Rivera	.50	.15
❑ 339 Robin Ventura	.30	.09
❑ 340 Yogi Berra	1.25	.35
❑ 341 Phil Rizzuto	.75	.23
❑ 342 Bernie Williams	.50	.15
❑ 343 Alfonso Soriano	.75	.23
❑ 344 Drew Henson	.30	.09
❑ 345 Erick Almonte	.30	.09
❑ 346 Rondell White	.30	.09
❑ 347 Christian Parker	.30	.09
❑ 348 Joe Torre MG Yankees	.75	.23
❑ 349 Nick Johnson	.30	.09
❑ 350 Raul Mondesi	.30	.09
❑ 351 Brandon Claussen	.30	.09
❑ 352 Reggie Jackson Yankees	.75	.23
❑ 353 Roger Clemens Yankees	1.50	.45
❑ 354 Don Mattingly	3.00	.90
❑ 355 Jason Giambi	.75	.23
❑ 356 Adrian Hernandez	.30	.09
❑ 357 Jeff Weaver	.30	.09
❑ 358 Mike Mussina	.75	.23
❑ 359 Brett Jodie	.30	.09
❑ 360 David Wells	.30	.09
❑ 361 Enos Slaughter Yankees	.50	.15
❑ 362 Whitey Ford	.75	.23
❑ 363 Eric Chavez	.30	.09
❑ 364 Miguel Tejada	.30	.09
❑ 365 Barry Zito	.75	.23
❑ 366 Bert Snow	.30	.09
❑ 367 Rickey Henderson A's	1.25	.35
❑ 368 Juan Pena	.30	.09
❑ 369 Terrence Long	.30	.09
❑ 370 Dennis Eckersley A's	.50	.15
❑ 371 Mark Ellis	.30	.09
❑ 372 Tim Hudson	.30	.09
❑ 373 Jose Canseco	1.25	.35
❑ 374 Reggie Jackson A's	.75	.23
❑ 375 Mark Mulder	.30	.09
❑ 376 David Justice	.30	.09
❑ 377 Jermaine Dye	.30	.09
❑ 378 Brett Myers	.30	.09
❑ 379 Lenny Dykstra	.50	.15
❑ 380 Vicente Padilla	.30	.09
❑ 381 Bobby Abreu	.30	.09
❑ 382 Pat Burrell	.30	.09
❑ 383 Jorge Padilla	.30	.09
❑ 384 Jeremy Giambi	.30	.09
❑ 385 Mike Lieberthal	.30	.09
❑ 386 Anderson Machado	.30	.09
❑ 387 Marlon Byrd	.30	.09
❑ 388 Bud Smith	.30	.09
❑ 389 Eric Valent	.30	.09
❑ 390 Elio Serrano	.30	.09
❑ 391 Jimmy Rollins	.30	.09
❑ 392 Brandon Duckworth	.30	.09
❑ 393 Robin Roberts	.50	.15
❑ 394 Marlon Anderson	.30	.09
❑ 395 Robert Person	.30	.09
❑ 396 Johnny Estrada	.30	.09
❑ 397 Mike Schmidt	3.00	.90
❑ 398 Eric Junge	.30	.09
❑ 399 Jason Michaels	.30	.09
❑ 400 Steve Carlton	.75	.23
❑ 401 Placido Polanco	.30	.09
❑ 402 John Grabow	.30	.09
❑ 403 Tomas De La Rosa	.30	.09
❑ 404 Tike Redman	.30	.09
❑ 405 Willie Stargell	.75	.23
❑ 406 Dave Williams	.30	.09
❑ 407 John Candelaria	.30	.09
❑ 408 Jack Wilson	.30	.09
❑ 409 Matt Guerrier	.30	.09
❑ 410 Jason Kendall	.30	.09
❑ 411 Josh Fogg	.30	.09
❑ 412 Aramis Ramirez	.30	.09
❑ 413 Dave Parker	.50	.15
❑ 414 Roberto Clemente	2.50	.75
❑ 415 Kip Wells	.30	.09
❑ 416 Brian Giles	.30	.09
❑ 417 Honus Wagner	1.25	.35
❑ 418 Ramon Vazquez	.30	.09
❑ 419 Oliver Perez	.30	.09
❑ 420 Ryan Klesko	.30	.09
❑ 421 Brian Lawrence	.30	.09
❑ 422 Ben Howard	.30	.09
❑ 423 Ozzie Smith Padres	1.25	.35
❑ 424 Dennis Tankersley	.30	.09
❑ 425 Tony Gwynn	1.00	.30
❑ 426 Sean Burroughs	.30	.09
❑ 427 Xavier Nady	.30	.09
❑ 428 Phil Nevin	.30	.09
❑ 429 Trevor Hoffman	.30	.09
❑ 430 Jake Peavy	.30	.09
❑ 431 Cody Ransom	.30	.09
❑ 432 Kenny Lofton	.30	.09
❑ 433 Mel Ott	.75	.23
❑ 434 Tsuyoshi Shinjo	.30	.09
❑ 435 Deivis Santos	.30	.09
❑ 436 Rich Aurilia	.30	.09
❑ 437 Will Clark Giants	1.25	.35
❑ 438 Pedro Feliz	.30	.09
❑ 439 J.T. Snow	.30	.09
❑ 440 Robb Nen	.30	.09
❑ 441 Carlos Valderrama	.30	.09
❑ 442 Willie McCovey	.50	.15
❑ 443 Jeff Kent	.30	.09
❑ 444 Orlando Cepeda	.50	.15
❑ 445 Barry Bonds	2.00	.60
❑ 446 Alex Rodriguez M's	1.50	.45
❑ 447 Allan Simpson	.30	.09
❑ 448 Antonio Perez	.30	.09
❑ 449 Edgar Martinez	.50	.15
❑ 450 Freddy Garcia	.30	.09
❑ 451 Chris Snelling	.30	.09
❑ 452 Matt Thornton	.30	.09
❑ 453 Kazuhiro Sasaki	.30	.09
❑ 454 Harold Reynolds	.50	.15
❑ 455 Randy Johnson M's	.75	.23
❑ 456 Bret Boone	.30	.09
❑ 457 Rafael Soriano	.30	.09
❑ 458 Luis Ugueto	.30	.09
❑ 459 Ken Griffey Jr. M's	1.25	.35
❑ 460 Ichiro Suzuki	1.50	.45
❑ 461 Jamie Moyer	.30	.09
❑ 462 Joel Pineiro	.30	.09
❑ 463 Jeff Cirillo	.30	.09
❑ 464 John Olerud	.30	.09
❑ 465 Mike Cameron	.30	.09
❑ 466 Ruben Sierra	.30	.09
❑ 467 Mark McLemore	.30	.09
❑ 468 Carlos Guillen	.30	.09
❑ 469 Dan Wilson	.30	.09
❑ 470 Shigetoshi Hasegawa	.30	.09
❑ 471 Ben Davis	.30	.09
❑ 472 Ozzie Smith Cards	1.25	.35
❑ 473 Matt Morris	.30	.09
❑ 474 Edgar Renteria	.30	.09
❑ 475 Les Walrond	.30	.09
❑ 476 Albert Pujols	1.50	.45
❑ 477 Stan Musial	2.00	.60
❑ 478 J.D. Drew	.30	.09
❑ 479 Josh Pearce	.30	.09
❑ 480 Enos Slaughter Cards	.50	.15
❑ 481 Jason Simontacchi	.30	.09
❑ 482 Jeremy Lambert	.30	.09
❑ 483 Tino Martinez	.50	.15
❑ 484 Rogers Hornsby	1.25	.35
❑ 485 Rick Ankiel	.30	.09
❑ 486 Jim Edmonds	.30	.09
❑ 487 Scott Rolen	.50	.15
❑ 488 Kevin Joseph	.30	.09
❑ 489 Fernando Vina	.30	.09
❑ 490 Jason Isringhausen	.30	.09
❑ 491 Lou Brock	.75	.23
❑ 492 Joe Torre Cards	.75	.23
❑ 493 Bob Gibson	.75	.23
❑ 494 Chuck Finley	.30	.09
❑ 495 So Taguchi	.30	.09
❑ 496 Ben Grieve	.30	.09
❑ 497 Toby Hall	.30	.09
❑ 498 Brent Abernathy	.30	.09
❑ 499 Brandon Backe	.30	.09
❑ 500 Felix Escalona	.30	.09
❑ 501 Matt White	.30	.09
❑ 502 Randy Winn	.30	.09
❑ 503 Carl Crawford	.30	.09
❑ 504 Dewon Brazelton	.30	.09
❑ 505 Joe Kennedy	.30	.09
❑ 506 Wade Boggs D-Rays	.75	.23
❑ 507 Aubrey Huff	.30	.09
❑ 508 Alex Rodriguez Rangers	1.50	.45
❑ 509 Ivan Rodriguez	.75	.23
❑ 510 Will Clark Rangers	1.25	.35
❑ 511 Hank Blalock	.50	.15
❑ 512 Travis Hughes	.30	.09
❑ 513 Travis Hafner	.30	.09
❑ 514 Ryan Ludwick	.30	.09
❑ 515 Doug Davis	.30	.09
❑ 516 Juan Gonzalez	.75	.23
❑ 517 Jason Hart	.30	.09
❑ 518 Mark Teixeira	.50	.15
❑ 519 Nolan Ryan Rangers	4.00	1.20
❑ 520 Rafael Palmeiro	.50	.15
❑ 521 Kevin Mench	.30	.09
❑ 522 Chan Ho Park	.30	.09
❑ 523 Kenny Rogers	.30	.09
❑ 524 Rusty Greer	.30	.09
❑ 525 Michael Young	.30	.09
❑ 526 Carlos Delgado	.30	.09
❑ 527 Vernon Wells	.30	.09
❑ 528 Orlando Hudson	.30	.09
❑ 529 Shannon Stewart	.30	.09
❑ 530 Joe Carter	.50	.15
❑ 531 Chris Baker	.30	.09
❑ 532 Eric Hinske	.30	.09
❑ 533 Corey Thurman	.30	.09
❑ 534 Josh Phelps	.30	.09
❑ 535 Reed Johnson	.30	.09
❑ 536 Brian Bowles	.30	.09
❑ 537 Roy Halladay	.30	.09
❑ 538 Jose Cruz Jr.	.30	.09
❑ 539 Kelvim Escobar	.30	.09
❑ 540 Chris Carpenter	.30	.09
❑ 541 Rickie Weeks RC	-	
❑ 542 Hideki Matsui RC	-	
❑ 543 Ramon Nivar RC	-	
❑ 544 Adam Loewen RC	-	
❑ 545 Brandon Webb RC	-	
❑ 546 Dan Haren RC	-	
❑ 547 Delmon Young RC	-	
❑ 548 Ryan Wagner RC	-	

2003 Timeless Treasures

	Nm-Mt	Ex-Mt
STATED PRINT RUN 900 SERIAL #'d SETS		-
PRODUCED BY DONRUSS/PLAYOFF		-
❑ 1 Adam Dunn	4.00	1.20
❑ 2 Al Kaline	6.00	1.80
❑ 3 Alan Trammell	4.00	1.20
❑ 4 Albert Pujols	12.00	3.60
❑ 5 Alex Rodriguez	12.00	3.60
❑ 6 Alfonso Soriano	6.00	1.80
❑ 7 Andre Dawson	4.00	1.20
❑ 8 Andruw Jones	4.00	1.20
❑ 9 Austin Kearns	4.00	1.20
❑ 10 Babe Ruth	15.00	4.50
❑ 11 Barry Bonds	15.00	4.50
❑ 12 Barry Larkin	6.00	1.80
❑ 13 Barry Zito	6.00	1.80
❑ 14 Bernie Williams	4.00	1.20

Card	Nm-Mt	Ex-Mt
❑ 15 Bo Jackson	6.00	1.80
❑ 16 Brooks Robinson	6.00	1.80
❑ 17 Cal Ripken	20.00	6.00
❑ 18 Carlton Fisk	4.00	1.20
❑ 19 Chipper Jones	6.00	1.80
❑ 20 Curt Schilling	4.00	1.20
❑ 21 Dale Murphy	6.00	1.80
❑ 22 Derek Jeter	15.00	4.50
❑ 23 Don Mattingly	15.00	4.50
❑ 24 Duke Snider	4.00	1.20
❑ 25 Eddie Mathews	6.00	1.80
❑ 26 Frank Robinson	4.00	1.20
❑ 27 Frank Thomas	6.00	1.80
❑ 28 Garret Anderson	4.00	1.20
❑ 29 Gary Carter	4.00	1.20
❑ 30 George Brett	15.00	4.50
❑ 31 Greg Maddux	12.00	3.60
❑ 32 Harmon Killebrew	6.00	1.80
❑ 33 Hideki Matsui RC	20.00	6.00
❑ 34 Hideo Nomo	6.00	1.80
❑ 35 Ichiro Suzuki	12.00	3.60
❑ 36 Ivan Rodriguez	6.00	1.80
❑ 37 Jackie Robinson	10.00	3.00
❑ 38 Jason Giambi	6.00	1.80
❑ 39 Jeff Bagwell	4.00	1.20
❑ 40 Jim Edmonds	4.00	1.20
❑ 41 Jim Palmer	4.00	1.20
❑ 42 Jim Thome	6.00	1.80
❑ 43 Joe Morgan	4.00	1.20
❑ 44 Jorge Posada	4.00	1.20
❑ 45 Jose Contreras RC	10.00	3.00
❑ 46 Juan Gonzalez	6.00	1.80
❑ 47 Kazuhisa Ishii	4.00	1.20
❑ 48 Ken Griffey Jr.	10.00	3.00
❑ 49 Kerry Wood	6.00	1.80
❑ 50 Kirby Puckett	6.00	1.80
❑ 51 Lance Berkman	4.00	1.20
❑ 52 Larry Walker	4.00	1.20
❑ 53 Lou Brock	4.00	1.20
❑ 54 Lou Gehrig	12.00	3.60
❑ 55 Magglio Ordonez	4.00	1.20
❑ 56 Mark Prior	12.00	3.60
❑ 57 Miguel Tejada	4.00	1.20
❑ 58 Mike Mussina	6.00	1.80
❑ 59 Mike Piazza	10.00	3.00
❑ 60 Mike Schmidt	12.00	3.60
❑ 61 Nolan Ryan	20.00	6.00
❑ 62 Nomar Garciaparra	12.00	3.60
❑ 63 Ozzie Smith	6.00	1.80
❑ 64 Pat Burrell	4.00	1.20
❑ 65 Pedro Martinez	6.00	1.80
❑ 66 Pee Wee Reese	4.00	1.20
❑ 67 Phil Rizzuto	4.00	1.20
❑ 68 Rafael Palmeiro	4.00	1.20
❑ 69 Randy Johnson	6.00	1.80
❑ 70 Reggie Jackson	4.00	1.20
❑ 71 Richie Ashburn	4.00	1.20
❑ 72 Rickey Henderson	10.00	3.00
❑ 73 Roberto Alomar	6.00	1.80
❑ 74 Roberto Clemente	12.00	3.60
❑ 75 Robin Yount	6.00	1.80
❑ 76 Rod Carew	4.00	1.20
❑ 77 Roger Clemens	12.00	3.60
❑ 78 Rogers Hornsby	6.00	1.80
❑ 79 Roy Oswalt	4.00	1.20
❑ 80 Ryan Klesko	4.00	1.20
❑ 81 Ryne Sandberg	12.00	3.60
❑ 82 Sammy Sosa	10.00	3.00
❑ 83 Scott Rolen	4.00	1.20
❑ 84 Shawn Green	4.00	1.20
❑ 85 Stan Musial	10.00	3.00
❑ 86 Steve Carlton	4.00	1.20
❑ 87 Thurman Munson	8.00	2.40
❑ 88 Todd Helton	4.00	1.20
❑ 89 Tom Glavine	6.00	1.80
❑ 90 Tom Seaver	6.00	1.80
❑ 91 Tony Gwynn	8.00	2.40
❑ 92 Tony Perez	4.00	1.20
❑ 93 Torii Hunter	4.00	1.20
❑ 94 Troy Glaus	4.00	1.20
❑ 95 Ty Cobb	10.00	3.00
❑ 96 Vernon Wells	4.00	1.20
❑ 97 Vladimir Guerrero	6.00	1.80
❑ 98 Warren Spahn	4.00	1.20
❑ 99 Willie McCovey	4.00	1.20
❑ 100 Yogi Berra	6.00	1.80

2001 eTopps

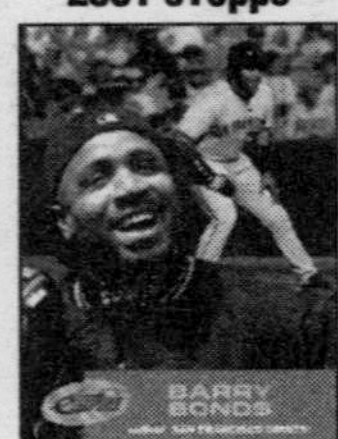

Card	Nm-Mt	Ex-Mt
❑ 1 Nomar Garciaparra/1315	-	-
❑ 2 Chipper Jones/674	-	-
❑ 3 Jeff Bagwell/485	-	-
❑ 4 Randy Johnson/1499	-	-
❑ 7 Adam Dunn/4197	-	-
❑ 8 J.D. Drew/767	-	-
❑ 9 Larry Walker/420	-	-
❑ 10 Edgardo Alfonzo/338	-	-
❑ 11 Lance Berkman/595	-	-
❑ 12 Tony Gwynn/828	-	-
❑ 13 Andruw Jones/908	-	-
❑ 15 Troy Glaus/862	-	-
❑ 17 Sammy Sosa/2487	-	-
❑ 21 Darin Erstad/664	-	-
❑ 22 Barry Bonds/1567	-	-
❑ 27 Derek Jeter/1041	-	-
❑ 29 Curt Schilling/2125	-	-
❑ 30 Roberto Alomar/448	-	-
❑ 31 Luis Gonzalez/1104	-	-
❑ 32 Jimmy Rollins/1307	15.00	4.50
❑ 34 Joe Crede/1050	-	-
❑ 39 Sean Casey/537	-	-
❑ 46 Alex Rodriguez/2212	-	-
❑ 47 Tom Glavine/437	-	-
❑ 50 Jose Ortiz/738	-	-
❑ 51 Cal Ripken/2201	-	-
❑ 52 Bob Abreu/677	-	-
❑ 55 Alex Escobar/931	-	-
❑ 56 Ivan Rodriguez/698	-	-
❑ 59 Jeff Kent/452	-	-
❑ 62 Rick Ankiel/752	-	-
❑ 65 Craig Biggio/410	-	-
❑ 66 Carlos Delgado/398	-	-
❑ 68 Greg Maddux/1031	-	-
❑ 69 Kerry Wood/1056	-	-
❑ 71 Todd Helton/978	-	-
❑ 72 Mariano Rivera/824	-	-
❑ 73 Jason Kendall/672	-	-
❑ 75 Scott Rolen/498	-	-
❑ 76 Kazuhiro Sasaki/5000	-	-
❑ 77 Roy Oswalt/915	-	-
❑ 78 C.C. Sabathia/1974	-	-
❑ 83 Brian Giles/400	-	-
❑ 87 Rafael Furcal/646	-	-
❑ 88 Mike Mussina/793	-	-
❑ 89 Gary Sheffield/359	-	-
❑ 92 Mark McGwire/2908	-	-
❑ 94 Tsuyoshi Shinjo/3000	-	-
❑ 99 Jose Vidro/443	-	-
❑ 100 Ichiro Suzuki/10000	20.00	6.00
❑ 105 Manny Ramirez/1074	-	-
❑ 109 Juan Gonzalez/558	-	-
❑ 112 Ken Griffey Jr./2398	-	-
❑ 114 Tim Hudson/663	-	-
❑ 115 Nick Johnson/1217	-	-
❑ 118 Jason Giambi/897	-	-
❑ 122 Rafael Palmeiro/464	-	-
❑ 124 V. Guerrero/854	-	-
❑ 125 Vernon Wells/349	-	-
❑ 127 Roger Clemens/1462	-	-
❑ 128 Frank Thomas/834	-	-
❑ 129 Carlos Beltran/489	-	-
❑ 130 Pat Burrell/1253	-	-
❑ 131 Pedro Martinez/1038	-	-
❑ 132 Mike Piazza/1379	-	-
❑ 135 Luis Montanez/5000	-	-
❑ 140 Sean Burroughs/5000	-	-
❑ 141 Barry Zito/843	-	-
❑ 142 Bobby Bradley/5000	-	-
❑ 143 Albert Pujols/5000	50.00	15.00
❑ 144 Ben Sheets/1713	-	-
❑ 145 Alfonso Soriano/1699	-	-
❑ 146 Josh Hamilton/5000	-	-
❑ 147 Eric Munson/5000	-	-
❑ 150 Mark Mulder/4335	-	-

2002 eTopps

Card	Nm-Mt	Ex-Mt
❑ 1 Ichiro Suzuki/9477	-	-
❑ 2 Jason Giambi/5142	-	-
❑ 3 Roberto Alomar/2711	-	-
❑ 4 Bret Boone/2000	-	-
❑ 5 Frank Catalanotto/2000	-	
❑ 6 Alex Rodriguez/6393	-	
❑ 7 Jim Thome/2927	-	
❑ 8 Toby Hall/2000	-	-
❑ 9 Troy Glaus/4323	-	
❑ 10 Derek Jeter/8000	-	
❑ 11 Alfonso Soriano/5000	-	
❑ 12 Eric Chavez/4334	-	
❑ 13 Preston Wilson/2000	-	-
❑ 14 Bernie Williams/4436	-	
❑ 15 Larry Walker/2546	-	
❑ 16 Todd Helton/3430	-	-
❑ 17 Moises Alou/2856	-	
❑ 18 Lance Berkman/5000	-	
❑ 19 Chipper Jones/4734	-	-
❑ 20 Andruw Jones/4849	-	
❑ 21 Barry Bonds/6658	-	-
❑ 22 Sammy Sosa/8000	-	
❑ 23 Luis Gonzalez/2671	-	-
❑ 24 Shawn Green/4438	-	
❑ 25 Jeff Bagwell/3359	-	
❑ 26 Albert Pujols/5531	-	
❑ 27 Rafael Palmeiro/2700	-	
❑ 28 Jimmy Rollins/5000	-	
❑ 29 Vladimir Guerrero/6000	-	
❑ 30 Jeff Kent/3000	-	
❑ 31 Ken Griffey Jr./4569	-	
❑ 32 Magglio Ordonez/4000	-	
❑ 33 Mike Piazza/4202	-	
❑ 34 Pedro Martinez/6000	-	
❑ 35 Mark Mulder/4000	-	
❑ 36 Roger Clemens/4567	-	
❑ 37 Freddy Garcia/4986	-	
❑ 38 Tim Hudson/2000	-	
❑ 39 Mike Mussina/3708	-	
❑ 40 Joe Mays/3000	-	
❑ 41 Barry Zito/3590	-	
❑ 42 Jermaine Dye/2693	-	
❑ 43 Mariano Rivera/3709	-	
❑ 44 Randy Johnson/6211	-	
❑ 45 Curt Schilling/5190	-	
❑ 46 Greg Maddux/4008	-	
❑ 47 Javier Vazquez/3000	-	
❑ 48 Kerry Wood/3346	-	
❑ 49 Wilson Betemit/2377	-	-
❑ 50 Adam Dunn/6000	-	
❑ 51 Josh Beckett/5000	-	
❑ 52 Paul LoDuca/3998	-	
❑ 53 Ben Sheets/3842	-	
❑ 54 Eric Valent/5000	-	

	Nm-Mt	Ex-Mt
❑ 55 Brian Giles/2000	-	
❑ 56 Mo Vaughn/2772	-	
❑ 57 C.C. Sabathia/2525	-	-
❑ 58 Nick Johnson/5000	-	
❑ 59 Miguel Tejada/4000	-	
❑ 60 Carlos Delgado/3604	-	
❑ 61 Tsuyoshi Shinjo/3000	-	
❑ 62 Juan Gonzalez/2361	-	
❑ 63 Mike Sweeney/3173	-	
❑ 64 Ivan Rodriguez/3000	-	
❑ 65 Bud Smith/3000	-	
❑ 66 Brandon Duckworth/2000	-	
❑ 67 Xavier Nady/4000	-	
❑ 68 D'Angelo Jimenez/1725	-	-
❑ 69 Roy Oswalt/3523	-	
❑ 70 J.D. Drew/3195	-	
❑ 71 Cliff Floyd/3725	-	
❑ 72 Kevin Brown/3000	-	
❑ 73 Gary Sheffield/3593	-	
❑ 74 Aramis Ramirez/3000	-	
❑ 75 Nomar Garciaparra/5090	-	
❑ 76 Phil Nevin/2348	-	
❑ 77 Juan Cruz/4000	-	
❑ 78 Hideo Nomo/2857	-	
❑ 79 Chris George/3000	-	
❑ 80 Matt Morris/3000	-	
❑ 81 Corey Patterson/4000	-	
❑ 82 Joel Pineiro/4776	-	
❑ 83 Mark Buehrle/3000	-	
❑ 84 Shannon Stewart/1992	-	-
❑ 85 Kazuhiro Sasaki/4000	-	
❑ 86 Carlos Pena/4000	-	
❑ 87 Brad Penny/3000	-	
❑ 88 Rich Aurilia/2795	-	
❑ 89 Wade Miller/4000	-	
❑ 90 Tim Raines Jr./5000	-	
❑ 91 Kazuhisa Ishii/6000	-	
❑ 92 Hank Blalock/5000	-	
❑ 93 So Taguchi/5000	-	
❑ 94 Mark Prior/5000	-	
❑ 95 Rickey Henderson/4013	-	
❑ 96 Austin Kearns/6000	-	
❑ 97 Tom Glavine/3000	-	
❑ 98 Manny Ramirez/4905	-	
❑ 99 Shea Hillenbrand/4000	-	
❑ 100 Junior Spivey/5000	-	
❑ 101 Derek Lowe/4911	-	
❑ 102 Torii Hunter/4000	-	
❑ 103 Juan Rivera/4000	-	
❑ 104 Eric Hinske/5000	-	
❑ 105 Bobby Hill/3000	-	
❑ 106 Rafael Soriano/4000	-	
❑ 107 Jim Edmonds/3851	-	

2003 eTopps

	Nm-Mt	Ex-Mt
❑ 1 Troy Glaus	-	
❑ 2 Manny Ramirez	-	
❑ 3 Magglio Ordonez	-	
❑ 4 Jim Thome	-	
❑ 5 Torii Hunter	-	
❑ 6 Jason Giambi	-	
❑ 7 Tim Hudson	-	
❑ 8 Ichiro Suzuki	-	
❑ 9 Aubrey Huff	-	
❑ 10 Alex Rodriguez	-	
❑ 11 Francisco Rodriguez	-	
❑ 13 Mark Teixeira	-	
❑ 15 Carlos Delgado	-	
❑ 16 Tom Glavine	-	
❑ 18 Mark Prior	-	
❑ 20 Todd Helton	-	
❑ 21 Jeff Bagwell	-	
❑ 22 Shawn Green	-	
❑ 23 Vladimir Guerrero	-	
❑ 26 Barry Bonds	-	
❑ 27 Albert Pujols	-	
❑ 28 Nomar Garciaparra	-	
❑ 29 Alfonso Soriano	-	
❑ 30 Barry Zito	-	
❑ 31 Edgar Martinez	-	
❑ 32 Ivan Rodriguez	-	
❑ 33 Greg Maddux	-	
❑ 35 Austin Kearns	-	
❑ 36 Craig Biggio	-	
❑ 38 Andruw Jones	-	
❑ 39 Jeff Kent	-	
❑ 40 Roy Oswalt	-	
❑ 41 Miguel Tejada	-	
❑ 42 Derek Jeter	-	
❑ 43 Pedro Martinez	-	
❑ 44 Jarrod Washburn	-	
❑ 46 Bernie Williams	-	
❑ 48 Gary Sheffield	-	
❑ 51 Garret Anderson	-	
❑ 52 Jason Schmidt	-	
❑ 55 Derek Lowe	-	
❑ 57 Paul Konerko	-	
❑ 58 Bartolo Colon	-	
❑ 59 Omar Vizquel	-	
❑ 60 Adam Dunn	-	
❑ 62 Richie Sexson	-	
❑ 63 Paul Byrd	-	
❑ 64 Eric Gagne	-	
❑ 67 Brandon Phillips	-	
❑ 69 Tim Salmon	-	
❑ 70 Roger Clemens	-	
❑ 71 Jake Peavy	-	
❑ 74 Fred McGriff	-	
❑ 75 John Smoltz	-	
❑ 76 Josh Phelps	-	
❑ 77 John Olerud	-	
❑ 78 Eric Chavez	-	
❑ 79 Jeff Weaver	-	
❑ 80 Scott Rolen	-	
❑ 84 Josh Beckett	-	
❑ 85 Jorge Posada	-	
❑ 86 Mark Mulder	-	
❑ 87 Eric Milton	-	
❑ 88 Angel Berroa	-	
❑ 90 Kerry Wood	-	
❑ 91 Brad Wilkerson	-	
❑ 92 Orlando Hudson	-	
❑ 93 Mike Mussina	-	
❑ 94 Hee Seop Choi	-	
❑ 95 Chris Snelling	-	
❑ 96 Tomo Ohka	-	
❑ 97 Andy Pettitte	-	
❑ 98 Drew Henson	-	
❑ 100 Jason Jennings	-	
❑ 101 Hideki Matsui	-	
❑ 102 Jose Contreras	-	
❑ 103 Rocco Baldelli	-	
❑ 104 Jeremy Bonderman	-	
❑ 105 Jesse Foppert	-	
❑ 106 Randy Wolf	-	
❑ 107 Kevin Millwood	-	
❑ 108 Eric Byrnes	-	
❑ 109 Edgar Renteria	-	
❑ 110 Jose Reyes	-	
❑ 111 Dontrelle Willis	-	

2001 E-X

	Nm-Mt	Ex-Mt
COMP.SET w/o SP's (100)	25.00	7.50
COMMON CARD (1-100)	.50	.15
COMMON (101-130)	8.00	2.40
COMMON (131-140)	15.00	4.50
❑ 1 Jason Kendall	.50	.15
❑ 2 Derek Jeter	3.00	.90
❑ 3 Greg Vaughn	.50	.15

	Nm-Mt	Ex-Mt
❑ 4 Eric Chavez	.50	.15
❑ 5 Nomar Garciaparra	2.50	.75
❑ 6 Roberto Alomar	1.25	.35
❑ 7 Barry Larkin	1.25	.35
❑ 8 Matt Lawton	.50	.15
❑ 9 Larry Walker	.75	.23
❑ 10 Chipper Jones	1.25	.35
❑ 11 Scott Rolen	.75	.23
❑ 12 Carlos Lee	.50	.15
❑ 13 Adrian Beltre	.50	.15
❑ 14 Ben Grieve	.50	.15
❑ 15 Mike Sweeney	.50	.15
❑ 16 John Olerud	.50	.15
❑ 17 Gabe Kapler	.50	.15
❑ 18 Brian Giles	.50	.15
❑ 19 Luis Gonzalez	.50	.15
❑ 20 Sammy Sosa	2.00	.60
❑ 21 Roger Clemens	2.50	.75
❑ 22 Vladimir Guerrero	1.25	.35
❑ 23 Ken Griffey Jr.	2.00	.60
❑ 24 Mark McGwire	3.00	.90
❑ 25 Orlando Hernandez	.50	.15
❑ 26 Shannon Stewart	.50	.15
❑ 27 Fred McGriff	.75	.23
❑ 28 Lance Berkman	.50	.15
❑ 29 Carlos Delgado	.50	.15
❑ 30 Mike Piazza	2.00	.60
❑ 31 Juan Encarnacion	.50	.15
❑ 32 David Justice	.50	.15
❑ 33 Greg Maddux	2.50	.75
❑ 34 Frank Thomas	1.25	.35
❑ 35 Jason Giambi	1.25	.35
❑ 36 Ruben Mateo	.50	.15
❑ 37 Todd Helton	.75	.23
❑ 38 Jim Edmonds	.50	.15
❑ 39 Steve Finley	.50	.15
❑ 40 Tom Glavine	1.25	.35
❑ 41 Mo Vaughn	.50	.15
❑ 42 Phil Nevin	.50	.15
❑ 43 Richie Sexson	.50	.15
❑ 44 Craig Biggio	.75	.23
❑ 45 Kerry Wood	1.25	.35
❑ 46 Pat Burrell	.50	.15
❑ 47 Edgar Martinez	.75	.23
❑ 48 Jim Thome	1.25	.35
❑ 49 Jeff Bagwell	.75	.23
❑ 50 Bernie Williams	.75	.23
❑ 51 Andruw Jones	.75	.23
❑ 52 Gary Sheffield	.50	.15
❑ 53 Johnny Damon	.50	.15
❑ 54 Rondell White	.50	.15
❑ 55 J.D. Drew	.50	.15
❑ 56 Tony Batista	.50	.15
❑ 57 Paul Konerko	.50	.15
❑ 58 Rafael Palmeiro	.75	.23
❑ 59 Cal Ripken	4.00	1.20
❑ 60 Darin Erstad	.50	.15
❑ 61 Ivan Rodriguez	1.25	.35
❑ 62 Barry Bonds	3.00	.90
❑ 63 Edgardo Alfonzo	.50	.15
❑ 64 Ellis Burks	.50	.15
❑ 65 Mike Lieberthal	.50	.15
❑ 66 Robin Ventura	.50	.15
❑ 67 Richard Hidalgo	.50	.15
❑ 68 Magglio Ordonez	.50	.15
❑ 69 Kazuhiro Sasaki	.50	.15
❑ 70 Miguel Tejada	.50	.15
❑ 71 David Wells	.50	.15

- ❑ 72 Troy Glaus .75 .23
- ❑ 73 Jose Vidro .50 .15
- ❑ 74 Shawn Green .50 .15
- ❑ 75 Barry Zito 1.25 .35
- ❑ 76 Jermaine Dye .50 .15
- ❑ 77 Geoff Jenkins .50 .15
- ❑ 78 Jeff Kent .50 .15
- ❑ 79 Al Leiter .50 .15
- ❑ 80 Deivi Cruz .50 .15
- ❑ 81 Eric Karros .50 .15
- ❑ 82 Albert Belle .50 .15
- ❑ 83 Pedro Martinez 1.25 .35
- ❑ 84 Raul Mondesi .50 .15
- ❑ 85 Preston Wilson .50 .15
- ❑ 86 Rafael Furcal .50 .15
- ❑ 87 Rick Ankiel .50 .15
- ❑ 88 Randy Johnson 1.25 .35
- ❑ 89 Kevin Brown .50 .15
- ❑ 90 Sean Casey .50 .15
- ❑ 91 Mike Mussina 1.25 .35
- ❑ 92 Alex Rodriguez 2.50 .75
- ❑ 93 Andres Galarraga .50 .15
- ❑ 94 Juan Gonzalez 1.25 .35
- ❑ 95 Manny Ramirez .50 .15
- ❑ 96 Mark Grace 1.25 .35
- ❑ 97 Carl Everett .50 .15
- ❑ 98 Tony Gwynn 1.50 .45
- ❑ 99 Mike Hampton .50 .15
- ❑ 100 Ken Caminiti .50 .15
- ❑ 101 Jason Hart/1749 8.00 2.40
- ❑ 102 Corey Patterson/1199 8.00 2.40
- ❑ 103 Timo Perez/1999 8.00 2.40
- ❑ 104 Marcus Giles/1999 8.00 2.40
- ❑ 105 I. Suzuki/1999 RC 60.00 18.00
- ❑ 106 Aubrey Huff/1499 8.00 2.40
- ❑ 107 Joe Crede/1999 8.00 2.40
- ❑ 108 Larry Barnes/1499 8.00 2.40
- ❑ 109 Esix Snead/1999 RC 8.00 2.40
- ❑ 110 Kenny Kelly/2249 8.00 2.40
- ❑ 111 Justin Miller/2249 8.00 2.40
- ❑ 112 Jack Cust/1999 8.00 2.40
- ❑ 113 Xavier Nady/999 8.00 2.40
- ❑ 114 Eric Munson/1499 8.00 2.40
- ❑ 115 E. Guzman/1749 RC 8.00 2.40
- ❑ 116 Juan Pierre/2189 8.00 2.40
- ❑ 117 W. Abreu/1749 RC 8.00 2.40
- ❑ 118 Keith Ginter/1999 8.00 2.40
- ❑ 119 Jace Brewer/2699 8.00 2.40
- ❑ 120 P. Crawford/2249 8.00 2.40
- ❑ 121 Jason Tyner/2249 8.00 2.40
- ❑ 122 Tike Redman/1999 8.00 2.40
- ❑ 123 John Riedling/2499 8.00 2.40
- ❑ 124 Jose Ortiz/1499 8.00 2.40
- ❑ 125 O. Mairena/2499 8.00 2.40
- ❑ 126 Eric Byrnes/2249 8.00 2.40
- ❑ 127 Brian Cole/999 8.00 2.40
- ❑ 128 Adam Piatt/2249 8.00 2.40
- ❑ 129 Nate Rolison/2499 8.00 2.40
- ❑ 130 Keith McDonald/2249 8.00 2.40
- ❑ 131 Albert Pujols/499 RC 100.00 30.00
- ❑ 132 Bud Smith/499 RC 15.00 4.50
- ❑ 133 T.Shinjo/499 RC 20.00 6.00
- ❑ 134 W.Betemit/499 RC 15.00 4.50
- ❑ 135 A.Hernandez/499 RC 15.00 4.50
- ❑ 136 J.Melian/499 RC 15.00 4.50
- ❑ 137 Jay Gibbons/499 RC 20.00 6.00
- ❑ 138 J.Estrada/499 RC 20.00 6.00
- ❑ 139 M.Ensberg/499 RC 25.00 7.50
- ❑ 140 Drew Henson/499 RC 25.00 7.50
- ❑ NNO Derek Jeter 150.00 45.00

Base Inks AU/500

- ❑ MM2 Derek Jeter 12.00 3.60

Monumental Moments

- ❑ NNO Derek Jeter 120.00 36.00

Monumental Moments AU/96

2002 E-X

	Nm-Mt	Ex-Mt
COMP.SET w/o SP's (100)	25.00	7.50
COMMON CARD (1-100)	.50	.15
COMMON CARD (101-120)	5.00	1.50
COMMON CARD (121-125)	5.00	1.50
COMMON CARD (126-140)	5.00	1.50

- ❑ 1 Alex Rodriguez 2.50 .75
- ❑ 2 Albert Pujols 2.50 .75
- ❑ 3 Ken Griffey Jr. 2.00 .60
- ❑ 4 Vladimir Guerrero 1.25 .35
- ❑ 5 Sammy Sosa 2.00 .60
- ❑ 6 Ichiro Suzuki 2.50 .75
- ❑ 7 Jorge Posada .75 .23
- ❑ 8 Matt Williams .50 .15
- ❑ 9 Adrian Beltre .50 .15
- ❑ 10 Pat Burrell .50 .15
- ❑ 11 Roger Cedeno .50 .15
- ❑ 12 Tony Clark .50 .15
- ❑ 13 Steve Finley .50 .15
- ❑ 14 Rafael Furcal .50 .15
- ❑ 15 Rickey Henderson 2.00 .60
- ❑ 16 Richard Hidalgo .50 .15
- ❑ 17 Jason Kendall .50 .15
- ❑ 18 Tino Martinez .75 .23
- ❑ 19 Scott Rolen .75 .23
- ❑ 20 Shannon Stewart .50 .15
- ❑ 21 Jose Vidro .50 .15
- ❑ 22 Preston Wilson .50 .15
- ❑ 23 Raul Mondesi .50 .15
- ❑ 24 Lance Berkman .50 .15
- ❑ 25 Rick Ankiel .50 .15
- ❑ 26 Kevin Brown .50 .15
- ❑ 27 Jeromy Burnitz .50 .15
- ❑ 28 Jeff Cirillo .50 .15
- ❑ 29 Carl Everett .50 .15
- ❑ 30 Eric Chavez .50 .15
- ❑ 31 Freddy Garcia .50 .15
- ❑ 32 Mark Grace 1.25 .35
- ❑ 33 David Justice .50 .15
- ❑ 34 Fred McGriff .75 .23
- ❑ 35 Mike Mussina 1.25 .35
- ❑ 36 John Olerud .50 .15
- ❑ 37 Magglio Ordonez .50 .15
- ❑ 38 Curt Schilling .75 .23
- ❑ 39 Aaron Sele .50 .15
- ❑ 40 Robin Ventura .50 .15
- ❑ 41 Adam Dunn .75 .23
- ❑ 42 Jeff Bagwell .75 .23
- ❑ 43 Barry Bonds 3.00 .90
- ❑ 44 Roger Clemens 2.50 .75
- ❑ 45 Cliff Floyd .50 .15
- ❑ 46 Jason Giambi 1.25 .35
- ❑ 47 Juan Gonzalez 1.25 .35
- ❑ 48 Luis Gonzalez .50 .15
- ❑ 49 Cristian Guzman .50 .15
- ❑ 50 Todd Helton .75 .23
- ❑ 51 Derek Jeter 3.00 .90
- ❑ 52 Rafael Palmeiro .75 .23
- ❑ 53 Mike Sweeney .50 .15
- ❑ 54 Ben Grieve .50 .15
- ❑ 55 Phil Nevin .50 .15
- ❑ 56 Mike Piazza 2.00 .60
- ❑ 57 Moises Alou .50 .15
- ❑ 58 Ivan Rodriguez 1.25 .35
- ❑ 59 Manny Ramirez .50 .15
- ❑ 60 Brian Giles .50 .15
- ❑ 61 Jim Thome 1.25 .35
- ❑ 62 Larry Walker .75 .23
- ❑ 63 Bobby Abreu .50 .15
- ❑ 64 Troy Glaus .75 .23
- ❑ 65 Garret Anderson .50 .15
- ❑ 66 Roberto Alomar 1.25 .35
- ❑ 67 Bret Boone .50 .15
- ❑ 68 Marty Cordova .50 .15
- ❑ 69 Craig Biggio .75 .23
- ❑ 70 Omar Vizquel .50 .15
- ❑ 71 Jermaine Dye .50 .15
- ❑ 72 Darin Erstad .50 .15
- ❑ 73 Carlos Delgado .50 .15
- ❑ 74 Nomar Garciaparra 2.50 .75
- ❑ 75 Greg Maddux 2.50 .75
- ❑ 76 Tom Glavine 1.25 .35
- ❑ 77 Frank Thomas 1.25 .35
- ❑ 78 Shawn Green .50 .15
- ❑ 79 Bobby Higginson .50 .15
- ❑ 80 Jeff Kent .50 .15
- ❑ 81 Chuck Knoblauch .50 .15
- ❑ 82 Paul Konerko .50 .15
- ❑ 83 Carlos Lee .50 .15
- ❑ 84 Jon Lieber .50 .15
- ❑ 85 Paul LoDuca .50 .15
- ❑ 86 Mike Lowell .50 .15
- ❑ 87 Edgar Martinez .75 .23
- ❑ 88 Doug Mientkiewicz .50 .15
- ❑ 89 Pedro Martinez 1.25 .35
- ❑ 90 Randy Johnson 1.25 .35
- ❑ 91 Aramis Ramirez .50 .15
- ❑ 92 J.D. Drew .50 .15
- ❑ 93 Chris Richard .50 .15
- ❑ 94 Jimmy Rollins .50 .15
- ❑ 95 Ryan Klesko .50 .15
- ❑ 96 Gary Sheffield .50 .15
- ❑ 97 Chipper Jones 1.25 .35
- ❑ 98 Greg Vaughn .50 .15
- ❑ 99 Mo Vaughn .50 .15
- ❑ 100 Bernie Williams .75 .23
- ❑ 101 John Foster NT/2999 RC 5.00 1.50
- ❑ 102 Jorge DeLaRosa NT/2999 RC 5.00 1.50
- ❑ 103 Edwin Almonte NT/2999 RC 5.00 1.50
- ❑ 104 Chris Booker NT/2999 RC 5.00 1.50
- ❑ 105 Victor Alvarez NT/2999 RC 5.00 1.50
- ❑ 106 Cliff Bartosh NT/2999 RC 5.00 1.50
- ❑ 107 Felix Escalona NT/2999 RC 5.00 1.50
- ❑ 108 Corey Thurman NT/2999 RC 5.00 1.50
- ❑ 109 Kazuhisa Ishii NT/2999 RC 10.00 3.00
- ❑ 110 Miguel Asencio NT/2999 RC 5.00 1.50
- ❑ 111 P.J. Bevis NT/2499 RC 5.00 1.50
- ❑ 112 Gustavo Chacin NT/2499 RC 5.00 1.50
- ❑ 113 Steve Kent NT/2499 RC 5.00 1.50
- ❑ 114 Takahito Nomura NT/2499 RC 5.00 1.50
- ❑ 115 Adam Walker NT/2499 RC 5.00 1.50
- ❑ 116 So Taguchi NT/2499 RC 8.00 2.40
- ❑ 117 Reed Johnson NT/2499 RC 8.00 2.40
- ❑ 118 Rod Rosario NT/2499 RC 5.00 1.50
- ❑ 119 Luis Martinez NT/2499 RC 8.00 2.40
- ❑ 120 Sat Komiyama NT/2499 RC 5.00 1.50
- ❑ 121 Sean Burroughs NT/1999 5.00 1.50
- ❑ 122 Hank Blalock NT/1999 8.00 2.40
- ❑ 123 Marlon Byrd NT/1999 5.00 1.50
- ❑ 124 Nick Johnson NT/1999 5.00 1.50
- ❑ 125 Mark Teixeira NT/1999 8.00 2.40
- ❑ 126 David Espinosa NT 5.00 1.50
- ❑ 127 Adrian Burnside NT RC 5.00 1.50
- ❑ 128 Mark Corey NT RC 5.00 1.50
- ❑ 129 Matt Thornton NT RC 5.00 1.50
- ❑ 130 Dane Sardinha NT 5.00 1.50
- ❑ 131 Juan Rivera NT 5.00 1.50
- ❑ 132 Austin Kearns NT 8.00 2.40
- ❑ 133 Does Not Exist - -
- ❑ 134 Ben Broussard NT 5.00 1.50
- ❑ 135 Orlando Hudson NT 5.00 1.50
- ❑ 136 Carlos Pena NT 5.00 1.50
- ❑ 137 Kenny Kelly NT 5.00 1.50
- ❑ 138 Bill Hall NT 5.00 1.50
- ❑ 139 Ron Chiavacci NT 5.00 1.50
- ❑ 140 Mark Prior NT 15.00 4.50

2003 E-X

	MINT	NRMT
COMP.SET w/o SP's (72)	40.00	18.00
COMMON CARD (1-72)	.50	.23
COMMON CARD (73-82)	5.00	2.20
COMMON CARD (83-86)	5.00	2.20
COMMON CARD (87-102)	5.00	2.20

- ❑ 1 Troy Glaus .75 .35
- ❑ 2 Darin Erstad .50 .23
- ❑ 3 Garret Anderson .50 .23
- ❑ 4 Curt Schilling .75 .35
- ❑ 5 Randy Johnson 1.25 .55

❑ 6 Luis Gonzalez	.50	.23
❑ 7 Greg Maddux	2.50	1.10
❑ 8 Chipper Jones	1.25	.55
❑ 9 Andruw Jones	.75	.35
❑ 10 Melvin Mora	.50	.23
❑ 11 Jay Gibbons	.50	.23
❑ 12 Nomar Garciaparra	2.50	1.10
❑ 13 Pedro Martinez	1.25	.55
❑ 14 Manny Ramirez	.50	.23
❑ 15 Sammy Sosa	2.00	.90
❑ 16 Kerry Wood	1.25	.55
❑ 17 Magglio Ordonez	.50	.23
❑ 18 Frank Thomas	1.25	.55
❑ 19 Roberto Alomar	1.25	.55
❑ 20 Barry Larkin	1.25	.55
❑ 21 Adam Dunn	.75	.35
❑ 22 Austin Kearns	.75	.35
❑ 23 Omar Vizquel	.50	.23
❑ 24 Larry Walker	.75	.35
❑ 25 Todd Helton	.75	.35
❑ 26 Preston Wilson	.50	.23
❑ 27 Dmitri Young	.50	.23
❑ 28 Ivan Rodriguez	1.25	.55
❑ 29 Mike Lowell	.50	.23
❑ 30 Jeff Kent	.50	.23
❑ 31 Jeff Bagwell	.75	.35
❑ 32 Roy Oswalt	.50	.23
❑ 33 Craig Biggio	.75	.35
❑ 34 Mike Sweeney	.50	.23
❑ 35 Carlos Beltran	.50	.23
❑ 36 Shawn Green	.50	.23
❑ 37 Kazuhisa Ishii	.50	.23
❑ 38 Richie Sexson	.50	.23
❑ 39 Torii Hunter	.50	.23
❑ 40 Jacque Jones	.50	.23
❑ 41 Jose Vidro	.50	.23
❑ 42 Vladimir Guerrero	1.25	.55
❑ 43 Mike Piazza	2.00	.90
❑ 44 Tom Glavine	1.25	.55
❑ 45 Roger Clemens	2.50	1.10
❑ 46 Jason Giambi	1.25	.55
❑ 47 Bernie Williams	.75	.35
❑ 48 Alfonso Soriano	1.25	.55
❑ 49 Mike Mussina	1.25	.55
❑ 50 Barry Zito	1.25	.55
❑ 51 Miguel Tejada	.50	.23
❑ 52 Eric Chavez	.50	.23
❑ 53 Eric Byrnes	.50	.23
❑ 54 Jim Thome	1.25	.55
❑ 55 Kevin Millwood	.50	.23
❑ 56 Brian Giles	.50	.23
❑ 57 Xavier Nady	.50	.23
❑ 58 Barry Bonds	3.00	1.35
❑ 59 Bret Boone	.50	.23
❑ 60 Edgar Martinez	.75	.35
❑ 61 Kazuhiro Sasaki	.50	.23
❑ 62 Edgar Renteria	.50	.23
❑ 63 J.D. Drew	.50	.23
❑ 64 Scott Rolen	.75	.35
❑ 65 Jim Edmonds	.50	.23
❑ 66 Aubrey Huff	.50	.23
❑ 67 Alex Rodriguez	2.50	1.10
❑ 68 Juan Gonzalez	1.25	.55
❑ 69 Hank Blalock	.75	.35
❑ 70 Mark Teixeira	.75	.35
❑ 71 Carlos Delgado	.50	.23
❑ 72 Vernon Wells	.50	.23
❑ 73 Shea Hillenbrand SP	5.00	2.20
❑ 74 Gary Sheffield SP	5.00	2.20
❑ 75 Mark Prior SP	15.00	6.75
❑ 76 Ken Griffey Jr. SP	12.00	5.50
❑ 77 Lance Berkman SP	5.00	2.20
❑ 78 Hideo Nomo SP	15.00	6.75
❑ 79 Derek Jeter SP	20.00	9.00
❑ 80 Ichiro Suzuki SP	15.00	6.75
❑ 81 Albert Pujols SP	15.00	6.75
❑ 82 Rafael Palmeiro SP	8.00	3.60
❑ 83 Jose Reyes ROO SP	8.00	3.60
❑ 84 Rocco Baldelli ROO SP	12.00	5.50
❑ 85 Hee Seop Choi ROO SP	5.00	2.20
❑ 86 Dontrelle Willis ROO SP	10.00	4.50
❑ 87 Robb Hammock ROO SP RC	8.00	3.60
❑ 88 Brandon Webb ROO SP RC	12.00	5.50
❑ 89 Matt Kata ROO SP RC	8.00	3.60
❑ 90 T.Wellemeyer ROO SP RC	8.00	3.60
❑ 91 Fran Cruceta ROO SP RC	5.00	2.20
❑ 92 Clint Barmes ROO SP RC	8.00	3.60
❑ 93 Jer Bonderman ROO SP RC	8.00	3.60
❑ 94 David Matranga ROO SP RC	5.00	2.20
❑ 95 Ryan Wagner ROO SP RC	10.00	4.50
❑ 96 Jeremy Griffiths ROO SP RC	8.00	3.60
❑ 97 Hideki Matsui ROO SP RC	25.00	11.00
❑ 98 Jose Contreras ROO SP RC	10.00	4.50
❑ 99 C.Wang ROO SP RC	10.00	4.50
❑ 100 Bo Hart ROO SP RC	10.00	4.50
❑ 101 Danny Haren ROO SP RC	8.00	3.60
❑ 102 Rickie Weeks ROO SP RC	20.00	9.00

1999 Finest

	Nm-Mt	Ex-Mt
COMPLETE SET (300)	100.00	30.00
COMP.SERIES 1 (150)	50.00	15.00
COMP.SERIES 2 (150)	50.00	15.00
COMP.SER.1 w/o SP's (100)	20.00	6.00
COMP.SER.2 w/o SP's (100)	20.00	6.00
COMMON (1-100/151-250)	.40	.12
COMMON (101-150/251-300)	.60	.18

❑ 1 Darin Erstad	.40	.12
❑ 2 Javy Lopez	.40	.12
❑ 3 Vinny Castilla	.40	.12
❑ 4 Jim Thome	1.00	.30
❑ 5 Tino Martinez	.60	.18
❑ 6 Mark Grace	1.00	.30
❑ 7 Shawn Green	.40	.12
❑ 8 Dustin Hermanson	.40	.12
❑ 9 Kevin Young	.40	.12
❑ 10 Tony Clark	.40	.12
❑ 11 Scott Brosius	.40	.12
❑ 12 Craig Biggio	.60	.18
❑ 13 Brian McRae	.40	.12
❑ 14 Chan Ho Park	.40	.12
❑ 15 Manny Ramirez	.40	.12
❑ 16 Chipper Jones	1.00	.30
❑ 17 Rico Brogna	.40	.12
❑ 18 Quinton McCracken	.40	.12
❑ 19 J.T. Snow	.40	.12
❑ 20 Tony Gwynn	1.25	.35
❑ 21 Juan Guzman	.40	.12
❑ 22 John Valentin	.40	.12
❑ 23 Rick Helling	.40	.12
❑ 24 Sandy Alomar Jr.	.40	.12
❑ 25 Frank Thomas	1.00	.30
❑ 26 Jorge Posada	.60	.18
❑ 27 Dmitri Young	.40	.12
❑ 28 Rick Reed	.40	.12
❑ 29 Kevin Tapani	.40	.12
❑ 30 Troy Glaus	.60	.18
❑ 31 Kenny Rogers	.40	.12
❑ 32 Jeromy Burnitz	.40	.12
❑ 33 Mark Grudzielanek	.40	.12
❑ 34 Mike Mussina	1.00	.30
❑ 35 Scott Rolen	.60	.18
❑ 36 Neifi Perez	.40	.12
❑ 37 Brad Radke	.40	.12
❑ 38 Darryl Strawberry	.60	.18
❑ 39 Robb Nen	.40	.12
❑ 40 Moises Alou	.40	.12
❑ 41 Eric Young	.40	.12
❑ 42 Livan Hernandez	.40	.12
❑ 43 John Wetteland	.40	.12
❑ 44 Matt Lawton	.40	.12
❑ 45 Ben Grieve	.40	.12
❑ 46 Fernando Tatis	.40	.12
❑ 47 Travis Fryman	.40	.12
❑ 48 David Segui	.40	.12
❑ 49 Bob Abreu	.40	.12
❑ 50 Nomar Garciaparra	2.00	.60
❑ 51 Paul O'Neill	.60	.18
❑ 52 Jeff King	.40	.12
❑ 53 Francisco Cordova	.40	.12
❑ 54 John Olerud	.40	.12
❑ 55 Vladimir Guerrero	1.00	.30
❑ 56 Fernando Vina	.40	.12
❑ 57 Shane Reynolds	.40	.12
❑ 58 Chuck Finley	.40	.12
❑ 59 Rondell White	.40	.12
❑ 60 Greg Vaughn	.40	.12
❑ 61 Ryan Minor	.40	.12
❑ 62 Tom Gordon	.40	.12
❑ 63 Damion Easley	.40	.12
❑ 64 Ray Durham	.40	.12
❑ 65 Orlando Hernandez	.40	.12
❑ 66 Bartolo Colon	.40	.12
❑ 67 Jaret Wright	.40	.12
❑ 68 Royce Clayton	.40	.12
❑ 69 Tim Salmon	.60	.18
❑ 70 Mark McGwire	2.50	.75
❑ 71 Alex Gonzalez	.40	.12
❑ 72 Tom Glavine	1.00	.30
❑ 73 David Justice	.40	.12
❑ 74 Omar Vizquel	.40	.12
❑ 75 Juan Gonzalez	1.00	.30
❑ 76 Bobby Higginson	.40	.12
❑ 77 Todd Walker	.40	.12
❑ 78 Dante Bichette	.40	.12
❑ 79 Kevin Millwood	.40	.12
❑ 80 Roger Clemens	2.00	.60
❑ 81 Kerry Wood	1.00	.30
❑ 82 Cal Ripken	3.00	.90
❑ 83 Jay Bell	.40	.12
❑ 84 Barry Bonds	2.50	.75
❑ 85 Alex Rodriguez	2.00	.60
❑ 86 Doug Glanville	.40	.12
❑ 87 Jason Kendall	.40	.12
❑ 88 Sean Casey	.40	.12
❑ 89 Aaron Sele	.40	.12
❑ 90 Derek Jeter	2.50	.75
❑ 91 Andy Ashby	.40	.12
❑ 92 Rusty Greer	.40	.12
❑ 93 Rod Beck	.40	.12
❑ 94 Matt Williams	.40	.12
❑ 95 Mike Piazza	1.50	.45
❑ 96 Wally Joyner	.40	.12
❑ 97 Barry Larkin	1.00	.30
❑ 98 Eric Milton	.40	.12
❑ 99 Gary Sheffield	.40	.12
❑ 100 Greg Maddux	2.00	.60
❑ 101 Ken Griffey Jr. GEM	2.50	.75
❑ 102 Frank Thomas GEM	1.50	.45
❑ 103 N.Garciaparra GEM	3.00	.90
❑ 104 Mark McGwire GEM	4.00	1.20
❑ 105 Alex Rodriguez GEM	3.00	.90
❑ 106 Tony Gwynn GEM	2.00	.60
❑ 107 Juan Gonzalez GEM	1.50	.45
❑ 108 Jeff Bagwell GEM	1.00	.30
❑ 109 Sammy Sosa GEM	2.50	.75
❑ 110 V.Guerrero GEM	1.50	.45
❑ 111 Roger Clemens GEM	3.00	.90
❑ 112 Barry Bonds GEM	4.00	1.20
❑ 113 Darin Erstad GEM	.60	.18

Card	Nm-Mt	Ex-Mt
❑ 114 Mike Piazza GEM	2.50	.75
❑ 115 Derek Jeter GEM	4.00	1.20
❑ 116 Chipper Jones GEM	1.50	.45
❑ 117 Larry Walker GEM	1.00	.30
❑ 118 Scott Rolen GEM	1.00	.30
❑ 119 Cal Ripken GEM	5.00	1.50
❑ 120 Greg Maddux GEM	3.00	.90
❑ 121 Troy Glaus SENS	1.00	.30
❑ 122 Ben Grieve SENS	.60	.18
❑ 123 Ryan Minor SENS	.60	.18
❑ 124 Kerry Wood SENS	1.50	.45
❑ 125 Travis Lee SENS	.60	.18
❑ 126 Adrian Beltre SENS	.60	.18
❑ 127 Brad Fullmer SENS	.60	.18
❑ 128 Aramis Ramirez SENS	.60	.18
❑ 129 Eric Chavez SENS	.60	.18
❑ 130 Todd Helton SENS	1.00	.30
❑ 131 Pat Burrell RC	6.00	1.80
❑ 132 Ryan Mills RC	.60	.18
❑ 133 Austin Kearns RC	10.00	3.00
❑ 134 Josh McKinley RC	.60	.18
❑ 135 Adam Everett RC	.60	.18
❑ 136 Marlon Anderson	.60	.18
❑ 137 Bruce Chen	.60	.18
❑ 138 Matt Clement	.60	.18
❑ 139 Alex Gonzalez	.60	.18
❑ 140 Roy Halladay	.60	.18
❑ 141 Calvin Pickering	.60	.18
❑ 142 Randy Wolf	.60	.18
❑ 143 Ryan Anderson	.60	.18
❑ 144 Ruben Mateo	.60	.18
❑ 145 Alex Escobar RC	.60	.18
❑ 146 Jeremy Giambi	.60	.18
❑ 147 Lance Berkman	.60	.18
❑ 148 Michael Barrett	.60	.18
❑ 149 Preston Wilson	.60	.18
❑ 150 Gabe Kapler	.60	.18
❑ 151 Roger Clemens	2.00	.60
❑ 152 Jay Buhner	.40	.12
❑ 153 Brad Fullmer	.40	.12
❑ 154 Ray Lankford	.40	.12
❑ 155 Jim Edmonds	.40	.12
❑ 156 Jason Giambi	1.00	.30
❑ 157 Bret Boone	.40	.12
❑ 158 Jeff Cirillo	.40	.12
❑ 159 Rickey Henderson	1.50	.45
❑ 160 Edgar Martinez	.60	.18
❑ 161 Ron Gant	.40	.12
❑ 162 Mark Kotsay	.40	.12
❑ 163 Trevor Hoffman	.40	.12
❑ 164 Jason Schmidt	.40	.12
❑ 165 Brett Tomko	.40	.12
❑ 166 David Ortiz	.40	.12
❑ 167 Dean Palmer	.40	.12
❑ 168 Hideki Irabu	.40	.12
❑ 169 Mike Cameron	.40	.12
❑ 170 Pedro Martinez	1.00	.30
❑ 171 Tom Goodwin	.40	.12
❑ 172 Brian Hunter	.40	.12
❑ 173 Al Leiter	.40	.12
❑ 174 Charles Johnson	.40	.12
❑ 175 Curt Schilling	.60	.18
❑ 176 Robin Ventura	.40	.12
❑ 177 Travis Lee	.40	.12
❑ 178 Jeff Shaw	.40	.12
❑ 179 Ugueth Urbina	.40	.12
❑ 180 Roberto Alomar	1.00	.30
❑ 181 Cliff Floyd	.40	.12
❑ 182 Adrian Beltre	.40	.12
❑ 183 Tony Womack	.40	.12
❑ 184 Brian Jordan	.40	.12
❑ 185 Randy Johnson	1.00	.30
❑ 186 Mickey Morandini	.40	.12
❑ 187 Todd Hundley	.40	.12
❑ 188 Jose Valentin	.40	.12
❑ 189 Eric Davis	.40	.12
❑ 190 Ken Caminiti	.40	.12
❑ 191 David Wells	.40	.12
❑ 192 Ryan Klesko	.40	.12
❑ 193 Garret Anderson	.40	.12
❑ 194 Eric Karros	.40	.12
❑ 195 Ivan Rodriguez	1.00	.30
❑ 196 Aramis Ramirez	.40	.12
❑ 197 Mike Lieberthal	.40	.12
❑ 198 Will Clark	1.00	.30
❑ 199 Rey Ordonez	.40	.12
❑ 200 Ken Griffey Jr.	1.50	.45
❑ 201 Jose Guillen	.40	.12
❑ 202 Scott Erickson	.40	.12
❑ 203 Paul Konerko	.40	.12
❑ 204 Johnny Damon	.40	.12
❑ 205 Larry Walker	.60	.18
❑ 206 Denny Neagle	.40	.12
❑ 207 Jose Offerman	.40	.12
❑ 208 Andy Pettitte	.60	.18
❑ 209 Bobby Jones	.40	.12
❑ 210 Kevin Brown	.60	.18
❑ 211 John Smoltz	.60	.18
❑ 212 Henry Rodriguez	.40	.12
❑ 213 Tim Belcher	.40	.12
❑ 214 Carlos Delgado	.40	.12
❑ 215 Andruw Jones	.60	.18
❑ 216 Andy Benes	.40	.12
❑ 217 Fred McGriff	.60	.18
❑ 218 Edgar Renteria	.40	.12
❑ 219 Miguel Tejada	.40	.12
❑ 220 Bernie Williams	.60	.18
❑ 221 Justin Thompson	.40	.12
❑ 222 Marty Cordova	.40	.12
❑ 223 Delino DeShields	.40	.12
❑ 224 Ellis Burks	.40	.12
❑ 225 Kenny Lofton	.40	.12
❑ 226 Steve Finley	.40	.12
❑ 227 Eric Chavez	.40	.12
❑ 228 Jose Cruz Jr.	.40	.12
❑ 229 Marquis Grissom	.40	.12
❑ 230 Jeff Bagwell	.60	.18
❑ 231 Jose Canseco	1.00	.30
❑ 232 Edgardo Alfonzo	.40	.12
❑ 233 Richie Sexson	.40	.12
❑ 234 Jeff Kent	.40	.12
❑ 235 Rafael Palmeiro	.60	.18
❑ 236 David Cone	.40	.12
❑ 237 Gregg Jefferies	.40	.12
❑ 238 Mike Lansing	.40	.12
❑ 239 Mariano Rivera	.60	.18
❑ 240 Albert Belle	.40	.12
❑ 241 Chuck Knoblauch	.40	.12
❑ 242 Derek Bell	.40	.12
❑ 243 Pat Hentgen	.40	.12
❑ 244 Andres Galarraga	.40	.12
❑ 245 Mo Vaughn	.40	.12
❑ 246 Wade Boggs	.60	.18
❑ 247 Devon White	.40	.12
❑ 248 Todd Helton	.60	.18
❑ 249 Raul Mondesi	.40	.12
❑ 250 Sammy Sosa	1.50	.45
❑ 251 Nomar Garciaparra ST	3.00	.90
❑ 252 Mark McGwire ST	4.00	1.20
❑ 253 Alex Rodriguez ST	3.00	.90
❑ 254 Juan Gonzalez ST	1.50	.45
❑ 255 Vladimir Guerrero ST	1.50	.45
❑ 256 Ken Griffey Jr. ST	2.50	.75
❑ 257 Mike Piazza ST	2.50	.75
❑ 258 Derek Jeter ST	4.00	1.20
❑ 259 Albert Belle ST	.60	.18
❑ 260 Greg Vaughn ST	.60	.18
❑ 261 Sammy Sosa ST	2.50	.75
❑ 262 Greg Maddux ST	3.00	.90
❑ 263 Frank Thomas ST	1.50	.45
❑ 264 Mark Grace ST	1.50	.45
❑ 265 Ivan Rodriguez ST	1.50	.45
❑ 266 Roger Clemens GM	3.00	.90
❑ 267 Mo Vaughn GM	.60	.18
❑ 268 Jim Thome GM	1.50	.45
❑ 269 Darin Erstad GM	.60	.18
❑ 270 Chipper Jones GM	1.50	.45
❑ 271 Larry Walker GM	1.00	.30
❑ 272 Cal Ripken GM	5.00	1.50
❑ 273 Scott Rolen GM	1.00	.30
❑ 274 Randy Johnson GM	1.50	.45
❑ 275 Tony Gwynn GM	2.00	.60
❑ 276 Barry Bonds GM	4.00	1.20
❑ 277 Sean Burroughs RC	5.00	1.50
❑ 278 J.M. Gold RC	.60	.18
❑ 279 Carlos Lee	.60	.18
❑ 280 George Lombard	.60	.18
❑ 281 Carlos Beltran	.60	.18
❑ 282 Fernando Seguignol	.60	.18
❑ 283 Eric Chavez	.60	.18
❑ 284 Carlos Pena RC	1.50	.45
❑ 285 Corey Patterson RC	6.00	1.80
❑ 286 Alfonso Soriano RC	15.00	4.50
❑ 287 Nick Johnson RC	3.00	.90
❑ 288 Jorge Toca RC	.60	.18
❑ 289 A.J. Burnett RC	1.00	.30
❑ 290 Andy Brown RC	.60	.18
❑ 291 D.Mientkiewicz RC	2.00	.60
❑ 292 Bobby Seay RC	.60	.18
❑ 293 Chip Ambres RC	.60	.18
❑ 294 C.C. Sabathia RC	1.50	.45
❑ 295 Choo Freeman RC	.60	.18
❑ 296 Eric Valent RC	.60	.18
❑ 297 Matt Belisle RC	.60	.18
❑ 298 Jason Tyner RC	.60	.18
❑ 299 Masao Kida RC	.60	.18
❑ 300 Hank Aaron	3.00	.90

Mark McGwire

2000 Finest

	Nm-Mt	Ex-Mt
COMP.SERIES 1 w/o SP's (100)	25.00	7.50
COMP.SERIES 2 w/o SP's (100)	25.00	7.50
COMMON (1-100/147-246)	.40	.12
COMMON (101-120)	5.00	1.50
COMMON (121-135)	1.50	.45
COMMON (136-145/277-286)	2.00	.60
COMMON (247-266)	5.00	1.50
COMMON (267-276)	1.00	.30

Card	Nm-Mt	Ex-Mt
❑ 1 Nomar Garciaparra	2.00	.60
❑ 2 Chipper Jones	1.00	.30
❑ 3 Erubiel Durazo	.40	.12
❑ 4 Robin Ventura	.60	.18
❑ 5 Garret Anderson	.40	.12
❑ 6 Dean Palmer	.40	.12
❑ 7 Mariano Rivera	.60	.18
❑ 8 Rusty Greer	.40	.12
❑ 9 Jim Thome	1.00	.30
❑ 10 Jeff Bagwell	.60	.18
❑ 11 Jason Giambi	1.00	.30
❑ 12 Jeromy Burnitz	.40	.12
❑ 13 Mark Grace	1.00	.30
❑ 14 Russ Ortiz	.40	.12
❑ 15 Kevin Brown	.60	.18
❑ 16 Kevin Millwood	.40	.12
❑ 17 Scott Williamson	.40	.12
❑ 18 Orlando Hernandez	.40	.12
❑ 19 Todd Walker	.40	.12
❑ 20 Carlos Beltran	.40	.12
❑ 21 Ruben Rivera	.40	.12
❑ 22 Curt Schilling	.60	.18
❑ 23 Brian Giles	.40	.12
❑ 24 Eric Karros	.40	.12
❑ 25 Preston Wilson	.40	.12
❑ 26 Al Leiter	.40	.12
❑ 27 Juan Encarnacion	.40	.12
❑ 28 Tim Salmon	.60	.18
❑ 29 B.J. Surhoff	.40	.12
❑ 30 Bernie Williams	.60	.18
❑ 31 Lee Stevens	.40	.12
❑ 32 Pokey Reese	.40	.12
❑ 33 Mike Sweeney	.40	.12
❑ 34 Corey Koskie	.40	.12
❑ 35 Roberto Alomar	1.00	.30
❑ 36 Tim Hudson	.60	.18
❑ 37 Tom Glavine	1.00	.30
❑ 38 Jeff Kent	.40	.12
❑ 39 Mike Lieberthal	.40	.12

☐ 40 Barry Larkin 1.00 .30
☐ 41 Paul O'Neill .60 .18
☐ 42 Rico Brogna .40 .12
☐ 43 Brian Daubach .40 .12
☐ 44 Rich Aurilia .40 .12
☐ 45 Vladimir Guerrero 1.00 .30
☐ 46 Luis Castillo .40 .12
☐ 47 Bartolo Colon .40 .12
☐ 48 Kevin Appier .40 .12
☐ 49 Mo Vaughn .40 .12
☐ 50 Alex Rodriguez 2.00 .60
☐ 51 Randy Johnson 1.00 .30
☐ 52 Kris Benson .40 .12
☐ 53 Tony Clark .40 .12
☐ 54 Chad Allen .40 .12
☐ 55 Larry Walker .60 .18
☐ 56 Freddy Garcia .40 .12
☐ 57 Paul Konerko .40 .12
☐ 58 Edgardo Alfonzo .40 .12
☐ 59 Brady Anderson .40 .12
☐ 60 Derek Jeter 2.50 .75
☐ 61 John Smoltz .60 .18
☐ 62 Doug Glanville .40 .12
☐ 63 Shannon Stewart .40 .12
☐ 64 Greg Maddux 2.00 .60
☐ 65 Mark McGwire 2.50 .75
☐ 66 Gary Sheffield .40 .12
☐ 67 Kevin Young .40 .12
☐ 68 Tony Gwynn 1.25 .35
☐ 69 Rey Ordonez .40 .12
☐ 70 Cal Ripken 3.00 .90
☐ 71 Todd Helton .60 .18
☐ 72 Brian Jordan .40 .12
☐ 73 Jose Canseco 1.00 .30
☐ 74 Luis Gonzalez .40 .12
☐ 75 Barry Bonds 2.50 .75
☐ 76 Jermaine Dye .40 .12
☐ 77 Jose Offerman .40 .12
☐ 78 Magglio Ordonez .40 .12
☐ 79 Fred McGriff .60 .18
☐ 80 Ivan Rodriguez 1.00 .30
☐ 81 Josh Hamilton .40 .12
☐ 82 Vernon Wells .40 .12
☐ 83 Mark Mulder .60 .18
☐ 84 John Patterson .40 .12
☐ 85 Nick Johnson .40 .12
☐ 86 Pablo Ozuna .40 .12
☐ 87 A.J. Burnett .40 .12
☐ 88 Jack Cust .40 .12
☐ 89 Adam Piatt .40 .12
☐ 90 Rob Ryan .40 .12
☐ 91 Sean Burroughs .60 .18
☐ 92 D'Angelo Jimenez .40 .12
☐ 93 Chad Hermansen .40 .12
☐ 94 Robert Fick .40 .12
☐ 95 Ruben Mateo .40 .12
☐ 96 Alex Escobar .40 .12
☐ 97 Wily Pena .40 .12
☐ 98 Corey Patterson .60 .18
☐ 99 Eric Munson .40 .12
☐ 100 Pat Burrell .60 .18
☐ 101 Michael Tejera RC 5.00 1.50
☐ 102 Bobby Bradley RC 5.00 1.50
☐ 103 Larry Bigbie RC 8.00 2.40
☐ 104 B.J. Garbe RC 5.00 1.50
☐ 105 Josh Kalinowski RC 5.00 1.50
☐ 106 Brett Myers RC 15.00 4.50
☐ 107 Chris Mears RC 5.00 1.50
☐ 108 Aaron Rowand RC 5.00 1.50
☐ 109 Corey Myers RC 5.00 1.50
☐ 110 John Sneed RC 5.00 1.50
☐ 111 Ryan Christianson RC 5.00 1.50
☐ 112 Kyle Snyder 5.00 1.50
☐ 113 Mike Paradis 5.00 1.50
☐ 114 Chance Caple RC 5.00 1.50
☐ 115 Ben Christensen RC 5.00 1.50
☐ 116 Brad Baker RC 5.00 1.50
☐ 117 Rob Purvis RC 5.00 1.50
☐ 118 Rick Asadoorian RC 5.00 1.50
☐ 119 Ruben Salazar RC 5.00 1.50
☐ 120 Julio Zuleta RC 5.00 1.50
☐ 121 Alex Rodriguez 5.00 1.50
Ken Griffey Jr.
☐ 122 Nomar Garciaparra 6.00 1.80
Derek Jeter
☐ 123 Mark Mcgwire 6.00 1.80
Sammy Sosa
☐ 124 Randy Johnson 2.50 .75
Pedro Martinez
☐ 125 Ivan Rodriguez 4.00 1.20
Mike Piazza
☐ 126 Manny Ramirez 2.50 .75
Roberto Alomar
☐ 127 Chipper Jones 2.50 .75
Andruw Jones
☐ 128 Cal Ripken 8.00 2.40
Tony Gwynn
☐ 129 Jeff Bagwell 1.50 .45
Craig Biggio
☐ 130 Barry Bonds 6.00 1.80
Vladimir Guerrero
☐ 131 Nick Johnson 4.00 1.20
Alfonso Soriano
☐ 132 Josh Hamilton 8.00 2.40
Pat Burrell
☐ 133 Corey Patterson 1.50 .45
Ruben Mateo
☐ 134 Larry Walker 1.50 .45
Todd Helton
☐ 135 Rey Ordonez 1.50 .45
Edgardo Alfonzo
☐ 136 Derek Jeter GEM 12.00 3.60
☐ 137 Alex Rodriguez GEM 10.00 3.00
☐ 138 Chipper Jones GEM 5.00 1.50
☐ 139 Mike Piazza GEM 8.00 2.40
☐ 140 Mark McGwire GEM 12.00 3.60
☐ 141 Ivan Rodriguez GEM 5.00 1.50
☐ 142 Cal Ripken GEM 15.00 4.50
☐ 143 V.Guerrero GEM 5.00 1.50
☐ 144 Randy Johnson GEM 5.00 1.50
☐ 145 Jeff Bagwell GEM 3.00 .90
☐ 146 K.Griffey Jr. ACTION 1.50 .45
☐ 146A Ken Griffey Jr. PORT 1.50 .45
☐ 147 Andruw Jones .60 .18
☐ 148 Kerry Wood 1.00 .30
☐ 149 Jim Edmonds .40 .12
☐ 150 Pedro Martinez 1.00 .30
☐ 151 Warren Morris .40 .12
☐ 152 Trevor Hoffman .40 .12
☐ 153 Ryan Klesko .40 .12
☐ 154 Andy Pettitte .60 .18
☐ 155 Frank Thomas 1.00 .30
☐ 156 Damion Easley .40 .12
☐ 157 Cliff Floyd .40 .12
☐ 158 Ben Davis .40 .12
☐ 159 John Valentin .40 .12
☐ 160 Rafael Palmeiro .60 .18
☐ 161 Andy Ashby .40 .12
☐ 162 J.D. Drew .40 .12
☐ 163 Jay Bell .40 .12
☐ 164 Adam Kennedy .40 .12
☐ 165 Manny Ramirez .40 .12
☐ 166 John Halama .40 .12
☐ 167 Octavio Dotel .40 .12
☐ 168 Darin Erstad .40 .12
☐ 169 Jose Lima .40 .12
☐ 170 Andres Galarraga .40 .12
☐ 171 Scott Rolen .60 .18
☐ 172 Delino DeShields .40 .12
☐ 173 J.T. Snow .40 .12
☐ 174 Tony Womack .40 .12
☐ 175 John Olerud .40 .12
☐ 176 Jason Kendall .40 .12
☐ 177 Carlos Lee .40 .12
☐ 178 Eric Milton .40 .12
☐ 179 Jeff Cirillo .40 .12
☐ 180 Gabe Kapler .40 .12
☐ 181 Greg Vaughn .40 .12
☐ 182 Denny Neagle .40 .12
☐ 183 Tino Martinez .60 .18
☐ 184 Doug Mientkiewicz .40 .12
☐ 185 Juan Gonzalez 1.00 .30
☐ 186 Ellis Burks .40 .12
☐ 187 Mike Hampton .40 .12
☐ 188 Royce Clayton .40 .12
☐ 189 Mike Mussina 1.00 .30
☐ 190 Carlos Delgado .40 .12
☐ 191 Ben Grieve .40 .12
☐ 192 Fernando Tatis .40 .12
☐ 193 Matt Williams .40 .12
☐ 194 Rondell White .40 .12
☐ 195 Shawn Green .40 .12
☐ 196 Hideki Irabu .40 .12
☐ 197 Troy Glaus .60 .18
☐ 198 Roger Cedeno .40 .12
☐ 199 Ray Lankford .40 .12
☐ 200 Sammy Sosa 1.50 .45
☐ 201 Kenny Lofton .40 .12
☐ 202 Edgar Martinez .60 .18
☐ 203 Mark Kotsay .40 .12
☐ 204 David Wells .40 .12
☐ 205 Craig Biggio .60 .18
☐ 206 Ray Durham .40 .12
☐ 207 Troy O'Leary .40 .12
☐ 208 Rickey Henderson 1.50 .45
☐ 209 Bob Abreu .40 .12
☐ 210 Neifi Perez .40 .12
☐ 211 Carlos Febles .40 .12
☐ 212 Chuck Knoblauch .40 .12
☐ 213 Moises Alou .40 .12
☐ 214 Omar Vizquel .40 .12
☐ 215 Vinny Castilla .40 .12
☐ 216 Javy Lopez .40 .12
☐ 217 Johnny Damon .40 .12
☐ 218 Roger Clemens 2.00 .60
☐ 219 Miguel Tejada .40 .12
☐ 220 Carl Everett .40 .12
☐ 221 Matt Lawton .40 .12
☐ 222 Albert Belle .40 .12
☐ 223 Adrian Beltre .40 .12
☐ 224 Dante Bichette .40 .12
☐ 225 Raul Mondesi .40 .12
☐ 226 Mike Piazza 1.50 .45
☐ 227 Brad Penny .40 .12
☐ 228 Kip Wells .40 .12
☐ 229 Adam Everett .40 .12
☐ 230 Eddie Yarnall .40 .12
☐ 231 Matt LeCroy .40 .12
☐ 232 Jason Tyner .40 .12
☐ 233 Rick Ankiel .40 .12
☐ 234 Lance Berkman .40 .12
☐ 235 Rafael Furcal .40 .12
☐ 236 Dee Brown .40 .12
☐ 237 Gookie Dawkins .40 .12
☐ 238 Eric Valent .40 .12
☐ 239 Peter Bergeron .40 .12
☐ 240 Alfonso Soriano 1.50 .45
☐ 241 Adam Dunn 1.00 .30
☐ 242 Jorge Toca .40 .12
☐ 243 Ryan Anderson .40 .12
☐ 244 Jason Dellaero .40 .12
☐ 245 Jason Grilli .40 .12
☐ 246 Milton Bradley .40 .12
☐ 247 Scott Downs RC 5.00 1.50
☐ 248 Keith Reed RC 5.00 1.50
☐ 249 Edgar Cruz RC 5.00 1.50
☐ 250 Wes Anderson RC 5.00 1.50
☐ 251 Lyle Overbay RC 6.00 1.80
☐ 252 Mike Lamb RC 5.00 1.50
☐ 253 Vince Faison RC 5.00 1.50
☐ 254 Chad Alexander 5.00 1.50
☐ 255 Chris Wakeland RC 5.00 1.50
☐ 256 Aaron McNeal RC 5.00 1.50
☐ 257 Tomo Ohka RC 5.00 1.50
☐ 258 Ty Howington RC 5.00 1.50
☐ 259 Javier Colina RC 5.00 1.50
☐ 260 Jason Jennings 5.00 1.50
☐ 261 Ramon Santiago RC 5.00 1.50
☐ 262 Johan Santana RC 15.00 4.50
☐ 263 Quincy Foster RC 5.00 1.50
☐ 264 Junior Brignac RC 5.00 1.50
☐ 265 Rico Washington RC 5.00 1.50
☐ 266 Scott Sobkowiak RC 5.00 1.50
☐ 267 Pedro Martinez 2.50 .75
Rick Ankiel
☐ 268 Manny Ramirez 2.50 .75
Vladimir Guerrero
☐ 269 A.J.Burnett 1.00 .30
Mark Mulder
☐ 270 Mike Piazza 4.00 1.20
Eric Munson
☐ 271 Josh Hamilton 1.00 .30
Corey Patterson
☐ 272 Ken Griffey Jr. 3.00 .90
Sammy Sosa
☐ 273 Derek Jeter 6.00 1.80
Alfonso Soriano
☐ 274 Mark McGwire 6.00 1.80

Pat Burrell
❑ 275 Chipper Jones 6.00 1.80
Cal Ripken
❑ 276 Nomar Garciaparra 6.00 1.80
Alex Rodriguez
❑ 277 Pedro Martinez GEM 5.00 1.50
❑ 278 Tony Gwynn GEM 6.00 1.80
❑ 279 Barry Bonds GEM 12.00 3.60
❑ 280 Juan Gonzalez GEM 5.00 1.50
❑ 281 Larry Walker GEM 3.00 .90
❑ 282 N.Garciaparra GEM 10.00 3.00
❑ 283 Ken Griffey Jr. GEM 8.00 2.40
❑ 284 Manny Ramirez GEM 2.00 .60
❑ 285 Shawn Green GEM 2.00 .60
❑ 286 Sammy Sosa GEM 8.00 2.40
❑ NNO Graded Gems Ser.1 EXCH/10 -
❑ NNO Graded Gems Ser.2 EXCH/10 -

2001 Finest

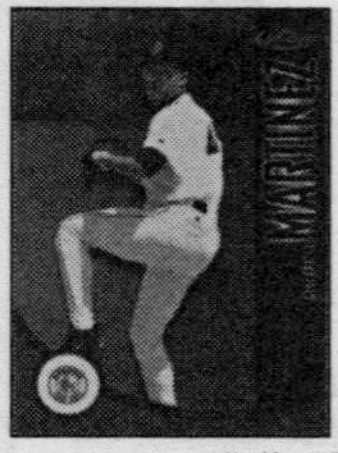

	Nm-Mt	Ex-Mt
COMP.SET w/o SP's	25.00	7.50
COMMON CARD (1-110)	.40	.12
COMMON SP	10.00	3.00
COMMON (111-140)	10.00	3.00

❑ 1 Mike Piazza SP 20.00 6.00
❑ 2 Andruw Jones .60 .18
❑ 3 Jason Giambi 1.00 .30
❑ 4 Fred McGriff .60 .18
❑ 5 Vladimir Guerrero SP 1.00 .30
❑ 6 Adrian Gonzalez .40 .12
❑ 7 Pedro Martinez 1.00 .30
❑ 8 Mike Lieberthal .40 .12
❑ 9 Warren Morris .40 .12
❑ 10 Juan Gonzalez 1.00 .30
❑ 11 Jose Canseco 1.00 .30
❑ 12 Jose Valentin .40 .12
❑ 13 Jeff Cirillo .40 .12
❑ 14 Pokey Reese .40 .12
❑ 15 Scott Rolen .60 .18
❑ 16 Greg Maddux 2.00 .60
❑ 17 Carlos Delgado .40 .12
❑ 18 Rick Ankiel .40 .12
❑ 19 Steve Finley .40 .12
❑ 20 Shawn Green .40 .12
❑ 21 Orlando Cabrera .40 .12
❑ 22 Roberto Alomar 1.00 .30
❑ 23 John Olerud .40 .12
❑ 24 Albert Belle .40 .12
❑ 25 Edgardo Alfonzo .40 .12
❑ 26 Rafael Palmeiro .60 .18
❑ 27 Mike Sweeney .40 .12
❑ 28 Bernie Williams .60 .18
❑ 29 Larry Walker .60 .18
❑ 30 Barry Bonds SP 25.00 7.50
❑ 31 Orlando Hernandez .40 .12
❑ 32 Randy Johnson 1.00 .30
❑ 33 Shannon Stewart .40 .12
❑ 34 Mark Grace 1.00 .30
❑ 35 Alex Rodriguez SP 25.00 7.50
❑ 36 Tino Martinez .60 .18
❑ 37 Carlos Febles .40 .12
❑ 38 Al Leiter .40 .12
❑ 39 Omar Vizquel .40 .12
❑ 40 Chuck Knoblauch .40 .12
❑ 41 Tim Salmon .60 .18
❑ 42 Brian Jordan .40 .12
❑ 43 Edgar Renteria .40 .12
❑ 44 Preston Wilson .40 .12
❑ 45 Mariano Rivera .60 .18
❑ 46 Gabe Kapler .40 .12
❑ 47 Jason Kendall .40 .12
❑ 48 Rickey Henderson 1.25 .35
❑ 49 Luis Gonzalez .40 .12
❑ 50 Tom Glavine 1.00 .30
❑ 51 Jeromy Burnitz .40 .12
❑ 52 Garret Anderson .40 .12
❑ 53 Craig Biggio .60 .18
❑ 54 Vinny Castilla .40 .12
❑ 55 Jeff Kent .40 .12
❑ 56 Gary Sheffield .40 .12
❑ 57 Jorge Posada .60 .18
❑ 58 Sean Casey .40 .12
❑ 59 Johnny Damon .40 .12
❑ 60 Dean Palmer .40 .12
❑ 61 Todd Helton .60 .18
❑ 62 Barry Larkin 1.00 .30
❑ 63 Robin Ventura .40 .12
❑ 64 Kenny Lofton .40 .12
❑ 65 Sammy Sosa SP 15.00 4.50
❑ 66 Rafael Furcal .40 .12
❑ 67 Jay Bell .40 .12
❑ 68 J.T. Snow .40 .12
❑ 69 Jose Vidro .40 .12
❑ 70 Ivan Rodriguez 1.00 .30
❑ 71 Jermaine Dye .40 .12
❑ 72 Chipper Jones SP 10.00 3.00
❑ 73 Fernando Vina .40 .12
❑ 74 Ben Grieve .40 .12
❑ 75 Mark McGwire SP 25.00 7.50
❑ 76 Matt Williams .40 .12
❑ 77 Mark Grudzielanek .40 .12
❑ 78 Mike Hampton .40 .12
❑ 79 Brian Giles .40 .12
❑ 80 Tony Gwynn 1.25 .35
❑ 81 Carlos Beltran .40 .12
❑ 82 Ray Durham .40 .12
❑ 83 Brad Radke .40 .12
❑ 84 David Justice .40 .12
❑ 85 Frank Thomas 1.00 .30
❑ 86 Todd Zeile .40 .12
❑ 87 Pat Burrell .40 .12
❑ 88 Jim Thome 1.00 .30
❑ 89 Greg Vaughn .40 .12
❑ 90 Ken Griffey Jr. SP 15.00 4.50
❑ 91 Mike Mussina 1.00 .30
❑ 92 Magglio Ordonez .40 .12
❑ 93 Bob Abreu .40 .12
❑ 94 Alex Gonzalez .40 .12
❑ 95 Kevin Brown .40 .12
❑ 96 Jay Buhner .40 .12
❑ 97 Roger Clemens 2.00 .60
❑ 98 Nomar Garciaparra SP 25.00 7.50
❑ 99 Derrek Lee .40 .12
❑ 100 Derek Jeter SP 25.00 7.50
❑ 101 Adrian Beltre .40 .12
❑ 102 Geoff Jenkins .40 .12
❑ 103 Javy Lopez .40 .12
❑ 104 Raul Mondesi .40 .12
❑ 105 Troy Glaus .60 .18
❑ 106 Jeff Bagwell .60 .18
❑ 107 Eric Karros .40 .12
❑ 108 Mo Vaughn .40 .12
❑ 109 Cal Ripken 3.00 .90
❑ 110 Manny Ramirez .40 .12
❑ 111 Scott Heard PROS 10.00 3.00
❑ 112 L. Montanez PROS RC 10.00 3.00
❑ 113 Ben Diggins PROS 10.00 3.00
❑ 114 Shaun Boyd PROS RC 10.00 3.00
❑ 115 Sean Burnett PROS 10.00 3.00
❑ 116 Carmen Cali PROS RC 10.00 3.00
❑ 117 D.Thompson PROS 10.00 3.00
❑ 118 D.Parrish PROS RC 10.00 3.00
❑ 119 D.Rich PROS RC 10.00 3.00
❑ 120 Chad Petty PROS RC 10.00 3.00
❑ 121 S.Smyth PROS RC 10.00 3.00
❑ 122 John Lackey PROS 10.00 3.00
❑ 123 M.Galante PROS RC 10.00 3.00
❑ 124 D.Borrell PROS RC 10.00 3.00
❑ 125 Bob Keppel PROS RC 10.00 3.00
❑ 126 J.Wayne PROS RC 15.00 4.50
❑ 127 J.R. House PROS 10.00 3.00
❑ 128 Brian Sellier PROS RC 10.00 3.00
❑ 129 Dan Moylan PROS RC 10.00 3.00
❑ 130 Scott Pratt PROS RC 10.00 3.00
❑ 131 Victor Hall PROS RC 10.00 3.00
❑ 132 Joel Pineiro PROS 20.00 6.00
❑ 133 J.Axelson PROS RC 10.00 3.00
❑ 134 Jose Reyes PROS RC 80.00 24.00
❑ 135 G. Runser PROS RC 10.00 3.00
❑ 136 B. Hebson PROS RC 10.00 3.00
❑ 137 S.Serrano PROS RC 10.00 3.00
❑ 138 K. Joseph PROS RC 10.00 3.00
❑ 139 J. Richardson PROS RC 10.00 3.00
❑ 140 M. Fischer PROS RC 10.00 3.00

2002 Finest

	Nm-Mt	Ex-Mt
COMP.SET w/o SP's (100)	25.00	7.50
COMMON CARD (1-100)	.50	.15
COMMON CARD (101-110)	10.00	3.00

❑ 1 Mike Mussina 1.25 .35
❑ 2 Steve Sparks .50 .15
❑ 3 Randy Johnson 1.25 .35
❑ 4 Orlando Cabrera .50 .15
❑ 5 Jeff Kent .50 .15
❑ 6 Carlos Delgado .50 .15
❑ 7 Ivan Rodriguez 1.25 .35
❑ 8 Jose Cruz .50 .15
❑ 9 Jason Giambi 1.25 .35
❑ 10 Brad Penny .50 .15
❑ 11 Moises Alou .50 .15
❑ 12 Mike Piazza 2.00 .60
❑ 13 Ben Grieve .50 .15
❑ 14 Derek Jeter 3.00 .90
❑ 15 Roy Oswalt .50 .15
❑ 16 Pat Burrell .50 .15
❑ 17 Preston Wilson .50 .15
❑ 18 Kevin Brown .50 .15
❑ 19 Barry Bonds 3.00 .90
❑ 20 Phil Nevin .50 .15
❑ 21 Aramis Ramirez .50 .15
❑ 22 Carlos Beltran .50 .15
❑ 23 Chipper Jones 1.25 .35
❑ 24 Curt Schilling .75 .23
❑ 25 Jorge Posada .75 .23
❑ 26 Alfonso Soriano 1.25 .35
❑ 27 Cliff Floyd .50 .15
❑ 28 Rafael Palmeiro .75 .23
❑ 29 Terrence Long .50 .15
❑ 30 Ken Griffey Jr. 2.00 .60
❑ 31 Jason Kendall .50 .15
❑ 32 Jose Vidro .50 .15
❑ 33 Jermaine Dye .50 .15
❑ 34 Bobby Higginson .50 .15
❑ 35 Albert Pujols 2.50 .75
❑ 36 Miguel Tejada .50 .15
❑ 37 Jim Edmonds .50 .15
❑ 38 Barry Zito 1.25 .35
❑ 39 Jimmy Rollins .50 .15
❑ 40 Rafael Furcal .50 .15
❑ 41 Omar Vizquel .50 .15
❑ 42 Kazuhiro Sasaki .50 .15
❑ 43 Brian Giles .50 .15
❑ 44 Darin Erstad .50 .15
❑ 45 Mariano Rivera .75 .23
❑ 46 Troy Percival .50 .15
❑ 47 Mike Sweeney .50 .15
❑ 48 Vladimir Guerrero 1.25 .35

❑ 49 Troy Glaus	.75	.23
❑ 50 So Taguchi RC	3.00	.90
❑ 51 Edgardo Alfonzo	.50	.15
❑ 52 Roger Clemens	2.50	.75
❑ 53 Eric Chavez	.50	.15
❑ 54 Alex Rodriguez	2.50	.75
❑ 55 Cristian Guzman	.50	.15
❑ 56 Jeff Bagwell	.75	.23
❑ 57 Bernie Williams	.75	.23
❑ 58 Kerry Wood	1.25	.35
❑ 59 Ryan Klesko	.50	.15
❑ 60 Ichiro Suzuki	2.50	.75
❑ 61 Larry Walker	.75	.23
❑ 62 Nomar Garciaparra	2.50	.75
❑ 63 Craig Biggio	.75	.23
❑ 64 J.D. Drew	.50	.15
❑ 65 Juan Pierre	.50	.15
❑ 66 Roberto Alomar	1.25	.35
❑ 67 Luis Gonzalez	.50	.15
❑ 68 Bud Smith	.50	.15
❑ 69 Magglio Ordonez	.50	.15
❑ 70 Scott Rolen	.75	.23
❑ 71 Tsuyoshi Shinjo	.50	.15
❑ 72 Paul Konerko	.50	.15
❑ 73 Garret Anderson	.50	.15
❑ 74 Tim Hudson	.50	.15
❑ 75 Adam Dunn	.75	.23
❑ 76 Gary Sheffield	.50	.15
❑ 77 Johnny Damon	.50	.15
❑ 78 Todd Helton	.75	.23
❑ 79 Geoff Jenkins	.50	.15
❑ 80 Shawn Green	.50	.15
❑ 81 C.C. Sabathia	.50	.15
❑ 82 Kazuhisa Ishii RC UER 2001 ERA is incorrect	4.00	1.20
❑ 83 Rich Aurilia	.50	.15
❑ 84 Mike Hampton	.50	.15
❑ 85 Ben Sheets	.50	.15
❑ 86 Andruw Jones	.75	.23
❑ 87 Richie Sexson	.50	.15
❑ 88 Jim Thome	1.25	.35
❑ 89 Sammy Sosa	2.00	.60
❑ 90 Greg Maddux	2.50	.75
❑ 91 Pedro Martinez	1.25	.35
❑ 92 Jeromy Burnitz	.50	.15
❑ 93 Raul Mondesi	.50	.15
❑ 94 Bret Boone	.50	.15
❑ 95 Jerry Hairston	.50	.15
❑ 96 Mike Rivera	.50	.15
❑ 97 Juan Cruz	.50	.15
❑ 98 Morgan Ensberg	.50	.15
❑ 99 Nathan Haynes	.50	.15
❑ 100 Xavier Nady	.50	.15
❑ 101 Nic Jackson FY AU RC	15.00	4.50
❑ 102 Mauricio Lara FY AU RC	10.00	3.00
❑ 103 Freddy Sanchez FY AU RC	15.00	4.50
❑ 104 Clint Nageotte FY AU RC	15.00	4.50
❑ 105 Beltran Perez FY AU RC	15.00	4.50
❑ 106 Garrett Gentry FY AU RC	15.00	4.50
❑ 107 Chad Qualls FY AU RC	10.00	3.00
❑ 108 Jason Bay FY AU RC	25.00	7.50
❑ 109 Michael Hill FY AU RC	10.00	3.00
❑ 110 Brian Tallet FY AU RC	15.00	4.50

2003 Finest

	Nm-Mt	Ex-Mt
COMP.SET w/o SP's (100)	25.00	7.50
COMMON CARD (1-100)	.50	.15
SEMISTARS 1-100	.75	.23
COMMON CARD (101-110)	15.00	4.50

❑ 1 Sammy Sosa	2.00	.60
❑ 2 Paul Konerko	.50	.15
❑ 3 Todd Helton	.75	.23
❑ 4 Mike Lowell	.50	.15
❑ 5 Lance Berkman	.50	.15
❑ 6 Kazuhisa Ishii	.50	.15
❑ 7 A.J. Pierzynski	.50	.15
❑ 8 Jose Vidro	.50	.15
❑ 9 Roberto Alomar	1.25	.35
❑ 10 Derek Jeter	3.00	.90
❑ 11 Barry Zito	1.25	.35
❑ 12 Jimmy Rollins	.50	.15
❑ 13 Brian Giles	.50	.15
❑ 14 Ryan Klesko	.50	.15
❑ 15 Rich Aurilia	.50	.15
❑ 16 Jim Edmonds	.50	.15
❑ 17 Aubrey Huff	.50	.15
❑ 18 Ivan Rodriguez	1.25	.35
❑ 19 Eric Hinske	.50	.15
❑ 20 Barry Bonds	3.00	.90
❑ 21 Darin Erstad	.50	.15
❑ 22 Curt Schilling	.75	.23
❑ 23 Andruw Jones	.75	.23
❑ 24 Jay Gibbons	.50	.15
❑ 25 Nomar Garciaparra	2.50	.75
❑ 26 Kerry Wood	1.25	.35
❑ 27 Magglio Ordonez	.50	.15
❑ 28 Austin Kearns	.75	.23
❑ 29 Jason Jennings	.50	.15
❑ 30 Jason Giambi	1.25	.35
❑ 31 Tim Hudson	.50	.15
❑ 32 Edgar Martinez	.75	.23
❑ 33 Carl Crawford	.50	.15
❑ 34 Hee Seop Choi	.50	.15
❑ 35 Vladimir Guerrero	1.25	.35
❑ 36 Jeff Kent	.50	.15
❑ 37 John Smoltz	.75	.23
❑ 38 Frank Thomas	1.25	.35
❑ 39 Cliff Floyd	.50	.15
❑ 40 Mike Piazza	2.00	.60
❑ 41 Mark Prior	2.50	.75
❑ 42 Tim Salmon	.75	.23
❑ 43 Shawn Green	.50	.15
❑ 44 Bernie Williams	.75	.23
❑ 45 Jim Thome	1.25	.35
❑ 46 John Olerud	.50	.15
❑ 47 Orlando Hudson	.50	.15
❑ 48 Mark Teixeira	.75	.23
❑ 49 Gary Sheffield	.50	.15
❑ 50 Ichiro Suzuki	2.50	.75
❑ 51 Tom Glavine	1.25	.35
❑ 52 Torii Hunter	.50	.15
❑ 53 Craig Biggio	.75	.23
❑ 54 Carlos Beltran	.50	.15
❑ 55 Bartolo Colon	.50	.15
❑ 56 Jorge Posada	.75	.23
❑ 57 Pat Burrell	.50	.15
❑ 58 Edgar Renteria	.50	.15
❑ 59 Rafael Palmeiro	.75	.23
❑ 60 Alfonso Soriano	1.25	.35
❑ 61 Brandon Phillips	.50	.15
❑ 62 Luis Gonzalez	.50	.15
❑ 63 Manny Ramirez	.50	.15
❑ 64 Garret Anderson	.50	.15
❑ 65 Ken Griffey Jr.	2.00	.60
❑ 66 A.J. Burnett	.50	.15
❑ 67 Mike Sweeney	.50	.15
❑ 68 Doug Mientkiewicz	.50	.15
❑ 69 Eric Chavez	.50	.15
❑ 70 Adam Dunn	.75	.23
❑ 71 Shea Hillenbrand	.50	.15
❑ 72 Troy Glaus	.75	.23
❑ 73 Rodrigo Lopez	.50	.15
❑ 74 Moises Alou	.50	.15
❑ 75 Chipper Jones	1.25	.35
❑ 76 Bobby Abreu	.50	.15
❑ 77 Mark Mulder	.50	.15
❑ 78 Kevin Brown	.50	.15
❑ 79 Josh Beckett	.75	.23
❑ 80 Larry Walker	.75	.23
❑ 81 Randy Johnson	1.25	.35
❑ 82 Greg Maddux	2.50	.75
❑ 83 Johnny Damon	.50	.15
❑ 84 Omar Vizquel	.50	.15
❑ 85 Jeff Bagwell	.75	.23
❑ 86 Carlos Pena	.50	.15
❑ 87 Roy Oswalt	.50	.15
❑ 88 Richie Sexson	.50	.15
❑ 89 Roger Clemens	2.50	.75
❑ 90 Miguel Tejada	.50	.15
❑ 91 Vicente Padilla	.50	.15
❑ 92 Phil Nevin	.50	.15
❑ 93 Edgardo Alfonzo	.50	.15
❑ 94 Bret Boone	.50	.15
❑ 95 Albert Pujols	2.50	.75
❑ 96 Carlos Delgado	.50	.15
❑ 97 Jose Contreras RC	2.50	.75
❑ 98 Scott Rolen	.75	.23
❑ 99 Pedro Martinez	1.25	.35
❑ 100 Alex Rodriguez	2.50	.75
❑ 101 Adam LaRoche AU	15.00	4.50
❑ 102 Andy Marte AU RC	40.00	12.00
❑ 103 Daryl Clark AU RC	15.00	4.50
❑ 104 J.D. Durbin AU RC	15.00	4.50
❑ 105 Craig Brazell AU RC	15.00	4.50
❑ 106 Brian Burgamy AU RC	10.00	3.00
❑ 107 Tyler Johnson AU RC	10.00	3.00
❑ 108 Joey Gomes AU RC	15.00	4.50
❑ 109 Bryan Bullington AU RC	30.00	9.00
❑ 110 Byron Gettis AU RC	15.00	4.50

1994 Flair

	Nm-Mt	Ex-Mt
COMPLETE SET (450)	80.00	24.00
COMP. SERIES 1 (250)	20.00	6.00
COMP. SERIES 2 (200)	60.00	18.00

❑ 1 Harold Baines	.50	.15
❑ 2 Jeffrey Hammonds	.25	.07
❑ 3 Chris Hoiles	.25	.07
❑ 4 Ben McDonald	.25	.07
❑ 5 Mark McLemore	.25	.07
❑ 6 Jamie Moyer	.50	.15
❑ 7 Jim Poole	.25	.07
❑ 8 Cal Ripken Jr.	4.00	1.20
❑ 9 Chris Sabo	.25	.07
❑ 10 Scott Bankhead	.25	.07
❑ 11 Scott Cooper	.25	.07
❑ 12 Danny Darwin	.25	.07
❑ 13 Andre Dawson	.50	.15
❑ 14 Billy Hatcher	.25	.07
❑ 15 Aaron Sele	.25	.07
❑ 16 John Valentin	.25	.07
❑ 17 Dave Valle	.25	.07
❑ 18 Mo Vaughn	.50	.15
❑ 19 Brian Anderson RC	.50	.15
❑ 20 Gary DiSarcina	.25	.07
❑ 21 Jim Edmonds	.75	.23
❑ 22 Chuck Finley	.50	.15
❑ 23 Bo Jackson	1.25	.35
❑ 24 Mark Leiter	.25	.07
❑ 25 Greg Myers	.25	.07
❑ 26 Eduardo Perez	.25	.07
❑ 27 Tim Salmon	.75	.23
❑ 28 Wilson Alvarez	.25	.07
❑ 29 Jason Bere	.25	.07
❑ 30 Alex Fernandez	.25	.07
❑ 31 Ozzie Guillen	.25	.07
❑ 32 Joe Hall RC	.25	.07

❑ 33 Darrin Jackson .25 .07
❑ 34 Kirk McCaskill .25 .07
❑ 35 Tim Raines .50 .15
❑ 36 Frank Thomas 1.25 .35
❑ 37 Carlos Baerga .25 .07
❑ 38 Albert Belle .50 .15
❑ 39 Mark Clark .25 .07
❑ 40 Wayne Kirby .25 .07
❑ 41 Dennis Martinez .50 .15
❑ 42 Charles Nagy .25 .07
❑ 43 Manny Ramirez .75 .23
❑ 44 Paul Sorrento .25 .07
❑ 45 Jim Thome 1.25 .35
❑ 46 Eric Davis .50 .15
❑ 47 John Doherty .25 .07
❑ 48 Junior Felix .25 .07
❑ 49 Cecil Fielder .50 .15
❑ 50 Kirk Gibson .50 .15
❑ 51 Mike Moore .25 .07
❑ 52 Tony Phillips .25 .07
❑ 53 Alan Trammell .75 .23
❑ 54 Kevin Appier .50 .15
❑ 55 Stan Belinda .25 .07
❑ 56 Vince Coleman .25 .07
❑ 57 Greg Gagne .25 .07
❑ 58 Bob Hamelin .25 .07
❑ 59 Dave Henderson .25 .07
❑ 60 Wally Joyner .50 .15
❑ 61 Mike Macfarlane .25 .07
❑ 62 Jeff Montgomery .25 .07
❑ 63 Ricky Bones .25 .07
❑ 64 Jeff Bronkey .25 .07
❑ 65 Alex Diaz RC .25 .07
❑ 66 Cal Eldred .25 .07
❑ 67 Darryl Hamilton .25 .07
❑ 68 John Jaha .25 .07
❑ 69 Mark Kiefer .25 .07
❑ 70 Kevin Seitzer .25 .07
❑ 71 Turner Ward .25 .07
❑ 72 Rich Becker .25 .07
❑ 73 Scott Erickson .25 .07
❑ 74 Keith Garagozzo RC .25 .07
❑ 75 Kent Hrbek .50 .15
❑ 76 Scott Leius .25 .07
❑ 77 Kirby Puckett 1.25 .35
❑ 78 Matt Walbeck .25 .07
❑ 79 Dave Winfield .75 .23
❑ 80 Mike Gallego .25 .07
❑ 81 Xavier Hernandez .25 .07
❑ 82 Jimmy Key .50 .15
❑ 83 Jim Leyritz .25 .07
❑ 84 Don Mattingly 3.00 .90
❑ 85 Matt Nokes .25 .07
❑ 86 Paul O'Neill .75 .23
❑ 87 Melido Perez .25 .07
❑ 88 Danny Tartabull .25 .07
❑ 89 Mike Bordick .25 .07
❑ 90 Ron Darling .25 .07
❑ 91 Dennis Eckersley .50 .15
❑ 92 Stan Javier .25 .07
❑ 93 Steve Karsay .25 .07
❑ 94 Mark McGwire 3.00 .90
❑ 95 Troy Neel .25 .07
❑ 96 Terry Steinbach .25 .07
❑ 97 Bill Taylor RC .50 .15
❑ 98 Eric Anthony .25 .07
❑ 99 Chris Bosio .25 .07
❑ 100 Tim Davis .25 .07
❑ 101 Felix Fermin .25 .07
❑ 102 Dave Fleming .25 .07
❑ 103 Ken Griffey Jr. 2.00 .60
❑ 104 Greg Hibbard .25 .07
❑ 105 Reggie Jefferson .25 .07
❑ 106 Tino Martinez .75 .23
❑ 107 Jack Armstrong .25 .07
❑ 108 Will Clark 1.25 .35
❑ 109 Juan Gonzalez 1.25 .35
❑ 110 Rick Helling .25 .07
❑ 111 Tom Henke .25 .07
❑ 112 David Hulse .25 .07
❑ 113 Manuel Lee .25 .07
❑ 114 Doug Strange .25 .07
❑ 115 Roberto Alomar 1.25 .35
❑ 116 Joe Carter .50 .15
❑ 117 Carlos Delgado .75 .23
❑ 118 Pat Hentgen .25 .07
❑ 119 Paul Molitor .75 .23
❑ 120 John Olerud .50 .15
❑ 121 Dave Stewart .50 .15
❑ 122 Todd Stottlemyre .25 .07
❑ 123 Mike Timlin .25 .07
❑ 124 Jeff Blauser .25 .07
❑ 125 Tom Glavine 1.25 .35
❑ 126 David Justice .50 .15
❑ 127 Mike Kelly .25 .07
❑ 128 Ryan Klesko .50 .15
❑ 129 Javier Lopez .50 .15
❑ 130 Greg Maddux 2.50 .75
❑ 131 Fred McGriff .75 .23
❑ 132 Kent Mercker .25 .07
❑ 133 Mark Wohlers .25 .07
❑ 134 Willie Banks .25 .07
❑ 135 Steve Buechele .25 .07
❑ 136 Shawon Dunston .25 .07
❑ 137 Jose Guzman .25 .07
❑ 138 Glenallen Hill .25 .07
❑ 139 Randy Myers .25 .07
❑ 140 Karl Rhodes .25 .07
❑ 141 Ryne Sandberg 2.00 .60
❑ 142 Steve Trachsel .25 .07
❑ 143 Bret Boone .50 .15
❑ 144 Tom Browning .25 .07
❑ 145 Hector Carrasco .25 .07
❑ 146 Barry Larkin 1.25 .35
❑ 147 Hal Morris .25 .07
❑ 148 Jose Rijo .25 .07
❑ 149 Reggie Sanders .50 .15
❑ 150 John Smiley .25 .07
❑ 151 Dante Bichette .50 .15
❑ 152 Ellis Burks .50 .15
❑ 153 Joe Girardi .25 .07
❑ 154 Mike Harkey .25 .07
❑ 155 Roberto Mejia .25 .07
❑ 156 Marcus Moore .25 .07
❑ 157 Armando Reynoso .25 .07
❑ 158 Bruce Ruffin .25 .07
❑ 159 Eric Young .25 .07
❑ 160 Kurt Abbott RC .50 .15
❑ 161 Jeff Conine .50 .15
❑ 162 Orestes Destrade .25 .07
❑ 163 Chris Hammond .25 .07
❑ 164 Bryan Harvey .25 .07
❑ 165 Dave Magadan .25 .07
❑ 166 Gary Sheffield .50 .15
❑ 167 David Weathers .25 .07
❑ 168 Andujar Cedeno .25 .07
❑ 169 Tom Edens .25 .07
❑ 170 Luis Gonzalez .50 .15
❑ 171 Pete Harnisch .25 .07
❑ 172 Todd Jones .25 .07
❑ 173 Darryl Kile .50 .15
❑ 174 James Mouton .25 .07
❑ 175 Scott Servais .25 .07
❑ 176 Mitch Williams .25 .07
❑ 177 Pedro Astacio .25 .07
❑ 178 Orel Hershiser .50 .15
❑ 179 Raul Mondesi .50 .15
❑ 180 Jose Offerman .25 .07
❑ 181 Chan Ho Park RC 1.50 .45
❑ 182 Mike Piazza 2.50 .75
❑ 183 Cory Snyder .25 .07
❑ 184 Tim Wallach .25 .07
❑ 185 Todd Worrell .25 .07
❑ 186 Sean Berry .25 .07
❑ 187 Wil Cordero .25 .07
❑ 188 Darrin Fletcher .25 .07
❑ 189 Cliff Floyd .50 .15
❑ 190 Marquis Grissom .25 .07
❑ 191 Rod Henderson .25 .07
❑ 192 Ken Hill .25 .07
❑ 193 Pedro Martinez 1.25 .35
❑ 194 Kirk Rueter .50 .15
❑ 195 Jeromy Burnitz .50 .15
❑ 196 John Franco .50 .15
❑ 197 Dwight Gooden .75 .23
❑ 198 Todd Hundley .25 .07
❑ 199 Bobby Jones .25 .07
❑ 200 Jeff Kent .50 .15
❑ 201 Mike Maddux .25 .07
❑ 202 Ryan Thompson .25 .07
❑ 203 Jose Vizcaino .25 .07
❑ 204 Darren Daulton .50 .15
❑ 205 Lenny Dykstra .50 .15
❑ 206 Jim Eisenreich .25 .07
❑ 207 Dave Hollins .25 .07
❑ 208 Danny Jackson .25 .07
❑ 209 Doug Jones .25 .07
❑ 210 Jeff Juden .25 .07
❑ 211 Ben Rivera .25 .07
❑ 212 Kevin Stocker .25 .07
❑ 213 Milt Thompson .25 .07
❑ 214 Jay Bell .50 .15
❑ 215 Steve Cooke .25 .07
❑ 216 Mark Dewey .25 .07
❑ 217 Al Martin .25 .07
❑ 218 Orlando Merced .25 .07
❑ 219 Don Slaught .25 .07
❑ 220 Zane Smith .25 .07
❑ 221 Rick White RC .25 .07
❑ 222 Kevin Young .25 .07
❑ 223 Rene Arocha .25 .07
❑ 224 Rheal Cormier .25 .07
❑ 225 Brian Jordan .50 .15
❑ 226 Ray Lankford .25 .07
❑ 227 Mike Perez .25 .07
❑ 228 Ozzie Smith 1.25 .35
❑ 229 Mark Whiten .25 .07
❑ 230 Todd Zeile .25 .07
❑ 231 Derek Bell .25 .07
❑ 232 Archi Cianfrocco .25 .07
❑ 233 Ricky Gutierrez .25 .07
❑ 234 Trevor Hoffman .50 .15
❑ 235 Phil Plantier .25 .07
❑ 236 Dave Staton .25 .07
❑ 237 Wally Whitehurst .25 .07
❑ 238 Todd Benzinger .25 .07
❑ 239 Barry Bonds 3.00 .90
❑ 240 John Burkett .25 .07
❑ 241 Royce Clayton .25 .07
❑ 242 Bryan Hickerson .25 .07
❑ 243 Mike Jackson .25 .07
❑ 244 Darren Lewis .25 .07
❑ 245 Kirt Manwaring .25 .07
❑ 246 Mark Portugal .25 .07
❑ 247 Salomon Torres .25 .07
❑ 248 Checklist .25 .07
❑ 249 Checklist .25 .07
❑ 250 Checklist .25 .07
❑ 251 Brady Anderson .50 .15
❑ 252 Mike Devereaux .25 .07
❑ 253 Sid Fernandez .25 .07
❑ 254 Leo Gomez .25 .07
❑ 255 Mike Mussina 1.25 .35
❑ 256 Mike Oquist .25 .07
❑ 257 Rafael Palmeiro .75 .23
❑ 258 Lee Smith .50 .15
❑ 259 Damon Berryhill .25 .07
❑ 260 Wes Chamberlain .25 .07
❑ 261 Roger Clemens 2.50 .75
❑ 262 Gar Finnvold RC .25 .07
❑ 263 Mike Greenwell .25 .07
❑ 264 Tim Naehring .25 .07
❑ 265 Otis Nixon .25 .07
❑ 266 Ken Ryan .25 .07
❑ 267 Chad Curtis .25 .07
❑ 268 Chili Davis .50 .15
❑ 269 Damion Easley .25 .07
❑ 270 Jorge Fabregas .25 .07
❑ 271 Mark Langston .25 .07
❑ 272 Phil Leftwich RC .25 .07
❑ 273 Harold Reynolds .50 .15
❑ 274 J.T. Snow .50 .15
❑ 275 Joey Cora .25 .07
❑ 276 Julio Franco .50 .15
❑ 277 Roberto Hernandez .25 .07
❑ 278 Lance Johnson .25 .07
❑ 279 Ron Karkovice .25 .07
❑ 280 Jack McDowell .25 .07
❑ 281 Robin Ventura .50 .15
❑ 282 Sandy Alomar Jr. .25 .07
❑ 283 Kenny Lofton .50 .15
❑ 284 Jose Mesa .25 .07
❑ 285 Jack Morris .50 .15
❑ 286 Eddie Murray 1.25 .35
❑ 287 Chad Ogea .25 .07
❑ 288 Eric Plunk .25 .07
❑ 289 Paul Shuey .25 .07
❑ 290 Omar Vizquel .50 .15

❑ 291 Danny Bautista .25 .07
❑ 292 Travis Fryman .50 .15
❑ 293 Greg Gohr .25 .07
❑ 294 Chris Gomez .25 .07
❑ 295 Mickey Tettleton .25 .07
❑ 296 Lou Whitaker .50 .15
❑ 297 David Cone .50 .15
❑ 298 Gary Gaetti .50 .15
❑ 299 Tom Gordon .25 .07
❑ 300 Felix Jose .25 .07
❑ 301 Jose Lind .25 .07
❑ 302 Brian McRae .25 .07
❑ 303 Mike Fetters .25 .07
❑ 304 Brian Harper .25 .07
❑ 305 Pat Listach .25 .07
❑ 306 Matt Mieske .25 .07
❑ 307 Dave Nilsson .25 .07
❑ 308 Jody Reed .25 .07
❑ 309 Greg Vaughn .50 .15
❑ 310 Bill Wegman .25 .07
❑ 311 Rick Aguilera .25 .07
❑ 312 Alex Cole .25 .07
❑ 313 Denny Hocking .25 .07
❑ 314 Chuck Knoblauch .50 .15
❑ 315 Shane Mack .25 .07
❑ 316 Pat Meares .25 .07
❑ 317 Kevin Tapani .25 .07
❑ 318 Jim Abbott 1.25 .35
❑ 319 Wade Boggs .75 .23
❑ 320 Sterling Hitchcock .25 .07
❑ 321 Pat Kelly .25 .07
❑ 322 Terry Mulholland .25 .07
❑ 323 Luis Polonia .25 .07
❑ 324 Mike Stanley .25 .07
❑ 325 Bob Wickman .25 .07
❑ 326 Bernie Williams .75 .23
❑ 327 Mark Acre RC .25 .07
❑ 328 Geronimo Berroa .25 .07
❑ 329 Scott Brosius .50 .15
❑ 330 Brent Gates .25 .07
❑ 331 Rickey Henderson 2.00 .60
❑ 332 Carlos Reyes RC .25 .07
❑ 333 Ruben Sierra .25 .07
❑ 334 Bobby Witt .25 .07
❑ 335 Bobby Ayala .25 .07
❑ 336 Jay Buhner .50 .15
❑ 337 Randy Johnson 1.25 .35
❑ 338 Edgar Martinez .75 .23
❑ 339 Bill Risley .25 .07
❑ 340 Alex Rodriguez RC 40.00 12.00
❑ 341 Roger Salkeld .25 .07
❑ 342 Dan Wilson .25 .07
❑ 343 Kevin Brown .50 .15
❑ 344 Jose Canseco 1.25 .35
❑ 345 Dean Palmer .50 .15
❑ 346 Ivan Rodriguez 1.25 .35
❑ 347 Kenny Rogers .50 .15
❑ 348 Pat Borders .25 .07
❑ 349 Juan Guzman .25 .07
❑ 350 Ed Sprague .25 .07
❑ 351 Devon White .25 .07
❑ 352 Steve Avery .25 .07
❑ 353 Roberto Kelly .25 .07
❑ 354 Mark Lemke .25 .07
❑ 355 Greg McMichael .25 .07
❑ 356 Terry Pendleton .50 .15
❑ 357 John Smoltz .75 .23
❑ 358 Mike Stanton .25 .07
❑ 359 Tony Tarasco .25 .07
❑ 360 Mark Grace 1.25 .35
❑ 361 Derrick May .25 .07
❑ 362 Rey Sanchez .25 .07
❑ 363 Sammy Sosa 2.00 .60
❑ 364 Rick Wilkins .25 .07
❑ 365 Jeff Brantley .25 .07
❑ 366 Tony Fernandez .25 .07
❑ 367 Chuck McElroy .25 .07
❑ 368 Kevin Mitchell .25 .07
❑ 369 John Roper .25 .07
❑ 370 Johnny Ruffin .25 .07
❑ 371 Deion Sanders .50 .15
❑ 372 Marvin Freeman .25 .07
❑ 373 Andres Galarraga .50 .15
❑ 374 Charlie Hayes .25 .07
❑ 375 Nelson Liriano .25 .07
❑ 376 David Nied .25 .07
❑ 377 Walt Weiss .25 .07
❑ 378 Bret Barberie .25 .07
❑ 379 Jerry Browne .25 .07
❑ 380 Chuck Carr .25 .07
❑ 381 Greg Colbrunn .25 .07
❑ 382 Charlie Hough .50 .15
❑ 383 Kurt Miller .25 .07
❑ 384 Benito Santiago .50 .15
❑ 385 Jeff Bagwell .75 .23
❑ 386 Craig Biggio .75 .23
❑ 387 Ken Caminiti .50 .15
❑ 388 Doug Drabek .25 .07
❑ 389 Steve Finley .50 .15
❑ 390 John Hudek RC .25 .07
❑ 391 Orlando Miller .25 .07
❑ 392 Shane Reynolds .25 .07
❑ 393 Brett Butler .50 .15
❑ 394 Tom Candiotti .25 .07
❑ 395 Delino DeShields .25 .07
❑ 396 Kevin Gross .25 .07
❑ 397 Eric Karros .50 .15
❑ 398 Ramon Martinez .25 .07
❑ 399 Henry Rodriguez .25 .07
❑ 400 Moises Alou .50 .15
❑ 401 Jeff Fassero .25 .07
❑ 402 Mike Lansing .25 .07
❑ 403 Mel Rojas .25 .07
❑ 404 Larry Walker .75 .23
❑ 405 John Wetteland .50 .15
❑ 406 Gabe White .25 .07
❑ 407 Bobby Bonilla .50 .15
❑ 408 Josias Manzanillo .25 .07
❑ 409 Bret Saberhagen .50 .15
❑ 410 David Segui .25 .07
❑ 411 Mariano Duncan .25 .07
❑ 412 Tommy Greene .25 .07
❑ 413 Billy Hatcher .25 .07
❑ 414 Ricky Jordan .25 .07
❑ 415 John Kruk .50 .15
❑ 416 Bobby Munoz .25 .07
❑ 417 Curt Schilling .75 .23
❑ 418 Fernando Valenzuela .50 .15
❑ 419 David West .25 .07
❑ 420 Carlos Garcia .25 .07
❑ 421 Brian Hunter .25 .07
❑ 422 Jeff King .25 .07
❑ 423 Jon Lieber .25 .07
❑ 424 Ravelo Manzanillo .25 .07
❑ 425 Denny Neagle .50 .15
❑ 426 Andy Van Slyke .50 .15
❑ 427 Bryan Eversgerd RC .25 .07
❑ 428 Bernard Gilkey .25 .07
❑ 429 Gregg Jefferies .25 .07
❑ 430 Tom Pagnozzi .25 .07
❑ 431 Bob Tewksbury .25 .07
❑ 432 Allen Watson .25 .07
❑ 433 Andy Ashby .25 .07
❑ 434 Andy Benes .25 .07
❑ 435 Donnie Elliott .25 .07
❑ 436 Tony Gwynn 1.50 .45
❑ 437 Joey Hamilton .25 .07
❑ 438 Tim Hyers RC .25 .07
❑ 439 Luis Lopez .25 .07
❑ 440 Bip Roberts .25 .07
❑ 441 Scott Sanders .25 .07
❑ 442 Rod Beck .25 .07
❑ 443 Dave Burba .25 .07
❑ 444 Darryl Strawberry .75 .23
❑ 445 Bill Swift .25 .07
❑ 446 Robby Thompson .25 .07
❑ 447 B.VanLandingham RC .25 .07
❑ 448 Matt Williams .50 .15
❑ 449 Checklist .25 .07
❑ 450 Checklist .25 .07
❑ P15 Aaron Sele Promo 1.00 .30

2002 Flair

	Nm-Mt	Ex-Mt
COMP.SET w/o SP's (100)	25.00	7.50
COMMON CARD (1-100)	.50	.15
COMMON CARD (101-138)	5.00	1.50

❑ 1 Scott Rolen .75 .23
❑ 2 Derek Jeter 3.00 .90
❑ 3 Sean Casey .50 .15

❑ 4 Hideo Nomo 1.25 .35
❑ 5 Craig Biggio .75 .23
❑ 6 Randy Johnson 1.25 .35
❑ 7 J.D. Drew .50 .15
❑ 8 Greg Maddux 2.50 .75
❑ 9 Paul LoDuca .50 .15
❑ 10 John Olerud .50 .15
❑ 11 Barry Larkin 1.25 .35
❑ 12 Mark Grace 1.25 .35
❑ 13 Jimmy Rollins .50 .15
❑ 14 Todd Helton .75 .23
❑ 15 Jim Edmonds .50 .15
❑ 16 Roy Oswalt .50 .15
❑ 17 Phil Nevin .50 .15
❑ 18 Tim Salmon .75 .23
❑ 19 Magglio Ordonez .50 .15
❑ 20 Roger Clemens 2.50 .75
❑ 21 Raul Mondesi .50 .15
❑ 22 Edgar Martinez .75 .23
❑ 23 Pedro Martinez 1.25 .35
❑ 24 Edgardo Alfonzo .50 .15
❑ 25 Bernie Williams .75 .23
❑ 26 Gary Sheffield .50 .15
❑ 27 D'Angelo Jimenez .50 .15
❑ 28 Toby Hall .50 .15
❑ 29 Joe Mays .50 .15
❑ 30 Alfonso Soriano 1.25 .35
❑ 31 Mike Piazza 2.00 .60
❑ 32 Lance Berkman .50 .15
❑ 33 Jim Thome 1.25 .35
❑ 34 Ben Sheets .50 .15
❑ 35 Brandon Inge .50 .15
❑ 36 Luis Gonzalez .50 .15
❑ 37 Jeff Kent .50 .15
❑ 38 Ben Grieve .50 .15
❑ 39 Carlos Delgado .50 .15
❑ 40 Pat Burrell .50 .15
❑ 41 Mark Buehrle .50 .15
❑ 42 Cristian Guzman .50 .15
❑ 43 Shawn Green .50 .15
❑ 44 Nomar Garciaparra 2.50 .75
❑ 45 Carlos Beltran .50 .15
❑ 46 Troy Glaus .75 .23
❑ 47 Paul Konerko .50 .15
❑ 48 Moises Alou .50 .15
❑ 49 Kerry Wood 1.25 .35
❑ 50 Jose Vidro .50 .15
❑ 51 Juan Encarnacion .50 .15
❑ 52 Bobby Abreu .50 .15
❑ 53 C.C. Sabathia .50 .15
❑ 54 Alex Rodriguez 2.50 .75
❑ 55 Albert Pujols 2.50 .75
❑ 56 Bret Boone .50 .15
❑ 57 Orlando Hernandez .50 .15
❑ 58 Jason Kendall .50 .15
❑ 59 Tim Hudson .50 .15
❑ 60 Darin Erstad .50 .15
❑ 61 Mike Mussina 1.25 .35
❑ 62 Ken Griffey Jr. 2.00 .60
❑ 63 Adrian Beltre .50 .15
❑ 64 Jeff Bagwell .75 .23
❑ 65 Vladimir Guerrero 1.25 .35
❑ 66 Mike Sweeney .50 .15
❑ 67 Sammy Sosa 2.00 .60
❑ 68 Andruw Jones .75 .23
❑ 69 Richie Sexson .50 .15
❑ 70 Matt Morris .50 .15
❑ 71 Ivan Rodriguez 1.25 .35

Card	Nm-Mt	Ex-Mt
❑ 72 Shannon Stewart	.50	.15
❑ 73 Barry Bonds	3.00	.90
❑ 74 Matt Williams	.50	.15
❑ 75 Jason Giambi	1.25	.35
❑ 76 Brian Giles	.50	.15
❑ 77 Cliff Floyd	.50	.15
❑ 78 Tino Martinez	.75	.23
❑ 79 Juan Gonzalez	1.25	.35
❑ 80 Frank Thomas	1.25	.35
❑ 81 Ichiro Suzuki	2.50	.75
❑ 82 Barry Zito	1.25	.35
❑ 83 Chipper Jones	1.25	.35
❑ 84 Adam Dunn	.75	.23
❑ 85 Kazuhiro Sasaki	.50	.15
❑ 86 Mark Quinn	.50	.15
❑ 87 Rafael Palmeiro	.75	.23
❑ 88 Jeromy Burnitz	.50	.15
❑ 89 Curt Schilling	.75	.23
❑ 90 Chris Richard	.50	.15
❑ 91 Jon Lieber	.50	.15
❑ 92 Doug Mientkiewicz	.50	.15
❑ 93 Roberto Alomar	1.25	.35
❑ 94 Rich Aurilia	.50	.15
❑ 95 Eric Chavez	.50	.15
❑ 96 Larry Walker	.75	.23
❑ 97 Manny Ramirez	.50	.15
❑ 98 Tony Clark	.50	.15
❑ 99 Tsuyoshi Shinjo	.50	.15
❑ 100 Josh Beckett	.75	.23
❑ 101 Dewon Brazelton FF	5.00	1.50
❑ 102 Jeremy Lambert FF RC	5.00	1.50
❑ 103 Andres Torres FF	5.00	1.50
❑ 104 Matt Childers FF RC	5.00	1.50
❑ 105 Wilson Betemit FF	5.00	1.50
❑ 106 Willie Harris FF	5.00	1.50
❑ 107 Drew Henson FF	5.00	1.50
❑ 108 Rafael Soriano FF	5.00	1.50
❑ 109 Carlos Valderrama FF	5.00	1.50
❑ 110 Victor Martinez FF	5.00	1.50
❑ 111 Juan Rivera FF	5.00	1.50
❑ 112 Felipe Lopez FF	5.00	1.50
❑ 113 Brandon Duckworth FF	5.00	1.50
❑ 114 Jeremy Owens FF	5.00	1.50
❑ 115 Aaron Cook FF RC	8.00	2.40
❑ 116 Derrick Lewis FF	5.00	1.50
❑ 117 Mark Teixeira FF	8.00	2.40
❑ 118 Ken Harvey FF	5.00	1.50
❑ 119 Tim Spooneybarger FF	5.00	1.50
❑ 120 Bill Hall FF	5.00	1.50
❑ 121 Adam Pettyjohn FF	5.00	1.50
❑ 122 Ramon Castro FF	5.00	1.50
❑ 123 Marlon Byrd FF	5.00	1.50
❑ 124 Matt White FF	5.00	1.50
❑ 125 Eric Cyr FF	5.00	1.50
❑ 126 Morgan Ensberg FF	5.00	1.50
❑ 127 Horacio Ramirez FF	5.00	1.50
❑ 128 Ron Calloway FF RC	5.00	1.50
❑ 129 Nick Punto FF	5.00	1.50
❑ 130 Joe Kennedy FF	5.00	1.50
❑ 131 So Taguchi FF RC	8.00	2.40
❑ 132 Austin Kearns FF	8.00	2.40
❑ 133 Mark Prior FF	15.00	4.50
❑ 134 Kazuhisa Ishii FF RC	10.00	3.00
❑ 135 Steve Torrealba FF	5.00	1.50
❑ 136 Adam Walker FF RC	5.00	1.50
❑ 137 Travis Hafner FF	5.00	1.50
❑ 138 Zach Day FF	5.00	1.50

2003 Flair

	Nm-Mt	Ex-Mt
COMP.LO SET w/o SP's (90)	25.00	7.50
COMMON CARD (1-	.50	.15
COMMON CARD (91-125)	8.00	2.40

Card	Nm-Mt	Ex-Mt
❑ 1 Hideo Nomo	1.25	.35
❑ 2 Derek Jeter	3.00	.90
❑ 3 Junior Spivey	.50	.15
❑ 4 Rich Aurilia	.50	.15
❑ 5 Luis Gonzalez	.50	.15
❑ 6 Sean Burroughs	.50	.15
❑ 7 Pedro Martinez	1.25	.35
❑ 8 Randy Winn	.50	.15
❑ 9 Carlos Delgado	.50	.15
❑ 10 Pat Burrell	.50	.15
❑ 11 Barry Larkin	1.25	.35
❑ 12 Roberto Alomar	1.25	.35
❑ 13 Tony Batista	.50	.15
❑ 14 Barry Bonds	3.00	.90
❑ 15 Craig Biggio	.75	.23
❑ 16 Ivan Rodriguez	1.25	.35
❑ 17 Javier Vazquez	.50	.15
❑ 18 Joe Borchard	.50	.15
❑ 19 Josh Phelps	.50	.15
❑ 20 Omar Vizquel	.50	.15
❑ 21 Tom Glavine	1.25	.35
❑ 22 Darin Erstad	.50	.15
❑ 23 Hee Seop Choi	.50	.15
❑ 24 Roger Clemens	2.50	.75
❑ 25 Michael Cuddyer	.50	.15
❑ 26 Mike Sweeney	.50	.15
❑ 27 Phil Nevin	.50	.15
❑ 28 Torii Hunter	.50	.15
❑ 29 Vladimir Guerrero	1.25	.35
❑ 30 Ellis Burks	.50	.15
❑ 31 Jimmy Rollins	.50	.15
❑ 32 Ken Griffey Jr.	2.00	.60
❑ 33 Magglio Ordonez	.50	.15
❑ 34 Mark Prior	2.50	.75
❑ 35 Mike Lieberthal	.50	.15
❑ 36 Jorge Posada	.75	.23
❑ 37 Rodrigo Lopez	.50	.15
❑ 38 Todd Helton	.75	.23
❑ 39 Adam Kennedy	.50	.15
❑ 40 Curt Schilling	.75	.23
❑ 41 Jim Thome	1.25	.35
❑ 42 Josh Beckett	.75	.23
❑ 43 Carlos Pena	.50	.15
❑ 44 Jason Kendall	.50	.15
❑ 45 Sammy Sosa	2.00	.60
❑ 46 Scott Rolen	.75	.23
❑ 47 Alex Rodriguez	2.50	.75
❑ 48 Aubrey Huff	.50	.15
❑ 49 Bobby Abreu	.50	.15
❑ 50 Jeff Kent	.50	.15
❑ 51 Joe Randa	.50	.15
❑ 52 Lance Berkman	.50	.15
❑ 53 Orlando Cabrera	.50	.15
❑ 54 Richie Sexson	.50	.15
❑ 55 Albert Pujols	2.00	.60
❑ 56 Alfonso Soriano	1.25	.35
❑ 57 Greg Maddux	2.50	.75
❑ 58 Jason Giambi	1.25	.35
❑ 59 Jeff Bagwell	.75	.23
❑ 60 Kerry Wood	1.25	.35
❑ 61 Manny Ramirez	.50	.15
❑ 62 Eric Chavez	.50	.15
❑ 63 Preston Wilson	.50	.15
❑ 64 Shawn Green	.50	.15
❑ 65 Shea Hillenbrand	.50	.15
❑ 66 Austin Kearns	.75	.23
❑ 67 Cliff Floyd	.50	.15
❑ 68 Edgardo Alfonzo	.50	.15
❑ 69 J.D. Drew	.50	.15
❑ 70 Larry Walker	.75	.23
❑ 71 Mike Piazza	2.00	.60
❑ 72 Andruw Jones	.75	.23
❑ 73 Ben Grieve	.50	.15
❑ 74 Eric Hinske	.50	.15
❑ 75 Geoff Jenkins	.50	.15
❑ 76 Kazuhiro Sasaki	.50	.15
❑ 77 Matt Morris	.50	.15
❑ 78 Miguel Tejada	.50	.15
❑ 79 Aramis Ramirez	.50	.15
❑ 80 Troy Glaus	.75	.23
❑ 81 Ichiro Suzuki	2.50	.75
❑ 82 Mark Teixeira	.75	.23
❑ 83 Nomar Garciaparra	2.50	.75
❑ 84 Chipper Jones	1.25	.35
❑ 85 Frank Thomas	1.25	.35
❑ 86 Paul Lo Duca	.50	.15
❑ 87 Bernie Williams	.75	.23
❑ 88 Adam Dunn	.75	.23
❑ 89 Randy Johnson	1.25	.35
❑ 90 Barry Zito	1.25	.35
❑ 91 Lew Ford FF RC	10.00	3.00
❑ 92 Joe Valentine FF RC	8.00	2.40
❑ 93 Jhonny Peralta FF RC	8.00	2.40
❑ 94 Hideki Matsui FF RC	25.00	7.50
❑ 95 Francisco Rosario FF RC	8.00	2.40
❑ 96 Adam LaRoche FF	8.00	2.40
❑ 97 Josh Hall FF RC	10.00	3.00
❑ 98 Chien-Ming Wang FF RC	15.00	4.50
❑ 99 Josh Willingham FF RC	15.00	4.50
❑ 100 Guillermo Quiroz FF RC	10.00	3.00
❑ 101 Termel Sledge FF RC	10.00	3.00
❑ 102 Prentice Redman FF RC	8.00	2.40
❑ 103 Matt Bruback FF RC	8.00	2.40
❑ 104 Alejandro Machado FF RC	8.00	2.40
❑ 105 Shane Victorino FF RC	8.00	2.40
❑ 106 Chris Waters FF RC	8.00	2.40
❑ 107 Jose Contreras FF RC	12.00	3.60
❑ 108 Pete LaForest FF RC	10.00	3.00
❑ 109 Nook Logan FF RC	8.00	2.40
❑ 110 Hector Luna FF RC	8.00	2.40
❑ 111 Daniel Cabrera FF RC	8.00	2.40
❑ 112 Matt Kata FF RC	10.00	3.00
❑ 113 Rontrez Johnson FF RC	8.00	2.40
❑ 114 Josh Stewart FF RC	8.00	2.40
❑ 115 Michael Hessman FF RC	8.00	2.40
❑ 116 Felix Sanchez FF RC	8.00	2.40
❑ 117 Michel Hernandez FF RC	8.00	2.40
❑ 118 Arnaldo Munoz FF RC	8.00	2.40
❑ 119 Ian Ferguson FF RC	8.00	2.40
❑ 120 Clint Barmes FF RC	10.00	3.00
❑ 121 Brian Stokes FF RC	8.00	2.40
❑ 122 Craig Brazell FF RC	10.00	3.00
❑ 123 John Webb FF	8.00	2.40
❑ 124 Tim Olson FF RC	10.00	3.00
❑ 125 Jeremy Bonderman FF RC	15.00	4.50
❑ 126 Jeff Duncan RC	-	
❑ 127 Rickie Weeks RC	-	
❑ 128 Brandon Webb RC	-	
❑ 129 Robby Hammock RC	-	
❑ 130 Jon Leicester RC	-	
❑ 131 Ryan Wagner RC	-	
❑ 132 Bo Hart RC	-	
❑ 133 Edwin Jackson RC	-	
❑ 134 Sergio Mitre RC	-	
❑ 135 Delmon Young RC	-	

2003 Flair Greats

	Nm-Mt	Ex-Mt
COMP.SET w/o SP's (95)	40.00	12.00
COMMON CARD (1-95)	1.00	.30
COMMON CARD (96-133)	5.00	1.50

Card	Nm-Mt	Ex-Mt
❑ 1 Ozzie Smith	2.50	.75
❑ 2 Red Schoendienst	1.00	.30
❑ 3 Harmon Killebrew	2.50	.75
❑ 4 Ralph Kiner	1.00	.30

❑ 5 Johnny Bench	2.50	.75
❑ 6 Al Kaline	2.50	.75
❑ 7 Bobby Doerr	1.00	.30
❑ 8 Cal Ripken	8.00	2.40
❑ 9 Enos Slaughter	1.00	.30
❑ 10 Phil Rizzuto	1.50	.45
❑ 11 Luis Aparicio	1.00	.30
❑ 12 Pee Wee Reese	1.50	.45
❑ 13 Richie Ashburn	1.50	.45
❑ 14 Ernie Banks	2.50	.75
❑ 15 Earl Weaver	1.00	.30
❑ 16 Whitey Ford	1.50	.45
❑ 17 Brooks Robinson	2.50	.75
❑ 18 Lou Boudreau	1.00	.30
❑ 19 Robin Yount	2.50	.75
❑ 20 Mike Schmidt	5.00	1.50
❑ 21 Bob Lemon	1.00	.30
❑ 22 Stan Musial	4.00	1.20
❑ 23 Joe Morgan	1.00	.30
❑ 24 Early Wynn	1.00	.30
❑ 25 Willie Stargell	1.50	.45
❑ 26 Yogi Berra	2.50	.75
❑ 27 Juan Marichal	1.00	.30
❑ 28 Rick Ferrell	1.00	.30
❑ 29 Rod Carew	1.50	.45
❑ 30 Jim Bunning	1.00	.30
❑ 31 Ferguson Jenkins	1.00	.30
❑ 32 Steve Carlton	1.50	.45
❑ 33 Larry Doby	1.00	.30
❑ 34 Nolan Ryan	8.00	2.40
❑ 35 Phil Niekro UER	1.00	.30
Career win total in blurb is wrong		
❑ 36 Billy Williams	1.00	.30
❑ 37 Hal Newhouser	1.00	.30
❑ 38 Bob Feller	1.50	.45
❑ 39 Lou Brock	1.50	.45
❑ 40 Monte Irvin	1.00	.30
❑ 41 Eddie Mathews	2.50	.75
❑ 42 Rollie Fingers	1.00	.30
❑ 43 Gaylord Perry	1.00	.30
❑ 44 Reggie Jackson	1.50	.45
❑ 45 Bob Gibson	1.50	.45
❑ 46 Robin Roberts	1.50	.45
❑ 47 Tom Seaver	2.50	.75
❑ 48 Willie McCovey	1.00	.30
❑ 49 Hoyt Wilhelm	1.00	.30
❑ 50 George Kell	1.00	.30
❑ 51 Warren Spahn	1.50	.45
❑ 52 Catfish Hunter	1.50	.45
❑ 53 Dom DiMaggio	1.00	.30
❑ 54 Joe Medwick	1.00	.30
❑ 55 Johnny Pesky	1.00	.30
❑ 56 Steve Garvey	1.00	.30
❑ 57 Harry Heilmann	1.00	.30
❑ 58 Dave Winfield	1.50	.45
❑ 59 Andre Dawson	1.00	.30
❑ 60 Jimmie Foxx	2.50	.75
❑ 61 Buddy Bell	1.00	.30
❑ 62 Gabby Hartnett	1.00	.30
❑ 63 Babe Ruth	8.00	2.40
❑ 64 Dizzy Dean	1.50	.45
❑ 65 Hank Greenberg	2.50	.75
❑ 66 Don Drysdale	2.50	.75
❑ 67 Gary Carter	1.50	.45
❑ 68 Wade Boggs	1.50	.45
❑ 69 Tony Perez	1.00	.30
❑ 70 Mickey Cochrane	1.50	.45
❑ 71 Bill Dickey	1.50	.45
❑ 72 George Brett	6.00	1.80
❑ 73 Honus Wagner	2.50	.75
❑ 74 George Sisler	1.00	.30
❑ 75 Walter Johnson	2.50	.75
❑ 76 Ron Santo	1.50	.45
❑ 77 Roy Campanella	2.50	.75
❑ 78 Roger Maris	3.00	.90
❑ 79 Kirby Puckett	2.50	.75
❑ 80 Alan Trammell	1.50	.45
❑ 81 Don Mattingly	6.00	1.80
❑ 82 Ty Cobb	3.00	.90
❑ 83 Lou Gehrig	5.00	1.50
❑ 84 Jackie Robinson	3.00	.90
❑ 85 Billy Martin	1.50	.45
❑ 86 Paul Molitor	1.50	.45
❑ 87 Duke Snider	1.50	.45
❑ 88 Thurman Munson	3.00	.90
❑ 89 Luke Appling	1.00	.30
❑ 90 Ernie Lombardi	1.00	.30
❑ 91 Rube Waddell	1.00	.30
❑ 92 Travis Jackson	1.00	.30
❑ 93 Joe Sewell	1.00	.30
❑ 94 King Kelly	1.50	.45
❑ 95 Heinie Manush	1.00	.30
❑ 96 Bobby Doerr HT	5.00	1.50
❑ 97 Johnny Pesky HT	5.00	1.50
❑ 98 Wade Boggs HT	8.00	2.40
❑ 99 Tony Conigliaro HT	8.00	2.40
❑ 100 Carlton Fisk HT	8.00	2.40
❑ 101 Rico Petrocelli HT	5.00	1.50
❑ 102 Jim Rice HT	5.00	1.50
❑ 103 Al Lopez HT	5.00	1.50
❑ 104 Pee Wee Reese HT	8.00	2.40
❑ 105 Tommy Lasorda HT	5.00	1.50
❑ 106 Gil Hodges HT	8.00	2.40
❑ 107 Jackie Robinson HT	10.00	3.00
❑ 108 Duke Snider HT	8.00	2.40
❑ 109 Don Drysdale HT	8.00	2.40
❑ 110 Steve Garvey HT	5.00	1.50
❑ 111 Hoyt Wilhelm HT	5.00	1.50
❑ 112 Juan Marichal HT	5.00	1.50
❑ 113 Monte Irvin HT	5.00	1.50
❑ 114 Willie McCovey HT	5.00	1.50
❑ 115 Travis Jackson HT	5.00	1.50
❑ 116 Bobby Bonds HT	5.00	1.50
❑ 117 Orlando Cepeda HT	5.00	1.50
❑ 118 Whitey Ford HT	8.00	2.40
❑ 119 Phil Rizzuto HT	8.00	2.40
❑ 120 Reggie Jackson HT	8.00	2.40
❑ 121 Yogi Berra HT	8.00	2.40
❑ 122 Roger Maris HT	10.00	3.00
❑ 123 Don Mattingly HT	25.00	7.50
❑ 124 Babe Ruth HT	15.00	4.50
❑ 125 Dave Winfield HT	8.00	2.40
❑ 126 Bob Gibson HT	8.00	2.40
❑ 127 Enos Slaughter HT	5.00	1.50
❑ 128 Joe Medwick HT	5.00	1.50
❑ 129 Lou Brock HT	8.00	2.40
❑ 130 Ozzie Smith HT	8.00	2.40
❑ 131 Stan Musial HT	10.00	3.00
❑ 132 Steve Carlton HT	8.00	2.40
❑ 133 Dizzy Dean HT	8.00	2.40
❑ P6 Al Kaline	2.00	.60
Promotional Sample		

1963 Fleer

	NM	Ex
COMPLETE SET (67)	2000.00	800.00
WRAPPER (5-CENT)	100.00	40.00
❑ 1 Steve Barber	25.00	7.50
❑ 2 Ron Hansen	15.00	6.00
❑ 3 Milt Pappas	20.00	8.00
❑ 4 Brooks Robinson	100.00	40.00
❑ 5 Willie Mays	200.00	80.00
❑ 6 Lou Clinton	15.00	6.00
❑ 7 Bill Monbouquette	15.00	6.00
❑ 8 Carl Yastrzemski	100.00	40.00
❑ 9 Ray Herbert	15.00	6.00
❑ 10 Jim Landis	15.00	6.00
❑ 11 Dick Donovan	15.00	6.00
❑ 12 Tito Francona	15.00	6.00
❑ 13 Jerry Kindall	15.00	6.00
❑ 14 Frank Lary	20.00	8.00
❑ 15 Dick Howser	20.00	8.00
❑ 16 Jerry Lumpe	15.00	6.00
❑ 17 Norm Siebern	15.00	6.00
❑ 18 Don Lee	15.00	6.00
❑ 19 Albie Pearson	20.00	8.00
❑ 20 Bob Rodgers	20.00	8.00
❑ 21 Leon Wagner	15.00	6.00
❑ 22 Jim Kaat	25.00	10.00
❑ 23 Vic Power	20.00	8.00
❑ 24 Rich Rollins	20.00	8.00
❑ 25 Bobby Richardson	25.00	10.00
❑ 26 Ralph Terry	20.00	8.00
❑ 27 Tom Cheney	15.00	6.00
❑ 28 Chuck Cottier	15.00	6.00
❑ 29 Jimmy Piersall	20.00	8.00
❑ 30 Dave Stenhouse	15.00	6.00
❑ 31 Glen Hobbie	15.00	6.00
❑ 32 Ron Santo	25.00	10.00
❑ 33 Gene Freese	15.00	6.00
❑ 34 Vada Pinson	25.00	10.00
❑ 35 Bob Purkey	15.00	6.00
❑ 36 Joe Amalfitano	15.00	6.00
❑ 37 Bob Aspromonte	15.00	6.00
❑ 38 Dick Farrell	15.00	6.00
❑ 39 Al Spangler	15.00	6.00
❑ 40 Tommy Davis	20.00	8.00
❑ 41 Don Drysdale	75.00	30.00
❑ 42 Sandy Koufax	200.00	80.00
❑ 43 Maury Wills RC	100.00	40.00
❑ 44 Frank Bolling	15.00	6.00
❑ 45 Warren Spahn	75.00	30.00
❑ 46 Joe Adcock SP	150.00	60.00
❑ 47 Roger Craig	20.00	8.00
❑ 48 Al Jackson	20.00	8.00
❑ 49 Rod Kanehl	20.00	8.00
❑ 50 Ruben Amaro	15.00	6.00
❑ 51 Johnny Callison	20.00	8.00
❑ 52 Clay Dalrymple	15.00	6.00
❑ 53 Don Demeter	15.00	6.00
❑ 54 Art Mahaffey	15.00	6.00
❑ 55 Smoky Burgess	20.00	8.00
❑ 56 Roberto Clemente	175.00	80.00
❑ 57 Roy Face	20.00	8.00
❑ 58 Vern Law	20.00	8.00
❑ 59 Bill Mazeroski	30.00	12.00
❑ 60 Ken Boyer	25.00	10.00
❑ 61 Bob Gibson	75.00	30.00
❑ 62 Gene Oliver	15.00	6.00
❑ 63 Bill White	20.00	8.00
❑ 64 Orlando Cepeda	30.00	12.00
❑ 65 Jim Davenport	15.00	6.00
❑ 66 Billy O'Dell	25.00	7.50
❑ NNO Checklist card	500.00	160.00

1981 Fleer

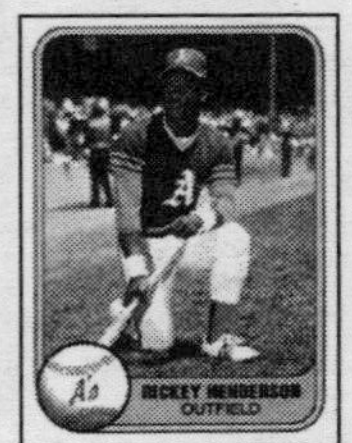

	Nm-Mt	Ex-Mt
COMPLETE SET (660)	40.00	16.00
❑ 1 Pete Rose UER	3.00	1.20
270 hits in 63 should be 170		
❑ 2 Larry Bowa	.25	.10
❑ 3 Manny Trillo	.10	.04
❑ 4 Bob Boone	.25	.10
❑ 5 Mike Schmidt	2.50	1.00
See also 640A		
❑ 6 Steve Carlton P1	.50	.20
Golden Arm		

Back 1066 Cardinals
Number on back 6
❑ 6B Steve Carlton P2 ... 1.50 .60
Pitcher of Year
Back 1066 Cardinals
❑ 6C Steve Carlton P3 ... 2.00 .80
1966 Cardinals
❑ 7 Tug McGraw ... .25 .10
See 657A
❑ 8 Larry Christenson ... .10 .04
❑ 9 Bake McBride ... .10 .04
❑ 10 Greg Luzinski ... .25 .10
❑ 11 Ron Reed ... .10 .04
❑ 12 Dickie Noles ... .10 .04
❑ 13 Keith Moreland ... .25 .10
❑ 14 Bob Walk RC ... .25 .10
❑ 15 Lonnie Smith ... .25 .10
❑ 16 Dick Ruthven ... .10 .04
❑ 17 Sparky Lyle ... .25 .10
❑ 18 Greg Gross ... .10 .04
❑ 19 Garry Maddox ... .10 .04
❑ 20 Nino Espinosa ... .10 .04
❑ 21 George Vukovich ... .10 .04
❑ 22 John Vukovich ... .10 .04
❑ 23 Ramon Aviles ... .10 .04
❑ 24A Kevin Saucier P1 ... .10 .04
Name on back Ken
❑ 24B Kevin Saucier P2 ... .10 .04
Name on back Ken
❑ 24C Kevin Saucier P3 ... 1.00 .40
Name on back Kevin
❑ 25 Randy Lerch ... .10 .04
❑ 26 Del Unser ... .10 .04
❑ 27 Tim McCarver ... .50 .20
❑ 28 George Brett ... 3.00 1.20
See also 655A
❑ 29 Willie Wilson ... .25 .10
See also 653A
❑ 30 Paul Splittorff ... .10 .04
❑ 31 Dan Quisenberry ... .25 .10
❑ 32A Amos Otis P1 ... .25 .10
(Batting Pose
Outfield
32 on back
❑ 32B Amos Otis P2 ... .25 .10
Series Starter
483 on back
❑ 33 Steve Busby ... .10 .04
❑ 34 U.L. Washington ... .10 .04
❑ 35 Dave Chalk ... .10 .04
❑ 36 Darrell Porter ... .10 .04
❑ 37 Marty Pattin ... .10 .04
❑ 38 Larry Gura ... .10 .04
❑ 39 Renie Martin ... .10 .04
❑ 40 Rich Gale ... .10 .04
❑ 41A Hal McRae P1 ... .50 .20
(Royals on front
in black letters
❑ 41B Hal McRae P2 ... .25 .10
(Royals on front
in blue letters
❑ 42 Dennis Leonard ... .10 .04
❑ 43 Willie Aikens ... .10 .04
❑ 44 Frank White ... .25 .10
❑ 45 Clint Hurdle ... .10 .04
❑ 46 John Wathan ... .10 .04
❑ 47 Pete LaCock ... .10 .04
❑ 48 Rance Mulliniks ... .10 .04
❑ 49 Jeff Twitty ... .10 .04
❑ 50 Jamie Quirk ... .10 .04
❑ 51 Art Howe ... .25 .10
❑ 52 Ken Forsch ... .10 .04
❑ 53 Vern Ruhle ... .10 .04
❑ 54 Joe Niekro ... .25 .10
❑ 55 Frank LaCorte ... .10 .04
❑ 56 J.R. Richard ... .25 .10
❑ 57 Nolan Ryan ... 5.00 2.00
❑ 58 Enos Cabell ... .10 .04
❑ 59 Cesar Cedeno ... .25 .10
❑ 60 Jose Cruz ... .25 .10
❑ 61 Bill Virdon MG ... .10 .04
❑ 62 Terry Puhl ... .10 .04
❑ 63 Joaquin Andujar ... .25 .10
❑ 64 Alan Ashby ... .10 .04
❑ 65 Joe Sambito ... .10 .04
❑ 66 Denny Walling ... .10 .04
❑ 67 Jeff Leonard ... .25 .10
❑ 68 Luis Pujols ... .10 .04
❑ 69 Bruce Bochy ... .10 .04
❑ 70 Rafael Landestoy ... .10 .04
❑ 71 Dave Smith RC ... .25 .10
❑ 72 Danny Heep ... .10 .04
❑ 73 Julio Gonzalez ... .10 .04
❑ 74 Craig Reynolds ... .10 .04
❑ 75 Gary Woods ... .10 .04
❑ 76 Dave Bergman ... .10 .04
❑ 77 Randy Niemann ... .10 .04
❑ 78 Joe Morgan ... .50 .20
❑ 79 Reggie Jackson ... .50 .20
See also 650A
❑ 80 Bucky Dent ... .25 .10
❑ 81 Tommy John ... .50 .20
❑ 82 Luis Tiant ... .25 .10
❑ 83 Rick Cerone ... .10 .04
❑ 84 Dick Howser MG ... .25 .10
❑ 85 Lou Piniella ... .25 .10
❑ 86 Ron Davis ... .10 .04
❑ 87A Graig Nettles ERR ... 5.00 2.00
Name on back spelled Craig
❑ 87B Graig Nettles COR ... .25 .10
Graig
❑ 88 Ron Guidry ... .25 .10
❑ 89 Rich Gossage ... .50 .20
❑ 90 Rudy May ... .10 .04
❑ 91 Gaylord Perry ... .25 .10
❑ 92 Eric Soderholm ... .10 .04
❑ 93 Bob Watson ... .25 .10
❑ 94 Bobby Murcer ... .25 .10
❑ 95 Bobby Brown ... .10 .04
❑ 96 Jim Spencer ... .10 .04
❑ 97 Tom Underwood ... .10 .04
❑ 98 Oscar Gamble ... .10 .04
❑ 99 Johnny Oates ... .25 .10
❑ 100 Fred Stanley ... .10 .04
❑ 101 Ruppert Jones ... .10 .04
❑ 102 Dennis Werth ... .10 .04
❑ 103 Joe Lefebvre ... .10 .04
❑ 104 Brian Doyle ... .10 .04
❑ 105 Aurelio Rodriguez ... .10 .04
❑ 106 Doug Bird ... .10 .04
❑ 107 Mike Griffin RC ... .10 .04
❑ 108 Tim Lollar ... .10 .04
❑ 109 Willie Randolph ... .25 .10
❑ 110 Steve Garvey ... .25 .10
❑ 111 Reggie Smith ... .25 .10
❑ 112 Don Sutton ... 1.00 .40
❑ 113 Burt Hooton ... .10 .04
❑ 114A Dave Lopes P1 ... .50 .20
Small hand on back
❑ 114B Dave Lopes P2 ... .25 .10
No hand
❑ 115 Dusty Baker ... .50 .20
❑ 116 Tom Lasorda MG ... .25 .10
❑ 117 Bill Russell ... .25 .10
❑ 118 Jerry Reuss UER ... .25 .10
Home omitted
❑ 119 Terry Forster ... .10 .04
❑ 120A Bob Welch P1 ... .25 .10
(Name on back is Bob
❑ 120B Bob Welch P2 ... .50 .20
Name on back is Robert
❑ 121 Don Stanhouse ... .10 .04
❑ 122 Rick Monday ... .25 .10
❑ 123 Derrel Thomas ... .10 .04
❑ 124 Joe Ferguson ... .10 .04
❑ 125 Rick Sutcliffe ... .25 .10
❑ 126A Ron Cey P1 ... .50 .20
Small hand on back
❑ 126B Ron Cey P2 ... .25 .10
No hand
❑ 127 Dave Goltz ... .10 .04
❑ 128 Jay Johnstone ... .25 .10
❑ 129 Steve Yeager ... .10 .04
❑ 130 Gary Weiss ... .10 .04
❑ 131 Mike Scioscia RC ... 1.50 .60
❑ 132 Vic Davalillo ... .10 .04
❑ 133 Doug Rau ... .10 .04
❑ 134 Pepe Frias ... .10 .04
❑ 135 Mickey Hatcher ... .25 .10
❑ 136 Steve Howe ... .25 .10
❑ 137 Robert Castillo ... .10 .04
❑ 138 Gary Thomasson ... .10 .04
❑ 139 Rudy Law ... .10 .04
❑ 140 F.Valenzuela RC UER ... 2.00 .80
Misspelled Fernand on card
❑ 141 Manny Mota ... .25 .10
❑ 142 Gary Carter ... .50 .20
❑ 143 Steve Rogers ... .10 .04
❑ 144 Warren Cromartie ... .10 .04
❑ 145 Andre Dawson ... .50 .20
❑ 146 Larry Parrish ... .10 .04
❑ 147 Rowland Office ... .10 .04
❑ 148 Ellis Valentine ... .10 .04
❑ 149 Dick Williams MG ... .10 .04
❑ 150 Bill Gullickson RC ... .50 .20
❑ 151 Elias Sosa ... .10 .04
❑ 152 John Tamargo ... .10 .04
❑ 153 Chris Speier ... .10 .04
❑ 154 Ron LeFlore ... .25 .10
❑ 155 Rodney Scott ... .10 .04
❑ 156 Stan Bahnsen ... .10 .04
❑ 157 Bill Lee ... .25 .10
❑ 158 Fred Norman ... .10 .04
❑ 159 Woodie Fryman ... .10 .04
❑ 160 David Palmer ... .10 .04
❑ 161 Jerry White ... .10 .04
❑ 162 Roberto Ramos ... .10 .04
❑ 163 John D'Acquisto ... .10 .04
❑ 164 Tommy Hutton ... .10 .04
❑ 165 Charlie Lea ... .10 .04
❑ 166 Scott Sanderson ... .10 .04
❑ 167 Ken Macha ... .10 .04
❑ 168 Tony Bernazard ... .10 .04
❑ 169 Jim Palmer ... .25 .10
❑ 170 Steve Stone ... .25 .10
❑ 171 Mike Flanagan ... .25 .10
❑ 172 Al Bumbry ... .25 .10
❑ 173 Doug DeCinces ... .25 .10
❑ 174 Scott McGregor ... .10 .04
❑ 175 Mark Belanger ... .25 .10
❑ 176 Tim Stoddard ... .10 .04
❑ 177A Rick Dempsey P1 ... .50 .20
Small hand on front
❑ 177B Rick Dempsey P2 ... .25 .10
No hand
❑ 178 Earl Weaver MG ... 1.00 .40
❑ 179 Tippy Martinez ... .10 .04
❑ 180 Dennis Martinez ... .50 .20
❑ 181 Sammy Stewart ... .10 .04
❑ 182 Rich Dauer ... .10 .04
❑ 183 Lee May ... .25 .10
❑ 184 Eddie Murray ... 1.50 .60
❑ 185 Benny Ayala ... .10 .04
❑ 186 John Lowenstein ... .10 .04
❑ 187 Gary Roenicke ... .10 .04
❑ 188 Ken Singleton ... .25 .10
❑ 189 Dan Graham ... .10 .04
❑ 190 Terry Crowley ... .10 .04
❑ 191 Kiko Garcia ... .10 .04
❑ 192 Dave Ford ... .10 .04
❑ 193 Mark Corey ... .10 .04
❑ 194 Lenn Sakata ... .10 .04
❑ 195 Doug DeCinces ... .25 .10
❑ 196 Johnny Bench ... 1.00 .40
❑ 197 Dave Concepcion ... .25 .10
❑ 198 Ray Knight ... .25 .10
❑ 199 Ken Griffey ... .50 .20
❑ 200 Tom Seaver ... 1.00 .40
❑ 201 Dave Collins ... .10 .04
❑ 202A George Foster P1 ... .50 .20
Slugger
Number on back 216
❑ 202B George Foster P2 ... .50 .20
Slugger
Number on back 202
❑ 203 Junior Kennedy ... .10 .04
❑ 204 Frank Pastore ... .10 .04
❑ 205 Dan Driessen ... .10 .04
❑ 206 Hector Cruz ... .10 .04
❑ 207 Paul Moskau ... .10 .04
❑ 208 Charlie Leibrandt RC ... .50 .20
❑ 209 Harry Spilman ... .10 .04
❑ 210 Joe Price ... .10 .04
❑ 211 Tom Hume ... .10 .04
❑ 212 Joe Nolan ... .10 .04
❑ 213 Doug Bair ... .10 .04
❑ 214 Mario Soto ... .10 .04
❑ 215A Bill Bonham P1 ... .50 .20

(Small hand on back)
❑ 215B Bill Bonham P2 .10 .04
(No hand)
❑ 216 George Foster .25 .10
(See 202)
❑ 217 Paul Householder .10 .04
❑ 218 Ron Oester .10 .04
❑ 219 Sam Mejias .10 .04
❑ 220 Sheldon Burnside .10 .04
❑ 221 Carl Yastrzemski 1.00 .40
❑ 222 Jim Rice .25 .10
❑ 223 Fred Lynn .25 .10
❑ 224 Carlton Fisk .50 .20
❑ 225 Rick Burleson .10 .04
❑ 226 Dennis Eckersley .50 .20
❑ 227 Butch Hobson .10 .04
❑ 228 Tom Burgmeier .10 .04
❑ 229 Garry Hancock .10 .04
❑ 230 Don Zimmer MG .25 .10
❑ 231 Steve Renko .10 .04
❑ 232 Dwight Evans .50 .20
❑ 233 Mike Torrez .10 .04
❑ 234 Bob Stanley .10 .04
❑ 235 Jim Dwyer .10 .04
❑ 236 Dave Stapleton .10 .04
❑ 237 Glenn Hoffman .10 .04
❑ 238 Jerry Remy .10 .04
❑ 239 Dick Drago .10 .04
❑ 240 Bill Campbell .10 .04
❑ 241 Tony Perez .50 .20
❑ 242 Phil Niekro .25 .10
❑ 243 Dale Murphy 1.00 .40
❑ 244 Bob Horner .25 .10
❑ 245 Jeff Burroughs .10 .04
❑ 246 Rick Camp .10 .04
❑ 247 Bobby Cox MG .25 .10
❑ 248 Bruce Benedict .10 .04
❑ 249 Gene Garber .10 .04
❑ 250 Jerry Royster .10 .04
❑ 251A Gary Matthews P1 .50 .20
Small hand on back
❑ 251B Gary Matthews P2 .25 .10
No hand
❑ 252 Chris Chambliss .25 .10
❑ 253 Luis Gomez .10 .04
❑ 254 Bill Nahorodny .10 .04
❑ 255 Doyle Alexander .10 .04
❑ 256 Brian Asselstine .10 .04
❑ 257 Biff Pocoroba .10 .04
❑ 258 Mike Lum .10 .04
❑ 259 Charlie Spikes .10 .04
❑ 260 Glenn Hubbard .10 .04
❑ 261 Tommy Boggs .10 .04
❑ 262 Al Hrabosky UER .10 .04
Card lists him as 5' 1"
❑ 263 Rick Matula .10 .04
❑ 264 Preston Hanna .10 .04
❑ 265 Larry Bradford .10 .04
❑ 266 Rafael Ramirez .10 .04
❑ 267 Larry McWilliams .10 .04
❑ 268 Rod Carew .50 .20
❑ 269 Bobby Grich .25 .10
❑ 270 Carney Lansford .25 .10
❑ 271 Don Baylor .50 .20
❑ 272 Joe Rudi .25 .10
❑ 273 Dan Ford .10 .04
❑ 274 Jim Fregosi MG .10 .04
❑ 275 Dave Frost .10 .04
❑ 276 Frank Tanana .25 .10
❑ 277 Dickie Thon .25 .10
❑ 278 Jason Thompson .10 .04
❑ 279 Rick Miller .10 .04
❑ 280 Bert Campaneris .25 .10
❑ 281 Tom Donohue .10 .04
❑ 282 Brian Downing .25 .10
❑ 283 Fred Patek .10 .04
❑ 284 Bruce Kison .10 .04
❑ 285 Dave LaRoche .10 .04
❑ 286 Don Aase .10 .04
❑ 287 Jim Barr .10 .04
❑ 288 Alfredo Martinez .10 .04
❑ 289 Larry Harlow .10 .04
❑ 290 Andy Hassler .10 .04
❑ 291 Dave Kingman .50 .20
❑ 292 Bill Buckner .25 .10
❑ 293 Rick Reuschel .25 .10
❑ 294 Bruce Sutter .25 .10
❑ 295 Jerry Martin .10 .04
❑ 296 Scot Thompson .10 .04
❑ 297 Ivan DeJesus .10 .04
❑ 298 Steve Dillard .10 .04
❑ 299 Dick Tidrow .10 .04
❑ 300 Randy Martz .10 .04
❑ 301 Lenny Randle .10 .04
❑ 302 Lynn McGlothen .10 .04
❑ 303 Cliff Johnson .10 .04
❑ 304 Tim Blackwell .10 .04
❑ 305 Dennis Lamp .10 .04
❑ 306 Bill Caudill .10 .04
❑ 307 Carlos Lezcano .10 .04
❑ 308 Jim Tracy RC .10 .04
❑ 309 Doug Capilla UER .10 .04
Cubs on front but
Braves on back
❑ 310 Willie Hernandez .25 .10
❑ 311 Mike Vail .10 .04
❑ 312 Mike Krukow .10 .04
❑ 313 Barry Foote .10 .04
❑ 314 Larry Biittner .10 .04
❑ 315 Mike Tyson .10 .04
❑ 316 Lee Mazzilli .10 .04
❑ 317 John Stearns .10 .04
❑ 318 Alex Trevino .10 .04
❑ 319 Craig Swan .10 .04
❑ 320 Frank Taveras .10 .04
❑ 321 Steve Henderson .10 .04
❑ 322 Neil Allen .10 .04
❑ 323 Mark Bomback .10 .04
❑ 324 Mike Jorgensen .10 .04
❑ 325 Joe Torre MG .25 .10
❑ 326 Elliott Maddox .10 .04
❑ 327 Pete Falcone .10 .04
❑ 328 Ray Burris .10 .04
❑ 329 Claudell Washington .10 .04
❑ 330 Doug Flynn .10 .04
❑ 331 Joel Youngblood .10 .04
❑ 332 Bill Almon .10 .04
❑ 333 Tom Hausman .10 .04
❑ 334 Pat Zachry .10 .04
❑ 335 Jeff Reardon RC 1.00 .40
❑ 336 Wally Backman .25 .10
❑ 337 Dan Norman .10 .04
❑ 338 Jerry Morales .10 .04
❑ 339 Ed Farmer .10 .04
❑ 340 Bob Molinaro .10 .04
❑ 341 Todd Cruz .10 .04
❑ 342A Britt Burns P1 .50 .20
Small hand on front
❑ 342B Britt Burns P2 .25 .10
No hand
❑ 343 Kevin Bell .10 .04
❑ 344 Tony LaRussa MG .25 .10
❑ 345 Steve Trout .10 .04
❑ 346 Harold Baines RC 5.00 2.00
❑ 347 Richard Wortham .10 .04
❑ 348 Wayne Nordhagen .10 .04
❑ 349 Mike Squires .10 .04
❑ 350 Lamar Johnson .10 .04
❑ 351 Rickey Henderson 3.00 1.20
Most Stolen Bases AL
❑ 352 Francisco Barrios .10 .04
❑ 353 Thad Bosley .10 .04
❑ 354 Chet Lemon .10 .04
❑ 355 Bruce Kimm .10 .04
❑ 356 Richard Dotson .10 .04
❑ 357 Jim Morrison .10 .04
❑ 358 Mike Proly .10 .04
❑ 359 Greg Pryor .10 .04
❑ 360 Dave Parker .25 .10
❑ 361 Omar Moreno .10 .04
❑ 362A Kent Tekulve P1 .25 .10
Back 1071 Waterbury
and 1078 Pirates
❑ 362B Kent Tekulve P2 .25 .10
1971 Waterbury and
1978 Pirates
❑ 363 Willie Stargell .50 .20
❑ 364 Phil Garner .25 .10
❑ 365 Ed Ott .10 .04
❑ 366 Don Robinson .10 .04
❑ 367 Chuck Tanner MG .25 .10
❑ 368 Jim Rooker .10 .04
❑ 369 Dale Berra .10 .04
❑ 370 Jim Bibby .10 .04
❑ 371 Steve Nicosia .10 .04
❑ 372 Mike Easler .10 .04
❑ 373 Bill Robinson .25 .10
❑ 374 Lee Lacy .10 .04
❑ 375 John Candelaria .25 .10
❑ 376 Manny Sanguillen .25 .10
❑ 377 Rick Rhoden .10 .04
❑ 378 Grant Jackson .10 .04
❑ 379 Tim Foli .10 .04
❑ 380 Rod Scurry .10 .04
❑ 381 Bill Madlock .25 .10
❑ 382A Kurt Bevacqua .25 .10
P1 ERR
P on cap backwards
❑ 382B Kurt Bevacqua P2 .10 .04
COR
❑ 383 Bert Blyleven .50 .20
❑ 384 Eddie Solomon .10 .04
❑ 385 Enrique Romo .10 .04
❑ 386 John Milner .10 .04
❑ 387 Mike Hargrove .25 .10
❑ 388 Jorge Orta .10 .04
❑ 389 Toby Harrah .25 .10
❑ 390 Tom Veryzer .10 .04
❑ 391 Miguel Dilone .10 .04
❑ 392 Dan Spillner .10 .04
❑ 393 Jack Brohamer .10 .04
❑ 394 Wayne Garland .10 .04
❑ 395 Sid Monge .10 .04
❑ 396 Rick Waits .10 .04
❑ 397 Joe Charboneau RC 1.00 .40
❑ 398 Gary Alexander .10 .04
❑ 399 Jerry Dybzinski .10 .04
❑ 400 Mike Stanton .10 .04
❑ 401 Mike Paxton .10 .04
❑ 402 Gary Gray .10 .04
❑ 403 Rick Manning .10 .04
❑ 404 Bo Diaz .10 .04
❑ 405 Ron Hassey .10 .04
❑ 406 Ross Grimsley .10 .04
❑ 407 Victor Cruz .10 .04
❑ 408 Len Barker .10 .04
❑ 409 Bob Bailor .10 .04
❑ 410 Otto Velez .10 .04
❑ 411 Ernie Whitt .10 .04
❑ 412 Jim Clancy .10 .04
❑ 413 Barry Bonnell .10 .04
❑ 414 Dave Stieb .25 .10
❑ 415 Damaso Garcia .10 .04
❑ 416 John Mayberry .10 .04
❑ 417 Roy Howell .10 .04
❑ 418 Danny Ainge RC 2.00 .80
❑ 419A Jesse Jefferson P1 .10 .04
Back says Pirates
❑ 419B Jesse Jefferson P2 .10 .04
Back says Pirates
❑ 419C Jesse Jefferson P3 1.00 .40
Back says Blue Jays
❑ 420 Joey McLaughlin .10 .04
❑ 421 Lloyd Moseby .25 .10
❑ 422 Alvis Woods .10 .04
❑ 423 Garth Iorg .10 .04
❑ 424 Doug Ault .10 .04
❑ 425 Ken Schrom .10 .04
❑ 426 Mike Willis .10 .04
❑ 427 Steve Braun .10 .04
❑ 428 Bob Davis .10 .04
❑ 429 Jerry Garvin .10 .04
❑ 430 Alfredo Griffin .10 .04
❑ 431 Bob Mattick MG .10 .04
❑ 432 Vida Blue .25 .10
❑ 433 Jack Clark .25 .10
❑ 434 Willie McCovey .25 .10
❑ 435 Mike Ivie .10 .04
❑ 436A Darrel Evans P1 ERR .50 .20
(Name on front Darrel
❑ 436B Darrell Evans P2 COR .50 .20
Name on front Darrell
❑ 437 Terry Whitfield .10 .04
❑ 438 Rennie Stennett .10 .04
❑ 439 John Montefusco .10 .04
❑ 440 Jim Wohlford .10 .04
❑ 441 Bill North .10 .04
❑ 442 Milt May .10 .04

❑ 443 Max Venable .10 .04
❑ 444 Ed Whitson .10 .04
❑ 445 Al Holland .10 .04
❑ 446 Randy Moffitt .10 .04
❑ 447 Bob Knepper .10 .04
❑ 448 Gary Lavelle .10 .04
❑ 449 Greg Minton .10 .04
❑ 450 Johnnie LeMaster .10 .04
❑ 451 Larry Herndon .10 .04
❑ 452 Rich Murray .10 .04
❑ 453 Joe Pettini .10 .04
❑ 454 Allen Ripley .10 .04
❑ 455 Dennis Littlejohn .10 .04
❑ 456 Tom Griffin .10 .04
❑ 457 Alan Hargesheimer .10 .04
❑ 458 Joe Strain .10 .04
❑ 459 Steve Kemp .10 .04
❑ 460 Sparky Anderson MG .25 .10
❑ 461 Alan Trammell .50 .20
❑ 462 Mark Fidrych 1.00 .40
❑ 463 Lou Whitaker 1.00 .40
❑ 464 Dave Rozema .10 .04
❑ 465 Milt Wilcox .10 .04
❑ 466 Champ Summers .10 .04
❑ 467 Lance Parrish .25 .10
❑ 468 Dan Petry .10 .04
❑ 469 Pat Underwood .10 .04
❑ 470 Rick Peters .10 .04
❑ 471 Al Cowens .10 .04
❑ 472 John Wockenfuss .10 .04
❑ 473 Tom Brookens .10 .04
❑ 474 Richie Hebner .10 .04
❑ 475 Jack Morris 1.00 .40
❑ 476 Jim Lentine .10 .04
❑ 477 Bruce Robbins .10 .04
❑ 478 Mark Wagner .10 .04
❑ 479 Tim Corcoran .10 .04
❑ 480A Stan Papi P1 .25 .10
Front as Pitcher
❑ 480B Stan Papi P2 .10 .04
Front as Shortstop
❑ 481 Kirk Gibson RC 2.00 .80
❑ 482 Dan Schatzeder .10 .04
❑ 483A Amos Otis P1 .25 .10
See card 32
❑ 483B Amos Otis P2 .25 .10
See card 32
❑ 484 Dave Winfield 1.00 .40
❑ 485 Rollie Fingers .25 .10
❑ 486 Gene Richards .10 .04
❑ 487 Randy Jones .10 .04
❑ 488 Ozzie Smith 3.00 1.20
❑ 489 Gene Tenace .25 .10
❑ 490 Bill Fahey .10 .04
❑ 491 John Curtis .10 .04
❑ 492 Dave Cash .10 .04
❑ 493A Tim Flannery P1 .25 .10
Batting right
❑ 493B Tim Flannery P2 .10 .04
Batting left
❑ 494 Jerry Mumphrey .10 .04
❑ 495 Bob Shirley .10 .04
❑ 496 Steve Mura .10 .04
❑ 497 Eric Rasmussen .10 .04
❑ 498 Broderick Perkins .10 .04
❑ 499 Barry Evans .10 .04
❑ 500 Chuck Baker .10 .04
❑ 501 Luis Salazar RC .10 .04
❑ 502 Gary Lucas .10 .04
❑ 503 Mike Armstrong .10 .04
❑ 504 Jerry Turner .10 .04
❑ 505 Dennis Kinney .10 .04
❑ 506 Willie Montanez UER .10 .04
Spelled Willy on card front
❑ 507 Gorman Thomas .25 .10
❑ 508 Ben Oglivie .25 .10
❑ 509 Larry Hisle .10 .04
❑ 510 Sal Bando .25 .10
❑ 511 Robin Yount 1.00 .40
❑ 512 Mike Caldwell .10 .04
❑ 513 Sixto Lezcano .10 .04
❑ 514A Bill Travers P1 ERR .25 .10
Jerry Augustine
with Augustine back
❑ 514B Bill Travers P2 COR .10 .04
❑ 515 Paul Molitor 2.00 .80
❑ 516 Moose Haas .10 .04
❑ 517 Bill Castro .10 .04
❑ 518 Jim Slaton .10 .04
❑ 519 Lary Sorensen .10 .04
❑ 520 Bob McClure .10 .04
❑ 521 Charlie Moore .10 .04
❑ 522 Jim Gantner .25 .10
❑ 523 Reggie Cleveland .10 .04
❑ 524 Don Money .10 .04
❑ 525 Bill Travers .10 .04
❑ 526 Buck Martinez .10 .04
❑ 527 Dick Davis .10 .04
❑ 528 Ted Simmons .25 .10
❑ 529 Garry Templeton .10 .04
❑ 530 Ken Reitz .10 .04
❑ 531 Tony Scott .10 .04
❑ 532 Ken Oberkfell .10 .04
❑ 533 Bob Sykes .10 .04
❑ 534 Keith Smith .10 .04
❑ 535 John Littlefield .10 .04
❑ 536 Jim Kaat .25 .10
❑ 537 Bob Forsch .10 .04
❑ 538 Mike Phillips .10 .04
❑ 539 Terry Landrum .10 .04
❑ 540 Leon Durham .25 .10
❑ 541 Terry Kennedy .10 .04
❑ 542 George Hendrick .10 .04
❑ 543 Dane Iorg .10 .04
❑ 544 Mark Littell .10 .04
❑ 545 Keith Hernandez .50 .20
❑ 546 Silvio Martinez .10 .04
❑ 547A Don Hood P1 ERR .25 .10
Pete Vuckovich
with Vuckovich back
❑ 547B Don Hood P2 COR .10 .04
❑ 548 Bobby Bonds .25 .10
❑ 549 Mike Ramsey RC .10 .04
❑ 550 Tom Herr .25 .10
❑ 551 Roy Smalley .10 .04
❑ 552 Jerry Koosman .25 .10
❑ 553 Ken Landreaux .10 .04
❑ 554 John Castino .10 .04
❑ 555 Doug Corbett .10 .04
❑ 556 Bombo Rivera .10 .04
❑ 557 Ron Jackson .10 .04
❑ 558 Butch Wynegar .10 .04
❑ 559 Hosken Powell .10 .04
❑ 560 Pete Redfern .10 .04
❑ 561 Roger Erickson .10 .04
❑ 562 Glenn Adams .10 .04
❑ 563 Rick Sofield .10 .04
❑ 564 Geoff Zahn .10 .04
❑ 565 Pete Mackanin .10 .04
❑ 566 Mike Cubbage .10 .04
❑ 567 Darrell Jackson .10 .04
❑ 568 Dave Edwards .10 .04
❑ 569 Rob Wilfong .10 .04
❑ 570 Sal Butera .10 .04
❑ 571 Jose Morales .10 .04
❑ 572 Rick Langford .10 .04
❑ 573 Mike Norris .10 .04
❑ 574 Rickey Henderson 6.00 2.40
❑ 575 Tony Armas .25 .10
❑ 576 Dave Revering .10 .04
❑ 577 Jeff Newman .10 .04
❑ 578 Bob Lacey .10 .04
❑ 579 Brian Kingman .10 .04
❑ 580 Mitchell Page .10 .04
❑ 581 Billy Martin MG .50 .20
❑ 582 Rob Picciolo .10 .04
❑ 583 Mike Heath .10 .04
❑ 584 Mickey Klutts .10 .04
❑ 585 Orlando Gonzalez .10 .04
❑ 586 Mike Davis .10 .04
❑ 587 Wayne Gross .10 .04
❑ 588 Matt Keough .10 .04
❑ 589 Steve McCatty .10 .04
❑ 590 Dwayne Murphy .10 .04
❑ 591 Mario Guerrero .10 .04
❑ 592 Dave McKay .10 .04
❑ 593 Jim Essian .10 .04
❑ 594 Dave Heaverlo .10 .04
❑ 595 Maury Wills MG .25 .10
❑ 596 Juan Beniquez .10 .04
❑ 597 Rodney Craig .10 .04
❑ 598 Jim Anderson .10 .04
❑ 599 Floyd Bannister .10 .04
❑ 600 Bruce Bochte .10 .04
❑ 601 Julio Cruz .10 .04
❑ 602 Ted Cox .10 .04
❑ 603 Dan Meyer .10 .04
❑ 604 Larry Cox .10 .04
❑ 605 Bill Stein .10 .04
❑ 606 Steve Garvey .25 .10
Most Hits NL
❑ 607 Dave Roberts .10 .04
❑ 608 Leon Roberts .10 .04
❑ 609 Reggie Walton .10 .04
❑ 610 Dave Edler .10 .04
❑ 611 Larry Milbourne .10 .04
❑ 612 Kim Allen .10 .04
❑ 613 Mario Mendoza .10 .04
❑ 614 Tom Paciorek .25 .10
❑ 615 Glenn Abbott .10 .04
❑ 616 Joe Simpson .10 .04
❑ 617 Mickey Rivers .25 .10
❑ 618 Jim Kern .10 .04
❑ 619 Jim Sundberg .25 .10
❑ 620 Richie Zisk .10 .04
❑ 621 Jon Matlack .10 .04
❑ 622 Ferguson Jenkins .25 .10
❑ 623 Pat Corrales MG .10 .04
❑ 624 Ed Figueroa .10 .04
❑ 625 Buddy Bell .25 .10
❑ 626 Al Oliver .25 .10
❑ 627 Doc Medich .10 .04
❑ 628 Bump Wills .10 .04
❑ 629 Rusty Staub .25 .10
❑ 630 Pat Putnam .10 .04
❑ 631 John Grubb .10 .04
❑ 632 Danny Darwin .10 .04
❑ 633 Ken Clay .10 .04
❑ 634 Jim Norris .10 .04
❑ 635 John Butcher .10 .04
❑ 636 Dave Roberts .10 .04
❑ 637 Billy Sample .10 .04
❑ 638 Carl Yastrzemski 1.00 .40
❑ 639 Cecil Cooper .25 .10
❑ 640 Mike Schmidt P1 2.50 1.00
Portrait
Third Base
number on back 5
❑ 640B Mike Schmidt P2 2.50 1.00
1980 Home Run King
640 on back
❑ 641A CL: Phils/Royals P1 .25 .10
41 is Hal McRae
❑ 641B CL: Phils/Royals P2 .25 .10
41 is Hal McRae
Double Threat
❑ 642 CL: Astros/Yankees .10 .04
❑ 643 CL: Expos/Dodgers .10 .04
❑ 644A CL: Reds/Orioles P1 .25 .10
202 is George Foster
Joe Nolan pitcher
should be catcher
❑ 644B CL: Reds/Orioles P2 .25 .10
202 is Foster Slugger
Joe Nolan pitcher
should be catcher
❑ 645 Pete Rose 1.50 .60
Larry Bowa
Mike Schmidt
Triple Threat P1
No number on back
❑ 645B Pete Rose 2.50 1.00
Larry Bowa
Mike Schmidt
Triple Threat P2
Back numbered 645
❑ 646 CL: Braves/Red Sox .10 .04
❑ 647 CL: Cubs/Angels .10 .04
❑ 648 CL: Mets/White Sox .10 .04
❑ 649 CL: Indians/Pirates .10 .04
❑ 650 Reggie Jackson .50 .20
Mr. Baseball P1
Number on back 79
❑ 650B Reggie Jackson .50 .20
Mr. Baseball P2
Number on back 650
❑ 651 CL: Giants/Blue Jays .10 .04
❑ 652A CL:Tigers/Padres P1 .25 .10

483 is listed
❑ 652B CL:Tigers/Padres P2 ...... .25 .10
483 is deleted
❑ 653A Willie Wilson P1 .... .25 .10
Most Hits Most Runs
Number on back 29
❑ 653B Willie Wilson P2 .... .25 .10
Most Hits Most Runs
Number on back 653
❑ 654A Checklist Brewers .... .25 .10
Cards P1
514 Jerry Augustine
547 Pete Vuckovich
❑ 654B Checklist Brewers .... .25 .10
Cards P2
514 Billy Travers
547 Don Hood
❑ 655 George Brett P1 .... 3.00 1.20
.390 Average
Number on back 28
❑ 655B George Brett P2 .... 4.00 1.60
.390 Average
Number on back 655
❑ 656 CL:Twins/Oakland A's ...... .25 .10
❑ 657A Tug McGraw P1 .... .25 .10
Game Saver
Number on back 7
❑ 657B Tug McGraw P2 .... .25 .10
Game Saver
Number on back 657
❑ 658 CL: Rangers/Mariners ...... .10 .04
❑ 659A Checklist P1 .... .10 .04
of Special Cards
Last lines on front
Wilson Most Hits
❑ 659B Checklist P2 .... .10 .04
of Special Cards
Last lines on front
Otis Series Starter
❑ 660 Steve Carlton P1 .... .50 .20
Golden Arm
(Number on back 660
Back 1066 Cardinals
❑ 660B Steve Carlton P2 .... 2.00 .80
Golden Arm
1966 Cardinals

1982 Fleer

	Nm-Mt	Ex-Mt
COMPLETE SET (660)	50.00	20.00

❑ 1 Dusty Baker .40 .16
❑ 2 Robert Castillo .10 .04
❑ 3 Ron Cey .20 .08
❑ 4 Terry Forster .10 .04
❑ 5 Steve Garvey .20 .08
❑ 6 Dave Goltz .10 .04
❑ 7 Pedro Guerrero .20 .08
❑ 8 Burt Hooton .10 .04
❑ 9 Steve Howe .10 .04
❑ 10 Jay Johnstone .20 .08
❑ 11 Ken Landreaux .10 .04
❑ 12 Dave Lopes .20 .08
❑ 13 Mike A. Marshall .20 .08
❑ 14 Bobby Mitchell .10 .04
❑ 15 Rick Monday .10 .04
❑ 16 Tom Niedenfuer .10 .04
❑ 17 Ted Power RC .10 .04
❑ 18 Jerry Reuss UER .20 .08
("Home:" omitted)
❑ 19 Ron Roenicke .10 .04
❑ 20 Bill Russell .10 .04
❑ 21 Steve Sax RC .75 .30
❑ 22 Mike Scioscia .20 .08
❑ 23 Reggie Smith .20 .08
❑ 24 Dave Stewart RC 1.00 .40
❑ 25 Rick Sutcliffe .20 .08
❑ 26 Derrel Thomas .10 .04
❑ 27 Fernando Valenzuela .75 .30
❑ 28 Bob Welch .20 .08
❑ 29 Steve Yeager .10 .04
❑ 30 Bobby Brown .10 .04
❑ 31 Rick Cerone .10 .04
❑ 32 Ron Davis .10 .04
❑ 33 Bucky Dent .20 .08
❑ 34 Barry Foote .10 .04
❑ 35 George Frazier .10 .04
❑ 36 Oscar Gamble .10 .04
❑ 37 Rich Gossage .40 .16
❑ 38 Ron Guidry .20 .08
❑ 39 Reggie Jackson .40 .16
❑ 40 Tommy John .40 .16
❑ 41 Rudy May .10 .04
❑ 42 Larry Milbourne .10 .04
❑ 43 Jerry Mumphrey .10 .04
❑ 44 Bobby Murcer .20 .08
❑ 45 Gene Nelson .10 .04
❑ 46 Graig Nettles .20 .08
❑ 47 Johnny Oates .20 .08
❑ 48 Lou Piniella .20 .08
❑ 49 Willie Randolph .20 .08
❑ 50 Rick Reuschel .20 .08
❑ 51 Dave Revering .10 .04
❑ 52 Dave Righetti RC .75 .30
❑ 53 Aurelio Rodriguez .10 .04
❑ 54 Bob Watson .20 .08
❑ 55 Dennis Werth .10 .04
❑ 56 Dave Winfield .40 .16
❑ 57 Johnny Bench .75 .30
❑ 58 Bruce Berenyi .10 .04
❑ 59 Larry Biittner .10 .04
❑ 60 Scott Brown .10 .04
❑ 61 Dave Collins .10 .04
❑ 62 Geoff Combe .10 .04
❑ 63 Dave Concepcion .20 .08
❑ 64 Dan Driessen .10 .04
❑ 65 Joe Edelen .10 .04
❑ 66 George Foster .20 .08
❑ 67 Ken Griffey .20 .08
❑ 68 Paul Householder .10 .04
❑ 69 Tom Hume .10 .04
❑ 70 Junior Kennedy .10 .04
❑ 71 Ray Knight .20 .08
❑ 72 Mike LaCoss .10 .04
❑ 73 Rafael Landestoy .10 .04
❑ 74 Charlie Leibrandt .10 .04
❑ 75 Sam Mejias .10 .04
❑ 76 Paul Moskau .10 .04
❑ 77 Joe Nolan .10 .04
❑ 78 Mike O'Berry .10 .04
❑ 79 Ron Oester .10 .04
❑ 80 Frank Pastore .10 .04
❑ 81 Joe Price .10 .04
❑ 82 Tom Seaver .75 .30
❑ 83 Mario Soto .10 .04
❑ 84 Mike Vail .10 .04
❑ 85 Tony Armas .10 .04
❑ 86 Shooty Babitt .10 .04
❑ 87 Dave Beard .10 .04
❑ 88 Rick Bosetti .10 .04
❑ 89 Keith Drumwright .10 .04
❑ 90 Wayne Gross .10 .04
❑ 91 Mike Heath .10 .04
❑ 92 Rickey Henderson 2.50 1.00
❑ 93 Cliff Johnson .10 .04
❑ 94 Jeff Jones .10 .04
❑ 95 Matt Keough .10 .04
❑ 96 Brian Kingman .10 .04
❑ 97 Mickey Klutts .10 .04
❑ 98 Rick Langford .10 .04
❑ 99 Steve McCatty .10 .04
❑ 100 Dave McKay .10 .04
❑ 101 Dwayne Murphy .10 .04
❑ 102 Jeff Newman .10 .04
❑ 103 Mike Norris .10 .04
❑ 104 Bob Owchinko .10 .04
❑ 105 Mitchell Page .10 .04
❑ 106 Rob Picciolo .10 .04
❑ 107 Jim Spencer .10 .04
❑ 108 Fred Stanley .10 .04
❑ 109 Tom Underwood .10 .04
❑ 110 Joaquin Andujar .20 .08
❑ 111 Steve Braun .10 .04
❑ 112 Bob Forsch .10 .04
❑ 113 George Hendrick .10 .04
❑ 114 Keith Hernandez .40 .16
❑ 115 Tom Herr .20 .08
❑ 116 Dane Iorg .10 .04
❑ 117 Jim Kaat .20 .08
❑ 118 Tito Landrum .10 .04
❑ 119 Sixto Lezcano .10 .04
❑ 120 Mark Littell .10 .04
❑ 121 John Martin RC .10 .04
❑ 122 Silvio Martinez .10 .04
❑ 123 Ken Oberkfell .10 .04
❑ 124 Darrell Porter .20 .08
❑ 125 Mike Ramsey .10 .04
❑ 126 Orlando Sanchez .10 .04
❑ 127 Bob Shirley .10 .04
❑ 128 Lary Sorensen .10 .04
❑ 129 Bruce Sutter .20 .08
❑ 130 Bob Sykes .10 .04
❑ 131 Garry Templeton .10 .04
❑ 132 Gene Tenace .20 .08
❑ 133 Jerry Augustine .10 .04
❑ 134 Sal Bando .20 .08
❑ 135 Mark Brouhard .10 .04
❑ 136 Mike Caldwell .10 .04
❑ 137 Reggie Cleveland .10 .04
❑ 138 Cecil Cooper .20 .08
❑ 139 Jamie Easterly .10 .04
❑ 140 Marshall Edwards .10 .04
❑ 141 Rollie Fingers .20 .08
❑ 142 Jim Gantner .20 .08
❑ 143 Moose Haas .10 .04
❑ 144 Larry Hisle .10 .04
❑ 145 Roy Howell .10 .04
❑ 146 Rickey Keeton .10 .04
❑ 147 Randy Lerch .10 .04
❑ 148 Paul Molitor 1.00 .40
❑ 149 Don Money .10 .04
❑ 150 Charlie Moore .10 .04
❑ 151 Ben Oglivie .20 .08
❑ 152 Ted Simmons .20 .08
❑ 153 Jim Slaton .10 .04
❑ 154 Gorman Thomas .20 .08
❑ 155 Robin Yount .75 .30
❑ 156 Pete Vuckovich .10 .04
(Should precede Yount
in the team order)
❑ 157 Benny Ayala .10 .04
❑ 158 Mark Belanger .10 .04
❑ 159 Al Bumbry .10 .04
❑ 160 Terry Crowley .10 .04
❑ 161 Rich Dauer .10 .04
❑ 162 Doug DeCinces .20 .08
❑ 163 Rick Dempsey .20 .08
❑ 164 Jim Dwyer .10 .04
❑ 165 Mike Flanagan .20 .08
❑ 166 Dave Ford .10 .04
❑ 167 Dan Graham .10 .04
❑ 168 Wayne Krenchicki .10 .04
❑ 169 John Lowenstein .10 .04
❑ 170 Dennis Martinez .40 .16
❑ 171 Tippy Martinez .10 .04
❑ 172 Scott McGregor .10 .04
❑ 173 Jose Morales .10 .04
❑ 174 Eddie Murray .75 .30
❑ 175 Jim Palmer .20 .08
❑ 176 Cal Ripken RC 40.00 16.00
Fleer Ripken cards from 1982
through 1993 erroneously have 22
games played in 1981;not 23.
❑ 177 Gary Roenicke .10 .04
❑ 178 Lenn Sakata .10 .04
❑ 179 Ken Singleton .20 .08
❑ 180 Sammy Stewart .10 .04
❑ 181 Tim Stoddard .10 .04
❑ 182 Steve Stone .20 .08

❑ 183 Stan Bahnsen .10 .04
❑ 184 Ray Burris .10 .04
❑ 185 Gary Carter .40 .16
❑ 186 Warren Cromartie .10 .04
❑ 187 Andre Dawson .20 .08
❑ 188 Terry Francona .40 .16
❑ 189 Woodie Fryman .10 .04
❑ 190 Bill Gullickson .10 .04
❑ 191 Grant Jackson .10 .04
❑ 192 Wallace Johnson .10 .04
❑ 193 Charlie Lea .10 .04
❑ 194 Bill Lee .20 .08
❑ 195 Jerry Manuel .10 .04
❑ 196 Brad Mills .10 .04
❑ 197 John Milner .10 .04
❑ 198 Rowland Office .10 .04
❑ 199 David Palmer .10 .04
❑ 200 Larry Parrish .10 .04
❑ 201 Mike Phillips .10 .04
❑ 202 Tim Raines .75 .30
❑ 203 Bobby Ramos .10 .04
❑ 204 Jeff Reardon .40 .16
❑ 205 Steve Rogers .10 .04
❑ 206 Scott Sanderson .10 .04
❑ 207 Rodney Scott UER .40 .16
(Photo actually Tim Raines)
❑ 208 Elias Sosa .10 .04
❑ 209 Chris Speier .10 .04
❑ 210 Tim Wallach RC .40 .16
❑ 211 Jerry White .10 .04
❑ 212 Alan Ashby .10 .04
❑ 213 Cesar Cedeno .20 .08
❑ 214 Jose Cruz .20 .08
❑ 215 Kiko Garcia .10 .04
❑ 216 Phil Garner .20 .08
❑ 217 Danny Heep .10 .04
❑ 218 Art Howe .20 .08
❑ 219 Bob Knepper .10 .04
❑ 220 Frank LaCorte .10 .04
❑ 221 Joe Niekro .20 .08
❑ 222 Joe Pittman .10 .04
❑ 223 Terry Puhl .10 .04
❑ 224 Luis Pujols .10 .04
❑ 225 Craig Reynolds .10 .04
❑ 226 J.R. Richard .20 .08
❑ 227 Dave Roberts .10 .04
❑ 228 Vern Ruhle .10 .04
❑ 229 Nolan Ryan 4.00 1.60
❑ 230 Joe Sambito .10 .04
❑ 231 Tony Scott .10 .04
❑ 232 Dave Smith .10 .04
❑ 233 Harry Spilman .10 .04
❑ 234 Don Sutton .75 .30
❑ 235 Dickie Thon .10 .04
❑ 236 Denny Walling .10 .04
❑ 237 Gary Woods .10 .04
❑ 238 Luis Aguayo .10 .04
❑ 239 Ramon Aviles .10 .04
❑ 240 Bob Boone .20 .08
❑ 241 Larry Bowa .20 .08
❑ 242 Warren Brusstar .10 .04
❑ 243 Steve Carlton .40 .16
❑ 244 Larry Christenson .10 .04
❑ 245 Dick Davis .10 .04
❑ 246 Greg Gross .10 .04
❑ 247 Sparky Lyle .20 .08
❑ 248 Garry Maddox .10 .04
❑ 249 Gary Matthews .20 .08
❑ 250 Bake McBride .10 .04
❑ 251 Tug McGraw .20 .08
❑ 252 Keith Moreland .10 .04
❑ 253 Dickie Noles .10 .04
❑ 254 Mike Proly .10 .04
❑ 255 Ron Reed .10 .04
❑ 256 Pete Rose 2.50 1.00
❑ 257 Dick Ruthven .10 .04
❑ 258 Mike Schmidt 2.00 .80
❑ 259 Lonnie Smith .20 .08
❑ 260 Manny Trillo .10 .04
❑ 261 Del Unser .10 .04
❑ 262 George Vukovich .10 .04
❑ 263 Tom Brookens .10 .04
❑ 264 George Cappuzzello .10 .04
❑ 265 Marty Castillo .10 .04
❑ 266 Al Cowens .10 .04
❑ 267 Kirk Gibson .75 .30
❑ 268 Richie Hebner .20 .08
❑ 269 Ron Jackson .10 .04
❑ 270 Lynn Jones .10 .04
❑ 271 Steve Kemp .10 .04
❑ 272 Rick Leach .10 .04
❑ 273 Aurelio Lopez .10 .04
❑ 274 Jack Morris .20 .08
❑ 275 Kevin Saucier .10 .04
❑ 276 Lance Parrish .40 .16
❑ 277 Rick Peters .10 .04
❑ 278 Dan Petry .10 .04
❑ 279 Dave Rozema .10 .04
❑ 280 Stan Papi .10 .04
❑ 281 Dan Schatzeder .10 .04
❑ 282 Champ Summers .10 .04
❑ 283 Alan Trammell .40 .16
❑ 284 Lou Whitaker .75 .30
❑ 285 Milt Wilcox .10 .04
❑ 286 John Wockenfuss .10 .04
❑ 287 Gary Allenson .10 .04
❑ 288 Tom Burgmeier .10 .04
❑ 289 Bill Campbell .10 .04
❑ 290 Mark Clear .10 .04
❑ 291 Steve Crawford .10 .04
❑ 292 Dennis Eckersley .40 .16
❑ 293 Dwight Evans .40 .16
❑ 294 Rich Gedman .20 .08
❑ 295 Garry Hancock .10 .04
❑ 296 Glenn Hoffman .10 .04
❑ 297 Bruce Hurst .10 .04
❑ 298 Carney Lansford .20 .08
❑ 299 Rick Miller .10 .04
❑ 300 Reid Nichols .10 .04
❑ 301 Bob Ojeda RC .40 .16
❑ 302 Tony Perez .40 .16
❑ 303 Chuck Rainey .10 .04
❑ 304 Jerry Remy .10 .04
❑ 305 Jim Rice .20 .08
❑ 306 Joe Rudi .10 .04
❑ 307 Bob Stanley .10 .04
❑ 308 Dave Stapleton .10 .04
❑ 309 Frank Tanana .20 .08
❑ 310 Mike Torrez .10 .04
❑ 311 John Tudor .10 .04
❑ 312 Carl Yastrzemski .75 .30
❑ 313 Buddy Bell .20 .08
❑ 314 Steve Comer .10 .04
❑ 315 Danny Darwin .10 .04
❑ 316 John Ellis .10 .04
❑ 317 John Grubb .10 .04
❑ 318 Rick Honeycutt .10 .04
❑ 319 Charlie Hough .20 .08
❑ 320 Ferguson Jenkins .20 .08
❑ 321 John Henry Johnson .10 .04
❑ 322 Jim Kern .10 .04
❑ 323 Jon Matlack .10 .04
❑ 324 Doc Medich .10 .04
❑ 325 Mario Mendoza .10 .04
❑ 326 Al Oliver .20 .08
❑ 327 Pat Putnam .10 .04
❑ 328 Mickey Rivers .10 .04
❑ 329 Leon Roberts .10 .04
❑ 330 Billy Sample .10 .04
❑ 331 Bill Stein .10 .04
❑ 332 Jim Sundberg .10 .04
❑ 333 Mark Wagner .10 .04
❑ 334 Bump Wills .10 .04
❑ 335 Bill Almon .10 .04
❑ 336 Harold Baines .75 .30
❑ 337 Ross Baumgarten .10 .04
❑ 338 Tony Bernazard .10 .04
❑ 339 Britt Burns .10 .04
❑ 340 Richard Dotson .10 .04
❑ 341 Jim Essian .10 .04
❑ 342 Ed Farmer .10 .04
❑ 343 Carlton Fisk .40 .16
❑ 344 Kevin Hickey RC .10 .04
❑ 345 LaMarr Hoyt .10 .04
❑ 346 Lamar Johnson .10 .04
❑ 347 Jerry Koosman .20 .08
❑ 348 Rusty Kuntz .10 .04
❑ 349 Dennis Lamp .10 .04
❑ 350 Ron LeFlore .20 .08
❑ 351 Chet Lemon .10 .04
❑ 352 Greg Luzinski .20 .08
❑ 353 Bob Molinaro .10 .04
❑ 354 Jim Morrison .10 .04
❑ 355 Wayne Nordhagen .10 .04
❑ 356 Greg Pryor .10 .04
❑ 357 Mike Squires .10 .04
❑ 358 Steve Trout .10 .04
❑ 359 Alan Bannister .10 .04
❑ 360 Len Barker .10 .04
❑ 361 Bert Blyleven .40 .16
❑ 362 Joe Charboneau .20 .08
❑ 363 John Denny .10 .04
❑ 364 Bo Diaz .10 .04
❑ 365 Miguel Dilone .10 .04
❑ 366 Jerry Dybzinski .10 .04
❑ 367 Wayne Garland .10 .04
❑ 368 Mike Hargrove .20 .08
❑ 369 Toby Harrah .20 .08
❑ 370 Ron Hassey .10 .04
❑ 371 Von Hayes .20 .08
❑ 372 Pat Kelly .10 .04
❑ 373 Duane Kuiper .10 .04
❑ 374 Rick Manning .10 .04
❑ 375 Sid Monge .10 .04
❑ 376 Jorge Orta .10 .04
❑ 377 Dave Rosello .10 .04
❑ 378 Dan Spillner .10 .04
❑ 379 Mike Stanton .10 .04
❑ 380 Andre Thornton .10 .04
❑ 381 Tom Veryzer .10 .04
❑ 382 Rick Waits .10 .04
❑ 383 Doyle Alexander .10 .04
❑ 384 Vida Blue .20 .08
❑ 385 Fred Breining .10 .04
❑ 386 Enos Cabell .10 .04
❑ 387 Jack Clark .20 .08
❑ 388 Darrell Evans .20 .08
❑ 389 Tom Griffin .10 .04
❑ 390 Larry Herndon .10 .04
❑ 391 Al Holland .10 .04
❑ 392 Gary Lavelle .10 .04
❑ 393 Johnnie LeMaster .10 .04
❑ 394 Jerry Martin .10 .04
❑ 395 Milt May .10 .04
❑ 396 Greg Minton .10 .04
❑ 397 Joe Morgan .40 .16
❑ 398 Joe Pettini .10 .04
❑ 399 Allen Ripley .10 .04
❑ 400 Billy Smith .10 .04
❑ 401 Rennie Stennett .10 .04
❑ 402 Ed Whitson .10 .04
❑ 403 Jim Wohlford .10 .04
❑ 404 Willie Aikens .10 .04
❑ 405 George Brett 2.50 1.00
❑ 406 Ken Brett .10 .04
❑ 407 Dave Chalk .10 .04
❑ 408 Rich Gale .10 .04
❑ 409 Cesar Geronimo .10 .04
❑ 410 Larry Gura .10 .04
❑ 411 Clint Hurdle .10 .04
❑ 412 Mike Jones .10 .04
❑ 413 Dennis Leonard .10 .04
❑ 414 Renie Martin .10 .04
❑ 415 Lee May .20 .08
❑ 416 Hal McRae .20 .08
❑ 417 Darryl Motley .10 .04
❑ 418 Rance Mulliniks .10 .04
❑ 419 Amos Otis .20 .08
❑ 420 Ken Phelps .10 .04
❑ 421 Jamie Quirk .10 .04
❑ 422 Dan Quisenberry .20 .08
❑ 423 Paul Splittorff .10 .04
❑ 424 U.L. Washington .10 .04
❑ 425 John Wathan .10 .04
❑ 426 Frank White .20 .08
❑ 427 Willie Wilson .20 .08
❑ 428 Brian Asselstine .10 .04
❑ 429 Bruce Benedict .10 .04
❑ 430 Tommy Boggs .10 .04
❑ 431 Larry Bradford .10 .04
❑ 432 Rick Camp .10 .04
❑ 433 Chris Chambliss .20 .08
❑ 434 Gene Garber .10 .04
❑ 435 Preston Hanna .10 .04
❑ 436 Bob Horner .20 .08
❑ 437 Glenn Hubbard .10 .04
❑ 438A Al Hrabosky ERR 8.00 3.20

	No.	Player		
		(Height 5'1" All on reverse)		
❑	438B	Al Hrabosky ERR	.40	.16
		(Height 5'1")		
❑	438C	Al Hrabosky	.20	.08
		(Height 5'10")		
❑	439	Rufino Linares	.10	.04
❑	440	Rick Mahler	.10	.04
❑	441	Ed Miller	.10	.04
❑	442	John Montefusco	.10	.04
❑	443	Dale Murphy	.75	.30
❑	444	Phil Niekro	.20	.08
❑	445	Gaylord Perry	.20	.08
❑	446	Biff Pocoroba	.10	.04
❑	447	Rafael Ramirez	.10	.04
❑	448	Jerry Royster	.10	.04
❑	449	Claudell Washington	.10	.04
❑	450	Don Aase	.10	.04
❑	451	Don Baylor	.40	.16
❑	452	Juan Beniquez	.10	.04
❑	453	Rick Burleson	.10	.04
❑	454	Bert Campaneris	.20	.08
❑	455	Rod Carew	.40	.16
❑	456	Bob Clark	.10	.04
❑	457	Brian Downing	.10	.04
❑	458	Dan Ford	.10	.04
❑	459	Ken Forsch	.10	.04
❑	460A	Dave Frost (5 mm space before ERA)	.10	.04
❑	460B	Dave Frost	.10	.04
		(1 mm space)		
❑	461	Bobby Grich	.20	.08
❑	462	Larry Harlow	.10	.04
❑	463	John Harris	.10	.04
❑	464	Andy Hassler	.10	.04
❑	465	Butch Hobson	.10	.04
❑	466	Jesse Jefferson	.10	.04
❑	467	Bruce Kison	.10	.04
❑	468	Fred Lynn	.20	.08
❑	469	Angel Moreno	.10	.04
❑	470	Ed Ott	.10	.04
❑	471	Fred Patek	.10	.04
❑	472	Steve Renko	.10	.04
❑	473	Mike Witt	.20	.08
❑	474	Geoff Zahn	.10	.04
❑	475	Gary Alexander	.10	.04
❑	476	Dale Berra	.10	.04
❑	477	Kurt Bevacqua	.10	.04
❑	478	Jim Bibby	.10	.04
❑	479	John Candelaria	.10	.04
❑	480	Victor Cruz	.10	.04
❑	481	Mike Easler	.10	.04
❑	482	Tim Foli	.10	.04
❑	483	Lee Lacy	.10	.04
❑	484	Vance Law	.10	.04
❑	485	Bill Madlock	.20	.08
❑	486	Willie Montanez	.10	.04
❑	487	Omar Moreno	.10	.04
❑	488	Steve Nicosia	.10	.04
❑	489	Dave Parker	.20	.08
❑	490	Tony Pena	.20	.08
❑	491	Pascual Perez	.10	.04
❑	492	Johnny Ray	.20	.08
❑	493	Rick Rhoden	.10	.04
❑	494	Bill Robinson	.10	.04
❑	495	Don Robinson	.10	.04
❑	496	Enrique Romo	.10	.04
❑	497	Rod Scurry	.10	.04
❑	498	Eddie Solomon	.10	.04
❑	499	Willie Stargell	.40	.16
❑	500	Kent Tekulve	.20	.08
❑	501	Jason Thompson	.10	.04
❑	502	Glenn Abbott	.10	.04
❑	503	Jim Anderson	.10	.04
❑	504	Floyd Bannister	.10	.04
❑	505	Bruce Bochte	.10	.04
❑	506	Jeff Burroughs	.10	.04
❑	507	Bryan Clark RC	.10	.04
❑	508	Ken Clay	.10	.04
❑	509	Julio Cruz	.10	.04
❑	510	Dick Drago	.10	.04
❑	511	Gary Gray	.10	.04
❑	512	Dan Meyer	.10	.04
❑	513	Jerry Narron	.10	.04
❑	514	Tom Paciorek	.20	.08
❑	515	Casey Parsons	.10	.04
❑	516	Lenny Randle	.10	.04
❑	517	Shane Rawley	.10	.04
❑	518	Joe Simpson	.10	.04
❑	519	Richie Zisk	.10	.04
❑	520	Neil Allen	.10	.04
❑	521	Bob Bailor	.10	.04
❑	522	Hubie Brooks	.20	.08
❑	523	Mike Cubbage	.10	.04
❑	524	Pete Falcone	.10	.04
❑	525	Doug Flynn	.10	.04
❑	526	Tom Hausman	.10	.04
❑	527	Ron Hodges	.10	.04
❑	528	Randy Jones	.10	.04
❑	529	Mike Jorgensen	.10	.04
❑	530	Dave Kingman	.20	.08
❑	531	Ed Lynch	.10	.04
❑	532	Mike G. Marshall	.10	.04
❑	533	Lee Mazzilli	.10	.04
❑	534	Dyar Miller	.10	.04
❑	535	Mike Scott	.20	.08
❑	536	Rusty Staub	.20	.08
❑	537	John Stearns	.10	.04
❑	538	Craig Swan	.10	.04
❑	539	Frank Taveras	.10	.04
❑	540	Alex Trevino	.10	.04
❑	541	Ellis Valentine	.10	.04
❑	542	Mookie Wilson	.20	.08
❑	543	Joel Youngblood	.10	.04
❑	544	Pat Zachry	.10	.04
❑	545	Glenn Adams	.10	.04
❑	546	Fernando Arroyo	.10	.04
❑	547	John Verhoeven	.10	.04
❑	548	Sal Butera	.10	.04
❑	549	John Castino	.10	.04
❑	550	Don Cooper	.10	.04
❑	551	Doug Corbett	.10	.04
❑	552	Dave Engle	.10	.04
❑	553	Roger Erickson	.10	.04
❑	554	Danny Goodwin	.10	.04
❑	555A	Darrell Jackson	.40	.16
		(Black cap)		
❑	555B	Darrell Jackson	.20	.08
		(Red cap with T)		
❑	555C	Darrell Jackson	3.00	1.20
		(Red cap, no emblem)		
❑	556	Pete Mackanin	.10	.04
❑	557	Jack O'Connor	.10	.04
❑	558	Hosken Powell	.10	.04
❑	559	Pete Redfern	.10	.04
❑	560	Roy Smalley	.10	.04
❑	561	Chuck Baker UER	.10	.04
		(Shortshop on front)		
❑	562	Gary Ward	.10	.04
❑	563	Rob Wilfong	.10	.04
❑	564	Al Williams	.10	.04
❑	565	Butch Wynegar	.10	.04
❑	566	Randy Bass RC	.10	.04
❑	567	Juan Bonilla RC	.10	.04
❑	568	Danny Boone	.10	.04
❑	569	John Curtis	.10	.04
❑	570	Juan Eichelberger	.10	.04
❑	571	Barry Evans	.10	.04
❑	572	Tim Flannery	.10	.04
❑	573	Ruppert Jones	.10	.04
❑	574	Terry Kennedy	.10	.04
❑	575	Joe Lefebvre	.10	.04
❑	576A	John Littlefield ERR	80.00	32.00
		(Left handed; reverse negative)		
❑	576B	John Littlefield COR	.20	.08
		(Right handed)		
❑	577	Gary Lucas	.10	.04
❑	578	Steve Mura	.10	.04
❑	579	Broderick Perkins	.10	.04
❑	580	Gene Richards	.10	.04
❑	581	Luis Salazar	.10	.04
❑	582	Ozzie Smith	1.50	.60
❑	583	John Urrea	.10	.04
❑	584	Chris Welsh	.10	.04
❑	585	Rick Wise	.10	.04
❑	586	Doug Bird	.10	.04
❑	587	Tim Blackwell	.10	.04
❑	588	Bobby Bonds	.20	.08
❑	589	Bill Buckner	.20	.08
❑	590	Bill Caudill	.10	.04
❑	591	Hector Cruz	.10	.04
❑	592	Jody Davis	.10	.04
❑	593	Ivan DeJesus	.10	.04
❑	594	Steve Dillard	.10	.04
❑	595	Leon Durham	.10	.04
❑	596	Rawly Eastwick	.10	.04
❑	597	Steve Henderson	.10	.04
❑	598	Mike Krukow	.10	.04
❑	599	Mike Lum	.10	.04
❑	600	Randy Martz	.10	.04
❑	601	Jerry Morales	.10	.04
❑	602	Ken Reitz	.10	.04
❑	603	Lee Smith RC ERR	2.00	.80
		(Cubs logo reversed)		
❑	603B	Lee Smith RC COR	6.00	2.40
❑	604	Dick Tidrow	.10	.04
❑	605	Jim Tracy	.10	.04
❑	606	Mike Tyson	.10	.04
❑	607	Ty Waller	.10	.04
❑	608	Danny Ainge	1.00	.40
❑	609	Jorge Bell RC	.75	.30
❑	610	Mark Bomback	.10	.04
❑	611	Barry Bonnell	.10	.04
❑	612	Jim Clancy	.10	.04
❑	613	Damaso Garcia	.10	.04
❑	614	Jerry Garvin	.10	.04
❑	615	Alfredo Griffin	.10	.04
❑	616	Garth Iorg	.10	.04
❑	617	Luis Leal	.10	.04
❑	618	Ken Macha	.10	.04
❑	619	John Mayberry	.10	.04
❑	620	Joey McLaughlin	.10	.04
❑	621	Lloyd Moseby	.10	.04
❑	622	Dave Stieb	.20	.08
❑	623	Jackson Todd	.10	.04
❑	624	Willie Upshaw	.10	.04
❑	625	Otto Velez	.10	.04
❑	626	Ernie Whitt	.10	.04
❑	627	Alvis Woods	.10	.04
❑	628	All Star Game	.20	.08
		Cleveland, Ohio		
❑	629	Frank White	.20	.08
		Bucky Dent		
❑	630	Dan Driessen	.20	.08
		Dave Concepcion		
		George Foster		
❑	631	Bruce Sutter	.10	.04
		Top NL Relief Pitcher		
❑	632	Steve Carlton	.20	.08
		Carlton Fisk		
❑	633	Carl Yastrzemski	.75	.30
		3000th Game		
❑	634	Johnny Bench	.75	.30
		Tom Seaver		
❑	635	Fernando Valenzuela	.20	.08
		Gary Carter		
❑	636A	Fernando Valenzuela:	.75	.30
		NL SO King "he" NL		
❑	636B	Fernando Valenzuela:	.75	.30
		NL SO King "the" NL		
❑	637	Mike Schmidt	.75	.30
		Home Run King		
❑	638	Gary Carter	.20	.08
		Dave Parker		
❑	639	Perfect Game UER	.20	.08
		Len Barker		
		Bo Diaz		
		(Catcher actually Ron Hassey)		
❑	640	Pete Rose	.75	.30
		Pete Rose Jr.		
❑	641	Lonnie Smith	.75	.30
		Mike Schmidt		
		Steve Carlton		
❑	642	Fred Lynn	.20	.08
		Dwight Evans		
❑	643	Rickey Henderson	1.25	.50
		Most Hits and Runs		
❑	644	Rollie Fingers	.20	.08
		Most Saves AL		
❑	645	Tom Seaver	.40	.16
		Most 1981 Wins		
❑	646	Yankee Powerhouse	.20	.08
		Reggie Jackson		
		Dave Winfield		
		(Comma on back after outfielder)		

❑ 646B Yankee Powerhouse .40 .16
Reggie Jackson
Dave Winfield
(No comma)
❑ 647 CL: Yankees/Dodgers .10 .04
❑ 648 CL: A's/Reds .10 .04
❑ 649 CL: Cards/Brewers .10 .04
❑ 650 CL: Expos/Orioles .10 .04
❑ 651 CL: Astros/Phillies .10 .04
❑ 652 CL: Tigers/Red Sox .10 .04
❑ 653 CL: Rangers/White Sox .10 .04
❑ 654 CL: Giants/Indians .10 .04
❑ 655 CL: Royals/Braves .10 .04
❑ 656 CL: Angels/Pirates .10 .04
❑ 657 CL: Mariners/Mets .10 .04
❑ 658 CL: Padres/Twins .10 .04
❑ 659 CL: Blue Jays/Cubs .10 .04
❑ 660 Specials Checklist .10 .04

1983 Fleer

	Nm-Mt	Ex-Mt
COMPLETE SET (660)	60.00	24.00

❑ 1 Joaquin Andujar .10 .04
❑ 2 Doug Bair .10 .04
❑ 3 Steve Braun .10 .04
❑ 4 Glenn Brummer .10 .04
❑ 5 Bob Forsch .10 .04
❑ 6 David Green RC .10 .04
❑ 7 George Hendrick .10 .04
❑ 8 Keith Hernandez .40 .16
❑ 9 Tom Herr .20 .08
❑ 10 Dane Iorg .10 .04
❑ 11 Jim Kaat .20 .08
❑ 12 Jeff Lahti .10 .04
❑ 13 Tito Landrum .10 .04
❑ 14 Dave LaPoint .10 .04
❑ 15 Willie McGee RC 1.50 .60
❑ 16 Steve Mura .10 .04
❑ 17 Ken Oberkfell .10 .04
❑ 18 Darrell Porter .10 .04
❑ 19 Mike Ramsey .10 .04
❑ 20 Gene Roof .10 .04
❑ 21 Lonnie Smith .10 .04
❑ 22 Ozzie Smith 1.25 .50
❑ 23 John Stuper .10 .04
❑ 24 Bruce Sutter .20 .08
❑ 25 Gene Tenace .20 .08
❑ 26 Jerry Augustine .10 .04
❑ 27 Dwight Bernard .10 .04
❑ 28 Mark Brouhard .10 .04
❑ 29 Mike Caldwell .10 .04
❑ 30 Cecil Cooper .20 .08
❑ 31 Jamie Easterly .10 .04
❑ 32 Marshall Edwards .10 .04
❑ 33 Rollie Fingers .20 .08
❑ 34 Jim Gantner .10 .04
❑ 35 Moose Haas .10 .04
❑ 36 Roy Howell .10 .04
❑ 37 Pete Ladd .10 .04
❑ 38 Bob McClure .10 .04
❑ 39 Doc Medich .10 .04
❑ 40 Paul Molitor 1.00 .40
❑ 41 Don Money .10 .04
❑ 42 Charlie Moore .10 .04
❑ 43 Ben Oglivie .10 .04
❑ 44 Ed Romero .10 .04
❑ 45 Ted Simmons .20 .08
❑ 46 Jim Slaton .10 .04
❑ 47 Don Sutton .75 .30
❑ 48 Gorman Thomas .10 .04
❑ 49 Pete Vuckovich .10 .04
❑ 50 Ned Yost .10 .04
❑ 51 Robin Yount .75 .30
❑ 52 Benny Ayala .10 .04
❑ 53 Bob Bonner .10 .04
❑ 54 Al Bumbry .10 .04
❑ 55 Terry Crowley .10 .04
❑ 56 Storm Davis RC .10 .04
❑ 57 Rich Dauer .10 .04
❑ 58 Rick Dempsey UER .20 .08
(Posing batting lefty)
❑ 59 Jim Dwyer .10 .04
❑ 60 Mike Flanagan .20 .08
❑ 61 Dan Ford .10 .04
❑ 62 Glenn Gulliver .10 .04
❑ 63 John Lowenstein .10 .04
❑ 64 Dennis Martinez .20 .08
❑ 65 Tippy Martinez .10 .04
❑ 66 Scott McGregor .10 .04
❑ 67 Eddie Murray .75 .30
❑ 68 Joe Nolan .10 .04
❑ 69 Jim Palmer .20 .08
❑ 70 Cal Ripken 6.00 2.40
❑ 71 Gary Roenicke .10 .04
❑ 72 Lenn Sakata .10 .04
❑ 73 Ken Singleton .10 .04
❑ 74 Sammy Stewart .10 .04
❑ 75 Tim Stoddard .10 .04
❑ 76 Don Aase .10 .04
❑ 77 Don Baylor .40 .16
❑ 78 Juan Beniquez .10 .04
❑ 79 Bob Boone .20 .08
❑ 80 Rick Burleson .10 .04
❑ 81 Rod Carew .40 .16
❑ 82 Bobby Clark .10 .04
❑ 83 Doug Corbett .10 .04
❑ 84 John Curtis .10 .04
❑ 85 Doug DeCinces .20 .08
❑ 86 Brian Downing .10 .04
❑ 87 Joe Ferguson .10 .04
❑ 88 Tim Foli .10 .04
❑ 89 Ken Forsch .10 .04
❑ 90 Dave Goltz .10 .04
❑ 91 Bobby Grich .20 .08
❑ 92 Andy Hassler .10 .04
❑ 93 Reggie Jackson .40 .16
❑ 94 Ron Jackson .10 .04
❑ 95 Tommy John .40 .16
❑ 96 Bruce Kison .10 .04
❑ 97 Fred Lynn .20 .08
❑ 98 Ed Ott .10 .04
❑ 99 Steve Renko .10 .04
❑ 100 Luis Sanchez .10 .04
❑ 101 Rob Wilfong .10 .04
❑ 102 Mike Witt .10 .04
❑ 103 Geoff Zahn .10 .04
❑ 104 Willie Aikens .10 .04
❑ 105 Mike Armstrong .10 .04
❑ 106 Vida Blue .20 .08
❑ 107 Bud Black RC .20 .08
❑ 108 George Brett 2.50 1.00
❑ 109 Bill Castro .10 .04
❑ 110 Onix Concepcion .10 .04
❑ 111 Dave Frost .10 .04
❑ 112 Cesar Geronimo .10 .04
❑ 113 Larry Gura .10 .04
❑ 114 Steve Hammond .10 .04
❑ 115 Don Hood .10 .04
❑ 116 Dennis Leonard .10 .04
❑ 117 Jerry Martin .10 .04
❑ 118 Lee May .20 .08
❑ 119 Hal McRae .20 .08
❑ 120 Amos Otis .20 .08
❑ 121 Greg Pryor .10 .04
❑ 122 Dan Quisenberry .20 .08
❑ 123 Don Slaught RC .40 .16
❑ 124 Paul Splittorff .10 .04
❑ 125 U.L. Washington .10 .04
❑ 126 John Wathan .10 .04
❑ 127 Frank White .20 .08
❑ 128 Willie Wilson .20 .08
❑ 129 Steve Bedrosian UER .20 .08
(Height 6'33")
❑ 130 Bruce Benedict .10 .04
❑ 131 Tommy Boggs .10 .04
❑ 132 Brett Butler .75 .30
❑ 133 Rick Camp .10 .04
❑ 134 Chris Chambliss .20 .08
❑ 135 Ken Dayley .10 .04
❑ 136 Gene Garber .10 .04
❑ 137 Terry Harper .10 .04
❑ 138 Bob Horner .10 .04
❑ 139 Glenn Hubbard .10 .04
❑ 140 Rufino Linares .10 .04
❑ 141 Rick Mahler .10 .04
❑ 142 Dale Murphy .75 .30
❑ 143 Phil Niekro .20 .08
❑ 144 Pascual Perez .10 .04
❑ 145 Biff Pocoroba .10 .04
❑ 146 Rafael Ramirez .10 .04
❑ 147 Jerry Royster .10 .04
❑ 148 Ken Smith .10 .04
❑ 149 Bob Walk .10 .04
❑ 150 Claudell Washington .10 .04
❑ 151 Bob Watson .20 .08
❑ 152 Larry Whisenton .10 .04
❑ 153 Porfirio Altamirano .10 .04
❑ 154 Marty Bystrom .10 .04
❑ 155 Steve Carlton .40 .16
❑ 156 Larry Christenson .10 .04
❑ 157 Ivan DeJesus .10 .04
❑ 158 John Denny .10 .04
❑ 159 Bob Dernier .10 .04
❑ 160 Bo Diaz .10 .04
❑ 161 Ed Farmer .10 .04
❑ 162 Greg Gross .10 .04
❑ 163 Mike Krukow .10 .04
❑ 164 Garry Maddox .10 .04
❑ 165 Gary Matthews .20 .08
❑ 166 Tug McGraw .20 .08
❑ 167 Bob Molinaro .10 .04
❑ 168 Sid Monge .10 .04
❑ 169 Ron Reed .10 .04
❑ 170 Bill Robinson .10 .04
❑ 171 Pete Rose 2.50 1.00
❑ 172 Dick Ruthven .10 .04
❑ 173 Mike Schmidt 2.00 .80
❑ 174 Manny Trillo .10 .04
❑ 175 Ozzie Virgil .10 .04
❑ 176 George Vukovich .10 .04
❑ 177 Gary Allenson .10 .04
❑ 178 Luis Aponte .10 .04
❑ 179 Wade Boggs RC 8.00 3.20
❑ 180 Tom Burgmeier .10 .04
❑ 181 Mark Clear .10 .04
❑ 182 Dennis Eckersley .40 .16
❑ 183 Dwight Evans .20 .08
❑ 184 Rich Gedman .10 .04
❑ 185 Glenn Hoffman .10 .04
❑ 186 Bruce Hurst .10 .04
❑ 187 Carney Lansford .20 .08
❑ 188 Rick Miller .10 .04
❑ 189 Reid Nichols .10 .04
❑ 190 Bob Ojeda .10 .04
❑ 191 Tony Perez .40 .16
❑ 192 Chuck Rainey .10 .04
❑ 193 Jerry Remy .10 .04
❑ 194 Jim Rice .20 .08
❑ 195 Bob Stanley .10 .04
❑ 196 Dave Stapleton .10 .04
❑ 197 Mike Torrez .10 .04
❑ 198 John Tudor .10 .04
❑ 199 Julio Valdez .10 .04
❑ 200 Carl Yastrzemski .75 .30
❑ 201 Dusty Baker .20 .08
❑ 202 Joe Beckwith .10 .04
❑ 203 Greg Brock .10 .04
❑ 204 Ron Cey .20 .08
❑ 205 Terry Forster .10 .04
❑ 206 Steve Garvey .20 .08
❑ 207 Pedro Guerrero .20 .08
❑ 208 Burt Hooton .10 .04
❑ 209 Steve Howe .10 .04
❑ 210 Ken Landreaux .10 .04
❑ 211 Mike Marshall .10 .04
❑ 212 Candy Maldonado RC .20 .08
❑ 213 Rick Monday .10 .04
❑ 214 Tom Niedenfuer .10 .04

❑ 215 Jorge Orta .10 .04
❑ 216 Jerry Reuss UER .20 .08
("Home:" omitted)
❑ 217 Ron Roenicke .10 .04
❑ 218 Vicente Romo .10 .04
❑ 219 Bill Russell .10 .04
❑ 220 Steve Sax .20 .08
❑ 221 Mike Scioscia .20 .08
❑ 222 Dave Stewart .20 .08
❑ 223 Derrel Thomas .10 .04
❑ 224 Fernando Valenzuela .40 .16
❑ 225 Bob Welch .20 .08
❑ 226 Ricky Wright .10 .04
❑ 227 Steve Yeager .10 .04
❑ 228 Bill Almon .10 .04
❑ 229 Harold Baines .75 .30
❑ 230 Salome Barojas .10 .04
❑ 231 Tony Bernazard .10 .04
❑ 232 Britt Burns .10 .04
❑ 233 Richard Dotson .10 .04
❑ 234 Ernesto Escarrega .10 .04
❑ 235 Carlton Fisk .40 .16
❑ 236 Jerry Hairston .10 .04
❑ 237 Kevin Hickey .10 .04
❑ 238 LaMarr Hoyt .20 .08
❑ 239 Steve Kemp .10 .04
❑ 240 Jim Kern .10 .04
❑ 241 Ron Kittle RC .40 .16
❑ 242 Jerry Koosman .20 .08
❑ 243 Dennis Lamp .10 .04
❑ 244 Rudy Law .10 .04
❑ 245 Vance Law .10 .04
❑ 246 Ron LeFlore .10 .04
❑ 247 Greg Luzinski .20 .08
❑ 248 Tom Paciorek .20 .08
❑ 249 Aurelio Rodriguez .10 .04
❑ 250 Mike Squires .10 .04
❑ 251 Steve Trout .10 .04
❑ 252 Jim Barr .10 .04
❑ 253 Dave Bergman .10 .04
❑ 254 Fred Breining .10 .04
❑ 255 Bob Brenly .10 .04
❑ 256 Jack Clark .20 .08
❑ 257 Chili Davis .75 .30
❑ 258 Darrell Evans .20 .08
❑ 259 Alan Fowlkes .10 .04
❑ 260 Rich Gale .10 .04
❑ 261 Atlee Hammaker .10 .04
❑ 262 Al Holland .10 .04
❑ 263 Duane Kuiper .10 .04
❑ 264 Bill Laskey .10 .04
❑ 265 Gary Lavelle .10 .04
❑ 266 Johnnie LeMaster .10 .04
❑ 267 Renie Martin .10 .04
❑ 268 Milt May .10 .04
❑ 269 Greg Minton .10 .04
❑ 270 Joe Morgan .40 .16
❑ 271 Tom O'Malley .10 .04
❑ 272 Reggie Smith .20 .08
❑ 273 Guy Sularz .10 .04
❑ 274 Champ Summers .10 .04
❑ 275 Max Venable .10 .04
❑ 276 Jim Wohlford .10 .04
❑ 277 Ray Burris .10 .04
❑ 278 Gary Carter .40 .16
❑ 279 Warren Cromartie .10 .04
❑ 280 Andre Dawson .20 .08
❑ 281 Terry Francona .10 .04
❑ 282 Doug Flynn .10 .04
❑ 283 Woodie Fryman .10 .04
❑ 284 Bill Gullickson .10 .04
❑ 285 Wallace Johnson .10 .04
❑ 286 Charlie Lea .10 .04
❑ 287 Randy Lerch .10 .04
❑ 288 Brad Mills .10 .04
❑ 289 Dan Norman .10 .04
❑ 290 Al Oliver .20 .08
❑ 291 David Palmer .10 .04
❑ 292 Tim Raines .75 .30
❑ 293 Jeff Reardon .20 .08
❑ 294 Steve Rogers .10 .04
❑ 295 Scott Sanderson .10 .04
❑ 296 Dan Schatzeder .10 .04
❑ 297 Bryn Smith .10 .04
❑ 298 Chris Speier .10 .04
❑ 299 Tim Wallach .20 .08
❑ 300 Jerry White .10 .04
❑ 301 Joel Youngblood .10 .04
❑ 302 Ross Baumgarten .10 .04
❑ 303 Dale Berra .10 .04
❑ 304 John Candelaria .10 .04
❑ 305 Dick Davis .10 .04
❑ 306 Mike Easler .10 .04
❑ 307 Richie Hebner .20 .08
❑ 308 Lee Lacy .10 .04
❑ 309 Bill Madlock .20 .08
❑ 310 Larry McWilliams .10 .04
❑ 311 John Milner .10 .04
❑ 312 Omar Moreno .10 .04
❑ 313 Jim Morrison .10 .04
❑ 314 Steve Nicosia .10 .04
❑ 315 Dave Parker .20 .08
❑ 316 Tony Pena .10 .04
❑ 317 Johnny Ray .10 .04
❑ 318 Rick Rhoden .10 .04
❑ 319 Don Robinson .10 .04
❑ 320 Enrique Romo .10 .04
❑ 321 Manny Sarmiento .10 .04
❑ 322 Rod Scurry .10 .04
❑ 323 Jimmy Smith .10 .04
❑ 324 Willie Stargell .40 .16
❑ 325 Jason Thompson .10 .04
❑ 326 Kent Tekulve .20 .08
❑ 327A Tom Brookens .10 .04
(Short .375" brown box shaded in on card back)
❑ 327B Tom Brookens .10 .04
(Longer 1.25" brown box shaded in on card back)
❑ 328 Enos Cabell .10 .04
❑ 329 Kirk Gibson .75 .30
❑ 330 Larry Herndon .10 .04
❑ 331 Mike Ivie .10 .04
❑ 332 Howard Johnson RC .75 .30
❑ 333 Lynn Jones .10 .04
❑ 334 Rick Leach .10 .04
❑ 335 Chet Lemon .10 .04
❑ 336 Jack Morris .20 .08
❑ 337 Lance Parrish .20 .08
❑ 338 Larry Pashnick .10 .04
❑ 339 Dan Petry .10 .04
❑ 340 Dave Rozema .10 .04
❑ 341 Dave Rucker .10 .04
❑ 342 Elias Sosa .10 .04
❑ 343 Dave Tobik .10 .04
❑ 344 Alan Trammell .40 .16
❑ 345 Jerry Turner .10 .04
❑ 346 Jerry Ujdur .10 .04
❑ 347 Pat Underwood .10 .04
❑ 348 Lou Whitaker .40 .16
❑ 349 Milt Wilcox .10 .04
❑ 350 Glenn Wilson .20 .08
❑ 351 John Wockenfuss .10 .04
❑ 352 Kurt Bevacqua .10 .04
❑ 353 Juan Bonilla .10 .04
❑ 354 Floyd Chiffer .10 .04
❑ 355 Luis DeLeon .10 .04
❑ 356 Dave Dravecky RC .75 .30
❑ 357 Dave Edwards .10 .04
❑ 358 Juan Eichelberger .10 .04
❑ 359 Tim Flannery .10 .04
❑ 360 Tony Gwynn RC 15.00 6.00
❑ 361 Ruppert Jones .10 .04
❑ 362 Terry Kennedy .10 .04
❑ 363 Joe Lefebvre .10 .04
❑ 364 Sixto Lezcano .10 .04
❑ 365 Tim Lollar .10 .04
❑ 366 Gary Lucas .10 .04
❑ 367 John Montefusco .10 .04
❑ 368 Broderick Perkins .10 .04
❑ 369 Joe Pittman .10 .04
❑ 370 Gene Richards .10 .04
❑ 371 Luis Salazar .10 .04
❑ 372 Eric Show .10 .04
❑ 373 Garry Templeton .10 .04
❑ 374 Chris Welsh .10 .04
❑ 375 Alan Wiggins .10 .04
❑ 376 Rick Cerone .10 .04
❑ 377 Dave Collins .10 .04
❑ 378 Roger Erickson .10 .04
❑ 379 George Frazier .10 .04
❑ 380 Oscar Gamble .10 .04
❑ 381 Rich Gossage .40 .16
❑ 382 Ken Griffey .20 .08
❑ 383 Ron Guidry .20 .08
❑ 384 Dave LaRoche .10 .04
❑ 385 Rudy May .10 .04
❑ 386 John Mayberry .10 .04
❑ 387 Lee Mazzilli .10 .04
❑ 388 Mike Morgan .10 .04
❑ 389 Jerry Mumphrey .10 .04
❑ 390 Bobby Murcer .20 .08
❑ 391 Graig Nettles .20 .08
❑ 392 Lou Piniella .20 .08
❑ 393 Willie Randolph .20 .08
❑ 394 Shane Rawley .10 .04
❑ 395 Dave Righetti .20 .08
❑ 396 Andre Robertson .10 .04
❑ 397 Roy Smalley .10 .04
❑ 398 Dave Winfield .40 .16
❑ 399 Butch Wynegar .10 .04
❑ 400 Chris Bando .10 .04
❑ 401 Alan Bannister .10 .04
❑ 402 Len Barker .10 .04
❑ 403 Tom Brennan .10 .04
❑ 404 Carmelo Castillo .10 .04
❑ 405 Miguel Dilone .10 .04
❑ 406 Jerry Dybzinski .10 .04
❑ 407 Mike Fischlin .10 .04
❑ 408 Ed Glynn UER .10 .04
(Photo actually Bud Anderson)
❑ 409 Mike Hargrove .20 .08
❑ 410 Toby Harrah .10 .04
❑ 411 Ron Hassey .10 .04
❑ 412 Von Hayes .20 .08
❑ 413 Rick Manning .10 .04
❑ 414 Bake McBride .10 .04
❑ 415 Larry Milbourne .10 .04
❑ 416 Bill Nahorodny .10 .04
❑ 417 Jack Perconte .10 .04
❑ 418 Lary Sorensen .10 .04
❑ 419 Dan Spillner .10 .04
❑ 420 Rick Sutcliffe .20 .08
❑ 421 Andre Thornton .10 .04
❑ 422 Rick Waits .10 .04
❑ 423 Eddie Whitson .10 .04
❑ 424 Jesse Barfield .20 .08
❑ 425 Barry Bonnell .10 .04
❑ 426 Jim Clancy .10 .04
❑ 427 Damaso Garcia .10 .04
❑ 428 Jerry Garvin .10 .04
❑ 429 Alfredo Griffin .10 .04
❑ 430 Garth Iorg .10 .04
❑ 431 Roy Lee Jackson .10 .04
❑ 432 Luis Leal .10 .04
❑ 433 Buck Martinez .10 .04
❑ 434 Joey McLaughlin .10 .04
❑ 435 Lloyd Moseby .10 .04
❑ 436 Rance Mulliniks .10 .04
❑ 437 Dale Murray .10 .04
❑ 438 Wayne Nordhagen .10 .04
❑ 439 Geno Petralli .20 .08
❑ 440 Hosken Powell .10 .04
❑ 441 Dave Stieb .20 .08
❑ 442 Willie Upshaw .10 .04
❑ 443 Ernie Whitt .10 .04
❑ 444 Alvis Woods .10 .04
❑ 445 Alan Ashby .10 .04
❑ 446 Jose Cruz .20 .08
❑ 447 Kiko Garcia .10 .04
❑ 448 Phil Garner .20 .08
❑ 449 Danny Heep .10 .04
❑ 450 Art Howe .20 .08
❑ 451 Bob Knepper .10 .04
❑ 452 Alan Knicely .10 .04
❑ 453 Ray Knight .20 .08
❑ 454 Frank LaCorte .10 .04
❑ 455 Mike LaCoss .10 .04
❑ 456 Randy Moffitt .10 .04
❑ 457 Joe Niekro .20 .08
❑ 458 Terry Puhl .10 .04
❑ 459 Luis Pujols .10 .04
❑ 460 Craig Reynolds .10 .04
❑ 461 Bert Roberge .10 .04
❑ 462 Vern Ruhle .10 .04
❑ 463 Nolan Ryan 4.00 1.60
❑ 464 Joe Sambito .10 .04

❑ 465 Tony Scott .10 .04
❑ 466 Dave Smith .10 .04
❑ 467 Harry Spilman .10 .04
❑ 468 Dickie Thon .10 .04
❑ 469 Denny Walling .10 .04
❑ 470 Larry Andersen .10 .04
❑ 471 Floyd Bannister .10 .04
❑ 472 Jim Beattie .10 .04
❑ 473 Bruce Bochte .10 .04
❑ 474 Manny Castillo .10 .04
❑ 475 Bill Caudill .10 .04
❑ 476 Bryan Clark .10 .04
❑ 477 Al Cowens .10 .04
❑ 478 Julio Cruz .10 .04
❑ 479 Todd Cruz .10 .04
❑ 480 Gary Gray .10 .04
❑ 481 Dave Henderson .10 .04
❑ 482 Mike Moore RC .20 .08
❑ 483 Gaylord Perry .20 .08
❑ 484 Dave Revering .10 .04
❑ 485 Joe Simpson .10 .04
❑ 486 Mike Stanton .10 .04
❑ 487 Rick Sweet .10 .04
❑ 488 Ed VandeBerg .10 .04
❑ 489 Richie Zisk .10 .04
❑ 490 Doug Bird .10 .04
❑ 491 Larry Bowa .20 .08
❑ 492 Bill Buckner .20 .08
❑ 493 Bill Campbell .10 .04
❑ 494 Jody Davis .10 .04
❑ 495 Leon Durham .10 .04
❑ 496 Steve Henderson .10 .04
❑ 497 Willie Hernandez .20 .08
❑ 498 Ferguson Jenkins .20 .08
❑ 499 Jay Johnstone .20 .08
❑ 500 Junior Kennedy .10 .04
❑ 501 Randy Martz .10 .04
❑ 502 Jerry Morales .10 .04
❑ 503 Keith Moreland .10 .04
❑ 504 Dickie Noles .10 .04
❑ 505 Mike Proly .10 .04
❑ 506 Allen Ripley .10 .04
❑ 507 R.Sandberg RC UER 10.00 4.00
Should say High School
in Spokane, Washington
❑ 508 Lee Smith .75 .30
❑ 509 Pat Tabler .10 .04
❑ 510 Dick Tidrow .10 .04
❑ 511 Bump Wills .10 .04
❑ 512 Gary Woods .10 .04
❑ 513 Tony Armas .10 .04
❑ 514 Dave Beard .10 .04
❑ 515 Jeff Burroughs .10 .04
❑ 516 John D'Acquisto .10 .04
❑ 517 Wayne Gross .10 .04
❑ 518 Mike Heath .10 .04
❑ 519 R.Henderson UER 1.50 .60
Brock record listed
as 120 steals
❑ 520 Cliff Johnson .10 .04
❑ 521 Matt Keough .10 .04
❑ 522 Brian Kingman .10 .04
❑ 523 Rick Langford .10 .04
❑ 524 Dave Lopes .20 .08
❑ 525 Steve McCatty .10 .04
❑ 526 Dave McKay .10 .04
❑ 527 Dan Meyer .10 .04
❑ 528 Dwayne Murphy .10 .04
❑ 529 Jeff Newman .10 .04
❑ 530 Mike Norris .10 .04
❑ 531 Bob Owchinko .10 .04
❑ 532 Joe Rudi .10 .04
❑ 533 Jimmy Sexton .10 .04
❑ 534 Fred Stanley .10 .04
❑ 535 Tom Underwood .10 .04
❑ 536 Neil Allen .10 .04
❑ 537 Wally Backman .10 .04
❑ 538 Bob Bailor .10 .04
❑ 539 Hubie Brooks .20 .08
❑ 540 Carlos Diaz RC .10 .04
❑ 541 Pete Falcone .10 .04
❑ 542 George Foster .20 .08
❑ 543 Ron Gardenhire .10 .04
❑ 544 Brian Giles .10 .04
❑ 545 Ron Hodges .10 .04
❑ 546 Randy Jones .10 .04
❑ 547 Mike Jorgensen .10 .04
❑ 548 Dave Kingman .40 .16
❑ 549 Ed Lynch .10 .04
❑ 550 Jesse Orosco .10 .04
❑ 551 Rick Ownbey .10 .04
❑ 552 Charlie Puleo .10 .04
❑ 553 Gary Rajsich .10 .04
❑ 554 Mike Scott .20 .08
❑ 555 Rusty Staub .20 .08
❑ 556 John Stearns .10 .04
❑ 557 Craig Swan .10 .04
❑ 558 Ellis Valentine .10 .04
❑ 559 Tom Veryzer .10 .04
❑ 560 Mookie Wilson .20 .08
❑ 561 Pat Zachry .10 .04
❑ 562 Buddy Bell .20 .08
❑ 563 John Butcher .10 .04
❑ 564 Steve Comer .10 .04
❑ 565 Danny Darwin .10 .04
❑ 566 Bucky Dent .20 .08
❑ 567 John Grubb .10 .04
❑ 568 Rick Honeycutt .10 .04
❑ 569 Dave Hostetler .10 .04
❑ 570 Charlie Hough .20 .08
❑ 571 Lamar Johnson .10 .04
❑ 572 Jon Matlack .10 .04
❑ 573 Paul Mirabella .10 .04
❑ 574 Larry Parrish .10 .04
❑ 575 Mike Richardt .10 .04
❑ 576 Mickey Rivers .10 .04
❑ 577 Billy Sample .10 .04
❑ 578 Dave Schmidt .10 .04
❑ 579 Bill Stein .10 .04
❑ 580 Jim Sundberg .20 .08
❑ 581 Frank Tanana .20 .08
❑ 582 Mark Wagner .10 .04
❑ 583 George Wright RC .10 .04
❑ 584 Johnny Bench .75 .30
❑ 585 Bruce Berenyi .10 .04
❑ 586 Larry Biittner .10 .04
❑ 587 Cesar Cedeno .20 .08
❑ 588 Dave Concepcion .20 .08
❑ 589 Dan Driessen .10 .04
❑ 590 Greg Harris .10 .04
❑ 591 Ben Hayes .10 .04
❑ 592 Paul Householder .10 .04
❑ 593 Tom Hume .10 .04
❑ 594 Wayne Krenchicki .10 .04
❑ 595 Rafael Landestoy .10 .04
❑ 596 Charlie Leibrandt .10 .04
❑ 597 Eddie Milner .10 .04
❑ 598 Ron Oester .10 .04
❑ 599 Frank Pastore .10 .04
❑ 600 Joe Price .10 .04
❑ 601 Tom Seaver .75 .30
❑ 602 Bob Shirley .10 .04
❑ 603 Mario Soto .10 .04
❑ 604 Alex Trevino .10 .04
❑ 605 Mike Vail .10 .04
❑ 606 Duane Walker .10 .04
❑ 607 Tom Brunansky .20 .08
❑ 608 Bobby Castillo .10 .04
❑ 609 John Castino .10 .04
❑ 610 Ron Davis .10 .04
❑ 611 Lenny Faedo .10 .04
❑ 612 Terry Felton .10 .04
❑ 613 Gary Gaetti RC .75 .30
❑ 614 Mickey Hatcher .10 .04
❑ 615 Brad Havens .10 .04
❑ 616 Kent Hrbek .20 .08
❑ 617 Randy Johnson .10 .04
❑ 618 Tim Laudner .10 .04
❑ 619 Jeff Little .10 .04
❑ 620 Bobby Mitchell .10 .04
❑ 621 Jack O'Connor .10 .04
❑ 622 John Pacella .10 .04
❑ 623 Pete Redfern .10 .04
❑ 624 Jesus Vega .10 .04
❑ 625 Frank Viola RC .75 .30
❑ 626 Ron Washington .10 .04
❑ 627 Gary Ward .10 .04
❑ 628 Al Williams .10 .04
❑ 629 Carl Yastrzemski .75 .30
Dennis Eckersley
Mark Clear
❑ 630 Gaylord Perry .10 .04
Terry Bulling 5/6/82
❑ 631 Dave Concepcion .20 .08
Manny Trillo
❑ 632 Robin Yount .75 .30
Buddy Bell
❑ 633 Dave Winfield .40 .16
Kent Hrbek
❑ 634 Willie Stargell .75 .30
Pete Rose
❑ 635 Toby Harrah .20 .08
Andre Thornton
❑ 636 Ozzie Smith .75 .30
Lonnie Smith
❑ 637 Bo Diaz .20 .08
Gary Carter
❑ 638 Carlton Fisk .20 .08
Gary Carter
❑ 639 Rickey Henderson IA .75 .30
❑ 640 Ben Oglivie .40 .16
Reggie Jackson
❑ 641 Joel Youngblood .10 .04
4-Aug-82
❑ 642 Ron Hassey .20 .08
Len Barker
❑ 643 Black and Blue .20 .08
Vida Blue
❑ 644 Black and Blue .10 .04
Bud Black
❑ 645 Reggie Jackson Power .... .20 .08
❑ 646 Rickey Henderson Speed.. .75 .30
❑ 647 CL: Cards/Brewers .10 .04
❑ 648 CL: Orioles/Angels .10 .04
❑ 649 CL: Royals/Braves .10 .04
❑ 650 CL: Phillies/Red Sox .10 .04
❑ 651 CL: Dodgers/White Sox .10 .04
❑ 652 CL: Giants/Expos .10 .04
❑ 653 CL: Pirates/Tigers .10 .04
❑ 654 CL: Padres/Yankees .10 .04
❑ 655 CL: Indians/Blue Jays .10 .04
❑ 656 CL: Astros/Mariners .10 .04
❑ 657 CL: Cubs/A's .10 .04
❑ 658 CL: Mets/Rangers .10 .04
❑ 659 CL: Reds/Twins .10 .04
❑ 660 CL: Specials/Teams .10 .04

1984 Fleer

	Nm-Mt	Ex-Mt
COMPLETE SET (660)	50.00	20.00
❑ 1 Mike Boddicker	.15	.06
❑ 2 Al Bumbry	.15	.06
❑ 3 Todd Cruz	.15	.06
❑ 4 Rich Dauer	.15	.06
❑ 5 Storm Davis	.15	.06
❑ 6 Rick Dempsey	.15	.06
❑ 7 Jim Dwyer	.15	.06
❑ 8 Mike Flanagan	.15	.06
❑ 9 Dan Ford	.15	.06
❑ 10 John Lowenstein	.15	.06
❑ 11 Dennis Martinez	.40	.16
❑ 12 Tippy Martinez	.15	.06
❑ 13 Scott McGregor	.15	.06
❑ 14 Eddie Murray	1.50	.60
❑ 15 Joe Nolan	.15	.06
❑ 16 Jim Palmer	.40	.16
❑ 17 Cal Ripken	10.00	4.00
❑ 18 Gary Roenicke	.15	.06

❑ 19 Lenn Sakata .15 .06
❑ 20 John Shelby .15 .06
❑ 21 Ken Singleton .15 .06
❑ 22 Sammy Stewart .15 .06
❑ 23 Tim Stoddard .15 .06
❑ 24 Marty Bystrom .15 .06
❑ 25 Steve Carlton .75 .30
❑ 26 Ivan DeJesus .15 .06
❑ 27 John Denny .15 .06
❑ 28 Bob Dernier .15 .06
❑ 29 Bo Diaz .15 .06
❑ 30 Kiko Garcia .15 .06
❑ 31 Greg Gross .15 .06
❑ 32 Kevin Gross RC .15 .06
❑ 33 Von Hayes .15 .06
❑ 34 Willie Hernandez .40 .16
❑ 35 Al Holland .15 .06
❑ 36 Charles Hudson .15 .06
❑ 37 Joe Lefebvre .15 .06
❑ 38 Sixto Lezcano .15 .06
❑ 39 Garry Maddox .15 .06
❑ 40 Gary Matthews .40 .16
❑ 41 Len Matuszek .15 .06
❑ 42 Tug McGraw .40 .16
❑ 43 Joe Morgan .75 .30
❑ 44 Tony Perez .75 .30
❑ 45 Ron Reed .15 .06
❑ 46 Pete Rose 5.00 2.00
❑ 47 Juan Samuel RC .75 .30
❑ 48 Mike Schmidt 4.00 1.60
❑ 49 Ozzie Virgil .15 .06
❑ 50 Juan Agosto .15 .06
❑ 51 Harold Baines 1.50 .60
❑ 52 Floyd Bannister .15 .06
❑ 53 Salome Barojas .15 .06
❑ 54 Britt Burns .15 .06
❑ 55 Julio Cruz .15 .06
❑ 56 Richard Dotson .15 .06
❑ 57 Jerry Dybzinski .15 .06
❑ 58 Carlton Fisk .75 .30
❑ 59 Scott Fletcher .15 .06
❑ 60 Jerry Hairston .15 .06
❑ 61 Kevin Hickey .15 .06
❑ 62 Marc Hill .15 .06
❑ 63 LaMarr Hoyt .15 .06
❑ 64 Ron Kittle .15 .06
❑ 65 Jerry Koosman .40 .16
❑ 66 Dennis Lamp .15 .06
❑ 67 Rudy Law .15 .06
❑ 68 Vance Law .15 .06
❑ 69 Greg Luzinski .40 .16
❑ 70 Tom Paciorek .40 .16
❑ 71 Mike Squires .15 .06
❑ 72 Dick Tidrow .15 .06
❑ 73 Greg Walker .40 .16
❑ 74 Glenn Abbott .15 .06
❑ 75 Howard Bailey .15 .06
❑ 76 Doug Bair .15 .06
❑ 77 Juan Berenguer .15 .06
❑ 78 Tom Brookens .40 .16
❑ 79 Enos Cabell .15 .06
❑ 80 Kirk Gibson 1.50 .60
❑ 81 John Grubb .15 .06
❑ 82 Larry Herndon .40 .16
❑ 83 Wayne Krenchicki .15 .06
❑ 84 Rick Leach .15 .06
❑ 85 Chet Lemon .15 .06
❑ 86 Aurelio Lopez .40 .16
❑ 87 Jack Morris 1.50 .60
❑ 88 Lance Parrish .75 .30
❑ 89 Dan Petry .40 .16
❑ 90 Dave Rozema .15 .06
❑ 91 Alan Trammell .75 .30
❑ 92 Lou Whitaker 1.50 .60
❑ 93 Milt Wilcox .15 .06
❑ 94 Glenn Wilson .40 .16
❑ 95 John Wockenfuss .15 .06
❑ 96 Dusty Baker .40 .16
❑ 97 Joe Beckwith .15 .06
❑ 98 Greg Brock .15 .06
❑ 99 Jack Fimple .15 .06
❑ 100 Pedro Guerrero .40 .16
❑ 101 Rick Honeycutt .15 .06
❑ 102 Burt Hooton .15 .06
❑ 103 Steve Howe .15 .06
❑ 104 Ken Landreaux .15 .06
❑ 105 Mike Marshall .15 .06
❑ 106 Rick Monday .15 .06
❑ 107 Jose Morales .15 .06
❑ 108 Tom Niedenfuer .15 .06
❑ 109 Alejandro Pena RC* .40 .16
❑ 110 Jerry Reuss UER .15 .06
("Home:" omitted)
❑ 111 Bill Russell .15 .06
❑ 112 Steve Sax .40 .16
❑ 113 Mike Scioscia .15 .06
❑ 114 Derrel Thomas .15 .06
❑ 115 Fernando Valenzuela .40 .16
❑ 116 Bob Welch .15 .06
❑ 117 Steve Yeager .15 .06
❑ 118 Pat Zachry .15 .06
❑ 119 Don Baylor .75 .30
❑ 120 Bert Campaneris .40 .16
❑ 121 Rick Cerone .15 .06
❑ 122 Ray Fontenot .15 .06
❑ 123 George Frazier .15 .06
❑ 124 Oscar Gamble .15 .06
❑ 125 Rich Gossage .75 .30
❑ 126 Ken Griffey .40 .16
❑ 127 Ron Guidry .40 .16
❑ 128 Jay Howell .15 .06
❑ 129 Steve Kemp .15 .06
❑ 130 Matt Keough .15 .06
❑ 131 Don Mattingly RC 20.00 8.00
❑ 132 John Montefusco .15 .06
❑ 133 Omar Moreno .15 .06
❑ 134 Dale Murray .15 .06
❑ 135 Graig Nettles .40 .16
❑ 136 Lou Piniella .40 .16
❑ 137 Willie Randolph .40 .16
❑ 138 Shane Rawley .15 .06
❑ 139 Dave Righetti .40 .16
❑ 140 Andre Robertson .15 .06
❑ 141 Bob Shirley .15 .06
❑ 142 Roy Smalley .15 .06
❑ 143 Dave Winfield .75 .30
❑ 144 Butch Wynegar .15 .06
❑ 145 Jim Acker .15 .06
❑ 146 Doyle Alexander .15 .06
❑ 147 Jesse Barfield .40 .16
❑ 148 Jorge Bell .40 .16
❑ 149 Barry Bonnell .15 .06
❑ 150 Jim Clancy .15 .06
❑ 151 Dave Collins .15 .06
❑ 152 Tony Fernandez RC 2.00 .80
❑ 153 Damaso Garcia .15 .06
❑ 154 Dave Geisel .15 .06
❑ 155 Jim Gott .15 .06
❑ 156 Alfredo Griffin .15 .06
❑ 157 Garth Iorg .15 .06
❑ 158 Roy Lee Jackson .15 .06
❑ 159 Cliff Johnson .15 .06
❑ 160 Luis Leal .15 .06
❑ 161 Buck Martinez .15 .06
❑ 162 Joey McLaughlin .15 .06
❑ 163 Randy Moffitt .15 .06
❑ 164 Lloyd Moseby .15 .06
❑ 165 Rance Mulliniks .15 .06
❑ 166 Jorge Orta .15 .06
❑ 167 Dave Stieb .15 .06
❑ 168 Willie Upshaw .15 .06
❑ 169 Ernie Whitt .15 .06
❑ 170 Len Barker .15 .06
❑ 171 Steve Bedrosian .15 .06
❑ 172 Bruce Benedict .15 .06
❑ 173 Brett Butler .75 .30
❑ 174 Rick Camp .15 .06
❑ 175 Chris Chambliss .40 .16
❑ 176 Ken Dayley .15 .06
❑ 177 Pete Falcone .15 .06
❑ 178 Terry Forster .15 .06
❑ 179 Gene Garber .15 .06
❑ 180 Terry Harper .15 .06
❑ 181 Bob Horner .15 .06
❑ 182 Glenn Hubbard .15 .06
❑ 183 Randy Johnson .15 .06
❑ 184 Craig McMurtry .15 .06
❑ 185 Donnie Moore .15 .06
❑ 186 Dale Murphy 1.50 .60
❑ 187 Phil Niekro .40 .16
❑ 188 Pascual Perez .15 .06
❑ 189 Biff Pocoroba .15 .06
❑ 190 Rafael Ramirez .15 .06
❑ 191 Jerry Royster .15 .06
❑ 192 Claudell Washington .15 .06
❑ 193 Bob Watson .40 .16
❑ 194 Jerry Augustine .15 .06
❑ 195 Mark Brouhard .15 .06
❑ 196 Mike Caldwell .15 .06
❑ 197 Tom Candiotti RC 1.50 .60
❑ 198 Cecil Cooper .40 .16
❑ 199 Rollie Fingers .40 .16
❑ 200 Jim Gantner .15 .06
❑ 201 Bob L. Gibson RC .15 .06
❑ 202 Moose Haas .15 .06
❑ 203 Roy Howell .15 .06
❑ 204 Pete Ladd .15 .06
❑ 205 Rick Manning .15 .06
❑ 206 Bob McClure .15 .06
❑ 207 Paul Molitor UER .75 .30
('83 stats should say .270 BA and 608 AB)
❑ 208 Don Money .15 .06
❑ 209 Charlie Moore .15 .06
❑ 210 Ben Oglivie .15 .06
❑ 211 Chuck Porter .15 .06
❑ 212 Ed Romero .15 .06
❑ 213 Ted Simmons .40 .16
❑ 214 Jim Slaton .15 .06
❑ 215 Don Sutton 1.50 .60
❑ 216 Tom Tellmann .15 .06
❑ 217 Pete Vuckovich .15 .06
❑ 218 Ned Yost .15 .06
❑ 219 Robin Yount 1.50 .60
❑ 220 Alan Ashby .15 .06
❑ 221 Kevin Bass .15 .06
❑ 222 Jose Cruz .40 .16
❑ 223 Bill Dawley .15 .06
❑ 224 Frank DiPino .15 .06
❑ 225 Bill Doran RC* .40 .16
❑ 226 Phil Garner .40 .16
❑ 227 Art Howe .40 .16
❑ 228 Bob Knepper .15 .06
❑ 229 Ray Knight .40 .16
❑ 230 Frank LaCorte .15 .06
❑ 231 Mike LaCoss .15 .06
❑ 232 Mike Madden .15 .06
❑ 233 Jerry Mumphrey .15 .06
❑ 234 Joe Niekro .40 .16
❑ 235 Terry Puhl .15 .06
❑ 236 Luis Pujols .15 .06
❑ 237 Craig Reynolds .15 .06
❑ 238 Vern Ruhle .15 .06
❑ 239 Nolan Ryan 8.00 3.20
❑ 240 Mike Scott .40 .16
❑ 241 Tony Scott .15 .06
❑ 242 Dave Smith .15 .06
❑ 243 Dickie Thon .15 .06
❑ 244 Denny Walling .15 .06
❑ 245 Dale Berra .15 .06
❑ 246 Jim Bibby .15 .06
❑ 247 John Candelaria .15 .06
❑ 248 Jose DeLeon RC .15 .06
❑ 249 Mike Easler .15 .06
❑ 250 Cecilio Guante .15 .06
❑ 251 Richie Hebner .15 .06
❑ 252 Lee Lacy .15 .06
❑ 253 Bill Madlock .40 .16
❑ 254 Milt May .15 .06
❑ 255 Lee Mazzilli .15 .06
❑ 256 Larry McWilliams .15 .06
❑ 257 Jim Morrison .15 .06
❑ 258 Dave Parker .40 .16
❑ 259 Tony Pena .15 .06
❑ 260 Johnny Ray .15 .06
❑ 261 Rick Rhoden .15 .06
❑ 262 Don Robinson .15 .06
❑ 263 Manny Sarmiento .15 .06
❑ 264 Rod Scurry .15 .06
❑ 265 Kent Tekulve .40 .16
❑ 266 Gene Tenace .40 .16
❑ 267 Jason Thompson .15 .06
❑ 268 Lee Tunnell .15 .06
❑ 269 Marvell Wynne .15 .06
❑ 270 Ray Burris .15 .06
❑ 271 Gary Carter .75 .30
❑ 272 Warren Cromartie .15 .06
❑ 273 Andre Dawson .40 .16

❑ 274 Doug Flynn .15 .06
❑ 275 Terry Francona .15 .06
❑ 276 Bill Gullickson .15 .06
❑ 277 Bob James .15 .06
❑ 278 Charlie Lea .15 .06
❑ 279 Bryan Little .15 .06
❑ 280 Al Oliver .40 .16
❑ 281 Tim Raines .75 .30
❑ 282 Bobby Ramos .15 .06
❑ 283 Jeff Reardon .40 .16
❑ 284 Steve Rogers .15 .06
❑ 285 Scott Sanderson .15 .06
❑ 286 Dan Schatzeder .15 .06
❑ 287 Bryn Smith .15 .06
❑ 288 Chris Speier .15 .06
❑ 289 Manny Trillo .15 .06
❑ 290 Mike Vail .15 .06
❑ 291 Tim Wallach .40 .16
❑ 292 Chris Welsh .15 .06
❑ 293 Jim Wohlford .15 .06
❑ 294 Kurt Bevacqua .15 .06
❑ 295 Juan Bonilla .15 .06
❑ 296 Bobby Brown .15 .06
❑ 297 Luis DeLeon .15 .06
❑ 298 Dave Dravecky .40 .16
❑ 299 Tim Flannery .15 .06
❑ 300 Steve Garvey .40 .16
❑ 301 Tony Gwynn 6.00 2.40
❑ 302 Andy Hawkins .15 .06
❑ 303 Ruppert Jones .15 .06
❑ 304 Terry Kennedy .15 .06
❑ 305 Tim Lollar .15 .06
❑ 306 Gary Lucas .15 .06
❑ 307 Kevin McReynolds RC .75 .30
❑ 308 Sid Monge .15 .06
❑ 309 Mario Ramirez .15 .06
❑ 310 Gene Richards .15 .06
❑ 311 Luis Salazar .15 .06
❑ 312 Eric Show .15 .06
❑ 313 Elias Sosa .15 .06
❑ 314 Garry Templeton .15 .06
❑ 315 Mark Thurmond .15 .06
❑ 316 Ed Whitson .15 .06
❑ 317 Alan Wiggins .15 .06
❑ 318 Neil Allen .15 .06
❑ 319 Joaquin Andujar .15 .06
❑ 320 Steve Braun .15 .06
❑ 321 Glenn Brummer .15 .06
❑ 322 Bob Forsch .15 .06
❑ 323 David Green .15 .06
❑ 324 George Hendrick .15 .06
❑ 325 Tom Herr .40 .16
❑ 326 Dane Iorg .15 .06
❑ 327 Jeff Lahti .15 .06
❑ 328 Dave LaPoint .15 .06
❑ 329 Willie McGee .75 .30
❑ 330 Ken Oberkfell .15 .06
❑ 331 Darrell Porter .15 .06
❑ 332 Jamie Quirk .15 .06
❑ 333 Mike Ramsey .15 .06
❑ 334 Floyd Rayford .15 .06
❑ 335 Lonnie Smith .15 .06
❑ 336 Ozzie Smith 2.00 .80
❑ 337 John Stuper .15 .06
❑ 338 Bruce Sutter .40 .16
❑ 339 A.Van Slyke RC UER 1.50 .60
Batting and throwing
both wrong on card back
❑ 340 Dave Von Ohlen .15 .06
❑ 341 Willie Aikens .15 .06
❑ 342 Mike Armstrong .15 .06
❑ 343 Bud Black .15 .06
❑ 344 George Brett 5.00 2.00
❑ 345 Onix Concepcion .15 .06
❑ 346 Keith Creel .15 .06
❑ 347 Larry Gura .15 .06
❑ 348 Don Hood .15 .06
❑ 349 Dennis Leonard .15 .06
❑ 350 Hal McRae .40 .16
❑ 351 Amos Otis .40 .16
❑ 352 Gaylord Perry .40 .16
❑ 353 Greg Pryor .15 .06
❑ 354 Dan Quisenberry .15 .06
❑ 355 Steve Renko .15 .06
❑ 356 Leon Roberts .15 .06
❑ 357 Pat Sheridan .15 .06
❑ 358 Joe Simpson .15 .06
❑ 359 Don Slaught .40 .16
❑ 360 Paul Splittorff .15 .06
❑ 361 U.L. Washington .15 .06
❑ 362 John Wathan .15 .06
❑ 363 Frank White .40 .16
❑ 364 Willie Wilson .15 .06
❑ 365 Jim Barr .15 .06
❑ 366 Dave Bergman .15 .06
❑ 367 Fred Breining .15 .06
❑ 368 Bob Brenly .15 .06
❑ 369 Jack Clark .40 .16
❑ 370 Chili Davis .75 .30
❑ 371 Mark Davis .15 .06
❑ 372 Darrell Evans .40 .16
❑ 373 Atlee Hammaker .15 .06
❑ 374 Mike Krukow .15 .06
❑ 375 Duane Kuiper .15 .06
❑ 376 Bill Laskey .15 .06
❑ 377 Gary Lavelle .15 .06
❑ 378 Johnnie LeMaster .15 .06
❑ 379 Jeff Leonard .15 .06
❑ 380 Randy Lerch .15 .06
❑ 381 Renie Martin .15 .06
❑ 382 Andy McGaffigan .15 .06
❑ 383 Greg Minton .15 .06
❑ 384 Tom O'Malley .15 .06
❑ 385 Max Venable .15 .06
❑ 386 Brad Wellman .15 .06
❑ 387 Joel Youngblood .15 .06
❑ 388 Gary Allenson .15 .06
❑ 389 Luis Aponte .15 .06
❑ 390 Tony Armas .15 .06
❑ 391 Doug Bird .15 .06
❑ 392 Wade Boggs 4.00 1.60
❑ 393 Dennis Boyd .40 .16
❑ 394 Mike Brown UER P .15 .06
(shown with record
of 31-104)
❑ 395 Mark Clear .15 .06
❑ 396 Dennis Eckersley .75 .30
❑ 397 Dwight Evans .40 .16
❑ 398 Rich Gedman .15 .06
❑ 399 Glenn Hoffman .15 .06
❑ 400 Bruce Hurst .15 .06
❑ 401 John Henry Johnson .15 .06
❑ 402 Ed Jurak .15 .06
❑ 403 Rick Miller .15 .06
❑ 404 Jeff Newman .15 .06
❑ 405 Reid Nichols .15 .06
❑ 406 Bob Ojeda .15 .06
❑ 407 Jerry Remy .15 .06
❑ 408 Jim Rice .40 .16
❑ 409 Bob Stanley .15 .06
❑ 410 Dave Stapleton .15 .06
❑ 411 John Tudor .15 .06
❑ 412 Carl Yastrzemski 1.50 .60
❑ 413 Buddy Bell .40 .16
❑ 414 Larry Biittner .15 .06
❑ 415 John Butcher .15 .06
❑ 416 Danny Darwin .15 .06
❑ 417 Bucky Dent .40 .16
❑ 418 Dave Hostetler .15 .06
❑ 419 Charlie Hough .40 .16
❑ 420 Bobby Johnson .15 .06
❑ 421 Odell Jones .15 .06
❑ 422 Jon Matlack .15 .06
❑ 423 Pete O'Brien RC* .40 .16
❑ 424 Larry Parrish .15 .06
❑ 425 Mickey Rivers .15 .06
❑ 426 Billy Sample .15 .06
❑ 427 Dave Schmidt .15 .06
❑ 428 Mike Smithson .15 .06
❑ 429 Bill Stein .15 .06
❑ 430 Dave Stewart .40 .16
❑ 431 Jim Sundberg .40 .16
❑ 432 Frank Tanana .40 .16
❑ 433 Dave Tobik .15 .06
❑ 434 Wayne Tolleson .15 .06
❑ 435 George Wright .15 .06
❑ 436 Bill Almon .15 .06
❑ 437 Keith Atherton .15 .06
❑ 438 Dave Beard .15 .06
❑ 439 Tom Burgmeier .15 .06
❑ 440 Jeff Burroughs .15 .06
❑ 441 Chris Codiroli .15 .06
❑ 442 Tim Conroy .15 .06
❑ 443 Mike Davis .15 .06
❑ 444 Wayne Gross .15 .06
❑ 445 Garry Hancock .15 .06
❑ 446 Mike Heath .15 .06
❑ 447 Rickey Henderson 3.00 1.20
❑ 448 Donnie Hill .15 .06
❑ 449 Bob Kearney .15 .06
❑ 450 Bill Krueger RC .15 .06
❑ 451 Rick Langford .15 .06
❑ 452 Carney Lansford .40 .16
❑ 453 Dave Lopes .40 .16
❑ 454 Steve McCatty .15 .06
❑ 455 Dan Meyer .15 .06
❑ 456 Dwayne Murphy .15 .06
❑ 457 Mike Norris .15 .06
❑ 458 Ricky Peters .15 .06
❑ 459 Tony Phillips RC 1.50 .60
❑ 460 Tom Underwood .15 .06
❑ 461 Mike Warren .15 .06
❑ 462 Johnny Bench 1.50 .60
❑ 463 Bruce Berenyi .15 .06
❑ 464 Dann Bilardello .15 .06
❑ 465 Cesar Cedeno .40 .16
❑ 466 Dave Concepcion .40 .16
❑ 467 Dan Driessen .15 .06
❑ 468 Nick Esasky .15 .06
❑ 469 Rich Gale .15 .06
❑ 470 Ben Hayes .15 .06
❑ 471 Paul Householder .15 .06
❑ 472 Tom Hume .15 .06
❑ 473 Alan Knicely .15 .06
❑ 474 Eddie Milner .15 .06
❑ 475 Ron Oester .15 .06
❑ 476 Kelly Paris .15 .06
❑ 477 Frank Pastore .15 .06
❑ 478 Ted Power .15 .06
❑ 479 Joe Price .15 .06
❑ 480 Charlie Puleo .15 .06
❑ 481 Gary Redus RC* .15 .06
❑ 482 Bill Scherrer .15 .06
❑ 483 Mario Soto .15 .06
❑ 484 Alex Trevino .15 .06
❑ 485 Duane Walker .15 .06
❑ 486 Larry Bowa .40 .16
❑ 487 Warren Brusstar .15 .06
❑ 488 Bill Buckner .40 .16
❑ 489 Bill Campbell .15 .06
❑ 490 Ron Cey .40 .16
❑ 491 Jody Davis .15 .06
❑ 492 Leon Durham .15 .06
❑ 493 Mel Hall .40 .16
❑ 494 Ferguson Jenkins .40 .16
❑ 495 Jay Johnstone .40 .16
❑ 496 Craig Lefferts RC .15 .06
❑ 497 Carmelo Martinez .15 .06
❑ 498 Jerry Morales .15 .06
❑ 499 Keith Moreland .15 .06
❑ 500 Dickie Noles .15 .06
❑ 501 Mike Proly .15 .06
❑ 502 Chuck Rainey .15 .06
❑ 503 Dick Ruthven .15 .06
❑ 504 Ryne Sandberg 6.00 2.40
❑ 505 Lee Smith 1.50 .60
❑ 506 Steve Trout .15 .06
❑ 507 Gary Woods .15 .06
❑ 508 Juan Beniquez .15 .06
❑ 509 Bob Boone .40 .16
❑ 510 Rick Burleson .15 .06
❑ 511 Rod Carew .75 .30
❑ 512 Bobby Clark .15 .06
❑ 513 John Curtis .15 .06
❑ 514 Doug DeCinces .15 .06
❑ 515 Brian Downing .15 .06
❑ 516 Tim Foli .15 .06
❑ 517 Ken Forsch .15 .06
❑ 518 Bobby Grich .40 .16
❑ 519 Andy Hassler .15 .06
❑ 520 Reggie Jackson .75 .30
❑ 521 Ron Jackson .15 .06
❑ 522 Tommy John .75 .30
❑ 523 Bruce Kison .15 .06
❑ 524 Steve Lubratich .15 .06
❑ 525 Fred Lynn .40 .16
❑ 526 Gary Pettis .15 .06
❑ 527 Luis Sanchez .15 .06

❑ 528 Daryl Sconiers .15 .06
❑ 529 Ellis Valentine .15 .06
❑ 530 Rob Wilfong .15 .06
❑ 531 Mike Witt .15 .06
❑ 532 Geoff Zahn .15 .06
❑ 533 Bud Anderson .15 .06
❑ 534 Chris Bando .15 .06
❑ 535 Alan Bannister .15 .06
❑ 536 Bert Blyleven .40 .16
❑ 537 Tom Brennan .15 .06
❑ 538 Jamie Easterly .15 .06
❑ 539 Juan Eichelberger .15 .06
❑ 540 Jim Essian .15 .06
❑ 541 Mike Fischlin .15 .06
❑ 542 Julio Franco .75 .30
❑ 543 Mike Hargrove .40 .16
❑ 544 Toby Harrah .40 .16
❑ 545 Ron Hassey .15 .06
❑ 546 Neal Heaton .15 .06
❑ 547 Bake McBride .15 .06
❑ 548 Broderick Perkins .15 .06
❑ 549 Lary Sorensen .15 .06
❑ 550 Dan Spillner .15 .06
❑ 551 Rick Sutcliffe .40 .16
❑ 552 Pat Tabler .15 .06
❑ 553 Gorman Thomas .15 .06
❑ 554 Andre Thornton .15 .06
❑ 555 George Vukovich .15 .06
❑ 556 Darrell Brown .15 .06
❑ 557 Tom Brunansky .40 .16
❑ 558 Randy Bush .15 .06
❑ 559 Bobby Castillo .15 .06
❑ 560 John Castino .15 .06
❑ 561 Ron Davis .15 .06
❑ 562 Dave Engle .15 .06
❑ 563 Lenny Faedo .15 .06
❑ 564 Pete Filson .15 .06
❑ 565 Gary Gaetti .75 .30
❑ 566 Mickey Hatcher .15 .06
❑ 567 Kent Hrbek .40 .16
❑ 568 Rusty Kuntz .15 .06
❑ 569 Tim Laudner .15 .06
❑ 570 Rick Lysander .15 .06
❑ 571 Bobby Mitchell .15 .06
❑ 572 Ken Schrom .15 .06
❑ 573 Ray Smith .15 .06
❑ 574 Tim Teufel RC .15 .06
❑ 575 Frank Viola .75 .30
❑ 576 Gary Ward .15 .06
❑ 577 Ron Washington .15 .06
❑ 578 Len Whitehouse .15 .06
❑ 579 Al Williams .15 .06
❑ 580 Bob Bailor .15 .06
❑ 581 Mark Bradley .15 .06
❑ 582 Hubie Brooks .15 .06
❑ 583 Carlos Diaz .15 .06
❑ 584 George Foster .40 .16
❑ 585 Brian Giles .15 .06
❑ 586 Danny Heep .15 .06
❑ 587 Keith Hernandez .75 .30
❑ 588 Ron Hodges .15 .06
❑ 589 Scott Holman .15 .06
❑ 590 Dave Kingman .75 .30
❑ 591 Ed Lynch .15 .06
❑ 592 Jose Oquendo RC .40 .16
❑ 593 Jesse Orosco .15 .06
❑ 594 Junior Ortiz .15 .06
❑ 595 Tom Seaver 1.50 .60
❑ 596 Doug Sisk .15 .06
❑ 597 Rusty Staub .40 .16
❑ 598 John Stearns .15 .06
❑ 599 Darryl Strawberry RC 3.00 1.20
❑ 600 Craig Swan .15 .06
❑ 601 Walt Terrell .15 .06
❑ 602 Mike Torrez .15 .06
❑ 603 Mookie Wilson .40 .16
❑ 604 Jamie Allen .15 .06
❑ 605 Jim Beattie .15 .06
❑ 606 Tony Bernazard .15 .06
❑ 607 Manny Castillo .15 .06
❑ 608 Bill Caudill .15 .06
❑ 609 Bryan Clark .15 .06
❑ 610 Al Cowens .15 .06
❑ 611 Dave Henderson .40 .16
❑ 612 Steve Henderson .15 .06
❑ 613 Orlando Mercado .15 .06
❑ 614 Mike Moore .15 .06
❑ 615 Ricky Nelson UER .15 .06
(Jamie Nelson's
stats on back)
❑ 616 Spike Owen RC .40 .16
❑ 617 Pat Putnam .15 .06
❑ 618 Ron Roenicke .15 .06
❑ 619 Mike Stanton .15 .06
❑ 620 Bob Stoddard .15 .06
❑ 621 Rick Sweet .15 .06
❑ 622 Roy Thomas .15 .06
❑ 623 Ed VandeBerg .15 .06
❑ 624 Matt Young .15 .06
❑ 625 Richie Zisk .15 .06
❑ 626 Fred Lynn IA .40 .16
❑ 627 Manny Trillo IA .15 .06
❑ 628 Steve Garvey IA .15 .06
❑ 629 Rod Carew IA .40 .16
❑ 630 Wade Boggs IA 1.50 .60
❑ 631 Tim Raines IA .40 .16
❑ 632 Al Oliver IA .40 .16
❑ 633 Steve Sax IA .15 .06
❑ 634 Dickie Thon IA .15 .06
❑ 635 Dan Quisenberry .15 .06
Tippy Martinez
❑ 636 Joe Morgan 1.50 .60
Pete Rose
Tony Perez
❑ 637 Lance Parrish .75 .30
Bob Boone
❑ 638 George Brett 3.00 1.20
Gaylord Perry
❑ 639 Dave Righetti .75 .30
Mike Warren
Bob Forsch
❑ 640 Johnny Bench 1.50 .60
Carl Yastrzemski
❑ 641 Gaylord Perry IA .15 .06
❑ 642 Steve Carlton IA .40 .16
❑ 643 Joe Altobelli MG .15 .06
Paul Owens MG
❑ 644 Rick Dempsey WS .40 .16
❑ 645 Mike Boddicker WS .15 .06
❑ 646 Scott McGregor WS .15 .06
❑ 647 CL: Orioles/Royals .15 .06
Joe Altobelli MG
❑ 648 CL: Phillies/Giants .15 .06
Paul Owens MG
❑ 649 CL: White Sox/Red Sox .75 .30
Tony LaRussa MG
❑ 650 CL: Tigers/Rangers .75 .30
Sparky Anderson MG
❑ 651 CL: Dodgers/A's .75 .30
Tommy Lasorda MG
❑ 652 CL: Yankees/Reds .75 .30
Billy Martin MG
❑ 653 CL: Blue Jays/Cubs .40 .16
Bobby Cox MG
❑ 654 CL: Braves/Angels .75 .30
Joe Torre MG
❑ 655 CL: Brewers/Indians .15 .06
Rene Lachemann MG
❑ 656 CL: Astros/Twins .15 .06
Bob Lillis MG
❑ 657 CL: Pirates/Mets .15 .06
Chuck Tanner MG
❑ 658 CL: Expos/Mariners .15 .06
Bill Virdon MG
❑ 659 CL: Padres/Specials .40 .16
Dick Williams MG
❑ 660 CL: Cardinals/Teams .75 .30
Whitey Herzog MG

1984 Fleer Update

	Nm-Mt	Ex-Mt
COMP.FACT.SET (132)	300.00	120.00

❑ 1 Willie Aikens 1.00 .40
❑ 2 Luis Aponte 1.00 .40
❑ 3 Mark Bailey 1.00 .40
❑ 4 Bob Bailor 1.00 .40
❑ 5 Dusty Baker 1.50 .60
❑ 6 Steve Balboni 1.00 .40
❑ 7 Alan Bannister 1.00 .40
❑ 8 Marty Barrett 1.50 .60

❑ 9 Dave Beard 1.00 .40
❑ 10 Joe Beckwith 1.00 .40
❑ 11 Dave Bergman 1.00 .40
❑ 12 Tony Bernazard 1.00 .40
❑ 13 Bruce Bochte 1.00 .40
❑ 14 Barry Bonnell 1.00 .40
❑ 15 Phil Bradley 1.50 .60
❑ 16 Fred Breining 1.00 .40
❑ 17 Mike C. Brown 1.00 .40
❑ 18 Bill Buckner 1.50 .60
❑ 19 Ray Burris 1.00 .40
❑ 20 John Butcher 1.00 .40
❑ 21 Brett Butler 2.50 1.00
❑ 22 Enos Cabell 1.00 .40
❑ 23 Bill Campbell 1.00 .40
❑ 24 Bill Caudill 1.00 .40
❑ 25 Bobby Clark 1.00 .40
❑ 26 Bryan Clark 1.00 .40
❑ 27 Roger Clemens XRC 200.00 80.00
❑ 28 Jaime Cocanower 1.00 .40
❑ 29 Ron Darling XRC* 2.50 1.00
❑ 30 Alvin Davis XRC 1.50 .60
❑ 31 Bob Dernier 1.00 .40
❑ 32 Carlos Diaz 1.00 .40
❑ 33 Mike Easler 1.00 .40
❑ 34 Dennis Eckersley 2.50 1.00
❑ 35 Jim Essian 1.00 .40
❑ 36 Darrell Evans 1.50 .60
❑ 37 Mike Fitzgerald 1.00 .40
❑ 38 Tim Foli 1.00 .40
❑ 39 John Franco XRC 8.00 3.20
❑ 40 George Frazier 1.00 .40
❑ 41 Rich Gale 1.00 .40
❑ 42 Barbaro Garbey 1.00 .40
❑ 43 Dwight Gooden XRC 15.00 6.00
❑ 44 Rich Gossage 2.50 1.00
❑ 45 Wayne Gross 1.00 .40
❑ 46 Mark Gubicza XRC 1.50 .60
❑ 47 Jackie Gutierrez 1.00 .40
❑ 48 Toby Harrah 1.50 .60
❑ 49 Ron Hassey 1.00 .40
❑ 50 Richie Hebner 1.00 .40
❑ 51 Willie Hernandez 1.50 .60
❑ 52 Ed Hodge 1.00 .40
❑ 53 Ricky Horton 1.00 .40
❑ 54 Art Howe 1.50 .60
❑ 55 Dane Iorg 1.00 .40
❑ 56 Brook Jacoby 1.50 .60
❑ 57 Dion James XRC* 1.00 .40
❑ 58 Mike Jeffcoat 1.00 .40
❑ 59 Ruppert Jones 1.00 .40
❑ 60 Bob Kearney 1.00 .40
❑ 61 Jimmy Key XRC 2.50 1.00
❑ 62 Dave Kingman 2.50 1.00
❑ 63 Brad Komminsk 1.00 .40
❑ 64 Jerry Koosman 1.50 .60
❑ 65 Wayne Krenchicki 1.00 .40
❑ 66 Rusty Kuntz 1.00 .40
❑ 67 Frank LaCorte 1.00 .40
❑ 68 Dennis Lamp 1.00 .40
❑ 69 Tito Landrum 1.00 .40
❑ 70 Mark Langston XRC 4.00 1.60
❑ 71 Rick Leach 1.00 .40
❑ 72 Craig Lefferts 1.50 .60
❑ 73 Gary Lucas 1.00 .40
❑ 74 Jerry Martin 1.00 .40
❑ 75 Carmelo Martinez 1.00 .40
❑ 76 Mike Mason XRC 1.00 .40

	No.	Player	Nm-Mt	Ex-Mt
❑	77	Gary Matthews	1.50	.60
❑	78	Andy McGaffigan	1.00	.40
❑	79	Joey McLaughlin	1.00	.40
❑	80	Joe Morgan	2.50	1.00
❑	81	Darryl Motley	1.00	.40
❑	82	Graig Nettles	1.50	.60
❑	83	Phil Niekro	1.50	.60
❑	84	Ken Oberkfell	1.00	.40
❑	85	Al Oliver	1.50	.60
❑	86	Jorge Orta	1.00	.40
❑	87	Amos Otis	1.50	.60
❑	88	Bob Owchinko	1.00	.40
❑	89	Dave Parker	1.50	.60
❑	90	Jack Perconte	1.00	.40
❑	91	Tony Perez	2.50	1.00
❑	92	Gerald Perry	1.50	.60
❑	93	Kirby Puckett XRC	80.00	32.00
❑	94	Shane Rawley	1.00	.40
❑	95	Floyd Rayford	1.00	.40
❑	96	Ron Reed	1.00	.40
❑	97	R.J. Reynolds	1.00	.40
❑	98	Gene Richards	1.00	.40
❑	99	Jose Rijo XRC	4.00	1.60
❑	100	Jeff D. Robinson	1.00	.40
❑	101	Ron Romanick	1.00	.40
❑	102	Pete Rose	12.00	4.80
❑	103	Bret Saberhagen XRC	10.00	4.00
❑	104	Scott Sanderson	1.00	.40
❑	105	Dick Schofield XRC*	1.50	.60
❑	106	Tom Seaver	4.00	1.60
❑	107	Jim Slaton	1.00	.40
❑	108	Mike Smithson	1.00	.40
❑	109	Lary Sorensen	1.00	.40
❑	110	Tim Stoddard	1.00	.40
❑	111	Jeff Stone	1.00	.40
❑	112	Champ Summers	1.00	.40
❑	113	Jim Sundberg	1.50	.60
❑	114	Rick Sutcliffe	1.50	.60
❑	115	Craig Swan	1.00	.40
❑	116	Derrel Thomas	1.00	.40
❑	117	Gorman Thomas	1.00	.40
❑	118	Alex Trevino	1.00	.40
❑	119	Manny Trillo	1.00	.40
❑	120	John Tudor	1.00	.40
❑	121	Tom Underwood	1.00	.40
❑	122	Mike Vail	1.00	.40
❑	123	Tom Waddell	1.00	.40
❑	124	Gary Ward	1.00	.40
❑	125	Terry Whitfield	1.00	.40
❑	126	Curtis Wilkerson	1.00	.40
❑	127	Frank Williams	1.00	.40
❑	128	Glenn Wilson	1.00	.40
❑	129	John Wockenfuss	1.00	.40
❑	130	Ned Yost	1.00	.40
❑	131	Mike Young RC	1.00	.40
❑	132	Checklist 1-132	1.00	.40

1985 Fleer

	Nm-Mt	Ex-Mt
COMPLETE SET (660)	80.00	32.00

	No.	Player	Nm-Mt	Ex-Mt
❑	1	Doug Bair	.15	.06
❑	2	Juan Berenguer	.15	.06
❑	3	Dave Bergman	.15	.06
❑	4	Tom Brookens	.15	.06
❑	5	Marty Castillo	.15	.06
❑	6	Darrell Evans	.40	.16
❑	7	Barbaro Garbey	.15	.06
❑	8	Kirk Gibson	.40	.16
❑	9	John Grubb	.15	.06
❑	10	Willie Hernandez	.15	.06
❑	11	Larry Herndon	.15	.06
❑	12	Howard Johnson	.40	.16
❑	13	Ruppert Jones	.15	.06
❑	14	Rusty Kuntz	.15	.06
❑	15	Chet Lemon	.15	.06
❑	16	Aurelio Lopez	.15	.06
❑	17	Sid Monge	.15	.06
❑	18	Jack Morris	.40	.16
❑	19	Lance Parrish	.40	.16
❑	20	Dan Petry	.15	.06
❑	21	Dave Rozema	.15	.06
❑	22	Bill Scherrer	.15	.06
❑	23	Alan Trammell	.75	.30
❑	24	Lou Whitaker	.75	.30
❑	25	Milt Wilcox	.15	.06
❑	26	Kurt Bevacqua	.15	.06
❑	27	Greg Booker	.15	.06
❑	28	Bobby Brown	.15	.06
❑	29	Luis DeLeon	.15	.06
❑	30	Dave Dravecky	.40	.16
❑	31	Tim Flannery	.15	.06
❑	32	Steve Garvey	.40	.16
❑	33	Rich Gossage	.40	.16
❑	34	Tony Gwynn	2.50	1.00
❑	35	Greg Harris	.15	.06
❑	36	Andy Hawkins	.15	.06
❑	37	Terry Kennedy	.15	.06
❑	38	Craig Lefferts	.15	.06
❑	39	Tim Lollar	.15	.06
❑	40	Carmelo Martinez	.15	.06
❑	41	Kevin McReynolds	.40	.16
❑	42	Graig Nettles	.40	.16
❑	43	Luis Salazar	.15	.06
❑	44	Eric Show	.15	.06
❑	45	Garry Templeton	.15	.06
❑	46	Mark Thurmond	.15	.06
❑	47	Ed Whitson	.15	.06
❑	48	Alan Wiggins	.15	.06
❑	49	Rich Bordi	.15	.06
❑	50	Larry Bowa	.40	.16
❑	51	Warren Brusstar	.15	.06
❑	52	Ron Cey	.40	.16
❑	53	Henry Cotto RC	.15	.06
❑	54	Jody Davis	.15	.06
❑	55	Bob Dernier	.15	.06
❑	56	Leon Durham	.15	.06
❑	57	Dennis Eckersley	.75	.30
❑	58	George Frazier	.15	.06
❑	59	Richie Hebner	.15	.06
❑	60	Dave Lopes	.40	.16
❑	61	Gary Matthews	.15	.06
❑	62	Keith Moreland	.15	.06
❑	63	Rick Reuschel	.15	.06
❑	64	Dick Ruthven	.15	.06
❑	65	Ryne Sandberg	2.50	1.00
❑	66	Scott Sanderson	.15	.06
❑	67	Lee Smith	.75	.30
❑	68	Tim Stoddard	.15	.06
❑	69	Rick Sutcliffe	.40	.16
❑	70	Steve Trout	.15	.06
❑	71	Gary Woods	.15	.06
❑	72	Wally Backman	.15	.06
❑	73	Bruce Berenyi	.15	.06
❑	74	Hubie Brooks UER (Kelvin Chapman's stats on card back)	.15	.06
❑	75	Kelvin Chapman	.15	.06
❑	76	Ron Darling	.40	.16
❑	77	Sid Fernandez	.40	.16
❑	78	Mike Fitzgerald	.15	.06
❑	79	George Foster	.40	.16
❑	80	Brent Gaff	.15	.06
❑	81	Ron Gardenhire	.15	.06
❑	82	Dwight Gooden RC	2.00	.80
❑	83	Tom Gorman	.15	.06
❑	84	Danny Heep	.15	.06
❑	85	Keith Hernandez	.75	.30
❑	86	Ray Knight	.15	.06
❑	87	Ed Lynch	.15	.06
❑	88	Jose Oquendo	.15	.06
❑	89	Jesse Orosco	.15	.06
❑	90	Rafael Santana	.15	.06
❑	91	Doug Sisk	.15	.06
❑	92	Rusty Staub	.40	.16
❑	93	Darryl Strawberry	1.25	.50
❑	94	Walt Terrell	.15	.06
❑	95	Mookie Wilson	.40	.16
❑	96	Jim Acker	.15	.06
❑	97	Willie Aikens	.15	.06
❑	98	Doyle Alexander	.15	.06
❑	99	Jesse Barfield	.15	.06
❑	100	George Bell	.40	.16
❑	101	Jim Clancy	.15	.06
❑	102	Dave Collins	.15	.06
❑	103	Tony Fernandez	.40	.16
❑	104	Damaso Garcia	.15	.06
❑	105	Jim Gott	.15	.06
❑	106	Alfredo Griffin	.15	.06
❑	107	Garth Iorg	.15	.06
❑	108	Roy Lee Jackson	.15	.06
❑	109	Cliff Johnson	.15	.06
❑	110	Jimmy Key RC	1.25	.50
❑	111	Dennis Lamp	.15	.06
❑	112	Rick Leach	.15	.06
❑	113	Luis Leal	.15	.06
❑	114	Buck Martinez	.15	.06
❑	115	Lloyd Moseby	.15	.06
❑	116	Rance Mulliniks	.15	.06
❑	117	Dave Stieb	.40	.16
❑	118	Willie Upshaw	.15	.06
❑	119	Ernie Whitt	.15	.06
❑	120	Mike Armstrong	.15	.06
❑	121	Don Baylor	.40	.16
❑	122	Marty Bystrom	.15	.06
❑	123	Rick Cerone	.15	.06
❑	124	Joe Cowley	.15	.06
❑	125	Brian Dayett	.15	.06
❑	126	Tim Foli	.15	.06
❑	127	Ray Fontenot	.15	.06
❑	128	Ken Griffey	.40	.16
❑	129	Ron Guidry	.40	.16
❑	130	Toby Harrah	.15	.06
❑	131	Jay Howell	.15	.06
❑	132	Steve Kemp	.15	.06
❑	133	Don Mattingly	5.00	2.00
❑	134	Bobby Meacham	.15	.06
❑	135	John Montefusco	.15	.06
❑	136	Omar Moreno	.15	.06
❑	137	Dale Murray	.15	.06
❑	138	Phil Niekro	.40	.16
❑	139	Mike Pagliarulo	.15	.06
❑	140	Willie Randolph	.40	.16
❑	141	Dennis Rasmussen	.15	.06
❑	142	Dave Righetti	.40	.16
❑	143	Jose Rijo RC	.75	.30
❑	144	Andre Robertson	.15	.06
❑	145	Bob Shirley	.15	.06
❑	146	Dave Winfield	.75	.30
❑	147	Butch Wynegar	.15	.06
❑	148	Gary Allenson	.15	.06
❑	149	Tony Armas	.15	.06
❑	150	Marty Barrett	.15	.06
❑	151	Wade Boggs	1.50	.60
❑	152	Dennis Boyd	.15	.06
❑	153	Bill Buckner	.40	.16
❑	154	Mark Clear	.15	.06
❑	155	Roger Clemens RC	40.00	16.00
❑	156	Steve Crawford	.15	.06
❑	157	Mike Easler	.15	.06
❑	158	Dwight Evans	.40	.16
❑	159	Rich Gedman	.15	.06
❑	160	Jackie Gutierrez (Wade Boggs shown on deck)	.40	.16
❑	161	Bruce Hurst	.15	.06
❑	162	John Henry Johnson	.15	.06
❑	163	Rick Miller	.15	.06
❑	164	Reid Nichols	.15	.06
❑	165	Al Nipper	.15	.06
❑	166	Bob Ojeda	.15	.06
❑	167	Jerry Remy	.15	.06
❑	168	Jim Rice	.40	.16
❑	169	Bob Stanley	.15	.06
❑	170	Mike Boddicker	.15	.06
❑	171	Al Bumbry	.15	.06
❑	172	Todd Cruz	.15	.06
❑	173	Rich Dauer	.15	.06
❑	174	Storm Davis	.15	.06

❑ 175 Rick Dempsey .15 .06
❑ 176 Jim Dwyer .15 .06
❑ 177 Mike Flanagan .15 .06
❑ 178 Dan Ford .15 .06
❑ 179 Wayne Gross .15 .06
❑ 180 John Lowenstein .15 .06
❑ 181 Dennis Martinez .40 .16
❑ 182 Tippy Martinez .15 .06
❑ 183 Scott McGregor .15 .06
❑ 184 Eddie Murray 1.25 .50
❑ 185 Joe Nolan .15 .06
❑ 186 Floyd Rayford .15 .06
❑ 187 Cal Ripken 5.00 2.00
❑ 188 Gary Roenicke .15 .06
❑ 189 Lenn Sakata .15 .06
❑ 190 John Shelby .15 .06
❑ 191 Ken Singleton .15 .06
❑ 192 Sammy Stewart .15 .06
❑ 193 Bill Swaggerty .15 .06
❑ 194 Tom Underwood .15 .06
❑ 195 Mike Young .15 .06
❑ 196 Steve Balboni .15 .06
❑ 197 Joe Beckwith .15 .06
❑ 198 Bud Black .15 .06
❑ 199 George Brett 4.00 1.60
❑ 200 Onix Concepcion .15 .06
❑ 201 Mark Gubicza RC* .40 .16
❑ 202 Larry Gura .15 .06
❑ 203 Mark Huismann .15 .06
❑ 204 Dane Iorg .15 .06
❑ 205 Danny Jackson .15 .06
❑ 206 Charlie Leibrandt .15 .06
❑ 207 Hal McRae .40 .16
❑ 208 Darryl Motley .15 .06
❑ 209 Jorge Orta .15 .06
❑ 210 Greg Pryor .15 .06
❑ 211 Dan Quisenberry .40 .16
❑ 212 Bret Saberhagen RC 1.25 .50
❑ 213 Pat Sheridan .15 .06
❑ 214 Don Slaught .15 .06
❑ 215 U.L. Washington .15 .06
❑ 216 John Wathan .15 .06
❑ 217 Frank White .40 .16
❑ 218 Willie Wilson .15 .06
❑ 219 Neil Allen .15 .06
❑ 220 Joaquin Andujar .15 .06
❑ 221 Steve Braun .15 .06
❑ 222 Danny Cox .15 .06
❑ 223 Bob Forsch .15 .06
❑ 224 David Green .15 .06
❑ 225 George Hendrick .15 .06
❑ 226 Tom Herr .15 .06
❑ 227 Ricky Horton .15 .06
❑ 228 Art Howe .15 .06
❑ 229 Mike Jorgensen .15 .06
❑ 230 Kurt Kepshire .15 .06
❑ 231 Jeff Lahti .15 .06
❑ 232 Tito Landrum .15 .06
❑ 233 Dave LaPoint .15 .06
❑ 234 Willie McGee .40 .16
❑ 235 Tom Nieto .15 .06
❑ 236 Terry Pendleton RC 1.25 .50
❑ 237 Darrell Porter .15 .06
❑ 238 Dave Rucker .15 .06
❑ 239 Lonnie Smith .15 .06
❑ 240 Ozzie Smith 1.25 .50
❑ 241 Bruce Sutter .40 .16
❑ 242 Andy Van Slyke UER .40 .16
(Bats Right, Throws Left)
❑ 243 Dave Von Ohlen .15 .06
❑ 244 Larry Andersen .15 .06
❑ 245 Bill Campbell .15 .06
❑ 246 Steve Carlton .75 .30
❑ 247 Tim Corcoran .15 .06
❑ 248 Ivan DeJesus .15 .06
❑ 249 John Denny .15 .06
❑ 250 Bo Diaz .15 .06
❑ 251 Greg Gross .15 .06
❑ 252 Kevin Gross .15 .06
❑ 253 Von Hayes .15 .06
❑ 254 Al Holland .15 .06
❑ 255 Charles Hudson .15 .06
❑ 256 Jerry Koosman .40 .16
❑ 257 Joe Lefebvre .15 .06
❑ 258 Sixto Lezcano .15 .06
❑ 259 Garry Maddox .15 .06
❑ 260 Len Matuszek .15 .06
❑ 261 Tug McGraw .40 .16
❑ 262 Al Oliver .40 .16
❑ 263 Shane Rawley .15 .06
❑ 264 Juan Samuel .15 .06
❑ 265 Mike Schmidt 3.00 1.20
❑ 266 Jeff Stone .15 .06
❑ 267 Ozzie Virgil .15 .06
❑ 268 Glenn Wilson .15 .06
❑ 269 John Wockenfuss .15 .06
❑ 270 Darrell Brown .15 .06
❑ 271 Tom Brunansky .40 .16
❑ 272 Randy Bush .15 .06
❑ 273 John Butcher .15 .06
❑ 274 Bobby Castillo .15 .06
❑ 275 Ron Davis .15 .06
❑ 276 Dave Engle .15 .06
❑ 277 Pete Filson .15 .06
❑ 278 Gary Gaetti .40 .16
❑ 279 Mickey Hatcher .15 .06
❑ 280 Ed Hodge .15 .06
❑ 281 Kent Hrbek .40 .16
❑ 282 Houston Jimenez .15 .06
❑ 283 Tim Laudner .15 .06
❑ 284 Rick Lysander .15 .06
❑ 285 Dave Meier .15 .06
❑ 286 Kirby Puckett RC 15.00 6.00
❑ 287 Pat Putnam .15 .06
❑ 288 Ken Schrom .15 .06
❑ 289 Mike Smithson .15 .06
❑ 290 Tim Teufel .15 .06
❑ 291 Frank Viola .40 .16
❑ 292 Ron Washington .15 .06
❑ 293 Don Aase .15 .06
❑ 294 Juan Beniquez .15 .06
❑ 295 Bob Boone .40 .16
❑ 296 Mike C. Brown .15 .06
❑ 297 Rod Carew .75 .30
❑ 298 Doug Corbett .15 .06
❑ 299 Doug DeCinces .15 .06
❑ 300 Brian Downing .15 .06
❑ 301 Ken Forsch .15 .06
❑ 302 Bobby Grich .40 .16
❑ 303 Reggie Jackson .75 .30
❑ 304 Tommy John .75 .30
❑ 305 Curt Kaufman .15 .06
❑ 306 Bruce Kison .15 .06
❑ 307 Fred Lynn .40 .16
❑ 308 Gary Pettis .15 .06
❑ 309 Ron Romanick .15 .06
❑ 310 Luis Sanchez .15 .06
❑ 311 Dick Schofield .15 .06
❑ 312 Daryl Sconiers .15 .06
❑ 313 Jim Slaton .15 .06
❑ 314 Derrel Thomas .15 .06
❑ 315 Rob Wilfong .15 .06
❑ 316 Mike Witt .15 .06
❑ 317 Geoff Zahn .15 .06
❑ 318 Len Barker .15 .06
❑ 319 Steve Bedrosian .15 .06
❑ 320 Bruce Benedict .15 .06
❑ 321 Rick Camp .15 .06
❑ 322 Chris Chambliss .40 .16
❑ 323 Jeff Dedmon .15 .06
❑ 324 Terry Forster .15 .06
❑ 325 Gene Garber .15 .06
❑ 326 Albert Hall .15 .06
❑ 327 Terry Harper .15 .06
❑ 328 Bob Horner .15 .06
❑ 329 Glenn Hubbard .15 .06
❑ 330 Randy Johnson .15 .06
❑ 331 Brad Komminsk .15 .06
❑ 332 Rick Mahler .15 .06
❑ 333 Craig McMurtry .15 .06
❑ 334 Donnie Moore .15 .06
❑ 335 Dale Murphy 1.25 .50
❑ 336 Ken Oberkfell .15 .06
❑ 337 Pascual Perez .15 .06
❑ 338 Gerald Perry .15 .06
❑ 339 Rafael Ramirez .15 .06
❑ 340 Jerry Royster .15 .06
❑ 341 Alex Trevino .15 .06
❑ 342 Claudell Washington .15 .06
❑ 343 Alan Ashby .15 .06
❑ 344 Mark Bailey .15 .06
❑ 345 Kevin Bass .15 .06
❑ 346 Enos Cabell .15 .06
❑ 347 Jose Cruz .40 .16
❑ 348 Bill Dawley .15 .06
❑ 349 Frank DiPino .15 .06
❑ 350 Bill Doran .15 .06
❑ 351 Phil Garner .40 .16
❑ 352 Bob Knepper .15 .06
❑ 353 Mike LaCoss .15 .06
❑ 354 Jerry Mumphrey .15 .06
❑ 355 Joe Niekro .15 .06
❑ 356 Terry Puhl .15 .06
❑ 357 Craig Reynolds .15 .06
❑ 358 Vern Ruhle .15 .06
❑ 359 Nolan Ryan 6.00 2.40
❑ 360 Joe Sambito .15 .06
❑ 361 Mike Scott .15 .06
❑ 362 Dave Smith .15 .06
❑ 363 Julio Solano .15 .06
❑ 364 Dickie Thon .15 .06
❑ 365 Denny Walling .15 .06
❑ 366 Dave Anderson .15 .06
❑ 367 Bob Bailor .15 .06
❑ 368 Greg Brock .15 .06
❑ 369 Carlos Diaz .15 .06
❑ 370 Pedro Guerrero .40 .16
❑ 371 Orel Hershiser RC 2.00 .80
❑ 372 Rick Honeycutt .15 .06
❑ 373 Burt Hooton .15 .06
❑ 374 Ken Howell .15 .06
❑ 375 Ken Landreaux .15 .06
❑ 376 Candy Maldonado .15 .06
❑ 377 Mike Marshall .15 .06
❑ 378 Tom Niedenfuer .15 .06
❑ 379 Alejandro Pena .15 .06
❑ 380 Jerry Reuss UER .15 .06
("Home:" omitted)
❑ 381 R.J. Reynolds .15 .06
❑ 382 German Rivera .15 .06
❑ 383 Bill Russell .15 .06
❑ 384 Steve Sax .15 .06
❑ 385 Mike Scioscia .15 .06
❑ 386 Franklin Stubbs .15 .06
❑ 387 Fernando Valenzuela .40 .16
❑ 388 Bob Welch .15 .06
❑ 389 Terry Whitfield .15 .06
❑ 390 Steve Yeager .15 .06
❑ 391 Pat Zachry .15 .06
❑ 392 Fred Breining .15 .06
❑ 393 Gary Carter .75 .30
❑ 394 Andre Dawson .40 .16
❑ 395 Miguel Dilone .15 .06
❑ 396 Dan Driessen .15 .06
❑ 397 Doug Flynn .15 .06
❑ 398 Terry Francona .15 .06
❑ 399 Bill Gullickson .15 .06
❑ 400 Bob James .15 .06
❑ 401 Charlie Lea .15 .06
❑ 402 Bryan Little .15 .06
❑ 403 Gary Lucas .15 .06
❑ 404 David Palmer .15 .06
❑ 405 Tim Raines .40 .16
❑ 406 Mike Ramsey .15 .06
❑ 407 Jeff Reardon .40 .16
❑ 408 Steve Rogers .15 .06
❑ 409 Dan Schatzeder .15 .06
❑ 410 Bryn Smith .15 .06
❑ 411 Mike Stenhouse .15 .06
❑ 412 Tim Wallach .40 .16
❑ 413 Jim Wohlford .15 .06
❑ 414 Bill Almon .15 .06
❑ 415 Keith Atherton .15 .06
❑ 416 Bruce Bochte .15 .06
❑ 417 Tom Burgmeier .15 .06
❑ 418 Ray Burris .15 .06
❑ 419 Bill Caudill .15 .06
❑ 420 Chris Codiroli .15 .06
❑ 421 Tim Conroy .15 .06
❑ 422 Mike Davis .15 .06
❑ 423 Jim Essian .15 .06
❑ 424 Mike Heath .15 .06
❑ 425 Rickey Henderson 2.50 1.00
❑ 426 Donnie Hill .15 .06
❑ 427 Dave Kingman .40 .16
❑ 428 Bill Krueger .15 .06
❑ 429 Carney Lansford .40 .16

❑ 430 Steve McCatty .15 .06
❑ 431 Joe Morgan .75 .30
❑ 432 Dwayne Murphy .15 .06
❑ 433 Tony Phillips .15 .06
❑ 434 Lary Sorensen .15 .06
❑ 435 Mike Warren .15 .06
❑ 436 Curt Young .15 .06
❑ 437 Luis Aponte .15 .06
❑ 438 Chris Bando .15 .06
❑ 439 Tony Bernazard .15 .06
❑ 440 Bert Blyleven .40 .16
❑ 441 Brett Butler .40 .16
❑ 442 Ernie Camacho .15 .06
❑ 443 Joe Carter 1.25 .50
❑ 444 Carmelo Castillo .15 .06
❑ 445 Jamie Easterly .15 .06
❑ 446 Steve Farr RC .40 .16
❑ 447 Mike Fischlin .15 .06
❑ 448 Julio Franco .75 .30
❑ 449 Mel Hall .15 .06
❑ 450 Mike Hargrove .40 .16
❑ 451 Neal Heaton .15 .06
❑ 452 Brook Jacoby .15 .06
❑ 453 Mike Jeffcoat .15 .06
❑ 454 Don Schulze .15 .06
❑ 455 Roy Smith .15 .06
❑ 456 Pat Tabler .15 .06
❑ 457 Andre Thornton .15 .06
❑ 458 George Vukovich .15 .06
❑ 459 Tom Waddell .15 .06
❑ 460 Jerry Willard .15 .06
❑ 461 Dale Berra .15 .06
❑ 462 John Candelaria .15 .06
❑ 463 Jose DeLeon .15 .06
❑ 464 Doug Frobel .15 .06
❑ 465 Cecilio Guante .15 .06
❑ 466 Brian Harper .15 .06
❑ 467 Lee Lacy .15 .06
❑ 468 Bill Madlock .40 .16
❑ 469 Lee Mazzilli .15 .06
❑ 470 Larry McWilliams .15 .06
❑ 471 Jim Morrison .15 .06
❑ 472 Tony Pena .15 .06
❑ 473 Johnny Ray .15 .06
❑ 474 Rick Rhoden .15 .06
❑ 475 Don Robinson .15 .06
❑ 476 Rod Scurry .15 .06
❑ 477 Kent Tekulve .15 .06
❑ 478 Jason Thompson .15 .06
❑ 479 John Tudor .15 .06
❑ 480 Lee Tunnell .15 .06
❑ 481 Marvell Wynne .15 .06
❑ 482 Salome Barojas .15 .06
❑ 483 Dave Beard .15 .06
❑ 484 Jim Beattie .15 .06
❑ 485 Barry Bonnell .15 .06
❑ 486 Phil Bradley .40 .16
❑ 487 Al Cowens .15 .06
❑ 488 Alvin Davis RC* .40 .16
❑ 489 Dave Henderson .15 .06
❑ 490 Steve Henderson .15 .06
❑ 491 Bob Kearney .15 .06
❑ 492 Mark Langston RC .75 .30
❑ 493 Larry Milbourne .15 .06
❑ 494 Paul Mirabella .15 .06
❑ 495 Mike Moore .15 .06
❑ 496 Edwin Nunez .15 .06
❑ 497 Spike Owen .15 .06
❑ 498 Jack Perconte .15 .06
❑ 499 Ken Phelps .15 .06
❑ 500 Jim Presley .40 .16
❑ 501 Mike Stanton .15 .06
❑ 502 Bob Stoddard .15 .06
❑ 503 Gorman Thomas .15 .06
❑ 504 Ed VandeBerg .15 .06
❑ 505 Matt Young .15 .06
❑ 506 Juan Agosto .15 .06
❑ 507 Harold Baines .40 .16
❑ 508 Floyd Bannister .15 .06
❑ 509 Britt Burns .15 .06
❑ 510 Julio Cruz .15 .06
❑ 511 Richard Dotson .15 .06
❑ 512 Jerry Dybzinski .15 .06
❑ 513 Carlton Fisk .75 .30
❑ 514 Scott Fletcher .15 .06
❑ 515 Jerry Hairston .15 .06
❑ 516 Marc Hill .15 .06
❑ 517 LaMarr Hoyt .15 .06
❑ 518 Ron Kittle .15 .06
❑ 519 Rudy Law .15 .06
❑ 520 Vance Law .15 .06
❑ 521 Greg Luzinski .40 .16
❑ 522 Gene Nelson .15 .06
❑ 523 Tom Paciorek .40 .16
❑ 524 Ron Reed .15 .06
❑ 525 Bert Roberge .15 .06
❑ 526 Tom Seaver 1.25 .50
❑ 527 Roy Smalley .15 .06
❑ 528 Dan Spillner .15 .06
❑ 529 Mike Squires .15 .06
❑ 530 Greg Walker .15 .06
❑ 531 Cesar Cedeno .40 .16
❑ 532 Dave Concepcion .40 .16
❑ 533 Eric Davis RC 2.00 .80
❑ 534 Nick Esasky .15 .06
❑ 535 Tom Foley .15 .06
❑ 536 John Franco RC UER 1.25 .50
(Koufax misspelled as Kofax on back)
❑ 537 Brad Gulden .15 .06
❑ 538 Tom Hume .15 .06
❑ 539 Wayne Krenchicki .15 .06
❑ 540 Andy McGaffigan .15 .06
❑ 541 Eddie Milner .15 .06
❑ 542 Ron Oester .15 .06
❑ 543 Bob Owchinko .15 .06
❑ 544 Dave Parker .40 .16
❑ 545 Frank Pastore .15 .06
❑ 546 Tony Perez .75 .30
❑ 547 Ted Power .15 .06
❑ 548 Joe Price .15 .06
❑ 549 Gary Redus .15 .06
❑ 550 Pete Rose 4.00 1.60
❑ 551 Jeff Russell .15 .06
❑ 552 Mario Soto .15 .06
❑ 553 Jay Tibbs .15 .06
❑ 554 Duane Walker .15 .06
❑ 555 Alan Bannister .15 .06
❑ 556 Buddy Bell .40 .16
❑ 557 Danny Darwin .15 .06
❑ 558 Charlie Hough .40 .16
❑ 559 Bobby Jones .15 .06
❑ 560 Odell Jones .15 .06
❑ 561 Jeff Kunkel .15 .06
❑ 562 Mike Mason RC .15 .06
❑ 563 Pete O'Brien .15 .06
❑ 564 Larry Parrish .15 .06
❑ 565 Mickey Rivers .15 .06
❑ 566 Billy Sample .15 .06
❑ 567 Dave Schmidt .15 .06
❑ 568 Donnie Scott .15 .06
❑ 569 Dave Stewart .40 .16
❑ 570 Frank Tanana .15 .06
❑ 571 Wayne Tolleson .15 .06
❑ 572 Gary Ward .15 .06
❑ 573 Curtis Wilkerson .15 .06
❑ 574 George Wright .15 .06
❑ 575 Ned Yost .15 .06
❑ 576 Mark Brouhard .15 .06
❑ 577 Mike Caldwell .15 .06
❑ 578 Bobby Clark .15 .06
❑ 579 Jaime Cocanower .15 .06
❑ 580 Cecil Cooper .40 .16
❑ 581 Rollie Fingers .40 .16
❑ 582 Jim Gantner .15 .06
❑ 583 Moose Haas .15 .06
❑ 584 Dion James .15 .06
❑ 585 Pete Ladd .15 .06
❑ 586 Rick Manning .15 .06
❑ 587 Bob McClure .15 .06
❑ 588 Paul Molitor .75 .30
❑ 589 Charlie Moore .15 .06
❑ 590 Ben Oglivie .15 .06
❑ 591 Chuck Porter .15 .06
❑ 592 Randy Ready RC* .15 .06
❑ 593 Ed Romero .15 .06
❑ 594 Bill Schroeder .15 .06
❑ 595 Ray Searage .15 .06
❑ 596 Ted Simmons .40 .16
❑ 597 Jim Sundberg .15 .06
❑ 598 Don Sutton 1.25 .50
❑ 599 Tom Tellmann .15 .06
❑ 600 Rick Waits .15 .06
❑ 601 Robin Yount 1.25 .50
❑ 602 Dusty Baker .40 .16
❑ 603 Bob Brenly .15 .06
❑ 604 Jack Clark .40 .16
❑ 605 Chili Davis .40 .16
❑ 606 Mark Davis .15 .06
❑ 607 Dan Gladden RC .40 .16
❑ 608 Atlee Hammaker .15 .06
❑ 609 Mike Krukow .15 .06
❑ 610 Duane Kuiper .15 .06
❑ 611 Bob Lacey .15 .06
❑ 612 Bill Laskey .15 .06
❑ 613 Gary Lavelle .15 .06
❑ 614 Johnnie LeMaster .15 .06
❑ 615 Jeff Leonard .15 .06
❑ 616 Randy Lerch .15 .06
❑ 617 Greg Minton .15 .06
❑ 618 Steve Nicosia .15 .06
❑ 619 Gene Richards .15 .06
❑ 620 Jeff D. Robinson .15 .06
❑ 621 Scot Thompson .15 .06
❑ 622 Manny Trillo .15 .06
❑ 623 Brad Wellman .15 .06
❑ 624 Frank Williams .15 .06
❑ 625 Joel Youngblood .15 .06
❑ 626 Cal Ripken IA 3.00 1.20
❑ 627 Mike Schmidt IA 1.25 .50
❑ 628 Sparky Anderson IA .40 .16
❑ 629 Dave Winfield .75 .30
Rickey Henderson
❑ 630 Mike Schmidt 2.00 .80
Ryne Sandberg
❑ 631 Darryl Strawberry .75 .30
Gary Carter
Steve Garvey
Ozzie Smith
❑ 632 Gary Carter .40 .16
Charlie Lea
❑ 633 Steve Garvey .40 .16
Rich Gossage
❑ 634 Dwight Gooden 1.25 .50
Juan Samuel
❑ 635 Willie Upshaw IA .15 .06
❑ 636 Lloyd Moseby IA .15 .06
❑ 637 HOLLAND: Al Holland .15 .06
❑ 638 TUNNELL .15 .06
Lee Tunnell
❑ 639 Reggie Jackson IA .75 .30
❑ 640 4000th Hit IA 1.25 .50
❑ 641 Cal Ripken Jr. 3.00 1.20
Cal Ripken Sr.
❑ 642 Cubs Division Champs .40 .16
❑ 643 Two Perfect Games .40 .16
and One No-Hitter:
Mike Witt
David Palmer
Jack Morris
❑ 644 Willie Lozado and .15 .06
Vic Mata
❑ 645 Kelly Gruber RC and .40 .16
Randy O'Neal
❑ 646 Jose Roman and .15 .06
Joel Skinner
❑ 647 Steve Kiefer RC and 1.25 .50
Danny Tartabull
❑ 648 Rob Dee RC and .40 .16
Alejandro Sanchez
❑ 649 Billy Hatcher RC and .75 .30
Shawon Dunston
❑ 650 Ron Robinson and .15 .06
Mike Bielecki
❑ 651 Zane Smith RC and .40 .16
Paul Zuvella
❑ 652 Joe Hesketh RC and .40 .16
Glenn Davis
❑ 653 John Russell and .15 .06
Steve Jeltz
❑ 654 CL: Tigers/Padres .15 .06
and Cubs/Mets
❑ 655 CL: Blue Jays/Yankees .15 .06
and Red Sox/Orioles
❑ 656 CL: Royals/Cardinals .15 .06
and Phillies/Twins
❑ 657 CL: Angels/Braves .15 .06
and Astros/Dodgers

	Card	Nm-Mt	Ex-Mt
❑	658 CL: Expos/A's and Indians/Pirates	.15	.06
❑	659 CL: Mariners/White Sox and Reds/Rangers	.15	.06
❑	660 CL: Brewers/Giants and Special Cards	.15	.06

1986 Fleer

	Nm-Mt	Ex-Mt
COMPLETE SET (660)	40.00	16.00
COMP.FACT.SET (660)	40.00	16.00

	Card	Nm-Mt	Ex-Mt
❑	1 Steve Balboni	.15	.06
❑	2 Joe Beckwith	.15	.06
❑	3 Buddy Biancalana	.15	.06
❑	4 Bud Black	.15	.06
❑	5 George Brett	2.50	1.00
❑	6 Onix Concepcion	.15	.06
❑	7 Steve Farr	.15	.06
❑	8 Mark Gubicza	.15	.06
❑	9 Dane Iorg	.15	.06
❑	10 Danny Jackson	.15	.06
❑	11 Lynn Jones	.15	.06
❑	12 Mike Jones	.15	.06
❑	13 Charlie Leibrandt	.15	.06
❑	14 Hal McRae	.25	.10
❑	15 Omar Moreno	.15	.06
❑	16 Darryl Motley	.15	.06
❑	17 Jorge Orta	.15	.06
❑	18 Dan Quisenberry	.15	.06
❑	19 Bret Saberhagen	.25	.10
❑	20 Pat Sheridan	.15	.06
❑	21 Lonnie Smith	.15	.06
❑	22 Jim Sundberg	.15	.06
❑	23 John Wathan	.15	.06
❑	24 Frank White	.25	.10
❑	25 Willie Wilson	.15	.06
❑	26 Joaquin Andujar	.15	.06
❑	27 Steve Braun	.15	.06
❑	28 Bill Campbell	.15	.06
❑	29 Cesar Cedeno	.25	.10
❑	30 Jack Clark	.25	.10
❑	31 Vince Coleman RC*	1.00	.40
❑	32 Danny Cox	.15	.06
❑	33 Ken Dayley	.15	.06
❑	34 Ivan DeJesus	.15	.06
❑	35 Bob Forsch	.15	.06
❑	36 Brian Harper	.15	.06
❑	37 Tom Herr	.15	.06
❑	38 Ricky Horton	.15	.06
❑	39 Kurt Kepshire	.15	.06
❑	40 Jeff Lahti	.15	.06
❑	41 Tito Landrum	.15	.06
❑	42 Willie McGee	.25	.10
❑	43 Tom Nieto	.15	.06
❑	44 Terry Pendleton	.25	.10
❑	45 Darrell Porter	.25	.10
❑	46 Ozzie Smith	.75	.30
❑	47 John Tudor	.15	.06
❑	48 Andy Van Slyke	.25	.10
❑	49 Todd Worrell RC	.50	.20
❑	50 Jim Acker	.15	.06
❑	51 Doyle Alexander	.15	.06
❑	52 Jesse Barfield	.15	.06
❑	53 George Bell	.25	.10
❑	54 Jeff Burroughs	.15	.06
❑	55 Bill Caudill	.15	.06
❑	56 Jim Clancy	.15	.06
❑	57 Tony Fernandez	.15	.06
❑	58 Tom Filer	.15	.06
❑	59 Damaso Garcia	.15	.06
❑	60 Tom Henke	.25	.10
❑	61 Garth Iorg	.15	.06
❑	62 Cliff Johnson	.15	.06
❑	63 Jimmy Key	.75	.30
❑	64 Dennis Lamp	.15	.06
❑	65 Gary Lavelle	.15	.06
❑	66 Buck Martinez	.15	.06
❑	67 Lloyd Moseby	.15	.06
❑	68 Rance Mulliniks	.15	.06
❑	69 Al Oliver	.25	.10
❑	70 Dave Stieb	.15	.06
❑	71 Louis Thornton	.15	.06
❑	72 Willie Upshaw	.15	.06
❑	73 Ernie Whitt	.15	.06
❑	74 Rick Aguilera RC	.50	.20
❑	75 Wally Backman	.15	.06
❑	76 Gary Carter	.50	.20
❑	77 Ron Darling	.15	.06
❑	78 Len Dykstra RC	1.50	.60
❑	79 Sid Fernandez	.25	.10
❑	80 George Foster	.25	.10
❑	81 Dwight Gooden	.75	.30
❑	82 Tom Gorman	.15	.06
❑	83 Danny Heep	.15	.06
❑	84 Keith Hernandez	.50	.20
❑	85 Howard Johnson	.25	.10
❑	86 Ray Knight	.25	.10
❑	87 Terry Leach	.15	.06
❑	88 Ed Lynch	.15	.06
❑	89 Roger McDowell RC*	.50	.20
❑	90 Jesse Orosco	.15	.06
❑	91 Tom Paciorek	.25	.10
❑	92 Ronn Reynolds	.15	.06
❑	93 Rafael Santana	.15	.06
❑	94 Doug Sisk	.15	.06
❑	95 Rusty Staub	.25	.10
❑	96 Darryl Strawberry	.50	.20
❑	97 Mookie Wilson	.25	.10
❑	98 Neil Allen	.15	.06
❑	99 Don Baylor	.50	.20
❑	100 Dale Berra	.15	.06
❑	101 Rich Bordi	.15	.06
❑	102 Marty Bystrom	.15	.06
❑	103 Joe Cowley	.15	.06
❑	104 Brian Fisher RC	.15	.06
❑	105 Ken Griffey	.25	.10
❑	106 Ron Guidry	.25	.10
❑	107 Ron Hassey	.15	.06
❑	108 R.Henderson UER SB Record of 120, sic	1.50	.60
❑	109 Don Mattingly	2.50	1.00
❑	110 Bobby Meacham	.15	.06
❑	111 John Montefusco	.15	.06
❑	112 Phil Niekro	.25	.10
❑	113 Mike Pagliarulo	.15	.06
❑	114 Dan Pasqua	.15	.06
❑	115 Willie Randolph	.25	.10
❑	116 Dave Righetti	.15	.06
❑	117 Andre Robertson	.15	.06
❑	118 Billy Sample	.15	.06
❑	119 Bob Shirley	.15	.06
❑	120 Ed Whitson	.15	.06
❑	121 Dave Winfield	.50	.20
❑	122 Butch Wynegar	.15	.06
❑	123 Dave Anderson	.15	.06
❑	124 Bob Bailor	.15	.06
❑	125 Greg Brock	.15	.06
❑	126 Enos Cabell	.15	.06
❑	127 Bobby Castillo	.15	.06
❑	128 Carlos Diaz	.15	.06
❑	129 Mariano Duncan RC*	.50	.20
❑	130 Pedro Guerrero	.25	.10
❑	131 Orel Hershiser	.50	.20
❑	132 Rick Honeycutt	.15	.06
❑	133 Ken Howell	.15	.06
❑	134 Ken Landreaux	.15	.06
❑	135 Bill Madlock	.15	.06
❑	136 Candy Maldonado	.15	.06
❑	137 Mike Marshall	.15	.06
❑	138 Len Matuszek	.15	.06
❑	139 Tom Niedenfuer	.15	.06
❑	140 Alejandro Pena	.15	.06
❑	141 Jerry Reuss	.15	.06
❑	142 Bill Russell	.15	.06
❑	143 Steve Sax	.15	.06
❑	144 Mike Scioscia	.15	.06
❑	145 Fernando Valenzuela	.25	.10
❑	146 Bob Welch	.15	.06
❑	147 Terry Whitfield	.15	.06
❑	148 Juan Beniquez	.15	.06
❑	149 Bob Boone	.25	.10
❑	150 John Candelaria	.15	.06
❑	151 Rod Carew	.50	.20
❑	152 Stu Cliburn	.15	.06
❑	153 Doug DeCinces	.15	.06
❑	154 Brian Downing	.15	.06
❑	155 Ken Forsch	.15	.06
❑	156 Craig Gerber	.15	.06
❑	157 Bobby Grich	.25	.10
❑	158 George Hendrick	.15	.06
❑	159 Al Holland	.15	.06
❑	160 Reggie Jackson	.50	.20
❑	161 Ruppert Jones	.15	.06
❑	162 Urbano Lugo	.15	.06
❑	163 Kirk McCaskill RC	.15	.06
❑	164 Donnie Moore	.15	.06
❑	165 Gary Pettis	.15	.06
❑	166 Ron Romanick	.15	.06
❑	167 Dick Schofield	.15	.06
❑	168 Daryl Sconiers	.15	.06
❑	169 Jim Slaton	.15	.06
❑	170 Don Sutton	.75	.30
❑	171 Mike Witt	.15	.06
❑	172 Buddy Bell	.25	.10
❑	173 Tom Browning	.15	.06
❑	174 Dave Concepcion	.25	.10
❑	175 Eric Davis	.50	.20
❑	176 Bo Diaz	.15	.06
❑	177 Nick Esasky	.15	.06
❑	178 John Franco	.75	.30
❑	179 Tom Hume	.15	.06
❑	180 Wayne Krenchicki	.15	.06
❑	181 Andy McGaffigan	.15	.06
❑	182 Eddie Milner	.15	.06
❑	183 Ron Oester	.15	.06
❑	184 Dave Parker	.25	.10
❑	185 Frank Pastore	.15	.06
❑	186 Tony Perez	.50	.20
❑	187 Ted Power	.15	.06
❑	188 Joe Price	.15	.06
❑	189 Gary Redus	.15	.06
❑	190 Ron Robinson	.15	.06
❑	191 Pete Rose	2.50	1.00
❑	192 Mario Soto	.15	.06
❑	193 John Stuper	.15	.06
❑	194 Jay Tibbs	.15	.06
❑	195 Dave Van Gorder	.15	.06
❑	196 Max Venable	.15	.06
❑	197 Juan Agosto	.15	.06
❑	198 Harold Baines	.50	.20
❑	199 Floyd Bannister	.15	.06
❑	200 Britt Burns	.15	.06
❑	201 Julio Cruz	.15	.06
❑	202 Joel Davis	.15	.06
❑	203 Richard Dotson	.15	.06
❑	204 Carlton Fisk	.50	.20
❑	205 Scott Fletcher	.15	.06
❑	206 Ozzie Guillen RC*	.50	.20
❑	207 Jerry Hairston	.15	.06
❑	208 Tim Hulett	.15	.06
❑	209 Bob James	.15	.06
❑	210 Ron Kittle	.15	.06
❑	211 Rudy Law	.15	.06
❑	212 Bryan Little	.15	.06
❑	213 Gene Nelson	.15	.06
❑	214 Reid Nichols	.15	.06
❑	215 Luis Salazar	.15	.06
❑	216 Tom Seaver	.75	.30
❑	217 Dan Spillner	.15	.06
❑	218 Bruce Tanner	.15	.06
❑	219 Greg Walker	.15	.06
❑	220 Dave Wehrmeister	.15	.06
❑	221 Juan Berenguer	.15	.06
❑	222 Dave Bergman	.15	.06
❑	223 Tom Brookens	.15	.06
❑	224 Darrell Evans	.25	.10
❑	225 Barbaro Garbey	.15	.06
❑	226 Kirk Gibson	.25	.10

❑ 227 John Grubb .15 .06
❑ 228 Willie Hernandez .15 .06
❑ 229 Larry Herndon .15 .06
❑ 230 Chet Lemon .15 .06
❑ 231 Aurelio Lopez .15 .06
❑ 232 Jack Morris .25 .10
❑ 233 Randy O'Neal .15 .06
❑ 234 Lance Parrish .25 .10
❑ 235 Dan Petry .15 .06
❑ 236 Alejandro Sanchez .15 .06
❑ 237 Bill Scherrer .15 .06
❑ 238 Nelson Simmons .15 .06
❑ 239 Frank Tanana .15 .06
❑ 240 Walt Terrell .15 .06
❑ 241 Alan Trammell .50 .20
❑ 242 Lou Whitaker .25 .10
❑ 243 Milt Wilcox .15 .06
❑ 244 Hubie Brooks .15 .06
❑ 245 Tim Burke .15 .06
❑ 246 Andre Dawson .25 .10
❑ 247 Mike Fitzgerald .15 .06
❑ 248 Terry Francona .15 .06
❑ 249 Bill Gullickson .15 .06
❑ 250 Joe Hesketh .15 .06
❑ 251 Bill Laskey .15 .06
❑ 252 Vance Law .15 .06
❑ 253 Charlie Lea .15 .06
❑ 254 Gary Lucas .15 .06
❑ 255 David Palmer .15 .06
❑ 256 Tim Raines .25 .10
❑ 257 Jeff Reardon .15 .06
❑ 258 Bert Roberge .15 .06
❑ 259 Dan Schatzeder .15 .06
❑ 260 Bryn Smith .15 .06
❑ 261 Randy St.Claire .15 .06
❑ 262 Scot Thompson .15 .06
❑ 263 Tim Wallach .15 .06
❑ 264 U.L. Washington .15 .06
❑ 265 Mitch Webster .15 .06
❑ 266 Herm Winningham .15 .06
❑ 267 Floyd Youmans .15 .06
❑ 268 Don Aase .15 .06
❑ 269 Mike Boddicker .15 .06
❑ 270 Rich Dauer .15 .06
❑ 271 Storm Davis .15 .06
❑ 272 Rick Dempsey .15 .06
❑ 273 Ken Dixon .15 .06
❑ 274 Jim Dwyer .15 .06
❑ 275 Mike Flanagan .15 .06
❑ 276 Wayne Gross .15 .06
❑ 277 Lee Lacy .15 .06
❑ 278 Fred Lynn .25 .10
❑ 279 Tippy Martinez .15 .06
❑ 280 Dennis Martinez .25 .10
❑ 281 Scott McGregor .15 .06
❑ 282 Eddie Murray .75 .30
❑ 283 Floyd Rayford .15 .06
❑ 284 Cal Ripken 3.00 1.20
❑ 285 Gary Roenicke .15 .06
❑ 286 Larry Sheets .15 .06
❑ 287 John Shelby .15 .06
❑ 288 Nate Snell .15 .06
❑ 289 Sammy Stewart .15 .06
❑ 290 Alan Wiggins .15 .06
❑ 291 Mike Young .15 .06
❑ 292 Alan Ashby .15 .06
❑ 293 Mark Bailey .15 .06
❑ 294 Kevin Bass .15 .06
❑ 295 Jeff Calhoun .15 .06
❑ 296 Jose Cruz .25 .10
❑ 297 Glenn Davis .25 .10
❑ 298 Bill Dawley .15 .06
❑ 299 Frank DiPino .15 .06
❑ 300 Bill Doran .15 .06
❑ 301 Phil Garner .25 .10
❑ 302 Jeff Heathcock .15 .06
❑ 303 Charlie Kerfeld .15 .06
❑ 304 Bob Knepper .15 .06
❑ 305 Ron Mathis .15 .06
❑ 306 Jerry Mumphrey .15 .06
❑ 307 Jim Pankovits .15 .06
❑ 308 Terry Puhl .15 .06
❑ 309 Craig Reynolds .15 .06
❑ 310 Nolan Ryan 4.00 1.60
❑ 311 Mike Scott .15 .06
❑ 312 Dave Smith .15 .06
❑ 313 Dickie Thon .15 .06
❑ 314 Denny Walling .15 .06
❑ 315 Kurt Bevacqua .15 .06
❑ 316 Al Bumbry .15 .06
❑ 317 Jerry Davis .15 .06
❑ 318 Luis DeLeon .15 .06
❑ 319 Dave Dravecky .25 .10
❑ 320 Tim Flannery .15 .06
❑ 321 Steve Garvey .25 .10
❑ 322 Rich Gossage .25 .10
❑ 323 Tony Gwynn 1.25 .50
❑ 324 Andy Hawkins .15 .06
❑ 325 LaMarr Hoyt .15 .06
❑ 326 Roy Lee Jackson .15 .06
❑ 327 Terry Kennedy .15 .06
❑ 328 Craig Lefferts .15 .06
❑ 329 Carmelo Martinez .15 .06
❑ 330 Lance McCullers .15 .06
❑ 331 Kevin McReynolds .15 .06
❑ 332 Graig Nettles .25 .10
❑ 333 Jerry Royster .15 .06
❑ 334 Eric Show .15 .06
❑ 335 Tim Stoddard .15 .06
❑ 336 Garry Templeton .15 .06
❑ 337 Mark Thurmond .15 .06
❑ 338 Ed Wojna .15 .06
❑ 339 Tony Armas .15 .06
❑ 340 Marty Barrett .15 .06
❑ 341 Wade Boggs .50 .20
❑ 342 Dennis Boyd .15 .06
❑ 343 Bill Buckner .25 .10
❑ 344 Mark Clear .15 .06
❑ 345 Roger Clemens 4.00 1.60
❑ 346 Steve Crawford .15 .06
❑ 347 Mike Easler .15 .06
❑ 348 Dwight Evans .25 .10
❑ 349 Rich Gedman .15 .06
❑ 350 Jackie Gutierrez .15 .06
❑ 351 Glenn Hoffman .15 .06
❑ 352 Bruce Hurst .15 .06
❑ 353 Bruce Kison .15 .06
❑ 354 Tim Lollar .15 .06
❑ 355 Steve Lyons .15 .06
❑ 356 Al Nipper .15 .06
❑ 357 Bob Ojeda .15 .06
❑ 358 Jim Rice .25 .10
❑ 359 Bob Stanley .15 .06
❑ 360 Mike Trujillo .15 .06
❑ 361 Thad Bosley .15 .06
❑ 362 Warren Brusstar .15 .06
❑ 363 Ron Cey .25 .10
❑ 364 Jody Davis .15 .06
❑ 365 Bob Dernier .15 .06
❑ 366 Shawon Dunston .25 .10
❑ 367 Leon Durham .15 .06
❑ 368 Dennis Eckersley .50 .20
❑ 369 Ray Fontenot .15 .06
❑ 370 George Frazier .15 .06
❑ 371 Billy Hatcher .15 .06
❑ 372 Dave Lopes .25 .10
❑ 373 Gary Matthews .15 .06
❑ 374 Ron Meridith .15 .06
❑ 375 Keith Moreland .15 .06
❑ 376 Reggie Patterson .15 .06
❑ 377 Dick Ruthven .15 .06
❑ 378 Ryne Sandberg 1.50 .60
❑ 379 Scott Sanderson .15 .06
❑ 380 Lee Smith .50 .20
❑ 381 Lary Sorensen .15 .06
❑ 382 Chris Speier .15 .06
❑ 383 Rick Sutcliffe .25 .10
❑ 384 Steve Trout .15 .06
❑ 385 Gary Woods .15 .06
❑ 386 Bert Blyleven .25 .10
❑ 387 Tom Brunansky .15 .06
❑ 388 Randy Bush .15 .06
❑ 389 John Butcher .15 .06
❑ 390 Ron Davis .15 .06
❑ 391 Dave Engle .15 .06
❑ 392 Frank Eufemia .15 .06
❑ 393 Pete Filson .15 .06
❑ 394 Gary Gaetti .25 .10
❑ 395 Greg Gagne .15 .06
❑ 396 Mickey Hatcher .15 .06
❑ 397 Kent Hrbek .25 .10
❑ 398 Tim Laudner .15 .06
❑ 399 Rick Lysander .15 .06
❑ 400 Dave Meier .15 .06
❑ 401 Kirby Puckett UER 2.00 .80
Card has him in NL, should be AL
❑ 402 Mark Salas .15 .06
❑ 403 Ken Schrom .15 .06
❑ 404 Roy Smalley .15 .06
❑ 405 Mike Smithson .15 .06
❑ 406 Mike Stenhouse .15 .06
❑ 407 Tim Teufel .15 .06
❑ 408 Frank Viola .25 .10
❑ 409 Ron Washington .15 .06
❑ 410 Keith Atherton .15 .06
❑ 411 Dusty Baker .25 .10
❑ 412 Tim Birtsas .15 .06
❑ 413 Bruce Bochte .15 .06
❑ 414 Chris Codiroli .15 .06
❑ 415 Dave Collins .15 .06
❑ 416 Mike Davis .15 .06
❑ 417 Alfredo Griffin .15 .06
❑ 418 Mike Heath .15 .06
❑ 419 Steve Henderson .15 .06
❑ 420 Donnie Hill .15 .06
❑ 421 Jay Howell .15 .06
❑ 422 Tommy John .75 .30
❑ 423 Dave Kingman .25 .10
❑ 424 Bill Krueger .15 .06
❑ 425 Rick Langford .15 .06
❑ 426 Carney Lansford .25 .10
❑ 427 Steve McCatty .15 .06
❑ 428 Dwayne Murphy .15 .06
❑ 429 Steve Ontiveros RC .15 .06
❑ 430 Tony Phillips .15 .06
❑ 431 Jose Rijo .15 .06
❑ 432 Mickey Tettleton RC .50 .20
❑ 433 Luis Aguayo .15 .06
❑ 434 Larry Andersen .15 .06
❑ 435 Steve Carlton .50 .20
❑ 436 Don Carman .15 .06
❑ 437 Tim Corcoran .15 .06
❑ 438 Darren Daulton RC 1.50 .60
❑ 439 John Denny .15 .06
❑ 440 Tom Foley .15 .06
❑ 441 Greg Gross .15 .06
❑ 442 Kevin Gross .15 .06
❑ 443 Von Hayes .15 .06
❑ 444 Charles Hudson .15 .06
❑ 445 Garry Maddox .15 .06
❑ 446 Shane Rawley .15 .06
❑ 447 Dave Rucker .15 .06
❑ 448 John Russell .15 .06
❑ 449 Juan Samuel .15 .06
❑ 450 Mike Schmidt 2.00 .80
❑ 451 Rick Schu .15 .06
❑ 452 Dave Shipanoff .15 .06
❑ 453 Dave Stewart .25 .10
❑ 454 Jeff Stone .15 .06
❑ 455 Kent Tekulve .15 .06
❑ 456 Ozzie Virgil .15 .06
❑ 457 Glenn Wilson .15 .06
❑ 458 Jim Beattie .15 .06
❑ 459 Karl Best .15 .06
❑ 460 Barry Bonnell .15 .06
❑ 461 Phil Bradley .15 .06
❑ 462 Ivan Calderon RC* .50 .20
❑ 463 Al Cowens .15 .06
❑ 464 Alvin Davis .15 .06
❑ 465 Dave Henderson .15 .06
❑ 466 Bob Kearney .15 .06
❑ 467 Mark Langston .15 .06
❑ 468 Bob Long .15 .06
❑ 469 Mike Moore .15 .06
❑ 470 Edwin Nunez .15 .06
❑ 471 Spike Owen .15 .06
❑ 472 Jack Perconte .15 .06
❑ 473 Jim Presley .15 .06
❑ 474 Donnie Scott .15 .06
❑ 475 Bill Swift .15 .06
❑ 476 Danny Tartabull .25 .10
❑ 477 Gorman Thomas .15 .06
❑ 478 Roy Thomas .15 .06
❑ 479 Ed VandeBerg .15 .06
❑ 480 Frank Wills .15 .06
❑ 481 Matt Young .15 .06
❑ 482 Ray Burris .15 .06

❑ 483 Jaime Cocanower .15 .06
❑ 484 Cecil Cooper .25 .10
❑ 485 Danny Darwin .15 .06
❑ 486 Rollie Fingers .25 .10
❑ 487 Jim Gantner .15 .06
❑ 488 Bob L. Gibson .15 .06
❑ 489 Moose Haas .15 .06
❑ 490 Teddy Higuera RC* .50 .20
❑ 491 Paul Householder .15 .06
❑ 492 Pete Ladd .15 .06
❑ 493 Rick Manning .15 .06
❑ 494 Bob McClure .15 .06
❑ 495 Paul Molitor .50 .20
❑ 496 Charlie Moore .15 .06
❑ 497 Ben Oglivie .15 .06
❑ 498 Randy Ready .15 .06
❑ 499 Earnie Riles .15 .06
❑ 500 Ed Romero .15 .06
❑ 501 Bill Schroeder .15 .06
❑ 502 Ray Searage .15 .06
❑ 503 Ted Simmons .25 .10
❑ 504 Pete Vuckovich .15 .06
❑ 505 Rick Waits .15 .06
❑ 506 Robin Yount .75 .30
❑ 507 Len Barker .15 .06
❑ 508 Steve Bedrosian .15 .06
❑ 509 Bruce Benedict .15 .06
❑ 510 Rick Camp .15 .06
❑ 511 Rick Cerone .15 .06
❑ 512 Chris Chambliss .25 .10
❑ 513 Jeff Dedmon .15 .06
❑ 514 Terry Forster .15 .06
❑ 515 Gene Garber .15 .06
❑ 516 Terry Harper .15 .06
❑ 517 Bob Horner .15 .06
❑ 518 Glenn Hubbard .15 .06
❑ 519 Joe Johnson .15 .06
❑ 520 Brad Komminsk .15 .06
❑ 521 Rick Mahler .15 .06
❑ 522 Dale Murphy .75 .30
❑ 523 Ken Oberkfell .15 .06
❑ 524 Pascual Perez .15 .06
❑ 525 Gerald Perry .15 .06
❑ 526 Rafael Ramirez .15 .06
❑ 527 Steve Shields .15 .06
❑ 528 Zane Smith .15 .06
❑ 529 Bruce Sutter .25 .10
❑ 530 Milt Thompson RC .15 .06
❑ 531 Claudell Washington .15 .06
❑ 532 Paul Zuvella .15 .06
❑ 533 Vida Blue .25 .10
❑ 534 Bob Brenly .15 .06
❑ 535 Chris Brown .15 .06
❑ 536 Chili Davis .50 .20
❑ 537 Mark Davis .15 .06
❑ 538 Rob Deer .15 .06
❑ 539 Dan Driessen .15 .06
❑ 540 Scott Garrelts .15 .06
❑ 541 Dan Gladden .15 .06
❑ 542 Jim Gott .15 .06
❑ 543 David Green .15 .06
❑ 544 Atlee Hammaker .15 .06
❑ 545 Mike Jeffcoat .15 .06
❑ 546 Mike Krukow .15 .06
❑ 547 Dave LaPoint .15 .06
❑ 548 Jeff Leonard .15 .06
❑ 549 Greg Minton .15 .06
❑ 550 Alex Trevino .15 .06
❑ 551 Manny Trillo .15 .06
❑ 552 Jose Uribe .15 .06
❑ 553 Brad Wellman .15 .06
❑ 554 Frank Williams .15 .06
❑ 555 Joel Youngblood .15 .06
❑ 556 Alan Bannister .15 .06
❑ 557 Glenn Brummer .15 .06
❑ 558 Steve Buechele RC .50 .20
❑ 559 Jose Guzman RC .15 .06
❑ 560 Toby Harrah .15 .06
❑ 561 Greg Harris .15 .06
❑ 562 Dwayne Henry .15 .06
❑ 563 Burt Hooton .15 .06
❑ 564 Charlie Hough .25 .10
❑ 565 Mike Mason .15 .06
❑ 566 Oddibe McDowell .15 .06
❑ 567 Dickie Noles .15 .06
❑ 568 Pete O'Brien .15 .06
❑ 569 Larry Parrish .15 .06
❑ 570 Dave Rozema .15 .06
❑ 571 Dave Schmidt .15 .06
❑ 572 Don Slaught .15 .06
❑ 573 Wayne Tolleson .15 .06
❑ 574 Duane Walker .15 .06
❑ 575 Gary Ward .15 .06
❑ 576 Chris Welsh .15 .06
❑ 577 Curtis Wilkerson .15 .06
❑ 578 George Wright .15 .06
❑ 579 Chris Bando .15 .06
❑ 580 Tony Bernazard .15 .06
❑ 581 Brett Butler .25 .10
❑ 582 Ernie Camacho .15 .06
❑ 583 Joe Carter .75 .30
❑ 584 Carmen Castillo .15 .06
❑ 585 Jamie Easterly .15 .06
❑ 586 Julio Franco .25 .10
❑ 587 Mel Hall .15 .06
❑ 588 Mike Hargrove .25 .10
❑ 589 Neal Heaton .15 .06
❑ 590 Brook Jacoby .15 .06
❑ 591 Otis Nixon RC .50 .20
❑ 592 Jerry Reed .15 .06
❑ 593 Vern Ruhle .15 .06
❑ 594 Pat Tabler .15 .06
❑ 595 Rich Thompson .15 .06
❑ 596 Andre Thornton .15 .06
❑ 597 Dave Von Ohlen .15 .06
❑ 598 George Vukovich .15 .06
❑ 599 Tom Waddell .15 .06
❑ 600 Curt Wardle .15 .06
❑ 601 Jerry Willard .15 .06
❑ 602 Bill Almon .15 .06
❑ 603 Mike Bielecki .15 .06
❑ 604 Sid Bream .15 .06
❑ 605 Mike C. Brown .15 .06
❑ 606 Pat Clements .15 .06
❑ 607 Jose DeLeon .15 .06
❑ 608 Denny Gonzalez .15 .06
❑ 609 Cecilio Guante .15 .06
❑ 610 Steve Kemp .15 .06
❑ 611 Sammy Khalifa .15 .06
❑ 612 Lee Mazzilli .15 .06
❑ 613 Larry McWilliams .15 .06
❑ 614 Jim Morrison .15 .06
❑ 615 Joe Orsulak RC* .15 .06
❑ 616 Tony Pena .15 .06
❑ 617 Johnny Ray .15 .06
❑ 618 Rick Reuschel .15 .06
❑ 619 R.J. Reynolds .15 .06
❑ 620 Rick Rhoden .15 .06
❑ 621 Don Robinson .15 .06
❑ 622 Jason Thompson .15 .06
❑ 623 Lee Tunnell .15 .06
❑ 624 Jim Winn .15 .06
❑ 625 Marvell Wynne .15 .06
❑ 626 Dwight Gooden IA .50 .20
❑ 627 Don Mattingly IA 1.25 .50
❑ 628 Pete Rose 4192 .50 .20
❑ 629 Rod Carew 3000 Hits .25 .10
❑ 630 Tom Seaver .50 .20
Phil Niekro
❑ 631 Don Baylor Ouch .25 .10
❑ 632 Darryl Strawberry .25 .10
Tim Raines
❑ 633 Cal Ripken 1.50 .60
Alan Trammell
❑ 634 Wade Boggs 1.50 .60
George Brett
❑ 635 Bob Horner .50 .20
Dale Murphy
❑ 636 Willie McGee .25 .10
Vince Coleman
❑ 637 Vince Coleman IA .25 .10
❑ 638 Pete Rose .75 .30
Dwight Gooden
❑ 639 Wade Boggs 1.25 .50
Don Mattingly
❑ 640 Dale Murphy .50 .20
Steve Garvey
Dave Parker
❑ 641 Fernando Valenzuela .50 .20
Dwight Gooden
❑ 642 Jimmy Key .25 .10
Dave Stieb
❑ 643 Carlton Fisk .25 .10
Rich Gedman
❑ 644 Gene Walter RC and 5.00 2.00
Benito Santiago
❑ 645 Mike Woodard and .15 .06
Colin Ward
❑ 646 Kal Daniels RC and 4.00 1.60
Paul O'Neill
❑ 647 Andres Galarraga RC 3.00 1.20
Fred Toliver
❑ 648 Bob Kipper and .15 .06
Curt Ford
❑ 649 Jose Canseco RC and 8.00 3.20
Eric Plunk
❑ 650 Mark McLemore RC 1.00 .40
Gus Polidor
❑ 651 Rob Woodward and .15 .06
Mickey Brantley
❑ 652 Billy Joe Robidoux .15 .06
Mark Funderburk
❑ 653 Cecil Fielder RC and 1.50 .60
Cory Snyder
❑ 654 CL: Royals/Cardinals .15 .06
Blue Jays/Mets
❑ 655 CL: Yankees/Dodgers .15 .06
Angels/Reds UER
(168 Darly Sconiers)
❑ 656 CL: White Sox/Tigers .15 .06
Expos/Orioles
(279 Dennis,
280 Tippy)
❑ 657 CL: Astros/Padres .15 .06
Red Sox/Cubs
❑ 658 CL: Twins/A's .15 .06
Phillies/Mariners
❑ 659 CL: Brewers/Braves .15 .06
Giants/Rangers
❑ 660 CL: Indians/Pirates .15 .06
Special Cards

1986 Fleer Update

	Nm-Mt	Ex-Mt
COMP.FACT.SET (132)	50.00	20.00

❑ 1 Mike Aldrete .15 .06
❑ 2 Andy Allanson .15 .06
❑ 3 Neil Allen .15 .06
❑ 4 Joaquin Andujar .15 .06
❑ 5 Paul Assenmacher .15 .06
❑ 6 Scott Bailes .15 .06
❑ 7 Jay Baller .15 .06
❑ 8 Scott Bankhead .15 .06
❑ 9 Bill Bathe .15 .06
❑ 10 Don Baylor .25 .10
❑ 11 Billy Beane XRC 1.00 .40
❑ 12 Steve Bedrosian .15 .06
❑ 13 Juan Beniquez .15 .06
❑ 14 Barry Bonds XRC 40.00 16.00
❑ 15 Bobby Bonilla UER 1.00 .40
(Wrong birthday) XRC
❑ 16 Rich Bordi .15 .06
❑ 17 Bill Campbell .15 .06
❑ 18 Tom Candiotti .15 .06
❑ 19 John Cangelosi .15 .06
❑ 20 Jose Canseco UER 1.50 .60
(Headings on back
for a pitcher)

❑ 21	Chuck Cary	.15	.06
❑ 22	Juan Castillo XRC	.15	.06
❑ 23	Rick Cerone	.15	.06
❑ 24	John Cerutti	.15	.06
❑ 25	Will Clark XRC	2.00	.80
❑ 26	Mark Clear	.15	.06
❑ 27	Darnell Coles	.15	.06
❑ 28	Dave Collins	.15	.06
❑ 29	Tim Conroy	.15	.06
❑ 30	Ed Correa	.15	.06
❑ 31	Joe Cowley	.15	.06
❑ 32	Bill Dawley	.15	.06
❑ 33	Rob Deer	.25	.10
❑ 34	John Denny	.15	.06
❑ 35	Jim Deshaies XRC	.15	.06
❑ 36	Doug Drabek XRC	1.00	.40
❑ 37	Mike Easler	.15	.06
❑ 38	Mark Eichhorn	.15	.06
❑ 39	Dave Engle	.15	.06
❑ 40	Mike Fischlin	.15	.06
❑ 41	Scott Fletcher	.15	.06
❑ 42	Terry Forster	.15	.06
❑ 43	Terry Francona	.15	.06
❑ 44	Andres Galarraga	1.25	.50
❑ 45	Lee Guetterman	.15	.06
❑ 46	Bill Gullickson	.15	.06
❑ 47	Jackie Gutierrez	.15	.06
❑ 48	Moose Haas	.15	.06
❑ 49	Billy Hatcher	.15	.06
❑ 50	Mike Heath	.15	.06
❑ 51	Guy Hoffman	.15	.06
❑ 52	Tom Hume	.15	.06
❑ 53	Pete Incaviglia XRC	.50	.20
❑ 54	Dane Iorg	.15	.06
❑ 55	Chris James XRC	.15	.06
❑ 56	Stan Javier XRC*	.50	.20
❑ 57	Tommy John	1.00	.40
❑ 58	Tracy Jones	.15	.06
❑ 59	Wally Joyner XRC	1.00	.40
❑ 60	Wayne Krenchicki	.15	.06
❑ 61	John Kruk XRC	1.50	.60
❑ 62	Mike LaCoss	.15	.06
❑ 63	Pete Ladd	.15	.06
❑ 64	Dave LaPoint	.15	.06
❑ 65	Mike LaValliere XRC	.50	.20
❑ 66	Rudy Law	.15	.06
❑ 67	Dennis Leonard	.15	.06
❑ 68	Steve Lombardozzi	.15	.06
❑ 69	Aurelio Lopez	.15	.06
❑ 70	Mickey Mahler	.15	.06
❑ 71	Candy Maldonado	.15	.06
❑ 72	Roger Mason XRC*	.15	.06
❑ 73	Greg Mathews	.15	.06
❑ 74	Andy McGaffigan	.15	.06
❑ 75	Joel McKeon	.15	.06
❑ 76	Kevin Mitchell XRC	1.00	.40
❑ 77	Bill Mooneyham	.15	.06
❑ 78	Omar Moreno	.15	.06
❑ 79	Jerry Mumphrey	.15	.06
❑ 80	Al Newman	.25	.10
❑ 81	Phil Niekro	.25	.10
❑ 82	Randy Niemann	.15	.06
❑ 83	Juan Nieves	.15	.06
❑ 84	Bob Ojeda	.15	.06
❑ 85	Rick Ownbey	.15	.06
❑ 86	Tom Paciorek	.25	.10
❑ 87	David Palmer	.15	.06
❑ 88	Jeff Parrett XRC	.15	.06
❑ 89	Pat Perry	.15	.06
❑ 90	Dan Plesac	.15	.06
❑ 91	Darrell Porter	.25	.10
❑ 92	Luis Quinones	.15	.06
❑ 93	Rey Quinones UER (Misspelled Quinonez)	.15	.06
❑ 94	Gary Redus	.15	.06
❑ 95	Jeff Reed	.15	.06
❑ 96	Bip Roberts XRC	.50	.20
❑ 97	Billy Joe Robidoux	.15	.06
❑ 98	Gary Roenicke	.15	.06
❑ 99	Ron Roenicke	.15	.06
❑ 100	Angel Salazar	.15	.06
❑ 101	Joe Sambito	.15	.06
❑ 102	Billy Sample	.15	.06
❑ 103	Dave Schmidt	.15	.06
❑ 104	Ken Schrom	.15	.06
❑ 105	Ruben Sierra XRC	1.50	.60
❑ 106	Ted Simmons	.25	.10
❑ 107	Sammy Stewart	.15	.06
❑ 108	Kurt Stillwell	.15	.06
❑ 109	Dale Sveum	.15	.06
❑ 110	Tim Teufel	.15	.06
❑ 111	Bob Tewksbury XRC	.50	.20
❑ 112	Andres Thomas	.15	.06
❑ 113	Jason Thompson	.15	.06
❑ 114	Milt Thompson	.25	.10
❑ 115	R. Thompson XRC	.50	.20
❑ 116	Jay Tibbs	.15	.06
❑ 117	Fred Toliver	.15	.06
❑ 118	Wayne Tolleson	.15	.06
❑ 119	Alex Trevino	.15	.06
❑ 120	Manny Trillo	.15	.06
❑ 121	Ed VandeBerg	.15	.06
❑ 122	Ozzie Virgil	.15	.06
❑ 123	Tony Walker	.15	.06
❑ 124	Gene Walter	.15	.06
❑ 125	Duane Ward XRC	.50	.20
❑ 126	Jerry Willard	.15	.06
❑ 127	Mitch Williams XRC	.50	.20
❑ 128	Reggie Williams	.15	.06
❑ 129	Bobby Witt XRC	.50	.20
❑ 130	Marvell Wynne	.15	.06
❑ 131	Steve Yeager	.15	.06
❑ 132	Checklist 1-132	.15	.06

1987 Fleer

	Nm-Mt	Ex-Mt
COMPLETE SET (660)	80.00	32.00
COMP.FACT.SET (672)	80.00	32.00

❑ 1	Rick Aguilera	.25	.10
❑ 2	Richard Anderson	.15	.06
❑ 3	Wally Backman	.15	.06
❑ 4	Gary Carter	.40	.16
❑ 5	Ron Darling	.15	.06
❑ 6	Len Dykstra	.40	.16
❑ 7	Kevin Elster RC	.50	.20
❑ 8	Sid Fernandez	.15	.06
❑ 9	Dwight Gooden	.40	.16
❑ 10	Ed Hearn	.15	.06
❑ 11	Danny Heep	.15	.06
❑ 12	Keith Hernandez	.40	.16
❑ 13	Howard Johnson	.15	.06
❑ 14	Ray Knight	.15	.06
❑ 15	Lee Mazzilli	.15	.06
❑ 16	Roger McDowell	.15	.06
❑ 17	Kevin Mitchell RC *	1.25	.50
❑ 18	Randy Niemann	.15	.06
❑ 19	Bob Ojeda	.15	.06
❑ 20	Jesse Orosco	.15	.06
❑ 21	Rafael Santana	.15	.06
❑ 22	Doug Sisk	.15	.06
❑ 23	Darryl Strawberry	.40	.16
❑ 24	Tim Teufel	.15	.06
❑ 25	Mookie Wilson	.25	.10
❑ 26	Tony Armas	.15	.06
❑ 27	Marty Barrett	.15	.06
❑ 28	Don Baylor	.25	.10
❑ 29	Wade Boggs	.40	.16
❑ 30	Oil Can Boyd	.15	.06
❑ 31	Bill Buckner	.25	.10
❑ 32	Roger Clemens	1.50	.60
❑ 33	Steve Crawford	.15	.06
❑ 34	Dwight Evans	.25	.10
❑ 35	Rich Gedman	.15	.06
❑ 36	Dave Henderson	.15	.06
❑ 37	Bruce Hurst	.15	.06
❑ 38	Tim Lollar	.15	.06
❑ 39	Al Nipper	.15	.06
❑ 40	Spike Owen	.15	.06
❑ 41	Jim Rice	.25	.10
❑ 42	Ed Romero	.15	.06
❑ 43	Joe Sambito	.15	.06
❑ 44	Calvin Schiraldi	.15	.06
❑ 45	Tom Seaver UER (Lifetime saves total 0, should be 1)	.60	.24
❑ 46	Jeff Sellers	.15	.06
❑ 47	Bob Stanley	.15	.06
❑ 48	Sammy Stewart	.15	.06
❑ 49	Larry Andersen	.15	.06
❑ 50	Alan Ashby	.15	.06
❑ 51	Kevin Bass	.15	.06
❑ 52	Jeff Calhoun	.15	.06
❑ 53	Jose Cruz	.25	.10
❑ 54	Danny Darwin	.15	.06
❑ 55	Glenn Davis	.15	.06
❑ 56	Jim Deshaies RC *	.25	.10
❑ 57	Bill Doran	.15	.06
❑ 58	Phil Garner	.15	.06
❑ 59	Billy Hatcher	.15	.06
❑ 60	Charlie Kerfeld	.15	.06
❑ 61	Bob Knepper	.15	.06
❑ 62	Dave Lopes	.25	.10
❑ 63	Aurelio Lopez	.15	.06
❑ 64	Jim Pankovits	.15	.06
❑ 65	Terry Puhl	.15	.06
❑ 66	Craig Reynolds	.15	.06
❑ 67	Nolan Ryan	3.00	1.20
❑ 68	Mike Scott	.15	.06
❑ 69	Dave Smith	.15	.06
❑ 70	Dickie Thon	.15	.06
❑ 71	Tony Walker	.15	.06
❑ 72	Denny Walling	.15	.06
❑ 73	Bob Boone	.25	.10
❑ 74	Rick Burleson	.15	.06
❑ 75	John Candelaria	.15	.06
❑ 76	Doug Corbett	.15	.06
❑ 77	Doug DeCinces	.15	.06
❑ 78	Brian Downing	.15	.06
❑ 79	Chuck Finley RC	1.25	.50
❑ 80	Terry Forster	.15	.06
❑ 81	Bob Grich	.25	.10
❑ 82	George Hendrick	.15	.06
❑ 83	Jack Howell	.15	.06
❑ 84	Reggie Jackson	.40	.16
❑ 85	Ruppert Jones	.15	.06
❑ 86	Wally Joyner RC	1.25	.50
❑ 87	Gary Lucas	.15	.06
❑ 88	Kirk McCaskill	.15	.06
❑ 89	Donnie Moore	.15	.06
❑ 90	Gary Pettis	.15	.06
❑ 91	Vern Ruhle	.15	.06
❑ 92	Dick Schofield	.15	.06
❑ 93	Don Sutton	.60	.24
❑ 94	Rob Wilfong	.15	.06
❑ 95	Mike Witt	.15	.06
❑ 96	Doug Drabek RC	.50	.20
❑ 97	Mike Easler	.15	.06
❑ 98	Mike Fischlin	.15	.06
❑ 99	Brian Fisher	.15	.06
❑ 100	Ron Guidry	.25	.10
❑ 101	Rickey Henderson	1.25	.50
❑ 102	Tommy John	.25	.10
❑ 103	Ron Kittle	.15	.06
❑ 104	Don Mattingly	2.00	.80
❑ 105	Bobby Meacham	.15	.06
❑ 106	Joe Niekro	.15	.06
❑ 107	Mike Pagliarulo	.15	.06
❑ 108	Dan Pasqua	.15	.06
❑ 109	Willie Randolph	.25	.10
❑ 110	Dennis Rasmussen	.15	.06
❑ 111	Dave Righetti	.15	.06
❑ 112	Gary Roenicke	.15	.06
❑ 113	Rod Scurry	.15	.06
❑ 114	Bob Shirley	.15	.06
❑ 115	Joel Skinner	.15	.06
❑ 116	Tim Stoddard	.15	.06
❑ 117	Bob Tewksbury RC *	.50	.20
❑ 118	Wayne Tolleson	.15	.06
❑ 119	Claudell Washington	.15	.06

❑ 120 Dave Winfield .40 .16
❑ 121 Steve Buechele .15 .06
❑ 122 Ed Correa .15 .06
❑ 123 Scott Fletcher .15 .06
❑ 124 Jose Guzman .15 .06
❑ 125 Toby Harrah .15 .06
❑ 126 Greg Harris .15 .06
❑ 127 Charlie Hough .25 .10
❑ 128 Pete Incaviglia RC * .50 .20
❑ 129 Mike Mason .15 .06
❑ 130 Oddibe McDowell .15 .06
❑ 131 Dale Mohorcic .15 .06
❑ 132 Pete O'Brien .15 .06
❑ 133 Tom Paciorek .25 .10
❑ 134 Larry Parrish .15 .06
❑ 135 Geno Petralli .15 .06
❑ 136 Darrell Porter .15 .06
❑ 137 Jeff Russell .15 .06
❑ 138 Ruben Sierra RC 1.25 .50
❑ 139 Don Slaught .15 .06
❑ 140 Gary Ward .15 .06
❑ 141 Curtis Wilkerson .15 .06
❑ 142 Mitch Williams RC * .50 .20
❑ 143 Bobby Witt RC UER .50 .20
(Tulsa misspelled as Tusla; ERA should be 6.43, not .643)
❑ 144 Dave Bergman .15 .06
❑ 145 Tom Brookens .15 .06
❑ 146 Bill Campbell .15 .06
❑ 147 Chuck Cary .15 .06
❑ 148 Darnell Coles .15 .06
❑ 149 Dave Collins .15 .06
❑ 150 Darrell Evans .25 .10
❑ 151 Kirk Gibson .25 .10
❑ 152 John Grubb .15 .06
❑ 153 Willie Hernandez .15 .06
❑ 154 Larry Herndon .15 .06
❑ 155 Eric King .15 .06
❑ 156 Chet Lemon .15 .06
❑ 157 Dwight Lowry .15 .06
❑ 158 Jack Morris .25 .10
❑ 159 Randy O'Neal .15 .06
❑ 160 Lance Parrish .25 .10
❑ 161 Dan Petry .15 .06
❑ 162 Pat Sheridan .15 .06
❑ 163 Jim Slaton .15 .06
❑ 164 Frank Tanana .15 .06
❑ 165 Walt Terrell .15 .06
❑ 166 Mark Thurmond .15 .06
❑ 167 Alan Trammell .40 .16
❑ 168 Lou Whitaker .25 .10
❑ 169 Luis Aguayo .15 .06
❑ 170 Steve Bedrosian .15 .06
❑ 171 Don Carman .15 .06
❑ 172 Darren Daulton .40 .16
❑ 173 Greg Gross .15 .06
❑ 174 Kevin Gross .15 .06
❑ 175 Von Hayes .15 .06
❑ 176 Charles Hudson .15 .06
❑ 177 Tom Hume .15 .06
❑ 178 Steve Jeltz .15 .06
❑ 179 Mike Maddux .15 .06
❑ 180 Shane Rawley .15 .06
❑ 181 Gary Redus .15 .06
❑ 182 Ron Roenicke .15 .06
❑ 183 Bruce Ruffin RC .25 .10
❑ 184 John Russell .15 .06
❑ 185 Juan Samuel .15 .06
❑ 186 Dan Schatzeder .15 .06
❑ 187 Mike Schmidt 1.50 .60
❑ 188 Rick Schu .15 .06
❑ 189 Jeff Stone .15 .06
❑ 190 Kent Tekulve .15 .06
❑ 191 Milt Thompson .15 .06
❑ 192 Glenn Wilson .15 .06
❑ 193 Buddy Bell .25 .10
❑ 194 Tom Browning .15 .06
❑ 195 Sal Butera .15 .06
❑ 196 Dave Concepcion .25 .10
❑ 197 Kal Daniels .15 .06
❑ 198 Eric Davis .40 .16
❑ 199 John Denny .15 .06
❑ 200 Bo Diaz .15 .06
❑ 201 Nick Esasky .15 .06
❑ 202 John Franco .25 .10
❑ 203 Bill Gullickson .15 .06
❑ 204 Barry Larkin RC 5.00 2.00
❑ 205 Eddie Milner .15 .06
❑ 206 Rob Murphy .15 .06
❑ 207 Ron Oester .15 .06
❑ 208 Dave Parker .25 .10
❑ 209 Tony Perez .40 .16
❑ 210 Ted Power .15 .06
❑ 211 Joe Price .15 .06
❑ 212 Ron Robinson .15 .06
❑ 213 Pete Rose 2.00 .80
❑ 214 Mario Soto .15 .06
❑ 215 Kurt Stillwell .15 .06
❑ 216 Max Venable .15 .06
❑ 217 Chris Welsh .15 .06
❑ 218 Carl Willis RC .25 .10
❑ 219 Jesse Barfield .15 .06
❑ 220 George Bell .15 .06
❑ 221 Bill Caudill .15 .06
❑ 222 John Cerutti .15 .06
❑ 223 Jim Clancy .15 .06
❑ 224 Mark Eichhorn .15 .06
❑ 225 Tony Fernandez .15 .06
❑ 226 Damaso Garcia .15 .06
❑ 227 Kelly Gruber ERR .15 .06
(Wrong birth year)
❑ 228 Tom Henke .15 .06
❑ 229 Garth Iorg .15 .06
❑ 230 Joe Johnson .15 .06
❑ 231 Cliff Johnson .15 .06
❑ 232 Jimmy Key .25 .10
❑ 233 Dennis Lamp .15 .06
❑ 234 Rick Leach .15 .06
❑ 235 Buck Martinez .15 .06
❑ 236 Lloyd Moseby .15 .06
❑ 237 Rance Mulliniks .15 .06
❑ 238 Dave Stieb .15 .06
❑ 239 Willie Upshaw .15 .06
❑ 240 Ernie Whitt .15 .06
❑ 241 Andy Allanson .15 .06
❑ 242 Scott Bailes .15 .06
❑ 243 Chris Bando .15 .06
❑ 244 Tony Bernazard .15 .06
❑ 245 John Butcher .15 .06
❑ 246 Brett Butler .25 .10
❑ 247 Ernie Camacho .15 .06
❑ 248 Tom Candiotti .15 .06
❑ 249 Joe Carter .60 .24
❑ 250 Carmen Castillo .15 .06
❑ 251 Julio Franco .25 .10
❑ 252 Mel Hall .15 .06
❑ 253 Brook Jacoby .15 .06
❑ 254 Phil Niekro .25 .10
❑ 255 Otis Nixon .15 .06
❑ 256 Dickie Noles .15 .06
❑ 257 Bryan Oelkers .15 .06
❑ 258 Ken Schrom .15 .06
❑ 259 Don Schulze .15 .06
❑ 260 Cory Snyder .15 .06
❑ 261 Pat Tabler .15 .06
❑ 262 Andre Thornton .15 .06
❑ 263 Rich Yett .15 .06
❑ 264 Mike Aldrete .15 .06
❑ 265 Juan Berenguer .15 .06
❑ 266 Vida Blue .25 .10
❑ 267 Bob Brenly .15 .06
❑ 268 Chris Brown .15 .06
❑ 269 Will Clark RC 3.00 1.20
❑ 270 Chili Davis .40 .16
❑ 271 Mark Davis .15 .06
❑ 272 Kelly Downs RC .25 .10
❑ 273 Scott Garrelts .15 .06
❑ 274 Dan Gladden .15 .06
❑ 275 Mike Krukow .15 .06
❑ 276 Randy Kutcher .15 .06
❑ 277 Mike LaCoss .15 .06
❑ 278 Jeff Leonard .15 .06
❑ 279 Candy Maldonado .15 .06
❑ 280 Roger Mason .15 .06
❑ 281 Bob Melvin .15 .06
❑ 282 Greg Minton .15 .06
❑ 283 Jeff D. Robinson .15 .06
❑ 284 Harry Spilman .15 .06
❑ 285 R.Thompson RC* .50 .20
❑ 286 Jose Uribe .15 .06
❑ 287 Frank Williams .15 .06
❑ 288 Joel Youngblood .15 .06
❑ 289 Jack Clark .25 .10
❑ 290 Vince Coleman .15 .06
❑ 291 Tim Conroy .15 .06
❑ 292 Danny Cox .15 .06
❑ 293 Ken Dayley .15 .06
❑ 294 Curt Ford .15 .06
❑ 295 Bob Forsch .15 .06
❑ 296 Tom Herr .15 .06
❑ 297 Ricky Horton .15 .06
❑ 298 Clint Hurdle .15 .06
❑ 299 Jeff Lahti .15 .06
❑ 300 Steve Lake .15 .06
❑ 301 Tito Landrum .15 .06
❑ 302 Mike LaValliere RC * .50 .20
❑ 303 Greg Mathews .15 .06
❑ 304 Willie McGee .25 .10
❑ 305 Jose Oquendo .15 .06
❑ 306 Terry Pendleton .25 .10
❑ 307 Pat Perry .15 .06
❑ 308 Ozzie Smith .60 .24
❑ 309 Ray Soff .15 .06
❑ 310 John Tudor .15 .06
❑ 311 Andy Van Slyke UER .25 .10
(Bats R, Throws L)
❑ 312 Todd Worrell .25 .10
❑ 313 Dann Bilardello .15 .06
❑ 314 Hubie Brooks .15 .06
❑ 315 Tim Burke .15 .06
❑ 316 Andre Dawson .25 .10
❑ 317 Mike Fitzgerald .15 .06
❑ 318 Tom Foley .15 .06
❑ 319 Andres Galarraga .40 .16
❑ 320 Joe Hesketh .15 .06
❑ 321 Wallace Johnson .15 .06
❑ 322 Wayne Krenchicki .15 .06
❑ 323 Vance Law .15 .06
❑ 324 Dennis Martinez .25 .10
❑ 325 Bob McClure .15 .06
❑ 326 Andy McGaffigan .15 .06
❑ 327 Al Newman .15 .06
❑ 328 Tim Raines .25 .10
❑ 329 Jeff Reardon .25 .10
❑ 330 Luis Rivera RC .25 .10
❑ 331 Bob Sebra .15 .06
❑ 332 Bryn Smith .15 .06
❑ 333 Jay Tibbs .15 .06
❑ 334 Tim Wallach .15 .06
❑ 335 Mitch Webster .15 .06
❑ 336 Jim Wohlford .15 .06
❑ 337 Floyd Youmans .15 .06
❑ 338 Chris Bosio RC .50 .20
❑ 339 Glenn Braggs RC .25 .10
❑ 340 Rick Cerone .15 .06
❑ 341 Mark Clear .15 .06
❑ 342 Bryan Clutterbuck .15 .06
❑ 343 Cecil Cooper .25 .10
❑ 344 Rob Deer .15 .06
❑ 345 Jim Gantner .15 .06
❑ 346 Ted Higuera .15 .06
❑ 347 John Henry Johnson .15 .06
❑ 348 Tim Leary .15 .06
❑ 349 Rick Manning .15 .06
❑ 350 Paul Molitor .40 .16
❑ 351 Charlie Moore .15 .06
❑ 352 Juan Nieves .15 .06
❑ 353 Ben Oglivie .15 .06
❑ 354 Dan Plesac .15 .06
❑ 355 Ernest Riles .15 .06
❑ 356 Billy Joe Robidoux .15 .06
❑ 357 Bill Schroeder .15 .06
❑ 358 Dale Sveum .15 .06
❑ 359 Gorman Thomas .15 .06
❑ 360 Bill Wegman .15 .06
❑ 361 Robin Yount .60 .24
❑ 362 Steve Balboni .15 .06
❑ 363 Scott Bankhead .15 .06
❑ 364 Buddy Biancalana .15 .06
❑ 365 Bud Black .15 .06
❑ 366 George Brett 2.00 .80
❑ 367 Steve Farr .15 .06
❑ 368 Mark Gubicza .15 .06
❑ 369 Bo Jackson RC 3.00 1.20
❑ 370 Danny Jackson .15 .06
❑ 371 Mike Kingery RC .25 .10
❑ 372 Rudy Law .15 .06

	No.	Player		
☐	373	Charlie Leibrandt	.15	.06
☐	374	Dennis Leonard	.15	.06
☐	375	Hal McRae	.25	.10
☐	376	Jorge Orta	.15	.06
☐	377	Jamie Quirk	.15	.06
☐	378	Dan Quisenberry	.15	.06
☐	379	Bret Saberhagen	.25	.10
☐	380	Angel Salazar	.15	.06
☐	381	Lonnie Smith	.15	.06
☐	382	Jim Sundberg	.15	.06
☐	383	Frank White	.25	.10
☐	384	Willie Wilson	.25	.10
☐	385	Joaquin Andujar	.15	.06
☐	386	Doug Bair	.15	.06
☐	387	Dusty Baker	.25	.10
☐	388	Bruce Bochte	.15	.06
☐	389	Jose Canseco	1.50	.60
☐	390	Chris Codiroli	.15	.06
☐	391	Mike Davis	.15	.06
☐	392	Alfredo Griffin	.15	.06
☐	393	Moose Haas	.15	.06
☐	394	Donnie Hill	.15	.06
☐	395	Jay Howell	.15	.06
☐	396	Dave Kingman	.25	.10
☐	397	Carney Lansford	.25	.10
☐	398	Dave Leiper	.15	.06
☐	399	Bill Mooneyham	.15	.06
☐	400	Dwayne Murphy	.15	.06
☐	401	Steve Ontiveros	.15	.06
☐	402	Tony Phillips	.15	.06
☐	403	Eric Plunk	.15	.06
☐	404	Jose Rijo	.15	.06
☐	405	Terry Steinbach RC	.50	.20
☐	406	Dave Stewart	.25	.10
☐	407	Mickey Tettleton	.15	.06
☐	408	Dave Von Ohlen	.15	.06
☐	409	Jerry Willard	.15	.06
☐	410	Curt Young	.15	.06
☐	411	Bruce Bochy	.15	.06
☐	412	Dave Dravecky	.25	.10
☐	413	Tim Flannery	.15	.06
☐	414	Steve Garvey	.25	.10
☐	415	Rich Gossage	.25	.10
☐	416	Tony Gwynn	1.00	.40
☐	417	Andy Hawkins	.15	.06
☐	418	LaMarr Hoyt	.15	.06
☐	419	Terry Kennedy	.15	.06
☐	420	John Kruk RC	1.25	.50
☐	421	Dave LaPoint	.15	.06
☐	422	Craig Lefferts	.15	.06
☐	423	Carmelo Martinez	.15	.06
☐	424	Lance McCullers	.15	.06
☐	425	Kevin McReynolds	.15	.06
☐	426	Graig Nettles	.25	.10
☐	427	Bip Roberts RC	.50	.20
☐	428	Jerry Royster	.15	.06
☐	429	Benito Santiago	.40	.16
☐	430	Eric Show	.15	.06
☐	431	Bob Stoddard	.15	.06
☐	432	Garry Templeton	.15	.06
☐	433	Gene Walter	.15	.06
☐	434	Ed Whitson	.15	.06
☐	435	Marvell Wynne	.15	.06
☐	436	Dave Anderson	.15	.06
☐	437	Greg Brock	.15	.06
☐	438	Enos Cabell	.15	.06
☐	439	Mariano Duncan	.15	.06
☐	440	Pedro Guerrero	.15	.06
☐	441	Orel Hershiser	.25	.10
☐	442	Rick Honeycutt	.15	.06
☐	443	Ken Howell	.15	.06
☐	444	Ken Landreaux	.15	.06
☐	445	Bill Madlock	.25	.10
☐	446	Mike Marshall	.15	.06
☐	447	Len Matuszek	.15	.06
☐	448	Tom Niedenfuer	.15	.06
☐	449	Alejandro Pena	.15	.06
☐	450	Dennis Powell	.15	.06
☐	451	Jerry Reuss	.15	.06
☐	452	Bill Russell	.15	.06
☐	453	Steve Sax	.15	.06
☐	454	Mike Scioscia	.15	.06
☐	455	Franklin Stubbs	.15	.06
☐	456	Alex Trevino	.15	.06
☐	457	Fernando Valenzuela	.25	.10
☐	458	Ed VandeBerg	.15	.06
☐	459	Bob Welch	.15	.06
☐	460	Reggie Williams	.15	.06
☐	461	Don Aase	.15	.06
☐	462	Juan Beniquez	.15	.06
☐	463	Mike Boddicker	.15	.06
☐	464	Juan Bonilla	.15	.06
☐	465	Rich Bordi	.15	.06
☐	466	Storm Davis	.15	.06
☐	467	Rick Dempsey	.25	.10
☐	468	Ken Dixon	.15	.06
☐	469	Jim Dwyer	.15	.06
☐	470	Mike Flanagan	.15	.06
☐	471	Jackie Gutierrez	.15	.06
☐	472	Brad Havens	.15	.06
☐	473	Lee Lacy	.15	.06
☐	474	Fred Lynn	.25	.10
☐	475	Scott McGregor	.15	.06
☐	476	Eddie Murray	.60	.24
☐	477	Tom O'Malley	.15	.06
☐	478	Cal Ripken Jr.	2.50	1.00
☐	479	Larry Sheets	.15	.06
☐	480	John Shelby	.15	.06
☐	481	Nate Snell	.15	.06
☐	482	Jim Traber	.15	.06
☐	483	Mike Young	.15	.06
☐	484	Neil Allen	.15	.06
☐	485	Harold Baines	.25	.10
☐	486	Floyd Bannister	.15	.06
☐	487	Daryl Boston	.15	.06
☐	488	Ivan Calderon	.15	.06
☐	489	John Cangelosi	.15	.06
☐	490	Steve Carlton	.40	.16
☐	491	Joe Cowley	.15	.06
☐	492	Julio Cruz	.15	.06
☐	493	Bill Dawley	.15	.06
☐	494	Jose DeLeon	.15	.06
☐	495	Richard Dotson	.15	.06
☐	496	Carlton Fisk	.40	.16
☐	497	Ozzie Guillen	.15	.06
☐	498	Jerry Hairston	.15	.06
☐	499	Ron Hassey	.15	.06
☐	500	Tim Hulett	.15	.06
☐	501	Bob James	.15	.06
☐	502	Steve Lyons	.15	.06
☐	503	Joel McKeon	.15	.06
☐	504	Gene Nelson	.15	.06
☐	505	Dave Schmidt	.15	.06
☐	506	Ray Searage	.15	.06
☐	507	Bobby Thigpen RC	.50	.20
☐	508	Greg Walker	.15	.06
☐	509	Jim Acker	.15	.06
☐	510	Doyle Alexander	.15	.06
☐	511	Paul Assenmacher	.40	.16
☐	512	Bruce Benedict	.15	.06
☐	513	Chris Chambliss	.25	.10
☐	514	Jeff Dedmon	.15	.06
☐	515	Gene Garber	.15	.06
☐	516	Ken Griffey	.25	.10
☐	517	Terry Harper	.15	.06
☐	518	Bob Horner	.15	.06
☐	519	Glenn Hubbard	.15	.06
☐	520	Rick Mahler	.15	.06
☐	521	Omar Moreno	.15	.06
☐	522	Dale Murphy	.60	.24
☐	523	Ken Oberkfell	.15	.06
☐	524	Ed Olwine	.15	.06
☐	525	David Palmer	.15	.06
☐	526	Rafael Ramirez	.15	.06
☐	527	Billy Sample	.15	.06
☐	528	Ted Simmons	.25	.10
☐	529	Zane Smith	.15	.06
☐	530	Bruce Sutter	.15	.06
☐	531	Andres Thomas	.15	.06
☐	532	Ozzie Virgil	.15	.06
☐	533	Allan Anderson	.15	.06
☐	534	Keith Atherton	.15	.06
☐	535	Billy Beane	.25	.10
☐	536	Bert Blyleven	.25	.10
☐	537	Tom Brunansky	.15	.06
☐	538	Randy Bush	.15	.06
☐	539	George Frazier	.15	.06
☐	540	Gary Gaetti	.25	.10
☐	541	Greg Gagne	.15	.06
☐	542	Mickey Hatcher	.15	.06
☐	543	Neal Heaton	.15	.06
☐	544	Kent Hrbek	.25	.10
☐	545	Roy Lee Jackson	.15	.06
☐	546	Tim Laudner	.15	.06
☐	547	Steve Lombardozzi	.15	.06
☐	548	Mark Portugal RC *	.25	.10
☐	549	Kirby Puckett	.60	.24
☐	550	Jeff Reed	.15	.06
☐	551	Mark Salas	.15	.06
☐	552	Roy Smalley	.15	.06
☐	553	Mike Smithson	.15	.06
☐	554	Frank Viola	.15	.06
☐	555	Thad Bosley	.15	.06
☐	556	Ron Cey	.25	.10
☐	557	Jody Davis	.15	.06
☐	558	Ron Davis	.15	.06
☐	559	Bob Dernier	.15	.06
☐	560	Frank DiPino	.15	.06
☐	561	Shawon Dunston UER (Wrong birth year listed on card back)	.15	.06
☐	562	Leon Durham	.15	.06
☐	563	Dennis Eckersley	.40	.16
☐	564	Terry Francona	.25	.10
☐	565	Dave Gumpert	.15	.06
☐	566	Guy Hoffman	.15	.06
☐	567	Ed Lynch	.15	.06
☐	568	Gary Matthews	.15	.06
☐	569	Keith Moreland	.15	.06
☐	570	Jamie Moyer RC	2.00	.80
☐	571	Jerry Mumphrey	.15	.06
☐	572	Ryne Sandberg	1.25	.50
☐	573	Scott Sanderson	.15	.06
☐	574	Lee Smith	.40	.16
☐	575	Chris Speier	.15	.06
☐	576	Rick Sutcliffe	.25	.10
☐	577	Manny Trillo	.15	.06
☐	578	Steve Trout	.15	.06
☐	579	Karl Best	.15	.06
☐	580	Scott Bradley	.15	.06
☐	581	Phil Bradley	.15	.06
☐	582	Mickey Brantley	.15	.06
☐	583	Mike G. Brown P	.15	.06
☐	584	Alvin Davis	.15	.06
☐	585	Lee Guetterman	.15	.06
☐	586	Mark Huismann	.15	.06
☐	587	Bob Kearney	.15	.06
☐	588	Pete Ladd	.15	.06
☐	589	Mark Langston	.15	.06
☐	590	Mike Moore	.15	.06
☐	591	Mike Morgan	.15	.06
☐	592	John Moses	.15	.06
☐	593	Ken Phelps	.15	.06
☐	594	Jim Presley	.15	.06
☐	595	Rey Quinones UER (Quinonez on front)	.15	.06
☐	596	Harold Reynolds	.25	.10
☐	597	Billy Swift	.15	.06
☐	598	Danny Tartabull	.15	.06
☐	599	Steve Yeager	.15	.06
☐	600	Matt Young	.15	.06
☐	601	Bill Almon	.15	.06
☐	602	Rafael Belliard RC	.50	.20
☐	603	Mike Bielecki	.15	.06
☐	604	Barry Bonds RC	50.00	20.00
☐	605	Bobby Bonilla RC	1.25	.50
☐	606	Sid Bream	.15	.06
☐	607	Mike C. Brown	.15	.06
☐	608	Pat Clements	.15	.06
☐	609	Mike Diaz	.15	.06
☐	610	Cecilio Guante	.15	.06
☐	611	Barry Jones	.15	.06
☐	612	Bob Kipper	.15	.06
☐	613	Larry McWilliams	.15	.06
☐	614	Jim Morrison	.15	.06
☐	615	Joe Orsulak	.15	.06
☐	616	Junior Ortiz	.15	.06
☐	617	Tony Pena	.15	.06
☐	618	Johnny Ray	.15	.06
☐	619	Rick Reuschel	.15	.06
☐	620	R.J. Reynolds	.15	.06
☐	621	Rick Rhoden	.15	.06
☐	622	Don Robinson	.15	.06
☐	623	Bob Walk	.15	.06
☐	624	Jim Winn	.15	.06
☐	625	Pete Incaviglia Jose Canseco	.60	.24
☐	626	Don Sutton	.25	.10

Phil Niekro
❑ 627 Dave Righetti .15 .06
Don Aase
❑ 628 Wally Joyner .60 .24
Jose Canseco
❑ 629 Gary Carter .40 .16
Sid Fernandez
Dwight Gooden
Keith Hernandez
Darryl Strawberry
❑ 630 Mike Scott .15 .06
Mike Krukow
❑ 631 Fernando Valenzuela .15 .06
John Franco
❑ 632 Bob Horner 4 Homers .15 .06
❑ 633 Jose Canseco .60 .24
Jim Rice
Kirby Puckett
❑ 634 Gary Carter .60 .24
Roger Clemens
❑ 635 Steve Carlton 4000K's .25 .10
❑ 636 Glenn Davis .60 .24
Eddie Murray
❑ 637 Wade Boggs .25 .10
Keith Hernandez
❑ 638 Don Mattingly 1.00 .40
Darryl Strawberry
❑ 639 Dave Parker .60 .24
Ryne Sandberg
❑ 640 Dwight Gooden .60 .24
Roger Clemens
❑ 641 Mike Witt .15 .06
Charlie Hough
❑ 642 Juan Samuel .25 .10
Tim Raines
❑ 643 Harold Baines .25 .10
Jesse Barfield
❑ 644 Dave Clark RC and .50 .20
Greg Swindell
❑ 645 Ron Karkovice RC .50 .20
Russ Morman
❑ 646 Devon White RC and 1.25 .50
Willie Fraser
❑ 647 Mike Stanley RC and .50 .20
Jerry Browne
❑ 648 Dave Magadan RC .50 .20
Phil Lombardi
❑ 649 Jose Gonzalez RC .25 .10
Ralph Bryant
❑ 650 Jimmy Jones RC and .25 .10
Randy Asadoor
❑ 651 Tracy Jones RC and .25 .10
Marvin Freeman
❑ 652 John Stefero and .50 .20
Kevin Seitzer RC
❑ 653 Rob Nelson and .25 .10
Steve Fireovid
❑ 654 CL: Mets/Red Sox .15 .06
Astros/Angels
❑ 655 CL: Yankees/Rangers .15 .06
Tigers/Phillies
❑ 656 CL: Reds/Blue Jays .15 .06
Indians/Giants
ERR (230/231 wrong)
❑ 657 CL: Cardinals/Expos .15 .06
Brewers/Royals
❑ 658 CL: A's/Padres .15 .06
Dodgers/Orioles
❑ 659 CL: White Sox/Braves .15 .06
Twins/Cubs
❑ 660 CL: Mariners/Pirates .15 .06
Special Cards
ER (580/581 wrong)

1987 Fleer Update

	Nm-Mt	Ex-Mt
COMP.FACT.SET (132)	15.00	6.00

❑ 1 Scott Bankhead .10 .04
❑ 2 Eric Bell .15 .06
❑ 3 Juan Beniquez .10 .04
❑ 4 Juan Berenguer .10 .04
❑ 5 Mike Birkbeck .15 .06
❑ 6 Randy Bockus .10 .04
❑ 7 Rod Booker .10 .04

❑ 8 Thad Bosley .10 .04
❑ 9 Greg Brock .10 .04
❑ 10 Bob Brower .10 .04
❑ 11 Chris Brown .10 .04
❑ 12 Jerry Browne .15 .06
❑ 13 Ralph Bryant .10 .04
❑ 14 DeWayne Buice .10 .04
❑ 15 Ellis Burks XRC .75 .30
❑ 16 Casey Candaele .10 .04
❑ 17 Steve Carlton .25 .10
❑ 18 Juan Castillo .15 .06
❑ 19 Chuck Crim .10 .04
❑ 20 Mark Davidson .10 .04
❑ 21 Mark Davis .10 .04
❑ 22 Storm Davis .10 .04
❑ 23 Bill Dawley .10 .04
❑ 24 Andre Dawson .15 .06
❑ 25 Brian Dayett .10 .04
❑ 26 Rick Dempsey .15 .06
❑ 27 Ken Dowell .10 .04
❑ 28 Dave Dravecky .15 .06
❑ 29 Mike Dunne .10 .04
❑ 30 Dennis Eckersley .25 .10
❑ 31 Cecil Fielder .25 .10
❑ 32 Brian Fisher .10 .04
❑ 33 Willie Fraser .15 .06
❑ 34 Ken Gerhart .10 .04
❑ 35 Jim Gott .10 .04
❑ 36 Dan Gladden .10 .04
❑ 37 Mike Greenwell XRC* .30 .12
❑ 38 Cecilio Guante .10 .04
❑ 39 Albert Hall .10 .04
❑ 40 Atlee Hammaker .10 .04
❑ 41 Mickey Hatcher .10 .04
❑ 42 Mike Heath .10 .04
❑ 43 Neal Heaton .10 .04
❑ 44 Mike Henneman XRC .30 .12
❑ 45 Guy Hoffman .10 .04
❑ 46 Charles Hudson .10 .04
❑ 47 Chuck Jackson .10 .04
❑ 48 Mike Jackson XRC .30 .12
❑ 49 Reggie Jackson .25 .10
❑ 50 Chris James .10 .04
❑ 51 Dion James .10 .04
❑ 52 Stan Javier .10 .04
❑ 53 Stan Jefferson .10 .04
❑ 54 Jimmy Jones .15 .06
❑ 55 Tracy Jones .10 .04
❑ 56 Terry Kennedy .10 .04
❑ 57 Mike Kingery .15 .06
❑ 58 Ray Knight .10 .04
❑ 59 Gene Larkin XRC .30 .12
❑ 60 Mike LaValliere .30 .12
❑ 61 Jack Lazorko .10 .04
❑ 62 Terry Leach .10 .04
❑ 63 Rick Leach .10 .04
❑ 64 Craig Lefferts .10 .04
❑ 65 Jim Lindeman .15 .06
❑ 66 Bill Long .10 .04
❑ 67 Mike Loynd .10 .04
❑ 68 Greg Maddux XRC 5.00 2.00
❑ 69 Bill Madlock .15 .06
❑ 70 Dave Magadan .30 .12
❑ 71 Joe Magrane XRC .15 .06
❑ 72 Fred Manrique .10 .04
❑ 73 Mike Mason .10 .04
❑ 74 Lloyd McClendon XRC .30 .12
❑ 75 Fred McGriff 1.00 .40
❑ 76 Mark McGwire 5.00 2.00
❑ 77 Mark McLemore .15 .06
❑ 78 Kevin McReynolds .10 .04
❑ 79 Dave Meads .10 .04
❑ 80 Greg Minton .10 .04
❑ 81 John Mitchell XRC .15 .06
❑ 82 Kevin Mitchell .25 .10
❑ 83 John Morris .10 .04
❑ 84 Jeff Musselman .10 .04
❑ 85 Randy Myers XRC .75 .30
❑ 86 Gene Nelson .10 .04
❑ 87 Joe Niekro .10 .04
❑ 88 Tom Nieto .10 .04
❑ 89 Reid Nichols .10 .04
❑ 90 Matt Nokes XRC .30 .12
❑ 91 Dickie Noles .10 .04
❑ 92 Edwin Nunez .10 .04
❑ 93 Jose Nunez .10 .04
❑ 94 Paul O'Neill .40 .16
❑ 95 Jim Paciorek .10 .04
❑ 96 Lance Parrish .15 .06
❑ 97 Bill Pecota XRC .15 .06
❑ 98 Tony Pena .10 .04
❑ 99 Luis Polonia XRC .15 .06
❑ 100 Randy Ready .10 .04
❑ 101 Jeff Reardon .15 .06
❑ 102 Gary Redus .10 .04
❑ 103 Rick Rhoden .10 .04
❑ 104 Wally Ritchie .10 .04
❑ 105 Jeff M. Robinson UER .10 .04
(Wrong Jeff's
stats on back)
❑ 106 Mark Salas .10 .04
❑ 107 Dave Schmidt .10 .04
❑ 108 Kevin Seitzer UER .30 .12
(Wrong birth year)
❑ 109 John Shelby .10 .04
❑ 110 John Smiley XRC .30 .12
❑ 111 Lary Sorensen .10 .04
❑ 112 Chris Speier .10 .04
❑ 113 Randy St.Claire .10 .04
❑ 114 Jim Sundberg .10 .04
❑ 115 B.J. Surhoff XRC .75 .30
❑ 116 Greg Swindell .30 .12
❑ 117 Danny Tartabull .10 .04
❑ 118 Dorn Taylor .10 .04
❑ 119 Lee Tunnell .10 .04
❑ 120 Ed VandeBerg .10 .04
❑ 121 Andy Van Slyke .15 .06
❑ 122 Gary Ward .10 .04
❑ 123 Devon White .75 .30
❑ 124 Alan Wiggins .10 .04
❑ 125 Bill Wilkinson .10 .04
❑ 126 Jim Winn .10 .04
❑ 127 Frank Williams .10 .04
❑ 128 Ken Williams XRC .10 .04
❑ 129 Matt Williams XRC 1.50 .60
❑ 130 Herm Winningham .10 .04
❑ 131 Matt Young .10 .04
❑ 132 Checklist 1-132 .10 .04

1988 Fleer

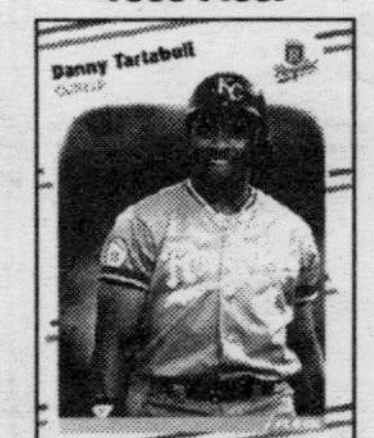

	Nm-Mt	Ex-Mt
COMPLETE SET (660)	15.00	6.00
COMP.RETAIL SET (660)	15.00	6.00
COMP.HOBBY SET (672)	15.00	6.00

❑ 1 Keith Atherton .10 .04
❑ 2 Don Baylor .15 .06
❑ 3 Juan Berenguer .10 .04
❑ 4 Bert Blyleven .15 .06
❑ 5 Tom Brunansky .10 .04
❑ 6 Randy Bush .10 .04
❑ 7 Steve Carlton .20 .08
❑ 8 Mark Davidson .10 .04
❑ 9 George Frazier .10 .04
❑ 10 Gary Gaetti .15 .06
❑ 11 Greg Gagne .10 .04
❑ 12 Dan Gladden .10 .04
❑ 13 Kent Hrbek .15 .06
❑ 14 Gene Larkin RC* .10 .04
❑ 15 Tim Laudner .10 .04
❑ 16 Steve Lombardozzi .10 .04
❑ 17 Al Newman .10 .04
❑ 18 Joe Niekro .10 .04
❑ 19 Kirby Puckett .30 .12
❑ 20 Jeff Reardon .15 .06
❑ 21A Dan Schatzeder ERR .15 .06
(Misspelled Schatzader on both sides of the card)
❑ 21B Dan Schatzeder COR .10 .04
❑ 22 Roy Smalley .10 .04
❑ 23 Mike Smithson .10 .04
❑ 24 Les Straker .10 .04
❑ 25 Frank Viola .10 .04
❑ 26 Jack Clark .15 .06
❑ 27 Vince Coleman .10 .04
❑ 28 Danny Cox .10 .04
❑ 29 Bill Dawley .10 .04
❑ 30 Ken Dayley .10 .04
❑ 31 Doug DeCinces .10 .04
❑ 32 Curt Ford .10 .04
❑ 33 Bob Forsch .10 .04
❑ 34 David Green .10 .04
❑ 35 Tom Herr .10 .04
❑ 36 Ricky Horton .10 .04
❑ 37 Lance Johnson RC .30 .12
❑ 38 Steve Lake .10 .04
❑ 39 Jim Lindeman .10 .04
❑ 40 Joe Magrane RC* .10 .04
❑ 41 Greg Mathews .10 .04
❑ 42 Willie McGee .15 .06
❑ 43 John Morris .10 .04
❑ 44 Jose Oquendo .10 .04
❑ 45 Tony Pena .10 .04
❑ 46 Terry Pendleton .15 .06
❑ 47 Ozzie Smith .30 .12
❑ 48 John Tudor .10 .04
❑ 49 Lee Tunnell .10 .04
❑ 50 Todd Worrell .15 .06
❑ 51 Doyle Alexander .10 .04
❑ 52 Dave Bergman .10 .04
❑ 53 Tom Brookens .10 .04
❑ 54 Darrell Evans .15 .06
❑ 55 Kirk Gibson .15 .06
❑ 56 Mike Heath .10 .04
❑ 57 Mike Henneman RC* .15 .06
❑ 58 Willie Hernandez .10 .04
❑ 59 Larry Herndon .10 .04
❑ 60 Eric King .10 .04
❑ 61 Chet Lemon .10 .04
❑ 62 Scott Lusader .10 .04
❑ 63 Bill Madlock .15 .06
❑ 64 Jack Morris .15 .06
❑ 65 Jim Morrison .10 .04
❑ 66 Matt Nokes RC* .10 .04
❑ 67 Dan Petry .10 .04
❑ 68A Jeff M. Robinson .30 .12
ERR, Stats for Jeff D. Robinson on card back
Born 12-13-60
❑ 68B Jeff M. Robinson .10 .04
COR, Born 12-14-61
❑ 69 Pat Sheridan .10 .04
❑ 70 Nate Snell .10 .04
❑ 71 Frank Tanana .10 .04
❑ 72 Walt Terrell .10 .04
❑ 73 Mark Thurmond .10 .04
❑ 74 Alan Trammell .20 .08
❑ 75 Lou Whitaker .15 .06
❑ 76 Mike Aldrete .10 .04
❑ 77 Bob Brenly .10 .04
❑ 78 Will Clark .30 .12
❑ 79 Chili Davis .20 .08
❑ 80 Kelly Downs .10 .04
❑ 81 Dave Dravecky .15 .06
❑ 82 Scott Garrelts .10 .04
❑ 83 Atlee Hammaker .10 .04
❑ 84 Dave Henderson .10 .04
❑ 85 Mike Krukow .10 .04
❑ 86 Mike LaCoss .10 .04
❑ 87 Craig Lefferts .10 .04
❑ 88 Jeff Leonard .10 .04
❑ 89 Candy Maldonado .10 .04
❑ 90 Eddie Milner .10 .04
❑ 91 Bob Melvin .10 .04
❑ 92 Kevin Mitchell .15 .06
❑ 93 Jon Perlman .10 .04
❑ 94 Rick Reuschel .10 .04
❑ 95 Don Robinson .10 .04
❑ 96 Chris Speier .10 .04
❑ 97 Harry Spilman .10 .04
❑ 98 Robby Thompson .10 .04
❑ 99 Jose Uribe .10 .04
❑ 100 Mark Wasinger .10 .04
❑ 101 Matt Williams RC 1.50 .60
❑ 102 Jesse Barfield .10 .04
❑ 103 George Bell .10 .04
❑ 104 Juan Beniquez .10 .04
❑ 105 John Cerutti .10 .04
❑ 106 Jim Clancy .10 .04
❑ 107 Rob Ducey .10 .04
❑ 108 Mark Eichhorn .10 .04
❑ 109 Tony Fernandez .10 .04
❑ 110 Cecil Fielder .20 .08
❑ 111 Kelly Gruber .10 .04
❑ 112 Tom Henke .10 .04
❑ 113A Garth Iorg ERR .30 .12
(Misspelled Iorq on card front)
❑ 113B Garth Iorg COR .10 .04
❑ 114 Jimmy Key .15 .06
❑ 115 Rick Leach .10 .04
❑ 116 Manny Lee .10 .04
❑ 117 Nelson Liriano .10 .04
❑ 118 Fred McGriff .30 .12
❑ 119 Lloyd Moseby .10 .04
❑ 120 Rance Mulliniks .10 .04
❑ 121 Jeff Musselman .10 .04
❑ 122 Jose Nunez .10 .04
❑ 123 Dave Stieb .10 .04
❑ 124 Willie Upshaw .10 .04
❑ 125 Duane Ward .10 .04
❑ 126 Ernie Whitt .10 .04
❑ 127 Rick Aguilera .15 .06
❑ 128 Wally Backman .10 .04
❑ 129 Mark Carreon RC .15 .06
❑ 130 Gary Carter .20 .08
❑ 131 David Cone .15 .06
❑ 132 Ron Darling .10 .04
❑ 133 Len Dykstra .15 .06
❑ 134 Sid Fernandez .10 .04
❑ 135 Dwight Gooden .20 .08
❑ 136 Keith Hernandez .20 .08
❑ 137 Gregg Jefferies RC .30 .12
❑ 138 Howard Johnson .10 .04
❑ 139 Terry Leach .10 .04
❑ 140 Barry Lyons .10 .04
❑ 141 Dave Magadan .10 .04
❑ 142 Roger McDowell .10 .04
❑ 143 Kevin McReynolds .10 .04
❑ 144 Keith A. Miller RC .10 .04
❑ 145 John Mitchell RC .10 .04
❑ 146 Randy Myers .20 .08
❑ 147 Bob Ojeda .10 .04
❑ 148 Jesse Orosco .10 .04
❑ 149 Rafael Santana .10 .04
❑ 150 Doug Sisk .10 .04
❑ 151 Darryl Strawberry .20 .08
❑ 152 Tim Teufel .10 .04
❑ 153 Gene Walter .10 .04
❑ 154 Mookie Wilson .15 .06
❑ 155 Jay Aldrich .10 .04
❑ 156 Chris Bosio .10 .04
❑ 157 Glenn Braggs .10 .04
❑ 158 Greg Brock .10 .04
❑ 159 Juan Castillo .10 .04
❑ 160 Mark Clear .10 .04
❑ 161 Cecil Cooper .15 .06
❑ 162 Chuck Crim .10 .04
❑ 163 Rob Deer .10 .04
❑ 164 Mike Felder .10 .04
❑ 165 Jim Gantner .10 .04
❑ 166 Ted Higuera .10 .04
❑ 167 Steve Kiefer .10 .04
❑ 168 Rick Manning .10 .04
❑ 169 Paul Molitor .20 .08
❑ 170 Juan Nieves .10 .04
❑ 171 Dan Plesac .10 .04
❑ 172 Earnest Riles .10 .04
❑ 173 Bill Schroeder .10 .04
❑ 174 Steve Stanicek .10 .04
❑ 175 B.J. Surhoff .15 .06
❑ 176 Dale Sveum .10 .04
❑ 177 Bill Wegman .10 .04
❑ 178 Robin Yount .30 .12
❑ 179 Hubie Brooks .10 .04
❑ 180 Tim Burke .10 .04
❑ 181 Casey Candaele .10 .04
❑ 182 Mike Fitzgerald .10 .04
❑ 183 Tom Foley .10 .04
❑ 184 Andres Galarraga .15 .06
❑ 185 Neal Heaton .10 .04
❑ 186 Wallace Johnson .10 .04
❑ 187 Vance Law .10 .04
❑ 188 Dennis Martinez .15 .06
❑ 189 Bob McClure .10 .04
❑ 190 Andy McGaffigan .10 .04
❑ 191 Reid Nichols .10 .04
❑ 192 Pascual Perez .10 .04
❑ 193 Tim Raines .15 .06
❑ 194 Jeff Reed .10 .04
❑ 195 Bob Sebra .10 .04
❑ 196 Bryn Smith .10 .04
❑ 197 Randy St.Claire .10 .04
❑ 198 Tim Wallach .10 .04
❑ 199 Mitch Webster .10 .04
❑ 200 Herm Winningham .10 .04
❑ 201 Floyd Youmans .10 .04
❑ 202 Brad Arnsberg .10 .04
❑ 203 Rick Cerone .10 .04
❑ 204 Pat Clements .10 .04
❑ 205 Henry Cotto .10 .04
❑ 206 Mike Easler .10 .04
❑ 207 Ron Guidry .15 .06
❑ 208 Bill Gullickson .10 .04
❑ 209 Rickey Henderson .60 .24
❑ 210 Charles Hudson .10 .04
❑ 211 Tommy John .15 .06
❑ 212 Roberto Kelly RC .30 .12
❑ 213 Ron Kittle .10 .04
❑ 214 Don Mattingly 1.00 .40
❑ 215 Bobby Meacham .10 .04
❑ 216 Mike Pagliarulo .10 .04
❑ 217 Dan Pasqua .10 .04
❑ 218 Willie Randolph .15 .06
❑ 219 Rick Rhoden .10 .04
❑ 220 Dave Righetti .10 .04
❑ 221 Jerry Royster .10 .04
❑ 222 Tim Stoddard .10 .04
❑ 223 Wayne Tolleson .10 .04
❑ 224 Gary Ward .10 .04
❑ 225 Claudell Washington .10 .04
❑ 226 Dave Winfield .20 .08
❑ 227 Buddy Bell .15 .06
❑ 228 Tom Browning .10 .04
❑ 229 Dave Concepcion .15 .06
❑ 230 Kal Daniels .10 .04
❑ 231 Eric Davis .15 .06
❑ 232 Bo Diaz .10 .04
❑ 233 Nick Esasky .10 .04
(Has a dollar sign before '87 SB totals)
❑ 234 John Franco .15 .06
❑ 235 Guy Hoffman .10 .04
❑ 236 Tom Hume .10 .04
❑ 237 Tracy Jones .10 .04
❑ 238 Bill Landrum .10 .04
❑ 239 Barry Larkin .30 .12
❑ 240 Terry McGriff .10 .04
❑ 241 Rob Murphy .10 .04
❑ 242 Ron Oester .10 .04
❑ 243 Dave Parker .15 .06
❑ 244 Pat Perry .10 .04
❑ 245 Ted Power .10 .04

❑ 246 Dennis Rasmussen .10 .04
❑ 247 Ron Robinson .10 .04
❑ 248 Kurt Stillwell .10 .04
❑ 249 Jeff Treadway RC .10 .04
❑ 250 Frank Williams .10 .04
❑ 251 Steve Balboni .10 .04
❑ 252 Bud Black .10 .04
❑ 253 Thad Bosley .10 .04
❑ 254 George Brett 1.00 .40
❑ 255 John Davis .10 .04
❑ 256 Steve Farr .10 .04
❑ 257 Gene Garber .10 .04
❑ 258 Jerry Don Gleaton .10 .04
❑ 259 Mark Gubicza .10 .04
❑ 260 Bo Jackson .30 .12
❑ 261 Danny Jackson .10 .04
❑ 262 Ross Jones .10 .04
❑ 263 Charlie Leibrandt .10 .04
❑ 264 Bill Pecota RC* .10 .04
❑ 265 Melido Perez RC .10 .04
❑ 266 Jamie Quirk .10 .04
❑ 267 Dan Quisenberry .10 .04
❑ 268 Bret Saberhagen .15 .06
❑ 269 Angel Salazar .10 .04
❑ 270 Kevin Seitzer UER .15 .06
(Wrong birth year)
❑ 271 Danny Tartabull .10 .04
❑ 272 Gary Thurman .10 .04
❑ 273 Frank White .15 .06
❑ 274 Willie Wilson .10 .04
❑ 275 Tony Bernazard .10 .04
❑ 276 Jose Canseco .30 .12
❑ 277 Mike Davis .10 .04
❑ 278 Storm Davis .10 .04
❑ 279 Dennis Eckersley .15 .06
❑ 280 Alfredo Griffin .10 .04
❑ 281 Rick Honeycutt .10 .04
❑ 282 Jay Howell .10 .04
❑ 283 Reggie Jackson .20 .08
❑ 284 Dennis Lamp .10 .04
❑ 285 Carney Lansford .15 .06
❑ 286 Mark McGwire 2.50 1.00
❑ 287 Dwayne Murphy .10 .04
❑ 288 Gene Nelson .10 .04
❑ 289 Steve Ontiveros .10 .04
❑ 290 Tony Phillips .10 .04
❑ 291 Eric Plunk .10 .04
❑ 292 Luis Polonia RC* .10 .04
❑ 293 Rick Rodriguez .10 .04
❑ 294 Terry Steinbach .15 .06
❑ 295 Dave Stewart .15 .06
❑ 296 Curt Young .10 .04
❑ 297 Luis Aguayo .10 .04
❑ 298 Steve Bedrosian .10 .04
❑ 299 Jeff Calhoun .10 .04
❑ 300 Don Carman .10 .04
❑ 301 Todd Frohwirth .10 .04
❑ 302 Greg Gross .10 .04
❑ 303 Kevin Gross .10 .04
❑ 304 Von Hayes .10 .04
❑ 305 Keith Hughes .10 .04
❑ 306 Mike Jackson RC* .15 .06
❑ 307 Chris James .10 .04
❑ 308 Steve Jeltz .10 .04
❑ 309 Mike Maddux .10 .04
❑ 310 Lance Parrish .10 .04
❑ 311 Shane Rawley .10 .04
❑ 312 Wally Ritchie .10 .04
❑ 313 Bruce Ruffin .10 .04
❑ 314 Juan Samuel .10 .04
❑ 315 Mike Schmidt .75 .30
❑ 316 Rick Schu .10 .04
❑ 317 Jeff Stone .10 .04
❑ 318 Kent Tekulve .10 .04
❑ 319 Milt Thompson .10 .04
❑ 320 Glenn Wilson .10 .04
❑ 321 Rafael Belliard .10 .04
❑ 322 Barry Bonds 3.00 1.20
❑ 323 Bobby Bonilla UER .15 .06
(Wrong birth year)
❑ 324 Sid Bream .10 .04
❑ 325 John Cangelosi .10 .04
❑ 326 Mike Diaz .10 .04
❑ 327 Doug Drabek .10 .04
❑ 328 Mike Dunne .10 .04
❑ 329 Brian Fisher .10 .04
❑ 330 Brett Gideon .10 .04
❑ 331 Terry Harper .10 .04
❑ 332 Bob Kipper .10 .04
❑ 333 Mike LaValliere .10 .04
❑ 334 Jose Lind RC .10 .04
❑ 335 Junior Ortiz .10 .04
❑ 336 Vicente Palacios .10 .04
❑ 337 Bob Patterson .10 .04
❑ 338 Al Pedrique .10 .04
❑ 339 R.J. Reynolds .10 .04
❑ 340 John Smiley RC* .15 .06
❑ 341 Andy Van Slyke UER .15 .06
(Wrong batting and throwing listed)
❑ 342 Bob Walk .10 .04
❑ 343 Marty Barrett .10 .04
❑ 344 Todd Benzinger RC* .10 .04
❑ 345 Wade Boggs .20 .08
❑ 346 Tom Bolton .10 .04
❑ 347 Oil Can Boyd .10 .04
❑ 348 Ellis Burks RC .75 .30
❑ 349 Roger Clemens .75 .30
❑ 350 Steve Crawford .10 .04
❑ 351 Dwight Evans .15 .06
❑ 352 Wes Gardner .10 .04
❑ 353 Rich Gedman .10 .04
❑ 354 Mike Greenwell .10 .04
❑ 355 Sam Horn RC .10 .04
❑ 356 Bruce Hurst .10 .04
❑ 357 John Marzano .10 .04
❑ 358 Al Nipper .10 .04
❑ 359 Spike Owen .10 .04
❑ 360 Jody Reed RC .15 .06
❑ 361 Jim Rice .15 .06
❑ 362 Ed Romero .10 .04
❑ 363 Kevin Romine .10 .04
❑ 364 Joe Sambito .10 .04
❑ 365 Calvin Schiraldi .10 .04
❑ 366 Jeff Sellers .10 .04
❑ 367 Bob Stanley .10 .04
❑ 368 Scott Bankhead .10 .04
❑ 369 Phil Bradley .10 .04
❑ 370 Scott Bradley .10 .04
❑ 371 Mickey Brantley .10 .04
❑ 372 Mike Campbell .10 .04
❑ 373 Alvin Davis .10 .04
❑ 374 Lee Guetterman .10 .04
❑ 375 Dave Hengel .10 .04
❑ 376 Mike Kingery .10 .04
❑ 377 Mark Langston .10 .04
❑ 378 Edgar Martinez RC 3.00 1.20
❑ 379 Mike Moore .10 .04
❑ 380 Mike Morgan .10 .04
❑ 381 John Moses .10 .04
❑ 382 Donell Nixon .10 .04
❑ 383 Edwin Nunez .10 .04
❑ 384 Ken Phelps .10 .04
❑ 385 Jim Presley .10 .04
❑ 386 Rey Quinones .10 .04
❑ 387 Jerry Reed .10 .04
❑ 388 Harold Reynolds .15 .06
❑ 389 Dave Valle .10 .04
❑ 390 Bill Wilkinson .10 .04
❑ 391 Harold Baines .15 .06
❑ 392 Floyd Bannister .10 .04
❑ 393 Daryl Boston .10 .04
❑ 394 Ivan Calderon .10 .04
❑ 395 Jose DeLeon .10 .04
❑ 396 Richard Dotson .10 .04
❑ 397 Carlton Fisk .20 .08
❑ 398 Ozzie Guillen .10 .04
❑ 399 Ron Hassey .10 .04
❑ 400 Donnie Hill .10 .04
❑ 401 Bob James .10 .04
❑ 402 Dave LaPoint .10 .04
❑ 403 Bill Lindsey .10 .04
❑ 404 Bill Long .10 .04
❑ 405 Steve Lyons .10 .04
❑ 406 Fred Manrique .10 .04
❑ 407 Jack McDowell RC .30 .12
❑ 408 Gary Redus .10 .04
❑ 409 Ray Searage .10 .04
❑ 410 Bobby Thigpen .10 .04
❑ 411 Greg Walker .10 .04
❑ 412 Ken Williams RC .10 .04
❑ 413 Jim Winn .10 .04
❑ 414 Jody Davis .10 .04
❑ 415 Andre Dawson .15 .06
❑ 416 Brian Dayett .10 .04
❑ 417 Bob Dernier .10 .04
❑ 418 Frank DiPino .10 .04
❑ 419 Shawon Dunston .10 .04
❑ 420 Leon Durham .10 .04
❑ 421 Les Lancaster .10 .04
❑ 422 Ed Lynch .10 .04
❑ 423 Greg Maddux 1.50 .60
❑ 424 Dave Martinez .10 .04
❑ 425A Keith Moreland ERR 1.50 .60
(Photo actually Jody Davis)
❑ 425B Keith Moreland COR .15 .06
(Bat on shoulder)
❑ 426 Jamie Moyer .30 .12
❑ 427 Jerry Mumphrey .10 .04
❑ 428 Paul Noce .10 .04
❑ 429 Rafael Palmeiro .60 .24
❑ 430 Wade Rowdon .10 .04
❑ 431 Ryne Sandberg .60 .24
❑ 432 Scott Sanderson .10 .04
❑ 433 Lee Smith .15 .06
❑ 434 Jim Sundberg .10 .04
❑ 435 Rick Sutcliffe .15 .06
❑ 436 Manny Trillo .10 .04
❑ 437 Juan Agosto .10 .04
❑ 438 Larry Andersen .10 .04
❑ 439 Alan Ashby .10 .04
❑ 440 Kevin Bass .10 .04
❑ 441 Ken Caminiti RC 1.00 .40
❑ 442 Rocky Childress .10 .04
❑ 443 Jose Cruz .10 .04
❑ 444 Danny Darwin .10 .04
❑ 445 Glenn Davis .10 .04
❑ 446 Jim Deshaies .10 .04
❑ 447 Bill Doran .10 .04
❑ 448 Ty Gainey .10 .04
❑ 449 Billy Hatcher .10 .04
❑ 450 Jeff Heathcock .10 .04
❑ 451 Bob Knepper .10 .04
❑ 452 Rob Mallicoat .10 .04
❑ 453 Dave Meads .10 .04
❑ 454 Craig Reynolds .10 .04
❑ 455 Nolan Ryan 1.50 .60
❑ 456 Mike Scott .10 .04
❑ 457 Dave Smith .10 .04
❑ 458 Denny Walling .10 .04
❑ 459 Robbie Wine .10 .04
❑ 460 Gerald Young .10 .04
❑ 461 Bob Brower .10 .04
❑ 462A Jerry Browne ERR 1.50 .60
(Photo actually Bob Brower, white player)
❑ 462B Jerry Browne COR .15 .06
(Black player)
❑ 463 Steve Buechele .10 .04
❑ 464 Edwin Correa .10 .04
❑ 465 Cecil Espy .10 .04
❑ 466 Scott Fletcher .10 .04
❑ 467 Jose Guzman .10 .04
❑ 468 Greg Harris .10 .04
❑ 469 Charlie Hough .15 .06
❑ 470 Pete Incaviglia .10 .04
❑ 471 Paul Kilgus .10 .04
❑ 472 Mike Loynd .10 .04
❑ 473 Oddibe McDowell .10 .04
❑ 474 Dale Mohorcic .10 .04
❑ 475 Pete O'Brien .10 .04
❑ 476 Larry Parrish .10 .04
❑ 477 Geno Petralli .10 .04
❑ 478 Jeff Russell .10 .04
❑ 479 Ruben Sierra .10 .04
❑ 480 Mike Stanley .15 .06
❑ 481 Curtis Wilkerson .10 .04
❑ 482 Mitch Williams .10 .04
❑ 483 Bobby Witt .10 .04
❑ 484 Tony Armas .10 .04
❑ 485 Bob Boone .15 .06
❑ 486 Bill Buckner .15 .06
❑ 487 DeWayne Buice .10 .04
❑ 488 Brian Downing .10 .04
❑ 489 Chuck Finley .20 .08
❑ 490 Willie Fraser UER .10 .04

(Wrong bio stats,
for George Hendrick)
❑ 491 Jack Howell .10 .04
❑ 492 Ruppert Jones .10 .04
❑ 493 Wally Joyner .20 .08
❑ 494 Jack Lazorko .10 .04
❑ 495 Gary Lucas .10 .04
❑ 496 Kirk McCaskill .10 .04
❑ 497 Mark McLemore .10 .04
❑ 498 Darrell Miller .10 .04
❑ 499 Greg Minton .10 .04
❑ 500 Donnie Moore .10 .04
❑ 501 Gus Polidor .10 .04
❑ 502 Johnny Ray .10 .04
❑ 503 Mark Ryal .10 .04
❑ 504 Dick Schofield .10 .04
❑ 505 Don Sutton .30 .12
❑ 506 Devon White .15 .06
❑ 507 Mike Witt .10 .04
❑ 508 Dave Anderson .10 .04
❑ 509 Tim Belcher .15 .06
❑ 510 Ralph Bryant .10 .04
❑ 511 Tim Crews RC .10 .04
❑ 512 Mike Devereaux RC .15 .06
❑ 513 Mariano Duncan .10 .04
❑ 514 Pedro Guerrero .10 .04
❑ 515 Jeff Hamilton .10 .04
❑ 516 Mickey Hatcher .10 .04
❑ 517 Brad Havens .10 .04
❑ 518 Orel Hershiser .15 .06
❑ 519 Shawn Hillegas .10 .04
❑ 520 Ken Howell .10 .04
❑ 521 Tim Leary .10 .04
❑ 522 Mike Marshall .10 .04
❑ 523 Steve Sax .10 .04
❑ 524 Mike Scioscia .10 .04
❑ 525 Mike Sharperson .10 .04
❑ 526 John Shelby .10 .04
❑ 527 Franklin Stubbs .10 .04
❑ 528 Fernando Valenzuela .15 .06
❑ 529 Bob Welch .10 .04
❑ 530 Matt Young .10 .04
❑ 531 Jim Acker .10 .04
❑ 532 Paul Assenmacher .10 .04
❑ 533 Jeff Blauser RC .30 .12
❑ 534 Joe Boever .10 .04
❑ 535 Martin Clary .10 .04
❑ 536 Kevin Coffman .10 .04
❑ 537 Jeff Dedmon .10 .04
❑ 538 Ron Gant RC .50 .20
❑ 539 Tom Glavine RC 4.00 1.60
❑ 540 Ken Griffey .15 .06
❑ 541 Albert Hall .10 .04
❑ 542 Glenn Hubbard .10 .04
❑ 543 Dion James .10 .04
❑ 544 Dale Murphy .30 .12
❑ 545 Ken Oberkfell .10 .04
❑ 546 David Palmer .10 .04
❑ 547 Gerald Perry .10 .04
❑ 548 Charlie Puleo .10 .04
❑ 549 Ted Simmons .15 .06
❑ 550 Zane Smith .10 .04
❑ 551 Andres Thomas .10 .04
❑ 552 Ozzie Virgil .10 .04
❑ 553 Don Aase .10 .04
❑ 554 Jeff Ballard .10 .04
❑ 555 Eric Bell .10 .04
❑ 556 Mike Boddicker .10 .04
❑ 557 Ken Dixon .10 .04
❑ 558 Jim Dwyer .10 .04
❑ 559 Ken Gerhart .10 .04
❑ 560 Rene Gonzales RC .10 .04
❑ 561 Mike Griffin .10 .04
❑ 562 John Habyan UER .10 .04
(Misspelled Hayban on
both sides of card)
❑ 563 Terry Kennedy .10 .04
❑ 564 Ray Knight .10 .04
❑ 565 Lee Lacy .10 .04
❑ 566 Fred Lynn .10 .04
❑ 567 Eddie Murray .30 .12
❑ 568 Tom Niedenfuer .10 .04
❑ 569 Bill Ripken RC* .10 .04
❑ 570 Cal Ripken 1.25 .50
❑ 571 Dave Schmidt .10 .04
❑ 572 Larry Sheets .10 .04
❑ 573 Pete Stanicek .10 .04
❑ 574 Mark Williamson .10 .04
❑ 575 Mike Young .10 .04
❑ 576 Shawn Abner .10 .04
❑ 577 Greg Booker .10 .04
❑ 578 Chris Brown .10 .04
❑ 579 Keith Comstock .10 .04
❑ 580 Joey Cora RC .30 .12
❑ 581 Mark Davis .10 .04
❑ 582 Tim Flannery .30 .12
(With surfboard)
❑ 583 Goose Gossage .20 .08
❑ 584 Mark Grant .10 .04
❑ 585 Tony Gwynn .50 .20
❑ 586 Andy Hawkins .10 .04
❑ 587 Stan Jefferson .10 .04
❑ 588 Jimmy Jones .10 .04
❑ 589 John Kruk .15 .06
❑ 590 Shane Mack .10 .04
❑ 591 Carmelo Martinez .10 .04
❑ 592 Lance McCullers UER .10 .04
(6'11" tall)
❑ 593 Eric Nolte .10 .04
❑ 594 Randy Ready .10 .04
❑ 595 Luis Salazar .10 .04
❑ 596 Benito Santiago .20 .08
❑ 597 Eric Show .10 .04
❑ 598 Garry Templeton .10 .04
❑ 599 Ed Whitson .10 .04
❑ 600 Scott Bailes .10 .04
❑ 601 Chris Bando .10 .04
❑ 602 Jay Bell RC .75 .30
❑ 603 Brett Butler .15 .06
❑ 604 Tom Candiotti .10 .04
❑ 605 Joe Carter .30 .12
❑ 606 Carmen Castillo .10 .04
❑ 607 Brian Dorsett .10 .04
❑ 608 John Farrell RC .10 .04
❑ 609 Julio Franco .10 .04
❑ 610 Mel Hall .10 .04
❑ 611 Tommy Hinzo .10 .04
❑ 612 Brook Jacoby .10 .04
❑ 613 Doug Jones RC .30 .12
❑ 614 Ken Schrom .10 .04
❑ 615 Cory Snyder .10 .04
❑ 616 Sammy Stewart .10 .04
❑ 617 Greg Swindell .10 .04
❑ 618 Pat Tabler .10 .04
❑ 619 Ed VandeBerg .10 .04
❑ 620 Eddie Williams RC .15 .06
❑ 621 Rich Yett .10 .04
❑ 622 Wally Joyner .15 .06
Cory Snyder
❑ 623 George Bell .10 .04
Pedro Guerrero
❑ 624 Mark McGwire 1.00 .40
Jose Canseco
❑ 625 Dave Righetti .10 .04
Dan Plesac
❑ 626 Bret Saberhagen .15 .06
Mike Witt
Jack Morris
❑ 627 John Franco .10 .04
Steve Bedrosian
❑ 628 Ozzie Smith .30 .12
Ryne Sandberg
❑ 629 Mark McGwire HL 1.25 .50
❑ 630 Mike Greenwell .30 .12
Ellis Burks
Todd Benzinger
❑ 631 Tony Gwynn .20 .08
Tim Raines
❑ 632 Mike Scott .15 .06
Orel Hershiser
❑ 633 Pat Tabler 1.25 .50
Mark McGwire
❑ 634 Tony Gwynn .20 .08
Vince Coleman
❑ 635 Tony Fernandez .50 .20
Cal Ripken
Alan Trammell
❑ 636 Mike Schmidt .30 .12
Gary Carter
❑ 637 Darryl Strawberry .15 .06
Eric Davis
❑ 638 AL All-Stars .20 .08
Matt Nokes
Kirby Puckett
❑ 639 NL All-Stars .20 .08
Keith Hernandez
Dale Murphy
❑ 640 The O's Brothers .75 .30
Billy Ripken
Cal Ripken
❑ 641 Mark Grace RC and 2.00 .80
Darrin Jackson
❑ 642 Damon Berryhill RC .30 .12
Jeff Montgomery RC
❑ 643 Felix Fermin and .10 .04
Jesse Reid
❑ 644 Greg Myers RC and .10 .04
Greg Tabor
❑ 645 Joey Meyer and .10 .04
Jim Eppard
❑ 646 Adam Peterson .50 .20
Randy Velarde RC
❑ 647 Pete Smith and .15 .06
Chris Gwynn RC
❑ 648 Tom Newell and .10 .04
Greg Jelks
❑ 649 Mario Diaz RC .10 .04
Clay Parker
❑ 650 Jack Savage and .10 .04
Todd Simmons
❑ 651 John Burkett RC and .30 .12
Kirt Manwaring
❑ 652 Dave Otto RC and .40 .16
Walt Weiss
❑ 653 Jeff King RC and .15 .06
Randell Byers
❑ 654 CL: Twins/Cards .10 .04
Tigers/Giants UER
(90 Bob Melvin,
91 Eddie Milner)
❑ 655 CL: Blue Jays/Mets .10 .04
Brewers/Expos UER
(Mets listed before
Blue Jays on card)
❑ 656 CL: Yankees/Reds .10 .04
Royals/A's
❑ 657 CL: Phillies/Pirates .10 .04
Red Sox/Mariners
❑ 658 CL: White Sox/Cubs .10 .04
Astros/Rangers
❑ 659 CL: Angels/Dodgers .10 .04
Braves/Orioles
❑ 660 CL: Padres/Indians .10 .04
Rookies/Specials

1988 Fleer Update

	Nm-Mt	Ex-Mt
COMP.FACT.SET (132)	8.00	3.20

❑ 1 Jose Bautista XRC .10 .04
❑ 2 Joe Orsulak .10 .04
❑ 3 Doug Sisk .10 .04
❑ 4 Craig Worthington .10 .04
❑ 5 Mike Boddicker .10 .04
❑ 6 Rick Cerone .10 .04
❑ 7 Larry Parrish .10 .04
❑ 8 Lee Smith .20 .08
❑ 9 Mike Smithson .10 .04
❑ 10 John Trautwein .10 .04

No.	Player	Nm-Mt	Ex-Mt
11	Sherman Corbett	.10	.04
12	Chili Davis	.30	.12
13	Jim Eppard	.10	.04
14	Bryan Harvey XRC	.20	.08
15	John Davis	.10	.04
16	Dave Gallagher	.10	.04
17	Ricky Horton	.10	.04
18	Dan Pasqua	.10	.04
19	Melido Perez	.10	.04
20	Jose Segura	.10	.04
21	Andy Allanson	.10	.04
22	Jon Perlman	.10	.04
23	Domingo Ramos	.10	.04
24	Rick Rodriguez	.10	.04
25	Willie Upshaw	.10	.04
26	Paul Gibson	.10	.04
27	Don Heinkel	.10	.04
28	Ray Knight	.10	.04
29	Gary Pettis	.10	.04
30	Luis Salazar	.10	.04
31	Mike Macfarlane XRC	.10	.04
32	Jeff Montgomery	.50	.20
33	Ted Power	.10	.04
34	Israel Sanchez	.10	.04
35	Kurt Stillwell	.10	.04
36	Pat Tabler	.10	.04
37	Don August	.10	.04
38	Darryl Hamilton XRC	.20	.08
39	Jeff Leonard	.10	.04
40	Joey Meyer	.10	.04
41	Allan Anderson	.10	.04
42	Brian Harper	.10	.04
43	Tom Herr	.10	.04
44	Charlie Lea	.10	.04
45	John Moses (Listed as Hohn on checklist card)	.10	.04
46	John Candelaria	.10	.04
47	Jack Clark	.20	.08
48	Richard Dotson	.10	.04
49	Al Leiter XRC*	1.00	.40
50	Rafael Santana	.10	.04
51	Don Slaught	.10	.04
52	Todd Burns	.10	.04
53	Dave Henderson	.10	.04
54	Doug Jennings	.10	.04
55	Dave Parker	.20	.08
56	Walt Weiss	.30	.12
57	Bob Welch	.10	.04
58	Henry Cotto	.10	.04
59	Mario Diaz UER (Listed as Marion on card front)	.10	.04
60	Mike Jackson	.20	.08
61	Bill Swift	.10	.04
62	Jose Cecena	.10	.04
63	Ray Hayward	.10	.04
64	Jim Steels UER (Listed as Jim Steele on card back)	.10	.04
65	Pat Borders XRC	.20	.08
66	Sil Campusano	.10	.04
67	Mike Flanagan	.10	.04
68	Todd Stottlemyre XRC	.50	.20
69	David Wells XRC	1.00	.40
70	Jose Alvarez XRC	.10	.04
71	Paul Runge	.10	.04
72	Cesar Jimenez (Card was intended for German Jiminez, it's his photo)	.10	.04
73	Pete Smith	.10	.04
74	John Smoltz XRC	3.00	1.20
75	Damon Berryhill	.10	.04
76	Goose Gossage	.30	.12
77	Mark Grace	1.50	.60
78	Darrin Jackson	.10	.04
79	Vance Law	.10	.04
80	Jeff Pico	.10	.04
81	Gary Varsho	.10	.04
82	Tim Birtsas	.10	.04
83	Rob Dibble XRC	.75	.30
84	Danny Jackson	.10	.04
85	Paul O'Neill	.30	.12
86	Jose Rijo	.10	.04
87	Chris Sabo XRC	.20	.08
88	John Fishel	.10	.04
89	Craig Biggio XRC	2.00	.80
90	Terry Puhl	.10	.04
91	Rafael Ramirez	.10	.04
92	Louie Meadows	.10	.04
93	Kirk Gibson	.50	.20
94	Alfredo Griffin	.10	.04
95	Jay Howell	.10	.04
96	Jesse Orosco	.10	.04
97	Alejandro Pena	.10	.04
98	Tracy Woodson XRC*	.10	.04
99	John Dopson	.10	.04
100	Brian Holman XRC	.10	.04
101	Rex Hudler	.10	.04
102	Jeff Parrett	.10	.04
103	Nelson Santovenia	.10	.04
104	Kevin Elster	.10	.04
105	Jeff Innis	.10	.04
106	Mackey Sasser XRC*	.10	.04
107	Phil Bradley	.10	.04
108	Danny Clay	.10	.04
109	Greg A.Harris	.10	.04
110	Ricky Jordan XRC	.20	.08
111	David Palmer	.10	.04
112	Jim Gott	.10	.04
113	Tommy Gregg UER (Photo actually Randy Milligan)	.10	.04
114	Barry Jones	.10	.04
115	Randy Milligan XRC*	.10	.04
116	Luis Alicea XRC	.20	.08
117	Tom Brunansky	.10	.04
118	John Costello	.10	.04
119	Jose DeLeon	.10	.04
120	Bob Horner	.10	.04
121	Scott Terry	.10	.04
122	Roberto Alomar XRC	3.00	1.20
123	Dave Leiper	.10	.04
124	Keith Moreland	.10	.04
125	Mark Parent	.10	.04
126	Dennis Rasmussen	.10	.04
127	Randy Bockus	.10	.04
128	Brett Butler	.20	.08
129	Donell Nixon	.10	.04
130	Earnest Riles	.10	.04
131	Roger Samuels	.10	.04
132	Checklist U1-U132	.10	.04

1989 Fleer

	Nm-Mt	Ex-Mt
COMPLETE SET (660)	15.00	6.00
COMP.FACT.SET (672)	15.00	6.00

No.	Player	Nm-Mt	Ex-Mt
1	Don Baylor	.10	.04
2	Lance Blankenship RC	.10	.04
3	Todd Burns UER (Wrong birthdate; before/after All-Star stats missing)	.05	.02
4	Greg Cadaret UER (All-Star Break stats show 3 losses, should be 2	.05	.02
5	Jose Canseco	.25	.10
6	Storm Davis	.05	.02
7	Dennis Eckersley	.10	.04
8	Mike Gallego	.05	.02
9	Ron Hassey	.05	.02
10	Dave Henderson	.05	.02
11	Rick Honeycutt	.05	.02
12	Glenn Hubbard	.05	.02
13	Stan Javier	.05	.02
14	Doug Jennings	.05	.02
15	Felix Jose RC	.10	.04
16	Carney Lansford	.10	.04
17	Mark McGwire	1.00	.40
18	Gene Nelson	.05	.02
19	Dave Parker	.10	.04
20	Eric Plunk	.05	.02
21	Luis Polonia	.05	.02
22	Terry Steinbach	.10	.04
23	Dave Stewart	.10	.04
24	Walt Weiss	.05	.02
25	Bob Welch	.05	.02
26	Curt Young	.05	.02
27	Rick Aguilera	.10	.04
28	Wally Backman	.05	.02
29	Mark Carreon UER (After All-Star Break batting 7.14)	.05	.02
30	Gary Carter	.15	.06
31	David Cone	.10	.04
32	Ron Darling	.05	.02
33	Len Dykstra	.10	.04
34	Kevin Elster	.05	.02
35	Sid Fernandez	.05	.02
36	Dwight Gooden	.15	.06
37	Keith Hernandez	.15	.06
38	Gregg Jefferies	.10	.04
39	Howard Johnson	.05	.02
40	Terry Leach	.05	.02
41	Dave Magadan UER (Bio says 15 doubles, should be 13)	.05	.02
42	Bob McClure	.05	.02
43	Roger McDowell UER (Led Mets with 58, should be 62)	.05	.02
44	Kevin McReynolds	.05	.02
45	Keith A. Miller	.05	.02
46	Randy Myers	.10	.04
47	Bob Ojeda	.05	.02
48	Mackey Sasser	.05	.02
49	Darryl Strawberry	.15	.06
50	Tim Teufel	.05	.02
51	Dave West RC	.10	.04
52	Mookie Wilson	.10	.04
53	Dave Anderson	.05	.02
54	Tim Belcher	.05	.02
55	Mike Davis	.05	.02
56	Mike Devereaux	.05	.02
57	Kirk Gibson	.10	.04
58	Alfredo Griffin	.05	.02
59	Chris Gwynn	.05	.02
60	Jeff Hamilton	.05	.02
61A	Danny Heep ERR Lake Hills	.25	.10
61B	Danny Heep COR San Antonio	.05	.02
62	Orel Hershiser	.10	.04
63	Brian Holton	.05	.02
64	Jay Howell	.05	.02
65	Tim Leary	.05	.02
66	Mike Marshall	.05	.02
67	Ramon Martinez RC	.25	.10
68	Jesse Orosco	.05	.02
69	Alejandro Pena	.05	.02
70	Steve Sax	.05	.02
71	Mike Scioscia	.05	.02
72	Mike Sharperson	.05	.02
73	John Shelby	.05	.02
74	Franklin Stubbs	.05	.02
75	John Tudor	.05	.02
76	Fernando Valenzuela	.10	.04
77	Tracy Woodson	.05	.02
78	Marty Barrett	.05	.02
79	Todd Benzinger	.05	.02
80	Mike Boddicker UER (Rochester in '76, should be '78)	.05	.02
81	Wade Boggs	.15	.06
82	Oil Can Boyd	.05	.02
83	Ellis Burks	.15	.06
84	Rick Cerone	.05	.02

❑ 85 Roger Clemens .50 .20
❑ 86 Steve Curry .05 .02
❑ 87 Dwight Evans .10 .04
❑ 88 Wes Gardner .05 .02
❑ 89 Rich Gedman .05 .02
❑ 90 Mike Greenwell .05 .02
❑ 91 Bruce Hurst .05 .02
❑ 92 Dennis Lamp .05 .02
❑ 93 Spike Owen .05 .02
❑ 94 Larry Parrish UER .05 .02
(Before All-Star Break batting 1.90)
❑ 95 Carlos Quintana RC .10 .04
❑ 96 Jody Reed .05 .02
❑ 97 Jim Rice .10 .04
❑ 98A Kevin Romine ERR .25 .10
(Photo actually Randy Kutcher batting)
❑ 98B Kevin Romine COR .05 .02
(Arms folded)
❑ 99 Lee Smith .10 .04
❑ 100 Mike Smithson .05 .02
❑ 101 Bob Stanley .05 .02
❑ 102 Allan Anderson .05 .02
❑ 103 Keith Atherton .05 .02
❑ 104 Juan Berenguer .05 .02
❑ 105 Bert Blyleven .10 .04
❑ 106 Eric Bullock UER .05 .02
Bats/Throws Right, should be Left
❑ 107 Randy Bush .05 .02
❑ 108 John Christensen .05 .02
❑ 109 Mark Davidson .05 .02
❑ 110 Gary Gaetti .10 .04
❑ 111 Greg Gagne .05 .02
❑ 112 Dan Gladden .05 .02
❑ 113 German Gonzalez .05 .02
❑ 114 Brian Harper .05 .02
❑ 115 Tom Herr .05 .02
❑ 116 Kent Hrbek .10 .04
❑ 117 Gene Larkin .05 .02
❑ 118 Tim Laudner .05 .02
❑ 119 Charlie Lea .05 .02
❑ 120 Steve Lombardozzi .05 .02
❑ 121A John Moses ERR .25 .10
Tempe
❑ 121B John Moses COR .05 .02
Phoenix
❑ 122 Al Newman .05 .02
❑ 123 Mark Portugal .05 .02
❑ 124 Kirby Puckett .25 .10
❑ 125 Jeff Reardon .10 .04
❑ 126 Fred Toliver .05 .02
❑ 127 Frank Viola .05 .02
❑ 128 Doyle Alexander .05 .02
❑ 129 Dave Bergman .05 .02
❑ 130A Tom Brookens ERR .75 .30
(Mike Heath back)
❑ 130B Tom Brookens COR .05 .02
❑ 131 Paul Gibson .05 .02
❑ 132A Mike Heath ERR .75 .30
(Tom Brookens back)
❑ 132B Mike Heath COR .05 .02
❑ 133 Don Heinkel .05 .02
❑ 134 Mike Henneman .05 .02
❑ 135 Guillermo Hernandez .05 .02
❑ 136 Eric King .05 .02
❑ 137 Chet Lemon .05 .02
❑ 138 Fred Lynn UER .05 .02
'74 and '75 stats missing
❑ 139 Jack Morris .10 .04
❑ 140 Matt Nokes .05 .02
❑ 141 Gary Pettis .05 .02
❑ 142 Ted Power .05 .02
❑ 143 Jeff M. Robinson .05 .02
❑ 144 Luis Salazar .05 .02
❑ 145 Steve Searcy .05 .02
❑ 146 Pat Sheridan .05 .02
❑ 147 Frank Tanana .05 .02
❑ 148 Alan Trammell .15 .06
❑ 149 Walt Terrell .05 .02
❑ 150 Jim Walewander .05 .02
❑ 151 Lou Whitaker .10 .04
❑ 152 Tim Birtsas .05 .02
❑ 153 Tom Browning .05 .02
❑ 154 Keith Brown .05 .02
❑ 155 Norm Charlton RC .25 .10
❑ 156 Dave Concepcion .10 .04
❑ 157 Kal Daniels .05 .02
❑ 158 Eric Davis .10 .04
❑ 159 Bo Diaz .05 .02
❑ 160 Rob Dibble RC .50 .20
❑ 161 Nick Esasky .05 .02
❑ 162 John Franco .10 .04
❑ 163 Danny Jackson .05 .02
❑ 164 Barry Larkin .25 .10
❑ 165 Rob Murphy .05 .02
❑ 166 Paul O'Neill .15 .06
❑ 167 Jeff Reed .05 .02
❑ 168 Jose Rijo .05 .02
❑ 169 Ron Robinson .05 .02
❑ 170 Chris Sabo RC .40 .16
❑ 171 Candy Sierra .05 .02
❑ 172 Van Snider .05 .02
❑ 173A Jeff Treadway 5.00 2.00
(Target registration mark above head on front in light blue)
❑ 173B Jeff Treadway .05 .02
(No target on front)
❑ 174 Frank Williams UER .05 .02
(After All-Star Break stats are jumbled)
❑ 175 Herm Winningham .05 .02
❑ 176 Jim Adduci .05 .02
❑ 177 Don August .05 .02
❑ 178 Mike Birkbeck .05 .02
❑ 179 Chris Bosio .05 .02
❑ 180 Glenn Braggs .05 .02
❑ 181 Greg Brock .05 .02
❑ 182 Mark Clear .05 .02
❑ 183 Chuck Crim .05 .02
❑ 184 Rob Deer .05 .02
❑ 185 Tom Filer .05 .02
❑ 186 Jim Gantner .05 .02
❑ 187 Darryl Hamilton RC .25 .10
❑ 188 Ted Higuera .05 .02
❑ 189 Odell Jones .05 .02
❑ 190 Jeffrey Leonard .05 .02
❑ 191 Joey Meyer .05 .02
❑ 192 Paul Mirabella .05 .02
❑ 193 Paul Molitor .15 .06
❑ 194 Charlie O'Brien .05 .02
❑ 195 Dan Plesac .05 .02
❑ 196 Gary Sheffield RC 1.50 .60
❑ 197 B.J. Surhoff .10 .04
❑ 198 Dale Sveum .05 .02
❑ 199 Bill Wegman .05 .02
❑ 200 Robin Yount .25 .10
❑ 201 Rafael Belliard .05 .02
❑ 202 Barry Bonds 1.25 .50
❑ 203 Bobby Bonilla .10 .04
❑ 204 Sid Bream .05 .02
❑ 205 Benny Distefano .05 .02
❑ 206 Doug Drabek .05 .02
❑ 207 Mike Dunne .05 .02
❑ 208 Felix Fermin .05 .02
❑ 209 Brian Fisher .05 .02
❑ 210 Jim Gott .05 .02
❑ 211 Bob Kipper .05 .02
❑ 212 Dave LaPoint .05 .02
❑ 213 Mike LaValliere .05 .02
❑ 214 Jose Lind .05 .02
❑ 215 Junior Ortiz .05 .02
❑ 216 Vicente Palacios .05 .02
❑ 217 Tom Prince .05 .02
❑ 218 Gary Redus .05 .02
❑ 219 R.J. Reynolds .05 .02
❑ 220 Jeff D. Robinson .05 .02
❑ 221 John Smiley .05 .02
❑ 222 Andy Van Slyke .10 .04
❑ 223 Bob Walk .05 .02
❑ 224 Glenn Wilson .05 .02
❑ 225 Jesse Barfield .05 .02
❑ 226 George Bell .05 .02
❑ 227 Pat Borders RC .25 .10
❑ 228 John Cerutti .05 .02
❑ 229 Jim Clancy .05 .02
❑ 230 Mark Eichhorn .05 .02
❑ 231 Tony Fernandez .05 .02
❑ 232 Cecil Fielder .10 .04
❑ 233 Mike Flanagan .05 .02
❑ 234 Kelly Gruber .05 .02
❑ 235 Tom Henke .05 .02
❑ 236 Jimmy Key .10 .04
❑ 237 Rick Leach .05 .02
❑ 238 Manny Lee UER .05 .02
(Bio says regular shortstop, sic, Tony Fernandez)
❑ 239 Nelson Liriano .05 .02
❑ 240 Fred McGriff .25 .10
❑ 241 Lloyd Moseby .05 .02
❑ 242 Rance Mulliniks .05 .02
❑ 243 Jeff Musselman .05 .02
❑ 244 Dave Stieb .05 .02
❑ 245 Todd Stottlemyre .15 .06
❑ 246 Duane Ward .05 .02
❑ 247 David Wells .10 .04
❑ 248 Ernie Whitt UER .05 .02
(HR total 21, should be 121)
❑ 249 Luis Aguayo .05 .02
❑ 250A Neil Allen ERR .75 .30
Sarasota, FL
❑ 250B Neil Allen COR .05 .02
Syosset, NY
❑ 251 John Candelaria .05 .02
❑ 252 Jack Clark .05 .02
❑ 253 Richard Dotson .05 .02
❑ 254 Rickey Henderson .40 .16
❑ 255 Tommy John .10 .04
❑ 256 Roberto Kelly .10 .04
❑ 257 Al Leiter .25 .10
❑ 258 Don Mattingly .60 .24
❑ 259 Dale Mohorcic .05 .02
❑ 260 Hal Morris RC .25 .10
❑ 261 Scott Nielsen .05 .02
❑ 262 Mike Pagliarulo UER .05 .02
(Wrong birthdate)
❑ 263 Hipolito Pena .05 .02
❑ 264 Ken Phelps .05 .02
❑ 265 Willie Randolph .10 .04
❑ 266 Rick Rhoden .05 .02
❑ 267 Dave Righetti .05 .02
❑ 268 Rafael Santana .05 .02
❑ 269 Steve Shields .05 .02
❑ 270 Joel Skinner .05 .02
❑ 271 Don Slaught .05 .02
❑ 272 Claudell Washington .05 .02
❑ 273 Gary Ward .05 .02
❑ 274 Dave Winfield .15 .06
❑ 275 Luis Aquino .05 .02
❑ 276 Floyd Bannister .05 .02
❑ 277 George Brett .60 .24
❑ 278 Bill Buckner .10 .04
❑ 279 Nick Capra .05 .02
❑ 280 Jose DeJesus .05 .02
❑ 281 Steve Farr .05 .02
❑ 282 Jerry Don Gleaton .05 .02
❑ 283 Mark Gubicza .05 .02
❑ 284 Tom Gordon RC UER .25 .10
(16.2 innings in '88, should be 15.2)
❑ 285 Bo Jackson .25 .10
❑ 286 Charlie Leibrandt .05 .02
❑ 287 Mike Macfarlane RC .25 .10
❑ 288 Jeff Montgomery .10 .04
❑ 289 Bill Pecota UER .05 .02
(Photo actually Brad Wellman)
❑ 290 Jamie Quirk .05 .02
❑ 291 Bret Saberhagen .10 .04
❑ 292 Kevin Seitzer .05 .02
❑ 293 Kurt Stillwell .05 .02
❑ 294 Pat Tabler .05 .02
❑ 295 Danny Tartabull .05 .02
❑ 296 Gary Thurman .05 .02
❑ 297 Frank White .10 .04
❑ 298 Willie Wilson .05 .02
❑ 299 Roberto Alomar .30 .12
❑ 300 S.Alomar Jr. RC UER .40 .16
Wrong birthdate, says 6/16/66, should say 6/18/66
❑ 301 Chris Brown .05 .02
❑ 302 Mike Brumley UER .05 .02

(133 hits in '88,
should be 134)
❑ 303 Mark Davis .05 .02
❑ 304 Mark Grant .05 .02
❑ 305 Tony Gwynn .30 .12
❑ 306 Greg W. Harris RC .10 .04
❑ 307 Andy Hawkins .05 .02
❑ 308 Jimmy Jones .05 .02
❑ 309 John Kruk .10 .04
❑ 310 Dave Leiper .05 .02
❑ 311 Carmelo Martinez .05 .02
❑ 312 Lance McCullers .05 .02
❑ 313 Keith Moreland .05 .02
❑ 314 Dennis Rasmussen .05 .02
❑ 315 Randy Ready UER .05 .02
(1214 games in '88,
should be 114)
❑ 316 Benito Santiago .10 .04
❑ 317 Eric Show .05 .02
❑ 318 Todd Simmons .05 .02
❑ 319 Garry Templeton .05 .02
❑ 320 Dickie Thon .05 .02
❑ 321 Ed Whitson .05 .02
❑ 322 Marvell Wynne .05 .02
❑ 323 Mike Aldrete .05 .02
❑ 324 Brett Butler .10 .04
❑ 325 Will Clark UER .25 .10
(Three consecutive
100 RBI seasons)
❑ 326 Kelly Downs UER .05 .02
('88 stats missing)
❑ 327 Dave Dravecky .10 .04
❑ 328 Scott Garrelts .05 .02
❑ 329 Atlee Hammaker .05 .02
❑ 330 Charlie Hayes RC .25 .10
❑ 331 Mike Krukow .05 .02
❑ 332 Craig Lefferts .05 .02
❑ 333 Candy Maldonado .05 .02
❑ 334 Kirt Manwaring UER .05 .02
(Bats Rights)
❑ 335 Bob Melvin .05 .02
❑ 336 Kevin Mitchell .10 .04
❑ 337 Donell Nixon .05 .02
❑ 338 Tony Perezchica .05 .02
❑ 339 Joe Price .05 .02
❑ 340 Rick Reuschel .05 .02
❑ 341 Earnest Riles .05 .02
❑ 342 Don Robinson .05 .02
❑ 343 Chris Speier .05 .02
❑ 344 Robby Thompson UER .05 .02
(West Plam Beach)
❑ 345 Jose Uribe .05 .02
❑ 346 Matt Williams .25 .10
❑ 347 Trevor Wilson RC .10 .04
❑ 348 Juan Agosto .05 .02
❑ 349 Larry Andersen .05 .02
❑ 350A Alan Ashby ERR 2.00 .80
(Throws Rig)
❑ 350B Alan Ashby COR .05 .02
❑ 351 Kevin Bass .05 .02
❑ 352 Buddy Bell .10 .04
❑ 353 Craig Biggio RC .75 .30
❑ 354 Danny Darwin .05 .02
❑ 355 Glenn Davis .05 .02
❑ 356 Jim Deshaies .05 .02
❑ 357 Bill Doran .05 .02
❑ 358 John Fishel .05 .02
❑ 359 Billy Hatcher .05 .02
❑ 360 Bob Knepper .05 .02
❑ 361 L.Meadows UER .05 .02
Bio says 10 EBH's
and 6 SB's in '88,
should be 3 and 4
❑ 362 Dave Meads .05 .02
❑ 363 Jim Pankovits .05 .02
❑ 364 Terry Puhl .05 .02
❑ 365 Rafael Ramirez .05 .02
❑ 366 Craig Reynolds .05 .02
❑ 367 Mike Scott .05 .02
(Card number listed
as 368 on Astros CL)
❑ 368 Nolan Ryan 1.00 .40
(Card number listed
as 367 on Astros CL)
❑ 369 Dave Smith .05 .02
❑ 370 Gerald Young .05 .02
❑ 371 Hubie Brooks .05 .02
❑ 372 Tim Burke .05 .02
❑ 373 John Dopson .05 .02
❑ 374 Mike R. Fitzgerald .05 .02
❑ 375 Tom Foley .05 .02
❑ 376 Andres Galarraga UER .10 .04
(Home: Caracus)
❑ 377 Neal Heaton .05 .02
❑ 378 Joe Hesketh .05 .02
❑ 379 Brian Holman RC .10 .04
❑ 380 Rex Hudler .05 .02
❑ 381 R.Johnson RC UER 3.00 1.20
Innings for '85 and
'86 shown as 27 and
120, should be 27.1
and 119.2
❑ 382 Wallace Johnson .05 .02
❑ 383 Tracy Jones .05 .02
❑ 384 Dave Martinez .05 .02
❑ 385 Dennis Martinez .10 .04
❑ 386 Andy McGaffigan .05 .02
❑ 387 Otis Nixon .05 .02
❑ 388 Johnny Paredes .05 .02
❑ 389 Jeff Parrett .05 .02
❑ 390 Pascual Perez .05 .02
❑ 391 Tim Raines .10 .04
❑ 392 Luis Rivera .05 .02
❑ 393 Nelson Santovenia .05 .02
❑ 394 Bryn Smith .05 .02
❑ 395 Tim Wallach .05 .02
❑ 396 Andy Allanson UER .05 .02
1214 hits in '88,
should be 114
❑ 397 Rod Allen .05 .02
❑ 398 Scott Bailes .05 .02
❑ 399 Tom Candiotti .05 .02
❑ 400 Joe Carter .15 .06
❑ 401 Carmen Castillo UER .05 .02
(After All-Star Break
batting 2.50)
❑ 402 Dave Clark UER .05 .02
(Card front shows
position as Rookie;
after All-Star Break
batting 3.14)
❑ 403 John Farrell UER .05 .02
(Typo in runs
allowed in '88)
❑ 404 Julio Franco .05 .02
❑ 405 Don Gordon .05 .02
❑ 406 Mel Hall .05 .02
❑ 407 Brad Havens .05 .02
❑ 408 Brook Jacoby .05 .02
❑ 409 Doug Jones .05 .02
❑ 410 Jeff Kaiser .05 .02
❑ 411 Luis Medina .05 .02
❑ 412 Cory Snyder .05 .02
❑ 413 Greg Swindell .05 .02
❑ 414 Ron Tingley UER .05 .02
(Hit HR in first ML
at-bat, should be
first AL at-bat)
❑ 415 Willie Upshaw .05 .02
❑ 416 Ron Washington .05 .02
❑ 417 Rich Yett .05 .02
❑ 418 Damon Berryhill .05 .02
❑ 419 Mike Bielecki .05 .02
❑ 420 Doug Dascenzo .05 .02
❑ 421 Jody Davis UER .05 .02
(Braves stats for
'88 missing)
❑ 422 Andre Dawson .10 .04
❑ 423 Frank DiPino .05 .02
❑ 424 Shawon Dunston .05 .02
❑ 425 Rich Gossage .10 .04
❑ 426 Mark Grace UER .25 .10
(Minor League stats
for '88 missing)
❑ 427 Mike Harkey RC .10 .04
❑ 428 Darrin Jackson .05 .02
❑ 429 Les Lancaster .05 .02
❑ 430 Vance Law .05 .02
❑ 431 Greg Maddux .60 .24
❑ 432 Jamie Moyer .10 .04
❑ 433 Al Nipper .05 .02
❑ 434 Rafael Palmeiro UER .25 .10
170 hits in '88,
should be 178
❑ 435 Pat Perry .05 .02
❑ 436 Jeff Pico .05 .02
❑ 437 Ryne Sandberg .40 .16
❑ 438 Calvin Schiraldi .05 .02
❑ 439 Rick Sutcliffe .10 .04
❑ 440A Manny Trillo ERR 2.00 .80
(Throws Rig)
❑ 440B Manny Trillo COR .05 .02
❑ 441 Gary Varsho UER .05 .02
(Wrong birthdate;
.303 should be .302;
11/28 should be 9/19)
❑ 442 Mitch Webster .05 .02
❑ 443 Luis Alicea RC .25 .10
❑ 444 Tom Brunansky .05 .02
❑ 445 Vince Coleman UER .05 .02
Third straight with 83
should be fourth straight with 81
❑ 446 John Costello UER .05 .02
(Home California,
should be New York)
❑ 447 Danny Cox .05 .02
❑ 448 Ken Dayley .05 .02
❑ 449 Jose DeLeon .05 .02
❑ 450 Curt Ford .05 .02
❑ 451 Pedro Guerrero .05 .02
❑ 452 Bob Horner .05 .02
❑ 453 Tim Jones .05 .02
❑ 454 Steve Lake .05 .02
❑ 455 Joe Magrane UER .05 .02
(Des Moines, IO)
❑ 456 Greg Mathews .05 .02
❑ 457 Willie McGee .10 .04
❑ 458 Larry McWilliams .05 .02
❑ 459 Jose Oquendo .05 .02
❑ 460 Tony Pena .05 .02
❑ 461 Terry Pendleton .10 .04
❑ 462 Steve Peters UER .05 .02
(Lives in Harrah,
not Harah)
❑ 463 Ozzie Smith .25 .10
❑ 464 Scott Terry .05 .02
❑ 465 Denny Walling .05 .02
❑ 466 Todd Worrell .05 .02
❑ 467 Tony Armas UER .05 .02
(Before All-Star Break
batting 2.39)
❑ 468 Dante Bichette RC .40 .16
❑ 469 Bob Boone .10 .04
❑ 470 Terry Clark .05 .02
❑ 471 Stu Cliburn .05 .02
❑ 472 Mike Cook UER .05 .02
(TM near Angels logo
missing from front)
❑ 473 Sherman Corbett .05 .02
❑ 474 Chili Davis .10 .04
❑ 475 Brian Downing .05 .02
❑ 476 Jim Eppard .05 .02
❑ 477 Chuck Finley .10 .04
❑ 478 Willie Fraser .05 .02
❑ 479 Bryan Harvey UER RC .25 .10
ML record shows 0-0,
should be 7-5
❑ 480 Jack Howell .05 .02
❑ 481 Wally Joyner UER .10 .04
(Yorba Linda, GA)
❑ 482 Jack Lazorko .05 .02
❑ 483 Kirk McCaskill .05 .02
❑ 484 Mark McLemore .05 .02
❑ 485 Greg Minton .05 .02
❑ 486 Dan Petry .05 .02
❑ 487 Johnny Ray .05 .02
❑ 488 Dick Schofield .05 .02
❑ 489 Devon White .10 .04
❑ 490 Mike Witt .05 .02
❑ 491 Harold Baines .10 .04
❑ 492 Daryl Boston .05 .02
❑ 493 Ivan Calderon UER .05 .02
('80 stats shifted)
❑ 494 Mike Diaz .05 .02
❑ 495 Carlton Fisk .15 .06
❑ 496 Dave Gallagher .05 .02
❑ 497 Ozzie Guillen .05 .02
❑ 498 Shawn Hillegas .05 .02

❑ 499 Lance Johnson .10 .04
❑ 500 Barry Jones .05 .02
❑ 501 Bill Long .05 .02
❑ 502 Steve Lyons .05 .02
❑ 503 Fred Manrique .05 .02
❑ 504 Jack McDowell .10 .04
❑ 505 Donn Pall .05 .02
❑ 506 Kelly Paris .05 .02
❑ 507 Dan Pasqua .05 .02
❑ 508 Ken Patterson .05 .02
❑ 509 Melido Perez .05 .02
❑ 510 Jerry Reuss .05 .02
❑ 511 Mark Salas .05 .02
❑ 512 Bobby Thigpen UER .05 .02
('86 ERA 4.69,
should be 4.68)
❑ 513 Mike Woodard .05 .02
❑ 514 Bob Brower .05 .02
❑ 515 Steve Buechele .05 .02
❑ 516 Jose Cecena .05 .02
❑ 517 Cecil Espy .05 .02
❑ 518 Scott Fletcher .05 .02
❑ 519 Cecilio Guante .05 .02
('87 Yankee stats
are off-centered)
❑ 520 Jose Guzman .05 .02
❑ 521 Ray Hayward .05 .02
❑ 522 Charlie Hough .10 .04
❑ 523 Pete Incaviglia .05 .02
❑ 524 Mike Jeffcoat .05 .02
❑ 525 Paul Kilgus .05 .02
❑ 526 Chad Kreuter RC .25 .10
❑ 527 Jeff Kunkel .05 .02
❑ 528 Oddibe McDowell .05 .02
❑ 529 Pete O'Brien .05 .02
❑ 530 Geno Petralli .05 .02
❑ 531 Jeff Russell .05 .02
❑ 532 Ruben Sierra .05 .02
❑ 533 Mike Stanley .05 .02
❑ 534A Ed VandeBerg ERR 2.00 .80
(Throws Lef)
❑ 534B Ed VandeBerg COR .05 .02
❑ 535 Curtis Wilkerson ERR .05 .02
(Pitcher headings
at bottom)
❑ 536 Mitch Williams .05 .02
❑ 537 Bobby Witt UER .05 .02
('85 ERA .643,
should be 6.43)
❑ 538 Steve Balboni .05 .02
❑ 539 Scott Bankhead .05 .02
❑ 540 Scott Bradley .05 .02
❑ 541 Mickey Brantley .05 .02
❑ 542 Jay Buhner .10 .04
❑ 543 Mike Campbell .05 .02
❑ 544 Darnell Coles .05 .02
❑ 545 Henry Cotto .05 .02
❑ 546 Alvin Davis .05 .02
❑ 547 Mario Diaz .05 .02
❑ 548 Ken Griffey Jr. RC 8.00 3.20
❑ 549 Erik Hanson RC .25 .10
❑ 550 Mike Jackson UER .05 .02
(Lifetime ERA 3.345,
should be 3.45)
❑ 551 Mark Langston .05 .02
❑ 552 Edgar Martinez .15 .06
❑ 553 Bill McGuire .05 .02
❑ 554 Mike Moore .05 .02
❑ 555 Jim Presley .05 .02
❑ 556 Rey Quinones .05 .02
❑ 557 Jerry Reed .05 .02
❑ 558 Harold Reynolds .10 .04
❑ 559 Mike Schooler .05 .02
❑ 560 Bill Swift .05 .02
❑ 561 Dave Valle .05 .02
❑ 562 Steve Bedrosian .05 .02
❑ 563 Phil Bradley .05 .02
❑ 564 Don Carman .05 .02
❑ 565 Bob Dernier .05 .02
❑ 566 Marvin Freeman .05 .02
❑ 567 Todd Frohwirth .05 .02
❑ 568 Greg Gross .05 .02
❑ 569 Kevin Gross .05 .02
❑ 570 Greg A. Harris .05 .02
❑ 571 Von Hayes .05 .02
❑ 572 Chris James .05 .02
❑ 573 Steve Jeltz .05 .02
❑ 574 Ron Jones UER .05 .02
(Led IL in '88 with
85, should be 75)
❑ 575 Ricky Jordan RC .25 .10
❑ 576 Mike Maddux .05 .02
❑ 577 David Palmer .05 .02
❑ 578 Lance Parrish .05 .02
❑ 579 Shane Rawley .05 .02
❑ 580 Bruce Ruffin .05 .02
❑ 581 Juan Samuel .05 .02
❑ 582 Mike Schmidt .50 .20
❑ 583 Kent Tekulve .05 .02
❑ 584 Milt Thompson UER .05 .02
(19 hits in '88,
should be 109)
❑ 585 Jose Alvarez RC .10 .04
❑ 586 Paul Assenmacher .05 .02
❑ 587 Bruce Benedict .05 .02
❑ 588 Jeff Blauser .10 .04
❑ 589 Terry Blocker .05 .02
❑ 590 Ron Gant .10 .04
❑ 591 Tom Glavine .25 .10
❑ 592 Tommy Gregg .05 .02
❑ 593 Albert Hall .05 .02
❑ 594 Dion James .05 .02
❑ 595 Rick Mahler .05 .02
❑ 596 Dale Murphy .25 .10
❑ 597 Gerald Perry .05 .02
❑ 598 Charlie Puleo .05 .02
❑ 599 Ted Simmons .10 .04
❑ 600 Pete Smith .05 .02
❑ 601 Zane Smith .05 .02
❑ 602 John Smoltz RC 1.00 .40
❑ 603 Bruce Sutter .05 .02
❑ 604 Andres Thomas .05 .02
❑ 605 Ozzie Virgil .05 .02
❑ 606 Brady Anderson RC .50 .20
❑ 607 Jeff Ballard .05 .02
❑ 608 Jose Bautista RC .10 .04
❑ 609 Ken Gerhart .05 .02
❑ 610 Terry Kennedy .05 .02
❑ 611 Eddie Murray .25 .10
❑ 612 Carl Nichols UER .05 .02
(Before All-Star Break
batting 1.88)
❑ 613 Tom Niedenfuer .05 .02
❑ 614 Joe Orsulak .05 .02
❑ 615 Oswald Peraza UER .05 .02
(Shown as Oswaldo)
❑ 616A Bill Ripken ERR 20.00 8.00
(Rick Face written
on knob of bat)
❑ 616B Bill Ripken 50.00 20.00
(Bat knob
whited out)
❑ 616C Bill Ripken 5.00 2.00
(Words on bat knob
scribbled out in White)
❑ 616D Bill Ripken 20.00 8.00
Words on Bat
scribbled out in Black
❑ 616E Bill Ripken DP .10 .04
(Black box covering
bat knob)
❑ 617 Cal Ripken .75 .30
❑ 618 Dave Schmidt .05 .02
❑ 619 Rick Schu .05 .02
❑ 620 Larry Sheets .05 .02
❑ 621 Doug Sisk .05 .02
❑ 622 Pete Stanicek .05 .02
❑ 623 Mickey Tettleton .05 .02
❑ 624 Jay Tibbs .05 .02
❑ 625 Jim Traber .05 .02
❑ 626 Mark Williamson .05 .02
❑ 627 Craig Worthington .05 .02
❑ 628 Jose Canseco 40/40 .10 .04
❑ 629 Tom Browning Perfect .05 .02
❑ 630 Roberto Alomar .25 .10
Sandy Alomar Jr. UER
(Names on card listed
in wrong order)
❑ 631 Will Clark .25 .10
Rafael Palmeiro UER
(Gallaraga, sic;
Clark 3 consecutive
100 RBI seasons;
third with 102 RBI's)
❑ 632 Darryl Strawberry .10 .04
Will Clark UER (Homeruns
should be two words)
❑ 633 Wade Boggs .10 .04
Carney Lansford UER
(Boggs hit .366 in
'86, should be '88)
❑ 634 Jose Canseco .50 .20
Terry Steinbach
Mark McGwire
❑ 635 Mark Davis .15 .06
Dwight Gooden
❑ 636 Danny Jackson .05 .02
David Cone UER
Hersheiser, sic
❑ 637 Chris Sabo .10 .04
Bobby Bonilla UER
Bobby Bonds, sic
❑ 638 Andres Galarraga UER .05 .02
(Misspelled Gallaraga
on card back)
Gerald Perry
❑ 639 Kirby Puckett .15 .06
Eric Davis
❑ 640 Steve Wilson and .05 .02
Cameron Drew
❑ 641 Kevin Brown and .25 .10
Kevin Reimer
❑ 642 Brad Pounders RC .10 .04
Jerald Clark
❑ 643 Mike Capel and .05 .02
Drew Hall
❑ 644 Joe Girardi RC and .40 .16
Rolando Roomes
❑ 645 Lenny Harris RC and .25 .10
Marty Brown
❑ 646 Luis DeLosSantos .05 .02
and Jim Campbell
❑ 647 Randy Kramer and .05 .02
Miguel Garcia
❑ 648 Torey Lovullo RC and .10 .04
Robert Palacios
❑ 649 Jim Corsi and .05 .02
Bob Milacki
❑ 650 Grady Hall and .05 .02
Mike Rochford
❑ 651 Terry Taylor RC .10 .04
Vance Lovelace
❑ 652 Ken Hill RC and .25 .10
Dennis Cook
❑ 653 Scott Service and .05 .02
Shane Turner
❑ 654 CL: Oakland/Mets .05 .02
Dodgers/Red Sox
(10 Henderson;
68 Jess Orosco)
❑ 655A CL: Twins/Tigers ERR .05 .02
Reds/Brewers
(179 Boslo and
Twins/Tigers positions
listed)
❑ 655B CL: Twins/Tigers COR .05 .02
Reds/Brewers
(179 Boslo but
Twins/Tigers positions
not listed)
❑ 656 CL: Pirates/Blue Jays .05 .02
Yankees/Royals
(225 Jess Barfield)
❑ 657 CL: Padres/Giants .05 .02
Astros/Expos
(367/368 wrong)
❑ 658 CL: Indians/Cubs .05 .02
Cardinals/Angels
(449 Deleon)
❑ 659 CL: White Sox/Rangers .05 .02
Mariners/Phillies
❑ 660 CL: Braves/Orioles .05 .02
Specials/Checklists
(632 hyphenated diff-
erently and 650 Hali;
595 Rich Mahler;
619 Rich Schu)

1990 Fleer

	Nm-Mt	Ex-Mt
COMPLETE SET (660)	15.00	4.50
COMP.RETAIL SET (660)	8.00	2.40
COMP.HOBBY SET (672)	15.00	4.50

❑ 1 Lance Blankenship .05 .02
❑ 2 Todd Burns .05 .02
❑ 3 Jose Canseco .25 .07
❑ 4 Jim Corsi .05 .02
❑ 5 Storm Davis .05 .02
❑ 6 Dennis Eckersley .10 .03
❑ 7 Mike Gallego .05 .02
❑ 8 Ron Hassey .05 .02
❑ 9 Dave Henderson .05 .02
❑ 10 Rickey Henderson .40 .12
❑ 11 Rick Honeycutt .05 .02
❑ 12 Stan Javier .05 .02
❑ 13 Felix Jose .05 .02
❑ 14 Carney Lansford .10 .03
❑ 15 Mark McGwire UER .60 .18
(1989 runs listed as 4, should be 74)
❑ 16 Mike Moore .05 .02
❑ 17 Gene Nelson .05 .02
❑ 18 Dave Parker .10 .03
❑ 19 Tony Phillips .05 .02
❑ 20 Terry Steinbach .05 .02
❑ 21 Dave Stewart .10 .03
❑ 22 Walt Weiss .05 .02
❑ 23 Bob Welch .05 .02
❑ 24 Curt Young .05 .02
❑ 25 Paul Assenmacher .05 .02
❑ 26 Damon Berryhill .05 .02
❑ 27 Mike Bielecki .05 .02
❑ 28 Kevin Blankenship .05 .02
❑ 29 Andre Dawson .10 .03
❑ 30 Shawon Dunston .05 .02
❑ 31 Joe Girardi .15 .04
❑ 32 Mark Grace .25 .07
❑ 33 Mike Harkey .05 .02
❑ 34 Paul Kilgus .05 .02
❑ 35 Les Lancaster .05 .02
❑ 36 Vance Law .05 .02
❑ 37 Greg Maddux .50 .15
❑ 38 Lloyd McClendon .05 .02
❑ 39 Jeff Pico .05 .02
❑ 40 Ryne Sandberg .40 .12
❑ 41 Scott Sanderson .05 .02
❑ 42 Dwight Smith .05 .02
❑ 43 Rick Sutcliffe .10 .03
❑ 44 Jerome Walton .05 .02
❑ 45 Mitch Webster .05 .02
❑ 46 Curt Wilkerson .05 .02
❑ 47 Dean Wilkins .05 .02
❑ 48 Mitch Williams .05 .02
❑ 49 Steve Wilson .05 .02
❑ 50 Steve Bedrosian .05 .02
❑ 51 Mike Benjamin RC .10 .03
❑ 52 Jeff Brantley .05 .02
❑ 53 Brett Butler .10 .03
❑ 54 Will Clark UER .10 .03
(Did You Know says first in runs, should say tied for first)
❑ 55 Kelly Downs .05 .02
❑ 56 Scott Garrelts .05 .02
❑ 57 Atlee Hammaker .05 .02
❑ 58 Terry Kennedy .05 .02
❑ 59 Mike LaCoss .05 .02
❑ 60 Craig Lefferts .05 .02
❑ 61 Greg Litton .05 .02
❑ 62 Candy Maldonado .05 .02
❑ 63 Kirt Manwaring UER .05 .02
(No '88 Phoenix stats as noted in box)
❑ 64 Randy McCament .05 .02
❑ 65 Kevin Mitchell .05 .02
❑ 66 Donell Nixon .05 .02
❑ 67 Ken Oberkfell .05 .02
❑ 68 Rick Reuschel .05 .02
❑ 69 Ernest Riles .05 .02
❑ 70 Don Robinson .05 .02
❑ 71 Pat Sheridan .05 .02
❑ 72 Chris Speier .05 .02
❑ 73 Robby Thompson .05 .02
❑ 74 Jose Uribe .05 .02
❑ 75 Matt Williams .10 .03
❑ 76 George Bell .05 .02
❑ 77 Pat Borders .05 .02
❑ 78 John Cerutti .05 .02
❑ 79 Junior Felix .05 .02
❑ 80 Tony Fernandez .05 .02
❑ 81 Mike Flanagan .05 .02
❑ 82 Mauro Gozzo .05 .02
❑ 83 Kelly Gruber .05 .02
❑ 84 Tom Henke .05 .02
❑ 85 Jimmy Key .10 .03
❑ 86 Manny Lee .05 .02
❑ 87 Nelson Liriano UER .05 .02
(Should say "led the IL" instead of "led the TL")
❑ 88 Lee Mazzilli .05 .02
❑ 89 Fred McGriff .25 .07
❑ 90 Lloyd Moseby .05 .02
❑ 91 Rance Mulliniks .05 .02
❑ 92 Alex Sanchez .05 .02
❑ 93 Dave Stieb .10 .03
❑ 94 Todd Stottlemyre .10 .03
❑ 95 Duane Ward UER .05 .02
(Double line of '87 Syracuse stats)
❑ 96 David Wells .10 .03
❑ 97 Ernie Whitt .05 .02
❑ 98 Frank Wills .05 .02
❑ 99 Mookie Wilson .10 .03
❑ 100 Kevin Appier .25 .07
❑ 101 Luis Aquino .05 .02
❑ 102 Bob Boone .10 .03
❑ 103 George Brett .60 .18
❑ 104 Jose DeJesus .05 .02
❑ 105 Luis De Los Santos .05 .02
❑ 106 Jim Eisenreich .05 .02
❑ 107 Steve Farr .05 .02
❑ 108 Tom Gordon .10 .03
❑ 109 Mark Gubicza .05 .02
❑ 110 Bo Jackson .25 .07
❑ 111 Terry Leach .05 .02
❑ 112 Charlie Leibrandt .05 .02
❑ 113 Rick Luecken .05 .02
❑ 114 Mike Macfarlane .05 .02
❑ 115 Jeff Montgomery .10 .03
❑ 116 Bret Saberhagen .10 .03
❑ 117 Kevin Seitzer .05 .02
❑ 118 Kurt Stillwell .05 .02
❑ 119 Pat Tabler .05 .02
❑ 120 Danny Tartabull .05 .02
❑ 121 Gary Thurman .05 .02
❑ 122 Frank White .10 .03
❑ 123 Willie Wilson .05 .02
❑ 124 Matt Winters .05 .02
❑ 125 Jim Abbott .25 .07
❑ 126 Tony Armas .05 .02
❑ 127 Dante Bichette .25 .07
❑ 128 Bert Blyleven .10 .03
❑ 129 Chili Davis .10 .03
❑ 130 Brian Downing .05 .02
❑ 131 Mike Fetters RC .25 .07
❑ 132 Chuck Finley .10 .03
❑ 133 Willie Fraser .05 .02
❑ 134 Bryan Harvey .05 .02
❑ 135 Jack Howell .05 .02
❑ 136 Wally Joyner .10 .03
❑ 137 Jeff Manto .05 .02
❑ 138 Kirk McCaskill .05 .02
❑ 139 Bob McClure .05 .02
❑ 140 Greg Minton .05 .02
❑ 141 Lance Parrish .05 .02
❑ 142 Dan Petry .05 .02
❑ 143 Johnny Ray .05 .02
❑ 144 Dick Schofield .05 .02
❑ 145 Lee Stevens .10 .03
❑ 146 Claudell Washington .05 .02
❑ 147 Devon White .05 .02
❑ 148 Mike Witt .05 .02
❑ 149 Roberto Alomar .25 .07
❑ 150 Sandy Alomar Jr. .10 .03
❑ 151 Andy Benes .10 .03
❑ 152 Jack Clark .10 .03
❑ 153 Pat Clements .05 .02
❑ 154 Joey Cora .10 .03
❑ 155 Mark Davis .05 .02
❑ 156 Mark Grant .05 .02
❑ 157 Tony Gwynn .30 .09
❑ 158 Greg W. Harris .05 .02
❑ 159 Bruce Hurst .05 .02
❑ 160 Darrin Jackson .05 .02
❑ 161 Chris James .05 .02
❑ 162 Carmelo Martinez .05 .02
❑ 163 Mike Pagliarulo .05 .02
❑ 164 Mark Parent .05 .02
❑ 165 Dennis Rasmussen .05 .02
❑ 166 Bip Roberts .05 .02
❑ 167 Benito Santiago .10 .03
❑ 168 Calvin Schiraldi .05 .02
❑ 169 Eric Show .05 .02
❑ 170 Garry Templeton .05 .02
❑ 171 Ed Whitson .05 .02
❑ 172 Brady Anderson .10 .03
❑ 173 Jeff Ballard .05 .02
❑ 174 Phil Bradley .05 .02
❑ 175 Mike Devereaux .05 .02
❑ 176 Steve Finley .10 .03
❑ 177 Pete Harnisch .05 .02
❑ 178 Kevin Hickey .05 .02
❑ 179 Brian Holton .05 .02
❑ 180 Ben McDonald RC .25 .07
❑ 181 Bob Melvin .05 .02
❑ 182 Bob Milacki .05 .02
❑ 183 Randy Milligan UER .05 .02
(Double line of '87 stats)
❑ 184 Gregg Olson .10 .03
❑ 185 Joe Orsulak .05 .02
❑ 186 Bill Ripken .05 .02
❑ 187 Cal Ripken .75 .23
❑ 188 Dave Schmidt .05 .02
❑ 189 Larry Sheets .05 .02
❑ 190 Mickey Tettleton .05 .02
❑ 191 Mark Thurmond .05 .02
❑ 192 Jay Tibbs .05 .02
❑ 193 Jim Traber .05 .02
❑ 194 Mark Williamson .05 .02
❑ 195 Craig Worthington .05 .02
❑ 196 Don Aase .05 .02
❑ 197 Blaine Beatty .05 .02
❑ 198 Mark Carreon .05 .02
❑ 199 Gary Carter .15 .04
❑ 200 David Cone .10 .03
❑ 201 Ron Darling .05 .02
❑ 202 Kevin Elster .05 .02
❑ 203 Sid Fernandez .05 .02
❑ 204 Dwight Gooden .15 .04
❑ 205 Keith Hernandez .15 .04
❑ 206 Jeff Innis .05 .02
❑ 207 Gregg Jefferies .10 .03
❑ 208 Howard Johnson .05 .02
❑ 209 Barry Lyons UER .05 .02
(Double line of '87 stats)
❑ 210 Dave Magadan .05 .02
❑ 211 Kevin McReynolds .05 .02
❑ 212 Jeff Musselman .05 .02
❑ 213 Randy Myers .10 .03
❑ 214 Bob Ojeda .05 .02
❑ 215 Juan Samuel .05 .02
❑ 216 Mackey Sasser .05 .02
❑ 217 Darryl Strawberry .15 .04

❑ 218 Tim Teufel .05 .02
❑ 219 Frank Viola .05 .02
❑ 220 Juan Agosto .05 .02
❑ 221 Larry Andersen .05 .02
❑ 222 Eric Anthony RC .10 .03
❑ 223 Kevin Bass .05 .02
❑ 224 Craig Biggio .15 .04
❑ 225 Ken Caminiti .10 .03
❑ 226 Jim Clancy .05 .02
❑ 227 Danny Darwin .05 .02
❑ 228 Glenn Davis .05 .02
❑ 229 Jim Deshaies .05 .02
❑ 230 Bill Doran .05 .02
❑ 231 Bob Forsch .05 .02
❑ 232 Brian Meyer .05 .02
❑ 233 Terry Puhl .05 .02
❑ 234 Rafael Ramirez .05 .02
❑ 235 Rick Rhoden .05 .02
❑ 236 Dan Schatzeder .05 .02
❑ 237 Mike Scott .05 .02
❑ 238 Dave Smith .05 .02
❑ 239 Alex Trevino .05 .02
❑ 240 Glenn Wilson .05 .02
❑ 241 Gerald Young .05 .02
❑ 242 Tom Brunansky .05 .02
❑ 243 Cris Carpenter .05 .02
❑ 244 Alex Cole RC .10 .03
❑ 245 Vince Coleman .05 .02
❑ 246 John Costello .05 .02
❑ 247 Ken Dayley .05 .02
❑ 248 Jose DeLeon .05 .02
❑ 249 Frank DiPino .05 .02
❑ 250 Pedro Guerrero .05 .02
❑ 251 Ken Hill .10 .03
❑ 252 Joe Magrane .05 .02
❑ 253 Willie McGee UER .10 .03
(No decimal point before 353)
❑ 254 John Morris .05 .02
❑ 255 Jose Oquendo .05 .02
❑ 256 Tony Pena .05 .02
❑ 257 Terry Pendleton .10 .03
❑ 258 Ted Power .05 .02
❑ 259 Dan Quisenberry .05 .02
❑ 260 Ozzie Smith .25 .07
❑ 261 Scott Terry .05 .02
❑ 262 Milt Thompson .05 .02
❑ 263 Denny Walling .05 .02
❑ 264 Todd Worrell .05 .02
❑ 265 Todd Zeile .10 .03
❑ 266 Marty Barrett .05 .02
❑ 267 Mike Boddicker .05 .02
❑ 268 Wade Boggs .15 .04
❑ 269 Ellis Burks .15 .04
❑ 270 Rick Cerone .05 .02
❑ 271 Roger Clemens .50 .15
❑ 272 John Dopson .05 .02
❑ 273 Nick Esasky .05 .02
❑ 274 Dwight Evans .10 .03
❑ 275 Wes Gardner .05 .02
❑ 276 Rich Gedman .05 .02
❑ 277 Mike Greenwell .05 .02
❑ 278 Danny Heep .05 .02
❑ 279 Eric Hetzel .05 .02
❑ 280 Dennis Lamp .05 .02
❑ 281 Rob Murphy UER .05 .02
('89 stats say Reds, should say Red Sox)
❑ 282 Joe Price .05 .02
❑ 283 Carlos Quintana .05 .02
❑ 284 Jody Reed .05 .02
❑ 285 Luis Rivera .05 .02
❑ 286 Kevin Romine .05 .02
❑ 287 Lee Smith .10 .03
❑ 288 Mike Smithson .05 .02
❑ 289 Bob Stanley .05 .02
❑ 290 Harold Baines .10 .03
❑ 291 Kevin Brown .10 .03
❑ 292 Steve Buechele .05 .02
❑ 293 Scott Coolbaugh .05 .02
❑ 294 Jack Daugherty .05 .02
❑ 295 Cecil Espy .05 .02
❑ 296 Julio Franco .05 .02
❑ 297 Juan Gonzalez RC 1.50 .45
❑ 298 Cecilio Guante .05 .02
❑ 299 Drew Hall .05 .02
❑ 300 Charlie Hough .10 .03
❑ 301 Pete Incaviglia .05 .02
❑ 302 Mike Jeffcoat .05 .02
❑ 303 Chad Kreuter .05 .02
❑ 304 Jeff Kunkel .05 .02
❑ 305 Rick Leach .05 .02
❑ 306 Fred Manrique .05 .02
❑ 307 Jamie Moyer .10 .03
❑ 308 Rafael Palmeiro .15 .04
❑ 309 Geno Petralli .05 .02
❑ 310 Kevin Reimer .05 .02
❑ 311 Kenny Rogers .10 .03
❑ 312 Jeff Russell .05 .02
❑ 313 Nolan Ryan 1.00 .30
❑ 314 Ruben Sierra .05 .02
❑ 315 Bobby Witt .05 .02
❑ 316 Chris Bosio .05 .02
❑ 317 Glenn Braggs UER .05 .02
(Stats say 111 K's, but bio says 117 K's)
❑ 318 Greg Brock .05 .02
❑ 319 Chuck Crim .05 .02
❑ 320 Rob Deer .05 .02
❑ 321 Mike Felder .05 .02
❑ 322 Tom Filer .05 .02
❑ 323 Tony Fossas .05 .02
❑ 324 Jim Gantner .05 .02
❑ 325 Darryl Hamilton .05 .02
❑ 326 Teddy Higuera .05 .02
❑ 327 Mark Knudson .05 .02
❑ 328 Bill Krueger UER .05 .02
('86 stats missing)
❑ 329 Tim McIntosh RC .10 .03
❑ 330 Paul Molitor .15 .04
❑ 331 Jaime Navarro .05 .02
❑ 332 Charlie O'Brien .05 .02
❑ 333 Jeff Peterek .05 .02
❑ 334 Dan Plesac .05 .02
❑ 335 Jerry Reuss .05 .02
❑ 336 Gary Sheffield UER .25 .07
(Bio says played for 3 teams in '87, but stats say in '88)
❑ 337 Bill Spiers .05 .02
❑ 338 B.J. Surhoff .10 .03
❑ 339 Greg Vaughn .10 .03
❑ 340 Robin Yount .25 .07
❑ 341 Hubie Brooks .05 .02
❑ 342 Tim Burke .05 .02
❑ 343 Mike Fitzgerald .05 .02
❑ 344 Tom Foley .05 .02
❑ 345 Andres Galarraga .10 .03
❑ 346 Damaso Garcia .05 .02
❑ 347 Marquis Grissom RC .25 .07
❑ 348 Kevin Gross .05 .02
❑ 349 Joe Hesketh .05 .02
❑ 350 Jeff Huson RC .05 .02
❑ 351 Wallace Johnson .05 .02
❑ 352 Mark Langston .05 .02
❑ 353A Dave Martinez 2.00 .60
(Yellow on front)
❑ 353B Dave Martinez .05 .02
(Red on front)
❑ 354 Dennis Martinez UER .10 .03
('87 ERA is 616, should be 6.16)
❑ 355 Andy McGaffigan .05 .02
❑ 356 Otis Nixon .05 .02
❑ 357 Spike Owen .05 .02
❑ 358 Pascual Perez .05 .02
❑ 359 Tim Raines .10 .03
❑ 360 Nelson Santovenia .05 .02
❑ 361 Bryn Smith .05 .02
❑ 362 Zane Smith .05 .02
❑ 363 Larry Walker RC 1.00 .30
❑ 364 Tim Wallach .05 .02
❑ 365 Rick Aguilera .10 .03
❑ 366 Allan Anderson .05 .02
❑ 367 Wally Backman .05 .02
❑ 368 Doug Baker .05 .02
❑ 369 Juan Berenguer .05 .02
❑ 370 Randy Bush .05 .02
❑ 371 Carmelo Castillo .05 .02
❑ 372 Mike Dyer .05 .02
❑ 373 Gary Gaetti .10 .03
❑ 374 Greg Gagne .05 .02
❑ 375 Dan Gladden .05 .02
❑ 376 G.Gonzalez UER .05 .02
Bio says 31 saves in '88, but stats say 30
❑ 377 Brian Harper .05 .02
❑ 378 Kent Hrbek .10 .03
❑ 379 Gene Larkin .05 .02
❑ 380 Tim Laudner UER .05 .02
(No decimal point before '85 BA of 238)
❑ 381 John Moses .05 .02
❑ 382 Al Newman .05 .02
❑ 383 Kirby Puckett .25 .07
❑ 384 Shane Rawley .05 .02
❑ 385 Jeff Reardon .10 .03
❑ 386 Roy Smith .05 .02
❑ 387 Gary Wayne .05 .02
❑ 388 Dave West .05 .02
❑ 389 Tim Belcher .05 .02
❑ 390 Tim Crews UER .05 .02
(Stats say 163 IP for '83, but bio says 136)
❑ 391 Mike Davis .05 .02
❑ 392 Rick Dempsey .05 .02
❑ 393 Kirk Gibson .10 .03
❑ 394 Jose Gonzalez .05 .02
❑ 395 Alfredo Griffin .05 .02
❑ 396 Jeff Hamilton .05 .02
❑ 397 Lenny Harris .05 .02
❑ 398 Mickey Hatcher .05 .02
❑ 399 Orel Hershiser .10 .03
❑ 400 Jay Howell .05 .02
❑ 401 Mike Marshall .05 .02
❑ 402 Ramon Martinez .05 .02
❑ 403 Mike Morgan .05 .02
❑ 404 Eddie Murray .25 .07
❑ 405 Alejandro Pena .05 .02
❑ 406 Willie Randolph .10 .03
❑ 407 Mike Scioscia .05 .02
❑ 408 Ray Searage .05 .02
❑ 409 Fernando Valenzuela .10 .03
❑ 410 Jose Vizcaino RC .25 .07
❑ 411 John Wetteland .25 .07
❑ 412 Jack Armstrong .05 .02
❑ 413 Todd Benzinger UER .05 .02
(Bio says .323 at Pawtucket, but stats say .321)
❑ 414 Tim Birtsas .05 .02
❑ 415 Tom Browning .05 .02
❑ 416 Norm Charlton .05 .02
❑ 417 Eric Davis .10 .03
❑ 418 Rob Dibble .10 .03
❑ 419 John Franco .10 .03
❑ 420 Ken Griffey Sr. .10 .03
❑ 421 Chris Hammond RC .10 .03
(No 1989 used for "Did Not Play" stat, actually did play for Nashville in 1989)
❑ 422 Danny Jackson .05 .02
❑ 423 Barry Larkin .25 .07
❑ 424 Tim Leary .05 .02
❑ 425 Rick Mahler .05 .02
❑ 426 Joe Oliver .05 .02
❑ 427 Paul O'Neill .15 .04
❑ 428 Luis Quinones UER .05 .02
('86-'88 stats are omitted from card but included in totals)
❑ 429 Jeff Reed .05 .02
❑ 430 Jose Rijo .05 .02
❑ 431 Ron Robinson .05 .02
❑ 432 Rolando Roomes .05 .02
❑ 433 Chris Sabo .05 .02
❑ 434 Scott Scudder .05 .02
❑ 435 Herm Winningham .05 .02
❑ 436 Steve Balboni .05 .02
❑ 437 Jesse Barfield .05 .02
❑ 438 Mike Blowers RC .10 .03
❑ 439 Tom Brookens .05 .02
❑ 440 Greg Cadaret .05 .02
❑ 441 Alvaro Espinoza UER .05 .02
(Career games say 218, should be 219)
❑ 442 Bob Geren .05 .02

	No.	Player		
❑	443	Lee Guetterman	.05	.02
❑	444	Mel Hall	.05	.02
❑	445	Andy Hawkins	.05	.02
❑	446	Roberto Kelly	.05	.02
❑	447	Don Mattingly	.60	.18
❑	448	Lance McCullers	.05	.02
❑	449	Hensley Meulens	.05	.02
❑	450	Dale Mohorcic	.05	.02
❑	451	Clay Parker	.05	.02
❑	452	Eric Plunk	.05	.02
❑	453	Dave Righetti	.05	.02
❑	454	Deion Sanders	.25	.07
❑	455	Steve Sax	.05	.02
❑	456	Don Slaught	.05	.02
❑	457	Walt Terrell	.05	.02
❑	458	Dave Winfield	.15	.04
❑	459	Jay Bell	.10	.03
❑	460	Rafael Belliard	.05	.02
❑	461	Barry Bonds	.60	.18
❑	462	Bobby Bonilla	.10	.03
❑	463	Sid Bream	.05	.02
❑	464	Benny Distefano	.05	.02
❑	465	Doug Drabek	.05	.02
❑	466	Jim Gott	.05	.02
❑	467	Billy Hatcher UER (.1 hits for Cubs in 1984)	.05	.02
❑	468	Neal Heaton	.05	.02
❑	469	Jeff King	.05	.02
❑	470	Bob Kipper	.05	.02
❑	471	Randy Kramer	.05	.02
❑	472	Bill Landrum	.05	.02
❑	473	Mike LaValliere	.05	.02
❑	474	Jose Lind	.05	.02
❑	475	Junior Ortiz	.05	.02
❑	476	Gary Redus	.05	.02
❑	477	Rick Reed RC	.25	.07
❑	478	R.J. Reynolds	.05	.02
❑	479	Jeff D. Robinson	.05	.02
❑	480	John Smiley	.05	.02
❑	481	Andy Van Slyke	.10	.03
❑	482	Bob Walk	.05	.02
❑	483	Andy Allanson	.05	.02
❑	484	Scott Bailes	.05	.02
❑	485	Joey Belle UER (Has Jay Bell "Did You Know")	.25	.07
❑	486	Bud Black	.05	.02
❑	487	Jerry Browne	.05	.02
❑	488	Tom Candiotti	.05	.02
❑	489	Joe Carter	.10	.03
❑	490	Dave Clark (No '84 stats)	.05	.02
❑	491	John Farrell	.05	.02
❑	492	Felix Fermin	.05	.02
❑	493	Brook Jacoby	.05	.02
❑	494	Dion James	.05	.02
❑	495	Doug Jones	.05	.02
❑	496	Brad Komminsk	.05	.02
❑	497	Rod Nichols	.05	.02
❑	498	Pete O'Brien	.05	.02
❑	499	Steve Olin RC	.10	.03
❑	500	Jesse Orosco	.05	.02
❑	501	Joel Skinner	.05	.02
❑	502	Cory Snyder	.05	.02
❑	503	Greg Swindell	.05	.02
❑	504	Rich Yett	.05	.02
❑	505	Scott Bankhead	.05	.02
❑	506	Scott Bradley	.05	.02
❑	507	Greg Briley UER (28 SB's in bio, but 27 in stats)	.05	.02
❑	508	Jay Buhner	.10	.03
❑	509	Darnell Coles	.05	.02
❑	510	Keith Comstock	.05	.02
❑	511	Henry Cotto	.05	.02
❑	512	Alvin Davis	.05	.02
❑	513	Ken Griffey Jr.	.75	.23
❑	514	Erik Hanson	.05	.02
❑	515	Gene Harris	.05	.02
❑	516	Brian Holman	.05	.02
❑	517	Mike Jackson	.05	.02
❑	518	Randy Johnson	.40	.12
❑	519	Jeffrey Leonard	.05	.02
❑	520	Edgar Martinez	.15	.04
❑	521	Dennis Powell	.05	.02
❑	522	Jim Presley	.05	.02
❑	523	Jerry Reed	.05	.02
❑	524	Harold Reynolds	.10	.03
❑	525	Mike Schooler	.05	.02
❑	526	Bill Swift	.05	.02
❑	527	Dave Valle	.05	.02
❑	528	Omar Vizquel	.25	.07
❑	529	Ivan Calderon	.05	.02
❑	530	Carlton Fisk UER (Bellow Falls, should be Bellows Falls)	.15	.04
❑	531	Scott Fletcher	.05	.02
❑	532	Dave Gallagher	.05	.02
❑	533	Ozzie Guillen	.05	.02
❑	534	Greg Hibbard RC	.10	.03
❑	535	Shawn Hillegas	.05	.02
❑	536	Lance Johnson	.05	.02
❑	537	Eric King	.05	.02
❑	538	Ron Kittle	.05	.02
❑	539	Steve Lyons	.05	.02
❑	540	Carlos Martinez	.05	.02
❑	541	Tom McCarthy	.05	.02
❑	542	Matt Merullo (Had 5 ML runs scored entering '90, not 6)	.05	.02
❑	543	Donn Pall UER (Stats say pro career began in '85, bio says '88)	.05	.02
❑	544	Dan Pasqua	.05	.02
❑	545	Ken Patterson	.05	.02
❑	546	Melido Perez	.05	.02
❑	547	Steve Rosenberg	.05	.02
❑	548	Sammy Sosa RC	8.00	2.40
❑	549	Bobby Thigpen	.05	.02
❑	550	Robin Ventura	.25	.07
❑	551	Greg Walker	.05	.02
❑	552	Don Carman	.05	.02
❑	553	Pat Combs (6 walks for Phillies in '89 in stats, brief bio says 4)	.05	.02
❑	554	Dennis Cook	.05	.02
❑	555	Darren Daulton	.10	.03
❑	556	Len Dykstra	.10	.03
❑	557	Curt Ford	.05	.02
❑	558	Charlie Hayes	.05	.02
❑	559	Von Hayes	.05	.02
❑	560	Tommy Herr	.05	.02
❑	561	Ken Howell	.05	.02
❑	562	Steve Jeltz	.05	.02
❑	563	Ron Jones	.05	.02
❑	564	Ricky Jordan UER (Duplicate line of statistics on back)	.05	.02
❑	565	John Kruk	.10	.03
❑	566	Steve Lake	.05	.02
❑	567	Roger McDowell	.05	.02
❑	568	Terry Mulholland UER (Did You Know refers to Dave Magadan)	.05	.02
❑	569	Dwayne Murphy	.05	.02
❑	570	Jeff Parrett	.05	.02
❑	571	Randy Ready	.05	.02
❑	572	Bruce Ruffin	.05	.02
❑	573	Dickie Thon	.05	.02
❑	574	Jose Alvarez UER ('78 and '79 stats are reversed)	.05	.02
❑	575	Geronimo Berroa	.05	.02
❑	576	Jeff Blauser	.05	.02
❑	577	Joe Boever	.05	.02
❑	578	Marty Clary UER (No comma between city and state)	.05	.02
❑	579	Jody Davis	.05	.02
❑	580	Mark Eichhorn	.05	.02
❑	581	Darrell Evans	.10	.03
❑	582	Ron Gant	.10	.03
❑	583	Tom Glavine	.25	.07
❑	584	Tommy Greene RC	.10	.03
❑	585	Tommy Gregg	.05	.02
❑	586	Dave Justice RC UER (Actually had 16 2B in Sumter in '86)	.50	.15
❑	587	Mark Lemke	.05	.02
❑	588	Derek Lilliquist	.05	.02
❑	589	Oddibe McDowell	.05	.02
❑	590	Kent Mercker RC ERA (Bio says 2.75 ERA, stats say 2.68 ERA)	.05	.02
❑	591	Dale Murphy	.25	.07
❑	592	Gerald Perry	.05	.02
❑	593	Lonnie Smith	.05	.02
❑	594	Pete Smith	.05	.02
❑	595	John Smoltz	.25	.07
❑	596	Mike Stanton RC UER (No comma between city and state)	.25	.07
❑	597	Andres Thomas	.05	.02
❑	598	Jeff Treadway	.05	.02
❑	599	Doyle Alexander	.05	.02
❑	600	Dave Bergman	.05	.02
❑	601	Brian DuBois	.05	.02
❑	602	Paul Gibson	.05	.02
❑	603	Mike Heath	.05	.02
❑	604	Mike Henneman	.05	.02
❑	605	Guillermo Hernandez	.05	.02
❑	606	Shawn Holman	.05	.02
❑	607	Tracy Jones	.05	.02
❑	608	Chet Lemon	.05	.02
❑	609	Fred Lynn	.05	.02
❑	610	Jack Morris	.10	.03
❑	611	Matt Nokes	.05	.02
❑	612	Gary Pettis	.05	.02
❑	613	Kevin Ritz	.05	.02
❑	614	Jeff M. Robinson ('88 stats are not in line)	.05	.02
❑	615	Steve Searcy	.05	.02
❑	616	Frank Tanana	.05	.02
❑	617	Alan Trammell	.15	.04
❑	618	Gary Ward	.05	.02
❑	619	Lou Whitaker	.10	.03
❑	620	Frank Williams	.05	.02
❑	621A	George Brett '80 ERR (Had 10 .390 hitting seasons)	2.00	.60
❑	621B	George Brett '80 COR	.25	.07
❑	622	Fern.Valenzuela '81	.05	.02
❑	623	Dale Murphy '82	.15	.04
❑	624A	Cal Ripken '83 ERR (Misspelled Ripkin on card back)	5.00	1.50
❑	624B	Cal Ripken '83 COR	.40	.12
❑	625	Ryne Sandberg '84	.25	.07
❑	626	Don Mattingly '85	.20	.06
❑	627	Roger Clemens '86	.25	.07
❑	628	George Bell '87	.05	.02
❑	629	J.Canseco '88 UER Reggie won MVP in '83, should say '73	.10	.03
❑	630A	Will Clark '89 ERR (32 total bases on card back)	1.00	.30
❑	630B	Will Clark '89 COR (321 total bases; technically still an error, listing only 24 runs)	.25	.07
❑	631	Game Savers Mark Davis Mitch Williams	.05	.02
❑	632	Boston Igniters Wade Boggs Mike Greenwell	.10	.03
❑	633	Starter and Stopper Mark Gubicza Jeff Russell	.05	.02
❑	634	League's Best Shortstops Tony Fernandez Cal Ripken	.25	.07
❑	635	Human Dynamos Kirby Puckett Bo Jackson	.15	.04
❑	636	300 Strikeout Club Nolan Ryan Mike Scott	.40	.12
❑	637	The Dynamic Duo Will Clark	.10	.03

No.	Card	Nm-Mt	Ex-Mt
	Kevin Mitchell		
❑ 638	AL All-Stars Don Mattingly Mark McGwire	.30	.09
❑ 639	NL East Rivals Howard Johnson Ryne Sandberg	.25	.07
❑ 640	Rudy Seanez RC Colin Charland	.10	.03
❑ 641	George Canale RC Kevin Maas UER (Canale listed as INF on front, 1B on back)	.25	.07
❑ 642	Kelly Mann and Dave Hansen RC	.25	.07
❑ 643	Greg Smith and Stu Tate	.10	.03
❑ 644	Tom Drees and Dann Howitt	.10	.03
❑ 645	Mike Roesler RC and Derrick May	.10	.03
❑ 646	Scott Hemond and Mark Gardner RC	.10	.03
❑ 647	John Orton and Scott Leius RC	.10	.03
❑ 648	Rich Monteleone and Dana Williams	.10	.03
❑ 649	Mike Huff and Steve Frey	.10	.03
❑ 650	Chuck McElroy and Moises Alou RC	.50	.15
❑ 651	Bobby Rose and Mike Hartley	.25	.07
❑ 652	Matt Kinzer and Wayne Edwards	.10	.03
❑ 653	Delino DeShields RC and Jason Grimsley	.25	.07
❑ 654	CL: A's/Cubs Giants/Blue Jays	.05	.02
❑ 655	CL: Royals/Angels Padres/Orioles	.05	.02
❑ 656	CL: Mets/Astros Cards/Red Sox	.05	.02
❑ 657	CL: Rangers/Brewers Expos/Twins	.05	.02
❑ 658	CL: Dodgers/Reds Yankees/Pirates	.05	.02
❑ 659	CL: Indians/Mariners White Sox/Phillies	.05	.02
❑ 660A	CL: Braves/Tigers Specials/Checklists (Checklist-660 in smaller print on card front)	.05	.02
❑ 660B	CL: Braves/Tigers Specials/Checklists (Checklist-660 in normal print on card front)	.05	.02

1992 Fleer Update

	Nm-Mt	Ex-Mt
COMP.FACT.SET (136)	100.00	30.00
COMPLETE SET (132)	100.00	30.00

No.	Card	Nm-Mt	Ex-Mt
❑ 1	Todd Frohwirth	.50	.15
❑ 2	Alan Mills	.50	.15
❑ 3	Rick Sutcliffe	1.00	.30
❑ 4	John Valentin RC	1.50	.45
❑ 5	Frank Viola	1.00	.30
❑ 6	Bob Zupcic RC	.50	.15
❑ 7	Mike Butcher	.50	.15
❑ 8	Chad Curtis RC	1.50	.45
❑ 9	Damion Easley RC	1.50	.45
❑ 10	Tim Salmon	2.50	.75
❑ 11	Julio Valera	.50	.15
❑ 12	George Bell	.50	.15
❑ 13	Roberto Hernandez	.50	.15
❑ 14	Shawn Jeter RC	.50	.15
❑ 15	Thomas Howard	.50	.15
❑ 16	Jesse Levis	.50	.15
❑ 17	Kenny Lofton	1.50	.45
❑ 18	Paul Sorrento	.50	.15
❑ 19	Rico Brogna	.50	.15
❑ 20	John Doherty RC	.50	.15
❑ 21	Dan Gladden	.50	.15
❑ 22	Buddy Groom RC	.50	.15
❑ 23	Shawn Hare RC	.50	.15
❑ 24	John Kiely	.50	.15
❑ 25	Kurt Knudsen	.50	.15
❑ 26	Gregg Jefferies	.50	.15
❑ 27	Wally Joyner	1.00	.30
❑ 28	Kevin Koslofski	.50	.15
❑ 29	Kevin McReynolds	.50	.15
❑ 30	Rusty Meacham	.50	.15
❑ 31	Keith Miller	.50	.15
❑ 32	Hipolito Pichardo RC	.50	.15
❑ 33	Jim Austin	.50	.15
❑ 34	Scott Fletcher	.50	.15
❑ 35	John Jaha RC	1.50	.45
❑ 36	Pat Listach RC	1.50	.45
❑ 37	Dave Nilsson	.50	.15
❑ 38	Kevin Seitzer	.50	.15
❑ 39	Tom Edens	.50	.15
❑ 40	Pat Mahomes RC	1.50	.45
❑ 41	John Smiley	.50	.15
❑ 42	Charlie Hayes	.50	.15
❑ 43	Sam Militello	.50	.15
❑ 44	Andy Stankiewicz	.50	.15
❑ 45	Danny Tartabull	.50	.15
❑ 46	Bob Wickman	.50	.15
❑ 47	Jerry Browne	.50	.15
❑ 48	Kevin Campbell	.50	.15
❑ 49	Vince Horsman	.50	.15
❑ 50	Troy Neel RC	.50	.15
❑ 51	Ruben Sierra	.50	.15
❑ 52	Bruce Walton	.50	.15
❑ 53	Willie Wilson	.50	.15
❑ 54	Bret Boone	2.50	.75
❑ 55	Dave Fleming	.50	.15
❑ 56	Kevin Mitchell	.50	.15
❑ 57	Jeff Nelson RC	2.50	.75
❑ 58	Shane Turner	.50	.15
❑ 59	Jose Canseco	2.50	.75
❑ 60	Jeff Frye RC	.50	.15
❑ 61	Danny Leon	.50	.15
❑ 62	Roger Pavlik RC	.50	.15
❑ 63	David Cone	1.00	.30
❑ 64	Pat Hentgen	.50	.15
❑ 65	Randy Knorr	.50	.15
❑ 66	Jack Morris	1.00	.30
❑ 67	Dave Winfield	1.50	.45
❑ 68	David Nied RC	.50	.15
❑ 69	Otis Nixon	.50	.15
❑ 70	Alejandro Pena	.50	.15
❑ 71	Jeff Reardon	1.00	.30
❑ 72	Alex Arias RC	.50	.15
❑ 73	Jim Bullinger	.50	.15
❑ 74	Mike Morgan	.50	.15
❑ 75	Rey Sanchez RC	1.50	.45
❑ 76	Bob Scanlan	.50	.15
❑ 77	Sammy Sosa	4.00	1.20
❑ 78	Scott Bankhead	.50	.15
❑ 79	Tim Belcher	.50	.15
❑ 80	Steve Foster	.50	.15
❑ 81	Willie Greene	.50	.15
❑ 82	Bip Roberts	.50	.15
❑ 83	Scott Ruskin	.50	.15
❑ 84	Greg Swindell	.50	.15
❑ 85	Juan Guerrero	.50	.15
❑ 86	Butch Henry	.50	.15
❑ 87	Doug Jones	.50	.15
❑ 88	Brian Williams RC	.50	.15
❑ 89	Tom Candiotti	.50	.15
❑ 90	Eric Davis	1.00	.30
❑ 91	Carlos Hernandez	.50	.15
❑ 92	Mike Piazza RC	60.00	18.00
❑ 93	Mike Sharperson	.50	.15
❑ 94	Eric Young RC	1.50	.45
❑ 95	Moises Alou	1.00	.30
❑ 96	Greg Colbrunn	.50	.15
❑ 97	Wil Cordero	.50	.15
❑ 98	Ken Hill	.50	.15
❑ 99	John Vander Wal RC	1.50	.45
❑ 100	John Wetteland	1.00	.30
❑ 101	Bobby Bonilla	1.00	.30
❑ 102	Eric Hillman RC	.50	.15
❑ 103	Pat Howell	.50	.15
❑ 104	Jeff Kent RC	10.00	3.00
❑ 105	Dick Schofield	.50	.15
❑ 106	Ryan Thompson RC	.50	.15
❑ 107	Chico Walker	.50	.15
❑ 108	Juan Bell	.50	.15
❑ 109	Mariano Duncan	.50	.15
❑ 110	Jeff Grotewold	.50	.15
❑ 111	Ben Rivera	.50	.15
❑ 112	Curt Schilling	1.50	.45
❑ 113	Victor Cole	.50	.15
❑ 114	Al Martin RC	1.50	.45
❑ 115	Roger Mason	.50	.15
❑ 116	Blas Minor	.50	.15
❑ 117	Tim Wakefield RC	4.00	1.20
❑ 118	Mark Clark RC	.50	.15
❑ 119	Rheal Cormier	.50	.15
❑ 120	Donovan Osborne	.50	.15
❑ 121	Todd Worrell	.50	.15
❑ 122	Jeremy Hernandez RC	.50	.15
❑ 123	Randy Myers	.50	.15
❑ 124	Frank Seminara RC	.50	.15
❑ 125	Gary Sheffield	1.00	.30
❑ 126	Dan Walters	.50	.15
❑ 127	Steve Hosey	.50	.15
❑ 128	Mike Jackson	.50	.15
❑ 129	Jim Pena	.50	.15
❑ 130	Cory Snyder	.50	.15
❑ 131	Bill Swift	.50	.15
❑ 132	Checklist U1-U132	.50	.15

1994 Fleer Update

	Nm-Mt	Ex-Mt
COMP.FACT.SET (210)	50.00	15.00
COMPLETE SET (200)	75.00	22.00

No.	Card	Nm-Mt	Ex-Mt
❑ 1	Mark Eichhorn	.25	.07
❑ 2	Sid Fernandez	.25	.07
❑ 3	Leo Gomez	.25	.07
❑ 4	Mike Oquist	.25	.07
❑ 5	Rafael Palmeiro	.75	.23
❑ 6	Chris Sabo	.25	.07
❑ 7	Dwight Smith	.25	.07
❑ 8	Lee Smith	.50	.15
❑ 9	Damon Berryhill	.25	.07
❑ 10	Wes Chamberlain	.25	.07
❑ 11	Gar Finnvold	.25	.07
❑ 12	Chris Howard	.25	.07
❑ 13	Tim Naehring	.25	.07
❑ 14	Otis Nixon	.25	.07
❑ 15	Brian Anderson RC	.50	.15
❑ 16	Jorge Fabregas	.25	.07
❑ 17	Rex Hudler	.25	.07
❑ 18	Bo Jackson	1.25	.35
❑ 19	Mark Leiter	.25	.07

❑ 20 Spike Owen .25 .07
❑ 21 Harold Reynolds .50 .15
❑ 22 Chris Turner .25 .07
❑ 23 Dennis Cook .25 .07
❑ 24 Jose DeLeon .25 .07
❑ 25 Julio Franco .50 .15
❑ 26 Joe Hall .25 .07
❑ 27 Darrin Jackson .25 .07
❑ 28 Dane Johnson .25 .07
❑ 29 Norberto Martin .25 .07
❑ 30 Scott Sanderson .25 .07
❑ 31 Jason Grimsley .25 .07
❑ 32 Dennis Martinez .50 .15
❑ 33 Jack Morris .50 .15
❑ 34 Eddie Murray 1.25 .35
❑ 35 Chad Ogea .25 .07
❑ 36 Tony Pena .25 .07
❑ 37 Paul Shuey .25 .07
❑ 38 Omar Vizquel .50 .15
❑ 39 Danny Bautista .25 .07
❑ 40 Tim Belcher .25 .07
❑ 41 Joe Boever .25 .07
❑ 42 Storm Davis .25 .07
❑ 43 Junior Felix .25 .07
❑ 44 Mike Gardiner .25 .07
❑ 45 Buddy Groom .25 .07
❑ 46 Juan Samuel .25 .07
❑ 47 Vince Coleman .25 .07
❑ 48 Bob Hamelin .25 .07
❑ 49 Dave Henderson .25 .07
❑ 50 Rusty Meacham .25 .07
❑ 51 Terry Shumpert .25 .07
❑ 52 Jeff Bronkey .25 .07
❑ 53 Alex Diaz .25 .07
❑ 54 Brian Harper .25 .07
❑ 55 Jose Mercedes .25 .07
❑ 56 Jody Reed .25 .07
❑ 57 Bob Scanlan .25 .07
❑ 58 Turner Ward .25 .07
❑ 59 Rich Becker .25 .07
❑ 60 Alex Cole .25 .07
❑ 61 Denny Hocking .25 .07
❑ 62 Scott Leius .25 .07
❑ 63 Pat Mahomes .25 .07
❑ 64 Carlos Pulido .25 .07
❑ 65 Dave Stevens .25 .07
❑ 66 Matt Walbeck .25 .07
❑ 67 Xavier Hernandez .25 .07
❑ 68 Sterling Hitchcock .25 .07
❑ 69 Terry Mulholland .25 .07
❑ 70 Luis Polonia .25 .07
❑ 71 Gerald Williams .25 .07
❑ 72 Mark Acre RC .25 .07
❑ 73 Geronimo Berroa .25 .07
❑ 74 Rickey Henderson 2.00 .60
❑ 75 Stan Javier .25 .07
❑ 76 Steve Karsay .25 .07
❑ 77 Carlos Reyes .25 .07
❑ 78 Bill Taylor RC .50 .15
❑ 79 Eric Anthony .25 .07
❑ 80 Bobby Ayala .25 .07
❑ 81 Tim Davis .25 .07
❑ 82 Felix Fermin .25 .07
❑ 83 Reggie Jefferson .25 .07
❑ 84 Keith Mitchell .25 .07
❑ 85 Bill Risley .25 .07
❑ 86 Alex Rodriguez RC 40.00 12.00
❑ 87 Roger Salkeld .25 .07
❑ 88 Dan Wilson .25 .07
❑ 89 Cris Carpenter .25 .07
❑ 90 Will Clark 1.25 .35
❑ 91 Jeff Frye .25 .07
❑ 92 Rick Helling .25 .07
❑ 93 Chris James .25 .07
❑ 94 Oddibe McDowell .25 .07
❑ 95 Billy Ripken .25 .07
❑ 96 Carlos Delgado .75 .23
❑ 97 Alex Gonzalez .25 .07
❑ 98 Shawn Green 1.25 .35
❑ 99 Darren Hall .25 .07
❑ 100 Mike Huff .25 .07
❑ 101 Mike Kelly .25 .07
❑ 102 Roberto Kelly .25 .07
❑ 103 Charlie O'Brien .25 .07
❑ 104 Jose Oliva .25 .07
❑ 105 Gregg Olson .25 .07
❑ 106 Willie Banks .25 .07
❑ 107 Jim Bullinger .25 .07
❑ 108 Chuck Crim .25 .07
❑ 109 Shawon Dunston .25 .07
❑ 110 Karl Rhodes .25 .07
❑ 111 Steve Trachsel .25 .07
❑ 112 Anthony Young .25 .07
❑ 113 Eddie Zambrano .25 .07
❑ 114 Bret Boone .50 .15
❑ 115 Jeff Brantley .25 .07
❑ 116 Hector Carrasco .25 .07
❑ 117 Tony Fernandez .25 .07
❑ 118 Tim Fortugno .25 .07
❑ 119 Erik Hanson .25 .07
❑ 120 Chuck McElroy .25 .07
❑ 121 Deion Sanders .50 .15
❑ 122 Ellis Burks .50 .15
❑ 123 Marvin Freeman .25 .07
❑ 124 Mike Harkey .25 .07
❑ 125 Howard Johnson .25 .07
❑ 126 Mike Kingery .25 .07
❑ 127 Nelson Liriano .25 .07
❑ 128 Marcus Moore .25 .07
❑ 129 Mike Munoz .25 .07
❑ 130 Kevin Ritz .25 .07
❑ 131 Walt Weiss .25 .07
❑ 132 Kurt Abbott RC .50 .15
❑ 133 Jerry Browne .25 .07
❑ 134 Greg Colbrunn .25 .07
❑ 135 Jeremy Hernandez .25 .07
❑ 136 Dave Magadan .25 .07
❑ 137 Kurt Miller .25 .07
❑ 138 Robb Nen .50 .15
❑ 139 Jesus Tavarez RC .25 .07
❑ 140 Sid Bream .25 .07
❑ 141 Tom Edens .25 .07
❑ 142 Tony Eusebio .25 .07
❑ 143 John Hudek RC .25 .07
❑ 144 Brian L. Hunter .25 .07
❑ 145 Orlando Miller .25 .07
❑ 146 James Mouton .25 .07
❑ 147 Shane Reynolds .25 .07
❑ 148 Rafael Bournigal .25 .07
❑ 149 Delino DeShields .25 .07
❑ 150 Garey Ingram RC .25 .07
❑ 151 Chan Ho Park RC 1.50 .45
❑ 152 Wil Cordero .25 .07
❑ 153 Pedro Martinez 1.25 .35
❑ 154 Randy Milligan .25 .07
❑ 155 Lenny Webster .25 .07
❑ 156 Rico Brogna .25 .07
❑ 157 Josias Manzanillo .25 .07
❑ 158 Kevin McReynolds .25 .07
❑ 159 Mike Remlinger .25 .07
❑ 160 David Segui .25 .07
❑ 161 Pete Smith .25 .07
❑ 162 Kelly Stinnett RC .50 .15
❑ 163 Jose Vizcaino .25 .07
❑ 164 Billy Hatcher .25 .07
❑ 165 Doug Jones .25 .07
❑ 166 Mike Lieberthal .50 .15
❑ 167 Tony Longmire .25 .07
❑ 168 Bobby Munoz .25 .07
❑ 169 Paul Quantrill .25 .07
❑ 170 Heathcliff Slocumb .25 .07
❑ 171 Fernando Valenzuela .50 .15
❑ 172 Mark Dewey .25 .07
❑ 173 Brian R. Hunter .25 .07
❑ 174 Jon Lieber .25 .07
❑ 175 Ravelo Manzanillo .25 .07
❑ 176 Dan Miceli .25 .07
❑ 177 Rick White .25 .07
❑ 178 Bryan Eversgerd .25 .07
❑ 179 John Habyan .25 .07
❑ 180 Terry McGriff .25 .07
❑ 181 Vicente Palacios .25 .07
❑ 182 Rich Rodriguez .25 .07
❑ 183 Rick Sutcliffe .50 .15
❑ 184 Donnie Elliott .25 .07
❑ 185 Joey Hamilton .25 .07
❑ 186 Tim Hyers RC .25 .07
❑ 187 Luis Lopez .25 .07
❑ 188 Ray McDavid .25 .07
❑ 189 Bip Roberts .25 .07
❑ 190 Scott Sanders .25 .07
❑ 191 Eddie Williams .25 .07
❑ 192 Steve Frey .25 .07
❑ 193 Pat Gomez .25 .07
❑ 194 Rich Monteleone .25 .07
❑ 195 Mark Portugal .25 .07
❑ 196 Darryl Strawberry .75 .23
❑ 197 Salomon Torres .25 .07
❑ 198 W.VanLandingham RC .25 .07
❑ 199 Checklist .25 .07
❑ 200 Checklist .25 .07

2002 Fleer

	Nm-Mt	Ex-Mt
COMPLETE SET (540)	100.00	30.00
COMMON CARD (1-540)	.25	.07
COMMON CARD (492-531)	.50	.15

❑ 1 Darin Erstad FP .25 .07
❑ 2 Randy Johnson FP .60 .18
❑ 3 Chipper Jones FP .60 .18
❑ 4 Jay Gibbons FP .25 .07
❑ 5 Nomar Garciaparra FP 1.00 .30
❑ 6 Sammy Sosa FP 1.00 .30
❑ 7 Frank Thomas FP .60 .18
❑ 8 Ken Griffey Jr. FP 1.00 .30
❑ 9 Jim Thome FP .60 .18
❑ 10 Todd Helton FP .40 .12
❑ 11 Jeff Weaver FP .25 .07
❑ 12 Cliff Floyd FP .25 .07
❑ 13 Jeff Bagwell FP .40 .12
❑ 14 Mike Sweeney FP .25 .07
❑ 15 Adrian Beltre FP .25 .07
❑ 16 Richie Sexson FP .25 .07
❑ 17 Brad Radke FP .25 .07
❑ 18 Vladimir Guerrero FP .60 .18
❑ 19 Mike Piazza FP 1.00 .30
❑ 20 Derek Jeter FP 1.25 .35
❑ 21 Eric Chavez FP .25 .07
❑ 22 Pat Burrell FP .25 .07
❑ 23 Brian Giles FP .25 .07
❑ 24 Trevor Hoffman FP .25 .07
❑ 25 Barry Bonds FP 1.00 .30
❑ 26 Ichiro Suzuki FP 1.00 .30
❑ 27 Albert Pujols FP 1.00 .30
❑ 28 Ben Grieve FP .25 .07
❑ 29 Alex Rodriguez FP 1.00 .30
❑ 30 Carlos Delgado FP .25 .07
❑ 31 Miguel Tejada .40 .12
❑ 32 Todd Hollandsworth .25 .07
❑ 33 Marlon Anderson .25 .07
❑ 34 Kerry Robinson .25 .07
❑ 35 Chris Richard .25 .07
❑ 36 Jamey Wright .25 .07
❑ 37 Ray Lankford .25 .07
❑ 38 Mike Bordick .40 .12
❑ 39 Danny Graves .25 .07
❑ 40 A.J. Pierzynski .40 .12
❑ 41 Shannon Stewart .40 .12
❑ 42 Tony Armas Jr. .25 .07
❑ 43 Brad Ausmus .25 .07
❑ 44 Alfonso Soriano 1.00 .30
❑ 45 Junior Spivey .25 .07
❑ 46 Brent Mayne .25 .07
❑ 47 Jim Thome 1.00 .30
❑ 48 Dan Wilson .25 .07
❑ 49 Geoff Jenkins .40 .12
❑ 50 Kris Benson .25 .07
❑ 51 Rafael Furcal .40 .12

☐ 52	Wiki Gonzalez	.25	.07
☐ 53	Jeff Kent	.40	.12
☐ 54	Curt Schilling	.60	.18
☐ 55	Ken Harvey	.25	.07
☐ 56	Roosevelt Brown	.25	.07
☐ 57	David Segui	.25	.07
☐ 58	Mario Valdez	.25	.07
☐ 59	Adam Dunn	.60	.18
☐ 60	Bob Howry	.25	.07
☐ 61	Michael Barrett	.25	.07
☐ 62	Garret Anderson	.40	.12
☐ 63	Kelvim Escobar	.25	.07
☐ 64	Ben Grieve	.25	.07
☐ 65	Randy Johnson	1.00	.30
☐ 66	Jose Offerman	.25	.07
☐ 67	Jason Kendall	.40	.12
☐ 68	Joel Pineiro	.40	.12
☐ 69	Alex Escobar	.25	.07
☐ 70	Chris George	.25	.07
☐ 71	Bobby Higginson	.40	.12
☐ 72	Nomar Garciaparra	2.00	.60
☐ 73	Pat Burrell	.40	.12
☐ 74	Lee Stevens	.25	.07
☐ 75	Felipe Lopez	.25	.07
☐ 76	Al Leiter	.40	.12
☐ 77	Jim Edmonds	.40	.12
☐ 78	Al Levine	.25	.07
☐ 79	Raul Mondesi	.40	.12
☐ 80	Jose Valentin	.25	.07
☐ 81	Matt Clement	.25	.07
☐ 82	Richard Hidalgo	.40	.12
☐ 83	Jamie Moyer	.40	.12
☐ 84	Brian Schneider	.25	.07
☐ 85	John Franco	.40	.12
☐ 86	Brian Buchanan	.25	.07
☐ 87	Roy Oswalt	.40	.12
☐ 88	Johnny Estrada	.25	.07
☐ 89	Marcus Giles	.40	.12
☐ 90	Carlos Valderrama	.25	.07
☐ 91	Mark Mulder	.40	.12
☐ 92	Mark Grace	1.00	.30
☐ 93	Andy Ashby	.25	.07
☐ 94	Woody Williams	.25	.07
☐ 95	Ben Petrick	.25	.07
☐ 96	Roy Halladay	.40	.12
☐ 97	Fred McGriff	.60	.18
☐ 98	Shawn Green	.40	.12
☐ 99	Todd Hundley	.25	.07
☐ 100	Carlos Febles	.25	.07
☐ 101	Jason Marquis	.25	.07
☐ 102	Mike Redmond	.25	.07
☐ 103	Shane Halter	.25	.07
☐ 104	Trot Nixon	.40	.12
☐ 105	Jeremy Giambi	.25	.07
☐ 106	Carlos Delgado	.40	.12
☐ 107	Richie Sexson	.40	.12
☐ 108	Russ Ortiz	.40	.12
☐ 109	David Ortiz	.40	.12
☐ 110	Curtis Leskanic	.25	.07
☐ 111	Jay Payton	.25	.07
☐ 112	Travis Phelps	.25	.07
☐ 113	J.T. Snow	.40	.12
☐ 114	Edgar Renteria	.40	.12
☐ 115	Freddy Garcia	.40	.12
☐ 116	Cliff Floyd	.40	.12
☐ 117	Charles Nagy	.25	.07
☐ 118	Tony Batista	.40	.12
☐ 119	Rafael Palmeiro	.60	.18
☐ 120	Darren Dreifort	.25	.07
☐ 121	Warren Morris	.25	.07
☐ 122	Augie Ojeda	.25	.07
☐ 123	Rusty Greer	.40	.12
☐ 124	Esteban Yan	.25	.07
☐ 125	Corey Patterson	.40	.12
☐ 126	Matt Ginter	.25	.07
☐ 127	Matt Lawton	.25	.07
☐ 128	Miguel Batista	.25	.07
☐ 129	Randy Winn	.25	.07
☐ 130	Eric Milton	.25	.07
☐ 131	Jack Wilson	.25	.07
☐ 132	Sean Casey	.40	.12
☐ 133	Mike Sweeney	.40	.12
☐ 134	Jason Tyner	.25	.07
☐ 135	Carlos Hernandez	.25	.07
☐ 136	Shea Hillenbrand	.40	.12
☐ 137	Shawn Wooten	.25	.07
☐ 138	Peter Bergeron	.25	.07
☐ 139	Travis Lee	.25	.07
☐ 140	Craig Wilson	.25	.07
☐ 141	Carlos Guillen	.25	.07
☐ 142	Chipper Jones	1.00	.30
☐ 143	Gabe Kapler	.25	.07
☐ 144	Raul Ibanez	.40	.12
☐ 145	Eric Chavez	.40	.12
☐ 146	D'Angelo Jimenez	.25	.07
☐ 147	Chad Hermansen	.25	.07
☐ 148	Joe Kennedy	.25	.07
☐ 149	Mariano Rivera	.60	.18
☐ 150	Jeff Bagwell	.60	.18
☐ 151	Joe McEwing	.25	.07
☐ 152	Ronnie Belliard	.25	.07
☐ 153	Desi Relaford	.25	.07
☐ 154	Vinny Castilla	.40	.12
☐ 155	Tim Hudson	.40	.12
☐ 156	Wilton Guerrero	.25	.07
☐ 157	Raul Casanova	.25	.07
☐ 158	Edgardo Alfonzo	.40	.12
☐ 159	Derrek Lee	.40	.12
☐ 160	Phil Nevin	.40	.12
☐ 161	Roger Clemens	2.00	.60
☐ 162	Jason LaRue	.25	.07
☐ 163	Brian Lawrence	.25	.07
☐ 164	Adrian Beltre	.40	.12
☐ 165	Troy Glaus	.60	.18
☐ 166	Jeff Weaver	.25	.07
☐ 167	B.J. Surhoff	.40	.12
☐ 168	Eric Byrnes	.25	.07
☐ 169	Mike Sirotka	.25	.07
☐ 170	Bill Haselman	.25	.07
☐ 171	Javier Vazquez	.40	.12
☐ 172	Sidney Ponson	.25	.07
☐ 173	Adam Everett	.25	.07
☐ 174	Bubba Trammell	.25	.07
☐ 175	Robb Nen	.40	.12
☐ 176	Barry Larkin	1.00	.30
☐ 177	Tony Graffanino	.25	.07
☐ 178	Rich Garces	.25	.07
☐ 179	Juan Uribe	.25	.07
☐ 180	Tom Glavine	1.00	.30
☐ 181	Eric Karros	.40	.12
☐ 182	Michael Cuddyer	.40	.12
☐ 183	Wade Miller	.40	.12
☐ 184	Matt Williams	.40	.12
☐ 185	Matt Morris	.40	.12
☐ 186	Rickey Henderson	1.50	.45
☐ 187	Trevor Hoffman	.40	.12
☐ 188	Wilson Betemit	.25	.07
☐ 189	Steve Karsay	.25	.07
☐ 190	Frank Catalanotto	.25	.07
☐ 191	Jason Schmidt	.40	.12
☐ 192	Roger Cedeno	.25	.07
☐ 193	Magglio Ordonez	.40	.12
☐ 194	Pat Hentgen	.25	.07
☐ 195	Mike Lieberthal	.40	.12
☐ 196	Andy Pettitte	.60	.18
☐ 197	Jay Gibbons	.40	.12
☐ 198	Rolando Arrojo	.25	.07
☐ 199	Joe Mays	.25	.07
☐ 200	Aubrey Huff	.40	.12
☐ 201	Nelson Figueroa	.25	.07
☐ 202	Paul Konerko	.40	.12
☐ 203	Ken Griffey Jr.	1.50	.45
☐ 204	Brandon Duckworth	.25	.07
☐ 205	Sammy Sosa	1.50	.45
☐ 206	Carl Everett	.40	.12
☐ 207	Scott Rolen	.60	.18
☐ 208	Orlando Hernandez	.40	.12
☐ 209	Todd Helton	.60	.18
☐ 210	Preston Wilson	.40	.12
☐ 211	Gil Meche	.40	.12
☐ 212	Bill Mueller	.40	.12
☐ 213	Craig Biggio	.60	.18
☐ 214	Dean Palmer	.40	.12
☐ 215	Randy Wolf	.40	.12
☐ 216	Jeff Suppan	.25	.07
☐ 217	Jimmy Rollins	.40	.12
☐ 218	Alexis Gomez	.25	.07
☐ 219	Ellis Burks	.40	.12
☐ 220	Ramon E. Martinez	.25	.07
☐ 221	Ramiro Mendoza	.25	.07
☐ 222	Einar Diaz	.25	.07
☐ 223	Brent Abernathy	.25	.07
☐ 224	Darin Erstad	.40	.12
☐ 225	Reggie Taylor	.25	.07
☐ 226	Jason Jennings	.25	.07
☐ 227	Ray Durham	.40	.12
☐ 228	John Parrish	.25	.07
☐ 229	Kevin Young	.25	.07
☐ 230	Xavier Nady	.40	.12
☐ 231	Juan Cruz	.25	.07
☐ 232	Greg Norton	.25	.07
☐ 233	Barry Bonds	2.50	.75
☐ 234	Kip Wells	.25	.07
☐ 235	Paul LoDuca	.40	.12
☐ 236	Javy Lopez	.40	.12
☐ 237	Luis Castillo	.40	.12
☐ 238	Tom Gordon	.25	.07
☐ 239	Mike Mordecai	.25	.07
☐ 240	Damian Rolls	.25	.07
☐ 241	Julio Lugo	.25	.07
☐ 242	Ichiro Suzuki	2.00	.60
☐ 243	Tony Womack	.25	.07
☐ 244	Matt Anderson	.25	.07
☐ 245	Carlos Lee	.40	.12
☐ 246	Alex Rodriguez	2.00	.60
☐ 247	Bernie Williams	.60	.18
☐ 248	Scott Sullivan	.25	.07
☐ 249	Mike Hampton	.40	.12
☐ 250	Orlando Cabrera	.25	.07
☐ 251	Benito Santiago	.40	.12
☐ 252	Steve Finley	.40	.12
☐ 253	Dave Williams	.25	.07
☐ 254	Adam Kennedy	.25	.07
☐ 255	Omar Vizquel	.40	.12
☐ 256	Garrett Stephenson	.25	.07
☐ 257	Fernando Tatis	.25	.07
☐ 258	Mike Piazza	1.50	.45
☐ 259	Scott Spiezio	.40	.12
☐ 260	Jacque Jones	.40	.12
☐ 261	Russell Branyan	.25	.07
☐ 262	Mark McLemore	.25	.07
☐ 263	Mitch Meluskey	.25	.07
☐ 264	Marlon Byrd	.40	.12
☐ 265	Kyle Farnsworth	.25	.07
☐ 266	Billy Sylvester	.25	.07
☐ 267	C.C. Sabathia	.40	.12
☐ 268	Mark Buehrle	.40	.12
☐ 269	Geoff Blum	.25	.07
☐ 270	Bret Prinz	.25	.07
☐ 271	Placido Polanco	.25	.07
☐ 272	John Olerud	.40	.12
☐ 273	Pedro Martinez	1.00	.30
☐ 274	Doug Mientkiewicz	.40	.12
☐ 275	Jason Bere	.25	.07
☐ 276	Bud Smith	.25	.07
☐ 277	Terrence Long	.40	.12
☐ 278	Troy Percival	.40	.12
☐ 279	Derek Jeter	2.50	.75
☐ 280	Eric Owens	.25	.07
☐ 281	Jay Bell	.40	.12
☐ 282	Mike Cameron	.40	.12
☐ 283	Joe Randa	.25	.07
☐ 284	Brian Roberts	.25	.07
☐ 285	Ryan Klesko	.40	.12
☐ 286	Ryan Dempster	.25	.07
☐ 287	Cristian Guzman	.40	.12
☐ 288	Tim Salmon	.60	.18
☐ 289	Mark Johnson	.25	.07
☐ 290	Brian Giles	.40	.12
☐ 291	Jon Lieber	.25	.07
☐ 292	Fernando Vina	.40	.12
☐ 293	Mike Mussina	1.00	.30
☐ 294	Juan Pierre	.40	.12
☐ 295	Carlos Beltran	.40	.12
☐ 296	Vladimir Guerrero	1.00	.30
☐ 297	Orlando Merced	.25	.07
☐ 298	Jose Hernandez	.25	.07
☐ 299	Mike Lamb	.25	.07
☐ 300	David Eckstein	.25	.07
☐ 301	Mark Loretta	.25	.07
☐ 302	Greg Vaughn	.40	.12
☐ 303	Jose Vidro	.40	.12
☐ 304	Jose Ortiz	.25	.07
☐ 305	Mark Grudzielanek	.25	.07
☐ 306	Rob Bell	.25	.07
☐ 307	Elmer Dessens	.25	.07
☐ 308	Tomas Perez	.25	.07
☐ 309	Jerry Hairston Jr.	.25	.07

	No.	Player	Nm-Mt	Ex-Mt
❑	310	Mike Stanton	.25	.07
❑	311	Todd Walker	.40	.12
❑	312	Jason Varitek	.40	.12
❑	313	Masato Yoshii	.25	.07
❑	314	Ben Sheets	.40	.12
❑	315	Roberto Hernandez	.25	.07
❑	316	Eli Marrero	.25	.07
❑	317	Josh Beckett	.60	.18
❑	318	Robert Fick	.40	.12
❑	319	Aramis Ramirez	.40	.12
❑	320	Bartolo Colon	.40	.12
❑	321	Kenny Kelly	.25	.07
❑	322	Luis Gonzalez	.40	.12
❑	323	John Smoltz	.60	.18
❑	324	Homer Bush	.25	.07
❑	325	Kevin Millwood	.40	.12
❑	326	Manny Ramirez	.40	.12
❑	327	Armando Benitez	.40	.12
❑	328	Luis Alicea	.25	.07
❑	329	Mark Kotsay	.25	.07
❑	330	Felix Rodriguez	.25	.07
❑	331	Eddie Taubensee	.25	.07
❑	332	John Burkett	.25	.07
❑	333	Ramon Ortiz	.25	.07
❑	334	Daryle Ward	.25	.07
❑	335	Jarrod Washburn	.40	.12
❑	336	Benji Gil	.25	.07
❑	337	Mike Lowell	.40	.12
❑	338	Larry Walker	.60	.18
❑	339	Andruw Jones	.60	.18
❑	340	Scott Elarton	.25	.07
❑	341	Tony McKnight	.25	.07
❑	342	Frank Thomas	1.00	.30
❑	343	Kevin Brown	.40	.12
❑	344	Jermaine Dye	.40	.12
❑	345	Luis Rivas	.25	.07
❑	346	Jeff Conine	.40	.12
❑	347	Bobby Kielty	.25	.07
❑	348	Jeffrey Hammonds	.25	.07
❑	349	Keith Foulke	.25	.07
❑	350	Dave Martinez	.25	.07
❑	351	Adam Eaton	.25	.07
❑	352	Brandon Inge	.25	.07
❑	353	Tyler Houston	.25	.07
❑	354	Bobby Abreu	.40	.12
❑	355	Ivan Rodriguez	1.00	.30
❑	356	Doug Glanville	.25	.07
❑	357	Jorge Julio	.25	.07
❑	358	Kerry Wood	1.00	.30
❑	359	Eric Munson	.25	.07
❑	360	Joe Crede	.25	.07
❑	361	Denny Neagle	.25	.07
❑	362	Vance Wilson	.25	.07
❑	363	Neifi Perez	.25	.07
❑	364	Darryl Kile	.40	.12
❑	365	Jose Macias	.25	.07
❑	366	Michael Coleman	.25	.07
❑	367	Erubiel Durazo	.40	.12
❑	368	Darrin Fletcher	.25	.07
❑	369	Matt White	.25	.07
❑	370	Marvin Benard	.25	.07
❑	371	Brad Penny	.25	.07
❑	372	Chuck Finley	.40	.12
❑	373	Delino DeShields	.25	.07
❑	374	Adrian Brown	.25	.07
❑	375	Corey Koskie	.40	.12
❑	376	Kazuhiro Sasaki	.40	.12
❑	377	Brent Butler	.25	.07
❑	378	Paul Wilson	.25	.07
❑	379	Scott Williamson	.25	.07
❑	380	Mike Young	.40	.12
❑	381	Toby Hall	.25	.07
❑	382	Shane Reynolds	.25	.07
❑	383	Tom Goodwin	.25	.07
❑	384	Seth Etherton	.25	.07
❑	385	Billy Wagner	.40	.12
❑	386	Josh Phelps	.40	.12
❑	387	Kyle Lohse	.25	.07
❑	388	Jeremy Fikac	.25	.07
❑	389	Jorge Posada	.60	.18
❑	390	Bret Boone	.40	.12
❑	391	Angel Berroa	.40	.12
❑	392	Matt Mantei	.25	.07
❑	393	Alex Gonzalez	.25	.07
❑	394	Scott Strickland	.25	.07
❑	395	Charles Johnson	.40	.12
❑	396	Ramon Hernandez	.25	.07
❑	397	Damian Jackson	.25	.07
❑	398	Albert Pujols	2.00	.60
❑	399	Gary Bennett	.25	.07
❑	400	Edgar Martinez	.60	.18
❑	401	Carl Pavano	.25	.07
❑	402	Chris Gomez	.25	.07
❑	403	Jaret Wright	.25	.07
❑	404	Lance Berkman	.40	.12
❑	405	Robert Person	.25	.07
❑	406	Brook Fordyce	.25	.07
❑	407	Adam Pettyjohn	.25	.07
❑	408	Chris Carpenter	.25	.07
❑	409	Rey Ordonez	.25	.07
❑	410	Eric Gagne	.60	.18
❑	411	Damion Easley	.25	.07
❑	412	A.J. Burnett	.25	.07
❑	413	Aaron Boone	.40	.12
❑	414	J.D. Drew	.40	.12
❑	415	Kelly Stinnett	.25	.07
❑	416	Mark Quinn	.25	.07
❑	417	Brad Radke	.40	.12
❑	418	Jose Cruz Jr.	.40	.12
❑	419	Greg Maddux	2.00	.60
❑	420	Steve Cox	.25	.07
❑	421	Torii Hunter	.40	.12
❑	422	Sandy Alomar	.25	.07
❑	423	Barry Zito	1.00	.30
❑	424	Bill Hall	.25	.07
❑	425	Marquis Grissom	.25	.07
❑	426	Rich Aurilia	.40	.12
❑	427	Royce Clayton	.25	.07
❑	428	Travis Fryman	.40	.12
❑	429	Pablo Ozuna	.25	.07
❑	430	David Dellucci	.25	.07
❑	431	Vernon Wells	.40	.12
❑	432	Gregg Zaun CP	.25	.07
❑	433	Alex Gonzalez CP	.25	.07
❑	434	Hideo Nomo CP	1.00	.30
❑	435	Jeromy Burnitz CP	.40	.12
❑	436	Gary Sheffield CP	.40	.12
❑	437	Tino Martinez CP	.60	.18
❑	438	Tsuyoshi Shinjo CP	.40	.12
❑	439	Chan Ho Park CP	.40	.12
❑	440	Tony Clark CP	.25	.07
❑	441	Brad Fullmer CP	.40	.12
❑	442	Jason Giambi CP	1.00	.30
❑	443	Billy Koch CP	.25	.07
❑	444	Mo Vaughn CP	.40	.12
❑	445	Alex Ochoa CP	.25	.07
❑	446	Darren Lewis CP	.25	.07
❑	447	John Rocker CP	.25	.07
❑	448	Scott Hatteberg CP	.25	.07
❑	449	Brady Anderson CP	.40	.12
❑	450	Chuck Knoblauch CP	.40	.12
❑	451	Pokey Reese CP	.25	.07
❑	452	Brian Jordan CP	.40	.12
❑	453	Albie Lopez CP	.25	.07
❑	454	David Bell CP	.25	.07
❑	455	Juan Gonzalez CP	1.00	.30
❑	456	Terry Adams CP	.25	.07
❑	457	Kenny Lofton CP	.40	.12
❑	458	Shawn Estes CP	.25	.07
❑	459	Josh Fogg CP	.25	.07
❑	460	Dmitri Young CP	.40	.12
❑	461	Johnny Damon CP	.40	.12
❑	462	Chris Singleton CP	.25	.07
❑	463	Ricky Ledee CP	.25	.07
❑	464	Dustin Hermanson CP	.25	.07
❑	465	Aaron Sele CP	.25	.07
❑	466	Chris Stynes CP	.25	.07
❑	467	Matt Stairs CP	.25	.07
❑	468	Kevin Appier CP	.40	.12
❑	469	Omar Daal CP	.25	.07
❑	470	Moises Alou CP	.40	.12
❑	471	Juan Encarnacion CP	.25	.07
❑	472	Robin Ventura CP	.40	.12
❑	473	Eric Hinske CP	.25	.07
❑	474	Rondell White CP	.40	.12
❑	475	Carlos Pena CP	.25	.07
❑	476	Craig Paquette CP	.25	.07
❑	477	Marty Cordova CP	.25	.07
❑	478	Brett Tomko CP	.25	.07
❑	479	Reggie Sanders CP	.40	.12
❑	480	Roberto Alomar CP	1.00	.30
❑	481	Jeff Cirillo CP	.40	.12
❑	482	Todd Zeile CP	.40	.12
❑	483	John Vander Wal CP	.25	.07
❑	484	Rick Helling CP	.25	.07
❑	485	Jeff D'Amico CP	.25	.07
❑	486	David Justice CP	.40	.12
❑	487	Jason Isringhausen CP	.40	.12
❑	488	Shigetoshi Hasegawa CP	.40	.12
❑	489	Eric Young CP	.25	.07
❑	490	David Wells CP	.40	.12
❑	491	Ruben Sierra CP	.25	.07
❑	492	Aaron Cook FF RC	1.25	.35
❑	493	Takahito Nomura FF RC	.75	.23
❑	494	Austin Kearns FF	1.25	.35
❑	495	Kazuhisa Ishii FF RC	4.00	1.20
❑	496	Mark Teixeira FF	2.00	.60
❑	497	Rene Reyes FF RC	.75	.23
❑	498	Tim Spooneybarger FF	.50	.15
❑	499	Ben Broussard FF	.50	.15
❑	500	Eric Cyr FF	.50	.15
❑	501	Anastacio Martinez FF RC	.75	.23
❑	502	Morgan Ensberg FF	.75	.23
❑	503	Steve Kent FF RC	.75	.23
❑	504	Franklin Nunez FF RC	.75	.23
❑	505	Adam Walker FF RC	.75	.23
❑	506	Anderson Machado FF RC	1.25	.35
❑	507	Ryan Drese FF	.50	.15
❑	508	Luis Ugueto FF RC	.75	.23
❑	509	Jorge Nunez FF RC	.75	.23
❑	510	Colby Lewis FF	.50	.15
❑	511	Ron Calloway FF RC	.75	.23
❑	512	Hansel Izquierdo FF RC	.75	.23
❑	513	Jason Lane FF	.50	.15
❑	514	Rafael Soriano FF	.75	.23
❑	515	Jackson Melian FF	.50	.15
❑	516	Edwin Almonte FF RC	.75	.23
❑	517	Satoru Komiyama FF RC	.75	.23
❑	518	Corey Thurman FF RC	.75	.23
❑	519	Jorge De La Rosa FF RC	.75	.23
❑	520	Victor Martinez FF	.75	.23
❑	521	Dewon Brazelton FF	.50	.15
❑	522	Marlon Byrd FF	.75	.23
❑	523	Jae Seo FF	.50	.15
❑	524	Orlando Hudson FF	.50	.15
❑	525	Sean Burroughs FF	.75	.23
❑	526	Ryan Langerhans FF	.50	.15
❑	527	David Kelton FF	.50	.15
❑	528	So Taguchi FF RC	1.25	.35
❑	529	Tyler Walker FF	.50	.15
❑	530	Hank Blalock FF	2.00	.60
❑	531	Mark Prior FF	5.00	1.50
❑	532	Yankee Stadium CL	.40	.12
❑	533	Fenway Park CL	.40	.12
❑	534	Wrigley Field CL	.40	.12
❑	535	Dodger Stadium CL	.40	.12
❑	536	Camden Yards CL	.40	.12
❑	537	PacBell Park CL	.25	.07
❑	538	Jacobs Field CL	.25	.07
❑	539	SAFECO Field CL	.25	.07
❑	540	Miller Field CL	.25	.07
❑	P279	Derek Jeter Promo	-	

2002 Fleer Authentix

	Nm-Mt	Ex-Mt
COMP.SET w/o SP's (150)	40.00	12.00
COMMON CARD (1-135)	.40	.12
COMMON CARD (136-150)	.60	.18
COMMON CARD (151-170)	5.00	1.50

❑ 1 Derek Jeter 2.50 .75
❑ 2 Tim Hudson .40 .12
❑ 3 Robert Fick .40 .12
❑ 4 Javy Lopez .40 .12
❑ 5 Alfonso Soriano 1.00 .30
❑ 6 Ken Griffey Jr. 1.50 .45
❑ 7 Rafael Palmeiro .60 .18
❑ 8 Bernie Williams .60 .18
❑ 9 Adam Dunn .60 .18
❑ 10 Ivan Rodriguez 1.00 .30
❑ 11 Vladimir Guerrero 1.00 .30
❑ 12 Pedro Martinez 1.00 .30
❑ 13 Bret Boone .40 .12
❑ 14 Paul LoDuca .40 .12
❑ 15 Tony Batista .40 .12
❑ 16 Barry Bonds 2.50 .75
❑ 17 Craig Biggio .60 .18
❑ 18 Garret Anderson .40 .12
❑ 19 Mark Mulder .40 .12
❑ 20 Frank Thomas 1.00 .30
❑ 21 Alex Rodriguez 2.00 .60
❑ 22 Cristian Guzman .40 .12
❑ 23 Sammy Sosa 1.50 .45
❑ 24 Ichiro Suzuki 2.00 .60
❑ 25 Carlos Beltran .40 .12
❑ 26 Edgardo Alfonzo .40 .12
❑ 27 Josh Beckett .60 .18
❑ 28 Eric Chavez .40 .12
❑ 29 Roberto Alomar 1.00 .30
❑ 30 Raul Mondesi .40 .12
❑ 31 Mike Piazza 1.50 .45
❑ 32 Barry Larkin 1.00 .30
❑ 33 Ruben Sierra .40 .12
❑ 34 Tsuyoshi Shinjo .40 .12
❑ 35 Magglio Ordonez .40 .12
❑ 36 Ben Grieve .40 .12
❑ 37 Richie Sexson .40 .12
❑ 38 Manny Ramirez .40 .12
❑ 39 Jeff Kent .40 .12
❑ 40 Shawn Green .40 .12
❑ 41 Andruw Jones .60 .18
❑ 42 Aramis Ramirez .40 .12
❑ 43 Cliff Floyd .40 .12
❑ 44 Juan Pierre .40 .12
❑ 45 Jose Vidro .40 .12
❑ 46 Paul Konerko .40 .12
❑ 47 Greg Vaughn .40 .12
❑ 48 Geoff Jenkins .40 .12
❑ 49 Greg Maddux 2.00 .60
❑ 50 Ryan Klesko .40 .12
❑ 51 Corey Koskie .40 .12
❑ 52 Nomar Garciaparra 2.00 .60
❑ 53 Edgar Martinez .60 .18
❑ 54 Gary Sheffield .40 .12
❑ 55 Randy Johnson 1.00 .30
❑ 56 Bobby Abreu .40 .12
❑ 57 Mike Sweeney .40 .12
❑ 58 Chipper Jones 1.00 .30
❑ 59 Brian Giles .40 .12
❑ 60 Charles Johnson .40 .12
❑ 61 Ben Sheets .40 .12
❑ 62 Jason Giambi 1.00 .30
❑ 63 Todd Helton .60 .18
❑ 64 David Eckstein .40 .12
❑ 65 Troy Glaus .60 .18
❑ 66 Sean Casey .40 .12
❑ 67 Gabe Kapler .40 .12
❑ 68 Doug Mientkiewicz .40 .12
❑ 69 Curt Schilling .60 .18
❑ 70 Pat Burrell .40 .12
❑ 71 Albert Pujols 2.00 .60
❑ 72 Jermaine Dye .40 .12
❑ 73 Miguel Tejada .40 .12
❑ 74 Jim Thome 1.00 .30
❑ 75 Carlos Delgado .40 .12
❑ 76 Fred McGriff .60 .18
❑ 77 Mike Cameron .40 .12
❑ 78 Jeromy Burnitz .40 .12
❑ 79 Jay Gibbons .40 .12
❑ 80 Rich Aurilia .40 .12
❑ 81 Lance Berkman .40 .12
❑ 82 Brian Jordan .40 .12
❑ 83 Phil Nevin .40 .12
❑ 84 Moises Alou .40 .12
❑ 85 Reggie Sanders .40 .12
❑ 86 Scott Rolen .60 .18
❑ 87 Larry Walker .60 .18
❑ 88 Matt Williams .40 .12
❑ 89 Roger Clemens 2.00 .60
❑ 90 Juan Gonzalez 1.00 .30
❑ 91 Jose Cruz Jr. .40 .12
❑ 92 Tino Martinez .60 .18
❑ 93 Kerry Wood 1.00 .30
❑ 94 Freddy Garcia .40 .12
❑ 95 Jeff Bagwell .60 .18
❑ 96 Luis Gonzalez .40 .12
❑ 97 Jimmy Rollins .40 .12
❑ 98 Bobby Higginson .40 .12
❑ 99 Rondell White .40 .12
❑ 100 Jorge Posada .60 .18
❑ 101 Trot Nixon .40 .12
❑ 102 Jason Kendall .40 .12
❑ 103 Preston Wilson .40 .12
❑ 104 Corey Patterson .40 .12
❑ 105 Jose Valentin .40 .12
❑ 106 Carlos Lee .40 .12
❑ 107 Chris Richard .40 .12
❑ 108 Todd Walker .40 .12
❑ 109 Ellis Burks .40 .12
❑ 110 Brady Anderson .40 .12
❑ 111 Kazuhiro Sasaki .40 .12
❑ 112 Roy Oswalt .40 .12
❑ 113 Kevin Brown .40 .12
❑ 114 Jeff Weaver .40 .12
❑ 115 Todd Hollandsworth .40 .12
❑ 116 Joe Crede .40 .12
❑ 117 Tom Glavine 1.00 .30
❑ 118 Mike Lieberthal .40 .12
❑ 119 Tim Salmon .60 .18
❑ 120 Johnny Damon .40 .12
❑ 121 Brad Fullmer .40 .12
❑ 122 Mo Vaughn .40 .12
❑ 123 Torii Hunter .40 .12
❑ 124 Jamie Moyer .40 .12
❑ 125 Terrence Long .40 .12
❑ 126 Travis Lee .40 .12
❑ 127 Jacque Jones .40 .12
❑ 128 Lee Stevens .40 .12
❑ 129 Russ Ortiz .40 .12
❑ 130 Jeremy Giambi .40 .12
❑ 131 Mike Mussina 1.00 .30
❑ 132 Orlando Cabrera .40 .12
❑ 133 Barry Zito 1.00 .30
❑ 134 Robert Person .40 .12
❑ 135 Andy Pettitte .60 .18
❑ 136 Drew Henson FS .60 .18
❑ 137 Mark Teixeira FS 1.50 .45
❑ 138 David Espinosa FS .60 .18
❑ 139 Orlando Hudson FS .60 .18
❑ 140 Colby Lewis FS .60 .18
❑ 141 Bill Hall FS .60 .18
❑ 142 Michael Restovich FS .60 .18
❑ 143 Angel Berroa FS .60 .18
❑ 144 Dewon Brazelton FS .60 .18
❑ 145 Joe Thurston FS .60 .18
❑ 146 Mark Prior FS 3.00 .90
❑ 147 Dane Sardinha FS .60 .18
❑ 148 Marlon Byrd FS .60 .18
❑ 149 Jeff Deardorff FS .60 .18
❑ 150 Austin Kearns FS 1.00 .30
❑ 151 Anderson Machado TM RC 8.00 2.40
❑ 152 Kazuhisa Ishii TM RC 10.00 3.00
❑ 153 Eric Junge TM RC 5.00 1.50
❑ 154 Mark Corey TM RC 5.00 1.50
❑ 155 So Taguchi TM RC 8.00 2.40
❑ 156 Jorge Padilla TM RC 8.00 2.40
❑ 157 Steve Kent TM RC 5.00 1.50
❑ 158 Jaime Cerda TM RC 5.00 1.50
❑ 159 Hansel Izquierdo TM RC 5.00 1.50
❑ 160 Rene Reyes TM RC 5.00 1.50
❑ 161 Jorge Nunez TM RC 5.00 1.50
❑ 162 Corey Thurman TM RC 5.00 1.50
❑ 163 Jorge Sosa TM RC 5.00 1.50
❑ 164 Franklin Nunez TM RC 5.00 1.50
❑ 165 Adam Walker TM RC 5.00 1.50
❑ 166 Ryan Baerlocher TM RC 5.00 1.50
❑ 167 Ron Calloway TM RC 5.00 1.50
❑ 168 Miguel Asencio TM RC 5.00 1.50
❑ 169 Luis Ugueto TM RC 5.00 1.50
❑ 170 Felix Escalona TM RC 5.00 1.50

2003 Fleer Authentix

	Nm-Mt	Ex-Mt
COMP.LO SET w/o SP's (110)	25.00	7.50
COMMON CARD (1-100)	.40	.12
COMMON CARD (101-110)	.60	.18
COMMON CARD (111-125)	5.00	1.50
COMMON CARD (126-132)	5.00	1.50
126-132 STATED PRINT RUN 1700 SETS		-
COMMON CARD (133-139/	8.00	2.40
133-139 STATED PRINT RUN 210 SETS		-
COMMON CARD (140-153)	5.00	1.50
140-153 STATED PRINT RUN 560 SETS		-
COMMON CARD (154-160)	8.00	2.40
154-160 STATED PRINT RUN 280 SETS		-

❑ 1 Derek Jeter 2.50 .75
❑ 2 Tom Glavine 1.00 .30
❑ 3 Jason Jennings .40 .12
❑ 4 Craig Biggio .60 .18
❑ 5 Miguel Tejada .40 .12
❑ 6 Barry Bonds 2.50 .75
❑ 7 Juan Gonzalez 1.00 .30
❑ 8 Luis Gonzalez .40 .12
❑ 9 Johnny Damon .40 .12
❑ 10 Ellis Burks .40 .12
❑ 11 Frank Thomas 1.00 .30
❑ 12 Richie Sexson .40 .12
❑ 13 Roger Clemens 2.00 .60
❑ 14 Matt Morris .40 .12
❑ 15 Troy Glaus .60 .18
❑ 16 Tony Batista .40 .12
❑ 17 Magglio Ordonez .40 .12
❑ 18 Jose Vidro .40 .12
❑ 19 Barry Zito 1.00 .30
❑ 20 Chipper Jones 1.00 .30
❑ 21 Moises Alou .40 .12
❑ 22 Lance Berkman .40 .12
❑ 23 Jacque Jones .40 .12
❑ 24 Alfonso Soriano 1.00 .30
❑ 25 Sean Burroughs .40 .12
❑ 26 Scott Rolen .60 .18
❑ 27 Mark Grace 1.00 .30
❑ 28 Manny Ramirez .40 .12
❑ 29 Ken Griffey Jr. 1.50 .45
❑ 30 Josh Beckett .60 .18
❑ 31 Kazuhisa Ishii .40 .12
❑ 32 Pat Burrell .40 .12
❑ 33 Edgar Martinez .60 .18
❑ 34 Tim Salmon .60 .18
❑ 35 Raul Ibanez .40 .12
❑ 36 Vladimir Guerrero 1.00 .30
❑ 37 Jermaine Dye .40 .12
❑ 38 Rich Aurilia .40 .12
❑ 39 Rafael Palmeiro .60 .18
❑ 40 Kerry Wood 1.00 .30
❑ 41 Omar Vizquel .40 .12
❑ 42 Fred McGriff .60 .18
❑ 43 Ben Sheets .40 .12
❑ 44 Bernie Williams .60 .18
❑ 45 Brian Giles .40 .12
❑ 46 Jim Edmonds .40 .12
❑ 47 Garret Anderson .40 .12
❑ 48 Pedro Martinez 1.00 .30
❑ 49 Adam Dunn .60 .18
❑ 50 A.J. Burnett .40 .12
❑ 51 Eric Gagne .60 .18
❑ 52 Mo Vaughn .40 .12

❑ 53	Bobby Abreu	.40	.12
❑ 54	Bret Boone	.40	.12
❑ 55	Carlos Delgado	.40	.12
❑ 56	Gary Sheffield	.40	.12
❑ 57	Sammy Sosa	1.50	.45
❑ 58	Jim Thome	1.00	.30
❑ 59	Jeff Bagwell	.60	.18
❑ 60	David Eckstein	.40	.12
❑ 61	Jason Kendall	.40	.12
❑ 62	Albert Pujols	2.00	.60
❑ 63	Curt Schilling	.60	.18
❑ 64	Nomar Garciaparra	2.00	.60
❑ 65	Sean Casey	.40	.12
❑ 66	Shawn Green	.40	.12
❑ 67	Mike Piazza	1.50	.45
❑ 68	Ichiro Suzuki	2.00	.60
❑ 69	Eric Hinske	.40	.12
❑ 70	Greg Maddux	2.00	.60
❑ 71	Larry Walker	.60	.18
❑ 72	Roy Oswalt	.40	.12
❑ 73	Alex Rodriguez	2.00	.60
❑ 74	Austin Kearns	.60	.18
❑ 75	Cliff Floyd	.40	.12
❑ 76	Kevin Brown	.40	.12
❑ 77	Jason Giambi	1.00	.30
❑ 78	Jorge Julio	.40	.12
❑ 79	Carlos Lee	.40	.12
❑ 80	Mike Sweeney	.40	.12
❑ 81	Edgardo Alfonzo	.40	.12
❑ 82	Eric Chavez	.40	.12
❑ 83	Andruw Jones	.60	.18
❑ 84	Mark Prior	2.00	.60
❑ 85	Todd Helton	.60	.18
❑ 86	Torii Hunter	.40	.12
❑ 87	Ryan Klesko	.40	.12
❑ 88	Aubrey Huff	.40	.12
❑ 89	Randy Johnson	1.00	.30
❑ 90	Barry Larkin	1.00	.30
❑ 91	Mike Lowell	.40	.12
❑ 92	Jimmy Rollins	.40	.12
❑ 93	Darin Erstad	.40	.12
❑ 94	Jay Gibbons	.40	.12
❑ 95	Paul Konerko	.40	.12
❑ 96	Bobby Higginson	.40	.12
❑ 97	Carlos Beltran	.40	.12
❑ 98	Bartolo Colon	.40	.12
❑ 99	Jeff Kent	.40	.12
❑ 100	Ivan Rodriguez	1.00	.30
❑ 101	Joe Borchard FS	.60	.18
❑ 102	Mark Teixeira FS	1.00	.30
❑ 103	Francisco Rodriguez FS	.60	.18
❑ 104	Chris Snelling FS	.60	.18
❑ 105	Hee Seop Choi FS	.60	.18
❑ 106	Hank Blalock FS	1.00	.30
❑ 107	Marlon Byrd FS	.60	.18
❑ 108	Michael Restovich FS	.60	.18
❑ 109	Victor Martinez FS	.60	.18
❑ 110	Lyle Overbay FS	.60	.18
❑ 111	Brian Stokes TM RC	5.00	1.50
❑ 112	Josh Hall TM RC	8.00	2.40
❑ 113	Chris Waters TM RC	5.00	1.50
❑ 114	Lew Ford TM RC	8.00	2.40
❑ 115	Ian Ferguson TM RC	5.00	1.50
❑ 116	Josh Willingham TM RC	10.00	3.00
❑ 117	Josh Stewart TM RC	5.00	1.50
❑ 118	Pete LaForest TM RC	8.00	2.40
❑ 119	Jose Contreras TM RC	10.00	3.00
❑ 120	Terrmel Sledge TM RC	8.00	2.40
❑ 121	Guillermo Quiroz TM RC	8.00	2.40
❑ 122	Alejandro Machado TM RC	5.00	1.50
❑ 123	Nook Logan TM RC	5.00	1.50
❑ 124	Rontrez Johnson TM RC	5.00	1.50
❑ 125	Hideki Matsui TM RC	20.00	6.00
❑ 126	Phil Rizzuto HT	8.00	2.40
❑ 127	Robin Ventura HT	5.00	1.50
❑ 128	Andy Pettitte HT	8.00	2.40
❑ 129	Mike Mussina HT	8.00	2.40
❑ 130	Mariano Rivera HT	8.00	2.40
❑ 131	Jeff Weaver HT	5.00	1.50
❑ 132	David Wells HT	5.00	1.50
❑ 133	Tommy Lasorda HT	8.00	2.40
❑ 134	Pee Wee Reese HT	10.00	3.00
❑ 135	Hideo Nomo HT	15.00	4.50
❑ 136	Adrian Beltre HT	8.00	2.40
❑ 137	Chin-Feng Chen HT	8.00	2.40
❑ 138	Odalis Perez HT	8.00	2.40
❑ 139	Dave Roberts HT	8.00	2.40
❑ 140	Bobby Doerr HT	5.00	1.50
❑ 141	Jason Varitek HT	5.00	1.50
❑ 142	Trot Nixon HT	5.00	1.50
❑ 143	Tim Wakefield HT	5.00	1.50
❑ 144	John Burkett HT	5.00	1.50
❑ 145	Jeremy Giambi HT	5.00	1.50
❑ 146	Casey Fossum HT	5.00	1.50
❑ 147	Phil Niekro HT	5.00	1.50
❑ 148	Warren Spahn HT	8.00	2.40
❑ 149	Rafael Furcal HT	5.00	1.50
❑ 150	Vinny Castilla HT	5.00	1.50
❑ 151	Javy Lopez HT	5.00	1.50
❑ 152	Jason Marquis HT	5.00	1.50
❑ 153	Mike Hampton HT	5.00	1.50
❑ 154	Gaylord Perry HT	8.00	2.40
❑ 155	Ruben Sierra HT	8.00	2.40
❑ 156	Mike Cameron HT	8.00	2.40
❑ 157	Freddy Garcia HT	8.00	2.40
❑ 158	Joel Pineiro HT	8.00	2.40
❑ 159	Jamie Moyer HT	8.00	2.40
❑ 160	Carlos Guillen HT	8.00	2.40
❑ 161	Chien-Ming Wang RC	-	
❑ 162	Rickie Weeks RC	-	
❑ 163	Brandon Webb RC	-	
❑ 164	Craig Brazell RC	-	
❑ 165	Michael Hessman RC	-	
❑ 166	Ryan Wagner RC	-	
❑ 167	Matt Kata RC	-	
❑ 168	Edwin Jackson RC	-	
❑ 169	Mike Ryan RC	-	
❑ 170	Delmon Young RC	-	
❑ 171	Bo Hart RC	-	
❑ 172	Jeff Duncan RC	-	
❑ 173	Robby Hammock RC	-	
❑ 174	Jeremy Bonderman RC	-	
❑ 175	Clint Barmes RC	-	

2001 Fleer Authority

	Nm-Mt	Ex-Mt
COMP.SET w/o SP's (100)	25.00	7.50
COMMON CARD (1-100)	.40	.12
COMMON (101-150)	5.00	1.50

		Nm-Mt	Ex-Mt
❑ 1	Mark Grace	1.00	.30
❑ 2	Paul Konerko	.40	.12
❑ 3	Sean Casey	.40	.12
❑ 4	Jim Thome	1.00	.30
❑ 5	Todd Helton	.60	.18
❑ 6	Tony Clark	.40	.12
❑ 7	Jeff Bagwell	.60	.18
❑ 8	Mike Sweeney	.40	.12
❑ 9	Eric Karros	.40	.12
❑ 10	Richie Sexson	.40	.12
❑ 11	Doug Mientkiewicz	.40	.12
❑ 12	Ryan Klesko	.40	.12
❑ 13	John Olerud	.40	.12
❑ 14	Mark McGwire	2.50	.75
❑ 15	Fred McGriff	.60	.18
❑ 16	Rafael Palmeiro	.60	.18
❑ 17	Carlos Delgado	.40	.12
❑ 18	Roberto Alomar	1.00	.30
❑ 19	Craig Biggio	.60	.18
❑ 20	Jose Vidro	.40	.12
❑ 21	Edgardo Alfonzo	.40	.12
❑ 22	Jeff Kent	.40	.12
❑ 23	Bret Boone	.40	.12
❑ 24	Rafael Furcal	.40	.12
❑ 25	Nomar Garciaparra	2.00	.60
❑ 26	Barry Larkin	1.00	.30
❑ 27	Cristian Guzman	.40	.12
❑ 28	Derek Jeter	2.50	.75
❑ 29	Miguel Tejada	.40	.12
❑ 30	Jimmy Rollins	.40	.12
❑ 31	Rich Aurilia	.40	.12
❑ 32	Alex Rodriguez	2.00	.60
❑ 33	Cal Ripken	3.00	.90
❑ 34	Troy Glaus	.60	.18
❑ 35	Matt Williams	.40	.12
❑ 36	Chipper Jones	1.00	.30
❑ 37	Jeff Cirillo	.40	.12
❑ 38	Robin Ventura	.40	.12
❑ 39	Eric Chavez	.40	.12
❑ 40	Scott Rolen	.60	.18
❑ 41	Phil Nevin	.40	.12
❑ 42	Mike Piazza	1.50	.45
❑ 43	Jorge Posada	.60	.18
❑ 44	Jason Kendall	.40	.12
❑ 45	Ivan Rodriguez	1.00	.30
❑ 46	Frank Thomas	1.00	.30
❑ 47	Edgar Martinez	.60	.18
❑ 48	Darin Erstad	.40	.12
❑ 49	Tim Salmon	.60	.18
❑ 50	Luis Gonzalez	.40	.12
❑ 51	Andruw Jones	.60	.18
❑ 52	Carl Everett	.40	.12
❑ 53	Manny Ramirez	.40	.12
❑ 54	Sammy Sosa	1.50	.45
❑ 55	Rondell White	.40	.12
❑ 56	Magglio Ordonez	.40	.12
❑ 57	Ken Griffey Jr.	1.50	.45
❑ 58	Juan Gonzalez	1.00	.30
❑ 59	Larry Walker	.60	.18
❑ 60	Bobby Higginson	.40	.12
❑ 61	Cliff Floyd	.40	.12
❑ 62	Preston Wilson	.40	.12
❑ 63	Moises Alou	.40	.12
❑ 64	Lance Berkman	.40	.12
❑ 65	Richard Hidalgo	.40	.12
❑ 66	Jermaine Dye	.40	.12
❑ 67	Mark Quinn	.40	.12
❑ 68	Shawn Green	.40	.12
❑ 69	Gary Sheffield	.40	.12
❑ 70	Jeromy Burnitz	.40	.12
❑ 71	Geoff Jenkins	.40	.12
❑ 72	Vladimir Guerrero	1.00	.30
❑ 73	Bernie Williams	.60	.18
❑ 74	Johnny Damon	.40	.12
❑ 75	Jason Giambi	1.00	.30
❑ 76	Bobby Abreu	.40	.12
❑ 77	Pat Burrell	.40	.12
❑ 78	Brian Giles	.40	.12
❑ 79	Tony Gwynn	1.25	.35
❑ 80	Barry Bonds	2.50	.75
❑ 81	J.D. Drew	.40	.12
❑ 82	Jim Edmonds	.40	.12
❑ 83	Greg Vaughn	.40	.12
❑ 84	Raul Mondesi	.40	.12
❑ 85	Shannon Stewart	.40	.12
❑ 86	Randy Johnson	1.00	.30
❑ 87	Curt Schilling	.60	.18
❑ 88	Tom Glavine	1.00	.30
❑ 89	Greg Maddux	2.00	.60
❑ 90	Pedro Martinez	1.00	.30
❑ 91	Kerry Wood	1.00	.30
❑ 92	David Wells	.40	.12
❑ 93	Bartolo Colon	.40	.12
❑ 94	Mike Hampton	.40	.12
❑ 95	Kevin Brown	.40	.12
❑ 96	Al Leiter	.40	.12
❑ 97	Roger Clemens	2.00	.60
❑ 98	Mike Mussina	1.00	.30
❑ 99	Tim Hudson	.40	.12
❑ 100	Kazuhiro Sasaki	.40	.12
❑ 101	Ichiro Suzuki RC	40.00	12.00
❑ 102	Albert Pujols RC	50.00	15.00
❑ 103	Drew Henson RC	8.00	2.40
❑ 104	Adam Pettyjohn RC	5.00	1.50
❑ 105	Adrian Hernandez RC	5.00	1.50
❑ 106	Andy Morales RC	5.00	1.50
❑ 107	Tsuyoshi Shinjo RC	8.00	2.40
❑ 108	Juan Uribe RC	5.00	1.50
❑ 109	Jack Wilson RC	5.00	1.50

❑ 110 Jason Smith RC	5.00	1.50
❑ 111 Junior Spivey RC	6.00	1.80
❑ 112 Wilson Betemit RC	5.00	1.50
❑ 113 Elpidio Guzman RC	5.00	1.50
❑ 114 Esix Snead RC	5.00	1.50
❑ 115 Winston Abreu RC	5.00	1.50
❑ 116 Jeremy Owens RC	5.00	1.50
❑ 117 Jay Gibbons RC	8.00	2.40
❑ 118 Luis Lopez	5.00	1.50
❑ 119 Ryan Freel RC	5.00	1.50
❑ 120 Rafael Soriano RC	8.00	2.40
❑ 121 Johnny Estrada RC	5.00	1.50
❑ 122 Bud Smith RC	5.00	1.50
❑ 123 Jackson Melian RC	5.00	1.50
❑ 124 Matt White RC	5.00	1.50
❑ 125 Travis Hafner RC	6.00	1.80
❑ 126 Morgan Ensberg RC	8.00	2.40
❑ 127 Endy Chavez RC	5.00	1.50
❑ 128 Brett Prinz RC	5.00	1.50
❑ 129 Juan Diaz RC	5.00	1.50
❑ 130 Erick Almonte RC	5.00	1.50
❑ 131 Rob Mackowiak RC	5.00	1.50
❑ 132 Carlos Valderrama RC	5.00	1.50
❑ 133 Wilkin Ruan RC	5.00	1.50
❑ 134 Angel Berroa RC	10.00	3.00
❑ 135 Henry Mateo RC	5.00	1.50
❑ 136 Bill Ortega RC	5.00	1.50
❑ 137 Billy Sylvester RC	5.00	1.50
❑ 138 Andres Torres RC	5.00	1.50
❑ 139 Nate Frese RC	5.00	1.50
❑ 140 Casey Fossum RC	5.00	1.50
❑ 141 Ricardo Rodriguez RC	5.00	1.50
❑ 142 Brian Roberts RC	5.00	1.50
❑ 143 Carlos Garcia RC	5.00	1.50
❑ 144 Brian Lawrence RC	5.00	1.50
❑ 145 Cory Aldridge RC	5.00	1.50
❑ 146 Mark Teixeira RC	25.00	7.50
❑ 147 Juan Cruz RC	5.00	1.50
❑ 148 B. Duckworth RC	5.00	1.50
❑ 149 Dewon Brazelton RC	5.00	1.50
❑ 150 Mark Prior RC	50.00	15.00
❑ MM4 Derek Jeter MM/2000	15.00	4.50
❑ MM4AU Derek Jeter MM AU/100	150.00	45.00
❑ NNO Derek Jeter 93 AU/500	150.00	45.00

2003 Fleer Avant

	MINT	NRMT
COMP.SET w/o SP's (65)	50.00	22.00
COMMON CARD (1-65)	1.00	.45
COMMON CARD (76-90)	8.00	3.60
❑ 1 Adam Dunn	1.50	.70
❑ 2 Barry Zito	2.50	1.10
❑ 3 Preston Wilson	1.00	.45
❑ 4 Barry Bonds	6.00	2.70
❑ 5 Hank Blalock	1.50	.70
❑ 6 Omar Vizquel	1.00	.45
❑ 7 Brian Giles	1.00	.45
❑ 8 Kerry Wood	2.50	1.10
❑ 9 Miguel Tejada	1.00	.45
❑ 10 Magglio Ordonez	1.00	.45
❑ 11 Randy Johnson	2.50	1.10
❑ 12 Jeff Bagwell	1.50	.70
❑ 13 Pat Burrell	1.00	.45
❑ 14 Jason Giambi	2.50	1.10
❑ 15 Mark Prior	5.00	2.20
❑ 16 Roger Clemens	5.00	2.20
❑ 17 Sammy Sosa	4.00	1.80
❑ 18 Jay Gibbons	1.00	.45
❑ 19 Torii Hunter	1.00	.45
❑ 20 Ichiro Suzuki	5.00	2.20
❑ 21 Derek Jeter	6.00	2.70
❑ 22 Tom Glavine	2.50	1.10
❑ 23 Alfonso Soriano	2.50	1.10
❑ 24 Manny Ramirez	1.00	.45
❑ 25 Frank Thomas	2.50	1.10
❑ 26 Carlos Pena	1.00	.45
❑ 27 Alex Rodriguez	5.00	2.20
❑ 28 Edgar Martinez	1.50	.70
❑ 29 Larry Walker	1.50	.70
❑ 30 Rafael Palmeiro	1.50	.70
❑ 31 Mike Piazza	4.00	1.80
❑ 32 Nomar Garciaparra	5.00	2.20
❑ 33 Lance Berkman	1.00	.45
❑ 34 Vladimir Guerrero	2.50	1.10
❑ 35 Troy Glaus	1.50	.70
❑ 36 Ivan Rodriguez	2.50	1.10
❑ 37 Mark Mulder	1.00	.45
❑ 38 Curt Schilling	1.50	.70
❑ 39 Mike Sweeney	1.00	.45
❑ 40 Albert Pujols	5.00	2.20
❑ 41 Tim Hudson	1.00	.45
❑ 42 Greg Maddux	5.00	2.20
❑ 43 Shawn Green	1.50	.70
❑ 44 Scott Rolen	1.50	.70
❑ 45 Gary Sheffield	1.00	.45
❑ 46 Richie Sexson	1.00	.45
❑ 47 Aubrey Huff	1.00	.45
❑ 48 Luis Gonzalez	1.00	.45
❑ 49 Todd Helton	1.50	.70
❑ 50 Xavier Nady	1.00	.45
❑ 51 Juan Gonzalez	2.50	1.10
❑ 52 Pedro Martinez	2.50	1.10
❑ 53 Garret Anderson	1.00	.45
❑ 54 Craig Biggio	1.50	.70
❑ 55 Bret Boone	1.00	.45
❑ 56 Ken Griffey Jr.	4.00	1.80
❑ 57 Kevin Millwood	1.00	.45
❑ 58 Carlos Delgado	1.00	.45
❑ 59 Chipper Jones	2.50	1.10
❑ 60 Hideo Nomo	2.50	1.10
❑ 61 Jim Edmonds	1.50	.70
❑ 62 Austin Kearns	1.50	.70
❑ 63 Jim Thome	2.50	1.10
❑ 64 Vernon Wells	1.00	.45
❑ 65 Mike Lowell	1.00	.45
❑ 66 Whitey Ford RET	8.00	3.60
❑ 67 Bob Gibson RET	8.00	3.60
❑ 68 Reggie Jackson RET	8.00	3.60
❑ 69 Willie McCovey RET	8.00	3.60
❑ 70 Phil Rizzuto RET	8.00	3.60
❑ 71 Al Kaline RET	8.00	3.60
❑ 72 Brooks Robinson RET	8.00	3.60
❑ 73 Nolan Ryan RET	15.00	6.75
❑ 74 Mike Schmidt RET	10.00	4.50
❑ 75 Tom Seaver RET	8.00	3.60
❑ 76 Hideki Matsui ROO RC	20.00	9.00
❑ 77 Rocco Baldelli ROO	15.00	6.75
❑ 78 Jose Contreras ROO RC	10.00	4.50
❑ 79 Hee Seop Choi ROO	8.00	3.60
❑ 80 Jeremy Bonderman ROO RC	10.00	4.50
❑ 81 Bo Hart ROO RC	10.00	4.50
❑ 82 Brandon Webb ROO RC	12.00	5.50
❑ 83 Ron Calloway ROO	8.00	3.60
❑ 84 Jesse Foppert ROO	8.00	3.60
❑ 85 Kyle Snyder ROO	8.00	3.60
❑ 86 Mark Teixeira ROO	8.00	3.60
❑ 87 Jose Reyes ROO	8.00	3.60
❑ 88 Dontrelle Willis ROO	10.00	4.50
❑ 89 Reed Johnson ROO	8.00	3.60
❑ 90 Rickie Weeks ROO RC	20.00	9.00
❑ P39 Derek Jeter Promo	2.00	.90

2002 Fleer Box Score

	Nm-Mt	Ex-Mt
COMP.SET w/o SP's (125)	25.00	7.50
COMMON CARD (1-125)	.40	.12
COMMON CARD (126-150)	5.00	1.50
COMP.RISING STAR SET (40)	25.00	7.50
COMMON CARD (151-190)	2.00	.60
COMP.INT'L SET (40)	25.00	7.50
COMMON CARD (191-230)	2.00	.60
COMP.ALL-STAR SET (40)	25.00	7.50
COMMON CARD (231-270)	2.00	.60
COMP.COOPERSTOWN SET (40)	40.00	12.00
COMMON CARD (271-310)	2.00	.60
❑ 1 Derek Jeter	2.50	.75
❑ 2 Kevin Brown	.40	.12
❑ 3 Nomar Garciaparra	2.00	.60
❑ 4 Mark Buehrle	.40	.12
❑ 5 Mike Piazza	1.50	.45
❑ 6 David Justice	.40	.12
❑ 7 Tino Martinez	.60	.18
❑ 8 Paul Konerko	.40	.12
❑ 9 Larry Walker	.60	.18
❑ 10 Ben Sheets	.40	.12
❑ 11 Mike Cameron	.40	.12
❑ 12 David Wells	.40	.12
❑ 13 Barry Zito	1.00	.30
❑ 14 Pat Burrell	.40	.12
❑ 15 Mike Mussina	1.00	.30
❑ 16 Bud Smith	.40	.12
❑ 17 Brian Jordan	.40	.12
❑ 18 Chris Singleton	.40	.12
❑ 19 Daryle Ward	.40	.12
❑ 20 Russ Ortiz	.40	.12
❑ 21 Jason Kendall	.40	.12
❑ 22 Kerry Wood	1.00	.30
❑ 23 Jeff Weaver	.40	.12
❑ 24 Tony Armas Jr.	.40	.12
❑ 25 Toby Hall	.40	.12
❑ 26 Brian Giles	.40	.12
❑ 27 Juan Pierre	.40	.12
❑ 28 Ken Griffey Jr.	1.50	.45
❑ 29 Mike Sweeney	.40	.12
❑ 30 John Smoltz	.60	.18
❑ 31 Sean Casey	.40	.12
❑ 32 Jeremy Giambi	.40	.12
❑ 33 Mike Lieberthal	.40	.12
❑ 34 Rich Aurilia	.40	.12
❑ 35 Matt Lawton	.40	.12
❑ 36 Dmitri Young	.40	.12
❑ 37 Wade Miller	.40	.12
❑ 38 Jason Giambi	1.00	.30
❑ 39 Jeff Cirillo	.40	.12
❑ 40 Mark Grace	1.00	.30
❑ 41 Frank Thomas	1.00	.30
❑ 42 Preston Wilson	.40	.12
❑ 43 Brad Radke	.40	.12
❑ 44 Greg Maddux	2.00	.60
❑ 45 Adam Dunn	.60	.18
❑ 46 Roy Oswalt	.40	.12
❑ 47 Troy Glaus	.60	.18
❑ 48 Edgar Martinez	.60	.18
❑ 49 Billy Koch	.40	.12
❑ 50 Chipper Jones	1.00	.30
❑ 51 Lance Berkman	.40	.12
❑ 52 Shannon Stewart	.40	.12
❑ 53 Eddie Guardado	.40	.12
❑ 54 C.C. Sabathia	.40	.12
❑ 55 Craig Biggio	.60	.18
❑ 56 Roger Clemens	2.00	.60
❑ 57 Jimmy Rollins	.40	.12
❑ 58 Carlos Delgado	.40	.12
❑ 59 Tony Clark	.40	.12
❑ 60 Mike Hampton	.40	.12

Card	Nm-Mt	Ex-Mt
❑ 61 Jeromy Burnitz	.40	.12
❑ 62 Jorge Posada	.60	.18
❑ 63 Todd Helton	.60	.18
❑ 64 Richie Sexson	.40	.12
❑ 65 Ryan Klesko	.40	.12
❑ 66 Cliff Floyd	.40	.12
❑ 67 Eric Milton	.40	.12
❑ 68 Scott Rolen	.60	.18
❑ 69 Steve Finley	.40	.12
❑ 70 Ray Durham	.40	.12
❑ 71 Jeff Bagwell	.60	.18
❑ 72 Geoff Jenkins	.40	.12
❑ 73 Jamie Moyer	.40	.12
❑ 74 David Eckstein	.40	.12
❑ 75 Johnny Damon	.40	.12
❑ 76 Pokey Reese	.40	.12
❑ 77 Mo Vaughn	.40	.12
❑ 78 Trevor Hoffman	.40	.12
❑ 79 Albert Pujols	2.00	.60
❑ 80 Ben Grieve	.40	.12
❑ 81 Matt Morris	.40	.12
❑ 82 Aubrey Huff	.40	.12
❑ 83 Darin Erstad	.40	.12
❑ 84 Garret Anderson	.40	.12
❑ 85 Jacque Jones	.40	.12
❑ 86 Matt Anderson	.40	.12
❑ 87 Jose Vidro	.40	.12
❑ 88 Carlos Lee	.40	.12
❑ 89 Jeff Suppan	.40	.12
❑ 90 Al Leiter	.40	.12
❑ 91 Jeff Kent	.40	.12
❑ 92 Randy Johnson	1.00	.30
❑ 93 Moises Alou	.40	.12
❑ 94 Bobby Higginson	.40	.12
❑ 95 Phil Nevin	.40	.12
❑ 96 Alex Rodriguez	2.00	.60
❑ 97 Luis Gonzalez	.40	.12
❑ 98 A.J. Burnett	.40	.12
❑ 99 Torii Hunter	.40	.12
❑ 100 Ivan Rodriguez	1.00	.30
❑ 101 Pedro Martinez	1.00	.30
❑ 102 Brady Anderson	.40	.12
❑ 103 Paul LoDuca	.40	.12
❑ 104 Eric Chavez	.40	.12
❑ 105 Tim Salmon	.60	.18
❑ 106 Javier Vazquez	.40	.12
❑ 107 Bret Boone	.40	.12
❑ 108 Greg Vaughn	.40	.12
❑ 109 J.D. Drew	.40	.12
❑ 110 Jay Gibbons	.40	.12
❑ 111 Jim Thome	1.00	.30
❑ 112 Shawn Green	.40	.12
❑ 113 Tim Hudson	.40	.12
❑ 114 John Olerud	.40	.12
❑ 115 Raul Mondesi	.40	.12
❑ 116 Curt Schilling	.60	.18
❑ 117 Corey Patterson	.40	.12
❑ 118 Robert Fick	.40	.12
❑ 119 Corey Koskie	.40	.12
❑ 120 Juan Gonzalez	1.00	.30
❑ 121 Jerry Hairston Jr.	.40	.12
❑ 122 Gary Sheffield	.40	.12
❑ 123 Mark Mulder	.40	.12
❑ 124 Barry Bonds	2.50	.75
❑ 125 Jim Edmonds	.40	.12
❑ 126 Franklyn German RP RC	5.00	1.50
❑ 127 Rodrigo Rosario RP RC	5.00	1.50
❑ 128 Ryan Ludwick RP	5.00	1.50
❑ 129 Jorge De La Rosa RP RC	5.00	1.50
❑ 130 Jason Lane RP	5.00	1.50
❑ 131 Brian Mallette RP RC	5.00	1.50
❑ 132 Chris Baker RP RC	5.00	1.50
❑ 133 Kyle Kane RP RC	5.00	1.50
❑ 134 Doug Devore RP RC	5.00	1.50
❑ 135 Raul Chavez RP RC	5.00	1.50
❑ 136 Miguel Asencio RP RC	5.00	1.50
❑ 137 Luis C.Garcia RP RC	5.00	1.50
❑ 138 Nick Johnson RP	5.00	1.50
❑ 139 Mike Crudale RP RC	5.00	1.50
❑ 140 P.J. Bevis RP RC	5.00	1.50
❑ 141 Josh Hancock RP RC	5.00	1.50
❑ 142 Jeremy Lambert RP RC	5.00	1.50
❑ 143 Ben Broussard RP	5.00	1.50
❑ 144 John Ennis RP RC	5.00	1.50
❑ 145 Wilson Valdez RP RC	5.00	1.50
❑ 146 Eric Good RP RC	5.00	1.50
❑ 147 Elio Serrano RP RC	5.00	1.50
❑ 148 Jaime Cerda RP RC	5.00	1.50
❑ 149 Hank Blalock RP	8.00	2.40
❑ 150 Brandon Duckworth RP	5.00	1.50
❑ 151 Drew Henson RS	2.00	.60
❑ 152 Kazuhisa Ishii RS RC	5.00	1.50
❑ 153 Earl Snyder RS RC	2.00	.60
❑ 154 J.M. Gold RS	2.00	.60
❑ 155 Satoru Komiyama RS RC	2.00	.60
❑ 156 Marlon Byrd RS	2.00	.60
❑ 157 So Taguchi RS RC	3.00	.90
❑ 158 Eric Hinske RS	2.00	.60
❑ 159 Mark Prior RS	10.00	3.00
❑ 160 Jorge Padilla RS RC	3.00	.90
❑ 161 Rene Reyes RS RC	2.00	.60
❑ 162 Jorge Nunez RS RC	2.00	.60
❑ 163 Nelson Castro RS RC	2.00	.60
❑ 164 Anderson Machado RS RC	3.00	.90
❑ 165 Mark Teixeira RS	3.00	.90
❑ 166 Orlando Hudson RS	2.00	.60
❑ 167 Edwin Almonte RS RC	2.00	.60
❑ 168 Luis Ugueto RS RC	2.00	.60
❑ 169 Felix Escalona RS RC	2.00	.60
❑ 170 Ron Calloway RS RC	2.00	.60
❑ 171 Kevin Mench RS	2.00	.60
❑ 172 Takahito Nomura RS RC	2.00	.60
❑ 173 Sean Burroughs RS	2.00	.60
❑ 174 Steve Kent RS RC	2.00	.60
❑ 175 Jorge Sosa RS RC	2.00	.60
❑ 176 Mike Moriarty RS RC	2.00	.60
❑ 177 Carlos Pena RS	2.00	.60
❑ 178 Anastacio Martinez RS RC	2.00	.60
❑ 179 Reed Johnson RS RC	3.00	.90
❑ 180 Juan Brito RS RC	2.00	.60
❑ 181 Wilson Betemit RS	2.00	.60
❑ 182 Mike Rivera RS	2.00	.60
❑ 183 David Espinosa RS	2.00	.60
❑ 184 Todd Donovan RS RC	2.00	.60
❑ 185 Morgan Ensberg RS	2.00	.60
❑ 186 Dewon Brazelton RS	2.00	.60
❑ 187 Ben Howard RS RC	2.00	.60
❑ 188 Austin Kearns RS	3.00	.90
❑ 189 Josh Beckett RS	3.00	.90
❑ 190 Brandon Backe RS RC	2.00	.60
❑ 191 Ichiro Suzuki IRT	8.00	2.40
❑ 192 Tsuyoshi Shinjo IRT	2.00	.60
❑ 193 Hideo Nomo IRT	4.00	1.20
❑ 194 Kazuhiro Sasaki IRT	2.00	.60
❑ 195 Edgardo Alfonzo IRT	2.00	.60
❑ 196 Chan Ho Park IRT	2.00	.60
❑ 197 Carlos Hernandez IRT	2.00	.60
❑ 198 Byung-Hyun Kim IRT	2.00	.60
❑ 199 Omar Vizquel IRT	2.00	.60
❑ 200 Freddy Garcia IRT	2.00	.60
❑ 201 Richard Hidalgo IRT	2.00	.60
❑ 202 Magglio Ordonez IRT	2.00	.60
❑ 203 Bob Abreu IRT	2.00	.60
❑ 204 Roger Cedeno IRT	2.00	.60
❑ 205 Andruw Jones IRT	2.50	.75
❑ 206 Mariano Rivera IRT	2.50	.75
❑ 207 Jose Macias IRT	2.00	.60
❑ 208 Orlando Hernandez IRT	2.00	.60
❑ 209 Rafael Palmeiro IRT	2.50	.75
❑ 210 Danys Baez IRT	2.00	.60
❑ 211 Bernie Williams IRT	2.50	.75
❑ 212 Carlos Beltran IRT	2.00	.60
❑ 213 Roberto Alomar IRT	4.00	1.20
❑ 214 Jose Cruz Jr. IRT	2.00	.60
❑ 215 Ryan Dempster IRT	2.00	.60
❑ 216 Erubiel Durazo IRT	2.00	.60
❑ 217 Carlos Pena IRT	2.00	.60
❑ 218 Sammy Sosa IRT	6.00	1.80
❑ 219 Adrian Beltre IRT	2.00	.60
❑ 220 Aramis Ramirez IRT	2.00	.60
❑ 221 Alfonso Soriano IRT	4.00	1.20
❑ 222 Vladimir Guerrero IRT	4.00	1.20
❑ 223 Juan Uribe IRT	2.00	.60
❑ 224 Cristian Guzman IRT	2.00	.60
❑ 225 Manny Ramirez IRT	2.00	.60
❑ 226 Juan Cruz IRT	2.00	.60
❑ 227 Ramon Ortiz IRT	2.00	.60
❑ 228 Juan Encarnacion IRT	2.00	.60
❑ 229 Bartolo Colon IRT	2.00	.60
❑ 230 Miguel Tejada IRT	2.00	.60
❑ 231 Cal Ripken AS	12.00	3.60
❑ 232 Derek Jeter AS	10.00	3.00
❑ 233 Pedro Martinez AS	4.00	1.20
❑ 234 Roberto Alomar AS	4.00	1.20
❑ 235 Sandy Alomar Jr. AS	2.00	.60
❑ 236 Mike Piazza AS	6.00	1.80
❑ 237 Jeff Conine AS	2.00	.60
❑ 238 Fred McGriff AS	2.50	.75
❑ 239 Kirby Puckett AS	4.00	1.20
❑ 240 Ken Griffey Jr. AS	6.00	1.80
❑ 241 Roger Clemens AS	8.00	2.40
❑ 242 Joe Morgan AS	2.00	.60
❑ 243 Willie McCovey AS	2.00	.60
❑ 244 Brooks Robinson AS	4.00	1.20
❑ 245 Juan Marichal AS	2.00	.60
❑ 246 Todd Helton AS	2.50	.75
❑ 247 Alex Rodriguez AS	8.00	2.40
❑ 248 Barry Bonds AS	10.00	3.00
❑ 249 Nomar Garciaparra AS	8.00	2.40
❑ 250 Jeff Bagwell AS	2.50	.75
❑ 251 Kenny Lofton AS	2.00	.60
❑ 252 Barry Larkin AS	4.00	1.20
❑ 253 Tom Glavine AS	4.00	1.20
❑ 254 Magglio Ordonez AS	2.00	.60
❑ 255 Randy Johnson AS	4.00	1.20
❑ 256 Chipper Jones AS	4.00	1.20
❑ 257 Kevin Brown AS	2.00	.60
❑ 258 Rickey Henderson AS	6.00	1.80
❑ 259 Greg Maddux AS	8.00	2.40
❑ 260 Jim Thome AS	4.00	1.20
❑ 261 Rafael Palmeiro AS	2.50	.75
❑ 262 Frank Thomas AS	4.00	1.20
❑ 263 Manny Ramirez AS	2.00	.60
❑ 264 Travis Fryman AS	2.00	.60
❑ 265 Gary Sheffield AS	2.00	.60
❑ 266 Bernie Williams AS	2.50	.75
❑ 267 Matt Williams AS	2.00	.60
❑ 268 Ivan Rodriguez AS	4.00	1.20
❑ 269 Mike Mussina AS	4.00	1.20
❑ 270 Larry Walker AS	2.50	.75
❑ 271 Jim Palmer CT	2.00	.60
❑ 272 Cal Ripken CT	15.00	4.50
❑ 273 Brooks Robinson CT	5.00	1.50
❑ 274 Bobby Doerr CT	2.00	.60
❑ 275 Ernie Banks CT	5.00	1.50
❑ 276 Fergie Jenkins CT	2.00	.60
❑ 277 Luis Aparicio CT	2.00	.60
❑ 278 Hoyt Wilhelm CT	2.00	.60
❑ 279 Tom Seaver CT	5.00	1.50
❑ 280 Joe Morgan CT	2.00	.60
❑ 281 Lou Boudreau CT	2.00	.60
❑ 282 Larry Doby CT	2.00	.60
❑ 283 Jim Bunning CT	2.00	.60
❑ 284 George Kell CT	2.00	.60
❑ 285 Pee Wee Reese CT	3.00	.90
❑ 286 Eddie Mathews CT	5.00	1.50
❑ 287 Robin Yount CT	5.00	1.50
❑ 288 Rod Carew CT	3.00	.90
❑ 289 Monte Irvin CT	2.00	.60
❑ 290 Yogi Berra CT	5.00	1.50
❑ 291 Whitey Ford CT	3.00	.90
❑ 292 Reggie Jackson CT	3.00	.90
❑ 293 Rollie Fingers CT	2.00	.60
❑ 294 Catfish Hunter CT	3.00	.90
❑ 295 Richie Ashburn CT	3.00	.90
❑ 296 Willie Stargell CT	3.00	.90
❑ 297 Ralph Kiner CT	3.00	.90
❑ 298 Orlando Cepeda CT	2.00	.60
❑ 299 Juan Marichal CT	2.00	.60
❑ 300 Gaylord Perry CT	2.00	.60
❑ 301 Willie McCovey CT	2.00	.60
❑ 302 Red Schoendienst CT	2.00	.60
❑ 303 Nolan Ryan CT	15.00	4.50
❑ 304 Bob Gibson CT	3.00	.90
❑ 305 Al Kaline CT	5.00	1.50
❑ 306 Harmon Killebrew CT	5.00	1.50
❑ 307 Stan Musial CT	8.00	2.40
❑ 308 Phil Rizzuto CT	3.00	.90
❑ 309 Mike Schmidt CT	12.00	3.60
❑ 310 Enos Slaughter CT	2.00	.60
❑ P124 Barry Bonds Promo	2.00	.60

2003 Fleer Box Score

	Nm-Mt	Ex-Mt
COMP.SET w/o SP's (100)	25.00	7.50
COMMON CARD (1-100)	.40	.12
COMMON CARD (101-110)	8.00	2.40

COMMON CARD (111-125)	3.00	.90
COMP.RS SET (30)	25.00	7.50
COMMON CARD (126-155)	2.00	.60
COMP.AS SET (30)	25.00	7.50
COMMON CARD (156-185)	2.00	.60
COMP.IRT SET (30)	25.00	7.50
COMMON CARD (186-215)	2.00	.60
COMP.BRX SET (29)	40.00	12.00
COMMON CARD (216-245)	2.00	.60

❑ 1	Troy Glaus	.60	.18
❑ 2	Derek Jeter	2.50	.75
❑ 3	Alex Rodriguez	2.00	.60
❑ 4	Barry Zito	1.00	.30
❑ 5	Darin Erstad	.40	.12
❑ 6	Tim Hudson	.40	.12
❑ 7	Josh Beckett	.60	.18
❑ 8	Adam Dunn	.60	.18
❑ 9	Tim Salmon	.40	.12
❑ 10	Ivan Rodriguez	1.00	.30
❑ 11	Mark Buehrle	.40	.12
❑ 12	Sammy Sosa	1.50	.45
❑ 13	Vicente Padilla	.40	.12
❑ 14	Randy Johnson	1.00	.30
❑ 15	Lance Berkman	.40	.12
❑ 16	Jim Thome	1.00	.30
❑ 17	Luis Gonzalez	.40	.12
❑ 18	Craig Biggio	.60	.18
❑ 19	Cliff Floyd	.40	.12
❑ 20	Pat Burrell	.40	.12
❑ 21	Matt Morris	.40	.12
❑ 22	Torii Hunter	.40	.12
❑ 23	Curt Schilling	.60	.18
❑ 24	Paul Konerko	.40	.12
❑ 25	Jeff Bagwell	.60	.18
❑ 26	Mike Piazza	1.50	.45
❑ 27	A.J. Burnett	.40	.12
❑ 28	Jimmy Rollins	.40	.12
❑ 29	Greg Maddux	2.00	.60
❑ 30	Jeff Kent	.40	.12
❑ 31	Bobby Abreu	.40	.12
❑ 32	Chipper Jones	1.00	.30
❑ 33	Mike Sweeney	.40	.12
❑ 34	Jason Kendall	.40	.12
❑ 35	Gary Sheffield	.40	.12
❑ 36	Carlos Beltran	.40	.12
❑ 37	Brian Giles	.40	.12
❑ 38	Jim Edmonds	.40	.12
❑ 39	Roger Clemens	2.00	.60
❑ 40	Andruw Jones	.60	.18
❑ 41	Paul Lo Duca	.40	.12
❑ 42	Ryan Klesko	.40	.12
❑ 43	Jay Gibbons	.40	.12
❑ 44	Shawn Green	.40	.12
❑ 45	Sean Burroughs	.40	.12
❑ 46	Magglio Ordonez	.40	.12
❑ 47	Tony Batista	.40	.12
❑ 48	J.D. Drew	.40	.12
❑ 49	Hideo Nomo	1.00	.30
❑ 50	Edgardo Alfonzo	.40	.12
❑ 51	Nomar Garciaparra	2.00	.60
❑ 52	Frank Thomas	1.00	.30
❑ 53	Kazuhisa Ishii	.40	.12
❑ 54	Rich Aurilia	.40	.12
❑ 55	Shea Hillenbrand	.40	.12
❑ 56	Tom Glavine	1.00	.30
❑ 57	Richie Sexson	.40	.12
❑ 58	Mo Vaughn	.40	.12
❑ 59	Barry Bonds	2.50	.75
❑ 60	Carlos Delgado	.40	.12
❑ 61	Pedro Martinez	1.00	.30
❑ 62	Jacque Jones	.40	.12
❑ 63	Edgar Martinez	.60	.18
❑ 64	Manny Ramirez	.40	.12
❑ 65	Bret Boone	.40	.12
❑ 66	Kerry Wood	1.00	.30
❑ 67	Roy Oswalt	.40	.12
❑ 68	Cristian Guzman	.40	.12
❑ 69	Moises Alou	.40	.12
❑ 70	Bartolo Colon	.40	.12
❑ 71	Ichiro Suzuki	2.00	.60
❑ 72	Jose Vidro	.40	.12
❑ 73	Scott Rolen	.60	.18
❑ 74	Mark Prior	2.00	.60
❑ 75	Vladimir Guerrero	1.00	.30
❑ 76	Albert Pujols	1.50	.45
❑ 77	Aubrey Huff	.40	.12
❑ 78	Ken Griffey Jr.	1.50	.45
❑ 79	Roberto Alomar	1.00	.30
❑ 80	Ben Grieve	.40	.12
❑ 81	Miguel Tejada	.40	.12
❑ 82	Austin Kearns	.60	.18
❑ 83	Jason Giambi	1.00	.30
❑ 84	John Olerud	.40	.12
❑ 85	Omar Vizquel	.40	.12
❑ 86	Juan Gonzalez	1.00	.30
❑ 87	Larry Walker	.60	.18
❑ 88	Jorge Posada	.60	.18
❑ 89	Rafael Palmeiro	.60	.18
❑ 90	Todd Helton	.60	.18
❑ 91	Bernie Williams	.60	.18
❑ 92	Garret Anderson	.40	.12
❑ 93	Eric Hinske	.40	.12
❑ 94	Mike Lowell	.40	.12
❑ 95	Jason Jennings	.40	.12
❑ 96	Eric Chavez	.40	.12
❑ 97	Alfonso Soriano	1.00	.30
❑ 98	David Eckstein	.40	.12
❑ 99	Bobby Higginson	.40	.12
❑ 100	Roy Halladay	.40	.12
❑ 101	Robby Hammock BSD RC	10.00	3.00
❑ 102	Hideki Matsui BSD RC	20.00	6.00
❑ 103	Chase Utley BSD	8.00	2.40
❑ 104	Oscar Villarreal BSD RC	8.00	2.40
❑ 105	Jose Contreras BSD RC	10.00	3.00
❑ 106	Rocco Baldelli BSD	15.00	4.50
❑ 107	Jesse Foppert BSD	8.00	2.40
❑ 108	Jeremy Bonderman BSD RC	10.00	3.00
❑ 109	Shane Victorino BSD RC	8.00	2.40
❑ 110	Ron Calloway BSD	8.00	2.40
❑ 111	Brandon Webb ROO RC	10.00	3.00
❑ 112	Guillermo Quiroz ROO RC	5.00	1.50
❑ 113	Clint Barmes ROO RC	5.00	1.50
❑ 114	Pete LaForest ROO RC	5.00	1.50
❑ 115	Craig Brazell ROO RC	5.00	1.50
❑ 116	Todd Wellemeyer ROO RC	5.00	1.50
❑ 117	Bernie Castro ROO RC	3.00	.90
❑ 118	Alejandro Machado ROO RC	3.00	.90
❑ 119	Termel Sledge ROO RC	5.00	1.50
❑ 120	Ian Ferguson ROO RC	3.00	.90
❑ 121	Lew Ford ROO RC	5.00	1.50
❑ 122	Nook Logan ROO RC	3.00	.90
❑ 123	Mike Nicolas ROO RC	3.00	.90
❑ 124	Jeff Duncan ROO RC	5.00	1.50
❑ 125	Tim Olson ROO RC	5.00	1.50
❑ 126	Michael Hessman RS RC	2.00	.60
❑ 127	Francisco Rosario RS RC	2.00	.60
❑ 128	Felix Sanchez RS RC	2.00	.60
❑ 129	Andrew Brown RS RC	2.00	.60
❑ 130	Matt Bruback RS RC	2.00	.60
❑ 131	Diegomar Markwell RS RC	2.00	.60
❑ 132	Josh Willingham RS RC	4.00	1.20
❑ 133	Wes Obermueller RS	2.00	.60
❑ 134	Phil Seibel RS RC	2.00	.60
❑ 135	Arnie Munoz RS RC	2.00	.60
❑ 136	Matt Kata RS RC	3.00	.90
❑ 137	Joe Valentine RS RC	2.00	.60
❑ 138	Ricardo Rodriguez RS	2.00	.60
❑ 139	Lyle Overbay RS	2.00	.60
❑ 140	Brian Stokes RS RC	2.00	.60
❑ 141	Josh Hall RS RC	3.00	.90
❑ 142	Kevin Hooper RS	2.00	.60
❑ 143	Chien-Ming Wang RS RC	6.00	1.80
❑ 144	Prentice Redman RS RC	2.00	.60
❑ 145	Chris Waters RS RC	2.00	.60
❑ 146	Jon Leicester RS RC	2.00	.60
❑ 147	Daniel Cabrera RS RC	2.00	.60
❑ 148	Alfredo Gonzalez RS RC	2.00	.60
❑ 149	Doug Waechter RS RC	3.00	.90
❑ 150	Brandon Larson RS	2.00	.60
❑ 151	Beau Kemp RS RC	2.00	.60
❑ 152	Cory Stewart RS RC	2.00	.60
❑ 153	Francisco Rodriguez RS	2.00	.60
❑ 154	Hee Seop Choi RS	2.00	.60
❑ 155	Mike Neu RS RC	2.00	.60
❑ 156	Derek Jeter AS	10.00	3.00
❑ 157	Alex Rodriguez AS	8.00	2.40
❑ 158	Nomar Garciaparra AS	8.00	2.40
❑ 159	Barry Bonds AS	10.00	3.00
❑ 160	Sammy Sosa AS	6.00	1.80
❑ 161	Vladimir Guerrero AS	4.00	1.20
❑ 162	Roger Clemens AS	8.00	2.40
❑ 163	Randy Johnson AS	4.00	1.20
❑ 164	Greg Maddux AS	8.00	2.40
❑ 165	Ken Griffey Jr. AS	6.00	1.80
❑ 166	Mike Piazza AS	6.00	1.80
❑ 167	Ichiro Suzuki AS	8.00	2.40
❑ 168	Barry Larkin AS	4.00	1.20
❑ 169	Lance Berkman AS	2.00	.60
❑ 170	Jim Thome AS	4.00	1.20
❑ 171	Jason Giambi AS	4.00	1.20
❑ 172	Gary Sheffield AS	2.00	.60
❑ 173	Ivan Rodriguez AS	4.00	1.20
❑ 174	Miguel Tejada AS	2.00	.60
❑ 175	Manny Ramirez AS	2.00	.60
❑ 176	Mike Sweeney AS	2.00	.60
❑ 177	Larry Walker AS	2.50	.75
❑ 178	Jeff Bagwell AS	2.50	.75
❑ 179	Chipper Jones AS	4.00	1.20
❑ 180	Craig Biggio AS	2.50	.75
❑ 181	Curt Schilling AS	2.50	.75
❑ 182	Pedro Martinez AS	4.00	1.20
❑ 183	Roberto Alomar AS	4.00	1.20
❑ 184	Bernie Williams AS	2.50	.75
❑ 185	Magglio Ordonez AS	2.00	.60
❑ 186	Jose Contreras IRT	6.00	1.80
❑ 187	Rafael Palmeiro IRT	2.50	.75
❑ 188	Andruw Jones IRT	2.50	.75
❑ 189	Bartolo Colon IRT	2.00	.60
❑ 190	Vladimir Guerrero IRT	4.00	1.20
❑ 191	Pedro Martinez IRT	4.00	1.20
❑ 192	Albert Pujols IRT	6.00	1.80
❑ 193	Manny Ramirez IRT	2.00	.60
❑ 194	Felix Rodriguez IRT	2.00	.60
❑ 195	Alfonso Soriano IRT	4.00	1.20
❑ 196	Sammy Sosa IRT	6.00	1.80
❑ 197	Miguel Tejada IRT	2.00	.60
❑ 198	Kazuhisa Ishii IRT	2.00	.60
❑ 199	Hideki Matsui IRT	15.00	4.50
❑ 200	Hideo Nomo IRT	4.00	1.20
❑ 201	Tomo Ohka IRT	2.00	.60
❑ 202	Kazuhiro Sasaki IRT	2.00	.60
❑ 203	Tsuyoshi Shinjo IRT	2.00	.60
❑ 204	Ichiro Suzuki IRT	8.00	2.40
❑ 205	Vicente Padilla IRT	2.00	.60
❑ 206	Carlos Beltran IRT	2.00	.60
❑ 207	Jose Cruz Jr. IRT	2.00	.60
❑ 208	Carlos Delgado IRT	2.00	.60
❑ 209	Juan Gonzalez IRT	4.00	1.20
❑ 210	Jorge Posada IRT	2.50	.75
❑ 211	Ivan Rodriguez IRT	4.00	1.20
❑ 212	Hee Seop Choi IRT	2.00	.60
❑ 213	Bobby Abreu IRT	2.00	.60
❑ 214	Magglio Ordonez IRT	2.00	.60
❑ 215	Francisco Rodriguez IRT	2.00	.60
❑ 216	Juan Acevedo BRX	2.00	.60
❑ 217	Erick Almonte BRX	2.00	.60
❑ 218	Yogi Berra BRX	4.00	1.20
❑ 219	Brandon Claussen BRX	2.00	.60
❑ 220	Roger Clemens BRX	8.00	2.40
❑ 221	Jose Contreras BRX	6.00	1.80
❑ 222	Whitey Ford BRX	2.50	.75
❑ 223	Jason Giambi BRX	4.00	1.20
❑ 224	Does Not Exist	-	
❑ 225	Michel Hernandez BRX RC	2.00	.60
❑ 226	Sterling Hitchcock BRX	2.00	.60
❑ 227	Catfish Hunter BRX	2.50	.75
❑ 228	Reggie Jackson BRX	2.50	.75
❑ 229	Derek Jeter BRX	10.00	3.00
❑ 230	Nick Johnson BRX	2.00	.60

❑ 231 Hideki Matsui BRX	15.00	4.50
❑ 232 Raul Mondesi BRX	2.00	.60
❑ 233 Mike Mussina BRX	4.00	1.20
❑ 234 Andy Pettitte BRX	2.50	.75
❑ 235 Jorge Posada BRX	2.50	.75
❑ 236 Mariano Rivera BRX	2.50	.75
❑ 237 Phil Rizzuto BRX	2.50	.75
❑ 238 Enos Slaughter BRX	2.00	.60
❑ 239 Alfonso Soriano BRX	4.00	1.20
❑ 240 Robin Ventura BRX	2.00	.60
❑ 241 Chien-Ming Wang BRX RC	6.00	1.80
❑ 242 Jeff Weaver BRX	2.00	.60
❑ 243 David Wells BRX	2.00	.60
❑ 244 Bernie Williams BRX	2.50	.75
❑ 245 Todd Zeile BRX	2.00	.60

2003 Fleer Double Header

	Nm-Mt	Ex-Mt
COMPLETE SET (240)	80.00	24.00
COMMON CARD (1-180)	.40	.12
COMMON CARD (181-270)	.50	.15
COMMON CARD (271-300)	1.00	.30

❑ 1 Ramon Vazquez	.40	.12
❑ 2 Derek Jeter	2.50	.75
❑ 3 Orlando Hudson	.40	.12
❑ 4 Miguel Tejada	.40	.12
❑ 5 Steve Finley	.40	.12
❑ 6 Brad Wilkerson	.40	.12
❑ 7 Craig Biggio	.60	.18
❑ 8 Marlon Anderson	.40	.12
❑ 9 Phil Nevin	.40	.12
❑ 10 Hideo Nomo	1.00	.30
❑ 11 Barry Larkin	1.00	.30
❑ 12 Alfonso Soriano	1.00	.30
❑ 13 Rodrigo Lopez	.40	.12
❑ 14 Paul Konerko	.40	.12
❑ 15 Carlos Beltran	.40	.12
❑ 16 Garret Anderson	.40	.12
❑ 17 Kazuhisa Ishii	.40	.12
❑ 18 Eddie Guardado	.40	.12
❑ 19 Juan Gonzalez	1.00	.30
❑ 20 Mark Mulder	.40	.12
❑ 21 Sammy Sosa	1.50	.45
❑ 22 Kazuhiro Sasaki	.40	.12
❑ 23 Jose Cruz Jr.	.40	.12
❑ 24 Tomo Ohka	.40	.12
❑ 25 Barry Bonds	2.50	.75
❑ 26 Carlos Delgado	.40	.12
❑ 27 Scott Rolen	.60	.18
❑ 28 Steve Cox	.40	.12
❑ 29 Mike Sweeney	.40	.12
❑ 30 Ryan Klesko	.40	.12
❑ 31 Greg Maddux	2.00	.60
❑ 32 Derek Lowe	.40	.12
❑ 33 David Wells	.40	.12
❑ 34 Kerry Wood	1.00	.30
❑ 35 Randall Simon	.40	.12
❑ 36 Ben Howard	.40	.12
❑ 37 Jeff Suppan	.40	.12
❑ 38 Curt Schilling	.60	.18
❑ 39 Eric Gagne	.60	.18
❑ 40 Raul Mondesi	.40	.12
❑ 41 Jeffrey Hammonds	.40	.12
❑ 42 Mo Vaughn	.40	.12
❑ 43 Sidney Ponson	.40	.12
❑ 44 Adam Dunn	.60	.18
❑ 45 Pedro Martinez	1.00	.30
❑ 46 Jason Simontacchi	.40	.12
❑ 47 Tom Glavine	1.00	.30
❑ 48 Torii Hunter	.40	.12
❑ 49 Gabe Kapler	.40	.12
❑ 50 Andy Van Hekken	.40	.12
❑ 51 Ichiro Suzuki	2.00	.60
❑ 52 Andruw Jones	.60	.18
❑ 53 Bobby Abreu	.40	.12
❑ 54 Junior Spivey	.40	.12
❑ 55 Ray Durham	.40	.12
❑ 56 Mark Buehrle	.40	.12
❑ 57 Drew Henson	.40	.12
❑ 58 Brandon Duckworth	.40	.12
❑ 59 Rob Mackowiak	.40	.12
❑ 60 Josh Beckett	.60	.18
❑ 61 Chan Ho Park	.40	.12
❑ 62 John Smoltz	.60	.18
❑ 63 Jimmy Rollins	.40	.12
❑ 64 Orlando Cabrera	.40	.12
❑ 65 Johnny Damon	.40	.12
❑ 66 Austin Kearns	.60	.18
❑ 67 Tsuyoshi Shinjo	.40	.12
❑ 68 Tim Hudson	.40	.12
❑ 69 Coco Crisp	.40	.12
❑ 70 Darin Erstad	.40	.12
❑ 71 Jacque Jones	.40	.12
❑ 72 Vicente Padilla	.40	.12
❑ 73 Hee Seop Choi	.40	.12
❑ 74 Shea Hillenbrand	.40	.12
❑ 75 Edgardo Alfonzo	.40	.12
❑ 76 Pat Burrell	.40	.12
❑ 77 Ben Sheets	.40	.12
❑ 78 Ivan Rodriguez	1.00	.30
❑ 79 Josh Phelps	.40	.12
❑ 80 Adam Kennedy	.40	.12
❑ 81 Eric Chavez	.40	.12
❑ 82 Bobby Higginson	.40	.12
❑ 83 Nomar Garciaparra	2.00	.60
❑ 84 J.D. Drew	.40	.12
❑ 85 Carl Crawford	.40	.12
❑ 86 Matt Morris	.40	.12
❑ 87 Chipper Jones	1.00	.30
❑ 88 Luis Gonzalez	.40	.12
❑ 89 Richie Sexson	.40	.12
❑ 90 Eric Milton	.40	.12
❑ 91 Andres Galarraga	.40	.12
❑ 92 Paul Lo Duca	.40	.12
❑ 93 Mark Grace	1.00	.30
❑ 94 Ben Grieve	.40	.12
❑ 95 Mike Lowell	.40	.12
❑ 96 Roberto Alomar	1.00	.30
❑ 97 Wade Miller	.40	.12
❑ 98 Sean Casey	.40	.12
❑ 99 Roger Clemens	2.00	.60
❑ 100 Matt Williams	.40	.12
❑ 101 Brian Giles	.40	.12
❑ 102 Jim Thome	1.00	.30
❑ 103 Troy Glaus	.60	.18
❑ 104 Joe Borchard	.40	.12
❑ 105 Vladimir Guerrero	1.00	.30
❑ 106 Kevin Mench	.40	.12
❑ 107 Omar Vizquel	.40	.12
❑ 108 Magglio Ordonez	.40	.12
❑ 109 Ken Griffey Jr.	1.50	.45
❑ 110 Mike Piazza	1.50	.45
❑ 111 Mark Teixeira	.60	.18
❑ 112 Jason Jennings	.40	.12
❑ 113 Ellis Burks	.40	.12
❑ 114 Jason Varitek	.40	.12
❑ 115 Larry Walker	.60	.18
❑ 116 Frank Thomas	1.00	.30
❑ 117 Ramon Ortiz	.40	.12
❑ 118 Mark Quinn	.40	.12
❑ 119 Preston Wilson	.40	.12
❑ 120 Carlos Lee	.40	.12
❑ 121 Brian Lawrence	.40	.12
❑ 122 Tim Salmon	.60	.18
❑ 123 Shawn Green	.40	.12
❑ 124 Randy Johnson	1.00	.30
❑ 125 Jeff Bagwell	.60	.18
❑ 126 C.C. Sabathia	.40	.12
❑ 127 Bernie Williams	.60	.18
❑ 128 Roy Oswalt	.40	.12
❑ 129 Albert Pujols	2.00	.60
❑ 130 Reggie Sanders	.40	.12
❑ 131 Jeff Conine	.40	.12
❑ 132 John Olerud	.40	.12
❑ 133 Lance Berkman	.40	.12
❑ 134 Geoff Jenkins	.40	.12
❑ 135 Jim Edmonds	.40	.12
❑ 136 Todd Helton	.60	.18
❑ 137 Jason Kendall	.40	.12
❑ 138 Robin Ventura	.40	.12
❑ 139 Randy Winn	.40	.12
❑ 140 Carl Everett	.40	.12
❑ 141 Jose Vidro	.40	.12
❑ 142 Pokey Reese	.40	.12
❑ 143 Edgar Renteria	.40	.12
❑ 144 Alex Rodriguez	2.00	.60
❑ 145 Doug Mientkiewicz	.40	.12
❑ 146 Aramis Ramirez	.40	.12
❑ 147 Bobby Hill	.40	.12
❑ 148 Jorge Posada	.60	.18
❑ 149 Sean Burroughs	.40	.12
❑ 150 Jeff Kent	.40	.12
❑ 151 Tino Martinez	.40	.12
❑ 152 Mark Prior	1.50	.45
❑ 153 Brad Radke	.40	.12
❑ 154 Al Leiter	.40	.12
❑ 155 Eric Karros	.40	.12
❑ 156 Manny Ramirez	.40	.12
❑ 157 Jason Lane	.40	.12
❑ 158 Mike Lieberthal	.40	.12
❑ 159 Shannon Stewart	.40	.12
❑ 160 Robert Fick	.40	.12
❑ 161 Derrek Lee	.40	.12
❑ 162 Jason Giambi	1.00	.30
❑ 163 Rafael Palmeiro	.60	.18
❑ 164 Jay Payton	.40	.12
❑ 165 Adrian Beltre	.40	.12
❑ 166 Marlon Byrd	.40	.12
❑ 167 Bret Boone	.40	.12
❑ 168 Roy Halladay	.40	.12
❑ 169 Freddy Garcia	.40	.12
❑ 170 Rich Aurilia	.40	.12
❑ 171 Jared Sandberg	.40	.12
❑ 172 Paul Byrd	.40	.12
❑ 173 Gary Sheffield	.40	.12
❑ 174 Edgar Martinez	.60	.18
❑ 175 Eric Hinske	.40	.12
❑ 176 Milton Bradley	.40	.12
❑ 177 David Eckstein	.40	.12
❑ 178 Jay Gibbons	.40	.12
❑ 179 Corey Patterson	.40	.12
❑ 180 Barry Zito	1.00	.30
❑ 181-82 Darin Erstad Troy Glaus	.75	.23
❑ 183-84 Curt Schilling Randy Johnson	1.25	.35
❑ 185-86 Andruw Jones Chipper Jones	1.25	.35
❑ 187-88 Tony Batista Jay Gibbons	.50	.15
❑ 189-90 Pedro Martinez Nomar Garciaparra	2.00	.60
❑ 191-92 Sammy Sosa Kerry Wood	2.00	.60
❑ 193-94 Paul Konerko Joe Borchard	.75	.23
❑ 195-96 Austin Kearns Adam Dunn	1.25	.35
❑ 197-98 Omar Vizquel Jim Thome	1.25	.35
❑ 199-00 Larry Walker Todd Helton	.75	.23
❑ 201-02 Josh Beckett Luis Castillo	1.25	.35
❑ 203-04 Craig Biggio Jeff Bagwell	.75	.23
❑ 205-06 Paul Byrd Mike Sweeney	.50	.15
❑ 207-08 Adrian Beltre Shawn Green	.75	.23
❑ 209-10 Jose Hernandez Richie Sexson	.50	.15
❑ 211-12 Jacque Jones Torii Hunter	.75	.23
❑ 213-14 Vladmir Guerrero Jose Vidro	1.25	.35
❑ 215-16 Edgardo Alfonzo	2.00	.60

Mike Piazza
❑ 217-18 Roger Clemens 2.50 .75
Derek Jeter
❑ 219-20 Eric Chavez .75 .23
Miguel Tejada
❑ 221-22 Marlon Byrd .75 .23
Pat Burrell
❑ 223-24 Jason Kendall .50 .15
Brian Giles
❑ 225-26 Phil Nevin .75 .23
Sean Burroughs
❑ 227-28 Jeff Kent 2.50 .75
Barry Bonds
❑ 229-30 Kazuhiro Sasaki 2.00 .60
Ichiro Suzuki
❑ 231-32 Albert Pujols 2.00 .60
J.D. Drew
❑ 233-34 Juan Gonzalez 2.00 .60
Ivan Rodriguez
❑ 235-36 Eric Hinske .50 .15
Orlando Hudson
❑ 237-38 Lance Berkman 1.25 .35
Chipper Jones
❑ 239-40 Alex Rodriguez 2.50 .75
Derek Jeter
❑ 241-42 Ichiro Suzuki 2.00 .60
Hideo Nomo
❑ 243-44 Manny Ramirez .75 .23
Bernie Williams
❑ 245-46 Tom Glavine 2.00 .60
Roger Clemens
❑ 247-48 Ken Griffey Jr. 2.00 .60
Barry Larkin
❑ 249-50 Mark Teixeira 3.00 .90
Mark Prior
❑ 251-52 Albert Pujols 2.00 .60
Drew Henson
❑ 253-54 Jason Giambi 2.00 .60
Todd Helton AS
❑ 255-56 Jose Vidro 1.25 .35
Alfonso Soriano AS
❑ 257-58 Shea Hillenbrand .75 .23
Scott Rolen AS
❑ 259-60 Jimmy Rollins 2.00 .60
Alex Rodriguez AS
❑ 261-62 Torii Hunter 1.25 .35
Vladmir Guerrero AS
❑ 263-64 Ichiro Suzuki AS 2.00 .60
Sammy Sosa AS
❑ 265-66 Barry Bonds 2.50 .75
Manny Ramirez AS
❑ 267-68 Mike Piazza 2.00 .60
Jorge Posada AS
❑ 269-70 Robin Yount 2.00 .60
Ozzie Smith AS
❑ 271-72 Josh Hancock 1.00 .30
Freddy Sanchez OD
❑ 273-74 Ryan Bukvich 1.00 .30
Shawn Sedlacek OD
❑ 275-76 Doug Devore 1.00 .30
Rene Reyes OD
❑ 277-78 Hank Blalock 1.50 .45
Travis Hafner OD
❑ 279-80 Eric Junge 1.00 .30
Brett Myers OD
❑ 281-82 Brad Lidge 1.00 .30
Jeriome Robertson OD
❑ 283-84 Miguel Asencio 1.00 .30
Runelvys Hernandez OD
❑ 285-86 Fernando Rodney 1.00 .30
Barry Wesson OD
❑ 287-88 Victor Alvarez 1.00 .30
David Ross OD
❑ 289-90 Tony Torcato 1.00 .30
Chris Snelling OD
❑ 291-92 Kirk Saarloos 1.00 .30
Morgan Ensberg OD
❑ 293-94 Josh Bard 1.00 .30
Wil Nieves OD
❑ 295-96 Jung Bong 1.00 .30
Trey Hodges OD
❑ 297-98 Kevin Cash 1.00 .30
Reed Johnson OD
❑ 299-00 Chone Figgins 1.00 .30
John Lackey OD
❑ P2 Derek Jeter Promo 3.00 .90

2002 Fleer Fall Classics

	Nm-Mt	Ex-Mt
COMPLETE SET (100)	30.00	9.00
COMMON CARD (1-100)	.50	.15
COMMON SP	5.00	1.50

❑ 1 Rabbit Maranville .50 .15
❑ 2 Tris Speaker .75 .23
❑ 3 Harmon Killebrew 1.25 .35
❑ 4 Lou Gehrig 3.00 .90
❑ 5 Lou Boudreau .50 .15
❑ 6 Al Kaline 1.25 .35
❑ 7A Paul Molitor Blue Jays .75 .23
❑ 7B Paul Molitor Brewers SP 8.00 2.40
❑ 8 Cal Ripken 4.00 1.20
❑ 9 Yogi Berra 1.25 .35
❑ 10 Phil Rizzuto .75 .23
❑ 11A Luis Aparicio W.Sox .50 .15
❑ 11B Luis Aparicio O's SP 5.00 1.50
❑ 12 Stan Musial 2.00 .60
❑ 13 Mel Ott 1.25 .35
❑ 14 Larry Doby .50 .15
❑ 15 Ozzie Smith 1.25 .35
❑ 16A Babe Ruth Yankees 5.00 1.50
❑ 16B Babe Ruth Red Sox SP 15.00 4.50
❑ 17A Red Schoendienst Braves .50 .15
❑ 17B Red Schoendienst Cards SP 5.00 1.50
❑ 18 Rollie Fingers .50 .15
❑ 19 Thurman Munson 2.00 .60
❑ 20 Lou Brock .75 .23
❑ 21A Paul O'Neill Yankees .75 .23
❑ 21B Paul O'Neill Reds SP 8.00 2.40
❑ 22 Jim Palmer .50 .15
❑ 23 Kirby Puckett 1.25 .35
❑ 24A Tony Perez Reds .50 .15
❑ 24B Tony Perez Phils SP 5.00 1.50
❑ 25 Don Larsen .50 .15
❑ 26A Steve Garvey Dodgers .50 .15
❑ 26B Steve Garvey Padres SP 5.00 1.50
❑ 27A Jim Hunter A's .75 .23
❑ 27B Jim Hunter Yankees SP 8.00 2.40
❑ 28 Juan Marichal .50 .15
❑ 29 Pee Wee Reese .75 .23
❑ 30 Orlando Cepeda .50 .15
❑ 31 Goose Gossage .50 .15
❑ 32 Ray Knight .50 .15
❑ 33 Eddie Murray 1.25 .35
❑ 34 Nolan Ryan 4.00 1.20
❑ 35 Alan Trammell .75 .23
❑ 36 Grover Alexander 1.25 .35
❑ 37 Joe Carter .50 .15
❑ 38 Rogers Hornsby 1.25 .35
❑ 39 Jimmie Foxx 1.25 .35
❑ 40 Mike Schmidt 2.50 .75
❑ 41 Eddie Mathews 1.25 .35
❑ 42 Jackie Robinson 2.00 .60
❑ 43A Eddie Collins A's .50 .15
❑ 43B Eddie Collins White Sox SP 5.00 1.50
❑ 44 Willie McCovey .50 .15
❑ 45 Bob Gibson .75 .23
❑ 46A Keith Hernandez Mets .75 .23
❑ 46B Keith Hernandez Cards SP 8.00 2.40
❑ 47 Brooks Robinson 1.25 .35
❑ 48 Mordecai Brown .50 .15
❑ 49 Gary Carter .75 .23
❑ 50A Kirk Gibson Dodgers .50 .15
❑ 50B Kirk Gibson Tigers SP 5.00 1.50
❑ 51 Johnny Mize .50 .15
❑ 52 Johnny Podres .50 .15
❑ 53 Darrell Porter .50 .15
❑ 54 Willie Stargell .75 .23
❑ 55A Lenny Dykstra Mets .50 .15
❑ 55B Lenny Dykstra Phillies SP 5.00 1.50
❑ 56 Christy Mathewson 1.25 .35
❑ 57 Walter Johnson 1.25 .35
❑ 58 Whitey Ford .75 .23
❑ 59 Lefty Grove .75 .23
❑ 60 Duke Snider .75 .23
❑ 61 Cy Young 1.25 .35
❑ 62A Dave Winfield Blue Jays .75 .23
❑ 62B Dave Winfield Yankees SP 8.00 2.40
❑ 63 Robin Yount 1.25 .35
❑ 64 Fred Lynn .50 .15
❑ 65 Ty Cobb 2.00 .60
❑ 66 Joe Morgan .50 .15
❑ 67 Bill Mazeroski .50 .15
❑ 68 Frank Baker .50 .15
❑ 69 Chief Bender .50 .15
❑ 70 Carlton Fisk .75 .23
❑ 71 Jerry Coleman .50 .15
❑ 72 Frankie Frisch .50 .15
❑ 73A Wade Boggs Red Sox .75 .23
❑ 73B Wade Boggs Yankees SP 8.00 2.40
❑ 74 Johnny Bench 1.25 .35
❑ 75A Roger Maris Yankees 1.50 .45
❑ 75B Roger Maris Cards SP 10.00 3.00
❑ 76 Dom DiMaggio .50 .15
❑ 77 George Brett 3.00 .90
❑ 78A Dave Parker Pirates .50 .15
❑ 78B Dave Parker A's SP 5.00 1.50
❑ 79 Hank Greenberg 1.25 .35
❑ 80 Pepper Martin .75 .23
❑ 81A Graig Nettles Yankees .50 .15
❑ 81B Graig Nettles Padres SP 5.00 1.50
❑ 82 Dennis Eckersley .50 .15
❑ 83 Donn Clendenon .50 .15
❑ 84 Tom Seaver 1.25 .35
❑ 85 Honus Wagner 2.00 .60
❑ 86A Reggie Jackson Yankees .75 .23
❑ 86B Reggie Jackson A's SP 8.00 2.40
❑ 87A Goose Goslin Senators .50 .15
❑ 87B Goose Goslin Tigers SP 5.00 1.50
❑ 88 Tony Kubek .75 .23
❑ 89 Roy Campanella 1.25 .35
❑ 90A Steve Carlton Phillies .75 .23
❑ 90B Steve Carlton Cards SP 8.00 2.40
❑ 91 Lou Gehrig 2.00 .60
Mel Ott
❑ 92 Eddie Collins .50 .15
Joe Morgan
❑ 93 George Brett 2.50 .75
Mike Schmidt
❑ 94 Cal Ripken 2.50 .75
Ozzie Smith
❑ 95 Thurman Munson 1.25 .35
Johnny Bench
❑ 96 Willie Stargell 1.25 .35
Stan Musial
Pepper Martin
❑ 97 Babe Ruth 3.00 .90
Kirby Puckett
Reggie Jackson
❑ 98 Cy Young .75 .23
Bob Gibson
❑ 99 Whitey Ford .75 .23
Steve Carlton
❑ 100 Paul Molitor .75 .23
Lou Brock

2003 Fleer Fall Classics

	MINT	NRMT
COMP. SET w/o SP's (87)	25.00	11.00
COMMON CARD (1-87)	.50	.23
COMMON SP1	5.00	2.20
SP1 STATED ODDS 1:18 H, 1:36 R	-	
COMMON SP2	5.00	2.20
SP2 STATED ODDS 1:1 LGD STAR	-	

❑ 1 Rod Carew .75 .35
❑ 2 Bobby Doerr .50 .23
❑ 3A Eddie Mathews Braves 1.25 .55
❑ 3B Eddie Mathews Tigers SP2 10.00 4.50

❑ 4 Tom Seaver 1.25 .55
❑ 5 Lou Brock .75 .35
❑ 6A Nolan Ryan Mets 4.00 1.80
❑ 6B Nolan Ryan Astros SP2 15.00 6.75
❑ 7 Pee Wee Reese .75 .35
❑ 8 Robin Yount 1.25 .55
❑ 9 Bob Feller .75 .35
❑ 10 Harmon Killebrew 1.25 .55
❑ 11 Hal Newhouser .50 .23
❑ 12 Al Kaline 1.25 .55
❑ 13 Hoyt Wilhelm .50 .23
❑ 14 Early Wynn .50 .23
❑ 15A Yogi Berra Yanks 1.25 .55
❑ 15B Yogi Berra Mets SP2 10.00 4.50
❑ 16 Billy Williams .50 .23
❑ 17 Rollie Fingers .50 .23
❑ 18A Sparky Anderson Tigers .50 .23
❑ 18B Sparky Anderson Reds SP1 5.00 2.20
❑ 19 Lou Boudreau .50 .23
❑ 20 Warren Spahn .75 .35
❑ 21 Enos Slaughter .50 .23
❑ 22 Luis Aparicio .50 .23
❑ 23 Phil Rizzuto .75 .35
❑ 24 Willie McCovey .50 .23
❑ 25 Joe Morgan .50 .23
❑ 26 Alan Trammell .50 .23
❑ 27 Eddie Plank .50 .23
❑ 28 Lefty Grove .75 .35
❑ 29 Walter Johnson 1.25 .55
❑ 30 Roy Campanella 1.25 .55
❑ 31 Carlton Fisk .75 .35
❑ 32 Bill Dickey .75 .35
❑ 33A Rogers Hornsby Cards 1.25 .55
❑ 33B Rogers Hornsby Cubs SP1 10.00 4.50
❑ 34 Wade Boggs .75 .35
❑ 35 Chick Stahl .50 .23
❑ 36A Don Drysdale Brooklyn 1.25 .55
❑ 36B Don Drysdale LA SP1 10.00 4.50
❑ 37 Jose Canseco 1.25 .55
❑ 38A Roger Maris Cards 1.50 .70
❑ 38B Roger Maris Yanks SP2 10.00 4.50
❑ 39 Cal Ripken 4.00 1.80
❑ 40A Kiki Cuyler Pirates .50 .23
❑ 40B Kiki Cuyler Cubs SP1 5.00 2.20
❑ 41 Hank Greenberg 1.25 .55
❑ 42 Bud Harrelson .50 .23
❑ 43A Eddie Murray O's 1.25 .55
❑ 43B Eddie Murray Indians SP2 10.00 4.50
❑ 44 Jimmy Sebring .50 .23
❑ 45 Ozzie Smith 1.25 .55
❑ 46A Darryl Strawberry Mets .75 .35
❑ 46B Darryl Strawberry Yanks SP2 8.00 3.60
❑ 47 Dave Parker .50 .23
❑ 48A Gil Hodges Dodgers .75 .35
❑ 48B Gil Hodges Mets SP2 8.00 3.60
❑ 49 Joe Carter .50 .23
❑ 50A Leo Durocher Cards .50 .23
❑ 50B Leo Durocher Giants SP1 5.00 2.20
❑ 51 Christy Mathewson 1.25 .55
❑ 52 Elston Howard .50 .23
❑ 53 Hughie Jennings .50 .23
❑ 54 Nellie Fox .75 .35
❑ 55 Carl Yastrzemski 2.00 .90
❑ 56A Frank Robinson O's .50 .23
❑ 56B Frank Robinson Reds SP2 5.00 2.20
❑ 57 Dennis Eckersley .50 .23
❑ 58A Grover Alexander Phils .75 .35
❑ 58B Grover Alexander Cards SP1 8.00 3.60
❑ 59 Carl Hubbell .75 .35
❑ 60 Dave Winfield .75 .35
❑ 61 Honus Wagner 2.00 .90
❑ 62A Duke Snider Brooklyn .75 .35
❑ 62B Duke Snider LA SP2 8.00 3.60
❑ 63A Frankie Frisch Giants .50 .23
❑ 63B Frankie Frisch Cards SP1 5.00 2.20
❑ 64 Dizzy Dean DF .75 .35
❑ 65 Bob Gibson DF .75 .35
❑ 66 Johnny Bench DF 1.25 .55
❑ 67 Ty Cobb DF 2.00 .90
❑ 68 Lou Gehrig DF 3.00 1.35
❑ 69 Catfish Hunter DF .75 .35
❑ 70 Willie Stargell DF .75 .35
❑ 71A Reggie Jackson A's GC .75 .35
❑ 71B Reggie Jackson Yanks GC SP2 8.00 3.60
❑ 72 George Brett GC 3.00 1.35
❑ 73A Babe Ruth Sox GC 5.00 2.20
❑ 73B Babe Ruth Yanks GC SP1 15.00 6.75
❑ 74 Cy Young GC 1.25 .55
❑ 75 Jim Palmer GC .50 .23
❑ 76 Mickey Lolich GC .50 .23
❑ 77 Stan Musial GC 2.00 .90
❑ 78 Steve Carlton GC .75 .35
❑ 79 Roberto Clemente GC 3.00 1.35
❑ 80 John McGraw GC .75 .35
❑ 81 Paul Molitor GC .75 .35
❑ 82 Red Ruffing GC .50 .23
❑ 83 Connie Mack GC .50 .23
❑ 84 Mike Schmidt GC 2.50 1.10
❑ 85A Mickey Cochrane A's GC .75 .35
❑ 85B Mickey Cochrane Tigers GC SP1 8.00 3.60
❑ 86 Brooks Robinson GC 1.25 .55
❑ 87 Whitey Ford GC .75 .35

2001 Fleer Focus

	Nm-Mt	Ex-Mt
COMP.SET w/o SP's (200)	25.00	7.50
COMMON CARD (1-200)	.30	.09
COMMON (201-240)	5.00	1.50
COMMON (241-250)	10.00	3.00

❑ 1 Derek Jeter 2.00 .60
❑ 2 Manny Ramirez .30 .09
❑ 3 Ken Griffey Jr. 1.25 .35
❑ 4 Ken Caminiti .30 .09
❑ 5 Joe Randa .30 .09
❑ 6 Jason Kendall .30 .09
❑ 7 Ron Coomer .30 .09
❑ 8 Rondell White .30 .09
❑ 9 Tino Martinez .50 .15
❑ 10 Nomar Garciaparra 1.50 .45
❑ 11 Tony Batista .30 .09
❑ 12 Todd Stottlemyre .30 .09
❑ 13 Ryan Klesko .30 .09
❑ 14 Darin Erstad .30 .09
❑ 15 Todd Walker .30 .09
❑ 16 Al Leiter .30 .09
❑ 17 Carl Everett .30 .09
❑ 18 Bobby Abreu .30 .09
❑ 19 Raul Mondesi .30 .09
❑ 20 Vladimir Guerrero .75 .23
❑ 21 Mike Bordick .30 .09
❑ 22 Aaron Sele .30 .09
❑ 23 Ray Lankford .30 .09
❑ 24 Roger Clemens 1.50 .45
❑ 25 Kevin Young .30 .09
❑ 26 Brad Radke .30 .09
❑ 27 Todd Hundley .30 .09
❑ 28 Ellis Burks .30 .09
❑ 29 Lee Stevens .30 .09
❑ 30 Eric Karros .30 .09
❑ 31 Darren Dreifort .30 .09
❑ 32 Ivan Rodriguez .75 .23
❑ 33 Pedro Martinez .75 .23
❑ 34 Travis Fryman .30 .09
❑ 35 Garret Anderson .30 .09
❑ 36 Rafael Palmeiro .50 .15
❑ 37 Jason Giambi .75 .23
❑ 38 Jeromy Burnitz .30 .09
❑ 39 Robin Ventura .30 .09
❑ 40 Derek Bell .30 .09
❑ 41 Carlos Guillen .30 .09
❑ 42 Albert Belle .30 .09
❑ 43 Henry Rodriguez .30 .09
❑ 44 Brian Jordan .30 .09
❑ 45 Mike Sweeney .30 .09
❑ 46 Ruben Rivera .30 .09
❑ 47 Greg Maddux 1.50 .45
❑ 48 Corey Koskie .30 .09
❑ 49 Sandy Alomar Jr. .30 .09
❑ 50 Mike Mussina .75 .23
❑ 51 Tom Glavine .75 .23
❑ 52 Aaron Boone .30 .09
❑ 53 Frank Thomas .75 .23
❑ 54 Kenny Lofton .30 .09
❑ 55 Danny Graves .30 .09
❑ 56 Jose Valentin .30 .09
❑ 57 Travis Lee .30 .09
❑ 58 Jim Edmonds .30 .09
❑ 59 Jim Thome .75 .23
❑ 60 Steve Finley .30 .09
❑ 61 Shawn Green .30 .09
❑ 62 Lance Berkman .30 .09
❑ 63 Mark Quinn .30 .09
❑ 64 Randy Johnson .75 .23
❑ 65 Dmitri Young .30 .09
❑ 66 Andy Pettitte .50 .15
❑ 67 Paul O'Neill .50 .15
❑ 68 Gil Heredia .30 .09
❑ 69 Russell Branyan .30 .09
❑ 70 Alex Rodriguez 1.50 .45
❑ 71 Geoff Jenkins .30 .09
❑ 72 Eric Chavez .30 .09
❑ 73 Cal Ripken 2.50 .75
❑ 74 Mark Kotsay .30 .09
❑ 75 Jeff D'Amico .30 .09
❑ 76 Tony Womack .30 .09
❑ 77 Eric Milton .30 .09
❑ 78 Joe Girardi .30 .09
❑ 79 Peter Bergeron .30 .09
❑ 80 Miguel Tejada .30 .09
❑ 81 Luis Gonzalez .30 .09
❑ 82 Doug Glanville .30 .09
❑ 83 Gerald Williams .30 .09
❑ 84 Troy O'Leary .30 .09
❑ 85 Brian Giles .30 .09
❑ 86 Miguel Cairo .30 .09
❑ 87 Magglio Ordonez .30 .09
❑ 88 Rick Helling .30 .09
❑ 89 Bruce Chen .30 .09
❑ 90 Jason Varitek .30 .09
❑ 91 Mike Lieberthal .30 .09
❑ 92 Shawn Estes .30 .09
❑ 93 Rick Ankiel .30 .09
❑ 94 Tim Salmon .50 .15
❑ 95 Jacque Jones .30 .09
❑ 96 Johnny Damon .30 .09
❑ 97 Larry Walker .50 .15
❑ 98 Ruben Mateo .30 .09
❑ 99 Brad Fullmer .30 .09
❑ 100 Edgardo Alfonzo .30 .09
❑ 101 Mark Mulder .30 .09
❑ 102 Tony Gwynn 1.00 .30
❑ 103 Mike Cameron .30 .09
❑ 104 Richie Sexson .30 .09
❑ 105 Barry Larkin .75 .23
❑ 106 Mike Piazza 1.25 .35
❑ 107 Eric Young .30 .09
❑ 108 Edgar Renteria .30 .09
❑ 109 Todd Zeile .30 .09
❑ 110 Luis Castillo .30 .09
❑ 111 Sammy Sosa 1.25 .35

❑ 112 David Justice .30 .09
❑ 113 Delino DeShields .30 .09
❑ 114 Mariano Rivera .50 .15
❑ 115 Edgar Martinez .30 .09
❑ 116 Ray Durham .30 .09
❑ 117 Brady Anderson .30 .09
❑ 118 Eric Owens .30 .09
❑ 119 Alex Gonzalez .30 .09
❑ 120 Jay Buhner .30 .09
❑ 121 Greg Vaughn .30 .09
❑ 122 Mike Lowell .30 .09
❑ 123 Marquis Grissom .30 .09
❑ 124 Matt Williams .30 .09
❑ 125 Dean Palmer .30 .09
❑ 126 Troy Glaus .50 .15
❑ 127 Bret Boone .30 .09
❑ 128 David Ortiz .30 .09
❑ 129 Glenallen Hill .30 .09
❑ 130 Chipper Jones .75 .23
❑ 131 Tony Clark .30 .09
❑ 132 Terrence Long .30 .09
❑ 133 Chuck Finley .30 .09
❑ 134 Jeff Bagwell .50 .15
❑ 135 J.T. Snow .30 .09
❑ 136 Andruw Jones .50 .15
❑ 137 Carlos Delgado .30 .09
❑ 138 Mo Vaughn .30 .09
❑ 139 Derrek Lee .30 .09
❑ 140 Bobby Estalella .30 .09
❑ 141 Kerry Wood .75 .23
❑ 142 Jose Vidro .30 .09
❑ 143 Ben Grieve .30 .09
❑ 144 Barry Bonds 2.00 .60
❑ 145 Javy Lopez .30 .09
❑ 146 Adam Kennedy .30 .09
❑ 147 Jeff Cirillo .30 .09
❑ 148 Cliff Floyd .30 .09
❑ 149 Carl Pavano .30 .09
❑ 150 Bobby Higginson .30 .09
❑ 151 Kevin Brown .30 .09
❑ 152 Fernando Tatis .30 .09
❑ 153 Matt Lawton .30 .09
❑ 154 Damion Easley .30 .09
❑ 155 Curt Schilling .50 .15
❑ 156 Mark McGwire 2.00 .60
❑ 157 Mark Grace .75 .23
❑ 158 Adrian Beltre .30 .09
❑ 159 Jorge Posada .50 .15
❑ 160 Richard Hidalgo .30 .09
❑ 161 Vinny Castilla .30 .09
❑ 162 Bernie Williams .50 .15
❑ 163 John Olerud .30 .09
❑ 164 Todd Helton .50 .15
❑ 165 Craig Biggio .50 .15
❑ 166 David Wells .30 .09
❑ 167 Phil Nevin .30 .09
❑ 168 Andres Galarraga .30 .09
❑ 169 Moises Alou .30 .09
❑ 170 Denny Neagle .30 .09
❑ 171 Jeffrey Hammonds .30 .09
❑ 172 Sean Casey .30 .09
❑ 173 Gary Sheffield .30 .09
❑ 174 Carlos Lee .30 .09
❑ 175 Juan Encarnacion .30 .09
❑ 176 Roberto Alomar .75 .23
❑ 177 Kenny Rogers .30 .09
❑ 178 Charles Johnson .30 .09
❑ 179 Shannon Stewart .30 .09
❑ 180 B.J. Surhoff .30 .09
❑ 181 Paul Konerko .30 .09
❑ 182 Jermaine Dye .30 .09
❑ 183 Scott Rolen .50 .15
❑ 184 Fred McGriff .50 .15
❑ 185 Juan Gonzalez .75 .23
❑ 186 Carlos Beltran .30 .09
❑ 187 Jay Payton .30 .09
❑ 188 Chad Hermansen .30 .09
❑ 189 Pat Burrell .30 .09
❑ 190 Omar Vizquel .30 .09
❑ 191 Trot Nixon .30 .09
❑ 192 Mike Hampton .30 .09
❑ 193 Kris Benson .30 .09
❑ 194 Gabe Kapler .30 .09
❑ 195 Rickey Henderson 1.25 .35
❑ 196 J.D. Drew .30 .09
❑ 197 Pokey Reese .30 .09
❑ 198 Jeff Kent .30 .09
❑ 199 Jose Cruz Jr. .30 .09
❑ 200 Preston Wilson .30 .09
❑ 201 Eric Munson/2499 5.00 1.50
❑ 202 Alex Cabrera/2499 5.00 1.50
❑ 203 Nate Rolison/2499 5.00 1.50
❑ 204 Julio Zuleta/2499 5.00 1.50
❑ 205 Chris Richard/2499 5.00 1.50
❑ 206 Dernell Stenson/2499 5.00 1.50
❑ 207 Aaron McNeal/2499 5.00 1.50
❑ 208 Aubrey Huff/2999 5.00 1.50
❑ 209 Mike Lamb/2999 5.00 1.50
❑ 210 Xavier Nady/2999 5.00 1.50
❑ 211 Joe Crede/2999 5.00 1.50
❑ 212 Ben Petrick/3499 5.00 1.50
❑ 213 M.Burkhart/1999 5.00 1.50
❑ 214 Jason Tyner/1999 5.00 1.50
❑ 215 Juan Pierre/1999 5.00 1.50
❑ 216 Adam Dunn/1999 8.00 2.40
❑ 217 Adam Piatt/1999 5.00 1.50
❑ 218 Eric Byrnes/1999 5.00 1.50
❑ 219 Corey Patterson/1999 5.00 1.50
❑ 220 Kenny Kelly/1999 5.00 1.50
❑ 221 Tike Redman/1999 5.00 1.50
❑ 222 Luis Matos/1999 5.00 1.50
❑ 223 Timo Perez/1999 5.00 1.50
❑ 224 Vernon Wells/1999 5.00 1.50
❑ 225 Barry Zito/4999 8.00 2.40
❑ 226 Adam Bernero/4999 5.00 1.50
❑ 227 Kazuhiro Sasaki/4999 5.00 1.50
❑ 228 O.Mairena/4999 5.00 1.50
❑ 229 Mark Buehrle/4999 5.00 1.50
❑ 230 Ryan Dempster/4999 5.00 1.50
❑ 231 Tim Hudson/4999 5.00 1.50
❑ 232 Scott Downs/4999 5.00 1.50
❑ 233 A.J. Burnett/4999 5.00 1.50
❑ 234 Adam Eaton/4999 5.00 1.50
❑ 235 P.Crawford/4999 5.00 1.50
❑ 236 Jace Brewer/3999 5.00 1.50
❑ 237 Jose Ortiz/3999 5.00 1.50
❑ 238 Rafael Furcal/3999 5.00 1.50
❑ 239 Julio Lugo/3999 5.00 1.50
❑ 240 T. De la Rosa/3999 5.00 1.50
❑ 241 T. Shinjo/999 RC 12.00 3.60
❑ 242 W. Betemit/999 RC 10.00 3.00
❑ 243 J. Owens/999 RC 10.00 3.00
❑ 244 Drew Henson/999 RC 12.00 3.60
❑ 245 Albert Pujols/999 RC 50.00 15.00
❑ 246 Travis Hafner/999 RC 10.00 3.00
❑ 247 Ichiro Suzuki/999 RC 40.00 12.00
❑ 248 E. Guzman/999 RC 10.00 3.00
❑ 249 Matt White/999 RC 10.00 3.00
❑ 250 Junior Spivey/999 RC 10.00 3.00

2002 Fleer Focus JE

	Nm-Mt	Ex-Mt
COMPLETE SET (260)	100.00	30.00
COMP.SET w/o SP's (225)	25.00	7.50
COMMON CARD (1-225)	.30	.09
COMMON CARD (226-260)	2.00	.60

❑ 1 Mike Piazza 1.25 .35
❑ 2 Jason Giambi .75 .23
❑ 3 Jim Thome .75 .23
❑ 4 John Olerud .30 .09
❑ 5 J.D. Drew .30 .09
❑ 6 Richard Hidalgo .30 .09
❑ 7 Rusty Greer .30 .09
❑ 8 Tony Batista .30 .09
❑ 9 Omar Vizquel .30 .09
❑ 10 Randy Johnson .75 .23
❑ 11 Cristian Guzman .30 .09
❑ 12 Mark Grace .75 .23
❑ 13 Jeff Cirillo .30 .09
❑ 14 Mike Cameron .30 .09
❑ 15 Jeromy Burnitz .30 .09
❑ 16 Pokey Reese .30 .09
❑ 17 Richie Sexson .30 .09
❑ 18 Joe Randa .30 .09
❑ 19 Aramis Ramirez .30 .09
❑ 20 Pedro Martinez .75 .23
❑ 21 Todd Hollandsworth .30 .09
❑ 22 Rondell White .30 .09
❑ 23 Tsuyoshi Shinjo .30 .09
❑ 24 Melvin Mora .30 .09
❑ 25 Tim Hudson .30 .09
❑ 26 Darrin Fletcher .30 .09
❑ 27 Bill Mueller .30 .09
❑ 28 Jeff Weaver .30 .09
❑ 29 Tony Clark .30 .09
❑ 30 Tom Glavine .75 .23
❑ 31 Jarrod Washburn .30 .09
❑ 32 Greg Vaughn .30 .09
❑ 33 Lee Stevens .30 .09
❑ 34 Charles Johnson .30 .09
❑ 35 Lance Berkman .30 .09
❑ 36 Bud Smith .30 .09
❑ 37 Keith Foulke .30 .09
❑ 38 Ben Davis .30 .09
❑ 39 Daryle Ward .30 .09
❑ 40 Bernie Williams .50 .15
❑ 41 Dean Palmer .30 .09
❑ 42 Mark Mulder .30 .09
❑ 43 Jason LaRue .30 .09
❑ 44 Jay Gibbons .30 .09
❑ 45 Brandon Duckworth .30 .09
❑ 46 Carlos Delgado .30 .09
❑ 47 Barry Zito .75 .23
❑ 48 Matt Morris .30 .09
❑ 49 J.T. Snow .30 .09
❑ 50 Albert Pujols 1.50 .45
❑ 51 Brad Fullmer .30 .09
❑ 52 Damion Easley .30 .09
❑ 53 Pat Burrell .30 .09
❑ 54 Kevin Brown .30 .09
❑ 55 Todd Walker .30 .09
❑ 56 Rich Garces .30 .09
❑ 57 Carlos Pena .30 .09
❑ 58 Paul LoDuca .30 .09
❑ 59 Mike Lieberthal .30 .09
❑ 60 Barry Larkin .75 .23
❑ 61 Jon Lieber .30 .09
❑ 62 Jose Cruz Jr. .30 .09
❑ 63 Mo Vaughn .30 .09
❑ 64 Ivan Rodriguez .75 .23
❑ 65 Jorge Posada .50 .15
❑ 66 Magglio Ordonez .30 .09
❑ 67 Juan Encarnacion .30 .09
❑ 68 Shawn Estes .30 .09
❑ 69 Kevin Appier .30 .09
❑ 70 Jeff Bagwell .50 .15
❑ 71 Tim Wakefield .30 .09
❑ 72 Shannon Stewart .30 .09
❑ 73 Scott Rolen .50 .15
❑ 74 Bobby Higginson .30 .09
❑ 75 Jim Edmonds .30 .09
❑ 76 Adam Dunn .50 .15
❑ 77 Eric Chavez .30 .09
❑ 78 Adrian Beltre .30 .09
❑ 79 Jason Varitek .30 .09
❑ 80 Barry Bonds 2.00 .60
❑ 81 Edgar Renteria .30 .09
❑ 82 Raul Mondesi .30 .09
❑ 83 Eric Karros .30 .09
❑ 84 Ken Griffey Jr. 1.25 .35
❑ 85 Jermaine Dye .30 .09
❑ 86 Carlos Beltran .30 .09
❑ 87 Mark Quinn .30 .09
❑ 88 Terrence Long .30 .09
❑ 89 Shawn Green .30 .09
❑ 90 Nomar Garciaparra 1.50 .45
❑ 91 Sean Casey .30 .09
❑ 92 Homer Bush .30 .09

Card	Nm-Mt	Ex-Mt
❑ 93 Bob Abreu	.30	.09
❑ 94 Jamey Wright	.30	.09
❑ 95 Tony Womack	.30	.09
❑ 96 Larry Walker	.50	.15
❑ 97 Doug Mientkiewicz	.30	.09
❑ 98 Jimmy Rollins	.30	.09
❑ 99 Brady Anderson	.30	.09
❑ 100 Derek Jeter	2.00	.60
❑ 101 Kevin Young	.30	.09
❑ 102 Juan Pierre	.30	.09
❑ 103 Edgar Martinez	.50	.15
❑ 104 Corey Koskie	.30	.09
❑ 105 Jeffrey Hammonds	.30	.09
❑ 106 Luis Gonzalez	.30	.09
❑ 107 Travis Fryman	.30	.09
❑ 108 Kerry Wood	.75	.23
❑ 109 Rafael Palmeiro	.50	.15
❑ 110 Ichiro Suzuki	1.50	.45
❑ 111 Russ Ortiz	.30	.09
❑ 112 Jeff Kent	.30	.09
❑ 113 Scott Erickson	.30	.09
❑ 114 Bruce Chen	.30	.09
❑ 115 Craig Biggio	.50	.15
❑ 116 Robin Ventura	.30	.09
❑ 117 Alex Rodriguez	1.50	.45
❑ 118 Roy Oswalt	.30	.09
❑ 119 Fred McGriff	.50	.15
❑ 120 Juan Gonzalez	.75	.23
❑ 121 David Justice	.30	.09
❑ 122 Pat Hentgen	.30	.09
❑ 123 Hideo Nomo	.75	.23
❑ 124 Ramon Ortiz	.30	.09
❑ 125 David Ortiz	.30	.09
❑ 126 Phil Nevin	.30	.09
❑ 127 Ryan Dempster	.30	.09
❑ 128 Toby Hall	.30	.09
❑ 129 Vladimir Guerrero	.75	.23
❑ 130 Chipper Jones	.75	.23
❑ 131 Russell Branyan	.30	.09
❑ 132 Jose Vidro	.30	.09
❑ 133 Bubba Trammell	.30	.09
❑ 134 Tino Martinez	.50	.15
❑ 135 Greg Maddux	1.50	.45
❑ 136 Derrek Lee	.30	.09
❑ 137 Troy Glaus	.50	.15
❑ 138 Joe Crede	.30	.09
❑ 139 Steve Cox	.30	.09
❑ 140 Sammy Sosa	1.25	.35
❑ 141 Corey Patterson	.30	.09
❑ 142 Vernon Wells	.30	.09
❑ 143 Matt Lawton	.30	.09
❑ 144 Gabe Kapler	.30	.09
❑ 145 Johnny Damon	.30	.09
❑ 146 Marty Cordova	.30	.09
❑ 147 Moises Alou	.30	.09
❑ 148 Fernando Tatis	.30	.09
❑ 149 Tanyon Sturtze	.30	.09
❑ 150 Roger Clemens	1.50	.45
❑ 151 Paul Konerko	.30	.09
❑ 152 Chan Ho Park	.30	.09
❑ 153 Marcus Giles	.30	.09
❑ 154 David Eckstein	.30	.09
❑ 155 Mike Lowell	.30	.09
❑ 156 Preston Wilson	.30	.09
❑ 157 John Vander Wal	.30	.09
❑ 158 Tim Salmon	.50	.15
❑ 159 Andy Pettitte	.50	.15
❑ 160 Mike Mussina	.75	.23
❑ 161 Doug Davis	.30	.09
❑ 162 Peter Bergeron	.30	.09
❑ 163 Rich Aurilia	.30	.09
❑ 164 Eric Milton	.30	.09
❑ 165 Geoff Jenkins	.30	.09
❑ 166 Todd Helton	.50	.15
❑ 167 Bret Boone	.30	.09
❑ 168 Kris Benson	.30	.09
❑ 169 Brian Anderson	.30	.09
❑ 170 Roberto Alomar	.75	.23
❑ 171 Javier Vazquez	.30	.09
❑ 172 Scott Schoeneweis	.30	.09
❑ 173 Ryan Klesko	.30	.09
❑ 174 Jacque Jones	.30	.09
❑ 175 Andruw Jones	.50	.15
❑ 176 Aubrey Huff	.30	.09
❑ 177 Mark Buehrle	.30	.09
❑ 178 Josh Beckett	.50	.15
❑ 179 Ben Sheets	.30	.09
❑ 180 Curt Schilling	.50	.15
❑ 181 C.C. Sabathia	.30	.09
❑ 182 Denny Neagle	.30	.09
❑ 183 Jamie Moyer	.30	.09
❑ 184 Jason Kendall	.30	.09
❑ 185 Dee Brown	.30	.09
❑ 186 Frank Thomas	.75	.23
❑ 187 Damian Rolls	.30	.09
❑ 188 Carlos Lee	.30	.09
❑ 189 Kevin Jarvis	.30	.09
❑ 190 Manny Ramirez	.30	.09
❑ 191 Cliff Floyd	.30	.09
❑ 192 Freddy Garcia	.30	.09
❑ 193 Orlando Cabrera	.30	.09
❑ 194 Mike Sweeney	.30	.09
❑ 195 Gary Sheffield	.30	.09
❑ 196 Rafael Furcal	.30	.09
❑ 197 Esteban Loaiza	.30	.09
❑ 198 Mike Hampton	.30	.09
❑ 199 Brian Giles	.30	.09
❑ 200 Darin Erstad	.30	.09
❑ 201 David Wells	.30	.09
❑ 202 Kenny Lofton	.30	.09
❑ 203 Aaron Sele	.30	.09
❑ 204 Jason Schmidt	.30	.09
❑ 205 Javy Lopez	.30	.09
❑ 206 Dmitri Young	.30	.09
❑ 207 Darryl Kile	.30	.09
❑ 208 Matt Williams	.30	.09
❑ 209 Joe Kennedy	.30	.09
❑ 210 Chuck Knoblauch	.30	.09
❑ 211 Brian Jordan	.30	.09
❑ 212 Robert Person	.30	.09
❑ 213 Alex Ochoa	.30	.09
❑ 214 Steve Finley	.30	.09
❑ 215 Ben Petrick	.30	.09
❑ 216 Al Leiter	.30	.09
❑ 217 Mark Kotsay	.30	.09
❑ 218 Miguel Tejada	.30	.09
❑ 219 David Segui	.30	.09
❑ 220 A.J. Burnett	.30	.09
❑ 221 Marlon Anderson	.30	.09
❑ 222 Wiki Gonzalez	.30	.09
❑ 223 Jeff Suppan	.30	.09
❑ 224 Dave Roberts	.30	.09
❑ 225 Jose Hernandez	.30	.09
❑ 226 Angel Berroa ROO	2.00	.60
❑ 227 Sean Burroughs ROO	2.00	.60
❑ 228 Luis Martinez ROO RC	3.00	.90
❑ 229 Adrian Burnside ROO RC	2.00	.60
❑ 230 John Ennis ROO RC	2.00	.60
❑ 231 Anastacio Martinez ROO RC	2.00	.60
❑ 232 Hank Blalock ROO	3.00	.90
❑ 233 Eric Hinske ROO	2.00	.60
❑ 234 Chris Booker ROO RC	2.00	.60
❑ 235 Colin Young ROO RC	2.00	.60
❑ 236 Mark Corey ROO RC	2.00	.60
❑ 237 Satoru Komiyama ROO RC	2.00	.60
❑ 238 So Taguchi ROO RC	3.00	.90
❑ 239 Elio Serrano ROO RC	2.00	.60
❑ 240 Reed Johnson ROO RC	3.00	.90
❑ 241 Jeremy Lambert ROO RC	2.00	.60
❑ 242 Chris Baker ROO RC	2.00	.60
❑ 243 Orlando Hudson ROO	2.00	.60
❑ 244 Travis Hughes ROO RC	3.00	.90
❑ 245 Kevin Frederick ROO RC	2.00	.60
❑ 246 Rodrigo Rosario ROO RC	2.00	.60
❑ 247 Jeremy Ward ROO RC	2.00	.60
❑ 248 Kazuhisa Ishii ROO RC	5.00	1.50
❑ 249 Austin Kearns ROO	3.00	.90
❑ 250 Kyle Kane ROO RC	2.00	.60
❑ 251 Cam Esslinger ROO RC	2.00	.60
❑ 252 Jeff Austin ROO RC	2.00	.60
❑ 253 Brian Mallette ROO RC	2.00	.60
❑ 254 Mark Prior ROO	10.00	3.00
❑ 255 Mark Teixeira ROO	3.00	.90
❑ 256 Carlos Valderrama ROO	2.00	.60
❑ 257 Jason Hart ROO	2.00	.60
❑ 258 Takahito Nomura ROO RC	2.00	.60
❑ 259 Matt Thornton ROO RC	2.00	.60
❑ 260 Marlon Byrd ROO	2.00	.60

2003 Fleer Focus JE

	Nm-Mt	Ex-Mt
COMPLETE SET (180)	50.00	15.00
COMP.SET w/o SP's (160)	20.00	6.00
COMMON CARD (1-160)	.30	.09
COMMON CARD (161-180)	2.00	.60
❑ 1 Derek Jeter	2.00	.60
❑ 2 Preston Wilson	.30	.09
❑ 3 Trevor Hoffman	.30	.09
❑ 4 Moises Alou	.30	.09
❑ 5 Roberto Alomar	.75	.23
❑ 6 Tim Salmon	.50	.15
❑ 7 Mike Lowell	.30	.09
❑ 8 Barry Bonds	2.00	.60
❑ 9 Fred McGriff	.50	.15
❑ 10 Mo Vaughn	.30	.09
❑ 11 Junior Spivey	.30	.09
❑ 12 Roy Oswalt	.30	.09
❑ 13 Ichiro Suzuki	1.50	.45
❑ 14 Magglio Ordonez	.30	.09
❑ 15 Adam Kennedy	.30	.09
❑ 16 Randy Johnson	.75	.23
❑ 17 Carlos Beltran	.30	.09
❑ 18 John Olerud	.30	.09
❑ 19 Joe Borchard	.30	.09
❑ 20 Alfonso Soriano	.75	.23
❑ 21 Curt Schilling	.50	.15
❑ 22 Mike Sweeney	.30	.09
❑ 23 Tino Martinez	.50	.15
❑ 24 Barry Larkin	.75	.23
❑ 25 Miguel Tejada	.30	.09
❑ 26 Chipper Jones	.75	.23
❑ 27 Kevin Brown	.30	.09
❑ 28 J.D. Drew	.30	.09
❑ 29 Sean Casey	.30	.09
❑ 30 Bernie Williams	.50	.15
❑ 31 Troy Percival	.30	.09
❑ 32 Jeff Bagwell	.50	.15
❑ 33 Kenny Lofton	.30	.09
❑ 34 Kerry Wood	.75	.23
❑ 35 Armando Benitez	.30	.09
❑ 36 David Eckstein	.30	.09
❑ 37 Wade Miller	.30	.09
❑ 38 Edgar Martinez	.50	.15
❑ 39 Mark Prior	1.50	.45
❑ 40 Mike Piazza	1.25	.35
❑ 41 Shea Hillenbrand	.30	.09
❑ 42 Bartolo Colon	.30	.09
❑ 43 Darin Erstad	.30	.09
❑ 44 A.J. Burnett	.30	.09
❑ 45 Jeff Kent	.30	.09
❑ 46 Corey Patterson	.30	.09
❑ 47 Ty Wigginton	.30	.09
❑ 48 Troy Glaus	.50	.15
❑ 49 Josh Beckett	.50	.15
❑ 50 Brian Lawrence	.30	.09
❑ 51 Frank Thomas	.75	.23
❑ 52 Jason Giambi	.75	.23
❑ 53 Luis Gonzalez	.30	.09
❑ 54 Raul Ibanez	.30	.09
❑ 55 Kazuhiro Sasaki	.30	.09
❑ 56 Mark Buehrle	.30	.09
❑ 57 Roger Clemens	1.50	.45
❑ 58 Matt Williams	.30	.09
❑ 59 Joe Randa	.30	.09
❑ 60 Jamie Moyer	.30	.09

❏ 61 Paul Konerko .30 .09
❏ 62 Mike Mussina .75 .23
❏ 63 Javy Lopez .30 .09
❏ 64 Brian Jordan .30 .09
❏ 65 Scott Rolen .50 .15
❏ 66 Aaron Boone .30 .09
❏ 67 Eric Chavez .30 .09
❏ 68 Mark Grace .75 .23
❏ 69 Shawn Green .30 .09
❏ 70 Albert Pujols 1.50 .45
❏ 71 Sammy Sosa 1.25 .35
❏ 72 Edgardo Alfonzo .30 .09
❏ 73 Garret Anderson .30 .09
❏ 74 Lance Berkman .30 .09
❏ 75 Bret Boone .30 .09
❏ 76 Joe Crede .30 .09
❏ 77 Al Leiter .30 .09
❏ 78 Jarrod Washburn .30 .09
❏ 79 Craig Biggio .50 .15
❏ 80 Rich Aurilia .30 .09
❏ 81 Adam Dunn .50 .15
❏ 82 Jermaine Dye .30 .09
❏ 83 Tom Glavine .75 .23
❏ 84 Eric Gagne .50 .15
❏ 85 Jared Sandberg .30 .09
❏ 86 Jim Thome .75 .23
❏ 87 Barry Zito .75 .23
❏ 88 Gary Sheffield .30 .09
❏ 89 Paul Lo Duca .30 .09
❏ 90 Matt Morris .30 .09
❏ 91 Juan Pierre .30 .09
❏ 92 Randy Wolf .30 .09
❏ 93 Jay Gibbons .30 .09
❏ 94 Brad Radke .30 .09
❏ 95 Carlos Delgado .30 .09
❏ 96 Carlos Pena .30 .09
❏ 97 Brian Giles .30 .09
❏ 98 Rodrigo Lopez .30 .09
❏ 99 Jacque Jones .30 .09
❏ 100 Juan Gonzalez .75 .23
❏ 101 Randall Simon .30 .09
❏ 102 Mike Williams .30 .09
❏ 103 Derek Lowe .30 .09
❏ 104 Brad Wilkerson .30 .09
❏ 105 Eric Hinske .30 .09
❏ 106 Luis Castillo .30 .09
❏ 107 Phil Nevin .30 .09
❏ 108 Manny Ramirez .30 .09
❏ 109 Vladimir Guerrero .75 .23
❏ 110 Roy Halladay .30 .09
❏ 111 Ellis Burks .30 .09
❏ 112 Bobby Abreu .30 .09
❏ 113 Tony Batista .30 .09
❏ 114 Richie Sexson .30 .09
❏ 115 Rafael Palmeiro .50 .15
❏ 116 Todd Helton .50 .15
❏ 117 Pat Burrell .30 .09
❏ 118 John Smoltz .50 .15
❏ 119 Ben Sheets .30 .09
❏ 120 Aubrey Huff .30 .09
❏ 121 Andruw Jones .50 .15
❏ 122 Kazuhisa Ishii .30 .09
❏ 123 Jim Edmonds .30 .09
❏ 124 Austin Kearns .50 .15
❏ 125 Mark Mulder .30 .09
❏ 126 Greg Maddux 1.50 .45
❏ 127 Jose Hernandez .30 .09
❏ 128 Ben Grieve .30 .09
❏ 129 Ken Griffey Jr. 1.25 .35
❏ 130 Tim Hudson .30 .09
❏ 131 Jorge Julio .30 .09
❏ 132 Torii Hunter .30 .09
❏ 133 Ivan Rodriguez .75 .23
❏ 134 Jason Jennings .30 .09
❏ 135 Jason Kendall .30 .09
❏ 136 Nomar Garciaparra 1.50 .45
❏ 137 Michael Cuddyer .30 .09
❏ 138 Shannon Stewart .30 .09
❏ 139 Larry Walker .50 .15
❏ 140 Aramis Ramirez .30 .09
❏ 141 Johnny Damon .30 .09
❏ 142 Orlando Cabrera .30 .09
❏ 143 Vernon Wells .30 .09
❏ 144 Bobby Higginson .30 .09
❏ 145 Sean Burroughs .30 .09
❏ 146 Pedro Martinez .75 .23
❏ 147 Jose Vidro .30 .09
❏ 148 Orlando Hudson .30 .09
❏ 149 Robert Fick .30 .09
❏ 150 Ryan Klesko .30 .09
❏ 151 Kevin Millwood .30 .09
❏ 152 Alex Sanchez .30 .09
❏ 153 Randy Winn .30 .09
❏ 154 Omar Vizquel .30 .09
❏ 155 Mike Lieberthal .30 .09
❏ 156 Marty Cordova .30 .09
❏ 157 Cristian Guzman .30 .09
❏ 158 Alex Rodriguez 1.50 .45
❏ 159 C.C. Sabathia .30 .09
❏ 160 Jimmy Rollins .30 .09
❏ 161 Josh Willingham HP RC 4.00 1.20
❏ 162 Lance Niekro HP 2.00 .60
❏ 163 Nook Logan HP RC 2.00 .60
❏ 164 Chase Utley HP 2.00 .60
❏ 165 Pete LaForest HP RC 3.00 .90
❏ 166 Victor Martinez HP 2.00 .60
❏ 167 Adam LaRoche HP 2.00 .60
❏ 168 Ian Ferguson HP RC 2.00 .60
❏ 169 Mark Teixeira HP 3.00 .90
❏ 170 Chris Waters HP RC 2.00 .60
❏ 171 Hideki Matsui HP RC 8.00 2.40
❏ 172 Alejandro Machado HP RC 2.00 .60
❏ 173 Francisco Rosario HP RC 2.00 .60
❏ 174 Termel Sledge HP RC 3.00 .90
❏ 175 Guillermo Quiroz HP RC 3.00 .90
❏ 176 Lew Ford HP RC 3.00 .90
❏ 177 Hank Blalock HP 3.00 .90
❏ 178 Lyle Overbay HP 2.00 .60
❏ 179 Matt Bruback HP RC 2.00 .60
❏ 180 Jose Contreras HP RC 4.00 1.20

2001 Fleer Futures

	Nm-Mt	Ex-Mt
COMPLETE SET (220)	25.00	7.50
COMMON CARD (1-220)	.30	.09
COMMON (221-230)	5.00	1.50

❏ 1 Darin Erstad .30 .09
❏ 2 Manny Ramirez .30 .09
❏ 3 Darryl Kile .30 .09
❏ 4 Troy O'Leary .30 .09
❏ 5 Mark Quinn .30 .09
❏ 6 Brian Giles .30 .09
❏ 7 Randy Johnson .75 .23
❏ 8 Todd Walker .30 .09
❏ 9 Mike Piazza 1.25 .35
❏ 10 Fred McGriff .50 .15
❏ 11 Sammy Sosa 1.25 .35
❏ 12 Chan Ho Park .30 .09
❏ 13 John Rocker .30 .09
❏ 14 Luis Castillo .30 .09
❏ 15 Eric Chavez .30 .09
❏ 16 Carlos Delgado .30 .09
❏ 17 Sean Casey .30 .09
❏ 18 Corey Koskie .30 .09
❏ 19 John Olerud .30 .09
❏ 20 Nomar Garciaparra 1.50 .45
❏ 21 Craig Biggio .50 .15
❏ 22 Pat Burrell .30 .09
❏ 23 Ben Molina .30 .09
❏ 24 Jim Thome .75 .23
❏ 25 Rey Ordonez .30 .09
❏ 26 Fernando Tatis .30 .09
❏ 27 Eric Young .30 .09
❏ 28 Eric Karros .30 .09
❏ 29 Adam Eaton .30 .09
❏ 30 Brian Jordan .30 .09
❏ 31 Jorge Posada .50 .15
❏ 32 Gabe Kapler .30 .09
❏ 33 Keith Foulke .30 .09
❏ 34 Ron Coomer .30 .09
❏ 35 Chipper Jones .75 .23
❏ 36 Miguel Tejada .30 .09
❏ 37 David Wells .30 .09
❏ 38 Carlos Lee .30 .09
❏ 39 Barry Bonds 2.00 .60
❏ 40 Derrek Lee .30 .09
❏ 41 Tim Hudson .30 .09
❏ 42 Billy Koch .30 .09
❏ 43 Dmitri Young .30 .09
❏ 44 Vladimir Guerrero .75 .23
❏ 45 Rickey Henderson 1.25 .35
❏ 46 Jeff Bagwell .50 .15
❏ 47 Robert Person .30 .09
❏ 48 Brady Anderson .30 .09
❏ 49 Lance Berkman .30 .09
❏ 50 Mike Lieberthal .30 .09
❏ 51 Adam Kennedy .30 .09
❏ 52 Russell Branyan .30 .09
❏ 53 Robin Ventura .30 .09
❏ 54 Mark McGwire 2.00 .60
❏ 55 Tony Gwynn 1.00 .30
❏ 56 Matt Williams .30 .09
❏ 57 Jeff Cirillo .30 .09
❏ 58 Roger Clemens 1.50 .45
❏ 59 Ivan Rodriguez .75 .23
❏ 60 Brad Radke .30 .09
❏ 61 Kazuhiro Sasaki .30 .09
❏ 62 Cal Ripken 2.50 .75
❏ 63 Ken Caminiti .30 .09
❏ 64 Bob Abreu .30 .09
❏ 65 Troy Glaus .50 .15
❏ 66 Sandy Alomar Jr. .30 .09
❏ 67 Jose Vidro .30 .09
❏ 68 Pedro Martinez .75 .23
❏ 69 Kevin Young .30 .09
❏ 70 Jay Bell .30 .09
❏ 71 Larry Walker .50 .15
❏ 72 Derek Jeter 2.00 .60
❏ 73 Miguel Cairo .30 .09
❏ 74 Magglio Ordonez .30 .09
❏ 75 Jeromy Burnitz .30 .09
❏ 76 J.T. Snow .30 .09
❏ 77 Andres Galarraga .30 .09
❏ 78 Ryan Dempster .30 .09
❏ 79 Ken Griffey Jr. 1.25 .35
❏ 80 Aaron Sele .30 .09
❏ 81 Tom Glavine .75 .23
❏ 82 Hideo Nomo .75 .23
❏ 83 Orlando Hernandez .30 .09
❏ 84 Tony Batista .30 .09
❏ 85 Aaron Boone .30 .09
❏ 86 Jacque Jones .30 .09
❏ 87 Delino DeShields .30 .09
❏ 88 Garret Anderson .30 .09
❏ 89 Fernando Seguignol .30 .09
❏ 90 Jim Edmonds .30 .09
❏ 91 Frank Thomas .75 .23
❏ 92 Adrian Beltre .30 .09
❏ 93 Ellis Burks .30 .09
❏ 94 Andruw Jones .50 .15
❏ 95 Tony Clark .30 .09
❏ 96 Danny Graves .30 .09
❏ 97 Alex Rodriguez 1.50 .45
❏ 98 Mike Mussina .75 .23
❏ 99 Scott Elarton .30 .09
❏ 100 Jason Giambi .75 .23
❏ 101 Jay Payton .30 .09
❏ 102 Gerald Williams .30 .09
❏ 103 Kerry Wood .75 .23
❏ 104 Shawn Green .30 .09
❏ 105 Greg Maddux 1.50 .45
❏ 106 Juan Encarnacion .30 .09
❏ 107 Bernie Williams .50 .15
❏ 108 Mike Lamb .30 .09
❏ 109 Charles Johnson .30 .09
❏ 110 Richie Sexson .30 .09
❏ 111 Jeff Kent .30 .09
❏ 112 Albert Belle .30 .09

❑ 113 Cliff Floyd .30 .09
❑ 114 Ben Grieve .30 .09
❑ 115 Tim Salmon .50 .15
❑ 116 Carl Pavano .30 .09
❑ 117 Rick Ankiel .30 .09
❑ 118 Dante Bichette .30 .09
❑ 119 Johnny Damon .30 .09
❑ 120 Brian Anderson .30 .09
❑ 121 Roberto Alomar .75 .23
❑ 122 Mike Hampton .30 .09
❑ 123 Greg Vaughn .30 .09
❑ 124 Carl Everett .30 .09
❑ 125 Moises Alou .30 .09
❑ 126 Jason Kendall .30 .09
❑ 127 Omar Vizquel .30 .09
❑ 128 Mark Grace .75 .23
❑ 129 Kevin Brown .30 .09
❑ 130 Phil Nevin .30 .09
❑ 131 Kevin Millwood .30 .09
❑ 132 Bobby Higginson .30 .09
❑ 133 Ruben Mateo .30 .09
❑ 134 Luis Gonzalez .30 .09
❑ 135 Dean Palmer .30 .09
❑ 136 Mariano Rivera .50 .15
❑ 137 Rick Helling .30 .09
❑ 138 Paul Konerko .30 .09
❑ 139 Marquis Grissom .30 .09
❑ 140 Robb Nen .30 .09
❑ 141 Javy Lopez .30 .09
❑ 142 Preston Wilson .30 .09
❑ 143 Terrence Long .30 .09
❑ 144 Shannon Stewart .30 .09
❑ 145 Barry Larkin .75 .23
❑ 146 Cristian Guzman .30 .09
❑ 147 Jay Buhner .30 .09
❑ 148 Jermaine Dye .30 .09
❑ 149 Kris Benson .30 .09
❑ 150 Curt Schilling .50 .15
❑ 151 Todd Helton .50 .15
❑ 152 Paul O'Neill .50 .15
❑ 153 Rafael Palmeiro .50 .15
❑ 154 Ray Durham .30 .09
❑ 155 Geoff Jenkins .30 .09
❑ 156 Livan Hernandez .30 .09
❑ 157 Rafael Furcal .30 .09
❑ 158 Juan Gonzalez .75 .23
❑ 159 Tino Martinez .50 .15
❑ 160 Raul Mondesi .30 .09
❑ 161 Matt Lawton .30 .09
❑ 162 Edgar Martinez .50 .15
❑ 163 Richard Hidalgo .30 .09
❑ 164 Scott Rolen .50 .15
❑ 165 Chuck Finley .30 .09
❑ 166 Edgardo Alfonzo .30 .09
❑ 167 J.D. Drew .30 .09
❑ 168 Trot Nixon .30 .09
❑ 169 Carlos Beltran .30 .09
❑ 170 Ryan Klesko .30 .09
❑ 171 Mo Vaughn .30 .09
❑ 172 Kenny Lofton .30 .09
❑ 173 Al Leiter .30 .09
❑ 174 Rondell White .30 .09
❑ 175 Mike Sweeney .30 .09
❑ 176 Trevor Hoffman .30 .09
❑ 177 Steve Finley .30 .09
❑ 178 Jeffrey Hammonds .30 .09
❑ 179 David Justice .30 .09
❑ 180 Gary Sheffield .30 .09
❑ 181 Eric Munson BF .30 .09
❑ 182 Luis Matos BF .30 .09
❑ 183 Alex Cabrera BF .30 .09
❑ 184 Randy Keisler BF .30 .09
❑ 185 Nate Rolison BF .30 .09
❑ 186 Jason Hart BF .30 .09
❑ 187 Timo Perez BF .30 .09
❑ 188 Adam Bernero BF .30 .09
❑ 189 Barry Zito BF .75 .23
❑ 190 Ryan Kohlmeier BF .30 .09
❑ 191 Joey Nation BF .30 .09
❑ 192 Oswaldo Mairena BF .30 .09
❑ 193 Aubrey Huff BF .30 .09
❑ 194 Mark Buehrle BF .30 .09
❑ 195 Jace Brewer BF .30 .09
❑ 196 Julio Zuleta BF .30 .09
❑ 197 Xavier Nady BF .30 .09
❑ 198 Vernon Wells BF .30 .09
❑ 199 Joe Crede BF .30 .09
❑ 200 Scott Downs BF .30 .09
❑ 201 Ben Petrick BF .30 .09
❑ 202 A.J. Burnett BF .30 .09
❑ 203 Esix Snead BF RC .30 .09
❑ 204 Dernell Stenson BF .30 .09
❑ 205 Jose Ortiz BF .30 .09
❑ 206 Paxton Crawford BF .30 .09
❑ 207 Jason Tyner BF .30 .09
❑ 208 Jimmy Rollins BF .30 .09
❑ 209 Juan Pierre BF .30 .09
❑ 210 Keith Ginter BF .30 .09
❑ 211 Adam Dunn BF .50 .15
❑ 212 Larry Barnes BF .30 .09
❑ 213 Adam Piatt BF .30 .09
❑ 214 Rodney Lindsey BF .30 .09
❑ 215 Eric Byrnes BF .30 .09
❑ 216 Julio Lugo BF .30 .09
❑ 217 Corey Patterson BF .30 .09
❑ 218 Reggie Taylor BF .30 .09
❑ 219 Kenny Kelly BF .30 .09
❑ 220 Tike Redman BF .30 .09
❑ 221 D.Henson/2499 RC 6.00 1.80
❑ 222 J.Estrada/2499 RC 5.00 1.50
❑ 223 E.Guzman/2499 RC 5.00 1.50
❑ 224 Albert Pujols/2499 RC 30.00 9.00
❑ 225 W.Betemit/2499 RC 5.00 1.50
❑ 226 M.Teixeira/2499 RC 15.00 4.50
❑ 227 T.Shinjo/2499 RC 6.00 1.80
❑ 228 Matt White/2499 RC 5.00 1.50
❑ 229 A.Hernandez/2499 RC 5.00 1.50
❑ 230 I.Suzuki/2499 RC 25.00 7.50

2001 Fleer Game Time

	Nm-Mt	Ex-Mt
COMP.SET w/o SP's (90)	25.00	7.50
COMMON CARD (1-90)	.40	.12
COMMON NG (91-121)	4.00	1.20

❑ 1 Derek Jeter 2.50 .75
❑ 2 Nomar Garciaparra 2.00 .60
❑ 3 Alex Rodriguez 2.00 .60
❑ 4 Jason Kendall .40 .12
❑ 5 Barry Bonds 2.50 .75
❑ 6 David Wells .40 .12
❑ 7 Craig Biggio .60 .18
❑ 8 Adrian Beltre .40 .12
❑ 9 Pat Burrell .40 .12
❑ 10 Rafael Palmeiro .60 .18
❑ 11 Jim Thome 1.00 .30
❑ 12 Mike Lowell .40 .12
❑ 13 Trevor Hoffman .40 .12
❑ 14 Pokey Reese .40 .12
❑ 15 Juan Encarnacion .40 .12
❑ 16 Shawn Green .40 .12
❑ 17 Kerry Wood 1.00 .30
❑ 18 Richard Hidalgo .40 .12
❑ 19 Scott Rolen .60 .18
❑ 20 Jeff Kent .40 .12
❑ 21 Alex Gonzalez .40 .12
❑ 22 Matt Williams .40 .12
❑ 23 Mike Sweeney .40 .12
❑ 24 Edgar Martinez .60 .18
❑ 25 Sammy Sosa 1.50 .45
❑ 26 Bobby Higginson .40 .12
❑ 27 Kevin Brown .40 .12
❑ 28 Mike Lieberthal .40 .12
❑ 29 Pedro Martinez 1.00 .30
❑ 30 Jeff Weaver .40 .12
❑ 31 Greg Maddux 2.00 .60
❑ 32 Mike Hampton .40 .12
❑ 33 Vladimir Guerrero 1.00 .30
❑ 34 Greg Vaughn .40 .12
❑ 35 Manny Ramirez .40 .12
❑ 36 Carlos Beltran .40 .12
❑ 37 Eric Chavez .40 .12
❑ 38 Troy Glaus .60 .18
❑ 39 Todd Helton .60 .18
❑ 40 Gary Sheffield .40 .12
❑ 41 Brady Anderson .40 .12
❑ 42 Juan Gonzalez 1.00 .30
❑ 43 Tim Hudson .40 .12
❑ 44 Kenny Lofton .40 .12
❑ 45 Al Leiter .40 .12
❑ 46 Eric Owens .40 .12
❑ 47 Roberto Alomar 1.00 .30
❑ 48 Preston Wilson .40 .12
❑ 49 Tony Gwynn 1.25 .35
❑ 50 Cal Ripken 3.00 .90
❑ 51 Ben Petrick .40 .12
❑ 52 Jason Giambi 1.00 .30
❑ 53 Ben Grieve .40 .12
❑ 54 Albert Belle .40 .12
❑ 55 Jose Vidro .40 .12
❑ 56 Barry Zito 1.00 .30
❑ 57 Ivan Rodriguez 1.00 .30
❑ 58 Jeff Bagwell .60 .18
❑ 59 Geoff Jenkins .40 .12
❑ 60 Roger Clemens 2.00 .60
❑ 61 John Olerud .40 .12
❑ 62 Randy Johnson 1.00 .30
❑ 63 Matt Lawton .40 .12
❑ 64 Mark McGwire 2.50 .75
❑ 65 Brad Radke .40 .12
❑ 66 Frank Thomas 1.00 .30
❑ 67 Edgardo Alfonzo .40 .12
❑ 68 Brian Giles .40 .12
❑ 69 J.T. Snow .40 .12
❑ 70 Carlos Delgado .40 .12
❑ 71 Chipper Jones 1.00 .30
❑ 72 Mark Quinn .40 .12
❑ 73 Mike Mussina 1.00 .30
❑ 74 Rick Ankiel .40 .12
❑ 75 Rafael Furcal .40 .12
❑ 76 Jim Edmonds .40 .12
❑ 77 Vinny Castilla .40 .12
❑ 78 Sean Casey .40 .12
❑ 79 Derrek Lee .40 .12
❑ 80 Mike Piazza 1.50 .45
❑ 81 Warren Morris .40 .12
❑ 82 Tim Salmon .60 .18
❑ 83 Jeromy Burnitz .40 .12
❑ 84 Freddy Garcia .40 .12
❑ 85 Ken Griffey Jr. 1.50 .45
❑ 86 Andruw Jones .60 .18
❑ 87 Darryl Kile .40 .12
❑ 88 Magglio Ordonez .40 .12
❑ 89 Bernie Williams .60 .18
❑ 90 Timo Perez .40 .12
❑ 91 Ichiro Suzuki NG RC 30.00 9.00
❑ 92 Larry Barnes 4.00 1.20
Darin Erstad
❑ 93 J. Randolph NG RC 4.00 1.20
❑ 94 Paul Phillips NG RC 4.00 1.20
❑ 95 Esix Snead NG RC 4.00 1.20
❑ 96 Matt White NG RC 4.00 1.20
❑ 97 Ryan Freel NG RC 4.00 1.20
❑ 98 Winston Abreu NG RC 4.00 1.20
❑ 99 Junior Spivey NG RC 5.00 1.50
❑ 100 Randy Keisler 8.00 2.40
Roger Clemens
❑ 101 Mike Piazza 6.00 1.80
Brian Cole
❑ 102 Aubrey Huff 5.00 1.50
Chipper Jones
❑ 103 Corey Patterson 5.00 1.50
Sammy Sosa
❑ 104 Sun Woo Kim 5.00 1.50
Pedro Martinez
❑ 105 Drew Henson NG RC 6.00 1.80
❑ 106 C. Vargas NG RC 4.00 1.20
❑ 107 Rafael Furcal 4.00 1.20
Cesar Izturis

❑ 108	Paxton Crawford	5.00	1.50
	Pedro Martinez		
❑ 109	A. Hernandez NG RC	4.00	1.20
❑ 110	Jace Brewer	10.00	3.00
	Derek Jeter		
❑ 111	Andy Morales NG RC	4.00	1.20
❑ 112	W. Betemit NG RC	4.00	1.20
❑ 113	Juan Diaz NG RC	4.00	1.20
❑ 114	Erick Almonte NG RC	4.00	1.20
❑ 115	Nick Punto NG RC	4.00	1.20
❑ 116	T. Shinjo NG RC	6.00	1.80
❑ 117	Jay Gibbons NG RC	6.00	1.80
❑ 118	Andres Torres NG RC	4.00	1.20
❑ 119	Alexis Gomez NG RC	4.00	1.20
❑ 120	Wilkin Ruan NG RC	4.00	1.20
❑ 121	Albert Pujols NG RC	40.00	12.00
❑ MM2	Derek Jeter/1996	12.00	3.60
❑ MM2	Derek Jeter AU/96	120.00	36.00

2001 Fleer Genuine

	Nm-Mt	Ex-Mt
COMP.SET w/o SP's (90)	25.00	7.50
COMMON CARD (1-100)	.50	.15
COMMON (101-130)	5.00	1.50

❑ 1	Derek Jeter	3.00	.90
❑ 2	Nomar Garciaparra	2.50	.75
❑ 3	Alex Rodriguez	2.50	.75
❑ 4	Frank Thomas	1.25	.35
❑ 5	Travis Fryman	.50	.15
❑ 6	Gary Sheffield	.50	.15
❑ 7	Jason Giambi	1.25	.35
❑ 8	Trevor Hoffman	.50	.15
❑ 9	Todd Helton	.75	.23
❑ 10	Ivan Rodriguez	1.25	.35
❑ 11	Roberto Alomar	1.25	.35
❑ 12	Barrry Zito	1.25	.35
❑ 13	Kevin Brown	.50	.15
❑ 14	Shawn Green	.50	.15
❑ 15	Kenny Lofton	.50	.15
❑ 16	Jeff Weaver	.50	.15
❑ 17	Geoff Jenkins	.50	.15
❑ 18	Carlos Delgado	.50	.15
❑ 19	Mark Grace	1.25	.35
❑ 20	Ken Griffey Jr.	2.00	.60
❑ 21	David Justice	.50	.15
❑ 22	Brian Giles	.50	.15
❑ 23	Scott Williamson	.50	.15
❑ 24	Richie Sexson	.50	.15
❑ 25	John Olerud	.50	.15
❑ 26	Sammy Sosa	2.00	.60
❑ 27	Bobby Higginson	.50	.15
❑ 28	Matt Lawton	.50	.15
❑ 29	Vinny Castilla	.50	.15
❑ 30	Alex Gonzalez	.50	.15
❑ 31	Manny Ramirez	.50	.15
❑ 32	Brad Radke	.50	.15
❑ 33	Cal Ripken	4.00	1.20
❑ 34	Richard Hidalgo	.50	.15
❑ 35	Al Leiter	.50	.15
❑ 36	Freddy Garcia	.50	.15
❑ 37	Juan Encarnacion	.50	.15
❑ 38	Corey Koskie	.50	.15
❑ 39	Greg Vaughn	.50	.15
❑ 40	Rafael Palmeiro	.75	.23
❑ 41	Vladimir Guerrero	1.25	.35
❑ 42	Troy Glaus	.75	.23
❑ 43	Mike Hampton	.50	.15
❑ 44	Jose Vidro	.50	.15
❑ 45	Ryan Rupe	.50	.15
❑ 46	Troy O'Leary	.50	.15
❑ 47	Ben Petrick	.50	.15
❑ 48	Mike Lieberthal	.50	.15
❑ 49	Mike Sweeney	.50	.15
❑ 50	Scott Rolen	.75	.23
❑ 51	Albert Belle	.75	.23
❑ 52	Mark Quinn	.50	.15
❑ 53	Mike Piazza	2.00	.60
❑ 54	Mark McGwire	3.00	.90
❑ 55	Brady Anderson	.50	.15
❑ 56	Carlos Beltran	.50	.15
❑ 57	Michael Barrett	.50	.15
❑ 58	Jason Kendall	.50	.15
❑ 59	Jim Edmonds	.50	.15
❑ 60	Matt Williams	.50	.15
❑ 61	Pokey Reese	.50	.15
❑ 62	Bernie Williams	.75	.23
❑ 63	Barry Bonds	3.00	.90
❑ 64	David Wells	.50	.15
❑ 65	Chipper Jones	1.25	.35
❑ 66	Jim Parque	.50	.15
❑ 67	Derrek Lee	.50	.15
❑ 68	Darin Erstad	.50	.15
❑ 69	Edgar Martinez	.75	.23
❑ 70	Kerry Wood	1.25	.35
❑ 71	Omar Vizquel	.50	.15
❑ 72	Jeromy Burnitz	.50	.15
❑ 73	Warren Morris	.50	.15
❑ 74	Rick Ankiel	.50	.15
❑ 75	Andruw Jones	.75	.23
❑ 76	Paul Konerko	.50	.15
❑ 77	Mike Lowell	.50	.15
❑ 78	Roger Clemens	2.50	.75
❑ 79	Tim Hudson	.50	.15
❑ 80	Rafael Furcal	.50	.15
❑ 81	Craig Biggio	.75	.23
❑ 82	Edgardo Alfonzo	.50	.15
❑ 83	Pat Burrell	.50	.15
❑ 84	Adrian Beltre	.50	.15
❑ 85	Tony Gwynn	1.50	.45
❑ 86	J.T. Snow	.50	.15
❑ 87	Randy Johnson	1.25	.35
❑ 88	Sean Casey	.50	.15
❑ 89	Preston Wilson	.50	.15
❑ 90	Mike Mussina	1.25	.35
❑ 91	Eric Chavez	.50	.15
❑ 92	Tim Salmon	.75	.23
❑ 93	Pedro Martinez	1.25	.35
❑ 94	Darryl Kile	.50	.15
❑ 95	Greg Maddux	2.50	.75
❑ 96	Magglio Ordonez	.50	.15
❑ 97	Jeff Bagwell	.75	.23
❑ 98	Timo Perez	.50	.15
❑ 99	Jeff Kent	.50	.15
❑ 100	Eric Owens	.50	.15
❑ 101	Ichiro Suzuki GU RC	40.00	12.00
❑ 102	E. Guzman GU RC	5.00	1.50
❑ 103	T. Shinjo GU RC	8.00	2.40
❑ 104	Travis Hafner GU RC	6.00	1.80
❑ 105	Larry Barnes GU	5.00	1.50
❑ 106	J. Randolph GU RC	5.00	1.50
❑ 107	Paul Phillips GU RC	5.00	1.50
❑ 108	Erick Almonte GU RC	5.00	1.50
❑ 109	Nick Punto GU RC	5.00	1.50
❑ 110	Jack Wilson GU RC	5.00	1.50
❑ 111	Jeremy Owens GU RC	5.00	1.50
❑ 112	Esix Snead GU RC	5.00	1.50
❑ 113	Jay Gibbons GU RC	8.00	2.40
❑ 114	A. Hernandez GU RC	5.00	1.50
❑ 115	Matt White GU RC	5.00	1.50
❑ 116	Ryan Freel GU RC	5.00	1.50
❑ 117	Martin Vargas GU RC	5.00	1.50
❑ 118	Winston Abreu GU RC	5.00	1.50
❑ 119	Junior Spivey GU RC	6.00	1.80
❑ 120	Paxton Crawford GU	5.00	1.50
❑ 121	Randy Keisler GU	5.00	1.50
❑ 122	Juan Diaz GU RC	5.00	1.50
❑ 123	Aaron Rowand GU	5.00	1.50
❑ 124	Toby Hall GU	5.00	1.50
❑ 125	Brian Cole GU	5.00	1.50
❑ 126	Aubrey Huff GU	5.00	1.50
❑ 127	Corey Patterson GU	5.00	1.50
❑ 128	Sun Woo Kim GU	5.00	1.50
❑ 129	Jace Brewer GU	5.00	1.50
❑ 130	Cesar Izturis GU	5.00	1.50
❑ NNO	Derek Jeter	120.00	36.00
	AU Sheet/500 EXCH		

2002 Fleer Genuine

	Nm-Mt	Ex-Mt
COMP.SET w/o SP's (100)	25.00	7.50
COMMON CARD (1-100)	.50	.15
COMMON CARD (101-140)	5.00	1.50

❑ 1	Alex Rodriguez	2.50	.75
❑ 2	Manny Ramirez	.50	.15
❑ 3	Jim Thome	1.25	.35
❑ 4	Eric Milton	.50	.15
❑ 5	Todd Helton	.75	.23
❑ 6	Mike Mussina	1.25	.35
❑ 7	Ichiro Suzuki	2.50	.75
❑ 8	Randy Johnson	1.25	.35
❑ 9	Mark Mulder	.50	.15
❑ 10	Johnny Damon	.50	.15
❑ 11	Sean Casey	.50	.15
❑ 12	Albert Pujols	2.50	.75
❑ 13	Mark Grace	1.25	.35
❑ 14	Moises Alou	.50	.15
❑ 15	Raul Mondesi	.50	.15
❑ 16	Cliff Floyd	.50	.15
❑ 17	Vladimir Guerrero	1.25	.35
❑ 18	Pat Burrell	.50	.15
❑ 19	Ryan Klesko	.50	.15
❑ 20	Mike Hampton	.50	.15
❑ 21	Shawn Green	.50	.15
❑ 22	Rich Aurilia	.50	.15
❑ 23	Matt Morris	.50	.15
❑ 24	Curt Schilling	.75	.23
❑ 25	Kevin Brown	.50	.15
❑ 26	Adrian Beltre	.50	.15
❑ 27	Joe Mays	.50	.15
❑ 28	Luis Gonzalez	.50	.15
❑ 29	Barry Larkin	1.25	.35
❑ 30	A.J. Burnett	.50	.15
❑ 31	Eric Munson	.50	.15
❑ 32	Juan Gonzalez	1.25	.35
❑ 33	Lance Berkman	.50	.15
❑ 34	Fred McGriff	.75	.23
❑ 35	Paul Konerko	.50	.15
❑ 36	Pedro Martinez	1.25	.35
❑ 37	Adam Dunn	.75	.23
❑ 38	Jeromy Burnitz	.50	.15
❑ 39	Mike Sweeney	.50	.15
❑ 40	Bret Boone	.50	.15
❑ 41	Ken Griffey Jr.	2.00	.60
❑ 42	Eric Chavez	.50	.15
❑ 43	Mark Quinn	.50	.15
❑ 44	Roberto Alomar	1.25	.35
❑ 45	Bobby Abreu	.50	.15
❑ 46	Bartolo Colon	.50	.15
❑ 47	Jimmy Rollins	.50	.15
❑ 48	Chipper Jones	1.25	.35
❑ 49	Ben Sheets	.50	.15
❑ 50	Freddy Garcia	.50	.15
❑ 51	Sammy Sosa	2.00	.60
❑ 52	Rafael Palmeiro	.75	.23
❑ 53	Preston Wilson	.50	.15
❑ 54	Troy Glaus	.75	.23
❑ 55	Josh Beckett	.75	.23
❑ 56	C.C. Sabathia	.50	.15

			MINT	NRMT
❑	57	Magglio Ordonez	.50	.15
❑	58	Brian Giles	.50	.15
❑	59	Darin Erstad	.50	.15
❑	60	Gary Sheffield	.50	.15
❑	61	Paul LoDuca	.50	.15
❑	62	Derek Jeter	3.00	.90
❑	63	Greg Maddux	2.50	.75
❑	64	Kerry Wood	1.25	.35
❑	65	Toby Hall	.50	.15
❑	66	Barry Bonds	3.00	.90
❑	67	Jeff Bagwell	.75	.23
❑	68	Jason Kendall	.50	.15
❑	69	Richard Hidalgo	.50	.15
❑	70	J.D. Drew	.50	.15
❑	71	Tom Glavine	1.25	.35
❑	72	Javier Vazquez	.50	.15
❑	73	Doug Mientkiewicz	.50	.15
❑	74	Jason Giambi	1.25	.35
❑	75	Carlos Delgado	.50	.15
❑	76	Aramis Ramirez	.50	.15
❑	77	Torii Hunter	.50	.15
❑	78	Ivan Rodriguez	1.25	.35
❑	79	Charles Johnson	.50	.15
❑	80	Jeff Kent	.50	.15
❑	81	Jacque Jones	.50	.15
❑	82	Larry Walker	.75	.23
❑	83	Cristian Guzman	.50	.15
❑	84	Jermaine Dye	.50	.15
❑	85	Roger Clemens	2.50	.75
❑	86	Mike Piazza	2.00	.60
❑	87	Craig Biggio	.75	.23
❑	88	Phil Nevin	.50	.15
❑	89	Jeff Cirillo	.50	.15
❑	90	Barry Zito	1.25	.35
❑	91	Ryan Dempster	.50	.15
❑	92	Mark Buehrle	.50	.15
❑	93	Nomar Garciaparra	2.50	.75
❑	94	Frank Thomas	1.25	.35
❑	95	Jim Edmonds	.50	.15
❑	96	Geoff Jenkins	.50	.15
❑	97	Scott Rolen	.75	.23
❑	98	Tim Hudson	.50	.15
❑	99	Shannon Stewart	.50	.15
❑	100	Richie Sexson	.50	.15
❑	101	Orlando Hudson UP	5.00	1.50
❑	102	Doug Devore UP RC	5.00	1.50
❑	103	Rene Reyes UP RC	5.00	1.50
❑	104	Steve Bechler UP RC	5.00	1.50
❑	105	Jorge Nunez UP RC	5.00	1.50
❑	106	Mitch Wylie UP RC	5.00	1.50
❑	107	Jaime Cerda UP RC	5.00	1.50
❑	108	Brandon Puffer UP RC	5.00	1.50
❑	109	Tyler Yates UP RC	5.00	1.50
❑	110	Bill Hall UP	5.00	1.50
❑	111	Pete Zamora UP RC	5.00	1.50
❑	112	Jeff Deardorff UP	5.00	1.50
❑	113	J.J. Putz UP RC	5.00	1.50
❑	114	Scotty Layfield UP RC	5.00	1.50
❑	115	Brandon Backe UP RC	5.00	1.50
❑	116	Andy Pratt UP RC	5.00	1.50
❑	117	Mark Prior UP	15.00	4.50
❑	118	Franklyn German UP RC	5.00	1.50
❑	119	Todd Donovan UP RC	5.00	1.50
❑	120	Franklin Nunez UP RC	5.00	1.50
❑	121	Adam Walker UP RC	5.00	1.50
❑	122	Ron Calloway UP RC	5.00	1.50
❑	123	Tim Kalita UP RC	5.00	1.50
❑	124	Kazuhisa Ishii UP RC	10.00	3.00
❑	125	Mark Teixeira UP	8.00	2.40
❑	126	Nate Field UP RC	5.00	1.50
❑	127	Nelson Castro UP RC	5.00	1.50
❑	128	So Taguchi UP RC	8.00	2.40
❑	129	Marlon Byrd UP	5.00	1.50
❑	130	Drew Henson UP	5.00	1.50
❑	131	Kenny Kelly UP	5.00	1.50
❑	132	John Ennis UP RC	5.00	1.50
❑	133	Anastacio Martinez UP RC	5.00	1.50
❑	134	Matt Guerrier UP	5.00	1.50
❑	135	Tom Wilson UP RC	5.00	1.50
❑	136	Ben Howard UP RC	5.00	1.50
❑	137	Chris Baker UP RC	5.00	1.50
❑	138	Kevin Frederick UP RC	5.00	1.50
❑	139	Wilson Valdez UP RC	5.00	1.50
❑	140	Austin Kearns UP	8.00	2.40

2003 Fleer Genuine

	MINT	NRMT
COMP.LO SET w/o SP's (100)	25.00	11.00
COMMON CARD (1-100)	.50	.23
COMMON CARD (101-130)	8.00	3.60

			MINT	NRMT
❑	1	Derek Jeter	3.00	1.35
❑	2	Mo Vaughn	.50	.23
❑	3	Adam Dunn	.75	.35
❑	4	Aubrey Huff	.50	.23
❑	5	Jacque Jones	.50	.23
❑	6	Kerry Wood	1.25	.55
❑	7	Barry Bonds	3.00	1.35
❑	8	Kevin Brown	.50	.23
❑	9	Sammy Sosa	2.00	.90
❑	10	Ray Durham	.50	.23
❑	11	Carlos Beltran	.50	.23
❑	12	Tony Batista	.50	.23
❑	13	Bobby Abreu	.50	.23
❑	14	Craig Biggio	.75	.35
❑	15	Gary Sheffield	.50	.23
❑	16	Jermaine Dye	.50	.23
❑	17	Carlos Pena	.50	.23
❑	18	Tim Salmon	.75	.35
❑	19	Mike Piazza	2.00	.90
❑	20	Moises Alou	.50	.23
❑	21	Edgardo Alfonzo	.50	.23
❑	22	Mike Sweeney	.50	.23
❑	23	Jay Gibbons	.50	.23
❑	24	Kevin Millwood	.50	.23
❑	25	A.J. Burnett	.50	.23
❑	26	Austin Kearns	.75	.35
❑	27	Rafael Palmeiro	.75	.35
❑	28	Vladimir Guerrero	1.25	.55
❑	29	Paul Konerko	.50	.23
❑	30	Scott Rolen	.75	.35
❑	31	Fred McGriff	.75	.35
❑	32	Frank Thomas	1.25	.55
❑	33	John Olerud	.50	.23
❑	34	Eric Gagne	.75	.35
❑	35	Nomar Garciaparra	2.50	1.10
❑	36	Ryan Klesko	.50	.23
❑	37	Lance Berkman	.50	.23
❑	38	Andruw Jones	.75	.35
❑	39	Pat Burrell	.50	.23
❑	40	Juan Encarnacion	.50	.23
❑	41	Curt Schilling	.75	.35
❑	42	Jason Giambi	1.25	.55
❑	43	Barry Larkin	1.25	.55
❑	44	Alex Rodriguez	2.50	1.10
❑	45	Kazuhisa Ishii	.50	.23
❑	46	Pedro Martinez	1.25	.55
❑	47	Sean Burroughs	.50	.23
❑	48	Roy Oswalt	.50	.23
❑	49	Chipper Jones	1.25	.55
❑	50	Barry Zito	1.25	.55
❑	51	Jeff Kent	.50	.23
❑	52	Rodrigo Lopez	.50	.23
❑	53	Jim Thome	1.25	.55
❑	54	Ivan Rodriguez	1.25	.55
❑	55	Luis Gonzalez	.50	.23
❑	56	Alfonso Soriano	1.25	.55
❑	57	Josh Beckett	.75	.35
❑	58	Junior Spivey	.50	.23
❑	59	Bernie Williams	.75	.35
❑	60	Omar Vizquel	.50	.23
❑	61	Eric Hinske	.50	.23

			MINT	NRMT
❑	62	Jose Vidro	.50	.23
❑	63	Bartolo Colon	.50	.23
❑	64	Jim Edmonds	.50	.23
❑	65	Ben Sheets	.50	.23
❑	66	Mark Prior	2.50	1.10
❑	67	Edgar Martinez	.75	.35
❑	68	Raul Ibanez	.50	.23
❑	69	Darin Erstad	.50	.23
❑	70	Roger Clemens	2.50	1.10
❑	71	C.C. Sabathia	.50	.23
❑	72	Carlos Delgado	.50	.23
❑	73	Tom Glavine	1.25	.55
❑	74	Magglio Ordonez	.50	.23
❑	75	Ichiro Suzuki	2.50	1.10
❑	76	Johnny Damon	.50	.23
❑	77	Brian Giles	.50	.23
❑	78	Jeff Bagwell	.75	.35
❑	79	Greg Maddux	2.50	1.10
❑	80	Eric Chavez	.50	.23
❑	81	Larry Walker	.75	.35
❑	82	Randy Johnson	1.25	.55
❑	83	Miguel Tejada	.50	.23
❑	84	Todd Helton	.75	.35
❑	85	Jarrod Washburn	.50	.23
❑	86	Troy Glaus	.75	.35
❑	87	Ken Griffey Jr.	2.00	.90
❑	88	Albert Pujols	2.50	1.10
❑	89	Torii Hunter	.50	.23
❑	90	Joe Crede	.50	.23
❑	91	Matt Morris	.50	.23
❑	92	Shawn Green	.50	.23
❑	93	Manny Ramirez	.50	.23
❑	94	Jason Kendall	.50	.23
❑	95	Preston Wilson	.50	.23
❑	96	Garret Anderson	.50	.23
❑	97	Cliff Floyd	.50	.23
❑	98	Sean Casey	.50	.23
❑	99	Juan Gonzalez	1.25	.55
❑	100	Richie Sexson	.50	.23
❑	101	Joe Borchard GU	8.00	3.60
❑	102	Josh Stewart GU RC	8.00	3.60
❑	103	Francisco Rodriguez GU	8.00	3.60
❑	104	Jeremy Bonderman GU RC	10.00	4.50
❑	105	Walter Young GU	8.00	3.60
❑	106	Brandon Webb GU RC	12.00	5.50
❑	107	Lyle Overbay GU	8.00	3.60
❑	108	Jose Contreras GU RC	10.00	4.50
❑	109	Victor Martinez GU	8.00	3.60
❑	110	Hideki Matsui GU RC	20.00	9.00
❑	111	Brian Stokes GU RC	8.00	3.60
❑	112	Daniel Cabrera GU RC	8.00	3.60
❑	113	Josh Willingham GU RC	10.00	4.50
❑	114	Mark Teixeira GU	10.00	4.50
❑	115	Pete LaForest GU RC	10.00	4.50
❑	116	Chris Waters GU RC	8.00	3.60
❑	117	Chien-Ming Wang GU RC	10.00	4.50
❑	118	Ian Ferguson GU RC	8.00	3.60
❑	119	Rocco Baldelli GU	15.00	6.75
❑	120	Terrmel Sledge GU RC	10.00	4.50
❑	121	Hank Blalock GU	10.00	4.50
❑	122	Alejandro Machado GU RC	8.00	3.60
❑	123	Hee Seop Choi GU	8.00	3.60
❑	124	Guillermo Quiroz GU RC	10.00	4.50
❑	125	Chase Utley GU	8.00	3.60
❑	126	Nook Logan GU RC	8.00	3.60
❑	127	Josh Hall GU RC	10.00	4.50
❑	128	Ryan Church GU	8.00	3.60
❑	129	Lew Ford GU RC	10.00	4.50
❑	130	Francisco Rosario GU RC	8.00	3.60
❑	131	Dan Haren RC	-	
❑	132	Rickie Weeks RC	-	
❑	133	Prentice Redman RC	-	
❑	134	Craig Brazell RC	-	
❑	135	Jon Leicester RC	-	
❑	136	Ryan Wagner RC	-	
❑	137	Matt Kata RC	-	
❑	138	Edwin Jackson RC	-	
❑	139	Mike Ryan RC	-	
❑	140	Delmon Young RC	-	
❑	141	Bo Hart RC	-	
❑	142	Jeff Duncan RC	-	
❑	143	Robby Hammock RC	-	
❑	144	Michael Hessman RC	-	
❑	145	Clint Barmes RC	-	

2002 Fleer Greats of the Game

	Nm-Mt	Ex-Mt
COMPLETE SET (100)	50.00	15.00
❑ 1 Cal Ripken	8.00	2.40
❑ 2 Paul Molitor	1.50	.45
❑ 3 Roberto Clemente	5.00	1.50
❑ 4 Cy Young	2.50	.75
❑ 5 Tris Speaker	2.50	.75
❑ 6 Lou Brock	1.50	.45
❑ 7 Fred Lynn	1.00	.30
❑ 8 Harmon Killebrew	2.50	.75
❑ 9 Ted Williams	6.00	1.80
❑ 10 Dave Winfield	1.50	.45
❑ 11 Orlando Cepeda	1.00	.30
❑ 12 Johnny Mize	1.50	.45
❑ 13 Walter Johnson	2.50	.75
❑ 14 Roy Campanella	2.50	.75
❑ 15 George Sisler	1.00	.30
❑ 16 Bo Jackson	2.50	.75
❑ 17 Rollie Fingers	1.00	.30
❑ 18 Brooks Robinson	2.50	.75
❑ 19 Billy Williams	1.00	.30
❑ 20 Maury Wills	1.00	.30
❑ 21 Jimmie Foxx	2.50	.75
❑ 22 Alan Trammell	1.50	.45
❑ 23 Rogers Hornsby	2.50	.75
❑ 24 Don Drysdale	2.50	.75
❑ 25 Bob Feller	1.50	.45
❑ 26 Jackie Robinson	4.00	1.20
❑ 27 Whitey Ford	1.50	.45
❑ 28 Enos Slaughter	1.00	.30
❑ 29 Rod Carew	1.50	.45
❑ 30 Eddie Mathews	2.50	.75
❑ 31 Ron Cey	1.00	.30
❑ 32 Thurman Munson	3.00	.90
❑ 33 Ty Cobb	4.00	1.20
❑ 34 Rocky Colavito	2.50	.75
❑ 35 Satchel Paige	2.50	.75
❑ 36 Andre Dawson	1.00	.30
❑ 37 Phil Rizzuto	2.50	.75
❑ 38 Roger Maris	3.00	.90
❑ 39 Earl Weaver	1.00	.30
❑ 40 Joe Carter	1.00	.30
❑ 41 Christy Mathewson	2.50	.75
❑ 42 Tony Lazzeri	1.00	.30
❑ 43 Gil Hodges	2.50	.75
❑ 44 Gaylord Perry	1.00	.30
❑ 45 Steve Carlton	1.50	.45
❑ 46 George Kell	1.50	.45
❑ 47 Mickey Cochrane	1.50	.45
❑ 48 Joe Morgan	1.00	.30
❑ 49 Steve Garvey	1.00	.30
❑ 50 Bob Gibson	1.50	.45
❑ 51 Lefty Grove	1.50	.45
❑ 52 Warren Spahn	1.50	.45
❑ 53 Willie McCovey	1.00	.30
❑ 54 Frank Robinson	1.50	.45
❑ 55 Rich Gossage	1.00	.30
❑ 56 Hank Bauer	1.00	.30
❑ 57 Hoyt Wilhelm	1.00	.30
❑ 58 Mel Ott	2.50	.75
❑ 59 Preacher Roe	1.00	.30
❑ 60 Yogi Berra	2.50	.75
❑ 61 Nolan Ryan	8.00	2.40
❑ 62 Dizzy Dean	2.50	.75
❑ 63 Ryne Sandberg	4.00	1.20
❑ 64 Frank Howard	1.00	.30
❑ 65 Hack Wilson	1.50	.45
❑ 66 Robin Yount	2.50	.75
❑ 67 Al Kaline	2.50	.75
❑ 68 Mike Schmidt	5.00	1.50
❑ 69 Vida Blue	1.00	.30
❑ 70 George Brett	6.00	1.80
❑ 71 Sparky Anderson	1.00	.30
❑ 72 Tom Seaver	2.50	.75
❑ 73 Bill Skowron	1.00	.30
❑ 74 Don Mattingly	6.00	1.80
❑ 75 Carl Yastrzemski	3.00	.90
❑ 76 Eddie Murray	2.50	.75
❑ 77 Jim Palmer	1.00	.30
❑ 78 Bill Dickey	1.50	.45
❑ 79 Ozzie Smith	2.50	.75
❑ 80 Dale Murphy	2.50	.75
❑ 81 Nap Lajoie	2.50	.75
❑ 82 Jim Hunter	1.50	.45
❑ 83 Duke Snider	1.50	.45
❑ 84 Luis Aparicio	1.00	.30
❑ 85 Reggie Jackson	1.50	.45
❑ 86 Honus Wagner	3.00	.90
❑ 87 Johnny Bench	2.50	.75
❑ 88 Stan Musial	4.00	1.20
❑ 89 Carlton Fisk	1.50	.45
❑ 90 Tony Oliva	1.00	.30
❑ 91 Wade Boggs	1.50	.45
❑ 92 Jim Rice	1.00	.30
❑ 93 Bill Mazeroski	1.50	.45
❑ 94 Ralph Kiner	1.00	.30
❑ 95 Tony Perez	1.00	.30
❑ 96 Kirby Puckett	2.50	.75
❑ 97 Bobby Bonds	1.00	.30
❑ 98 Bill Terry	1.00	.30
❑ 99 Juan Marichal	1.00	.30
❑ 100 Hank Greenberg	2.50	.75

2003 Fleer Hardball

	Nm-Mt	Ex-Mt
COMPLETE SET (280)	150.00	45.00
COMP.SET w/o SP's (240)	80.00	24.00
COMMON CARD (1-240)	.40	.12
COMMON CARD (241-265)	1.50	.45
COMMON CARD (266-280)	1.50	.45
❑ 1 Barry Bonds	2.50	.75
❑ 2 Derek Jeter	2.50	.75
❑ 3 Jason Varitek	.40	.12
❑ 4 Magglio Ordonez	.40	.12
❑ 5 Ryan Dempster	.40	.12
❑ 6 Adam Everett	.40	.12
❑ 7 Paul LoDuca	.40	.12
❑ 8 Brad Wilkerson	.40	.12
❑ 9 Al Leiter	.40	.12
❑ 10 Jermaine Dye	.40	.12
❑ 11 Rob Mackowiak	.40	.12
❑ 12 J.T. Snow	.40	.12
❑ 13 Juan Gonzalez	1.00	.30
❑ 14 Eric Hinske	.40	.12
❑ 15 Greg Maddux	2.00	.60
❑ 16 Moises Alou	.40	.12
❑ 17 Carlos Lee	.40	.12
❑ 18 Richard Hidalgo	.40	.12
❑ 19 Jorge Posada	.60	.18
❑ 20 Mike Lieberthal	.40	.12
❑ 21 Jeff Cirillo	.40	.12
❑ 22 Corey Patterson	.40	.12
❑ 23 C.C. Sabathia	.40	.12
❑ 24 Brian Giles	.40	.12
❑ 25 Edgar Martinez	.60	.18
❑ 26 Trot Nixon	.40	.12
❑ 27 Kerry Wood	1.00	.30
❑ 28 Austin Kearns	.60	.18
❑ 29 Lance Berkman	.40	.12
❑ 30 Hideo Nomo	1.00	.30
❑ 31 Brad Radke	.40	.12
❑ 32 John Valentin	.40	.12
❑ 33 Tim Hudson	.40	.12
❑ 34 Aramis Ramirez	.40	.12
❑ 35 Kevin Mench	.40	.12
❑ 36 Kevin Appier	.40	.12
❑ 37 Chris Richard	.40	.12
❑ 38 Ruben Mateo	.40	.12
❑ 39 Juan Pierre	.40	.12
❑ 40 Nick Neugebauer	.40	.12
❑ 41 Mike Mussina	1.00	.30
❑ 42 Rich Aurilia	.40	.12
❑ 43 Albert Pujols	2.00	.60
❑ 44 Carlos Delgado	.40	.12
❑ 45 Junior Spivey	.40	.12
❑ 46 Marcus Giles	.40	.12
❑ 47 Johnny Damon	.40	.12
❑ 48 Mark Prior	2.00	.60
❑ 49 Omar Vizquel	.40	.12
❑ 50 Craig Biggio	.60	.18
❑ 51 Chuck Knoblauch	.40	.12
❑ 52 Eric Milton	.40	.12
❑ 53 Jeromy Burnitz	.40	.12
❑ 54 Jim Thome	1.00	.30
❑ 55 Steve Finley	.40	.12
❑ 56 Kevin Millwood	.40	.12
❑ 57 Alex Gonzalez	.40	.12
❑ 58 Ben Broussard	.40	.12
❑ 59 Derrek Lee	.40	.12
❑ 60 Joe Randa	.40	.12
❑ 61 Doug Mientkiewicz	.40	.12
❑ 62 Jason Phillips	.40	.12
❑ 63 Brett Myers	.40	.12
❑ 64 Josh Fogg	.40	.12
❑ 65 Reggie Sanders	.40	.12
❑ 66 Chipper Jones	1.00	.30
❑ 67 Roosevelt Brown	.40	.12
❑ 68 Matt Lawton	.40	.12
❑ 69 Charles Johnson	.40	.12
❑ 70 Mark Quinn	.40	.12
❑ 71 Jacque Jones	.40	.12
❑ 72 Armando Benitez	.40	.12
❑ 73 Bobby Abreu	.40	.12
❑ 74 Jason Kendall	.40	.12
❑ 75 Jeff Kent	.40	.12
❑ 76 Mark Teixeira	.60	.18
❑ 77 Garret Anderson	.40	.12
❑ 78 Jerry Hairston Jr.	.40	.12
❑ 79 Tony Graffanino	.40	.12
❑ 80 Josh Beckett	.60	.18
❑ 81 Eric Gagne	.60	.18
❑ 82 Fernando Tatis	.40	.12
❑ 83 Brett Tomko	.40	.12
❑ 84 Fernando Vina	.40	.12
❑ 85 Rafael Palmeiro	.60	.18
❑ 86 Luis Gonzalez	.40	.12
❑ 87 Javy Lopez	.40	.12
❑ 88 Shea Hillenbrand	.40	.12
❑ 89 Hee Seop Choi	.40	.12
❑ 90 Preston Wilson	.40	.12
❑ 91 Neifi Perez	.40	.12
❑ 92 Ray Lankford	.40	.12
❑ 93 Tsuyoshi Shinjo	.40	.12
❑ 94 Ben Grieve	.40	.12
❑ 95 Jarrod Washburn	.40	.12
❑ 96 Gary Sheffield	.40	.12
❑ 97 Derek Lowe	.40	.12
❑ 98 Tony Womack	.40	.12
❑ 99 Milton Bradley	.40	.12
❑ 100 Brad Penny	.40	.12
❑ 101 Mike Sweeney	.40	.12
❑ 102 A.J. Pierzynski	.40	.12
❑ 103 Edgardo Alfonzo	.40	.12
❑ 104 Marlon Byrd	.40	.12
❑ 105 Sean Burroughs	.40	.12
❑ 106 Kazuhiro Sasaki	.40	.12
❑ 107 Damian Rolls	.40	.12
❑ 108 Troy Glaus	.60	.18
❑ 109 Rafael Furcal	.40	.12
❑ 110 Nomar Garciaparra	2.00	.60

❑ 111 Josh Bard .40 .12
❑ 112 Alex Gonzalez .40 .12
❑ 113 Cristian Guzman .40 .12
❑ 114 Roger Cedeno .40 .12
❑ 115 Freddy Garcia .40 .12
❑ 116 Travis Phelps .40 .12
❑ 117 Juan Cruz .40 .12
❑ 118 Frank Thomas 1.00 .30
❑ 119 Jaret Wright .40 .12
❑ 120 Carlos Beltran .40 .12
❑ 121 Ronnie Belliard .40 .12
❑ 122 Roger Clemens 2.00 .60
❑ 123 Vicente Padilla .40 .12
❑ 124 Joel Pineiro .40 .12
❑ 125 Jared Sandberg .40 .12
❑ 126 Tom Glavine 1.00 .30
❑ 127 Matt Clement .40 .12
❑ 128 Aaron Rowand .40 .12
❑ 129 Alex Escobar .40 .12
❑ 130 Randy Wolf .40 .12
❑ 131 Ichiro Suzuki 2.00 .60
❑ 132 Toby Hall .40 .12
❑ 133 Scott Spiezio .40 .12
❑ 134 Bobby Higginson .40 .12
❑ 135 A.J. Burnett .40 .12
❑ 136 Cesar Izturis .40 .12
❑ 137 Roberto Alomar 1.00 .30
❑ 138 Trevor Hoffman .40 .12
❑ 139 Edgar Renteria .40 .12
❑ 140 Rusty Greer .40 .12
❑ 141 David Eckstein .40 .12
❑ 142 Pedro Martinez 1.00 .30
❑ 143 Joe Crede .40 .12
❑ 144 Robert Fick .40 .12
❑ 145 Mike Lowell .40 .12
❑ 146 Brian Jordan .40 .12
❑ 147 Mark Mulder .40 .12
❑ 148 Scott Rolen .60 .18
❑ 149 Eddie Guardado .40 .12
❑ 150 Adam Kennedy .40 .12
❑ 151 Ken Griffey Jr. 1.50 .45
❑ 152 Larry Walker .60 .18
❑ 153 Carlos Pena .40 .12
❑ 154 Geoff Jenkins .40 .12
❑ 155 Bartolo Colon .40 .12
❑ 156 Mariano Rivera .60 .18
❑ 157 Robb Nen .40 .12
❑ 158 Bret Boone .40 .12
❑ 159 Shannon Stewart .40 .12
❑ 160 Chris Singleton .40 .12
❑ 161 Todd Walker .40 .12
❑ 162 Jay Payton .40 .12
❑ 163 Zach Day .40 .12
❑ 164 Bernie Williams .60 .18
❑ 165 Bubba Trammell .40 .12
❑ 166 Matt Morris .40 .12
❑ 167 Jose Cruz Jr. .40 .12
❑ 168 Mark Grace 1.00 .30
❑ 169 Andruw Jones .60 .18
❑ 170 Cliff Floyd .40 .12
❑ 171 Antonio Alfonseca .40 .12
❑ 172 Jeff Bagwell .60 .18
❑ 173 Shawn Green .40 .12
❑ 174 Joe Mays .40 .12
❑ 175 Mike Piazza 1.50 .45
❑ 176 Adam Piatt .40 .12
❑ 177 Pokey Reese .40 .12
❑ 178 Carl Everett .40 .12
❑ 179 Tim Salmon .60 .18
❑ 180 Rodrigo Lopez .40 .12
❑ 181 Brandon Inge .40 .12
❑ 182 Kazuhisa Ishii .40 .12
❑ 183 Jose Vidro .40 .12
❑ 184 Barry Zito 1.00 .30
❑ 185 Phil Nevin .40 .12
❑ 186 J.D. Drew .40 .12
❑ 187 Vernon Wells .40 .12
❑ 188 Darin Erstad .40 .12
❑ 189 Barry Larkin 1.00 .30
❑ 190 Jason Jennings .40 .12
❑ 191 Luis Castillo .40 .12
❑ 192 Adrian Beltre .40 .12
❑ 193 Tony Armas .40 .12
❑ 194 Terrence Long .40 .12
❑ 195 Mark Kotsay .40 .12
❑ 196 Tino Martinez .60 .18
❑ 197 Jayson Werth .40 .12
❑ 198 Eric Chavez .40 .12
❑ 199 Matt Williams .40 .12
❑ 200 Jon Lieber .40 .12
❑ 201 Eddie Taubensee .40 .12
❑ 202 Shane Reynolds .40 .12
❑ 203 Alex Sanchez .40 .12
❑ 204 Jason Giambi 1.00 .30
❑ 205 Jimmy Rollins .40 .12
❑ 206 Jamie Moyer .40 .12
❑ 207 Francisco Rodriguez .40 .12
❑ 208 Marty Cordova .40 .12
❑ 209 Aaron Boone .40 .12
❑ 210 Mike Hampton .40 .12
❑ 211 Mark Redman .40 .12
❑ 212 Richie Sexson .40 .12
❑ 213 Andy Pettitte .60 .18
❑ 214 Livan Hernandez .40 .12
❑ 215 Jason Isringhausen .40 .12
❑ 216 Curt Schilling .60 .18
❑ 217 Manny Ramirez .40 .12
❑ 218 Jose Valentin .40 .12
❑ 219 Brent Butler .40 .12
❑ 220 Billy Wagner .40 .12
❑ 221 Ben Sheets .40 .12
❑ 222 Jeff Weaver .40 .12
❑ 223 Brent Abernathy .40 .12
❑ 224 Jay Gibbons .40 .12
❑ 225 Sean Casey .40 .12
❑ 226 Greg Norton .40 .12
❑ 227 Andy Van Hekken .40 .12
❑ 228 Kevin Brown .40 .12
❑ 229 Orlando Cabrera .40 .12
❑ 230 Scott Hatteberg .40 .12
❑ 231 Ryan Klesko .40 .12
❑ 232 Roy Halladay .40 .12
❑ 233 Randy Johnson 1.00 .30
❑ 234 Mark Buehrle .40 .12
❑ 235 Todd Helton .60 .18
❑ 236 Jeffrey Hammonds .40 .12
❑ 237 Sidney Ponson .40 .12
❑ 238 Kip Wells .40 .12
❑ 239 John Olerud .40 .12
❑ 240 Aubrey Huff .40 .12
❑ 241 Derek Jeter AAS 4.00 1.20
❑ 242 Barry Bonds AAS 4.00 1.20
❑ 243 Ichiro Suzuki AAS 3.00 .90
❑ 244 Troy Glaus AAS 1.50 .45
❑ 245 Alex Rodriguez AAS 3.00 .90
❑ 246 Sammy Sosa AAS 2.50 .75
❑ 247 Lance Berkman AAS 1.50 .45
❑ 248 Jason Giambi AAS 2.00 .60
❑ 249 Nomar Garciaparra AAS 3.00 .90
❑ 250 Miguel Tejada AAS 1.50 .45
❑ 251 Albert Pujols AAS 3.00 .90
❑ 252 Mike Piazza AAS 2.50 .75
❑ 253 Vladimir Guerrero AAS 2.00 .60
❑ 254 Shawn Green AAS 1.50 .45
❑ 255 Todd Helton AAS 1.50 .45
❑ 256 Ken Griffey Jr. AAS 2.50 .75
❑ 257 Torii Hunter AAS 1.50 .45
❑ 258 Chipper Jones AAS 2.00 .60
❑ 259 Alfonso Soriano AAS 2.00 .60
❑ 260 Luis Gonzalez AAS 1.50 .45
❑ 261 Pedro Martinez AAS 2.00 .60
❑ 262 Tim Hudson AAS 1.50 .45
❑ 263 Roger Clemens AAS 3.00 .90
❑ 264 Greg Maddux AAS 3.00 .90
❑ 265 Randy Johnson AAS 2.00 .60
❑ 266 Vinny Chulk OD 1.50 .45
❑ 267 Jose Castillo OD 1.50 .45
❑ 268 Craig Brazell OD RC 3.00 .90
❑ 269 Felix Sanchez OD RC 1.50 .45
❑ 270 John Webb OD 1.50 .45
❑ 271 Josh Hall OD RC 2.00 .60
❑ 272 Alexis Rios OD 1.50 .45
❑ 273 Phil Seibel OD RC 1.50 .45
❑ 274 Prentice Redman OD RC 1.50 .45
❑ 275 Walter Young OD 1.50 .45
❑ 276 Nic Jackson OD 1.50 .45
❑ 277 Adam Morrissey OD 1.50 .45
❑ 278 Bobby Jenks OD 1.50 .45
❑ 279 Rodrigo Rosario OD 1.50 .45
❑ 280 Chin-Feng Chen OD 1.50 .45

2002 Fleer Hot Prospects

	Nm-Mt	Ex-Mt
COMP.SET w/o SP's (80)	30.00	9.00
COMMON CARD (1-80)	.50	.15
COMMON CARD (81-105)	10.00	3.00
COMMON CARD (106-125)	5.00	1.50

❑ 1 Derek Jeter 3.00 .90
❑ 2 Garret Anderson .50 .15
❑ 3 Scott Rolen .75 .23
❑ 4 Bret Boone .50 .15
❑ 5 Lance Berkman .50 .15
❑ 6 Andruw Jones .75 .23
❑ 7 Ivan Rodriguez 1.25 .35
❑ 8 Bernie Williams .75 .23
❑ 9 Cristian Guzman .50 .15
❑ 10 Mo Vaughn .50 .15
❑ 11 Troy Glaus .75 .23
❑ 12 Tim Salmon .75 .23
❑ 13 Jason Giambi 1.25 .35
❑ 14 Cliff Floyd .50 .15
❑ 15 Tim Hudson .50 .15
❑ 16 Curt Schilling .75 .23
❑ 17 Sammy Sosa 2.00 .60
❑ 18 Alex Rodriguez 2.50 .75
❑ 19 Chuck Knoblauch .50 .15
❑ 20 Jason Kendall .50 .15
❑ 21 Ben Sheets .50 .15
❑ 22 Nomar Garciaparra 2.50 .75
❑ 23 Ryan Klesko .50 .15
❑ 24 Greg Vaughn .50 .15
❑ 25 Rafael Palmeiro .75 .23
❑ 26 Miguel Tejada .50 .15
❑ 27 Shea Hillenbrand .50 .15
❑ 28 Jim Thome 1.25 .35
❑ 29 Randy Johnson 1.25 .35
❑ 30 Barry Larkin 1.25 .35
❑ 31 Paul LoDuca .50 .15
❑ 32 Pedro Martinez 1.25 .35
❑ 33 Luis Gonzalez .50 .15
❑ 34 Carlos Delgado .50 .15
❑ 35 Richie Sexson .50 .15
❑ 36 Albert Pujols 2.50 .75
❑ 37 Bobby Abreu .50 .15
❑ 38 Gary Sheffield .50 .15
❑ 39 Magglio Ordonez .50 .15
❑ 40 Eric Chavez .50 .15
❑ 41 Jeff Bagwell .75 .23
❑ 42 Doug Mientkiewicz .50 .15
❑ 43 Moises Alou .50 .15
❑ 44 Todd Helton .75 .23
❑ 45 Ichiro Suzuki 2.50 .75
❑ 46 Jose Cruz Jr. .50 .15
❑ 47 Freddy Garcia .50 .15
❑ 48 Tino Martinez .75 .23
❑ 49 Roger Clemens 2.50 .75
❑ 50 Greg Maddux 2.50 .75
❑ 51 Mike Piazza 2.00 .60
❑ 52 Roberto Alomar 1.25 .35
❑ 53 Adam Dunn .75 .23
❑ 54 Kerry Wood 1.25 .35
❑ 55 Edgar Martinez .75 .23
❑ 56 Ken Griffey Jr. 2.00 .60
❑ 57 Juan Gonzalez 1.25 .35
❑ 58 Pat Burrell .50 .15
❑ 59 Corey Koskie .50 .15

❑ 60 Jose Vidro .50 .15
❑ 61 Ben Grieve .50 .15
❑ 62 Barry Bonds 3.00 .90
❑ 63 Raul Mondesi .50 .15
❑ 64 Jimmy Rollins .50 .15
❑ 65 Mike Sweeney .50 .15
❑ 66 Josh Beckett .75 .23
❑ 67 Chipper Jones 1.25 .35
❑ 68 Jeff Kent .50 .15
❑ 69 Tony Batista .50 .15
❑ 70 Phil Nevin .50 .15
❑ 71 Brian Jordan .50 .15
❑ 72 Rich Aurilia .50 .15
❑ 73 Brian Giles .50 .15
❑ 74 Frank Thomas 1.25 .35
❑ 75 Larry Walker .75 .23
❑ 76 Shawn Green .50 .15
❑ 77 Manny Ramirez .50 .15
❑ 78 Craig Biggio .75 .23
❑ 79 Vladimir Guerrero 1.25 .35
❑ 80 Jeromy Burnitz .50 .15
❑ 81 Mark Teixeira FS Pants 15.00 4.50
❑ 82 Corey Thurman FS Pants RC 10.00 3.00
❑ 83 Mark Prior FS Bat 25.00 7.50
❑ 84 Marlon Byrd FS Pants 10.00 3.00
❑ 85 Austin Kearns FS Pants 12.00 3.60
❑ 86 Satoru Komiyama FS Jsy RC 10.00 3.00
❑ 87 So Taguchi FS Bat RC 12.00 3.60
❑ 88 Jorge Padilla FS Pants RC 12.00 3.60
❑ 89 Rene Reyes FS Pants RC 10.00 3.00
❑ 90 Jorge Nunez FS Pants RC 10.00 3.00
❑ 91 Ron Calloway FS Pants RC 10.00 3.00
❑ 92 Kazuhisa Ishii FS Jsy RC 15.00 4.50
❑ 93 Dewon Brazelton FS Pants 10.00 3.00
❑ 94 Angel Berroa FS Pants 10.00 3.00
❑ 95 Felix Escalona FS Pants RC 10.00 3.00
❑ 96 Sean Burroughs FS Bat 10.00 3.00
❑ 97 Brandon Duckworth FS Pants 10.00 3.00
❑ 98 Hank Blalock FS Pants 15.00 4.50
❑ 99 Eric Hinske FS Pants 10.00 3.00
❑ 100 Carlos Pena FS Jsy 10.00 3.00
❑ 101 Morgan Ensberg FS Pants 10.00 3.00
❑ 102 Ryan Ludwick FS Pants 10.00 3.00
❑ 103 Chris Snelling FS Pants RC 12.00 3.60
❑ 104 Jason Lane FS Pants 10.00 3.00
❑ 105 Drew Henson FS Bat 10.00 3.00
❑ 106 Bobby Kielty HP 5.00 1.50
❑ 107 Earl Snyder HP RC 5.00 1.50
❑ 108 Nate Field HP RC 5.00 1.50
❑ 109 Juan Diaz HP 5.00 1.50
❑ 110 Ryan Anderson HP 5.00 1.50
❑ 111 Esteban German HP 5.00 1.50
❑ 112 Takahito Nomura HP RC 5.00 1.50
❑ 113 David Kelton HP 5.00 1.50
❑ 114 Steve Kent HP RC 5.00 1.50
❑ 115 Colby Lewis HP 5.00 1.50
❑ 116 Jason Simontacchi HP RC 8.00 2.40
❑ 117 Rodrigo Rosario HP RC 5.00 1.50
❑ 118 Ben Howard HP RC 5.00 1.50
❑ 119 Hansel Izquierdo HP RC 5.00 1.50
❑ 120 John Ennis HP RC 5.00 1.50
❑ 121 Anderson Machado HP RC 8.00 2.40
❑ 122 Luis Ugueto HP RC 5.00 1.50
❑ 123 Anastacio Martinez HP RC 5.00 1.50
❑ 124 Reed Johnson HP RC 8.00 2.40
❑ 125 Juan Cruz HP 5.00 1.50

2003 Fleer Hot Prospects

	MINT	NRMT
COMP.LO SET w/o SP's (80)	30.00	13.50
COMMON CARD (1-80)	.50	.23
FS BAT/JSY PRINT RUN 1250 #'d SETS	-	
CUT AU PRINT RUN 500 SERIAL #'d SETS	-	
GG AU PRINT RUN 400 SERIAL #'d SETS	-	
81-119 RANDOM INSERTS IN PACKS	-	
ONE CUT AU OR GG AU PER HOBBY BOX	-	

❑ 1 Derek Jeter 3.00 1.35
❑ 2 Ryan Klesko .50 .23
❑ 3 Troy Glaus .75 .35
❑ 4 Jeff Kent .50 .23
❑ 5 Frank Thomas 1.25 .55
❑ 6 Gary Sheffield .50 .23

❑ 7 Jim Edmonds .50 .23
❑ 8 Pat Burrell .50 .23
❑ 9 Jacque Jones .50 .23
❑ 10 Jason Jennings .50 .23
❑ 11 Pedro Martinez 1.25 .55
❑ 12 Rafael Palmeiro .75 .35
❑ 13 Jason Kendall .50 .23
❑ 14 Tom Glavine 1.25 .55
❑ 15 Josh Beckett .75 .35
❑ 16 Luis Gonzalez .50 .23
❑ 17 Edgar Martinez .75 .35
❑ 18 Miguel Tejada .50 .23
❑ 19 Fred McGriff .75 .35
❑ 20 Adam Dunn .75 .35
❑ 21 Lance Berkman .50 .23
❑ 22 Maggio Ordonez .50 .23
❑ 23 Darin Erstad .50 .23
❑ 24 Rich Aurilia .50 .23
❑ 25 Mike Piazza 2.00 .90
❑ 26 Shawn Green .50 .23
❑ 27 Larry Walker .75 .35
❑ 28 Manny Ramirez .50 .23
❑ 29 Juan Gonzalez 1.25 .55
❑ 30 Eric Chavez .50 .23
❑ 31 Torii Hunter .50 .23
❑ 32 A.J. Burnett .50 .23
❑ 33 Sammy Sosa 2.00 .90
❑ 34 Eric Hinske .50 .23
❑ 35 Brian Giles .50 .23
❑ 36 Mike Sweeney .50 .23
❑ 37 Sean Casey .50 .23
❑ 38 Chipper Jones 1.25 .55
❑ 39 Scott Rolen .75 .35
❑ 40 Jason Giambi 1.25 .55
❑ 41 Mo Vaughn .50 .23
❑ 42 Roy Oswalt .50 .23
❑ 43 Paul Konerko .50 .23
❑ 44 Tim Salmon .75 .35
❑ 45 Edgardo Alfonzo .50 .23
❑ 46 Jermaine Dye .50 .23
❑ 47 Ben Sheets .50 .23
❑ 48 Todd Helton .75 .35
❑ 49 Greg Maddux 2.50 1.10
❑ 50 Albert Pujols 2.50 1.10
❑ 51 Jim Thome 1.25 .55
❑ 52 Vladimir Guerrero 1.25 .55
❑ 53 Ivan Rodriguez 1.25 .55
❑ 54 Nomar Garciaparra 2.50 1.10
❑ 55 Alex Rodriguez 2.50 1.10
❑ 56 Alfonso Soriano 1.25 .55
❑ 57 Kazuhisa Ishii .50 .23
❑ 58 Austin Kearns .75 .35
❑ 59 Curt Schilling .75 .35
❑ 60 Bret Boone .50 .23
❑ 61 Mark Prior 2.50 1.10
❑ 62 Garret Anderson .50 .23
❑ 63 Barry Bonds 3.00 1.35
❑ 64 Roger Clemens 2.50 1.10
❑ 65 Jeff Bagwell .75 .35
❑ 66 Omar Vizquel .50 .23
❑ 67 Jay Gibbons .50 .23
❑ 68 Aubrey Huff .50 .23
❑ 69 Bobby Abreu .50 .23
❑ 70 Richie Sexson .50 .23
❑ 71 Bobby Higginson .50 .23
❑ 72 Kerry Wood 1.25 .55
❑ 73 Carlos Delgado .50 .23
❑ 74 Sean Burroughs .50 .23
❑ 75 Jose Vidro .50 .23
❑ 76 Ken Griffey Jr. 2.00 .90
❑ 77 Randy Johnson 1.25 .55
❑ 78 Ichiro Suzuki 2.50 1.10
❑ 79 Barry Zito 1.25 .55
❑ 80 Carlos Beltran .50 .23
❑ 81 Joe Borchard FS Jsy 10.00 4.50
❑ 82 Mark Teixeira FS Bat 10.00 4.50
❑ 83 Brandon Webb FS Jsy RC 15.00 6.75
❑ 84 Shane Victorino Pants AU RC 15.00 6.75
❑ 85 Hee Seop Choi FS Jsy 10.00 4.50
❑ 86 Hank Blalock FS Bat 10.00 4.50
❑ 87 Brett Myers FS Jsy 10.00 4.50
❑ 88 Does Not Exist -
❑ 89 Jesse Foppert FS Jsy 10.00 4.50
❑ 90 Lyle Overbay FS Jsy 10.00 4.50
❑ 91 Brian Stokes Pants AU RC 15.00 6.75
❑ 92 Josh Hall Bat AU RC 25.00 11.00
❑ 93 Chris Waters Pants AU RC 15.00 6.75
❑ 94 Lew Ford Pants AU RC 25.00 11.00
❑ 95 Ian Ferguson AU RC 10.00 4.50
❑ 96 Does Not Exist -
❑ 97 Josh Stewart AU RC 10.00 4.50
❑ 98 Pete LaForest AU RC 15.00 6.75
❑ 99 Jose Contreras Jsy AU/300 RC 50.00 22.00
❑ 100 Termel Sledge AU RC 15.00 6.75
❑ 101 Guillermo Quiroz AU RC 15.00 6.75
❑ 102 Alejandro Machado AU RC 10.00 4.50
❑ 103 Nook Logan Pants AU RC 15.00 6.75
❑ 104 Rob Hammock Pants AU RC 25.00 11.00
❑ 105 Hideki Matsui FS Base RC 25.00 11.00
❑ 106 Does Not Exist -
❑ 107 Rocco Baldelli FS Jsy 15.00 6.75
❑ 108 Does Not Exist -
❑ 109 T.Wellemeyer Pants AU RC 25.00 11.00
❑ 110 Mike Hessman Pants AU RC 15.00 6.75
❑ 111 J.Bonderman Pants AU RC 25.00 11.00
❑ 112 Craig Brazell Pants AU RC 25.00 11.00
❑ 113 Franc Rosario Pants AU RC 15.00 6.75
❑ 114 Jeff Duncan Pants AU RC 25.00 11.00
❑ 115 Daniel Cabrera Pants AU RC 15.00 6.75
❑ 116 Dontrelle Willis Pants AU 60.00 27.00
❑ 117 Cory Stewart AU RC 10.00 4.50
❑ 118 Tim Olson Pants AU RC 25.00 11.00
❑ 119 C.Wang Pants AU/500 RC 50.00 22.00
❑ 120 Josh Willingham Pants RC -
❑ 121 Rickie Weeks Bat RC -
❑ 122 Prentice Redman Pants RC -
❑ 123 Mike Ryan Pants RC -
❑ 124 Oscar Villarreal Pants RC -
❑ 125 Ryan Wagner Pants RC -
❑ 126 Bo Hart Pants RC -
❑ 127 Edwin Jackson Pants RC -

2001 Fleer Legacy

	Nm-Mt	Ex-Mt
COMP.SET w/o SP's (90)	40.00	12.00
COMMON CARD (1-90)	1.00	.30
COMMON AUTO (91-100)	15.00	4.50
COMMON CARD (101-105)	10.00	3.00

❑ 1 Pedro Martinez 2.50 .75
❑ 2 Andruw Jones 1.50 .45
❑ 3 Mike Hampton 1.00 .30
❑ 4 Gary Sheffield 1.00 .30
❑ 5 Barry Zito 2.50 .75
❑ 6 J.D. Drew 1.00 .30

❑ 7 Charles Johnson	1.00	.30
❑ 8 David Wells	1.00	.30
❑ 9 Kazuhiro Sasaki	1.00	.30
❑ 10 Vladimir Guerrero	2.50	.75
❑ 11 Pat Burrell	1.00	.30
❑ 12 Ruben Mateo	1.00	.30
❑ 13 Greg Maddux	5.00	1.50
❑ 14 Sean Casey	1.00	.30
❑ 15 Craig Biggio	1.50	.45
❑ 16 Bernie Williams	1.50	.45
❑ 17 Jeff Kent	1.00	.30
❑ 18 Nomar Garciaparra	5.00	1.50
❑ 19 Cal Ripken	8.00	2.40
❑ 20 Larry Walker	1.50	.45
❑ 21 Adrian Beltre	1.00	.30
❑ 22 Johnny Damon	1.00	.30
❑ 23 Rick Ankiel	1.00	.30
❑ 24 Matt Williams	1.00	.30
❑ 25 Magglio Ordonez	1.00	.30
❑ 26 Richard Hidalgo	1.00	.30
❑ 27 Robin Ventura	1.00	.30
❑ 28 Jason Kendall	1.00	.30
❑ 29 Tony Batista	1.00	.30
❑ 30 Chipper Jones	2.50	.75
❑ 31 Jim Thome	2.50	.75
❑ 32 Kevin Brown	1.00	.30
❑ 33 Mike Mussina	2.50	.75
❑ 34 Mark McGwire	6.00	1.80
❑ 35 Darin Erstad	1.00	.30
❑ 36 Manny Ramirez	1.00	.30
❑ 37 Bobby Higginson	1.00	.30
❑ 38 Richie Sexson	1.00	.30
❑ 39 Jason Giambi	2.50	.75
❑ 40 Alex Rodriguez	5.00	1.50
❑ 41 Mark Grace	2.50	.75
❑ 42 Ken Griffey Jr.	4.00	1.20
❑ 43 Moises Alou	1.00	.30
❑ 44 Edgardo Alfonzo	1.00	.30
❑ 45 Phil Nevin	1.00	.30
❑ 46 Rafael Palmeiro	1.50	.45
❑ 47 Javy Lopez	1.00	.30
❑ 48 Juan Gonzalez	2.50	.75
❑ 49 Jermaine Dye	1.00	.30
❑ 50 Roger Clemens	5.00	1.50
❑ 51 Barry Bonds	6.00	1.80
❑ 52 Carl Everett	1.00	.30
❑ 53 Ben Sheets	1.00	.30
❑ 54 Juan Encarnacion	1.00	.30
❑ 55 Jeromy Burnitz	1.00	.30
❑ 56 Miguel Tejada	1.00	.30
❑ 57 Ben Grieve	1.00	.30
❑ 58 Randy Johnson	2.50	.75
❑ 59 Frank Thomas	2.50	.75
❑ 60 Preston Wilson	1.00	.30
❑ 61 Mike Piazza	4.00	1.20
❑ 62 Brian Giles	1.00	.30
❑ 63 Carlos Delgado	1.00	.30
❑ 64 Tom Glavine	2.50	.75
❑ 65 Roberto Alomar	2.50	.75
❑ 66 Mike Sweeney	1.00	.30
❑ 67 Orlando Hernandez	1.00	.30
❑ 68 Edgar Martinez	1.50	.45
❑ 69 Tim Salmon	1.50	.45
❑ 70 Kerry Wood	2.50	.75
❑ 71 Jack Wilson RC	1.00	.30
❑ 72 Matt Lawton	1.00	.30
❑ 73 Scott Rolen	1.50	.45
❑ 74 Ivan Rodriguez	2.50	.75
❑ 75 Steve Finley	1.00	.30
❑ 76 Barry Larkin	2.50	.75
❑ 77 Jeff Bagwell	1.50	.45
❑ 78 Derek Jeter	6.00	1.80
❑ 79 Tony Gwynn	3.00	.90
❑ 80 Raul Mondesi	1.00	.30
❑ 81 Rafael Furcal	1.00	.30
❑ 82 Todd Helton	1.50	.45
❑ 83 Shawn Green	1.00	.30
❑ 84 Tim Hudson	1.00	.30
❑ 85 Jim Edmonds	1.00	.30
❑ 86 Troy Glaus	1.50	.45
❑ 87 Sammy Sosa	4.00	1.20
❑ 88 Cliff Floyd	1.00	.30
❑ 89 Jose Vidro	1.00	.30
❑ 90 Bob Abreu	1.00	.30
❑ 91 Drew Henson AU RC	40.00	12.00
❑ 92 Andy Morales AU RC	15.00	4.50
❑ 93 Wilson Betemit AU RC	15.00	4.50
❑ 94 Elpidio Guzman AU RC	15.00	4.50
❑ 95 Esix Snead AU RC	15.00	4.50
❑ 96 Winston Abreu AU RC	15.00	4.50
❑ 97 Jeremy Owens AU RC	15.00	4.50
❑ 98 Does Not Exist	-	
❑ 99 Junior Spivey AU RC	25.00	7.50
❑ 100 J. Randolph AU RC	15.00	4.50
❑ 101 Ichiro Suzuki RC	50.00	15.00
❑ 102 Albert Pujols RC/499	80.00	24.00
❑ 102AU Albert Pujols AU/300	300.00	90.00
❑ 103 Tsuyoshi Shinjo RC	15.00	4.50
❑ 104 Jay Gibbons RC	15.00	4.50
❑ 105 Juan Uribe RC	10.00	3.00

1999 Fleer Mystique

	Nm-Mt	Ex-Mt
COMPLETE SET (160)	400.00	120.00
COMP.SHORT SET (100)	40.00	12.00
COMMON CARD (1-100)	.40	.12
COMMON SP (1-100)	1.00	.30
COMMON (101-150)	5.00	1.50
COMMON (151-160)	5.00	1.50

Card	Nm-Mt	Ex-Mt
❑ 1 Ken Griffey Jr. SP	2.50	.75
❑ 2 Livan Hernandez	.40	.12
❑ 3 Jeff Kent	.40	.12
❑ 4 Brian Jordan	.40	.12
❑ 5 Kevin Young	.40	.12
❑ 6 Vinny Castilla	.40	.12
❑ 7 Orlando Hernandez SP	1.00	.30
❑ 8 Bobby Abreu	.40	.12
❑ 9 Vladimir Guerrero SP	1.50	.45
❑ 10 Chuck Knoblauch	.40	.12
❑ 11 Nomar Garciaparra SP	3.00	.90
❑ 12 Jeff Bagwell	.60	.18
❑ 13 Todd Walker	.40	.12
❑ 14 Johnny Damon	.40	.12
❑ 15 Mike Caruso	.40	.12
❑ 16 Cliff Floyd	.40	.12
❑ 17 Andy Pettitte	.60	.18
❑ 18 Cal Ripken SP	5.00	1.50
❑ 19 Brian Giles	.40	.12
❑ 20 Robin Ventura	.40	.12
❑ 21 Alex Gonzalez	.40	.12
❑ 22 Randy Johnson	1.00	.30
❑ 23 Raul Mondesi	.40	.12
❑ 24 Ken Caminiti	.40	.12
❑ 25 Tom Glavine	1.00	.30
❑ 26 Derek Jeter SP	4.00	1.20
❑ 27 Carlos Delgado	.40	.12
❑ 28 Adrian Beltre	.40	.12
❑ 29 Tino Martinez	.60	.18
❑ 30 Todd Helton	.60	.18
❑ 31 Juan Gonzalez SP	1.50	.45
❑ 32 Henry Rodriguez	.40	.12
❑ 33 Jim Thome	1.00	.30
❑ 34 Paul O'Neill	.60	.18
❑ 35 Scott Rolen SP	1.00	.30
❑ 36 Rafael Palmeiro	.60	.18
❑ 37 Will Clark	1.00	.30
❑ 38 Todd Hundley	.40	.12
❑ 39 Andruw Jones SP	1.00	.30
❑ 40 Rolando Arrojo	.40	.12
❑ 41 Barry Larkin	1.00	.30
❑ 42 Tim Salmon	.60	.18
❑ 43 Rondell White	.40	.12
❑ 44 Curt Schilling	.60	.18
❑ 45 Chipper Jones SP	1.50	.45
❑ 46 Jeromy Burnitz	.40	.12
❑ 47 Mo Vaughn	.40	.12
❑ 48 Tony Clark	.40	.12
❑ 49 Fernando Tatis	.40	.12
❑ 50 Dmitri Young	.40	.12
❑ 51 Wade Boggs	.60	.18
❑ 52 Rickey Henderson	1.50	.45
❑ 53 Manny Ramirez SP	1.00	.30
❑ 54 Edgar Martinez	.60	.18
❑ 55 Jason Giambi	1.00	.30
❑ 56 Jason Kendall	.40	.12
❑ 57 Eric Karros	.40	.12
❑ 58 Jose Canseco SP	1.50	.45
❑ 59 Shawn Green	.40	.12
❑ 60 Ellis Burks	.40	.12
❑ 61 Derek Bell	.40	.12
❑ 62 Shannon Stewart	.40	.12
❑ 63 Roger Clemens SP	3.00	.90
❑ 64 Sean Casey SP	1.00	.30
❑ 65 Jose Offerman	.40	.12
❑ 66 Sammy Sosa SP	2.50	.75
❑ 67 Frank Thomas SP	1.50	.45
❑ 68 Tony Gwynn SP	1.50	.45
❑ 69 Roberto Alomar	1.00	.30
❑ 70 Mark McGwire SP	4.00	1.20
❑ 71 Troy Glaus	.60	.18
❑ 72 Ray Durham	.40	.12
❑ 73 Jeff Cirillo	.40	.12
❑ 74 Alex Rodriguez SP	3.00	.90
❑ 75 Jose Cruz Jr.	.40	.12
❑ 76 Juan Encarnacion	.40	.12
❑ 77 Mark Grace	1.00	.30
❑ 78 Barry Bonds SP	4.00	1.20
❑ 79 Ivan Rodriguez SP	1.50	.45
❑ 80 Greg Vaughn	.40	.12
❑ 81 Greg Maddux SP	3.00	.90
❑ 82 Albert Belle	.40	.12
❑ 83 John Olerud	.40	.12
❑ 84 Kenny Lofton	.40	.12
❑ 85 Bernie Williams	.60	.18
❑ 86 Matt Williams	.40	.12
❑ 87 Ray Lankford	.40	.12
❑ 88 Darin Erstad	.40	.12
❑ 89 Ben Grieve	.40	.12
❑ 90 Craig Biggio	.60	.18
❑ 91 Dean Palmer	.40	.12
❑ 92 Reggie Sanders	.40	.12
❑ 93 Dante Bichette	.40	.12
❑ 94 Pedro Martinez SP	1.50	.45
❑ 95 Larry Walker	.60	.18
❑ 96 David Wells	.40	.12
❑ 97 Travis Lee SP	1.00	.30
❑ 98 Mike Piazza SP	2.50	.75
❑ 99 Mike Mussina	1.00	.30
❑ 100 Kevin Brown	.60	.18
❑ 101 Ruben Mateo PROS	5.00	1.50
❑ 102 Rob. Ramirez RC	5.00	1.50
❑ 103 Glen Barker PROS RC	5.00	1.50
❑ 104 C. Bellinger PROS RC	5.00	1.50
❑ 105 Carlos Guillen PROS	5.00	1.50
❑ 106 S.Schoeneweis PROS	5.00	1.50
❑ 107 C.Gubanich PROS RC	5.00	1.50
❑ 108 S.Williamson PROS	5.00	1.50
❑ 109 E.Guzman PROS RC	5.00	1.50
❑ 110 A.J. Burnett PROS RC	8.00	2.40
❑ 111 Jeremy Giambi PROS	5.00	1.50
❑ 112 Trot Nixon PROS	5.00	1.50
❑ 113 J.D. Drew PROS	5.00	1.50
❑ 114 Roy Halladay PROS	5.00	1.50
❑ 115 J.Macias PROS RC	5.00	1.50
❑ 116 Corey Koskie PROS	5.00	1.50
❑ 117 Ryan Rupe PROS RC	5.00	1.50
❑ 118 S.Hunter PROS RC	5.00	1.50
❑ 119 Rob Fick PROS	5.00	1.50
❑ 120 M.Christensen PROS	5.00	1.50
❑ 121 Carlos Febles PROS	5.00	1.50
❑ 122 Gabe Kapler PROS	5.00	1.50
❑ 123 Jeff Liefer PROS	5.00	1.50
❑ 124 Warren Morris PROS	5.00	1.50
❑ 125 Chris Pritchett PROS	5.00	1.50
❑ 126 Torii Hunter PROS	5.00	1.50
❑ 127 Armando Rios PROS	5.00	1.50
❑ 128 Ricky Ledee PROS	5.00	1.50
❑ 129 K.Dransfeldt RC	5.00	1.50

❑ 130 J.Zimmerman RC	5.00	1.50
❑ 131 Eric Chavez PROS	5.00	1.50
❑ 132 F.Garcia PROS RC	15.00	4.50
❑ 133 Jose Jimenez PROS	5.00	1.50
❑ 134 Pat Burrell PROS RC	50.00	15.00
❑ 135 J.McEwing PROS RC	5.00	1.50
❑ 136 Kris Benson PROS	5.00	1.50
❑ 137 Joe Mays PROS RC	8.00	2.40
❑ 138 R.Roque PROS RC	5.00	1.50
❑ 139 C.Guzman PROS	5.00	1.50
❑ 140 Michael Barrett PROS	5.00	1.50
❑ 141 D.Mientkiewicz RC	12.00	3.60
❑ 142 Jeff Weaver PROS RC	8.00	2.40
❑ 143 Mike Lowell PROS	5.00	1.50
❑ 144 J.Phillips PROS RC	5.00	1.50
❑ 145 M.Anderson PROS	5.00	1.50
❑ 146 B.Hinchliffe PROS RC	5.00	1.50
❑ 147 Matt Clement PROS	5.00	1.50
❑ 148 Terrence Long PROS	5.00	1.50
❑ 149 Carlos Beltran PROS	5.00	1.50
❑ 150 Preston Wilson PROS	5.00	1.50
❑ 151 Ken Griffey Jr. STAR	8.00	2.40
❑ 152 Mark McGwire STAR	12.00	3.60
❑ 153 Sammy Sosa STAR	8.00	2.40
❑ 154 Mike Piazza STAR	8.00	2.40
❑ 155 Alex Rodriguez STAR	10.00	3.00
❑ 156 N.Garciaparra STAR	10.00	3.00
❑ 157 Cal Ripken STAR	15.00	4.50
❑ 158 Greg Maddux STAR	10.00	3.00
❑ 159 Derek Jeter STAR	12.00	3.60
❑ 160 Juan Gonzalez STAR	5.00	1.50
❑ P113 J.D. Drew Promo	1.00	.30

2003 Fleer Mystique

	MINT	NRMT
COMP.SET w/o SP's (80)	40.00	18.00
COMMON CARD (1-80)	.50	.23
COMMON CARD (81-130)	8.00	3.60

❑ 1 Alex Rodriguez	2.50	1.10
❑ 2 Derek Jeter	3.00	1.35
❑ 3 Jose Vidro	.50	.23
❑ 4 Miguel Tejada	.50	.23
❑ 5 Albert Pujols	2.50	1.10
❑ 6 Rocco Baldelli	2.50	1.10
❑ 7 Jose Reyes	.75	.35
❑ 8 Hideo Nomo	1.25	.55
❑ 9 Hank Blalock	.75	.35
❑ 10 Chipper Jones	1.25	.55
❑ 11 Barry Larkin	1.25	.55
❑ 12 Alfonso Soriano	1.25	.55
❑ 13 Aramis Ramirez	.50	.23
❑ 14 Darin Erstad	.50	.23
❑ 15 Jim Edmonds	.50	.23
❑ 16 Garret Anderson	.50	.23
❑ 17 Todd Helton	.75	.35
❑ 18 Jason Kendall	.50	.23
❑ 19 Aubrey Huff	.50	.23
❑ 20 Troy Glaus	.75	.35
❑ 21 Sammy Sosa	2.00	.90
❑ 22 Roger Clemens	2.50	1.10
❑ 23 Mark Teixeira	.75	.35
❑ 24 Barry Bonds	3.00	1.35
❑ 25 Jim Thome	1.25	.55
❑ 26 Carlos Delgado	.50	.23
❑ 27 Vladimir Guerrero	1.25	.55
❑ 28 Austin Kearns	.75	.35
❑ 29 Pat Burrell	.50	.23
❑ 30 Ken Griffey Jr.	2.00	.90
❑ 31 Greg Maddux	2.50	1.10
❑ 32 Corey Patterson	.50	.23
❑ 33 Larry Walker	.75	.35
❑ 34 Kerry Wood	1.25	.55
❑ 35 Frank Thomas	1.25	.55
❑ 36 Dontrelle Willis	2.00	.90
❑ 37 Randy Johnson	1.25	.55
❑ 38 Curt Schilling	.75	.35
❑ 39 Jay Gibbons	.50	.23
❑ 40 Dmitri Young	.50	.23
❑ 41 Edgar Martinez	.75	.35
❑ 42 Kevin Brown	.50	.23
❑ 43 Scott Rolen	.75	.35
❑ 44 Adam Dunn	.75	.35
❑ 45 Pedro Martinez	1.25	.55
❑ 46 Corey Koskie	.50	.23
❑ 47 Tom Glavine	1.25	.55
❑ 48 Torii Hunter	.50	.23
❑ 49 Shawn Green	.50	.23
❑ 50 Nomar Garciaparra	2.50	1.10
❑ 51 Bernie Williams	.75	.35
❑ 52 Milton Bradley	.50	.23
❑ 53 Jason Giambi	1.25	.55
❑ 54 Mike Lieberthal	.50	.23
❑ 55 Jeff Bagwell	.75	.35
❑ 56 Carlos Pena	.50	.23
❑ 57 Lance Berkman	.50	.23
❑ 58 Jose Cruz Jr.	.50	.23
❑ 59 Josh Beckett	.75	.35
❑ 60 Mark Mulder	.50	.23
❑ 61 Mike Piazza	2.00	.90
❑ 62 Mark Prior	2.50	1.10
❑ 63 Sean Burroughs	.50	.23
❑ 64 Angel Berroa	.50	.23
❑ 65 Geoff Jenkins	.50	.23
❑ 66 Magglio Ordonez	.50	.23
❑ 67 Craig Biggio	.75	.35
❑ 68 Roberto Alomar	1.25	.55
❑ 69 Hee Seop Choi	.50	.23
❑ 70 J.D. Drew	.50	.23
❑ 71 Richie Sexson	.50	.23
❑ 72 Brian Giles	.50	.23
❑ 73 Gary Sheffield	.50	.23
❑ 74 Manny Ramirez	.50	.23
❑ 75 Barry Zito	1.25	.55
❑ 76 Andruw Jones	.75	.35
❑ 77 Ivan Rodriguez	1.25	.55
❑ 78 Ichiro Suzuki	2.50	1.10
❑ 79 Mike Sweeney	.50	.23
❑ 80 Vernon Wells	.50	.23
❑ 81 Craig Brazell RU RC	8.00	3.60
❑ 82 Wilfredo Ledezma RU RC	8.00	3.60
❑ 83 Josh Willingham RU RC	10.00	4.50
❑ 84 Chien-Ming Wang RU RC	10.00	4.50
❑ 85 Mike Ryan RU RC	8.00	3.60
❑ 86 Mike Gallo RU RC	8.00	3.60
❑ 87 Rickie Weeks RU RC	20.00	9.00
❑ 88 Brian Stokes RU RC	8.00	3.60
❑ 89 Humberto Quintero RU RC	8.00	3.60
❑ 90 Ramon Nivar RU RC	10.00	4.50
❑ 91 Jeremy Griffiths RU RC	8.00	3.60
❑ 92 Termel Sledge RU RC	8.00	3.60
❑ 93 Brandon Webb RU RC	12.00	5.50
❑ 94 David DeJesus RU RC	8.00	3.60
❑ 95 Doug Waechter RU RC	8.00	3.60
❑ 96 Jeremy Bonderman RU RC	10.00	4.50
❑ 97 Felix Sanchez RU RC	8.00	3.60
❑ 98 Colin Porter RU RC	8.00	3.60
❑ 99 Francisco Cruceta RU RC	8.00	3.60
❑ 100 Hideki Matsui RU RC	20.00	9.00
❑ 101 Chris Waters RU RC	8.00	3.60
❑ 102 Dan Haren RU RC	10.00	4.50
❑ 103 Lew Ford RU RC	8.00	3.60
❑ 104 Oscar Villarreal RU RC	8.00	3.60
❑ 105 Ryan Wagner RU RC	10.00	4.50
❑ 106 Prentice Redman RU RC	8.00	3.60
❑ 107 Josh Stewart RU RC	8.00	3.60
❑ 108 Carlos Mendez RU RC	8.00	3.60
❑ 109 Michael Hessman RU RC	8.00	3.60
❑ 110 Josh Hall RU RC	8.00	3.60
❑ 111 Daniel Garcia RU RC	8.00	3.60
❑ 112 Matt Kata RU RC	8.00	3.60
❑ 113 Michel Hernandez RU RC	8.00	3.60
❑ 114 Sergio Mitre RU RC	8.00	3.60
❑ 115 Pete LaForest RU RC	8.00	3.60
❑ 116 Edwin Jackson RU RC	15.00	6.75
❑ 117 Matt Diaz RU RC	8.00	3.60
❑ 118 Greg Aquino RU RC	8.00	3.60
❑ 119 Jose Contreras RU RC	10.00	4.50
❑ 120 Jeff Duncan RU RC	8.00	3.60
❑ 121 Richard Fischer RU RC	8.00	3.60
❑ 122 Todd Wellemeyer RU RC	8.00	3.60
❑ 123 Robby Hammock RU RC	8.00	3.60
❑ 124 Delmon Young RU RC	40.00	18.00
❑ 125 Clint Barmes RU RC	8.00	3.60
❑ 126 Phil Seibel RU RC	8.00	3.60
❑ 127 Bo Hart RU RC	10.00	4.50
❑ 128 Jon Leicester RU RC	8.00	3.60
❑ 129 Chad Gaudin RU RC	8.00	3.60
❑ 130 Guillermo Quiroz RU RC	8.00	3.60

2001 Fleer Platinum

	Nm-Mt	Ex-Mt
COMP. SERIES 1 (301)	200.00	60.00
COMP. SERIES 2 (300)	200.00	60.00
COMP.SER.1 w/o SP's (250)	40.00	12.00
COMP.SER.2 w/o SP's (200)	40.00	12.00
COMMON (1-250/302-501)	.40	.12
COMMON (251-280)	2.00	.60
COMMON AS (281-300)	2.00	.60
COMMON (502-601)	2.00	.60

❑ 1 Bobby Abreu	.40	.12
❑ 2 Brad Radke	.40	.12
❑ 3 Bill Mueller	.40	.12
❑ 4 Adam Eaton	.40	.12
❑ 5 Antonio Alfonseca	.40	.12
❑ 6 Manny Ramirez	.40	.12
❑ 7 Adam Kennedy	.40	.12
❑ 8 Jose Valentin	.40	.12
❑ 9 Jaret Wright	.40	.12
❑ 10 Aramis Ramirez	.40	.12
❑ 11 Jeff Kent	.40	.12
❑ 12 Juan Encarnacion	.40	.12
❑ 13 Sandy Alomar Jr.	.40	.12
❑ 14 Joe Randa	.40	.12
❑ 15 Darryl Kile	.40	.12
❑ 16 Darren Dreifort	.40	.12
❑ 17 Matt Kinney	.40	.12
❑ 18 Pokey Reese	.40	.12
❑ 19 Ryan Klesko	.40	.12
❑ 20 Shawn Estes	.40	.12
❑ 21 Moises Alou	.40	.12
❑ 22 Edgar Renteria	.40	.12
❑ 23 Chuck Knoblauch	.40	.12
❑ 24 Carl Everett	.40	.12
❑ 25 Garret Anderson	.40	.12
❑ 26 Shane Reynolds	.40	.12
❑ 27 Billy Koch	.40	.12
❑ 28 Carlos Febles	.40	.12
❑ 29 Brian Anderson	.40	.12
❑ 30 Armando Rios	.40	.12
❑ 31 Ryan Kohlmeier	.40	.12
❑ 32 Steve Finley	.40	.12
❑ 33 Brady Anderson	.40	.12
❑ 34 Cal Ripken	3.00	.90
❑ 35 Paul Konerko	.40	.12
❑ 36 Chuck Finley	.40	.12
❑ 37 Rick Ankiel	.40	.12
❑ 38 Mariano Rivera	.60	.18
❑ 39 Corey Koskie	.40	.12

❑ 40 Cliff Floyd .40 .12
❑ 41 Kevin Appier .40 .12
❑ 42 Henry Rodriguez .40 .12
❑ 43 Mark Kotsay .40 .12
❑ 44 Brook Fordyce .40 .12
❑ 45 Brad Ausmus .40 .12
❑ 46 Alfonso Soriano 1.00 .30
❑ 47 Ray Lankford .40 .12
❑ 48 Keith Foulke .40 .12
❑ 49 Rich Aurilia .40 .12
❑ 50 Alex Rodriguez 2.00 .60
❑ 51 Eric Byrnes .40 .12
❑ 52 Travis Fryman .40 .12
❑ 53 Jeff Bagwell .60 .18
❑ 54 Scott Rolen .60 .18
❑ 55 Matt Lawton .40 .12
❑ 56 Brad Fullmer .40 .12
❑ 57 Tony Batista .40 .12
❑ 58 Nate Rolison .40 .12
❑ 59 Carlos Lee .40 .12
❑ 60 Rafael Furcal .40 .12
❑ 61 Jay Bell .40 .12
❑ 62 Jimmy Rollins .40 .12
❑ 63 Derrek Lee .40 .12
❑ 64 Andres Galarraga .40 .12
❑ 65 Derek Bell .40 .12
❑ 66 Tim Salmon .60 .18
❑ 67 Travis Lee .40 .12
❑ 68 Kevin Millwood .40 .12
❑ 69 Albert Belle .40 .12
❑ 70 Kazuhiro Sasaki .40 .12
❑ 71 Al Leiter .40 .12
❑ 72 Britt Reames .40 .12
❑ 73 Carlos Beltran .40 .12
❑ 74 Curt Schilling .60 .18
❑ 75 Curtis Leskanic .40 .12
❑ 76 Jeremy Giambi .40 .12
❑ 77 Adrian Beltre .40 .12
❑ 78 David Segui .40 .12
❑ 79 Mike Lieberthal .40 .12
❑ 80 Brian Giles .40 .12
❑ 81 Marvin Benard .40 .12
❑ 82 Aaron Sele .40 .12
❑ 83 Kenny Lofton .40 .12
❑ 84 Doug Glanville .40 .12
❑ 85 Kris Benson .40 .12
❑ 86 Richie Sexson .40 .12
❑ 87 Javy Lopez .40 .12
❑ 88 Doug Mientkiewicz .40 .12
❑ 89 Peter Bergeron .40 .12
❑ 90 Gary Sheffield .40 .12
❑ 91 Derek Lowe .40 .12
❑ 92 Tom Glavine 1.00 .30
❑ 93 Lance Berkman .40 .12
❑ 94 Chris Singleton .40 .12
❑ 95 Mike Lowell .40 .12
❑ 96 Luis Gonzalez .40 .12
❑ 97 Dante Bichette .40 .12
❑ 98 Mike Sirotka .40 .12
❑ 99 Julio Lugo .40 .12
❑ 100 Juan Gonzalez 1.00 .30
❑ 101 Craig Biggio .60 .18
❑ 102 Armando Benitez .40 .12
❑ 103 Greg Maddux 2.00 .60
❑ 104 Mark Grace 1.00 .30
❑ 105 John Smoltz .60 .18
❑ 106 J.T. Snow .40 .12
❑ 107 Al Martin .40 .12
❑ 108 Danny Graves .40 .12
❑ 109 Barry Bonds 2.50 .75
❑ 110 Lee Stevens .40 .12
❑ 111 Pedro Martinez 1.00 .30
❑ 112 Shawn Green .40 .12
❑ 113 Bret Boone .40 .12
❑ 114 Matt Stairs .40 .12
❑ 115 Tino Martinez .60 .18
❑ 116 Rusty Greer .40 .12
❑ 117 Mike Bordick .40 .12
❑ 118 Garrett Stephenson .40 .12
❑ 119 Edgar Martinez .60 .18
❑ 120 Ben Grieve .40 .12
❑ 121 Milton Bradley .40 .12
❑ 122 Aaron Boone .40 .12
❑ 123 Ruben Mateo .40 .12
❑ 124 Ken Griffey Jr. 1.50 .45
❑ 125 Russell Branyan .40 .12
❑ 126 Shannon Stewart .40 .12
❑ 127 Fred McGriff .60 .18
❑ 128 Ben Petrick .40 .12
❑ 129 Kevin Brown .40 .12
❑ 130 B.J. Surhoff .40 .12
❑ 131 Mark McGwire 2.50 .75
❑ 132 Carlos Guillen .40 .12
❑ 133 Adrian Brown .40 .12
❑ 134 Mike Sweeney .40 .12
❑ 135 Eric Milton .40 .12
❑ 136 Cristian Guzman .40 .12
❑ 137 Ellis Burks .40 .12
❑ 138 Fernando Tatis .40 .12
❑ 139 Bengie Molina .40 .12
❑ 140 Tony Gwynn 1.25 .35
❑ 141 Jeromy Burnitz .40 .12
❑ 142 Miguel Tejada .40 .12
❑ 143 Raul Mondesi .40 .12
❑ 144 Jeffrey Hammonds .40 .12
❑ 145 Pat Burrell .40 .12
❑ 146 Frank Thomas 1.00 .30
❑ 147 Eric Munson .40 .12
❑ 148 Mike Hampton .40 .12
❑ 149 Mike Cameron .40 .12
❑ 150 Jim Thome 1.00 .30
❑ 151 Mike Mussina 1.00 .30
❑ 152 Rick Helling .40 .12
❑ 153 Ken Caminiti .40 .12
❑ 154 John VanderWal .40 .12
❑ 155 Denny Neagle .40 .12
❑ 156 Robb Nen .40 .12
❑ 157 Jose Canseco 1.00 .30
❑ 158 Mo Vaughn .40 .12
❑ 159 Phil Nevin .40 .12
❑ 160 Pat Hentgen .40 .12
❑ 161 Sean Casey .40 .12
❑ 162 Greg Vaughn .40 .12
❑ 163 Trot Nixon .40 .12
❑ 164 Roberto Hernandez .40 .12
❑ 165 Vinny Castilla .40 .12
❑ 166 Robin Ventura .40 .12
❑ 167 Alex Ochoa .40 .12
❑ 168 Orlando Hernandez .40 .12
❑ 169 Luis Castillo .40 .12
❑ 170 Quilvio Veras .40 .12
❑ 171 Troy O'Leary .40 .12
❑ 172 Livan Hernandez .40 .12
❑ 173 Roger Cedeno .40 .12
❑ 174 Jose Vidro .40 .12
❑ 175 John Olerud .40 .12
❑ 176 Richard Hidalgo .40 .12
❑ 177 Eric Chavez .40 .12
❑ 178 Fernando Vina .40 .12
❑ 179 Chris Stynes .40 .12
❑ 180 Bobby Higginson .40 .12
❑ 181 Bruce Chen .40 .12
❑ 182 Omar Vizquel .40 .12
❑ 183 Rey Ordonez .40 .12
❑ 184 Trevor Hoffman .40 .12
❑ 185 Jeff Cirillo .40 .12
❑ 186 Billy Wagner .40 .12
❑ 187 David Ortiz .40 .12
❑ 188 Tim Hudson .40 .12
❑ 189 Tony Clark .40 .12
❑ 190 Larry Walker .60 .18
❑ 191 Eric Owens .40 .12
❑ 192 Aubrey Huff .40 .12
❑ 193 Royce Clayton .40 .12
❑ 194 Todd Walker .40 .12
❑ 195 Rafael Palmeiro .60 .18
❑ 196 Todd Hundley .40 .12
❑ 197 Roger Clemens 2.00 .60
❑ 198 Jeff Weaver .40 .12
❑ 199 Dean Palmer .40 .12
❑ 200 Geoff Jenkins .40 .12
❑ 201 Matt Clement .40 .12
❑ 202 David Wells .40 .12
❑ 203 Chan Ho Park .40 .12
❑ 204 Hideo Nomo 1.00 .30
❑ 205 Bartolo Colon .40 .12
❑ 206 John Wetteland .40 .12
❑ 207 Corey Patterson .40 .12
❑ 208 Freddy Garcia .40 .12
❑ 209 David Cone .40 .12
❑ 210 Rondell White .40 .12
❑ 211 Carl Pavano .40 .12
❑ 212 Charles Johnson .40 .12
❑ 213 Ron Coomer .40 .12
❑ 214 Matt Williams .40 .12
❑ 215 Jay Payton .40 .12
❑ 216 Nick Johnson .40 .12
❑ 217 Deivi Cruz .40 .12
❑ 218 Scott Elarton .40 .12
❑ 219 Neifi Perez .40 .12
❑ 220 Jason Isringhausen .40 .12
❑ 221 Jose Cruz Jr. .40 .12
❑ 222 Gerald Williams .40 .12
❑ 223 Timo Perez .40 .12
❑ 224 Damion Easley .40 .12
❑ 225 Jeff D'Amico .40 .12
❑ 226 Preston Wilson .40 .12
❑ 227 Robert Person .40 .12
❑ 228 Jacque Jones .40 .12
❑ 229 Johnny Damon .40 .12
❑ 230 Tony Womack .40 .12
❑ 231 Adam Piatt .40 .12
❑ 232 Brian Jordan .40 .12
❑ 233 Ben Davis .40 .12
❑ 234 Kerry Wood 1.00 .30
❑ 235 Mike Piazza 1.50 .45
❑ 236 David Justice .40 .12
❑ 237 Dave Veres .40 .12
❑ 238 Eric Young .40 .12
❑ 239 Juan Pierre .40 .12
❑ 240 Gabe Kapler .40 .12
❑ 241 Ryan Dempster .40 .12
❑ 242 Dmitri Young .40 .12
❑ 243 Jorge Posada .60 .18
❑ 244 Eric Karros .40 .12
❑ 245 J.D. Drew .40 .12
❑ 246 Todd Zeile .40 .12
❑ 247 Mark Quinn .40 .12
❑ 248 Kenny Kelly UER .40 .12
Listed as a Mariner on the front
❑ 249 Jermaine Dye .40 .12
❑ 250 Barry Zito 1.00 .30
❑ 251 Jason Hart 2.00 .60
Larry Barnes
❑ 252 Ichiro Suzuki RC 30.00 9.00
Elpidio Guzman RC
❑ 253 Tsuyoshi Shinjo RC 5.00 1.50
Brian Cole
❑ 254 John Barnes 2.00 .60
Adrian Hernandez RC
❑ 255 Jason Tyner 2.00 .60
Jace Brewer
❑ 256 Brian Buchanan 2.00 .60
Luis Rivas
❑ 257 Brent Abernathy 2.00 .60
Jose Ortiz
❑ 258 Marcus Giles 2.00 .60
Keith Ginter
❑ 259 Tike Redman 2.00 .60
Jaisen Randolph RC
❑ 260 Dane Sardinha 2.00 .60
David Espinosa
❑ 261 Josh Beckett 3.00 .90
Craig House
❑ 262 Jack Cust 2.00 .60
Hiram Bocachica
❑ 263 Alex Escobar 2.00 .60
Esix Snead RC
❑ 264 Chris Richard 2.00 .60
Vernon Wells
❑ 265 Pedro Feliz 2.00 .60
Xavier Nady
❑ 266 Brandon Inge 2.00 .60
Joe Crede
❑ 267 Ben Sheets 3.00 .90
Roy Oswalt
❑ 268 Drew Henson RC 6.00 1.80
Andy Morales RC
❑ 269 C.C. Sabathia 2.00 .60
Justin Miller
❑ 270 David Eckstein 2.00 .60
Jason Grabowski
❑ 271 Dee Brown 2.00 .60
Chris Wakeland
❑ 272 Junior Spivey RC 4.00 1.20
Alex Cintron
❑ 273 Elvis Pena 2.00 .60
Juan Uribe RC

	No.	Player		
❑	274	Carlos Pena	2.00	.60
		Jason Romano		
❑	275	Winston Abreu	2.00	.60
		Wilson Betemit		
❑	276	Jose Mieses RC	2.00	.60
		Nick Neugebauer		
❑	277	Shea Hillenbrand	2.00	.60
		Dernell Stenson		
❑	278	Jared Sandberg	2.00	.60
		Toby Hall		
❑	279	Jay Gibbons RC	5.00	1.50
		Ivanon Coffie		
❑	280	Pablo Ozuna	2.00	.60
		Santiago Perez		
❑	281	N.Garciaparra AS	10.00	3.00
❑	282	Derek Jeter AS	12.00	3.60
❑	283	Jason Giambi AS	5.00	1.50
❑	284	Maggilo Ordonez AS	2.00	.60
❑	285	Ivan Rodriguez AS	5.00	1.50
❑	286	Troy Glaus AS	3.00	.90
❑	287	Carlos Delgado AS	2.00	.60
❑	288	Darin Erstad AS	2.00	.60
❑	289	Bernie Williams AS	3.00	.90
❑	290	Roberto Alomar AS	5.00	1.50
❑	291	Barry Larkin AS	5.00	1.50
❑	292	Chipper Jones AS	5.00	1.50
❑	293	Vladimir Guerrero AS	5.00	1.50
❑	294	Sammy Sosa AS	8.00	2.40
❑	295	Todd Helton AS	3.00	.90
❑	296	Randy Johnson AS	5.00	1.50
❑	297	Jason Kendall AS	2.00	.60
❑	298	Jim Edmonds AS	2.00	.60
❑	299	Andruw Jones AS	3.00	.90
❑	300	Edgardo Alfonzo AS	2.00	.60
❑	301	Albert Pujols RC	50.00	15.00
		Donaldo Mendez RC/1500		
❑	302	Shawn Wooten	.40	.12
❑	303	Todd Walker	.40	.12
❑	304	Brian Buchanan	.40	.12
❑	305	Jim Edmonds	.40	.12
❑	306	Jarrod Washburn	.40	.12
❑	307	Jose Rijo	.40	.12
❑	308	Tim Raines	.40	.12
❑	309	Matt Morris	.40	.12
❑	310	Troy Glaus	.60	.18
❑	311	Barry Larkin	1.00	.30
❑	312	Javier Vazquez	.40	.12
❑	313	Placido Polanco	.40	.12
❑	314	Darin Erstad	.40	.12
❑	315	Marty Cordova	.40	.12
❑	316	Vladimir Guerrero	1.00	.30
❑	317	Kerry Robinson	.40	.12
❑	318	Byung-Hyun Kim	.40	.12
❑	319	C.C. Sabathia	.40	.12
❑	320	Edgardo Alfonzo	.40	.12
❑	321	Jason Tyner	.40	.12
❑	322	Reggie Sanders	.40	.12
❑	323	Roberto Alomar	1.00	.30
❑	324	Matt Lawton	.40	.12
❑	325	Brent Abernathy	.40	.12
❑	326	Randy Johnson	1.00	.30
❑	327	Todd Helton	.60	.18
❑	328	Andy Pettitte	.60	.18
❑	329	Josh Beckett	.60	.18
❑	330	Mark DeRosa	.40	.12
❑	331	Jose Ortiz	.40	.12
❑	332	Derek Jeter	2.50	.75
❑	333	Toby Hall	.40	.12
❑	334	Wes Helms	.40	.12
❑	335	Jose Macias	.40	.12
❑	336	Bernie Williams	.60	.18
❑	337	Ivan Rodriguez	1.00	.30
❑	338	Chipper Jones	1.00	.30
❑	339	Brandon Inge	.40	.12
❑	340	Jason Giambi	1.00	.30
❑	341	Frank Catalanotto	.40	.12
❑	342	Andruw Jones	.60	.18
❑	343	Carlos Hernandez	.40	.12
❑	344	Jermaine Dye	.40	.12
❑	345	Mike Lamb	.40	.12
❑	346	Ken Caminiti	.40	.12
❑	347	A.J. Burnett	.40	.12
❑	348	Terrence Long	.40	.12
❑	349	Ruben Sierra	.40	.12
❑	350	Marcus Giles UER	.40	.12
		Listed as a pitcher on the back		
❑	351	Wade Miller	.40	.12
❑	352	Mark Mulder	.40	.12
❑	353	Carlos Delgado	.40	.12
❑	354	Chris Richard	.40	.12
❑	355	Daryle Ward	.40	.12
❑	356	Brad Penny	.40	.12
❑	357	Vernon Wells	.40	.12
❑	358	Jason Johnson	.40	.12
❑	359	Tim Redding	.40	.12
❑	360	Marlon Anderson	.40	.12
❑	361	Carlos Pena	.40	.12
❑	362	Nomar Garciaparra	2.00	.60
❑	363	Roy Oswalt	.60	.18
❑	364	Todd Ritchie	.40	.12
❑	365	Jose Mesa	.40	.12
❑	366	Shea Hillenbrand	.40	.12
❑	367	Dee Brown	.40	.12
❑	368	Jason Kendall	.40	.12
❑	369	Vinny Castilla	.40	.12
❑	370	Fred McGriff	.60	.18
❑	371	Neifi Perez	.40	.12
❑	372	Xavier Nady	.40	.12
❑	373	Abraham Nunez	.40	.12
❑	374	Jon Lieber	.40	.12
❑	375	Paul LoDuca	.40	.12
❑	376	Bubba Trammell	.40	.12
❑	377	Brady Clark	.40	.12
❑	378	Joel Pineiro	1.00	.30
❑	379	Mark Grudzielanek	.40	.12
❑	380	D'Angelo Jimenez	.40	.12
❑	381	Junior Herndon	.40	.12
❑	382	Magglio Ordonez	.40	.12
❑	383	Ben Sheets	.40	.12
❑	384	John Vander Wal	.40	.12
❑	385	Pedro Astacio	.40	.12
❑	386	Jose Canseco	1.00	.30
❑	387	Jose Hernandez	.40	.12
❑	388	Eric Davis	.40	.12
❑	389	Sammy Sosa	1.50	.45
❑	390	Mark Buehrle	.40	.12
❑	391	Mark Loretta	.40	.12
❑	392	Andres Galarraga	.40	.12
❑	393	Scott Spiezio	.40	.12
❑	394	Joe Crede	.40	.12
❑	395	Luis Rivas	.40	.12
❑	396	David Bell	.40	.12
❑	397	Einar Diaz	.40	.12
❑	398	Adam Dunn	.60	.18
❑	399	A.J. Pierzynski	.40	.12
❑	400	Jamie Moyer	.40	.12
❑	401	Nick Johnson	.40	.12
❑	402	Freddy Garcia CT SP	10.00	3.00
❑	403	Hideo Nomo CT	.40	.12
❑	404	Mark Mulder CT	.40	.12
❑	405	Steve Sparks CT	.40	.12
❑	406	Mariano Rivera CT	.40	.12
❑	407	Mark Buerhle	.60	.18
		Mike Mussina CT		
❑	408	Randy Johnson CT	.60	.18
❑	409	Randy Johnson CT	.60	.18
❑	410	Curt Schilling	.40	.12
		Matt Morris CT		
❑	411	Greg Maddux CT	1.00	.30
❑	412	Robb Nen CT	.40	.12
❑	413	Randy Johnson CT	.60	.18
❑	414	Barry Bonds CT	1.00	.30
❑	415	Jason Giambi CT	.40	.12
❑	416	Ichiro Suzuki CT	5.00	1.50
❑	417	Ichiro Suzuki CT	5.00	1.50
❑	418	Alex Rodriguez CT	1.00	.30
❑	419	Bret Boone CT	.40	.12
❑	420	Ichiro Suzuki CT	5.00	1.50
❑	421	Alex Rodriguez CT	1.00	.30
❑	422	Jason Giambi CT	.40	.12
❑	423	Alex Rodriguez CT	1.00	.30
❑	424	Larry Walker CT	.40	.12
❑	425	Rich Aurilia CT	.40	.12
❑	426	Barry Bonds CT	1.00	.30
❑	427	Sammy Sosa CT	1.00	.30
❑	428	Jimmy Rollins	.40	.12
		Juan Pierre CT		
❑	429	Sammy Sosa CT	1.00	.30
❑	430	Lance Berkman CT	.40	.12
❑	431	Sammy Sosa CT	1.00	.30
❑	432	Carlos Delgado TL	.40	.12
❑	433	Alex Rodriguez TL	1.00	.30
❑	434	Greg Vaughn TL	.40	.12
❑	435	Albert Pujols TL	15.00	4.50
❑	436	Ichiro Suzuki TL	5.00	1.50
❑	437	Barry Bonds TL	1.00	.30
❑	438	Phil Nevin TL	.40	.12
❑	439	Brian Giles TL	.40	.12
❑	440	Bobby Abreu TL	.40	.12
❑	441	Jason Giambi TL	.40	.12
❑	442	Derek Jeter TL	1.25	.35
❑	443	Mike Piazza TL	1.00	.30
❑	444	Vladimir Guerrero TL	.60	.18
❑	445	Corey Koskie TL	.40	.12
❑	446	Richie Sexson TL	.40	.12
❑	447	Shawn Green TL	.40	.12
❑	448	Mike Sweeney TL	.40	.12
❑	449	Jeff Bagwell TL	.40	.12
❑	450	Cliff Floyd TL	.40	.12
❑	451	Roger Cedeno TL	.40	.12
❑	452	Todd Helton TL	.40	.12
❑	453	Juan Gonzalez TL	.60	.18
❑	454	Sean Casey TL	.40	.12
❑	455	Magglio Ordonez TL	.40	.12
❑	456	Sammy Sosa TL	1.00	.30
❑	457	Manny Ramirez TL	.40	.12
❑	458	Jeff Conine TL	.40	.12
❑	459	Chipper Jones TL	.60	.18
❑	460	Luis Gonzalez TL	.40	.12
❑	461	Troy Glaus TL	.40	.12
❑	462	Ivan Rodriguez	.60	.18
		Jason Romano FF		
❑	463	Luis Gonzalez	.40	.12
		Jack Cust FF		
❑	464	Jim Thome	.40	.12
		C.C. Sabathia FF		
❑	465	Jason Giambi	.40	.12
		Jason Hart FF		
❑	466	Jeff Bagwell	.60	.18
		Roy Oswalt FF		
❑	467	Sammy Sosa	1.00	.30
		Corey Patterson FF		
❑	468	Mike Piazza	1.00	.30
		Alex Escobar FF		
❑	469	Ken Griffey Jr.	1.00	.30
		Adam Dunn FF		
❑	470	Roger Clemens	1.00	.30
		Nick Johnson FF		
❑	471	Cliff Floyd	.40	.12
		Josh Beckett FF		
❑	472	Cal Ripken Jr.	1.50	.45
		Jerry Hairston Jr. FF		
❑	473	Phil Nevin	.40	.12
		Xavier Nady FF		
❑	474	Scott Rolen	.40	.12
		Jimmy Rollins FF		
❑	475	Barry Larkin	.60	.18
		David Espinosa FF		
❑	476	Larry Walker	.60	.18
		Jose Ortiz FF		
❑	477	Chipper Jones	.60	.18
		Marcus Giles FF		
❑	478	Craig Biggio	.40	.12
		Keith Ginter FF		
❑	479	Magglio Ordonez	.40	.12
		Aaron Rowand FF		
❑	480	Alex Rodriguez	1.00	.30
		Carlos Pena FF		
❑	481	Derek Jeter	1.25	.35
		Alfonso Soriano FF		
❑	482	Erubiel Durazo PG	.40	.12
❑	483	Bernie Williams PG	.40	.12
❑	484	Team Photo PG	.40	.12
❑	485	Team Photo PG	.40	.12
❑	486	Andy Pettitte PG	.40	.12
❑	487	Curt Schilling PG	.40	.12
❑	488	Randy Johnson PG	.60	.18
❑	489	Rudolph Guiliani PG	1.00	.30
		Mayor of New York City		
❑	490	George W. Bush PG	2.50	.45
		President of United States		
❑	491	Roger Clemens PG	1.00	.30
❑	492	Mariano Rivera PG	.60	.18
❑	493	Tino Martinez PG	.40	.12
❑	494	Derek Jeter PG	1.25	.35
❑	495	Scott Brosius PG	.40	.12
❑	496	Alfonso Soriano PG	.60	.18
❑	497	Matt Williams PG	.40	.12

❑ 498 Tony Womack PG .40 .12
❑ 499 Luis Gonzalez PG .40 .12
❑ 500 Arizona Diamondbacks PG 1.00 .30
❑ 501 Randy Johnson .60 .18
Curt Schilling
Co-MVP's PG
❑ 502 Josh Fogg RC 2.00 .60
❑ 503 Elpidio Guzman 2.00 .60
❑ 504 Corky Miller RC 2.00 .60
❑ 505 Cesar Crespo RC 2.00 .60
❑ 506 Carlos Garcia RC 2.00 .60
❑ 507 Carlos Valderrama RC 2.00 .60
❑ 508 Joe Kennedy RC 2.00 .60
❑ 509 Henry Mateo RC 2.00 .60
❑ 510 B. Duckworth RC 2.00 .60
❑ 511 Ichiro Suzuki 15.00 4.50
❑ 512 Zach Day RC 3.00 .90
❑ 513 Ryan Freel RC 2.00 .60
❑ 514 Brian Lawrence RC 2.00 .60
❑ 515 Alexis Gomez RC 2.00 .60
❑ 516 Will Ohman RC 2.00 .60
❑ 517 Juan Diaz RC 2.00 .60
❑ 518 Juan Moreno RC 2.00 .60
❑ 519 Rob Mackowiak RC 2.00 .60
❑ 520 Horacio Ramirez RC 3.00 .90
❑ 521 Albert Pujols 30.00 9.00
❑ 522 Tsuyoshi Shinjo 4.00 1.20
❑ 523 Ryan Drese RC 2.00 .60
❑ 524 Angel Berroa RC 5.00 1.50
❑ 525 Josh Towers RC 2.00 .60
❑ 526 Junior Spivey 3.00 .90
❑ 527 Greg Miller RC 2.00 .60
❑ 528 Esix Snead 2.00 .60
❑ 529 Mark Prior DP RC 25.00 7.50
❑ 530 Drew Henson 4.00 1.20
❑ 531 Brian Reith RC 2.00 .60
❑ 532 Andres Torres RC 2.00 .60
❑ 533 Casey Fossum RC 2.00 .60
❑ 534 Wilmy Caceres RC 2.00 .60
❑ 535 Matt White RC 2.00 .60
❑ 536 Wilkin Ruan RC 2.00 .60
❑ 537 Rick Bauer RC 2.00 .60
❑ 538 Morgan Ensberg RC 4.00 1.20
❑ 539 Geronimo Gil RC 2.00 .60
❑ 540 Dewon Brazelton RC 2.00 .60
❑ 541 Johnny Estrada RC 3.00 .90
❑ 542 Claudio Vargas RC 2.00 .60
❑ 543 Donaldo Mendez 2.00 .60
❑ 544 Kyle Lohse RC 3.00 .90
❑ 545 Nate Frese RC 2.00 .60
❑ 546 Christian Parker RC 2.00 .60
❑ 547 Blaine Neal RC 2.00 .60
❑ 548 Travis Hafner RC 3.00 .90
❑ 549 Billy Sylvester RC 2.00 .60
❑ 550 Adam Pettyjohn RC 2.00 .60
❑ 551 Bill Ortega RC 2.00 .60
❑ 552 Jose Acevedo RC 2.00 .60
❑ 553 Steve Green RC 2.00 .60
❑ 554 Jay Gibbons 4.00 1.20
❑ 555 Bert Snow RC 2.00 .60
❑ 556 Erick Almonte RC 2.00 .60
❑ 557 Jeremy Owens RC 2.00 .60
❑ 558 Sean Douglass RC 2.00 .60
❑ 559 Jason Smith RC 2.00 .60
❑ 560 Ricardo Rodriguez RC 2.00 .60
❑ 561 Mark Teixeira RC 12.00 3.60
❑ 562 Tyler Walker RC 2.00 .60
❑ 563 Juan Uribe 2.00 .60
❑ 564 Bud Smith RC 2.00 .60
❑ 565 Angel Santos RC 2.00 .60
❑ 566 Brandon Lyon RC 2.00 .60
❑ 567 Eric Hinske RC UER 3.00 .90
Front says he is a pitcher
❑ 568 Nick Punto RC 2.00 .60
❑ 569 Winston Abreu 2.00 .60
❑ 570 Jason Phillips RC 25.00 7.50
❑ 571 Rafael Soriano RC 4.00 1.20
❑ 572 Wilson Betemit 2.00 .60
❑ 573 Endy Chavez RC 2.00 .60
❑ 574 Juan Cruz RC 2.00 .60
❑ 575 Cory Aldridge RC 2.00 .60
❑ 576 Adrian Hernandez 2.00 .60
❑ 577 Brandon Larson RC 2.00 .60
❑ 578 Bret Prinz RC 2.00 .60
❑ 579 Jackson Melian RC 2.00 .60
❑ 580 Dave Maurer RC 2.00 .60
❑ 581 Jason Michaels RC 2.00 .60
❑ 582 Travis Phelps RC 2.00 .60
❑ 583 Cody Ransom RC 2.00 .60
❑ 584 Benito Baez RC 2.00 .60
❑ 585 Brian Roberts RC 2.00 .60
❑ 586 Nate Teut RC 2.00 .60
❑ 587 Jack Wilson RC 2.00 .60
❑ 588 Willie Harris RC 2.00 .60
❑ 589 Martin Vargas RC 2.00 .60
❑ 590 Steve Torrealba RC 2.00 .60
❑ 591 Stubby Clapp RC 2.00 .60
❑ 592 Dan Wright 2.00 .60
❑ 593 Mike Rivera RC 2.00 .60
❑ 594 Luis Pineda RC 2.00 .60
❑ 595 Lance Davis RC 2.00 .60
❑ 596 Ramon Vazquez RC 2.00 .60
❑ 597 Dustan Mohr RC 2.00 .60
❑ 598 Troy Mattes RC 2.00 .60
❑ 599 Grant Balfour RC 2.00 .60
❑ 600 Jared Fernandez RC 2.00 .60
❑ 601 Jorge Julio RC 2.00 .60

2002 Fleer Platinum

	Nm-Mt	Ex-Mt
COMPLETE SET (301)	200.00	60.00
COMP.SET w/o SP's (250)	30.00	9.00
COMMON CARD (1-250)	.40	.12
COMMON CARD (251-260)	3.00	.90
COMMON CARD (261-270)	3.00	.90
COMMON CARD (271-302)	3.00	.90

❑ 1 Garret Anderson .40 .12
❑ 2 Randy Johnson 1.00 .30
❑ 3 Chipper Jones 1.00 .30
❑ 4 David Cone .40 .12
❑ 5 Corey Patterson .40 .12
❑ 6 Carlos Lee .40 .12
❑ 7 Barry Larkin 1.00 .30
❑ 8 Jim Thome 1.00 .30
❑ 9 Larry Walker .60 .18
❑ 10 Randall Simon .40 .12
❑ 11 Charles Johnson .40 .12
❑ 12 Richard Hidalgo .40 .12
❑ 13 Mark Quinn .40 .12
❑ 14 Paul LoDuca .40 .12
❑ 15 Cristian Guzman .40 .12
❑ 16 Orlando Cabrera .40 .12
❑ 17 Al Leiter .40 .12
❑ 18 Nick Johnson .40 .12
❑ 19 Eric Chavez .40 .12
❑ 20 Miguel Tejada .40 .12
❑ 21 Mike Lieberthal .40 .12
❑ 22 Rob Mackowiak .40 .12
❑ 23 Ryan Klesko .40 .12
❑ 24 Jeff Kent .40 .12
❑ 25 Edgar Martinez .60 .18
❑ 26 Steve Kline .40 .12
❑ 27 Toby Hall .40 .12
❑ 28 Rusty Greer .40 .12
❑ 29 Jose Cruz Jr. .40 .12
❑ 30 Darin Erstad .40 .12
❑ 31 Reggie Sanders .40 .12
❑ 32 Javy Lopez .40 .12
❑ 33 Carl Everett .40 .12
❑ 34 Sammy Sosa 1.50 .45
❑ 35 Magglio Ordonez .40 .12
❑ 36 Todd Walker .40 .12
❑ 37 Omar Vizquel .40 .12
❑ 38 Matt Anderson .40 .12
❑ 39 Jeff Weaver .40 .12
❑ 40 Derrek Lee .40 .12
❑ 41 Julio Lugo .40 .12
❑ 42 Joe Randa .40 .12
❑ 43 Chan Ho Park .40 .12
❑ 44 Torii Hunter .40 .12
❑ 45 Vladimir Guerrero 1.00 .30
❑ 46 Rey Ordonez .40 .12
❑ 47 Tino Martinez .60 .18
❑ 48 Johnny Damon .40 .12
❑ 49 Barry Zito 1.00 .30
❑ 50 Robert Person .40 .12
❑ 51 Aramis Ramirez .40 .12
❑ 52 Mark Kotsay .40 .12
❑ 53 Jason Schmidt .40 .12
❑ 54 Jamie Moyer .40 .12
❑ 55 David Justice .40 .12
❑ 56 Aubrey Huff .40 .12
❑ 57 Rick Helling .40 .12
❑ 58 Carlos Delgado .40 .12
❑ 59 Troy Glaus .60 .18
❑ 60 Curt Schilling .60 .18
❑ 61 Greg Maddux 2.00 .60
❑ 62 Nomar Garciaparra 2.00 .60
❑ 63 Kerry Wood 1.00 .30
❑ 64 Frank Thomas 1.00 .30
❑ 65 Dmitri Young .40 .12
❑ 66 Alex Ochoa .40 .12
❑ 67 Jose Macias .40 .12
❑ 68 Antonio Alfonseca .40 .12
❑ 69 Mike Lowell .40 .12
❑ 70 Wade Miller .40 .12
❑ 71 Mike Sweeney .40 .12
❑ 72 Gary Sheffield .40 .12
❑ 73 Corey Koskie .40 .12
❑ 74 Lee Stevens .40 .12
❑ 75 Jay Payton .40 .12
❑ 76 Mike Mussina 1.00 .30
❑ 77 Jermaine Dye .40 .12
❑ 78 Bobby Abreu .40 .12
❑ 79 Scott Rolen .60 .18
❑ 80 Todd Ritchie .40 .12
❑ 81 D'Angelo Jimenez .40 .12
❑ 82 Robb Nen .40 .12
❑ 83 John Olerud .40 .12
❑ 84 Matt Morris .40 .12
❑ 85 Joe Kennedy .40 .12
❑ 86 Gabe Kapler .40 .12
❑ 87 Chris Carpenter .40 .12
❑ 88 David Eckstein .40 .12
❑ 89 Matt Williams .40 .12
❑ 90 John Smoltz .60 .18
❑ 91 Pedro Martinez 1.00 .30
❑ 92 Eric Young .40 .12
❑ 93 Jose Valentin .40 .12
❑ 94 Erubiel Durazo .40 .12
❑ 95 Jeff Cirillo .40 .12
❑ 96 Brandon Inge .40 .12
❑ 97 Josh Beckett .60 .18
❑ 98 Preston Wilson .40 .12
❑ 99 Damian Jackson .40 .12
❑ 100 Adrian Beltre .40 .12
❑ 101 Jeromy Burnitz .40 .12
❑ 102 Joe Mays .40 .12
❑ 103 Michael Barrett .40 .12
❑ 104 Mike Piazza 1.50 .45
❑ 105 Brady Anderson .40 .12
❑ 106 Jason Giambi Yankees 1.00 .30
❑ 107 Marlon Anderson .40 .12
❑ 108 Jimmy Rollins .40 .12
❑ 109 Jack Wilson .40 .12
❑ 110 Brian Lawrence .40 .12
❑ 111 Russ Ortiz .40 .12
❑ 112 Kazuhiro Sasaki .40 .12
❑ 113 Placido Polanco .40 .12
❑ 114 Damian Rolls .40 .12
❑ 115 Rafael Palmeiro .60 .18
❑ 116 Brad Fullmer .40 .12
❑ 117 Tim Salmon .60 .18
❑ 118 Tony Womack .40 .12
❑ 119 Tony Batista .40 .12
❑ 120 Trot Nixon .40 .12
❑ 121 Mark Buehrle .40 .12
❑ 122 Derek Jeter 2.50 .75

❑ 123 Ellis Burks .40 .12
❑ 124 Mike Hampton .40 .12
❑ 125 Roger Cedeno .40 .12
❑ 126 A.J. Burnett .40 .12
❑ 127 Moises Alou .40 .12
❑ 128 Billy Wagner .40 .12
❑ 129 Kevin Brown .40 .12
❑ 130 Jose Hernandez .40 .12
❑ 131 Doug Mientkiewicz .40 .12
❑ 132 Javier Vazquez .40 .12
❑ 133 Tsuyoshi Shinjo .40 .12
❑ 134 Andy Pettitte .60 .18
❑ 135 Tim Hudson .40 .12
❑ 136 Pat Burrell .40 .12
❑ 137 Brian Giles .40 .12
❑ 138 Kevin Young .40 .12
❑ 139 Xavier Nady .40 .12
❑ 140 J.T. Snow .40 .12
❑ 141 Aaron Sele .40 .12
❑ 142 Albert Pujols 2.00 .60
❑ 143 Jason Tyner .40 .12
❑ 144 Ivan Rodriguez 1.00 .30
❑ 145 Raul Mondesi .40 .12
❑ 146 Matt Lawton .40 .12
❑ 147 Rafael Furcal .40 .12
❑ 148 Jeff Conine .40 .12
❑ 149 Hideo Nomo 1.00 .30
❑ 150 Jose Canseco 1.00 .30
❑ 151 Aaron Boone .40 .12
❑ 152 Bartolo Colon .40 .12
❑ 153 Todd Helton .60 .18
❑ 154 Tony Clark .40 .12
❑ 155 Pablo Ozuna .40 .12
❑ 156 Jeff Bagwell .60 .18
❑ 157 Carlos Beltran .40 .12
❑ 158 Shawn Green .40 .12
❑ 159 Geoff Jenkins .40 .12
❑ 160 Eric Milton .40 .12
❑ 161 Jose Vidro .40 .12
❑ 162 Robin Ventura .40 .12
❑ 163 Jorge Posada .60 .18
❑ 164 Terrence Long .40 .12
❑ 165 Brandon Duckworth .40 .12
❑ 166 Chad Hermansen .40 .12
❑ 167 Ben Davis .40 .12
❑ 168 Phil Nevin .40 .12
❑ 169 Bret Boone .40 .12
❑ 170 J.D. Drew .40 .12
❑ 171 Edgar Renteria .40 .12
❑ 172 Randy Winn .40 .12
❑ 173 Alex Rodriguez 2.00 .60
❑ 174 Shannon Stewart .40 .12
❑ 175 Steve Finley .40 .12
❑ 176 Marcus Giles .40 .12
❑ 177 Jay Gibbons .40 .12
❑ 178 Manny Ramirez .40 .12
❑ 179 Ray Durham .40 .12
❑ 180 Sean Casey .40 .12
❑ 181 Travis Fryman .40 .12
❑ 182 Denny Neagle .40 .12
❑ 183 Deivi Cruz .40 .12
❑ 184 Luis Castillo .40 .12
❑ 185 Lance Berkman .40 .12
❑ 186 Dee Brown .40 .12
❑ 187 Jeff Shaw .40 .12
❑ 188 Mark Loretta .40 .12
❑ 189 David Ortiz .40 .12
❑ 190 Edgardo Alfonzo .40 .12
❑ 191 Roger Clemens 2.00 .60
❑ 192 Mariano Rivera .60 .18
❑ 193 Jeremy Giambi .40 .12
❑ 194 Johnny Estrada .40 .12
❑ 195 Craig Wilson .40 .12
❑ 196 Adam Eaton .40 .12
❑ 197 Rich Aurilia .40 .12
❑ 198 Mike Cameron .40 .12
❑ 199 Jim Edmonds .40 .12
❑ 200 Fernando Vina .40 .12
❑ 201 Greg Vaughn .40 .12
❑ 202 Mike Young .40 .12
❑ 203 Vernon Wells .40 .12
❑ 204 Luis Gonzalez .40 .12
❑ 205 Tom Glavine 1.00 .30
❑ 206 Chris Richard .40 .12
❑ 207 Jon Lieber .40 .12
❑ 208 Keith Foulke .40 .12
❑ 209 Rondell White .40 .12
❑ 210 Bernie Williams .60 .18
❑ 211 Juan Pierre .40 .12
❑ 212 Juan Encarnacion .40 .12
❑ 213 Ryan Dempster .40 .12
❑ 214 Tim Redding .40 .12
❑ 215 Jeff Suppan .40 .12
❑ 216 Mark Grudzielanek .40 .12
❑ 217 Richie Sexson .40 .12
❑ 218 Brad Radke .40 .12
❑ 219 Armando Benitez .40 .12
❑ 220 Orlando Hernandez .40 .12
❑ 221 Alfonso Soriano 1.00 .30
❑ 222 Mark Mulder .40 .12
❑ 223 Travis Lee .40 .12
❑ 224 Jason Kendall .40 .12
❑ 225 Trevor Hoffman .40 .12
❑ 226 Barry Bonds 2.50 .75
❑ 227 Freddy Garcia .40 .12
❑ 228 Darryl Kile .40 .12
❑ 229 Ben Grieve .40 .12
❑ 230 Frank Catalanotto .40 .12
❑ 231 Ruben Sierra .40 .12
❑ 232 Homer Bush .40 .12
❑ 233 Mark Grace 1.00 .30
❑ 234 Andruw Jones .60 .18
❑ 235 Brian Roberts .40 .12
❑ 236 Fred McGriff .60 .18
❑ 237 Paul Konerko .40 .12
❑ 238 Ken Griffey Jr. 1.50 .45
❑ 239 John Burkett .40 .12
❑ 240 Juan Uribe .40 .12
❑ 241 Bobby Higginson .40 .12
❑ 242 Cliff Floyd .40 .12
❑ 243 Craig Biggio .60 .18
❑ 244 Neifi Perez .40 .12
❑ 245 Eric Karros .40 .12
❑ 246 Ben Sheets .40 .12
❑ 247 Tony Armas Jr. .40 .12
❑ 248 Mo Vaughn .40 .12
❑ 249 David Wells .40 .12
❑ 250 Juan Gonzalez 1.00 .30
❑ 251 Barry Bonds DD 8.00 2.40
❑ 252 Sammy Sosa DD 5.00 1.50
❑ 253 Ken Griffey Jr. DD 5.00 1.50
❑ 254 Roger Clemens DD 6.00 1.80
❑ 255 Greg Maddux DD 6.00 1.80
❑ 256 Chipper Jones DD 3.00 .90
❑ 257 Alex Rodriguez 8.00 2.40
Derek Jeter
Nomar Garciaparra DD
❑ 258 Roberto Alomar DD 3.00 .90
❑ 259 Jeff Bagwell DD 3.00 .90
❑ 260 Mike Piazza DD 5.00 1.50
❑ 261 Mark Teixeira BB 4.00 1.20
❑ 262 Mark Prior BB 6.00 1.80
❑ 263 Alex Escobar BB 3.00 .90
❑ 264 C.C. Sabathia BB 3.00 .90
❑ 265 Drew Henson BB 3.00 .90
❑ 266 Wilson Betemit BB 3.00 .90
❑ 267 Roy Oswalt BB 3.00 .90
❑ 268 Adam Dunn BB 3.00 .90
❑ 269 Bud Smith BB 3.00 .90
❑ 270 Dewon Brazelton BB 3.00 .90
❑ 271 Brandon Backe RC 3.00 .90
Jason Standridge
❑ 272 Wilfredo Rodriguez 3.00 .90
Carlos Hernandez
❑ 273 Geronimo Gil 3.00 .90
Luis Rivera
❑ 274 Carlos Pena 3.00 .90
Jovanny Cedeno
❑ 275 Austin Kearns 3.00 .90
Ben Broussard
❑ 276 Jorge De La RosaRC 3.00 .90
Kenny Kelly
❑ 277 Ryan Drese 3.00 .90
Victor Martinez
❑ 278 Joel Pinero 3.00 .90
Nate Cornejo
❑ 279 David Kelton 3.00 .90
Carlos Zambrano
❑ 280 Bill Ortega -
Satoru Komiyama ERR
Not intended for public release
Card features large cut out square
over Komiyama image
❑ 281 Donnie Bridges 3.00 .90
Wilkin Ruan
❑ 282 Wily Mo Pena 4.00 1.20
Brandon Claussen
❑ 283 Jason Jennings 3.00 .90
Rene Reyes RC
❑ 284 Steve Green 3.00 .90
Alfredo Amezaga
❑ 285 Eric Hinske 3.00 .90
Felipe Lopez
❑ 286 Anderson Machado RC 3.00 .90
Brad Baisley
❑ 287 Carlos Garcia 3.00 .90
Sean Douglass
❑ 288 Pat Strange 3.00 .90
Jae Weong Seo
❑ 289 Marcus Thames 3.00 .90
Alex Graman
❑ 290 Matt Childers RC 3.00 .90
Hansel Izquierdo RC
❑ 291 Ron Calloway RC 3.00 .90
Adam Walker RC
❑ 292 J.R. House 3.00 .90
J.J. Davis
❑ 293 Ryan Anderson 3.00 .90
Rafael Soriano
❑ 294 Mike Bynum 3.00 .90
Dennis Tankersley
❑ 295 Kurt Ainsworth 3.00 .90
Carlos Valderrama
❑ 296 Billy Hall 3.00 .90
Cristian Guerrero
❑ 297 Miguel Olivo 3.00 .90
Danny Wright
❑ 298 Marlon Byrd 3.00 .90
Jorge Padilla RC
❑ 299 Juan Cruz 3.00 .90
Ben Christensen
❑ 300 Adam Johnson 3.00 .90
Michael Restovich
❑ 301 So Taguchi SP RC 3.00 .90
❑ 302 Kazuhisa Ishii SP RC 4.00 1.20
❑ NNO Barry Bonds 1986 AU/73 500.00 150.00

2003 Fleer Patchworks

	Nm-Mt	Ex-Mt
COMP.SET w/o SP's (90)	15.00	4.50
COMMON CARD (1-90)	.40	.12
COMMON CARD (91-115)	5.00	1.50

❑ 1 Luis Castillo .40 .12
❑ 2 Derek Jeter 2.50 .75
❑ 3 Vladimir Guerrero 1.00 .30
❑ 4 Bobby Higginson .40 .12
❑ 5 Pat Burrell .40 .12
❑ 6 Ivan Rodriguez 1.00 .30
❑ 7 Craig Biggio .60 .18
❑ 8 Troy Glaus .60 .18
❑ 9 Barry Bonds 2.50 .75
❑ 10 Hideo Nomo 1.00 .30
❑ 11 Barry Larkin 1.00 .30
❑ 12 Roberto Alomar 1.00 .30
❑ 13 Rodrigo Lopez .40 .12
❑ 14 Eric Chavez .40 .12
❑ 15 Shawn Green .40 .12
❑ 16 Joe Randa .40 .12

❑ 17 Mark Grace 1.00 .30
❑ 18 Jason Kendall .40 .12
❑ 19 Hee Seop Choi .40 .12
❑ 20 Luis Gonzalez .40 .12
❑ 21 Sammy Sosa 1.50 .45
❑ 22 Larry Walker .60 .18
❑ 23 Phil Nevin .40 .12
❑ 24 Manny Ramirez .40 .12
❑ 25 Jim Thome 1.00 .30
❑ 26 Randy Johnson 1.00 .30
❑ 27 Jose Vidro .40 .12
❑ 28 Austin Kearns .60 .18
❑ 29 Mike Sweeney .40 .12
❑ 30 Magglio Ordonez .40 .12
❑ 31 Mike Piazza 1.50 .45
❑ 32 Eric Hinske .40 .12
❑ 33 Alex Rodriguez 2.00 .60
❑ 34 Kerry Wood 1.00 .30
❑ 35 Matt Morris .40 .12
❑ 36 Lance Berkman .40 .12
❑ 37 Michael Cuddyer .40 .12
❑ 38 Curt Schilling .60 .18
❑ 39 Sean Burroughs .40 .12
❑ 40 Ken Griffey Jr. 1.50 .45
❑ 41 Edgardo Alfonzo .40 .12
❑ 42 Carlos Pena .40 .12
❑ 43 Adam Dunn .60 .18
❑ 44 Pedro Martinez 1.00 .30
❑ 45 Miguel Tejada .40 .12
❑ 46 Tom Glavine 1.00 .30
❑ 47 Torii Hunter .40 .12
❑ 48 Jason Giambi 1.00 .30
❑ 49 Tony Batista .40 .12
❑ 50 Ben Grieve .40 .12
❑ 51 Ichiro Suzuki 2.00 .60
❑ 52 Bobby Abreu .40 .12
❑ 53 Todd Helton .60 .18
❑ 54 Kazuhiro Sasaki .40 .12
❑ 55 Nomar Garciaparra 2.00 .60
❑ 56 Francisco Rodriguez .40 .12
❑ 57 Ellis Burks .40 .12
❑ 58 Frank Thomas 1.00 .30
❑ 59 Greg Maddux 2.00 .60
❑ 60 Josh Beckett .60 .18
❑ 61 Brad Wilkerson .40 .12
❑ 62 Joe Borchard .40 .12
❑ 63 Carlos Delgado .40 .12
❑ 64 Alfonso Soriano 1.00 .30
❑ 65 Chipper Jones 1.00 .30
❑ 66 J.D. Drew .40 .12
❑ 67 Mark Prior 2.00 .60
❑ 68 Rafael Palmeiro .60 .18
❑ 69 Jeff Kent .40 .12
❑ 70 Adrian Beltre .40 .12
❑ 71 Marlon Byrd .40 .12
❑ 72 Orlando Hudson .40 .12
❑ 73 Junior Spivey .40 .12
❑ 74 Jeff Bagwell .60 .18
❑ 75 Barry Zito 1.00 .30
❑ 76 Roger Clemens 2.00 .60
❑ 77 Aubrey Huff .40 .12
❑ 78 Geoff Jenkins .40 .12
❑ 79 Andruw Jones .60 .18
❑ 80 Scott Rolen .60 .18
❑ 81 Omar Vizquel .40 .12
❑ 82 Darin Erstad .40 .12
❑ 83 Bernie Williams .60 .18
❑ 84 Freddy Garcia .40 .12
❑ 85 Richie Sexson .40 .12
❑ 86 Josh Phelps .40 .12
❑ 87 Albert Pujols 2.00 .60
❑ 88 Aramis Ramirez .40 .12
❑ 89 Shea Hillenbrand .40 .12
❑ 90 Cristian Guzman .40 .12
❑ 91 Adam LaRoche RR 5.00 1.50
❑ 92 David Pember RR RC 5.00 1.50
❑ 93 Terrmel Sledge RR RC 8.00 2.40
❑ 94 Hideki Matsui RR RC 20.00 6.00
❑ 95 Nook Logan RR RC 5.00 1.50
❑ 96 Jose Contreras RR RC 10.00 3.00
❑ 97 Pete LaForest RR RC 8.00 2.40
❑ 98 Rich Fischer RR RC 5.00 1.50
❑ 99 Francisco Rosario RR RC 5.00 1.50
❑ 100 Josh Willingham RR RC 10.00 3.00
❑ 101 Alejandro Machado RR RC 5.00 1.50
❑ 102 Lew Ford RR RC 8.00 2.40
❑ 103 Joe Valentine RR RC 5.00 1.50
❑ 104 Guillermo Quiroz RR RC 8.00 2.40
❑ 105 Chien-Ming Wang RR RC 10.00 3.00
❑ 106 Jhonny Peralta RR RC 5.00 1.50
❑ 107 Shane Victorino RR RC 5.00 1.50
❑ 108 Prentice Redman RR RC 5.00 1.50
❑ 109 Matt Bruback RR RC 5.00 1.50
❑ 110 Lance Niekro RR 5.00 1.50
❑ 111 Travis Hughes RR 5.00 1.50
❑ 112 Nic Jackson RR 5.00 1.50
❑ 113 Hector Luna RR RC 5.00 1.50
❑ 114 Cliff Lee RR 5.00 1.50
❑ 115 Tim Olson RR RC 8.00 2.40

2003 Fleer Platinum

	Nm-Mt	Ex-Mt
COMP.SET w/o SP's (220)	30.00	9.00
COMMON CARD (1-220)	.30	.09
COMMON CARD (221-235)	2.00	.60
221-235 ODDS 1:4 WAX, 1:2 JUMBO, 1:1 RACK		
COMMON CARD (236-240)	2.00	.60
236-240 ODDS 1:12 WAX	-	
COMMON CARD (241-245)	3.00	.90
241-245 ODDS 1:6 JUMBO	-	
COMMON CARD (246-250)	3.00	.90
246-250 ODDS 1:2 RACK	-	

❑ 1 Barry Bonds 2.00 .60
❑ 2 Sean Casey .30 .09
❑ 3 Todd Walker .30 .09
❑ 4 Tony Batista .30 .09
❑ 5 Todd Zeile .30 .09
❑ 6 Ruben Sierra .30 .09
❑ 7 Jose Cruz Jr. .30 .09
❑ 8 Ben Grieve .30 .09
❑ 9 Rob Mackowiak .30 .09
❑ 10 Gary Sheffield .30 .09
❑ 11 Armando Benitez .30 .09
❑ 12 Tim Hudson .30 .09
❑ 13 Eric Milton .30 .09
❑ 14 Andy Pettitte .50 .15
❑ 15 Jeff Bagwell .50 .15
❑ 16 Jeff Kent .30 .09
❑ 17 Joe Randa .30 .09
❑ 18 Benito Santiago .30 .09
❑ 19 Russell Branyan .30 .09
❑ 20 Cliff Floyd .30 .09
❑ 21 Chris Richard .30 .09
❑ 22 Randy Winn .30 .09
❑ 23 Freddy Garcia .30 .09
❑ 24 Derek Lowe .30 .09
❑ 25 Ben Sheets .30 .09
❑ 26 Fred McGriff .50 .15
❑ 27 Bret Boone .30 .09
❑ 28 Jose Hernandez .30 .09
❑ 29 Phil Nevin .30 .09
❑ 30 Mike Piazza 1.25 .35
❑ 31 Bobby Abreu .30 .09
❑ 32 Darin Erstad .30 .09
❑ 33 Andruw Jones .50 .15
❑ 34 Brad Wilkerson .30 .09
❑ 35 Brian Lawrence .30 .09
❑ 36 Vladimir Nunez .30 .09
❑ 37 Kazuhiro Sasaki .30 .09
❑ 38 Carlos Delgado .30 .09
❑ 39 Steve Cox .30 .09
❑ 40 Adrian Beltre .30 .09
❑ 41 Josh Bard .30 .09
❑ 42 Randall Simon .30 .09
❑ 43 Johnny Damon .30 .09
❑ 44 Ken Griffey Jr. 1.25 .35
❑ 45 Sammy Sosa 1.25 .35
❑ 46 Kevin Brown .30 .09
❑ 47 Kazuhisa Ishii .30 .09
❑ 48 Matt Morris .30 .09
❑ 49 Mark Prior 1.50 .45
❑ 50 Kip Wells .30 .09
❑ 51 Hee Seop Choi .30 .09
❑ 52 Craig Biggio .50 .15
❑ 53 Derek Jeter 2.00 .60
❑ 54 Albert Pujols 1.50 .45
❑ 55 Joe Borchard .30 .09
❑ 56 Robert Fick .30 .09
❑ 57 Jacque Jones .30 .09
❑ 58 Juan Pierre .30 .09
❑ 59 Bernie Williams .50 .15
❑ 60 Elmer Dessens .30 .09
❑ 61 Al Leiter .30 .09
❑ 62 Curt Schilling .50 .15
❑ 63 Carlos Pena .30 .09
❑ 64 Tino Martinez .50 .15
❑ 65 Fernando Vina .30 .09
❑ 66 Aaron Boone .30 .09
❑ 67 Michael Barrett .30 .09
❑ 68 Frank Thomas .75 .23
❑ 69 J.D. Drew .30 .09
❑ 70 Vladimir Guerrero .75 .23
❑ 71 Shannon Stewart .30 .09
❑ 72 Mark Buehrle .30 .09
❑ 73 Jamie Moyer .30 .09
❑ 74 Brad Radke .30 .09
❑ 75 Mike Williams .30 .09
❑ 76 Ryan Klesko .30 .09
❑ 77 Roberto Alomar .75 .23
❑ 78 Edgardo Alfonzo .30 .09
❑ 79 Matt Williams .30 .09
❑ 80 Edgar Martinez .50 .15
❑ 81 Shawn Green .30 .09
❑ 82 Kenny Lofton .30 .09
❑ 83 Josh Beckett .50 .15
❑ 84 Trevor Hoffman .30 .09
❑ 85 Kevin Millwood .30 .09
❑ 86 Odalis Perez .30 .09
❑ 87 Jarrod Washburn .30 .09
❑ 88 Jason Giambi .75 .23
❑ 89 Eric Young .30 .09
❑ 90 Barry Larkin .75 .23
❑ 91 Aramis Ramirez .30 .09
❑ 92 Ivan Rodriguez .75 .23
❑ 93 Steve Finley .30 .09
❑ 94 Brian Jordan .30 .09
❑ 95 Manny Ramirez .30 .09
❑ 96 Preston Wilson .30 .09
❑ 97 Rodrigo Lopez .30 .09
❑ 98 Ramon Ortiz .30 .09
❑ 99 Jim Thome .75 .23
❑ 100 Luis Castillo .30 .09
❑ 101 Alex Rodriguez 1.50 .45
❑ 102 Jared Sandberg .30 .09
❑ 103 Ellis Burks .30 .09
❑ 104 Pat Burrell .30 .09
❑ 105 Brian Giles .30 .09
❑ 106 Mark Kotsay .30 .09
❑ 107 Dave Roberts .30 .09
❑ 108 Roy Halladay .30 .09
❑ 109 Chan Ho Park .30 .09
❑ 110 Erubiel Durazo .30 .09
❑ 111 Bobby Hill .30 .09
❑ 112 Cristian Guzman .30 .09
❑ 113 Troy Glaus .50 .15
❑ 114 Lance Berkman .30 .09
❑ 115 Juan Encarnacion .30 .09
❑ 116 Chipper Jones .75 .23
❑ 117 Corey Patterson .30 .09
❑ 118 Vernon Wells .30 .09
❑ 119 Matt Clement .30 .09
❑ 120 Billy Koch .30 .09
❑ 121 Hideo Nomo .75 .23
❑ 122 Derrek Lee .30 .09
❑ 123 Todd Helton .50 .15
❑ 124 Sean Burroughs .30 .09
❑ 125 Jason Kendall .30 .09
❑ 126 Dmitri Young .30 .09

❑ 127 Adam Dunn .50 .15
❑ 128 Bobby Higginson .30 .09
❑ 129 Raul Mondesi .30 .09
❑ 130 Bubba Trammell .30 .09
❑ 131 A.J. Burnett .30 .09
❑ 132 Randy Johnson .75 .23
❑ 133 Mark Mulder .30 .09
❑ 134 Mariano Rivera .50 .15
❑ 135 Kerry Wood .75 .23
❑ 136 Mo Vaughn .30 .09
❑ 137 Jimmy Rollins .30 .09
❑ 138 Jose Valentin .30 .09
❑ 139 Brad Fullmer .30 .09
❑ 140 Mike Cameron .30 .09
❑ 141 Luis Gonzalez .30 .09
❑ 142 Kevin Appier .30 .09
❑ 143 Mike Hampton .30 .09
❑ 144 Pedro Martinez .75 .23
❑ 145 Javier Vazquez .30 .09
❑ 146 Doug Mientkiewicz .30 .09
❑ 147 Adam Kennedy .30 .09
❑ 148 Rafael Furcal .30 .09
❑ 149 Eric Chavez .30 .09
❑ 150 Mike Lieberthal .30 .09
❑ 151 Moises Alou .30 .09
❑ 152 Jermaine Dye .30 .09
❑ 153 Torii Hunter .30 .09
❑ 154 Trot Nixon .30 .09
❑ 155 Larry Walker .50 .15
❑ 156 Jorge Julio .30 .09
❑ 157 Mike Mussina .75 .23
❑ 158 Kirk Rueter .30 .09
❑ 159 Rafael Palmeiro .50 .15
❑ 160 Pokey Reese .30 .09
❑ 161 Miguel Tejada .30 .09
❑ 162 Robin Ventura .30 .09
❑ 163 Raul Ibanez .30 .09
❑ 164 Roger Cedeno .30 .09
❑ 165 Juan Gonzalez .75 .23
❑ 166 Carlos Lee .30 .09
❑ 167 Tim Salmon .50 .15
❑ 168 Orlando Hernandez .30 .09
❑ 169 Wade Miller .30 .09
❑ 170 Troy Percival .30 .09
❑ 171 Billy Wagner .30 .09
❑ 172 Jeff Conine .30 .09
❑ 173 Junior Spivey .30 .09
❑ 174 Edgar Renteria .30 .09
❑ 175 Scott Rolen .50 .15
❑ 176 Jason Varitek .30 .09
❑ 177 Ben Broussard .30 .09
❑ 178 Jeremy Giambi .30 .09
❑ 179 Gabe Kapler .30 .09
❑ 180 Armando Rios .30 .09
❑ 181 Ichiro Suzuki 1.50 .45
❑ 182 Tom Glavine .75 .23
❑ 183 Greg Maddux 1.50 .45
❑ 184 Roy Oswalt .30 .09
❑ 185 John Smoltz .50 .15
❑ 186 Eric Karros .30 .09
❑ 187 Alfonso Soriano .75 .23
❑ 188 Nomar Garciaparra 1.50 .45
❑ 189 Joe Crede .30 .09
❑ 190 Javy Lopez .30 .09
❑ 191 Carlos Beltran .30 .09
❑ 192 Jim Edmonds .30 .09
❑ 193 Geoff Jenkins .30 .09
❑ 194 Magglio Ordonez .30 .09
❑ 195 Daryle Ward .30 .09
❑ 196 Roger Clemens 1.50 .45
❑ 197 Byung-Hyun Kim .30 .09
❑ 198 Robb Nen .30 .09
❑ 199 C.C. Sabathia .30 .09
❑ 200 Barry Zito .75 .23
❑ 201 Mark Grace UH .50 .15
❑ 202 Paul Konerko UH .30 .09
❑ 203 Mike Sweeney UH .30 .09
❑ 204 John Olerud UH .30 .09
❑ 205 Jose Vidro UH .30 .09
❑ 206 Ray Durham UH .30 .09
❑ 207 Omar Vizquel UH .30 .09
❑ 208 Shea Hillenbrand UH .30 .09
❑ 209 Mike Lowell UH .30 .09
❑ 210 Aubrey Huff UH .30 .09
❑ 211 Eric Hinske UH .30 .09
❑ 212 Paul Lo Duca UH .30 .09
❑ 213 Jay Gibbons UH .30 .09
❑ 214 Austin Kearns UH .50 .15
❑ 215 Richie Sexson UH .30 .09
❑ 216 Garret Anderson UH .30 .09
❑ 217 Eric Gagne UH .30 .09
❑ 218 Jason Jennings UH .30 .09
❑ 219 Damian Moss UH .30 .09
❑ 220 David Eckstein UH .30 .09
❑ 221 Mark Teixeira PROS 3.00 .90
❑ 222 Bill Hall PROS 2.00 .60
❑ 223 Bobby Jenks PROS 2.00 .60
❑ 224 Adam Morrissey PROS 2.00 .60
❑ 225 Rodrigo Rosario PROS 2.00 .60
❑ 226 Brett Myers PROS 2.00 .60
❑ 227 Tony Alvarez PROS 2.00 .60
❑ 228 Willie Bloomquist PROS 2.00 .60
❑ 229 Ben Howard PROS 2.00 .60
❑ 230 Nic Jackson PROS 2.00 .60
❑ 231 Carl Crawford PROS 2.00 .60
❑ 232 Omar Infante PROS 2.00 .60
❑ 233 Francisco Rodriguez PROS 2.00 .60
❑ 234 Andy Van Hekken PROS 2.00 .60
❑ 235 Kirk Saarloos PROS 2.00 .60
❑ 236 Dusty Wathan PROS RC 2.00 .60
❑ 237 Jamey Carroll PROS 2.00 .60
❑ 238 Jason Phillips PROS 2.00 .60
❑ 239 Jose Castillo PROS 2.00 .60
❑ 240 Arnaldo Munoz PROS RC 2.00 .60
❑ 241 Orlando Hudson PROS 3.00 .90
❑ 242 Drew Henson PROS 3.00 .90
❑ 243 Jason Lane PROS 3.00 .90
❑ 244 Vinny Chulk PROS 3.00 .90
❑ 245 Prentice Redman PROS RC 3.00 .90
❑ 246 Marlon Byrd PROS 3.00 .90
❑ 247 Chin-Feng Chen PROS 3.00 .90
❑ 248 Craig Brazell PROS RC 8.00 2.40
❑ 249 John Webb PROS 3.00 .90
❑ 250 Adam LaRoche PROS 3.00 .90

2001 Fleer Premium

	Nm-Mt	Ex-Mt
COMP.SET w/o SP's (200)	30.00	9.00
COMMON CARD (1-200)	.40	.12
COMMON (201-230)	8.00	2.40
COMMON (231-235)	8.00	2.40

❑ 1 Cal Ripken 3.00 .90
❑ 2 Derek Jeter 2.50 .75
❑ 3 Edgardo Alfonzo .40 .12
❑ 4 Luis Castillo .40 .12
❑ 5 Mike Lieberthal .40 .12
❑ 6 Kazuhiro Sasaki .40 .12
❑ 7 Jeff Kent .40 .12
❑ 8 Eric Karros .40 .12
❑ 9 Tom Glavine 1.00 .30
❑ 10 Jeromy Burnitz .40 .12
❑ 11 Travis Fryman .40 .12
❑ 12 Ron Coomer .40 .12
❑ 13 Jeff D'Amico .40 .12
❑ 14 Carlos Febles .40 .12
❑ 15 Kevin Brown .40 .12
❑ 16 Deivi Cruz .40 .12
❑ 17 Tino Martinez .60 .18
❑ 18 Bobby Abreu .40 .12
❑ 19 Roger Clemens 2.00 .60
❑ 20 Jeffrey Hammonds .40 .12
❑ 21 Peter Bergeron .40 .12
❑ 22 Ray Lankford .40 .12
❑ 23 Scott Rolen .60 .18
❑ 24 Jermaine Dye .40 .12
❑ 25 Rusty Greer .40 .12
❑ 26 Frank Thomas 1.00 .30
❑ 27 Jeff Bagwell .60 .18
❑ 28 Cliff Floyd .40 .12
❑ 29 Chris Singleton .40 .12
❑ 30 Steve Finley .40 .12
❑ 31 Orlando Hernandez .40 .12
❑ 32 Tom Goodwin .40 .12
❑ 33 Larry Walker .60 .18
❑ 34 Mike Sweeney .40 .12
❑ 35 Tim Hudson .40 .12
❑ 36 Kerry Wood 1.00 .30
❑ 37 Mike Lowell .40 .12
❑ 38 Andruw Jones .75 .23
❑ 39 Alex Gonzalez .40 .12
❑ 40 Juan Gonzalez .75 .23
❑ 41 J.D. Drew .40 .12
❑ 42 Mark McLemore .40 .12
❑ 43 Royce Clayton .40 .12
❑ 44 Paul O'Neill .60 .18
❑ 45 Carlos Beltran .40 .12
❑ 46 Phil Nevin .40 .12
❑ 47 Rondell White .40 .12
❑ 48 Gerald Williams .40 .12
❑ 49 Geoff Jenkins .40 .12
❑ 50 Marvin Benard .40 .12
❑ 51 Alex Rodriguez 2.00 .60
❑ 52 Moises Alou .40 .12
❑ 53 Mike Lansing .40 .12
❑ 54 Omar Vizquel .40 .12
❑ 55 Eric Chavez .40 .12
❑ 56 Mark Quinn .40 .12
❑ 57 Mike Lamb .40 .12
❑ 58 Rick Ankiel .40 .12
❑ 59 Lance Berkman .40 .12
❑ 60 Jeff Conine .40 .12
❑ 61 B.J. Surhoff .40 .12
❑ 62 Todd Helton .60 .18
❑ 63 J.T. Snow .40 .12
❑ 64 John VanderWal .40 .12
❑ 65 Johnny Damon .40 .12
❑ 66 Bobby Higginson .40 .12
❑ 67 Carlos Delgado .75 .23
❑ 68 Shawn Green .40 .12
❑ 69 Mike Redmond .40 .12
❑ 70 Mike Piazza 1.50 .45
❑ 71 Adrian Beltre .40 .12
❑ 72 Juan Encarnacion .40 .12
❑ 73 Chipper Jones 1.00 .30
❑ 74 Garret Anderson .40 .12
❑ 75 Paul Konerko .40 .12
❑ 76 Barry Larkin 1.00 .30
❑ 77 Tony Gwynn 1.25 .35
❑ 78 Rafael Palmeiro .60 .18
❑ 79 Randy Johnson 1.00 .30
❑ 80 Mark Grace .75 .23
❑ 81 Javy Lopez .40 .12
❑ 82 Gabe Kapler .40 .12
❑ 83 Henry Rodriguez .40 .12
❑ 84 Raul Mondesi .40 .12
❑ 85 Adam Piatt .40 .12
❑ 86 Marquis Grissom .40 .12
❑ 87 Charles Johnson .40 .12
❑ 88 Sean Casey .40 .12
❑ 89 Manny Ramirez .40 .12
❑ 90 Curt Schilling .60 .18
❑ 91 Fernando Tatis .40 .12
❑ 92 Derek Bell .40 .12
❑ 93 Tony Clark .40 .12
❑ 94 Homer Bush .40 .12
❑ 95 Nomar Garciaparra 2.00 .60
❑ 96 Vinny Castilla .40 .12
❑ 97 Ben Davis .40 .12
❑ 98 Carl Everett .40 .12
❑ 99 Damion Easley .40 .12
❑ 100 Craig Biggio .60 .18
❑ 101 Todd Hollandsworth .40 .12
❑ 102 Jay Payton .40 .12
❑ 103 Gary Sheffield .40 .12
❑ 104 Sandy Alomar Jr. .40 .12
❑ 105 Doug Glanville .40 .12
❑ 106 Barry Bonds 2.50 .75
❑ 107 Tim Salmon .60 .18

❑ 108 Terrence Long .40 .12
❑ 109 Jorge Posada .60 .18
❑ 110 Jose Offerman .40 .12
❑ 111 Edgar Martinez .60 .18
❑ 112 Jeremy Giambi .40 .12
❑ 113 Dean Palmer .40 .12
❑ 114 Roberto Alomar .75 .23
❑ 115 Aaron Boone .40 .12
❑ 116 Adam Kennedy .40 .12
❑ 117 Joe Randa .40 .12
❑ 118 Jose Vidro .40 .12
❑ 119 Tony Batista .40 .12
❑ 120 Kevin Young .40 .12
❑ 121 Preston Wilson .40 .12
❑ 122 Jason Kendall .40 .12
❑ 123 Mark Kotsay .40 .12
❑ 124 Timo Perez .40 .12
❑ 125 Eric Young .40 .12
❑ 126 Greg Maddux 2.00 .60
❑ 127 Richard Hidalgo .40 .12
❑ 128 Brian Giles .40 .12
❑ 129 Fred McGriff .60 .18
❑ 130 Troy Glaus .60 .18
❑ 131 Todd Walker .40 .12
❑ 132 Brady Anderson .40 .12
❑ 133 Jim Edmonds .40 .12
❑ 134 Ben Grieve .40 .12
❑ 135 Greg Vaughn .40 .12
❑ 136 Robin Ventura .40 .12
❑ 137 Sammy Sosa 1.50 .45
❑ 138 Rich Aurilia .40 .12
❑ 139 Jose Valentin .40 .12
❑ 140 Trot Nixon .40 .12
❑ 141 Troy Percival .40 .12
❑ 142 Bernie Williams .60 .18
❑ 143 Warren Morris .40 .12
❑ 144 Jacque Jones .40 .12
❑ 145 Danny Bautista .40 .12
❑ 146 A.J. Pierzynski .40 .12
❑ 147 Mark McGwire 2.50 .75
❑ 148 Rafael Furcal .40 .12
❑ 149 Ray Durham .40 .12
❑ 150 Mike Mussina .75 .23
❑ 151 Jay Bell .40 .12
❑ 152 David Wells .40 .12
❑ 153 Ken Caminiti .40 .12
❑ 154 Jim Thome 1.00 .30
❑ 155 Ivan Rodriguez 1.00 .30
❑ 156 Milton Bradley .40 .12
❑ 157 Ken Griffey Jr. 1.50 .45
❑ 158 Al Leiter .40 .12
❑ 159 Corey Koskie .40 .12
❑ 160 Shannon Stewart .40 .12
❑ 161 Mo Vaughn .40 .12
❑ 162 Pedro Martinez 1.00 .30
❑ 163 Todd Hundley .40 .12
❑ 164 Darin Erstad .75 .23
❑ 165 Ruben Rivera .40 .12
❑ 166 Richie Sexson .40 .12
❑ 167 Andres Galarraga .40 .12
❑ 168 Darryl Kile .40 .12
❑ 169 Jose Cruz Jr. .40 .12
❑ 170 David Justice .40 .12
❑ 171 Vladimir Guerrero 1.00 .30
❑ 172 Jeff Cirillo .40 .12
❑ 173 John Olerud .40 .12
❑ 174 Devon White .40 .12
❑ 175 Ron Belliard .40 .12
❑ 176 Pokey Reese .40 .12
❑ 177 Mike Hampton .40 .12
❑ 178 David Ortiz .40 .12
❑ 179 Magglio Ordonez .40 .12
❑ 180 Ruben Mateo .40 .12
❑ 181 Carlos Lee .40 .12
❑ 182 Matt Williams .40 .12
❑ 183 Miguel Tejada .40 .12
❑ 184 Scott Elarton .40 .12
❑ 185 Bret Boone .40 .12
❑ 186 Pat Burrell .40 .12
❑ 187 Brad Radke .40 .12
❑ 188 Brian Jordan .40 .12
❑ 189 Matt Lawton .40 .12
❑ 190 Al Martin .40 .12
❑ 191 Albert Belle .40 .12
❑ 192 Tony Womack .40 .12
❑ 193 Roger Cedeno .40 .12
❑ 194 Travis Lee .40 .12
❑ 195 Dmitri Young .40 .12
❑ 196 Jay Buhner .40 .12
❑ 197 Jason Giambi .75 .23
❑ 198 Jason Tyner .40 .12
❑ 199 Ben Petrick .40 .12
❑ 200 Jose Canseco .75 .23
❑ 201 Nick Johnson 8.00 2.40
❑ 202 Jace Brewer 8.00 2.40
❑ 203 Ryan Freel RC 8.00 2.40
❑ 204 Jaisen Randolph RC 8.00 2.40
❑ 205 Marcus Giles 8.00 2.40
❑ 206 Claudio Vargas RC 8.00 2.40
❑ 207 Brian Cole 8.00 2.40
❑ 208 Scott Hodges 8.00 2.40
❑ 209 Winston Abreu RC 8.00 2.40
❑ 210 Shea Hillenbrand 8.00 2.40
❑ 211 Larry Barnes 8.00 2.40
❑ 212 Paul Phillips RC 8.00 2.40
❑ 213 Pedro Santana RC 8.00 2.40
❑ 214 Ivanon Coffie 8.00 2.40
❑ 215 Junior Spivey RC 10.00 3.00
❑ 216 Donzell McDonald 8.00 2.40
❑ 217 Vernon Wells 8.00 2.40
❑ 218 Corey Patterson 8.00 2.40
❑ 219 Sang-Hoon Lee 8.00 2.40
❑ 220 Jack Cust 8.00 2.40
❑ 221 Jason Romano 8.00 2.40
❑ 222 Jack Wilson RC 8.00 2.40
❑ 223 Adam Everett 8.00 2.40
❑ 224 Esix Snead RC 8.00 2.40
❑ 225 Jason Hart 8.00 2.40
❑ 226 Joe Lawrence 8.00 2.40
❑ 227 Brandon Inge 8.00 2.40
❑ 228 Alex Escobar 8.00 2.40
❑ 229 Abraham Nunez 8.00 2.40
❑ 230 Jared Sandberg 8.00 2.40
❑ 231 Ichiro Suzuki RC 40.00 12.00
❑ 232 Tsuyoshi Shinjo RC 12.00 3.60
❑ 233 Albert Pujols RC 60.00 18.00
❑ 234 Wilson Betemit RC 8.00 2.40
❑ 235 Drew Henson RC 20.00 6.00
❑ MM1 D.Jeter MM/1995 12.00 3.60
❑ NNO D.Jeter MM AU/95 EX 120.00 36.00

2001 Fleer Showcase

	Nm-Mt	Ex-Mt
COMP.SET w/o SP's (100)	30.00	9.00
COMMON CARD (1-100)	.50	.15
COMMON (101-115)	5.00	1.50
COMMON (116-125)	15.00	4.50
COMMON (126-160)	8.00	2.40

❑ 1 Tony Gwynn 1.50 .45
❑ 2 Barry Larkin 1.25 .35
❑ 3 Chan Ho Park .50 .15
❑ 4 Darin Erstad .50 .15
❑ 5 Rafael Furcal .50 .15
❑ 6 Roger Cedeno .50 .15
❑ 7 Timo Perez .50 .15
❑ 8 Rick Ankiel .50 .15
❑ 9 Pokey Reese .50 .15
❑ 10 Jeromy Burnitz .50 .15
❑ 11 Phil Nevin .50 .15
❑ 12 Matt Williams .50 .15
❑ 13 Mike Hampton .50 .15
❑ 14 Fernando Tatis .50 .15
❑ 15 Kazuhiro Sasaki .50 .15
❑ 16 Jim Thome 1.25 .35
❑ 17 Geoff Jenkins .50 .15
❑ 18 Jeff Kent .50 .15
❑ 19 Tom Glavine 1.25 .35
❑ 20 Dean Palmer .50 .15
❑ 21 Todd Zeile .50 .15
❑ 22 Edgar Renteria .50 .15
❑ 23 Andruw Jones .75 .23
❑ 24 Juan Encarnacion .50 .15
❑ 25 Robin Ventura .50 .15
❑ 26 J.D. Drew .50 .15
❑ 27 Ray Durham .50 .15
❑ 28 Richard Hidalgo .50 .15
❑ 29 Eric Chavez .50 .15
❑ 30 Rafael Palmeiro .75 .23
❑ 31 Steve Finley .50 .15
❑ 32 Jeff Weaver .50 .15
❑ 33 Al Leiter .50 .15
❑ 34 Jim Edmonds .50 .15
❑ 35 Garret Anderson .50 .15
❑ 36 Larry Walker .75 .23
❑ 37 Jose Vidro .50 .15
❑ 38 Mike Cameron .50 .15
❑ 39 Brady Anderson .50 .15
❑ 40 Mike Lowell .50 .15
❑ 41 Bernie Williams .75 .23
❑ 42 Gary Sheffield .50 .15
❑ 43 John Smoltz .75 .23
❑ 44 Mike Mussina 1.25 .35
❑ 45 Greg Vaughn .50 .15
❑ 46 Juan Gonzalez 1.25 .35
❑ 47 Matt Lawton .50 .15
❑ 48 Robb Nen .50 .15
❑ 49 Brad Radke .50 .15
❑ 50 Edgar Martinez .75 .23
❑ 51 Mike Bordick .50 .15
❑ 52 Shawn Green .50 .15
❑ 53 Carl Everett .50 .15
❑ 54 Adrian Beltre .50 .15
❑ 55 Kerry Wood 1.25 .35
❑ 56 Kevin Brown .50 .15
❑ 57 Brian Giles .50 .15
❑ 58 Greg Maddux 2.50 .75
❑ 59 Preston Wilson .50 .15
❑ 60 Orlando Hernandez .50 .15
❑ 61 Ben Grieve .50 .15
❑ 62 Jermaine Dye .50 .15
❑ 63 Travis Lee .50 .15
❑ 64 Jose Cruz Jr. .50 .15
❑ 65 Rondell White .50 .15
❑ 66 Carlos Beltran .50 .15
❑ 67 Scott Rolen .75 .23
❑ 68 Brad Fullmer .50 .15
❑ 69 David Wells .50 .15
❑ 70 Mike Sweeney .50 .15
❑ 71 Barry Zito 1.25 .35
❑ 72 Tony Batista .50 .15
❑ 73 Curt Schilling .75 .23
❑ 74 Jeff Cirillo .50 .15
❑ 75 Edgardo Alfonzo .50 .15
❑ 76 John Olerud .50 .15
❑ 77 Carlos Lee .50 .15
❑ 78 Moises Alou .50 .15
❑ 79 Tim Hudson .50 .15
❑ 80 Andres Galarraga .50 .15
❑ 81 Roberto Alomar 1.25 .35
❑ 82 Richie Sexson .50 .15
❑ 83 Trevor Hoffman .50 .15
❑ 84 Omar Vizquel .50 .15
❑ 85 Jacque Jones .50 .15
❑ 86 J.T. Snow .50 .15
❑ 87 Sean Casey .50 .15
❑ 88 Craig Biggio .75 .23
❑ 89 Mariano Rivera .75 .23
❑ 90 Rusty Greer .50 .15
❑ 91 Barry Bonds 3.00 .90
❑ 92 Pedro Martinez 1.25 .35
❑ 93 Cal Ripken 4.00 1.20
❑ 94 Pat Burrell .50 .15
❑ 95 Chipper Jones 1.25 .35
❑ 96 Magglio Ordonez .50 .15
❑ 97 Jeff Bagwell .75 .23
❑ 98 Randy Johnson 1.25 .35
❑ 99 Frank Thomas 1.25 .35
❑ 100 Jason Kendall .50 .15

Card	Nm-Mt	Ex-Mt
❑ 101 N.Garciaparra AC	15.00	4.50
❑ 102 Mark McGwire AC	20.00	6.00
❑ 103 Troy Glaus AC	5.00	1.50
❑ 104 Ivan Rodriguez AC	8.00	2.40
❑ 105 Manny Ramirez AC	5.00	1.50
❑ 106 Derek Jeter AC	20.00	6.00
❑ 107 Alex Rodriguez AC	15.00	4.50
❑ 108 Ken Griffey Jr. AC	12.00	3.60
❑ 109 Todd Helton AC	5.00	1.50
❑ 110 Sammy Sosa AC	12.00	3.60
❑ 111 Vladimir Guerrero AC	8.00	2.40
❑ 112 Mike Piazza AC	12.00	3.60
❑ 113 Roger Clemens AC	15.00	4.50
❑ 114 Jason Giambi AC	8.00	2.40
❑ 115 Carlos Delgado AC	5.00	1.50
❑ 116 Ichiro Suzuki AC RC	80.00	24.00
❑ 117 M.Ensberg AC RC	25.00	7.50
❑ 118 C. Valderrama AC RC	15.00	4.50
❑ 119 Erick Almonte AC RC	15.00	4.50
❑ 120 T.Shinjo AC RC	25.00	7.50
❑ 121 Albert Pujols AC RC	100.00	30.00
❑ 122 Wilson Betemit AC RC	15.00	4.50
❑ 123 A.Hernandez AC RC	15.00	4.50
❑ 124 J.Melian AC RC	15.00	4.50
❑ 125 Drew Henson AC RC	25.00	7.50
❑ 126 Paul Phillips RS RC	8.00	2.40
❑ 127 Esix Snead RS RC	8.00	2.40
❑ 128 Ryan Freel RS RC	8.00	2.40
❑ 129 Junior Spivey RS RC	10.00	3.00
❑ 130 E.Guzman RS RC	8.00	2.40
❑ 131 Juan Diaz RS RC	8.00	2.40
❑ 132 Andres Torres RS RC	8.00	2.40
❑ 133 Jay Gibbons RS RC	12.00	3.60
❑ 134 Bill Ortega RS RC	8.00	2.40
❑ 135 Alexis Gomez RS RC	8.00	2.40
❑ 136 Wilkin Ruan RS RC	8.00	2.40
❑ 137 Henry Mateo RS RC	8.00	2.40
❑ 138 Juan Uribe RS RC	8.00	2.40
❑ 139 J.Estrada RS RC	10.00	3.00
❑ 140 J.Randolph RS RC	8.00	2.40
❑ 141 Eric Hinske RS RC	10.00	3.00
❑ 142 Jack Wilson RS RC	8.00	2.40
❑ 143 Cody Ransom RS RC	8.00	2.40
❑ 144 Nate Frese RS RC	8.00	2.40
❑ 145 John Grabow RS RC	8.00	2.40
❑ 146 C.Parker RS RC	8.00	2.40
❑ 147 B.Lawrence RS RC	8.00	2.40
❑ 148 B. Duckworth RS RC	8.00	2.40
❑ 149 Winston Abreu RS RC	8.00	2.40
❑ 150 H.Ramirez RS RC	10.00	3.00
❑ 151 Nick Maness RS RC	8.00	2.40
❑ 152 Blaine Neal RS RC	8.00	2.40
❑ 153 Billy Sylvester RS RC	8.00	2.40
❑ 154 David Elder RS RC	8.00	2.40
❑ 155 Bert Snow RS RC	8.00	2.40
❑ 156 Claudio Vargas RS RC	8.00	2.40
❑ 157 Martin Vargas RS RC	8.00	2.40
❑ 158 Grant Balfour RS RC	8.00	2.40
❑ 159 Randy Keisler RS	8.00	2.40
❑ 160 Zach Day RS RC	10.00	3.00
❑ P1 Tony Gwynn Promo	2.00	.60
❑ MM5 D.Jeter MM/2000	12.00	3.60
❑ NNO D.Jeter MM AU/100	120.00	36.00

2002 Fleer Showcase

	Nm-Mt	Ex-Mt
COMP.SET w/o SP's (125)	30.00	9.00
COMMON CARD (1-125)	.50	.15
COMMON CARD (126-135)	8.00	2.40
COMMON CARD (136-141)	10.00	3.00
COMMON CARD (142-166)	8.00	2.40
❑ 1 Albert Pujols	2.50	.75
❑ 2 Pedro Martinez	1.25	.35
❑ 3 Frank Thomas	1.25	.35
❑ 4 Gary Sheffield	.50	.15
❑ 5 Roberto Alomar	1.25	.35
❑ 6 Luis Gonzalez	.50	.15
❑ 7 Bobby Abreu	.50	.15
❑ 8 Carlos Lee	.50	.15
❑ 9 Preston Wilson	.50	.15
❑ 10 Todd Helton	.75	.23
❑ 11 Juan Gonzalez	1.25	.35
❑ 12 Chuck Knoblauch	.50	.15
❑ 13 Jason Kendall	.50	.15
❑ 14 Aaron Sele	.50	.15
❑ 15 Greg Vaughn	.50	.15
❑ 16 Fred McGriff	.75	.23
❑ 17 Doug Mientkiewicz	.50	.15
❑ 18 Richard Hidalgo	.50	.15
❑ 19 Alfonso Soriano	1.25	.35
❑ 20 Matt Williams	.50	.15
❑ 21 Bobby Higginson	.50	.15
❑ 22 Mo Vaughn	.50	.15
❑ 23 Andruw Jones	.75	.23
❑ 24 Omar Vizquel	.50	.15
❑ 25 Bret Boone	.50	.15
❑ 26 Bernie Williams	.75	.23
❑ 27 Rafael Furcal	.50	.15
❑ 28 Jeff Bagwell	.75	.23
❑ 29 Marty Cordova	.50	.15
❑ 30 Lance Berkman	.50	.15
❑ 31 Vernon Wells	.50	.15
❑ 32 Garret Anderson	.50	.15
❑ 33 Larry Bigbie	.50	.15
❑ 34 Steve Finley	.50	.15
❑ 35 Barry Bonds	3.00	.90
❑ 36 Eric Chavez	.50	.15
❑ 37 Tony Clark	.50	.15
❑ 38 Roger Clemens	2.50	.75
❑ 39 Adam Dunn	.75	.23
❑ 40 Roger Cedeno	.50	.15
❑ 41 Carlos Delgado	.50	.15
❑ 42 Jermaine Dye	.50	.15
❑ 43 Brian Jordan	.50	.15
❑ 44 Darin Erstad	.50	.15
❑ 45 Paul LoDuca	.50	.15
❑ 46 Jim Edmonds	.50	.15
❑ 47 Tom Glavine	1.25	.35
❑ 48 Cliff Floyd	.50	.15
❑ 49 Jon Lieber	.50	.15
❑ 50 Adrian Beltre	.50	.15
❑ 51 Joel Pineiro	.50	.15
❑ 52 Jim Thome	1.25	.35
❑ 53 Jimmy Rollins	.50	.15
❑ 54 Pat Burrell	.50	.15
❑ 55 Jeromy Burnitz	.50	.15
❑ 56 Larry Walker	.75	.23
❑ 57 Damon Minor	.50	.15
❑ 58 John Olerud	.50	.15
❑ 59 Carlos Beltran	.50	.15
❑ 60 Vladimir Guerrero	1.25	.35
❑ 61 David Justice	.50	.15
❑ 62 Phil Nevin	.50	.15
❑ 63 Tino Martinez	.75	.23
❑ 64 Curt Schilling	.75	.23
❑ 65 Corey Patterson	.50	.15
❑ 66 Aubrey Huff	.50	.15
❑ 67 Mark Grace	1.25	.35
❑ 68 Rafael Palmeiro	.75	.23
❑ 69 Jorge Posada	.75	.23
❑ 70 Craig Biggio	.75	.23
❑ 71 Manny Ramirez	.50	.15
❑ 72 Mark Quinn	.50	.15
❑ 73 Raul Mondesi	.50	.15
❑ 74 Shawn Green	.50	.15
❑ 75 Brian Giles	.50	.15
❑ 76 Paul Konerko	.50	.15
❑ 77 Troy Glaus	.75	.23
❑ 78 Mike Mussina	1.25	.35
❑ 79 Greg Maddux	2.50	.75
❑ 80 Edgar Martinez	.75	.23
❑ 81 Jose Vidro	.50	.15
❑ 82 Scott Rolen	.75	.23
❑ 83 Ben Grieve	.50	.15
❑ 84 Jeff Kent	.50	.15
❑ 85 Magglio Ordonez	.50	.15
❑ 86 Freddy Garcia	.50	.15
❑ 87 Ivan Rodriguez	1.25	.35
❑ 88 Pokey Reese	.50	.15
❑ 89 Shannon Stewart	.50	.15
❑ 90 Randy Johnson	1.25	.35
❑ 91 Cristian Guzman	.50	.15
❑ 92 Tsuyoshi Shinjo	.50	.15
❑ 93 Steve Cox	.50	.15
❑ 94 Mike Sweeney	.50	.15
❑ 95 Robert Fick	.50	.15
❑ 96 Sean Casey	.50	.15
❑ 97 Tim Hudson	.50	.15
❑ 98 Bud Smith	.50	.15
❑ 99 Corey Koskie	.50	.15
❑ 100 Richie Sexson	.50	.15
❑ 101 Aramis Ramirez	.50	.15
❑ 102 Barry Larkin	1.25	.35
❑ 103 Rich Aurilia	.50	.15
❑ 104 Charles Johnson	.50	.15
❑ 105 Ryan Klesko	.50	.15
❑ 106 Ben Sheets	.50	.15
❑ 107 J.D. Drew	.50	.15
❑ 108 Jay Gibbons	.50	.15
❑ 109 Kerry Wood	1.25	.35
❑ 110 C.C. Sabathia	.50	.15
❑ 111 Eric Munson	.50	.15
❑ 112 Josh Beckett	.75	.23
❑ 113 Javier Vazquez	.50	.15
❑ 114 Barry Zito	1.25	.35
❑ 115 Kazuhiro Sasaki	.50	.15
❑ 116 Bubba Trammell	.50	.15
❑ 117 Russell Branyan	.50	.15
❑ 118 Todd Walker	.50	.15
❑ 119 Mike Hampton	.50	.15
❑ 120 Jeff Weaver	.50	.15
❑ 121 Geoff Jenkins	.50	.15
❑ 122 Edgardo Alfonzo	.50	.15
❑ 123 Mike Lieberthal	.50	.15
❑ 124 Mike Lowell	.50	.15
❑ 125 Kevin Brown	.50	.15
❑ 126 Derek Jeter AC	20.00	6.00
❑ 127 Ichiro Suzuki AC	15.00	4.50
❑ 128 Nomar Garciaparra AC	15.00	4.50
❑ 129 Ken Griffey Jr. AC	12.00	3.60
❑ 130 Jason Giambi AC	8.00	2.40
❑ 131 Alex Rodriguez AC	15.00	4.50
❑ 132 Chipper Jones AC	8.00	2.40
❑ 133 Mike Piazza AC	12.00	3.60
❑ 134 Sammy Sosa AC	12.00	3.60
❑ 135 Hideo Nomo AC	8.00	2.40
❑ 136 Kazuhisa Ishii AC RC	15.00	4.50
❑ 137 Satoru Komiyama AC RC	10.00	3.00
❑ 138 So Taguchi AC RC	15.00	4.50
❑ 139 Jorge Padilla AC RC	15.00	4.50
❑ 140 Rene Reyes AC RC	10.00	3.00
❑ 141 Jorge Nunez AC RC	10.00	3.00
❑ 142 Nelson Castro RS	8.00	2.40
❑ 143 Anderson Machado RS RC	10.00	3.00
❑ 144 Edwin Almonte RS RC	8.00	2.40
❑ 145 Luis Ugueto RS RC	8.00	2.40
❑ 146 Felix Escalona RS RC	8.00	2.40
❑ 147 Ron Calloway RS RC	8.00	2.40
❑ 148 Hansel Izquierdo RS RC	8.00	2.40
❑ 149 Mark Teixeira RS	10.00	3.00
❑ 150 Orlando Hudson RS	8.00	2.40
❑ 151 Aaron Cook RS RC	10.00	3.00
❑ 152 Aaron Taylor RS RC	8.00	2.40
❑ 153 Takahito Nomura RS RC	8.00	2.40
❑ 154 Matt Thornton RS RC	8.00	2.40
❑ 155 Mark Prior RS	15.00	4.50
❑ 156 Reed Johnson RS RC	10.00	3.00
❑ 157 Doug DeVore RS RC	8.00	2.40
❑ 158 Ben Howard RS RC	8.00	2.40
❑ 159 Francis Beltran RS RC	8.00	2.40
❑ 160 Brian Mallette RS RC	8.00	2.40
❑ 161 Sean Burroughs RS	8.00	2.40
❑ 162 Michael Restovich RS	8.00	2.40
❑ 163 Austin Kearns RS	10.00	3.00
❑ 164 Marlon Byrd RS	8.00	2.40
❑ 165 Hank Blalock RS	10.00	3.00
❑ 166 Mike Rivera RS	8.00	2.40

2003 Fleer Showcase

	Nm-Mt	Ex-Mt
COMP.LO SET w/o SP's (105)	25.00	7.50
COMMON CARD (1-95)	.50	.15
COMMON CARD (96-105)	1.00	.30
COMMON CARD (106-135)	3.00	.90

Card	Nm-Mt	Ex-Mt
❑ 1 David Eckstein	.50	.15
❑ 2 Curt Schilling	.75	.23
❑ 3 Jay Gibbons	.50	.15
❑ 4 Kerry Wood	1.25	.35
❑ 5 Jeff Bagwell	.75	.23
❑ 6 Hideo Nomo	1.25	.35
❑ 7 Tim Hudson	.50	.15
❑ 8 J.D. Drew	.50	.15
❑ 9 Josh Phelps	.50	.15
❑ 10 Bartolo Colon	.50	.15
❑ 11 Bobby Abreu	.50	.15
❑ 12 Matt Morris	.50	.15
❑ 13 Kazuhiro Sasaki	.50	.15
❑ 14 Sean Burroughs	.50	.15
❑ 15 Vicente Padilla	.50	.15
❑ 16 Jorge Posada	.75	.23
❑ 17 Torii Hunter	.50	.15
❑ 18 Richie Sexson	.50	.15
❑ 19 Lance Berkman	.50	.15
❑ 20 Todd Helton	.75	.23
❑ 21 Paul Konerko	.50	.15
❑ 22 Pedro Martinez	1.25	.35
❑ 23 Rodrigo Lopez	.50	.15
❑ 24 Gary Sheffield	.50	.15
❑ 25 Darin Erstad	.50	.15
❑ 26 Nomar Garciaparra	2.50	.75
❑ 27 Adam Dunn	.75	.23
❑ 28 Jason Giambi	1.25	.35
❑ 29 Miguel Tejada	.50	.15
❑ 30 Chipper Jones	1.25	.35
❑ 31 Alex Rodriguez	2.50	.75
❑ 32 Barry Bonds	3.00	.90
❑ 33 Roger Clemens	2.50	.75
❑ 34 Sammy Sosa	2.00	.60
❑ 35 Randy Johnson	1.25	.35
❑ 36 Tim Salmon	.75	.23
❑ 37 Shea Hillenbrand	.50	.15
❑ 38 Larry Walker	.75	.23
❑ 39 A.J. Burnett	.50	.15
❑ 40 Shawn Green	.50	.15
❑ 41 Cristian Guzman	.50	.15
❑ 42 Bernie Williams	.75	.23
❑ 43 Mark Mulder	.50	.15
❑ 44 Brian Giles	.50	.15
❑ 45 Bret Boone	.50	.15
❑ 46 Juan Gonzalez	1.25	.35
❑ 47 Roy Halladay	.50	.15
❑ 48 Wade Miller	.50	.15
❑ 49 Jeff Kent	.50	.15
❑ 50 Carlos Delgado	.50	.15
❑ 51 Mike Lowell	.50	.15
❑ 52 Jim Edmonds	.50	.15
❑ 53 Ivan Rodriguez	1.25	.35
❑ 54 Aubrey Huff	.50	.15
❑ 55 Ryan Klesko	.50	.15
❑ 56 Paul Lo Duca	.50	.15
❑ 57 Roy Oswalt	.50	.15
❑ 58 Omar Vizquel	.50	.15
❑ 59 Manny Ramirez	.50	.15
❑ 60 Andruw Jones	.75	.23
❑ 61 Troy Glaus	.75	.23
❑ 62 Ichiro Suzuki	2.50	.75
❑ 63 Albert Pujols	2.50	.75
❑ 64 Derek Jeter	3.00	.90
❑ 65 Mark Prior	2.50	.75
❑ 66 Ken Griffey Jr.	2.00	.60
❑ 67 Vladimir Guerrero	1.25	.35
❑ 68 Mike Piazza	2.00	.60
❑ 69 Alfonso Soriano	1.25	.35
❑ 70 Greg Maddux	2.50	.75
❑ 71 Adam Kennedy	.50	.15
❑ 72 Junior Spivey	.50	.15
❑ 73 Tom Glavine	1.25	.35
❑ 74 Derek Lowe	.50	.15
❑ 75 Magglio Ordonez	.50	.15
❑ 76 Jim Thome	1.25	.35
❑ 77 Robert Fick	.50	.15
❑ 78 Josh Beckett	.75	.23
❑ 79 Mike Sweeney	.50	.15
❑ 80 Kazuhisa Ishii	.50	.15
❑ 81 Roberto Alomar	1.25	.35
❑ 82 Barry Zito	1.25	.35
❑ 83 Pat Burrell	.50	.15
❑ 84 Scott Rolen	.75	.23
❑ 85 John Olerud	.50	.15
❑ 86 Eric Hinske	.50	.15
❑ 87 Rafael Palmeiro	.75	.23
❑ 88 Edgar Martinez	.75	.23
❑ 89 Eric Chavez	.50	.15
❑ 90 Jose Vidro	.50	.15
❑ 91 Craig Biggio	.75	.23
❑ 92 Rich Aurilia	.50	.15
❑ 93 Austin Kearns	.75	.23
❑ 94 Luis Gonzalez	.50	.15
❑ 95 Garret Anderson	.50	.15
❑ 96 Yogi Berra	2.00	.60
❑ 97 Al Kaline	2.00	.60
❑ 98 Robin Yount	2.00	.60
❑ 99 Reggie Jackson	1.50	.45
❑ 100 Harmon Killebrew	2.00	.60
❑ 101 Eddie Mathews	2.00	.60
❑ 102 Willie McCovey	1.00	.30
❑ 103 Nolan Ryan	5.00	1.50
❑ 104 Mike Schmidt	2.50	.75
❑ 105 Tom Seaver	2.00	.60
❑ 106 Francisco Rodriguez ST	3.00	.90
❑ 107 Carl Crawford ST	3.00	.90
❑ 108 Ben Howard ST	3.00	.90
❑ 109 Hank Blalock ST	5.00	1.50
❑ 110 Hee Seop Choi ST	3.00	.90
❑ 111 Kirk Saarloos ST	3.00	.90
❑ 112 Lew Ford ST RC	5.00	1.50
❑ 113 Andy Van Hekken ST	3.00	.90
❑ 114 Drew Henson ST	3.00	.90
❑ 115 Marlon Byrd ST	3.00	.90
❑ 116 Jayson Werth ST	3.00	.90
❑ 117 Willie Bloomquist ST	3.00	.90
❑ 118 Joe Borchard ST	3.00	.90
❑ 119 Mark Teixeira ST	5.00	1.50
❑ 120 Bobby Hill ST	3.00	.90
❑ 121 Jason Lane ST	3.00	.90
❑ 122 Omar Infante ST	3.00	.90
❑ 123 Victor Martinez ST	3.00	.90
❑ 124 Jorge Padilla ST	3.00	.90
❑ 125 John Lackey ST	3.00	.90
❑ 126 Anderson Machado ST	3.00	.90
❑ 127 Rodrigo Rosario ST	3.00	.90
❑ 128 Freddy Sanchez ST	3.00	.90
❑ 129 Tony Alvarez ST	3.00	.90
❑ 130 Matt Thornton ST	3.00	.90
❑ 131 Joe Thurston ST	3.00	.90
❑ 132 Brett Myers ST	3.00	.90
❑ 133 Nook Logan ST RC	3.00	.90
❑ 134 Chris Snelling ST	3.00	.90
❑ 135 Terrmel Sledge ST RC	5.00	1.50
❑ 136 Chien-Ming Wang RC	-	
❑ 137 Rickie Weeks RC	-	
❑ 138 Brandon Webb RC	-	
❑ 139 Hideki Matsui RC	-	
❑ 140 Michael Hessman RC	-	
❑ 141 Ryan Wagner RC	-	
❑ 142 Bo Hart RC	-	
❑ 143 Edwin Jackson RC	-	
❑ 144 Jose Contreras RC	-	
❑ 145 Delmon Young RC	-	

2003 Fleer Splendid Splinters

	Nm-Mt	Ex-Mt
COMP.SET w/o SP's (90)	15.00	4.50
COMMON CARD (1-90)	.30	.09
COMMON CARD (91-110)	10.00	3.00
COMMON CARD (111-140)	3.00	.90
COMMON CARD (141-150)	8.00	2.40

Card	Nm-Mt	Ex-Mt
❑ 1 David Eckstein	.30	.09
❑ 2 Barry Larkin	.75	.23
❑ 3 Edgardo Alfonzo	.30	.09
❑ 4 Darin Erstad	.30	.09
❑ 5 Ellis Burks	.30	.09
❑ 6 Omar Vizquel	.30	.09
❑ 7 Bartolo Colon	.30	.09
❑ 8 Roberto Alomar	.75	.23
❑ 9 Garret Anderson	.30	.09
❑ 10 Al Leiter	.30	.09
❑ 11 Tim Salmon	.50	.15
❑ 12 Larry Walker	.50	.15
❑ 13 Jorge Posada	.50	.15
❑ 14 Curt Schilling	.50	.15
❑ 15 Jason Jennings	.30	.09
❑ 16 Jason Giambi	.75	.23
❑ 17 Robert Fick	.30	.09
❑ 18 Kazuhiro Sasaki	.30	.09
❑ 19 Bernie Williams	.50	.15
❑ 20 Junior Spivey	.30	.09
❑ 21 Mike Lowell	.30	.09
❑ 22 Luis Gonzalez	.30	.09
❑ 23 Josh Beckett	.50	.15
❑ 24 John Smoltz	.50	.15
❑ 25 Mike Mussina	.75	.23
❑ 26 Gary Sheffield	.30	.09
❑ 27 Tom Glavine	.75	.23
❑ 28 Tim Hudson	.30	.09
❑ 29 Austin Kearns	.50	.15
❑ 30 Andruw Jones	.50	.15
❑ 31 Roger Clemens	1.50	.45
❑ 32 Mark Mulder	.30	.09
❑ 33 Jay Gibbons	.30	.09
❑ 34 Jeff Kent	.30	.09
❑ 35 Barry Zito	.75	.23
❑ 36 Rodrigo Lopez	.30	.09
❑ 37 Jeff Bagwell	.50	.15
❑ 38 Eric Chavez	.30	.09
❑ 39 Pedro Martinez	.75	.23
❑ 40 Lance Berkman	.30	.09
❑ 41 Bobby Abreu	.30	.09
❑ 42 Wade Miller	.30	.09
❑ 43 Bret Boone	.30	.09
❑ 44 Vicente Padilla	.30	.09
❑ 45 Shea Hillenbrand	.30	.09
❑ 46 Roy Oswalt	.30	.09
❑ 47 Pat Burrell	.30	.09
❑ 48 Manny Ramirez	.30	.09
❑ 49 Craig Biggio	.50	.15
❑ 50 Randy Wolf	.30	.09
❑ 51 Kerry Wood	.75	.23
❑ 52 Mike Sweeney	.30	.09
❑ 53 Brian Giles	.30	.09
❑ 54 Kazuhisa Ishii	.30	.09
❑ 55 Jason Kendall	.30	.09
❑ 56 Hideo Nomo	.75	.23
❑ 57 Josh Phelps	.30	.09
❑ 58 Sean Burroughs	.30	.09

	Player	Nm-Mt	Ex-Mt
❑ 59	Paul Konerko	.30	.09
❑ 60	Shawn Green	.30	.09
❑ 61	Ryan Klesko	.30	.09
❑ 62	Magglio Ordonez	.30	.09
❑ 63	Paul Lo Duca	.30	.09
❑ 64	Edgar Martinez	.30	.09
❑ 65	J.D. Drew	.30	.09
❑ 66	Phil Nevin	.30	.09
❑ 67	Jim Edmonds	.30	.09
❑ 68	Matt Morris	.30	.09
❑ 69	Aubrey Huff	.30	.09
❑ 70	Adam Dunn	.50	.15
❑ 71	John Olerud	.30	.09
❑ 72	Juan Gonzalez	.75	.23
❑ 73	Scott Rolen	.50	.15
❑ 74	Rafael Palmeiro	.50	.15
❑ 75	Roy Halladay	.30	.09
❑ 76	Kevin Brown	.30	.09
❑ 77	Ivan Rodriguez	.75	.23
❑ 78	Eric Hinske	.30	.09
❑ 79	Frank Thomas	.75	.23
❑ 80	Carlos Delgado	.30	.09
❑ 81	Bobby Higginson	.30	.09
❑ 82	Trevor Hoffman	.30	.09
❑ 83	Cliff Floyd	.30	.09
❑ 84	Derek Lowe	.30	.09
❑ 85	Richie Sexson	.30	.09
❑ 86	Rich Aurilia	.30	.09
❑ 87	Sean Casey	.30	.09
❑ 88	Cristian Guzman	.30	.09
❑ 89	Randy Winn	.30	.09
❑ 90	Jose Vidro	.30	.09
❑ 91	Mark Prior Wood	15.00	4.50
❑ 92	Derek Jeter Wood	20.00	6.00
❑ 93	Alex Rodriguez Wood	15.00	4.50
❑ 94	Greg Maddux Wood	15.00	4.50
❑ 95	Troy Glaus Wood	10.00	3.00
❑ 96	Vladimir Guerrero Wood	10.00	3.00
❑ 97	Todd Helton Wood	10.00	3.00
❑ 98	Albert Pujols Wood	15.00	4.50
❑ 99	Torii Hunter Wood	10.00	3.00
❑ 100	Mike Piazza Wood	15.00	4.50
❑ 101	Ichiro Suzuki Wood	15.00	4.50
❑ 102	Sammy Sosa Wood	15.00	4.50
❑ 103	Ken Griffey Jr. Wood	15.00	4.50
❑ 104	Nomar Garciaparra Wood	15.00	4.50
❑ 105	Barry Bonds Wood	20.00	6.00
❑ 106	Chipper Jones Wood	10.00	3.00
❑ 107	Jim Thome Wood	10.00	3.00
❑ 108	Miguel Tejada Wood	10.00	3.00
❑ 109	Randy Johnson Wood	10.00	3.00
❑ 110	Alfonso Soriano Wood	10.00	3.00
❑ 111	Guillermo Quiroz BB RC	5.00	1.50
❑ 112	Josh Willingham BB RC	6.00	1.80
❑ 113	Alejandro Machado BB RC	3.00	.90
❑ 114	Chris Waters BB RC	3.00	.90
❑ 115	Adam LaRoche BB	3.00	.90
❑ 116	Prentice Redman BB RC	3.00	.90
❑ 117	Jhonny Peralta BB RC	3.00	.90
❑ 118	Francisco Rosario BB RC	3.00	.90
❑ 119	Shane Victorino BB RC	3.00	.90
❑ 120	Chien-Ming Wang BB RC	8.00	2.40
❑ 121	Matt Bruback BB RC	3.00	.90
❑ 122	Rontrez Johnson BB RC	3.00	.90
❑ 123	Josh Hall BB RC	5.00	1.50
❑ 124	Matt Kata BB RC	5.00	1.50
❑ 125	Hector Luna BB RC	3.00	.90
❑ 126	Josh Stewart BB RC	3.00	.90
❑ 127	Craig Brazell BB RC	5.00	1.50
❑ 128	Tim Olson BB RC	5.00	1.50
❑ 129	Michel Hernandez BB RC	3.00	.90
❑ 130	Michael Hessman BB RC	3.00	.90
❑ 131	Clint Barmes BB RC	5.00	1.50
❑ 132	Justin Morneau BB	3.00	.90
❑ 133	Chris Snelling BB	3.00	.90
❑ 134	Bobby Jenks BB	3.00	.90
❑ 135	Tim Hummell BB	3.00	.90
❑ 136	Adam Morrissey BB	3.00	.90
❑ 137	Carl Crawford BB	3.00	.90
❑ 138	Garrett Atkins BB	3.00	.90
❑ 139	Jung Bong BB	3.00	.90
❑ 140	Ken Harvey BB	3.00	.90
❑ 141	Chin-Feng Chen Wood	15.00	4.50
❑ 142	Hee Seop Choi Wood	8.00	2.40
❑ 143	Lance Niekro Wood	8.00	2.40
❑ 144	Mark Teixeira Wood	10.00	3.00
❑ 145	Nook Logan Wood RC	8.00	2.40
❑ 146	Terrmel Sledge Wood RC	10.00	3.00
❑ 147	Lew Ford Wood RC	10.00	3.00
❑ 148	Ian Ferguson Wood RC	8.00	2.40
❑ 149	Hid Matsui Wood/499 RC	25.00	7.50
❑ 150	Jose Contreras Wood RC	10.00	3.00

1998 Fleer Tradition Update

		Nm-Mt	Ex-Mt
COMP.FACT.SET (100)		25.00	7.50
❑ U1	Mark McGwire HL	1.25	.35
❑ U2	Sammy Sosa HL	.75	.23
❑ U3	Roger Clemens HL	1.00	.30
❑ U4	Barry Bonds HL	1.25	.35
❑ U5	Kerry Wood HL	.50	.15
❑ U6	Paul Molitor HL	.30	.09
❑ U7	Ken Griffey Jr. HL	.75	.23
❑ U8	Cal Ripken HL	1.50	.45
❑ U9	David Wells HL	.20	.06
❑ U10	Alex Rodriguez HL	1.00	.30
❑ U11	Angel Pena RC	.25	.07
❑ U12	Bruce Chen	.20	.06
❑ U13	Craig Wilson	.20	.06
❑ U14	O.Hernandez RC	1.25	.35
❑ U15	Aramis Ramirez	.20	.06
❑ U16	Aaron Boone	.20	.06
❑ U17	Bob Henley	.20	.06
❑ U18	Juan Guzman	.20	.06
❑ U19	Darryl Hamilton	.20	.06
❑ U20	Jay Payton	.20	.06
❑ U21	Jeremy Powell	.20	.06
❑ U22	Ben Davis	.20	.06
❑ U23	Preston Wilson	.20	.06
❑ U24	Jim Parque RC	.40	.12
❑ U25	Odalis Perez RC	.60	.18
❑ U26	Ronnie Belliard	.20	.06
❑ U27	Royce Clayton	.20	.06
❑ U28	George Lombard	.20	.06
❑ U29	Tony Phillips	.20	.06
❑ U30	F.Seguignol RC	.25	.07
❑ U31	Armando Rios RC	.40	.12
❑ U32	Jerry Hairston Jr. RC	.40	.12
❑ U33	Justin Baughman RC	.25	.07
❑ U34	Seth Greisinger	.20	.06
❑ U35	Alex Gonzalez	.20	.06
❑ U36	Michael Barrett	.20	.06
❑ U37	Carlos Beltran	.20	.06
❑ U38	Ellis Burks	.20	.06
❑ U39	Jose Jimenez RC	.60	.18
❑ U40	Carlos Guillen	.20	.06
❑ U41	Marlon Anderson	.20	.06
❑ U42	Scott Elarton	.20	.06
❑ U43	Glenallen Hill	.20	.06
❑ U44	Shane Monahan	.20	.06
❑ U45	Dennis Martinez	.20	.06
❑ U46	Carlos Febles RC	.40	.12
❑ U47	Carlos Perez	.20	.06
❑ U48	Wilton Guerrero	.20	.06
❑ U49	Randy Johnson	.50	.15
❑ U50	Brian Simmons RC	.25	.07
❑ U51	Carlton Loewer	.20	.06
❑ U52	Mark DeRosa RC	.40	.12
❑ U53	Tim Young RC	.25	.07
❑ U54	Gary Gaetti	.20	.06
❑ U55	Eric Chavez	.30	.09
❑ U56	Carl Pavano	.20	.06
❑ U57	Mike Stanley	.20	.06
❑ U58	Todd Stottlemyre	.20	.06
❑ U59	Gabe Kapler RC	.60	.18
❑ U60	Mike Jerzembeck RC	.25	.07
❑ U61	Mitch Meluskey RC	.40	.12
❑ U62	Bill Pulsipher	.20	.06
❑ U63	Derrick Gibson	.20	.06
❑ U64	John Rocker RC	.40	.12
❑ U65	Calvin Pickering	.20	.06
❑ U66	Blake Stein	.20	.06
❑ U67	Fernando Tatis	.20	.06
❑ U68	Gabe Alvarez	.20	.06
❑ U69	Jeffrey Hammonds	.20	.06
❑ U70	Adrian Beltre	.20	.06
❑ U71	Ryan Bradley RC	.25	.07
❑ U72	Edgard Clemente	.20	.06
❑ U73	Rick Croushore RC	.25	.07
❑ U74	Matt Clement	.20	.06
❑ U75	Dermal Brown	.20	.06
❑ U76	Paul Bako	.20	.06
❑ U77	Placido Polanco RC	.40	.12
❑ U78	Jay Tessmer	.20	.06
❑ U79	Jarrod Washburn	.20	.06
❑ U80	Kevin Witt	.20	.06
❑ U81	Mike Metcalfe	.20	.06
❑ U82	Daryle Ward	.20	.06
❑ U83	Benj Sampson RC	.25	.07
❑ U84	Mike Kinkade RC	.25	.07
❑ U85	Randy Winn	.20	.06
❑ U86	Jeff Shaw	.20	.06
❑ U87	Troy Glaus RC	5.00	1.50
❑ U88	Hideo Nomo	.50	.15
❑ U89	Mark Grudzielanek	.20	.06
❑ U90	Mike Frank RC	.25	.07
❑ U91	Bobby Howry RC	.40	.12
❑ U92	Ryan Minor RC	.25	.07
❑ U93	Corey Koskie RC	1.25	.35
❑ U94	Matt Anderson RC	.40	.12
❑ U95	Joe Carter	.20	.06
❑ U96	Paul Konerko	.20	.06
❑ U97	Sidney Ponson	.20	.06
❑ U98	Jeremy Giambi RC	.40	.12
❑ U99	Jeff Kubenka RC	.25	.07
❑ U100	J.D. Drew RC	2.50	.75

1999 Fleer Tradition Update

		Nm-Mt	Ex-Mt
COMP.FACT.SET (150)		40.00	12.00
❑ U1	Rick Ankiel RC	.75	.23
❑ U2	Peter Bergeron RC	.30	.09
❑ U3	Pat Burrell RC	2.50	.75
❑ U4	Eric Munson RC	.60	.18
❑ U5	Alfonso Soriano RC	10.00	3.00
❑ U6	Tim Hudson RC	2.50	.75
❑ U7	Erubiel Durazo RC	1.00	.30
❑ U8	Chad Hermansen	.20	.06
❑ U9	Jeff Zimmerman RC	.30	.09
❑ U10	Jesus Pena RC	.30	.09
❑ U11	Ramon Hernandez	.30	.09
❑ U12	Trent Durrington RC	.30	.09
❑ U13	Tony Armas Jr.	.20	.06
❑ U14	Mike Fyhrie RC	.30	.09
❑ U15	Danny Kolb RC	.30	.09
❑ U16	Mike Porzio RC	.30	.09

- ❑ U17 Will Brunson RC .30 .09
- ❑ U18 Mike Duvall RC .30 .09
- ❑ U19 D.Mientkiewicz RC .75 .23
- ❑ U20 Gabe Molina RC .30 .09
- ❑ U21 Luis Vizcaino RC .30 .09
- ❑ U22 Robinson Cancel RC .30 .09
- ❑ U23 Brett Laxton RC .30 .09
- ❑ U24 Joe McEwing RC .30 .09
- ❑ U25 Justin Speier RC .30 .09
- ❑ U26 Kip Wells RC .50 .15
- ❑ U27 Armando Almanza RC .30 .09
- ❑ U28 Joe Davenport RC .30 .09
- ❑ U29 Yamid Haad RC .30 .09
- ❑ U30 John Halama .20 .06
- ❑ U31 Adam Kennedy .20 .06
- ❑ U32 Micah Bowie RC .30 .09
- ❑ U33 Gookie Dawkins RC .30 .09
- ❑ U34 Ryan Rupe RC .30 .09
- ❑ U35 B.J. Ryan RC .30 .09
- ❑ U36 Chance Sanford RC .30 .09
- ❑ U37 A.Shumaker RC .30 .09
- ❑ U38 Ryan Glynn RC .30 .09
- ❑ U39 Roosevelt Brown RC .30 .09
- ❑ U40 Ben Molina RC .60 .18
- ❑ U41 Scott Williamson .20 .06
- ❑ U42 Eric Gagne RC 8.00 2.40
- ❑ U43 John McDonald RC .30 .09
- ❑ U44 Scott Sauerbeck RC .30 .09
- ❑ U45 Mike Venafro RC .30 .09
- ❑ U46 Edwards Guzman RC .30 .09
- ❑ U47 Richard Barker RC .30 .09
- ❑ U48 Braden Looper .20 .06
- ❑ U49 Chad Meyers RC .30 .09
- ❑ U50 Scott Strickland RC .30 .09
- ❑ U51 Billy Koch .20 .06
- ❑ U52 David Newhan RC .30 .09
- ❑ U53 David Riske RC .30 .09
- ❑ U54 Jose Santiago RC .30 .09
- ❑ U55 Miguel Del Toro RC .30 .09
- ❑ U56 Orber Moreno RC .30 .09
- ❑ U57 Dave Roberts RC .50 .15
- ❑ U58 Tim Byrdak RC .30 .09
- ❑ U59 David Lee RC .30 .09
- ❑ U60 Guillermo Mota RC .30 .09
- ❑ U61 Wilton Veras RC .30 .09
- ❑ U62 Joe Mays RC .50 .15
- ❑ U63 Jose Fernandez RC .30 .09
- ❑ U64 Ray King RC .30 .09
- ❑ U65 Chris Petersen RC .30 .09
- ❑ U66 Vernon Wells .20 .06
- ❑ U67 Ruben Mateo .20 .06
- ❑ U68 Ben Petrick .20 .06
- ❑ U69 Chris Tremie RC .30 .09
- ❑ U70 Lance Berkman .20 .06
- ❑ U71 Dan Smith RC .30 .09
- ❑ U72 Carlos E. Hernandez RC .30 .09
- ❑ U73 Chad Harville RC .30 .09
- ❑ U74 Damaso Marte RC .30 .09
- ❑ U75 Aaron Myette RC .30 .09
- ❑ U76 Willis Roberts RC .30 .09
- ❑ U77 Erik Sabel RC .30 .09
- ❑ U78 Hector Almonte RC .30 .09
- ❑ U79 Kris Benson .20 .06
- ❑ U80 Pat Daneker RC .30 .09
- ❑ U81 Freddy Garcia RC 1.00 .30
- ❑ U82 Byung-Hyun Kim RC 2.00 .60
- ❑ U83 Wily Pena RC 1.25 .35
- ❑ U84 Dan Wheeler RC .30 .09
- ❑ U85 Tim Harikkala RC .30 .09
- ❑ U86 Derrin Ebert RC .30 .09
- ❑ U87 Horacio Estrada RC .30 .09
- ❑ U88 Liu Rodriguez RC .30 .09
- ❑ U89 J.Zimmerman RC .30 .09
- ❑ U90 A.J. Burnett RC .50 .15
- ❑ U91 Doug Davis RC .30 .09
- ❑ U92 Rob Ramsay RC .30 .09
- ❑ U93 Clay Bellinger RC .30 .09
- ❑ U94 Charlie Greene RC .30 .09
- ❑ U95 Bo Porter RC .30 .09
- ❑ U96 Jorge Toca RC .30 .09
- ❑ U97 Casey Blake RC .30 .09
- ❑ U98 Amaury Garcia RC .30 .09
- ❑ U99 Jose Molina RC .30 .09
- ❑ U100 Melvin Mora RC 1.25 .35
- ❑ U101 Joe Nathan RC .30 .09
- ❑ U102 Juan Pena RC .30 .09
- ❑ U103 Dave Borkowski RC .30 .09
- ❑ U104 Eddie Gaillard RC .30 .09
- ❑ U105 Glen Barker RC .30 .09
- ❑ U106 Brett Hinchliffe RC .30 .09
- ❑ U107 Carlos Lee .20 .06
- ❑ U108 Rob Ryan RC .30 .09
- ❑ U109 Jeff Weaver RC .50 .15
- ❑ U110 Ed Yarnall .20 .06
- ❑ U111 Nelson Cruz RC .30 .09
- ❑ U112 C.Davidson RC .30 .09
- ❑ U113 Tim Kubinski RC .30 .09
- ❑ U114 Sean Spencer RC .30 .09
- ❑ U115 Joe Winkelsas RC .30 .09
- ❑ U116 Mike Colangelo RC .30 .09
- ❑ U117 Tom Davey RC .30 .09
- ❑ U118 Warren Morris .20 .06
- ❑ U119 Dan Murray RC .30 .09
- ❑ U120 Jose Nieves RC .30 .09
- ❑ U121 Mark Quinn RC .30 .09
- ❑ U122 Josh Beckett RC 15.00 4.50
- ❑ U123 Chad Allen RC .30 .09
- ❑ U124 Mike Figga .30 .09
- ❑ U125 Beiker Graterol RC .30 .09
- ❑ U126 Aaron Scheffer RC .30 .09
- ❑ U127 Wiki Gonzalez RC .30 .09
- ❑ U128 Ramon E.Martinez RC .30 .09
- ❑ U129 Matt Riley RC .30 .09
- ❑ U130 Chris Woodward RC .30 .09
- ❑ U131 Albert Belle .20 .06
- ❑ U132 Roger Cedeno .20 .06
- ❑ U133 Roger Clemens 1.00 .30
- ❑ U134 Brian Giles .20 .06
- ❑ U135 Rickey Henderson .75 .23
- ❑ U136 Randy Johnson .50 .15
- ❑ U137 Brian Jordan .20 .06
- ❑ U138 Paul Konerko .20 .06
- ❑ U139 Hideo Nomo .50 .15
- ❑ U140 Kenny Rogers .20 .06
- ❑ U141 Wade Boggs HL .30 .09
- ❑ U142 Jose Canseco HL .20 .06
- ❑ U143 Roger Clemens HL 1.00 .30
- ❑ U144 David Cone HL .20 .06
- ❑ U145 Tony Gwynn HL .60 .18
- ❑ U146 Mark McGwire HL 1.25 .35
- ❑ U147 Cal Ripken HL 1.50 .45
- ❑ U148 Alex Rodriguez HL 1.00 .30
- ❑ U149 Fernando Tatis HL .20 .06
- ❑ U150 Robin Ventura HL .20 .06

2000 Fleer Tradition Glossy

	Nm-Mt	Ex-Mt
COMP.FACT.SET (455)	60.00	18.00
*STARS 1-450: .75X TO 2X BASIC		-
*ROOKIES 1-450: .75X TO 2X BASIC		-

- ❑ 451 Carlos Casimiro RC 10.00 3.00
- ❑ 452 Adam Melhuse RC 10.00 3.00
- ❑ 453 Adam Bernero RC 10.00 3.00
- ❑ 454 Dusty Allen RC 10.00 3.00
- ❑ 455 Chan Perry RC 10.00 3.00
- ❑ 456 Damian Rolls RC 10.00 3.00
- ❑ 457 Josh Phelps RC 40.00 12.00
- ❑ 458 Barry Zito 40.00 12.00
- ❑ 459 Hector Ortiz RC 10.00 3.00
- ❑ 460 Juan Pierre RC 25.00 7.50
- ❑ 461 Jose Ortiz RC 10.00 3.00
- ❑ 462 Chad Zerbe RC 10.00 3.00
- ❑ 463 Julio Zuleta RC 10.00 3.00
- ❑ 464 Eric Byrnes 15.00 4.50
- ❑ 465 Wilf. Rodriguez RC 10.00 3.00
- ❑ 466 Wascar Serrano RC 10.00 3.00
- ❑ 467 Aaron McNeal RC 10.00 3.00
- ❑ 468 Paul Rigdon RC 10.00 3.00
- ❑ 469 John Snyder RC 10.00 3.00
- ❑ 470 J.C. Romero RC 10.00 3.00
- ❑ 471 Talmadge Nunnari RC 10.00 3.00
- ❑ 472 Mike Lamb 10.00 3.00
- ❑ 473 Ryan Kohlmeier RC 10.00 3.00
- ❑ 474 Rodney Lindsey RC 10.00 3.00
- ❑ 475 Elvis Pena RC 10.00 3.00
- ❑ 476 Alex Cabrera 10.00 3.00
- ❑ 477 Chris Richard 10.00 3.00
- ❑ 478 Pedro Feliz RC 10.00 3.00
- ❑ 479 Ross Gload RC 10.00 3.00
- ❑ 480 Timo Perez RC 10.00 3.00
- ❑ 481 Jason Woolf RC 10.00 3.00
- ❑ 482 Kenny Kelly RC 10.00 3.00
- ❑ 483 Sang-Hoon Lee 10.00 3.00
- ❑ 484 John Riedling RC 10.00 3.00
- ❑ 485 Chris Wakeland RC 10.00 3.00
- ❑ 486 Britt Reames RC 10.00 3.00
- ❑ 487 Greg LaRocca RC 10.00 3.00
- ❑ 488 Randy Keisler RC 10.00 3.00
- ❑ 489 Xavier Nady RC 20.00 6.00
- ❑ 490 Keith Ginter RC 10.00 3.00
- ❑ 491 Joey Nation RC 10.00 3.00
- ❑ 492 Kazuhiro Sasaki 20.00 6.00
- ❑ 493 Lesli Brea RC 10.00 3.00
- ❑ 494 Jace Brewer 10.00 3.00
- ❑ 495 Yohanny Valera RC 10.00 3.00
- ❑ 496 Adam Piatt 10.00 3.00
- ❑ 497 Nate Rolison 10.00 3.00
- ❑ 498 Aubrey Huff 10.00 3.00
- ❑ 499 Jason Tyner 10.00 3.00
- ❑ 500 Corey Patterson 15.00 4.50

2000 Fleer Tradition Update

	Nm-Mt	Ex-Mt
COMP.FACT.SET (149)	15.00	4.50

- ❑ 1 Ken Griffey Jr. SH .75 .23
- ❑ 2 Cal Ripken SH 1.00 .30
- ❑ 3 Randy Velarde SH .30 .09
- ❑ 4 Fred McGriff SH .30 .09
- ❑ 5 Derek Jeter SH .75 .23
- ❑ 6 Tom Glavine SH .30 .09
- ❑ 7 Brent Mayne SH .30 .09
- ❑ 8 Alex Ochoa SH .30 .09
- ❑ 9 Scott Sheldon SH .30 .09
- ❑ 10 Randy Johnson SH .50 .15
- ❑ 11 Daniel Garibay RC .30 .09
- ❑ 12 Brad Fullmer .30 .09
- ❑ 13 Kazuhiro Sasaki RC 1.25 .35
- ❑ 14 Andy Tracy RC .30 .09
- ❑ 15 Bret Boone .30 .09
- ❑ 16 Chad Durbin RC .40 .12
- ❑ 17 Mark Buehrle RC 1.25 .35
- ❑ 18 Julio Zuleta RC .40 .12
- ❑ 19 Jeremy Giambi .30 .09
- ❑ 20 Gene Stechschulte RC .30 .09
- ❑ 21 Lou Pote .30 .09

Bengie Molina

❑ 22 Darrell Einertson RC .30 .09
❑ 23 Ken Griffey Jr. 1.25 .35
❑ 24 Jeff Sparks RC .30 .09
Dan Wheeler
❑ 25 Aaron Fultz RC .30 .09
❑ 26 Derek Bell .30 .09
❑ 27 Rob Bell .30 .09
D.T. Cromer
❑ 28 Robert Fick .30 .09
❑ 29 Darryl Kile .30 .09
❑ 30 Clayton Andrews .30 .09
John Bale RC
❑ 31 Dave Veres .30 .09
❑ 32 Hector Mercado RC .30 .09
❑ 33 Willie Morales RC .30 .09
❑ 34 Kelly Wunsch .30 .09
Kip Wells
❑ 35 Hideki Irabu .30 .09
❑ 36 Sean DePaula RC .30 .09
❑ 37 DeWayne Wise .30 .09
Chris Woodward
❑ 38 Curt Schilling .50 .15
❑ 39 Mark Johnson .30 .09
❑ 40 Mike Cameron .30 .09
❑ 41 Scott Sheldon .30 .09
Tom Evans
❑ 42 Brett Tomko .30 .09
❑ 43 Johan Santana RC 2.00 .60
❑ 44 Andy Benes .30 .09
❑ 45 Matt LeCroy .30 .09
Mark Redman
❑ 46 Ryan Klesko .30 .09
❑ 47 Andy Ashby .30 .09
❑ 48 Octavio Dotel .30 .09
❑ 49 Eric Byrnes RC 1.00 .30
❑ 50 Does Not Exist -
❑ 51 Kenny Rogers .30 .09
❑ 52 Ben Weber RC .40 .12
❑ 53 Matt Blank .30 .09
Scott Strickland
❑ 54 Tom Goodwin .30 .09
❑ 55 Jim Edmonds Cards .30 .09
❑ 56 Derrick Turnbow RC .40 .12
❑ 57 Mark Mulder .50 .15
❑ 58 Tarrick Brock .30 .09
Ruben Quevedo
❑ 59 Danny Young RC .30 .09
❑ 60 Fernando Vina .30 .09
❑ 61 Justin Brunette RC .30 .09
❑ 62 Jimmy Anderson .30 .09
❑ 63 Reggie Sanders .30 .09
❑ 64 Adam Kennedy .30 .09
❑ 65 Jesse Garcia .30 .09
B.J. Ryan
❑ 66 Al Martin .30 .09
❑ 67 Kevin Walker RC .30 .09
❑ 68 Brad Penny .30 .09
❑ 69 B.J. Surhoff .30 .09
❑ 70 Geoff Blum .30 .09
Trace Coquillette RC
❑ 71 Jose Jimenez .30 .09
❑ 72 Chuck Finley .30 .09
❑ 73 Valerio De Los Santos .30 .09
Everett Stull
❑ 74 Terry Adams .30 .09
❑ 75 Rafael Furcal .30 .09
❑ 76 John Roskos .30 .09
Mike Darr
❑ 77 Quilvio Veras .30 .09
❑ 78 Armando Almanza .30 .09
Nate Rolison
❑ 79 Greg Vaughn .30 .09
❑ 80 Keith McDonald RC .30 .09
❑ 81 Eric Cammack RC .30 .09
❑ 82 Horacio Estrada .30 .09
Ray King
❑ 83 Kory DeHaan .30 .09
❑ 84 Kevin Hodges RC .30 .09
❑ 85 Mike Lamb RC .40 .12
❑ 86 Shawn Green .30 .09
❑ 87 Dan Reichert .30 .09
Jason Rakers
❑ 88 Adam Piatt .30 .09
❑ 89 Mike Garcia .30 .09
❑ 90 Rodrigo Lopez RC .60 .18
❑ 91 John Olerud .30 .09
❑ 92 Barry Zito RC 3.00 .90
Terrence Long
❑ 93 Jimmy Rollins .30 .09
❑ 94 Denny Neagle .30 .09
❑ 95 Rickey Henderson 1.25 .35
❑ 96 Adam Eaton .30 .09
Buddy Carlyle
❑ 97 Brian O'Connor RC .30 .09
❑ 98 Andy Thompson RC .30 .09
❑ 99 Jason Boyd RC .30 .09
❑ 100 Joel Pineiro RC 4.00 1.20
Carlos Guillen
❑ 101 Raul Gonzalez RC .30 .09
❑ 102 Brandon Kolb RC .30 .09
❑ 103 Jason Maxwell .30 .09
Mike Lincoln
❑ 104 Luis Matos RC 1.50 .45
❑ 105 Morgan Burkhart RC .30 .09
❑ 106 Ismael Villegas RC .30 .09
Steve Sisco RC
❑ 107 David Justice Yankees .30 .09
❑ 108 Pablo Ozuna .30 .09
❑ 109 Jose Canseco .75 .23
❑ 110 Alex Cora .30 .09
Shawn Gilbert
❑ 111 Will Clark Cardinals .75 .23
❑ 112 Keith Luuloa .30 .09
Eric Weaver
❑ 113 Bruce Chen .30 .09
❑ 114 Adam Hyzdu .30 .09
❑ 115 Scott Forster RC .30 .09
Yovanny Lara RC
❑ 116 Allen McDill RC .30 .09
Jose Macias
❑ 117 Kevin Nicholson .30 .09
❑ 118 Israel Alcantara .30 .09
Tim Young
❑ 119 Juan Alvarez RC .30 .09
❑ 120 Julio Lugo .30 .09
Mitch Meluskey
❑ 121 B.J. Waszgis RC .30 .09
❑ 122 Jeff M. D'Amico RC .30 .09
Brett Laxton
❑ 123 Ricky Ledee .30 .09
❑ 124 Mark DeRosa .30 .09
Jason Marquis
❑ 125 Alex Cabrera RC .40 .12
❑ 126 Augie Ojeda RC .30 .09
Gary Matthews Jr.
❑ 127 Richie Sexson .30 .09
❑ 128 Santiago Perez RC .30 .09
Hector Ramirez RC
❑ 129 Rondell White .30 .09
❑ 130 Craig House RC .30 .09
❑ 131 Kevin Beirne .30 .09
Jon Garland
❑ 132 Wayne Franklin RC .30 .09
❑ 133 Henry Rodriguez .30 .09
❑ 134 Jay Payton .30 .09
Jim Mann
❑ 135 Ron Gant .30 .09
❑ 136 Paxton Crawford RC .30 .09
Sang-Hoon Lee RC
❑ 137 Kent Bottenfield .30 .09
❑ 138 Rocky Biddle RC .30 .09
❑ 139 Travis Lee .30 .09
❑ 140 Ryan Vogelsong RC .40 .12
❑ 141 Jason Conti .30 .09
Geraldo Guzman RC
❑ 142 Tim Drew .30 .09
Mark Watson RC
❑ 143 John Parrish RC .40 .12
Chris Richard RC
❑ 144 Javier Cardona RC .30 .09
Brandon Villafuerte RC
❑ 145 Tike Redman RC .40 .12
Steve Sparks RC
❑ 146 Brian Schneider .30 .09
Matt Skrmetta RC
❑ 147 Pasqual Coco RC .30 .09
❑ 148 Lorenzo Barcelo RC .30 .09
Joe Crede
❑ 149 Jace Brewer RC .40 .12
❑ 150 Milton Bradley .40 .12
Tomas De La Rosa RC
❑ MP1 Mickey Mantle 200.00 60.00

2001 Fleer Tradition

	Nm-Mt	Ex-Mt
COMP.FACT.SET (485)	50.00	15.00
COMPLETE SET (450)	25.00	7.50
COMMON CARD (1-450)	.30	.09
COMMON (451-485)	.50	.15

❑ 1 Andres Galarraga .30 .09
❑ 2 Armando Rios .30 .09
❑ 3 Julio Lugo .30 .09
❑ 4 Darryl Hamilton .30 .09
❑ 5 Dave Veres .30 .09
❑ 6 Edgardo Alfonzo .30 .09
❑ 7 Brook Fordyce .30 .09
❑ 8 Eric Karros .30 .09
❑ 9 Neifi Perez .30 .09
❑ 10 Jim Edmonds .30 .09
❑ 11 Barry Larkin .75 .23
❑ 12 Trot Nixon .30 .09
❑ 13 Andy Pettitte .50 .15
❑ 14 Jose Guillen .30 .09
❑ 15 David Wells .30 .09
❑ 16 Magglio Ordonez .30 .09
❑ 17 David Segui .30 .09
❑ 17A David Segui ERR .30 .09
Card has no number on the back
❑ 18 Juan Encarnacion .30 .09
❑ 19 Robert Person .30 .09
❑ 20 Quilvio Veras .30 .09
❑ 21 Mo Vaughn .30 .09
❑ 22 B.J. Surhoff .30 .09
❑ 23 Ken Caminiti .30 .09
❑ 24 Frank Catalanotto .30 .09
❑ 25 Luis Gonzalez .30 .09
❑ 26 Pete Harnisch .30 .09
❑ 27 Alex Gonzalez .30 .09
❑ 28 Mark Quinn .30 .09
❑ 29 Luis Castillo .30 .09
❑ 30 Rick Helling .30 .09
❑ 31 Barry Bonds 2.00 .60
❑ 32 Warren Morris .30 .09
❑ 33 Aaron Boone .30 .09
❑ 34 Ricky Gutierrez .30 .09
❑ 35 Preston Wilson .30 .09
❑ 36 Erubiel Durazo .30 .09
❑ 37 Jermaine Dye .30 .09
❑ 38 John Rocker .30 .09
❑ 39 Mark Grudzielanek .30 .09
❑ 40 Pedro Martinez .75 .23
❑ 41 Phil Nevin .30 .09
❑ 42 Luis Matos .30 .09
❑ 43 Orlando Hernandez .30 .09
❑ 44 Steve Cox .30 .09
❑ 45 James Baldwin .30 .09
❑ 46 Rafael Furcal .30 .09
❑ 47 Todd Zeile .30 .09
❑ 48 Elmer Dessens .30 .09
❑ 49 Russell Branyan .30 .09
❑ 50 Juan Gonzalez .75 .23
❑ 51 Mac Suzuki .30 .09
❑ 52 Adam Kennedy .30 .09
❑ 53 Randy Velarde .30 .09
❑ 54 David Bell .30 .09
❑ 55 Royce Clayton .30 .09
❑ 56 Greg Colbrunn .30 .09
❑ 57 Rey Ordonez .30 .09
❑ 58 Kevin Millwood .30 .09

❑ 59 Fernando Vina .30 .09
❑ 60 Eddie Taubensee .30 .09
❑ 61 Enrique Wilson .30 .09
❑ 62 Jay Bell .30 .09
❑ 63 Brian Moehler .30 .09
❑ 64 Brad Fullmer .30 .09
❑ 65 Ben Petrick .30 .09
❑ 66 Orlando Cabrera .30 .09
❑ 67 Shane Reynolds .30 .09
❑ 68 Mitch Meluskey .30 .09
❑ 69 Jeff Shaw .30 .09
❑ 70 Chipper Jones .75 .23
❑ 71 Tomo Ohka .30 .09
❑ 72 Ruben Rivera .30 .09
❑ 73 Mike Sirotka .30 .09
❑ 74 Scott Rolen .50 .15
❑ 75 Glendon Rusch .30 .09
❑ 76 Miguel Tejada .30 .09
❑ 77 Brady Anderson .30 .09
❑ 78 Bartolo Colon .30 .09
❑ 79 Ron Coomer .30 .09
❑ 80 Gary DiSarcina .30 .09
❑ 81 Geoff Jenkins .30 .09
❑ 82 Billy Koch .30 .09
❑ 83 Mike Lamb .30 .09
❑ 84 Alex Rodriguez 1.50 .45
❑ 85 Denny Neagle .30 .09
❑ 86 Michael Tucker .30 .09
❑ 87 Edgar Renteria .30 .09
❑ 88 Brian Anderson .30 .09
❑ 89 Glenallen Hill .30 .09
❑ 90 Aramis Ramirez .30 .09
❑ 91 Rondell White .30 .09
❑ 92 Tony Womack .30 .09
❑ 93 Jeffrey Hammonds .30 .09
❑ 94 Freddy Garcia .30 .09
❑ 95 Bill Mueller .30 .09
❑ 96 Mike Lieberthal .30 .09
❑ 97 Michael Barrett .30 .09
❑ 98 Derrek Lee .30 .09
❑ 99 Bill Spiers .30 .09
❑ 100 Derek Lowe .30 .09
❑ 101 Javy Lopez .30 .09
❑ 102 Adrian Beltre .30 .09
❑ 103 Jim Parque .30 .09
❑ 104 Marquis Grissom .30 .09
❑ 105 Eric Chavez .30 .09
❑ 106 Todd Jones .30 .09
❑ 107 Eric Owens .30 .09
❑ 108 Roger Clemens 1.50 .45
❑ 109 Denny Hocking .30 .09
❑ 110 Roberto Hernandez .30 .09
❑ 111 Albert Belle .30 .09
❑ 112 Troy Glaus .50 .15
❑ 113 Ivan Rodriguez .75 .23
❑ 114 Carlos Guillen .30 .09
❑ 115 Chuck Finley .30 .09
❑ 116 Dmitri Young .30 .09
❑ 117 Paul Konerko .30 .09
❑ 118 Damon Buford .30 .09
❑ 119 Fernando Tatis .30 .09
❑ 120 Larry Walker .50 .15
❑ 121 Jason Kendall .30 .09
❑ 122 Matt Williams .30 .09
❑ 123 Henry Rodriguez .30 .09
❑ 124 Placido Polanco .30 .09
❑ 125 Bobby Estalella .30 .09
❑ 126 Pat Burrell .30 .09
❑ 127 Mark Loretta .30 .09
❑ 128 Moises Alou .30 .09
❑ 129 Tino Martinez .50 .15
❑ 130 Milton Bradley .30 .09
❑ 131 Todd Hundley .30 .09
❑ 132 Keith Foulke .30 .09
❑ 133 Robert Fick .30 .09
❑ 134 Cristian Guzman .30 .09
❑ 135 Rusty Greer .30 .09
❑ 136 John Olerud .30 .09
❑ 137 Mariano Rivera .50 .15
❑ 138 Jeromy Burnitz .30 .09
❑ 139 Dave Burba .30 .09
❑ 140 Ken Griffey Jr. 1.25 .35
❑ 141 Tony Gwynn 1.00 .30
❑ 142 Carlos Delgado .30 .09
❑ 143 Edgar Martinez .50 .15
❑ 144 Ramon Hernandez .30 .09
❑ 145 Pedro Astacio .30 .09
❑ 146 Ray Lankford .30 .09
❑ 147 Mike Mussina .75 .23
❑ 148 Ray Durham .30 .09
❑ 149 Lee Stevens .30 .09
❑ 150 Jay Canizaro .30 .09
❑ 151 Adrian Brown .30 .09
❑ 152 Mike Piazza 1.25 .35
❑ 153 Cliff Floyd .30 .09
❑ 154 Jose Vidro .30 .09
❑ 155 Jason Giambi .75 .23
❑ 156 Andruw Jones .50 .15
❑ 157 Robin Ventura .30 .09
❑ 158 Gary Sheffield .30 .09
❑ 159 Jeff D'Amico .30 .09
❑ 160 Chuck Knoblauch .30 .09
❑ 161 Roger Cedeno .30 .09
❑ 162 Jim Thome .75 .23
❑ 163 Peter Bergeron .30 .09
❑ 164 Kerry Wood .75 .23
❑ 165 Gabe Kapler .30 .09
❑ 166 Corey Koskie .30 .09
❑ 167 Doug Glanville .30 .09
❑ 168 Brent Mayne .30 .09
❑ 169 Scott Spiezio .30 .09
❑ 170 Steve Karsay .30 .09
❑ 171 Al Martin .30 .09
❑ 172 Fred McGriff .50 .15
❑ 173 Gabe White .30 .09
❑ 174 Alex Gonzalez .30 .09
❑ 175 Mike Darr .30 .09
❑ 176 Bengie Molina .30 .09
❑ 177 Ben Grieve .30 .09
❑ 178 Marlon Anderson .30 .09
❑ 179 Brian Giles .30 .09
❑ 180 Jose Valentin .30 .09
❑ 181 Brian Jordan .30 .09
❑ 182 Randy Johnson .75 .23
❑ 183 Ricky Ledee .30 .09
❑ 184 Russ Ortiz .30 .09
❑ 185 Mike Lowell .30 .09
❑ 186 Curtis Leskanic .30 .09
❑ 187 Bob Abreu .30 .09
❑ 188 Derek Jeter 2.00 .60
❑ 189 Lance Berkman .30 .09
❑ 190 Roberto Alomar .75 .23
❑ 191 Darin Erstad .30 .09
❑ 192 Richie Sexson .30 .09
❑ 193 Alex Ochoa .30 .09
❑ 194 Carlos Febles .30 .09
❑ 195 David Ortiz .30 .09
❑ 196 Shawn Green .30 .09
❑ 197 Mike Sweeney .30 .09
❑ 198 Vladimir Guerrero .75 .23
❑ 199 Jose Jimenez .30 .09
❑ 200 Travis Lee .30 .09
❑ 201 Rickey Henderson 1.25 .35
❑ 202 Bob Wickman .30 .09
❑ 203 Miguel Cairo .30 .09
❑ 204 Steve Finley .30 .09
❑ 205 Tony Batista .30 .09
❑ 206 Jamey Wright .30 .09
❑ 207 Terrence Long .30 .09
❑ 208 Trevor Hoffman .30 .09
❑ 209 John VanderWal .30 .09
❑ 210 Greg Maddux 1.50 .45
❑ 211 Tim Salmon .50 .15
❑ 212 Herbert Perry .30 .09
❑ 213 Marvin Benard .30 .09
❑ 214 Jose Offerman .30 .09
❑ 215 Jay Payton .30 .09
❑ 216 Jon Lieber .30 .09
❑ 217 Mark Kotsay .30 .09
❑ 218 Scott Brosius .30 .09
❑ 219 Scott Williamson .30 .09
❑ 220 Omar Vizquel .30 .09
❑ 221 Mike Hampton .30 .09
❑ 222 Richard Hidalgo .30 .09
❑ 223 Rey Sanchez .30 .09
❑ 224 Matt Lawton .30 .09
❑ 225 Bruce Chen .30 .09
❑ 226 Ryan Klesko .30 .09
❑ 227 Garret Anderson .30 .09
❑ 228 Kevin Brown .30 .09
❑ 229 Mike Cameron .30 .09
❑ 230 Tony Clark .30 .09
❑ 231 Curt Schilling .50 .15
❑ 232 Vinny Castilla .30 .09
❑ 233 Carl Pavano .30 .09
❑ 234 Eric Davis .30 .09
❑ 235 Darrin Fletcher .30 .09
❑ 236 Matt Stairs .30 .09
❑ 237 Octavio Dotel .30 .09
❑ 238 Mark Grace .75 .23
❑ 239 John Smoltz .50 .15
❑ 240 Matt Clement .30 .09
❑ 241 Ellis Burks .30 .09
❑ 242 Charles Johnson .30 .09
❑ 243 Jeff Bagwell .50 .15
❑ 244 Derek Bell .30 .09
❑ 245 Nomar Garciaparra 1.50 .45
❑ 246 Jorge Posada .50 .15
❑ 247 Ryan Dempster .30 .09
❑ 248 J.T. Snow .30 .09
❑ 249 Eric Young .30 .09
❑ 250 Daryle Ward .30 .09
❑ 251 Joe Randa .30 .09
❑ 252 Travis Fryman .30 .09
❑ 253 Mike Williams .30 .09
❑ 254 Jacque Jones .30 .09
❑ 255 Scott Elarton .30 .09
❑ 256 Mark McGwire 2.00 .60
❑ 257 Jay Buhner .30 .09
❑ 258 Randy Wolf .30 .09
❑ 259 Sammy Sosa 1.25 .35
❑ 260 Chan Ho Park .30 .09
❑ 261 Damion Easley .30 .09
❑ 262 Rick Ankiel .30 .09
❑ 263 Frank Thomas .75 .23
❑ 264 Kris Benson .30 .09
❑ 265 Luis Alicea .30 .09
❑ 266 Jeromy Burnitz .30 .09
❑ 267 Geoff Blum .30 .09
❑ 268 Joe Girardi .30 .09
❑ 269 Livan Hernandez .30 .09
❑ 270 Jeff Conine .30 .09
❑ 271 Danny Graves .30 .09
❑ 272 Craig Biggio .50 .15
❑ 273 Jose Canseco .75 .23
❑ 274 Tom Glavine .75 .23
❑ 275 Ruben Mateo .30 .09
❑ 276 Jeff Kent .30 .09
❑ 277 Kevin Young .30 .09
❑ 278 A.J. Burnett .30 .09
❑ 279 Dante Bichette .30 .09
❑ 280 Sandy Alomar Jr. .30 .09
❑ 281 John Wetteland .30 .09
❑ 282 Torii Hunter .30 .09
❑ 283 Jarrod Washburn .30 .09
❑ 284 Rich Aurilia .30 .09
❑ 285 Jeff Cirillo .30 .09
❑ 286 Fernando Seguignol .30 .09
❑ 287 Darren Dreifort .30 .09
❑ 288 Deivi Cruz .30 .09
❑ 289 Pokey Reese .30 .09
❑ 290 Garrett Stephenson .30 .09
❑ 291 Bret Boone .30 .09
❑ 292 Tim Hudson .30 .09
❑ 293 John Flaherty .30 .09
❑ 294 Shannon Stewart .30 .09
❑ 295 Shawn Estes .30 .09
❑ 296 Wilton Guerrero .30 .09
❑ 297 Delino DeShields .30 .09
❑ 298 David Justice .30 .09
❑ 299 Harold Baines .30 .09
❑ 300 Al Leiter .30 .09
❑ 301 Wil Cordero .30 .09
❑ 302 Antonio Alfonseca .30 .09
❑ 303 Sean Casey .30 .09
❑ 304 Carlos Beltran .30 .09
❑ 305 Brad Radke .30 .09
❑ 306 Jason Varitek .30 .09
❑ 307 Shigetoshi Hasegawa .30 .09
❑ 308 Todd Stottlemyre .30 .09
❑ 309 Raul Mondesi .30 .09
❑ 310 Mike Bordick .30 .09
❑ 311 Darryl Kile .30 .09
❑ 312 Dean Palmer .30 .09
❑ 313 Johnny Damon .30 .09
❑ 314 Todd Helton .50 .15
❑ 315 Chad Hermansen .30 .09
❑ 316 Kevin Appier .30 .09

❑ 317 Greg Vaughn .30 .09
❑ 318 Robb Nen .30 .09
❑ 319 Jose Cruz Jr. .30 .09
❑ 320 Ron Belliard .30 .09
❑ 321 Bernie Williams .50 .15
❑ 322 Melvin Mora .30 .09
❑ 323 Kenny Lofton .30 .09
❑ 324 Armando Benitez .30 .09
❑ 325 Carlos Lee .30 .09
❑ 326 Damian Jackson .30 .09
❑ 327 Eric Milton .30 .09
❑ 328 J.D. Drew .30 .09
❑ 329 Byung-Hyun Kim .30 .09
❑ 330 Chris Stynes .30 .09
❑ 331 Kazuhiro Sasaki .30 .09
❑ 332 Troy O'Leary .30 .09
❑ 333 Pat Hentgen .30 .09
❑ 334 Brad Ausmus .30 .09
❑ 335 Todd Walker .30 .09
❑ 336 Jason Isringhausen .30 .09
❑ 337 Gerald Williams .30 .09
❑ 338 Aaron Sele .30 .09
❑ 339 Paul O'Neill .50 .15
❑ 340 Cal Ripken 2.50 .75
❑ 341 Manny Ramirez .30 .09
❑ 342 Will Clark .75 .23
❑ 343 Mark Redman .30 .09
❑ 344 Bubba Trammell .30 .09
❑ 345 Troy Percival .30 .09
❑ 346 Chris Singleton .30 .09
❑ 347 Rafael Palmeiro .50 .15
❑ 348 Carl Everett .30 .09
❑ 349 Andy Benes .30 .09
❑ 350 Bobby Higginson .30 .09
❑ 351 Alex Cabrera .30 .09
❑ 352 Barry Zito .75 .23
❑ 353 Jace Brewer .30 .09
❑ 354 Paxton Crawford .30 .09
❑ 355 Oswaldo Mairena .30 .09
❑ 356 Joe Crede .30 .09
❑ 357 A.J. Pierzynski .30 .09
❑ 358 Daniel Garibay .30 .09
❑ 359 Jason Tyner .30 .09
❑ 360 Nate Rolison .30 .09
❑ 361 Scott Downs .30 .09
❑ 362 Keith Ginter .30 .09
❑ 363 Juan Pierre .30 .09
❑ 364 Adam Bernero .30 .09
❑ 365 Chris Richard .30 .09
❑ 366 Joey Nation .30 .09
❑ 367 Aubrey Huff .30 .09
❑ 368 Adam Eaton .30 .09
❑ 369 Jose Ortiz .30 .09
❑ 370 Eric Munson .30 .09
❑ 371 Matt Kinney .30 .09
❑ 372 Eric Byrnes .30 .09
❑ 373 Keith McDonald .30 .09
❑ 374 Matt Wise .30 .09
❑ 375 Timo Perez .30 .09
❑ 376 Julio Zuleta .30 .09
❑ 377 Jimmy Rollins .30 .09
❑ 378 Xavier Nady .30 .09
❑ 379 Ryan Kohlmeier .30 .09
❑ 380 Corey Patterson .30 .09
❑ 381 Todd Helton LL .30 .09
❑ 382 Moises Alou LL .30 .09
❑ 383 Vladimir Guerrero LL .50 .15
❑ 384 Luis Castillo LL .30 .09
❑ 385 Jeffrey Hammonds LL .30 .09
❑ 386 Nomar Garciaparra LL .75 .23
❑ 387 Carlos Delgado LL .30 .09
❑ 388 Darin Erstad LL .30 .09
❑ 389 Manny Ramirez LL .30 .09
❑ 390 Mike Sweeney LL .30 .09
❑ 391 Sammy Sosa LL .75 .23
❑ 392 Barry Bonds LL .75 .23
❑ 393 Jeff Bagwell LL .30 .09
❑ 394 Richard Hidalgo LL .30 .09
❑ 395 Vladimir Guerrero LL .50 .15
❑ 396 Troy Glaus LL .50 .15
❑ 397 Frank Thomas LL .50 .15
❑ 398 Carlos Delgado LL .30 .09
❑ 399 David Justice LL .30 .09
❑ 400 Jason Giambi LL .30 .09
❑ 401 Randy Johnson LL .50 .15
❑ 402 Kevin Brown LL .30 .09
❑ 403 Greg Maddux LL .75 .23
❑ 404 Al Leiter LL .30 .09
❑ 405 Mike Hampton LL .30 .09
❑ 406 Pedro Martinez LL .50 .15
❑ 407 Roger Clemens LL .75 .23
❑ 408 Mike Sirotka LL .30 .09
❑ 409 Mike Mussina LL .50 .15
❑ 410 Bartolo Colon LL .30 .09
❑ 411 Subway Series WS .50 .15
❑ 412 Jose Vizcaino WS .50 .15
❑ 413 Jose Vizcaino WS .50 .15
❑ 414 Roger Clemens WS .75 .23
❑ 415 Armando Benitez .30 .09
Edgardo Alfonzo
Timo Perez WS
❑ 416 Al Leiter WS .50 .15
❑ 417 Luis Sojo WS .50 .15
❑ 418 Yankees 3-Peat WS .75 .23
❑ 419 Derek Jeter WS 1.00 .30
❑ 420 Toast of the Town WS .50 .15
❑ 421 Rafael Furcal .30 .09
Chipper Jones
Greg Maddux
John Rocker
Tom Glavine CL
❑ 422 Armando Benitez .75 .23
Mike Piazza
Mike Hampton
Al Leiter CL
❑ 423 Ryan Dempster .50 .15
Luis Castillo
Antonio Alfonseca
Preston Wilson CL
❑ 424 Robert Person .50 .15
Scott Rolen
Randy Wolf
Bob Abreu
Doug Glanville CL
❑ 425 Vladimir Guerrero .50 .15
Peter Bergeron CL
❑ 426 Fernando Vina .30 .09
Dave Veres
Jim Edmonds
Rick Ankiel
Edgar Renteria
Darryl Kile CL
❑ 427 Danny Graves .30 .09
Ken Griffey Jr.
Sean Casey
Pokey Reese CL
❑ 428 Jon Lieber .50 .15
Sammy Sosa
Eric Young CL
❑ 429 Curtis Leskanic .50 .15
Geoff Jenkins
Jeff D'Amico
Jeromy Burnitz
Marquis Grissom CL
❑ 430 Scott Elarton .30 .09
Jeff Bagwell
Octavio Dotel
Moises Alou
Roger Cedeno CL
❑ 431 Mike Williams .50 .15
Jason Kendall
Kris Benson
Brian Giles CL
❑ 432 Livan Hernandez .30 .09
Jeff Kent
Robb Nen
Barry Bonds
Marvin Benard CL
❑ 433 Luis Gonzalez .30 .09
Steve Finley
Tony Womack
Randy Johnson CL
❑ 434 Jeff Shaw .30 .09
Gary Sheffield
Kevin Brown
Shawn Green
Chan Ho Park CL UER
B.Shaw should be J.Shaw
❑ 435 Jose Jimenez .30 .09
Todd Helton
Brian Bohanon
Tom Goodwin CL UER
C.Goodwin should be T.Goodwin
❑ 436 Trevor Hoffman .50 .15
Phil Nevin
Matt Clement
Eric Owens CL
❑ 437 Mariano Rivera .75 .23
Derek Jeter
Roger Clemens
Bernie Williams
Andy Pettitte CL
❑ 438 Pedro Martinez .50 .15
Nomar Garciaparra
Derek Lowe
Carl Everett CL
❑ 439 Ryan Kohlmeier .50 .15
Delino DeShields
Mike Mussina
Albert Belle CL
❑ 440 David Wells .30 .09
Carlos Delgado
Billy Koch
Raul Mondesi CL
❑ 441 Ramon Hernandez .30 .09
Fred McGriff
Miguel Cairo
Greg Vaughn CL
❑ 442 Mike Sirotka .50 .15
Frank Thomas
Keith Foulke
Ray Durham CL
❑ 443 Steve Karsay .30 .09
Manny Ramirez
Bartolo Colon
Roberto Alomar CL
❑ 444 Brian Moehler .30 .09
Deivi Cruz
Juan Encarnacion
Todd Jones
Bobby Higginson CL
❑ 445 Mac Suzuki .50 .15
Mike Sweeney
Johnny Damon
Jermaine Dye CL
❑ 446 Brad Radke .30 .09
Matt Lawton
Eric Milton
Jacque Jones
Cristian Guzman CL
❑ 447 Kazuhiro Sasaki .30 .09
Edgar Martinez
Aaron Sele
Rickey Henderson CL
❑ 448 Jason Isringhausen .30 .09
Jason Giambi
Tim Hudson
Randy Velarde CL
❑ 449 Shigetoshi Hasegawa .30 .09
Darin Erstad
Troy Percival
Troy Glaus CL
❑ 450 Rick Helling .30 .09
Rafael Palmeiro
John Wetteland
Luis Alicea CL
❑ 451 Albert Pujols RC 20.00 6.00
❑ 452 Ichiro Suzuki RC 10.00 3.00
❑ 453 Tsuyoshi Shinjo RC 1.50 .45
❑ 454 Johnny Estrada RC .75 .23
❑ 455 Elpidio Guzman RC .50 .15
❑ 456 Adrian Hernandez RC .50 .15
❑ 457 Rafael Soriano RC 1.50 .45
❑ 458 Drew Henson RC 1.50 .45
❑ 459 Juan Uribe RC .50 .15
❑ 460 Matt White RC .50 .15
❑ 461 Endy Chavez RC .50 .15
❑ 462 Bud Smith RC .50 .15
❑ 463 Morgan Ensberg RC 1.50 .45
❑ 464 Jay Gibbons RC 1.50 .45
❑ 465 Jackson Melian RC .50 .15
❑ 466 Junior Spivey RC 1.25 .35
❑ 467 Juan Cruz RC .50 .15
❑ 468 Wilson Betemit RC .50 .15
❑ 469 Alexis Gomez RC .50 .15
❑ 470 Mark Teixeira RC 8.00 2.40
❑ 471 Erick Almonte RC .50 .15
❑ 472 Travis Hafner RC 1.25 .35

❑ 473 Carlos Valderrama RC ...... .50 .15
❑ 474 Brandon Duckworth RC .... .50 .15
❑ 475 Ryan Freel RC .... .50 .15
❑ 476 Wilkin Ruan RC .... .50 .15
❑ 477 Andres Torres RC .... .50 .15
❑ 478 Josh Towers RC .... .50 .15
❑ 479 Kyle Lohse RC .... 1.25 .35
❑ 480 Jason Michaels RC .... .50 .15
❑ 481 Alfonso Soriano .... 1.25 .35
❑ 482 C.C. Sabathia .... .50 .15
❑ 483 Roy Oswalt .... .75 .23
❑ 484 Ben Sheets UER .... .50 .15
Wrong team logo on the front
❑ 485 Adam Dunn .... .75 .23
❑ NNO Uncut Sheet EXCH/100 2.00 .60

2002 Fleer Tradition

	Nm-Mt	Ex-Mt
COMPLETE SET (500)	250.00	75.00
COMP.SET w/o SP's (400)	50.00	15.00
COMMON CARD (101-500)	.30	.09
COMMON SP (1-100)	3.00	.90
COMMON CARD (436-470)	.50	.15

❑ 1 Barry Bonds SP 12.00 3.60
❑ 2 Cal Ripken SP 15.00 4.50
❑ 3 Tony Gwynn SP 6.00 1.80
❑ 4 Brad Radke SP .... 3.00 .90
❑ 5 Jose Ortiz SP .... 3.00 .90
❑ 6 Mark Mulder SP .... 3.00 .90
❑ 7 Jon Lieber SP .... 3.00 .90
❑ 8 John Olerud SP .... 3.00 .90
❑ 9 Phil Nevin SP .... 3.00 .90
❑ 10 Craig Biggio SP .... 3.00 .90
❑ 11 Pedro Martinez SP 5.00 1.50
❑ 12 Fred McGriff SP .... 3.00 .90
❑ 13 Vladimir Guerrero SP 5.00 1.50
❑ 14 Jason Giambi SP 5.00 1.50
❑ 15 Mark Kotsay SP .... 3.00 .90
❑ 16 Bud Smith SP .... 3.00 .90
❑ 17 Kevin Brown SP .... 3.00 .90
❑ 18 Darin Erstad SP .... 3.00 .90
❑ 19 Julio Franco SP .... 3.00 .90
❑ 20 C.C. Sabathia SP .... 3.00 .90
❑ 21 Larry Walker SP .... 3.00 .90
❑ 22 Doug Mientkiewicz SP .... 3.00 .90
❑ 23 Luis Gonzalez SP .... 3.00 .90
❑ 24 Albert Pujols SP 10.00 3.00
❑ 25 Brian Lawrence SP .... 3.00 .90
❑ 26 Al Leiter SP .... 3.00 .90
❑ 27 Mike Sweeney SP .... 3.00 .90
❑ 28 Jeff Weaver SP .... 3.00 .90
❑ 29 Matt Morris SP .... 3.00 .90
❑ 30 Hideo Nomo SP 5.00 1.50
❑ 31 Tom Glavine SP 5.00 1.50
❑ 32 Magglio Ordonez SP .... 3.00 .90
❑ 33 Roberto Alomar SP 5.00 1.50
❑ 34 Roger Cedeno SP .... 3.00 .90
❑ 35 Greg Vaughn SP .... 3.00 .90
❑ 36 Chan Ho Park SP .... 3.00 .90
❑ 37 Rich Aurilia SP .... 3.00 .90
❑ 38 Tsuyoshi Shinjo SP .... 3.00 .90
❑ 39 Eric Young SP .... 3.00 .90
❑ 40 Bobby Higginson SP .... 3.00 .90
❑ 41 Marlon Anderson SP .... 3.00 .90
❑ 42 Mark Grace SP 5.00 1.50
❑ 43 Steve Cox SP .... 3.00 .90
❑ 44 Cliff Floyd SP .... 3.00 .90
❑ 45 Brian Roberts SP .... 3.00 .90
❑ 46 Paul Konerko SP .... 3.00 .90
❑ 47 Brandon Duckworth SP .... 3.00 .90
❑ 48 Josh Beckett SP .... 3.00 .90
❑ 49 David Ortiz SP .... 3.00 .90
❑ 50 Geoff Jenkins SP .... 3.00 .90
❑ 51 Ruben Sierra SP .... 3.00 .90
❑ 52 John Franco SP .... 3.00 .90
❑ 53 Einar Diaz SP .... 3.00 .90
❑ 54 Luis Castillo SP .... 3.00 .90
❑ 55 Mark Quinn SP .... 3.00 .90
❑ 56 Shea Hillenbrand SP .... 3.00 .90
❑ 57 Rafael Palmeiro SP .... 3.00 .90
❑ 58 Paul O'Neill SP .... 3.00 .90
❑ 59 Andruw Jones SP .... 3.00 .90
❑ 60 Lance Berkman SP .... 3.00 .90
❑ 61 Jimmy Rollins SP .... 3.00 .90
❑ 62 Jose Hernandez SP .... 3.00 .90
❑ 63 Rusty Greer SP .... 3.00 .90
❑ 64 Wade Miller SP .... 3.00 .90
❑ 65 David Eckstein SP .... 3.00 .90
❑ 66 Jose Valentin SP .... 3.00 .90
❑ 67 Javier Vazquez SP .... 3.00 .90
❑ 68 Roger Clemens SP 10.00 3.00
❑ 69 Omar Vizquel SP .... 3.00 .90
❑ 70 Roy Oswalt SP .... 3.00 .90
❑ 71 Shannon Stewart SP .... 3.00 .90
❑ 72 Byung-Hyun Kim SP .... 3.00 .90
❑ 73 Jay Gibbons SP .... 3.00 .90
❑ 74 Barry Larkin SP 5.00 1.50
❑ 75 Brian Giles SP .... 3.00 .90
❑ 76 Andres Galarraga SP .... 3.00 .90
❑ 77 Sammy Sosa SP 8.00 2.40
❑ 78 Manny Ramirez SP .... 3.00 .90
❑ 79 Carlos Delgado SP .... 3.00 .90
❑ 80 Jorge Posada SP .... 3.00 .90
❑ 81 Todd Ritchie SP .... 3.00 .90
❑ 82 Russ Ortiz SP .... 3.00 .90
❑ 83 Brent Mayne SP .... 3.00 .90
❑ 84 Mike Mussina SP 5.00 1.50
❑ 85 Raul Mondesi SP .... 3.00 .90
❑ 86 Mark Loretta SP .... 3.00 .90
❑ 87 Tim Raines SP .... 3.00 .90
❑ 88 Ichiro Suzuki SP 10.00 3.00
❑ 89 Juan Pierre SP .... 3.00 .90
❑ 90 Adam Dunn SP .... 3.00 .90
❑ 91 Jason Tyner SP .... 3.00 .90
❑ 92 Miguel Tejada SP .... 3.00 .90
❑ 93 Elpidio Guzman SP .... 3.00 .90
❑ 94 Freddy Garcia SP .... 3.00 .90
❑ 95 Marcus Giles SP .... 3.00 .90
❑ 96 Junior Spivey SP .... 3.00 .90
❑ 97 Aramis Ramirez SP .... 3.00 .90
❑ 98 Jose Rijo SP .... 3.00 .90
❑ 99 Paul LoDuca SP .... 3.00 .90
❑ 100 Mike Cameron SP .... 3.00 .90
❑ 101 Alex Hernandez .... .30 .09
❑ 102 Benji Gil .... .30 .09
❑ 103 Benito Santiago .... .30 .09
❑ 104 Bobby Abreu .... .30 .09
❑ 105 Brad Penny .... .30 .09
❑ 106 Calvin Murray .... .30 .09
❑ 107 Chad Durbin .... .30 .09
❑ 108 Chris Singleton .... .30 .09
❑ 109 Chris Carpenter .... .30 .09
❑ 110 David Justice .... .30 .09
❑ 111 Eric Chavez .... .30 .09
❑ 112 Fernando Tatis .... .30 .09
❑ 113 Frank Castillo .... .30 .09
❑ 114 Jason LaRue .... .30 .09
❑ 115 Jim Edmonds .... .30 .09
❑ 116 Joe Kennedy .... .30 .09
❑ 117 Jose Jimenez .... .30 .09
❑ 118 Josh Towers .... .30 .09
❑ 119 Junior Herndon .... .30 .09
❑ 120 Luke Prokopec .... .30 .09
❑ 121 Mac Suzuki .... .30 .09
❑ 122 Mark DeRosa .... .30 .09
❑ 123 Marty Cordova .... .30 .09
❑ 124 Michael Tucker .... .30 .09
❑ 125 Michael Young .... .30 .09
❑ 126 Robin Ventura .... .30 .09
❑ 127 Shane Halter .... .30 .09
❑ 128 Shane Reynolds .... .30 .09
❑ 129 Tony Womack .... .30 .09
❑ 130 A.J. Pierzynski .... .30 .09
❑ 131 Aaron Rowand .... .30 .09
❑ 132 Antonio Alfonseca .... .30 .09
❑ 133 Arthur Rhodes .... .30 .09
❑ 134 Bob Wickman .... .30 .09
❑ 135 Brady Clark .... .30 .09
❑ 136 Chad Hermansen .... .30 .09
❑ 137 Marlon Byrd .... .30 .09
❑ 138 Dan Wilson .... .30 .09
❑ 139 David Cone .... .30 .09
❑ 140 Dean Palmer .... .30 .09
❑ 141 Denny Neagle .... .30 .09
❑ 142 Derek Jeter .... 2.00 .60
❑ 143 Erubiel Durazo .... .30 .09
❑ 144 Felix Rodriguez .... .30 .09
❑ 145 Jason Hart .... .30 .09
❑ 146 Jay Bell .... .30 .09
❑ 147 Jeff Suppan .... .30 .09
❑ 148 Jeff Zimmerman .... .30 .09
❑ 149 Kerry Wood .... .75 .23
❑ 150 Kerry Robinson .... .30 .09
❑ 151 Kevin Appier .... .30 .09
❑ 152 Michael Barrett .... .30 .09
❑ 153 Mo Vaughn .... .30 .09
❑ 154 Rafael Furcal .... .30 .09
❑ 155 Sidney Ponson .... .30 .09
❑ 156 Terry Adams .... .30 .09
❑ 157 Tim Redding .... .30 .09
❑ 158 Toby Hall .... .30 .09
❑ 159 Aaron Sele .... .30 .09
❑ 160 Bartolo Colon .... .30 .09
❑ 161 Brad Ausmus .... .30 .09
❑ 162 Carlos Pena .... .30 .09
❑ 163 Jace Brewer .... .30 .09
❑ 164 David Wells .... .30 .09
❑ 165 David Segui .... .30 .09
❑ 166 Derek Lowe .... .30 .09
❑ 167 Derek Bell .... .30 .09
❑ 168 Jason Grabowski .... .30 .09
❑ 169 Johnny Damon .... .30 .09
❑ 170 Jose Mesa .... .30 .09
❑ 171 Juan Encarnacion .... .30 .09
❑ 172 Ken Caminiti .... .30 .09
❑ 173 Ken Griffey Jr. .... 1.25 .35
❑ 174 Luis Rivas .... .30 .09
❑ 175 Mariano Rivera .... .50 .15
❑ 176 Mark Grudzielanek .... .30 .09
❑ 177 Mark McGwire .... 2.00 .60
❑ 178 Mike Bordick .... .30 .09
❑ 179 Mike Hampton .... .30 .09
❑ 180 Nick Bierbrodt .... .30 .09
❑ 181 Paul Byrd .... .30 .09
❑ 182 Robb Nen .... .30 .09
❑ 183 Ryan Dempster .... .30 .09
❑ 184 Ryan Klesko .... .30 .09
❑ 185 Scott Spiezio .... .30 .09
❑ 186 Scott Strickland .... .30 .09
❑ 187 Todd Zeile .... .30 .09
❑ 188 Tom Gordon .... .30 .09
❑ 189 Troy Glaus .... .50 .15
❑ 190 Matt Williams .... .30 .09
❑ 191 Wes Helms .... .30 .09
❑ 192 Jerry Hairston Jr. .... .30 .09
❑ 193 Brook Fordyce .... .30 .09
❑ 194 Nomar Garciaparra .... 1.50 .45
❑ 195 Kevin Tapani .... .30 .09
❑ 196 Mark Buehrle .... .30 .09
❑ 197 Dmitri Young .... .30 .09
❑ 198 John Rocker .... .30 .09
❑ 199 Juan Uribe .... .30 .09
❑ 200 Matt Anderson .... .30 .09
❑ 201 Alex Gonzalez .... .30 .09
❑ 202 Julio Lugo .... .30 .09
❑ 203 Roberto Hernandez .... .30 .09
❑ 204 Richie Sexson .... .30 .09
❑ 205 Corey Koskie .... .30 .09
❑ 206 Tony Armas Jr. .... .30 .09
❑ 207 Rey Ordonez .... .30 .09
❑ 208 Orlando Hernandez .... .30 .09
❑ 209 Pokey Reese .... .30 .09
❑ 210 Mike Lieberthal .... .30 .09
❑ 211 Kris Benson .... .30 .09
❑ 212 Jermaine Dye .... .30 .09
❑ 213 Livan Hernandez .... .30 .09
❑ 214 Bret Boone .... .30 .09
❑ 215 Dustin Hermanson .... .30 .09

❑ 216 Placido Polanco .30 .09
❑ 217 Jesus Colome .30 .09
❑ 218 Alex Gonzalez .30 .09
❑ 219 Adam Everett .30 .09
❑ 220 Adam Piatt .30 .09
❑ 221 Brad Fullmer .30 .09
❑ 222 Brian Buchanan .30 .09
❑ 223 Chipper Jones .75 .23
❑ 224 Chuck Finley .30 .09
❑ 225 David Bell .30 .09
❑ 226 Jack Wilson .30 .09
❑ 227 Jason Bere .30 .09
❑ 228 Jeff Conine .30 .09
❑ 229 Jeff Bagwell .50 .15
❑ 230 Joe McEwing .30 .09
❑ 231 Kip Wells .30 .09
❑ 232 Mike Lansing .30 .09
❑ 233 Neifi Perez .30 .09
❑ 234 Omar Daal .30 .09
❑ 235 Reggie Sanders .30 .09
❑ 236 Shawn Wooten .30 .09
❑ 237 Shawn Chacon .30 .09
❑ 238 Shawn Estes .30 .09
❑ 239 Steve Sparks .30 .09
❑ 240 Steve Kline .30 .09
❑ 241 Tino Martinez .50 .15
❑ 242 Tyler Houston .30 .09
❑ 243 Xavier Nady .30 .09
❑ 244 Bengie Molina .30 .09
❑ 245 Ben Davis .30 .09
❑ 246 Casey Fossum .30 .09
❑ 247 Chris Stynes .30 .09
❑ 248 Danny Graves .30 .09
❑ 249 Pedro Feliz .30 .09
❑ 250 Darren Oliver .30 .09
❑ 251 Dave Veres .30 .09
❑ 252 Deivi Cruz .30 .09
❑ 253 Desi Relaford .30 .09
❑ 254 Devon White .30 .09
❑ 255 Edgar Martinez .50 .15
❑ 256 Eric Munson .30 .09
❑ 257 Eric Karros .30 .09
❑ 258 Homer Bush .30 .09
❑ 259 Jason Kendall .30 .09
❑ 260 Javy Lopez .30 .09
❑ 261 Keith Foulke .30 .09
❑ 262 Keith Ginter .30 .09
❑ 263 Nick Johnson .30 .09
❑ 264 Pat Burrell .30 .09
❑ 265 Ricky Gutierrez .30 .09
❑ 266 Russ Johnson .30 .09
❑ 267 Steve Finley .30 .09
❑ 268 Terrence Long .30 .09
❑ 269 Tony Batista .30 .09
❑ 270 Torii Hunter .30 .09
❑ 271 Vinny Castilla .30 .09
❑ 272 A.J. Burnett .30 .09
❑ 273 Adrian Beltre .30 .09
❑ 274 Alex Rodriguez 1.50 .45
❑ 275 Armando Benitez .30 .09
❑ 276 Billy Koch .30 .09
❑ 277 Brady Anderson .30 .09
❑ 278 Brian Jordan .30 .09
❑ 279 Carlos Febles .30 .09
❑ 280 Daryle Ward .30 .09
❑ 281 Eli Marrero .30 .09
❑ 282 Garret Anderson .30 .09
❑ 283 Jack Cust .30 .09
❑ 284 Jacque Jones .30 .09
❑ 285 Jamie Moyer .30 .09
❑ 286 Jeffrey Hammonds .30 .09
❑ 287 Jim Thome .75 .23
❑ 288 Jon Garland .30 .09
❑ 289 Jose Offerman .30 .09
❑ 290 Matt Stairs .30 .09
❑ 291 Orlando Cabrera .30 .09
❑ 292 Ramiro Mendoza .30 .09
❑ 293 Ray Durham .30 .09
❑ 294 Rickey Henderson 1.25 .35
❑ 295 Rob Mackowiak .30 .09
❑ 296 Scott Rolen .50 .15
❑ 297 Tim Hudson .30 .09
❑ 298 Todd Helton .50 .15
❑ 299 Tony Clark .30 .09
❑ 300 B.J. Surhoff .30 .09
❑ 301 Bernie Williams .50 .15
❑ 302 Bill Mueller .30 .09
❑ 303 Chris Richard .30 .09
❑ 304 Craig Paquette .30 .09
❑ 305 Curt Schilling .50 .15
❑ 306 Damian Jackson .30 .09
❑ 307 Derrek Lee .30 .09
❑ 308 Eric Milton .30 .09
❑ 309 Frank Catalanotto .30 .09
❑ 310 J.T. Snow .30 .09
❑ 311 Jared Sandberg .30 .09
❑ 312 Jason Varitek .30 .09
❑ 313 Jeff Cirillo .30 .09
❑ 314 Jeromy Burnitz .30 .09
❑ 315 Joe Crede .30 .09
❑ 316 Joel Pineiro .30 .09
❑ 317 Jose Cruz Jr. .30 .09
❑ 318 Kevin Young .30 .09
❑ 319 Marquis Grissom .30 .09
❑ 320 Moises Alou .30 .09
❑ 321 Randall Simon .30 .09
❑ 322 Royce Clayton .30 .09
❑ 323 Tim Salmon .50 .15
❑ 324 Travis Fryman .30 .09
❑ 325 Travis Lee .30 .09
❑ 326 Vance Wilson .30 .09
❑ 327 Jarrod Washburn .30 .09
❑ 328 Ben Petrick .30 .09
❑ 329 Ben Grieve .30 .09
❑ 330 Carl Everett .30 .09
❑ 331 Eric Byrnes .30 .09
❑ 332 Doug Glanville .30 .09
❑ 333 Edgardo Alfonzo .30 .09
❑ 334 Ellis Burks .30 .09
❑ 335 Gabe Kapler .30 .09
❑ 336 Gary Sheffield .30 .09
❑ 337 Greg Maddux 1.50 .45
❑ 338 J.D. Drew .30 .09
❑ 339 Jamey Wright .30 .09
❑ 340 Jeff Kent .30 .09
❑ 341 Jeremy Giambi .30 .09
❑ 342 Joe Randa .30 .09
❑ 343 Joe Mays .30 .09
❑ 344 Jose Macias .30 .09
❑ 345 Kazuhiro Sasaki .30 .09
❑ 346 Mike Kinkade .30 .09
❑ 347 Mike Lowell .30 .09
❑ 348 Randy Johnson .75 .23
❑ 349 Randy Wolf .30 .09
❑ 350 Richard Hidalgo .30 .09
❑ 351 Ron Coomer .30 .09
❑ 352 Sandy Alomar Jr. .30 .09
❑ 353 Sean Casey .30 .09
❑ 354 Trevor Hoffman .30 .09
❑ 355 Adam Eaton .30 .09
❑ 356 Alfonso Soriano .75 .23
❑ 357 Barry Zito .75 .23
❑ 358 Billy Wagner .30 .09
❑ 359 Brent Abernathy .30 .09
❑ 360 Bret Prinz .30 .09
❑ 361 Carlos Beltran .30 .09
❑ 362 Carlos Guillen .30 .09
❑ 363 Charles Johnson .30 .09
❑ 364 Cristian Guzman .30 .09
❑ 365 Damion Easley .30 .09
❑ 366 Darryl Kile .30 .09
❑ 367 Delino DeShields .30 .09
❑ 368 Eric Davis .30 .09
❑ 369 Frank Thomas .75 .23
❑ 370 Ivan Rodriguez .75 .23
❑ 371 Jay Payton .30 .09
❑ 372 Jeff D'Amico .30 .09
❑ 373 John Burkett .30 .09
❑ 374 Melvin Mora .30 .09
❑ 375 Ramon Ortiz .30 .09
❑ 376 Robert Person .30 .09
❑ 377 Russell Branyan .30 .09
❑ 378 Shawn Green .30 .09
❑ 379 Todd Hollandsworth .30 .09
❑ 380 Tony McKnight .30 .09
❑ 381 Trot Nixon .30 .09
❑ 382 Vernon Wells .30 .09
❑ 383 Troy Percival .30 .09
❑ 384 Albie Lopez .30 .09
❑ 385 Alex Ochoa .30 .09
❑ 386 Andy Pettitte .50 .15
❑ 387 Brandon Inge .30 .09
❑ 388 Bubba Trammell .30 .09
❑ 389 Corey Patterson .30 .09
❑ 390 Damian Rolls .30 .09
❑ 391 Dee Brown .30 .09
❑ 392 Edgar Renteria .30 .09
❑ 393 Eric Gagne .50 .15
❑ 394 Jason Johnson .30 .09
❑ 395 Jeff Nelson .30 .09
❑ 396 John Vander Wal .30 .09
❑ 397 Johnny Estrada .30 .09
❑ 398 Jose Canseco .75 .23
❑ 399 Juan Gonzalez .75 .23
❑ 400 Kevin Millwood .30 .09
❑ 401 Lee Stevens .30 .09
❑ 402 Matt Lawton .30 .09
❑ 403 Mike Lamb .30 .09
❑ 404 Octavio Dotel .30 .09
❑ 405 Ramon Hernandez .30 .09
❑ 406 Ruben Quevedo .30 .09
❑ 407 Todd Walker .30 .09
❑ 408 Troy O'Leary .30 .09
❑ 409 Wascar Serrano .30 .09
❑ 410 Aaron Boone .30 .09
❑ 411 Aubrey Huff .30 .09
❑ 412 Ben Sheets .30 .09
❑ 413 Carlos Lee .30 .09
❑ 414 Chuck Knoblauch .30 .09
❑ 415 Steve Karsay .30 .09
❑ 416 Dante Bichette .30 .09
❑ 417 David Dellucci .30 .09
❑ 418 Esteban Loaiza .30 .09
❑ 419 Fernando Vina .30 .09
❑ 420 Ismael Valdes .30 .09
❑ 421 Jason Isringhausen .30 .09
❑ 422 Jeff Shaw .30 .09
❑ 423 John Smoltz .50 .15
❑ 424 Jose Vidro .30 .09
❑ 425 Kenny Lofton .30 .09
❑ 426 Mark Little .30 .09
❑ 427 Mark McLemore .30 .09
❑ 428 Marvin Benard .30 .09
❑ 429 Mike Piazza 1.25 .35
❑ 430 Pat Hentgen .30 .09
❑ 431 Preston Wilson .30 .09
❑ 432 Rick Helling .30 .09
❑ 433 Robert Fick .30 .09
❑ 434 Rondell White .30 .09
❑ 435 Adam Kennedy .30 .09
❑ 436 David Espinosa PROS .50 .15
❑ 437 Dewon Brazelton PROS .50 .15
❑ 438 Drew Henson PROS .50 .15
❑ 439 Juan Cruz PROS .50 .15
❑ 440 Jason Jennings PROS .50 .15
❑ 441 Carlos Garcia PROS .50 .15
❑ 442 Carlos Hernandez PROS .50 .15
❑ 443 Wilkin Ruan PROS .50 .15
❑ 444 Wilson Betemit PROS .50 .15
❑ 445 Horacio Ramirez PROS .50 .15
❑ 446 Danys Baez PROS .50 .15
❑ 447 Abraham Nunez PROS .50 .15
❑ 448 Josh Hamilton PROS .50 .15
❑ 449 Chris George PROS .50 .15
❑ 450 Rick Bauer PROS .50 .15
❑ 451 Donnie Bridges PROS .50 .15
❑ 452 Erick Almonte PROS .50 .15
❑ 453 Cory Aldridge PROS .50 .15
❑ 454 Ryan Drese PROS .50 .15
❑ 455 Jason Romano PROS .50 .15
❑ 456 Corky Miller PROS .50 .15
❑ 457 Rafael Soriano PROS .50 .15
❑ 458 Mark Prior PROS 2.50 .75
❑ 459 Mark Teixeira PROS 1.25 .35
❑ 460 Adrian Hernandez PROS .50 .15
❑ 461 Tim Spooneybarger PROS .50 .15
❑ 462 Bill Ortega PROS .50 .15
❑ 463 D'Angelo Jimenez PROS .50 .15
❑ 464 Andres Torres PROS .50 .15
❑ 465 Alexis Gomez PROS .50 .15
❑ 466 Angel Berroa PROS .50 .15
❑ 467 Henry Mateo PROS .50 .15
❑ 468 Endy Chavez PROS .50 .15
❑ 469 Billy Sylvester PROS .50 .15
❑ 470 Nate Frese PROS .50 .15
❑ 471 Luis Gonzalez BNR .30 .09
❑ 472 Barry Bonds BNR 2.00 .60
❑ 473 Rich Aurilia BNR .30 .09

		Nm-Mt	Ex-Mt
❑ 474	Albert Pujols BNR	1.50	.45
❑ 475	Todd Helton BNR	.50	.15
❑ 476	Moises Alou BNR	.30	.09
❑ 477	Lance Berkman BNR	.30	.09
❑ 478	Brian Giles BNR	.30	.09
❑ 479	Cliff Floyd BNR	.30	.09
❑ 480	Sammy Sosa BNR	1.25	.35
❑ 481	Shawn Green BNR	.30	.09
❑ 482	Jon Lieber BNR	.30	.09
❑ 483	Matt Morris BNR	.30	.09
❑ 484	Curt Schilling BNR	.50	.15
❑ 485	Randy Johnson BNR	.50	.15
❑ 486	Manny Ramirez BNR	.30	.09
❑ 487	Ichiro Suzuki BNR	1.50	.45
❑ 488	Juan Gonzalez BNR	.75	.23
❑ 489	Derek Jeter BNR	2.00	.60
❑ 490	Alex Rodriguez BNR	1.50	.45
❑ 491	Bret Boone BNR	.30	.09
❑ 492	Roberto Alomar BNR	.75	.23
❑ 493	Jason Giambi BNR	.75	.23
❑ 494	Rafael Palmeiro BNR	.50	.15
❑ 495	Doug Mientkiewicz BNR	.30	.09
❑ 496	Jim Thome BNR	.50	.15
❑ 497	Freddy Garcia BNR	.30	.09
❑ 498	Mark Buehrle BNR	.30	.09
❑ 499	Mark Mulder BNR	.30	.09
❑ 500	Roger Clemens BNR	1.50	.45

2002 Fleer Tradition Update

	Nm-Mt	Ex-Mt
COMPLETE SET (400)	120.00	36.00
COMP.SET w/o SP's (300)	40.00	12.00
COMMON CARD (U101-U400)	.30	.09
COMMON CARD (U1-U100)	1.00	.30

		Nm-Mt	Ex-Mt
❑ U1	P.J. Bevis SP RC	1.00	.30
❑ U2	Mike Crudale SP RC	1.00	.30
❑ U3	Ben Howard SP RC	1.00	.30
❑ U4	Travis Driskill SP RC	1.00	.30
❑ U5	Reed Johnson SP RC	1.25	.35
❑ U6	Kyle Kane SP RC	1.00	.30
❑ U7	Deivis Santos SP	1.00	.30
❑ U8	Tim Kalita SP RC	1.00	.30
❑ U9	Brandon Puffer SP RC	1.00	.30
❑ U10	Chris Snelling SP RC	2.50	.75
❑ U11	Juan Brito SP RC	1.00	.30
❑ U12	Tyler Yates SP RC	1.00	.30
❑ U13	Victor Alvarez SP RC	1.00	.30
❑ U14	Takahito Nomura SP RC	1.00	.30
❑ U15	Ron Calloway SP RC	1.00	.30
❑ U16	Satoru Komiyama SP RC	1.00	.30
❑ U17	Julius Matos SP RC	1.00	.30
❑ U18	Jorge Nunez SP RC	1.00	.30
❑ U19	Anderson Machado SP RC	1.25	.35
❑ U20	Scott Layfield SP RC	1.00	.30
❑ U21	Aaron Cook SP RC	1.25	.35
❑ U22	Alex Pelaez SP RC	1.00	.30
❑ U23	Corey Thurman SP RC	1.00	.30
❑ U24	Nelson Castro SP RC	1.00	.30
❑ U25	Jeff Austin SP RC	1.00	.30
❑ U26	Felix Escalona SP RC	1.00	.30
❑ U27	Luis Ugueto SP RC	1.00	.30
❑ U28	Jaime Cerda SP RC	1.00	.30
❑ U29	J.J. Trujillo SP RC	1.00	.30
❑ U30	Rodrigo Rosario SP RC	1.00	.30
❑ U31	Jorge Padilla SP RC	1.25	.35
❑ U32	Shawn Sedlacek SP RC	1.00	.30
❑ U33	Nate Field SP RC	1.00	.30
❑ U34	Earl Snyder SP RC	1.00	.30
❑ U35	Miguel Asencio SP RC	1.00	.30
❑ U36	Ken Huckaby SP RC	1.00	.30
❑ U37	Valentino Pascucci SP	1.00	.30
❑ U38	So Taguchi SP RC	1.25	.35
❑ U39	Brian Mallette SP RC	1.00	.30
❑ U40	Kazuhisa Ishii SP RC	3.00	.90
❑ U41	Matt Thornton SP RC	1.00	.30
❑ U42	Mark Corey SP RC	1.00	.30
❑ U43	Kirk Saarloos SP RC	2.00	.60
❑ U44	Josh Bard SP RC	1.00	.30
❑ U45	Hansel Izquierdo SP RC	1.00	.30
❑ U46	Rene Reyes SP RC	1.00	.30
❑ U47	Luis Garcia SP	1.00	.30
❑ U48	Jason Simontacchi SP RC	1.25	.35
❑ U49	John Ennis SP RC	1.00	.30
❑ U50	Franklyn German SP RC	1.00	.30
❑ U51	Aaron Guiel SP RC	1.25	.35
❑ U52	Howie Clark SP RC	1.00	.30
❑ U53	David Ross SP RC	1.00	.30
❑ U54	Jason Davis SP RC	2.00	.60
❑ U55	Francis Beltran SP RC	1.00	.30
❑ U56	Barry Wesson SP RC	1.00	.30
❑ U57	Runelvys Hernandez SP RC	2.00	.60
❑ U58	Oliver Perez SP RC	2.50	.75
❑ U59	Ryan Bukvich SP RC	1.00	.30
❑ U60	Steve Kent SP RC	1.00	.30
❑ U61	Julio Mateo SP RC	1.00	.30
❑ U62	Jason Jimenez SP RC	1.00	.30
❑ U63	Jayson Durocher SP RC	1.00	.30
❑ U64	Kevin Frederick SP RC	1.00	.30
❑ U65	Kevin Gryboski SP RC	1.00	.30
❑ U66	Edwin Almonte SP RC	1.00	.30
❑ U67	John Foster SP RC	1.00	.30
❑ U68	Doug Devore SP RC	1.00	.30
❑ U69	Tom Shearn SP RC	1.00	.30
❑ U70	Colin Young SP RC	1.00	.30
❑ U71	Jon Adkins SP RC	1.00	.30
❑ U72	Wilbert Nieves SP RC	1.00	.30
❑ U73	Matt Duff SP RC	1.00	.30
❑ U74	Carl Sadler SP RC	1.00	.30
❑ U75	Jason Kershner SP RC	1.00	.30
❑ U76	Brandon Backe SP RC	1.00	.30
❑ U77	Josh Hancock SP RC	1.00	.30
❑ U78	Chris Baker SP RC	1.00	.30
❑ U79	Travis Hughes SP RC	1.00	.30
❑ U80	Steve Bechler SP RC	1.00	.30
❑ U81	Allan Simpson SP RC	1.00	.30
❑ U82	Aaron Taylor SP RC	1.00	.30
❑ U83	Kevin Cash SP RC	1.00	.30
❑ U84	Chone Figgins SP RC	1.00	.30
❑ U85	Clay Condrey SP RC	1.00	.30
❑ U86	Shane Nance SP RC	1.00	.30
❑ U87	Freddy Sanchez SP RC	2.00	.60
❑ U88	Jim Rushford SP RC	1.00	.30
❑ U89	Jeriome Robertson SP RC	1.25	.35
❑ U90	Trey Lunsford SP RC	1.00	.30
❑ U91	Cody McKay SP RC	1.00	.30
❑ U92	Trey Hodges SP RC	1.25	.35
❑ U93	Hee Seop Choi SP	1.25	.35
❑ U94	Joe Borchard SP	1.00	.30
❑ U95	Orlando Hudson SP	1.00	.30
❑ U96	Carl Crawford SP	1.00	.30
❑ U97	Mark Prior SP	5.00	1.50
❑ U98	Brett Myers SP	1.00	.30
❑ U99	Kenny Lofton SP	1.00	.30
❑ U100	Cliff Floyd SP	1.00	.30
❑ U101	Randy Winn	.30	.09
❑ U102	Ryan Dempster	.30	.09
❑ U103	Josh Phelps	.30	.09
❑ U104	Marcus Giles	.30	.09
❑ U105	Rickey Henderson	1.25	.35
❑ U106	Jose Leon	.30	.09
❑ U107	Tino Martinez	.50	.15
❑ U108	Greg Norton	.30	.09
❑ U109	Odalis Perez	.30	.09
❑ U110	J.C. Romero	.30	.09
❑ U111	Gary Sheffield	.30	.09
❑ U112	Ismael Valdes	.30	.09
❑ U113	Juan Acevedo	.30	.09
❑ U114	Ben Broussard	.30	.09
❑ U115	Deivi Cruz	.30	.09
❑ U116	Geronimo Gil	.30	.09
❑ U117	Eric Hinske	.30	.09
❑ U118	Ted Lilly	.30	.09
❑ U119	Quinton McCracken	.30	.09
❑ U120	Antonio Alfonseca	.30	.09
❑ U121	Brent Abernathy	.30	.09
❑ U122	Johnny Damon	.30	.09
❑ U123	Francisco Cordero	.30	.09
❑ U124	Sterling Hitchcock	.30	.09
❑ U125	Vladimir Nunez	.30	.09
❑ U126	Andres Galarraga	.30	.09
❑ U127	Timo Perez	.30	.09
❑ U128	Tsuyoshi Shinjo	.30	.09
❑ U129	Joe Girardi	.30	.09
❑ U130	Roberto Alomar	.75	.23
❑ U131	Ellis Burks	.30	.09
❑ U132	Mike DeJean	.30	.09
❑ U133	Alex Gonzalez	.30	.09
❑ U134	Johan Santana	.30	.09
❑ U135	Kenny Lofton	.30	.09
❑ U136	Juan Encarnacion	.30	.09
❑ U137	Dewon Brazelton	.30	.09
❑ U138	Jeromy Burnitz	.30	.09
❑ U139	Elmer Dessens	.30	.09
❑ U140	Juan Gonzalez	.75	.23
❑ U141	Todd Hundley	.30	.09
❑ U142	Tomo Ohka	.30	.09
❑ U143	Robin Ventura	.30	.09
❑ U144	Rodrigo Lopez	.30	.09
❑ U145	Ruben Sierra	.30	.09
❑ U146	Jason Phillips	.30	.09
❑ U147	Ryan Rupe	.30	.09
❑ U148	Kevin Appier	.30	.09
❑ U149	Sean Burroughs	.30	.09
❑ U150	Masato Yoshii	.30	.09
❑ U151	Juan Diaz	.30	.09
❑ U152	Tony Graffanino	.30	.09
❑ U153	Raul Ibanez	.30	.09
❑ U154	Kevin Mench	.30	.09
❑ U155	Pedro Astacio	.30	.09
❑ U156	Brent Butler	.30	.09
❑ U157	Kirk Rueter	.30	.09
❑ U158	Eddie Guardado	.30	.09
❑ U159	Hideki Irabu	.30	.09
❑ U160	Wendell Magee	.30	.09
❑ U161	Antonio Osuna	.30	.09
❑ U162	Jose Vizcaino	.30	.09
❑ U163	Danny Bautista	.30	.09
❑ U164	Vinny Castilla	.30	.09
❑ U165	Chris Singleton	.30	.09
❑ U166	Mark Redman	.30	.09
❑ U167	Olmedo Saenz	.30	.09
❑ U168	Scott Erickson	.30	.09
❑ U169	Ty Wigginton	.30	.09
❑ U170	Jason Isringhausen	.30	.09
❑ U171	Andy Van Hekken	.30	.09
❑ U172	Chris Magruder	.30	.09
❑ U173	Brandon Berger	.30	.09
❑ U174	Roger Cedeno	.30	.09
❑ U175	Kelvim Escobar	.30	.09
❑ U176	Jose Guillen	.30	.09
❑ U177	Damian Jackson	.30	.09
❑ U178	Eric Owens	.30	.09
❑ U179	Angel Berroa	.30	.09
❑ U180	Alex Cintron	.30	.09
❑ U181	Jeff Weaver	.30	.09
❑ U182	Damon Minor	.30	.09
❑ U183	Bobby Estalella	.30	.09
❑ U184	David Justice	.30	.09
❑ U185	Roy Halladay	.30	.09
❑ U186	Brian Jordan	.30	.09
❑ U187	Mike Maroth	.30	.09
❑ U188	Pokey Reese	.30	.09
❑ U189	Rey Sanchez	.30	.09
❑ U190	Hank Blalock	.75	.23
❑ U191	Jeff Cirillo	.30	.09
❑ U192	Dmitri Young	.30	.09
❑ U193	Carl Everett	.30	.09
❑ U194	Joey Hamilton	.30	.09
❑ U195	Jorge Julio	.30	.09
❑ U196	Pablo Ozuna	.30	.09
❑ U197	Jason Marquis	.30	.09
❑ U198	Dustan Mohr	.30	.09
❑ U199	Joe Borowski	.30	.09
❑ U200	Tony Clark	.30	.09
❑ U201	David Wells	.30	.09
❑ U202	Josh Fogg	.30	.09
❑ U203	Aaron Harang	.30	.09

❑ U204 John McDonald .30 .09
❑ U205 John Stephens .30 .09
❑ U206 Chris Reitsma .30 .09
❑ U207 Alex Sanchez .30 .09
❑ U208 Milton Bradley .30 .09
❑ U209 Matt Clement .30 .09
❑ U210 Brad Fullmer .30 .09
❑ U211 Shigetoshi Hasegawa .30 .09
❑ U212 Austin Kearns .50 .15
❑ U213 Damaso Marte .30 .09
❑ U214 Vicente Padilla .30 .09
❑ U215 Raul Mondesi .30 .09
❑ U216 Russell Branyan .30 .09
❑ U217 Bartolo Colon .30 .09
❑ U218 Moises Alou .30 .09
❑ U219 Scott Hatteberg .30 .09
❑ U220 Bobby Kielty .30 .09
❑ U221 Kip Wells .30 .09
❑ U222 Scott Stewart .30 .09
❑ U223 Victor Martinez .30 .09
❑ U224 Marty Cordova .30 .09
❑ U225 Desi Relaford .30 .09
❑ U226 Reggie Sanders .30 .09
❑ U227 Jason Giambi .75 .23
❑ U228 Jimmy Haynes .30 .09
❑ U229 Billy Koch .30 .09
❑ U230 Damian Moss .30 .09
❑ U231 Chan Ho Park .30 .09
❑ U232 Cliff Floyd .30 .09
❑ U233 Todd Zeile .30 .09
❑ U234 Jeremy Giambi .30 .09
❑ U235 Rick Helling .30 .09
❑ U236 Matt Lawton .30 .09
❑ U237 Ramon Martinez .30 .09
❑ U238 Rondell White .30 .09
❑ U239 Scott Sullivan .30 .09
❑ U240 Hideo Nomo .75 .23
❑ U241 Todd Ritchie .30 .09
❑ U242 Ramon Santiago .30 .09
❑ U243 Jake Peavy .30 .09
❑ U244 Brad Wilkerson .30 .09
❑ U245 Reggie Taylor .30 .09
❑ U246 Carlos Pena .30 .09
❑ U247 Willis Roberts .30 .09
❑ U248 Jason Schmidt .30 .09
❑ U249 Mike Williams .30 .09
❑ U250 Alan Zinter .30 .09
❑ U251 Michael Tejera .30 .09
❑ U252 Dave Roberts .30 .09
❑ U253 Scott Schoeneweis .30 .09
❑ U254 Woody Williams .30 .09
❑ U255 John Thomson .30 .09
❑ U256 Ricardo Rodriguez .30 .09
❑ U257 Aaron Sele .30 .09
❑ U258 Paul Wilson .30 .09
❑ U259 Brett Tomko .30 .09
❑ U260 Kenny Rogers .30 .09
❑ U261 Mo Vaughn .30 .09
❑ U262 John Burkett .30 .09
❑ U263 Dennis Stark .30 .09
❑ U264 Ray Durham .30 .09
❑ U265 Scott Rolen .50 .15
❑ U266 Gabe Kapler .30 .09
❑ U267 Todd Hollandsworth .30 .09
❑ U268 Bud Smith .30 .09
❑ U269 Jay Payton .30 .09
❑ U270 Tyler Houston .30 .09
❑ U271 Brian Moehler .30 .09
❑ U272 David Espinosa .30 .09
❑ U273 Placido Polanco .30 .09
❑ U274 John Patterson .30 .09
❑ U275 Adam Hyzdu .30 .09
❑ U276 Albert Pujols DS .75 .23
❑ U277 Larry Walker DS .30 .09
❑ U278 Magglio Ordonez DS .30 .09
❑ U279 Ryan Klesko DS .30 .09
❑ U280 Darin Erstad DS .30 .09
❑ U281 Jeff Kent DS .30 .09
❑ U282 Paul Lo Duca DS .30 .09
❑ U283 Jim Edmonds DS .30 .09
❑ U284 Chipper Jones DS .50 .15
❑ U285 Bernie Williams DS .30 .09
❑ U286 Pat Burrell DS .30 .09
❑ U287 Cliff Floyd DS .30 .09
❑ U288 Troy Glaus DS .30 .09
❑ U289 Brian Giles DS .30 .09
❑ U290 Jim Thome DS .50 .15
❑ U291 Greg Maddux DS .75 .23
❑ U292 Roberto Alomar DS .50 .15
❑ U293 Jeff Bagwell DS .30 .09
❑ U294 Rafael Furcal DS .30 .09
❑ U295 Josh Beckett DS .30 .09
❑ U296 Carlos Delgado DS .30 .09
❑ U297 Ken Griffey Jr. DS .75 .23
❑ U298 Jason Giambi AS .50 .15
❑ U299 Paul Konerko AS .30 .09
❑ U300 Mike Sweeney AS .30 .09
❑ U301 Alfonso Soriano AS .50 .15
❑ U302 Shea Hillenbrand AS .30 .09
❑ U303 Tony Batista AS .30 .09
❑ U304 Robin Ventura AS .30 .09
❑ U305 Alex Rodriguez AS .75 .23
❑ U306 Nomar Garciaparra AS .75 .23
❑ U307 Derek Jeter AS 1.00 .30
❑ U308 Miguel Tejada AS .30 .09
❑ U309 Omar Vizquel AS .30 .09
❑ U310 Jorge Posada AS .30 .09
❑ U311 A.J. Pierzynski AS .30 .09
❑ U312 Ichiro Suzuki AS .75 .23
❑ U313 Manny Ramirez AS .30 .09
❑ U314 Torii Hunter AS .30 .09
❑ U315 Garret Anderson AS .30 .09
❑ U316 Robert Fick AS .30 .09
❑ U317 Randy Winn AS .30 .09
❑ U318 Mark Buehrle AS .30 .09
❑ U319 Freddy Garcia AS .30 .09
❑ U320 Eddie Guardado AS .30 .09
❑ U321 Roy Halladay AS .30 .09
❑ U322 Derek Lowe AS .30 .09
❑ U323 Pedro Martinez AS .50 .15
❑ U324 Mariano Rivera AS .30 .09
❑ U325 Kazuhiro Sasaki AS .30 .09
❑ U326 Barry Zito AS .50 .15
❑ U327 Johnny Damon AS .30 .09
❑ U328 Ugueth Urbina AS .30 .09
❑ U329 Todd Helton AS .30 .09
❑ U330 Richie Sexson AS .30 .09
❑ U331 Jose Vidro AS .30 .09
❑ U332 Luis Castillo AS .30 .09
❑ U333 Junior Spivey AS .30 .09
❑ U334 Scott Rolen AS .30 .09
❑ U335 Mike Lowell AS .30 .09
❑ U336 Jimmy Rollins AS .30 .09
❑ U337 Jose Hernandez AS .30 .09
❑ U338 Mike Piazza AS .75 .23
❑ U339 Benito Santiago AS .30 .09
❑ U340 Sammy Sosa AS .75 .23
❑ U341 Barry Bonds AS 1.00 .30
❑ U342 Vladimir Guerrero AS .50 .15
❑ U343 Lance Berkman AS .30 .09
❑ U344 Adam Dunn AS .30 .09
❑ U345 Shawn Green AS .30 .09
❑ U346 Luis Gonzalez AS .30 .09
❑ U347 Eric Gagne AS .30 .09
❑ U348 Tom Glavine AS .50 .15
❑ U349 Trevor Hoffman AS .30 .09
❑ U350 Randy Johnson AS .50 .15
❑ U351 Byung-Hyun Kim AS .30 .09
❑ U352 Matt Morris AS .30 .09
❑ U353 Odalis Perez AS .30 .09
❑ U354 Curt Schilling AS .30 .09
❑ U355 John Smoltz AS .30 .09
❑ U356 Mike Williams AS .30 .09
❑ U357 Andruw Jones AS .30 .09
❑ U358 Vicente Padilla AS .30 .09
❑ U359 Mike Remlinger AS .30 .09
❑ U360 Robb Nen AS .30 .09
❑ U361 Shawn Green CC .30 .09
❑ U362 Derek Jeter CC 1.00 .30
❑ U363 Troy Glaus CC .30 .09
❑ U364 Ken Griffey Jr. CC .75 .23
❑ U365 Mike Piazza CC .75 .23
❑ U366 Jason Giambi CC .50 .15
❑ U367 Greg Maddux CC .75 .23
❑ U368 Albert Pujols CC .75 .23
❑ U369 Pedro Martinez CC .50 .15
❑ U370 Barry Zito CC .50 .15
❑ U371 Ichiro Suzuki CC .75 .23
❑ U372 Nomar Garciaparra CC .75 .23
❑ U373 Vladimir Guerrero CC .50 .15
❑ U374 Randy Johnson CC .50 .15
❑ U375 Barry Bonds CC 1.00 .30
❑ U376 Sammy Sosa CC .75 .23
❑ U377 Hideo Nomo CC .50 .15
❑ U378 Jeff Bagwell CC .30 .09
❑ U379 Curt Schilling CC .30 .09
❑ U380 Jim Thome CC .50 .15
❑ U381 Todd Helton CC .30 .09
❑ U382 Roger Clemens CC .75 .23
❑ U383 Chipper Jones CC .50 .15
❑ U384 Alex Rodriguez CC .75 .23
❑ U385 Manny Ramirez CC .30 .09
❑ U386 Barry Bonds TT 1.00 .30
❑ U387 Jim Thome TT .50 .15
❑ U388 Adam Dunn TT .30 .09
❑ U389 Alex Rodriguez TT .75 .23
❑ U390 Shawn Green TT .30 .09
❑ U391 Jason Giambi TT .50 .15
❑ U392 Lance Berkman TT .30 .09
❑ U393 Pat Burrell TT .30 .09
❑ U394 Eric Chavez TT .30 .09
❑ U395 Mike Piazza TT .75 .23
❑ U396 Vladimir Guerrero TT .50 .15
❑ U397 Paul Konerko TT .30 .09
❑ U398 Sammy Sosa TT .75 .23
❑ U399 Richie Sexson TT .30 .09
❑ U400 Torii Hunter TT .30 .09

2003 Fleer Tradition

	Nm-Mt	Ex-Mt
COMPLETE SET (485)	150.00	45.00
COMP.SET w/o SP's (385)	40.00	12.00
COMMON CARD (1-30)	1.00	.30
COMM.SP (31-66/86-100)	1.00	.30
COMMON ML (67-85)	1.50	.45
COMMON CARD (	.30	.09
COMMON PR (426-460)	.30	.09

❑ 1 Jarrod Washburn 1.00 .30
Troy Glaus
Garret Anderson
Ramon Ortiz TL SP
❑ 2 Luis Gonzalez 1.50 .45
Randy Johnson TL SP
❑ 3 Andruw Jones 1.50 .45
Chipper Jones
Tom Glavine
Kevin Millwood TL SP
❑ 4 Tony Batista 1.00 .30
Rodrigo Lopez TL SP
❑ 5 Manny Ramirez 2.50 .75
Nomar Garciaparra
Derek Lowe
Pedro Martinez TL SP
❑ 6 Sammy Sosa 2.50 .75
Matt Clement
Kerry Wood TL SP
❑ 7 Matt Buehrle 1.00 .30
Magglio Ordonez
Danny Wright TL SP
❑ 8 Adam Dunn 1.00 .30
Aaron Boone
Jimmy Haynes TL SP
❑ 9 C.C. Sabathia 1.50 .45
Jim Thome TL SP
❑ 10 Todd Helton 1.00 .30
Jason Jennings TL SP
❑ 11 Randall Simon 1.00 .30
Steve Sparks

Mark Redman TL SP
❑ 12 Derrek Lee 1.00 .30
Mike Lowell
A.J. Burnett TL SP
❑ 13 Lance Berkman 1.00 .30
Roy Oswalt TL SP
❑ 14 Paul Byrd 1.00 .30
Carlos Beltran TL SP
❑ 15 Shawn Green 1.50 .45
Hideo Nomo TL SP
❑ 16 Richie Sexson 1.00 .30
Ben Sheets TL SP
❑ 17 Torii Hunter 1.00 .30
Kyle Lohse
Johan Santana TL SP
❑ 18 Vladimir Guerrrero 1.50 .45
Tomo Ohka
Javier Vazquez TL SP
❑ 19 Mike Piazza 2.50 .75
Al Leiter TL SP
❑ 20 Jason Giambi 2.50 .75
David Wells
Roger Clemens TL SP
❑ 21 Eric Chavez 1.50 .45
Miguel Tejada
Barry Zito TL SP
❑ 22 Pat Burrell 1.00 .30
Vicente Padilla
Randy Wolf TL SP
❑ 23 Brian Giles 1.00 .30
Josh Fogg
Kip Wells TL SP
❑ 24 Ryan Klesko 1.00 .30
Brian Lawrence TL SP
❑ 25 Barry Bonds 2.50 .75
Russ Ortiz
Jason Schmidt TL SP
❑ 26 Mike Cameron 1.00 .30
Bret Boone
Freddy Garcia TL SP
❑ 27 Albert Pujols 2.50 .75
Matt Morris TL SP
❑ 28 Aubry Huff 1.00 .30
Randy Winn
Joe Kennedy
Tanyon Sturtze TL SP
❑ 29 Alex Rodriguez 2.50 .75
Kenny Rogers
Chan Ho Park TL SP
❑ 30 Carlos Delgado 1.00 .30
Roy Halladay TL SP
❑ 31 Greg Maddux SP 5.00 1.50
❑ 32 Nick Neugebauer SP 1.00 .30
❑ 33 Larry Walker SP 1.50 .45
❑ 34 Freddy Garcia SP 1.00 .30
❑ 35 Rich Aurilia SP 1.00 .30
❑ 36 Craig Wilson SP 1.00 .30
❑ 37 Jeff Suppan SP 1.00 .30
❑ 38 Joel Pineiro SP 1.00 .30
❑ 39 Pedro Feliz SP 1.00 .30
❑ 40 Bartolo Colon SP 1.00 .30
❑ 41 Pete Walker SP 1.00 .30
❑ 42 Mo Vaughn SP 1.00 .30
❑ 43 Sidney Ponson SP 1.00 .30
❑ 44 Jason Isringhausen SP 1.00 .30
❑ 45 Hideki Irabu SP 1.00 .30
❑ 46 Pedro Martinez SP 2.50 .75
❑ 47 Tom Glavine SP 2.50 .75
❑ 48 Matt Lawton SP 1.00 .30
❑ 49 Kyle Lohse SP 1.00 .30
❑ 50 Corey Patterson SP 1.00 .30
❑ 51 Ichiro Suzuki SP UER 5.00 1.50
RBI total for 2002 incorrect
❑ 52 Wade Miller SP 1.00 .30
❑ 53 Ben Diggins SP 1.00 .30
❑ 54 Jayson Werth SP 1.00 .30
❑ 55 Masato Yoshii SP 1.00 .30
❑ 56 Mark Buehrle SP 1.00 .30
❑ 57 Drew Henson SP 1.00 .30
❑ 58 Dave Williams SP 1.00 .30
❑ 59 Juan Rivera SP 1.00 .30
❑ 60 Scott Schoeneweis SP 1.00 .30
❑ 61 Josh Beckett SP 1.50 .45
❑ 62 Vinny Castilla SP 1.00 .30
❑ 63 Barry Zito SP 2.50 .75
❑ 64 Jose Valentin SP 1.00 .30
❑ 65 Jon Lieber SP 1.00 .30
❑ 66 Jorge Padilla SP 1.00 .30
❑ 67 Luis Aparicio ML SP 1.50 .45
❑ 68 Boog Powell ML SP 2.50 .75
❑ 69 Dick Radatz ML SP 1.50 .45
❑ 70 Frank Malzone ML SP 1.50 .45
❑ 71 Lou Brock ML SP 2.50 .75
❑ 72 Billy Williams ML SP 1.50 .45
❑ 73 Early Wynn ML SP 1.50 .45
❑ 74 Jim Bunning ML SP 2.50 .75
❑ 75 Al Kaline ML SP 4.00 1.20
❑ 76 Eddie Mathews ML SP 4.00 1.20
❑ 77 Harmon Killebrew ML SP 4.00 1.20
❑ 78 Gil Hodges ML SP 2.50 .75
❑ 79 Duke Snider ML SP 2.50 .75
❑ 80 Yogi Berra ML SP 4.00 1.20
❑ 81 Whitey Ford ML SP 2.50 .75
❑ 82 Willie Stargell ML SP 2.50 .75
❑ 83 Willie McCovey ML SP 1.50 .45
❑ 84 Gaylord Perry ML SP 1.50 .45
❑ 85 Red Schoendienst ML SP 1.50 .45
❑ 86 Luis Castillo SP 1.00 .30
❑ 87 Derek Jeter SP 6.00 1.80
❑ 88 Orlando Hudson SP 1.00 .30
❑ 89 Bobby Higginson SP 1.00 .30
❑ 90 Brent Butler SP 1.00 .30
❑ 91 Brad Wilkerson SP 1.00 .30
❑ 92 Craig Biggio SP 1.50 .45
❑ 93 Marlon Anderson SP 1.00 .30
❑ 94 Ty Wigginton SP 1.00 .30
❑ 95 Hideo Nomo SP 2.50 .75
❑ 96 Barry Larkin SP 2.50 .75
❑ 97 Roberto Alomar SP 2.50 .75
❑ 98 Omar Vizquel SP 1.00 .30
❑ 99 Andres Galarraga SP 1.00 .30
❑ 100 Shawn Green SP 1.00 .30
❑ 101 Rafael Furcal .30 .09
❑ 102 Bill Selby .30 .09
❑ 103 Brent Abernathy .30 .09
❑ 104 Nomar Garciaparra 1.50 .45
❑ 105 Michael Barrett .30 .09
❑ 106 Travis Hafner .30 .09
❑ 107 Carl Crawford .30 .09
❑ 108 Jeff Cirillo .30 .09
❑ 109 Mike Hampton .30 .09
❑ 110 Kip Wells .30 .09
❑ 111 Luis Alicea .30 .09
❑ 112 Ellis Burks .30 .09
❑ 113 Matt Anderson .30 .09
❑ 114 Carlos Beltran .30 .09
❑ 115 Paul Lo Duca .30 .09
❑ 116 Lance Berkman .30 .09
❑ 117 Moises Alou .30 .09
❑ 118 Roger Cedeno .30 .09
❑ 119 Brad Fullmer .30 .09
❑ 120 Sean Burroughs .30 .09
❑ 121 Eric Byrnes .30 .09
❑ 122 Milton Bradley .30 .09
❑ 123 Jason Giambi .75 .23
❑ 124 Brook Fordyce .30 .09
❑ 125 Kevin Appier .30 .09
❑ 126 Steve Cox .30 .09
❑ 127 Danny Bautista .30 .09
❑ 128 Edgardo Alfonzo .30 .09
❑ 129 Matt Clement .30 .09
❑ 130 Robb Nen .30 .09
❑ 131 Roy Halladay .30 .09
❑ 132 Brian Jordan .30 .09
❑ 133 A.J. Burnett .30 .09
❑ 134 Aaron Cook .30 .09
❑ 135 Paul Byrd .30 .09
❑ 136 Ramon Ortiz .30 .09
❑ 137 Adam Hyzdu .30 .09
❑ 138 Rafael Soriano .30 .09
❑ 139 Marty Cordova .30 .09
❑ 140 Nelson Cruz .30 .09
❑ 141 Jamie Moyer .30 .09
❑ 142 Raul Mondesi .30 .09
❑ 143 Josh Bard .30 .09
❑ 144 Elmer Dessens .30 .09
❑ 145 Rickey Henderson 1.25 .35
❑ 146 Joe McEwing .30 .09
❑ 147 Luis Rivas .30 .09
❑ 148 Armando Benitez .30 .09
❑ 149 Keith Foulke .30 .09
❑ 150 Zach Day .30 .09
❑ 151 Trey Lunsford .30 .09
❑ 152 Bobby Abreu .30 .09
❑ 153 Juan Cruz .30 .09
❑ 154 Ramon Hernandez .30 .09
❑ 155 Brandon Duckworth .30 .09
❑ 156 Matt Ginter .30 .09
❑ 157 Rob Mackowiak .30 .09
❑ 158 Josh Pearce .30 .09
❑ 159 Marlon Byrd .30 .09
❑ 160 Todd Walker .30 .09
❑ 161 Chad Hermansen .30 .09
❑ 162 Felix Escalona .30 .09
❑ 163 Ruben Mateo .30 .09
❑ 164 Mark Johnson .30 .09
❑ 165 Juan Pierre .30 .09
❑ 166 Gary Sheffield .30 .09
❑ 167 Edgar Martinez .50 .15
❑ 168 Randy Winn .30 .09
❑ 169 Pokey Reese .30 .09
❑ 170 Kevin Mench .30 .09
❑ 171 Albert Pujols 1.50 .45
❑ 172 J.T. Snow .30 .09
❑ 173 Dean Palmer .30 .09
❑ 174 Jay Payton .30 .09
❑ 175 Abraham Nunez .30 .09
❑ 176 Richie Sexson .30 .09
❑ 177 Jose Vidro .30 .09
❑ 178 Geoff Jenkins .30 .09
❑ 179 Dan Wilson .30 .09
❑ 180 John Olerud .30 .09
❑ 181 Javy Lopez .30 .09
❑ 182 Carl Everett .30 .09
❑ 183 Vernon Wells .30 .09
❑ 184 Juan Gonzalez .75 .23
❑ 185 Jorge Posada .50 .15
❑ 186 Mike Sweeney .30 .09
❑ 187 Cesar Izturis .30 .09
❑ 188 Jason Schmidt .30 .09
❑ 189 Chris Richard .30 .09
❑ 190 Jason Phillips .30 .09
❑ 191 Fred McGriff .50 .15
❑ 192 Shea Hillenbrand .30 .09
❑ 193 Ivan Rodriguez .75 .23
❑ 194 Mike Lowell .30 .09
❑ 195 Neifi Perez .30 .09
❑ 196 Kenny Lofton .30 .09
❑ 197 A.J. Pierzynski .30 .09
❑ 198 Larry Bigbie .30 .09
❑ 199 Juan Uribe .30 .09
❑ 200 Jeff Bagwell .50 .15
❑ 201 Timo Perez .30 .09
❑ 202 Jeremy Giambi .30 .09
❑ 203 Deivi Cruz .30 .09
❑ 204 Marquis Grissom .30 .09
❑ 205 Chipper Jones .75 .23
❑ 206 Alex Gonzalez .30 .09
❑ 207 Steve Finley .30 .09
❑ 208 Ben Davis .30 .09
❑ 209 Mike Bordick .30 .09
❑ 210 Casey Fossum .30 .09
❑ 211 Aramis Ramirez .30 .09
❑ 212 Aaron Boone .30 .09
❑ 213 Orlando Cabrera .30 .09
❑ 214 Hee Seop Choi .30 .09
❑ 215 Jeromy Burnitz .30 .09
❑ 216 Todd Hollandsworth .30 .09
❑ 217 Rey Sanchez .30 .09
❑ 218 Jose Cruz .30 .09
❑ 219 Roosevelt Brown .30 .09
❑ 220 Odalis Perez .30 .09
❑ 221 Carlos Delgado .30 .09
❑ 222 Orlando Hernandez .30 .09
❑ 223 Adam Everett .30 .09
❑ 224 Adrian Beltre .30 .09
❑ 225 Ken Griffey Jr. 1.25 .35
❑ 226 Brad Penny .30 .09
❑ 227 Carlos Lee .30 .09
❑ 228 J.C. Romero .30 .09
❑ 229 Ramon Martinez .30 .09
❑ 230 Matt Morris .30 .09
❑ 231 Ben Howard .30 .09
❑ 232 Damon Minor .30 .09
❑ 233 Jason Marquis .30 .09
❑ 234 Paul Wilson .30 .09
❑ 235 Ryan Dempster .30 .09
❑ 236 Jeffrey Hammonds .30 .09

No.	Player	Mint	NrMt
❑ 237	Jaret Wright	.30	.09
❑ 238	Carlos Pena	.30	.09
❑ 239	Toby Hall	.30	.09
❑ 240	Rick Helling	.30	.09
❑ 241	Alex Escobar	.30	.09
❑ 242	Trevor Hoffman	.30	.09
❑ 243	Bernie Williams	.50	.15
❑ 244	Jorge Julio	.30	.09
❑ 245	Byung-Hyun Kim	.30	.09
❑ 246	Mike Redmond	.30	.09
❑ 247	Tony Armas	.30	.09
❑ 248	Aaron Rowand	.30	.09
❑ 249	Rusty Greer	.30	.09
❑ 250	Aaron Harang	.30	.09
❑ 251	Jeremy Fikac	.30	.09
❑ 252	Jay Gibbons	.30	.09
❑ 253	Brandon Puffer	.30	.09
❑ 254	Dewayne Wise	.30	.09
❑ 255	Chan Ho Park	.30	.09
❑ 256	David Bell	.30	.09
❑ 257	Kenny Rogers	.30	.09
❑ 258	Mark Quinn	.30	.09
❑ 259	Greg LaRocca	.30	.09
❑ 260	Reggie Taylor	.30	.09
❑ 261	Brett Tomko	.30	.09
❑ 262	Jack Wilson	.30	.09
❑ 263	Billy Wagner	.30	.09
❑ 264	Greg Norton	.30	.09
❑ 265	Tim Salmon	.50	.15
❑ 266	Joe Randa	.30	.09
❑ 267	Geronimo Gil	.30	.09
❑ 268	Johnny Damon	.30	.09
❑ 269	Robin Ventura	.30	.09
❑ 270	Frank Thomas	.75	.23
❑ 271	Terrence Long	.30	.09
❑ 272	Mark Redman	.30	.09
❑ 273	Mark Kotsay	.30	.09
❑ 274	Ben Sheets	.30	.09
❑ 275	Reggie Sanders	.30	.09
❑ 276	Mark Grace	.75	.23
❑ 277	Eddie Guardado	.30	.09
❑ 278	Julio Mateo	.30	.09
❑ 279	Bengie Molina	.30	.09
❑ 280	Bill Hall	.30	.09
❑ 281	Eric Chavez	.30	.09
❑ 282	Joe Kennedy	.30	.09
❑ 283	John Valentin	.30	.09
❑ 284	Ray Durham	.30	.09
❑ 285	Trot Nixon	.30	.09
❑ 286	Rondell White	.30	.09
❑ 287	Alex Gonzalez	.30	.09
❑ 288	Tomas Perez	.30	.09
❑ 289	Jared Sandberg	.30	.09
❑ 290	Jacque Jones	.30	.09
❑ 291	Cliff Floyd	.30	.09
❑ 292	Ryan Klesko	.30	.09
❑ 293	Morgan Ensberg	.30	.09
❑ 294	Jerry Hairston	.30	.09
❑ 295	Doug Mientkiewicz	.30	.09
❑ 296	Darin Erstad	.30	.09
❑ 297	Jeff Conine	.30	.09
❑ 298	Johnny Estrada	.30	.09
❑ 299	Mark Mulder	.30	.09
❑ 300	Jeff Kent	.30	.09
❑ 301	Roger Clemens	1.50	.45
❑ 302	Endy Chavez	.30	.09
❑ 303	Joe Crede	.30	.09
❑ 304	J.D. Drew	.30	.09
❑ 305	David Dellucci	.30	.09
❑ 306	Eli Marrero	.30	.09
❑ 307	Josh Fogg	.30	.09
❑ 308	Mike Crudale	.30	.09
❑ 309	Bret Boone	.30	.09
❑ 310	Mariano Rivera	.50	.15
❑ 311	Mike Piazza	1.25	.35
❑ 312	Jason Jennings	.30	.09
❑ 313	Jason Varitek	.30	.09
❑ 314	Vicente Padilla	.30	.09
❑ 315	Kevin Millwood	.30	.09
❑ 316	Nick Johnson	.30	.09
❑ 317	Shane Reynolds	.30	.09
❑ 318	Joe Thurston	.30	.09
❑ 319	Mike Lamb	.30	.09
❑ 320	Aaron Sele	.30	.09
❑ 321	Fernando Tatis	.30	.09
❑ 322	Randy Wolf	.30	.09
❑ 323	David Justice	.30	.09
❑ 324	Andy Pettitte	.50	.15
❑ 325	Freddy Sanchez	.30	.09
❑ 326	Scott Spiezio	.30	.09
❑ 327	Randy Johnson	.75	.23
❑ 328	Karim Garcia	.30	.09
❑ 329	Eric Milton	.30	.09
❑ 330	Jermaine Dye	.30	.09
❑ 331	Kevin Brown	.30	.09
❑ 332	Adam Pettyjohn	.30	.09
❑ 333	Jason Lane	.30	.09
❑ 334	Mark Prior	1.50	.45
❑ 335	Mike Lieberthal	.30	.09
❑ 336	Matt White	.30	.09
❑ 337	John Patterson	.30	.09
❑ 338	Marcus Giles	.30	.09
❑ 339	Kazuhisa Ishii	.30	.09
❑ 340	Willie Harris	.30	.09
❑ 341	Travis Phelps	.30	.09
❑ 342	Randall Simon	.30	.09
❑ 343	Manny Ramirez	.30	.09
❑ 344	Kerry Wood	.75	.23
❑ 345	Shannon Stewart	.30	.09
❑ 346	Mike Mussina	.75	.23
❑ 347	Joe Borchard	.30	.09
❑ 348	Tyler Walker	.30	.09
❑ 349	Preston Wilson	.30	.09
❑ 350	Damian Moss	.30	.09
❑ 351	Eric Karros	.30	.09
❑ 352	Bobby Kielty	.30	.09
❑ 353	Jason LaRue	.30	.09
❑ 354	Phil Nevin	.30	.09
❑ 355	Tony Graffanino	.30	.09
❑ 356	Antonio Alfonseca	.30	.09
❑ 357	Eddie Taubensee	.30	.09
❑ 358	Luis Ugueto	.30	.09
❑ 359	Greg Vaughn	.30	.09
❑ 360	Corey Thurman	.30	.09
❑ 361	Omar Infante	.30	.09
❑ 362	Alex Cintron	.30	.09
❑ 363	Esteban Loaiza	.30	.09
❑ 364	Tino Martinez	.50	.15
❑ 365	David Eckstein	.30	.09
❑ 366	Dave Pember RC	.30	.09
❑ 367	Damian Rolls	.30	.09
❑ 368	Richard Hidalgo	.30	.09
❑ 369	Brad Radke	.30	.09
❑ 370	Alex Sanchez	.30	.09
❑ 371	Ben Grieve	.30	.09
❑ 372	Brandon Inge	.30	.09
❑ 373	Adam Piatt	.30	.09
❑ 374	Charles Johnson	.30	.09
❑ 375	Rafael Palmeiro	.50	.15
❑ 376	Joe Mays	.30	.09
❑ 377	Derrek Lee	.30	.09
❑ 378	Fernando Vina	.30	.09
❑ 379	Andruw Jones	.50	.15
❑ 380	Troy Glaus	.50	.15
❑ 381	Bobby Hill	.30	.09
❑ 382	C.C. Sabathia	.30	.09
❑ 383	Jose Hernandez	.30	.09
❑ 384	Al Leiter	.30	.09
❑ 385	Jarrod Washburn	.30	.09
❑ 386	Cody Ransom	.30	.09
❑ 387	Matt Stairs	.30	.09
❑ 388	Edgar Renteria	.30	.09
❑ 389	Tsuyoshi Shinjo	.30	.09
❑ 390	Matt Williams	.30	.09
❑ 391	Bubba Trammell	.30	.09
❑ 392	Jason Kendall	.30	.09
❑ 393	Scott Rolen	.50	.15
❑ 394	Chuck Knoblauch	.30	.09
❑ 395	Jimmy Rollins	.30	.09
❑ 396	Gary Bennett	.30	.09
❑ 397	David Wells	.30	.09
❑ 398	Ronnie Belliard	.30	.09
❑ 399	Austin Kearns	.50	.15
❑ 400	Tim Hudson	.30	.09
❑ 401	Andy Van Hekken	.30	.09
❑ 402	Ray Lankford	.30	.09
❑ 403	Todd Helton	.50	.15
❑ 404	Jeff Weaver	.30	.09
❑ 405	Gabe Kapler	.30	.09
❑ 406	Luis Gonzalez	.30	.09
❑ 407	Sean Casey	.30	.09
❑ 408	Kazuhiro Sasaki	.30	.09
❑ 409	Mark Teixeira	.50	.15
❑ 410	Brian Giles	.30	.09
❑ 411	Robert Fick	.30	.09
❑ 412	Wilkin Ruan	.30	.09
❑ 413	Jose Rijo	.30	.09
❑ 414	Ben Broussard	.30	.09
❑ 415	Aubrey Huff	.30	.09
❑ 416	Magglio Ordonez	.30	.09
❑ 417	Barry Bonds AW	1.00	.30
❑ 418	Miguel Tejada AW	.30	.09
❑ 419	Randy Johnson AW	.50	.15
❑ 420	Barry Zito AW	.50	.15
❑ 421	Jason Jennings AW	.30	.09
❑ 422	Eric Hinske AW	.30	.09
❑ 423	Benito Santiago AW	.30	.09
❑ 424	Adam Kennedy AW	.30	.09
❑ 425	Troy Glaus AW	.30	.09
❑ 426	Brandon Phillips PR	.30	.09
❑ 427	Jake Peavy PR	.30	.09
❑ 428	Jason Romano PR	.30	.09
❑ 429	Jeriome Robertson PR	.30	.09
❑ 430	Aaron Guiel PR	.30	.09
❑ 431	Hank Blalock PR	.50	.15
❑ 432	Brad Lidge PR	.30	.09
❑ 433	Francisco Rodriguez PR	.30	.09
❑ 434	Jaime Cerda PR	.30	.09
❑ 435	Jung Bong PR	.30	.09
❑ 436	Reed Johnson PR	.30	.09
❑ 437	Rene Reyes PR	.30	.09
❑ 438	Chris Snelling PR	.30	.09
❑ 439	Miguel Olivo PR	.30	.09
❑ 440	Brian Banks PR	.30	.09
❑ 441	Eric Junge PR	.30	.09
❑ 442	Kirk Saarloos PR	.30	.09
❑ 443	Jamey Carroll PR	.30	.09
❑ 444	Josh Hancock PR	.30	.09
❑ 445	Michael Restovich PR	.30	.09
❑ 446	Willie Bloomquist PR	.30	.09
❑ 447	John Lackey PR	.30	.09
❑ 448	Marcus Thames PR	.30	.09
❑ 449	Victor Martinez PR	.30	.09
❑ 450	Brett Myers PR	.30	.09
❑ 451	Wes Obermueller PR	.30	.09
❑ 452	Hansel Izquierdo PR	.30	.09
❑ 453	Brian Tallet PR	.30	.09
❑ 454	Craig Monroe PR	.30	.09
❑ 455	Doug Devore PR	.30	.09
❑ 456	John Buck PR	.30	.09
❑ 457	Tony Alvarez PR	.30	.09
❑ 458	Wily Mo Pena PR	.30	.09
❑ 459	John Stephens PR	.30	.09
❑ 460	Tony Torcato PR	.30	.09
❑ 461	Adam Kennedy BNR	.30	.09
❑ 462	Alex Rodriguez BNR	.75	.23
❑ 463	Derek Lowe BNR	.30	.09
❑ 464	Garret Anderson BNR	.30	.09
❑ 465	Pat Burrell BNR	.30	.09
❑ 466	Eric Gagne BNR	.30	.09
❑ 467	Tomo Ohka BNR	.30	.09
❑ 468	Josh Phelps BNR	.30	.09
❑ 469	Sammy Sosa BNR	.75	.23
❑ 470	Jim Thome BNR	.50	.15
❑ 471	Vladimir Guerrero BNR	.50	.15
❑ 472	Jason Simontacchi BNR	.30	.09
❑ 473	Adam Dunn BNR	.30	.09
❑ 474	Jim Edmonds BNR	.30	.09
❑ 475	Barry Bonds BNR	1.00	.30
❑ 476	Paul Konerko BNR	.30	.09
❑ 477	Alfonso Soriano BNR	.50	.15
❑ 478	Curt Schilling BNR	.30	.09
❑ 479	John Smoltz BNR	.30	.09
❑ 480	Torii Hunter BNR	.30	.09
❑ 481	Rodrigo Lopez BNR	.30	.09
❑ 482	Miguel Tejada BNR	.30	.09
❑ 483	Eric Hinske BNR	.30	.09
❑ 484	Roy Oswalt BNR	.30	.09
❑ 485	Junior Spivey BNR	.30	.09
❑ P1	Barry Bonds Pin	8.00	2.40
❑ P87	Derek Jeter Promo	2.00	.60

2003 Fleer Tradition Update

	MINT	NRMT
COMP.SET w/o SP's (285)	40.00	18.00

COMMON CARD (1-285)	.30	.14
COMMON CARD (286-299)	1.00	.45
COMMON RC (286-299)	1.00	.45
286-299 STATED ODDS 1:4 HOB/RET		-
COMMON CARD (300-398)	1.00	.45
COMMON RC (300-398)	1.00	.45
300-398 ISSUED IN MINI-BOXES	-	
ONE MINI-BOX PER UPDATE BOX	-	
25 CARDS PER MINI-BOX	-	

☐	1 Aaron Boone	.30	.14
☐	2 Carl Everett	.30	.14
☐	3 Eduardo Perez	.30	.14
☐	4 Jason Michaels	.30	.14
☐	5 Karim Garcia	.30	.14
☐	6 Rainer Olmedo	.30	.14
☐	7 Scott Williamson	.30	.14
☐	8 Adam Kennedy	.30	.14
☐	9 Carl Pavano	.30	.14
☐	10 Eli Marrero	.30	.14
☐	11 Jason Simontacchi	.30	.14
☐	12 Keith Foulke	.30	.14
☐	13 Preston Wilson	.30	.14
☐	14 Scott Hatteberg	.30	.14
☐	15 Adam Dunn	.50	.23
☐	16 Carlos Baerga	.30	.14
☐	17 Elmer Dessens	.30	.14
☐	18 Javier Vazquez	.30	.14
☐	19 Kenny Rogers	.30	.14
☐	20 Quinton McCracken	.30	.14
☐	21 Shane Reynolds	.30	.14
☐	22 Adam Eaton	.30	.14
☐	23 Carlos Zambrano	.30	.14
☐	24 Enrique Wilson	.30	.14
☐	25 Jeff DaVanon	.30	.14
☐	26 Kenny Lofton	.30	.14
☐	27 Ramon Castro	.30	.14
☐	28 Shannon Stewart	.30	.14
☐	29 Al Martin	.30	.14
☐	30 Carlos Guillen	.30	.14
☐	31 Eric Karros	.30	.14
☐	32 Tim Worrell	.30	.14
☐	33 Kevin Millwood	.30	.14
☐	34 Randall Simon	.30	.14
☐	35 Shawn Chacon	.30	.14
☐	36 Alex Rodriguez	1.50	.70
☐	37 Casey Blake	.30	.14
☐	38 Eric Munson	.30	.14
☐	39 Jeff Kent	.30	.14
☐	40 Kris Benson	.30	.14
☐	41 Randy Winn	.30	.14
☐	42 Shea Hillenbrand	.30	.14
☐	43 Alfonso Soriano	.75	.35
☐	44 Chris George	.30	.14
☐	45 Eric Bruntlett	.30	.14
☐	46 Jeromy Burnitz	.30	.14
☐	47 Kyle Farnsworth	.30	.14
☐	48 Torii Hunter	.30	.14
☐	49 Sidney Ponson	.30	.14
☐	50 Andres Galarraga	.30	.14
☐	51 Chris Singleton	.30	.14
☐	52 Eric Gagne	.50	.23
☐	53 Jesse Foppert	.30	.14
☐	54 Lance Carter	.30	.14
☐	55 Ray Durham	.30	.14
☐	56 Tanyon Sturtze	.30	.14
☐	57 Andy Ashby	.30	.14
☐	58 Cliff Floyd	.30	.14
☐	59 Eric Young	.30	.14
☐	60 Jhonny Peralta RC	.50	.23
☐	61 Livan Hernandez	.30	.14
☐	62 Reggie Sanders	.30	.14
☐	63 Tim Spooneybarger	.30	.14
☐	64 Angel Berroa	.30	.14
☐	65 Coco Crisp	.30	.14
☐	66 Eric Hinske	.30	.14
☐	67 Jim Edmonds	.30	.14
☐	68 Luis Matos	.30	.14
☐	69 Rickey Henderson	1.25	.55
☐	70 Todd Walker	.30	.14
☐	71 Antonio Alfonseca	.30	.14
☐	72 Corey Koskie	.30	.14
☐	73 Erubiel Durazo	.30	.14
☐	74 Jim Thome	.75	.35
☐	75 Lyle Overbay	.30	.14
☐	76 Robert Fick	.30	.14
☐	77 Todd Hollandsworth	.30	.14
☐	78 Aramis Ramirez	.30	.14
☐	79 Cristian Guzman	.30	.14
☐	80 Esteban Loaiza	.30	.14
☐	81 Jody Gerut	.30	.14
☐	82 Mark Grudzielanek	.30	.14
☐	83 Roberto Alomar	.75	.35
☐	84 Todd Hundley	.30	.14
☐	85 Mike Hampton	.30	.14
☐	86 Curt Schilling	.50	.23
☐	87 Francisco Rodriguez	.30	.14
☐	88 John Lackey	.30	.14
☐	89 Mark Redman	.30	.14
☐	90 Robin Ventura	.30	.14
☐	91 Todd Zeile	.30	.14
☐	92 B.J. Surhoff	.30	.14
☐	93 Raul Mondesi	.30	.14
☐	94 Frank Catalanotto	.30	.14
☐	95 John Smoltz	.50	.23
☐	96 Mark Ellis	.30	.14
☐	97 Rocco Baldelli	1.50	.70
☐	98 Todd Pratt	.30	.14
☐	99 Barry Bonds	2.00	.90
☐	100 Danny Graves	.30	.14
☐	101 Fred McGriff	.50	.23
☐	102 John Burkett	.30	.14
☐	103 Marquis Grissom	.30	.14
☐	104 Rocky Biddle	.30	.14
☐	105 Tom Glavine	.75	.35
☐	106 Bartolo Colon	.30	.14
☐	107 Darren Bragg	.30	.14
☐	108 Gabe Kapler	.30	.14
☐	109 John Franco	.30	.14
☐	110 Matt Mantei	.30	.14
☐	111 Rod Beck	.30	.14
☐	112 Tomo Ohka	.30	.14
☐	113 Ben Petrick	.30	.14
☐	114 Darren Dreifort	.30	.14
☐	115 Garret Anderson	.30	.14
☐	116 John Vander Wal	.30	.14
☐	117 Melvin Mora	.30	.14
☐	118 Rodrigo Lopez	.30	.14
☐	119 Raul Ibanez	.30	.14
☐	120 Benito Santiago	.30	.14
☐	121 David Ortiz	.30	.14
☐	122 Gary Bennett	.30	.14
☐	123 Jon Garland	.30	.14
☐	124 Michael Young	.30	.14
☐	125 Rodrigo Rosario	.30	.14
☐	126 Travis Lee	.30	.14
☐	127 Bill Mueller	.30	.14
☐	128 Derek Lowe	.30	.14
☐	129 Gil Meche	.30	.14
☐	130 Jose Guillen	.30	.14
☐	131 Miguel Cabrera	1.50	.70
☐	132 Ron Calloway	.30	.14
☐	133 Troy Percival	.30	.14
☐	134 Billy Koch	.30	.14
☐	135 Dmitri Young	.30	.14
☐	136 Glendon Rusch	.30	.14
☐	137 Jose Jimenez	.30	.14
☐	138 Miguel Tejada	.30	.14
☐	139 John Thomson	.30	.14
☐	140 Troy O'Leary	.30	.14
☐	141 Bobby Kielty	.30	.14
☐	142 Dontrelle Willis	1.25	.55
☐	143 Greg Myers	.30	.14
☐	144 Jose Vizcaino	.30	.14
☐	145 Mike MacDougal	.30	.14
☐	146 Ronnie Belliard	.30	.14
☐	147 Tyler Houston	.30	.14
☐	148 Brady Clark	.30	.14
☐	149 Edgardo Alfonzo	.30	.14
☐	150 Guillermo Mota	.30	.14
☐	151 Jose Lima	.30	.14
☐	152 Mike Williams	.30	.14
☐	153 Roy Oswalt	.30	.14
☐	154 Scott Podsednik	8.00	3.60
☐	155 Brandon Lyon	.30	.14
☐	156 Henry Mateo	.30	.14
☐	157 Jose Macias	.30	.14
☐	158 Mike Bordick	.30	.14
☐	159 Royce Clayton	.30	.14
☐	160 Vance Wilson	.30	.14
☐	161 Brent Abernathy	.30	.14
☐	162 Horacio Ramirez	.30	.14
☐	163 Jose Reyes	.50	.23
☐	164 Nick Punto	.30	.14
☐	165 Ruben Sierra	.30	.14
☐	166 Victor Zambrano	.30	.14
☐	167 Brett Tomko	.30	.14
☐	168 Ivan Rodriguez	.75	.35
☐	169 Jose Mesa	.30	.14
☐	170 Octavio Dotel	.30	.14
☐	171 Russ Ortiz	.30	.14
☐	172 Vladimir Guerrero	.75	.35
☐	173 Brian Lawrence	.30	.14
☐	174 Jae Weong Seo	.30	.14
☐	175 Jose Cruz Jr.	.30	.14
☐	176 Pat Burrell	.30	.14
☐	177 Russell Branyan	.30	.14
☐	178 Warren Morris	.30	.14
☐	179 Brian Boehringer	.30	.14
☐	180 Jason Johnson	.30	.14
☐	181 Josh Phelps	.30	.14
☐	182 Paul Konerko	.30	.14
☐	183 Ryan Franklin	.30	.14
☐	184 Wes Helms	.30	.14
☐	185 Brooks Kieschnick	.30	.14
☐	186 Jason Davis	.30	.14
☐	187 Juan Pierre	.30	.14
☐	188 Paul Wilson	.30	.14
☐	189 Sammy Sosa	1.25	.55
☐	190 Wil Cordero	.30	.14
☐	191 Byung-Hyun Kim	.30	.14
☐	192 Juan Encarnacion	.30	.14
☐	193 Placido Polanco	.30	.14
☐	194 Sandy Alomar Jr.	.30	.14
☐	195 Julio Lugo	.30	.14
☐	196 Junior Spivey	.30	.14
☐	197 Woody Williams	.30	.14
☐	198 Xavier Nady	.30	.14
☐	199 Mark Loretta	.30	.14
☐	200 Deivi Cruz	.30	.14
☐	201 Jorge Posada AS	.30	.14
☐	202 Carlos Delgado AS	.30	.14
☐	203 Alfonso Soriano AS	.50	.23
☐	204 Alex Rodriguez AS	.75	.35
☐	205 Troy Glaus AS	.30	.14
☐	206 Garret Anderson AS	.30	.14
☐	207 Hideki Matsui AS	2.50	1.10
☐	208 Ichiro Suzuki AS	.75	.35
☐	209 Esteban Loaiza AS	.30	.14
☐	210 Manny Ramirez AS	.30	.14
☐	211 Roger Clemens AS	.75	.35
☐	212 Roy Halladay AS	.30	.14
☐	213 Jason Giambi AS	.50	.23
☐	214 Edgar Martinez AS	.30	.14
☐	215 Bret Boone AS	.30	.14
☐	216 Hank Blalock AS	.30	.14
☐	217 Nomar Garciaparra AS	.75	.35
☐	218 Vernon Wells AS	.30	.14
☐	219 Melvin Mora AS	.30	.14
☐	220 Magglio Ordonez AS	.30	.14
☐	221 Mike Sweeney AS	.30	.14
☐	222 Barry Zito AS	.50	.23
☐	223 Carl Everett AS	.30	.14
☐	224 Shigetoshi Hasegawa AS	.30	.14
☐	225 Jamie Moyer AS	.30	.14
☐	226 Mark Mulder AS	.30	.14
☐	227 Eddie Guardado AS	.30	.14
☐	228 Ramon Hernandez AS	.30	.14
☐	229 Keith Foulke AS	.30	.14
☐	230 Javy Lopez AS	.30	.14

❑ 231 Todd Helton AS .30 .14
❑ 232 Marcus Giles AS .30 .14
❑ 233 Edgar Renteria AS .30 .14
❑ 234 Scott Rolen AS .30 .14
❑ 235 Barry Bonds AS 1.00 .45
❑ 236 Albert Pujols AS .75 .35
❑ 237 Gary Sheffield AS .30 .14
❑ 238 Jim Edmonds AS .30 .14
❑ 239 Jason Schmidt AS .30 .14
❑ 240 Mark Prior AS .75 .35
❑ 241 Dontrelle Willis AS .75 .35
❑ 242 Kerry Wood AS .50 .23
❑ 243 Kevin Brown AS .30 .14
❑ 244 Woody Williams AS .30 .14
❑ 245 Paul Lo Duca AS .30 .14
❑ 246 Richie Sexson AS .30 .14
❑ 247 Jose Vidro AS .30 .14
❑ 248 Luis Castillo AS .30 .14
❑ 249 Aaron Boone AS .30 .14
❑ 250 Mike Lowell AS .30 .14
❑ 251 Rafael Furcal AS .30 .14
❑ 252 Andruw Jones AS .30 .14
❑ 253 Preston Wilson AS .30 .14
❑ 254 John Smoltz AS .30 .14
❑ 255 Eric Gagne AS .30 .14
❑ 256 Randy Wolf AS .30 .14
❑ 257 Billy Wagner AS .30 .14
❑ 258 Luis Gonzalez AS .30 .14
❑ 259 Russ Ortiz AS .30 .14
❑ 260 Jim Thome .50 .23
Pedro Martinez IL
❑ 261 Alfonso Soriano .50 .23
Jeff Bagwell IL
❑ 262 Dontrelle Willis 1.00 .45
Rocco Baldelli IL
❑ 263 Carlos Delgado .50 .23
Vladimir Guerrero IL
❑ 264 Sammy Sosa .75 .35
Magglio Ordonez IL
❑ 265 Jason Giambi .50 .23
Adam Dunn IL
❑ 266 Mike Sweeney .75 .35
Albert Pujols IL
❑ 267 Barry Bonds 1.00 .45
Torii Hunter IL
❑ 268 Ichiro Suzuki .75 .35
Andruw Jones IL
❑ 269 Chipper Jones .50 .23
Hank Blalock IL
❑ 270 Mark Prior .75 .35
Vernon Wells IL
❑ 271 Nomar Garciaparra .75 .35
Scott Rolen IL
❑ 272 Alex Rodriguez .75 .35
Lance Berkman IL
❑ 273 Roger Clemens .75 .35
Kerry Wood IL
❑ 274 Derek Jeter 1.00 .45
Jose Reyes IL
❑ 275 Greg Maddux .75 .35
Barry Zito IL
❑ 276 Carlos Delgado TT .30 .14
❑ 277 J.D. Drew TT .30 .14
❑ 278 Barry Bonds TT 1.00 .45
❑ 279 Albert Pujols TT .75 .35
❑ 280 Jim Thome TT .50 .23
❑ 281 Sammy Sosa TT .75 .35
❑ 282 Alfonso Soriano TT .50 .23
❑ 283 Hideki Matsui TT 2.50 1.10
❑ 284 Mike Piazza TT .75 .35
❑ 285 Vladimir Guerrero TT .50 .23
❑ 286 Rich Harden ROO 2.50 1.10
❑ 287 Chin-Hui Tsao ROO 1.00 .45
❑ 288 Edwin Jackson ROO RC 6.00 2.70
❑ 289 Chien-Ming Wang ROO RC 4.00 1.80
❑ 290 Josh Willingham ROO RC 3.00 1.35
❑ 291 Matt Kata ROO RC 2.50 1.10
❑ 292 Jose Contreras ROO RC 4.00 1.80
❑ 293 Chris Bootcheck ROO 1.00 .45
❑ 294 Javier Lopez ROO RC 1.00 .45
❑ 295 Delmon Young ROO RC 15.00 6.75
❑ 296 Pedro Liriano ROO 1.00 .45
❑ 297 Noah Lowry ROO 1.00 .45
❑ 298 Khalil Greene ROO 1.50 .70
❑ 299 Rob Bowen ROO 1.00 .45
❑ 300 Bo Hart ROO RC 4.00 1.80
❑ 301 Beau Kemp ROO RC 1.00 .45
❑ 302 Gerald Laird ROO 1.00 .45
❑ 303 Miguel Ojeda ROO RC 1.00 .45
❑ 304 Todd Wellemeyer ROO RC 1.50 .70
❑ 305 Ryan Wagner ROO RC 3.00 1.35
❑ 306 Jeff Duncan ROO RC 1.50 .70
❑ 307 Wilfredo Ledezma ROO RC 1.00 .45
❑ 308 Wes Obermueller ROO 1.00 .45
❑ 309 Bernie Castro ROO RC 1.00 .45
❑ 310 Tim Olson ROO RC 1.50 .70
❑ 311 Colin Porter ROO RC 1.00 .45
❑ 312 Francisco Cruceta ROO RC 1.00 .45
❑ 313 Guillermo Quiroz ROO RC 2.50 1.10
❑ 314 Brian Stokes ROO RC 1.00 .45
❑ 315 Robby Hammock ROO RC 2.00 .90
❑ 316 Lew Ford ROO RC 1.50 .70
❑ 317 Todd Linden ROO 1.00 .45
❑ 318 Mike Gallo ROO RC 1.00 .45
❑ 319 Francisco Rosario ROO RC 1.00 .45
❑ 320 Rosman Garcia ROO RC 1.00 .45
❑ 321 Felix Sanchez ROO RC 1.00 .45
❑ 322 Chad Gaudin ROO RC 1.50 .70
❑ 323 Phil Seibel ROO RC 1.00 .45
❑ 324 Jason Gilfillan ROO RC 1.00 .45
❑ 325 Termel Sledge ROO RC 1.50 .70
❑ 326 Alfredo Gonzalez ROO RC 1.00 .45
❑ 327 Josh Stewart ROO RC 1.00 .45
❑ 328 Jeremy Griffiths ROO RC 1.50 .70
❑ 329 Cory Stewart ROO RC 1.00 .45
❑ 330 Josh Hall ROO RC 1.50 .70
❑ 331 Arnie Munoz ROO RC 1.00 .45
❑ 332 Garrett Atkins ROO 1.00 .45
❑ 333 Neal Cotts ROO 1.00 .45
❑ 334 Dan Haren ROO RC 2.50 1.10
❑ 335 Shane Victorino ROO RC 1.00 .45
❑ 336 David Sanders ROO RC 1.00 .45
❑ 337 Oscar Villarreal ROO RC 1.00 .45
❑ 338 Michael Hessman ROO RC 1.00 .45
❑ 339 Andrew Brown ROO RC 1.00 .45
❑ 340 Kevin Hooper ROO 1.00 .45
❑ 341 Prentice Redman ROO RC 1.00 .45
❑ 342 Brandon Webb ROO RC 5.00 2.20
❑ 343 Jimmy Gobble ROO 1.00 .45
❑ 344 Pete LaForest ROO RC 1.50 .70
❑ 345 Chris Waters ROO RC 1.00 .45
❑ 346 Hideki Matsui ROO RC 10.00 4.50
❑ 347 Chris Capuano ROO RC 1.00 .45
❑ 348 Jon Leicester ROO RC 1.00 .45
❑ 349 Mike Nicolas ROO RC 1.00 .45
❑ 350 Nook Logan ROO RC 1.00 .45
❑ 351 Craig Brazell ROO RC 2.00 .90
❑ 352 Aaron Looper ROO RC 1.00 .45
❑ 353 D.J. Carrasco ROO RC 1.00 .45
❑ 354 Clint Barmes ROO RC 2.00 .90
❑ 355 Doug Waechter ROO RC 2.00 .90
❑ 356 Julio Manon ROO RC 1.00 .45
❑ 357 Jeremy Bonderman ROO RC 3.00 1.35
❑ 358 Diegomar Markwell ROO RC 1.00 .45
❑ 359 Dave Matranga ROO RC 1.00 .45
❑ 360 Luis Ayala ROO RC 1.00 .45
❑ 361 Jason Stanford ROO 1.00 .45
❑ 362 Roger Deago ROO RC 1.00 .45
❑ 363 Geoff Geary ROO RC 1.00 .45
❑ 364 Edgar Gonzalez ROO RC 1.00 .45
❑ 365 Michel Hernandez ROO RC 1.00 .45
❑ 366 Aquilino Lopez ROO RC 1.00 .45
❑ 367 David Manning ROO 1.00 .45
❑ 368 Carlos Mendez ROO RC 1.00 .45
❑ 369 Matt Miller ROO RC 1.00 .45
❑ 370 Michael Nakamura ROO RC 1.00 .45
❑ 371 Mike Neu ROO RC 1.00 .45
❑ 372 Ramon Nivar ROO RC 2.50 1.10
❑ 373 Kevin Ohme ROO RC 1.00 .45
❑ 374 Alex Prieto ROO RC 1.00 .45
❑ 375 Stephen Randolph ROO RC 1.00 .45
❑ 376 Brian Sweeney ROO RC 1.00 .45
❑ 377 Matt Diaz ROO RC 2.00 .90
❑ 378 Mike Gonzalez ROO 1.00 .45
❑ 379 Daniel Cabrera ROO RC 1.00 .45
❑ 380 Fernando Cabrera ROO RC 1.50 .70
❑ 381 David DeJesus ROO RC 2.00 .90
❑ 382 Mike Ryan ROO RC 1.50 .70
❑ 383 Rick Roberts ROO RC 1.00 .45
❑ 384 Seung Song ROO 1.00 .45
❑ 385 Rickie Weeks ROO RC 15.00 6.75
❑ 386 Humberto Quintero ROO RC 1.00 .45
❑ 387 Alexis Rios ROO 1.00 .45
❑ 388 Aaron Miles ROO RC 1.00 .45
❑ 389 Tom Gregorio ROO RC 1.00 .45
❑ 390 Anthony Ferrari ROO RC 1.00 .45
❑ 391 Kevin Correia ROO RC 1.00 .45
❑ 392 Rafael Betancourt ROO RC 1.50 .70
❑ 393 Rett Johnson ROO RC 1.50 .70
❑ 394 Richard Fischer ROO RC 1.00 .45
❑ 395 Greg Aquino ROO RC 1.00 .45
❑ 396 Daniel Garcia ROO RC 1.00 .45
❑ 397 Sergio Mitre ROO RC 1.00 .45
❑ 398 Edwin Almonte ROO 1.00 .45

2001 Fleer Triple Crown

	Nm-Mt	Ex-Mt
COMPLETE SET (300)	30.00	9.00
COMMON CARD (1-300)	.30	.09
COMMON (301-310)	5.00	1.50

❑ 1 Derek Jeter 2.00 .60
❑ 2 Vladimir Guerrero .75 .23
❑ 3 Henry Rodriguez .30 .09
❑ 4 Jason Giambi .75 .23
❑ 5 Nomar Garciaparra 1.50 .45
❑ 6 Jeff Kent .30 .09
❑ 7 Garret Anderson .30 .09
❑ 8 Todd Helton .50 .15
❑ 9 Barry Bonds 2.00 .60
❑ 10 Preston Wilson .30 .09
❑ 11 Troy Glaus .50 .15
❑ 12 Geoff Jenkins .30 .09
❑ 13 Jim Edmonds .30 .09
❑ 14 Bobby Higginson .30 .09
❑ 15 Mark Quinn .30 .09
❑ 16 Barry Larkin .75 .23
❑ 17 Richie Sexson .30 .09
❑ 18 Fernando Tatis .30 .09
❑ 19 John VanderWal .30 .09
❑ 20 Darin Erstad .30 .09
❑ 21 Shawn Green .30 .09
❑ 22 Scott Rolen .50 .15
❑ 23 Tony Batista .30 .09
❑ 24 Phil Nevin .30 .09
❑ 25 Tim Salmon .50 .15
❑ 26 Gary Sheffield .30 .09
❑ 27 Ben Grieve .30 .09
❑ 28 Jermaine Dye .30 .09
❑ 29 Andres Galarraga .30 .09
❑ 30 Adrian Beltre .30 .09
❑ 31 Rafael Palmeiro .50 .15
❑ 32 J.T. Snow .30 .09
❑ 33 Edgardo Alfonzo .30 .09
❑ 34 Paul Konerko .30 .09
❑ 35 Jim Thome .75 .23
❑ 36 Andruw Jones .50 .15
❑ 37 Mike Sweeney .30 .09
❑ 38 Jose Cruz Jr. .30 .09
❑ 39 David Ortiz .30 .09
❑ 40 Pat Burrell .30 .09
❑ 41 Chipper Jones .75 .23
❑ 42 Jeff Bagwell .50 .15
❑ 43 Raul Mondesi .30 .09
❑ 44 Rondell White .30 .09
❑ 45 Edgar Martinez .50 .15
❑ 46 Cal Ripken 2.50 .75
❑ 47 Moises Alou .30 .09
❑ 48 Shannon Stewart .30 .09

❑ 49 Tino Martinez .50 .15
❑ 50 Jason Kendall .30 .09
❑ 51 Richard Hidalgo .30 .09
❑ 52 Albert Belle .30 .09
❑ 53 Jay Payton .30 .09
❑ 54 Cliff Floyd .30 .09
❑ 55 Rusty Greer .30 .09
❑ 56 Matt Williams .30 .09
❑ 57 Sammy Sosa 1.25 .35
❑ 58 Carl Everett .30 .09
❑ 59 Carlos Delgado .30 .09
❑ 60 Jeremy Giambi .30 .09
❑ 61 Jose Canseco .75 .23
❑ 62 David Segui .30 .09
❑ 63 Jose Vidro .30 .09
❑ 64 Matt Stairs .30 .09
❑ 65 Travis Fryman .30 .09
❑ 66 Ken Griffey Jr. 1.25 .35
❑ 67 Mike Piazza 1.25 .35
❑ 68 Mark McGwire 2.00 .60
❑ 69 Craig Biggio .50 .15
❑ 70 Eric Chavez .30 .09
❑ 71 Mo Vaughn .30 .09
❑ 72 Matt Lawton .30 .09
❑ 73 Miguel Tejada .30 .09
❑ 74 Brian Giles .30 .09
❑ 75 Sean Casey .30 .09
❑ 76 Robin Ventura .30 .09
❑ 77 Ivan Rodriguez .75 .23
❑ 78 Dean Palmer .30 .09
❑ 79 Frank Thomas .75 .23
❑ 80 Bernie Williams .50 .15
❑ 81 Juan Encarnacion .30 .09
❑ 82 John Olerud .30 .09
❑ 83 Rich Aurilia .30 .09
❑ 84 Juan Gonzalez .75 .23
❑ 85 Ray Durham .30 .09
❑ 86 Steve Finley .30 .09
❑ 87 Ken Caminiti .30 .09
❑ 88 Roberto Alomar .75 .23
❑ 89 Jeromy Burnitz .30 .09
❑ 90 J.D. Drew .30 .09
❑ 91 Lance Berkman .30 .09
❑ 92 Gabe Kapler .30 .09
❑ 93 Larry Walker .50 .15
❑ 94 Alex Rodriguez 1.50 .45
❑ 95 Jeffrey Hammonds .30 .09
❑ 96 Magglio Ordonez .30 .09
❑ 97 David Justice .30 .09
❑ 98 Eric Karros .30 .09
❑ 99 Manny Ramirez .30 .09
❑ 100 Paul O'Neill .50 .15
❑ 101 Ron Gant .30 .09
❑ 102 Erubiel Durazo .30 .09
❑ 103 Jason Varitek .30 .09
❑ 104 Chan Ho Park .30 .09
❑ 105 Corey Koskie .30 .09
❑ 106 Jeff Conine .30 .09
❑ 107 Kevin Tapani .30 .09
❑ 108 Mike Lowell .30 .09
❑ 109 Tim Hudson .30 .09
❑ 110 Bobby Abreu .30 .09
❑ 111 Bret Boone .30 .09
❑ 112 David Wells .30 .09
❑ 113 Brian Jordan .30 .09
❑ 114 Mitch Meluskey .30 .09
❑ 115 Terrence Long .30 .09
❑ 116 Matt Clement .30 .09
❑ 117 Fernando Vina .30 .09
❑ 118 Luis Alicea .30 .09
❑ 119 Jay Bell .30 .09
❑ 120 Mark Grace .75 .23
❑ 121 Carlos Febles .30 .09
❑ 122 Mark Redman .30 .09
❑ 123 Kevin Jordan .30 .09
❑ 124 Pat Meares .30 .09
❑ 125 Mark McLemore .30 .09
❑ 126 Chris Singleton .30 .09
❑ 127 Trot Nixon .30 .09
❑ 128 Carlos Beltran .30 .09
❑ 129 Lee Stevens .30 .09
❑ 130 Kris Benson .30 .09
❑ 131 Jay Buhner .30 .09
❑ 132 Greg Vaughn .30 .09
❑ 133 Eric Young .30 .09
❑ 134 Tony Womack .30 .09
❑ 135 Roger Cedeno .30 .09
❑ 136 Travis Lee .30 .09
❑ 137 Marvin Benard .30 .09
❑ 138 Aaron Sele .30 .09
❑ 139 Rick Ankiel .30 .09
❑ 140 Ruben Mateo .30 .09
❑ 141 Randy Johnson .75 .23
❑ 142 Jason Tyner .30 .09
❑ 143 Mike Redmond .30 .09
❑ 144 Ron Coomer .30 .09
❑ 145 Scott Elarton .30 .09
❑ 146 Javy Lopez .30 .09
❑ 147 Carlos Lee .30 .09
❑ 148 Tony Clark .30 .09
❑ 149 Roger Clemens 1.50 .45
❑ 150 Mike Lieberthal .30 .09
❑ 151 Shawn Estes .30 .09
❑ 152 Vinny Castilla .30 .09
❑ 153 Alex Gonzalez .30 .09
❑ 154 Troy Percival .30 .09
❑ 155 Pokey Reese .30 .09
❑ 156 Todd Hollandsworth .30 .09
❑ 157 Marquis Grissom .30 .09
❑ 158 Greg Maddux 1.50 .45
❑ 159 Dante Bichette .30 .09
❑ 160 Hideo Nomo .75 .23
❑ 161 Jacque Jones .30 .09
❑ 162 Kevin Young .30 .09
❑ 163 B.J. Surhoff .30 .09
❑ 164 Eddie Taubensee .30 .09
❑ 165 Neifi Perez .30 .09
❑ 166 Orlando Hernandez .30 .09
❑ 167 Francisco Cordova .30 .09
❑ 168 Miguel Cairo .30 .09
❑ 169 Rafael Furcal .30 .09
❑ 170 Sandy Alomar Jr. .30 .09
❑ 171 Jeff Cirillo .30 .09
❑ 172 A.J. Pierzynski .30 .09
❑ 173 Fred McGriff .50 .15
❑ 174 Mike Mussina .75 .23
❑ 175 Aaron Boone .30 .09
❑ 176 Nick Johnson .30 .09
❑ 177 Kent Bottenfield .30 .09
❑ 178 Felipe Crespo .30 .09
❑ 179 Ryan Minor .30 .09
❑ 180 Charles Johnson .30 .09
❑ 181 Damion Easley .30 .09
❑ 182 Michael Barrett .30 .09
❑ 183 Doug Glanville .30 .09
❑ 184 Ben Davis .30 .09
❑ 185 Rickey Henderson 1.25 .35
❑ 186 Edgard Clemente .30 .09
❑ 187 Dmitri Young .30 .09
❑ 188 Tom Goodwin .30 .09
❑ 189 Mike Hampton .30 .09
❑ 190 Gerald Williams .30 .09
❑ 191 Omar Vizquel .30 .09
❑ 192 Ben Petrick .30 .09
❑ 193 Brad Radke .30 .09
❑ 194 Russ Davis .30 .09
❑ 195 Milton Bradley .30 .09
❑ 196 John Parrish .30 .09
❑ 197 Todd Hundley .30 .09
❑ 198 Carl Pavano .30 .09
❑ 199 Bruce Chen .30 .09
❑ 200 Royce Clayton .30 .09
❑ 201 Homer Bush .30 .09
❑ 202 Mark Grudzielanek .30 .09
❑ 203 Mike Lansing .30 .09
❑ 204 Daryle Ward .30 .09
❑ 205 Jeff D'Amico .30 .09
❑ 206 Ray Lankford .30 .09
❑ 207 Curt Schilling .50 .15
❑ 208 Pedro Martinez .75 .23
❑ 209 Johnny Damon .30 .09
❑ 210 Al Leiter .30 .09
❑ 211 Ruben Rivera .30 .09
❑ 212 Kazuhiro Sasaki .30 .09
❑ 213 Will Clark .75 .23
❑ 214 Rick Helling .30 .09
❑ 215 Adam Piatt .30 .09
❑ 216 Joe Girardi .30 .09
❑ 217 A.J. Burnett .30 .09
❑ 218 Mike Bordick .30 .09
❑ 219 Mike Cameron .30 .09
❑ 220 Tony Gwynn 1.00 .30
❑ 221 Deivi Cruz .30 .09
❑ 222 Bubba Trammell .30 .09
❑ 223 Scott Erickson .30 .09
❑ 224 Kerry Wood .75 .23
❑ 225 Derrek Lee .30 .09
❑ 226 Peter Bergeron .30 .09
❑ 227 Chris Gomez .30 .09
❑ 228 Al Martin .30 .09
❑ 229 Brady Anderson .30 .09
❑ 230 Ramon Martinez .30 .09
❑ 231 Darryl Kile .30 .09
❑ 232 Devon White .30 .09
❑ 233 Charlie Hayes .30 .09
❑ 234 Aramis Ramirez .30 .09
❑ 235 Mike Lamb .30 .09
❑ 236 Tom Glavine .75 .23
❑ 237 Troy O'Leary .30 .09
❑ 238 Joe Randa .30 .09
❑ 239 Dustin Hermanson .30 .09
❑ 240 Adam Kennedy .30 .09
❑ 241 Jose Valentin .30 .09
❑ 242 Derek Bell .30 .09
❑ 243 Mark Kotsay .30 .09
❑ 244 Ron Belliard .30 .09
❑ 245 Warren Morris .30 .09
❑ 246 Ozzie Guillen .30 .09
❑ 247 Andy Ashby .30 .09
❑ 248 Jose Offerman .30 .09
❑ 249 Kevin Brown .30 .09
❑ 250 Jorge Posada .50 .15
❑ 251 Alex Cabrera .30 .09
❑ 252 Chan Perry .30 .09
❑ 253 Augie Ojeda .30 .09
❑ 254 Santiago Perez .30 .09
❑ 255 Grant Roberts .30 .09
❑ 256 Dusty Allen .30 .09
❑ 257 Elvis Pena .30 .09
❑ 258 Matt Kinney .30 .09
❑ 259 Timo Perez .30 .09
❑ 260 Adam Eaton .30 .09
❑ 261 Geraldo Guzman .30 .09
❑ 262 Damian Rolls .30 .09
❑ 263 Alfonso Soriano .75 .23
❑ 264 Corey Patterson .30 .09
❑ 265 Juan Alvarez .30 .09
❑ 266 Shawn Gilbert .30 .09
❑ 267 Adam Bernero .30 .09
❑ 268 Ben Weber .30 .09
❑ 269 Tike Redman .30 .09
❑ 270 Willie Morales .30 .09
❑ 271 Tomas De la Rosa .30 .09
❑ 272 Rodney Lindsey .30 .09
❑ 273 Carlos Casimiro .30 .09
❑ 274 Jim Mann .30 .09
❑ 275 Pasqual Coco .30 .09
❑ 276 Julio Zuleta .30 .09
❑ 277 Damon Minor .30 .09
❑ 278 Jose Ortiz .30 .09
❑ 279 Eric Munson .30 .09
❑ 280 Andy Thompson .30 .09
❑ 281 Aubrey Huff .30 .09
❑ 282 Chris Richard .30 .09
❑ 283 Ross Gload .30 .09
❑ 284 Travis Dawkins .30 .09
❑ 285 Tim Drew .30 .09
❑ 286 Barry Zito .75 .23
❑ 287 Andy Tracy .30 .09
❑ 288 Julio Lugo .30 .09
❑ 289 Greg LaRocca .30 .09
❑ 290 Keith McDonald .30 .09
❑ 291 J.C. Romero .30 .09
❑ 292 Adam Melhuse .30 .09
❑ 293 Ryan Kohlmeier .30 .09
❑ 294 John Bale .30 .09
❑ 295 Eric Cammack .30 .09
❑ 296 Morgan Burkhart .30 .09
❑ 297 Kory DeHaan .30 .09
❑ 298 Mike Mahoney .30 .09
❑ 299 Hector Ortiz .30 .09
❑ 300 Talmadge Nunnari .30 .09
❑ 301 E.Guzman/2999 RC 5.00 1.50
❑ 302 D.Henson/2999 RC 6.00 1.80
❑ 303 Bud Smith/2999 RC 5.00 1.50
❑ 304 C.Valderrama/2999 RC 5.00 1.50
❑ 305 T.Shinjo/2999 RC 6.00 1.80
❑ 306 I.Suzuki/2999 RC 20.00 6.00

❑ 307 J.Melian/2999 RC	5.00	1.50
❑ 308 M.Ensberg/2999 RC	6.00	1.80
❑ 309 Albert Pujols/2999 RC	25.00	7.50
❑ 310 J.Estrada/2999 RC	5.00	1.50

1949 Leaf

	NM	Ex
COMPLETE SET (98)	30000.00	15000.00
COMMON CARD (1-168)	25.00	12.50
COMMON SP's	300.00	150.00
WRAPPER (1-CENT)	160.00	80.00

❑ 1 Joe DiMaggio	3000.00	1200.00
❑ 3 Babe Ruth	2500.00	1250.00
❑ 4 Stan Musial	1000.00	500.00
❑ 5 Virgil Trucks SP RC	400.00	200.00
❑ 8 Satchel Paige SP RC	10000.00	5000.00
❑ 10 Dizzy Trout	40.00	20.00
❑ 11 Phil Rizzuto	300.00	150.00
❑ 13 Cass Michaels SP	300.00	150.00
❑ 14 Billy Johnson	40.00	20.00
❑ 17 Frank Overmire	25.00	12.50
❑ 19 Johnny Wyrostek SP	300.00	150.00
❑ 20 Hank Sauer SP	400.00	200.00
❑ 22 Al Evans	25.00	12.50
❑ 26 Sam Chapman	40.00	20.00
❑ 27 Mickey Harris	25.00	12.50
❑ 28 Jim Hegan RC	40.00	20.00
❑ 29 Elmer Valo RC	40.00	20.00
❑ 30 Billy Goodman SP RC	400.00	200.00
❑ 31 Lou Brissie	25.00	12.50
❑ 32 Warren Spahn	300.00	150.00
❑ 33 Peanuts Lowrey SP	300.00	150.00
❑ 36 Al Zarilla SP	300.00	150.00
❑ 38 Ted Kluszewski RC	200.00	100.00
❑ 39 Ewell Blackwell	60.00	30.00
❑ 42 Kent Peterson	25.00	12.50
❑ 43 Ed Stevens SP	300.00	150.00
❑ 45 Ken Keltner SP	300.00	150.00
❑ 46 Johnny Mize	100.00	50.00
❑ 47 George Vico	25.00	12.50
❑ 48 Johnny Schmitz SP	300.00	150.00
❑ 49 Del Ennis RC	60.00	30.00
❑ 50 Dick Wakefield	25.00	12.50
❑ 51 Al Dark SP RC	500.00	250.00
❑ 53 Johnny VanderMeer	100.00	50.00
❑ 54 Bobby Adams SP	300.00	150.00
❑ 55 Tommy Henrich SP	500.00	250.00
❑ 56 Larry Jansen RC UER (Misspelled Jensen)	40.00	20.00
❑ 57 Bob McCall	25.00	12.50
❑ 59 Luke Appling	100.00	50.00
❑ 61 Jake Early	25.00	12.50
❑ 62 Eddie Joost SP	300.00	150.00
❑ 63 Barney McCosky SP	300.00	150.00
❑ 65 Robert Elliott RC UER (Misspelled Elliot on card front)	100.00	50.00
❑ 66 Orval Grove SP	300.00	150.00
❑ 68 Eddie Miller SP	300.00	150.00
❑ 70 Honus Wagner CO	300.00	150.00
❑ 72 Hank Edwards	25.00	12.50
❑ 73 Pat Seerey	25.00	12.50
❑ 75 Dom DiMaggio SP	550.00	275.00
❑ 76 Ted Williams	1200.00	600.00
❑ 77 Roy Smalley RC	25.00	12.50
❑ 78 Hoot Evers SP	300.00	150.00
❑ 79 Jackie Robinson RC	1600.00	800.00
❑ 81 Whitey Kurowski SP	300.00	150.00
❑ 82 Johnny Lindell	40.00	20.00
❑ 83 Bobby Doerr	100.00	50.00
❑ 84 Sid Hudson	25.00	12.50
❑ 85 Dave Philley SP RC	400.00	200.00
❑ 86 Ralph Weigel	25.00	12.50
❑ 88 Frank Gustine SP	300.00	150.00
❑ 91 Ralph Kiner	200.00	100.00
❑ 93 Bob Feller SP	1800.00	900.00
❑ 95 George Stirnweiss RC	40.00	20.00
❑ 97 Marty Marion	60.00	30.00
❑ 98 Hal Newhouser SP RC	600.00	300.00
❑ 102A Gene Hermansk ERR	250.00	125.00
❑ 102B G.Hermanski COR	40.00	20.00
❑ 104 Eddie Stewart SP	300.00	150.00
❑ 106 Lou Boudreau	100.00	50.00
❑ 108 Matt Batts SP	300.00	150.00
❑ 111 Jerry Priddy	25.00	12.50
❑ 113 Dutch Leonard SP	300.00	150.00
❑ 117 Joe Gordon	40.00	20.00
❑ 120 George Kell SP RC	600.00	300.00
❑ 121 Johnny Pesky SP RC	400.00	200.00
❑ 123 Cliff Fannin SP	300.00	150.00
❑ 125 Andy Pafko RC	25.00	12.50
❑ 127 Enos Slaughter SP	800.00	400.00
❑ 128 Buddy Rosar	25.00	12.50
❑ 129 Kirby Higbe SP	300.00	150.00
❑ 131 Sid Gordon SP	300.00	150.00
❑ 133 Tommy Holmes SP	500.00	250.00
❑ 136A Cliff Aberson (Full sleeve)	25.00	12.50
❑ 136B Cliff Aberson (Short sleeve)	250.00	125.00
❑ 137 Harry Walker SP	400.00	200.00
❑ 138 Larry Doby SP RC	650.00	325.00
❑ 139 Johnny Hopp RC	25.00	12.50
❑ 142 D.Murtaugh SP RC	400.00	200.00
❑ 143 Dick Sisler SP	300.00	150.00
❑ 144 Bob Dillinger SP	300.00	150.00
❑ 146 Pete Reiser SP	500.00	250.00
❑ 149 Hank Majeski SP	300.00	150.00
❑ 153 Floyd Baker SP	300.00	150.00
❑ 158 H. Brecheen SP RC	400.00	200.00
❑ 159 Mizell Platt	25.00	12.50
❑ 160 Bob Scheffing SP	300.00	150.00
❑ 161 Vern Stephens SP RC	400.00	200.00
❑ 163 F.Hutchinson SP RC	400.00	200.00
❑ 165 Dale Mitchell SP RC	400.00	200.00
❑ 168 P.Cavarretta SP UER (Name spelled Cavaretta)	500.00	200.00
❑ NNO Album	-	

1990 Leaf

	Nm-Mt	Ex-Mt
COMPLETE SET (528)	100.00	30.00
COMPLETE SERIES 1 (264)	60.00	18.00
COMPLETE SERIES 2 (264)	40.00	12.00
COMP. BERRA PUZZLE	1.00	.30

❑ 1 Introductory Card	.40	.12
❑ 2 Mike Henneman	.40	.12
❑ 3 Steve Bedrosian	.40	.12
❑ 4 Mike Scott	.40	.12
❑ 5 Allan Anderson	.40	.12
❑ 6 Rick Sutcliffe	.60	.18
❑ 7 Gregg Olson	.60	.18
❑ 8 Kevin Elster	.40	.12
❑ 9 Pete O'Brien	.40	.12
❑ 10 Carlton Fisk	1.00	.30
❑ 11 Joe Magrane	.40	.12
❑ 12 Roger Clemens	3.00	.90
❑ 13 Tom Glavine	1.50	.45
❑ 14 Tom Gordon	.60	.18
❑ 15 Todd Benzinger	.40	.12
❑ 16 Hubie Brooks	.40	.12
❑ 17 Roberto Kelly	.40	.12
❑ 18 Barry Larkin	1.50	.45
❑ 19 Mike Boddicker	.40	.12
❑ 20 Roger McDowell	.40	.12
❑ 21 Nolan Ryan	5.00	1.50
❑ 22 John Farrell	.40	.12
❑ 23 Bruce Hurst	.40	.12
❑ 24 Wally Joyner	.60	.18
❑ 25 Greg Maddux	8.00	2.40
❑ 26 Chris Bosio	.40	.12
❑ 27 John Cerutti	.40	.12
❑ 28 Tim Burke	.40	.12
❑ 29 Dennis Eckersley	.60	.18
❑ 30 Glenn Davis	.40	.12
❑ 31 Jim Abbott	1.50	.45
❑ 32 Mike LaValliere	.40	.12
❑ 33 Andres Thomas	.40	.12
❑ 34 Lou Whitaker	.60	.18
❑ 35 Alvin Davis	.40	.12
❑ 36 Melido Perez	.40	.12
❑ 37 Craig Biggio	1.00	.30
❑ 38 Rick Aguilera	.60	.18
❑ 39 Pete Harnisch	.40	.12
❑ 40 David Cone	.60	.18
❑ 41 Scott Garrelts	.40	.12
❑ 42 Jay Howell	.40	.12
❑ 43 Eric King	.40	.12
❑ 44 Pedro Guerrero	.40	.12
❑ 45 Mike Bielecki	.40	.12
❑ 46 Bob Boone	.60	.18
❑ 47 Kevin Brown	.60	.18
❑ 48 Jerry Browne	.40	.12
❑ 49 Mike Scioscia	.40	.12
❑ 50 Chuck Cary	.40	.12
❑ 51 Wade Boggs	1.00	.30
❑ 52 Von Hayes	.40	.12
❑ 53 Tony Fernandez	.40	.12
❑ 54 Dennis Martinez	.60	.18
❑ 55 Tom Candiotti	.40	.12
❑ 56 Andy Benes	.60	.18
❑ 57 Rob Dibble	.60	.18
❑ 58 Chuck Crim	.40	.12
❑ 59 John Smoltz	1.50	.45
❑ 60 Mike Heath	.40	.12
❑ 61 Kevin Gross	.40	.12
❑ 62 Mark McGwire	4.00	1.20
❑ 63 Bert Blyleven	.60	.18
❑ 64 Bob Walk	.40	.12
❑ 65 Mickey Tettleton	.40	.12
❑ 66 Sid Fernandez	.40	.12
❑ 67 Terry Kennedy	.40	.12
❑ 68 Fernando Valenzuela	.60	.18
❑ 69 Don Mattingly	4.00	1.20
❑ 70 Paul O'Neill	1.00	.30
❑ 71 Robin Yount	1.50	.45
❑ 72 Bret Saberhagen	.60	.18
❑ 73 Geno Petralli	.40	.12
❑ 74 Brook Jacoby	.40	.12
❑ 75 Roberto Alomar	1.50	.45
❑ 76 Devon White	.40	.12
❑ 77 Jose Lind	.40	.12
❑ 78 Pat Combs	.40	.12
❑ 79 Dave Stieb	.60	.18
❑ 80 Tim Wallach	.40	.12
❑ 81 Dave Stewart	.60	.18
❑ 82 Eric Anthony RC	.40	.12
❑ 83 Randy Bush	.40	.12
❑ 84 Rickey Henderson CL	1.50	.45
❑ 85 Jaime Navarro	.40	.12
❑ 86 Tommy Gregg	.40	.12
❑ 87 Frank Tanana	.40	.12
❑ 88 Omar Vizquel	1.50	.45
❑ 89 Ivan Calderon	.40	.12
❑ 90 Vince Coleman	.40	.12
❑ 91 Barry Bonds	4.00	1.20
❑ 92 Randy Milligan	.40	.12
❑ 93 Frank Viola	.40	.12

❑ 94 Matt Williams .60 .18
❑ 95 Alfredo Griffin .40 .12
❑ 96 Steve Sax .40 .12
❑ 97 Gary Gaetti .60 .18
❑ 98 Ryne Sandberg 3.00 .90
❑ 99 Danny Tartabull .40 .12
❑ 100 Rafael Palmeiro 1.00 .30
❑ 101 Jesse Orosco .40 .12
❑ 102 Garry Templeton .40 .12
❑ 103 Frank DiPino .40 .12
❑ 104 Tony Pena .40 .12
❑ 105 Dickie Thon .40 .12
❑ 106 Kelly Gruber .40 .12
❑ 107 Marquis Grissom RC 1.00 .30
❑ 108 Jose Canseco 1.50 .45
❑ 109 Mike Blowers RC .40 .12
❑ 110 Tom Browning .40 .12
❑ 111 Greg Vaughn .60 .18
❑ 112 Oddibe McDowell .40 .12
❑ 113 Gary Ward .40 .12
❑ 114 Jay Buhner .60 .18
❑ 115 Eric Show .40 .12
❑ 116 Bryan Harvey .40 .12
❑ 117 Andy Van Slyke .60 .18
❑ 118 Jeff Ballard .40 .12
❑ 119 Barry Lyons .40 .12
❑ 120 Kevin Mitchell .40 .12
❑ 121 Mike Gallego .40 .12
❑ 122 Dave Smith .40 .12
❑ 123 Kirby Puckett 1.50 .45
❑ 124 Jerome Walton .40 .12
❑ 125 Bo Jackson 1.50 .45
❑ 126 Harold Baines .60 .18
❑ 127 Scott Bankhead .40 .12
❑ 128 Ozzie Guillen .40 .12
❑ 129 Jose Oquendo UER .40 .12
(League misspelled as Legue)
❑ 130 John Dopson .40 .12
❑ 131 Charlie Hayes .40 .12
❑ 132 Fred McGriff 1.50 .45
❑ 133 Chet Lemon .40 .12
❑ 134 Gary Carter 1.00 .30
❑ 135 Rafael Ramirez .40 .12
❑ 136 Shane Mack .40 .12
❑ 137 Mark Grace UER 1.50 .45
(Card back has OB:L, should be B:L)
❑ 138 Phil Bradley .40 .12
❑ 139 Dwight Gooden 1.00 .30
❑ 140 Harold Reynolds .60 .18
❑ 141 Scott Fletcher .40 .12
❑ 142 Ozzie Smith 1.50 .45
❑ 143 Mike Greenwell .40 .12
❑ 144 Pete Smith .40 .12
❑ 145 Mark Gubicza .40 .12
❑ 146 Chris Sabo .40 .12
❑ 147 Ramon Martinez .40 .12
❑ 148 Tim Leary .40 .12
❑ 149 Randy Myers .60 .18
❑ 150 Jody Reed .40 .12
❑ 151 Bruce Ruffin .40 .12
❑ 152 Jeff Russell .40 .12
❑ 153 Doug Jones .40 .12
❑ 154 Tony Gwynn 2.00 .60
❑ 155 Mark Langston .40 .12
❑ 156 Mitch Williams .40 .12
❑ 157 Gary Sheffield 1.50 .45
❑ 158 Tom Henke .40 .12
❑ 159 Oil Can Boyd .40 .12
❑ 160 Rickey Henderson 2.50 .75
❑ 161 Bill Doran .40 .12
❑ 162 Chuck Finley .60 .18
❑ 163 Jeff King .40 .12
❑ 164 Nick Esasky .40 .12
❑ 165 Cecil Fielder .60 .18
❑ 166 Dave Valle .40 .12
❑ 167 Robin Ventura 1.50 .45
❑ 168 Jim Deshaies .40 .12
❑ 169 Juan Berenguer .40 .12
❑ 170 Craig Worthington .40 .12
❑ 171 Gregg Jefferies .60 .18
❑ 172 Will Clark 1.50 .45
❑ 173 Kirk Gibson .60 .18
❑ 174 Carlton Fisk CL .60 .18
❑ 175 Bobby Thigpen .40 .12
❑ 176 John Tudor .40 .12
❑ 177 Andre Dawson .60 .18
❑ 178 George Brett 4.00 1.20
❑ 179 Steve Buechele .40 .12
❑ 180 Joey Belle 1.50 .45
❑ 181 Eddie Murray 1.50 .45
❑ 182 Bob Geren .40 .12
❑ 183 Rob Murphy .40 .12
❑ 184 Tom Herr .40 .12
❑ 185 George Bell .40 .12
❑ 186 Spike Owen .40 .12
❑ 187 Cory Snyder .40 .12
❑ 188 Fred Lynn .40 .12
❑ 189 Eric Davis .60 .18
❑ 190 Dave Parker .60 .18
❑ 191 Jeff Blauser .40 .12
❑ 192 Matt Nokes .40 .12
❑ 193 Delino DeShields RC 1.00 .30
❑ 194 Scott Sanderson .40 .12
❑ 195 Lance Parrish .40 .12
❑ 196 Bobby Bonilla .60 .18
❑ 197 Cal Ripken UER 5.00 1.50
(Reistertown, should be Reisterstown)
❑ 198 Kevin McReynolds .40 .12
❑ 199 Robby Thompson .40 .12
❑ 200 Tim Belcher .40 .12
❑ 201 Jesse Barfield .40 .12
❑ 202 Mariano Duncan .40 .12
❑ 203 Bill Spiers .40 .12
❑ 204 Frank White .60 .18
❑ 205 Julio Franco .40 .12
❑ 206 Greg Swindell .40 .12
❑ 207 Benito Santiago .60 .18
❑ 208 Johnny Ray .40 .12
❑ 209 Gary Redus .40 .12
❑ 210 Jeff Parrett .40 .12
❑ 211 Jimmy Key .60 .18
❑ 212 Tim Raines .60 .18
❑ 213 Carney Lansford .60 .18
❑ 214 Gerald Young .40 .12
❑ 215 Gene Larkin .40 .12
❑ 216 Dan Plesac .40 .12
❑ 217 Lonnie Smith .40 .12
❑ 218 Alan Trammell 1.00 .30
❑ 219 Jeffrey Leonard .40 .12
❑ 220 Sammy Sosa RC 50.00 15.00
❑ 221 Todd Zeile .60 .18
❑ 222 Bill Landrum .40 .12
❑ 223 Mike Devereaux .40 .12
❑ 224 Mike Marshall .40 .12
❑ 225 Jose Uribe .40 .12
❑ 226 Juan Samuel .40 .12
❑ 227 Mel Hall .40 .12
❑ 228 Kent Hrbek .60 .18
❑ 229 Shawon Dunston .40 .12
❑ 230 Kevin Seitzer .40 .12
❑ 231 Pete Incaviglia .40 .12
❑ 232 Sandy Alomar Jr. .60 .18
❑ 233 Bip Roberts .40 .12
❑ 234 Scott Terry .40 .12
❑ 235 Dwight Evans .60 .18
❑ 236 Ricky Jordan .40 .12
❑ 237 John Olerud RC 5.00 1.50
❑ 238 Zane Smith .40 .12
❑ 239 Walt Weiss .40 .12
❑ 240 Alvaro Espinoza .40 .12
❑ 241 Billy Hatcher .40 .12
❑ 242 Paul Molitor 1.00 .30
❑ 243 Dale Murphy 1.50 .45
❑ 244 Dave Bergman .40 .12
❑ 245 Ken Griffey Jr. 6.00 1.80
❑ 246 Ed Whitson .40 .12
❑ 247 Kirk McCaskill .40 .12
❑ 248 Jay Bell .60 .18
❑ 249 Ben McDonald RC 1.00 .30
❑ 250 Darryl Strawberry 1.00 .30
❑ 251 Brett Butler .60 .18
❑ 252 Terry Steinbach .40 .12
❑ 253 Ken Caminiti 1.50 .45
❑ 254 Dan Gladden .40 .12
❑ 255 Dwight Smith .40 .12
❑ 256 Kurt Stillwell .40 .12
❑ 257 Ruben Sierra .40 .12
❑ 258 Mike Schooler .40 .12
❑ 259 Lance Johnson .40 .12
❑ 260 Terry Pendleton .60 .18
❑ 261 Ellis Burks 1.00 .30
❑ 262 Len Dykstra .60 .18
❑ 263 Mookie Wilson .60 .18
❑ 264 Nolan Ryan CL UER 1.50 .45
No TM after Ranger logo
❑ 265 Nolan Ryan 2.50 .75
No Hit King
❑ 266 Brian DuBois .40 .12
❑ 267 Don Robinson .40 .12
❑ 268 Glenn Wilson .40 .12
❑ 269 Kevin Tapani RC 1.00 .30
❑ 270 Marvell Wynne .40 .12
❑ 271 Bill Ripken .40 .12
❑ 272 Howard Johnson .40 .12
❑ 273 Brian Holman .40 .12
❑ 274 Dan Pasqua .40 .12
❑ 275 Ken Dayley .40 .12
❑ 276 Jeff Reardon .60 .18
❑ 277 Jim Presley .40 .12
❑ 278 Jim Eisenreich .40 .12
❑ 279 Danny Jackson .40 .12
❑ 280 Orel Hershiser .60 .18
❑ 281 Andy Hawkins .40 .12
❑ 282 Jose Rijo .40 .12
❑ 283 Luis Rivera .40 .12
❑ 284 John Kruk .60 .18
❑ 285 Jeff Huson RC .40 .12
❑ 286 Joel Skinner .40 .12
❑ 287 Jack Clark .60 .18
❑ 288 Chili Davis .60 .18
❑ 289 Joe Girardi 1.00 .30
❑ 290 B.J. Surhoff .60 .18
❑ 291 Luis Sojo .40 .12
❑ 292 Tom Foley .40 .12
❑ 293 Mike Moore .40 .12
❑ 294 Ken Oberkfell .40 .12
❑ 295 Luis Polonia .40 .12
❑ 296 Doug Drabek .40 .12
❑ 297 Dave Justice RC 5.00 1.50
❑ 298 Paul Gibson .40 .12
❑ 299 Edgar Martinez 1.00 .30
❑ 300 F.Thomas RC UER 25.00 7.50
No B in front of birthdate
❑ 301 Eric Yelding .40 .12
❑ 302 Greg Gagne .40 .12
❑ 303 Brad Komminsk .40 .12
❑ 304 Ron Darling .40 .12
❑ 305 Kevin Bass .40 .12
❑ 306 Jeff Hamilton .40 .12
❑ 307 Ron Karkovice .40 .12
❑ 308 Milt Thompson UER .60 .18
(Ray Lankford pictured on card back)
❑ 309 Mike Harkey .40 .12
❑ 310 Mel Stottlemyre Jr. .40 .12
❑ 311 Kenny Rogers .60 .18
❑ 312 Mitch Webster .40 .12
❑ 313 Kal Daniels .40 .12
❑ 314 Matt Nokes .40 .12
❑ 315 Dennis Lamp .40 .12
❑ 316 Ken Howell .40 .12
❑ 317 Glenallen Hill .40 .12
❑ 318 Dave Martinez .40 .12
❑ 319 Chris James .40 .12
❑ 320 Mike Pagliarulo .40 .12
❑ 321 Hal Morris .40 .12
❑ 322 Rob Deer .40 .12
❑ 323 Greg Olson .40 .12
❑ 324 Tony Phillips .40 .12
❑ 325 Larry Walker RC 10.00 3.00
❑ 326 Ron Hassey .40 .12
❑ 327 Jack Howell .40 .12
❑ 328 John Smiley .40 .12
❑ 329 Steve Finley .60 .18
❑ 330 Dave Magadan .40 .12
❑ 331 Greg Litton .40 .12
❑ 332 Mickey Hatcher .40 .12
❑ 333 Lee Guetterman .40 .12
❑ 334 Norm Charlton .40 .12
❑ 335 Edgar Diaz .40 .12
❑ 336 Willie Wilson .40 .12
❑ 337 Bobby Witt .40 .12
❑ 338 Candy Maldonado .40 .12
❑ 339 Craig Lefferts .40 .12

❑ 340	Dante Bichette	1.50	.45
❑ 341	Wally Backman	.40	.12
❑ 342	Dennis Cook	.40	.12
❑ 343	Pat Borders	.40	.12
❑ 344	Wallace Johnson	.40	.12
❑ 345	Willie Randolph	.60	.18
❑ 346	Danny Darwin	.40	.12
❑ 347	Al Newman	.40	.12
❑ 348	Mark Knudson	.40	.12
❑ 349	Joe Boever	.40	.12
❑ 350	Larry Sheets	.40	.12
❑ 351	Mike Jackson	.40	.12
❑ 352	Wayne Edwards	.40	.12
❑ 353	Bernard Gilkey RC	1.00	.30
❑ 354	Don Slaught	.40	.12
❑ 355	Joe Orsulak	.40	.12
❑ 356	John Franco	.60	.18
❑ 357	Jeff Brantley	.40	.12
❑ 358	Mike Morgan	.40	.12
❑ 359	Deion Sanders	1.50	.45
❑ 360	Terry Leach	.40	.12
❑ 361	Les Lancaster	.40	.12
❑ 362	Storm Davis	.40	.12
❑ 363	Scott Coolbaugh	.40	.12
❑ 364	Ozzie Smith CL	.60	.18
❑ 365	Cecilio Guante	.40	.12
❑ 366	Joey Cora	.60	.18
❑ 367	Willie McGee	.60	.18
❑ 368	Jerry Reed	.40	.12
❑ 369	Darren Daulton	.60	.18
❑ 370	Manny Lee	.40	.12
❑ 371	Mark Gardner	.40	.12
❑ 372	Rick Honeycutt	.40	.12
❑ 373	Steve Balboni	.40	.12
❑ 374	Jack Armstrong	.40	.12
❑ 375	Charlie O'Brien	.40	.12
❑ 376	Ron Gant	.60	.18
❑ 377	Lloyd Moseby	.40	.12
❑ 378	Gene Harris	.40	.12
❑ 379	Joe Carter	.60	.18
❑ 380	Scott Bailes	.40	.12
❑ 381	R.J. Reynolds	.40	.12
❑ 382	Bob Melvin	.40	.12
❑ 383	Tim Teufel	.40	.12
❑ 384	John Burkett	.40	.12
❑ 385	Felix Jose	.40	.12
❑ 386	Larry Andersen	.40	.12
❑ 387	David West	.40	.12
❑ 388	Luis Salazar	.40	.12
❑ 389	Mike Macfarlane	.40	.12
❑ 390	Charlie Hough	.60	.18
❑ 391	Greg Briley	.40	.12
❑ 392	Donn Pall	.40	.12
❑ 393	Bryn Smith	.40	.12
❑ 394	Carlos Quintana	.40	.12
❑ 395	Steve Lake	.40	.12
❑ 396	Mark Whiten RC	1.00	.30
❑ 397	Edwin Nunez	.40	.12
❑ 398	Rick Parker	.40	.12
❑ 399	Mark Portugal	.40	.12
❑ 400	Roy Smith	.40	.12
❑ 401	Hector Villanueva	.40	.12
❑ 402	Bob Milacki	.40	.12
❑ 403	Alejandro Pena	.40	.12
❑ 404	Scott Bradley	.40	.12
❑ 405	Ron Kittle	.40	.12
❑ 406	Bob Tewksbury	.40	.12
❑ 407	Wes Gardner	.40	.12
❑ 408	Ernie Whitt	.40	.12
❑ 409	Terry Shumpert	.40	.12
❑ 410	Tim Layana	.40	.12
❑ 411	Chris Gwynn	.40	.12
❑ 412	Jeff D. Robinson	.40	.12
❑ 413	Scott Scudder	.40	.12
❑ 414	Kevin Romine	.40	.12
❑ 415	Jose DeJesus	.40	.12
❑ 416	Mike Jeffcoat	.40	.12
❑ 417	Rudy Seanez	.40	.12
❑ 418	Mike Dunne	.40	.12
❑ 419	Dick Schofield	.40	.12
❑ 420	Steve Wilson	.40	.12
❑ 421	Bill Krueger	.40	.12
❑ 422	Junior Felix	.40	.12
❑ 423	Drew Hall	.40	.12
❑ 424	Curt Young	.40	.12
❑ 425	Franklin Stubbs	.40	.12
❑ 426	Dave Winfield	1.00	.30
❑ 427	Rick Reed RC	1.00	.30
❑ 428	Charlie Leibrandt	.40	.12
❑ 429	Jeff M. Robinson	.40	.12
❑ 430	Erik Hanson	.40	.12
❑ 431	Barry Jones	.40	.12
❑ 432	Alex Trevino	.40	.12
❑ 433	John Moses	.40	.12
❑ 434	Dave Johnson	.40	.12
❑ 435	Mackey Sasser	.40	.12
❑ 436	Rick Leach	.40	.12
❑ 437	Lenny Harris	.40	.12
❑ 438	Carlos Martinez	.40	.12
❑ 439	Rex Hudler	.40	.12
❑ 440	Domingo Ramos	.40	.12
❑ 441	Gerald Perry	.40	.12
❑ 442	Jeff Russell	.40	.12
❑ 443	Carlos Baerga RC	1.00	.30
❑ 444	Will Clark CL	.60	.18
❑ 445	Stan Javier	.40	.12
❑ 446	Kevin Maas RC	1.00	.30
❑ 447	Tom Brunansky	.40	.12
❑ 448	Carmelo Martinez	.40	.12
❑ 449	Willie Blair RC	.40	.12
❑ 450	Andres Galarraga	.60	.18
❑ 451	Bud Black	.40	.12
❑ 452	Greg W. Harris	.40	.12
❑ 453	Joe Oliver	.40	.12
❑ 454	Greg Brock	.40	.12
❑ 455	Jeff Treadway	.40	.12
❑ 456	Lance McCullers	.40	.12
❑ 457	Dave Schmidt	.40	.12
❑ 458	Todd Burns	.40	.12
❑ 459	Max Venable	.40	.12
❑ 460	Neal Heaton	.40	.12
❑ 461	Mark Williamson	.40	.12
❑ 462	Keith Miller	.40	.12
❑ 463	Mike LaCoss	.40	.12
❑ 464	Jose Offerman RC	1.00	.30
❑ 465	Jim Leyritz RC	1.00	.30
❑ 466	Glenn Braggs	.40	.12
❑ 467	Ron Robinson	.40	.12
❑ 468	Mark Davis	.40	.12
❑ 469	Gary Pettis	.40	.12
❑ 470	Keith Hernandez	1.00	.30
❑ 471	Dennis Rasmussen	.40	.12
❑ 472	Mark Eichhorn	.40	.12
❑ 473	Ted Power	.40	.12
❑ 474	Terry Mulholland	.40	.12
❑ 475	Todd Stottlemyre	.60	.18
❑ 476	Jerry Goff	.40	.12
❑ 477	Gene Nelson	.40	.12
❑ 478	Rich Gedman	.40	.12
❑ 479	Brian Harper	.40	.12
❑ 480	Mike Felder	.40	.12
❑ 481	Steve Avery	1.50	.45
❑ 482	Jack Morris	.60	.18
❑ 483	Randy Johnson	2.50	.75
❑ 484	Scott Radinsky RC	.40	.12
❑ 485	Jose DeLeon	.40	.12
❑ 486	Stan Belinda RC	.40	.12
❑ 487	Brian Holton	.40	.12
❑ 488	Mark Carreon	.40	.12
❑ 489	Trevor Wilson	.40	.12
❑ 490	Mike Sharperson	.40	.12
❑ 491	Alan Mills RC	.40	.12
❑ 492	John Candelaria	.40	.12
❑ 493	Paul Assenmacher	.40	.12
❑ 494	Steve Crawford	.40	.12
❑ 495	Brad Arnsberg	.40	.12
❑ 496	Sergio Valdez	.40	.12
❑ 497	Mark Parent	.40	.12
❑ 498	Tom Pagnozzi	.40	.12
❑ 499	Greg A. Harris	.40	.12
❑ 500	Randy Ready	.40	.12
❑ 501	Duane Ward	.40	.12
❑ 502	Nelson Santovenia	.40	.12
❑ 503	Joe Klink	.40	.12
❑ 504	Eric Plunk	.40	.12
❑ 505	Jeff Reed	.40	.12
❑ 506	Ted Higuera	.40	.12
❑ 507	Joe Hesketh	.40	.12
❑ 508	Dan Petry	.40	.12
❑ 509	Matt Young	.40	.12
❑ 510	Jerald Clark	.40	.12
❑ 511	John Orton	.40	.12
❑ 512	Scott Ruskin	.40	.12
❑ 513	Chris Hoiles RC	1.00	.30
❑ 514	Daryl Boston	.40	.12
❑ 515	Francisco Oliveras	.40	.12
❑ 516	Ozzie Canseco	.40	.12
❑ 517	Xavier Hernandez RC	.40	.12
❑ 518	Fred Manrique	.40	.12
❑ 519	Shawn Boskie RC	.40	.12
❑ 520	Jeff Montgomery	.60	.18
❑ 521	Jack Daugherty	.40	.12
❑ 522	Keith Comstock	.40	.12
❑ 523	Greg Hibbard RC	.40	.12
❑ 524	Lee Smith	.60	.18
❑ 525	Dana Kiecker	.40	.12
❑ 526	Darrel Akerfelds	.40	.12
❑ 527	Greg Myers	.40	.12
❑ 528	Ryne Sandberg CL	1.50	.45

2002 Leaf

	Nm-Mt	Ex-Mt
COMP.SET w/o SP's (149)	25.00	7.50
COMMON (1-41/43-150)	.30	.09
COMMON CARD (151-200)	4.00	1.20

		Nm-Mt	Ex-Mt
❑ 1	Tim Salmon	.50	.15
❑ 2	Troy Glaus	.50	.15
❑ 3	Curt Schilling	.50	.15
❑ 4	Luis Gonzalez	.30	.09
❑ 5	Mark Grace	.75	.23
❑ 6	Matt Williams	.30	.09
❑ 7	Randy Johnson	.75	.23
❑ 8	Tom Glavine	.75	.23
❑ 9	Brady Anderson	.30	.09
❑ 10	Hideo Nomo	.75	.23
❑ 11	Pedro Martinez	.75	.23
❑ 12	Corey Patterson	.30	.09
❑ 13	Paul Konerko	.30	.09
❑ 14	Jon Lieber	.30	.09
❑ 15	Carlos Lee	.30	.09
❑ 16	Magglio Ordonez	.30	.09
❑ 17	Adam Dunn	.50	.15
❑ 18	Ken Griffey Jr.	1.25	.35
❑ 19	C.C. Sabathia	.30	.09
❑ 20	Jim Thome	.75	.23
❑ 21	Juan Gonzalez	.75	.23
❑ 22	Kenny Lofton	.30	.09
❑ 23	Juan Encarnacion	.30	.09
❑ 24	Tony Clark	.30	.09
❑ 25	A.J. Burnett	.30	.09
❑ 26	Josh Beckett	.50	.15
❑ 27	Lance Berkman	.30	.09
❑ 28	Eric Karros	.30	.09
❑ 29	Shawn Green	.30	.09
❑ 30	Brad Radke	.30	.09
❑ 31	Joe Mays	.30	.09
❑ 32	Javier Vazquez	.30	.09
❑ 33	Alfonso Soriano	.75	.23
❑ 34	Jorge Posada	.50	.15
❑ 35	Eric Chavez	.30	.09
❑ 36	Mark Mulder	.30	.09
❑ 37	Miguel Tejada	.30	.09
❑ 38	Tim Hudson	.30	.09
❑ 39	Bob Abreu	.30	.09
❑ 40	Pat Burrell	.30	.09
❑ 41	Ryan Klesko	.30	.09
❑ 43	John Olerud	.30	.09
❑ 44	Ellis Burks	.30	.09

❑ 45 Mike Cameron .30 .09
❑ 46 Jim Edmonds .30 .09
❑ 47 Ben Grieve .30 .09
❑ 48 Carlos Pena .30 .09
❑ 49 Alex Rodriguez 1.50 .45
❑ 50 Raul Mondesi .30 .09
❑ 51 Billy Koch .30 .09
❑ 52 Manny Ramirez .30 .09
❑ 53 Darin Erstad .30 .09
❑ 54 Troy Percival .30 .09
❑ 55 Andruw Jones .50 .15
❑ 56 Chipper Jones .75 .23
❑ 57 David Segui .30 .09
❑ 58 Chris Stynes .30 .09
❑ 59 Trot Nixon .30 .09
❑ 60 Sammy Sosa 1.25 .35
❑ 61 Kerry Wood .75 .23
❑ 62 Frank Thomas .75 .23
❑ 63 Barry Larkin .75 .23
❑ 64 Bartolo Colon .30 .09
❑ 65 Kazuhiro Sasaki .30 .09
❑ 66 Roberto Alomar .75 .23
❑ 67 Mike Hampton .30 .09
❑ 68 Roger Cedeno .30 .09
❑ 69 Cliff Floyd .30 .09
❑ 70 Mike Lowell .30 .09
❑ 71 Billy Wagner .30 .09
❑ 72 Craig Biggio .50 .15
❑ 73 Jeff Bagwell .50 .15
❑ 74 Carlos Beltran .30 .09
❑ 75 Mark Quinn .30 .09
❑ 76 Mike Sweeney .30 .09
❑ 77 Gary Sheffield .30 .09
❑ 78 Kevin Brown .30 .09
❑ 79 Paul LoDuca .30 .09
❑ 80 Ben Sheets .30 .09
❑ 81 Jeromy Burnitz .30 .09
❑ 82 Richie Sexson .30 .09
❑ 83 Corey Koskie .30 .09
❑ 84 Eric Milton .30 .09
❑ 85 Jose Vidro .30 .09
❑ 86 Mike Piazza 1.25 .35
❑ 87 Robin Ventura .30 .09
❑ 88 Andy Pettitte .50 .15
❑ 89 Mike Mussina .75 .23
❑ 90 Orlando Hernandez .30 .09
❑ 91 Roger Clemens 1.50 .45
❑ 92 Barry Zito .75 .23
❑ 93 Jermaine Dye .30 .09
❑ 94 Jimmy Rollins .30 .09
❑ 95 Jason Kendall .30 .09
❑ 96 Rickey Henderson 1.25 .35
❑ 97 Andres Galarraga .30 .09
❑ 98 Bret Boone .30 .09
❑ 99 Freddy Garcia .30 .09
❑ 100 J.D. Drew .30 .09
❑ 101 Jose Cruz Jr. .30 .09
❑ 102 Greg Maddux 1.50 .45
❑ 103 Javy Lopez .30 .09
❑ 104 Nomar Garciaparra 1.50 .45
❑ 105 Fred McGriff .50 .15
❑ 106 Keith Foulke .30 .09
❑ 107 Ray Durham .30 .09
❑ 108 Sean Casey .30 .09
❑ 109 Todd Walker .30 .09
❑ 110 Omar Vizquel .30 .09
❑ 111 Travis Fryman .30 .09
❑ 112 Larry Walker .50 .15
❑ 113 Todd Helton .50 .15
❑ 114 Bobby Higginson .30 .09
❑ 115 Charles Johnson .30 .09
❑ 116 Moises Alou .30 .09
❑ 117 Richard Hidalgo .30 .09
❑ 118 Roy Oswalt .30 .09
❑ 119 Neifi Perez .30 .09
❑ 120 Adrian Beltre .30 .09
❑ 121 Chan Ho Park .30 .09
❑ 122 Geoff Jenkins .30 .09
❑ 123 Doug Mientkiewicz .30 .09
❑ 124 Torii Hunter .30 .09
❑ 125 Vladimir Guerrero .75 .23
❑ 126 Matt Lawton .30 .09
❑ 127 Tsuyoshi Shinjo .30 .09
❑ 128 Bernie Williams .50 .15
❑ 129 Derek Jeter 2.00 .60
❑ 130 Mariano Rivera .50 .15
❑ 131 Tino Martinez .50 .15
❑ 132 Jason Giambi .75 .23
❑ 133 Scott Rolen .50 .15
❑ 134 Brian Giles .30 .09
❑ 135 Phil Nevin .30 .09
❑ 136 Trevor Hoffman .30 .09
❑ 137 Barry Bonds 2.00 .60
❑ 138 Jeff Kent .30 .09
❑ 139 Shannon Stewart .30 .09
❑ 140 Shawn Estes .30 .09
❑ 141 Edgar Martinez .50 .15
❑ 142 Ichiro Suzuki 2.00 .60
❑ 143 Albert Pujols 1.50 .45
❑ 144 Bud Smith .30 .09
❑ 145 Matt Morris .30 .09
❑ 146 Frank Catalanotto .30 .09
❑ 147 Gabe Kapler .30 .09
❑ 148 Ivan Rodriguez .75 .23
❑ 149 Rafael Palmeiro .50 .15
❑ 150 Carlos Delgado .30 .09
❑ 151 Marlon Byrd ROO 4.00 1.20
❑ 152 Alex Herrera ROO 4.00 1.20
❑ 153 Brandon Backe ROO RC 4.00 1.20
❑ 154 Jorge De La Rosa ROO RC 4.00 1.20
❑ 155 Corky Miller ROO 4.00 1.20
❑ 156 Dennis Tankersley ROO 4.00 1.20
❑ 157 Kyle Kane ROO RC 4.00 1.20
❑ 158 Justin Duchscherer ROO 4.00 1.20
❑ 159 Brian Mallette ROO RC 4.00 1.20
❑ 160 Eric Hinske ROO 4.00 1.20
❑ 161 Jason Lane ROO 4.00 1.20
❑ 162 Hee Seop Choi ROO 5.00 1.50
❑ 163 Juan Cruz ROO 4.00 1.20
❑ 164 Rodrigo Rosario ROO RC 4.00 1.20
❑ 165 Matt Guerrier ROO 4.00 1.20
❑ 166 Anderson Machado ROO RC 5.00 1.50
❑ 167 Geronimo Gil ROO 4.00 1.20
❑ 168 Dewon Brazelton ROO 4.00 1.20
❑ 169 Mark Prior ROO 15.00 4.50
❑ 170 Bill Hall ROO 4.00 1.20
❑ 171 Jorge Padilla ROO RC 5.00 1.50
❑ 172 Josh Pearce ROO 4.00 1.20
❑ 173 Allan Simpson ROO RC 4.00 1.20
❑ 174 Doug Devore ROO RC 4.00 1.20
❑ 175 Luis Garcia ROO 4.00 1.20
❑ 176 Angel Berroa ROO 4.00 1.20
❑ 177 Steve Bechler ROO RC 4.00 1.20
❑ 178 Antonio Perez ROO 4.00 1.20
❑ 179 Mark Teixeira ROO 8.00 2.40
❑ 180 Mark Ellis ROO 4.00 1.20
❑ 181 Michael Cuddyer ROO 4.00 1.20
❑ 182 Michael Rivera ROO 4.00 1.20
❑ 183 Raul Chavez ROO RC 4.00 1.20
❑ 184 Juan Pena ROO 4.00 1.20
❑ 185 Austin Kearns ROO 5.00 1.50
❑ 186 Ryan Ludwick ROO 4.00 1.20
❑ 187 Ed Rogers ROO 4.00 1.20
❑ 188 Wilson Betemit ROO 4.00 1.20
❑ 189 Nick Neugebauer ROO 4.00 1.20
❑ 190 Tom Shearn ROO RC 4.00 1.20
❑ 191 Eric Cyr ROO 4.00 1.20
❑ 192 Victor Martinez ROO 4.00 1.20
❑ 193 Brandon Berger ROO 4.00 1.20
❑ 194 Erik Bedard ROO 4.00 1.20
❑ 195 Franklyn German ROO RC 4.00 1.20
❑ 196 Joe Thurston ROO 4.00 1.20
❑ 197 John Buck ROO 4.00 1.20
❑ 198 Jeff Deardorff ROO 4.00 1.20
❑ 199 Ryan Jamison ROO 4.00 1.20
❑ 200 Alfredo Amezaga ROO 4.00 1.20
❑ 201 So Taguchi ROO/500 RC 15.00 4.50
❑ 202 Kazuhisa Ishii ROO/250 RC 25.00 7.50

2003 Leaf

	Nm-Mt	Ex-Mt
COMPLETE SET (329)	50.00	15.00
COMMON CARD (1-270)	.30	.09
COMMON CARD (271-320)	.50	.15
HIGGINSON AND PENA ARE BOTH CARD 41	-	

❑ 1 Brad Fullmer .30 .09
❑ 2 Darin Erstad .30 .09
❑ 3 David Eckstein .30 .09
❑ 4 Garret Anderson .30 .09
❑ 5 Jarrod Washburn .30 .09

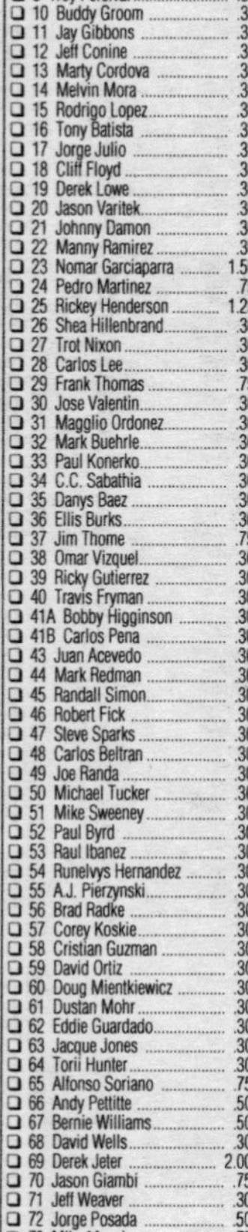

❑ 6 Kevin Appier .30 .09
❑ 7 Tim Salmon .50 .15
❑ 8 Troy Glaus .50 .15
❑ 9 Troy Percival .30 .09
❑ 10 Buddy Groom .30 .09
❑ 11 Jay Gibbons .30 .09
❑ 12 Jeff Conine .30 .09
❑ 13 Marty Cordova .30 .09
❑ 14 Melvin Mora .30 .09
❑ 15 Rodrigo Lopez .30 .09
❑ 16 Tony Batista .30 .09
❑ 17 Jorge Julio .30 .09
❑ 18 Cliff Floyd .30 .09
❑ 19 Derek Lowe .30 .09
❑ 20 Jason Varitek .30 .09
❑ 21 Johnny Damon .30 .09
❑ 22 Manny Ramirez .30 .09
❑ 23 Nomar Garciaparra 1.50 .45
❑ 24 Pedro Martinez .75 .23
❑ 25 Rickey Henderson 1.25 .35
❑ 26 Shea Hillenbrand .30 .09
❑ 27 Trot Nixon .30 .09
❑ 28 Carlos Lee .30 .09
❑ 29 Frank Thomas .75 .23
❑ 30 Jose Valentin .30 .09
❑ 31 Magglio Ordonez .30 .09
❑ 32 Mark Buehrle .30 .09
❑ 33 Paul Konerko .30 .09
❑ 34 C.C. Sabathia .30 .09
❑ 35 Danys Baez .30 .09
❑ 36 Ellis Burks .30 .09
❑ 37 Jim Thome .75 .23
❑ 38 Omar Vizquel .30 .09
❑ 39 Ricky Gutierrez .30 .09
❑ 40 Travis Fryman .30 .09
❑ 41A Bobby Higginson .30 .09
❑ 41B Carlos Pena .30 .09
❑ 43 Juan Acevedo .30 .09
❑ 44 Mark Redman .30 .09
❑ 45 Randall Simon .30 .09
❑ 46 Robert Fick .30 .09
❑ 47 Steve Sparks .30 .09
❑ 48 Carlos Beltran .30 .09
❑ 49 Joe Randa .30 .09
❑ 50 Michael Tucker .30 .09
❑ 51 Mike Sweeney .30 .09
❑ 52 Paul Byrd .30 .09
❑ 53 Raul Ibanez .30 .09
❑ 54 Runelvys Hernandez .30 .09
❑ 55 A.J. Pierzynski .30 .09
❑ 56 Brad Radke .30 .09
❑ 57 Corey Koskie .30 .09
❑ 58 Cristian Guzman .30 .09
❑ 59 David Ortiz .30 .09
❑ 60 Doug Mientkiewicz .30 .09
❑ 61 Dustan Mohr .30 .09
❑ 62 Eddie Guardado .30 .09
❑ 63 Jacque Jones .30 .09
❑ 64 Torii Hunter .30 .09
❑ 65 Alfonso Soriano .75 .23
❑ 66 Andy Pettitte .50 .15
❑ 67 Bernie Williams .50 .15
❑ 68 David Wells .30 .09
❑ 69 Derek Jeter 2.00 .60
❑ 70 Jason Giambi .75 .23
❑ 71 Jeff Weaver .30 .09
❑ 72 Jorge Posada .50 .15
❑ 73 Mike Mussina .75 .23

❑ 74 Nick Johnson .30 .09
❑ 75 Raul Mondesi .30 .09
❑ 76 Robin Ventura .30 .09
❑ 77 Roger Clemens 1.50 .45
❑ 78 Barry Zito .75 .23
❑ 79 Billy Koch .30 .09
❑ 80 David Justice .30 .09
❑ 81 Eric Chavez .30 .09
❑ 82 Jermaine Dye .30 .09
❑ 83 Mark Mulder .30 .09
❑ 84 Miguel Tejada .30 .09
❑ 85 Ray Durham .30 .09
❑ 86 Scott Hatteberg .30 .09
❑ 87 Ted Lilly .30 .09
❑ 88 Tim Hudson .30 .09
❑ 89 Bret Boone .30 .09
❑ 90 Carlos Guillen .30 .09
❑ 91 Chris Snelling .30 .09
❑ 92 Dan Wilson .30 .09
❑ 93 Edgar Martinez .50 .15
❑ 94 Freddy Garcia .30 .09
❑ 95 Ichiro Suzuki 1.50 .45
❑ 96 Jamie Moyer .30 .09
❑ 97 Joel Pineiro .30 .09
❑ 98 John Olerud .30 .09
❑ 99 Mark McLemore .30 .09
❑ 100 Mike Cameron .30 .09
❑ 101 Kazuhiro Sasaki .30 .09
❑ 102 Aubrey Huff .30 .09
❑ 103 Ben Grieve .30 .09
❑ 104 Joe Kennedy .30 .09
❑ 105 Paul Wilson .30 .09
❑ 106 Randy Winn .30 .09
❑ 107 Steve Cox .30 .09
❑ 108 Alex Rodriguez 1.50 .45
❑ 109 Chan Ho Park .30 .09
❑ 110 Hank Blalock .50 .15
❑ 111 Herbert Perry .30 .09
❑ 112 Ivan Rodriguez .75 .23
❑ 113 Juan Gonzalez .75 .23
❑ 114 Kenny Rogers .30 .09
❑ 115 Kevin Mench .30 .09
❑ 116 Rafael Palmeiro .50 .15
❑ 117 Carlos Delgado .30 .09
❑ 118 Eric Hinske .30 .09
❑ 119 Jose Cruz .30 .09
❑ 120 Josh Phelps .30 .09
❑ 121 Roy Halladay .30 .09
❑ 122 Shannon Stewart .30 .09
❑ 123 Vernon Wells .30 .09
❑ 124 Curt Schilling .50 .15
❑ 125 Junior Spivey .30 .09
❑ 126 Luis Gonzalez .30 .09
❑ 127 Mark Grace .75 .23
❑ 128 Randy Johnson .75 .23
❑ 129 Steve Finley .30 .09
❑ 130 Tony Womack .30 .09
❑ 131 Andruw Jones .50 .15
❑ 132 Chipper Jones .75 .23
❑ 133 Gary Sheffield .30 .09
❑ 134 Greg Maddux 1.50 .45
❑ 135 John Smoltz .50 .15
❑ 136 Kevin Millwood .30 .09
❑ 137 Rafael Furcal .30 .09
❑ 138 Tom Glavine .75 .23
❑ 139 Alex Gonzalez .30 .09
❑ 140 Corey Patterson .30 .09
❑ 141 Fred McGriff .50 .15
❑ 142 Jon Lieber .30 .09
❑ 143 Kerry Wood .75 .23
❑ 144 Mark Prior 1.50 .45
❑ 145 Matt Clement .30 .09
❑ 146 Moises Alou .30 .09
❑ 147 Sammy Sosa 1.25 .35
❑ 148 Aaron Boone .30 .09
❑ 149 Adam Dunn .50 .15
❑ 150 Austin Kearns .50 .15
❑ 151 Barry Larkin .75 .23
❑ 152 Danny Graves .30 .09
❑ 153 Elmer Dessens .30 .09
❑ 154 Ken Griffey Jr. 1.25 .35
❑ 155 Sean Casey .30 .09
❑ 156 Todd Walker .30 .09
❑ 157 Gabe Kapler .30 .09
❑ 158 Jason Jennings .30 .09
❑ 159 Jay Payton .30 .09
❑ 160 Larry Walker .50 .15
❑ 161 Mike Hampton .30 .09
❑ 162 Todd Helton .50 .15
❑ 163 Todd Zeile .30 .09
❑ 164 A.J. Burnett .30 .09
❑ 165 Derrek Lee .30 .09
❑ 166 Josh Beckett .50 .15
❑ 167 Juan Encarnacion .30 .09
❑ 168 Luis Castillo .30 .09
❑ 169 Mike Lowell .30 .09
❑ 170 Preston Wilson .30 .09
❑ 171 Billy Wagner .30 .09
❑ 172 Craig Biggio .50 .15
❑ 173 Daryle Ward .30 .09
❑ 174 Jeff Bagwell .50 .15
❑ 175 Lance Berkman .30 .09
❑ 176 Octavio Dotel .30 .09
❑ 177 Richard Hidalgo .30 .09
❑ 178 Roy Oswalt .30 .09
❑ 179 Adrian Beltre .30 .09
❑ 180 Eric Gagne .50 .15
❑ 181 Eric Karros .30 .09
❑ 182 Hideo Nomo .75 .23
❑ 183 Kazuhisa Ishii .30 .09
❑ 184 Kevin Brown .30 .09
❑ 185 Mark Grudzielanek .30 .09
❑ 186 Odalis Perez .30 .09
❑ 187 Paul Lo Duca .30 .09
❑ 188 Shawn Green .30 .09
❑ 189 Alex Sanchez .30 .09
❑ 190 Ben Sheets .30 .09
❑ 191 Jeffrey Hammonds .30 .09
❑ 192 Jose Hernandez .30 .09
❑ 193 Takahito Nomura .30 .09
❑ 194 Richie Sexson .30 .09
❑ 195 Andres Galarraga .30 .09
❑ 196 Bartolo Colon .30 .09
❑ 197 Brad Wilkerson .30 .09
❑ 198 Javier Vazquez .30 .09
❑ 199 Jose Vidro .30 .09
❑ 200 Michael Barrett .30 .09
❑ 201 Tomo Ohka .30 .09
❑ 202 Vladimir Guerrero .75 .23
❑ 203 Al Leiter .30 .09
❑ 204 Armando Benitez .30 .09
❑ 205 Edgardo Alfonzo .30 .09
❑ 206 Mike Piazza 1.25 .35
❑ 207 Mo Vaughn .30 .09
❑ 208 Pedro Astacio .30 .09
❑ 209 Roberto Alomar .75 .23
❑ 210 Roger Cedeno .30 .09
❑ 211 Timo Perez .30 .09
❑ 212 Bobby Abreu .30 .09
❑ 213 Jimmy Rollins .30 .09
❑ 214 Mike Lieberthal .30 .09
❑ 215 Pat Burrell .30 .09
❑ 216 Randy Wolf .30 .09
❑ 217 Travis Lee .30 .09
❑ 218 Vicente Padilla .30 .09
❑ 219 Aramis Ramirez .30 .09
❑ 220 Brian Giles .30 .09
❑ 221 Craig Wilson .30 .09
❑ 222 Jason Kendall .30 .09
❑ 223 Josh Fogg .30 .09
❑ 224 Kevin Young .30 .09
❑ 225 Kip Wells .30 .09
❑ 226 Mike Williams .30 .09
❑ 227 Brett Tomko .30 .09
❑ 228 Brian Lawrence .30 .09
❑ 229 Mark Kotsay .30 .09
❑ 230 Oliver Perez .30 .09
❑ 231 Phil Nevin .30 .09
❑ 232 Ryan Klesko .30 .09
❑ 233 Sean Burroughs .30 .09
❑ 234 Trevor Hoffman .30 .09
❑ 235 Barry Bonds 2.00 .60
❑ 236 Benito Santiago .30 .09
❑ 237 Jeff Kent .30 .09
❑ 238 Kirk Rueter .30 .09
❑ 239 Livan Hernandez .30 .09
❑ 240 Kenny Lofton .30 .09
❑ 241 Rich Aurilia .30 .09
❑ 242 Russ Ortiz .30 .09
❑ 243 Albert Pujols 1.50 .45
❑ 244 Edgar Renteria .30 .09
❑ 245 J.D. Drew .30 .09
❑ 246 Jason Isringhausen .30 .09
❑ 247 Jim Edmonds .30 .09
❑ 248 Matt Morris .30 .09
❑ 249 Tino Martinez .50 .15
❑ 250 Scott Rolen .50 .15
❑ 251 Curt Schilling PT .30 .09
❑ 252 Ivan Rodriguez PT .50 .15
❑ 253 Mike Piazza PT .75 .23
❑ 254 Sammy Sosa PT .75 .23
❑ 255 Matt Williams PT .30 .09
❑ 256 Frank Thomas PT .50 .15
❑ 257 Barry Bonds PT 1.00 .30
❑ 258 Roger Clemens PT .75 .23
❑ 259 Rickey Henderson PT .75 .23
❑ 260 Ken Griffey Jr. PT .75 .23
❑ 261 Greg Maddux PT .75 .23
❑ 262 Randy Johnson PT .50 .15
❑ 263 Jeff Bagwell PT .30 .09
❑ 264 Roberto Alomar PT .50 .15
❑ 265 Tom Glavine PT .50 .15
❑ 266 Juan Gonzalez PT .50 .15
❑ 267 Mark Grace PT .50 .15
❑ 268 Mike Mussina PT .50 .15
❑ 269 Ryan Klesko PT .30 .09
❑ 270 Fred McGriff PT .30 .09
❑ 271 Joe Borchard ROO .40 .12
❑ 272 Chris Snelling ROO .40 .12
❑ 273 Brian Tallet ROO .50 .15
❑ 274 Cliff Lee ROO .40 .12
❑ 275 Freddy Sanchez ROO .40 .12
❑ 276 Chone Figgins ROO .50 .15
❑ 277 Kevin Cash ROO .50 .15
❑ 278 Josh Bard ROO .50 .15
❑ 279 Jeriome Robertson ROO .50 .15
❑ 280 Jeremy Hill ROO .50 .15
❑ 281 Shane Nance ROO .50 .15
❑ 282 Jeff Baker ROO .40 .12
❑ 283 Trey Hodges ROO .50 .15
❑ 284 Eric Eckenstahler ROO .50 .15
❑ 285 Jim Rushford ROO .50 .15
❑ 286 Carlos Rivera ROO .50 .15
❑ 287 Josh Bonifay ROO .40 .12
❑ 288 Garrett Atkins ROO .40 .12
❑ 289 Nic Jackson ROO .50 .15
❑ 290 Corwin Malone ROO .50 .15
❑ 291 Jimmy Gobble ROO .40 .12
❑ 292 Josh Wilson ROO .50 .15
❑ 293 Clint Barmes ROO RC .60 .18
❑ 294 Jon Adkins ROO .50 .15
❑ 295 Tim Kalita ROO .50 .15
❑ 296 Nelson Castro ROO .50 .15
❑ 297 Colin Young ROO .50 .15
❑ 298 Adrian Burnside ROO .50 .15
❑ 299 Luis Martinez ROO .50 .15
❑ 300 Termel Sledge ROO RC .60 .18
❑ 301 Todd Donovan ROO .50 .15
❑ 302 Jeremy Ward ROO .50 .15
❑ 303 Wilson Valdez ROO .50 .15
❑ 304 Jose Contreras ROO RC 2.00 .60
❑ 305 Marshall McDougall ROO .50 .15
❑ 306 Mitch Wylie ROO .50 .15
❑ 307 Ron Calloway ROO .50 .15
❑ 308 Jose Valverde ROO .50 .15
❑ 309 Jason Davis ROO .40 .12
❑ 310 Scotty Layfield ROO .50 .15
❑ 311 Matt Thornton ROO .50 .15
❑ 312 Adam Walker ROO .50 .15
❑ 313 Gustavo Chacin ROO .50 .15
❑ 314 Ron Chiavacci ROO .50 .15
❑ 315 Wilbert Nieves ROO .50 .15
❑ 316 Cliff Bartosh ROO .50 .15
❑ 317 Mike Gonzalez ROO .50 .15
❑ 318 Jeremy Guthrie ROO .40 .12
❑ 319 Eric Junge ROO .50 .15
❑ 320 Ben Kozlowski ROO .50 .15
❑ 321 Hideki Matsui ROO RC -
❑ 322 Ramon Nivar ROO RC -
❑ 323 Adam Loewen ROO RC -
❑ 324 Brandon Webb ROO RC -
❑ 325 Chien-Ming Wang ROO RC -
❑ 326 Delmon Young ROO RC -
❑ 327 Ryan Wagner ROO RC -
❑ 328 Dan Haren ROO RC -
❑ 329 Rickie Weeks ROO RC -

2001 Leaf Certified Materials

	Nm-Mt	Ex-Mt
COMP.SET w/o SP's (110)	40.00	12.00
COMMON CARD (1-110)	1.00	.30
COMMON (111-160)	20.00	6.00

Card	Nm-Mt	Ex-Mt
❑ 1 Alex Rodriguez	5.00	1.50
❑ 2 Barry Bonds	6.00	1.80
❑ 3 Cal Ripken	8.00	2.40
❑ 4 Chipper Jones	2.50	.75
❑ 5 Derek Jeter	6.00	1.80
❑ 6 Troy Glaus	1.50	.45
❑ 7 Frank Thomas	2.50	.75
❑ 8 Greg Maddux	5.00	1.50
❑ 9 Ivan Rodriguez	2.50	.75
❑ 10 Jeff Bagwell	1.50	.45
❑ 11 Eric Karros	1.00	.30
❑ 12 Todd Helton	1.50	.45
❑ 13 Ken Griffey Jr.	4.00	1.20
❑ 14 Manny Ramirez	1.00	.30
❑ 15 Mark McGwire	6.00	1.80
❑ 16 Mike Piazza	4.00	1.20
❑ 17 Nomar Garciaparra	6.00	1.80
❑ 18 Pedro Martinez	2.50	.75
❑ 19 Randy Johnson	2.50	.75
❑ 20 Rick Ankiel	1.00	.30
❑ 21 Rickey Henderson	4.00	1.20
❑ 22 Roger Clemens	5.00	1.50
❑ 23 Sammy Sosa	4.00	1.20
❑ 24 Tony Gwynn	3.00	.90
❑ 25 Vladimir Guerrero	2.50	.75
❑ 26 Kazuhiro Sasaki	1.00	.30
❑ 27 Roberto Alomar	2.50	.75
❑ 28 Barry Zito	2.50	.75
❑ 29 Pat Burrell	1.00	.30
❑ 30 Harold Baines	1.00	.30
❑ 31 Carlos Delgado	1.00	.30
❑ 32 J.D. Drew	1.00	.30
❑ 33 Jim Edmonds	1.00	.30
❑ 34 Darin Erstad	1.00	.30
❑ 35 Jason Giambi	2.50	.75
❑ 36 Tom Glavine	2.50	.75
❑ 37 Juan Gonzalez	2.50	.75
❑ 38 Mark Grace	2.50	.75
❑ 39 Shawn Green	1.00	.30
❑ 40 Tim Hudson	1.00	.30
❑ 41 Andruw Jones	1.50	.45
❑ 42 Jeff Kent	1.00	.30
❑ 43 Barry Larkin	2.50	.75
❑ 44 Rafael Furcal	1.00	.30
❑ 45 Mike Mussina	2.50	.75
❑ 46 Hideo Nomo	2.50	.75
❑ 47 Rafael Palmeiro	1.50	.45
❑ 48 Scott Rolen	1.50	.45
❑ 49 Gary Sheffield	1.00	.30
❑ 50 Bernie Williams	1.50	.45
❑ 51 Bob Abreu	1.00	.30
❑ 52 Edgardo Alfonzo	1.00	.30
❑ 53 Edgar Martinez	1.50	.45
❑ 54 Magglio Ordonez	1.00	.30
❑ 55 Kerry Wood	2.50	.75
❑ 56 Adrian Beltre	1.00	.30
❑ 57 Lance Berkman	1.00	.30
❑ 58 Kevin Brown	1.00	.30
❑ 59 Sean Casey	1.00	.30
❑ 60 Eric Chavez	1.00	.30
❑ 61 Bartolo Colon	1.00	.30
❑ 62 Johnny Damon	1.00	.30
❑ 63 Jermaine Dye	1.00	.30
❑ 64 Juan Encarnacion UER Card has him playing for Detroit Lions	1.00	.30
❑ 65 Carl Everett	1.00	.30
❑ 66 Brian Giles	1.00	.30
❑ 67 Mike Hampton	1.00	.30
❑ 68 Richard Hidalgo	1.00	.30
❑ 69 Geoff Jenkins	1.00	.30
❑ 70 Jacque Jones	1.00	.30
❑ 71 Jason Kendall	1.00	.30
❑ 72 Ryan Klesko	1.00	.30
❑ 73 Chan Ho Park	1.00	.30
❑ 74 Richie Sexson	1.00	.30
❑ 75 Mike Sweeney	1.00	.30
❑ 76 Fernando Tatis	1.00	.30
❑ 77 Miguel Tejada	1.00	.30
❑ 78 Jose Vidro	1.00	.30
❑ 79 Larry Walker	1.50	.45
❑ 80 Preston Wilson	1.00	.30
❑ 81 Craig Biggio	1.50	.45
❑ 82 Fred McGriff	1.50	.45
❑ 83 Jim Thome	2.50	.75
❑ 84 Garret Anderson	1.00	.30
❑ 85 Russell Branyan	1.00	.30
❑ 86 Tony Batista	1.00	.30
❑ 87 Terrence Long	1.00	.30
❑ 88 Deion Sanders	1.00	.30
❑ 89 Rusty Greer	1.00	.30
❑ 90 Orlando Hernandez	1.00	.30
❑ 91 Gabe Kapler	1.00	.30
❑ 92 Paul Konerko	1.00	.30
❑ 93 Carlos Lee	1.00	.30
❑ 94 Kenny Lofton	1.00	.30
❑ 95 Raul Mondesi	1.00	.30
❑ 96 Jorge Posada	1.50	.45
❑ 97 Tim Salmon	1.50	.45
❑ 98 Greg Vaughn	1.00	.30
❑ 99 Mo Vaughn	1.00	.30
❑ 100 Omar Vizquel	1.00	.30
❑ 101 Ray Durham	1.00	.30
❑ 102 Jeff Cirillo	1.00	.30
❑ 103 Dean Palmer	1.00	.30
❑ 104 Ryan Dempster	1.00	.30
❑ 105 Carlos Beltran	1.00	.30
❑ 106 Timo Perez	1.00	.30
❑ 107 Robin Ventura	1.00	.30
❑ 108 Andy Pettitte	1.50	.45
❑ 109 Aramis Ramirez	1.00	.30
❑ 110 Phil Nevin	1.00	.30
❑ 111 Alex Escobar FF	20.00	6.00
❑ 112 Johnny Estrada FF RC	25.00	7.50
❑ 113 Pedro Feliz FF	20.00	6.00
❑ 114 Nate Frese FF RC	20.00	6.00
❑ 115 Joe Kennedy FF RC	20.00	6.00
❑ 116 B. Larson FF RC	20.00	6.00
❑ 117 Alexis Gomez FF RC	20.00	6.00
❑ 118 Jason Hart FF	20.00	6.00
❑ 119 Jason Michaels FF RC	20.00	6.00
❑ 120 Marcus Giles FF	20.00	6.00
❑ 121 C. Parker FF RC	20.00	6.00
❑ 122 Jackson Melian FF RC	20.00	6.00
❑ 123 D. Mendez FF RC	20.00	6.00
❑ 124 A. Hernandez FF RC	20.00	6.00
❑ 125 Bud Smith FF RC	20.00	6.00
❑ 126 Jose Mieses FF RC	20.00	6.00
❑ 127 Roy Oswalt FF	25.00	7.50
❑ 128 Eric Munson FF	20.00	6.00
❑ 129 Xavier Nady FF	20.00	6.00
❑ 130 H. Ramirez FF RC	25.00	7.50
❑ 131 Abraham Nunez FF	20.00	6.00
❑ 132 Jose Ortiz FF	20.00	6.00
❑ 133 Jeremy Owens FF RC	20.00	6.00
❑ 134 Claudio Vargas FF RC	20.00	6.00
❑ 135 R. Rodriguez FF RC	20.00	6.00
❑ 136 Aubrey Huff FF	20.00	6.00
❑ 137 Ben Sheets FF	20.00	6.00
❑ 138 Adam Dunn FF	25.00	7.50
❑ 139 Andres Torres FF RC	20.00	6.00
❑ 140 Elpidio Guzman FF RC	20.00	6.00
❑ 141 Jay Gibbons FF RC	25.00	7.50
❑ 142 Wilkin Ruan FF RC	20.00	6.00
❑ 143 T. Shinjo FF RC	25.00	7.50
❑ 144 Alfonso Soriano FF	25.00	7.50
❑ 145 Josh Towers FF RC	20.00	6.00
❑ 146 Ichiro Suzuki FF RC	120.00	36.00
❑ 147 Juan Uribe FF RC	20.00	6.00
❑ 148 Joe Crede FF	20.00	6.00
❑ 149 C. Valderrama FF RC	20.00	6.00
❑ 150 Matt White FF RC	20.00	6.00
❑ 151 Dee Brown FF	20.00	6.00
❑ 152 Juan Cruz FF RC	20.00	6.00
❑ 153 Cory Aldridge FF RC	20.00	6.00
❑ 154 Wilmy Caceres FF RC	20.00	6.00
❑ 155 Josh Beckett FF	25.00	7.50
❑ 156 Wilson Betemit FF RC	20.00	6.00
❑ 157 Corey Patterson FF	20.00	6.00
❑ 158 Albert Pujols FF RC	200.00	60.00
❑ 159 Rafael Soriano FF RC	30.00	9.00
❑ 160 Jack Wilson FF RC	20.00	6.00

2002 Leaf Certified

	Nm-Mt	Ex-Mt
COMP.SET w/o SP's (150)	80.00	24.00
COMMON CARD (1-150)	1.00	.30
COMMON CARD (151-200)	10.00	3.00

Card	Nm-Mt	Ex-Mt
❑ 1 Alex Rodriguez	5.00	1.50
❑ 2 Luis Gonzalez	1.00	.30
❑ 3 Javier Vazquez	1.00	.30
❑ 4 Juan Uribe	1.00	.30
❑ 5 Ben Sheets	1.00	.30
❑ 6 George Brett	6.00	1.80
❑ 7 Magglio Ordonez	1.00	.30
❑ 8 Randy Johnson	2.50	.75
❑ 9 Joe Kennedy	1.00	.30
❑ 10 Richie Sexson	1.00	.30
❑ 11 Larry Walker	1.50	.45
❑ 12 Lance Berkman	1.00	.30
❑ 13 Jose Cruz Jr.	1.00	.30
❑ 14 Doug Davis	1.00	.30
❑ 15 Cliff Floyd	1.00	.30
❑ 16 Ryan Klesko	1.00	.30
❑ 17 Troy Glaus	1.50	.45
❑ 18 Robert Person	1.00	.30
❑ 19 Bartolo Colon	1.00	.30
❑ 20 Adam Dunn	1.50	.45
❑ 21 Kevin Brown	1.00	.30
❑ 22 John Smoltz	1.50	.45
❑ 23 Edgar Martinez	1.50	.45
❑ 24 Eric Karros	1.00	.30
❑ 25 Tony Gwynn	3.00	.90
❑ 26 Mark Mulder	1.00	.30
❑ 27 Don Mattingly	6.00	1.80
❑ 28 Brandon Duckworth	1.00	.30
❑ 29 C.C. Sabathia	1.00	.30
❑ 30 Nomar Garciaparra	5.00	1.50
❑ 31 Adam Johnson	1.00	.30
❑ 32 Miguel Tejada	1.00	.30
❑ 33 Ryne Sandberg	5.00	1.50
❑ 34 Roger Clemens	5.00	1.50
❑ 35 Edgardo Alfonzo	1.00	.30
❑ 36 Jason Jennings	1.00	.30
❑ 37 Todd Helton	1.50	.45
❑ 38 Nolan Ryan	8.00	2.40
❑ 39 Paul LoDuca	1.00	.30
❑ 40 Cal Ripken	8.00	2.40
❑ 41 Terrence Long	1.00	.30
❑ 42 Mike Sweeney	1.00	.30
❑ 43 Carlos Lee	1.00	.30
❑ 44 Ben Grieve	1.00	.30
❑ 45 Tony Armas Jr.	1.00	.30

Card	Player	Mint	Nrmt
❑ 46	Joe Mays	1.00	.30
❑ 47	Jeff Kent	1.00	.30
❑ 48	Andy Pettitte	1.50	.45
❑ 49	Kirby Puckett	2.50	.75
❑ 50	Aramis Ramirez	1.00	.30
❑ 51	Tim Redding	1.00	.30
❑ 52	Freddy Garcia	1.00	.30
❑ 53	Javy Lopez	1.00	.30
❑ 54	Mike Schmidt	6.00	1.80
❑ 55	Wade Miller	1.00	.30
❑ 56	Ramon Ortiz	1.00	.30
❑ 57	Ray Durham	1.00	.30
❑ 58	J.D. Drew	1.00	.30
❑ 59	Bret Boone	1.00	.30
❑ 60	Mark Buehrle	1.00	.30
❑ 61	Geoff Jenkins	1.00	.30
❑ 62	Greg Maddux	5.00	1.50
❑ 63	Mark Grace	2.50	.75
❑ 64	Toby Hall	1.00	.30
❑ 65	A.J. Burnett	1.00	.30
❑ 66	Bernie Williams	1.50	.45
❑ 67	Roy Oswalt	1.00	.30
❑ 68	Shannon Stewart	1.00	.30
❑ 69	Barry Zito	2.50	.75
❑ 70	Juan Pierre	1.00	.30
❑ 71	Preston Wilson	1.00	.30
❑ 72	Rafael Furcal	1.00	.30
❑ 73	Sean Casey	1.00	.30
❑ 74	John Olerud	1.00	.30
❑ 75	Paul Konerko	1.00	.30
❑ 76	Vernon Wells	1.00	.30
❑ 77	Juan Gonzalez	2.50	.75
❑ 78	Ellis Burks	1.00	.30
❑ 79	Jim Edmonds	1.00	.30
❑ 80	Robert Fick	1.00	.30
❑ 81	Michael Cuddyer	1.00	.30
❑ 82	Tim Hudson	1.00	.30
❑ 83	Phil Nevin	1.00	.30
❑ 84	Curt Schilling	1.50	.45
❑ 85	Juan Cruz	1.00	.30
❑ 86	Jeff Bagwell	1.50	.45
❑ 87	Raul Mondesi	1.00	.30
❑ 88	Bud Smith	1.00	.30
❑ 89	Omar Vizquel	1.00	.30
❑ 90	Vladimir Guerrero	2.50	.75
❑ 91	Garret Anderson	1.00	.30
❑ 92	Mike Piazza	4.00	1.20
❑ 93	Josh Beckett	1.50	.45
❑ 94	Carlos Delgado	1.00	.30
❑ 95	Kazuhiro Sasaki	1.00	.30
❑ 96	Chipper Jones	2.50	.75
❑ 97	Jacque Jones	1.00	.30
❑ 98	Pedro Martinez	2.50	.75
❑ 99	Marcus Giles	1.00	.30
❑ 100	Craig Biggio	1.50	.45
❑ 101	Orlando Cabrera	1.00	.30
❑ 102	Al Leiter	1.00	.30
❑ 103	Michael Barrett	1.00	.30
❑ 104	Hideo Nomo	2.50	.75
❑ 105	Mike Mussina	2.50	.75
❑ 106	Jeremy Giambi	1.00	.30
❑ 107	Cristian Guzman	1.00	.30
❑ 108	Frank Thomas	2.50	.75
❑ 109	Carlos Beltran	1.00	.30
❑ 110	Jorge Posada	1.50	.45
❑ 111	Roberto Alomar	2.50	.75
❑ 112	Bob Abreu	1.00	.30
❑ 113	Robin Ventura	1.00	.30
❑ 114	Pat Burrell	1.00	.30
❑ 115	Kenny Lofton	1.00	.30
❑ 116	Adrian Beltre	1.00	.30
❑ 117	Gary Sheffield	1.00	.30
❑ 118	Jermaine Dye	1.00	.30
❑ 119	Manny Ramirez	1.00	.30
❑ 120	Brian Giles	1.00	.30
❑ 121	Tsuyoshi Shinjo	1.00	.30
❑ 122	Rafael Palmeiro	1.50	.45
❑ 123	Mo Vaughn UER Yankee Logo on back	1.00	.30
❑ 124	Kerry Wood	2.50	.75
❑ 125	Moises Alou	1.00	.30
❑ 126	Rickey Henderson	4.00	1.20
❑ 127	Corey Patterson	1.00	.30
❑ 128	Jim Thome	2.50	.75
❑ 129	Richard Hidalgo	1.00	.30
❑ 130	Darin Erstad	1.00	.30
❑ 131	Johnny Damon	1.00	.30
❑ 132	Juan Encarnacion	1.00	.30
❑ 133	Scott Rolen	1.50	.45
❑ 134	Tom Glavine	2.50	.75
❑ 135	Ivan Rodriguez	2.50	.75
❑ 136	Jay Gibbons	1.00	.30
❑ 137	Trot Nixon	1.00	.30
❑ 138	Nick Neugebauer	1.00	.30
❑ 139	Barry Larkin	2.50	.75
❑ 140	Andruw Jones	1.50	.45
❑ 141	Shawn Green	1.00	.30
❑ 142	Jose Vidro	1.00	.30
❑ 143	Derek Jeter	6.00	1.80
❑ 144	Ichiro Suzuki	5.00	1.50
❑ 145	Ken Griffey Jr.	4.00	1.20
❑ 146	Barry Bonds	6.00	1.80
❑ 147	Albert Pujols	5.00	1.50
❑ 148	Sammy Sosa	4.00	1.20
❑ 149	Jason Giambi	2.50	.75
❑ 150	Alfonso Soriano	2.50	.75
❑ 151	Drew Henson NG Bat	10.00	3.00
❑ 152	Luis Garcia NG Bat	10.00	3.00
❑ 153	Geronimo Gil NG Jsy	10.00	3.00
❑ 154	Corky Miller NG Jsy	10.00	3.00
❑ 155	Mike Rivera NG Bat	10.00	3.00
❑ 156	Mark Ellis NG Jsy	10.00	3.00
❑ 157	Josh Pearce NG Bat	10.00	3.00
❑ 158	Ryan Ludwick NG Bat	10.00	3.00
❑ 159	So Taguchi NG Bat RC	15.00	4.50
❑ 160	Cody Ransom NG Jsy	10.00	3.00
❑ 161	Jeff Deardorff NG Bat	10.00	3.00
❑ 162	Franklyn German NG Bat RC	10.00	3.00
❑ 163	Ed Rogers NG Jsy	10.00	3.00
❑ 164	Eric Cyr NG Jsy	10.00	3.00
❑ 165	Victor Alvarez NG Jsy RC	10.00	3.00
❑ 166	Victor Martinez NG Jsy	10.00	3.00
❑ 167	Brandon Berger NG Jsy	10.00	3.00
❑ 168	Juan Diaz NG Jsy	10.00	3.00
❑ 169	Kevin Frederick NG Jsy RC	10.00	3.00
❑ 170	Earl Snyder NG Bat RC	10.00	3.00
❑ 171	Morgan Ensberg NG Bat	10.00	3.00
❑ 172	Ryan Jamison NG Jsy	10.00	3.00
❑ 173	Rodrigo Rosario NG Jsy RC	10.00	3.00
❑ 174	Willie Harris NG Bat	10.00	3.00
❑ 175	Ramon Vazquez NG Bat	10.00	3.00
❑ 176	Kazuhisa Ishii NG Bat RC	20.00	6.00
❑ 177	Hank Blalock NG Jsy	15.00	4.50
❑ 178	Mark Prior NG Bat	25.00	7.50
❑ 179	Dewon Brazelton NG Jsy	10.00	3.00
❑ 180	Doug Devore NG Jsy RC	10.00	3.00
❑ 181	Jorge Padilla NG Bat RC	15.00	4.50
❑ 182	Mark Teixeira NG Jsy	15.00	4.50
❑ 183	Orlando Hudson NG Bat	10.00	3.00
❑ 184	John Buck NG Jsy	10.00	3.00
❑ 185	Erik Bedard NG Jsy	10.00	3.00
❑ 186	Allan Simpson NG Jsy RC	10.00	3.00
❑ 187	Travis Hafner NG Jsy	10.00	3.00
❑ 188	Jason Lane NG Jsy	10.00	3.00
❑ 189	Marlon Byrd NG Jsy	10.00	3.00
❑ 190	Joe Thurston NG Jsy	10.00	3.00
❑ 191	Brandon Backe NG Jsy RC	10.00	3.00
❑ 192	Josh Phelps NG Jsy	10.00	3.00
❑ 193	Bill Hall NG Bat	10.00	3.00
❑ 194	Chris Snelling NG Bat RC	15.00	4.50
❑ 195	Austin Kearns NG Jsy	15.00	4.50
❑ 196	Antonio Perez NG Bat	10.00	3.00
❑ 197	Angel Berroa NG Bat	10.00	3.00
❑ 198	Andy Machado NG Jsy RC	15.00	4.50
❑ 199	Alfredo Amezaga NG Jsy	10.00	3.00
❑ 200	Eric Hinske NG Bat	10.00	3.00

2003 Leaf Certified Materials

	MINT	NRMT
COMP.SET w/o SP's (200)	60.00	27.00
COMMON CARD (1-200)	1.00	.45
COMMON CARD (201-205)	10.00	4.50
COMMON CARD (206-250)	10.00	4.50
201-250 RANDOM INSERTS IN PACKS		-
201-219/221-250 PRINT RUN 400 #'d SETS		-
CARD 220 PRINT RUN 100 #'d CARDS		-

Card	Player	Mint	Nrmt
❑ 1	Troy Glaus	1.50	.70
❑ 2	Alfredo Amezaga	1.00	.45
❑ 3	Garret Anderson	1.00	.45
❑ 4	Nolan Ryan Angels	8.00	3.60
❑ 5	Darin Erstad	1.00	.45
❑ 6	Junior Spivey	1.00	.45
❑ 7	Randy Johnson	2.50	1.10
❑ 8	Curt Schilling	1.50	.70
❑ 9	Luis Gonzalez	1.00	.45
❑ 10	Steve Finley	1.00	.45
❑ 11	Matt Williams	1.00	.45
❑ 12	Greg Maddux	5.00	2.20
❑ 13	Chipper Jones	2.50	1.10
❑ 14	Gary Sheffield	1.00	.45
❑ 15	Adam LaRoche	1.00	.45
❑ 16	Andruw Jones	1.50	.70
❑ 17	Robert Fick	1.00	.45
❑ 18	John Smoltz	1.50	.70
❑ 19	Javy Lopez	1.00	.45
❑ 20	Jay Gibbons	1.00	.45
❑ 21	Geronimo Gil	1.00	.45
❑ 22	Cal Ripken	8.00	3.60
❑ 23	Nomar Garciaparra	5.00	2.20
❑ 24	Pedro Martinez	2.50	1.10
❑ 25	Freddy Sanchez	1.00	.45
❑ 26	Rickey Henderson	4.00	1.80
❑ 27	Manny Ramirez	1.00	.45
❑ 28	Casey Fossum	1.00	.45
❑ 29	Sammy Sosa	4.00	1.80
❑ 30	Kerry Wood	2.50	1.10
❑ 31	Corey Patterson	1.00	.45
❑ 32	Nic Jackson	1.00	.45
❑ 33	Mark Prior	5.00	2.20
❑ 34	Juan Cruz	1.00	.45
❑ 35	Steve Smyth	1.00	.45
❑ 36	Magglio Ordonez	1.00	.45
❑ 37	Joe Borchard	1.00	.45
❑ 38	Frank Thomas	2.50	1.10
❑ 39	Mark Buehrle	1.00	.45
❑ 40	Joe Crede	1.00	.45
❑ 41	Carlos Lee	1.00	.45
❑ 42	Paul Konerko	1.00	.45
❑ 43	Adam Dunn	1.50	.70
❑ 44	Corky Miller	1.00	.45
❑ 45	Brandon Larson	1.00	.45
❑ 46	Ken Griffey Jr.	4.00	1.80
❑ 47	Barry Larkin	2.50	1.10
❑ 48	Sean Casey	1.00	.45
❑ 49	Wily Mo Pena	1.00	.45
❑ 50	Austin Kearns	1.50	.70
❑ 51	Victor Martinez	1.00	.45
❑ 52	Brian Tallet	1.00	.45
❑ 53	Cliff Lee	1.00	.45
❑ 54	Jeremy Guthrie	1.00	.45
❑ 55	C.C. Sabathia	1.00	.45
❑ 56	Ricardo Rodriguez	1.00	.45
❑ 57	Omar Vizquel	1.00	.45
❑ 58	Travis Hafner	1.00	.45
❑ 59	Todd Helton	1.50	.70
❑ 60	Jason Jennings	1.00	.45
❑ 61	Jeff Baker	1.00	.45
❑ 62	Larry Walker	1.50	.70
❑ 63	Travis Chapman	1.00	.45
❑ 64	Mike Maroth	1.00	.45
❑ 65	Josh Beckett	1.50	.70
❑ 66	Ivan Rodriguez	2.50	1.10
❑ 67	Brad Penny	1.00	.45
❑ 68	A.J. Burnett	1.00	.45
❑ 69	Craig Biggio	1.50	.70
❑ 70	Roy Oswalt	1.00	.45

❑ 71 Jason Lane 1.00 .45
❑ 72 Nolan Ryan Astros 8.00 3.60
❑ 73 Wade Miller 1.00 .45
❑ 74 Richard Hidalgo 1.00 .45
❑ 75 Jeff Bagwell 1.50 .70
❑ 76 Lance Berkman 1.00 .45
❑ 77 Rodrigo Rosario 1.00 .45
❑ 78 Jeff Kent 1.00 .45
❑ 79 John Buck 1.00 .45
❑ 80 Angel Berroa 1.00 .45
❑ 81 Mike Sweeney 1.00 .45
❑ 82 Mac Suzuki 1.00 .45
❑ 83 Alexis Gomez 1.00 .45
❑ 84 Carlos Beltran 1.00 .45
❑ 85 Runelvys Hernandez 1.00 .45
❑ 86 Hideo Nomo 2.50 1.10
❑ 87 Paul Lo Duca 1.00 .45
❑ 88 Cesar Izturis 1.00 .45
❑ 89 Kazuhisa Ishii 1.00 .45
❑ 90 Shawn Green 1.00 .45
❑ 91 Joe Thurston 1.00 .45
❑ 92 Adrian Beltre 1.00 .45
❑ 93 Kevin Brown 1.00 .45
❑ 94 Richie Sexson 1.00 .45
❑ 95 Ben Sheets 1.00 .45
❑ 96 Takahito Nomura 1.00 .45
❑ 97 Geoff Jenkins 1.00 .45
❑ 98 Bill Hall 1.00 .45
❑ 99 Torii Hunter 1.00 .45
❑ 100 A.J. Pierzynski 1.00 .45
❑ 101 Michael Cuddyer 1.00 .45
❑ 102 Jose Morban 1.00 .45
❑ 103 Brad Radke 1.00 .45
❑ 104 Jacque Jones 1.00 .45
❑ 105 Eric Milton 1.00 .45
❑ 106 Joe Mays 1.00 .45
❑ 107 Adam Johnson 1.00 .45
❑ 108 Javier Vazquez 1.00 .45
❑ 109 Vladimir Guerrero 2.50 1.10
❑ 110 Jose Vidro 1.00 .45
❑ 111 Michael Barrett 1.00 .45
❑ 112 Orlando Cabrera 1.00 .45
❑ 113 Tom Glavine 2.50 1.10
❑ 114 Roberto Alomar 2.50 1.10
❑ 115 Tsuyoshi Shinjo 1.00 .45
❑ 116 Cliff Floyd 1.00 .45
❑ 117 Mike Piazza 4.00 1.80
❑ 118 Al Leiter 1.00 .45
❑ 119 Don Mattingly 6.00 2.70
❑ 120 Roger Clemens 5.00 2.20
❑ 121 Derek Jeter 6.00 2.70
❑ 122 Alfonso Soriano 2.50 1.10
❑ 123 Drew Henson 1.00 .45
❑ 124 Brandon Claussen 1.00 .45
❑ 125 Christian Parker 1.00 .45
❑ 126 Jason Giambi 2.50 1.10
❑ 127 Mike Mussina 2.50 1.10
❑ 128 Bernie Williams 1.50 .70
❑ 129 Jason Anderson 1.00 .45
❑ 130 Nick Johnson 1.00 .45
❑ 131 Jorge Posada 1.50 .70
❑ 132 Andy Pettitte 1.50 .70
❑ 133 Barry Zito 2.50 1.10
❑ 134 Miguel Tejada 1.00 .45
❑ 135 Eric Chavez 1.00 .45
❑ 136 Tim Hudson 1.00 .45
❑ 137 Mark Mulder 1.00 .45
❑ 138 Terrence Long 1.00 .45
❑ 139 Mark Ellis 1.00 .45
❑ 140 Jim Thome 2.50 1.10
❑ 141 Pat Burrell 1.00 .45
❑ 142 Marlon Byrd 1.00 .45
❑ 143 Bobby Abreu 1.00 .45
❑ 144 Brandon Duckworth 1.00 .45
❑ 145 Robert Person 1.00 .45
❑ 146 Anderson Machado 1.00 .45
❑ 147 Aramis Ramirez 1.00 .45
❑ 148 Jack Wilson 1.00 .45
❑ 149 Carlos Rivera 1.00 .45
❑ 150 Jose Castillo 1.00 .45
❑ 151 Walter Young 1.00 .45
❑ 152 Brian Giles 1.00 .45
❑ 153 Jason Kendall 1.00 .45
❑ 154 Ryan Klesko 1.00 .45
❑ 155 Mike Rivera 1.00 .45
❑ 156 Sean Burroughs 1.00 .45
❑ 157 Brian Lawrence 1.00 .45
❑ 158 Xavier Nady 1.00 .45
❑ 159 Dennis Tankersley 1.00 .45
❑ 160 Phil Nevin 1.00 .45
❑ 161 Barry Bonds 6.00 2.70
❑ 162 Kenny Lofton 1.00 .45
❑ 163 Rich Aurilia 1.00 .45
❑ 164 Ichiro Suzuki 5.00 2.20
❑ 165 Edgar Martinez 1.50 .70
❑ 166 Chris Snelling 1.00 .45
❑ 167 Rafael Soriano 1.00 .45
❑ 168 John Olerud 1.00 .45
❑ 169 Bret Boone 1.00 .45
❑ 170 Freddy Garcia 1.00 .45
❑ 171 Aaron Sele 1.00 .45
❑ 172 Kazuhiro Sasaki 1.00 .45
❑ 173 Albert Pujols 5.00 2.20
❑ 174 Scott Rolen 1.50 .70
❑ 175 So Taguchi 1.00 .45
❑ 176 Jim Edmonds 1.00 .45
❑ 177 Edgar Renteria 1.00 .45
❑ 178 J.D. Drew 1.00 .45
❑ 179 Antonio Perez 1.00 .45
❑ 180 Dewon Brazelton 1.00 .45
❑ 181 Aubrey Huff 1.00 .45
❑ 182 Toby Hall 1.00 .45
❑ 183 Ben Grieve 1.00 .45
❑ 184 Joe Kennedy 1.00 .45
❑ 185 Alex Rodriguez 5.00 2.20
❑ 186 Rafael Palmeiro 1.50 .70
❑ 187 Hank Blalock 1.50 .70
❑ 188 Mark Teixeira 1.50 .70
❑ 189 Juan Gonzalez 2.50 1.10
❑ 190 Kevin Mench 1.00 .45
❑ 191 Nolan Ryan Rgr 8.00 3.60
❑ 192 Doug Davis 1.00 .45
❑ 193 Eric Hinske 1.00 .45
❑ 194 Vinny Chulk 1.00 .45
❑ 195 Alexis Rios 1.00 .45
❑ 196 Carlos Delgado 1.00 .45
❑ 197 Shannon Stewart 1.00 .45
❑ 198 Josh Phelps 1.00 .45
❑ 199 Vernon Wells 1.00 .45
❑ 200 Roy Halladay 1.00 .45
❑ 201 Babe Ruth RET 20.00 9.00
❑ 202 Lou Gehrig RET 15.00 6.75
❑ 203 Jackie Robinson RET 15.00 6.75
❑ 204 Ty Cobb RET 15.00 6.75
❑ 205 Thurman Munson RET 10.00 4.50
❑ 206 Prentice Redman NG AU RC 10.00 4.50
❑ 207 Craig Brazell NG AU RC 15.00 6.75
❑ 208 Nook Logan NG AU RC 10.00 4.50
❑ 209 Hong-Chih Kuo NG AU RC 25.00 11.00
❑ 210 Matt Kata NG AU RC 15.00 6.75
❑ 211 C.Wang NG AU RC 40.00 18.00
❑ 212 Alej Machado NG AU RC 10.00 4.50
❑ 213 Mike Hessman NG AU RC 10.00 4.50
❑ 214 Franc Rosario NG AU RC 10.00 4.50
❑ 215 Pedro Liriano NG AU 10.00 4.50
❑ 216 J.Bonderman NG AU RC 20.00 9.00
❑ 217 Oscar Villarreal NG AU RC 10.00 4.50
❑ 218 Arnie Munoz NG AU RC 10.00 4.50
❑ 219 Tim Olson NG AU RC 15.00 6.75
❑ 220 J.Contreras NG AU/100 RC 50.00 22.00
❑ 221 Franc Cruceta NG AU RC 10.00 4.50
❑ 222 John Webb NG AU 10.00 4.50
❑ 223 Phil Seibel NG AU RC 10.00 4.50
❑ 224 Aaron Looper NG AU RC 10.00 4.50
❑ 225 Brian Stokes NG AU RC 10.00 4.50
❑ 226 Guillermo Quiroz NG AU RC 15.00 6.75
❑ 227 Fern Cabrera NG AU RC 15.00 6.75
❑ 228 Josh Hall NG AU RC 15.00 6.75
❑ 229 Diego Markwell NG AU RC 10.00 4.50
❑ 230 Andrew Brown NG AU RC 10.00 4.50
❑ 231 Doug Waechter NG AU RC 15.00 6.75
❑ 232 Felix Sanchez NG AU RC 10.00 4.50
❑ 233 Gerardo Garcia NG AU 10.00 4.50
❑ 234 Matt Bruback NG AU RC 10.00 4.50
❑ 235 Michel Hernandez NG AU RC 10.00 4.50
❑ 236 Rett Johnson NG AU RC 15.00 6.75
❑ 237 Ryan Cameron NG AU RC 10.00 4.50
❑ 238 Rob Hammock NG AU RC 15.00 6.75
❑ 239 Clint Barmes NG AU RC 15.00 6.75
❑ 240 Brandon Webb NG AU RC 50.00 22.00
❑ 241 Jon Leicester NG AU RC 10.00 4.50
❑ 242 Shane Bazzell NG AU RC 10.00 4.50
❑ 243 Joe Valentine NG AU RC 10.00 4.50
❑ 244 Josh Stewart NG AU RC 10.00 4.50
❑ 245 Pete LaForest NG AU RC 15.00 6.75
❑ 246 Shane Victorino NG AU RC 10.00 4.50
❑ 247 Terrmel Sledge NG AU RC 15.00 6.75
❑ 248 Lew Ford NG AU RC 15.00 6.75
❑ 249 Todd Wellemeyer NG AU RC 15.00 6.75
❑ 250 Hideki Matsui NG RC 30.00 13.50
❑ 251 Adam Loewen NG RC -
❑ 252 Dan Haren NG RC -
❑ 253 Dontrelle Willis NG -
❑ 254 Ramon Nivar NG RC -
❑ 255 Chad Gaudin NG RC -
❑ 256 Kevin Correia NG RC -
❑ 257 Rickie Weeks NG RC -
❑ 258 Ryan Wagner NG RC -
❑ 259 Delmon Young NG RC -

2001 Leaf Limited

	Nm-Mt	Ex-Mt
COMP.SET w/o SP'S (150)	100.00	30.00
COMMON CARD (1-150)	1.00	.30
COMMON LUM/500 (151-200)	10.00	3.00
COMMON LUM/250 (151-200)	15.00	4.50
COMMON LUM/100 (151-200)	40.00	12.00
COMMON (201-250)	6.00	1.80
COMMON (251-300)	8.00	2.40
COMMON (301-325)	15.00	4.50
COMMON BASE (326-375)	25.00	7.50
COMMON BAT (326-375)	10.00	3.00
COMMON HAT (326-375)	40.00	12.00
COMMON JSY (326-375)	10.00	3.00
COMMON PANTS (326-375)	10.00	3.00
COMMON SPIKES (326-375)	40.00	12.00

❑ 1 Curt Schilling 1.50 .45
❑ 2 Craig Biggio 1.50 .45
❑ 3 Brian Giles 1.00 .30
❑ 4 Scott Brosius 1.00 .30
❑ 5 Barry Larkin 2.50 .75
❑ 6 Bartolo Colon 1.00 .30
❑ 7 John Olerud 1.00 .30
❑ 8 Cal Ripken 8.00 2.40
❑ 9 Moises Alou 1.00 .30
❑ 10 Barry Zito 2.50 .75
❑ 11 Ken Griffey Jr. 4.00 1.20
❑ 12 Garret Anderson 1.00 .30
❑ 13 Andy Pettitte 1.50 .45
❑ 14 Jim Edmonds 1.00 .30
❑ 15 Tom Glavine 2.50 .75
❑ 16 Jose Canseco 2.50 .75
❑ 17 Fred McGriff 1.50 .45
❑ 18 Robin Ventura 1.00 .30
❑ 19 Tony Gwynn 3.00 .90
❑ 20 Jeff Cirillo 1.00 .30
❑ 21 Brad Radke 1.00 .30
❑ 22 Ellis Burks 1.00 .30
❑ 23 Scott Rolen 1.50 .45
❑ 24 Rickey Henderson 4.00 1.20
❑ 25 Edgar Martinez 1.50 .45
❑ 26 Kerry Wood 2.50 .75
❑ 27 Al Leiter 1.00 .30
❑ 28 Jose Cruz Jr. 1.00 .30
❑ 29 Sean Casey 1.00 .30
❑ 30 Eric Chavez 1.00 .30
❑ 31 Jarrod Washburn 1.00 .30
❑ 32 Gary Sheffield 1.00 .30
❑ 33 Jermaine Dye 1.00 .30

❑ 34 Bernie Williams 1.50 .45
❑ 35 Tony Armas Jr. 1.00 .30
❑ 36 Carlos Beltran 1.00 .30
❑ 37 Geoff Jenkins 1.00 .30
❑ 38 Shawn Green 1.00 .30
❑ 39 Ryan Klesko 1.00 .30
❑ 40 Richie Sexson 1.00 .30
❑ 41 Pat Burrell 1.00 .30
❑ 42 J.D. Drew 1.00 .30
❑ 43 Larry Walker 1.50 .45
❑ 44 Andres Galarraga 1.00 .30
❑ 45 Tino Martinez 1.50 .45
❑ 46 Rafael Furcal 1.00 .30
❑ 47 Cristian Guzman 1.00 .30
❑ 48 Omar Vizquel 1.00 .30
❑ 49 Bret Boone 1.00 .30
❑ 50 Wade Miller 1.00 .30
❑ 51 Eric Milton 1.00 .30
❑ 52 Gabe Kapler 1.00 .30
❑ 53 Johnny Damon 1.00 .30
❑ 54 Shannon Stewart 1.00 .30
❑ 55 Kenny Lofton 1.00 .30
❑ 56 Raul Mondesi 1.00 .30
❑ 57 Jorge Posada 1.50 .45
❑ 58 Mark Grace 2.50 .75
❑ 59 Robert Fick 1.00 .30
❑ 60 Phil Nevin 1.00 .30
❑ 61 Mike Mussina 2.50 .75
❑ 62 Joe Mays 1.00 .30
❑ 63 Todd Helton 1.50 .45
❑ 64 Tim Hudson 1.00 .30
❑ 65 Manny Ramirez 1.00 .30
❑ 66 Sammy Sosa 4.00 1.20
❑ 67 Darin Erstad 1.00 .30
❑ 68 Roberto Alomar 2.50 .75
❑ 69 Jeff Bagwell 1.50 .45
❑ 70 Mark McGwire 6.00 1.80
❑ 71 Jason Giambi 2.50 .75
❑ 72 Cliff Floyd 1.00 .30
❑ 73 Barry Bonds 6.00 1.80
❑ 74 Juan Gonzalez 2.50 .75
❑ 75 Jeremy Giambi 1.00 .30
❑ 76 Carlos Lee 1.00 .30
❑ 77 Randy Johnson 2.50 .75
❑ 78 Frank Thomas 2.50 .75
❑ 79 Carlos Delgado 1.00 .30
❑ 80 Pedro Martinez 2.50 .75
❑ 81 Rusty Greer 1.00 .30
❑ 82 Brian Jordan 1.00 .30
❑ 83 Vladimir Guerrero 2.50 .75
❑ 84 Mike Sweeney 1.00 .30
❑ 85 Jose Vidro 1.00 .30
❑ 86 Paul LoDuca 1.00 .30
❑ 87 Matt Morris 1.00 .30
❑ 88 Adrian Beltre 1.00 .30
❑ 89 Aramis Ramirez 1.00 .30
❑ 90 Derek Jeter 6.00 1.80
❑ 91 Rich Aurilia 1.00 .30
❑ 92 Freddy Garcia 1.00 .30
❑ 93 Preston Wilson 1.00 .30
❑ 94 Greg Maddux 5.00 1.50
❑ 95 Miguel Tejada 1.00 .30
❑ 96 Luis Gonzalez 1.00 .30
❑ 97 Torii Hunter 1.00 .30
❑ 98 Nomar Garciaparra 5.00 1.50
❑ 99 Jamie Moyer 1.00 .30
❑ 100 Javier Vazquez 1.00 .30
❑ 101 Ben Grieve 1.00 .30
❑ 102 Mike Piazza 4.00 1.20
❑ 103 Paul O'Neill 1.50 .45
❑ 104 Terrence Long 1.00 .30
❑ 105 Charles Johnson 1.00 .30
❑ 106 Rafael Palmeiro 1.50 .45
❑ 107 David Cone 1.00 .30
❑ 108 Alex Rodriguez 5.00 1.50
❑ 109 John Burkett 1.00 .30
❑ 110 Chipper Jones 2.50 .75
❑ 111 Ryan Dempster 1.00 .30
❑ 112 Bobby Abreu 1.00 .30
❑ 113 Brad Fullmer 1.00 .30
❑ 114 Kazuhiro Sasaki 1.00 .30
❑ 115 Mariano Rivera 1.50 .45
❑ 116 Edgardo Alfonzo 1.00 .30
❑ 117 Ray Durham 1.00 .30
❑ 118 Richard Hidalgo 1.00 .30
❑ 119 Jeff Weaver 1.00 .30
❑ 120 Paul Konerko 1.00 .30
❑ 121 Jon Lieber 1.00 .30
❑ 122 Mike Hampton 1.00 .30
❑ 123 Mike Cameron 1.00 .30
❑ 124 Kevin Brown 1.00 .30
❑ 125 Doug Mientkiewicz 1.00 .30
❑ 126 Jim Thome 2.50 .75
❑ 127 Corey Koskie 1.00 .30
❑ 128 Trot Nixon 1.00 .30
❑ 129 Darryl Kile 1.00 .30
❑ 130 Ivan Rodriguez 2.50 .75
❑ 131 Carl Everett 1.00 .30
❑ 132 Jeff Kent 1.00 .30
❑ 133 Rondell White 1.00 .30
❑ 134 Chan Ho Park 1.00 .30
❑ 135 Robert Person 1.00 .30
❑ 136 Troy Glaus 1.50 .45
❑ 137 Aaron Sele 1.00 .30
❑ 138 Roger Clemens 5.00 1.50
❑ 139 Tony Clark 1.00 .30
❑ 140 Mark Buehrle 1.00 .30
❑ 141 David Justice 1.00 .30
❑ 142 Magglio Ordonez 1.00 .30
❑ 143 Bobby Higginson 1.00 .30
❑ 144 Hideo Nomo 2.50 .75
❑ 145 Tim Salmon 1.50 .45
❑ 146 Mark Mulder 1.00 .30
❑ 147 Troy Percival 1.00 .30
❑ 148 Lance Berkman 1.00 .30
❑ 149 Russ Ortiz 1.00 .30
❑ 150 Andruw Jones 1.50 .45
❑ 151 Mike Piazza LUM/500 25.00 7.50
❑ 152 M.Ramirez LUM/500 10.00 3.00
❑ 153 B.Williams LUM/500 15.00 4.50
❑ 154 N.Garciaparra LUM/500 30.00 9.00
❑ 155 A.Galarraga LUM/500 10.00 3.00
❑ 156 K.Lofton LUM/500 10.00 3.00
❑ 157 Scott Rolen LUM/250 20.00 6.00
❑ 158 Jim Thome LUM/500 15.00 4.50
❑ 159 Darin Erstad LUM/500 10.00 3.00
❑ 160 G.Anderson LUM/500 10.00 3.00
❑ 161 A.Jones LUM/500 15.00 4.50
❑ 162 J.Gonzalez LUM/500 15.00 4.50
❑ 163 R.Palmeiro LUM/500 15.00 4.50
❑ 164 M.Ordonez LUM/500 10.00 3.00
❑ 165 Jeff Bagwell LUM/250 20.00 6.00
❑ 166 Eric Chavez LUM/500 10.00 3.00
❑ 167 Brian Giles LUM/500 10.00 3.00
❑ 168 A.Beltre LUM/500 10.00 3.00
❑ 169 T.Gwynn LUM/500 20.00 6.00
❑ 170 S.Green LUM/500 10.00 3.00
❑ 171 Todd Helton LUM/500 15.00 4.50
❑ 172 Troy Glaus LUM/100 40.00 12.00
❑ 173 L.Berkman LUM/500 10.00 3.00
❑ 174 I.Rodriguez LUM/500 15.00 4.50
❑ 175 Sean Casey LUM/500 10.00 3.00
❑ 176 A.Ramirez LUM/100 40.00 12.00
❑ 177 J.D. Drew LUM/500 10.00 3.00
❑ 178 Barry Bonds LUM/250 40.00 12.00
❑ 179 Barry Larkin LUM/500 15.00 4.50
❑ 180 Cal Ripken LUM/500 50.00 15.00
❑ 181 F.Thomas LUM/500 15.00 4.50
❑ 182 Craig Biggio LUM/250 20.00 6.00
❑ 183 Carlos Lee LUM/500 10.00 3.00
❑ 184 C. Jones LUM/500 15.00 4.50
❑ 185 Miguel Tejada LUM/250 15.00 4.50
❑ 186 Jose Vidro LUM/500 10.00 3.00
❑ 187 T.Long LUM/500 10.00 3.00
❑ 188 Moises Alou LUM/500 10.00 3.00
❑ 189 Trot Nixon LUM/500 10.00 3.00
❑ 190 S.Stewart LUM/500 10.00 3.00
❑ 191 Ryan Klesko LUM/500 10.00 3.00
❑ 192 C.Beltran LUM/500 10.00 3.00
❑ 193 V.Guerrero LUM/500 15.00 4.50
❑ 194 E.Martinez LUM/500 15.00 4.50
❑ 195 L.Gonzalez LUM/500 10.00 3.00
❑ 196 R.Hidalgo LUM/500 10.00 3.00
❑ 197 R.Alomar LUM/500 15.00 4.50
❑ 198 M.Sweeney LUM/100 40.00 12.00
❑ 199 B.Abreu LUM/250 15.00 4.50
❑ 200 Cliff Floyd LUM/500 10.00 3.00
❑ 201 Jackson Melian RC 6.00 1.80
❑ 202 Jason Jennings 6.00 1.80
❑ 203 Toby Hall 6.00 1.80
❑ 204 Jason Karnuth RC 6.00 1.80
❑ 205 Jason Smith RC 6.00 1.80
❑ 206 Mike Maroth RC 6.00 1.80
❑ 207 Sean Douglass RC 6.00 1.80
❑ 208 Adam Johnson 6.00 1.80
❑ 209 Luke Hudson RC 6.00 1.80
❑ 210 Nick Maness RC 6.00 1.80
❑ 211 Les Walrond RC 6.00 1.80
❑ 212 Travis Phelps RC 6.00 1.80
❑ 213 Carlos Garcia RC 6.00 1.80
❑ 214 Bill Ortega RC 6.00 1.80
❑ 215 Gene Altman RC 6.00 1.80
❑ 216 Nate Frese RC 6.00 1.80
❑ 217 Bob File RC 6.00 1.80
❑ 218 Steve Green RC 6.00 1.80
❑ 219 Kris Keller RC 6.00 1.80
❑ 220 Matt White RC 6.00 1.80
❑ 221 Nate Teut RC 6.00 1.80
❑ 222 Nick Johnson 6.00 1.80
❑ 223 Jeremy Fikac RC 6.00 1.80
❑ 224 Abraham Nunez 6.00 1.80
❑ 225 Mike Penney RC 6.00 1.80
❑ 226 Roy Smith RC 6.00 1.80
❑ 227 Tim Christman RC 6.00 1.80
❑ 228 Carlos Pena 6.00 1.80
❑ 229 Joe Beimel RC 6.00 1.80
❑ 230 Mike Koplove RC 6.00 1.80
❑ 231 Scott MacRae RC 6.00 1.80
❑ 232 Kyle Lohse RC 8.00 2.40
❑ 233 Jerrod Riggan RC 6.00 1.80
❑ 234 Scott Podsednik RC 30.00 9.00
❑ 235 Winston Abreu RC 6.00 1.80
❑ 236 Ryan Freel RC 6.00 1.80
❑ 237 Ken Vining RC 6.00 1.80
❑ 238 Bret Prinz RC 6.00 1.80
❑ 239 Paul Phillips RC 6.00 1.80
❑ 240 Josh Fogg RC 6.00 1.80
❑ 241 Saul Rivera RC 6.00 1.80
❑ 242 Esix Snead RC 6.00 1.80
❑ 243 John Grabow RC 6.00 1.80
❑ 244 Tony Cogan RC 6.00 1.80
❑ 245 Pedro Santana RC 6.00 1.80
❑ 246 Jack Cust 6.00 1.80
❑ 247 Joe Crede 6.00 1.80
❑ 248 Juan Moreno RC 6.00 1.80
❑ 249 Kevin Joseph RC 6.00 1.80
❑ 250 Scott Stewart RC 6.00 1.80
❑ 251 Rob Mackowiak RC 8.00 2.40
❑ 252 Luis Pineda RC 8.00 2.40
❑ 253 Bert Snow RC 8.00 2.40
❑ 254 Dustan Mohr RC 8.00 2.40
❑ 255 Justin Kaye RC 8.00 2.40
❑ 256 Chad Paronto RC 8.00 2.40
❑ 257 Nick Punto RC 8.00 2.40
❑ 258 Brian Roberts RC 8.00 2.40
❑ 259 Eric Hinske RC 10.00 3.00
❑ 260 Victor Zambrano RC 8.00 2.40
❑ 261 Juan Pena RC 8.00 2.40
❑ 262 Rick Bauer RC 8.00 2.40
❑ 263 Jorge Julio RC 8.00 2.40
❑ 264 Craig Monroe RC 8.00 2.40
❑ 265 Stubby Clapp RC 8.00 2.40
❑ 266 Martin Vargas RC 8.00 2.40
❑ 267 Josue Perez RC 8.00 2.40
❑ 268 Cody Ransom RC 8.00 2.40
❑ 269 Will Ohman RC 8.00 2.40
❑ 270 Juan Diaz RC 8.00 2.40
❑ 271 Ramon Vazquez RC 8.00 2.40
❑ 272 Grant Balfour RC 8.00 2.40
❑ 273 Ryan Jensen RC 8.00 2.40
❑ 274 Benito Baez RC 8.00 2.40
❑ 275 Angel Santos RC 8.00 2.40
❑ 276 Brian Reith RC 8.00 2.40
❑ 277 Brandon Lyon RC 8.00 2.40
❑ 278 Erik Hiljus RC 8.00 2.40
❑ 279 Brandon Knight RC 8.00 2.40
❑ 280 Jose Acevedo RC 8.00 2.40
❑ 281 Cesar Crespo RC 8.00 2.40
❑ 282 Kevin Olsen RC 8.00 2.40
❑ 283 Duaner Sanchez RC 8.00 2.40
❑ 284 Endy Chavez RC 8.00 2.40
❑ 285 Blaine Neal RC 8.00 2.40
❑ 286 Brett Jodie RC 8.00 2.40
❑ 287 Brad Voyles RC 8.00 2.40
❑ 288 Doug Nickle RC 8.00 2.40
❑ 289 Junior Spivey RC 10.00 3.00
❑ 290 Henry Mateo RC 8.00 2.40
❑ 291 Xavier Nady 8.00 2.40

	Card	Mint	NrMt
❑ 292	Lance Davis RC	8.00	2.40
❑ 293	Willie Harris RC	8.00	2.40
❑ 294	Mark Lukasiewicz RC	8.00	2.40
❑ 295	Ryan Drese RC	8.00	2.40
❑ 296	Morgan Ensberg RC	12.00	3.60
❑ 297	Jose Mieses RC	8.00	2.40
❑ 298	Jason Michaels RC	8.00	2.40
❑ 299	Kris Foster RC	8.00	2.40
❑ 300	J.Duchscherer RC	8.00	2.40
❑ 301	Elpidio Guzman AU RC	15.00	4.50
❑ 302	Cory Aldridge AU RC	15.00	4.50
❑ 303	A.Berroa AU/500 RC	40.00	12.00
❑ 304	Travis Hafner AU RC	20.00	6.00
❑ 305	H.Ramirez AU RC	20.00	6.00
❑ 306	Juan Uribe AU RC	15.00	4.50
❑ 307	M.Prior AU/500 RC	200.00	60.00
❑ 308	B.Larson AU RC	15.00	4.50
❑ 309	N.Neugebauer AU/750	15.00	4.50
❑ 310	Zach Day AU/750 RC	20.00	6.00
❑ 311	Jeremy Owens AU RC	15.00	4.50
❑ 312	D.Brazelton AU/500 RC	15.00	4.50
❑ 313	B.Duckworth AU/750 RC	15.00	4.50
❑ 314	A.Hernandez AU RC	15.00	4.50
❑ 315	M.Teixeira AU/500 RC	100.00	30.00
❑ 316	Brian Rogers AU RC	15.00	4.50
❑ 317	D.Brous AU/750 RC	15.00	4.50
❑ 318	Geronimo Gil AU RC	15.00	4.50
❑ 319	Erick Almonte AU RC	15.00	4.50
❑ 320	Claudio Vargas AU RC	15.00	4.50
❑ 321	Wilkin Ruan AU RC	15.00	4.50
❑ 322	David Williams AU RC	15.00	4.50
❑ 323	Alexis Gomez AU RC	15.00	4.50
❑ 324	Mike Rivera AU RC	15.00	4.50
❑ 325	B.Berger AU RC	15.00	4.50
❑ 326	Keith Ginter Bat/125	40.00	12.00
❑ 327	Brandon Inge Bat/700	10.00	3.00
❑ 328	B.Abernathy Bat/700	10.00	3.00
❑ 329	B.Sylvester Bat/700 RC	10.00	3.00
❑ 330	B.Miadich Jsy/500 RC	10.00	3.00
❑ 331	T.Shinjo Jsy/500 RC	15.00	4.50
❑ 332	E.Valent Spikes/125	40.00	12.00
❑ 333	Dee Brown Jsy/500	10.00	3.00
❑ 334	A.Torres Spikes/125 RC	40.00	12.00
❑ 335	Timo Perez Bat/700	10.00	3.00
❑ 336	C.Izturis Pants/650	10.00	3.00
❑ 337	P.Feliz Spikes/125	40.00	12.00
❑ 338	Jason Hart Bat/200	15.00	4.50
❑ 339	G.Miller Bat/700 RC	10.00	3.00
❑ 340	Eric Munson Bat/700	10.00	3.00
❑ 341	Aubrey Huff Jsy/450	10.00	3.00
❑ 342	W.Caceres Bat/700 RC	10.00	3.00
❑ 343	A.Escobar Pants/650	10.00	3.00
❑ 344	B.Lawrence Bat/700 RC	10.00	3.00
❑ 345	Adam Pettyjohn Pants/650 RC	10.00	3.00
❑ 346	D.Mendez Bat/700 RC	10.00	3.00
❑ 347	Carlos Valderrama Jsy/250 RC	15.00	4.50
❑ 348	C.Parker Pants/650 RC	10.00	3.00
❑ 349	C.Miller Jsy/500 RC	10.00	3.00
❑ 350	M.Cuddyer Jsy/500	10.00	3.00
❑ 351	Adam Dunn Bat/500	30.00	9.00
❑ 352	J.Beckett Pants/650	15.00	4.50
❑ 353	Juan Cruz Jsy/500 RC	10.00	3.00
❑ 354	Ben Sheets Jsy/400	10.00	3.00
❑ 355	Roy Oswalt Bat/100	40.00	12.00
❑ 356	R.Soriano Pants/650 RC	15.00	4.50
❑ 357	R.Rodriguez Pants/650 RC	10.00	3.00
❑ 358	J.Rollins Base/300	25.00	7.50
❑ 359	C.C. Sabathia Jsy/500	10.00	3.00
❑ 360	B.Smith Jsy/500 RC	10.00	3.00
❑ 361	Jose Ortiz Hat/100	40.00	12.00
❑ 362	Marcus Giles Jsy/400	10.00	3.00
❑ 363	J.Wilson Hat/100 RC	40.00	12.00
❑ 364	W.Betemit Hat/100 RC	40.00	12.00
❑ 365	C.Patterson Pants/650	10.00	3.00
❑ 366	J.Gibbons Spikes/125 RC	60.00	18.00
❑ 367	A.Pujols Jsy/250 RC	150.00	45.00
❑ 368	J.Kennedy Hat/100 RC	40.00	12.00
❑ 369	A.Soriano Hat/100	60.00	18.00
❑ 370	D.James Pants/650 RC	10.00	3.00
❑ 371	J.Towers Pants/650 RC	10.00	3.00
❑ 372	J.Affeldt Pants/650 RC	10.00	3.00
❑ 373	Tim Redding Jsy/500	10.00	3.00
❑ 374	I.Suzuki Base/100 RC	600.00	180.00
❑ 375	J.Estrada Bat/100 RC	40.00	12.00

2003 Leaf Limited

	MINT	NRMT
COMMON CARD (1-151)	3.00	1.35
1-151 PRINT RUN 999 SERIAL #'d SETS	-	
COMMON CARD (151-170)	6.00	2.70
151-170 RANDOM INSERTS IN PACKS	-	
151-170 PRINT RUN 399 SERIAL #'d SETS	-	
COMMON AU GU (171-200)	25.00	11.00
AU GU 171-200 PRINT 99 SERIAL #'d SETS	-	
GU 174/199 PRINT RUN 99 SERIAL #'d SETS	-	
COMMON AU (171-200) p/r 99	15.00	6.75
AU 171-200 PRINT B/WN 49-99 COPIES PER	-	
171-200 RANDOM INSERTS IN PACKS	-	
A EQUALS AWAY UNIFORM IMAGE	-	
H EQUALS HOME UNIFORM IMAGE	-	

	Card	Mint	NrMt
❑ 1	Derek Jeter Btg	10.00	4.50
❑ 2	Eric Chavez	3.00	1.35
❑ 3	Alex Rodriguez Rgr A	8.00	3.60
❑ 4	Miguel Tejada Fldg	3.00	1.35
❑ 5	Nomar Garciaparra H	8.00	3.60
❑ 6	Jeff Bagwell H	3.00	1.35
❑ 7	Jim Thome Phils A	4.00	1.80
❑ 8	Pat Burrell w/Bat	3.00	1.35
❑ 9	Albert Pujols H	8.00	3.60
❑ 10	Juan Gonzalez Rgr Btg	4.00	1.80
❑ 11	Shawn Green Jays	3.00	1.35
❑ 12	Craig Biggio H	3.00	1.35
❑ 13	Chipper Jones H	4.00	1.80
❑ 14	H.Nomo Dodgers	4.00	1.80
❑ 15	Vernon Wells	3.00	1.35
❑ 16	Gary Sheffield	3.00	1.35
❑ 17	Barry Larkin	4.00	1.80
❑ 18	Josh Beckett White	3.00	1.35
❑ 19	Edgar Martinez A	3.00	1.35
❑ 20	I.Rodriguez Marlins	4.00	1.80
❑ 21	Jeff Kent Astros	3.00	1.35
❑ 22	Roberto Alomar Mets A	4.00	1.80
❑ 23	Alfonso Soriano A	4.00	1.80
❑ 24	Jim Thome Indians H	4.00	1.80
❑ 25	J.Gonzalez Indians Btg	4.00	1.80
❑ 26	Carlos Beltran	3.00	1.35
❑ 27	S.Green Dodgers H	3.00	1.35
❑ 28	Tim Hudson H	3.00	1.35
❑ 29	Deion Sanders	4.00	1.80
❑ 30	Rafael Palmeiro O's	3.00	1.35
❑ 31	Todd Helton H	3.00	1.35
❑ 32	L.Berkman No Socks	3.00	1.35
❑ 33	M.Mussina Yanks H	4.00	1.80
❑ 34	Kazuhisa Ishii H	3.00	1.35
❑ 35	Pat Burrell Run	3.00	1.35
❑ 36	Miguel Tejada Btg	3.00	1.35
❑ 37	J.Gonzalez Rgr Stand	4.00	1.80
❑ 38	Roberto Alomar Mets H	4.00	1.80
❑ 39	R.Alom Indians Bunt	4.00	1.80
❑ 40	Luis Gonzalez	3.00	1.35
❑ 41	Jorge Posada	3.00	1.35
❑ 42	Mark Mulder Leg	3.00	1.35
❑ 43	Sammy Sosa H	6.00	2.70
❑ 44	Mark Prior H	8.00	3.60
❑ 45	R.Clemens Yanks H	8.00	3.60
❑ 46	Tom Glavine Mets H	4.00	1.80
❑ 47	Mark Teixeira A	3.00	1.35
❑ 48	Manny Ramirez H	3.00	1.35
❑ 49	Frank Thomas Swing	4.00	1.80
❑ 50	Troy Glaus White	3.00	1.35
❑ 51	Andruw Jones H	3.00	1.35
❑ 52	J.Giambi Yanks H	4.00	1.80
❑ 53	Jim Thome Phils H	4.00	1.80
❑ 54	Barry Bonds H	10.00	4.50
❑ 55	R.Palmeiro Rgr A	3.00	1.35
❑ 56	Edgar Martinez H	3.00	1.35
❑ 57	Vladimir Guerrero H	4.00	1.80
❑ 58	Roberto Alomar O's	4.00	1.80
❑ 59	Mike Sweeney	3.00	1.35
❑ 60	Magglio Ordonez A	3.00	1.35
❑ 61	Ken Griffey Jr. Btg	6.00	2.70
❑ 62	Craig Biggio A	3.00	1.35
❑ 63	Greg Maddux H	8.00	3.60
❑ 64	Mike Piazza Mets H	6.00	2.70
❑ 65	T.Glavine Braves A	4.00	1.80
❑ 66	Kerry Wood H	4.00	1.80
❑ 67	Frank Thomas Arms	4.00	1.80
❑ 68	M.Mussina Yanks A	4.00	1.80
❑ 69	Nick Johnson H	3.00	1.35
❑ 70	Bernie Williams H	3.00	1.35
❑ 71	Scott Rolen	3.00	1.35
❑ 72	C.Schill D'backs Leg	3.00	1.35
❑ 73	Adam Dunn A	3.00	1.35
❑ 74	Roy Oswalt A	3.00	1.35
❑ 75	P.Martinez Sox H	4.00	1.80
❑ 76	Tom Glavine Mets A	4.00	1.80
❑ 77	Torii Hunter Swing	3.00	1.35
❑ 78	Austin Kearns	3.00	1.35
❑ 79	R.Johnson D'backs A	4.00	1.80
❑ 80	Bernie Williams A	3.00	1.35
❑ 81	Ichiro Suzuki Btg	8.00	3.60
❑ 82	Kerry Wood A	4.00	1.80
❑ 83	Kazuhisa Ishii A	3.00	1.35
❑ 84	R.Johnson Astros	4.00	1.80
❑ 85	Nick Johnson A	3.00	1.35
❑ 86	J.Beckett Pinstripe	3.00	1.35
❑ 87	Curt Schilling Phils	3.00	1.35
❑ 88	Mike Mussina O's	4.00	1.80
❑ 89	P.Martinez Dodgers	4.00	1.80
❑ 90	Barry Zito A	4.00	1.80
❑ 91	Jim Edmonds	3.00	1.35
❑ 92	R.Henderson Sox	6.00	2.70
❑ 93	R.Henderson Padres	6.00	2.70
❑ 94	R.Henderson M's	6.00	2.70
❑ 95	R.Henderson Mets	6.00	2.70
❑ 96	R.Henderson Jays	6.00	2.70
❑ 97	R.Johnson M's Arm Up	4.00	1.80
❑ 98	Mark Grace	4.00	1.80
❑ 99	P.Martinez Expos	4.00	1.80
❑ 100	Hee Seop Choi	3.00	1.35
❑ 101	Ivan Rodriguez Rgr	4.00	1.80
❑ 102	Jeff Kent Giants	3.00	1.35
❑ 103	Hideo Nomo Sox	4.00	1.80
❑ 104	Hideo Nomo Mets	4.00	1.80
❑ 105	Mike Piazza Dodgers	6.00	2.70
❑ 106	T.Glavine Braves H	4.00	1.80
❑ 107	R.Alom Indians Swing	4.00	1.80
❑ 108	Roger Clemens Sox	8.00	3.60
❑ 109	Jason Giambi A's H	4.00	1.80
❑ 110	Jim Thome Indians A	4.00	1.80
❑ 111	Alex Rodriguez M's H	8.00	3.60
❑ 112	J.Gonz Indians Hands	4.00	1.80
❑ 113	Torii Hunter Crouch	3.00	1.35
❑ 114	Roy Oswalt H	3.00	1.35
❑ 115	C.Schill D'backs Throw	3.00	1.35
❑ 116	Magglio Ordonez H	3.00	1.35
❑ 117	R.Palmeiro Rgr H	3.00	1.35
❑ 118	Andruw Jones A	3.00	1.35
❑ 119	Manny Ramirez A	3.00	1.35
❑ 120	Mark Teixeira H	3.00	1.35
❑ 121	Mark Mulder Stance	3.00	1.35
❑ 122	Garret Anderson	3.00	1.35
❑ 123	Tim Hudson A	3.00	1.35
❑ 124	Todd Helton A	3.00	1.35
❑ 125	Troy Glaus Pinstripe	3.00	1.35
❑ 126	Derek Jeter Run	10.00	4.50
❑ 127	Barry Bonds A	10.00	4.50
❑ 128	Greg Maddux A	8.00	3.60
❑ 129	R.Clemens Yanks A	8.00	3.60
❑ 130	Nomar Garciaparra A	8.00	3.60
❑ 131	Mike Piazza Mets A	6.00	2.70
❑ 132	Alex Rodriguez Rgr H	8.00	3.60
❑ 133	Ichiro Suzuki Run	8.00	3.60
❑ 134	R.Johnson D'backs H	4.00	1.80
❑ 135	Sammy Sosa A	6.00	2.70
❑ 136	Ken Griffey Jr. Fldg	6.00	2.70
❑ 137	Alfonso Soriano H	4.00	1.80

❑ 138 J.Giambi Yanks A 4.00 1.80
❑ 139 Albert Pujols A 8.00 3.60
❑ 140 Chipper Jones A 4.00 1.80
❑ 141 Adam Dunn H 3.00 1.35
❑ 142 P.Martinez Sox A.......... 4.00 1.80
❑ 143 Vladimir Guerrero A 4.00 1.80
❑ 144 Mark Prior A 8.00 3.60
❑ 145 Barry Zito H.......... 4.00 1.80
❑ 146 Jeff Bagwell A 3.00 1.35
❑ 147 Lance Berkman Socks.... 3.00 1.35
❑ 148 S.Green Dodgers A 3.00 1.35
❑ 149 Jason Giambi A's A....... 4.00 1.80
❑ 150 R.Johnson M's Arm Out 4.00 1.80
❑ 151 Alex Rodriguez M's A 8.00 3.60
❑ 152 Babe Ruth 15.00 6.75
❑ 153 Ty Cobb 8.00 3.60
❑ 154 Jackie Robinson 8.00 3.60
❑ 155 Lou Gehrig 10.00 4.50
❑ 156 Thurman Munson 8.00 3.60
❑ 157 Roberto Clemente 12.00 5.50
❑ 158 Nolan Ryan Rgr 15.00 6.75
❑ 159 Nolan Ryan Angels 15.00 6.75
❑ 160 Nolan Ryan Astros....... 15.00 6.75
❑ 161 Cal Ripken.......... 20.00 9.00
❑ 162 Don Mattingly 15.00 6.75
❑ 163 Stan Musial.......... 10.00 4.50
❑ 164 Tony Gwynn 8.00 3.60
❑ 165 Yogi Berra.......... 6.00 2.70
❑ 166 Johnny Bench 6.00 2.70
❑ 167 Mike Schmidt 12.00 5.50
❑ 168 George Brett 15.00 6.75
❑ 169 Ryne Sandberg 12.00 5.50
❑ 170 Ernie Banks.......... 6.00 2.70
❑ 171 J.Bonder A PH AU Jsy RC 40.00 18.00
❑ 172 J.Contreras A PH AU RC 80.00 36.00
❑ 173 C.Wang PH AU RC 80.00 36.00
❑ 174 H.Matsui H PH Base RC 50.00 22.00
❑ 175 H.Kuo PH AU Bat RC.... 50.00 22.00
❑ 176 B.Webb A PH AU Bat RC 60.00 27.00
❑ 177 Rich Fischer PH AU RC 15.00 6.75
❑ 178 R.Hammock PH AU Bat RC 30.00 13.50
❑ 179 T.Welle Stance PH AU/49 RC 25.00 11.00
❑ 180 P.Redman PH AU Bat RC 25.00 11.00
❑ 181 Nook Logan PH AU RC 15.00 6.75
❑ 182 Craig Brazell PH AU RC 20.00 9.00
❑ 183 Tim Olson PH AU Bat RC 30.00 13.50
❑ 184 Matt Kata PH AU Bat RC 30.00 13.50
❑ 185 Alej Machado PH AU RC 15.00 6.75
❑ 186 Mike Hessman PH AU RC 15.00 6.75
❑ 187 Oscar Villarreal PH AU RC 15.00 6.75
❑ 188 G.Quiroz PH AU Bat RC 30.00 13.50
❑ 189 M.Hernandez PH AU RC 15.00 6.75
❑ 190 C.Barmes H PH AU Bat RC 30.00 13.50
❑ 191 P.LaForest PH AU Bat RC 25.00 11.00
❑ 192 Adam Loewen PH AU RC 120.00 55.00
❑ 193 T.Sledge PH AU Bat RC 25.00 11.00
❑ 194 Lew Ford PH AU Bat RC 25.00 11.00
❑ 195 T.Welle Throw PH AU/49 RC 25.00 11.00
❑ 196 C.Barmes A PH AU Bat RC 30.00 13.50
❑ 197 J.Bonder H PH AU Jsy RC 40.00 18.00
❑ 198 B.Webb H PH AU Jsy RC 60.00 27.00
❑ 199 H.Matsui A PH Base RC 50.00 22.00
❑ 200 J.Contreras H PH AU RC 80.00 36.00
❑ 201 Delmon Young PH AU .. -
❑ 202 Rickie Weeks PH AU...... -
❑ 203 Edwin Jackson PH AU .. -
❑ 204 Dan Haren PH AU.......... -
❑ 205 Chad Cordero PH .... -

1998 Leaf Rookies and Stars

	Nm-Mt	Ex-Mt
COMPLETE SET (339)	400.00	120.00
COMP.SET w/o SP's (200)	25.00	7.50
COMMON (1-130/231-300)	.30	.09
COMMON (131-190)	1.00	.30
COMMON (191-230)	2.00	.60
COMMON RC (191-230)	2.50	.75
COMMON (301-339)	2.50	.75
COMMON RC (301-339)	4.00	1.20

❑ 2 Roberto Alomar .... .75 .23
❑ 3 Randy Johnson .... .75 .23
❑ 4 Manny Ramirez .... .30 .09

❑ 5 Paul Molitor .... .50 .15
❑ 6 Mike Mussina .... .75 .23
❑ 7 Jim Thome .... .75 .23
❑ 8 Tino Martinez .... .50 .15
❑ 9 Gary Sheffield .... .30 .09
❑ 10 Chuck Knoblauch .... .30 .09
❑ 11 Bernie Williams.......... .50 .15
❑ 12 Tim Salmon.......... .50 .15
❑ 13 Sammy Sosa.......... 1.25 .35
❑ 14 Wade Boggs .... .50 .15
❑ 15 Andres Galarraga.......... .30 .09
❑ 16 Pedro Martinez .... .75 .23
❑ 17 David Justice.......... .30 .09
❑ 18 Chan Ho Park .... .30 .09
❑ 19 Jay Buhner .... .30 .09
❑ 20 Ryan Klesko .... .30 .09
❑ 21 Barry Larkin.......... .75 .23
❑ 22 Will Clark .... .75 .23
❑ 23 Raul Mondesi .... .30 .09
❑ 24 Rickey Henderson .... 1.25 .35
❑ 25 Jim Edmonds .... .30 .09
❑ 26 Ken Griffey Jr. .... 1.25 .35
❑ 27 Frank Thomas .... .75 .23
❑ 28 Cal Ripken.......... 2.50 .75
❑ 29 Alex Rodriguez .... 1.50 .45
❑ 30 Mike Piazza.......... 1.25 .35
❑ 31 Greg Maddux .... 1.50 .45
❑ 32 Chipper Jones.......... .75 .23
❑ 33 Tony Gwynn .... 1.00 .30
❑ 34 Derek Jeter .... 2.00 .60
❑ 35 Jeff Bagwell.......... .50 .15
❑ 36 Juan Gonzalez.......... .75 .23
❑ 37 Nomar Garciaparra .... 1.50 .45
❑ 38 Andruw Jones .... .50 .15
❑ 39 Hideo Nomo .... .75 .23
❑ 40 Roger Clemens .... 1.50 .45
❑ 41 Mark McGwire.......... 2.00 .60
❑ 42 Scott Rolen .... .50 .15
❑ 43 Vladimir Guerrero .... .75 .23
❑ 44 Barry Bonds .... 2.00 .60
❑ 45 Darin Erstad .... .30 .09
❑ 46 Albert Belle .... .30 .09
❑ 47 Kenny Lofton.......... .30 .09
❑ 48 Mo Vaughn .... .30 .09
❑ 49 Ivan Rodriguez .... .75 .23
❑ 50 Jose Cruz Jr. .... .30 .09
❑ 51 Tony Clark.......... .30 .09
❑ 52 Larry Walker .... .50 .15
❑ 53 Mark Grace .... .75 .23
❑ 54 Edgar Martinez .... .50 .15
❑ 55 Fred McGriff .... .50 .15
❑ 56 Rafael Palmeiro.......... .50 .15
❑ 57 Matt Williams .... .30 .09
❑ 58 Craig Biggio .... .50 .15
❑ 59 Ken Caminiti .... .30 .09
❑ 60 Jose Canseco .... .75 .23
❑ 61 Brady Anderson.......... .30 .09
❑ 62 Moises Alou .... .30 .09
❑ 63 Justin Thompson .... .30 .09
❑ 64 John Smoltz .... .50 .15
❑ 65 Carlos Delgado .... .30 .09
❑ 66 J.T. Snow .... .30 .09
❑ 67 Jason Giambi .... .75 .23
❑ 68 Garret Anderson .... .30 .09
❑ 69 Rondell White .... .30 .09
❑ 70 Eric Karros .... .30 .09
❑ 71 Javier Lopez .... .30 .09
❑ 72 Pat Hentgen.......... .30 .09
❑ 73 Dante Bichette.......... .30 .09
❑ 74 Charles Johnson.......... .30 .09
❑ 75 Tom Glavine .... .75 .23
❑ 76 Rusty Greer .... .30 .09
❑ 77 Travis Fryman .... .30 .09
❑ 78 Todd Hundley .... .30 .09
❑ 79 Ray Lankford.......... .30 .09
❑ 80 Denny Neagle .... .30 .09
❑ 81 Henry Rodriguez .... .30 .09
❑ 82 Sandy Alomar Jr. .... .30 .09
❑ 83 Robin Ventura .... .30 .09
❑ 84 John Olerud .... .30 .09
❑ 85 Omar Vizquel.......... .30 .09
❑ 86 Darren Dreifort .... .30 .09
❑ 87 Kevin Brown .... .30 .09
❑ 88 Curt Schilling .... .50 .15
❑ 89 Francisco Cordova .... .30 .09
❑ 90 Brad Radke .... .30 .09
❑ 91 David Cone .... .30 .09
❑ 92 Paul O'Neill.......... .50 .15
❑ 93 Vinny Castilla .... .30 .09
❑ 94 Marquis Grissom .... .30 .09
❑ 95 Brian L.Hunter.......... .30 .09
❑ 96 Kevin Appier .... .30 .09
❑ 97 Bobby Bonilla .... .30 .09
❑ 98 Eric Young .... .30 .09
❑ 99 Jason Kendall .... .30 .09
❑ 100 Shawn Green.......... .30 .09
❑ 101 Edgardo Alfonzo .... .30 .09
❑ 102 Alan Benes .... .30 .09
❑ 103 Bobby Higginson .... .30 .09
❑ 104 Todd Greene .... .30 .09
❑ 105 Jose Guillen .... .30 .09
❑ 106 Neifi Perez.......... .30 .09
❑ 107 Edgar Renteria.......... .30 .09
❑ 108 Chris Stynes .... .30 .09
❑ 109 Todd Walker .... .30 .09
❑ 110 Brian Jordan .... .30 .09
❑ 111 Joe Carter .... .30 .09
❑ 112 Ellis Burks.......... .30 .09
❑ 113 Brett Tomko.......... .30 .09
❑ 114 Mike Cameron.......... .30 .09
❑ 115 Shannon Stewart.......... .30 .09
❑ 116 Kevin Orie .... .30 .09
❑ 117 Brian Giles .... .30 .09
❑ 118 Hideki Irabu.......... .30 .09
❑ 119 Delino DeShields .... .30 .09
❑ 120 David Segui.......... .30 .09
❑ 121 Dustin Hermanson .... .30 .09
❑ 122 Kevin Young .... .30 .09
❑ 123 Jay Bell .... .30 .09
❑ 124 Doug Glanville .... .30 .09
❑ 125 John Roskos RC .... .30 .09
❑ 126 Damon Hollins .... .30 .09
❑ 127 Matt Stairs.......... .30 .09
❑ 128 Cliff Floyd .... .30 .09
❑ 129 Derek Bell .... .30 .09
❑ 130 Darryl Strawberry .... .50 .15
❑ 131 Ken Griffey Jr. PT SP...... 4.00 1.20
❑ 132 Tim Salmon PT SP .... 1.50 .45
❑ 133 M.Ramirez PT SP .... 1.00 .30
❑ 134 Paul Konerko PT SP ...... 1.00 .30
❑ 135 Frank Thomas PT SP...... 2.50 .75
❑ 136 Todd Helton PT SP ...... 1.50 .45
❑ 137 Larry Walker PT SP...... 1.50 .45
❑ 138 Mo Vaughn PT SP.......... 1.00 .30
❑ 139 Travis Lee PT SP.......... 1.00 .30
❑ 140 Ivan Rodriguez PT SP .... 2.50 .75
❑ 141 Ben Grieve PT SP .... 1.00 .30
❑ 142 Brad Fullmer PT SP.......... 1.00 .30
❑ 143 Alex Rodriguez PT SP 5.00 1.50
❑ 144 Mike Piazza PT SP 4.00 1.20
❑ 145 Greg Maddux PT SP 5.00 1.50
❑ 146 Chipper Jones PT SP .... 2.50 .75
❑ 147 Kenny Lofton PT SP ...... 1.00 .30
❑ 148 Albert Belle PT SP.......... 1.00 .30
❑ 149 Barry Bonds PT SP 6.00 1.80
❑ 150 V.Guerrero PT SP .... 2.50 .75
❑ 151 Tony Gwynn PT SP.......... 3.00 .90
❑ 152 Derek Jeter PT SP 6.00 1.80
❑ 153 Jeff Bagwell PT SP .... 1.50 .45
❑ 154 Juan Gonzalez PT SP .... 2.50 .75
❑ 155 N.Garciaparra PT SP 5.00 1.50
❑ 156 Andruw Jones PT SP...... 1.50 .45
❑ 157 Hideo Nomo PT SP .... 2.50 .75
❑ 158 Roger Clemens PT SP.... 5.00 1.50

❑ 159 Mark McGwire PT SP 6.00 1.80
❑ 160 Scott Rolen PT SP 1.50 .45
❑ 161 Travis Lee TLU SP 1.00 .30
❑ 162 Ben Grieve TLU SP 1.00 .30
❑ 163 Jose Guillen TLU SP 1.00 .30
❑ 164 Mike Piazza TLU SP 4.00 1.20
❑ 165 Kevin Appier TLU SP 1.00 .30
❑ 166 M.Grissom TLU SP 1.00 .30
❑ 167 Rusty Greer TLU SP 1.00 .30
❑ 168 Ken Caminiti TLU SP 1.00 .30
❑ 169 Craig Biggio TLU SP 1.50 .45
❑ 170 K.Griffey Jr. TLU SP 4.00 1.20
❑ 171 Larry Walker TLU SP 1.50 .45
❑ 172 Barry Larkin TLU SP 2.50 .75
❑ 173 A.Galarraga TLU SP 1.00 .30
❑ 174 Wade Boggs TLU SP 1.50 .45
❑ 175 Sammy Sosa TLU SP 4.00 1.20
❑ 176 T.Dunwoody TLU SP 1.00 .30
❑ 177 Jim Thome TLU SP 2.50 .75
❑ 178 Paul Molitor TLU SP 1.50 .45
❑ 179 Tony Clark TLU SP 1.00 .30
❑ 180 Jose Cruz Jr. TLU SP 1.00 .30
❑ 181 Darin Erstad TLU SP 1.00 .30
❑ 182 Barry Bonds TLU SP 6.00 1.80
❑ 183 Vlad.Guerrero TLU SP 2.50 .75
❑ 184 Scott Rolen TLU SP 1.50 .45
❑ 185 M.McGwire TLU SP 6.00 1.80
❑ 186 N.Garciaparra TLU SP 5.00 1.50
❑ 187 Gary Sheffield TLU SP 1.00 .30
❑ 188 Cal Ripken TLU SP 8.00 2.40
❑ 189 F.Thomas TLU SP 2.50 .75
❑ 190 Andy Pettitte TLU SP 1.50 .45
❑ 191 Paul Konerko SP 2.00 .60
❑ 192 Todd Helton SP 3.00 .90
❑ 193 Mark Kotsay SP 2.00 .60
❑ 194 Brad Fullmer SP 2.00 .60
❑ 195 K.Millwood SP RC 15.00 4.50
❑ 196 David Ortiz SP 2.00 .60
❑ 197 Kerry Wood SP 5.00 1.50
❑ 198 Miguel Tejada SP 3.00 .90
❑ 199 Fernando Tatis SP 2.00 .60
❑ 200 Jaret Wright SP 2.00 .60
❑ 201 Ben Grieve SP 2.00 .60
❑ 202 Travis Lee SP 2.00 .60
❑ 203 Wes Helms SP 2.00 .60
❑ 204 Geoff Jenkins SP 10.00 3.00
❑ 205 Russell Branyan SP 2.00 .60
❑ 206 Esteban Yan SP RC 4.00 1.20
❑ 207 Ben Ford SP RC 2.50 .75
❑ 208 Rich Butler SP RC 2.50 .75
❑ 209 Ryan Jackson SP RC 2.50 .75
❑ 210 A.J. Hinch SP 2.00 .60
❑ 211 M.Ordonez SP RC 40.00 12.00
❑ 212 Dave Dellucci SP RC 2.50 .75
❑ 213 Billy McMillon SP 2.00 .60
❑ 214 Mike Lowell SP RC 15.00 4.50
❑ 215 Todd Erdos SP RC 2.50 .75
❑ 216 C.Mendoza SP RC 2.50 .75
❑ 217 F.Catalanotto SP RC 6.00 1.80
❑ 218 Julio Ramirez SP RC 4.00 1.20
❑ 219 John Halama SP RC 4.00 1.20
❑ 220 Wilson Delgado SP 2.00 .60
❑ 221 Mike Judd SP RC 4.00 1.20
❑ 222 Rolando Arrojo SP RC 4.00 1.20
❑ 223 Jason LaRue SP RC 4.00 1.20
❑ 224 Manny Aybar SP RC 4.00 1.20
❑ 225 Jorge Velandia SP 2.00 .60
❑ 226 Mike Kinkade SP RC 4.00 1.20
❑ 227 Carlos Lee SP RC 12.00 3.60
❑ 228 Bobby Hughes SP 2.00 .60
❑ 229 R.Christenson SP RC 2.50 .75
❑ 230 Masato Yoshii SP RC 6.00 1.80
❑ 231 Richard Hidalgo .30 .09
❑ 232 Rafael Medina .30 .09
❑ 233 Damian Jackson .30 .09
❑ 234 Derek Lowe .30 .09
❑ 235 Mario Valdez .30 .09
❑ 236 Eli Marrero .30 .09
❑ 237 Juan Encarnacion .30 .09
❑ 238 Livan Hernandez .30 .09
❑ 239 Bruce Chen .30 .09
❑ 240 Eric Milton .30 .09
❑ 241 Jason Varitek .30 .09
❑ 242 Scott Elarton .30 .09
❑ 243 Manuel Barrios RC .30 .09
❑ 244 Mike Caruso .30 .09
❑ 245 Tom Evans .30 .09
❑ 246 Pat Cline .30 .09
❑ 247 Matt Clement .30 .09
❑ 248 Karim Garcia .30 .09
❑ 249 Richie Sexson .30 .09
❑ 250 Sidney Ponson .30 .09
❑ 251 Randall Simon .30 .09
❑ 252 Tony Saunders .30 .09
❑ 253 Javier Valentin .30 .09
❑ 254 Danny Clyburn .30 .09
❑ 255 Michael Coleman .30 .09
❑ 256 Hanley Frias RC .30 .09
❑ 257 Miguel Cairo .30 .09
❑ 258 Rob Stanifer RC .30 .09
❑ 259 Lou Collier .30 .09
❑ 260 Abraham Nunez .30 .09
❑ 261 Ricky Ledee .30 .09
❑ 262 Carl Pavano .30 .09
❑ 263 Derrek Lee .30 .09
❑ 264 Jeff Abbott .30 .09
❑ 265 Bob Abreu .30 .09
❑ 266 Bartolo Colon .30 .09
❑ 267 Mike Drumright .30 .09
❑ 268 Daryle Ward .30 .09
❑ 269 Gabe Alvarez .30 .09
❑ 270 Josh Booty .30 .09
❑ 271 Damian Moss .30 .09
❑ 272 Brian Rose .30 .09
❑ 273 Jarrod Washburn .30 .09
❑ 274 Bobby Estalella .30 .09
❑ 275 Enrique Wilson .30 .09
❑ 276 Derrick Gibson .30 .09
❑ 277 Ken Cloude .30 .09
❑ 278 Kevin Witt .30 .09
❑ 279 Donnie Sadler .30 .09
❑ 280 Sean Casey .30 .09
❑ 281 Jacob Cruz .30 .09
❑ 282 Ron Wright .30 .09
❑ 283 Jeremi Gonzalez .30 .09
❑ 284 Desi Relaford .30 .09
❑ 285 Bobby Smith .30 .09
❑ 286 Javier Vazquez .50 .09
❑ 287 Steve Woodard .30 .09
❑ 288 Greg Norton .30 .09
❑ 289 Cliff Politte .30 .09
❑ 290 Felix Heredia .30 .09
❑ 291 Braden Looper .30 .09
❑ 292 Felix Martinez .30 .09
❑ 293 Brian Meadows .30 .09
❑ 294 Edwin Diaz .30 .09
❑ 295 Pat Watkins .30 .09
❑ 296 Marc Pisciotta RC .30 .09
❑ 297 Rick Gorecki .30 .09
❑ 298 DaRond Stovall .30 .09
❑ 299 Andy Larkin .30 .09
❑ 300 Felix Rodriguez .30 .09
❑ 301 Blake Stein SP 2.50 .75
❑ 302 John Rocker SP RC 6.00 1.80
❑ 303 J.Baughman SP RC 4.00 1.20
❑ 304 Jesus Sanchez SP RC 6.00 1.80
❑ 305 Randy Winn SP 2.50 .75
❑ 306 Lou Merloni SP 2.50 .75
❑ 307 Jim Parque SP RC 6.00 1.80
❑ 308 Dennis Reyes SP 2.50 .75
❑ 309 O.Hernandez SP RC 15.00 4.50
❑ 310 Jason Johnson SP 2.50 .75
❑ 311 Torii Hunter SP 2.50 .75
❑ 312 M.Piazza Marlins SP 10.00 3.00
❑ 313 Mike Frank SP RC 4.00 1.20
❑ 314 Troy Glaus SP RC 150.00 45.00
❑ 315 Jin Ho Cho SP RC 6.00 1.80
❑ 316 Ruben Mateo SP RC 6.00 1.80
❑ 317 Ryan Minor SP RC 6.00 1.80
❑ 318 Aramis Ramirez SP 2.50 .75
❑ 319 Adrian Beltre SP 2.50 .75
❑ 320 Matt Anderson SP RC 6.00 1.80
❑ 321 Gabe Kapler SP RC 10.00 3.00
❑ 322 Jeremy Giambi SP RC 6.00 1.80
❑ 323 Carlos Beltran SP 2.50 .75
❑ 324 Dermal Brown SP 2.50 .75
❑ 325 Ben Davis SP 2.50 .75
❑ 326 Eric Chavez SP 4.00 1.20
❑ 327 Bobby Howry SP RC 6.00 1.80
❑ 328 Roy Halladay SP 4.00 1.20
❑ 329 George Lombard SP 2.50 .75
❑ 330 Michael Barrett SP 2.50 .75
❑ 331 F. Seguignol SP RC 4.00 1.20
❑ 332 J.D. Drew SP RC 40.00 12.00
❑ 333 Odalis Perez SP RC 10.00 3.00
❑ 334 Alex Cora SP RC 6.00 1.80
❑ 335 P.Polanco SP RC 6.00 1.80
❑ 336 Armando Rios SP RC 6.00 1.80
❑ 337 Sammy Sosa HR SP 10.00 3.00
❑ 338 Mark McGwire HR SP 15.00 4.50
❑ 339 Sammy Sosa 12.00 3.60
Mark McGwire CL SP

2001 Leaf Rookies and Stars

	Nm-Mt	Ex-Mt
COMP.SET w/o SP'S (100)	20.00	6.00
COMMON CARD (1-100)	.30	.09
COMMON (101-200)	3.00	.90
COMMON (201-300)	10.00	3.00

❑ 1 Alex Rodriguez 1.50 .45
❑ 2 Derek Jeter 2.00 .60
❑ 3 Aramis Ramirez .30 .09
❑ 4 Cliff Floyd .30 .09
❑ 5 Nomar Garciaparra 1.50 .45
❑ 6 Craig Biggio .50 .15
❑ 7 Ivan Rodriguez .75 .23
❑ 8 Cal Ripken 2.50 .75
❑ 9 Fred McGriff .50 .15
❑ 10 Chipper Jones .75 .23
❑ 11 Roberto Alomar .75 .23
❑ 12 Moises Alou .30 .09
❑ 13 Freddy Garcia .30 .09
❑ 14 Bobby Abreu .30 .09
❑ 15 Shawn Green .30 .09
❑ 16 Jason Giambi .75 .23
❑ 17 Todd Helton .50 .15
❑ 18 Robert Fick .30 .09
❑ 19 Tony Gwynn 1.00 .30
❑ 20 Luis Gonzalez .30 .09
❑ 21 Sean Casey .30 .09
❑ 22 Roger Clemens 1.50 .45
❑ 23 Brian Giles .30 .09
❑ 24 Manny Ramirez .30 .09
❑ 25 Barry Bonds 2.00 .60
❑ 26 Richard Hidalgo .30 .09
❑ 27 Vladimir Guerrero .75 .23
❑ 28 Kevin Brown UER .30 .09
Batting headers for stats
❑ 29 Mike Sweeney .30 .09
❑ 30 Ken Griffey Jr. 1.25 .35
❑ 31 Mike Piazza 1.25 .35
❑ 32 Richie Sexson .30 .09
❑ 33 Matt Morris .30 .09
❑ 34 Jorge Posada .50 .15
❑ 35 Eric Chavez .30 .09
❑ 36 Mark Buehrle .30 .09
❑ 37 Jeff Bagwell .50 .15
❑ 38 Curt Schilling .50 .15
❑ 39 Bartolo Colon .30 .09
❑ 40 Mark Quinn .30 .09
❑ 41 Tony Clark .30 .09
❑ 42 Brad Radke .30 .09
❑ 43 Gary Sheffield .30 .09
❑ 44 Doug Mientkiewicz .30 .09
❑ 45 Pedro Martinez .75 .23
❑ 46 Carlos Lee .30 .09
❑ 47 Troy Glaus .50 .15

	No.	Player		
❑	48	Preston Wilson	.30	.09
❑	49	Phil Nevin	.30	.09
❑	50	Chan Ho Park	.30	.09
❑	51	Randy Johnson	.75	.23
❑	52	Jermaine Dye	.30	.09
❑	53	Terrence Long	.30	.09
❑	54	Joe Mays	.30	.09
❑	55	Scott Rolen	.50	.15
❑	56	Miguel Tejada	.30	.09
❑	57	Jim Thome	.75	.23
❑	58	Jose Vidro	.30	.09
❑	59	Gabe Kapler	.30	.09
❑	60	Darin Erstad	.30	.09
❑	61	Jim Edmonds	.30	.09
❑	62	Jarrod Washburn	.30	.09
❑	63	Tom Glavine	.75	.23
❑	64	Adrian Beltre	.30	.09
❑	65	Sammy Sosa	1.25	.35
❑	66	Juan Gonzalez	.75	.23
❑	67	Rafael Furcal	.30	.09
❑	68	Mike Mussina	.75	.23
❑	69	Mark McGwire	2.00	.60
❑	70	Ryan Klesko	.30	.09
❑	71	Raul Mondesi	.30	.09
❑	72	Trot Nixon	.30	.09
❑	73	Barry Larkin	.75	.23
❑	74	Rafael Palmeiro	.50	.15
❑	75	Mark Mulder	.30	.09
❑	76	Carlos Delgado	.30	.09
❑	77	Mike Hampton	.30	.09
❑	78	Carl Everett	.30	.09
❑	79	Paul Konerko	.30	.09
❑	80	Larry Walker	.50	.15
❑	81	Kerry Wood	.75	.23
❑	82	Frank Thomas	.75	.23
❑	83	Andruw Jones	.50	.15
❑	84	Eric Milton	.30	.09
❑	85	Ben Grieve	.30	.09
❑	86	Carlos Beltran	.30	.09
❑	87	Tim Hudson	.30	.09
❑	88	Hideo Nomo	.75	.23
❑	89	Greg Maddux	1.50	.45
❑	90	Edgar Martinez	.50	.15
❑	91	Lance Berkman	.30	.09
❑	92	Pat Burrell	.30	.09
❑	93	Jeff Kent	.30	.09
❑	94	Magglio Ordonez	.30	.09
❑	95	Cristian Guzman	.30	.09
❑	96	Jose Canseco	.75	.23
❑	97	J.D. Drew	.30	.09
❑	98	Bernie Williams	.50	.15
❑	99	Kazuhiro Sasaki	.30	.09
❑	100	Rickey Henderson	1.25	.35
❑	101	Wilson Guzman RC	3.00	.90
❑	102	Nick Neugebauer	3.00	.90
❑	103	Lance Davis RC	3.00	.90
❑	104	Felipe Lopez	3.00	.90
❑	105	Toby Hall	3.00	.90
❑	106	Jack Cust	3.00	.90
❑	107	Jason Karnuth RC	3.00	.90
❑	108	Bart Miadich RC	3.00	.90
❑	109	Brian Roberts RC	3.00	.90
❑	110	Brandon Larson RC	3.00	.90
❑	111	Sean Douglass RC	3.00	.90
❑	112	Joe Crede	3.00	.90
❑	113	Tim Redding	3.00	.90
❑	114	Adam Johnson	3.00	.90
❑	115	Marcus Giles	3.00	.90
❑	116	Jose Ortiz	3.00	.90
❑	117	Jose Mieses RC	3.00	.90
❑	118	Nick Maness RC	3.00	.90
❑	119	Les Walrond RC	3.00	.90
❑	120	Travis Phelps RC	3.00	.90
❑	121	Troy Mattes RC	3.00	.90
❑	122	Carlos Garcia RC	3.00	.90
❑	123	Bill Ortega RC	3.00	.90
❑	124	Gene Altman RC	3.00	.90
❑	125	Nate Frese RC	3.00	.90
❑	126	Alfonso Soriano	5.00	1.50
❑	127	Jose Nunez RC	3.00	.90
❑	128	Bob File RC	3.00	.90
❑	129	Dan Wright	3.00	.90
❑	130	Nick Johnson	3.00	.90
❑	131	Brent Abernathy	3.00	.90
❑	132	Steve Green RC	3.00	.90
❑	133	Billy Sylvester RC	3.00	.90
❑	134	Scott MacRae RC	3.00	.90
❑	135	Kris Keller RC	3.00	.90
❑	136	Scott Stewart RC	3.00	.90
❑	137	Henry Mateo RC	3.00	.90
❑	138	Timo Perez	3.00	.90
❑	139	Nate Teut RC	3.00	.90
❑	140	Jason Michaels RC	3.00	.90
❑	141	Junior Spivey RC	5.00	1.50
❑	142	Carlos Pena	3.00	.90
❑	143	Wilmy Caceres RC	3.00	.90
❑	144	David Lundquist	3.00	.90
❑	145	Jack Wilson RC	3.00	.90
❑	146	Jeremy Fikac RC	3.00	.90
❑	147	Alex Escobar	3.00	.90
❑	148	Abraham Nunez	3.00	.90
❑	149	Xavier Nady	3.00	.90
❑	150	Michael Cuddyer	3.00	.90
❑	151	Greg Miller RC	3.00	.90
❑	152	Eric Munson	3.00	.90
❑	153	Aubrey Huff	3.00	.90
❑	154	Tim Christman RC	3.00	.90
❑	155	Erick Almonte RC	3.00	.90
❑	156	Mike Penney RC	3.00	.90
❑	157	Delvin James RC	3.00	.90
❑	158	Ben Sheets	3.00	.90
❑	159	Jason Hart	3.00	.90
❑	160	Jose Acevedo RC	3.00	.90
❑	161	Will Ohman RC	3.00	.90
❑	162	Erik Hiljus RC	3.00	.90
❑	163	Juan Moreno RC	3.00	.90
❑	164	Mike Koplove RC	3.00	.90
❑	165	Pedro Santana RC	3.00	.90
❑	166	Jimmy Rollins	3.00	.90
❑	167	Matt White RC	3.00	.90
❑	168	Cesar Crespo RC	3.00	.90
❑	169	Carlos Hernandez	3.00	.90
❑	170	Chris George	3.00	.90
❑	171	Brad Voyles RC	3.00	.90
❑	172	Luis Pineda RC	3.00	.90
❑	173	Carlos Zambrano RC	3.00	.90
❑	174	Nate Cornejo	3.00	.90
❑	175	Jason Smith RC	3.00	.90
❑	176	Craig Monroe RC	3.00	.90
❑	177	Cody Ransom RC	3.00	.90
❑	178	John Grabow RC	3.00	.90
❑	179	Pedro Feliz	3.00	.90
❑	180	Jeremy Owens RC	3.00	.90
❑	181	Kurt Ainsworth	3.00	.90
❑	182	Luis Lopez	3.00	.90
❑	183	Stubby Clapp RC	3.00	.90
❑	184	Ryan Freel RC	3.00	.90
❑	185	Duaner Sanchez RC	3.00	.90
❑	186	Jason Jennings	3.00	.90
❑	187	Kyle Lohse RC	5.00	1.50
❑	188	Jerrod Riggan RC	3.00	.90
❑	189	Joe Beimel RC	3.00	.90
❑	190	Nick Punto RC	3.00	.90
❑	191	Willie Harris RC	3.00	.90
❑	192	Ryan Jensen RC	3.00	.90
❑	193	Adam Pettyjohn RC	3.00	.90
❑	194	Donaldo Mendez RC	3.00	.90
❑	195	Bret Prinz RC	3.00	.90
❑	196	Paul Phillips RC	3.00	.90
❑	197	Brian Lawrence RC	3.00	.90
❑	198	Cesar Izturis	3.00	.90
❑	199	Blaine Neal RC	3.00	.90
❑	200	Josh Fogg RC	10.00	3.00
❑	201	Josh Towers RC	10.00	3.00
❑	202	T.Spooneybarger RC	10.00	3.00
❑	203	Michael Rivera RC	10.00	3.00
❑	204	Juan Cruz RC	10.00	3.00
❑	205	Albert Pujols RC	100.00	30.00
❑	206	Josh Beckett	12.00	3.60
❑	207	Roy Oswalt	12.00	3.60
❑	208	Elpidio Guzman RC	10.00	3.00
❑	209	Horacio Ramirez RC	12.00	3.60
❑	210	Corey Patterson	10.00	3.00
❑	211	Geronimo Gil RC	10.00	3.00
❑	212	Jay Gibbons RC	15.00	4.50
❑	213	O.Woodards RC	10.00	3.00
❑	214	David Espinosa	10.00	3.00
❑	215	Angel Berroa RC	20.00	6.00
❑	216	B.Duckworth RC	10.00	3.00
❑	217	Brian Reith RC	10.00	3.00
❑	218	David Brous RC	10.00	3.00
❑	219	Bud Smith RC	10.00	3.00
❑	220	Ramon Vazquez RC	10.00	3.00
❑	221	Mark Teixeira RC	50.00	15.00
❑	222	Justin Atchley RC	10.00	3.00
❑	223	Tony Cogan RC	10.00	3.00
❑	224	Grant Balfour RC	10.00	3.00
❑	225	Ricardo Rodriguez RC	10.00	3.00
❑	226	Brian Rogers RC	10.00	3.00
❑	227	Adam Dunn	12.00	3.60
❑	228	Wilson Betemit RC	10.00	3.00
❑	229	Juan Diaz RC	10.00	3.00
❑	230	Jackson Melian RC	10.00	3.00
❑	231	Claudio Vargas RC	10.00	3.00
❑	232	Wilkin Ruan RC	10.00	3.00
❑	233	J.Duchscherer RC	10.00	3.00
❑	234	Kevin Olsen RC	10.00	3.00
❑	235	Tony Fiore RC	10.00	3.00
❑	236	Jeremy Affeldt RC	10.00	3.00
❑	237	Mike Maroth RC	10.00	3.00
❑	238	C.C. Sabathia	10.00	3.00
❑	239	Cory Aldridge RC	10.00	3.00
❑	240	Zach Day RC	12.00	3.60
❑	241	Brett Jodie RC	10.00	3.00
❑	242	Winston Abreu RC	10.00	3.00
❑	243	Travis Hafner RC	12.00	3.60
❑	244	Joe Kennedy RC	10.00	3.00
❑	245	Rick Bauer RC	10.00	3.00
❑	246	Mike Young	10.00	3.00
❑	247	Ken Vining RC	10.00	3.00
❑	248	Doug Nickle RC	10.00	3.00
❑	249	Pablo Ozuna	10.00	3.00
❑	250	Dustan Mohr RC	10.00	3.00
❑	251	Ichiro Suzuki RC	60.00	18.00
❑	252	Ryan Drese RC	10.00	3.00
❑	253	Morgan Ensberg RC	15.00	4.50
❑	254	George Perez RC	10.00	3.00
❑	255	Roy Smith RC	10.00	3.00
❑	256	Juan Uribe RC	10.00	3.00
❑	257	Dewon Brazelton RC	10.00	3.00
❑	258	Endy Chavez RC	10.00	3.00
❑	259	Kris Foster	10.00	3.00
❑	260	Eric Knott RC	10.00	3.00
❑	261	Corky Miller RC	10.00	3.00
❑	262	Larry Bigbie	10.00	3.00
❑	263	Andres Torres RC	10.00	3.00
❑	264	Adrian Hernandez RC	10.00	3.00
❑	265	Johnny Estrada RC	12.00	3.60
❑	266	David Williams RC	10.00	3.00
❑	267	Steve Lomasney	10.00	3.00
❑	268	Victor Zambrano RC	10.00	3.00
❑	269	Keith Ginter	10.00	3.00
❑	270	Casey Fossum RC	10.00	3.00
❑	271	Josue Perez RC	10.00	3.00
❑	272	Josh Phelps	10.00	3.00
❑	273	Mark Prior RC	80.00	24.00
❑	274	Brandon Berger RC	10.00	3.00
❑	275	Scott Podsednik RC	40.00	12.00
❑	276	Jorge Julio RC	10.00	3.00
❑	277	Esix Snead RC	10.00	3.00
❑	278	Brandon Knight RC	10.00	3.00
❑	279	Saul Rivera RC	10.00	3.00
❑	280	Benito Baez RC	10.00	3.00
❑	281	Rob MacKowiak RC	10.00	3.00
❑	282	Eric Hinske RC	12.00	3.60
❑	283	Juan Rivera	10.00	3.00
❑	284	Kevin Joseph RC	10.00	3.00
❑	285	Juan A. Pena RC	10.00	3.00
❑	286	Brandon Lyon RC	10.00	3.00
❑	287	Adam Everett	10.00	3.00
❑	288	Eric Valent	10.00	3.00
❑	289	Ken Harvey	10.00	3.00
❑	290	Bert Snow RC	10.00	3.00
❑	291	Wily Mo Pena	10.00	3.00
❑	292	Rafael Soriano RC	15.00	4.50
❑	293	Carlos Valderrama RC	10.00	3.00
❑	294	Christian Parker RC	10.00	3.00
❑	295	Tsuyoshi Shinjo RC	15.00	4.50
❑	296	Martin Vargas RC	10.00	3.00
❑	297	Luke Hudson RC	10.00	3.00
❑	298	Dee Brown	10.00	3.00
❑	299	Alexis Gomez RC	10.00	3.00
❑	300	Angel Santos RC	10.00	3.00

2002 Leaf Rookies and Stars

	Nm-Mt	Ex-Mt
COMMON CARD (1-300)	.30	.09
COMMON SP (1-300)	2.00	.60
COMMON CARD (301-400)	1.00	.30
❑ 1 Darin Erstad	.30	.09
❑ 2 Garret Anderson	.30	.09
❑ 3 Troy Glaus	.50	.15
❑ 4 David Eckstein	.30	.09
❑ 5 Adam Kennedy	.30	.09
❑ 6 Kevin Appier Angels	.30	.09
❑ 6A Kevin Appier Mets SP	2.00	.60
❑ 6B Kevin Appier Royals SP	2.00	.60
❑ 7 Jarrod Washburn	.30	.09
❑ 8 David Segui	.30	.09
❑ 9 Jay Gibbons	.30	.09
❑ 10 Tony Batista	.30	.09
❑ 11 Scott Erickson	.30	.09
❑ 12 Jeff Conine	.30	.09
❑ 13 Melvin Mora	.30	.09
❑ 14 Shea Hillenbrand	.30	.09
❑ 15 Manny Ramirez Red Sox	.30	.09
❑ 15A Manny Ramirez Indians SP	2.00	.60
❑ 16 Pedro Martinez Red Sox	.75	.23
❑ 16A Pedro Martinez Dodgers SP	4.00	1.20
❑ 16B Pedro Martinez Expos SP	4.00	1.20
❑ 17 Nomar Garciaparra	1.50	.45
❑ 18 Rickey Henderson Red Sox	1.25	.35
❑ 18A Rickey Henderson Angels SP	6.00	1.80
❑ 18B Rickey Henderson A's SP	6.00	1.80
❑ 18C Rickey Henderson Bl.Jays SP	6.00	1.80
❑ 18D Rickey Henderson M's SP	6.00	1.80
❑ 18E Rickey Henderson Mets SP	6.00	1.80
❑ 18F Rickey Henderson Padres SP	6.00	1.80
❑ 18G Rickey Henderson Yanks SP	6.00	1.80
❑ 19 Johnny Damon Red Sox	.30	.09
❑ 19A Johnny Damon A's SP	2.00	.60
❑ 19B Johnny Damon Royals SP	2.00	.60
❑ 20 Trot Nixon	.30	.09
❑ 21 Derek Lowe	.30	.09
❑ 22 Jason Varitek	.30	.09
❑ 23 Tim Wakefield	.30	.09
❑ 24 Frank Thomas	.75	.23
❑ 25 Kenny Lofton White Sox	.30	.09
❑ 25A Kenny Lofton Indians SP	2.00	.60
❑ 26 Magglio Ordonez	.30	.09
❑ 27 Ray Durham	.30	.09
❑ 28 Mark Buehrle	.30	.09
❑ 29 Paul Konerko White Sox	.30	.09
❑ 29A Paul Konerko Dodgers SP	2.00	.60
❑ 29B Paul Konerko Reds SP	2.00	.60
❑ 30 Jose Valentin	.30	.09
❑ 31 C.C. Sabathia	.30	.09
❑ 32 Ellis Burks Indians	.30	.09
❑ 32A Ellis Burks Giants SP	2.00	.60
❑ 32B Ellis Burks Red Sox SP	2.00	.60
❑ 32C Ellis Burks Rockies SP	2.00	.60
❑ 33 Omar Vizquel Indians	.30	.09
❑ 33A Omar Vizquel Mariners SP	2.00	.60
❑ 34 Jim Thome	.75	.23
❑ 35 Matt Lawton	.30	.09
❑ 36 Travis Fryman Indians	.30	.09
❑ 36A Travis Fryman Tigers SP	2.00	.60
❑ 37 Robert Fick	.30	.09
❑ 38 Bobby Higginson	.30	.09
❑ 39 Steve Sparks	.30	.09
❑ 40 Mike Rivera	.30	.09
❑ 41 Wendell Magee	.30	.09
❑ 42 Randall Simon	.30	.09
❑ 43 Carlos Pena Yankees	.30	.09
❑ 43A Carlos Pena A's SP	2.00	.60
❑ 43B Carlos Pena Rangers SP	2.00	.60
❑ 44 Mike Sweeney	.30	.09
❑ 45 Chuck Knoblauch	.30	.09
❑ 46 Carlos Beltran	.30	.09
❑ 47 Joe Randa	.30	.09
❑ 48 Paul Byrd	.30	.09
❑ 49 Mac Suzuki	.30	.09
❑ 50 Torii Hunter	.30	.09
❑ 51 Jacque Jones	.30	.09
❑ 52 David Ortiz	.30	.09
❑ 53 Corey Koskie	.30	.09
❑ 54 Brad Radke	.30	.09
❑ 55 Doug Mientkiewicz	.30	.09
❑ 56 A.J. Pierzynski	.30	.09
❑ 57 Dustan Mohr	.30	.09
❑ 58 Derek Jeter	2.00	.60
❑ 59 Bernie Williams	.50	.15
❑ 60 Roger Clemens Yankees	1.50	.45
❑ 60A Roger Clemens Blue Jays SP	8.00	2.40
❑ 60B Roger Clemens Red Sox SP	8.00	2.40
❑ 61 Mike Mussina Yankees	.75	.23
❑ 61A Mike Mussina Orioles SP	4.00	1.20
❑ 62 Jorge Posada	.50	.15
❑ 63 Alfonso Soriano	.75	.23
❑ 64 Jason Giambi Yankees	.75	.23
❑ 64A Jason Giambi A's SP	4.00	1.20
❑ 65 Robin Ventura Yankees	.30	.09
❑ 65A Robin Ventura Mets SP	2.00	.60
❑ 65B Robin Ventura White Sox SP	2.00	.60
❑ 66 Andy Pettitte	.50	.15
❑ 67 David Wells Yankees	.30	.09
❑ 67A David Wells Blue Jays SP	2.00	.60
❑ 67B David Wells Tigers SP	2.00	.60
❑ 68 Nick Johnson	.30	.09
❑ 69 Jeff Weaver Yankees	.30	.09
❑ 69A Jeff Weaver Tigers SP	2.00	.60
❑ 70 Raul Mondesi Yankees	.30	.09
❑ 70A Raul Mondesi Blue Jays SP	2.00	.60
❑ 70B Raul Mondesi Dodgers SP	2.00	.60
❑ 71 Tim Hudson	.30	.09
❑ 72 Barry Zito	.75	.23
❑ 73 Mark Mulder	.30	.09
❑ 74 Miguel Tejada	.30	.09
❑ 75 Eric Chavez	.30	.09
❑ 76 Billy Koch A's	.30	.09
❑ 76A Billy Koch Blue Jays SP	2.00	.60
❑ 77 Jermaine Dye A's	.30	.09
❑ 77A Jermaine Dye Royals SP	2.00	.60
❑ 78 Scott Hatteberg	.30	.09
❑ 79 Ichiro Suzuki	1.50	.45
❑ 80 Edgar Martinez	.50	.15
❑ 81 Mike Cameron Mariners	.30	.09
❑ 81A Mike Cameron White Sox SP	2.00	.60
❑ 82 John Olerud Mariners	.30	.09
❑ 82A John Olerud Blue Jays SP	2.00	.60
❑ 82B John Olerud Mets SP	2.00	.60
❑ 83 Bret Boone	.30	.09
❑ 84 Dan Wilson	.30	.09
❑ 85 Freddy Garcia	.30	.09
❑ 86 Jamie Moyer	.30	.09
❑ 87 Carlos Guillen	.30	.09
❑ 88 Ruben Sierra	.30	.09
❑ 89 Kazuhiro Sasaki	.30	.09
❑ 90 Mark McLemore	.30	.09
❑ 91 Ben Grieve	.30	.09
❑ 92 Aubrey Huff	.30	.09
❑ 93 Steve Cox	.30	.09
❑ 94 Toby Hall	.30	.09
❑ 95 Randy Winn	.30	.09
❑ 96 Brent Abernathy	.30	.09
❑ 97 Chan Ho Park Rangers	.30	.09
❑ 97A Chan Ho Park Dodgers SP	2.00	.60
❑ 98 Alex Rodriguez Rangers	1.50	.45
❑ 98A Alex Rodriguez Mariners SP	8.00	2.40
❑ 99 Juan Gonzalez Rangers	.75	.23
❑ 99A Juan Gonzalez Indians SP	4.00	1.20
❑ 99B Juan Gonzalez Tigers SP	4.00	1.20
❑ 100 Rafael Palmeiro Rangers	.50	.15
❑ 100A Rafael Palmeiro Cubs SP	2.50	.75
❑ 100B Rafael Palmeiro Orioles SP	2.50	.75
❑ 101 Ivan Rodriguez	.75	.23
❑ 102 Rusty Greer	.30	.09
❑ 103 Kenny Rogers Rangers	.30	.09
❑ 103A Kenny Rogers A's SP	2.00	.60
❑ 103B Kenny Rogers Yankees SP	2.00	.60
❑ 104 Hank Blalock	.75	.23
❑ 105 Mark Teixeira	.75	.23
❑ 106 Carlos Delgado	.30	.09
❑ 107 Shannon Stewart	.30	.09
❑ 108 Eric Hinske	.30	.09
❑ 109 Roy Halladay	.30	.09
❑ 110 Felipe Lopez	.30	.09
❑ 111 Vernon Wells	.30	.09
❑ 112 Curt Schilling D'backs	.50	.15
❑ 112A Curt Schilling Phillies SP	2.50	.75
❑ 113 Randy Johnson D'backs	.75	.23
❑ 113A Randy Johnson Astros SP	4.00	1.20
❑ 113B Randy Johnson Expos SP	4.00	1.20
❑ 113C Randy Johnson Mariners SP	4.00	1.20
❑ 114 Luis Gonzalez D'backs	.30	.09
❑ 114A Luis Gonzalez Astros SP	2.00	.60
❑ 114B Luis Gonzalez Cubs SP	2.00	.60
❑ 115 Mark Grace D'backs	.75	.23
❑ 115A Mark Grace Cubs SP	4.00	1.20
❑ 116 Junior Spivey	.30	.09
❑ 117 Tony Womack	.30	.09
❑ 118 Matt Williams D'backs	.30	.09
❑ 118A Matt Williams Giants SP	2.00	.60
❑ 118B Matt Williams Indians SP	2.00	.60
❑ 119 Danny Bautista	.30	.09
❑ 120 Byung-Hyun Kim	.30	.09
❑ 121 Craig Counsell	.30	.09
❑ 122 Greg Maddux Braves	1.50	.45
❑ 122A Greg Maddux Cubs SP	8.00	2.40
❑ 123 Tom Glavine	.75	.23
❑ 124 John Smoltz Braves	.50	.15
❑ 124A John Smoltz Tigers SP	2.50	.75
❑ 125 Chipper Jones	.75	.23
❑ 126 Gary Sheffield	.30	.09
❑ 127 Andruw Jones	.50	.15
❑ 128 Vinny Castilla	.30	.09
❑ 129 Damian Moss	.30	.09
❑ 130 Rafael Furcal	.30	.09
❑ 131 Kerry Wood	.75	.23
❑ 132 Fred McGriff Cubs	.50	.15
❑ 132A Fred McGriff Blue Jays SP	2.50	.75
❑ 132B Fred McGriff Braves SP	2.50	.75
❑ 132C Fred McGriff Devil Rays SP	2.50	.75
❑ 132D Fred McGriff Padres SP	2.50	.75
❑ 133 Sammy Sosa Cubs	1.25	.35
❑ 133A Sammy Sosa Rangers SP	6.00	1.80
❑ 133B Sammy Sosa White Sox SP	6.00	1.80
❑ 134 Alex Gonzalez	.30	.09
❑ 135 Corey Patterson	.30	.09
❑ 136 Moises Alou	.30	.09
❑ 137 Mark Prior	1.50	.45
❑ 138 Jon Lieber	.30	.09
❑ 139 Matt Clement	.30	.09
❑ 140 Ken Griffey Jr. Reds	1.25	.35
❑ 140A Ken Griffey Jr. Mariners SP	6.00	1.80
❑ 141 Barry Larkin	.75	.23
❑ 142 Adam Dunn	.50	.15
❑ 143 Sean Casey Reds	.30	.09
❑ 143A Sean Casey Indians SP	2.00	.60
❑ 144 Jose Rijo	.30	.09
❑ 145 Elmer Dessens	.30	.09
❑ 146 Austin Kearns	.50	.15
❑ 147 Corky Miller	.30	.09
❑ 148 Todd Walker Reds	.30	.09
❑ 148A Todd Walker Rockies SP	2.00	.60
❑ 149 Chris Reitsma	.30	.09
❑ 150 Ryan Dempster	.30	.09
❑ 151 Larry Walker Rockies	.50	.15
❑ 151A Larry Walker Expos SP	2.50	.75
❑ 152 Todd Helton	.50	.15
❑ 153 Juan Uribe	.30	.09
❑ 154 Juan Pierre	.30	.09
❑ 155 Mike Hampton	.30	.09
❑ 156 Todd Zeile	.30	.09
❑ 157 Josh Beckett	.50	.15
❑ 158 Mike Lowell Marlins	.30	.09
❑ 158A Mike Lowell Yankees SP	2.00	.60
❑ 159 Derrek Lee	.30	.09
❑ 160 A.J. Burnett	.30	.09
❑ 161 Luis Castillo	.30	.09
❑ 162 Tim Raines	.30	.09

❑ 163 Preston Wilson .30 .09
❑ 164 Juan Encarnacion .30 .09
❑ 165 Jeff Bagwell .50 .15
❑ 166 Craig Biggio .50 .15
❑ 167 Lance Berkman .30 .09
❑ 168 Wade Miller .30 .09
❑ 169 Roy Oswalt .30 .09
❑ 170 Richard Hidalgo .30 .09
❑ 171 Carlos Hernandez .30 .09
❑ 172 Daryle Ward .30 .09
❑ 173 Shawn Green Dodgers .30 .09
❑ 173A Shawn Green Blue Jays SP 2.00 .60
❑ 174 Adrian Beltre .30 .09
❑ 175 Paul Lo Duca .30 .09
❑ 176 Eric Karros .30 .09
❑ 177 Kevin Brown .30 .09
❑ 178 Hideo Nomo Dodgers .75 .23
❑ 178A Hideo Nomo Brewers SP 4.00 1.20
❑ 178B Hideo Nomo Mets SP 4.00 1.20
❑ 178C Hideo Nomo Red Sox SP 4.00 1.20
❑ 178D Hideo Nomo Tigers SP 4.00 1.20
❑ 179 Odalis Perez .30 .09
❑ 180 Eric Gagne .50 .15
❑ 181 Brian Jordan .30 .09
❑ 182 Cesar Izturis .30 .09
❑ 183 Geoff Jenkins .30 .09
❑ 184 Richie Sexson Brewers .30 .09
❑ 184A Richie Sexson Indians SP 2.00 .60
❑ 185 Jose Hernandez .30 .09
❑ 186 Ben Sheets .30 .09
❑ 187 Ruben Quevedo .30 .09
❑ 188 Jeffrey Hammonds .30 .09
❑ 189 Alex Sanchez .30 .09
❑ 190 Vladimir Guerrero .75 .23
❑ 191 Jose Vidro .30 .09
❑ 192 Orlando Cabrera .30 .09
❑ 193 Michael Barrett .30 .09
❑ 194 Javier Vazquez .30 .09
❑ 195 Tony Armas Jr. .30 .09
❑ 196 Andres Galarraga .30 .09
❑ 197 Tomo Ohka .30 .09
❑ 198 Bartolo Colon Expos .30 .09
❑ 198A Bartolo Colon Indians SP 2.00 .60
❑ 199 Cliff Floyd Expos .30 .09
❑ 199A Cliff Floyd Marlins SP 2.00 .60
❑ 200 Mike Piazza Mets 1.25 .35
❑ 200A Mike Piazza Dodgers SP 6.00 1.80
❑ 200B Mike Piazza Marlins SP 6.00 1.80
❑ 201 Jeromy Burnitz .30 .09
❑ 202 Roberto Alomar Mets .75 .23
❑ 202A Roberto Alomar Bl.Jays SP 4.00 1.20
❑ 202B Roberto Alomar Indians SP 4.00 1.20
❑ 202C Roberto Alomar Orioles SP 4.00 1.20
❑ 202D Roberto Alomar Padres SP 4.00 1.20
❑ 203 Mo Vaughn Mets .30 .09
❑ 203A Mo Vaughn Angels SP 2.00 .60
❑ 203B Mo Vaughn Red Sox SP 2.00 .60
❑ 204 Al Leiter Mets .30 .09
❑ 204A Al Leiter Blue Jays SP 2.00 .60
❑ 205 Pedro Astacio .30 .09
❑ 206 Edgardo Alfonzo .30 .09
❑ 207 Armando Benitez .30 .09
❑ 208 Scott Rolen .50 .15
❑ 209 Pat Burrell .30 .09
❑ 210 Bobby Abreu Phillies .30 .09
❑ 210A Bobby Abreu Astros SP 2.00 .60
❑ 211 Mike Lieberthal .30 .09
❑ 212 Brandon Duckworth .30 .09
❑ 213 Jimmy Rollins .30 .09
❑ 214 Jeremy Giambi .30 .09
❑ 215 Vicente Padilla .30 .09
❑ 216 Travis Lee .30 .09
❑ 217 Jason Kendall .30 .09
❑ 218 Brian Giles Pirates .30 .09
❑ 218A Brian Giles Indians SP 2.00 .60
❑ 219 Aramis Ramirez .30 .09
❑ 220 Pokey Reese .30 .09
❑ 221 Kip Wells .30 .09
❑ 222 Josh Fogg Pirates .30 .09
❑ 222A Josh Fogg White Sox SP 2.00 .60
❑ 223 Mike Williams .30 .09
❑ 224 Ryan Klesko Padres .30 .09
❑ 224A Ryan Klesko Braves SP 2.00 .60
❑ 225 Phil Nevin Padres .30 .09
❑ 225A Phil Nevin Tigers SP 2.00 .60
❑ 226 Brian Lawrence .30 .09
❑ 227 Mark Kotsay .30 .09
❑ 228 Brett Tomko .30 .09
❑ 229 Trevor Hoffman Padres .30 .09
❑ 229A Trevor Hoffman Marlins SP 2.00 .60
❑ 230 Barry Bonds Giants 2.00 .60
❑ 230A Barry Bonds Pirates SP 10.00 3.00
❑ 231 Jeff Kent Giants .30 .09
❑ 231A Jeff Kent Blue Jays SP 2.00 .60
❑ 232 Rich Aurilia .30 .09
❑ 233 Tsuyoshi Shinjo Giants .30 .09
❑ 233A Tsuyoshi Shinjo Mets SP 2.00 .60
❑ 234 Benito Santiago Giants .30 .09
❑ 234A Benito Santiago Padres SP 2.00 .60
❑ 235 Kirk Rueter .30 .09
❑ 236 Kurt Ainsworth .30 .09
❑ 237 Livan Hernandez .30 .09
❑ 238 Russ Ortiz .30 .09
❑ 239 David Bell .30 .09
❑ 240 Jason Schmidt .30 .09
❑ 241 Reggie Sanders .30 .09
❑ 242 Jim Edmonds Cardinals .30 .09
❑ 242A Jim Edmonds Angels SP 2.00 .60
❑ 243 J.D. Drew .30 .09
❑ 244 Albert Pujols 1.50 .45
❑ 245 Fernando Vina .30 .09
❑ 246 Tino Martinez Cardinals .50 .15
❑ 246A Tino Martinez Mariners SP 2.50 .75
❑ 246B Tino Martinez Yankees SP 2.50 .75
❑ 247 Edgar Renteria .30 .09
❑ 248 Matt Morris .30 .09
❑ 249 Woody Williams .30 .09
❑ 250 Jason Isringhausen Cards .30 .09
❑ 250A Jason Isringhausen A's SP 2.00 .60
❑ 251 Cal Ripken 82 ROY 2.50 .75
❑ 252 Cal Ripken 83 MVP 2.50 .75
❑ 253 Cal Ripken 91 MVP 2.50 .75
❑ 254 Cal Ripken 91 AS 2.50 .75
❑ 255 Ryne Sandberg 84 MVP 1.50 .45
❑ 256 Don Mattingly 85 MVP 2.00 .60
❑ 257 Don Mattingly 85-94 GLV 2.00 .60
❑ 258 Roger Clemens 01 CY 1.50 .45
❑ 259 Roger Clemens 87 CY 1.50 .45
❑ 260 Roger Clemens 91 CY 1.50 .45
❑ 261 Roger Clemens 97 CY 1.50 .45
❑ 262 Roger Clemens 98 CY 1.50 .45
❑ 263 Roger Clemens 86 CY 1.50 .45
❑ 264 Roger Clemens 86 MVP 1.50 .45
❑ 265 Rickey Henderson 90 MVP 1.25 .35
❑ 266 Rickey Henderson 81 GLV 1.25 .35
❑ 267 Jose Canseco 88 MVP .50 .15
❑ 268 Barry Bonds 01 MVP 2.00 .60
❑ 269 Barry Bonds 90 MVP 2.00 .60
❑ 270 Barry Bonds 92 MVP 2.00 .60
❑ 271 Barry Bonds 93 MVP 2.00 .60
❑ 272 Jeff Bagwell 94 MVP .30 .09
❑ 273 Kirby Puckett 91 ALCS .75 .23
❑ 274 Kirby Puckett 93 AS .75 .23
❑ 275 Greg Maddux 95 CY 1.50 .45
❑ 276 Greg Maddux 92 CY 1.50 .45
❑ 277 Greg Maddux 93 CY 1.50 .45
❑ 278 Greg Maddux 94 CY 1.50 .45
❑ 279 Ken Griffey Jr. 97 MVP 1.25 .35
❑ 280 Mike Piazza 93 ROY 1.25 .35
❑ 281 Kirby Puckett 86-89 GLV .75 .23
❑ 282 Mike Piazza 96 AS 1.25 .35
❑ 283 Frank Thomas 93 MVP .50 .15
❑ 284 Hideo Nomo 95 ROY .50 .15
❑ 285 Randy Johnson 01 CY .50 .15
❑ 286 Juan Gonzalez 96 MVP .50 .15
❑ 287 Derek Jeter 96 ROY 2.00 .60
❑ 288 Derek Jeter 00 WS 2.00 .60
❑ 289 Derek Jeter 00 AS 2.00 .60
❑ 290 Nomar Garciaparra 97 ROY 1.50 .45
❑ 291 Pedro Martinez 00 CY .50 .15
❑ 292 Kerry Wood 98 ROY .50 .15
❑ 293 Sammy Sosa 98 MVP 1.25 .35
❑ 294 Chipper Jones 99 MVP .50 .15
❑ 295 Ivan Rodriguez 99 MVP .50 .15
❑ 296 Ivan Rodriguez 92-01 GLV .50 .15
❑ 297 Albert Pujols 01 ROY 1.50 .45
❑ 298 Ichiro Suzuki 01 ROY 1.50 .45
❑ 299 Ichiro Suzuki 01 MVP 1.50 .45
❑ 300 Ichiro Suzuki 01 GLV 1.50 .45
❑ 301 So Taguchi RS RC 1.25 .35
❑ 302 Kazuhisa Ishii RS RC 3.00 .90
❑ 303 Jeremy Lambert RS RC 1.00 .30
❑ 304 Sean Burroughs RS 1.00 .30
❑ 305 P.J. Bevis RS RC 1.00 .30
❑ 306 Jon Rauch RS 1.00 .30
❑ 307 Scotty Layfield RS RC 1.00 .30
❑ 308 Miguel Asencio RS RC 1.00 .30
❑ 309 Franklyn German RS RC 1.00 .30
❑ 310 Luis Ugueto RS RC 1.00 .30
❑ 311 Jorge Sosa RS RC 1.00 .30
❑ 312 Felix Escalona RS RC 1.00 .30
❑ 313 Jose Valverde RS RC 1.25 .35
❑ 314 Jeremy Ward RS RC 1.00 .30
❑ 315 Kevin Gryboski RS RC 1.00 .30
❑ 316 Francis Beltran RS RC 1.00 .30
❑ 317 Joe Thurston RS 1.00 .30
❑ 318 Cliff Lee RS RC 2.00 .60
❑ 319 Takahito Nomura RS RC 1.00 .30
❑ 320 Bill Hall RS 1.00 .30
❑ 321 Marlon Byrd RS 1.00 .30
❑ 322 Andy Shibilo RS RC 1.00 .30
❑ 323 Edwin Almonte RS RC 1.00 .30
❑ 324 Brandon Backe RS RC 1.00 .30
❑ 325 Chone Figgins RS RC 1.00 .30
❑ 326 Brian Mallette RS RC 1.00 .30
❑ 327 Rodrigo Rosario RS RC 1.00 .30
❑ 328 Anderson Machado RS RC 1.25 .35
❑ 329 Jorge Padilla RS RC 1.25 .35
❑ 330 Allan Simpson RS RC 1.00 .30
❑ 331 Doug Devore RS RC 1.00 .30
❑ 332 Drew Henson RS 1.00 .30
❑ 333 Raul Chavez RS RC 1.00 .30
❑ 334 Tom Shearn RS RC 1.00 .30
❑ 335 Ben Howard RS RC 1.00 .30
❑ 336 Chris Baker RS RC 1.00 .30
❑ 337 Travis Hughes RS RC 1.25 .35
❑ 338 Kevin Mench RS 1.00 .30
❑ 339 Brian Tallet RS RC 1.25 .35
❑ 340 Mike Moriarty RS RC 1.00 .30
❑ 341 Corey Thurman RS RC 1.00 .30
❑ 342 Terry Pearson RS RC 1.00 .30
❑ 343 Steve Kent RS RC 1.00 .30
❑ 344 Satoru Komiyama RS RC 1.00 .30
❑ 345 Jason Lane RS 1.00 .30
❑ 346 Freddy Sanchez RS RC 2.00 .60
❑ 347 Brandon Puffer RS RC 1.00 .30
❑ 348 Clay Condrey RS RC 1.00 .30
❑ 349 Rene Reyes RS RC 1.00 .30
❑ 350 Hee Seop Choi RS 1.25 .35
❑ 351 Rodrigo Lopez RS 1.00 .30
❑ 352 Colin Young RS RC 1.00 .30
❑ 353 Jason Simontacchi RS RC 1.25 .35
❑ 354 Oliver Perez RS RC 2.50 .75
❑ 355 Kirk Saarloos RS RC 2.00 .60
❑ 356 Marcus Thames RS 1.00 .30
❑ 357 Jeff Austin RS RC 1.00 .30
❑ 358 Justin Kaye RS 1.00 .30
❑ 359 Julio Mateo RS RC 1.00 .30
❑ 360 Mike A. Smith RS RC 1.00 .30
❑ 361 Chris Snelling RS RC 2.50 .75
❑ 362 Dennis Tankersley RS 1.00 .30
❑ 363 Runelvys Hernandez RS RC 2.00 .60
❑ 364 Aaron Cook RS RC 1.25 .35
❑ 365 Joe Borchard RS 1.00 .30
❑ 366 Earl Snyder RS RC 1.00 .30
❑ 367 Shane Nance RS RC 1.00 .30
❑ 368 Aaron Guiel RS RC 1.25 .35
❑ 369 Steve Bechler RS RC 1.00 .30
❑ 370 Tim Kalita RS RC 1.00 .30
❑ 371 Shawn Sedlacek RS RC 1.00 .30
❑ 372 Eric Good RS RC 1.00 .30
❑ 373 Eric Junge RS RC 1.00 .30
❑ 374 Matt Thornton RS RC 1.00 .30
❑ 375 Travis Driskill RS RC 1.00 .30
❑ 376 Mitch Wylie RS RC 1.00 .30
❑ 377 John Ennis RS RC 1.00 .30
❑ 378 Reed Johnson RS RC 1.25 .35
❑ 379 Juan Brito RS RC 1.00 .30
❑ 380 Ron Calloway RS RC 1.00 .30
❑ 381 Adrian Burnside RS RC 1.00 .30
❑ 382 Josh Bard RS RC 1.00 .30
❑ 383 Matt Childers RS RC 1.00 .30
❑ 384 Gustavo Chacin RS RC 1.00 .30
❑ 385 Luis Martinez RS RC 1.25 .35
❑ 386 Trey Hodges RS RC 1.25 .35
❑ 387 Hansel Izquierdo RS RC 1.00 .30
❑ 388 Jeriome Robertson RS RC 1.25 .35
❑ 389 Victor Alvarez RS RC 1.00 .30

Card	MINT	NRMT
❑ 390 David Ross RS RC	1.00	.30
❑ 391 Ron Chiavacci RS	1.00	.30
❑ 392 Adam Walker RS RC	1.00	.30
❑ 393 Mike Gonzalez RS RC	1.00	.30
❑ 394 John Foster RS RC	1.00	.30
❑ 395 Kyle Kane RS RC	1.00	.30
❑ 396 Cam Esslinger RS RC	1.00	.30
❑ 397 Kevin Frederick RS RC	1.00	.30
❑ 398 Franklin Nunez RS RC	1.00	.30
❑ 399 Todd Donovan RS RC	1.00	.30
❑ 400 Kevin Cash RS RC	1.00	.30

2003 MLB Showdown Pennant Run

	MINT	NRMT
COMP.SET w/o SP's (100)	40.00	18.00
COMMON CARD (1-125)	.50	.23
COMMON FOIL	3.00	1.35
FOIL STATED ODDS 1:3		
❑ 1 Jeremy Bonderman RC	3.00	1.35
❑ 2 Tom Goodwin	.50	.23
❑ 3 Terry Mulholland	.50	.23
❑ 4 Jake Westbrook	.50	.23
❑ 5 Jake Peavy	1.00	.45
❑ 6 Felix Rodriguez	.50	.23
❑ 7 Marlon Byrd	1.00	.45
❑ 8 Toby Hall	.50	.23
❑ 9 Roberto Hernandez	.50	.23
❑ 10 Carlos Silva	.50	.23
❑ 11 Chris Hammond	.50	.23
❑ 12 David Dellucci	.50	.23
❑ 13 R.A. Dickey	.50	.23
❑ 14 Cliff Politte	.50	.23
❑ 15 Russ Springer	.50	.23
❑ 16 Vance Wilson	.50	.23
❑ 17 Scott Williamson	.50	.23
❑ 18 Ryan Franklin	.50	.23
❑ 19 Juan Castro	.50	.23
❑ 20 Craig Monroe	.50	.23
❑ 21 Joe Beimel	.50	.23
❑ 22 John Halama	.50	.23
❑ 23 Eli Marrero	.50	.23
❑ 24 Felipe Lopez	.50	.23
❑ 25 Mike MacDougal	.50	.23
❑ 26 Kris Benson	.50	.23
❑ 27 Josh Beckett	1.50	.70
❑ 28 Carlos Febles	.50	.23
❑ 29 Luis Rivas	.50	.23
❑ 30 Scott Sullivan	.50	.23
❑ 31 John Thomson	.50	.23
❑ 32 Lance Carter	.50	.23
❑ 33 Chris George	.50	.23
❑ 34 Rocky Biddle	.50	.23
❑ 35 Brandon Lyon	.50	.23
❑ 36 Eric Munson	.50	.23
❑ 37 Kirk Rueter	.50	.23
❑ 38 Scott Schoeneweis	.50	.23
❑ 39 Casey Blake	.50	.23
❑ 40 Francisco Cordero	.50	.23
❑ 41 Tom Gordon	.50	.23
❑ 42 Neifi Perez	.50	.23
❑ 43 Chad Bradford	.50	.23
❑ 44 Miguel Cairo	.50	.23
❑ 45 Mike Matheny	.50	.23
❑ 46 Mike Timlin	.50	.23
❑ 47 D.J. Carrasco RC	.50	.23
❑ 48 Eddie Perez	.50	.23
❑ 49 Gregg Zaun	.50	.23
❑ 50 Ronnie Belliard	.50	.23
❑ 51 Ricardo Rodriguez	.50	.23
❑ 52 B.J. Ryan	.50	.23
❑ 53 Michael Tucker	.50	.23
❑ 54 Rheal Cormier	.50	.23
❑ 55 Felix Heredia	.50	.23
❑ 56 Alex Cora	.50	.23
❑ 57 Travis Lee	.50	.23
❑ 58 Ted Lilly	.50	.23
❑ 59 Tom Wilson	.50	.23
❑ 60 Jeff D'Amico	.50	.23
❑ 61 Adam Eaton	.50	.23
❑ 62 Travis Harper	.50	.23
❑ 63 Mark Loretta	.50	.23
❑ 64 Ricky Stone	.50	.23
❑ 65 Wil Cordero	.50	.23
❑ 66 Cliff Floyd	1.00	.45
❑ 67 Livan Hernandez	.50	.23
❑ 68 Paul Quantrill	.50	.23
❑ 69 Ben Davis	.50	.23
❑ 70 Shawn Estes	.50	.23
❑ 71 Chris Stynes	.50	.23
❑ 72 Jay Payton	.50	.23
❑ 73 Ramon Hernandez	.50	.23
❑ 74 Jason Johnson	.50	.23
❑ 75 John Vander Wal	.50	.23
❑ 76 Shawn Chacon FOIL	3.00	1.35
❑ 77 D'Angelo Jimenez	.50	.23
❑ 78 Desi Relaford	.50	.23
❑ 79 Rich Aurilia	1.00	.45
❑ 80 Rod Barajas	.50	.23
❑ 81 Jose Cruz FOIL	5.00	2.20
❑ 82 Kyle Lohse	.50	.23
❑ 83 Rondell White	1.00	.45
❑ 84 Gil Meche FOIL	5.00	2.20
❑ 85 Jose Guillen	.50	.23
❑ 86 Kenny Lofton	1.00	.45
❑ 87 Zach Day FOIL	3.00	1.35
❑ 88 Mark Redman	.50	.23
❑ 89 Melvin Mora FOIL	5.00	2.20
❑ 90 Todd Walker	1.00	.45
❑ 91 Torii Hunter	1.00	.45
❑ 92 Frank Catalanotto	.50	.23
❑ 93 Andres Galarraga	1.00	.45
❑ 94 Jason Schmidt	1.00	.45
❑ 95 Eric Byrnes	.50	.23
❑ 96 Hank Blalock FOIL	8.00	3.60
❑ 97 Jacque Jones FOIL	5.00	2.20
❑ 98 Michael Young	1.00	.45
❑ 99 Carl Everett	1.00	.45
❑ 100 Preston Wilson	1.00	.45
❑ 101 Esteban Loaiza	1.00	.45
❑ 102 Raul Mondesi FOIL	5.00	2.20
❑ 103 Carlos Delgado FOIL	5.00	2.20
❑ 104 Gary Sheffield FOIL	5.00	2.20
❑ 105 Kevin Appier	1.00	.45
❑ 106 Jesse Orosco SS	.50	.23
❑ 107 Pat Hentgen SS	.50	.23
❑ 108 Matt Williams SS	1.00	.45
❑ 109 David Cone SS FOIL	5.00	2.20
❑ 110 Mark Grace SS FOIL	10.00	4.50
❑ 111 Carlos Baerga SS FOIL	3.00	1.35
❑ 112 Greg Maddux SS FOIL	10.00	4.50
❑ 113 Kevin Brown SS FOIL	8.00	3.60
❑ 114 Ivan Rodriguez SS FOIL	15.00	6.75
❑ 115 John Olerud SS FOIL	5.00	2.20
❑ 116 Larry Doby CC	1.00	.45
❑ 117 Yogi Berra CC FOIL	10.00	4.50
❑ 118 Hoyt Wilhelm CC FOIL	15.00	6.75
❑ 119 Pee Wee Reese CC	1.50	.70
❑ 120 Brooks Robinson CC FOIL	10.00	4.50
❑ 121 Robin Yount CC FOIL	10.00	4.50
❑ 122 Reggie Jackson CC FOIL	15.00	6.75
❑ 123 Harmon Killebrew CC FOIL	15.00	6.75
❑ 124 Rod Carew CC FOIL	15.00	6.75
❑ 125 Nolan Ryan CC FOIL	20.00	9.00

2003 MLB Showdown Trading Deadline

	MINT	NRMT
COMP.SET w/o SP's (120)	40.00	18.00
COMMON CARD (1-145)	.50	.23
COMMON FOIL	3.00	1.35
FOIL STATED ODDS 1:3		
❑ 1 So Taguchi	1.00	.45
❑ 2 Ryan Drese	.50	.23
❑ 3 Mike Hampton	1.00	.45
❑ 4 Sandy Alomar Jr.	.50	.23
❑ 5 Steve Sparks	.50	.23
❑ 6 Chan Ho Park	1.00	.45
❑ 7 Roger Cedeno	.50	.23
❑ 8 Antonio Osuna	.50	.23
❑ 9 Ryan Dempster	.50	.23
❑ 10 Jesse Orosco	.50	.23
❑ 11 Angel Berroa	1.00	.45
❑ 12 Sean Burroughs	1.00	.45
❑ 13 Matt Mantei	.50	.23
❑ 14 Einar Diaz	.50	.23
❑ 15 Ken Griffey Jr.	4.00	1.80
❑ 16 Rey Sanchez	.50	.23
❑ 17 Antonio Alfonseca	.50	.23
❑ 18 Carl Crawford	1.00	.45
❑ 19 Rey Ordonez	.50	.23
❑ 20 Brandon Inge	.50	.23
❑ 21 Hank Blalock	1.50	.70
❑ 22 Albie Lopez	.50	.23
❑ 23 Aaron Sele	.50	.23
❑ 24 Willie Bloomquist	1.00	.45
❑ 25 Shigetoshi Hasegawa	1.00	.45
❑ 26 Steve Kline	.50	.23
❑ 27 Ramiro Mendoza	.50	.23
❑ 28 Mike Stanton	.50	.23
❑ 29 Carlos Zambrano	1.00	.45
❑ 30 Dean Palmer	.50	.23
❑ 31 Mark Grudzielanek	.50	.23
❑ 32 Matt Williams	1.00	.45
❑ 33 Michael Cuddyer	1.00	.45
❑ 34 Glendon Rusch	.50	.23
❑ 35 Hee Seop Choi	1.00	.45
❑ 36 Mike Bordick	1.00	.45
❑ 37 Ray King	.50	.23
❑ 38 Bill Mueller	1.00	.45
❑ 39 John McDonald	.50	.23
❑ 40 Brent Butler	.50	.23
❑ 41 Josh Bard	.50	.23
❑ 42 Xavier Nady	1.00	.45
❑ 43 J.C. Romero	.50	.23
❑ 44 Paul Shuey	.50	.23
❑ 45 Eric Karros	1.00	.45
❑ 46 Runelvys Hernandez	1.00	.45
❑ 47 Braden Looper	.50	.23
❑ 48 Dave Roberts	.50	.23
❑ 49 Deivi Cruz	.50	.23
❑ 50 Todd Hollandsworth	.50	.23
❑ 51 Billy Koch	.50	.23
❑ 52 Brandon Villafuerte	.50	.23
❑ 53 Ricardo Rincon	.50	.23
❑ 54 Joe Crede	.50	.23
❑ 55 Juan Pierre	1.00	.45
❑ 56 Tsuyoshi Shinjo	1.00	.45
❑ 57 Ugueth Urbina	.50	.23
❑ 58 Luis Vizcaino FOIL	3.00	1.35
❑ 59 Ben Weber	.50	.23
❑ 60A Kerry Wood	2.50	1.10
❑ 60B Kerry Wood FOIL	10.00	4.50
❑ 61 Tim Worrell	.50	.23
❑ 62 Royce Clayton	.50	.23
❑ 63 Chone Figgins	.50	.23
❑ 64 Ken Huckaby	.50	.23
❑ 65 Brian Anderson	.50	.23
❑ 66 Aramis Ramirez	1.00	.45

❑ 67 Edgar Martinez 1.50 .70
❑ 68 Keith Foulke .50 .23
❑ 69 LaTroy Hawkins .50 .23
❑ 70 Mike Remlinger .50 .23
❑ 71 Lyle Overbay .50 .23
❑ 72 Buddy Groom .50 .23
❑ 73 Orlando Hudson .50 .23
❑ 74 Francisco Rodriguez FOIL 5.00 2.20
❑ 75 Craig Biggio 1.50 .70
❑ 76 Todd Zeile 1.00 .45
❑ 77 Vernon Wells 1.00 .45
❑ 78 Casey Fossum .50 .23
❑ 79 Wes Helms .50 .23
❑ 80 Robert Fick 1.00 .45
❑ 81 Scott Spiezio 1.00 .45
❑ 82 Ty Wigginton 1.00 .45
❑ 83 Elmer Dessens .50 .23
❑ 84 Arthur Rhodes .50 .23
❑ 85 Matt Stairs .50 .23
❑ 86 Miguel Olivo .50 .23
❑ 87 Tino Martinez 1.50 .70
❑ 88 Travis Hafner .50 .23
❑ 89 Octavio Dotel .50 .23
❑ 90 Jimmy Rollins 1.00 .45
❑ 91 Placido Polanco .50 .23
❑ 92 Kevin Brown 1.00 .45
❑ 93 John Patterson .50 .23
❑ 94 Andy Pettitte 1.50 .70
❑ 95 Bobby Kielty .50 .23
❑ 96 Jeremy Giambi .50 .23
❑ 97 Brandon Phillips .50 .23
❑ 98 Fred McGriff 1.50 .70
❑ 99 Damian Moss .50 .23
❑ 100 Russ Ortiz 1.00 .45
❑ 101 Mark Teixeira 1.50 .70
❑ 102 Tom Glavine FOIL 10.00 4.50
❑ 103 Chris Woodward .50 .23
❑ 104 Brad Radke 1.00 .45
❑ 105 Edgardo Alfonzo 1.00 .45
❑ 106 Jose Contreras FOIL RC 8.00 3.60
❑ 107 Josh Beckett 1.50 .70
❑ 108 Johan Santana 1.00 .45
❑ 109 Brandon Larson .50 .23
❑ 110 Randall Simon .50 .23
❑ 111 Randy Winn FOIL 3.00 1.35
❑ 112 Ray Durham 1.00 .45
❑ 113 Omar Daal FOIL 3.00 1.35
❑ 114 David Wells FOIL 5.00 2.20
❑ 115 Wade Miller 1.00 .45
❑ 116 Bartolo Colon FOIL 5.00 2.20
❑ 117 Ryan Klesko FOIL 5.00 2.20
❑ 118 Jeff Bagwell 1.50 .70
❑ 119 Roy Oswalt FOIL 5.00 2.20
❑ 120 Orlando Hernandez FOIL 5.00 2.20
❑ 121 Ivan Rodriguez FOIL 10.00 4.50
❑ 122 Tim Wakefield 1.00 .45
❑ 123 Josh Phelps 1.00 .45
❑ 124 Woody Williams .50 .23
❑ 125 Chipper Jones FOIL 10.00 4.50
❑ 126 Randy Wolf 1.00 .45
❑ 127 Kevin Millwood FOIL 5.00 2.20
❑ 128 Jeff Kent FOIL 5.00 2.20
❑ 129 Rocco Baldelli FOIL 10.00 4.50
❑ 130 Hideki Matsui FOIL RC 15.00 6.75
❑ 131 Jim Thome FOIL 10.00 4.50
❑ 132 Kazuhiro Sasaki RS 1.00 .45
❑ 133 Jason Jennings RS FOIL 3.00 1.35
❑ 134 Rafael Furcal RS 1.00 .45
❑ 135 Derek Jeter RS FOIL 15.00 6.75
❑ 136 Benito Santiago RS 1.00 .45
❑ 137 Jeff Bagwell RS 1.50 .70
❑ 138 Carlos Beltran RS 1.00 .45
❑ 139 Scott Rolen RS FOIL 8.00 3.60
❑ 141 Tim Salmon RS 1.00 .45
❑ 142 Ichiro Suzuki RS FOIL 15.00 6.75
❑ 143 Mike Piazza RS FOIL 10.00 4.50
❑ 144 Albert Pujols RS 5.00 2.20
❑ 145 Nomar Garciaparra RS FOIL 15.00 6.75

2003 MLB Showdown

	Nm-Mt	Ex-Mt
COMP.SET w/o FOIL (252)	60.00	18.00
COMMON CARD (1-304)	.50	.15
COMMON FOIL	3.00	.90

❑ 1 Garret Anderson FOIL 5.00 1.50
❑ 2 David Eckstein FOIL 3.00 .90
❑ 3 Darin Erstad 1.00 .30
❑ 4 Brad Fullmer 1.00 .30
❑ 5 Troy Glaus 1.50 .45
❑ 6 Adam Kennedy .50 .15
❑ 7 Bengie Molina .50 .15
❑ 8 Ramon Ortiz .50 .15
❑ 9 Orlando Palmeiro .50 .15
❑ 10 Troy Percival 1.00 .30
❑ 11 Tim Salmon 1.50 .45
❑ 12 Jarrod Washburn FOIL 5.00 1.50
❑ 13 Miguel Batista .50 .15
❑ 14 Danny Bautista .50 .15
❑ 15 Craig Counsell .50 .15
❑ 16 Steve Finley 1.00 .30
❑ 17 Luis Gonzalez FOIL 5.00 1.50
❑ 18 Mark Grace 2.50 .75
❑ 19 Randy Johnson FOIL 10.00 3.00
❑ 20 Byung-Hyun Kim 1.00 .30
❑ 21 Quinton McCracken .50 .15
❑ 22 Curt Schilling FOIL 20.00 6.00
❑ 23 Junior Spivey FOIL 3.00 .90
❑ 24 Tony Womack .50 .15
❑ 25 Vinny Castilla 1.00 .30
❑ 26 Julio Franco .50 .15
❑ 27 Rafael Furcal FOIL 5.00 1.50
❑ 28 Marcus Giles 1.00 .30
❑ 29 Tom Glavine FOIL 10.00 3.00
❑ 30 Andruw Jones FOIL 8.00 2.40
❑ 31 Keith Lockhart .50 .15
❑ 32 Javy Lopez 1.00 .30
❑ 33 Greg Maddux FOIL 10.00 3.00
❑ 34 Kevin Millwood 1.00 .30
❑ 35 Gary Sheffield 1.00 .30
❑ 36 John Smoltz FOIL 8.00 2.40
❑ 37 Tony Batista 1.00 .30
❑ 38 Mike Bordick 1.00 .30
❑ 39 Jeff Conine 1.00 .30
❑ 40 Marty Cordova .50 .15
❑ 41 Jay Gibbons 1.00 .30
❑ 42 Geronimo Gil .50 .15
❑ 43 Jerry Hairston .50 .15
❑ 44 Jorge Julio .50 .15
❑ 45 Rodrigo Lopez .50 .15
❑ 46 Gary Matthews Jr. .50 .15
❑ 47 Melvin Mora .50 .15
❑ 48 Sidney Ponson .50 .15
❑ 49 Chris Singleton .50 .15
❑ 50 John Burkett .50 .15
❑ 51 Tony Clark .50 .15
❑ 52 Johnny Damon 1.00 .30
❑ 53 Alan Embree .50 .15
❑ 54 Nomar Garciaparra FOIL 15.00 4.50
❑ 55 Shea Hillenbrand 1.00 .30
❑ 56 Derek Lowe FOIL 5.00 1.50
❑ 57 Pedro Martinez FOIL 10.00 3.00
❑ 58 Trot Nixon 1.00 .30
❑ 59 Manny Ramirez 1.00 .30
❑ 60 Rey Sanchez .50 .15
❑ 61 Ugueth Urbina .50 .15
❑ 62 Jason Varitek 1.00 .30
❑ 63 Moises Alou 1.00 .30
❑ 64 Mark Bellhorn .50 .15
❑ 65 Roosevelt Brown .50 .15
❑ 66 Matt Clement .50 .15
❑ 67 Joe Girardi .50 .15
❑ 68 Alex Gonzalez .50 .15
❑ 69 Todd Hundley .50 .15
❑ 70 Jon Lieber .50 .15
❑ 71 Fred McGriff 1.50 .45
❑ 72 Bill Mueller 1.00 .30
❑ 73 Corey Patterson 1.00 .30
❑ 74 Mark Prior FOIL 10.00 3.00
❑ 75 Sammy Sosa FOIL 15.00 4.50
❑ 76 Mark Buehrle FOIL 5.00 1.50
❑ 77 Jon Garland .50 .15
❑ 78 Tony Graffanino .50 .15
❑ 79 Paul Konerko FOIL 5.00 1.50
❑ 80 Carlos Lee 1.00 .30
❑ 81 Magglio Ordonez FOIL 5.00 1.50
❑ 82 Frank Thomas 2.50 .75
❑ 83 Dan Wright .50 .15
❑ 84 Aaron Boone 1.00 .30
❑ 85 Sean Casey 1.00 .30
❑ 86 Elmer Dessens .50 .15
❑ 87 Adam Dunn 1.50 .45
❑ 88 Danny Graves .50 .15
❑ 89 Joey Hamilton .50 .15
❑ 90 Jimmy Haynes .50 .15
❑ 91 Austin Kearns FOIL 8.00 2.40
❑ 92 Barry Larkin 2.50 .75
❑ 93 Jason LaRue .50 .15
❑ 94 Reggie Taylor .50 .15
❑ 95 Todd Walker 1.00 .30
❑ 96 Danys Baez .50 .15
❑ 97 Milton Bradley 1.00 .30
❑ 98 Ellis Burks 1.00 .30
❑ 99 Einar Diaz .50 .15
❑ 100 Ricky Gutierrez .50 .15
❑ 101 Matt Lawton .50 .15
❑ 102 Chris Magruder .50 .15
❑ 103 C. C. Sabathia 1.00 .30
❑ 104 Lee Stevens .50 .15
❑ 105 Jim Thome FOIL 10.00 3.00
❑ 106 Omar Vizquel 1.00 .30
❑ 107 Bob Wickman .50 .15
❑ 108 Gary Bennett .50 .15
❑ 109 Mike Hampton 1.00 .30
❑ 110 Todd Helton 1.50 .45
❑ 111 Jose Jimenez .50 .15
❑ 112 Denny Neagle .50 .15
❑ 113 Jose Ortiz .50 .15
❑ 114 Juan Pierre 1.00 .30
❑ 115 Juan Uribe .50 .15
❑ 116 Larry Walker FOIL 1.50 .45
❑ 117 Todd Zeile 1.00 .30
❑ 118 Juan Acevedo .50 .15
❑ 119 Robert Fick 1.00 .30
❑ 120 Bobby Higginson 1.00 .30
❑ 121 Damian Jackson .50 .15
❑ 122 Craig Paquette .50 .15
❑ 123 Carlos Pena .50 .15
❑ 124 Mark Redman .50 .15
❑ 125 Randall Simon .50 .15
❑ 126 Steve Sparks .50 .15
❑ 127 Dmitri Young 1.00 .30
❑ 128 A. J. Burnett .50 .15
❑ 129 Luis Castillo 1.00 .30
❑ 130 Juan Encarnacion .50 .15
❑ 131 Alex Gonzalez .50 .15
❑ 132 Charles Johnson 1.00 .30
❑ 133 Derrek Lee 1.00 .30
❑ 134 Mike Lowell 1.00 .30
❑ 135 Vladimir Nunez .50 .15
❑ 136 Eric Owens .50 .15
❑ 137 Preston Wilson 1.00 .30
❑ 138 Brad Ausmus .50 .15
❑ 139 Lance Berkman FOIL 5.00 1.50
❑ 140 Craig Biggio 1.50 .45
❑ 141 Geoff Blum .50 .15
❑ 142 Richard Hidalgo 1.00 .30
❑ 143 Julio Lugo .50 .15
❑ 144 Orlando Merced .50 .15
❑ 145 Billy Wagner 1.00 .30
❑ 146 Carlos Beltran 1.00 .30
❑ 147 Paul Byrd .50 .15
❑ 148 Raul Ibanez 1.00 .30
❑ 149 Chuck Knoblauch 1.00 .30
❑ 150 Brent Mayne .50 .15
❑ 151 Neifi Perez .50 .15
❑ 152 Joe Randa .50 .15
❑ 153 Mike Sweeney 1.00 .30
❑ 154 Adrian Beltre 1.00 .30

❑ 155 Eric Gagne FOIL 5.00 1.50
❑ 156 Shawn Green 1.00 .30
❑ 157 Marquis Grissom .50 .15
❑ 158 Mark Grudzielanek .50 .15
❑ 159 Kazuhisha Ishii FOIL 5.00 1.50
❑ 160 Cesar Izturis .50 .15
❑ 161 Brian Jordan 1.00 .30
❑ 162 Eric Karros 1.00 .30
❑ 163 Paul Lo Duca FOIL 5.00 1.50
❑ 164 Hideo Nomo 2.50 .75
❑ 165 Jesse Orosco .50 .15
❑ 166 Odalis Perez .50 .15
❑ 167 Mike DeJean .50 .15
❑ 168 Jose Hernandez .50 .15
❑ 169 Geoff Jenkins 1.00 .30
❑ 170 Alex Sanchez .50 .15
❑ 171 Richie Sexson 1.00 .30
❑ 172 Ben Sheets 1.00 .30
❑ 173 Eric Young .50 .15
❑ 174 Eddie Guardado 1.00 .30
❑ 175 Cristian Guzman 1.00 .30
❑ 176 Torii Hunter FOIL 5.00 1.50
❑ 177 Jacque Jones 1.00 .30
❑ 178 Corey Koskie 1.00 .30
❑ 179 Doug Mientkiewicz 1.00 .30
❑ 180 Eric Milton .50 .15
❑ 181 A. J. Pierzynski 1.00 .30
❑ 182 Michael Barrett .50 .15
❑ 183 Orlando Cabrera .50 .15
❑ 184 Cliff Floyd 1.00 .30
❑ 185 Vladimir Guerrero FOIL 15.00 4.50
❑ 186 Tomo Ohka .50 .15
❑ 187 Fernando Tatis .50 .15
❑ 188 Javier Vazquez 1.00 .30
❑ 189 Jose Vidro FOIL 5.00 1.50
❑ 190 Brad Wilkerson .50 .15
❑ 191 Edgardo Alfonzo 1.00 .30
❑ 192 Roberto Alomar 2.50 .75
❑ 193 Pedro Astacio .50 .15
❑ 194 Armando Benitez 1.00 .30
❑ 195 Jeromy Burnitz 1.00 .30
❑ 196 Al Leiter 1.00 .30
❑ 197 Rey Ordonez .50 .15
❑ 198 Timo Perez .50 .15
❑ 199 Mike Piazza FOIL 12.00 3.60
❑ 200 Steve Trachsel .50 .15
❑ 201 Mo Vaughn 1.00 .30
❑ 202 Roger Clemens 5.00 1.50
❑ 203 Jason Giambi FOIL 10.00 3.00
❑ 204 Derek Jeter 6.00 1.80
❑ 205 Nick Johnson 1.00 .30
❑ 206 Steve Karsay .50 .15
❑ 207 Mike Mussina FOIL 10.00 3.00
❑ 208 Jorge Posada 1.50 .45
❑ 209 Mariano Rivera FOIL 8.00 2.40
❑ 210 Alfonso Soriano FOIL 10.00 3.00
❑ 211 Mike Stanton .50 .15
❑ 212 Robin Ventura 1.00 .30
❑ 213 Jeff Weaver .50 .15
❑ 214 Rondell White 1.00 .30
❑ 215 Bernie Williams FOIL 8.00 2.40
❑ 216 Eric Chavez 1.00 .30
❑ 217 Jermaine Dye 1.00 .30
❑ 218 Scott Hatteberg .50 .15
❑ 219 Tim Hudson 1.00 .30
❑ 220 Billy Koch 1.00 .30
❑ 221 Terrence Long 1.00 .30
❑ 222 Mark Mulder 1.00 .30
❑ 223 Miguel Tejada FOIL 5.00 1.50
❑ 224 Barry Zito FOIL 10.00 3.00
❑ 225 Bobby Abreu 1.00 .30
❑ 226 Marlon Anderson .50 .15
❑ 227 Pat Burrell 1.00 .30
❑ 228 Brandon Duckworth .50 .15
❑ 229 Jeremy Giambi .50 .15
❑ 230 Doug Glanville .50 .15
❑ 231 Mike Lieberthal 1.00 .30
❑ 232 Jose Mesa .50 .15
❑ 233 Vicente Padilla .50 .15
❑ 234 Jimmy Rollins 1.00 .30
❑ 235 Adrian Brown .50 .15
❑ 236 Josh Fogg .50 .15
❑ 237 Brian Giles 1.00 .30
❑ 238 Jason Kendall 1.00 .30
❑ 239 Pokey Reese .50 .15
❑ 240 Kip Wells .50 .15
❑ 241 Mike Williams FOIL 3.00 .90
❑ 242 Craig Wilson .50 .15
❑ 243 Jack Wilson .50 .15
❑ 244 Kevin Young .50 .15
❑ 245 Trevor Hoffman FOIL 5.00 1.50
❑ 246 Mark Kotsay .50 .15
❑ 247 Ray Lankford .50 .15
❑ 248 Brian Lawrence .50 .15
❑ 249 Phil Nevin 1.00 .30
❑ 250 Kurt Ainsworth .50 .15
❑ 251 David Bell .50 .15
❑ 252 Barry Bonds FOIL 30.00 9.00
❑ 253 Ryan Jensen .50 .15
❑ 254 Jeff Kent FOIL 5.00 1.50
❑ 255 Robb Nen 1.00 .30
❑ 256 Reggie Sanders .50 .15
❑ 257 Benito Santiago 1.00 .30
❑ 258 Tsuyoshi Shinjo 1.00 .30
❑ 259 J. T. Snow 1.00 .30
❑ 260 Bret Boone 1.00 .30
❑ 261 Mike Cameron 1.00 .30
❑ 262 Jeff Cirillo 1.00 .30
❑ 263 Freddy Garcia 1.00 .30
❑ 264 Carlos Guillen .50 .15
❑ 265 Mark McLemore .50 .15
❑ 266 Jamie Moyer 1.00 .30
❑ 267 John Olerud 1.00 .30
❑ 268 Joel Pineiro FOIL 5.00 1.50
❑ 269 Kazuhiro Sasaki FOIL 5.00 1.50
❑ 270 Ruben Sierra .50 .15
❑ 271 Dan Wilson .50 .15
❑ 272 Ichiro Suzuki FOIL 15.00 4.50
❑ 273 J.D. Drew 1.00 .30
❑ 274 Jim Edmonds FOIL 5.00 1.50
❑ 275 Jason Isringhausen 1.00 .30
❑ 276 Matt Morris FOIL 5.00 1.50
❑ 277 Albert Pujols FOIL 12.00 3.60
❑ 278 Edgar Renteria 1.00 .30
❑ 279 Scott Rolen FOIL 8.00 2.40
❑ 280 Jason Simontacchi .50 .15
❑ 281 Fernando Vina 1.00 .30
❑ 282 Brent Abernathy .50 .15
❑ 283 Steve Cox .50 .15
❑ 284 Chris Gomez .50 .15
❑ 285 Ben Grieve .50 .15
❑ 286 Joe Kennedy .50 .15
❑ 287 Tanyon Sturtze .50 .15
❑ 288 Paul Wilson .50 .15
❑ 289 Randy Winn FOIL 3.00 .90
❑ 290 Juan Gonzalez 2.50 .75
❑ 291 Hideki Irabu .50 .15
❑ 292 Rafael Palmeiro FOIL 8.00 2.40
❑ 293 Herbert Perry .50 .15
❑ 294 Alex Rodriguez FOIL 20.00 6.00
❑ 295 Ivan Rodriguez 2.50 .75
❑ 296 Kenny Rogers 1.00 .30
❑ 297 Ismael Valdes .50 .15
❑ 298 Mike Young 1.00 .30
❑ 299 Dave Berg .50 .15
❑ 300 Carlos Delgado 1.00 .30
❑ 301 Kelvim Escobar .50 .15
❑ 302 Roy Halladay FOIL 5.00 1.50
❑ 303 Eric Hinske FOIL 3.00 .90
❑ 304 Shannon Stewart 1.00 .30

2000 Pacific Omega

	Nm-Mt	Ex-Mt
COMP.SET w/o SP's (150)	20.00	6.00
COMMON CARD (1-150)	.30	.09
COMMON (151-255)	5.00	1.50

❑ 1 Garret Anderson .30 .09
❑ 2 Darin Erstad .30 .09
❑ 3 Troy Glaus .50 .15
❑ 4 Tim Salmon .50 .15
❑ 5 Mo Vaughn .30 .09
❑ 6 Jay Bell .30 .09
❑ 7 Steve Finley .30 .09
❑ 8 Luis Gonzalez .30 .09
❑ 9 Randy Johnson .75 .23
❑ 10 Matt Williams .30 .09
❑ 11 Andres Galarraga .30 .09
❑ 12 Andruw Jones .50 .15
❑ 13 Chipper Jones .75 .23
❑ 14 Brian Jordan .30 .09
❑ 15 Greg Maddux 1.50 .45
❑ 16 B.J. Surhoff .30 .09
❑ 17 Brady Anderson .30 .09
❑ 18 Albert Belle .30 .09
❑ 19 Mike Mussina .75 .23
❑ 20 Cal Ripken 2.50 .75
❑ 21 Carl Everett .30 .09
❑ 22 Nomar Garciaparra 1.50 .45
❑ 23 Pedro Martinez .75 .23
❑ 24 Jason Varitek .30 .09
❑ 25 Mark Grace .75 .23
❑ 26 Sammy Sosa 1.25 .35
❑ 27 Rondell White .30 .09
❑ 28 Kerry Wood .75 .23
❑ 29 Eric Young .30 .09
❑ 30 Ray Durham .30 .09
❑ 31 Carlos Lee .30 .09
❑ 32 Magglio Ordonez .30 .09
❑ 33 Frank Thomas .75 .23
❑ 34 Sean Casey .30 .09
❑ 35 Ken Griffey Jr. 1.25 .35
❑ 36 Barry Larkin .75 .23
❑ 37 Pokey Reese .30 .09
❑ 38 Roberto Alomar .75 .23
❑ 39 Kenny Lofton .30 .09
❑ 40 Manny Ramirez .30 .09
❑ 41 David Segui .30 .09
❑ 42 Jim Thome .75 .23
❑ 43 Omar Vizquel .30 .09
❑ 44 Jeff Cirillo .30 .09
❑ 45 Jeffrey Hammonds .30 .09
❑ 46 Todd Helton .50 .15
❑ 47 Todd Hollandsworth .30 .09
❑ 48 Larry Walker .50 .15
❑ 49 Tony Clark .30 .09
❑ 50 Juan Encarnacion .30 .09
❑ 51 Juan Gonzalez .75 .23
❑ 52 Bobby Higginson .30 .09
❑ 53 Hideo Nomo .75 .23
❑ 54 Dean Palmer .30 .09
❑ 55 Luis Castillo .30 .09
❑ 56 Cliff Floyd .30 .09
❑ 57 Derrek Lee .30 .09
❑ 58 Mike Lowell .30 .09
❑ 59 Henry Rodriguez .30 .09
❑ 60 Preston Wilson .30 .09
❑ 61 Moises Alou .30 .09
❑ 62 Jeff Bagwell .50 .15
❑ 63 Craig Biggio .50 .15
❑ 64 Ken Caminiti .30 .09
❑ 65 Richard Hidalgo .30 .09
❑ 66 Carlos Beltran .30 .09
❑ 67 Johnny Damon .30 .09
❑ 68 Jermaine Dye .30 .09
❑ 69 Joe Randa .30 .09
❑ 70 Mike Sweeney .30 .09
❑ 71 Adrian Beltre .30 .09
❑ 72 Kevin Brown .30 .09
❑ 73 Shawn Green .30 .09
❑ 74 Eric Karros .30 .09
❑ 75 Chan Ho Park .30 .09
❑ 76 Gary Sheffield .30 .09
❑ 77 Ron Belliard .30 .09
❑ 78 Jeromy Burnitz .30 .09
❑ 79 Geoff Jenkins .30 .09
❑ 80 Richie Sexson .30 .09
❑ 81 Ron Coomer .30 .09

❑ 82 Jacque Jones .30 .09
❑ 83 Corey Koskie .30 .09
❑ 84 Matt Lawton .30 .09
❑ 85 Vladimir Guerrero .75 .23
❑ 86 Lee Stevens .30 .09
❑ 87 Jose Vidro .30 .09
❑ 88 Edgardo Alfonzo .30 .09
❑ 89 Derek Bell .30 .09
❑ 90 Mike Bordick .30 .09
❑ 91 Mike Piazza 1.25 .35
❑ 92 Robin Ventura .30 .09
❑ 93 Jose Canseco .75 .23
❑ 94 Roger Clemens 1.50 .45
❑ 95 Orlando Hernandez .30 .09
❑ 96 Derek Jeter 2.00 .60
❑ 97 David Justice .30 .09
❑ 98 Tino Martinez .50 .15
❑ 99 Jorge Posada .50 .15
❑ 100 Bernie Williams .50 .15
❑ 101 Eric Chavez .30 .09
❑ 102 Jason Giambi .75 .23
❑ 103 Ben Grieve .30 .09
❑ 104 Miguel Tejada .30 .09
❑ 105 Bobby Abreu .30 .09
❑ 106 Doug Glanville .30 .09
❑ 107 Travis Lee .30 .09
❑ 108 Mike Lieberthal .30 .09
❑ 109 Scott Rolen .50 .15
❑ 110 Brian Giles .30 .09
❑ 111 Jason Kendall .30 .09
❑ 112 Warren Morris .30 .09
❑ 113 Kevin Young .30 .09
❑ 114 Will Clark .75 .23
❑ 115 J.D. Drew .30 .09
❑ 116 Jim Edmonds .30 .09
❑ 117 Mark McGwire 2.00 .60
❑ 118 Edgar Renteria .30 .09
❑ 119 Fernando Tatis .30 .09
❑ 120 Fernando Vina .30 .09
❑ 121 Bret Boone .30 .09
❑ 122 Tony Gwynn 1.00 .30
❑ 123 Trevor Hoffman .30 .09
❑ 124 Phil Nevin .30 .09
❑ 125 Eric Owens .30 .09
❑ 126 Barry Bonds 2.00 .60
❑ 127 Ellis Burks .30 .09
❑ 128 Jeff Kent .30 .09
❑ 129 J.T. Snow .30 .09
❑ 130 Jay Buhner .30 .09
❑ 131 Mike Cameron .30 .09
❑ 132 Rickey Henderson 1.25 .35
❑ 133 Edgar Martinez .30 .09
❑ 134 John Olerud .30 .09
❑ 135 Alex Rodriguez 1.50 .45
❑ 136 Kazuhiro Sasaki RC 1.25 .35
❑ 137 Fred McGriff .50 .15
❑ 138 Greg Vaughn .30 .09
❑ 139 Gerald Williams .30 .09
❑ 140 Rusty Greer .30 .09
❑ 141 Gabe Kapler .30 .09
❑ 142 Ricky Ledee .30 .09
❑ 143 Rafael Palmeiro .50 .15
❑ 144 Ivan Rodriguez .75 .23
❑ 145 Tony Batista .30 .09
❑ 146 Jose Cruz Jr. .30 .09
❑ 147 Carlos Delgado .30 .09
❑ 148 Brad Fullmer .30 .09
❑ 149 Shannon Stewart .30 .09
❑ 150 David Wells .30 .09
❑ 151 Juan Alvarez RC 5.00 1.50
Jeff DaVanon RC
❑ 152 Seth Etherton 5.00 1.50
Adam Kennedy
❑ 153 Ramon Ortiz 5.00 1.50
Lou Pote
❑ 154 Derrick Turnbow RC 5.00 1.50
Eric Weaver
❑ 155 Rod Barajas 5.00 1.50
Jason Conti
❑ 156 Byung-Hyun Kim .30 .09
Rob Ryan
❑ 157 David Cortes RC 5.00 1.50
George Lombard
❑ 158 Ivanon Coffie 5.00 1.50
Melvin Mora
❑ 159 Ryan Kohlmeier RC 10.00 3.00
Luis Matos RC
❑ 160 Willie Morales RC 5.00 1.50
John Parrish RC
❑ 161 Chris Richard RC 5.00 1.50
Jay Spurgeon RC
❑ 162 Israel Alcantara 5.00 1.50
Tomokazu Ohka RC
❑ 163 Paxton Crawford RC 5.00 1.50
Sang-Hoon Lee RC
❑ 164 Mike Mahoney RC 5.00 1.50
Wilton Veras
❑ 165 Daniel Garibay RC 5.00 1.50
Ross Gload RC
❑ 166 Gary Matthews Jr. 5.00 1.50
Phil Norton
❑ 167 Roosevelt Brown 5.00 1.50
Ruben Quevedo
❑ 168 Lorenzo Barcelo RC 5.00 1.50
Rocky Biddle RC
❑ 169 Mark Buehrle 10.00 3.00
John Garland
❑ 170 Aaron Myette 5.00 1.50
Josh Paul
❑ 171 Kip Wells 5.00 1.50
Kelly Wunsch
❑ 172 Rob Bell 5.00 1.50
Travis Dawkins
❑ 173 Hector Mercado RC 5.00 1.50
John Riedling RC
❑ 174 Russell Branyan 5.00 1.50
Sean DePaula RC
❑ 175 Tim Drew 5.00 1.50
Mark Watson RC
❑ 176 Craig House RC 5.00 1.50
Ben Petrick
❑ 177 Robert Fick 5.00 1.50
Jose Macias
❑ 178 Javier Cardona RC 5.00 1.50
Brandon Villafuerte RC
❑ 179 Armando Almanza 5.00 1.50
A.J. Burnett
❑ 180 Ramon Castro 5.00 1.50
Pablo Ozuna
❑ 181 Lance Berkman 5.00 1.50
Jason Green
❑ 182 Julio Lugo 5.00 1.50
Tony McKnight
❑ 183 Mitch Meluskey 5.00 1.50
Wade Miller
❑ 184 Chad Durbin RC 5.00 1.50
Hector Ortiz RC
❑ 185 Dermal Brown 5.00 1.50
Mark Quinn
❑ 186 Eric Gagne 8.00 2.40
Mike Judd
❑ 187 Kane Davis RC 5.00 1.50
Valerio De Los Santos
❑ 188 Santiago Perez RC 5.00 1.50
Paul Rigdon RC
❑ 189 Matt Kinney 5.00 1.50
Matt LeCroy
❑ 190 Jason Maxwell 5.00 1.50
A.J. Pierzynski
❑ 191 J.C. Romero RC 20.00 6.00
Johan Santana RC
❑ 192 Tony Armas Jr. 5.00 1.50
Peter Bergeron
❑ 193 Matt Blank 5.00 1.50
Milton Bradley
❑ 194 T.De La Rosa RC 5.00 1.50
Scott Forster RC
❑ 195 Yovanny Lara RC 5.00 1.50
Talmadge Nunnari RC
❑ 196 Brian Schneider 5.00 1.50
Andy Tracy RC
❑ 197 Scott Strickland 5.00 1.50
T.J. Tucker
❑ 198 Eric Cammack RC 5.00 1.50
Jim Mann RC
❑ 199 Grant Roberts 5.00 1.50
Jorge Toca
❑ 200 Alfonso Soriano 12.00 3.60
Jay Tessmer
❑ 201 Terrence Long 8.00 2.40
Mark Mulder
❑ 202 Pat Burrell 8.00 2.40
Cliff Politte
❑ 203 Jimmy Anderson 5.00 1.50
Bronson Arroyo
❑ 204 Mike Darr 5.00 1.50
Kory DeHaan
❑ 205 Adam Eaton 5.00 1.50
Wiki Gonzalez
❑ 206 Brandon Kolb RC 5.00 1.50
Kevin Walker RC
❑ 207 Damon Minor 5.00 1.50
Calvin Murray
❑ 208 Kevin Hodges RC 100.00 30.00
Joel Pineiro RC
❑ 209 Rob Ramsay 10.00 3.00
Kazuhiro Sasaki
❑ 210 Rick Ankiel 5.00 1.50
Mike Matthews
❑ 211 Steve Cox 5.00 1.50
Travis Harper
❑ 212 Kenny Kelly RC 5.00 1.50
Damian Rolls RC
❑ 213 Doug Davis 5.00 1.50
Scott Sheldon
❑ 214 Brian Sikorski 5.00 1.50
Pedro Valdes
❑ 215 Francisco Cordero 5.00 1.50
B.J. Waszgis RC
❑ 216 Matt DeWitt RC 10.00 3.00
Josh Phelps RC
❑ 217 Vernon Wells 5.00 1.50
Dewayne Wise
❑ 218 Geraldo Guzman RC 5.00 1.50
Jason Marquis
❑ 219 Rafael Furcal 5.00 1.50
Steve Sisco RC
❑ 220 B.J. Ryan 5.00 1.50
Kevin Beirne
❑ 221 Matt Ginter RC 5.00 1.50
Brad Penny
❑ 222 Julio Zuleta RC 5.00 1.50
Eric Munson
❑ 223 Dan Reichert 5.00 1.50
Jeff Williams RC
❑ 224 Jason LaRue 5.00 1.50
Danny Ardoin RC
❑ 225 Ray King 5.00 1.50
Mark Redman
❑ 226 Joe Crede 5.00 1.50
Mike Bell
❑ 227 Juan Pierre RC 10.00 3.00
Jay Payton
❑ 228 Wayne Franklin RC 5.00 1.50
Randy Choate RC
❑ 229 Chris Truby 5.00 1.50
Adam Piatt
❑ 230 Kevin Nicholson 5.00 1.50
Chris Woodward
❑ 231 Barry Zito RC 25.00 7.50
Jason Boyd RC
❑ 232 Brian O'Connor RC 5.00 1.50
Miguel Del Toro
❑ 233 Carlos Guillen 5.00 1.50
Aubrey Huff
❑ 234 Chad Hermansen 5.00 1.50
Jason Tyner
❑ 235 Aaron Fultz RC 5.00 1.50
Ryan Vogelsong RC
❑ 236 Shawn Wooten 5.00 1.50
Vance Wilson
❑ 237 Danny Klassen 5.00 1.50
Mike Lamb RC
❑ 238 Chad Bradford 5.00 1.50
Gene Stechshulte RC
❑ 239 Ismael Villegas RC 5.00 1.50
Hector Ramirez RC
Matt T.Williams RC
Luis Vizcaino
❑ 240 Mike Garcia RC 5.00 1.50
Domingo Guzman RC
Justin Brunette RC
Pasqual Coco RC
❑ 241 Frank Charles RC 5.00 1.50
Keith McDonald RC
❑ 242 Carlos Casimiro RC 5.00 1.50
Morgan Burkhart RC
❑ 243 Raul Gonzalez RC 5.00 1.50

Card	Nm-Mt	Ex-Mt
Shawn Gilbert		
❑ 244 Darrell Einertson RC	5.00	1.50
Jeff Sparks RC		
❑ 245 Augie Ojeda RC	8.00	2.40
Brady Clark		
Todd Belitz		
Eric Byrnes RC		
❑ 246 Leo Estrella RC	5.00	1.50
Charlie Greene		
❑ 247 Trace Coquillette RC	5.00	1.50
Pedro Feliz RC		
❑ 248 Tike Redman RC	5.00	1.50
David Newhan		
❑ 249 Rodrigo Lopez RC	8.00	2.40
John Bale RC		
❑ 250 Corey Patterson	8.00	2.40
Jose Ortiz RC		
❑ 251 Britt Reames RC	5.00	1.50
Oswaldo Mairena RC		
❑ 252 Xavier Nady RC	10.00	3.00
Timo Perez RC		
❑ 253 Tom Jacquez RC	8.00	2.40
Vicente Padilla RC		
❑ 254 Elvis Pena RC	5.00	1.50
Adam Melhuse RC		
❑ 255 Ben Weber RC	5.00	1.50
Alex Cabrera RC		

1993 Pinnacle

	Nm-Mt	Ex-Mt
COMPLETE SET (620)	45.00	13.50
COMP. SERIES 1 (310)	15.00	4.50
COMP. SERIES 2 (310)	30.00	9.00

Card	Nm-Mt	Ex-Mt
❑ 1 Gary Sheffield	.30	.09
❑ 2 Cal Eldred	.15	.04
❑ 3 Larry Walker	.50	.15
❑ 4 Deion Sanders	.30	.09
❑ 5 Dave Fleming	.15	.04
❑ 6 Carlos Baerga	.15	.04
❑ 7 Bernie Williams	.50	.15
❑ 8 John Kruk	.30	.09
❑ 9 Jimmy Key	.30	.09
❑ 10 Jeff Bagwell	.50	.15
❑ 11 Jim Abbott	.75	.23
❑ 12 Terry Steinbach	.15	.04
❑ 13 Bob Tewksbury	.15	.04
❑ 14 Eric Karros	.30	.09
❑ 15 Ryne Sandberg	1.25	.35
❑ 16 Will Clark	.75	.23
❑ 17 Edgar Martinez	.50	.15
❑ 18 Eddie Murray	.75	.23
❑ 19 Andy Van Slyke	.30	.09
❑ 20 Cal Ripken Jr.	2.50	.75
❑ 21 Ivan Rodriguez	.75	.23
❑ 22 Barry Larkin	.75	.23
❑ 23 Don Mattingly	2.00	.60
❑ 24 Gregg Jefferies	.15	.04
❑ 25 Roger Clemens	1.50	.45
❑ 26 Cecil Fielder	.30	.09
❑ 27 Kent Hrbek	.30	.09
❑ 28 Robin Ventura	.30	.09
❑ 29 Rickey Henderson	1.25	.35
❑ 30 Roberto Alomar	.75	.23
❑ 31 Luis Polonia	.15	.04
❑ 32 Andujar Cedeno	.15	.04
❑ 33 Pat Listach	.15	.04
❑ 34 Mark Grace	.75	.23
❑ 35 Otis Nixon	.15	.04
❑ 36 Felix Jose	.15	.04
❑ 37 Mike Sharperson	.15	.04
❑ 38 Dennis Martinez	.30	.09
❑ 39 Willie McGee	.30	.09
❑ 40 Kenny Lofton	.30	.09
❑ 41 Randy Johnson	.75	.23
❑ 42 Andy Benes	.15	.04
❑ 43 Bobby Bonilla	.30	.09
❑ 44 Mike Mussina	.75	.23
❑ 45 Len Dykstra	.30	.09
❑ 46 Ellis Burks	.30	.09
❑ 47 Chris Sabo	.15	.04
❑ 48 Jay Bell	.30	.09
❑ 49 Jose Canseco	.75	.23
❑ 50 Craig Biggio	.50	.15
❑ 51 Wally Joyner	.30	.09
❑ 52 Mickey Tettleton	.15	.04
❑ 53 Tim Raines	.30	.09
❑ 54 Brian Harper	.15	.04
❑ 55 Rene Gonzales	.15	.04
❑ 56 Mark Langston	.15	.04
❑ 57 Jack Morris	.30	.09
❑ 58 Mark McGwire	2.00	.60
❑ 59 Ken Caminiti	.30	.09
❑ 60 Terry Pendleton	.30	.09
❑ 61 Dave Nilsson	.15	.04
❑ 62 Tom Pagnozzi	.15	.04
❑ 63 Mike Morgan	.15	.04
❑ 64 Darryl Strawberry	.50	.15
❑ 65 Charles Nagy	.15	.04
❑ 66 Ken Hill	.15	.04
❑ 67 Matt Williams	.30	.09
❑ 68 Jay Buhner	.30	.09
❑ 69 Vince Coleman	.15	.04
❑ 70 Brady Anderson	.30	.09
❑ 71 Fred McGriff	.50	.15
❑ 72 Ben McDonald	.15	.04
❑ 73 Terry Mulholland	.15	.04
❑ 74 Randy Tomlin	.15	.04
❑ 75 Nolan Ryan	3.00	.90
❑ 76 Frank Viola UER	.30	.09
(Card incorrectly states he has a surgically repaired elbow)		
❑ 77 Jose Rijo	.15	.04
❑ 78 Shane Mack	.15	.04
❑ 79 Travis Fryman	.30	.09
❑ 80 Jack McDowell	.15	.04
❑ 81 Mark Gubicza	.15	.04
❑ 82 Matt Nokes	.15	.04
❑ 83 Bert Blyleven	.30	.09
❑ 84 Eric Anthony	.15	.04
❑ 85 Mike Bordick	.15	.04
❑ 86 John Olerud	.30	.09
❑ 87 B.J. Surhoff	.30	.09
❑ 88 Bernard Gilkey	.15	.04
❑ 89 Shawon Dunston	.15	.04
❑ 90 Tom Glavine	.75	.23
❑ 91 Brett Butler	.30	.09
❑ 92 Moises Alou	.30	.09
❑ 93 Albert Belle	.30	.09
❑ 94 Darren Lewis	.15	.04
❑ 95 Omar Vizquel	.30	.09
❑ 96 Dwight Gooden	.50	.15
❑ 97 Gregg Olson	.15	.04
❑ 98 Tony Gwynn	1.00	.30
❑ 99 Darren Daulton	.30	.09
❑ 100 Dennis Eckersley	.30	.09
❑ 101 Rob Dibble	.30	.09
❑ 102 Mike Greenwell	.15	.04
❑ 103 Jose Lind	.15	.04
❑ 104 Julio Franco	.30	.09
❑ 105 Tom Gordon	.15	.04
❑ 106 Scott Livingstone	.15	.04
❑ 107 Chuck Knoblauch	.30	.09
❑ 108 Frank Thomas	.75	.23
❑ 109 Melido Perez	.15	.04
❑ 110 Ken Griffey Jr.	1.25	.35
❑ 111 Harold Baines	.30	.09
❑ 112 Gary Gaetti	.30	.09
❑ 113 Pete Harnisch	.15	.04
❑ 114 David Wells	.30	.09
❑ 115 Charlie Leibrandt	.15	.04
❑ 116 Ray Lankford	.15	.04
❑ 117 Kevin Seitzer	.15	.04
❑ 118 Robin Yount	.75	.23
❑ 119 Lenny Harris	.15	.04
❑ 120 Chris James	.15	.04
❑ 121 Delino DeShields	.15	.04
❑ 122 Kirt Manwaring	.15	.04
❑ 123 Glenallen Hill	.15	.04
❑ 124 Hensley Meulens	.15	.04
❑ 125 Darrin Jackson	.15	.04
❑ 126 Todd Hundley	.15	.04
❑ 127 Dave Hollins	.15	.04
❑ 128 Sam Horn	.15	.04
❑ 129 Roberto Hernandez	.15	.04
❑ 130 Vicente Palacios	.15	.04
❑ 131 George Brett	2.00	.60
❑ 132 Dave Martinez	.15	.04
❑ 133 Kevin Appier	.30	.09
❑ 134 Pat Kelly	.15	.04
❑ 135 Pedro Munoz	.15	.04
❑ 136 Mark Carreon	.15	.04
❑ 137 Lance Johnson	.15	.04
❑ 138 Devon White	.15	.04
❑ 139 Julio Valera	.15	.04
❑ 140 Eddie Taubensee	.15	.04
❑ 141 Willie Wilson	.15	.04
❑ 142 Stan Belinda	.15	.04
❑ 143 John Smoltz	.50	.15
❑ 144 Darryl Hamilton	.15	.04
❑ 145 Sammy Sosa	1.25	.35
❑ 146 Carlos Hernandez	.15	.04
❑ 147 Tom Candiotti	.15	.04
❑ 148 Mike Felder	.15	.04
❑ 149 Rusty Meacham	.15	.04
❑ 150 Ivan Calderon	.15	.04
❑ 151 Pete O'Brien	.15	.04
❑ 152 Erik Hanson	.15	.04
❑ 153 Billy Ripken	.15	.04
❑ 154 Kurt Stillwell	.15	.04
❑ 155 Jeff Kent	.75	.23
❑ 156 Mickey Morandini	.15	.04
❑ 157 Randy Milligan	.15	.04
❑ 158 Reggie Sanders	.30	.09
❑ 159 Luis Rivera	.15	.04
❑ 160 Orlando Merced	.15	.04
❑ 161 Dean Palmer	.30	.09
❑ 162 Mike Perez	.15	.04
❑ 163 Scott Erickson	.15	.04
❑ 164 Kevin McReynolds	.15	.04
❑ 165 Kevin Maas	.15	.04
❑ 166 Ozzie Guillen	.15	.04
❑ 167 Rob Deer	.15	.04
❑ 168 Danny Tartabull	.15	.04
❑ 169 Lee Stevens	.15	.04
❑ 170 Dave Henderson	.15	.04
❑ 171 Derek Bell	.15	.04
❑ 172 Steve Finley	.30	.09
❑ 173 Greg Olson	.15	.04
❑ 174 Geronimo Pena	.15	.04
❑ 175 Paul Quantrill	.15	.04
❑ 176 Steve Buechele	.15	.04
❑ 177 Kevin Gross	.15	.04
❑ 178 Tim Wallach	.15	.04
❑ 179 Dave Valle	.15	.04
❑ 180 Dave Silvestri	.15	.04
❑ 181 Bud Black	.15	.04
❑ 182 Henry Rodriguez	.15	.04
❑ 183 Tim Teufel	.15	.04
❑ 184 Mark McLemore	.15	.04
❑ 185 Bret Saberhagen	.30	.09
❑ 186 Chris Hoiles	.15	.04
❑ 187 Ricky Jordan	.15	.04
❑ 188 Don Slaught	.15	.04
❑ 189 Mo Vaughn	.30	.09
❑ 190 Joe Oliver	.15	.04
❑ 191 Juan Gonzalez	.75	.23
❑ 192 Scott Leius	.15	.04
❑ 193 Milt Cuyler	.15	.04
❑ 194 Chris Haney	.15	.04
❑ 195 Ron Karkovice	.15	.04
❑ 196 Steve Farr	.15	.04
❑ 197 John Orton	.15	.04
❑ 198 Kelly Gruber	.15	.04
❑ 199 Ron Darling	.15	.04
❑ 200 Ruben Sierra	.15	.04
❑ 201 Chuck Finley	.30	.09
❑ 202 Mike Moore	.15	.04

- ❑ 203 Pat Borders .15 .04
- ❑ 204 Sid Bream .15 .04
- ❑ 205 Todd Zeile .15 .04
- ❑ 206 Rick Wilkins .15 .04
- ❑ 207 Jim Gantner .15 .04
- ❑ 208 Frank Castillo .15 .04
- ❑ 209 Dave Hansen .15 .04
- ❑ 210 Trevor Wilson .15 .04
- ❑ 211 Sandy Alomar Jr. .15 .04
- ❑ 212 Sean Berry .15 .04
- ❑ 213 Tino Martinez .50 .15
- ❑ 214 Chito Martinez .15 .04
- ❑ 215 Dan Walters .15 .04
- ❑ 216 John Franco .30 .09
- ❑ 217 Glenn Davis .15 .04
- ❑ 218 Mariano Duncan .15 .04
- ❑ 219 Mike LaValliere .15 .04
- ❑ 220 Rafael Palmeiro .50 .15
- ❑ 221 Jack Clark .30 .09
- ❑ 222 Hal Morris .15 .04
- ❑ 223 Ed Sprague .15 .04
- ❑ 224 John Valentin .15 .04
- ❑ 225 Sam Militello .15 .04
- ❑ 226 Bob Wickman .15 .04
- ❑ 227 Damion Easley .15 .04
- ❑ 228 John Jaha .15 .04
- ❑ 229 Bob Ayrault .15 .04
- ❑ 230 Mo Sanford .15 .04
- ❑ 231 Walt Weiss .15 .04
- ❑ 232 Dante Bichette .30 .09
- ❑ 233 Steve Decker .15 .04
- ❑ 234 Jerald Clark .15 .04
- ❑ 235 Bryan Harvey .15 .04
- ❑ 236 Joe Girardi .15 .04
- ❑ 237 Dave Magadan .15 .04
- ❑ 238 David Nied .15 .04
- ❑ 239 Eric Wedge RC .15 .04
- ❑ 240 Rico Brogna .15 .04
- ❑ 241 J.T. Bruett .15 .04
- ❑ 242 Jonathan Hurst .15 .04
- ❑ 243 Bret Boone .50 .15
- ❑ 244 Manny Alexander .15 .04
- ❑ 245 Scooter Tucker .15 .04
- ❑ 246 Troy Neel .15 .04
- ❑ 247 Eddie Zosky .15 .04
- ❑ 248 Melvin Nieves .15 .04
- ❑ 249 Ryan Thompson .15 .04
- ❑ 250 Shawn Barton RC .15 .04
- ❑ 251 Ryan Klesko .30 .09
- ❑ 252 Mike Piazza 2.00 .60
- ❑ 253 Steve Hosey .15 .04
- ❑ 254 Shane Reynolds .15 .04
- ❑ 255 Dan Wilson .30 .09
- ❑ 256 Tom Marsh .15 .04
- ❑ 257 Barry Manuel .15 .04
- ❑ 258 Paul Miller .15 .04
- ❑ 259 Pedro Martinez 1.50 .45
- ❑ 260 Steve Cooke .15 .04
- ❑ 261 Johnny Guzman .15 .04
- ❑ 262 Mike Butcher .15 .04
- ❑ 263 Bien Figueroa .15 .04
- ❑ 264 Rich Rowland .15 .04
- ❑ 265 Shawn Jeter .15 .04
- ❑ 266 Gerald Williams .15 .04
- ❑ 267 Derek Parks .15 .04
- ❑ 268 Henry Mercedes .15 .04
- ❑ 269 David Hulse RC .15 .04
- ❑ 270 Tim Pugh RC .15 .04
- ❑ 271 William Suero .15 .04
- ❑ 272 Ozzie Canseco .15 .04
- ❑ 273 Fernando Ramsey RC .15 .04
- ❑ 274 Bernardo Brito .15 .04
- ❑ 275 Dave Mlicki .15 .04
- ❑ 276 Tim Salmon .50 .15
- ❑ 277 Mike Raczka .15 .04
- ❑ 278 Ken Ryan RC .15 .04
- ❑ 279 Rafael Bournigal .15 .04
- ❑ 280 Wil Cordero .15 .04
- ❑ 281 Billy Ashley .15 .04
- ❑ 282 Paul Wagner .15 .04
- ❑ 283 Blas Minor .15 .04
- ❑ 284 Rick Trlicek .15 .04
- ❑ 285 Willie Greene .15 .04
- ❑ 286 Ted Wood .15 .04
- ❑ 287 Phil Clark .15 .04
- ❑ 288 Jesse Levis .15 .04
- ❑ 289 Tony Gwynn NT .50 .15
- ❑ 290 Nolan Ryan NT 1.50 .45
- ❑ 291 Dennis Martinez NT .15 .04
- ❑ 292 Eddie Murray NT .50 .15
- ❑ 293 Robin Yount NT .30 .09
- ❑ 294 George Brett NT .75 .23
- ❑ 295 Dave Winfield NT .30 .09
- ❑ 296 Bert Blyleven NT .15 .04
- ❑ 297 Jeff Bagwell .75 .23
  Carl Yastrzemski
- ❑ 298 John Smoltz .30 .09
  Jack Morris
- ❑ 299 Larry Walker .50 .15
  Mike Bossy
- ❑ 300 Gary Sheffield .30 .09
  Barry Larkin
- ❑ 301 Ivan Rodriguez .50 .15
  Carlton Fisk
- ❑ 302 Delino DeShields .75 .23
  Malcolm X
- ❑ 303 Tim Salmon .50 .15
  Dwight Evans
- ❑ 304 Bernard Gilkey HH .15 .04
- ❑ 305 Cal Ripken Jr. HH 1.25 .35
- ❑ 306 Barry Larkin HH .30 .09
- ❑ 307 Kent Hrbek HH .15 .04
- ❑ 308 Rickey Henderson HH .75 .23
- ❑ 309 Darryl Strawberry HH .30 .09
- ❑ 310 John Franco HH .15 .04
- ❑ 311 Todd Stottlemyre .15 .04
- ❑ 312 Luis Gonzalez .30 .09
- ❑ 313 Tommy Greene .15 .04
- ❑ 314 Randy Velarde .15 .04
- ❑ 315 Steve Avery .15 .04
- ❑ 316 Jose Oquendo .15 .04
- ❑ 317 Rey Sanchez .15 .04
- ❑ 318 Greg Vaughn .30 .09
- ❑ 319 Orel Hershiser .30 .09
- ❑ 320 Paul Sorrento .15 .04
- ❑ 321 Royce Clayton .15 .04
- ❑ 322 John Vander Wal .15 .04
- ❑ 323 Henry Cotto .15 .04
- ❑ 324 Pete Schourek .15 .04
- ❑ 325 David Segui .15 .04
- ❑ 326 Arthur Rhodes .15 .04
- ❑ 327 Bruce Hurst .15 .04
- ❑ 328 Wes Chamberlain .15 .04
- ❑ 329 Ozzie Smith .75 .23
- ❑ 330 Scott Cooper .15 .04
- ❑ 331 Felix Fermin .15 .04
- ❑ 332 Mike Macfarlane .15 .04
- ❑ 333 Dan Gladden .15 .04
- ❑ 334 Kevin Tapani .15 .04
- ❑ 335 Steve Sax .15 .04
- ❑ 336 Jeff Montgomery .15 .04
- ❑ 337 Gary DiSarcina .15 .04
- ❑ 338 Lance Blankenship .15 .04
- ❑ 339 Brian Williams .15 .04
- ❑ 340 Duane Ward .15 .04
- ❑ 341 Chuck McElroy .15 .04
- ❑ 342 Joe Magrane .15 .04
- ❑ 343 Jaime Navarro .15 .04
- ❑ 344 Dave Justice .30 .09
- ❑ 345 Jose Offerman .15 .04
- ❑ 346 Marquis Grissom .15 .04
- ❑ 347 Bill Swift .15 .04
- ❑ 348 Jim Thome .75 .23
- ❑ 349 Archi Cianfrocco .15 .04
- ❑ 350 Anthony Young .15 .04
- ❑ 351 Leo Gomez .15 .04
- ❑ 352 Bill Gullickson .15 .04
- ❑ 353 Alan Trammell .50 .15
- ❑ 354 Dan Pasqua .15 .04
- ❑ 355 Jeff King .15 .04
- ❑ 356 Kevin Brown .30 .09
- ❑ 357 Tim Belcher .15 .04
- ❑ 358 Bip Roberts .15 .04
- ❑ 359 Brent Mayne .15 .04
- ❑ 360 Rheal Cormier .15 .04
- ❑ 361 Mark Guthrie .15 .04
- ❑ 362 Craig Grebeck .15 .04
- ❑ 363 Andy Stankiewicz .15 .04
- ❑ 364 Juan Guzman .15 .04
- ❑ 365 Bobby Witt .15 .04
- ❑ 366 Mark Portugal .15 .04
- ❑ 367 Brian McRae .15 .04
- ❑ 368 Mark Lemke .15 .04
- ❑ 369 Bill Wegman .15 .04
- ❑ 370 Donovan Osborne .15 .04
- ❑ 371 Derrick May .15 .04
- ❑ 372 Carl Willis .15 .04
- ❑ 373 Chris Nabholz .15 .04
- ❑ 374 Mark Lewis .15 .04
- ❑ 375 John Burkett .15 .04
- ❑ 376 Luis Mercedes .15 .04
- ❑ 377 Ramon Martinez .15 .04
- ❑ 378 Kyle Abbott .15 .04
- ❑ 379 Mark Wohlers .15 .04
- ❑ 380 Bob Walk .15 .04
- ❑ 381 Kenny Rogers .30 .09
- ❑ 382 Tim Naehring .15 .04
- ❑ 383 Alex Fernandez .15 .04
- ❑ 384 Keith Miller .15 .04
- ❑ 385 Mike Henneman .15 .04
- ❑ 386 Rick Aguilera .15 .04
- ❑ 387 George Bell .15 .04
- ❑ 388 Mike Gallego .15 .04
- ❑ 389 Howard Johnson .15 .04
- ❑ 390 Kim Batiste .15 .04
- ❑ 391 Jerry Browne .15 .04
- ❑ 392 Damon Berryhill .15 .04
- ❑ 393 Ricky Bones .15 .04
- ❑ 394 Omar Olivares .15 .04
- ❑ 395 Mike Harkey .15 .04
- ❑ 396 Pedro Astacio .15 .04
- ❑ 397 John Wetteland .30 .09
- ❑ 398 Rod Beck .15 .04
- ❑ 399 Thomas Howard .15 .04
- ❑ 400 Mike Devereaux .15 .04
- ❑ 401 Tim Wakefield .30 .09
- ❑ 402 Curt Schilling .50 .15
- ❑ 403 Zane Smith .15 .04
- ❑ 404 Bob Zupcic .15 .04
- ❑ 405 Tom Browning .15 .04
- ❑ 406 Tony Phillips .15 .04
- ❑ 407 John Doherty .15 .04
- ❑ 408 Pat Mahomes .15 .04
- ❑ 409 John Habyan .15 .04
- ❑ 410 Steve Olin .15 .04
- ❑ 411 Chad Curtis .15 .04
- ❑ 412 Joe Grahe .15 .04
- ❑ 413 John Patterson .15 .04
- ❑ 414 Brian Hunter .15 .04
- ❑ 415 Doug Henry .15 .04
- ❑ 416 Lee Smith .30 .09
- ❑ 417 Bob Scanlan .15 .04
- ❑ 418 Kent Mercker .15 .04
- ❑ 419 Mel Rojas .15 .04
- ❑ 420 Mark Whiten .15 .04
- ❑ 421 Carlton Fisk .50 .15
- ❑ 422 Candy Maldonado .15 .04
- ❑ 423 Doug Drabek .15 .04
- ❑ 424 Wade Boggs .50 .15
- ❑ 425 Mark Davis .15 .04
- ❑ 426 Kirby Puckett .75 .23
- ❑ 427 Joe Carter .30 .09
- ❑ 428 Paul Molitor .50 .15
- ❑ 429 Eric Davis .30 .09
- ❑ 430 Darryl Kile .30 .09
- ❑ 431 Jeff Parrett .15 .04
- ❑ 432 Jeff Blauser .15 .04
- ❑ 433 Dan Plesac .15 .04
- ❑ 434 Andres Galarraga .30 .09
- ❑ 435 Jim Gott .15 .04
- ❑ 436 Jose Mesa .15 .04
- ❑ 437 Ben Rivera .15 .04
- ❑ 438 Dave Winfield .50 .15
- ❑ 439 Norm Charlton .15 .04
- ❑ 440 Chris Bosio .15 .04
- ❑ 441 Wilson Alvarez .15 .04
- ❑ 442 Dave Stewart .30 .09
- ❑ 443 Doug Jones .15 .04
- ❑ 444 Jeff Russell .15 .04
- ❑ 445 Ron Gant .30 .09
- ❑ 446 Paul O'Neill .50 .15
- ❑ 447 Charlie Hayes .15 .04
- ❑ 448 Joe Hesketh .15 .04
- ❑ 449 Chris Hammond .15 .04
- ❑ 450 Hipolito Pichardo .15 .04
- ❑ 451 Scott Radinsky .15 .04
- ❑ 452 Bobby Thigpen .15 .04
- ❑ 453 Xavier Hernandez .15 .04

			Nm-Mt	Ex-Mt
❑	454	Lonnie Smith	.15	.04
❑	455	Jamie Arnold DP RC	.15	.04
❑	456	B.J. Wallace DP	.15	.04
❑	457	Derek Jeter DP RC	15.00	4.50
❑	458	Jason Kendall DP RC	1.00	.30
❑	459	Rick Helling DP	.15	.04
❑	460	Derek Wallace DP RC	.15	.04
❑	461	Sean Lowe DP RC	.15	.04
❑	462	S. Stewart DP RC	1.00	.30
❑	463	Benji Grigsby DP RC	.15	.04
❑	464	T. Steverson DP RC	.15	.04
❑	465	Dan Serafini DP RC	.15	.04
❑	466	Michael Tucker DP	.15	.04
❑	467	Chris Roberts DP	.15	.04
❑	468	Pete Janicki DP RC	.15	.04
❑	469	Jeff Schmidt DP RC	.15	.04
❑	470	Don Mattingly NT	1.00	.30
❑	471	Cal Ripken Jr. NT	1.25	.35
❑	472	Jack Morris NT	.15	.04
❑	473	Terry Pendleton NT	.15	.04
❑	474	Dennis Eckersley NT	.30	.09
❑	475	Carlton Fisk NT	.30	.09
❑	476	Wade Boggs NT	.30	.09
❑	477	Len Dykstra Ken Stabler	.30	.09
❑	478	Danny Tartabull Jose Tartabull	.15	.04
❑	479	Jeff Conine Dale Murphy	.50	.15
❑	480	Gregg Jefferies Ron Cey	.15	.04
❑	481	Paul Molitor Harmon Killebrew	.30	.09
❑	482	John Valentin Dave Concepcion	.15	.04
❑	483	Alex Arias Dave Winfield	.30	.09
❑	484	Barry Bonds HH	1.00	.30
❑	485	Doug Drabek HH	.15	.04
❑	486	Dave Winfield HH	.30	.09
❑	487	Brett Butler HH	.15	.04
❑	488	Harold Baines HH	.15	.04
❑	489	David Cone HH	.15	.04
❑	490	Willie McGee HH	.15	.04
❑	491	Robby Thompson	.15	.04
❑	492	Pete Incaviglia	.15	.04
❑	493	Manuel Lee	.15	.04
❑	494	Rafael Belliard	.15	.04
❑	495	Scott Fletcher	.15	.04
❑	496	Jeff Frye	.15	.04
❑	497	Andre Dawson	.30	.09
❑	498	Mike Scioscia	.15	.04
❑	499	Spike Owen	.15	.04
❑	500	Sid Fernandez	.15	.04
❑	501	Joe Orsulak	.15	.04
❑	502	Benito Santiago	.30	.09
❑	503	Dale Murphy	.75	.23
❑	504	Barry Bonds	2.00	.60
❑	505	Jose Guzman	.15	.04
❑	506	Tony Pena	.15	.04
❑	507	Greg Swindell	.15	.04
❑	508	Mike Pagliarulo	.15	.04
❑	509	Lou Whitaker	.30	.09
❑	510	Greg Gagne	.15	.04
❑	511	Butch Henry	.15	.04
❑	512	Jeff Brantley	.15	.04
❑	513	Jack Armstrong	.15	.04
❑	514	Danny Jackson	.15	.04
❑	515	Junior Felix	.15	.04
❑	516	Milt Thompson	.15	.04
❑	517	Greg Maddux	1.50	.45
❑	518	Eric Young	.15	.04
❑	519	Jody Reed	.15	.04
❑	520	Roberto Kelly	.15	.04
❑	521	Darren Holmes	.15	.04
❑	522	Craig Lefferts	.15	.04
❑	523	Charlie Hough	.30	.09
❑	524	Bo Jackson	.75	.23
❑	525	Bill Spiers	.15	.04
❑	526	Orestes Destrade	.15	.04
❑	527	Greg Hibbard	.15	.04
❑	528	Roger McDowell	.15	.04
❑	529	Cory Snyder	.15	.04
❑	530	Harold Reynolds	.30	.09
❑	531	Kevin Reimer	.15	.04
❑	532	Rick Sutcliffe	.30	.09
❑	533	Tony Fernandez	.15	.04
❑	534	Tom Brunansky	.15	.04
❑	535	Jeff Reardon	.30	.09
❑	536	Chili Davis	.30	.09
❑	537	Bob Ojeda	.15	.04
❑	538	Greg Colbrunn	.15	.04
❑	539	Phil Plantier	.15	.04
❑	540	Brian Jordan	.30	.09
❑	541	Pete Smith	.15	.04
❑	542	Frank Tanana	.15	.04
❑	543	John Smiley	.15	.04
❑	544	David Cone	.30	.09
❑	545	Daryl Boston	.15	.04
❑	546	Tom Henke	.15	.04
❑	547	Bill Krueger	.15	.04
❑	548	Freddie Benavides	.15	.04
❑	549	Randy Myers	.15	.04
❑	550	Reggie Jefferson	.15	.04
❑	551	Kevin Mitchell	.15	.04
❑	552	Dave Stieb	.15	.04
❑	553	Bret Barberie	.15	.04
❑	554	Tim Crews	.15	.04
❑	555	Doug Dascenzo	.15	.04
❑	556	Alex Cole	.15	.04
❑	557	Jeff Innis	.15	.04
❑	558	Carlos Garcia	.15	.04
❑	559	Steve Howe	.15	.04
❑	560	Kirk McCaskill	.15	.04
❑	561	Frank Seminara	.15	.04
❑	562	Cris Carpenter	.15	.04
❑	563	Mike Stanley	.15	.04
❑	564	Carlos Quintana	.15	.04
❑	565	Mitch Williams	.15	.04
❑	566	Juan Bell	.15	.04
❑	567	Eric Fox	.15	.04
❑	568	Al Leiter	.30	.09
❑	569	Mike Stanton	.15	.04
❑	570	Scott Kamieniecki	.15	.04
❑	571	Ryan Bowen	.15	.04
❑	572	Andy Ashby	.15	.04
❑	573	Bob Welch	.15	.04
❑	574	Scott Sanderson	.15	.04
❑	575	Joe Kmak	.15	.04
❑	576	Scott Pose RC	.15	.04
❑	577	Ricky Gutierrez	.15	.04
❑	578	Mike Trombley	.15	.04
❑	579	Sterling Hitchcock RC	.30	.09
❑	580	Rodney Bolton	.15	.04
❑	581	Tyler Green	.15	.04
❑	582	Tim Costo	.15	.04
❑	583	Tim Laker RC	.15	.04
❑	584	Steve Reed RC	.15	.04
❑	585	Tom Kramer RC	.15	.04
❑	586	Robb Nen	.30	.09
❑	587	Jim Tatum RC	.15	.04
❑	588	Frank Bolick	.15	.04
❑	589	Kevin Young	.30	.09
❑	590	Matt Whiteside RC	.15	.04
❑	591	Cesar Hernandez	.15	.04
❑	592	Mike Mohler RC	.15	.04
❑	593	Alan Embree	.15	.04
❑	594	Terry Jorgensen	.15	.04
❑	595	John Cummings RC	.15	.04
❑	596	Domingo Martinez RC	.15	.04
❑	597	Benji Gil	.15	.04
❑	598	Todd Pratt RC	.30	.09
❑	599	Rene Arocha RC	.30	.09
❑	600	Dennis Moeller	.15	.04
❑	601	Jeff Conine	.30	.09
❑	602	Trevor Hoffman	.30	.09
❑	603	Daniel Smith	.15	.04
❑	604	Lee Tinsley	.15	.04
❑	605	Dan Peltier	.15	.04
❑	606	Billy Brewer	.15	.04
❑	607	Matt Walbeck RC	.15	.04
❑	608	Richie Lewis RC	.15	.04
❑	609	J.T. Snow RC	.75	.23
❑	610	Pat Gomez RC	.15	.04
❑	611	Phil Hiatt	.15	.04
❑	612	Alex Arias	.15	.04
❑	613	Kevin Rogers	.15	.04
❑	614	Al Martin	.15	.04
❑	615	Greg Gohr	.15	.04
❑	616	Graeme Lloyd RC	.30	.09
❑	617	Kent Bottenfield	.15	.04
❑	618	Chuck Carr	.15	.04
❑	619	Darrell Sherman RC	.15	.04
❑	620	Mike Lansing RC	.30	.09

2001 Playoff Absolute Memorabilia

	Nm-Mt	Ex-Mt
COMP.SET w/o SP's (150)	40.00	12.00
COMMON CARD (1-150)	.75	.23
COMMON RPM (151-200)	10.00	3.00

			Nm-Mt	Ex-Mt
❑	1	Alex Rodriguez	4.00	1.20
❑	2	Barry Bonds	5.00	1.50
❑	3	Cal Ripken	6.00	1.80
❑	4	Chipper Jones	2.00	.60
❑	5	Derek Jeter	5.00	1.50
❑	6	Troy Glaus	1.25	.35
❑	7	Frank Thomas	2.00	.60
❑	8	Greg Maddux	4.00	1.20
❑	9	Ivan Rodriguez	2.00	.60
❑	10	Jeff Bagwell	1.25	.35
❑	11	Ryan Dempster	.75	.23
❑	12	Todd Helton	1.25	.35
❑	13	Ken Griffey Jr.	4.00	1.20
❑	14	Manny Ramirez	.75	.23
❑	15	Mark McGwire	5.00	1.50
❑	16	Mike Piazza	3.00	.90
❑	17	Nomar Garciaparra	4.00	1.20
❑	18	Pedro Martinez	2.00	.60
❑	19	Randy Johnson	2.00	.60
❑	20	Rick Ankiel	.75	.23
❑	21	Rickey Henderson	3.00	.90
❑	22	Roger Clemens	4.00	1.20
❑	23	Sammy Sosa	3.00	.90
❑	24	Tony Gwynn	2.50	.75
❑	25	Vladimir Guerrero	2.00	.60
❑	26	Kazuhiro Sasaki	.75	.23
❑	27	Roberto Alomar	2.00	.60
❑	28	Barry Zito	2.00	.60
❑	29	Pat Burrell	.75	.23
❑	30	Harold Baines	.75	.23
❑	31	Carlos Delgado	.75	.23
❑	32	J.D. Drew	.75	.23
❑	33	Jim Edmonds	.75	.23
❑	34	Darin Erstad	.75	.23
❑	35	Jason Giambi	2.00	.60
❑	36	Tom Glavine	2.00	.60
❑	37	Juan Gonzalez	2.00	.60
❑	38	Mark Grace	2.00	.60
❑	39	Shawn Green	.75	.23
❑	40	Tim Hudson	.75	.23
❑	41	Andruw Jones	1.25	.35
❑	42	David Justice	.75	.23
❑	43	Jeff Kent	.75	.23
❑	44	Barry Larkin	2.00	.60
❑	45	Rafael Furcal	.75	.23
❑	46	Mike Mussina	2.00	.60
❑	47	Hideo Nomo	2.00	.60
❑	48	Rafael Palmeiro	1.25	.35
❑	49	Adam Piatt	.75	.23
❑	50	Scott Rolen	1.25	.35
❑	51	Gary Sheffield	.75	.23
❑	52	Bernie Williams	1.25	.35
❑	53	Bob Abreu	.75	.23
❑	54	Edgardo Alfonzo	.75	.23
❑	55	Edgar Renteria	.75	.23
❑	56	Phil Nevin	.75	.23
❑	57	Craig Biggio	1.25	.35

❑ 58 Andres Galarraga	.75	.23
❑ 59 Edgar Martinez	1.25	.35
❑ 60 Fred McGriff	1.25	.35
❑ 61 Maggio Ordonez	.75	.23
❑ 62 Jim Thome	2.00	.60
❑ 63 Matt Williams	.75	.23
❑ 64 Kerry Wood	2.00	.60
❑ 65 Moises Alou	.75	.23
❑ 66 Brady Anderson	.75	.23
❑ 67 Garret Anderson	.75	.23
❑ 68 Russell Branyan	.75	.23
❑ 69 Tony Batista	.75	.23
❑ 70 Vernon Wells	.75	.23
❑ 71 Carlos Beltran	.75	.23
❑ 72 Adrian Beltre	.75	.23
❑ 73 Kris Benson	.75	.23
❑ 74 Lance Berkman	.75	.23
❑ 75 Kevin Brown	.75	.23
❑ 76 Dee Brown	.75	.23
❑ 77 Jeromy Burnitz	.75	.23
❑ 78 Timo Perez	.75	.23
❑ 79 Sean Casey	.75	.23
❑ 80 Luis Castillo	.75	.23
❑ 81 Eric Chavez	.75	.23
❑ 82 Jeff Cirillo	.75	.23
❑ 83 Bartolo Colon	.75	.23
❑ 84 David Cone	.75	.23
❑ 85 Freddy Garcia	.75	.23
❑ 86 Johnny Damon	.75	.23
❑ 87 Ray Durham	.75	.23
❑ 88 Jermaine Dye	.75	.23
❑ 89 Juan Encarnacion	.75	.23
❑ 90 Terrence Long	.75	.23
❑ 91 Carl Everett	.75	.23
❑ 92 Steve Finley	.75	.23
❑ 93 Cliff Floyd	.75	.23
❑ 94 Brad Fullmer	.75	.23
❑ 95 Brian Giles	.75	.23
❑ 96 Luis Gonzalez	.75	.23
❑ 97 Rusty Greer	.75	.23
❑ 98 Jeffrey Hammonds	.75	.23
❑ 99 Mike Hampton	.75	.23
❑ 100 Orlando Hernandez	.75	.23
❑ 101 Richard Hidalgo	.75	.23
❑ 102 Geoff Jenkins	.75	.23
❑ 103 Jacque Jones	.75	.23
❑ 104 Brian Jordan	.75	.23
❑ 105 Gabe Kapler	.75	.23
❑ 106 Eric Karros	.75	.23
❑ 107 Jason Kendall	.75	.23
❑ 108 Adam Kennedy	.75	.23
❑ 109 Deion Sanders	.75	.23
❑ 110 Ryan Klesko	.75	.23
❑ 111 Chuck Knoblauch	.75	.23
❑ 112 Paul Konerko	.75	.23
❑ 113 Carlos Lee	.75	.23
❑ 114 Kenny Lofton	.75	.23
❑ 115 Javy Lopez	.75	.23
❑ 116 Tino Martinez	1.25	.35
❑ 117 Ruben Mateo	.75	.23
❑ 118 Kevin Millwood	.75	.23
❑ 119 Jimmy Rollins	.75	.23
❑ 120 Raul Mondesi	.75	.23
❑ 121 Trot Nixon	.75	.23
❑ 122 John Olerud	.75	.23
❑ 123 Paul O' Neill	1.25	.35
❑ 124 Chan Ho Park	.75	.23
❑ 125 Andy Pettitte	1.25	.35
❑ 126 Jorge Posada	1.25	.35
❑ 127 Mark Quinn	.75	.23
❑ 128 Aramis Ramirez	.75	.23
❑ 129 Mariano Rivera	1.25	.35
❑ 130 Tim Salmon	1.25	.35
❑ 131 Curt Schilling	1.25	.35
❑ 132 Richie Sexson	.75	.23
❑ 133 John Smoltz	1.25	.35
❑ 134 J.T. Snow	.75	.23
❑ 135 Jay Payton	.75	.23
❑ 136 Shannon Stewart	.75	.23
❑ 137 B.J. Surhoff	.75	.23
❑ 138 Mike Sweeney	.75	.23
❑ 139 Fernando Tatis	.75	.23
❑ 140 Miguel Tejada	.75	.23
❑ 141 Jason Varitek	.75	.23
❑ 142 Greg Vaughn	.75	.23
❑ 143 Mo Vaughn	.75	.23
❑ 144 Robin Ventura	.75	.23
❑ 145 Jose Vidro	.75	.23
❑ 146 Omar Vizquel	.75	.23
❑ 147 Larry Walker	1.25	.35
❑ 148 David Wells	.75	.23
❑ 149 Rondell White	.75	.23
❑ 150 Preston Wilson	.75	.23
❑ 151 Bud Smith RPM RC	10.00	3.00
❑ 152 C. Aldridge RPM RC	10.00	3.00
❑ 153 W.Caceres RPM RC	10.00	3.00
❑ 154 Josh Beckett RPM	12.00	3.60
❑ 155 W.Betemit RPM RC	10.00	3.00
❑ 156 J.Michaels RPM RC	10.00	3.00
❑ 157 Albert Pujols RPM RC	60.00	18.00
❑ 158 A.Torres RPM RC	10.00	3.00
❑ 159 Jack Wilson RPM RC	10.00	3.00
❑ 160 Alex Escobar RPM	10.00	3.00
❑ 161 Ben Sheets RPM	10.00	3.00
❑ 162 R.Soriano RPM RC	12.00	3.60
❑ 163 Nate Frese RPM RC	10.00	3.00
❑ 164 C. Garcia RPM EXCH	10.00	3.00
❑ 165 B.Larson RPM RC	10.00	3.00
❑ 166 A.Gomez RPM RC	10.00	3.00
❑ 167 Jason Hart RPM	10.00	3.00
❑ 168 Nick Johnson RPM	10.00	3.00
❑ 169 Donaldo Mendez RPM	10.00	3.00
❑ 170 C. Parker RPM RC	10.00	3.00
❑ 171 Jackson Melian RPM	10.00	3.00
❑ 172 Jack Cust RPM	10.00	3.00
❑ 173 Adrian Hernandez RPM	10.00	3.00
❑ 174 Joe Crede RPM	10.00	3.00
❑ 175 Jose Mieses RPM RC	10.00	3.00
❑ 176 Roy Oswalt RPM	12.00	3.60
❑ 177 Eric Munson RPM	10.00	3.00
❑ 178 Xavier Nady RPM	10.00	3.00
❑ 179 H. Ramirez RPM RC	12.00	3.60
❑ 180 Abraham Nunez RPM	10.00	3.00
❑ 181 Jose Ortiz RPM	10.00	3.00
❑ 182 J. Owens RPM RC	10.00	3.00
❑ 183 C. Vargas RPM RC	10.00	3.00
❑ 184 Marcus Giles RPM	10.00	3.00
❑ 185 Aubrey Huff RPM	10.00	3.00
❑ 186 C.C. Sabathia RPM	10.00	3.00
❑ 187 Adam Dunn RPM	12.00	3.60
❑ 188 Adam Pettyjohn RPM	10.00	3.00
❑ 189 El. Guzman RPM RC	10.00	3.00
❑ 190 Jay Gibbons RPM RC	12.00	3.60
❑ 191 Wilkin Ruan RPM RC	10.00	3.00
❑ 192 T. Shinjo RPM RC	12.00	3.60
❑ 193 Alfonso Soriano RPM	12.00	3.60
❑ 194 Corey Patterson RPM	10.00	3.00
❑ 195 Ichiro Suzuki RPM RC	50.00	15.00
❑ 196 Billy Sylvester RPM	10.00	3.00
❑ 197 Juan Uribe RPM RC	10.00	3.00
❑ 198 J. Estrada RPM RC	12.00	3.60
❑ 199 C. Valderrama RPM RC	10.00	3.00
❑ 200 Matt White RPM	10.00	3.00

2002 Playoff Absolute Memorabilia

	Nm-Mt	Ex-Mt
COMP.SET w/o SP's (150)	40.00	12.00
COMMON CARD (1-150)	.75	.23
COMMON CARD (151-200)	5.00	1.50
❑ 1 David Eckstein	.75	.23
❑ 2 Darin Erstad	.75	.23
❑ 3 Troy Glaus	1.25	.35
❑ 4 Garret Anderson	.75	.23
❑ 5 Tim Salmon	1.25	.35
❑ 6 Curt Schilling	1.25	.35
❑ 7 Randy Johnson	2.00	.60
❑ 8 Luis Gonzalez	.75	.23
❑ 9 Mark Grace	2.00	.60
❑ 10 Tom Glavine	2.00	.60
❑ 11 Greg Maddux	4.00	1.20
❑ 12 Chipper Jones	2.00	.60
❑ 13 Gary Sheffield	.75	.23
❑ 14 John Smoltz	1.25	.35
❑ 15 Andruw Jones	1.25	.35
❑ 16 Wilson Betemit	.75	.23
❑ 17 Tony Batista	.75	.23
❑ 18 Javier Vazquez	.75	.23
❑ 19 Scott Erickson	.75	.23
❑ 20 Josh Towers	.75	.23
❑ 21 Pedro Martinez	2.00	.60
❑ 22 Johnny Damon	.75	.23
❑ 23 Manny Ramirez	.75	.23
❑ 24 Rickey Henderson	3.00	.90
❑ 25 Trot Nixon	.75	.23
❑ 26 Nomar Garciaparra	4.00	1.20
❑ 27 Juan Cruz	.75	.23
❑ 28 Kerry Wood	2.00	.60
❑ 29 Fred McGriff	1.25	.35
❑ 30 Moises Alou	.75	.23
❑ 31 Sammy Sosa	3.00	.90
❑ 32 Corey Patterson	.75	.23
❑ 33 Mark Buehrle	.75	.23
❑ 34 Keith Foulke	.75	.23
❑ 35 Frank Thomas	2.00	.60
❑ 36 Kenny Lofton	.75	.23
❑ 37 Magglio Ordonez	.75	.23
❑ 38 Barry Larkin	2.00	.60
❑ 39 Ken Griffey Jr.	3.00	.90
❑ 40 Adam Dunn	1.25	.35
❑ 41 Juan Encarnacion	.75	.23
❑ 42 Sean Casey	.75	.23
❑ 43 Bartolo Colon	.75	.23
❑ 44 C.C. Sabathia	.75	.23
❑ 45 Travis Fryman	.75	.23
❑ 46 Jim Thome	2.00	.60
❑ 47 Omar Vizquel	.75	.23
❑ 48 Ellis Burks	.75	.23
❑ 49 Russell Branyan	.75	.23
❑ 50 Mike Hampton	.75	.23
❑ 51 Todd Helton	1.25	.35
❑ 52 Jose Ortiz	.75	.23
❑ 53 Juan Uribe	.75	.23
❑ 54 Juan Pierre	.75	.23
❑ 55 Larry Walker	1.25	.35
❑ 56 Mike Rivera	.75	.23
❑ 57 Robert Fick	.75	.23
❑ 58 Bobby Higginson	.75	.23
❑ 59 Josh Beckett	1.25	.35
❑ 60 Richard Hidalgo	.75	.23
❑ 61 Cliff Floyd	.75	.23
❑ 62 Mike Lowell	.75	.23
❑ 63 Roy Oswalt	.75	.23
❑ 64 Morgan Ensberg	.75	.23
❑ 65 Jeff Bagwell	1.25	.35
❑ 66 Craig Biggio	1.25	.35
❑ 67 Lance Berkman	.75	.23
❑ 68 Carlos Beltran	.75	.23
❑ 69 Mike Sweeney	.75	.23
❑ 70 Neifi Perez	.75	.23
❑ 71 Kevin Brown	.75	.23
❑ 72 Hideo Nomo	2.00	.60
❑ 73 Paul Lo Duca	.75	.23
❑ 74 Adrian Beltre	.75	.23
❑ 75 Shawn Green	.75	.23
❑ 76 Eric Karros	.75	.23
❑ 77 Brad Radke	.75	.23
❑ 78 Corey Koskie	.75	.23
❑ 79 Doug Mientkiewicz	.75	.23
❑ 80 Torii Hunter	.75	.23
❑ 81 Jacque Jones	.75	.23
❑ 82 Ben Sheets	.75	.23
❑ 83 Richie Sexson	.75	.23
❑ 84 Geoff Jenkins	.75	.23
❑ 85 Tony Armas Jr.	.75	.23
❑ 86 Michael Barrett	.75	.23
❑ 87 Jose Vidro	.75	.23
❑ 88 Vladimir Guerrero	2.00	.60

❑ 89 Roger Clemens 4.00 1.20
❑ 90 Derek Jeter 5.00 1.50
❑ 91 Bernie Williams 1.25 .35
❑ 92 Jason Giambi 2.00 .60
❑ 93 Jorge Posada 1.25 .35
❑ 94 Mike Mussina 2.00 .60
❑ 95 Andy Pettitte 1.25 .35
❑ 96 Nick Johnson .75 .23
❑ 97 Alfonso Soriano 2.00 .60
❑ 98 Shawn Estes .75 .23
❑ 99 Al Leiter .75 .23
❑ 100 Mike Piazza 3.00 .90
❑ 101 Roberto Alomar 2.00 .60
❑ 102 Mo Vaughn .75 .23
❑ 103 Jeromy Burnitz .75 .23
❑ 104 Tim Hudson .75 .23
❑ 105 Barry Zito 2.00 .60
❑ 106 Mark Mulder .75 .23
❑ 107 Eric Chavez .75 .23
❑ 108 Miguel Tejada .75 .23
❑ 109 Carlos Pena .75 .23
❑ 110 Jermaine Dye .75 .23
❑ 111 Mike Lieberthal .75 .23
❑ 112 Scott Rolen 1.25 .35
❑ 113 Pat Burrell .75 .23
❑ 114 Brandon Duckworth .75 .23
❑ 115 Bobby Abreu .75 .23
❑ 116 Jason Kendall .75 .23
❑ 117 Aramis Ramirez .75 .23
❑ 118 Brian Giles .75 .23
❑ 119 Pokey Reese .75 .23
❑ 120 Phil Nevin .75 .23
❑ 121 Ryan Klesko .75 .23
❑ 122 Jeremy Giambi .75 .23
❑ 123 Trevor Hoffman .75 .23
❑ 124 Barry Bonds 5.00 1.50
❑ 125 Rich Aurilia .75 .23
❑ 126 Jeff Kent .75 .23
❑ 127 Tsuyoshi Shinjo .75 .23
❑ 128 Ichiro Suzuki 4.00 1.20
❑ 129 Edgar Martinez 1.25 .35
❑ 130 Freddy Garcia .75 .23
❑ 131 Bret Boone .75 .23
❑ 132 Matt Morris .75 .23
❑ 133 Tino Martinez 1.25 .35
❑ 134 Albert Pujols 4.00 1.20
❑ 135 J.D. Drew .75 .23
❑ 136 Jim Edmonds .75 .23
❑ 137 Gabe Kapler .75 .23
❑ 138 Paul Wilson .75 .23
❑ 139 Ben Grieve .75 .23
❑ 140 Wade Miller .75 .23
❑ 141 Chan Ho Park .75 .23
❑ 142 Alex Rodriguez 4.00 1.20
❑ 143 Rafael Palmeiro 1.25 .35
❑ 144 Juan Gonzalez 2.00 .60
❑ 145 Ivan Rodriguez 2.00 .60
❑ 146 Carlos Delgado .75 .23
❑ 147 Jose Cruz Jr. .75 .23
❑ 148 Shannon Stewart .75 .23
❑ 149 Raul Mondesi .75 .23
❑ 150 Vernon Wells .75 .23
❑ 151 So Taguchi RP RC 8.00 2.40
❑ 152 Kazuhisa Ishii RP RC 10.00 3.00
❑ 153 Hank Blalock RP 8.00 2.40
❑ 154 Sean Burroughs RP 5.00 1.50
❑ 155 Geronimo Gil RP 5.00 1.50
❑ 156 Jon Rauch RP 5.00 1.50
❑ 157 Fernando Rodney RP 5.00 1.50
❑ 158 Miguel Asencio RP RC 5.00 1.50
❑ 159 Franklyn German RP RC 5.00 1.50
❑ 160 Luis Ugueto RP RC 5.00 1.50
❑ 161 Jorge Sosa RP RC 5.00 1.50
❑ 162 Felix Escalona RP RC 5.00 1.50
❑ 163 Colby Lewis RP 5.00 1.50
❑ 164 Mark Teixeira RP 8.00 2.40
❑ 165 Mark Prior RP 15.00 4.50
❑ 166 Francis Beltran RP RC 5.00 1.50
❑ 167 Joe Thurston RP 5.00 1.50
❑ 168 Earl Snyder RP RC 5.00 1.50
❑ 169 Takahito Nomura RP RC 5.00 1.50
❑ 170 Bill Hall RP 5.00 1.50
❑ 171 Marlon Byrd RP 5.00 1.50
❑ 172 Dave Williams RP 5.00 1.50
❑ 173 Yorvit Torrealba RP 5.00 1.50
❑ 174 Brandon Backe RP RC 5.00 1.50
❑ 175 Jorge De La Rosa RP RC 5.00 1.50
❑ 176 Brian Mallette RP RC 5.00 1.50
❑ 177 Rodrigo Rosario RP RC 5.00 1.50
❑ 178 Anderson Machado RP RC 8.00 2.40
❑ 179 Jorge Padilla RP RC 8.00 2.40
❑ 180 Allan Simpson RP RC 5.00 1.50
❑ 181 Doug Devore RP RC 5.00 1.50
❑ 182 Steve Bechler RP RC 5.00 1.50
❑ 183 Raul Chavez RP RC 5.00 1.50
❑ 184 Tom Shearn RP RC 5.00 1.50
❑ 185 Ben Howard RP RC 5.00 1.50
❑ 186 Chris Baker RP RC 5.00 1.50
❑ 187 Travis Hughes RP RC 8.00 2.40
❑ 188 Kevin Mench RP 5.00 1.50
❑ 189 Drew Henson RP 5.00 1.50
❑ 190 Mike Moriarty RP RC 5.00 1.50
❑ 191 Corey Thurman RP RC 5.00 1.50
❑ 192 Bobby Hill RP 5.00 1.50
❑ 193 Steve Kent RP RC 5.00 1.50
❑ 194 Satoru Komiyama RP RC 5.00 1.50
❑ 195 Jason Lane RP 5.00 1.50
❑ 196 Angel Berroa RP 5.00 1.50
❑ 197 Brandon Puffer RP RC 5.00 1.50
❑ 198 Brian Fitzgerald RP RC 5.00 1.50
❑ 199 Rene Reyes RP RC 5.00 1.50
❑ 200 Hee Seop Choi RP 8.00 2.40

2003 Playoff Absolute Memorabilia

	MINT	NRMT
COMP.SET w/o SP's (150)	40.00	18.00
COMMON CARD (1-150)	.75	.35
COMMON CARD (151-200)	5.00	2.20

151-200 RANDOM INSERTS IN PACKS
151-200 PRINT RUN 1500 SERIAL #'d SETS

❑ 1 Nomar Garciaparra 4.00 1.80
❑ 2 Barry Bonds 5.00 2.20
❑ 3 Greg Maddux 4.00 1.80
❑ 4 Roger Clemens 4.00 1.80
❑ 5 Derek Jeter 5.00 2.20
❑ 6 Alex Rodriguez 4.00 1.80
❑ 7 Chipper Jones 2.00 .90
❑ 8 Sammy Sosa 3.00 1.35
❑ 9 Alfonso Soriano 2.00 .90
❑ 10 Albert Pujols 4.00 1.80
❑ 11 Adam Dunn 1.25 .55
❑ 12 Tom Glavine 2.00 .90
❑ 13 Pedro Martinez 2.00 .90
❑ 14 Jim Thome 2.00 .90
❑ 15 Hideo Nomo 2.00 .90
❑ 16 Roberto Alomar 2.00 .90
❑ 17 Barry Zito 2.00 .90
❑ 18 Troy Glaus 1.25 .55
❑ 19 Kerry Wood 2.00 .90
❑ 20 Magglio Ordonez .75 .35
❑ 21 Todd Helton 1.25 .55
❑ 22 Craig Biggio 1.25 .55
❑ 23 Roy Oswalt .75 .35
❑ 24 Torii Hunter .75 .35
❑ 25 Miguel Tejada .75 .35
❑ 26 Tsuyoshi Shinjo .75 .35
❑ 27 Scott Rolen 1.25 .55
❑ 28 Rafael Palmeiro 1.25 .55
❑ 29 Victor Martinez .75 .35
❑ 30 Hank Blalock 1.25 .55
❑ 31 Jason Lane .75 .35
❑ 32 Junior Spivey .75 .35
❑ 33 Gary Sheffield .75 .35
❑ 34 Corey Patterson .75 .35
❑ 35 Corky Miller .75 .35
❑ 36 Brian Tallet .75 .35
❑ 37 Cliff Lee .75 .35
❑ 38 Jason Jennings .75 .35
❑ 39 Kirk Saarloos .75 .35
❑ 40 Wade Miller .75 .35
❑ 41 Angel Berroa .75 .35
❑ 42 Mike Sweeney .75 .35
❑ 43 Paul Lo Duca .75 .35
❑ 44 A.J. Pierzynski .75 .35
❑ 45 Drew Henson .75 .35
❑ 46 Eric Chavez .75 .35
❑ 47 Tim Hudson .75 .35
❑ 48 Aramis Ramirez .75 .35
❑ 49 Jack Wilson .75 .35
❑ 50 Ryan Klesko .75 .35
❑ 51 Antonio Perez .75 .35
❑ 52 Dewon Brazelton .75 .35
❑ 53 Mark Teixeira 1.25 .55
❑ 54 Eric Hinske .75 .35
❑ 55 Freddy Sanchez .75 .35
❑ 56 Mike Rivera .75 .35
❑ 57 Alfredo Amezaga .75 .35
❑ 58 Cliff Floyd .75 .35
❑ 59 Brandon Larson .75 .35
❑ 60 Richard Hidalgo .75 .35
❑ 61 Cesar Izturis .75 .35
❑ 62 Richie Sexson .75 .35
❑ 63 Michael Cuddyer .75 .35
❑ 64 Javier Vazquez .75 .35
❑ 65 Brandon Claussen .75 .35
❑ 66 Carlos Rivera .75 .35
❑ 67 Vernon Wells .75 .35
❑ 68 Kenny Lofton .75 .35
❑ 69 Aubrey Huff .75 .35
❑ 70 Adam LaRoche .75 .35
❑ 71 Jeff Baker .75 .35
❑ 72 Jose Castillo .75 .35
❑ 73 Joe Borchard .75 .35
❑ 74 Walter Young .75 .35
❑ 75 Jose Morban .75 .35
❑ 76 Vinnie Chulk .75 .35
❑ 77 Christian Parker .75 .35
❑ 78 Mike Piazza 3.00 1.35
❑ 79 Ichiro Suzuki 4.00 1.80
❑ 80 Kazuhisa Ishii .75 .35
❑ 81 Rickey Henderson 3.00 1.35
❑ 82 Ken Griffey Jr. 3.00 1.35
❑ 83 Jason Giambi 2.00 .90
❑ 84 Randy Johnson 2.00 .90
❑ 85 Curt Schilling 1.25 .55
❑ 86 Manny Ramirez .75 .35
❑ 87 Barry Larkin 2.00 .90
❑ 88 Jeff Bagwell 1.25 .55
❑ 89 Vladimir Guerrero 2.00 .90
❑ 90 Mike Mussina 2.00 .90
❑ 91 Juan Gonzalez 2.00 .90
❑ 92 Andruw Jones 1.25 .55
❑ 93 Frank Thomas 2.00 .90
❑ 94 Sean Casey .75 .35
❑ 95 Josh Beckett 1.25 .55
❑ 96 Lance Berkman .75 .35
❑ 97 Shawn Green .75 .35
❑ 98 Bernie Williams 1.25 .55
❑ 99 Pat Burrell .75 .35
❑ 100 Edgar Martinez 1.25 .55
❑ 101 Ivan Rodriguez 2.00 .90
❑ 102 Jeremy Guthrie .75 .35
❑ 103 Alexis Rios .75 .35
❑ 104 Nic Jackson .75 .35
❑ 105 Jason Anderson .75 .35
❑ 106 Travis Chapman .75 .35
❑ 107 Mac Suzuki .75 .35
❑ 108 Toby Hall .75 .35
❑ 109 Mark Prior 4.00 1.80
❑ 110 So Taguchi .75 .35
❑ 111 Marlon Byrd .75 .35
❑ 112 Garret Anderson .75 .35
❑ 113 Luis Gonzalez .75 .35
❑ 114 Jay Gibbons .75 .35
❑ 115 Mark Buehrle .75 .35
❑ 116 Wily Mo Pena .75 .35
❑ 117 C.C. Sabathia .75 .35
❑ 118 Ricardo Rodriguez .75 .35

❑ 119 Robert Fick .75 .35
❑ 120 Rodrigo Rosario .75 .35
❑ 121 Alexis Gomez .75 .35
❑ 122 Carlos Beltran .75 .35
❑ 123 Joe Thurston .75 .35
❑ 124 Ben Sheets .75 .35
❑ 125 Jose Vidro .75 .35
❑ 126 Nick Johnson .75 .35
❑ 127 Mark Mulder .75 .35
❑ 128 Bobby Abreu .75 .35
❑ 129 Brian Giles .75 .35
❑ 130 Brian Lawrence .75 .35
❑ 131 Jeff Kent .75 .35
❑ 132 Chris Snelling .75 .35
❑ 133 Kevin Mench .75 .35
❑ 134 Carlos Delgado .75 .35
❑ 135 Orlando Hudson .75 .35
❑ 136 Juan Cruz .75 .35
❑ 137 Jim Edmonds .75 .35
❑ 138 Geronimo Gil .75 .35
❑ 139 Joe Crede .75 .35
❑ 140 Wilson Valdez .75 .35
❑ 141 Runelvys Hernandez .75 .35
❑ 142 Nick Neugebauer .75 .35
❑ 143 Takahito Nomura .75 .35
❑ 144 Andres Galarraga .75 .35
❑ 145 Mark Grace 2.00 .90
❑ 146 Brandon Duckworth .75 .35
❑ 147 Oliver Perez .75 .35
❑ 148 Xavier Nady .75 .35
❑ 149 Rafael Soriano .75 .35
❑ 150 Ben Kozlowski .75 .35
❑ 151 Prentice Redman ROO RC 5.00 2.20
❑ 152 Craig Brazell ROO RC 8.00 3.60
❑ 153 Nook Logan ROO RC 5.00 2.20
❑ 154 Greg Aquino ROO RC 5.00 2.20
❑ 155 Matt Kata ROO RC 8.00 3.60
❑ 156 Ian Ferguson ROO RC 5.00 2.20
❑ 157 Chien-Ming Wang ROO RC 10.00 4.50
❑ 158 Beau Kemp ROO RC 5.00 2.20
❑ 159 Alejandro Machado ROO RC 5.00 2.20
❑ 160 Michael Hessman ROO RC 5.00 2.20
❑ 161 Francisco Rosario ROO RC 5.00 2.20
❑ 162 Pedro Liriano ROO 5.00 2.20
❑ 163 Rich Fischer ROO RC 5.00 2.20
❑ 164 Franklin Perez ROO RC 5.00 2.20
❑ 165 Oscar Villarreal ROO RC 5.00 2.20
❑ 166 Arnie Munoz ROO RC 5.00 2.20
❑ 167 Tim Olson ROO RC 8.00 3.60
❑ 168 Jose Contreras ROO RC 10.00 4.50
❑ 169 Francisco Cruceta ROO RC 5.00 2.20
❑ 170 Jeremy Bonderman ROO RC 8.00 3.60
❑ 171 Jeremy Griffiths ROO RC 8.00 3.60
❑ 172 John Webb ROO 5.00 2.20
❑ 173 Phil Seibel ROO RC 5.00 2.20
❑ 174 Aaron Looper ROO RC 5.00 2.20
❑ 175 Brian Stokes ROO RC 5.00 2.20
❑ 176 Guillermo Quiroz ROO RC 8.00 3.60
❑ 177 Fernando Cabrera ROO RC 8.00 3.60
❑ 178 Josh Hall ROO RC 8.00 3.60
❑ 179 Diegomar Markwell ROO RC 5.00 2.20
❑ 180 Andrew Brown ROO RC 5.00 2.20
❑ 181 Doug Waechter ROO RC 8.00 3.60
❑ 182 Felix Sanchez ROO RC 5.00 2.20
❑ 183 Gerardo Garcia ROO 5.00 2.20
❑ 184 Matt Bruback ROO RC 5.00 2.20
❑ 185 Michel Hernandez ROO RC 5.00 2.20
❑ 186 Rett Johnson ROO RC 8.00 3.60
❑ 187 Ryan Cameron ROO RC 5.00 2.20
❑ 188 Rob Hammock ROO RC 8.00 3.60
❑ 189 Clint Barmes ROO RC 8.00 3.60
❑ 190 Brandon Webb ROO RC 12.00 5.50
❑ 191 Jon Leicester ROO RC 5.00 2.20
❑ 192 Shane Bazzell ROO RC 5.00 2.20
❑ 193 Joe Valentine ROO RC 5.00 2.20
❑ 194 Josh Stewart ROO RC 5.00 2.20
❑ 195 Pete LaForest ROO RC 8.00 3.60
❑ 196 Shane Victorino ROO RC 5.00 2.20
❑ 197 Termel Sledge ROO RC 8.00 3.60
❑ 198 Lew Ford ROO RC 8.00 3.60
❑ 199 Todd Wellemeyer ROO RC 8.00 3.60
❑ 200 Hideki Matsui ROO RC 20.00 9.00
❑ 201 Adam Loewen ROO RC
❑ 202 Ramon Nivar ROO RC
❑ 203 Dan Haren ROO RC
❑ 204 Dontrelle Willis ROO
❑ 205 Chad Gaudin ROO RC
❑ 206 Rickie Weeks ROO RC
❑ 207 Ryan Wagner ROO RC
❑ 208 Delmon Young ROO RC

2002 Playoff Piece of the Game

	Nm-Mt	Ex-Mt
COMP.SET w/o SP's (50)	40.00	12.00
COMMON CARD (1-50)	.75	.23
COMMON CARD (51-100)	8.00	2.40

❑ 1 Vladimir Guerrero 2.00 .60
❑ 2 Troy Glaus 1.25 .35
❑ 3 Ichiro Suzuki 4.00 1.20
❑ 4 Chipper Jones 2.00 .60
❑ 5 Roberto Alomar 2.00 .60
❑ 6 Scott Rolen 1.25 .35
❑ 7 Randy Johnson 2.00 .60
❑ 8 Roger Clemens 4.00 1.20
❑ 9 Nomar Garciaparra 4.00 1.20
❑ 10 Greg Maddux 4.00 1.20
❑ 11 Barry Bonds 5.00 1.50
❑ 12 Derek Jeter 5.00 1.50
❑ 13 Albert Pujols 4.00 1.20
❑ 14 Kerry Wood 2.00 .60
❑ 15 Jim Thome 2.00 .60
❑ 16 Manny Ramirez .75 .23
❑ 17 Carlos Delgado .75 .23
❑ 18 Magglio Ordonez .75 .23
❑ 19 Torii Hunter .75 .23
❑ 20 Garret Anderson .75 .23
❑ 21 Eric Chavez .75 .23
❑ 22 Rafael Palmeiro 1.25 .35
❑ 23 Andruw Jones 1.25 .35
❑ 24 Cliff Floyd .75 .23
❑ 25 Sammy Sosa 3.00 .90
❑ 26 Mike Mussina 2.00 .60
❑ 27 Jeff Bagwell 1.25 .35
❑ 28 Miguel Tejada .75 .23
❑ 29 Curt Schilling 1.25 .35
❑ 30 Tom Glavine 2.00 .60
❑ 31 Frank Thomas 2.00 .60
❑ 32 Jim Edmonds .75 .23
❑ 33 Juan Gonzalez 2.00 .60
❑ 34 Todd Helton 1.25 .35
❑ 35 Shawn Green .75 .23
❑ 36 Alfonso Soriano 2.00 .60
❑ 37 Lance Berkman .75 .23
❑ 38 Barry Zito 2.00 .60
❑ 39 Ryan Klesko .75 .23
❑ 40 Larry Walker 1.25 .35
❑ 41 Craig Biggio 1.25 .35
❑ 42 Luis Gonzalez .75 .23
❑ 43 Ivan Rodriguez 2.00 .60
❑ 44 J.D. Drew .75 .23
❑ 45 Roy Oswalt .75 .23
❑ 46 Jason Giambi 2.00 .60
❑ 47 Brian Giles .75 .23
❑ 48 Richie Sexson .75 .23
❑ 49 Pat Burrell .75 .23
❑ 50 Alex Rodriguez 4.00 1.20
❑ 51 So Taguchi ROO RC 10.00 3.00
❑ 52 Allan Simpson ROO RC 8.00 2.40
❑ 53 Oliver Perez ROO RC 10.00 3.00
❑ 54 Ben Howard ROO RC 8.00 2.40
❑ 55 Kirk Saarloos ROO RC 10.00 3.00
❑ 56 Francis Beltran ROO RC 8.00 2.40
❑ 57 Jorge Padilla ROO RC 10.00 3.00
❑ 58 Brandon Puffer ROO RC 8.00 2.40
❑ 59 Brian Mallette ROO RC 8.00 2.40
❑ 60 Kyle Kane ROO RC 8.00 2.40
❑ 61 Travis Driskill ROO RC 8.00 2.40
❑ 62 Jeremy Lambert ROO RC 8.00 2.40
❑ 63 Steve Kent ROO RC 8.00 2.40
❑ 64 Julius Matos ROO RC 8.00 2.40
❑ 65 Julio Mateo ROO RC 8.00 2.40
❑ 66 Kazuhisa Ishii ROO RC 12.00 3.60
❑ 67 Franklyn German ROO RC 8.00 2.40
❑ 68 John Foster ROO RC 8.00 2.40
❑ 69 Luis Ugueto ROO RC 8.00 2.40
❑ 70 Shawn Sedlacek ROO RC 8.00 2.40
❑ 71 Earl Snyder ROO RC 8.00 2.40
❑ 72 Jason Simontacchi ROO RC 10.00 3.00
❑ 73 Victor Alvarez ROO RC 8.00 2.40
❑ 74 Tom Shearn ROO RC 8.00 2.40
❑ 75 Corey Thurman ROO RC 8.00 2.40
❑ 76 Eric Junge ROO RC 8.00 2.40
❑ 77 Hansel Izquierdo ROO RC 8.00 2.40
❑ 78 Elio Serrano ROO RC 8.00 2.40
❑ 79 J.J. Trujillo ROO RC 8.00 2.40
❑ 80 Chris Snelling ROO RC 10.00 3.00
❑ 81 Satoru Komiyama ROO RC 8.00 2.40
❑ 82 Brandon Backe ROO RC 8.00 2.40
❑ 83 Anderson Machado ROO RC 10.00 3.00
❑ 84 Doug Devore ROO RC 8.00 2.40
❑ 85 Steve Bechler ROO RC 8.00 2.40
❑ 86 John Ennis ROO RC 8.00 2.40
❑ 87 Rodrigo Rosario ROO RC 8.00 2.40
❑ 88 Jorge Sosa ROO RC 8.00 2.40
❑ 89 Ken Huckaby ROO RC 8.00 2.40
❑ 90 Mike Moriarty ROO RC 8.00 2.40
❑ 91 Mike Crudale ROO RC 8.00 2.40
❑ 92 Kevin Frederick ROO RC 8.00 2.40
❑ 93 Aaron Guiel ROO RC 10.00 3.00
❑ 94 Jose Rodriguez ROO RC 8.00 2.40
❑ 95 Andy Shibilo ROO RC 8.00 2.40
❑ 96 Deivis Santos ROO 8.00 2.40
❑ 97 Felix Escalona ROO RC 8.00 2.40
❑ 98 Miguel Asencio ROO RC 8.00 2.40
❑ 99 Takahito Nomura ROO RC 8.00 2.40
❑ 100 Cam Esslinger ROO RC 8.00 2.40

2003 Playoff Piece of the Game

	MINT	NRMT
STATED ODDS 1:1.5		
SERIAL #'d PRINTS B/WN 10-200 COPIES PER		
NO PRICING ON QTY OF 25 OR LESS		

❑ 1A Adam Dunn Bat 10.00 4.50
❑ 1B Adam Dunn Btg Glv/40 25.00 11.00
❑ 2 Adam Dunn Jsy 10.00 4.50
❑ 3A Adrian Beltre Bat 8.00 3.60
❑ 3B Adrian Beltre Jsy/100 10.00 4.50
❑ 3C Adrian Beltre Hat/50 15.00 6.75
❑ 3D Adrian Beltre Shoe/50 15.00 6.75
❑ 4 Albert Pujols Jsy 20.00 9.00
❑ 5 Albert Pujols Bat 20.00 9.00
❑ 6 Alex Rodriguez Bat 10.00 4.50
❑ 7 Alex Rodriguez Blue Jsy 10.00 4.50
❑ 8 Alex Rodriguez White Jsy 10.00 4.50
❑ 9 Alfonso Soriano Bat 10.00 4.50
❑ 10 Alfonso Soriano Gray Jsy 10.00 4.50
❑ 11 Alfonso Soriano White Jsy 10.00 4.50

❑ 12 Brett Myers Jsy/50 .... 15.00 6.75
❑ 13 Andruw Jones Jsy 10.00 4.50
❑ 14A Austin Kearns Jsy 10.00 4.50
❑ 14B Austin Kearns Bat/195 10.00 4.50
❑ 15A Barry Larkin Jsy 10.00 4.50
❑ 15B Barry Larkin Bat/200 .... 10.00 4.50
❑ 16A Barry Zito Jsy 10.00 4.50
❑ 16B Barry Zito Hat/40.......... 25.00 11.00
❑ 17A Bernie Williams Jsy 10.00 4.50
❑ 17B Bernie Williams Bat/95 15.00 6.75
❑ 17C Bernie Williams Shoe/45 25.00 11.00
❑ 18A Brian Giles Bat 8.00 3.60
❑ 18B Brian Giles Hat/85........ 10.00 4.50
❑ 18C Brian Giles Btg Glv/40 15.00 6.75
❑ 18D Brian Giles Shoe/45 .... 15.00 6.75
❑ 19 Zach Day Jsy/50 .... 15.00 6.75
❑ 20A Carlos Beltran Bat.......... 8.00 3.60
❑ 20B Carlos Beltran Jsy/75 .. 10.00 4.50
❑ 20C Carlos Beltran Hat/45 .. 15.00 6.75
❑ 20D Carlos Beltran Shoe/25......
❑ 21 Brandon Phillips Bat/50 15.00 6.75
❑ 22 Carlos Lee Bat/50 .... 15.00 6.75
❑ 23A Casey Fossum Jsy/75 .. 10.00 4.50
❑ 23B Casey Fossum Hat/25........
❑ 23C Casey Fossum Fld Glv/25..
❑ 23D Casey Fossum Shoe/25 ....
❑ 24A Chipper Jones Jsy 10.00 4.50
❑ 24B Chipper Jones Bat/195 10.00 4.50
❑ 25 Marcus Giles Jsy/50 ...... 15.00 6.75
❑ 26A Craig Biggio Bat 10.00 4.50
❑ 26B Craig Biggio Jsy/100 .. 15.00 6.75
❑ 26C Craig Biggio Hat/50 .... 25.00 11.00
❑ 26D Craig Biggio Shoe/50 .. 25.00 11.00
❑ 27 Curt Schilling Jsy 10.00 4.50
❑ 28 Derek Jeter Base 20.00 9.00
❑ 29A Edgar Martinez Jsy 10.00 4.50
❑ 29B Edgar Martinez Bat/150 10.00 4.50
❑ 30A Eric Chavez Jsy............. 8.00 3.60
❑ 30B Eric Chavez Bat/175 ...... 8.00 3.60
❑ 31A Eric Hinske Bat/25 ....
❑ 31B Eric Hinske Hat/25 ....
❑ 31C Eric Hinske Shoe/10 ....
❑ 32A Frank Thomas Jsy........ 10.00 4.50
❑ 32B Frank Thomas Bat/190 10.00 4.50
❑ 33 Aubrey Huff Jsy/50 .... 15.00 6.75
❑ 34A Gary Carter Jacket.......... 8.00 3.60
❑ 34B Gary Carter Fld Glv/40 25.00 11.00
❑ 34C Gary Carter Bat/40 ...... 25.00 11.00
❑ 35 Greg Maddux Gray Jsy .. 10.00 4.50
❑ 36 Greg Maddux White Jsy 10.00 4.50
❑ 37 Hideki Matsui Base RC .. 20.00 9.00
❑ 38 Hideo Nomo White Jsy .. 15.00 6.75
❑ 39A Rod Carew Jacket 10.00 4.50
❑ 39B Rod Carew Shoe/100 .. 15.00 6.75
❑ 39C Rod Carew Hat/50........ 25.00 11.00
❑ 40 Ichiro Suzuki Base.......... 15.00 6.75
❑ 41A Ivan Rodriguez Bat 10.00 4.50
❑ 41B Ivan Rodriguez Btg Glv/10
❑ 41C Ivan Rodriguez Fld Glv/25
❑ 41D Ivan Rodriguez Shoe/25 ....
❑ 42A Jason Giambi A's Bat .. 10.00 4.50
❑ 42B Jason Giambi A's Hat/200 .. 10.00 4.50
❑ 43 Jason Giambi Yanks Bat 10.00 4.50
❑ 44 J.C. Romero Jsy/50........ 15.00 6.75
❑ 45 Jason Giambi Yanks Jsy 10.00 4.50
❑ 46A Jeff Bagwell Jsy 10.00 4.50
❑ 46B Jeff Bagwell Bat/195 .... 10.00 4.50
❑ 47 Josh Bard Jsy/50 .... 15.00 6.75
❑ 48A Jim Thome Jsy 10.00 4.50
❑ 48B Jim Thome Bat/200...... 10.00 4.50
❑ 49 Jay Gibbons Jsy/200........ 8.00 3.60
❑ 50A Jorge Posada Jsy 10.00 4.50
❑ 50B Jorge Posada Bat/200.. 10.00 4.50
❑ 51A Juan Gonzalez Bat........ 10.00 4.50
❑ 51B Juan Gonzalez Jsy/40 .. 25.00 11.00
❑ 52A Kazuhisa Ishii Bat 8.00 3.60
❑ 52B Kazuhisa Ishii Jsy/200 .. 8.00 3.60
❑ 53 George Brett Bat 15.00 6.75
❑ 54A Kenny Lofton Bat.......... 10.00 4.50
❑ 54B Kenny Lofton Hat/90.... 15.00 6.75
❑ 54C Kenny Lofton Fld Glv/45 25.00 11.00
❑ 54D Kenny Lofton Shoe/45 25.00 11.00
❑ 55A Kerry Wood Jsy............ 10.00 4.50
❑ 55B Kerry Wood Hat/90 ...... 15.00 6.75
❑ 55C Kerry Wood Fld Glv/45 25.00 11.00
❑ 55D Kerry Wood Shoe/45 .. 25.00 11.00
❑ 56 Kevin Brown Jsy 8.00 3.60
❑ 57 Kirk Saarloos Jsy 8.00 3.60
❑ 58A Lance Berkman Jsy 8.00 3.60
❑ 58B Lance Berkman Bat/90 10.00 4.50
❑ 58C Lance Berkman Btg Glv/45.. 15.00 6.75
❑ 58D Lance Berkman Shoe/45 15.00 6.75
❑ 59A Larry Walker Jsy 10.00 4.50
❑ 59B Larry Walker Bat/200 .. 10.00 4.50
❑ 60A Magglio Ordonez Jsy 8.00 3.60
❑ 60B Magglio Ordonez Hat/100 10.00 4.50
❑ 60C Magglio Ordonez Bat/50 15.00 6.75
❑ 60D Magglio Ordonez Shoe/50.. 15.00 6.75
❑ 61A Manny Ramirez Jsy........ 8.00 3.60
❑ 61B Manny Ramirez Bat/200 8.00 3.60
❑ 62 Mark Mulder Jsy.............. 8.00 3.60
❑ 63A Mark Prior Jsy 20.00 9.00
❑ 63B Mark Prior Hat/95........ 30.00 13.50
❑ 63C Mark Prior Fld Glv/45.. 60.00 27.00
❑ 63D Mark Prior Shoe/45 .... 40.00 18.00
❑ 64 Matt Williams Jsy/50 .... 25.00 11.00
❑ 65A Miguel Tejada Jsy.......... 8.00 3.60
❑ 65B Miguel Tejada Bat/100 10.00 4.50
❑ 65C Miguel Tejada Hat/50 .. 15.00 6.75
❑ 66A Mike Mussina Jsy........ 10.00 4.50
❑ 66B Mike Mussina Fld Glv/45 25.00 11.00
❑ 67 Mike Piazza Bat 10.00 4.50
❑ 68 Mike Piazza Black Jsy 10.00 4.50
❑ 69 Mike Piazza White Jsy.... 10.00 4.50
❑ 70 Nomar Garciaparra Bat .. 15.00 6.75
❑ 71 Nomar Garciaparra Gray Jsy.. 15.00 6.75
❑ 72 Nomar Garciaparra White Jsy 15.00 6.75
❑ 73 Paul Lo Duca Jsy/50...... 15.00 6.75
❑ 74 Pedro Martinez Jsy 10.00 4.50
❑ 75A Rafael Palmeiro Jsy...... 10.00 4.50
❑ 75B Rafael Palmeiro Hat/95 15.00 6.75
❑ 75C Rafael Palmeiro Fld Glv/45.. 25.00 11.00
❑ 75D Rafael Palmeiro Btg Glv/45 25.00 11.00
❑ 76 Randy Johnson Gray Jsy 10.00 4.50
❑ 77 Randy Johnson White Jsy 10.00 4.50
❑ 78A Rickey Henderson Jsy .. 10.00 4.50
❑ 78B Rickey Henderson Bat/195 .. 10.00 4.50
❑ 79A Roberto Alomar Jsy...... 10.00 4.50
❑ 79B Roberto Alomar Bat/90 15.00 6.75
❑ 79C Roberto Alomar Btg Glv/45 25.00 11.00
❑ 80 Rod Carew Pants............ 10.00 4.50
❑ 81 Roger Clemens Gray Jsy 15.00 6.75
❑ 82 Roger Clemens White Jsy 15.00 6.75
❑ 83 Cal Ripken Jsy 25.00 11.00
❑ 84A Roy Oswalt Jsy 8.00 3.60
❑ 84B Roy Oswalt Fld Glv/95 10.00 4.50
❑ 84C Roy Oswalt Shoe/45 .... 15.00 6.75
❑ 85 Jer Bonderman Jsy/50 RC 15.00 6.75
❑ 86 Ryne Sandberg Bat 15.00 6.75
❑ 87 Sammy Sosa Bat............ 15.00 6.75
❑ 88 Sammy Sosa Gray Jsy.... 15.00 6.75
❑ 89 Sammy Sosa White Jsy.. 15.00 6.75
❑ 90A Scott Rolen Jsy............ 10.00 4.50
❑ 90B Scott Rolen Bat/185 .... 10.00 4.50
❑ 91 Frank Catalanotto Jsy/50 15.00 6.75
❑ 92A Shawn Green Jsy 8.00 3.60
❑ 92B Shawn Green Bat/195 .... 8.00 3.60
❑ 93A Tim Hudson Jsy 8.00 3.60
❑ 93B Tim Hudson Hat/100.... 10.00 4.50
❑ 93C Tim Hudson Shoe/50 .. 15.00 6.75
❑ 94A Todd Helton Jsy 10.00 4.50
❑ 94B Todd Helton Bat/195.... 10.00 4.50
❑ 95A Tony Gwynn Pants 10.00 4.50
❑ 95B Tony Gwynn Bat/95...... 15.00 6.75
❑ 95C Tony Gwynn Btg Glv/45 30.00 13.50
❑ 95D Tony Gwynn Hat/45 ....
❑ 96A Torii Hunter Jsy 8.00 3.60
❑ 96B Torii Hunter Bat/150 ...... 8.00 3.60
❑ 97A Troy Glaus Jsy 10.00 4.50
❑ 97B Troy Glaus Bat/195 ...... 10.00 4.50
❑ 98 Runelvys Hernandez Jsy/50 .. 15.00 6.75
❑ 99 Vernon Wells Jsy 8.00 3.60
❑ 100A Vladimir Guerrero Jsy 10.00 4.50
❑ 100B Vladimir Guerrero Bat/150 10.00 4.50

2003 Playoff Portraits

MINT NRMT
COMPLETE SET (144) 50.00 22.00

❑ 1 Vladimir Guerrero .... 2.00 .90
❑ 2 Luis Gonzalez .... .75 .35

❑ 3 Andruw Jones .... 1.25 .55
❑ 4 Manny Ramirez .... .75 .35
❑ 5 Derek Jeter 5.00 2.20
❑ 6 Eric Hinske .... .75 .35
❑ 7 Curt Schilling .... 1.25 .55
❑ 8 Adam Dunn .... 1.25 .55
❑ 9 Jason Jennings........................ .75 .35
❑ 10 Mike Piazza Mets 3.00 1.35
❑ 11 Jason Giambi Yanks .... 2.00 .90
❑ 12 Jeff Bagwell...................... 1.25 .55
❑ 13 Rickey Henderson Sox 3.00 1.35
❑ 14 Randy Johnson D'backs .. 2.00 .90
❑ 15 Roger Clemens Yanks 4.00 1.80
❑ 16 Troy Glaus........................ 1.25 .55
❑ 17 Hideo Nomo Dodgers ...... 2.00 .90
❑ 18 Joe Borchard........................ .75 .35
❑ 19 Torii Hunter.......................... .75 .35
❑ 20 Lance Berkman .... .75 .35
❑ 21 Todd Helton .... 1.25 .55
❑ 22 Mike Mussina .... 2.00 .90
❑ 23 Vernon Wells........................ .75 .35
❑ 24 Pat Burrell............................ .75 .35
❑ 25 Ichiro Suzuki 4.00 1.80
❑ 26 Shawn Green........................ .75 .35
❑ 27 Frank Thomas .... 2.00 .90
❑ 28 Barry Zito .... 2.00 .90
❑ 29 Barry Bonds 5.00 2.20
❑ 30 Ken Griffey Jr. 3.00 1.35
❑ 31 Albert Pujols 4.00 1.80
❑ 32 Roberto Alomar .... 2.00 .90
❑ 33 Barry Larkin........................ 2.00 .90
❑ 34 Tony Gwynn 3.00 1.35
❑ 35 Chipper Jones .... 2.00 .90
❑ 36 Pedro Martinez Sox............ 2.00 .90
❑ 37 Juan Gonzalez .... 2.00 .90
❑ 38 Greg Maddux 4.00 1.80
❑ 39 Tim Hudson .... .75 .35
❑ 40 Sammy Sosa...................... 3.00 1.35
❑ 41 Victor Martinez .... .75 .35
❑ 42 Mark Buehrle........................ .75 .35
❑ 43 Austin Kearns .... 1.25 .55
❑ 44 Kerry Wood .... 2.00 .90
❑ 45 Nomar Garciaparra 4.00 1.80
❑ 46 Alfonso Soriano .... 2.00 .90
❑ 47 Mark Prior.......................... 4.00 1.80
❑ 48 Richie Sexson .... .75 .35
❑ 49 Mark Teixeira .... 1.25 .55
❑ 50 Craig Biggio .... 1.25 .55
❑ 51 Rafael Palmeiro .... 1.25 .55
❑ 52 Carlos Beltran .... .75 .35
❑ 53 Bernie Williams.................. 1.25 .55
❑ 54 Eric Chavez .... .75 .35
❑ 55 Paul Konerko.......................... .75 .35
❑ 56 Nolan Ryan Rgr 8.00 3.60
❑ 57 Mark Mulder .... .75 .35
❑ 58 Miguel Tejada .... .75 .35
❑ 59 Roy Oswalt .... .75 .35
❑ 60 Jim Edmonds .... .75 .35
❑ 61 Ryan Klesko .... .75 .35
❑ 62 Cal Ripken.......................... 8.00 3.60
❑ 63 Josh Beckett .... 1.25 .55
❑ 64 Kazuhisa Ishii .... .75 .35
❑ 65 Alex Rodriguez Rgr 4.00 1.80
❑ 66 Mike Sweeney........................ .75 .35
❑ 67 C.C. Sabathia .... .75 .35
❑ 68 Jose Vidro.............................. .75 .35
❑ 69 Magglio Ordonez.................... .75 .35
❑ 70 Carlos Delgado .... .75 .35

Card	Nm-Mt	Ex-Mt
❑ 71 Jorge Posada	1.25	.55
❑ 72 Bobby Abreu	.75	.35
❑ 73 Brian Giles	.75	.35
❑ 74 Kirby Puckett	2.50	1.10
❑ 75 Yogi Berra	2.50	1.10
❑ 76 Ryne Sandberg	5.00	2.20
❑ 77 Tom Glavine	2.00	.90
❑ 78 Jim Thome	2.00	.90
❑ 79 Chris Snelling	.75	.35
❑ 80 Drew Henson	.75	.35
❑ 81 Junior Spivey	.75	.35
❑ 82 Mike Schmidt	5.00	2.20
❑ 83 Jeff Kent	.75	.35
❑ 84 Stan Musial	4.00	1.80
❑ 85 Garret Anderson	.75	.35
❑ 86 Jose Contreras RC	5.00	2.20
❑ 87 Ivan Rodriguez	2.00	.90
❑ 88 Hideki Matsui RC	10.00	4.50
❑ 89 Don Mattingly	6.00	2.70
❑ 90 Angel Berroa	.75	.35
❑ 91 George Brett	6.00	2.70
❑ 92 Jermaine Dye	.75	.35
❑ 93 John Olerud	.75	.35
❑ 94 Josh Phelps	.75	.35
❑ 95 Sean Casey	.75	.35
❑ 96 Larry Walker	1.25	.55
❑ 97 Jason Lane	.75	.35
❑ 98 Travis Hafner	.75	.35
❑ 99 Terrence Long	.75	.35
❑ 100 Shannon Stewart	.75	.35
❑ 101 Richard Hidalgo	.75	.35
❑ 102 Joe Thurston	.75	.35
❑ 103 Ben Sheets	.75	.35
❑ 104 Orlando Cabrera	.75	.35
❑ 105 Aramis Ramirez	.75	.35
❑ 106 So Taguchi	.75	.35
❑ 107 Frank Robinson	1.50	.70
❑ 108 Phil Nevin	.75	.35
❑ 109 Dennis Tankersley	.75	.35
❑ 110 J.D. Drew	.75	.35
❑ 111 Paul Lo Duca	.75	.35
❑ 112 Ozzie Smith	2.50	1.10
❑ 113 Carlos Lee	.75	.35
❑ 114 Nick Johnson	.75	.35
❑ 115 Edgar Martinez	1.25	.55
❑ 116 Hank Blalock	1.25	.55
❑ 117 Orlando Hudson	.75	.35
❑ 118 Corey Patterson	.75	.35
❑ 119 Steve Carlton	1.50	.70
❑ 120 Wade Miller	.75	.35
❑ 121 Adrian Beltre	.75	.35
❑ 122 Scott Rolen	1.25	.55
❑ 123 Brian Lawrence	.75	.35
❑ 124 Rich Aurilia	.75	.35
❑ 125 Tsuyoshi Shinjo	.75	.35
❑ 126 John Buck	.75	.35
❑ 127 Marlon Byrd	.75	.35
❑ 128 Michael Cuddyer	.75	.35
❑ 129 Marshall McDougall	.75	.35
❑ 130 Travis Chapman	.75	.35
❑ 131 Jose Morban	.75	.35
❑ 132 Adam LaRoche	.75	.35
❑ 133 Jose Castillo	.75	.35
❑ 134 Walter Young	.75	.35
❑ 135 Jeff Baker	.75	.35
❑ 136 Jeremy Guthrie	.75	.35
❑ 137 Pedro Martinez Expos	2.00	.90
❑ 138 Randy Johnson M's	2.00	.90
❑ 139 Alex Rodriguez M's	4.00	1.80
❑ 140 Hideo Nomo Mets	2.00	.90
❑ 141 Roger Clemens Sox	4.00	1.80
❑ 142 Rickey Henderson A's	3.00	1.35
❑ 143 Jason Giambi A's	2.00	.90
❑ 144 Mike Piazza Dodgers	3.00	1.35
❑ NNO Original Artwork EXCH/144		

2003 Playoff Prestige

	Nm-Mt	Ex-Mt
COMPLETE SET (210)	40.00	12.00
COMP.SET w/o SP's (180)	25.00	7.50
COMMON CARD (1-180)	.50	.15
COMMON CARD (181-200)	1.50	.45

Card	Nm-Mt	Ex-Mt
❑ 1 Darin Erstad	.50	.15
❑ 2 David Eckstein	.50	.15
❑ 3 Garret Anderson	.50	.15
❑ 4 Jarrod Washburn	.50	.15
❑ 5 Tim Salmon	.75	.23
❑ 6 Troy Glaus	.75	.23
❑ 7 Jay Gibbons	.50	.15
❑ 8 Marty Cordova	.50	.15
❑ 9 Melvin Mora	.50	.15
❑ 10 Rodrigo Lopez	.50	.15
❑ 11 Tony Batista	.50	.15
❑ 12 Cliff Floyd	.50	.15
❑ 13 Derek Lowe	.50	.15
❑ 14 Johnny Damon	.50	.15
❑ 15 Manny Ramirez	.50	.15
❑ 16 Nomar Garciaparra	2.50	.75
❑ 17 Pedro Martinez	1.25	.35
❑ 18 Rickey Henderson	2.00	.60
❑ 19 Shea Hillenbrand	.50	.15
❑ 20 Carlos Lee	.50	.15
❑ 21 Frank Thomas	1.25	.35
❑ 22 Magglio Ordonez	.50	.15
❑ 23 Mark Buehrle	.50	.15
❑ 24 Paul Konerko	.50	.15
❑ 25 C.C. Sabathia	.50	.15
❑ 26 Danys Baez	.50	.15
❑ 27 Ellis Burks	.50	.15
❑ 28 Travis Hafner	.50	.15
❑ 29 Omar Vizquel	.50	.15
❑ 30 Bobby Higginson	.50	.15
❑ 31 Carlos Pena	.50	.15
❑ 32 Mark Redman	.50	.15
❑ 33 Robert Fick	.50	.15
❑ 34 Steve Sparks	.50	.15
❑ 35 Carlos Beltran	.50	.15
❑ 36 Joe Randa	.50	.15
❑ 37 Mike Sweeney	.50	.15
❑ 38 Paul Byrd	.50	.15
❑ 39 Raul Ibanez	.50	.15
❑ 40 Runelvys Hernandez	.50	.15
❑ 41 Brad Radke	.50	.15
❑ 42 Corey Koskie	.50	.15
❑ 43 Cristian Guzman	.50	.15
❑ 44 David Ortiz	.50	.15
❑ 45 Doug Mientkiewicz	.50	.15
❑ 46 Dustin Mohr	.50	.15
❑ 47 Jacque Jones	.50	.15
❑ 48 Torii Hunter	.50	.15
❑ 49 Alfonso Soriano	1.25	.35
❑ 50 Andy Pettitte	.75	.23
❑ 51 Bernie Williams	.75	.23
❑ 52 David Wells	.50	.15
❑ 53 Derek Jeter	3.00	.90
❑ 54 Jason Giambi	1.25	.35
❑ 55 Jeff Weaver	.50	.15
❑ 56 Jorge Posada	.75	.23
❑ 57 Mike Mussina	1.25	.35
❑ 58 Roger Clemens	2.50	.75
❑ 59 Barry Zito	1.25	.35
❑ 60 David Justice	.50	.15
❑ 61 Eric Chavez	.50	.15
❑ 62 Jermaine Dye	.50	.15
❑ 63 Mark Mulder	.50	.15
❑ 64 Miguel Tejada	.50	.15
❑ 65 Ray Durham	.50	.15
❑ 66 Tim Hudson	.50	.15
❑ 67 Bret Boone	.50	.15
❑ 68 Chris Snelling	.50	.15
❑ 69 Edgar Martinez	.50	.15
❑ 70 Freddy Garcia	.50	.15
❑ 71 Ichiro Suzuki	2.50	.75
❑ 72 Jamie Moyer	.50	.15
❑ 73 John Olerud	.50	.15
❑ 74 Kazuhiro Sasaki	.50	.15
❑ 75 Aubrey Huff	.50	.15
❑ 76 Joe Kennedy	.50	.15
❑ 77 Paul Wilson	.50	.15
❑ 78 Alex Rodriguez	2.50	.75
❑ 79 Chan Ho Park	.50	.15
❑ 80 Hank Blalock	.75	.23
❑ 81 Ivan Rodriguez	1.25	.35
❑ 82 Juan Gonzalez	.75	.23
❑ 83 Kevin Mench	.50	.15
❑ 84 Rafael Palmeiro	.75	.23
❑ 85 Carlos Delgado	.50	.15
❑ 86 Eric Hinske	.50	.15
❑ 87 Jose Cruz Jr.	.50	.15
❑ 88 Josh Phelps	.50	.15
❑ 89 Roy Halladay	.50	.15
❑ 90 Shannon Stewart	.50	.15
❑ 91 Vernon Wells	.50	.15
❑ 92 Curt Schilling	.75	.23
❑ 93 Junior Spivey	.50	.15
❑ 94 Luis Gonzalez	.50	.15
❑ 95 Mark Grace	1.25	.35
❑ 96 Randy Johnson	1.25	.35
❑ 97 Andruw Jones	.75	.23
❑ 98 Chipper Jones	1.25	.35
❑ 99 Gary Sheffield	.50	.15
❑ 100 Greg Maddux	2.50	.75
❑ 101 John Smoltz	.75	.23
❑ 102 Kevin Millwood	.50	.15
❑ 103 Mike Hampton	.50	.15
❑ 104 Corey Patterson	.50	.15
❑ 105 Fred McGriff	.75	.23
❑ 106 Kerry Wood	1.25	.35
❑ 107 Mark Prior	2.50	.75
❑ 108 Moises Alou	.50	.15
❑ 109 Sammy Sosa	2.00	.60
❑ 110 Adam Dunn	.75	.23
❑ 111 Austin Kearns	.75	.23
❑ 112 Barry Larkin	1.25	.35
❑ 113 Ken Griffey Jr.	2.00	.60
❑ 114 Sean Casey	.50	.15
❑ 115 Jason Jennings	.50	.15
❑ 116 Jay Payton	.50	.15
❑ 117 Larry Walker	.75	.23
❑ 118 Todd Helton	.75	.23
❑ 119 A.J. Burnett	.50	.15
❑ 120 Josh Beckett	.75	.23
❑ 121 Juan Encarnacion	.50	.15
❑ 122 Mike Lowell	.50	.15
❑ 123 Craig Biggio	.75	.23
❑ 124 Daryle Ward	.50	.15
❑ 125 Jeff Bagwell	.75	.23
❑ 126 Lance Berkman	.50	.15
❑ 127 Roy Oswalt	.50	.15
❑ 128 Adrian Beltre	.50	.15
❑ 129 Hideo Nomo	1.25	.35
❑ 130 Kazuhisa Ishii	.50	.15
❑ 131 Kevin Brown	.50	.15
❑ 132 Odalis Perez	.50	.15
❑ 133 Paul Lo Duca	.50	.15
❑ 134 Shawn Green	.50	.15
❑ 135 Jeff Kent	.50	.15
❑ 136 Ben Sheets	.50	.15
❑ 137 Jeffrey Hammonds	.50	.15
❑ 138 Jose Hernandez	.50	.15
❑ 139 Richie Sexson	.50	.15
❑ 140 Bartolo Colon	.50	.15
❑ 141 Brad Wilkerson	.50	.15
❑ 142 Javier Vazquez	.50	.15
❑ 143 Jose Vidro	.50	.15
❑ 144 Michael Barrett	.50	.15
❑ 145 Vladimir Guerrero	1.25	.35
❑ 146 Al Leiter	.50	.15
❑ 147 Mike Piazza	2.00	.60
❑ 148 Mo Vaughn	.50	.15
❑ 149 Pedro Astacio	.50	.15
❑ 150 Roberto Alomar	1.25	.35
❑ 151 Roger Cedeno	.50	.15
❑ 152 Tom Glavine	1.25	.35
❑ 153 Bobby Abreu	.50	.15
❑ 154 Jimmy Rollins	.50	.15
❑ 155 Mike Lieberthal	.50	.15
❑ 156 Pat Burrell	.50	.15

❑ 157 Vicente Padilla	.50	.15
❑ 158 Jim Thome	1.25	.35
❑ 159 Aramis Ramirez	.50	.15
❑ 160 Brian Giles	.50	.15
❑ 161 Jason Kendall	.50	.15
❑ 162 Josh Fogg	.50	.15
❑ 163 Kip Wells	.50	.15
❑ 164 Mark Kotsay	.50	.15
❑ 165 Oliver Perez	.50	.15
❑ 166 Phil Nevin	.50	.15
❑ 167 Ryan Klesko	.50	.15
❑ 168 Sean Burroughs	.50	.15
❑ 169 Trevor Hoffman	.50	.15
❑ 170 Barry Bonds	3.00	.90
❑ 171 Benito Santiago	.50	.15
❑ 172 Reggie Sanders	.50	.15
❑ 173 Rich Aurilia	.50	.15
❑ 174 Russ Ortiz	.50	.15
❑ 175 Albert Pujols	2.50	.75
❑ 176 J.D. Drew	.50	.15
❑ 177 Jim Edmonds	.50	.15
❑ 178 Matt Morris	.50	.15
❑ 179 Tino Martinez	.75	.23
❑ 180 Scott Rolen	.75	.23
❑ 181 Joe Borchard ROO	1.50	.45
❑ 182 Freddy Sanchez ROO	1.50	.45
❑ 183 Jose Contreras ROO RC	3.00	.90
❑ 184 Jeff Baker ROO	1.50	.45
❑ 185 Ryan Church ROO	1.50	.45
❑ 186 Mario Ramos ROO	1.50	.45
❑ 187 Corwin Malone ROO	1.50	.45
❑ 188 Jimmy Gobble ROO	1.50	.45
❑ 189 Jon Adkins ROO	1.50	.45
❑ 190 Tim Kalita ROO	1.50	.45
❑ 191 Nelson Castro ROO	1.50	.45
❑ 192 Colin Young ROO	1.50	.45
❑ 193 Luis Martinez ROO	1.50	.45
❑ 194 Todd Donovan ROO	1.50	.45
❑ 195 Jeremy Ward ROO	1.50	.45
❑ 196 Wilson Valdez ROO	1.50	.45
❑ 197 Hideki Matsui ROO RC	6.00	1.80
❑ 198 Mitch Wylie ROO	1.50	.45
❑ 199 Adam Walker ROO	1.50	.45
❑ 200 Cliff Bartosh ROO	1.50	.45
❑ 201 Jeremy Bonderman ROO RC		
❑ 202 Brandon Webb ROO RC		
❑ 203 Adam Loewen ROO RC		
❑ 204 Chien-Ming Wang ROO RC		
❑ 205 Hong-Chih Kuo ROO RC		
❑ 206 Delmon Young ROO RC		
❑ 207 Ryan Wagner ROO RC		
❑ 208 Dan Haren ROO RC		
❑ 209 Rickie Weeks ROO RC		
❑ 210 Ramon Nivar ROO RC		

2004 Playoff Prime Cuts

	MINT	NRMT
COMPLETE SET (50)	225.00	100.00
STATED PRINT RUN 949 SERIAL #'d SETS		
B.RUTH SANTA STATED ODDS 1:15		
❑ 1 Roger Clemens Yanks	10.00	4.50
❑ 2 Nomar Garciaparra	10.00	4.50
❑ 3 Albert Pujols	10.00	4.50
❑ 4 Sammy Sosa	8.00	3.60
❑ 5 Greg Maddux Braves	10.00	4.50
❑ 6 Jason Giambi	5.00	2.20
❑ 7 Hideo Nomo Dodgers	5.00	2.20
❑ 8 Mike Piazza Mets	8.00	3.60
❑ 9 Ichiro Suzuki	10.00	4.50
❑ 10 Jeff Bagwell	5.00	2.20
❑ 11 Derek Jeter	12.00	5.50
❑ 12 Manny Ramirez	5.00	2.20
❑ 13 R.Henderson Dodgers	8.00	3.60
❑ 14 Alex Rodriguez Rgr	10.00	4.50
❑ 15 Troy Glaus	5.00	2.20
❑ 16 Mike Mussina	5.00	2.20
❑ 17 Kerry Wood	5.00	2.20
❑ 18 Kazuhisa Ishii	5.00	2.20
❑ 19 Hideki Matsui	15.00	6.75
❑ 20 Frank Thomas	5.00	2.20
❑ 21 Barry Bonds Giants	12.00	5.50
❑ 22 Adam Dunn	5.00	2.20
❑ 23 Randy Johnson D'backs	5.00	2.20
❑ 24 Alfonso Soriano	5.00	2.20
❑ 25 Pedro Martinez Sox	5.00	2.20
❑ 26 Andruw Jones	5.00	2.20
❑ 27 Mark Prior	10.00	4.50
❑ 28 Vladimir Guerrero	5.00	2.20
❑ 29 Chipper Jones	5.00	2.20
❑ 30 Todd Helton	5.00	2.20
❑ 31 Rafael Palmeiro	5.00	2.20
❑ 32 Mark Grace	5.00	2.20
❑ 33 Pedro Martinez Dodgers	5.00	2.20
❑ 34 Randy Johnson M's	5.00	2.20
❑ 35 Randy Johnson Astros	5.00	2.20
❑ 36 Roger Clemens Sox	10.00	4.50
❑ 37 Roger Clemens Jays	10.00	4.50
❑ 38 Alex Rodriguez M's	10.00	4.50
❑ 39 Greg Maddux Cubs	10.00	4.50
❑ 40 Mike Piazza Dodgers	8.00	3.60
❑ 41 Mike Piazza Marlins	8.00	3.60
❑ 42 Hideo Nomo Mets	5.00	2.20
❑ 43 R.Henderson Yanks	8.00	3.60
❑ 44 Rickey Henderson A's	8.00	3.60
❑ 45 Barry Bonds Pirates	12.00	5.50
❑ 46 Ivan Rodriguez	5.00	2.20
❑ 47 George Brett	10.00	4.50
❑ 48 Cal Ripken	12.00	5.50
❑ 49 Nolan Ryan	12.00	5.50
❑ 50 Don Mattingly	10.00	4.50
❑ BRS1 Babe Ruth Santa	15.00	6.75

1988 Score Rookie/Traded

	Nm-Mt	Ex-Mt
COMP.FACT.SET (110)	40.00	16.00
❑ 1T Jack Clark	.75	.30
❑ 2T Danny Jackson	.25	.10
❑ 3T Brett Butler	.75	.30
❑ 4T Kurt Stillwell	.25	.10
❑ 5T Tom Brunansky	.25	.10
❑ 6T Dennis Lamp	.25	.10
❑ 7T Jose DeLeon	.25	.10
❑ 8T Tom Herr	.25	.10
❑ 9T Keith Moreland	.25	.10
❑ 10T Kirk Gibson	2.00	.80
❑ 11T Bud Black	.25	.10
❑ 12T Rafael Ramirez	.25	.10
❑ 13T Luis Salazar	.25	.10
❑ 14T Goose Gossage	1.25	.50
❑ 15T Bob Welch	.25	.10
❑ 16T Vance Law	.25	.10
❑ 17T Ray Knight	.25	.10
❑ 18T Dan Quisenberry	.25	.10
❑ 19T Don Slaught	.25	.10
❑ 20T Lee Smith	.75	.30
❑ 21T Rick Cerone	.25	.10
❑ 22T Pat Tabler	.25	.10
❑ 23T Larry McWilliams	.25	.10
❑ 24T Ricky Horton	.25	.10
❑ 25T Graig Nettles	.75	.30
❑ 26T Dan Petry	.25	.10
❑ 27T Jose Rijo	.25	.10
❑ 28T Chili Davis	1.25	.50
❑ 29T Dickie Thon	.25	.10
❑ 30T Mackey Sasser	.25	.10
❑ 31T Mickey Tettleton	.25	.10
❑ 32T Rick Dempsey	.25	.10
❑ 33T Ron Hassey	.25	.10
❑ 34T Phil Bradley	.25	.10
❑ 35T Jay Howell	.25	.10
❑ 36T Bill Buckner	.75	.30
❑ 37T Alfredo Griffin	.25	.10
❑ 38T Gary Pettis	.25	.10
❑ 39T Calvin Schiraldi	.25	.10
❑ 40T John Candelaria	.25	.10
❑ 41T Joe Orsulak	.25	.10
❑ 42T Willie Upshaw	.25	.10
❑ 43T Herm Winningham	.25	.10
❑ 44T Ron Kittle	.25	.10
❑ 45T Bob Dernier	.25	.10
❑ 46T Steve Balboni	.25	.10
❑ 47T Steve Shields	.25	.10
❑ 48T Henry Cotto	.25	.10
❑ 49T Dave Henderson	.25	.10
❑ 50T Dave Parker	.75	.30
❑ 51T Mike Young	.25	.10
❑ 52T Mark Salas	.25	.10
❑ 53T Mike Davis	.25	.10
❑ 54T Rafael Santana	.25	.10
❑ 55T Don Baylor	.75	.30
❑ 56T Dan Pasqua	.25	.10
❑ 57T Ernest Riles	.25	.10
❑ 58T Glenn Hubbard	.25	.10
❑ 59T Mike Smithson	.25	.10
❑ 60T Richard Dotson	.25	.10
❑ 61T Jerry Reuss	.25	.10
❑ 62T Mike Jackson	.75	.30
❑ 63T Floyd Bannister	.25	.10
❑ 64T Jesse Orosco	.25	.10
❑ 65T Larry Parrish	.25	.10
❑ 66T Jeff Bittiger	.25	.10
❑ 67T Ray Hayward	.25	.10
❑ 68T Ricky Jordan XRC	.75	.30
❑ 69T Tommy Gregg	.25	.10
❑ 70T Brady Anderson XRC	1.50	.60
❑ 71T Jeff Montgomery	2.00	.80
❑ 72T Darryl Hamilton XRC	.75	.30
❑ 73T Cecil Espy	.25	.10
❑ 74T Greg Briley XRC	.25	.10
❑ 75T Joey Meyer	.25	.10
❑ 76T Mike Macfarlane XRC	.25	.10
❑ 77T Oswald Peraza	.25	.10
❑ 78T Jack Armstrong XRC	.25	.10
❑ 79T Don Heinkel	.25	.10
❑ 80T Mark Grace XRC	8.00	3.20
❑ 81T Steve Curry	.25	.10
❑ 82T Damon Berryhill XRC	.25	.10
❑ 83T Steve Ellsworth	.25	.10
❑ 84T Pete Smith XRC*	.25	.10
❑ 85T Jack McDowell XRC	2.00	.80
❑ 86T Rob Dibble XRC	1.50	.60
❑ 87T Bryan Harvey UER (Games Pitched 47, Innings 5) XRC	.75	.30
❑ 88T John Dopson	.25	.10
❑ 89T Dave Gallagher	.25	.10
❑ 90T Todd Stottlemyre XRC	1.25	.50
❑ 91T Mike Schooler	.25	.10
❑ 92T Don Gordon	.25	.10
❑ 93T Sil Campusano	.25	.10
❑ 94T Jeff Pico	.25	.10
❑ 95T Jay Buhner XRC	3.00	1.20
❑ 96T Nelson Santovenia	.25	.10
❑ 97T Al Leiter XRC*	2.00	.80
❑ 98T Luis Alicea XRC	.75	.30
❑ 99T Pat Borders XRC	.75	.30
❑ 100T Chris Sabo XRC	.75	.30
❑ 101T Tim Belcher	.75	.30

❑ 102T Walt Weiss XRC*	.75	.30
❑ 103T Craig Biggio XRC	8.00	3.20
❑ 104T Don August	.25	.10
❑ 105T Roberto Alomar XRC	20.00	8.00
❑ 106T Todd Burns	.25	.10
❑ 107T John Costello	.25	.10
❑ 108T Melido Perez XRC*	.25	.10
❑ 109T Darrin Jackson XRC	.25	.10
❑ 110T O.Destrade XRC	.75	.30

1989 Score Rookie/Traded

	Nm-Mt	Ex-Mt
COMP.FACT.SET (110)	15.00	6.00
❑ 1T Rafael Palmeiro	.25	.10
❑ 2T Nolan Ryan	1.50	.60
❑ 3T Jack Clark	.05	.02
❑ 4T Dave LaPoint	.05	.02
❑ 5T Mike Moore	.05	.02
❑ 6T Pete O'Brien	.05	.02
❑ 7T Jeffrey Leonard	.05	.02
❑ 8T Rob Murphy	.05	.02
❑ 9T Tom Herr	.05	.02
❑ 10T Claudell Washington	.05	.02
❑ 11T Mike Pagliarulo	.05	.02
❑ 12T Steve Lake	.05	.02
❑ 13T Spike Owen	.05	.02
❑ 14T Andy Hawkins	.05	.02
❑ 15T Todd Benzinger	.05	.02
❑ 16T Mookie Wilson	.10	.04
❑ 17T Bert Blyleven	.10	.04
❑ 18T Jeff Treadway	.05	.02
❑ 19T Bruce Hurst	.05	.02
❑ 20T Steve Sax	.05	.02
❑ 21T Juan Samuel	.05	.02
❑ 22T Jesse Barfield	.05	.02
❑ 23T Carmen Castillo	.05	.02
❑ 24T Terry Leach	.05	.02
❑ 25T Mark Langston	.05	.02
❑ 26T Eric King	.05	.02
❑ 27T Steve Balboni	.05	.02
❑ 28T Len Dykstra	.10	.04
❑ 29T Keith Moreland	.05	.02
❑ 30T Terry Kennedy	.05	.02
❑ 31T Eddie Murray	.25	.10
❑ 32T Mitch Williams	.05	.02
❑ 33T Jeff Parrett	.05	.02
❑ 34T Wally Backman	.05	.02
❑ 35T Julio Franco	.05	.02
❑ 36T Lance Parrish	.05	.02
❑ 37T Nick Esasky	.05	.02
❑ 38T Luis Polonia	.05	.02
❑ 39T Kevin Gross	.05	.02
❑ 40T John Dopson	.05	.02
❑ 41T Willie Randolph	.10	.04
❑ 42T Jim Clancy	.05	.02
❑ 43T Tracy Jones	.05	.02
❑ 44T Phil Bradley	.05	.02
❑ 45T Milt Thompson	.05	.02
❑ 46T Chris James	.05	.02
❑ 47T Scott Fletcher	.05	.02
❑ 48T Kal Daniels	.05	.02
❑ 49T Steve Bedrosian	.05	.02
❑ 50T Rickey Henderson	.40	.16
❑ 51T Dion James	.05	.02
❑ 52T Tim Leary	.05	.02
❑ 53T Roger McDowell	.05	.02
❑ 54T Mel Hall	.05	.02
❑ 55T Dickie Thon	.05	.02
❑ 56T Zane Smith	.05	.02
❑ 57T Danny Heep	.05	.02
❑ 58T Bob McClure	.05	.02
❑ 59T Brian Holton	.05	.02
❑ 60T Randy Ready	.05	.02
❑ 61T Bob Melvin	.05	.02
❑ 62T Harold Baines	.10	.04
❑ 63T Lance McCullers	.05	.02
❑ 64T Jody Davis	.05	.02
❑ 65T Darrell Evans	.10	.04
❑ 66T Joel Youngblood	.05	.02
❑ 67T Frank Viola	.05	.02
❑ 68T Mike Aldrete	.05	.02
❑ 69T Greg Cadaret	.05	.02
❑ 70T John Kruk	.10	.04
❑ 71T Pat Sheridan	.05	.02
❑ 72T Oddibe McDowell	.05	.02
❑ 73T Tom Brookens	.05	.02
❑ 74T Bob Boone	.10	.04
❑ 75T Walt Terrell	.05	.02
❑ 76T Joel Skinner	.05	.02
❑ 77T Randy Johnson	2.00	.80
❑ 78T Felix Fermin	.05	.02
❑ 79T Rick Mahler	.05	.02
❑ 80T Richard Dotson	.05	.02
❑ 81T Cris Carpenter RC *	.10	.04
❑ 82T Bill Spiers RC	.25	.10
❑ 83T Junior Felix RC	.10	.04
❑ 84T Joe Girardi RC	.40	.16
❑ 85T Jerome Walton	.25	.10
❑ 86T Greg Litton	.05	.02
❑ 87T Greg W.Harris RC	.10	.04
❑ 88T Jim Abbott RC*	.50	.20
❑ 89T Kevin Brown	.25	.10
❑ 90T John Wetteland RC	.40	.16
❑ 91T Gary Wayne	.05	.02
❑ 92T Rich Monteleone	.05	.02
❑ 93T Bob Geren	.05	.02
❑ 94T Clay Parker	.05	.02
❑ 95T Steve Finley RC	.50	.20
❑ 96T Gregg Olson RC	.25	.10
❑ 97T Ken Patterson	.05	.02
❑ 98T Ken Hill RC	.25	.10
❑ 99T Scott Scudder RC	.10	.04
❑ 100T Ken Griffey Jr. RC	8.00	3.20
❑ 101T Jeff Brantley RC	.25	.10
❑ 102T Donn Pall	.05	.02
❑ 103T Carlos Martinez RC	.10	.04
❑ 104T Joe Oliver RC	.25	.10
❑ 105T Omar Vizquel RC	.50	.20
❑ 106T Joey Belle RC	.75	.30
❑ 107T Kenny Rogers RC	.50	.20
❑ 108T Mark Carreon	.05	.02
❑ 109T Rolando Roomes	.05	.02
❑ 110T Pete Harnisch RC	.25	.10

1990 Score

	Nm-Mt	Ex-Mt
COMPLETE SET (704)	15.00	4.50
COMP.RETAIL SET (704)	15.00	4.50
COMP.HOBBY SET (714)	15.00	4.50
❑ 1 Don Mattingly	.60	.18
❑ 2 Cal Ripken	.75	.23
❑ 3 Dwight Evans	.10	.03
❑ 4 Barry Bonds	.60	.18
❑ 5 Kevin McReynolds	.05	.02
❑ 6 Ozzie Guillen	.05	.02
❑ 7 Terry Kennedy	.05	.02
❑ 8 Bryan Harvey	.05	.02
❑ 9 Alan Trammell	.15	.04
❑ 10 Cory Snyder	.05	.02
❑ 11 Jody Reed	.05	.02
❑ 12 Roberto Alomar	.25	.07
❑ 13 Pedro Guerrero	.05	.02
❑ 14 Gary Redus	.05	.02
❑ 15 Marty Barrett	.05	.02
❑ 16 Ricky Jordan	.05	.02
❑ 17 Joe Magrane	.05	.02
❑ 18 Sid Fernandez	.05	.02
❑ 19 Richard Dotson	.05	.02
❑ 20 Jack Clark	.10	.03
❑ 21 Bob Walk	.05	.02
❑ 22 Ron Karkovice	.05	.02
❑ 23 Lenny Harris	.05	.02
❑ 24 Phil Bradley	.05	.02
❑ 25 Andres Galarraga	.10	.03
❑ 26 Brian Downing	.05	.02
❑ 27 Dave Martinez	.05	.02
❑ 28 Eric King	.05	.02
❑ 29 Barry Lyons	.05	.02
❑ 30 Dave Schmidt	.05	.02
❑ 31 Mike Boddicker	.05	.02
❑ 32 Tom Foley	.05	.02
❑ 33 Brady Anderson	.10	.03
❑ 34 Jim Presley	.05	.02
❑ 35 Lance Parrish	.05	.02
❑ 36 Von Hayes	.05	.02
❑ 37 Lee Smith	.10	.03
❑ 38 Herm Winningham	.05	.02
❑ 39 Alejandro Pena	.05	.02
❑ 40 Mike Scott	.05	.02
❑ 41 Joe Orsulak	.05	.02
❑ 42 Rafael Ramirez	.05	.02
❑ 43 Gerald Young	.05	.02
❑ 44 Dick Schofield	.05	.02
❑ 45 Dave Smith	.05	.02
❑ 46 Dave Magadan	.05	.02
❑ 47 Dennis Martinez	.10	.03
❑ 48 Greg Minton	.05	.02
❑ 49 Milt Thompson	.05	.02
❑ 50 Orel Hershiser	.10	.03
❑ 51 Bip Roberts	.05	.02
❑ 52 Jerry Browne	.05	.02
❑ 53 Bob Ojeda	.05	.02
❑ 54 Fernando Valenzuela	.10	.03
❑ 55 Matt Nokes	.05	.02
❑ 56 Brook Jacoby	.05	.02
❑ 57 Frank Tanana	.05	.02
❑ 58 Scott Fletcher	.05	.02
❑ 59 Ron Oester	.05	.02
❑ 60 Bob Boone	.10	.03
❑ 61 Dan Gladden	.05	.02
❑ 62 Darnell Coles	.05	.02
❑ 63 Gregg Olson	.10	.03
❑ 64 Todd Burns	.05	.02
❑ 65 Todd Benzinger	.05	.02
❑ 66 Dale Murphy	.25	.07
❑ 67 Mike Flanagan	.05	.02
❑ 68 Jose Oquendo	.05	.02
❑ 69 Cecil Espy	.05	.02
❑ 70 Chris Sabo	.05	.02
❑ 71 Shane Rawley	.05	.02
❑ 72 Tom Brunansky	.05	.02
❑ 73 Vance Law	.05	.02
❑ 74 B.J. Surhoff	.10	.03
❑ 75 Lou Whitaker	.10	.03
❑ 76 Ken Caminiti UER Euclid and Ohio should be Hanford and California	.10	.03
❑ 77 Nelson Liriano	.05	.02
❑ 78 Tommy Gregg	.05	.02
❑ 79 Don Slaught	.05	.02
❑ 80 Eddie Murray	.25	.07
❑ 81 Joe Boever	.05	.02
❑ 82 Charlie Leibrandt	.05	.02
❑ 83 Jose Lind	.05	.02
❑ 84 Tony Phillips	.05	.02
❑ 85 Mitch Webster	.05	.02
❑ 86 Dan Plesac	.05	.02

❑ 87 Rick Mahler	.05	.02
❑ 88 Steve Lyons	.05	.02
❑ 89 Tony Fernandez	.05	.02
❑ 90 Ryne Sandberg	.40	.12
❑ 91 Nick Esasky	.05	.02
❑ 92 Luis Salazar	.05	.02
❑ 93 Pete Incaviglia	.05	.02
❑ 94 Ivan Calderon	.05	.02
❑ 95 Jeff Treadway	.05	.02
❑ 96 Kurt Stillwell	.05	.02
❑ 97 Gary Sheffield	.25	.07
❑ 98 Jeffrey Leonard	.05	.02
❑ 99 Andres Thomas	.05	.02
❑ 100 Roberto Kelly	.05	.02
❑ 101 Alvaro Espinoza	.05	.02
❑ 102 Greg Gagne	.05	.02
❑ 103 John Farrell	.05	.02
❑ 104 Willie Wilson	.05	.02
❑ 105 Glenn Braggs	.05	.02
❑ 106 Chet Lemon	.05	.02
❑ 107A Jamie Moyer ERR	.10	.03
(Scintilating)		
❑ 107B Jamie Moyer COR	.50	.15
(Scintillating)		
❑ 108 Chuck Crim	.05	.02
❑ 109 Dave Valle	.05	.02
❑ 110 Walt Weiss	.05	.02
❑ 111 Larry Sheets	.05	.02
❑ 112 Don Robinson	.05	.02
❑ 113 Danny Heep	.05	.02
❑ 114 Carmelo Martinez	.05	.02
❑ 115 Dave Gallagher	.05	.02
❑ 116 Mike LaValliere	.05	.02
❑ 117 Bob McClure	.05	.02
❑ 118 Rene Gonzales	.05	.02
❑ 119 Mark Parent	.05	.02
❑ 120 Wally Joyner	.10	.03
❑ 121 Mark Gubicza	.05	.02
❑ 122 Tony Pena	.05	.02
❑ 123 Carmelo Castillo	.05	.02
❑ 124 Howard Johnson	.05	.02
❑ 125 Steve Sax	.05	.02
❑ 126 Tim Belcher	.05	.02
❑ 127 Tim Burke	.05	.02
❑ 128 Al Newman	.05	.02
❑ 129 Dennis Rasmussen	.05	.02
❑ 130 Doug Jones	.05	.02
❑ 131 Fred Lynn	.05	.02
❑ 132 Jeff Hamilton	.05	.02
❑ 133 German Gonzalez	.05	.02
❑ 134 John Morris	.05	.02
❑ 135 Dave Parker	.10	.03
❑ 136 Gary Pettis	.05	.02
❑ 137 Dennis Boyd	.05	.02
❑ 138 Candy Maldonado	.05	.02
❑ 139 Rick Cerone	.05	.02
❑ 140 George Brett	.60	.18
❑ 141 Dave Clark	.05	.02
❑ 142 Dickie Thon	.05	.02
❑ 143 Junior Ortiz	.05	.02
❑ 144 Don August	.05	.02
❑ 145 Gary Gaetti	.10	.03
❑ 146 Kirt Manwaring	.05	.02
❑ 147 Jeff Reed	.05	.02
❑ 148 Jose Alvarez	.05	.02
❑ 149 Mike Schooler	.05	.02
❑ 150 Mark Grace	.25	.07
❑ 151 Geronimo Berroa	.05	.02
❑ 152 Barry Jones	.05	.02
❑ 153 Geno Petralli	.05	.02
❑ 154 Jim Deshaies	.05	.02
❑ 155 Barry Larkin	.25	.07
❑ 156 Alfredo Griffin	.05	.02
❑ 157 Tom Henke	.05	.02
❑ 158 Mike Jeffcoat	.05	.02
❑ 159 Bob Welch	.05	.02
❑ 160 Julio Franco	.05	.02
❑ 161 Henry Cotto	.05	.02
❑ 162 Terry Steinbach	.05	.02
❑ 163 Damon Berryhill	.05	.02
❑ 164 Tim Crews	.05	.02
❑ 165 Tom Browning	.05	.02
❑ 166 Fred Manrique	.05	.02
❑ 167 Harold Reynolds	.10	.03
❑ 168A Ron Hassey ERR	.05	.02
(27 on back)		
❑ 168B Ron Hassey COR	.50	.15
(24 on back)		
❑ 169 Shawon Dunston	.05	.02
❑ 170 Bobby Bonilla	.10	.03
❑ 171 Tommy Herr	.05	.02
❑ 172 Mike Heath	.05	.02
❑ 173 Rich Gedman	.05	.02
❑ 174 Bill Ripken	.05	.02
❑ 175 Pete O'Brien	.05	.02
❑ 176A L.McClendon ERR	.05	.02
Uniform number on back listed as 1		
❑ 176B L.McClendon COR	.50	.15
Uniform number on back listed as 10		
❑ 177 Brian Holton	.05	.02
❑ 178 Jeff Blauser	.05	.02
❑ 179 Jim Eisenreich	.05	.02
❑ 180 Bert Blyleven	.10	.03
❑ 181 Rob Murphy	.05	.02
❑ 182 Bill Doran	.05	.02
❑ 183 Curt Ford	.05	.02
❑ 184 Mike Henneman	.05	.02
❑ 185 Eric Davis	.10	.03
❑ 186 Lance McCullers	.05	.02
❑ 187 Steve Davis	.05	.02
❑ 188 Bill Wegman	.05	.02
❑ 189 Brian Harper	.05	.02
❑ 190 Mike Moore	.05	.02
❑ 191 Dale Mohorcic	.05	.02
❑ 192 Tim Wallach	.05	.02
❑ 193 Keith Hernandez	.15	.04
❑ 194 Dave Righetti	.05	.02
❑ 195A B.Saberhagen ERR	.10	.03
Joke		
❑ 195B B.Saberhagen COR	.50	.15
Joker		
❑ 196 Paul Kilgus	.05	.02
❑ 197 Bud Black	.05	.02
❑ 198 Juan Samuel	.05	.02
❑ 199 Kevin Seitzer	.05	.02
❑ 200 Darryl Strawberry	.15	.04
❑ 201 Dave Stieb	.10	.03
❑ 202 Charlie Hough	.10	.03
❑ 203 Jack Morris	.10	.03
❑ 204 Rance Mulliniks	.05	.02
❑ 205 Alvin Davis	.05	.02
❑ 206 Jack Howell	.05	.02
❑ 207 Ken Patterson	.05	.02
❑ 208 Terry Pendleton	.10	.03
❑ 209 Craig Lefferts	.05	.02
❑ 210 Kevin Brown UER	.10	.03
(First mention of '89 Rangers should be '88)		
❑ 211 Dan Petry	.05	.02
❑ 212 Dave Leiper	.05	.02
❑ 213 Daryl Boston	.05	.02
❑ 214 Kevin Hickey	.05	.02
❑ 215 Mike Krukow	.05	.02
❑ 216 Terry Francona	.10	.03
❑ 217 Kirk McCaskill	.05	.02
❑ 218 Scott Bailes	.05	.02
❑ 219 Bob Forsch	.05	.02
❑ 220A Mike Aldrete ERR	.05	.02
(25 on back)		
❑ 220B Mike Aldrete COR	.50	.15
(24 on back)		
❑ 221 Steve Buechele	.05	.02
❑ 222 Jesse Barfield	.05	.02
❑ 223 Juan Berenguer	.05	.02
❑ 224 Andy McGaffigan	.05	.02
❑ 225 Pete Smith	.05	.02
❑ 226 Mike Witt	.05	.02
❑ 227 Jay Howell	.05	.02
❑ 228 Scott Bradley	.05	.02
❑ 229 Jerome Walton	.05	.02
❑ 230 Greg Swindell	.05	.02
❑ 231 Atlee Hammaker	.05	.02
❑ 232A Mike Devereaux ERR	.05	.02
(RF on front)		
❑ 232B M.Devereaux COR	.50	.15
CF on front		
❑ 233 Ken Hill	.10	.03
❑ 234 Craig Worthington	.05	.02
❑ 235 Scott Terry	.05	.02
❑ 236 Brett Butler	.10	.03
❑ 237 Doyle Alexander	.05	.02
❑ 238 Dave Anderson	.05	.02
❑ 239 Bob Milacki	.05	.02
❑ 240 Dwight Smith	.05	.02
❑ 241 Otis Nixon	.05	.02
❑ 242 Pat Tabler	.05	.02
❑ 243 Derek Lilliquist	.05	.02
❑ 244 Danny Tartabull	.05	.02
❑ 245 Wade Boggs	.15	.04
❑ 246 Scott Garrelts	.05	.02
(Should say Relief Pitcher on front)		
❑ 247 Spike Owen	.05	.02
❑ 248 Norm Charlton	.05	.02
❑ 249 Gerald Perry	.05	.02
❑ 250 Nolan Ryan	1.00	.30
❑ 251 Kevin Gross	.05	.02
❑ 252 Randy Milligan	.05	.02
❑ 253 Mike LaCoss	.05	.02
❑ 254 Dave Bergman	.05	.02
❑ 255 Tony Gwynn	.30	.09
❑ 256 Felix Fermin	.05	.02
❑ 257 Greg W. Harris	.05	.02
❑ 258 Junior Felix	.05	.02
❑ 259 Mark Davis	.05	.02
❑ 260 Vince Coleman	.05	.02
❑ 261 Paul Gibson	.05	.02
❑ 262 Mitch Williams	.05	.02
❑ 263 Jeff Russell	.05	.02
❑ 264 Omar Vizquel	.25	.07
❑ 265 Andre Dawson	.10	.03
❑ 266 Storm Davis	.05	.02
❑ 267 Guillermo Hernandez	.05	.02
❑ 268 Mike Felder	.05	.02
❑ 269 Tom Candiotti	.05	.02
❑ 270 Bruce Hurst	.05	.02
❑ 271 Fred McGriff	.25	.07
❑ 272 Glenn Davis	.05	.02
❑ 273 John Franco	.10	.03
❑ 274 Rich Yett	.05	.02
❑ 275 Craig Biggio	.15	.04
❑ 276 Gene Larkin	.05	.02
❑ 277 Rob Dibble	.10	.03
❑ 278 Randy Bush	.05	.02
❑ 279 Kevin Bass	.05	.02
❑ 280A Bo Jackson ERR	.25	.07
(Watham)		
❑ 280B Bo Jackson COR	.75	.23
(Wathan)		
❑ 281 Wally Backman	.05	.02
❑ 282 Larry Andersen	.05	.02
❑ 283 Chris Bosio	.05	.02
❑ 284 Juan Agosto	.05	.02
❑ 285 Ozzie Smith	.25	.07
❑ 286 George Bell	.05	.02
❑ 287 Rex Hudler	.05	.02
❑ 288 Pat Borders	.05	.02
❑ 289 Danny Jackson	.05	.02
❑ 290 Carlton Fisk	.15	.04
❑ 291 Tracy Jones	.05	.02
❑ 292 Allan Anderson	.05	.02
❑ 293 Johnny Ray	.05	.02
❑ 294 Lee Guetterman	.05	.02
❑ 295 Paul O'Neill	.15	.04
❑ 296 Carney Lansford	.10	.03
❑ 297 Tom Brookens	.05	.02
❑ 298 Claudell Washington	.05	.02
❑ 299 Hubie Brooks	.05	.02
❑ 300 Will Clark	.25	.07
❑ 301 Kenny Rogers	.10	.03
❑ 302 Darrell Evans	.10	.03
❑ 303 Greg Briley	.05	.02
❑ 304 Donn Pall	.05	.02
❑ 305 Teddy Higuera	.05	.02
❑ 306 Dan Pasqua	.05	.02
❑ 307 Dave Winfield	.15	.04
❑ 308 Dennis Powell	.05	.02
❑ 309 Jose DeLeon	.05	.02
❑ 310 Roger Clemens UER	.50	.15
(Dominate, should say dominant)		
❑ 311 Melido Perez	.05	.02
❑ 312 Devon White	.05	.02
❑ 313 Dwight Gooden	.15	.04
❑ 314 Carlos Martinez	.05	.02
❑ 315 Dennis Eckersley	.10	.03

No.	Player		
316	Clay Parker UER (Height 6'11")	.05	.02
317	Rick Honeycutt	.05	.02
318	Tim Laudner	.05	.02
319	Joe Carter	.10	.03
320	Robin Yount	.25	.07
321	Felix Jose	.05	.02
322	Mickey Tettleton	.05	.02
323	Mike Gallego	.05	.02
324	Edgar Martinez	.15	.04
325	Dave Henderson	.05	.02
326	Chili Davis	.10	.03
327	Steve Balboni	.05	.02
328	Jody Davis	.05	.02
329	Shawn Hillegas	.05	.02
330	Jim Abbott	.25	.07
331	John Dopson	.05	.02
332	Mark Williamson	.05	.02
333	Jeff D. Robinson	.05	.02
334	John Smiley	.05	.02
335	Bobby Thigpen	.05	.02
336	Garry Templeton	.05	.02
337	Marvell Wynne	.05	.02
338A	Ken Griffey Sr. ERR (Uniform number on back listed as 25)	.10	.03
338B	Ken Griffey Sr. COR (Uniform number on back listed as 30)	.50	.15
339	Steve Finley	.10	.03
340	Ellis Burks	.15	.04
341	Frank Williams	.05	.02
342	Mike Morgan	.05	.02
343	Kevin Mitchell	.05	.02
344	Joel Youngblood	.05	.02
345	Mike Greenwell	.05	.02
346	Glenn Wilson	.05	.02
347	John Costello	.05	.02
348	Wes Gardner	.05	.02
349	Jeff Ballard	.05	.02
350	Mark Thurmond UER (ERA is 192, should be 1.92)	.05	.02
351	Randy Myers	.10	.03
352	Shawn Abner	.05	.02
353	Jesse Orosco	.05	.02
354	Greg Walker	.05	.02
355	Pete Harnisch	.05	.02
356	Steve Farr	.05	.02
357	Dave LaPoint	.05	.02
358	Willie Fraser	.05	.02
359	Mickey Hatcher	.05	.02
360	Rickey Henderson	.40	.12
361	Mike Fitzgerald	.05	.02
362	Bill Schroeder	.05	.02
363	Mark Carreon	.05	.02
364	Ron Jones	.05	.02
365	Jeff Montgomery	.10	.03
366	Bill Krueger	.05	.02
367	John Cangelosi	.05	.02
368	Jose Gonzalez	.05	.02
369	Greg Hibbard RC	.10	.03
370	John Smoltz	.25	.07
371	Jeff Brantley	.05	.02
372	Frank White	.10	.03
373	Ed Whitson	.05	.02
374	Willie McGee	.10	.03
375	Jose Canseco	.25	.07
376	Randy Ready	.05	.02
377	Don Aase	.05	.02
378	Tony Armas	.05	.02
379	Steve Bedrosian	.05	.02
380	Chuck Finley	.10	.03
381	Kent Hrbek	.10	.03
382	Jim Gantner	.05	.02
383	Mel Hall	.05	.02
384	Mike Marshall	.05	.02
385	Mark McGwire	.60	.18
386	Wayne Tolleson	.05	.02
387	Brian Holman	.05	.02
388	John Wetteland	.25	.07
389	Darren Daulton	.10	.03
390	Rob Deer	.05	.02
391	John Moses	.05	.02
392	Todd Worrell	.05	.02
393	Chuck Cary	.05	.02
394	Stan Javier	.05	.02
395	Willie Randolph	.10	.03
396	Bill Buckner	.05	.02
397	Robby Thompson	.05	.02
398	Mike Scioscia	.05	.02
399	Lonnie Smith	.05	.02
400	Kirby Puckett	.25	.07
401	Mark Langston	.05	.02
402	Danny Darwin	.05	.02
403	Greg Maddux	.50	.15
404	Lloyd Moseby	.05	.02
405	Rafael Palmeiro	.15	.04
406	Chad Kreuter	.05	.02
407	Jimmy Key	.10	.03
408	Tim Birtsas	.05	.02
409	Tim Raines	.10	.03
410	Dave Stewart	.10	.03
411	Eric Yelding	.05	.02
412	Kent Anderson	.05	.02
413	Les Lancaster	.05	.02
414	Rick Dempsey	.05	.02
415	Randy Johnson	.40	.12
416	Gary Carter	.15	.04
417	Rolando Roomes	.05	.02
418	Dan Schatzeder	.05	.02
419	Bryn Smith	.05	.02
420	Ruben Sierra	.05	.02
421	Steve Jeltz	.05	.02
422	Ken Oberkfell	.05	.02
423	Sid Bream	.05	.02
424	Jim Clancy	.05	.02
425	Kelly Gruber	.05	.02
426	Rick Leach	.05	.02
427	Len Dykstra	.10	.03
428	Jeff Pico	.05	.02
429	John Cerutti	.05	.02
430	David Cone	.10	.03
431	Jeff Kunkel	.05	.02
432	Luis Aquino	.05	.02
433	Ernie Whitt	.05	.02
434	Bo Diaz	.05	.02
435	Steve Lake	.05	.02
436	Pat Perry	.05	.02
437	Mike Davis	.05	.02
438	Cecilio Guante	.05	.02
439	Duane Ward	.05	.02
440	Andy Van Slyke	.10	.03
441	Gene Nelson	.05	.02
442	Luis Polonia	.05	.02
443	Kevin Elster	.05	.02
444	Keith Moreland	.05	.02
445	Roger McDowell	.05	.02
446	Ron Darling	.05	.02
447	Ernest Riles	.05	.02
448	Mookie Wilson	.10	.03
449A	Billy Spiers ERR (No birth year)	.05	.02
449B	Billy Spiers COR (Born in 1966)	.50	.15
450	Rick Sutcliffe	.10	.03
451	Nelson Santovenia	.05	.02
452	Andy Allanson	.05	.02
453	Bob Melvin	.05	.02
454	Benito Santiago	.10	.03
455	Jose Uribe	.05	.02
456	Bill Landrum	.05	.02
457	Bobby Witt	.05	.02
458	Kevin Romine	.05	.02
459	Lee Mazzilli	.05	.02
460	Paul Molitor	.15	.04
461	Ramon Martinez	.05	.02
462	Frank DiPino	.05	.02
463	Walt Terrell	.05	.02
464	Bob Geren	.05	.02
465	Rick Reuschel	.05	.02
466	Mark Grant	.05	.02
467	John Kruk	.10	.03
468	Gregg Jefferies	.10	.03
469	R.J. Reynolds	.05	.02
470	Harold Baines	.10	.03
471	Dennis Lamp	.05	.02
472	Tom Gordon	.10	.03
473	Terry Puhl	.05	.02
474	Curt Wilkerson	.05	.02
475	Dan Quisenberry	.05	.02
476	Oddibe McDowell	.05	.02
477A	Zane Smith ERR (Career ERA .393)	.05	.02
477B	Zane Smith COR (career ERA 3.93)	.50	.15
478	Franklin Stubbs	.05	.02
479	Wallace Johnson	.05	.02
480	Jay Tibbs	.05	.02
481	Tom Glavine	.25	.07
482	Manny Lee	.05	.02
483	Joe Hesketh UER Says Rookiess on back, should say Rookies	.05	.02
484	Mike Bielecki	.05	.02
485	Greg Brock	.05	.02
486	Pascual Perez	.05	.02
487	Kirk Gibson	.10	.03
488	Scott Sanderson	.05	.02
489	Domingo Ramos	.05	.02
490	Kal Daniels	.05	.02
491A	David Wells ERR (Reverse negative photo on card back)	.10	.03
491B	David Wells COR	.50	.15
492	Jerry Reed	.05	.02
493	Eric Show	.05	.02
494	Mike Pagliarulo	.05	.02
495	Ron Robinson	.05	.02
496	Brad Komminsk	.05	.02
497	Greg Litton	.05	.02
498	Chris James	.05	.02
499	Luis Quinones	.05	.02
500	Frank Viola	.05	.02
501	Tim Teufel UER (Twins '85, the s is lower case, should be upper case)	.05	.02
502	Terry Leach	.05	.02
503	Matt Williams UER (Wearing 10 on front, listed as 9 on back)	.10	.03
504	Tim Leary	.05	.02
505	Doug Drabek	.05	.02
506	Mariano Duncan	.05	.02
507	Charlie Hayes	.05	.02
508	Joey Belle	.15	.04
509	Pat Sheridan	.05	.02
510	Mackey Sasser	.05	.02
511	Jose Rijo	.05	.02
512	Mike Smithson	.05	.02
513	Gary Ward	.05	.02
514	Dion James	.05	.02
515	Jim Gott	.05	.02
516	Drew Hall	.05	.02
517	Doug Bair	.05	.02
518	Scott Scudder	.05	.02
519	Rick Aguilera	.10	.03
520	Rafael Belliard	.05	.02
521	Jay Buhner	.10	.03
522	Jeff Reardon	.10	.03
523	Steve Rosenberg	.05	.02
524	Randy Velarde	.05	.02
525	Jeff Musselman	.05	.02
526	Bill Long	.05	.02
527	Gary Wayne	.05	.02
528	Dave Johnson (P)	.05	.02
529	Ron Kittle	.05	.02
530	Erik Hanson UER (5th line on back says seson, should say season)	.05	.02
531	Steve Wilson	.05	.02
532	Joey Meyer	.05	.02
533	Curt Young	.05	.02
534	Kelly Downs	.05	.02
535	Joe Girardi	.15	.04
536	Lance Blankenship	.05	.02
537	Greg Mathews	.05	.02
538	Donell Nixon	.05	.02
539	Mark Knudson	.05	.02
540	Jeff Wetherby	.05	.02
541	Darrin Jackson	.05	.02
542	Terry Mulholland	.05	.02
543	Eric Hetzel	.05	.02
544	Rick Reed RC	.25	.07
545	Dennis Cook	.05	.02
546	Mike Jackson	.05	.02

Card	Nm-Mt	Ex-Mt
❑ 547 Brian Fisher	.05	.02
❑ 548 Gene Harris	.05	.02
❑ 549 Jeff King	.05	.02
❑ 550 Dave Dravecky	.25	.07
❑ 551 Randy Kutcher	.05	.02
❑ 552 Mark Portugal	.05	.02
❑ 553 Jim Corsi	.05	.02
❑ 554 Todd Stottlemyre	.10	.03
❑ 555 Scott Bankhead	.05	.02
❑ 556 Ken Dayley	.05	.02
❑ 557 Rick Wrona	.05	.02
❑ 558 Sammy Sosa RC	8.00	2.40
❑ 559 Keith Miller	.05	.02
❑ 560 Ken Griffey Jr.	.75	.23
❑ 561A R.Sandberg HL ERR	8.00	2.40
Position on front listed as 3B		
❑ 561B R.Sandberg HL COR	.25	.07
❑ 562 Billy Hatcher	.05	.02
❑ 563 Jay Bell	.10	.03
❑ 564 Jack Daugherty	.05	.02
❑ 565 Rich Monteleone	.05	.02
❑ 566 Bo Jackson AS-MVP	.10	.03
❑ 567 Tony Fossas	.05	.02
❑ 568 Roy Smith	.05	.02
❑ 569 Jaime Navarro	.05	.02
❑ 570 Lance Johnson	.05	.02
❑ 571 Mike Dyer	.05	.02
❑ 572 Kevin Ritz	.05	.02
❑ 573 Dave West	.05	.02
❑ 574 Gary Mielke	.05	.02
❑ 575 Scott Lusader	.05	.02
❑ 576 Joe Oliver	.05	.02
❑ 577 Sandy Alomar Jr.	.10	.03
❑ 578 Andy Benes UER	.10	.03
(Extra comma between day and year)		
❑ 579 Tim Jones	.05	.02
❑ 580 Randy McCament	.05	.02
❑ 581 Curt Schilling	1.00	.30
❑ 582 John Orton RC	.10	.03
❑ 583A Milt Cuyler ERR RC	.10	.03
(998 games)		
❑ 583B Milt Cuyler RC COR	.50	.15
(98 games; the extra 9 was ghosted out and may still be visible)		
❑ 584 Eric Anthony RC	.10	.03
❑ 585 Greg Vaughn	.10	.03
❑ 586 Deion Sanders	.25	.07
❑ 587 Jose DeJesus	.05	.02
❑ 588 Chip Hale	.05	.02
❑ 589 John Olerud RC	.50	.15
❑ 590 Steve Olin RC	.25	.07
❑ 591 Marquis Grissom RC	.25	.07
❑ 592 Moises Alou RC	.50	.15
❑ 593 Mark Lemke	.05	.02
❑ 594 Dean Palmer RC	.25	.07
❑ 595 Robin Ventura	.25	.07
❑ 596 Tino Martinez	.25	.07
❑ 597 Mike Huff	.05	.02
❑ 598 Scott Hemond RC	.10	.03
❑ 599 Wally Whitehurst	.05	.02
❑ 600 Todd Zeile	.10	.03
❑ 601 Glenallen Hill	.05	.02
❑ 602 Hal Morris	.05	.02
❑ 603 Juan Bell	.05	.02
❑ 604 Bobby Rose	.05	.02
❑ 605 Matt Merullo	.05	.02
❑ 606 Kevin Maas RC	.25	.07
❑ 607 Randy Nosek	.05	.02
❑ 608A Billy Bates	.05	.02
(Text mentions 12 triples in tenth line)		
❑ 608B Billy Bates	.05	.02
(Text has no mention of triples)		
❑ 609 Mike Stanton RC	.25	.07
❑ 610 Mauro Gozzo	.05	.02
❑ 611 Charles Nagy	.05	.02
❑ 612 Scott Coolbaugh	.05	.02
❑ 613 Jose Vizcaino RC	.25	.07
❑ 614 Greg Smith	.05	.02
❑ 615 Jeff Huson RC	.10	.03
❑ 616 Mickey Weston	.05	.02
❑ 617 John Pawlowski	.05	.02
❑ 618A Joe Skalski ERR	.05	.02
(27 on back)		
❑ 618B Joe Skalski COR	.50	.15
(67 on back)		
❑ 619 Bernie Williams RC	1.00	.30
❑ 620 Shawn Holman	.05	.02
❑ 621 Gary Eave	.05	.02
❑ 622 Darrin Fletcher UER	.10	.03
Elmherst, should be Elmhurst		
❑ 623 Pat Combs	.05	.02
❑ 624 Mike Blowers RC	.10	.03
❑ 625 Kevin Appier	.25	.07
❑ 626 Pat Austin	.05	.02
❑ 627 Kelly Mann	.05	.02
❑ 628 Matt Kinzer	.05	.02
❑ 629 Chris Hammond RC	.10	.03
❑ 630 Dean Wilkins	.05	.02
❑ 631 Larry Walker RC UER	1.00	.30
Uniform number 55 on front and 33 on back; Home is Maple Ridge, not Maple River		
❑ 632 Blaine Beatty	.05	.02
❑ 633A Tommy Barrett ERR	.05	.02
(29 on back)		
❑ 633B Tommy Barrett COR	.50	.15
(14 on back)		
❑ 634 Stan Belinda RC	.10	.03
❑ 635 Mike (Tex) Smith	.05	.02
❑ 636 Hensley Meulens	.05	.02
❑ 637 J.Gonzalez RC UER	1.50	.45
Sarasots on back, should be Sarasota		
❑ 638 Lenny Webster RC	.10	.03
❑ 639 Mark Gardner RC	.10	.03
❑ 640 Tommy Greene RC	.10	.03
❑ 641 Mike Hartley	.05	.02
❑ 642 Phil Stephenson	.05	.02
❑ 643 Kevin Mmahat	.05	.02
❑ 644 Ed Whited	.05	.02
❑ 645 Delino DeShields RC	.25	.07
❑ 646 Kevin Blankenship	.05	.02
❑ 647 Paul Sorrento RC	.25	.07
❑ 648 Mike Roesler	.05	.02
❑ 649 Jason Grimsley RC	.10	.03
❑ 650 Dave Justice RC	.50	.15
❑ 651 Scott Cooper RC	.10	.03
❑ 652 Dave Eiland	.05	.02
❑ 653 Mike Munoz	.05	.02
❑ 654 Jeff Fischer	.05	.02
❑ 655 Terry Jorgensen	.05	.02
❑ 656 George Canale	.05	.02
❑ 657 Brian DuBois UER	.05	.02
(Misspelled Dubois on card)		
❑ 658 Carlos Quintana	.05	.02
❑ 659 Luis de los Santos	.05	.02
❑ 660 Jerald Clark	.05	.02
❑ 661 Donald Harris DC	.05	.02
❑ 662 Paul Coleman DC RC	.10	.03
❑ 663 Frank Thomas DC RC	1.50	.45
❑ 664 Brent Mayne DC RC	.25	.07
❑ 665 Eddie Zosky DC RC	.10	.03
❑ 666 Steve Hosey DC RC	.10	.03
❑ 667 Scott Bryant DC	.10	.03
❑ 668 Tom Goodwin DC RC	.25	.07
❑ 669 Cal Eldred DC RC	.25	.07
❑ 670 E.Cunningham DC RC	.10	.03
❑ 671 Alan Zinter DC RC	.10	.03
❑ 672 C.Knoblauch DC RC	.40	.12
❑ 673 Kyle Abbott DC	.05	.02
❑ 674 Roger Salkeld DC RC	.05	.02
❑ 675 M.Vaughn DC RC	.50	.15
❑ 676 Keith (Kiki) Jones DC	.05	.02
❑ 677 Tyler Houston DC RC	.25	.07
❑ 678 Jeff Jackson DC RC	.10	.03
❑ 679 Greg Gohr DC RC	.10	.03
❑ 680 Ben McDonald DC RC	.25	.07
❑ 681 Greg Blosser DC RC	.10	.03
❑ 682 W.Greene RC DC UER	.25	.07
Name spelled as Green		
❑ 683A W.Boggs DT ERR	.10	.03
Text says 215 hits in '89, should be 205		
❑ 683B W.Boggs DT COR	.50	.15
Text says 205 hits in '89		
❑ 684 Will Clark DT	.10	.03
❑ 685 Tony Gwynn DT UER	.15	.04
(Text reads battling instead of batting)		
❑ 686 Rickey Henderson DT	.25	.07
❑ 687 Bo Jackson DT	.10	.03
❑ 688 Mark Langston DT	.05	.02
❑ 689 Barry Larkin DT	.10	.03
❑ 690 Kirby Puckett DT	.15	.04
❑ 691 Ryne Sandberg DT	.25	.07
❑ 692 Mike Scott DT	.05	.02
❑ 693A Terry Steinbach DT	.05	.02
ERR (cathers)		
❑ 693B Terry Steinbach DT	.05	.02
COR (catchers)		
❑ 694 Bobby Thigpen DT	.05	.02
❑ 695 Mitch Williams DT	.05	.02
❑ 696 Nolan Ryan HL	.25	.07
❑ 697 Bo Jackson FB/BB	.50	.15
❑ 698 Rickey Henderson	.25	.07
ALCS-MVP		
❑ 699 Will Clark	.10	.03
NLCS-MVP		
❑ 700 Dave Stewart	.10	.03
Mike Moore WS		
❑ 701 Lights Out	.25	.07
❑ 702 Carney Lansford	.25	.07
Rickey Henderson Jose Canseco Dave Henderson WS		
❑ 703 WS Game 4/Wrap-up	.05	.02
❑ 704 Wade Boggs HL	.10	.03

1991 Score

	Nm-Mt	Ex-Mt
COMPLETE SET (893)	20.00	6.00
COMP.FACT.SET (900)	25.00	7.50

Card	Nm-Mt	Ex-Mt
❑ 1 Jose Canseco	.25	.07
❑ 2 Ken Griffey Jr.	.50	.15
❑ 3 Ryne Sandberg	.40	.12
❑ 4 Nolan Ryan	1.00	.30
❑ 5 Bo Jackson	.25	.07
❑ 6 Bret Saberhagen UER	.05	.02
(In bio, missed misspelled as mised)		
❑ 7 Will Clark	.25	.07
❑ 8 Ellis Burks	.10	.03
❑ 9 Joe Carter	.10	.03
❑ 10 Rickey Henderson	.40	.12
❑ 11 Ozzie Guillen	.05	.02
❑ 12 Wade Boggs	.15	.04
❑ 13 Jerome Walton	.05	.02
❑ 14 John Franco	.10	.03
❑ 15 Ricky Jordan UER	.05	.02
(League misspelled as legue)		
❑ 16 Wally Backman	.05	.02
❑ 17 Rob Dibble	.10	.03
❑ 18 Glenn Braggs	.05	.02
❑ 19 Cory Snyder	.05	.02
❑ 20 Kal Daniels	.05	.02
❑ 21 Mark Langston	.05	.02
❑ 22 Kevin Gross	.05	.02
❑ 23 Don Mattingly UER	.60	.18
First line, ' is missing from Yankee		
❑ 24 Dave Righetti	.10	.03

❑ 25 Roberto Alomar .25 .07
❑ 26 Robby Thompson .05 .02
❑ 27 Jack McDowell .05 .02
❑ 28 Bip Roberts UER .05 .02
(Bio reads playd)
❑ 29 Jay Howell .05 .02
❑ 30 Dave Stieb UER .05 .02
(17 wins in bio,
18 in stats)
❑ 31 Johnny Ray .05 .02
❑ 32 Steve Sax .05 .02
❑ 33 Terry Mulholland .05 .02
❑ 34 Lee Guetterman .05 .02
❑ 35 Tim Raines .10 .03
❑ 36 Scott Fletcher .05 .02
❑ 37 Lance Parrish .10 .03
❑ 38 Tony Phillips UER .05 .02
(Born 4/15
should be 4/25)
❑ 39 Todd Stottlemyre .05 .02
❑ 40 Alan Trammell .15 .04
❑ 41 Todd Burns .05 .02
❑ 42 Mookie Wilson .10 .03
❑ 43 Chris Bosio .05 .02
❑ 44 Jeffrey Leonard .05 .02
❑ 45 Doug Jones .05 .02
❑ 46 Mike Scott UER .05 .02
(In first line,
dominate should
read dominating)
❑ 47 Andy Hawkins .05 .02
❑ 48 Harold Reynolds .10 .03
❑ 49 Paul Molitor .15 .04
❑ 50 John Farrell .05 .02
❑ 51 Danny Darwin .05 .02
❑ 52 Jeff Blauser .05 .02
❑ 53 John Tudor UER .05 .02
(41 wins in '81)
❑ 54 Milt Thompson .05 .02
❑ 55 Dave Justice .10 .03
❑ 56 Greg Olson .05 .02
❑ 57 Willie Blair .05 .02
❑ 58 Rick Parker .05 .02
❑ 59 Shawn Boskie .05 .02
❑ 60 Kevin Tapani .05 .02
❑ 61 Dave Hollins .05 .02
❑ 62 Scott Radinsky .05 .02
❑ 63 Francisco Cabrera .05 .02
❑ 64 Tim Layana .05 .02
❑ 65 Jim Leyritz .05 .02
❑ 66 Wayne Edwards .05 .02
❑ 67 Lee Stevens .05 .02
❑ 68 Bill Sampen UER .05 .02
Fourth line, long is spelled along
❑ 69 Craig Grebeck UER .05 .02
Born in Cerritos, not Johnstown
❑ 70 John Burkett .05 .02
❑ 71 Hector Villanueva .05 .02
❑ 72 Oscar Azocar .05 .02
❑ 73 Alan Mills .05 .02
❑ 74 Carlos Baerga .05 .02
❑ 75 Charles Nagy .05 .02
❑ 76 Tim Drummond .05 .02
❑ 77 Dana Kiecker .05 .02
❑ 78 Tom Edens .05 .02
❑ 79 Kent Mercker .05 .02
❑ 80 Steve Avery .05 .02
❑ 81 Lee Smith .10 .03
❑ 82 Dave Martinez .05 .02
❑ 83 Dave Winfield .15 .04
❑ 84 Bill Spiers .05 .02
❑ 85 Dan Pasqua .05 .02
❑ 86 Randy Milligan .05 .02
❑ 87 Tracy Jones .05 .02
❑ 88 Greg Myers .05 .02
❑ 89 Keith Hernandez .15 .04
❑ 90 Todd Benzinger .05 .02
❑ 91 Mike Jackson .05 .02
❑ 92 Mike Stanley .05 .02
❑ 93 Candy Maldonado .05 .02
❑ 94 John Kruk UER .10 .03
(No decimal point
before 1990 BA)
❑ 95 Cal Ripken UER .75 .23
(Genius spelled genuis)
❑ 96 Willie Fraser .05 .02
❑ 97 Mike Felder .05 .02
❑ 98 Bill Landrum .05 .02
❑ 99 Chuck Crim .05 .02
❑ 100 Chuck Finley .10 .03
❑ 101 Kirt Manwaring .05 .02
❑ 102 Jaime Navarro .05 .02
❑ 103 Dickie Thon .05 .02
❑ 104 Brian Downing .05 .02
❑ 105 Jim Abbott .25 .07
❑ 106 Tom Brookens .05 .02
❑ 107 Darryl Hamilton UER .05 .02
(Bio info is for
Jeff Hamilton)
❑ 108 Bryan Harvey .05 .02
❑ 109 Greg A. Harris UER .05 .02
Shown pitching lefty, bio says righty
❑ 110 Greg Swindell .05 .02
❑ 111 Juan Berenguer .05 .02
❑ 112 Mike Heath .05 .02
❑ 113 Scott Bradley .05 .02
❑ 114 Jack Morris .10 .03
❑ 115 Barry Jones .05 .02
❑ 116 Kevin Romine .05 .02
❑ 117 Garry Templeton .05 .02
❑ 118 Scott Sanderson .05 .02
❑ 119 Roberto Kelly .05 .02
❑ 120 George Brett .60 .18
❑ 121 Oddibe McDowell .05 .02
❑ 122 Jim Acker .05 .02
❑ 123 Bill Swift UER .05 .02
(Born 12/27/61,
should be 10/27)
❑ 124 Eric King .05 .02
❑ 125 Jay Buhner .10 .03
❑ 126 Matt Young .05 .02
❑ 127 Alvaro Espinoza .05 .02
❑ 128 Greg Hibbard .05 .02
❑ 129 Jeff M. Robinson .05 .02
❑ 130 Mike Greenwell .05 .02
❑ 131 Dion James .05 .02
❑ 132 Donn Pall UER .05 .02
(1988 ERA in stats 0.00)
❑ 133 Lloyd Moseby .05 .02
❑ 134 Randy Velarde .05 .02
❑ 135 Allan Anderson .05 .02
❑ 136 Mark Davis .05 .02
❑ 137 Eric Davis .10 .03
❑ 138 Phil Stephenson .05 .02
❑ 139 Felix Fermin .05 .02
❑ 140 Pedro Guerrero .10 .03
❑ 141 Charlie Hough .10 .03
❑ 142 Mike Henneman .05 .02
❑ 143 Jeff Montgomery .05 .02
❑ 144 Lenny Harris .05 .02
❑ 145 Bruce Hurst .05 .02
❑ 146 Eric Anthony .05 .02
❑ 147 Paul Assenmacher .05 .02
❑ 148 Jesse Barfield .05 .02
❑ 149 Carlos Quintana .05 .02
❑ 150 Dave Stewart .10 .03
❑ 151 Roy Smith .05 .02
❑ 152 Paul Gibson .05 .02
❑ 153 Mickey Hatcher .05 .02
❑ 154 Jim Eisenreich .05 .02
❑ 155 Kenny Rogers .10 .03
❑ 156 Dave Schmidt .05 .02
❑ 157 Lance Johnson .05 .02
❑ 158 Dave West .05 .02
❑ 159 Steve Balboni .05 .02
❑ 160 Jeff Brantley .05 .02
❑ 161 Craig Biggio .15 .04
❑ 162 Brook Jacoby .05 .02
❑ 163 Dan Gladden .05 .02
❑ 164 Jeff Reardon UER .10 .03
(Total IP shown as
943.2, should be 943.1)
❑ 165 Mark Carreon .05 .02
❑ 166 Mel Hall .05 .02
❑ 167 Gary Mielke .05 .02
❑ 168 Cecil Fielder .10 .03
❑ 169 Darrin Jackson .05 .02
❑ 170 Rick Aguilera .10 .03
❑ 171 Walt Weiss .05 .02
❑ 172 Steve Farr .05 .02
❑ 173 Jody Reed .05 .02
❑ 174 Mike Jeffcoat .05 .02
❑ 175 Mark Grace .25 .07
❑ 176 Larry Sheets .05 .02
❑ 177 Bill Gullickson .05 .02
❑ 178 Chris Gwynn .05 .02
❑ 179 Melido Perez .05 .02
❑ 180 Sid Fernandez UER .05 .02
(779 runs in 1990)
❑ 181 Tim Burke .05 .02
❑ 182 Gary Pettis .05 .02
❑ 183 Rob Murphy .05 .02
❑ 184 Craig Lefferts .05 .02
❑ 185 Howard Johnson .05 .02
❑ 186 Ken Caminiti .10 .03
❑ 187 Tim Belcher .05 .02
❑ 188 Greg Cadaret .05 .02
❑ 189 Matt Williams .10 .03
❑ 190 Dave Magadan .05 .02
❑ 191 Geno Petralli .05 .02
❑ 192 Jeff D. Robinson .05 .02
❑ 193 Jim Deshaies .05 .02
❑ 194 Willie Randolph .10 .03
❑ 195 George Bell .05 .02
❑ 196 Hubie Brooks .05 .02
❑ 197 Tom Gordon .05 .02
❑ 198 Mike Fitzgerald .05 .02
❑ 199 Mike Pagliarulo .05 .02
❑ 200 Kirby Puckett .25 .07
❑ 201 Shawon Dunston .05 .02
❑ 202 Dennis Boyd .05 .02
❑ 203 Junior Felix UER .05 .02
(Text has him in NL)
❑ 204 Alejandro Pena .05 .02
❑ 205 Pete Smith .05 .02
❑ 206 Tom Glavine UER .25 .07
(Lefty spelled leftie)
❑ 207 Luis Salazar .05 .02
❑ 208 John Smoltz .15 .04
❑ 209 Doug Dascenzo .05 .02
❑ 210 Tim Wallach .05 .02
❑ 211 Greg Gagne .05 .02
❑ 212 Mark Gubicza .05 .02
❑ 213 Mark Parent .05 .02
❑ 214 Ken Oberkfell .05 .02
❑ 215 Gary Carter .15 .04
❑ 216 Rafael Palmeiro .15 .04
❑ 217 Tom Niedenfuer .05 .02
❑ 218 Dave LaPoint .05 .02
❑ 219 Jeff Treadway .05 .02
❑ 220 Mitch Williams UER .05 .02
('89 ERA shown as 2.76,
should be 2.64)
❑ 221 Jose DeLeon .05 .02
❑ 222 Mike LaValliere .05 .02
❑ 223 Darrel Akerfelds .05 .02
❑ 224A Kent Anderson ERR .10 .03
(First line& flachy
should read flashy)
❑ 224B Kent Anderson COR .10 .03
(Corrected in
factory sets)
❑ 225 Dwight Evans .10 .03
❑ 226 Gary Redus .05 .02
❑ 227 Paul O'Neill .15 .04
❑ 228 Marty Barrett .05 .02
❑ 229 Tom Browning .05 .02
❑ 230 Terry Pendleton .10 .03
❑ 231 Jack Armstrong .05 .02
❑ 232 Mike Boddicker .05 .02
❑ 233 Neal Heaton .05 .02
❑ 234 Marquis Grissom .05 .02
❑ 235 Bert Blyleven .10 .03
❑ 236 Curt Young .05 .02
❑ 237 Don Carman .05 .02
❑ 238 Charlie Hayes .05 .02
❑ 239 Mark Knudson .05 .02
❑ 240 Todd Zeile .05 .02
❑ 241 Larry Walker UER .25 .07
(Maple River, should
be Maple Ridge)
❑ 242 Jerald Clark .05 .02
❑ 243 Jeff Ballard .05 .02
❑ 244 Jeff King .05 .02
❑ 245 Tom Brunansky .05 .02
❑ 246 Darren Daulton .10 .03
❑ 247 Scott Terry .05 .02
❑ 248 Rob Deer .05 .02

❑ 249 Brady Anderson UER .10 .03
(1990 Hagerstown 1 hit, should say 13 hits)
❑ 250 Len Dykstra .10 .03
❑ 251 Greg W. Harris .05 .02
❑ 252 Mike Hartley .05 .02
❑ 253 Joey Cora .05 .02
❑ 254 Ivan Calderon .05 .02
❑ 255 Ted Power .05 .02
❑ 256 Sammy Sosa .50 .15
❑ 257 Steve Buechele .05 .02
❑ 258 Mike Devereaux UER .05 .02
(No comma between city and state)
❑ 259 Brad Komminsk UER .05 .02
(Last text line, Ba should be BA)
❑ 260 Ted Higuera .05 .02
❑ 261 Shawn Abner .05 .02
❑ 262 Dave Valle .05 .02
❑ 263 Jeff Huson .05 .02
❑ 264 Edgar Martinez .15 .04
❑ 265 Carlton Fisk .15 .04
❑ 266 Steve Finley .10 .03
❑ 267 John Wetteland .10 .03
❑ 268 Kevin Appier .10 .03
❑ 269 Steve Lyons .05 .02
❑ 270 Mickey Tettleton .05 .02
❑ 271 Luis Rivera .05 .02
❑ 272 Steve Jeltz .05 .02
❑ 273 R.J. Reynolds .05 .02
❑ 274 Carlos Martinez .05 .02
❑ 275 Dan Plesac .05 .02
❑ 276 Mike Morgan UER .05 .02
Total IP shown as 1149.1, should be 1149
❑ 277 Jeff Russell .05 .02
❑ 278 Pete Incaviglia .05 .02
❑ 279 Kevin Seitzer UER .05 .02
Bio has 200 hits twice and .300 four times, should be once and three times
❑ 280 Bobby Thigpen .05 .02
❑ 281 Stan Javier UER .05 .02
(Born 1/9, should say 9/1)
❑ 282 Henry Cotto .05 .02
❑ 283 Gary Wayne .05 .02
❑ 284 Shane Mack .05 .02
❑ 285 Brian Holman .05 .02
❑ 286 Gerald Perry .05 .02
❑ 287 Steve Crawford .05 .02
❑ 288 Nelson Liriano .05 .02
❑ 289 Don Aase .05 .02
❑ 290 Randy Johnson .30 .09
❑ 291 Harold Baines .10 .03
❑ 292 Kent Hrbek .10 .03
❑ 293A Les Lancaster ERR .05 .02
(No comma between Dallas and Texas)
❑ 293B Les Lancaster COR .05 .02
(Corrected in factory sets)
❑ 294 Jeff Musselman .05 .02
❑ 295 Kurt Stillwell .05 .02
❑ 296 Stan Belinda .05 .02
❑ 297 Lou Whitaker .10 .03
❑ 298 Glenn Wilson .05 .02
❑ 299 Omar Vizquel UER .10 .03
Born 5/15, should be 4/24, there is a decimal before GP total for '90
❑ 300 Ramon Martinez .05 .02
❑ 301 Dwight Smith .05 .02
❑ 302 Tim Crews .05 .02
❑ 303 Lance Blankenship .05 .02
❑ 304 Sid Bream .05 .02
❑ 305 Rafael Ramirez .05 .02
❑ 306 Steve Wilson .05 .02
❑ 307 Mackey Sasser .05 .02
❑ 308 Franklin Stubbs .05 .02
❑ 309 Jack Daugherty UER .05 .02
(Born 6/3/60, should say July)
❑ 310 Eddie Murray .25 .07
❑ 311 Bob Welch .05 .02
❑ 312 Brian Harper .05 .02
❑ 313 Lance McCullers .05 .02
❑ 314 Dave Smith .05 .02
❑ 315 Bobby Bonilla .10 .03
❑ 316 Jerry Don Gleaton .05 .02
❑ 317 Greg Maddux .50 .15
❑ 318 Keith Miller .05 .02
❑ 319 Mark Portugal .05 .02
❑ 320 Robin Ventura .10 .03
❑ 321 Bob Ojeda .05 .02
❑ 322 Mike Harkey .05 .02
❑ 323 Jay Bell .10 .03
❑ 324 Mark McGwire .60 .18
❑ 325 Gary Gaetti .10 .03
❑ 326 Jeff Pico .05 .02
❑ 327 Kevin McReynolds .05 .02
❑ 328 Frank Tanana .05 .02
❑ 329 Eric Yelding UER .05 .02
(Listed as 6'3" should be 5'11")
❑ 330 Barry Bonds .60 .18
❑ 331 Brian McRae RC UER .25 .07
(No comma between city and state)
❑ 332 Pedro Munoz RC .10 .03
❑ 333 Daryl Irvine .05 .02
❑ 334 Chris Hoiles .05 .02
❑ 335 Thomas Howard .05 .02
❑ 336 Jeff Schulz .05 .02
❑ 337 Jeff Manto .05 .02
❑ 338 Beau Allred .05 .02
❑ 339 Mike Bordick RC .40 .12
❑ 340 Todd Hundley .05 .02
❑ 341 Jim Vatcher UER .05 .02
(Height 6'9", should be 5'9")
❑ 342 Luis Sojo .05 .02
❑ 343 Jose Offerman UER .05 .02
(Born 1969, should say 1968)
❑ 344 Pete Coachman .05 .02
❑ 345 Mike Benjamin .05 .02
❑ 346 Ozzie Canseco .05 .02
❑ 347 Tim McIntosh .05 .02
❑ 348 Phil Plantier RC .10 .03
❑ 349 Terry Shumpert .05 .02
❑ 350 Darren Lewis .05 .02
❑ 351 David Walsh .05 .02
❑ 352A Scott Chiamparino .10 .03
ERR
Bats left, should be right
❑ 352B Scott Chiamparino .10 .03
COR
corrected in factory sets
❑ 353 Julio Valera .05 .02
UER (Progressed mis-spelled as progessed)
❑ 354 Anthony Telford .05 .02
❑ 355 Kevin Wickander .05 .02
❑ 356 Tim Naehring .05 .02
❑ 357 Jim Poole .05 .02
❑ 358 Mark Whiten UER .05 .02
Shown hitting lefty, bio says righty
❑ 359 Terry Wells .05 .02
❑ 360 Rafael Valdez .05 .02
❑ 361 Mel Stottlemyre Jr. .05 .02
❑ 362 David Segui .05 .02
❑ 363 Paul Abbott RC .10 .03
❑ 364 Steve Howard .05 .02
❑ 365 Karl Rhodes .05 .02
❑ 366 Rafael Novoa .05 .02
❑ 367 Joe Grahe RC .05 .02
❑ 368 Darren Reed .05 .02
❑ 369 Jeff McKnight .05 .02
❑ 370 Scott Leius .05 .02
❑ 371 Mark Dewey .05 .02
❑ 372 Mark Lee UER RC .10 .03
(Shown hitting left, bio says righty, born in Dakota, should say North Dakota
❑ 373 Rosario Rodriguez UER .05 .02
Shown hitting lefty, bio says righty
❑ 374 Chuck McElroy .05 .02
❑ 375 Mike Bell .05 .02
❑ 376 Mickey Morandini .05 .02
❑ 377 Bill Haselman .05 .02
❑ 378 Dave Pavlas .05 .02
❑ 379 Derrick May .05 .02
❑ 380 J.Burnitz FDP RC .40 .12
❑ 381 Donald Peters FDP .05 .02
❑ 382 Alex Fernandez FDP .05 .02
❑ 383 Mike Mussina FDP RC 1.50 .45
❑ 384 Dan Smith FDP RC .10 .03
❑ 385 L.Dickson FDP RC .10 .03
❑ 386 Carl Everett FDP RC .50 .15
❑ 387 Tom Nevers FDP RC .10 .03
❑ 388 Adam Hyzdu FDP RC .25 .07
❑ 389 T.Van Poppel FDP RC .25 .07
❑ 390 R.White FDP RC .40 .12
❑ 391 M.Newfield FDP RC .10 .03
❑ 392 Julio Franco AS .05 .02
❑ 393 Wade Boggs AS .10 .03
❑ 394 Ozzie Guillen AS .05 .02
❑ 395 Cecil Fielder AS .05 .02
❑ 396 Ken Griffey Jr. AS .25 .07
❑ 397 Rickey Henderson AS .25 .07
❑ 398 Jose Canseco AS .10 .03
❑ 399 Roger Clemens AS .25 .07
❑ 400 Sandy Alomar Jr. AS .05 .02
❑ 401 Bobby Thigpen AS .05 .02
❑ 402 Bobby Bonilla MB .05 .02
❑ 403 Eric Davis MB .05 .02
❑ 404 Fred McGriff MB .10 .03
❑ 405 Glenn Davis MB .05 .02
❑ 406 Kevin Mitchell MB .05 .02
❑ 407 Rob Dibble KM .05 .02
❑ 408 Ramon Martinez KM .05 .02
❑ 409 David Cone KM .05 .02
❑ 410 Bobby Witt KM .05 .02
❑ 411 Mark Langston KM .05 .02
❑ 412 Bo Jackson RIF .10 .03
❑ 413 Shawon Dunston RIF .05 .02
UER
In the baseball, should say in baseball
❑ 414 Jesse Barfield RIF .05 .02
❑ 415 Ken Caminiti RIF .05 .02
❑ 416 Benito Santiago RIF .05 .02
❑ 417 Nolan Ryan HL .50 .15
❑ 418 B.Thigpen HL UER .05 .02
Back refers to Hal McRae Jr., should say Brian McRae
❑ 419 Ramon Martinez HL .05 .02
❑ 420 Bo Jackson HL .10 .03
❑ 421 Carlton Fisk HL .10 .03
❑ 422 Jimmy Key .10 .03
❑ 423 Junior Noboa .05 .02
❑ 424 Al Newman .05 .02
❑ 425 Pat Borders .05 .02
❑ 426 Von Hayes .05 .02
❑ 427 Tim Teufel .05 .02
❑ 428 Eric Plunk UER .05 .02
Text says Eric's had, no apostrophe needed
❑ 429 John Moses .05 .02
❑ 430 Mike Witt .05 .02
❑ 431 Otis Nixon .05 .02
❑ 432 Tony Fernandez .05 .02
❑ 433 Rance Mulliniks .05 .02
❑ 434 Dan Petry .05 .02
❑ 435 Bob Geren .05 .02
❑ 436 Steve Frey .05 .02
❑ 437 Jamie Moyer .10 .03
❑ 438 Junior Ortiz .05 .02
❑ 439 Tom O'Malley .05 .02
❑ 440 Pat Combs .05 .02
❑ 441 Jose Canseco DT .25 .07
❑ 442 Alfredo Griffin .05 .02
❑ 443 Andres Galarraga .10 .03
❑ 444 Bryn Smith .05 .02
❑ 445 Andre Dawson .10 .03
❑ 446 Juan Samuel .05 .02
❑ 447 Mike Aldrete .05 .02
❑ 448 Ron Gant .10 .03
❑ 449 Fernando Valenzuela .10 .03
❑ 450 Vince Coleman UER .05 .02
Should say topped majors in steals four times, not three times
❑ 451 Kevin Mitchell .05 .02

	No.	Player		
❑	452	Spike Owen	.05	.02
❑	453	Mike Bielecki	.05	.02
❑	454	Dennis Martinez	.10	.03
❑	455	Brett Butler	.10	.03
❑	456	Ron Darling	.05	.02
❑	457	Dennis Rasmussen	.05	.02
❑	458	Ken Howell	.05	.02
❑	459	Steve Bedrosian	.05	.02
❑	460	Frank Viola	.10	.03
❑	461	Jose Lind	.05	.02
❑	462	Chris Sabo	.05	.02
❑	463	Dante Bichette	.10	.03
❑	464	Rick Mahler	.05	.02
❑	465	John Smiley	.05	.02
❑	466	Devon White	.05	.02
❑	467	John Orton	.05	.02
❑	468	Mike Stanton	.05	.02
❑	469	Billy Hatcher	.05	.02
❑	470	Wally Joyner	.10	.03
❑	471	Gene Larkin	.05	.02
❑	472	Doug Drabek	.05	.02
❑	473	Gary Sheffield	.10	.03
❑	474	David Wells	.10	.03
❑	475	Andy Van Slyke	.10	.03
❑	476	Mike Gallego	.05	.02
❑	477	B.J. Surhoff	.10	.03
❑	478	Gene Nelson	.05	.02
❑	479	Mariano Duncan	.05	.02
❑	480	Fred McGriff	.15	.04
❑	481	Jerry Browne	.05	.02
❑	482	Alvin Davis	.05	.02
❑	483	Bill Wegman	.05	.02
❑	484	Dave Parker	.10	.03
❑	485	Dennis Eckersley	.10	.03
❑	486	Erik Hanson UER (Basketball misspelled as baseketball)	.05	.02
❑	487	Bill Ripken	.05	.02
❑	488	Tom Candiotti	.05	.02
❑	489	Mike Schooler	.05	.02
❑	490	Gregg Olson	.05	.02
❑	491	Chris James	.05	.02
❑	492	Pete Harnisch	.05	.02
❑	493	Julio Franco	.10	.03
❑	494	Greg Briley	.05	.02
❑	495	Ruben Sierra	.05	.02
❑	496	Steve Olin	.05	.02
❑	497	Mike Fetters	.05	.02
❑	498	Mark Williamson	.05	.02
❑	499	Bob Tewksbury	.05	.02
❑	500	Tony Gwynn	.30	.09
❑	501	Randy Myers	.05	.02
❑	502	Keith Comstock	.05	.02
❑	503	C.Worthington UER DeCinces misspelled DiCinces on back	.05	.02
❑	504	Mark Eichhorn UER Stats incomplete, doesn't have '89 Braves stint	.05	.02
❑	505	Barry Larkin	.25	.07
❑	506	Dave Johnson	.05	.02
❑	507	Bobby Witt	.05	.02
❑	508	Joe Orsulak	.05	.02
❑	509	Pete O'Brien	.05	.02
❑	510	Brad Arnsberg	.05	.02
❑	511	Storm Davis	.05	.02
❑	512	Bob Milacki	.05	.02
❑	513	Bill Pecota	.05	.02
❑	514	Glenallen Hill	.05	.02
❑	515	Danny Tartabull	.05	.02
❑	516	Mike Moore	.05	.02
❑	517	Ron Robinson UER (577 K's in 1990)	.05	.02
❑	518	Mark Gardner	.05	.02
❑	519	Rick Wrona	.05	.02
❑	520	Mike Scioscia	.05	.02
❑	521	Frank Wills	.05	.02
❑	522	Greg Brock	.05	.02
❑	523	Jack Clark	.10	.03
❑	524	Bruce Ruffin	.05	.02
❑	525	Robin Yount	.25	.07
❑	526	Tom Foley	.05	.02
❑	527	Pat Perry	.05	.02
❑	528	Greg Vaughn	.10	.03
❑	529	Wally Whitehurst	.05	.02
❑	530	Norm Charlton	.05	.02
❑	531	Marvell Wynne	.05	.02
❑	532	Jim Gantner	.05	.02
❑	533	Greg Litton	.05	.02
❑	534	Manny Lee	.05	.02
❑	535	Scott Bailes	.05	.02
❑	536	Charlie Leibrandt	.05	.02
❑	537	Roger McDowell	.05	.02
❑	538	Andy Benes	.05	.02
❑	539	Rick Honeycutt	.05	.02
❑	540	Dwight Gooden	.15	.04
❑	541	Scott Garrelts	.05	.02
❑	542	Dave Clark	.05	.02
❑	543	Lonnie Smith	.05	.02
❑	544	Rick Reuschel	.05	.02
❑	545	Delino DeShields UER (Rockford misspelled as Rock Ford in '88)	.10	.03
❑	546	Mike Sharperson	.05	.02
❑	547	Mike Kingery	.05	.02
❑	548	Terry Kennedy	.05	.02
❑	549	David Cone	.10	.03
❑	550	Orel Hershiser	.10	.03
❑	551	Matt Nokes	.05	.02
❑	552	Eddie Williams	.05	.02
❑	553	Frank DiPino	.05	.02
❑	554	Fred Lynn	.05	.02
❑	555	Alex Cole	.05	.02
❑	556	Terry Leach	.05	.02
❑	557	Chet Lemon	.05	.02
❑	558	Paul Mirabella	.05	.02
❑	559	Bill Long	.05	.02
❑	560	Phil Bradley	.05	.02
❑	561	Duane Ward	.05	.02
❑	562	Dave Bergman	.05	.02
❑	563	Eric Show	.05	.02
❑	564	Xavier Hernandez	.05	.02
❑	565	Jeff Parrett	.05	.02
❑	566	Chuck Cary	.05	.02
❑	567	Ken Hill	.05	.02
❑	568	Bob Welch Hand (Complement should be compliment) UER	.05	.02
❑	569	John Mitchell	.05	.02
❑	570	Travis Fryman	.10	.03
❑	571	Derek Lilliquist	.05	.02
❑	572	Steve Lake	.05	.02
❑	573	John Barfield	.05	.02
❑	574	Randy Bush	.05	.02
❑	575	Joe Magrane	.05	.02
❑	576	Eddie Diaz	.05	.02
❑	577	Casey Candaele	.05	.02
❑	578	Jesse Orosco	.05	.02
❑	579	Tom Henke	.05	.02
❑	580	Rick Cerone UER (Actually his third go-round with Yankees)	.05	.02
❑	581	Drew Hall	.05	.02
❑	582	Tony Castillo	.05	.02
❑	583	Jimmy Jones	.05	.02
❑	584	Rick Reed	.05	.02
❑	585	Joe Girardi	.05	.02
❑	586	Jeff Gray	.05	.02
❑	587	Luis Polonia	.05	.02
❑	588	Joe Klink	.05	.02
❑	589	Rex Hudler	.05	.02
❑	590	Kirk McCaskill	.05	.02
❑	591	Juan Agosto	.05	.02
❑	592	Wes Gardner	.05	.02
❑	593	Rich Rodriguez	.05	.02
❑	594	Mitch Webster	.05	.02
❑	595	Kelly Gruber	.05	.02
❑	596	Dale Mohorcic	.05	.02
❑	597	Willie McGee	.10	.03
❑	598	Bill Krueger	.05	.02
❑	599	Bob Walk UER Cards says he's 33, but actually he's 34	.05	.02
❑	600	Kevin Maas	.05	.02
❑	601	Danny Jackson	.05	.02
❑	602	Craig McMurtry UER (Anonymously misspelled anonimously)	.05	.02
❑	603	Curtis Wilkerson	.05	.02
❑	604	Adam Peterson	.05	.02
❑	605	Sam Horn	.05	.02
❑	606	Tommy Gregg	.05	.02
❑	607	Ken Dayley	.05	.02
❑	608	Carmelo Castillo	.05	.02
❑	609	John Shelby	.05	.02
❑	610	Don Slaught	.05	.02
❑	611	Calvin Schiraldi	.05	.02
❑	612	Dennis Lamp	.05	.02
❑	613	Andres Thomas	.05	.02
❑	614	Jose Gonzalez	.05	.02
❑	615	Randy Ready	.05	.02
❑	616	Kevin Bass	.05	.02
❑	617	Mike Marshall	.05	.02
❑	618	Daryl Boston	.05	.02
❑	619	Andy McGaffigan	.05	.02
❑	620	Joe Oliver	.05	.02
❑	621	Jim Gott	.05	.02
❑	622	Jose Oquendo	.05	.02
❑	623	Jose DeJesus	.05	.02
❑	624	Mike Brumley	.05	.02
❑	625	John Olerud	.10	.03
❑	626	Ernest Riles	.05	.02
❑	627	Gene Harris	.05	.02
❑	628	Jose Uribe	.05	.02
❑	629	Darnell Coles	.05	.02
❑	630	Carney Lansford	.10	.03
❑	631	Tim Leary	.05	.02
❑	632	Tim Hulett	.05	.02
❑	633	Kevin Elster	.05	.02
❑	634	Tony Fossas	.05	.02
❑	635	Francisco Oliveras	.05	.02
❑	636	Bob Patterson	.05	.02
❑	637	Gary Ward	.05	.02
❑	638	Rene Gonzales	.05	.02
❑	639	Don Robinson	.05	.02
❑	640	Darryl Strawberry	.15	.04
❑	641	Dave Anderson	.05	.02
❑	642	Scott Scudder	.05	.02
❑	643	Reggie Harris UER (Hepatitis misspelled as hepititis)	.05	.02
❑	644	Dave Henderson	.05	.02
❑	645	Ben McDonald	.05	.02
❑	646	Bob Kipper	.05	.02
❑	647	Hal Morris UER (It's should be its)	.05	.02
❑	648	Tim Birtsas	.05	.02
❑	649	Steve Searcy	.05	.02
❑	650	Dale Murphy	.25	.07
❑	651	Ron Oester	.05	.02
❑	652	Mike LaCoss	.05	.02
❑	653	Ron Jones	.05	.02
❑	654	Kelly Downs	.05	.02
❑	655	Roger Clemens	.50	.15
❑	656	Herm Winningham	.05	.02
❑	657	Trevor Wilson	.05	.02
❑	658	Jose Rijo	.05	.02
❑	659	Dann Bilardello UER Bio has 13 games, 1 hit, and 32 AB, stats show 19, 2, and 37	.05	.02
❑	660	Gregg Jefferies	.05	.02
❑	661	Doug Drabek AS UER (Through is misspelled though)	.05	.02
❑	662	Randy Myers AS	.05	.02
❑	663	Benny Santiago AS	.05	.02
❑	664	Will Clark AS	.10	.03
❑	665	Ryne Sandberg AS	.25	.07
❑	666	Barry Larkin AS UER Line 13, coolly misspelled cooly	.10	.03
❑	667	Matt Williams AS	.05	.02
❑	668	Barry Bonds AS	.30	.09
❑	669	Eric Davis AS	.05	.02
❑	670	Bobby Bonilla AS	.05	.02
❑	671	C.Jones FDP RC	4.00	1.20
❑	672	E.Christopherson RC FDP	.10	.03
❑	673	R.Beckett FDP RC	.10	.03
❑	674	S.Andrews FDP RC	.25	.07
❑	675	Steve Karsay FDP RC	.25	.07
❑	676	Aaron Holbert FDP RC	.10	.03
❑	677	D.Osborne FDP RC	.10	.03
❑	678	Todd Ritchie FDP RC	.25	.07
❑	679	Ron Walden FDP RC	.10	.03
❑	680	Tim Costo FDP RC	.10	.03
❑	681	Dan Wilson FDP RC	.25	.07
❑	682	Kurt Miller FDP RC	.10	.03
❑	683	M.Lieberthal FDP RC	.40	.12

❑ 684 Roger Clemens KM .25 .07
❑ 685 Dwight Gooden KM .10 .03
❑ 686 Nolan Ryan KM .50 .15
❑ 687 Frank Viola KM .05 .02
❑ 688 Erik Hanson KM .05 .02
❑ 689 Matt Williams MB .05 .02
❑ 690 J.Canseco MB UER .10 .03
Mammoth misspelled
as monmouth
❑ 691 Darryl Strawberry MB .10 .03
❑ 692 Bo Jackson MB .10 .03
❑ 693 Cecil Fielder MB .05 .02
❑ 694 Sandy Alomar Jr. RF .05 .02
❑ 695 Cory Snyder RF .05 .02
❑ 696 Eric Davis RF .05 .02
❑ 697 Ken Griffey Jr. RF .25 .07
❑ 698 A.Van Slyke RF UER .05 .02
Line 2, outfielders
does not need
❑ 699 Mark Langston NH .05 .02
Mike Witt
❑ 700 Randy Johnson NH .15 .04
❑ 701 Nolan Ryan NH .50 .15
❑ 702 Dave Stewart NH .05 .02
❑ 703 F.Valenzuela NH .05 .02
❑ 704 Andy Hawkins NH .05 .02
❑ 705 Melido Perez NH .05 .02
❑ 706 Terry Mulholland NH .05 .02
❑ 707 Dave Stieb NH .05 .02
❑ 708 Brian Barnes RC .05 .02
❑ 709 Bernard Gilkey .05 .02
❑ 710 Steve Decker .05 .02
❑ 711 Paul Faries .05 .02
❑ 712 Paul Marak .05 .02
❑ 713 Wes Chamberlain RC .10 .03
❑ 714 Kevin Belcher .05 .02
❑ 715 Dan Boone UER .05 .02
(IP adds up to 101,
but card has 101.2)
❑ 716 Steve Adkins .05 .02
❑ 717 Geronimo Pena .05 .02
❑ 718 Howard Farmer .05 .02
❑ 719 Mark Leonard .05 .02
❑ 720 Tom Lampkin .05 .02
❑ 721 Mike Gardiner .05 .02
❑ 722 Jeff Conine RC .50 .15
❑ 723 Efrain Valdez .05 .02
❑ 724 Chuck Malone .05 .02
❑ 725 Leo Gomez .05 .02
❑ 726 Paul McClellan .05 .02
❑ 727 Mark Leiter RC .10 .03
❑ 728 Rich DeLucia UER .05 .02
(Line 2, all told
is written alltold)
❑ 729 Mel Rojas .05 .02
❑ 730 Hector Wagner .05 .02
❑ 731 Ray Lankford .05 .02
❑ 732 Turner Ward RC .10 .03
❑ 733 Gerald Alexander .05 .02
❑ 734 Scott Anderson .05 .02
❑ 735 Tony Perezchica .05 .02
❑ 736 Jimmy Kremers .05 .02
❑ 737 American Flag .25 .07
(Pray for Peace)
❑ 738 Mike York .05 .02
❑ 739 Mike Rochford .05 .02
❑ 740 Scott Aldred .05 .02
❑ 741 Rico Brogna .05 .02
❑ 742 Dave Burba RC .25 .07
❑ 743 Ray Stephens .05 .02
❑ 744 Eric Gunderson .05 .02
❑ 745 Troy Afenir .05 .02
❑ 746 Jeff Shaw .05 .02
❑ 747 Orlando Merced RC .10 .03
❑ 748 O.Olivares UER RC .10 .03
Line 9, league is
misspelled legaue
❑ 749 Jerry Kutzler .05 .02
❑ 750 Mo Vaughn UER .10 .03
(44 SB's in 1990)
❑ 751 Matt Stark .05 .02
❑ 752 Randy Hennis .05 .02
❑ 753 Andujar Cedeno .05 .02
❑ 754 Kelvin Torve .05 .02
❑ 755 Joe Kraemer .05 .02
❑ 756 Phil Clark RC .10 .03
❑ 757 Ed Vosberg .05 .02
❑ 758 Mike Perez RC .10 .03
❑ 759 Scott Lewis .05 .02
❑ 760 Steve Chitren .05 .02
❑ 761 Ray Young .05 .02
❑ 762 Andres Santana .05 .02
❑ 763 Rodney McCray .05 .02
❑ 764 Sean Berry UER RC .10 .03
(Name misspelled
Barry on card front)
❑ 765 Brent Mayne .05 .02
❑ 766 Mike Simms .05 .02
❑ 767 Glenn Sutko .05 .02
❑ 768 Gary DiSarcina .05 .02
❑ 769 George Brett HL .25 .07
❑ 770 Cecil Fielder HL .05 .02
❑ 771 Jim Presley .05 .02
❑ 772 John Dopson .05 .02
❑ 773 Bo Jackson Breaker .10 .03
❑ 774 Brent Knackert UER .05 .02
Born in 1954,
shown throwing righty,
but bio says lefty
❑ 775 Bill Doran UER .05 .02
(Reds in NL East)
❑ 776 Dick Schofield .05 .02
❑ 777 Nelson Santovenia .05 .02
❑ 778 Mark Guthrie .05 .02
❑ 779 Mark Lemke .05 .02
❑ 780 Terry Steinbach .05 .02
❑ 781 Tom Bolton .05 .02
❑ 782 Randy Tomlin RC .10 .03
❑ 783 Jeff Kunkel .05 .02
❑ 784 Felix Jose .05 .02
❑ 785 Rick Sutcliffe .10 .03
❑ 786 John Cerutti .05 .02
❑ 787 Jose Vizcaino UER .05 .02
(Offerman, not Opperman)
❑ 788 Curt Schilling .15 .04
❑ 789 Ed Whitson .05 .02
❑ 790 Tony Pena .05 .02
❑ 791 John Candelaria .05 .02
❑ 792 Carmelo Martinez .05 .02
❑ 793 Sandy Alomar Jr. UER .05 .02
(Indian's should
say Indians')
❑ 794 Jim Neidlinger .05 .02
❑ 795 Barry Larkin WS .10 .03
and Chris Sabo
❑ 796 Paul Sorrento .05 .02
❑ 797 Tom Pagnozzi .05 .02
❑ 798 Tino Martinez .15 .04
❑ 799 Scott Ruskin UER .05 .02
(Text says first three
seasons but lists
averages for four)
❑ 800 Kirk Gibson .10 .03
❑ 801 Walt Terrell .05 .02
❑ 802 John Russell .05 .02
❑ 803 Chili Davis .10 .03
❑ 804 Chris Nabholz .05 .02
❑ 805 Juan Gonzalez .25 .07
❑ 806 Ron Hassey .05 .02
❑ 807 Todd Worrell .05 .02
❑ 808 Tommy Greene .05 .02
❑ 809 Joel Skinner UER .05 .02
Joel, not Bob, was drafted in 1979
❑ 810 Benito Santiago .10 .03
❑ 811 Pat Tabler UER .05 .02
Line 3, always misspelled alway
❑ 812 Scott Erickson UER .05 .02
(Record spelled rcord)
❑ 813 Moises Alou .10 .03
❑ 814 Dale Sveum .05 .02
❑ 815 R.Sandberg MANYR .25 .07
❑ 816 Rick Dempsey .05 .02
❑ 817 Scott Bankhead .05 .02
❑ 818 Jason Grimsley .05 .02
❑ 819 Doug Jennings .05 .02
❑ 820 Tom Herr .05 .02
❑ 821 Rob Ducey .05 .02
❑ 822 Luis Quinones .05 .02
❑ 823 Greg Minton .05 .02
❑ 824 Mark Grant .05 .02
❑ 825 Ozzie Smith UER .25 .07
(Shortstop misspelled
shortsop)
❑ 826 Dave Eiland .05 .02
❑ 827 Danny Heep .05 .02
❑ 828 Hensley Meulens .05 .02
❑ 829 Charlie O'Brien .05 .02
❑ 830 Glenn Davis .05 .02
❑ 831 John Marzano UER .05 .02
(International mis-
spelled Internaional)
❑ 832 Steve Ontiveros .05 .02
❑ 833 Ron Karkovice .05 .02
❑ 834 Jerry Goff .05 .02
❑ 835 Ken Griffey Sr. .10 .03
❑ 836 Kevin Reimer .05 .02
❑ 837 Randy Kutcher UER .05 .02
(Infectious mis-
spelled infectous)
❑ 838 Mike Blowers .05 .02
❑ 839 Mike Macfarlane .05 .02
❑ 840 Frank Thomas UER .25 .07
1989 Sarasota stats,
15 games but 188 AB
❑ 841 The Griffeys .40 .12
Ken Griffey Jr.
Ken Griffey Sr.
❑ 842 Jack Howell .05 .02
❑ 843 Goose Gozzo .05 .02
❑ 844 Gerald Young .05 .02
❑ 845 Zane Smith .05 .02
❑ 846 Kevin Brown .10 .03
❑ 847 Sil Campusano .05 .02
❑ 848 Larry Andersen .05 .02
❑ 849 Cal Ripken FRAN .40 .12
❑ 850 Roger Clemens FRAN .25 .07
❑ 851 S.Alomar Jr. FRAN .05 .02
❑ 852 Alan Trammell FRAN .10 .03
❑ 853 George Brett FRAN .25 .07
❑ 854 Robin Yount FRAN .10 .03
❑ 855 Kirby Puckett FRAN .15 .04
❑ 856 Don Mattingly FRAN .30 .09
❑ 857 R.Henderson FRAN .25 .07
❑ 858 Ken Griffey Jr. FRAN .25 .07
❑ 859 Ruben Sierra FRAN .05 .02
❑ 860 John Olerud FRAN .05 .02
❑ 861 Dave Justice FRAN .05 .02
❑ 862 Ryne Sandberg FRAN .25 .07
❑ 863 Eric Davis FRAN .05 .02
❑ 864 D.Strawberry FRAN .10 .03
❑ 865 Tim Wallach FRAN .05 .02
❑ 866 Dwight Gooden FRAN .10 .03
❑ 867 Len Dykstra FRAN .05 .02
❑ 868 Barry Bonds FRAN .30 .09
❑ 869 Todd Zeile FRAN UER .05 .02
(Powerful misspelled
as poweful)
❑ 870 Benito Santiago FRAN .05 .02
❑ 871 Will Clark FRAN .10 .03
❑ 872 Craig Biggio FRAN .10 .03
❑ 873 Wally Joyner FRAN .05 .02
❑ 874 Frank Thomas FRAN .15 .04
❑ 875 R.Henderson MVP .25 .07
❑ 876 Barry Bonds MVP .30 .09
❑ 877 Bob Welch CY .05 .02
❑ 878 Doug Drabek CY .05 .02
❑ 879 S.Alomar Jr. ROY .05 .02
❑ 880 Dave Justice ROY .05 .02
❑ 881 Damon Berryhill .05 .02
❑ 882 Frank Viola DT .05 .02
❑ 883 Dave Stewart DT .05 .02
❑ 884 Doug Jones DT .05 .02
❑ 885 Randy Myers DT .05 .02
❑ 886 Will Clark DT .10 .03
❑ 887 Roberto Alomar DT .10 .03
❑ 888 Barry Larkin DT .10 .03
❑ 889 Wade Boggs DT .15 .04
❑ 890 Rickey Henderson DT .40 .12
❑ 891 Kirby Puckett DT .15 .04
❑ 892 Ken Griffey Jr DT .50 .15
❑ 893 Benny Santiago DT .10 .03

1993 Score

	Nm-Mt	Ex-Mt
COMPLETE SET (660)	40.00	12.00

No.	Player		
❑ 1	Ken Griffey Jr.	.75	.23
❑ 2	Gary Sheffield	.20	.06
❑ 3	Frank Thomas	.50	.15
❑ 4	Ryne Sandberg	.75	.23
❑ 5	Larry Walker	.30	.09
❑ 6	Cal Ripken Jr.	1.50	.45
❑ 7	Roger Clemens	1.00	.30
❑ 8	Bobby Bonilla	.20	.06
❑ 9	Carlos Baerga	.10	.03
❑ 10	Darren Daulton	.20	.06
❑ 11	Travis Fryman	.20	.06
❑ 12	Andy Van Slyke	.20	.06
❑ 13	Jose Canseco	.50	.15
❑ 14	Roberto Alomar	.50	.15
❑ 15	Tom Glavine	.50	.15
❑ 16	Barry Larkin	.50	.15
❑ 17	Gregg Jefferies	.10	.03
❑ 18	Craig Biggio	.30	.09
❑ 19	Shane Mack	.10	.03
❑ 20	Brett Butler	.20	.06
❑ 21	Dennis Eckersley	.20	.06
❑ 22	Will Clark	.50	.15
❑ 23	Don Mattingly	1.25	.35
❑ 24	Tony Gwynn	.60	.18
❑ 25	Ivan Rodriguez	.50	.15
❑ 26	Shawon Dunston	.10	.03
❑ 27	Mike Mussina	.50	.15
❑ 28	Marquis Grissom	.10	.03
❑ 29	Charles Nagy	.10	.03
❑ 30	Len Dykstra	.20	.06
❑ 31	Cecil Fielder	.20	.06
❑ 32	Jay Bell	.20	.06
❑ 33	B.J. Surhoff	.20	.06
❑ 34	Bob Tewksbury	.10	.03
❑ 35	Danny Tartabull	.10	.03
❑ 36	Terry Pendleton	.20	.06
❑ 37	Jack Morris	.20	.06
❑ 38	Hal Morris	.10	.03
❑ 39	Luis Polonia	.10	.03
❑ 40	Ken Caminiti	.20	.06
❑ 41	Robin Ventura	.20	.06
❑ 42	Darryl Strawberry	.30	.09
❑ 43	Wally Joyner	.20	.06
❑ 44	Fred McGriff	.30	.09
❑ 45	Kevin Tapani	.10	.03
❑ 46	Matt Williams	.20	.06
❑ 47	Robin Yount	.50	.15
❑ 48	Ken Hill	.10	.03
❑ 49	Edgar Martinez	.30	.09
❑ 50	Mark Grace	.50	.15
❑ 51	Juan Gonzalez	.50	.15
❑ 52	Curt Schilling	.30	.09
❑ 53	Dwight Gooden	.30	.09
❑ 54	Chris Hoiles	.10	.03
❑ 55	Frank Viola	.20	.06
❑ 56	Ray Lankford	.10	.03
❑ 57	George Brett	1.25	.35
❑ 58	Kenny Lofton	.20	.06
❑ 59	Nolan Ryan	2.00	.60
❑ 60	Mickey Tettleton	.10	.03
❑ 61	John Smoltz	.30	.09
❑ 62	Howard Johnson	.10	.03
❑ 63	Eric Karros	.20	.06
❑ 64	Rick Aguilera	.10	.03
❑ 65	Steve Finley	.20	.06
❑ 66	Mark Langston	.10	.03
❑ 67	Bill Swift	.10	.03
❑ 68	John Olerud	.20	.06
❑ 69	Kevin McReynolds	.10	.03
❑ 70	Jack McDowell	.10	.03
❑ 71	Rickey Henderson	.75	.23
❑ 72	Brian Harper	.10	.03
❑ 73	Mike Morgan	.10	.03
❑ 74	Rafael Palmeiro	.30	.09
❑ 75	Dennis Martinez	.20	.06
❑ 76	Tino Martinez	.30	.09
❑ 77	Eddie Murray	.50	.15
❑ 78	Ellis Burks	.20	.06
❑ 79	John Kruk	.20	.06
❑ 80	Gregg Olson	.10	.03
❑ 81	Bernard Gilkey	.10	.03
❑ 82	Milt Cuyler	.10	.03
❑ 83	Mike LaValliere	.10	.03
❑ 84	Albert Belle	.20	.06
❑ 85	Bip Roberts	.10	.03
❑ 86	Melido Perez	.10	.03
❑ 87	Otis Nixon	.10	.03
❑ 88	Bill Spiers	.10	.03
❑ 89	Jeff Bagwell	.30	.09
❑ 90	Orel Hershiser	.20	.06
❑ 91	Andy Benes	.10	.03
❑ 92	Devon White	.10	.03
❑ 93	Willie McGee	.20	.06
❑ 94	Ozzie Guillen	.10	.03
❑ 95	Ivan Calderon	.10	.03
❑ 96	Keith Miller	.10	.03
❑ 97	Steve Buechele	.10	.03
❑ 98	Kent Hrbek	.20	.06
❑ 99	Dave Hollins	.10	.03
❑ 100	Mike Bordick	.10	.03
❑ 101	Randy Tomlin	.10	.03
❑ 102	Omar Vizquel	.20	.06
❑ 103	Lee Smith	.20	.06
❑ 104	Leo Gomez	.10	.03
❑ 105	Jose Rijo	.10	.03
❑ 106	Mark Whiten	.10	.03
❑ 107	Dave Justice	.20	.06
❑ 108	Eddie Taubensee	.10	.03
❑ 109	Lance Johnson	.10	.03
❑ 110	Felix Jose	.10	.03
❑ 111	Mike Harkey	.10	.03
❑ 112	Randy Milligan	.10	.03
❑ 113	Anthony Young	.10	.03
❑ 114	Rico Brogna	.10	.03
❑ 115	Bret Saberhagen	.20	.06
❑ 116	Sandy Alomar Jr.	.10	.03
❑ 117	Terry Mulholland	.10	.03
❑ 118	Darryl Hamilton	.10	.03
❑ 119	Todd Zeile	.10	.03
❑ 120	Bernie Williams	.30	.09
❑ 121	Zane Smith	.10	.03
❑ 122	Derek Bell	.10	.03
❑ 123	Deion Sanders	.20	.06
❑ 124	Luis Sojo	.10	.03
❑ 125	Joe Oliver	.10	.03
❑ 126	Craig Grebeck	.10	.03
❑ 127	Andujar Cedeno	.10	.03
❑ 128	Brian McRae	.10	.03
❑ 129	Jose Offerman	.10	.03
❑ 130	Pedro Munoz	.10	.03
❑ 131	Bud Black	.10	.03
❑ 132	Mo Vaughn	.20	.06
❑ 133	Bruce Hurst	.10	.03
❑ 134	Dave Henderson	.10	.03
❑ 135	Tom Pagnozzi	.10	.03
❑ 136	Erik Hanson	.10	.03
❑ 137	Orlando Merced	.10	.03
❑ 138	Dean Palmer	.20	.06
❑ 139	John Franco	.20	.06
❑ 140	Brady Anderson	.20	.06
❑ 141	Ricky Jordan	.10	.03
❑ 142	Jeff Blauser	.10	.03
❑ 143	Sammy Sosa	.75	.23
❑ 144	Bob Walk	.10	.03
❑ 145	Delino DeShields	.10	.03
❑ 146	Kevin Brown	.20	.06
❑ 147	Mark Lemke	.10	.03
❑ 148	Chuck Knoblauch	.20	.06
❑ 149	Chris Sabo	.10	.03
❑ 150	Bobby Witt	.10	.03
❑ 151	Luis Gonzalez	.20	.06
❑ 152	Ron Karkovice	.10	.03
❑ 153	Jeff Brantley	.10	.03
❑ 154	Kevin Appier	.20	.06
❑ 155	Darrin Jackson	.10	.03
❑ 156	Kelly Gruber	.10	.03
❑ 157	Royce Clayton	.10	.03
❑ 158	Chuck Finley	.20	.06
❑ 159	Jeff King	.10	.03
❑ 160	Greg Vaughn	.20	.06
❑ 161	Geronimo Pena	.10	.03
❑ 162	Steve Farr	.10	.03
❑ 163	Jose Oquendo	.10	.03
❑ 164	Mark Lewis	.10	.03
❑ 165	John Wetteland	.20	.06
❑ 166	Mike Henneman	.10	.03
❑ 167	Todd Hundley	.10	.03
❑ 168	Wes Chamberlain	.10	.03
❑ 169	Steve Avery	.10	.03
❑ 170	Mike Devereaux	.10	.03
❑ 171	Reggie Sanders	.20	.06
❑ 172	Jay Buhner	.20	.06
❑ 173	Eric Anthony	.10	.03
❑ 174	John Burkett	.10	.03
❑ 175	Tom Candiotti	.10	.03
❑ 176	Phil Plantier	.10	.03
❑ 177	Doug Henry	.10	.03
❑ 178	Scott Leius	.10	.03
❑ 179	Kirt Manwaring	.10	.03
❑ 180	Jeff Parrett	.10	.03
❑ 181	Don Slaught	.10	.03
❑ 182	Scott Radinsky	.10	.03
❑ 183	Luis Alicea	.10	.03
❑ 184	Tom Gordon	.10	.03
❑ 185	Rick Wilkins	.10	.03
❑ 186	Todd Stottlemyre	.10	.03
❑ 187	Moises Alou	.20	.06
❑ 188	Joe Grahe	.10	.03
❑ 189	Jeff Kent	.50	.15
❑ 190	Bill Wegman	.10	.03
❑ 191	Kim Batiste	.10	.03
❑ 192	Matt Nokes	.10	.03
❑ 193	Mark Wohlers	.10	.03
❑ 194	Paul Sorrento	.10	.03
❑ 195	Chris Hammond	.10	.03
❑ 196	Scott Livingstone	.10	.03
❑ 197	Doug Jones	.10	.03
❑ 198	Scott Cooper	.10	.03
❑ 199	Ramon Martinez	.10	.03
❑ 200	Dave Valle	.10	.03
❑ 201	Mariano Duncan	.10	.03
❑ 202	Ben McDonald	.10	.03
❑ 203	Darren Lewis	.10	.03
❑ 204	Kenny Rogers	.20	.06
❑ 205	Manuel Lee	.10	.03
❑ 206	Scott Erickson	.10	.03
❑ 207	Dan Gladden	.10	.03
❑ 208	Bob Welch	.10	.03
❑ 209	Greg Olson	.10	.03
❑ 210	Dan Pasqua	.10	.03
❑ 211	Tim Wallach	.10	.03
❑ 212	Jeff Montgomery	.10	.03
❑ 213	Derrick May	.10	.03
❑ 214	Ed Sprague	.10	.03
❑ 215	David Haas	.10	.03
❑ 216	Darrin Fletcher	.10	.03
❑ 217	Brian Jordan	.20	.06
❑ 218	Jaime Navarro	.10	.03
❑ 219	Randy Velarde	.10	.03
❑ 220	Ron Gant	.20	.06
❑ 221	Paul Quantrill	.10	.03
❑ 222	Damion Easley	.10	.03
❑ 223	Charlie Hough	.20	.06
❑ 224	Brad Brink	.10	.03
❑ 225	Barry Manuel	.10	.03
❑ 226	Kevin Koslofski	.10	.03
❑ 227	Ryan Thompson	.10	.03
❑ 228	Mike Munoz	.10	.03
❑ 229	Dan Wilson	.20	.06
❑ 230	Peter Hoy	.10	.03
❑ 231	Pedro Astacio	.10	.03
❑ 232	Matt Stairs	.10	.03
❑ 233	Jeff Reboulet	.10	.03
❑ 234	Manny Alexander	.10	.03
❑ 235	Willie Banks	.10	.03
❑ 236	John Jaha	.10	.03
❑ 237	Scooter Tucker	.10	.03
❑ 238	Russ Springer	.10	.03
❑ 239	Paul Miller	.10	.03
❑ 240	Dan Peltier	.10	.03

❑ 241 Ozzie Canseco .10 .03
❑ 242 Ben Rivera .10 .03
❑ 243 John Valentin .10 .03
❑ 244 Henry Rodriguez .10 .03
❑ 245 Derek Parks .10 .03
❑ 246 Carlos Garcia .10 .03
❑ 247 Tim Pugh RC .10 .03
❑ 248 Melvin Nieves .10 .03
❑ 249 Rich Amaral .10 .03
❑ 250 Willie Greene .10 .03
❑ 251 Tim Scott .10 .03
❑ 252 Dave Silvestri .10 .03
❑ 253 Rob Mallicoat .10 .03
❑ 254 Donald Harris .10 .03
❑ 255 Craig Colbert .10 .03
❑ 256 Jose Guzman .10 .03
❑ 257 Domingo Martinez RC .10 .03
❑ 258 William Suero .10 .03
❑ 259 Juan Guerrero .10 .03
❑ 260 J.T. Snow RC .50 .15
❑ 261 Tony Pena .10 .03
❑ 262 Tim Fortugno .10 .03
❑ 263 Tom Marsh .10 .03
❑ 264 Kurt Knudsen .10 .03
❑ 265 Tim Costo .10 .03
❑ 266 Steve Shifflett .10 .03
❑ 267 Billy Ashley .10 .03
❑ 268 Jerry Nielsen .10 .03
❑ 269 Pete Young .10 .03
❑ 270 Johnny Guzman .10 .03
❑ 271 Greg Colbrunn .10 .03
❑ 272 Jeff Nelson .10 .03
❑ 273 Kevin Young .20 .06
❑ 274 Jeff Frye .10 .03
❑ 275 J.T. Bruett .10 .03
❑ 276 Todd Pratt RC .20 .06
❑ 277 Mike Butcher .10 .03
❑ 278 John Flaherty .10 .03
❑ 279 John Patterson .10 .03
❑ 280 Eric Hillman .10 .03
❑ 281 Bien Figueroa .10 .03
❑ 282 Shane Reynolds .10 .03
❑ 283 Rich Rowland .10 .03
❑ 284 Steve Foster .10 .03
❑ 285 Dave Mlicki .10 .03
❑ 286 Mike Piazza 1.25 .35
❑ 287 Mike Trombley .10 .03
❑ 288 Jim Pena .10 .03
❑ 289 Bob Ayrault .10 .03
❑ 290 Henry Mercedes .10 .03
❑ 291 Bob Wickman .10 .03
❑ 292 Jacob Brumfield .10 .03
❑ 293 David Hulse RC .10 .03
❑ 294 Ryan Klesko .20 .06
❑ 295 Doug Linton .10 .03
❑ 296 Steve Cooke .10 .03
❑ 297 Eddie Zosky .10 .03
❑ 298 Gerald Williams .10 .03
❑ 299 Jonathan Hurst .10 .03
❑ 300 Larry Carter RC .10 .03
❑ 301 William Pennyfeather .10 .03
❑ 302 Cesar Hernandez .10 .03
❑ 303 Steve Hosey .10 .03
❑ 304 Blas Minor .10 .03
❑ 305 Jeff Grotewald .10 .03
❑ 306 Bernardo Brito .10 .03
❑ 307 Rafael Bournigal .10 .03
❑ 308 Jeff Branson .10 .03
❑ 309 Tom Quinlan RC .10 .03
❑ 310 Pat Gomez RC .10 .03
❑ 311 Sterling Hitchcock RC .20 .06
❑ 312 Kent Bottenfield .10 .03
❑ 313 Alan Trammell .30 .09
❑ 314 Cris Colon .10 .03
❑ 315 Paul Wagner .10 .03
❑ 316 Matt Maysey .10 .03
❑ 317 Mike Stanton .10 .03
❑ 318 Rick Trlicek .10 .03
❑ 319 Kevin Rogers .10 .03
❑ 320 Mark Clark .10 .03
❑ 321 Pedro Martinez 1.00 .30
❑ 322 Al Martin .10 .03
❑ 323 Mike Macfarlane .10 .03
❑ 324 Rey Sanchez .10 .03
❑ 325 Roger Pavlik .10 .03
❑ 326 Troy Neel .10 .03
❑ 327 Kerry Woodson .10 .03
❑ 328 Wayne Kirby .10 .03
❑ 329 Ken Ryan RC .10 .03
❑ 330 Jesse Levis .10 .03
❑ 331 Jim Austin .10 .03
❑ 332 Dan Walters .10 .03
❑ 333 Brian Williams .10 .03
❑ 334 Wil Cordero .10 .03
❑ 335 Bret Boone .30 .09
❑ 336 Hipolito Pichardo .10 .03
❑ 337 Pat Mahomes .10 .03
❑ 338 Andy Stankiewicz .10 .03
❑ 339 Jim Bullinger .10 .03
❑ 340 Archi Cianfrocco .10 .03
❑ 341 Ruben Amaro .10 .03
❑ 342 Frank Seminara .10 .03
❑ 343 Pat Hentgen .10 .03
❑ 344 Dave Nilsson .10 .03
❑ 345 Mike Perez .10 .03
❑ 346 Tim Salmon .30 .09
❑ 347 Tim Wakefield .20 .06
❑ 348 Carlos Hernandez .10 .03
❑ 349 Donovan Osborne .10 .03
❑ 350 Denny Neagle .20 .06
❑ 351 Sam Militello .10 .03
❑ 352 Eric Fox .10 .03
❑ 353 John Doherty .10 .03
❑ 354 Chad Curtis .10 .03
❑ 355 Jeff Tackett .10 .03
❑ 356 Dave Fleming .10 .03
❑ 357 Pat Listach .10 .03
❑ 358 Kevin Wickander .10 .03
❑ 359 John Vander Wal .10 .03
❑ 360 Arthur Rhodes .10 .03
❑ 361 Bob Scanlan .10 .03
❑ 362 Bob Zupcic .10 .03
❑ 363 Mel Rojas .10 .03
❑ 364 Jim Thome .50 .15
❑ 365 Bill Pecota .10 .03
❑ 366 Mark Carreon .10 .03
❑ 367 Mitch Williams .10 .03
❑ 368 Cal Eldred .10 .03
❑ 369 Stan Belinda .10 .03
❑ 370 Pat Kelly .10 .03
❑ 371 Rheal Cormier .10 .03
❑ 372 Juan Guzman .10 .03
❑ 373 Damon Berryhill .10 .03
❑ 374 Gary DiSarcina .10 .03
❑ 375 Norm Charlton .10 .03
❑ 376 Roberto Hernandez .10 .03
❑ 377 Scott Kamieniecki .10 .03
❑ 378 Rusty Meacham .10 .03
❑ 379 Kurt Stillwell .10 .03
❑ 380 Lloyd McClendon .10 .03
❑ 381 Mark Leonard .10 .03
❑ 382 Jerry Browne .10 .03
❑ 383 Glenn Davis .10 .03
❑ 384 Randy Johnson .50 .15
❑ 385 Mike Greenwell .10 .03
❑ 386 Scott Chiamparino .10 .03
❑ 387 George Bell .10 .03
❑ 388 Steve Olin .10 .03
❑ 389 Chuck McElroy .10 .03
❑ 390 Mark Gardner .10 .03
❑ 391 Rod Beck .10 .03
❑ 392 Dennis Rasmussen .10 .03
❑ 393 Charlie Leibrandt .10 .03
❑ 394 Julio Franco .20 .06
❑ 395 Pete Harnisch .10 .03
❑ 396 Sid Bream .10 .03
❑ 397 Milt Thompson .10 .03
❑ 398 Glenallen Hill .10 .03
❑ 399 Chico Walker .10 .03
❑ 400 Alex Cole .10 .03
❑ 401 Trevor Wilson .10 .03
❑ 402 Jeff Conine .20 .06
❑ 403 Kyle Abbott .10 .03
❑ 404 Tom Browning .10 .03
❑ 405 Jerald Clark .10 .03
❑ 406 Vince Horsman .10 .03
❑ 407 Kevin Mitchell .10 .03
❑ 408 Pete Smith .10 .03
❑ 409 Jeff Innis .10 .03
❑ 410 Mike Timlin .10 .03
❑ 411 Charlie Hayes .10 .03
❑ 412 Alex Fernandez .10 .03
❑ 413 Jeff Russell .10 .03
❑ 414 Jody Reed .10 .03
❑ 415 Mickey Morandini .10 .03
❑ 416 Darnell Coles .10 .03
❑ 417 Xavier Hernandez .10 .03
❑ 418 Steve Sax .10 .03
❑ 419 Joe Girardi .10 .03
❑ 420 Mike Fetters .10 .03
❑ 421 Danny Jackson .10 .03
❑ 422 Jim Gott .10 .03
❑ 423 Tim Belcher .10 .03
❑ 424 Jose Mesa .10 .03
❑ 425 Junior Felix .10 .03
❑ 426 Thomas Howard .10 .03
❑ 427 Julio Valera .10 .03
❑ 428 Dante Bichette .20 .06
❑ 429 Mike Sharperson .10 .03
❑ 430 Darryl Kile .20 .06
❑ 431 Lonnie Smith .10 .03
❑ 432 Monty Fariss .10 .03
❑ 433 Reggie Jefferson .10 .03
❑ 434 Bob McClure .10 .03
❑ 435 Craig Lefferts .10 .03
❑ 436 Duane Ward .10 .03
❑ 437 Shawn Abner .10 .03
❑ 438 Roberto Kelly .10 .03
❑ 439 Paul O'Neill .30 .09
❑ 440 Alan Mills .10 .03
❑ 441 Roger Mason .10 .03
❑ 442 Gary Pettis .10 .03
❑ 443 Steve Lake .10 .03
❑ 444 Gene Larkin .10 .03
❑ 445 Larry Andersen .10 .03
❑ 446 Doug Dascenzo .10 .03
❑ 447 Daryl Boston .10 .03
❑ 448 John Candelaria .10 .03
❑ 449 Storm Davis .10 .03
❑ 450 Tom Edens .10 .03
❑ 451 Mike Maddux .10 .03
❑ 452 Tim Naehring .10 .03
❑ 453 John Orton .10 .03
❑ 454 Joey Cora .10 .03
❑ 455 Chuck Crim .10 .03
❑ 456 Dan Plesac .10 .03
❑ 457 Mike Bielecki .10 .03
❑ 458 Terry Jorgensen .10 .03
❑ 459 John Habyan .10 .03
❑ 460 Pete O'Brien .10 .03
❑ 461 Jeff Treadway .10 .03
❑ 462 Frank Castillo .10 .03
❑ 463 Jimmy Jones .10 .03
❑ 464 Tommy Greene .10 .03
❑ 465 Tracy Woodson .10 .03
❑ 466 Rich Rodriguez .10 .03
❑ 467 Joe Hesketh .10 .03
❑ 468 Greg Myers .10 .03
❑ 469 Kirk McCaskill .10 .03
❑ 470 Ricky Bones .10 .03
❑ 471 Lenny Webster .10 .03
❑ 472 Francisco Cabrera .10 .03
❑ 473 Turner Ward .10 .03
❑ 474 Dwayne Henry .10 .03
❑ 475 Al Osuna .10 .03
❑ 476 Craig Wilson .10 .03
❑ 477 Chris Nabholz .10 .03
❑ 478 Rafael Belliard .10 .03
❑ 479 Terry Leach .10 .03
❑ 480 Tim Teufel .10 .03
❑ 481 Dennis Eckersley AW .20 .06
❑ 482 Barry Bonds AW .60 .18
❑ 483 Dennis Eckersley AW .20 .06
❑ 484 Greg Maddux AW .50 .15
❑ 485 Pat Listach AW .10 .03
❑ 486 Eric Karros AW .10 .03
❑ 487 Jamie Arnold DP RC .10 .03
❑ 488 B.J. Wallace DP .10 .03
❑ 489 Derek Jeter DP RC 10.00 3.00
❑ 490 Jason Kendall DP RC .75 .23
❑ 491 Rick Helling DP .10 .03
❑ 492 Derek Wallace DP RC .10 .03
❑ 493 Sean Lowe DP RC .10 .03
❑ 494 S.Stewart DP RC .75 .23
❑ 495 Benji Grigsby DP RC .10 .03
❑ 496 T.Steverson DP RC .10 .03
❑ 497 Dan Serafini DP RC .10 .03
❑ 498 Michael Tucker DP .10 .03

❑ 499	Chris Roberts DP	.10	.03
❑ 500	Pete Janicki DP RC	.10	.03
❑ 501	Jeff Schmidt DP RC	.10	.03
❑ 502	Edgar Martinez AS	.20	.06
❑ 503	Omar Vizquel AS	.20	.06
❑ 504	Ken Griffey Jr. AS	.50	.15
❑ 505	Kirby Puckett AS	.30	.09
❑ 506	Joe Carter AS	.10	.03
❑ 507	Ivan Rodriguez AS	.30	.09
❑ 508	Jack Morris AS	.10	.03
❑ 509	Dennis Eckersley AS	.20	.06
❑ 510	Frank Thomas AS	.30	.09
❑ 511	Roberto Alomar AS	.20	.06
❑ 512	Mickey Morandini AS	.10	.03
❑ 513	Dennis Eckersley HL	.20	.06
❑ 514	Jeff Reardon HL	.10	.03
❑ 515	Danny Tartabull HL	.10	.03
❑ 516	Bip Roberts HL	.10	.03
❑ 517	George Brett HL	.50	.15
❑ 518	Robin Yount HL	.20	.06
❑ 519	Kevin Gross HL	.10	.03
❑ 520	Ed Sprague WS	.10	.03
❑ 521	Dave Winfield WS	.20	.06
❑ 522	Ozzie Smith AS	.30	.09
❑ 523	Barry Bonds AS	.60	.18
❑ 524	Andy Van Slyke AS	.10	.03
❑ 525	Tony Gwynn AS	.30	.09
❑ 526	Darren Daulton AS	.10	.03
❑ 527	Greg Maddux AS	.50	.15
❑ 528	Fred McGriff AS	.30	.09
❑ 529	Lee Smith AS	.10	.03
❑ 530	Ryne Sandberg AS	.50	.15
❑ 531	Gary Sheffield AS	.10	.03
❑ 532	Ozzie Smith DT	.30	.09
❑ 533	Kirby Puckett DT	.30	.09
❑ 534	Gary Sheffield DT	.10	.03
❑ 535	Andy Van Slyke DT	.10	.03
❑ 536	Ken Griffey Jr. DT	.50	.15
❑ 537	Ivan Rodriguez DT	.30	.09
❑ 538	Charles Nagy DT	.10	.03
❑ 539	Tom Glavine DT	.20	.06
❑ 540	Dennis Eckersley DT	.20	.06
❑ 541	Frank Thomas DT	.30	.09
❑ 542	Roberto Alomar DT	.20	.06
❑ 543	Sean Berry	.10	.03
❑ 544	Mike Schooler	.10	.03
❑ 545	Chuck Carr	.10	.03
❑ 546	Lenny Harris	.10	.03
❑ 547	Gary Scott	.10	.03
❑ 548	Derek Lilliquist	.10	.03
❑ 549	Brian Hunter	.10	.03
❑ 550	Kirby Puckett MOY	.30	.09
❑ 551	Jim Eisenreich	.10	.03
❑ 552	Andre Dawson	.20	.06
❑ 553	David Nied	.10	.03
❑ 554	Spike Owen	.10	.03
❑ 555	Greg Gagne	.10	.03
❑ 556	Sid Fernandez	.10	.03
❑ 557	Mark McGwire	1.25	.35
❑ 558	Bryan Harvey	.10	.03
❑ 559	Harold Reynolds	.20	.06
❑ 560	Barry Bonds	1.25	.35
❑ 561	Eric Wedge RC	.10	.03
❑ 562	Ozzie Smith	.50	.15
❑ 563	Rick Sutcliffe	.20	.06
❑ 564	Jeff Reardon	.20	.06
❑ 565	Alex Arias	.10	.03
❑ 566	Greg Swindell	.10	.03
❑ 567	Brook Jacoby	.10	.03
❑ 568	Pete Incaviglia	.10	.03
❑ 569	Butch Henry	.10	.03
❑ 570	Eric Davis	.20	.06
❑ 571	Kevin Seitzer	.10	.03
❑ 572	Tony Fernandez	.10	.03
❑ 573	Steve Reed RC	.10	.03
❑ 574	Cory Snyder	.10	.03
❑ 575	Joe Carter	.20	.06
❑ 576	Greg Maddux	1.00	.30
❑ 577	Bert Blyleven UER (Should say 3701 career strikeouts)	.20	.06
❑ 578	Kevin Bass	.10	.03
❑ 579	Carlton Fisk	.30	.09
❑ 580	Doug Drabek	.10	.03
❑ 581	Mark Gubicza	.10	.03
❑ 582	Bobby Thigpen	.10	.03
❑ 583	Chili Davis	.20	.06
❑ 584	Scott Bankhead	.10	.03
❑ 585	Harold Baines	.20	.06
❑ 586	Eric Young	.10	.03
❑ 587	Lance Parrish	.20	.06
❑ 588	Juan Bell	.10	.03
❑ 589	Bob Ojeda	.10	.03
❑ 590	Joe Orsulak	.10	.03
❑ 591	Benito Santiago	.20	.06
❑ 592	Wade Boggs	.30	.09
❑ 593	Robby Thompson	.10	.03
❑ 594	Eric Plunk	.10	.03
❑ 595	Hensley Meulens	.10	.03
❑ 596	Lou Whitaker	.20	.06
❑ 597	Dale Murphy	.50	.15
❑ 598	Paul Molitor	.30	.09
❑ 599	Greg W. Harris	.10	.03
❑ 600	Darren Holmes	.10	.03
❑ 601	Dave Martinez	.10	.03
❑ 602	Tom Henke	.10	.03
❑ 603	Mike Benjamin	.10	.03
❑ 604	Rene Gonzales	.10	.03
❑ 605	Roger McDowell	.10	.03
❑ 606	Kirby Puckett	.50	.15
❑ 607	Randy Myers	.10	.03
❑ 608	Ruben Sierra	.10	.03
❑ 609	Wilson Alvarez	.10	.03
❑ 610	David Segui	.10	.03
❑ 611	Juan Samuel	.10	.03
❑ 612	Tom Brunansky	.10	.03
❑ 613	Willie Randolph	.20	.06
❑ 614	Tony Phillips	.10	.03
❑ 615	Candy Maldonado	.10	.03
❑ 616	Chris Bosio	.10	.03
❑ 617	Bret Barberie	.10	.03
❑ 618	Scott Sanderson	.10	.03
❑ 619	Ron Darling	.10	.03
❑ 620	Dave Winfield	.30	.09
❑ 621	Mike Felder	.10	.03
❑ 622	Greg Hibbard	.10	.03
❑ 623	Mike Scioscia	.10	.03
❑ 624	John Smiley	.10	.03
❑ 625	Alejandro Pena	.10	.03
❑ 626	Terry Steinbach	.10	.03
❑ 627	Freddie Benavides	.10	.03
❑ 628	Kevin Reimer	.10	.03
❑ 629	Braulio Castillo	.10	.03
❑ 630	Dave Stieb	.10	.03
❑ 631	Dave Magadan	.10	.03
❑ 632	Scott Fletcher	.10	.03
❑ 633	Cris Carpenter	.10	.03
❑ 634	Kevin Maas	.10	.03
❑ 635	Todd Worrell	.10	.03
❑ 636	Rob Deer	.10	.03
❑ 637	Dwight Smith	.10	.03
❑ 638	Chito Martinez	.10	.03
❑ 639	Jimmy Key	.20	.06
❑ 640	Greg A. Harris	.10	.03
❑ 641	Mike Moore	.10	.03
❑ 642	Pat Borders	.10	.03
❑ 643	Bill Gullickson	.10	.03
❑ 644	Gary Gaetti	.20	.06
❑ 645	David Howard	.10	.03
❑ 646	Jim Abbott	.50	.15
❑ 647	Willie Wilson	.10	.03
❑ 648	David Wells	.20	.06
❑ 649	Andres Galarraga	.20	.06
❑ 650	Vince Coleman	.10	.03
❑ 651	Rob Dibble	.20	.06
❑ 652	Frank Tanana	.10	.03
❑ 653	Steve Decker	.10	.03
❑ 654	David Cone	.20	.06
❑ 655	Jack Armstrong	.10	.03
❑ 656	Dave Stewart	.20	.06
❑ 657	Billy Hatcher	.10	.03
❑ 658	Tim Raines	.20	.06
❑ 659	Walt Weiss	.10	.03
❑ 660	Jose Lind	.10	.03

1994 Score Rookie/Traded

	Nm-Mt	Ex-Mt
COMPLETE SET (165)	15.00	4.50

❑ RT1	Will Clark	.75	.23
❑ RT2	Lee Smith	.30	.09
❑ RT3	Bo Jackson	.75	.23
❑ RT4	Ellis Burks	.30	.09
❑ RT5	Eddie Murray	.75	.23
❑ RT6	Delino DeShields	.15	.04
❑ RT7	Erik Hanson	.15	.04
❑ RT8	Rafael Palmeiro	.50	.15
❑ RT9	Luis Polonia	.15	.04
❑ RT10	Omar Vizquel	.30	.09
❑ RT11	Kurt Abbott	.30	.09
❑ RT12	Vince Coleman	.15	.04
❑ RT13	Rickey Henderson	1.25	.35
❑ RT14	Terry Mulholland	.15	.04
❑ RT15	Greg Hibbard	.15	.04
❑ RT16	Walt Weiss	.15	.04
❑ RT17	Chris Sabo	.15	.04
❑ RT18	Dave Henderson	.15	.04
❑ RT19	Rick Sutcliffe	.30	.09
❑ RT20	Harold Reynolds	.30	.09
❑ RT21	Jack Morris	.30	.09
❑ RT22	Dan Wilson	.15	.04
❑ RT23	Dave Magadan	.15	.04
❑ RT24	Dennis Martinez	.30	.09
❑ RT25	Wes Chamberlain	.15	.04
❑ RT26	Otis Nixon	.15	.04
❑ RT27	Eric Anthony	.15	.04
❑ RT28	Randy Milligan	.15	.04
❑ RT29	Julio Franco	.30	.09
❑ RT30	Kevin McReynolds	.15	.04
❑ RT31	Anthony Young	.15	.04
❑ RT32	Brian Harper	.15	.04
❑ RT33	Gene Harris	.15	.04
❑ RT34	Eddie Taubensee	.15	.04
❑ RT35	David Segui	.15	.04
❑ RT36	Stan Javier	.15	.04
❑ RT37	Felix Fermin	.15	.04
❑ RT38	Darrin Jackson	.15	.04
❑ RT39	Tony Fernandez	.15	.04
❑ RT40	Jose Vizcaino	.15	.04
❑ RT41	Willie Banks	.15	.04
❑ RT42	Brian Hunter	.15	.04
❑ RT43	Reggie Jefferson	.15	.04
❑ RT44	Junior Felix	.15	.04
❑ RT45	Jack Armstrong	.15	.04
❑ RT46	Bip Roberts	.15	.04
❑ RT47	Jerry Browne	.15	.04
❑ RT48	Marvin Freeman	.15	.04
❑ RT49	Jody Reed	.15	.04
❑ RT50	Alex Cole	.15	.04
❑ RT51	Sid Fernandez	.15	.04
❑ RT52	Pete Smith	.15	.04
❑ RT53	Xavier Hernandez	.15	.04
❑ RT54	Scott Sanderson	.15	.04
❑ RT55	Turner Ward	.15	.04
❑ RT56	Rex Hudler	.15	.04
❑ RT57	Deion Sanders	.30	.09
❑ RT58	Sid Bream	.15	.04
❑ RT59	Tony Pena	.15	.04
❑ RT60	Bret Boone	.30	.09
❑ RT61	Bobby Ayala	.15	.04
❑ RT62	Pedro Martinez	.75	.23
❑ RT63	Howard Johnson	.15	.04
❑ RT64	Mark Portugal	.15	.04
❑ RT65	Roberto Kelly	.15	.04
❑ RT66	Spike Owen	.15	.04
❑ RT67	Jeff Treadway	.15	.04
❑ RT68	Mike Harkey	.15	.04

Card	Nm-Mt	Ex-Mt
❑ RT69 Doug Jones	.15	.04
❑ RT70 Steve Farr	.15	.04
❑ RT71 Billy Taylor RC	.15	.04
❑ RT72 Manny Ramirez	.50	.15
❑ RT73 Bob Hamelin	.15	.04
❑ RT74 Steve Karsay	.15	.04
❑ RT75 Ryan Klesko	.30	.09
❑ RT76 Cliff Floyd	.30	.09
❑ RT77 Jeffrey Hammonds	.15	.04
❑ RT78 Javier Lopez	.30	.09
❑ RT79 Roger Salkeld	.15	.04
❑ RT80 Hector Carrasco	.15	.04
❑ RT81 Gerald Williams	.15	.04
❑ RT82 Raul Mondesi	.30	.09
❑ RT83 Sterling Hitchcock	.15	.04
❑ RT84 Danny Bautista	.15	.04
❑ RT85 Chris Turner	.15	.04
❑ RT86 Shane Reynolds	.15	.04
❑ RT87 Rondell White	.30	.09
❑ RT88 Salomon Torres	.15	.04
❑ RT89 Turk Wendell	.15	.04
❑ RT90 Tony Tarasco	.15	.04
❑ RT91 Shawn Green	.75	.23
❑ RT92 Greg Colbrunn	.15	.04
❑ RT93 Eddie Zambrano	.15	.04
❑ RT94 Rich Becker	.15	.04
❑ RT95 Chris Gomez	.15	.04
❑ RT96 John Patterson	.15	.04
❑ RT97 Derek Parks	.15	.04
❑ RT98 Rich Rowland	.15	.04
❑ RT99 James Mouton	.15	.04
❑ RT100 Tim Hyers RC	.15	.04
❑ RT101 Jose Valentin	.15	.04
❑ RT102 Carlos Delgado	.50	.15
❑ RT103 Robert Eenhoorn	.15	.04
❑ RT104 John Hudek RC	.15	.04
❑ RT105 Domingo Cedeno	.15	.04
❑ RT106 Denny Hocking	.15	.04
❑ RT107 Greg Pirkl	.15	.04
❑ RT108 Mark Smith	.15	.04
❑ RT109 Paul Shuey	.15	.04
❑ RT110 Jorge Fabregas	.15	.04
❑ RT111 Rikkert Faneyte RC	.15	.04
❑ RT112 Rob Butler	.15	.04
❑ RT113 Darren Oliver RC	.30	.09
❑ RT114 Troy O'Leary	.15	.04
❑ RT115 Scott Brow	.15	.04
❑ RT116 Tony Eusebio	.15	.04
❑ RT117 Carlos Reyes	.15	.04
❑ RT118 J.R. Phillips	.15	.04
❑ RT119 Alex Diaz	.15	.04
❑ RT120 Charles Johnson	.30	.09
❑ RT121 Nate Minchey	.15	.04
❑ RT122 Scott Sanders	.15	.04
❑ RT123 Daryl Boston	.15	.04
❑ RT124 Joey Hamilton	.15	.04
❑ RT125 Brian Anderson	.30	.09
❑ RT126 Dan Miceli	.15	.04
❑ RT127 Tom Brunansky	.15	.04
❑ RT128 Dave Staton	.15	.04
❑ RT129 Mike Oquist	.15	.04
❑ RT130 John Mabry RC	.30	.09
❑ RT131 Norberto Martin	.15	.04
❑ RT132 Hector Fajardo	.15	.04
❑ RT133 Mark Hutton	.15	.04
❑ RT134 Fernando Vina	.50	.15
❑ RT135 Lee Tinsley	.15	.04
❑ RT136 Chan Ho Park RC	.75	.23
❑ RT137 Paul Spoljaric	.15	.04
❑ RT138 Matias Carrillo	.15	.04
❑ RT139 Mark Kiefer	.15	.04
❑ RT140 Stan Royer	.15	.04
❑ RT141 Bryan Eversgerd	.15	.04
❑ RT142 Brian L. Hunter	.15	.04
❑ RT143 Joe Hall	.15	.04
❑ RT144 Johnny Ruffin	.15	.04
❑ RT145 Alex Gonzalez	.15	.04
❑ RT146 Keith Lockhart RC	.30	.09
❑ RT147 Tom Marsh	.15	.04
❑ RT148 Tony Longmire	.15	.04
❑ RT149 Keith Mitchell	.15	.04
❑ RT150 Melvin Nieves	.15	.04
❑ RT151 Kelly Stinnett RC	.15	.04
❑ RT152 Miguel Jimenez	.15	.04
❑ RT153 Jeff Juden	.15	.04
❑ RT154 Matt Walbeck	.15	.04
❑ RT155 Marc Newfield	.15	.04
❑ RT156 Matt Mieske	.15	.04
❑ RT157 Marcus Moore	.15	.04
❑ RT158 Jose Lima RC SP	5.00	1.50
❑ RT159 Mike Kelly	.15	.04
❑ RT160 Jim Edmonds	.50	.15
❑ RT161 Steve Trachsel	.15	.04
❑ RT162 Greg Blosser	.15	.04
❑ RT163 Marc Acre RC	.15	.04
❑ RT164 AL Checklist	.15	.04
❑ RT165 NL Checklist	.15	.04
❑ HC1 Alex Rodriguez Call-Up Redemption	300.00	90.00
❑ NNO Sept. Call-Up Trade EXP	2.00	.60

1993 Select

	Nm-Mt	Ex-Mt
COMPLETE SET (405)	25.00	7.50

Card	Nm-Mt	Ex-Mt
❑ 1 Barry Bonds	1.25	.35
❑ 2 Ken Griffey Jr.	.75	.23
❑ 3 Will Clark	.50	.15
❑ 4 Kirby Puckett	.50	.15
❑ 5 Tony Gwynn	.60	.18
❑ 6 Frank Thomas	.50	.15
❑ 7 Tom Glavine	.50	.15
❑ 8 Roberto Alomar	.50	.15
❑ 9 Andre Dawson	.20	.06
❑ 10 Ron Darling	.15	.04
❑ 11 Bobby Bonilla	.20	.06
❑ 12 Danny Tartabull	.15	.04
❑ 13 Darren Daulton	.20	.06
❑ 14 Roger Clemens	1.00	.30
❑ 15 Ozzie Smith	.50	.15
❑ 16 Mark McGwire	1.25	.35
❑ 17 Terry Pendleton	.20	.06
❑ 18 Cal Ripken	1.50	.45
❑ 19 Fred McGriff	.30	.09
❑ 20 Cecil Fielder	.20	.06
❑ 21 Darryl Strawberry	.30	.09
❑ 22 Robin Yount	.50	.15
❑ 23 Barry Larkin	.50	.15
❑ 24 Don Mattingly	1.25	.35
❑ 25 Craig Biggio	.30	.09
❑ 26 Sandy Alomar Jr.	.15	.04
❑ 27 Larry Walker	.30	.09
❑ 28 Junior Felix	.15	.04
❑ 29 Eddie Murray	.50	.15
❑ 30 Robin Ventura	.20	.06
❑ 31 Greg Maddux	1.00	.30
❑ 32 Dave Winfield	.30	.09
❑ 33 John Kruk	.20	.06
❑ 34 Wally Joyner	.20	.06
❑ 35 Andy Van Slyke	.20	.06
❑ 36 Chuck Knoblauch	.20	.06
❑ 37 Tom Pagnozzi	.15	.04
❑ 38 Dennis Eckersley	.20	.06
❑ 39 Dave Justice	.20	.06
❑ 40 Juan Gonzalez	.50	.15
❑ 41 Gary Sheffield	.20	.06
❑ 42 Paul Molitor	.30	.09
❑ 43 Delino DeShields	.15	.04
❑ 44 Travis Fryman	.20	.06
❑ 45 Hal Morris	.15	.04
❑ 46 Greg Olson	.15	.04
❑ 47 Ken Caminiti	.20	.06
❑ 48 Wade Boggs	.30	.09
❑ 49 Orel Hershiser	.20	.06
❑ 50 Albert Belle	.20	.06
❑ 51 Bill Swift	.15	.04
❑ 52 Mark Langston	.15	.04
❑ 53 Joe Girardi	.15	.04
❑ 54 Keith Miller	.15	.04
❑ 55 Gary Carter	.30	.09
❑ 56 Brady Anderson	.20	.06
❑ 57 Dwight Gooden	.30	.09
❑ 58 Julio Franco	.20	.06
❑ 59 Lenny Dykstra	.20	.06
❑ 60 Mickey Tettleton	.15	.04
❑ 61 Randy Tomlin	.15	.04
❑ 62 B.J. Surhoff	.20	.06
❑ 63 Todd Zeile	.15	.04
❑ 64 Roberto Kelly	.15	.04
❑ 65 Rob Dibble	.20	.06
❑ 66 Leo Gomez	.15	.04
❑ 67 Doug Jones	.15	.04
❑ 68 Ellis Burks	.20	.06
❑ 69 Mike Scioscia	.15	.04
❑ 70 Charles Nagy	.15	.04
❑ 71 Cory Snyder	.15	.04
❑ 72 Devon White	.15	.04
❑ 73 Mark Grace	.50	.15
❑ 74 Luis Polonia	.15	.04
❑ 75 John Smiley 2X	.15	.04
❑ 76 Carlton Fisk	.30	.09
❑ 77 Luis Sojo	.15	.04
❑ 78 George Brett	1.25	.35
❑ 79 Mitch Williams	.15	.04
❑ 80 Kent Hrbek	.20	.06
❑ 81 Jay Bell	.20	.06
❑ 82 Edgar Martinez	.30	.09
❑ 83 Lee Smith	.20	.06
❑ 84 Deion Sanders	.20	.06
❑ 85 Bill Gullickson	.15	.04
❑ 86 Paul O'Neill	.30	.09
❑ 87 Kevin Seitzer	.15	.04
❑ 88 Steve Finley	.20	.06
❑ 89 Mel Hall	.15	.04
❑ 90 Nolan Ryan	2.00	.60
❑ 91 Eric Davis	.20	.06
❑ 92 Mike Mussina	.50	.15
❑ 93 Tony Fernandez	.15	.04
❑ 94 Frank Viola	.20	.06
❑ 95 Matt Williams	.20	.06
❑ 96 Joe Carter	.20	.06
❑ 97 Ryne Sandberg	.75	.23
❑ 98 Jim Abbott	.50	.15
❑ 99 Marquis Grissom	.15	.04
❑ 100 George Bell	.15	.04
❑ 101 Howard Johnson	.15	.04
❑ 102 Kevin Appier	.20	.06
❑ 103 Dale Murphy	.50	.15
❑ 104 Shane Mack	.15	.04
❑ 105 Jose Lind	.15	.04
❑ 106 Rickey Henderson	.75	.23
❑ 107 Bob Tewksbury	.15	.04
❑ 108 Kevin Mitchell	.15	.04
❑ 109 Steve Avery	.15	.04
❑ 110 Candy Maldonado	.15	.04
❑ 111 Bip Roberts	.15	.04
❑ 112 Lou Whitaker	.20	.06
❑ 113 Jeff Bagwell	.30	.09
❑ 114 Dante Bichette	.20	.06
❑ 115 Brett Butler	.20	.06
❑ 116 Melido Perez	.15	.04
❑ 117 Andy Benes	.15	.04
❑ 118 Randy Johnson	.50	.15
❑ 119 Willie McGee	.20	.06
❑ 120 Jody Reed	.15	.04
❑ 121 Shawon Dunston	.15	.04
❑ 122 Carlos Baerga	.15	.04
❑ 123 Bret Saberhagen	.20	.06
❑ 124 John Olerud	.20	.06
❑ 125 Ivan Calderon	.15	.04
❑ 126 Bryan Harvey	.15	.04
❑ 127 Terry Mulholland	.15	.04
❑ 128 Ozzie Guillen	.15	.04
❑ 129 Steve Buechele	.15	.04
❑ 130 Kevin Tapani	.15	.04
❑ 131 Felix Jose	.15	.04
❑ 132 Terry Steinbach	.15	.04
❑ 133 Ron Gant	.20	.06
❑ 134 Harold Reynolds	.20	.06

❑ 135 Chris Sabo .15 .04
❑ 136 Ivan Rodriguez .50 .15
❑ 137 Eric Anthony .15 .04
❑ 138 Mike Henneman .15 .04
❑ 139 Robby Thompson .15 .04
❑ 140 Scott Fletcher .15 .04
❑ 141 Bruce Hurst .15 .04
❑ 142 Kevin Maas .15 .04
❑ 143 Tom Candiotti .15 .04
❑ 144 Chris Hoiles .15 .04
❑ 145 Mike Morgan .15 .04
❑ 146 Mark Whiten .15 .04
❑ 147 Dennis Martinez .20 .06
❑ 148 Tony Pena .15 .04
❑ 149 Dave Magadan .15 .04
❑ 150 Mark Lewis .15 .04
❑ 151 Mariano Duncan .15 .04
❑ 152 Gregg Jefferies .15 .04
❑ 153 Doug Drabek .15 .04
❑ 154 Brian Harper .15 .04
❑ 155 Ray Lankford .15 .04
❑ 156 Carney Lansford .20 .06
❑ 157 Mike Sharperson .15 .04
❑ 158 Jack Morris .20 .06
❑ 159 Otis Nixon .15 .04
❑ 160 Steve Sax .15 .04
❑ 161 Mark Lemke .15 .04
❑ 162 Rafael Palmeiro .30 .09
❑ 163 Jose Rijo .15 .04
❑ 164 Omar Vizquel .20 .06
❑ 165 Sammy Sosa .75 .23
❑ 166 Milt Cuyler .15 .04
❑ 167 John Franco .20 .06
❑ 168 Darryl Hamilton .15 .04
❑ 169 Ken Hill .15 .04
❑ 170 Mike Devereaux .15 .04
❑ 171 Don Slaught .15 .04
❑ 172 Steve Farr .15 .04
❑ 173 Bernard Gilkey .15 .04
❑ 174 Mike Fetters .15 .04
❑ 175 Vince Coleman .15 .04
❑ 176 Kevin McReynolds .15 .04
❑ 177 John Smoltz .30 .09
❑ 178 Greg Gagne .15 .04
❑ 179 Greg Swindell .15 .04
❑ 180 Juan Guzman .15 .04
❑ 181 Kal Daniels .15 .04
❑ 182 Rick Sutcliffe .20 .06
❑ 183 Orlando Merced .15 .04
❑ 184 Bill Wegman .15 .04
❑ 185 Mark Gardner .15 .04
❑ 186 Rob Deer .15 .04
❑ 187 Dave Hollins .15 .04
❑ 188 Jack Clark .20 .06
❑ 189 Brian Hunter .15 .04
❑ 190 Tim Wallach .15 .04
❑ 191 Tim Belcher .15 .04
❑ 192 Walt Weiss .15 .04
❑ 193 Kurt Stillwell .15 .04
❑ 194 Charlie Hayes .15 .04
❑ 195 Willie Randolph .20 .06
❑ 196 Jack McDowell .15 .04
❑ 197 Jose Offerman .15 .04
❑ 198 Chuck Finley .20 .06
❑ 199 Darrin Jackson .15 .04
❑ 200 Kelly Gruber .15 .04
❑ 201 John Wetteland .20 .06
❑ 202 Jay Buhner .20 .06
❑ 203 Mike LaValliere .15 .04
❑ 204 Kevin Brown .20 .06
❑ 205 Luis Gonzalez .20 .06
❑ 206 Rick Aguilera .15 .04
❑ 207 Norm Charlton .15 .04
❑ 208 Mike Bordick .15 .04
❑ 209 Charlie Leibrandt .15 .04
❑ 210 Tom Brunansky .15 .04
❑ 211 Tom Henke .15 .04
❑ 212 Randy Milligan .15 .04
❑ 213 Ramon Martinez .15 .04
❑ 214 Mo Vaughn .20 .06
❑ 215 Randy Myers .15 .04
❑ 216 Greg Hibbard .15 .04
❑ 217 Wes Chamberlain .15 .04
❑ 218 Tony Phillips .15 .04
❑ 219 Pete Harnisch .15 .04
❑ 220 Mike Gallego .15 .04
❑ 221 Bud Black .15 .04
❑ 222 Greg Vaughn .20 .06
❑ 223 Milt Thompson .15 .04
❑ 224 Ben McDonald .15 .04
❑ 225 Billy Hatcher .15 .04
❑ 226 Paul Sorrento .15 .04
❑ 227 Mark Gubicza .15 .04
❑ 228 Mike Greenwell .15 .04
❑ 229 Curt Schilling .30 .09
❑ 230 Alan Trammell .30 .09
❑ 231 Zane Smith .15 .04
❑ 232 Bobby Thigpen .15 .04
❑ 233 Greg Olson .15 .04
❑ 234 Joe Orsulak .15 .04
❑ 235 Joe Oliver .15 .04
❑ 236 Tim Raines .20 .06
❑ 237 Juan Samuel .15 .04
❑ 238 Chili Davis .20 .06
❑ 239 Spike Owen .15 .04
❑ 240 Dave Stewart .20 .06
❑ 241 Jim Eisenreich .15 .04
❑ 242 Phil Plantier .15 .04
❑ 243 Sid Fernandez .15 .04
❑ 244 Dan Gladden .15 .04
❑ 245 Mickey Morandini .15 .04
❑ 246 Tino Martinez .30 .09
❑ 247 Kirt Manwaring .15 .04
❑ 248 Dean Palmer .20 .06
❑ 249 Tom Browning .15 .04
❑ 250 Brian McRae .15 .04
❑ 251 Scott Leius .15 .04
❑ 252 Bert Blyleven .20 .06
❑ 253 Scott Erickson .15 .04
❑ 254 Bob Welch .15 .04
❑ 255 Pat Kelly .15 .04
❑ 256 Felix Fermin .15 .04
❑ 257 Harold Baines .20 .06
❑ 258 Duane Ward .15 .04
❑ 259 Bill Spiers .15 .04
❑ 260 Jaime Navarro .15 .04
❑ 261 Scott Sanderson .15 .04
❑ 262 Gary Gaetti .20 .06
❑ 263 Bob Ojeda .15 .04
❑ 264 Jeff Montgomery .15 .04
❑ 265 Scott Bankhead .15 .04
❑ 266 Lance Johnson .15 .04
❑ 267 Rafael Belliard .15 .04
❑ 268 Kevin Reimer .15 .04
❑ 269 Benito Santiago .20 .06
❑ 270 Mike Moore .15 .04
❑ 271 Dave Fleming .15 .04
❑ 272 Moises Alou .20 .06
❑ 273 Pat Listach .15 .04
❑ 274 Reggie Sanders .20 .06
❑ 275 Kenny Lofton .20 .06
❑ 276 Donovan Osborne .15 .04
❑ 277 Rusty Meacham .15 .04
❑ 278 Eric Karros .20 .06
❑ 279 Andy Stankiewicz .15 .04
❑ 280 Brian Jordan .20 .06
❑ 281 Gary DiSarcina .15 .04
❑ 282 Mark Wohlers .15 .04
❑ 283 Dave Nilsson .15 .04
❑ 284 Anthony Young .15 .04
❑ 285 Jim Bullinger .15 .04
❑ 286 Derek Bell .15 .04
❑ 287 Brian Williams .15 .04
❑ 288 Julio Valera .15 .04
❑ 289 Dan Walters .15 .04
❑ 290 Chad Curtis .15 .04
❑ 291 Michael Tucker DP .15 .04
❑ 292 Bob Zupcic .15 .04
❑ 293 Todd Hundley .15 .04
❑ 294 Jeff Tackett .15 .04
❑ 295 Greg Colbrunn .15 .04
❑ 296 Cal Eldred .15 .04
❑ 297 Chris Roberts DP .15 .04
❑ 298 John Doherty .15 .04
❑ 299 Denny Neagle .20 .06
❑ 300 Arthur Rhodes .15 .04
❑ 301 Mark Clark .15 .04
❑ 302 Scott Cooper .15 .04
❑ 303 Jamie Arnold DP RC .15 .04
❑ 304 Jim Thome .50 .15
❑ 305 Frank Seminara .15 .04
❑ 306 Kurt Knudsen .15 .04
❑ 307 Tim Wakefield .20 .06
❑ 308 John Jaha .15 .04
❑ 309 Pat Hentgen .15 .04
❑ 310 B.J. Wallace DP .15 .04
❑ 311 Roberto Hernandez .15 .04
❑ 312 Hipolito Pichardo .15 .04
❑ 313 Eric Fox .15 .04
❑ 314 Willie Banks .15 .04
❑ 315 Sam Militello .15 .04
❑ 316 Vince Horsman .15 .04
❑ 317 Carlos Hernandez .15 .04
❑ 318 Jeff Kent .50 .15
❑ 319 Mike Perez .15 .04
❑ 320 Scott Livingstone .15 .04
❑ 321 Jeff Conine .20 .06
❑ 322 Jim Austin .15 .04
❑ 323 John Vander Wal .15 .04
❑ 324 Pat Mahomes .15 .04
❑ 325 Pedro Astacio .15 .04
❑ 326 Bret Boone UER .30 .09
(Misspelled Brett)
❑ 327 Matt Stairs .15 .04
❑ 328 Damion Easley .15 .04
❑ 329 Ben Rivera .15 .04
❑ 330 Reggie Jefferson .15 .04
❑ 331 Luis Mercedes .15 .04
❑ 332 Kyle Abbott .15 .04
❑ 333 Eddie Taubensee .15 .04
❑ 334 Tim McIntosh .15 .04
❑ 335 Phil Clark .15 .04
❑ 336 Wil Cordero .15 .04
❑ 337 Russ Springer .15 .04
❑ 338 Craig Colbert .15 .04
❑ 339 Tim Salmon .30 .09
❑ 340 Braulio Castillo .15 .04
❑ 341 Donald Harris .15 .04
❑ 342 Eric Young .15 .04
❑ 343 Bob Wickman .15 .04
❑ 344 John Valentin .15 .04
❑ 345 Dan Wilson .20 .06
❑ 346 Steve Hosey .15 .04
❑ 347 Mike Piazza 1.25 .35
❑ 348 Willie Greene .15 .04
❑ 349 Tom Goodwin .15 .04
❑ 350 Eric Hillman .15 .04
❑ 351 Steve Reed RC .15 .04
❑ 352 Dan Serafini DP RC .15 .04
❑ 353 T.Steverson DP RC .15 .04
❑ 354 Benji Grigsby DP RC .15 .04
❑ 355 S.Stewart DP RC .75 .23
❑ 356 Sean Lowe DP RC .15 .04
❑ 357 Derek Wallace DP RC .15 .04
❑ 358 Rick Helling DP .15 .04
❑ 359 Jason Kendall DP RC .75 .23
❑ 360 Derek Jeter DP RC 10.00 3.00
❑ 361 David Cone .20 .06
❑ 362 Jeff Reardon .20 .06
❑ 363 Bobby Witt .15 .04
❑ 364 Jose Canseco .50 .15
❑ 365 Jeff Russell .15 .04
❑ 366 Ruben Sierra .15 .04
❑ 367 Alan Mills .15 .04
❑ 368 Matt Nokes .15 .04
❑ 369 Pat Borders .15 .04
❑ 370 Pedro Munoz .15 .04
❑ 371 Danny Jackson .15 .04
❑ 372 Geronimo Pena .15 .04
❑ 373 Craig Lefferts .15 .04
❑ 374 Joe Grahe .15 .04
❑ 375 Roger McDowell .15 .04
❑ 376 Jimmy Key .20 .06
❑ 377 Steve Olin .15 .04
❑ 378 Glenn Davis .15 .04
❑ 379 Rene Gonzales .15 .04
❑ 380 Manuel Lee .15 .04
❑ 381 Ron Karkovice .15 .04
❑ 382 Sid Bream .15 .04
❑ 383 Gerald Williams .15 .04
❑ 384 Lenny Harris .15 .04
❑ 385 J.T. Snow RC .50 .15
❑ 386 Dave Stieb .15 .04
❑ 387 Kirk McCaskill .15 .04
❑ 388 Lance Parrish .20 .06
❑ 389 Craig Grebeck .15 .04
❑ 390 Rick Wilkins .15 .04
❑ 391 Manny Alexander .15 .04

❑ 392 Mike Schooler	.15	.04
❑ 393 Bernie Williams	.30	.09
❑ 394 Kevin Koslofski	.15	.04
❑ 395 Willie Wilson	.15	.04
❑ 396 Jeff Parrett	.15	.04
❑ 397 Mike Harkey	.15	.04
❑ 398 Frank Tanana	.15	.04
❑ 399 Doug Henry	.15	.04
❑ 400 Royce Clayton	.15	.04
❑ 401 Eric Wedge RC	.15	.04
❑ 402 Derrick May	.15	.04
❑ 403 Carlos Garcia	.15	.04
❑ 404 Henry Rodriguez	.15	.04
❑ 405 Ryan Klesko	.20	.06

1993 SP

	Nm-Mt	Ex-Mt
COMPLETE SET (290)	120.00	36.00
COMMON CARD (1-270)	.50	.15
COMMON FOIL (271-290)	1.00	.30

	Nm-Mt	Ex-Mt
❑ 1 Roberto Alomar AS	2.00	.60
❑ 2 Wade Boggs AS	1.25	.35
❑ 3 Joe Carter AS	.50	.15
❑ 4 Ken Griffey Jr. AS	3.00	.90
❑ 5 Mark Langston AS	.50	.15
❑ 6 John Olerud AS	.75	.23
❑ 7 Kirby Puckett AS	2.00	.60
❑ 8 Cal Ripken Jr. AS	6.00	1.80
❑ 9 Ivan Rodriguez AS	2.00	.60
❑ 10 Barry Bonds AS	5.00	1.50
❑ 11 Darren Daulton AS	.75	.23
❑ 12 Marquis Grissom AS	.50	.15
❑ 13 David Justice AS	.75	.23
❑ 14 John Kruk AS	.75	.23
❑ 15 Barry Larkin AS	2.00	.60
❑ 16 Terry Mulholland AS	.50	.15
❑ 17 Ryne Sandberg AS	3.00	.90
❑ 18 Gary Sheffield AS	.75	.23
❑ 19 Chad Curtis	.50	.15
❑ 20 Chili Davis	.75	.23
❑ 21 Gary DiSarcina	.50	.15
❑ 22 Damion Easley	.50	.15
❑ 23 Chuck Finley	.75	.23
❑ 24 Luis Polonia	.50	.15
❑ 25 Tim Salmon	1.25	.35
❑ 26 J.T. Snow RC	2.00	.60
❑ 27 Russ Springer	.50	.15
❑ 28 Jeff Bagwell	1.25	.35
❑ 29 Craig Biggio	1.25	.35
❑ 30 Ken Caminiti	.75	.23
❑ 31 Andujar Cedeno	.50	.15
❑ 32 Doug Drabek	.50	.15
❑ 33 Steve Finley	.75	.23
❑ 34 Luis Gonzalez	.75	.23
❑ 35 Pete Harnisch	.50	.15
❑ 36 Darryl Kile	.75	.23
❑ 37 Mike Bordick	.50	.15
❑ 38 Dennis Eckersley	.75	.23
❑ 39 Brent Gates	.50	.15
❑ 40 Rickey Henderson	3.00	.90
❑ 41 Mark McGwire	5.00	1.50
❑ 42 Craig Paquette	.50	.15
❑ 43 Ruben Sierra	.50	.15
❑ 44 Terry Steinbach	.50	.15
❑ 45 Todd Van Poppel	.50	.15
❑ 46 Pat Borders	.50	.15
❑ 47 Tony Fernandez	.50	.15
❑ 48 Juan Guzman	.50	.15
❑ 49 Pat Hentgen	.50	.15
❑ 50 Paul Molitor	1.25	.35
❑ 51 Jack Morris	.75	.23
❑ 52 Ed Sprague	.50	.15
❑ 53 Duane Ward	.50	.15
❑ 54 Devon White	.50	.15
❑ 55 Steve Avery	.50	.15
❑ 56 Jeff Blauser	.50	.15
❑ 57 Ron Gant	.75	.23
❑ 58 Tom Glavine	2.00	.60
❑ 59 Greg Maddux	4.00	1.20
❑ 60 Fred McGriff	1.25	.35
❑ 61 Terry Pendleton	.75	.23
❑ 62 Deion Sanders	.75	.23
❑ 63 John Smoltz	1.25	.35
❑ 64 Cal Eldred	.50	.15
❑ 65 Darryl Hamilton	.50	.15
❑ 66 John Jaha	.50	.15
❑ 67 Pat Listach	.50	.15
❑ 68 Jaime Navarro	.50	.15
❑ 69 Kevin Reimer	.50	.15
❑ 70 B.J. Surhoff	.75	.23
❑ 71 Greg Vaughn	.75	.23
❑ 72 Robin Yount	2.00	.60
❑ 73 Rene Arocha RC	.75	.23
❑ 74 Bernard Gilkey	.50	.15
❑ 75 Gregg Jefferies	.50	.15
❑ 76 Ray Lankford	.50	.15
❑ 77 Tom Pagnozzi	.50	.15
❑ 78 Lee Smith	.75	.23
❑ 79 Ozzie Smith	2.00	.60
❑ 80 Bob Tewksbury	.50	.15
❑ 81 Mark Whiten	.50	.15
❑ 82 Steve Buechele	.50	.15
❑ 83 Mark Grace	2.00	.60
❑ 84 Jose Guzman	.50	.15
❑ 85 Derrick May	.50	.15
❑ 86 Mike Morgan	.50	.15
❑ 87 Randy Myers	.50	.15
❑ 88 Kevin Roberson RC	.50	.15
❑ 89 Sammy Sosa	3.00	.90
❑ 90 Rick Wilkins	.50	.15
❑ 91 Brett Butler	.75	.23
❑ 92 Eric Davis	.75	.23
❑ 93 Orel Hershiser	.75	.23
❑ 94 Eric Karros	.75	.23
❑ 95 Ramon Martinez	.50	.15
❑ 96 Raul Mondesi	.75	.23
❑ 97 Jose Offerman	.50	.15
❑ 98 Mike Piazza	5.00	1.50
❑ 99 Darryl Strawberry	1.25	.35
❑ 100 Moises Alou	.75	.23
❑ 101 Wil Cordero	.50	.15
❑ 102 Delino DeShields	.50	.15
❑ 103 Darrin Fletcher	.50	.15
❑ 104 Ken Hill	.50	.15
❑ 105 Mike Lansing RC	.75	.23
❑ 106 Dennis Martinez	.75	.23
❑ 107 Larry Walker	1.25	.35
❑ 108 John Wetteland	.75	.23
❑ 109 Rod Beck	.50	.15
❑ 110 John Burkett	.50	.15
❑ 111 Will Clark	2.00	.60
❑ 112 Royce Clayton	.50	.15
❑ 113 Darren Lewis	.50	.15
❑ 114 Willie McGee	.75	.23
❑ 115 Bill Swift	.50	.15
❑ 116 Robby Thompson	.50	.15
❑ 117 Matt Williams	.75	.23
❑ 118 Sandy Alomar Jr.	.50	.15
❑ 119 Carlos Baerga	.50	.15
❑ 120 Albert Belle	.75	.23
❑ 121 Reggie Jefferson	.50	.15
❑ 122 Wayne Kirby	.50	.15
❑ 123 Kenny Lofton	.75	.23
❑ 124 Carlos Martinez	.50	.15
❑ 125 Charles Nagy	.50	.15
❑ 126 Paul Sorrento	.50	.15
❑ 127 Rich Amaral	.50	.15
❑ 128 Jay Buhner	.75	.23
❑ 129 Norm Charlton	.50	.15
❑ 130 Dave Fleming	.50	.15
❑ 131 Erik Hanson	.50	.15
❑ 132 Randy Johnson	2.00	.60
❑ 133 Edgar Martinez	1.25	.35
❑ 134 Tino Martinez	1.25	.35
❑ 135 Omar Vizquel	.75	.23
❑ 136 Bret Barberie	.50	.15
❑ 137 Chuck Carr	.50	.15
❑ 138 Jeff Conine	.75	.23
❑ 139 Orestes Destrade	.50	.15
❑ 140 Chris Hammond	.50	.15
❑ 141 Bryan Harvey	.50	.15
❑ 142 Benito Santiago	.75	.23
❑ 143 Walt Weiss	.50	.15
❑ 144 Darrell Whitmore RC	.50	.15
❑ 145 Tim Bogar RC	.50	.15
❑ 146 Bobby Bonilla	.75	.23
❑ 147 Jeromy Burnitz	.75	.23
❑ 148 Vince Coleman	.50	.15
❑ 149 Dwight Gooden	1.25	.35
❑ 150 Todd Hundley	.50	.15
❑ 151 Howard Johnson	.50	.15
❑ 152 Eddie Murray	2.00	.60
❑ 153 Bret Saberhagen	.75	.23
❑ 154 Brady Anderson	.75	.23
❑ 155 Mike Devereaux	.50	.15
❑ 156 Jeffrey Hammonds	.50	.15
❑ 157 Chris Hoiles	.50	.15
❑ 158 Ben McDonald	.50	.15
❑ 159 Mark McLemore	.50	.15
❑ 160 Mike Mussina	2.00	.60
❑ 161 Gregg Olson	.50	.15
❑ 162 David Segui	.50	.15
❑ 163 Derek Bell	.50	.15
❑ 164 Andy Benes	.50	.15
❑ 165 Archi Cianfrocco	.50	.15
❑ 166 Ricky Gutierrez	.50	.15
❑ 167 Tony Gwynn	2.50	.75
❑ 168 Gene Harris	.50	.15
❑ 169 Trevor Hoffman	.75	.23
❑ 170 Ray McDavid RC	.50	.15
❑ 171 Phil Plantier	.50	.15
❑ 172 Mariano Duncan	.50	.15
❑ 173 Len Dykstra	.75	.23
❑ 174 Tommy Greene	.50	.15
❑ 175 Dave Hollins	.50	.15
❑ 176 Pete Incaviglia	.50	.15
❑ 177 Mickey Morandini	.50	.15
❑ 178 Curt Schilling	1.25	.35
❑ 179 Kevin Stocker	.50	.15
❑ 180 Mitch Williams	.50	.15
❑ 181 Stan Belinda	.50	.15
❑ 182 Jay Bell	.75	.23
❑ 183 Steve Cooke	.50	.15
❑ 184 Carlos Garcia	.50	.15
❑ 185 Jeff King	.50	.15
❑ 186 Orlando Merced	.50	.15
❑ 187 Don Slaught	.50	.15
❑ 188 Andy Van Slyke	.75	.23
❑ 189 Kevin Young	.75	.23
❑ 190 Kevin Brown	.75	.23
❑ 191 Jose Canseco	2.00	.60
❑ 192 Julio Franco	.75	.23
❑ 193 Benji Gil	.50	.15
❑ 194 Juan Gonzalez	2.00	.60
❑ 195 Tom Henke	.50	.15
❑ 196 Rafael Palmeiro	1.25	.35
❑ 197 Dean Palmer	.75	.23
❑ 198 Nolan Ryan	8.00	2.40
❑ 199 Roger Clemens	4.00	1.20
❑ 200 Scott Cooper	.50	.15
❑ 201 Andre Dawson	.75	.23
❑ 202 Mike Greenwell	.50	.15
❑ 203 Carlos Quintana	.50	.15
❑ 204 Jeff Russell	.50	.15
❑ 205 Aaron Sele	.50	.15
❑ 206 Mo Vaughn	.75	.23
❑ 207 Frank Viola	.75	.23
❑ 208 Rob Dibble	.75	.23
❑ 209 Roberto Kelly	.50	.15
❑ 210 Kevin Mitchell	.50	.15
❑ 211 Hal Morris	.50	.15
❑ 212 Joe Oliver	.50	.15
❑ 213 Jose Rijo	.50	.15
❑ 214 Bip Roberts	.50	.15
❑ 215 Chris Sabo	.50	.15
❑ 216 Reggie Sanders	.75	.23
❑ 217 Dante Bichette	.75	.23
❑ 218 Jerald Clark	.50	.15

❑ 219 Alex Cole .50 .15
❑ 220 Andres Galarraga .75 .23
❑ 221 Joe Girardi .50 .15
❑ 222 Charlie Hayes .50 .15
❑ 223 Roberto Mejia RC .50 .15
❑ 224 Armando Reynoso .50 .15
❑ 225 Eric Young .50 .15
❑ 226 Kevin Appier .75 .23
❑ 227 George Brett 5.00 1.50
❑ 228 David Cone .75 .23
❑ 229 Phil Hiatt .50 .15
❑ 230 Felix Jose .50 .15
❑ 231 Wally Joyner .75 .23
❑ 232 Mike Macfarlane .50 .15
❑ 233 Brian McRae .50 .15
❑ 234 Jeff Montgomery .50 .15
❑ 235 Rob Deer .50 .15
❑ 236 Cecil Fielder .75 .23
❑ 237 Travis Fryman .75 .23
❑ 238 Mike Henneman .50 .15
❑ 239 Tony Phillips .50 .15
❑ 240 Mickey Tettleton .50 .15
❑ 241 Alan Trammell 1.25 .35
❑ 242 David Wells .75 .23
❑ 243 Lou Whitaker .75 .23
❑ 244 Rick Aguilera .50 .15
❑ 245 Scott Erickson .50 .15
❑ 246 Brian Harper .50 .15
❑ 247 Kent Hrbek .75 .23
❑ 248 Chuck Knoblauch .75 .23
❑ 249 Shane Mack .50 .15
❑ 250 David McCarty .50 .15
❑ 251 Pedro Munoz .50 .15
❑ 252 Dave Winfield 1.25 .35
❑ 253 Alex Fernandez .50 .15
❑ 254 Ozzie Guillen .50 .15
❑ 255 Bo Jackson 2.00 .60
❑ 256 Lance Johnson .50 .15
❑ 257 Ron Karkovice .50 .15
❑ 258 Jack McDowell .50 .15
❑ 259 Tim Raines .75 .23
❑ 260 Frank Thomas 2.00 .60
❑ 261 Robin Ventura .75 .23
❑ 262 Jim Abbott 2.00 .60
❑ 263 Steve Farr .50 .15
❑ 264 Jimmy Key .75 .23
❑ 265 Don Mattingly 5.00 1.50
❑ 266 Paul O'Neill 1.25 .35
❑ 267 Mike Stanley .50 .15
❑ 268 Danny Tartabull .50 .15
❑ 269 Bob Wickman .50 .15
❑ 270 Bernie Williams 1.25 .35
❑ 271 Jason Bere FOIL 1.00 .30
❑ 272 R.Cedeno FOIL RC 1.50 .45
❑ 273 J.Damon FOIL RC 8.00 2.40
❑ 274 Russ Davis FOIL RC 1.50 .45
❑ 275 Carlos Delgado FOIL 4.00 1.20
❑ 276 Carl Everett FOIL 1.50 .45
❑ 277 Cliff Floyd FOIL 2.50 .75
❑ 278 Alex Gonzalez FOIL 1.00 .30
❑ 279 Derek Jeter FOIL RC 80.00 24.00
❑ 280 Chipper Jones FOIL 4.00 1.20
❑ 281 Javier Lopez FOIL 1.25 .35
❑ 282 Chad Mottola FOIL RC 1.00 .30
❑ 283 Marc Newfield FOIL 1.00 .30
❑ 284 Eduardo Perez FOIL 1.00 .30
❑ 285 Manny Ramirez FOIL 4.00 1.20
❑ 286 T.Steverson FOIL RC 1.00 .30
❑ 287 Michael Tucker FOIL 1.00 .30
❑ 288 Allen Watson FOIL 1.00 .30
❑ 289 Rondell White FOIL 1.50 .45
❑ 290 Dmitri Young FOIL 1.50 .45

1994 SP

	Nm-Mt	Ex-Mt
COMPLETE SET (200)	120.00	36.00
COMMON CARD (21-200)	.20	.06
COMMON FOIL (1-20)	.50	.15

❑ 1 Mike Bell FOIL RC .50 .15
❑ 2 D.J. Boston FOIL RC .50 .15
❑ 3 Johnny Damon FOIL .75 .23
❑ 4 Brad Fullmer FOIL RC 2.00 .60
❑ 5 Joey Hamilton FOIL .50 .15
❑ 6 T.Hollandsworth FOIL .50 .15

❑ 7 Brian L. Hunter FOIL .50 .15
❑ 8 L.Hawkins FOIL RC .75 .23
❑ 9 B.Kieschnick FOIL RC .75 .23
❑ 10 Derrek Lee FOIL RC 2.00 .60
❑ 11 Trot Nixon FOIL RC 2.00 .60
❑ 12 Alex Ochoa FOIL .50 .15
❑ 13 Chan Ho Park FOIL RC 2.00 .60
❑ 14 Kirk Presley FOIL RC .50 .15
❑ 15 A.Rodriguez FOIL RC 100.00 30.00
❑ 16 Jose Silva FOIL RC .50 .15
❑ 17 Terrell Wade FOIL RC .50 .15
❑ 18 Billy Wagner FOIL RC 2.00 .60
❑ 19 G.Williams FOIL RC .50 .15
❑ 20 Preston Wilson FOIL 1.25 .35
❑ 21 Brian Anderson RC .40 .12
❑ 22 Chad Curtis .20 .06
❑ 23 Chili Davis .40 .12
❑ 24 Bo Jackson 1.00 .30
❑ 25 Mark Langston .20 .06
❑ 26 Tim Salmon .60 .18
❑ 27 Jeff Bagwell .60 .18
❑ 28 Craig Biggio .60 .18
❑ 29 Ken Caminiti .40 .12
❑ 30 Doug Drabek .20 .06
❑ 31 John Hudek RC .20 .06
❑ 32 Greg Swindell .20 .06
❑ 33 Brent Gates .20 .06
❑ 34 Rickey Henderson 1.50 .45
❑ 35 Steve Karsay .20 .06
❑ 36 Mark McGwire 2.50 .75
❑ 37 Ruben Sierra .20 .06
❑ 38 Terry Steinbach .20 .06
❑ 39 Roberto Alomar 1.00 .30
❑ 40 Joe Carter .40 .12
❑ 41 Carlos Delgado .60 .18
❑ 42 Alex Gonzalez .20 .06
❑ 43 Juan Guzman .20 .06
❑ 44 Paul Molitor .60 .18
❑ 45 John Olerud .40 .12
❑ 46 Devon White .20 .06
❑ 47 Steve Avery .20 .06
❑ 48 Jeff Blauser .20 .06
❑ 49 Tom Glavine 1.00 .30
❑ 50 David Justice .40 .12
❑ 51 Roberto Kelly .20 .06
❑ 52 Ryan Klesko .40 .12
❑ 53 Javier Lopez .40 .12
❑ 54 Greg Maddux 2.00 .60
❑ 55 Fred McGriff .60 .18
❑ 56 Ricky Bones .20 .06
❑ 57 Cal Eldred .20 .06
❑ 58 Brian Harper .20 .06
❑ 59 Pat Listach .20 .06
❑ 60 B.J. Surhoff .40 .12
❑ 61 Greg Vaughn .40 .12
❑ 62 Bernard Gilkey .20 .06
❑ 63 Gregg Jefferies .20 .06
❑ 64 Ray Lankford .20 .06
❑ 65 Ozzie Smith 1.00 .30
❑ 66 Bob Tewksbury .20 .06
❑ 67 Mark Whiten .20 .06
❑ 68 Todd Zeile .20 .06
❑ 69 Mark Grace 1.00 .30
❑ 70 Randy Myers .20 .06
❑ 71 Ryne Sandberg 1.50 .45
❑ 72 Sammy Sosa 1.50 .45
❑ 73 Steve Trachsel .20 .06
❑ 74 Rick Wilkins .20 .06
❑ 75 Brett Butler .40 .12
❑ 76 Delino DeShields .20 .06
❑ 77 Orel Hershiser .40 .12
❑ 78 Eric Karros .40 .12
❑ 79 Raul Mondesi .40 .12
❑ 80 Mike Piazza 2.00 .60
❑ 81 Tim Wallach .20 .06
❑ 82 Moises Alou .40 .12
❑ 83 Cliff Floyd .40 .12
❑ 84 Marquis Grissom .20 .06
❑ 85 Pedro Martinez 1.00 .30
❑ 86 Larry Walker .60 .18
❑ 87 John Wetteland .40 .12
❑ 88 Rondell White .40 .12
❑ 89 Rod Beck .20 .06
❑ 90 Barry Bonds 2.50 .75
❑ 91 John Burkett .20 .06
❑ 92 Royce Clayton .20 .06
❑ 93 Billy Swift .20 .06
❑ 94 Robby Thompson .20 .06
❑ 95 Matt Williams .40 .12
❑ 96 Carlos Baerga .20 .06
❑ 97 Albert Belle .40 .12
❑ 98 Kenny Lofton .40 .12
❑ 99 Dennis Martinez .40 .12
❑ 100 Eddie Murray 1.00 .30
❑ 101 Manny Ramirez .60 .18
❑ 102 Eric Anthony .20 .06
❑ 103 Chris Bosio .20 .06
❑ 104 Jay Buhner .40 .12
❑ 105 Ken Griffey Jr. 1.50 .45
❑ 106 Randy Johnson 1.00 .30
❑ 107 Edgar Martinez .60 .18
❑ 108 Chuck Carr .20 .06
❑ 109 Jeff Conine .40 .12
❑ 110 Carl Everett .40 .12
❑ 111 Chris Hammond .20 .06
❑ 112 Bryan Harvey .20 .06
❑ 113 Charles Johnson .40 .12
❑ 114 Gary Sheffield .40 .12
❑ 115 Bobby Bonilla .40 .12
❑ 116 Dwight Gooden .60 .18
❑ 117 Todd Hundley .20 .06
❑ 118 Bobby Jones .20 .06
❑ 119 Jeff Kent .40 .12
❑ 120 Bret Saberhagen .40 .12
❑ 121 Jeffrey Hammonds .20 .06
❑ 122 Chris Hoiles .20 .06
❑ 123 Ben McDonald .20 .06
❑ 124 Mike Mussina 1.00 .30
❑ 125 Rafael Palmeiro .60 .18
❑ 126 Cal Ripken Jr. 3.00 .90
❑ 127 Lee Smith .40 .12
❑ 128 Derek Bell .20 .06
❑ 129 Andy Benes .20 .06
❑ 130 Tony Gwynn 1.25 .35
❑ 131 Trevor Hoffman .40 .12
❑ 132 Phil Plantier .20 .06
❑ 133 Bip Roberts .20 .06
❑ 134 Darren Daulton .40 .12
❑ 135 Lenny Dykstra .40 .12
❑ 136 Dave Hollins .20 .06
❑ 137 Danny Jackson .20 .06
❑ 138 John Kruk .40 .12
❑ 139 Kevin Stocker .20 .06
❑ 140 Jay Bell .40 .12
❑ 141 Carlos Garcia .20 .06
❑ 142 Jeff King .20 .06
❑ 143 Orlando Merced .20 .06
❑ 144 Andy Van Slyke .40 .12
❑ 145 Rick White .20 .06
❑ 146 Jose Canseco 1.00 .30
❑ 147 Will Clark 1.00 .30
❑ 148 Juan Gonzalez 1.00 .30
❑ 149 Rick Helling .20 .06
❑ 150 Dean Palmer .40 .12
❑ 151 Ivan Rodriguez 1.00 .30
❑ 152 Roger Clemens 2.00 .60
❑ 153 Scott Cooper .20 .06
❑ 154 Andre Dawson .40 .12
❑ 155 Mike Greenwell .20 .06
❑ 156 Aaron Sele .20 .06
❑ 157 Mo Vaughn .40 .12
❑ 158 Bret Boone .40 .12
❑ 159 Barry Larkin 1.00 .30
❑ 160 Kevin Mitchell .20 .06

Card	Nm-Mt	Ex-Mt
161 Jose Rijo	.20	.06
162 Deion Sanders	.40	.12
163 Reggie Sanders	.40	.12
164 Dante Bichette	.40	.12
165 Ellis Burks	.40	.12
166 Andres Galarraga	.40	.12
167 Charlie Hayes	.20	.06
168 David Nied	.20	.06
169 Walt Weiss	.20	.06
170 Kevin Appier	.40	.12
171 David Cone	.40	.12
172 Jeff Granger	.20	.06
173 Felix Jose	.20	.06
174 Wally Joyner	.40	.12
175 Brian McRae	.20	.06
176 Cecil Fielder	.40	.12
177 Travis Fryman	.40	.12
178 Mike Henneman	.20	.06
179 Tony Phillips	.20	.06
180 Mickey Tettleton	.20	.06
181 Alan Trammell	.60	.18
182 Rick Aguilera	.20	.06
183 Rich Becker	.20	.06
184 Scott Erickson	.20	.06
185 Chuck Knoblauch	.40	.12
186 Kirby Puckett	1.00	.30
187 Dave Winfield	.60	.18
188 Wilson Alvarez	.20	.06
189 Jason Bere	.20	.06
190 Alex Fernandez	.20	.06
191 Julio Franco	.40	.12
192 Jack McDowell	.20	.06
193 Frank Thomas	1.00	.30
194 Robin Ventura	.40	.12
195 Jim Abbott	1.00	.30
196 Wade Boggs	.60	.18
197 Jimmy Key	.40	.12
198 Don Mattingly	2.50	.75
199 Paul O'Neill	.60	.18
200 Danny Tartabull	.20	.06
P24 Ken Griffey Jr. Promo	2.00	.60

2000 SP Authentic

	Nm-Mt	Ex-Mt
COMP.BASIC w/o SP's (90)	25.00	7.50
COMP.UPDATE w/o SP'S (30)	10.00	3.00
COMMON CARD (1-90)	.40	.12
COMMON SUP (91-105)	3.00	.90
COMMON FW (106-135)	5.00	1.50
COMMON FW (136-164)	6.00	1.80
COMMON (166-195)	.60	.18

Card	Nm-Mt	Ex-Mt
1 Mo Vaughn	.40	.12
2 Troy Glaus	.60	.18
3 Jason Giambi	1.00	.30
4 Tim Hudson	.60	.18
5 Eric Chavez	.40	.12
6 Shannon Stewart	.40	.12
7 Raul Mondesi	.40	.12
8 Carlos Delgado	.40	.12
9 Jose Canseco	1.00	.30
10 Vinny Castilla	.40	.12
11 Greg Vaughn	.40	.12
12 Manny Ramirez	.40	.12
13 Roberto Alomar	1.00	.30
14 Jim Thome	1.00	.30
15 Richie Sexson	.40	.12
16 Alex Rodriguez	2.00	.60
17 Freddy Garcia	.40	.12
18 John Olerud	.40	.12
19 Albert Belle	.40	.12
20 Cal Ripken	3.00	.90
21 Mike Mussina	1.00	.30
22 Ivan Rodriguez	1.00	.30
23 Gabe Kapler	.40	.12
24 Rafael Palmeiro	.60	.18
25 Nomar Garciaparra	2.00	.60
26 Pedro Martinez	1.00	.30
27 Carl Everett	.40	.12
28 Carlos Beltran	.40	.12
29 Jermaine Dye	.40	.12
30 Juan Gonzalez	1.00	.30
31 Dean Palmer	.40	.12
32 Corey Koskie	.40	.12
33 Jacque Jones	.40	.12
34 Frank Thomas	1.00	.30
35 Paul Konerko	.40	.12
36 Magglio Ordonez	.40	.12
37 Bernie Williams	.60	.18
38 Derek Jeter	2.50	.75
39 Roger Clemens	2.00	.60
40 Mariano Rivera	.60	.18
41 Jeff Bagwell	.60	.18
42 Craig Biggio	.60	.18
43 Jose Lima	.40	.12
44 Moises Alou	.40	.12
45 Chipper Jones	1.00	.30
46 Greg Maddux	2.00	.60
47 Andruw Jones	.60	.18
48 Andres Galarraga	.40	.12
49 Jeromy Burnitz	.40	.12
50 Geoff Jenkins	.40	.12
51 Mark McGwire	2.50	.75
52 Fernando Tatis	.40	.12
53 J.D. Drew	.40	.12
54 Sammy Sosa	1.50	.45
55 Kerry Wood	1.00	.30
56 Mark Grace	1.00	.30
57 Matt Williams	.40	.12
58 Randy Johnson	1.00	.30
59 Erubiel Durazo	.40	.12
60 Gary Sheffield	.40	.12
61 Kevin Brown	.60	.18
62 Shawn Green	.40	.12
63 Vladimir Guerrero	1.00	.30
64 Michael Barrett	.40	.12
65 Barry Bonds	2.50	.75
66 Jeff Kent	.40	.12
67 Russ Ortiz	.40	.12
68 Preston Wilson	.40	.12
69 Mike Lowell	.40	.12
70 Mike Piazza	1.50	.45
71 Mike Hampton	.40	.12
72 Robin Ventura	.40	.12
73 Edgardo Alfonzo	.40	.12
74 Tony Gwynn	1.25	.35
75 Ryan Klesko	.40	.12
76 Trevor Hoffman	.40	.12
77 Scott Rolen	.60	.18
78 Bob Abreu	.40	.12
79 Mike Lieberthal	.40	.12
80 Curt Schilling	.60	.18
81 Jason Kendall	.40	.12
82 Brian Giles	.40	.12
83 Kris Benson	.40	.12
84 Ken Griffey Jr.	1.50	.45
85 Sean Casey	.40	.12
86 Pokey Reese	.40	.12
87 Barry Larkin	1.00	.30
88 Larry Walker	.60	.18
89 Todd Helton	.60	.18
90 Jeff Cirillo	.40	.12
91 Ken Griffey Jr. SUP	8.00	2.40
92 Mark McGwire SUP	12.00	3.60
93 Chipper Jones SUP	5.00	1.50
94 Derek Jeter SUP	12.00	3.60
95 Shawn Green SUP	3.00	.90
96 Pedro Martinez SUP	5.00	1.50
97 Mike Piazza SUP	8.00	2.40
98 Alex Rodriguez SUP	10.00	3.00
99 Jeff Bagwell SUP	3.00	.90
100 Cal Ripken SUP	15.00	4.50
101 Sammy Sosa SUP	8.00	2.40
102 Barry Bonds SUP	12.00	3.60
103 Jose Canseco SUP	5.00	1.50
104 N.Garciaparra SUP	10.00	3.00
105 Ivan Rodriguez SUP	5.00	1.50
106 Rick Ankiel FW	5.00	1.50
107 Pat Burrell FW	3.00	.90
108 Vernon Wells FW	5.00	1.50
109 Nick Johnson FW	5.00	1.50
110 Kip Wells FW	5.00	1.50
111 Matt Riley FW	5.00	1.50
112 Alfonso Soriano FW	15.00	4.50
113 Josh Beckett FW	20.00	6.00
114 Danys Baez FW RC	8.00	2.40
115 Travis Dawkins FW	5.00	1.50
116 Eric Gagne FW	10.00	3.00
117 Mike Lamb FW RC	5.00	1.50
118 Eric Munson FW	5.00	1.50
119 W.Rodriguez FW RC	5.00	1.50
120 K.Sasaki FW RC	10.00	3.00
121 Chad Hutchinson FW	5.00	1.50
122 Peter Bergeron FW	5.00	1.50
123 W.Serrano FW RC	5.00	1.50
124 Tony Armas Jr. FW	5.00	1.50
125 Ramon Ortiz FW	5.00	1.50
126 Adam Kennedy FW	5.00	1.50
127 Joe Crede FW	5.00	1.50
128 Roosevelt Brown FW	5.00	1.50
129 Mark Mulder FW	8.00	2.40
130 Brad Penny FW	5.00	1.50
131 Terrence Long FW	5.00	1.50
132 Ruben Mateo FW	5.00	1.50
133 Wily Mo Pena FW	5.00	1.50
134 Rafael Furcal FW	5.00	1.50
135 M.Encarnacion FW	5.00	1.50
136 Barry Zito FW RC	50.00	15.00
137 Aaron McNeal FW RC	6.00	1.80
138 Timo Perez FW RC	6.00	1.80
139 Sun Woo Kim FW RC	6.00	1.80
140 Xavier Nady FW RC	10.00	3.00
141 M.Wheatland FW RC	6.00	1.80
142 B.Abernathy FW RC	6.00	1.80
143 Cory Vance FW RC	6.00	1.80
144 Scott Heard FW RC	6.00	1.80
145 Mike Meyers FW RC	6.00	1.80
146 Ben Diggins FW RC	6.00	1.80
147 Luis Matos FW RC	10.00	3.00
148 Ben Sheets FW RC	10.00	3.00
149 K.Ainsworth FW RC	10.00	3.00
150 Dave Krynzel FW RC	6.00	1.80
151 Alex Cabrera FW RC	6.00	1.80
152 Mike Tonis FW RC	10.00	3.00
153 Dane Sardinha FW RC	6.00	1.80
154 Keith Ginter FW RC	6.00	1.80
155 D.Espinosa FW RC	6.00	1.80
156 Joe Torres FW RC	6.00	1.80
157 Daylan Holt FW RC	6.00	1.80
158 Koyie Hill FW RC	10.00	3.00
159 B.Wilkerson FW RC	10.00	3.00
160 Juan Pierre FW RC	10.00	3.00
161 Matt Ginter FW RC	6.00	1.80
162 Dane Artman FW RC	6.00	1.80
163 Jon Rauch FW RC	6.00	1.80
164 Sean Burnett FW RC	10.00	3.00
165 Does Not Exist		
166 Darin Erstad	.60	.18
167 Ben Grieve	.60	.18
168 David Wells	.60	.18
169 Fred McGriff	1.00	.30
170 Bob Wickman	.60	.18
171 Al Martin	.60	.18
172 Melvin Mora	.60	.18
173 Ricky Ledee	.60	.18
174 Dante Bichette	.60	.18
175 Mike Sweeney	.60	.18
176 Bobby Higginson	.60	.18
177 Matt Lawton	.60	.18
178 Charles Johnson	.60	.18
179 David Justice	.60	.18
180 Richard Hidalgo	.60	.18
181 B.J. Surhoff	.60	.18
182 Richie Sexson	.60	.18
183 Jim Edmonds	.60	.18
184 Rondell White	.60	.18
185 Curt Schilling	1.00	.30
186 Tom Goodwin	.60	.18
187 Jose Vidro	.60	.18

- ❑ 188 Ellis Burks .60 .18
- ❑ 189 Henry Rodriguez .60 .18
- ❑ 190 Mike Bordick .60 .18
- ❑ 191 Eric Owens .60 .18
- ❑ 192 Travis Lee .60 .18
- ❑ 193 Kevin Young .60 .18
- ❑ 194 Aaron Boone .60 .18
- ❑ 195 Todd Hollandsworth .60 .18
- ❑ SPA K.Griffey Jr. Sample 2.00 .60

2001 SP Authentic

	Nm-Mt	Ex-Mt
COMP.BASIC w/o SP's (90)	25.00	7.50
COMP.UPDATE w/o SP's (30)	10.00	3.00
COMMON CARD (1-90)	.40	.12
COMMON FW (91-135)	8.00	2.40
COMMON SS (136-180)	5.00	1.50
COMMON (181-210)	.60	.18
COMMON (211-240)	6.00	1.80

- ❑ 1 Troy Glaus .60 .18
- ❑ 2 Darin Erstad .40 .12
- ❑ 3 Jason Giambi 1.00 .30
- ❑ 4 Tim Hudson .40 .12
- ❑ 5 Eric Chavez .40 .12
- ❑ 6 Miguel Tejada .40 .12
- ❑ 7 Jose Ortiz .40 .12
- ❑ 8 Carlos Delgado .40 .12
- ❑ 9 Tony Batista .40 .12
- ❑ 10 Raul Mondesi .40 .12
- ❑ 11 Aubrey Huff .40 .12
- ❑ 12 Greg Vaughn .40 .12
- ❑ 13 Roberto Alomar 1.00 .30
- ❑ 14 Juan Gonzalez 1.00 .30
- ❑ 15 Jim Thome 1.00 .30
- ❑ 16 Omar Vizquel .40 .12
- ❑ 17 Edgar Martinez .60 .18
- ❑ 18 Freddy Garcia .40 .12
- ❑ 19 Cal Ripken 3.00 .90
- ❑ 20 Ivan Rodriguez 1.00 .30
- ❑ 21 Rafael Palmeiro .60 .18
- ❑ 22 Alex Rodriguez 2.00 .60
- ❑ 23 Manny Ramirez .40 .12
- ❑ 24 Pedro Martinez 1.00 .30
- ❑ 25 Nomar Garciaparra 2.00 .60
- ❑ 26 Mike Sweeney .40 .12
- ❑ 27 Jermaine Dye .40 .12
- ❑ 28 Bobby Higginson .40 .12
- ❑ 29 Dean Palmer .40 .12
- ❑ 30 Matt Lawton .40 .12
- ❑ 31 Eric Milton .40 .12
- ❑ 32 Frank Thomas 1.00 .30
- ❑ 33 Magglio Ordonez .40 .12
- ❑ 34 David Wells .40 .12
- ❑ 35 Paul Konerko .40 .12
- ❑ 36 Derek Jeter 2.50 .75
- ❑ 37 Bernie Williams .60 .18
- ❑ 38 Roger Clemens 2.00 .60
- ❑ 39 Mike Mussina 1.00 .30
- ❑ 40 Jorge Posada .60 .18
- ❑ 41 Jeff Bagwell .60 .18
- ❑ 42 Richard Hidalgo .40 .12
- ❑ 43 Craig Biggio .60 .18
- ❑ 44 Greg Maddux 2.00 .60
- ❑ 45 Chipper Jones 1.00 .30
- ❑ 46 Andruw Jones .60 .18
- ❑ 47 Rafael Furcal .40 .12
- ❑ 48 Tom Glavine 1.00 .30
- ❑ 49 Jeromy Burnitz .40 .12
- ❑ 50 Jeffrey Hammonds .40 .12
- ❑ 51 Mark McGwire 2.50 .75
- ❑ 52 Jim Edmonds .40 .12
- ❑ 53 Rick Ankiel .40 .12
- ❑ 54 J.D. Drew .40 .12
- ❑ 55 Sammy Sosa 1.50 .45
- ❑ 56 Corey Patterson .40 .12
- ❑ 57 Kerry Wood 1.00 .30
- ❑ 58 Randy Johnson 1.00 .30
- ❑ 59 Luis Gonzalez .40 .12
- ❑ 60 Curt Schilling .60 .18
- ❑ 61 Gary Sheffield .40 .12
- ❑ 62 Shawn Green .40 .12
- ❑ 63 Kevin Brown .40 .12
- ❑ 64 Vladimir Guerrero 1.00 .30
- ❑ 65 Jose Vidro .40 .12
- ❑ 66 Barry Bonds 2.50 .75
- ❑ 67 Jeff Kent .40 .12
- ❑ 68 Livan Hernandez .40 .12
- ❑ 69 Preston Wilson .40 .12
- ❑ 70 Charles Johnson .40 .12
- ❑ 71 Ryan Dempster .40 .12
- ❑ 72 Mike Piazza 1.50 .45
- ❑ 73 Al Leiter .40 .12
- ❑ 74 Edgardo Alfonzo .40 .12
- ❑ 75 Robin Ventura .40 .12
- ❑ 76 Tony Gwynn 1.25 .35
- ❑ 77 Phil Nevin .40 .12
- ❑ 78 Trevor Hoffman .40 .12
- ❑ 79 Scott Rolen .60 .18
- ❑ 80 Pat Burrell .40 .12
- ❑ 81 Bob Abreu .40 .12
- ❑ 82 Jason Kendall .40 .12
- ❑ 83 Brian Giles .40 .12
- ❑ 84 Kris Benson .40 .12
- ❑ 85 Ken Griffey Jr. 1.50 .45
- ❑ 86 Barry Larkin 1.00 .30
- ❑ 87 Sean Casey .40 .12
- ❑ 88 Todd Helton .60 .18
- ❑ 89 Mike Hampton .40 .12
- ❑ 90 Larry Walker .60 .18
- ❑ 91 Ichiro Suzuki FW RC 100.00 30.00
- ❑ 92 Wilson Betemit FW RC 8.00 2.40
- ❑ 93 A. Hernandez FW RC 8.00 2.40
- ❑ 94 Juan Uribe FW RC 8.00 2.40
- ❑ 95 Travis Hafner FW RC 12.00 3.60
- ❑ 96 M. Ensberg FW RC 15.00 4.50
- ❑ 97 Sean Douglass FW RC 8.00 2.40
- ❑ 98 Juan Diaz FW RC 8.00 2.40
- ❑ 99 Erick Almonte FW RC 8.00 2.40
- ❑ 100 Ryan Freel FW RC 8.00 2.40
- ❑ 101 E. Guzman FW RC 8.00 2.40
- ❑ 102 C. Parker FW RC 8.00 2.40
- ❑ 103 Josh Fogg FW RC 8.00 2.40
- ❑ 104 Bert Snow FW RC 8.00 2.40
- ❑ 105 H. Ramirez FW RC 12.00 3.60
- ❑ 106 R. Rodriguez FW RC 8.00 2.40
- ❑ 107 Tyler Walker FW RC 8.00 2.40
- ❑ 108 Jose Mieses FW RC 8.00 2.40
- ❑ 109 Billy Sylvester FW RC 8.00 2.40
- ❑ 110 Martin Vargas FW RC 8.00 2.40
- ❑ 111 Andres Torres FW RC 8.00 2.40
- ❑ 112 Greg Miller FW RC 8.00 2.40
- ❑ 113 Alexis Gomez FW RC 8.00 2.40
- ❑ 114 Grant Balfour FW RC 8.00 2.40
- ❑ 115 Henry Mateo FW RC 8.00 2.40
- ❑ 116 Esix Snead FW RC 8.00 2.40
- ❑ 117 J. Melian FW RC 8.00 2.40
- ❑ 118 Nate Teut FW RC 8.00 2.40
- ❑ 119 T. Shinjo FW RC 15.00 4.50
- ❑ 120 C. Valderrama FW RC 8.00 2.40
- ❑ 121 J. Estrada FW RC 10.00 3.00
- ❑ 122 J. Michaels FW RC 8.00 2.40
- ❑ 123 William Ortega FW RC 8.00 2.40
- ❑ 124 Jason Smith FW RC 8.00 2.40
- ❑ 125 B. Lawrence FW RC 8.00 2.40
- ❑ 126 Albert Pujols FW RC 200.00 60.00
- ❑ 127 Wilkin Ruan FW RC 8.00 2.40
- ❑ 128 Josh Towers FW RC 8.00 2.40
- ❑ 129 Kris Keller FW RC 8.00 2.40
- ❑ 130 Nick Maness FW RC 8.00 2.40
- ❑ 131 Jack Wilson FW RC 8.00 2.40
- ❑ 132 B. Duckworth FW RC 8.00 2.40
- ❑ 133 Mike Penney FW RC 8.00 2.40
- ❑ 134 Jay Gibbons FW RC 15.00 4.50
- ❑ 135 Cesar Crespo FW RC 8.00 2.40
- ❑ 136 Ken Griffey Jr. SS 10.00 3.00
- ❑ 137 Mark McGwire SS 15.00 4.50
- ❑ 138 Derek Jeter SS 15.00 4.50
- ❑ 139 Alex Rodriguez SS 12.00 3.60
- ❑ 140 Sammy Sosa SS 10.00 3.00
- ❑ 141 Carlos Delgado SS 5.00 1.50
- ❑ 142 Cal Ripken SS 20.00 6.00
- ❑ 143 Pedro Martinez SS 6.00 1.80
- ❑ 144 Frank Thomas SS 6.00 1.80
- ❑ 145 Juan Gonzalez SS 6.00 1.80
- ❑ 146 Troy Glaus SS 5.00 1.50
- ❑ 147 Jason Giambi SS 6.00 1.80
- ❑ 148 Ivan Rodriguez SS 6.00 1.80
- ❑ 149 Chipper Jones SS 6.00 1.80
- ❑ 150 Vladimir Guerrero SS 6.00 1.80
- ❑ 151 Mike Piazza SS 10.00 3.00
- ❑ 152 Jeff Bagwell SS 5.00 1.50
- ❑ 153 Randy Johnson SS 6.00 1.80
- ❑ 154 Todd Helton SS 5.00 1.50
- ❑ 155 Gary Sheffield SS 5.00 1.50
- ❑ 156 Tony Gwynn SS 8.00 2.40
- ❑ 157 Barry Bonds SS 15.00 4.50
- ❑ 158 N. Garciaparra SS 12.00 3.60
- ❑ 159 Bernie Williams SS 5.00 1.50
- ❑ 160 Greg Vaughn SS 5.00 1.50
- ❑ 161 David Wells SS 5.00 1.50
- ❑ 162 Roberto Alomar SS 6.00 1.80
- ❑ 163 Jermaine Dye SS 5.00 1.50
- ❑ 164 Rafael Palmeiro SS 5.00 1.50
- ❑ 165 Andruw Jones SS 5.00 1.50
- ❑ 166 Preston Wilson SS 5.00 1.50
- ❑ 167 Edgardo Alfonzo SS 5.00 1.50
- ❑ 168 Pat Burrell SS 5.00 1.50
- ❑ 169 Jim Edmonds SS 5.00 1.50
- ❑ 170 Mike Hampton SS 5.00 1.50
- ❑ 171 Jeff Kent SS 5.00 1.50
- ❑ 172 Kevin Brown SS 5.00 1.50
- ❑ 173 Manny Ramirez SS 5.00 1.50
- ❑ 174 Magglio Ordonez SS 5.00 1.50
- ❑ 175 Roger Clemens SS 12.00 3.60
- ❑ 176 Jim Thome SS 6.00 1.80
- ❑ 177 Barry Zito SS 6.00 1.80
- ❑ 178 Brian Giles SS 5.00 1.50
- ❑ 179 Rick Ankiel SS 5.00 1.50
- ❑ 180 Corey Patterson SS 5.00 1.50
- ❑ 181 Garret Anderson .60 .18
- ❑ 182 Jermaine Dye .60 .18
- ❑ 183 Shannon Stewart .60 .18
- ❑ 184 Ben Grieve .60 .18
- ❑ 185 Ellis Burks .60 .18
- ❑ 186 John Olerud .60 .18
- ❑ 187 Tony Batista .60 .18
- ❑ 188 Ruben Sierra .60 .18
- ❑ 189 Carl Everett .60 .18
- ❑ 190 Neifi Perez .60 .18
- ❑ 191 Tony Clark .60 .18
- ❑ 192 Doug Mientkiewicz .60 .18
- ❑ 193 Carlos Lee .60 .18
- ❑ 194 Jorge Posada 1.00 .30
- ❑ 195 Lance Berkman 5.00 1.50
- ❑ 196 Ken Caminiti .60 .18
- ❑ 197 Ben Sheets .60 .18
- ❑ 198 Matt Morris .60 .18
- ❑ 199 Fred McGriff 1.00 .30
- ❑ 200 Mark Grace 1.50 .45
- ❑ 201 Paul LoDuca .60 .18
- ❑ 202 Tony Armas Jr. .60 .18
- ❑ 203 Andres Galarraga .60 .18
- ❑ 204 Cliff Floyd .60 .18
- ❑ 205 Matt Lawton .60 .18
- ❑ 206 Ryan Klesko .60 .18
- ❑ 207 Jimmy Rollins .60 .18
- ❑ 208 Aramis Ramirez .60 .18
- ❑ 209 Aaron Boone .60 .18
- ❑ 210 Jose Ortiz .60 .18
- ❑ 211 Mark Prior FW RC 180.00 55.00
- ❑ 212 Mark Teixeira FW RC 60.00 18.00
- ❑ 213 Bud Smith FW RC 6.00 1.80
- ❑ 214 W.Caceres FW RC 6.00 1.80
- ❑ 215 Dave Williams FW RC 6.00 1.80
- ❑ 216 Delvin James FW RC 6.00 1.80
- ❑ 217 Endy Chavez FW RC 6.00 1.80
- ❑ 218 Doug Nickle FW RC 6.00 1.80
- ❑ 219 Bret Prinz FW RC 6.00 1.80

Card	Nm-Mt	Ex-Mt
❑ 220 Troy Mattes FW RC	6.00	1.80
❑ 221 D.Sanchez FW RC	6.00	1.80
❑ 222 D.Brazelton FW RC	6.00	1.80
❑ 223 Brian Bowles FW RC	6.00	1.80
❑ 224 D.Mendez FW RC	6.00	1.80
❑ 225 Jorge Julio FW RC	6.00	1.80
❑ 226 Matt White FW RC	6.00	1.80
❑ 227 Casey Fossum FW RC	6.00	1.80
❑ 228 Mike Rivera FW RC	6.00	1.80
❑ 229 Joe Kennedy FW RC	6.00	1.80
❑ 230 Kyle Lohse FW RC	10.00	3.00
❑ 231 Juan Cruz FW RC	6.00	1.80
❑ 232 Jeremy Affeldt FW RC	6.00	1.80
❑ 233 Brandon Lyon FW RC	6.00	1.80
❑ 234 Brian Roberts FW RC	6.00	1.80
❑ 235 Willie Harris FW RC	6.00	1.80
❑ 236 Pedro Santana FW RC	6.00	1.80
❑ 237 Rafael Soriano FW RC	12.00	3.60
❑ 238 Steve Green FW RC	6.00	1.80
❑ 239 Junior Spivey FW RC	10.00	3.00
❑ 240 R.Mackowiak FW RC	6.00	1.80
❑ NNO K.Griffey Jr. Promo	2.00	.60

2002 SP Authentic

	Nm-Mt	Ex-Mt
COMP.LOW w/o SP's (90)	15.00	4.50
COMP.UPDATE w/o SP's (30)	10.00	3.00
COMMON CARD (1-90)	.40	.12
COMMON (91-135/201-230)	8.00	2.40
COMMON CARD (136-170)	15.00	4.50
COMMON CARD (171-200)	.60	.18

Card	Nm-Mt	Ex-Mt
❑ 1 Troy Glaus	.60	.18
❑ 2 Darin Erstad	.40	.12
❑ 3 Barry Zito	1.00	.30
❑ 4 Eric Chavez	.40	.12
❑ 5 Tim Hudson	.40	.12
❑ 6 Miguel Tejada	.40	.12
❑ 7 Carlos Delgado	.40	.12
❑ 8 Shannon Stewart	.40	.12
❑ 9 Ben Grieve	.40	.12
❑ 10 Jim Thome	1.00	.30
❑ 11 C.C. Sabathia	.40	.12
❑ 12 Ichiro Suzuki	2.00	.60
❑ 13 Freddy Garcia	.40	.12
❑ 14 Edgar Martinez	.60	.18
❑ 15 Bret Boone	.40	.12
❑ 16 Jeff Conine	.40	.12
❑ 17 Alex Rodriguez	2.00	.60
❑ 18 Juan Gonzalez	1.00	.30
❑ 19 Ivan Rodriguez	1.00	.30
❑ 20 Rafael Palmeiro	.60	.18
❑ 21 Hank Blalock	1.00	.30
❑ 22 Pedro Martinez	1.00	.30
❑ 23 Manny Ramirez	.40	.12
❑ 24 Nomar Garciaparra	2.00	.60
❑ 25 Carlos Beltran	.40	.12
❑ 26 Mike Sweeney	.40	.12
❑ 27 Randall Simon	.40	.12
❑ 28 Dmitri Young	.40	.12
❑ 29 Bobby Higginson	.40	.12
❑ 30 Corey Koskie	.40	.12
❑ 31 Eric Milton	.40	.12
❑ 32 Torii Hunter	.40	.12
❑ 33 Joe Mays	.40	.12
❑ 34 Frank Thomas	1.00	.30
❑ 35 Mark Buehrle	.40	.12
❑ 36 Magglio Ordonez	.40	.12
❑ 37 Kenny Lofton	.40	.12
❑ 38 Roger Clemens	2.00	.60
❑ 39 Derek Jeter	2.50	.75
❑ 40 Jason Giambi	1.00	.30
❑ 41 Bernie Williams	.60	.18
❑ 42 Alfonso Soriano	1.00	.30
❑ 43 Lance Berkman	.40	.12
❑ 44 Roy Oswalt	.40	.12
❑ 45 Jeff Bagwell	.60	.18
❑ 46 Craig Biggio	.60	.18
❑ 47 Chipper Jones	1.00	.30
❑ 48 Greg Maddux	2.00	.60
❑ 49 Gary Sheffield	.40	.12
❑ 50 Andruw Jones	.60	.18
❑ 51 Ben Sheets	.40	.12
❑ 52 Richie Sexson	.40	.12
❑ 53 Albert Pujols	2.00	.60
❑ 54 Matt Morris	.40	.12
❑ 55 J.D. Drew	.40	.12
❑ 56 Sammy Sosa	1.50	.45
❑ 57 Kerry Wood	1.00	.30
❑ 58 Corey Patterson	.40	.12
❑ 59 Mark Prior	2.00	.60
❑ 60 Randy Johnson	1.00	.30
❑ 61 Luis Gonzalez	.40	.12
❑ 62 Curt Schilling	.60	.18
❑ 63 Shawn Green	.40	.12
❑ 64 Kevin Brown	.40	.12
❑ 65 Hideo Nomo	1.00	.30
❑ 66 Vladimir Guerrero	1.00	.30
❑ 67 Jose Vidro	.40	.12
❑ 68 Barry Bonds	2.50	.75
❑ 69 Jeff Kent	.40	.12
❑ 70 Rich Aurilia	.40	.12
❑ 71 Preston Wilson	.40	.12
❑ 72 Josh Beckett	.60	.18
❑ 73 Mike Lowell	.40	.12
❑ 74 Roberto Alomar	1.00	.30
❑ 75 Mo Vaughn	.40	.12
❑ 76 Jeromy Burnitz	.40	.12
❑ 77 Mike Piazza	1.50	.45
❑ 78 Sean Burroughs	.40	.12
❑ 79 Phil Nevin	.40	.12
❑ 80 Bobby Abreu	.40	.12
❑ 81 Pat Burrell	.40	.12
❑ 82 Scott Rolen	.60	.18
❑ 83 Jason Kendall	.40	.12
❑ 84 Brian Giles	.40	.12
❑ 85 Ken Griffey Jr.	1.50	.45
❑ 86 Adam Dunn	.60	.18
❑ 87 Sean Casey	.40	.12
❑ 88 Todd Helton	.60	.18
❑ 89 Larry Walker	.60	.18
❑ 90 Mike Hampton	.40	.12
❑ 91 Brandon Puffer FW	8.00	2.40
❑ 92 Tom Shearn FW RC	8.00	2.40
❑ 93 Chris Baker FW RC	8.00	2.40
❑ 94 Gustavo Chacin FW RC	8.00	2.40
❑ 95 Joe Orloski FW RC	8.00	2.40
❑ 96 Mike Smith FW RC	8.00	2.40
❑ 97 John Ennis FW RC	8.00	2.40
❑ 98 John Foster FW RC	8.00	2.40
❑ 99 Kevin Gryboski FW RC	8.00	2.40
❑ 100 Brian Mallette FW RC	8.00	2.40
❑ 101 Takahito Nomura FW RC	8.00	2.40
❑ 102 So Taguchi FW RC	10.00	3.00
❑ 103 Jeremy Lambert FW RC	8.00	2.40
❑ 104 Jason Simontacchi FW RC	10.00	3.00
❑ 105 Jorge Sosa FW RC	8.00	2.40
❑ 106 Brandon Backe FW RC	8.00	2.40
❑ 107 P.J. Bevis FW RC	8.00	2.40
❑ 108 Jeremy Ward FW RC	8.00	2.40
❑ 109 Doug Devore FW RC	8.00	2.40
❑ 110 Ron Chiavacci FW	8.00	2.40
❑ 111 Ron Calloway FW RC	8.00	2.40
❑ 112 Nelson Castro FW RC	8.00	2.40
❑ 113 Deivis Santos FW	8.00	2.40
❑ 114 Earl Snyder FW RC	8.00	2.40
❑ 115 Julio Mateo FW RC	8.00	2.40
❑ 116 J.J. Putz FW RC	8.00	2.40
❑ 117 Allan Simpson FW RC	8.00	2.40
❑ 118 Satoru Komiyama FW RC	8.00	2.40
❑ 119 Adam Walker FW RC	8.00	2.40
❑ 120 Oliver Perez FW RC	10.00	3.00
❑ 121 Cliff Bartosh FW RC	8.00	2.40
❑ 122 Todd Donovan FW RC	8.00	2.40
❑ 123 Elio Serrano FW RC	8.00	2.40
❑ 124 Pete Zamora FW RC	8.00	2.40
❑ 125 Mike Gonzalez FW RC	8.00	2.40
❑ 126 Travis Hughes FW RC	8.00	2.40
❑ 127 Jorge De La Rosa FW RC	8.00	2.40
❑ 128 Anastacio Martinez FW RC	8.00	2.40
❑ 129 Colin Young FW RC	8.00	2.40
❑ 130 Nate Field FW RC	8.00	2.40
❑ 131 Tim Kalita FW RC	8.00	2.40
❑ 132 Julius Matos FW RC	8.00	2.40
❑ 133 Terry Pearson FW RC	8.00	2.40
❑ 134 Kyle Kane FW RC	8.00	2.40
❑ 135 Mitch Wylie FW RC	8.00	2.40
❑ 136 Rodrigo Rosario AU RC	15.00	4.50
❑ 137 Franklyn German AU RC	15.00	4.50
❑ 138 Reed Johnson AU RC	20.00	6.00
❑ 139 Luis Martinez AU RC	20.00	6.00
❑ 140 Michael Crudale AU RC	15.00	4.50
❑ 141 Francis Beltran AU RC	15.00	4.50
❑ 142 Steve Kent AU RC	15.00	4.50
❑ 143 Felix Escalona AU RC	15.00	4.50
❑ 144 Jose Valverde AU RC	20.00	6.00
❑ 145 Victor Alvarez AU RC	15.00	4.50
❑ 146 Kazuhisa Ishii AU/249 RC	50.00	15.00
❑ 147 Jorge Nunez AU RC	15.00	4.50
❑ 148 Eric Good AU RC	15.00	4.50
❑ 149 Luis Ugueto AU RC	15.00	4.50
❑ 150 Matt Thornton AU RC	15.00	4.50
❑ 151 Wilson Valdez AU RC	15.00	4.50
❑ 152 Han Izquierdo AU/249 RC	40.00	12.00
❑ 153 Jaime Cerda AU RC	15.00	4.50
❑ 154 Mark Corey AU RC	15.00	4.50
❑ 155 Tyler Yates AU RC	15.00	4.50
❑ 156 Steve Bechler AU RC	15.00	4.50
❑ 157 Ben Howard AU/249 RC	40.00	12.00
❑ 158 Anderson Machado AU RC	20.00	6.00
❑ 159 Jorge Padilla AU RC	20.00	6.00
❑ 160 Eric Junge AU RC	15.00	4.50
❑ 161 Adrian Burnside AU RC	15.00	4.50
❑ 162 Josh Hancock AU RC	15.00	4.50
❑ 163 Chris Booker AU RC	15.00	4.50
❑ 164 Cam Esslinger AU RC	15.00	4.50
❑ 165 Rene Reyes AU RC	15.00	4.50
❑ 166 Aaron Cook AU RC	20.00	6.00
❑ 167 Juan Brito AU RC	15.00	4.50
❑ 168 Miguel Ascencio AU RC	15.00	4.50
❑ 169 Kevin Frederick AU RC	15.00	4.50
❑ 170 Edwin Almonte AU RC	15.00	4.50
❑ 171 Erubiel Durazo	.60	.18
❑ 172 Junior Spivey	.60	.18
❑ 173 Geronimo Gil	.60	.18
❑ 174 Cliff Floyd	.60	.18
❑ 175 Brandon Larson	.60	.18
❑ 176 Aaron Boone	.60	.18
❑ 177 Shawn Estes	.60	.18
❑ 178 Austin Kearns	1.00	.30
❑ 179 Joe Borchard	.60	.18
❑ 180 Russell Branyan	.60	.18
❑ 181 Jay Payton	.60	.18
❑ 182 Andres Torres	.60	.18
❑ 183 Andy Van Hekken	.60	.18
❑ 184 Alex Sanchez	.60	.18
❑ 185 Endy Chavez	.60	.18
❑ 186 Bartolo Colon	.60	.18
❑ 187 Raul Mondesi	.60	.18
❑ 188 Robin Ventura	.60	.18
❑ 189 Mike Mussina	1.50	.45
❑ 190 Jorge Posada	1.00	.30
❑ 191 Ted Lilly	.60	.18
❑ 192 Ray Durham	.60	.18
❑ 193 Brett Myers	.60	.18
❑ 194 Marlon Byrd	.60	.18
❑ 195 Vicente Padilla	.60	.18
❑ 196 Josh Fogg	.60	.18
❑ 197 Kenny Lofton	.60	.18
❑ 198 Scott Rolen	1.00	.30
❑ 199 Jason Lane	.60	.18
❑ 200 Josh Phelps	.60	.18
❑ 201 Travis Driskill FW RC	8.00	2.40
❑ 202 Howie Clark FW RC	8.00	2.40
❑ 203 Mike Mahoney FW	8.00	2.40
❑ 204 Brian Tallet FW RC	10.00	3.00
❑ 205 Kirk Saarloos FW RC	10.00	3.00
❑ 206 Barry Wesson FW RC	8.00	2.40
❑ 207 Aaron Guiel FW RC	10.00	3.00

Card	Nm-Mt	Ex-Mt
❑ 208 Shawn Sedlacek FW RC	8.00	2.40
❑ 209 Jose Diaz FW RC	8.00	2.40
❑ 210 Jorge Nunez FW	8.00	2.40
❑ 211 Danny Mota FW RC	8.00	2.40
❑ 212 David Ross FW RC	8.00	2.40
❑ 213 Jayson Durocher FW RC	8.00	2.40
❑ 214 Shane Nance FW RC	8.00	2.40
❑ 215 Wil Nieves FW RC	8.00	2.40
❑ 216 Freddy Sanchez FW RC	10.00	3.00
❑ 217 Alex Pelaez FW RC	8.00	2.40
❑ 218 Jamey Carroll FW RC	8.00	2.40
❑ 219 J.J. Trujillo FW RC	8.00	2.40
❑ 220 Kevin Pickford FW RC	8.00	2.40
❑ 221 Clay Condrey FW RC	8.00	2.40
❑ 222 Chris Snelling FW RC	10.00	3.00
❑ 223 Cliff Lee FW RC	10.00	3.00
❑ 224 Jeremy Hill FW RC	8.00	2.40
❑ 225 Jose Rodriguez FW RC	8.00	2.40
❑ 226 Lance Carter FW RC	8.00	2.40
❑ 227 Ken Huckaby FW RC	8.00	2.40
❑ 228 Scott Wiggins FW RC	8.00	2.40
❑ 229 Corey Thurman FW RC	8.00	2.40
❑ 230 Kevin Cash FW RC	8.00	2.40
❑ RJ-D Joe DiMaggio Poster AU EX	200.00	60.00

2003 SP Authentic

	Nm-Mt	Ex-Mt
COMP.SET w/o SP's (90)	15.00	4.50
COMMON CARD (1-90)	.40	.12
COMMON CARD (91-123)	3.00	.90
COMMON CARD (124-150)	3.00	.90
COMMON CARD (151-180)	8.00	2.40
COMMON CARD (181-189)	15.00	4.50
91-189 RANDOM INSERTS IN PACKS		
❑ 1 Darin Erstad	.40	.12
❑ 2 Garret Anderson	.40	.12
❑ 3 Troy Glaus	.60	.18
❑ 4 Eric Chavez	.40	.12
❑ 5 Barry Zito	1.00	.30
❑ 6 Miguel Tejada	.40	.12
❑ 7 Eric Hinske	.40	.12
❑ 8 Carlos Delgado	.40	.12
❑ 9 Josh Phelps	.40	.12
❑ 10 Ben Grieve	.40	.12
❑ 11 Carl Crawford	.40	.12
❑ 12 Omar Vizquel	.40	.12
❑ 13 Matt Lawton	.40	.12
❑ 14 C.C. Sabathia	.40	.12
❑ 15 Ichiro Suzuki	2.00	.60
❑ 16 John Olerud	.40	.12
❑ 17 Freddy Garcia	.40	.12
❑ 18 Jay Gibbons	.40	.12
❑ 19 Tony Batista	.40	.12
❑ 20 Melvin Mora	.40	.12
❑ 21 Alex Rodriguez	2.00	.60
❑ 22 Rafael Palmeiro	.60	.18
❑ 23 Hank Blalock	.60	.18
❑ 24 Nomar Garciaparra	2.00	.60
❑ 25 Pedro Martinez	1.00	.30
❑ 26 Johnny Damon	.40	.12
❑ 27 Mike Sweeney	.40	.12
❑ 28 Carlos Febles	.40	.12
❑ 29 Carlos Beltran	.40	.12
❑ 30 Carlos Pena	.40	.12
❑ 31 Eric Munson	.40	.12
❑ 32 Bobby Higginson	.40	.12
❑ 33 Torii Hunter	.40	.12
❑ 34 Doug Mientkiewicz	.40	.12
❑ 35 Jacque Jones	.40	.12
❑ 36 Paul Konerko	.40	.12
❑ 37 Bartolo Colon	.40	.12
❑ 38 Magglio Ordonez	.40	.12
❑ 39 Derek Jeter	2.50	.75
❑ 40 Bernie Williams	.60	.18
❑ 41 Jason Giambi	1.00	.30
❑ 42 Alfonso Soriano	1.00	.30
❑ 43 Roger Clemens	2.00	.60
❑ 44 Jeff Bagwell	.60	.18
❑ 45 Jeff Kent	.40	.12
❑ 46 Lance Berkman	.40	.12
❑ 47 Chipper Jones	1.00	.30
❑ 48 Andruw Jones	.60	.18
❑ 49 Gary Sheffield	.40	.12
❑ 50 Ben Sheets	.40	.12
❑ 51 Richie Sexson	.40	.12
❑ 52 Geoff Jenkins	.40	.12
❑ 53 Jim Edmonds	.40	.12
❑ 54 Albert Pujols	2.00	.60
❑ 55 Scott Rolen	.60	.18
❑ 56 Sammy Sosa	1.50	.45
❑ 57 Kerry Wood	1.00	.30
❑ 58 Eric Karros	.40	.12
❑ 59 Luis Gonzalez	.40	.12
❑ 60 Randy Johnson	1.00	.30
❑ 61 Curt Schilling	.60	.18
❑ 62 Fred McGriff	.60	.18
❑ 63 Shawn Green	.40	.12
❑ 64 Paul Lo Duca	.40	.12
❑ 65 Vladimir Guerrero	1.00	.30
❑ 66 Jose Vidro	.40	.12
❑ 67 Barry Bonds	2.50	.75
❑ 68 Rich Aurilia	.40	.12
❑ 69 Edgardo Alfonzo	.40	.12
❑ 70 Ivan Rodriguez	1.00	.30
❑ 71 Mike Lowell	.40	.12
❑ 72 Derrek Lee	.40	.12
❑ 73 Tom Glavine	1.00	.30
❑ 74 Mike Piazza	1.50	.45
❑ 75 Roberto Alomar	1.00	.30
❑ 76 Ryan Klesko	.40	.12
❑ 77 Phil Nevin	.40	.12
❑ 78 Mark Kotsay	.40	.12
❑ 79 Jim Thome	1.00	.30
❑ 80 Pat Burrell	.40	.12
❑ 81 Bobby Abreu	.40	.12
❑ 82 Jason Kendall	.40	.12
❑ 83 Brian Giles	.40	.12
❑ 84 Aramis Ramirez	.40	.12
❑ 85 Austin Kearns	.60	.18
❑ 86 Ken Griffey Jr.	1.50	.45
❑ 87 Adam Dunn	.60	.18
❑ 88 Larry Walker	.60	.18
❑ 89 Todd Helton	.60	.18
❑ 90 Preston Wilson	.40	.12
❑ 91 Derek Jeter RA	8.00	2.40
❑ 92 Johnny Damon RA	3.00	.90
❑ 93 Chipper Jones RA	3.00	.90
❑ 94 Manny Ramirez RA	3.00	.90
❑ 95 Trot Nixon RA	3.00	.90
❑ 96 Alex Rodriguez RA	6.00	1.80
❑ 97 Chan Ho Park RA	3.00	.90
❑ 98 Brad Fullmer RA	3.00	.90
❑ 99 Billy Wagner RA	3.00	.90
❑ 100 Hideo Nomo RA	3.00	.90
❑ 101 Freddy Garcia RA	3.00	.90
❑ 102 Darin Erstad RA	3.00	.90
❑ 103 Jose Cruz Jr. RA	3.00	.90
❑ 104 Nomar Garciaparra RA	6.00	1.80
❑ 105 Magglio Ordonez RA	3.00	.90
❑ 106 Kerry Wood RA	3.00	.90
❑ 107 Troy Glaus RA	3.00	.90
❑ 108 J.D. Drew RA	3.00	.90
❑ 109 Alfonso Soriano RA	3.00	.90
❑ 110 Danys Baez RA	3.00	.90
❑ 111 Kazuhiro Sasaki RA	3.00	.90
❑ 112 Barry Zito RA	3.00	.90
❑ 113 Brent Abernathy RA	3.00	.90
❑ 114 Ben Diggins RA	3.00	.90
❑ 115 Ben Sheets RA	3.00	.90
❑ 116 Brad Wilkerson RA	3.00	.90
❑ 117 Juan Pierre RA	3.00	.90
❑ 118 Jon Rauch RA	3.00	.90
❑ 119 Ichiro Suzuki RA	6.00	1.80
❑ 120 Albert Pujols RA	6.00	1.80
❑ 121 Mark Prior RA	6.00	1.80
❑ 122 Mark Teixeira RA	3.00	.90
❑ 123 Kazuhisa Ishii RA	3.00	.90
❑ 124 Troy Glaus B93	3.00	.90
❑ 125 Randy Johnson B93	3.00	.90
❑ 126 Curt Schilling B93	3.00	.90
❑ 127 Chipper Jones B93	3.00	.90
❑ 128 Greg Maddux B93	6.00	1.80
❑ 129 Nomar Garciaparra B93	6.00	1.80
❑ 130 Pedro Martinez B93	3.00	.90
❑ 131 Sammy Sosa B93	5.00	1.50
❑ 132 Mark Prior B93	6.00	1.80
❑ 133 Ken Griffey Jr. B93	5.00	1.50
❑ 134 Adam Dunn B93	3.00	.90
❑ 135 Jeff Bagwell B93	3.00	.90
❑ 136 Vladimir Guerrero B93	3.00	.90
❑ 137 Mike Piazza B93	5.00	1.50
❑ 138 Tom Glavine B93	3.00	.90
❑ 139 Derek Jeter B93	8.00	2.40
❑ 140 Roger Clemens B93	6.00	1.80
❑ 141 Jason Giambi B93	3.00	.90
❑ 142 Alfonso Soriano B93	3.00	.90
❑ 143 Miguel Tejada B93	3.00	.90
❑ 144 Barry Zito B93	3.00	.90
❑ 145 Jim Thome B93	3.00	.90
❑ 146 Barry Bonds B93	8.00	2.40
❑ 147 Ichiro Suzuki B93	6.00	1.80
❑ 148 Albert Pujols B93	6.00	1.80
❑ 149 Alex Rodriguez B93	6.00	1.80
❑ 150 Carlos Delgado B93	3.00	.90
❑ 151 Rich Fischer FW RC	8.00	2.40
❑ 152 Brandon Webb FW RC	20.00	6.00
❑ 153 Rob Hammock FW RC	10.00	3.00
❑ 154 Matt Kata FW RC	10.00	3.00
❑ 155 Tim Olson FW RC	10.00	3.00
❑ 156 Oscar Villarreal FW RC	8.00	2.40
❑ 157 Michael Hessman FW RC	8.00	2.40
❑ 158 Daniel Cabrera FW RC	8.00	2.40
❑ 159 Jon Leicester FW RC	8.00	2.40
❑ 160 Todd Wellemeyer FW RC	10.00	3.00
❑ 161 Felix Sanchez FW RC	8.00	2.40
❑ 162 David Sanders FW RC	8.00	2.40
❑ 163 Josh Stewart FW RC	8.00	2.40
❑ 164 Arnie Munoz FW RC	8.00	2.40
❑ 165 Ryan Cameron FW RC	8.00	2.40
❑ 166 Clint Barmes FW RC	10.00	3.00
❑ 167 Josh Willingham FW RC	12.00	3.60
❑ 169 Willie Eyre FW RC	8.00	2.40
❑ 170 Brent Hoard FW RC	8.00	2.40
❑ 171 Terrmel Sledge FW RC	10.00	3.00
❑ 172 Phil Seibel FW RC	8.00	2.40
❑ 173 Craig Brazell FW RC	10.00	3.00
❑ 174 Jeff Duncan FW RC	10.00	3.00
❑ 176 Bernie Castro FW RC	8.00	2.40
❑ 177 Mike Nicolas FW RC	8.00	2.40
❑ 178 Rett Johnson FW RC	10.00	3.00
❑ 179 Bobby Madritsch FW RC	8.00	2.40
❑ 180 Chris Capuano FW RC	8.00	2.40
❑ 181 Hideki Matsui FW AU RC	300.00	90.00
❑ 182 Jose Contreras FW AU RC	50.00	15.00
❑ 183 Lew Ford FW AU RC	25.00	7.50
❑ 184 Jeremy Griffiths FW AU RC	25.00	7.50
❑ 185 Guillermo Quiroz FW AU RC	40.00	12.00
❑ 186 Alej Machado FW AU RC	15.00	4.50
❑ 187 Fran Cruceta FW AU RC	15.00	4.50
❑ 188 Prentice Redman FW AU RC	15.00	4.50
❑ 189 Shane Bazzell FW AU RC	15.00	4.50
❑ 190 Aaron Looper FW RC		
❑ 191 Alex Prieto FW RC		
❑ 192 Alfredo Gonzalez FW RC		
❑ 193 Andrew Brown FW RC		
❑ 194 Anthony Ferrari FW RC		
❑ 195 Aquilino Lopez FW RC		
❑ 196 Beau Kemp FW RC		
❑ 197 Bo Hart FW RC		
❑ 198 Chad Gaudin FW RC		
❑ 199 Colin Porter FW RC		
❑ 200 D.J. Carrasco FW RC		
❑ 201 Dan Haren FW RC		
❑ 202 Danny Garcia FW RC		
❑ 203 Jon Switzer FW		
❑ 204 Edwin Jackson FW RC		
❑ 205 Fernando Cabrera FW RC		
❑ 206 Garrett Atkins FW		
❑ 207 Gerald Laird FW		

❑ 208 Greg Jones FW RC
❑ 209 Ian Ferguson FW RC
❑ 210 Jason Roach FW RC
❑ 211 Jason Shiell FW RC
❑ 212 Jeremy Bonderman FW RC
❑ 213 Jeremy Wedel FW RC
❑ 214 Jhonny Peralta FW RC
❑ 215 Delmon Young FW RC
❑ 216 Julio DePaula FW
❑ 217 Josh Hall FW RC
❑ 218 Julio Manon FW RC
❑ 219 Kevin Correia FW RC
❑ 220 Kevin Ohme FW RC
❑ 221 Kevin Tolar FW RC
❑ 222 Luis Ayala FW RC
❑ 223 Luis De Los Santos FW
❑ 224 Chad Cordero FW RC
❑ 225 Mark Malaska FW RC
❑ 226 Khalil Greene FW
❑ 227 Michael Nakamura FW RC
❑ 228 Michel Hernandez FW RC
❑ 229 Miguel Ojeda FW RC
❑ 230 Mike Neu FW RC
❑ 231 Nate Bland FW RC
❑ 232 Pete LaForest FW RC
❑ 233 Rickie Weeks FW RC
❑ 234 Rosman Garcia FW RC
❑ 235 Ryan Wagner FW RC
❑ 236 Lance Niekro FW
❑ 237 Tom Gregorio FW RC
❑ 238 Tommy Phelps FW RC
❑ 239 Wilfredo Ledezma FW RC

2001 SP Game Bat Milestone

	Nm-Mt	Ex-Mt
COMP.SET w/o SP's (90)	80.00	24.00
COMMON CARD (1-90)	1.00	.30
COMMON BAT (91-96)	10.00	3.00

❑ 1 Troy Glaus	1.50	.45
❑ 2 Darin Erstad	1.00	.30
❑ 3 Jason Giambi	2.50	.75
❑ 4 Jermaine Dye	1.00	.30
❑ 5 Eric Chavez	1.00	.30
❑ 6 Carlos Delgado	1.00	.30
❑ 7 Raul Mondesi	1.00	.30
❑ 8 Shannon Stewart	1.00	.30
❑ 9 Greg Vaughn	1.00	.30
❑ 10 Aubrey Huff	1.00	.30
❑ 11 Juan Gonzalez	2.50	.75
❑ 12 Roberto Alomar	2.50	.75
❑ 13 Jim Thome	2.50	.75
❑ 14 Omar Vizquel	1.00	.30
❑ 15 Mike Cameron	1.00	.30
❑ 16 Edgar Martinez	1.50	.45
❑ 17 John Olerud	1.00	.30
❑ 18 Bret Boone	1.00	.30
❑ 19 Cal Ripken	8.00	2.40
❑ 20 Tony Batista	1.00	.30
❑ 21 Alex Rodriguez	5.00	1.50
❑ 22 Ivan Rodriguez	2.50	.75
❑ 23 Rafael Palmeiro	1.50	.45
❑ 24 Manny Ramirez	1.00	.30
❑ 25 Pedro Martinez	2.50	.75
❑ 26 Nomar Garciaparra	5.00	1.50
❑ 27 Carl Everett	1.00	.30
❑ 28 Mike Sweeney	1.00	.30
❑ 29 Neifi Perez	1.00	.30
❑ 30 Mark Quinn	1.00	.30
❑ 31 Bobby Higginson	1.00	.30
❑ 32 Tony Clark	1.00	.30
❑ 33 Doug Mientkiewicz	1.00	.30
❑ 34 Cristian Guzman	1.00	.30
❑ 35 Joe Mays	1.00	.30
❑ 36 David Ortiz	1.00	.30
❑ 37 Frank Thomas	2.50	.75
❑ 38 Magglio Ordonez	1.00	.30
❑ 39 Carlos Lee	1.00	.30
❑ 40 Alfonso Soriano	2.50	.75
❑ 41 Bernie Williams	1.50	.45
❑ 42 Derek Jeter	6.00	1.80
❑ 43 Roger Clemens	5.00	1.50
❑ 44 Jeff Bagwell	1.50	.45
❑ 45 Richard Hidalgo	1.00	.30
❑ 46 Moises Alou	1.00	.30
❑ 47 Chipper Jones	2.50	.75
❑ 48 Greg Maddux	5.00	1.50
❑ 49 Rafael Furcal	1.00	.30
❑ 50 Andruw Jones	1.50	.45
❑ 51 Jeromy Burnitz	1.00	.30
❑ 52 Geoff Jenkins	1.00	.30
❑ 53 Richie Sexson	1.00	.30
❑ 54 Edgar Renteria	1.00	.30
❑ 55 Mark McGwire	6.00	1.80
❑ 56 Jim Edmonds	1.00	.30
❑ 57 J.D. Drew	1.00	.30
❑ 58 Sammy Sosa	4.00	1.20
❑ 59 Fred McGriff	1.50	.45
❑ 60 Luis Gonzalez	1.00	.30
❑ 61 Randy Johnson	2.50	.75
❑ 62 Gary Sheffield	1.00	.30
❑ 63 Shawn Green	1.00	.30
❑ 64 Kevin Brown	1.00	.30
❑ 65 Vladimir Guerrero	2.50	.75
❑ 66 Jose Vidro	1.00	.30
❑ 67 Fernando Tatis	1.00	.30
❑ 68 Barry Bonds	6.00	1.80
❑ 69 Jeff Kent	1.00	.30
❑ 70 Rich Aurilia	1.00	.30
❑ 71 Preston Wilson	1.00	.30
❑ 72 Charles Johnson	1.00	.30
❑ 73 Cliff Floyd	1.00	.30
❑ 74 Mike Piazza	4.00	1.20
❑ 75 Matt Lawton	1.00	.30
❑ 76 Edgardo Alfonzo	1.00	.30
❑ 77 Tony Gwynn	3.00	.90
❑ 78 Phil Nevin	1.00	.30
❑ 79 Scott Rolen	1.50	.45
❑ 80 Pat Burrell	1.00	.30
❑ 81 Bobby Abreu	1.00	.30
❑ 82 Brian Giles	1.00	.30
❑ 83 Jason Kendall	1.00	.30
❑ 84 Aramis Ramirez	1.00	.30
❑ 85 Sean Casey	1.00	.30
❑ 86 Ken Griffey Jr.	4.00	1.20
❑ 87 Barry Larkin	2.50	.75
❑ 88 Todd Helton	1.50	.45
❑ 89 Mike Hampton	1.00	.30
❑ 90 Larry Walker	1.50	.45
❑ 91 Ichiro Suzuki BAT RC	40.00	12.00
❑ 92 Albert Pujols BAT RC	50.00	15.00
❑ 93 T. Shinjo BAT RC	15.00	4.50
❑ 94 Jack Wilson BAT RC	10.00	3.00
❑ 95 D. Mendez BAT RC	10.00	3.00
❑ 96 Junior Spivey BAT RC	15.00	4.50

2001 SP Game-Used Edition

	Nm-Mt	Ex-Mt
COMP.SET w/o SP's (60)	80.00	24.00
COMMON CARD (1-60)	1.25	.35
COMMON CARD (61-90)	10.00	3.00

❑ 1 Garret Anderson	1.25	.35
❑ 2 Troy Glaus	2.00	.60
❑ 3 Darin Erstad	1.25	.35
❑ 4 Jason Giambi	3.00	.90
❑ 5 Tim Hudson	1.25	.35
❑ 6 Johnny Damon	1.25	.35
❑ 7 Carlos Delgado	1.25	.35

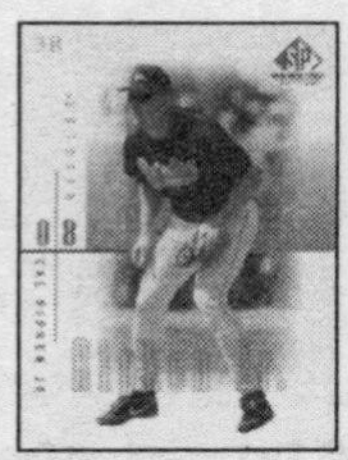

❑ 8 Greg Vaughn	1.25	.35
❑ 9 Juan Gonzalez	3.00	.90
❑ 10 Roberto Alomar	3.00	.90
❑ 11 Jim Thome	3.00	.90
❑ 12 Edgar Martinez	2.00	.60
❑ 13 Cal Ripken	10.00	3.00
❑ 14 Andres Galarraga	1.25	.35
❑ 15 Alex Rodriguez	6.00	1.80
❑ 16 Rafael Palmeiro	2.00	.60
❑ 17 Ivan Rodriguez	3.00	.90
❑ 18 Manny Ramirez	1.25	.35
❑ 19 Nomar Garciaparra	6.00	1.80
❑ 20 Pedro Martinez	3.00	.90
❑ 21 Jermaine Dye	1.25	.35
❑ 22 Dean Palmer	1.25	.35
❑ 23 Matt Lawton	1.25	.35
❑ 24 Frank Thomas	3.00	.90
❑ 25 David Wells	1.25	.35
❑ 26 Magglio Ordonez	1.25	.35
❑ 27 Derek Jeter	8.00	2.40
❑ 28 Bernie Williams	2.00	.60
❑ 29 Roger Clemens	6.00	1.80
❑ 30 Jeff Bagwell	2.00	.60
❑ 31 Richard Hidalgo	1.25	.35
❑ 32 Chipper Jones	3.00	.90
❑ 33 Andruw Jones	2.00	.60
❑ 34 Greg Maddux	6.00	1.80
❑ 35 Jeffrey Hammonds	1.25	.35
❑ 36 Mark McGwire	8.00	2.40
❑ 37 Jim Edmonds	1.25	.35
❑ 38 Sammy Sosa	5.00	1.50
❑ 39 Corey Patterson	1.25	.35
❑ 40 Randy Johnson	3.00	.90
❑ 41 Luis Gonzalez	1.25	.35
❑ 42 Gary Sheffield	1.25	.35
❑ 43 Shawn Green	1.25	.35
❑ 44 Kevin Brown	1.25	.35
❑ 45 Vladimir Guerrero	3.00	.90
❑ 46 Barry Bonds	8.00	2.40
❑ 47 Jeff Kent	1.25	.35
❑ 48 Preston Wilson	1.25	.35
❑ 49 Charles Johnson	1.25	.35
❑ 50 Mike Piazza	5.00	1.50
❑ 51 Edgardo Alfonzo	1.25	.35
❑ 52 Tony Gwynn	4.00	1.20
❑ 53 Scott Rolen	2.00	.60
❑ 54 Pat Burrell	1.25	.35
❑ 55 Brian Giles	1.25	.35
❑ 56 Jason Kendall	1.25	.35
❑ 57 Ken Griffey Jr.	5.00	1.50
❑ 58 Mike Hampton	1.25	.35
❑ 59 Todd Helton	2.00	.60
❑ 60 Larry Walker	2.00	.60
❑ 61 Wilson Betemit RC	10.00	3.00
❑ 62 Travis Hafner RC	15.00	4.50
❑ 63 Ichiro Suzuki RC	80.00	24.00
❑ 64 Juan Diaz RC	10.00	3.00
❑ 65 Morgan Ensberg RC	15.00	4.50
❑ 66 Horacio Ramirez RC	15.00	4.50
❑ 67 Ricardo Rodriguez RC	10.00	3.00
❑ 68 Sean Douglass RC	10.00	3.00
❑ 69 Brandon Duckworth RC	10.00	3.00
❑ 70 Jackson Melian RC	10.00	3.00
❑ 71 Adrian Hernandez RC	10.00	3.00
❑ 72 Kyle Kessel RC	10.00	3.00
❑ 73 Jason Michaels RC	10.00	3.00
❑ 74 Esix Snead RC	10.00	3.00
❑ 75 Jason Smith RC	10.00	3.00

❑ 76 Tyler Walker RC	10.00	3.00
❑ 77 Juan Uribe RC	10.00	3.00
❑ 78 Adam Pettyjohn RC	10.00	3.00
❑ 79 Tsuyoshi Shinjo RC	15.00	4.50
❑ 80 Mike Penney RC	10.00	3.00
❑ 81 Josh Towers RC	10.00	3.00
❑ 82 Erick Almonte RC	10.00	3.00
❑ 83 Ryan Freel RC	10.00	3.00
❑ 84 Juan Pena	10.00	3.00
❑ 85 Albert Pujols RC	80.00	24.00
❑ 86 Henry Mateo RC	10.00	3.00
❑ 87 Greg Miller RC	10.00	3.00
❑ 88 Jose Mieses RC	10.00	3.00
❑ 89 Jack Wilson RC	10.00	3.00
❑ 90 Carlos Valderrama RC	10.00	3.00

2002 SP Legendary Cuts

	Nm-Mt	Ex-Mt
COMPLETE SET (90)	30.00	9.00
❑ 1 Al Kaline	1.50	.45
❑ 2 Alvin Dark	.60	.18
❑ 3 Andre Dawson	.60	.18
❑ 4 Babe Ruth	5.00	1.50
❑ 5 Ernie Banks	1.50	.45
❑ 6 Bob Lemon	1.00	.30
❑ 7 Bobby Bonds	.60	.18
❑ 8 Carl Erskine	.60	.18
❑ 9 Carl Hubbell	1.00	.30
❑ 10 Casey Stengel	1.50	.45
❑ 11 Charlie Gehringer	1.00	.30
❑ 12 Christy Mathewson	1.50	.45
❑ 13 Dale Murphy	1.50	.45
❑ 14 Dave Concepcion	.60	.18
❑ 15 Dave Parker	.60	.18
❑ 16 Dazzy Vance	.60	.18
❑ 17 Dizzy Dean	1.00	.30
❑ 18 Don Baylor	.60	.18
❑ 19 Don Drysdale	1.50	.45
❑ 20 Duke Snider	1.00	.30
❑ 21 Earl Averill	.60	.18
❑ 22 Early Wynn	.60	.18
❑ 23 Edd Roush	.60	.18
❑ 24 Elston Howard	.60	.18
❑ 25 Ferguson Jenkins	.60	.18
❑ 26 Frank Crosetti	.60	.18
❑ 27 Frankie Frisch	.60	.18
❑ 28 Gaylord Perry	.60	.18
❑ 29 George Foster	.60	.18
❑ 30 George Kell	.60	.18
❑ 31 Gil Hodges	1.00	.30
❑ 32 Hank Greenberg	1.50	.45
❑ 33 Phil Niekro	.60	.18
❑ 34 Harvey Haddix	.60	.18
❑ 35 Harvey Kuenn	.60	.18
❑ 36 Honus Wagner	2.50	.75
❑ 37 Jackie Robinson	2.50	.75
❑ 38 Orlando Cepeda	.60	.18
❑ 39 Joe Adcock	.60	.18
❑ 40 Joe Cronin	.60	.18
❑ 41 Joe DiMaggio	4.00	1.20
❑ 42 Joe Morgan	.60	.18
❑ 43 Johnny Mize	.60	.18
❑ 44 Lefty Gomez	1.00	.30
❑ 45 Lefty Grove	1.00	.30
❑ 46 Jim Palmer	.60	.18
❑ 47 Lou Boudreau	.60	.18
❑ 48 Lou Gehrig	4.00	1.20
❑ 49 Luke Appling	.60	.18
❑ 50 Mark McGwire	5.00	1.50
❑ 51 Mel Ott	1.50	.45
❑ 52 Mickey Cochrane	1.00	.30
❑ 53 Mickey Mantle	6.00	1.80
❑ 54 Minnie Minoso	.60	.18
❑ 55 Brooks Robinson	1.50	.45
❑ 56 Nellie Fox	1.00	.30
❑ 57 Nolan Ryan	5.00	1.50
❑ 58 Rollie Fingers	.60	.18
❑ 59 Pee Wee Reese	1.00	.30
❑ 60 Phil Rizzuto	1.00	.30
❑ 61 Ralph Kiner	.60	.18
❑ 62 Ray Dandridge	.60	.18
❑ 63 Richie Ashburn	1.00	.30
❑ 64 Robin Yount	1.50	.45
❑ 65 Rocky Colavito	1.00	.30
❑ 66 Roger Maris	2.00	.60
❑ 67 Rogers Hornsby	1.50	.45
❑ 68 Ron Santo	.60	.18
❑ 69 Ryne Sandberg	3.00	.90
❑ 70 Stan Musial	2.50	.75
❑ 71 Sam McDowell	.60	.18
❑ 72 Satchel Paige	1.50	.45
❑ 73 Willie McCovey	.60	.18
❑ 74 Steve Garvey	.60	.18
❑ 75 Ted Kluszewski	1.00	.30
❑ 76 Catfish Hunter	1.00	.30
❑ 77 Terry Moore	.40	.12
❑ 78 Thurman Munson	2.00	.60
❑ 79 Tom Seaver	1.50	.45
❑ 80 Tommy John	.60	.18
❑ 81 Tony Gwynn	2.00	.60
❑ 82 Tony Kubek	1.00	.30
❑ 83 Tony Lazzeri	.60	.18
❑ 84 Ty Cobb	2.50	.75
❑ 85 Wade Boggs	1.00	.30
❑ 86 Waite Hoyt	.60	.18
❑ 87 Walter Johnson	1.50	.45
❑ 88 Willie Stargell	1.00	.30
❑ 89 Yogi Berra	1.50	.45
❑ 90 Zack Wheat	.60	.18
❑ MM M.McGwire AU/100 EX	600.00	180.00

2003 SP Legendary Cuts

	MINT	NRMT
COMP.SET w/o SP's (100)	40.00	18.00
COMMON CARD	.40	.18
COMMON SP	8.00	3.60
SP STATED ODDS 1:12		
SP PRINT RUN 1299 SERIAL #'d SETS		
❑ 1 Luis Aparicio	.60	.25
❑ 2 Al Barlick	.40	.18
❑ 3 Al Lopez	.60	.25
❑ 4 Ernie Banks	1.50	.70
❑ 5 Alexander Cartwright	.60	.25
❑ 6 Lou Brock	1.00	.45
❑ 7 Babe Ruth/1299	15.00	6.75
❑ 8 Bill Dickey	1.00	.45
❑ 9 Bill Mazeroski	1.00	.45
❑ 10 Bob Feller	1.00	.45
❑ 11 Billy Herman	.60	.25
❑ 12 Billy Williams	.60	.25
❑ 13 Bob Gibson/1299	10.00	4.50
❑ 14 Bob Lemon	.60	.25
❑ 15 Bobby Doerr	.60	.25
❑ 16 Branch Rickey	.60	.25
❑ 17 Gary Carter	.60	.25
❑ 18 Burleigh Grimes	.60	.25
❑ 19 Cap Anson	1.00	.45
❑ 20 Carl Hubbell	1.00	.45
❑ 21 Carlton Fisk	1.00	.45
❑ 22 Casey Stengel	1.00	.45
❑ 23 Charlie Gehringer	.60	.25
❑ 24 Chief Bender	.60	.25
❑ 25 Christy Mathewson/1299	10.00	4.50
❑ 26 Cy Young	1.50	.70
❑ 27 Dave Winfield	1.00	.45
❑ 28 Dazzy Vance	.60	.25
❑ 29 Dizzy Dean/1299	10.00	4.50
❑ 30 Don Drysdale/1299	10.00	4.50
❑ 31 Duke Snider/1299	10.00	4.50
❑ 32 Earl Averill	.60	.25
❑ 33 Earle Combs	.60	.25
❑ 34 Edd Roush	.60	.25
❑ 35 Earl Weaver	.60	.25
❑ 36 Eddie Collins	.60	.25
❑ 37 Eddie Plank	.60	.25
❑ 38 Elmer Flick	.60	.25
❑ 39 Enos Slaughter	.60	.25
❑ 40 Ernie Lombardi	.60	.25
❑ 41 Ford Frick	.40	.18
❑ 42 Jim Hunter	1.00	.45
❑ 43 Frankie Frisch	.60	.25
❑ 44 Gabby Hartnett	.60	.25
❑ 45 George Kell	.60	.25
❑ 46 Early Wynn	.60	.25
❑ 47 Ferguson Jenkins	.60	.25
❑ 48 Al Kaline	1.50	.70
❑ 49 Harmon Killebrew	1.50	.70
❑ 50 Hal Newhouser	.60	.25
❑ 51 Hank Greenberg/1299	10.00	4.50
❑ 52 Harry Caray	1.00	.45
❑ 53 Tommy Lasorda	.60	.25
❑ 54 Honus Wagner/1299	10.00	4.50
❑ 55 Hoyt Wilhelm/1299	8.00	3.60
❑ 56 Jackie Robinson/1299	10.00	4.50
❑ 57 Jim Bottomley	.60	.25
❑ 58 Jim Bunning/1299	10.00	4.50
❑ 59 Jimmie Foxx/1299	10.00	4.50
❑ 60 Eddie Mathews	1.50	.70
❑ 61 Joe Cronin	.60	.25
❑ 62 Joe DiMaggio/1299	10.00	4.50
❑ 63 Joe McCarthy/1299	8.00	3.60
❑ 64 Joe Morgan/1299	8.00	3.60
❑ 65 Willie McCovey	1.00	.45
❑ 66 Joe Tinker	.60	.25
❑ 67 Johnny Bench/1299	10.00	4.50
❑ 68 Johnny Evers/1299	8.00	3.60
❑ 69 Johnny Mize/1299	8.00	3.60
❑ 70 Josh Gibson/1299	10.00	4.50
❑ 71 Juan Marichal	.60	.25
❑ 72 Judy Johnson	.60	.25
❑ 73 Stan Musial	2.50	1.10
❑ 74 Kiki Cuyler	.60	.25
❑ 75 Larry Doby	.60	.25
❑ 76 Nap Lajoie	1.00	.45
❑ 77 Larry MacPhail	.40	.18
❑ 78 Phil Niekro	.60	.25
❑ 79 Lefty Gomez/1299	10.00	4.50
❑ 80 Lefty Grove/1299	10.00	4.50
❑ 81 Leo Durocher/1299	8.00	3.60
❑ 82 Leon Day	.60	.25
❑ 83 Gaylord Perry/1299	8.00	3.60
❑ 84 Lou Boudreau	.60	.25
❑ 85 Lou Gehrig	4.00	1.80
❑ 86 Luke Appling	.60	.25
❑ 87 Max Carey	.60	.25
❑ 88 Mel Allen/1299	8.00	3.60
❑ 89 Mel Ott/1299	10.00	4.50
❑ 90 Mickey Cochrane	.60	.25
❑ 91 Mickey Mantle	5.00	2.20
❑ 92 Brooks Robinson	1.50	.70
❑ 93 Monte Irvin	.60	.25
❑ 94 Nellie Fox	1.00	.45
❑ 95 Nolan Ryan/1299	15.00	6.75
❑ 96 Ozzie Smith/1299	10.00	4.50
❑ 97 Mike Schmidt	3.00	1.35
❑ 98 Pee Wee Reese/1299	10.00	4.50
❑ 99 Phil Rizzuto	1.00	.45
❑ 100 Ralph Kiner	.60	.25
❑ 101 Ray Dandridge	.60	.25

Card	Nm-Mt	Ex-Mt
❑ 102 Richie Ashburn	1.00	.45
❑ 103 Rick Ferrell	.60	.25
❑ 104 Roberto Clemente	4.00	1.80
❑ 105 Robin Roberts	.60	.25
❑ 106 Robin Yount	1.50	.70
❑ 107 Rogers Hornsby	1.50	.70
❑ 108 Rollie Fingers	.60	.25
❑ 109 Roy Campanella	1.50	.70
❑ 110 Rube Marquard	.60	.25
❑ 111 Sam Crawford	.60	.25
❑ 112 Steve Carlton	1.00	.45
❑ 113 Satchel Paige/1299	10.00	4.50
❑ 114 Sparky Anderson	.60	.25
❑ 115 Stan Coveleski	.60	.25
❑ 116 Red Schoendienst	1.00	.45
❑ 117 Ted Williams	4.00	1.80
❑ 118 Tom Seaver	1.50	.70
❑ 119 Tom Yawkey	.40	.18
❑ 120 Tony Lazzeri	.60	.25
❑ 121 Tony Perez	.60	.25
❑ 122 Tris Speaker	1.50	.70
❑ 123 Ty Cobb	2.50	1.10
❑ 124 Waite Hoyt/1299	8.00	3.60
❑ 125 Walter Alston	.60	.25
❑ 126 Walter Johnson	1.50	.70
❑ 127 Warren Spahn	1.00	.45
❑ 128 Whitey Ford	1.00	.45
❑ 129 Willie Stargell	1.00	.45
❑ 130 Yogi Berra	1.50	.70

1986 Sportflics Rookies

	Nm-Mt	Ex-Mt
COMP.FACT.SET (50)	25.00	10.00
❑ 1 John Kruk	.75	.30
❑ 2 Edwin Correa	.10	.04
❑ 3 Pete Incaviglia	.25	.10
❑ 4 Dale Sveum	.10	.04
❑ 5 Juan Nieves	.10	.04
❑ 6 Will Clark	2.00	.80
❑ 7 Wally Joyner	.40	.16
❑ 8 Lance McCullers	.10	.04
❑ 9 Scott Bailes	.10	.04
❑ 10 Dan Plesac	.25	.10
❑ 11 Jose Canseco	2.00	.80
❑ 12 Bobby Witt	.25	.10
❑ 13 Barry Bonds	20.00	8.00
❑ 14 Andres Thomas	.10	.04
❑ 15 Jim Deshaies	.10	.04
❑ 16 Ruben Sierra	.75	.30
❑ 17 Steve Lombardozzi	.10	.04
❑ 18 Cory Snyder	.10	.04
❑ 19 Reggie Williams	.10	.04
❑ 20 Mitch Williams	.25	.10
❑ 21 Glenn Braggs	.10	.04
❑ 22 Danny Tartabull	.10	.04
❑ 23 Charlie Kerfeld	.10	.04
❑ 24 Paul Assenmacher	.10	.04
❑ 25 Robby Thompson	.25	.10
❑ 26 Bobby Bonilla	.40	.16
❑ 27 Andres Galarraga	1.00	.40
❑ 28 Billy Joe Robidoux	.10	.04
❑ 29 Bruce Ruffin	.10	.04
❑ 30 Greg Swindell	.25	.10
❑ 31 John Cangelosi	.10	.04
❑ 32 Jim Traber	.10	.04
❑ 33 Russ Morman	.10	.04
❑ 34 Barry Larkin	2.00	.80
❑ 35 Todd Worrell	.25	.10
❑ 36 John Cerutti	.10	.04
❑ 37 Mike Kingery	.10	.04
❑ 38 Mark Eichhorn	.10	.04
❑ 39 Scott Bankhead	.10	.04
❑ 40 Bo Jackson	2.00	.80
❑ 41 Greg Mathews	.10	.04
❑ 42 Eric King	.10	.04
❑ 43 Kal Daniels	.25	.10
❑ 44 Calvin Schiraldi	.10	.04
❑ 45 Mickey Brantley	.10	.04
❑ 46 Willie Mays Pete Rose Fred Lynn	.75	.30
❑ 47 Tom Seaver Fernando Valenzuela Dwight Gooden	.40	.16
❑ 48 Eddie Murray Lou Whitaker Dave Righetti Steve Sax Cal Ripken Darryl Strawberry	.75	.30
❑ 49 Kevin Mitchell	.40	.16
❑ 50 Mike Diaz	.10	.04

1994 Sportflics Rookie/Traded

	Nm-Mt	Ex-Mt
COMPLETE SET (150)	25.00	7.50
❑ 1 Will Clark	1.25	.35
❑ 2 Sid Fernandez	.25	.07
❑ 3 Joe Magrane	.25	.07
❑ 4 Pete Smith	.25	.07
❑ 5 Roberto Kelly	.25	.07
❑ 6 Delino DeShields	.25	.07
❑ 7 Brian Harper	.25	.07
❑ 8 Darrin Jackson	.25	.07
❑ 9 Omar Vizquel	.50	.15
❑ 10 Luis Polonia	.25	.07
❑ 11 Reggie Jefferson	.25	.07
❑ 12 Geronimo Berroa	.25	.07
❑ 13 Mike Harkey	.25	.07
❑ 14 Bret Boone	.50	.15
❑ 15 Dave Henderson	.25	.07
❑ 16 Pedro Martinez	1.25	.35
❑ 17 Jose Vizcaino	.25	.07
❑ 18 Xavier Hernandez	.25	.07
❑ 19 Eddie Taubensee	.25	.07
❑ 20 Ellis Burks	.50	.15
❑ 21 Turner Ward	.25	.07
❑ 22 Terry Mulholland	.25	.07
❑ 23 Howard Johnson	.25	.07
❑ 24 Vince Coleman	.25	.07
❑ 25 Deion Sanders	.50	.15
❑ 26 Rafael Palmeiro	.75	.23
❑ 27 Dave Weathers	.25	.07
❑ 28 Kent Mercker	.25	.07
❑ 29 Gregg Olson	.25	.07
❑ 30 Cory Bailey RC	.25	.07
❑ 31 Brian L. Hunter	.25	.07
❑ 32 Garey Ingram RC	.25	.07
❑ 33 Daniel Smith	.25	.07
❑ 34 Denny Hocking	.25	.07
❑ 35 Charles Johnson	.50	.15
❑ 36 Otis Nixon	.25	.07
❑ 37 Hector Fajardo	.25	.07
❑ 38 Lee Smith	.50	.15
❑ 39 Phil Stidham	.25	.07
❑ 40 Melvin Nieves	.25	.07
❑ 41 Julio Franco	.50	.15
❑ 42 Greg Gohr	.25	.07
❑ 43 Steve Dunn	.25	.07
❑ 44 Tony Fernandez	.25	.07
❑ 45 Toby Borland RC	.25	.07
❑ 46 Paul Shuey	.25	.07
❑ 47 Shawn Hare	.25	.07
❑ 48 Shawn Green	1.25	.35
❑ 49 Julian Tavarez RC	.50	.15
❑ 50 Ernie Young RC	.50	.15
❑ 51 Chris Sabo	.25	.07
❑ 52 Greg O'Halloran	.25	.07
❑ 53 Donnie Elliott	.25	.07
❑ 54 Jim Converse	.25	.07
❑ 55 Ray Holbert	.25	.07
❑ 56 Keith Lockhart RC	.50	.15
❑ 57 Tony Longmire	.25	.07
❑ 58 Jorge Fabregas	.25	.07
❑ 59 Ravelo Manzanillo	.25	.07
❑ 60 Marcus Moore	.25	.07
❑ 61 Carlos Rodriguez	.25	.07
❑ 62 Mark Portugal	.25	.07
❑ 63 Yorkis Perez	.25	.07
❑ 64 Dan Miceli	.25	.07
❑ 65 Chris Turner	.25	.07
❑ 66 Mike Oquist	.25	.07
❑ 67 Tom Quinlan	.25	.07
❑ 68 Matt Walbeck	.25	.07
❑ 69 Dave Staton	.25	.07
❑ 70 W.VanLandingham RC	.25	.07
❑ 71 Dave Stevens	.25	.07
❑ 72 Domingo Cedeno	.25	.07
❑ 73 Alex Diaz	.25	.07
❑ 74 Darren Bragg RC	.25	.07
❑ 75 James Hurst	.25	.07
❑ 76 Alex Gonzalez	.25	.07
❑ 77 Steve Dreyer	.25	.07
❑ 78 Robert Eenhoorn	.25	.07
❑ 79 Derek Parks	.25	.07
❑ 80 Jose Valentin	.25	.07
❑ 81 Wes Chamberlain	.25	.07
❑ 82 Tony Tarasco	.25	.07
❑ 83 Steve Traschel	.25	.07
❑ 84 Willie Banks	.25	.07
❑ 85 Rob Butler	.25	.07
❑ 86 Miguel Jimenez	.25	.07
❑ 87 Gerald Williams	.25	.07
❑ 88 Aaron Small	.25	.07
❑ 89 Matt Mieske	.25	.07
❑ 90 Tim Hyers RC	.25	.07
❑ 91 Eddie Murray	1.25	.35
❑ 92 Dennis Martinez	.50	.15
❑ 93 Tony Eusebio	.25	.07
❑ 94 Brian Anderson RC	.50	.15
❑ 95 Blaise Ilsley	.25	.07
❑ 96 Johnny Ruffin	.25	.07
❑ 97 Carlos Reyes	.25	.07
❑ 98 Greg Pirkl	.25	.07
❑ 99 Jack Morris	.50	.15
❑ 100 John Mabry RC	.50	.15
❑ 101 Mike Kelly	.25	.07
❑ 102 Rich Becker	.25	.07
❑ 103 Chris Gomez	.25	.07
❑ 104 Jim Edmonds	.75	.23
❑ 105 Rich Rowland	.25	.07
❑ 106 Damon Buford	.25	.07
❑ 107 Mark Kiefer	.25	.07
❑ 108 Matias Carrillo	.25	.07
❑ 109 James Mouton	.25	.07
❑ 110 Kelly Stinnett RC	.25	.07
❑ 111 Billy Ashley	.25	.07
❑ 112 Fausto Cruz RC	.25	.07
❑ 113 Roberto Petagine	.25	.07
❑ 114 Joe Hall	.25	.07
❑ 115 Brian Johnson RC	.25	.07
❑ 116 Kevin Jarvis	.25	.07
❑ 117 Tim Davis	.25	.07
❑ 118 John Patterson	.25	.07
❑ 119 Stan Royer	.25	.07
❑ 120 Jeff Juden	.25	.07
❑ 121 Bryan Eversgerd	.25	.07

Card	Nm-Mt	Ex-Mt
❑ 122 Chan Ho Park RC	1.50	.45
❑ 123 Shane Reynolds	.25	.07
❑ 124 Danny Bautista	.25	.07
❑ 125 Rikkert Faneyte RC	.25	.07
❑ 126 Carlos Pulido	.25	.07
❑ 127 Mike Matheny RC	.50	.15
❑ 128 Hector Carrasco	.25	.07
❑ 129 Eddie Zambrano	.25	.07
❑ 130 Lee Tinsley	.25	.07
❑ 131 Roger Salkeld	.25	.07
❑ 132 Carlos Delgado	.75	.23
❑ 133 Troy O'Leary	.25	.07
❑ 134 Keith Mitchell	.25	.07
❑ 135 Lance Painter	.25	.07
❑ 136 Nate Minchey	.25	.07
❑ 137 Eric Anthony	.25	.07
❑ 138 Rafael Bournigal	.25	.07
❑ 139 Joey Hamilton	.25	.07
❑ 140 Bobby Munoz	.25	.07
❑ 141 Rex Hudler	.25	.07
❑ 142 Alex Cole	.25	.07
❑ 143 Stan Javier	.25	.07
❑ 144 Jose Oliva	.25	.07
❑ 145 Tom Brunansky	.25	.07
❑ 146 Greg Colbrunn	.25	.07
❑ 147 Luis Lopez	.25	.07
❑ 148 Alex Rodriguez RC	15.00	4.50
❑ 149 Darryl Strawberry	.75	.23
❑ 150 Bo Jackson	1.25	.35
❑ R01 Ryan Klesko ROY Manny Ramirez	4.00	1.20

1996 SPx

	Nm-Mt	Ex-Mt
COMPLETE SET (60)	50.00	15.00
❑ 1 Greg Maddux	4.00	1.20
❑ 2 Chipper Jones	2.00	.60
❑ 3 Fred McGriff	1.25	.35
❑ 4 Tom Glavine	2.00	.60
❑ 5 Cal Ripken	6.00	1.80
❑ 6 Roberto Alomar	2.00	.60
❑ 7 Rafael Palmeiro	1.25	.35
❑ 8 Jose Canseco	2.00	.60
❑ 9 Roger Clemens	4.00	1.20
❑ 10 Mo Vaughn	.75	.23
❑ 11 Jim Edmonds	.75	.23
❑ 12 Tim Salmon	1.25	.35
❑ 13 Sammy Sosa	3.00	.90
❑ 14 Ryne Sandberg	3.00	.90
❑ 15 Mark Grace	2.00	.60
❑ 16 Frank Thomas	2.00	.60
❑ 17 Barry Larkin	2.00	.60
❑ 18 Kenny Lofton	.75	.23
❑ 19 Albert Belle	.75	.23
❑ 20 Eddie Murray	2.00	.60
❑ 21 Manny Ramirez	.75	.23
❑ 22 Dante Bichette	.75	.23
❑ 23 Larry Walker	1.25	.35
❑ 24 Vinny Castilla	.75	.23
❑ 25 Andres Galarraga	.75	.23
❑ 26 Cecil Fielder	.75	.23
❑ 27 Gary Sheffield	.75	.23
❑ 28 Craig Biggio	1.25	.35
❑ 29 Jeff Bagwell	1.25	.35
❑ 30 Derek Bell	.75	.23
❑ 31 Johnny Damon	.75	.23
❑ 32 Eric Karros	.75	.23
❑ 33 Mike Piazza	3.00	.90
❑ 34 Raul Mondesi	.75	.23
❑ 35 Hideo Nomo	2.00	.60
❑ 36 Kirby Puckett	2.00	.60
❑ 37 Paul Molitor	1.25	.35
❑ 38 Marty Cordova	.75	.23
❑ 39 Rondell White	.75	.23
❑ 40 Jason Isringhausen	.75	.23
❑ 41 Paul Wilson	.75	.23
❑ 42 Rey Ordonez	.75	.23
❑ 43 Derek Jeter	5.00	1.50
❑ 44 Wade Boggs	1.25	.35
❑ 45 Mark McGwire	5.00	1.50
❑ 46 Jason Kendall	.75	.23
❑ 47 Ron Gant	.75	.23
❑ 48 Ozzie Smith	2.00	.60
❑ 49 Tony Gwynn	2.50	.75
❑ 50 Ken Caminiti	.75	.23
❑ 51 Barry Bonds	5.00	1.50
❑ 52 Matt Williams	.75	.23
❑ 53 Osvaldo Fernandez	.75	.23
❑ 54 Jay Buhner	.75	.23
❑ 55 Ken Griffey Jr.	3.00	.90
❑ 56 Randy Johnson	2.00	.60
❑ 57 Alex Rodriguez	4.00	1.20
❑ 58 Juan Gonzalez	2.00	.60
❑ 59 Joe Carter	.75	.23
❑ 60 Carlos Delgado	.75	.23
❑ KG1 K.Griffey Jr. Comm.	5.00	1.50
❑ MP1 Mike Piazza Trib.	5.00	1.50
❑ KGA1 Ken Griffey Jr. Auto.	150.00	45.00
❑ MPA1 Mike Piazza Auto.	300.00	90.00

1999 SPx

	Nm-Mt	Ex-Mt
COMPLETE SET (120)	-	-
COMP.SET w/o SP's (80)	25.00	7.50
COMMON (1-10)	1.50	.45
COMMON CARD (11-80)	.50	.15
COMMON SP (81-120)	10.00	3.00
❑ 1 Mark McGwire 61	3.00	.90
❑ 2 Mark McGwire 62	3.00	.90
❑ 3 Mark McGwire 63	1.50	.45
❑ 4 Mark McGwire 64	1.50	.45
❑ 5 Mark McGwire 65	1.50	.45
❑ 6 Mark McGwire 66	1.50	.45
❑ 7 Mark McGwire 67	1.50	.45
❑ 8 Mark McGwire 68	1.50	.45
❑ 9 Mark McGwire 69	1.50	.45
❑ 10 Mark McGwire 70	4.00	1.20
❑ 11 Mo Vaughn	.50	.15
❑ 12 Darin Erstad	.50	.15
❑ 13 Travis Lee	.50	.15
❑ 14 Randy Johnson	1.25	.35
❑ 15 Matt Williams	.50	.15
❑ 16 Chipper Jones	1.25	.35
❑ 17 Greg Maddux	2.50	.75
❑ 18 Andruw Jones	.75	.23
❑ 19 Andres Galarraga	.50	.15
❑ 20 Cal Ripken	4.00	1.20
❑ 21 Albert Belle	.50	.15
❑ 22 Mike Mussina	1.25	.35
❑ 23 Nomar Garciaparra	2.50	.75
❑ 24 Pedro Martinez	1.25	.35
❑ 25 John Valentin	.50	.15
❑ 26 Kerry Wood	1.25	.35
❑ 27 Sammy Sosa	2.00	.60
❑ 28 Mark Grace	1.25	.35
❑ 29 Frank Thomas	1.25	.35
❑ 30 Mike Caruso	.50	.15
❑ 31 Barry Larkin	1.25	.35
❑ 32 Sean Casey	.50	.15
❑ 33 Jim Thome	1.25	.35
❑ 34 Kenny Lofton	.50	.15
❑ 35 Manny Ramirez	.50	.15
❑ 36 Larry Walker	.75	.23
❑ 37 Todd Helton	.75	.23
❑ 38 Vinny Castilla	.50	.15
❑ 39 Tony Clark	.50	.15
❑ 40 Derrek Lee	.50	.15
❑ 41 Mark Kotsay	.50	.15
❑ 42 Jeff Bagwell	.75	.23
❑ 43 Craig Biggio	.75	.23
❑ 44 Moises Alou	.50	.15
❑ 45 Larry Sutton	.50	.15
❑ 46 Johnny Damon	.50	.15
❑ 47 Gary Sheffield	.50	.15
❑ 48 Raul Mondesi	.50	.15
❑ 49 Jeromy Burnitz	.50	.15
❑ 50 Todd Walker	.50	.15
❑ 51 David Ortiz	.50	.15
❑ 52 Vladimir Guerrero	1.25	.35
❑ 53 Rondell White	.50	.15
❑ 54 Mike Piazza	2.00	.60
❑ 55 Derek Jeter	3.00	.90
❑ 56 Tino Martinez	.75	.23
❑ 57 Roger Clemens	2.50	.75
❑ 58 Ben Grieve	.50	.15
❑ 59 A.J. Hinch	.50	.15
❑ 60 Scott Rolen	.75	.23
❑ 61 Doug Glanville	.50	.15
❑ 62 Aramis Ramirez	.50	.15
❑ 63 Jose Guillen	.50	.15
❑ 64 Tony Gwynn	1.50	.45
❑ 65 Greg Vaughn	.50	.15
❑ 66 Ruben Rivera	.50	.15
❑ 67 Barry Bonds	3.00	.90
❑ 68 J.T. Snow	.50	.15
❑ 69 Alex Rodriguez	2.50	.75
❑ 70 Ken Griffey Jr.	2.00	.60
❑ 71 Jay Buhner	.50	.15
❑ 72 Mark McGwire	3.00	.90
❑ 73 Fernando Tatis	.50	.15
❑ 74 Quinton McCracken	.50	.15
❑ 75 Wade Boggs	.75	.23
❑ 76 Ivan Rodriguez	1.25	.35
❑ 77 Juan Gonzalez	1.25	.35
❑ 78 Rafael Palmeiro	.75	.23
❑ 79 Jose Cruz Jr.	.50	.15
❑ 80 Carlos Delgado	.50	.15
❑ 81 Troy Glaus SP	15.00	4.50
❑ 82 Vladimir Nunez SP	10.00	3.00
❑ 83 George Lombard SP	10.00	3.00
❑ 84 Bruce Chen SP	10.00	3.00
❑ 85 Ryan Minor SP	10.00	3.00
❑ 86 Calvin Pickering SP	10.00	3.00
❑ 87 Jin Ho Cho SP	10.00	3.00
❑ 88 Russ Branyan SP	10.00	3.00
❑ 89 Derrick Gibson SP	10.00	3.00
❑ 90 Gabe Kapler SP AU	25.00	7.50
❑ 91 Matt Anderson SP	10.00	3.00
❑ 92 Robert Fick SP	10.00	3.00
❑ 93 Juan Encarnacion SP	10.00	3.00
❑ 94 Preston Wilson SP	10.00	3.00
❑ 95 Alex Gonzalez SP	10.00	3.00
❑ 96 Carlos Beltran SP	10.00	3.00
❑ 97 Jeremy Giambi SP	10.00	3.00
❑ 98 Dee Brown SP	10.00	3.00
❑ 99 Adrian Beltre SP	10.00	3.00
❑ 100 Alex Cora SP	10.00	3.00
❑ 101 Angel Pena SP	10.00	3.00
❑ 102 Geoff Jenkins SP	10.00	3.00
❑ 103 Ronnie Belliard SP	10.00	3.00
❑ 104 Corey Koskie SP	10.00	3.00
❑ 105 A.J. Pierzynski SP	10.00	3.00
❑ 106 Michael Barrett SP	10.00	3.00
❑ 107 Fern.Seguignol SP	10.00	3.00
❑ 108 Mike Kinkade SP	10.00	3.00
❑ 109 Mike Lowell SP	10.00	3.00
❑ 110 Ricky Ledee SP	10.00	3.00
❑ 111 Eric Chavez SP	10.00	3.00

Card	Nm-Mt	Ex-Mt
❑ 112 Abraham Nunez SP	10.00	3.00
❑ 113 Matt Clement SP	10.00	3.00
❑ 114 Ben Davis SP	10.00	3.00
❑ 115 Mike Darr SP	10.00	3.00
❑ 116 Ramon E.Martinez SP RC	10.00	3.00
❑ 117 Carlos Guillen SP	10.00	3.00
❑ 118 Shane Monahan SP	10.00	3.00
❑ 119 J.D. Drew SP AU	25.00	7.50
❑ 120 Kevin Witt SP	10.00	3.00
❑ 24EAST K.Griffey Jr. SAMP	2.00	.60

2000 SPx

	Nm-Mt	Ex-Mt
COMP.BASIC w/o SP's (90)	25.00	7.50
COMP.UPDATE w/o SP's (30)	10.00	3.00
COMMON CARD (1-90)	.50	.15
COMMON AU/1500 (91-120)	15.00	4.50
COMMON (121-135/182-196)	10.00	3.00
COMMON (136-151)	15.00	4.50
COMMON (152-181)	.75	.23

Card	Nm-Mt	Ex-Mt
❑ 1 Troy Glaus	.75	.23
❑ 2 Mo Vaughn	.50	.15
❑ 3 Ramon Ortiz	.50	.15
❑ 4 Jeff Bagwell	.75	.23
❑ 5 Moises Alou	.50	.15
❑ 6 Craig Biggio	.75	.23
❑ 7 Jose Lima	.50	.15
❑ 8 Jason Giambi	1.25	.35
❑ 9 John Jaha	.50	.15
❑ 10 Matt Stairs	.50	.15
❑ 11 Chipper Jones	1.25	.35
❑ 12 Greg Maddux	2.50	.75
❑ 13 Andres Galarraga	.50	.15
❑ 14 Andruw Jones	.75	.23
❑ 15 Jeromy Burnitz	.50	.15
❑ 16 Ron Belliard	.50	.15
❑ 17 Carlos Delgado	.50	.15
❑ 18 David Wells	.50	.15
❑ 19 Tony Batista	.50	.15
❑ 20 Shannon Stewart	.50	.15
❑ 21 Sammy Sosa	2.00	.60
❑ 22 Mark Grace	1.25	.35
❑ 23 Henry Rodriguez	.50	.15
❑ 24 Mark McGwire	3.00	.90
❑ 25 J.D. Drew	.50	.15
❑ 26 Luis Gonzalez	.50	.15
❑ 27 Randy Johnson	1.25	.35
❑ 28 Matt Williams	.50	.15
❑ 29 Steve Finley	.50	.15
❑ 30 Shawn Green	.50	.15
❑ 31 Kevin Brown	.75	.23
❑ 32 Gary Sheffield	.50	.15
❑ 33 Jose Canseco	1.25	.35
❑ 34 Greg Vaughn	.50	.15
❑ 35 Vladimir Guerrero	1.25	.35
❑ 36 Michael Barrett	.50	.15
❑ 37 Russ Ortiz	.50	.15
❑ 38 Barry Bonds	3.00	.90
❑ 39 Jeff Kent	.50	.15
❑ 40 Richie Sexson	.50	.15
❑ 41 Manny Ramirez	.50	.15
❑ 42 Jim Thome	1.25	.35
❑ 43 Roberto Alomar	1.25	.35
❑ 44 Edgar Martinez	.75	.23
❑ 45 Alex Rodriguez	2.50	.75
❑ 46 John Olerud	.50	.15
❑ 47 Alex Gonzalez	.50	.15
❑ 48 Cliff Floyd	.50	.15
❑ 49 Mike Piazza	2.00	.60
❑ 50 Al Leiter	.50	.15
❑ 51 Robin Ventura	.75	.23
❑ 52 Edgardo Alfonzo	.50	.15
❑ 53 Albert Belle	.50	.15
❑ 54 Cal Ripken	4.00	1.20
❑ 55 B.J. Surhoff	.50	.15
❑ 56 Tony Gwynn	1.50	.45
❑ 57 Trevor Hoffman	.50	.15
❑ 58 Brian Giles	.50	.15
❑ 59 Jason Kendall	.50	.15
❑ 60 Kris Benson	.50	.15
❑ 61 Bob Abreu	.50	.15
❑ 62 Scott Rolen	.75	.23
❑ 63 Curt Schilling	.75	.23
❑ 64 Mike Lieberthal	.50	.15
❑ 65 Sean Casey	.50	.15
❑ 66 Dante Bichette	.50	.15
❑ 67 Ken Griffey Jr.	2.00	.60
❑ 68 Pokey Reese	.50	.15
❑ 69 Mike Sweeney	.50	.15
❑ 70 Carlos Febles	.50	.15
❑ 71 Ivan Rodriguez	1.25	.35
❑ 72 Ruben Mateo	.50	.15
❑ 73 Rafael Palmeiro	.75	.23
❑ 74 Larry Walker	.75	.23
❑ 75 Todd Helton	.75	.23
❑ 76 Nomar Garciaparra	2.50	.75
❑ 77 Pedro Martinez	1.25	.35
❑ 78 Troy O'Leary	.50	.15
❑ 79 Jacque Jones	.50	.15
❑ 80 Corey Koskie	.50	.15
❑ 81 Juan Gonzalez	1.25	.35
❑ 82 Dean Palmer	.50	.15
❑ 83 Juan Encarnacion	.50	.15
❑ 84 Frank Thomas	1.25	.35
❑ 85 Magglio Ordonez	.50	.15
❑ 86 Paul Konerko	.50	.15
❑ 87 Bernie Williams	.75	.23
❑ 88 Derek Jeter	3.00	.90
❑ 89 Roger Clemens	2.50	.75
❑ 90 Orlando Hernandez	.50	.15
❑ 91 Vernon Wells/1500 AU	25.00	7.50
❑ 92 Rick Ankiel/1500 AU	15.00	4.50
❑ 93 Eric Chavez/1500 AU	25.00	7.50
❑ 94 A.Soriano/1500 AU	80.00	24.00
❑ 95 Eric Gagne/1500 AU	60.00	18.00
❑ 96 Rob Bell/1500 AU	15.00	4.50
❑ 97 Matt Riley/1500 AU	15.00	4.50
❑ 98 Josh Beckett/1500 AU	80.00	24.00
❑ 99 Ben Petrick/1500 AU	15.00	4.50
❑ 100 Rob Ramsay/1500 AU	15.00	4.50
❑ 101 Scott Williamson 1500 AU	15.00	4.50
❑ 102 Doug Davis/1500 AU	15.00	4.50
❑ 103 E.Munson/1500 AU*	15.00	4.50
❑ 104 Pat Burrell/500 AU	60.00	18.00
❑ 105 Jim Morris/1500 AU	25.00	7.50
❑ 106 Gabe Kapler/500 AU	25.00	7.50
❑ 107 Lance Berkman/1000	10.00	3.00
❑ 108 E.Durazo/1500 AU	25.00	7.50
❑ 109 Tim Hudson/1500 AU	40.00	12.00
❑ 110 Ben Davis/1500 AU*	15.00	4.50
❑ 111 N.Johnson/1500 AU	25.00	7.50
❑ 112 O.Dotel/1500 AU	15.00	4.50
❑ 113 Jerry Hairston/1000	10.00	3.00
❑ 114 Ruben Mateo/1000	10.00	3.00
❑ 115 Chris Singleton/1000	10.00	3.00
❑ 116 Bruce Chen/1500 AU	15.00	4.50
❑ 117 Derrick Gibson/1000	10.00	3.00
❑ 118 Carlos Beltran/500 AU	40.00	12.00
❑ 119 F.Garcia/1500 AU	25.00	7.50
❑ 120 P.Wilson/1500 AU	25.00	7.50
❑ 121 B.Wilkerson/1600 RC	15.00	4.50
❑ 122 Roy Oswalt/1600 RC	60.00	18.00
❑ 123 W.Serrano/1600 RC	10.00	3.00
❑ 124 Sean Burnett/1600 RC	15.00	4.50
❑ 125 Alex Cabrera/1600 RC	10.00	3.00
❑ 126 Timo Perez/1600 RC	10.00	3.00
❑ 127 Juan Pierre/1600 RC	15.00	4.50
❑ 128 Daylan Holt/1600 RC	10.00	3.00
❑ 129 T.Ohka/1600 RC	10.00	3.00
❑ 130 K.Sasaki/1600 RC	15.00	4.50
❑ 131 K.Ainsworth/1600 RC	15.00	4.50
❑ 132 B.Abernathy/1600 RC	10.00	3.00
❑ 133 Danys Baez/1600 RC	15.00	4.50
❑ 134 Brad Cresse/1600 RC	10.00	3.00
❑ 135 R.Franklin/1600 RC	10.00	3.00
❑ 136 M.Lamb/1500 AU RC	15.00	4.50
❑ 137 David Espinosa 1500 AU RC	15.00	4.50
❑ 138 Matt Wheatland 1500 AU RC	15.00	4.50
❑ 139 X.Nady/1500 AU RC	40.00	12.00
❑ 140 S.Heard/1500 AU RC	15.00	4.50
❑ 141 P.Coco/1500 AU RC Card erroneously numbered 54 instead of 141	15.00	4.50
❑ 142 J.Miller/1500 AU RC	15.00	4.50
❑ 143 Dave Krynzel 1500 AU RC	15.00	4.50
❑ 144 Dane Sardinha 1500 AU RC	15.00	4.50
❑ 145 B.Sheets/1500 AU RC	25.00	7.50
❑ 146 L.Estrella/1500 AU RC	15.00	4.50
❑ 147 Ben Diggins 1500 AU RC	15.00	4.50
❑ 148 B.Zito/1500 AU RC	100.00	30.00
❑ 149 J.Torres/1500 AU RC	15.00	4.50
❑ 150 Mike Meyers 1500 AU RC	15.00	4.50
❑ 151 K.Wilson/1500 AU RC	15.00	4.50
❑ 152 Darin Erstad	.75	.23
❑ 153 Richard Hidalgo	.75	.23
❑ 154 Eric Chavez	.75	.23
❑ 155 B.J. Surhoff	.75	.23
❑ 156 Richie Sexson	.75	.23
❑ 157 Raul Mondesi	.75	.23
❑ 158 Rondell White	.75	.23
❑ 159 Jim Edmonds	.75	.23
❑ 160 Curt Schilling	1.25	.35
❑ 161 Tom Goodwin	.75	.23
❑ 162 Fred McGriff	1.25	.35
❑ 163 Jose Vidro	.75	.23
❑ 164 Ellis Burks	.75	.23
❑ 165 David Segui	.75	.23
❑ 166 Aaron Sele	.75	.23
❑ 167 Henry Rodriguez	.75	.23
❑ 168 Mike Bordick	.75	.23
❑ 169 Mike Mussina	2.00	.60
❑ 170 Ryan Klesko	.75	.23
❑ 171 Kevin Young	.75	.23
❑ 172 Travis Lee	.75	.23
❑ 173 Aaron Boone	.75	.23
❑ 174 Jermaine Dye	.75	.23
❑ 175 Ricky Ledee	.75	.23
❑ 176 Jeffrey Hammonds	.75	.23
❑ 177 Carl Everett	.75	.23
❑ 178 Matt Lawton	.75	.23
❑ 179 Bobby Higginson	.75	.23
❑ 180 Charles Johnson	.75	.23
❑ 181 David Justice	.75	.23
❑ 182 Joey Nation/1600 RC	10.00	3.00
❑ 183 Rico Washington 1600 RC	10.00	3.00
❑ 184 Luis Matos/1600 RC	15.00	4.50
❑ 185 C.Wakeland/1600 RC	10.00	3.00
❑ 186 SW Kim/1600 RC	10.00	3.00
❑ 187 Keith Ginter/1600 RC	10.00	3.00
❑ 188 G.Guzman/1600 RC	10.00	3.00
❑ 189 J.Spurgeon/1600 RC	10.00	3.00
❑ 190 Jace Brewer/1600 RC	10.00	3.00
❑ 191 J.Guzman/1600 RC	10.00	3.00
❑ 192 Ross Gload/1600 RC	10.00	3.00
❑ 193 P.Crawford/1600 RC	10.00	3.00
❑ 194 R.Kohlmeier/1600 RC	10.00	3.00
❑ 195 Julio Zuleta/1600 RC	10.00	3.00
❑ 196 Matt Ginter/1600 RC	10.00	3.00

2001 SPx

	Nm-Mt	Ex-Mt
COMP.BASIC w/o SP's (90)	25.00	7.50
COMP.UPDATE w/o SP's (30)	10.00	3.00
COMMON CARD (1-90)	.50	.15
COMMON YS (91-120)	8.00	2.40
COMMON JSY (121-135)	10.00	3.00
COMMON (136-150)	15.00	4.50
COMMON (151-180)	.75	.23
COMMON (181-210)	5.00	1.50

❑ 1 Darin Erstad .50 .15
❑ 2 Troy Glaus .75 .23
❑ 3 Mo Vaughn .50 .15
❑ 4 Johnny Damon .50 .15
❑ 5 Jason Giambi 1.25 .35
❑ 6 Tim Hudson .50 .15
❑ 7 Miguel Tejada .50 .15
❑ 8 Carlos Delgado .50 .15
❑ 9 Raul Mondesi .50 .15
❑ 10 Tony Batista .50 .15
❑ 11 Ben Grieve .50 .15
❑ 12 Greg Vaughn .50 .15
❑ 13 Juan Gonzalez 1.25 .35
❑ 14 Jim Thome 1.25 .35
❑ 15 Roberto Alomar 1.25 .35
❑ 16 John Olerud .50 .15
❑ 17 Edgar Martinez .75 .23
❑ 18 Albert Belle .50 .15
❑ 19 Cal Ripken 4.00 1.20
❑ 20 Ivan Rodriguez 1.25 .35
❑ 21 Rafael Palmeiro .75 .23
❑ 22 Alex Rodriguez 2.50 .75
❑ 23 Nomar Garciaparra 2.50 .75
❑ 24 Pedro Martinez 1.25 .35
❑ 25 Manny Ramirez .50 .15
❑ 26 Jermaine Dye .50 .15
❑ 27 Mark Quinn .50 .15
❑ 28 Carlos Beltran .50 .15
❑ 29 Tony Clark .50 .15
❑ 30 Bobby Higginson .50 .15
❑ 31 Eric Milton .50 .15
❑ 32 Matt Lawton .50 .15
❑ 33 Frank Thomas 1.25 .35
❑ 34 Magglio Ordonez .50 .15
❑ 35 Ray Durham .50 .15
❑ 36 David Wells .50 .15
❑ 37 Derek Jeter 3.00 .90
❑ 38 Bernie Williams .75 .23
❑ 39 Roger Clemens UER 2.50 .75
Wrong uniform number on card
❑ 40 David Justice .50 .15
❑ 41 Jeff Bagwell .75 .23
❑ 42 Richard Hidalgo .50 .15
❑ 43 Moises Alou .50 .15
❑ 44 Chipper Jones 1.25 .35
❑ 45 Andruw Jones .75 .23
❑ 46 Greg Maddux 2.50 .75
❑ 47 Rafael Furcal .50 .15
❑ 48 Jeromy Burnitz .50 .15
❑ 49 Geoff Jenkins .50 .15
❑ 50 Mark McGwire 3.00 .90
❑ 51 Jim Edmonds .50 .15
❑ 52 Rick Ankiel .50 .15
❑ 53 Edgar Renteria .50 .15
❑ 54 Sammy Sosa 2.00 .60
❑ 55 Kerry Wood 1.25 .35
❑ 56 Rondell White .50 .15
❑ 57 Randy Johnson 1.25 .35
❑ 58 Steve Finley .50 .15
❑ 59 Matt Williams .50 .15
❑ 60 Luis Gonzalez .50 .15
❑ 61 Kevin Brown .50 .15
❑ 62 Gary Sheffield .50 .15
❑ 63 Shawn Green .50 .15
❑ 64 Vladimir Guerrero 1.25 .35
❑ 65 Jose Vidro .50 .15
❑ 66 Barry Bonds 3.00 .90
❑ 67 Jeff Kent .50 .15
❑ 68 Livan Hernandez .50 .15
❑ 69 Preston Wilson .50 .15
❑ 70 Charles Johnson .50 .15
❑ 71 Cliff Floyd .50 .15
❑ 72 Mike Piazza 2.00 .60
❑ 73 Edgardo Alfonzo .50 .15
❑ 74 Jay Payton .50 .15
❑ 75 Robin Ventura .50 .15
❑ 76 Tony Gwynn 1.50 .45
❑ 77 Phil Nevin .50 .15
❑ 78 Ryan Klesko .50 .15
❑ 79 Scott Rolen .75 .23
❑ 80 Pat Burrell .50 .15
❑ 81 Bob Abreu .50 .15
❑ 82 Brian Giles .50 .15
❑ 83 Kris Benson .50 .15
❑ 84 Jason Kendall .50 .15
❑ 85 Ken Griffey Jr. 2.00 .60
❑ 86 Barry Larkin 1.25 .35
❑ 87 Sean Casey .50 .15
❑ 88 Todd Helton .75 .23
❑ 89 Larry Walker .75 .23
❑ 90 Mike Hampton .50 .15
❑ 91 Billy Sylvester YS RC 8.00 2.40
❑ 92 Josh Towers YS RC 8.00 2.40
❑ 93 Zach Day YS RC 8.00 2.40
❑ 94 Martin Vargas YS RC 8.00 2.40
❑ 95 Adam Pettyjohn YS RC 8.00 2.40
❑ 96 Andres Torres YS RC 8.00 2.40
❑ 97 Kris Keller YS RC 8.00 2.40
❑ 98 Blaine Neal YS RC 8.00 2.40
❑ 99 Kyle Kessel YS RC 8.00 2.40
❑ 100 Greg Miller YS RC 8.00 2.40
❑ 101 Shawn Sonnier YS 8.00 2.40
❑ 102 Alexis Gomez YS RC 8.00 2.40
❑ 103 Grant Balfour YS RC 8.00 2.40
❑ 104 Henry Mateo YS RC 8.00 2.40
❑ 105 Wilken Ruan YS RC 8.00 2.40
❑ 106 Nick Maness YS RC 8.00 2.40
❑ 107 J. Michaels YS RC 8.00 2.40
❑ 108 Esix Snead YS RC 8.00 2.40
❑ 109 William Ortega YS RC 8.00 2.40
❑ 110 David Elder YS RC 8.00 2.40
❑ 111 J. Melian YS RC 8.00 2.40
❑ 112 Nate Teut YS RC 8.00 2.40
❑ 113 Jason Smith YS RC 8.00 2.40
❑ 114 Mike Penney YS RC 8.00 2.40
❑ 115 Jose Mieses YS RC 8.00 2.40
❑ 116 Juan Pena YS 8.00 2.40
❑ 117 B. Lawrence YS RC 8.00 2.40
❑ 118 Jeremy Owens YS RC 8.00 2.40
❑ 119 C. Valderrama YS RC 8.00 2.40
❑ 120 Rafael Soriano YS RC 12.00 3.60
❑ 121 H. Ramirez JSY RC 15.00 4.50
❑ 122 R. Rodriguez JSY RC 10.00 3.00
❑ 123 Juan Diaz JSY RC 10.00 3.00
❑ 124 Donnie Bridges JSY 10.00 3.00
❑ 125 Tyler Walker JSY RC 10.00 3.00
❑ 126 Erick Almonte JSY RC 10.00 3.00
❑ 127 Jesus Colome JSY 10.00 3.00
❑ 128 Ryan Freel JSY RC 10.00 3.00
❑ 129 Elpidio Guzman JSY RC 10.00 3.00
❑ 130 Jack Cust JSY 10.00 3.00
❑ 131 Eric Hinske JSY RC 15.00 4.50
❑ 132 Josh Fogg JSY RC 10.00 3.00
❑ 133 Juan Uribe JSY RC 10.00 3.00
❑ 134 Bert Snow JSY RC 10.00 3.00
❑ 135 Pedro Feliz JSY 10.00 3.00
❑ 136 W. Betemit JSY AU RC 15.00 4.50
❑ 137 S. Douglass JSY AU RC 15.00 4.50
❑ 138 D. Stenson JSY AU 15.00 4.50
❑ 139 Brandon Inge JSY AU 15.00 4.50
❑ 140 M. Ensberg JSY AU RC 40.00 12.00
❑ 141 Brian Cole JSY AU 15.00 4.50
❑ 142 A. Hernandez JSY AU RC 15.00 4.50
❑ 143 Brandon Duckworth 15.00 4.50
JSY AU RC
❑ 144 J. Wilson JSY AU RC 15.00 4.50
❑ 145 T. Hafner JSY AU RC 25.00 7.50
❑ 146 Carlos Pena JSY AU 15.00 4.50
❑ 147 C. Patterson JSY AU 15.00 4.50
❑ 148 Xavier Nady JSY AU 15.00 4.50
❑ 149 Jason Hart JSY AU 15.00 4.50
❑ 150 I. Suzuki JSY AU RC 500.00 150.00
❑ 151 Garret Anderson .75 .23
❑ 152 Jermaine Dye .75 .23
❑ 153 Shannon Stewart .75 .23
❑ 154 Toby Hall .75 .23
❑ 155 C.C. Sabathia .75 .23
❑ 156 Bret Boone .75 .23
❑ 157 Tony Batista .75 .23
❑ 158 Gabe Kapler .75 .23
❑ 159 Carl Everett .75 .23
❑ 160 Mike Sweeney .75 .23
❑ 161 Dean Palmer .75 .23
❑ 162 Doug Mientkiewicz .75 .23
❑ 163 Carlos Lee .75 .23
❑ 164 Mike Mussina 2.00 .60
❑ 165 Lance Berkman .75 .23
❑ 166 Ken Caminiti .75 .23
❑ 167 Ben Sheets .75 .23
❑ 168 Matt Morris .75 .23
❑ 169 Fred McGriff 1.25 .35
❑ 170 Curt Schilling 1.25 .35
❑ 171 Paul LoDuca .75 .23
❑ 172 Javier Vazquez .75 .23
❑ 173 Rich Aurilia .75 .23
❑ 174 A.J. Burnett .75 .23
❑ 175 Al Leiter .75 .23
❑ 176 Mark Kotsay .75 .23
❑ 177 Jimmy Rollins .75 .23
❑ 178 Aramis Ramirez .75 .23
❑ 179 Aaron Boone .75 .23
❑ 180 Jeff Cirillo .75 .23
❑ 181 J.Estrada YS RC 6.00 1.80
❑ 182 Dave Williams YS RC 5.00 1.50
❑ 183 D.Mendez YS RC 5.00 1.50
❑ 184 Junior Spivey YS RC 10.00 3.00
❑ 185 Jay Gibbons YS RC 12.00 3.60
❑ 186 Kyle Lohse YS RC 10.00 3.00
❑ 187 Willie Harris YS RC 5.00 1.50
❑ 188 Juan Cruz YS RC 5.00 1.50
❑ 189 Joe Kennedy YS RC 5.00 1.50
❑ 190 D.Sanchez YS RC 5.00 1.50
❑ 191 Jorge Julio YS RC 5.00 1.50
❑ 192 Cesar Crespo YS RC 5.00 1.50
❑ 193 Casey Fossum YS RC 5.00 1.50
❑ 194 Brian Roberts YS RC 5.00 1.50
❑ 195 Troy Mattes YS RC 5.00 1.50
❑ 196 R.Mackowiak YS RC 5.00 1.50
❑ 197 T.Shinjo YS RC 12.00 3.60
❑ 198 Nick Punto YS RC 5.00 1.50
❑ 199 Wilmy Caceres YS RC 5.00 1.50
❑ 200 Jeremy Affeldt YS RC 5.00 1.50
❑ 201 Bret Prinz YS RC 5.00 1.50
❑ 202 Delvin James YS RC 5.00 1.50
❑ 203 Luis Pineda YS RC 5.00 1.50
❑ 204 Matt White YS RC 5.00 1.50
❑ 205 B.Knight YS RC 5.00 1.50
❑ 206 Albert Pujols YS AU RC 350.00 105.00
❑ 207 M.Teixeira YS AU RC 100.00 30.00
❑ 208 Mark Prior YS AU RC 250.00 75.00
❑ 209 D.Brazelton YS AU RC 15.00 4.50
❑ 210 Bud Smith YS AU RC 15.00 4.50

2002 SPx

	Nm-Mt	Ex-Mt
COMP.LOW w/o SP's (90)	25.00	7.50
COMP.UPDATE w/o SP's (30)	10.00	3.00
COMMON CARD (1-90)	.50	.15
COMMON ROOKIE (91A-	10.00	3.00
COMMON CARD (121-150)	15.00	4.50
COMMON CARD (151-190)	10.00	3.00

Card	Nrmt	Ex
COMMON CARD (191-220)	.75	.23
COMMON CARD (221-250)	15.00	4.50
❑ 1 Troy Glaus	.75	.23
❑ 2 Darin Erstad	.50	.15
❑ 3 David Justice	.50	.15
❑ 4 Tim Hudson	.50	.15
❑ 5 Miguel Tejada	.50	.15
❑ 6 Barry Zito	1.25	.35
❑ 7 Carlos Delgado	.50	.15
❑ 8 Shannon Stewart	.50	.15
❑ 9 Greg Vaughn	.75	.23
❑ 10 Toby Hall	.50	.15
❑ 11 Jim Thome	1.25	.35
❑ 12 C.C. Sabathia	.50	.15
❑ 13 Ichiro Suzuki	2.50	.75
❑ 14 Edgar Martinez	.75	.23
❑ 15 Freddy Garcia	.50	.15
❑ 16 Mike Cameron	.50	.15
❑ 17 Jeff Conine	.50	.15
❑ 18 Tony Batista	.50	.15
❑ 19 Alex Rodriguez	2.50	.75
❑ 20 Rafael Palmeiro	.75	.23
❑ 21 Ivan Rodriguez	1.25	.35
❑ 22 Carl Everett	.50	.15
❑ 23 Pedro Martinez	1.25	.35
❑ 24 Manny Ramirez	.50	.15
❑ 25 Nomar Garciaparra	2.50	.75
❑ 26 Johnny Damon	.50	.15
❑ 27 Mike Sweeney	.50	.15
❑ 28 Carlos Beltran	.50	.15
❑ 29 Dmitri Young	.50	.15
❑ 30 Joe Mays	.50	.15
❑ 31 Doug Mientkiewicz	.50	.15
❑ 32 Cristian Guzman	.50	.15
❑ 33 Corey Koskie	.50	.15
❑ 34 Frank Thomas	1.25	.35
❑ 35 Magglio Ordonez	.50	.15
❑ 36 Mark Buehrle	.50	.15
❑ 37 Bernie Williams	.75	.23
❑ 38 Roger Clemens	2.50	.75
❑ 39 Derek Jeter	3.00	.90
❑ 40 Jason Giambi	1.25	.35
❑ 41 Mike Mussina	1.25	.35
❑ 42 Lance Berkman	.50	.15
❑ 43 Jeff Bagwell	.75	.23
❑ 44 Roy Oswalt	.50	.15
❑ 45 Greg Maddux	2.50	.75
❑ 46 Chipper Jones	1.25	.35
❑ 47 Andruw Jones	.75	.23
❑ 48 Gary Sheffield	.50	.15
❑ 49 Geoff Jenkins	.50	.15
❑ 50 Richie Sexson	.50	.15
❑ 51 Ben Sheets	.50	.15
❑ 52 Albert Pujols	2.50	.75
❑ 53 J.D. Drew	.50	.15
❑ 54 Jim Edmonds	.50	.15
❑ 55 Sammy Sosa	2.00	.60
❑ 56 Moises Alou	.50	.15
❑ 57 Kerry Wood	1.25	.35
❑ 58 Jon Lieber	.50	.15
❑ 59 Fred McGriff	.75	.23
❑ 60 Randy Johnson	1.25	.35
❑ 61 Luis Gonzalez	.50	.15
❑ 62 Curt Schilling	.75	.23
❑ 63 Kevin Brown	.50	.15
❑ 64 Hideo Nomo	1.25	.35
❑ 65 Shawn Green	.50	.15
❑ 66 Vladimir Guerrero	1.25	.35
❑ 67 Jose Vidro	.50	.15
❑ 68 Barry Bonds	3.00	.90
❑ 69 Jeff Kent	.50	.15
❑ 70 Rich Aurilia	.50	.15
❑ 71 Cliff Floyd	.50	.15
❑ 72 Josh Beckett	.75	.23
❑ 73 Preston Wilson	.50	.15
❑ 74 Mike Piazza	2.00	.60
❑ 75 Mo Vaughn	.50	.15
❑ 76 Jeromy Burnitz	.50	.15
❑ 77 Roberto Alomar	1.25	.35
❑ 78 Phil Nevin	.50	.15
❑ 79 Ryan Klesko	.50	.15
❑ 80 Scott Rolen	.75	.23
❑ 81 Bobby Abreu	.50	.15
❑ 82 Jimmy Rollins	.50	.15
❑ 83 Brian Giles	.50	.15
❑ 84 Aramis Ramirez	.50	.15
❑ 85 Ken Griffey Jr.	2.00	.60
❑ 86 Sean Casey	.50	.15
❑ 87 Barry Larkin	1.25	.35
❑ 88 Mike Hampton	.50	.15
❑ 89 Larry Walker	.75	.23
❑ 90 Todd Helton	.75	.23
❑ 91A Ron Calloway YS RC	10.00	3.00
❑ 91P Ron Calloway YS RC	10.00	3.00
❑ 92A Joe Orloski YS RC	10.00	3.00
❑ 92P Joe Orloski YS RC	10.00	3.00
❑ 93A Anderson Machado YS RC	10.00	3.00
❑ 93P Anderson Machado YS RC	10.00	3.00
❑ 94A Eric Good YS RC	10.00	3.00
❑ 94P Eric Good YS RC	10.00	3.00
❑ 95A Reed Johnson YS RC	10.00	3.00
❑ 95P Reed Johnson YS RC	10.00	3.00
❑ 96A Brendan Donnelly YS RC	10.00	3.00
❑ 96P Brendan Donnelly YS RC	10.00	3.00
❑ 97A Chris Baker YS RC	10.00	3.00
❑ 97P Chris Baker YS RC	10.00	3.00
❑ 98A Wilson Valdez YS RC	10.00	3.00
❑ 98P Wilson Valdez YS RC	10.00	3.00
❑ 99A Scotty Layfield YS RC	10.00	3.00
❑ 99P Scotty Layfield YS RC	10.00	3.00
❑ 100A P.J. Bevis YS RC	10.00	3.00
❑ 100P P.J. Bevis YS RC	10.00	3.00
❑ 101A Edwin Almonte YS RC	10.00	3.00
❑ 101P Edwin Almonte YS RC	10.00	3.00
❑ 102A Francis Beltran YS RC	10.00	3.00
❑ 102P Francis Beltran YS RC	10.00	3.00
❑ 103A Val Pascucci YS	10.00	3.00
❑ 103P Val Pascucci YS	10.00	3.00
❑ 104A Nelson Castro YS RC	10.00	3.00
❑ 104P Nelson Castro YS RC	10.00	3.00
❑ 105A Michael Crudale YS RC	10.00	3.00
❑ 105P Michael Crudale YS RC	10.00	3.00
❑ 106A Colin Young YS RC	10.00	3.00
❑ 106P Colin Young YS RC	10.00	3.00
❑ 107A Todd Donovan YS RC	10.00	3.00
❑ 107P Todd Donovan YS RC	10.00	3.00
❑ 108A Felix Escalona YS RC	10.00	3.00
❑ 108P Felix Escalona YS RC	10.00	3.00
❑ 109A Brandon Backe YS RC	10.00	3.00
❑ 109P Brandon Backe YS RC	10.00	3.00
❑ 110A Corey Thurman YS RC	10.00	3.00
❑ 110P Corey Thurman YS RC	10.00	3.00
❑ 111A Kyle Kane YS RC	10.00	3.00
❑ 111P Kyle Kane YS RC	10.00	3.00
❑ 112A Allan Simpson YS RC	10.00	3.00
❑ 112P Allan Simpson YS RC	10.00	3.00
❑ 113A Jose Valverde YS RC	10.00	3.00
❑ 113P Jose Valverde YS RC	10.00	3.00
❑ 114A Chris Booker YS RC	10.00	3.00
❑ 114P Chris Booker YS RC	10.00	3.00
❑ 115A Brandon Puffer YS RC	10.00	3.00
❑ 115P Brandon Puffer YS RC	10.00	3.00
❑ 116A John Foster YS RC	10.00	3.00
❑ 116P John Foster YS RC	10.00	3.00
❑ 117A Cliff Bartosh YS RC	10.00	3.00
❑ 117P Cliff Bartosh YS RC	10.00	3.00
❑ 118A Gustavo Chacin YS RC	10.00	3.00
❑ 118P Gustavo Chacin YS RC	10.00	3.00
❑ 119A Steve Kent YS RC	10.00	3.00
❑ 119P Steve Kent YS RC	10.00	3.00
❑ 120A Nate Field YS RC	10.00	3.00
❑ 120P Nate Field YS RC	10.00	3.00
❑ 121 Victor Alvarez AU RC	15.00	4.50
❑ 122 Steve Bechler AU RC	15.00	4.50
❑ 123 Adrian Burnside AU RC	15.00	4.50
❑ 124 Marlon Byrd AU	15.00	4.50
❑ 125 Jaime Cerda AU RC	15.00	4.50
❑ 126 Brandon Claussen AU	25.00	7.50
❑ 127 Mark Corey AU RC	15.00	4.50
❑ 128 Doug Devore AU RC	15.00	4.50
❑ 129 Kazuhisa Ishii AU SP RC	100.00	30.00
❑ 130 John Ennis AU RC	15.00	4.50
❑ 131 Kevin Frederick AU RC	15.00	4.50
❑ 132 Josh Hancock AU RC	15.00	4.50
❑ 133 Ben Howard AU RC	15.00	4.50
❑ 134 Orlando Hudson AU	15.00	4.50
❑ 135 Hansel Izquierdo AU RC	15.00	4.50
❑ 136 Eric Junge AU RC	15.00	4.50
❑ 137 Austin Kearns AU	25.00	7.50
❑ 138 Victor Martinez AU	15.00	4.50
❑ 139 Luis Martinez AU RC	15.00	4.50
❑ 140 Danny Mota AU RC	15.00	4.50
❑ 141 Jorge Padilla AU RC	15.00	4.50
❑ 142 Andy Pratt AU RC	15.00	4.50
❑ 143 Rene Reyes AU RC	15.00	4.50
❑ 144 Rodrigo Rosario AU RC	15.00	4.50
❑ 145 Tom Shearn AU RC	15.00	4.50
❑ 146 So Taguchi AU SP RC	40.00	12.00
❑ 147 Dennis Tankersley AU	15.00	4.50
❑ 148 Matt Thornton AU RC	15.00	4.50
❑ 149 Jeremy Ward AU RC	15.00	4.50
❑ 150 Mitch Wylie AU RC	15.00	4.50
❑ 151 Pedro Martinez JSY/800	15.00	4.50
❑ 152 Cal Ripken JSY/800	40.00	12.00
❑ 153 Roger Clemens JSY/800	25.00	7.50
❑ 154 Bernie Williams JSY/800	15.00	4.50
❑ 155 Jason Giambi JSY/700	25.00	7.50
❑ 156 Robin Ventura JSY/800	10.00	3.00
❑ 157 Carlos Delgado JSY/800	10.00	3.00
❑ 158 Frank Thomas JSY/800	15.00	4.50
❑ 159 Magglio Ordonez JSY/800	10.00	3.00
❑ 160 Jim Thome JSY/800	15.00	4.50
❑ 161 Darin Erstad JSY/800	10.00	3.00
❑ 162 Tim Salmon JSY/800	15.00	4.50
❑ 163 Tim Hudson JSY/800	10.00	3.00
❑ 164 Barry Zito JSY/800	15.00	4.50
❑ 165 Ichiro Suzuki JSY/800	50.00	15.00
❑ 166 Edgar Martinez JSY/800	15.00	4.50
❑ 167 Alex Rodriguez JSY/800	25.00	7.50
❑ 168 Ivan Rodriguez JSY/800	15.00	4.50
❑ 169 Juan Gonzalez JSY/800	15.00	4.50
❑ 170 Greg Maddux JSY/800	25.00	7.50
❑ 171 Chipper Jones JSY/800	15.00	4.50
❑ 172 Andruw Jones JSY/800	15.00	4.50
❑ 173 Tom Glavine JSY/800	15.00	4.50
❑ 174 Mike Piazza JSY/800	20.00	6.00
❑ 175 Roberto Alomar JSY/800	15.00	4.50
❑ 176 Scott Rolen JSY/800	15.00	4.50
❑ 177 Sammy Sosa JSY/800	25.00	7.50
❑ 178 Moises Alou JSY/800	10.00	3.00
❑ 179 Ken Griffey Jr. JSY/700	25.00	7.50
❑ 180 Jeff Bagwell JSY/800	15.00	4.50
❑ 181 Jim Edmonds JSY/800	10.00	3.00
❑ 182 J.D. Drew JSY/800	10.00	3.00
❑ 183 Brian Giles JSY/800	10.00	3.00
❑ 184 Randy Johnson JSY/800	15.00	4.50
❑ 185 Curt Schilling JSY/800	15.00	4.50
❑ 186 Luis Gonzalez JSY/800	10.00	3.00
❑ 187 Todd Helton JSY/800	15.00	4.50
❑ 188 Shawn Green JSY/800	10.00	3.00
❑ 189 David Wells JSY/800	10.00	3.00
❑ 190 Jeff Kent JSY/800	10.00	3.00
❑ 191 Tom Glavine	2.00	.60
❑ 192 Cliff Floyd	.75	.23
❑ 193 Mark Prior	4.00	1.20
❑ 194 Corey Patterson	.75	.23
❑ 195 Paul Konerko	.75	.23
❑ 196 Adam Dunn	1.25	.35
❑ 197 Joe Borchard	.75	.23
❑ 198 Carlos Pena	.75	.23
❑ 199 Juan Encarnacion	.75	.23
❑ 200 Luis Castillo	.75	.23
❑ 201 Torii Hunter	.75	.23
❑ 202 Hee Seop Choi	1.25	.35
❑ 203 Bartolo Colon	.75	.23
❑ 204 Raul Mondesi	.75	.23
❑ 205 Jeff Weaver	.75	.23
❑ 206 Eric Munson	.75	.23
❑ 207 Alfonso Soriano	2.00	.60
❑ 208 Ray Durham	.75	.23
❑ 209 Eric Chavez	.75	.23
❑ 210 Brett Myers	.75	.23
❑ 211 Jeremy Giambi	.75	.23
❑ 212 Vicente Padilla	.75	.23
❑ 213 Felipe Lopez	.75	.23
❑ 214 Sean Burroughs	.75	.23
❑ 215 Kenny Lofton	.75	.23
❑ 216 Scott Rolen	1.25	.35
❑ 217 Carl Crawford	.75	.23
❑ 218 Juan Gonzalez	2.00	.60
❑ 219 Orlando Hudson	.75	.23
❑ 220 Eric Hinske	.75	.23
❑ 221 Adam Walker AU RC	15.00	4.50
❑ 222 Aaron Cook AU RC	20.00	6.00
❑ 223 Cam Esslinger AU RC	15.00	4.50
❑ 224 Kirk Saarloos AU RC	20.00	6.00
❑ 225 Jose Diaz AU RC	15.00	4.50

❑ 226 David Ross AU RC 15.00 4.50
❑ 227 Jayson Durocher AU RC 15.00 4.50
❑ 228 Brian Mallette AU RC .. 15.00 4.50
❑ 229 Aaron Guiel AU RC 20.00 6.00
❑ 230 Jorge Nunez AU RC...... 15.00 4.50
❑ 231 Satoru Komiyama AU RC 30.00 9.00
❑ 232 Tyler Yates AU RC........ 15.00 4.50
❑ 233 Pete Zamora AU RC...... 15.00 4.50
❑ 234 Mike Gonzalez AU RC .. 15.00 4.50
❑ 235 Oliver Perez AU RC 25.00 7.50
❑ 236 Julius Matos AU RC 15.00 4.50
❑ 237 Andy Shibilo AU RC 15.00 4.50
❑ 238 Jason Simontacchi AU RC .. 20.00 6.00
❑ 239 Ron Chiavacci AU 15.00 4.50
❑ 240 Deivis Santos AU 15.00 4.50
❑ 241 Travis Driskill AU RC .. 15.00 4.50
❑ 242 Jorge De La Rosa AU RC 15.00 4.50
❑ 243 Anastacio Martinez AU RC .. 15.00 4.50
❑ 244 Earl Snyder AU RC 15.00 4.50
❑ 245 Freddy Sanchez AU RC 20.00 6.00
❑ 246 Miguel Asencio AU RC 15.00 4.50
❑ 247 Juan Brito AU RC 15.00 4.50
❑ 248 Franklyn German AU RC 15.00 4.50
❑ 249 Chris Snelling AU RC .. 25.00 7.50
❑ 250 Ken Huckaby AU RC 15.00 4.50

2003 SPx

	MINT	NRMT
COMP.SET w/o SP's (100)........	25.00	11.00
COMP.SET w/ SP's (125)........	100.00	45.00
COMMON CARD (1-125)............	.50	.23
COMMON SP (1-125)	4.00	1.80
COMMON CARD (126-160).......	10.00	4.50
126-160 PRINT RUN 999 SERIAL #'d SETS		
CARD 161 PRINT RUN 864 SERIAL #'d COPIES		
CARD 162 PRINT RUN 800 SERIAL #'d COPIES		
COMMON CARD (163-178)......	15.00	6.75
163-178 PRINT RUN 1224 SERIAL #'d SETS		
126-178 RANDOM INSERTS IN PACKS		

❑ 1 Darin Erstad .... .50 .23
❑ 2 Garret Anderson .... .50 .23
❑ 3 Tim Salmon.......................... .75 .35
❑ 4 Troy Glaus SP 4.00 1.80
❑ 5 Luis Gonzalez .... .50 .23
❑ 6 Randy Johnson .... 1.25 .55
❑ 7 Curt Schilling .... .75 .35
❑ 8 Lyle Overbay .... .50 .23
❑ 9 Andruw Jones SP 4.00 1.80
❑ 10 Gary Sheffield .... .50 .23
❑ 11 Rafael Furcal .... .50 .23
❑ 12 Greg Maddux 2.50 1.10
❑ 13 Chipper Jones SP 5.00 2.20
❑ 14 Tony Batista .... .50 .23
❑ 15 Rodrigo Lopez...................... .50 .23
❑ 16 Jay Gibbons .... .50 .23
❑ 17 Byung-Hyun Kim................ .50 .23
❑ 18 Johnny Damon .... .50 .23
❑ 19 Derek Lowe.......................... .50 .23
❑ 20 Nomar Garciaparra SP.... 10.00 4.50
❑ 21 Pedro Martinez .... 1.25 .55
❑ 22 Manny Ramirez SP 4.00 1.80
❑ 23 Mark Prior.......................... 2.50 1.10
❑ 24 Kerry Wood.......................... 1.25 .55
❑ 25 Corey Patterson.................. .50 .23
❑ 26 Sammy Sosa SP 8.00 3.60
❑ 27 Moises Alou .... .50 .23
❑ 28 Magglio Ordonez................ .50 .23
❑ 29 Frank Thomas .... 1.25 .55
❑ 30 Paul Konerko...................... .50 .23
❑ 31 Bartolo Colon .... .50 .23
❑ 32 Adam Dunn .... .75 .35
❑ 33 Austin Kearns .... .75 .35
❑ 34 Aaron Boone .... .50 .23
❑ 35 Ken Griffey Jr. SP 8.00 3.60
❑ 36 Omar Vizquel...................... .50 .23
❑ 37 C.C. Sabathia .... .50 .23
❑ 38 Jason Davis.......................... .50 .23
❑ 39 Travis Hafner...................... .50 .23
❑ 40 Brandon Phillips .... .50 .23
❑ 41 Larry Walker .... .75 .35
❑ 42 Preston Wilson .... .50 .23
❑ 43 Jay Payton............................ .50 .23
❑ 44 Todd Helton .... .75 .35
❑ 45 Carlos Pena.......................... .50 .23
❑ 46 Eric Munson .... .50 .23
❑ 47 Ivan Rodriguez .... 1.25 .55
❑ 48 Josh Beckett .... .75 .35
❑ 49 Alex Gonzalez .... .50 .23
❑ 50 Roy Oswalt .... .50 .23
❑ 51 Craig Biggio .... .75 .35
❑ 52 Jeff Bagwell.......................... .75 .35
❑ 53 Dontrelle Willis SP 8.00 3.60
❑ 54 Mike Sweeney...................... .50 .23
❑ 55 Carlos Beltran...................... .50 .23
❑ 56 Brent Mayne .... .50 .23
❑ 57 Hideo Nomo .... 1.25 .55
❑ 58 Rickey Henderson .... 2.00 .90
❑ 59 Adrian Beltre .... .50 .23
❑ 60 Miguel Cabrera SP 10.00 4.50
❑ 61 Kazuhisa Ishii .... .50 .23
❑ 62 Ben Sheets .... .50 .23
❑ 63 Richie Sexson .... .50 .23
❑ 64 Torii Hunter SP 4.00 1.80
❑ 65 Jacque Jones .... .50 .23
❑ 66 Joe Mays.............................. .50 .23
❑ 67 Corey Koskie........................ .50 .23
❑ 68 A.J. Pierzynski.................... .50 .23
❑ 69 Jose Vidro............................ .50 .23
❑ 70 Vladimir Guerrero SP 5.00 2.20
❑ 71 Tom Glavine .... 1.25 .55
❑ 72 Jose Reyes SP.................... 4.00 1.80
❑ 73 Aaron Heilman .... .50 .23
❑ 74 Mike Piazza........................ 2.00 .90
❑ 75 Jorge Posada .... .75 .35
❑ 76 Mike Mussina .... 1.25 .55
❑ 77 Robin Ventura...................... .50 .23
❑ 78 Mariano Rivera .... .75 .35
❑ 79 Roger Clemens SP 10.00 4.50
❑ 80 Jason Giambi .... 1.25 .55
❑ 81 Bernie Williams.................... .75 .35
❑ 82 Alfonso Soriano SP.......... 5.00 2.20
❑ 83 Derek Jeter SP.................. 12.00 5.50
❑ 84 Miguel Tejada SP 4.00 1.80
❑ 85 Eric Chavez .... .50 .23
❑ 86 Tim Hudson .... .50 .23
❑ 87 Barry Zito .... 1.25 .55
❑ 88 Mark Mulder........................ .50 .23
❑ 89 Erubiel Durazo.................... .50 .23
❑ 90 Pat Burrell............................ .50 .23
❑ 91 Jim Thome SP.................... 5.00 2.20
❑ 92 Bobby Abreu .... .50 .23
❑ 93 Brian Giles .... .50 .23
❑ 94 Reggie Sanders SP 4.00 1.80
❑ 95 Kenny Lofton........................ .50 .23
❑ 96 Ryan Klesko .... .50 .23
❑ 97 Sean Burroughs .... .50 .23
❑ 98 Edgardo Alfonzo .... .50 .23
❑ 99 Rich Aurilia .... .50 .23
❑ 100 Jose Cruz Jr. .... .50 .23
❑ 101 Barry Bonds SP.............. 12.00 5.50
❑ 102 Mike Cameron.................... .50 .23
❑ 103 Kazuhiro Sasaki.................. .50 .23
❑ 104 Bret Boone .... .50 .23
❑ 105 Ichiro Suzuki SP 10.00 4.50
❑ 106 J.D. Drew .... .50 .23
❑ 107 Jim Edmonds .... .50 .23
❑ 108 Scott Rolen SP 4.00 1.80
❑ 109 Matt Morris.......................... .50 .23
❑ 110 Tino Martinez .... .75 .35
❑ 111 Albert Pujols SP 10.00 4.50
❑ 112 Damian Rolls...................... .50 .23
❑ 113 Carl Crawford .... .50 .23
❑ 114 Rocco Baldelli SP 10.00 4.50
❑ 115 Hank Blalock...................... .75 .35
❑ 116 Alex Rodriguez SP........ 10.00 4.50
❑ 117 Kevin Mench...................... .50 .23
❑ 118 Rafael Palmeiro .... .75 .35
❑ 119 Mark Teixeira .... .75 .35
❑ 120 Shannon Stewart .... .50 .23
❑ 121 Vernon Wells...................... .50 .23
❑ 122 Josh Phelps .... .50 .23
❑ 123 Eric Hinske .... .50 .23
❑ 124 Orlando Hudson .... .50 .23
❑ 125 Carlos Delgado SP 4.00 1.80
❑ 126 Jason Roach ROO RC .. 10.00 4.50
❑ 127 Dan Haren ROO RC...... 12.00 5.50
❑ 128 Luis Ayala ROO RC 10.00 4.50
❑ 129 Bo Hart ROO RC 40.00 18.00
❑ 130 Wilfredo Ledezma ROO RC.. 10.00 4.50
❑ 131 Rick Roberts ROO RC .. 10.00 4.50
❑ 132 Miguel Ojeda ROO RC.. 10.00 4.50
❑ 133 Aquilino Lopez ROO RC 10.00 4.50
❑ 134 Roger Deago ROO RC .. 10.00 4.50
❑ 135 Arnie Munoz ROO RC .. 10.00 4.50
❑ 136 Brent Hoard ROO RC 10.00 4.50
❑ 137 Terrmel Sledge ROO RC 10.00 4.50
❑ 138 Ryan Cameron ROO RC 10.00 4.50
❑ 139 Prentice Redman ROO RC .. 10.00 4.50
❑ 140 Clint Barmes ROO RC .. 10.00 4.50
❑ 141 Jeremy Griffiths ROO RC 10.00 4.50
❑ 142 Jon Leicester ROO RC.. 10.00 4.50
❑ 143 Brandon Webb ROO RC 20.00 9.00
❑ 144 Todd Wellemeyer ROO RC .. 10.00 4.50
❑ 145 Felix Sanchez ROO RC 10.00 4.50
❑ 146 Anthony Ferrari ROO RC 10.00 4.50
❑ 147 Ian Ferguson ROO RC .. 10.00 4.50
❑ 148 Michael Nakamura ROO RC 10.00 4.50
❑ 149 Lew Ford ROO RC 10.00 4.50
❑ 150 Nate Bland ROO RC...... 10.00 4.50
❑ 151 David Matranga ROO RC 10.00 4.50
❑ 152 Edgar Gonzalez ROO RC 10.00 4.50
❑ 153 Carlos Mendez ROO RC 10.00 4.50
❑ 154 Jason Gilfillan ROO RC 10.00 4.50
❑ 155 Mike Neu ROO RC........ 10.00 4.50
❑ 156 Jason Shiell ROO RC .. 10.00 4.50
❑ 157 Jeff Duncan ROO RC 10.00 4.50
❑ 158 Oscar Villarreal ROO RC 10.00 4.50
❑ 159 Diegomar Markwell ROO RC 10.00 4.50
❑ 160 Joe Valentine ROO RC.. 10.00 4.50
❑ 161 Hideki Matsui AU JSY RC 300.00 135.00
❑ 162 Jose Contreras AU RC.. 50.00 22.00
❑ 163 Willie Eyre AU JSY RC 15.00 6.75
❑ 164 Matt Bruback AU JSY RC 15.00 6.75
❑ 165 Rett Johnson AU JSY RC 15.00 6.75
❑ 166 Jeremy Griffiths AU JSY 15.00 6.75
❑ 167 Fran Cruceta AU JSY RC 15.00 6.75
❑ 168 Fern Cabrera AU JSY RC 15.00 6.75
❑ 169 Jhonny Peralta AU JSY RC.. 15.00 6.75
❑ 170 Shane Bazzell AU JSY RC.... 15.00 6.75
❑ 171 Bob Madritsch AU JSY RC.. 15.00 6.75
❑ 172 Phil Seibel AU JSY RC 15.00 6.75
❑ 173 J.Willingham AU JSY RC 40.00 18.00
❑ 174 Rob Hammock AU JSY RC 20.00 9.00
❑ 175 A.Machado AU JSY RC 15.00 6.75
❑ 176 David Sanders AU JSY RC.. 15.00 6.75
❑ 177 Matt Kata AU JSY RC .. 25.00 11.00
❑ 178 Heath Bell AU JSY RC.. 15.00 6.75
❑ 179 Chad Gaudin ROO RC ....
❑ 180 Chris Capuano ROO RC ....
❑ 181 Danny Garcia ROO RC........
❑ 182 Delmon Young ROO RC ....
❑ 183 Edwin Jackson ROO RC ....
❑ 184 Greg Jones ROO RC ....
❑ 185 Jeremy Bonderman ROO RC
❑ 186 Julio DePaula ROO ....
❑ 187 Khalil Greene ROO ....
❑ 188 Chad Cordero ROO RC ......
❑ 189 Miguel Cabrera ROO..........
❑ 190 Rich Harden ROO ....
❑ 191 Rickie Weeks ROO RC........
❑ 192 Rosman Garcia ROO RC ....
❑ 193 Tom Gregorio ROO RC ......
❑ 381 Andrew Brown AU JSY RC
❑ 382 Delmon Young AU JSY RC
❑ 383 Colin Porter AU JSY RC ....
❑ 385 Rickie Weeks AU JSY RC ..
❑ 386 David Matranga AU JSY RC
❑ 387 Bo Hart AU JSY..................

1992 Stadium Club Dome

	Nm-Mt	Ex-Mt
COMP.FACT.SET (200)	15.00	4.50
❑ 1 Terry Adams RC	.50	.15
❑ 2 Tommy Adams RC	.25	.07
❑ 3 Rick Aguilera	.15	.04
❑ 4 Ron Allen RC	.25	.07
❑ 5 Roberto Alomar	.50	.15
❑ 6 Sandy Alomar Jr.	.10	.03
❑ 7 Greg Anthony RC	.25	.07
❑ 8 James Austin RC	.25	.07
❑ 9 Steve Avery	.10	.03
❑ 10 Harold Baines	.15	.04
❑ 11 Brian Barber RC	.25	.07
❑ 12 Jon Barnes RC	.25	.07
❑ 13 George Bell	.10	.03
❑ 14 Doug Bennett RC	.25	.07
❑ 15 Sean Bergman RC	.50	.15
❑ 16 Craig Biggio	.25	.07
❑ 17 Bill Bliss RC	.25	.07
❑ 18 Wade Boggs	.25	.07
❑ 19 Bobby Bonilla	.15	.04
❑ 20 Russell Brock RC	.25	.07
❑ 21 Tarrik Brock RC	.25	.07
❑ 22 Tom Browning	.10	.03
❑ 23 Brett Butler	.15	.04
❑ 24 Ivan Calderon	.10	.03
❑ 25 Joe Carter	.15	.04
❑ 26 Joe Caruso RC	.25	.07
❑ 27 Dan Cholowsky RC	.25	.07
❑ 28 Will Clark	.50	.15
❑ 29 Roger Clemens	1.00	.30
❑ 30 Shawn Curran RC	.25	.07
❑ 31 Chris Curtis RC	.25	.07
❑ 32 Chili Davis	.15	.04
❑ 33 Andre Dawson	.15	.04
❑ 34 Joe DeBerry RC	.25	.07
❑ 35 John Dettmer	.10	.03
❑ 36 Rob Dibble	.15	.04
❑ 37 John Donati RC	.25	.07
❑ 38 Dave Doorneweerd RC	.25	.07
❑ 39 Darren Dreifort	.15	.04
❑ 40 Mike Durant RC	.25	.07
❑ 41 Chris Durkin RC	.25	.07
❑ 42 Dennis Eckersley	.15	.04
❑ 43 Brian Edmondson RC	.25	.07
❑ 44 Vaughn Eshelman RC	.25	.07
❑ 45 Shawn Estes RC	.50	.15
❑ 46 Jorge Fabregas RC	.50	.15
❑ 47 Jon Farrell RC	.25	.07
❑ 48 Cecil Fielder	.15	.04
❑ 49 Carlton Fisk	.25	.07
❑ 50 Tim Flannelly RC	.25	.07
❑ 51 Cliff Floyd RC	1.25	.35
❑ 52 Julio Franco	.15	.04
❑ 53 Greg Gagne	.10	.03
❑ 54 Chris Gambs RC	.25	.07
❑ 55 Ron Gant	.15	.04
❑ 56 Brent Gates RC	.25	.07
❑ 57 Dwayne Gerald RC	.25	.07
❑ 58 Jason Giambi	4.00	1.20
❑ 59 Benji Gil RC	.50	.15
❑ 60 Mark Gipner RC	.25	.07
❑ 61 Danny Gladden	.10	.03
❑ 62 Tom Glavine	.50	.15
❑ 63 Jimmy Gonzalez RC	.25	.07
❑ 64 Jeff Granger	.10	.03
❑ 65 Dan Grapenthien RC	.25	.07
❑ 66 Dennis Gray RC	.25	.07
❑ 67 Shawn Green RC	4.00	1.20
❑ 68 Tyler Green RC	.25	.07
❑ 69 Todd Greene	.10	.03
❑ 70 Ken Griffey Jr.	.75	.23
❑ 71 Kelly Gruber	.10	.03
❑ 72 Ozzie Guillen	.10	.03
❑ 73 Tony Gwynn	.60	.18
❑ 74 Shane Halter RC	.25	.07
❑ 75 Jeffrey Hammonds	.15	.04
❑ 76 Larry Hanlon RC	.25	.07
❑ 77 Pete Harnisch	.10	.03
❑ 78 Mike Harrison RC	.25	.07
❑ 79 Bryan Harvey	.10	.03
❑ 80 Scott Hatteberg RC	.50	.15
❑ 81 Rick Helling	.10	.03
❑ 82 Dave Henderson	.10	.03
❑ 83 Rickey Henderson	.75	.23
❑ 84 Tyrone Hill RC	.25	.07
❑ 85 T.Hollandsworth RC	.50	.15
❑ 86 Brian Holliday RC	.25	.07
❑ 87 Terry Horn RC	.25	.07
❑ 88 Jeff Hostetler RC	.25	.07
❑ 89 Kent Hrbek	.15	.04
❑ 90 Mark Hubbard RC	.25	.07
❑ 91 Charles Johnson	.15	.04
❑ 92 Howard Johnson	.10	.03
❑ 93 Todd Johnson	.10	.03
❑ 94 Bobby Jones RC	.50	.15
❑ 95 Dan Jones RC	.25	.07
❑ 96 Felix Jose	.10	.03
❑ 97 David Justice	.10	.03
❑ 98 Jimmy Key	.15	.04
❑ 99 Marc Kroon RC	.25	.07
❑ 100 John Kruk	.15	.04
❑ 101 Mark Langston	.10	.03
❑ 102 Barry Larkin	.50	.15
❑ 103 Mike LaValliere	.10	.03
❑ 104 Scott Leius	.10	.03
❑ 105 Mark Lemke	.10	.03
❑ 106 Donnie Leshnock	.10	.03
❑ 107 Jimmy Lewis RC	.25	.07
❑ 108 Shane Livesy RC	.25	.07
❑ 109 Ryan Long RC	.25	.07
❑ 110 Trevor Mallory RC	.25	.07
❑ 111 Dennis Martinez	.15	.04
❑ 112 Justin Mashore RC	.25	.07
❑ 113 Jason McDonald	.10	.03
❑ 114 Jack McDowell	.10	.03
❑ 115 Tom McKinnon RC	.25	.07
❑ 116 Billy McMillon	.10	.03
❑ 117 Buck McNabb RC	.25	.07
❑ 118 Jim Mecir RC	.25	.07
❑ 119 Dan Melendez	.25	.07
❑ 120 Shawn Miller RC	.25	.07
❑ 121 Trever Miller RC	.25	.07
❑ 122 Paul Molitor	.25	.07
❑ 123 Vincent Moore RC	.25	.07
❑ 124 Mike Morgan	.10	.03
❑ 125 Jack Morris WS	.10	.03
❑ 126 Jack Morris AS	.10	.03
❑ 127 Sean Mulligan RC	.25	.07
❑ 128 Eddie Murray AS	.50	.15
❑ 129 Mike Neill RC	.50	.15
❑ 130 Phil Nevin	1.00	.30
❑ 131 Mark O'Brien RC	.25	.07
❑ 132 Alex Ochoa RC	.50	.15
❑ 133 Chad Ogea RC	.25	.07
❑ 134 Greg Olson	.10	.03
❑ 135 Paul O'Neill	.25	.07
❑ 136 Jared Osentowski RC	.25	.07
❑ 137 Mike Pagliarulo	.10	.03
❑ 138 Rafael Palmeiro	.25	.07
❑ 139 Rodney Pedraza RC	.25	.07
❑ 140 Tony Phillips (P)	.10	.03
❑ 141 Scott Pisciotta RC	.25	.07
❑ 142 C.Pritchett RC	.25	.07
❑ 143 Jason Pruitt RC	.25	.07
❑ 144 K.Puckett WS UER Championship series AB and BA is wrong	.50	.15
❑ 145 Kirby Puckett AS	.50	.15
❑ 146 Manny Ramirez RC	4.00	1.20
❑ 147 Eddie Ramos RC	.25	.07
❑ 148 Mark Ratekin RC	.25	.07
❑ 149 Jeff Reardon	.15	.04
❑ 150 Sean Rees RC	.25	.07
❑ 151 Pokey Reese RC	.50	.15
❑ 152 Desmond Relaford RC	.50	.15
❑ 153 Eric Richardson RC	.25	.07
❑ 154 Cal Ripken	1.50	.45
❑ 155 Chris Roberts	.10	.03
❑ 156 Mike Robertson RC	.25	.07
❑ 157 Steve Rodriguez	.10	.03
❑ 158 Mike Rossiter RC	.25	.07
❑ 159 Scott Ruffcorn RC	.25	.07
❑ 160 Chris Sabo	.10	.03
❑ 161 Juan Samuel	.10	.03
❑ 162 Ryne Sandberg UER (On 5th line, prior misspelled as prilor)	.75	.23
❑ 163 Scott Sanderson	.10	.03
❑ 164 Benny Santiago	.15	.04
❑ 165 Gene Schall RC	.25	.07
❑ 166 Chad Schoenvogel RC	.25	.07
❑ 167 Chris Seelbach RC	.25	.07
❑ 168 Aaron Sele RC	.75	.23
❑ 169 Basil Shabazz RC	.25	.07
❑ 170 Al Shirley RC	.25	.07
❑ 171 Paul Shuey	.10	.03
❑ 172 Ruben Sierra	.10	.03
❑ 173 John Smiley	.10	.03
❑ 174 Lee Smith	.15	.04
❑ 175 Ozzie Smith	.50	.15
❑ 176 Tim Smith RC	.25	.07
❑ 177 Zane Smith	.10	.03
❑ 178 John Smoltz	.25	.07
❑ 179 Scott Stahoviak RC	.25	.07
❑ 180 Kennie Steenstra	.10	.03
❑ 181 Kevin Stocker RC	.25	.07
❑ 182 Chris Stynes RC	.50	.15
❑ 183 Danny Tartabull	.10	.03
❑ 184 Brien Taylor RC	.50	.15
❑ 185 Todd Taylor	.10	.03
❑ 186 Larry Thomas RC	.25	.07
❑ 187 Ozzie Timmons RC (See also 188)	.25	.07
❑ 188 David Tuttle UER (Mistakenly numbered as 187 on card)	.10	.03
❑ 189 Andy Van Slyke	.15	.04
❑ 190 Frank Viola	.15	.04
❑ 191 Michael Walkden RC	.25	.07
❑ 192 Jeff Ware	.10	.03
❑ 193 Allen Watson RC	.25	.07
❑ 194 Steve Whitaker RC	.25	.07
❑ 195 Jerry Willard	.10	.03
❑ 196 Craig Wilson	.10	.03
❑ 197 Chris Wimmer	.10	.03
❑ 198 S.Wojciechowski RC	.25	.07
❑ 199 Joel Wolfe RC	.25	.07
❑ 200 Ivan Zweig	.10	.03

1993 Stadium Club Murphy

	Nm-Mt	Ex-Mt
COMP.FACT.SET (212)	50.00	15.00
COMPLETE SET (200)	25.00	7.50

COMMON RC .15 .04

❑ 1 Dave Winfield .30 .09
❑ 2 Juan Guzman .15 .04
❑ 3 Tony Gwynn 1.00 .30
❑ 4 Chris Roberts .15 .04
❑ 5 Benny Santiago .30 .09
❑ 6 Sherard Clinkscales RC .15 .04
❑ 7 Jon Nunnally RC .50 .15
❑ 8 Chuck Knoblauch .30 .09
❑ 9 Bob Wolcott RC .15 .04
❑ 10 Steve Rodriguez .15 .04
❑ 11 Mark Williams RC .15 .04
❑ 12 Danny Clyburn RC .15 .04
❑ 13 Darren Dreifort .30 .09
❑ 14 Andy Van Slyke .30 .09
❑ 15 Wade Boggs .50 .15
❑ 16 Scott Patton RC .15 .04
❑ 17 Gary Sheffield .30 .09
❑ 18 Ron Villone .15 .04
❑ 19 Roberto Alomar .75 .23
❑ 20 Marc Valdes .15 .04
❑ 21 Daron Kirkreit .15 .04
❑ 22 Jeff Granger .15 .04
❑ 23 Levon Largusa RC .15 .04
❑ 24 Jimmy Key .30 .09
❑ 25 Kevin Pearson RC .15 .04
❑ 26 Michael Moore RC .15 .04
❑ 27 Preston Wilson RC 5.00 1.50
❑ 28 Kirby Puckett .75 .23
❑ 29 Tim Crabtree RC .15 .04
❑ 30 Bip Roberts .15 .04
❑ 31 Kelly Gruber .15 .04
❑ 32 Tony Fernandez .15 .04
❑ 33 Jason Angel RC .15 .04
❑ 34 Calvin Murray .15 .04
❑ 35 Chad McConnell .15 .04
❑ 36 Jason Moler .15 .04
❑ 37 Mark Lemke .15 .04
❑ 38 Tom Knauss RC .15 .04
❑ 39 Larry Mitchell RC .15 .04
❑ 40 Doug Mirabelli RC .15 .04
❑ 41 Everett Stull II RC .15 .04
❑ 42 Chris Wimmer .15 .04
❑ 43 Dan Serafini RC .15 .04
❑ 44 Ryne Sandberg 1.25 .35
❑ 45 Steve Lyons RC .15 .04
❑ 46 Ryan Freeburg RC .15 .04
❑ 47 Ruben Sierra .15 .04
❑ 48 David Mysel RC .15 .04
❑ 49 Joe Hamilton RC .15 .04
❑ 50 Steve Rodriguez .15 .04
❑ 51 Tim Wakefield .30 .09
❑ 52 Scott Gentile RC .15 .04
❑ 53 Doug Jones .15 .04
❑ 54 Willie Brown RC .15 .04
❑ 55 Chad Mottola RC .50 .15
❑ 56 Ken Griffey Jr. 1.25 .35
❑ 57 Jon Lieber RC .50 .15
❑ 58 Dennis Martinez .30 .09
❑ 59 Joe Petcka RC .15 .04
❑ 60 Benji Simonton RC .15 .04
❑ 61 Brett Backlund RC .15 .04
❑ 62 Damon Berryhill .15 .04
❑ 63 Juan Guzman .15 .04
❑ 64 Doug Hecker RC .15 .04
❑ 65 Jamie Arnold RC .15 .04
❑ 66 Bob Tewksbury .15 .04
❑ 67 Tim Leger RC .15 .04
❑ 68 Todd Etler RC .15 .04
❑ 69 Lloyd McClendon .15 .04
❑ 70 Kurt Ehmann RC .15 .04
❑ 71 Rick Magdaleno RC .15 .04
❑ 72 Tom Pagnozzi .15 .04
❑ 73 Jeffrey Hammonds .15 .04
❑ 74 Joe Carter .30 .09
❑ 75 Chris Holt RC .30 .09
❑ 76 Charles Johnson .30 .09
❑ 77 Bob Walk .15 .04
❑ 78 Fred McGriff .50 .15
❑ 79 Tom Evans RC .15 .04
❑ 80 Scott Klingenbeck RC .15 .04
❑ 81 Chad McConnell .15 .04
❑ 82 Chris Eddy RC .15 .04
❑ 83 Phil Nevin .30 .09
❑ 84 John Kruk .30 .09
❑ 85 Tony Sheffield RC .15 .04
❑ 86 John Smoltz .50 .15
❑ 87 Trevor Humphry RC .15 .04
❑ 88 Charles Nagy .15 .04
❑ 89 Sean Runyan RC .15 .04
❑ 90 Mike Gulan RC .15 .04
❑ 91 Darren Daulton .30 .09
❑ 92 Otis Nixon .15 .04
❑ 93 Nomar Garciaparra 15.00 4.50
❑ 94 Larry Walker .50 .15
❑ 95 Hut Smith RC .15 .04
❑ 96 Rick Helling .15 .04
❑ 97 Roger Clemens 1.50 .45
❑ 98 Ron Gant .30 .09
❑ 99 Kenny Felder RC .15 .04
❑ 100 Steve Murphy RC .15 .04
❑ 101 Mike Smith RC .15 .04
❑ 102 Terry Pendleton .30 .09
❑ 103 Tim Davis .15 .04
❑ 104 Jeff Patzke RC .15 .04
❑ 105 Craig Wilson .15 .04
❑ 106 Tom Glavine .75 .23
❑ 107 Mark Langston .15 .04
❑ 108 Mark Thompson RC .15 .04
❑ 109 Eric Owens RC 1.00 .30
❑ 110 Keith Johnson RC .15 .04
❑ 111 Robin Ventura .30 .09
❑ 112 Ed Sprague .15 .04
❑ 113 Jeff Schmidt RC .15 .04
❑ 114 Don Wengert RC .15 .04
❑ 115 Craig Biggio .50 .15
❑ 116 Kenny Carlyle RC .15 .04
❑ 117 Derek Jeter RC 25.00 7.50
❑ 118 Manuel Lee .15 .04
❑ 119 Jeff Haas RC .15 .04
❑ 120 Roger Bailey RC .15 .04
❑ 121 Sean Lowe RC .15 .04
❑ 122 Rick Aguilera .15 .04
❑ 123 Sandy Alomar Jr. .15 .04
❑ 124 Derek Wallace RC .15 .04
❑ 125 B.J. Wallace .15 .04
❑ 126 Greg Maddux 1.50 .45
❑ 127 Tim Moore RC .15 .04
❑ 128 Lee Smith .30 .09
❑ 129 Todd Steverson RC .15 .04
❑ 130 Chris Widger RC .50 .15
❑ 131 Paul Molitor .50 .15
❑ 132 Chris Smith RC .15 .04
❑ 133 Chris Gomez RC .50 .15
❑ 134 Jimmy Baron RC .15 .04
❑ 135 John Smoltz .50 .15
❑ 136 Pat Borders .15 .04
❑ 137 Donnie Leshnock .15 .04
❑ 138 Gus Gandarillos RC .15 .04
❑ 139 Will Clark .75 .23
❑ 140 Ryan Luzinski RC .15 .04
❑ 141 Cal Ripken 2.50 .75
❑ 142 B.J. Wallace .15 .04
❑ 143 Trey Beamon RC .50 .15
❑ 144 Norm Charlton .15 .04
❑ 145 Mike Mussina .75 .23
❑ 146 Billy Owens RC .15 .04
❑ 147 Ozzie Smith .75 .23
❑ 148 Jason Kendall RC 2.00 .60
❑ 149 Mike Matthews RC .15 .04
❑ 150 David Spykstra RC .15 .04
❑ 151 Benji Grigsby RC .15 .04
❑ 152 Sean Smith RC .15 .04
❑ 153 Mark McGwire 2.00 .60
❑ 154 David Cone .30 .09
❑ 155 Shon Walker RC .15 .04
❑ 156 Jason Giambi 1.50 .45
❑ 157 Jack McDowell .15 .04
❑ 158 Paxton Briley RC .15 .04
❑ 159 Edgar Martinez .50 .15
❑ 160 Brian Sackinsky RC .15 .04
❑ 161 Barry Bonds 2.00 .60
❑ 162 Roberto Kelly .15 .04
❑ 163 Jeff Alkire .15 .04
❑ 164 Mike Sharperson .15 .04
❑ 165 Jamie Taylor RC .15 .04
❑ 166 John Saffer UER RC .15 .04
❑ 167 Jerry Browne .15 .04
❑ 168 Travis Fryman .30 .09
❑ 169 Brady Anderson .30 .09
❑ 170 Chris Roberts .15 .04
❑ 171 Lloyd Peever RC .15 .04
❑ 172 Francisco Cabrera .15 .04
❑ 173 Ramiro Martinez RC .15 .04
❑ 174 Jeff Alkire .15 .04
❑ 175 Ivan Rodriguez .75 .23
❑ 176 Kevin Brown .30 .09
❑ 177 Chad Roper RC .15 .04
❑ 178 Rod Henderson RC .15 .04
❑ 179 Dennis Eckersley .30 .09
❑ 180 Shannon Stewart RC 2.00 .60
❑ 181 DeShawn Warren RC .15 .04
❑ 182 Lonnie Smith .15 .04
❑ 183 Willie Adams .15 .04
❑ 184 Jeff Montgomery .15 .04
❑ 185 Damon Hollins RC .15 .04
❑ 186 Byron Mathews RC .15 .04
❑ 187 Harold Baines .30 .09
❑ 188 Rick Greene .15 .04
❑ 189 Carlos Baerga .15 .04
❑ 190 Brandon Cromer RC .15 .04
❑ 191 Roberto Alomar .75 .23
❑ 192 Rich Ireland RC .15 .04
❑ 193 S.Montgomery RC .15 .04
❑ 194 Brant Brown RC .15 .04
❑ 195 Ritchie Moody RC .15 .04
❑ 196 Michael Tucker .15 .04
❑ 197 Jason Varitek .50 .15
❑ 198 David Manning RC .15 .04
❑ 199 Marquis Riley RC .15 .04
❑ 200 Jason Giambi 2.00 .60

1994 Stadium Club Draft Picks

	Nm-Mt	Ex-Mt
COMPLETE SET (90)	15.00	4.50

❑ 1 Jacob Shumate XRC .25 .07
❑ 2 C.J. Nitkowski XRC .25 .07
❑ 3 Doug Million XRC .25 .07
❑ 4 Matt Smith XRC .25 .07
❑ 5 Kevin Lovinger XRC .25 .07
❑ 6 Alberto Castillo XRC .25 .07
❑ 7 Mike Russell XRC .25 .07
❑ 8 Dan Lock XRC .25 .07
❑ 9 Tom Szimanski XRC .25 .07
❑ 10 Aaron Boone XRC 2.50 .75
❑ 11 Jayson Peterson XRC .25 .07
❑ 12 Mark Johnson XRC .25 .07
❑ 13 Cade Gaspar XRC .25 .07
❑ 14 George Lombard XRC .40 .12
❑ 15 Russ Johnson .25 .07
❑ 16 Travis Miller XRC .25 .07
❑ 17 Jay Payton XRC .50 .15
❑ 18 Brian Buchanan XRC .25 .07
❑ 19 Jacob Cruz XRC .40 .12
❑ 20 Gary Rath XRC .25 .07
❑ 21 Ramon Castro XRC .25 .07
❑ 22 Tommy Davis XRC .25 .07
❑ 23 Tony Terry XRC .25 .07
❑ 24 Jerry Whittaker XRC .25 .07
❑ 25 Mike Darr XRC .40 .12
❑ 26 Doug Webb XRC .25 .07
❑ 27 Jason Camilli XRC .25 .07
❑ 28 Brad Rigby XRC .25 .07
❑ 29 Ryan Nye XRC .25 .07
❑ 30 Carl Dale XRC .25 .07
❑ 31 Andy Taulbee XRC .25 .07

		Nm-Mt	Ex-Mt
32	Trey Moore XRC	.25	.07
33	John Crowther XRC	.25	.07
34	Joe Giuliano XRC	.25	.07
35	Brian Rose XRC	.25	.07
36	Paul Failla XRC	.25	.07
37	Brian Meadows XRC	.25	.07
38	Oscar Robles XRC	.25	.07
39	Mike Metcalfe XRC	.25	.07
40	Larry Barnes XRC	.25	.07
41	Paul Ottavinia XRC	.25	.07
42	Chris McBride XRC	.25	.07
43	Ricky Stone XRC	.25	.07
44	Billy Blythe XRC	.25	.07
45	Eddie Priest XRC	.25	.07
46	Scott Forster XRC	.25	.07
47	Eric Pickett XRC	.25	.07
48	Matt Beaumont	.25	.07
49	Darrell Nicholas XRC	.25	.07
50	Mike A. Hampton XRC	.25	.07
51	Paul O'Malley XRC	.25	.07
52	Steve Shoemaker XRC	.25	.07
53	Jason Sikes XRC	.25	.07
54	Bryan Farson XRC	.25	.07
55	Yates Hall XRC	.25	.07
56	Troy Brohawn XRC	.25	.07
57	Dan Hower XRC	.25	.07
58	Clay Caruthers XRC	.25	.07
59	Pepe McNeal XRC	.25	.07
60	Ray Ricken XRC	.25	.07
61	Scott Shores XRC	.25	.07
62	Eddie Brooks XRC	.25	.07
63	Dave Kauflin XRC	.25	.07
64	David Meyer XRC	.25	.07
65	Geoff Blum XRC	.40	.12
66	Roy Marsh XRC	.25	.07
67	Ryan Beeney XRC	.25	.07
68	Derek Dukart XRC	.25	.07
69	Nomar Garciaparra	4.00	1.20
70	Jason Kelly XRC	.25	.07
71	Jesse Ibarra XRC	.25	.07
72	Bucky Buckles XRC	.25	.07
73	Mark Little XRC	.25	.07
74	Heath Murray XRC	.25	.07
75	Greg Morris XRC	.25	.07
76	Mike Halperlin XRC	.25	.07
77	Wes Helms XRC	.50	.15
78	Ray Brown XRC	.25	.07
79	Kevin L.Brown XRC	.40	.12
80	Paul Konerko XRC	1.50	.45
81	Mike Thurman XRC	.25	.07
82	Paul Wilson	.25	.07
83	Terrence Long XRC	1.50	.45
84	Ben Grieve XRC	.50	.15
85	Mark Farris XRC	.25	.07
86	Bret Wagner	.25	.07
87	Dustin Hermanson	.40	.12
88	Kevin Witt XRC	.40	.12
89	Corey Pointer XRC	.25	.07
90	Tim Grieve XRC	.25	.07

2001 Stadium Club

	Nm-Mt	Ex-Mt
COMPLETE SET (200)	120.00	36.00
COMP.SET w/o SP's (175)	25.00	7.50
COMMON CARD (1-150)	.30	.09
COMMON SP (151-200)	3.00	.90

		Nm-Mt	Ex-Mt
1	Nomar Garciaparra	1.50	.45
2	Chipper Jones	.75	.23
3	Jeff Bagwell	.50	.15
4	Chad Kreuter	.30	.09
5	Randy Johnson	.75	.23
6	Mike Hampton	.30	.09
7	Barry Larkin	.75	.23
8	Bernie Williams	.50	.15
9	Chris Singleton	.30	.09
10	Larry Walker	.50	.15
11	Brad Ausmus	.30	.09
12	Ron Coomer	.30	.09
13	Edgardo Alfonzo	.30	.09
14	Delino DeShields	.30	.09
15	Tony Gwynn	1.00	.30
16	Andruw Jones	.50	.15
17	Raul Mondesi	.30	.09
18	Troy Glaus	.50	.15
19	Ben Grieve	.30	.09
20	Sammy Sosa	1.25	.35
21	Fernando Vina	.30	.09
22	Jeromy Burnitz	.30	.09
23	Jay Bell	.30	.09
24	Pete Harnisch	.30	.09
25	Barry Bonds	2.00	.60
26	Eric Karros	.30	.09
27	Alex Gonzalez	.30	.09
28	Mike Lieberthal	.30	.09
29	Juan Encarnacion	.30	.09
30	Derek Jeter	2.00	.60
31	Luis Sojo	.30	.09
32	Eric Milton	.30	.09
33	Aaron Boone	.30	.09
34	Roberto Alomar	.75	.23
35	John Olerud	.30	.09
36	Orlando Cabrera	.30	.09
37	Shawn Green	.30	.09
38	Roger Cedeno	.30	.09
39	Garret Anderson	.30	.09
40	Jim Thome	.75	.23
41	Gabe Kapler	.30	.09
42	Mo Vaughn	.30	.09
43	Sean Casey	.30	.09
44	Preston Wilson	.30	.09
45	Javy Lopez	.30	.09
46	Ryan Klesko	.30	.09
47	Ray Durham	.30	.09
48	Dean Palmer	.30	.09
49	Jorge Posada	.50	.15
50	Alex Rodriguez	1.50	.45
51	Tom Glavine	.75	.23
52	Ray Lankford	.30	.09
53	Jose Canseco	.75	.23
54	Tim Salmon	.50	.15
55	Cal Ripken	2.50	.75
56	Bob Abreu	.30	.09
57	Robin Ventura	.30	.09
58	Damion Easley	.30	.09
59	Paul O'Neill	.50	.15
60	Ivan Rodriguez	.75	.23
61	Carl Everett	.30	.09
62	Doug Glanville	.30	.09
63	Jeff Kent	.30	.09
64	Jay Buhner	.30	.09
65	Cliff Floyd	.30	.09
66	Rick Ankiel	.30	.09
67	Mark Grace	.75	.23
68	Brian Jordan	.30	.09
69	Craig Biggio	.50	.15
70	Carlos Delgado	.30	.09
71	Brad Radke	.30	.09
72	Greg Maddux	1.50	.45
73	Al Leiter	.30	.09
74	Pokey Reese	.30	.09
75	Todd Helton	.50	.15
76	Mariano Rivera	.50	.15
77	Shane Spencer	.30	.09
78	Jason Kendall	.30	.09
79	Chuck Knoblauch	.30	.09
80	Scott Rolen	.50	.15
81	Jose Offerman	.30	.09
82	J.T. Snow	.30	.09
83	Pat Meares	.30	.09
84	Quilvio Veras	.30	.09
85	Edgar Renteria	.30	.09
86	Luis Matos	.30	.09
87	Adrian Beltre	.30	.09
88	Luis Gonzalez	.30	.09
89	Rickey Henderson	1.25	.35
90	Brian Giles	.30	.09
91	Carlos Febles	.30	.09
92	Tino Martinez	.50	.15
93	Magglio Ordonez	.30	.09
94	Rafael Furcal	.30	.09
95	Mike Mussina	.75	.23
96	Gary Sheffield	.30	.09
97	Kenny Lofton	.30	.09
98	Fred McGriff	.50	.15
99	Ken Caminiti	.30	.09
100	Mark McGwire	2.00	.60
101	Tom Goodwin	.30	.09
102	Mark Grudzielanek	.30	.09
103	Derek Bell	.30	.09
104	Mike Lowell	.30	.09
105	Jeff Cirillo	.30	.09
106	Orlando Hernandez	.30	.09
107	Jose Valentin	.30	.09
108	Warren Morris	.30	.09
109	Mike Williams	.30	.09
110	Greg Zaun	.30	.09
111	Jose Vidro	.30	.09
112	Omar Vizquel	.30	.09
113	Vinny Castilla	.30	.09
114	Gregg Jefferies	.30	.09
115	Kevin Brown	.30	.09
116	Shannon Stewart	.30	.09
117	Marquis Grissom	.30	.09
118	Manny Ramirez	.30	.09
119	Albert Belle	.30	.09
120	Bret Boone	.30	.09
121	Johnny Damon	.30	.09
122	Juan Gonzalez	.75	.23
123	David Justice	.30	.09
124	Jeffrey Hammonds	.30	.09
125	Ken Griffey Jr.	1.25	.35
126	Mike Sweeney	.30	.09
127	Tony Clark	.30	.09
128	Todd Zeile	.30	.09
129	Mark Johnson	.30	.09
130	Matt Williams	.30	.09
131	Geoff Jenkins	.30	.09
132	Jason Giambi	.75	.23
133	Steve Finley	.30	.09
134	Derek Lee	.30	.09
135	Royce Clayton	.30	.09
136	Joe Randa	.30	.09
137	Rafael Palmeiro	.50	.15
138	Kevin Young	.30	.09
139	Mike Redmond	.30	.09
140	Vladimir Guerrero	.75	.23
141	Greg Vaughn	.30	.09
142	Jermaine Dye	.30	.09
143	Roger Clemens	1.50	.45
144	Denny Hocking	.30	.09
145	Frank Thomas	.75	.23
146	Carlos Beltran	.30	.09
147	Eric Young	.30	.09
148	Pat Burrell	.30	.09
149	Pedro Martinez	.75	.23
150	Mike Piazza	1.25	.35
151	Adrian Gonzalez	.50	.15
152	Adam Johnson	.50	.15
153	Luis Montanez SP RC	3.00	.90
154	Mike Stodolka	.50	.15
155	Phil Dumatrait	.50	.15
156	Sean Burnett SP	3.00	.90
157	Dominic Rich SP RC	3.00	.90
158	Adam Wainwright	.50	.15
159	Scott Thorman	.50	.15
160	Scott Heard SP	3.00	.90
161	Chad Petty SP RC	3.00	.90
162	Matt Wheatland	.50	.15
163	Bryan Digby	.50	.15
164	Rocco Baldelli	3.00	.90
165	Grady Sizemore	1.00	.30
166	Brian Sellier SP RC	3.00	.90
167	Rick Brosseau SP RC	3.00	.90
168	Shawn Fagan SP RC	3.00	.90
169	Sean Smith SP	3.00	.90
170	Chris Bass SP RC	3.00	.90
171	Corey Patterson	.50	.15
172	Sean Burroughs	.50	.15

❑ 173 Ben Petrick .50 .15
❑ 174 Mike Glendenning .50 .15
❑ 175 Barry Zito 1.00 .30
❑ 176 Milton Bradley .50 .15
❑ 177 Bobby Bradley .50 .15
❑ 178 Jason Hart .50 .15
❑ 179 Ryan Anderson .50 .15
❑ 180 Ben Sheets .50 .15
❑ 181 Adam Everett .50 .15
❑ 182 Alfonso Soriano .75 .23
❑ 183 Josh Hamilton .50 .15
❑ 184 Eric Munson .50 .15
❑ 185 Chin-Feng Chen .50 .15
❑ 186 Tim Christman SP RC 3.00 .90
❑ 187 J.R. House SP 3.00 .90
❑ 188 B.Parker SP RC 3.00 .90
❑ 189 Sean Fesh SP RC 3.00 .90
❑ 190 Joel Pineiro SP 4.00 1.20
❑ 191 Oscar Ramirez SP RC 3.00 .90
❑ 192 Alex Santos SP RC 3.00 .90
❑ 193 Eddy Reyes SP RC 3.00 .90
❑ 194 Mike Jacobs SP RC 3.00 .90
❑ 195 Erick Almonte SP RC 3.00 .90
❑ 196 B.Claussen SP RC 15.00 4.50
❑ 197 Kris Keller SP RC 3.00 .90
❑ 198 Wilson Betemit SP RC 3.00 .90
❑ 199 Andy Phillips SP RC 3.00 .90
❑ 200 A.Pettyjohn SP RC 3.00 .90

2002 Stadium Club

	Nm-Mt	Ex-Mt
COMP.SET w/o SP's (100)	25.00	7.50
COMMON CARD (1-100)	.30	.09
COMMON (101-125)	20.00	6.00

❑ 1 Pedro Martinez .75 .23
❑ 2 Derek Jeter 2.00 .60
❑ 3 Chipper Jones .75 .23
❑ 4 Roberto Alomar .75 .23
❑ 5 Albert Pujols 1.50 .45
❑ 6 Bret Boone .30 .09
❑ 7 Alex Rodriguez 1.50 .45
❑ 8 Jose Cruz Jr. .30 .09
❑ 9 Mike Hampton .30 .09
❑ 10 Vladimir Guerrero .75 .23
❑ 11 Jim Edmonds .30 .09
❑ 12 Luis Gonzalez .30 .09
❑ 13 Jeff Kent .30 .09
❑ 14 Mike Piazza 1.25 .35
❑ 15 Ben Sheets .30 .09
❑ 16 Tsuyoshi Shinjo .30 .09
❑ 17 Pat Burrell UER .30 .09
Card has a photo of Scott Rolen
❑ 18 Jermaine Dye .30 .09
❑ 19 Rafael Furcal .30 .09
❑ 20 Randy Johnson .75 .23
❑ 21 Carlos Delgado .30 .09
❑ 22 Roger Clemens 1.50 .45
❑ 23 Eric Chavez .30 .09
❑ 24 Nomar Garciaparra 1.50 .45
❑ 25 Ivan Rodriguez .75 .23
❑ 26 Juan Gonzalez .75 .23
❑ 27 Reggie Sanders .30 .09
❑ 28 Jeff Bagwell .50 .15
❑ 29 Kazuhiro Sasaki .30 .09
❑ 30 Larry Walker .50 .15
❑ 31 Ben Grieve .30 .09
❑ 32 David Justice .30 .09
❑ 33 David Wells .30 .09
❑ 34 Kevin Brown .30 .09
❑ 35 Miguel Tejada .30 .09
❑ 36 Jorge Posada .50 .15
❑ 37 Javy Lopez .30 .09
❑ 38 Cliff Floyd .30 .09
❑ 39 Carlos Lee .30 .09
❑ 40 Manny Ramirez .30 .09
❑ 41 Jim Thome .75 .23
❑ 42 Pokey Reese .30 .09
❑ 43 Scott Rolen .50 .15
❑ 44 Richie Sexson .30 .09
❑ 45 Dean Palmer .30 .09
❑ 46 Rafael Palmeiro .50 .15
❑ 47 Alfonso Soriano .75 .23
❑ 48 Craig Biggio .50 .15
❑ 49 Troy Glaus .50 .15
❑ 50 Andruw Jones .50 .15
❑ 51 Ichiro Suzuki 1.50 .45
❑ 52 Kenny Lofton .30 .09
❑ 53 Hideo Nomo .75 .23
❑ 54 Magglio Ordonez .30 .09
❑ 55 Brad Penny .30 .09
❑ 56 Omar Vizquel .30 .09
❑ 57 Mike Sweeney .30 .09
❑ 58 Gary Sheffield .30 .09
❑ 59 Ken Griffey Jr. 1.25 .35
❑ 60 Curt Schilling .50 .15
❑ 61 Bobby Higginson .30 .09
❑ 62 Terrence Long .30 .09
❑ 63 Moises Alou .30 .09
❑ 64 Sandy Alomar Jr. .30 .09
❑ 65 Cristian Guzman .30 .09
❑ 66 Sammy Sosa 1.25 .35
❑ 67 Jose Vidro .30 .09
❑ 68 Edgar Martinez .50 .15
❑ 69 Jason Giambi .75 .23
❑ 70 Mark McGwire 2.00 .60
❑ 71 Barry Bonds 2.00 .60
❑ 72 Greg Vaughn .30 .09
❑ 73 Phil Nevin .30 .09
❑ 74 Jason Kendall .30 .09
❑ 75 Greg Maddux 1.50 .45
❑ 76 Jeromy Burnitz .30 .09
❑ 77 Mike Mussina .75 .23
❑ 78 Johnny Damon .30 .09
❑ 79 Shawn Green .30 .09
❑ 80 Jimmy Rollins .30 .09
❑ 81 Edgardo Alfonzo .30 .09
❑ 82 Barry Larkin .75 .23
❑ 83 Raul Mondesi .30 .09
❑ 84 Preston Wilson .30 .09
❑ 85 Mike Lieberthal .30 .09
❑ 86 J.D. Drew .30 .09
❑ 87 Ryan Klesko .30 .09
❑ 88 David Segui .30 .09
❑ 89 Derek Bell .30 .09
❑ 90 Bernie Williams .50 .15
❑ 91 Doug Mientkiewicz .30 .09
❑ 92 Rich Aurilia .30 .09
❑ 93 Ellis Burks .30 .09
❑ 94 Placido Polanco .30 .09
❑ 95 Darin Erstad .30 .09
❑ 96 Brian Giles .30 .09
❑ 97 Geoff Jenkins .30 .09
❑ 98 Kerry Wood .75 .23
❑ 99 Mariano Rivera .50 .15
❑ 100 Todd Helton .50 .15
❑ 101 Adam Dunn FS 20.00 6.00
❑ 102 Grant Balfour FS 20.00 6.00
❑ 103 Jae Seo FS 20.00 6.00
❑ 104 Hank Blalock FS 25.00 7.50
❑ 105 Chris George FS 20.00 6.00
❑ 106 Jack Cust FS 20.00 6.00
❑ 107 Juan Cruz FS 20.00 6.00
❑ 108 Adrian Gonzalez FS 20.00 6.00
❑ 109 Nick Johnson FS 20.00 6.00
❑ 110 Jeff DaVanon FS 20.00 6.00
❑ 111 Juan Diaz FS 20.00 6.00
❑ 112 B. Duckworth FS 20.00 6.00
❑ 113 Jason Lane FS 20.00 6.00
❑ 114 Seung Song FS 20.00 6.00
❑ 115 Morgan Ensberg FS 20.00 6.00
❑ 116 Marlyn Tisdale FY RC 20.00 6.00
❑ 117 Jason Botts FY RC 20.00 6.00
❑ 118 Henry Pichardo FY RC 20.00 6.00
❑ 119 J. Rodriguez FY RC 20.00 6.00
❑ 120 Mike Peeples FY RC 20.00 6.00
❑ 121 Rob Bowen EFY RC 20.00 6.00
❑ 122 Jeremy Affeldt EFY 20.00 6.00
❑ 123 Jorge Buret EFY RC 20.00 6.00
❑ 124 Manny Ravelo EFY RC 20.00 6.00
❑ 125 Eudy Lajara EFY RC 20.00 6.00
❑ NNO B.Bonds AU Ball EXCH 150.00 45.00

2003 Stadium Club

	Nm-Mt	Ex-Mt
COMP.MASTER SET (150)	60.00	18.00
COMPLETE SET (125)	40.00	12.00
COMMON CARD (1-100)	.30	.09
COMMON CARD (101-115)	.50	.15
COMMON CARD (116-125)	1.00	.30

❑ 1 Rafael Furcal .30 .09
❑ 2 Randy Winn .30 .09
❑ 3 Eric Chavez .30 .09
❑ 4 Fernando Vina .30 .09
❑ 5 Pat Burrell .30 .09
❑ 6 Derek Jeter 2.00 .60
❑ 7 Ivan Rodriguez .75 .23
❑ 8 Eric Hinske .30 .09
❑ 9 Roberto Alomar .75 .23
❑ 10 Tony Batista .30 .09
❑ 11 Jacque Jones .30 .09
❑ 12 Alfonso Soriano .75 .23
❑ 13 Omar Vizquel .30 .09
❑ 14 Paul Konerko .30 .09
❑ 15 Shawn Green .30 .09
❑ 16 Garret Anderson .30 .09
❑ 17 Darin Erstad .30 .09
❑ 18 Johnny Damon .30 .09
❑ 19 Juan Gonzalez .75 .23
❑ 20 Luis Gonzalez .30 .09
❑ 21 Sean Burroughs .30 .09
❑ 22 Mark Prior 1.50 .45
❑ 23 Javier Vazquez .30 .09
❑ 24 Shannon Stewart .30 .09
❑ 25 Jay Gibbons .30 .09
❑ 26 A.J. Pierzynski .30 .09
❑ 27 Vladimir Guerrero .75 .23
❑ 28 Austin Kearns .50 .15
❑ 29 Shea Hillenbrand .30 .09
❑ 30 Magglio Ordonez .30 .09
❑ 31 Mike Cameron .30 .09
❑ 32 Tim Salmon .50 .15
❑ 33 Brian Jordan .30 .09
❑ 34 Moises Alou .30 .09
❑ 35 Rich Aurilia .30 .09
❑ 36 Nick Johnson .30 .09
❑ 37 Junior Spivey .30 .09
❑ 38 Curt Schilling .50 .15
❑ 39 Jose Vidro .30 .09
❑ 40 Orlando Cabrera .30 .09
❑ 41 Jeff Bagwell .50 .15
❑ 42 Mo Vaughn .30 .09
❑ 43 Luis Castillo .30 .09
❑ 44 Vicente Padilla .30 .09
❑ 45 Pedro Martinez .75 .23
❑ 46 John Olerud .30 .09
❑ 47 Tom Glavine .75 .23
❑ 48 Torii Hunter .30 .09
❑ 49 J.D. Drew .30 .09

❑ 50 Alex Rodriguez 1.50 .45
❑ 51 Randy Johnson .75 .23
❑ 52 Richie Sexson .30 .09
❑ 53 Jimmy Rollins .30 .09
❑ 54 Cristian Guzman .30 .09
❑ 55 Tim Hudson .30 .09
❑ 56 Mark Buehrle .30 .09
❑ 57 Paul Lo Duca .30 .09
❑ 58 Aramis Ramirez .30 .09
❑ 59 Todd Helton .50 .15
❑ 60 Lance Berkman .30 .09
❑ 61 Josh Beckett .50 .15
❑ 62 Bret Boone .30 .09
❑ 63 Miguel Tejada .30 .09
❑ 64 Nomar Garciaparra 1.50 .45
❑ 65 Albert Pujols 1.50 .45
❑ 66 Chipper Jones .75 .23
❑ 67 Scott Rolen .50 .15
❑ 68 Kerry Wood .75 .23
❑ 69 Jorge Posada .50 .15
❑ 70 Ichiro Suzuki 1.50 .45
❑ 71 Jeff Kent .30 .09
❑ 72 David Eckstein .30 .09
❑ 73 Phil Nevin .30 .09
❑ 74 Brian Giles .30 .09
❑ 75 Barry Zito .75 .23
❑ 76 Andruw Jones .50 .15
❑ 77 Jim Thome .75 .23
❑ 78 Robert Fick .30 .09
❑ 79 Rafael Palmeiro .50 .15
❑ 80 Barry Bonds 2.00 .60
❑ 81 Gary Sheffield .30 .09
❑ 82 Jim Edmonds .30 .09
❑ 83 Kazuhisa Ishii .30 .09
❑ 84 Jose Hernandez .30 .09
❑ 85 Jason Giambi .75 .23
❑ 86 Mark Mulder .30 .09
❑ 87 Roger Clemens 1.50 .45
❑ 88 Troy Glaus .50 .15
❑ 89 Carlos Delgado .30 .09
❑ 90 Mike Sweeney .30 .09
❑ 91 Ken Griffey Jr. 1.25 .35
❑ 92 Manny Ramirez .30 .09
❑ 93 Ryan Klesko .30 .09
❑ 94 Larry Walker .50 .15
❑ 95 Adam Dunn .50 .15
❑ 96 Raul Ibanez .30 .09
❑ 97 Preston Wilson .30 .09
❑ 98 Roy Oswalt .30 .09
❑ 99 Sammy Sosa 1.25 .35
❑ 100 Mike Piazza 1.25 .35
❑ 101H Jose Reyes FS 1.00 .30
❑ 101R Jose Reyes FS 1.00 .30
❑ 102H Ed Rogers FS .50 .15
❑ 102R Ed Rogers FS .50 .15
❑ 103H Hank Blalock FS 1.00 .30
❑ 103R Hank Blalock FS 1.00 .30
❑ 104H Mark Teixeira FS 1.00 .30
❑ 104R Mark Teixeira FS 1.00 .30
❑ 105H Orlando Hudson FS .50 .15
❑ 105R Orlando Hudson FS .50 .15
❑ 106H Drew Henson FS .75 .23
❑ 106R Drew Henson FS .75 .23
❑ 107H Joe Mauer FS 1.50 .45
❑ 107R Joe Mauer FS 1.50 .45
❑ 108H Carl Crawford FS .75 .23
❑ 108R Carl Crawford FS .75 .23
❑ 109H Marlon Byrd FS .75 .23
❑ 109R Marlon Byrd FS .75 .23
❑ 110H Jason Stokes FS 1.50 .45
❑ 110R Jason Stokes FS 1.50 .45
❑ 111H Miguel Cabrera FS 4.00 1.20
❑ 111R Miguel Cabrera FS 4.00 1.20
❑ 112H Wilson Betemit FS .50 .15
❑ 112R Wilson Betemit FS .50 .15
❑ 113H Jerome Williams FS .75 .23
❑ 113R Jerome Williams FS .75 .23
❑ 114H Walter Young FYP 1.00 .30
❑ 114R Walter Young FYP 1.00 .30
❑ 115H Juan Camacho FYP RC 1.00 .30
❑ 115R Juan Camacho FYP RC 1.00 .30
❑ 116H Chris Duncan FYP RC 1.00 .30
❑ 116R Chris Duncan FYP RC 1.00 .30
❑ 117H F.Gutierrez FYP RC 5.00 1.20
❑ 117R Franklin Gutierrez FYP RC 5.00 1.20
❑ 118H Adam LaRoche FYP 1.00 .30
❑ 118R Adam LaRoche FYP RC 1.00 .30
❑ 119H Manuel Ramirez FYP RC 2.00 .60
❑ 119R Manuel Ramirez FYP RC 2.00 .60
❑ 120H Il Kim FYP RC 1.00 .30
❑ 120R Il Kim FYP RC 1.00 .30
❑ 121H Wayne Lydon FYP RC 1.50 .45
❑ 121R Wayne Lydon FYP RC 1.50 .45
❑ 122H Daryl Clark FYP RC 1.50 .45
❑ 122R Daryl Clark FYP RC 1.50 .45
❑ 123H Sean Pierce FYP 1.00 .30
❑ 123R Sean Pierce FYP 1.00 .30
❑ 124H Andy Marte FYP RC 5.00 1.50
❑ 124R Andy Marte FYP RC 5.00 1.50
❑ 125H Matthew Peterson FYP RC 1.00 .30
❑ 125R Matthew Peterson FYP RC 1.00 .30

2001 Studio

	Nm-Mt	Ex-Mt
COMP.SET w/o SP's (150)	40.00	12.00
COMMON CARD (1-150)	.50	.15
COMMON (151-200)	8.00	2.40

❑ 1 Alex Rodriguez 2.50 .75
❑ 2 Barry Bonds 3.00 .90
❑ 3 Cal Ripken 4.00 1.20
❑ 4 Chipper Jones 1.25 .35
❑ 5 Derek Jeter 3.00 .90
❑ 6 Troy Glaus .75 .23
❑ 7 Frank Thomas 1.25 .35
❑ 8 Greg Maddux 2.50 .75
❑ 9 Ivan Rodriguez 1.25 .35
❑ 10 Jeff Bagwell .75 .23
❑ 11 Mark Quinn .50 .15
❑ 12 Todd Helton .75 .23
❑ 13 Ken Griffey Jr. 2.00 .60
❑ 14 Manny Ramirez .50 .15
❑ 15 Mark McGwire 3.00 .90
❑ 16 Mike Piazza 2.00 .60
❑ 17 Nomar Garciaparra 2.50 .75
❑ 18 Robin Ventura .50 .15
❑ 19 Aramis Ramirez .50 .15
❑ 20 J.T. Snow .50 .15
❑ 21 Pat Burrell .50 .15
❑ 22 Curt Schilling .75 .23
❑ 23 Carlos Delgado .50 .15
❑ 24 J.D. Drew .50 .15
❑ 25 Cliff Floyd .50 .15
❑ 26 Brian Jordan .50 .15
❑ 27 Roberto Alomar 1.25 .35
❑ 28 Barry Zito 1.25 .35
❑ 29 Harold Baines .50 .15
❑ 30 Brad Penny .50 .15
❑ 31 Jose Cruz Jr. .50 .15
❑ 32 Andy Pettitte .75 .23
❑ 33 Jim Edmonds .50 .15
❑ 34 Darin Erstad .50 .15
❑ 35 Jason Giambi 1.25 .35
❑ 36 Tom Glavine 1.25 .35
❑ 37 Juan Gonzalez 1.25 .35
❑ 38 Mark Grace 1.25 .35
❑ 39 Shawn Green .50 .15
❑ 40 Tim Hudson .50 .15
❑ 41 Andruw Jones .75 .23
❑ 42 Jeff Kent .50 .15
❑ 43 Barry Larkin 1.25 .35
❑ 44 Rafael Furcal .50 .15
❑ 45 Mike Mussina 1.25 .35
❑ 46 Hideo Nomo 1.25 .35
❑ 47 Rafael Palmeiro .75 .23
❑ 48 Scott Rolen .75 .23
❑ 49 Gary Sheffield .50 .15
❑ 50 Bernie Williams .75 .23
❑ 51 Bob Abreu .50 .15
❑ 52 Edgardo Alfonzo .50 .15
❑ 53 Edgar Martinez .75 .23
❑ 54 Magglio Ordonez .50 .15
❑ 55 Kerry Wood 1.25 .35
❑ 56 Matt Morris .50 .15
❑ 57 Lance Berkman .50 .15
❑ 58 Kevin Brown .50 .15
❑ 59 Sean Casey .50 .15
❑ 60 Eric Chavez .50 .15
❑ 61 Bartolo Colon .50 .15
❑ 62 Johnny Damon .50 .15
❑ 63 Jermaine Dye .50 .15
❑ 64 Juan Encarnacion .50 .15
❑ 65 Carl Everett .50 .15
❑ 66 Brian Giles .50 .15
❑ 67 Mike Hampton .50 .15
❑ 68 Richard Hidalgo .50 .15
❑ 69 Geoff Jenkins .50 .15
❑ 70 Jacque Jones .50 .15
❑ 71 Jason Kendall .50 .15
❑ 72 Ryan Klesko .50 .15
❑ 73 Chan Ho Park .50 .15
❑ 74 Richie Sexson .50 .15
❑ 75 Mike Sweeney .50 .15
❑ 76 Fernando Tatis .50 .15
❑ 77 Miguel Tejada .50 .15
❑ 78 Jose Vidro .50 .15
❑ 79 Larry Walker 2.00 .60
❑ 80 Preston Wilson .50 .15
❑ 81 Craig Biggio .75 .23
❑ 82 Fred McGriff .75 .23
❑ 83 Jim Thome 1.25 .35
❑ 84 Garret Anderson .50 .15
❑ 85 Mark Mulder .50 .15
❑ 86 Tony Batista .50 .15
❑ 87 Terrence Long .50 .15
❑ 88 Brad Fullmer .50 .15
❑ 89 Rusty Greer .50 .15
❑ 90 Orlando Hernandez .50 .15
❑ 91 Gabe Kapler .50 .15
❑ 92 Paul Konerko .50 .15
❑ 93 Carlos Lee .50 .15
❑ 94 Kenny Lofton .50 .15
❑ 95 Raul Mondesi .50 .15
❑ 96 Jorge Posada .75 .23
❑ 97 Tim Salmon .75 .23
❑ 98 Greg Vaughn .50 .15
❑ 99 Mo Vaughn .50 .15
❑ 100 Omar Vizquel .50 .15
❑ 101 Ben Grieve .50 .15
❑ 102 Luis Gonzalez .50 .15
❑ 103 Ray Durham .50 .15
❑ 104 Ryan Dempster .50 .15
❑ 105 Eric Karros .50 .15
❑ 106 David Justice .50 .15
❑ 107 Pedro Martinez 1.25 .35
❑ 108 Randy Johnson 1.25 .35
❑ 109 Rick Ankiel .50 .15
❑ 110 Rickey Henderson 2.00 .60
❑ 111 Roger Clemens 2.50 .75
❑ 112 Sammy Sosa 2.00 .60
❑ 113 Tony Gwynn 1.50 .45
❑ 114 Vladimir Guerrero 1.25 .35
❑ 115 Kazuhiro Sasaki .50 .15
❑ 116 Phil Nevin .50 .15
❑ 117 Ruben Mateo .50 .15
❑ 118 Shannon Stewart .50 .15
❑ 119 Matt Williams .50 .15
❑ 120 Tino Martinez .75 .23
❑ 121 Ken Caminiti .50 .15
❑ 122 Edgar Renteria .50 .15
❑ 123 Charles Johnson .50 .15
❑ 124 Aaron Sele .50 .15
❑ 125 Javy Lopez .50 .15
❑ 126 Mariano Rivera .75 .23
❑ 127 Shea Hillenbrand .50 .15
❑ 128 Jeff D'Amico .50 .15
❑ 129 Brady Anderson .50 .15
❑ 130 Kevin Millwood .50 .15
❑ 131 Trot Nixon .50 .15

❑ 132 Mike Lieberthal .50 .15
❑ 133 Juan Pierre .50 .15
❑ 134 Russ Ortiz .50 .15
❑ 135 Jose Macias .50 .15
❑ 136 John Smoltz .75 .23
❑ 137 Jason Varitek .50 .15
❑ 138 Dean Palmer .50 .15
❑ 139 Jeff Cirillo .50 .15
❑ 140 Paul O'Neill .75 .23
❑ 141 Andres Galarraga .50 .15
❑ 142 David Wells .50 .15
❑ 143 Brad Radke .50 .15
❑ 144 Wade Miller .50 .15
❑ 145 John Olerud .50 .15
❑ 146 Moises Alou .50 .15
❑ 147 Carlos Beltran .50 .15
❑ 148 Jeromy Burnitz .50 .15
❑ 149 Steve Finley .50 .15
❑ 150 Joe Mays .50 .15
❑ 151 Alex Escobar ROO 8.00 2.40
❑ 152 J. Estrada ROO RC 10.00 3.00
❑ 153 Pedro Feliz ROO 8.00 2.40
❑ 154 Nate Frese ROO RC 8.00 2.40
❑ 155 Dee Brown ROO 8.00 2.40
❑ 156 B. Larson ROO RC 8.00 2.40
❑ 157 A. Gomez ROO RC 8.00 2.40
❑ 158 Jason Hart ROO 8.00 2.40
❑ 159 C.C. Sabathia ROO 8.00 2.40
❑ 160 Josh Towers ROO RC 8.00 2.40
❑ 161 C. Parker ROO RC 8.00 2.40
❑ 162 J. Melian ROO RC 8.00 2.40
❑ 163 Joe Kennedy ROO RC 8.00 2.40
❑ 164 A. Hernandez ROO RC 8.00 2.40
❑ 165 Jimmy Rollins ROO 8.00 2.40
❑ 166 Jose Mieses ROO RC 8.00 2.40
❑ 167 Roy Oswalt ROO 10.00 3.00
❑ 168 Eric Munson ROO 8.00 2.40
❑ 169 Xavier Nady ROO 8.00 2.40
❑ 170 H. Ramirez ROO RC 10.00 3.00
❑ 171 Abraham Nunez ROO 8.00 2.40
❑ 172 Jose Ortiz ROO 8.00 2.40
❑ 173 Jeremy Owens ROO RC UER 8.00 2.40
Eric Owens pictured on front
❑ 174 C. Vargas ROO RC 8.00 2.40
❑ 175 Corey Patterson ROO 8.00 2.40
❑ 176 Carlos Pena ROO 8.00 2.40
❑ 177 Bud Smith ROO RC 8.00 2.40
❑ 178 Adam Dunn ROO 10.00 3.00
❑ 179 A. Pettyjohn ROO RC 8.00 2.40
❑ 180 E. Guzman ROO RC 8.00 2.40
❑ 181 Jay Gibbons ROO RC 10.00 3.00
❑ 182 Wilkin Ruan ROO RC 8.00 2.40
❑ 183 T. Shinjo ROO RC 10.00 3.00
❑ 184 Alfonso Soriano ROO 10.00 3.00
❑ 185 Marcus Giles ROO 8.00 2.40
❑ 186 Ichiro Suzuki ROO RC 50.00 15.00
❑ 187 Juan Uribe ROO RC 8.00 2.40
❑ 188 D. Williams ROO RC 8.00 2.40
❑ 189 Carlos Valderrama ROO RC 8.00 2.40
❑ 190 Matt White ROO RC 8.00 2.40
❑ 191 Albert Pujols ROO RC 60.00 18.00
❑ 192 D. Mendez ROO RC 8.00 2.40
❑ 193 C. Aldridge ROO RC 8.00 2.40
❑ 194 Endy Chavez ROO RC 8.00 2.40
❑ 195 Josh Beckett ROO 10.00 3.00
❑ 196 W. Betemit ROO RC 8.00 2.40
❑ 197 Ben Sheets ROO 8.00 2.40
❑ 198 A. Torres ROO RC 8.00 2.40
❑ 199 Aubrey Huff ROO 8.00 2.40
❑ 200 Jack Wilson ROO RC 8.00 2.40

2002 Studio

	Nm-Mt	Ex-Mt
COMP.LOW SET w/o SP's (200)	50.00	15.00
COMMON CARD (1-200)	.50	.15
COMMON ROOKIE (1-200)	.50	.15
COMMON CARD (201-275)	5.00	1.50

❑ 1 Vladimir Guerrero 1.25 .35
❑ 2 Chipper Jones 1.25 .35
❑ 3 Bob Abreu .50 .15
❑ 4 Barry Zito 1.25 .35
❑ 5 Larry Walker .75 .23
❑ 6 Miguel Tejada .50 .15

❑ 7 Mike Sweeney .50 .15
❑ 8 Shannon Stewart .50 .15
❑ 9 Sammy Sosa 2.00 .60
❑ 10 Bud Smith .50 .15
❑ 11 Wilson Betemit .50 .15
❑ 12 Kevin Brown .50 .15
❑ 13 Ellis Burks .50 .15
❑ 14 Pat Burrell .50 .15
❑ 15 Cliff Floyd .50 .15
❑ 16 Marcus Giles .50 .15
❑ 17 Troy Glaus .75 .23
❑ 18 Barry Larkin 1.25 .35
❑ 19 Carlos Lee .50 .15
❑ 20 Brian Lawrence .50 .15
❑ 21 Paul Lo Duca .50 .15
❑ 22 Ben Grieve .50 .15
❑ 23 Shawn Green .50 .15
❑ 24 Mike Cameron .50 .15
❑ 25 Roger Clemens 2.50 .75
❑ 26 Joe Crede .50 .15
❑ 27 Jose Cruz Jr. .50 .15
❑ 28 Jeremy Affeldt .50 .15
❑ 29 Adrian Beltre .50 .15
❑ 30 Josh Beckett .75 .23
❑ 31 Roberto Alomar 1.25 .35
❑ 32 Toby Hall .50 .15
❑ 33 Mike Hampton .50 .15
❑ 34 Eric Milton .50 .15
❑ 35 Eric Munson .50 .15
❑ 36 Trot Nixon .50 .15
❑ 37 Roy Oswalt .50 .15
❑ 38 Chan Ho Park .50 .15
❑ 39 Charles Johnson .50 .15
❑ 40 Nick Johnson .50 .15
❑ 41 Tim Hudson .50 .15
❑ 42 Cristian Guzman .50 .15
❑ 43 Drew Henson .50 .15
❑ 44 Mark Grace 1.25 .35
❑ 45 Luis Gonzalez .50 .15
❑ 46 Pedro Martinez 1.25 .35
❑ 47 Joe Mays .50 .15
❑ 48 Jorge Posada .75 .23
❑ 49 Aramis Ramirez .50 .15
❑ 50 Kip Wells .50 .15
❑ 51 Moises Alou .50 .15
❑ 52 Omar Vizquel .50 .15
❑ 53 Ichiro Suzuki 2.50 .75
❑ 54 Jimmy Rollins .50 .15
❑ 55 Freddy Garcia .50 .15
❑ 56 Steve Green .50 .15
❑ 57 Brian Jordan .50 .15
❑ 58 Paul Konerko .50 .15
❑ 59 Jack Cust .50 .15
❑ 60 Sean Casey .50 .15
❑ 61 Bret Boone .50 .15
❑ 62 Hideo Nomo 1.25 .35
❑ 63 Magglio Ordonez .50 .15
❑ 64 Frank Thomas 1.25 .35
❑ 65 Josh Towers .50 .15
❑ 66 Javier Vazquez .50 .15
❑ 67 Robin Ventura .50 .15
❑ 68 Aubrey Huff .50 .15
❑ 69 Richard Hidalgo .50 .15
❑ 70 Brandon Claussen 1.25 .35
❑ 71 Bartolo Colon .50 .15
❑ 72 John Buck .50 .15
❑ 73 Dee Brown .50 .15
❑ 74 Barry Bonds 3.00 .90
❑ 75 Jason Giambi 1.25 .35
❑ 76 Erick Almonte .50 .15
❑ 77 Ryan Dempster .50 .15
❑ 78 Jim Edmonds .50 .15
❑ 79 Jay Gibbons .50 .15
❑ 80 Shigetoshi Hasegawa .50 .15
❑ 81 Todd Helton .75 .23
❑ 82 Erik Bedard .50 .15
❑ 83 Carlos Beltran .50 .15
❑ 84 Rafael Soriano .50 .15
❑ 85 Gary Sheffield .50 .15
❑ 86 Richie Sexson .50 .15
❑ 87 Mike Rivera .50 .15
❑ 88 Jose Ortiz .50 .15
❑ 89 Abraham Nunez .50 .15
❑ 90 Dave Williams .50 .15
❑ 91 Preston Wilson .50 .15
❑ 92 Jason Jennings .50 .15
❑ 93 Juan Diaz .50 .15
❑ 94 Steve Smyth .50 .15
❑ 95 Phil Nevin .50 .15
❑ 96 John Olerud .50 .15
❑ 97 Brad Penny .50 .15
❑ 98 Andy Pettitte .75 .23
❑ 99 Juan Pierre .50 .15
❑ 100 Manny Ramirez .50 .15
❑ 101 Edgardo Alfonzo .50 .15
❑ 102 Michael Cuddyer .50 .15
❑ 103 Johnny Damon .50 .15
❑ 104 Carlos Zambrano .50 .15
❑ 105 Jose Vidro .50 .15
❑ 106 Tsuyoshi Shinjo .50 .15
❑ 107 Ed Rogers .50 .15
❑ 108 Scott Rolen .75 .23
❑ 109 Mariano Rivera .75 .23
❑ 110 Tim Redding .50 .15
❑ 111 Josh Phelps .50 .15
❑ 112 Gabe Kapler .50 .15
❑ 113 Edgar Martinez .75 .23
❑ 114 Fred McGriff .75 .23
❑ 115 Raul Mondesi .50 .15
❑ 116 Wade Miller .50 .15
❑ 117 Mike Mussina 1.25 .35
❑ 118 Rafael Palmeiro .75 .23
❑ 119 Adam Johnson .50 .15
❑ 120 Rickey Henderson 2.00 .60
❑ 121 Bill Hall .50 .15
❑ 122 Ken Griffey Jr. 2.00 .60
❑ 123 Geronimo Gil .50 .15
❑ 124 Robert Fick .50 .15
❑ 125 Darin Erstad .50 .15
❑ 126 Brandon Duckworth .50 .15
❑ 127 Garret Anderson .50 .15
❑ 128 Pedro Feliz .50 .15
❑ 129 Jeff Cirillo .50 .15
❑ 130 Brian Giles .50 .15
❑ 131 Craig Biggio .75 .23
❑ 132 Willie Harris .50 .15
❑ 133 Doug Davis .50 .15
❑ 134 Jeff Kent .50 .15
❑ 135 Terrence Long .50 .15
❑ 136 Carlos Delgado .50 .15
❑ 137 Tino Martinez .75 .23
❑ 138 Donaldo Mendez .50 .15
❑ 139 Sean Douglass .50 .15
❑ 140 Eric Chavez .50 .15
❑ 141 Rick Ankiel .50 .15
❑ 142 Jeremy Giambi .50 .15
❑ 143 Juan Pena .50 .15
❑ 144 Bernie Williams .75 .23
❑ 145 Craig Wilson .50 .15
❑ 146 Ricardo Rodriguez .50 .15
❑ 147 Albert Pujols 2.50 .75
❑ 148 Antonio Perez .50 .15
❑ 149 Russ Ortiz .50 .15
❑ 150 Corky Miller .50 .15
❑ 151 Rich Aurilia .50 .15
❑ 152 Kerry Wood 1.25 .35
❑ 153 Joe Thurston .50 .15
❑ 154 Jeff Deardorff .50 .15
❑ 155 Jermaine Dye .50 .15
❑ 156 Andruw Jones .75 .23
❑ 157 Victor Martinez .50 .15
❑ 158 Nick Neugebauer .50 .15
❑ 159 Matt Morris .50 .15
❑ 160 Casey Fossum .50 .15

Card	Nm-Mt	Ex-Mt
❑ 161 J.D. Drew	.50	.15
❑ 162 Matt Childers	.50	.15
❑ 163 Mark Buehrle	.50	.15
❑ 164 Jeff Bagwell	.75	.23
❑ 165 Kazuhiro Sasaki	.50	.15
❑ 166 Ben Sheets	.50	.15
❑ 167 Alex Rodriguez	2.50	.75
❑ 168 Adam Pettyjohn	.50	.15
❑ 169 Chris Snelling RC	1.50	.45
❑ 170 Robert Person	.50	.15
❑ 171 Juan Uribe	.50	.15
❑ 172 Mo Vaughn	.50	.15
❑ 173 Alfredo Amezaga	.50	.15
❑ 174 Ryan Drese	.50	.15
❑ 175 Corey Thurman RC	.50	.15
❑ 176 Jim Thome	1.25	.35
❑ 177 Orlando Cabrera	.50	.15
❑ 178 Eric Cyr	.50	.15
❑ 179 Greg Maddux	2.50	.75
❑ 180 Earl Snyder RC	.50	.15
❑ 181 C.C. Sabathia	.50	.15
❑ 182 Mark Mulder	.50	.15
❑ 183 Jose Mieses	.50	.15
❑ 184 Joe Kennedy	.50	.15
❑ 185 Randy Johnson	1.25	.35
❑ 186 Tom Glavine	1.25	.35
❑ 187 Eric Junge RC	.50	.15
❑ 188 Mike Piazza	2.00	.60
❑ 189 Corey Patterson	.50	.15
❑ 190 Carlos Pena	.50	.15
❑ 191 Curt Schilling	.75	.23
❑ 192 Nomar Garciaparra	2.50	.75
❑ 193 Lance Berkman	.50	.15
❑ 194 Ryan Klesko	.50	.15
❑ 195 Ivan Rodriguez	1.25	.35
❑ 196 Alfonso Soriano	1.25	.35
❑ 197 Derek Jeter	3.00	.90
❑ 198 David Justice	.50	.15
❑ 199 Juan Gonzalez	1.25	.35
❑ 200 Adam Dunn	.75	.23
❑ 201 Victor Alvarez ROO RC	5.00	1.50
❑ 202 Miguel Asencio ROO RC	5.00	1.50
❑ 203 Brandon Backe ROO RC	5.00	1.50
❑ 204 Chris Baker ROO RC	5.00	1.50
❑ 205 Steve Bechler ROO RC	5.00	1.50
❑ 206 Francis Beltran ROO RC	5.00	1.50
❑ 207 Angel Berroa ROO	5.00	1.50
❑ 208 Hank Blalock ROO	8.00	2.40
❑ 209 Dewon Brazelton ROO	5.00	1.50
❑ 210 Sean Burroughs ROO	5.00	1.50
❑ 211 Marlon Byrd ROO	5.00	1.50
❑ 212 Raul Chavez ROO RC	5.00	1.50
❑ 213 Juan Cruz ROO	5.00	1.50
❑ 214 Jorge De La Rosa ROO RC	5.00	1.50
❑ 215 Doug Devore ROO RC	5.00	1.50
❑ 216 John Ennis ROO RC	5.00	1.50
❑ 217 Felix Escalona ROO RC	5.00	1.50
❑ 218 Morgan Ensberg ROO	5.00	1.50
❑ 219 Cam Esslinger ROO RC	5.00	1.50
❑ 220 Kevin Frederick ROO RC	5.00	1.50
❑ 221 Franklyn German ROO RC	5.00	1.50
❑ 222 Eric Hinske ROO	5.00	1.50
❑ 223 Ben Howard ROO RC	5.00	1.50
❑ 224 Orlando Hudson ROO	5.00	1.50
❑ 225 Travis Hughes ROO RC	8.00	2.40
❑ 226 Kazuhisa Ishii ROO RC	10.00	3.00
❑ 227 Ryan Jamison ROO	5.00	1.50
❑ 228 Reed Johnson ROO RC	8.00	2.40
❑ 229 Kyle Kane ROO RC	5.00	1.50
❑ 230 Austin Kearns ROO	8.00	2.40
❑ 231 Satoru Komiyama ROO RC	5.00	1.50
❑ 232 Jason Lane ROO	5.00	1.50
❑ 233 Jeremy Lambert ROO RC	5.00	1.50
❑ 234 Anderson Machado ROO RC	8.00	2.40
❑ 235 Brian Mallette ROO RC	5.00	1.50
❑ 236 Takahito Nomura ROO RC	5.00	1.50
❑ 237 Jorge Padilla ROO RC	8.00	2.40
❑ 238 Luis Ugueto ROO RC	5.00	1.50
❑ 239 Mark Prior ROO	15.00	4.50
❑ 240 Rene Reyes ROO RC	5.00	1.50
❑ 241 Deivis Santos ROO	5.00	1.50
❑ 242 Elio Serrano ROO RC	5.00	1.50
❑ 243 Tom Shearn ROO RC	5.00	1.50
❑ 244 Allan Simpson ROO RC	5.00	1.50
❑ 245 So Taguchi ROO RC	8.00	2.40
❑ 246 Dennis Tankersley ROO	5.00	1.50
❑ 247 Mark Teixeira ROO	8.00	2.40
❑ 248 Matt Thornton ROO RC	5.00	1.50
❑ 249 Bobby Hill ROO	5.00	1.50
❑ 250 Ramon Vazquez ROO	5.00	1.50
❑ 251 Freddy Sanchez ROO RC	8.00	2.40
❑ 252 Josh Bard ROO RC	5.00	1.50
❑ 253 Trey Hodges ROO RC	8.00	2.40
❑ 254 Jorge Sosa ROO RC	5.00	1.50
❑ 255 Ben Kozlowski ROO RC	5.00	1.50
❑ 256 Eric Good ROO RC	5.00	1.50
❑ 257 Brian Tallet ROO RC	8.00	2.40
❑ 258 P.J. Bevis ROO RC	5.00	1.50
❑ 259 Rodrigo Rosario ROO RC	5.00	1.50
❑ 260 Kirk Saarloos ROO RC	8.00	2.40
❑ 261 Runelvys Hernandez ROO RC	8.00	2.40
❑ 262 Josh Hancock ROO RC	5.00	1.50
❑ 263 Tim Kalita ROO RC	5.00	1.50
❑ 264 Jason Simontacchi ROO RC	8.00	2.40
❑ 265 Clay Condrey ROO RC	5.00	1.50
❑ 266 Cliff Lee ROO RC	8.00	2.40
❑ 267 Aaron Guiel ROO RC	8.00	2.40
❑ 268 Andy Pratt ROO RC	5.00	1.50
❑ 269 Wilson Valdez ROO RC	5.00	1.50
❑ 270 Oliver Perez ROO RC	8.00	2.40
❑ 271 Joe Borchard ROO	5.00	1.50
❑ 272 Jeriome Robertson ROO RC	8.00	2.40
❑ 273 Aaron Cook ROO RC	8.00	2.40
❑ 274 Kevin Cash ROO RC	5.00	1.50
❑ 275 Chone Figgins ROO RC	5.00	1.50

2003 Studio

	Nm-Mt	Ex-Mt
COMPLETE SET (211)	50.00	15.00
❑ 1 Darin Erstad	.50	.15
❑ 2 David Eckstein	.50	.15
❑ 3 Garret Anderson	.50	.15
❑ 4 Jarrod Washburn	.50	.15
❑ 5 Tim Salmon	.75	.23
❑ 6 Troy Glaus	.75	.23
❑ 7 Jay Gibbons	.50	.15
❑ 8 Melvin Mora	.50	.15
❑ 9 Rodrigo Lopez	.50	.15
❑ 10 Tony Batista	.50	.15
❑ 11 Freddy Sanchez	.50	.15
❑ 12 Derek Lowe	.50	.15
❑ 13 Johnny Damon	.50	.15
❑ 14 Manny Ramirez	.50	.15
❑ 15 Nomar Garciaparra	2.50	.75
❑ 16 Pedro Martinez	1.25	.35
❑ 17 Rickey Henderson	2.00	.60
❑ 18 Shea Hillenbrand	.50	.15
❑ 19 Carlos Lee	.50	.15
❑ 20 Frank Thomas	1.25	.35
❑ 21 Magglio Ordonez	.50	.15
❑ 22 Bartolo Colon	.50	.15
❑ 23 Paul Konerko	.50	.15
❑ 24 Josh Stewart RC	.60	.18
❑ 25 C.C. Sabathia	.50	.15
❑ 26 Jeremy Guthrie	.50	.15
❑ 27 Ellis Burks	.50	.15
❑ 28 Omar Vizquel	.50	.15
❑ 29 Victor Martinez	.50	.15
❑ 30 Cliff Lee	.50	.15
❑ 31 Jhonny Peralta RC	.60	.18
❑ 32 Brian Tallet	.50	.15
❑ 33 Bobby Higginson	.50	.15
❑ 34 Carlos Pena	.50	.15
❑ 35 Nook Logan RC	.60	.18
❑ 36 Steve Sparks	.50	.15
❑ 37 Travis Chapman	.50	.15
❑ 38 Carlos Beltran	.50	.15
❑ 39 Joe Randa	.50	.15
❑ 40 Mike Sweeney	.50	.15
❑ 41 Jimmy Gobble	.50	.15
❑ 42 Michael Tucker	.50	.15
❑ 43 Runelvys Hernandez	.50	.15
❑ 44 Brad Radke	.50	.15
❑ 45 Corey Koskie	.50	.15
❑ 46 Cristian Guzman	.50	.15
❑ 47 J.C. Romero	.50	.15
❑ 48 Doug Mientkiewicz	.50	.15
❑ 49 Lew Ford RC	1.00	.30
❑ 50 Jacque Jones	.50	.15
❑ 51 Torii Hunter	.50	.15
❑ 52 Alfonso Soriano	1.25	.35
❑ 53 Nick Johnson	.50	.15
❑ 54 Bernie Williams	.75	.23
❑ 55 Jose Contreras RC	3.00	.90
❑ 56 Derek Jeter	3.00	.90
❑ 57 Jason Giambi	1.25	.35
❑ 58 Brandon Claussen	.50	.15
❑ 59 Jorge Posada	.75	.23
❑ 60 Mike Mussina	1.25	.35
❑ 61 Roger Clemens	2.50	.75
❑ 62 Hideki Matsui RC	6.00	1.80
❑ 63 Barry Zito	1.25	.35
❑ 64 Adam Morrissey	.50	.15
❑ 65 Eric Chavez	.50	.15
❑ 66 Jermaine Dye	.50	.15
❑ 67 Mark Mulder	.50	.15
❑ 68 Miguel Tejada	.50	.15
❑ 69 Joe Valentine RC	.60	.18
❑ 70 Tim Hudson	.50	.15
❑ 71 Bret Boone	.50	.15
❑ 72 Chris Snelling	.50	.15
❑ 73 Edgar Martinez	.75	.23
❑ 74 Freddy Garcia	.50	.15
❑ 75 Ichiro Suzuki	2.50	.75
❑ 76 Jamie Moyer	.50	.15
❑ 77 John Olerud	.50	.15
❑ 78 Kazuhiro Sasaki	.50	.15
❑ 79 Aubrey Huff	.50	.15
❑ 80 Joe Kennedy	.50	.15
❑ 81 Dewon Brazelton	.50	.15
❑ 82 Pete LaForest RC	1.00	.30
❑ 83 Alex Rodriguez	2.50	.75
❑ 84 Chan Ho Park	.50	.15
❑ 85 Hank Blalock	.75	.23
❑ 86 Juan Gonzalez	1.25	.35
❑ 87 Kevin Mench	.50	.15
❑ 88 Rafael Palmeiro	.75	.23
❑ 89 Carlos Delgado	.50	.15
❑ 90 Eric Hinske	.50	.15
❑ 91 Josh Phelps	.50	.15
❑ 92 Roy Halladay	.50	.15
❑ 93 Shannon Stewart	.50	.15
❑ 94 Vernon Wells	.50	.15
❑ 95 Vinny Chulk	.50	.15
❑ 96 Curt Schilling	.75	.23
❑ 97 Junior Spivey	.50	.15
❑ 98 Luis Gonzalez	.50	.15
❑ 99 Mark Grace	1.25	.35
❑ 100 Randy Johnson	1.25	.35
❑ 101 Andruw Jones	.75	.23
❑ 102 Chipper Jones	1.25	.35
❑ 103 Gary Sheffield	.50	.15
❑ 104 Greg Maddux	2.50	.75
❑ 105 John Smoltz	.75	.23
❑ 106 Mike Hampton	.50	.15
❑ 107 Adam LaRoche	.50	.15
❑ 108 Michael Hessman RC	.60	.18
❑ 109 Corey Patterson	.50	.15
❑ 110 Kerry Wood	1.25	.35
❑ 111 Mark Prior	2.50	.75
❑ 112 Moises Alou	.50	.15
❑ 113 Sammy Sosa	2.00	.60
❑ 114 Adam Dunn	.75	.23
❑ 115 Austin Kearns	.75	.23
❑ 116 Barry Larkin	1.25	.35
❑ 117 Ken Griffey Jr.	2.00	.60
❑ 118 Sean Casey	.50	.15
❑ 119 Jason Jennings	.50	.15

❑ 120 Jay Payton .50 .15
❑ 121 Larry Walker .75 .23
❑ 122 Todd Helton .75 .23
❑ 123 Jeff Baker .50 .15
❑ 124 Clint Barmes RC 1.00 .30
❑ 125 Ivan Rodriguez 1.25 .35
❑ 126 Josh Beckett .75 .23
❑ 127 Juan Encarnacion .50 .15
❑ 128 Mike Lowell .50 .15
❑ 129 Craig Biggio .75 .23
❑ 130 Jason Lane .50 .15
❑ 131 Jeff Bagwell .75 .23
❑ 132 Lance Berkman .50 .15
❑ 133 Roy Oswalt .50 .15
❑ 134 Jeff Kent .50 .15
❑ 135 Hideo Nomo 1.25 .35
❑ 136 Kazuhisa Ishii .50 .15
❑ 137 Kevin Brown .50 .15
❑ 138 Odalis Perez .50 .15
❑ 139 Paul Lo Duca .50 .15
❑ 140 Shawn Green .50 .15
❑ 141 Adrian Beltre .50 .15
❑ 142 Ben Sheets .50 .15
❑ 143 Bill Hall .50 .15
❑ 144 Jeffrey Hammonds .50 .15
❑ 145 Richie Sexson .50 .15
❑ 146 Termel Sledge RC 1.00 .30
❑ 147 Brad Wilkerson .50 .15
❑ 148 Javier Vazquez .50 .15
❑ 149 Jose Vidro .50 .15
❑ 150 Michael Barrett .50 .15
❑ 151 Vladimir Guerrero 1.25 .35
❑ 152 Al Leiter .50 .15
❑ 153 Mike Piazza 2.00 .60
❑ 154 Mo Vaughn .50 .15
❑ 155 Cliff Floyd .50 .15
❑ 156 Roberto Alomar 1.25 .35
❑ 157 Roger Cedeno .50 .15
❑ 158 Tom Glavine 1.25 .35
❑ 159 Prentice Redman RC .60 .18
❑ 160 Bobby Abreu .50 .15
❑ 161 Jimmy Rollins .50 .15
❑ 162 Mike Lieberthal .50 .15
❑ 163 Pat Burrell .50 .15
❑ 164 Vicente Padilla .50 .15
❑ 165 Jim Thome 1.25 .35
❑ 166 Kevin Millwood .50 .15
❑ 167 Aramis Ramirez .50 .15
❑ 168 Brian Giles .50 .15
❑ 169 Jason Kendall .50 .15
❑ 170 Josh Fogg .50 .15
❑ 171 Kip Wells .50 .15
❑ 172 Jose Castillo .50 .15
❑ 173 Mark Kotsay .50 .15
❑ 174 Oliver Perez .50 .15
❑ 175 Phil Nevin .50 .15
❑ 176 Ryan Klesko .50 .15
❑ 177 Sean Burroughs .50 .15
❑ 178 Brian Lawrence .50 .15
❑ 179 Shane Victorino RC .60 .18
❑ 180 Barry Bonds 3.00 .90
❑ 181 Benito Santiago .50 .15
❑ 182 Ray Durham .50 .15
❑ 183 Rich Aurilla .50 .15
❑ 184 Damian Moss .50 .15
❑ 185 Albert Pujols 2.50 .75
❑ 186 J.D. Drew .50 .15
❑ 187 Jim Edmonds .50 .15
❑ 188 Matt Morris .50 .15
❑ 189 Tino Martinez .75 .23
❑ 190 Scott Rolen .75 .23
❑ 191 Troy Glaus 1.50 .45
Tim Salmon
❑ 192 Sean Casey 1.00 .30
Corky Miller
❑ 193 Carlos Lee 1.50 .45
Frank Thomas
❑ 194 Lance Berkman 1.00 .30
Jeff Kent
❑ 195 Jose Contreras 1.50 .45
Mariano Rivera
❑ 196 Alex Rodriguez 2.00 .60
Juan Gonzalez
❑ 197 Andy Pettitte 1.50 .45
David Wells
❑ 198 Shawn Green 1.00 .30
Dave Roberts
❑ 199 Mike Lieberthal 1.00 .30
Jimmy Rollins
❑ 200 Mike Mussina 3.00 .90
Hideki Matsui
❑ 201 Adam Loewen ROO RC
❑ 202 Jeremy Bonderman ROO RC
❑ 203 Brandon Webb ROO RC
❑ 204 Chien-Ming Wang ROO RC
❑ 205 Chad Gaudin ROO RC
❑ 206 Ryan Wagner ROO RC
❑ 207 Hong-Chih Kuo ROO RC
❑ 208 Dan Haren ROO RC
❑ 209 Rickie Weeks ROO RC
❑ 210 Ramon Nivar ROO RC
❑ 211 Delmon Young ROO RC

2001 Sweet Spot

	Nm-Mt	Ex-Mt
COMP.BASIC w/o SP's (60)	25.00	7.50
COMP.UPDATE w/o SP's (30)	10.00	3.00
COMMON CARD (1-60)	.40	.12
COMMON CARD (61-90)	10.00	3.00
COMMON CARD (91-120)	.60	.18
COMMON (121-150)	5.00	1.50

❑ 1 Troy Glaus .60 .18
❑ 2 Darin Erstad .40 .12
❑ 3 Jason Giambi 1.00 .30
❑ 4 Tim Hudson .40 .12
❑ 5 Ben Grieve .40 .12
❑ 6 Carlos Delgado .40 .12
❑ 7 David Wells .40 .12
❑ 8 Greg Vaughn .40 .12
❑ 9 Roberto Alomar 1.00 .30
❑ 10 Jim Thome 1.00 .30
❑ 11 John Olerud .40 .12
❑ 12 Edgar Martinez .60 .18
❑ 13 Cal Ripken 3.00 .90
❑ 14 Albert Belle .40 .12
❑ 15 Ivan Rodriguez 1.00 .30
❑ 16 Alex Rodriguez Rangers 4.00 1.20
❑ 17 Pedro Martinez 1.00 .30
❑ 18 Nomar Garciaparra 2.00 .60
❑ 19 Manny Ramirez .40 .12
❑ 20 Jermaine Dye .40 .12
❑ 21 Juan Gonzalez 1.00 .30
❑ 22 Dean Palmer .40 .12
❑ 23 Matt Lawton .40 .12
❑ 24 Eric Milton .40 .12
❑ 25 Frank Thomas 1.00 .30
❑ 26 Magglio Ordonez .40 .12
❑ 27 Derek Jeter 2.50 .75
❑ 28 Bernie Williams .60 .18
❑ 29 Roger Clemens 2.00 .60
❑ 30 Jeff Bagwell .60 .18
❑ 31 Richard Hidalgo .40 .12
❑ 32 Chipper Jones 1.00 .30
❑ 33 Greg Maddux 2.00 .60
❑ 34 Richie Sexson .40 .12
❑ 35 Jeromy Burnitz .40 .12
❑ 36 Mark McGwire 2.50 .75
❑ 37 Jim Edmonds .40 .12
❑ 38 Sammy Sosa 1.50 .45
❑ 39 Randy Johnson 1.00 .30
❑ 40 Steve Finley .40 .12
❑ 41 Gary Sheffield .40 .12
❑ 42 Shawn Green .40 .12
❑ 43 Vladimir Guerrero 1.00 .30
❑ 44 Jose Vidro .40 .12
❑ 45 Barry Bonds 2.50 .75
❑ 46 Jeff Kent .40 .12
❑ 47 Preston Wilson .40 .12
❑ 48 Luis Castillo .40 .12
❑ 49 Mike Piazza 1.50 .45
❑ 50 Edgardo Alfonzo .40 .12
❑ 51 Tony Gwynn 1.25 .35
❑ 52 Ryan Klesko .40 .12
❑ 53 Scott Rolen .60 .18
❑ 54 Bob Abreu .40 .12
❑ 55 Jason Kendall .40 .12
❑ 56 Brian Giles .40 .12
❑ 57 Ken Griffey Jr. 1.50 .45
❑ 58 Barry Larkin 1.00 .30
❑ 59 Todd Helton .60 .18
❑ 60 Mike Hampton .40 .12
Card back has batting header lines UER
❑ 61 Corey Patterson SB 10.00 3.00
❑ 62 Ichiro Suzuki SB RC 150.00 45.00
❑ 63 Jason Grilli SB 10.00 3.00
❑ 64 Brian Cole SB 10.00 3.00
❑ 65 Juan Pierre SB 10.00 3.00
❑ 66 Matt Ginter SB 10.00 3.00
❑ 67 Jimmy Rollins SB 10.00 3.00
❑ 68 Jason Smith SB RC 10.00 3.00
❑ 69 Israel Alcantara SB 10.00 3.00
❑ 70 Adam Pettyjohn SB RC 10.00 3.00
❑ 71 Luke Prokopec SB 10.00 3.00
❑ 72 Barry Zito SB 12.00 3.60
❑ 73 Keith Ginter SB 10.00 3.00
❑ 74 Sun Woo Kim SB 10.00 3.00
❑ 75 Ross Gload SB 10.00 3.00
❑ 76 Matt Wise SB 10.00 3.00
❑ 77 Aubrey Huff SB 10.00 3.00
❑ 78 Ryan Franklin SB 10.00 3.00
❑ 79 Brandon Inge SB 10.00 3.00
❑ 80 Wes Helms SB 10.00 3.00
❑ 81 Junior Spivey SB RC 12.00 3.60
❑ 82 Ryan Vogelsong SB 10.00 3.00
❑ 83 John Parrish SB 10.00 3.00
❑ 84 Joe Crede SB 10.00 3.00
❑ 85 Damian Rolls SB 10.00 3.00
❑ 86 Esix Snead SB RC 10.00 3.00
❑ 87 Rocky Biddle SB 10.00 3.00
❑ 88 Brady Clark SB 10.00 3.00
❑ 89 Timo Perez SB 10.00 3.00
❑ 90 Jay Spurgeon SB 10.00 3.00
❑ 91 Garret Anderson .60 .18
❑ 92 Jermaine Dye .60 .18
❑ 93 Shannon Stewart .60 .18
❑ 94 Ben Grieve .60 .18
❑ 95 Juan Gonzalez 1.50 .45
❑ 96 Brett Boone .60 .18
❑ 97 Tony Batista .60 .18
❑ 98 Rafael Palmeiro 1.00 .30
❑ 99 Carl Everett .60 .18
❑ 100 Mike Sweeney .60 .18
❑ 101 Tony Clark .60 .18
❑ 102 Doug Mientkiewicz .60 .18
❑ 103 Jose Canseco 1.50 .45
❑ 104 Mike Mussina 1.50 .45
❑ 105 Lance Berkman .60 .18
❑ 106 Andruw Jones 1.00 .30
❑ 107 Geoff Jenkins .60 .18
❑ 108 Matt Morris .60 .18
❑ 109 Fred McGriff 1.00 .30
❑ 110 Luis Gonzalez .60 .18
❑ 111 Kevin Brown .60 .18
❑ 112 Tony Armas Jr. .60 .18
❑ 113 John Vander Wal .60 .18
❑ 114 Cliff Floyd .60 .18
❑ 115 Matt Lawton .60 .18
❑ 116 Phil Nevin .60 .18
❑ 117 Pat Burrell .60 .18
❑ 118 Aramis Ramirez .60 .18
❑ 119 Sean Casey .60 .18
❑ 120 Larry Walker 1.00 .30
❑ 121 Albert Pujols SB RC 100.00 30.00
❑ 122 J.Estrada SB RC 5.00 1.50
❑ 123 Wilson Betemit SB RC 5.00 1.50
❑ 124 A.Hernandez SB RC 5.00 1.50
❑ 125 M.Ensberg SB RC 10.00 3.00
❑ 126 H.Ramirez SB RC 8.00 2.40

❑ 127 Josh Towers SB RC	5.00	1.50
❑ 128 Juan Uribe SB RC	5.00	1.50
❑ 129 Wilken Ruan SB RC	5.00	1.50
❑ 130 Andres Torres SB RC	5.00	1.50
❑ 131 B.Lawrence SB RC	5.00	1.50
❑ 132 Ryan Freel SB RC	5.00	1.50
❑ 133 B.Duckworth SB RC	5.00	1.50
❑ 134 Juan Diaz SB RC	5.00	1.50
❑ 135 Rafael Soriano SB RC	10.00	3.00
❑ 136 R.Rodriguez SB RC	5.00	1.50
❑ 137 Bud Smith SB RC	5.00	1.50
❑ 138 Mark Teixeira SB RC	40.00	12.00
❑ 139 Mark Prior SB RC	80.00	24.00
❑ 140 J.Melian SB RC	5.00	1.50
❑ 141 D.Brazelton SB RC	5.00	1.50
❑ 142 Greg Miller SB RC	5.00	1.50
❑ 143 Billy Sylvester SB RC	5.00	1.50
❑ 144 E.Guzman SB RC	5.00	1.50
❑ 145 Jack Wilson SB RC	5.00	1.50
❑ 146 Jose Mieses SB RC	5.00	1.50
❑ 147 Brandon Lyon SB RC	5.00	1.50
❑ 148 T.Shinjo SB RC	10.00	3.00
❑ 149 Juan Cruz SB RC	5.00	1.50
❑ 150 Jay Gibbons SB RC	10.00	3.00

2002 Sweet Spot

	Nm-Mt	Ex-Mt
COMP.SET w/o SP's (90)	25.00	7.50
COMMON CARD (1-90)	.40	.12
COMMON CARD (91-130)	5.00	1.50
COMMON TIER 1 AU (131-145)	15.00	4.50
COMMON TIER 2 AU (131-145)	25.00	7.50
COMMON CARD (146-175)	10.00	3.00

❑ 1 Troy Glaus	.60	.18
❑ 2 Darin Erstad	.40	.12
❑ 3 Tim Hudson	.40	.12
❑ 4 Eric Chavez	.40	.12
❑ 5 Barry Zito	1.00	.30
❑ 6 Miguel Tejada	.40	.12
❑ 7 Carlos Delgado	.40	.12
❑ 8 Eric Hinske	.40	.12
❑ 9 Ben Grieve	.40	.12
❑ 10 Jim Thome	1.00	.30
❑ 11 C.C. Sabathia	.40	.12
❑ 12 Omar Vizquel	.40	.12
❑ 13 Ichiro Suzuki	2.00	.60
❑ 14 Edgar Martinez	.60	.18
❑ 15 Bret Boone	.40	.12
❑ 16 Freddy Garcia	.40	.12
❑ 17 Tony Batista	.40	.12
❑ 18 Geronimo Gil	.40	.12
❑ 19 Alex Rodriguez	2.00	.60
❑ 20 Rafael Palmeiro	.60	.18
❑ 21 Ivan Rodriguez	1.00	.30
❑ 22 Hank Blalock	1.00	.30
❑ 23 Juan Gonzalez	1.00	.30
❑ 24 Nomar Garciaparra	2.00	.60
❑ 25 Pedro Martinez	1.00	.30
❑ 26 Manny Ramirez	.40	.12
❑ 27 Mike Sweeney	.40	.12
❑ 28 Carlos Beltran	.40	.12
❑ 29 Dmitri Young	.40	.12
❑ 30 Torii Hunter	.40	.12
❑ 31 Eric Milton	.40	.12
❑ 32 Corey Koskie	.40	.12
❑ 33 Frank Thomas	1.00	.30
❑ 34 Mark Buehrle	.40	.12
❑ 35 Magglio Ordonez	.40	.12
❑ 36 Roger Clemens	2.00	.60
❑ 37 Derek Jeter	2.50	.75
❑ 38 Jason Giambi	1.00	.30
❑ 39 Alfonso Soriano	1.00	.30
❑ 40 Bernie Williams	.60	.18
❑ 41 Jeff Bagwell	.60	.18
❑ 42 Roy Oswalt	.40	.12
❑ 43 Lance Berkman	.40	.12
❑ 44 Greg Maddux	2.00	.60
❑ 45 Chipper Jones	1.00	.30
❑ 46 Gary Sheffield	.40	.12
❑ 47 Andruw Jones	.60	.18
❑ 48 Richie Sexson	.40	.12
❑ 49 Ben Sheets	.40	.12
❑ 50 Albert Pujols	2.00	.60
❑ 51 Matt Morris	.40	.12
❑ 52 J.D. Drew	.40	.12
❑ 53 Sammy Sosa	1.50	.45
❑ 54 Kerry Wood	1.00	.30
❑ 55 Mark Prior	2.00	.60
❑ 56 Moises Alou	.40	.12
❑ 57 Corey Patterson	.40	.12
❑ 58 Randy Johnson	1.00	.30
❑ 59 Luis Gonzalez	.40	.12
❑ 60 Curt Schilling	.60	.18
❑ 61 Shawn Green	.40	.12
❑ 62 Kevin Brown	.40	.12
❑ 63 Paul Lo Duca	.40	.12
❑ 64 Adrian Beltre	.40	.12
❑ 65 Vladimir Guerrero	1.00	.30
❑ 66 Jose Vidro	.40	.12
❑ 67 Javier Vazquez	.40	.12
❑ 68 Barry Bonds	2.50	.75
❑ 69 Jeff Kent	.40	.12
❑ 70 Rich Aurilia	.40	.12
❑ 71 Mike Lowell	.40	.12
❑ 72 Josh Beckett	.60	.18
❑ 73 Brad Penny	.40	.12
❑ 74 Roberto Alomar	1.00	.30
❑ 75 Mike Piazza	1.50	.45
❑ 76 Jeromy Burnitz	.40	.12
❑ 77 Mo Vaughn	.40	.12
❑ 78 Phil Nevin	.40	.12
❑ 79 Sean Burroughs	.40	.12
❑ 80 Jeremy Giambi	.40	.12
❑ 81 Bobby Abreu	.40	.12
❑ 82 Jimmy Rollins	.40	.12
❑ 83 Pat Burrell	.40	.12
❑ 84 Brian Giles	.40	.12
❑ 85 Aramis Ramirez	.40	.12
❑ 86 Ken Griffey Jr.	1.50	.45
❑ 87 Adam Dunn	.60	.18
❑ 88 Austin Kearns	.60	.18
❑ 89 Todd Helton	.60	.18
❑ 90 Larry Walker	.60	.18
❑ 91 Earl Snyder SB RC	5.00	1.50
❑ 92 Jorge Padilla SB RC	8.00	2.40
❑ 93 Felix Escalona SB RC	5.00	1.50
❑ 94 John Foster SB RC	5.00	1.50
❑ 95 Brandon Puffer SB RC	5.00	1.50
❑ 96 Steve Bechler SB RC	5.00	1.50
❑ 97 Hansel Izquierdo SB RC	5.00	1.50
❑ 98 Chris Baker SB RC	5.00	1.50
❑ 99 Jeremy Ward SB RC	5.00	1.50
❑ 100 Kevin Frederick SB RC	5.00	1.50
❑ 101 Josh Hancock SB RC	5.00	1.50
❑ 102 Allan Simpson SB RC	5.00	1.50
❑ 103 Mitch Wylie SB RC	5.00	1.50
❑ 104 Mark Corey SB RC	5.00	1.50
❑ 105 Victor Alvarez SB RC	5.00	1.50
❑ 106 Todd Donovan SB RC	5.00	1.50
❑ 107 Nelson Castro SB RC	5.00	1.50
❑ 108 Chris Booker SB RC	5.00	1.50
❑ 109 Corey Thurman SB RC	5.00	1.50
❑ 110 Kirk Saarloos SB RC	8.00	2.40
❑ 111 Michael Crudale SB RC	5.00	1.50
❑ 112 Jason Simontacchi SB RC	8.00	2.40
❑ 113 Ron Calloway SB RC	5.00	1.50
❑ 114 Brandon Backe SB RC	5.00	1.50
❑ 115 Tom Shearn SB RC	5.00	1.50
❑ 116 Oliver Perez SB RC	8.00	2.40
❑ 117 Kyle Kane SB RC	5.00	1.50
❑ 118 Francis Beltran SB RC	5.00	1.50
❑ 119 So Taguchi SB RC	8.00	2.40
❑ 120 Doug Devore SB RC	5.00	1.50
❑ 121 Juan Brito SB RC	5.00	1.50
❑ 122 Cliff Bartosh SB RC	5.00	1.50
❑ 123 Eric Junge SB RC	5.00	1.50
❑ 124 Joe Orloski SB RC	5.00	1.50
❑ 125 Scotty Layfield SB RC	5.00	1.50
❑ 126 Jorge Sosa SB RC	5.00	1.50
❑ 127 Satoru Komiyama SB RC	5.00	1.50
❑ 128 Edwin Almonte SB RC	5.00	1.50
❑ 129 Takahito Nomura SB RC	5.00	1.50
❑ 130 John Ennis SB RC	5.00	1.50
❑ 131 Kazuhisa Ishii T2 AU RC	120.00	36.00
❑ 132 Ben Howard T2 AU RC	25.00	7.50
❑ 133 Aaron Cook T1 AU RC	20.00	6.00
❑ 134 Andy Machado T1 AU RC	20.00	6.00
❑ 135 Luis Ugueto T1 AU RC	15.00	4.50
❑ 136 Tyler Yates T1 AU RC	15.00	4.50
❑ 137 Rodrigo Rosario T1 AU RC	15.00	4.50
❑ 138 Jaime Cerda T1 AU RC	15.00	4.50
❑ 139 Luis Martinez T1 AU RC	20.00	6.00
❑ 140 Rene Reyes T1 AU RC	15.00	4.50
❑ 141 Eric Good T1 AU RC	15.00	4.50
❑ 142 Matt Thornton T2 AU RC	25.00	7.50
❑ 143 Steve Kent T1 AU RC	15.00	4.50
❑ 144 Jose Valverde T1 AU RC	20.00	6.00
❑ 145 Adrian Burnside T1 AU RC	15.00	4.50
❑ 146 Barry Bonds GF	25.00	7.50
❑ 147 Ken Griffey Jr. GF	15.00	4.50
❑ 148 Alex Rodriguez GF	20.00	6.00
❑ 149 Jason Giambi GF	8.00	2.40
❑ 150 Chipper Jones GF	10.00	3.00
❑ 151 Nomar Garciaparra GF	20.00	6.00
❑ 152 Mike Piazza GF	15.00	4.50
❑ 153 Sammy Sosa GF	15.00	4.50
❑ 154 Derek Jeter GF	25.00	7.50
❑ 155 Jeff Bagwell GF	10.00	3.00
❑ 156 Albert Pujols GF	20.00	6.00
❑ 157 Ichiro Suzuki GF	20.00	6.00
❑ 158 Randy Johnson GF	10.00	3.00
❑ 159 Frank Thomas GF	10.00	3.00
❑ 160 Greg Maddux GF	20.00	6.00
❑ 161 Jim Thome GF	10.00	3.00
❑ 162 Scott Rolen GF	10.00	3.00
❑ 163 Shawn Green GF	10.00	3.00
❑ 164 Vladimir Guerrero GF	10.00	3.00
❑ 165 Troy Glaus GF	10.00	3.00
❑ 166 Carlos Delgado GF	10.00	3.00
❑ 167 Luis Gonzalez GF	10.00	3.00
❑ 168 Roger Clemens GF	20.00	6.00
❑ 169 Todd Helton GF	10.00	3.00
❑ 170 Eric Chavez GF	10.00	3.00
❑ 171 Rafael Palmeiro GF	10.00	3.00
❑ 172 Pedro Martinez GF	10.00	3.00
❑ 173 Lance Berkman GF	10.00	3.00
❑ 174 Josh Beckett GF	10.00	3.00
❑ 175 Sean Burroughs GF	10.00	3.00
❑ MM Mark McGwire AU EXCH/100	600.00	180.00

2003 Sweet Spot

	MINT	NRMT
COMP.SET w/o SP's (100)	25.00	11.00
COMP.SET w/SP's (130)	120.00	55.00
COMMON CARD (1-130)	.50	.23
COMMON SP (1-130)	3.00	1.35
COMMON CARD (131-190)	5.00	2.20
131-190 STATED ODDS 1:3		

131-190 PRINT RUN 2003 SERIAL #'d SETS
COMMON P1 (191-232) 10.00 4.50
P1 191-232 PRINT RUN 500 SERIAL #'d SETS
COMMON P2-P3 (191-232)......... 8.00 3.60
P2 191-232 PRINT RUN 1200 SERIAL #'d SETS
P3 191-232 PRINT RUN 1430 SERIAL #'d SETS
❑ 1 Darin Erstad .50 .23
❑ 2 Garret Anderson .50 .23
❑ 3 Tim Salmon .75 .35
❑ 4 Troy Glaus .75 .35
❑ 5 Luis Gonzalez .50 .23
❑ 6 Randy Johnson 1.25 .55
❑ 7 Curt Schilling .75 .35
❑ 8 Lyle Overbay .50 .23
❑ 9 Andruw Jones SP 5.00 2.20
❑ 10 Gary Sheffield SP 3.00 1.35
❑ 11 Rafael Furcal SP 3.00 1.35
❑ 12 Greg Maddux SP 8.00 3.60
❑ 13 Chipper Jones SP 5.00 2.20
❑ 14 Tony Batista .50 .23
❑ 15 Rodrigo Lopez .50 .23
❑ 16 Jay Gibbons .50 .23
❑ 17 Jason Johnson .50 .23
❑ 18 Byung-Hyun Kim SP 3.00 1.35
❑ 19 Johnny Damon SP 3.00 1.35
❑ 20 Derek Lowe SP 3.00 1.35
❑ 21 Nomar Garciaparra SP 8.00 3.60
❑ 22 Pedro Martinez SP 5.00 2.20
❑ 23 Manny Ramirez SP 3.00 1.35
❑ 24 Mark Prior 2.50 1.10
❑ 25 Kerry Wood 1.25 .55
❑ 26 Corey Patterson .50 .23
❑ 27 Sammy Sosa 2.00 .90
❑ 28 Moises Alou .50 .23
❑ 29 Magglio Ordonez .50 .23
❑ 30 Frank Thomas 1.25 .55
❑ 31 Paul Konerko .50 .23
❑ 32 Roberto Alomar 1.25 .55
❑ 33 Adam Dunn .75 .35
❑ 34 Austin Kearns .75 .35
❑ 35 Ryan Wagner RC 4.00 1.80
❑ 36 Ken Griffey Jr. 2.00 .90
❑ 37 Sean Casey .50 .23
❑ 38 Omar Vizquel .50 .23
❑ 39 C.C. Sabathia .50 .23
❑ 40 Jason Davis .50 .23
❑ 41 Travis Hafner .50 .23
❑ 42 Brandon Phillips .50 .23
❑ 43 Larry Walker .75 .35
❑ 44 Preston Wilson .50 .23
❑ 45 Jay Payton .50 .23
❑ 46 Todd Helton .75 .35
❑ 47 Carlos Pena .50 .23
❑ 48 Eric Munson .50 .23
❑ 49 Ivan Rodriguez 1.25 .55
❑ 50 Josh Beckett .75 .35
❑ 51 Alex Gonzalez .50 .23
❑ 52 Roy Oswalt .50 .23
❑ 53 Craig Biggio .75 .35
❑ 54 Jeff Bagwell .75 .35
❑ 55 Lance Berkman .50 .23
❑ 56 Mike Sweeney .50 .23
❑ 57 Carlos Beltran .50 .23
❑ 58 Brent Mayne .50 .23
❑ 59 Mike MacDougal .50 .23
❑ 60 Hideo Nomo 1.25 .55
❑ 61 Dave Roberts .50 .23
❑ 62 Adrian Beltre .50 .23
❑ 63 Shawn Green .50 .23
❑ 64 Kazuhisa Ishii .50 .23
❑ 65 Rickey Henderson 2.00 .90
❑ 66 Richie Sexson .50 .23
❑ 67 Torii Hunter .50 .23
❑ 68 Jacque Jones .50 .23
❑ 69 Joe Mays .50 .23
❑ 70 Corey Koskie .50 .23
❑ 71 A.J. Pierzynski .50 .23
❑ 72 Jose Vidro .50 .23
❑ 73 Vladimir Guerrero 1.25 .55
❑ 74 Tom Glavine 1.25 .55
❑ 75 Mike Piazza 2.00 .90
❑ 76 Jose Reyes .75 .35
❑ 77 Jae Weong Seo .50 .23
❑ 78 Jorge Posada SP 5.00 2.20
❑ 79 Mike Mussina SP 5.00 2.20
❑ 80 Robin Ventura SP 3.00 1.35
❑ 81 Mariano Rivera SP 5.00 2.20
❑ 82 Roger Clemens SP 8.00 3.60
❑ 83 Jason Giambi SP 5.00 2.20
❑ 84 Bernie Williams SP 5.00 2.20
❑ 85 Alfonso Soriano SP 5.00 2.20
❑ 86 Derek Jeter 3.00 1.35
❑ 87 Miguel Tejada .50 .23
❑ 88 Eric Chavez .50 .23
❑ 89 Tim Hudson .50 .23
❑ 90 Barry Zito 1.25 .55
❑ 91 Mark Mulder .50 .23
❑ 92 Erubiel Durazo .50 .23
❑ 93 Pat Burrell .50 .23
❑ 94 Jim Thome 1.25 .55
❑ 95 Bobby Abreu .50 .23
❑ 96 Brian Giles .50 .23
❑ 97 Reggie Sanders .50 .23
❑ 98 Jose Hernandez .50 .23
❑ 99 Ryan Klesko .50 .23
❑ 100 Sean Burroughs .50 .23
❑ 101 Edgardo Alfonzo SP 3.00 1.35
❑ 102 Rich Aurilia SP 3.00 1.35
❑ 103 Jose Cruz Jr. SP 3.00 1.35
❑ 104 Barry Bonds SP 10.00 4.50
❑ 105 Andres Galarraga SP 3.00 1.35
❑ 106 Mike Cameron .50 .23
❑ 107 Kazuhiro Sasaki .50 .23
❑ 108 Bret Boone .50 .23
❑ 109 Ichiro Suzuki 2.50 1.10
❑ 110 John Olerud .50 .23
❑ 111 J.D. Drew SP 3.00 1.35
❑ 112 Jim Edmonds SP 3.00 1.35
❑ 113 Scott Rolen SP 5.00 2.20
❑ 114 Matt Morris SP 3.00 1.35
❑ 115 Tino Martinez SP 5.00 2.20
❑ 116 Albert Pujols SP 8.00 3.60
❑ 117 Jared Sandberg .50 .23
❑ 118 Carl Crawford .50 .23
❑ 119 Rafael Palmeiro .75 .35
❑ 120 Hank Blalock .75 .35
❑ 121 Alex Rodriguez 8.00 3.60
❑ 122 Kevin Mench .50 .23
❑ 123 Juan Gonzalez 1.25 .55
❑ 124 Mark Teixeira .75 .35
❑ 125 Shannon Stewart .50 .23
❑ 126 Vernon Wells .50 .23
❑ 127 Josh Phelps .50 .23
❑ 128 Eric Hinske .50 .23
❑ 129 Orlando Hudson .50 .23
❑ 130 Carlos Delgado .50 .23
❑ 131 Jason Shiell SB RC 5.00 2.20
❑ 132 Kevin Tolar SB RC 5.00 2.20
❑ 133 Nathan Bland SB RC 5.00 2.20
❑ 134 Brent Hoard SB RC 5.00 2.20
❑ 135 Jon Pridie SB RC 5.00 2.20
❑ 136 Mike Ryan SB RC 8.00 3.60
❑ 137 Francisco Rosario SB RC 5.00 2.20
❑ 138 Runelvys Hernandez SB 5.00 2.20
❑ 139 Guillermo Quiroz SB RC 8.00 3.60
❑ 140 Chin-Hui Tsao SB 5.00 2.20
❑ 141 Rett Johnson SB RC 8.00 3.60
❑ 142 Colin Porter SB RC 5.00 2.20
❑ 143 Jose Castillo SB 5.00 2.20
❑ 144 Chris Waters SB RC 5.00 2.20
❑ 145 Jeremy Guthrie SB 5.00 2.20
❑ 146 Pedro Liriano SB 5.00 2.20
❑ 147 Joe Borowski SB 5.00 2.20
❑ 148 Felix Sanchez SB RC 5.00 2.20
❑ 149 Todd Wellemeyer SB RC 8.00 3.60
❑ 150 Gerald Laird SB 5.00 2.20
❑ 151 Brandon Webb SB RC 10.00 4.50
❑ 152 Tommy Whiteman SB 5.00 2.20
❑ 153 Carlos Rivera SB 5.00 2.20
❑ 154 Rick Roberts SB RC 5.00 2.20
❑ 155 Termel Sledge SB RC 8.00 3.60
❑ 156 Jeff Duncan SB RC 8.00 3.60
❑ 157 Craig Brazell SB RC 8.00 3.60
❑ 158 Bernie Castro SB RC 5.00 2.20
❑ 159 Cory Stewart SB RC 5.00 2.20
❑ 160 Brandon Villafuerte SB 5.00 2.20
❑ 161 Tommy Phelps SB 5.00 2.20
❑ 162 Josh Hall SB RC 8.00 3.60
❑ 163 Ryan Cameron SB RC 5.00 2.20
❑ 164 Garret Atkins SB 5.00 2.20
❑ 165 Brian Stokes SB RC 5.00 2.20
❑ 166 Rafael Betancourt SB RC 8.00 3.60
❑ 167 Jaime Cerda SB 5.00 2.20
❑ 168 D.J. Carrasco SB RC 5.00 2.20
❑ 169 Ian Ferguson SB RC 5.00 2.20
❑ 170 Jorge Cordova SB RC 5.00 2.20
❑ 171 Eric Munson SB 5.00 2.20
❑ 172 Nook Logan SB RC 5.00 2.20
❑ 173 Jeremy Bonderman SB RC 8.00 3.60
❑ 174 Kyle Snyder SB 5.00 2.20
❑ 175 Rich Harden SB 8.00 3.60
❑ 176 Kevin Ohme SB RC 5.00 2.20
❑ 177 Roger Deago SB RC 5.00 2.20
❑ 178 Marlon Byrd SB 5.00 2.20
❑ 179 Dontrelle Willis SB 10.00 4.50
❑ 180 Bobby Hill SB 5.00 2.20
❑ 181 Jesse Foppert SB 5.00 2.20
❑ 182 Andrew Good SB 5.00 2.20
❑ 183 Chase Utley SB 5.00 2.20
❑ 184 Bo Hart SB RC 10.00 4.50
❑ 185 Dan Haren SB RC 8.00 3.60
❑ 186 Tim Olson SB RC 8.00 3.60
❑ 187 Joe Thurston SB 5.00 2.20
❑ 188 Jason Anderson SB 5.00 2.20
❑ 189 Jason Gilfillan SB RC 5.00 2.20
❑ 190 Rickie Weeks SB RC 15.00 6.75
❑ 191 Hideki Matsui SB P1 RC 50.00 22.00
❑ 192 Jose Contreras SB P3 RC 15.00 6.75
❑ 193 Willie Eyre SB P3 RC 8.00 3.60
❑ 194 Matt Bruback SB P3 RC 8.00 3.60
❑ 195 Heath Bell SB P3 RC 8.00 3.60
❑ 196 Lew Ford SB P3 RC 10.00 4.50
❑ 197 Jeremy Griffiths SB P3 RC 10.00 4.50
❑ 198 Oscar Villarreal SB P1 RC 10.00 4.50
❑ 199 Francisco Cruceta SB P3 RC 8.00 3.60
❑ 200 Fern Cabrera SB P3 RC 10.00 4.50
❑ 201 Jhonny Peralta SB P3 RC 8.00 3.60
❑ 202 Shane Bazzell SB P3 RC 8.00 3.60
❑ 203 Bobby Madritsch SB P1 RC 10.00 4.50
❑ 204 Phil Seibel SB P3 RC 8.00 3.60
❑ 205 Josh Willingham SB P3 RC 12.00 5.50
❑ 206 Rob Hammock SB P1 RC 15.00 6.75
❑ 207 Alejandro Machado SB P3 RC 8.00 3.60
❑ 208 David Sanders SB P3 RC 8.00 3.60
❑ 209 Mike Neu SB P1 RC 10.00 4.50
❑ 210 Andrew Brown SB P3 RC 8.00 3.60
❑ 211 Nate Robertson SB P3 RC 8.00 3.60
❑ 212 Miguel Ojeda SB P3 RC 8.00 3.60
❑ 213 Beau Kemp SB P3 RC 8.00 3.60
❑ 214 Aaron Looper SB P3 RC 8.00 3.60
❑ 215 Alfredo Gonzalez SB P3 RC 8.00 3.60
❑ 216 Rich Fischer SB P1 RC 10.00 4.50
❑ 218 Jeremy Wedel SB P3 RC 8.00 3.60
❑ 219 Prentice Redman SB P3 RC 8.00 3.60
❑ 220 Michel Hernandez SB P3 RC 8.00 3.60
❑ 221 Rocco Baldelli SB P1 25.00 11.00
❑ 222 Luis Ayala SB P3 RC 8.00 3.60
❑ 223 Arnaldo Munoz SB P3 RC 8.00 3.60
❑ 224 Wilfredo Ledezma SB P3 RC 8.00 3.60
❑ 225 Chris Capuano SB P3 RC 8.00 3.60
❑ 226 Aquilino Lopez SB P3 RC 8.00 3.60
❑ 227 Joe Valentine SB P1 RC 10.00 4.50
❑ 228 Matt Kata SB P2 RC 10.00 4.50
❑ 229 Diegomar Markwell SB P2 RC 8.00 3.60
❑ 230 Clint Barmes SB P2 RC 10.00 4.50
❑ 231 Mike Nicolas SB P1 RC 10.00 4.50
❑ 232 Jon Leicester SB P2 RC 8.00 3.60

2002 Sweet Spot Classics

	Nm-Mt	Ex-Mt
COMPLETE SET (90)	40.00	12.00
❑ 1 Mickey Mantle	6.00	1.80
❑ 2 Joe DiMaggio	4.00	1.20
❑ 3 Babe Ruth	5.00	1.50
❑ 4 Ty Cobb	2.50	.75
❑ 5 Nolan Ryan	5.00	1.50
❑ 6 Sandy Koufax	3.00	.90
❑ 7 Cy Young	1.50	.45
❑ 8 Roberto Clemente	4.00	1.20
❑ 9 Lefty Grove	1.00	.30
❑ 10 Lou Gehrig	3.00	.90
❑ 11 Walter Johnson	1.50	.45
❑ 12 Honus Wagner	2.00	.60
❑ 13 Christy Mathewson	1.50	.45
❑ 14 Jackie Robinson	2.50	.75
❑ 15 Joe Morgan	1.00	.30
❑ 16 Reggie Jackson	1.00	.30
❑ 17 Eddie Collins	1.00	.30
❑ 18 Cal Ripken	5.00	1.50
❑ 19 Hank Greenberg	1.50	.45
❑ 20 Harmon Killebrew	1.50	.45
❑ 21 Johnny Bench	1.50	.45
❑ 22 Ernie Banks	1.50	.45
❑ 23 Willie McCovey	1.00	.30
❑ 24 Mel Ott	1.50	.45
❑ 25 Tom Seaver	1.50	.45
❑ 26 Tony Gwynn	2.00	.60
❑ 27 Dave Winfield	1.00	.30
❑ 28 Willie Stargell	1.00	.30
❑ 29 Mark McGwire	4.00	1.20
❑ 30 Al Kaline	1.50	.45
❑ 31 Jimmie Foxx	1.50	.45
❑ 32 Satchel Paige	1.50	.45
❑ 33 Eddie Murray	1.50	.45
❑ 34 Lou Boudreau	1.00	.30
❑ 35 Joe Jackson	3.00	.90
❑ 36 Luke Appling	1.00	.30
❑ 37 Ralph Kiner	1.00	.30
❑ 38 Robin Yount	1.50	.45
❑ 39 Paul Molitor	1.00	.30
❑ 40 Juan Marichal	1.00	.30
❑ 41 Brooks Robinson	1.50	.45
❑ 42 Wade Boggs	1.00	.30
❑ 43 Kirby Puckett	1.50	.45
❑ 44 Yogi Berra	1.50	.45
❑ 45 George Sisler	1.00	.30
❑ 46 Buck Leonard	1.00	.30
❑ 47 Billy Williams	1.00	.30
❑ 48 Duke Snider	1.00	.30
❑ 49 Don Drysdale	1.50	.45
❑ 50 Bill Mazeroski	1.00	.30
❑ 51 Tony Oliva	1.00	.30
❑ 52 Luis Aparicio	1.00	.30
❑ 53 Carlton Fisk	1.00	.30
❑ 54 Kirk Gibson	1.00	.30
❑ 55 Catfish Hunter	1.00	.30
❑ 56 Joe Carter	1.00	.30
❑ 57 Gaylord Perry	1.00	.30
❑ 58 Don Mattingly	4.00	1.20
❑ 59 Eddie Mathews	1.50	.45
❑ 60 Fergie Jenkins	1.00	.30
❑ 61 Roy Campanella	1.50	.45
❑ 62 Orlando Cepeda	1.00	.30
❑ 63 Tony Perez	1.00	.30
❑ 64 Dave Parker	1.00	.30
❑ 65 Richie Ashburn	1.00	.30
❑ 66 Andre Dawson	1.00	.30
❑ 67 Dwight Evans	1.00	.30
❑ 68 Rollie Fingers	1.00	.30
❑ 69 Dale Murphy	1.50	.45
❑ 70 Ron Santo	1.00	.30
❑ 71 Steve Garvey	1.00	.30
❑ 72 Monte Irvin	1.00	.30
❑ 73 Alan Trammell	1.00	.30
❑ 74 Ryne Sandberg	2.50	.75
❑ 75 Gary Carter	1.00	.30
❑ 76 Fred Lynn	1.00	.30
❑ 77 Maury Wills	1.00	.30
❑ 78 Ozzie Smith	1.50	.45
❑ 79 Bobby Bonds	1.00	.30
❑ 80 Mickey Cochrane	1.00	.30
❑ 81 Dizzy Dean	1.50	.45
❑ 82 Graig Nettles	1.00	.30
❑ 83 Keith Hernandez	1.00	.30
❑ 84 Boog Powell	1.00	.30
❑ 85 Jack Clark	1.00	.30
❑ 86 Dave Stewart	1.00	.30
❑ 87 Tommy Lasorda	1.00	.30
❑ 88 Dennis Eckersley	1.00	.30
❑ 89 Ken Griffey Sr.	1.00	.30
❑ 90 Bucky Dent	1.00	.30

2003 Sweet Spot Classics

	Nm-Mt	Ex-Mt
COMP.SET w/o SP's (89)	40.00	12.00
COMMON (1-74/76-90)	.75	.23
COMMON CARD (91-120)	8.00	2.40
COMMON CARD (121-150)	5.00	1.50
❑ 1 Al Hrabosky	.75	.23
❑ 2 Al Lopez	.75	.23
❑ 3 Andre Dawson	.75	.23
❑ 4 Bill Buckner	.75	.23
❑ 5 Billy Williams	.75	.23
❑ 6 Bob Feller	.75	.23
❑ 7 Bob Lemon	.75	.23
❑ 8 Bobby Doerr	.75	.23
❑ 9 Cecil Cooper	.75	.23
❑ 10 Cal Ripken	6.00	1.80
❑ 11 Carlton Fisk	1.25	.35
❑ 12 Catfish Hunter	1.25	.35
❑ 13 Chris Chambliss	.75	.23
❑ 14 Dale Murphy	2.00	.60
❑ 15 Gaylord Perry	.75	.23
❑ 16 Dave Kingman	.75	.23
❑ 17 Dave Parker	.75	.23
❑ 18 Dave Stewart	.75	.23
❑ 19 David Cone	.75	.23
❑ 20 Dennis Eckersley	.75	.23
❑ 21 Don Baylor	.75	.23
❑ 22 Don Sutton	.75	.23
❑ 23 Duke Snider	1.25	.35
❑ 24 Dwight Evans	.75	.23
❑ 25 Dwight Gooden	1.25	.35
❑ 26 Earl Weaver MG	.75	.23
❑ 27 Early Wynn	.75	.23
❑ 28 Eddie Mathews	2.00	.60
❑ 29 Enos Slaughter	1.25	.35
❑ 30 Ernie Banks	2.00	.60
❑ 31 Fred Lynn	.75	.23
❑ 32 Fred Stanley	.75	.23
❑ 33 Gary Carter	1.25	.35
❑ 34 George Foster	.75	.23
❑ 35 Hal Newhouser	.75	.23
❑ 36 George Kell	.75	.23
❑ 37 Harmon Killebrew	2.00	.60
❑ 38 Hoyt Wilhelm	.75	.23
❑ 39 Jack Morris	.75	.23
❑ 40 Jim Bunning	.75	.23
❑ 41 Jim Gilliam	.75	.23
❑ 42 Jim Leyritz	.75	.23
❑ 43 Jimmy Key	.75	.23
❑ 44 Joe Carter	.75	.23
❑ 45 Joe Morgan	.75	.23
❑ 46 John Montefusco	.75	.23
❑ 47 Johnny Bench	2.00	.60
❑ 48 Johnny Podres	.75	.23
❑ 49 Jose Canseco	2.00	.60
❑ 50 Juan Marichal	.75	.23
❑ 51 Keith Hernandez	.75	.23
❑ 52 Ken Griffey Sr.	.75	.23
❑ 53 Kirby Puckett	2.00	.60
❑ 54 Kirk Gibson	.75	.23
❑ 55 Larry Doby	.75	.23
❑ 56 Lee May	.75	.23
❑ 57 Lee Mazzilli	.75	.23
❑ 58 Lou Boudreau	.75	.23
❑ 59 Mark McGwire	5.00	1.50
❑ 60 Maury Wills	.75	.23
❑ 61 Mike Pagliarulo	.75	.23
❑ 62 Monte Irvin	.75	.23
❑ 63 Nolan Ryan	6.00	1.80
❑ 64 Orlando Cepeda	.75	.23
❑ 65 Ozzie Smith	2.00	.60
❑ 66 Paul O'Neill	1.25	.35
❑ 67 Pee Wee Reese	1.25	.35
❑ 68 Phil Niekro	.75	.23
❑ 69 Ralph Kiner	.75	.23
❑ 70 Red Schoendienst	.75	.23
❑ 71 Richie Ashburn	1.25	.35
❑ 72 Rick Ferrell	.75	.23
❑ 73 Robin Roberts	.75	.23
❑ 74 Robin Yount	2.00	.60
❑ 75 Hideki Matsui/1999 XRC	25.00	7.50
❑ 75B Rod Carew ERR ......Not Intended for Public Release		
❑ 76 Rollie Fingers	.75	.23
❑ 77 Ron Cey	.75	.23
❑ 78 Tom Seaver	2.00	.60
❑ 79 Sparky Anderson MG	.75	.23
❑ 80 Stan Musial	3.00	.90
❑ 81 Steve Garvey	.75	.23
❑ 82 Ted Williams	5.00	1.50
❑ 83 Tommy Lasorda	.75	.23
❑ 84 Tony Gwynn	2.50	.75
❑ 85 Tony Perez	.75	.23
❑ 86 Vida Blue	.75	.23
❑ 87 Warren Spahn	1.25	.35
❑ 88 Bob Gibson	1.25	.35
❑ 89 Willie McCovey	.75	.23
❑ 90 Willie Stargell	1.25	.35
❑ 91 Ted Williams TB	8.00	2.40
❑ 92 Ted Williams TB	8.00	2.40
❑ 93 Ted Williams TB	8.00	2.40
❑ 94 Ted Williams TB	8.00	2.40
❑ 95 Ted Williams TB	8.00	2.40
❑ 96 Ted Williams TB	8.00	2.40
❑ 97 Ted Williams TB	8.00	2.40
❑ 98 Ted Williams TB	8.00	2.40
❑ 99 Ted Williams TB	8.00	2.40
❑ 100 Ted Williams TB	8.00	2.40
❑ 101 Ted Williams TB	8.00	2.40
❑ 102 Ted Williams TB	8.00	2.40
❑ 103 Ted Williams TB	8.00	2.40
❑ 104 Ted Williams TB	8.00	2.40
❑ 105 Ted Williams TB	8.00	2.40
❑ 106 Ted Williams TB	8.00	2.40
❑ 107 Ted Williams TB	8.00	2.40
❑ 108 Ted Williams TB	8.00	2.40
❑ 109 Ted Williams TB	8.00	2.40
❑ 110 Ted Williams TB	8.00	2.40
❑ 111 Ted Williams TB	8.00	2.40
❑ 112 Ted Williams TB	8.00	2.40
❑ 113 Ted Williams TB	8.00	2.40
❑ 114 Ted Williams TB	8.00	2.40
❑ 115 Ted Williams TB	8.00	2.40
❑ 116 Ted Williams TB	8.00	2.40
❑ 117 Ted Williams TB	8.00	2.40
❑ 118 Ted Williams TB	8.00	2.40
❑ 119 Ted Williams TB	8.00	2.40
❑ 120 Ted Williams TB	8.00	2.40
❑ 121 Babe Ruth YH	15.00	4.50
❑ 122 Bucky Dent YH	5.00	1.50
❑ 123 Casey Stengel YH	5.00	1.50
❑ 124 Dave Righetti YH	5.00	1.50
❑ 125 Dave Winfield YH	5.00	1.50
❑ 126 Dick Tidrow YH	5.00	1.50
❑ 127 Dock Ellis YH	5.00	1.50
❑ 128 Don Mattingly YH	15.00	4.50
❑ 129 Hank Bauer YH	5.00	1.50
❑ 130 Jim Bouton YH	5.00	1.50
❑ 131 Jim Kaat YH	5.00	1.50
❑ 132 Joe DiMaggio YH	12.00	3.60
❑ 133 Joe Torre YH	8.00	2.40
❑ 134 Lou Piniella YH	5.00	1.50
❑ 135 Mel Stottlemyre YH	5.00	1.50

❑ 136 Mickey Mantle YH	20.00	6.00
❑ 137 Mickey Rivers YH	5.00	1.50
❑ 138 Phil Rizzuto YH	5.00	1.50
❑ 139 Ralph Branca YH	5.00	1.50
❑ 140 Ralph Houk YH	5.00	1.50
❑ 141 Roger Maris YH	10.00	3.00
❑ 142 Ron Guidry YH	5.00	1.50
❑ 143 Ruben Amaro Sr. YH	5.00	1.50
❑ 144 Sparky Lyle YH	5.00	1.50
❑ 145 Thurman Munson YH	10.00	3.00
❑ 146 Tommy Henrich YH	5.00	1.50
❑ 147 Tommy John YH	5.00	1.50
❑ 148 Tony Kubek YH	5.00	1.50
❑ 149 Whitey Ford YH	5.00	1.50
❑ 150 Yogi Berra YH	8.00	2.40

1952 Topps

	NM	Ex
COMP.MASTER SET (487)	80000.00	40000.00
COMPLETE SET (407)	65000.00	32500.00
COMMON CARD (1-80)	60.00	30.00
COMMON CARD (81-250)	40.00	20.00
COMMON (251-310)	50.00	25.00
COMMON (311-407)	250.00	125.00
WRAPPER (1-cent)	250.00	125.00
WRAPPER (5-cent)	100.00	50.00

❑ 1 Andy Pafko	4000.00	400.00
❑ 1A Andy Pafko Black	3000.00	1500.00
❑ 2 Pete Runnels RC	250.00	125.00
❑ 2A Pete Runnels RC Black	250.00	125.00
❑ 3 Hank Thompson	70.00	35.00
❑ 3A Hank Thompson Black	70.00	35.00
❑ 4 Don Lenhardt	60.00	30.00
❑ 4A Don Lenhardt Black	60.00	30.00
❑ 5 Larry Jansen	70.00	35.00
❑ 5A Larry Jansen Black	70.00	35.00
❑ 6 Grady Hatton	60.00	30.00
❑ 6A Grady Hatton Black	60.00	30.00
❑ 7 Wayne Terwilliger	60.00	30.00
❑ 7A W. Terwilliger Black	60.00	30.00
❑ 8 Fred Marsh	60.00	30.00
❑ 8A Fred Marsh Black	60.00	30.00
❑ 9 Robert Hogue	60.00	30.00
❑ 9A Robert Hogue Black	60.00	30.00
❑ 10 Al Rosen	70.00	35.00
❑ 10A Al Rosen Black	70.00	35.00
❑ 11 Phil Rizzuto	350.00	180.00
❑ 11A Phil Rizzuto Black	350.00	180.00
❑ 12 Monty Basgall	60.00	30.00
❑ 12A Monty Basgall Black	60.00	30.00
❑ 13 Johnny Wyrostek	60.00	30.00
❑ 13A J. Wyrostek Black	60.00	30.00
❑ 14 Bob Elliott	70.00	35.00
❑ 14A Bob Elliott Black	70.00	35.00
❑ 15 Johnny Pesky	70.00	35.00
❑ 15A Johnny Pesky Black	70.00	35.00
❑ 16 Gene Hermanski	60.00	30.00
❑ 16A G. Hermanski Black	60.00	30.00
❑ 17 Jim Hegan	70.00	35.00
❑ 17A Jim Hegan Black	70.00	35.00
❑ 18 Merrill Combs	60.00	30.00
❑ 18A Merrill Combs Black	60.00	30.00
❑ 19 Johnny Bucha	60.00	30.00
❑ 19A Johnny Bucha Black	60.00	30.00
❑ 20 Billy Loes RC	125.00	60.00
❑ 20A Billy Loes RC Black	125.00	60.00

❑ 21 Ferris Fain	70.00	35.00
❑ 21A Ferris Fain Black	70.00	35.00
❑ 22 Dom DiMaggio	100.00	50.00
❑ 22A Dom DiMaggio Black	100.00	50.00
❑ 23 Billy Goodman	70.00	35.00
❑ 23A Billy Goodman Black	70.00	35.00
❑ 24 Luke Easter	80.00	40.00
❑ 24A Luke Easter Black	80.00	40.00
❑ 25 Johnny Groth	60.00	30.00
❑ 25A Johnny Groth Black	60.00	30.00
❑ 26 Monte Irvin	150.00	75.00
❑ 26A Monte Irvin Black	125.00	60.00
❑ 27 Sam Jethroe	70.00	35.00
❑ 27A Sam Jethroe Black	70.00	35.00
❑ 28 Jerry Priddy	60.00	30.00
❑ 28A Jerry Priddy Black	60.00	30.00
❑ 29 Ted Kluszewski	125.00	60.00
❑ 29A Ted Kluszewski Black	125.00	60.00
❑ 30 Mel Parnell	70.00	35.00
❑ 30A Mel Parnell Black	70.00	35.00
❑ 31 Gus Zernial Posed with seven baseballs	80.00	40.00
❑ 31A Gus Zernial Black Posed with seven baseballs	80.00	40.00
❑ 32 Eddie Robinson	60.00	30.00
❑ 32A Eddie Robinson Black	60.00	30.00
❑ 33 Warren Spahn	250.00	125.00
❑ 33A Warren Spahn Black	250.00	125.00
❑ 34 Elmer Valo	60.00	30.00
❑ 34A Elmer Valo Black	60.00	30.00
❑ 35 Hank Sauer	70.00	35.00
❑ 35A Hank Sauer Black	70.00	35.00
❑ 36 Gil Hodges	250.00	125.00
❑ 36A Gil Hodges Black	250.00	125.00
❑ 37 Duke Snider	450.00	220.00
❑ 37A Duke Snider Black	400.00	200.00
❑ 38 Wally Westlake	60.00	30.00
❑ 38A Wally Westlake Black	60.00	30.00
❑ 39 Dizzy Trout	70.00	35.00
❑ 39A Dizzy Trout Black	70.00	35.00
❑ 40 Irv Noren	70.00	35.00
❑ 40A Irv Noren Black	70.00	35.00
❑ 41 Bob Wellman	60.00	30.00
❑ 41A Bob Wellman Black	60.00	30.00
❑ 42 Lou Kretlow	60.00	30.00
❑ 42A Lou Kretlow Black	60.00	30.00
❑ 43 Ray Scarborough	60.00	30.00
❑ 43A R. Scarbourough Black	60.00	30.00
❑ 44 Con Dempsey	60.00	30.00
❑ 44A Con Dempsey Black	60.00	30.00
❑ 45 Eddie Joost	60.00	30.00
❑ 45A Eddie Joost Black	60.00	30.00
❑ 46 Gordon Goldsberry	60.00	30.00
❑ 46A G. Goldsberry Black	60.00	30.00
❑ 47 Willie Jones	70.00	35.00
❑ 47A Willie Jones Black	70.00	35.00
❑ 48A Joe Page ERR Bio for Sain Black Back	400.00	200.00
❑ 48B Joe Page COR Black Back	125.00	60.00
❑ 48C Joe Page COR Red Back	125.00	60.00
❑ 49A John Sain ERR Bio for Page Black Back	400.00	200.00
❑ 49B John Sain COR Black Back	125.00	60.00
❑ 49C John Sain COR Red Back	125.00	60.00
❑ 50 Marv Rickert	60.00	30.00
❑ 50A Marv Richert Black	60.00	30.00
❑ 51 Jim Russell	60.00	30.00
❑ 51A Jim Russell Black	60.00	30.00
❑ 52 Don Mueller	70.00	35.00
❑ 52A Don Mueller Black	70.00	35.00
❑ 53 Chris Van Cuyk	60.00	30.00
❑ 53A Chris Van Cuyk Black	60.00	30.00
❑ 54 Leo Kiely	60.00	30.00
❑ 54A Leo Kiely Black	60.00	30.00
❑ 55 Ray Boone	80.00	40.00
❑ 55A Ray Boone Black	80.00	40.00
❑ 56 Tommy Glaviano	60.00	30.00
❑ 56A T. Glaviano Black	60.00	30.00
❑ 57 Ed Lopat	100.00	50.00
❑ 57A Ed Lopat Black	100.00	50.00

❑ 58 Bob Mahoney	60.00	30.00
❑ 58A Bob Mahoney Black	60.00	30.00
❑ 59 Robin Roberts	175.00	90.00
❑ 59A Robin Roberts Black	175.00	90.00
❑ 60 Sid Hudson	60.00	30.00
❑ 60A Sid Hudson Black	60.00	30.00
❑ 61 Tookie Gilbert	60.00	30.00
❑ 61A Tookie Gilbert Black	60.00	30.00
❑ 62 Chuck Stobbs	60.00	30.00
❑ 62A Chuck Stobbs Black	60.00	30.00
❑ 63 Howie Pollet	60.00	30.00
❑ 63A Howie Pollet Black	60.00	30.00
❑ 64 Roy Sievers	70.00	35.00
❑ 64A Roy Sievers Black	70.00	35.00
❑ 65 Enos Slaughter	175.00	90.00
❑ 65A Enos Slaughter Black	175.00	90.00
❑ 66 Preacher Roe	100.00	50.00
❑ 66A Preacher Roe Black	100.00	50.00
❑ 67 Allie Reynolds	100.00	50.00
❑ 67A Allie Reynolds Black	100.00	50.00
❑ 68 Cliff Chambers	60.00	30.00
❑ 68A Cliff Chambers Black	60.00	30.00
❑ 69 Virgil Stallcup	60.00	30.00
❑ 69A Virgil Stallcup Black	60.00	30.00
❑ 70 Al Zarilla	60.00	30.00
❑ 70A Al Zarilla Black	60.00	30.00
❑ 71 Tom Upton	60.00	30.00
❑ 71A Tom Upton Black	60.00	30.00
❑ 72 Karl Olson	60.00	30.00
❑ 72A Karl Olson Black	60.00	30.00
❑ 73 Bill Werle	60.00	30.00
❑ 73A Bill Werle Black	60.00	30.00
❑ 74 Andy Hansen	60.00	30.00
❑ 74A Andy Hansen Black	60.00	30.00
❑ 75 Wes Westrum	70.00	35.00
❑ 75A Wes Westrum Black	70.00	35.00
❑ 76 Eddie Stanky	70.00	35.00
❑ 76A Eddie Stanky Black	70.00	35.00
❑ 77 Bob Kennedy	70.00	35.00
❑ 77A Bob Kennedy Black	70.00	35.00
❑ 78 Ellis Kinder	60.00	30.00
❑ 78A Ellis Kinder Black	60.00	30.00
❑ 79 Gerry Staley	60.00	30.00
❑ 79A Gerry Staley Black	60.00	30.00
❑ 80 Herman Wehmeier	80.00	40.00
❑ 80A H. Wehmeier Black	80.00	40.00
❑ 81 Vernon Law	80.00	40.00
❑ 82 Duane Pillette	40.00	20.00
❑ 83 Billy Johnson	40.00	20.00
❑ 84 Vern Stephens	50.00	25.00
❑ 85 Bob Kuzava	50.00	25.00
❑ 86 Ted Gray	40.00	20.00
❑ 87 Dale Coogan	40.00	20.00
❑ 88 Bob Feller	250.00	125.00
❑ 89 Johnny Lipon	40.00	20.00
❑ 90 Mickey Grasso	40.00	20.00
❑ 91 Red Schoendienst	100.00	50.00
❑ 92 Dale Mitchell	50.00	25.00
❑ 93 Al Sima	40.00	20.00
❑ 94 Sam Mele	40.00	20.00
❑ 95 Ken Holcombe	40.00	20.00
❑ 96 Willard Marshall	40.00	20.00
❑ 97 Earl Torgeson	40.00	20.00
❑ 98 Billy Pierce	50.00	25.00
❑ 99 Gene Woodling	60.00	30.00
❑ 100 Del Rice	40.00	20.00
❑ 101 Max Lanier	40.00	20.00
❑ 102 Bill Kennedy	40.00	20.00
❑ 103 Cliff Mapes	40.00	20.00
❑ 104 Don Kolloway	40.00	20.00
❑ 105 Johnny Pramesa	40.00	20.00
❑ 106 Mickey Vernon	60.00	30.00
❑ 107 Connie Ryan	40.00	20.00
❑ 108 Jim Konstanty	60.00	30.00
❑ 109 Ted Wilks	40.00	20.00
❑ 110 Dutch Leonard	40.00	20.00
❑ 111 Peanuts Lowrey	40.00	20.00
❑ 112 Hank Majeski	40.00	20.00
❑ 113 Dick Sisler	50.00	25.00
❑ 114 Willard Ramsdell	40.00	20.00
❑ 115 Red Munger	40.00	20.00
❑ 116 Carl Scheib	40.00	20.00
❑ 117 Sherm Lollar	50.00	25.00
❑ 118 Ken Raffensberger	40.00	20.00
❑ 119 Mickey McDermott	40.00	20.00
❑ 120 Bob Chakales	40.00	20.00

❑ 121 Gus Niarhos 40.00 20.00
❑ 122 Jackie Jensen 80.00 40.00
❑ 123 Eddie Yost 50.00 25.00
❑ 124 Monte Kennedy 40.00 20.00
❑ 125 Bill Rigney 40.00 20.00
❑ 126 Fred Hutchinson 50.00 25.00
❑ 127 Paul Minner 40.00 20.00
❑ 128 Don Bollweg 40.00 20.00
❑ 129 Johnny Mize 150.00 75.00
❑ 130 Sheldon Jones 40.00 20.00
❑ 131 Morrie Martin 40.00 20.00
❑ 132 Clyde Kluttz 40.00 20.00
❑ 133 Al Widmar 40.00 20.00
❑ 134 Joe Tipton 40.00 20.00
❑ 135 Dixie Howell 40.00 20.00
❑ 136 Johnny Schmitz 40.00 20.00
❑ 137 Roy McMillan RC 50.00 25.00
❑ 138 Bill MacDonald 40.00 20.00
❑ 139 Ken Wood 40.00 20.00
❑ 140 Johnny Antonelli 60.00 30.00
❑ 141 Clint Hartung 40.00 20.00
❑ 142 Harry Perkowski 40.00 20.00
❑ 143 Les Moss 40.00 20.00
❑ 144 Ed Blake 40.00 20.00
❑ 145 Joe Haynes 40.00 20.00
❑ 146 Frank House 40.00 20.00
❑ 147 Bob Young 40.00 20.00
❑ 148 Johnny Klippstein 40.00 20.00
❑ 149 Dick Kryhoski 40.00 20.00
❑ 150 Ted Beard 40.00 20.00
❑ 151 Wally Post RC 50.00 25.00
❑ 152 Al Evans 40.00 20.00
❑ 153 Bob Rush 40.00 20.00
❑ 154 Joe Muir 40.00 20.00
❑ 155 Frank Overmire 40.00 20.00
❑ 156 Frank Hiller 40.00 20.00
❑ 157 Bob Usher 40.00 20.00
❑ 158 Eddie Waitkus 40.00 20.00
❑ 159 Saul Rogovin 40.00 20.00
❑ 160 Owen Friend 40.00 20.00
❑ 161 Bud Byerly 40.00 20.00
❑ 162 Del Crandall 50.00 25.00
❑ 163 Stan Rojek 40.00 20.00
❑ 164 Walt Dubiel 40.00 20.00
❑ 165 Eddie Kazak 40.00 20.00
❑ 166 Paul LaPalme 40.00 20.00
❑ 167 Bill Howerton 40.00 20.00
❑ 168 Charlie Silvera RC 60.00 30.00
❑ 169 Howie Judson 40.00 20.00
❑ 170 Gus Bell 50.00 25.00
❑ 171 Ed Erautt 40.00 20.00
❑ 172 Eddie Miksis 40.00 20.00
❑ 173 Roy Smalley 40.00 20.00
❑ 174 Clarence Marshall 60.00 30.00
❑ 175 Billy Martin RC 450.00 220.00
❑ 176 Hank Edwards 40.00 20.00
❑ 177 Bill Wight 40.00 20.00
❑ 178 Cass Michaels 40.00 20.00
❑ 179 Frank Smith 40.00 20.00
❑ 180 Charlie Maxwell RC 50.00 25.00
❑ 181 Bob Swift 40.00 20.00
❑ 182 Billy Hitchcock 40.00 20.00
❑ 183 Erv Dusak 40.00 20.00
❑ 184 Bob Ramazzotti 40.00 20.00
❑ 185 Bill Nicholson 50.00 25.00
❑ 186 Walt Masterson 40.00 20.00
❑ 187 Bob Miller 40.00 20.00
❑ 188 Clarence Podbielan 40.00 20.00
❑ 189 Pete Reiser 60.00 30.00
❑ 190 Don Johnson 40.00 20.00
❑ 191 Yogi Berra 800.00 350.00
❑ 192 Myron Ginsberg 40.00 20.00
❑ 193 Harry Simpson 50.00 25.00
❑ 194 Joe Hatton 40.00 20.00
❑ 195 Minnie Minoso RC 150.00 75.00
❑ 196 Solly Hemus RC 60.00 30.00
❑ 197 George Strickland 40.00 20.00
❑ 198 Phil Haugstad 40.00 20.00
❑ 199 George Zuverink 40.00 20.00
❑ 200 Ralph Houk RC 80.00 40.00
❑ 201 Alex Kellner 40.00 20.00
❑ 202 Joe Collins RC 60.00 30.00
❑ 203 Curt Simmons 60.00 30.00
❑ 204 Ron Northey 40.00 20.00
❑ 205 Clyde King 60.00 30.00
❑ 206 Joe Ostrowski 40.00 20.00
❑ 207 Mickey Harris 40.00 20.00
❑ 208 Marlin Stuart 40.00 20.00
❑ 209 Howie Fox 40.00 20.00
❑ 210 Dick Fowler 40.00 20.00
❑ 211 Ray Coleman 40.00 20.00
❑ 212 Ned Garver 40.00 20.00
❑ 213 Nippy Jones 40.00 20.00
❑ 214 Johnny Hopp 50.00 25.00
❑ 215 Hank Bauer 100.00 50.00
❑ 216 Richie Ashburn 200.00 100.00
❑ 217 Snuffy Stirnweiss 50.00 25.00
❑ 218 Clyde McCullough 40.00 20.00
❑ 219 Bobby Shantz 60.00 30.00
❑ 220 Joe Presko 40.00 20.00
❑ 221 Granny Hamner 40.00 20.00
❑ 222 Hoot Evers 40.00 20.00
❑ 223 Del Ennis 50.00 25.00
❑ 224 Bruce Edwards 40.00 20.00
❑ 225 Frank Baumholtz 40.00 20.00
❑ 226 Dave Philley 40.00 20.00
❑ 227 Joe Garagiola 80.00 40.00
❑ 228 Al Brazle 40.00 20.00
❑ 229 Gene Bearden UER 40.00 20.00
(Misspelled Beardon)
❑ 230 Matt Batts 40.00 20.00
❑ 231 Sam Zoldak 40.00 20.00
❑ 232 Billy Cox 50.00 25.00
❑ 233 Bob Friend RC 80.00 40.00
❑ 234 Steve Souchock 40.00 20.00
❑ 235 Walt Dropo 40.00 20.00
❑ 236 Ed Fitzgerald 40.00 20.00
❑ 237 Jerry Coleman 60.00 30.00
❑ 238 Art Houtteman 40.00 20.00
❑ 239 Rocky Bridges 50.00 25.00
❑ 240 Jack Phillips 40.00 20.00
❑ 241 Tommy Byrne 40.00 20.00
❑ 242 Tom Poholsky 40.00 20.00
❑ 243 Larry Doby 80.00 40.00
❑ 244 Vic Wertz 40.00 20.00
❑ 245 Sherry Robertson 40.00 20.00
❑ 246 George Kell 80.00 40.00
❑ 247 Randy Gumpert 40.00 20.00
❑ 248 Frank Shea 40.00 20.00
❑ 249 Bobby Adams 40.00 20.00
❑ 250 Carl Erskine 100.00 50.00
❑ 251 Chico Carrasquel 50.00 25.00
❑ 252 Vern Bickford 50.00 25.00
❑ 253 Johnny Berardino 100.00 50.00
❑ 254 Joe Dobson 50.00 25.00
❑ 255 Clyde Vollmer 50.00 25.00
❑ 256 Pete Suder 50.00 25.00
❑ 257 Bobby Avila 60.00 30.00
❑ 258 Steve Gromek 60.00 30.00
❑ 259 Bob Addis 50.00 25.00
❑ 260 Pete Castiglione 50.00 25.00
❑ 261 Willie Mays 2500.00 1250.00
❑ 262 Virgil Trucks 60.00 30.00
❑ 263 Harry Brecheen 60.00 30.00
❑ 264 Roy Hartsfield 50.00 25.00
❑ 265 Chuck Diering 50.00 25.00
❑ 266 Murry Dickson 50.00 25.00
❑ 267 Sid Gordon 60.00 30.00
❑ 268 Bob Lemon 150.00 75.00
❑ 269 Willard Nixon 50.00 25.00
❑ 270 Lou Brissie 50.00 25.00
❑ 271 Jim Delsing 60.00 30.00
❑ 272 Mike Garcia 75.00 38.00
❑ 273 Erv Palica 50.00 25.00
❑ 274 Ralph Branca 125.00 60.00
❑ 275 Pat Mullin 50.00 25.00
❑ 276 Jim Wilson RC 50.00 25.00
❑ 277 Early Wynn 150.00 75.00
❑ 278 Allie Clark 50.00 25.00
❑ 279 Eddie Stewart 50.00 25.00
❑ 280 Cloyd Boyer 75.00 38.00
❑ 281 Tommy Brown SP 75.00 38.00
❑ 282 Birdie Tebbetts SP 75.00 38.00
❑ 283 Phil Masi SP 60.00 30.00
❑ 284 Hank Arft SP 60.00 30.00
❑ 285 Cliff Fannin SP 60.00 30.00
❑ 286 Joe DeMaestri SP 60.00 30.00
❑ 287 Steve Bilko SP 60.00 30.00
❑ 288 Chet Nichols SP 75.00 38.00
❑ 289 Tommy Holmes SP 90.00 45.00
❑ 290 Joe Astroth SP 60.00 30.00
❑ 291 Gil Coan SP 60.00 30.00
❑ 292 Floyd Baker SP 60.00 30.00
❑ 293 Sibby Sisti SP 60.00 30.00
❑ 294 Walker Cooper SP 60.00 30.00
❑ 295 Phil Cavarretta SP 75.00 38.00
❑ 296 Red Rolfe MG SP 60.00 30.00
❑ 297 Andy Seminick SP 60.00 30.00
❑ 298 Bob Ross SP 60.00 30.00
❑ 299 Ray Murray SP 75.00 38.00
❑ 300 Barney McCosky SP 75.00 38.00
❑ 301 Bob Porterfield 50.00 25.00
❑ 302 Max Surkont 50.00 25.00
❑ 303 Harry Dorish 50.00 25.00
❑ 304 Sam Dente 50.00 25.00
❑ 305 Paul Richards MG 60.00 30.00
❑ 306 Lou Sleater 50.00 25.00
❑ 307 Frank Campos 50.00 25.00
❑ 307A Frank Campos
Black Star on Back
❑ 308 Luis Aloma 50.00 25.00
❑ 309 Jim Busby 60.00 30.00
❑ 310 George Metkovich 90.00 45.00
❑ 311 Mickey Mantle DP 18000.00 9000.00
❑ 312 Jackie Robinson DP 2000.00 1000.00
❑ 313 Bobby Thomson DP 350.00 180.00
❑ 314 Roy Campanella 2200.00 1100.00
❑ 315 Leo Durocher MG 600.00 300.00
❑ 316 Dave Williams RC 300.00 150.00
❑ 317 Conrado Marrero 300.00 150.00
❑ 318 Harold Gregg 300.00 150.00
❑ 319 Al Walker 250.00 125.00
❑ 320 John Rutherford RC 300.00 150.00
❑ 321 Joe Black RC 350.00 180.00
❑ 322 Randy Jackson 300.00 150.00
❑ 323 Bubba Church 250.00 125.00
❑ 324 Warren Hacker 250.00 125.00
❑ 325 Bill Serena 300.00 150.00
❑ 326 George Shuba RC 400.00 200.00
❑ 327 Al Wilson 250.00 125.00
❑ 328 Bob Borkowski 300.00 150.00
❑ 329 Ike Delock 300.00 150.00
❑ 330 Turk Lown 300.00 150.00
❑ 331 Tom Morgan 300.00 150.00
❑ 332 Anthony Bartirome 300.00 150.00
❑ 333 Pee Wee Reese 1600.00 800.00
❑ 334 Wilmer Mizell RC 300.00 150.00
❑ 335 Ted Lepcio 250.00 125.00
❑ 336 Dave Koslo 250.00 125.00
❑ 337 Jim Hearn 300.00 150.00
❑ 338 Sal Yvars 300.00 150.00
❑ 339 Russ Meyer 300.00 150.00
❑ 340 Bob Hooper 300.00 150.00
❑ 341 Hal Jeffcoat 300.00 150.00
❑ 342 Clem Labine RC 400.00 200.00
❑ 343 Dick Gernert 250.00 125.00
❑ 344 Ewell Blackwell 300.00 150.00
❑ 345 Sammy White 250.00 125.00
❑ 346 George Spencer 250.00 125.00
❑ 347 Joe Adcock 300.00 150.00
❑ 348 Robert Kelly 250.00 125.00
❑ 349 Bob Cain 300.00 150.00
❑ 350 Cal Abrams 300.00 150.00
❑ 351 Alvin Dark 300.00 150.00
❑ 352 Karl Drews 300.00 150.00
❑ 353 Bobby Del Greco 300.00 150.00
❑ 354 Fred Hatfield 300.00 150.00
❑ 355 Bobby Morgan 300.00 150.00
❑ 356 Toby Atwell 300.00 150.00
❑ 357 Smoky Burgess 300.00 150.00
❑ 358 John Kucab 300.00 150.00
❑ 359 Dee Fondy 250.00 125.00
❑ 360 George Crowe RC 300.00 150.00
❑ 361 William Posedel CO 250.00 125.00
❑ 362 Ken Heintzelman 300.00 150.00
❑ 363 Dick Rozek 300.00 150.00
❑ 364 Clyde Sukeforth CO 300.00 150.00
❑ 365 Cookie Lavagetto CO 350.00 180.00
❑ 366 Dave Madison 250.00 125.00
❑ 367 Ben Thorpe 300.00 150.00
❑ 368 Ed Wright 300.00 150.00
❑ 369 Dick Groat RC 400.00 200.00
❑ 370 Billy Hoeft RC 300.00 150.00
❑ 371 Bobby Hofman 250.00 125.00
❑ 372 Gil McDougald RC 450.00 220.00
❑ 373 Jim Turner RC CO 400.00 200.00
❑ 374 John Benton 250.00 125.00
❑ 375 John Merson 250.00 125.00

Card	NM	Ex
❑ 376 Faye Throneberry	250.00	125.00
❑ 377 Chuck Dressen MG	350.00	180.00
❑ 378 Leroy Fusselman	300.00	150.00
❑ 379 Joe Rossi	250.00	125.00
❑ 380 Clem Koshorek	250.00	125.00
❑ 381 Milton Stock CO	300.00	150.00
❑ 382 Sam Jones RC	350.00	180.00
❑ 383 Del Wilber	250.00	125.00
❑ 384 Frank Crosetti CO	450.00	220.00
❑ 385 H.Franks CO RC	250.00	125.00
❑ 386 John Yuhas	300.00	150.00
❑ 387 Billy Meyer MG	250.00	125.00
❑ 388 Bob Chipman	250.00	125.00
❑ 389 Ben Wade	300.00	150.00
❑ 390 Glenn Nelson	300.00	150.00
❑ 391 B.Chapman UER CO Photo actually Sam Chapman	250.00	125.00
❑ 392 Hoyt Wilhelm RC	800.00	400.00
❑ 393 Ebba St.Claire	300.00	150.00
❑ 394 Billy Herman CO	400.00	200.00
❑ 395 Jake Pitler CO	300.00	150.00
❑ 396 Dick Williams RC	400.00	200.00
❑ 397 Forrest Main	250.00	125.00
❑ 398 Hal Rice	250.00	125.00
❑ 399 Jim Fridley	250.00	125.00
❑ 400 Bill Dickey CO	1000.00	500.00
❑ 401 Bob Schultz	300.00	150.00
❑ 402 Earl Harrist	300.00	150.00
❑ 403 Bill Miller	300.00	150.00
❑ 404 Dick Brodowski	300.00	150.00
❑ 405 Eddie Pellagrini	300.00	150.00
❑ 406 Joe Nuxhall RC	400.00	200.00
❑ 407 Eddie Mathews RC	8000.00	2000.00

1953 Topps

	NM	Ex
COMPLETE SET (274)	15000.00	7500.00
COMMON CARD (1-165)	30.00	15.00
COMMON (166-220)	25.00	12.50
COMMON DP (1-220)	15.00	7.50
COMMON (221-280)	100.00	50.00
NOT ISSUED (253/261/267)		
NOT ISSUED (268/271/275)		
WRAP.(1-CENT, DATED)	200.00	100.00
WRAP.(1-CENT, UNDATED)	300.00	150.00
WRAP.(5-CENT, DATED)	400.00	200.00
WRAP.(5-CENT, UNDATED)	350.00	180.00

Card	NM	Ex
❑ 1 Jackie Robinson DP	750.00	210.00
❑ 2 Luke Easter DP	20.00	10.00
❑ 3 George Crowe	40.00	20.00
❑ 4 Ben Wade	30.00	15.00
❑ 5 Joe Dobson	30.00	15.00
❑ 6 Sam Jones	40.00	20.00
❑ 7 Bob Borkowski DP	15.00	7.50
❑ 8 Clem Koshorek DP	15.00	7.50
❑ 9 Joe Collins	60.00	30.00
❑ 10 Smoky Burgess SP	70.00	35.00
❑ 11 Sal Yvars	30.00	15.00
❑ 12 Howie Judson DP	15.00	7.50
❑ 13 Conrado Marrero DP	15.00	7.50
❑ 14 Clem Labine DP	20.00	10.00
❑ 15 Bobo Newsom DP	20.00	10.00
❑ 16 Peanuts Lowrey DP	15.00	7.50
❑ 17 Billy Hitchcock	30.00	15.00
❑ 18 Ted Lepcio DP	15.00	7.50
❑ 19 Mel Parnell DP	20.00	10.00
❑ 20 Hank Thompson	40.00	20.00
❑ 21 Billy Johnson	30.00	15.00
❑ 22 Howie Fox	30.00	15.00
❑ 23 Toby Atwell DP	15.00	7.50
❑ 24 Ferris Fain	40.00	20.00
❑ 25 Ray Boone	40.00	20.00
❑ 26 Dale Mitchell DP	20.00	10.00
❑ 27 Roy Campanella DP	200.00	100.00
❑ 28 Eddie Pellagrini	30.00	15.00
❑ 29 Hal Jeffcoat	30.00	15.00
❑ 30 Willard Nixon	30.00	15.00
❑ 31 Ewell Blackwell	60.00	30.00
❑ 32 Clyde Vollmer	30.00	15.00
❑ 33 Bob Kennedy DP	15.00	7.50
❑ 34 George Shuba	40.00	20.00
❑ 35 Irv Noren DP	15.00	7.50
❑ 36 Johnny Groth DP	15.00	7.50
❑ 37 Eddie Mathews DP	150.00	75.00
❑ 38 Jim Hearn DP	15.00	7.50
❑ 39 Eddie Miksis	30.00	15.00
❑ 40 John Lipon	30.00	15.00
❑ 41 Enos Slaughter	80.00	40.00
❑ 42 Gus Zernial DP	20.00	10.00
❑ 43 Gil McDougald	60.00	30.00
❑ 44 Ellis Kinder SP	35.00	17.50
❑ 45 Grady Hatton DP	15.00	7.50
❑ 46 Johnny Klippstein DP	15.00	7.50
❑ 47 Bubba Church DP	15.00	7.50
❑ 48 Bob Del Greco DP	15.00	7.50
❑ 49 Faye Throneberry DP	15.00	7.50
❑ 50 Chuck Dressen MG DP	20.00	10.00
❑ 51 Frank Campos DP	15.00	7.50
❑ 52 Ted Gray DP	15.00	7.50
❑ 53 Sherm Lollar DP	20.00	10.00
❑ 54 Bob Feller DP	125.00	60.00
❑ 55 Maurice McDermott DP	15.00	7.50
❑ 56 Gerry Staley DP	15.00	7.50
❑ 57 Carl Scheib	30.00	15.00
❑ 58 George Metkovich	30.00	15.00
❑ 59 Karl Drews DP	15.00	7.50
❑ 60 Cloyd Boyer DP	15.00	7.50
❑ 61 Early Wynn SP	110.00	55.00
❑ 62 Monte Irvin DP	35.00	17.50
❑ 63 Gus Niarhos DP	15.00	7.50
❑ 64 Dave Philley	30.00	15.00
❑ 65 Earl Harrist	30.00	15.00
❑ 66 Minnie Minoso	60.00	30.00
❑ 67 Roy Sievers DP	20.00	10.00
❑ 68 Del Rice	30.00	15.00
❑ 69 Dick Brodowski	30.00	15.00
❑ 70 Ed Yuhas	30.00	15.00
❑ 71 Tony Bartirome	30.00	15.00
❑ 72 F.Hutchinson MG SP	50.00	25.00
❑ 73 Eddie Robinson	30.00	15.00
❑ 74 Joe Rossi	30.00	15.00
❑ 75 Mike Garcia	40.00	20.00
❑ 76 Pee Wee Reese	175.00	90.00
❑ 77 Johnny Mize DP	80.00	40.00
❑ 78 Red Schoendienst	80.00	40.00
❑ 79 Johnny Wyrostek	30.00	15.00
❑ 80 Jim Hegan	40.00	20.00
❑ 81 Joe Black SP	70.00	35.00
❑ 82 Mickey Mantle	3000.00	1500.00
❑ 83 Howie Pollet	30.00	15.00
❑ 84 Bob Hooper DP	15.00	7.50
❑ 85 Bobby Morgan DP	15.00	7.50
❑ 86 Billy Martin	125.00	60.00
❑ 87 Ed Lopat	60.00	30.00
❑ 88 Willie Jones DP	15.00	7.50
❑ 89 Chuck Stobbs DP	15.00	7.50
❑ 90 Hank Edwards DP	15.00	7.50
❑ 91 Ebba St.Claire DP	15.00	7.50
❑ 92 Paul Minner DP	15.00	7.50
❑ 93 Hal Rice DP	15.00	7.50
❑ 94 Bill Kennedy DP	15.00	7.50
❑ 95 Willard Marshall DP	15.00	7.50
❑ 96 Virgil Trucks	40.00	20.00
❑ 97 Don Kolloway DP	15.00	7.50
❑ 98 Cal Abrams DP	15.00	7.50
❑ 99 Dave Madison	30.00	15.00
❑ 100 Bill Miller	30.00	15.00
❑ 101 Ted Wilks	30.00	15.00
❑ 102 Connie Ryan DP	15.00	7.50
❑ 103 Joe Astroth DP	15.00	7.50
❑ 104 Yogi Berra	300.00	150.00
❑ 105 Joe Nuxhall DP	20.00	10.00
❑ 106 Johnny Antonelli	40.00	20.00
❑ 107 Danny O'Connell DP	15.00	7.50
❑ 108 Bob Porterfield DP	15.00	7.50
❑ 109 Alvin Dark	60.00	30.00
❑ 110 Herman Wehmeier DP	15.00	7.50
❑ 111 Hank Sauer DP	15.00	7.50
❑ 112 Ned Garver DP	15.00	7.50
❑ 113 Jerry Priddy	30.00	15.00
❑ 114 Phil Rizzuto	175.00	90.00
❑ 115 George Spencer	30.00	15.00
❑ 116 Frank Smith DP	15.00	7.50
❑ 117 Sid Gordon DP	15.00	7.50
❑ 118 Gus Bell DP	20.00	10.00
❑ 119 Johnny Sain SP	60.00	25.00
❑ 120 Davey Williams	40.00	20.00
❑ 121 Walt Dropo	40.00	20.00
❑ 122 Elmer Valo	30.00	15.00
❑ 123 Tommy Byrne DP	15.00	7.50
❑ 124 Sibby Sisti DP	15.00	7.50
❑ 125 Dick Williams DP	25.00	12.50
❑ 126 Bill Connelly DP	15.00	7.50
❑ 127 Clint Courtney DP	15.00	7.50
❑ 128 Wilmer Mizell DP (Inconsistent design, logo on front with black birds)	20.00	10.00
❑ 129 Keith Thomas	30.00	15.00
❑ 130 Turk Lown DP	15.00	7.50
❑ 131 Harry Byrd DP	15.00	7.50
❑ 132 Tom Morgan	30.00	15.00
❑ 133 Gil Coan	30.00	15.00
❑ 134 Rube Walker	40.00	20.00
❑ 135 Al Rosen DP	25.00	12.50
❑ 136 Ken Heintzelman DP	15.00	7.50
❑ 137 John Rutherford DP	15.00	7.50
❑ 138 George Kell	80.00	40.00
❑ 139 Sammy White	30.00	15.00
❑ 140 Tommy Glaviano	30.00	15.00
❑ 141 Allie Reynolds DP	35.00	15.00
❑ 142 Vic Wertz	40.00	20.00
❑ 143 Billy Pierce	60.00	30.00
❑ 144 Bob Schultz DP	15.00	7.50
❑ 145 Harry Dorish DP	15.00	7.50
❑ 146 Granny Hamner	30.00	15.00
❑ 147 Warren Spahn	150.00	75.00
❑ 148 Mickey Grasso	30.00	15.00
❑ 149 Dom DiMaggio DP	35.00	17.50
❑ 150 Harry Simpson DP	15.00	7.50
❑ 151 Hoyt Wilhelm	80.00	40.00
❑ 152 Bob Adams DP	15.00	7.50
❑ 153 Andy Seminick DP	15.00	7.50
❑ 154 Dick Groat	40.00	20.00
❑ 155 Dutch Leonard	30.00	15.00
❑ 156 Jim Rivera DP	20.00	10.00
❑ 157 Bob Addis DP	15.00	7.50
❑ 158 Johnny Logan RC	40.00	20.00
❑ 159 Wayne Terwilliger DP	15.00	7.50
❑ 160 Bob Young	30.00	15.00
❑ 161 Vern Bickford DP	15.00	7.50
❑ 162 Ted Kluszewski	60.00	30.00
❑ 163 Fred Hatfield DP	15.00	7.50
❑ 164 Frank Shea DP	15.00	7.50
❑ 165 Billy Hoeft	30.00	15.00
❑ 166 Billy Hunter	25.00	12.50
❑ 167 Art Schult	25.00	12.50
❑ 168 Willard Schmidt	25.00	12.50
❑ 169 Dizzy Trout	30.00	15.00
❑ 170 Bill Werle	25.00	12.50
❑ 171 Bill Glynn	25.00	12.50
❑ 172 Rip Repulski	25.00	12.50
❑ 173 Preston Ward	25.00	12.50
❑ 174 Billy Loes	30.00	15.00
❑ 175 Ron Kline	25.00	12.50
❑ 176 Don Hoak RC	40.00	20.00
❑ 177 Jim Dyck	25.00	12.50
❑ 178 Jim Waugh	25.00	12.50
❑ 179 Gene Hermanski	25.00	12.50
❑ 180 Virgil Stallcup	25.00	12.50
❑ 181 Al Zarilla	25.00	12.50
❑ 182 Bobby Hofman	25.00	12.50
❑ 183 Stu Miller RC	40.00	20.00
❑ 184 Hal Brown	25.00	12.50
❑ 185 Jim Pendleton	25.00	12.50
❑ 186 Charlie Bishop	25.00	12.50
❑ 187 Jim Fridley	25.00	12.50

	No.	Player	NM	Ex
❑	188	Andy Carey RC	40.00	20.00
❑	189	Ray Jablonski	25.00	12.50
❑	190	Dixie Walker CO	30.00	15.00
❑	191	Ralph Kiner	80.00	40.00
❑	192	Wally Westlake	25.00	12.50
❑	193	Mike Clark	25.00	12.50
❑	194	Eddie Kazak	25.00	12.50
❑	195	Ed McGhee	25.00	12.50
❑	196	Bob Keegan	25.00	12.50
❑	197	Del Crandall	40.00	20.00
❑	198	Forrest Main	25.00	12.50
❑	199	Marion Fricano	25.00	12.50
❑	200	Gordon Goldsberry	25.00	12.50
❑	201	Paul LaPalme	25.00	12.50
❑	202	Carl Sawatski	25.00	12.50
❑	203	Cliff Fannin	25.00	12.50
❑	204	Dick Bokelman	25.00	12.50
❑	205	Vern Benson	25.00	12.50
❑	206	Ed Bailey RC	30.00	15.00
❑	207	Whitey Ford	200.00	100.00
❑	208	Jim Wilson	25.00	12.50
❑	209	Jim Greengrass	25.00	12.50
❑	210	Bob Cerv RC	40.00	20.00
❑	211	J.W. Porter	25.00	12.50
❑	212	Jack Dittmer	25.00	12.50
❑	213	Ray Scarborough	25.00	12.50
❑	214	Bill Bruton RC	40.00	20.00
❑	215	Gene Conley RC	30.00	15.00
❑	216	Jim Hughes	25.00	12.50
❑	217	Murray Wall	25.00	12.50
❑	218	Les Fusselman	25.00	12.50
❑	219	Pete Runnels UER (Photo actually Don Johnson)	30.00	15.00
❑	220	Satchel Paige UER (Misspelled Satchell on card front)	600.00	300.00
❑	221	Bob Milliken	100.00	50.00
❑	222	Vic Janowicz DP RC	60.00	30.00
❑	223	Johnny O'Brien DP	50.00	25.00
❑	224	Lou Sleater DP	50.00	25.00
❑	225	Bobby Shantz	120.00	60.00
❑	226	Ed Erautt	100.00	50.00
❑	227	Morrie Martin	100.00	50.00
❑	228	Hal Newhouser	150.00	75.00
❑	229	Rocky Krsnich	100.00	50.00
❑	230	Johnny Lindell DP	50.00	25.00
❑	231	Solly Hemus DP	50.00	25.00
❑	232	Dick Kokos	100.00	50.00
❑	233	Al Aber	100.00	50.00
❑	234	Ray Murray DP	50.00	25.00
❑	235	John Hetki DP	50.00	25.00
❑	236	Harry Perkowski DP	50.00	25.00
❑	237	Bud Podbielan DP	50.00	25.00
❑	238	Cal Hogue DP	50.00	25.00
❑	239	Jim Delsing	100.00	50.00
❑	240	Fred Marsh	100.00	50.00
❑	241	Al Sima DP	50.00	25.00
❑	242	Charlie Silvera	120.00	60.00
❑	243	Carlos Bernier DP	50.00	25.00
❑	244	Willie Mays	2700.00	1350.00
❑	245	Bill Norman CO	100.00	50.00
❑	246	Roy Face DP RC	80.00	40.00
❑	247	Mike Sandlock DP	50.00	25.00
❑	248	Gene Stephens DP	50.00	25.00
❑	249	Eddie O'Brien	100.00	50.00
❑	250	Bob Wilson	100.00	50.00
❑	251	Sid Hudson	100.00	50.00
❑	252	Hank Foiles	100.00	50.00
❑	253	Does not exist		
❑	254	Preacher Roe DP	80.00	40.00
❑	255	Dixie Howell	100.00	50.00
❑	256	Les Peden	100.00	50.00
❑	257	Bob Boyd	100.00	50.00
❑	258	Jim Gilliam RC	300.00	150.00
❑	259	Roy McMillan DP	50.00	25.00
❑	260	Sam Calderone	100.00	50.00
❑	261	Does not exist		
❑	262	Bob Oldis	100.00	50.00
❑	263	Johnny Podres RC	300.00	150.00
❑	264	Gene Woodling DP	60.00	30.00
❑	265	Jackie Jensen	120.00	60.00
❑	266	Bob Cain	100.00	50.00
❑	267	Does not exist		
❑	268	Does not exist		
❑	269	Duane Pillette	100.00	50.00
❑	270	Vern Stephens	120.00	60.00
❑	271	Does not exist		
❑	272	Bill Antonello	100.00	50.00
❑	273	Harvey Haddix RC	150.00	75.00
❑	274	John Riddle CO	100.00	50.00
❑	275	Does not exist		
❑	276	Ken Raffensberger	100.00	50.00
❑	277	Don Lund	100.00	50.00
❑	278	Willie Miranda	100.00	50.00
❑	279	Joe Coleman DP	50.00	25.00
❑	280	Milt Bolling RC	350.00	57.50

1954 Topps

	NM	Ex
COMPLETE SET (250)	8000.00	4000.00
COMMON (1-50/76-250)	15.00	7.50
COMMON CARD (51-75)	25.00	12.50
WRAP.(1-CENT, DATED)	200.00	100.00
WRAP.(1-CENT, UNDATED)	150.00	75.00
WRAP.(5-CENT, DATED)	300.00	150.00
WRAP.(5-CENT, UNDATED)	250.00	125.00

	No.	Player	NM	Ex
❑	1	Ted Williams	800.00	275.00
❑	2	Gus Zernial	25.00	12.50
❑	3	Monte Irvin	50.00	25.00
❑	4	Hank Sauer	25.00	12.50
❑	5	Ed Lopat	25.00	12.50
❑	6	Pete Runnels	25.00	12.50
❑	7	Ted Kluszewski	50.00	25.00
❑	8	Bob Young	15.00	7.50
❑	9	Harvey Haddix	25.00	12.50
❑	10	Jackie Robinson	300.00	150.00
❑	11	Paul Leslie Smith	15.00	7.50
❑	12	Del Crandall	25.00	12.50
❑	13	Billy Martin	100.00	50.00
❑	14	Preacher Roe	25.00	12.50
❑	15	Al Rosen	25.00	12.50
❑	16	Vic Janowicz	25.00	12.50
❑	17	Phil Rizzuto	100.00	50.00
❑	18	Walt Dropo	25.00	12.50
❑	19	Johnny Lipon (Orioles Team Name on Front White Sox team on Back Wearing a Red Sox cap)	15.00	7.50
❑	20	Warren Spahn	100.00	50.00
❑	21	Bobby Shantz	25.00	12.50
❑	22	Jim Greengrass	15.00	7.50
❑	23	Luke Easter	25.00	12.50
❑	24	Granny Hamner	15.00	7.50
❑	25	Harvey Kuenn RC	40.00	20.00
❑	26	Ray Jablonski	15.00	7.50
❑	27	Ferris Fain	25.00	12.50
❑	28	Paul Minner	15.00	7.50
❑	29	Jim Hegan	25.00	12.50
❑	30	Eddie Mathews	100.00	50.00
❑	31	Johnny Klippstein	15.00	7.50
❑	32	Duke Snider	175.00	90.00
❑	33	Johnny Schmitz	15.00	7.50
❑	34	Jim Rivera	15.00	7.50
❑	35	Jim Gilliam	50.00	25.00
❑	36	Hoyt Wilhelm	50.00	25.00
❑	37	Whitey Ford	125.00	60.00
❑	38	Eddie Stanky MG	25.00	12.50
❑	39	Sherm Lollar	25.00	12.50
❑	40	Mel Parnell	25.00	12.50
❑	41	Willie Jones	15.00	7.50
❑	42	Don Mueller	25.00	12.50
❑	43	Dick Groat	25.00	12.50
❑	44	Ned Garver	15.00	7.50
❑	45	Richie Ashburn	80.00	40.00
❑	46	Ken Raffensberger	15.00	7.50
❑	47	Ellis Kinder	15.00	7.50
❑	48	Billy Hunter	25.00	12.50
❑	49	Ray Murray	15.00	7.50
❑	50	Yogi Berra	200.00	100.00
❑	51	Johnny Lindell	25.00	12.50
❑	52	Vic Power RC	30.00	15.00
❑	53	Jack Dittmer	25.00	12.50
❑	54	Vern Stephens	30.00	15.00
❑	55	Phil Cavarretta MG	30.00	15.00
❑	56	Willie Miranda	25.00	12.50
❑	57	Luis Aloma	25.00	12.50
❑	58	Bob Wilson	25.00	12.50
❑	59	Gene Conley	30.00	15.00
❑	60	Frank Baumholtz	25.00	12.50
❑	61	Bob Cain	25.00	12.50
❑	62	Eddie Robinson	25.00	12.50
❑	63	Johnny Pesky	30.00	15.00
❑	64	Hank Thompson	25.00	12.50
❑	65	Bob Swift CO	25.00	12.50
❑	66	Ted Lepcio	25.00	12.50
❑	67	Jim Willis	25.00	12.50
❑	68	Sam Calderone	25.00	12.50
❑	69	Bud Podbielan	25.00	12.50
❑	70	Larry Doby	60.00	30.00
❑	71	Frank Smith	25.00	12.50
❑	72	Preston Ward	25.00	12.50
❑	73	Wayne Terwilliger	25.00	12.50
❑	74	Bill Taylor	25.00	12.50
❑	75	Fred Haney MG	25.00	12.50
❑	76	Bob Scheffing CO	15.00	7.50
❑	77	Ray Boone	25.00	12.50
❑	78	Ted Kazanski	15.00	7.50
❑	79	Andy Pafko	25.00	12.50
❑	80	Jackie Jensen	25.00	12.50
❑	81	Dave Hoskins	15.00	7.50
❑	82	Milt Bolling	15.00	7.50
❑	83	Joe Collins	25.00	12.50
❑	84	Dick Cole	15.00	7.50
❑	85	Bob Turley RC	40.00	20.00
❑	86	Billy Herman CO	25.00	12.50
❑	87	Roy Face	25.00	12.50
❑	88	Matt Batts	15.00	7.50
❑	89	Howie Pollet	15.00	7.50
❑	90	Willie Mays	500.00	250.00
❑	91	Bob Oldis	15.00	7.50
❑	92	Wally Westlake	15.00	7.50
❑	93	Sid Hudson	15.00	7.50
❑	94	Ernie Banks RC	800.00	400.00
❑	95	Hal Rice	15.00	7.50
❑	96	Charlie Silvera	25.00	12.50
❑	97	Jerald Hal Lane	15.00	7.50
❑	98	Joe Black	40.00	20.00
❑	99	Bobby Hofman	15.00	7.50
❑	100	Bob Keegan	15.00	7.50
❑	101	Gene Woodling	25.00	12.50
❑	102	Gil Hodges	80.00	40.00
❑	103	Jim Lemon RC	15.00	7.50
❑	104	Mike Sandlock	15.00	7.50
❑	105	Andy Carey	25.00	12.50
❑	106	Dick Kokos	15.00	7.50
❑	107	Duane Pillette	15.00	7.50
❑	108	Thornton Kipper	15.00	7.50
❑	109	Bill Bruton	25.00	12.50
❑	110	Harry Dorish	15.00	7.50
❑	111	Jim Delsing	15.00	7.50
❑	112	Bill Renna	15.00	7.50
❑	113	Bob Boyd	15.00	7.50
❑	114	Dean Stone	15.00	7.50
❑	115	Rip Repulski	15.00	7.50
❑	116	Steve Bilko	15.00	7.50
❑	117	Solly Hemus	15.00	7.50
❑	118	Carl Scheib	15.00	7.50
❑	119	Johnny Antonelli	25.00	12.50
❑	120	Roy McMillan	25.00	12.50
❑	121	Clem Labine	25.00	12.50
❑	122	Johnny Logan	25.00	12.50
❑	123	Bobby Adams	15.00	7.50
❑	124	Marion Fricano	15.00	7.50
❑	125	Harry Perkowski	15.00	7.50
❑	126	Ben Wade	15.00	7.50
❑	127	Steve O'Neill MG	15.00	7.50
❑	128	Hank Aaron RC	1400.00	700.00

❑ 129 Forrest Jacobs 15.00 7.50
❑ 130 Hank Bauer 25.00 12.50
❑ 131 Reno Bertoia 25.00 12.50
❑ 132 Tommy Lasorda RC 200.00 100.00
❑ 133 Del Baker CO 15.00 7.50
❑ 134 Cal Hogue 15.00 7.50
❑ 135 Joe Presko 15.00 7.50
❑ 136 Connie Ryan 15.00 7.50
❑ 137 Wally Moon RC 40.00 20.00
❑ 138 Bob Borkowski 15.00 7.50
❑ 139 The O'Briens 50.00 25.00
Johnny O'Brien
Eddie O'Brien
❑ 140 Tom Wright 15.00 7.50
❑ 141 Joey Jay RC 25.00 12.50
❑ 142 Tom Poholsky 15.00 7.50
❑ 143 Rollie Hemsley CO 15.00 7.50
❑ 144 Bill Werle 15.00 7.50
❑ 145 Elmer Valo 15.00 7.50
❑ 146 Don Johnson 15.00 7.50
❑ 147 Johnny Riddle CO 15.00 7.50
❑ 148 Bob Trice 15.00 7.50
❑ 149 Al Robertson 15.00 7.50
❑ 150 Dick Kryhoski 15.00 7.50
❑ 151 Alex Grammas 15.00 7.50
❑ 152 Michael Blyzka 15.00 7.50
❑ 153 Al Walker 25.00 12.50
❑ 154 Mike Fornieles 15.00 7.50
❑ 155 Bob Kennedy 25.00 12.50
❑ 156 Joe Coleman 25.00 12.50
❑ 157 Don Lenhardt 25.00 12.50
❑ 158 Peanuts Lowrey 15.00 7.50
❑ 159 Dave Philley 15.00 7.50
❑ 160 Ralph Kress CO 15.00 7.50
❑ 161 John Hetki 15.00 7.50
❑ 162 Herman Wehmeier 15.00 7.50
❑ 163 Frank House 15.00 7.50
❑ 164 Stu Miller 25.00 12.50
❑ 165 Jim Pendleton 15.00 7.50
❑ 166 Johnny Podres 40.00 20.00
❑ 167 Don Lund 15.00 7.50
❑ 168 Morrie Martin 25.00 12.50
❑ 169 Jim Hughes 40.00 20.00
❑ 170 Dusty Rhodes RC 25.00 12.50
❑ 171 Leo Kiely 15.00 7.50
❑ 172 Harold Brown 15.00 7.50
❑ 173 Jack Harshman 15.00 7.50
❑ 174 Tom Qualters 15.00 7.50
❑ 175 Frank Leja RC 25.00 12.50
❑ 176 Robert Keely CO 15.00 7.50
❑ 177 Bob Milliken 15.00 7.50
❑ 178 Bill Glynn UER 15.00 7.50
Spelled Gylnn on the front
❑ 179 Gair Allie 15.00 7.50
❑ 180 Wes Westrum 25.00 12.50
❑ 181 Mel Roach 15.00 7.50
❑ 182 Chuck Harmon 15.00 7.50
❑ 183 Earle Combs CO 25.00 12.50
❑ 184 Ed Bailey 15.00 7.50
❑ 185 Chuck Stobbs 15.00 7.50
❑ 186 Karl Olson 15.00 7.50
❑ 187 Heinie Manush CO 25.00 12.50
❑ 188 Dave Jolly 15.00 7.50
❑ 189 Bob Ross 15.00 7.50
❑ 190 Ray Herbert 15.00 7.50
❑ 191 John(Dick) Schofield RC 25.00 12.50
❑ 192 Ellis Deal CO 15.00 7.50
❑ 193 Johnny Hopp CO 25.00 12.50
❑ 194 Bill Sarni 15.00 7.50
❑ 195 Billy Consolo RC 15.00 7.50
❑ 196 Stan Jok 15.00 7.50
❑ 197 Lynwood Rowe CO 25.00 12.50
("Schoolboy")
❑ 198 Carl Sawatski 15.00 7.50
❑ 199 Glenn(Rocky) Nelson 15.00 7.50
❑ 200 Larry Jansen 25.00 12.50
❑ 201 Al Kaline RC 600.00 300.00
❑ 202 Bob Purkey RC 25.00 12.50
❑ 203 Harry Brecheen CO 25.00 12.50
❑ 204 Angel Scull 15.00 7.50
❑ 205 Johnny Sain 40.00 20.00
❑ 206 Ray Crone 15.00 7.50
❑ 207 Tom Oliver CO 15.00 7.50
❑ 208 Grady Hatton 15.00 7.50
❑ 209 Chuck Thompson 15.00 7.50
❑ 210 Bob Buhl RC 25.00 12.50
❑ 211 Don Hoak 25.00 12.50
❑ 212 Bob Micelotta 15.00 7.50
❑ 213 Johnny Fitzpatrick CO 15.00 7.50
❑ 214 Arnie Portocarrero 15.00 7.50
❑ 215 Ed McGhee 25.00 12.50
❑ 216 Al Sima 15.00 7.50
❑ 217 Paul Schreiber CO 15.00 7.50
❑ 218 Fred Marsh 15.00 7.50
❑ 219 Chuck Kress 15.00 7.50
❑ 220 Ruben Gomez 25.00 12.50
❑ 221 Dick Brodowski 15.00 7.50
❑ 222 Bill Wilson 15.00 7.50
❑ 223 Joe Haynes CO 15.00 7.50
❑ 224 Dick Weik 15.00 7.50
❑ 225 Don Liddle 15.00 7.50
❑ 226 Jehosie Heard 25.00 12.50
❑ 227 Colonel Mills CO 15.00 7.50
❑ 228 Gene Hermanski 15.00 7.50
❑ 229 Bob Talbot 15.00 7.50
❑ 230 Bob Kuzava 25.00 12.50
❑ 231 Roy Smalley 15.00 7.50
❑ 232 Lou Limmer 15.00 7.50
❑ 233 Augie Galan CO 15.00 7.50
❑ 234 Jerry Lynch RC 15.00 7.50
❑ 235 Vern Law 25.00 12.50
❑ 236 Paul Penson 15.00 7.50
❑ 237 Mike Ryba CO 15.00 7.50
❑ 238 Al Aber 15.00 7.50
❑ 239 Bill Skowron RC 100.00 50.00
❑ 240 Sam Mele 25.00 12.50
❑ 241 Robert Miller 15.00 7.50
❑ 242 Curt Roberts 15.00 7.50
❑ 243 Ray Blades CO 15.00 7.50
❑ 244 Leroy Wheat 15.00 7.50
❑ 245 Roy Sievers 25.00 12.50
❑ 246 Howie Fox 15.00 7.50
❑ 247 Ed Mayo CO 15.00 7.50
❑ 248 Al Smith RC 25.00 12.50
❑ 249 Wilmer Mizell 25.00 12.50
❑ 250 Ted Williams 800.00 325.00

1955 Topps

	NM	Ex
COMPLETE SET (206)	8000.00	4000.00
COMMON CARD (1-150)	12.00	6.00
COMMON (151-160)	20.00	10.00
COMMON (161-210)	30.00	15.00
NOT ISSUED (175/186/203/209)		
WRAP.(1-CENT, DATED)	150.00	75.00
WRAP.(1-CENT, UNDATED)	50.00	25.00
WRAP.(5-CENT, DATED)	150.00	75.00
WRAP.(5-CENT, DATED)	100.00	50.00

❑ 1 Dusty Rhodes 100.00 20.00
❑ 2 Ted Williams 600.00 300.00
❑ 3 Art Fowler 15.00 7.50
❑ 4 Al Kaline 150.00 75.00
❑ 5 Jim Gilliam 40.00 20.00
❑ 6 Stan Hack MG 25.00 12.50
❑ 7 Jim Hegan 15.00 7.50
❑ 8 Harold Smith 12.00 6.00
❑ 9 Robert Miller 12.00 6.00
❑ 10 Bob Keegan 12.00 6.00
❑ 11 Ferris Fain 15.00 7.50
❑ 12 Vernon(Jake) Thies 12.00 6.00
❑ 13 Fred Marsh 12.00 6.00
❑ 14 Jim Finigan 12.00 6.00
❑ 15 Jim Pendleton 12.00 6.00
❑ 16 Roy Sievers 15.00 7.50
❑ 17 Bobby Hofman 12.00 6.00
❑ 18 Russ Kemmerer 12.00 6.00
❑ 19 Billy Herman CO 15.00 7.50
❑ 20 Andy Carey 15.00 7.50
❑ 21 Alex Grammas 12.00 6.00
❑ 22 Bill Skowron 40.00 20.00
❑ 23 Jack Parks 12.00 6.00
❑ 24 Hal Newhouser 40.00 20.00
❑ 25 Johnny Podres 25.00 12.50
❑ 26 Dick Groat 15.00 7.50
❑ 27 Billy Gardner RC 15.00 7.50
❑ 28 Ernie Banks 175.00 90.00
❑ 29 Herman Wehmeier 12.00 6.00
❑ 30 Vic Power 15.00 7.50
❑ 31 Warren Spahn 100.00 50.00
❑ 32 Warren McGhee 12.00 6.00
❑ 33 Tom Qualters 12.00 6.00
❑ 34 Wayne Terwilliger 12.00 6.00
❑ 35 Dave Jolly 12.00 6.00
❑ 36 Leo Kiely 12.00 6.00
❑ 37 Joe Cunningham RC 15.00 7.50
❑ 38 Bob Turley 15.00 7.50
❑ 39 Bill Glynn 12.00 6.00
❑ 40 Don Hoak 15.00 7.50
❑ 41 Chuck Stobbs 12.00 6.00
❑ 42 John(Windy) McCall 12.00 6.00
❑ 43 Harvey Haddix 15.00 7.50
❑ 44 Harold Valentine 12.00 6.00
❑ 45 Hank Sauer 15.00 7.50
❑ 46 Ted Kazanski 12.00 6.00
❑ 47 Hank Aaron UER 350.00 180.00
(Birth incorrectly listed as 2/10)
❑ 48 Bob Kennedy 15.00 7.50
❑ 49 J.W. Porter 12.00 6.00
❑ 50 Jackie Robinson 350.00 180.00
❑ 51 Jim Hughes 15.00 7.50
❑ 52 Bill Tremel 12.00 6.00
❑ 53 Bill Taylor 12.00 6.00
❑ 54 Lou Limmer 12.00 6.00
❑ 55 Rip Repulski 12.00 6.00
❑ 56 Ray Jablonski 12.00 6.00
❑ 57 Billy O'Dell 12.00 6.00
❑ 58 Jim Rivera 12.00 6.00
❑ 59 Gair Allie 12.00 6.00
❑ 60 Dean Stone 12.00 6.00
❑ 61 Forrest Jacobs 12.00 6.00
❑ 62 Thornton Kipper 12.00 6.00
❑ 63 Joe Collins 15.00 7.50
❑ 64 Gus Triandos RC 15.00 7.50
❑ 65 Ray Boone 15.00 7.50
❑ 66 Ron Jackson RC 12.00 6.00
❑ 67 Wally Moon 15.00 7.50
❑ 68 Jim Davis 12.00 6.00
❑ 69 Ed Bailey 15.00 7.50
❑ 70 Al Rosen 15.00 7.50
❑ 71 Ruben Gomez 12.00 6.00
❑ 72 Karl Olson 12.00 6.00
❑ 73 Jack Shepard 12.00 6.00
❑ 74 Bob Borkowski 12.00 6.00
❑ 75 Sandy Amoros RC 40.00 20.00
❑ 76 Howie Pollet 12.00 6.00
❑ 77 Arnie Portocarrero 12.00 6.00
❑ 78 Gordon Jones 12.00 6.00
❑ 79 Clyde(Danny) Schell 12.00 6.00
❑ 80 Bob Grim RC 15.00 7.50
❑ 81 Gene Conley 15.00 7.50
❑ 82 Chuck Harmon 12.00 6.00
❑ 83 Tom Brewer 12.00 6.00
❑ 84 Camilo Pascual RC 15.00 7.50
❑ 85 Don Mossi RC 25.00 12.50
❑ 86 Bill Wilson 12.00 6.00
❑ 87 Frank House 12.00 6.00
❑ 88 Bob Skinner RC 15.00 7.50
❑ 89 Joe Frazier 15.00 7.50
❑ 90 Karl Spooner RC 15.00 7.50
❑ 91 Milt Bolling 12.00 6.00
❑ 92 Don Zimmer RC 25.00 12.50
❑ 93 Steve Bilko 12.00 6.00
❑ 94 Reno Bertoia 12.00 6.00
❑ 95 Preston Ward 12.00 6.00
❑ 96 Chuck Bishop 12.00 6.00
❑ 97 Carlos Paula 12.00 6.00

Card	NM	Ex
❑ 98 John Riddle CO	12.00	6.00
❑ 99 Frank Leja	12.00	6.00
❑ 100 Monte Irvin	40.00	20.00
❑ 101 Johnny Gray	12.00	6.00
❑ 102 Wally Westlake	12.00	6.00
❑ 103 Chuck White	12.00	6.00
❑ 104 Jack Harshman	12.00	6.00
❑ 105 Chuck Diering	12.00	6.00
❑ 106 Frank Sullivan	12.00	6.00
❑ 107 Curt Roberts	12.00	6.00
❑ 108 Al Walker	15.00	7.50
❑ 109 Ed Lopat	15.00	7.50
❑ 110 Gus Zernial	15.00	7.50
❑ 111 Bob Milliken	15.00	7.50
❑ 112 Nelson King	12.00	6.00
❑ 113 Harry Brecheen CO	15.00	7.50
❑ 114 Louis Ortiz	12.00	6.00
❑ 115 Ellis Kinder	12.00	6.00
❑ 116 Tom Hurd	12.00	6.00
❑ 117 Mel Roach	12.00	6.00
❑ 118 Bob Purkey	12.00	6.00
❑ 119 Bob Lennon	12.00	6.00
❑ 120 Ted Kluszewski	75.00	38.00
❑ 121 Bill Renna	12.00	6.00
❑ 122 Carl Sawatski	12.00	6.00
❑ 123 Sandy Koufax RC	800.00	400.00
❑ 124 Harmon Killebrew RC	250.00	125.00
❑ 125 Ken Boyer RC	60.00	30.00
❑ 126 Dick Hall	12.00	6.00
❑ 127 Dale Long RC	15.00	7.50
❑ 128 Ted Lepcio	12.00	6.00
❑ 129 Elvin Tappe	15.00	7.50
❑ 130 Mayo Smith MG	12.00	6.00
❑ 131 Grady Hatton	12.00	6.00
❑ 132 Bob Trice	12.00	6.00
❑ 133 Dave Hoskins	12.00	6.00
❑ 134 Joey Jay	15.00	7.50
❑ 135 Johnny O'Brien	15.00	7.50
❑ 136 Veston(Bunky)Stewart	12.00	6.00
❑ 137 Harry Elliott	12.00	6.00
❑ 138 Ray Herbert	12.00	6.00
❑ 139 Steve Kraly	12.00	6.00
❑ 140 Mel Parnell	15.00	7.50
❑ 141 Tom Wright	12.00	6.00
❑ 142 Jerry Lynch	15.00	7.50
❑ 143 John(Dick) Schofield	15.00	7.50
❑ 144 John(Joe) Amalfitano RC	12.00	6.00
❑ 145 Elmer Valo	12.00	6.00
❑ 146 Dick Donovan RC	12.00	6.00
❑ 147 Hugh Pepper	12.00	6.00
❑ 148 Hector Brown	12.00	6.00
❑ 149 Ray Crone	12.00	6.00
❑ 150 Mike Higgins MG	12.00	6.00
❑ 151 Ralph Kress CO	20.00	10.00
❑ 152 Harry Agganis RC	90.00	45.00
❑ 153 Bud Podbielan	25.00	12.50
❑ 154 Willie Miranda	20.00	10.00
❑ 155 Eddie Mathews	125.00	60.00
❑ 156 Joe Black	50.00	25.00
❑ 157 Robert Miller	20.00	10.00
❑ 158 Tommy Carroll	25.00	12.50
❑ 159 Johnny Schmitz	20.00	10.00
❑ 160 Ray Narleski RC	20.00	10.00
❑ 161 Chuck Tanner RC	40.00	20.00
❑ 162 Joe Coleman	30.00	15.00
❑ 163 Faye Throneberry	30.00	15.00
❑ 164 Roberto Clemente RC	2000.00	1000.00
❑ 165 Don Johnson	30.00	15.00
❑ 166 Hank Bauer	75.00	38.00
❑ 167 Tom Casagrande	30.00	15.00
❑ 168 Duane Pillette	30.00	15.00
❑ 169 Bob Oldis	40.00	20.00
❑ 170 Jim Pearce DP	15.00	7.50
❑ 171 Dick Brodowski	30.00	15.00
❑ 172 Frank Baumholtz DP	15.00	7.50
❑ 173 Bob Kline	30.00	15.00
❑ 174 Rudy Minarcin	30.00	15.00
❑ 175 Does not exist		
❑ 176 Norm Zauchin	30.00	15.00
❑ 177 Al Robertson	30.00	15.00
❑ 178 Bobby Adams	30.00	15.00
❑ 179 Jim Bolger	30.00	15.00
❑ 180 Clem Labine	60.00	30.00
❑ 181 Roy McMillan	40.00	20.00
❑ 182 Humberto Robinson	30.00	15.00
❑ 183 Anthony Jacobs	30.00	15.00
❑ 184 Harry Perkowski DP	15.00	7.50
❑ 185 Don Ferrarese	30.00	15.00
❑ 186 Does not exist		
❑ 187 Gil Hodges	150.00	75.00
❑ 188 Charlie Silvera DP	15.00	7.50
❑ 189 Phil Rizzuto	150.00	75.00
❑ 190 Gene Woodling	40.00	20.00
❑ 191 Eddie Stanky MG	40.00	20.00
❑ 192 Jim Delsing	40.00	20.00
❑ 193 Johnny Sain	60.00	30.00
❑ 194 Willie Mays	500.00	250.00
❑ 195 Ed Roebuck RC	60.00	30.00
❑ 196 Gale Wade	30.00	15.00
❑ 197 Al Smith	60.00	30.00
❑ 198 Yogi Berra	250.00	125.00
❑ 199 Odbert Hamric	40.00	20.00
❑ 200 Jackie Jensen	60.00	30.00
❑ 201 Sherman Lollar	40.00	20.00
❑ 202 Jim Owens	30.00	15.00
❑ 203 Does not exist		
❑ 204 Frank Smith	30.00	15.00
❑ 205 Gene Freese RC	40.00	20.00
❑ 206 Pete Daley	30.00	15.00
❑ 207 Billy Consolo	30.00	15.00
❑ 208 Ray Moore	40.00	20.00
❑ 209 Does not exist		
❑ 210 Duke Snider	500.00	150.00

1956 Topps

	NM	Ex
COMPLETE SET (340)	8000.00	4000.00
COMMON CARD (1-100)	10.00	5.00
COMMON (101-180)	12.00	6.00
COMMON (261-340)	12.00	6.00
COMMON (181-260)	15.00	7.50
WRAPPER (1-CENT)	250.00	125.00
WRAP.(1-CENT, REPEAT)	100.00	50.00
WRAPPER (5-CENT)	200.00	100.00

Card	NM	Ex
❑ 1 W.Harridge PRES RC	100.00	28.00
❑ 2 W. Giles PRES RC DP	50.00	25.00
❑ 3 Elmer Valo	15.00	7.50
❑ 4 Carlos Paula	15.00	7.50
❑ 5 Ted Williams	400.00	200.00
❑ 6 Ray Boone	25.00	12.50
❑ 7 Ron Negray	10.00	5.00
❑ 8 Walter Alston MG RC	40.00	20.00
❑ 9 Ruben Gomez DP	9.00	4.50
❑ 10 Warren Spahn	80.00	40.00
❑ 11A Chicago Cubs (Centered)	30.00	15.00
❑ 11B Cubs Team (Dated 1955)	80.00	40.00
❑ 11C Cubs Team (Name at far left)	30.00	15.00
❑ 12 Andy Carey	15.00	7.50
❑ 13 Roy Face	15.00	7.50
❑ 14 Ken Boyer DP	15.00	7.50
❑ 15 Ernie Banks DP	90.00	45.00
❑ 16 Hector Lopez RC	15.00	7.50
❑ 17 Gene Conley	15.00	7.50
❑ 18 Dick Donovan	10.00	5.00
❑ 19 Chuck Diering DP	10.00	5.00
❑ 20 Al Kaline	100.00	50.00
❑ 21 Joe Collins DP	15.00	7.50
❑ 22 Jim Finigan	10.00	5.00
❑ 23 Fred Marsh	10.00	5.00
❑ 24 Dick Groat	15.00	7.50
❑ 25 Ted Kluszewski	75.00	38.00
❑ 26 Grady Hatton	10.00	5.00
❑ 27 Nelson Burbrink DP	10.00	5.00
❑ 28 Bobby Hofman	10.00	5.00
❑ 29 Jack Harshman	10.00	5.00
❑ 30 Jackie Robinson DP	200.00	100.00
❑ 31 Hank Aaron UER DP (Small photo actually Willie Mays)	300.00	150.00
❑ 32 Frank House	10.00	5.00
❑ 33 Roberto Clemente	375.00	190.00
❑ 34 Tom Brewer DP	10.00	5.00
❑ 35 Al Rosen	15.00	7.50
❑ 36 Rudy Minarcin	15.00	7.50
❑ 37 Alex Grammas	10.00	5.00
❑ 38 Bob Kennedy	15.00	7.50
❑ 39 Don Mossi	15.00	7.50
❑ 40 Bob Turley	15.00	7.50
❑ 41 Hank Sauer	15.00	7.50
❑ 42 Sandy Amoros	25.00	12.50
❑ 43 Ray Moore	10.00	5.00
❑ 44 Windy McCall	10.00	5.00
❑ 45 Gus Zernial	15.00	7.50
❑ 46 Gene Freese DP	9.00	4.50
❑ 47 Art Fowler	10.00	5.00
❑ 48 Jim Hegan	15.00	7.50
❑ 49 Pedro Ramos	10.00	5.00
❑ 50 Dusty Rhodes DP	15.00	7.50
❑ 51 Ernie Oravetz	10.00	5.00
❑ 52 Bob Grim DP	15.00	7.50
❑ 53 Arnie Portocarrero	10.00	5.00
❑ 54 Bob Keegan	10.00	5.00
❑ 55 Wally Moon	15.00	7.50
❑ 56 Dale Long	15.00	7.50
❑ 57 Duke Maas	10.00	5.00
❑ 58 Ed Roebuck	25.00	12.50
❑ 59 Jose Santiago	10.00	5.00
❑ 60 Mayo Smith MG DP	9.00	4.50
❑ 61 Bill Skowron	25.00	12.50
❑ 62 Hal Smith	15.00	7.50
❑ 63 Roger Craig RC	40.00	20.00
❑ 64 Luis Arroyo RC	10.00	5.00
❑ 65 Johnny O'Brien	15.00	7.50
❑ 66 Bob Speake DP	10.00	5.00
❑ 67 Vic Power	15.00	7.50
❑ 68 Chuck Stobbs	10.00	5.00
❑ 69 Chuck Tanner	15.00	7.50
❑ 70 Jim Rivera	10.00	5.00
❑ 71 Frank Sullivan	10.00	5.00
❑ 72A Phillies Team (Centered)	30.00	15.00
❑ 72B Phillies Team (Dated 1955)	80.00	40.00
❑ 72C Phillies Team DP (Name at far left)	30.00	15.00
❑ 73 Wayne Terwilliger	10.00	5.00
❑ 74 Jim King	10.00	5.00
❑ 75 Roy Sievers DP	15.00	7.50
❑ 76 Ray Crone	10.00	5.00
❑ 77 Harvey Haddix	15.00	7.50
❑ 78 Herman Wehmeier	10.00	5.00
❑ 79 Sandy Koufax	350.00	180.00
❑ 80 Gus Triandos DP	9.00	4.50
❑ 81 Wally Westlake	10.00	5.00
❑ 82 Bill Renna DP	10.00	5.00
❑ 83 Karl Spooner	15.00	7.50
❑ 84 Babe Birrer	10.00	5.00
❑ 85A Cleveland Indians (Centered)	30.00	15.00
❑ 85B Indians Team (Dated 1955)	80.00	40.00
❑ 85C Indians Team (Name at far left)	30.00	15.00
❑ 86 Ray Jablonski DP	9.00	4.50
❑ 87 Dean Stone	10.00	5.00
❑ 88 Johnny Kucks RC	15.00	7.50
❑ 89 Norm Zauchin	10.00	5.00
❑ 90A Cincinnati Redlegs Team (Centered)	30.00	15.00
❑ 90B Reds Team (Dated 1955)	80.00	40.00
❑ 90C Reds Team (Name at far left)	30.00	15.00
❑ 91 Gail Harris	10.00	5.00
❑ 92 Bob(Red) Wilson	10.00	5.00

❑ 93 George Susce 10.00 5.00
❑ 94 Ron Kline 10.00 5.00
❑ 95A Milwaukee Braves 40.00 20.00 Team (Centered)
❑ 95B Braves Team 80.00 40.00 (Dated 1955)
❑ 95C Braves Team 40.00 20.00 (Name at far left)
❑ 96 Bill Tremel 10.00 5.00
❑ 97 Jerry Lynch 15.00 7.50
❑ 98 Camilo Pascual 15.00 7.50
❑ 99 Don Zimmer 25.00 12.50
❑ 100A Baltimore Orioles 35.00 17.50 Team (centered)
❑ 100B Orioles Team 80.00 40.00 (Dated 1955)
❑ 100C Orioles Team 35.00 17.50 (Name at far left)
❑ 101 Roy Campanella 150.00 75.00
❑ 102 Jim Davis 12.00 6.00
❑ 103 Willie Miranda 12.00 6.00
❑ 104 Bob Lennon 12.00 6.00
❑ 105 Al Smith 12.00 6.00
❑ 106 Joe Astroth 12.00 6.00
❑ 107 Eddie Mathews 80.00 40.00
❑ 108 Laurin Pepper 12.00 6.00
❑ 109 Enos Slaughter 40.00 20.00
❑ 110 Yogi Berra 150.00 75.00
❑ 111 Boston Red Sox 35.00 17.50 Team Card
❑ 112 Dee Fondy 12.00 6.00
❑ 113 Phil Rizzuto 125.00 60.00
❑ 114 Jim Owens 15.00 7.50
❑ 115 Jackie Jensen 15.00 7.50
❑ 116 Eddie O'Brien 12.00 6.00
❑ 117 Virgil Trucks 15.00 7.50
❑ 118 Nellie Fox 60.00 30.00
❑ 119 Larry Jackson RC 15.00 7.50
❑ 120 Richie Ashburn 60.00 30.00
❑ 121 Pittsburgh Pirates 35.00 17.50 Team Card
❑ 122 Willard Nixon 12.00 6.00
❑ 123 Roy McMillan 15.00 7.50
❑ 124 Don Kaiser 12.00 6.00
❑ 125 Minnie Minoso 40.00 20.00
❑ 126 Jim Brady 12.00 6.00
❑ 127 Willie Jones 15.00 7.50
❑ 128 Eddie Yost 15.00 7.50
❑ 129 Jake Martin 12.00 6.00
❑ 130 Willie Mays 300.00 150.00
❑ 131 Bob Roselli 12.00 6.00
❑ 132 Bobby Avila 12.00 6.00
❑ 133 Ray Narleski 12.00 6.00
❑ 134 St. Louis Cardinals 35.00 17.50 Team Card
❑ 135 Mickey Mantle 1400.00 700.00
❑ 136 Johnny Logan 15.00 7.50
❑ 137 Al Silvera 12.00 6.00
❑ 138 Johnny Antonelli 15.00 7.50
❑ 139 Tommy Carroll 15.00 7.50
❑ 140 Herb Score RC 60.00 30.00
❑ 141 Joe Frazier 12.00 6.00
❑ 142 Gene Baker 12.00 6.00
❑ 143 Jim Piersall 15.00 7.50
❑ 144 Leroy Powell 12.00 6.00
❑ 145 Gil Hodges 60.00 30.00
❑ 146 Washington Nationals 35.00 17.50 Team Card
❑ 147 Earl Torgeson 12.00 6.00
❑ 148 Alvin Dark 15.00 7.50
❑ 149 Dixie Howell 12.00 6.00
❑ 150 Duke Snider 125.00 60.00
❑ 151 Spook Jacobs 15.00 7.50
❑ 152 Billy Hoeft 15.00 7.50
❑ 153 Frank Thomas 15.00 7.50
❑ 154 Dave Pope 12.00 6.00
❑ 155 Harvey Kuenn 15.00 7.50
❑ 156 Wes Westrum 15.00 7.50
❑ 157 Dick Brodowski 12.00 6.00
❑ 158 Wally Post 15.00 7.50
❑ 159 Clint Courtney 12.00 6.00
❑ 160 Billy Pierce 15.00 7.50
❑ 161 Joe DeMaestri 12.00 6.00
❑ 162 Dave(Gus) Bell 15.00 7.50
❑ 163 Gene Woodling 15.00 7.50
❑ 164 Harmon Killebrew 100.00 50.00
❑ 165 Red Schoendienst 40.00 20.00
❑ 166 Brooklyn Dodgers 200.00 100.00 Team Card
❑ 167 Harry Dorish 12.00 6.00
❑ 168 Sammy White 12.00 6.00
❑ 169 Bob Nelson 12.00 6.00
❑ 170 Bill Virdon 15.00 7.50
❑ 171 Jim Wilson 12.00 6.00
❑ 172 Frank Torre RC 15.00 7.50
❑ 173 Johnny Podres 25.00 12.50
❑ 174 Glen Gorbous 12.00 6.00
❑ 175 Del Crandall 15.00 7.50
❑ 176 Alex Kellner 12.00 6.00
❑ 177 Hank Bauer 25.00 12.50
❑ 178 Joe Black 15.00 7.50
❑ 179 Harry Chiti 12.00 6.00
❑ 180 Robin Roberts 50.00 25.00
❑ 181 Billy Martin 60.00 30.00
❑ 182 Paul Minner 15.00 7.50
❑ 183 Stan Lopata 20.00 10.00
❑ 184 Don Bessent 20.00 10.00
❑ 185 Bill Bruton 20.00 10.00
❑ 186 Ron Jackson 15.00 7.50
❑ 187 Early Wynn 50.00 25.00
❑ 188 Chicago White Sox 50.00 25.00 Team Card
❑ 189 Ned Garver 15.00 7.50
❑ 190 Carl Furillo 30.00 15.00
❑ 191 Frank Lary 20.00 10.00
❑ 192 Smoky Burgess 20.00 10.00
❑ 193 Wilmer Mizell 20.00 10.00
❑ 194 Monte Irvin 30.00 15.00
❑ 195 George Kell 30.00 15.00
❑ 196 Tom Poholsky 15.00 7.50
❑ 197 Granny Hamner 15.00 7.50
❑ 198 Ed Fitzgerald 15.00 7.50
❑ 199 Hank Thompson 20.00 10.00
❑ 200 Bob Feller 125.00 60.00
❑ 201 Rip Repulski 15.00 7.50
❑ 202 Jim Hearn 15.00 7.50
❑ 203 Bill Tuttle 15.00 7.50
❑ 204 Art Swanson 15.00 7.50
❑ 205 Whitey Lockman 20.00 10.00
❑ 206 Erv Palica 15.00 7.50
❑ 207 Jim Small 15.00 7.50
❑ 208 Elston Howard 60.00 30.00
❑ 209 Max Surkont 15.00 7.50
❑ 210 Mike Garcia 20.00 10.00
❑ 211 Murry Dickson 15.00 7.50
❑ 212 Johnny Temple 15.00 7.50
❑ 213 Detroit Tigers 60.00 30.00 Team Card
❑ 214 Bob Rush 15.00 7.50
❑ 215 Tommy Byrne 20.00 10.00
❑ 216 Jerry Schoonmaker 15.00 7.50
❑ 217 Billy Klaus 15.00 7.50
❑ 218 Joe Nuxhall UER 20.00 10.00 (Misspelled Nuxall)
❑ 219 Lew Burdette 20.00 10.00
❑ 220 Del Ennis 20.00 10.00
❑ 221 Bob Friend 20.00 10.00
❑ 222 Dave Philley 15.00 7.50
❑ 223 Randy Jackson 15.00 7.50
❑ 224 Bud Podbielan 15.00 7.50
❑ 225 Gil McDougald 50.00 25.00
❑ 226 New York Giants 75.00 38.00 Team Card
❑ 227 Russ Meyer 15.00 7.50
❑ 228 Mickey Vernon 20.00 10.00
❑ 229 Harry Brecheen CO 20.00 10.00
❑ 230 Chico Carrasquel 15.00 7.50
❑ 231 Bob Hale 15.00 7.50
❑ 232 Toby Atwell 15.00 7.50
❑ 233 Carl Erskine 30.00 15.00
❑ 234 Pete Runnels 15.00 7.50
❑ 235 Don Newcombe 50.00 25.00
❑ 236 Kansas City Athletics 35.00 17.50 Team Card
❑ 237 Jose Valdivielso 15.00 7.50
❑ 238 Walt Dropo 20.00 10.00
❑ 239 Harry Simpson 15.00 7.50
❑ 240 Whitey Ford 125.00 60.00
❑ 241 Don Mueller UER 20.00 10.00 (6~ tall)
❑ 242 Hershell Freeman 15.00 7.50
❑ 243 Sherm Lollar 20.00 10.00
❑ 244 Bob Buhl 30.00 15.00
❑ 245 Billy Goodman 20.00 10.00
❑ 246 Tom Gorman 15.00 7.50
❑ 247 Bill Sarni 15.00 7.50
❑ 248 Bob Porterfield 15.00 7.50
❑ 249 Johnny Klippstein 15.00 7.50
❑ 250 Larry Doby 30.00 15.00
❑ 251 New York Yankees 250.00 125.00 Team Card UER (Don Larsen misspelled as Larson on front)
❑ 252 Vern Law 20.00 10.00
❑ 253 Irv Noren 30.00 15.00
❑ 254 George Crowe 15.00 7.50
❑ 255 Bob Lemon 50.00 25.00
❑ 256 Tom Hurd 15.00 7.50
❑ 257 Bobby Thomson 30.00 15.00
❑ 258 Art Ditmar 15.00 7.50
❑ 259 Sam Jones 20.00 10.00
❑ 260 Pee Wee Reese 125.00 60.00
❑ 261 Bobby Shantz 15.00 7.50
❑ 262 Howie Pollet 12.00 6.00
❑ 263 Bob Miller 12.00 6.00
❑ 264 Ray Monzant 12.00 6.00
❑ 265 Sandy Consuegra 12.00 6.00
❑ 266 Don Ferrarese 12.00 6.00
❑ 267 Bob Nieman 12.00 6.00
❑ 268 Dale Mitchell 15.00 7.50
❑ 269 Jack Meyer 12.00 6.00
❑ 270 Billy Loes 15.00 7.50
❑ 271 Foster Castleman 12.00 6.00
❑ 272 Danny O'Connell 12.00 6.00
❑ 273 Walker Cooper 12.00 6.00
❑ 274 Frank Baumholtz 12.00 6.00
❑ 275 Jim Greengrass 12.00 6.00
❑ 276 George Zuverink 12.00 6.00
❑ 277 Daryl Spencer 12.00 6.00
❑ 278 Chet Nichols 12.00 6.00
❑ 279 Johnny Groth 12.00 6.00
❑ 280 Jim Gilliam 40.00 20.00
❑ 281 Art Houtteman 12.00 6.00
❑ 282 Warren Hacker 12.00 6.00
❑ 283 Hal Smith RC 15.00 7.50
❑ 284 Ike Delock 12.00 6.00
❑ 285 Eddie Miksis 12.00 6.00
❑ 286 Bill Wight 12.00 6.00
❑ 287 Bobby Adams 12.00 6.00
❑ 288 Bob Cerv 40.00 20.00
❑ 289 Hal Jeffcoat 12.00 6.00
❑ 290 Curt Simmons 15.00 7.50
❑ 291 Frank Kellert 12.00 6.00
❑ 292 Luis Aparicio RC 150.00 75.00
❑ 293 Stu Miller 25.00 12.50
❑ 294 Ernie Johnson 15.00 7.50
❑ 295 Clem Labine 15.00 7.50
❑ 296 Andy Seminick 12.00 6.00
❑ 297 Bob Skinner 15.00 7.50
❑ 298 Johnny Schmitz 12.00 6.00
❑ 299 Charlie Neal 40.00 20.00
❑ 300 Vic Wertz 15.00 7.50
❑ 301 Marv Grissom 12.00 6.00
❑ 302 Eddie Robinson 12.00 6.00
❑ 303 Jim Dyck 12.00 6.00
❑ 304 Frank Malzone 15.00 7.50
❑ 305 Brooks Lawrence 12.00 6.00
❑ 306 Curt Roberts 12.00 6.00
❑ 307 Hoyt Wilhelm 40.00 20.00
❑ 308 Chuck Harmon 12.00 6.00
❑ 309 Don Blasingame RC 15.00 7.50
❑ 310 Steve Gromek 12.00 6.00
❑ 311 Hal Naragon 12.00 6.00
❑ 312 Andy Pafko 15.00 7.50
❑ 313 Gene Stephens 12.00 6.00
❑ 314 Hobie Landrith 12.00 6.00
❑ 315 Milt Bolling 12.00 6.00
❑ 316 Jerry Coleman 15.00 7.50
❑ 317 Al Aber 12.00 6.00
❑ 318 Fred Hatfield 12.00 6.00
❑ 319 Jack Crimian 12.00 6.00
❑ 320 Joe Adcock 15.00 7.50
❑ 321 Jim Konstanty 15.00 7.50
❑ 322 Karl Olson 12.00 6.00
❑ 323 Willard Schmidt 12.00 6.00
❑ 324 Rocky Bridges 15.00 7.50
❑ 325 Don Liddle 12.00 6.00
❑ 326 Connie Johnson 12.00 6.00

Card	NM	Ex
❑ 327 Bob Wiesler	12.00	6.00
❑ 328 Preston Ward	12.00	6.00
❑ 329 Lou Berberet	12.00	6.00
❑ 330 Jim Busby	15.00	7.50
❑ 331 Dick Hall	12.00	6.00
❑ 332 Don Larsen	60.00	30.00
❑ 333 Rube Walker	12.00	6.00
❑ 334 Bob Miller	15.00	7.50
❑ 335 Don Hoak	15.00	7.50
❑ 336 Ellis Kinder	12.00	6.00
❑ 337 Bobby Morgan	12.00	6.00
❑ 338 Jim Delsing	12.00	6.00
❑ 339 Rance Pless	12.00	6.00
❑ 340 Mickey McDermott	60.00	12.00
❑ NNO Checklist 1/3	275.00	90.00
❑ NNO Checklist 2/4	275.00	90.00

1957 Topps

	NM	Ex
COMPLETE SET (407)	10000.00	5000.00
COMMON CARD (1-88)	10.00	5.00
COMMON CARD (89-176)	8.00	4.00
COMMON (177-264)	8.00	4.00
COMMON (265-352)	20.00	10.00
COMMON (353-407)	8.00	4.00
COMMON DP (265-352)	13.00	6.50
WRAPPER (1-CENT)	300.00	150.00
WRAPPER (5-CENT)	200.00	100.00

Card	NM	Ex
❑ 1 Ted Williams	500.00	150.00
❑ 2 Yogi Berra	135.00	70.00
❑ 3 Dale Long	20.00	10.00
❑ 4 Johnny Logan	20.00	10.00
❑ 5 Sal Maglie	20.00	10.00
❑ 6 Hector Lopez	15.00	7.50
❑ 7 Luis Aparicio	30.00	15.00
❑ 8 Don Mossi	15.00	7.50
❑ 9 Johnny Temple	15.00	7.50
❑ 10 Willie Mays	225.00	110.00
❑ 11 George Zuverink	10.00	5.00
❑ 12 Dick Groat	20.00	10.00
❑ 13 Wally Burnette	10.00	5.00
❑ 14 Bob Nieman	10.00	5.00
❑ 15 Robin Roberts	30.00	15.00
❑ 16 Walt Moryn	10.00	5.00
❑ 17 Billy Gardner	10.00	5.00
❑ 18 Don Drysdale RC	225.00	110.00
❑ 19 Bob Wilson	10.00	5.00
❑ 20 Hank Aaron UER (Reverse negative photo on front)	250.00	125.00
❑ 21 Frank Sullivan	10.00	5.00
❑ 22 Jerry Snyder UER Photo actually Ed Fitzgerald	10.00	5.00
❑ 23 Sherm Lollar	15.00	7.50
❑ 24 Bill Mazeroski RC	75.00	38.00
❑ 25 Whitey Ford	100.00	50.00
❑ 26 Bob Boyd	10.00	5.00
❑ 27 Ted Kazanski	10.00	5.00
❑ 28 Gene Conley	15.00	7.50
❑ 29 Whitey Herzog RC	30.00	15.00
❑ 30 Pee Wee Reese	75.00	38.00
❑ 31 Ron Northey	10.00	5.00
❑ 32 Hershell Freeman	10.00	5.00
❑ 33 Jim Small	10.00	5.00
❑ 34 Tom Sturdivant	15.00	7.50
❑ 35 Frank Robinson RC	200.00	100.00
❑ 36 Bob Grim	10.00	5.00
❑ 37 Frank Torre	15.00	7.50
❑ 38 Nellie Fox	50.00	25.00
❑ 39 Al Worthington	10.00	5.00
❑ 40 Early Wynn	30.00	15.00
❑ 41 Hal W. Smith	10.00	5.00
❑ 42 Dee Fondy	10.00	5.00
❑ 43 Connie Johnson	10.00	5.00
❑ 44 Joe DeMaestri	10.00	5.00
❑ 45 Carl Furillo	30.00	15.00
❑ 46 Robert J. Miller	10.00	5.00
❑ 47 Don Blasingame	10.00	5.00
❑ 48 Bill Bruton	15.00	7.50
❑ 49 Daryl Spencer	10.00	5.00
❑ 50 Herb Score	30.00	15.00
❑ 51 Clint Courtney	10.00	5.00
❑ 52 Lee Walls	10.00	5.00
❑ 53 Clem Labine	20.00	10.00
❑ 54 Elmer Valo	10.00	5.00
❑ 55 Ernie Banks	125.00	60.00
❑ 56 Dave Sisler	10.00	5.00
❑ 57 Jim Lemon	15.00	7.50
❑ 58 Ruben Gomez	10.00	5.00
❑ 59 Dick Williams	15.00	7.50
❑ 60 Billy Hoeft	15.00	7.50
❑ 61 Dusty Rhodes	15.00	7.50
❑ 62 Billy Martin	50.00	25.00
❑ 63 Ike Delock	10.00	5.00
❑ 64 Pete Runnels	15.00	7.50
❑ 65 Wally Moon	15.00	7.50
❑ 66 Brooks Lawrence	10.00	5.00
❑ 67 Chico Carrasquel	10.00	5.00
❑ 68 Ray Crone	10.00	5.00
❑ 69 Roy McMillan	15.00	7.50
❑ 70 Richie Ashburn	50.00	25.00
❑ 71 Murry Dickson	10.00	5.00
❑ 72 Bill Tuttle	10.00	5.00
❑ 73 George Crowe	10.00	5.00
❑ 74 Vito Valentinetti	10.00	5.00
❑ 75 Jimmy Piersall	15.00	7.50
❑ 76 Roberto Clemente	300.00	150.00
❑ 77 Paul Foytack	10.00	5.00
❑ 78 Vic Wertz	15.00	7.50
❑ 79 Lindy McDaniel RC	15.00	7.50
❑ 80 Gil Hodges	50.00	25.00
❑ 81 Herman Wehmeier	10.00	5.00
❑ 82 Elston Howard	30.00	15.00
❑ 83 Lou Skizas	10.00	5.00
❑ 84 Moe Drabowsky	15.00	7.50
❑ 85 Larry Doby	30.00	15.00
❑ 86 Bill Sarni	10.00	5.00
❑ 87 Tom Gorman	10.00	5.00
❑ 88 Harvey Kuenn	15.00	7.50
❑ 89 Roy Sievers	15.00	7.50
❑ 90 Warren Spahn	90.00	45.00
❑ 91 Mack Burk	8.00	4.00
❑ 92 Mickey Vernon	15.00	7.50
❑ 93 Hal Jeffcoat	8.00	4.00
❑ 94 Bobby Del Greco	8.00	4.00
❑ 95 Mickey Mantle	1000.00	500.00
❑ 96 Hank Aguirre	8.00	4.00
❑ 97 New York Yankees Team Card	90.00	45.00
❑ 98 Alvin Dark	15.00	7.50
❑ 99 Bob Keegan	8.00	4.00
❑ 100 Warren Giles PRES Will Harridge PRES	15.00	7.50
❑ 101 Chuck Stobbs	8.00	4.00
❑ 102 Ray Boone	15.00	7.50
❑ 103 Joe Nuxhall	15.00	7.50
❑ 104 Hank Foiles	8.00	4.00
❑ 105 Johnny Antonelli	15.00	7.50
❑ 106 Ray Moore	8.00	4.00
❑ 107 Jim Rivera	8.00	4.00
❑ 108 Tommy Byrne	15.00	7.50
❑ 109 Hank Thompson	8.00	4.00
❑ 110 Bill Virdon	15.00	7.50
❑ 111 Hal R. Smith	8.00	4.00
❑ 112 Tom Brewer	8.00	4.00
❑ 113 Wilmer Mizell	15.00	7.50
❑ 114 Milwaukee Braves Team Card	20.00	10.00
❑ 115 Jim Gilliam	15.00	7.50
❑ 116 Mike Fornieles	8.00	4.00
❑ 117 Joe Adcock	20.00	10.00
❑ 118 Bob Porterfield	8.00	4.00
❑ 119 Stan Lopata	8.00	4.00
❑ 120 Bob Lemon	30.00	15.00
❑ 121 Clete Boyer RC	30.00	15.00
❑ 122 Ken Boyer	20.00	10.00
❑ 123 Steve Ridzik	8.00	4.00
❑ 124 Dave Philley	8.00	4.00
❑ 125 Al Kaline	100.00	50.00
❑ 126 Bob Wiesler	8.00	4.00
❑ 127 Bob Buhl	15.00	7.50
❑ 128 Ed Bailey	15.00	7.50
❑ 129 Saul Rogovin	8.00	4.00
❑ 130 Don Newcombe	20.00	10.00
❑ 131 Milt Bolling	8.00	4.00
❑ 132 Art Ditmar	15.00	7.50
❑ 133 Del Crandall	15.00	7.50
❑ 134 Don Kaiser	8.00	4.00
❑ 135 Bill Skowron	20.00	10.00
❑ 136 Jim Hegan	15.00	7.50
❑ 137 Bob Rush	8.00	4.00
❑ 138 Minnie Minoso	20.00	10.00
❑ 139 Lou Kretlow	8.00	4.00
❑ 140 Frank Thomas	15.00	7.50
❑ 141 Al Aber	8.00	4.00
❑ 142 Charley Thompson	8.00	4.00
❑ 143 Andy Pafko	15.00	7.50
❑ 144 Ray Narleski	8.00	4.00
❑ 145 Al Smith	8.00	4.00
❑ 146 Don Ferrarese	8.00	4.00
❑ 147 Al Walker	8.00	4.00
❑ 148 Don Mueller	15.00	7.50
❑ 149 Bob Kennedy	15.00	7.50
❑ 150 Bob Friend	15.00	7.50
❑ 151 Willie Miranda	8.00	4.00
❑ 152 Jack Harshman	8.00	4.00
❑ 153 Karl Olson	8.00	4.00
❑ 154 Red Schoendienst	30.00	15.00
❑ 155 Jim Brosnan	15.00	7.50
❑ 156 Gus Triandos	15.00	7.50
❑ 157 Wally Post	15.00	7.50
❑ 158 Curt Simmons	15.00	7.50
❑ 159 Solly Drake	8.00	4.00
❑ 160 Billy Pierce	15.00	7.50
❑ 161 Pittsburgh Pirates Team Card	15.00	7.50
❑ 162 Jack Meyer	8.00	4.00
❑ 163 Sammy White	8.00	4.00
❑ 164 Tommy Carroll	8.00	4.00
❑ 165 Ted Kluszewski	90.00	45.00
❑ 166 Roy Face	15.00	7.50
❑ 167 Vic Power	15.00	7.50
❑ 168 Frank Lary	15.00	7.50
❑ 169 Herb Plews	8.00	4.00
❑ 170 Duke Snider	125.00	60.00
❑ 171 Boston Red Sox Team Card	15.00	7.50
❑ 172 Gene Woodling	15.00	7.50
❑ 173 Roger Craig	15.00	7.50
❑ 174 Willie Jones	8.00	4.00
❑ 175 Don Larsen	30.00	15.00
❑ 176A Gene Baker ERR (Misspelled Bakep on card back)	350.00	180.00
❑ 176B Gene Baker COR	15.00	7.50
❑ 177 Eddie Yost	15.00	7.50
❑ 178 Don Bessent	8.00	4.00
❑ 179 Ernie Oravetz	8.00	4.00
❑ 180 Gus Bell	15.00	7.50
❑ 181 Dick Donovan	8.00	4.00
❑ 182 Hobie Landrith	8.00	4.00
❑ 183 Chicago Cubs Team Card	15.00	7.50
❑ 184 Tito Francona RC	8.00	4.00
❑ 185 Johnny Kucks	15.00	7.50
❑ 186 Jim King	15.00	7.50
❑ 187 Virgil Trucks	15.00	7.50
❑ 188 Felix Mantilla RC	15.00	7.50
❑ 189 Willard Nixon	8.00	4.00
❑ 190 Randy Jackson	8.00	4.00
❑ 191 Joe Margoneri	8.00	4.00
❑ 192 Jerry Coleman	15.00	7.50
❑ 193 Del Rice	8.00	4.00
❑ 194 Hal Brown	8.00	4.00
❑ 195 Bobby Avila	8.00	4.00
❑ 196 Larry Jackson	15.00	7.50
❑ 197 Hank Sauer	15.00	7.50
❑ 198 Detroit Tigers	15.00	7.50

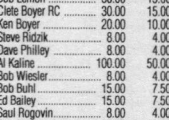

		Team Card		
❑	199	Vern Law	15.00	7.50
❑	200	Gil McDougald	15.00	7.50
❑	201	Sandy Amoros	15.00	7.50
❑	202	Dick Gernert	8.00	4.00
❑	203	Hoyt Wilhelm	30.00	15.00
❑	204	Kansas City Athletics	15.00	7.50
		Team Card		
❑	205	Charlie Maxwell	15.00	7.50
❑	206	Willard Schmidt	8.00	4.00
❑	207	Gordon(Billy) Hunter	8.00	4.00
❑	208	Lou Burdette	15.00	7.50
❑	209	Bob Skinner	15.00	7.50
❑	210	Roy Campanella	150.00	75.00
❑	211	Camilo Pascual	15.00	7.50
❑	212	Rocky Colavito RC	150.00	75.00
❑	213	Les Moss	8.00	4.00
❑	214	Philadelphia Phillies	15.00	7.50
		Team Card		
❑	215	Enos Slaughter	30.00	15.00
❑	216	Marv Grissom	8.00	4.00
❑	217	Gene Stephens	8.00	4.00
❑	218	Ray Jablonski	8.00	4.00
❑	219	Tom Acker	8.00	4.00
❑	220	Jackie Jensen	20.00	10.00
❑	221	Dixie Howell	8.00	4.00
❑	222	Alex Grammas	8.00	4.00
❑	223	Frank House	8.00	4.00
❑	224	Marv Blaylock	8.00	4.00
❑	225	Harry Simpson	8.00	4.00
❑	226	Preston Ward	8.00	4.00
❑	227	Gerry Staley	8.00	4.00
❑	228	Smoky Burgess UER	15.00	7.50
		(Misspelled Smokey on card back)		
❑	229	George Susce	8.00	4.00
❑	230	George Kell	30.00	15.00
❑	231	Solly Hemus	8.00	4.00
❑	232	Whitey Lockman	15.00	7.50
❑	233	Art Fowler	8.00	4.00
❑	234	Dick Cole	8.00	4.00
❑	235	Tom Poholsky	8.00	4.00
❑	236	Joe Ginsberg	8.00	4.00
❑	237	Foster Castleman	8.00	4.00
❑	238	Eddie Robinson	8.00	4.00
❑	239	Tom Morgan	8.00	4.00
❑	240	Hank Bauer	15.00	7.50
❑	241	Joe Lonnett	8.00	4.00
❑	242	Charlie Neal	15.00	7.50
❑	243	St. Louis Cardinals	15.00	7.50
		Team Card		
❑	244	Billy Loes	15.00	7.50
❑	245	Rip Repulski	8.00	4.00
❑	246	Jose Valdivielso	8.00	4.00
❑	247	Turk Lown	8.00	4.00
❑	248	Jim Finigan	8.00	4.00
❑	249	Dave Pope	8.00	4.00
❑	250	Eddie Mathews	50.00	25.00
❑	251	Baltimore Orioles	15.00	7.50
		Team Card		
❑	252	Carl Erskine	15.00	7.50
❑	253	Gus Zernial	15.00	7.50
❑	254	Ron Negray	8.00	4.00
❑	255	Charlie Silvera	15.00	7.50
❑	256	Ron Kline	8.00	4.00
❑	257	Walt Dropo	8.00	4.00
❑	258	Steve Gromek	8.00	4.00
❑	259	Eddie O'Brien	8.00	4.00
❑	260	Del Ennis	15.00	7.50
❑	261	Bob Chakales	8.00	4.00
❑	262	Bobby Thomson	15.00	7.50
❑	263	George Strickland	8.00	4.00
❑	264	Bob Turley	15.00	7.50
❑	265	Harvey Haddix DP	13.00	6.50
❑	266	Ken Kuhn DP	13.00	6.50
❑	267	Danny Kravitz	20.00	10.00
❑	268	Jack Collum	20.00	10.00
❑	269	Bob Cerv	30.00	15.00
❑	270	Washington Senators	60.00	30.00
		Team Card		
❑	271	Danny O'Connell DP	13.00	6.50
❑	272	Bobby Shantz	30.00	15.00
❑	273	Jim Davis	20.00	10.00
❑	274	Don Hoak	15.00	7.50
❑	275	Cleveland Indians	60.00	30.00
		Team Card UER		
		(Text on back credits Tribe with winning AL title in '28. The Yankees won that year.)		
❑	276	Jim Pyburn	20.00	10.00
❑	277	Johnny Podres DP	45.00	22.00
❑	278	Fred Hatfield DP	13.00	6.50
❑	279	Bob Thurman	20.00	10.00
❑	280	Alex Kellner	20.00	10.00
❑	281	Gail Harris	20.00	10.00
❑	282	Jack Dittmer DP	13.00	6.50
❑	283	Wes Covington DP	13.00	6.50
❑	284	Don Zimmer	45.00	22.00
❑	285	Ned Garver	20.00	10.00
❑	286	Bobby Richardson RC	125.00	60.00
❑	287	Sam Jones	20.00	10.00
❑	288	Ted Lepcio	20.00	10.00
❑	289	Jim Bolger DP	13.00	6.50
❑	290	Andy Carey DP	40.00	20.00
❑	291	Windy McCall	20.00	10.00
❑	292	Billy Klaus	20.00	10.00
❑	293	Ted Abernathy	20.00	10.00
❑	294	Rocky Bridges DP	13.00	6.50
❑	295	Joe Collins DP	40.00	20.00
❑	296	Johnny Klippstein	20.00	10.00
❑	297	Jack Crimian	20.00	10.00
❑	298	Irv Noren DP	13.00	6.50
❑	299	Chuck Harmon	20.00	10.00
❑	300	Mike Garcia	30.00	15.00
❑	301	Sammy Esposito DP	20.00	10.00
❑	302	Sandy Koufax DP	300.00	150.00
❑	303	Billy Goodman	30.00	15.00
❑	304	Joe Cunningham	30.00	15.00
❑	305	Chico Fernandez	20.00	10.00
❑	306	Darrell Johnson DP	13.00	6.50
❑	307	Jack D. Phillips DP	13.00	6.50
❑	308	Dick Hall	20.00	10.00
❑	309	Jim Busby DP	13.00	6.50
❑	310	Max Surkont DP	13.00	6.50
❑	311	Al Pilarcik DP	13.00	6.50
❑	312	Tony Kubek DP RC	90.00	45.00
❑	313	Mel Parnell	15.00	7.50
❑	314	Ed Bouchee DP	13.00	6.50
❑	315	Lou Berberet DP	13.00	6.50
❑	316	Billy O'Dell	20.00	10.00
❑	317	New York Giants	75.00	38.00
		Team Card		
❑	318	Mickey McDermott	20.00	10.00
❑	319	Gino Cimoli RC	20.00	10.00
❑	320	Neil Chrisley	20.00	10.00
❑	321	John(Red) Murff	20.00	10.00
❑	322	Cincinnati Reds	75.00	38.00
		Team Card		
❑	323	Wes Westrum	30.00	15.00
❑	324	Brooklyn Dodgers	125.00	60.00
		Team Card		
❑	325	Frank Bolling	20.00	10.00
❑	326	Pedro Ramos	20.00	10.00
❑	327	Jim Pendleton	20.00	10.00
❑	328	Brooks Robinson RC	350.00	180.00
❑	329	Chicago White Sox	60.00	30.00
		Team Card		
❑	330	Jim Wilson	20.00	10.00
❑	331	Ray Katt	20.00	10.00
❑	332	Bob Bowman	20.00	10.00
❑	333	Ernie Johnson	20.00	10.00
❑	334	Jerry Schoonmaker	20.00	10.00
❑	335	Granny Hamner	20.00	10.00
❑	336	Haywood Sullivan RC	40.00	20.00
❑	337	Rene Valdes	20.00	10.00
❑	338	Jim Bunning RC	125.00	60.00
❑	339	Bob Speake	20.00	10.00
❑	340	Bill Wight	20.00	10.00
❑	341	Don Gross	20.00	10.00
❑	342	Gene Mauch	30.00	15.00
❑	343	Taylor Phillips	15.00	7.50
❑	344	Paul LaPalme	20.00	10.00
❑	345	Paul Smith	20.00	10.00
❑	346	Dick Littlefield	20.00	10.00
❑	347	Hal Naragon	20.00	10.00
❑	348	Jim Hearn	20.00	10.00
❑	349	Nellie King	20.00	10.00
❑	350	Eddie Miksis	20.00	10.00
❑	351	Dave Hillman	20.00	10.00
❑	352	Ellis Kinder	20.00	10.00
❑	353	Cal Neeman	8.00	4.00
❑	354	Rip Coleman	8.00	4.00
❑	355	Frank Malzone	15.00	7.50
❑	356	Faye Throneberry	8.00	4.00
❑	357	Earl Torgeson	8.00	4.00
❑	358	Jerry Lynch	15.00	7.50
❑	359	Tom Cheney	8.00	4.00
❑	360	Johnny Groth	8.00	4.00
❑	361	Curt Barclay	8.00	4.00
❑	362	Roman Mejias	15.00	7.50
❑	363	Eddie Kasko	8.00	4.00
❑	364	Cal McLish	15.00	7.50
❑	365	Ozzie Virgil	8.00	4.00
❑	366	Ken Lehman	8.00	4.00
❑	367	Ed Fitzgerald	8.00	4.00
❑	368	Bob Purkey	8.00	4.00
❑	369	Milt Graff	8.00	4.00
❑	370	Warren Hacker	8.00	4.00
❑	371	Bob Lennon	8.00	4.00
❑	372	Norm Zauchin	8.00	4.00
❑	373	Pete Whisenant	8.00	4.00
❑	374	Don Cardwell	8.00	4.00
❑	375	Jim Landis	15.00	7.50
❑	376	Don Elston	8.00	4.00
❑	377	Andre Rodgers	8.00	4.00
❑	378	Elmer Singleton	8.00	4.00
❑	379	Don Lee	8.00	4.00
❑	380	Walker Cooper	8.00	4.00
❑	381	Dean Stone	8.00	4.00
❑	382	Jim Brideweser	8.00	4.00
❑	383	Juan Pizarro	8.00	4.00
❑	384	Bobby G. Smith	8.00	4.00
❑	385	Art Houtteman	8.00	4.00
❑	386	Lyle Luttrell	8.00	4.00
❑	387	Jack Sanford RC	15.00	7.50
❑	388	Pete Daley	8.00	4.00
❑	389	Dave Jolly	8.00	4.00
❑	390	Reno Bertoia	8.00	4.00
❑	391	Ralph Terry RC	15.00	7.50
❑	392	Chuck Tanner	15.00	7.50
❑	393	Raul Sanchez	8.00	4.00
❑	394	Luis Arroyo	15.00	7.50
❑	395	Bubba Phillips	8.00	4.00
❑	396	Casey Wise	8.00	4.00
❑	397	Roy Smalley	8.00	4.00
❑	398	Al Cicotte	15.00	7.50
❑	399	Billy Consolo	8.00	4.00
❑	400	Carl Furillo	250.00	125.00
		Gil Hodges		
		Roy Campanella		
		Duke Snider		
❑	401	Earl Battey RC	15.00	7.50
❑	402	Jim Pisoni	8.00	4.00
❑	403	Dick Hyde	8.00	4.00
❑	404	Harry Anderson	8.00	4.00
❑	405	Duke Maas	8.00	4.00
❑	406	Bob Hale	8.00	4.00
❑	407	Mickey Mantle	500.00	150.00
		Yogi Berra		
❑	CC1	Contest Card	90.00	22.00
		Saturday, May 4th		
		Boston Red Sox		
		vs. Cleveland Indians		
		Cincinnati Redlegs		
		vs. New York Giants		
❑	CC2	Contest Card	90.00	22.00
		Saturday, May 25th		
		Detroit Tigers		
		vs. Kansas City Athletics		
		Pittsburgh Pirates		
		vs. Philadelphia Phillies		
❑	CC3	Contest Card	120.00	30.00
		Saturday, June 22nd		
		Brooklyn Dodgers		
		vs. St. Louis Cardinals		
		Chicago White Sox		
		vs. New York Yankees		
❑	CC4	Contest Card	120.00	30.00
		Saturday, July 19th		
		Milwaukee Braves		
		vs. New York Giants		
		Baltimore Orioles		
		vs. Kansas City Athletics		
❑	NNO	Checklist 1/2	250.00	75.00
		Bazooka Back		
❑	NNO	Checklist 1/2	250.00	125.00
		Blony Back		
❑	NNO	Checklist 2/3	400.00	100.00

	NM	Ex
Bazooka Back		
❑ NNO Checklist 2/3	400.00	200.00
Blony Back		
❑ NNO Checklist 3/4	750.00	170.00
Bazooka Back		
❑ NNO Checklist 3/4	750.00	375.00
Blony Back		
❑ NNO Checklist 4/5	900.00	200.00
Bazooka Back		
❑ NNO Checklist 4/5	900.00	450.00
Blony Back		
❑ NNO Lucky Penny Charm and Key Chain offer card	100.00	50.00

1958 Topps

	NM	Ex
COMP. MASTER (534)	12000.00	6000.00
COMPLETE SET (494)	6000.00	3000.00
COMMON CARD (1-110)	12.00	6.00
COMMON (111-495)	8.00	4.00
WRAPPER (1-CENT)	100.00	50.00
WRAPPER (5-CENT)	125.00	60.00

	NM	Ex
❑ 1 Ted Williams	500.00	180.00
❑ 2A Bob Lemon	30.00	15.00
❑ 2B Bob Lemon YT	60.00	30.00
❑ 3 Alex Kellner	12.00	6.00
❑ 4 Hank Foiles	12.00	6.00
❑ 5 Willie Mays	250.00	125.00
❑ 6 George Zuverink	12.00	6.00
❑ 7 Dale Long	15.00	7.50
❑ 8A Eddie Kasko	12.00	6.00
❑ 8B Eddie Kasko YN	45.00	22.00
❑ 9 Hank Bauer	20.00	10.00
❑ 10 Lou Burdette	20.00	10.00
❑ 11A Jim Rivera	12.00	6.00
❑ 11B Jim Rivera YT	45.00	22.00
❑ 12 George Crowe	12.00	6.00
❑ 13A Billy Hoeft	12.00	6.00
❑ 13B Billy Hoeft YN	45.00	22.00
❑ 14 Rip Repulski	12.00	6.00
❑ 15 Jim Lemon	15.00	7.50
❑ 16 Charlie Neal	15.00	7.50
❑ 17 Felix Mantilla	12.00	6.00
❑ 18 Frank Sullivan	12.00	6.00
❑ 19 Giants Team Card CL	40.00	8.00
❑ 20A Gil McDougald	20.00	10.00
❑ 20B Gil McDougald YN	60.00	30.00
❑ 21 Curt Barclay	12.00	6.00
❑ 22 Hal Naragon	12.00	6.00
❑ 23A Bill Tuttle	12.00	6.00
❑ 23B Bill Tuttle YN	45.00	22.00
❑ 24A Hobie Landrith	12.00	6.00
❑ 24B Hobie Landrith YN	45.00	22.00
❑ 25 Don Drysdale	75.00	38.00
❑ 26 Ron Jackson	12.00	6.00
❑ 27 Bud Freeman	12.00	6.00
❑ 28 Jim Busby	12.00	6.00
❑ 29 Ted Lepcio	12.00	6.00
❑ 30A Hank Aaron	200.00	100.00
❑ 30B Hank Aaron YN	500.00	250.00
❑ 31 Tex Clevenger	12.00	6.00
❑ 32A J.W. Porter	12.00	6.00
❑ 32B J.W. Porter YN	45.00	22.00
❑ 33A Cal Neeman	12.00	6.00
❑ 33B Cal Neeman YT	45.00	22.00
❑ 34 Bob Thurman	12.00	6.00
❑ 35A Don Mossi	15.00	7.50
❑ 35B Don Mossi YT	45.00	22.00
❑ 36 Ted Kazanski	12.00	6.00
❑ 37 Mike McCormick RC UER Photo actually Ray Monzant	15.00	7.50
❑ 38 Dick Gernert	12.00	6.00
❑ 39 Bob Martyn	12.00	6.00
❑ 40 George Kell	30.00	15.00
❑ 41 Dave Hillman	12.00	6.00
❑ 42 John Roseboro RC	30.00	15.00
❑ 43 Sal Maglie	15.00	7.50
❑ 44 Washington Senators Team Card CL	20.00	4.00
❑ 45 Dick Groat	15.00	7.50
❑ 46A Lou Sleater	12.00	6.00
❑ 46B Lou Sleater YN	45.00	22.00
❑ 47 Roger Maris RC	400.00	200.00
❑ 48 Chuck Harmon	12.00	6.00
❑ 49 Smoky Burgess	15.00	7.50
❑ 50A Billy Pierce	15.00	7.50
❑ 50B Billy Pierce YT	45.00	22.00
❑ 51 Del Rice	12.00	6.00
❑ 52A Roberto Clemente	300.00	150.00
❑ 52B Roberto Clemente YT	500.00	250.00
❑ 53A Morrie Martin	12.00	6.00
❑ 53B Morrie Martin YN	45.00	22.00
❑ 54 Norm Siebern RC	20.00	10.00
❑ 55 Chico Carrasquel	12.00	6.00
❑ 56 Bill Fischer	12.00	6.00
❑ 57A Tim Thompson	12.00	6.00
❑ 57B Tim Thompson YN	45.00	22.00
❑ 58A Art Schult	12.00	6.00
❑ 58B Art Schult YT	45.00	22.00
❑ 59 Dave Sisler	12.00	6.00
❑ 60A Del Ennis	15.00	7.50
❑ 60B Del Ennis YN	45.00	22.00
❑ 61A Darrell Johnson	12.00	6.00
❑ 61B Darrell Johnson YN	45.00	22.00
❑ 62 Joe DeMaestri	12.00	6.00
❑ 63 Joe Nuxhall	15.00	7.50
❑ 64 Joe Lonnett	12.00	6.00
❑ 65A Von McDaniel RC	12.00	6.00
❑ 65B Von McDaniel YL RC	45.00	22.00
❑ 66 Lee Walls	12.00	6.00
❑ 67 Joe Ginsberg	12.00	6.00
❑ 68 Daryl Spencer	12.00	6.00
❑ 69 Wally Burnette	12.00	6.00
❑ 70A Al Kaline	100.00	50.00
❑ 70B Al Kaline YN	250.00	125.00
❑ 71 Dodgers Team CL	60.00	12.00
❑ 72 Bud Byerly	12.00	6.00
❑ 73 Pete Daley	12.00	6.00
❑ 74 Roy Face	15.00	7.50
❑ 75 Gus Bell	15.00	7.50
❑ 76A Dick Farrell	12.00	6.00
❑ 76B Dick Farrell YT	45.00	22.00
❑ 77A Don Zimmer	15.00	7.50
❑ 77B Don Zimmer YT	45.00	22.00
❑ 78A Ernie Johnson	15.00	7.50
❑ 78B Ernie Johnson YN	45.00	22.00
❑ 79A Dick Williams	15.00	7.50
❑ 79B Dick Williams YT	45.00	22.00
❑ 80 Dick Drott	12.00	6.00
❑ 81A Steve Boros RC	12.00	6.00
❑ 81B Steve Boros YT RC	45.00	22.00
❑ 82 Ron Kline	12.00	6.00
❑ 83 Bob Hazle RC	12.00	6.00
❑ 84 Billy O'Dell	12.00	6.00
❑ 85A Luis Aparicio	30.00	15.00
❑ 85B Luis Aparicio YT	75.00	38.00
❑ 86 Valmy Thomas	12.00	6.00
❑ 87 Johnny Kucks	12.00	6.00
❑ 88 Duke Snider	75.00	38.00
❑ 89 Billy Klaus	12.00	6.00
❑ 90 Robin Roberts	30.00	15.00
❑ 91 Chuck Tanner	15.00	7.50
❑ 92A Clint Courtney	12.00	6.00
❑ 92B Clint Courtney YN	45.00	22.00
❑ 93 Sandy Amoros	15.00	7.50
❑ 94 Bob Skinner	15.00	7.50
❑ 95 Frank Bolling	12.00	6.00
❑ 96 Joe Durham	12.00	6.00
❑ 97A Larry Jackson	12.00	6.00
❑ 97B Larry Jackson YN	45.00	22.00
❑ 98A Billy Hunter	12.00	6.00
❑ 98B Billy Hunter YN	45.00	22.00
❑ 99 Bobby Adams	12.00	6.00
❑ 100A Early Wynn	30.00	15.00
❑ 100B Early Wynn YT	75.00	38.00
❑ 101A Bobby Richardson	30.00	15.00
❑ 101B B.Richardson YN	60.00	30.00
❑ 102 George Strickland	12.00	6.00
❑ 103 Jerry Lynch	15.00	7.50
❑ 104 Jim Pendleton	12.00	6.00
❑ 105 Billy Gardner	12.00	6.00
❑ 106 Dick Schofield	15.00	7.50
❑ 107 Ossie Virgil	12.00	6.00
❑ 108A Jim Landis	12.00	6.00
❑ 108B Jim Landis YT	45.00	22.00
❑ 109 Herb Plews	12.00	6.00
❑ 110 Johnny Logan	15.00	7.50
❑ 111 Stu Miller	10.00	5.00
❑ 112 Gus Zernial	10.00	5.00
❑ 113 Jerry Walker RC	8.00	4.00
❑ 114 Irv Noren	10.00	5.00
❑ 115 Jim Bunning	30.00	15.00
❑ 116 Dave Philley	8.00	4.00
❑ 117 Frank Torre	10.00	5.00
❑ 118 Harvey Haddix	10.00	5.00
❑ 119 Harry Chiti	8.00	4.00
❑ 120 Johnny Podres	10.00	5.00
❑ 121 Eddie Miksis	8.00	4.00
❑ 122 Walt Moryn	8.00	4.00
❑ 123 Dick Tomanek	8.00	4.00
❑ 124 Bobby Usher	8.00	4.00
❑ 125 Alvin Dark	10.00	5.00
❑ 126 Stan Palys	8.00	4.00
❑ 127 Tom Sturdivant	10.00	5.00
❑ 128 Willie Kirkland	8.00	4.00
❑ 129 Jim Derrington	8.00	4.00
❑ 130 Jackie Jensen	10.00	5.00
❑ 131 Bob Henrich	8.00	4.00
❑ 132 Vern Law	10.00	5.00
❑ 133 Russ Nixon RC	8.00	4.00
❑ 134 Philadelphia Phillies Team Card CL	15.00	3.00
❑ 135 Mike(Moe)Drabowsky	10.00	5.00
❑ 136 Jim Finigan	8.00	4.00
❑ 137 Russ Kemmerer	8.00	4.00
❑ 138 Earl Torgeson	8.00	4.00
❑ 139 George Brunet	8.00	4.00
❑ 140 Wes Covington	10.00	5.00
❑ 141 Ken Lehman	8.00	4.00
❑ 142 Enos Slaughter	25.00	12.50
❑ 143 Billy Muffett RC	8.00	4.00
❑ 144 Bobby Morgan	8.00	4.00
❑ 145 Never issued	-	-
❑ 146 Dick Gray	8.00	4.00
❑ 147 Don McMahon RC	8.00	4.00
❑ 148 Billy Consolo	8.00	4.00
❑ 149 Tom Acker	8.00	4.00
❑ 150 Mickey Mantle	800.00	400.00
❑ 151 Buddy Pritchard	8.00	4.00
❑ 152 Johnny Antonelli	10.00	5.00
❑ 153 Les Moss	8.00	4.00
❑ 154 Harry Byrd	8.00	4.00
❑ 155 Hector Lopez	10.00	5.00
❑ 156 Dick Hyde	8.00	4.00
❑ 157 Dee Fondy	8.00	4.00
❑ 158 Cleveland Indians Team Card CL	15.00	3.00
❑ 159 Taylor Phillips	8.00	4.00
❑ 160 Don Hoak	10.00	5.00
❑ 161 Don Larsen	15.00	7.50
❑ 162 Gil Hodges	40.00	20.00
❑ 163 Jim Wilson	8.00	4.00
❑ 164 Bob Taylor	8.00	4.00
❑ 165 Bob Nieman	8.00	4.00
❑ 166 Danny O'Connell	8.00	4.00
❑ 167 Frank Baumann	8.00	4.00
❑ 168 Joe Cunningham	8.00	4.00
❑ 169 Ralph Terry	10.00	5.00
❑ 170 Vic Wertz	10.00	5.00
❑ 171 Harry Anderson	8.00	4.00
❑ 172 Don Gross	8.00	4.00
❑ 173 Eddie Yost	8.00	4.00
❑ 174 K.C. Athletics Team CL	15.00	3.00
❑ 175 Marv Throneberry RC	15.00	7.50
❑ 176 Bob Buhl	10.00	5.00
❑ 177 Al Smith	8.00	4.00

❑ 178 Ted Kluszewski 25.00 12.50
❑ 179 Willie Miranda 8.00 4.00
❑ 180 Lindy McDaniel 10.00 5.00
❑ 181 Willie Jones 8.00 4.00
❑ 182 Joe Caffie 8.00 4.00
❑ 183 Dave Jolly 8.00 4.00
❑ 184 Elvin Tappe 8.00 4.00
❑ 185 Ray Boone 10.00 5.00
❑ 186 Jack Meyer 8.00 4.00
❑ 187 Sandy Koufax 225.00 110.00
❑ 188 Milt Bolling UER 8.00 4.00
(Photo actually
Lou Berberet)
❑ 189 George Susce 8.00 4.00
❑ 190 Red Schoendienst 25.00 12.50
❑ 191 Art Ceccarelli 8.00 4.00
❑ 192 Milt Graff 8.00 4.00
❑ 193 Jerry Lumpe RC 8.00 4.00
❑ 194 Roger Craig 10.00 5.00
❑ 195 Whitey Lockman 10.00 5.00
❑ 196 Mike Garcia 10.00 5.00
❑ 197 Haywood Sullivan 10.00 5.00
❑ 198 Bill Virdon 10.00 5.00
❑ 199 Don Blasingame 8.00 4.00
❑ 200 Bob Keegan 8.00 4.00
❑ 201 Jim Bolger 8.00 4.00
❑ 202 Woody Held RC 8.00 4.00
❑ 203 Al Walker 8.00 4.00
❑ 204 Leo Kiely 8.00 4.00
❑ 205 Johnny Temple 10.00 5.00
❑ 206 Bob Shaw RC 8.00 4.00
❑ 207 Solly Hemus 8.00 4.00
❑ 208 Cal McLish 8.00 4.00
❑ 209 Bob Anderson 8.00 4.00
❑ 210 Wally Moon 10.00 5.00
❑ 211 Pete Burnside 8.00 4.00
❑ 212 Bubba Phillips 8.00 4.00
❑ 213 Red Wilson 8.00 4.00
❑ 214 Willard Schmidt 8.00 4.00
❑ 215 Jim Gilliam 15.00 7.50
❑ 216 St. Louis Cardinals 15.00 3.00
Team Card CL
❑ 217 Jack Harshman 8.00 4.00
❑ 218 Dick Rand 8.00 4.00
❑ 219 Camilo Pascual 10.00 5.00
❑ 220 Tom Brewer 8.00 4.00
❑ 221 Jerry Kindall RC 8.00 4.00
❑ 222 Bud Daley 8.00 4.00
❑ 223 Andy Pafko 10.00 5.00
❑ 224 Bob Grim 10.00 5.00
❑ 225 Billy Goodman 10.00 5.00
❑ 226 Bob Smith 8.00 4.00
❑ 227 Gene Stephens 8.00 4.00
❑ 228 Duke Maas 8.00 4.00
❑ 229 Frank Zupo 8.00 4.00
❑ 230 Richie Ashburn 40.00 20.00
❑ 231 Lloyd Merritt 8.00 4.00
❑ 232 Reno Bertoia 8.00 4.00
❑ 233 Mickey Vernon 10.00 5.00
❑ 234 Carl Sawatski 8.00 4.00
❑ 235 Tom Gorman 8.00 4.00
❑ 236 Ed Fitzgerald 8.00 4.00
❑ 237 Bill Wight 8.00 4.00
❑ 238 Bill Mazeroski 30.00 15.00
❑ 239 Chuck Stobbs 8.00 4.00
❑ 240 Bill Skowron 25.00 12.50
❑ 241 Dick Littlefield 8.00 4.00
❑ 242 Johnny Klippstein 8.00 4.00
❑ 243 Larry Raines 8.00 4.00
❑ 244 Don Demeter 8.00 4.00
❑ 245 Frank Lary 10.00 5.00
❑ 246 New York Yankees 100.00 20.00
Team Card CL
❑ 247 Casey Wise 8.00 4.00
❑ 248 Herman Wehmeier 8.00 4.00
❑ 249 Ray Moore 8.00 4.00
❑ 250 Roy Sievers 10.00 5.00
❑ 251 Warren Hacker 8.00 4.00
❑ 252 Bob Trowbridge 8.00 4.00
❑ 253 Don Mueller 10.00 5.00
❑ 254 Alex Grammas 8.00 4.00
❑ 255 Bob Turley 10.00 5.00
❑ 256 Chicago White Sox 15.00 3.00
Team Card CL
❑ 257 Hal Smith 8.00 4.00
❑ 258 Carl Erskine 15.00 7.50
❑ 259 Al Pilarcik 8.00 4.00
❑ 260 Frank Malzone 10.00 5.00
❑ 261 Turk Lown 8.00 4.00
❑ 262 Johnny Groth 8.00 4.00
❑ 263 Eddie Bressoud 10.00 5.00
❑ 264 Jack Sanford 10.00 5.00
❑ 265 Pete Runnels 10.00 5.00
❑ 266 Connie Johnson 8.00 4.00
❑ 267 Sherm Lollar 10.00 5.00
❑ 268 Granny Hamner 8.00 4.00
❑ 269 Paul Smith 8.00 4.00
❑ 270 Warren Spahn 60.00 30.00
❑ 271 Billy Martin 40.00 20.00
❑ 272 Ray Crone 8.00 4.00
❑ 273 Hal Smith 8.00 4.00
❑ 274 Rocky Bridges 8.00 4.00
❑ 275 Elston Howard 15.00 7.50
❑ 276 Bobby Avila 8.00 4.00
❑ 277 Virgil Trucks 10.00 5.00
❑ 278 Mack Burk 8.00 4.00
❑ 279 Bob Boyd 8.00 4.00
❑ 280 Jim Piersall 10.00 5.00
❑ 281 Sammy Taylor 8.00 4.00
❑ 282 Paul Foytack 8.00 4.00
❑ 283 Ray Shearer 8.00 4.00
❑ 284 Ray Katt 8.00 4.00
❑ 285 Frank Robinson 100.00 50.00
❑ 286 Gino Cimoli 8.00 4.00
❑ 287 Sam Jones 10.00 5.00
❑ 288 Harmon Killebrew 90.00 45.00
❑ 289 Lou Burdette 10.00 5.00
Bobby Shantz
❑ 290 Dick Donovan 8.00 4.00
❑ 291 Don Landrum 8.00 4.00
❑ 292 Ned Garver 8.00 4.00
❑ 293 Gene Freese 8.00 4.00
❑ 294 Hal Jeffcoat 8.00 4.00
❑ 295 Minnie Minoso 25.00 12.50
❑ 296 Ryne Duren RC 15.00 7.50
❑ 297 Don Buddin 8.00 4.00
❑ 298 Jim Hearn 8.00 4.00
❑ 299 Harry Simpson 8.00 4.00
❑ 300 Will Harridge PRES 15.00 7.50
Warren Giles
❑ 301 Randy Jackson 8.00 4.00
❑ 302 Mike Baxes 8.00 4.00
❑ 303 Neil Chrisley 8.00 4.00
❑ 304 Harvey Kuenn 25.00 12.50
Al Kaline
❑ 305 Clem Labine 10.00 5.00
❑ 306 Whammy Douglas 8.00 4.00
❑ 307 Brooks Robinson 100.00 50.00
❑ 308 Paul Giel 10.00 5.00
❑ 309 Gail Harris 8.00 4.00
❑ 310 Ernie Banks 100.00 50.00
❑ 311 Bob Purkey 8.00 4.00
❑ 312 Boston Red Sox 15.00 3.00
Team Card CL
❑ 313 Bob Rush 8.00 4.00
❑ 314 Duke Snider 50.00 25.00
Walt Alston MG
❑ 315 Bob Friend 10.00 5.00
❑ 316 Tito Francona 10.00 5.00
❑ 317 Albie Pearson 10.00 5.00
❑ 318 Frank House 8.00 4.00
❑ 319 Lou Skizas 8.00 4.00
❑ 320 Whitey Ford 60.00 30.00
❑ 321 Ted Kluszewski 75.00 38.00
Ted Williams
❑ 322 Harding Peterson 10.00 5.00
❑ 323 Elmer Valo 8.00 4.00
❑ 324 Hoyt Wilhelm 25.00 12.50
❑ 325 Joe Adcock 10.00 5.00
❑ 326 Bob Miller 8.00 4.00
❑ 327 Chicago Cubs 15.00 3.00
Team Card CL
❑ 328 Ike Delock 8.00 4.00
❑ 329 Bob Cerv 10.00 5.00
❑ 330 Ed Bailey 10.00 5.00
❑ 331 Pedro Ramos 8.00 4.00
❑ 332 Jim King 8.00 4.00
❑ 333 Andy Carey 10.00 5.00
❑ 334 Bob Friend 10.00 5.00
Billy Pierce
❑ 335 Ruben Gomez 8.00 4.00
❑ 336 Bert Hamric 8.00 4.00
❑ 337 Hank Aguirre 8.00 4.00
❑ 338 Walt Dropo 10.00 5.00
❑ 339 Fred Hatfield 8.00 4.00
❑ 340 Don Newcombe 15.00 7.50
❑ 341 Pittsburgh Pirates 15.00 3.00
Team Card CL
❑ 342 Jim Brosnan 10.00 5.00
❑ 343 Orlando Cepeda RC 100.00 50.00
❑ 344 Bob Porterfield 8.00 4.00
❑ 345 Jim Hegan 10.00 5.00
❑ 346 Steve Bilko 8.00 4.00
❑ 347 Don Rudolph 8.00 4.00
❑ 348 Chico Fernandez 8.00 4.00
❑ 349 Murry Dickson 8.00 4.00
❑ 350 Ken Boyer 25.00 12.50
❑ 351 Del Crandall 40.00 20.00
Eddie Mathews
Hank Aaron
Joe Adcock
❑ 352 Herb Score 15.00 7.50
❑ 353 Stan Lopata 8.00 4.00
❑ 354 Art Ditmar 10.00 5.00
❑ 355 Bill Bruton 10.00 5.00
❑ 356 Bob Malkmus 8.00 4.00
❑ 357 Danny McDevitt 8.00 4.00
❑ 358 Gene Baker 8.00 4.00
❑ 359 Billy Loes 10.00 5.00
❑ 360 Roy McMillan 10.00 5.00
❑ 361 Mike Fornieles 8.00 4.00
❑ 362 Ray Jablonski 8.00 4.00
❑ 363 Don Elston 8.00 4.00
❑ 364 Earl Battey 8.00 4.00
❑ 365 Tom Morgan 8.00 4.00
❑ 366 Gene Green 8.00 4.00
❑ 367 Jack Urban 8.00 4.00
❑ 368 Rocky Colavito 50.00 25.00
❑ 369 Ralph Lumenti 8.00 4.00
❑ 370 Yogi Berra 100.00 50.00
❑ 371 Marty Keough 8.00 4.00
❑ 372 Don Cardwell 8.00 4.00
❑ 373 Joe Pignatano 8.00 4.00
❑ 374 Brooks Lawrence 8.00 4.00
❑ 375 Pee Wee Reese 75.00 38.00
❑ 376 Charley Rabe 8.00 4.00
❑ 377A Milwaukee Braves 15.00 7.50
Team Card
(Alphabetical)
❑ 377B Milwaukee Team 100.00 20.00
numerical checklist
❑ 378 Hank Sauer 10.00 5.00
❑ 379 Ray Herbert 8.00 4.00
❑ 380 Charlie Maxwell 10.00 5.00
❑ 381 Hal Brown 8.00 4.00
❑ 382 Al Cicotte 8.00 4.00
❑ 383 Lou Berberet 8.00 4.00
❑ 384 John Goryl 8.00 4.00
❑ 385 Wilmer Mizell 10.00 5.00
❑ 386 Ed Bailey 15.00 7.50
Birdie Tebbetts MG
Frank Robinson
❑ 387 Wally Post 10.00 5.00
❑ 388 Billy Moran 8.00 4.00
❑ 389 Bill Taylor 8.00 4.00
❑ 390 Del Crandall 10.00 5.00
❑ 391 Dave Melton 8.00 4.00
❑ 392 Bennie Daniels 8.00 4.00
❑ 393 Tony Kubek 30.00 15.00
❑ 394 Jim Grant RC 8.00 4.00
❑ 395 Willard Nixon 8.00 4.00
❑ 396 Dutch Dotterer 8.00 4.00
❑ 397A Detroit Tigers 15.00 7.50
Team Card
(Alphabetical)
❑ 397B Detroit Team 100.00 20.00
numerical checklist
❑ 398 Gene Woodling 10.00 5.00
❑ 399 Marv Grissom 8.00 4.00
❑ 400 Nellie Fox 30.00 15.00
❑ 401 Don Bessent 8.00 4.00
❑ 402 Bobby Gene Smith 8.00 4.00
❑ 403 Steve Korcheck 8.00 4.00
❑ 404 Curt Simmons 10.00 5.00
❑ 405 Ken Aspromonte 8.00 4.00
❑ 406 Vic Power 10.00 5.00
❑ 407 Carlton Willey 10.00 5.00
❑ 408A Baltimore Orioles 15.00 7.50

Card	NM	Ex
Team Card		
(Alphabetical)		
❑ 408B Baltimore Team	100.00	20.00
numerical checklist		
❑ 409 Frank Thomas	10.00	5.00
❑ 410 Murray Wall	8.00	4.00
❑ 411 Tony Taylor RC	10.00	5.00
❑ 412 Gerry Staley	8.00	4.00
❑ 413 Jim Davenport RC	8.00	4.00
❑ 414 Sammy White	8.00	4.00
❑ 415 Bob Bowman	8.00	4.00
❑ 416 Foster Castleman	8.00	4.00
❑ 417 Carl Furillo	15.00	7.50
❑ 418 Mickey Mantle	350.00	180.00
Hank Aaron		
❑ 419 Bobby Shantz	10.00	5.00
❑ 420 Vada Pinson RC	40.00	20.00
❑ 421 Dixie Howell	8.00	4.00
❑ 422 Norm Zauchin	8.00	4.00
❑ 423 Phil Clark	8.00	4.00
❑ 424 Larry Doby	25.00	12.50
❑ 425 Sammy Esposito	8.00	4.00
❑ 426 Johnny O'Brien	10.00	5.00
❑ 427 Al Worthington	8.00	4.00
❑ 428A Cincinnati Reds	15.00	7.50
Team Card		
(Alphabetical)		
❑ 428B Cincinnati Team	100.00	20.00
numerical checklist		
❑ 429 Gus Triandos	10.00	5.00
❑ 430 Bobby Thomson	10.00	5.00
❑ 431 Gene Conley	10.00	5.00
❑ 432 John Powers	8.00	4.00
❑ 433A Pancho Herrer ERR	650.00	325.00
❑ 433B Pancho Herrera COR	10.00	5.00
❑ 434 Harvey Kuenn	10.00	5.00
❑ 435 Ed Roebuck	10.00	5.00
❑ 436 Willie Mays	75.00	38.00
Duke Snider		
❑ 437 Bob Speake	8.00	4.00
❑ 438 Whitey Herzog	10.00	5.00
❑ 439 Ray Narleski	8.00	4.00
❑ 440 Eddie Mathews	75.00	30.00
❑ 441 Jim Marshall	10.00	5.00
❑ 442 Phil Paine	8.00	4.00
❑ 443 Billy Harrell SP	20.00	10.00
❑ 444 Danny Kravitz	8.00	4.00
❑ 445 Bob Smith	8.00	4.00
❑ 446 Carroll Hardy SP	20.00	10.00
❑ 447 Ray Monzant	8.00	4.00
❑ 448 Charlie Lau RC	10.00	5.00
❑ 449 Gene Fodge	8.00	4.00
❑ 450 Preston Ward SP	20.00	10.00
❑ 451 Joe Taylor	8.00	4.00
❑ 452 Roman Mejias	8.00	4.00
❑ 453 Tom Qualters	8.00	4.00
❑ 454 Harry Hanebrink	8.00	4.00
❑ 455 Hal Griggs	8.00	4.00
❑ 456 Dick Brown	8.00	4.00
❑ 457 Milt Pappas RC	10.00	5.00
❑ 458 Julio Becquer	8.00	4.00
❑ 459 Ron Blackburn	8.00	4.00
❑ 460 Chuck Essegian	8.00	4.00
❑ 461 Ed Mayer	8.00	4.00
❑ 462 Gary Geiger SP	20.00	10.00
❑ 463 Vito Valentinetti	8.00	4.00
❑ 464 Curt Flood RC	30.00	15.00
❑ 465 Arnie Portocarrero	8.00	4.00
❑ 466 Pete Whisenant	8.00	4.00
❑ 467 Glen Hobbie	8.00	4.00
❑ 468 Bob Schmidt	8.00	4.00
❑ 469 Don Ferrarese	8.00	4.00
❑ 470 R.C. Stevens	8.00	4.00
❑ 471 Lenny Green	8.00	4.00
❑ 472 Joey Jay	10.00	5.00
❑ 473 Bill Renna	8.00	4.00
❑ 474 Roman Semproch	8.00	4.00
❑ 475 Fred Haney AS MG	25.00	7.50
Casey Stengel AS MG CL		
❑ 476 Stan Musial AS TP	50.00	25.00
❑ 477 Bill Skowron AS	10.00	5.00
❑ 478 J.Temple AS UER	8.00	4.00
Card says record vs American League		
Temple was NL AS		
❑ 479 Nellie Fox AS	15.00	7.50
❑ 480 Eddie Mathews AS	30.00	15.00
❑ 481 Frank Malzone AS	8.00	4.00
❑ 482 Ernie Banks AS	40.00	20.00
❑ 483 Luis Aparicio AS	15.00	7.50
❑ 484 Frank Robinson AS	30.00	15.00
❑ 485 Ted Williams AS	125.00	60.00
❑ 486 Willie Mays AS	60.00	30.00
❑ 487 Mickey Mantle AS TP	175.00	90.00
❑ 488 Hank Aaron AS	60.00	30.00
❑ 489 Jackie Jensen AS	10.00	5.00
❑ 490 Ed Bailey AS	8.00	4.00
❑ 491 Sherm Lollar AS	8.00	4.00
❑ 492 Bob Friend AS	8.00	4.00
❑ 493 Bob Turley AS	10.00	5.00
❑ 494 Warren Spahn AS	25.00	12.50
❑ 495 Herb Score AS	15.00	3.00
❑ NNO Contest Cards	40.00	20.00

1959 Topps

	NM	Ex
COMPLETE SET (572)	5000.00	2500.00
COMMON CARD (1-110)	6.00	3.00
COMMON (111-506)	4.00	2.00
COMMON (507-572)	16.00	8.00
WRAPPER (1-CENT)	125.00	60.00
WRAPPER (5-CENT)	100.00	50.00

Card	NM	Ex
❑ 1 Ford Frick COMM RC	60.00	16.50
❑ 2 Eddie Yost	8.00	4.00
❑ 3 Don McMahon	8.00	4.00
❑ 4 Albie Pearson	8.00	4.00
❑ 5 Dick Donovan	8.00	4.00
❑ 6 Alex Grammas	6.00	3.00
❑ 7 Al Pilarcik	6.00	3.00
❑ 8 Phillies Team CL	75.00	15.00
❑ 9 Paul Giel	8.00	4.00
❑ 10 Mickey Mantle	700.00	350.00
❑ 11 Billy Hunter	8.00	4.00
❑ 12 Vern Law	8.00	4.00
❑ 13 Dick Gernert	6.00	3.00
❑ 14 Pete Whisenant	6.00	3.00
❑ 15 Dick Drott	6.00	3.00
❑ 16 Joe Pignatano	6.00	3.00
❑ 17 Frank Thomas	8.00	4.00
Danny Murtaugh MG		
Ted Kluszewski		
❑ 18 Jack Urban	6.00	3.00
❑ 19 Eddie Bressoud	6.00	3.00
❑ 20 Duke Snider	60.00	30.00
❑ 21 Connie Johnson	6.00	3.00
❑ 22 Al Smith	8.00	4.00
❑ 23 Murry Dickson	8.00	4.00
❑ 24 Red Wilson	6.00	3.00
❑ 25 Don Hoak	8.00	4.00
❑ 26 Chuck Stobbs	6.00	3.00
❑ 27 Andy Pafko	8.00	4.00
❑ 28 Al Worthington	6.00	3.00
❑ 29 Jim Bolger	6.00	3.00
❑ 30 Nellie Fox	30.00	15.00
❑ 31 Ken Lehman	6.00	3.00
❑ 32 Don Buddin	6.00	3.00
❑ 33 Ed Fitzgerald	6.00	3.00
❑ 34 Al Kaline	20.00	10.00
Charley Maxwell		
❑ 35 Ted Kluszewski	12.00	6.00
❑ 36 Hank Aguirre	6.00	3.00
❑ 37 Gene Green	6.00	3.00
❑ 38 Morrie Martin	6.00	3.00
❑ 39 Ed Bouchee	6.00	3.00
❑ 40A Warren Spahn ERR	75.00	38.00
(Born 1931)		
❑ 40B Warren Spahn ERR	100.00	50.00
(Born 1931, but three		
is partially obscured)		
❑ 40C Warren Spahn COR	60.00	30.00
(Born 1921)		
❑ 41 Bob Martyn	6.00	3.00
❑ 42 Murray Wall	6.00	3.00
❑ 43 Steve Bilko	6.00	3.00
❑ 44 Vito Valentinetti	6.00	3.00
❑ 45 Andy Carey	8.00	4.00
❑ 46 Bill R. Henry	6.00	3.00
❑ 47 Jim Finigan	6.00	3.00
❑ 48 Orioles Team CL	24.00	4.80
❑ 49 Bill Hall	6.00	3.00
❑ 50 Willie Mays	125.00	60.00
❑ 51 Rip Coleman	6.00	3.00
❑ 52 Coot Veal	6.00	3.00
❑ 53 Stan Williams RC	8.00	4.00
❑ 54 Mel Roach	6.00	3.00
❑ 55 Tom Brewer	6.00	3.00
❑ 56 Carl Sawatski	6.00	3.00
❑ 57 Al Cicotte	6.00	3.00
❑ 58 Eddie Miksis	6.00	3.00
❑ 59 Irv Noren	8.00	4.00
❑ 60 Bob Turley	8.00	4.00
❑ 61 Dick Brown	6.00	3.00
❑ 62 Tony Taylor	8.00	4.00
❑ 63 Jim Hearn	6.00	3.00
❑ 64 Joe DeMaestri	6.00	3.00
❑ 65 Frank Torre	8.00	4.00
❑ 66 Joe Ginsberg	6.00	3.00
❑ 67 Brooks Lawrence	6.00	3.00
❑ 68 Dick Schofield	8.00	4.00
❑ 69 Giants Team CL	24.00	4.80
❑ 70 Harvey Kuenn	8.00	4.00
❑ 71 Don Bessent	6.00	3.00
❑ 72 Bill Renna	6.00	3.00
❑ 73 Ron Jackson	8.00	4.00
❑ 74 Jim Lemon	8.00	4.00
Cookie Lavagetto MG		
Roy Sievers		
❑ 75 Sam Jones	8.00	4.00
❑ 76 Bobby Richardson	20.00	10.00
❑ 77 John Goryl	6.00	3.00
❑ 78 Pedro Ramos	6.00	3.00
❑ 79 Harry Chiti	6.00	3.00
❑ 80 Minnie Minoso	12.00	6.00
❑ 81 Hal Jeffcoat	6.00	3.00
❑ 82 Bob Boyd	6.00	3.00
❑ 83 Bob Smith	6.00	3.00
❑ 84 Reno Bertoia	6.00	3.00
❑ 85 Harry Anderson	6.00	3.00
❑ 86 Bob Keegan	8.00	4.00
❑ 87 Danny O'Connell	6.00	3.00
❑ 88 Herb Score	12.00	6.00
❑ 89 Billy Gardner	6.00	3.00
❑ 90 Bill Skowron	12.00	6.00
❑ 91 Herb Moford	6.00	3.00
❑ 92 Dave Philley	6.00	3.00
❑ 93 Julio Becquer	6.00	3.00
❑ 94 White Sox Team CL	40.00	8.00
❑ 95 Carl Willey	6.00	3.00
❑ 96 Lou Berberet	6.00	3.00
❑ 97 Jerry Lynch	8.00	4.00
❑ 98 Arnie Portocarrero	6.00	3.00
❑ 99 Ted Kazanski	6.00	3.00
❑ 100 Bob Cerv	8.00	4.00
❑ 101 Alex Kellner	6.00	3.00
❑ 102 Felipe Alou RC	30.00	15.00
❑ 103 Billy Goodman	8.00	4.00
❑ 104 Del Rice	8.00	4.00
❑ 105 Lee Walls	6.00	3.00
❑ 106 Hal Woodeshick	6.00	3.00
❑ 107 Norm Larker	8.00	4.00
❑ 108 Zack Monroe	8.00	4.00
❑ 109 Bob Schmidt	6.00	3.00
❑ 110 George Witt	8.00	4.00
❑ 111 Redlegs Team CL	15.00	3.00
❑ 112 Billy Consolo	4.00	2.00
❑ 113 Taylor Phillips	4.00	2.00
❑ 114 Earl Battey	8.00	4.00
❑ 115 Mickey Vernon	8.00	4.00
❑ 116 Bob Allison RP RC	12.00	6.00

No.	Player		
❑ 117	J.Blanchard RP RC	12.00	6.00
❑ 118	John Buzhardt RP	5.00	2.50
❑ 119	John Callison RP RC	12.00	6.00
❑ 120	Chuck Coles RP	5.00	2.50
❑ 121	Bob Conley RP	5.00	2.50
❑ 122	Bennie Daniels RP	5.00	2.50
❑ 123	Don Dillard RP	5.00	2.50
❑ 124	Dan Dobbek RP	5.00	2.50
❑ 125	Ron Fairly RP RC	12.00	6.00
❑ 126	Eddie Haas RP	5.00	2.50
❑ 127	Kent Hadley RP	5.00	2.50
❑ 128	Bob Hartman RP	5.00	2.50
❑ 129	Frank Herrera RP	5.00	2.50
❑ 130	Lou Jackson RP	5.00	2.50
❑ 131	Deron Johnson RP RC	12.00	6.00
❑ 132	Don Lee RP	5.00	2.50
❑ 133	Bob Lillis RP RC	5.00	2.50
❑ 134	Jim McDaniel RP	5.00	2.50
❑ 135	Gene Oliver RP	5.00	2.50
❑ 136	Jim O'Toole RP RC	5.00	2.50
❑ 137	Dick Ricketts RP	5.00	2.50
❑ 138	John Romano RP RC	5.00	2.50
❑ 139	Ed Sadowski RP	5.00	2.50
❑ 140	Charlie Secrest RP	5.00	2.50
❑ 141	Joe Shipley RP	5.00	2.50
❑ 142	Dick Stigman RP	5.00	2.50
❑ 143	Willie Tasby RP RC	5.00	2.50
❑ 144	Jerry Walker RP	5.00	2.50
❑ 145	Dom Zanni RP	5.00	2.50
❑ 146	Jerry Zimmerman RP	5.00	2.50
❑ 147	Dale Long	30.00	15.00
	Ernie Banks		
	Walt Moryn		
❑ 148	Mike McCormick	8.00	4.00
❑ 149	Jim Bunning	20.00	10.00
❑ 150	Stan Musial	125.00	60.00
❑ 151	Bob Malkmus	4.00	2.00
❑ 152	Johnny Klippstein	4.00	2.00
❑ 153	Jim Marshall	4.00	2.00
❑ 154	Ray Herbert	4.00	2.00
❑ 155	Enos Slaughter	20.00	10.00
❑ 156	Billy Pierce	12.00	6.00
	Robin Roberts		
❑ 157	Felix Mantilla	4.00	2.00
❑ 158	Walt Dropo	4.00	2.00
❑ 159	Bob Shaw	8.00	4.00
❑ 160	Dick Groat	8.00	4.00
❑ 161	Frank Baumann	4.00	2.00
❑ 162	Bobby G. Smith	4.00	2.00
❑ 163	Sandy Koufax	150.00	75.00
❑ 164	Johnny Groth	4.00	2.00
❑ 165	Bill Bruton	4.00	2.00
❑ 166	Minnie Minoso	30.00	15.00
	Rocky Colavito		
	(Misspelled Colovito		
	on card back)		
	Larry Doby		
❑ 167	Duke Maas	4.00	2.00
❑ 168	Carroll Hardy	4.00	2.00
❑ 169	Ted Abernathy	4.00	2.00
❑ 170	Gene Woodling	8.00	4.00
❑ 171	Willard Schmidt	4.00	2.00
❑ 172	Athletics Team CL	15.00	3.00
❑ 173	Bill Monbouquette	8.00	4.00
❑ 174	Jim Pendleton	4.00	2.00
❑ 175	Dick Farrell	8.00	4.00
❑ 176	Preston Ward	4.00	2.00
❑ 177	John Briggs	4.00	2.00
❑ 178	Ruben Amaro RC	12.00	6.00
❑ 179	Don Rudolph	4.00	2.00
❑ 180	Yogi Berra	80.00	40.00
❑ 181	Bob Porterfield	4.00	2.00
❑ 182	Milt Graff	4.00	2.00
❑ 183	Stu Miller	8.00	4.00
❑ 184	Harvey Haddix	8.00	4.00
❑ 185	Jim Busby	4.00	2.00
❑ 186	Mudcat Grant	8.00	4.00
❑ 187	Bubba Phillips	8.00	4.00
❑ 188	Juan Pizarro	4.00	2.00
❑ 189	Neil Chrisley	4.00	2.00
❑ 190	Bill Virdon	8.00	4.00
❑ 191	Russ Kemmerer	4.00	2.00
❑ 192	Charlie Beamon	4.00	2.00
❑ 193	Sammy Taylor	4.00	2.00
❑ 194	Jim Brosnan	8.00	4.00
❑ 195	Rip Repulski	4.00	2.00
❑ 196	Billy Moran	4.00	2.00
❑ 197	Ray Semproch	4.00	2.00
❑ 198	Jim Davenport	8.00	4.00
❑ 199	Leo Kiely	4.00	2.00
❑ 200	W.Giles NL PRES	8.00	4.00
❑ 201	Tom Acker	4.00	2.00
❑ 202	Roger Maris	125.00	60.00
❑ 203	Ossie Virgil	4.00	2.00
❑ 204	Casey Wise	4.00	2.00
❑ 205	Don Larsen	8.00	4.00
❑ 206	Carl Furillo	12.00	6.00
❑ 207	George Strickland	4.00	2.00
❑ 208	Willie Jones	4.00	2.00
❑ 209	Lenny Green	4.00	2.00
❑ 210	Ed Bailey	4.00	2.00
❑ 211	Bob Blaylock	4.00	2.00
❑ 212	Hank Aaron	75.00	38.00
	Eddie Mathews		
❑ 213	Jim Rivera	8.00	4.00
❑ 214	Marcelino Solis	4.00	2.00
❑ 215	Jim Lemon	8.00	4.00
❑ 216	Andre Rodgers	4.00	2.00
❑ 217	Carl Erskine	12.00	6.00
❑ 218	Roman Mejias	4.00	2.00
❑ 219	George Zuverink	4.00	2.00
❑ 220	Frank Malzone	8.00	4.00
❑ 221	Bob Bowman	4.00	2.00
❑ 222	Bobby Shantz	8.00	4.00
❑ 223	Cardinals Team CL	15.00	3.00
❑ 224	Claude Osteen RC	8.00	4.00
❑ 225	Johnny Logan	8.00	4.00
❑ 226	Art Ceccarelli	4.00	2.00
❑ 227	Hal W. Smith	4.00	2.00
❑ 228	Don Gross	4.00	2.00
❑ 229	Vic Power	8.00	4.00
❑ 230	Bill Fischer	4.00	2.00
❑ 231	Ellis Burton	4.00	2.00
❑ 232	Eddie Kasko	4.00	2.00
❑ 233	Paul Foytack	4.00	2.00
❑ 234	Chuck Tanner	8.00	4.00
❑ 235	Valmy Thomas	4.00	2.00
❑ 236	Ted Bowsfield	4.00	2.00
❑ 237	Gil McDougald	12.00	6.00
	Bob Turley		
	Bobby Richardson		
❑ 238	Gene Baker	4.00	2.00
❑ 239	Bob Trowbridge	4.00	2.00
❑ 240	Hank Bauer	12.00	6.00
❑ 241	Billy Muffett	4.00	2.00
❑ 242	Ron Samford	4.00	2.00
❑ 243	Marv Grissom	4.00	2.00
❑ 244	Ted Gray	4.00	2.00
❑ 245	Ned Garver	4.00	2.00
❑ 246	J.W. Porter	4.00	2.00
❑ 247	Don Ferrarese	4.00	2.00
❑ 248	Red Sox Team CL	15.00	3.00
❑ 249	Bobby Adams	4.00	2.00
❑ 250	Billy O'Dell	4.00	2.00
❑ 251	Clete Boyer	12.00	6.00
❑ 252	Ray Boone	8.00	4.00
❑ 253	Seth Morehead	4.00	2.00
❑ 254	Zeke Bella	4.00	2.00
❑ 255	Del Ennis	8.00	4.00
❑ 256	Jerry Davie	4.00	2.00
❑ 257	Leon Wagner RC	8.00	4.00
❑ 258	Fred Kipp	4.00	2.00
❑ 259	Jim Pisoni	4.00	2.00
❑ 260	Early Wynn UER	20.00	10.00
	1957 Cleevland		
❑ 261	Gene Stephens	4.00	2.00
❑ 262	Johnny Podres	12.00	6.00
	Clem Labine		
	Don Drysdale		
❑ 263	Bud Daley	4.00	2.00
❑ 264	Chico Carrasquel	4.00	2.00
❑ 265	Ron Kline	4.00	2.00
❑ 266	Woody Held	4.00	2.00
❑ 267	John Romonosky	4.00	2.00
❑ 268	Tito Francona	8.00	4.00
❑ 269	Jack Meyer	4.00	2.00
❑ 270	Gil Hodges	30.00	15.00
❑ 271	Orlando Pena	4.00	2.00
❑ 272	Jerry Lumpe	4.00	2.00
❑ 273	Joey Jay	8.00	4.00
❑ 274	Jerry Kindall	8.00	4.00
❑ 275	Jack Sanford	8.00	4.00
❑ 276	Pete Daley	4.00	2.00
❑ 277	Turk Lown	8.00	4.00
❑ 278	Chuck Essegian	4.00	2.00
❑ 279	Ernie Johnson	4.00	2.00
❑ 280	Frank Bolling	4.00	2.00
❑ 281	Walt Craddock	4.00	2.00
❑ 282	R.C. Stevens	4.00	2.00
❑ 283	Russ Heman	4.00	2.00
❑ 284	Steve Korcheck	4.00	2.00
❑ 285	Joe Cunningham	4.00	2.00
❑ 286	Dean Stone	4.00	2.00
❑ 287	Don Zimmer	12.00	6.00
❑ 288	Dutch Dotterer	4.00	2.00
❑ 289	Johnny Kucks	8.00	4.00
❑ 290	Wes Covington	4.00	2.00
❑ 291	Pedro Ramos	4.00	2.00
	Camilo Pascual		
❑ 292	Dick Williams	8.00	4.00
❑ 293	Ray Moore	4.00	2.00
❑ 294	Hank Foiles	4.00	2.00
❑ 295	Billy Martin	30.00	15.00
❑ 296	Ernie Broglio RC	4.00	2.00
❑ 297	Jackie Brandt	4.00	2.00
❑ 298	Tex Clevenger	4.00	2.00
❑ 299	Billy Klaus	4.00	2.00
❑ 300	Richie Ashburn	30.00	15.00
❑ 301	Earl Averill	4.00	2.00
❑ 302	Don Mossi	8.00	4.00
❑ 303	Marty Keough	4.00	2.00
❑ 304	Cubs Team CL	15.00	3.00
❑ 305	Curt Raydon	4.00	2.00
❑ 306	Jim Gilliam	8.00	4.00
❑ 307	Curt Barclay	4.00	2.00
❑ 308	Norm Siebern	4.00	2.00
❑ 309	Sal Maglie	8.00	4.00
❑ 310	Luis Aparicio	20.00	10.00
❑ 311	Norm Zauchin	4.00	2.00
❑ 312	Don Newcombe	8.00	4.00
❑ 313	Frank House	4.00	2.00
❑ 314	Don Cardwell	4.00	2.00
❑ 315	Joe Adcock	8.00	4.00
❑ 316A	Ralph Lumenti UER	4.00	2.00
	(Option)		
	(Photo actually		
	Camilo Pascual)		
❑ 316B	Ralph Lumenti UER	80.00	40.00
	(No option)		
	(Photo actually		
	Camilo Pascual)		
❑ 317	Willie Mays	75.00	38.00
	Richie Ashburn		
❑ 318	Rocky Bridges	4.00	2.00
❑ 319	Dave Hillman	4.00	2.00
❑ 320	Bob Skinner	8.00	4.00
❑ 321A	Bob Giallombardo	8.00	4.00
	(Option)		
❑ 321B	Bob Giallombardo	80.00	40.00
	(No option)		
❑ 322A	Harry Hanebrink	8.00	4.00
	(Traded)		
❑ 322B	Harry Hanebrink	80.00	40.00
	(No trade)		
❑ 323	Frank Sullivan	4.00	2.00
❑ 324	Don Demeter	4.00	2.00
❑ 325	Ken Boyer	12.00	6.00
❑ 326	Marv Throneberry	8.00	4.00
❑ 327	Gary Bell	4.00	2.00
❑ 328	Lou Skizas	4.00	2.00
❑ 329	Tigers Team CL	15.00	3.00
❑ 330	Gus Triandos	8.00	4.00
❑ 331	Steve Boros	4.00	2.00
❑ 332	Ray Monzant	4.00	2.00
❑ 333	Harry Simpson	4.00	2.00
❑ 334	Glen Hobbie	4.00	2.00
❑ 335	Johnny Temple	8.00	4.00
❑ 336A	Billy Loes	8.00	4.00
	(With traded line)		
❑ 336B	Billy Loes	80.00	40.00
	(No trade)		
❑ 337	George Crowe	4.00	2.00
❑ 338	Sparky Anderson RC	60.00	30.00
❑ 339	Roy Face	8.00	4.00
❑ 340	Roy Sievers	8.00	4.00
❑ 341	Tom Qualters	4.00	2.00
❑ 342	Ray Jablonski	4.00	2.00
❑ 343	Billy Hoeft	4.00	2.00

❑ 344 Russ Nixon 4.00 2.00
❑ 345 Gil McDougald 12.00 6.00
❑ 346 Dave Sisler 4.00 2.00
Tom Brewer
❑ 347 Bob Buhl 4.00 2.00
❑ 348 Ted Lepcio 4.00 2.00
❑ 349 Hoyt Wilhelm 20.00 10.00
❑ 350 Ernie Banks 75.00 38.00
❑ 351 Earl Torgeson 4.00 2.00
❑ 352 Robin Roberts 20.00 10.00
❑ 353 Curt Flood 8.00 4.00
❑ 354 Pete Burnside 4.00 2.00
❑ 355 Jimmy Piersall 8.00 4.00
❑ 356 Bob Mabe 4.00 2.00
❑ 357 Dick Stuart RC 8.00 4.00
❑ 358 Ralph Terry 8.00 4.00
❑ 359 Bill White RC 20.00 10.00
❑ 360 Al Kaline 60.00 30.00
❑ 361 Willard Nixon 4.00 2.00
❑ 362A Dolan Nichols 4.00 2.00
(With option line)
❑ 362B Dolan Nichols 80.00 40.00
(No option)
❑ 363 Bobby Avila 4.00 2.00
❑ 364 Danny McDevitt 4.00 2.00
❑ 365 Gus Bell 8.00 4.00
❑ 366 Humberto Robinson 4.00 2.00
❑ 367 Cal Neeman 4.00 2.00
❑ 368 Don Mueller 8.00 4.00
❑ 369 Dick Tomanek 4.00 2.00
❑ 370 Pete Runnels 8.00 4.00
❑ 371 Dick Brodowski 4.00 2.00
❑ 372 Jim Hegan 8.00 4.00
❑ 373 Herb Plews 4.00 2.00
❑ 374 Art Ditmar 8.00 4.00
❑ 375 Bob Nieman 4.00 2.00
❑ 376 Hal Naragon 4.00 2.00
❑ 377 John Antonelli 8.00 4.00
❑ 378 Gail Harris 4.00 2.00
❑ 379 Bob Miller 4.00 2.00
❑ 380 Hank Aaron 125.00 60.00
❑ 381 Mike Baxes 4.00 2.00
❑ 382 Curt Simmons 8.00 4.00
❑ 383 Don Larsen 12.00 6.00
Casey Stengel MG
❑ 384 Dave Sisler 4.00 2.00
❑ 385 Sherm Lollar 8.00 4.00
❑ 386 Jim Delsing 4.00 2.00
❑ 387 Don Drysdale 50.00 25.00
❑ 388 Bob Will 4.00 2.00
❑ 389 Joe Nuxhall 8.00 4.00
❑ 390 Orlando Cepeda 20.00 10.00
❑ 391 Milt Pappas 8.00 4.00
❑ 392 Whitey Herzog 8.00 4.00
❑ 393 Frank Lary 8.00 4.00
❑ 394 Randy Jackson 4.00 2.00
❑ 395 Elston Howard 12.00 6.00
❑ 396 Bob Rush 4.00 2.00
❑ 397 Senators Team CL 15.00 3.00
❑ 398 Wally Post 8.00 4.00
❑ 399 Larry Jackson 4.00 2.00
❑ 400 Jackie Jensen 8.00 4.00
❑ 401 Ron Blackburn 4.00 2.00
❑ 402 Hector Lopez 8.00 4.00
❑ 403 Clem Labine 8.00 4.00
❑ 404 Hank Sauer 8.00 4.00
❑ 405 Roy McMillan 8.00 4.00
❑ 406 Solly Drake 4.00 2.00
❑ 407 Moe Drabowsky 8.00 4.00
❑ 408 Nellie Fox 35.00 17.50
Luis Aparicio
❑ 409 Gus Zernial 8.00 4.00
❑ 410 Billy Pierce 8.00 4.00
❑ 411 Whitey Lockman 8.00 4.00
❑ 412 Stan Lopata 4.00 2.00
❑ 413 Camilo Pascual UER 8.00 4.00
(Listed as Camillo
on front and Pasqual
on back)
❑ 414 Dale Long 8.00 4.00
❑ 415 Bill Mazeroski 12.00 6.00
❑ 416 Haywood Sullivan 8.00 4.00
❑ 417 Virgil Trucks 8.00 4.00
❑ 418 Gino Cimoli 4.00 2.00
❑ 419 Braves Team CL 15.00 3.00
❑ 420 Rocky Colavito 30.00 15.00
❑ 421 Herman Wehmeier 4.00 2.00
❑ 422 Hobie Landrith 4.00 2.00
❑ 423 Bob Grim 8.00 4.00
❑ 424 Ken Aspromonte 4.00 2.00
❑ 425 Del Crandall 8.00 4.00
❑ 426 Jerry Staley 8.00 4.00
❑ 427 Charlie Neal 8.00 4.00
❑ 428 Ron Kline 4.00 2.00
Bob Friend
Vernon Law
Roy Face
❑ 429 Bobby Thomson 8.00 4.00
❑ 430 Whitey Ford 60.00 30.00
❑ 431 Whammy Douglas 4.00 2.00
❑ 432 Smoky Burgess 8.00 4.00
❑ 433 Billy Harrell 4.00 2.00
❑ 434 Hal Griggs 4.00 2.00
❑ 435 Frank Robinson 50.00 25.00
❑ 436 Granny Hamner 4.00 2.00
❑ 437 Ike Delock 4.00 2.00
❑ 438 Sammy Esposito 4.00 2.00
❑ 439 Brooks Robinson 50.00 25.00
❑ 440 Lou Burdette 8.00 4.00
(Posing as if
lefthanded)
❑ 441 John Roseboro 8.00 4.00
❑ 442 Ray Narleski 4.00 2.00
❑ 443 Daryl Spencer 4.00 2.00
❑ 444 Ron Hansen RC 8.00 4.00
❑ 445 Cal McLish 4.00 2.00
❑ 446 Rocky Nelson 4.00 2.00
❑ 447 Bob Anderson 4.00 2.00
❑ 448 Vada Pinson UER 12.00 6.00
(Born: 8/8/38
should be 8/11/38)
❑ 449 Tom Gorman 4.00 2.00
❑ 450 Eddie Mathews 35.00 17.50
❑ 451 Jimmy Constable 4.00 2.00
❑ 452 Chico Fernandez 4.00 2.00
❑ 453 Les Moss 4.00 2.00
❑ 454 Phil Clark 4.00 2.00
❑ 455 Larry Doby 12.00 6.00
❑ 456 Jerry Casale 4.00 2.00
❑ 457 Dodgers Team CL 30.00 6.00
❑ 458 Gordon Jones 4.00 2.00
❑ 459 Bill Tuttle 4.00 2.00
❑ 460 Bob Friend 8.00 4.00
❑ 461 Mickey Mantle HL 125.00 60.00
❑ 462 Rocky Colavito HL 12.00 6.00
❑ 463 Al Kaline HL 30.00 15.00
❑ 464 Willie Mays HL 40.00 20.00
54 World Series Catch
❑ 465 Roy Sievers HL 8.00 4.00
❑ 466 Billy Pierce HL 8.00 4.00
❑ 467 Hank Aaron HL 40.00 20.00
❑ 468 Duke Snider HL 20.00 10.00
❑ 469 Ernie Banks HL 20.00 10.00
❑ 470 Stan Musial HL 30.00 15.00
3,000 Hits
❑ 471 Tom Sturdivant 4.00 2.00
❑ 472 Gene Freese 4.00 2.00
❑ 473 Mike Fornieles 4.00 2.00
❑ 474 Moe Thacker 4.00 2.00
❑ 475 Jack Harshman 4.00 2.00
❑ 476 Indians Team CL 15.00 3.00
❑ 477 Barry Latman 4.00 2.00
❑ 478 Roberto Clemente 175.00 90.00
❑ 479 Lindy McDaniel 8.00 4.00
❑ 480 Red Schoendienst 12.00 6.00
❑ 481 Charlie Maxwell 8.00 4.00
❑ 482 Russ Meyer 4.00 2.00
❑ 483 Clint Courtney 4.00 2.00
❑ 484 Willie Kirkland 4.00 2.00
❑ 485 Ryne Duren 8.00 4.00
❑ 486 Sammy White 4.00 2.00
❑ 487 Hal Brown 4.00 2.00
❑ 488 Walt Moryn 4.00 2.00
❑ 489 John Powers 4.00 2.00
❑ 490 Frank Thomas 8.00 4.00
❑ 491 Don Blasingame 4.00 2.00
❑ 492 Gene Conley 8.00 4.00
❑ 493 Jim Landis 8.00 4.00
❑ 494 Don Pavletich 4.00 2.00
❑ 495 Johnny Podres 12.00 6.00
❑ 496 W.Terwilliger UER 4.00 2.00
Athlftics on front
❑ 497 Hal R. Smith 4.00 2.00
❑ 498 Dick Hyde 4.00 2.00
❑ 499 Johnny O'Brien 8.00 4.00
❑ 500 Vic Wertz 8.00 4.00
❑ 501 Bob Tiefenauer 4.00 2.00
❑ 502 Alvin Dark 8.00 4.00
❑ 503 Jim Owens 4.00 2.00
❑ 504 Ossie Alvarez 4.00 2.00
❑ 505 Tony Kubek 12.00 6.00
❑ 506 Bob Purkey 4.00 2.00
❑ 507 Bob Hale 16.00 8.00
❑ 508 Art Fowler 16.00 8.00
❑ 509 Norm Cash RC 80.00 40.00
❑ 510 Yankees Team CL 125.00 25.00
❑ 511 George Susce 16.00 8.00
❑ 512 George Altman 16.00 8.00
❑ 513 Tommy Carroll 16.00 8.00
❑ 514 Bob Gibson RC 225.00 110.00
❑ 515 Harmon Killebrew 125.00 60.00
❑ 516 Mike Garcia 20.00 10.00
❑ 517 Joe Koppe 16.00 8.00
❑ 518 Mike Cueller UER RC 30.00 15.00
Sic, Cuellar
❑ 519 Pete Runnels 20.00 10.00
Dick Gernert
Frank Malzone
❑ 520 Don Elston 16.00 8.00
❑ 521 Gary Geiger 16.00 8.00
❑ 522 Gene Snyder 16.00 8.00
❑ 523 Harry Bright 16.00 8.00
❑ 524 Larry Osborne 16.00 8.00
❑ 525 Jim Coates 20.00 10.00
❑ 526 Bob Speake 16.00 8.00
❑ 527 Solly Hemus 16.00 8.00
❑ 528 Pirates Team CL 75.00 15.00
❑ 529 G.Bamberger RC 20.00 10.00
❑ 530 Wally Moon 20.00 10.00
❑ 531 Ray Webster 16.00 8.00
❑ 532 Mark Freeman 16.00 8.00
❑ 533 Darrell Johnson 20.00 10.00
❑ 534 Faye Throneberry 16.00 8.00
❑ 535 Ruben Gomez 16.00 8.00
❑ 536 Danny Kravitz 16.00 8.00
❑ 537 Rudolph Arias 16.00 8.00
❑ 538 Chick King 16.00 8.00
❑ 539 Gary Blaylock 16.00 8.00
❑ 540 Willie Miranda 16.00 8.00
❑ 541 Bob Thurman 16.00 8.00
❑ 542 Jim Perry RC 30.00 15.00
❑ 543 Bob Skinner 150.00 75.00
Bill Virdon
Roberto Clemente
❑ 544 Lee Tate 16.00 8.00
❑ 545 Tom Morgan 16.00 8.00
❑ 546 Al Schroll 16.00 8.00
❑ 547 Jim Baxes 16.00 8.00
❑ 548 Elmer Singleton 16.00 8.00
❑ 549 Howie Nunn 16.00 8.00
❑ 550 Roy Campanella 150.00 75.00
(Symbol of Courage)
❑ 551 Fred Haney AS MG 16.00 8.00
❑ 552 Casey Stengel AS MG 30.00 15.00
❑ 553 Orlando Cepeda AS 30.00 15.00
❑ 554 Bill Skowron AS 20.00 10.00
❑ 555 Bill Mazeroski AS 30.00 15.00
❑ 556 Nellie Fox AS 40.00 20.00
❑ 557 Ken Boyer AS 30.00 15.00
❑ 558 Frank Malzone AS 16.00 8.00
❑ 559 Ernie Banks AS 60.00 30.00
❑ 560 Luis Aparicio AS 40.00 20.00
❑ 561 Hank Aaron AS 125.00 60.00
❑ 562 Al Kaline AS 60.00 30.00
❑ 563 Willie Mays AS 125.00 60.00
❑ 564 Mickey Mantle AS 250.00 125.00
❑ 565 Wes Covington AS 20.00 10.00
❑ 566 Roy Sievers AS 16.00 8.00
❑ 567 Del Crandall AS 16.00 8.00
❑ 568 Gus Triandos AS 16.00 8.00
❑ 569 Bob Friend AS 16.00 8.00
❑ 570 Bob Turley AS 16.00 8.00
❑ 571 Warren Spahn AS 50.00 25.00
❑ 572 Billy Pierce AS 40.00 13.00

1960 Topps

	NM	Ex
COMPLETE SET (572)	5000.00	2000.00
COMMON CARD (1-440)	4.00	1.60
COMMON (441-506)	7.00	2.80
COMMON (507-572)	16.00	6.50
WRAPPER (1-CENT)	900.00	350.00
WRAP. (1-CENT REPEAT)	500.00	200.00
WRAPPER (5-CENT)	40.00	16.00

No.	Card	NM	Ex
❑ 1	Early Wynn	35.00	8.75
❑ 2	Roman Mejias	4.00	1.60
❑ 3	Joe Adcock	6.00	2.40
❑ 4	Bob Purkey	4.00	1.60
❑ 5	Wally Moon	6.00	2.40
❑ 6	Lou Berberet	4.00	1.60
❑ 7	Willie Mays Bill Rigney MG	25.00	10.00
❑ 8	Bud Daley	4.00	1.60
❑ 9	Faye Throneberry	4.00	1.60
❑ 10	Ernie Banks	50.00	20.00
❑ 11	Norm Siebern	4.00	1.60
❑ 12	Milt Pappas	6.00	2.40
❑ 13	Wally Post	6.00	2.40
❑ 14	Jim Grant	6.00	2.40
❑ 15	Pete Runnels	6.00	2.40
❑ 16	Ernie Broglio	6.00	2.40
❑ 17	Johnny Callison	6.00	2.40
❑ 18	Dodgers Team CL	50.00	10.00
❑ 19	Felix Mantilla	4.00	1.60
❑ 20	Roy Face	6.00	2.40
❑ 21	Dutch Dotterer	4.00	1.60
❑ 22	Rocky Bridges	4.00	1.60
❑ 23	Eddie Fisher	4.00	1.60
❑ 24	Dick Gray	4.00	1.60
❑ 25	Roy Sievers	6.00	2.40
❑ 26	Wayne Terwilliger	4.00	1.60
❑ 27	Dick Drott	4.00	1.60
❑ 28	Brooks Robinson	50.00	20.00
❑ 29	Clem Labine	6.00	2.40
❑ 30	Tito Francona	4.00	1.60
❑ 31	Sammy Esposito	4.00	1.60
❑ 32	Jim O'Toole Vada Pinson	4.00	1.60
❑ 33	Tom Morgan	4.00	1.60
❑ 34	Sparky Anderson	15.00	6.00
❑ 35	Whitey Ford	50.00	20.00
❑ 36	Russ Nixon	4.00	1.60
❑ 37	Bill Bruton	4.00	1.60
❑ 38	Jerry Casale	4.00	1.60
❑ 39	Earl Averill	4.00	1.60
❑ 40	Joe Cunningham	4.00	1.60
❑ 41	Barry Latman	4.00	1.60
❑ 42	Hobie Landrith	4.00	1.60
❑ 43	Senators Team CL	10.00	2.00
❑ 44	Bobby Locke	4.00	1.60
❑ 45	Roy McMillan	6.00	2.40
❑ 46	Jerry Fisher	4.00	1.60
❑ 47	Don Zimmer	6.00	2.40
❑ 48	Hal W. Smith	4.00	1.60
❑ 49	Curt Raydon	4.00	1.60
❑ 50	Al Kaline	50.00	20.00
❑ 51	Jim Coates	6.00	2.40
❑ 52	Dave Philley	4.00	1.60
❑ 53	Jackie Brandt	4.00	1.60
❑ 54	Mike Fornieles	4.00	1.60
❑ 55	Bill Mazeroski	15.00	6.00
❑ 56	Steve Korcheck	4.00	1.60
❑ 57	Turk Lown Gerry Staley	4.00	1.60
❑ 58	Gino Cimoli	4.00	1.60
❑ 58A	Gino Cimoli Cardinals Team Logo		
❑ 59	Juan Pizarro	4.00	1.60
❑ 60	Gus Triandos	6.00	2.40
❑ 61	Eddie Kasko	4.00	1.60
❑ 62	Roger Craig	6.00	2.40
❑ 63	George Strickland	4.00	1.60
❑ 64	Jack Meyer	4.00	1.60
❑ 65	Elston Howard	6.00	2.40
❑ 66	Bob Trowbridge	4.00	1.60
❑ 67	Jose Pagan	4.00	1.60
❑ 68	Dave Hillman	4.00	1.60
❑ 69	Billy Goodman	6.00	2.40
❑ 70	Lew Burdette Card spelled as Lou on front and back	6.00	2.40
❑ 71	Marty Keough	4.00	1.60
❑ 72	Tigers Team CL	25.00	5.00
❑ 73	Bob Gibson	50.00	20.00
❑ 74	Walt Moryn	4.00	1.60
❑ 75	Vic Power	6.00	2.40
❑ 76	Bill Fischer	4.00	1.60
❑ 77	Hank Foiles	4.00	1.60
❑ 78	Bob Grim	4.00	1.60
❑ 79	Walt Dropo	4.00	1.60
❑ 80	Johnny Antonelli	6.00	2.40
❑ 81	Russ Snyder	4.00	1.60
❑ 82	Ruben Gomez	4.00	1.60
❑ 83	Tony Kubek	15.00	6.00
❑ 84	Hal R. Smith	4.00	1.60
❑ 85	Frank Lary	6.00	2.40
❑ 86	Dick Gernert	4.00	1.60
❑ 87	John Romonosky	4.00	1.60
❑ 88	John Roseboro	6.00	2.40
❑ 89	Hal Brown	4.00	1.60
❑ 90	Bobby Avila	4.00	1.60
❑ 91	Bennie Daniels	4.00	1.60
❑ 92	Whitey Herzog	6.00	2.40
❑ 93	Art Schult	4.00	1.60
❑ 94	Leo Kiely	4.00	1.60
❑ 95	Frank Thomas	6.00	2.40
❑ 96	Ralph Terry	6.00	2.40
❑ 97	Ted Lepcio	4.00	1.60
❑ 98	Gordon Jones	4.00	1.60
❑ 99	Lenny Green	4.00	1.60
❑ 100	Nellie Fox	20.00	8.00
❑ 101	Bob Miller	4.00	1.60
❑ 102	Kent Hadley	4.00	1.60
❑ 102A	Kent Hadley Athletics Team Logo		
❑ 103	Dick Farrell	6.00	2.40
❑ 104	Dick Schofield	6.00	2.40
❑ 105	Larry Sherry RC	6.00	2.40
❑ 106	Billy Gardner	4.00	1.60
❑ 107	Carlton Willey	4.00	1.60
❑ 108	Pete Daley	4.00	1.60
❑ 109	Clete Boyer	15.00	6.00
❑ 110	Cal McLish	4.00	1.60
❑ 111	Vic Wertz	6.00	2.40
❑ 112	Jack Harshman	4.00	1.60
❑ 113	Bob Skinner	4.00	1.60
❑ 114	Ken Aspromonte	4.00	1.60
❑ 115	Roy Face Hoyt Wilhelm	6.00	2.40
❑ 116	Jim Rivera	4.00	1.60
❑ 117	Tom Borland RP	4.00	1.60
❑ 118	Bob Bruce RP	4.00	1.60
❑ 119	Chico Cardenas RP	6.00	2.40
❑ 120	Duke Carmel RP	4.00	1.60
❑ 121	Camilo Carreon RP	4.00	1.60
❑ 122	Don Dillard RP	4.00	1.60
❑ 123	Dan Dobbek RP	4.00	1.60
❑ 124	Jim Donohue RP	4.00	1.60
❑ 125	Dick Ellsworth RP RC	6.00	2.40
❑ 126	Chuck Estrada RP RC	4.00	1.60
❑ 127	Ron Hansen RP	6.00	2.40
❑ 128	Bill Harris RP	4.00	1.60
❑ 129	Bob Hartman RP	4.00	1.60
❑ 130	Frank Herrera RP	4.00	1.60
❑ 131	Ed Hobaugh RP	4.00	1.60
❑ 132	Frank Howard RP RC	25.00	10.00
❑ 133	Manuel Javier RC RP (Sic, Julian)	6.00	2.40
❑ 134	Deron Johnson RP	6.00	2.40
❑ 135	Ken Johnson RP	4.00	1.60
❑ 136	Jim Kaat RP RC	40.00	16.00
❑ 137	Lou Klimchock RP	4.00	1.60
❑ 138	Art Mahaffey RP RC	6.00	2.40
❑ 139	Carl Mathias RP	4.00	1.60
❑ 140	Julio Navarro RP RC	4.00	1.60
❑ 141	Jim Proctor RP	4.00	1.60
❑ 142	Bill Short RP	4.00	1.60
❑ 143	Al Spangler RP	4.00	1.60
❑ 144	Al Stieglitz RP	4.00	1.60
❑ 145	Jim Umbricht RP	4.00	1.60
❑ 146	Ted Wieand RP	4.00	1.60
❑ 147	Bob Will RP	4.00	1.60
❑ 148	C.Yastrzemski RP RC	150.00	60.00
❑ 149	Bob Nieman	4.00	1.60
❑ 150	Billy Pierce	6.00	2.40
❑ 151	Giants Team CL	10.00	2.00
❑ 152	Gail Harris	4.00	1.60
❑ 153	Bobby Thomson	6.00	2.40
❑ 154	Jim Davenport	6.00	2.40
❑ 155	Charlie Neal	6.00	2.40
❑ 156	Art Ceccarelli	4.00	1.60
❑ 157	Rocky Nelson	6.00	2.40
❑ 158	Wes Covington	6.00	2.40
❑ 159	Jim Piersall	6.00	2.40
❑ 160	Mickey Mantle Ken Boyer	125.00	50.00
❑ 161	Ray Narleski	4.00	1.60
❑ 162	Sammy Taylor	4.00	1.60
❑ 163	Hector Lopez	6.00	2.40
❑ 164	Reds Team CL	10.00	2.00
❑ 165	Jack Sanford	6.00	2.40
❑ 166	Chuck Essegian	4.00	1.60
❑ 167	Valmy Thomas	4.00	1.60
❑ 168	Alex Grammas	4.00	1.60
❑ 169	Jake Striker	4.00	1.60
❑ 170	Del Crandall	6.00	2.40
❑ 171	Johnny Groth	4.00	1.60
❑ 172	Willie Kirkland	4.00	1.60
❑ 173	Billy Martin	20.00	8.00
❑ 174	Indians Team CL	10.00	2.00
❑ 175	Pedro Ramos	4.00	1.60
❑ 176	Vada Pinson	6.00	2.40
❑ 177	Johnny Kucks	4.00	1.60
❑ 178	Woody Held	4.00	1.60
❑ 179	Rip Coleman	4.00	1.60
❑ 180	Harry Simpson	4.00	1.60
❑ 181	Billy Loes	6.00	2.40
❑ 182	Glen Hobbie	4.00	1.60
❑ 183	Eli Grba	4.00	1.60
❑ 184	Gary Geiger	4.00	1.60
❑ 185	Jim Owens	4.00	1.60
❑ 186	Dave Sisler	4.00	1.60
❑ 187	Jay Hook	4.00	1.60
❑ 188	Dick Williams	6.00	2.40
❑ 189	Don McMahon	4.00	1.60
❑ 190	Gene Woodling	6.00	2.40
❑ 191	Johnny Klippstein	4.00	1.60
❑ 192	Danny O'Connell	4.00	1.60
❑ 193	Dick Hyde	4.00	1.60
❑ 194	Bobby Gene Smith	4.00	1.60
❑ 195	Lindy McDaniel	6.00	2.40
❑ 196	Andy Carey	6.00	2.40
❑ 197	Ron Kline	4.00	1.60
❑ 198	Jerry Lynch	6.00	2.40
❑ 199	Dick Donovan	6.00	2.40
❑ 200	Willie Mays	125.00	50.00
❑ 201	Larry Osborne	4.00	1.60
❑ 202	Fred Kipp	4.00	1.60
❑ 203	Sammy White	4.00	1.60
❑ 204	Ryne Duren	6.00	2.40
❑ 205	Johnny Logan	6.00	2.40
❑ 206	Claude Osteen	6.00	2.40
❑ 207	Bob Boyd	4.00	1.60
❑ 208	White Sox Team CL	10.00	2.00
❑ 209	Ron Blackburn	4.00	1.60
❑ 210	Harmon Killebrew	40.00	12.00
❑ 211	Taylor Phillips	4.00	1.60
❑ 212	Walter Alston MG	10.00	4.00
❑ 213	Chuck Dressen MG	6.00	2.40
❑ 214	Jimmy Dykes MG	6.00	2.40
❑ 215	Bob Elliott MG	6.00	2.40
❑ 216	Joe Gordon MG	6.00	2.40
❑ 217	Charlie Grimm MG	6.00	2.40
❑ 218	Solly Hemus MG	4.00	1.60

❑ 219 Fred Hutchinson MG 6.00 2.40
❑ 220 Billy Jurges MG 4.00 1.60
❑ 221 Cookie Lavagetto MG 4.00 1.60
❑ 222 Al Lopez MG 10.00 4.00
❑ 223 Danny Murtaugh MG 6.00 2.40
❑ 224 Paul Richards MG 6.00 2.40
❑ 225 Bill Rigney MG 4.00 1.60
❑ 226 Eddie Sawyer MG 4.00 1.60
❑ 227 Casey Stengel MG 15.00 6.00
❑ 228 Ernie Johnson 6.00 2.40
❑ 229 Joe M. Morgan 4.00 1.60
❑ 230 Lou Burdette 10.00 4.00
Warren Spahn
Bob Buhl
❑ 231 Hal Naragon 4.00 1.60
❑ 232 Jim Busby 4.00 1.60
❑ 233 Don Elston 4.00 1.60
❑ 234 Don Demeter 4.00 1.60
❑ 235 Gus Bell 6.00 2.40
❑ 236 Dick Ricketts 4.00 1.60
❑ 237 Elmer Valo 4.00 1.60
❑ 238 Danny Kravitz 4.00 1.60
❑ 239 Joe Shipley 4.00 1.60
❑ 240 Luis Aparicio 15.00 6.00
❑ 241 Albie Pearson 6.00 2.40
❑ 242 Cardinals Team CL 10.00 2.00
❑ 243 Bubba Phillips 4.00 1.60
❑ 244 Hal Griggs 4.00 1.60
❑ 245 Eddie Yost 6.00 2.40
❑ 246 Lee Maye 6.00 2.40
❑ 247 Gil McDougald 10.00 4.00
❑ 248 Del Rice 4.00 1.60
❑ 249 Earl Wilson RC 6.00 2.40
❑ 250 Stan Musial 100.00 40.00
❑ 251 Bob Malkmus 4.00 1.60
❑ 252 Ray Herbert 4.00 1.60
❑ 253 Eddie Bressoud 4.00 1.60
❑ 254 Arnie Portocarrero 4.00 1.60
❑ 255 Jim Gilliam 6.00 2.40
❑ 256 Dick Brown 4.00 1.60
❑ 257 Gordy Coleman RC 4.00 1.60
❑ 258 Dick Groat 6.00 2.40
❑ 259 George Altman 4.00 1.60
❑ 260 Rocky Colavito 15.00 6.00
Tito Francona
❑ 261 Pete Burnside 4.00 1.60
❑ 262 Hank Bauer 6.00 2.40
❑ 263 Darrell Johnson 4.00 1.60
❑ 264 Robin Roberts 15.00 6.00
❑ 265 Rip Repulski 4.00 1.60
❑ 266 Joey Jay 6.00 2.40
❑ 267 Jim Marshall 4.00 1.60
❑ 268 Al Worthington 4.00 1.60
❑ 269 Gene Green 4.00 1.60
❑ 270 Bob Turley 6.00 2.40
❑ 271 Julio Becquer 4.00 1.60
❑ 272 Fred Green 6.00 2.40
❑ 273 Neil Chrisley 4.00 1.60
❑ 274 Tom Acker 4.00 1.60
❑ 275 Curt Flood 6.00 2.40
❑ 276 Ken McBride 4.00 1.60
❑ 277 Harry Bright 4.00 1.60
❑ 278 Stan Williams 6.00 2.40
❑ 279 Chuck Tanner 6.00 2.40
❑ 280 Frank Sullivan 4.00 1.60
❑ 281 Ray Boone 6.00 2.40
❑ 282 Joe Nuxhall 6.00 2.40
❑ 283 John Blanchard 6.00 2.40
❑ 284 Don Gross 4.00 1.60
❑ 285 Harry Anderson 4.00 1.60
❑ 286 Ray Semproch 4.00 1.60
❑ 287 Felipe Alou 6.00 2.40
❑ 288 Bob Mabe 4.00 1.60
❑ 289 Willie Jones 4.00 1.60
❑ 290 Jerry Lumpe 4.00 1.60
❑ 291 Bob Keegan 4.00 1.60
❑ 292 Joe Pignatano 6.00 2.40
John Roseboro
❑ 293 Gene Conley 6.00 2.40
❑ 294 Tony Taylor 6.00 2.40
❑ 295 Gil Hodges 25.00 10.00
❑ 296 Nelson Chittum 4.00 1.60
❑ 297 Reno Bertoia 4.00 1.60
❑ 298 George Witt 4.00 1.60
❑ 299 Earl Torgeson 4.00 1.60
❑ 300 Hank Aaron 100.00 40.00
❑ 301 Jerry Davie 4.00 1.60
❑ 302 Phillies Team CL 10.00 2.00
❑ 303 Billy O'Dell 4.00 1.60
❑ 304 Joe Ginsberg 4.00 1.60
❑ 305 Richie Ashburn 20.00 8.00
❑ 306 Frank Baumann 4.00 1.60
❑ 307 Gene Oliver 4.00 1.60
❑ 308 Dick Hall 4.00 1.60
❑ 309 Bob Hale 4.00 1.60
❑ 310 Frank Malzone 6.00 2.40
❑ 311 Raul Sanchez 4.00 1.60
❑ 312 Charley Lau 6.00 2.40
❑ 313 Turk Lown 4.00 1.60
❑ 314 Chico Fernandez 4.00 1.60
❑ 315 Bobby Shantz 10.00 4.00
❑ 316 Willie McCovey RC 125.00 50.00
❑ 317 Pumpsie Green 6.00 2.40
❑ 318 Jim Baxes 6.00 2.40
❑ 319 Joe Koppe 6.00 2.40
❑ 320 Bob Allison 6.00 2.40
❑ 321 Ron Fairly 6.00 2.40
❑ 322 Willie Tasby 6.00 2.40
❑ 323 John Romano 6.00 2.40
❑ 324 Jim Perry 6.00 2.40
❑ 325 Jim O'Toole 6.00 2.40
❑ 326 Roberto Clemente 175.00 70.00
❑ 327 Ray Sadecki RC 4.00 1.60
❑ 328 Earl Battey 4.00 1.60
❑ 329 Zack Monroe 4.00 1.60
❑ 330 Harvey Kuenn 6.00 2.40
❑ 331 Henry Mason 4.00 1.60
❑ 332 Yankees Team CL 75.00 15.00
❑ 333 Danny McDevitt 4.00 1.60
❑ 334 Ted Abernathy 4.00 1.60
❑ 335 Red Schoendienst 15.00 6.00
❑ 336 Ike Delock 4.00 1.60
❑ 337 Cal Neeman 4.00 1.60
❑ 338 Ray Monzant 4.00 1.60
❑ 339 Harry Chiti 4.00 1.60
❑ 340 Harvey Haddix 6.00 2.40
❑ 341 Carroll Hardy 4.00 1.60
❑ 342 Casey Wise 4.00 1.60
❑ 343 Sandy Koufax 125.00 50.00
❑ 344 Clint Courtney 4.00 1.60
❑ 345 Don Newcombe 6.00 2.40
❑ 346 J.C. Martin UER 6.00 2.40
(Face actually
Gary Peters)
❑ 347 Ed Bouchee 4.00 1.60
❑ 348 Barry Shetrone 4.00 1.60
❑ 349 Moe Drabowsky 6.00 2.40
❑ 350 Mickey Mantle 400.00 160.00
❑ 351 Don Nottebart 4.00 1.60
❑ 352 Gus Bell 10.00 4.00
Frank Robinson
Jerry Lynch
❑ 353 Don Larsen 6.00 2.40
❑ 354 Bob Lillis 4.00 1.60
❑ 355 Bill White 6.00 2.40
❑ 356 Joe Amalfitano 4.00 1.60
❑ 357 Al Schroll 4.00 1.60
❑ 358 Joe DeMaestri 4.00 1.60
❑ 359 Buddy Gilbert 4.00 1.60
❑ 360 Herb Score 6.00 2.40
❑ 361 Bob Oldis 6.00 2.40
❑ 362 Russ Kemmerer 4.00 1.60
❑ 363 Gene Stephens 4.00 1.60
❑ 364 Paul Foytack 4.00 1.60
❑ 365 Minnie Minoso 10.00 4.00
❑ 366 Dallas Green RC 10.00 4.00
❑ 367 Bill Tuttle 4.00 1.60
❑ 368 Daryl Spencer 4.00 1.60
❑ 369 Billy Hoeft 4.00 1.60
❑ 370 Bill Skowron 10.00 4.00
❑ 371 Bud Byerly 4.00 1.60
❑ 372 Frank House 4.00 1.60
❑ 373 Don Hoak 6.00 2.40
❑ 374 Bob Buhl 6.00 2.40
❑ 375 Dale Long 10.00 4.00
❑ 376 John Briggs 4.00 1.60
❑ 377 Roger Maris 100.00 40.00
❑ 378 Stu Miller 6.00 2.40
❑ 379 Red Wilson 4.00 1.60
❑ 380 Bob Shaw 4.00 1.60
❑ 381 Braves Team CL 10.00 2.00
❑ 382 Ted Bowsfield 4.00 1.60
❑ 383 Leon Wagner 4.00 1.60
❑ 384 Don Cardwell 4.00 1.60
❑ 385 Charlie Neal WS 7.00 2.80
❑ 386 Charlie Neal WS 7.00 2.80
❑ 387 Carl Furillo WS 7.00 2.80
❑ 388 Gil Hodges WS 10.00 4.00
❑ 389 Luis Aparicio WS 12.00 4.80
Maury Wills
❑ 390 World Series Game 6 7.00 2.80
❑ 391 WS Summary 7.00 2.80
The Champs Celebrate
❑ 392 Tex Clevenger 4.00 1.60
❑ 393 Smoky Burgess 6.00 2.40
❑ 394 Norm Larker 6.00 2.40
❑ 395 Hoyt Wilhelm 15.00 6.00
❑ 396 Steve Bilko 4.00 1.60
❑ 397 Don Blasingame 4.00 1.60
❑ 398 Mike Cuellar 6.00 2.40
❑ 399 Milt Pappas 6.00 2.40
Jack Fisher
Jerry Walker
❑ 400 Rocky Colavito 20.00 8.00
❑ 401 Bob Duliba 4.00 1.60
❑ 402 Dick Stuart 15.00 6.00
❑ 403 Ed Sadowski 4.00 1.60
❑ 404 Bob Rush 4.00 1.60
❑ 405 Bobby Richardson 15.00 6.00
❑ 406 Billy Klaus 4.00 1.60
❑ 407 Gary Peters RC UER 6.00 2.40
(Face actually
J.C. Martin)
❑ 408 Carl Furillo 10.00 4.00
❑ 409 Ron Samford 4.00 1.60
❑ 410 Sam Jones 6.00 2.40
❑ 411 Ed Bailey 4.00 1.60
❑ 412 Bob Anderson 4.00 1.60
❑ 413 Athletics Team CL 10.00 2.00
❑ 414 Don Williams 4.00 1.60
❑ 415 Bob Cerv 4.00 1.60
❑ 416 Humberto Robinson 4.00 1.60
❑ 417 Chuck Cottier RC 4.00 1.60
❑ 418 Don Mossi 6.00 2.40
❑ 419 George Crowe 4.00 1.60
❑ 420 Eddie Mathews 40.00 16.00
❑ 421 Duke Maas 4.00 1.60
❑ 422 John Powers 4.00 1.60
❑ 423 Ed Fitzgerald 4.00 1.60
❑ 424 Pete Whisenant 4.00 1.60
❑ 425 Johnny Podres 6.00 2.40
❑ 426 Ron Jackson 4.00 1.60
❑ 427 Al Grunwald 4.00 1.60
❑ 428 Al Smith 4.00 1.60
❑ 429 Nellie Fox 10.00 4.00
Harvey Kuenn
❑ 430 Art Ditmar 4.00 1.60
❑ 431 Andre Rodgers 4.00 1.60
❑ 432 Chuck Stobbs 4.00 1.60
❑ 433 Irv Noren 4.00 1.60
❑ 434 Brooks Lawrence 6.00 2.40
❑ 435 Gene Freese 4.00 1.60
❑ 436 Marv Throneberry 6.00 2.40
❑ 437 Bob Friend 6.00 2.40
❑ 438 Jim Coker 4.00 1.60
❑ 439 Tom Brewer 4.00 1.60
❑ 440 Jim Lemon 6.00 2.40
❑ 441 Gary Bell 10.00 4.00
❑ 442 Joe Pignatano 7.00 2.80
❑ 443 Charlie Maxwell 7.00 2.80
❑ 444 Jerry Kindall 7.00 2.80
❑ 445 Warren Spahn 50.00 20.00
❑ 446 Ellis Burton 7.00 2.80
❑ 447 Ray Moore 7.00 2.80
❑ 448 Jim Gentile RC 15.00 6.00
❑ 449 Jim Brosnan 7.00 2.80
❑ 450 Orlando Cepeda 25.00 10.00
❑ 451 Curt Simmons 7.00 2.80
❑ 452 Ray Webster 7.00 2.80
❑ 453 Vern Law 25.00 10.00
❑ 454 Hal Woodeshick 7.00 2.80
❑ 455 Eddie Robinson CO 7.00 2.80
Harry Brecheen CO
Luman Harris CO
❑ 456 Rudy York CO 10.00 4.00
Billy Herman CO
Sal Maglie CO
Del Baker CO

❑ 457 Charlie Root CO	7.00	2.80
Lou Klein CO		
Elvin Tappe CO		
❑ 458 Johnny Cooney CO	7.00	2.80
Don Gutteridge CO		
Tony Cuccinello CO		
Ray Berres CO		
❑ 459 Reggie Otero CO	7.00	2.80
Cot Deal CO		
Wally Moses CO		
❑ 460 Mel Harder CO	15.00	6.00
Jo-Jo White CO		
Bob Lemon CO		
Ralph(Red) Kress CO		
❑ 461 Tom Ferrick CO	10.00	4.00
Luke Appling CO		
Billy Hitchcock CO		
❑ 462 Fred Fitzsimmons CO	7.00	2.80
Don Heffner CO		
Walker Cooper CO		
❑ 463 Bobby Bragan CO	7.00	2.80
Pete Reiser CO		
Joe Becker CO		
Greg Mulleavy CO		
❑ 464 Bob Scheffing CO	7.00	2.80
Whitlow Wyatt CO		
Andy Pafko CO		
George Myatt CO		
❑ 465 Bill Dickey CO	25.00	10.00
Ralph Houk CO		
Frank Crosetti CO		
Ed Lopat CO		
❑ 466 Ken Silvestri CO	7.00	2.80
Dick Carter CO		
Andy Cohen CO		
❑ 467 Mickey Vernon CO	7.00	2.80
Frank Oceak CO		
Sam Narron CO		
Bill Burwell CO		
❑ 468 Johnny Keane CO	7.00	2.80
Howie Pollet CO		
Ray Katt CO		
Harry Walker CO		
❑ 469 Wes Westrum CO	7.00	2.80
Salty Parker CO		
Bill Posedel CO		
❑ 470 Bob Swift CO	7.00	2.80
Ellis Clary CO		
Sam Mele CO		
❑ 471 Ned Garver	7.00	2.80
❑ 472 Alvin Dark	7.00	2.80
❑ 473 Al Cicotte	7.00	2.80
❑ 474 Haywood Sullivan	7.00	2.80
❑ 475 Don Drysdale	40.00	16.00
❑ 476 Lou Johnson	7.00	2.80
❑ 477 Don Ferrarese	7.00	2.80
❑ 478 Frank Torre	7.00	2.80
❑ 479 Georges Maranda	7.00	2.80
❑ 480 Yogi Berra	75.00	30.00
❑ 481 Wes Stock	7.00	2.80
❑ 482 Frank Bolling	7.00	2.80
❑ 483 Camilo Pascual	7.00	2.80
❑ 484 Pirates Team CL	40.00	8.00
❑ 485 Ken Boyer	15.00	6.00
❑ 486 Bobby Del Greco	7.00	2.80
❑ 487 Tom Sturdivant	7.00	2.80
❑ 488 Norm Cash	25.00	10.00
Shown with Indians Cap but listed as a Tiger		
❑ 489 Steve Ridzik	7.00	2.80
❑ 490 Frank Robinson	50.00	20.00
❑ 491 Mel Roach	7.00	2.80
❑ 492 Larry Jackson	7.00	2.80
❑ 493 Duke Snider	50.00	20.00
❑ 494 Orioles Team CL	25.00	5.00
❑ 495 Sherm Lollar	7.00	2.80
❑ 496 Bill Virdon	10.00	4.00
❑ 497 John Tsitouris	7.00	2.80
❑ 498 Al Pilarcik	7.00	2.80
❑ 499 Johnny James	10.00	4.00
❑ 500 Johnny Temple	7.00	2.80
❑ 501 Bob Schmidt	7.00	2.80
❑ 502 Jim Bunning	25.00	10.00
❑ 503 Don Lee	7.00	2.80
❑ 504 Seth Morehead	7.00	2.80
❑ 505 Ted Kluszewski	25.00	10.00
❑ 506 Lee Walls	7.00	2.80
❑ 507 Dick Stigman	16.00	6.50
❑ 508 Billy Consolo	16.00	6.50
❑ 509 Tommy Davis RC	25.00	10.00
❑ 510 Gerry Staley	16.00	6.50
❑ 511 Ken Walters	16.00	6.50
❑ 512 Joe Gibbon	16.00	6.50
❑ 513 Chicago Cubs Team Card CL	30.00	6.00
❑ 514 Steve Barber RC	16.00	6.50
❑ 515 Stan Lopata	16.00	6.50
❑ 516 Marty Kutyna	16.00	6.50
❑ 517 Charlie James	25.00	10.00
❑ 518 Tony Gonzalez	16.00	6.50
❑ 519 Ed Roebuck	16.00	6.50
❑ 520 Don Buddin	16.00	6.50
❑ 521 Mike Lee	16.00	6.50
❑ 522 Ken Hunt	30.00	12.00
❑ 523 Clay Dalrymple	16.00	6.50
❑ 524 Bill Henry	16.00	6.50
❑ 525 Marv Breeding	16.00	6.50
❑ 526 Paul Giel	25.00	10.00
❑ 527 Jose Valdivielso	25.00	10.00
❑ 528 Ben Johnson	16.00	6.50
❑ 529 Norm Sherry RC	20.00	8.00
❑ 530 Mike McCormick	16.00	6.50
❑ 531 Sandy Amoros	20.00	8.00
❑ 532 Mike Garcia	20.00	8.00
❑ 533 Lu Clinton	16.00	6.50
❑ 534 Ken MacKenzie	16.00	6.50
❑ 535 Whitey Lockman	16.00	6.50
❑ 536 Wynn Hawkins	16.00	6.50
❑ 537 Boston Red Sox Team Card CL	30.00	6.00
❑ 538 Frank Barnes	16.00	6.50
❑ 539 Gene Baker	16.00	6.50
❑ 540 Jerry Walker	16.00	6.50
❑ 541 Tony Curry	16.00	6.50
❑ 542 Ken Hamlin	16.00	6.50
❑ 543 Elio Chacon	16.00	6.50
❑ 544 Bill Monbouquette	20.00	8.00
❑ 545 Carl Sawatski	16.00	6.50
❑ 546 Hank Aguirre	16.00	6.50
❑ 547 Bob Aspromonte	20.00	8.00
❑ 548 Don Mincher	16.00	6.50
❑ 549 John Buzhardt	16.00	6.50
❑ 550 Jim Landis	16.00	6.50
❑ 551 Ed Rakow	16.00	6.50
❑ 552 Walt Bond	16.00	6.50
❑ 553 Bill Skowron AS	20.00	8.00
❑ 554 Willie McCovey AS	35.00	14.00
❑ 555 Nellie Fox AS	30.00	12.00
❑ 556 Charlie Neal AS	16.00	6.50
❑ 557 Frank Malzone AS	16.00	6.50
❑ 558 Eddie Mathews AS	35.00	14.00
❑ 559 Luis Aparicio AS	30.00	12.00
❑ 560 Ernie Banks AS	60.00	24.00
❑ 561 Al Kaline AS	60.00	24.00
❑ 562 Joe Cunningham AS	16.00	6.50
❑ 563 Mickey Mantle AS	250.00	100.00
❑ 564 Willie Mays AS	100.00	40.00
❑ 565 Roger Maris AS	100.00	40.00
❑ 566 Hank Aaron AS	100.00	40.00
❑ 567 Sherm Lollar AS	16.00	6.50
❑ 568 Del Crandall AS	16.00	6.50
❑ 569 Camilo Pascual AS	16.00	6.50
❑ 570 Don Drysdale AS	35.00	14.00
❑ 571 Billy Pierce AS	16.00	6.50
❑ 572 Johnny Antonelli AS	30.00	9.00
❑ NNO Iron-on team transfer	4.00	1.60

1961 Topps

	NM	Ex
COMPLETE SET (587)	7000.00	2800.00
COMMON CARD (1-370)	3.00	1.20
COMMON (371-446)	4.00	1.60
COMMON (447-522)	7.00	2.80
COMMON (523-589)	30.00	12.00
NOT ISSUED (587/588)		
WRAPPER (1-CENT)	200.00	80.00
WRAP.(1-CENT, REPEAT)	100.00	40.00
WRAPPER (5-CENT)	40.00	16.00
❑ 1 Dick Groat	30.00	6.00

❑ 2 Roger Maris	175.00	70.00
❑ 3 John Buzhardt	3.00	1.20
❑ 4 Lenny Green	3.00	1.20
❑ 5 John Romano	3.00	1.20
❑ 6 Ed Roebuck	3.00	1.20
❑ 7 White Sox Team	8.00	3.20
❑ 8 Dick Williams	6.00	2.40
❑ 9 Bob Purkey	3.00	1.20
❑ 10 Brooks Robinson	50.00	20.00
❑ 11 Curt Simmons	6.00	2.40
❑ 12 Moe Thacker	3.00	1.20
❑ 13 Chuck Cottier	3.00	1.20
❑ 14 Don Mossi	6.00	2.40
❑ 15 Willie Kirkland	3.00	1.20
❑ 16 Billy Muffett	3.00	1.20
❑ 17 Checklist 1	10.00	2.00
❑ 18 Jim Grant	6.00	2.40
❑ 19 Clete Boyer	8.00	3.20
❑ 20 Robin Roberts	15.00	6.00
❑ 21 Zorro Versalles	8.00	3.20
UER RC		
First name should be Zoilo		
❑ 22 Clem Labine	6.00	2.40
❑ 23 Don Demeter	3.00	1.20
❑ 24 Ken Johnson	6.00	2.40
❑ 25 Vada Pinson	8.00	3.20
Gus Bell		
Frank Robinson		
❑ 26 Wes Stock	3.00	1.20
❑ 27 Jerry Kindall	3.00	1.20
❑ 28 Hector Lopez	6.00	2.40
❑ 29 Don Nottebart	3.00	1.20
❑ 30 Nellie Fox	15.00	6.00
❑ 31 Bob Schmidt	3.00	1.20
❑ 32 Ray Sadecki	3.00	1.20
❑ 33 Gary Geiger	3.00	1.20
❑ 34 Wynn Hawkins	3.00	1.20
❑ 35 Ron Santo RC	40.00	16.00
❑ 36 Jack Kralick	3.00	1.20
❑ 37 Charley Maxwell	6.00	2.40
❑ 38 Bob Lillis	3.00	1.20
❑ 39 Leo Posada	3.00	1.20
❑ 40 Bob Turley	6.00	2.40
❑ 41 Dick Groat	35.00	14.00
Norm Larker		
Willie Mays		
Roberto Clemente LL		
❑ 42 Pete Runnels	8.00	3.20
Al Smith		
Minnie Minoso		
Bill Skowron LL		
❑ 43 Ernie Banks	30.00	12.00
Hank Aaron		
Ed Mathews		
Ken Boyer LL		
❑ 44 Mickey Mantle	80.00	32.00
Roger Maris		
Jim Lemon		
Rocky Colavito LL		
❑ 45 Mike McCormick	8.00	3.20
Ernie Broglio		
Don Drysdale		
Bob Friend		
Stan Williams LL		
❑ 46 Frank Baumann	8.00	3.20
Jim Bunning		
Art Ditmar		

Hal Brown LL
❑ 47 Ernie Broglio 8.00 3.20
Warren Spahn
Vern Law
Lou Burdette LL
❑ 48 Chuck Estrada 8.00 3.20
Jim Perry UER
(Listed as an Oriole)
Bud Daley
Art Ditmar
Frank Lary
Milt Pappas LL
❑ 49 Don Drysdale 20.00 8.00
Sandy Koufax
Sam Jones
Ernie Broglio LL
❑ 50 Jim Bunning 8.00 3.20
Pedro Ramos
Early Wynn
Frank Lary LL
❑ 51 Detroit Tigers 8.00 3.20
Team Card
❑ 52 George Crowe 3.00 1.20
❑ 53 Russ Nixon 3.00 1.20
❑ 54 Earl Francis 3.00 1.20
❑ 55 Jim Davenport 6.00 2.40
❑ 56 Russ Kemmerer 3.00 1.20
❑ 57 Marv Throneberry 6.00 2.40
❑ 58 Joe Schaffernoth 3.00 1.20
❑ 59 Jim Woods 3.00 1.20
❑ 60 Woody Held 3.00 1.20
❑ 61 Ron Piche 3.00 1.20
❑ 62 Al Pilarcik 3.00 1.20
❑ 63 Jim Kaat 8.00 3.20
❑ 64 Alex Grammas 3.00 1.20
❑ 65 Ted Kluszewski 8.00 3.20
❑ 66 Bill Henry 3.00 1.20
❑ 67 Ossie Virgil 3.00 1.20
❑ 68 Deron Johnson 6.00 2.40
❑ 69 Earl Wilson 6.00 2.40
❑ 70 Bill Virdon 6.00 2.40
❑ 71 Jerry Adair 3.00 1.20
❑ 72 Stu Miller 6.00 2.40
❑ 73 Al Spangler 3.00 1.20
❑ 74 Joe Pignatano 3.00 1.20
❑ 75 Lindy McDaniel 6.00 2.40
Larry Jackson
❑ 76 Harry Anderson 3.00 1.20
❑ 77 Dick Stigman 3.00 1.20
❑ 78 Lee Walls 6.00 2.40
❑ 79 Joe Ginsberg 3.00 1.20
❑ 80 Harmon Killebrew 20.00 8.00
❑ 81 Tracy Stallard 3.00 1.20
❑ 82 Joe Christopher 3.00 1.20
❑ 83 Bob Bruce 3.00 1.20
❑ 84 Lee Maye 3.00 1.20
❑ 85 Jerry Walker 3.00 1.20
❑ 86 Los Angeles Dodgers 8.00 3.20
Team Card
❑ 87 Joe Amalfitano 3.00 1.20
❑ 88 Richie Ashburn 15.00 6.00
❑ 89 Billy Martin 15.00 6.00
❑ 90 Gerry Staley 3.00 1.20
❑ 91 Walt Moryn 3.00 1.20
❑ 92 Hal Naragon 3.00 1.20
❑ 93 Tony Gonzalez 3.00 1.20
❑ 94 Johnny Kucks 3.00 1.20
❑ 95 Norm Cash 8.00 3.20
❑ 96 Billy O'Dell 3.00 1.20
❑ 97 Jerry Lynch 6.00 2.40
❑ 98A Checklist 2 10.00 2.00
(Red "Checklist"
98 black on white)
❑ 98B Checklist 2 10.00 2.00
(Yellow "Checklist"
98 black on white)
❑ 98C Checklist 2 10.00 2.00
(Yellow "Checklist"
98 white on black
no copyright)
❑ 99 Don Buddin UER 3.00 1.20
(66 HR's)
❑ 100 Harvey Haddix 6.00 2.40
❑ 101 Bubba Phillips 3.00 1.20
❑ 102 Gene Stephens 3.00 1.20
❑ 103 Ruben Amaro 3.00 1.20

❑ 104 John Blanchard 8.00 3.20
❑ 105 Carl Willey 3.00 1.20
❑ 106 Whitey Herzog 3.00 1.20
❑ 107 Seth Morehead 3.00 1.20
❑ 108 Dan Dobbek 3.00 1.20
❑ 109 Johnny Podres 8.00 3.20
❑ 110 Vada Pinson 8.00 3.20
❑ 111 Jack Meyer 3.00 1.20
❑ 112 Chico Fernandez 3.00 1.20
❑ 113 Mike Fornieles 3.00 1.20
❑ 114 Hobie Landrith 3.00 1.20
❑ 115 Johnny Antonelli 6.00 2.40
❑ 116 Joe DeMaestri 3.00 1.20
❑ 117 Dale Long 6.00 2.40
❑ 118 Chris Cannizzaro 3.00 1.20
❑ 119 Norm Siebern 6.00 2.40
Hank Bauer
Jerry Lumpe
❑ 120 Eddie Mathews 30.00 12.00
❑ 121 Eli Grba 6.00 2.40
❑ 122 Chicago Cubs 8.00 3.20
Team Card
❑ 123 Billy Gardner 3.00 1.20
❑ 124 J.C. Martin 3.00 1.20
❑ 125 Steve Barber 3.00 1.20
❑ 126 Dick Stuart 6.00 2.40
❑ 127 Ron Kline 3.00 1.20
❑ 128 Rip Repulski 3.00 1.20
❑ 129 Ed Hobaugh 3.00 1.20
❑ 130 Norm Larker 3.00 1.20
❑ 131 Paul Richards MG 6.00 2.40
❑ 132 Al Lopez MG 8.00 3.20
❑ 133 Ralph Houk MG 6.00 2.40
❑ 134 Mickey Vernon MG 6.00 2.40
❑ 135 Fred Hutchinson MG 6.00 2.40
❑ 136 Walter Alston MG 8.00 3.20
❑ 137 Chuck Dressen MG 6.00 2.40
❑ 138 Danny Murtaugh MG 6.00 2.40
❑ 139 Solly Hemus MG 6.00 2.40
❑ 140 Gus Triandos 6.00 2.40
❑ 141 Billy Williams RC 60.00 24.00
❑ 142 Luis Arroyo 6.00 2.40
❑ 143 Russ Snyder 3.00 1.20
❑ 144 Jim Coker 3.00 1.20
❑ 145 Bob Buhl 6.00 2.40
❑ 146 Marty Keough 3.00 1.20
❑ 147 Ed Rakow 3.00 1.20
❑ 148 Julian Javier 6.00 2.40
❑ 149 Bob Oldis 3.00 1.20
❑ 150 Willie Mays 100.00 40.00
❑ 151 Jim Donohue 3.00 1.20
❑ 152 Earl Torgeson 3.00 1.20
❑ 153 Don Lee 3.00 1.20
❑ 154 Bobby Del Greco 3.00 1.20
❑ 155 Johnny Temple 6.00 2.40
❑ 156 Ken Hunt 6.00 2.40
❑ 157 Cal McLish 3.00 1.20
❑ 158 Pete Daley 3.00 1.20
❑ 159 Orioles Team 8.00 3.20
❑ 160 Whitey Ford UER 50.00 20.00
Incorrectly listed
as 5'0" tall
❑ 161 Sherman Jones UER 3.00 1.20
(Photo actually
Eddie Fisher)
❑ 162 Jay Hook 3.00 1.20
❑ 163 Ed Sadowski 3.00 1.20
❑ 164 Felix Mantilla 3.00 1.20
❑ 165 Gino Cimoli 3.00 1.20
❑ 166 Danny Kravitz 3.00 1.20
❑ 167 San Francisco Giants 8.00 3.20
Team Card
❑ 168 Tommy Davis 8.00 3.20
❑ 169 Don Elston 3.00 1.20
❑ 170 Al Smith 3.00 1.20
❑ 171 Paul Foytack 3.00 1.20
❑ 172 Don Dillard 3.00 1.20
❑ 173 Frank Malzone 6.00 2.40
Vic Wertz
Jackie Jensen
❑ 174 Ray Semproch 3.00 1.20
❑ 175 Gene Freese 3.00 1.20
❑ 176 Ken Aspromonte 3.00 1.20
❑ 177 Don Larsen 6.00 2.40
❑ 178 Bob Nieman 3.00 1.20
❑ 179 Joe Koppe 3.00 1.20

❑ 180 Bobby Richardson 12.00 4.80
❑ 181 Fred Green 3.00 1.20
❑ 182 Dave Nicholson 3.00 1.20
❑ 183 Andre Rodgers 3.00 1.20
❑ 184 Steve Bilko 6.00 2.40
❑ 185 Herb Score 6.00 2.40
❑ 186 Elmer Valo 6.00 2.40
❑ 187 Billy Klaus 3.00 1.20
❑ 188 Jim Marshall 3.00 1.20
❑ 189A Checklist 3 10.00 2.00
(Copyright symbol
almost adjacent to
263 Ken Hamlin)
❑ 189B Checklist 3 10.00 2.00
(Copyright symbol
adjacent to
264 Glen Hobbie)
❑ 190 Stan Williams 6.00 2.40
❑ 191 Mike de la Hoz 3.00 1.20
❑ 192 Dick Brown 3.00 1.20
❑ 193 Gene Conley 6.00 2.40
❑ 194 Gordy Coleman 6.00 2.40
❑ 195 Jerry Casale 3.00 1.20
❑ 196 Ed Bouchee 3.00 1.20
❑ 197 Dick Hall 3.00 1.20
❑ 198 Carl Sawatski 3.00 1.20
❑ 199 Bob Boyd 3.00 1.20
❑ 200 Warren Spahn 40.00 16.00
❑ 201 Pete Whisenant 3.00 1.20
❑ 202 Al Neiger 3.00 1.20
❑ 203 Eddie Bressoud 3.00 1.20
❑ 204 Bob Skinner 6.00 2.40
❑ 205 Billy Pierce 6.00 2.40
❑ 206 Gene Green 3.00 1.20
❑ 207 Sandy Koufax 30.00 12.00
Johnny Podres
❑ 208 Larry Osborne 3.00 1.20
❑ 209 Ken McBride 3.00 1.20
❑ 210 Pete Runnels 6.00 2.40
❑ 211 Bob Gibson 40.00 16.00
❑ 212 Haywood Sullivan 6.00 2.40
❑ 213 Bill Stafford 3.00 1.20
❑ 214 Danny Murphy 6.00 2.40
❑ 215 Gus Bell 6.00 2.40
❑ 216 Ted Bowsfield 3.00 1.20
❑ 217 Mel Roach 3.00 1.20
❑ 218 Hal Brown 3.00 1.20
❑ 219 Gene Mauch MG 6.00 2.40
❑ 220 Alvin Dark MG 6.00 2.40
❑ 221 Mike Higgins MG 3.00 1.20
❑ 222 Jimmy Dykes MG 6.00 2.40
❑ 223 Bob Scheffing MG 3.00 1.20
❑ 224 Joe Gordon MG 6.00 2.40
❑ 225 Bill Rigney MG 6.00 2.40
❑ 226 Cookie Lavagetto MG 6.00 2.40
❑ 227 Juan Pizarro 3.00 1.20
❑ 228 New York Yankees 60.00 24.00
Team Card
❑ 229 Rudy Hernandez 3.00 1.20
❑ 230 Don Hoak 6.00 2.40
❑ 231 Dick Drott 3.00 1.20
❑ 232 Bill White 6.00 2.40
❑ 233 Joey Jay 6.00 2.40
❑ 234 Ted Lepcio 3.00 1.20
❑ 235 Camilo Pascual 6.00 2.40
❑ 236 Don Gile 3.00 1.20
❑ 237 Billy Loes 6.00 2.40
❑ 238 Jim Gilliam 6.00 2.40
❑ 239 Dave Sisler 3.00 1.20
❑ 240 Ron Hansen 3.00 1.20
❑ 241 Al Cicotte 3.00 1.20
❑ 242 Hal Smith 3.00 1.20
❑ 243 Frank Lary 6.00 2.40
❑ 244 Chico Cardenas 6.00 2.40
❑ 245 Joe Adcock 6.00 2.40
❑ 246 Bob Davis 3.00 1.20
❑ 247 Billy Goodman 6.00 2.40
❑ 248 Ed Keegan 3.00 1.20
❑ 249 Cincinnati Reds 8.00 3.20
Team Card
❑ 250 Vern Law 6.00 2.40
Roy Face
❑ 251 Bill Bruton 3.00 1.20
❑ 252 Bill Short 3.00 1.20
❑ 253 Sammy Taylor 3.00 1.20
❑ 254 Ted Sadowski 6.00 2.40

❑ 255 Vic Power 6.00 2.40
❑ 256 Billy Hoeft 3.00 1.20
❑ 257 Carroll Hardy 3.00 1.20
❑ 258 Jack Sanford 6.00 2.40
❑ 259 John Schaive 3.00 1.20
❑ 260 Don Drysdale 30.00 12.00
❑ 261 Charlie Lau 6.00 2.40
❑ 262 Tony Curry 3.00 1.20
❑ 263 Ken Hamlin 3.00 1.20
❑ 264 Glen Hobbie 3.00 1.20
❑ 265 Tony Kubek 12.00 4.80
❑ 266 Lindy McDaniel 6.00 2.40
❑ 267 Norm Siebern 3.00 1.20
❑ 268 Ike Delock 3.00 1.20
❑ 269 Harry Chiti 3.00 1.20
❑ 270 Bob Friend 6.00 2.40
❑ 271 Jim Landis 3.00 1.20
❑ 272 Tom Morgan 3.00 1.20
❑ 273A Checklist 4 .... 16.00 3.20
(Copyright symbol
adjacent to
336 Don Mincher)
❑ 273B Checklist 4 .... 10.00 2.00
(Copyright symbol
adjacent to
339 Gene Baker)
❑ 274 Gary Bell 3.00 1.20
❑ 275 Gene Woodling 6.00 2.40
❑ 276 Ray Rippelmeyer 3.00 1.20
❑ 277 Hank Foiles 3.00 1.20
❑ 278 Don McMahon 3.00 1.20
❑ 279 Jose Pagan 3.00 1.20
❑ 280 Frank Howard 8.00 3.20
❑ 281 Frank Sullivan 3.00 1.20
❑ 282 Faye Throneberry 3.00 1.20
❑ 283 Bob Anderson 3.00 1.20
❑ 284 Dick Gernert 3.00 1.20
❑ 285 Sherm Lollar 6.00 2.40
❑ 286 George Witt 3.00 1.20
❑ 287 Carl Yastrzemski 50.00 20.00
❑ 288 Albie Pearson 6.00 2.40
❑ 289 Ray Moore 3.00 1.20
❑ 290 Stan Musial 100.00 40.00
❑ 291 Tex Clevenger 3.00 1.20
❑ 292 Jim Baumer 3.00 1.20
❑ 293 Tom Sturdivant 3.00 1.20
❑ 294 Don Blasingame 3.00 1.20
❑ 295 Milt Pappas 6.00 2.40
❑ 296 Wes Covington 6.00 2.40
❑ 297 Athletics Team 8.00 3.20
❑ 298 Jim Golden 3.00 1.20
❑ 299 Clay Dalrymple 3.00 1.20
❑ 300 Mickey Mantle 400.00 160.00
❑ 301 Chet Nichols 3.00 1.20
❑ 302 Al Heist 3.00 1.20
❑ 303 Gary Peters 6.00 2.40
❑ 304 Rocky Nelson 3.00 1.20
❑ 305 Mike McCormick 6.00 2.40
❑ 306 Bill Virdon WS 9.00 3.60
❑ 307 Mickey Mantle WS 80.00 32.00
❑ 308 B.Richardson WS 12.00 4.80
❑ 309 Gino Cimoli WS 9.00 3.60
❑ 310 Roy Face WS 9.00 3.60
❑ 311 Whitey Ford WS 16.00 6.50
❑ 312 Bill Mazeroski WS 20.00 8.00
Mazeroski Homer Wins it
❑ 313 WS Summary 16.00 6.50
Pirates Celebrate
❑ 314 Bob Miller 3.00 1.20
❑ 315 Earl Battey 6.00 2.40
❑ 316 Bobby Gene Smith 3.00 1.20
❑ 317 Jim Brewer 3.00 1.20
❑ 318 Danny O'Connell 3.00 1.20
❑ 319 Valmy Thomas 3.00 1.20
❑ 320 Lou Burdette 6.00 2.40
❑ 321 Marv Breeding 3.00 1.20
❑ 322 Bill Kunkel 6.00 2.40
❑ 323 Sammy Esposito 3.00 1.20
❑ 324 Hank Aguirre 3.00 1.20
❑ 325 Wally Moon 6.00 2.40
❑ 326 Dave Hillman 3.00 1.20
❑ 327 Matty Alou RC 12.00 4.80
❑ 328 Jim O'Toole 6.00 2.40
❑ 329 Julio Becquer 3.00 1.20
❑ 330 Rocky Colavito 20.00 8.00
❑ 331 Ned Garver 3.00 1.20
❑ 332 Dutch Dotterer UER 3.00 1.20
(Photo actually
Tommy Dotterer
Dutch's brother)
❑ 333 Fritz Brickell 3.00 1.20
❑ 334 Walt Bond 3.00 1.20
❑ 335 Frank Bolling 3.00 1.20
❑ 336 Don Mincher 6.00 2.40
❑ 337 Early Wynn 8.00 3.20
Al Lopez
Herb Score
❑ 338 Don Landrum 3.00 1.20
❑ 339 Gene Baker 3.00 1.20
❑ 340 Vic Wertz 6.00 2.40
❑ 341 Jim Owens 3.00 1.20
❑ 342 Clint Courtney 3.00 1.20
❑ 343 Earl Robinson 3.00 1.20
❑ 344 Sandy Koufax 100.00 40.00
❑ 345 Jimmy Piersall 8.00 3.20
❑ 346 Howie Nunn 3.00 1.20
❑ 347 St. Louis Cardinals 8.00 3.20
Team Card
❑ 348 Steve Boros 3.00 1.20
❑ 349 Danny McDevitt 3.00 1.20
❑ 350 Ernie Banks 40.00 16.00
❑ 351 Jim King 3.00 1.20
❑ 352 Bob Shaw 3.00 1.20
❑ 353 Howie Bedell 3.00 1.20
❑ 354 Billy Harrell 6.00 2.40
❑ 355 Bob Allison 8.00 3.20
❑ 356 Ryne Duren 3.00 1.20
❑ 357 Daryl Spencer 3.00 1.20
❑ 358 Earl Averill 6.00 2.40
❑ 359 Dallas Green 3.00 1.20
❑ 360 Frank Robinson 40.00 16.00
❑ 361A Checklist 5 .... 16.00 3.20
(No ad on back)
❑ 361B Checklist 5 .... 16.00 3.20
(Special Feature
ad on back)
❑ 362 Frank Funk 3.00 1.20
❑ 363 John Roseboro 6.00 2.40
❑ 364 Moe Drabowsky 6.00 2.40
❑ 365 Jerry Lumpe 3.00 1.20
❑ 366 Eddie Fisher 3.00 1.20
❑ 367 Jim Rivera 3.00 1.20
❑ 368 Bennie Daniels 3.00 1.20
❑ 369 Dave Philley 3.00 1.20
❑ 370 Roy Face 6.00 2.40
❑ 371 Bill Skowron SP 50.00 20.00
❑ 372 Bob Hendley 4.00 1.60
❑ 373 Boston Red Sox 8.00 3.20
Team Card
❑ 374 Paul Giel 4.00 1.60
❑ 375 Ken Boyer 12.00 4.80
❑ 376 Mike Roarke RC 6.00 2.40
❑ 377 Ruben Gomez 4.00 1.60
❑ 378 Wally Post 6.00 2.40
❑ 379 Bobby Shantz 4.00 1.60
❑ 380 Minnie Minoso 8.00 3.20
❑ 381 Dave Wickersham 4.00 1.60
❑ 382 Frank Thomas 6.00 2.40
❑ 383 Mike McCormick 6.00 2.40
Jack Sanford
Billy O'Dell
❑ 384 Chuck Essegian 4.00 1.60
❑ 385 Jim Perry 6.00 2.40
❑ 386 Joe Hicks 4.00 1.60
❑ 387 Duke Maas 4.00 1.60
❑ 388 Roberto Clemente 125.00 50.00
❑ 389 Ralph Terry 6.00 2.40
❑ 390 Del Crandall 8.00 3.20
❑ 391 Winston Brown 4.00 1.60
❑ 392 Reno Bertoia 4.00 1.60
❑ 393 Don Cardwell 4.00 1.60
Glen Hobbie
❑ 394 Ken Walters 4.00 1.60
❑ 395 Chuck Estrada 6.00 2.40
❑ 396 Bob Aspromonte 4.00 1.60
❑ 397 Hal Woodeshick 4.00 1.60
❑ 398 Hank Bauer 6.00 2.40
❑ 399 Cliff Cook 4.00 1.60
❑ 400 Vern Law 6.00 2.40
❑ 401 Babe Ruth HL 60.00 24.00
60th HR
❑ 402 Don Larsen HL SP 25.00 10.00
WS Perfect Game
❑ 403 Joe Oeschger HL 7.00 2.80
Leon Cadore
26 Inning Tie
❑ 404 Rogers Hornsby HL 12.00 4.80
.424 Season BA
❑ 405 Lou Gehrig HL 75.00 30.00
Consecutive Game Streak
❑ 406 Mickey Mantle HL 100.00 40.00
565 foot HR
❑ 407 Jack Chesbro HL 7.00 2.80
41 victories
❑ 408 C. Mathewson HL SP 20.00 8.00
267 Strikeouts
❑ 409 Walter Johnson SL 12.00 4.80
3 Shutouts in 4 days
❑ 410 Harvey Haddix HL 7.00 2.80
12 Perfect Innings
❑ 411 Tony Taylor 6.00 2.40
❑ 412 Larry Sherry 6.00 2.40
❑ 413 Eddie Yost 6.00 2.40
❑ 414 Dick Donovan 6.00 2.40
❑ 415 Hank Aaron 125.00 50.00
❑ 416 Dick Howser RC 8.00 3.20
❑ 417 Juan Marichal SP RC 100.00 40.00
❑ 418 Ed Bailey 6.00 2.40
❑ 419 Tom Borland 4.00 1.60
❑ 420 Ernie Broglio 6.00 2.40
❑ 421 Ty Cline SP 18.00 7.25
❑ 422 Bud Daley 4.00 1.60
❑ 423 Charlie Neal SP 18.00 7.25
❑ 424 Turk Lown 4.00 1.60
❑ 425 Yogi Berra 80.00 32.00
❑ 426 Milwaukee Braves 12.00 4.80
Team Card
(Back numbered 463)
❑ 427 Dick Ellsworth 6.00 2.40
❑ 428 Ray Barker SP 18.00 7.25
❑ 429 Al Kaline 50.00 20.00
❑ 430 Bill Mazeroski SP 50.00 20.00
❑ 431 Chuck Stobbs 4.00 1.60
❑ 432 Coot Veal 6.00 2.40
❑ 433 Art Mahaffey 4.00 1.60
❑ 434 Tom Brewer 4.00 1.60
❑ 435 Orlando Cepeda UER 12.00 4.80
(San Francis on
card front)
❑ 436 Jim Maloney SP RC 20.00 8.00
❑ 437A Checklist 6 .... 16.00 3.20
440 Louis Aparicio
❑ 437B Checklist 6 .... 16.00 3.20
440 Luis Aparicio
❑ 438 Curt Flood 8.00 3.20
❑ 439 Phil Regan RC 6.00 2.40
❑ 440 Luis Aparicio 12.00 4.80
❑ 441 Dick Bertell 4.00 1.60
❑ 442 Gordon Jones 4.00 1.60
❑ 443 Duke Snider 50.00 16.00
❑ 444 Joe Nuxhall 6.00 2.40
❑ 445 Frank Malzone 6.00 2.40
❑ 446 Bob Taylor 4.00 1.60
❑ 447 Harry Bright 7.00 2.80
❑ 448 Del Rice 15.00 6.00
❑ 449 Bob Bolin 7.00 2.80
❑ 450 Jim Lemon 7.00 2.80
❑ 451 Daryl Spencer 7.00 2.80
Bill White
Ernie Broglio
❑ 452 Bob Allen 7.00 2.80
❑ 453 Dick Schofield 7.00 2.80
❑ 454 Pumpsie Green 7.00 2.80
❑ 455 Early Wynn 15.00 6.00
❑ 456 Hal Bevan 7.00 2.80
❑ 457 Johnny James 7.00 2.80
(Listed as Angel,
but wearing Yankee
uniform and cap)
❑ 458 Willie Tasby 7.00 2.80
❑ 459 Terry Fox RC 10.00 4.00
❑ 460 Gil Hodges 25.00 10.00
❑ 461 Smoky Burgess 15.00 6.00
❑ 462 Lou Klimchock 7.00 2.80
❑ 463 Jack Fisher 7.00 2.80
(See also 426)
❑ 464 Lee Thomas RC 10.00 4.00
(Pictured with Yankee

Card	NM	Ex
cap but listed as		
Los Angeles Angel)		
❑ 465 Roy McMillan	15.00	6.00
❑ 466 Ron Moeller	7.00	2.80
❑ 467 Cleveland Indians	12.00	4.80
Team Card		
❑ 468 John Callison	10.00	4.00
❑ 469 Ralph Lumenti	7.00	2.80
❑ 470 Roy Sievers	10.00	4.00
❑ 471 Phil Rizzuto MVP	25.00	10.00
❑ 472 Yogi Berra MVP	50.00	20.00
❑ 473 Bob Shantz MVP	8.00	3.20
❑ 474 Al Rosen MVP	10.00	4.00
❑ 475 Mickey Mantle MVP	175.00	70.00
❑ 476 Jackie Jensen MVP	10.00	4.00
❑ 477 Nellie Fox MVP	15.00	6.00
❑ 478 Roger Maris MVP	60.00	24.00
❑ 479 Jim Konstanty MVP	8.00	3.20
❑ 480 Roy Campanella MVP	40.00	16.00
❑ 481 Hank Sauer MVP	8.00	3.20
❑ 482 Willie Mays MVP	50.00	20.00
❑ 483 Don Newcombe MVP	10.00	4.00
❑ 484 Hank Aaron MVP	50.00	20.00
❑ 485 Ernie Banks MVP	40.00	16.00
❑ 486 Dick Groat MVP	10.00	4.00
❑ 487 Gene Oliver	7.00	2.80
❑ 488 Joe McClain	10.00	4.00
❑ 489 Walt Dropo	7.00	2.80
❑ 490 Jim Bunning	25.00	10.00
❑ 491 Philadelphia Phillies	12.00	4.80
Team Card		
❑ 492 Ron Fairly	10.00	4.00
❑ 493 Don Zimmer UER	10.00	4.00
(Brooklyn A.L.)		
❑ 494 Tom Cheney	15.00	6.00
❑ 495 Elston Howard	10.00	4.00
❑ 496 Ken MacKenzie	7.00	2.80
❑ 497 Willie Jones	7.00	2.80
❑ 498 Ray Herbert	7.00	2.80
❑ 499 Chuck Schilling RC	7.00	2.80
❑ 500 Harvey Kuenn	10.00	4.00
❑ 501 John DeMerit	7.00	2.80
❑ 502 Clarence Coleman RC	10.00	4.00
❑ 503 Tito Francona	7.00	2.80
❑ 504 Billy Consolo	7.00	2.80
❑ 505 Red Schoendienst	15.00	6.00
❑ 506 Willie Davis RC	15.00	6.00
❑ 507 Pete Burnside	7.00	2.80
❑ 508 Rocky Bridges	7.00	2.80
❑ 509 Camilo Carreon	7.00	2.80
❑ 510 Art Ditmar	7.00	2.80
❑ 511 Joe M. Morgan	7.00	2.80
❑ 512 Bob Will	7.00	2.80
❑ 513 Jim Brosnan	7.00	2.80
❑ 514 Jake Wood	7.00	2.80
❑ 515 Jackie Brandt	7.00	2.80
❑ 516 Checklist 7	16.00	3.20
❑ 517 Willie McCovey	40.00	16.00
❑ 518 Andy Carey	7.00	2.80
❑ 519 Jim Pagliaroni	7.00	2.80
❑ 520 Joe Cunningham	7.00	2.80
❑ 521 Norm Sherry	7.00	2.80
Larry Sherry		
❑ 522 Dick Farrell UER	15.00	6.00
(Phillies cap but		
listed on Dodgers)		
❑ 523 Joe Gibbon	30.00	12.00
❑ 524 Johnny Logan	30.00	12.00
❑ 525 Ron Perranoski RC	60.00	24.00
❑ 526 R.C. Stevens	30.00	12.00
❑ 527 Gene Leek	30.00	12.00
❑ 528 Pedro Ramos	30.00	12.00
❑ 529 Bob Roselli	30.00	12.00
❑ 530 Bob Malkmus	30.00	12.00
❑ 531 Jim Coates	50.00	20.00
❑ 532 Bob Hale	30.00	12.00
❑ 533 Jack Curtis	30.00	12.00
❑ 534 Eddie Kasko	40.00	16.00
❑ 535 Larry Jackson	30.00	12.00
❑ 536 Bill Tuttle	30.00	12.00
❑ 537 Bobby Locke	30.00	12.00
❑ 538 Chuck Hiller	30.00	12.00
❑ 539 Johnny Klippstein	30.00	12.00
❑ 540 Jackie Jensen	40.00	16.00
❑ 541 Roland Sheldon RC	50.00	20.00
❑ 542 Minnesota Twins	60.00	24.00
Team Card		
❑ 543 Roger Craig	40.00	16.00
❑ 544 George Thomas	50.00	20.00
❑ 545 Hoyt Wilhelm	60.00	24.00
❑ 546 Marty Kutyna	30.00	12.00
❑ 547 Leon Wagner	30.00	12.00
❑ 548 Ted Wills	30.00	12.00
❑ 549 Hal R. Smith	30.00	12.00
❑ 550 Frank Baumann	30.00	12.00
❑ 551 George Altman	40.00	16.00
❑ 552 Jim Archer	30.00	12.00
❑ 553 Bill Fischer	30.00	12.00
❑ 554 Pittsburgh Pirates	70.00	28.00
Team Card		
❑ 555 Sam Jones	30.00	12.00
❑ 556 Ken R. Hunt	30.00	12.00
❑ 557 Jose Valdivielso	30.00	12.00
❑ 558 Don Ferrarese	30.00	12.00
❑ 559 Jim Gentile	60.00	24.00
❑ 560 Barry Latman	40.00	16.00
❑ 561 Charley James	30.00	12.00
❑ 562 Bill Monbouquette	30.00	12.00
❑ 563 Bob Cerv	60.00	24.00
❑ 564 Don Cardwell	30.00	12.00
❑ 565 Felipe Alou	50.00	20.00
❑ 566 Paul Richards AS MG	30.00	12.00
❑ 567 D.Murtaugh AS MG	30.00	12.00
❑ 568 Bill Skowron AS	50.00	20.00
❑ 569 Frank Herrera AS	40.00	16.00
❑ 570 Nellie Fox AS	60.00	24.00
❑ 571 Bill Mazeroski AS	60.00	24.00
❑ 572 Brooks Robinson AS	80.00	32.00
❑ 573 Ken Boyer AS	50.00	20.00
❑ 574 Luis Aparicio AS	60.00	24.00
❑ 575 Ernie Banks AS	80.00	32.00
❑ 576 Roger Maris AS	175.00	70.00
❑ 577 Hank Aaron AS	150.00	60.00
❑ 578 Mickey Mantle AS	400.00	160.00
❑ 579 Willie Mays AS	150.00	60.00
❑ 580 Al Kaline AS	80.00	32.00
❑ 581 Frank Robinson AS	80.00	32.00
❑ 582 Earl Battey AS	30.00	12.00
❑ 583 Del Crandall AS	30.00	12.00
❑ 584 Jim Perry AS	30.00	12.00
❑ 585 Bob Friend AS	30.00	12.00
❑ 586 Whitey Ford AS	100.00	40.00
❑ 589 Warren Spahn AS	100.00	30.00

1962 Topps

	NM	Ex
COMP. MASTER (688)	7000.00	2800.00
COMPLETE SET (598)	6000.00	2400.00
COMMON CARD (1-370)	5.00	2.00
COMMON (371-446)	6.00	2.40
COMMON (447-522)	12.00	4.80
COMMON (523-598)	20.00	8.00
WRAPPER (1-CENT)	100.00	40.00
WRAPPER (5-CENT)	30.00	12.00

Card	NM	Ex
❑ 1 Roger Maris	300.00	75.00
❑ 2 Jim Brosnan	5.00	2.00
❑ 3 Pete Runnels	5.00	2.00
❑ 4 John DeMerit	8.00	3.20
❑ 5 Sandy Koufax UER	135.00	55.00
Struck ou 18		
❑ 6 Marv Breeding	5.00	2.00
❑ 7 Frank Thomas	10.00	4.00
❑ 8 Ray Herbert	5.00	2.00
❑ 9 Jim Davenport	8.00	3.20
❑ 10 Roberto Clemente	175.00	70.00
❑ 11 Tom Morgan	5.00	2.00
❑ 12 Harry Craft MG	8.00	3.20
❑ 13 Dick Howser	8.00	3.20
❑ 14 Bill White	8.00	3.20
❑ 15 Dick Donovan	5.00	2.00
❑ 16 Darrell Johnson	5.00	2.00
❑ 17 Johnny Callison	8.00	3.20
❑ 18 Mickey Mantle	175.00	70.00
Willie Mays		
❑ 19 Ray Washburn	5.00	2.00
❑ 20 Rocky Colavito	15.00	6.00
❑ 21 Jim Kaat	8.00	3.20
❑ 22A Checklist 1 ERR	12.00	2.40
(121-176 on back)		
❑ 22B Checklist 1 COR	12.00	2.40
❑ 23 Norm Larker	5.00	2.00
❑ 24 Tigers Team	10.00	4.00
❑ 25 Ernie Banks	50.00	20.00
❑ 26 Chris Cannizzaro	8.00	3.20
❑ 27 Chuck Cottier	5.00	2.00
❑ 28 Minnie Minoso	10.00	4.00
❑ 29 Casey Stengel MG	20.00	8.00
❑ 30 Eddie Mathews	40.00	16.00
❑ 31 Tom Tresh RC	15.00	6.00
❑ 32 John Roseboro	8.00	3.20
❑ 33 Don Larsen	8.00	3.20
❑ 34 Johnny Temple	8.00	3.20
❑ 35 Don Schwall	10.00	4.00
❑ 36 Don Leppert	5.00	2.00
❑ 37 Barry Latman	5.00	2.00
Dick Sligman		
Jim Perry		
❑ 38 Gene Stephens	5.00	2.00
❑ 39 Joe Koppe	5.00	2.00
❑ 40 Orlando Cepeda	15.00	6.00
❑ 41 Cliff Cook	5.00	2.00
❑ 42 Jim King	5.00	2.00
❑ 43 Los Angeles Dodgers	10.00	4.00
Team Card		
❑ 44 Don Taussig	5.00	2.00
❑ 45 Brooks Robinson	50.00	20.00
❑ 46 Jack Baldschun	5.00	2.00
❑ 47 Bob Will	5.00	2.00
❑ 48 Ralph Terry	8.00	3.20
❑ 49 Hal Jones	5.00	2.00
❑ 50 Stan Musial	100.00	40.00
❑ 51 Norm Cash	8.00	3.20
Jim Piersall		
Al Kaline		
Elston Howard LL		
❑ 52 Roberto Clemente	20.00	8.00
Vada Pinson		
Ken Boyer		
Wally Moon LL		
❑ 53 Roger Maris	100.00	40.00
Mickey Mantle		
Jim Gentile		
Harmon Killebrew LL		
❑ 54 Orlando Cepeda	20.00	8.00
Willie Mays		
Frank Robinson LL		
❑ 55 Dick Donovan	8.00	3.20
Bill Stafford		
Don Mossi		
Milt Pappas LL		
❑ 56 Warren Spahn	8.00	3.20
Jim O'Toole		
Curt Simmons		
Mike McCormick LL		
❑ 57 Whitey Ford	8.00	3.20
Frank Lary		
Steve Barber		
Jim Bunning LL		
❑ 58 Warren Spahn	8.00	3.20
Joe Jay		
Jim O'Toole LL		
❑ 59 Camilo Pascual	8.00	3.20
Whitey Ford		
Jim Bunning		
Juan Pizzaro LL		
❑ 60 Sandy Koufax	20.00	8.00
Stan Williams		
Don Drysdale		

Jim O'Toole LL
❑ 61 Cardinals Team 10.00 4.00
❑ 62 Steve Boros 5.00 2.00
❑ 63 Tony Cloninger RC 8.00 3.20
❑ 64 Russ Snyder 5.00 2.00
❑ 65 Bobby Richardson 10.00 4.00
❑ 66 Cuno Barragan 5.00 2.00
❑ 67 Harvey Haddix 8.00 3.20
❑ 68 Ken Hunt 5.00 2.00
❑ 69 Phil Ortega 5.00 2.00
❑ 70 Harmon Killebrew 25.00 10.00
❑ 71 Dick LeMay 5.00 2.00
❑ 72 Steve Boros 5.00 2.00
Bob Scheffing MG
Jake Wood
❑ 73 Nellie Fox 20.00 8.00
❑ 74 Bob Lillis 8.00 3.20
❑ 75 Milt Pappas 8.00 3.20
❑ 76 Howie Bedell 5.00 2.00
❑ 77 Tony Taylor 8.00 3.20
❑ 78 Gene Green 5.00 2.00
❑ 79 Ed Hobaugh 5.00 2.00
❑ 80 Vada Pinson 8.00 3.20
❑ 81 Jim Pagliaroni 5.00 2.00
❑ 82 Deron Johnson 8.00 3.20
❑ 83 Larry Jackson 5.00 2.00
❑ 84 Lenny Green 5.00 2.00
❑ 85 Gil Hodges 20.00 8.00
❑ 86 Donn Clendenon RC 8.00 3.20
❑ 87 Mike Roarke 5.00 2.00
❑ 88 Ralph Houk MG 8.00 3.20
(Berra in background)
❑ 89 Barney Schultz 5.00 2.00
❑ 90 Jimmy Piersall 8.00 3.20
❑ 91 J.C. Martin 5.00 2.00
❑ 92 Sam Jones 5.00 2.00
❑ 93 John Blanchard 8.00 3.20
❑ 94 Jay Hook 8.00 3.20
❑ 95 Don Hoak 8.00 3.20
❑ 96 Eli Grba 5.00 2.00
❑ 97 Tito Francona 5.00 2.00
❑ 98 Checklist 2 12.00 2.40
❑ 99 John (Boog) Powell RC 30.00 12.00
❑ 100 Warren Spahn 40.00 16.00
❑ 101 Carroll Hardy 5.00 2.00
❑ 102 Al Schroll 5.00 2.00
❑ 103 Don Blasingame 5.00 2.00
❑ 104 Ted Savage 5.00 2.00
❑ 105 Don Mossi 8.00 3.20
❑ 106 Carl Sawatski 5.00 2.00
❑ 107 Mike McCormick 8.00 3.20
❑ 108 Willie Davis 8.00 3.20
❑ 109 Bob Shaw 5.00 2.00
❑ 110 Bill Skowron 8.00 3.20
❑ 110A Bill Skowron 8.00 3.20
Green Tint
❑ 111 Dallas Green 8.00 3.20
❑ 111A Dallas Green 8.00 3.20
Green Tint
❑ 112 Hank Foiles 5.00 2.00
❑ 112A Hank Foiles 5.00 2.00
Green Tint
❑ 113 Chicago White Sox 10.00 4.00
Team Card
❑ 113A Chicago White Sox 10.00 4.00
Team Card
Green Tint
❑ 114 Howie Koplitz 5.00 2.00
❑ 114A Howie Koplitz 5.00 2.00
Green Tint
❑ 115 Bob Skinner 8.00 3.20
❑ 115A Bob Skinner 8.00 3.20
Green Tint
❑ 116 Herb Score 8.00 3.20
❑ 116A Herb Score 8.00 3.20
Green Tint
❑ 117 Gary Geiger 8.00 3.20
❑ 117A Gary Geiger 8.00 3.20
Green Tint
❑ 118 Julian Javier 8.00 3.20
❑ 118A Julian Javier 8.00 3.20
Green Tint
❑ 119 Danny Murphy 5.00 2.00
❑ 119A Danny Murphy 5.00 2.00
Green Tint
❑ 120 Bob Purkey 5.00 2.00
❑ 120A Bob Purkey 5.00 2.00
Green Tint
❑ 121 Billy Hitchcock MG 5.00 2.00
❑ 121A Billy Hitchcock 5.00 2.00
Green Tint
❑ 122 Norm Bass 5.00 2.00
❑ 122A Norm Bass 5.00 2.00
Green Tint
❑ 123 Mike de la Hoz 5.00 2.00
❑ 123A Mike de la Hoz 5.00 2.00
Green Tint
❑ 124 Bill Pleis 5.00 2.00
❑ 124A Bill Pleis 5.00 2.00
Green Tint
❑ 125 Gene Woodling 8.00 3.20
❑ 125A Gene Woodling 8.00 3.20
Green Tint
❑ 126 Al Cicotte 5.00 2.00
❑ 126A Al Cicotte 5.00 2.00
Green Tint
❑ 127 Norm Siebern 5.00 2.00
Hank Bauer MG
Jerry Lumpe
❑ 127A Norm Siebern 5.00 2.00
Hank Bauer MG
Jerry Lumpe
Green Tint
❑ 128 Art Fowler 5.00 2.00
❑ 128A Art Fowler 5.00 2.00
Green Tint
❑ 129A Lee Walls 5.00 2.00
(Facing right)
❑ 129B Lee Walls 30.00 12.00
(Facing left)
❑ 130 Frank Bolling 5.00 2.00
❑ 130A Frank Bolling 5.00 2.00
Green Tint
❑ 131 Pete Richert 5.00 2.00
❑ 131A Pete Richert 5.00 2.00
Green Tint
❑ 132A Angels Team 10.00 4.00
(Without photo)
❑ 132B Angels Team 30.00 12.00
(With photo)
❑ 133 Felipe Alou 8.00 3.20
❑ 133A Felipe Alou 8.00 3.20
Green Tint
❑ 134A Billy Hoeft 5.00 2.00
❑ 134B Billy Hoeft 30.00 12.00
Green Tint
❑ 135 Babe Ruth Special 1 20.00 8.00
Babe as a Boy
❑ 135A Babe Ruth Special 20.00 8.00
Base as a Boy
❑ 136 Babe Ruth Special 2 20.00 8.00
Jacob Ruppert OWN
Babe Joins Yanks
❑ 136A Babe Ruth Special 20.00 8.00
Jacob Ruppert OWN
Babe Joins Yanks
Green Tint
❑ 137 Babe Ruth Special 3 20.00 8.00
With Miller Huggins
❑ 137A Babe Ruth Special 20.00 8.00
With Miller Huggins
Green Tint
❑ 138 Babe Ruth Special 4 20.00 8.00
Famous Slugger
❑ 138A Babe Ruth Special 20.00 8.00
Famous Slugger
Green Tint
❑ 139A Babe Ruth Special 5 30.00 12.00
Babe Hits 60
❑ 139B Hal Reniff PORT RC 15.00 6.00
❑ 139C Hal Reniff RC 65.00 26.00
Pitching
❑ 140 Babe Ruth Special 6 60.00 24.00
With Lou Gehrig
❑ 140A Babe Ruth Special 60.00 24.00
Lou Gehrig
Green Tint
❑ 141 Babe Ruth Special 7 20.00 8.00
Twilight Years
❑ 141A Babe Ruth Special 20.00 8.00
Twilight Years
Green Tint
❑ 142 Babe Ruth Special 8 20.00 8.00
Coaching Dodgers
❑ 142A Babe Ruth Special 20.00 8.00
Coaching Dodgers
Green Tint
❑ 143 Babe Ruth Special 9 20.00 8.00
Greatest Sports Hero
❑ 143A Babe Ruth Special 20.00 8.00
Greatest Sports Hero
Green Tint
❑ 144 Babe Ruth Special 10 20.00 8.00
Farewell Speech
❑ 144A Babe Ruth Special 20.00 8.00
Babe Ruth Special
Farewell Speech
❑ 145 Barry Latman 5.00 2.00
❑ 145A Barry Latman 5.00 2.00
Green Tint
❑ 146 Don Demeter 5.00 2.00
❑ 146A Don Demeter 5.00 2.00
Green Tint
❑ 147A Bill Kunkel PORT 5.00 2.00
❑ 147B Bill Kunkel 30.00 12.00
(Pitching pose)
❑ 148 Wally Post 5.00 2.00
❑ 148A Wally Post 5.00 2.00
Green Tint
❑ 149 Bob Duliba 5.00 2.00
❑ 149A Bob Duliba 5.00 2.00
Green Tint
❑ 150 Al Kaline 50.00 20.00
❑ 150A Al Kaline 50.00 20.00
Green Tint
❑ 151 Johnny Klippstein 5.00 2.00
❑ 151A Johnny Klippstein 5.00 2.00
Green Tint
❑ 152 Mickey Vernon MG 8.00 3.20
❑ 152A Mickey Vernon MG 8.00 3.20
Green Tint
❑ 153 Pumpsie Green 6.00 2.40
❑ 153A Pumpsie Green 6.00 2.40
Green Tint
❑ 154 Lee Thomas 6.00 2.40
❑ 154A Lee Thomas 6.00 2.40
Green Tint
❑ 155 Stu Miller 6.00 2.40
❑ 155A Stu Miller 6.00 2.40
Green Tint
❑ 156 Merritt Ranew 5.00 2.00
❑ 156A Merritt Ranew 5.00 2.00
Green Tint
❑ 157 Wes Covington 8.00 3.20
❑ 157A Wes Covington 8.00 3.20
Green Tint
❑ 158 Braves Team 10.00 4.00
❑ 158A Braves Team 15.00 6.00
Green Tint
❑ 159 Hal Reniff RC 8.00 3.20
❑ 160 Dick Stuart 8.00 3.20
❑ 160A Dick Stuart 8.00 3.20
Green Tint
❑ 161 Frank Baumann 5.00 2.00
❑ 161A Frank Baumann 5.00 2.00
Green Tint
❑ 162 Sammy Drake 5.00 2.00
❑ 162A Sammy Drake 5.00 2.00
Green Tint
❑ 163 Billy Gardner 8.00 3.20
Cletis Boyer
❑ 163A Billy Gardner 8.00 3.20
Clete Boyer
Green Tint
❑ 164 Hal Naragon 5.00 2.00
❑ 164A Hal Naragon 5.00 2.00
Green Tint
❑ 165 Jackie Brandt 5.00 2.00
❑ 165A Jackie Brandt 5.00 2.00
Green Tint
❑ 166 Don Lee 5.00 2.00
❑ 166A Don Lee 5.00 2.00
Green Tint
❑ 167 Tim McCarver RC 30.00 12.00
❑ 167A Tim McCarver RC 30.00 12.00
Green Tint
❑ 168 Leo Posada 5.00 2.00
❑ 168A Leo Posada 5.00 2.00

Green Tint
❑ 169 Bob Cerv 10.00 4.00
❑ 169A Bob Cerv 10.00 4.00
Green Tint
❑ 170 Ron Santo 15.00 6.00
❑ 170A Ron Santo 15.00 6.00
Green Tint
❑ 171 Dave Sisler 5.00 2.00
❑ 171A Dave Sisler 5.00 2.00
Green Tint
❑ 172 Fred Hutchinson MG 8.00 3.20
❑ 172A Fred Hutchinson MG 8.00 3.20
Green Tint
❑ 173 Chico Fernandez 5.00 2.00
❑ 173A Chico Fernandez 5.00 2.00
Green Tint
❑ 174A Carl Willey 5.00 2.00
(Capless)
❑ 174B Carl Willey 30.00 12.00
(With cap)
❑ 175 Frank Howard 10.00 4.00
❑ 175A Frank Howard 10.00 4.00
Green Tint
❑ 176A Eddie Yost PORT 5.00 2.00
❑ 176B Eddie Yost BATTING 30.00 12.00
❑ 177 Bobby Shantz 8.00 3.20
❑ 177A Bobby Shantz 8.00 3.20
Green Tint
❑ 178 Camilo Carreon 5.00 2.00
❑ 178A Camilo Carreon 5.00 2.00
Green Tint
❑ 179 Tom Sturdivant 5.00 2.00
❑ 179A Tom Sturdivant 5.00 2.00
Green Tint
❑ 180 Bob Allison 10.00 4.00
❑ 180A Bob Allison 10.00 4.00
Green Tint
❑ 181 Paul Brown 5.00 2.00
❑ 181A Paul Brown 5.00 2.00
Green Tint
❑ 182 Bob Nieman 5.00 2.00
❑ 182A Bob Nieman 5.00 2.00
Green Tint
❑ 183 Roger Craig 8.00 3.20
❑ 183A Roger Craig 8.00 3.20
Green Tint
❑ 184 Haywood Sullivan 8.00 3.20
❑ 184A Haywood Sullivan 8.00 3.20
Green Tint
❑ 185 Roland Sheldon 10.00 4.00
❑ 185A Roland Sheldon 10.00 4.00
Green Tint
❑ 186 Mack Jones 5.00 2.00
❑ 186A Mack Jones 5.00 2.00
Green Tint
❑ 187 Gene Conley 5.00 2.00
❑ 187A Gene Conley 5.00 2.00
Green Tint
❑ 188 Chuck Hiller 5.00 2.00
❑ 188A Chuck Hiller 5.00 2.00
Green Tint
❑ 189 Dick Hall 5.00 2.00
❑ 189A Dick Hall 5.00 2.00
Green Tint
❑ 190A Wally Moon PORT 8.00 3.20
❑ 190B W.Moon BATTING 30.00 12.00
❑ 191 Jim Brewer 5.00 2.00
❑ 191A Jim Brewer 5.00 2.00
Green Tint
❑ 192A Checklist 3 12.00 2.40
(Without comma)
❑ 192B Checklist 3 16.00 3.20
(Comma after
Checklist)
❑ 193 Eddie Kasko 5.00 2.00
❑ 193A Eddie Kasko 5.00 2.00
Green Tint
❑ 194 Dean Chance RC 8.00 3.20
❑ 194A Dean Chance RC 8.00 3.20
Green Tint
❑ 195 Joe Cunningham 5.00 2.00
❑ 195A Joe Cunningham 5.00 2.00
Green Tint
❑ 196 Terry Fox 5.00 2.00
❑ 196A Terry Fox 5.00 2.00
Green Tint

❑ 197 Daryl Spencer 5.00 2.00
❑ 198 Johnny Keane MG 5.00 2.00
❑ 199 Gaylord Perry RC 80.00 32.00
❑ 200 Mickey Mantle 500.00 200.00
❑ 201 Ike Delock 5.00 2.00
❑ 202 Carl Warwick 5.00 2.00
❑ 203 Jack Fisher 5.00 2.00
❑ 204 Johnny Weekly 5.00 2.00
❑ 205 Gene Freese 5.00 2.00
❑ 206 Senators Team 10.00 4.00
❑ 207 Pete Burnside 5.00 2.00
❑ 208 Billy Martin 20.00 8.00
❑ 209 Jim Fregosi RC 15.00 6.00
❑ 210 Roy Face 8.00 3.20
❑ 211 Frank Bolling 5.00 2.00
Roy McMillan
❑ 212 Jim Owens 5.00 2.00
❑ 213 Richie Ashburn 20.00 8.00
❑ 214 Dom Zanni 5.00 2.00
❑ 215 Woody Held 5.00 2.00
❑ 216 Ron Kline 5.00 2.00
❑ 217 Walter Alston MG 10.00 4.00
❑ 218 Joe Torre RC 40.00 16.00
❑ 219 Al Downing RC 8.00 3.20
❑ 220 Roy Sievers 8.00 3.20
❑ 221 Bill Short 5.00 2.00
❑ 222 Jerry Zimmerman 5.00 2.00
❑ 223 Alex Grammas 5.00 2.00
❑ 224 Don Rudolph 5.00 2.00
❑ 225 Frank Malzone 8.00 3.20
❑ 226 San Francisco Giants 10.00 4.00
Team Card
❑ 227 Bob Tiefenauer 5.00 2.00
❑ 228 Dale Long 10.00 4.00
❑ 229 Jesus McFarlane 5.00 2.00
❑ 230 Camilo Pascual 8.00 3.20
❑ 231 Ernie Bowman 5.00 2.00
❑ 232 World Series Game 1 10.00 4.00
Yanks win opener
❑ 233 Joey Jay WS 10.00 4.00
❑ 234 Roger Maris WS 25.00 10.00
❑ 235 Whitey Ford WS 15.00 6.00
sets new mark
❑ 236 World Series Game 5 10.00 4.00
Yanks crush Reds
❑ 237 WS Summary 10.00 4.00
Yanks celebrate
❑ 238 Norm Sherry 5.00 2.00
❑ 239 Cecil Butler 5.00 2.00
❑ 240 George Altman 5.00 2.00
❑ 241 Johnny Kucks 5.00 2.00
❑ 242 Mel McGaha MG 5.00 2.00
❑ 243 Robin Roberts 15.00 6.00
❑ 244 Don Gile 5.00 2.00
❑ 245 Ron Hansen 5.00 2.00
❑ 246 Art Ditmar 5.00 2.00
❑ 247 Joe Pignatano 5.00 2.00
❑ 248 Bob Aspromonte 8.00 3.20
❑ 249 Ed Keegan 5.00 2.00
❑ 250 Norm Cash 10.00 4.00
❑ 251 New York Yankees 50.00 20.00
Team Card
❑ 252 Earl Francis 5.00 2.00
❑ 253 Harry Chiti CO 5.00 2.00
❑ 254 Gordon Windhorn 5.00 2.00
❑ 255 Juan Pizarro 5.00 2.00
❑ 256 Elio Chacon 8.00 3.20
❑ 257 Jack Spring 5.00 2.00
❑ 258 Marty Keough 5.00 2.00
❑ 259 Lou Klimchock 5.00 2.00
❑ 260 Billy Pierce 8.00 3.20
❑ 261 George Alusik 5.00 2.00
❑ 262 Bob Schmidt 5.00 2.00
❑ 263 Bob Purkey 5.00 2.00
Jim Turner CO
Joe Jay
❑ 264 Dick Ellsworth 8.00 3.20
❑ 265 Joe Adcock 8.00 3.20
❑ 266 John Anderson 5.00 2.00
❑ 267 Dan Dobbek 5.00 2.00
❑ 268 Ken McBride 5.00 2.00
❑ 269 Bob Oldis 5.00 2.00
❑ 270 Dick Groat 8.00 3.20
❑ 271 Ray Rippelmeyer 5.00 2.00
❑ 272 Earl Robinson 5.00 2.00
❑ 273 Gary Bell 5.00 2.00

❑ 274 Sammy Taylor 5.00 2.00
❑ 275 Norm Siebern 5.00 2.00
❑ 276 Hal Kolstad 5.00 2.00
❑ 277 Checklist 4 16.00 3.20
❑ 278 Ken Johnson 8.00 3.20
❑ 279 Hobie Landrith UER 8.00 3.20
(Wrong birthdate)
❑ 280 Johnny Podres 8.00 3.20
❑ 281 Jake Gibbs 10.00 4.00
❑ 282 Dave Hillman 5.00 2.00
❑ 283 Charlie Smith 5.00 2.00
❑ 284 Ruben Amaro 5.00 2.00
❑ 285 Curt Simmons 8.00 3.20
❑ 286 Al Lopez MG 10.00 4.00
❑ 287 George Witt 5.00 2.00
❑ 288 Billy Williams 30.00 12.00
❑ 289 Mike Krsnich 5.00 2.00
❑ 290 Jim Gentile 8.00 3.20
❑ 291 Hal Stowe 5.00 2.00
❑ 292 Jerry Kindall 5.00 2.00
❑ 293 Bob Miller 8.00 3.20
❑ 294 Phillies Team 10.00 4.00
❑ 295 Vern Law 8.00 3.20
❑ 296 Ken Hamlin 5.00 2.00
❑ 297 Ron Perranoski 8.00 3.20
❑ 298 Bill Tuttle 5.00 2.00
❑ 299 Don Wert 5.00 2.00
❑ 300 Willie Mays 150.00 60.00
❑ 301 Galen Cisco RC 5.00 2.00
❑ 302 Johnny Edwards 5.00 2.00
❑ 303 Frank Torre 8.00 3.20
❑ 304 Dick Farrell 8.00 3.20
❑ 305 Jerry Lumpe 5.00 2.00
❑ 306 Lindy McDaniel 5.00 2.00
Larry Jackson
❑ 307 Jim Grant 8.00 3.20
❑ 308 Neil Chrisley 8.00 3.20
❑ 309 Moe Morhardt 5.00 2.00
❑ 310 Whitey Ford 50.00 20.00
❑ 311 Tony Kubek IA 8.00 3.20
❑ 312 Warren Spahn IA 15.00 6.00
❑ 313 Roger Maris IA 75.00 30.00
Blasts 61th
❑ 314 Rocky Colavito IA 8.00 3.20
❑ 315 Whitey Ford IA 15.00 6.00
❑ 316 Harmon Killebrew IA 15.00 6.00
❑ 317 Stan Musial IA 20.00 8.00
❑ 318 Mickey Mantle IA 125.00 50.00
❑ 319 Mike McCormick IA 5.00 2.00
❑ 320 Hank Aaron 150.00 60.00
❑ 321 Lee Stange 5.00 2.00
❑ 322 Alvin Dark MG 8.00 3.20
❑ 323 Don Landrum 5.00 2.00
❑ 324 Joe McClain 5.00 2.00
❑ 325 Luis Aparicio 15.00 6.00
❑ 326 Tom Parsons 5.00 2.00
❑ 327 Ozzie Virgil 5.00 2.00
❑ 328 Ken Walters 5.00 2.00
❑ 329 Bob Bolin 5.00 2.00
❑ 330 John Romano 5.00 2.00
❑ 331 Moe Drabowsky 8.00 3.20
❑ 332 Don Buddin 5.00 2.00
❑ 333 Frank Cipriani 5.00 2.00
❑ 334 Boston Red Sox 10.00 4.00
Team Card
❑ 335 Bill Bruton 5.00 2.00
❑ 336 Billy Muffett 5.00 2.00
❑ 337 Jim Marshall 8.00 3.20
❑ 338 Billy Gardner 5.00 2.00
❑ 339 Jose Valdivielso 5.00 2.00
❑ 340 Don Drysdale 50.00 20.00
❑ 341 Mike Hershberger 5.00 2.00
❑ 342 Ed Rakow 5.00 2.00
❑ 343 Albie Pearson 8.00 3.20
❑ 344 Ed Bauta 5.00 2.00
❑ 345 Chuck Schilling 5.00 2.00
❑ 346 Jack Kralick 5.00 2.00
❑ 347 Chuck Hinton 5.00 2.00
❑ 348 Larry Burright 8.00 3.20
❑ 349 Paul Foytack 5.00 2.00
❑ 350 Frank Robinson 50.00 20.00
❑ 351 Joe Torre 8.00 3.20
Del Crandall
❑ 352 Frank Sullivan 5.00 2.00
❑ 353 Bill Mazeroski 15.00 6.00
❑ 354 Roman Mejias 8.00 3.20

❑ 355 Steve Barber 5.00 2.00
❑ 356 Tom Haller RC 5.00 2.00
❑ 357 Jerry Walker 5.00 2.00
❑ 358 Tommy Davis 8.00 3.20
❑ 359 Bobby Locke 5.00 2.00
❑ 360 Yogi Berra 80.00 32.00
❑ 361 Bob Hendley 5.00 2.00
❑ 362 Ty Cline 5.00 2.00
❑ 363 Bob Roselli 5.00 2.00
❑ 364 Ken Hunt 5.00 2.00
❑ 365 Charlie Neal 8.00 3.20
❑ 366 Phil Regan 8.00 3.20
❑ 367 Checklist 5 16.00 3.20
❑ 368 Bob Tillman 5.00 2.00
❑ 369 Ted Bowsfield 5.00 2.00
❑ 370 Ken Boyer 10.00 4.00
❑ 371 Earl Battey 6.00 2.40
❑ 372 Jack Curtis 6.00 2.40
❑ 373 Al Heist 6.00 2.40
❑ 374 Gene Mauch MG 10.00 4.00
❑ 375 Ron Fairly 10.00 4.00
❑ 376 Bud Daley 8.00 3.20
❑ 377 John Orsino 6.00 2.40
❑ 378 Bennie Daniels 6.00 2.40
❑ 379 Chuck Essegian 6.00 2.40
❑ 380 Lou Burdette 10.00 4.00
❑ 381 Chico Cardenas 10.00 4.00
❑ 382 Dick Williams 8.00 3.20
❑ 383 Ray Sadecki 6.00 2.40
❑ 384 K.C. Athletics 10.00 4.00
Team Card
❑ 385 Early Wynn 15.00 6.00
❑ 386 Don Mincher 8.00 3.20
❑ 387 Lou Brock RC 125.00 50.00
❑ 388 Ryne Duren 8.00 3.20
❑ 389 Smoky Burgess 10.00 4.00
❑ 390 Orlando Cepeda AS 10.00 4.00
❑ 391 Bill Mazeroski AS 10.00 4.00
❑ 392 Ken Boyer AS UER 8.00 3.20
Batting Average mistakenly listed as .392
❑ 393 Roy McMillan AS 6.00 2.40
❑ 394 Hank Aaron AS 50.00 20.00
❑ 395 Willie Mays AS 50.00 20.00
❑ 396 Frank Robinson AS 15.00 6.00
❑ 397 John Roseboro AS 6.00 2.40
❑ 398 Don Drysdale AS 15.00 6.00
❑ 399 Warren Spahn AS 15.00 6.00
❑ 400 Elston Howard 10.00 4.00
❑ 401 Roger Maris 60.00 24.00
Orlando Cepeda
❑ 402 Gino Cimoli 6.00 2.40
❑ 403 Chet Nichols 6.00 2.40
❑ 404 Tim Harkness 8.00 3.20
❑ 405 Jim Perry 8.00 3.20
❑ 406 Bob Taylor 6.00 2.40
❑ 407 Hank Aguirre 6.00 2.40
❑ 408 Gus Bell 8.00 3.20
❑ 409 Pittsburgh Pirates 10.00 4.00
Team Card
❑ 410 Al Smith 6.00 2.40
❑ 411 Danny O'Connell 6.00 2.40
❑ 412 Charlie James 6.00 2.40
❑ 413 Matty Alou 10.00 4.00
❑ 414 Joe Gaines 6.00 2.40
❑ 415 Bill Virdon 10.00 4.00
❑ 416 Bob Scheffing MG 6.00 2.40
❑ 417 Joe Azcue 6.00 2.40
❑ 418 Andy Carey 6.00 2.40
❑ 419 Bob Bruce 8.00 3.20
❑ 420 Gus Triandos 8.00 3.20
❑ 421 Ken MacKenzie 8.00 3.20
❑ 422 Steve Bilko 6.00 2.40
❑ 423 Roy Face 10.00 4.00
Hoyt Wilhelm
❑ 424 Al McBean RC 6.00 2.40
❑ 425 Carl Yastrzemski 125.00 50.00
❑ 426 Bob Farley 6.00 2.40
❑ 427 Jake Wood 6.00 2.40
❑ 428 Joe Hicks 6.00 2.40
❑ 429 Billy O'Dell 6.00 2.40
❑ 430 Tony Kubek 15.00 6.00
❑ 431 Bob Rodgers RC 8.00 3.20
❑ 432 Jim Pendleton 6.00 2.40
❑ 433 Jim Archer 6.00 2.40
❑ 434 Clay Dalrymple 6.00 2.40
❑ 435 Larry Sherry 8.00 3.20
❑ 436 Felix Mantilla 8.00 3.20
❑ 437 Ray Moore 6.00 2.40
❑ 438 Dick Brown 6.00 2.40
❑ 439 Jerry Buchek 6.00 2.40
❑ 440 Joey Jay 6.00 2.40
❑ 441 Checklist 6 16.00 6.50
❑ 442 Wes Stock 6.00 2.40
❑ 443 Del Crandall 8.00 3.20
❑ 444 Ted Wills 6.00 2.40
❑ 445 Vic Power 8.00 3.20
❑ 446 Don Elston 6.00 2.40
❑ 447 Willie Kirkland 12.00 4.80
❑ 448 Joe Gibbon 12.00 4.80
❑ 449 Jerry Adair 12.00 4.80
❑ 450 Jim O'Toole 15.00 6.00
❑ 451 Jose Tartabull RC 15.00 6.00
❑ 452 Earl Averill Jr. 12.00 4.80
❑ 453 Cal McLish 12.00 4.80
❑ 454 Floyd Robinson 12.00 4.80
❑ 455 Luis Arroyo 15.00 6.00
❑ 456 Joe Amalfitano 15.00 6.00
❑ 457 Lou Clinton 12.00 4.80
❑ 458A Bob Buhl 15.00 6.00
(Braves emblem on cap)
❑ 458B Bob Buhl 50.00 20.00
(No emblem on cap)
❑ 459 Ed Bailey 12.00 4.80
❑ 460 Jim Bunning 20.00 8.00
❑ 461 Ken Hubbs RC 35.00 14.00
❑ 462A Willie Tasby 12.00 4.80
(Senators emblem on cap)
❑ 462B Willie Tasby 50.00 20.00
(No emblem on cap)
❑ 463 Hank Bauer MG 15.00 6.00
❑ 464 Al Jackson RC 12.00 4.80
❑ 465 Reds Team 20.00 8.00
❑ 466 Norm Cash AS 15.00 6.00
❑ 467 Chuck Schilling AS 12.00 4.80
❑ 468 Brooks Robinson AS 25.00 10.00
❑ 469 Luis Aparicio AS 15.00 6.00
❑ 470 Al Kaline AS 25.00 10.00
❑ 471 Mickey Mantle AS 200.00 80.00
❑ 472 Rocky Colavito AS 15.00 6.00
❑ 473 Elston Howard AS 15.00 6.00
❑ 474 Frank Lary AS 12.00 4.80
❑ 475 Whitey Ford AS 15.00 6.00
❑ 476 Orioles Team 20.00 8.00
❑ 477 Andre Rodgers 12.00 4.80
❑ 478 Don Zimmer 20.00 8.00
Shown with Mets cap, but listed with Cincinnati
❑ 479 Joel Horlen RC 12.00 4.80
❑ 480 Harvey Kuenn 15.00 6.00
❑ 481 Vic Wertz 15.00 6.00
❑ 482 Sam Mele MG 12.00 4.80
❑ 483 Don McMahon 12.00 4.80
❑ 484 Dick Schofield 12.00 4.80
❑ 485 Pedro Ramos 12.00 4.80
❑ 486 Jim Gilliam 15.00 6.00
❑ 487 Jerry Lynch 12.00 4.80
❑ 488 Hal Brown 12.00 4.80
❑ 489 Julio Gotay 12.00 4.80
❑ 490 Clete Boyer UER 15.00 6.00
Reversed Negative
❑ 491 Leon Wagner 12.00 4.80
❑ 492 Hal W. Smith 15.00 6.00
❑ 493 Danny McDevitt 12.00 4.80
❑ 494 Sammy White 12.00 4.80
❑ 495 Don Cardwell 12.00 4.80
❑ 496 Wayne Causey 12.00 4.80
❑ 497 Ed Bouchee 15.00 6.00
❑ 498 Jim Donohue 12.00 4.80
❑ 499 Zoilo Versalles 15.00 6.00
❑ 500 Duke Snider 60.00 24.00
❑ 501 Claude Osteen 15.00 6.00
❑ 502 Hector Lopez 15.00 6.00
❑ 503 Danny Murtaugh MG 15.00 6.00
❑ 504 Eddie Bressoud 12.00 4.80
❑ 505 Juan Marichal 40.00 16.00
❑ 506 Charlie Maxwell 15.00 6.00
❑ 507 Ernie Broglio 15.00 6.00
❑ 508 Gordy Coleman 15.00 6.00
❑ 509 Dave Giusti RC 15.00 6.00
❑ 510 Jim Lemon 12.00 4.80
❑ 511 Bubba Phillips 12.00 4.80
❑ 512 Mike Fornieles 12.00 4.80
❑ 513 Whitey Herzog 15.00 6.00
❑ 514 Sherm Lollar 15.00 6.00
❑ 515 Stan Williams 15.00 6.00
❑ 516A Checklist 7 16.00 3.20
White Boxes
❑ 516B Checklist 7 16.00 6.50
Yellow Boxes
❑ 517 Dave Wickersham 12.00 4.80
❑ 518 Lee Maye 12.00 4.80
❑ 519 Bob Johnson 12.00 4.80
❑ 520 Bob Friend 15.00 6.00
❑ 521 Jacke Davis UER 12.00 4.80
(Listed as OF on front and P on back)
❑ 522 Lindy McDaniel 15.00 6.00
❑ 523 Russ Nixon SP 30.00 12.00
❑ 524 Howie Nunn SP 30.00 12.00
❑ 525 George Thomas 20.00 8.00
❑ 526 Hal Woodeshick SP 30.00 12.00
❑ 527 Dick McAuliffe RC 30.00 12.00
❑ 528 Turk Lown 20.00 8.00
❑ 529 John Schaive SP 30.00 12.00
❑ 530 Bob Gibson SP 125.00 50.00
❑ 531 Bobby G. Smith 20.00 8.00
❑ 532 Dick Stigman 20.00 8.00
❑ 533 Charley Lau SP 30.00 12.00
❑ 534 Tony Gonzalez SP 30.00 12.00
❑ 535 Ed Roebuck 20.00 8.00
❑ 536 Dick Gernert 20.00 8.00
❑ 537 Cleveland Indians 50.00 20.00
Team Card
❑ 538 Jack Sanford 20.00 8.00
❑ 539 Billy Moran 20.00 8.00
❑ 540 Jim Landis SP 30.00 12.00
❑ 541 Don Nottebart SP 30.00 12.00
❑ 542 Dave Philley 20.00 8.00
❑ 543 Bob Allen SP 30.00 12.00
❑ 544 Willie McCovey SP 125.00 50.00
❑ 545 Hoyt Wilhelm SP 50.00 20.00
❑ 546 Moe Thacker SP 30.00 12.00
❑ 547 Don Ferrarese 20.00 8.00
❑ 548 Bobby Del Greco 20.00 8.00
❑ 549 Bill Rigney MG SP 30.00 12.00
❑ 550 Art Mahaffey SP 30.00 12.00
❑ 551 Harry Bright 20.00 8.00
❑ 552 Chicago Cubs SP 50.00 20.00
Team Card
❑ 553 Jim Coates 30.00 12.00
❑ 554 Bubba Morton SP 30.00 12.00
❑ 555 John Buzhardt SP 30.00 12.00
❑ 556 Al Spangler 20.00 8.00
❑ 557 Bob Anderson SP 30.00 12.00
❑ 558 John Goryl 20.00 8.00
❑ 559 Mike Higgins MG 20.00 8.00
❑ 560 Chuck Estrada SP 30.00 12.00
❑ 561 Gene Oliver SP 30.00 12.00
❑ 562 Bill Henry 20.00 8.00
❑ 563 Ken Aspromonte 20.00 8.00
❑ 564 Bob Grim 20.00 8.00
❑ 565 Jose Pagan 20.00 8.00
❑ 566 Marty Kutyna SP 30.00 12.00
❑ 567 Tracy Stallard SP 30.00 12.00
❑ 568 Jim Golden 20.00 8.00
❑ 569 Ed Sadowski SP 30.00 12.00
❑ 570 Bill Stafford SP 30.00 12.00
❑ 571 Billy Klaus SP 30.00 12.00
❑ 572 Bob G. Miller SP 30.00 12.00
❑ 573 Johnny Logan 20.00 8.00
❑ 574 Dean Stone 20.00 8.00
❑ 575 Red Schoendienst SP 50.00 20.00
❑ 576 Russ Kemmerer SP 30.00 12.00
❑ 577 Dave Nicholson SP 30.00 12.00
❑ 578 Jim Duffalo 20.00 8.00
❑ 579 Jim Schaffer SP 30.00 12.00
❑ 580 Bill Monbouquette 20.00 8.00
❑ 581 Mel Roach 20.00 8.00
❑ 582 Ron Piche 20.00 8.00
❑ 583 Larry Osborne 20.00 8.00
❑ 584 Minnesota Twins SP 60.00 24.00
Team Card
❑ 585 Glen Hobbie SP 30.00 12.00
❑ 586 Sammy Esposito SP 30.00 12.00
❑ 587 Frank Funk SP 30.00 12.00

❑ 588 Birdie Tebbetts MG 20.00 8.00
❑ 589 Bob Turley 30.00 12.00
❑ 590 Curt Flood 30.00 12.00
❑ 591 Sam McDowell RC 70.00 28.00
Ron Taylor
Ron Nischwitz
Art Quirk
Dick Radatz SP
❑ 592 Dan Pfister 70.00 28.00
Bo Belinsky
Dave Stenhouse
Jim Bouton RC
Joe Bonikowski SP
❑ 593 Jack Lamabe 50.00 20.00
Craig Anderson
Jack Hamilton
Bob Moorhead
Bob Veale SP
❑ 594 Doc Edwards 75.00 30.00
Ken Retzer
Bob Uecker RC
Doug Camilli
Don Pavletich SP
❑ 595 Bob Sadowski 50.00 20.00
Felix Torres
Marlan Coughtry
Ed Charles SP
❑ 596 Bernie Allen 70.00 28.00
Joe Pepitone RC
Phil Linz
Rich Rollins SP
❑ 597 Jim McKnight 50.00 20.00
Rod Kanehl
Amado Samuel
Denis Menke RC SP
❑ 598 Al Luplow 80.00 23.00
Manny Jimenez
Howie Goss
Jim Hickman
Ed Olivares SP

1963 Topps

	NM	Ex
COMPLETE SET (576)	5000.00	2000.00
COMMON CARD (1-196)	4.00	1.60
COMMON (197-283)	5.00	2.00
COMMON (284-370)	5.00	2.00
COMMON (371-446)	5.00	2.00
COMMON (447-522)	25.00	10.00
COMMON (523-576)	15.00	6.00
WRAPPER (1-CENT)	40.00	16.00
WRAPPER (5-CENT)	30.00	12.00

❑ 1 Tommy Davis 40.00 8.00
Frank Robinson
Stan Musial
Hank Aaron
Bill White LL
❑ 2 Pete Runnels 50.00 20.00
Mickey Mantle
Floyd Robinson
Norm Siebern
Chuck Hinton LL
❑ 3 Willie Mays 40.00 16.00
Hank Aaron
Frank Robinson
Orlando Cepeda
Ernie Banks LL
❑ 4 Harmon Killebrew 20.00 8.00
Norm Cash
Rocky Colavito
Roger Maris
Jim Gentile
Leon Wagner LL
❑ 5 Sandy Koufax 25.00 10.00
Bob Shaw
Bob Purkey
Bob Gibson
Don Drysdale LL
❑ 6 Hank Aguirre 10.00 4.00
Robin Roberts
Whitey Ford
Eddie Fisher
Dean Chance LL
❑ 7 Don Drysdale 10.00 4.00
Jack Sanford
Bob Purkey
Billy O'Dell
Art Mahaffey
Joe Jay LL
❑ 8 Ralph Terry 8.00 3.20
Dick Donovan
Ray Herbert
Jim Bunning
Camilo Pascual LL
❑ 9 Don Drysdale 30.00 12.00
Sandy Koufax
Bob Gibson
Billy O'Dell
Dick Farrell LL
❑ 10 Camilo Pascual 8.00 3.20
Jim Bunning
Ralph Terry
Juan Pizarro
Jim Kaat LL
❑ 11 Lee Walls 4.00 1.60
❑ 12 Steve Barber 4.00 1.60
❑ 13 Philadelphia Phillies 8.00 3.20
Team Card
❑ 14 Pedro Ramos 4.00 1.60
❑ 15 Ken Hubbs UER 10.00 4.00
(No position listed
on front of card)
❑ 16 Al Smith 4.00 1.60
❑ 17 Ryne Duren 8.00 3.20
❑ 18 Smoky Burgess 80.00 32.00
Dick Stuart
Bob Clemente
Bob Skinner
❑ 19 Pete Burnside 4.00 1.60
❑ 20 Tony Kubek 10.00 4.00
❑ 21 Marty Keough 4.00 1.60
❑ 22 Curt Simmons 8.00 3.20
❑ 23 Ed Lopat MG 8.00 3.20
❑ 24 Bob Bruce 4.00 1.60
❑ 25 Al Kaline 45.00 18.00
❑ 26 Ray Moore 4.00 1.60
❑ 27 Choo Choo Coleman 8.00 3.20
❑ 28 Mike Fornieles 4.00 1.60
❑ 29A 1962 Rookie Stars 10.00 4.00
Sammy Ellis
Ray Culp
John Boozer
Jesse Gonder
❑ 29B 1963 Rookie Stars 4.00 1.60
Sammy Ellis
Ray Culp
John Boozer
Jesse Gonder
❑ 30 Harvey Kuenn 8.00 3.20
❑ 31 Cal Koonce 4.00 1.60
❑ 32 Tony Gonzalez 4.00 1.60
❑ 33 Bo Belinsky 8.00 3.20
❑ 34 Dick Schofield 4.00 1.60
❑ 35 John Buzhardt 4.00 1.60
❑ 36 Jerry Kindall 4.00 1.60
❑ 37 Jerry Lynch 4.00 1.60
❑ 38 Bud Daley 8.00 3.20
❑ 39 Angels Team 8.00 3.20
❑ 40 Vic Power 8.00 3.20
❑ 41 Charley Lau 8.00 3.20
❑ 42 Stan Williams 8.00 3.20
(Listed as Yankee on
card but LA cap)
❑ 43 Casey Stengel MG 8.00 3.20
Gene Woodling
❑ 44 Terry Fox 4.00 1.60
❑ 45 Bob Aspromonte 4.00 1.60
❑ 46 Tommie Aaron RC 8.00 3.20
❑ 47 Don Lock 4.00 1.60
❑ 48 Birdie Tebbetts MG 8.00 3.20
❑ 49 Dal Maxvill RC 8.00 3.20
❑ 50 Billy Pierce 8.00 3.20
❑ 51 George Alusik 4.00 1.60
❑ 52 Chuck Schilling 4.00 1.60
❑ 53 Joe Moeller 8.00 3.20
❑ 54A 1962 Rookie Stars 15.00 6.00
Nelson Mathews
Harry Fanok
Jack Cullen
Dave DeBusschere RC
❑ 54B 1963 Rookie Stars 8.00 3.20
Nelson Mathews
Harry Fanok
Jack Cullen
Dave DeBusschere RC
❑ 55 Bill Virdon 8.00 3.20
❑ 56 Dennis Bennett 4.00 1.60
❑ 57 Billy Moran 4.00 1.60
❑ 58 Bob Will 4.00 1.60
❑ 59 Craig Anderson 4.00 1.60
❑ 60 Elston Howard 8.00 3.20
❑ 61 Ernie Bowman 4.00 1.60
❑ 62 Bob Hendley 4.00 1.60
❑ 63 Reds Team 8.00 3.20
❑ 64 Dick McAuliffe 8.00 3.20
❑ 65 Jackie Brandt 4.00 1.60
❑ 66 Mike Joyce 4.00 1.60
❑ 67 Ed Charles 4.00 1.60
❑ 68 Duke Snider 25.00 10.00
Gil Hodges
❑ 69 Bud Zipfel 4.00 1.60
❑ 70 Jim O'Toole 8.00 3.20
❑ 71 Bobby Wine 8.00 3.20
❑ 72 Johnny Romano 4.00 1.60
❑ 73 Bobby Bragan MG RC 8.00 3.20
❑ 74 Denny Lemaster 4.00 1.60
❑ 75 Bob Allison 8.00 3.20
❑ 76 Earl Wilson 8.00 3.20
❑ 77 Al Spangler 4.00 1.60
❑ 78 Marv Throneberry 8.00 3.20
❑ 79 Checklist 1 ...... 12.00 2.40
❑ 80 Jim Gilliam 8.00 3.20
❑ 81 Jim Schaffer 4.00 1.60
❑ 82 Ed Rakow 4.00 1.60
❑ 83 Charley James 4.00 1.60
❑ 84 Ron Kline 4.00 1.60
❑ 85 Tom Haller 8.00 3.20
❑ 86 Charley Maxwell 8.00 3.20
❑ 87 Bob Veale 8.00 3.20
❑ 88 Ron Hansen 4.00 1.60
❑ 89 Dick Stigman 4.00 1.60
❑ 90 Gordy Coleman 8.00 3.20
❑ 91 Dallas Green 8.00 3.20
❑ 92 Hector Lopez 8.00 3.20
❑ 93 Galen Cisco 4.00 1.60
❑ 94 Bob Schmidt 4.00 1.60
❑ 95 Larry Jackson 4.00 1.60
❑ 96 Lou Clinton 4.00 1.60
❑ 97 Bob Duliba 4.00 1.60
❑ 98 George Thomas 4.00 1.60
❑ 99 Jim Umbricht 4.00 1.60
❑ 100 Joe Cunningham 4.00 1.60
❑ 101 Joe Gibbon 4.00 1.60
❑ 102A Checklist 2 ...... 12.00 2.40
(Red on yellow)
❑ 102B Checklist 2 ...... 12.00 2.40
(White on red)
❑ 103 Chuck Essegian 4.00 1.60
❑ 104 Lew Krausse 4.00 1.60
❑ 105 Ron Fairly 8.00 3.20
❑ 106 Bobby Bolin 4.00 1.60
❑ 107 Jim Hickman 8.00 3.20
❑ 108 Hoyt Wilhelm 10.00 4.00
❑ 109 Lee Maye 4.00 1.60
❑ 110 Rich Rollins 8.00 3.20
❑ 111 Al Jackson 4.00 1.60
❑ 112 Dick Brown 4.00 1.60
❑ 113 Don Landrum UER 4.00 1.60

	(Photo actually Ron Santo)		
❑ 114	Dan Osinski	4.00	1.60
❑ 115	Carl Yastrzemski	40.00	16.00
❑ 116	Jim Brosnan	8.00	3.20
❑ 117	Jacke Davis	4.00	1.60
❑ 118	Sherm Lollar	4.00	1.60
❑ 119	Bob Lillis	4.00	1.60
❑ 120	Roger Maris	80.00	32.00
❑ 121	Jim Hannan	4.00	1.60
❑ 122	Julio Gotay	4.00	1.60
❑ 123	Frank Howard	8.00	3.20
❑ 124	Dick Howser	8.00	3.20
❑ 125	Robin Roberts	15.00	6.00
❑ 126	Bob Uecker	15.00	6.00
❑ 127	Bill Tuttle	4.00	1.60
❑ 128	Matty Alou	8.00	3.20
❑ 129	Gary Bell	4.00	1.60
❑ 130	Dick Groat	8.00	3.20
❑ 131	Washington Senators Team Card	8.00	3.20
❑ 132	Jack Hamilton	4.00	1.60
❑ 133	Gene Freese	4.00	1.60
❑ 134	Bob Scheffing MG	4.00	1.60
❑ 135	Richie Ashburn	20.00	8.00
❑ 136	Ike Delock	4.00	1.60
❑ 137	Mack Jones	4.00	1.60
❑ 138	Willie Mays Stan Musial	70.00	28.00
❑ 139	Earl Averill	4.00	1.60
❑ 140	Frank Lary	8.00	3.20
❑ 141	Manny Mota RC	8.00	3.20
❑ 142	Whitey Ford WS	10.00	4.00
❑ 143	Jack Sanford WS	8.00	3.20
❑ 144	Roger Maris WS	15.00	6.00
❑ 145	Chuck Hiller WS	8.00	3.20
❑ 146	Tom Tresh WS	8.00	3.20
❑ 147	Billy Pierce WS	8.00	3.20
❑ 148	Ralph Terry WS	8.00	3.20
❑ 149	Marv Breeding	4.00	1.60
❑ 150	Johnny Podres	8.00	3.20
❑ 151	Pirates Team	8.00	3.20
❑ 152	Ron Nischwitz	4.00	1.60
❑ 153	Hal Smith	4.00	1.60
❑ 154	Walter Alston MG	8.00	3.20
❑ 155	Bill Stafford	4.00	1.60
❑ 156	Roy McMillan	8.00	3.20
❑ 157	Diego Segui RC	8.00	3.20
❑ 158	Rogelio Alvares Dave Roberts Tommy Harper RC Bob Saverine	8.00	3.20
❑ 159	Jim Pagliaroni	4.00	1.60
❑ 160	Juan Pizarro	4.00	1.60
❑ 161	Frank Torre	8.00	3.20
❑ 162	Twins Team	8.00	3.20
❑ 163	Don Larsen	8.00	3.20
❑ 164	Bubba Morton	4.00	1.60
❑ 165	Jim Kaat	8.00	3.20
❑ 166	Johnny Keane MG	4.00	1.60
❑ 167	Jim Fregosi	8.00	3.20
❑ 168	Russ Nixon	4.00	1.60
❑ 169	Dick Egan Julio Navarro Tommie Sisk Gaylord Perry	25.00	10.00
❑ 170	Joe Adcock	8.00	3.20
❑ 171	Steve Hamilton	4.00	1.60
❑ 172	Gene Oliver	4.00	1.60
❑ 173	Tom Tresh Mickey Mantle Bobby Richardson	150.00	60.00
❑ 174	Larry Burright	4.00	1.60
❑ 175	Bob Buhl	8.00	3.20
❑ 176	Jim King	4.00	1.60
❑ 177	Bubba Phillips	4.00	1.60
❑ 178	Johnny Edwards	4.00	1.60
❑ 179	Ron Piche	4.00	1.60
❑ 180	Bill Skowron	8.00	3.20
❑ 181	Sammy Esposito	4.00	1.60
❑ 182	Albie Pearson	8.00	3.20
❑ 183	Joe Pepitone	8.00	3.20
❑ 184	Vern Law	8.00	3.20
❑ 185	Chuck Hiller	4.00	1.60
❑ 186	Jerry Zimmerman	4.00	1.60
❑ 187	Willie Kirkland	4.00	1.60
❑ 188	Eddie Bressoud	4.00	1.60
❑ 189	Dave Giusti	8.00	3.20
❑ 190	Minnie Minoso	8.00	3.20
❑ 191	Checklist 3	12.00	2.40
❑ 192	Clay Dalrymple	4.00	1.60
❑ 193	Andre Rodgers	4.00	1.60
❑ 194	Joe Nuxhall	8.00	3.20
❑ 195	Manny Jimenez	4.00	1.60
❑ 196	Doug Camilli	4.00	1.60
❑ 197	Roger Craig	8.00	3.20
❑ 198	Lenny Green	5.00	2.00
❑ 199	Joe Amalfitano	5.00	2.00
❑ 200	Mickey Mantle	450.00	180.00
❑ 201	Cecil Butler	5.00	2.00
❑ 202	Boston Red Sox Team Card	8.00	3.20
❑ 203	Chico Cardenas	8.00	3.20
❑ 204	Don Nottebart	5.00	2.00
❑ 205	Luis Aparicio	15.00	6.00
❑ 206	Ray Washburn	5.00	2.00
❑ 207	Ken Hunt	5.00	2.00
❑ 208	Ron Herbel John Miller Wally Wolf Ron Taylor	5.00	2.00
❑ 209	Hobie Landrith	5.00	2.00
❑ 210	Sandy Koufax	150.00	60.00
❑ 211	Fred Whitfield	5.00	2.00
❑ 212	Glen Hobbie	5.00	2.00
❑ 213	Billy Hitchcock MG	5.00	2.00
❑ 214	Orlando Pena	5.00	2.00
❑ 215	Bob Skinner	8.00	3.20
❑ 216	Gene Conley	8.00	3.20
❑ 217	Joe Christopher	5.00	2.00
❑ 218	Frank Lary Don Mossi Jim Bunning	8.00	3.20
❑ 219	Chuck Cottier	5.00	2.00
❑ 220	Camilo Pascual	8.00	3.20
❑ 221	Cookie Rojas RC	8.00	3.20
❑ 222	Cubs Team	8.00	3.20
❑ 223	Eddie Fisher	5.00	2.00
❑ 224	Mike Roarke	5.00	2.00
❑ 225	Joey Jay	5.00	2.00
❑ 226	Julian Javier	8.00	3.20
❑ 227	Jim Grant	8.00	3.20
❑ 228	Max Alvis Bob Bailey Tony Oliva (Listed as Pedro) Ed Kranepool RC	50.00	20.00
❑ 229	Willie Davis	8.00	3.20
❑ 230	Pete Runnels	8.00	3.20
❑ 231	Eli Grba UER (Large photo is Ryne Duren)	5.00	2.00
❑ 232	Frank Malzone	8.00	3.20
❑ 233	Casey Stengel MG	20.00	8.00
❑ 234	Dave Nicholson	5.00	2.00
❑ 235	Billy O'Dell	5.00	2.00
❑ 236	Bill Bryan	5.00	2.00
❑ 237	Jim Coates	8.00	3.20
❑ 238	Lou Johnson	5.00	2.00
❑ 239	Harvey Haddix	8.00	3.20
❑ 240	Rocky Colavito	15.00	6.00
❑ 241	Bob Smith	5.00	2.00
❑ 242	Ernie Banks Hank Aaron	60.00	24.00
❑ 243	Don Leppert	5.00	2.00
❑ 244	John Tsitouris	5.00	2.00
❑ 245	Gil Hodges	20.00	8.00
❑ 246	Lee Stange	5.00	2.00
❑ 247	Yankees Team	50.00	20.00
❑ 248	Tito Francona	5.00	2.00
❑ 249	Leo Burke	5.00	2.00
❑ 250	Stan Musial	100.00	40.00
❑ 251	Jack Lamabe	5.00	2.00
❑ 252	Ron Santo	10.00	4.00
❑ 253	Len Gabrielson Pete Jernigan John Wojcik Deacon Jones	5.00	2.00
❑ 254	Mike Hershberger	5.00	2.00
❑ 255	Bob Shaw	5.00	2.00
❑ 256	Jerry Lumpe	5.00	2.00
❑ 257	Hank Aguirre	5.00	2.00
❑ 258	Alvin Dark MG	8.00	3.20
❑ 259	Johnny Logan	8.00	3.20
❑ 260	Jim Gentile	8.00	3.20
❑ 261	Bob Miller	5.00	2.00
❑ 262	Ellis Burton	5.00	2.00
❑ 263	Dave Stenhouse	5.00	2.00
❑ 264	Phil Linz	5.00	2.00
❑ 265	Vada Pinson	8.00	3.20
❑ 266	Bob Allen	5.00	2.00
❑ 267	Carl Sawatski	5.00	2.00
❑ 268	Don Demeter	5.00	2.00
❑ 269	Don Mincher	5.00	2.00
❑ 270	Felipe Alou	8.00	3.20
❑ 271	Dean Stone	5.00	2.00
❑ 272	Danny Murphy	5.00	2.00
❑ 273	Sammy Taylor	5.00	2.00
❑ 274	Checklist 4	12.00	2.40
❑ 275	Eddie Mathews	30.00	12.00
❑ 276	Barry Shetrone	5.00	2.00
❑ 277	Dick Farrell	5.00	2.00
❑ 278	Chico Fernandez	5.00	2.00
❑ 279	Wally Moon	8.00	3.20
❑ 280	Bob Rodgers	5.00	2.00
❑ 281	Tom Sturdivant	5.00	2.00
❑ 282	Bobby Del Greco	5.00	2.00
❑ 283	Roy Sievers	8.00	3.20
❑ 284	Dave Sisler	5.00	2.00
❑ 285	Dick Stuart	8.00	3.20
❑ 286	Stu Miller	8.00	3.20
❑ 287	Dick Bertell	5.00	2.00
❑ 288	Chicago White Sox Team Card	10.00	4.00
❑ 289	Hal Brown	5.00	2.00
❑ 290	Bill White	8.00	3.20
❑ 291	Don Rudolph	5.00	2.00
❑ 292	Pumpsie Green	8.00	3.20
❑ 293	Bill Pleis	5.00	2.00
❑ 294	Bill Rigney MG	5.00	2.00
❑ 295	Ed Roebuck	5.00	2.00
❑ 296	Doc Edwards	5.00	2.00
❑ 297	Jim Golden	5.00	2.00
❑ 298	Don Dillard	5.00	2.00
❑ 299	Dave Morehead Bob Dustal Tom Butters Dan Schneider	8.00	3.20
❑ 300	Willie Mays	150.00	60.00
❑ 301	Bill Fischer	5.00	2.00
❑ 302	Whitey Herzog	8.00	3.20
❑ 303	Earl Francis	5.00	2.00
❑ 304	Harry Bright	5.00	2.00
❑ 305	Don Hoak	5.00	2.00
❑ 306	Earl Battey Elston Howard	10.00	4.00
❑ 307	Chet Nichols	5.00	2.00
❑ 308	Camilo Carreon	5.00	2.00
❑ 309	Jim Brewer	5.00	2.00
❑ 310	Tommy Davis	8.00	3.20
❑ 311	Joe McClain	5.00	2.00
❑ 312	Houston Colts Team Card	25.00	10.00
❑ 313	Ernie Broglio	5.00	2.00
❑ 314	John Goryl	5.00	2.00
❑ 315	Ralph Terry	8.00	3.20
❑ 316	Norm Sherry	8.00	3.20
❑ 317	Sam McDowell	8.00	3.20
❑ 318	Gene Mauch MG	8.00	3.20
❑ 319	Joe Gaines	5.00	2.00
❑ 320	Warren Spahn	60.00	24.00
❑ 321	Gino Cimoli	5.00	2.00
❑ 322	Bob Turley	8.00	3.20
❑ 323	Bill Mazeroski	15.00	6.00
❑ 324	George Williams Pete Ward Phil Roof Vic Davalillo	8.00	3.20
❑ 325	Jack Sanford	5.00	2.00
❑ 326	Hank Foiles	5.00	2.00
❑ 327	Paul Foytack	5.00	2.00
❑ 328	Dick Williams	8.00	3.20
❑ 329	Lindy McDaniel	8.00	3.20
❑ 330	Chuck Hinton	5.00	2.00
❑ 331	Bill Stafford Bill Pierce	8.00	3.20
❑ 332	Joel Horlen	8.00	3.20
❑ 333	Carl Warwick	5.00	2.00

❑ 334 Wynn Hawkins	5.00	2.00
❑ 335 Leon Wagner	5.00	2.00
❑ 336 Ed Bauta	5.00	2.00
❑ 337 Dodgers Team	25.00	10.00
❑ 338 Russ Kemmerer	5.00	2.00
❑ 339 Ted Bowsfield	5.00	2.00
❑ 340 Yogi Berra P/CO	80.00	32.00
❑ 341 Jack Baldschun	5.00	2.00
❑ 342 Gene Woodling	8.00	3.20
❑ 343 Johnny Pesky MG	8.00	3.20
❑ 344 Don Schwall	5.00	2.00
❑ 345 Brooks Robinson	60.00	24.00
❑ 346 Billy Hoeft	5.00	2.00
❑ 347 Joe Torre	15.00	6.00
❑ 348 Vic Wertz	8.00	3.20
❑ 349 Zoilo Versalles	8.00	3.20
❑ 350 Bob Purkey	5.00	2.00
❑ 351 Al Luplow	5.00	2.00
❑ 352 Ken Johnson	5.00	2.00
❑ 353 Billy Williams	30.00	12.00
❑ 354 Dom Zanni	5.00	2.00
❑ 355 Dean Chance	8.00	3.20
❑ 356 John Schaive	5.00	2.00
❑ 357 George Altman	5.00	2.00
❑ 358 Milt Pappas	8.00	3.20
❑ 359 Haywood Sullivan	8.00	3.20
❑ 360 Don Drysdale	60.00	24.00
❑ 361 Clete Boyer	10.00	4.00
❑ 362 Checklist 5	12.00	2.40
❑ 363 Dick Radatz	8.00	3.20
❑ 364 Howie Goss	5.00	2.00
❑ 365 Jim Bunning	20.00	8.00
❑ 366 Tony Taylor	8.00	3.20
❑ 367 Tony Cloninger	5.00	2.00
❑ 368 Ed Bailey	5.00	2.00
❑ 369 Jim Lemon	5.00	2.00
❑ 370 Dick Donovan	5.00	2.00
❑ 371 Rod Kanehl	8.00	3.20
❑ 372 Don Lee	5.00	2.00
❑ 373 Jim Campbell	5.00	2.00
❑ 374 Claude Osteen	8.00	3.20
❑ 375 Ken Boyer	15.00	6.00
❑ 376 John Wyatt	5.00	2.00
❑ 377 Baltimore Orioles	10.00	4.00
Team Card		
❑ 378 Bill Henry	5.00	2.00
❑ 379 Bob Anderson	5.00	2.00
❑ 380 Ernie Banks UER	80.00	32.00
(Back has career Major		
and Minor, but he		
never played in Minors)		
❑ 381 Frank Baumann	5.00	2.00
❑ 382 Ralph Houk MG	10.00	4.00
❑ 383 Pete Richert	5.00	2.00
❑ 384 Bob Tillman	5.00	2.00
❑ 385 Art Mahaffey	5.00	2.00
❑ 386 Ed Kirkpatrick	5.00	2.00
John Bateman RC		
Larry Bearnarth		
Garry Roggenburk		
❑ 387 Al McBean	5.00	2.00
❑ 388 Jim Davenport	8.00	3.20
❑ 389 Frank Sullivan	5.00	2.00
❑ 390 Hank Aaron	125.00	50.00
❑ 391 Bill Dailey	5.00	2.00
❑ 392 Johnny Romano	5.00	2.00
Tito Francona		
❑ 393 Ken MacKenzie	8.00	3.20
❑ 394 Tim McCarver	15.00	6.00
❑ 395 Don McMahon	5.00	2.00
❑ 396 Joe Koppe	5.00	2.00
❑ 397 Kansas City Athletics	10.00	4.00
Team Card		
❑ 398 Boog Powell	25.00	10.00
❑ 399 Dick Ellsworth	5.00	2.00
❑ 400 Frank Robinson	60.00	24.00
❑ 401 Jim Bouton	15.00	6.00
❑ 402 Mickey Vernon MG	8.00	3.20
❑ 403 Ron Perranoski	8.00	3.20
❑ 404 Bob Oldis	5.00	2.00
❑ 405 Floyd Robinson	5.00	2.00
❑ 406 Howie Koplitz	5.00	2.00
❑ 407 Frank Kostro	8.00	3.20
Chico Ruiz		
Larry Elliot		
Dick Simpson		
❑ 408 Billy Gardner	5.00	2.00
❑ 409 Roy Face	8.00	3.20
❑ 410 Earl Battey	5.00	2.00
❑ 411 Jim Constable	5.00	2.00
❑ 412 Johnny Podres	50.00	20.00
Don Drysdale		
Sandy Koufax		
❑ 413 Jerry Walker	5.00	2.00
❑ 414 Ty Cline	5.00	2.00
❑ 415 Bob Gibson	60.00	24.00
❑ 416 Alex Grammas	5.00	2.00
❑ 417 Giants Team	10.00	4.00
❑ 418 John Orsino	5.00	2.00
❑ 419 Tracy Stallard	5.00	2.00
❑ 420 Bobby Richardson	15.00	6.00
❑ 421 Tom Morgan	5.00	2.00
❑ 422 Fred Hutchinson MG	8.00	3.20
❑ 423 Ed Hobaugh	5.00	2.00
❑ 424 Charlie Smith	5.00	2.00
❑ 425 Smoky Burgess	8.00	3.20
❑ 426 Barry Latman	5.00	2.00
❑ 427 Bernie Allen	5.00	2.00
❑ 428 Carl Boles	5.00	2.00
❑ 429 Lou Burdette	8.00	3.20
❑ 430 Norm Siebern	5.00	2.00
❑ 431A Checklist 6	12.00	2.40
(White on red)		
❑ 431B Checklist 6	30.00	6.00
(Black on orange)		
❑ 432 Roman Mejias	5.00	2.00
❑ 433 Denis Menke	5.00	2.00
❑ 434 John Callison	8.00	3.20
❑ 435 Woody Held	5.00	2.00
❑ 436 Tim Harkness	8.00	3.20
❑ 437 Bill Bruton	5.00	2.00
❑ 438 Wes Stock	5.00	2.00
❑ 439 Don Zimmer	8.00	3.20
❑ 440 Juan Marichal	30.00	12.00
❑ 441 Lee Thomas	8.00	3.20
❑ 442 J.C. Hartman	5.00	2.00
❑ 443 Jimmy Piersall	8.00	3.20
❑ 444 Jim Maloney	8.00	3.20
❑ 445 Norm Cash	10.00	4.00
❑ 446 Whitey Ford	60.00	24.00
❑ 447 Felix Mantilla	25.00	10.00
❑ 448 Jack Kralick	25.00	10.00
❑ 449 Jose Tartabull	25.00	10.00
❑ 450 Bob Friend	30.00	12.00
❑ 451 Indians Team	40.00	16.00
❑ 452 Barney Schultz	25.00	10.00
❑ 453 Jake Wood	25.00	10.00
❑ 454A Art Fowler	25.00	10.00
(Card number on		
white background)		
❑ 454B Art Fowler	30.00	12.00
(Card number on		
orange background)		
❑ 455 Ruben Amaro	25.00	10.00
❑ 456 Jim Coker	25.00	10.00
❑ 457 Tex Clevenger	25.00	10.00
❑ 458 Al Lopez MG	30.00	12.00
❑ 459 Dick LeMay	25.00	10.00
❑ 460 Del Crandall	30.00	12.00
❑ 461 Norm Bass	25.00	10.00
❑ 462 Wally Post	25.00	10.00
❑ 463 Joe Schaffernoth	25.00	10.00
❑ 464 Ken Aspromonte	25.00	10.00
❑ 465 Chuck Estrada	25.00	10.00
❑ 466 Nate Oliver	60.00	24.00
Tony Martinez		
Bill Freehan RC		
Jerry Robinson SP		
❑ 467 Phil Ortega	25.00	10.00
❑ 468 Carroll Hardy	30.00	12.00
❑ 469 Jay Hook	30.00	12.00
❑ 470 Tom Tresh SP	60.00	24.00
❑ 471 Ken Retzer	25.00	10.00
❑ 472 Lou Brock	80.00	32.00
❑ 473 New York Mets	100.00	40.00
Team Card		
❑ 474 Jack Fisher	25.00	10.00
❑ 475 Gus Triandos	30.00	12.00
❑ 476 Frank Funk	25.00	10.00
❑ 477 Donn Clendenon	30.00	12.00
❑ 478 Paul Brown	25.00	10.00
❑ 479 Ed Brinkman	25.00	10.00
❑ 480 Bill Monbouquette	25.00	10.00
❑ 481 Bob Taylor	25.00	10.00
❑ 482 Felix Torres	25.00	10.00
❑ 483 Jim Owens UER	25.00	10.00
(Stat column for Wins		
has an R instead)		
❑ 484 Dale Long SP	30.00	12.00
❑ 485 Jim Landis	25.00	10.00
❑ 486 Ray Sadecki	25.00	10.00
❑ 487 John Roseboro	30.00	12.00
❑ 488 Jerry Adair	25.00	10.00
❑ 489 Paul Toth	25.00	10.00
❑ 490 Willie McCovey	100.00	40.00
❑ 491 Harry Craft MG	25.00	10.00
❑ 492 Dave Wickersham	25.00	10.00
❑ 493 Walt Bond	25.00	10.00
❑ 494 Phil Regan	25.00	10.00
❑ 495 Frank Thomas SP	30.00	12.00
❑ 496 Steve Dalkowski RC	30.00	12.00
Fred Newman		
Jack Smith		
Carl Bouldin		
❑ 497 Bennie Daniels	25.00	10.00
❑ 498 Eddie Kasko	25.00	10.00
❑ 499 J.C. Martin	25.00	10.00
❑ 500 Harmon Killebrew SP	150.00	60.00
❑ 501 Joe Azcue	25.00	10.00
❑ 502 Daryl Spencer	25.00	10.00
❑ 503 Braves Team	40.00	16.00
❑ 504 Bob Johnson	25.00	10.00
❑ 505 Curt Flood	40.00	16.00
❑ 506 Gene Green	25.00	10.00
❑ 507 Roland Sheldon	30.00	12.00
❑ 508 Ted Savage	25.00	10.00
❑ 509A Checklist 7	30.00	6.00
(Copyright centered)		
❑ 509B Checklist 7	30.00	6.00
(Copyright to right)		
❑ 510 Ken McBride	25.00	10.00
❑ 511 Charlie Neal	30.00	12.00
❑ 512 Cal McLish	25.00	10.00
❑ 513 Gary Geiger	25.00	10.00
❑ 514 Larry Osborne	25.00	10.00
❑ 515 Don Elston	25.00	10.00
❑ 516 Purnell Goldy	25.00	10.00
❑ 517 Hal Woodeshick	25.00	10.00
❑ 518 Don Blasingame	25.00	10.00
❑ 519 Claude Raymond RC	25.00	10.00
❑ 520 Orlando Cepeda	40.00	16.00
❑ 521 Dan Pfister	25.00	10.00
❑ 522 Mel Nelson	30.00	12.00
Gary Peters		
Jim Roland		
Art Quirk		
❑ 523 Bill Kunkel	15.00	6.00
❑ 524 Cardinals Team	30.00	12.00
❑ 525 Nellie Fox	50.00	20.00
❑ 526 Dick Hall	15.00	6.00
❑ 527 Ed Sadowski	15.00	6.00
❑ 528 Carl Willey	15.00	6.00
❑ 529 Wes Covington	15.00	6.00
❑ 530 Don Mossi	20.00	8.00
❑ 531 Sam Mele MG	15.00	6.00
❑ 532 Steve Boros	15.00	6.00
❑ 533 Bobby Shantz	20.00	8.00
❑ 534 Ken Walters	15.00	6.00
❑ 535 Jim Perry	20.00	8.00
❑ 536 Norm Larker	15.00	6.00
❑ 537 Pedro Gonzalez	800.00	325.00
Ken McMullen		
Al Weis		
Pete Rose RC		
❑ 538 George Brunet	15.00	6.00
❑ 539 Wayne Causey	15.00	6.00
❑ 540 Roberto Clemente	250.00	100.00
❑ 541 Ron Moeller	15.00	6.00
❑ 542 Lou Klimchock	15.00	6.00
❑ 543 Russ Snyder	15.00	6.00
❑ 544 Duke Carmel	50.00	20.00
Bill Haas		
Rusty Staub RC		
Dick Phillips		
❑ 545 Jose Pagan	15.00	6.00
❑ 546 Hal Reniff	20.00	8.00
❑ 547 Gus Bell	15.00	6.00
❑ 548 Tom Satriano	15.00	6.00

Card	NM	Ex
❑ 549 Marcelino Lopez	15.00	6.00
Pete Lovrich		
Paul Ratliff		
Elmo Plaskett		
❑ 550 Duke Snider	80.00	32.00
❑ 551 Billy Klaus	15.00	6.00
❑ 552 Detroit Tigers	50.00	20.00
Team Card		
❑ 553 Brock Davis	125.00	50.00
Jim Gosger		
Willie Stargell RC		
John Herrnstein		
❑ 554 Hank Fischer	15.00	6.00
❑ 555 John Blanchard	20.00	8.00
❑ 556 Al Worthington	15.00	6.00
❑ 557 Cuno Barragan	15.00	6.00
❑ 558 Bill Faul	20.00	8.00
Ron Hunt RC		
Al Moran		
Bob Lipski		
❑ 559 Danny Murtaugh MG	15.00	6.00
❑ 560 Ray Herbert	15.00	6.00
❑ 561 Mike De La Hoz	15.00	6.00
❑ 562 Randy Cardinal	30.00	12.00
Dave McNally RC		
Ken Rowe		
Don Rowe		
❑ 563 Mike McCormick	15.00	6.00
❑ 564 George Banks	15.00	6.00
❑ 565 Larry Sherry	15.00	6.00
❑ 566 Cliff Cook	15.00	6.00
❑ 567 Jim Duffalo	15.00	6.00
❑ 568 Bob Sadowski	15.00	6.00
❑ 569 Luis Arroyo	20.00	8.00
❑ 570 Frank Bolling	15.00	6.00
❑ 571 Johnny Klippstein	15.00	6.00
❑ 572 Jack Spring	15.00	6.00
❑ 573 Coot Veal	15.00	6.00
❑ 574 Hal Kolstad	15.00	6.00
❑ 575 Don Cardwell	15.00	6.00
❑ 576 Johnny Temple	30.00	11.00

1964 Topps

	NM	Ex
COMPLETE SET (587)	4500.00	1800.00
COMMON CARD (1-196)	3.00	1.20
COMMON (197-370)	4.00	1.60
COMMON (371-522)	7.00	2.80
COMMON (523-587)	16.00	6.50
WRAPPER (1-CENT)	100.00	40.00
WRAP. (1-CENT, REPEAT)	125.00	50.00
WRAPPER (5-CENT)	30.00	12.00
WRAP.(5-CENT, COIN)	40.00	16.00

Card	NM	Ex
❑ 1 Sandy Koufax	30.00	9.00
Dick Ellsworth		
Bob Friend LL		
❑ 2 Gary Peters	8.00	3.20
Juan Pizarro		
Camilo Pascual LL		
❑ 3 Sandy Koufax	20.00	8.00
Juan Marichal		
Warren Spahn		
Jim Maloney LL		
❑ 4 Whitey Ford	8.00	3.20
Camilo Pascual		
Jim Bouton LL		
❑ 5 Sandy Koufax	15.00	6.00
Jim Maloney		
Don Drysdale LL		
❑ 6 Camilo Pascual	8.00	3.20
Jim Bunning		
Dick Stigman LL		
❑ 7 Tommy Davis	20.00	8.00
Roberto Clemente		
Dick Groat		
Hank Aaron LL		
❑ 8 Carl Yastrzemski	15.00	6.00
Al Kaline		
Rich Rollins LL		
❑ 9 Hank Aaron	30.00	12.00
Willie McCovey		
Willie Mays		
Orlando Cepeda LL		
❑ 10 Harmon Killebrew	8.00	3.20
Dick Stuart		
Bob Allison LL		
❑ 11 Hank Aaron	15.00	6.00
Ken Boyer		
Bill White LL		
❑ 12 Dick Stuart	8.00	3.20
Al Kaline		
Harmon Killebrew LL		
❑ 13 Hoyt Wilhelm	12.00	4.80
❑ 14 Dick Nen RC	3.00	1.20
Nick Willhite		
❑ 15 Zoilo Versalles	6.00	2.40
❑ 16 John Boozer	3.00	1.20
❑ 17 Willie Kirkland	3.00	1.20
❑ 18 Billy O'Dell	3.00	1.20
❑ 19 Don Wert	3.00	1.20
❑ 20 Bob Friend	6.00	2.40
❑ 21 Yogi Berra MG	35.00	14.00
❑ 22 Jerry Adair	3.00	1.20
❑ 23 Chris Zachary	3.00	1.20
❑ 24 Carl Sawatski	3.00	1.20
❑ 25 Bill Monbouquette	3.00	1.20
❑ 26 Gino Cimoli	3.00	1.20
❑ 27 New York Mets	8.00	3.20
Team Card		
❑ 28 Claude Osteen	6.00	2.40
❑ 29 Lou Brock	35.00	14.00
❑ 30 Ron Perranoski	6.00	2.40
❑ 31 Dave Nicholson	3.00	1.20
❑ 32 Dean Chance	6.00	2.40
❑ 33 Sammy Ellis	6.00	2.40
Mel Queen		
❑ 34 Jim Perry	6.00	2.40
❑ 35 Eddie Mathews	20.00	8.00
❑ 36 Hal Reniff	3.00	1.20
❑ 37 Smoky Burgess	6.00	2.40
❑ 38 Jim Wynn RC	8.00	3.20
❑ 39 Hank Aguirre	3.00	1.20
❑ 40 Dick Groat	6.00	2.40
❑ 41 Willie McCovey	8.00	3.20
Leon Wagner		
❑ 42 Moe Drabowsky	6.00	2.40
❑ 43 Roy Sievers	6.00	2.40
❑ 44 Duke Carmel	3.00	1.20
❑ 45 Milt Pappas	6.00	2.40
❑ 46 Ed Brinkman	3.00	1.20
❑ 47 Jesus Alou RC	6.00	2.40
Ron Herbel		
❑ 48 Bob Perry	3.00	1.20
❑ 49 Bill Henry	3.00	1.20
❑ 50 Mickey Mantle	300.00	120.00
❑ 51 Pete Richert	3.00	1.20
❑ 52 Chuck Hinton	3.00	1.20
❑ 53 Denis Menke	3.00	1.20
❑ 54 Sam Mele MG	3.00	1.20
❑ 55 Ernie Banks	35.00	14.00
❑ 56 Hal Brown	3.00	1.20
❑ 57 Tim Harkness	6.00	2.40
❑ 58 Don Demeter	6.00	2.40
❑ 59 Ernie Broglio	3.00	1.20
❑ 60 Frank Malzone	6.00	2.40
❑ 61 Bob Rodgers	6.00	2.40
Ed Sadowski		
❑ 62 Ted Savage	3.00	1.20
❑ 63 John Orsino	3.00	1.20
❑ 64 Ted Abernathy	3.00	1.20
❑ 65 Felipe Alou	6.00	2.40
❑ 66 Eddie Fisher	3.00	1.20
❑ 67 Tigers Team	6.00	2.40
❑ 68 Willie Davis	6.00	2.40
❑ 69 Clete Boyer	6.00	2.40
❑ 70 Joe Torre	8.00	3.20
❑ 71 Jack Spring	3.00	1.20
❑ 72 Chico Cardenas	6.00	2.40
❑ 73 Jimmie Hall	8.00	3.20
❑ 74 Bob Priddy	3.00	1.20
Tom Butters		
❑ 75 Wayne Causey	3.00	1.20
❑ 76 Checklist 1	10.00	2.00
❑ 77 Jerry Walker	3.00	1.20
❑ 78 Merritt Ranew	3.00	1.20
❑ 79 Bob Heffner	3.00	1.20
❑ 80 Vada Pinson	8.00	3.20
❑ 81 Nellie Fox	12.00	4.80
Harmon Killebrew		
❑ 82 Jim Davenport	6.00	2.40
❑ 83 Gus Triandos	6.00	2.40
❑ 84 Carl Willey	3.00	1.20
❑ 85 Pete Ward	3.00	1.20
❑ 86 Al Downing	6.00	2.40
❑ 87 St. Louis Cardinals	6.00	2.40
Team Card		
❑ 88 John Roseboro	6.00	2.40
❑ 89 Boog Powell	6.00	2.40
❑ 90 Earl Battey	3.00	1.20
❑ 91 Bob Bailey	6.00	2.40
❑ 92 Steve Ridzik	3.00	1.20
❑ 93 Gary Geiger	3.00	1.20
❑ 94 Jim Britton	3.00	1.20
Larry Maxie		
❑ 95 George Altman	3.00	1.20
❑ 96 Bob Buhl	6.00	2.40
❑ 97 Jim Fregosi	6.00	2.40
❑ 98 Bill Bruton	3.00	1.20
❑ 99 Al Stanek	3.00	1.20
❑ 100 Elston Howard	6.00	2.40
❑ 101 Walt Alston MG	8.00	3.20
❑ 102 Checklist 2	10.00	2.00
❑ 103 Curt Flood	6.00	2.40
❑ 104 Art Mahaffey	6.00	2.40
❑ 105 Woody Held	3.00	1.20
❑ 106 Joe Nuxhall	6.00	2.40
❑ 107 Bruce Howard	3.00	1.20
Frank Kreutzer		
❑ 108 John Wyatt	3.00	1.20
❑ 109 Rusty Staub	6.00	2.40
❑ 110 Albie Pearson	6.00	2.40
❑ 111 Don Elston	3.00	1.20
❑ 112 Bob Tillman	3.00	1.20
❑ 113 Grover Powell	6.00	2.40
❑ 114 Don Lock	3.00	1.20
❑ 115 Frank Bolling	3.00	1.20
❑ 116 Jay Ward	12.00	4.80
Tony Oliva		
❑ 117 Earl Francis	3.00	1.20
❑ 118 John Blanchard	6.00	2.40
❑ 119 Gary Kolb	3.00	1.20
❑ 120 Don Drysdale	20.00	8.00
❑ 121 Pete Runnels	6.00	2.40
❑ 122 Don McMahon	3.00	1.20
❑ 123 Jose Pagan	3.00	1.20
❑ 124 Orlando Pena	3.00	1.20
❑ 125 Pete Rose	175.00	60.00
❑ 126 Russ Snyder	3.00	1.20
❑ 127 Aubrey Gatewood	3.00	1.20
Dick Simpson		
❑ 128 Mickey Lolich RC	20.00	8.00
❑ 129 Amado Samuel	3.00	1.20
❑ 130 Gary Peters	6.00	2.40
❑ 131 Steve Boros	3.00	1.20
❑ 132 Braves Team	6.00	2.40
❑ 133 Jim Grant	6.00	2.40
❑ 134 Don Zimmer	6.00	2.40
❑ 135 Johnny Callison	6.00	2.40
❑ 136 Sandy Koufax WS	20.00	8.00
strikes out 15		
❑ 137 Willie Davis WS	8.00	3.20
❑ 138 Ron Fairly WS	8.00	3.20
❑ 139 Frank Howard WS	8.00	3.20
❑ 140 WS Summary	8.00	3.20
Dodgers celebrate		
❑ 141 Danny Murtaugh MG	6.00	2.40
❑ 142 John Bateman	3.00	1.20
❑ 143 Bubba Phillips	3.00	1.20

	No.	Player	Price 1	Price 2
❑	144	Al Worthington	3.00	1.20
❑	145	Norm Siebern	3.00	1.20
❑	146	Tommy John RC	30.00	12.00
		Bob Chance		
❑	147	Ray Sadecki	3.00	1.20
❑	148	J.C. Martin	3.00	1.20
❑	149	Paul Foytack	3.00	1.20
❑	150	Willie Mays	100.00	40.00
❑	151	Athletics Team	6.00	2.40
❑	152	Denny Lemaster	3.00	1.20
❑	153	Dick Williams	6.00	2.40
❑	154	Dick Tracewski RC	6.00	2.40
❑	155	Duke Snider	30.00	12.00
❑	156	Bill Dailey	3.00	1.20
❑	157	Gene Mauch MG	6.00	2.40
❑	158	Ken Johnson	3.00	1.20
❑	159	Charlie Dees	3.00	1.20
❑	160	Ken Boyer	6.00	2.40
❑	161	Dave McNally	6.00	2.40
❑	162	Dick Sisler CO	6.00	2.40
		Vada Pinson		
❑	163	Donn Clendenon	6.00	2.40
❑	164	Bud Daley	3.00	1.20
❑	165	Jerry Lumpe	3.00	1.20
❑	166	Marty Keough	3.00	1.20
❑	167	Mike Brumley	30.00	12.00
		Lou Piniella RC		
❑	168	Al Weis	3.00	1.20
❑	169	Del Crandall	6.00	2.40
❑	170	Dick Radatz	6.00	2.40
❑	171	Ty Cline	3.00	1.20
❑	172	Indians Team	6.00	2.40
❑	173	Ryne Duren	6.00	2.40
❑	174	Doc Edwards	3.00	1.20
❑	175	Billy Williams	12.00	4.80
❑	176	Tracy Stallard	3.00	1.20
❑	177	Harmon Killebrew	20.00	8.00
❑	178	Hank Bauer MG	6.00	2.40
❑	179	Carl Warwick	3.00	1.20
❑	180	Tommy Davis	6.00	2.40
❑	181	Dave Wickersham	3.00	1.20
❑	182	Carl Yastrzemski	15.00	6.00
		Chuck Schilling		
❑	183	Ron Taylor	3.00	1.20
❑	184	Al Luplow	3.00	1.20
❑	185	Jim O'Toole	6.00	2.40
❑	186	Roman Mejias	3.00	1.20
❑	187	Ed Roebuck	3.00	1.20
❑	188	Checklist 3	10.00	2.00
❑	189	Bob Hendley	3.00	1.20
❑	190	Bobby Richardson	8.00	3.20
❑	191	Clay Dalrymple	6.00	2.40
❑	192	John Boccabella	3.00	1.20
		Billy Cowan		
❑	193	Jerry Lynch	3.00	1.20
❑	194	John Goryl	3.00	1.20
❑	195	Floyd Robinson	3.00	1.20
❑	196	Jim Gentile	3.00	1.20
❑	197	Frank Lary	6.00	2.40
❑	198	Len Gabrielson	4.00	1.60
❑	199	Joe Azcue	4.00	1.60
❑	200	Sandy Koufax	100.00	40.00
❑	201	Sam Bowens	6.00	2.40
		Wally Bunker		
❑	202	Galen Cisco	6.00	2.40
❑	203	John Kennedy	6.00	2.40
❑	204	Matty Alou	6.00	2.40
❑	205	Nellie Fox	12.00	4.80
❑	206	Steve Hamilton	6.00	2.40
❑	207	Fred Hutchinson MG	6.00	2.40
❑	208	Wes Covington	6.00	2.40
❑	209	Bob Allen	4.00	1.60
❑	210	Carl Yastrzemski	40.00	16.00
❑	211	Jim Coker	4.00	1.60
❑	212	Pete Lovrich	4.00	1.60
❑	213	Angels Team	6.00	2.40
❑	214	Ken McMullen	6.00	2.40
❑	215	Ray Herbert	4.00	1.60
❑	216	Mike de la Hoz	4.00	1.60
❑	217	Jim King	4.00	1.60
❑	218	Hank Fischer	4.00	1.60
❑	219	Al Downing	6.00	2.40
		Jim Bouton		
❑	220	Dick Ellsworth	6.00	2.40
❑	221	Bob Saverine	4.00	1.60
❑	222	Billy Pierce	6.00	2.40
❑	223	George Banks	4.00	1.60
❑	224	Tommie Sisk	4.00	1.60
❑	225	Roger Maris	60.00	24.00
❑	226	Jerry Grote RC	6.00	2.40
		Larry Yellen		
❑	227	Barry Latman	4.00	1.60
❑	228	Felix Mantilla	4.00	1.60
❑	229	Charley Lau	6.00	2.40
❑	230	Brooks Robinson	40.00	16.00
❑	231	Dick Calmus	4.00	1.60
❑	232	Al Lopez MG	8.00	3.20
❑	233	Hal Smith	4.00	1.60
❑	234	Gary Bell	4.00	1.60
❑	235	Ron Hunt	4.00	1.60
❑	236	Bill Faul	4.00	1.60
❑	237	Cubs Team	6.00	2.40
❑	238	Roy McMillan	6.00	2.40
❑	239	Herm Starrette	4.00	1.60
❑	240	Bill White	6.00	2.40
❑	241	Jim Owens	4.00	1.60
❑	242	Harvey Kuenn	6.00	2.40
❑	243	Richie Allen RC	30.00	12.00
		John Herrnstein		
❑	244	Tony LaRussa RC	30.00	12.00
❑	245	Dick Stigman	4.00	1.60
❑	246	Manny Mota	6.00	2.40
❑	247	Dave DeBusschere	6.00	2.40
❑	248	Johnny Pesky MG	6.00	2.40
❑	249	Doug Camilli	4.00	1.60
❑	250	Al Kaline	40.00	16.00
❑	251	Choo Choo Coleman	6.00	2.40
❑	252	Ken Aspromonte	4.00	1.60
❑	253	Wally Post	6.00	2.40
❑	254	Don Hoak	6.00	2.40
❑	255	Lee Thomas	6.00	2.40
❑	256	Johnny Weekly	4.00	1.60
❑	257	San Francisco Giants	6.00	2.40
		Team Card		
❑	258	Garry Roggenburk	4.00	1.60
❑	259	Harry Bright	4.00	1.60
❑	260	Frank Robinson	40.00	16.00
❑	261	Jim Hannan	4.00	1.60
❑	262	Mike Shannon RC	8.00	3.20
		Harry Fanok		
❑	263	Chuck Estrada	4.00	1.60
❑	264	Jim Landis	4.00	1.60
❑	265	Jim Bunning	12.00	4.80
❑	266	Gene Freese	4.00	1.60
❑	267	Wilbur Wood RC	6.00	2.40
❑	268	Danny Murtaugh MG	6.00	2.40
		Bill Virdon		
❑	269	Ellis Burton	4.00	1.60
❑	270	Rich Rollins	6.00	2.40
❑	271	Bob Sadowski	4.00	1.60
❑	272	Jake Wood	4.00	1.60
❑	273	Mel Nelson	4.00	1.60
❑	274	Checklist 4	10.00	2.00
❑	275	John Tsitouris	4.00	1.60
❑	276	Jose Tartabull	6.00	2.40
❑	277	Ken Retzer	4.00	1.60
❑	278	Bobby Shantz	6.00	2.40
❑	279	Joe Koppe UER	4.00	1.60
		(Glove on wrong hand)		
❑	280	Juan Marichal	15.00	4.80
❑	281	Jake Gibbs	6.00	2.40
		Tom Metcalf		
❑	282	Bob Bruce	4.00	1.60
❑	283	Tom McCraw RC	4.00	1.60
❑	284	Dick Schofield	4.00	1.60
❑	285	Robin Roberts	15.00	4.80
❑	286	Don Landrum	4.00	1.60
❑	287	Tony Conigliaro RC	50.00	20.00
		Bill Spanswick		
❑	288	Al Moran	4.00	1.60
❑	289	Frank Funk	4.00	1.60
❑	290	Bob Allison	6.00	2.40
❑	291	Phil Ortega	4.00	1.60
❑	292	Mike Roarke	4.00	1.60
❑	293	Phillies Team	6.00	2.40
❑	294	Ken L. Hunt	4.00	1.60
❑	295	Roger Craig	6.00	2.40
❑	296	Ed Kirkpatrick	4.00	1.60
❑	297	Ken MacKenzie	4.00	1.60
❑	298	Harry Craft MG	4.00	1.60
❑	299	Bill Stafford	4.00	1.60
❑	300	Hank Aaron	100.00	40.00
❑	301	Larry Brown	4.00	1.60
❑	302	Dan Pfister	4.00	1.60
❑	303	Jim Campbell	4.00	1.60
❑	304	Bob Johnson	4.00	1.60
❑	305	Jack Lamabe	4.00	1.60
❑	306	Willie Mays	40.00	16.00
		Orlando Cepeda		
❑	307	Joe Gibbon	4.00	1.60
❑	308	Gene Stephens	4.00	1.60
❑	309	Paul Toth	4.00	1.60
❑	310	Jim Gilliam	6.00	2.40
❑	311	Tom Brown RC	6.00	2.40
❑	312	Fritz Fisher	4.00	1.60
		Fred Gladding		
❑	313	Chuck Hiller	4.00	1.60
❑	314	Jerry Buchek	4.00	1.60
❑	315	Bo Belinsky	6.00	2.40
❑	316	Gene Oliver	4.00	1.60
❑	317	Al Smith	4.00	1.60
❑	318	Minnesota Twins	6.00	2.40
		Team Card		
❑	319	Paul Brown	4.00	1.60
❑	320	Rocky Colavito	12.00	4.80
❑	321	Bob Lillis	4.00	1.60
❑	322	George Brunet	4.00	1.60
❑	323	John Buzhardt	4.00	1.60
❑	324	Casey Stengel MG	15.00	6.00
❑	325	Hector Lopez	6.00	2.40
❑	326	Ron Brand	4.00	1.60
❑	327	Don Blasingame	4.00	1.60
❑	328	Bob Shaw	4.00	1.60
❑	329	Russ Nixon	4.00	1.60
❑	330	Tommy Harper	6.00	2.40
❑	331	Roger Maris	150.00	60.00
		Norm Cash		
		Mickey Mantle		
		Al Kaline		
❑	332	Ray Washburn	4.00	1.60
❑	333	Billy Moran	4.00	1.60
❑	334	Lew Krausse	4.00	1.60
❑	335	Don Mossi	6.00	2.40
❑	336	Andre Rodgers	4.00	1.60
❑	337	Al Ferrara	6.00	2.40
		Jeff Torborg RC		
❑	338	Jack Kralick	4.00	1.60
❑	339	Walt Bond	4.00	1.60
❑	340	Joe Cunningham	4.00	1.60
❑	341	Jim Roland	4.00	1.60
❑	342	Willie Stargell	30.00	12.00
❑	343	Senators Team	6.00	2.40
❑	344	Phil Linz	6.00	2.40
❑	345	Frank Thomas	8.00	3.20
❑	346	Joey Jay	4.00	1.60
❑	347	Bobby Wine	6.00	2.40
❑	348	Ed Lopat MG	6.00	2.40
❑	349	Art Fowler	4.00	1.60
❑	350	Willie McCovey	25.00	10.00
❑	351	Dan Schneider	4.00	1.60
❑	352	Eddie Bressoud	4.00	1.60
❑	353	Wally Moon	6.00	2.40
❑	354	Dave Giusti	4.00	1.60
❑	355	Vic Power	6.00	2.40
❑	356	Bill McCool	6.00	2.40
		Chico Ruiz		
❑	357	Charley James	4.00	1.60
❑	358	Ron Kline	4.00	1.60
❑	359	Jim Schaffer	4.00	1.60
❑	360	Joe Pepitone	12.00	4.80
❑	361	Jay Hook	4.00	1.60
❑	362	Checklist 5	10.00	2.00
❑	363	Dick McAuliffe	6.00	2.40
❑	364	Joe Gaines	4.00	1.60
❑	365	Cal McLish	6.00	2.40
❑	366	Nelson Mathews	4.00	1.60
❑	367	Fred Whitfield	4.00	1.60
❑	368	Fritz Ackley	6.00	2.40
		Don Buford RC		
❑	369	Jerry Zimmerman	4.00	1.60
❑	370	Hal Woodeshick	4.00	1.60
❑	371	Frank Howard	8.00	3.20
❑	372	Howie Koplitz	7.00	2.80
❑	373	Pirates Team	12.00	4.80
❑	374	Bobby Bolin	7.00	2.80
❑	375	Ron Santo	10.00	4.00
❑	376	Dave Morehead	7.00	2.80
❑	377	Bob Skinner	7.00	2.80

❑ 378 Woody Woodward RC 10.00 4.00
Jack Smith
❑ 379 Tony Gonzalez 7.00 2.80
❑ 380 Whitey Ford 40.00 16.00
❑ 381 Bob Taylor 7.00 2.80
❑ 382 Wes Stock 7.00 2.80
❑ 383 Bill Rigney MG 7.00 2.80
❑ 384 Ron Hansen 7.00 2.80
❑ 385 Curt Simmons 10.00 4.00
❑ 386 Lenny Green 7.00 2.80
❑ 387 Terry Fox 7.00 2.80
❑ 388 John O'Donoghue RC 10.00 4.00
George Williams
❑ 389 Jim Umbricht 10.00 4.00
(Card back mentions his death)
❑ 390 Orlando Cepeda 25.00 10.00
❑ 391 Sam McDowell 10.00 4.00
❑ 392 Jim Pagliaroni 7.00 2.80
❑ 393 Casey Stengel MG 15.00 6.00
Ed Kranepool
❑ 394 Bob Miller 7.00 2.80
❑ 395 Tom Tresh 10.00 4.00
❑ 396 Dennis Bennett 7.00 2.80
❑ 397 Chuck Cottier 7.00 2.80
❑ 398 Bill Haas 10.00 4.00
Dick Smith
❑ 399 Jackie Brandt 7.00 2.80
❑ 400 Warren Spahn 40.00 16.00
❑ 401 Charlie Maxwell 7.00 2.80
❑ 402 Tom Sturdivant 7.00 2.80
❑ 403 Reds Team 12.00 4.80
❑ 404 Tony Martinez 7.00 2.80
❑ 405 Ken McBride 7.00 2.80
❑ 406 Al Spangler 7.00 2.80
❑ 407 Bill Freehan 10.00 4.00
❑ 408 Jim Stewart 7.00 2.80
Fred Burdette
❑ 409 Bill Fischer 7.00 2.80
❑ 410 Dick Stuart 10.00 4.00
❑ 411 Lee Walls 7.00 2.80
❑ 412 Ray Culp 10.00 4.00
❑ 413 Johnny Keane MG 7.00 2.80
❑ 414 Jack Sanford 7.00 2.80
❑ 415 Tony Kubek 15.00 6.00
❑ 416 Lee Maye 7.00 2.80
❑ 417 Don Cardwell 7.00 2.80
❑ 418 Darold Knowles 10.00 4.00
Buster Narum
❑ 419 Ken Harrelson RC 15.00 6.00
❑ 420 Jim Maloney 10.00 4.00
❑ 421 Camilo Carreon 7.00 2.80
❑ 422 Jack Fisher 7.00 2.80
❑ 423 Hank Aaron 125.00 50.00
Willie Mays
❑ 424 Dick Bertell 7.00 2.80
❑ 425 Norm Cash 10.00 4.00
❑ 426 Bob Rodgers 7.00 2.80
❑ 427 Don Rudolph 7.00 2.80
❑ 428 Archie Skeen 7.00 2.80
Pete Smith
(Back states Archie has retired)
❑ 429 Tim McCarver 10.00 4.00
❑ 430 Juan Pizarro 7.00 2.80
❑ 431 George Alusik 7.00 2.80
❑ 432 Ruben Amaro 10.00 4.00
❑ 433 Yankees Team 40.00 16.00
❑ 434 Don Nottebart 7.00 2.80
❑ 435 Vic Davalillo 7.00 2.80
❑ 436 Charlie Neal 10.00 4.00
❑ 437 Ed Bailey 7.00 2.80
❑ 438 Checklist 6 16.00 3.20
❑ 439 Harvey Haddix 10.00 4.00
❑ 440 R.Clemente UER 250.00 100.00
1960 Pittsburfh
❑ 441 Bob Duliba 7.00 2.80
❑ 442 Pumpsie Green 10.00 4.00
❑ 443 Chuck Dressen MG 10.00 4.00
❑ 444 Larry Jackson 7.00 2.80
❑ 445 Bill Skowron 10.00 4.00
❑ 446 Julian Javier 15.00 6.00
❑ 447 Ted Bowsfield 7.00 2.80
❑ 448 Cookie Rojas 10.00 4.00
❑ 449 Deron Johnson 10.00 4.00
❑ 450 Steve Barber 7.00 2.80
❑ 451 Joe Amalfitano 7.00 2.80
❑ 452 Gil Garrido 10.00 4.00
Jim Ray Hart RC
❑ 453 Frank Baumann 7.00 2.80
❑ 454 Tommie Aaron 10.00 4.00
❑ 455 Bernie Allen 7.00 2.80
❑ 456 Wes Parker RC 10.00 4.00
John Werhas
❑ 457 Jesse Gonder 7.00 2.80
❑ 458 Ralph Terry 10.00 4.00
❑ 459 Pete Charton 7.00 2.80
Dalton Jones
❑ 460 Bob Gibson 40.00 16.00
❑ 461 George Thomas 7.00 2.80
❑ 462 Birdie Tebbetts MG 7.00 2.80
❑ 463 Don Leppert 7.00 2.80
❑ 464 Dallas Green 15.00 6.00
❑ 465 Mike Hershberger 7.00 2.80
❑ 466 Dick Green 10.00 4.00
Aurelio Monteagudo
❑ 467 Bob Aspromonte 7.00 2.80
❑ 468 Gaylord Perry 40.00 16.00
❑ 469 Fred Norman 10.00 4.00
Sterling Slaughter
❑ 470 Jim Bouton 10.00 4.00
❑ 471 Gates Brown RC 10.00 4.00
❑ 472 Vern Law 10.00 4.00
❑ 473 Baltimore Orioles 12.00 4.80
Team Card
❑ 474 Larry Sherry 10.00 4.00
❑ 475 Ed Charles 7.00 2.80
❑ 476 Rico Carty RC 15.00 6.00
Dick Kelley
❑ 477 Mike Joyce 7.00 2.80
❑ 478 Dick Howser 10.00 4.00
❑ 479 Dave Bakenhaster 7.00 2.80
Johnny Lewis
❑ 480 Bob Purkey 7.00 2.80
❑ 481 Chuck Schilling 7.00 2.80
❑ 482 John Briggs 10.00 4.00
Danny Cater
❑ 483 Fred Valentine 7.00 2.80
❑ 484 Bill Pleis 7.00 2.80
❑ 485 Tom Haller 7.00 2.80
❑ 486 Bob Kennedy MG 7.00 2.80
❑ 487 Mike McCormick 10.00 4.00
❑ 488 Pete Mikkelsen 15.00 6.00
Bob Meyer
❑ 489 Julio Navarro 7.00 2.80
❑ 490 Ron Fairly 10.00 4.00
❑ 491 Ed Rakow 7.00 2.80
❑ 492 Jim Beauchamp RC 7.00 2.80
Mike White
❑ 493 Don Lee 7.00 2.80
❑ 494 Al Jackson 7.00 2.80
❑ 495 Bill Virdon 10.00 4.00
❑ 496 White Sox Team 12.00 4.80
❑ 497 Jeoff Long 7.00 2.80
❑ 498 Dave Stenhouse 7.00 2.80
❑ 499 Chico Salmon 7.00 2.80
Gordon Seyfried
❑ 500 Camilo Pascual 10.00 4.00
❑ 501 Bob Veale 10.00 4.00
❑ 502 Bobby Knoop RC 7.00 2.80
Bob Lee
❑ 503 Earl Wilson 7.00 2.80
❑ 504 Claude Raymond 7.00 2.80
❑ 505 Stan Williams 7.00 2.80
❑ 506 Bobby Bragan MG 7.00 2.80
❑ 507 Johnny Edwards 7.00 2.80
❑ 508 Diego Segui 7.00 2.80
❑ 509 Gene Alley RC 10.00 4.00
Orlando McFarlane
❑ 510 Lindy McDaniel 10.00 4.00
❑ 511 Lou Jackson 10.00 4.00
❑ 512 Willie Horton RC 15.00 6.00
Joe Sparma
❑ 513 Don Larsen 10.00 4.00
❑ 514 Jim Hickman 10.00 4.00
❑ 515 Johnny Romano 7.00 2.80
❑ 516 Jerry Arrigo 7.00 2.80
Dwight Siebler
❑ 517A Checklist 7 ERR 25.00 5.00
(Incorrect numbering sequence on back)
❑ 517B Checklist 7 COR 16.00 3.20
(Correct numbering on back)
❑ 518 Carl Bouldin 7.00 2.80
❑ 519 Charlie Smith 7.00 2.80
❑ 520 Jack Baldschun 10.00 4.00
❑ 521 Tom Satriano 7.00 2.80
❑ 522 Bob Tiefenauer 7.00 2.80
❑ 523 Lou Burdette UER 20.00 8.00
(Pitching lefty)
❑ 524 Jim Dickson 16.00 6.50
Bobby Klaus
❑ 525 Al McBean 16.00 6.50
❑ 526 Lou Clinton 16.00 6.50
❑ 527 Larry Bearnarth 16.00 6.50
❑ 528 Dave Duncan RC 20.00 8.00
Tommie Reynolds
❑ 529 Alvin Dark MG 20.00 8.00
❑ 530 Leon Wagner 16.00 6.50
❑ 531 Los Angeles Dodgers 25.00 10.00
Team Card
❑ 532 Bud Bloomfield 16.00 6.50
(Bloomfield photo actually Jay Ward)
Joe Nossek RC
❑ 533 Johnny Klippstein 16.00 6.50
❑ 534 Gus Bell 16.00 6.50
❑ 535 Phil Regan 16.00 6.50
❑ 536 Larry Elliot 16.00 6.50
John Stephenson
❑ 537 Dan Osinski 16.00 6.50
❑ 538 Minnie Minoso 20.00 8.00
❑ 539 Roy Face 20.00 8.00
❑ 540 Luis Aparicio 40.00 16.00
❑ 541 Phil Roof 80.00 32.00
Phil Niekro RC
❑ 542 Don Mincher 16.00 6.50
❑ 543 Bob Uecker 40.00 16.00
❑ 544 Steve Hertz 16.00 6.50
Joe Hoerner
❑ 545 Max Alvis 16.00 6.50
❑ 546 Joe Christopher 16.00 6.50
❑ 547 Gil Hodges MG 30.00 12.00
❑ 548 Wayne Schurr 20.00 8.00
Paul Speckenbach
❑ 549 Joe Moeller 16.00 6.50
❑ 550 Ken Hubbs MEM 40.00 16.00
❑ 551 Billy Hoeft 16.00 6.50
❑ 552 Tom Kelley 16.00 6.50
Sonny Siebert
❑ 553 Jim Brewer 16.00 6.50
❑ 554 Hank Foiles 16.00 6.50
❑ 555 Lee Stange 16.00 6.50
❑ 556 Steve Dillon 16.00 6.50
Ron Locke
❑ 557 Leo Burke 16.00 6.50
❑ 558 Don Schwall 16.00 6.50
❑ 559 Dick Phillips 16.00 6.50
❑ 560 Dick Farrell 16.00 6.50
❑ 561 Dave Bennett UER 20.00 8.00
(19 ... is 18)
Rick Wise RC
❑ 562 Pedro Ramos 16.00 6.50
❑ 563 Dal Maxvill 20.00 8.00
❑ 564 Joe McCabe 20.00 8.00
Jerry McNertney
❑ 565 Stu Miller 16.00 6.50
❑ 566 Ed Kranepool 20.00 8.00
❑ 567 Jim Kaat 20.00 8.00
❑ 568 Phil Gagliano 16.00 6.50
Cap Peterson
❑ 569 Fred Newman 16.00 6.50
❑ 570 Bill Mazeroski 40.00 16.00
❑ 571 Gene Conley 16.00 6.50
❑ 572 Dave Gray 16.00 6.50
Dick Egan
❑ 573 Jim Duffalo 16.00 6.50
❑ 574 Manny Jimenez 16.00 6.50
❑ 575 Tony Cloninger 16.00 6.50
❑ 576 Jerry Hinsley 16.00 6.50
Bill Wakefield
❑ 577 Gordy Coleman 16.00 6.50
❑ 578 Glen Hobbie 16.00 6.50
❑ 579 Red Sox Team 25.00 10.00
❑ 580 Johnny Podres 20.00 8.00
❑ 581 Pedro Gonzalez 20.00 8.00
Archie Moore

Card	NM	Ex
❑ 582 Rod Kanehl	20.00	8.00
❑ 583 Tito Francona	16.00	6.50
❑ 584 Joel Horlen	16.00	6.50
❑ 585 Tony Taylor	20.00	8.00
❑ 586 Jimmy Piersall	20.00	8.00
❑ 587 Bennie Daniels	20.00	8.00

1965 Topps

	NM	Ex
COMPLETE SET (598)	4500.00	1800.00
COMMON CARD (1-196)	2.00	.80
COMMON (197-283)	2.50	1.00
COMMON (284-370)	4.00	1.60
COMMON (371-598)	7.00	2.80
WRAPPER (1-CENT)	125.00	50.00
WRAPPER (5-CENT)	100.00	40.00

Card	NM	Ex
❑ 1 Tony Oliva	20.00	6.00
Elston Howard		
Brooks Robinson LL		
❑ 2 Roberto Clemente	25.00	10.00
Hank Aaron		
Rico Carty LL		
❑ 3 Harmon Killebrew	50.00	20.00
Mickey Mantle		
Boog Powell LL		
❑ 4 Willie Mays	15.00	6.00
Billy Williams		
Jim Ray Hart		
Orlando Cepeda		
Johnny Callison LL		
❑ 5 Brooks Robinson	40.00	16.00
Harmon Killebrew		
Mickey Mantle		
Dick Stuart LL		
❑ 6 Ken Boyer	12.00	4.80
Willie Mays		
Ron Santo LL		
❑ 7 Dean Chance	5.00	2.00
Joel Horlen LL		
❑ 8 Sandy Koufax	20.00	8.00
Don Drysdale LL		
❑ 9 Dean Chance	5.00	2.00
Gary Peters		
Dave Wickersham		
Juan Pizarro		
Wally Bunker LL		
❑ 10 Larry Jackson	5.00	2.00
Ray Sadecki		
Juan Marichal LL		
❑ 11 Al Downing	5.00	2.00
Dean Chance		
Camilo Pascual LL		
❑ 12 Bob Veale	10.00	4.00
Don Drysdale		
Bob Gibson LL		
❑ 13 Pedro Ramos	4.00	1.60
❑ 14 Len Gabrielson	2.00	.80
❑ 15 Robin Roberts	10.00	4.00
❑ 16 Joe Morgan RC	60.00	24.00
Sonny Jackson DP		
❑ 17 Johnny Romano	2.00	.80
❑ 18 Bill McCool	2.00	.80
❑ 19 Gates Brown	4.00	1.60
❑ 20 Jim Bunning	10.00	4.00
❑ 21 Don Blasingame	2.00	.80
❑ 22 Charlie Smith	2.00	.80
❑ 23 Bob Tiefenauer	2.00	.80
❑ 24 Minnesota Twins	6.00	2.40
Team Card		
❑ 25 Al McBean	2.00	.80
❑ 26 Bobby Knoop	2.00	.80
❑ 27 Dick Bertell	2.00	.80
❑ 28 Barney Schultz	2.00	.80
❑ 29 Felix Mantilla	2.00	.80
❑ 30 Jim Bouton	6.00	2.40
❑ 31 Mike White	2.00	.80
❑ 32 Herman Franks MG	2.00	.80
❑ 33 Jackie Brandt	2.00	.80
❑ 34 Cal Koonce	2.00	.80
❑ 35 Ed Charles	2.00	.80
❑ 36 Bobby Wine	2.00	.80
❑ 37 Fred Gladding	2.00	.80
❑ 38 Jim King	2.00	.80
❑ 39 Gerry Arrigo	2.00	.80
❑ 40 Frank Howard	6.00	2.40
❑ 41 Bruce Howard	2.00	.80
Marv Staehle		
❑ 42 Earl Wilson	4.00	1.60
❑ 43 Mike Shannon	4.00	1.60
(Name in red, other		
Cardinals in yellow)		
❑ 44 Wade Blasingame	2.00	.80
❑ 45 Roy McMillan	4.00	1.60
❑ 46 Bob Lee	2.00	.80
❑ 47 Tommy Harper	4.00	1.60
❑ 48 Claude Raymond	4.00	1.60
❑ 49 Curt Blefary RC	4.00	1.60
John Miller		
❑ 50 Juan Marichal	10.00	4.00
❑ 51 Bill Bryan	2.00	.80
❑ 52 Ed Roebuck	2.00	.80
❑ 53 Dick McAuliffe	4.00	1.60
❑ 54 Joe Gibbon	2.00	.80
❑ 55 Tony Conigliaro	15.00	6.00
❑ 56 Ron Kline	2.00	.80
❑ 57 Cardinals Team	6.00	2.40
❑ 58 Fred Talbot	2.00	.80
❑ 59 Nate Oliver	2.00	.80
❑ 60 Jim O'Toole	4.00	1.60
❑ 61 Chris Cannizzaro	2.00	.80
❑ 62 Jim Kaat UER DP	6.00	2.40
(Misspelled Katt)		
❑ 63 Ty Cline	2.00	.80
❑ 64 Lou Burdette	4.00	1.60
❑ 65 Tony Kubek	10.00	4.00
❑ 66 Bill Rigney MG	2.00	.80
❑ 67 Harvey Haddix	4.00	1.60
❑ 68 Del Crandall	4.00	1.60
❑ 69 Bill Virdon	4.00	1.60
❑ 70 Bill Skowron	6.00	2.40
❑ 71 John O'Donoghue	2.00	.80
❑ 72 Tony Gonzalez	2.00	.80
❑ 73 Dennis Ribant	2.00	.80
❑ 74 Rico Petrocelli RC	10.00	4.00
Jerry Stephenson		
❑ 75 Deron Johnson	4.00	1.60
❑ 76 Sam McDowell	6.00	2.40
❑ 77 Doug Camilli	2.00	.80
❑ 78 Dal Maxvill	2.00	.80
❑ 79A Checklist 1	10.00	2.00
(61 Cannizzaro)		
❑ 79B Checklist 1	10.00	2.00
(61 C.Cannizzaro)		
❑ 80 Turk Farrell	2.00	.80
❑ 81 Don Buford	4.00	1.60
❑ 82 Santos Alomar RC	6.00	2.40
John Braun		
❑ 83 George Thomas	2.00	.80
❑ 84 Ron Herbel	2.00	.80
❑ 85 Willie Smith	2.00	.80
❑ 86 Buster Narum	2.00	.80
❑ 87 Nelson Mathews	2.00	.80
❑ 88 Jack Lamabe	2.00	.80
❑ 89 Mike Hershberger	2.00	.80
❑ 90 Rich Rollins	4.00	1.60
❑ 91 Cubs Team	6.00	2.40
❑ 92 Dick Howser	4.00	1.60
❑ 93 Jack Fisher	2.00	.80
❑ 94 Charlie Lau	4.00	1.60
❑ 95 Bill Mazeroski DP	6.00	2.40
❑ 96 Sonny Siebert	4.00	1.60
❑ 97 Pedro Gonzalez	2.00	.80
❑ 98 Bob Miller	2.00	.80
❑ 99 Gil Hodges MG	6.00	2.40
❑ 100 Ken Boyer	10.00	4.00
❑ 101 Fred Newman	2.00	.80
❑ 102 Steve Boros	2.00	.80
❑ 103 Harvey Kuenn	4.00	1.60
❑ 104 Checklist 2	10.00	2.00
❑ 105 Chico Salmon	2.00	.80
❑ 106 Gene Oliver	2.00	.80
❑ 107 Pat Corrales RC	4.00	1.60
Costen Shockley		
❑ 108 Don Mincher	2.00	.80
❑ 109 Walt Bond	2.00	.80
❑ 110 Ron Santo	6.00	2.40
❑ 111 Lee Thomas	4.00	1.60
❑ 112 Derrell Griffith	2.00	.80
❑ 113 Steve Barber	2.00	.80
❑ 114 Jim Hickman	4.00	1.60
❑ 115 Bobby Richardson	10.00	4.00
❑ 116 Dave Dowling	4.00	1.60
Bob Tolan RC		
❑ 117 Wes Stock	2.00	.80
❑ 118 Hal Lanier	4.00	1.60
❑ 119 John Kennedy	2.00	.80
❑ 120 Frank Robinson	35.00	14.00
❑ 121 Gene Alley	4.00	1.60
❑ 122 Bill Pleis	2.00	.80
❑ 123 Frank Thomas	4.00	1.60
❑ 124 Tom Satriano	2.00	.80
❑ 125 Juan Pizarro	2.00	.80
❑ 126 Dodgers Team	6.00	2.40
❑ 127 Frank Lary	2.00	.80
❑ 128 Vic Davalillo	2.00	.80
❑ 129 Bennie Daniels	2.00	.80
❑ 130 Al Kaline	35.00	14.00
❑ 131 Johnny Keane MG	2.00	.80
❑ 132 Mike Shannon WS	10.00	4.00
❑ 133 Mel Stottlemyre WS	6.00	2.40
❑ 134 Mickey Mantle WS	80.00	32.00
Mantle's Clutch HR UER		
Mantle is shown wearing a road uniform		
That game was played in New York		
❑ 135 Ken Boyer WS	10.00	4.00
❑ 136 Tim McCarver WS	6.00	2.40
❑ 137 Jim Bouton WS	6.00	2.40
❑ 138 Bob Gibson WS	12.00	4.80
❑ 139 WS Summary	6.00	2.40
Cards celebrate		
❑ 140 Dean Chance	4.00	1.60
❑ 141 Charlie James	2.00	.80
❑ 142 Bill Monbouquette	2.00	.80
❑ 143 John Gelnar	2.00	.80
Jerry May		
❑ 144 Ed Kranepool	4.00	1.60
❑ 145 Luis Tiant RC	10.00	4.00
❑ 146 Ron Hansen	2.00	.80
❑ 147 Dennis Bennett	2.00	.80
❑ 148 Willie Kirkland	2.00	.80
❑ 149 Wayne Schurr	2.00	.80
❑ 150 Brooks Robinson	40.00	16.00
❑ 151 Athletics Team	6.00	2.40
❑ 152 Phil Ortega	2.00	.80
❑ 153 Norm Cash	6.00	2.40
❑ 154 Bob Humphreys	2.00	.80
❑ 155 Roger Maris	60.00	24.00
❑ 156 Bob Sadowski	2.00	.80
❑ 157 Zoilo Versalles	4.00	1.60
❑ 158 Dick Sisler	2.00	.80
❑ 159 Jim Duffalo	2.00	.80
❑ 160 R.Clemente UER	175.00	70.00
1960 Pittsburfh		
❑ 161 Frank Baumann	2.00	.80
❑ 162 Russ Nixon	2.00	.80
❑ 163 Johnny Briggs	2.00	.80
❑ 164 Al Spangler	2.00	.80
❑ 165 Dick Ellsworth	2.00	.80
❑ 166 George Culver	4.00	1.60
Tommie Agee RC		
❑ 167 Bill Wakefield	2.00	.80
❑ 168 Dick Green	2.00	.80
❑ 169 Dave Vineyard	2.00	.80
❑ 170 Hank Aaron	100.00	40.00
❑ 171 Jim Roland	2.00	.80
❑ 172 Jimmy Piersall	6.00	2.40
❑ 173 Detroit Tigers	6.00	2.40

	No.	Card		
		Team Card		
❑	174	Joey Jay	2.00	.80
❑	175	Bob Aspromonte	2.00	.80
❑	176	Willie McCovey	20.00	8.00
❑	177	Pete Mikkelsen	2.00	.80
❑	178	Dalton Jones	2.00	.80
❑	179	Hal Woodeshick	2.00	.80
❑	180	Bob Allison	4.00	1.60
❑	181	Don Loun	2.00	.80
		Joe McCabe		
❑	182	Mike de la Hoz	2.00	.80
❑	183	Dave Nicholson	2.00	.80
❑	184	John Boozer	2.00	.80
❑	185	Max Alvis	2.00	.80
❑	186	Billy Cowan	2.00	.80
❑	187	Casey Stengel MG	15.00	6.00
❑	188	Sam Bowens	2.00	.80
❑	189	Checklist 3	10.00	2.00
❑	190	Bill White	6.00	2.40
❑	191	Phil Regan	4.00	1.60
❑	192	Jim Coker	2.00	.80
❑	193	Gaylord Perry	15.00	6.00
❑	194	Bill Kelso	2.00	.80
		Rick Reichardt		
❑	195	Bob Veale	4.00	1.60
❑	196	Ron Fairly	4.00	1.60
❑	197	Diego Segui	2.50	1.00
❑	198	Smoky Burgess	4.00	1.60
❑	199	Bob Heffner	2.50	1.00
❑	200	Joe Torre	6.00	2.40
❑	201	Sandy Valdespino	4.00	1.60
		Cesar Tovar RC		
❑	202	Leo Burke	2.50	1.00
❑	203	Dallas Green	4.00	1.60
❑	204	Russ Snyder	2.50	1.00
❑	205	Warren Spahn	30.00	12.00
❑	206	Willie Horton	4.00	1.60
❑	207	Pete Rose	125.00	50.00
❑	208	Tommy John	6.00	2.40
❑	209	Pirates Team	6.00	2.40
❑	210	Jim Fregosi	4.00	1.60
❑	211	Steve Ridzik	2.50	1.00
❑	212	Ron Brand	2.50	1.00
❑	213	Jim Davenport	2.50	1.00
❑	214	Bob Purkey	2.50	1.00
❑	215	Pete Ward	2.50	1.00
❑	216	Al Worthington	2.50	1.00
❑	217	Walter Alston MG	6.00	2.40
❑	218	Dick Schofield	2.50	1.00
❑	219	Bob Meyer	2.50	1.00
❑	220	Billy Williams	10.00	4.00
❑	221	John Tsitouris	2.50	1.00
❑	222	Bob Tillman	2.50	1.00
❑	223	Dan Osinski	2.50	1.00
❑	224	Bob Chance	2.50	1.00
❑	225	Bo Belinsky	4.00	1.60
❑	226	Elvio Jimenez	6.00	2.40
		Jake Gibbs		
❑	227	Bobby Klaus	2.50	1.00
❑	228	Jack Sanford	2.50	1.00
❑	229	Lou Clinton	2.50	1.00
❑	230	Ray Sadecki	2.50	1.00
❑	231	Jerry Adair	2.50	1.00
❑	232	Steve Blass RC	4.00	1.60
❑	233	Don Zimmer	4.00	1.60
❑	234	White Sox Team	6.00	2.40
❑	235	Chuck Hinton	2.50	1.00
❑	236	Denny McLain RC	25.00	10.00
❑	237	Bernie Allen	2.50	1.00
❑	238	Joe Moeller	2.50	1.00
❑	239	Doc Edwards	2.50	1.00
❑	240	Bob Bruce	2.50	1.00
❑	241	Mack Jones	2.50	1.00
❑	242	George Brunet	2.50	1.00
❑	243	Ted Davidson	4.00	1.60
		Tommy Helms RC		
❑	244	Lindy McDaniel	4.00	1.60
❑	245	Joe Pepitone	6.00	2.40
❑	246	Tom Butters	4.00	1.60
❑	247	Wally Moon	4.00	1.60
❑	248	Gus Triandos	4.00	1.60
❑	249	Dave McNally	4.00	1.60
❑	250	Willie Mays	100.00	40.00
❑	251	Billy Herman MG	4.00	1.60
❑	252	Pete Richert	2.50	1.00
❑	253	Danny Cater	2.50	1.00
❑	254	Roland Sheldon	2.50	1.00
❑	255	Camilo Pascual	4.00	1.60
❑	256	Tito Francona	2.50	1.00
❑	257	Jim Wynn	4.00	1.60
❑	258	Larry Bearnarth	2.50	1.00
❑	259	Jim Northrup RC	6.00	2.40
		Ray Oyler		
❑	260	Don Drysdale	20.00	8.00
❑	261	Duke Carmel	2.50	1.00
❑	262	Bud Daley	2.50	1.00
❑	263	Marty Keough	2.50	1.00
❑	264	Bob Buhl	4.00	1.60
❑	265	Jim Pagliaroni	2.50	1.00
❑	266	Bert Campaneris RC	10.00	4.00
❑	267	Senators Team	6.00	2.40
❑	268	Ken McBride	2.50	1.00
❑	269	Frank Bolling	2.50	1.00
❑	270	Milt Pappas	4.00	1.60
❑	271	Don Wert	4.00	1.60
❑	272	Chuck Schilling	2.50	1.00
❑	273	Checklist 4	10.00	2.00
❑	274	Lum Harris MG	2.50	1.00
❑	275	Dick Groat	6.00	2.40
❑	276	Hoyt Wilhelm	10.00	4.00
❑	277	Johnny Lewis	2.50	1.00
❑	278	Ken Retzer	2.50	1.00
❑	279	Dick Tracewski	2.50	1.00
❑	280	Dick Stuart	4.00	1.60
❑	281	Bill Stafford	2.50	1.00
❑	282	Dick Estelle	40.00	16.00
		Masanori Murakami RC		
❑	283	Fred Whitfield	2.50	1.00
❑	284	Nick Willhite	4.00	1.60
❑	285	Ron Hunt	4.00	1.60
❑	286	Jim Dickson	4.00	1.60
		Aurelio Monteagudo		
❑	287	Gary Kolb	4.00	1.60
❑	288	Jack Hamilton	4.00	1.60
❑	289	Gordy Coleman	6.00	2.40
❑	290	Wally Bunker	6.00	2.40
❑	291	Jerry Lynch	4.00	1.60
❑	292	Larry Yellen	4.00	1.60
❑	293	Angels Team	6.00	2.40
❑	294	Tim McCarver	10.00	4.00
❑	295	Dick Radatz	6.00	2.40
❑	296	Tony Taylor	6.00	2.40
❑	297	Dave DeBusschere	10.00	4.00
❑	298	Jim Stewart	4.00	1.60
❑	299	Jerry Zimmerman	4.00	1.60
❑	300	Sandy Koufax	100.00	40.00
❑	301	Birdie Tebbetts MG	6.00	2.40
❑	302	Al Stanek	4.00	1.60
❑	303	John Orsino	4.00	1.60
❑	304	Dave Stenhouse	4.00	1.60
❑	305	Rico Carty	6.00	2.40
❑	306	Bubba Phillips	4.00	1.60
❑	307	Barry Latman	4.00	1.60
❑	308	Cleon Jones RC	6.00	2.40
		Tom Parsons		
❑	309	Steve Hamilton	6.00	2.40
❑	310	Johnny Callison	6.00	2.40
❑	311	Orlando Pena	4.00	1.60
❑	312	Joe Nuxhall	4.00	1.60
❑	313	Jim Schaffer	4.00	1.60
❑	314	Sterling Slaughter	4.00	1.60
❑	315	Frank Malzone	6.00	2.40
❑	316	Reds Team	6.00	2.40
❑	317	Don McMahon	4.00	1.60
❑	318	Matty Alou	6.00	2.40
❑	319	Ken McMullen	4.00	1.60
❑	320	Bob Gibson	50.00	20.00
❑	321	Rusty Staub	10.00	4.00
❑	322	Rick Wise	6.00	2.40
❑	323	Hank Bauer MG	6.00	2.40
❑	324	Bobby Locke	4.00	1.60
❑	325	Donn Clendenon	6.00	2.40
❑	326	Dwight Siebler	4.00	1.60
❑	327	Denis Menke	4.00	1.60
❑	328	Eddie Fisher	4.00	1.60
❑	329	Hawk Taylor	4.00	1.60
❑	330	Whitey Ford	40.00	16.00
❑	331	Al Ferrara	6.00	2.40
		John Purdin		
❑	332	Ted Abernathy	4.00	1.60
❑	333	Tom Reynolds	4.00	1.60
❑	334	Vic Roznovsky	4.00	1.60
❑	335	Mickey Lolich	6.00	2.40
❑	336	Woody Held	4.00	1.60
❑	337	Mike Cuellar	6.00	2.40
❑	338	Philadelphia Phillies	6.00	2.40
		Team Card		
❑	339	Ryne Duren	6.00	2.40
❑	340	Tony Oliva	20.00	8.00
❑	341	Bob Bolin	4.00	1.60
❑	342	Bob Rodgers	6.00	2.40
❑	343	Mike McCormick	6.00	2.40
❑	344	Wes Parker	6.00	2.40
❑	345	Floyd Robinson	4.00	1.60
❑	346	Bobby Bragan MG	4.00	1.60
❑	347	Roy Face	6.00	2.40
❑	348	George Banks	4.00	1.60
❑	349	Larry Miller	4.00	1.60
❑	350	Mickey Mantle	450.00	180.00
❑	351	Jim Perry	6.00	2.40
❑	352	Alex Johnson RC	6.00	2.40
❑	353	Jerry Lumpe	4.00	1.60
❑	354	Billy Ott	4.00	1.60
		Jack Warner		
❑	355	Vada Pinson	10.00	4.00
❑	356	Bill Spanswick	4.00	1.60
❑	357	Carl Warwick	4.00	1.60
❑	358	Albie Pearson	6.00	2.40
❑	359	Ken Johnson	4.00	1.60
❑	360	Orlando Cepeda	15.00	6.00
❑	361	Checklist 5	12.00	2.40
❑	362	Don Schwall	4.00	1.60
❑	363	Bob Johnson	4.00	1.60
❑	364	Galen Cisco	4.00	1.60
❑	365	Jim Gentile	6.00	2.40
❑	366	Dan Schneider	4.00	1.60
❑	367	Leon Wagner	4.00	1.60
❑	368	Ken Berry	6.00	2.40
		Joel Gibson		
❑	369	Phil Linz	6.00	2.40
❑	370	Tommy Davis	6.00	2.40
❑	371	Frank Kreutzer	7.00	2.80
❑	372	Clay Dalrymple	7.00	2.80
❑	373	Curt Simmons	7.00	2.80
❑	374	Jose Cardenal RC	7.00	2.80
		Dick Simpson		
❑	375	Dave Wickersham	7.00	2.80
❑	376	Jim Landis	7.00	2.80
❑	377	Willie Stargell	25.00	10.00
❑	378	Chuck Estrada	7.00	2.80
❑	379	Giants Team	7.00	2.80
❑	380	Rocky Colavito	25.00	10.00
❑	381	Al Jackson	7.00	2.80
❑	382	J.C. Martin	7.00	2.80
❑	383	Felipe Alou	15.00	6.00
❑	384	Johnny Klippstein	7.00	2.80
❑	385	Carl Yastrzemski	60.00	24.00
❑	386	Paul Jaeckel	7.00	2.80
		Fred Norman		
❑	387	Johnny Podres	15.00	6.00
❑	388	John Blanchard	15.00	6.00
❑	389	Don Larsen	15.00	6.00
❑	390	Bill Freehan	15.00	6.00
❑	391	Mel McGaha MG	7.00	2.80
❑	392	Bob Friend	15.00	6.00
❑	393	Ed Kirkpatrick	7.00	2.80
❑	394	Jim Hannan	7.00	2.80
❑	395	Jim Ray Hart	7.00	2.80
❑	396	Frank Bertaina	7.00	2.80
❑	397	Jerry Buchek	7.00	2.80
❑	398	Dan Neville	15.00	6.00
		Art Shamsky		
❑	399	Ray Herbert	7.00	2.80
❑	400	Harmon Killebrew	50.00	20.00
❑	401	Carl Willey	7.00	2.80
❑	402	Joe Amalfitano	7.00	2.80
❑	403	Boston Red Sox	7.00	2.80
		Team Card		
❑	404	Stan Williams	7.00	2.80
		(Listed as Indian		
		but Yankee cap)		
❑	405	John Roseboro	20.00	8.00
❑	406	Ralph Terry	15.00	6.00
❑	407	Lee Maye	7.00	2.80
❑	408	Larry Sherry	7.00	2.80
❑	409	Jim Beauchamp	15.00	6.00
		Larry Dierker RC		
❑	410	Luis Aparicio	25.00	10.00

No.	Card	NM	Ex
❑ 411	Roger Craig	15.00	6.00
❑ 412	Bob Bailey	7.00	2.80
❑ 413	Hal Reniff	7.00	2.80
❑ 414	Al Lopez MG	15.00	6.00
❑ 415	Curt Flood	15.00	6.00
❑ 416	Jim Brewer	7.00	2.80
❑ 417	Ed Brinkman	7.00	2.80
❑ 418	Johnny Edwards	7.00	2.80
❑ 419	Ruben Amaro	7.00	2.80
❑ 420	Larry Jackson	7.00	2.80
❑ 421	Gary Dotter	7.00	2.80
	Jay Ward		
❑ 422	Aubrey Gatewood	7.00	2.80
❑ 423	Jesse Gonder	7.00	2.80
❑ 424	Gary Bell	7.00	2.80
❑ 425	Wayne Causey	7.00	2.80
❑ 426	Braves Team	7.00	2.80
❑ 427	Bob Saverine	7.00	2.80
❑ 428	Bob Shaw	7.00	2.80
❑ 429	Don Demeter	7.00	2.80
❑ 430	Gary Peters	7.00	2.80
❑ 431	Nelson Briles RC	15.00	6.00
	Wayne Spiezio		
❑ 432	Jim Grant	15.00	6.00
❑ 433	John Bateman	7.00	2.80
❑ 434	Dave Morehead	7.00	2.80
❑ 435	Willie Davis	15.00	6.00
❑ 436	Don Elston	7.00	2.80
❑ 437	Chico Cardenas	15.00	6.00
❑ 438	Harry Walker MG	7.00	2.80
❑ 439	Moe Drabowsky	15.00	6.00
❑ 440	Tom Tresh	15.00	6.00
❑ 441	Denny Lemaster	7.00	2.80
❑ 442	Vic Power	7.00	2.80
❑ 443	Checklist 6	12.00	2.40
❑ 444	Bob Hendley	7.00	2.80
❑ 445	Don Lock	7.00	2.80
❑ 446	Art Mahaffey	7.00	2.80
❑ 447	Julian Javier	15.00	6.00
❑ 448	Lee Stange	7.00	2.80
❑ 449	Jerry Hinsley	15.00	6.00
	Gary Kroll		
❑ 450	Elston Howard	15.00	6.00
❑ 451	Jim Owens	7.00	2.80
❑ 452	Gary Geiger	7.00	2.80
❑ 453	Willie Crawford	15.00	6.00
	John Werhas		
❑ 454	Ed Rakow	7.00	2.80
❑ 455	Norm Siebern	7.00	2.80
❑ 456	Bill Henry	7.00	2.80
❑ 457	Bob Kennedy MG	15.00	6.00
❑ 458	John Buzhardt	7.00	2.80
❑ 459	Frank Kostro	7.00	2.80
❑ 460	Richie Allen	40.00	16.00
❑ 461	Clay Carroll RC	50.00	20.00
	Phil Niekro		
❑ 462	Lew Krausse UER	7.00	2.80
	(Photo actually		
	Pete Lovrich)		
❑ 463	Manny Mota	15.00	6.00
❑ 464	Ron Piche	7.00	2.80
❑ 465	Tom Haller	15.00	6.00
❑ 466	Pete Craig	7.00	2.80
	Dick Nen		
❑ 467	Ray Washburn	7.00	2.80
❑ 468	Larry Brown	7.00	2.80
❑ 469	Don Nottebart	7.00	2.80
❑ 470	Yogi Berra P/CO	50.00	20.00
❑ 471	Billy Hoeft	7.00	2.80
❑ 472	Don Pavletich UER	7.00	2.80
	Listed as a pitcher		
❑ 473	Paul Blair	15.00	6.00
	Davey Johnson RC		
❑ 474	Cookie Rojas	15.00	6.00
❑ 475	Clete Boyer	15.00	6.00
❑ 476	Billy O'Dell	7.00	2.80
❑ 477	Fritz Ackley	150.00	60.00
	Steve Carlton RC		
❑ 478	Wilbur Wood	15.00	6.00
❑ 479	Ken Harrelson	15.00	6.00
❑ 480	Joel Horlen	7.00	2.80
❑ 481	Cleveland Indians	10.00	4.00
	Team Card		
❑ 482	Bob Priddy	7.00	2.80
❑ 483	George Smith	7.00	2.80
❑ 484	Ron Perranoski	20.00	8.00
❑ 485	Nellie Fox P/CO	25.00	10.00
❑ 486	Tom Egan	7.00	2.80
	Pat Rogan		
❑ 487	Woody Woodward	15.00	6.00
❑ 488	Ted Wills	7.00	2.80
❑ 489	Gene Mauch MG	15.00	6.00
❑ 490	Earl Battey	7.00	2.80
❑ 491	Tracy Stallard	7.00	2.80
❑ 492	Gene Freese	7.00	2.80
❑ 493	Bill Roman	7.00	2.80
	Bruce Brubaker		
❑ 494	Jay Ritchie	7.00	2.80
❑ 495	Joe Christopher	7.00	2.80
❑ 496	Joe Cunningham	7.00	2.80
❑ 497	Ken Henderson	15.00	6.00
	Jack Hiatt		
❑ 498	Gene Stephens	7.00	2.80
❑ 499	Stu Miller	15.00	6.00
❑ 500	Eddie Mathews	40.00	16.00
❑ 501	Ralph Gagliano	7.00	2.80
	Jim Rittwage		
❑ 502	Don Cardwell	7.00	2.80
❑ 503	Phil Gagliano	7.00	2.80
❑ 504	Jerry Grote	15.00	6.00
❑ 505	Ray Culp	7.00	2.80
❑ 506	Sam Mele MG	7.00	2.80
❑ 507	Sammy Ellis	7.00	2.80
❑ 508	Checklist 7	12.00	2.40
❑ 509	Bob Guindon	7.00	2.80
	Gerry Vezendy		
❑ 510	Ernie Banks	80.00	32.00
❑ 511	Ron Locke	7.00	2.80
❑ 512	Cap Peterson	7.00	2.80
❑ 513	New York Yankees	40.00	16.00
	Team Card		
❑ 514	Joe Azcue	7.00	2.80
❑ 515	Vern Law	15.00	6.00
❑ 516	Al Weis	7.00	2.80
❑ 517	Paul Schaal	15.00	6.00
	Jack Warner		
❑ 518	Ken Rowe	7.00	2.80
❑ 519	Bob Uecker UER	30.00	12.00
	(Posing as a left-		
	handed batter)		
❑ 520	Tony Cloninger	7.00	2.80
❑ 521	Dave Bennett	7.00	2.80
	Morrie Stevens		
❑ 522	Hank Aguirre	7.00	2.80
❑ 523	Mike Brumley SP	12.00	4.80
❑ 524	Dave Giusti SP	12.00	4.80
❑ 525	Eddie Bressoud	7.00	2.80
❑ 526	Rene Lachemann	80.00	32.00
	Johnny Odom		
	Jim Hunter RC UER		
	(Tim on back)		
	Skip Lockwood SP		
❑ 527	Jeff Torborg SP	12.00	4.80
❑ 528	George Altman	7.00	2.80
❑ 529	Jerry Fosnow SP	12.00	4.80
❑ 530	Jim Maloney	15.00	6.00
❑ 531	Chuck Hiller	7.00	2.80
❑ 532	Hector Lopez	15.00	6.00
❑ 533	Dan Napoleon	25.00	10.00
	Ron Swoboda RC		
	Tug McGraw RC		
	Jim Bethke SP		
❑ 534	John Herrnstein	7.00	2.80
❑ 535	Jack Kralick SP	12.00	4.80
❑ 536	Andre Rodgers SP	12.00	4.80
❑ 537	Marcelino Lopez	7.00	2.80
	Phil Roof		
	Rudy May RC		
❑ 538	C.Dressen SP MG	12.00	4.80
❑ 539	Herm Starrette	7.00	2.80
❑ 540	Lou Brock SP	50.00	20.00
❑ 541	Greg Bollo	7.00	2.80
	Bob Locker		
❑ 542	Lou Klimchock	7.00	2.80
❑ 543	Ed Connolly SP	12.00	4.80
❑ 544	Howie Reed	7.00	2.80
❑ 545	Jesus Alou SP	14.00	5.50
❑ 546	Bill Davis	7.00	2.80
	Mike Hedlund		
	Ray Barker		
	Floyd Weaver		
❑ 547	Jake Wood SP	12.00	4.80
❑ 548	Dick Stigman	7.00	2.80
❑ 549	Roberto Pena	20.00	8.00
	Glenn Beckert RC		
❑ 550	M.Stottlemyre RC SP	30.00	12.00
❑ 551	New York Mets SP	30.00	12.00
	Team Card		
❑ 552	Julio Gotay	7.00	2.80
❑ 553	Dan Coombs	7.00	2.80
	Gene Ratliff		
	Jack McClure		
❑ 554	Chico Ruiz SP	12.00	4.80
❑ 555	Jack Baldschun SP	12.00	4.80
❑ 556	Red Schoendienst	24.00	9.50
	SP MG		
❑ 557	Jose Santiago	7.00	2.80
❑ 558	Tommie Sisk	7.00	2.80
❑ 559	Ed Bailey SP	12.00	4.80
❑ 560	Boog Powell SP	24.00	9.50
❑ 561	Dennis Daboll	15.00	6.00
	Mike Kekich		
	Hector Valle		
	Jim Lefebvre RC		
❑ 562	Billy Moran	7.00	2.80
❑ 563	Julio Navarro	7.00	2.80
❑ 564	Mel Nelson	7.00	2.80
❑ 565	Ernie Broglio SP	12.00	4.80
❑ 566	Gil Blanco	12.00	4.80
	Ross Moschitto		
	Art Lopez SP		
❑ 567	Tommie Aaron	7.00	2.80
❑ 568	Ron Taylor SP	12.00	4.80
❑ 569	Gino Cimoli SP	12.00	4.80
❑ 570	Claude Osteen SP	15.00	6.00
❑ 571	Ossie Virgil SP	12.00	4.80
❑ 572	Baltimore Orioles SP	25.00	10.00
	Team Card		
❑ 573	Jim Lonborg RC	24.00	9.50
	Gerry Moses		
	Bill Schlesinger		
	Mike Ryan SP		
❑ 574	Roy Sievers	15.00	6.00
❑ 575	Jose Pagan	7.00	2.80
❑ 576	Terry Fox SP	12.00	4.80
❑ 577	Darold Knowles	12.00	4.80
	Don Buschhorn		
	Richie Scheinblum SP		
❑ 578	Camilo Carreon SP	12.00	4.80
❑ 579	Dick Smith SP	12.00	4.80
❑ 580	Jimmie Hall SP	12.00	4.80
❑ 581	Tony Perez RC	80.00	32.00
	Dave Ricketts		
	Kevin Collins SP		
❑ 582	Bob Schmidt SP	12.00	4.80
❑ 583	Wes Covington SP	12.00	4.80
❑ 584	Harry Bright	15.00	6.00
❑ 585	Hank Fischer	7.00	2.80
❑ 586	Tom McCraw SP	12.00	4.80
❑ 587	Joe Sparma	7.00	2.80
❑ 588	Lenny Green	7.00	2.80
❑ 589	Frank Linzy	12.00	4.80
	Bob Schroder SP		
❑ 590	John Wyatt	7.00	2.80
❑ 591	Bob Skinner SP	12.00	4.80
❑ 592	Frank Bork SP	12.00	4.80
❑ 593	Jackie Moore RC	12.00	4.80
	John Sullivan SP		
❑ 594	Joe Gaines	7.00	2.80
❑ 595	Don Lee	7.00	2.80
❑ 596	Don Landrum SP	12.00	4.80
❑ 597	Joe Nossek	7.00	2.80
	John Sevcik		
	Dick Reese		
❑ 598	Al Downing SP	24.00	7.25

1966 Topps

	NM	Ex
COMPLETE SET (598)	4000.00	1600.00
COMMON CARD (1-109)	1.50	.60
COMMON (110-283)	2.00	.80
COMMON (284-370)	3.00	1.20
COMMON (371-446)	5.00	2.00
COMMON (447-522)	9.00	3.60
COMMON (523-598)	15.00	6.00
COMMON SP (523-598)	30.00	12.00
WRAPPER (5-CENT)	25.00	10.00

❑ 1 Willie Mays 150.00 47.50
❑ 2 Ted Abernathy 1.50 .60
❑ 3 Sam Mele MG 1.50 .60
❑ 4 Ray Culp 1.50 .60
❑ 5 Jim Fregosi 2.00 .80
❑ 6 Chuck Schilling 1.50 .60
❑ 7 Tracy Stallard 1.50 .60
❑ 8 Floyd Robinson 1.50 .60
❑ 9 Clete Boyer 2.00 .80
❑ 10 Tony Cloninger 1.50 .60
❑ 11 Brant Alyea 1.50 .60
Pete Craig
❑ 12 John Tsitouris 1.50 .60
❑ 13 Lou Johnson 2.00 .80
❑ 14 Norm Siebern 1.50 .60
❑ 15 Vern Law 2.00 .80
❑ 16 Larry Brown 1.50 .60
❑ 17 John Stephenson 1.50 .60
❑ 18 Roland Sheldon 1.50 .60
❑ 19 San Francisco Giants 5.00 2.00
Team Card
❑ 20 Willie Horton 2.00 .80
❑ 21 Don Nottebart 1.50 .60
❑ 22 Joe Nossek 1.50 .60
❑ 23 Jack Sanford 1.50 .60
❑ 24 Don Kessinger RC 4.00 1.60
❑ 25 Pete Ward 1.50 .60
❑ 26 Ray Sadecki 1.50 .60
❑ 27 Darold Knowles 1.50 .60
Andy Etchebarren
❑ 28 Phil Niekro 20.00 8.00
❑ 29 Mike Brumley 1.50 .60
❑ 30 Pete Rose DP 80.00 24.00
❑ 31 Jack Cullen 2.00 .80
❑ 32 Adolfo Phillips 1.50 .60
❑ 33 Jim Pagliaroni 1.50 .60
❑ 34 Checklist 1 8.00 1.60
❑ 35 Ron Swoboda 4.00 1.60
❑ 36 Jim Hunter UER 20.00 8.00
Stats say 1963 and 1964
should be 1964 and 1965
❑ 37 Billy Herman MG 2.00 .80
❑ 38 Ron Nischwitz 1.50 .60
❑ 39 Ken Henderson 1.50 .60
❑ 40 Jim Grant 1.50 .60
❑ 41 Don LeJohn 1.50 .60
❑ 42 Aubrey Gatewood 1.50 .60
❑ 43A Don Landrum 2.00 .80
(Dark button on pants
showing)
❑ 43B Don Landrum 20.00 8.00
(Button on pants
partially airbrushed)
❑ 43C Don Landrum 2.00 .80
(Button on pants
not showing)
❑ 44 Bill Davis 1.50 .60
Tom Kelley
❑ 45 Jim Gentile 2.00 .80
❑ 46 Howie Koplitz 1.50 .60
❑ 47 J.C. Martin 1.50 .60
❑ 48 Paul Blair 2.00 .80
❑ 49 Woody Woodward 2.00 .80
❑ 50 Mickey Mantle DP 250.00 100.00
❑ 51 Gordon Richardson 1.50 .60
❑ 52 Wes Covington 4.00 1.60
Johnny Callison
❑ 53 Bob Duliba 1.50 .60
❑ 54 Jose Pagan 1.50 .60
❑ 55 Ken Harrelson 2.00 .80
❑ 56 Sandy Valdespino 1.50 .60
❑ 57 Jim Lefebvre 2.00 .80
❑ 58 Dave Wickersham 1.50 .60
❑ 59 Reds Team 5.00 2.00
❑ 60 Curt Flood 4.00 1.60
❑ 61 Bob Bolin 1.50 .60
❑ 62A Merritt Ranew 2.00 .80
(With sold line)
❑ 62B Merritt Ranew 30.00 12.00
(Without sold line)
❑ 63 Jim Stewart 1.50 .60
❑ 64 Bob Bruce 1.50 .60
❑ 65 Leon Wagner 1.50 .60
❑ 66 Al Weis 1.50 .60
❑ 67 Cleon Jones 4.00 1.60
Dick Selma
❑ 68 Hal Reniff 1.50 .60
❑ 69 Ken Hamlin 1.50 .60
❑ 70 Carl Yastrzemski 30.00 12.00
❑ 71 Frank Carpin 1.50 .60
❑ 72 Tony Perez 25.00 10.00
❑ 73 Jerry Zimmerman 1.50 .60
❑ 74 Don Mossi 2.00 .80
❑ 75 Tommy Davis 2.00 .80
❑ 76 Red Schoendienst MG 4.00 1.60
❑ 77 John Orsino 1.50 .60
❑ 78 Frank Linzy 1.50 .60
❑ 79 Joe Pepitone 4.00 1.60
❑ 80 Richie Allen 6.00 2.40
❑ 81 Ray Oyler 1.50 .60
❑ 82 Bob Hendley 1.50 .60
❑ 83 Albie Pearson 2.00 .80
❑ 84 Jim Beauchamp 1.50 .60
Dick Kelley
❑ 85 Eddie Fisher 1.50 .60
❑ 86 John Bateman 1.50 .60
❑ 87 Dan Napoleon 1.50 .60
❑ 88 Fred Whitfield 1.50 .60
❑ 89 Ted Davidson 1.50 .60
❑ 90 Luis Aparicio 8.00 3.20
❑ 91A Bob Uecker TR 10.00 4.00
❑ 91B Bob Uecker NTR 40.00 16.00
❑ 92 Yankees Team 14.00 5.50
❑ 93 Jim Lonborg 2.00 .80
❑ 94 Matty Alou 2.00 .80
❑ 95 Pete Richert 1.50 .60
❑ 96 Felipe Alou 4.00 1.60
❑ 97 Jim Merritt 1.50 .60
❑ 98 Don Demeter 1.50 .60
❑ 99 Willie Stargell 6.00 2.40
Donn Clendenon
❑ 100 Sandy Koufax 75.00 30.00
❑ 101A Checklist 2 16.00 3.20
(115 W. Spahn) ERR
❑ 101B Checklist 2 10.00 2.00
(115 Bill Henry) COR
❑ 102 Ed Kirkpatrick 1.50 .60
❑ 103A Dick Groat TR 2.00 .80
❑ 103B Dick Groat NTR 40.00 16.00
❑ 104A Alex Johnson TR 2.00 .80
❑ 104B Alex Johnson NTR 30.00 12.00
❑ 105 Milt Pappas 2.00 .80
❑ 106 Rusty Staub 4.00 1.60
❑ 107 Larry Stahl 1.50 .60
Ron Tompkins
❑ 108 Bobby Klaus 1.50 .60
❑ 109 Ralph Terry 2.00 .80
❑ 110 Ernie Banks 30.00 12.00
❑ 111 Gary Peters 2.00 .80
❑ 112 Manny Mota 4.00 1.60
❑ 113 Hank Aguirre 2.00 .80
❑ 114 Jim Gosger 2.00 .80
❑ 115 Bill Henry 2.00 .80
❑ 116 Walter Alston MG 6.00 2.40
❑ 117 Jake Gibbs 2.00 .80
❑ 118 Mike McCormick 2.00 .80
❑ 119 Art Shamsky 2.00 .80
❑ 120 Harmon Killebrew 15.00 6.00
❑ 121 Ray Herbert 2.00 .80
❑ 122 Joe Gaines 2.00 .80
❑ 123 Frank Bork 2.00 .80
Jerry May
❑ 124 Tug McGraw 4.00 1.60
❑ 125 Lou Brock 20.00 8.00
❑ 126 Jim Palmer RC UER 100.00 40.00
Described as a
lefthander on
card back
❑ 127 Ken Berry 2.00 .80
❑ 128 Jim Landis 2.00 .80
❑ 129 Jack Kralick 2.00 .80
❑ 130 Joe Torre 6.00 2.40
❑ 131 Angels Team 5.00 2.00
❑ 132 Orlando Cepeda 8.00 3.20
❑ 133 Don McMahon 2.00 .80
❑ 134 Wes Parker 4.00 1.60
❑ 135 Dave Morehead 2.00 .80
❑ 136 Woody Held 2.00 .80
❑ 137 Pat Corrales 2.00 .80
❑ 138 Roger Repoz 2.00 .80
❑ 139 Byron Browne 2.00 .80
Don Young
❑ 140 Jim Maloney 4.00 1.60
❑ 141 Tom McCraw 2.00 .80
❑ 142 Don Dennis 2.00 .80
❑ 143 Jose Tartabull 4.00 1.60
❑ 144 Don Schwall 2.00 .80
❑ 145 Bill Freehan 4.00 1.60
❑ 146 George Altman 2.00 .80
❑ 147 Lum Harris MG 2.00 .80
❑ 148 Bob Johnson 2.00 .80
❑ 149 Dick Nen 2.00 .80
❑ 150 Rocky Colavito 8.00 3.20
❑ 151 Gary Wagner 2.00 .80
❑ 152 Frank Malzone 4.00 1.60
❑ 153 Rico Carty 4.00 1.60
❑ 154 Chuck Hiller 2.00 .80
❑ 155 Marcelino Lopez 2.00 .80
❑ 156 Dick Schofield 2.00 .80
Hal Lanier
❑ 157 Rene Lachemann 2.00 .80
❑ 158 Jim Brewer 2.00 .80
❑ 159 Chico Ruiz 2.00 .80
❑ 160 Whitey Ford 30.00 10.00
❑ 161 Jerry Lumpe 2.00 .80
❑ 162 Lee Maye 2.00 .80
❑ 163 Tito Francona 2.00 .80
❑ 164 Tommie Agee 4.00 1.60
Marv Staehle
❑ 165 Don Lock 2.00 .80
❑ 166 Chris Krug 2.00 .80
❑ 167 Boog Powell 6.00 2.40
❑ 168 Dan Osinski 2.00 .80
❑ 169 Duke Sims 2.00 .80
❑ 170 Cookie Rojas 4.00 1.60
❑ 171 Nick Willhite 2.00 .80
❑ 172 Mets Team 5.00 2.00
❑ 173 Al Spangler 2.00 .80
❑ 174 Ron Taylor 2.00 .80
❑ 175 Bert Campaneris 4.00 1.60
❑ 176 Jim Davenport 2.00 .80
❑ 177 Hector Lopez 2.00 .80
❑ 178 Bob Tillman 2.00 .80
❑ 179 Dennis Aust 4.00 1.60
Bob Tolan
❑ 180 Vada Pinson 4.00 1.60
❑ 181 Al Worthington 2.00 .80
❑ 182 Jerry Lynch 2.00 .80
❑ 183A Checklist 3 8.00 1.60
(Large print
on front)
❑ 183B Checklist 3 8.00 1.60
(Small print
on front)
❑ 184 Denis Menke 2.00 .80
❑ 185 Bob Buhl 4.00 1.60
❑ 186 Ruben Amaro 2.00 .80
❑ 187 Chuck Dressen MG 4.00 1.60
❑ 188 Al Luplow 2.00 .80
❑ 189 John Roseboro 4.00 1.60
❑ 190 Jimmie Hall 2.00 .80
❑ 191 Darrell Sutherland 2.00 .80
❑ 192 Vic Power 4.00 1.60
❑ 193 Dave McNally 4.00 1.60
❑ 194 Senators Team 5.00 2.00
❑ 195 Joe Morgan 15.00 6.00
❑ 196 Don Pavletich 2.00 .80
❑ 197 Sonny Siebert 2.00 .80
❑ 198 Mickey Stanley RC 6.00 2.40
❑ 199 Bill Skowron 4.00 1.60

	No.	Card	NRMT	VG-E
		Johnny Romano		
		Floyd Robinson		
❏	200	Eddie Mathews	15.00	6.00
❏	201	Jim Dickson	2.00	.80
❏	202	Clay Dalrymple	2.00	.80
❏	203	Jose Santiago	2.00	.80
❏	204	Cubs Team	5.00	2.00
❏	205	Tom Tresh	4.00	1.60
❏	206	Al Jackson	2.00	.80
❏	207	Frank Quilici	2.00	.80
❏	208	Bob Miller	2.00	.80
❏	209	Fritz Fisher	4.00	1.60
		John Hiller RC		
❏	210	Bill Mazeroski	8.00	3.20
❏	211	Frank Kreutzer	2.00	.80
❏	212	Ed Kranepool	4.00	1.60
❏	213	Fred Newman	2.00	.80
❏	214	Tommy Harper	4.00	1.60
❏	215	Bob Clemente	50.00	20.00
		Hank Aaron		
		Willie Mays LL		
❏	216	Tony Oliva	5.00	2.00
		Carl Yastrzemski		
		Vic Davalillo LL		
❏	217	Willie Mays	20.00	8.00
		Willie McCovey		
		Billy Williams LL		
❏	218	Tony Conigliaro	5.00	2.00
		Norm Cash		
		Willie Horton LL		
❏	219	Deron Johnson	12.00	4.80
		Frank Robinson		
		Willie Mays LL		
❏	220	Rocky Colavito	5.00	2.00
		Willie Horton		
		Tony Oliva LL		
❏	221	Sandy Koufax	12.00	4.80
		Juan Marichal		
		Vern Law LL		
❏	222	Sam McDowell	5.00	2.00
		Eddie Fisher		
		Sonny Siebert LL		
❏	223	Sandy Koufax	12.00	4.80
		Tony Cloninger		
		Don Drysdale LL		
❏	224	Jim Grant	5.00	2.00
		Mel Stottlemyre		
		Jim Kaat LL		
❏	225	Sandy Koufax	12.00	4.80
		Bob Veale		
		Bob Gibson LL		
❏	226	Sam McDowell	5.00	2.00
		Mickey Lolich		
		Dennis McLain		
		Sonny Siebert LL		
❏	227	Russ Nixon	2.00	.80
❏	228	Larry Dierker	4.00	1.60
❏	229	Hank Bauer MG	4.00	1.60
❏	230	Johnny Callison	4.00	1.60
❏	231	Floyd Weaver	2.00	.80
❏	232	Glenn Beckert	4.00	1.60
❏	233	Dom Zanni	2.00	.80
❏	234	Rich Beck	8.00	3.20
		Roy White RC		
❏	235	Don Cardwell	2.00	.80
❏	236	Mike Hershberger	2.00	.80
❏	237	Billy O'Dell	2.00	.80
❏	238	Dodgers Team	5.00	2.00
❏	239	Orlando Pena	2.00	.80
❏	240	Earl Battey	2.00	.80
❏	241	Dennis Ribant	2.00	.80
❏	242	Jesus Alou	2.00	.80
❏	243	Nelson Briles	4.00	1.60
❏	244	Chuck Harrison	2.00	.80
		Sonny Jackson		
❏	245	John Buzhardt	2.00	.80
❏	246	Ed Bailey	2.00	.80
❏	247	Carl Warwick	2.00	.80
❏	248	Pete Mikkelsen	2.00	.80
❏	249	Bill Rigney MG	2.00	.80
❏	250	Sammy Ellis	2.00	.80
❏	251	Ed Brinkman	2.00	.80
❏	252	Denny Lemaster	2.00	.80
❏	253	Don Wert	2.00	.80
❏	254	Fergie Jenkins RC	70.00	28.00
		Bill Sorrell		
❏	255	Willie Stargell	20.00	8.00
❏	256	Lew Krausse	2.00	.80
❏	257	Jeff Torborg	4.00	1.60
❏	258	Dave Giusti	2.00	.80
❏	259	Boston Red Sox	5.00	2.00
		Team Card		
❏	260	Bob Shaw	2.00	.80
❏	261	Ron Hansen	2.00	.80
❏	262	Jack Hamilton	2.00	.80
❏	263	Tom Egan	2.00	.80
❏	264	Andy Kosco	2.00	.80
		Ted Uhlaender		
❏	265	Stu Miller	4.00	1.60
❏	266	Pedro Gonzalez UER	2.00	.80
		(Misspelled Gonzales		
		on card back)		
❏	267	Joe Sparma	2.00	.80
❏	268	John Blanchard	2.00	.80
❏	269	Don Heffner MG	2.00	.80
❏	270	Claude Osteen	4.00	1.60
❏	271	Hal Lanier	2.00	.80
❏	272	Jack Baldschun	2.00	.80
❏	273	Bob Aspromonte	4.00	1.60
		Rusty Staub		
❏	274	Buster Narum	2.00	.80
❏	275	Tim McCarver	4.00	1.60
❏	276	Jim Bouton	4.00	1.60
❏	277	George Thomas	2.00	.80
❏	278	Cal Koonce	2.00	.80
❏	279A	Checklist 4	8.00	1.60
		(Player's cap black)		
❏	279B	Checklist 4	8.00	1.60
		(Player's cap red)		
❏	280	Bobby Knoop	2.00	.80
❏	281	Bruce Howard	2.00	.80
❏	282	Johnny Lewis	2.00	.80
❏	283	Jim Perry	4.00	1.60
❏	284	Bobby Wine	3.00	1.20
❏	285	Luis Tiant	5.00	2.00
❏	286	Gary Geiger	3.00	1.20
❏	287	Jack Aker	3.00	1.20
❏	288	Bill Singer	50.00	20.00
		Don Sutton RC		
❏	289	Larry Sherry	3.00	1.20
❏	290	Ron Santo	5.00	2.00
❏	291	Moe Drabowsky	5.00	2.00
❏	292	Jim Coker	3.00	1.20
❏	293	Mike Shannon	5.00	2.00
❏	294	Steve Ridzik	3.00	1.20
❏	295	Jim Ray Hart	5.00	2.00
❏	296	Johnny Keane MG	5.00	2.00
❏	297	Jim Owens	3.00	1.20
❏	298	Rico Petrocelli	5.00	2.00
❏	299	Lou Burdette	5.00	2.00
❏	300	Bob Clemente	150.00	60.00
❏	301	Greg Bollo	3.00	1.20
❏	302	Ernie Bowman	3.00	1.20
❏	303	Cleveland Indians	5.00	2.00
		Team Card		
❏	304	John Herrnstein	3.00	1.20
❏	305	Camilo Pascual	5.00	2.00
❏	306	Ty Cline	3.00	1.20
❏	307	Clay Carroll	5.00	2.00
❏	308	Tom Haller	5.00	2.00
❏	309	Diego Segui	3.00	1.20
❏	310	Frank Robinson	40.00	16.00
❏	311	Tommy Helms	5.00	2.00
		Dick Simpson		
❏	312	Bob Saverine	3.00	1.20
❏	313	Chris Zachary	3.00	1.20
❏	314	Hector Valle	3.00	1.20
❏	315	Norm Cash	5.00	2.00
❏	316	Jack Fisher	3.00	1.20
❏	317	Dalton Jones	3.00	1.20
❏	318	Harry Walker MG	3.00	1.20
❏	319	Gene Freese	3.00	1.20
❏	320	Bob Gibson	25.00	10.00
❏	321	Rick Reichardt	3.00	1.20
❏	322	Bill Faul	3.00	1.20
❏	323	Ray Barker	3.00	1.20
❏	324	John Boozer	3.00	1.20
❏	325	Vic Davalillo	3.00	1.20
❏	326	Braves Team	5.00	2.00
❏	327	Bernie Allen	3.00	1.20
❏	328	Jerry Grote	5.00	2.00
❏	329	Pete Charton	3.00	1.20
❏	330	Ron Fairly	5.00	2.00
❏	331	Ron Herbel	3.00	1.20
❏	332	Bill Bryan	3.00	1.20
❏	333	Joe Coleman RC	3.00	1.20
		Jim French		
❏	334	Marty Keough	3.00	1.20
❏	335	Juan Pizarro	3.00	1.20
❏	336	Gene Alley	5.00	2.00
❏	337	Fred Gladding	3.00	1.20
❏	338	Dal Maxvill	3.00	1.20
❏	339	Del Crandall	5.00	2.00
❏	340	Dean Chance	5.00	2.00
❏	341	Wes Westrum MG	5.00	2.00
❏	342	Bob Humphreys	3.00	1.20
❏	343	Joe Christopher	3.00	1.20
❏	344	Steve Blass	5.00	2.00
❏	345	Bob Allison	5.00	2.00
❏	346	Mike de la Hoz	3.00	1.20
❏	347	Phil Regan	5.00	2.00
❏	348	Orioles Team	8.00	3.20
❏	349	Cap Peterson	3.00	1.20
❏	350	Mel Stottlemyre	8.00	3.20
❏	351	Fred Valentine	3.00	1.20
❏	352	Bob Aspromonte	3.00	1.20
❏	353	Al McBean	3.00	1.20
❏	354	Smoky Burgess	5.00	2.00
❏	355	Wade Blasingame	3.00	1.20
❏	356	Owen Johnson	3.00	1.20
		Ken Sanders		
❏	357	Gerry Arrigo	3.00	1.20
❏	358	Charlie Smith	3.00	1.20
❏	359	Johnny Briggs	3.00	1.20
❏	360	Ron Hunt	3.00	1.20
❏	361	Tom Satriano	3.00	1.20
❏	362	Gates Brown	5.00	2.00
❏	363	Checklist 5	10.00	2.00
❏	364	Nate Oliver	3.00	1.20
❏	365	Roger Maris UER	50.00	20.00
		Wrong birth year listed on card		
❏	366	Wayne Causey	3.00	1.20
❏	367	Mel Nelson	3.00	1.20
❏	368	Charlie Lau	5.00	2.00
❏	369	Jim King	3.00	1.20
❏	370	Chico Cardenas	3.00	1.20
❏	371	Lee Stange	5.00	2.00
❏	372	Harvey Kuenn	8.00	3.20
❏	373	Jack Hiatt	8.00	3.20
		Dick Estelle		
❏	374	Bob Locker	5.00	2.00
❏	375	Donn Clendenon	8.00	3.20
❏	376	Paul Schaal	5.00	2.00
❏	377	Turk Farrell	5.00	2.00
❏	378	Dick Tracewski	5.00	2.00
❏	379	Cardinal Team	10.00	4.00
❏	380	Tony Conigliaro	10.00	4.00
❏	381	Hank Fischer	5.00	2.00
❏	382	Phil Roof	5.00	2.00
❏	383	Jackie Brandt	5.00	2.00
❏	384	Al Downing	8.00	3.20
❏	385	Ken Boyer	10.00	4.00
❏	386	Gil Hodges MG	8.00	3.20
❏	387	Howie Reed	5.00	2.00
❏	388	Don Mincher	5.00	2.00
❏	389	Jim O'Toole	8.00	3.20
❏	390	Brooks Robinson	50.00	20.00
❏	391	Chuck Hinton	5.00	2.00
❏	392	Bill Hands	8.00	3.20
		Randy Hundley RC		
❏	393	George Brunet	5.00	2.00
❏	394	Ron Brand	5.00	2.00
❏	395	Len Gabrielson	5.00	2.00
❏	396	Jerry Stephenson	5.00	2.00
❏	397	Bill White	8.00	3.20
❏	398	Danny Cater	5.00	2.00
❏	399	Ray Washburn	5.00	2.00
❏	400	Zoilo Versalles	8.00	3.20
❏	401	Ken McMullen	5.00	2.00
❏	402	Jim Hickman	5.00	2.00
❏	403	Fred Talbot	5.00	2.00
❏	404	Pittsburgh Pirates	10.00	4.00
		Team Card		
❏	405	Elston Howard	8.00	3.20
❏	406	Joey Jay	5.00	2.00
❏	407	John Kennedy	5.00	2.00
❏	408	Lee Thomas	8.00	3.20
❏	409	Billy Hoeft	5.00	2.00

❑ 410 Al Kaline 40.00 16.00
❑ 411 Gene Mauch MG 5.00 2.00
❑ 412 Sam Bowens 5.00 2.00
❑ 413 Johnny Romano 5.00 2.00
❑ 414 Dan Coombs 5.00 2.00
❑ 415 Max Alvis 5.00 2.00
❑ 416 Phil Ortega 5.00 2.00
❑ 417 Jim McGlothlin 5.00 2.00
Ed Sukla
❑ 418 Phil Gagliano 5.00 2.00
❑ 419 Mike Ryan 5.00 2.00
❑ 420 Juan Marichal 15.00 6.00
❑ 421 Roy McMillan 8.00 3.20
❑ 422 Ed Charles 5.00 2.00
❑ 423 Ernie Broglio 5.00 2.00
❑ 424 Lee May RC 10.00 4.00
Darrell Osteen
❑ 425 Bob Veale 8.00 3.20
❑ 426 White Sox Team 10.00 4.00
❑ 427 John Miller 5.00 2.00
❑ 428 Sandy Alomar 5.00 2.00
❑ 429 Bill Monbouquette 5.00 2.00
❑ 430 Don Drysdale 20.00 8.00
❑ 431 Walt Bond 5.00 2.00
❑ 432 Bob Heffner 5.00 2.00
❑ 433 Alvin Dark MG 8.00 3.20
❑ 434 Willie Kirkland 5.00 2.00
❑ 435 Jim Bunning 15.00 6.00
❑ 436 Julian Javier 8.00 3.20
❑ 437 Al Stanek 5.00 2.00
❑ 438 Willie Smith 5.00 2.00
❑ 439 Pedro Ramos 5.00 2.00
❑ 440 Deron Johnson 8.00 3.20
❑ 441 Tommie Sisk 5.00 2.00
❑ 442 Ed Barnowski 5.00 2.00
Eddie Watt
❑ 443 Bill Wakefield 3.00 1.20
❑ 444 Checklist 6 10.00 2.00
❑ 445 Jim Kaat 10.00 4.00
❑ 446 Mack Jones 5.00 2.00
❑ 447 Dick Ellsworth UER 15.00 6.00
(Photo actually
Ken Hubbs)
❑ 448 Eddie Stanky MG 9.00 3.60
❑ 449 Joe Moeller 9.00 3.60
❑ 450 Tony Oliva 15.00 6.00
❑ 451 Barry Latman 9.00 3.60
❑ 452 Joe Azcue 9.00 3.60
❑ 453 Ron Kline 9.00 3.60
❑ 454 Jerry Buchek 9.00 3.60
❑ 455 Mickey Lolich 15.00 6.00
❑ 456 Darrell Brandon 9.00 3.60
Joe Foy
❑ 457 Joe Gibbon 9.00 3.60
❑ 458 Manny Jiminez 9.00 3.60
❑ 459 Bill McCool 9.00 3.60
❑ 460 Curt Blefary 9.00 3.60
❑ 461 Roy Face 15.00 6.00
❑ 462 Bob Rodgers 9.00 3.60
❑ 463 Philadelphia Phillies 15.00 6.00
Team Card
❑ 464 Larry Bearnarth 9.00 3.60
❑ 465 Don Buford 9.00 3.60
❑ 466 Ken Johnson 9.00 3.60
❑ 467 Vic Roznovsky 9.00 3.60
❑ 468 Johnny Podres 15.00 6.00
❑ 469 Bobby Murcer RC 30.00 12.00
Dooley Womack
❑ 470 Sam McDowell 15.00 6.00
❑ 471 Bob Skinner 9.00 3.60
❑ 472 Terry Fox 9.00 3.60
❑ 473 Rich Rollins 9.00 3.60
❑ 474 Dick Schofield 9.00 3.60
❑ 475 Dick Radatz 9.00 3.60
❑ 476 Bobby Bragan MG 9.00 3.60
❑ 477 Steve Barber 9.00 3.60
❑ 478 Tony Gonzalez 9.00 3.60
❑ 479 Jim Hannan 9.00 3.60
❑ 480 Dick Stuart 9.00 3.60
❑ 481 Bob Lee 9.00 3.60
❑ 482 John Boccabella 9.00 3.60
Dave Dowling
❑ 483 Joe Nuxhall 9.00 3.60
❑ 484 Wes Covington 9.00 3.60
❑ 485 Bob Bailey 9.00 3.60
❑ 486 Tommy John 15.00 6.00
❑ 487 Al Ferrara 9.00 3.60
❑ 488 George Banks 9.00 3.60
❑ 489 Curt Simmons 9.00 3.60
❑ 490 Bobby Richardson 25.00 10.00
❑ 491 Dennis Bennett 9.00 3.60
❑ 492 Athletics Team 15.00 6.00
❑ 493 Johnny Klippstein 9.00 3.60
❑ 494 Gordy Coleman 9.00 3.60
❑ 495 Dick McAuliffe 15.00 6.00
❑ 496 Lindy McDaniel 9.00 3.60
❑ 497 Chris Cannizzaro 9.00 3.60
❑ 498 Luke Walker 9.00 3.60
Woody Fryman
❑ 499 Wally Bunker 9.00 3.60
❑ 500 Hank Aaron 125.00 50.00
❑ 501 John O'Donoghue 9.00 3.60
❑ 502 Lenny Green UER 9.00 3.60
Born: aJn. 6, 1933
❑ 503 Steve Hamilton 15.00 6.00
❑ 504 Grady Hatton MG 9.00 3.60
❑ 505 Jose Cardenal 9.00 3.60
❑ 506 Bo Belinsky 15.00 6.00
❑ 507 Johnny Edwards 9.00 3.60
❑ 508 Steve Hargan RC 15.00 6.00
❑ 509 Jake Wood 9.00 3.60
❑ 510 Hoyt Wilhelm 25.00 10.00
❑ 511 Bob Barton 9.00 3.60
Tito Fuentes RC
❑ 512 Dick Stigman 9.00 3.60
❑ 513 Camilo Carreon 9.00 3.60
❑ 514 Hal Woodeshick 9.00 3.60
❑ 515 Frank Howard 15.00 6.00
❑ 516 Eddie Bressoud 9.00 3.60
❑ 517A Checklist 7 16.00 3.20
529 White Sox Rookies
544 Cardinals Rookies
❑ 517B Checklist 7 16.00 3.20
529 W. Sox Rookies
544 Cards Rookies
❑ 518 Herb Hippauf 9.00 3.60
Arnie Umbach
❑ 519 Bob Friend 15.00 6.00
❑ 520 Jim Wynn 15.00 6.00
❑ 521 John Wyatt 9.00 3.60
❑ 522 Phil Linz 9.00 3.60
❑ 523 Bob Sadowski 9.00 3.60
❑ 524 Ollie Brown 30.00 12.00
Don Mason SP
❑ 525 Gary Bell SP 30.00 12.00
❑ 526 Twins Team SP 100.00 40.00
❑ 527 Julio Navarro 15.00 6.00
❑ 528 Jesse Gonder SP 30.00 12.00
❑ 529 Lee Elia 15.00 6.00
Dennis Higgins
Bill Voss
❑ 530 Robin Roberts 50.00 20.00
❑ 531 Joe Cunningham 15.00 6.00
❑ 532 A.Monteagudo SP 30.00 12.00
❑ 533 Jerry Adair SP 30.00 12.00
❑ 534 Dave Eilers 15.00 6.00
Rob Gardner
❑ 535 Willie Davis SP 40.00 16.00
❑ 536 Dick Egan 15.00 6.00
❑ 537 Herman Franks MG 15.00 6.00
❑ 538 Bob Allen SP 30.00 12.00
❑ 539 Bill Heath 25.00 10.00
Carroll Sembera
❑ 540 Denny McLain SP 60.00 24.00
❑ 541 Gene Oliver SP 30.00 12.00
❑ 542 George Smith 15.00 6.00
❑ 543 Roger Craig SP 30.00 12.00
❑ 544 Joe Hoerner 30.00 12.00
George Kernek
Jimy Williams RC UER SP
(Misspelled Jimmy
on card)
❑ 545 Dick Green SP 30.00 12.00
❑ 546 Dwight Siebler 25.00 10.00
❑ 547 Horace Clarke RC SP 40.00 16.00
❑ 548 Gary Kroll SP 30.00 12.00
❑ 549 Al Closter 15.00 6.00
Casey Cox
❑ 550 Willie McCovey SP 100.00 40.00
❑ 551 Bob Purkey SP 30.00 12.00
❑ 552 Birdie Tebbetts 30.00 12.00
MG SP
❑ 553 Pat Garrett 15.00 6.00
Jackie Warner
❑ 554 Jim Northrup SP 30.00 12.00
❑ 555 Ron Perranoski SP 30.00 12.00
❑ 556 Mel Queen SP 30.00 12.00
❑ 557 Felix Mantilla SP 30.00 12.00
❑ 558 Guido Grilli 20.00 8.00
Pete Magrini
George Scott RC
❑ 559 Roberto Pena SP 30.00 12.00
❑ 560 Joel Horlen 15.00 6.00
❑ 561 Choo Choo Coleman SP 30.00 12.00
❑ 562 Russ Snyder 25.00 10.00
❑ 563 Pete Cimino 15.00 6.00
Cesar Tovar
❑ 564 Bob Chance SP 30.00 12.00
❑ 565 Jimmy Piersall SP 40.00 16.00
❑ 566 Mike Cuellar SP 30.00 12.00
❑ 567 Dick Howser SP 40.00 16.00
❑ 568 Paul Lindblad 15.00 6.00
Ron Stone
❑ 569 Orlando McFarlane SP 30.00 12.00
❑ 570 Art Mahaffey SP 30.00 12.00
❑ 571 Dave Roberts SP 30.00 12.00
❑ 572 Bob Priddy 15.00 6.00
❑ 573 Derrell Griffith 15.00 6.00
❑ 574 Bill Hepler 15.00 6.00
Bill Murphy
❑ 575 Earl Wilson 15.00 6.00
❑ 576 Dave Nicholson SP 30.00 12.00
❑ 577 Jack Lamabe SP 30.00 12.00
❑ 578 Chi Chi Olivo SP 30.00 12.00
❑ 579 Frank Bertaina 20.00 8.00
Gene Brabender
Dave Johnson
❑ 580 Billy Williams SP 60.00 24.00
❑ 581 Tony Martinez 15.00 6.00
❑ 582 Garry Roggenburk 15.00 6.00
❑ 583 Tigers Team SP UER 125.00 50.00
Text on back states Tigers
finished third in 1965 instead
of fourth
❑ 584 Frank Fernandez 15.00 6.00
Fritz Peterson
❑ 585 Tony Taylor 25.00 10.00
❑ 586 Claude Raymond SP 30.00 12.00
❑ 587 Dick Bertell 15.00 6.00
❑ 588 Chuck Dobson 15.00 6.00
Ken Suarez
❑ 589 Lou Klimchock SP 30.00 12.00
❑ 590 Bill Skowron SP 40.00 16.00
❑ 591 Bart Shirley 40.00 16.00
Grant Jackson RC SP
❑ 592 Andre Rodgers 15.00 6.00
❑ 593 Doug Camilli SP 30.00 12.00
❑ 594 Chico Salmon 15.00 6.00
❑ 595 Larry Jackson 15.00 6.00
❑ 596 Nate Colbert RC 30.00 12.00
Greg Sims SP
❑ 597 John Sullivan 15.00 6.00
❑ 598 Gaylord Perry SP 175.00 50.00

1967 Topps

	NM	Ex
COMPLETE SET (609)	5000.00	2000.00
COMMON CARD (1-109)	1.50	.60
COMMON (110-283)	2.00	.80

COMMON (284-370) 2.50 1.00
COMMON (371-457) 4.00 1.60
COMMON (458-533) 6.00 2.40
COMMON (534-609) 16.00 6.50
COMMON DP (534-609) 9.00 3.60
WRAPPER (5-CENT) 25.00 10.00

❑ 1 Frank Robinson 25.00 7.50
Hank Bauer MG
Brooks Robinson DP
❑ 2 Jack Hamilton 1.50 .60
❑ 3 Duke Sims 1.50 .60
❑ 4 Hal Lanier 1.50 .60
❑ 5 Whitey Ford UER 20.00 8.00
(1953 listed as
1933 in stats on back)
❑ 6 Dick Simpson 1.50 .60
❑ 7 Don McMahon 1.50 .60
❑ 8 Chuck Harrison 1.50 .60
❑ 9 Ron Hansen 1.50 .60
❑ 10 Matty Alou 4.00 1.60
❑ 11 Barry Moore 1.50 .60
❑ 12 Jim Campanis 4.00 1.60
Bill Singer
❑ 13 Joe Sparma 1.50 .60
❑ 14 Phil Linz 4.00 1.60
❑ 15 Earl Battey 1.50 .60
❑ 16 Bill Hands 1.50 .60
❑ 17 Jim Gosger 1.50 .60
❑ 18 Gene Oliver 1.50 .60
❑ 19 Jim McGlothlin 1.50 .60
❑ 20 Orlando Cepeda 8.00 3.20
❑ 21 Dave Bristol MG 1.50 .60
❑ 22 Gene Brabender 1.50 .60
❑ 23 Larry Elliot 1.50 .60
❑ 24 Bob Allen 1.50 .60
❑ 25 Elston Howard 4.00 1.60
❑ 26A Bob Priddy NTR 30.00 12.00
❑ 26B Bob Priddy TR 4.00 1.60
❑ 27 Bob Saverine 1.50 .60
❑ 28 Barry Latman 1.50 .60
❑ 29 Tom McCraw 1.50 .60
❑ 30 Al Kaline DP 20.00 8.00
❑ 31 Jim Brewer 1.50 .60
❑ 32 Bob Bailey 4.00 1.60
❑ 33 Sal Bando RC 6.00 2.40
Randy Schwartz
❑ 34 Pete Cimino 1.50 .60
❑ 35 Rico Carty 4.00 1.60
❑ 36 Bob Tillman 1.50 .60
❑ 37 Rick Wise 4.00 1.60
❑ 38 Bob Johnson 1.50 .60
❑ 39 Curt Simmons 4.00 1.60
❑ 40 Rick Reichardt 1.50 .60
❑ 41 Joe Hoerner 1.50 .60
❑ 42 Mets Team 10.00 4.00
❑ 43 Chico Salmon 1.50 .60
❑ 44 Joe Nuxhall 4.00 1.60
❑ 45 Roger Maris 50.00 20.00
❑ 45A Roger Maris 1000.00 400.00
Yankees listed as team
Blank Back
❑ 46 Lindy McDaniel 4.00 1.60
❑ 47 Ken McMullen 1.50 .60
❑ 48 Bill Freehan 4.00 1.60
❑ 49 Roy Face 4.00 1.60
❑ 50 Tony Oliva 6.00 2.40
❑ 51 Dave Adlesh 1.50 .60
Wes Bales
❑ 52 Dennis Higgins 1.50 .60
❑ 53 Clay Dalrymple 1.50 .60
❑ 54 Dick Green 1.50 .60
❑ 55 Don Drysdale 16.00 6.50
❑ 56 Jose Tartabull 4.00 1.60
❑ 57 Pat Jarvis RC 4.00 1.60
❑ 58A Paul Schaal 20.00 8.00
Green Bat
❑ 58B Paul Schaal 1.50 .60
Normal Colored Bat
❑ 59 Ralph Terry 4.00 1.60
❑ 60 Luis Aparicio 8.00 3.20
❑ 61 Gordy Coleman 1.50 .60
❑ 62 Frank Robinson CL 8.00 1.60
❑ 63 Lou Brock 8.00 3.20
Curt Flood
❑ 64 Fred Valentine 1.50 .60
❑ 65 Tom Haller 4.00 1.60
❑ 66 Manny Mota 4.00 1.60
❑ 67 Ken Berry 1.50 .60
❑ 68 Bob Buhl 4.00 1.60
❑ 69 Vic Davalillo 1.50 .60
❑ 70 Ron Santo 6.00 2.40
❑ 71 Camilo Pascual 4.00 1.60
❑ 72 George Korince 1.50 .60
(Photo actually
James Murray Brown)
John (Tom) Matchick
❑ 73 Rusty Staub 6.00 2.40
❑ 74 Wes Stock 1.50 .60
❑ 75 George Scott 4.00 1.60
❑ 76 Jim Barbieri 1.50 .60
❑ 77 Dooley Womack 4.00 1.60
❑ 78 Pat Corrales 1.50 .60
❑ 79 Bubba Morton 1.50 .60
❑ 80 Jim Maloney 4.00 1.60
❑ 81 Eddie Stanky MG 4.00 1.60
❑ 82 Steve Barber 1.50 .60
❑ 83 Ollie Brown 1.50 .60
❑ 84 Tommie Sisk 1.50 .60
❑ 85 Johnny Callison 4.00 1.60
❑ 86A Mike McCormick NTR 30.00 12.00
(Senators on front
and Senators on back)
❑ 86B Mike McCormick TR 4.00 1.60
(Traded line
at end of bio;
Senators on front,
but Giants on back)
❑ 87 George Altman 1.50 .60
❑ 88 Mickey Lolich 4.00 1.60
❑ 89 Felix Millan 4.00 1.60
❑ 90 Jim Nash 1.50 .60
❑ 91 Johnny Lewis 1.50 .60
❑ 92 Ray Washburn 1.50 .60
❑ 93 Stan Bahnsen RC 4.00 1.60
Bobby Murcer
❑ 94 Ron Fairly 4.00 1.60
❑ 95 Sonny Siebert 1.50 .60
❑ 96 Art Shamsky 1.50 .60
❑ 97 Mike Cuellar 4.00 1.60
❑ 98 Rich Rollins 1.50 .60
❑ 99 Lee Stange 1.50 .60
❑ 100 Frank Robinson DP 14.00 5.50
❑ 101 Ken Johnson 1.50 .60
❑ 102 Philadelphia Phillies 4.00 1.60
Team Card
❑ 103 Mickey Mantle CL 20.00 4.00
❑ 104 Minnie Rojas 1.50 .60
❑ 105 Ken Boyer 6.00 2.40
❑ 106 Randy Hundley 4.00 1.60
❑ 107 Joel Horlen 1.50 .60
❑ 108 Alex Johnson 4.00 1.60
❑ 109 Rocky Colavito 6.00 2.40
Leon Wagner
❑ 110 Jack Aker 4.00 1.60
❑ 111 John Kennedy 2.00 .80
❑ 112 Dave Wickersham 2.00 .80
❑ 113 Dave Nicholson 2.00 .80
❑ 114 Jack Baldschun 2.00 .80
❑ 115 Paul Casanova 2.00 .80
❑ 116 Herman Franks MG 2.00 .80
❑ 117 Darrell Brandon 2.00 .80
❑ 118 Bernie Allen 2.00 .80
❑ 119 Wade Blasingame 2.00 .80
❑ 120 Floyd Robinson 2.00 .80
❑ 121 Eddie Bressoud 2.00 .80
❑ 122 George Brunet 2.00 .80
❑ 123 Jim Price 4.00 1.60
Luke Walker
❑ 124 Jim Stewart 2.00 .80
❑ 125 Moe Drabowsky 4.00 1.60
❑ 126 Tony Taylor 2.00 .80
❑ 127 John O'Donoghue 2.00 .80
❑ 128 Ed Spiezio 2.00 .80
❑ 129 Phil Roof 2.00 .80
❑ 130 Phil Regan 4.00 1.60
❑ 131 Yankees Team 10.00 4.00
❑ 132 Ozzie Virgil 2.00 .80
❑ 133 Ron Kline 2.00 .80
❑ 134 Gates Brown 6.00 2.40
❑ 135 Deron Johnson 4.00 1.60
❑ 136 Carroll Sembera 2.00 .80
❑ 137 Ron Clark 2.00 .80
Jim Ollum
❑ 138 Dick Kelley 2.00 .80
❑ 139 Dalton Jones 4.00 1.60
❑ 140 Willie Stargell 20.00 8.00
❑ 141 John Miller 2.00 .80
❑ 142 Jackie Brandt 2.00 .80
❑ 143 Pete Ward 2.00 .80
Don Buford
❑ 144 Bill Hepler 2.00 .80
❑ 145 Larry Brown 2.00 .80
❑ 146 Steve Carlton 50.00 20.00
❑ 147 Tom Egan 2.00 .80
❑ 148 Adolfo Phillips 2.00 .80
❑ 149 Joe Moeller 2.00 .80
❑ 150 Mickey Mantle 250.00 100.00
❑ 151 Moe Drabowsky WS 5.00 2.00
❑ 152 Jim Palmer WS 8.00 3.20
❑ 153 Paul Blair WS 5.00 2.00
❑ 154 Brooks Robinson WS 5.00 2.00
Dave McNally
❑ 155 WS Summary 5.00 2.00
Winners celebrate
❑ 156 Ron Herbel 2.00 .80
❑ 157 Danny Cater 2.00 .80
❑ 158 Jimmie Coker 2.00 .80
❑ 159 Bruce Howard 2.00 .80
❑ 160 Willie Davis 4.00 1.60
❑ 161 Dick Williams MG 4.00 1.60
❑ 162 Billy O'Dell 2.00 .80
❑ 163 Vic Roznovsky 2.00 .80
❑ 164 Dwight Siebler UER 2.00 .80
(Last line of stats
shows 1960 Minnesota)
❑ 165 Cleon Jones 4.00 1.60
❑ 166 Eddie Mathews 15.00 6.00
❑ 167 Joe Coleman 2.00 .80
Tim Cullen
❑ 168 Ray Culp 2.00 .80
❑ 169 Horace Clarke 4.00 1.60
❑ 170 Dick McAuliffe 4.00 1.60
❑ 171 Cal Koonce 2.00 .80
❑ 172 Bill Heath 2.00 .80
❑ 173 St. Louis Cardinals 4.00 1.60
Team Card
❑ 174 Dick Radatz 4.00 1.60
❑ 175 Bobby Knoop 2.00 .80
❑ 176 Sammy Ellis 2.00 .80
❑ 177 Tito Fuentes 1.50 .60
❑ 178 John Buzhardt 2.00 .80
❑ 179 Charles Vaughan 4.00 1.60
Cecil Upshaw
❑ 180 Curt Blefary 2.00 .80
❑ 181 Terry Fox 2.00 .80
❑ 182 Ed Charles 2.00 .80
❑ 183 Jim Pagliaroni 2.00 .80
❑ 184 George Thomas 2.00 .80
❑ 185 Ken Holtzman RC 4.00 1.60
❑ 186 Ed Kranepool 4.00 1.60
Ron Swoboda
❑ 187 Pedro Ramos 2.00 .80
❑ 188 Ken Harrelson 4.00 1.60
❑ 189 Chuck Hinton 2.00 .80
❑ 190 Turk Farrell 2.00 .80
❑ 191A Willie Mays CL 10.00 2.00
214 Tom Kelley
❑ 191B Willie Mays CL 12.00 2.40
214 Dick Kelley
❑ 192 Fred Gladding 2.00 .80
❑ 193 Jose Cardenal 4.00 1.60
❑ 194 Bob Allison 4.00 1.60
❑ 195 Al Jackson 2.00 .80
❑ 196 Johnny Romano 2.00 .80
❑ 197 Ron Perranoski 4.00 1.60
❑ 198 Chuck Hiller 2.00 .80
❑ 199 Billy Hitchcock MG 2.00 .80
❑ 200 Willie Mays UER 80.00 32.00
('63 Sna Francisco
on card back stats)
❑ 201 Hal Reniff 4.00 1.60
❑ 202 Johnny Edwards 2.00 .80
❑ 203 Al McBean 2.00 .80
❑ 204 Mike Epstein 6.00 2.40
Tom Phoebus
❑ 205 Dick Groat 4.00 1.60
❑ 206 Dennis Bennett 2.00 .80

❑ 207 John Orsino	2.00	.80
❑ 208 Jack Lamabe	2.00	.80
❑ 209 Joe Nossek	2.00	.80
❑ 210 Bob Gibson	20.00	8.00
❑ 211 Twins Team	4.00	1.60
❑ 212 Chris Zachary	2.00	.80
❑ 213 Jay Johnstone RC	4.00	1.60
❑ 214 Dick Kelley	2.00	.80
❑ 215 Ernie Banks	20.00	8.00
❑ 216 Norm Cash	8.00	3.20
Al Kaline		
❑ 217 Rob Gardner	2.00	.80
❑ 218 Wes Parker	4.00	1.60
❑ 219 Clay Carroll	4.00	1.60
❑ 220 Jim Ray Hart	4.00	1.60
❑ 221 Woody Fryman	4.00	1.60
❑ 222 Darrell Osteen	4.00	1.60
Lee May		
❑ 223 Mike Ryan	4.00	1.60
❑ 224 Walt Bond	2.00	.80
❑ 225 Mel Stottlemyre	6.00	2.40
❑ 226 Julian Javier	4.00	1.60
❑ 227 Paul Lindblad	2.00	.80
❑ 228 Gil Hodges MG	6.00	2.40
❑ 229 Larry Jackson	2.00	.80
❑ 230 Boog Powell	6.00	2.40
❑ 231 John Bateman	2.00	.80
❑ 232 Don Buford	2.00	.80
❑ 233 Gary Peters	4.00	1.60
Joel Horlen		
Steve Hargan LL		
❑ 234 Sandy Koufax	15.00	6.00
Mike Cuellar		
Juan Marichal LL		
❑ 235 Jim Kaat	6.00	2.40
Denny McLain		
Earl Wilson LL		
❑ 236 Sandy Koufax	25.00	10.00
Juan Marichal		
Bob Gibson		
Gaylord Perry LL		
❑ 237 Sam McDowell	6.00	2.40
Jim Kaat		
Earl Wilson LL		
❑ 238 Sandy Koufax	12.00	4.80
Jim Bunning		
Bob Veale LL		
❑ 239 Frank Robinson	9.00	3.60
Tony Oliva		
Al Kaline LL		
❑ 240 Matty Alou	6.00	2.40
Felipe Alou		
Rico Carty LL		
❑ 241 Frank Robinson	9.00	3.60
Harmon Killebrew		
Boog Powell LL		
❑ 242 Hank Aaron	25.00	10.00
Bob Clemente		
Richie Allen LL		
❑ 243 Frank Robinson	9.00	3.60
Harmon Killebrew		
Boog Powell LL		
❑ 244 Hank Aaron	20.00	8.00
Richie Allen		
Willie Mays LL		
❑ 245 Curt Flood	6.00	2.40
❑ 246 Jim Perry	4.00	1.60
❑ 247 Jerry Lumpe	2.00	.80
❑ 248 Gene Mauch MG	4.00	1.60
❑ 249 Nick Willhite	2.00	.80
❑ 250 Hank Aaron UER	80.00	32.00
(Second 1961 in stats		
should be 1962)		
❑ 251 Woody Held	2.00	.80
❑ 252 Bob Bolin	2.00	.80
❑ 253 Bill Davis	2.00	.80
Gus Gil		
❑ 254 Milt Pappas	4.00	1.60
(No facsimile auto-		
graph on card front)		
❑ 255 Frank Howard	4.00	1.60
❑ 256 Bob Hendley	2.00	.80
❑ 257 Charlie Smith	2.00	.80
❑ 258 Lee Maye	2.00	.80
❑ 259 Don Dennis	2.00	.80
❑ 260 Jim Lefebvre	4.00	1.60
❑ 261 John Wyatt	2.00	.80
❑ 262 Athletics Team	4.00	1.60
❑ 263 Hank Aguirre	2.00	.80
❑ 264 Ron Swoboda	4.00	1.60
❑ 265 Lou Burdette	4.00	1.60
❑ 266 Willie Stargell	4.00	1.60
Donn Clendenon		
❑ 267 Don Schwall	2.00	.80
❑ 268 Johnny Briggs	2.00	.80
❑ 269 Don Nottebart	2.00	.80
❑ 270 Zoilo Versalles	2.00	.80
❑ 271 Eddie Watt	2.00	.80
❑ 272 Bill Connors RC	4.00	1.60
Dave Dowling		
❑ 273 Dick Lines	2.00	.80
❑ 274 Bob Aspromonte	2.00	.80
❑ 275 Fred Whitfield	2.00	.80
❑ 276 Bruce Brubaker	2.00	.80
❑ 277 Steve Whitaker	6.00	2.40
❑ 278 Jim Kaat CL	8.00	1.60
❑ 279 Frank Linzy	2.00	.80
❑ 280 Tony Conigliaro	8.00	3.20
❑ 281 Bob Rodgers	2.00	.80
❑ 282 John Odom	2.00	.80
❑ 283 Gene Alley	4.00	1.60
❑ 284 Johnny Podres	4.00	1.60
❑ 285 Lou Brock	20.00	8.00
❑ 286 Wayne Causey	2.50	1.00
❑ 287 Greg Goossen	2.50	1.00
Bart Shirley		
❑ 288 Denny Lemaster	2.50	1.00
❑ 289 Tom Tresh	5.00	2.00
❑ 290 Bill White	5.00	2.00
❑ 291 Jim Hannan	2.50	1.00
❑ 292 Don Pavletich	2.50	1.00
❑ 293 Ed Kirkpatrick	2.50	1.00
❑ 294 Walter Alston MG	8.00	3.20
❑ 295 Sam McDowell	5.00	2.00
❑ 296 Glenn Beckert	5.00	2.00
❑ 297 Dave Morehead	5.00	2.00
❑ 298 Ron Davis	2.50	1.00
❑ 299 Norm Siebern	2.50	1.00
❑ 300 Jim Kaat	5.00	2.00
❑ 301 Jesse Gonder	2.50	1.00
❑ 302 Orioles Team	8.00	3.20
❑ 303 Gil Blanco	2.50	1.00
❑ 304 Phil Gagliano	2.50	1.00
❑ 305 Earl Wilson	5.00	2.00
❑ 306 Bud Harrelson RC	5.00	2.00
❑ 307 Jim Beauchamp	2.50	1.00
❑ 308 Al Downing	5.00	2.00
❑ 309 Johnny Callison	5.00	2.00
Richie Allen		
❑ 310 Gary Peters	2.50	1.00
❑ 311 Ed Brinkman	2.50	1.00
❑ 312 Don Mincher	2.50	1.00
❑ 313 Bob Lee	2.50	1.00
❑ 314 Mike Andrews	8.00	3.20
Reggie Smith RC		
❑ 315 Billy Williams	15.00	6.00
❑ 316 Jack Kralick	2.50	1.00
❑ 317 Cesar Tovar	2.50	1.00
❑ 318 Dave Giusti	2.50	1.00
❑ 319 Paul Blair	5.00	2.00
❑ 320 Gaylord Perry	15.00	6.00
❑ 321 Mayo Smith MG	2.50	1.00
❑ 322 Jose Pagan	2.50	1.00
❑ 323 Mike Hershberger	2.50	1.00
❑ 324 Hal Woodeshick	2.50	1.00
❑ 325 Chico Cardenas	5.00	2.00
❑ 326 Bob Uecker	10.00	4.00
❑ 327 California Angels	8.00	3.20
Team Card		
❑ 328 Clete Boyer UER	5.00	2.00
(Stats only go up		
through 1965)		
❑ 329 Charlie Lau	5.00	2.00
❑ 330 Claude Osteen	5.00	2.00
❑ 331 Joe Foy	5.00	2.00
❑ 332 Jesus Alou	2.50	1.00
❑ 333 Fergie Jenkins	20.00	8.00
❑ 334 Bob Allison	10.00	4.00
Harmon Killebrew		
❑ 335 Bob Veale	5.00	2.00
❑ 336 Joe Azcue	2.50	1.00
❑ 337 Joe Morgan	15.00	6.00
❑ 338 Bob Locker	2.50	1.00
❑ 339 Chico Ruiz	2.50	1.00
❑ 340 Joe Pepitone	8.00	3.20
❑ 341 Dick Dietz	2.50	1.00
Bill Sorrell		
❑ 342 Hank Fischer	2.50	1.00
❑ 343 Tom Satriano	2.50	1.00
❑ 344 Ossie Chavarria	2.50	1.00
❑ 345 Stu Miller	5.00	2.00
❑ 346 Jim Hickman	2.50	1.00
❑ 347 Grady Hatton MG	2.50	1.00
❑ 348 Tug McGraw	5.00	2.00
❑ 349 Bob Chance	2.50	1.00
❑ 350 Joe Torre	8.00	3.20
❑ 351 Vern Law	5.00	2.00
❑ 352 Ray Oyler	2.50	1.00
❑ 353 Bill McCool	2.50	1.00
❑ 354 Cubs Team	8.00	3.20
❑ 355 Carl Yastrzemski	50.00	20.00
❑ 356 Larry Jaster	2.50	1.00
❑ 357 Bill Skowron	5.00	2.00
❑ 358 Ruben Amaro	2.50	1.00
❑ 359 Dick Ellsworth	2.50	1.00
❑ 360 Leon Wagner	2.50	1.00
❑ 361 Roberto Clemente CL	15.00	3.00
❑ 362 Darold Knowles	2.50	1.00
❑ 363 Davey Johnson	5.00	2.00
❑ 364 Claude Raymond	2.50	1.00
❑ 365 John Roseboro	5.00	2.00
❑ 366 Andy Kosco	2.50	1.00
❑ 367 Bill Kelso	2.50	1.00
Don Wallace		
❑ 368 Jack Hiatt	2.50	1.00
❑ 369 Jim Hunter	15.00	6.00
❑ 370 Tommy Davis	5.00	2.00
❑ 371 Jim Lonborg	8.00	3.20
❑ 372 Mike de la Hoz	4.00	1.60
❑ 373 Duane Josephson	4.00	1.60
Fred Klages DP		
❑ 374A Mel Queen ERR DP	20.00	8.00
(Incomplete stat		
line on back)		
❑ 374B Mel Queen COR DP	4.00	1.60
(Complete stat		
line on back)		
❑ 375 Jake Gibbs	8.00	3.20
❑ 376 Don Lock DP	4.00	1.60
❑ 377 Luis Tiant	8.00	3.20
❑ 378 Detroit Tigers	8.00	3.20
Team Card UER		
(Willie Horton with		
262 RBI's in 1966)		
❑ 379 Jerry May DP	4.00	1.60
❑ 380 Dean Chance DP	4.00	1.60
❑ 381 Dick Schofield DP	4.00	1.60
❑ 382 Dave McNally	8.00	3.20
❑ 383 Ken Henderson DP	4.00	1.60
❑ 384 Jim Cosman	4.00	1.60
Dick Hughes		
❑ 385 Jim Fregosi	8.00	3.20
(Batting wrong)		
❑ 386 Dick Selma DP	4.00	1.60
❑ 387 Cap Peterson DP	4.00	1.60
❑ 388 Arnold Earley DP	4.00	1.60
❑ 389 Alvin Dark MG DP	8.00	3.20
❑ 390 Jim Wynn DP	8.00	3.20
❑ 391 Wilbur Wood DP	8.00	3.20
❑ 392 Tommy Harper DP	8.00	3.20
❑ 393 Jim Bouton DP	8.00	3.20
❑ 394 Jake Wood DP	4.00	1.60
❑ 395 Chris Short	8.00	3.20
❑ 396 Denis Menke	4.00	1.60
Tony Cloninger		
❑ 397 Willie Smith DP	4.00	1.60
❑ 398 Jeff Torborg	8.00	3.20
❑ 399 Al Worthington DP	4.00	1.60
❑ 400 Bob Clemente DP	100.00	40.00
❑ 401 Jim Coates	4.00	1.60
❑ 402A Phillies Rookies DP	20.00	8.00
Grant Jackson		
Billy Wilson		
Incomplete stat line		
❑ 402B Phillies Rookies DP	8.00	3.20
Grant Jackson		
Billy Wilson		
❑ 403 Dick Nen	4.00	1.60

❑ 404 Nelson Briles	8.00	3.20
❑ 405 Russ Snyder	4.00	1.60
❑ 406 Lee Elia DP	4.00	1.60
❑ 407 Reds Team	8.00	3.20
❑ 408 Jim Northrup DP	8.00	3.20
❑ 409 Ray Sadecki	4.00	1.60
❑ 410 Lou Johnson DP	4.00	1.60
❑ 411 Dick Howser DP	4.00	1.60
❑ 412 Norm Miller	8.00	3.20
Doug Rader RC		
❑ 413 Jerry Grote	4.00	1.60
❑ 414 Casey Cox	4.00	1.60
❑ 415 Sonny Jackson	4.00	1.60
❑ 416 Roger Repoz	4.00	1.60
❑ 417A Bob Bruce ERR DP	30.00	12.00
(RBAVES on back)		
❑ 417B Bob Bruce COR DP	4.00	1.60
❑ 418 Sam Mele MG	4.00	1.60
❑ 419 Don Kessinger DP	8.00	3.20
❑ 420 Denny McLain	12.00	4.80
❑ 421 Dal Maxvill DP	4.00	1.60
❑ 422 Hoyt Wilhelm	15.00	6.00
❑ 423 Willie Mays	25.00	10.00
Willie McCovey DP		
❑ 424 Pedro Gonzalez	4.00	1.60
❑ 425 Pete Mikkelsen	4.00	1.60
❑ 426 Lou Clinton	4.00	1.60
❑ 427A R.Gomez ERR DP	20.00	8.00
Incomplete stat line on back		
❑ 427B R.Gomez COR DP	4.00	1.60
Complete stat line on back		
❑ 428 Tom Hutton RC	8.00	3.20
Gene Michael DP		
❑ 429 Garry Roggenburk DP	4.00	1.60
❑ 430 Pete Rose	80.00	32.00
❑ 431 Ted Uhlaender	4.00	1.60
❑ 432 Jimmie Hall DP	4.00	1.60
❑ 433 Al Luplow DP	4.00	1.60
❑ 434 Eddie Fisher DP	4.00	1.60
❑ 435 Mack Jones DP	4.00	1.60
❑ 436 Pete Ward	4.00	1.60
❑ 437 Senators Team	8.00	3.20
❑ 438 Chuck Dobson	4.00	1.60
❑ 439 Byron Browne	4.00	1.60
❑ 440 Steve Hargan	4.00	1.60
❑ 441 Jim Davenport	4.00	1.60
❑ 442 Bill Robinson RC	8.00	3.20
Joe Verbanic DP		
❑ 443 Tito Francona DP	4.00	1.60
❑ 444 George Smith	4.00	1.60
❑ 445 Don Sutton	25.00	10.00
❑ 446 Russ Nixon DP	4.00	1.60
❑ 447A Bo Belinsky ERR DP	5.00	2.00
(Incomplete stat line on back)		
❑ 447B Bo Belinsky COR DP	8.00	3.20
(Complete stat line on back)		
❑ 448 Harry Walker DP MG	4.00	1.60
❑ 449 Orlando Pena	4.00	1.60
❑ 450 Richie Allen	8.00	3.20
❑ 451 Fred Newman DP	4.00	1.60
❑ 452 Ed Kranepool	8.00	3.20
❑ 453 A.Monteagudo DP	4.00	1.60
❑ 454A Juan Marichal CL	12.00	2.40
Missing left ear		
❑ 454B Juan Marichal CL	12.00	2.40
left ear showing		
❑ 455 Tommie Agee	8.00	3.20
❑ 456 Phil Niekro	15.00	6.00
❑ 457 Andy Etchebarren DP	8.00	3.20
❑ 458 Lee Thomas	6.00	2.40
❑ 459 Dick Bosman RC	6.00	2.40
Pete Craig		
❑ 460 Harmon Killebrew	60.00	24.00
❑ 461 Bob Miller	12.00	4.80
❑ 462 Bob Barton	6.00	2.40
❑ 463 Sam McDowell	12.00	4.80
Sonny Siebert		
❑ 464 Dan Coombs	6.00	2.40
❑ 465 Willie Horton	12.00	4.80
❑ 466 Bobby Wine	6.00	2.40
❑ 467 Jim O'Toole	6.00	2.40
❑ 468 Ralph Houk MG	6.00	2.40
❑ 469 Len Gabrielson	6.00	2.40
❑ 470 Bob Shaw	6.00	2.40
❑ 471 Rene Lachemann	6.00	2.40
❑ 472 John Gelnar	6.00	2.40
George Spriggs		
❑ 473 Jose Santiago	6.00	2.40
❑ 474 Bob Tolan	6.00	2.40
❑ 475 Jim Palmer	80.00	32.00
❑ 476 Tony Perez SP	60.00	24.00
❑ 477 Braves Team	15.00	6.00
❑ 478 Bob Humphreys	6.00	2.40
❑ 479 Gary Bell	6.00	2.40
❑ 480 Willie McCovey	40.00	16.00
❑ 481 Leo Durocher MG	20.00	8.00
❑ 482 Bill Monbouquette	6.00	2.40
❑ 483 Jim Landis	6.00	2.40
❑ 484 Jerry Adair	6.00	2.40
❑ 485 Tim McCarver	25.00	10.00
❑ 486 Rich Reese	6.00	2.40
Bill Whitby		
❑ 487 Tommie Reynolds	6.00	2.40
❑ 488 Gerry Arrigo	6.00	2.40
❑ 489 Doug Clemens	6.00	2.40
❑ 490 Tony Cloninger	6.00	2.40
❑ 491 Sam Bowens	6.00	2.40
❑ 492 Pittsburgh Pirates	15.00	6.00
Team Card		
❑ 493 Phil Ortega	6.00	2.40
❑ 494 Bill Rigney MG	6.00	2.40
❑ 495 Fritz Peterson	6.00	2.40
❑ 496 Orlando McFarlane	6.00	2.40
❑ 497 Ron Campbell	6.00	2.40
❑ 498 Larry Dierker	12.00	4.80
❑ 499 George Culver	6.00	2.40
Jose Vidal		
❑ 500 Juan Marichal	25.00	10.00
❑ 501 Jerry Zimmerman	6.00	2.40
❑ 502 Derrell Griffith	6.00	2.40
❑ 503 Los Angeles Dodgers	20.00	8.00
Team Card		
❑ 504 Orlando Martinez	6.00	2.40
❑ 505 Tommy Helms	12.00	4.80
❑ 506 Smoky Burgess	6.00	2.40
❑ 507 Ed Barnowski	6.00	2.40
Larry Haney RC		
❑ 508 Dick Hall	6.00	2.40
❑ 509 Jim King	6.00	2.40
❑ 510 Bill Mazeroski	25.00	10.00
❑ 511 Don Wert	6.00	2.40
❑ 512 Red Schoendienst MG	25.00	10.00
❑ 513 Marcelino Lopez	6.00	2.40
❑ 514 John Werhas	6.00	2.40
❑ 515 Bert Campaneris	12.00	4.80
❑ 516 Giants Team	15.00	6.00
❑ 517 Fred Talbot	12.00	4.80
❑ 518 Denis Menke	6.00	2.40
❑ 519 Ted Davidson	6.00	2.40
❑ 520 Max Alvis	6.00	2.40
❑ 521 Boog Powell	12.00	4.80
Curt Blefary		
❑ 522 John Stephenson	6.00	2.40
❑ 523 Jim Merritt	6.00	2.40
❑ 524 Felix Mantilla	6.00	2.40
❑ 525 Ron Hunt	6.00	2.40
❑ 526 Pat Dobson RC	6.00	2.40
George Korince (See 67T-72)		
❑ 527 Dennis Ribant	6.00	2.40
❑ 528 Rico Petrocelli	20.00	8.00
❑ 529 Gary Wagner	6.00	2.40
❑ 530 Felipe Alou	12.00	4.80
❑ 531 Brooks Robinson CL	14.00	2.80
❑ 532 Jim Hicks	6.00	2.40
❑ 533 Jack Fisher	6.00	2.40
❑ 534 Hank Bauer MG DP	9.00	3.60
❑ 535 Donn Clendenon	25.00	10.00
❑ 536 Joe Niekro RC	50.00	20.00
Paul Popovich		
❑ 537 Chuck Estrada DP	9.00	3.60
❑ 538 J.C. Martin	16.00	6.50
❑ 539 Dick Egan DP	9.00	3.60
❑ 540 Norm Cash	50.00	20.00
❑ 541 Joe Gibbon	16.00	6.50
❑ 542 Rick Monday RC	15.00	6.00
Tony Pierce DP		
❑ 543 Dan Schneider	16.00	6.50
❑ 544 Cleveland Indians	30.00	12.00
Team Card		
❑ 545 Jim Grant	25.00	10.00
❑ 546 Woody Woodward	25.00	10.00
❑ 547 Russ Gibson	9.00	3.60
Bill Rohr DP		
❑ 548 Tony Gonzalez DP	9.00	3.60
❑ 549 Jack Sanford	16.00	6.50
❑ 550 Vada Pinson DP	10.00	4.00
❑ 551 Doug Camilli DP	9.00	3.60
❑ 552 Ted Savage	25.00	10.00
❑ 553 Mike Hegan RC	40.00	16.00
Thad Tillotson		
❑ 554 Andre Rodgers DP	9.00	3.60
❑ 555 Don Cardwell	25.00	10.00
❑ 556 Al Weis DP	9.00	3.60
❑ 557 Al Ferrara	25.00	10.00
❑ 558 Mark Belanger RC	50.00	20.00
Bill Dillman		
❑ 559 Dick Tracewski DP	9.00	3.60
❑ 560 Jim Bunning	60.00	24.00
❑ 561 Sandy Alomar	40.00	16.00
❑ 562 Steve Blass DP	9.00	3.60
❑ 563 Joe Adcock	40.00	16.00
❑ 564 Alonzo Harris	9.00	3.60
Aaron Pointer		
❑ 565 Lew Krausse	25.00	10.00
❑ 566 Gary Geiger DP	9.00	3.60
❑ 567 Steve Hamilton	40.00	16.00
❑ 568 John Sullivan	40.00	16.00
❑ 569 Rod Carew RC	200.00	80.00
Hank Allen DP		
❑ 570 Maury Wills	90.00	36.00
❑ 571 Larry Sherry	25.00	10.00
❑ 572 Don Demeter	25.00	10.00
❑ 573 Chicago White Sox	30.00	12.00
Team Card UER (Indians team stats on back)		
❑ 574 Jerry Buchek	25.00	10.00
❑ 575 Dave Boswell	16.00	6.50
❑ 576 Ramon Hernandez	40.00	16.00
Norm Gigon RC		
❑ 577 Bill Short	16.00	6.50
❑ 578 John Boccabella	16.00	6.50
❑ 579 Bill Henry	16.00	6.50
❑ 580 Rocky Colavito	125.00	50.00
❑ 581 Bill Denehy	500.00	200.00
Tom Seaver RC		
❑ 582 Jim Owens DP	9.00	3.60
❑ 583 Ray Barker	40.00	16.00
❑ 584 Jimmy Piersall	40.00	16.00
❑ 585 Wally Bunker	25.00	10.00
❑ 586 Manny Jimenez	16.00	6.50
❑ 587 Don Shaw	40.00	16.00
Gary Sutherland RC		
❑ 588 Johnny Klippstein DP	9.00	3.60
❑ 589 Dave Ricketts DP	9.00	3.60
❑ 590 Pete Richert	16.00	6.50
❑ 591 Ty Cline	25.00	10.00
❑ 592 Jim Shellenback	25.00	10.00
Ron Willis RC		
❑ 593 Wes Westrum MG	50.00	20.00
❑ 594 Dan Osinski	40.00	16.00
❑ 595 Cookie Rojas	25.00	10.00
❑ 596 Galen Cisco DP	9.00	3.60
❑ 597 Ted Abernathy	16.00	6.50
❑ 598 Walt Williams	25.00	10.00
Ed Stroud		
❑ 599 Bob Duliba DP	9.00	3.60
❑ 600 Brooks Robinson	250.00	100.00
❑ 601 Bill Bryan DP	9.00	3.60
❑ 602 Juan Pizarro	40.00	16.00
❑ 603 Tim Talton	25.00	10.00
Ramon Webster		
❑ 604 Red Sox Team	125.00	50.00
❑ 605 Mike Shannon	50.00	20.00
❑ 606 Ron Taylor	25.00	10.00
❑ 607 Mickey Stanley	50.00	20.00
❑ 608 Rich Nye	9.00	3.60
John Upham DP		
❑ 609 Tommy John	80.00	27.00

1968 Topps

	NM	Ex
COMPLETE SET (598)	3000.00	1200.00
COMMON CARD (1-457)	1.75	.70
COMMON (458-598)	3.50	1.40
WRAPPER (5-CENT)	25.00	10.00
❑ 1 Roberto Clemente	30.00	12.00
Tony Gonzalez		
Matty Alou LL		
❑ 2 Carl Yastrzemski	14.00	5.50
Frank Robinson		
Al Kaline LL		
❑ 3 Orlando Cepeda	20.00	8.00
Roberto Clemente		
Hank Aaron LL		
❑ 4 Carl Yastrzemski	14.00	5.50
Harmon Killebrew		
Frank Robinson LL		
❑ 5 Hank Aaron	8.00	3.20
Jim Wynn		
Ron Santo		
Willie McCovey LL		
❑ 6 Carl Yastrzemski	8.00	3.20
Harmon Killebrew		
Frank Howard LL		
❑ 7 Phil Niekro	4.00	1.60
Jim Bunning		
Chris Short LL		
❑ 8 Joel Horlen	4.00	1.60
Gary Peters		
Sonny Siebert LL		
❑ 9 Mike McCormick	4.00	1.60
Ferguson Jenkins		
Jim Bunning		
Claude Osteen LL		
❑ 10A Jim Lonborg ERR	4.00	1.60
(Misspelled Lonberg on card back)		
Earl Wilson		
Dean Chance LL		
❑ 10B Jim Lonborg COR	4.00	1.60
Earl Wilson		
Dean Chance LL		
❑ 11 Jim Bunning	6.00	2.40
Ferguson Jenkins		
Gaylord Perry LL		
❑ 12 Jim Lonborg UER	4.00	1.60
(Misspelled Longberg on card back)		
Sam McDowell		
Dean Chance LL		
❑ 13 Chuck Hartenstein	1.75	.70
❑ 14 Jerry McNertney	1.75	.70
❑ 15 Ron Hunt	1.75	.70
❑ 16 Lou Piniella	6.00	2.40
Richie Scheinblum		
❑ 17 Dick Hall	1.75	.70
❑ 18 Mike Hershberger	1.75	.70
❑ 19 Juan Pizarro	1.75	.70
❑ 20 Brooks Robinson	25.00	10.00
❑ 21 Ron Davis	1.75	.70
❑ 22 Pat Dobson	4.00	1.60
❑ 23 Chico Cardenas	4.00	1.60
❑ 24 Bobby Locke	1.75	.70
❑ 25 Julian Javier	4.00	1.60
❑ 26 Darrell Brandon	1.75	.70
❑ 27 Gil Hodges MG	8.00	3.20
❑ 28 Ted Uhlaender	1.75	.70
❑ 29 Joe Verbanic	1.75	.70
❑ 30 Joe Torre	6.00	2.40
❑ 31 Ed Stroud	1.75	.70
❑ 32 Joe Gibbon	1.75	.70
❑ 33 Pete Ward	1.75	.70
❑ 34 Al Ferrara	1.75	.70
❑ 35 Steve Hargan	1.75	.70
❑ 36 Bob Moose	4.00	1.60
Bob Robertson		
❑ 37 Billy Williams	8.00	3.20
❑ 38 Tony Pierce	1.75	.70
❑ 39 Cookie Rojas	1.75	.70
❑ 40 Denny McLain	8.00	3.20
❑ 41 Julio Gotay	1.75	.70
❑ 42 Larry Haney	1.75	.70
❑ 43 Gary Bell	1.75	.70
❑ 44 Frank Kostro	1.75	.70
❑ 45 Tom Seaver	50.00	20.00
❑ 46 Dave Ricketts	1.75	.70
❑ 47 Ralph Houk MG	4.00	1.60
❑ 48 Ted Davidson	1.75	.70
❑ 49A Eddie Brinkman	1.75	.70
(White team name)		
❑ 49B Eddie Brinkman	50.00	20.00
(Yellow team name)		
❑ 50 Willie Mays	60.00	24.00
❑ 51 Bob Locker	1.75	.70
❑ 52 Hawk Taylor	1.75	.70
❑ 53 Gene Alley	4.00	1.60
❑ 54 Stan Williams	1.75	.70
❑ 55 Felipe Alou	4.00	1.60
❑ 56 Dave Leonhard	1.75	.70
Dave May RC		
❑ 57 Dan Schneider	1.75	.70
❑ 58 Eddie Mathews	15.00	6.00
❑ 59 Don Lock	1.75	.70
❑ 60 Ken Holtzman	4.00	1.60
❑ 61 Reggie Smith	4.00	1.60
❑ 62 Chuck Dobson	1.75	.70
❑ 63 Dick Kenworthy	1.75	.70
❑ 64 Jim Merritt	1.75	.70
❑ 65 John Roseboro	4.00	1.60
❑ 66A Casey Cox	1.75	.70
(White team name)		
❑ 66B Casey Cox	100.00	40.00
(Yellow team name)		
❑ 67 Jim Kaat CL	6.00	1.20
❑ 68 Ron Willis	1.75	.70
❑ 69 Tom Tresh	4.00	1.60
❑ 70 Bob Veale	4.00	1.60
❑ 71 Vern Fuller	1.75	.70
❑ 72 Tommy John	6.00	2.40
❑ 73 Jim Ray Hart	4.00	1.60
❑ 74 Milt Pappas	4.00	1.60
❑ 75 Don Mincher	1.75	.70
❑ 76 Jim Britton	4.00	1.60
Ron Reed		
❑ 77 Don Wilson	4.00	1.60
❑ 78 Jim Northrup	6.00	2.40
❑ 79 Ted Kubiak	1.75	.70
❑ 80 Rod Carew	50.00	20.00
❑ 81 Larry Jackson	1.75	.70
❑ 82 Sam Bowens	1.75	.70
❑ 83 John Stephenson	1.75	.70
❑ 84 Bob Tolan	1.75	.70
❑ 85 Gaylord Perry	8.00	3.20
❑ 86 Willie Stargell	8.00	3.20
❑ 87 Dick Williams MG	4.00	1.60
❑ 88 Phil Regan	4.00	1.60
❑ 89 Jake Gibbs	4.00	1.60
❑ 90 Vada Pinson	4.00	1.60
❑ 91 Jim Ollom	1.75	.70
❑ 92 Ed Kranepool	4.00	1.60
❑ 93 Tony Cloninger	1.75	.70
❑ 94 Lee Maye	1.75	.70
❑ 95 Bob Aspromonte	1.75	.70
❑ 96 Frank Coggins	1.75	.70
Dick Nold		
❑ 97 Tom Phoebus	1.75	.70
❑ 98 Gary Sutherland	1.75	.70
❑ 99 Rocky Colavito	8.00	3.20
❑ 100 Bob Gibson	25.00	10.00
❑ 101 Glenn Beckert	4.00	1.60
❑ 102 Jose Cardenal	4.00	1.60
❑ 103 Don Sutton	8.00	3.20
❑ 104 Dick Dietz	1.75	.70
❑ 105 Al Downing	4.00	1.60
❑ 106 Dalton Jones	1.75	.70
❑ 107A Juan Marichal CL	6.00	1.20
Tan wide mesh		
❑ 107B Juan Marichal CL	6.00	1.20
Brown fine mesh		
❑ 108 Don Pavletich	1.75	.70
❑ 109 Bert Campaneris	4.00	1.60
❑ 110 Hank Aaron	60.00	24.00
❑ 111 Rich Reese	1.75	.70
❑ 112 Woody Fryman	1.75	.70
❑ 113 Tom Matchick	4.00	1.60
Daryl Patterson		
❑ 114 Ron Swoboda	4.00	1.60
❑ 115 Sam McDowell	4.00	1.60
❑ 116 Ken McMullen	1.75	.70
❑ 117 Larry Jaster	1.75	.70
❑ 118 Mark Belanger	4.00	1.60
❑ 119 Ted Savage	1.75	.70
❑ 120 Mel Stottlemyre	4.00	1.60
❑ 121 Jimmie Hall	1.75	.70
❑ 122 Gene Mauch MG	4.00	1.60
❑ 123 Jose Santiago	1.75	.70
❑ 124 Nate Oliver	1.75	.70
❑ 125 Joel Horlen	1.75	.70
❑ 126 Bobby Etheridge	1.75	.70
❑ 127 Paul Lindblad	1.75	.70
❑ 128 Tom Dukes	1.75	.70
Alonzo Harris		
❑ 129 Mickey Stanley	6.00	2.40
❑ 130 Tony Perez	8.00	3.20
❑ 131 Frank Bertaina	1.75	.70
❑ 132 Bud Harrelson	4.00	1.60
❑ 133 Fred Whitfield	1.75	.70
❑ 134 Pat Jarvis	1.75	.70
❑ 135 Paul Blair	4.00	1.60
❑ 136 Randy Hundley	4.00	1.60
❑ 137 Twins Team	4.00	1.60
❑ 138 Ruben Amaro	1.75	.70
❑ 139 Chris Short	1.75	.70
❑ 140 Tony Conigliaro	8.00	3.20
❑ 141 Dal Maxvill	1.75	.70
❑ 142 Buddy Bradford	1.75	.70
Bill Voss		
❑ 143 Pete Cimino	1.75	.70
❑ 144 Joe Morgan	12.00	4.80
❑ 145 Don Drysdale	12.00	4.80
❑ 146 Sal Bando	4.00	1.60
❑ 147 Frank Linzy	1.75	.70
❑ 148 Dave Bristol MG	1.75	.70
❑ 149 Bob Saverine	1.75	.70
❑ 150 Roberto Clemente	75.00	30.00
❑ 151 Lou Brock WS	10.00	4.00
❑ 152 Carl Yastrzemski WS	10.00	4.00
❑ 153 Nellie Briles WS	5.00	2.00
❑ 154 Bob Gibson WS	10.00	4.00
❑ 155 Jim Lonborg WS	5.00	2.00
❑ 156 Rico Petrocelli WS	5.00	2.00
❑ 157 World Series Game 7	5.00	2.00
St. Louis wins it		
❑ 158 WS Summary	5.00	2.00
Cardinals celebrate		
❑ 159 Don Kessinger	4.00	1.60
❑ 160 Earl Wilson	4.00	1.60
❑ 161 Norm Miller	1.75	.70
❑ 162 Hal Gilson	4.00	1.60
Mike Torrez		
❑ 163 Gene Brabender	1.75	.70
❑ 164 Ramon Webster	1.75	.70
❑ 165 Tony Oliva	6.00	2.40
❑ 166 Claude Raymond	1.75	.70
❑ 167 Elston Howard	6.00	2.40
❑ 168 Dodgers Team	4.00	1.60
❑ 169 Bob Bolin	1.75	.70
❑ 170 Jim Fregosi	4.00	1.60
❑ 171 Don Nottebart	1.75	.70
❑ 172 Walt Williams	1.75	.70
❑ 173 John Boozer	1.75	.70
❑ 174 Bob Tillman	1.75	.70
❑ 175 Maury Wills	6.00	2.40
❑ 176 Bob Allen	1.75	.70
❑ 177 Jerry Koosman RC	600.00	240.00
Nolan Ryan RC		
❑ 178 Don Wert	4.00	1.60

❑ 179 Bill Stoneman 1.75 .70
❑ 180 Curt Flood 6.00 2.40
❑ 181 Jerry Zimmerman 1.75 .70
❑ 182 Dave Giusti 1.75 .70
❑ 183 Bob Kennedy MG 4.00 1.60
❑ 184 Lou Johnson 1.75 .70
❑ 185 Tom Haller 1.75 .70
❑ 186 Eddie Watt 1.75 .70
❑ 187 Sonny Jackson 1.75 .70
❑ 188 Cap Peterson 1.75 .70
❑ 189 Bill Landis 1.75 .70
❑ 190 Bill White 4.00 1.60
❑ 191 Dan Frisella 1.75 .70
❑ 192A Carl Yastrzemski CL 8.00 1.60
Special Baseball Playing Card
❑ 192B Carl Yastrzemski CL 8.00 1.60
Special Baseball
Playing Card Game
❑ 193 Jack Hamilton 1.75 .70
❑ 194 Don Buford 1.75 .70
❑ 195 Joe Pepitone 4.00 1.60
❑ 196 Gary Nolan 4.00 1.60
❑ 197 Larry Brown 1.75 .70
❑ 198 Roy Face 4.00 1.60
❑ 199 Roberto Rodriquez 1.75 .70
Darrell Osteen
❑ 200 Orlando Cepeda 8.00 3.20
❑ 201 Mike Marshall RC 4.00 1.60
❑ 202 Adolfo Phillips 1.75 .70
❑ 203 Dick Kelley 1.75 .70
❑ 204 Andy Etchebarren 1.75 .70
❑ 205 Juan Marichal 8.00 3.20
❑ 206 Cal Ermer MG 1.75 .70
❑ 207 Carroll Sembera 1.75 .70
❑ 208 Willie Davis 4.00 1.60
❑ 209 Tim Cullen 1.75 .70
❑ 210 Gary Peters 1.75 .70
❑ 211 J.C. Martin 1.75 .70
❑ 212 Dave Morehead 1.75 .70
❑ 213 Chico Ruiz 1.75 .70
❑ 214 Stan Bahnsen 4.00 1.60
Frank Fernandez
❑ 215 Jim Bunning 8.00 3.20
❑ 216 Bubba Morton 1.75 .70
❑ 217 Dick Farrell 1.75 .70
❑ 218 Ken Suarez 1.75 .70
❑ 219 Rob Gardner 1.75 .70
❑ 220 Harmon Killebrew 15.00 6.00
❑ 221 Braves Team 4.00 1.60
❑ 222 Jim Hardin 1.75 .70
❑ 223 Ollie Brown 1.75 .70
❑ 224 Jack Aker 1.75 .70
❑ 225 Richie Allen 6.00 2.40
❑ 226 Jimmie Price 1.75 .70
❑ 227 Joe Hoerner 1.75 .70
❑ 228 Jack Billingham 4.00 1.60
Jim Fairey
❑ 229 Fred Klages 1.75 .70
❑ 230 Pete Rose 60.00 24.00
❑ 231 Dave Baldwin 1.75 .70
❑ 232 Denis Menke 1.75 .70
❑ 233 George Scott 4.00 1.60
❑ 234 Bill Monbouquette 1.75 .70
❑ 235 Ron Santo 8.00 3.20
❑ 236 Tug McGraw 6.00 2.40
❑ 237 Alvin Dark MG 4.00 1.60
❑ 238 Tom Satriano 1.75 .70
❑ 239 Bill Henry 1.75 .70
❑ 240 Al Kaline 25.00 10.00
❑ 241 Felix Millan 1.75 .70
❑ 242 Moe Drabowsky 4.00 1.60
❑ 243 Rich Rollins 1.75 .70
❑ 244 John Donaldson 1.75 .70
❑ 245 Tony Gonzalez 1.75 .70
❑ 246 Fritz Peterson 4.00 1.60
❑ 247 Johnny Bench RC 125.00 50.00
Ron Tompkins
❑ 248 Fred Valentine 1.75 .70
❑ 249 Bill Singer 1.75 .70
❑ 250 Carl Yastrzemski 30.00 12.00
❑ 251 Manny Sanguillen RC 6.00 2.40
❑ 252 Angels Team 4.00 1.60
❑ 253 Dick Hughes 1.75 .70
❑ 254 Cleon Jones 4.00 1.60
❑ 255 Dean Chance 4.00 1.60
❑ 256 Norm Cash 6.00 2.40
❑ 257 Phil Niekro 8.00 3.20
❑ 258 Jose Arcia 1.75 .70
Bill Schlesinger
❑ 259 Ken Boyer 6.00 2.40
❑ 260 Jim Wynn 4.00 1.60
❑ 261 Dave Duncan 4.00 1.60
❑ 262 Rick Wise 4.00 1.60
❑ 263 Horace Clarke 4.00 1.60
❑ 264 Ted Abernathy 1.75 .70
❑ 265 Tommy Davis 4.00 1.60
❑ 266 Paul Popovich 1.75 .70
❑ 267 Herman Franks MG 1.75 .70
❑ 268 Bob Humphreys 1.75 .70
❑ 269 Bob Tiefenauer 1.75 .70
❑ 270 Matty Alou 4.00 1.60
❑ 271 Bobby Knoop 1.75 .70
❑ 272 Ray Culp 1.75 .70
❑ 273 Dave Johnson 4.00 1.60
❑ 274 Mike Cuellar 4.00 1.60
❑ 275 Tim McCarver 6.00 2.40
❑ 276 Jim Roland 1.75 .70
❑ 277 Jerry Buchek 1.75 .70
❑ 278 Orlando Cepeda CL 6.00 1.20
❑ 279 Bill Hands 1.75 .70
❑ 280 Mickey Mantle 250.00 100.00
❑ 281 Jim Campanis 1.75 .70
❑ 282 Rick Monday 4.00 1.60
❑ 283 Mel Queen 1.75 .70
❑ 284 Johnny Briggs 1.75 .70
❑ 285 Dick McAuliffe 6.00 2.40
❑ 286 Cecil Upshaw 1.75 .70
❑ 287 Mickey Abarbanel 1.75 .70
Cisco Carlos
❑ 288 Dave Wickersham 1.75 .70
❑ 289 Woody Held 1.75 .70
❑ 290 Willie McCovey 12.00 4.80
❑ 291 Dick Lines 1.75 .70
❑ 292 Art Shamsky 1.75 .70
❑ 293 Bruce Howard 1.75 .70
❑ 294 Red Schoendienst MG 6.00 2.40
❑ 295 Sonny Siebert 1.75 .70
❑ 296 Byron Browne 1.75 .70
❑ 297 Russ Gibson 1.75 .70
❑ 298 Jim Brewer 1.75 .70
❑ 299 Gene Michael 4.00 1.60
❑ 300 Rusty Staub 4.00 1.60
❑ 301 George Mitterwald 1.75 .70
Rick Renick
❑ 302 Gerry Arrigo 1.75 .70
❑ 303 Dick Green 4.00 1.60
❑ 304 Sandy Valdespino 1.75 .70
❑ 305 Minnie Rojas 1.75 .70
❑ 306 Mike Ryan 1.75 .70
❑ 307 John Hiller 4.00 1.60
❑ 308 Pirates Team 4.00 1.60
❑ 309 Ken Henderson 1.75 .70
❑ 310 Luis Aparicio 8.00 3.20
❑ 311 Jack Lamabe 1.75 .70
❑ 312 Curt Blefary 1.75 .70
❑ 313 Al Weis 1.75 .70
❑ 314 Bill Rohr 1.75 .70
George Spriggs
❑ 315 Zoilo Versalles 1.75 .70
❑ 316 Steve Barber 1.75 .70
❑ 317 Ron Brand 1.75 .70
❑ 318 Chico Salmon 1.75 .70
❑ 319 George Culver 1.75 .70
❑ 320 Frank Howard 4.00 1.60
❑ 321 Leo Durocher MG 6.00 2.40
❑ 322 Dave Boswell 1.75 .70
❑ 323 Deron Johnson 4.00 1.60
❑ 324 Jim Nash 1.75 .70
❑ 325 Manny Mota 4.00 1.60
❑ 326 Dennis Ribant 1.75 .70
❑ 327 Tony Taylor 4.00 1.60
❑ 328 Chuck Vinson 1.75 .70
Jim Weaver
❑ 329 Duane Josephson 1.75 .70
❑ 330 Roger Maris 50.00 20.00
❑ 331 Dan Osinski 1.75 .70
❑ 332 Doug Rader 4.00 1.60
❑ 333 Ron Herbel 1.75 .70
❑ 334 Orioles Team 4.00 1.60
❑ 335 Bob Allison 4.00 1.60
❑ 336 John Purdin 1.75 .70
❑ 337 Bill Robinson 4.00 1.60
❑ 338 Bob Johnson 1.75 .70
❑ 339 Rich Nye 1.75 .70
❑ 340 Max Alvis 1.75 .70
❑ 341 Jim Lemon MG 1.75 .70
❑ 342 Ken Johnson 1.75 .70
❑ 343 Jim Gosger 1.75 .70
❑ 344 Donn Clendenon 4.00 1.60
❑ 345 Bob Hendley 1.75 .70
❑ 346 Jerry Adair 1.75 .70
❑ 347 George Brunet 1.75 .70
❑ 348 Larry Colton 1.75 .70
Dick Thoenen
❑ 349 Ed Spiezio 4.00 1.60
❑ 350 Hoyt Wilhelm 8.00 3.20
❑ 351 Bob Barton 1.75 .70
❑ 352 Jackie Hernandez 1.75 .70
❑ 353 Mack Jones 1.75 .70
❑ 354 Pete Richert 1.75 .70
❑ 355 Ernie Banks 25.00 10.00
❑ 356A Ken Holtzman CL 6.00 1.20
Head centered within circle
❑ 356B Ken Holtzman 6.00 1.20
Head shifted right
within circle
❑ 357 Len Gabrielson 1.75 .70
❑ 358 Mike Epstein 1.75 .70
❑ 359 Joe Moeller 1.75 .70
❑ 360 Willie Horton 6.00 2.40
❑ 361 Harmon Killebrew AS 8.00 3.20
❑ 362 Orlando Cepeda AS 6.00 2.40
❑ 363 Rod Carew AS 8.00 3.20
❑ 364 Joe Morgan AS 8.00 3.20
❑ 365 Brooks Robinson AS 8.00 3.20
❑ 366 Ron Santo AS 6.00 2.40
❑ 367 Jim Fregosi AS 4.00 1.60
❑ 368 Gene Alley AS 4.00 1.60
❑ 369 Carl Yastrzemski AS 10.00 4.00
❑ 370 Hank Aaron AS 20.00 8.00
❑ 371 Tony Oliva AS 6.00 2.40
❑ 372 Lou Brock AS 8.00 3.20
❑ 373 Frank Robinson AS 8.00 3.20
❑ 374 Bob Clemente AS 30.00 12.00
❑ 375 Bill Freehan AS 4.00 1.60
❑ 376 Tim McCarver AS 4.00 1.60
❑ 377 Joel Horlen AS 4.00 1.60
❑ 378 Bob Gibson AS 8.00 3.20
❑ 379 Gary Peters AS 4.00 1.60
❑ 380 Ken Holtzman AS 4.00 1.60
❑ 381 Boog Powell 4.00 1.60
❑ 382 Ramon Hernandez 1.75 .70
❑ 383 Steve Whitaker 1.75 .70
❑ 384 Bill Henry 6.00 2.40
Hal McRae RC
❑ 385 Jim Hunter 10.00 4.00
❑ 386 Greg Goossen 1.75 .70
❑ 387 Joe Foy 1.75 .70
❑ 388 Ray Washburn 1.75 .70
❑ 389 Jay Johnstone 4.00 1.60
❑ 390 Bill Mazeroski 8.00 3.20
❑ 391 Bob Priddy 1.75 .70
❑ 392 Grady Hatton MG 1.75 .70
❑ 393 Jim Perry 4.00 1.60
❑ 394 Tommie Aaron 6.00 2.40
❑ 395 Camilo Pascual 4.00 1.60
❑ 396 Bobby Wine 1.75 .70
❑ 397 Vic Davalillo 1.75 .70
❑ 398 Jim Grant 1.75 .70
❑ 399 Ray Oyler 4.00 1.60
❑ 400A Mike McCormick 4.00 1.60
(Yellow letters)
❑ 400B Mike McCormick 150.00 60.00
(Team name in
white letters)
❑ 401 Mets Team 4.00 1.60
❑ 402 Mike Hegan 4.00 1.60
❑ 403 John Buzhardt 1.75 .70
❑ 404 Floyd Robinson 1.75 .70
❑ 405 Tommy Helms 4.00 1.60
❑ 406 Dick Ellsworth 1.75 .70
❑ 407 Gary Kolb 1.75 .70
❑ 408 Steve Carlton 30.00 12.00
❑ 409 Frank Peters 1.75 .70
Ron Stone
❑ 410 Ferguson Jenkins 10.00 4.00
❑ 411 Ron Hansen 1.75 .70
❑ 412 Clay Carroll 4.00 1.60

Card	NM	Ex
❑ 413 Tom McCraw	1.75	.70
❑ 414 Mickey Lolich	8.00	3.20
❑ 415 Johnny Callison	4.00	1.60
❑ 416 Bill Rigney MG	1.75	.70
❑ 417 Willie Crawford	1.75	.70
❑ 418 Eddie Fisher	1.75	.70
❑ 419 Jack Hiatt	1.75	.70
❑ 420 Cesar Tovar	1.75	.70
❑ 421 Ron Taylor	1.75	.70
❑ 422 Rene Lachemann	1.75	.70
❑ 423 Fred Gladding	1.75	.70
❑ 424 Chicago White Sox Team Card	4.00	1.60
❑ 425 Jim Maloney	4.00	1.60
❑ 426 Hank Allen	1.75	.70
❑ 427 Dick Calmus	1.75	.70
❑ 428 Vic Roznovsky	1.75	.70
❑ 429 Tommie Sisk	1.75	.70
❑ 430 Rico Petrocelli	4.00	1.60
❑ 431 Dooley Womack	1.75	.70
❑ 432 Bill Davis Jose Vidal	1.75	.70
❑ 433 Bob Rodgers	1.75	.70
❑ 434 Ricardo Joseph	1.75	.70
❑ 435 Ron Perranoski	4.00	1.60
❑ 436 Hal Lanier	1.75	.70
❑ 437 Don Cardwell	1.75	.70
❑ 438 Lee Thomas	4.00	1.60
❑ 439 Lum Harris MG	1.75	.70
❑ 440 Claude Osteen	4.00	1.60
❑ 441 Alex Johnson	4.00	1.60
❑ 442 Dick Bosman	1.75	.70
❑ 443 Joe Azcue	1.75	.70
❑ 444 Jack Fisher	1.75	.70
❑ 445 Mike Shannon	4.00	1.60
❑ 446 Ron Kline	1.75	.70
❑ 447 George Korince Fred Lasher	4.00	1.60
❑ 448 Gary Wagner	1.75	.70
❑ 449 Gene Oliver	1.75	.70
❑ 450 Jim Kaat	6.00	2.40
❑ 451 Al Spangler	1.75	.70
❑ 452 Jesus Alou	1.75	.70
❑ 453 Sammy Ellis	1.75	.70
❑ 454A Frank Robinson CL Cap complete within circle	8.00	1.60
❑ 454B Frank Robinson CL Cap partially within circle	8.00	1.60
❑ 455 Rico Carty	4.00	1.60
❑ 456 John O'Donoghue	1.75	.70
❑ 457 Jim Lefebvre	4.00	1.60
❑ 458 Lew Krausse	6.00	2.40
❑ 459 Dick Simpson	3.50	1.40
❑ 460 Jim Lonborg	6.00	2.40
❑ 461 Chuck Hiller	3.50	1.40
❑ 462 Barry Moore	3.50	1.40
❑ 463 Jim Schaffer	3.50	1.40
❑ 464 Don McMahon	3.50	1.40
❑ 465 Tommie Agee	10.00	4.00
❑ 466 Bill Dillman	3.50	1.40
❑ 467 Dick Howser	10.00	4.00
❑ 468 Larry Sherry	3.50	1.40
❑ 469 Ty Cline	3.50	1.40
❑ 470 Bill Freehan	10.00	4.00
❑ 471 Orlando Pena	3.50	1.40
❑ 472 Walter Alston MG	6.00	2.40
❑ 473 Al Worthington	3.50	1.40
❑ 474 Paul Schaal	3.50	1.40
❑ 475 Joe Niekro	6.00	2.40
❑ 476 Woody Woodward	3.50	1.40
❑ 477 Philadelphia Phillies Team Card	7.00	2.80
❑ 478 Dave McNally	6.00	2.40
❑ 479 Phil Gagliano	6.00	2.40
❑ 480 Tony Oliva Chico Cardenas Bob Clemente	80.00	32.00
❑ 481 John Wyatt	3.50	1.40
❑ 482 Jose Pagan	3.50	1.40
❑ 483 Darold Knowles	3.50	1.40
❑ 484 Phil Roof	3.50	1.40
❑ 485 Ken Berry	6.00	2.40
❑ 486 Cal Koonce	3.50	1.40
❑ 487 Lee May	10.00	4.00
❑ 488 Dick Tracewski	6.00	2.40
❑ 489 Wally Bunker	3.50	1.40
❑ 490 Harmon Killebrew Willie Mays Mickey Mantle	175.00	70.00
❑ 491 Denny Lemaster	3.50	1.40
❑ 492 Jeff Torborg	6.00	2.40
❑ 493 Jim McGlothlin	3.50	1.40
❑ 494 Ray Sadecki	3.50	1.40
❑ 495 Leon Wagner	3.50	1.40
❑ 496 Steve Hamilton	6.00	2.40
❑ 497 Cardinals Team	7.00	2.80
❑ 498 Bill Bryan	6.00	2.40
❑ 499 Steve Blass	6.00	2.40
❑ 500 Frank Robinson	30.00	12.00
❑ 501 John Odom	6.00	2.40
❑ 502 Mike Andrews	3.50	1.40
❑ 503 Al Jackson	6.00	2.40
❑ 504 Russ Snyder	3.50	1.40
❑ 505 Joe Sparma	10.00	4.00
❑ 506 Clarence Jones RC	3.50	1.40
❑ 507 Wade Blasingame	3.50	1.40
❑ 508 Duke Sims	3.50	1.40
❑ 509 Dennis Higgins	3.50	1.40
❑ 510 Ron Fairly	10.00	4.00
❑ 511 Bill Kelso	3.50	1.40
❑ 512 Grant Jackson	3.50	1.40
❑ 513 Hank Bauer MG	6.00	2.40
❑ 514 Al McBean	3.50	1.40
❑ 515 Russ Nixon	3.50	1.40
❑ 516 Pete Mikkelsen	3.50	1.40
❑ 517 Diego Segui	6.00	2.40
❑ 518A Clete Boyer CL ERR 539 AL Rookies	12.00	2.40
❑ 518B Clete Boyer CL COR 539 ML Rookies	12.00	2.40
❑ 519 Jerry Stephenson	3.50	1.40
❑ 520 Lou Brock	25.00	10.00
❑ 521 Don Shaw	3.50	1.40
❑ 522 Wayne Causey	3.50	1.40
❑ 523 John Tsitouris	3.50	1.40
❑ 524 Andy Kosco	6.00	2.40
❑ 525 Jim Davenport	3.50	1.40
❑ 526 Bill Denehy	3.50	1.40
❑ 527 Tito Francona	3.50	1.40
❑ 528 Tigers Team	60.00	24.00
❑ 529 Bruce Von Hoff	3.50	1.40
❑ 530 Brooks Robinson Frank Robinson	40.00	16.00
❑ 531 Chuck Hinton	3.50	1.40
❑ 532 Luis Tiant	6.00	2.40
❑ 533 Wes Parker	6.00	2.40
❑ 534 Bob Miller	6.00	2.40
❑ 535 Danny Cater	6.00	2.40
❑ 536 Bill Short	3.50	1.40
❑ 537 Norm Siebern	6.00	2.40
❑ 538 Manny Jimenez	6.00	2.40
❑ 539 Jim Ray Mike Ferraro	3.50	1.40
❑ 540 Nelson Briles	6.00	2.40
❑ 541 Sandy Alomar	6.00	2.40
❑ 542 John Boccabella	3.50	1.40
❑ 543 Bob Lee	3.50	1.40
❑ 544 Mayo Smith MG	12.00	4.80
❑ 545 Lindy McDaniel	6.00	2.40
❑ 546 Roy White	6.00	2.40
❑ 547 Dan Coombs	3.50	1.40
❑ 548 Bernie Allen	3.50	1.40
❑ 549 Curt Motton Roger Nelson	3.50	1.40
❑ 550 Clete Boyer	6.00	2.40
❑ 551 Darrell Sutherland	3.50	1.40
❑ 552 Ed Kirkpatrick	3.50	1.40
❑ 553 Hank Aguirre	3.50	1.40
❑ 554 A's Team	10.00	4.00
❑ 555 Jose Tartabull	6.00	2.40
❑ 556 Dick Selma	3.50	1.40
❑ 557 Frank Quilici	6.00	2.40
❑ 558 Johnny Edwards	3.50	1.40
❑ 559 Carl Taylor Luke Walker	3.50	1.40
❑ 560 Paul Casanova	3.50	1.40
❑ 561 Lee Elia	3.50	1.40
❑ 562 Jim Bouton	6.00	2.40
❑ 563 Ed Charles	3.50	1.40
❑ 564 Eddie Stanky MG	6.00	2.40
❑ 565 Larry Dierker	6.00	2.40
❑ 566 Ken Harrelson	6.00	2.40
❑ 567 Clay Dalrymple	3.50	1.40
❑ 568 Willie Smith	3.50	1.40
❑ 569 Ivan Murrell Les Rohr	3.50	1.40
❑ 570 Rick Reichardt	3.50	1.40
❑ 571 Tony LaRussa	12.00	4.80
❑ 572 Don Bosch	3.50	1.40
❑ 573 Joe Coleman	3.50	1.40
❑ 574 Cincinnati Reds Team Card	10.00	4.00
❑ 575 Jim Palmer	40.00	16.00
❑ 576 Dave Adlesh	3.50	1.40
❑ 577 Fred Talbot	3.50	1.40
❑ 578 Orlando Martinez	3.50	1.40
❑ 579 Larry Hisle RC Mike Lum	10.00	4.00
❑ 580 Bob Bailey	3.50	1.40
❑ 581 Garry Roggenburk	3.50	1.40
❑ 582 Jerry Grote	10.00	4.00
❑ 583 Gates Brown	10.00	4.00
❑ 584 Larry Shepard MG	3.50	1.40
❑ 585 Wilbur Wood	6.00	2.40
❑ 586 Jim Pagliaroni	6.00	2.40
❑ 587 Roger Repoz	3.50	1.40
❑ 588 Dick Schofield	3.50	1.40
❑ 589 Ron Clark Moe Ogier	3.50	1.40
❑ 590 Tommy Harper	6.00	2.40
❑ 591 Dick Nen	3.50	1.40
❑ 592 John Bateman	3.50	1.40
❑ 593 Lee Stange	3.50	1.40
❑ 594 Phil Linz	6.00	2.40
❑ 595 Phil Ortega	3.50	1.40
❑ 596 Charlie Smith	3.50	1.40
❑ 597 Bill McCool	3.50	1.40
❑ 598 Jerry May	6.00	1.85

1969 Topps

	NM	Ex
COMP. MASTER (695)	5000.00	2000.00
COMPLETE SET (664)	2800.00	1100.00
COMMON (1-218/328-512)	1.50	.60
COMMON (219-327)	2.50	1.00
COMMON (513-588)	2.00	.80
COMMON (589-664)	3.00	1.20
WRAPPER (5-CENT)	20.00	8.00

Card	NM	Ex
❑ 1 Carl Yastrzemski Danny Cater Tony Oliva LL	15.00	5.25
❑ 2 Pete Rose Matty Alou Felipe Alou LL	7.00	2.80
❑ 3 Ken Harrelson Frank Howard Jim Northrup LL	3.50	1.40
❑ 4 Willie McCovey Ron Santo Billy Williams LL	6.00	2.40
❑ 5 Frank Howard Willie Horton Ken Harrelson LL	3.50	1.40
❑ 6 Willie McCovey Richie Allen Ernie Banks LL	6.00	2.40
❑ 7 Luis Tiant Sam McDowell	3.50	1.40

Dave McNally LL
❑ 8 Bob Gibson 6.00 2.40
Bobby Bolin
Bob Veale LL
❑ 9 Denny McLain 3.50 1.40
Dave McNally
Luis Tiant
Mel Stottlemyre LL
❑ 10 Juan Marichal 7.00 2.80
Bob Gibson
Fergie Jenkins LL
❑ 11 Sam McDowell 3.50 1.40
Denny McLain
Luis Tiant LL
❑ 12 Bob Gibson 4.00 1.60
Fergie Jenkins
Bill Singer LL
❑ 13 Mickey Stanley 2.50 1.00
❑ 14 Al McBean 1.50 .60
❑ 15 Boog Powell 4.00 1.60
❑ 16 Cesar Gutierrez 1.50 .60
Rich Robertson
❑ 17 Mike Marshall 2.50 1.00
❑ 18 Dick Schofield 1.50 .60
❑ 19 Ken Suarez 1.50 .60
❑ 20 Ernie Banks 20.00 8.00
❑ 21 Jose Santiago 1.50 .60
❑ 22 Jesus Alou 2.50 1.00
❑ 23 Lew Krausse 1.50 .60
❑ 24 Walt Alston MG 4.00 1.60
❑ 25 Roy White 2.50 1.00
❑ 26 Clay Carroll 2.50 1.00
❑ 27 Bernie Allen 1.50 .60
❑ 28 Mike Ryan 1.50 .60
❑ 29 Dave Morehead 1.50 .60
❑ 30 Bob Allison 2.50 1.00
❑ 31 Gary Gentry RC 2.50 1.00
Amos Otis RC
❑ 32 Sammy Ellis 1.50 .60
❑ 33 Wayne Causey 1.50 .60
❑ 34 Gary Peters 1.50 .60
❑ 35 Joe Morgan 10.00 4.00
❑ 36 Luke Walker 1.50 .60
❑ 37 Curt Motton 1.50 .60
❑ 38 Zoilo Versalles 2.50 1.00
❑ 39 Dick Hughes 1.50 .60
❑ 40 Mayo Smith MG 1.50 .60
❑ 41 Bob Barton 1.50 .60
❑ 42 Tommy Harper 2.50 1.00
❑ 43 Joe Niekro 2.50 1.00
❑ 44 Danny Cater 1.50 .60
❑ 45 Maury Wills 2.50 1.00
❑ 46 Fritz Peterson 2.50 1.00
❑ 47A Paul Popovich 1.50 .60
(No helmet emblem)
❑ 47B Paul Popovich 25.00 10.00
(C emblem on helmet)
❑ 48 Brant Alyea 1.50 .60
❑ 49A Royals Rookies ERR 25.00 10.00
Steve Jones
E. Rodriquez
❑ 49B Royals Rookies COR 1.50 .60
Steve Jones
E. Rodriguez
❑ 50 Roberto Clemente UER 60.00 24.00
Bats Right listed twice
❑ 51 Woody Fryman 2.50 1.00
❑ 52 Mike Andrews 1.50 .60
❑ 53 Sonny Jackson 1.50 .60
❑ 54 Cisco Carlos 1.50 .60
❑ 55 Jerry Grote 2.50 1.00
❑ 56 Rich Reese 1.50 .60
❑ 57 Denny McLain CL 6.00 1.20
❑ 58 Fred Gladding 1.50 .60
❑ 59 Jay Johnstone 2.50 1.00
❑ 60 Nelson Briles 2.50 1.00
❑ 61 Jimmie Hall 1.50 .60
❑ 62 Chico Salmon 1.50 .60
❑ 63 Jim Hickman 2.50 1.00
❑ 64 Bill Monbouquette 1.50 .60
❑ 65 Willie Davis 2.50 1.00
❑ 66 Mike Adamson 1.50 .60
Merv Rettenmund
❑ 67 Bill Stoneman 2.50 1.00
❑ 68 Dave Duncan 2.50 1.00
❑ 69 Steve Hamilton 2.50 1.00

❑ 70 Tommy Helms 2.50 1.00
❑ 71 Steve Whitaker 2.50 1.00
❑ 72 Ron Taylor 1.50 .60
❑ 73 Johnny Briggs 1.50 .60
❑ 74 Preston Gomez MG 2.50 1.00
❑ 75 Luis Aparicio 6.00 2.40
❑ 76 Norm Miller 1.50 .60
❑ 77A Ron Perranoski 2.50 1.00
(No emblem on cap)
❑ 77B Ron Perranoski 25.00 10.00
(LA on cap)
❑ 78 Tom Satriano 1.50 .60
❑ 79 Milt Pappas 2.50 1.00
❑ 80 Norm Cash 2.50 1.00
❑ 81 Mel Queen 1.50 .60
❑ 82 Rich Hebner RC 8.00 3.20
Al Oliver RC
❑ 83 Mike Ferraro 2.50 1.00
❑ 84 Bob Humphreys 1.50 .60
❑ 85 Lou Brock 20.00 8.00
❑ 86 Pete Richert 1.50 .60
❑ 87 Horace Clarke 2.50 1.00
❑ 88 Rich Nye 1.50 .60
❑ 89 Russ Gibson 1.50 .60
❑ 90 Jerry Koosman 2.50 1.00
❑ 91 Alvin Dark MG 2.50 1.00
❑ 92 Jack Billingham 2.50 1.00
❑ 93 Joe Foy 2.50 1.00
❑ 94 Hank Aguirre 1.50 .60
❑ 95 Johnny Bench 50.00 20.00
❑ 96 Denny Lemaster 1.50 .60
❑ 97 Buddy Bradford 1.50 .60
❑ 98 Dave Giusti 1.50 .60
❑ 99A Twins Rookies 15.00 6.00
Danny Morris
Graig Nettles RC
(No loop)
❑ 99B Twins Rookies 15.00 6.00
Danny Morris
Graig Nettles RC
(Errant loop in
upper left corner
of obverse)
❑ 100 Hank Aaron 40.00 16.00
❑ 101 Daryl Patterson 1.50 .60
❑ 102 Jim Davenport 1.50 .60
❑ 103 Roger Repoz 1.50 .60
❑ 104 Steve Blass 1.50 .60
❑ 105 Rick Monday 2.50 1.00
❑ 106 Jim Hannan 1.50 .60
❑ 107A Bob Gibson CL ERR 6.00 1.20
161 Jim Purdin
❑ 107B Bob Gibson CL COR 7.50 1.50
161 John Purdin
❑ 108 Tony Taylor 2.50 1.00
❑ 109 Jim Lonborg 2.50 1.00
❑ 110 Mike Shannon 2.50 1.00
❑ 111 John Morris RC 1.50 .60
❑ 112 J.C. Martin 2.50 1.00
❑ 113 Dave May 1.50 .60
❑ 114 Alan Closter 2.50 1.00
John Cumberland
❑ 115 Bill Hands 1.50 .60
❑ 116 Chuck Harrison 1.50 .60
❑ 117 Jim Fairey 2.50 1.00
❑ 118 Stan Williams 1.50 .60
❑ 119 Doug Rader 2.50 1.00
❑ 120 Pete Rose 40.00 16.00
❑ 121 Joe Grzenda 1.50 .60
❑ 122 Ron Fairly 2.50 1.00
❑ 123 Wilbur Wood 2.50 1.00
❑ 124 Hank Bauer MG 2.50 1.00
❑ 125 Ray Sadecki 1.50 .60
❑ 126 Dick Tracewski 1.50 .60
❑ 127 Kevin Collins 2.50 1.00
❑ 128 Tommie Aaron 2.50 1.00
❑ 129 Bill McCool 1.50 .60
❑ 130 Carl Yastrzemski 20.00 8.00
❑ 131 Chris Cannizzaro 1.50 .60
❑ 132 Dave Baldwin 1.50 .60
❑ 133 Johnny Callison 2.50 1.00
❑ 134 Jim Weaver 1.50 .60
❑ 135 Tommy Davis 2.50 1.00
❑ 136 Steve Huntz 1.50 .60
Mike Torrez
❑ 137 Wally Bunker 1.50 .60

❑ 138 John Bateman 1.50 .60
❑ 139 Andy Kosco 1.50 .60
❑ 140 Jim Lefebvre 2.50 1.00
❑ 141 Bill Dillman 1.50 .60
❑ 142 Woody Woodward 1.50 .60
❑ 143 Joe Nossek 1.50 .60
❑ 144 Bob Hendley 2.50 1.00
❑ 145 Max Alvis 1.50 .60
❑ 146 Jim Perry 2.50 1.00
❑ 147 Leo Durocher MG 4.00 1.60
❑ 148 Lee Stange 1.50 .60
❑ 149 Ollie Brown 2.50 1.00
❑ 150 Denny McLain 4.00 1.60
❑ 151A Clay Dalrymple 1.50 .60
Portrait, Orioles
❑ 151B Clay Dalrymple 15.00 6.00
Catching, Phillies
❑ 152 Tommie Sisk 1.50 .60
❑ 153 Ed Brinkman 1.50 .60
❑ 154 Jim Britton 1.50 .60
❑ 155 Pete Ward 1.50 .60
❑ 156 Hal Gilson 1.50 .60
Leon McFadden
❑ 157 Bob Rodgers 2.50 1.00
❑ 158 Joe Gibbon 1.50 .60
❑ 159 Jerry Adair 1.50 .60
❑ 160 Vada Pinson 2.50 1.00
❑ 161 John Purdin 1.50 .60
❑ 162 Bob Gibson WS 8.00 3.20
Fans 17
❑ 163 Willie Horton WS 6.00 2.40
❑ 164 Tim McCarver WS 12.00 4.80
Roger Maris
❑ 165 Lou Brock WS 8.00 3.20
❑ 166 Al Kaline WS 8.00 3.20
❑ 167 Jim Northrup WS 6.00 2.40
❑ 168 Mickey Lolich WS 8.00 3.20
Bob Gibson
❑ 169 Dick McAuliffe WS 6.00 2.40
Denny McLain
Willie Horton
❑ 170 Frank Howard 2.50 1.00
❑ 171 Glenn Beckert 2.50 1.00
❑ 172 Jerry Stephenson 1.50 .60
❑ 173 Bob Christian 1.50 .60
Gerry Nyman
❑ 174 Grant Jackson 1.50 .60
❑ 175 Jim Bunning 6.00 2.40
❑ 176 Joe Azcue 1.50 .60
❑ 177 Ron Reed 1.50 .60
❑ 178 Ray Oyler 2.50 1.00
❑ 179 Don Pavletich 1.50 .60
❑ 180 Willie Horton 2.50 1.00
❑ 181 Mel Nelson 1.50 .60
❑ 182 Bill Rigney MG 1.50 .60
❑ 183 Don Shaw 2.50 1.00
❑ 184 Roberto Pena 1.50 .60
❑ 185 Tom Phoebus 1.50 .60
❑ 186 Johnny Edwards 1.50 .60
❑ 187 Leon Wagner 1.50 .60
❑ 188 Rick Wise 2.50 1.00
❑ 189 Joe Lahoud 1.50 .60
John Thibodeau
❑ 190 Willie Mays 60.00 24.00
❑ 191 Lindy McDaniel 2.50 1.00
❑ 192 Jose Pagan 1.50 .60
❑ 193 Don Cardwell 2.50 1.00
❑ 194 Ted Uhlaender 1.50 .60
❑ 195 John Odom 1.50 .60
❑ 196 Lum Harris MG 1.50 .60
❑ 197 Dick Selma 1.50 .60
❑ 198 Willie Smith 1.50 .60
❑ 199 Jim French 1.50 .60
❑ 200 Bob Gibson 12.00 4.80
❑ 201 Russ Snyder 1.50 .60
❑ 202 Don Wilson 2.50 1.00
❑ 203 Dave Johnson 2.50 1.00
❑ 204 Jack Hiatt 1.50 .60
❑ 205 Rick Reichardt 1.50 .60
❑ 206 Larry Hisle 2.50 1.00
Barry Lersch
❑ 207 Roy Face 2.50 1.00
❑ 208A Donn Clendenon 2.50 1.00
Houston
❑ 208B Donn Clendenon 15.00 6.00
Expos

❑ 209 Larry Haney UER 1.50 .60
(Reverse negative)
❑ 210 Felix Millan 1.50 .60
❑ 211 Galen Cisco 1.50 .60
❑ 212 Tom Tresh 2.50 1.00
❑ 213 Gerry Arrigo 1.50 .60
❑ 214 Checklist 3 6.00 1.20
With 69T deckle CL
on back (no player)
❑ 215 Rico Petrocelli 2.50 1.00
❑ 216 Don Sutton 6.00 2.40
❑ 217 John Donaldson 1.50 .60
❑ 218 John Roseboro 2.50 1.00
❑ 219 Freddie Patek RC 4.00 1.60
❑ 220 Sam McDowell 4.00 1.60
❑ 221 Art Shamsky 4.00 1.60
❑ 222 Duane Josephson 2.50 1.00
❑ 223 Tom Dukes 4.00 1.60
❑ 224 Bill Harrelson 2.50 1.00
Steve Kealey
❑ 225 Don Kessinger 4.00 1.60
❑ 226 Bruce Howard 2.50 1.00
❑ 227 Frank Johnson 2.50 1.00
❑ 228 Dave Leonhard 2.50 1.00
❑ 229 Don Lock 2.50 1.00
❑ 230 Rusty Staub UER 4.00 1.60
For 1966 stats, Houston spelled
Huoston
❑ 231 Pat Dobson 4.00 1.60
❑ 232 Dave Ricketts 2.50 1.00
❑ 233 Steve Barber 4.00 1.60
❑ 234 Dave Bristol MG 2.50 1.00
❑ 235 Jim Hunter 10.00 4.00
❑ 236 Manny Mota 4.00 1.60
❑ 237 Bobby Cox RC 10.00 4.00
❑ 238 Ken Johnson 2.50 1.00
❑ 239 Bob Taylor 4.00 1.60
❑ 240 Ken Harrelson 4.00 1.60
❑ 241 Jim Brewer 2.50 1.00
❑ 242 Frank Kostro 2.50 1.00
❑ 243 Ron Kline 2.50 1.00
❑ 244 Ray Fosse RC 4.00 1.60
George Woodson
❑ 245 Ed Charles 4.00 1.60
❑ 246 Joe Coleman 2.50 1.00
❑ 247 Gene Oliver 2.50 1.00
❑ 248 Bob Priddy 2.50 1.00
❑ 249 Ed Spiezio 4.00 1.60
❑ 250 Frank Robinson 20.00 8.00
❑ 251 Ron Herbel 2.50 1.00
❑ 252 Chuck Cottier 2.50 1.00
❑ 253 Jerry Johnson 2.50 1.00
❑ 254 Joe Schultz MG 4.00 1.60
❑ 255 Steve Carlton 30.00 12.00
❑ 256 Gates Brown 4.00 1.60
❑ 257 Jim Ray 2.50 1.00
❑ 258 Jackie Hernandez 4.00 1.60
❑ 259 Bill Short 2.50 1.00
❑ 260 Reggie Jackson RC 250.00 100.00
❑ 261 Bob Johnson 2.50 1.00
❑ 262 Mike Kekich 4.00 1.60
❑ 263 Jerry May 2.50 1.00
❑ 264 Bill Landis 2.50 1.00
❑ 265 Chico Cardenas 4.00 1.60
❑ 266 Tom Hutton 4.00 1.60
Alan Foster
❑ 267 Vicente Romo 2.50 1.00
❑ 268 Al Spangler 2.50 1.00
❑ 269 Al Weis 4.00 1.60
❑ 270 Mickey Lolich 4.00 1.60
❑ 271 Larry Stahl 4.00 1.60
❑ 272 Ed Stroud 2.50 1.00
❑ 273 Ron Willis 2.50 1.00
❑ 274 Clyde King MG 2.50 1.00
❑ 275 Vic Davalillo 2.50 1.00
❑ 276 Gary Wagner 2.50 1.00
❑ 277 Elrod Hendricks RC 2.50 1.00
❑ 278 Gary Geiger UER 2.50 1.00
(Batting wrong)
❑ 279 Roger Nelson 4.00 1.60
❑ 280 Alex Johnson 4.00 1.60
❑ 281 Ted Kubiak 2.50 1.00
❑ 282 Pat Jarvis 2.50 1.00
❑ 283 Sandy Alomar 4.00 1.60
❑ 284 Jerry Robertson 4.00 1.60
Mike Wegener

❑ 285 Don Mincher 4.00 1.60
❑ 286 Dock Ellis RC 4.00 1.60
❑ 287 Jose Tartabull 4.00 1.60
❑ 288 Ken Holtzman 4.00 1.60
❑ 289 Bart Shirley 2.50 1.00
❑ 290 Jim Kaat 4.00 1.60
❑ 291 Vern Fuller 2.50 1.00
❑ 292 Al Downing 4.00 1.60
❑ 293 Dick Dietz 2.50 1.00
❑ 294 Jim Lemon MG 2.50 1.00
❑ 295 Tony Perez 12.00 4.80
❑ 296 Andy Messersmith RC 4.00 1.60
❑ 297 Deron Johnson 2.50 1.00
❑ 298 Dave Nicholson 4.00 1.60
❑ 299 Mark Belanger 4.00 1.60
❑ 300 Felipe Alou 4.00 1.60
❑ 301 Darrell Brandon 4.00 1.60
❑ 302 Jim Pagliaroni 2.50 1.00
❑ 303 Cal Koonce 4.00 1.60
❑ 304 Bill Davis 6.00 2.40
Clarence Gaston RC
❑ 305 Dick McAuliffe 4.00 1.60
❑ 306 Jim Grant 4.00 1.60
❑ 307 Gary Kolb 2.50 1.00
❑ 308 Wade Blasingame 2.50 1.00
❑ 309 Walt Williams 2.50 1.00
❑ 310 Tom Haller 2.50 1.00
❑ 311 Sparky Lyle RC 10.00 4.00
❑ 312 Lee Elia 2.50 1.00
❑ 313 Bill Robinson 4.00 1.60
❑ 314 Don Drysdale CL 6.00 1.20
❑ 315 Eddie Fisher 2.50 1.00
❑ 316 Hal Lanier 2.50 1.00
❑ 317 Bruce Look 2.50 1.00
❑ 318 Jack Fisher 2.50 1.00
❑ 319 Ken McMullen UER 2.50 1.00
(Headings on back
are for a pitcher)
❑ 320 Dal Maxvill 2.50 1.00
❑ 321 Jim McAndrew 4.00 1.60
❑ 322 Jose Vidal 4.00 1.60
❑ 323 Larry Miller 2.50 1.00
❑ 324 Les Cain 4.00 1.60
Dave Campbell RC
❑ 325 Jose Cardenal 4.00 1.60
❑ 326 Gary Sutherland 4.00 1.60
❑ 327 Willie Crawford 2.50 1.00
❑ 328 Joel Horlen 1.50 .60
❑ 329 Rick Joseph 1.50 .60
❑ 330 Tony Conigliaro 4.00 1.60
❑ 331 Gil Garrido 2.50 1.00
Tom House RC
❑ 332 Fred Talbot 1.50 .60
❑ 333 Ivan Murrell 1.50 .60
❑ 334 Phil Roof 1.50 .60
❑ 335 Bill Mazeroski 6.00 2.40
❑ 336 Jim Roland 1.50 .60
❑ 337 Marty Martinez 1.50 .60
❑ 338 Del Unser 1.50 .60
❑ 339 Steve Mingori 1.50 .60
Jose Pena
❑ 340 Dave McNally 2.50 1.00
❑ 341 Dave Adlesh 1.50 .60
❑ 342 Bubba Morton 1.50 .60
❑ 343 Dan Frisella 1.50 .60
❑ 344 Tom Matchick 1.50 .60
❑ 345 Frank Linzy 1.50 .60
❑ 346 Wayne Comer 1.50 .60
❑ 347 Randy Hundley 2.50 1.00
❑ 348 Steve Hargan 1.50 .60
❑ 349 Dick Williams MG 2.50 1.00
❑ 350 Richie Allen 4.00 1.60
❑ 351 Carroll Sembera 1.50 .60
❑ 352 Paul Schaal 2.50 1.00
❑ 353 Jeff Torborg 2.50 1.00
❑ 354 Nate Oliver 1.50 .60
❑ 355 Phil Niekro 6.00 2.40
❑ 356 Frank Quilici 1.50 .60
❑ 357 Carl Taylor 1.50 .60
❑ 358 George Lauzerique 1.50 .60
Roberto Rodriquez
❑ 359 Dick Kelley 1.50 .60
❑ 360 Jim Wynn 2.50 1.00
❑ 361 Gary Holman 1.50 .60
❑ 362 Jim Maloney 2.50 1.00
❑ 363 Russ Nixon 1.50 .60

❑ 364 Tommie Agee 4.00 1.60
❑ 365 Jim Fregosi 2.50 1.00
❑ 366 Bo Belinsky 2.50 1.00
❑ 367 Lou Johnson 2.50 1.00
❑ 368 Vic Roznovsky 1.50 .60
❑ 369 Bob Skinner MG 2.50 1.00
❑ 370 Juan Marichal 8.00 3.20
❑ 371 Sal Bando 2.50 1.00
❑ 372 Adolfo Phillips 1.50 .60
❑ 373 Fred Lasher 1.50 .60
❑ 374 Bob Tillman 1.50 .60
❑ 375 Harmon Killebrew 15.00 6.00
❑ 376 Mike Fiore 1.50 .60
Jim Rooker RC
❑ 377 Gary Bell 2.50 1.00
❑ 378 Jose Herrera 1.50 .60
❑ 379 Ken Boyer 2.50 1.00
❑ 380 Stan Bahnsen 2.50 1.00
❑ 381 Ed Kranepool 2.50 1.00
❑ 382 Pat Corrales 2.50 1.00
❑ 383 Casey Cox 1.50 .60
❑ 384 Larry Shepard MG 1.50 .60
❑ 385 Orlando Cepeda 6.00 2.40
❑ 386 Jim McGlothlin 1.50 .60
❑ 387 Bobby Klaus 1.50 .60
❑ 388 Tom McCraw 1.50 .60
❑ 389 Dan Coombs 1.50 .60
❑ 390 Bill Freehan 2.50 1.00
❑ 391 Ray Culp 1.50 .60
❑ 392 Bob Burda 1.50 .60
❑ 393 Gene Brabender 2.50 1.00
❑ 394 Lou Piniella 6.00 2.40
Marv Staehle
❑ 395 Chris Short 1.50 .60
❑ 396 Jim Campanis 1.50 .60
❑ 397 Chuck Dobson 1.50 .60
❑ 398 Tito Francona 1.50 .60
❑ 399 Bob Bailey 2.50 1.00
❑ 400 Don Drysdale 16.00 6.50
❑ 401 Jake Gibbs 2.50 1.00
❑ 402 Ken Boswell 2.50 1.00
❑ 403 Bob Miller 1.50 .60
❑ 404 Vic LaRose 2.50 1.00
Gary Ross
❑ 405 Lee May 2.50 1.00
❑ 406 Phil Ortega 1.50 .60
❑ 407 Tom Egan 1.50 .60
❑ 408 Nate Colbert 1.50 .60
❑ 409 Bob Moose 1.50 .60
❑ 410 Al Kaline 25.00 10.00
❑ 411 Larry Dierker 2.50 1.00
❑ 412 Mickey Mantle CL DP 15.00 3.00
❑ 413 Roland Sheldon 2.50 1.00
❑ 414 Duke Sims 1.50 .60
❑ 415 Ray Washburn 1.50 .60
❑ 416 Willie McCovey AS 7.00 2.80
❑ 417 Ken Harrelson AS 3.00 1.20
❑ 418 Tommy Helms AS 3.00 1.20
❑ 419 Rod Carew AS 10.00 4.00
❑ 420 Ron Santo AS 4.00 1.60
❑ 421 Brooks Robinson AS 7.00 2.80
❑ 422 Don Kessinger AS 3.00 1.20
❑ 423 Bert Campaneris AS 4.00 1.60
❑ 424 Pete Rose AS 14.00 5.50
❑ 425 Carl Yastrzemski AS 10.00 4.00
❑ 426 Curt Flood AS 4.00 1.60
❑ 427 Tony Oliva AS 4.00 1.60
❑ 428 Lou Brock AS 6.00 2.40
❑ 429 Willie Horton AS 3.00 1.20
❑ 430 Johnny Bench AS 10.00 4.00
❑ 431 Bill Freehan AS 4.00 1.60
❑ 432 Bob Gibson AS 6.00 2.40
❑ 433 Denny McLain AS 3.00 1.20
❑ 434 Jerry Koosman AS 3.00 1.20
❑ 435 Sam McDowell AS 2.50 1.00
❑ 436 Gene Alley 2.50 1.00
❑ 437 Luis Alcaraz 1.50 .60
❑ 438 Gary Waslewski 1.50 .60
❑ 439 Ed Herrmann 1.50 .60
Dan Lazar
❑ 440A Willie McCovey 15.00 6.00
❑ 440B Willie McCovey WL 100.00 40.00
(McCovey white)
❑ 441A Dennis Higgins 1.50 .60
❑ 441B Dennis Higgins WL 25.00 10.00
(Higgins white)

❑ 442 Ty Cline 1.50 .60
❑ 443 Don Wert 1.50 .60
❑ 444A Joe Moeller 1.50 .60
❑ 444B Joe Moeller WL 25.00 10.00
(Moeller white)
❑ 445 Bobby Knoop 1.50 .60
❑ 446 Claude Raymond 1.50 .60
❑ 447A Ralph Houk MG 2.50 1.00
❑ 447B Ralph Houk WL 25.00 10.00
MG (Houk white)
❑ 448 Bob Tolan 2.50 1.00
❑ 449 Paul Lindblad 1.50 .60
❑ 450 Billy Williams 7.00 2.80
❑ 451A Rich Rollins 2.50 1.00
❑ 451B Rich Rollins WL 25.00 10.00
(Rich and 3B white)
❑ 452A Al Ferrara 1.50 .60
❑ 452B Al Ferrara WL 25.00 10.00
(Al and OF white)
❑ 453 Mike Cuellar 2.50 1.00
❑ 454A Phillies Rookies 2.50 1.00
Larry Colton
Don Money
❑ 454B Phillies Rookies WL 25.00 10.00
Larry Colton
Don Money
(Names in white)
❑ 455 Sonny Siebert 1.50 .60
❑ 456 Bud Harrelson 2.50 1.00
❑ 457 Dalton Jones 1.50 .60
❑ 458 Curt Blefary 1.50 .60
❑ 459 Dave Boswell 1.50 .60
❑ 460 Joe Torre 4.00 1.60
❑ 461A Mike Epstein 1.50 .60
❑ 461B Mike Epstein WL 25.00 10.00
(Epstein white)
❑ 462 Red Schoendienst 2.50 1.00
MG
❑ 463 Dennis Ribant 1.50 .60
❑ 464A Dave Marshall 1.50 .60
❑ 464B Dave Marshall WL 25.00 10.00
(Marshall white)
❑ 465 Tommy John 4.00 1.60
❑ 466 John Boccabella 2.50 1.00
❑ 467 Tommie Reynolds 1.50 .60
❑ 468A Pirates Rookies 1.50 .60
Bruce Dal Canton
Bob Robertson
❑ 468B Pirates Rookies WL 25.00 10.00
Bruce Dal Canton
Bob Robertson
(Names in white)
❑ 469 Chico Ruiz 1.50 .60
❑ 470A Mel Stottlemyre 2.50 1.00
❑ 470B Mel Stottlemyre WL 30.00 12.00
(Stottlemyre white)
❑ 471A Ted Savage 1.50 .60
❑ 471B Ted Savage WL 25.00 10.00
(Savage white)
❑ 472 Jim Price 1.50 .60
❑ 473A Jose Arcia 1.50 .60
❑ 473B Jose Arcia WL 25.00 10.00
(Jose and 2B white)
❑ 474 Tom Murphy 1.50 .60
❑ 475 Tim McCarver 4.00 1.60
❑ 476A Boston Rookies 3.00 1.20
Ken Brett RC
Gerry Moses
❑ 476B Boston Rookies WL 30.00 12.00
Ken Brett RC
Gerry Moses
(Names in white)
❑ 477 Jeff James 1.50 .60
❑ 478 Don Buford 1.50 .60
❑ 479 Richie Scheinblum 1.50 .60
❑ 480 Tom Seaver 70.00 28.00
❑ 481 Bill Melton 2.50 1.00
❑ 482A Jim Gosger 1.50 .60
❑ 482B Jim Gosger WL 25.00 10.00
(Jim and OF white)
❑ 483 Ted Abernathy 1.50 .60
❑ 484 Joe Gordon MG 2.50 1.00
❑ 485A Gaylord Perry 10.00 4.00
❑ 485B Gaylord Perry WL 85.00 34.00
(Perry white)
❑ 486A Paul Casanova 1.50 .60
❑ 486B Paul Casanova WL 25.00 10.00
(Casanova white)
❑ 487 Denis Menke 1.50 .60
❑ 488 Joe Sparma 1.50 .60
❑ 489 Clete Boyer 2.50 1.00
❑ 490 Matty Alou 2.50 1.00
❑ 491A Twins Rookies 1.50 .60
Jerry Crider
George Mitterwald
❑ 491B Twins Rookies WL 25.00 10.00
Jerry Crider
George Mitterwald
(Names in white)
❑ 492 Tony Cloninger 1.50 .60
❑ 493A Wes Parker 2.50 1.00
❑ 493B Wes Parker WL 25.00 10.00
(Parker white)
❑ 494 Ken Berry 1.50 .60
❑ 495 Bert Campaneris 2.50 1.00
❑ 496 Larry Jaster 1.50 .60
❑ 497 Julian Javier 2.50 1.00
❑ 498 Juan Pizarro 2.50 1.00
❑ 499 Astro Rookies 1.50 .60
Don Bryant
Steve Shea
❑ 500A Mickey Mantle UER 300.00 120.00
(No Topps copy-
right on card back)
❑ 500B Mickey Mantle WL 1200.00 475.00
(Mantle in white;
no Topps copyright
on card back) UER
❑ 501A Tony Gonzalez 2.50 1.00
❑ 501B Tony Gonzalez WL 25.00 10.00
(Tony and OF white)
❑ 502 Minnie Rojas 1.50 .60
❑ 503 Larry Brown 1.50 .60
❑ 504 Brooks Robinson CL 7.00 1.40
❑ 505A Bobby Bolin 1.50 .60
❑ 505B Bobby Bolin WL 25.00 10.00
(Bolin white)
❑ 506 Paul Blair 2.50 1.00
❑ 507 Cookie Rojas 2.50 1.00
❑ 508 Moe Drabowsky 2.50 1.00
❑ 509 Manny Sanguillen 2.50 1.00
❑ 510 Rod Carew 40.00 16.00
❑ 511A Diego Segui 2.50 1.00
❑ 511B Diego Segui WL 25.00 10.00
(Diego and P white)
❑ 512 Cleon Jones 2.50 1.00
❑ 513 Camilo Pascual 3.00 1.20
❑ 514 Mike Lum 2.00 .80
❑ 515 Dick Green 2.00 .80
❑ 516 Earl Weaver RC MG 20.00 8.00
❑ 517 Mike McCormick 3.00 1.20
❑ 518 Fred Whitfield 2.00 .80
❑ 519 Yankees Rookies 2.00 .80
Jerry Kenney
Len Boehmer
❑ 520 Bob Veale 3.00 1.20
❑ 521 George Thomas 2.00 .80
❑ 522 Joe Hoerner 2.00 .80
❑ 523 Bob Chance 2.00 .80
❑ 524 Jose Laboy 3.00 1.20
Floyd Wicker
❑ 525 Earl Wilson 3.00 1.20
❑ 526 Hector Torres 2.00 .80
❑ 527 Al Lopez MG 5.00 2.00
❑ 528 Claude Osteen 3.00 1.20
❑ 529 Ed Kirkpatrick 3.00 1.20
❑ 530 Cesar Tovar 2.00 .80
❑ 531 Dick Farrell 2.00 .80
❑ 532 Tom Phoebus 3.00 1.20
Jim Hardin
Dave McNally
Mike Cuellar
❑ 533 Nolan Ryan 250.00 100.00
❑ 534 Jerry McNertney 3.00 1.20
❑ 535 Phil Regan 3.00 1.20
❑ 536 Danny Breeden 2.00 .80
Dave Roberts
❑ 537 Mike Paul 2.00 .80
❑ 538 Charlie Smith 2.00 .80
❑ 539 Mike Epstein 12.00 4.80
Ted Williams MG
❑ 540 Curt Flood 3.00 1.20
❑ 541 Joe Verbanic 2.00 .80
❑ 542 Bob Aspromonte 2.00 .80
❑ 543 Fred Newman 2.00 .80
❑ 544 Mike Kilkenny 2.00 .80
Ron Woods
❑ 545 Willie Stargell 12.00 4.80
❑ 546 Jim Nash 2.00 .80
❑ 547 Billy Martin MG 5.00 2.00
❑ 548 Bob Locker 2.00 .80
❑ 549 Ron Brand 2.00 .80
❑ 550 Brooks Robinson 30.00 12.00
❑ 551 Wayne Granger 2.00 .80
❑ 552 Ted Sizemore RC 3.00 1.20
Bill Sudakis
❑ 553 Ron Davis 2.00 .80
❑ 554 Frank Bertaina 2.00 .80
❑ 555 Jim Ray Hart 3.00 1.20
❑ 556 Sal Bando 3.00 1.20
Bert Campaneris
Danny Cater
❑ 557 Frank Fernandez 2.00 .80
❑ 558 Tom Burgmeier 3.00 1.20
❑ 559 Joe Hague 2.00 .80
Jim Hicks
❑ 560 Luis Tiant 3.00 1.20
❑ 561 Ron Clark 2.00 .80
❑ 562 Bob Watson RC 8.00 3.20
❑ 563 Marty Pattin 3.00 1.20
❑ 564 Gil Hodges MG 10.00 4.00
❑ 565 Hoyt Wilhelm 8.00 3.20
❑ 566 Ron Hansen 2.00 .80
❑ 567 Elvio Jimenez 2.00 .80
Jim Shellenback
❑ 568 Cecil Upshaw 2.00 .80
❑ 569 Billy Harris 1.50 .60
❑ 570 Ron Santo 8.00 3.20
❑ 571 Cap Peterson 2.00 .80
❑ 572 Willie McCovey 16.00 6.50
Juan Marichal
❑ 573 Jim Palmer 30.00 12.00
❑ 574 George Scott 3.00 1.20
❑ 575 Bill Singer 3.00 1.20
❑ 576 Ron Stone 2.00 .80
Bill Wilson
❑ 577 Mike Hegan 3.00 1.20
❑ 578 Don Bosch 2.00 .80
❑ 579 Dave Nelson 2.00 .80
❑ 580 Jim Northrup 3.00 1.20
❑ 581 Gary Nolan 3.00 1.20
❑ 582A Tony Oliva CL 6.00 1.20
White circle on back
❑ 582B Tony Oliva CL 7.50 1.50
Red circle on back
❑ 583 Clyde Wright 2.00 .80
❑ 584 Don Mason 2.00 .80
❑ 585 Ron Swoboda 3.00 1.20
❑ 586 Tim Cullen 2.00 .80
❑ 587 Joe Rudi RC 8.00 3.20
❑ 588 Bill White 3.00 1.20
❑ 589 Joe Pepitone 5.00 2.00
❑ 590 Rico Carty 5.00 2.00
❑ 591 Mike Hedlund 3.00 1.20
❑ 592 Rafael Robles 5.00 2.00
Al Santorini
❑ 593 Don Nottebart 3.00 1.20
❑ 594 Dooley Womack 3.00 1.20
❑ 595 Lee Maye 3.00 1.20
❑ 596 Chuck Hartenstein 3.00 1.20
❑ 597 Bob Floyd 40.00 16.00
Larry Burchart
Rollie Fingers RC
❑ 598 Ruben Amaro 3.00 1.20
❑ 599 John Boozer 3.00 1.20
❑ 600 Tony Oliva 8.00 3.20
❑ 601 Tug McGraw 8.00 3.20
❑ 602 Alec Distaso 5.00 2.00
Don Young
Jim Qualls
❑ 603 Joe Keough 3.00 1.20
❑ 604 Bobby Etheridge 3.00 1.20
❑ 605 Dick Ellsworth 3.00 1.20
❑ 606 Gene Mauch MG 5.00 2.00
❑ 607 Dick Bosman 3.00 1.20
❑ 608 Dick Simpson 3.00 1.20
❑ 609 Phil Gagliano 3.00 1.20
❑ 610 Jim Hardin 3.00 1.20

		NM	Ex
❑ 611	Bob Didier	5.00	2.00
	Walt Hriniak RC		
	Gary Neibauer		
❑ 612	Jack Aker	5.00	2.00
❑ 613	Jim Beauchamp	3.00	1.20
❑ 614	Tom Griffin	3.00	1.20
	Skip Guinn		
❑ 615	Len Gabrielson	3.00	1.20
❑ 616	Don McMahon	3.00	1.20
❑ 617	Jesse Gonder	3.00	1.20
❑ 618	Ramon Webster	3.00	1.20
❑ 619	Bill Butler	5.00	2.00
	Pat Kelly		
	Juan Rios		
❑ 620	Dean Chance	5.00	2.00
❑ 621	Bill Voss	3.00	1.20
❑ 622	Dan Osinski	3.00	1.20
❑ 623	Hank Allen	3.00	1.20
❑ 624	Darrel Chaney	5.00	2.00
	Duffy Dyer RC		
	Terry Harmon		
❑ 625	Mack Jones UER	5.00	2.00
	(Batting wrong)		
❑ 626	Gene Michael	5.00	2.00
❑ 627	George Stone	3.00	1.20
❑ 628	Bill Conigliaro RC	5.00	2.00
	Syd O'Brien		
	Fred Wenz		
❑ 629	Jack Hamilton	3.00	1.20
❑ 630	Bobby Bonds RC	30.00	12.00
❑ 631	John Kennedy	5.00	2.00
❑ 632	Jon Warden	3.00	1.20
❑ 633	Harry Walker MG	3.00	1.20
❑ 634	Andy Etchebarren	3.00	1.20
❑ 635	George Culver	3.00	1.20
❑ 636	Woody Held	3.00	1.20
❑ 637	Jerry DaVanon	5.00	2.00
	Frank Reberger		
	Clay Kirby		
❑ 638	Ed Sprague RC	3.00	1.20
❑ 639	Barry Moore	3.00	1.20
❑ 640	Ferguson Jenkins	20.00	8.00
❑ 641	Bobby Darwin	5.00	2.00
	John Miller		
	Tommy Dean		
❑ 642	John Hiller	3.00	1.20
❑ 643	Billy Cowan	3.00	1.20
❑ 644	Chuck Hinton	3.00	1.20
❑ 645	George Brunet	3.00	1.20
❑ 646	Dan McGinn	5.00	2.00
	Carl Morton		
❑ 647	Dave Wickersham	3.00	1.20
❑ 648	Bobby Wine	5.00	2.00
❑ 649	Al Jackson	3.00	1.20
❑ 650	Ted Williams MG	20.00	8.00
❑ 651	Gus Gil	5.00	2.00
❑ 652	Eddie Watt	3.00	1.20
❑ 653	A.Rodriguez RC UER	5.00	2.00
	Photo actually		
	Angels' batboy		
❑ 654	Carlos May RC	5.00	2.00
	Don Secrist		
	Rich Morales		
❑ 655	Mike Hershberger	3.00	1.20
❑ 656	Dan Schneider	3.00	1.20
❑ 657	Bobby Murcer	8.00	3.20
❑ 658	Tom Hall	3.00	1.20
	Bill Burbach		
	Jim Miles		
❑ 659	Johnny Podres	5.00	2.00
❑ 660	Reggie Smith	5.00	2.00
❑ 661	Jim Merritt	3.00	1.20
❑ 662	Dick Drago	5.00	2.00
	George Spriggs		
	Bob Oliver		
❑ 663	Dick Radatz	5.00	2.00
❑ 664	Ron Hunt	5.00	1.35

1970 Topps

	NM	Ex
COMPLETE SET (720)	2500.00	1000.00
COMMON CARD (1-132)	.75	.30
COMMON (373-459)	1.00	.40
COMMON CARD (373-459)	1.50	.60
COMMON (460-546)	2.00	.80
COMMON (547-633)	4.00	1.60
COMMON (634-720)	10.00	4.00
WRAPPER (10-CENT)	20.00	8.00

		NM	Ex
❑ 1	New York Mets	30.00	9.50
	Team Card		
❑ 2	Diego Segui	1.00	.40
❑ 3	Darrel Chaney	.75	.30
❑ 4	Tom Egan	.75	.30
❑ 5	Wes Parker	1.00	.40
❑ 6	Grant Jackson	.75	.30
❑ 7	Gary Boyd	.75	.30
	Russ Nagelson		
❑ 8	Jose Martinez	.75	.30
❑ 9	Checklist 1	12.00	2.40
❑ 10	Carl Yastrzemski	20.00	8.00
❑ 11	Nate Colbert	.75	.30
❑ 12	John Hiller	.75	.30
❑ 13	Jack Hiatt	.75	.30
❑ 14	Hank Allen	.75	.30
❑ 15	Larry Dierker	.75	.30
❑ 16	Charlie Metro MG	.75	.30
❑ 17	Hoyt Wilhelm	4.00	1.60
❑ 18	Carlos May	1.00	.40
❑ 19	John Boccabella	.75	.30
❑ 20	Dave McNally	1.00	.40
❑ 21	Vida Blue RC	4.00	1.60
	Gene Tenace RC		
❑ 22	Ray Washburn	.75	.30
❑ 23	Bill Robinson	1.00	.40
❑ 24	Dick Selma	.75	.30
❑ 25	Cesar Tovar	.75	.30
❑ 26	Tug McGraw	2.00	.80
❑ 27	Chuck Hinton	.75	.30
❑ 28	Billy Wilson	.75	.30
❑ 29	Sandy Alomar	1.00	.40
❑ 30	Matty Alou	1.00	.40
❑ 31	Marty Pattin	1.00	.40
❑ 32	Harry Walker MG	.75	.30
❑ 33	Don Wert	.75	.30
❑ 34	Willie Crawford	.75	.30
❑ 35	Joel Horlen	.75	.30
❑ 36	Danny Breeden	1.00	.40
	Bernie Carbo		
❑ 37	Dick Drago	.75	.30
❑ 38	Mack Jones	.75	.30
❑ 39	Mike Nagy	.75	.30
❑ 40	Rich Allen	2.00	.80
❑ 41	George Lauzerique	.75	.30
❑ 42	Tito Fuentes	.75	.30
❑ 43	Jack Aker	.75	.30
❑ 44	Roberto Pena	.75	.30
❑ 45	Dave Johnson	1.00	.40
❑ 46	Ken Rudolph	.75	.30
❑ 47	Bob Miller	.75	.30
❑ 48	Gil Garrido	.75	.30
❑ 49	Tim Cullen	.75	.30
❑ 50	Tommie Agee	1.00	.40
❑ 51	Bob Christian	.75	.30
❑ 52	Bruce Dal Canton	.75	.30
❑ 53	John Kennedy	.75	.30
❑ 54	Jeff Torborg	1.00	.40
❑ 55	John Odom	.75	.30
❑ 56	Joe Lis	.75	.30
	Scott Reid		
❑ 57	Pat Kelly	.75	.30
❑ 58	Dave Marshall	.75	.30
❑ 59	Dick Ellsworth	.75	.30
❑ 60	Jim Wynn	1.00	.40
❑ 61	Pete Rose	12.00	4.80
	Bob Clemente		
	Cleon Jones LL		
❑ 62	Rod Carew	2.00	.80
	Reggie Smith		
	Tony Oliva LL		
❑ 63	Willie McCovey	2.00	.80
	Ron Santo		
	Tony Perez LL		
❑ 64	Harmon Killebrew	4.00	1.60
	Boog Powell		
	Reggie Jackson LL		
❑ 65	Willie McCovey	4.00	1.60
	Hank Aaron		
	Lee May LL		
❑ 66	Harmon Killebrew	4.00	1.60
	Frank Howard		
	Reggie Jackson LL		
❑ 67	Juan Marichal	4.00	1.60
	Steve Carlton		
	Bob Gibson LL		
❑ 68	Dick Bosman	1.00	.40
	Jim Palmer		
	Mike Cuellar LL		
❑ 69	Tom Seaver	4.00	1.60
	Phil Niekro		
	Fergie Jenkins		
	Juan Marichal LL		
❑ 70	Dennis McLain	1.00	.40
	Mike Cuellar		
	Dave Boswell		
	Dave McNally		
	Jim Perry		
	Mel Stottlemyre LL		
❑ 71	Fergie Jenkins	2.00	.80
	Bob Gibson		
	Bill Singer LL		
❑ 72	Sam McDowell	1.00	.40
	Mickey Lolich		
	Andy Messersmith LL		
❑ 73	Wayne Granger	.75	.30
❑ 74	Greg Washburn	.75	.30
	Wally Wolf		
❑ 75	Jim Kaat	1.00	.40
❑ 76	Carl Taylor	.75	.30
❑ 77	Frank Linzy	.75	.30
❑ 78	Joe Lahoud	.75	.30
❑ 79	Clay Kirby	.75	.30
❑ 80	Don Kessinger	1.00	.40
❑ 81	Dave May	.75	.30
❑ 82	Frank Fernandez	.75	.30
❑ 83	Don Cardwell	.75	.30
❑ 84	Paul Casanova	.75	.30
❑ 85	Max Alvis	.75	.30
❑ 86	Lum Harris MG	.75	.30
❑ 87	Steve Renko RC	.75	.30
❑ 88	Miguel Fuentes	1.00	.40
	Dick Baney		
❑ 89	Juan Rios	.75	.30
❑ 90	Tim McCarver	1.00	.40
❑ 91	Rich Morales	.75	.30
❑ 92	George Culver	.75	.30
❑ 93	Rick Renick	.75	.30
❑ 94	Freddie Patek	1.00	.40
❑ 95	Earl Wilson	1.00	.40
❑ 96	Leron Lee	1.00	.40
	Jerry Reuss RC		
❑ 97	Joe Moeller	.75	.30
❑ 98	Gates Brown	1.00	.40
❑ 99	Bobby Pfeil	.75	.30
❑ 100	Mel Stottlemyre	1.00	.40
❑ 101	Bobby Floyd	.75	.30
❑ 102	Joe Rudi	1.00	.40
❑ 103	Frank Reberger	.75	.30
❑ 104	Gerry Moses	.75	.30
❑ 105	Tony Gonzalez	.75	.30
❑ 106	Darold Knowles	.75	.30
❑ 107	Bobby Etheridge	.75	.30
❑ 108	Tom Burgmeier	.75	.30
❑ 109	Garry Jestadt	.75	.30
	Carl Morton		
❑ 110	Bob Moose	.75	.30
❑ 111	Mike Hegan	1.00	.40
❑ 112	Dave Nelson	.75	.30
❑ 113	Jim Ray	.75	.30

❑ 114 Gene Michael 1.00 .40
❑ 115 Alex Johnson 1.00 .40
❑ 116 Sparky Lyle 1.00 .40
❑ 117 Don Young .75 .30
❑ 118 George Mitterwald .75 .30
❑ 119 Chuck Taylor .75 .30
❑ 120 Sal Bando 1.00 .40
❑ 121 Fred Beene .75 .30
Terry Crowley
❑ 122 George Stone .75 .30
❑ 123 Don Gutteridge MG .75 .30
❑ 124 Larry Jaster .75 .30
❑ 125 Deron Johnson .75 .30
❑ 126 Marty Martinez .75 .30
❑ 127 Joe Coleman .75 .30
❑ 128A Checklist 2 ERR 6.00 1.20
(226 R Perranoski)
❑ 128B Checklist 2 COR 6.00 1.20
(226 R. Perranoski)
❑ 129 Jimmie Price .75 .30
❑ 130 Ollie Brown .75 .30
❑ 131 Ray Lamb .75 .30
Bob Stinson
❑ 132 Jim McGlothlin .75 .30
❑ 133 Clay Carroll 1.00 .40
❑ 134 Danny Walton 1.00 .40
❑ 135 Dick Dietz 1.00 .40
❑ 136 Steve Hargan 1.00 .40
❑ 137 Art Shamsky 1.00 .40
❑ 138 Joe Foy 1.00 .40
❑ 139 Rich Nye 1.00 .40
❑ 140 Reggie Jackson 50.00 20.00
❑ 141 Dave Cash RC 1.50 .60
Johnny Jeter
❑ 142 Fritz Peterson 1.00 .40
❑ 143 Phil Gagliano 1.00 .40
❑ 144 Ray Culp 1.00 .40
❑ 145 Rico Carty 1.50 .60
❑ 146 Danny Murphy 1.00 .40
❑ 147 Angel Hermoso 1.00 .40
❑ 148 Earl Weaver MG 3.00 1.20
❑ 149 Billy Champion 1.00 .40
❑ 150 Harmon Killebrew 8.00 3.20
❑ 151 Dave Roberts 1.00 .40
❑ 152 Ike Brown 1.00 .40
❑ 153 Gary Gentry 1.00 .40
❑ 154 Jim Miles 1.00 .40
Jan Dukes
❑ 155 Denis Menke 1.00 .40
❑ 156 Eddie Fisher 1.00 .40
❑ 157 Manny Mota 1.50 .60
❑ 158 Jerry McNertney 1.50 .60
❑ 159 Tommy Helms 1.50 .60
❑ 160 Phil Niekro 5.00 2.00
❑ 161 Richie Scheinblum 1.00 .40
❑ 162 Jerry Johnson 1.00 .40
❑ 163 Syd O'Brien 1.00 .40
❑ 164 Ty Cline 1.00 .40
❑ 165 Ed Kirkpatrick 1.00 .40
❑ 166 Al Oliver 3.00 1.20
❑ 167 Bill Burbach 1.00 .40
❑ 168 Dave Watkins 1.00 .40
❑ 169 Tom Hall 1.00 .40
❑ 170 Billy Williams 5.00 2.00
❑ 171 Jim Nash 1.00 .40
❑ 172 Garry Hill 1.50 .60
Ralph Garr RC
❑ 173 Jim Hicks 1.00 .40
❑ 174 Ted Sizemore 1.50 .60
❑ 175 Dick Bosman 1.00 .40
❑ 176 Jim Ray Hart 1.50 .60
❑ 177 Jim Northrup 1.50 .60
❑ 178 Denny Lemaster 1.00 .40
❑ 179 Ivan Murrell 1.00 .40
❑ 180 Tommy John 1.50 .60
❑ 181 Sparky Anderson MG 5.00 2.00
❑ 182 Dick Hall 1.00 .40
❑ 183 Jerry Grote 1.50 .60
❑ 184 Ray Fosse 1.00 .40
❑ 185 Don Mincher 1.50 .60
❑ 186 Rick Joseph 1.00 .40
❑ 187 Mike Hedlund 1.00 .40
❑ 188 Manny Sanguillen 1.50 .60
❑ 189 Thurman Munson RC 60.00 24.00
Dave McDonald
❑ 190 Joe Torre 3.00 1.20
❑ 191 Vicente Romo 1.00 .40
❑ 192 Jim Qualls 1.00 .40
❑ 193 Mike Wegener 1.00 .40
❑ 194 Chuck Manuel 1.00 .40
❑ 195 Tom Seaver NLCS 15.00 6.00
❑ 196 Ken Boswell NLCS 2.00 .80
❑ 197 Nolan Ryan NLCS 30.00 12.00
❑ 198 NL Playoff Summary 15.00 6.00
Mets celebrate
(Nolan Ryan)
❑ 199 Mike Cuellar ALCS 2.00 .80
❑ 200 Boog Powell ALCS 3.00 1.20
❑ 201 Boog Powell ALCS 2.00 .80
Andy Etchebarren)
❑ 202 AL Playoff Summary 2.00 .80
Orioles celebrate
❑ 203 Rudy May 1.00 .40
❑ 204 Len Gabrielson 1.00 .40
❑ 205 Bert Campaneris 1.50 .60
❑ 206 Clete Boyer 1.50 .60
❑ 207 Norman McRae 1.00 .40
Bob Reed
❑ 208 Fred Gladding 1.00 .40
❑ 209 Ken Suarez 1.00 .40
❑ 210 Juan Marichal 5.00 2.00
❑ 211 Ted Williams MG UER 15.00 6.00
Throwing information on back incorrect
❑ 212 Al Santorini 1.00 .40
❑ 213 Andy Etchebarren 1.00 .40
❑ 214 Ken Boswell 1.00 .40
❑ 215 Reggie Smith 1.50 .60
❑ 216 Chuck Hartenstein 1.00 .40
❑ 217 Ron Hansen 1.00 .40
❑ 218 Ron Stone 1.00 .40
❑ 219 Jerry Kenney 1.00 .40
❑ 220 Steve Carlton 15.00 6.00
❑ 221 Ron Brand 1.00 .40
❑ 222 Jim Rooker 1.00 .40
❑ 223 Nate Oliver 1.00 .40
❑ 224 Steve Barber 1.50 .60
❑ 225 Lee May 1.50 .60
❑ 226 Ron Perranoski 1.00 .40
❑ 227 John Mayberry RC 1.50 .60
Bob Watkins
❑ 228 Aurelio Rodriguez 1.00 .40
❑ 229 Rich Robertson 1.00 .40
❑ 230 Brooks Robinson 15.00 6.00
❑ 231 Luis Tiant 1.50 .60
❑ 232 Bob Didier 1.00 .40
❑ 233 Lew Krausse 1.00 .40
❑ 234 Tommy Dean 1.00 .40
❑ 235 Mike Epstein 1.00 .40
❑ 236 Bob Veale 1.00 .40
❑ 237 Russ Gibson 1.00 .40
❑ 238 Jose Laboy 1.00 .40
❑ 239 Ken Berry 1.00 .40
❑ 240 Ferguson Jenkins 5.00 2.00
❑ 241 Al Fitzmorris 1.00 .40
Scott Northey
❑ 242 Walter Alston MG 3.00 1.20
❑ 243 Joe Sparma 1.00 .40
❑ 244A Checklist 3 6.00 1.20
(Red bat on front)
❑ 244B Checklist 3 6.00 1.20
(Brown bat on front)
❑ 245 Leo Cardenas 1.00 .40
❑ 246 Jim McAndrew 1.00 .40
❑ 247 Lou Klimchock 1.00 .40
❑ 248 Jesus Alou 1.00 .40
❑ 249 Bob Locker 1.00 .40
❑ 250 Willie McCovey UER 10.00 4.00
(1963 San Francisci)
❑ 251 Dick Schofield 1.00 .40
❑ 252 Lowell Palmer 1.00 .40
❑ 253 Ron Woods 1.00 .40
❑ 254 Camilo Pascual 1.00 .40
❑ 255 Jim Spencer 1.00 .40
❑ 256 Vic Davalillo 1.00 .40
❑ 257 Dennis Higgins 1.00 .40
❑ 258 Paul Popovich 1.00 .40
❑ 259 Tommie Reynolds 1.00 .40
❑ 260 Claude Osteen 1.00 .40
❑ 261 Curt Motton 1.00 .40
❑ 262 Jerry Morales 1.00 .40
Jim Williams
❑ 263 Duane Josephson 1.00 .40
❑ 264 Rich Hebner 1.00 .40
❑ 265 Randy Hundley 1.00 .40
❑ 266 Wally Bunker 1.00 .40
❑ 267 Herman Hill 1.00 .40
Paul Ratliff
❑ 268 Claude Raymond 1.00 .40
❑ 269 Cesar Gutierrez 1.00 .40
❑ 270 Chris Short 1.00 .40
❑ 271 Greg Goossen 1.50 .60
❑ 272 Hector Torres 1.00 .40
❑ 273 Ralph Houk MG 1.50 .60
❑ 274 Gerry Arrigo 1.00 .40
❑ 275 Duke Sims 1.00 .40
❑ 276 Ron Hunt 1.00 .40
❑ 277 Paul Doyle 1.00 .40
❑ 278 Tommie Aaron 1.00 .40
❑ 279 Bill Lee RC 1.50 .60
❑ 280 Donn Clendenon 1.50 .60
❑ 281 Casey Cox 1.00 .40
❑ 282 Steve Huntz 1.00 .40
❑ 283 Angel Bravo 1.00 .40
❑ 284 Jack Baldschun 1.00 .40
❑ 285 Paul Blair 1.50 .60
❑ 286 Jack Jenkins 5.00 2.00
Bill Buckner RC
❑ 287 Fred Talbot 1.00 .40
❑ 288 Larry Hisle 1.50 .60
❑ 289 Gene Brabender 1.00 .40
❑ 290 Rod Carew 18.00 7.25
❑ 291 Leo Durocher MG 3.00 1.20
❑ 292 Eddie Leon 1.00 .40
❑ 293 Bob Bailey 1.50 .60
❑ 294 Jose Azcue 1.00 .40
❑ 295 Cecil Upshaw 1.00 .40
❑ 296 Woody Woodward 1.00 .40
❑ 297 Curt Blefary 1.00 .40
❑ 298 Ken Henderson 1.00 .40
❑ 299 Buddy Bradford 1.00 .40
❑ 300 Tom Seaver 30.00 12.00
❑ 301 Chico Salmon 1.00 .40
❑ 302 Jeff James 1.00 .40
❑ 303 Brant Alyea 1.00 .40
❑ 304 Bill Russell RC 5.00 2.00
❑ 305 Don Buford WS 4.00 1.60
❑ 306 Donn Clendenon WS 4.00 1.60
❑ 307 Tommie Agee WS 4.00 1.60
❑ 308 J.C. Martin WS 4.00 1.60
❑ 309 Jerry Koosman WS 4.00 1.60
❑ 310 WS Summary 5.00 2.00
Mets whoop it up
❑ 311 Dick Green 1.00 .40
❑ 312 Mike Torrez 1.00 .40
❑ 313 Mayo Smith MG 1.00 .40
❑ 314 Bill McCool 1.00 .40
❑ 315 Luis Aparicio 5.00 2.00
❑ 316 Skip Guinn 1.00 .40
❑ 317 Billy Conigliaro 1.50 .60
Luis Alvarado
❑ 318 Willie Smith 1.00 .40
❑ 319 Clay Dalrymple 1.00 .40
❑ 320 Jim Maloney 1.50 .60
❑ 321 Lou Piniella 1.50 .60
❑ 322 Luke Walker 1.00 .40
❑ 323 Wayne Comer 1.00 .40
❑ 324 Tony Taylor 1.50 .60
❑ 325 Dave Boswell 1.00 .40
❑ 326 Bill Voss 1.00 .40
❑ 327 Hal King 1.00 .40
❑ 328 George Brunet 1.00 .40
❑ 329 Chris Cannizzaro 1.00 .40
❑ 330 Lou Brock 10.00 4.00
❑ 331 Chuck Dobson 1.00 .40
❑ 332 Bobby Wine 1.00 .40
❑ 333 Bobby Murcer 1.50 .60
❑ 334 Phil Regan 1.00 .40
❑ 335 Bill Freehan 1.50 .60
❑ 336 Del Unser 1.00 .40
❑ 337 Mike McCormick 1.50 .60
❑ 338 Paul Schaal 1.00 .40
❑ 339 Johnny Edwards 1.00 .40
❑ 340 Tony Conigliaro 3.00 1.20
❑ 341 Bill Sudakis 1.00 .40
❑ 342 Wilbur Wood 1.50 .60
❑ 343A Checklist 4 6.00 1.20
(Red bat on front)
❑ 343B Checklist 4 6.00 1.20

(Brown bat on front)
❑ 344 Marcelino Lopez 1.00 .40
❑ 345 Al Ferrara 1.00 .40
❑ 346 Red Schoendienst MG 1.50 .60
❑ 347 Russ Snyder 1.00 .40
❑ 348 Mike Jorgensen 1.50 .60
Jesse Hudson
❑ 349 Steve Hamilton 1.00 .40
❑ 350 Roberto Clemente 60.00 24.00
❑ 351 Tom Murphy 1.00 .40
❑ 352 Bob Barton 1.00 .40
❑ 353 Stan Williams 1.00 .40
❑ 354 Amos Otis 1.50 .60
❑ 355 Doug Rader 1.00 .40
❑ 356 Fred Lasher 1.00 .40
❑ 357 Bob Burda 1.00 .40
❑ 358 Pedro Borbon RC 1.50 .60
❑ 359 Phil Roof 1.00 .40
❑ 360 Curt Flood 1.50 .60
❑ 361 Ray Jarvis 1.00 .40
❑ 362 Joe Hague 1.00 .40
❑ 363 Tom Shopay 1.00 .40
❑ 364 Dan McGinn 1.00 .40
❑ 365 Zoilo Versalles 1.00 .40
❑ 366 Barry Moore 1.00 .40
❑ 367 Mike Lum 1.00 .40
❑ 368 Ed Herrmann 1.00 .40
❑ 369 Alan Foster 1.00 .40
❑ 370 Tommy Harper 1.50 .60
❑ 371 Rod Gaspar 1.00 .40
❑ 372 Dave Giusti 1.00 .40
❑ 373 Roy White 2.00 .80
❑ 374 Tommie Sisk 1.50 .60
❑ 375 Johnny Callison 2.00 .80
❑ 376 Lefty Phillips MG 1.50 .60
❑ 377 Bill Butler 1.50 .60
❑ 378 Jim Davenport 1.50 .60
❑ 379 Tom Tischinski 1.50 .60
❑ 380 Tony Perez 6.00 2.40
❑ 381 Bobby Brooks 1.50 .60
Mike Olivo
❑ 382 Jack DiLauro 1.50 .60
❑ 383 Mickey Stanley 2.00 .80
❑ 384 Gary Neibauer 1.50 .60
❑ 385 George Scott 2.00 .80
❑ 386 Bill Dillman 1.50 .60
❑ 387 Baltimore Orioles 3.00 1.20
Team Card
❑ 388 Byron Browne 1.50 .60
❑ 389 Jim Shellenback 1.50 .60
❑ 390 Willie Davis 2.00 .80
❑ 391 Larry Brown 1.50 .60
❑ 392 Walt Hriniak 2.00 .80
❑ 393 John Gelnar 1.50 .60
❑ 394 Gil Hodges MG 4.00 1.60
❑ 395 Walt Williams 1.50 .60
❑ 396 Steve Blass 2.00 .80
❑ 397 Roger Repoz 1.50 .60
❑ 398 Bill Stoneman 1.50 .60
❑ 399 New York Yankees 3.00 1.20
Team Card
❑ 400 Denny McLain 4.00 1.60
❑ 401 John Harrell 1.50 .60
Bernie Williams
❑ 402 Ellie Rodriguez 1.50 .60
❑ 403 Jim Bunning 6.00 2.40
❑ 404 Rich Reese 1.50 .60
❑ 405 Bill Hands 1.50 .60
❑ 406 Mike Andrews 1.50 .60
❑ 407 Bob Watson 2.00 .80
❑ 408 Paul Lindblad 1.50 .60
❑ 409 Bob Tolan 1.50 .60
❑ 410 Boog Powell 4.00 1.60
❑ 411 Los Angeles Dodgers 3.00 1.20
Team Card
❑ 412 Larry Burchart 1.50 .60
❑ 413 Sonny Jackson 1.50 .60
❑ 414 Paul Edmondson 1.50 .60
❑ 415 Julian Javier 2.00 .80
❑ 416 Joe Verbanic 1.50 .60
❑ 417 John Bateman 1.50 .60
❑ 418 John Donaldson 1.50 .60
❑ 419 Ron Taylor 1.50 .60
❑ 420 Ken McMullen 2.00 .80
❑ 421 Pat Dobson 2.00 .80
❑ 422 Royals Team 3.00 1.20
❑ 423 Jerry May 1.50 .60
❑ 424 Mike Kilkenny 1.50 .60
(Inconsistent design card number in white circle)
❑ 425 Bobby Bonds 6.00 2.40
❑ 426 Bill Rigney MG 1.50 .60
❑ 427 Fred Norman 1.50 .60
❑ 428 Don Buford 1.50 .60
❑ 429 Randy Bobb 1.50 .60
Jim Cosman
❑ 430 Andy Messersmith 2.00 .80
❑ 431 Ron Swoboda 2.00 .80
❑ 432A Checklist 5 6.00 1.20
(Baseball in yellow letters)
❑ 432B Checklist 5 6.00 1.20
(Baseball in white letters)
❑ 433 Ron Bryant 1.50 .60
❑ 434 Felipe Alou 2.00 .80
❑ 435 Nelson Briles 2.00 .80
❑ 436 Philadelphia Phillies 3.00 1.20
Team Card
❑ 437 Danny Cater 1.50 .60
❑ 438 Pat Jarvis 1.50 .60
❑ 439 Lee Maye 1.50 .60
❑ 440 Bill Mazeroski 6.00 2.40
❑ 441 John O'Donoghue 1.50 .60
❑ 442 Gene Mauch MG 2.00 .80
❑ 443 Al Jackson 1.50 .60
❑ 444 Billy Farmer 1.50 .60
John Matias
❑ 445 Vada Pinson 2.00 .80
❑ 446 Billy Grabarkewitz 1.50 .60
❑ 447 Lee Stange 1.50 .60
❑ 448 Houston Astros 3.00 1.20
Team Card
❑ 449 Jim Palmer 12.00 4.80
❑ 450 Willie McCovey AS 6.00 2.40
❑ 451 Boog Powell AS 4.00 1.60
❑ 452 Felix Millan AS 2.00 .80
❑ 453 Rod Carew AS 6.00 2.40
❑ 454 Ron Santo AS 4.00 1.60
❑ 455 Brooks Robinson AS 6.00 2.40
❑ 456 Don Kessinger AS 2.00 .80
❑ 457 Rico Petrocelli AS 4.00 1.60
❑ 458 Pete Rose AS 14.00 5.50
❑ 459 Reggie Jackson AS 12.00 4.80
❑ 460 Matty Alou AS 3.00 1.20
❑ 461 Carl Yastrzemski AS 10.00 4.00
❑ 462 Hank Aaron AS 15.00 6.00
❑ 463 Frank Robinson AS 7.00 2.80
❑ 464 Johnny Bench AS 15.00 6.00
❑ 465 Bill Freehan AS 3.00 1.20
❑ 466 Juan Marichal AS 5.00 2.00
❑ 467 Denny McLain AS 3.00 1.20
❑ 468 Jerry Koosman AS 3.00 1.20
❑ 469 Sam McDowell AS 3.00 1.20
❑ 470 Willie Stargell 10.00 4.00
❑ 471 Chris Zachary 2.00 .80
❑ 472 Braves Team 3.50 1.40
❑ 473 Don Bryant 2.00 .80
❑ 474 Dick Kelley 2.00 .80
❑ 475 Dick McAuliffe 3.00 1.20
❑ 476 Don Shaw 2.00 .80
❑ 477 Al Severinsen 2.00 .80
Roger Freed
❑ 478 Bobby Heise 2.00 .80
❑ 479 Dick Woodson 2.00 .80
❑ 480 Glenn Beckert 3.00 1.20
❑ 481 Jose Tartabull 2.00 .80
❑ 482 Tom Hilgendorf 2.00 .80
❑ 483 Gail Hopkins 2.00 .80
❑ 484 Gary Nolan 3.00 1.20
❑ 485 Jay Johnstone 3.00 1.20
❑ 486 Terry Harmon 2.00 .80
❑ 487 Cisco Carlos 2.00 .80
❑ 488 J.C. Martin 2.00 .80
❑ 489 Eddie Kasko MG 2.00 .80
❑ 490 Bill Singer 3.00 1.20
❑ 491 Graig Nettles 5.00 2.00
❑ 492 Keith Lampard 2.00 .80
Scipio Spinks
❑ 493 Lindy McDaniel 3.00 1.20
❑ 494 Larry Stahl 2.00 .80
❑ 495 Dave Morehead 2.00 .80
❑ 496 Steve Whitaker 2.00 .80
❑ 497 Eddie Watt 2.00 .80
❑ 498 Al Weis 2.00 .80
❑ 499 Skip Lockwood 3.00 1.20
❑ 500 Hank Aaron 50.00 20.00
❑ 501 Chicago White Sox 3.50 1.40
Team Card
❑ 502 Rollie Fingers 10.00 4.00
❑ 503 Dal Maxvill 2.00 .80
❑ 504 Don Pavletich 2.00 .80
❑ 505 Ken Holtzman 3.00 1.20
❑ 506 Ed Stroud 2.00 .80
❑ 507 Pat Corrales 2.00 .80
❑ 508 Joe Niekro 3.00 1.20
❑ 509 Montreal Expos 3.50 1.40
Team Card
❑ 510 Tony Oliva 5.00 2.00
❑ 511 Joe Hoerner 2.00 .80
❑ 512 Billy Harris 2.00 .80
❑ 513 Preston Gomez MG 2.00 .80
❑ 514 Steve Hovley 2.00 .80
❑ 515 Don Wilson 3.00 1.20
❑ 516 John Ellis 2.00 .80
Jim Lyttle
❑ 517 Joe Gibbon 2.00 .80
❑ 518 Bill Melton 2.00 .80
❑ 519 Don McMahon 2.00 .80
❑ 520 Willie Horton 3.00 1.20
❑ 521 Cal Koonce 2.00 .80
❑ 522 Angels Team 3.50 1.40
❑ 523 Jose Pena 2.00 .80
❑ 524 Alvin Dark MG 3.00 1.20
❑ 525 Jerry Adair 2.00 .80
❑ 526 Ron Herbel 2.00 .80
❑ 527 Don Bosch 2.00 .80
❑ 528 Elrod Hendricks 2.00 .80
❑ 529 Bob Aspromonte 2.00 .80
❑ 530 Bob Gibson 14.00 5.50
❑ 531 Ron Clark 2.00 .80
❑ 532 Danny Murtaugh MG 3.00 1.20
❑ 533 Buzz Stephen 2.00 .80
❑ 534 Minnesota Twins 3.50 1.40
Team Card
❑ 535 Andy Kosco 2.00 .80
❑ 536 Mike Kekich 2.00 .80
❑ 537 Joe Morgan 10.00 4.00
❑ 538 Bob Humphreys 2.00 .80
❑ 539 Denny Doyle 8.00 3.20
Larry Bowa RC
❑ 540 Gary Peters 2.00 .80
❑ 541 Bill Heath 2.00 .80
❑ 542 Checklist 6 6.00 1.20
❑ 543 Clyde Wright 2.00 .80
❑ 544 Cincinnati Reds 3.50 1.40
Team Card
❑ 545 Ken Harrelson 3.00 1.20
❑ 546 Ron Reed 2.00 .80
❑ 547 Rick Monday 6.00 2.40
❑ 548 Howie Reed 4.00 1.60
❑ 549 St. Louis Cardinals 6.00 2.40
Team Card
❑ 550 Frank Howard 6.00 2.40
❑ 551 Dock Ellis 6.00 2.40
❑ 552 Don O'Riley 4.00 1.60
Dennis Paepke
Fred Rico
❑ 553 Jim Lefebvre 6.00 2.40
❑ 554 Tom Timmermann 4.00 1.60
❑ 555 Orlando Cepeda 12.00 4.80
❑ 556 Dave Bristol MG 6.00 2.40
❑ 557 Ed Kranepool 6.00 2.40
❑ 558 Vern Fuller 4.00 1.60
❑ 559 Tommy Davis 6.00 2.40
❑ 560 Gaylord Perry 12.00 4.80
❑ 561 Tom McCraw 4.00 1.60
❑ 562 Ted Abernathy 4.00 1.60
❑ 563 Boston Red Sox 6.00 2.40
Team Card
❑ 564 Johnny Briggs 4.00 1.60
❑ 565 Jim Hunter 12.00 4.80
❑ 566 Gene Alley 6.00 2.40
❑ 567 Bob Oliver 4.00 1.60
❑ 568 Stan Bahnsen 6.00 2.40
❑ 569 Cookie Rojas 6.00 2.40
❑ 570 Jim Fregosi 6.00 2.40

	NM	Ex
White Chevy Pick-Up in Background		
❑ 571 Jim Brewer	4.00	1.60
❑ 572 Frank Quilici	4.00	1.60
❑ 573 Mike Corkins	4.00	1.60
Rafael Robles		
Ron Slocum		
❑ 574 Bobby Bolin	6.00	2.40
❑ 575 Cleon Jones	6.00	2.40
❑ 576 Milt Pappas	6.00	2.40
❑ 577 Bernie Allen	4.00	1.60
❑ 578 Tom Griffin	4.00	1.60
❑ 579 Detroit Tigers	6.00	2.40
Team Card		
❑ 580 Pete Rose	50.00	20.00
❑ 581 Tom Satriano	4.00	1.60
❑ 582 Mike Paul	4.00	1.60
❑ 583 Hal Lanier	4.00	1.60
❑ 584 Al Downing	6.00	2.40
❑ 585 Rusty Staub	8.00	3.20
❑ 586 Rickey Clark	4.00	1.60
❑ 587 Jose Arcia	4.00	1.60
❑ 588A Checklist 7 ERR	8.00	1.60
(666 Adolfo)		
❑ 588B Checklist 7 COR	6.00	1.20
(666 Adolpho)		
❑ 589 Joe Keough	4.00	1.60
❑ 590 Mike Cuellar	6.00	2.40
❑ 591 Mike Ryan UER	4.00	1.60
(Pitching Record		
header on card back)		
❑ 592 Daryl Patterson	4.00	1.60
❑ 593 Chicago Cubs	8.00	3.20
Team Card		
❑ 594 Jake Gibbs	4.00	1.60
❑ 595 Maury Wills	8.00	3.20
❑ 596 Mike Hershberger	6.00	2.40
❑ 597 Sonny Siebert	4.00	1.60
❑ 598 Joe Pepitone	6.00	2.40
❑ 599 Dick Stelmaszek	4.00	1.60
Gene Martin		
Dick Such		
❑ 600 Willie Mays	70.00	28.00
❑ 601 Pete Richert	4.00	1.60
❑ 602 Ted Savage	4.00	1.60
❑ 603 Ray Oyler	4.00	1.60
❑ 604 Clarence Gaston	6.00	2.40
❑ 605 Rick Wise	6.00	2.40
❑ 606 Chico Ruiz	4.00	1.60
❑ 607 Gary Waslewski	4.00	1.60
❑ 608 Pittsburgh Pirates	6.00	2.40
Team Card		
❑ 609 Buck Martinez RC	6.00	2.40
(Inconsistent design		
card number in		
white circle)		
❑ 610 Jerry Koosman	8.00	3.20
❑ 611 Norm Cash	6.00	2.40
❑ 612 Jim Hickman	6.00	2.40
❑ 613 Dave Baldwin	6.00	2.40
❑ 614 Mike Shannon	6.00	2.40
❑ 615 Mark Belanger	6.00	2.40
❑ 616 Jim Merritt	4.00	1.60
❑ 617 Jim French	4.00	1.60
❑ 618 Billy Wynne	4.00	1.60
❑ 619 Norm Miller	4.00	1.60
❑ 620 Jim Perry	6.00	2.40
❑ 621 Mike McQueen	12.00	4.80
Darrell Evans RC		
Rick Kester		
❑ 622 Don Sutton	12.00	4.80
❑ 623 Horace Clarke	6.00	2.40
❑ 624 Clyde King MG	4.00	1.60
❑ 625 Dean Chance	4.00	1.60
❑ 626 Dave Ricketts	4.00	1.60
❑ 627 Gary Wagner	4.00	1.60
❑ 628 Wayne Garrett	4.00	1.60
❑ 629 Merv Rettenmund	4.00	1.60
❑ 630 Ernie Banks	50.00	20.00
❑ 631 Oakland Athletics	6.00	2.40
Team Card		
❑ 632 Gary Sutherland	4.00	1.60
❑ 633 Roger Nelson	4.00	1.60
❑ 634 Bud Harrelson	15.00	6.00
❑ 635 Bob Allison	15.00	6.00
❑ 636 Jim Stewart	10.00	4.00
❑ 637 Cleveland Indians	12.00	4.80
Team Card		
❑ 638 Frank Bertaina	10.00	4.00
❑ 639 Dave Campbell	15.00	6.00
❑ 640 Al Kaline	50.00	20.00
❑ 641 Al McBean	10.00	4.00
❑ 642 Greg Garrett	10.00	4.00
Gordon Lund		
Jarvis Tatum		
❑ 643 Jose Pagan	10.00	4.00
❑ 644 Gerry Nyman	10.00	4.00
❑ 645 Don Money	15.00	6.00
❑ 646 Jim Britton	10.00	4.00
❑ 647 Tom Matchick	10.00	4.00
❑ 648 Larry Haney	10.00	4.00
❑ 649 Jimmie Hall	10.00	4.00
❑ 650 Sam McDowell	15.00	6.00
❑ 651 Jim Gosger	10.00	4.00
❑ 652 Rich Rollins	15.00	6.00
❑ 653 Moe Drabowsky	10.00	4.00
❑ 654 Oscar Gamble RC	15.00	6.00
Boots Day		
Angel Mangual		
❑ 655 John Roseboro	15.00	6.00
❑ 656 Jim Hardin	10.00	4.00
❑ 657 San Diego Padres	12.00	4.80
Team Card		
❑ 658 Ken Tatum	10.00	4.00
❑ 659 Pete Ward	10.00	4.00
❑ 660 Johnny Bench	80.00	32.00
❑ 661 Jerry Robertson	10.00	4.00
❑ 662 Frank Lucchesi MG	10.00	4.00
❑ 663 Tito Francona	10.00	4.00
❑ 664 Bob Robertson	10.00	4.00
❑ 665 Jim Lonborg	15.00	6.00
❑ 666 Adolpho Phillips	10.00	4.00
❑ 667 Bob Meyer	15.00	6.00
❑ 668 Bob Tillman	10.00	4.00
❑ 669 Bart Johnson	10.00	4.00
Dan Lazar		
Mickey Scott		
❑ 670 Ron Santo	15.00	6.00
❑ 671 Jim Campanis	10.00	4.00
❑ 672 Leon McFadden	10.00	4.00
❑ 673 Ted Uhlaender	10.00	4.00
❑ 674 Dave Leonhard	10.00	4.00
❑ 675 Jose Cardenal	15.00	6.00
❑ 676 Washington Senators	12.00	4.80
Team Card		
❑ 677 Woodie Fryman	10.00	4.00
❑ 678 Dave Duncan	15.00	6.00
❑ 679 Ray Sadecki	10.00	4.00
❑ 680 Rico Petrocelli	15.00	6.00
❑ 681 Bob Garibaldi	10.00	4.00
❑ 682 Dalton Jones	10.00	4.00
❑ 683 Vern Geishert	15.00	6.00
Hal McRae		
Wayne Simpson		
❑ 684 Jack Fisher	10.00	4.00
❑ 685 Tom Haller	10.00	4.00
❑ 686 Jackie Hernandez	10.00	4.00
❑ 687 Bob Priddy	10.00	4.00
❑ 688 Ted Kubiak	15.00	6.00
❑ 689 Frank Tepedino	15.00	6.00
❑ 690 Ron Fairly	15.00	6.00
❑ 691 Joe Grzenda	10.00	4.00
❑ 692 Duffy Dyer	10.00	4.00
❑ 693 Bob Johnson	10.00	4.00
❑ 694 Gary Ross	10.00	4.00
❑ 695 Bobby Knoop	10.00	4.00
❑ 696 San Francisco Giants	12.00	4.80
Team Card		
❑ 697 Jim Hannan	10.00	4.00
❑ 698 Tom Tresh	15.00	6.00
❑ 699 Hank Aguirre	10.00	4.00
❑ 700 Frank Robinson	50.00	20.00
❑ 701 Jack Billingham	10.00	4.00
❑ 702 Bob Johnson	10.00	4.00
Ron Klimkowski		
Bill Zepp		
❑ 703 Lou Marone	10.00	4.00
❑ 704 Frank Baker	10.00	4.00
❑ 705 Tony Cloninger UER	10.00	4.00
(Batter headings		
on card back)		
❑ 706 John McNamara MG	10.00	4.00
❑ 707 Kevin Collins	10.00	4.00
❑ 708 Jose Santiago	10.00	4.00
❑ 709 Mike Fiore	10.00	4.00
❑ 710 Felix Millan	10.00	4.00
❑ 711 Ed Brinkman	10.00	4.00
❑ 712 Nolan Ryan	225.00	90.00
❑ 713 Seattle Pilots	25.00	10.00
Team Card		
❑ 714 Al Spangler	10.00	4.00
❑ 715 Mickey Lolich	15.00	6.00
❑ 716 Sal Campisi	15.00	6.00
Reggie Cleveland		
Santiago Guzman		
❑ 717 Tom Phoebus	10.00	4.00
❑ 718 Ed Spiezio	10.00	4.00
❑ 719 Jim Roland	10.00	4.00
❑ 720 Rick Reichardt	15.00	5.00

1971 Topps

	NM	Ex
COMPLETE SET (752)	2800.00	1100.00
COMMON CARD (1-393)	1.50	.60
COMMON (394-523)	2.50	1.00
COMMON (524-643)	4.00	1.60
COMMON (644-752)	8.00	3.20
COMMON SP (644-752)	12.00	4.80
WRAPPER (10-CENT)	15.00	6.00
❑ 1 Baltimore Orioles	20.00	6.75
Team Card		
❑ 2 Dock Ellis	1.50	.60
❑ 3 Dick McAuliffe	2.00	.80
❑ 4 Vic Davalillo	1.50	.60
❑ 5 Thurman Munson	50.00	20.00
❑ 6 Ed Spiezio	1.50	.60
❑ 7 Jim Holt	1.50	.60
❑ 8 Mike McQueen	1.50	.60
❑ 9 George Scott	2.00	.80
❑ 10 Claude Osteen	2.00	.80
❑ 11 Elliott Maddox	1.50	.60
❑ 12 Johnny Callison	2.00	.80
❑ 13 Charlie Brinkman	1.50	.60
Dick Moloney		
❑ 14 Dave Concepcion RC	15.00	6.00
❑ 15 Andy Messersmith	2.00	.80
❑ 16 Ken Singleton RC	4.00	1.60
❑ 17 Billy Sorrell	1.50	.60
❑ 18 Norm Miller	1.50	.60
❑ 19 Skip Pitlock	1.50	.60
❑ 20 Reggie Jackson	50.00	20.00
❑ 21 Dan McGinn	1.50	.60
❑ 22 Phil Roof	1.50	.60
❑ 23 Oscar Gamble	1.50	.60
❑ 24 Rich Hand	1.50	.60
❑ 25 Clarence Gaston	2.00	.80
❑ 26 Bert Blyleven RC	15.00	6.00
❑ 27 Fred Cambria	1.50	.60
Gene Clines		
❑ 28 Ron Klimkowski	1.50	.60
❑ 29 Don Buford	1.50	.60
❑ 30 Phil Niekro	6.00	2.40
❑ 31 Eddie Kasko MG	1.50	.60
❑ 32 Jerry DaVanon	1.50	.60
❑ 33 Del Unser	1.50	.60
❑ 34 Sandy Vance	1.50	.60
❑ 35 Lou Piniella	2.00	.80
❑ 36 Dean Chance	2.00	.80
❑ 37 Rich McKinney	1.50	.60

❑ 38 Jim Colborn 1.50 .60
❑ 39 Lerrin LaGrow 2.00 .80
Gene Lamont RC
❑ 40 Lee May 2.00 .80
❑ 41 Rick Austin 1.50 .60
❑ 42 Boots Day 1.50 .60
❑ 43 Steve Kealey 1.50 .60
❑ 44 Johnny Edwards 1.50 .60
❑ 45 Jim Hunter 6.00 2.40
❑ 46 Dave Campbell 2.00 .80
❑ 47 Johnny Jeter 1.50 .60
❑ 48 Dave Baldwin 1.50 .60
❑ 49 Don Money 1.50 .60
❑ 50 Willie McCovey 10.00 4.00
❑ 51 Steve Kline 1.50 .60
❑ 52 Oscar Brown 1.50 .60
Earl Williams RC
❑ 53 Paul Blair 2.00 .80
❑ 54 Checklist 1 11.00 2.20
❑ 55 Steve Carlton 20.00 8.00
❑ 56 Duane Josephson 1.50 .60
❑ 57 Von Joshua 1.50 .60
❑ 58 Bill Lee 2.00 .80
❑ 59 Gene Mauch MG 2.00 .80
❑ 60 Dick Bosman 1.50 .60
❑ 61 Alex Johnson 4.00 1.60
Carl Yastrzemski
Tony Oliva LL
❑ 62 Rico Carty 2.00 .80
Joe Torre
Manny Sanguillen LL
❑ 63 Frank Howard 4.00 1.60
Tony Conigliaro
Boog Powell LL
❑ 64 Johnny Bench 6.00 2.40
Tony Perez
Billy Williams LL
❑ 65 Frank Howard 4.00 1.60
Harmon Killebrew
Carl Yastrzemski LL
❑ 66 Johnny Bench 6.00 2.40
Billy Williams
Tony Perez LL
❑ 67 Diego Segui 4.00 1.60
Jim Palmer
Clyde Wright LL
❑ 68 Tom Seaver 4.00 1.60
Wayne Simpson
Luke Walker LL
❑ 69 Mike Cuellar 2.00 .80
Dave McNally
Jim Perry LL
❑ 70 Bob Gibson 6.00 2.40
Gaylord Perry
Fergie Jenkins LL
❑ 71 Sam McDowell 2.00 .80
Mickey Lolich
Bob Johnson LL
❑ 72 Tom Seaver 6.00 2.40
Bob Gibson
Fergie Jenkins LL
❑ 73 George Brunet 1.50 .60
❑ 74 Pete Hamm 1.50 .60
Jim Nettles
❑ 75 Gary Nolan 2.00 .80
❑ 76 Ted Savage 1.50 .60
❑ 77 Mike Compton 1.50 .60
❑ 78 Jim Spencer 1.50 .60
❑ 79 Wade Blasingame 1.50 .60
❑ 80 Bill Melton 1.50 .60
❑ 81 Felix Millan 1.50 .60
❑ 82 Casey Cox 1.50 .60
❑ 83 Tim Foli RC 2.00 .80
Randy Bobb
❑ 84 Marcel Lachemann RC 1.50 .60
❑ 85 Billy Grabarkewitz 1.50 .60
❑ 86 Mike Kilkenny 1.50 .60
❑ 87 Jack Heidemann 1.50 .60
❑ 88 Hal King 1.50 .60
❑ 89 Ken Brett 1.50 .60
❑ 90 Joe Pepitone 2.00 .80
❑ 91 Bob Lemon MG 2.00 .80
❑ 92 Fred Wenz 1.50 .60
❑ 93 Norm McRae 1.50 .60
Denny Riddleberger
❑ 94 Don Hahn 1.50 .60
❑ 95 Luis Tiant 2.00 .80
❑ 96 Joe Hague 1.50 .60
❑ 97 Floyd Wicker 1.50 .60
❑ 98 Joe Decker 1.50 .60
❑ 99 Mark Belanger 2.00 .80
❑ 100 Pete Rose 80.00 32.00
❑ 101 Les Cain 1.50 .60
❑ 102 Ken Forsch 2.00 .80
Larry Howard
❑ 103 Rich Severson 1.50 .60
❑ 104 Dan Frisella 1.50 .60
❑ 105 Tony Conigliaro 2.00 .80
❑ 106 Tom Dukes 1.50 .60
❑ 107 Roy Foster 1.50 .60
❑ 108 John Cumberland 1.50 .60
❑ 109 Steve Hovley 1.50 .60
❑ 110 Bill Mazeroski 6.00 2.40
❑ 111 Loyd Colson 1.50 .60
Bobby Mitchell
❑ 112 Manny Mota 2.00 .80
❑ 113 Jerry Crider 1.50 .60
❑ 114 Billy Conigliaro 2.00 .80
❑ 115 Donn Clendenon 2.00 .80
❑ 116 Ken Sanders 1.50 .60
❑ 117 Ted Simmons RC 8.00 3.20
❑ 118 Cookie Rojas 2.00 .80
❑ 119 Frank Lucchesi MG 1.50 .60
❑ 120 Willie Horton 2.00 .80
❑ 121 Jim Dunegan 1.50 .60
Roe Skidmore
❑ 122 Eddie Watt 1.50 .60
❑ 123A Checklist 2 11.00 2.20
(Card number
at bottom right)
❑ 123B Checklist 2 11.00 2.20
(Card number
centered)
❑ 124 Don Gullett RC 2.00 .80
❑ 125 Ray Fosse 1.50 .60
❑ 126 Danny Coombs 1.50 .60
❑ 127 Danny Thompson 2.00 .80
❑ 128 Frank Johnson 1.50 .60
❑ 129 Aurelio Monteagudo 1.50 .60
❑ 130 Denis Menke 1.50 .60
❑ 131 Curt Blefary 1.50 .60
❑ 132 Jose Laboy 1.50 .60
❑ 133 Mickey Lolich 2.00 .80
❑ 134 Jose Arcia 1.50 .60
❑ 135 Rick Monday 2.00 .80
❑ 136 Duffy Dyer 1.50 .60
❑ 137 Marcelino Lopez 1.50 .60
❑ 138 Joe Lis 2.00 .80
Willie Montanez
❑ 139 Paul Casanova 1.50 .60
❑ 140 Gaylord Perry 6.00 2.40
❑ 141 Frank Quilici 1.50 .60
❑ 142 Mack Jones 1.50 .60
❑ 143 Steve Blass 2.00 .80
❑ 144 Jackie Hernandez 1.50 .60
❑ 145 Bill Singer 2.00 .80
❑ 146 Ralph Houk MG 2.00 .80
❑ 147 Bob Priddy 1.50 .60
❑ 148 John Mayberry 2.00 .80
❑ 149 Mike Hershberger 1.50 .60
❑ 150 Sam McDowell 2.00 .80
❑ 151 Tommy Davis 2.00 .80
❑ 152 Lloyd Allen 1.50 .60
Winston Llenas
❑ 153 Gary Ross 1.50 .60
❑ 154 Cesar Gutierrez 1.50 .60
❑ 155 Ken Henderson 1.50 .60
❑ 156 Bart Johnson 1.50 .60
❑ 157 Bob Bailey 2.00 .80
❑ 158 Jerry Reuss 2.00 .80
❑ 159 Jarvis Tatum 1.50 .60
❑ 160 Tom Seaver 30.00 12.00
❑ 161 Coin Checklist 11.00 2.20
❑ 162 Jack Billingham 1.50 .60
❑ 163 Buck Martinez 2.00 .80
❑ 164 Frank Duffy 2.00 .80
Milt Wilcox
❑ 165 Cesar Tovar 1.50 .60
❑ 166 Joe Hoerner 1.50 .60
❑ 167 Tom Grieve RC 2.00 .80
❑ 168 Bruce Dal Canton 1.50 .60
❑ 169 Ed Herrmann 1.50 .60
❑ 170 Mike Cuellar 2.00 .80
❑ 171 Bobby Wine 1.50 .60
❑ 172 Duke Sims 1.50 .60
❑ 173 Gil Garrido 1.50 .60
❑ 174 Dave LaRoche 1.50 .60
❑ 175 Jim Hickman 1.50 .60
❑ 176 Bob Montgomery RC 2.00 .80
Doug Griffin
❑ 177 Hal McRae 2.00 .80
❑ 178 Dave Duncan 2.00 .80
❑ 179 Mike Corkins 1.50 .60
❑ 180 Al Kaline UER 20.00 8.00
(Home instead
of Birth)
❑ 181 Hal Lanier 1.50 .60
❑ 182 Al Downing 2.00 .80
❑ 183 Gil Hodges MG 4.00 1.60
❑ 184 Stan Bahnsen 1.50 .60
❑ 185 Julian Javier 1.50 .60
❑ 186 Bob Spence 1.50 .60
❑ 187 Ted Abernathy 1.50 .60
❑ 188 Bob Valentine RC 6.00 2.40
Mike Strahler
❑ 189 George Mitterwald 1.50 .60
❑ 190 Bob Tolan 1.50 .60
❑ 191 Mike Andrews 1.50 .60
❑ 192 Billy Wilson 1.50 .60
❑ 193 Bob Grich RC 4.00 1.60
❑ 194 Mike Lum 1.50 .60
❑ 195 Boog Powell ALCS 2.00 .80
❑ 196 Dave McNally ALCS 2.00 .80
❑ 197 Jim Palmer ALCS 4.00 1.60
❑ 198 AL Playoff Summary 2.00 .80
Orioles celebrate
❑ 199 Ty Cline NLCS 2.00 .80
❑ 200 Bobby Tolan NLCS 2.00 .80
❑ 201 Ty Cline NLCS 2.00 .80
❑ 202 NL Playoff Summary 2.00 .80
Reds celebrate
❑ 203 Larry Gura 2.00 .80
❑ 204 Bernie Smith 1.50 .60
George Kopacz
❑ 205 Gerry Moses 1.50 .60
❑ 206 Checklist 3 11.00 2.20
❑ 207 Alan Foster 1.50 .60
❑ 208 Billy Martin MG 4.00 1.60
❑ 209 Steve Renko 1.50 .60
❑ 210 Rod Carew 15.00 6.00
❑ 211 Phil Hennigan 1.50 .60
❑ 212 Rich Hebner 2.00 .80
❑ 213 Frank Baker 1.50 .60
❑ 214 Al Ferrara 1.50 .60
❑ 215 Diego Segui 1.50 .60
❑ 216 Reggie Cleveland 1.50 .60
Luis Melendez
❑ 217 Ed Stroud 1.50 .60
❑ 218 Tony Cloninger 1.50 .60
❑ 219 Elrod Hendricks 1.50 .60
❑ 220 Ron Santo 4.00 1.60
❑ 221 Dave Morehead 1.50 .60
❑ 222 Bob Watson 2.00 .80
❑ 223 Cecil Upshaw 1.50 .60
❑ 224 Alan Gallagher 1.50 .60
❑ 225 Gary Peters 1.50 .60
❑ 226 Bill Russell 2.00 .80
❑ 227 Floyd Weaver 1.50 .60
❑ 228 Wayne Garrett 1.50 .60
❑ 229 Jim Hannan 1.50 .60
❑ 230 Willie Stargell 15.00 6.00
❑ 231 Vince Colbert 2.00 .80
John Lowenstein RC
❑ 232 John Strohmayer 1.50 .60
❑ 233 Larry Bowa 2.00 .80
❑ 234 Jim Lyttle 1.50 .60
❑ 235 Nate Colbert 1.50 .60
❑ 236 Bob Humphreys 1.50 .60
❑ 237 Cesar Cedeno RC 2.00 .80
❑ 238 Chuck Dobson 1.50 .60
❑ 239 Red Schoendienst MG 2.00 .80
❑ 240 Clyde Wright 1.50 .60
❑ 241 Dave Nelson 1.50 .60
❑ 242 Jim Ray 1.50 .60
❑ 243 Carlos May 1.50 .60
❑ 244 Bob Tillman 1.50 .60
❑ 245 Jim Kaat 2.00 .80
❑ 246 Tony Taylor 1.50 .60

❑ 247 Jerry Cram 2.00 .80
Paul Splittorff
❑ 248 Hoyt Wilhelm 6.00 2.40
❑ 249 Chico Salmon 1.50 .60
❑ 250 Johnny Bench 40.00 16.00
❑ 251 Frank Reberger 1.50 .60
❑ 252 Eddie Leon 1.50 .60
❑ 253 Bill Sudakis 1.50 .60
❑ 254 Cal Koonce 1.50 .60
❑ 255 Bob Robertson 2.00 .80
❑ 256 Tony Gonzalez 1.50 .60
❑ 257 Nelson Briles 2.00 .80
❑ 258 Dick Green 1.50 .60
❑ 259 Dave Marshall 1.50 .60
❑ 260 Tommy Harper 2.00 .80
❑ 261 Darold Knowles 1.50 .60
❑ 262 Jim Williams 1.50 .60
Dave Robinson
❑ 263 John Ellis 1.50 .60
❑ 264 Joe Morgan 8.00 3.20
❑ 265 Jim Northrup 2.00 .80
❑ 266 Bill Stoneman 1.50 .60
❑ 267 Rich Morales 1.50 .60
❑ 268 Philadelphia Phillies 4.00 1.60
Team Card
❑ 269 Gail Hopkins 1.50 .60
❑ 270 Rico Carty 2.00 .80
❑ 271 Bill Zepp 1.50 .60
❑ 272 Tommy Helms 2.00 .80
❑ 273 Pete Richert 1.50 .60
❑ 274 Ron Slocum 1.50 .60
❑ 275 Vada Pinson 2.00 .80
❑ 276 Mike Davison 8.00 3.20
George Foster RC
❑ 277 Gary Waslewski 1.50 .60
❑ 278 Jerry Grote 2.00 .80
❑ 279 Lefty Phillips MG 1.50 .60
❑ 280 Ferguson Jenkins 6.00 2.40
❑ 281 Danny Walton 1.50 .60
❑ 282 Jose Pagan 1.50 .60
❑ 283 Dick Such 1.50 .60
❑ 284 Jim Gosger 1.50 .60
❑ 285 Sal Bando 2.00 .80
❑ 286 Jerry McNertney 1.50 .60
❑ 287 Mike Fiore 1.50 .60
❑ 288 Joe Moeller 1.50 .60
❑ 289 Chicago White Sox 4.00 1.60
Team Card
❑ 290 Tony Oliva 4.00 1.60
❑ 291 George Culver 1.50 .60
❑ 292 Jay Johnstone 2.00 .80
❑ 293 Pat Corrales 2.00 .80
❑ 294 Steve Dunning 1.50 .60
❑ 295 Bobby Bonds 4.00 1.60
❑ 296 Tom Timmermann 1.50 .60
❑ 297 Johnny Briggs 1.50 .60
❑ 298 Jim Nelson 1.50 .60
❑ 299 Ed Kirkpatrick 1.50 .60
❑ 300 Brooks Robinson 20.00 8.00
❑ 301 Earl Wilson 1.50 .60
❑ 302 Phil Gagliano 1.50 .60
❑ 303 Lindy McDaniel 2.00 .80
❑ 304 Ron Brand 1.50 .60
❑ 305 Reggie Smith 2.00 .80
❑ 306 Jim Nash 1.50 .60
❑ 307 Don Wert 1.50 .60
❑ 308 St. Louis Cardinals 4.00 1.60
Team Card
❑ 309 Dick Ellsworth 1.50 .60
❑ 310 Tommie Agee 2.00 .80
❑ 311 Lee Stange 1.50 .60
❑ 312 Harry Walker MG 1.50 .60
❑ 313 Tom Hall 1.50 .60
❑ 314 Jeff Torborg 2.00 .80
❑ 315 Ron Fairly 2.00 .80
❑ 316 Fred Scherman 1.50 .60
❑ 317 Jim Driscoll 1.50 .60
Angel Mangual
❑ 318 Rudy May 1.50 .60
❑ 319 Ty Cline 1.50 .60
❑ 320 Dave McNally 2.00 .80
❑ 321 Tom Matchick 1.50 .60
❑ 322 Jim Beauchamp 1.50 .60
❑ 323 Billy Champion 1.50 .60
❑ 324 Graig Nettles 2.00 .80
❑ 325 Juan Marichal 8.00 3.20
❑ 326 Richie Scheinblum 1.50 .60
❑ 327 Boog Powell WS 2.00 .80
❑ 328 Don Buford WS 2.00 .80
❑ 329 Frank Robinson WS 4.00 1.60
❑ 330 World Series Game 4 2.00 .80
Reds stay alive
❑ 331 Brooks Robinson WS 6.00 2.40
commits robbery
❑ 332 WS Summary 2.00 .80
Orioles celebrate
❑ 333 Clay Kirby 1.50 .60
❑ 334 Roberto Pena 1.50 .60
❑ 335 Jerry Koosman 2.00 .80
❑ 336 Detroit Tigers 4.00 1.60
Team Card
❑ 337 Jesus Alou 1.50 .60
❑ 338 Gene Tenace 2.00 .80
❑ 339 Wayne Simpson 1.50 .60
❑ 340 Rico Petrocelli 2.00 .80
❑ 341 Steve Garvey RC 35.00 14.00
❑ 342 Frank Tepedino 2.00 .80
❑ 343 Ed Acosta 2.00 .80
Milt May RC
❑ 344 Ellie Rodriguez 1.50 .60
❑ 345 Joel Horlen 1.50 .60
❑ 346 Lum Harris MG 1.50 .60
❑ 347 Ted Uhlaender 1.50 .60
❑ 348 Fred Norman 1.50 .60
❑ 349 Rich Reese 1.50 .60
❑ 350 Billy Williams 6.00 2.40
❑ 351 Jim Shellenback 1.50 .60
❑ 352 Denny Doyle 1.50 .60
❑ 353 Carl Taylor 1.50 .60
❑ 354 Don McMahon 1.50 .60
❑ 355 Bud Harrelson 4.00 1.60
(Nolan Ryan in photo)
❑ 356 Bob Locker 1.50 .60
❑ 357 Cincinnati Reds 4.00 1.60
Team Card
❑ 358 Danny Cater 1.50 .60
❑ 359 Ron Reed 1.50 .60
❑ 360 Jim Fregosi 2.00 .80
❑ 361 Don Sutton 6.00 2.40
❑ 362 Mike Adamson 1.50 .60
Roger Freed
❑ 363 Mike Nagy 1.50 .60
❑ 364 Tommy Dean 1.50 .60
❑ 365 Bob Johnson 1.50 .60
❑ 366 Ron Stone 1.50 .60
❑ 367 Dalton Jones 1.50 .60
❑ 368 Bob Veale 2.00 .80
❑ 369 Checklist 4 11.00 2.20
❑ 370 Joe Torre 4.00 1.60
❑ 371 Jack Hiatt 1.50 .60
❑ 372 Lew Krausse 1.50 .60
❑ 373 Tom McCraw 1.50 .60
❑ 374 Clete Boyer 2.00 .80
❑ 375 Steve Hargan 1.50 .60
❑ 376 Clyde Mashore 1.50 .60
Ernie McAnally
❑ 377 Greg Garrett 1.50 .60
❑ 378 Tito Fuentes 1.50 .60
❑ 379 Wayne Granger 1.50 .60
❑ 380 Ted Williams MG 12.00 4.80
❑ 381 Fred Gladding 1.50 .60
❑ 382 Jake Gibbs 1.50 .60
❑ 383 Rod Gaspar 1.50 .60
❑ 384 Rollie Fingers 6.00 2.40
❑ 385 Maury Wills 4.00 1.60
❑ 386 Boston Red Sox 2.00 .80
Team Card
❑ 387 Ron Herbel 1.50 .60
❑ 388 Al Oliver 4.00 1.60
❑ 389 Ed Brinkman 1.50 .60
❑ 390 Glenn Beckert 2.00 .80
❑ 391 Steve Brye 2.00 .80
Cotton Nash
❑ 392 Grant Jackson 1.50 .60
❑ 393 Merv Rettenmund 2.00 .80
❑ 394 Clay Carroll 2.50 1.00
❑ 395 Roy White 4.00 1.60
❑ 396 Dick Schofield 2.50 1.00
❑ 397 Alvin Dark MG 4.00 1.60
❑ 398 Howie Reed 2.50 1.00
❑ 399 Jim French 2.50 1.00
❑ 400 Hank Aaron 60.00 24.00
❑ 401 Tom Murphy 2.50 1.00
❑ 402 Los Angeles Dodgers 6.00 2.40
Team Card
❑ 403 Joe Coleman 2.50 1.00
❑ 404 Buddy Harris 2.50 1.00
Roger Metzger
❑ 405 Leo Cardenas 2.50 1.00
❑ 406 Ray Sadecki 2.50 1.00
❑ 407 Joe Rudi 4.00 1.60
❑ 408 Rafael Robles 2.50 1.00
❑ 409 Don Pavletich 2.50 1.00
❑ 410 Ken Holtzman 4.00 1.60
❑ 411 George Spriggs 2.50 1.00
❑ 412 Jerry Johnson 2.50 1.00
❑ 413 Pat Kelly 2.50 1.00
❑ 414 Woodie Fryman 2.50 1.00
❑ 415 Mike Hegan 2.50 1.00
❑ 416 Gene Alley 2.50 1.00
❑ 417 Dick Hall 2.50 1.00
❑ 418 Adolfo Phillips 2.50 1.00
❑ 419 Ron Hansen 2.50 1.00
❑ 420 Jim Merritt 2.50 1.00
❑ 421 John Stephenson 2.50 1.00
❑ 422 Frank Bertaina 2.50 1.00
❑ 423 Dennis Saunders 2.50 1.00
Tim Marting
❑ 424 Roberto Rodriquez 2.50 1.00
❑ 425 Doug Rader 4.00 1.60
❑ 426 Chris Cannizzaro 2.50 1.00
❑ 427 Bernie Allen 2.50 1.00
❑ 428 Jim McAndrew 2.50 1.00
❑ 429 Chuck Hinton 2.50 1.00
❑ 430 Wes Parker 4.00 1.60
❑ 431 Tom Burgmeier 2.50 1.00
❑ 432 Bob Didier 2.50 1.00
❑ 433 Skip Lockwood 2.50 1.00
❑ 434 Gary Sutherland 2.50 1.00
❑ 435 Jose Cardenal 4.00 1.60
❑ 436 Wilbur Wood 4.00 1.60
❑ 437 Danny Murtaugh MG 4.00 1.60
❑ 438 Mike McCormick 4.00 1.60
❑ 439 Greg Luzinski RC 6.00 2.40
Scott Reid
❑ 440 Bert Campaneris 4.00 1.60
❑ 441 Milt Pappas 4.00 1.60
❑ 442 California Angels 4.00 1.60
Team Card
❑ 443 Rich Robertson 2.50 1.00
❑ 444 Jimmie Price 2.50 1.00
❑ 445 Art Shamsky 2.50 1.00
❑ 446 Bobby Bolin 2.50 1.00
❑ 447 Cesar Geronimo 4.00 1.60
❑ 448 Dave Roberts 2.50 1.00
❑ 449 Brant Alyea 2.50 1.00
❑ 450 Bob Gibson 15.00 6.00
❑ 451 Joe Keough 2.50 1.00
❑ 452 John Boccabella 2.50 1.00
❑ 453 Terry Crowley 2.50 1.00
❑ 454 Mike Paul 2.50 1.00
❑ 455 Don Kessinger 4.00 1.60
❑ 456 Bob Meyer 2.50 1.00
❑ 457 Willie Smith 2.50 1.00
❑ 458 Ron Lolich 2.50 1.00
Dave Lemonds
❑ 459 Jim Lefebvre 2.50 1.00
❑ 460 Fritz Peterson 2.50 1.00
❑ 461 Jim Ray Hart 2.50 1.00
❑ 462 Washington Senators 6.00 2.40
Team Card
❑ 463 Tom Kelley 2.50 1.00
❑ 464 Aurelio Rodriguez 2.50 1.00
❑ 465 Tim McCarver 6.00 2.40
❑ 466 Ken Berry 2.50 1.00
❑ 467 Al Santorini 2.50 1.00
❑ 468 Frank Fernandez 2.50 1.00
❑ 469 Bob Aspromonte 2.50 1.00
❑ 470 Bob Oliver 2.50 1.00
❑ 471 Tom Griffin 2.50 1.00
❑ 472 Ken Rudolph 2.50 1.00
❑ 473 Gary Wagner 2.50 1.00
❑ 474 Jim Fairey 2.50 1.00
❑ 475 Ron Perranoski 2.50 1.00
❑ 476 Dal Maxvill 2.50 1.00
❑ 477 Earl Weaver MG 6.00 2.40
❑ 478 Bernie Carbo 2.50 1.00
❑ 479 Dennis Higgins 2.50 1.00

❑ 480 Manny Sanguillen 4.00 1.60
❑ 481 Daryl Patterson 2.50 1.00
❑ 482 San Diego Padres 6.00 2.40
Team Card
❑ 483 Gene Michael 2.50 1.00
❑ 484 Don Wilson 2.50 1.00
❑ 485 Ken McMullen 2.50 1.00
❑ 486 Steve Huntz 2.50 1.00
❑ 487 Paul Schaal 2.50 1.00
❑ 488 Jerry Stephenson 2.50 1.00
❑ 489 Luis Alvarado 2.50 1.00
❑ 490 Deron Johnson 2.50 1.00
❑ 491 Jim Hardin 2.50 1.00
❑ 492 Ken Boswell 2.50 1.00
❑ 493 Dave May 2.50 1.00
❑ 494 Ralph Garr 4.00 1.60
Rick Kester
❑ 495 Felipe Alou 4.00 1.60
❑ 496 Woody Woodward 2.50 1.00
❑ 497 Horacio Pina 2.50 1.00
❑ 498 John Kennedy 2.50 1.00
❑ 499 Checklist 5 11.00 2.20
❑ 500 Jim Perry 4.00 1.60
❑ 501 Andy Etchebarren 2.50 1.00
❑ 502 Chicago Cubs 6.00 2.40
Team Card
❑ 503 Gates Brown 4.00 1.60
❑ 504 Ken Wright 2.50 1.00
❑ 505 Ollie Brown 2.50 1.00
❑ 506 Bobby Knoop 2.50 1.00
❑ 507 George Stone 2.50 1.00
❑ 508 Roger Repoz 2.50 1.00
❑ 509 Jim Grant 2.50 1.00
❑ 510 Ken Harrelson 4.00 1.60
❑ 511 Chris Short 4.00 1.60
(Pete Rose leading off second)
❑ 512 Dick Mills 2.50 1.00
Mike Garman
❑ 513 Nolan Ryan 150.00 60.00
❑ 514 Ron Woods 2.50 1.00
❑ 515 Carl Morton 2.50 1.00
❑ 516 Ted Kubiak 2.50 1.00
❑ 517 Charlie Fox MG 2.50 1.00
❑ 518 Joe Grzenda 2.50 1.00
❑ 519 Willie Crawford 2.50 1.00
❑ 520 Tommy John 6.00 2.40
❑ 521 Leron Lee 2.50 1.00
❑ 522 Minnesota Twins 6.00 2.40
Team Card
❑ 523 John Odom 2.50 1.00
❑ 524 Mickey Stanley 6.00 2.40
❑ 525 Ernie Banks 50.00 20.00
❑ 526 Ray Jarvis 4.00 1.60
❑ 527 Cleon Jones 6.00 2.40
❑ 528 Wally Bunker 4.00 1.60
❑ 529 Enzo Hernandez 6.00 2.40
Bill Buckner
Marty Perez
❑ 530 Carl Yastrzemski 30.00 12.00
❑ 531 Mike Torrez 4.00 1.60
❑ 532 Bill Rigney MG 4.00 1.60
❑ 533 Mike Ryan 4.00 1.60
❑ 534 Luke Walker 4.00 1.60
❑ 535 Curt Flood 6.00 2.40
❑ 536 Claude Raymond 4.00 1.60
❑ 537 Tom Egan 4.00 1.60
❑ 538 Angel Bravo 4.00 1.60
❑ 539 Larry Brown 4.00 1.60
❑ 540 Larry Dierker 6.00 2.40
❑ 541 Bob Burda 4.00 1.60
❑ 542 Bob Miller 4.00 1.60
❑ 543 New York Yankees 10.00 4.00
Team Card
❑ 544 Vida Blue 6.00 2.40
❑ 545 Dick Dietz 4.00 1.60
❑ 546 John Matias 4.00 1.60
❑ 547 Pat Dobson 6.00 2.40
❑ 548 Don Mason 4.00 1.60
❑ 549 Jim Brewer 6.00 2.40
❑ 550 Harmon Killebrew 25.00 10.00
❑ 551 Frank Linzy 4.00 1.60
❑ 552 Buddy Bradford 4.00 1.60
❑ 553 Kevin Collins 4.00 1.60
❑ 554 Lowell Palmer 4.00 1.60
❑ 555 Walt Williams 4.00 1.60
❑ 556 Jim McGlothlin 4.00 1.60
❑ 557 Tom Satriano 4.00 1.60
❑ 558 Hector Torres 4.00 1.60
❑ 559 Terry Cox 4.00 1.60
Bill Gogolewski
Gary Jones
❑ 560 Rusty Staub 6.00 2.40
❑ 561 Syd O'Brien 4.00 1.60
❑ 562 Dave Giusti 4.00 1.60
❑ 563 San Francisco Giants 8.00 3.20
Team Card
❑ 564 Al Fitzmorris 4.00 1.60
❑ 565 Jim Wynn 6.00 2.40
❑ 566 Tim Cullen 4.00 1.60
❑ 567 Walt Alston MG 8.00 3.20
❑ 568 Sal Campisi 4.00 1.60
❑ 569 Ivan Murrell 4.00 1.60
❑ 570 Jim Palmer 30.00 12.00
❑ 571 Ted Sizemore 4.00 1.60
❑ 572 Jerry Kenney 4.00 1.60
❑ 573 Ed Kranepool 6.00 2.40
❑ 574 Jim Bunning 8.00 3.20
❑ 575 Bill Freehan 6.00 2.40
❑ 576 Adrian Garrett 4.00 1.60
Brock Davis
Garry Jestadt
❑ 577 Jim Lonborg 6.00 2.40
❑ 578 Ron Hunt 4.00 1.60
❑ 579 Marty Pattin 4.00 1.60
❑ 580 Tony Perez 20.00 8.00
❑ 581 Roger Nelson 4.00 1.60
❑ 582 Dave Cash 6.00 2.40
❑ 583 Ron Cook 4.00 1.60
❑ 584 Cleveland Indians 8.00 3.20
Team Card
❑ 585 Willie Davis 6.00 2.40
❑ 586 Dick Woodson 4.00 1.60
❑ 587 Sonny Jackson 4.00 1.60
❑ 588 Tom Bradley 4.00 1.60
❑ 589 Bob Barton 4.00 1.60
❑ 590 Alex Johnson 6.00 2.40
❑ 591 Jackie Brown 4.00 1.60
❑ 592 Randy Hundley 6.00 2.40
❑ 593 Jack Aker 4.00 1.60
❑ 594 Bob Chlupsa 6.00 2.40
Bob Stinson
Al Hrabosky RC
❑ 595 Dave Johnson 6.00 2.40
❑ 596 Mike Jorgensen 4.00 1.60
❑ 597 Ken Suarez 4.00 1.60
❑ 598 Rick Wise 6.00 2.40
❑ 599 Norm Cash 6.00 2.40
❑ 600 Willie Mays 100.00 40.00
❑ 601 Ken Tatum 4.00 1.60
❑ 602 Marty Martinez 4.00 1.60
❑ 603 Pittsburgh Pirates 8.00 3.20
Team Card
❑ 604 John Gelnar 4.00 1.60
❑ 605 Orlando Cepeda 8.00 3.20
❑ 606 Chuck Taylor 4.00 1.60
❑ 607 Paul Ratliff 4.00 1.60
❑ 608 Mike Wegener 4.00 1.60
❑ 609 Leo Durocher MG 8.00 3.20
❑ 610 Amos Otis 6.00 2.40
❑ 611 Tom Phoebus 4.00 1.60
❑ 612 Lou Camilli 4.00 1.60
Ted Ford
Steve Mingori
❑ 613 Pedro Borbon 4.00 1.60
❑ 614 Billy Cowan 4.00 1.60
❑ 615 Mel Stottlemyre 6.00 2.40
❑ 616 Larry Hisle 6.00 2.40
❑ 617 Clay Dalrymple 4.00 1.60
❑ 618 Tug McGraw 6.00 2.40
❑ 619A Checklist 6 ERR 11.00 2.20
(No copyright)
❑ 619B Checklist 6 COR 6.00 1.20
(Copyright on back)
❑ 620 Frank Howard 6.00 2.40
❑ 621 Ron Bryant 4.00 1.60
❑ 622 Joe Lahoud 4.00 1.60
❑ 623 Pat Jarvis 4.00 1.60
❑ 624 Oakland Athletics 8.00 3.20
Team Card
❑ 625 Lou Brock 30.00 12.00
❑ 626 Freddie Patek 6.00 2.40
❑ 627 Steve Hamilton 4.00 1.60
❑ 628 John Bateman 4.00 1.60
❑ 629 John Hiller 6.00 2.40
❑ 630 Roberto Clemente 125.00 50.00
❑ 631 Eddie Fisher 4.00 1.60
❑ 632 Darrel Chaney 4.00 1.60
❑ 633 Bobby Brooks 4.00 1.60
Pete Koegel
Scott Northey
❑ 634 Phil Regan 4.00 1.60
❑ 635 Bobby Murcer 6.00 2.40
❑ 636 Denny Lemaster 4.00 1.60
❑ 637 Dave Bristol MG 4.00 1.60
❑ 638 Stan Williams 4.00 1.60
❑ 639 Tom Haller 4.00 1.60
❑ 640 Frank Robinson 40.00 16.00
❑ 641 New York Mets 15.00 6.00
Team Card
❑ 642 Jim Roland 4.00 1.60
❑ 643 Rick Reichardt 4.00 1.60
❑ 644 Jim Stewart SP 12.00 4.80
❑ 645 Jim Maloney SP 15.00 6.00
❑ 646 Bobby Floyd SP 12.00 4.80
❑ 647 Juan Pizarro 8.00 3.20
❑ 648 Rich Folkers 25.00 10.00
Ted Martinez
John Matlack RC SP
❑ 649 Sparky Lyle SP 15.00 6.00
❑ 650 Rich Allen SP 30.00 12.00
❑ 651 Jerry Robertson SP 12.00 4.80
❑ 652 Atlanta Braves 12.00 4.80
Team Card
❑ 653 Russ Snyder SP 12.00 4.80
❑ 654 Don Shaw SP 12.00 4.80
❑ 655 Mike Epstein SP 12.00 4.80
❑ 656 Gerry Nyman SP 12.00 4.80
❑ 657 Jose Azcue 8.00 3.20
❑ 658 Paul Lindblad SP 12.00 4.80
❑ 659 Byron Browne SP 12.00 4.80
❑ 660 Ray Culp 8.00 3.20
❑ 661 Chuck Tanner MG SP 15.00 6.00
❑ 662 Mike Hedlund SP 12.00 4.80
❑ 663 Marv Staehle 8.00 3.20
❑ 664 Archie Reynolds 12.00 4.80
Bob Reynolds
Ken Reynolds SP
❑ 665 Ron Swoboda SP 15.00 6.00
❑ 666 Gene Brabender SP 12.00 4.80
❑ 667 Pete Ward 8.00 3.20
❑ 668 Gary Neibauer 8.00 3.20
❑ 669 Ike Brown SP 12.00 4.80
❑ 670 Bill Hands 8.00 3.20
❑ 671 Bill Voss SP 12.00 4.80
❑ 672 Ed Crosby SP 12.00 4.80
❑ 673 Gerry Janeski SP 12.00 4.80
❑ 674 Montreal Expos 12.00 4.80
Team Card
❑ 675 Dave Boswell 8.00 3.20
❑ 676 Tommie Reynolds 8.00 3.20
❑ 677 Jack DiLauro SP 12.00 4.80
❑ 678 George Thomas 8.00 3.20
❑ 679 Don O'Riley 8.00 3.20
❑ 680 Don Mincher SP 12.00 4.80
❑ 681 Bill Butler 8.00 3.20
❑ 682 Terry Harmon 8.00 3.20
❑ 683 Bill Burbach SP 12.00 4.80
❑ 684 Curt Motton 8.00 3.20
❑ 685 Moe Drabowsky 8.00 3.20
❑ 686 Chico Ruiz SP 12.00 4.80
❑ 687 Ron Taylor SP 12.00 4.80
❑ 688 S.Anderson MG SP 30.00 12.00
❑ 689 Frank Baker 8.00 3.20
❑ 690 Bob Moose 8.00 3.20
❑ 691 Bobby Heise 8.00 3.20
❑ 692 Hal Haydel 12.00 4.80
Rogelio Moret
Wayne Twitchell SP
❑ 693 Jose Pena SP 12.00 4.80
❑ 694 Rick Renick SP 12.00 4.80
❑ 695 Joe Niekro 12.00 4.80
❑ 696 Jerry Morales 8.00 3.20
❑ 697 Rickey Clark SP 12.00 4.80
❑ 698 M. Brewers SP 20.00 8.00
Team Card
❑ 699 Jim Britton 8.00 3.20
❑ 700 Boog Powell SP 25.00 10.00
❑ 701 Bob Garibaldi 8.00 3.20

❑ 702 Milt Ramirez 8.00 3.20
❑ 703 Mike Kekich 8.00 3.20
❑ 704 J.C. Martin SP 12.00 4.80
❑ 705 Dick Selma SP 12.00 4.80
❑ 706 Joe Foy SP 12.00 4.80
❑ 707 Fred Lasher 8.00 3.20
❑ 708 Russ Nagelson SP 12.00 4.80
❑ 709 Dusty Baker RC 80.00 32.00
Don Baylor RC
Tom Paciorek RC SP
❑ 710 Sonny Siebert 8.00 3.20
❑ 711 Larry Stahl SP 12.00 4.80
❑ 712 Jose Martinez 8.00 3.20
❑ 713 Mike Marshall SP 15.00 6.00
❑ 714 Dick Williams MG SP 15.00 6.00
❑ 715 Horace Clarke SP 15.00 6.00
❑ 716 Dave Leonhard 8.00 3.20
❑ 717 Tommie Aaron SP 12.00 4.80
❑ 718 Billy Wynne 8.00 3.20
❑ 719 Jerry May SP 12.00 4.80
❑ 720 Matty Alou 12.00 4.80
❑ 721 John Morris 8.00 3.20
❑ 722 Houston Astros SP 20.00 8.00
Team Card
❑ 723 Vicente Romo SP 12.00 4.80
❑ 724 Tom Tischinski SP 12.00 4.80
❑ 725 Gary Gentry SP 12.00 4.80
❑ 726 Paul Popovich 8.00 3.20
❑ 727 Ray Lamb SP 12.00 4.80
❑ 728 Wayne Redmond 8.00 3.20
Keith Lampard
Bernie Williams
❑ 729 Dick Billings 8.00 3.20
❑ 730 Jim Rooker 8.00 3.20
❑ 731 Jim Qualls SP 12.00 4.80
❑ 732 Bob Reed 8.00 3.20
❑ 733 Lee Maye SP 12.00 4.80
❑ 734 Rob Gardner SP 12.00 4.80
❑ 735 Mike Shannon SP 15.00 6.00
❑ 736 Mel Queen SP 12.00 4.80
❑ 737 P.Gomez SP MG 12.00 4.80
❑ 738 Russ Gibson SP 12.00 4.80
❑ 739 Barry Lersch SP 12.00 4.80
❑ 740 Luis Aparicio SP UER 30.00 12.00
(Led AL in steals
from 1965 to 1964,
should be 1956 to 1964)
❑ 741 Skip Guinn 8.00 3.20
❑ 742 Kansas City Royals 12.00 4.80
Team Card
❑ 743 John O'Donoghue SP 12.00 4.80
❑ 744 Chuck Manuel SP 12.00 4.80
❑ 745 Sandy Alomar SP 12.00 4.80
❑ 746 Andy Kosco 8.00 3.20
❑ 747 Al Severinsen 8.00 3.20
Scipio Spinks
Balor Moore
❑ 748 John Purdin SP 12.00 4.80
❑ 749 Ken Szotkiewicz 8.00 3.20
❑ 750 Denny McLain SP 25.00 10.00
❑ 751 Al Weis SP 15.00 6.00
❑ 752 Dick Drago 12.00 2.90

1972 Topps

	NM	Ex
COMPLETE SET (787)	1800.00	700.00
COMMON CARD (1-132)	.60	.24
COMMON (133-263)	1.00	.40
COMMON (264-394)	1.25	.50
COMMON (395-525)	1.50	.60
COMMON (526-656)	4.00	1.60
COMMON (657-787)	12.00	4.80
WRAPPER (10-CENT)	15.00	6.00

❑ 1 Pittsburgh Pirates 8.00 2.90
Team Card
❑ 2 Ray Culp .60 .24
❑ 3 Bob Tolan .60 .24
❑ 4 Checklist 1-132 6.00 1.20
❑ 5 John Bateman .60 .24
❑ 6 Fred Scherman .60 .24
❑ 7 Enzo Hernandez .60 .24
❑ 8 Ron Swoboda 1.25 .50
❑ 9 Stan Williams .60 .24
❑ 10 Amos Otis 1.25 .50
❑ 11 Bobby Valentine 1.25 .50
❑ 12 Jose Cardenal .60 .24
❑ 13 Joe Grzenda .60 .24
❑ 14 Pete Koegel .60 .24
Mike Anderson
Wayne Twitchell
❑ 15 Walt Williams .60 .24
❑ 16 Mike Jorgensen .60 .24
❑ 17 Dave Duncan 1.25 .50
❑ 18A Juan Pizarro .60 .24
(Yellow underline
C and S of Cubs)
❑ 18B Juan Pizarro 5.00 2.00
(Green underline
C and S of Cubs)
❑ 19 Billy Cowan .60 .24
❑ 20 Don Wilson .60 .24
❑ 21 Atlanta Braves 1.50 .60
Team Card
❑ 22 Rob Gardner .60 .24
❑ 23 Ted Kubiak .60 .24
❑ 24 Ted Ford .60 .24
❑ 25 Bill Singer .60 .24
❑ 26 Andy Etchebarren .60 .24
❑ 27 Bob Johnson .60 .24
❑ 28 Bob Gebhard .60 .24
Steve Brye
Hal Haydel
❑ 29A Bill Bonham .60 .24
(Yellow underline
C and S of Cubs)
❑ 29B Bill Bonham 5.00 2.00
(Green underline
C and S of Cubs)
❑ 30 Rico Petrocelli 1.25 .50
❑ 31 Cleon Jones 1.25 .50
❑ 32 Cleon Jones IA .60 .24
❑ 33 Billy Martin MG 4.00 1.60
❑ 34 Billy Martin IA 2.50 1.00
❑ 35 Jerry Johnson .60 .24
❑ 36 Jerry Johnson IA .60 .24
❑ 37 Carl Yastrzemski 10.00 4.00
❑ 38 Carl Yastrzemski IA 6.00 2.40
❑ 39 Bob Barton .60 .24
❑ 40 Bob Barton IA .60 .24
❑ 41 Tommy Davis 1.25 .50
❑ 42 Tommy Davis IA .60 .24
❑ 43 Rick Wise 1.25 .50
❑ 44 Rick Wise IA .60 .24
❑ 45A Glenn Beckert 1.25 .50
(Yellow underline
C and S of Cubs)
❑ 45B Glenn Beckert 5.00 2.00
(Green underline
C and S of Cubs)
❑ 46 Glenn Beckert IA .60 .24
❑ 47 John Ellis .60 .24
❑ 48 John Ellis IA .60 .24
❑ 49 Willie Mays 30.00 12.00
❑ 50 Willie Mays IA 14.00 5.50
❑ 51 Harmon Killebrew 7.00 2.80
❑ 52 Harmon Killebrew IA 4.00 1.60
❑ 53 Bud Harrelson 1.25 .50
❑ 54 Bud Harrelson IA .60 .24
❑ 55 Clyde Wright .60 .24
❑ 56 Rich Chiles .60 .24
❑ 57 Bob Oliver .60 .24
❑ 58 Ernie McAnally .60 .24
❑ 59 Fred Stanley .60 .24
❑ 60 Manny Sanguillen 1.25 .50
❑ 61 Burt Hooton RC 1.25 .50
Gene Hiser
Earl Stephenson
❑ 62 Angel Mangual .60 .24
❑ 63 Duke Sims .60 .24
❑ 64 Pete Broberg .60 .24
❑ 65 Cesar Cedeno 1.25 .50
❑ 66 Ray Corbin .60 .24
❑ 67 Red Schoendienst MG 2.50 1.00
❑ 68 Jim York .60 .24
❑ 69 Roger Freed .60 .24
❑ 70 Mike Cuellar 1.25 .50
❑ 71 California Angels 1.50 .60
Team Card
❑ 72 Bruce Kison RC .60 .24
❑ 73 Steve Huntz .60 .24
❑ 74 Cecil Upshaw .60 .24
❑ 75 Bert Campaneris 1.25 .50
❑ 76 Don Carrithers .60 .24
❑ 77 Ron Theobald .60 .24
❑ 78 Steve Arlin .60 .24
❑ 79 Mike Garman 50.00 20.00
Cecil Cooper RC
Carlton Fisk RC
❑ 80 Tony Perez 4.00 1.60
❑ 81 Mike Hedlund .60 .24
❑ 82 Ron Woods .60 .24
❑ 83 Dalton Jones .60 .24
❑ 84 Vince Colbert .60 .24
❑ 85 Joe Torre 2.50 1.00
Ralph Garr
Glenn Beckert LL
❑ 86 Tony Oliva 2.50 1.00
Bobby Murcer
Merv Rettenmund LL
❑ 87 Joe Torre 4.00 1.60
Willie Stargell
Hank Aaron LL
❑ 88 Harmon Killebrew 4.00 1.60
Frank Robinson
Reggie Smith LL
❑ 89 Willie Stargell 2.50 1.00
Hank Aaron
Lee May LL
❑ 90 Bill Melton 2.50 1.00
Norm Cash
Reggie Jackson LL
❑ 91 Tom Seaver 2.50 1.00
Dave Roberts UER
(Photo actually
Danny Coombs)
Don Wilson LL
❑ 92 Vida Blue 2.50 1.00
Wilbur Wood
Jim Palmer LL
❑ 93 Fergie Jenkins 4.00 1.60
Steve Carlton
Al Downing
Tom Seaver LL
❑ 94 Mickey Lolich 2.50 1.00
Vida Blue
Wilbur Wood LL
❑ 95 Tom Seaver 4.00 1.60
Fergie Jenkins
Bill Stoneman LL
❑ 96 Mickey Lolich 2.50 1.00
Vida Blue
Joe Coleman LL
❑ 97 Tom Kelley .60 .24
❑ 98 Chuck Tanner MG 1.25 .50
❑ 99 Ross Grimsley .60 .24
❑ 100 Frank Robinson 8.00 3.20
❑ 101 Bill Greif 2.50 1.00
J.R. Richard RC
Ray Busse
❑ 102 Lloyd Allen .60 .24
❑ 103 Checklist 133-263 6.00 1.20
❑ 104 Toby Harrah RC 1.25 .50
❑ 105 Gary Gentry .60 .24
❑ 106 Milwaukee Brewers 1.50 .60
Team Card
❑ 107 Jose Cruz RC 1.25 .50
❑ 108 Gary Waslewski .60 .24
❑ 109 Jerry May .60 .24

❑ 110 Ron Hunt .60 .24
❑ 111 Jim Grant .60 .24
❑ 112 Greg Luzinski 1.25 .50
❑ 113 Rogelio Moret .60 .24
❑ 114 Bill Buckner 1.25 .50
❑ 115 Jim Fregosi 1.25 .50
❑ 116 Ed Farmer .60 .24
❑ 117A Cleo James .60 .24
(Yellow underline
C and S of Cubs)
❑ 117B Cleo James 5.00 2.00
(Green underline
C and S of Cubs)
❑ 118 Skip Lockwood .60 .24
❑ 119 Marty Perez .60 .24
❑ 120 Bill Freehan 1.25 .50
❑ 121 Ed Sprague .60 .24
❑ 122 Larry Biittner .60 .24
❑ 123 Ed Acosta .60 .24
❑ 124 Alan Closter .60 .24
Rusty Torres
Roger Hambright
❑ 125 Dave Cash 1.25 .50
❑ 126 Bart Johnson .60 .24
❑ 127 Duffy Dyer .60 .24
❑ 128 Eddie Watt .60 .24
❑ 129 Charlie Fox MG .60 .24
❑ 130 Bob Gibson 8.00 3.20
❑ 131 Jim Nettles .60 .24
❑ 132 Joe Morgan 6.00 2.40
❑ 133 Joe Keough 1.00 .40
❑ 134 Carl Morton 1.00 .40
❑ 135 Vada Pinson 2.00 .80
❑ 136 Darrel Chaney 1.00 .40
❑ 137 Dick Williams MG 2.00 .80
❑ 138 Mike Kekich 1.00 .40
❑ 139 Tim McCarver 2.00 .80
❑ 140 Pat Dobson 2.00 .80
❑ 141 Buzz Capra 2.00 .80
Lee Stanton
Jon Matlack
❑ 142 Chris Chambliss RC 4.00 1.60
❑ 143 Garry Jestadt 1.00 .40
❑ 144 Marty Pattin 1.00 .40
❑ 145 Don Kessinger 2.00 .80
❑ 146 Steve Kealey 1.00 .40
❑ 147 Dave Kingman RC 6.00 2.40
❑ 148 Dick Billings 1.00 .40
❑ 149 Gary Neibauer 1.00 .40
❑ 150 Norm Cash 2.00 .80
❑ 151 Jim Brewer 1.00 .40
❑ 152 Gene Clines 1.00 .40
❑ 153 Rick Auerbach 1.00 .40
❑ 154 Ted Simmons 4.00 1.60
❑ 155 Larry Dierker 1.00 .40
❑ 156 Minnesota Twins 2.00 .80
Team Card
❑ 157 Don Gullett 1.00 .40
❑ 158 Jerry Kenney 1.00 .40
❑ 159 John Boccabella 1.00 .40
❑ 160 Andy Messersmith 2.00 .80
❑ 161 Brock Davis 1.00 .40
❑ 162 Jerry Bell 2.00 .80
Darrell Porter RC
Bob Reynolds UER
(Porter and Bell
photos switched)
❑ 163 Tug McGraw 4.00 1.60
❑ 164 Tug McGraw IA 2.00 .80
❑ 165 Chris Speier RC 2.00 .80
❑ 166 Chris Speier IA 1.00 .40
❑ 167 Deron Johnson 1.00 .40
❑ 168 Deron Johnson IA 1.00 .40
❑ 169 Vida Blue 4.00 1.60
❑ 170 Vida Blue IA 2.00 .80
❑ 171 Darrell Evans 4.00 1.60
❑ 172 Darrell Evans IA 2.00 .80
❑ 173 Clay Kirby 1.00 .40
❑ 174 Clay Kirby IA 1.00 .40
❑ 175 Tom Haller 1.00 .40
❑ 176 Tom Haller IA 1.00 .40
❑ 177 Paul Schaal 1.00 .40
❑ 178 Paul Schaal IA 1.00 .40
❑ 179 Dock Ellis 1.00 .40
❑ 180 Dock Ellis IA 1.00 .40
❑ 181 Ed Kranepool 2.00 .80
❑ 182 Ed Kranepool IA 1.00 .40
❑ 183 Bill Melton 1.00 .40
❑ 184 Bill Melton IA 1.00 .40
❑ 185 Ron Bryant 1.00 .40
❑ 186 Ron Bryant IA 1.00 .40
❑ 187 Gates Brown 1.00 .40
❑ 188 Frank Lucchesi MG 1.00 .40
❑ 189 Gene Tenace 2.00 .80
❑ 190 Dave Giusti 1.00 .40
❑ 191 Jeff Burroughs RC 4.00 1.60
❑ 192 Chicago Cubs 2.00 .80
Team Card
❑ 193 Kurt Bevacqua 1.00 .40
❑ 194 Fred Norman 1.00 .40
❑ 195 Orlando Cepeda 6.00 2.40
❑ 196 Mel Queen 1.00 .40
❑ 197 Johnny Briggs 1.00 .40
❑ 198 Charlie Hough RC 6.00 2.40
Bob O'Brien
Mike Strahler
❑ 199 Mike Fiore 1.00 .40
❑ 200 Lou Brock 7.00 2.80
❑ 201 Phil Roof 1.00 .40
❑ 202 Scipio Spinks 1.00 .40
❑ 203 Ron Blomberg 1.00 .40
❑ 204 Tommy Helms 1.00 .40
❑ 205 Dick Drago 1.00 .40
❑ 206 Dal Maxvill 1.00 .40
❑ 207 Tom Egan 1.00 .40
❑ 208 Milt Pappas 2.00 .80
❑ 209 Joe Rudi 2.00 .80
❑ 210 Denny McLain 2.00 .80
❑ 211 Gary Sutherland 1.00 .40
❑ 212 Grant Jackson 1.00 .40
❑ 213 Billy Parker 1.00 .40
Art Kusnyer
Tom Silverio
❑ 214 Mike McQueen 1.00 .40
❑ 215 Alex Johnson 2.00 .80
❑ 216 Joe Niekro 2.00 .80
❑ 217 Roger Metzger 1.00 .40
❑ 218 Eddie Kasko MG 1.00 .40
❑ 219 Rennie Stennett 2.00 .80
❑ 220 Jim Perry 2.00 .80
❑ 221 NL Playoffs 2.00 .80
Bucs champs
❑ 222 Br. Robinson ALCS 4.00 1.60
❑ 223 Dave McNally WS 2.00 .80
❑ 224 Dave Johnson WS 2.00 .80
Mark Belanger
❑ 225 Manny Sanguillen WS 2.00 .80
❑ 226 Roberto Clemente WS 8.00 3.20
❑ 227 Nellie Briles WS 2.00 .80
❑ 228 Frank Robinson WS 2.00 .80
Manny Sanguillen
❑ 229 Steve Blass WS 2.00 .80
❑ 230 WS Summary 2.00 .80
Pirates celebrate
❑ 231 Casey Cox 1.00 .40
❑ 232 Chris Arnold 1.00 .40
Jim Barr
Dave Rader
❑ 233 Jay Johnstone 2.00 .80
❑ 234 Ron Taylor 1.00 .40
❑ 235 Merv Rettenmund 1.00 .40
❑ 236 Jim McGlothlin 1.00 .40
❑ 237 New York Yankees 2.00 .80
Team Card
❑ 238 Leron Lee 1.00 .40
❑ 239 Tom Timmermann 1.00 .40
❑ 240 Rich Allen 2.00 .80
❑ 241 Rollie Fingers 6.00 2.40
❑ 242 Don Mincher 1.00 .40
❑ 243 Frank Linzy 1.00 .40
❑ 244 Steve Braun 1.00 .40
❑ 245 Tommie Agee 2.00 .80
❑ 246 Tom Burgmeier 1.00 .40
❑ 247 Milt May 1.00 .40
❑ 248 Tom Bradley 1.00 .40
❑ 249 Harry Walker MG 1.00 .40
❑ 250 Boog Powell 2.00 .80
❑ 251 Checklist 264-394 6.00 1.20
❑ 252 Ken Reynolds 1.00 .40
❑ 253 Sandy Alomar 2.00 .80
❑ 254 Boots Day 1.00 .40
❑ 255 Jim Lonborg 2.00 .80
❑ 256 George Foster 2.00 .80
❑ 257 Jim Foor 1.00 .40
Tim Hosley
Paul Jata
❑ 258 Randy Hundley 1.00 .40
❑ 259 Sparky Lyle 2.00 .80
❑ 260 Ralph Garr 2.00 .80
❑ 261 Steve Mingori 1.00 .40
❑ 262 San Diego Padres 2.00 .80
Team Card
❑ 263 Felipe Alou 2.00 .80
❑ 264 Tommy John 2.00 .80
❑ 265 Wes Parker 2.00 .80
❑ 266 Bobby Bolin 1.25 .50
❑ 267 Dave Concepcion 4.00 1.60
❑ 268 Dwain Anderson 1.25 .50
Chris Floethe
❑ 269 Don Hahn 1.25 .50
❑ 270 Jim Palmer 8.00 3.20
❑ 271 Ken Rudolph 1.25 .50
❑ 272 Mickey Rivers RC 2.00 .80
❑ 273 Bobby Floyd 1.25 .50
❑ 274 Al Severinsen 1.25 .50
❑ 275 Cesar Tovar 1.25 .50
❑ 276 Gene Mauch MG 2.00 .80
❑ 277 Elliott Maddox 1.25 .50
❑ 278 Dennis Higgins 1.25 .50
❑ 279 Larry Brown 1.25 .50
❑ 280 Willie McCovey 7.00 2.80
❑ 281 Bill Parsons 1.25 .50
❑ 282 Houston Astros 2.00 .80
Team Card
❑ 283 Darrell Brandon 1.25 .50
❑ 284 Ike Brown 1.25 .50
❑ 285 Gaylord Perry 6.00 2.40
❑ 286 Gene Alley 1.25 .50
❑ 287 Jim Hardin 1.25 .50
❑ 288 Johnny Jeter 1.25 .50
❑ 289 Syd O'Brien 1.25 .50
❑ 290 Sonny Siebert 1.25 .50
❑ 291 Hal McRae 2.00 .80
❑ 292 Hal McRae IA 1.25 .50
❑ 293 Dan Frisella 1.25 .50
❑ 294 Dan Frisella IA 1.25 .50
❑ 295 Dick Dietz 1.25 .50
❑ 296 Dick Dietz IA 1.25 .50
❑ 297 Claude Osteen 2.00 .80
❑ 298 Claude Osteen IA 1.25 .50
❑ 299 Hank Aaron 40.00 16.00
❑ 300 Hank Aaron IA 20.00 8.00
❑ 301 George Mitterwald 1.25 .50
❑ 302 George Mitterwald IA 1.25 .50
❑ 303 Joe Pepitone 2.00 .80
❑ 304 Joe Pepitone IA 1.25 .50
❑ 305 Ken Boswell 1.25 .50
❑ 306 Ken Boswell IA 1.25 .50
❑ 307 Steve Renko 1.25 .50
❑ 308 Steve Renko IA 1.25 .50
❑ 309 Roberto Clemente 50.00 20.00
❑ 310 Roberto Clemente IA 30.00 12.00
❑ 311 Clay Carroll 1.25 .50
❑ 312 Clay Carroll IA 1.25 .50
❑ 313 Luis Aparicio 6.00 2.40
❑ 314 Luis Aparicio IA 2.00 .80
❑ 315 Paul Splittorff 1.25 .50
❑ 316 Jim Bibby 2.00 .80
Jorge Roque
Santiago Guzman
❑ 317 Rich Hand 1.25 .50
❑ 318 Sonny Jackson 1.25 .50
❑ 319 Aurelio Rodriguez 1.25 .50
❑ 320 Steve Blass 2.00 .80
❑ 321 Joe Lahoud 1.25 .50
❑ 322 Jose Pena 1.25 .50
❑ 323 Earl Weaver MG 4.00 1.60
❑ 324 Mike Ryan 1.25 .50
❑ 325 Mel Stottlemyre 2.00 .80
❑ 326 Pat Kelly 1.25 .50
❑ 327 Steve Stone RC 2.00 .80
❑ 328 Boston Red Sox 2.00 .80
Team Card
❑ 329 Roy Foster 1.25 .50
❑ 330 Jim Hunter 6.00 2.40
❑ 331 Stan Swanson 1.25 .50
❑ 332 Buck Martinez 1.25 .50
❑ 333 Steve Barber 1.25 .50

❑ 334 Bill Fahey 1.25 .50
Jim Mason
Tom Ragland
❑ 335 Bill Hands 1.25 .50
❑ 336 Marty Martinez 1.25 .50
❑ 337 Mike Kilkenny 1.25 .50
❑ 338 Bob Grich 2.00 .80
❑ 339 Ron Cook 1.25 .50
❑ 340 Roy White 2.00 .80
❑ 341 Joe Torre KP 1.25 .50
❑ 342 Wilbur Wood KP 1.25 .50
❑ 343 Willie Stargell KP 2.00 .80
❑ 344 Dave McNally KP 1.25 .50
❑ 345 Rick Wise KP 1.25 .50
❑ 346 Jim Fregosi KP 1.25 .50
❑ 347 Tom Seaver KP 4.00 1.60
❑ 348 Sal Bando KP 1.25 .50
❑ 349 Al Fitzmorris 1.25 .50
❑ 350 Frank Howard 2.00 .80
❑ 351 Tom House 2.00 .80
Rick Kester
Jimmy Britton
❑ 352 Dave LaRoche 1.25 .50
❑ 353 Art Shamsky 1.25 .50
❑ 354 Tom Murphy 1.25 .50
❑ 355 Bob Watson 2.00 .80
❑ 356 Gerry Moses 1.25 .50
❑ 357 Woody Fryman 1.25 .50
❑ 358 Sparky Anderson MG 4.00 1.60
❑ 359 Don Pavletich 1.25 .50
❑ 360 Dave Roberts 1.25 .50
❑ 361 Mike Andrews 1.25 .50
❑ 362 New York Mets 2.00 .80
Team Card
❑ 363 Ron Klimkowski 1.25 .50
❑ 364 Johnny Callison 2.00 .80
❑ 365 Dick Bosman 2.00 .80
❑ 366 Jimmy Rosario 1.25 .50
❑ 367 Ron Perranoski 1.25 .50
❑ 368 Danny Thompson 1.25 .50
❑ 369 Jim Lefebvre 2.00 .80
❑ 370 Don Buford 1.25 .50
❑ 371 Denny Lemaster 1.25 .50
❑ 372 Lance Clemons 1.25 .50
Monty Montgomery
❑ 373 John Mayberry 2.00 .80
❑ 374 Jack Heidemann 1.25 .50
❑ 375 Reggie Cleveland 1.25 .50
❑ 376 Andy Kosco 1.25 .50
❑ 377 Terry Harmon 1.25 .50
❑ 378 Checklist 395-525 6.00 1.20
❑ 379 Ken Berry 1.25 .50
❑ 380 Earl Williams 1.25 .50
❑ 381 Chicago White Sox 2.00 .80
Team Card
❑ 382 Joe Gibbon 1.25 .50
❑ 383 Brant Alyea 1.25 .50
❑ 384 Dave Campbell 2.00 .80
❑ 385 Mickey Stanley 2.00 .80
❑ 386 Jim Colborn 1.25 .50
❑ 387 Horace Clarke 2.00 .80
❑ 388 Charlie Williams 1.25 .50
❑ 389 Bill Rigney MG 1.25 .50
❑ 390 Willie Davis 2.00 .80
❑ 391 Ken Sanders 1.25 .50
❑ 392 Fred Cambria 2.00 .80
Richie Zisk RC
❑ 393 Curt Motton 1.25 .50
❑ 394 Ken Forsch 2.00 .80
❑ 395 Matty Alou 2.00 .80
❑ 396 Paul Lindblad 1.50 .60
❑ 397 Philadelphia Phillies 2.00 .80
Team Card
❑ 398 Larry Hisle 2.00 .80
❑ 399 Milt Wilcox 2.00 .80
❑ 400 Tony Oliva 4.00 1.60
❑ 401 Jim Nash 1.50 .60
❑ 402 Bobby Heise 1.50 .60
❑ 403 John Cumberland 1.50 .60
❑ 404 Jeff Torborg 2.00 .80
❑ 405 Ron Fairly 2.00 .80
❑ 406 George Hendrick RC 2.00 .80
❑ 407 Chuck Taylor 1.50 .60
❑ 408 Jim Northrup 2.00 .80
❑ 409 Frank Baker 1.50 .60
❑ 410 Ferguson Jenkins 6.00 2.40
❑ 411 Bob Montgomery 1.50 .60
❑ 412 Dick Kelley 1.50 .60
❑ 413 Don Eddy 1.50 .60
Dave Lemonds
❑ 414 Bob Miller 1.50 .60
❑ 415 Cookie Rojas 2.00 .80
❑ 416 Johnny Edwards 1.50 .60
❑ 417 Tom Hall 1.50 .60
❑ 418 Tom Shopay 1.50 .60
❑ 419 Jim Spencer 1.50 .60
❑ 420 Steve Carlton 18.00 7.25
❑ 421 Ellie Rodriguez 1.50 .60
❑ 422 Ray Lamb 1.50 .60
❑ 423 Oscar Gamble 2.00 .80
❑ 424 Bill Gogolewski 1.50 .60
❑ 425 Ken Singleton 2.00 .80
❑ 426 Ken Singleton IA 1.50 .60
❑ 427 Tito Fuentes 1.50 .60
❑ 428 Tito Fuentes IA 1.50 .60
❑ 429 Bob Robertson 1.50 .60
❑ 430 Bob Robertson IA 1.50 .60
❑ 431 Clarence Gaston 2.00 .80
❑ 432 Clarence Gaston IA 2.00 .80
❑ 433 Johnny Bench 25.00 10.00
❑ 434 Johnny Bench IA 15.00 6.00
❑ 435 Reggie Jackson 30.00 12.00
❑ 436 Reggie Jackson IA 12.00 4.80
❑ 437 Maury Wills 2.00 .80
❑ 438 Maury Wills IA 2.00 .80
❑ 439 Billy Williams 6.00 2.40
❑ 440 Billy Williams IA 4.00 1.60
❑ 441 Thurman Munson 15.00 6.00
❑ 442 Thurman Munson IA 8.00 3.20
❑ 443 Ken Henderson 1.50 .60
❑ 444 Ken Henderson IA 1.50 .60
❑ 445 Tom Seaver 30.00 12.00
❑ 446 Tom Seaver IA 15.00 6.00
❑ 447 Willie Stargell 8.00 3.20
❑ 448 Willie Stargell IA 4.00 1.60
❑ 449 Bob Lemon MG 2.00 .80
❑ 450 Mickey Lolich 2.00 .80
❑ 451 Tony LaRussa 4.00 1.60
❑ 452 Ed Herrmann 1.50 .60
❑ 453 Barry Lersch 1.50 .60
❑ 454 Oakland A's 2.00 .80
Team Card
❑ 455 Tommy Harper 2.00 .80
❑ 456 Mark Belanger 2.00 .80
❑ 457 Darcy Fast 1.50 .60
Derrel Thomas
Mike Ivie
❑ 458 Aurelio Monteagudo 1.50 .60
❑ 459 Rick Renick 1.50 .60
❑ 460 Al Downing 1.50 .60
❑ 461 Tim Cullen 1.50 .60
❑ 462 Rickey Clark 1.50 .60
❑ 463 Bernie Carbo 1.50 .60
❑ 464 Jim Roland 1.50 .60
❑ 465 Gil Hodges MG 4.00 1.60
❑ 466 Norm Miller 1.50 .60
❑ 467 Steve Kline 1.50 .60
❑ 468 Richie Scheinblum 1.50 .60
❑ 469 Ron Herbel 1.50 .60
❑ 470 Ray Fosse 1.50 .60
❑ 471 Luke Walker 1.50 .60
❑ 472 Phil Gagliano 1.50 .60
❑ 473 Dan McGinn 1.50 .60
❑ 474 Don Baylor 15.00 6.00
Roric Harrison
Johnny Oates RC
❑ 475 Gary Nolan 2.00 .80
❑ 476 Lee Richard 1.50 .60
❑ 477 Tom Phoebus 1.50 .60
❑ 478 Checklist 526-656 6.00 1.20
❑ 479 Don Shaw 1.50 .60
❑ 480 Lee May 2.00 .80
❑ 481 Billy Conigliaro 2.00 .80
❑ 482 Joe Hoerner 1.50 .60
❑ 483 Ken Suarez 1.50 .60
❑ 484 Lum Harris MG 1.50 .60
❑ 485 Phil Regan 2.00 .80
❑ 486 John Lowenstein 1.50 .60
❑ 487 Detroit Tigers 2.00 .80
Team Card
❑ 488 Mike Nagy 1.50 .60
❑ 489 Terry Humphrey 1.50 .60
Keith Lampard
❑ 490 Dave McNally 2.00 .80
❑ 491 Lou Piniella KP 2.00 .80
❑ 492 Mel Stottlemyre KP 2.00 .80
❑ 493 Bob Bailey KP 2.00 .80
❑ 494 Willie Horton KP 2.00 .80
❑ 495 Bill Melton KP 2.00 .80
❑ 496 Bud Harrelson KP 2.00 .80
❑ 497 Jim Perry KP 2.00 .80
❑ 498 Brooks Robinson KP 4.00 1.60
❑ 499 Vicente Romo 1.50 .60
❑ 500 Joe Torre 4.00 1.60
❑ 501 Pete Hamm 1.50 .60
❑ 502 Jackie Hernandez 1.50 .60
❑ 503 Gary Peters 1.50 .60
❑ 504 Ed Spiezio 1.50 .60
❑ 505 Mike Marshall 2.00 .80
❑ 506 Terry Ley 1.50 .60
Jim Moyer
Dick Tidrow RC
❑ 507 Fred Gladding 1.50 .60
❑ 508 Elrod Hendricks 1.50 .60
❑ 509 Don McMahon 1.50 .60
❑ 510 Ted Williams MG 12.00 4.80
❑ 511 Tony Taylor 2.00 .80
❑ 512 Paul Popovich 1.50 .60
❑ 513 Lindy McDaniel 2.00 .80
❑ 514 Ted Sizemore 1.50 .60
❑ 515 Bert Blyleven 4.00 1.60
❑ 516 Oscar Brown 1.50 .60
❑ 517 Ken Brett 1.50 .60
❑ 518 Wayne Garrett 1.50 .60
❑ 519 Ted Abernathy 1.50 .60
❑ 520 Larry Bowa 2.00 .80
❑ 521 Alan Foster 1.50 .60
❑ 522 Los Angeles Dodgers 2.00 .80
Team Card
❑ 523 Chuck Dobson 1.50 .60
❑ 524 Ed Armbrister 1.50 .60
Mel Behney
❑ 525 Carlos May 2.00 .80
❑ 526 Bob Bailey 6.00 2.40
❑ 527 Dave Leonhard 4.00 1.60
❑ 528 Ron Stone 4.00 1.60
❑ 529 Dave Nelson 6.00 2.40
❑ 530 Don Sutton 12.00 4.80
❑ 531 Freddie Patek 6.00 2.40
❑ 532 Fred Kendall 4.00 1.60
❑ 533 Ralph Houk MG 6.00 2.40
❑ 534 Jim Hickman 6.00 2.40
❑ 535 Ed Brinkman 4.00 1.60
❑ 536 Doug Rader 6.00 2.40
❑ 537 Bob Locker 4.00 1.60
❑ 538 Charlie Sands 4.00 1.60
❑ 539 Terry Forster RC 6.00 2.40
❑ 540 Felix Millan 4.00 1.60
❑ 541 Roger Repoz 4.00 1.60
❑ 542 Jack Billingham 4.00 1.60
❑ 543 Duane Josephson 4.00 1.60
❑ 544 Ted Martinez 4.00 1.60
❑ 545 Wayne Granger 4.00 1.60
❑ 546 Joe Hague 4.00 1.60
❑ 547 Cleveland Indians 8.00 3.20
Team Card
❑ 548 Frank Reberger 4.00 1.60
❑ 549 Dave May 4.00 1.60
❑ 550 Brooks Robinson 25.00 10.00
❑ 551 Ollie Brown 4.00 1.60
❑ 552 Ollie Brown IA 4.00 1.60
❑ 553 Wilbur Wood 6.00 2.40
❑ 554 Wilbur Wood IA 4.00 1.60
❑ 555 Ron Santo 8.00 3.20
❑ 556 Ron Santo IA 6.00 2.40
❑ 557 John Odom 4.00 1.60
❑ 558 John Odom IA 4.00 1.60
❑ 559 Pete Rose 50.00 20.00
❑ 560 Pete Rose IA 20.00 8.00
❑ 561 Leo Cardenas 4.00 1.60
❑ 562 Leo Cardenas IA 4.00 1.60
❑ 563 Ray Sadecki 4.00 1.60
❑ 564 Ray Sadecki IA 4.00 1.60
❑ 565 Reggie Smith 6.00 2.40
❑ 566 Reggie Smith IA 4.00 1.60
❑ 567 Juan Marichal 12.00 4.80
❑ 568 Juan Marichal IA 6.00 2.40
❑ 569 Ed Kirkpatrick 4.00 1.60

❑	No.	Card	NM	Ex
❑	570	Ed Kirkpatrick IA	4.00	1.60
❑	571	Nate Colbert	4.00	1.60
❑	572	Nate Colbert IA	4.00	1.60
❑	573	Fritz Peterson	4.00	1.60
❑	574	Fritz Peterson IA	4.00	1.60
❑	575	Al Oliver	8.00	3.20
❑	576	Leo Durocher MG	6.00	2.40
❑	577	Mike Paul	6.00	2.40
❑	578	Billy Grabarkewitz	4.00	1.60
❑	579	Doyle Alexander RC	6.00	2.40
❑	580	Lou Piniella	6.00	2.40
❑	581	Wade Blasingame	4.00	1.60
❑	582	Montreal Expos	8.00	3.20
		Team Card		
❑	583	Darold Knowles	4.00	1.60
❑	584	Jerry McNertney	4.00	1.60
❑	585	George Scott	6.00	2.40
❑	586	Denis Menke	4.00	1.60
❑	587	Billy Wilson	4.00	1.60
❑	588	Jim Holt	4.00	1.60
❑	589	Hal Lanier	4.00	1.60
❑	590	Graig Nettles	8.00	3.20
❑	591	Paul Casanova	4.00	1.60
❑	592	Lew Krausse	4.00	1.60
❑	593	Rich Morales	4.00	1.60
❑	594	Jim Beauchamp	4.00	1.60
❑	595	Nolan Ryan	100.00	40.00
❑	596	Manny Mota	6.00	2.40
❑	597	Jim Magnuson	4.00	1.60
❑	598	Hal King	6.00	2.40
❑	599	Billy Champion	4.00	1.60
❑	600	Al Kaline	25.00	10.00
❑	601	George Stone	4.00	1.60
❑	602	Dave Bristol MG	4.00	1.60
❑	603	Jim Ray	4.00	1.60
❑	604A	Checklist 657-787	12.00	2.40
		(Copyright on back		
		bottom right)		
❑	604B	Checklist 657-787	12.00	2.40
		(Copyright on back		
		bottom left)		
❑	605	Nelson Briles	6.00	2.40
❑	606	Luis Melendez	4.00	1.60
❑	607	Frank Duffy	4.00	1.60
❑	608	Mike Corkins	4.00	1.60
❑	609	Tom Grieve	6.00	2.40
❑	610	Bill Stoneman	6.00	2.40
❑	611	Rich Reese	4.00	1.60
❑	612	Joe Decker	4.00	1.60
❑	613	Mike Ferraro	4.00	1.60
❑	614	Ted Uhlaender	4.00	1.60
❑	615	Steve Hargan	4.00	1.60
❑	616	Joe Ferguson RC	6.00	2.40
❑	617	Kansas City Royals	8.00	3.20
		Team Card		
❑	618	Rich Robertson	4.00	1.60
❑	619	Rich McKinney	4.00	1.60
❑	620	Phil Niekro	12.00	4.80
❑	621	Comm. Award	8.00	3.20
❑	622	MVP Award	8.00	3.20
❑	623	Cy Young Award	8.00	3.20
❑	624	Minor League Player	8.00	3.20
		of the Year		
❑	625	Rookie of the Year	8.00	3.20
❑	626	Babe Ruth Award	8.00	3.20
❑	627	Moe Drabowsky	4.00	1.60
❑	628	Terry Crowley	4.00	1.60
❑	629	Paul Doyle	4.00	1.60
❑	630	Rich Hebner	6.00	2.40
❑	631	John Strohmayer	4.00	1.60
❑	632	Mike Hegan	4.00	1.60
❑	633	Jack Hiatt	4.00	1.60
❑	634	Dick Woodson	4.00	1.60
❑	635	Don Money	6.00	2.40
❑	636	Bill Lee	6.00	2.40
❑	637	Preston Gomez MG	4.00	1.60
❑	638	Ken Wright	4.00	1.60
❑	639	J.C. Martin	4.00	1.60
❑	640	Joe Coleman	4.00	1.60
❑	641	Mike Lum	4.00	1.60
❑	642	Dennis Riddleberger	4.00	1.60
❑	643	Russ Gibson	4.00	1.60
❑	644	Bernie Allen	4.00	1.60
❑	645	Jim Maloney	6.00	2.40
❑	646	Chico Salmon	4.00	1.60
❑	647	Bob Moose	4.00	1.60

❑	No.	Card	NM	Ex
❑	648	Jim Lyttle	4.00	1.60
❑	649	Pete Richert	4.00	1.60
❑	650	Sal Bando	6.00	2.40
❑	651	Cincinnati Reds	8.00	3.20
		Team Card		
❑	652	Marcelino Lopez	4.00	1.60
❑	653	Jim Fairey	4.00	1.60
❑	654	Horacio Pina	6.00	2.40
❑	655	Jerry Grote	4.00	1.60
❑	656	Rudy May	4.00	1.60
❑	657	Bobby Wine	12.00	4.80
❑	658	Steve Dunning	12.00	4.80
❑	659	Bob Aspromonte	12.00	4.80
❑	660	Paul Blair	15.00	6.00
❑	661	Bill Virdon MG	12.00	4.80
❑	662	Stan Bahnsen	12.00	4.80
❑	663	Fran Healy	15.00	6.00
❑	664	Bobby Knoop	12.00	4.80
❑	665	Chris Short	12.00	4.80
❑	666	Hector Torres	12.00	4.80
❑	667	Ray Newman	12.00	4.80
❑	668	Texas Rangers	30.00	12.00
		Team Card		
❑	669	Willie Crawford	12.00	4.80
❑	670	Ken Holtzman	15.00	6.00
❑	671	Donn Clendenon	15.00	6.00
❑	672	Archie Reynolds	12.00	4.80
❑	673	Dave Marshall	12.00	4.80
❑	674	John Kennedy	12.00	4.80
❑	675	Pat Jarvis	12.00	4.80
❑	676	Danny Cater	12.00	4.80
❑	677	Ivan Murrell	12.00	4.80
❑	678	Steve Luebber	12.00	4.80
❑	679	Bob Fenwick	12.00	4.80
		Bob Stinson		
❑	680	Dave Johnson	15.00	6.00
❑	681	Bobby Pfeil	12.00	4.80
❑	682	Mike McCormick	15.00	6.00
❑	683	Steve Hovley	12.00	4.80
❑	684	Hal Breeden	12.00	4.80
❑	685	Joel Horlen	12.00	4.80
❑	686	Steve Garvey	40.00	16.00
❑	687	Del Unser	12.00	4.80
❑	688	St. Louis Cardinals	20.00	8.00
		Team Card		
❑	689	Eddie Fisher	12.00	4.80
❑	690	Willie Montanez	15.00	6.00
❑	691	Curt Blefary	12.00	4.80
❑	692	Curt Blefary IA	12.00	4.80
❑	693	Alan Gallagher	12.00	4.80
❑	694	Alan Gallagher IA	12.00	4.80
❑	695	Rod Carew	50.00	20.00
❑	696	Rod Carew IA	30.00	12.00
❑	697	Jerry Koosman	15.00	6.00
❑	698	Jerry Koosman IA	15.00	6.00
❑	699	Bobby Murcer	15.00	6.00
❑	700	Bobby Murcer IA	15.00	6.00
❑	701	Jose Pagan	12.00	4.80
❑	702	Jose Pagan IA	12.00	4.80
❑	703	Doug Griffin	12.00	4.80
❑	704	Doug Griffin IA	12.00	4.80
❑	705	Pat Corrales	15.00	6.00
❑	706	Pat Corrales IA	12.00	4.80
❑	707	Tim Foli	12.00	4.80
❑	708	Tim Foli IA	12.00	4.80
❑	709	Jim Kaat	15.00	6.00
❑	710	Jim Kaat IA	15.00	6.00
❑	711	Bobby Bonds	20.00	8.00
❑	712	Bobby Bonds IA	15.00	6.00
❑	713	Gene Michael	20.00	8.00
❑	714	Gene Michael IA	15.00	6.00
❑	715	Mike Epstein	12.00	4.80
❑	716	Jesus Alou	12.00	4.80
❑	717	Bruce Dal Canton	12.00	4.80
❑	718	Del Rice MG	12.00	4.80
❑	719	Cesar Geronimo	12.00	4.80
❑	720	Sam McDowell	15.00	6.00
❑	721	Eddie Leon	12.00	4.80
❑	722	Bill Sudakis	12.00	4.80
❑	723	Al Santorini	12.00	4.80
❑	724	John Curtis	12.00	4.80
		Rich Hinton		
		Mickey Scott RC		
❑	725	Dick McAuliffe	15.00	6.00
❑	726	Dick Selma	12.00	4.80
❑	727	Jose Laboy	12.00	4.80

❑	No.	Card	NM	Ex
❑	728	Gail Hopkins	12.00	4.80
❑	729	Bob Veale	15.00	6.00
❑	730	Rick Monday	15.00	6.00
❑	731	Baltimore Orioles	20.00	8.00
		Team Card		
❑	732	George Culver	12.00	4.80
❑	733	Jim Ray Hart	15.00	6.00
❑	734	Bob Burda	12.00	4.80
❑	735	Diego Segui	12.00	4.80
❑	736	Bill Russell	15.00	6.00
❑	737	Len Randle	15.00	6.00
❑	738	Jim Merritt	12.00	4.80
❑	739	Don Mason	12.00	4.80
❑	740	Rico Carty	15.00	6.00
❑	741	Tom Hutton	15.00	6.00
		John Milner		
		Rick Miller RC		
❑	742	Jim Rooker	12.00	4.80
❑	743	Cesar Gutierrez	12.00	4.80
❑	744	Jim Slaton	12.00	4.80
❑	745	Julian Javier	15.00	6.00
❑	746	Lowell Palmer	12.00	4.80
❑	747	Jim Stewart	12.00	4.80
❑	748	Phil Hennigan	12.00	4.80
❑	749	Walter Alston MG	20.00	8.00
❑	750	Willie Horton	15.00	6.00
❑	751	Steve Carlton TR	40.00	16.00
❑	752	Joe Morgan TR	45.00	18.00
❑	753	Denny McLain TR	20.00	8.00
❑	754	Frank Robinson TR	45.00	18.00
❑	755	Jim Fregosi TR	15.00	6.00
❑	756	Rick Wise TR	15.00	6.00
❑	757	Jose Cardenal TR	15.00	6.00
❑	758	Gil Garrido	12.00	4.80
❑	759	Chris Cannizzaro	12.00	4.80
❑	760	Bill Mazeroski	25.00	10.00
❑	761	Ben Oglivie RC	25.00	10.00
		Ron Cey RC		
		Bernie Williams		
❑	762	Wayne Simpson	12.00	4.80
❑	763	Ron Hansen	12.00	4.80
❑	764	Dusty Baker	20.00	8.00
❑	765	Ken McMullen	12.00	4.80
❑	766	Steve Hamilton	12.00	4.80
❑	767	Tom McCraw	15.00	6.00
❑	768	Denny Doyle	12.00	4.80
❑	769	Jack Aker	12.00	4.80
❑	770	Jim Wynn	15.00	6.00
❑	771	San Francisco Giants	20.00	8.00
		Team Card		
❑	772	Ken Tatum	12.00	4.80
❑	773	Ron Brand	12.00	4.80
❑	774	Luis Alvarado	12.00	4.80
❑	775	Jerry Reuss	15.00	6.00
❑	776	Bill Voss	12.00	4.80
❑	777	Hoyt Wilhelm	25.00	10.00
❑	778	Vic Albury	20.00	8.00
		Rick Dempsey RC		
		Jim Strickland		
❑	779	Tony Cloninger	12.00	4.80
❑	780	Dick Green	12.00	4.80
❑	781	Jim McAndrew	12.00	4.80
❑	782	Larry Stahl	12.00	4.80
❑	783	Les Cain	12.00	4.80
❑	784	Ken Aspromonte	12.00	4.80
❑	785	Vic Davalillo	12.00	4.80
❑	786	Chuck Brinkman	12.00	4.80
❑	787	Ron Reed	15.00	5.25

1973 Topps

	NM	Ex
COMPLETE SET (660)	700.00	275.00
COMMON CARD (1-264)	.50	.20
COMMON (265-396)	.75	.30
COMMON (397-528)	1.25	.50
COMMON (529-660)	3.50	1.40
WRAP. (10-CENT, BAT)	15.00	6.00
WRAPPER (10-CENT)	15.00	6.00

❑	No.	Card	NM	Ex
❑	1	Babe Ruth 714	40.00	11.50
		Hank Aaron 673		
		Willie Mays 654 ATL		
❑	2	Rich Hebner	1.50	.60
❑	3	Jim Lonborg	1.50	.60

❑ 4	John Milner	.50	.20
❑ 5	Ed Brinkman	.50	.20
❑ 6	Mac Scarce	.50	.20
❑ 7	Texas Rangers	2.00	.80
	Team Card		
❑ 8	Tom Hall	.50	.20
❑ 9	Johnny Oates	1.50	.60
❑ 10	Don Sutton	4.00	1.60
❑ 11	Chris Chambliss	1.50	.60
❑ 12A	Don Zimmer MG	3.00	1.20
	Dave Garcia CO		
	Johnny Podres CO		
	Bob Skinner CO		
	Whitey Wietelmann CO		
	(Podres no right ear)		
❑ 12B	Padres Leaders	.75	.30
	(Podres has right ear)		
❑ 13	George Hendrick	1.50	.60
❑ 14	Sonny Siebert	.50	.20
❑ 15	Ralph Garr	1.50	.60
❑ 16	Steve Braun	.50	.20
❑ 17	Fred Gladding	.50	.20
❑ 18	Leroy Stanton	.50	.20
❑ 19	Tim Foli	.50	.20
❑ 20	Stan Bahnsen	.50	.20
❑ 21	Randy Hundley	1.50	.60
❑ 22	Ted Abernathy	.50	.20
❑ 23	Dave Kingman	1.50	.60
❑ 24	Al Santorini	.50	.20
❑ 25	Roy White	1.50	.60
❑ 26	Pittsburgh Pirates	2.00	.80
	Team Card		
❑ 27	Bill Gogolewski	.50	.20
❑ 28	Hal McRae	1.50	.60
❑ 29	Tony Taylor	1.50	.60
❑ 30	Tug McGraw	1.50	.60
❑ 31	Buddy Bell RC	2.50	1.00
❑ 32	Fred Norman	.50	.20
❑ 33	Jim Breazeale	.50	.20
❑ 34	Pat Dobson	.50	.20
❑ 35	Willie Davis	1.50	.60
❑ 36	Steve Barber	.50	.20
❑ 37	Bill Robinson	1.50	.60
❑ 38	Mike Epstein	.50	.20
❑ 39	Dave Roberts	.50	.20
❑ 40	Reggie Smith	1.50	.60
❑ 41	Tom Walker	.50	.20
❑ 42	Mike Andrews	.50	.20
❑ 43	Randy Moffitt	.50	.20
❑ 44	Rick Monday	1.50	.60
❑ 45	Ellie Rodriguez UER	.50	.20
	(Photo actually		
	John Felske)		
❑ 46	Lindy McDaniel	1.50	.60
❑ 47	Luis Melendez	.50	.20
❑ 48	Paul Splittorff	.50	.20
❑ 49A	Frank Quilici MG	3.00	1.20
	Vern Morgan CO		
	Bob Rodgers CO		
	Ralph Rowe CO		
	Al Worthington CO		
	(Solid backgrounds)		
❑ 49B	Twins Leaders	.75	.30
	(Natural backgrounds)		
❑ 50	Roberto Clemente	50.00	20.00
❑ 51	Chuck Seelbach	.50	.20
❑ 52	Denis Menke	.50	.20
❑ 53	Steve Dunning	.50	.20
❑ 54	Checklist 1-132	3.00	.60
❑ 55	Jon Matlack	1.50	.60
❑ 56	Merv Rettenmund	.50	.20
❑ 57	Derrel Thomas	.50	.20
❑ 58	Mike Paul	.50	.20
❑ 59	Steve Yeager RC	1.50	.60
❑ 60	Ken Holtzman	1.50	.60
❑ 61	Billy Williams	2.50	1.00
	Rod Carew LL		
❑ 62	Johnny Bench	2.50	1.00
	Dick Allen LL		
	Home Run Leaders		
❑ 63	Johnny Bench	2.50	1.00
	Dick Allen		
	RBI Leaders		
❑ 64	Lou Brock	1.50	.60
	Bert Campaneris LL		
❑ 65	Steve Carlton	1.50	.60
	Luis Tiant LL		
❑ 66	Steve Carlton	1.50	.60
	Gaylord Perry		
	Wilbur Wood LL		
❑ 67	Steve Carlton	25.00	10.00
	Nolan Ryan LL		
❑ 68	Clay Carroll	1.50	.60
	Sparky Lyle LL		
❑ 69	Phil Gagliano	.50	.20
❑ 70	Milt Pappas	1.50	.60
❑ 71	Johnny Briggs	.50	.20
❑ 72	Ron Reed	.50	.20
❑ 73	Ed Herrmann	.50	.20
❑ 74	Billy Champion	.50	.20
❑ 75	Vada Pinson	1.50	.60
❑ 76	Doug Rader	.50	.20
❑ 77	Mike Torrez	1.50	.60
❑ 78	Richie Scheinblum	.50	.20
❑ 79	Jim Willoughby	.50	.20
❑ 80	Tony Oliva UER	2.50	1.00
	(Minnseota on front)		
❑ 81A	Whitey Lockman MG	1.50	.60
	Hank Aguirre CO		
	Ernie Banks CO		
	Larry Jansen CO		
	Pete Reiser CO		
	(Solid backgrounds)		
❑ 81B	Cubs Leaders	1.50	.60
	(Natural backgrounds)		
❑ 82	Fritz Peterson	.50	.20
❑ 83	Leron Lee	.50	.20
❑ 84	Rollie Fingers	4.00	1.60
❑ 85	Ted Simmons	1.50	.60
❑ 86	Tom McCraw	.50	.20
❑ 87	Ken Boswell	.50	.20
❑ 88	Mickey Stanley	1.50	.60
❑ 89	Jack Billingham	.50	.20
❑ 90	Brooks Robinson	7.00	2.80
❑ 91	Los Angeles Dodgers	2.00	.80
	Team Card		
❑ 92	Jerry Bell	.50	.20
❑ 93	Jesus Alou	.50	.20
❑ 94	Dick Billings	.50	.20
❑ 95	Steve Blass	1.50	.60
❑ 96	Doug Griffin	.50	.20
❑ 97	Willie Montanez	1.50	.60
❑ 98	Dick Woodson	.50	.20
❑ 99	Carl Taylor	.50	.20
❑ 100	Hank Aaron	25.00	10.00
❑ 101	Ken Henderson	.50	.20
❑ 102	Rudy May	.50	.20
❑ 103	Celerino Sanchez	.50	.20
❑ 104	Reggie Cleveland	.50	.20
❑ 105	Carlos May	.50	.20
❑ 106	Terry Humphrey	.50	.20
❑ 107	Phil Hennigan	.50	.20
❑ 108	Bill Russell	1.50	.60
❑ 109	Doyle Alexander	1.50	.60
❑ 110	Bob Watson	1.50	.60
❑ 111	Dave Nelson	.50	.20
❑ 112	Gary Ross	.50	.20
❑ 113	Jerry Grote	1.50	.60
❑ 114	Lynn McGlothen	.50	.20
❑ 115	Ron Santo	1.50	.60
❑ 116A	Ralph Houk MG	3.00	1.20
	Jim Hegan CO		
	Elston Howard CO		
	Dick Howser CO		
	Jim Turner CO		
	(Solid backgrounds)		
❑ 116B	Yankees Leaders	.75	.30
	(Natural backgrounds)		
❑ 117	Ramon Hernandez	.50	.20
❑ 118	John Mayberry	1.50	.60
❑ 119	Larry Bowa	1.50	.60
❑ 120	Joe Coleman	.50	.20
❑ 121	Dave Rader	.50	.20
❑ 122	Jim Strickland	.50	.20
❑ 123	Sandy Alomar	1.50	.60
❑ 124	Jim Hardin	.50	.20
❑ 125	Ron Fairly	1.50	.60
❑ 126	Jim Brewer	.50	.20
❑ 127	Milwaukee Brewers	2.00	.80
	Team Card		
❑ 128	Ted Sizemore	.50	.20
❑ 129	Terry Forster	1.50	.60
❑ 130	Pete Rose	20.00	8.00
❑ 131A	Eddie Kasko MG	3.00	1.20
	Doug Camilli CO		
	Don Lenhardt CO		
	Eddie Popowski CO		
	(No right ear)		
	Lee Stange CO		
❑ 131B	Red Sox Leaders	1.50	.60
	(Popowski has right		
	ear showing)		
❑ 132	Matty Alou	1.50	.60
❑ 133	Dave Roberts RC	.50	.20
❑ 134	Milt Wilcox	.50	.20
❑ 135	Lee May UER	1.50	.60
	(Career average .000)		
❑ 136A	Earl Weaver MG	2.00	.80
	George Bamberger CO		
	Jim Frey CO		
	Billy Hunter CO		
	George Staller CO		
	(Orange backgrounds)		
❑ 136B	Orioles Leaders	3.00	1.20
	(Dark pale		
	backgrounds)		
❑ 137	Jim Beauchamp	.50	.20
❑ 138	Horacio Pina	.50	.20
❑ 139	Carmen Fanzone	.50	.20
❑ 140	Lou Piniella	2.50	1.00
❑ 141	Bruce Kison	.50	.20
❑ 142	Thurman Munson	6.00	2.40
❑ 143	John Curtis	.50	.20
❑ 144	Marty Perez	.50	.20
❑ 145	Bobby Bonds	2.50	1.00
❑ 146	Woodie Fryman	.50	.20
❑ 147	Mike Anderson	.50	.20
❑ 148	Dave Goltz	.50	.20
❑ 149	Ron Hunt	.50	.20
❑ 150	Wilbur Wood	1.50	.60
❑ 151	Wes Parker	1.50	.60
❑ 152	Dave May	.50	.20
❑ 153	Al Hrabosky	1.50	.60
❑ 154	Jeff Torborg	1.50	.60
❑ 155	Sal Bando	1.50	.60
❑ 156	Cesar Geronimo	.50	.20
❑ 157	Denny Riddleberger	.50	.20
❑ 158	Houston Astros	2.00	.80
	Team Card		
❑ 159	Clarence Gaston	1.50	.60
❑ 160	Jim Palmer	7.00	2.80
❑ 161	Ted Martinez	.50	.20
❑ 162	Pete Broberg	.50	.20
❑ 163	Vic Davalillo	.50	.20
❑ 164	Monty Montgomery	.50	.20
❑ 165	Luis Aparicio	4.00	1.60
❑ 166	Terry Harmon	.50	.20
❑ 167	Steve Stone	1.50	.60
❑ 168	Jim Northrup	1.50	.60
❑ 169	Ron Schueler RC	1.50	.60
❑ 170	Harmon Killebrew	5.00	2.00
❑ 171	Bernie Carbo	.50	.20
❑ 172	Steve Kline	.50	.20
❑ 173	Hal Breeden	.50	.20
❑ 174	Goose Gossage RC	6.00	2.40
❑ 175	Frank Robinson	7.00	2.80
❑ 176	Chuck Taylor	.50	.20
❑ 177	Bill Plummer	.50	.20
❑ 178	Don Rose	.50	.20
❑ 179A	Dick Williams MG	4.00	1.60

Jerry Adair CO
Vern Hoscheit CO
Irv Noren CO
Wes Stock CO
(Hoscheit left ear showing)

❑ 179B A's Leaders .... 1.50 .60
(Hoscheit left ear not showing)

❑ 180 Ferguson Jenkins 4.00 1.60
❑ 181 Jack Brohamer .... .50 .20
❑ 182 Mike Caldwell RC .... 1.50 .60
❑ 183 Don Buford .... .50 .20
❑ 184 Jerry Koosman .... 1.50 .60
❑ 185 Jim Wynn .... 1.50 .60
❑ 186 Bill Fahey .... .50 .20
❑ 187 Luke Walker .... .50 .20
❑ 188 Cookie Rojas .... 1.50 .60
❑ 189 Greg Luzinski 2.50 1.00
❑ 190 Bob Gibson 8.00 3.20
❑ 191 Detroit Tigers 2.50 1.00
Team Card
❑ 192 Pat Jarvis .... .50 .20
❑ 193 Carlton Fisk 10.00 4.00
❑ 194 Jorge Orta .... .50 .20
❑ 195 Clay Carroll .... .50 .20
❑ 196 Ken McMullen .... .50 .20
❑ 197 Ed Goodson .... .50 .20
❑ 198 Horace Clarke .... .50 .20
❑ 199 Bert Blyleven 2.50 1.00
❑ 200 Billy Williams 4.00 1.60
❑ 201 G. Hendrick ALCS .... 1.50 .60
❑ 202 George Foster NLCS .... 1.50 .60
❑ 203 Gene Tenace WS .... 1.50 .60
❑ 204 World Series Game 2 .... 1.50 .60
A's two straight
❑ 205 Tony Perez WS 2.50 1.00
❑ 206 Gene Tenace WS .... 1.50 .60
❑ 207 Blue Moon Odom WS .... 1.50 .60
❑ 208 Johnny Bench WS6 .... 5.00 2.00
❑ 209 Bert Campaneris WS .... 1.50 .60
❑ 210 W.S. Summary .... .50 .20
World champions:
A's Win
❑ 211 Balor Moore .... .50 .20
❑ 212 Joe Lahoud .... .50 .20
❑ 213 Steve Garvey 5.00 2.00
❑ 214 Dave Hamilton .... .50 .20
❑ 215 Dusty Baker 2.50 1.00
❑ 216 Toby Harrah .... 1.50 .60
❑ 217 Don Wilson .... .50 .20
❑ 218 Aurelio Rodriguez .... .50 .20
❑ 219 St. Louis Cardinals 2.50 1.00
Team Card
❑ 220 Nolan Ryan 60.00 24.00
❑ 221 Fred Kendall .... .50 .20
❑ 222 Rob Gardner .... .50 .20
❑ 223 Bud Harrelson .... 1.50 .60
❑ 224 Bill Lee .... 1.50 .60
❑ 225 Al Oliver .... 1.50 .60
❑ 226 Ray Fosse .... .50 .20
❑ 227 Wayne Twitchell .... .50 .20
❑ 228 Bobby Darwin .... .50 .20
❑ 229 Roric Harrison .... .50 .20
❑ 230 Joe Morgan 6.00 2.40
❑ 231 Bill Parsons .... .50 .20
❑ 232 Ken Singleton .... 1.50 .60
❑ 233 Ed Kirkpatrick .... .50 .20
❑ 234 Bill North .... .50 .20
❑ 235 Jim Hunter 4.00 1.60
❑ 236 Tito Fuentes .... .50 .20
❑ 237A Eddie Mathews MG .... 1.50 .60
Lew Burdette CO
Jim Busby CO
Roy Hartsfield CO
Ken Silvestri CO
(Burdette right ear showing)
❑ 237B Braves Leaders 3.00 1.20
(Burdette right ear not showing)
❑ 238 Tony Muser .... .50 .20
❑ 239 Pete Richert .... .50 .20
❑ 240 Bobby Murcer .... 1.50 .60
❑ 241 Dwain Anderson .... .50 .20
❑ 242 George Culver .... .50 .20

❑ 243 California Angels 2.50 1.00
Team Card
❑ 244 Ed Acosta .... .50 .20
❑ 245 Carl Yastrzemski 8.00 3.20
❑ 246 Ken Sanders .... .50 .20
❑ 247 Del Unser .... .50 .20
❑ 248 Jerry Johnson .... .50 .20
❑ 249 Larry Biittner .... .50 .20
❑ 250 Manny Sanguillen .... 1.50 .60
❑ 251 Roger Nelson .... .50 .20
❑ 252A Charlie Fox MG 4.00 1.60
Joe Amalfitano CO
Andy Gilbert CO
Don McMahon CO
John McNamara CO
(Orange backgrounds)
❑ 252B Giants Leaders .... 1.50 .60
(Dark pale backgrounds)
❑ 253 Mark Belanger .... 1.50 .60
❑ 254 Bill Stoneman .... .50 .20
❑ 255 Reggie Jackson 15.00 6.00
❑ 256 Chris Zachary .... .50 .20
❑ 257A Yogi Berra MG 2.50 1.00
Roy McMillan CO
Joe Pignatano CO
Rube Walker CO
Eddie Yost CO
(Orange backgrounds)
❑ 257B Mets Leaders 5.00 2.00
(Dark pale backgrounds)
❑ 258 Tommy John .... 1.50 .60
❑ 259 Jim Holt .... .50 .20
❑ 260 Gary Nolan .... 1.50 .60
❑ 261 Pat Kelly .... .50 .20
❑ 262 Jack Aker .... .50 .20
❑ 263 George Scott .... 1.50 .60
❑ 264 Checklist 133-264 .... 3.00 .60
❑ 265 Gene Michael .... 1.50 .60
❑ 266 Mike Lum .... .75 .30
❑ 267 Lloyd Allen .... .75 .30
❑ 268 Jerry Morales .... .75 .30
❑ 269 Tim McCarver .... 1.50 .60
❑ 270 Luis Tiant .... 1.50 .60
❑ 271 Tom Hutton .... .75 .30
❑ 272 Ed Farmer .... .75 .30
❑ 273 Chris Speier .... .75 .30
❑ 274 Darold Knowles .... .75 .30
❑ 275 Tony Perez 4.00 1.60
❑ 276 Joe Lovitto .... .75 .30
❑ 277 Bob Miller .... .75 .30
❑ 278 Baltimore Orioles .... 1.50 .60
Team Card
❑ 279 Mike Strahler .... .75 .30
❑ 280 Al Kaline 7.00 2.80
❑ 281 Mike Jorgensen .... .75 .30
❑ 282 Steve Hovley .... .75 .30
❑ 283 Ray Sadecki .... .75 .30
❑ 284 Glenn Borgmann .... .75 .30
❑ 285 Don Kessinger .... 1.50 .60
❑ 286 Frank Linzy .... .75 .30
❑ 287 Eddie Leon .... .75 .30
❑ 288 Gary Gentry .... .75 .30
❑ 289 Bob Oliver .... .75 .30
❑ 290 Cesar Cedeno .... 1.50 .60
❑ 291 Rogelio Moret .... .75 .30
❑ 292 Jose Cruz .... 1.50 .60
❑ 293 Bernie Allen .... .75 .30
❑ 294 Steve Arlin .... .75 .30
❑ 295 Bert Campaneris .... 1.50 .60
❑ 296 Sparky Anderson MG 2.50 1.00
Alex Grammas CO
Ted Kluszewski CO
George Scherger CO
Larry Shepard CO
❑ 297 Walt Williams .... .75 .30
❑ 298 Ron Bryant .... .75 .30
❑ 299 Ted Ford .... .75 .30
❑ 300 Steve Carlton 10.00 4.00
❑ 301 Billy Grabarkewitz .... .75 .30
❑ 302 Terry Crowley .... .75 .30
❑ 303 Nelson Briles .... .75 .30
❑ 304 Duke Sims .... .75 .30
❑ 305 Willie Mays 40.00 16.00
❑ 306 Tom Burgmeier .... .75 .30

❑ 307 Boots Day .... .75 .30
❑ 308 Skip Lockwood .... .75 .30
❑ 309 Paul Popovich .... .75 .30
❑ 310 Dick Allen .... 1.50 .60
❑ 311 Joe Decker .... .75 .30
❑ 312 Oscar Brown .... .75 .30
❑ 313 Jim Ray .... .75 .30
❑ 314 Ron Swoboda .... 1.50 .60
❑ 315 John Odom .... .75 .30
❑ 316 San Diego Padres .... 1.50 .60
Team Card
❑ 317 Danny Cater .... .75 .30
❑ 318 Jim McGlothlin .... .75 .30
❑ 319 Jim Spencer .... .75 .30
❑ 320 Lou Brock 7.00 2.80
❑ 321 Rich Hinton .... .75 .30
❑ 322 Garry Maddox RC .... 1.50 .60
❑ 323 Billy Martin MG .... 1.50 .60
Art Fowler CO
Charlie Silvera CO
Dick Tracewski CO
Joe Schultz CO ERR
Schult's name not printed on card
❑ 324 Al Downing .... .75 .30
❑ 325 Boog Powell .... 1.50 .60
❑ 326 Darrell Brandon .... .75 .30
❑ 327 John Lowenstein .... .75 .30
❑ 328 Bill Bonham .... .75 .30
❑ 329 Ed Kranepool .... 1.50 .60
❑ 330 Rod Carew 7.00 2.80
❑ 331 Carl Morton .... .75 .30
❑ 332 John Felske .... .75 .30
❑ 333 Gene Clines .... .75 .30
❑ 334 Freddie Patek .... .75 .30
❑ 335 Bob Tolan .... .75 .30
❑ 336 Tom Bradley .... .75 .30
❑ 337 Dave Duncan .... 1.50 .60
❑ 338 Checklist 265-396 .... 3.00 .60
❑ 339 Dick Tidrow .... .75 .30
❑ 340 Nate Colbert .... .75 .30
❑ 341 Jim Palmer KP 2.50 1.00
❑ 342 Sam McDowell KP .... .75 .30
❑ 343 Bobby Murcer KP .... .75 .30
❑ 344 Jim Hunter KP 2.50 1.00
❑ 345 Chris Speier KP .... .75 .30
❑ 346 Gaylord Perry KP .... 1.50 .60
❑ 347 Kansas City Royals .... 1.50 .60
Team Card
❑ 348 Rennie Stennett .... .75 .30
❑ 349 Dick McAuliffe .... .75 .30
❑ 350 Tom Seaver 12.00 4.80
❑ 351 Jimmy Stewart .... .75 .30
❑ 352 Don Stanhouse .... .75 .30
❑ 353 Steve Brye .... .75 .30
❑ 354 Billy Parker .... .75 .30
❑ 355 Mike Marshall .... 1.50 .60
❑ 356 Chuck Tanner MG 4.00 1.60
Joe Lonnett CO
Jim Mahoney CO
Al Monchak CO
Johnny Sain CO
❑ 357 Ross Grimsley .... .75 .30
❑ 358 Jim Nettles .... .75 .30
❑ 359 Cecil Upshaw .... .75 .30
❑ 360 Joe Rudi UER .... 1.50 .60
(Photo actually Gene Tenace)
❑ 361 Fran Healy .... .75 .30
❑ 362 Eddie Watt .... .75 .30
❑ 363 Jackie Hernandez .... .75 .30
❑ 364 Rick Wise .... .75 .30
❑ 365 Rico Petrocelli .... 1.50 .60
❑ 366 Brock Davis .... .75 .30
❑ 367 Burt Hooton .... 1.50 .60
❑ 368 Bill Buckner .... 1.50 .60
❑ 369 Lerrin LaGrow .... .75 .30
❑ 370 Willie Stargell 5.00 2.00
❑ 371 Mike Kekich .... .75 .30
❑ 372 Oscar Gamble .... .75 .30
❑ 373 Clyde Wright .... .75 .30
❑ 374 Darrell Evans .... 1.50 .60
❑ 375 Larry Dierker .... 1.50 .60
❑ 376 Frank Duffy .... .75 .30
❑ 377 Gene Mauch MG 4.00 1.60
Dave Bristol CO
Larry Doby CO

Cal McLish CO
Jerry Zimmerman CO
❑ 378 Len Randle .75 .30
❑ 379 Cy Acosta .75 .30
❑ 380 Johnny Bench 12.00 4.80
❑ 381 Vicente Romo .75 .30
❑ 382 Mike Hegan .75 .30
❑ 383 Diego Segui .75 .30
❑ 384 Don Baylor 4.00 1.60
❑ 385 Jim Perry 1.50 .60
❑ 386 Don Money .75 .30
❑ 387 Jim Barr .75 .30
❑ 388 Ben Oglivie 1.50 .60
❑ 389 New York Mets 4.00 1.60
Team Card
❑ 390 Mickey Lolich 1.50 .60
❑ 391 Lee Lacy RC 1.50 .60
❑ 392 Dick Drago .75 .30
❑ 393 Jose Cardenal .75 .30
❑ 394 Sparky Lyle 1.50 .60
❑ 395 Roger Metzger .75 .30
❑ 396 Grant Jackson .75 .30
❑ 397 Dave Cash 1.25 .50
❑ 398 Rich Hand 1.25 .50
❑ 399 George Foster 2.00 .80
❑ 400 Gaylord Perry 5.00 2.00
❑ 401 Clyde Mashore 1.25 .50
❑ 402 Jack Hiatt 1.25 .50
❑ 403 Sonny Jackson 1.25 .50
❑ 404 Chuck Brinkman 1.25 .50
❑ 405 Cesar Tovar 1.25 .50
❑ 406 Paul Lindblad 1.25 .50
❑ 407 Felix Millan 1.25 .50
❑ 408 Jim Colborn 1.25 .50
❑ 409 Ivan Murrell 1.25 .50
❑ 410 Willie McCovey 6.00 2.40
(Bench behind plate)
❑ 411 Ray Corbin 1.25 .50
❑ 412 Manny Mota 2.00 .80
❑ 413 Tom Timmermann 1.25 .50
❑ 414 Ken Rudolph 1.25 .50
❑ 415 Marty Pattin 1.25 .50
❑ 416 Paul Schaal 1.25 .50
❑ 417 Scipio Spinks 1.25 .50
❑ 418 Bob Grich 2.00 .80
❑ 419 Casey Cox 1.25 .50
❑ 420 Tommie Agee 1.25 .50
❑ 421A Bobby Winkles MG 1.50 .60
Tom Morgan CO
Salty Parker CO
Jimmie Reese CO
John Roseboro CO
(Orange backgrounds)
❑ 421B Angels Leaders 3.00 1.20
(Dark pale
backgrounds)
❑ 422 Bob Robertson 1.25 .50
❑ 423 Johnny Jeter 1.25 .50
❑ 424 Denny Doyle 1.25 .50
❑ 425 Alex Johnson 1.25 .50
❑ 426 Dave LaRoche 1.25 .50
❑ 427 Rick Auerbach 1.25 .50
❑ 428 Wayne Simpson 1.25 .50
❑ 429 Jim Fairey 1.25 .50
❑ 430 Vida Blue 2.00 .80
❑ 431 Gerry Moses 1.25 .50
❑ 432 Dan Frisella 1.25 .50
❑ 433 Willie Horton 2.00 .80
❑ 434 San Francisco Giants 3.00 1.20
Team Card
❑ 435 Rico Carty 2.00 .80
❑ 436 Jim McAndrew 1.25 .50
❑ 437 John Kennedy 1.25 .50
❑ 438 Enzo Hernandez 1.25 .50
❑ 439 Eddie Fisher 1.25 .50
❑ 440 Glenn Beckert 1.25 .50
❑ 441 Gail Hopkins 1.25 .50
❑ 442 Dick Dietz 1.25 .50
❑ 443 Danny Thompson 1.25 .50
❑ 444 Ken Brett 1.25 .50
❑ 445 Ken Berry 1.25 .50
❑ 446 Jerry Reuss 2.00 .80
❑ 447 Joe Hague 1.25 .50
❑ 448 John Hiller 1.25 .50
❑ 449A Ken Aspromonte MG 4.00 1.60
Rocky Colavito CO
Joe Lutz CO
Warren Spahn CO
(Spahn's right
ear pointed)
❑ 449B Indians Leaders 4.00 1.60
(Spahn's right
ear round)
❑ 450 Joe Torre 3.00 1.20
❑ 451 John Vukovich 1.25 .50
❑ 452 Paul Casanova 1.25 .50
❑ 453 Checklist 397-528 3.00 .60
❑ 454 Tom Haller 1.25 .50
❑ 455 Bill Melton 1.25 .50
❑ 456 Dick Green 1.25 .50
❑ 457 John Strohmayer 1.25 .50
❑ 458 Jim Mason 1.25 .50
❑ 459 Jimmy Howarth 1.25 .50
❑ 460 Bill Freehan 2.00 .80
❑ 461 Mike Corkins 1.25 .50
❑ 462 Ron Blomberg 1.25 .50
❑ 463 Ken Tatum 1.25 .50
❑ 464 Chicago Cubs 3.00 1.20
Team Card
❑ 465 Dave Giusti 1.25 .50
❑ 466 Jose Arcia 1.25 .50
❑ 467 Mike Ryan 1.25 .50
❑ 468 Tom Griffin 1.25 .50
❑ 469 Dan Monzon 1.25 .50
❑ 470 Mike Cuellar 2.00 .80
❑ 471 Ty Cobb ATL 10.00 4.00
4191 Hits
❑ 472 Lou Gehrig ATL 15.00 6.00
23 Grand Slams
❑ 473 Hank Aaron ATL 10.00 4.00
6172 Total Bases
❑ 474 Babe Ruth ATL 20.00 8.00
2209 RBI
❑ 475 Ty Cobb ATL 8.00 3.20
.367 Batting Average
❑ 476 Walter Johnson ATL 3.00 1.20
113 Shutouts
❑ 477 Cy Young ATL 3.00 1.20
511 Victories
❑ 478 Walter Johnson ATL 3.00 1.20
3508 Strikeouts
❑ 479 Hal Lanier 1.25 .50
❑ 480 Juan Marichal 5.00 2.00
❑ 481 Chicago White Sox 3.00 1.20
Team Card
❑ 482 Rick Reuschel RC 3.00 1.20
❑ 483 Dal Maxvill 1.25 .50
❑ 484 Ernie McAnally 1.25 .50
❑ 485 Norm Cash 2.00 .80
❑ 486A Danny Ozark MG 1.50 .60
Carroll Beringer CO
Billy DeMars CO
Ray Rippelmeyer CO
Bobby Wine CO
(Orange backgrounds)
❑ 486B Phillies Leaders 3.00 1.20
(Dark pale
backgrounds)
❑ 487 Bruce Dal Canton 1.25 .50
❑ 488 Dave Campbell 2.00 .80
❑ 489 Jeff Burroughs 2.00 .80
❑ 490 Claude Osteen 2.00 .80
❑ 491 Bob Montgomery 1.25 .50
❑ 492 Pedro Borbon 1.25 .50
❑ 493 Duffy Dyer 1.25 .50
❑ 494 Rich Morales 1.25 .50
❑ 495 Tommy Helms 1.25 .50
❑ 496 Ray Lamb 1.25 .50
❑ 497A Red Schoendienst MG 2.00 .80
Vern Benson CO
George Kissell CO
Barney Schultz CO
(Orange backgrounds)
❑ 497B Cardinals Leaders 3.00 1.20
(Dark pale
backgrounds)
❑ 498 Graig Nettles 3.00 1.20
❑ 499 Bob Moose 1.25 .50
❑ 500 Oakland A's 3.00 1.20
Team Card
❑ 501 Larry Gura 1.25 .50
❑ 502 Bobby Valentine 3.00 1.20
❑ 503 Phil Niekro 5.00 2.00
❑ 504 Earl Williams 1.25 .50
❑ 505 Bob Bailey 1.25 .50
❑ 506 Bart Johnson 1.25 .50
❑ 507 Darrel Chaney 1.25 .50
❑ 508 Gates Brown 1.25 .50
❑ 509 Jim Nash 1.25 .50
❑ 510 Amos Otis 2.00 .80
❑ 511 Sam McDowell 2.00 .80
❑ 512 Dalton Jones 1.25 .50
❑ 513 Dave Marshall 1.25 .50
❑ 514 Jerry Kenney 1.25 .50
❑ 515 Andy Messersmith 2.00 .80
❑ 516 Danny Walton 1.25 .50
❑ 517A Bill Virdon MG 1.50 .60
Don Leppert CO
Bill Mazeroski CO
Dave Ricketts CO
Mel Wright CO
(Mazeroski has
no right ear)
❑ 517B Pirates Leaders 3.00 1.20
(Mazeroski has
right ear)
❑ 518 Bob Veale 1.25 .50
❑ 519 Johnny Edwards 1.25 .50
❑ 520 Mel Stottlemyre 2.00 .80
❑ 521 Atlanta Braves 3.00 1.20
Team Card
❑ 522 Leo Cardenas 1.25 .50
❑ 523 Wayne Granger 1.25 .50
❑ 524 Gene Tenace 2.00 .80
❑ 525 Jim Fregosi 2.00 .80
❑ 526 Ollie Brown 1.25 .50
❑ 527 Dan McGinn 1.25 .50
❑ 528 Paul Blair 1.25 .50
❑ 529 Milt May 3.50 1.40
❑ 530 Jim Kaat 5.00 2.00
❑ 531 Ron Woods 3.50 1.40
❑ 532 Steve Mingori 3.50 1.40
❑ 533 Larry Stahl 3.50 1.40
❑ 534 Dave Lemonds 3.50 1.40
❑ 535 Johnny Callison 5.00 2.00
❑ 536 Philadelphia Phillies 6.00 2.40
Team Card
❑ 537 Bill Slayback 3.50 1.40
❑ 538 Jim Ray Hart 5.00 2.00
❑ 539 Tom Murphy 3.50 1.40
❑ 540 Cleon Jones 5.00 2.00
❑ 541 Bob Bolin 3.50 1.40
❑ 542 Pat Corrales 5.00 2.00
❑ 543 Alan Foster 3.50 1.40
❑ 544 Von Joshua 3.50 1.40
❑ 545 Orlando Cepeda 8.00 3.20
❑ 546 Jim York 3.50 1.40
❑ 547 Bobby Heise 3.50 1.40
❑ 548 Don Durham 3.50 1.40
❑ 549 Whitey Herzog MG 5.00 2.00
Chuck Estrada CO
Chuck Hiller CO
Jackie Moore CO
❑ 550 Dave Johnson 5.00 2.00
❑ 551 Mike Kilkenny 3.50 1.40
❑ 552 J.C. Martin 3.50 1.40
❑ 553 Mickey Scott 3.50 1.40
❑ 554 Dave Concepcion 5.00 2.00
❑ 555 Bill Hands 3.50 1.40
❑ 556 New York Yankees 8.00 3.20
Team Card
❑ 557 Bernie Williams 3.50 1.40
❑ 558 Jerry May 3.50 1.40
❑ 559 Barry Lersch 3.50 1.40
❑ 560 Frank Howard 5.00 2.00
❑ 561 Jim Geddes 3.50 1.40
❑ 562 Wayne Garrett 3.50 1.40
❑ 563 Larry Haney 3.50 1.40
❑ 564 Mike Thompson 3.50 1.40
❑ 565 Jim Hickman 3.50 1.40
❑ 566 Lew Krausse 3.50 1.40
❑ 567 Bob Fenwick 3.50 1.40
❑ 568 Ray Newman 3.50 1.40
❑ 569 Walt Alston MG 8.00 3.20
Red Adams CO
Monty Basgall CO
Jim Gilliam CO
Tom Lasorda CO

❑ 570 Bill Singer 5.00 2.00
❑ 571 Rusty Torres 3.50 1.40
❑ 572 Gary Sutherland 3.50 1.40
❑ 573 Fred Beene 3.50 1.40
❑ 574 Bob Didier 3.50 1.40
❑ 575 Dock Ellis 3.50 1.40
❑ 576 Montreal Expos 6.00 2.40
Team Card
❑ 577 Eric Soderholm 3.50 1.40
❑ 578 Ken Wright 3.50 1.40
❑ 579 Tom Grieve 5.00 2.00
❑ 580 Joe Pepitone 5.00 2.00
❑ 581 Steve Kealey 3.50 1.40
❑ 582 Darrell Porter 5.00 2.00
❑ 583 Bill Grief 3.50 1.40
❑ 584 Chris Arnold 3.50 1.40
❑ 585 Joe Niekro 5.00 2.00
❑ 586 Bill Sudakis 3.50 1.40
❑ 587 Rich McKinney 3.50 1.40
❑ 588 Checklist 529-660 20.00 4.00
❑ 589 Ken Forsch 3.50 1.40
❑ 590 Deron Johnson 3.50 1.40
❑ 591 Mike Hedlund 3.50 1.40
❑ 592 John Boccabella 3.50 1.40
❑ 593 Jack McKeon MG 3.50 1.40
Galen Cisco CO
Harry Dunlop CO
Charlie Lau CO
❑ 594 Vic Harris 3.50 1.40
❑ 595 Don Gullett 5.00 2.00
❑ 596 Boston Red Sox 6.00 2.40
Team Card
❑ 597 Mickey Rivers 5.00 2.00
❑ 598 Phil Roof 3.50 1.40
❑ 599 Ed Crosby 3.50 1.40
❑ 600 Dave McNally 5.00 2.00
❑ 601 Sergio Robles 5.00 2.00
George Pena
Rick Stelmaszek
❑ 602 Mel Behney 5.00 2.00
Ralph Garcia
Doug Rau
❑ 603 Terry Hughes 5.00 2.00
Bill McNulty
Ken Reitz RC
❑ 604 Jesse Jefferson 5.00 2.00
Dennis O'Toole
Bob Strampe
❑ 605 Enos Cabell RC 5.00 2.00
Pat Bourque
Gonzalo Marquez
❑ 606 Gary Matthews RC 5.00 2.00
Tom Paciorek
Jorge Roque
❑ 607 Pepe Frias 5.00 2.00
Ray Busse
Mario Guerrero
❑ 608 Steve Busby RC 5.00 2.00
Dick Colpaert
George Medich RC
❑ 609 Larvell Blanks 5.00 2.00
Pedro Garcia
Dave Lopes RC
❑ 610 Jimmy Freeman 5.00 2.00
Charlie Hough
Hank Webb
❑ 611 Rich Coggins 5.00 2.00
Jim Wohlford
Richie Zisk
❑ 612 Steve Lawson 5.00 2.00
Bob Reynolds
Brent Strom
❑ 613 Bob Boone RC 15.00 6.00
Skip Jutze
Mike Ivie
❑ 614 Al Bumbry RC 18.00 7.25
Dwight Evans RC
Charlie Spikes
❑ 615 Ron Cey 150.00 60.00
John Hilton
Mike Schmidt RC
❑ 616 Norm Angelini 5.00 2.00
Steve Blateric
Mike Garman
❑ 617 Rich Chiles 3.50 1.40
❑ 618 Andy Etchebarren 3.50 1.40
❑ 619 Billy Wilson 3.50 1.40
❑ 620 Tommy Harper 5.00 2.00
❑ 621 Joe Ferguson 5.00 2.00
❑ 622 Larry Hisle 5.00 2.00
❑ 623 Steve Renko 3.50 1.40
❑ 624 Leo Durocher MG 5.00 2.00
Preston Gomez CO
Grady Hatton CO
Hub Kittle CO
Jim Owens CO
❑ 625 Angel Mangual 3.50 1.40
❑ 626 Bob Barton 3.50 1.40
❑ 627 Luis Alvarado 3.50 1.40
❑ 628 Jim Slaton 3.50 1.40
❑ 629 Cleveland Indians 6.00 2.40
Team Card
❑ 630 Denny McLain 8.00 3.20
❑ 631 Tom Matchick 3.50 1.40
❑ 632 Dick Selma 3.50 1.40
❑ 633 Ike Brown 3.50 1.40
❑ 634 Alan Closter 3.50 1.40
❑ 635 Gene Alley 5.00 2.00
❑ 636 Rickey Clark 3.50 1.40
❑ 637 Norm Miller 3.50 1.40
❑ 638 Ken Reynolds 3.50 1.40
❑ 639 Willie Crawford 3.50 1.40
❑ 640 Dick Bosman 3.50 1.40
❑ 641 Cincinnati Reds 6.00 2.40
Team Card
❑ 642 Jose Laboy 3.50 1.40
❑ 643 Al Fitzmorris 3.50 1.40
❑ 644 Jack Heidemann 3.50 1.40
❑ 645 Bob Locker 3.50 1.40
❑ 646 Del Crandall MG 3.50 1.40
Harvey Kuenn CO
Joe Nossek CO
Bob Shaw CO
Jim Walton CO
❑ 647 George Stone 3.50 1.40
❑ 648 Tom Egan 3.50 1.40
❑ 649 Rich Folkers 3.50 1.40
❑ 650 Felipe Alou 5.00 2.00
❑ 651 Don Carrithers 3.50 1.40
❑ 652 Ted Kubiak 3.50 1.40
❑ 653 Joe Hoerner 3.50 1.40
❑ 654 Minnesota Twins 6.00 2.40
Team Card
❑ 655 Clay Kirby 3.50 1.40
❑ 656 John Ellis 3.50 1.40
❑ 657 Bob Johnson 3.50 1.40
❑ 658 Elliott Maddox 3.50 1.40
❑ 659 Jose Pagan 3.50 1.40
❑ 660 Fred Scherman 5.00 1.95

1974 Topps

	NM	Ex
COMPLETE SET (660)	400.00	160.00
COMP.FACT.SET (660)	600.00	240.00
WRAPPERS (10-CENTS)	10.00	4.00

❑ 1 Hank Aaron 715 40.00 12.00
❑ 2 Hank Aaron 54-57 8.00 3.20
❑ 3 Hank Aaron 58-61 8.00 3.20
❑ 4 Hank Aaron 62-65 8.00 3.20
❑ 5 Hank Aaron 66-69 8.00 3.20
❑ 6 Hank Aaron 70-73 8.00 3.20
❑ 7 Jim Hunter 4.00 1.60
❑ 8 George Theodore .50 .20
❑ 9 Mickey Lolich 1.00 .40
❑ 10 Johnny Bench 15.00 6.00
❑ 11 Jim Bibby .50 .20
❑ 12 Dave May .50 .20
❑ 13 Tom Hilgendorf .50 .20
❑ 14 Paul Popovich .50 .20
❑ 15 Joe Torre 2.00 .80
❑ 16 Baltimore Orioles 1.00 .40
Team Card
❑ 17 Doug Bird .50 .20
❑ 18 Gary Thomasson .50 .20
❑ 19 Gerry Moses .50 .20
❑ 20 Nolan Ryan 40.00 16.00
❑ 21 Bob Gallagher .50 .20
❑ 22 Cy Acosta .50 .20
❑ 23 Craig Robinson .50 .20
❑ 24 John Hiller 1.00 .40
❑ 25 Ken Singleton 1.00 .40
❑ 26 Bill Campbell .50 .20
❑ 27 George Scott 1.00 .40
❑ 28 Manny Sanguillen 1.00 .40
❑ 29 Phil Niekro 3.00 1.20
❑ 30 Bobby Bonds 2.00 .80
❑ 31 Preston Gomez MG 1.00 .40
Roger Craig CO
Hub Kittle CO
Grady Hatton CO
Bob Lillis CO
❑ 32A Johnny Grubb SD 1.00 .40
❑ 32B Johnny Grubb WASH 4.00 1.60
❑ 33 Don Newhauser .50 .20
❑ 34 Andy Kosco .50 .20
❑ 35 Gaylord Perry 3.00 1.20
❑ 36 St. Louis Cardinals 1.00 .40
Team Card
❑ 37 Dave Sells .50 .20
❑ 38 Don Kessinger 1.00 .40
❑ 39 Ken Suarez .50 .20
❑ 40 Jim Palmer 8.00 3.20
❑ 41 Bobby Floyd .50 .20
❑ 42 Claude Osteen 1.00 .40
❑ 43 Jim Wynn 1.00 .40
❑ 44 Mel Stottlemyre 1.00 .40
❑ 45 Dave Johnson 1.00 .40
❑ 46 Pat Kelly .50 .20
❑ 47 Dick Ruthven .50 .20
❑ 48 Dick Sharon .50 .20
❑ 49 Steve Renko .50 .20
❑ 50 Rod Carew 8.00 3.20
❑ 51 Bobby Heise .50 .20
❑ 52 Al Oliver 1.00 .40
❑ 53A Fred Kendall SD 1.00 .40
❑ 53B Fred Kendall WASH 4.00 1.60
❑ 54 Elias Sosa .50 .20
❑ 55 Frank Robinson 8.00 3.20
❑ 56 New York Mets 1.00 .40
Team Card
❑ 57 Darold Knowles .50 .20
❑ 58 Charlie Spikes .50 .20
❑ 59 Ross Grimsley .50 .20
❑ 60 Lou Brock 6.00 2.40
❑ 61 Luis Aparicio 3.00 1.20
❑ 62 Bob Locker .50 .20
❑ 63 Bill Sudakis .50 .20
❑ 64 Doug Rau .50 .20
❑ 65 Amos Otis 1.00 .40
❑ 66 Sparky Lyle 1.00 .40
❑ 67 Tommy Helms .50 .20
❑ 68 Grant Jackson .50 .20
❑ 69 Del Unser .50 .20
❑ 70 Dick Allen 2.00 .80
❑ 71 Dan Frisella .50 .20
❑ 72 Aurelio Rodriguez .50 .20
❑ 73 Mike Marshall 2.00 .80
❑ 74 Minnesota Twins 1.00 .40
Team Card
❑ 75 Jim Colborn .50 .20
❑ 76 Mickey Rivers 1.00 .40
❑ 77A Rich Troedson SD 1.00 .40
❑ 77B Rich Troedson WASH 4.00 1.60
❑ 78 Charlie Fox MG 1.00 .40
John McNamara CO
Joe Amalfitano CO
Andy Gilbert CO
Don McMahon CO

❑ 79 Gene Tenace 1.00 .40
❑ 80 Tom Seaver 12.00 4.80
❑ 81 Frank Duffy .50 .20
❑ 82 Dave Giusti .50 .20
❑ 83 Orlando Cepeda 3.00 1.20
❑ 84 Rick Wise .50 .20
❑ 85 Joe Morgan 8.00 3.20
❑ 86 Joe Ferguson 1.00 .40
❑ 87 Fergie Jenkins 3.00 1.20
❑ 88 Freddie Patek 1.00 .40
❑ 89 Jackie Brown .50 .20
❑ 90 Bobby Murcer 1.00 .40
❑ 91 Ken Forsch .50 .20
❑ 92 Paul Blair 1.00 .40
❑ 93 Rod Gilbreath .50 .20
❑ 94 Detroit Tigers 1.00 .40
Team Card
❑ 95 Steve Carlton 8.00 3.20
❑ 96 Jerry Hairston .50 .20
❑ 97 Bob Bailey .50 .20
❑ 98 Bert Blyleven 2.00 .80
❑ 99 Del Crandall MG 1.00 .40
Harvey Kuenn CO
Joe Nossek CO
Jim Walton CO
Al Widmar CO
❑ 100 Willie Stargell 6.00 2.40
❑ 101 Bobby Valentine 1.00 .40
❑ 102A Bill Greif SD 1.00 .40
❑ 102B Bill Greif WASH 4.00 1.60
❑ 103 Sal Bando 1.00 .40
❑ 104 Ron Bryant .50 .20
❑ 105 Carlton Fisk 12.00 4.80
❑ 106 Harry Parker .50 .20
❑ 107 Alex Johnson .50 .20
❑ 108 Al Hrabosky 1.00 .40
❑ 109 Bob Grich 1.00 .40
❑ 110 Billy Williams 3.00 1.20
❑ 111 Clay Carroll .50 .20
❑ 112 Dave Lopes 2.00 .80
❑ 113 Dick Drago .50 .20
❑ 114 Angels Team 1.00 .40
❑ 115 Willie Horton 1.00 .40
❑ 116 Jerry Reuss 1.00 .40
❑ 117 Ron Blomberg .50 .20
❑ 118 Bill Lee 1.00 .40
❑ 119 Danny Ozark MG 1.00 .40
Ray Ripplemeyer CO
Bobby Wine CO
Carroll Beringer CO
Billy DeMars CO
❑ 120 Wilbur Wood .50 .20
❑ 121 Larry Lintz .50 .20
❑ 122 Jim Holt .50 .20
❑ 123 Nelson Briles 1.00 .40
❑ 124 Bobby Coluccio .50 .20
❑ 125A Nate Colbert SD 1.00 .40
❑ 125B Nate Colbert WASH 4.00 1.60
❑ 126 Checklist 1-132 3.00 .60
❑ 127 Tom Paciorek 1.00 .40
❑ 128 John Ellis .50 .20
❑ 129 Chris Speier .50 .20
❑ 130 Reggie Jackson 15.00 6.00
❑ 131 Bob Boone 2.00 .80
❑ 132 Felix Millan .50 .20
❑ 133 David Clyde 1.00 .40
❑ 134 Denis Menke .50 .20
❑ 135 Roy White 1.00 .40
❑ 136 Rick Reuschel 1.00 .40
❑ 137 Al Bumbry 1.00 .40
❑ 138 Eddie Brinkman .50 .20
❑ 139 Aurelio Monteagudo .50 .20
❑ 140 Darrell Evans 2.00 .80
❑ 141 Pat Bourque .50 .20
❑ 142 Pedro Garcia .50 .20
❑ 143 Dick Woodson .50 .20
❑ 144 Walter Alston MG 3.00 1.20
Tom Lasorda CO
Jim Gilliam CO
Red Adams CO
Monty Basgall CO
❑ 145 Dock Ellis .50 .20
❑ 146 Ron Fairly 1.00 .40
❑ 147 Bart Johnson .50 .20
❑ 148A Dave Hilton SD 1.00 .40
❑ 148B Dave Hilton WASH 4.00 1.60
❑ 149 Mac Scarce .50 .20
❑ 150 John Mayberry 1.00 .40
❑ 151 Diego Segui .50 .20
❑ 152 Oscar Gamble 1.00 .40
❑ 153 Jon Matlack 1.00 .40
❑ 154 Houston Astros 1.00 .40
Team Card
❑ 155 Bert Campaneris 1.00 .40
❑ 156 Randy Moffitt .50 .20
❑ 157 Vic Harris .50 .20
❑ 158 Jack Billingham .50 .20
❑ 159 Jim Ray Hart .50 .20
❑ 160 Brooks Robinson 8.00 3.20
❑ 161 Ray Burris UER 1.00 .40
(Card number is
printed sideways)
❑ 162 Bill Freehan 1.00 .40
❑ 163 Ken Berry .50 .20
❑ 164 Tom House .50 .20
❑ 165 Willie Davis 1.00 .40
❑ 166 Jack McKeon MG 1.00 .40
Charlie Lau CO
Harry Dunlop CO
Galen Cisco CO
❑ 167 Luis Tiant 2.00 .80
❑ 168 Danny Thompson .50 .20
❑ 169 Steve Rogers RC 2.00 .80
❑ 170 Bill Melton .50 .20
❑ 171 Eduardo Rodriguez .50 .20
❑ 172 Gene Clines .50 .20
❑ 173A Randy Jones SD RC 2.00 .80
❑ 173B Randy Jones WASH 5.00 2.00
❑ 174 Bill Robinson 1.00 .40
❑ 175 Reggie Cleveland .50 .20
❑ 176 John Lowenstein .50 .20
❑ 177 Dave Roberts .50 .20
❑ 178 Garry Maddox 1.00 .40
❑ 179 Yogi Berra MG 5.00 2.00
Rube Walker CO
Eddie Yost CO
Roy McMillan CO
Joe Pignatano CO
❑ 180 Ken Holtzman 1.00 .40
❑ 181 Cesar Geronimo .50 .20
❑ 182 Lindy McDaniel 1.00 .40
❑ 183 Johnny Oates 1.00 .40
❑ 184 Texas Rangers 1.00 .40
Team Card
❑ 185 Jose Cardenal .50 .20
❑ 186 Fred Scherman .50 .20
❑ 187 Don Baylor 2.00 .80
❑ 188 Rudy Meoli .50 .20
❑ 189 Jim Brewer .50 .20
❑ 190 Tony Oliva 2.00 .80
❑ 191 Al Fitzmorris .50 .20
❑ 192 Mario Guerrero .50 .20
❑ 193 Tom Walker .50 .20
❑ 194 Darrell Porter 1.00 .40
❑ 195 Carlos May .50 .20
❑ 196 Jim Fregosi 1.00 .40
❑ 197A Vicente Romo SD 1.00 .40
❑ 197B V.Romo WASH 4.00 1.60
❑ 198 Dave Cash .50 .20
❑ 199 Mike Kekich .50 .20
❑ 200 Cesar Cedeno 1.00 .40
❑ 201 Rod Carew 6.00 2.40
Pete Rose LL
❑ 202 Reggie Jackson 5.00 2.00
Willie Stargell LL
❑ 203 Reggie Jackson 5.00 2.00
Willie Stargell LL
❑ 204 Tommy Harper 2.00 .80
Lou Brock LL
❑ 205 Wilbur Wood 1.00 .40
Ron Bryant LL
❑ 206 Jim Palmer 5.00 2.00
Tom Seaver LL
❑ 207 Nolan Ryan 12.00 4.80
Tom Seaver LL
❑ 208 John Hiller 1.00 .40
Mike Marshall LL
❑ 209 Ted Sizemore .50 .20
❑ 210 Bill Singer .50 .20
❑ 211 Chicago Cubs 1.00 .40
Team Card
❑ 212 Rollie Fingers 3.00 1.20
❑ 213 Dave Rader .50 .20
❑ 214 Billy Grabarkewitz .50 .20
❑ 215 Al Kaline UER 10.00 4.00
(No copyright on back)
❑ 216 Ray Sadecki .50 .20
❑ 217 Tim Foli .50 .20
❑ 218 Johnny Briggs .50 .20
❑ 219 Doug Griffin .50 .20
❑ 220 Don Sutton 3.00 1.20
❑ 221 Chuck Tanner MG 1.00 .40
Jim Mahoney CO
Alex Monchak CO
Johnny Sain CO
Joe Lonnett CO
❑ 222 Ramon Hernandez .50 .20
❑ 223 Jeff Burroughs 2.00 .80
❑ 224 Roger Metzger .50 .20
❑ 225 Paul Splittorff .50 .20
❑ 226A San Diego Padres 2.00 .80
Team Card San Diego Variation
❑ 226B San Diego Padres 8.00 3.20
Team Card Washington Variation
❑ 227 Mike Lum .50 .20
❑ 228 Ted Kubiak .50 .20
❑ 229 Fritz Peterson .50 .20
❑ 230 Tony Perez 4.00 1.60
❑ 231 Dick Tidrow .50 .20
❑ 232 Steve Brye .50 .20
❑ 233 Jim Barr .50 .20
❑ 234 John Milner .50 .20
❑ 235 Dave McNally 1.00 .40
❑ 236 Red Schoendienst MG 3.00 1.20
Barney Schultz CO
George Kissell CO
Johnny Lewis CO
Vern Benson CO
❑ 237 Ken Brett .50 .20
❑ 238 Fran Healy HOR .50 .20
(Munson sliding
in background)
❑ 239 Bill Russell 1.00 .40
❑ 240 Joe Coleman .50 .20
❑ 241A Glenn Beckert SD 1.00 .40
❑ 241B G.Beckert WASH 4.00 1.60
❑ 242 Bill Gogolewski .50 .20
❑ 243 Bob Oliver .50 .20
❑ 244 Carl Morton .50 .20
❑ 245 Cleon Jones .50 .20
❑ 246 Oakland Athletics 2.00 .80
Team Card
❑ 247 Rick Miller .50 .20
❑ 248 Tom Hall .50 .20
❑ 249 George Mitterwald .50 .20
❑ 250A Willie McCovey SD 8.00 3.20
❑ 250B W.McCovey WASH 25.00 10.00
❑ 251 Graig Nettles 2.00 .80
❑ 252 Dave Parker RC 10.00 4.00
❑ 253 John Boccabella .50 .20
❑ 254 Stan Bahnsen .50 .20
❑ 255 Larry Bowa 1.00 .40
❑ 256 Tom Griffin .50 .20
❑ 257 Buddy Bell 2.00 .80
❑ 258 Jerry Morales .50 .20
❑ 259 Bob Reynolds .50 .20
❑ 260 Ted Simmons 2.00 .80
❑ 261 Jerry Bell .50 .20
❑ 262 Ed Kirkpatrick .50 .20
❑ 263 Checklist 133-264 3.00 .60
❑ 264 Joe Rudi 1.00 .40
❑ 265 Tug McGraw 2.00 .80
❑ 266 Jim Northrup 1.00 .40
❑ 267 Andy Messersmith 1.00 .40
❑ 268 Tom Grieve 1.00 .40
❑ 269 Bob Johnson .50 .20
❑ 270 Ron Santo 2.00 .80
❑ 271 Bill Hands .50 .20
❑ 272 Paul Casanova .50 .20
❑ 273 Checklist 265-396 3.00 .60
❑ 274 Fred Beene .50 .20
❑ 275 Ron Hunt .50 .20
❑ 276 Bobby Winkles MG 1.00 .40
John Roseboro CO
Tom Morgan CO
Jimmie Reese CO
Salty Parker CO
❑ 277 Gary Nolan 1.00 .40

No.	Card	Price	Price
❑ 278	Cookie Rojas	1.00	.40
❑ 279	Jim Crawford	.50	.20
❑ 280	Carl Yastrzemski	12.00	4.80
❑ 281	San Francisco Giants	1.00	.40
	Team Card		
❑ 282	Doyle Alexander	1.00	.40
❑ 283	Mike Schmidt	20.00	8.00
❑ 284	Dave Duncan	1.00	.40
❑ 285	Reggie Smith	1.00	.40
❑ 286	Tony Muser	.50	.20
❑ 287	Clay Kirby	.50	.20
❑ 288	Gorman Thomas RC	2.00	.80
❑ 289	Rick Auerbach	.50	.20
❑ 290	Vida Blue	1.00	.40
❑ 291	Don Hahn	.50	.20
❑ 292	Chuck Seelbach	.50	.20
❑ 293	Milt May	.50	.20
❑ 294	Steve Foucault	.50	.20
❑ 295	Rick Monday	1.00	.40
❑ 296	Ray Corbin	.50	.20
❑ 297	Hal Breeden	.50	.20
❑ 298	Roric Harrison	.50	.20
❑ 299	Gene Michael	.50	.20
❑ 300	Pete Rose	25.00	10.00
❑ 301	Bob Montgomery	.50	.20
❑ 302	Rudy May	.50	.20
❑ 303	George Hendrick	1.00	.40
❑ 304	Don Wilson	.50	.20
❑ 305	Tito Fuentes	.50	.20
❑ 306	Earl Weaver MG	3.00	1.20
	Jim Frey CO		
	George Bamberger CO		
	Billy Hunter CO		
	George Staller CO		
❑ 307	Luis Melendez	.50	.20
❑ 308	Bruce Dal Canton	.50	.20
❑ 309A	Dave Roberts SD	1.00	.40
❑ 309B	Dave Roberts WASH	6.00	2.40
❑ 310	Terry Forster	1.00	.40
❑ 311	Jerry Grote	1.00	.40
❑ 312	Deron Johnson	.50	.20
❑ 313	Barry Lersch	.50	.20
❑ 314	Milwaukee Brewers	1.00	.40
	Team Card		
❑ 315	Ron Cey	2.00	.80
❑ 316	Jim Perry	1.00	.40
❑ 317	Richie Zisk	1.00	.40
❑ 318	Jim Merritt	.50	.20
❑ 319	Randy Hundley	.50	.20
❑ 320	Dusty Baker	2.00	.80
❑ 321	Steve Braun	.50	.20
❑ 322	Ernie McAnally	.50	.20
❑ 323	Richie Scheinblum	.50	.20
❑ 324	Steve Kline	.50	.20
❑ 325	Tommy Harper	1.00	.40
❑ 326	Sparky Anderson MG	3.00	1.20
	Larry Shepard CO		
	George Scherger CO		
	Alex Grammas CO		
	Ted Kluszewski CO		
❑ 327	Tom Timmermann	.50	.20
❑ 328	Skip Jutze	.50	.20
❑ 329	Mark Belanger	1.00	.40
❑ 330	Juan Marichal	5.00	2.00
❑ 331	Carlton Fisk	5.00	2.00
	Johnny Bench AS		
❑ 332	Dick Allen	8.00	3.20
	Hank Aaron AS		
❑ 333	Rod Carew	4.00	1.60
	Joe Morgan AS		
❑ 334	Brooks Robinson	3.00	1.20
	Ron Santo AS		
❑ 335	Bert Campaneris	1.00	.40
	Chris Speier AS		
❑ 336	Bobby Murcer	5.00	2.00
	Pete Rose AS		
❑ 337	Amos Otis	1.00	.40
	Cesar Cedeno AS		
❑ 338	Reggie Jackson	5.00	2.00
	Billy Williams AS		
❑ 339	Jim Hunter	3.00	1.20
	Rick Wise AS		
❑ 340	Thurman Munson	8.00	3.20
❑ 341	Dan Driessen RC	1.00	.40
❑ 342	Jim Lonborg	1.00	.40
❑ 343	Royals Team	1.00	.40
❑ 344	Mike Caldwell	.50	.20
❑ 345	Bill North	.50	.20
❑ 346	Ron Reed	.50	.20
❑ 347	Sandy Alomar	1.00	.40
❑ 348	Pete Richert	.50	.20
❑ 349	John Vukovich	.50	.20
❑ 350	Bob Gibson	8.00	3.20
❑ 351	Dwight Evans	3.00	1.20
❑ 352	Bill Stoneman	.50	.20
❑ 353	Rich Coggins	.50	.20
❑ 354	Whitey Lockman MG	1.00	.40
	J.C. Martin CO		
	Hank Aguirre CO		
	Al Spangler CO		
	Jim Marshall CO		
❑ 355	Dave Nelson	.50	.20
❑ 356	Jerry Koosman	1.00	.40
❑ 357	Buddy Bradford	.50	.20
❑ 358	Dal Maxvill	.50	.20
❑ 359	Brent Strom	.50	.20
❑ 360	Greg Luzinski	2.00	.80
❑ 361	Don Carrithers	.50	.20
❑ 362	Hal King	.50	.20
❑ 363	New York Yankees	2.00	.80
	Team Card		
❑ 364A	Cito Gaston SD	2.00	.80
❑ 364B	Cito Gaston WASH	8.00	3.20
❑ 365	Steve Busby	1.00	.40
❑ 366	Larry Hisle	1.00	.40
❑ 367	Norm Cash	2.00	.80
❑ 368	Manny Mota	1.00	.40
❑ 369	Paul Lindblad	.50	.20
❑ 370	Bob Watson	1.00	.40
❑ 371	Jim Slaton	.50	.20
❑ 372	Ken Reitz	.50	.20
❑ 373	John Curtis	.50	.20
❑ 374	Marty Perez	.50	.20
❑ 375	Earl Williams	.50	.20
❑ 376	Jorge Orta	.50	.20
❑ 377	Ron Woods	.50	.20
❑ 378	Burt Hooton	1.00	.40
❑ 379	Billy Martin MG	2.00	.80
	Frank Lucchesi CO		
	Art Fowler CO		
	Charlie Silvera CO		
	Jackie Moore CO		
❑ 380	Bud Harrelson	1.00	.40
❑ 381	Charlie Sands	.50	.20
❑ 382	Bob Moose	.50	.20
❑ 383	Philadelphia Phillies	1.00	.40
	Team Card		
❑ 384	Chris Chambliss	1.00	.40
❑ 385	Don Gullett	1.00	.40
❑ 386	Gary Matthews	2.00	.80
❑ 387A	Rich Morales SD	1.00	.40
❑ 387B	Rich Morales WASH	6.00	2.40
❑ 388	Phil Roof	.50	.20
❑ 389	Gates Brown	.50	.20
❑ 390	Lou Piniella	2.00	.80
❑ 391	Billy Champion	.50	.20
❑ 392	Dick Green	.50	.20
❑ 393	Orlando Pena	.50	.20
❑ 394	Ken Henderson	.50	.20
❑ 395	Doug Rader	.50	.20
❑ 396	Tommy Davis	1.00	.40
❑ 397	George Stone	.50	.20
❑ 398	Duke Sims	.50	.20
❑ 399	Mike Paul	.50	.20
❑ 400	Harmon Killebrew	6.00	2.40
❑ 401	Elliott Maddox	.50	.20
❑ 402	Jim Rooker	.50	.20
❑ 403	Darrell Johnson MG	1.00	.40
	Eddie Popowski CO		
	Lee Stange CO		
	Don Zimmer CO		
	Don Bryant CO		
❑ 404	Jim Howarth	.50	.20
❑ 405	Ellie Rodriguez	.50	.20
❑ 406	Steve Arlin	.50	.20
❑ 407	Jim Wohlford	.50	.20
❑ 408	Charlie Hough	1.00	.40
❑ 409	Ike Brown	.50	.20
❑ 410	Pedro Borbon	.50	.20
❑ 411	Frank Baker	.50	.20
❑ 412	Chuck Taylor	.50	.20
❑ 413	Don Money	1.00	.40
❑ 414	Checklist 397-528	3.00	.60
❑ 415	Gary Gentry	.50	.20
❑ 416	Chicago White Sox	1.00	.40
	Team Card		
❑ 417	Rich Folkers	.50	.20
❑ 418	Walt Williams	.50	.20
❑ 419	Wayne Twitchell	.50	.20
❑ 420	Ray Fosse	.50	.20
❑ 421	Dan Fife	.50	.20
❑ 422	Gonzalo Marquez	.50	.20
❑ 423	Fred Stanley	.50	.20
❑ 424	Jim Beauchamp	.50	.20
❑ 425	Pete Broberg	.50	.20
❑ 426	Rennie Stennett	.50	.20
❑ 427	Bobby Bolin	.50	.20
❑ 428	Gary Sutherland	.50	.20
❑ 429	Dick Lange	.50	.20
❑ 430	Matty Alou	1.00	.40
❑ 431	Gene Garber RC	1.00	.40
❑ 432	Chris Arnold	.50	.20
❑ 433	Lerrin LaGrow	.50	.20
❑ 434	Ken McMullen	.50	.20
❑ 435	Dave Concepcion	2.00	.80
❑ 436	Don Hood	.50	.20
❑ 437	Jim Lyttle	.50	.20
❑ 438	Ed Herrmann	.50	.20
❑ 439	Norm Miller	.50	.20
❑ 440	Jim Kaat	2.00	.80
❑ 441	Tom Ragland	.50	.20
❑ 442	Alan Foster	.50	.20
❑ 443	Tom Hutton	.50	.20
❑ 444	Vic Davalillo	.50	.20
❑ 445	George Medich	.50	.20
❑ 446	Len Randle	.50	.20
❑ 447	Frank Quilici MG	1.00	.40
	Ralph Rowe CO		
	Bob Rodgers CO		
	Vern Morgan CO		
❑ 448	Ron Hodges	.50	.20
❑ 449	Tom McCraw	.50	.20
❑ 450	Rich Hebner	1.00	.40
❑ 451	Tommy John	2.00	.80
❑ 452	Gene Hiser	.50	.20
❑ 453	Balor Moore	.50	.20
❑ 454	Kurt Bevacqua	.50	.20
❑ 455	Tom Bradley	.50	.20
❑ 456	Dave Winfield RC	40.00	16.00
❑ 457	Chuck Goggin	.50	.20
❑ 458	Jim Ray	.50	.20
❑ 459	Cincinnati Reds	2.00	.80
	Team Card		
❑ 460	Boog Powell	2.00	.80
❑ 461	John Odom	.50	.20
❑ 462	Luis Alvarado	.50	.20
❑ 463	Pat Dobson	.50	.20
❑ 464	Jose Cruz	2.00	.80
❑ 465	Dick Bosman	.50	.20
❑ 466	Dick Billings	.50	.20
❑ 467	Winston Llenas	.50	.20
❑ 468	Pepe Frias	.50	.20
❑ 469	Joe Decker	.50	.20
❑ 470	Reggie Jackson ALCS	5.00	2.00
❑ 471	Jon Matlack NLCS	1.00	.40
❑ 472	Darold Knowles WS1	1.00	.40
❑ 473	Willie Mays WS	8.00	3.20
❑ 474	Bert Campaneris WS3	1.00	.40
❑ 475	Rusty Staub WS4	1.00	.40
❑ 476	Cleon Jones WS5	1.00	.40
❑ 477	Reggie Jackson WS	5.00	2.00
❑ 478	Bert Campaneris WS7	1.00	.40
❑ 479	WS Summary	1.00	.40
	A's celebrate; win		
	2nd consecutive		
	championship		
❑ 480	Willie Crawford	.50	.20
❑ 481	Jerry Terrell	.50	.20
❑ 482	Bob Didier	.50	.20
❑ 483	Atlanta Braves	1.00	.40
	Team Card		
❑ 484	Carmen Fanzone	.50	.20
❑ 485	Felipe Alou	2.00	.80
❑ 486	Steve Stone	1.00	.40
❑ 487	Ted Martinez	.50	.20
❑ 488	Andy Etchebarren	.50	.20
❑ 489	Danny Murtaugh MG	1.00	.40
	Don Osborn CO		

Don Leppert CO
Bill Mazeroski CO
Bob Skinner CO
❑ 490 Vada Pinson .... 2.00 .80
❑ 491 Roger Nelson .... .50 .20
❑ 492 Mike Rogodzinski .... .50 .20
❑ 493 Joe Hoerner .... .50 .20
❑ 494 Ed Goodson .... .50 .20
❑ 495 Dick McAuliffe .... 1.00 .40
❑ 496 Tom Murphy .... .50 .20
❑ 497 Bobby Mitchell .... .50 .20
❑ 498 Pat Corrales .... .50 .20
❑ 499 Rusty Torres .... .50 .20
❑ 500 Lee May .... 1.00 .40
❑ 501 Eddie Leon .... .50 .20
❑ 502 Dave LaRoche .... .50 .20
❑ 503 Eric Soderholm .... .50 .20
❑ 504 Joe Niekro .... 1.00 .40
❑ 505 Bill Buckner .... 1.00 .40
❑ 506 Ed Farmer .... .50 .20
❑ 507 Larry Stahl .... .50 .20
❑ 508 Montreal Expos .... 1.00 .40
Team Card
❑ 509 Jesse Jefferson .... .50 .20
❑ 510 Wayne Garrett .... .50 .20
❑ 511 Toby Harrah .... 1.00 .40
❑ 512 Joe Lahoud .... .50 .20
❑ 513 Jim Campanis .... .50 .20
❑ 514 Paul Schaal .... .50 .20
❑ 515 Willie Montanez .... .50 .20
❑ 516 Horacio Pina .... .50 .20
❑ 517 Mike Hegan .... .50 .20
❑ 518 Derrel Thomas .... .50 .20
❑ 519 Bill Sharp .... .50 .20
❑ 520 Tim McCarver .... 2.00 .80
❑ 521 Ken Aspromonte MG .... 1.00 .40
Clay Bryant CO
Tony Pacheco CO
❑ 522 J.R. Richard .... 2.00 .80
❑ 523 Cecil Cooper .... 2.00 .80
❑ 524 Bill Plummer .... .50 .20
❑ 525 Clyde Wright .... .50 .20
❑ 526 Frank Tepedino .... 1.00 .40
❑ 527 Bobby Darwin .... .50 .20
❑ 528 Bill Bonham .... .50 .20
❑ 529 Horace Clarke .... 1.00 .40
❑ 530 Mickey Stanley .... 1.00 .40
❑ 531 Gene Mauch MG .... 1.00 .40
Dave Bristol CO
Cal McLish CO
Larry Doby CO
Jerry Zimmerman CO
❑ 532 Skip Lockwood .... .50 .20
❑ 533 Mike Phillips .... .50 .20
❑ 534 Eddie Watt .... .50 .20
❑ 535 Bob Tolan .... .50 .20
❑ 536 Duffy Dyer .... .50 .20
❑ 537 Steve Mingori .... .50 .20
❑ 538 Cesar Tovar .... .50 .20
❑ 539 Lloyd Allen .... .50 .20
❑ 540 Bob Robertson .... .50 .20
❑ 541 Cleveland Indians .... 1.00 .40
Team Card
❑ 542 Goose Gossage .... 2.00 .80
❑ 543 Danny Cater .... .50 .20
❑ 544 Ron Schueler .... .50 .20
❑ 545 Billy Conigliaro .... 1.00 .40
❑ 546 Mike Corkins .... .50 .20
❑ 547 Glenn Borgmann .... .50 .20
❑ 548 Sonny Siebert .... .50 .20
❑ 549 Mike Jorgensen .... .50 .20
❑ 550 Sam McDowell .... 1.00 .40
❑ 551 Von Joshua .... .50 .20
❑ 552 Denny Doyle .... .50 .20
❑ 553 Jim Willoughby .... .50 .20
❑ 554 Tim Johnson .... .50 .20
❑ 555 Woodie Fryman .... .50 .20
❑ 556 Dave Campbell .... 1.00 .40
❑ 557 Jim McGlothlin .... .50 .20
❑ 558 Bill Fahey .... .50 .20
❑ 559 Darrel Chaney .... .50 .20
❑ 560 Mike Cuellar .... 1.00 .40
❑ 561 Ed Kranepool .... 1.00 .40
❑ 562 Jack Aker .... .50 .20
❑ 563 Hal McRae .... 1.00 .40
❑ 564 Mike Ryan .... .50 .20
❑ 565 Milt Wilcox .... .50 .20
❑ 566 Jackie Hernandez .... .50 .20
❑ 567 Boston Red Sox .... 1.00 .40
Team Card
❑ 568 Mike Torrez .... 1.00 .40
❑ 569 Rick Dempsey .... 1.00 .40
❑ 570 Ralph Garr .... 1.00 .40
❑ 571 Rich Hand .... .50 .20
❑ 572 Enzo Hernandez .... .50 .20
❑ 573 Mike Adams .... .50 .20
❑ 574 Bill Parsons .... .50 .20
❑ 575 Steve Garvey 3.00 1.20
❑ 576 Scipio Spinks .... .50 .20
❑ 577 Mike Sadek .... .50 .20
❑ 578 Ralph Houk MG .... 1.00 .40
❑ 579 Cecil Upshaw .... .50 .20
❑ 580 Jim Spencer .... .50 .20
❑ 581 Fred Norman .... .50 .20
❑ 582 Bucky Dent RC 4.00 1.60
❑ 583 Marty Pattin .... .50 .20
❑ 584 Ken Rudolph .... .50 .20
❑ 585 Merv Rettenmund .... .50 .20
❑ 586 Jack Brohamer .... .50 .20
❑ 587 Larry Christenson .... .50 .20
❑ 588 Hal Lanier .... .50 .20
❑ 589 Boots Day .... .50 .20
❑ 590 Roger Moret .... .50 .20
❑ 591 Sonny Jackson .... .50 .20
❑ 592 Ed Bane .... .50 .20
❑ 593 Steve Yeager .... 1.00 .40
❑ 594 Leroy Stanton .... .50 .20
❑ 595 Steve Blass .... 1.00 .40
❑ 596 Wayne Garland .... .50 .20
Fred Holdsworth
Mark Littell
Dick Pole
❑ 597 Dave Chalk .... 1.00 .40
John Gamble
Pete MacKanin
Manny Trillo RC
❑ 598 Dave Augustine 12.00 4.80
Ken Griffey RC
Steve Ontiveros
Jim Tyrone
❑ 599A Rookie Pitchers WAS .. 2.00 .80
Ron Diorio
Dave Freisleben
Frank Riccelli
Greg Shanahan
❑ 599B Rookie Pitchers SD 3.00 1.20
(SD in large print)
❑ 599C Rookie Pitchers SD 6.00 2.40
(SD in small print)
❑ 600 Ron Cash 5.00 2.00
Jim Cox
Bill Madlock RC
Reggie Sanders
❑ 601 Ed Armbrister 3.00 1.20
Rich Bladt
Brian Downing RC
Bake McBride RC
❑ 602 Glen Abbott .... 1.00 .40
Rick Henninger
Craig Swan
Dan Vossler
❑ 603 Barry Foote .... 1.00 .40
Tom Lundstedt
Charlie Moore RC
Sergio Robles
❑ 604 Terry Hughes 5.00 2.00
John Knox
Andre Thornton RC
Frank White RC
❑ 605 Vic Albury 4.00 1.60
Ken Frailing
Kevin Kobel
Frank Tanana RC
❑ 606 Jim Fuller .... 1.00 .40
Wilbur Howard
Tommy Smith
Otto Velez
❑ 607 Leo Foster .... 1.00 .40
Tom Heintzelman
Dave Rosello
Frank Taveras RC
❑ 608A Rookie Pitchers ERR .... 2.00 .80
Bob Apodaco (sic)
Dick Baney
John D'Acquisto
Mike Wallace
❑ 608B Rookie Pitchers COR .... 1.00 .40
Bob Apodaca
Dick Baney
John D'Acquisto
Mike Wallace
❑ 609 Rico Petrocelli .... 1.00 .40
❑ 610 Dave Kingman .... 2.00 .80
❑ 611 Rich Stelmaszek .... .50 .20
❑ 612 Luke Walker .... .50 .20
❑ 613 Dan Monzon .... .50 .20
❑ 614 Adrian Devine .... .50 .20
❑ 615 Johnny Jeter UER .... .50 .20
(Misspelled Johnnie
on card back)
❑ 616 Larry Gura .... .50 .20
❑ 617 Ted Ford .... .50 .20
❑ 618 Jim Mason .... .50 .20
❑ 619 Mike Anderson .... .50 .20
❑ 620 Al Downing .... .50 .20
❑ 621 Bernie Carbo .... .50 .20
❑ 622 Phil Gagliano .... .50 .20
❑ 623 Celerino Sanchez .... .50 .20
❑ 624 Bob Miller .... .50 .20
❑ 625 Ollie Brown .... .50 .20
❑ 626 Pittsburgh Pirates .... 1.00 .40
Team Card
❑ 627 Carl Taylor .... .50 .20
❑ 628 Ivan Murrell .... .50 .20
❑ 629 Rusty Staub .... 2.00 .80
❑ 630 Tommie Agee .... 1.00 .40
❑ 631 Steve Barber .... .50 .20
❑ 632 George Culver .... .50 .20
❑ 633 Dave Hamilton .... .50 .20
❑ 634 Eddie Mathews MG 3.00 1.20
Herm Starrette CO
Connie Ryan CO
Jim Busby CO
Ken Silvestri CO
❑ 635 Johnny Edwards .... .50 .20
❑ 636 Dave Goltz .... .50 .20
❑ 637 Checklist 529-660 .... 3.00 .60
❑ 638 Ken Sanders .... .50 .20
❑ 639 Joe Lovitto .... .50 .20
❑ 640 Milt Pappas .... 1.00 .40
❑ 641 Chuck Brinkman .... .50 .20
❑ 642 Terry Harmon .... .50 .20
❑ 643 Dodgers Team .... 1.00 .40
❑ 644 Wayne Granger .... .50 .20
❑ 645 Ken Boswell .... .50 .20
❑ 646 George Foster .... 2.00 .80
❑ 647 Juan Beniquez .... .50 .20
❑ 648 Terry Crowley .... .50 .20
❑ 649 Fernando Gonzalez RC .... .50 .20
❑ 650 Mike Epstein .... .50 .20
❑ 651 Leron Lee .... .50 .20
❑ 652 Gail Hopkins .... .50 .20
❑ 653 Bob Stinson .... .50 .20
❑ 654A Jesus Alou ERR 4.00 1.60
(No position)
❑ 654B Jesus Alou COR .... 1.00 .40
(Outfield)
❑ 655 Mike Tyson .... .50 .20
❑ 656 Adrian Garrett .... .50 .20
❑ 657 Jim Shellenback .... .50 .20
❑ 658 Lee Lacy .... .50 .20
❑ 659 Joe Lis .... .50 .20
❑ 660 Larry Dierker .... 2.00 .50

1975 Topps

	NM	Ex
COMPLETE SET (660)	700.00	275.00
WRAPPER (15-CENT)	8.00	3.20

❑ 1 Hank Aaron HL 30.00 10.00
❑ 2 Lou Brock HL 3.00 1.20
❑ 3 Bob Gibson HL 3.00 1.20
❑ 4 Al Kaline HL 6.00 2.40
❑ 5 Nolan Ryan HL 15.00 6.00
❑ 6 Mike Marshall HL .... 1.00 .40
❑ 7 Steve Busby HL 8.00 3.20
Dick Bosman

Nolan Ryan
❑ 8 Rogelio Moret .50 .20
❑ 9 Frank Tepedino 1.00 .40
❑ 10 Willie Davis 1.00 .40
❑ 11 Bill Melton .50 .20
❑ 12 David Clyde .50 .20
❑ 13 Gene Locklear RC 1.00 .40
❑ 14 Milt Wilcox .50 .20
❑ 15 Jose Cardenal 1.00 .40
❑ 16 Frank Tanana 2.00 .80
❑ 17 Dave Concepcion 2.00 .80
❑ 18 Tigers Team CL 2.00 .40
Ralph Houk MG
❑ 19 Jerry Koosman 1.00 .40
❑ 20 Thurman Munson 8.00 3.20
❑ 21 Rollie Fingers 3.00 1.20
❑ 22 Dave Cash .50 .20
❑ 23 Bill Russell 1.00 .40
❑ 24 Al Fitzmorris .50 .20
❑ 25 Lee May 1.00 .40
❑ 26 Dave McNally 1.00 .40
❑ 27 Ken Reitz .50 .20
❑ 28 Tom Murphy .50 .20
❑ 29 Dave Parker 3.00 1.20
❑ 30 Bert Blyleven 2.00 .80
❑ 31 Dave Rader .50 .20
❑ 32 Reggie Cleveland .50 .20
❑ 33 Dusty Baker 2.00 .80
❑ 34 Steve Renko .50 .20
❑ 35 Ron Santo 1.00 .40
❑ 36 Joe Lovitto .50 .20
❑ 37 Dave Freisleben .50 .20
❑ 38 Buddy Bell 2.00 .80
❑ 39 Andre Thornton 1.00 .40
❑ 40 Bill Singer .50 .20
❑ 41 Cesar Geronimo 1.00 .40
❑ 42 Joe Coleman .50 .20
❑ 43 Cleon Jones 1.00 .40
❑ 44 Pat Dobson .50 .20
❑ 45 Joe Rudi 1.00 .40
❑ 46 Phillies Team CL 2.00 .40
Danny Ozark MG UER
Terry Harmon listed as 339
instead of 399
❑ 47 Tommy John 2.00 .80
❑ 48 Freddie Patek 1.00 .40
❑ 49 Larry Dierker 1.00 .40
❑ 50 Brooks Robinson 8.00 3.20
❑ 51 Bob Forsch RC 1.00 .40
❑ 52 Darrell Porter 1.00 .40
❑ 53 Dave Giusti .50 .20
❑ 54 Eric Soderholm .50 .20
❑ 55 Bobby Bonds 2.00 .80
❑ 56 Rick Wise 1.00 .40
❑ 57 Dave Johnson 1.00 .40
❑ 58 Chuck Taylor .50 .20
❑ 59 Ken Henderson .50 .20
❑ 60 Fergie Jenkins 3.00 1.20
❑ 61 Dave Winfield 15.00 6.00
❑ 62 Fritz Peterson .50 .20
❑ 63 Steve Swisher .50 .20
❑ 64 Dave Chalk .50 .20
❑ 65 Don Gullett 1.00 .40
❑ 66 Willie Horton 1.00 .40
❑ 67 Tug McGraw 1.00 .40
❑ 68 Ron Blomberg .50 .20
❑ 69 John Odom .50 .20
❑ 70 Mike Schmidt 20.00 8.00
❑ 71 Charlie Hough 1.00 .40
❑ 72 Royals Team CL 2.00 .40
Jack McKeon MG
❑ 73 J.R. Richard 1.00 .40
❑ 74 Mark Belanger 1.00 .40
❑ 75 Ted Simmons 2.00 .80
❑ 76 Ed Sprague .50 .20
❑ 77 Richie Zisk 1.00 .40
❑ 78 Ray Corbin .50 .20
❑ 79 Gary Matthews 1.00 .40
❑ 80 Carlton Fisk 8.00 3.20
❑ 81 Ron Reed .50 .20
❑ 82 Pat Kelly .50 .20
❑ 83 Jim Merritt .50 .20
❑ 84 Enzo Hernandez .50 .20
❑ 85 Bill Bonham .50 .20
❑ 86 Joe Lis .50 .20
❑ 87 George Foster 2.00 .80
❑ 88 Tom Egan .50 .20
❑ 89 Jim Ray .50 .20
❑ 90 Rusty Staub 2.00 .80
❑ 91 Dick Green .50 .20
❑ 92 Cecil Upshaw .50 .20
❑ 93 Dave Lopes 2.00 .80
❑ 94 Jim Lonborg 1.00 .40
❑ 95 John Mayberry 1.00 .40
❑ 96 Mike Cosgrove .50 .20
❑ 97 Earl Williams .50 .20
❑ 98 Rich Folkers .50 .20
❑ 99 Mike Hegan .50 .20
❑ 100 Willie Stargell 4.00 1.60
❑ 101 Expos Team CL 2.00 .40
Gene Mauch MG
❑ 102 Joe Decker .50 .20
❑ 103 Rick Miller .50 .20
❑ 104 Bill Madlock 2.00 .80
❑ 105 Buzz Capra .50 .20
❑ 106 M. Hargrove RC UER 3.00 1.20
Gastonia At-bats are wrong
❑ 107 Jim Barr .50 .20
❑ 108 Tom Hall .50 .20
❑ 109 George Hendrick 1.00 .40
❑ 110 Wilbur Wood .50 .20
❑ 111 Wayne Garrett .50 .20
❑ 112 Larry Hardy .50 .20
❑ 113 Elliott Maddox .50 .20
❑ 114 Dick Lange .50 .20
❑ 115 Joe Ferguson .50 .20
❑ 116 Lerrin LaGrow .50 .20
❑ 117 Orioles Team CL 3.00 .60
Earl Weaver MG
❑ 118 Mike Anderson .50 .20
❑ 119 Tommy Helms .50 .20
❑ 120 Steve Busby UER 1.00 .40
(Photo actually
Fran Healy)
❑ 121 Bill North .50 .20
❑ 122 Al Hrabosky 1.00 .40
❑ 123 Johnny Briggs .50 .20
❑ 124 Jerry Reuss 1.00 .40
❑ 125 Ken Singleton 1.00 .40
❑ 126 Checklist 1-132 3.00 .60
❑ 127 Glenn Borgmann .50 .20
❑ 128 Bill Lee 1.00 .40
❑ 129 Rick Monday 1.00 .40
❑ 130 Phil Niekro 3.00 1.20
❑ 131 Toby Harrah 1.00 .40
❑ 132 Randy Moffitt .50 .20
❑ 133 Dan Driessen 1.00 .40
❑ 134 Ron Hodges .50 .20
❑ 135 Charlie Spikes .50 .20
❑ 136 Jim Mason .50 .20
❑ 137 Terry Forster 1.00 .40
❑ 138 Del Unser .50 .20
❑ 139 Horacio Pina .50 .20
❑ 140 Steve Garvey 3.00 1.20
❑ 141 Mickey Stanley 1.00 .40
❑ 142 Bob Reynolds .50 .20
❑ 143 Cliff Johnson 1.00 .40
❑ 144 Jim Wohlford .50 .20
❑ 145 Ken Holtzman 1.00 .40
❑ 146 Padres Team CL 2.00 .40
John McNamara MG
❑ 147 Pedro Garcia .50 .20
❑ 148 Jim Rooker .50 .20
❑ 149 Tim Foli .50 .20
❑ 150 Bob Gibson 6.00 2.40
❑ 151 Steve Brye .50 .20
❑ 152 Mario Guerrero .50 .20
❑ 153 Rick Reuschel 1.00 .40
❑ 154 Mike Lum .50 .20
❑ 155 Jim Bibby .50 .20
❑ 156 Dave Kingman 2.00 .80
❑ 157 Pedro Borbon 1.00 .40
❑ 158 Jerry Grote .50 .20
❑ 159 Steve Arlin .50 .20
❑ 160 Graig Nettles 2.00 .80
❑ 161 Stan Bahnsen .50 .20
❑ 162 Willie Montanez .50 .20
❑ 163 Jim Brewer .50 .20
❑ 164 Mickey Rivers 1.00 .40
❑ 165 Doug Rader 1.00 .40
❑ 166 Woodie Fryman .50 .20
❑ 167 Rich Coggins .50 .20
❑ 168 Bill Greif .50 .20
❑ 169 Cookie Rojas .50 .20
❑ 170 Bert Campaneris 1.00 .40
❑ 171 Ed Kirkpatrick .50 .20
❑ 172 Red Sox Team CL 3.00 .60
Darrell Johnson MG
❑ 173 Steve Rogers 1.00 .40
❑ 174 Bake McBride 1.00 .40
❑ 175 Don Money 1.00 .40
❑ 176 Burt Hooton 1.00 .40
❑ 177 Vic Correll .50 .20
❑ 178 Cesar Tovar .50 .20
❑ 179 Tom Bradley .50 .20
❑ 180 Joe Morgan 6.00 2.40
❑ 181 Fred Beene .50 .20
❑ 182 Don Hahn .50 .20
❑ 183 Mel Stottlemyre 1.00 .40
❑ 184 Jorge Orta .50 .20
❑ 185 Steve Carlton 8.00 3.20
❑ 186 Willie Crawford .50 .20
❑ 187 Denny Doyle .50 .20
❑ 188 Tom Griffin .50 .20
❑ 189 Larry (Yogi) Berra 4.00 1.60
Roy Campanella MVP
Campanella card never issued
❑ 190 Bobby Shantz 2.00 .80
Hank Sauer MVP
❑ 191 Al Rosen 2.00 .80
Roy Campanella MVP
❑ 192 Yogi Berra 4.00 1.60
Willie Mays MVP
❑ 193 Yogi Berra 3.00 1.20
Roy Campanella MVP
Campanella card never issued
he is pictured with LA cap
❑ 194 Mickey Mantle 10.00 4.00
Don Newcombe MVP
❑ 195 Mickey Mantle 12.00 4.80
Hank Aaron MVP
❑ 196 Jackie Jensen 3.00 1.20
Ernie Banks MVP
❑ 197 Nellie Fox 2.00 .80
Ernie Banks MVP
❑ 198 Roger Maris 2.00 .80
Dick Groat MVP
❑ 199 Roger Maris 3.00 1.20
Frank Robinson MVP
❑ 200 Mickey Mantle 10.00 4.00
Maury Wills MVP
(Wills card never issued)
❑ 201 Elston Howard 2.00 .80
Sandy Koufax MVP
❑ 202 Brooks Robinson 2.00 .80
Ken Boyer MVP
❑ 203 Zoilo Versalles 2.00 .80
Willie Mays MVP
❑ 204 Frank Robinson 6.00 2.40
Bob Clemente MVP
❑ 205 Carl Yastrzemski 2.00 .80
Orlando Cepeda MVP
❑ 206 Denny McLain UER 2.00 .80
Bob Gibson MVP
On the back McLain is spelled McClain
❑ 207 Harmon Killebrew 2.00 .80
Willie McCovey MVP
❑ 208 Boog Powell 2.00 .80
Johnny Bench MVP
❑ 209 Vida Blue 2.00 .80

Joe Torre MVP
❑ 210 Rich Allen 2.00 .80
Johnny Bench MVP
❑ 211 Reggie Jackson 5.00 2.00
Pete Rose MVP
❑ 212 Jeff Burroughs 2.00 .80
Steve Garvey MVP
❑ 213 Oscar Gamble 1.00 .40
❑ 214 Harry Parker .50 .20
❑ 215 Bobby Valentine 1.00 .40
❑ 216 Giants Team CL 2.00 .40
Wes Westrum MG
❑ 217 Lou Piniella 2.00 .80
❑ 218 Jerry Johnson .50 .20
❑ 219 Ed Herrmann .50 .20
❑ 220 Don Sutton 3.00 1.20
❑ 221 Aurelio Rodriguez .50 .20
❑ 222 Dan Spillner .50 .20
❑ 223 Robin Yount RC 50.00 20.00
❑ 224 Ramon Hernandez .50 .20
❑ 225 Bob Grich 1.00 .40
❑ 226 Bill Campbell .50 .20
❑ 227 Bob Watson 1.00 .40
❑ 228 George Brett RC 80.00 32.00
❑ 229 Barry Foote .50 .20
❑ 230 Jim Hunter 4.00 1.60
❑ 231 Mike Tyson .50 .20
❑ 232 Diego Segui .50 .20
❑ 233 Billy Grabarkewitz .50 .20
❑ 234 Tom Grieve 1.00 .40
❑ 235 Jack Billingham 1.00 .40
❑ 236 Angels Team CL 2.00 .40
Dick Williams MG
❑ 237 Carl Morton 1.00 .40
❑ 238 Dave Duncan 1.00 .40
❑ 239 George Stone .50 .20
❑ 240 Garry Maddox 1.00 .40
❑ 241 Dick Tidrow .50 .20
❑ 242 Jay Johnstone 1.00 .40
❑ 243 Jim Kaat 2.00 .80
❑ 244 Bill Buckner 1.00 .40
❑ 245 Mickey Lolich 2.00 .80
❑ 246 Cardinals Team CL 2.00 .40
Red Schoendienst MG
❑ 247 Enos Cabell .50 .20
❑ 248 Randy Jones 2.00 .80
❑ 249 Danny Thompson .50 .20
❑ 250 Ken Brett .50 .20
❑ 251 Fran Healy .50 .20
❑ 252 Fred Scherman .50 .20
❑ 253 Jesus Alou .50 .20
❑ 254 Mike Torrez 1.00 .40
❑ 255 Dwight Evans 2.00 .80
❑ 256 Billy Champion .50 .20
❑ 257 Checklist: 133-264 3.00 .60
❑ 258 Dave LaRoche .50 .20
❑ 259 Len Randle .50 .20
❑ 260 Johnny Bench 15.00 6.00
❑ 261 Andy Hassler .50 .20
❑ 262 Rowland Office .50 .20
❑ 263 Jim Perry 1.00 .40
❑ 264 John Milner .50 .20
❑ 265 Ron Bryant .50 .20
❑ 266 Sandy Alomar 1.00 .40
❑ 267 Dick Ruthven .50 .20
❑ 268 Hal McRae 1.00 .40
❑ 269 Doug Rau .50 .20
❑ 270 Ron Fairly 1.00 .40
❑ 271 Gerry Moses .50 .20
❑ 272 Lynn McGlothen .50 .20
❑ 273 Steve Braun .50 .20
❑ 274 Vicente Romo .50 .20
❑ 275 Paul Blair 1.00 .40
❑ 276 White Sox Team CL 2.00 .40
Chuck Tanner MG
❑ 277 Frank Taveras .50 .20
❑ 278 Paul Lindblad .50 .20
❑ 279 Milt May .50 .20
❑ 280 Carl Yastrzemski 12.00 4.80
❑ 281 Jim Slaton .50 .20
❑ 282 Jerry Morales .50 .20
❑ 283 Steve Foucault .50 .20
❑ 284 Ken Griffey 4.00 1.60
❑ 285 Ellie Rodriguez .50 .20
❑ 286 Mike Jorgensen .50 .20
❑ 287 Roric Harrison .50 .20
❑ 288 Bruce Ellingsen .50 .20
❑ 289 Ken Rudolph .50 .20
❑ 290 Jon Matlack .50 .20
❑ 291 Bill Sudakis .50 .20
❑ 292 Ron Schueler .50 .20
❑ 293 Dick Sharon .50 .20
❑ 294 Geoff Zahn .50 .20
❑ 295 Vada Pinson 2.00 .80
❑ 296 Alan Foster .50 .20
❑ 297 Craig Kusick .50 .20
❑ 298 Johnny Grubb .50 .20
❑ 299 Bucky Dent 2.00 .80
❑ 300 Reggie Jackson 15.00 6.00
❑ 301 Dave Roberts .50 .20
❑ 302 Rick Burleson 1.00 .40
❑ 303 Grant Jackson .50 .20
❑ 304 Pirates Team CL 2.00 .40
Danny Murtaugh MG
❑ 305 Jim Colborn .50 .20
❑ 306 Rod Carew 2.00 .80
Ralph Garr LL
❑ 307 Dick Allen 4.00 1.60
Mike Schmidt LL
❑ 308 Jeff Burroughs 2.00 .80
Johnny Bench LL
❑ 309 Bill North 2.00 .80
Lou Brock LL
❑ 310 Jim Hunter 2.00 .80
Fergie Jenkins
Andy Messersmith
Phil Niekro LL
❑ 311 Jim Hunter 2.00 .80
Buzz Capra LL
❑ 312 Nolan Ryan 12.00 4.80
Steve Carlton LL
❑ 313 Terry Forster 1.00 .40
Mike Marshall LL
❑ 314 Buck Martinez .50 .20
❑ 315 Don Kessinger 1.00 .40
❑ 316 Jackie Brown .50 .20
❑ 317 Joe Lahoud .50 .20
❑ 318 Ernie McAnally .50 .20
❑ 319 Johnny Oates 1.00 .40
❑ 320 Pete Rose 30.00 12.00
❑ 321 Rudy May .50 .20
❑ 322 Ed Goodson .50 .20
❑ 323 Fred Holdsworth .50 .20
❑ 324 Ed Kranepool 1.00 .40
❑ 325 Tony Oliva 2.00 .80
❑ 326 Wayne Twitchell .50 .20
❑ 327 Jerry Hairston .50 .20
❑ 328 Sonny Siebert .50 .20
❑ 329 Ted Kubiak .50 .20
❑ 330 Mike Marshall 1.00 .40
❑ 331 Indians Team CL 2.00 .40
Frank Robinson MG
❑ 332 Fred Kendall .50 .20
❑ 333 Dick Drago .50 .20
❑ 334 Greg Gross .50 .20
❑ 335 Jim Palmer 6.00 2.40
❑ 336 Rennie Stennett .50 .20
❑ 337 Kevin Kobel .50 .20
❑ 338 Rich Stelmaszek .50 .20
❑ 339 Jim Fregosi 1.00 .40
❑ 340 Paul Splittorff .50 .20
❑ 341 Hal Breeden .50 .20
❑ 342 Leroy Stanton .50 .20
❑ 343 Danny Frisella .50 .20
❑ 344 Ben Oglivie 1.00 .40
❑ 345 Clay Carroll 1.00 .40
❑ 346 Bobby Darwin .50 .20
❑ 347 Mike Caldwell .50 .20
❑ 348 Tony Muser .50 .20
❑ 349 Ray Sadecki .50 .20
❑ 350 Bobby Murcer 1.00 .40
❑ 351 Bob Boone 2.00 .80
❑ 352 Darold Knowles .50 .20
❑ 353 Luis Melendez .50 .20
❑ 354 Dick Bosman .50 .20
❑ 355 Chris Cannizzaro .50 .20
❑ 356 Rico Petrocelli 1.00 .40
❑ 357 Ken Forsch UER .50 .20
Forsch is misspelled in blurb
❑ 358 Al Bumbry 1.00 .40
❑ 359 Paul Popovich .50 .20
❑ 360 George Scott 1.00 .40
❑ 361 Dodgers Team CL 2.00 .40
Walter Alston MG
❑ 362 Steve Hargan .50 .20
❑ 363 Carmen Fanzone .50 .20
❑ 364 Doug Bird .50 .20
❑ 365 Bob Bailey .50 .20
❑ 366 Ken Sanders .50 .20
❑ 367 Craig Robinson .50 .20
❑ 368 Vic Albury .50 .20
❑ 369 Merv Rettenmund .50 .20
❑ 370 Tom Seaver 12.00 4.80
❑ 371 Gates Brown .50 .20
❑ 372 John D'Acquisto .50 .20
❑ 373 Bill Sharp .50 .20
❑ 374 Eddie Watt .50 .20
❑ 375 Roy White 1.00 .40
❑ 376 Steve Yeager 1.00 .40
❑ 377 Tom Hilgendorf .50 .20
❑ 378 Derrel Thomas .50 .20
❑ 379 Bernie Carbo .50 .20
❑ 380 Sal Bando 1.00 .40
❑ 381 John Curtis .50 .20
❑ 382 Don Baylor 2.00 .80
❑ 383 Jim York .50 .20
❑ 384 Brewers Team 2.00 .40
Del Crandall MG
❑ 385 Dock Ellis .50 .20
❑ 386 Checklist: 265-396 UER 3.00 .60
Dick Sharon's name is misspelled
❑ 387 Jim Spencer .50 .20
❑ 388 Steve Stone 1.00 .40
❑ 389 Tony Solaita .50 .20
❑ 390 Ron Cey 2.00 .80
❑ 391 Don DeMola .50 .20
❑ 392 Bruce Bochte RC 1.00 .40
❑ 393 Gary Gentry .50 .20
❑ 394 Larvell Blanks .50 .20
❑ 395 Bud Harrelson 1.00 .40
❑ 396 Fred Norman 1.00 .40
❑ 397 Bill Freehan 1.00 .40
❑ 398 Elias Sosa .50 .20
❑ 399 Terry Harmon .50 .20
❑ 400 Dick Allen 2.00 .80
❑ 401 Mike Wallace .50 .20
❑ 402 Bob Tolan .50 .20
❑ 403 Tom Buskey .50 .20
❑ 404 Ted Sizemore .50 .20
❑ 405 John Montague .50 .20
❑ 406 Bob Gallagher .50 .20
❑ 407 Herb Washington RC 2.00 .80
❑ 408 Clyde Wright UER .50 .20
Listed with wrong 1974 team
❑ 409 Bob Robertson .50 .20
❑ 410 Mike Cueller UER 1.00 .40
Sic, Cuellar
❑ 411 George Mitterwald .50 .20
❑ 412 Bill Hands .50 .20
❑ 413 Marty Pattin .50 .20
❑ 414 Manny Mota 1.00 .40
❑ 415 John Hiller 1.00 .40
❑ 416 Larry Lintz .50 .20
❑ 417 Skip Lockwood .50 .20
❑ 418 Leo Foster .50 .20
❑ 419 Dave Goltz .50 .20
❑ 420 Larry Bowa 2.00 .80
❑ 421 Mets Team CL 3.00 .60
Yogi Berra MG
❑ 422 Brian Downing 1.00 .40
❑ 423 Clay Kirby .50 .20
❑ 424 John Lowenstein .50 .20
❑ 425 Tito Fuentes .50 .20
❑ 426 George Medich .50 .20
❑ 427 Clarence Gaston 1.00 .40
❑ 428 Dave Hamilton .50 .20
❑ 429 Jim Dwyer .50 .20
❑ 430 Luis Tiant 2.00 .80
❑ 431 Rod Gilbreath .50 .20
❑ 432 Ken Berry .50 .20
❑ 433 Larry Demery .50 .20
❑ 434 Bob Locker .50 .20
❑ 435 Dave Nelson .50 .20
❑ 436 Ken Frailing .50 .20
❑ 437 Al Cowens 1.00 .40
❑ 438 Don Carrithers .50 .20
❑ 439 Ed Brinkman .50 .20
❑ 440 Andy Messersmith 1.00 .40

❑ 441 Bobby Heise	.50	.20
❑ 442 Maximino Leon	.50	.20
❑ 443 Twins Team CL	2.00	.40
Frank Quilici MG		
❑ 444 Gene Garber	1.00	.40
❑ 445 Felix Millan	.50	.20
❑ 446 Bart Johnson	.50	.20
❑ 447 Terry Crowley	.50	.20
❑ 448 Frank Duffy	.50	.20
❑ 449 Charlie Williams	.50	.20
❑ 450 Willie McCovey	6.00	2.40
❑ 451 Rick Dempsey	1.00	.40
❑ 452 Angel Mangual	.50	.20
❑ 453 Claude Osteen	1.00	.40
❑ 454 Doug Griffin	.50	.20
❑ 455 Don Wilson	.50	.20
❑ 456 Bob Coluccio	.50	.20
❑ 457 Mario Mendoza	.50	.20
❑ 458 Ross Grimsley	.50	.20
❑ 459 1974 AL Champs	1.00	.40
A's over Orioles		
(Second base action		
pictured)		
❑ 460 Steve Garvey NLCS	2.00	.80
Frank Taveras		
❑ 461 Reggie Jackson WS	5.00	2.00
❑ 462 World Series Game 2	1.00	.40
(Dodger dugout)		
❑ 463 Rollie Fingers WS	2.00	.80
❑ 464 World Series Game 4	1.00	.40
(A's batter)		
❑ 465 Joe Rudi WS5	1.00	.40
❑ 466 WS Summary	2.00	.80
A's do it again;		
win third straight		
A's group picture		
❑ 467 Ed Halicki	.50	.20
❑ 468 Bobby Mitchell	.50	.20
❑ 469 Tom Dettore	.50	.20
❑ 470 Jeff Burroughs	1.00	.40
❑ 471 Bob Stinson	.50	.20
❑ 472 Bruce Dal Canton	.50	.20
❑ 473 Ken McMullen	.50	.20
❑ 474 Luke Walker	.50	.20
❑ 475 Darrell Evans	1.00	.40
❑ 476 Ed Figueroa	.50	.20
❑ 477 Tom Hutton	.50	.20
❑ 478 Tom Burgmeier	.50	.20
❑ 479 Ken Boswell	.50	.20
❑ 480 Carlos May	.50	.20
❑ 481 Will McEnaney	1.00	.40
❑ 482 Tom McCraw	.50	.20
❑ 483 Steve Ontiveros	.50	.20
❑ 484 Glenn Beckert	1.00	.40
❑ 485 Sparky Lyle	1.00	.40
❑ 486 Ray Fosse	.50	.20
❑ 487 Astros Team CL	2.00	.40
Preston Gomez MG		
❑ 488 Bill Travers	.50	.20
❑ 489 Cecil Cooper	2.00	.80
❑ 490 Reggie Smith	1.00	.40
❑ 491 Doyle Alexander	1.00	.40
❑ 492 Rich Hebner	1.00	.40
❑ 493 Don Stanhouse	.50	.20
❑ 494 Pete LaCock	.50	.20
❑ 495 Nelson Briles	1.00	.40
❑ 496 Pepe Frias	.50	.20
❑ 497 Jim Nettles	.50	.20
❑ 498 Al Downing	.50	.20
❑ 499 Marty Perez	.50	.20
❑ 500 Nolan Ryan	50.00	20.00
❑ 501 Bill Robinson	1.00	.40
❑ 502 Pat Bourque	.50	.20
❑ 503 Fred Stanley	.50	.20
❑ 504 Buddy Bradford	.50	.20
❑ 505 Chris Speier	.50	.20
❑ 506 Leron Lee	.50	.20
❑ 507 Tom Carroll	.50	.20
❑ 508 Bob Hansen	.50	.20
❑ 509 Dave Hilton	.50	.20
❑ 510 Vida Blue	1.00	.40
❑ 511 Rangers Team CL	2.00	.40
Billy Martin MG		
❑ 512 Larry Milbourne	.50	.20
❑ 513 Dick Pole	.50	.20
❑ 514 Jose Cruz	2.00	.80
❑ 515 Manny Sanguillen	1.00	.40
❑ 516 Don Hood	.50	.20
❑ 517 Checklist: 397-528	3.00	.60
❑ 518 Leo Cardenas	.50	.20
❑ 519 Jim Todd	.50	.20
❑ 520 Amos Otis	1.00	.40
❑ 521 Dennis Blair	.50	.20
❑ 522 Gary Sutherland	.50	.20
❑ 523 Tom Paciorek	1.00	.40
❑ 524 John Doherty	.50	.20
❑ 525 Tom House	.50	.20
❑ 526 Larry Hisle	1.00	.40
❑ 527 Mac Scarce	.50	.20
❑ 528 Eddie Leon	.50	.20
❑ 529 Gary Thomasson	.50	.20
❑ 530 Gaylord Perry	3.00	1.20
❑ 531 Reds Team CL	5.00	1.00
Sparky Anderson MG		
❑ 532 Gorman Thomas	1.00	.40
❑ 533 Rudy Meoli	.50	.20
❑ 534 Alex Johnson	.50	.20
❑ 535 Gene Tenace	1.00	.40
❑ 536 Bob Moose	.50	.20
❑ 537 Tommy Harper	1.00	.40
❑ 538 Duffy Dyer	.50	.20
❑ 539 Jesse Jefferson	.50	.20
❑ 540 Lou Brock	6.00	2.40
❑ 541 Roger Metzger	.50	.20
❑ 542 Pete Broberg	.50	.20
❑ 543 Larry Biittner	.50	.20
❑ 544 Steve Mingori	.50	.20
❑ 545 Billy Williams	3.00	1.20
❑ 546 John Knox	.50	.20
❑ 547 Von Joshua	.50	.20
❑ 548 Charlie Sands	.50	.20
❑ 549 Bill Butler	.50	.20
❑ 550 Ralph Garr	1.00	.40
❑ 551 Larry Christenson	.50	.20
❑ 552 Jack Brohamer	.50	.20
❑ 553 John Boccabella	.50	.20
❑ 554 Goose Gossage	2.00	.80
❑ 555 Al Oliver	2.00	.80
❑ 556 Tim Johnson	.50	.20
❑ 557 Larry Gura	.50	.20
❑ 558 Dave Roberts	.50	.20
❑ 559 Bob Montgomery	.50	.20
❑ 560 Tony Perez	4.00	1.60
❑ 561 A's Team CL	2.00	.40
Alvin Dark MG		
❑ 562 Gary Nolan	1.00	.40
❑ 563 Wilbur Howard	.50	.20
❑ 564 Tommy Davis	1.00	.40
❑ 565 Joe Torre	2.00	.80
❑ 566 Ray Burris	.50	.20
❑ 567 Jim Sundberg RC	2.00	.80
❑ 568 Dale Murray	.50	.20
❑ 569 Frank White	1.00	.40
❑ 570 Jim Wynn	1.00	.40
❑ 571 Dave Lemanczyk	.50	.20
❑ 572 Roger Nelson	.50	.20
❑ 573 Orlando Pena	.50	.20
❑ 574 Tony Taylor	.50	.20
❑ 575 Gene Clines	.50	.20
❑ 576 Phil Roof	.50	.20
❑ 577 John Morris	.50	.20
❑ 578 Dave Tomlin	.50	.20
❑ 579 Skip Pitlock	.50	.20
❑ 580 Frank Robinson	6.00	2.40
❑ 581 Darrel Chaney	.50	.20
❑ 582 Eduardo Rodriguez	.50	.20
❑ 583 Andy Etchebarren	.50	.20
❑ 584 Mike Garman	.50	.20
❑ 585 Chris Chambliss	1.00	.40
❑ 586 Tim McCarver	2.00	.80
❑ 587 Chris Ward	.50	.20
❑ 588 Rick Auerbach	.50	.20
❑ 589 Braves Team CL	2.00	.40
Clyde King MG		
❑ 590 Cesar Cedeno	1.00	.40
❑ 591 Glenn Abbott	.50	.20
❑ 592 Balor Moore	.50	.20
❑ 593 Gene Lamont	.50	.20
❑ 594 Jim Fuller	.50	.20
❑ 595 Joe Niekro	1.00	.40
❑ 596 Ollie Brown	.50	.20
❑ 597 Winston Llenas	.50	.20
❑ 598 Bruce Kison	.50	.20
❑ 599 Nate Colbert	.50	.20
❑ 600 Rod Carew	8.00	3.20
❑ 601 Juan Beniquez	.50	.20
❑ 602 John Vukovich	.50	.20
❑ 603 Lew Krausse	.50	.20
❑ 604 Oscar Zamora	.50	.20
❑ 605 John Ellis	.50	.20
❑ 606 Bruce Miller	.50	.20
❑ 607 Jim Holt	.50	.20
❑ 608 Gene Michael	.50	.20
❑ 609 Elrod Hendricks	.50	.20
❑ 610 Ron Hunt	.50	.20
❑ 611 Yankees Team CL	2.00	.40
Bill Virdon MG		
❑ 612 Terry Hughes	.50	.20
❑ 613 Bill Parsons	.50	.20
❑ 614 Jack Kucek	1.00	.40
Dyar Miller		
Vern Ruhle		
Paul Siebert		
❑ 615 Pat Darcy	2.00	.80
Dennis Leonard RC		
Tom Underwood		
Hank Webb		
❑ 616 Dave Augustine	15.00	6.00
Pepe Mangual		
Jim Rice RC		
John Scott		
❑ 617 Mike Cubbage	2.00	.80
Doug DeCinces RC		
Reggie Sanders		
Manny Trillo		
❑ 618 Jamie Easterly	1.00	.40
Tom Johnson		
Scott McGregor RC		
Rick Rhoden		
❑ 619 Benny Ayala	1.00	.40
Nyls Nyman		
Tommy Smith		
Jerry Turner		
❑ 620 Gary Carter RC	15.00	6.00
Marc Hill		
Danny Meyer		
Leon Roberts		
❑ 621 John Denny RC	2.00	.80
Rawly Eastwick		
Jim Kern		
Juan Veintidos		
❑ 622 Ed Armbrister	8.00	3.20
Fred Lynn RC		
Tom Poquette		
Terry Whitfield UER		
(Listed as Ney York)		
❑ 623 Phil Garner	6.00	2.40
Keith Hernandez RC UER		
(Sic, bats right)		
Bob Sheldon		
Tom Veryzer		
❑ 624 Doug Konieczny	1.00	.40
Gary Lavelle		
Jim Otten		
Eddie Solomon		
❑ 625 Boog Powell	2.00	.80
❑ 626 Larry Haney UER	.50	.20
Photo actually		
Dave Duncan		
❑ 627 Tom Walker	.50	.20
❑ 628 Ron LeFlore RC	1.00	.40
❑ 629 Joe Hoerner	.50	.20
❑ 630 Greg Luzinski	2.00	.80
❑ 631 Lee Lacy	.50	.20
❑ 632 Morris Nettles	.50	.20
❑ 633 Paul Casanova	.50	.20
❑ 634 Cy Acosta	.50	.20
❑ 635 Chuck Dobson	.50	.20
❑ 636 Charlie Moore	.50	.20
❑ 637 Ted Martinez	.50	.20
❑ 638 Cubs Team CL	2.00	.40
Jim Marshall MG		
❑ 639 Steve Kline	.50	.20
❑ 640 Harmon Killebrew	6.00	2.40
❑ 641 Jim Northrup	1.00	.40
❑ 642 Mike Phillips	.50	.20
❑ 643 Brent Strom	.50	.20
❑ 644 Bill Fahey	.50	.20

❑ 645 Danny Cater .50 .20
❑ 646 Checklist: 529-660 3.00 .60
❑ 647 Cl. Washington RC 2.00 .80
❑ 648 Dave Pagan .50 .20
❑ 649 Jack Heidemann .50 .20
❑ 650 Dave May .50 .20
❑ 651 John Morlan .50 .20
❑ 652 Lindy McDaniel 1.00 .40
❑ 653 Lee Richard UER .50 .20
(Listed as Richards on card front)
❑ 654 Jerry Terrell .50 .20
❑ 655 Rico Carty 1.00 .40
❑ 656 Bill Plummer .50 .20
❑ 657 Bob Oliver .50 .20
❑ 658 Vic Harris .50 .20
❑ 659 Bob Apodaca .50 .20
❑ 660 Hank Aaron 30.00 9.00

1976 Topps

	NM	Ex
COMPLETE SET (660)	300.00	120.00

❑ 1 Hank Aaron RB 15.00 4.70
❑ 2 Bobby Bonds RB 1.50 .60
❑ 3 Mickey Lolich RB .75 .30
❑ 4 Dave Lopes RB .75 .30
❑ 5 Tom Seaver RB 5.00 2.00
❑ 6 Rennie Stennett RB .75 .30
❑ 7 Jim Umbarger .40 .16
❑ 8 Tito Fuentes .40 .16
❑ 9 Paul Lindblad .40 .16
❑ 10 Lou Brock 5.00 2.00
❑ 11 Jim Hughes .40 .16
❑ 12 Richie Zisk .75 .30
❑ 13 John Wockenfuss .40 .16
❑ 14 Gene Garber .75 .30
❑ 15 George Scott .75 .30
❑ 16 Bob Apodaca .40 .16
❑ 17 New York Yankees 1.50 .30
Team Card CL
Billy Martin MG
❑ 18 Dale Murray .40 .16
❑ 19 George Brett 30.00 12.00
❑ 20 Bob Watson .75 .30
❑ 21 Dave LaRoche .40 .16
❑ 22 Bill Russell .75 .30
❑ 23 Brian Downing .40 .16
❑ 24 Cesar Geronimo .75 .30
❑ 25 Mike Torrez .75 .30
❑ 26 Andre Thornton .75 .30
❑ 27 Ed Figueroa .40 .16
❑ 28 Dusty Baker 1.50 .60
❑ 29 Rick Burleson .75 .30
❑ 30 John Montefusco .75 .30
❑ 31 Len Randle .40 .16
❑ 32 Danny Frisella .40 .16
❑ 33 Bill North .40 .16
❑ 34 Mike Garman .40 .16
❑ 35 Tony Oliva 1.50 .60
❑ 36 Frank Taveras .40 .16
❑ 37 John Hiller .75 .30
❑ 38 Garry Maddox .75 .30
❑ 39 Pete Broberg .40 .16
❑ 40 Dave Kingman 1.50 .60
❑ 41 Tippy Martinez .75 .30
❑ 42 Barry Foote .40 .16
❑ 43 Paul Splittorff .40 .16
❑ 44 Doug Rader .75 .30
❑ 45 Boog Powell 1.50 .60
❑ 46 Los Angeles Dodgers 1.50 .30
Team Card CL
Walter Alston MG
❑ 47 Jesse Jefferson .40 .16
❑ 48 Dave Concepcion 1.50 .60
❑ 49 Dave Duncan .75 .30
❑ 50 Fred Lynn 1.50 .60
❑ 51 Ray Burris .40 .16
❑ 52 Dave Chalk .40 .16
❑ 53 Mike Beard .40 .16
❑ 54 Dave Rader .40 .16
❑ 55 Gaylord Perry 2.50 1.00
❑ 56 Bob Tolan .40 .16
❑ 57 Phil Garner .75 .30
❑ 58 Ron Reed .40 .16
❑ 59 Larry Hisle .75 .30
❑ 60 Jerry Reuss .75 .30
❑ 61 Ron LeFlore .75 .30
❑ 62 Johnny Oates .75 .30
❑ 63 Bobby Darwin .40 .16
❑ 64 Jerry Koosman .75 .30
❑ 65 Chris Chambliss .75 .30
❑ 66 Gus Bell FS .75 .30
Buddy Bell
❑ 67 Ray Boone FS .75 .30
Bob Boone
❑ 68 Joe Coleman FS .40 .16
Joe Coleman Jr.
❑ 69 Jim Hegan FS .40 .16
Mike Hegan
❑ 70 Roy Smalley FS .75 .30
Roy Smalley Jr.
❑ 71 Steve Rogers .75 .30
❑ 72 Hal McRae .75 .30
❑ 73 Baltimore Orioles 1.50 .30
Team Card CL
Earl Weaver MG
❑ 74 Oscar Gamble .75 .30
❑ 75 Larry Dierker .75 .30
❑ 76 Willie Crawford .40 .16
❑ 77 Pedro Borbon .75 .30
❑ 78 Cecil Cooper .75 .30
❑ 79 Jerry Morales .40 .16
❑ 80 Jim Kaat 1.50 .60
❑ 81 Darrell Evans .75 .30
❑ 82 Von Joshua .40 .16
❑ 83 Jim Spencer .40 .16
❑ 84 Brent Strom .40 .16
❑ 85 Mickey Rivers .75 .30
❑ 86 Mike Tyson .40 .16
❑ 87 Tom Burgmeier .40 .16
❑ 88 Duffy Dyer .40 .16
❑ 89 Vern Ruhle .40 .16
❑ 90 Sal Bando .75 .30
❑ 91 Tom Hutton .40 .16
❑ 92 Eduardo Rodriguez .40 .16
❑ 93 Mike Phillips .40 .16
❑ 94 Jim Dwyer .40 .16
❑ 95 Brooks Robinson 6.00 2.40
❑ 96 Doug Bird .40 .16
❑ 97 Wilbur Howard .40 .16
❑ 98 Dennis Eckersley RC 25.00 10.00
❑ 99 Lee Lacy .40 .16
❑ 100 Jim Hunter 3.00 1.20
❑ 101 Pete LaCock .40 .16
❑ 102 Jim Willoughby .40 .16
❑ 103 Biff Pocoroba .40 .16
❑ 104 Cincinnati Reds 2.50 .50
Team Card CL
Sparky Anderson MG
❑ 105 Gary Lavelle .40 .16
❑ 106 Tom Grieve .75 .30
❑ 107 Dave Roberts .40 .16
❑ 108 Don Kirkwood .40 .16
❑ 109 Larry Lintz .40 .16
❑ 110 Carlos May .40 .16
❑ 111 Danny Thompson .40 .16
❑ 112 Kent Tekulve RC 1.50 .60
❑ 113 Gary Sutherland .40 .16
❑ 114 Jay Johnstone .75 .30
❑ 115 Ken Holtzman .75 .30
❑ 116 Charlie Moore .40 .16
❑ 117 Mike Jorgensen .40 .16
❑ 118 Boston Red Sox 1.50 .30
Team Card CL
Darrell Johnson MG
❑ 119 Checklist 1-132 1.50 .30
❑ 120 Rusty Staub .75 .30
❑ 121 Tony Solaita .40 .16
❑ 122 Mike Cosgrove .40 .16
❑ 123 Walt Williams .40 .16
❑ 124 Doug Rau .40 .16
❑ 125 Don Baylor 1.50 .60
❑ 126 Tom Dettore .40 .16
❑ 127 Larvell Blanks .40 .16
❑ 128 Ken Griffey Sr. 2.50 1.00
❑ 129 Andy Etchebarren .40 .16
❑ 130 Luis Tiant 1.50 .60
❑ 131 Bill Stein .40 .16
❑ 132 Don Hood .40 .16
❑ 133 Gary Matthews .75 .30
❑ 134 Mike Ivie .40 .16
❑ 135 Bake McBride .75 .30
❑ 136 Dave Goltz .40 .16
❑ 137 Bill Robinson .75 .30
❑ 138 Lerrin LaGrow .40 .16
❑ 139 Gorman Thomas .75 .30
❑ 140 Vida Blue .75 .30
❑ 141 Larry Parrish RC 1.50 .60
❑ 142 Dick Drago .40 .16
❑ 143 Jerry Grote .40 .16
❑ 144 Al Fitzmorris .40 .16
❑ 145 Larry Bowa .75 .30
❑ 146 George Medich .40 .16
❑ 147 Houston Astros 1.50 .30
Team Card CL
Bill Virdon MG
❑ 148 Stan Thomas .40 .16
❑ 149 Tommy Davis .75 .30
❑ 150 Steve Garvey 2.50 1.00
❑ 151 Bill Bonham .40 .16
❑ 152 Leroy Stanton .40 .16
❑ 153 Buzz Capra .40 .16
❑ 154 Bucky Dent .75 .30
❑ 155 Jack Billingham .75 .30
❑ 156 Rico Carty .75 .30
❑ 157 Mike Caldwell .40 .16
❑ 158 Ken Reitz .40 .16
❑ 159 Jerry Terrell .40 .16
❑ 160 Dave Winfield 10.00 4.00
❑ 161 Bruce Kison .40 .16
❑ 162 Jack Pierce .40 .16
❑ 163 Jim Slaton .40 .16
❑ 164 Pepe Mangual .40 .16
❑ 165 Gene Tenace .75 .30
❑ 166 Skip Lockwood .40 .16
❑ 167 Freddie Patek .75 .30
❑ 168 Tom Hilgendorf .40 .16
❑ 169 Graig Nettles 1.50 .60
❑ 170 Rick Wise .40 .16
❑ 171 Greg Gross .40 .16
❑ 172 Texas Rangers 1.50 .30
Team Card CL
Frank Lucchesi MG
❑ 173 Steve Swisher .40 .16
❑ 174 Charlie Hough .75 .30
❑ 175 Ken Singleton .75 .30
❑ 176 Dick Lange .40 .16
❑ 177 Marty Perez .40 .16
❑ 178 Tom Buskey .40 .16
❑ 179 George Foster 1.50 .60
❑ 180 Goose Gossage 1.50 .60
❑ 181 Willie Montanez .40 .16
❑ 182 Harry Rasmussen .40 .16
❑ 183 Steve Braun .40 .16
❑ 184 Bill Greif .40 .16
❑ 185 Dave Parker 1.50 .60
❑ 186 Tom Walker .40 .16
❑ 187 Pedro Garcia .40 .16
❑ 188 Fred Scherman .40 .16
❑ 189 Claudell Washington .75 .30
❑ 190 Jon Matlack .40 .16
❑ 191 Bill Madlock .75 .30
Ted Simmons
Manny Sanguillen LL
❑ 192 Rod Carew 2.50 1.00
Fred Lynn
Thurman Munson LL
❑ 193 Mike Schmidt 3.00 1.20

Dave Kingman
Greg Luzinski LL
❑ 194 Reggie Jackson 3.00 1.20
George Scott
John Mayberry LL
❑ 195 Greg Luzinski 1.50 .60
Johnny Bench
Tony Perez LL
❑ 196 George Scott .75 .30
John Mayberry
Fred Lynn LL
❑ 197 Dave Lopes 1.50 .60
Joe Morgan
Lou Brock LL
❑ 198 Mickey Rivers .75 .30
Claudell Washington
Amos Otis LL
❑ 199 Tom Seaver 2.50 1.00
Randy Jones
Andy Messersmith LL
❑ 200 Jim Hunter 1.50 .60
Jim Palmer
Vida Blue LL
❑ 201 Randy Jones 1.50 .60
Andy Messersmith
Tom Seaver LL
❑ 202 Jim Palmer 3.00 1.20
Jim Hunter
Dennis Eckersley LL
❑ 203 Tom Seaver 2.50 1.00
John Montefusco
Andy Messersmith LL
❑ 204 Frank Tanana .75 .30
Bert Blyleven
Gaylord Perry LL
❑ 205 Al Hrabosky .75 .30
Rich Gossage LL
❑ 206 Manny Trillo .40 .16
❑ 207 Andy Hassler .40 .16
❑ 208 Mike Lum .40 .16
❑ 209 Alan Ashby .75 .30
❑ 210 Lee May .75 .30
❑ 211 Clay Carroll .75 .30
❑ 212 Pat Kelly .40 .16
❑ 213 Dave Heaverlo .40 .16
❑ 214 Eric Soderholm .40 .16
❑ 215 Reggie Smith .75 .30
❑ 216 Montreal Expos 1.50 .30
Team Card CL
Karl Kuehl MG
❑ 217 Dave Freisleben .40 .16
❑ 218 John Knox .40 .16
❑ 219 Tom Murphy .40 .16
❑ 220 Manny Sanguillen .75 .30
❑ 221 Jim Todd .40 .16
❑ 222 Wayne Garrett .40 .16
❑ 223 Ollie Brown .40 .16
❑ 224 Jim York .40 .16
❑ 225 Roy White .75 .30
❑ 226 Jim Sundberg .75 .30
❑ 227 Oscar Zamora .40 .16
❑ 228 John Hale .40 .16
❑ 229 Jerry Remy .40 .16
❑ 230 Carl Yastrzemski 10.00 4.00
❑ 231 Tom House .40 .16
❑ 232 Frank Duffy .40 .16
❑ 233 Grant Jackson .40 .16
❑ 234 Mike Sadek .40 .16
❑ 235 Bert Blyleven 1.50 .60
❑ 236 Kansas City Royals 1.50 .30
Team Card CL
Whitey Herzog MG
❑ 237 Dave Hamilton .40 .16
❑ 238 Larry Biittner .40 .16
❑ 239 John Curtis .40 .16
❑ 240 Pete Rose 25.00 10.00
❑ 241 Hector Torres .40 .16
❑ 242 Dan Meyer .40 .16
❑ 243 Jim Rooker .40 .16
❑ 244 Bill Sharp .40 .16
❑ 245 Felix Millan .40 .16
❑ 246 Cesar Tovar .40 .16
❑ 247 Terry Harmon .40 .16
❑ 248 Dick Tidrow .40 .16
❑ 249 Cliff Johnson .75 .30
❑ 250 Fergie Jenkins 2.50 1.00
❑ 251 Rick Monday .75 .30
❑ 252 Tim Nordbrook .40 .16
❑ 253 Bill Buckner .75 .30
❑ 254 Rudy Meoli .40 .16
❑ 255 Fritz Peterson .40 .16
❑ 256 Rowland Office .40 .16
❑ 257 Ross Grimsley .40 .16
❑ 258 Nyls Nyman .40 .16
❑ 259 Darrel Chaney .40 .16
❑ 260 Steve Busby .40 .16
❑ 261 Gary Thomasson .40 .16
❑ 262 Checklist 133-264 1.50 .30
❑ 263 Lyman Bostock RC 1.50 .60
❑ 264 Steve Renko .40 .16
❑ 265 Willie Davis .75 .30
❑ 266 Alan Foster .40 .16
❑ 267 Aurelio Rodriguez .40 .16
❑ 268 Del Unser .40 .16
❑ 269 Rick Austin .40 .16
❑ 270 Willie Stargell 3.00 1.20
❑ 271 Jim Lonborg .75 .30
❑ 272 Rick Dempsey .75 .30
❑ 273 Joe Niekro .75 .30
❑ 274 Tommy Harper .75 .30
❑ 275 Rick Manning .40 .16
❑ 276 Mickey Scott .40 .16
❑ 277 Chicago Cubs 1.50 .30
Team Card CL
Jim Marshall MG
❑ 278 Bernie Carbo .40 .16
❑ 279 Roy Howell .40 .16
❑ 280 Burt Hooton .75 .30
❑ 281 Dave May .40 .16
❑ 282 Dan Osborn .40 .16
❑ 283 Merv Rettenmund .40 .16
❑ 284 Steve Ontiveros .40 .16
❑ 285 Mike Cuellar .75 .30
❑ 286 Jim Wohlford .40 .16
❑ 287 Pete Mackanin .40 .16
❑ 288 Bill Campbell .40 .16
❑ 289 Enzo Hernandez .40 .16
❑ 290 Ted Simmons .75 .30
❑ 291 Ken Sanders .40 .16
❑ 292 Leon Roberts .40 .16
❑ 293 Bill Castro .40 .16
❑ 294 Ed Kirkpatrick .40 .16
❑ 295 Dave Cash .40 .16
❑ 296 Pat Dobson .40 .16
❑ 297 Roger Metzger .40 .16
❑ 298 Dick Bosman .40 .16
❑ 299 Champ Summers .40 .16
❑ 300 Johnny Bench 12.00 4.80
❑ 301 Jackie Brown .40 .16
❑ 302 Rick Miller .40 .16
❑ 303 Steve Foucault .40 .16
❑ 304 California Angels 1.50 .30
Team Card CL
Dick Williams MG
❑ 305 Andy Messersmith .75 .30
❑ 306 Rod Gilbreath .40 .16
❑ 307 Al Bumbry .75 .30
❑ 308 Jim Barr .40 .16
❑ 309 Bill Melton .40 .16
❑ 310 Randy Jones .75 .30
❑ 311 Cookie Rojas .40 .16
❑ 312 Don Carrithers .40 .16
❑ 313 Dan Ford .40 .16
❑ 314 Ed Kranepool .40 .16
❑ 315 Al Hrabosky .75 .30
❑ 316 Robin Yount 15.00 6.00
❑ 317 John Candelaria RC 1.50 .60
❑ 318 Bob Boone 1.50 .60
❑ 319 Larry Gura .40 .16
❑ 320 Willie Horton .75 .30
❑ 321 Jose Cruz 1.50 .60
❑ 322 Glenn Abbott .40 .16
❑ 323 Rob Sperring .40 .16
❑ 324 Jim Bibby .40 .16
❑ 325 Tony Perez 3.00 1.20
❑ 326 Dick Pole .40 .16
❑ 327 Dave Moates .40 .16
❑ 328 Carl Morton .40 .16
❑ 329 Joe Ferguson .40 .16
❑ 330 Nolan Ryan 25.00 10.00
❑ 331 San Diego Padres 1.50 .30
Team Card CL
John McNamara MG
❑ 332 Charlie Williams .40 .16
❑ 333 Bob Coluccio .40 .16
❑ 334 Dennis Leonard .75 .30
❑ 335 Bob Grich .75 .30
❑ 336 Vic Albury .40 .16
❑ 337 Bud Harrelson .75 .30
❑ 338 Bob Bailey .40 .16
❑ 339 John Denny .75 .30
❑ 340 Jim Rice 4.00 1.60
❑ 341 Lou Gehrig ATG 12.00 4.80
❑ 342 Rogers Hornsby ATG 3.00 1.20
❑ 343 Pie Traynor ATG 1.50 .60
❑ 344 Honus Wagner ATG 5.00 2.00
❑ 345 Babe Ruth ATG 15.00 6.00
❑ 346 Ty Cobb ATG 12.00 4.80
❑ 347 Ted Williams ATG 12.00 4.80
❑ 348 Mickey Cochrane ATG 1.50 .60
❑ 349 Walter Johnson ATG 5.00 2.00
❑ 350 Lefty Grove ATG 1.50 .60
❑ 351 Randy Hundley .75 .30
❑ 352 Dave Giusti .40 .16
❑ 353 Sixto Lezcano .75 .30
❑ 354 Ron Blomberg .40 .16
❑ 355 Steve Carlton 6.00 2.40
❑ 356 Ted Martinez .40 .16
❑ 357 Ken Forsch .40 .16
❑ 358 Buddy Bell .75 .30
❑ 359 Rick Reuschel .75 .30
❑ 360 Jeff Burroughs .75 .30
❑ 361 Detroit Tigers 1.50 .30
Team Card CL
Ralph Houk MG
❑ 362 Will McEnaney .75 .30
❑ 363 Dave Collins RC .75 .30
❑ 364 Elias Sosa .40 .16
❑ 365 Carlton Fisk 6.00 2.40
❑ 366 Bobby Valentine .75 .30
❑ 367 Bruce Miller .40 .16
❑ 368 Wilbur Wood .40 .16
❑ 369 Frank White .75 .30
❑ 370 Ron Cey .75 .30
❑ 371 Elrod Hendricks .40 .16
❑ 372 Rick Baldwin .40 .16
❑ 373 Johnny Briggs .40 .16
❑ 374 Dan Warthen .40 .16
❑ 375 Ron Fairly .75 .30
❑ 376 Rich Hebner .75 .30
❑ 377 Mike Hegan .40 .16
❑ 378 Steve Stone .75 .30
❑ 379 Ken Boswell .40 .16
❑ 380 Bobby Bonds 1.50 .60
❑ 381 Denny Doyle .40 .16
❑ 382 Matt Alexander .40 .16
❑ 383 John Ellis .40 .16
❑ 384 Philadelphia Phillies 1.50 .30
Team Card CL
Danny Ozark MG
❑ 385 Mickey Lolich .75 .30
❑ 386 Ed Goodson .40 .16
❑ 387 Mike Miley .40 .16
❑ 388 Stan Perzanowski .40 .16
❑ 389 Glenn Adams .40 .16
❑ 390 Don Gullett .75 .30
❑ 391 Jerry Hairston .40 .16
❑ 392 Checklist 265-396 1.50 .30
❑ 393 Paul Mitchell .40 .16
❑ 394 Fran Healy .40 .16
❑ 395 Jim Wynn .75 .30
❑ 396 Bill Lee .40 .16
❑ 397 Tim Foli .40 .16
❑ 398 Dave Tomlin .40 .16
❑ 399 Luis Melendez .40 .16
❑ 400 Rod Carew 6.00 2.40
❑ 401 Ken Brett .40 .16
❑ 402 Don Money .75 .30
❑ 403 Geoff Zahn .40 .16
❑ 404 Enos Cabell .40 .16
❑ 405 Rollie Fingers 2.50 1.00
❑ 406 Ed Herrmann .40 .16
❑ 407 Tom Underwood .40 .16
❑ 408 Charlie Spikes .40 .16
❑ 409 Dave Lemanczyk .40 .16
❑ 410 Ralph Garr .75 .30
❑ 411 Bill Singer .40 .16
❑ 412 Toby Harrah .75 .30

❑ 413 Pete Varney .40 .16
❑ 414 Wayne Garland .40 .16
❑ 415 Vada Pinson 1.50 .60
❑ 416 Tommy John 1.50 .60
❑ 417 Gene Clines .40 .16
❑ 418 Jose Morales RC .40 .16
❑ 419 Reggie Cleveland .40 .16
❑ 420 Joe Morgan 5.00 2.00
❑ 421 Oakland A's 1.50 .30
Team Card CL
(No MG on front
❑ 422 Johnny Grubb .40 .16
❑ 423 Ed Halicki .40 .16
❑ 424 Phil Roof .40 .16
❑ 425 Rennie Stennett .40 .16
❑ 426 Bob Forsch .40 .16
❑ 427 Kurt Bevacqua .40 .16
❑ 428 Jim Crawford .40 .16
❑ 429 Fred Stanley .40 .16
❑ 430 Jose Cardenal .75 .30
❑ 431 Dick Ruthven .40 .16
❑ 432 Tom Veryzer .40 .16
❑ 433 Rick Waits .40 .16
❑ 434 Morris Nettles .40 .16
❑ 435 Phil Niekro 2.50 1.00
❑ 436 Bill Fahey .40 .16
❑ 437 Terry Forster .40 .16
❑ 438 Doug DeCinces .75 .30
❑ 439 Rick Rhoden .75 .30
❑ 440 John Mayberry .75 .30
❑ 441 Gary Carter 4.00 1.60
❑ 442 Hank Webb .40 .16
❑ 443 San Francisco Giants 1.50 .30
Team Card CL
(No MG on front
❑ 444 Gary Nolan .75 .30
❑ 445 Rico Petrocelli .75 .30
❑ 446 Larry Haney .40 .16
❑ 447 Gene Locklear .75 .30
❑ 448 Tom Johnson .40 .16
❑ 449 Bob Robertson .40 .16
❑ 450 Jim Palmer 5.00 2.00
❑ 451 Buddy Bradford .40 .16
❑ 452 Tom Hausman .40 .16
❑ 453 Lou Piniella 1.50 .60
❑ 454 Tom Griffin .40 .16
❑ 455 Dick Allen 1.50 .60
❑ 456 Joe Coleman .40 .16
❑ 457 Ed Crosby .40 .16
❑ 458 Earl Williams .40 .16
❑ 459 Jim Brewer .40 .16
❑ 460 Cesar Cedeno .75 .30
❑ 461 NL and AL Champs .75 .30
Reds sweep Bucs,
Bosox surprise A's
❑ 462 '75 World Series .75 .30
Reds Champs
❑ 463 Steve Hargan .40 .16
❑ 464 Ken Henderson .40 .16
❑ 465 Mike Marshall .75 .30
❑ 466 Bob Stinson .40 .16
❑ 467 Woodie Fryman .40 .16
❑ 468 Jesus Alou .40 .16
❑ 469 Rawly Eastwick .75 .30
❑ 470 Bobby Murcer .75 .30
❑ 471 Jim Burton .40 .16
❑ 472 Bob Davis .40 .16
❑ 473 Paul Blair .75 .30
❑ 474 Ray Corbin .40 .16
❑ 475 Joe Rudi .75 .30
❑ 476 Bob Moose .40 .16
❑ 477 Cleveland Indians 1.50 .30
Team Card CL
Frank Robinson MG
❑ 478 Lynn McGlothen .40 .16
❑ 479 Bobby Mitchell .40 .16
❑ 480 Mike Schmidt 15.00 6.00
❑ 481 Rudy May .40 .16
❑ 482 Tim Hosley .40 .16
❑ 483 Mickey Stanley .40 .16
❑ 484 Eric Raich .40 .16
❑ 485 Mike Hargrove .75 .30
❑ 486 Bruce Dal Canton .40 .16
❑ 487 Leron Lee .40 .16
❑ 488 Claude Osteen .75 .30
❑ 489 Skip Jutze .40 .16
❑ 490 Frank Tanana .75 .30
❑ 491 Terry Crowley .40 .16
❑ 492 Marty Pattin .40 .16
❑ 493 Derrel Thomas .40 .16
❑ 494 Craig Swan .75 .30
❑ 495 Nate Colbert .40 .16
❑ 496 Juan Beniquez .40 .16
❑ 497 Joe McIntosh .40 .16
❑ 498 Glenn Borgmann .40 .16
❑ 499 Mario Guerrero .40 .16
❑ 500 Reggie Jackson 12.00 4.80
❑ 501 Billy Champion .40 .16
❑ 502 Tim McCarver 1.50 .60
❑ 503 Elliott Maddox .40 .16
❑ 504 Pittsburgh Pirates 1.50 .30
Team Card CL
Danny Murtaugh MG
❑ 505 Mark Belanger .75 .30
❑ 506 George Mitterwald .40 .16
❑ 507 Ray Bare .40 .16
❑ 508 Duane Kuiper .40 .16
❑ 509 Bill Hands .40 .16
❑ 510 Amos Otis .75 .30
❑ 511 Jamie Easterley .40 .16
❑ 512 Ellie Rodriguez .40 .16
❑ 513 Bart Johnson .40 .16
❑ 514 Dan Driessen .75 .30
❑ 515 Steve Yeager .75 .30
❑ 516 Wayne Granger .40 .16
❑ 517 John Milner .40 .16
❑ 518 Doug Flynn .40 .16
❑ 519 Steve Brye .40 .16
❑ 520 Willie McCovey 5.00 2.00
❑ 521 Jim Colborn .40 .16
❑ 522 Ted Sizemore .40 .16
❑ 523 Bob Montgomery .40 .16
❑ 524 Pete Falcone .40 .16
❑ 525 Billy Williams 2.50 1.00
❑ 526 Checklist 397-528 1.50 .30
❑ 527 Mike Anderson .40 .16
❑ 528 Dock Ellis .40 .16
❑ 529 Deron Johnson .40 .16
❑ 530 Don Sutton 2.50 1.00
❑ 531 New York Mets 1.50 .30
Team Card CL
Joe Frazier MG
❑ 532 Milt May .40 .16
❑ 533 Lee Richard .40 .16
❑ 534 Stan Bahnsen .40 .16
❑ 535 Dave Nelson .40 .16
❑ 536 Mike Thompson .40 .16
❑ 537 Tony Muser .40 .16
❑ 538 Pat Darcy .40 .16
❑ 539 John Balaz .40 .16
❑ 540 Bill Freehan .75 .30
❑ 541 Steve Mingori .40 .16
❑ 542 Keith Hernandez 1.50 .60
❑ 543 Wayne Twitchell .40 .16
❑ 544 Pepe Frias .40 .16
❑ 545 Sparky Lyle .75 .30
❑ 546 Dave Rosello .40 .16
❑ 547 Roric Harrison .40 .16
❑ 548 Manny Mota .75 .30
❑ 549 Randy Tate .40 .16
❑ 550 Hank Aaron 25.00 10.00
❑ 551 Jerry DaVanon .40 .16
❑ 552 Terry Humphrey .40 .16
❑ 553 Randy Moffitt .40 .16
❑ 554 Ray Fosse .40 .16
❑ 555 Dyar Miller .40 .16
❑ 556 Minnesota Twins 1.50 .30
Team Card CL
Gene Mauch MG
❑ 557 Dan Spillner .40 .16
❑ 558 Clarence Gaston .75 .30
❑ 559 Clyde Wright .40 .16
❑ 560 Jorge Orta .40 .16
❑ 561 Tom Carroll .40 .16
❑ 562 Adrian Garrett .40 .16
❑ 563 Larry Demery .40 .16
❑ 564 Bubble Gum Champ 1.50 .60
Kurt Bevacqua
❑ 565 Tug McGraw .75 .30
❑ 566 Ken McMullen .40 .16
❑ 567 George Stone .40 .16
❑ 568 Rob Andrews .40 .16
❑ 569 Nelson Briles .75 .30
❑ 570 George Hendrick .75 .30
❑ 571 Don DeMola .40 .16
❑ 572 Rich Coggins .40 .16
❑ 573 Bill Travers .40 .16
❑ 574 Don Kessinger .75 .30
❑ 575 Dwight Evans 1.50 .60
❑ 576 Maximino Leon .40 .16
❑ 577 Marc Hill .40 .16
❑ 578 Ted Kubiak .40 .16
❑ 579 Clay Kirby .40 .16
❑ 580 Bert Campaneris .75 .30
❑ 581 St. Louis Cardinals 1.50 .30
Team Card CL
Red Schoendienst MG
❑ 582 Mike Kekich .40 .16
❑ 583 Tommy Helms .40 .16
❑ 584 Stan Wall .40 .16
❑ 585 Joe Torre 1.50 .60
❑ 586 Ron Schueler .40 .16
❑ 587 Leo Cardenas .40 .16
❑ 588 Kevin Kobel .40 .16
❑ 589 Santo Alcala 1.50 .60
Mike Flanagan RC
Joe Pactwa
Pablo Torrealba
❑ 590 Henry Cruz .75 .30
Chet Lemon RC
Ellis Valentine
Terry Whitfield
❑ 591 Steve Grilli .75 .30
Craig Mitchell
Jose Sosa
George Throop
❑ 592 Willie Randolph RC 6.00 2.40
Dave McKay
Jerry Royster
Roy Staiger
❑ 593 Larry Anderson .75 .30
Ken Crosby
Mark Littell
Butch Metzger
❑ 594 Andy Merchant .75 .30
Ed Ott
Royle Stillman
Jerry White
❑ 595 Art DeFillipis .75 .30
Randy Lerch
Sid Monge
Steve Barr
❑ 596 Craig Reynolds .75 .30
Lamar Johnson
Johnnie LeMaster
Jerry Manuel RC
❑ 597 Don Aase .75 .30
Jack Kucek
Frank LaCorte
Mike Pazik
❑ 598 Hector Cruz .75 .30
Jamie Quirk
Jerry Turner
Joe Wallis
❑ 599 Rob Dressler 6.00 2.40
Ron Guidry RC
Bob McClure
Pat Zachry
❑ 600 Tom Seaver 10.00 4.00
❑ 601 Ken Rudolph .40 .16
❑ 602 Doug Konieczny .40 .16
❑ 603 Jim Holt .40 .16
❑ 604 Joe Lovitto .40 .16
❑ 605 Al Downing .40 .16
❑ 606 Milwaukee Brewers 1.50 .30
Team Card CL
Alex Grammas MG
❑ 607 Rich Hinton .40 .16
❑ 608 Vic Correll .40 .16
❑ 609 Fred Norman .40 .16
❑ 610 Greg Luzinski 1.50 .60
❑ 611 Rich Folkers .40 .16
❑ 612 Joe Lahoud .40 .16
❑ 613 Tim Johnson .40 .16
❑ 614 Fernando Arroyo .40 .16
❑ 615 Mike Cubbage .40 .16
❑ 616 Buck Martinez .40 .16
❑ 617 Darold Knowles .40 .16

Card	NM	Ex
❑ 618 Jack Brohamer	.40	.16
❑ 619 Bill Butler	.40	.16
❑ 620 Al Oliver	.75	.30
❑ 621 Tom Hall	.40	.16
❑ 622 Rick Auerbach	.40	.16
❑ 623 Bob Allietta	.40	.16
❑ 624 Tony Taylor	.40	.16
❑ 625 J.R. Richard	.75	.30
❑ 626 Bob Sheldon	.40	.16
❑ 627 Bill Plummer	.40	.16
❑ 628 John D'Acquisto	.40	.16
❑ 629 Sandy Alomar	.75	.30
❑ 630 Chris Speier	.40	.16
❑ 631 Atlanta Braves	1.50	.30
Team Card CL		
Dave Bristol MG		
❑ 632 Rogelio Moret	.40	.16
❑ 633 John Stearns RC	.75	.30
❑ 634 Larry Christenson	.40	.16
❑ 635 Jim Fregosi	.75	.30
❑ 636 Joe Decker	.40	.16
❑ 637 Bruce Bochte	.40	.16
❑ 638 Doyle Alexander	.75	.30
❑ 639 Fred Kendall	.40	.16
❑ 640 Bill Madlock	1.50	.60
❑ 641 Tom Paciorek	.75	.30
❑ 642 Dennis Blair	.40	.16
❑ 643 Checklist 529-660	1.50	.30
❑ 644 Tom Bradley	.40	.16
❑ 645 Darrell Porter	.75	.30
❑ 646 John Lowenstein	.40	.16
❑ 647 Ramon Hernandez	.40	.16
❑ 648 Al Cowens	.40	.16
❑ 649 Dave Roberts	.40	.16
❑ 650 Thurman Munson	6.00	2.40
❑ 651 John Odom	.40	.16
❑ 652 Ed Armbrister	.40	.16
❑ 653 Mike Norris RC	.75	.30
❑ 654 Doug Griffin	.40	.16
❑ 655 Mike Vail	.40	.16
❑ 656 Chicago White Sox	1.50	.30
Team Card CL		
Chuck Tanner MG		
❑ 657 Roy Smalley RC	.75	.30
❑ 658 Jerry Johnson	.40	.16
❑ 659 Ben Oglivie	.75	.30
❑ 660 Dave Lopes	1.50	.30

1977 Topps

	NM	Ex
COMPLETE SET (660)	250.00	100.00
❑ 1 George Brett	8.00	2.30
Bill Madlock LL		
❑ 2 Graig Nettles	2.50	1.00
Mike Schmidt LL		
❑ 3 Lee May	1.50	.60
George Foster LL		
❑ 4 Bill North	.75	.30
Dave Lopes LL		
❑ 5 Jim Palmer	1.50	.60
Randy Jones LL		
❑ 6 Nolan Ryan	15.00	6.00
Tom Seaver LL		
❑ 7 Mark Fidrych	.75	.30
John Denny LL		
❑ 8 Bill Campbell	.75	.30
Rawly Eastwick LL		
❑ 9 Doug Rader	.30	.12
❑ 10 Reggie Jackson	10.00	4.00
❑ 11 Rob Dressler	.30	.12
❑ 12 Larry Haney	.30	.12
❑ 13 Luis Gomez	.30	.12
❑ 14 Tommy Smith	.30	.12
❑ 15 Don Gullett	.75	.30
❑ 16 Bob Jones	.30	.12
❑ 17 Steve Stone	.75	.30
❑ 18 Indians Team CL	1.50	.30
Frank Robinson MG		
❑ 19 John D'Acquisto	.30	.12
❑ 20 Graig Nettles	1.50	.60
❑ 21 Ken Forsch	.30	.12
❑ 22 Bill Freehan	.75	.30
❑ 23 Dan Driessen	.30	.12
❑ 24 Carl Morton	.30	.12
❑ 25 Dwight Evans	1.50	.60
❑ 26 Ray Sadecki	.30	.12
❑ 27 Bill Buckner	.75	.30
❑ 28 Woodie Fryman	.30	.12
❑ 29 Bucky Dent	.75	.30
❑ 30 Greg Luzinski	1.50	.60
❑ 31 Jim Todd	.30	.12
❑ 32 Checklist 1-132	1.50	.30
❑ 33 Wayne Garland	.30	.12
❑ 34 Angels Team CL	1.50	.30
Norm Sherry MG		
❑ 35 Rennie Stennett	.30	.12
❑ 36 John Ellis	.30	.12
❑ 37 Steve Hargan	.30	.12
❑ 38 Craig Kusick	.30	.12
❑ 39 Tom Griffin	.30	.12
❑ 40 Bobby Murcer	.75	.30
❑ 41 Jim Kern	.30	.12
❑ 42 Jose Cruz	.75	.30
❑ 43 Ray Bare	.30	.12
❑ 44 Bud Harrelson	.75	.30
❑ 45 Rawly Eastwick	.30	.12
❑ 46 Buck Martinez	.30	.12
❑ 47 Lynn McGlothen	.30	.12
❑ 48 Tom Paciorek	.75	.30
❑ 49 Grant Jackson	.30	.12
❑ 50 Ron Cey	.75	.30
❑ 51 Brewers Team CL	1.50	.30
Alex Grammas MG		
❑ 52 Ellis Valentine	.30	.12
❑ 53 Paul Mitchell	.30	.12
❑ 54 Sandy Alomar	.75	.30
❑ 55 Jeff Burroughs	.75	.30
❑ 56 Rudy May	.30	.12
❑ 57 Marc Hill	.30	.12
❑ 58 Chet Lemon	.75	.30
❑ 59 Larry Christenson	.30	.12
❑ 60 Jim Rice	2.50	1.00
❑ 61 Manny Sanguillen	.75	.30
❑ 62 Eric Raich	.30	.12
❑ 63 Tito Fuentes	.30	.12
❑ 64 Larry Biittner	.30	.12
❑ 65 Skip Lockwood	.30	.12
❑ 66 Roy Smalley	.75	.30
❑ 67 Joaquin Andujar RC	.75	.30
❑ 68 Bruce Bochte	.30	.12
❑ 69 Jim Crawford	.30	.12
❑ 70 Johnny Bench	10.00	4.00
❑ 71 Dock Ellis	.30	.12
❑ 72 Mike Anderson	.30	.12
❑ 73 Charlie Williams	.30	.12
❑ 74 A's Team CL	1.50	.30
Jack McKeon MG		
❑ 75 Dennis Leonard	.75	.30
❑ 76 Tim Foli	.30	.12
❑ 77 Dyar Miller	.30	.12
❑ 78 Bob Davis	.30	.12
❑ 79 Don Money	.75	.30
❑ 80 Andy Messersmith	.75	.30
❑ 81 Juan Beniquez	.30	.12
❑ 82 Jim Rooker	.30	.12
❑ 83 Kevin Bell	.30	.12
❑ 84 Ollie Brown	.30	.12
❑ 85 Duane Kuiper	.30	.12
❑ 86 Pat Zachry	.30	.12
❑ 87 Glenn Borgmann	.30	.12
❑ 88 Stan Wall	.30	.12
❑ 89 Butch Hobson RC	.75	.30
❑ 90 Cesar Cedeno	.75	.30
❑ 91 John Verhoeven	.30	.12
❑ 92 Dave Rosello	.30	.12
❑ 93 Tom Poquette	.30	.12
❑ 94 Craig Swan	.30	.12
❑ 95 Keith Hernandez	.75	.30
❑ 96 Lou Piniella	.75	.30
❑ 97 Dave Heaverlo	.30	.12
❑ 98 Milt May	.30	.12
❑ 99 Tom Hausman	.30	.12
❑ 100 Joe Morgan	4.00	1.60
❑ 101 Dick Bosman	.30	.12
❑ 102 Jose Morales	.30	.12
❑ 103 Mike Bacsik	.30	.12
❑ 104 Omar Moreno	.75	.30
❑ 105 Steve Yeager	.75	.30
❑ 106 Mike Flanagan	.75	.30
❑ 107 Bill Melton	.30	.12
❑ 108 Alan Foster	.30	.12
❑ 109 Jorge Orta	.30	.12
❑ 110 Steve Carlton	5.00	2.00
❑ 111 Rico Petrocelli	.75	.30
❑ 112 Bill Greif	.30	.12
❑ 113 Blue Jays Leaders	1.50	.30
Roy Hartsfield MG		
Don Leppert CO		
Bob Miller CO		
Jackie Moore CO		
Harry Warner CO		
❑ 114 Bruce Dal Canton	.30	.12
❑ 115 Rick Manning	.30	.12
❑ 116 Joe Niekro	.75	.30
❑ 117 Frank White	.75	.30
❑ 118 Rick Jones	.30	.12
❑ 119 John Stearns	.30	.12
❑ 120 Rod Carew	5.00	2.00
❑ 121 Gary Nolan	.30	.12
❑ 122 Ben Oglivie	.75	.30
❑ 123 Fred Stanley	.30	.12
❑ 124 George Mitterwald	.30	.12
❑ 125 Bill Travers	.30	.12
❑ 126 Rod Gilbreath	.30	.12
❑ 127 Ron Fairly	.75	.30
❑ 128 Tommy John	1.50	.60
❑ 129 Mike Sadek	.30	.12
❑ 130 Al Oliver	.75	.30
❑ 131 Orlando Ramirez	.30	.12
❑ 132 Chip Lang	.30	.12
❑ 133 Ralph Garr	.75	.30
❑ 134 Padres Team CL	1.50	.30
John McNamara MG		
❑ 135 Mark Belanger	.75	.30
❑ 136 Jerry Mumphrey	.75	.30
❑ 137 Jeff Terpko	.30	.12
❑ 138 Bob Stinson	.30	.12
❑ 139 Fred Norman	.30	.12
❑ 140 Mike Schmidt	12.00	4.80
❑ 141 Mark Littell	.30	.12
❑ 142 Steve Dillard	.30	.12
❑ 143 Ed Herrmann	.30	.12
❑ 144 Bruce Sutter RC	3.00	1.20
❑ 145 Tom Veryzer	.30	.12
❑ 146 Dusty Baker	1.50	.60
❑ 147 Jackie Brown	.30	.12
❑ 148 Fran Healy	.30	.12
❑ 149 Mike Cubbage	.30	.12
❑ 150 Tom Seaver	8.00	3.20
❑ 151 Johnny LeMaster	.30	.12
❑ 152 Gaylord Perry	2.50	1.00
❑ 153 Ron Jackson RC	.30	.12
❑ 154 Dave Giusti	.30	.12
❑ 155 Joe Rudi	.75	.30
❑ 156 Pete Mackanin	.30	.12
❑ 157 Ken Brett	.30	.12
❑ 158 Ted Kubiak	.30	.12
❑ 159 Bernie Carbo	.30	.12
❑ 160 Will McEnaney	.30	.12
❑ 161 Garry Templeton RC	1.50	.60
❑ 162 Mike Cuellar	.75	.30
❑ 163 Dave Hilton	.30	.12
❑ 164 Tug McGraw	.75	.30
❑ 165 Jim Wynn	.75	.30
❑ 166 Bill Campbell	.30	.12
❑ 167 Rich Hebner	.75	.30
❑ 168 Charlie Spikes	.30	.12
❑ 169 Darold Knowles	.30	.12

❑ 170 Thurman Munson 5.00 2.00
❑ 171 Ken Sanders .30 .12
❑ 172 John Milner .30 .12
❑ 173 Chuck Scrivener .30 .12
❑ 174 Nelson Briles .75 .30
❑ 175 Butch Wynegar .75 .30
❑ 176 Bob Robertson .30 .12
❑ 177 Bart Johnson .30 .12
❑ 178 Bombo Rivera .30 .12
❑ 179 Paul Hartzell .30 .12
❑ 180 Dave Lopes .75 .30
❑ 181 Ken McMullen .30 .12
❑ 182 Dan Spillner .30 .12
❑ 183 Cardinals Team CL 1.50 .30
Vern Rapp MG
❑ 184 Bo McLaughlin .30 .12
❑ 185 Sixto Lezcano .30 .12
❑ 186 Doug Flynn .30 .12
❑ 187 Dick Pole .30 .12
❑ 188 Bob Tolan .30 .12
❑ 189 Rick Dempsey .75 .30
❑ 190 Ray Burris .30 .12
❑ 191 Doug Griffin .30 .12
❑ 192 Clarence Gaston .75 .30
❑ 193 Larry Gura .30 .12
❑ 194 Gary Matthews .75 .30
❑ 195 Ed Figueroa .30 .12
❑ 196 Len Randle .30 .12
❑ 197 Ed Ott .30 .12
❑ 198 Wilbur Wood .30 .12
❑ 199 Pepe Frias .30 .12
❑ 200 Frank Tanana .75 .30
❑ 201 Ed Kranepool .30 .12
❑ 202 Tom Johnson .30 .12
❑ 203 Ed Armbrister .30 .12
❑ 204 Jeff Newman .30 .12
❑ 205 Pete Falcone .30 .12
❑ 206 Boog Powell 1.50 .60
❑ 207 Glenn Abbott .30 .12
❑ 208 Checklist 133-264 1.50 .30
❑ 209 Rob Andrews .30 .12
❑ 210 Fred Lynn .75 .15
❑ 211 Giants Team CL 1.50 .60
Joe Altobelli MG
❑ 212 Jim Mason .30 .12
❑ 213 Maximino Leon .30 .12
❑ 214 Darrell Porter .75 .30
❑ 215 Butch Metzger .30 .12
❑ 216 Doug DeCinces .75 .30
❑ 217 Tom Underwood .30 .12
❑ 218 John Wathan RC .75 .30
❑ 219 Joe Coleman .30 .12
❑ 220 Chris Chambliss .75 .30
❑ 221 Bob Bailey .30 .12
❑ 222 Francisco Barrios .30 .12
❑ 223 Earl Williams .30 .12
❑ 224 Rusty Torres .30 .12
❑ 225 Bob Apodaca .30 .12
❑ 226 Leroy Stanton .75 .30
❑ 227 Joe Sambito .30 .12
❑ 228 Twins Team CL 1.50 .30
Gene Mauch MG
❑ 229 Don Kessinger .75 .30
❑ 230 Vida Blue .75 .30
❑ 231 George Brett RB 8.00 3.20
❑ 232 Minnie Minoso RB .75 .30
❑ 233 Jose Morales RB .30 .12
❑ 234 Nolan Ryan RB 15.00 6.00
❑ 235 Cecil Cooper .75 .30
❑ 236 Tom Buskey .30 .12
❑ 237 Gene Clines .30 .12
❑ 238 Tippy Martinez .30 .12
❑ 239 Bill Plummer .30 .12
❑ 240 Ron LeFlore .75 .30
❑ 241 Dave Tomlin .30 .12
❑ 242 Ken Henderson .30 .12
❑ 243 Ron Reed .30 .12
❑ 244 John Mayberry .75 .30
(Cartoon mentions
T206 Wagner)
❑ 245 Rick Rhoden .75 .30
❑ 246 Mike Vail .30 .12
❑ 247 Chris Knapp .30 .12
❑ 248 Wilbur Howard .30 .12
❑ 249 Pete Redfern .30 .12
❑ 250 Bill Madlock .75 .30
❑ 251 Tony Muser .30 .12
❑ 252 Dale Murray .30 .12
❑ 253 John Hale .30 .12
❑ 254 Doyle Alexander .30 .12
❑ 255 George Scott .75 .30
❑ 256 Joe Hoerner .30 .12
❑ 257 Mike Miley .30 .12
❑ 258 Luis Tiant .75 .30
❑ 259 Mets Team CL 1.50 .30
Joe Frazier MG
❑ 260 J.R. Richard .75 .30
❑ 261 Phil Garner .75 .30
❑ 262 Al Cowens .30 .12
❑ 263 Mike Marshall .75 .30
❑ 264 Tom Hutton .30 .12
❑ 265 Mark Fidrych RC 3.00 1.20
❑ 266 Derrel Thomas .30 .12
❑ 267 Ray Fosse .30 .12
❑ 268 Rick Sawyer .30 .12
❑ 269 Joe Lis .30 .12
❑ 270 Dave Parker 1.50 .60
❑ 271 Terry Forster .30 .12
❑ 272 Lee Lacy .30 .12
❑ 273 Eric Soderholm .30 .12
❑ 274 Don Stanhouse .30 .12
❑ 275 Mike Hargrove .75 .30
❑ 276 C.Chambliss ALCS 1.50 .60
homer decides it
❑ 277 Pete Rose NLCS 5.00 2.00
❑ 278 Danny Frisella .30 .12
❑ 279 Joe Wallis .30 .12
❑ 280 Jim Hunter 2.50 1.00
❑ 281 Roy Staiger .30 .12
❑ 282 Sid Monge .30 .12
❑ 283 Jerry DaVanon .30 .12
❑ 284 Mike Norris .30 .12
❑ 285 Brooks Robinson 5.00 2.00
❑ 286 Johnny Grubb .30 .06
❑ 287 Reds Team CL 1.50 .60
Sparky Anderson MG
❑ 288 Bob Montgomery .30 .12
❑ 289 Gene Garber .75 .30
❑ 290 Amos Otis .75 .30
❑ 291 Jason Thompson RC .75 .30
❑ 292 Rogelio Moret .30 .12
❑ 293 Jack Brohamer .30 .12
❑ 294 George Medich .30 .12
❑ 295 Gary Carter 2.50 1.00
❑ 296 Don Hood .30 .12
❑ 297 Ken Reitz .30 .12
❑ 298 Charlie Hough .75 .30
❑ 299 Otto Velez .75 .30
❑ 300 Jerry Koosman .75 .30
❑ 301 Toby Harrah .75 .30
❑ 302 Mike Garman .30 .12
❑ 303 Gene Tenace .75 .30
❑ 304 Jim Hughes .30 .12
❑ 305 Mickey Rivers .75 .30
❑ 306 Rick Waits .30 .12
❑ 307 Gary Sutherland .30 .12
❑ 308 Gene Pentz .30 .12
❑ 309 Red Sox Team CL 1.50 .30
Don Zimmer MG
❑ 310 Larry Bowa .75 .30
❑ 311 Vern Ruhle .30 .12
❑ 312 Rob Belloir .30 .12
❑ 313 Paul Blair .75 .30
❑ 314 Steve Mingori .30 .12
❑ 315 Dave Chalk .30 .12
❑ 316 Steve Rogers .30 .12
❑ 317 Kurt Bevacqua .30 .12
❑ 318 Duffy Dyer .30 .12
❑ 319 Goose Gossage 1.50 .60
❑ 320 Ken Griffey Sr. 1.50 .60
❑ 321 Dave Goltz .30 .12
❑ 322 Bill Russell .75 .30
❑ 323 Larry Lintz .30 .12
❑ 324 John Curtis .30 .12
❑ 325 Mike Ivie .30 .12
❑ 326 Jesse Jefferson .30 .12
❑ 327 Astros Team CL 1.50 .30
Bill Virdon MG
❑ 328 Tommy Boggs .30 .12
❑ 329 Ron Hodges .30 .12
❑ 330 George Hendrick .75 .30
❑ 331 Jim Colborn .30 .12
❑ 332 Elliott Maddox .30 .12
❑ 333 Paul Reuschel .30 .12
❑ 334 Bill Stein .30 .12
❑ 335 Bill Robinson .75 .30
❑ 336 Denny Doyle .30 .12
❑ 337 Ron Schueler .30 .12
❑ 338 Dave Duncan .75 .30
❑ 339 Adrian Devine .30 .12
❑ 340 Hal McRae .75 .30
❑ 341 Joe Kerrigan .30 .12
❑ 342 Jerry Remy .30 .12
❑ 343 Ed Halicki .30 .12
❑ 344 Brian Downing .75 .30
❑ 345 Reggie Smith .75 .30
❑ 346 Bill Singer .30 .12
❑ 347 George Foster 1.50 .60
❑ 348 Brent Strom .30 .12
❑ 349 Jim Holt .30 .12
❑ 350 Larry Dierker .75 .30
❑ 351 Jim Sundberg .75 .30
❑ 352 Mike Phillips .30 .12
❑ 353 Stan Thomas .30 .12
❑ 354 Pirates Team CL 1.50 .30
Chuck Tanner MG
❑ 355 Lou Brock 4.00 1.60
❑ 356 Checklist 265-396 1.50 .30
❑ 357 Tim McCarver 1.50 .60
❑ 358 Tom House .30 .12
❑ 359 Willie Randolph 1.50 .60
❑ 360 Rick Monday .75 .30
❑ 361 Eduardo Rodriguez .30 .12
❑ 362 Tommy Davis .75 .30
❑ 363 Dave Roberts .30 .12
❑ 364 Vic Correll .30 .12
❑ 365 Mike Torrez .75 .30
❑ 366 Ted Sizemore .30 .12
❑ 367 Dave Hamilton .30 .12
❑ 368 Mike Jorgensen .30 .12
❑ 369 Terry Humphrey .30 .12
❑ 370 John Montefusco .30 .12
❑ 371 Royals Team CL 1.50 .30
Whitey Herzog MG
❑ 372 Rich Folkers .30 .12
❑ 373 Bert Campaneris .75 .30
❑ 374 Kent Tekulve .75 .30
❑ 375 Larry Hisle .75 .30
❑ 376 Nino Espinosa .30 .12
❑ 377 Dave McKay .30 .12
❑ 378 Jim Umbarger .30 .12
❑ 379 Larry Cox .30 .12
❑ 380 Lee May .75 .30
❑ 381 Bob Forsch .30 .12
❑ 382 Charlie Moore .30 .12
❑ 383 Stan Bahnsen .30 .12
❑ 384 Darrel Chaney .30 .12
❑ 385 Dave LaRoche .30 .12
❑ 386 Manny Mota .75 .30
❑ 387 Yankees Team CL 2.50 .50
Billy Martin MG
❑ 388 Terry Harmon .30 .12
❑ 389 Ken Kravec .30 .12
❑ 390 Dave Winfield 6.00 2.40
❑ 391 Dan Warthen .30 .12
❑ 392 Phil Roof .30 .12
❑ 393 John Lowenstein .30 .12
❑ 394 Bill Laxton .30 .12
❑ 395 Manny Trillo .30 .12
❑ 396 Tom Murphy .30 .12
❑ 397 Larry Herndon RC .75 .30
❑ 398 Tom Burgmeier .30 .12
❑ 399 Bruce Boisclair .30 .12
❑ 400 Steve Garvey 2.50 1.00
❑ 401 Mickey Scott .30 .12
❑ 402 Tommy Helms .30 .12
❑ 403 Tom Grieve .75 .30
❑ 404 Eric Rasmussen .30 .12
❑ 405 Claudell Washington .75 .30
❑ 406 Tim Johnson .30 .12
❑ 407 Dave Freisleben .30 .12
❑ 408 Cesar Tovar .30 .12
❑ 409 Pete Broberg .30 .12
❑ 410 Willie Montanez .30 .12
❑ 411 Joe Morgan WS 2.50 1.00
Johnny Bench
❑ 412 Johnny Bench WS 2.50 1.00
❑ 413 WS Summary .75 .30

Cincy wins 2nd
straight series
❑ 414 Tommy Harper .75 .30
❑ 415 Jay Johnstone .75 .30
❑ 416 Chuck Hartenstein .30 .12
❑ 417 Wayne Garrett .30 .12
❑ 418 White Sox Team CL 1.50 .30
Bob Lemon MG
❑ 419 Steve Swisher .30 .12
❑ 420 Rusty Staub 1.50 .60
❑ 421 Doug Rau .30 .12
❑ 422 Freddie Patek .75 .30
❑ 423 Gary Lavelle .30 .12
❑ 424 Steve Brye .30 .12
❑ 425 Joe Torre 1.50 .60
❑ 426 Dick Drago .30 .12
❑ 427 Dave Rader .30 .12
❑ 428 Rangers Team CL 1.50 .30
Frank Lucchesi
❑ 429 Ken Boswell .30 .12
❑ 430 Fergie Jenkins 2.50 1.00
❑ 431 Dave Collins UER .75 .30
(Photo actually
Bobby Jones)
❑ 432 Buzz Capra .30 .12
❑ 433 Nate Colbert TBC .30 .12
(5 HR, 13 RBI)
❑ 434 Carl Yastrzemski TBC 1.50 .60
'67 Triple Crown
❑ 435 Maury Wills TBC .75 .30
104 steals
❑ 436 Bob Keegan TBC .30 .12
Majors' only no-hitter
❑ 437 Ralph Kiner TBC 1.50 .60
Leads NL in HR's
7th straight year
❑ 438 Marty Perez .30 .12
❑ 439 Gorman Thomas .75 .30
❑ 440 Jon Matlack .30 .12
❑ 441 Larvell Blanks .30 .12
❑ 442 Braves Team CL 1.50 .30
Dave Bristol MG
❑ 443 Lamar Johnson .30 .12
❑ 444 Wayne Twitchell .30 .12
❑ 445 Ken Singleton .75 .30
❑ 446 Bill Bonham .30 .12
❑ 447 Jerry Turner .30 .12
❑ 448 Ellie Rodriguez .30 .12
❑ 449 Al Fitzmorris .30 .12
❑ 450 Pete Rose 20.00 8.00
❑ 451 Checklist 397-528 1.50 .30
❑ 452 Mike Caldwell .30 .12
❑ 453 Pedro Garcia .30 .12
❑ 454 Andy Etchebarren .30 .12
❑ 455 Rick Wise .30 .12
❑ 456 Leon Roberts .30 .12
❑ 457 Steve Luebber .30 .12
❑ 458 Leo Foster .30 .12
❑ 459 Steve Foucault .30 .12
❑ 460 Willie Stargell 2.50 1.00
❑ 461 Dick Tidrow .30 .12
❑ 462 Don Baylor 1.50 .60
❑ 463 Jamie Quirk .30 .12
❑ 464 Randy Moffitt .30 .12
❑ 465 Rico Carty .75 .30
❑ 466 Fred Holdsworth .30 .12
❑ 467 Phillies Team CL 1.50 .30
Danny Ozark MG
❑ 468 Ramon Hernandez .30 .12
❑ 469 Pat Kelly .30 .12
❑ 470 Ted Simmons .75 .30
❑ 471 Del Unser .30 .12
❑ 472 Don Aase .30 .12
Bob McClure
Gil Patterson
Dave Wehrmeister
Sheldon Gill pictured instead of Gil
Patterson
❑ 473 Andre Dawson RC 20.00 8.00
Gene Richards
John Scott
Denny Walling
❑ 474 Bob Bailor .75 .30
Kiko Garcia
Craig Reynolds
Alex Taveras
❑ 475 Chris Batton .75 .30
Rick Camp
Scott McGregor
Manny Sarmiento
❑ 476 Gary Alexander 20.00 8.00
Rick Cerone
Dale Murphy RC
Kevin Pasley
❑ 477 Doug Ault .75 .30
Rich Dauer
Orlando Gonzalez
Phil Mankowski
❑ 478 Jim Gideon .75 .30
Leon Hooten
Dave Johnson
Mark Lemongello
❑ 479 Brian Asselstine .75 .30
Wayne Gross
Sam Mejias
Alvis Woods
❑ 480 Carl Yastrzemski 8.00 3.20
❑ 481 Roger Metzger .30 .12
❑ 482 Tony Solaita .30 .12
❑ 483 Richie Zisk .30 .12
❑ 484 Burt Hooton .75 .30
❑ 485 Roy White .75 .30
❑ 486 Ed Bane .30 .12
❑ 487 Larry Anderson .75 .30
Ed Glynn
Joe Henderson
Greg Terlecky
❑ 488 Jack Clark RC 3.00 1.20
Ruppert Jones RC
Lee Mazzilli RC
Dan Thomas
❑ 489 Len Barker RC .75 .30
Randy Lerch
Greg Minton
Mike Overy
❑ 490 Billy Almon .75 .30
Mickey Klutts
Tommy McMillan
Mark Wagner
❑ 491 Mike Dupree 5.00 2.00
Dennis Martinez RC
Craig Mitchell
Bob Sykes
❑ 492 Tony Armas RC .75 .30
Steve Kemp RC
Carlos Lopez
Gary Woods
❑ 493 Mike Krukow .75 .30
Jim Otten
Gary Wheelock
Mike Willis
❑ 494 Juan Bernhardt 1.50 .60
Mike Champion
Jim Gantner RC
Bump Wills
❑ 495 Al Hrabosky .30 .12
❑ 496 Gary Thomasson .30 .12
❑ 497 Clay Carroll .30 .12
❑ 498 Sal Bando .75 .30
❑ 499 Pablo Torrealba .30 .12
❑ 500 Dave Kingman 1.50 .60
❑ 501 Jim Bibby .30 .12
❑ 502 Randy Hundley .30 .12
❑ 503 Bill Lee .30 .12
❑ 504 Dodgers Team CL 1.50 .30
Tom Lasorda MG
❑ 505 Oscar Gamble .75 .30
❑ 506 Steve Grilli .30 .12
❑ 507 Mike Hegan .30 .12
❑ 508 Dave Pagan .30 .12
❑ 509 Cookie Rojas .75 .30
❑ 510 John Candelaria .30 .12
❑ 511 Bill Fahey .30 .12
❑ 512 Jack Billingham .30 .12
❑ 513 Jerry Terrell .30 .12
❑ 514 Cliff Johnson .30 .12
❑ 515 Chris Speier .30 .12
❑ 516 Bake McBride .75 .30
❑ 517 Pete Vuckovich RC .75 .30
❑ 518 Cubs Team CL 1.50 .30
Herman Franks MG
❑ 519 Don Kirkwood .30 .12
❑ 520 Garry Maddox .30 .12
❑ 521 Bob Grich .75 .30
Only card in set with no date of birth
❑ 522 Enzo Hernandez .30 .12
❑ 523 Rollie Fingers 2.50 1.00
❑ 524 Rowland Office .30 .12
❑ 525 Dennis Eckersley 5.00 2.00
❑ 526 Larry Parrish .75 .30
❑ 527 Dan Meyer .75 .30
❑ 528 Bill Castro .30 .12
❑ 529 Jim Essian .30 .12
❑ 530 Rick Reuschel .75 .30
❑ 531 Lyman Bostock .75 .30
❑ 532 Jim Willoughby .30 .12
❑ 533 Mickey Stanley .30 .12
❑ 534 Paul Splittorff .30 .12
❑ 535 Cesar Geronimo .30 .12
❑ 536 Vic Albury .30 .12
❑ 537 Dave Roberts .30 .12
❑ 538 Frank Taveras .30 .12
❑ 539 Mike Wallace .30 .12
❑ 540 Bob Watson .75 .30
❑ 541 John Denny .75 .30
❑ 542 Frank Duffy .30 .12
❑ 543 Ron Blomberg .30 .12
❑ 544 Gary Ross .30 .12
❑ 545 Bob Boone .75 .30
❑ 546 Oriole Team CL 1.50 .30
Earl Weaver MG
❑ 547 Willie McCovey 4.00 1.60
❑ 548 Joel Youngblood .30 .12
❑ 549 Jerry Royster .30 .12
❑ 550 Randy Jones .30 .12
❑ 551 Bill North .30 .12
❑ 552 Pepe Mangual .30 .12
❑ 553 Jack Heidemann .30 .12
❑ 554 Bruce Kimm .30 .12
❑ 555 Dan Ford .30 .12
❑ 556 Doug Bird .30 .12
❑ 557 Jerry White .30 .12
❑ 558 Elias Sosa .30 .12
❑ 559 Alan Bannister .30 .12
❑ 560 Dave Concepcion 1.50 .60
❑ 561 Pete LaCock .30 .12
❑ 562 Checklist 529-660 1.50 .30
❑ 563 Bruce Kison .30 .12
❑ 564 Alan Ashby .75 .30
❑ 565 Mickey Lolich .75 .30
❑ 566 Rick Miller .30 .12
❑ 567 Enos Cabell .30 .12
❑ 568 Carlos May .30 .12
❑ 569 Jim Lonborg .75 .30
❑ 570 Bobby Bonds 1.50 .60
❑ 571 Darrell Evans .75 .30
❑ 572 Ross Grimsley .30 .12
❑ 573 Joe Ferguson .30 .12
❑ 574 Aurelio Rodriguez .30 .12
❑ 575 Dick Ruthven .30 .12
❑ 576 Fred Kendall .30 .12
❑ 577 Jerry Augustine .30 .12
❑ 578 Bob Randall .30 .12
❑ 579 Don Carrithers .30 .12
❑ 580 George Brett 15.00 6.00
❑ 581 Pedro Borbon .30 .12
❑ 582 Ed Kirkpatrick .30 .12
❑ 583 Paul Lindblad .30 .12
❑ 584 Ed Goodson .30 .12
❑ 585 Rick Burleson .75 .30
❑ 586 Steve Renko .30 .12
❑ 587 Rick Baldwin .30 .12
❑ 588 Dave Moates .30 .12
❑ 589 Mike Cosgrove .30 .12
❑ 590 Buddy Bell .75 .30
❑ 591 Chris Arnold .30 .12
❑ 592 Dan Briggs .30 .12
❑ 593 Dennis Blair .30 .12
❑ 594 Biff Pocoroba .30 .12
❑ 595 John Hiller .30 .12
❑ 596 Jerry Martin .30 .12
❑ 597 Mariners Leaders CL 1.50 .30
Darrell Johnson MG
Don Bryant CO
Jim Busby CO
Vada Pinson CO
Wes Stock CO
❑ 598 Sparky Lyle .75 .30

Card	NM	Ex
❑ 599 Mike Tyson	.30	.12
❑ 600 Jim Palmer	4.00	1.60
❑ 601 Mike Lum	.30	.12
❑ 602 Andy Hassler	.30	.12
❑ 603 Willie Davis	.75	.30
❑ 604 Jim Slaton	.30	.12
❑ 605 Felix Millan	.30	.12
❑ 606 Steve Braun	.30	.12
❑ 607 Larry Demery	.30	.12
❑ 608 Roy Howell	.30	.12
❑ 609 Jim Barr	.30	.12
❑ 610 Jose Cardenal	.75	.30
❑ 611 Dave Lemanczyk	.30	.12
❑ 612 Barry Foote	.30	.12
❑ 613 Reggie Cleveland	.30	.12
❑ 614 Greg Gross	.30	.12
❑ 615 Phil Niekro	2.50	1.00
❑ 616 Tommy Sandt	.30	.12
❑ 617 Bobby Darwin	.30	.12
❑ 618 Pat Dobson	.30	.12
❑ 619 Johnny Oates	.75	.30
❑ 620 Don Sutton	2.50	1.00
❑ 621 Tigers Team CL	1.50	.30
Ralph Houk MG		
❑ 622 Jim Wohlford	.30	.12
❑ 623 Jack Kucek	.30	.12
❑ 624 Hector Cruz	.30	.12
❑ 625 Ken Holtzman	.75	.30
❑ 626 Al Bumbry	.75	.30
❑ 627 Bob Myrick	.30	.12
❑ 628 Mario Guerrero	.30	.12
❑ 629 Bobby Valentine	.75	.30
❑ 630 Bert Blyleven	1.50	.60
❑ 631 George Brett	6.00	2.40
Ken Brett		
❑ 632 Bob Forsch	.75	.30
Ken Forsch		
❑ 633 Lee May	.75	.30
Carlos May		
❑ 634 Paul Reuschel	.75	.30
Rick Reuschel UER		
(Photos switched)		
❑ 635 Robin Yount	8.00	3.20
❑ 636 Santo Alcala	.30	.12
❑ 637 Alex Johnson	.30	.12
❑ 638 Jim Kaat	1.50	.60
❑ 639 Jerry Morales	.30	.12
❑ 640 Carlton Fisk	5.00	2.00
❑ 641 Dan Larson	.30	.12
❑ 642 Willie Crawford	.30	.12
❑ 643 Mike Pazik	.30	.12
❑ 644 Matt Alexander	.30	.12
❑ 645 Jerry Reuss	.75	.30
❑ 646 Andres Mora	.30	.12
❑ 647 Expos Team CL	1.50	.30
Dick Williams MG		
❑ 648 Jim Spencer	.30	.12
❑ 649 Dave Cash	.30	.12
❑ 650 Nolan Ryan	30.00	12.00
❑ 651 Von Joshua	.30	.12
❑ 652 Tom Walker	.30	.12
❑ 653 Diego Segui	.75	.30
❑ 654 Ron Pruitt	.30	.12
❑ 655 Tony Perez	2.50	1.00
❑ 656 Ron Guidry	1.50	.60
❑ 657 Mick Kelleher	.30	.12
❑ 658 Marty Pattin	.30	.12
❑ 659 Merv Rettenmund	.30	.12
❑ 660 Willie Horton	1.50	.30

1978 Topps

	NM	Ex
COMPLETE SET (726)	200.00	80.00
COMMON CARD (1-726)	.25	.10
COMMON CARD DP	.15	.06

Card	NM	Ex
❑ 1 Lou Brock RB	3.00	.90
❑ 2 Sparky Lyle RB	.60	.24
❑ 3 Willie McCovey RB	2.50	1.00
❑ 4 Brooks Robinson RB	2.50	1.00
❑ 5 Pete Rose RB	8.00	3.20
❑ 6 Nolan Ryan RB	15.00	6.00
❑ 7 Reggie Jackson RB	4.00	1.60
❑ 8 Mike Sadek	.25	.10

Card	NM	Ex
❑ 9 Doug DeCinces	.60	.24
❑ 10 Phil Niekro	2.50	1.00
❑ 11 Rick Manning	.25	.10
❑ 12 Don Aase	.25	.10
❑ 13 Art Howe RC	.60	.24
❑ 14 Lerrin LaGrow	.25	.10
❑ 15 Tony Perez DP	1.25	.50
❑ 16 Roy White	.60	.24
❑ 17 Mike Krukow	.25	.10
❑ 18 Bob Grich	.60	.24
❑ 19 Darrell Porter	.60	.24
❑ 20 Pete Rose DP	12.00	4.80
❑ 21 Steve Kemp	.25	.10
❑ 22 Charlie Hough	.60	.24
❑ 23 Bump Wills	.25	.10
❑ 24 Don Money DP	.15	.06
❑ 25 Jon Matlack	.25	.10
❑ 26 Rich Hebner	.60	.24
❑ 27 Geoff Zahn	.25	.10
❑ 28 Ed Ott	.25	.10
❑ 29 Bob Lacey	.25	.10
❑ 30 George Hendrick	.60	.24
❑ 31 Glenn Abbott	.25	.10
❑ 32 Garry Templeton	.60	.24
❑ 33 Dave Lemanczyk	.25	.10
❑ 34 Willie McCovey	3.00	1.20
❑ 35 Sparky Lyle	.60	.24
❑ 36 Eddie Murray RC	80.00	32.00
❑ 37 Rick Waits	.25	.10
❑ 38 Willie Montanez	.25	.10
❑ 39 Floyd Bannister RC	.25	.10
❑ 40 Carl Yastrzemski	6.00	2.40
❑ 41 Burt Hooton	.60	.24
❑ 42 Jorge Orta	.25	.10
❑ 43 Bill Atkinson	.25	.10
❑ 44 Toby Harrah	.60	.24
❑ 45 Mark Fidrych	2.50	1.00
❑ 46 Al Cowens	.25	.10
❑ 47 Jack Billingham	.25	.10
❑ 48 Don Baylor	1.25	.50
❑ 49 Ed Kranepool	.60	.24
❑ 50 Rick Reuschel	.60	.24
❑ 51 Charlie Moore DP	.15	.06
❑ 52 Jim Lonborg	.60	.24
❑ 53 Phil Garner DP	.25	.10
❑ 54 Tom Johnson	.25	.10
❑ 55 Mitchell Page	.25	.10
❑ 56 Randy Jones	.25	.10
❑ 57 Dan Meyer	.25	.10
❑ 58 Bob Forsch	.25	.10
❑ 59 Otto Velez	.25	.10
❑ 60 Thurman Munson	4.00	1.60
❑ 61 Larvell Blanks	.25	.10
❑ 62 Jim Barr	.25	.10
❑ 63 Don Zimmer MG	.60	.24
❑ 64 Gene Pentz	.25	.10
❑ 65 Ken Singleton	.60	.24
❑ 66 Chicago White Sox	1.25	.25
Team Card CL		
❑ 67 Claudell Washington	.60	.24
❑ 68 Steve Foucault DP	.15	.06
❑ 69 Mike Vail	.25	.10
❑ 70 Goose Gossage	1.25	.50
❑ 71 Terry Humphrey	.25	.10
❑ 72 Andre Dawson	4.00	1.60
❑ 73 Andy Hassler	.25	.10
❑ 74 Checklist 1-121	1.25	.25
❑ 75 Dick Ruthven	.25	.10
❑ 76 Steve Ontiveros	.25	.10
❑ 77 Ed Kirkpatrick	.25	.10
❑ 78 Pablo Torrealba	.25	.10
❑ 79 Da.Johnson DP MG	.15	.06
❑ 80 Ken Griffey Sr.	1.25	.50
❑ 81 Pete Redfern	.25	.10
❑ 82 San Francisco Giants	1.25	.25
Team Card CL		
❑ 83 Bob Montgomery	.25	.10
❑ 84 Kent Tekulve	.60	.24
❑ 85 Ron Fairly	.60	.24
❑ 86 Dave Tomlin	.25	.10
❑ 87 John Lowenstein	.25	.10
❑ 88 Mike Phillips	.25	.10
❑ 89 Ken Clay	.25	.10
❑ 90 Larry Bowa	1.25	.50
❑ 91 Oscar Zamora	.25	.10
❑ 92 Adrian Devine	.25	.10
❑ 93 Bobby Cox DP	.15	.06
❑ 94 Chuck Scrivener	.25	.10
❑ 95 Jamie Quirk	.25	.10
❑ 96 Baltimore Orioles	1.25	.25
Team Card CL		
❑ 97 Stan Bahnsen	.25	.10
❑ 98 Jim Essian	.60	.24
❑ 99 Willie Hernandez RC	1.25	.50
❑ 100 George Brett	15.00	6.00
❑ 101 Sid Monge	.25	.10
❑ 102 Matt Alexander	.25	.10
❑ 103 Tom Murphy	.25	.10
❑ 104 Lee Lacy	.25	.10
❑ 105 Reggie Cleveland	.25	.10
❑ 106 Bill Plummer	.25	.10
❑ 107 Ed Halicki	.25	.10
❑ 108 Von Joshua	.25	.10
❑ 109 Joe Torre MG	.60	.24
❑ 110 Richie Zisk	.25	.10
❑ 111 Mike Tyson	.25	.10
❑ 112 Houston Astros	1.25	.25
Team Card CL		
❑ 113 Don Carrithers	.25	.10
❑ 114 Paul Blair	.60	.24
❑ 115 Gary Nolan	.25	.10
❑ 116 Tucker Ashford	.25	.10
❑ 117 John Montague	.25	.10
❑ 118 Terry Harmon	.25	.10
❑ 119 Dennis Martinez	2.50	1.00
❑ 120 Gary Carter	2.50	1.00
❑ 121 Alvis Woods	.25	.10
❑ 122 Dennis Eckersley	3.00	1.20
❑ 123 Manny Trillo	.25	.10
❑ 124 Dave Rozema	.25	.10
❑ 125 George Scott	.60	.24
❑ 126 Paul Moskau	.25	.10
❑ 127 Chet Lemon	.60	.24
❑ 128 Bill Russell	.60	.24
❑ 129 Jim Colborn	.25	.10
❑ 130 Jeff Burroughs	.60	.24
❑ 131 Bert Blyleven	1.25	.50
❑ 132 Enos Cabell	.25	.10
❑ 133 Jerry Augustine	.25	.10
❑ 134 Steve Henderson	.25	.10
❑ 135 Ron Guidry DP	1.25	.50
❑ 136 Ted Sizemore	.25	.10
❑ 137 Craig Kusick	.25	.10
❑ 138 Larry Demery	.25	.10
❑ 139 Wayne Gross	.25	.10
❑ 140 Rollie Fingers	2.50	1.00
❑ 141 Ruppert Jones	.25	.10
❑ 142 John Montefusco	.25	.10
❑ 143 Keith Hernandez	.60	.24
❑ 144 Jesse Jefferson	.25	.10
❑ 145 Rick Monday	.60	.24
❑ 146 Doyle Alexander	.60	.24
❑ 147 Lee Mazzilli	.25	.10
❑ 148 Andre Thornton	.60	.24
❑ 149 Dale Murray	.25	.10
❑ 150 Bobby Bonds	1.25	.50
❑ 151 Milt Wilcox	.25	.10
❑ 152 Ivan DeJesus	.25	.10
❑ 153 Steve Stone	.60	.24
❑ 154 Cecil Cooper DP	.25	.10
❑ 155 Butch Hobson	.25	.10
❑ 156 Andy Messersmith	.60	.24
❑ 157 Pete LaCock DP	.15	.06
❑ 158 Joaquin Andujar	.60	.24

- ❑ 159 Lou Piniella .60 .24
- ❑ 160 Jim Palmer 3.00 1.20
- ❑ 161 Bob Boone 1.25 .50
- ❑ 162 Paul Thormodsgard .25 .10
- ❑ 163 Bill North .25 .10
- ❑ 164 Bob Owchinko .25 .10
- ❑ 165 Rennie Stennett .25 .10
- ❑ 166 Carlos Lopez .25 .10
- ❑ 167 Tim Foli .25 .10
- ❑ 168 Reggie Smith .60 .24
- ❑ 169 Jerry Johnson .25 .10
- ❑ 170 Lou Brock 3.00 1.20
- ❑ 171 Pat Zachry .25 .10
- ❑ 172 Mike Hargrove .60 .24
- ❑ 173 Robin Yount UER 5.00 2.00
  (Played for Newark
  in 1973, not 1971)
- ❑ 174 Wayne Garland .25 .10
- ❑ 175 Jerry Morales .25 .10
- ❑ 176 Milt May .25 .10
- ❑ 177 Gene Garber DP .25 .10
- ❑ 178 Dave Chalk .25 .10
- ❑ 179 Dick Tidrow .25 .10
- ❑ 180 Dave Concepcion 1.25 .50
- ❑ 181 Ken Forsch .25 .10
- ❑ 182 Jim Spencer .25 .10
- ❑ 183 Doug Bird .25 .10
- ❑ 184 Checklist 122-242 1.25 .25
- ❑ 185 Ellis Valentine .25 .10
- ❑ 186 Bob Stanley DP .15 .06
- ❑ 187 Jerry Royster DP .15 .06
- ❑ 188 Al Bumbry .60 .24
- ❑ 189 Tom Lasorda MG 2.50 1.00
- ❑ 190 John Candelaria .60 .24
- ❑ 191 Rodney Scott .25 .10
- ❑ 192 San Diego Padres 1.25 .25
  Team Card CL
- ❑ 193 Rich Chiles .25 .10
- ❑ 194 Derrel Thomas .25 .10
- ❑ 195 Larry Dierker .60 .24
- ❑ 196 Bob Bailor .25 .10
- ❑ 197 Nino Espinosa .25 .10
- ❑ 198 Ron Pruitt .25 .10
- ❑ 199 Craig Reynolds .25 .10
- ❑ 200 Reggie Jackson 8.00 3.20
- ❑ 201 Dave Parker 1.25 .50
  Rod Carew LL
- ❑ 202 George Foster .60 .24
  Jim Rice LL DP
- ❑ 203 George Foster .60 .24
  Larry Hisle LL
- ❑ 204 Frank Taveras .25 .10
  Freddie Patek LL DP
- ❑ 205 Steve Carlton 2.50 1.00
  Dave Goltz
  Dennis Leonard
  Jim Palmer LL
- ❑ 206 Phil Niekro 6.00 2.40
  Nolan Ryan LL DP
- ❑ 207 John Candelaria .60 .24
  Frank Tanana LL DP
- ❑ 208 Rollie Fingers 1.25 .50
  Bill Campbell LL
- ❑ 209 Dock Ellis .25 .10
- ❑ 210 Jose Cardenal .25 .10
- ❑ 211 Earl Weaver MG DP 1.25 .50
- ❑ 212 Mike Caldwell .25 .10
- ❑ 213 Alan Bannister .25 .10
- ❑ 214 California Angels 1.25 .25
  Team Card CL
- ❑ 215 Darrell Evans .60 .24
- ❑ 216 Mike Paxton .25 .10
- ❑ 217 Rod Gilbreath .25 .10
- ❑ 218 Marty Pattin .25 .10
- ❑ 219 Mike Cubbage .25 .10
- ❑ 220 Pedro Borbon .25 .10
- ❑ 221 Chris Speier .25 .10
- ❑ 222 Jerry Martin .25 .10
- ❑ 223 Bruce Kison .25 .10
- ❑ 224 Jerry Tabb .25 .10
- ❑ 225 Don Gullett DP .25 .10
- ❑ 226 Joe Ferguson .25 .10
- ❑ 227 Al Fitzmorris .25 .10
- ❑ 228 Manny Mota DP .25 .10
- ❑ 229 Leo Foster .25 .10
- ❑ 230 Al Hrabosky .25 .10
- ❑ 231 Wayne Nordhagen .25 .10
- ❑ 232 Mickey Stanley .25 .10
- ❑ 233 Dick Pole .25 .10
- ❑ 234 Herman Franks MG .25 .10
- ❑ 235 Tim McCarver .60 .24
- ❑ 236 Terry Whitfield .25 .10
- ❑ 237 Rich Dauer .25 .10
- ❑ 238 Juan Beniquez .25 .10
- ❑ 239 Dyar Miller .25 .10
- ❑ 240 Gene Tenace .60 .24
- ❑ 241 Pete Vuckovich .60 .24
- ❑ 242 Barry Bonnell DP .15 .06
- ❑ 243 Bob McClure .25 .10
- ❑ 244 Montreal Expos .60 .12
  Team Card CL DP
- ❑ 245 Rick Burleson .60 .24
- ❑ 246 Dan Driessen .25 .10
- ❑ 247 Larry Christenson .25 .10
- ❑ 248 Frank White DP .60 .24
- ❑ 249 Dave Goltz DP .15 .06
- ❑ 250 Graig Nettles DP .60 .24
- ❑ 251 Don Kirkwood .25 .10
- ❑ 252 Steve Swisher DP .15 .06
- ❑ 253 Jim Kern .25 .10
- ❑ 254 Dave Collins .60 .24
- ❑ 255 Jerry Reuss .60 .24
- ❑ 256 Joe Altobelli MG .25 .10
- ❑ 257 Hector Cruz .25 .10
- ❑ 258 John Hiller .25 .10
- ❑ 259 Los Angeles Dodgers 1.25 .25
  Team Card CL
- ❑ 260 Bert Campaneris .60 .24
- ❑ 261 Tim Hosley .25 .10
- ❑ 262 Rudy May .25 .10
- ❑ 263 Danny Walton .25 .10
- ❑ 264 Jamie Easterly .25 .10
- ❑ 265 Sal Bando DP .60 .24
- ❑ 266 Bob Shirley .25 .10
- ❑ 267 Doug Ault .25 .10
- ❑ 268 Gil Flores .25 .10
- ❑ 269 Wayne Twitchell .25 .10
- ❑ 270 Carlton Fisk 4.00 1.60
- ❑ 271 Randy Lerch DP .15 .06
- ❑ 272 Royle Stillman .25 .10
- ❑ 273 Fred Norman .25 .10
- ❑ 274 Freddie Patek .60 .24
- ❑ 275 Dan Ford .25 .10
- ❑ 276 Bill Bonham DP .15 .06
- ❑ 277 Bruce Boisclair .25 .10
- ❑ 278 Enrique Romo .25 .10
- ❑ 279 Bill Virdon MG .25 .10
- ❑ 280 Buddy Bell .60 .24
- ❑ 281 Eric Rasmussen DP .15 .06
- ❑ 282 New York Yankees 2.50 .50
  Team Card CL
- ❑ 283 Omar Moreno .25 .10
- ❑ 284 Randy Moffitt .25 .10
- ❑ 285 Steve Yeager DP .60 .24
- ❑ 286 Ben Oglivie .60 .24
- ❑ 287 Kiko Garcia .25 .10
- ❑ 288 Dave Hamilton .25 .10
- ❑ 289 Checklist 243-363 1.25 .25
- ❑ 290 Willie Horton .60 .24
- ❑ 291 Gary Ross .25 .10
- ❑ 292 Gene Richards .25 .10
- ❑ 293 Mike Willis .25 .10
- ❑ 294 Larry Parrish .60 .24
- ❑ 295 Bill Lee .25 .10
- ❑ 296 Biff Pocoroba .25 .10
- ❑ 297 Warren Brusstar DP .15 .06
- ❑ 298 Tony Armas .60 .24
- ❑ 299 Whitey Herzog MG .60 .24
- ❑ 300 Joe Morgan 3.00 1.20
- ❑ 301 Buddy Schultz .25 .10
- ❑ 302 Chicago Cubs 1.25 .25
  Team Card CL
- ❑ 303 Sam Hinds .25 .10
- ❑ 304 John Milner .25 .10
- ❑ 305 Rico Carty .60 .24
- ❑ 306 Joe Niekro .60 .24
- ❑ 307 Glenn Borgmann .25 .10
- ❑ 308 Jim Rooker .25 .10
- ❑ 309 Cliff Johnson .25 .10
- ❑ 310 Don Sutton 2.50 1.00
- ❑ 311 Jose Baez DP .15 .06
- ❑ 312 Greg Minton .25 .10
- ❑ 313 Andy Etchebarren .25 .10
- ❑ 314 Paul Lindblad .25 .10
- ❑ 315 Mark Belanger .60 .24
- ❑ 316 Henry Cruz DP .15 .06
- ❑ 317 Dave Johnson .25 .10
- ❑ 318 Tom Griffin .25 .10
- ❑ 319 Alan Ashby .25 .10
- ❑ 320 Fred Lynn .60 .24
- ❑ 321 Santo Alcala .25 .10
- ❑ 322 Tom Paciorek .60 .24
- ❑ 323 Jim Fregosi DP .25 .10
- ❑ 324 Vern Rapp MG .25 .10
- ❑ 325 Bruce Sutter 1.25 .50
- ❑ 326 Mike Lum DP .15 .06
- ❑ 327 Rick Langford DP .15 .06
- ❑ 328 Milwaukee Brewers 1.25 .25
  Team Card CL
- ❑ 329 John Verhoeven .25 .10
- ❑ 330 Bob Watson .60 .24
- ❑ 331 Mark Littell .25 .10
- ❑ 332 Duane Kuiper .25 .10
- ❑ 333 Jim Todd .25 .10
- ❑ 334 John Stearns .25 .10
- ❑ 335 Bucky Dent .60 .24
- ❑ 336 Steve Busby .25 .10
- ❑ 337 Tom Grieve .60 .24
- ❑ 338 Dave Heaverlo .25 .10
- ❑ 339 Mario Guerrero .25 .10
- ❑ 340 Bake McBride .60 .24
- ❑ 341 Mike Flanagan .60 .24
- ❑ 342 Aurelio Rodriguez .25 .10
- ❑ 343 John Wathan DP .15 .06
- ❑ 344 Sam Ewing .25 .10
- ❑ 345 Luis Tiant .60 .24
- ❑ 346 Larry Biittner .25 .10
- ❑ 347 Terry Forster .25 .10
- ❑ 348 Del Unser .25 .10
- ❑ 349 Rick Camp DP .15 .06
- ❑ 350 Steve Garvey 2.50 1.00
- ❑ 351 Jeff Torborg .60 .24
- ❑ 352 Tony Scott .25 .10
- ❑ 353 Doug Bair .25 .10
- ❑ 354 Cesar Geronimo .25 .10
- ❑ 355 Bill Travers .25 .10
- ❑ 356 New York Mets 1.25 .25
  Team Card CL
- ❑ 357 Tom Poquette .25 .10
- ❑ 358 Mark Lemongello .25 .10
- ❑ 359 Marc Hill .25 .10
- ❑ 360 Mike Schmidt 10.00 4.00
- ❑ 361 Chris Knapp .25 .10
- ❑ 362 Dave May .25 .10
- ❑ 363 Bob Randall .25 .10
- ❑ 364 Jerry Turner .25 .10
- ❑ 365 Ed Figueroa .25 .10
- ❑ 366 Larry Milbourne DP .15 .06
- ❑ 367 Rick Dempsey .60 .24
- ❑ 368 Balor Moore .25 .10
- ❑ 369 Tim Nordbrook .25 .10
- ❑ 370 Rusty Staub 1.25 .50
- ❑ 371 Ray Burris .25 .10
- ❑ 372 Brian Asselstine .25 .10
- ❑ 373 Jim Willoughby .25 .10
- ❑ 374 Jose Morales .25 .10
- ❑ 375 Tommy John 1.25 .50
- ❑ 376 Jim Wohlford .25 .10
- ❑ 377 Manny Sarmiento .25 .10
- ❑ 378 Bobby Winkles MG .25 .10
- ❑ 379 Skip Lockwood .25 .10
- ❑ 380 Ted Simmons .60 .24
- ❑ 381 Philadelphia Phillies 1.25 .25
  Team Card CL
- ❑ 382 Joe Lahoud .25 .10
- ❑ 383 Mario Mendoza .25 .10
- ❑ 384 Jack Clark 1.25 .50
- ❑ 385 Tito Fuentes .25 .10
- ❑ 386 Bob Gorinski .25 .10
- ❑ 387 Ken Holtzman .60 .24
- ❑ 388 Bill Fahey DP .15 .06
- ❑ 389 Julio Gonzalez .25 .10
- ❑ 390 Oscar Gamble .60 .24
- ❑ 391 Larry Haney .25 .10
- ❑ 392 Billy Almon .25 .10
- ❑ 393 Tippy Martinez .60 .24
- ❑ 394 Roy Howell DP .15 .06
- ❑ 395 Jim Hughes .25 .10

❑ 396 Bob Stinson DP .15 .06
❑ 397 Greg Gross .25 .10
❑ 398 Don Hood .25 .10
❑ 399 Pete Mackanin .25 .10
❑ 400 Nolan Ryan 30.00 12.00
❑ 401 Sparky Anderson MG .60 .24
❑ 402 Dave Campbell .25 .10
❑ 403 Bud Harrelson .60 .24
❑ 404 Detroit Tigers 1.25 .25
Team Card CL
❑ 405 Rawly Eastwick .25 .10
❑ 406 Mike Jorgensen .25 .10
❑ 407 Odell Jones .25 .10
❑ 408 Joe Zdeb .25 .10
❑ 409 Ron Schueler .25 .10
❑ 410 Bill Madlock .60 .24
❑ 411 Willie Randolph ALCS .60 .24
❑ 412 Davey Lopes NLCS .60 .24
❑ 413 Reggie Jackson WS 4.00 1.60
❑ 414 Darold Knowles DP .15 .06
❑ 415 Ray Fosse .25 .10
❑ 416 Jack Brohamer .25 .10
❑ 417 Mike Garman DP .15 .06
❑ 418 Tony Muser .25 .10
❑ 419 Jerry Garvin .25 .10
❑ 420 Greg Luzinski 1.25 .50
❑ 421 Junior Moore .25 .10
❑ 422 Steve Braun .25 .10
❑ 423 Dave Rosello .25 .10
❑ 424 Boston Red Sox 1.25 .25
Team Card CL
❑ 425 Steve Rogers DP .25 .10
❑ 426 Fred Kendall .25 .10
❑ 427 Mario Soto RC .60 .24
❑ 428 Joel Youngblood .25 .10
❑ 429 Mike Barlow .25 .10
❑ 430 Al Oliver .60 .24
❑ 431 Butch Metzger .25 .10
❑ 432 Terry Bulling .25 .10
❑ 433 Fernando Gonzalez .25 .10
❑ 434 Mike Norris .25 .10
❑ 435 Checklist 364-484 1.25 .25
❑ 436 Vic Harris DP .15 .06
❑ 437 Bo McLaughlin .25 .10
❑ 438 John Ellis .25 .10
❑ 439 Ken Kravec .25 .10
❑ 440 Dave Lopes .60 .24
❑ 441 Larry Gura .25 .10
❑ 442 Elliott Maddox .25 .10
❑ 443 Darrel Chaney .25 .10
❑ 444 Roy Hartsfield MG .25 .10
❑ 445 Mike Ivie .25 .10
❑ 446 Tug McGraw .60 .24
❑ 447 Leroy Stanton .25 .10
❑ 448 Bill Castro .25 .10
❑ 449 Tim Blackwell DP .15 .06
❑ 450 Tom Seaver 6.00 2.40
❑ 451 Minnesota Twins 1.25 .25
Team Card CL
❑ 452 Jerry Mumphrey .25 .10
❑ 453 Doug Flynn .25 .10
❑ 454 Dave LaRoche .25 .10
❑ 455 Bill Robinson .60 .24
❑ 456 Vern Ruhle .25 .10
❑ 457 Bob Bailey .25 .10
❑ 458 Jeff Newman .25 .10
❑ 459 Charlie Spikes .25 .10
❑ 460 Jim Hunter 2.50 1.00
❑ 461 Rob Andrews DP .15 .06
❑ 462 Rogelio Moret .25 .10
❑ 463 Kevin Bell .25 .10
❑ 464 Jerry Grote .25 .10
❑ 465 Hal McRae .60 .24
❑ 466 Dennis Blair .25 .10
❑ 467 Alvin Dark MG .60 .24
❑ 468 Warren Cromartie RC .60 .24
❑ 469 Rick Cerone .60 .24
❑ 470 J.R. Richard .60 .24
❑ 471 Roy Smalley .60 .24
❑ 472 Ron Reed .25 .10
❑ 473 Bill Buckner .60 .24
❑ 474 Jim Slaton .25 .10
❑ 475 Gary Matthews .60 .24
❑ 476 Bill Stein .25 .10
❑ 477 Doug Capilla .25 .10
❑ 478 Jerry Remy .25 .10
❑ 479 St. Louis Cardinals 1.25 .25
Team Card CL
❑ 480 Ron LeFlore .60 .24
❑ 481 Jackson Todd .25 .10
❑ 482 Rick Miller .25 .10
❑ 483 Ken Macha RC .25 .10
❑ 484 Jim Norris .25 .10
❑ 485 Chris Chambliss .60 .24
❑ 486 John Curtis .25 .10
❑ 487 Jim Tyrone .25 .10
❑ 488 Dan Spillner .25 .10
❑ 489 Rudy Meoli .25 .10
❑ 490 Amos Otis .60 .24
❑ 491 Scott McGregor .60 .24
❑ 492 Jim Sundberg .60 .24
❑ 493 Steve Renko .25 .10
❑ 494 Chuck Tanner MG .60 .24
❑ 495 Dave Cash .25 .10
❑ 496 Jim Clancy DP .15 .06
❑ 497 Glenn Adams .25 .10
❑ 498 Joe Sambito .25 .10
❑ 499 Seattle Mariners 1.25 .25
Team Card CL
❑ 500 George Foster 1.25 .50
❑ 501 Dave Roberts .25 .10
❑ 502 Pat Rockett .25 .10
❑ 503 Ike Hampton .25 .10
❑ 504 Roger Freed .25 .10
❑ 505 Felix Millan .25 .10
❑ 506 Ron Blomberg .25 .10
❑ 507 Willie Crawford .25 .10
❑ 508 Johnny Oates .60 .24
❑ 509 Brent Strom .25 .10
❑ 510 Willie Stargell 2.50 1.00
❑ 511 Frank Duffy .25 .10
❑ 512 Larry Herndon .25 .10
❑ 513 Barry Foote .25 .10
❑ 514 Rob Sperring .25 .10
❑ 515 Tim Corcoran .25 .10
❑ 516 Gary Beare .25 .10
❑ 517 Andres Mora .25 .10
❑ 518 Tommy Boggs DP .15 .06
❑ 519 Brian Downing .60 .24
❑ 520 Larry Hisle .25 .10
❑ 521 Steve Staggs .25 .10
❑ 522 Dick Williams MG .60 .24
❑ 523 Donnie Moore RC .25 .10
❑ 524 Bernie Carbo .25 .10
❑ 525 Jerry Terrell .25 .10
❑ 526 Cincinnati Reds 1.25 .25
Team Card CL
❑ 527 Vic Correll .25 .10
❑ 528 Rob Picciolo .25 .10
❑ 529 Paul Hartzell .25 .10
❑ 530 Dave Winfield 4.00 1.60
❑ 531 Tom Underwood .25 .10
❑ 532 Skip Jutze .25 .10
❑ 533 Sandy Alomar .60 .24
❑ 534 Wilbur Howard .25 .10
❑ 535 Checklist 485-605 1.25 .25
❑ 536 Roric Harrison .25 .10
❑ 537 Bruce Bochte .25 .10
❑ 538 Johnny LeMaster .25 .10
❑ 539 Vic Davalillo DP .15 .06
❑ 540 Steve Carlton 4.00 1.60
❑ 541 Larry Cox .25 .10
❑ 542 Tim Johnson .25 .10
❑ 543 Larry Harlow DP .15 .06
❑ 544 Len Randle DP .15 .06
❑ 545 Bill Campbell .25 .10
❑ 546 Ted Martinez .25 .10
❑ 547 John Scott .25 .10
❑ 548 Billy Hunter DP MG .15 .06
❑ 549 Joe Kerrigan .25 .10
❑ 550 John Mayberry .60 .24
❑ 551 Atlanta Braves 1.25 .25
Team Card CL
❑ 552 Francisco Barrios .25 .10
❑ 553 Terry Puhl .60 .24
❑ 554 Joe Coleman .25 .10
❑ 555 Butch Wynegar .25 .10
❑ 556 Ed Armbrister .25 .10
❑ 557 Tony Solaita .25 .10
❑ 558 Paul Mitchell .25 .10
❑ 559 Phil Mankowski .25 .10
❑ 560 Dave Parker 1.25 .50
❑ 561 Charlie Williams .25 .10
❑ 562 Glenn Burke .25 .10
❑ 563 Dave Rader .25 .10
❑ 564 Mick Kelleher .25 .10
❑ 565 Jerry Koosman .60 .24
❑ 566 Merv Rettenmund .25 .10
❑ 567 Dick Drago .25 .10
❑ 568 Tom Hutton .25 .10
❑ 569 Lary Sorensen .25 .10
❑ 570 Dave Kingman 1.25 .50
❑ 571 Buck Martinez .25 .10
❑ 572 Rick Wise .25 .10
❑ 573 Luis Gomez .25 .10
❑ 574 Bob Lemon MG 1.25 .50
❑ 575 Pat Dobson .25 .10
❑ 576 Sam Mejias .25 .10
❑ 577 Oakland A's 1.25 .25
Team Card CL
❑ 578 Buzz Capra .25 .10
❑ 579 Rance Mulliniks .25 .10
❑ 580 Rod Carew 4.00 1.60
❑ 581 Lynn McGlothen .25 .10
❑ 582 Fran Healy .25 .10
❑ 583 George Medich .25 .10
❑ 584 John Hale .25 .10
❑ 585 Woodie Fryman DP .15 .06
❑ 586 Ed Goodson .25 .10
❑ 587 John Urrea .25 .10
❑ 588 Jim Mason .25 .10
❑ 589 Bob Knepper .25 .10
❑ 590 Bobby Murcer .60 .24
❑ 591 George Zeber .25 .10
❑ 592 Bob Apodaca .25 .10
❑ 593 Dave Skaggs .25 .10
❑ 594 Dave Freisleben .25 .10
❑ 595 Sixto Lezcano .25 .10
❑ 596 Gary Wheelock .25 .10
❑ 597 Steve Dillard .25 .10
❑ 598 Eddie Solomon .25 .10
❑ 599 Gary Woods .25 .10
❑ 600 Frank Tanana .60 .24
❑ 601 Gene Mauch MG .60 .24
❑ 602 Eric Soderholm .25 .10
❑ 603 Will McEnaney .25 .10
❑ 604 Earl Williams .25 .10
❑ 605 Rick Rhoden .60 .24
❑ 606 Pittsburgh Pirates 1.25 .25
Team Card CL
❑ 607 Fernando Arroyo .25 .10
❑ 608 Johnny Grubb .25 .10
❑ 609 John Denny .25 .10
❑ 610 Garry Maddox .60 .24
❑ 611 Pat Scanlon .25 .10
❑ 612 Ken Henderson .25 .10
❑ 613 Marty Perez .25 .10
❑ 614 Joe Wallis .25 .10
❑ 615 Clay Carroll .25 .10
❑ 616 Pat Kelly .25 .10
❑ 617 Joe Nolan .25 .10
❑ 618 Tommy Helms .25 .10
❑ 619 Thad Bosley DP .15 .06
❑ 620 Willie Randolph 1.25 .50
❑ 621 Craig Swan DP .15 .06
❑ 622 Champ Summers .25 .10
❑ 623 Eduardo Rodriguez .25 .10
❑ 624 Gary Alexander DP .15 .06
❑ 625 Jose Cruz .60 .24
❑ 626 Toronto Blue Jays 1.25 .25
Team Card CL DP
❑ 627 David Johnson .25 .10
❑ 628 Ralph Garr .60 .24
❑ 629 Don Stanhouse .25 .10
❑ 630 Ron Cey 1.25 .50
❑ 631 Danny Ozark MG .25 .10
❑ 632 Rowland Office .25 .10
❑ 633 Tom Veryzer .25 .10
❑ 634 Len Barker .25 .10
❑ 635 Joe Rudi .60 .24
❑ 636 Jim Bibby .25 .10
❑ 637 Duffy Dyer .25 .10
❑ 638 Paul Splittorff .25 .10
❑ 639 Gene Clines .25 .10
❑ 640 Lee May DP .25 .10
❑ 641 Doug Rau .25 .10
❑ 642 Denny Doyle .25 .10
❑ 643 Tom House .25 .10

❑ 644	Jim Dwyer	.25	.10
❑ 645	Mike Torrez	.60	.24
❑ 646	Rick Auerbach DP	.15	.06
❑ 647	Steve Dunning	.25	.10
❑ 648	Gary Thomasson	.25	.10
❑ 649	Moose Haas	.25	.10
❑ 650	Cesar Cedeno	.60	.24
❑ 651	Doug Rader	.25	.10
❑ 652	Checklist 606-726	1.25	.25
❑ 653	Ron Hodges DP	.15	.06
❑ 654	Pepe Frias	.25	.10
❑ 655	Lyman Bostock	.60	.24
❑ 656	Dave Garcia MG	.25	.10
❑ 657	Bombo Rivera	.25	.10
❑ 658	Manny Sanguillen	.60	.24
❑ 659	Texas Rangers Team Card CL	1.25	.25
❑ 660	Jason Thompson	.60	.24
❑ 661	Grant Jackson	.25	.10
❑ 662	Paul Dade	.25	.10
❑ 663	Paul Reuschel	.25	.10
❑ 664	Fred Stanley	.25	.10
❑ 665	Dennis Leonard	.60	.24
❑ 666	Billy Smith RC	.25	.10
❑ 667	Jeff Byrd	.25	.10
❑ 668	Dusty Baker	1.25	.50
❑ 669	Pete Falcone	.25	.10
❑ 670	Jim Rice	1.25	.50
❑ 671	Gary Lavelle	.25	.10
❑ 672	Don Kessinger	.60	.24
❑ 673	Steve Brye	.25	.10
❑ 674	Ray Knight RC	2.50	1.00
❑ 675	Jay Johnstone	.60	.24
❑ 676	Bob Myrick	.25	.10
❑ 677	Ed Herrmann	.25	.10
❑ 678	Tom Burgmeier	.25	.10
❑ 679	Wayne Garrett	.25	.10
❑ 680	Vida Blue	.60	.24
❑ 681	Rob Belloir	.25	.10
❑ 682	Ken Brett	.25	.10
❑ 683	Mike Champion	.25	.10
❑ 684	Ralph Houk MG	.60	.24
❑ 685	Frank Taveras	.25	.10
❑ 686	Gaylord Perry	2.50	1.00
❑ 687	Julio Cruz RC	.25	.10
❑ 688	George Mitterwald	.25	.10
❑ 689	Cleveland Indians Team Card CL	1.25	.25
❑ 690	Mickey Rivers	.60	.24
❑ 691	Ross Grimsley	.25	.10
❑ 692	Ken Reitz	.25	.10
❑ 693	Lamar Johnson	.25	.10
❑ 694	Elias Sosa	.25	.10
❑ 695	Dwight Evans	1.25	.50
❑ 696	Steve Mingori	.25	.10
❑ 697	Roger Metzger	.25	.10
❑ 698	Juan Bernhardt	.25	.10
❑ 699	Jackie Brown	.25	.10
❑ 700	Johnny Bench	8.00	3.20
❑ 701	Tom Hume Larry Landreth Steve McCatty Bruce Taylor	.60	.24
❑ 702	Bill Nahorodny Kevin Pasley Rick Sweet Don Werner	.60	.24
❑ 703	Larry Andersen Tim Jones Mickey Mahler Jack Morris RC DP	5.00	2.00
❑ 704	Garth Iorg Dave Oliver Sam Perlozzo Lou Whitaker RC	8.00	3.20
❑ 705	Dave Bergman Miguel Dilone Clint Hurdle Willie Norwood	1.25	.50
❑ 706	Wayne Cage Ted Cox Pat Putnam Dave Revering	.60	.24
❑ 707	Mickey Klutts Paul Molitor RC Alan Trammell RC U.L. Washington	80.00	32.00
❑ 708	Bo Diaz Dale Murphy Lance Parrish RC Ernie Whitt	4.00	1.60
❑ 709	Steve Burke Matt Keough Lance Rautzhan Dan Schatzeder	.60	.24
❑ 710	Dell Alston Rick Bosetti Mike Easler RC Keith Smith	1.25	.50
❑ 711	Cardell Camper Dennis Lamp Craig Mitchell Roy Thomas DP	.25	.10
❑ 712	Bobby Valentine	.60	.24
❑ 713	Bob Davis	.25	.10
❑ 714	Mike Anderson	.25	.10
❑ 715	Jim Kaat	1.25	.50
❑ 716	Clarence Gaston	.60	.24
❑ 717	Nelson Briles	.25	.10
❑ 718	Ron Jackson	.25	.10
❑ 719	Randy Elliott	.25	.10
❑ 720	Fergie Jenkins	2.50	1.00
❑ 721	Billy Martin MG	1.25	.50
❑ 722	Pete Broberg	.25	.10
❑ 723	John Wockenfuss	.25	.10
❑ 724	Kansas City Royals Team Card CL	1.25	.25
❑ 725	Kurt Bevacqua	.25	.10
❑ 726	Wilbur Wood	1.25	.30

1979 Topps

	NM	Ex
COMPLETE SET (726)	150.00	60.00
COMMON CARD (1-726)	.25	.10
COMMON CARD DP	.10	.04

❑ 1	Rod Carew Dave Parker LL	2.50	.50
❑ 2	Jim Rice George Foster LL	1.00	.40
❑ 3	Jim Rice George Foster LL	1.00	.40
❑ 4	Ron LeFlore Omar Moreno LL	.50	.20
❑ 5	Ron Guidry Gaylord Perry LL	.50	.20
❑ 6	Nolan Ryan J.R. Richard LL	5.00	2.00
❑ 7	Ron Guidry Craig Swan LL	.50	.20
❑ 8	Rich Gossage Rollie Fingers LL	1.00	.40
❑ 9	Dave Campbell	.25	.10
❑ 10	Lee May	.50	.20
❑ 11	Marc Hill	.25	.10
❑ 12	Dick Drago	.25	.10
❑ 13	Paul Dade	.25	.10
❑ 14	Rafael Landestoy	.25	.10
❑ 15	Ross Grimsley	.25	.10
❑ 16	Fred Stanley	.25	.10
❑ 17	Donnie Moore	.25	.10
❑ 18	Tony Solaita	.25	.10
❑ 19	Larry Gura DP	.10	.04
❑ 20	Joe Morgan DP	2.00	.80
❑ 21	Kevin Kobel	.25	.10
❑ 22	Mike Jorgensen	.25	.10
❑ 23	Terry Forster	.25	.10
❑ 24	Paul Molitor	12.00	4.80
❑ 25	Steve Carlton	3.00	1.20
❑ 26	Jamie Quirk	.25	.10
❑ 27	Dave Goltz	.25	.10
❑ 28	Steve Brye	.25	.10
❑ 29	Rick Langford	.25	.10
❑ 30	Dave Winfield	4.00	1.60
❑ 31	Tom House DP	.10	.04
❑ 32	Jerry Mumphrey	.25	.10
❑ 33	Dave Rozema	.25	.10
❑ 34	Rob Andrews	.25	.10
❑ 35	Ed Figueroa	.25	.10
❑ 36	Alan Ashby	.25	.10
❑ 37	Joe Kerrigan DP	.10	.04
❑ 38	Bernie Carbo	.25	.10
❑ 39	Dale Murphy	3.00	1.20
❑ 40	Dennis Eckersley	2.00	.80
❑ 41	Twins Team CL Gene Mauch MG	1.00	.20
❑ 42	Ron Blomberg	.25	.10
❑ 43	Wayne Twitchell	.25	.10
❑ 44	Kurt Bevacqua	.25	.10
❑ 45	Al Hrabosky	.25	.10
❑ 46	Ron Hodges	.25	.10
❑ 47	Fred Norman	.25	.10
❑ 48	Merv Rettenmund	.25	.10
❑ 49	Vern Ruhle	.25	.10
❑ 50	Steve Garvey DP	1.00	.40
❑ 51	Ray Fosse DP	.10	.04
❑ 52	Randy Lerch	.25	.10
❑ 53	Mick Kelleher	.25	.10
❑ 54	Dell Alston DP	.10	.04
❑ 55	Willie Stargell	2.00	.80
❑ 56	John Hale	.25	.10
❑ 57	Eric Rasmussen	.25	.10
❑ 58	Bob Randall DP	.10	.04
❑ 59	John Denny DP	.25	.10
❑ 60	Mickey Rivers	.50	.20
❑ 61	Bo Diaz	.25	.10
❑ 62	Randy Moffitt	.25	.10
❑ 63	Jack Brohamer	.25	.10
❑ 64	Tom Underwood	.25	.10
❑ 65	Mark Belanger	.50	.20
❑ 66	Tigers Team CL Les Moss MG	1.00	.20
❑ 67	Jim Mason DP	.10	.04
❑ 68	Joe Niekro DP	.25	.10
❑ 69	Elliott Maddox	.25	.10
❑ 70	John Candelaria	.50	.20
❑ 71	Brian Downing	.50	.20
❑ 72	Steve Mingori	.25	.10
❑ 73	Ken Henderson	.25	.10
❑ 74	Shane Rawley	.25	.10
❑ 75	Steve Yeager	.50	.20
❑ 76	Warren Cromartie	.50	.20
❑ 77	Dan Briggs DP	.10	.04
❑ 78	Elias Sosa	.25	.10
❑ 79	Ted Cox	.25	.10
❑ 80	Jason Thompson	.50	.20
❑ 81	Roger Erickson	.25	.10
❑ 82	Mets Team CL Joe Torre MG	1.00	.20
❑ 83	Fred Kendall	.25	.10
❑ 84	Greg Minton	.25	.10
❑ 85	Gary Matthews	.50	.20
❑ 86	Rodney Scott	.25	.10
❑ 87	Pete Falcone	.25	.10
❑ 88	Bob Molinaro	.25	.10
❑ 89	Dick Tidrow	.25	.10
❑ 90	Bob Boone	1.00	.40
❑ 91	Terry Crowley	.25	.10
❑ 92	Jim Bibby	.25	.10
❑ 93	Phil Mankowski	.25	.10
❑ 94	Len Barker	.25	.10
❑ 95	Robin Yount	5.00	2.00
❑ 96	Indians Team CL Jeff Torborg	1.00	.20
❑ 97	Sam Mejias	.25	.10
❑ 98	Ray Burris	.25	.10
❑ 99	John Wathan	.50	.20
❑ 100	Tom Seaver DP	4.00	1.60
❑ 101	Roy Howell	.25	.10

❑ 102 Mike Anderson .25 .10
❑ 103 Jim Todd .25 .10
❑ 104 Johnny Oates DP .25 .10
❑ 105 Rick Camp DP .10 .04
❑ 106 Frank Duffy .25 .10
❑ 107 Jesus Alou DP .10 .04
❑ 108 Eduardo Rodriguez .25 .10
❑ 109 Joel Youngblood .25 .10
❑ 110 Vida Blue .50 .20
❑ 111 Roger Freed .25 .10
❑ 112 Phillies Team 1.00 .20
Danny Ozark MG
❑ 113 Pete Redfern .25 .10
❑ 114 Cliff Johnson .25 .10
❑ 115 Nolan Ryan 20.00 8.00
❑ 116 Ozzie Smith RC 80.00 32.00
❑ 117 Grant Jackson .25 .10
❑ 118 Bud Harrelson .50 .20
❑ 119 Don Stanhouse .25 .10
❑ 120 Jim Sundberg .50 .20
❑ 121 Checklist 1-121 DP .50 .10
❑ 122 Mike Paxton .25 .10
❑ 123 Lou Whitaker 2.50 1.00
❑ 124 Dan Schatzeder .25 .10
❑ 125 Rick Burleson .25 .10
❑ 126 Doug Bair .25 .10
❑ 127 Thad Bosley .25 .10
❑ 128 Ted Martinez .25 .10
❑ 129 Marty Pattin DP .10 .04
❑ 130 Bob Watson DP .25 .10
❑ 131 Jim Clancy .25 .10
❑ 132 Rowland Office .25 .10
❑ 133 Bill Castro .25 .10
❑ 134 Alan Bannister .25 .10
❑ 135 Bobby Murcer .50 .20
❑ 136 Jim Kaat .50 .20
❑ 137 Larry Wolfe DP .10 .04
❑ 138 Mark Lee RC .25 .10
❑ 139 Luis Pujols .25 .10
❑ 140 Don Gullett .50 .20
❑ 141 Tom Paciorek .50 .20
❑ 142 Charlie Williams .25 .10
❑ 143 Tony Scott .25 .10
❑ 144 Sandy Alomar .25 .10
❑ 145 Rick Rhoden .25 .10
❑ 146 Duane Kuiper .25 .10
❑ 147 Dave Hamilton .25 .10
❑ 148 Bruce Boisclair .25 .10
❑ 149 Manny Sarmiento .25 .10
❑ 150 Wayne Cage .25 .10
❑ 151 John Hiller .25 .10
❑ 152 Rick Cerone .25 .10
❑ 153 Dennis Lamp .25 .10
❑ 154 Jim Gantner DP .25 .10
❑ 155 Dwight Evans 1.00 .40
❑ 156 Buddy Solomon .25 .10
❑ 157 U.L. Washington UER .25 .10
(Sic, bats left, should be right)
❑ 158 Joe Sambito .25 .10
❑ 159 Roy White .50 .20
❑ 160 Mike Flanagan 1.00 .40
❑ 161 Barry Foote .25 .10
❑ 162 Tom Johnson .25 .10
❑ 163 Glenn Burke .25 .10
❑ 164 Mickey Lolich .50 .20
❑ 165 Frank Taveras .25 .10
❑ 166 Leon Roberts .25 .10
❑ 167 Roger Metzger DP .10 .04
❑ 168 Dave Freisleben .25 .10
❑ 169 Bill Nahorodny .25 .10
❑ 170 Don Sutton 2.00 .80
❑ 171 Gene Clines .25 .10
❑ 172 Mike Bruhert .25 .10
❑ 173 John Lowenstein .25 .10
❑ 174 Rick Auerbach .25 .10
❑ 175 George Hendrick 1.00 .40
❑ 176 Aurelio Rodriguez .25 .10
❑ 177 Ron Reed .25 .10
❑ 178 Alvis Woods .25 .10
❑ 179 Jim Beattie DP .10 .04
❑ 180 Larry Hisle .25 .10
❑ 181 Mike Garman .25 .10
❑ 182 Tim Johnson .25 .10
❑ 183 Paul Splittorff .25 .10
❑ 184 Darrel Chaney .25 .10
❑ 185 Mike Torrez .50 .20
❑ 186 Eric Soderholm .25 .10
❑ 187 Mark Lemongello .25 .10
❑ 188 Pat Kelly .25 .10
❑ 189 Eddie Whitson RC .25 .10
❑ 190 Ron Cey .50 .20
❑ 191 Mike Norris .25 .10
❑ 192 Cardinals Team CL 1.00 .20
Ken Boyer MG
❑ 193 Glenn Adams .25 .10
❑ 194 Randy Jones .25 .10
❑ 195 Bill Madlock .50 .20
❑ 196 Steve Kemp DP .25 .10
❑ 197 Bob Apodaca .25 .10
❑ 198 Johnny Grubb .25 .10
❑ 199 Larry Milbourne .25 .10
❑ 200 Johnny Bench DP 5.00 2.00
❑ 201 Mike Edwards RB .25 .10
❑ 202 Ron Guidry RB .50 .20
❑ 203 J.R. Richard RB .25 .10
❑ 204 Pete Rose RB 5.00 2.00
❑ 205 John Stearns RB .25 .10
❑ 206 Sammy Stewart RB .25 .10
❑ 207 Dave Lemanczyk .25 .10
❑ 208 Clarence Gaston .25 .10
❑ 209 Reggie Cleveland .25 .10
❑ 210 Larry Bowa .50 .20
❑ 211 Denny Martinez 2.00 .80
❑ 212 Carney Lansford RC 1.00 .40
❑ 213 Bill Travers .25 .10
❑ 214 Red Sox Team CL 1.00 .20
Don Zimmer MG
❑ 215 Willie McCovey 2.50 1.00
❑ 216 Wilbur Wood .25 .10
❑ 217 Steve Dillard .25 .10
❑ 218 Dennis Leonard .50 .20
❑ 219 Roy Smalley .50 .20
❑ 220 Cesar Geronimo .25 .10
❑ 221 Jesse Jefferson .25 .10
❑ 222 Bob Beall .25 .10
❑ 223 Kent Tekulve .50 .20
❑ 224 Dave Revering .25 .10
❑ 225 Goose Gossage 1.00 .40
❑ 226 Ron Pruitt .25 .10
❑ 227 Steve Stone .50 .20
❑ 228 Vic Davalillo .25 .10
❑ 229 Doug Flynn .25 .10
❑ 230 Bob Forsch .25 .10
❑ 231 John Wockenfuss .25 .10
❑ 232 Jimmy Sexton .25 .10
❑ 233 Paul Mitchell .25 .10
❑ 234 Toby Harrah .50 .20
❑ 235 Steve Rogers .25 .10
❑ 236 Jim Dwyer .25 .10
❑ 237 Billy Smith .25 .10
❑ 238 Balor Moore .25 .10
❑ 239 Willie Horton .50 .20
❑ 240 Rick Reuschel .50 .20
❑ 241 Checklist 122-242 DP .50 .10
❑ 242 Pablo Torrealba .25 .10
❑ 243 Buck Martinez DP .10 .04
❑ 244 Pirates Team CL 1.00 .20
Chuck Tanner MG
❑ 245 Jeff Burroughs .50 .20
❑ 246 Darrell Jackson .25 .10
❑ 247 Tucker Ashford DP .10 .04
❑ 248 Pete LaCock .25 .10
❑ 249 Paul Thormodsgard .25 .10
❑ 250 Willie Randolph .50 .20
❑ 251 Jack Morris 2.00 .80
❑ 252 Bob Stinson .25 .10
❑ 253 Rick Wise .25 .10
❑ 254 Luis Gomez .25 .10
❑ 255 Tommy John 1.00 .40
❑ 256 Mike Sadek .25 .10
❑ 257 Adrian Devine .25 .10
❑ 258 Mike Phillips .25 .10
❑ 259 Reds Team CL 1.00 .20
Sparky Anderson MG
❑ 260 Richie Zisk .25 .10
❑ 261 Mario Guerrero .25 .10
❑ 262 Nelson Briles .25 .10
❑ 263 Oscar Gamble .50 .20
❑ 264 Don Robinson RC .25 .10
❑ 265 Don Money .25 .10
❑ 266 Jim Willoughby .25 .10
❑ 267 Joe Rudi .50 .20
❑ 268 Julio Gonzalez .25 .10
❑ 269 Woodie Fryman .25 .10
❑ 270 Butch Hobson .50 .20
❑ 271 Rawly Eastwick .25 .10
❑ 272 Tim Corcoran .25 .10
❑ 273 Jerry Terrell .25 .10
❑ 274 Willie Norwood .25 .10
❑ 275 Junior Moore .25 .10
❑ 276 Jim Colborn .25 .10
❑ 277 Tom Grieve .50 .20
❑ 278 Andy Messersmith .50 .20
❑ 279 Jerry Grote DP .10 .04
❑ 280 Andre Thornton .50 .20
❑ 281 Vic Correll DP .10 .04
❑ 282 Blue Jays Team CL .50 .10
Roy Hartsfield MG
❑ 283 Ken Kravec .25 .10
❑ 284 Johnnie LeMaster .25 .10
❑ 285 Bobby Bonds 1.00 .40
❑ 286 Duffy Dyer .25 .10
❑ 287 Andres Mora .25 .10
❑ 288 Milt Wilcox .25 .10
❑ 289 Jose Cruz 1.00 .40
❑ 290 Dave Lopes .50 .20
❑ 291 Tom Griffin .25 .10
❑ 292 Don Reynolds .25 .10
❑ 293 Jerry Garvin .25 .10
❑ 294 Pepe Frias .25 .10
❑ 295 Mitchell Page .25 .10
❑ 296 Preston Hanna .25 .10
❑ 297 Ted Sizemore .25 .10
❑ 298 Rich Gale .25 .10
❑ 299 Steve Ontiveros .25 .10
❑ 300 Rod Carew 3.00 1.20
❑ 301 Tom Hume .25 .10
❑ 302 Braves Team CL 1.00 .20
Bobby Cox MG
❑ 303 Lary Sorensen DP .10 .04
❑ 304 Steve Swisher .25 .10
❑ 305 Willie Montanez .25 .10
❑ 306 Floyd Bannister .25 .10
❑ 307 Larvell Blanks .25 .10
❑ 308 Bert Blyleven 1.00 .40
❑ 309 Ralph Garr .50 .20
❑ 310 Thurman Munson 3.00 1.20
❑ 311 Gary Lavelle .25 .10
❑ 312 Bob Robertson .25 .10
❑ 313 Dyar Miller .25 .10
❑ 314 Larry Harlow .25 .10
❑ 315 Jon Matlack .25 .10
❑ 316 Milt May .25 .10
❑ 317 Jose Cardenal .50 .20
❑ 318 Bob Welch RC 2.00 .80
❑ 319 Wayne Garrett .25 .10
❑ 320 Carl Yastrzemski 5.00 2.00
❑ 321 Gaylord Perry 2.00 .80
❑ 322 Danny Goodwin .25 .10
❑ 323 Lynn McGlothen .25 .10
❑ 324 Mike Tyson .25 .10
❑ 325 Cecil Cooper .50 .20
❑ 326 Pedro Borbon .25 .10
❑ 327 Art Howe DP .25 .10
❑ 328 A's Team CL 1.00 .20
Jack McKeon MG
❑ 329 Joe Coleman .25 .10
❑ 330 George Brett 10.00 4.00
❑ 331 Mickey Mahler .25 .10
❑ 332 Gary Alexander .25 .10
❑ 333 Chet Lemon .50 .20
❑ 334 Craig Swan .25 .10
❑ 335 Chris Chambliss .50 .20
❑ 336 Bobby Thompson .25 .10
❑ 337 John Montague .25 .10
❑ 338 Vic Harris .25 .10
❑ 339 Ron Jackson .25 .10
❑ 340 Jim Palmer 2.50 1.00
❑ 341 Willie Upshaw .50 .20
❑ 342 Dave Roberts .25 .10
❑ 343 Ed Glynn .25 .10
❑ 344 Jerry Royster .25 .10
❑ 345 Tug McGraw .50 .20
❑ 346 Bill Buckner .50 .20
❑ 347 Doug Rau .25 .10
❑ 348 Andre Dawson 3.00 1.20
❑ 349 Jim Wright .25 .10

❑ 350 Garry Templeton .50 .20
❑ 351 Wayne Nordhagen DP .10 .04
❑ 352 Steve Renko .25 .10
❑ 353 Checklist 243-363 1.00 .20
❑ 354 Bill Bonham .25 .10
❑ 355 Lee Mazzilli .25 .10
❑ 356 Giants Team CL 1.00 .20
Joe Altobelli MG
❑ 357 Jerry Augustine .25 .10
❑ 358 Alan Trammell 3.00 1.20
❑ 359 Dan Spillner DP .10 .04
❑ 360 Amos Otis .50 .20
❑ 361 Tom Dixon .25 .10
❑ 362 Mike Cubbage .25 .10
❑ 363 Craig Skok .25 .10
❑ 364 Gene Richards .25 .10
❑ 365 Sparky Lyle .50 .20
❑ 366 Juan Bernhardt .25 .10
❑ 367 Dave Skaggs .25 .10
❑ 368 Don Aase .25 .10
❑ 369A Bump Wills ERR 3.00 1.20
(Blue Jays)
❑ 369B Bump Wills COR 3.00 1.20
(Rangers)
❑ 370 Dave Kingman 1.00 .40
❑ 371 Jeff Holly .25 .10
❑ 372 Lamar Johnson .25 .10
❑ 373 Lance Rautzhan .25 .10
❑ 374 Ed Herrmann .25 .10
❑ 375 Bill Campbell .25 .10
❑ 376 Gorman Thomas .50 .20
❑ 377 Paul Moskau .25 .10
❑ 378 Rob Picciolo DP .10 .04
❑ 379 Dale Murray .25 .10
❑ 380 John Mayberry .50 .20
❑ 381 Astros Team CL 1.00 .20
Bill Virdon MG
❑ 382 Jerry Martin .25 .10
❑ 383 Phil Garner .50 .20
❑ 384 Tommy Boggs .25 .10
❑ 385 Dan Ford .25 .10
❑ 386 Francisco Barrios .25 .10
❑ 387 Gary Thomasson .25 .10
❑ 388 Jack Billingham .25 .10
❑ 389 Joe Zdeb .25 .10
❑ 390 Rollie Fingers 2.00 .80
❑ 391 Al Oliver .50 .20
❑ 392 Doug Ault .25 .10
❑ 393 Scott McGregor .50 .20
❑ 394 Randy Stein .25 .10
❑ 395 Dave Cash .25 .10
❑ 396 Bill Plummer .25 .10
❑ 397 Sergio Ferrer .25 .10
❑ 398 Ivan DeJesus .25 .10
❑ 399 David Clyde .25 .10
❑ 400 Jim Rice 1.00 .40
❑ 401 Ray Knight .50 .20
❑ 402 Paul Hartzell .25 .10
❑ 403 Tim Foli .25 .10
❑ 404 White Sox Team CL 1.00 .20
Don Kessinger MG
❑ 405 Butch Wynegar DP .10 .04
❑ 406 Joe Wallis DP .10 .04
❑ 407 Pete Vuckovich .50 .20
❑ 408 Charlie Moore DP .10 .04
❑ 409 Willie Wilson RC 1.00 .40
❑ 410 Darrell Evans 1.00 .40
❑ 411 George Sisler ATL 2.50 1.00
Ty Cobb
❑ 412 Hack Wilson ATL 2.50 1.00
Hank Aaron
❑ 413 Roger Maris ATL 4.00 1.60
Hank Aaron
❑ 414 Rogers Hornsby ATL 2.50 1.00
Ty Cobb
❑ 415 Lou Brock ATL 1.00 .40
❑ 416 Jack Chesbro ATL .50 .20
Cy Young
❑ 417 Nolan Ryan ATL DP 5.00 2.00
Walter Johnson
❑ 418 D.Leonard ATL DP .25 .10
Walter Johnson
❑ 419 Dick Ruthven .25 .10
❑ 420 Ken Griffey Sr. .50 .20
❑ 421 Doug DeCinces .50 .20
❑ 422 Ruppert Jones .25 .10
❑ 423 Bob Montgomery .25 .10
❑ 424 Angels Team CL 1.00 .20
Jim Fregosi MG
❑ 425 Rick Manning .25 .10
❑ 426 Chris Speier .25 .10
❑ 427 Andy Replogle .25 .10
❑ 428 Bobby Valentine .50 .20
❑ 429 John Urrea DP .10 .04
❑ 430 Dave Parker .50 .20
❑ 431 Glenn Borgmann .25 .10
❑ 432 Dave Heaverlo .25 .10
❑ 433 Larry Biittner .25 .10
❑ 434 Ken Clay .25 .10
❑ 435 Gene Tenace .50 .20
❑ 436 Hector Cruz .25 .10
❑ 437 Rick Williams .25 .10
❑ 438 Horace Speed .25 .10
❑ 439 Frank White .50 .20
❑ 440 Rusty Staub 1.00 .40
❑ 441 Lee Lacy .25 .10
❑ 442 Doyle Alexander .25 .10
❑ 443 Bruce Bochte .25 .10
❑ 444 Aurelio Lopez .25 .10
❑ 445 Steve Henderson .25 .10
❑ 446 Jim Lonborg .50 .20
❑ 447 Manny Sanguillen .50 .20
❑ 448 Moose Haas .25 .10
❑ 449 Bombo Rivera .25 .10
❑ 450 Dave Concepcion 1.00 .40
❑ 451 Royals Team CL 1.00 .20
Whitey Herzog MG
❑ 452 Jerry Morales .25 .10
❑ 453 Chris Knapp .25 .10
❑ 454 Len Randle .25 .10
❑ 455 Bill Lee DP .10 .04
❑ 456 Chuck Baker .25 .10
❑ 457 Bruce Sutter .50 .20
❑ 458 Jim Essian .25 .10
❑ 459 Sid Monge .25 .10
❑ 460 Graig Nettles 1.00 .40
❑ 461 Jim Barr DP .10 .04
❑ 462 Otto Velez .25 .10
❑ 463 Steve Comer .25 .10
❑ 464 Joe Nolan .25 .10
❑ 465 Reggie Smith .50 .20
❑ 466 Mark Littell .25 .10
❑ 467 Don Kessinger DP .25 .10
❑ 468 Stan Bahnsen DP .10 .04
❑ 469 Lance Parrish 1.00 .40
❑ 470 Garry Maddox DP .25 .10
❑ 471 Joaquin Andujar .50 .20
❑ 472 Craig Kusick .25 .10
❑ 473 Dave Roberts .25 .10
❑ 474 Dick Davis .25 .10
❑ 475 Dan Driessen .25 .10
❑ 476 Tom Poquette .25 .10
❑ 477 Bob Grich .50 .20
❑ 478 Juan Beniquez .25 .10
❑ 479 Padres Team CL 1.00 .20
Roger Craig MG
❑ 480 Fred Lynn .50 .20
❑ 481 Skip Lockwood .25 .10
❑ 482 Craig Reynolds .25 .10
❑ 483 Checklist 364-484 DP .50 .10
❑ 484 Rick Waits .25 .10
❑ 485 Bucky Dent .50 .20
❑ 486 Bob Knepper .25 .10
❑ 487 Miguel Dilone .25 .10
❑ 488 Bob Owchinko .25 .10
❑ 489 Larry Cox UER .25 .10
(Photo actually
Dave Rader)
❑ 490 Al Cowens .25 .10
❑ 491 Tippy Martinez .25 .10
❑ 492 Bob Bailor .25 .10
❑ 493 Larry Christenson .25 .10
❑ 494 Jerry White .25 .10
❑ 495 Tony Perez 2.00 .80
❑ 496 Barry Bonnell DP .10 .04
❑ 497 Glenn Abbott .25 .10
❑ 498 Rich Chiles .25 .10
❑ 499 Rangers Team CL 1.00 .20
Pat Corrales MG
❑ 500 Ron Guidry .50 .20
❑ 501 Junior Kennedy .25 .10
❑ 502 Steve Braun .25 .10
❑ 503 Terry Humphrey .25 .10
❑ 504 Larry McWilliams .25 .10
❑ 505 Ed Kranepool .25 .10
❑ 506 John D'Acquisto .25 .10
❑ 507 Tony Armas .50 .20
❑ 508 Charlie Hough .50 .20
❑ 509 Mario Mendoza UER .25 .10
(Career BA .278,
should say .204)
❑ 510 Ted Simmons 1.00 .40
❑ 511 Paul Reuschel DP .10 .04
❑ 512 Jack Clark .50 .20
❑ 513 Dave Johnson .50 .20
❑ 514 Mike Proly .25 .10
❑ 515 Enos Cabell .25 .10
❑ 516 Champ Summers DP .10 .04
❑ 517 Al Bumbry .50 .20
❑ 518 Jim Umbarger .25 .10
❑ 519 Ben Oglivie .50 .20
❑ 520 Gary Carter 2.00 .80
❑ 521 Sam Ewing .25 .10
❑ 522 Ken Holtzman .50 .20
❑ 523 John Milner .25 .10
❑ 524 Tom Burgmeier .25 .10
❑ 525 Freddie Patek .25 .10
❑ 526 Dodgers Team CL 1.00 .20
Tom Lasorda MG
❑ 527 Lerrin LaGrow .25 .10
❑ 528 Wayne Gross DP .10 .04
❑ 529 Brian Asselstine .25 .10
❑ 530 Frank Tanana .50 .20
❑ 531 Fernando Gonzalez .25 .10
❑ 532 Buddy Schultz .25 .10
❑ 533 Leroy Stanton .25 .10
❑ 534 Ken Forsch .25 .10
❑ 535 Ellis Valentine .25 .10
❑ 536 Jerry Reuss .50 .20
❑ 537 Tom Veryzer .25 .10
❑ 538 Mike Ivie DP .10 .04
❑ 539 John Ellis .25 .10
❑ 540 Greg Luzinski .50 .20
❑ 541 Jim Slaton .25 .10
❑ 542 Rick Bosetti .25 .10
❑ 543 Kiko Garcia .25 .10
❑ 544 Fergie Jenkins 2.00 .80
❑ 545 John Stearns .25 .10
❑ 546 Bill Russell .50 .20
❑ 547 Clint Hurdle .25 .10
❑ 548 Enrique Romo .25 .10
❑ 549 Bob Bailey .25 .10
❑ 550 Sal Bando .50 .20
❑ 551 Cubs Team CL 1.00 .20
Herman Franks MG
❑ 552 Jose Morales .25 .10
❑ 553 Denny Walling .25 .10
❑ 554 Matt Keough .25 .10
❑ 555 Biff Pocoroba .25 .10
❑ 556 Mike Lum .25 .10
❑ 557 Ken Brett .25 .10
❑ 558 Jay Johnstone .50 .20
❑ 559 Greg Pryor .25 .10
❑ 560 John Montefusco .25 .10
❑ 561 Ed Ott .25 .10
❑ 562 Dusty Baker 1.00 .40
❑ 563 Roy Thomas .25 .10
❑ 564 Jerry Turner .25 .10
❑ 565 Rico Carty .50 .20
❑ 566 Nino Espinosa .25 .10
❑ 567 Richie Hebner .50 .20
❑ 568 Carlos Lopez .25 .10
❑ 569 Bob Sykes .25 .10
❑ 570 Cesar Cedeno .50 .20
❑ 571 Darrell Porter .50 .20
❑ 572 Rod Gilbreath .25 .10
❑ 573 Jim Kern .25 .10
❑ 574 Claudell Washington .50 .20
❑ 575 Luis Tiant .50 .20
❑ 576 Mike Parrott .25 .10
❑ 577 Brewers Team CL 1.00 .20
George Bamberger MG
❑ 578 Pete Broberg .25 .10
❑ 579 Greg Gross .25 .10
❑ 580 Ron Fairly .50 .20
❑ 581 Darold Knowles .25 .10
❑ 582 Paul Blair .50 .20
❑ 583 Julio Cruz .25 .10

Card	NM	Ex
❑ 584 Jim Rooker	.25	.10
❑ 585 Hal McRae	1.00	.40
❑ 586 Bob Horner RC	1.00	.40
❑ 587 Ken Reitz	.25	.10
❑ 588 Tom Murphy	.25	.10
❑ 589 Terry Whitfield	.25	.10
❑ 590 J.R. Richard	.50	.20
❑ 591 Mike Hargrove	.50	.20
❑ 592 Mike Krukow	.25	.10
❑ 593 Rick Dempsey	.50	.20
❑ 594 Bob Shirley	.25	.10
❑ 595 Phil Niekro	2.00	.80
❑ 596 Jim Wohlford	.25	.10
❑ 597 Bob Stanley	.25	.10
❑ 598 Mark Wagner	.25	.10
❑ 599 Jim Spencer	.25	.10
❑ 600 George Foster	.50	.20
❑ 601 Dave LaRoche	.25	.10
❑ 602 Checklist 485-605	1.00	.20
❑ 603 Rudy May	.25	.10
❑ 604 Jeff Newman	.25	.10
❑ 605 Rick Monday DP	.25	.10
❑ 606 Expos Team CL	1.00	.20
Dick Williams MG		
❑ 607 Omar Moreno	.25	.10
❑ 608 Dave McKay	.25	.10
❑ 609 Silvio Martinez	.25	.10
❑ 610 Mike Schmidt	8.00	3.20
❑ 611 Jim Norris	.25	.10
❑ 612 Rick Honeycutt RC	.50	.20
❑ 613 Mike Edwards	.25	.10
❑ 614 Willie Hernandez	.50	.20
❑ 615 Ken Singleton	.50	.20
❑ 616 Billy Almon	.25	.10
❑ 617 Terry Puhl	.25	.10
❑ 618 Jerry Remy	.25	.10
❑ 619 Ken Landreaux	.50	.20
❑ 620 Bert Campaneris	.50	.20
❑ 621 Pat Zachry	.25	.10
❑ 622 Dave Collins	.50	.20
❑ 623 Bob McClure	.25	.10
❑ 624 Larry Herndon	.25	.10
❑ 625 Mark Fidrych	2.00	.80
❑ 626 Yankees Team CL	1.00	.20
Bob Lemon MG		
❑ 627 Gary Serum	.25	.10
❑ 628 Del Unser	.25	.10
❑ 629 Gene Garber	.50	.20
❑ 630 Bake McBride	.50	.20
❑ 631 Jorge Orta	.25	.10
❑ 632 Don Kirkwood	.25	.10
❑ 633 Rob Wilfong DP	.10	.04
❑ 634 Paul Lindblad	.25	.10
❑ 635 Don Baylor	1.00	.40
❑ 636 Wayne Garland	.25	.10
❑ 637 Bill Robinson	.50	.20
❑ 638 Al Fitzmorris	.25	.10
❑ 639 Manny Trillo	.25	.10
❑ 640 Eddie Murray	12.00	4.80
❑ 641 Bobby Castillo	.25	.10
❑ 642 Wilbur Howard DP	.10	.04
❑ 643 Tom Hausman	.25	.10
❑ 644 Manny Mota	.50	.20
❑ 645 George Scott DP	.25	.10
❑ 646 Rick Sweet	.25	.10
❑ 647 Bob Lacey	.25	.10
❑ 648 Lou Piniella	.50	.20
❑ 649 John Curtis	.25	.10
❑ 650 Pete Rose	12.00	4.80
❑ 651 Mike Caldwell	.25	.10
❑ 652 Stan Papi	.25	.10
❑ 653 Warren Brusstar DP	.10	.04
❑ 654 Rick Miller	.25	.10
❑ 655 Jerry Koosman	.50	.20
❑ 656 Hosken Powell	.25	.10
❑ 657 George Medich	.25	.10
❑ 658 Taylor Duncan	.25	.10
❑ 659 Mariners Team CL	1.00	.20
Darrell Johnson MG		
❑ 660 Ron LeFlore DP	.25	.10
❑ 661 Bruce Kison	.25	.10
❑ 662 Kevin Bell	.25	.10
❑ 663 Mike Vail	.25	.10
❑ 664 Doug Bird	.25	.10
❑ 665 Lou Brock	2.50	1.00
❑ 666 Rich Dauer	.25	.10

Card	NM	Ex
❑ 667 Don Hood	.25	.10
❑ 668 Bill North	.25	.10
❑ 669 Checklist 606-726	1.00	.20
❑ 670 Jim Hunter DP	1.00	.40
❑ 671 Joe Ferguson DP	.10	.04
❑ 672 Ed Halicki	.25	.10
❑ 673 Tom Hutton	.25	.10
❑ 674 Dave Tomlin	.25	.10
❑ 675 Tim McCarver	1.00	.40
❑ 676 Johnny Sutton	.25	.10
❑ 677 Larry Parrish	.50	.20
❑ 678 Geoff Zahn	.25	.10
❑ 679 Derrel Thomas	.25	.10
❑ 680 Carlton Fisk	3.00	1.20
❑ 681 John Henry Johnson	.25	.10
❑ 682 Dave Chalk	.25	.10
❑ 683 Dan Meyer DP	.10	.04
❑ 684 Jamie Easterly DP	.10	.04
❑ 685 Sixto Lezcano	.25	.10
❑ 686 Ron Schueler DP	.10	.04
❑ 687 Rennie Stennett	.25	.10
❑ 688 Mike Willis	.25	.10
❑ 689 Orioles Team CL	1.00	.20
Earl Weaver MG		
❑ 690 Buddy Bell DP	.25	.10
❑ 691 Dock Ellis DP	.10	.04
❑ 692 Mickey Stanley	.25	.10
❑ 693 Dave Rader	.25	.10
❑ 694 Burt Hooton	.50	.20
❑ 695 Keith Hernandez	1.00	.40
❑ 696 Andy Hassler	.25	.10
❑ 697 Dave Bergman	.25	.10
❑ 698 Bill Stein	.25	.10
❑ 699 Hal Dues	.25	.10
❑ 700 Reggie Jackson DP	5.00	2.00
❑ 701 Mark Corey	.50	.20
John Flinn		
Sammy Stewart		
❑ 702 Joel Finch	.50	.20
Garry Hancock		
Allen Ripley		
❑ 703 Jim Anderson	.50	.20
Dave Frost		
Bob Slater		
❑ 704 Ross Baumgarten	.50	.20
Mike Colbern		
Mike Squires		
❑ 705 Alfredo Griffin RC	1.00	.40
Tim Norrid		
Dave Oliver		
❑ 706 Dave Stegman	.50	.20
Dave Tobik		
Kip Young		
❑ 707 Randy Bass RC	1.00	.40
Jim Gaudet		
Randy McGilberry		
❑ 708 Kevin Bass RC	1.00	.40
Eddie Romero		
Ned Yost RC		
❑ 709 Sam Perlozzo	.50	.20
Rick Sofield		
Kevin Stanfield		
❑ 710 Brian Doyle	.50	.20
Mike Heath		
Dave Rajsich		
❑ 711 Dwayne Murphy RC	1.00	.40
Bruce Robinson		
Alan Wirth		
❑ 712 Bud Anderson	.50	.20
Greg Biercevicz		
Byron McLaughlin		
❑ 713 Danny Darwin RC	1.00	.40
Pat Putnam		
Billy Sample		
❑ 714 Victor Cruz	.50	.20
Pat Kelly		
Ernie Whitt		
❑ 715 Bruce Benedict	1.00	.40
Glenn Hubbard RC		
Larry Whisenton		
❑ 716 Dave Geisel	.50	.20
Karl Pagel		
Scot Thompson		
❑ 717 Mike LaCoss	.50	.20
Ron Oester RC		
Harry Spilman		

Card	NM	Ex
❑ 718 Bruce Bochy	.50	.20
Mike Fischlin		
Don Pisker		
❑ 719 Pedro Guerrero RC	1.00	.40
Rudy Law		
Joe Simpson		
❑ 720 Jerry Fry	1.00	.40
Jerry Pirtle		
Scott Sanderson RC		
❑ 721 Juan Berenguer	.50	.20
Dwight Bernard		
Dan Norman		
❑ 722 Jim Morrison	1.00	.40
Lonnie Smith RC		
Jim Wright		
❑ 723 Dale Berra RC	.50	.20
Eugenio Cotes		
Ben Wiltbank		
❑ 724 Tom Bruno	1.00	.40
George Frazier		
Terry Kennedy RC		
❑ 725 Jim Beswick	.50	.20
Steve Mura		
Broderick Perkins		
❑ 726 Greg Johnston	.50	.10
Joe Strain		
John Tamargo		

1980 Topps

	NM	Ex
COMPLETE SET (726)	120.00	47.50
COMMON CARD (1-726)	.25	.10
COMMON CARD DP	.10	.04
❑ 1 Lou Brock HL	2.50	.50
Carl Yastrzemski		
❑ 2 Willie McCovey HL	.75	.30
❑ 3 Manny Mota HL	.25	.10
❑ 4 Pete Rose HL	3.00	1.20
❑ 5 Garry Templeton HL	.25	.10
❑ 6 Del Unser HL	.25	.10
❑ 7 Mike Lum	.25	.10
❑ 8 Craig Swan	.25	.10
❑ 9 Steve Braun	.25	.10
❑ 10 Dennis Martinez	1.25	.50
❑ 11 Jimmy Sexton	.25	.10
❑ 12 John Curtis DP	.10	.04
❑ 13 Ron Pruitt	.25	.10
❑ 14 Dave Cash	.25	.10
❑ 15 Bill Campbell	.25	.10
❑ 16 Jerry Narron	.25	.10
❑ 17 Bruce Sutter	.75	.30
❑ 18 Ron Jackson	.25	.10
❑ 19 Balor Moore	.25	.10
❑ 20 Dan Ford	.25	.10
❑ 21 Manny Sarmiento	.25	.10
❑ 22 Pat Putnam	.25	.10
❑ 23 Derrel Thomas	.25	.10
❑ 24 Jim Slaton	.25	.10
❑ 25 Lee Mazzilli	.40	.16
❑ 26 Marty Pattin	.25	.10
❑ 27 Del Unser	.25	.10
❑ 28 Bruce Kison	.25	.10
❑ 29 Mark Wagner	.25	.10
❑ 30 Vida Blue	.75	.30
❑ 31 Jay Johnstone	.40	.16
❑ 32 Julio Cruz DP	.10	.04

❑ 33 Tony Scott .25 .10
❑ 34 Jeff Newman DP .10 .04
❑ 35 Luis Tiant .40 .16
❑ 36 Rusty Torres .25 .10
❑ 37 Kiko Garcia .25 .10
❑ 38 Dan Spillner DP .10 .04
❑ 39 Rowland Office .25 .10
❑ 40 Carlton Fisk 2.00 .80
❑ 41 Rangers Team CL .75 .15
Pat Corrales MG
❑ 42 David Palmer .25 .10
❑ 43 Bombo Rivera .25 .10
❑ 44 Bill Fahey .25 .10
❑ 45 Frank White .75 .30
❑ 46 Rico Carty .40 .16
❑ 47 Bill Bonham DP .10 .04
❑ 48 Rick Miller .25 .10
❑ 49 Mario Guerrero .25 .10
❑ 50 J.R. Richard .40 .16
❑ 51 Joe Ferguson DP .10 .04
❑ 52 Warren Brusstar .25 .10
❑ 53 Ben Oglivie .40 .16
❑ 54 Dennis Lamp .25 .10
❑ 55 Bill Madlock .40 .16
❑ 56 Bobby Valentine .40 .16
❑ 57 Pete Vuckovich .25 .10
❑ 58 Doug Flynn .25 .10
❑ 59 Eddy Putman .25 .10
❑ 60 Bucky Dent .40 .16
❑ 61 Gary Serum .25 .10
❑ 62 Mike Ivie .25 .10
❑ 63 Bob Stanley .25 .10
❑ 64 Joe Nolan .25 .10
❑ 65 Al Bumbry .40 .16
❑ 66 Royals Team CL .75 .15
Jim Frey MG
❑ 67 Doyle Alexander .25 .10
❑ 68 Larry Harlow .25 .10
❑ 69 Rick Williams .25 .10
❑ 70 Gary Carter 1.25 .50
❑ 71 John Milner DP .10 .04
❑ 72 Fred Howard DP .10 .04
❑ 73 Dave Collins .25 .10
❑ 74 Sid Monge .25 .10
❑ 75 Bill Russell .40 .16
❑ 76 John Stearns .25 .10
❑ 77 Dave Stieb RC 1.25 .50
❑ 78 Ruppert Jones .25 .10
❑ 79 Bob Owchinko .25 .10
❑ 80 Ron LeFlore .40 .16
❑ 81 Ted Sizemore .25 .10
❑ 82 Astros Team CL .75 .15
Bill Virdon MG
❑ 83 Steve Trout .25 .10
❑ 84 Gary Lavelle .25 .10
❑ 85 Ted Simmons .40 .16
❑ 86 Dave Hamilton .25 .10
❑ 87 Pepe Frias .25 .10
❑ 88 Ken Landreaux .25 .10
❑ 89 Don Hood .25 .10
❑ 90 Manny Trillo .40 .16
❑ 91 Rick Dempsey .40 .16
❑ 92 Rick Rhoden .25 .10
❑ 93 Dave Roberts DP .10 .04
❑ 94 Neil Allen .40 .16
❑ 95 Cecil Cooper .40 .16
❑ 96 A's Team CL .75 .15
Jim Marshall MG
❑ 97 Bill Lee .40 .16
❑ 98 Jerry Terrell .25 .10
❑ 99 Victor Cruz .25 .10
❑ 100 Johnny Bench 4.00 1.60
❑ 101 Aurelio Lopez .25 .10
❑ 102 Rich Dauer .25 .10
❑ 103 Bill Caudill .25 .10
❑ 104 Manny Mota .40 .16
❑ 105 Frank Tanana .40 .16
❑ 106 Jeff Leonard RC .75 .30
❑ 107 Francisco Barrios .25 .10
❑ 108 Bob Horner .40 .16
❑ 109 Bill Travers .25 .10
❑ 110 Fred Lynn DP .40 .16
❑ 111 Bob Knepper .25 .10
❑ 112 White Sox Team CL .75 .15
Tony LaRussa MG
❑ 113 Geoff Zahn .25 .10
❑ 114 Juan Beniquez .25 .10
❑ 115 Sparky Lyle .40 .16
❑ 116 Larry Cox .25 .10
❑ 117 Dock Ellis .25 .10
❑ 118 Phil Garner .40 .16
❑ 119 Sammy Stewart .25 .10
❑ 120 Greg Luzinski .40 .16
❑ 121 Checklist 1-121 .75 .15
❑ 122 Dave Rosello DP .10 .04
❑ 123 Lynn Jones .25 .10
❑ 124 Dave Lemanczyk .25 .10
❑ 125 Tony Perez 1.25 .50
❑ 126 Dave Tomlin .25 .10
❑ 127 Gary Thomasson .25 .10
❑ 128 Tom Burgmeier .25 .10
❑ 129 Craig Reynolds .25 .10
❑ 130 Amos Otis .40 .16
❑ 131 Paul Mitchell .25 .10
❑ 132 Biff Pocoroba .25 .10
❑ 133 Jerry Turner .25 .10
❑ 134 Matt Keough .25 .10
❑ 135 Bill Buckner .40 .16
❑ 136 Dick Ruthven .25 .10
❑ 137 John Castino .25 .10
❑ 138 Ross Baumgarten .25 .10
❑ 139 Dane Iorg .25 .10
❑ 140 Rich Gossage .75 .30
❑ 141 Gary Alexander .25 .10
❑ 142 Phil Huffman .25 .10
❑ 143 Bruce Bochte DP .10 .04
❑ 144 Steve Comer .25 .10
❑ 145 Darrell Evans .40 .16
❑ 146 Bob Welch .40 .16
❑ 147 Terry Puhl .25 .10
❑ 148 Manny Sanguillen .40 .16
❑ 149 Tom Hume .25 .10
❑ 150 Jason Thompson .25 .10
❑ 151 Tom Hausman DP .10 .04
❑ 152 John Fulgham .25 .10
❑ 153 Tim Blackwell .25 .10
❑ 154 Lary Sorensen .25 .10
❑ 155 Jerry Remy .25 .10
❑ 156 Tony Brizzolara .25 .10
❑ 157 Willie Wilson DP .40 .16
❑ 158 Rob Picciolo DP .10 .04
❑ 159 Ken Clay .25 .10
❑ 160 Eddie Murray 5.00 2.00
❑ 161 Larry Christenson .25 .10
❑ 162 Bob Randall .25 .10
❑ 163 Steve Swisher .25 .10
❑ 164 Greg Pryor .25 .10
❑ 165 Omar Moreno .25 .10
❑ 166 Glenn Abbott .25 .10
❑ 167 Jack Clark .40 .16
❑ 168 Rick Waits .25 .10
❑ 169 Luis Gomez .25 .10
❑ 170 Burt Hooton .40 .16
❑ 171 Fernando Gonzalez .25 .10
❑ 172 Ron Hodges .25 .10
❑ 173 John Henry Johnson .25 .10
❑ 174 Ray Knight .40 .16
❑ 175 Rick Reuschel .40 .16
❑ 176 Champ Summers .25 .10
❑ 177 Dave Heaverlo .25 .10
❑ 178 Tim McCarver .75 .30
❑ 179 Ron Davis .25 .10
❑ 180 Warren Cromartie .25 .10
❑ 181 Moose Haas .25 .10
❑ 182 Ken Reitz .25 .10
❑ 183 Jim Anderson DP .10 .04
❑ 184 Steve Renko DP .10 .04
❑ 185 Hal McRae .40 .16
❑ 186 Junior Moore .25 .10
❑ 187 Alan Ashby .25 .10
❑ 188 Terry Crowley .25 .10
❑ 189 Kevin Kobel .25 .10
❑ 190 Buddy Bell .40 .16
❑ 191 Ted Martinez .25 .10
❑ 192 Braves Team CL .75 .15
Bobby Cox MG
❑ 193 Dave Goltz .25 .10
❑ 194 Mike Easler .25 .10
❑ 195 John Montefusco .25 .10
❑ 196 Lance Parrish .40 .16
❑ 197 Byron McLaughlin .25 .10
❑ 198 Dell Alston DP .10 .04
❑ 199 Mike LaCoss .25 .10
❑ 200 Jim Rice .40 .16
❑ 201 Keith Hernandez .75 .30
Fred Lynn LL
❑ 202 Dave Kingman .75 .30
Gorman Thomas LL
❑ 203 Dave Winfield 1.25 .50
Don Baylor LL
❑ 204 Omar Moreno .40 .16
Willie Wilson LL
❑ 205 Joe Niekro .75 .30
Phil Niekro
Mike Flanagan LL
❑ 206 J.R. Richard 5.00 2.00
Nolan Ryan LL
❑ 207 J.R. Richard .75 .30
Ron Guidry LL
❑ 208 Wayne Cage .25 .10
❑ 209 Von Joshua .25 .10
❑ 210 Steve Carlton 2.00 .80
❑ 211 Dave Skaggs DP .10 .04
❑ 212 Dave Roberts .25 .10
❑ 213 Mike Jorgensen DP .10 .04
❑ 214 Angels Team CL .75 .15
Jim Fregosi MG
❑ 215 Sixto Lezcano .25 .10
❑ 216 Phil Mankowski .25 .10
❑ 217 Ed Halicki .25 .10
❑ 218 Jose Morales .25 .10
❑ 219 Steve Mingori .25 .10
❑ 220 Dave Concepcion .75 .30
❑ 221 Joe Cannon .25 .10
❑ 222 Ron Hassey .25 .10
❑ 223 Bob Sykes .25 .10
❑ 224 Willie Montanez .25 .10
❑ 225 Lou Piniella .75 .30
❑ 226 Bill Stein .25 .10
❑ 227 Len Barker .25 .10
❑ 228 Johnny Oates .40 .16
❑ 229 Jim Bibby .25 .10
❑ 230 Dave Winfield 2.50 1.00
❑ 231 Steve McCatty .25 .10
❑ 232 Alan Trammell 1.25 .50
❑ 233 LaRue Washington .25 .10
❑ 234 Vern Ruhle .25 .10
❑ 235 Andre Dawson 1.50 .60
❑ 236 Marc Hill .25 .10
❑ 237 Scott McGregor .25 .10
❑ 238 Rob Wilfong .25 .10
❑ 239 Don Aase .25 .10
❑ 240 Dave Kingman .75 .30
❑ 241 Checklist 122-242 .75 .15
❑ 242 Lamar Johnson .25 .10
❑ 243 Jerry Augustine .25 .10
❑ 244 Cardinals Team CL .75 .15
Ken Boyer MG
❑ 245 Phil Niekro 1.25 .50
❑ 246 Tim Foli DP .10 .04
❑ 247 Frank Riccelli .25 .10
❑ 248 Jamie Quirk .25 .10
❑ 249 Jim Clancy .25 .10
❑ 250 Jim Kaat .75 .30
❑ 251 Kip Young .25 .10
❑ 252 Ted Cox .25 .10
❑ 253 John Montague .25 .10
❑ 254 Paul Dade DP .10 .04
❑ 255 Dusty Baker DP .40 .16
❑ 256 Roger Erickson .25 .10
❑ 257 Larry Herndon .25 .10
❑ 258 Paul Moskau .25 .10
❑ 259 Mets Team CL .75 .15
Joe Torre MG
❑ 260 Al Oliver .75 .30
❑ 261 Dave Chalk .25 .10
❑ 262 Benny Ayala .25 .10
❑ 263 Dave LaRoche DP .10 .04
❑ 264 Bill Robinson .25 .10
❑ 265 Robin Yount 3.00 1.20
❑ 266 Bernie Carbo .25 .10
❑ 267 Dan Schatzeder .25 .10
❑ 268 Rafael Landestoy .25 .10
❑ 269 Dave Tobik .25 .10
❑ 270 Mike Schmidt DP 3.00 1.20
❑ 271 Dick Drago DP .40 .16
❑ 272 Ralph Garr .40 .16
❑ 273 Eduardo Rodriguez .25 .10

❑ 274 Dale Murphy 1.25 .50
❑ 275 Jerry Koosman .40 .16
❑ 276 Tom Veryzer .25 .10
❑ 277 Rick Bosetti .25 .10
❑ 278 Jim Spencer .25 .10
❑ 279 Rob Andrews .25 .10
❑ 280 Gaylord Perry 1.25 .50
❑ 281 Paul Blair .40 .16
❑ 282 Mariners Team CL .75 .15
Darrell Johnson MG
❑ 283 John Ellis .25 .10
❑ 284 Larry Murray DP .10 .04
❑ 285 Don Baylor .75 .30
❑ 286 Darold Knowles DP .10 .04
❑ 287 John Lowenstein .25 .10
❑ 288 Dave Rozema .25 .10
❑ 289 Bruce Bochy .25 .10
❑ 290 Steve Garvey 1.25 .50
❑ 291 Randy Scarberry .25 .10
❑ 292 Dale Berra .25 .10
❑ 293 Elias Sosa .25 .10
❑ 294 Charlie Spikes .25 .10
❑ 295 Larry Gura .25 .10
❑ 296 Dave Rader .25 .10
❑ 297 Tim Johnson .25 .10
❑ 298 Ken Holtzman .40 .16
❑ 299 Steve Henderson .25 .10
❑ 300 Ron Guidry .40 .16
❑ 301 Mike Edwards .25 .10
❑ 302 Dodgers Team CL .75 .15
Tom Lasorda MG
❑ 303 Bill Castro .25 .10
❑ 304 Butch Wynegar .25 .10
❑ 305 Randy Jones .25 .10
❑ 306 Denny Walling .25 .10
❑ 307 Rick Honeycutt .25 .10
❑ 308 Mike Hargrove .40 .16
❑ 309 Larry McWilliams .25 .10
❑ 310 Dave Parker .75 .30
❑ 311 Roger Metzger .25 .10
❑ 312 Mike Barlow .25 .10
❑ 313 Johnny Grubb .25 .10
❑ 314 Tim Stoddard .25 .10
❑ 315 Steve Kemp .25 .10
❑ 316 Bob Lacey .25 .10
❑ 317 Mike Anderson DP .10 .04
❑ 318 Jerry Reuss .40 .16
❑ 319 Chris Speier .25 .10
❑ 320 Dennis Eckersley .75 .30
❑ 321 Keith Hernandez .40 .16
❑ 322 Claudell Washington .40 .16
❑ 323 Mick Kelleher .25 .10
❑ 324 Tom Underwood .25 .10
❑ 325 Dan Driessen .25 .10
❑ 326 Bo McLaughlin .25 .10
❑ 327 Ray Fosse DP .10 .04
❑ 328 Twins Team CL .75 .15
Gene Mauch MG
❑ 329 Bert Roberge .25 .10
❑ 330 Al Cowens .25 .10
❑ 331 Richie Hebner .40 .16
❑ 332 Enrique Romo .25 .10
❑ 333 Jim Norris DP .10 .04
❑ 334 Jim Beattie .25 .10
❑ 335 Willie McCovey 1.50 .60
❑ 336 George Medich .25 .10
❑ 337 Carney Lansford .40 .16
❑ 338 John Wockenfuss .25 .10
❑ 339 John D'Acquisto .25 .10
❑ 340 Ken Singleton .40 .16
❑ 341 Jim Essian .25 .10
❑ 342 Odell Jones .25 .10
❑ 343 Mike Vail .25 .10
❑ 344 Randy Lerch .25 .10
❑ 345 Larry Parrish .40 .16
❑ 346 Buddy Solomon .25 .10
❑ 347 Harry Chappas .25 .10
❑ 348 Checklist 243-363 .75 .15
❑ 349 Jack Brohamer .25 .10
❑ 350 George Hendrick .40 .16
❑ 351 Bob Davis .25 .10
❑ 352 Dan Briggs .25 .10
❑ 353 Andy Hassler .25 .10
❑ 354 Rick Auerbach .25 .10
❑ 355 Gary Matthews .40 .16
❑ 356 Padres Team CL .75 .15
Jerry Coleman MG
❑ 357 Bob McClure .25 .10
❑ 358 Lou Whitaker 1.25 .50
❑ 359 Randy Moffitt .25 .10
❑ 360 Darrell Porter DP .25 .10
❑ 361 Wayne Garland .25 .10
❑ 362 Danny Goodwin .25 .10
❑ 363 Wayne Gross .25 .10
❑ 364 Ray Burris .25 .10
❑ 365 Bobby Murcer .40 .16
❑ 366 Rob Dressler .25 .10
❑ 367 Billy Smith .25 .10
❑ 368 Willie Aikens .25 .10
❑ 369 Jim Kern .25 .10
❑ 370 Cesar Cedeno .40 .16
❑ 371 Jack Morris .75 .30
❑ 372 Joel Youngblood .25 .10
❑ 373 Dan Petry RC DP .25 .10
❑ 374 Jim Gantner .40 .16
❑ 375 Ross Grimsley .25 .10
❑ 376 Gary Allenson .25 .10
❑ 377 Junior Kennedy .25 .10
❑ 378 Jerry Mumphrey .25 .10
❑ 379 Kevin Bell .25 .10
❑ 380 Garry Maddox .40 .16
❑ 381 Cubs Team CL .75 .15
Preston Gomez MG
❑ 382 Dave Freisleben .25 .10
❑ 383 Ed Ott .25 .10
❑ 384 Joey McLaughlin .25 .10
❑ 385 Enos Cabell .25 .10
❑ 386 Darrell Jackson .25 .10
❑ 387A Fred Stanley YL 2.00 .80
❑ 387B Fred Stanley .25 .10
(Red name on front)
❑ 388 Mike Paxton .25 .10
❑ 389 Pete LaCock .25 .10
❑ 390 Fergie Jenkins 1.25 .50
❑ 391 Tony Armas DP .25 .10
❑ 392 Milt Wilcox .25 .10
❑ 393 Ozzie Smith 10.00 4.00
❑ 394 Reggie Cleveland .25 .10
❑ 395 Ellis Valentine .25 .10
❑ 396 Dan Meyer .25 .10
❑ 397 Roy Thomas DP .10 .04
❑ 398 Barry Foote .25 .10
❑ 399 Mike Proly DP .10 .04
❑ 400 George Foster .40 .16
❑ 401 Pete Falcone .25 .10
❑ 402 Merv Rettenmund .25 .10
❑ 403 Pete Redfern DP .10 .04
❑ 404 Orioles Team CL .75 .15
Earl Weaver MG
❑ 405 Dwight Evans .40 .16
❑ 406 Paul Molitor 5.00 2.00
❑ 407 Tony Solaita .25 .10
❑ 408 Bill North .25 .10
❑ 409 Paul Splittorff .25 .10
❑ 410 Bobby Bonds .75 .30
❑ 411 Frank LaCorte .25 .10
❑ 412 Thad Bosley .25 .10
❑ 413 Allen Ripley .25 .10
❑ 414 George Scott .40 .16
❑ 415 Bill Atkinson .25 .10
❑ 416 Tom Brookens .25 .10
❑ 417 Craig Chamberlain DP .10 .04
❑ 418 Roger Freed DP .10 .04
❑ 419 Vic Correll .25 .10
❑ 420 Butch Hobson .25 .10
❑ 421 Doug Bird .25 .10
❑ 422 Larry Milbourne .25 .10
❑ 423 Dave Frost .25 .10
❑ 424 Yankees Team CL .75 .15
Dick Howser MG
❑ 424A Yankees Team CL
Billy Martin MG
Card is believed to be a pre-production issue
❑ 425 Mark Belanger .40 .16
❑ 426 Grant Jackson .25 .10
❑ 427 Tom Hutton DP .10 .04
❑ 428 Pat Zachry .25 .10
❑ 429 Duane Kuiper .25 .10
❑ 430 Larry Hisle DP .10 .04
❑ 431 Mike Krukow .25 .10
❑ 432 Willie Norwood .25 .10
❑ 433 Rich Gale .25 .10
❑ 434 Johnnie LeMaster .25 .10
❑ 435 Don Gullett .40 .16
❑ 436 Billy Almon .25 .10
❑ 437 Joe Niekro .40 .16
❑ 438 Dave Revering .25 .10
❑ 439 Mike Phillips .25 .10
❑ 440 Don Sutton 1.25 .50
❑ 441 Eric Soderholm .25 .10
❑ 442 Jorge Orta .25 .10
❑ 443 Mike Parrott .25 .10
❑ 444 Alvis Woods .25 .10
❑ 445 Mark Fidrych 1.25 .50
❑ 446 Duffy Dyer .25 .10
❑ 447 Nino Espinosa .25 .10
❑ 448 Jim Wohlford .25 .10
❑ 449 Doug Bair .25 .10
❑ 450 George Brett 8.00 3.20
❑ 451 Indians Team CL .40 .08
Dave Garcia MG
❑ 452 Steve Dillard .25 .10
❑ 453 Mike Bacsik .25 .10
❑ 454 Tom Donohue .25 .10
❑ 455 Mike Torrez .25 .10
❑ 456 Frank Taveras .25 .10
❑ 457 Bert Blyleven .75 .30
❑ 458 Billy Sample .25 .10
❑ 459 Mickey Lolich DP .25 .10
❑ 460 Willie Randolph .40 .16
❑ 461 Dwayne Murphy .25 .10
❑ 462 Mike Sadek DP .10 .04
❑ 463 Jerry Royster .25 .10
❑ 464 John Denny .25 .10
❑ 465 Rick Monday .25 .10
❑ 466 Mike Squires .25 .10
❑ 467 Jesse Jefferson .25 .10
❑ 468 Aurelio Rodriguez .25 .10
❑ 469 Randy Niemann DP .10 .04
❑ 470 Bob Boone .75 .30
❑ 471 Hosken Powell DP .10 .04
❑ 472 Willie Hernandez .40 .16
❑ 473 Bump Wills .25 .10
❑ 474 Steve Busby .25 .10
❑ 475 Cesar Geronimo .25 .10
❑ 476 Bob Shirley .25 .10
❑ 477 Buck Martinez .25 .10
❑ 478 Gil Flores .25 .10
❑ 479 Expos Team CL .75 .15
Dick Williams MG
❑ 480 Bob Watson .40 .16
❑ 481 Tom Paciorek .40 .16
❑ 482 R.Henderson RC UER 70.00 28.00
7 steals at Modesto, should be at Fresno
❑ 483 Bo Diaz .25 .10
❑ 484 Checklist 364-484 .75 .15
❑ 485 Mickey Rivers .40 .16
❑ 486 Mike Tyson DP .10 .04
❑ 487 Wayne Nordhagen .25 .10
❑ 488 Roy Howell .25 .10
❑ 489 Preston Hanna DP .10 .04
❑ 490 Lee May .40 .16
❑ 491 Steve Mura DP .10 .04
❑ 492 Todd Cruz .25 .10
❑ 493 Jerry Martin .25 .10
❑ 494 Craig Minetto .25 .10
❑ 495 Bake McBride .25 .10
❑ 496 Silvio Martinez .25 .10
❑ 497 Jim Mason .25 .10
❑ 498 Danny Darwin .25 .10
❑ 499 Giants Team CL .75 .15
Dave Bristol MG
❑ 500 Tom Seaver 3.00 1.20
❑ 501 Rennie Stennett .25 .10
❑ 502 Rich Wortham DP .10 .04
❑ 503 Mike Cubbage .25 .10
❑ 504 Gene Garber .40 .16
❑ 505 Bert Campaneris .40 .16
❑ 506 Tom Buskey .25 .10
❑ 507 Leon Roberts .25 .10
❑ 508 U.L. Washington .25 .10
❑ 509 Ed Glynn .25 .10
❑ 510 Ron Cey .75 .30
❑ 511 Eric Wilkins .25 .10
❑ 512 Jose Cardenal .25 .10
❑ 513 Tom Dixon DP .10 .04

❑ 514 Steve Ontiveros .25 .10
❑ 515 Mike Caldwell UER .25 .10
1979 loss total reads
96 instead of 6#
❑ 516 Hector Cruz .25 .10
❑ 517 Don Stanhouse .25 .10
❑ 518 Nelson Norman .25 .10
❑ 519 Steve Nicosia .25 .10
❑ 520 Steve Rogers .25 .10
❑ 521 Ken Brett .25 .10
❑ 522 Jim Morrison .25 .10
❑ 523 Ken Henderson .25 .10
❑ 524 Jim Wright DP .10 .04
❑ 525 Clint Hurdle .25 .10
❑ 526 Phillies Team CL .75 .15
Dallas Green MG
❑ 527 Doug Rau DP .10 .04
❑ 528 Adrian Devine .25 .10
❑ 529 Jim Barr .25 .10
❑ 530 Jim Sundberg DP .25 .10
❑ 531 Eric Rasmussen .25 .10
❑ 532 Willie Horton .40 .16
❑ 533 Checklist 485-605 .75 .15
❑ 534 Andre Thornton .40 .16
❑ 535 Bob Forsch .25 .10
❑ 536 Lee Lacy .25 .10
❑ 537 Alex Trevino .25 .10
❑ 538 Joe Strain .25 .10
❑ 539 Rudy May .25 .10
❑ 540 Pete Rose 8.00 3.20
❑ 541 Miguel Dilone .25 .10
❑ 542 Joe Coleman .25 .10
❑ 543 Pat Kelly .25 .10
❑ 544 Rick Sutcliffe RC .75 .30
❑ 545 Jeff Burroughs .40 .16
❑ 546 Rick Langford .25 .10
❑ 547 John Wathan .25 .10
❑ 548 Dave Rajsich .25 .10
❑ 549 Larry Wolfe .25 .10
❑ 550 Ken Griffey Sr. .75 .30
❑ 551 Pirates Team CL .75 .15
Chuck Tanner MG
❑ 552 Bill Nahorodny .25 .10
❑ 553 Dick Davis .25 .10
❑ 554 Art Howe .40 .16
❑ 555 Ed Figueroa .25 .10
❑ 556 Joe Rudi .40 .16
❑ 557 Mark Lee .25 .10
❑ 558 Alfredo Griffin .25 .10
❑ 559 Dale Murray .25 .10
❑ 560 Dave Lopes .40 .16
❑ 561 Eddie Whitson .25 .10
❑ 562 Joe Wallis .25 .10
❑ 563 Will McEnaney .25 .10
❑ 564 Rick Manning .25 .10
❑ 565 Dennis Leonard .40 .16
❑ 566 Bud Harrelson .40 .16
❑ 567 Skip Lockwood .25 .10
❑ 568 Gary Roenicke .40 .16
❑ 569 Terry Kennedy .40 .16
❑ 570 Roy Smalley .25 .10
❑ 571 Joe Sambito .25 .10
❑ 572 Jerry Morales DP .10 .04
❑ 573 Kent Tekulve .40 .16
❑ 574 Scot Thompson .25 .10
❑ 575 Ken Kravec .25 .10
❑ 576 Jim Dwyer .25 .10
❑ 577 Blue Jays Team CL .75 .15
Bobby Mattick MG
❑ 578 Scott Sanderson .40 .16
❑ 579 Charlie Moore .25 .10
❑ 580 Nolan Ryan 15.00 6.00
❑ 581 Bob Bailor .25 .10
❑ 582 Brian Doyle .25 .10
❑ 583 Bob Stinson .25 .10
❑ 584 Kurt Bevacqua .25 .10
❑ 585 Al Hrabosky .25 .10
❑ 586 Mitchell Page .25 .10
❑ 587 Garry Templeton .25 .10
❑ 588 Greg Minton .25 .10
❑ 589 Chet Lemon .40 .16
❑ 590 Jim Palmer 1.50 .60
❑ 591 Rick Cerone .25 .10
❑ 592 Jon Matlack .25 .10
❑ 593 Jesus Alou .25 .10
❑ 594 Dick Tidrow .25 .10
❑ 595 Don Money .25 .10
❑ 596 Rick Matula .25 .10
❑ 597 Tom Poquette .25 .10
❑ 598 Fred Kendall DP .10 .04
❑ 599 Mike Norris .25 .10
❑ 600 Reggie Jackson 4.00 1.60
❑ 601 Buddy Schultz .25 .10
❑ 602 Brian Downing .25 .10
❑ 603 Jack Billingham DP .10 .04
❑ 604 Glenn Adams .25 .10
❑ 605 Terry Forster .25 .10
❑ 606 Reds Team CL .75 .15
John McNamara MG
❑ 607 Woodie Fryman .25 .10
❑ 608 Alan Bannister .25 .10
❑ 609 Ron Reed .25 .10
❑ 610 Willie Stargell 1.25 .50
❑ 611 Jerry Garvin DP .10 .04
❑ 612 Cliff Johnson .25 .10
❑ 613 Randy Stein .25 .10
❑ 614 John Hiller .25 .10
❑ 615 Doug DeCinces .40 .16
❑ 616 Gene Richards .25 .10
❑ 617 Joaquin Andujar .40 .16
❑ 618 Bob Montgomery DP .40 .16
❑ 619 Sergio Ferrer .25 .10
❑ 620 Richie Zisk .25 .10
❑ 621 Bob Grich .40 .16
❑ 622 Mario Soto .25 .10
❑ 623 Gorman Thomas .40 .16
❑ 624 Lerrin LaGrow .25 .10
❑ 625 Chris Chambliss .40 .16
❑ 626 Tigers Team CL .75 .15
Sparky Anderson MG
❑ 627 Pedro Borbon .25 .10
❑ 628 Doug Capilla .25 .10
❑ 629 Jim Todd .25 .10
❑ 630 Larry Bowa .40 .16
❑ 631 Mark Littell .25 .10
❑ 632 Barry Bonnell .25 .10
❑ 633 Bob Apodaca .25 .10
❑ 634 Glenn Borgmann DP .10 .04
❑ 635 John Candelaria .40 .16
❑ 636 Toby Harrah .40 .16
❑ 637 Joe Simpson .25 .10
❑ 638 Mark Clear .25 .10
❑ 639 Larry Biittner .25 .10
❑ 640 Mike Flanagan .40 .16
❑ 641 Ed Kranepool .25 .10
❑ 642 Ken Forsch DP .10 .04
❑ 643 John Mayberry .40 .16
❑ 644 Charlie Hough .40 .16
❑ 645 Rick Burleson .25 .10
❑ 646 Checklist 606-726 .75 .15
❑ 647 Milt May .25 .10
❑ 648 Roy White .40 .16
❑ 649 Tom Griffin .25 .10
❑ 650 Joe Morgan 1.50 .60
❑ 651 Rollie Fingers 1.25 .50
❑ 652 Mario Mendoza .25 .10
❑ 653 Stan Bahnsen .25 .10
❑ 654 Bruce Boisclair DP .10 .04
❑ 655 Tug McGraw .40 .16
❑ 656 Larvell Blanks .25 .10
❑ 657 Dave Edwards .25 .10
❑ 658 Chris Knapp .25 .10
❑ 659 Brewers Team CL .75 .15
George Bamberger MG
❑ 660 Rusty Staub .40 .16
❑ 661 Mark Corey .40 .16
Dave Ford
Wayne Krenchicki
❑ 662 Joel Finch .40 .16
Mike O'Berry
Chuck Rainey
❑ 663 Ralph Botting .75 .30
Bob Clark
Dickie Thon RC
❑ 664 Mike Colbern .40 .16
Guy Hoffman
Dewey Robinson
❑ 665 Larry Andersen .75 .30
Bobby Cuellar
Sandy Wihtol
❑ 666 Mike Chris .40 .16
Al Greene
Bruce Robbins
❑ 667 Renie Martin .75 .30
Bill Paschall
Dan Quisenberry RC
❑ 668 Danny Boitano .40 .16
Willie Mueller
Lenn Sakata
❑ 669 Dan Graham .40 .16
Rick Sofield
Gary Ward RC
❑ 670 Bobby Brown .40 .16
Brad Gulden
Darryl Jones
❑ 671 Derek Bryant 1.25 .50
Brian Kingman
Mike Morgan RC
❑ 672 Charlie Beamon .40 .16
Rodney Craig
Rafael Vasquez
❑ 673 Brian Allard .40 .16
Jerry Don Gleaton
Greg Mahlberg
❑ 674 Butch Edge .40 .16
Pat Kelly
Ted Wilborn
❑ 675 Bruce Benedict .40 .16
Larry Bradford
Eddie Miller
❑ 676 Dave Geisel .40 .16
Steve Macko
Karl Pagel
❑ 677 Art DeFreites .40 .16
Frank Pastore
Harry Spilman
❑ 678 Reggie Baldwin .40 .16
Alan Knicely
Pete Ladd
❑ 679 Joe Beckwith .75 .30
Mickey Hatcher RC
Dave Patterson
❑ 680 Tony Bernazard .75 .30
Randy Miller
John Tamargo
❑ 681 Dan Norman .40 .16
Jesse Orosco RC
Mike Scott RC
❑ 682 Ramon Aviles .40 .16
Dickie Noles
Kevin Saucier
❑ 683 Dorian Boyland .40 .16
Alberto Lois
Harry Saferight
❑ 684 George Frazier .75 .30
Tom Herr RC
Dan O'Brien
❑ 685 Tim Flannery .40 .16
Brian Greer
Jim Wilhelm
❑ 686 Greg Johnston .40 .16
Dennis Littlejohn
Phil Nastu
❑ 687 Mike Heath DP .10 .04
❑ 688 Steve Stone .40 .16
❑ 689 Red Sox Team CL .75 .15
Don Zimmer MG
❑ 690 Tommy John .75 .30
❑ 691 Ivan DeJesus .25 .10
❑ 692 Rawly Eastwick DP .10 .04
❑ 693 Craig Kusick .25 .10
❑ 694 Jim Rooker .25 .10
❑ 695 Reggie Smith .40 .16
❑ 696 Julio Gonzalez .25 .10
❑ 697 David Clyde .25 .10
❑ 698 Oscar Gamble .40 .16
❑ 699 Floyd Bannister .25 .10
❑ 700 Rod Carew DP 1.50 .60
❑ 701 Ken Oberkfell .25 .10
❑ 702 Ed Farmer .25 .10
❑ 703 Otto Velez .25 .10
❑ 704 Gene Tenace .40 .16
❑ 705 Freddie Patek .25 .10
❑ 706 Tippy Martinez .25 .10
❑ 707 Elliott Maddox .25 .10
❑ 708 Bob Tolan .25 .10
❑ 709 Pat Underwood .25 .10
❑ 710 Graig Nettles .75 .30

❑ 711 Bob Galasso .25 .10
❑ 712 Rodney Scott .25 .10
❑ 713 Terry Whitfield .25 .10
❑ 714 Fred Norman .25 .10
❑ 715 Sal Bando .40 .16
❑ 716 Lynn McGlothen .25 .10
❑ 717 Mickey Klutts DP .10 .04
❑ 718 Greg Gross .25 .10
❑ 719 Don Robinson .40 .16
❑ 720 Carl Yastrzemski DP 2.00 .80
❑ 721 Paul Hartzell .25 .10
❑ 722 Jose Cruz .40 .16
❑ 723 Shane Rawley .25 .10
❑ 724 Jerry White .25 .10
❑ 725 Rick Wise .25 .10
❑ 726 Steve Yeager .75 .15

1981 Topps

	Nm-Mt	Ex-Mt
COMPLETE SET (726)	60.00	24.00
COMMON CARD (1-726)	.15	.06
COMMON CARD DP	.07	.03

❑ 1 George Brett 3.00 1.20
Bill Buckner LL
❑ 2 Reggie Jackson 1.50 .60
Ben Oglivie
Mike Schmidt LL
❑ 3 Cecil Cooper 1.50 .60
Mike Schmidt LL
❑ 4 Rickey Henderson 3.00 1.20
Ron LeFlore LL
❑ 5 Steve Stone .40 .16
Steve Carlton LL
❑ 6 Len Barker .40 .16
Steve Carlton LL
❑ 7 Rudy May .75 .30
Don Sutton LL
❑ 8 Dan Quisenberry .40 .16
Rollie Fingers
Tom Hume LL
❑ 9 Pete LaCock DP .07 .03
❑ 10 Mike Flanagan .40 .16
❑ 11 Jim Wohlford DP .07 .03
❑ 12 Mark Clear .15 .06
❑ 13 Joe Charboneau RC 1.50 .60
❑ 14 John Tudor RC .40 .16
❑ 15 Larry Parrish .15 .06
❑ 16 Ron Davis .15 .06
❑ 17 Cliff Johnson .15 .06
❑ 18 Glenn Adams .15 .06
❑ 19 Jim Clancy .15 .06
❑ 20 Jeff Burroughs .15 .06
❑ 21 Ron Oester .15 .06
❑ 22 Danny Darwin .15 .06
❑ 23 Alex Trevino .15 .06
❑ 24 Don Stanhouse .15 .06
❑ 25 Sixto Lezcano .15 .06
❑ 26 U.L. Washington .15 .06
❑ 27 Champ Summers DP .07 .03
❑ 28 Enrique Romo .15 .06
❑ 29 Gene Tenace .40 .16
❑ 30 Jack Clark .40 .16
❑ 31 Checklist 1-121 DP .15 .06
❑ 32 Ken Oberkfell .15 .06
❑ 33 Rick Honeycutt .15 .06
❑ 34 Aurelio Rodriguez .15 .06
❑ 35 Mitchell Page .15 .06
❑ 36 Ed Farmer .15 .06
❑ 37 Gary Roenicke .15 .06
❑ 38 Win Remmerswaal .15 .06
❑ 39 Tom Veryzer .15 .06
❑ 40 Tug McGraw .40 .16
❑ 41 Bob Babcock .15 .06
John Butcher
Jerry Don Gleaton
❑ 42 Jerry White DP .07 .03
❑ 43 Jose Morales .15 .06
❑ 44 Larry McWilliams .15 .06
❑ 45 Enos Cabell .15 .06
❑ 46 Rick Bosetti .15 .06
❑ 47 Ken Brett .15 .06
❑ 48 Dave Skaggs .15 .06
❑ 49 Bob Shirley .15 .06
❑ 50 Dave Lopes .40 .16
❑ 51 Bill Robinson DP .15 .06
❑ 52 Hector Cruz .15 .06
❑ 53 Kevin Saucier .15 .06
❑ 54 Ivan DeJesus .15 .06
❑ 55 Mike Norris .15 .06
❑ 56 Buck Martinez .15 .06
❑ 57 Dave Roberts .15 .06
❑ 58 Joel Youngblood .15 .06
❑ 59 Dan Petry .15 .06
❑ 60 Willie Randolph .40 .16
❑ 61 Butch Wynegar .15 .06
❑ 62 Joe Pettini .15 .06
❑ 63 Steve Renko DP .07 .03
❑ 64 Brian Asselstine .15 .06
❑ 65 Scott McGregor .15 .06
❑ 66 Manny Castillo .15 .06
Tim Ireland
Mike Jones
❑ 67 Ken Kravec .15 .06
❑ 68 Matt Alexander DP .07 .03
❑ 69 Ed Halicki .15 .06
❑ 70 Al Oliver DP .40 .16
❑ 71 Hal Dues .15 .06
❑ 72 Barry Evans DP .07 .03
❑ 73 Doug Bair .15 .06
❑ 74 Mike Hargrove .40 .16
❑ 75 Reggie Smith .40 .16
❑ 76 Mario Mendoza .15 .06
❑ 77 Mike Barlow .15 .06
❑ 78 Steve Dillard .15 .06
❑ 79 Bruce Robbins .15 .06
❑ 80 Rusty Staub .40 .16
❑ 81 Dave Stapleton .15 .06
❑ 82 Danny Heep .15 .06
Alan Knicely
Bobby Sprowl
❑ 83 Mike Proly .15 .06
❑ 84 Johnnie LeMaster .15 .06
❑ 85 Mike Caldwell .15 .06
❑ 86 Wayne Gross .15 .06
❑ 87 Rick Camp .15 .06
❑ 88 Joe Lefebvre .15 .06
❑ 89 Darrell Jackson .15 .06
❑ 90 Bake McBride .15 .06
❑ 91 Tim Stoddard DP .07 .03
❑ 92 Mike Easler .15 .06
❑ 93 Ed Glynn DP .07 .03
❑ 94 Harry Spilman DP .07 .03
❑ 95 Jim Sundberg .40 .16
❑ 96 Dave Beard .15 .06
Ernie Camacho
Pat Dempsey
❑ 97 Chris Speier .15 .06
❑ 98 Clint Hurdle .15 .06
❑ 99 Eric Wilkins .15 .06
❑ 100 Rod Carew .75 .30
❑ 101 Benny Ayala .15 .06
❑ 102 Dave Tobik .15 .06
❑ 103 Jerry Martin .15 .06
❑ 104 Terry Forster .15 .06
❑ 105 Jose Cruz .40 .16
❑ 106 Don Money .15 .06
❑ 107 Rich Wortham .15 .06
❑ 108 Bruce Benedict .15 .06
❑ 109 Mike Scott .40 .16
❑ 110 Carl Yastrzemski 1.50 .60
❑ 111 Greg Minton .15 .06
❑ 112 Rusty Kuntz .15 .06
Fran Mullins
Leo Sutherland
❑ 113 Mike Phillips .15 .06
❑ 114 Tom Underwood .15 .06
❑ 115 Roy Smalley .15 .06
❑ 116 Joe Simpson .15 .06
❑ 117 Pete Falcone .15 .06
❑ 118 Kurt Bevacqua .15 .06
❑ 119 Tippy Martinez .15 .06
❑ 120 Larry Bowa .40 .16
❑ 121 Larry Harlow .15 .06
❑ 122 John Denny .15 .06
❑ 123 Al Cowens .15 .06
❑ 124 Jerry Garvin .15 .06
❑ 125 Andre Dawson .75 .30
❑ 126 Charlie Leibrandt RC .75 .30
❑ 127 Rudy Law .15 .06
❑ 128 Gary Allenson DP .07 .03
❑ 129 Art Howe .40 .16
❑ 130 Larry Gura .15 .06
❑ 131 Keith Moreland .40 .16
❑ 132 Tommy Boggs .15 .06
❑ 133 Jeff Cox .15 .06
❑ 134 Steve Mura .15 .06
❑ 135 Gorman Thomas .40 .16
❑ 136 Doug Capilla .15 .06
❑ 137 Hosken Powell .15 .06
❑ 138 Rich Dotson DP .15 .06
❑ 139 Oscar Gamble .15 .06
❑ 140 Bob Forsch .15 .06
❑ 141 Miguel Dilone .15 .06
❑ 142 Jackson Todd .15 .06
❑ 143 Dan Meyer .15 .06
❑ 144 Allen Ripley .15 .06
❑ 145 Mickey Rivers .40 .16
❑ 146 Bobby Castillo .15 .06
❑ 147 Dale Berra .15 .06
❑ 148 Randy Niemann .15 .06
❑ 149 Joe Nolan .15 .06
❑ 150 Mark Fidrych 1.50 .60
❑ 151 Claudell Washington .15 .06
❑ 152 John Urrea .15 .06
❑ 153 Tom Poquette .15 .06
❑ 154 Rick Langford .15 .06
❑ 155 Chris Chambliss .40 .16
❑ 156 Bob McClure .15 .06
❑ 157 John Wathan .15 .06
❑ 158 Fergie Jenkins .40 .16
❑ 159 Brian Doyle .15 .06
❑ 160 Garry Maddox .15 .06
❑ 161 Dan Graham .15 .06
❑ 162 Doug Corbett .15 .06
❑ 163 Bill Almon .15 .06
❑ 164 LaMarr Hoyt RC .40 .16
❑ 165 Tony Scott .15 .06
❑ 166 Floyd Bannister .15 .06
❑ 167 Terry Whitfield .15 .06
❑ 168 Don Robinson DP .07 .03
❑ 169 John Mayberry .15 .06
❑ 170 Ross Grimsley .15 .06
❑ 171 Gene Richards .15 .06
❑ 172 Gary Woods .15 .06
❑ 173 Bump Wills .15 .06
❑ 174 Doug Rau .15 .06
❑ 175 Dave Collins .15 .06
❑ 176 Mike Krukow .15 .06
❑ 177 Rick Peters .15 .06
❑ 178 Jim Essian DP .07 .03
❑ 179 Rudy May .15 .06
❑ 180 Pete Rose 5.00 2.00
❑ 181 Elias Sosa .15 .06
❑ 182 Bob Grich .40 .16
❑ 183 Dick Davis DP .07 .03
❑ 184 Jim Dwyer .15 .06
❑ 185 Dennis Leonard .15 .06
❑ 186 Wayne Nordhagen .15 .06
❑ 187 Mike Parrott .15 .06
❑ 188 Doug DeCinces .40 .16
❑ 189 Craig Swan .15 .06
❑ 190 Cesar Cedeno .40 .16
❑ 191 Rick Sutcliffe .40 .16
❑ 192 Terry Harper .40 .16
Ed Miller
Rafael Ramirez
❑ 193 Pete Vuckovich .40 .16
❑ 194 Rod Scurry .15 .06

- ☐ 195 Rich Murray .15 .06
- ☐ 196 Duffy Dyer .15 .06
- ☐ 197 Jim Kern .15 .06
- ☐ 198 Jerry Dybzinski .15 .06
- ☐ 199 Chuck Rainey .15 .06
- ☐ 200 George Foster .40 .16
- ☐ 201 Johnny Bench RB .75 .30
- ☐ 202 Steve Carlton RB .40 .16
- ☐ 203 Bill Gullickson RB .75 .30
- ☐ 204 Ron LeFlore RB .40 .16
  Rodney Scott
- ☐ 205 Pete Rose RB 1.50 .60
- ☐ 206 Mike Schmidt RB 1.50 .60
- ☐ 207 Ozzie Smith RB 2.00 .80
- ☐ 208 Willie Wilson RB .40 .16
- ☐ 209 Dickie Thon DP .40 .16
- ☐ 210 Jim Palmer .40 .16
- ☐ 211 Derrel Thomas .15 .06
- ☐ 212 Steve Nicosia .15 .06
- ☐ 213 Al Holland .15 .06
- ☐ 214 Ralph Botting .15 .06
  Jim Dorsey
  John Harris
- ☐ 215 Larry Hisle .15 .06
- ☐ 216 John Henry Johnson .15 .06
- ☐ 217 Rich Hebner .15 .06
- ☐ 218 Paul Splittorff .15 .06
- ☐ 219 Ken Landreaux .15 .06
- ☐ 220 Tom Seaver 1.50 .60
- ☐ 221 Bob Davis .15 .06
- ☐ 222 Jorge Orta .15 .06
- ☐ 223 Roy Lee Jackson .15 .06
- ☐ 224 Pat Zachry .15 .06
- ☐ 225 Ruppert Jones .15 .06
- ☐ 226 Manny Sanguillen DP .07 .03
- ☐ 227 Fred Martinez .15 .06
- ☐ 228 Tom Paciorek .40 .16
- ☐ 229 Rollie Fingers .40 .16
- ☐ 230 George Hendrick .40 .16
- ☐ 231 Joe Beckwith .15 .06
- ☐ 232 Mickey Klutts .15 .06
- ☐ 233 Skip Lockwood .15 .06
- ☐ 234 Lou Whitaker 1.50 .60
- ☐ 235 Scott Sanderson .15 .06
- ☐ 236 Mike Ivie .15 .06
- ☐ 237 Charlie Moore .15 .06
- ☐ 238 Willie Hernandez .40 .16
- ☐ 239 Rick Miller DP .07 .03
- ☐ 240 Nolan Ryan 8.00 3.20
- ☐ 241 Checklist 122-242 DP .15 .06
- ☐ 242 Chet Lemon .15 .06
- ☐ 243 Sal Butera .15 .06
- ☐ 244 Tito Landrum .15 .06
  Al Olmsted
  Andy Rincon
- ☐ 245 Ed Figueroa .15 .06
- ☐ 246 Ed Ott DP .07 .03
- ☐ 247 Glenn Hubbard DP .07 .03
- ☐ 248 Joey McLaughlin .15 .06
- ☐ 249 Larry Cox .15 .06
- ☐ 250 Ron Guidry .40 .16
- ☐ 251 Tom Brookens .15 .06
- ☐ 252 Victor Cruz .15 .06
- ☐ 253 Dave Bergman .15 .06
- ☐ 254 Ozzie Smith 5.00 2.00
- ☐ 255 Mark Littell .15 .06
- ☐ 256 Bombo Rivera .15 .06
- ☐ 257 Rennie Stennett .15 .06
- ☐ 258 Joe Price .15 .06
- ☐ 259 Juan Berenguer 1.50 .60
  Hubie Brooks RC
  Mookie Wilson
- ☐ 260 Ron Cey .40 .16
- ☐ 261 Rickey Henderson 10.00 4.00
- ☐ 262 Sammy Stewart .15 .06
- ☐ 263 Brian Downing .40 .16
- ☐ 264 Jim Norris .15 .06
- ☐ 265 John Candelaria .40 .16
- ☐ 266 Tom Herr .40 .16
- ☐ 267 Stan Bahnsen .15 .06
- ☐ 268 Jerry Royster .15 .06
- ☐ 269 Ken Forsch .15 .06
- ☐ 270 Greg Luzinski .40 .16
- ☐ 271 Bill Castro .15 .06
- ☐ 272 Bruce Kimm .15 .06
- ☐ 273 Stan Papi .15 .06
- ☐ 274 Craig Chamberlain .15 .06
- ☐ 275 Dwight Evans .75 .30
- ☐ 276 Dan Spillner .15 .06
- ☐ 277 Alfredo Griffin .15 .06
- ☐ 278 Rick Sofield .15 .06
- ☐ 279 Bob Knepper .15 .06
- ☐ 280 Ken Griffey .75 .30
- ☐ 281 Fred Stanley .15 .06
- ☐ 282 Rick Anderson .15 .06
  Greg Biercevicz
  Rodney Craig
- ☐ 283 Billy Sample .15 .06
- ☐ 284 Brian Kingman .15 .06
- ☐ 285 Jerry Turner .15 .06
- ☐ 286 Dave Frost .15 .06
- ☐ 287 Lenn Sakata .15 .06
- ☐ 288 Bob Clark .15 .06
- ☐ 289 Mickey Hatcher .40 .16
- ☐ 290 Bob Boone DP .40 .16
- ☐ 291 Aurelio Lopez .15 .06
- ☐ 292 Mike Squires .15 .06
- ☐ 293 Charlie Lea .15 .06
- ☐ 294 Mike Tyson DP .07 .03
- ☐ 295 Hal McRae .40 .16
- ☐ 296 Bill Nahorodny DP .07 .03
- ☐ 297 Bob Bailor .15 .06
- ☐ 298 Buddy Solomon .15 .06
- ☐ 299 Elliott Maddox .15 .06
- ☐ 300 Paul Molitor 3.00 1.20
- ☐ 301 Matt Keough .15 .06
- ☐ 302 Jack Perconte 5.00 2.00
  Mike Scioscia RC
  Fernando Valenzuela RC
- ☐ 303 Johnny Oates .40 .16
- ☐ 304 John Castino .15 .06
- ☐ 305 Ken Clay .15 .06
- ☐ 306 Juan Beniquez DP .07 .03
- ☐ 307 Gene Garber .15 .06
- ☐ 308 Rick Manning .15 .06
- ☐ 309 Luis Salazar RC .15 .06
- ☐ 310 Vida Blue DP .15 .06
- ☐ 311 Freddie Patek .15 .06
- ☐ 312 Rick Rhoden .15 .06
- ☐ 313 Luis Pujols .15 .06
- ☐ 314 Rich Dauer .15 .06
- ☐ 315 Kirk Gibson RC 3.00 1.20
- ☐ 316 Craig Minetto .15 .06
- ☐ 317 Lonnie Smith .40 .16
- ☐ 318 Steve Yeager .15 .06
- ☐ 319 Rowland Office .15 .06
- ☐ 320 Tom Burgmeier .15 .06
- ☐ 321 Leon Durham .40 .16
- ☐ 322 Neil Allen .15 .06
- ☐ 323 Jim Morrison DP .07 .03
- ☐ 324 Mike Willis .15 .06
- ☐ 325 Ray Knight .40 .16
- ☐ 326 Biff Pocoroba .15 .06
- ☐ 327 Moose Haas .15 .06
- ☐ 328 Dave Engle .15 .06
  Greg Johnston
  Gary Ward
- ☐ 329 Joaquin Andujar .40 .16
- ☐ 330 Frank White .40 .16
- ☐ 331 Dennis Lamp .15 .06
- ☐ 332 Lee Lacy DP .07 .03
- ☐ 333 Sid Monge .15 .06
- ☐ 334 Dane Iorg .15 .06
- ☐ 335 Rick Cerone .15 .06
- ☐ 336 Eddie Whitson .15 .06
- ☐ 337 Lynn Jones .15 .06
- ☐ 338 Checklist 243-363 .75 .30
- ☐ 339 John Ellis .15 .06
- ☐ 340 Bruce Kison .15 .06
- ☐ 341 Dwayne Murphy .15 .06
- ☐ 342 Eric Rasmussen DP .07 .03
- ☐ 343 Frank Taveras .15 .06
- ☐ 344 Byron McLaughlin .15 .06
- ☐ 345 Warren Cromartie .15 .06
- ☐ 346 Larry Christenson DP .07 .03
- ☐ 347 Harold Baines RC 8.00 3.20
- ☐ 348 Bob Sykes .15 .06
- ☐ 349 Glenn Hoffman .15 .06
- ☐ 350 J.R. Richard .40 .16
- ☐ 351 Otto Velez .15 .06
- ☐ 352 Dick Tidrow DP .07 .03
- ☐ 353 Terry Kennedy .15 .06
- ☐ 354 Mario Soto .15 .06
- ☐ 355 Bob Horner .40 .16
- ☐ 356 George Stablein .15 .06
  Craig Stimac
  Tom Tellmann
- ☐ 357 Jim Slaton .15 .06
- ☐ 358 Mark Wagner .15 .06
- ☐ 359 Tom Hausman .15 .06
- ☐ 360 Willie Wilson .40 .16
- ☐ 361 Joe Strain .15 .06
- ☐ 362 Bo Diaz .15 .06
- ☐ 363 Geoff Zahn .15 .06
- ☐ 364 Mike Davis .15 .06
- ☐ 365 Graig Nettles DP .40 .16
- ☐ 366 Mike Ramsey RC .15 .06
- ☐ 367 Dennis Martinez .75 .30
- ☐ 368 Leon Roberts .15 .06
- ☐ 369 Frank Tanana .40 .16
- ☐ 370 Dave Winfield 1.50 .60
- ☐ 371 Charlie Hough .40 .16
- ☐ 372 Jay Johnstone .40 .16
- ☐ 373 Pat Underwood .15 .06
- ☐ 374 Tommy Hutton .15 .06
- ☐ 375 Dave Concepcion .40 .16
- ☐ 376 Ron Reed .15 .06
- ☐ 377 Jerry Morales .15 .06
- ☐ 378 Dave Rader .15 .06
- ☐ 379 Lary Sorensen .15 .06
- ☐ 380 Willie Stargell .75 .30
- ☐ 381 Carlos Lezcano .15 .06
  Steve Macko
  Randy Martz
- ☐ 382 Paul Mirabella .15 .06
- ☐ 383 Eric Soderholm DP .07 .03
- ☐ 384 Mike Sadek .15 .06
- ☐ 385 Joe Sambito .15 .06
- ☐ 386 Dave Edwards .15 .06
- ☐ 387 Phil Niekro .40 .16
- ☐ 388 Andre Thornton .40 .16
- ☐ 389 Marty Pattin .15 .06
- ☐ 390 Cesar Geronimo .15 .06
- ☐ 391 Dave Lemanczyk DP .07 .03
- ☐ 392 Lance Parrish .40 .16
- ☐ 393 Broderick Perkins .15 .06
- ☐ 394 Woodie Fryman .15 .06
- ☐ 395 Scot Thompson .15 .06
- ☐ 396 Bill Campbell .15 .06
- ☐ 397 Julio Cruz .15 .06
- ☐ 398 Ross Baumgarten .15 .06
- ☐ 399 Mike Boddicker RC 1.50 .60
  Mark Corey
  Floyd Rayford
- ☐ 400 Reggie Jackson .75 .30
- ☐ 401 George Brett ALCS 2.50 1.00
- ☐ 402 NL Champs .75 .30
  Phillies squeak
  past Astros
  (Phillies celebrating)
- ☐ 403 Larry Bowa WS .75 .30
- ☐ 404 Tug McGraw WS .75 .30
- ☐ 405 Nino Espinosa .15 .06
- ☐ 406 Dickie Noles .15 .06
- ☐ 407 Ernie Whitt .15 .06
- ☐ 408 Fernando Arroyo .15 .06
- ☐ 409 Larry Herndon .15 .06
- ☐ 410 Bert Campaneris .40 .16
- ☐ 411 Terry Puhl .15 .06
- ☐ 412 Britt Burns .15 .06
- ☐ 413 Tony Bernazard .15 .06
- ☐ 414 John Pacella DP .07 .03
- ☐ 415 Ben Oglivie .40 .16
- ☐ 416 Gary Alexander .15 .06
- ☐ 417 Dan Schatzeder .15 .06
- ☐ 418 Bobby Brown .15 .06
- ☐ 419 Tom Hume .15 .06
- ☐ 420 Keith Hernandez .75 .30
- ☐ 421 Bob Stanley .15 .06
- ☐ 422 Dan Ford .15 .06
- ☐ 423 Shane Rawley .15 .06
- ☐ 424 Tim Lollar .15 .06
  Bruce Robinson
  Dennis Werth
- ☐ 425 Al Bumbry .40 .16
- ☐ 426 Warren Brusstar .15 .06
- ☐ 427 John D'Acquisto .15 .06
- ☐ 428 John Stearns .15 .06

	No.	Player		
❑	429	Mick Kelleher	.15	.06
❑	430	Jim Bibby	.15	.06
❑	431	Dave Roberts	.15	.06
❑	432	Len Barker	.15	.06
❑	433	Rance Mulliniks	.15	.06
❑	434	Roger Erickson	.15	.06
❑	435	Jim Spencer	.15	.06
❑	436	Gary Lucas	.15	.06
❑	437	Mike Heath DP	.07	.03
❑	438	John Montefusco	.15	.06
❑	439	Denny Walling	.15	.06
❑	440	Jerry Reuss	.40	.16
❑	441	Ken Reitz	.15	.06
❑	442	Ron Pruitt	.15	.06
❑	443	Jim Beattie DP	.07	.03
❑	444	Garth Iorg	.15	.06
❑	445	Ellis Valentine	.15	.06
❑	446	Checklist 364-484	.75	.30
❑	447	Junior Kennedy DP	.07	.03
❑	448	Tim Corcoran	.15	.06
❑	449	Paul Mitchell	.15	.06
❑	450	Dave Kingman DP	.40	.16
❑	451	Chris Bando	.15	.06
		Tom Brennan		
		Sandy Wihtol		
❑	452	Renie Martin	.15	.06
❑	453	Rob Wilfong DP	.40	.16
❑	454	Andy Hassler	.15	.06
❑	455	Rick Burleson	.15	.06
❑	456	Jeff Reardon RC	1.50	.60
❑	457	Mike Lum	.15	.06
❑	458	Randy Jones	.15	.06
❑	459	Greg Gross	.15	.06
❑	460	Rich Gossage	.75	.30
❑	461	Dave McKay	.15	.06
❑	462	Jack Brohamer	.15	.06
❑	463	Milt May	.15	.06
❑	464	Adrian Devine	.15	.06
❑	465	Bill Russell	.40	.16
❑	466	Bob Molinaro	.15	.06
❑	467	Dave Stieb	.40	.16
❑	468	John Wockenfuss	.15	.06
❑	469	Jeff Leonard	.40	.16
❑	470	Manny Trillo	.15	.06
❑	471	Mike Vail	.15	.06
❑	472	Dyar Miller DP	.07	.03
❑	473	Jose Cardenal	.15	.06
❑	474	Mike LaCoss	.15	.06
❑	475	Buddy Bell	.40	.16
❑	476	Jerry Koosman	.40	.16
❑	477	Luis Gomez	.15	.06
❑	478	Juan Eichelberger	.15	.06
❑	479	Tim Raines RC	3.00	1.20
		Roberto Ramos		
		Bobby Pate		
❑	480	Carlton Fisk	.75	.30
❑	481	Bob Lacey DP	.07	.03
❑	482	Jim Gantner	.40	.16
❑	483	Mike Griffin RC	.15	.06
❑	484	Max Venable DP	.07	.03
❑	485	Garry Templeton	.15	.06
❑	486	Marc Hill	.15	.06
❑	487	Dewey Robinson	.15	.06
❑	488	Damaso Garcia	.15	.06
❑	489	John Littlefield	.15	.06
		Photo on card believed to be Mark Riggins		
❑	490	Eddie Murray	2.50	1.00
❑	491	Gordy Pladson	.15	.06
❑	492	Barry Foote	.15	.06
❑	493	Dan Quisenberry	.40	.16
❑	494	Bob Walk RC	.40	.16
❑	495	Dusty Baker	.75	.30
❑	496	Paul Dade	.15	.06
❑	497	Fred Norman	.15	.06
❑	498	Pat Putnam	.15	.06
❑	499	Frank Pastore	.15	.06
❑	500	Jim Rice	.40	.16
❑	501	Tim Foli DP	.40	.16
❑	502	Chris Bourjos	.15	.06
		Al Hargesheimer		
		Mike Rowland		
❑	503	Steve McCatty	.15	.06
❑	504	Dale Murphy	1.50	.60
❑	505	Jason Thompson	.15	.06
❑	506	Phil Huffman	.15	.06
❑	507	Jamie Quirk	.15	.06
❑	508	Rob Dressler	.15	.06
❑	509	Pete Mackanin	.15	.06
❑	510	Lee Mazzilli	.15	.06
❑	511	Wayne Garland	.15	.06
❑	512	Gary Thomasson	.15	.06
❑	513	Frank LaCorte	.15	.06
❑	514	George Riley	.15	.06
❑	515	Robin Yount	1.50	.60
❑	516	Doug Bird	.15	.06
❑	517	Richie Zisk	.15	.06
❑	518	Grant Jackson	.15	.06
❑	519	John Tamargo DP	.40	.16
❑	520	Steve Stone	.40	.16
❑	521	Sam Mejias	.15	.06
❑	522	Mike Colbern	.15	.06
❑	523	John Fulgham	.15	.06
❑	524	Willie Aikens	.15	.06
❑	525	Mike Torrez	.15	.06
❑	526	Marty Bystrom	.15	.06
		Jay Loviglio		
		Jim Wright		
❑	527	Danny Goodwin	.15	.06
❑	528	Gary Matthews	.40	.16
❑	529	Dave LaRoche	.15	.06
❑	530	Steve Garvey	.40	.16
❑	531	John Curtis	.15	.06
❑	532	Bill Stein	.15	.06
❑	533	Jesus Figueroa	.15	.06
❑	534	Dave Smith RC	.40	.16
❑	535	Omar Moreno	.15	.06
❑	536	Bob Owchinko DP	.07	.03
❑	537	Ron Hodges	.15	.06
❑	538	Tom Griffin	.15	.06
❑	539	Rodney Scott	.15	.06
❑	540	Mike Schmidt DP	2.50	1.00
❑	541	Steve Swisher	.15	.06
❑	542	Larry Bradford DP	.07	.03
❑	543	Terry Crowley	.15	.06
❑	544	Rich Gale	.15	.06
❑	545	Johnny Grubb	.15	.06
❑	546	Paul Moskau	.15	.06
❑	547	Mario Guerrero	.15	.06
❑	548	Dave Goltz	.15	.06
❑	549	Jerry Remy	.15	.06
❑	550	Tommy John	.75	.30
❑	551	Vance Law	1.50	.60
		Tony Pena RC		
		Pascual Perez RC		
❑	552	Steve Trout	.15	.06
❑	553	Tim Blackwell	.15	.06
❑	554	Bert Blyleven UER	.75	.30
		(1 is missing from 1980 on card back)		
❑	555	Cecil Cooper	.40	.16
❑	556	Jerry Mumphrey	.15	.06
❑	557	Chris Knapp	.15	.06
❑	558	Barry Bonnell	.15	.06
❑	559	Willie Montanez	.15	.06
❑	560	Joe Morgan	.75	.30
❑	561	Dennis Littlejohn	.15	.06
❑	562	Checklist 485-605	.75	.30
❑	563	Jim Kaat	.40	.16
❑	564	Ron Hassey DP	.07	.03
❑	565	Burt Hooton	.15	.06
❑	566	Del Unser	.15	.06
❑	567	Mark Bomback	.15	.06
❑	568	Dave Revering	.15	.06
❑	569	Al Williams DP	.07	.03
❑	570	Ken Singleton	.40	.16
❑	571	Todd Cruz	.15	.06
❑	572	Jack Morris	1.50	.60
❑	573	Phil Garner	.40	.16
❑	574	Bill Caudill	.15	.06
❑	575	Tony Perez	.75	.30
❑	576	Reggie Cleveland	.15	.06
❑	577	Luis Leal	.15	.06
		Brian Milner		
		Ken Schrom		
❑	578	Bill Gullickson RC	.75	.30
❑	579	Tim Flannery	.15	.06
❑	580	Don Baylor	.75	.30
❑	581	Roy Howell	.15	.06
❑	582	Gaylord Perry	.40	.16
❑	583	Larry Milbourne	.15	.06
❑	584	Randy Lerch	.15	.06
❑	585	Amos Otis	.40	.16
❑	586	Silvio Martinez	.15	.06
❑	587	Jeff Newman	.15	.06
❑	588	Gary Lavelle	.15	.06
❑	589	Lamar Johnson	.15	.06
❑	590	Bruce Sutter	.40	.16
❑	591	John Lowenstein	.15	.06
❑	592	Steve Comer	.15	.06
❑	593	Steve Kemp	.15	.06
❑	594	Preston Hanna DP	.07	.03
❑	595	Butch Hobson	.15	.06
❑	596	Jerry Augustine	.15	.06
❑	597	Rafael Landestoy	.15	.06
❑	598	George Vukovich DP	.07	.03
❑	599	Dennis Kinney	.15	.06
❑	600	Johnny Bench	1.50	.60
❑	601	Don Aase	.15	.06
❑	602	Bobby Murcer	.40	.16
❑	603	John Verhoeven	.15	.06
❑	604	Rob Picciolo	.15	.06
❑	605	Don Sutton	1.50	.60
❑	606	Bruce Berenyi	.15	.06
		Geoff Combe		
		Paul Householder		
❑	607	David Palmer	.15	.06
❑	608	Greg Pryor	.15	.06
❑	609	Lynn McGlothen	.15	.06
❑	610	Darrell Porter	.15	.06
❑	611	Rick Matula DP	.07	.03
❑	612	Duane Kuiper	.15	.06
❑	613	Jim Anderson	.15	.06
❑	614	Dave Rozema	.15	.06
❑	615	Rick Dempsey	.40	.16
❑	616	Rick Wise	.15	.06
❑	617	Craig Reynolds	.15	.06
❑	618	John Milner	.15	.06
❑	619	Steve Henderson	.15	.06
❑	620	Dennis Eckersley	.75	.30
❑	621	Tom Donohue	.15	.06
❑	622	Randy Moffitt	.15	.06
❑	623	Sal Bando	.40	.16
❑	624	Bob Welch	.40	.16
❑	625	Bill Buckner	.40	.16
❑	626	Dave Steffen	.15	.06
		Jerry Ujdur		
		Roger Weaver		
❑	627	Luis Tiant	.40	.16
❑	628	Vic Correll	.15	.06
❑	629	Tony Armas	.40	.16
❑	630	Steve Carlton	.75	.30
❑	631	Ron Jackson	.15	.06
❑	632	Alan Bannister	.15	.06
❑	633	Bill Lee	.40	.16
❑	634	Doug Flynn	.15	.06
❑	635	Bobby Bonds	.40	.16
❑	636	Al Hrabosky	.15	.06
❑	637	Jerry Narron	.15	.06
❑	638	Checklist 606-726	.75	.30
❑	639	Carney Lansford	.40	.16
❑	640	Dave Parker	.40	.16
❑	641	Mark Belanger	.40	.16
❑	642	Vern Ruhle	.15	.06
❑	643	Lloyd Moseby	.40	.16
❑	644	Ramon Aviles DP	.07	.03
❑	645	Rick Reuschel	.40	.16
❑	646	Marvis Foley	.15	.06
❑	647	Dick Drago	.15	.06
❑	648	Darrell Evans	.40	.16
❑	649	Manny Sarmiento	.15	.06
❑	650	Bucky Dent	.40	.16
❑	651	Pedro Guerrero	.75	.30
❑	652	John Montague	.15	.06
❑	653	Bill Fahey	.15	.06
❑	654	Ray Burris	.15	.06
❑	655	Dan Driessen	.15	.06
❑	656	Jon Matlack	.15	.06
❑	657	Mike Cubbage DP	.07	.03
❑	658	Milt Wilcox	.15	.06
❑	659	John Flinn	.15	.06
		Ed Romero		
		Ned Yost		
❑	660	Gary Carter	.75	.30
❑	661	Orioles Team CL	.75	.30
		Earl Weaver MG		
❑	662	Red Sox Team CL	.75	.30
		Ralph Houk MG		

❑ 663 Angels Team CL .75 .30
Jim Fregosi MG
❑ 664 White Sox CL .75 .30
Tony LaRussa MG
❑ 665 Indians Team CL .75 .30
Dave Garcia MG
❑ 666 Tigers Team CL .75 .30
Sparky Anderson MG
❑ 667 Royals Team CL .75 .30
Jim Frey MG
❑ 668 Brewers Team CL .75 .30
Bob Rodgers MG
❑ 669 Twins Team CL .75 .30
John Goryl MG
❑ 670 Yankees Team CL .75 .30
Gene Michael MG
❑ 671 A's Team CL .75 .30
Billy Martin MG
❑ 672 Mariners Team CL .75 .30
Maury Wills MG
❑ 673 Rangers Team CL .75 .30
Don Zimmer MG
❑ 674 Blue Jays Team CL .75 .30
Bobby Mattick MG
❑ 675 Braves Team CL .75 .30
Bobby Cox MG
❑ 676 Cubs Team CL .75 .30
Joe Amalfitano MG
❑ 677 Reds Team CL .75 .30
John McNamara MG
❑ 678 Astros Team CL .75 .30
Bill Virdon MG
❑ 679 Dodgers Team CL .75 .30
Tom Lasorda MG
❑ 680 Expos Team CL .75 .30
Dick Williams MG
❑ 681 Mets Team CL .75 .30
Joe Torre MG
❑ 682 Phillies Team CL .75 .30
Dallas Green MG
❑ 683 Pirates Team CL .75 .30
Chuck Tanner MG
❑ 684 Cardinals Team CL .75 .30
Whitey Herzog MG
❑ 685 Padres Team CL .75 .30
Frank Howard MG
❑ 686 Giants Team CL .75 .30
Dave Bristol MG
❑ 687 Jeff Jones .15 .06
❑ 688 Kiko Garcia .15 .06
❑ 689 Bruce Hurst RC 1.50 .60
Keith MacWhorter
Reid Nichols
❑ 690 Bob Watson .40 .16
❑ 691 Dick Ruthven .15 .06
❑ 692 Lenny Randle .15 .06
❑ 693 Steve Howe .40 .16
❑ 694 Bud Harrelson DP .15 .06
❑ 695 Kent Tekulve .40 .16
❑ 696 Alan Ashby .15 .06
❑ 697 Rick Waits .15 .06
❑ 698 Mike Jorgensen .15 .06
❑ 699 Glenn Abbott .15 .06
❑ 700 George Brett 5.00 2.00
❑ 701 Joe Rudi .40 .16
❑ 702 George Medich .15 .06
❑ 703 Alvis Woods .15 .06
❑ 704 Bill Travers DP .07 .03
❑ 705 Ted Simmons .40 .16
❑ 706 Dave Ford .15 .06
❑ 707 Dave Cash .15 .06
❑ 708 Doyle Alexander .15 .06
❑ 709 Alan Trammell DP .75 .30
❑ 710 Ron LeFlore DP .15 .06
❑ 711 Joe Ferguson .15 .06
❑ 712 Bill Bonham .15 .06
❑ 713 Bill North .15 .06
❑ 714 Pete Redfern .15 .06
❑ 715 Bill Madlock .40 .16
❑ 716 Glenn Borgmann .15 .06
❑ 717 Jim Barr DP .07 .03
❑ 718 Larry Biittner .15 .06
❑ 719 Sparky Lyle .40 .16
❑ 720 Fred Lynn .40 .16
❑ 721 Toby Harrah .40 .16
❑ 722 Joe Niekro .40 .16
❑ 723 Bruce Bochte .15 .06
❑ 724 Lou Piniella .40 .16
❑ 725 Steve Rogers .15 .06
❑ 726 Rick Monday .40 .16

1981 Topps Traded

	Nm-Mt	Ex-Mt
COMP.FACT.SET (132)	30.00	12.00

❑ 727 Danny Ainge XRC 5.00 2.00
❑ 728 Doyle Alexander .25 .10
❑ 729 Gary Alexander .25 .10
❑ 730 Bill Almon .25 .10
❑ 731 Joaquin Andujar 1.00 .40
❑ 732 Bob Bailor .25 .10
❑ 733 Juan Beniquez .25 .10
❑ 734 Dave Bergman .25 .10
❑ 735 Tony Bernazard .25 .10
❑ 736 Larry Biittner .25 .10
❑ 737 Doug Bird .25 .10
❑ 738 Bert Blyleven 1.50 .60
❑ 739 Mark Bomback .25 .10
❑ 740 Bobby Bonds 1.00 .40
❑ 741 Rick Bosetti .25 .10
❑ 742 Hubie Brooks 1.00 .40
❑ 743 Rick Burleson .25 .10
❑ 744 Ray Burris .25 .10
❑ 745 Jeff Burroughs .25 .10
❑ 746 Enos Cabell .25 .10
❑ 747 Ken Clay .25 .10
❑ 748 Mark Clear .25 .10
❑ 749 Larry Cox .25 .10
❑ 750 Hector Cruz .25 .10
❑ 751 Victor Cruz .25 .10
❑ 752 Mike Cubbage .25 .10
❑ 753 Dick Davis .25 .10
❑ 754 Brian Doyle .25 .10
❑ 755 Dick Drago .25 .10
❑ 756 Leon Durham 1.00 .40
❑ 757 Jim Dwyer .25 .10
❑ 758 Dave Edwards UER .25 .10
No birthdate on card
❑ 759 Jim Essian .25 .10
❑ 760 Bill Fahey .25 .10
❑ 761 Rollie Fingers 1.00 .40
❑ 762 Carlton Fisk 4.00 1.60
❑ 763 Barry Foote .25 .10
❑ 764 Ken Forsch .25 .10
❑ 765 Kiko Garcia .25 .10
❑ 766 Cesar Geronimo .25 .10
❑ 767 Gary Gray .25 .10
❑ 768 Mickey Hatcher 1.00 .40
❑ 769 Steve Henderson .25 .10
❑ 770 Marc Hill .25 .10
❑ 771 Butch Hobson .25 .10
❑ 772 Rick Honeycutt .25 .10
❑ 773 Roy Howell .25 .10
❑ 774 Mike Ivie .25 .10
❑ 775 Roy Lee Jackson .25 .10
❑ 776 Cliff Johnson .25 .10
❑ 777 Randy Jones .25 .10
❑ 778 Ruppert Jones .25 .10
❑ 779 Mick Kelleher .25 .10
❑ 780 Terry Kennedy .25 .10
❑ 781 Dave Kingman 1.50 .60
❑ 782 Bob Knepper .25 .10
❑ 783 Ken Kravec .25 .10
❑ 784 Bob Lacey .25 .10
❑ 785 Dennis Lamp .25 .10
❑ 786 Rafael Landestoy .25 .10
❑ 787 Ken Landreaux .25 .10
❑ 788 Carney Lansford 1.00 .40
❑ 789 Dave LaRoche .25 .10
❑ 790 Joe Lefebvre .25 .10
❑ 791 Ron LeFlore 1.00 .40
❑ 792 Randy Lerch .25 .10
❑ 793 Sixto Lezcano .25 .10
❑ 794 John Littlefield .25 .10
❑ 795 Mike Lum .25 .10
❑ 796 Greg Luzinski 1.00 .40
❑ 797 Fred Lynn 1.00 .40
❑ 798 Jerry Martin .25 .10
❑ 799 Buck Martinez .25 .10
❑ 800 Gary Matthews 1.00 .40
❑ 801 Mario Mendoza .25 .10
❑ 802 Larry Milbourne .25 .10
❑ 803 Rick Miller .25 .10
❑ 804 John Montefusco .25 .10
❑ 805 Jerry Morales .25 .10
❑ 806 Jose Morales .25 .10
❑ 807 Joe Morgan 1.50 .60
❑ 808 Jerry Mumphrey .25 .10
❑ 809 Gene Nelson .25 .10
❑ 810 Ed Ott .25 .10
❑ 811 Bob Owchinko .25 .10
❑ 812 Gaylord Perry 1.00 .40
❑ 813 Mike Phillips .25 .10
❑ 814 Darrell Porter .25 .10
❑ 815 Mike Proly .25 .10
❑ 816 Tim Raines 5.00 2.00
❑ 817 Lenny Randle .25 .10
❑ 818 Doug Rau .25 .10
❑ 819 Jeff Reardon 2.50 1.00
❑ 820 Ken Reitz .25 .10
❑ 821 Steve Renko .25 .10
❑ 822 Rick Reuschel 1.00 .40
❑ 823 Dave Revering .25 .10
❑ 824 Dave Roberts .25 .10
❑ 825 Leon Roberts .25 .10
❑ 826 Joe Rudi 1.00 .40
❑ 827 Kevin Saucier .25 .10
❑ 828 Tony Scott .25 .10
❑ 829 Bob Shirley .25 .10
❑ 830 Ted Simmons 1.00 .40
❑ 831 Lary Sorensen .25 .10
❑ 832 Jim Spencer .25 .10
❑ 833 Harry Spilman .25 .10
❑ 834 Fred Stanley .25 .10
❑ 835 Rusty Staub 1.00 .40
❑ 836 Bill Stein .25 .10
❑ 837 Joe Strain .25 .10
❑ 838 Bruce Sutter 1.00 .40
❑ 839 Don Sutton 2.50 1.00
❑ 840 Steve Swisher .25 .10
❑ 841 Frank Tanana 1.00 .40
❑ 842 Gene Tenace 1.00 .40
❑ 843 Jason Thompson .25 .10
❑ 844 Dickie Thon 1.00 .40
❑ 845 Bill Travers .25 .10
❑ 846 Tom Underwood .25 .10
❑ 847 John Urrea .25 .10
❑ 848 Mike Vail .25 .10
❑ 849 Ellis Valentine .25 .10
❑ 850 Fernando Valenzuela 5.00 2.00
❑ 851 Pete Vuckovich 1.00 .40
❑ 852 Mark Wagner .25 .10
❑ 853 Bob Walk 1.00 .40
❑ 854 Claudell Washington .25 .10
❑ 855 Dave Winfield 5.00 2.00
❑ 856 Geoff Zahn .25 .10
❑ 857 Richie Zisk .25 .10
❑ 858 Checklist 727-858 .25 .10

1982 Topps

	Nm-Mt	Ex-Mt
COMPLETE SET (792)	100.00	40.00

❑ 1 Steve Carlton HL .30 .12
❑ 2 Ron Davis HL .15 .06
❑ 3 Tim Raines HL .60 .24
❑ 4 Pete Rose HL .60 .24
❑ 5 Nolan Ryan HL 3.00 1.20

❑ 6 Fernando Valenzuela HL .60 .24
❑ 7 Scott Sanderson .15 .06
❑ 8 Rich Dauer .15 .06
❑ 9 Ron Guidry .30 .12
❑ 10 Ron Guidry SA .15 .06
❑ 11 Gary Alexander .15 .06
❑ 12 Moose Haas .15 .06
❑ 13 Lamar Johnson .15 .06
❑ 14 Steve Howe .15 .06
❑ 15 Ellis Valentine .15 .06
❑ 16 Steve Comer .15 .06
❑ 17 Darrell Evans .30 .12
❑ 18 Fernando Arroyo .15 .06
❑ 19 Ernie Whitt .15 .06
❑ 20 Garry Maddox .15 .06
❑ 21 Bob Bonner 50.00 20.00
Cal Ripken RC
Jeff Schneider
Birthdate for Jeff Scheider is wrong
❑ 22 Jim Beattie .15 .06
❑ 23 Willie Hernandez .30 .12
❑ 24 Dave Frost .15 .06
❑ 25 Jerry Remy .15 .06
❑ 26 Jorge Orta .15 .06
❑ 27 Tom Herr .30 .12
❑ 28 John Urrea .15 .06
❑ 29 Dwayne Murphy .15 .06
❑ 30 Tom Seaver 1.25 .50
❑ 31 Tom Seaver SA .60 .24
❑ 32 Gene Garber .15 .06
❑ 33 Jerry Morales .15 .06
❑ 34 Joe Sambito .15 .06
❑ 35 Willie Aikens .15 .06
❑ 36 Al Oliver .60 .24
Doc Medich TL
❑ 37 Dan Graham .15 .06
❑ 38 Charlie Lea .15 .06
❑ 39 Lou Whitaker 1.25 .50
❑ 40 Dave Parker .30 .12
❑ 41 Dave Parker SA .15 .06
❑ 42 Rick Sofield .15 .06
❑ 43 Mike Cubbage .15 .06
❑ 44 Britt Burns .15 .06
❑ 45 Rick Cerone .15 .06
❑ 46 Jerry Augustine .15 .06
❑ 47 Jeff Leonard .15 .06
❑ 48 Bobby Castillo .15 .06
❑ 49 Alvis Woods .15 .06
❑ 50 Buddy Bell .30 .12
❑ 51 Jay Howell RC .60 .24
Carlos Lezcano
Ty Waller
❑ 52 Larry Andersen .15 .06
❑ 53 Greg Gross .15 .06
❑ 54 Ron Hassey .15 .06
❑ 55 Rick Burleson .15 .06
❑ 56 Mark Littell .15 .06
❑ 57 Craig Reynolds .15 .06
❑ 58 John D'Acquisto .15 .06
❑ 59 Rich Gedman .30 .12
❑ 60 Tony Armas .15 .06
❑ 61 Tommy Boggs .15 .06
❑ 62 Mike Tyson .15 .06
❑ 63 Mario Soto .15 .06
❑ 64 Lynn Jones .15 .06
❑ 65 Terry Kennedy .15 .06
❑ 66 Art Howe 2.00 .80
Nolan Ryan TL

❑ 67 Rich Gale .15 .06
❑ 68 Roy Howell .15 .06
❑ 69 Al Williams .15 .06
❑ 70 Tim Raines 1.25 .50
❑ 71 Roy Lee Jackson .15 .06
❑ 72 Rick Auerbach .15 .06
❑ 73 Buddy Solomon .15 .06
❑ 74 Bob Clark .15 .06
❑ 75 Tommy John .60 .24
❑ 76 Greg Pryor .15 .06
❑ 77 Miguel Dilone .15 .06
❑ 78 George Medich .15 .06
❑ 79 Bob Bailor .15 .06
❑ 80 Jim Palmer .30 .12
❑ 81 Jim Palmer SA .15 .06
❑ 82 Bob Welch .30 .12
❑ 83 Steve Balboni RC .60 .24
Andy McGaffigan
Andre Robertson
❑ 84 Rennie Stennett .15 .06
❑ 85 Lynn McGlothen .15 .06
❑ 86 Dane Iorg .15 .06
❑ 87 Matt Keough .15 .06
❑ 88 Biff Pocoroba .15 .06
❑ 89 Steve Henderson .15 .06
❑ 90 Nolan Ryan 6.00 2.40
❑ 91 Carney Lansford .30 .12
❑ 92 Brad Havens .15 .06
❑ 93 Larry Hisle .15 .06
❑ 94 Andy Hassler .15 .06
❑ 95 Ozzie Smith 2.50 1.00
❑ 96 George Brett 1.25 .50
Larry Gura TL
❑ 97 Paul Moskau .15 .06
❑ 98 Terry Bulling .15 .06
❑ 99 Barry Bonnell .15 .06
❑ 100 Mike Schmidt 3.00 1.20
❑ 101 Mike Schmidt SA 1.25 .50
❑ 102 Dan Briggs .15 .06
❑ 103 Bob Lacey .15 .06
❑ 104 Rance Mulliniks .15 .06
❑ 105 Kirk Gibson 1.25 .50
❑ 106 Enrique Romo .15 .06
❑ 107 Wayne Krenchicki .15 .06
❑ 108 Bob Sykes .15 .06
❑ 109 Dave Revering .15 .06
❑ 110 Carlton Fisk .60 .24
❑ 111 Carlton Fisk SA .30 .12
❑ 112 Billy Sample .15 .06
❑ 113 Steve McCatty .15 .06
❑ 114 Ken Landreaux .15 .06
❑ 115 Gaylord Perry .30 .12
❑ 116 Jim Wohlford .15 .06
❑ 117 Rawly Eastwick .15 .06
❑ 118 Terry Francona RC .30 .12
Brad Mills
Bryn Smith RC
❑ 119 Joe Pittman .15 .06
❑ 120 Gary Lucas .15 .06
❑ 121 Ed Lynch .15 .06
❑ 122 Jamie Easterly UER .15 .06
(Photo actually
Reggie Cleveland)
❑ 123 Danny Goodwin .15 .06
❑ 124 Reid Nichols .15 .06
❑ 125 Danny Ainge 1.50 .60
❑ 126 Claudell Washington .60 .24
Rick Mahler TL
❑ 127 Lonnie Smith .30 .12
❑ 128 Frank Pastore .15 .06
❑ 129 Checklist 1-132 .60 .24
❑ 130 Julio Cruz .15 .06
❑ 131 Stan Bahnsen .15 .06
❑ 132 Lee May .30 .12
❑ 133 Pat Underwood .15 .06
❑ 134 Dan Ford .15 .06
❑ 135 Andy Rincon .15 .06
❑ 136 Lenn Sakata .15 .06
❑ 137 George Cappuzzello .15 .06
❑ 138 Tony Pena .30 .12
❑ 139 Jeff Jones .15 .06
❑ 140 Ron LeFlore .30 .12
❑ 141 Chris Bando .30 .12
Tom Brennan
Von Hayes RC
❑ 142 Dave LaRoche .15 .06

❑ 143 Mookie Wilson .30 .12
❑ 144 Fred Breining .15 .06
❑ 145 Bob Horner .30 .12
❑ 146 Mike Griffin .15 .06
❑ 147 Denny Walling .15 .06
❑ 148 Mickey Klutts .15 .06
❑ 149 Pat Putnam .15 .06
❑ 150 Ted Simmons .30 .12
❑ 151 Dave Edwards .15 .06
❑ 152 Ramon Aviles .15 .06
❑ 153 Roger Erickson .15 .06
❑ 154 Dennis Werth .15 .06
❑ 155 Otto Velez .15 .06
❑ 156 Rickey Henderson 1.25 .50
Steve McCatty TL
❑ 157 Steve Crawford .15 .06
❑ 158 Brian Downing .15 .06
❑ 159 Larry Biittner .15 .06
❑ 160 Luis Tiant .30 .12
❑ 161 Bill Madlock .30 .12
Carney Lansford LL
❑ 162 Mike Schmidt 1.25 .50
Tony Armas
Dwight Evans
Bobby Grich
Eddie Murray LL
❑ 163 Mike Schmidt 1.25 .50
Eddie Murray LL
❑ 164 Tim Raines 1.25 .50
Rickey Henderson LL
❑ 165 Tom Seaver .30 .12
Denny Martinez
Steve McCatty
Jack Morris
Pete Vuckovich LL
❑ 166 Fernando Valenzuela .30 .12
Len Barker LL
❑ 167 Nolan Ryan 2.00 .80
Steve McCatty LL
❑ 168 Bruce Sutter .30 .12
Rollie Fingers LL
❑ 169 Charlie Leibrandt .15 .06
❑ 170 Jim Bibby .15 .06
❑ 171 Bob Brenly RC 3.00 1.20
Chili Davis RC
Bob Tufts
❑ 172 Bill Gullickson .15 .06
❑ 173 Jamie Quirk .15 .06
❑ 174 Dave Ford .15 .06
❑ 175 Jerry Mumphrey .15 .06
❑ 176 Dewey Robinson .15 .06
❑ 177 John Ellis .15 .06
❑ 178 Dyar Miller .15 .06
❑ 179 Steve Garvey .30 .12
❑ 180 Steve Garvey SA .15 .06
❑ 181 Silvio Martinez .15 .06
❑ 182 Larry Herndon .15 .06
❑ 183 Mike Proly .15 .06
❑ 184 Mick Kelleher .15 .06
❑ 185 Phil Niekro .30 .12
❑ 186 Keith Hernandez/Bob Forsch TL .60 .24
❑ 187 Jeff Newman .15 .06
❑ 188 Randy Martz .15 .06
❑ 189 Glenn Hoffman .15 .06
❑ 190 J.R. Richard .30 .12
❑ 191 Tim Wallach RC .60 .24
❑ 192 Broderick Perkins .15 .06
❑ 193 Darrell Jackson .15 .06
❑ 194 Mike Vail .15 .06
❑ 195 Paul Molitor 1.50 .60
❑ 196 Willie Upshaw .15 .06
❑ 197 Shane Rawley .15 .06
❑ 198 Chris Speier .15 .06
❑ 199 Don Aase .15 .06
❑ 200 George Brett 4.00 1.60
❑ 201 George Brett SA 1.25 .50
❑ 202 Rick Manning .15 .06
❑ 203 Jesse Barfield RC .60 .24
Brian Milner
Boomer Wells
❑ 204 Gary Roenicke .15 .06
❑ 205 Neil Allen .15 .06
❑ 206 Tony Bernazard .15 .06
❑ 207 Rod Scurry .15 .06
❑ 208 Bobby Murcer .30 .12
❑ 209 Gary Lavelle .15 .06

❑ 210 Keith Hernandez .60 .24
❑ 211 Dan Petry .15 .06
❑ 212 Mario Mendoza .15 .06
❑ 213 Dave Stewart RC 1.50 .60
❑ 214 Brian Asselstine .15 .06
❑ 215 Mike Krukow .15 .06
❑ 216 Chet Lemon .60 .24
Dennis Lamp TL
❑ 217 Bo McLaughlin .15 .06
❑ 218 Dave Roberts .15 .06
❑ 219 John Curtis .15 .06
❑ 220 Manny Trillo .15 .06
❑ 221 Jim Slaton .15 .06
❑ 222 Butch Wynegar .15 .06
❑ 223 Lloyd Moseby .15 .06
❑ 224 Bruce Bochte .15 .06
❑ 225 Mike Torrez .15 .06
❑ 226 Checklist 133-264 .60 .24
❑ 227 Ray Burris .15 .06
❑ 228 Sam Mejias .15 .06
❑ 229 Geoff Zahn .15 .06
❑ 230 Willie Wilson .30 .12
❑ 231 Mark Davis RC .60 .24
Bob Dernier
Ozzie Virgil
❑ 232 Terry Crowley .15 .06
❑ 233 Duane Kuiper .15 .06
❑ 234 Ron Hodges .15 .06
❑ 235 Mike Easler .15 .06
❑ 236 John Martin RC .15 .06
❑ 237 Rusty Kuntz .15 .06
❑ 238 Kevin Saucier .15 .06
❑ 239 Jon Matlack .15 .06
❑ 240 Bucky Dent .30 .12
❑ 241 Bucky Dent SA .15 .06
❑ 242 Milt May .15 .06
❑ 243 Bob Owchinko .15 .06
❑ 244 Rufino Linares .15 .06
❑ 245 Ken Reitz .15 .06
❑ 246 Hubie Brooks .60 .24
Mike Scott TL
❑ 247 Pedro Guerrero .30 .12
❑ 248 Frank LaCorte .15 .06
❑ 249 Tim Flannery .15 .06
❑ 250 Tug McGraw .30 .12
❑ 251 Fred Lynn .30 .12
❑ 252 Fred Lynn SA .15 .06
❑ 253 Chuck Baker .15 .06
❑ 254 Jorge Bell RC 1.25 .50
❑ 255 Tony Perez .60 .24
❑ 256 Tony Perez SA .30 .12
❑ 257 Larry Harlow .15 .06
❑ 258 Bo Diaz .15 .06
❑ 259 Rodney Scott .15 .06
❑ 260 Bruce Sutter .30 .12
❑ 261 Howard Bailey .15 .06
Marty Castillo
Dave Rucker UER
(Rucker photo actally Roger Weaver)
❑ 262 Doug Bair .15 .06
❑ 263 Victor Cruz .15 .06
❑ 264 Dan Quisenberry .30 .12
❑ 265 Al Bumbry .15 .06
❑ 266 Rick Leach .15 .06
❑ 267 Kurt Bevacqua .15 .06
❑ 268 Rickey Keeton .15 .06
❑ 269 Jim Essian .15 .06
❑ 270 Rusty Staub .30 .12
❑ 271 Larry Bradford .15 .06
❑ 272 Bump Wills .15 .06
❑ 273 Doug Bird .15 .06
❑ 274 Bob Ojeda RC .60 .24
❑ 275 Bob Watson .30 .12
❑ 276 Rod Carew .60 .24
Ken Forsch TL
❑ 277 Terry Puhl .15 .06
❑ 278 John Littlefield .15 .06
❑ 279 Bill Russell .15 .06
❑ 280 Ben Oglivie .30 .12
❑ 281 John Verhoeven .15 .06
❑ 282 Ken Macha .15 .06
❑ 283 Brian Allard .15 .06
❑ 284 Bobby Grich .30 .12
❑ 285 Sparky Lyle .30 .12
❑ 286 Bill Fahey .15 .06
❑ 287 Alan Bannister .15 .06
❑ 288 Garry Templeton .15 .06
❑ 289 Bob Stanley .15 .06
❑ 290 Ken Singleton .30 .12
❑ 291 Vance Law .30 .12
Bob Long
Johnny Ray RC
❑ 292 David Palmer .15 .06
❑ 293 Rob Picciolo .15 .06
❑ 294 Mike LaCoss .15 .06
❑ 295 Jason Thompson .15 .06
❑ 296 Bob Walk .15 .06
❑ 297 Clint Hurdle .15 .06
❑ 298 Danny Darwin .15 .06
❑ 299 Steve Trout .15 .06
❑ 300 Reggie Jackson .60 .24
❑ 301 Reggie Jackson SA .30 .12
❑ 302 Doug Flynn .15 .06
❑ 303 Bill Caudill .15 .06
❑ 304 Johnnie LeMaster .15 .06
❑ 305 Don Sutton 1.25 .50
❑ 306 Don Sutton SA .60 .24
❑ 307 Randy Bass RC .15 .06
❑ 308 Charlie Moore .15 .06
❑ 309 Pete Redfern .15 .06
❑ 310 Mike Hargrove .30 .12
❑ 311 Dusty Baker .60 .24
Burt Hooton TL
❑ 312 Lenny Randle .15 .06
❑ 313 John Harris .15 .06
❑ 314 Buck Martinez .15 .06
❑ 315 Burt Hooton .15 .06
❑ 316 Steve Braun .15 .06
❑ 317 Dick Ruthven .15 .06
❑ 318 Mike Heath .15 .06
❑ 319 Dave Rozema .15 .06
❑ 320 Chris Chambliss .30 .12
❑ 321 Chris Chambliss SA .15 .06
❑ 322 Garry Hancock .15 .06
❑ 323 Bill Lee .30 .12
❑ 324 Steve Dillard .15 .06
❑ 325 Jose Cruz .30 .12
❑ 326 Pete Falcone .15 .06
❑ 327 Joe Nolan .15 .06
❑ 328 Ed Farmer .15 .06
❑ 329 U.L. Washington .15 .06
❑ 330 Rick Wise .15 .06
❑ 331 Benny Ayala .15 .06
❑ 332 Don Robinson .15 .06
❑ 333 Frank DiPino .15 .06
Marshall Edwards
Chuck Porter
❑ 334 Aurelio Rodriguez .15 .06
❑ 335 Jim Sundberg .15 .06
❑ 336 Tom Paciorek .60 .24
Glenn Abbott TL
❑ 337 Pete Rose AS .60 .24
❑ 338 Dave Lopes AS .15 .06
❑ 339 Mike Schmidt AS 1.25 .50
❑ 340 Dave Concepcion AS .15 .06
❑ 341 Andre Dawson AS .15 .06
❑ 342A George Foster AS .30 .12
(With autograph)
❑ 342B George Foster AS 1.25 .50
(W/o autograph)
❑ 343 Dave Parker AS .15 .06
❑ 344 Gary Carter AS .30 .12
❑ 345 F. Valenzuela AS .60 .24
❑ 346 Tom Seaver AS ERR .60 .24
("t ed")
❑ 346B Tom Seaver AS COR .60 .24
("tied")
❑ 347 Bruce Sutter AS .15 .06
❑ 348 Derrel Thomas .15 .06
❑ 349 George Frazier .15 .06
❑ 350 Thad Bosley .15 .06
❑ 351 Scott Brown .15 .06
Geoff Combe
Paul Householder
❑ 352 Dick Davis .15 .06
❑ 353 Jack O'Connor .15 .06
❑ 354 Roberto Ramos .15 .06
❑ 355 Dwight Evans .60 .24
❑ 356 Denny Lewallyn .15 .06
❑ 357 Butch Hobson .15 .06
❑ 358 Mike Parrott .15 .06
❑ 359 Jim Dwyer .15 .06
❑ 360 Len Barker .15 .06
❑ 361 Rafael Landestoy .15 .06
❑ 362 Jim Wright UER .15 .06
(Wrong Jim Wright pictured)
❑ 363 Bob Molinaro .15 .06
❑ 364 Doyle Alexander .15 .06
❑ 365 Bill Madlock .30 .12
❑ 366 Luis Salazar .60 .24
Juan Eichelberger TL
❑ 367 Jim Kaat .30 .12
❑ 368 Alex Trevino .15 .06
❑ 369 Champ Summers .15 .06
❑ 370 Mike Norris .15 .06
❑ 371 Jerry Don Gleaton .15 .06
❑ 372 Luis Gomez .15 .06
❑ 373 Gene Nelson .15 .06
❑ 374 Tim Blackwell .15 .06
❑ 375 Dusty Baker .60 .24
❑ 376 Chris Welsh .15 .06
❑ 377 Kiko Garcia .15 .06
❑ 378 Mike Caldwell .15 .06
❑ 379 Rob Wilfong .15 .06
❑ 380 Dave Stieb .30 .12
❑ 381 Bruce Hurst .30 .12
Dave Schmidt
Julio Valdez
❑ 382 Joe Simpson .15 .06
❑ 383A Pascual Perez ERR 40.00 16.00
(No position on front)
❑ 383B Pascual Perez COR .30 .12
❑ 384 Keith Moreland .15 .06
❑ 385 Ken Forsch .15 .06
❑ 386 Jerry White .15 .06
❑ 387 Tom Veryzer .15 .06
❑ 388 Joe Rudi .15 .06
❑ 389 George Vukovich .15 .06
❑ 390 Eddie Murray 1.25 .50
❑ 391 Dave Tobik .15 .06
❑ 392 Rick Bosetti .15 .06
❑ 393 Al Hrabosky .15 .06
❑ 394 Checklist 265-396 .60 .24
❑ 395 Omar Moreno .15 .06
❑ 396 John Castino .60 .24
Fernando Arroyo TL
❑ 397 Ken Brett .15 .06
❑ 398 Mike Squires .15 .06
❑ 399 Pat Zachry .15 .06
❑ 400 Johnny Bench 1.25 .50
❑ 401 Johnny Bench SA .60 .24
❑ 402 Bill Stein .15 .06
❑ 403 Jim Tracy .15 .06
❑ 404 Dickie Thon .15 .06
❑ 405 Rick Reuschel .30 .12
❑ 406 Al Holland .15 .06
❑ 407 Danny Boone .15 .06
❑ 408 Ed Romero .15 .06
❑ 409 Don Cooper .15 .06
❑ 410 Ron Cey .30 .12
❑ 411 Ron Cey SA .15 .06
❑ 412 Luis Leal .15 .06
❑ 413 Dan Meyer .15 .06
❑ 414 Elias Sosa .15 .06
❑ 415 Don Baylor .60 .24
❑ 416 Marty Bystrom .15 .06
❑ 417 Pat Kelly .15 .06
❑ 418 John Butcher .15 .06
Bobby Johnson
Dave Schmidt
❑ 419 Steve Stone .30 .12
❑ 420 George Hendrick .15 .06
❑ 421 Mark Clear .15 .06
❑ 422 Cliff Johnson .15 .06
❑ 423 Stan Papi .15 .06
❑ 424 Bruce Benedict .15 .06
❑ 425 John Candelaria .15 .06
❑ 426 Eddie Murray .60 .24
Sammy Stewart
❑ 427 Ron Oester .15 .06
❑ 428 LaMarr Hoyt .15 .06
❑ 429 John Wathan .15 .06
❑ 430 Vida Blue .30 .12
❑ 431 Vida Blue SA .15 .06
❑ 432 Mike Scott .30 .12

❑ 433 Alan Ashby .15 .06
❑ 434 Joe Lefebvre .15 .06
❑ 435 Robin Yount 1.25 .50
❑ 436 Joe Strain .15 .06
❑ 437 Juan Berenguer .15 .06
❑ 438 Pete Mackanin .15 .06
❑ 439 Dave Righetti RC 1.25 .50
❑ 440 Jeff Burroughs .15 .06
❑ 441 Danny Heep .15 .06
Billy Smith
Bobby Sprowl
❑ 442 Bruce Kison .15 .06
❑ 443 Mark Wagner .15 .06
❑ 444 Terry Forster .15 .06
❑ 445 Larry Parrish .15 .06
❑ 446 Wayne Garland .15 .06
❑ 447 Darrell Porter .30 .12
❑ 448 Darrell Porter SA .15 .06
❑ 449 Luis Aguayo .15 .06
❑ 450 Jack Morris .30 .12
❑ 451 Ed Miller .15 .06
❑ 452 Lee Smith RC 3.00 1.20
❑ 453 Art Howe .30 .12
❑ 454 Rick Langford .15 .06
❑ 455 Tom Burgmeier .15 .06
❑ 456 Bill Buckner .60 .24
Randy Martz TL
❑ 457 Tim Stoddard .15 .06
❑ 458 Willie Montanez .15 .06
❑ 459 Bruce Berenyi .15 .06
❑ 460 Jack Clark .30 .12
❑ 461 Rich Dotson .15 .06
❑ 462 Dave Chalk .15 .06
❑ 463 Jim Kern .15 .06
❑ 464 Juan Bonilla RC .15 .06
❑ 465 Lee Mazzilli .15 .06
❑ 466 Randy Lerch .15 .06
❑ 467 Mickey Hatcher .15 .06
❑ 468 Floyd Bannister .15 .06
❑ 469 Ed Ott .15 .06
❑ 470 John Mayberry .15 .06
❑ 471 Atlee Hammaker .15 .06
Mike Jones
Darryl Motley
❑ 472 Oscar Gamble .15 .06
❑ 473 Mike Stanton .15 .06
❑ 474 Ken Oberkfell .15 .06
❑ 475 Alan Trammell .60 .24
❑ 476 Brian Kingman .15 .06
❑ 477 Steve Yeager .15 .06
❑ 478 Ray Searage .15 .06
❑ 479 Rowland Office .15 .06
❑ 480 Steve Carlton .60 .24
❑ 481 Steve Carlton SA .30 .12
❑ 482 Glenn Hubbard .15 .06
❑ 483 Gary Woods .15 .06
❑ 484 Ivan DeJesus .15 .06
❑ 485 Kent Tekulve .30 .12
❑ 486 Jerry Mumphrey .30 .12
Tommy John TL
❑ 487 Bob McClure .15 .06
❑ 488 Ron Jackson .15 .06
❑ 489 Rick Dempsey .30 .12
❑ 490 Dennis Eckersley .60 .24
❑ 491 Checklist 397-528 .60 .24
❑ 492 Joe Price .15 .06
❑ 493 Chet Lemon .15 .06
❑ 494 Hubie Brooks .30 .12
❑ 495 Dennis Leonard .15 .06
❑ 496 Johnny Grubb .15 .06
❑ 497 Jim Anderson .15 .06
❑ 498 Dave Bergman .15 .06
❑ 499 Paul Mirabella .15 .06
❑ 500 Rod Carew .60 .24
❑ 501 Rod Carew SA .60 .24
❑ 502 Steve Bedrosian RC UER 1.50 .60
Photo actually Larry Owen)
Brett Butler RC
Larry Owen
❑ 503 Julio Gonzalez .15 .06
❑ 504 Rick Peters .15 .06
❑ 505 Graig Nettles .30 .12
❑ 506 Graig Nettles SA .15 .06
❑ 507 Terry Harper .15 .06
❑ 508 Jody Davis .15 .06
❑ 509 Harry Spilman .15 .06
❑ 510 Fernando Valenzuela 1.25 .50
❑ 511 Ruppert Jones .15 .06
❑ 512 Jerry Dybzinski .15 .06
❑ 513 Rick Rhoden .15 .06
❑ 514 Joe Ferguson .15 .06
❑ 515 Larry Bowa .30 .12
❑ 516 Larry Bowa SA .15 .06
❑ 517 Mark Brouhard .15 .06
❑ 518 Garth Iorg .15 .06
❑ 519 Glenn Adams .15 .06
❑ 520 Mike Flanagan .30 .12
❑ 521 Bill Almon .15 .06
❑ 522 Chuck Rainey .15 .06
❑ 523 Gary Gray .15 .06
❑ 524 Tom Hausman .15 .06
❑ 525 Ray Knight .30 .12
❑ 526 Warren Cromartie .60 .24
Bill Gullickson TL
❑ 527 John Henry Johnson .15 .06
❑ 528 Matt Alexander .15 .06
❑ 529 Allen Ripley .15 .06
❑ 530 Dickie Noles .15 .06
❑ 531 Rich Bordi .15 .06
Mark Budaska
Kelvin Moore
❑ 532 Toby Harrah .30 .12
❑ 533 Joaquin Andujar .30 .12
❑ 534 Dave McKay .15 .06
❑ 535 Lance Parrish .60 .24
❑ 536 Rafael Ramirez .15 .06
❑ 537 Doug Capilla .15 .06
❑ 538 Lou Piniella .30 .12
❑ 539 Vern Ruhle .15 .06
❑ 540 Andre Dawson .30 .12
❑ 541 Barry Evans .15 .06
❑ 542 Ned Yost .15 .06
❑ 543 Bill Robinson .15 .06
❑ 544 Larry Christenson .15 .06
❑ 545 Reggie Smith .30 .12
❑ 546 Reggie Smith SA .15 .06
❑ 547 Rod Carew AS .30 .12
❑ 548 Willie Randolph AS .30 .12
❑ 549 George Brett AS 1.25 .50
❑ 550 Bucky Dent AS .15 .06
❑ 551 Reggie Jackson AS .30 .12
❑ 552 Ken Singleton AS .15 .06
❑ 553 Dave Winfield AS .30 .12
❑ 554 Carlton Fisk AS .60 .24
❑ 555 Scott McGregor AS .15 .06
❑ 556 Jack Morris AS .15 .06
❑ 557 Rich Gossage AS .30 .12
❑ 558 John Tudor .15 .06
❑ 559 Mike Hargrove .30 .12
Bert Blyleven TL
❑ 560 Doug Corbett .15 .06
❑ 561 Glenn Brummer .15 .06
Luis DeLeon
Gene Roof
❑ 562 Mike O'Berry .15 .06
❑ 563 Ross Baumgarten .15 .06
❑ 564 Doug DeCinces .30 .12
❑ 565 Jackson Todd .15 .06
❑ 566 Mike Jorgensen .15 .06
❑ 567 Bob Babcock .15 .06
❑ 568 Joe Pettini .15 .06
❑ 569 Willie Randolph .30 .12
❑ 570 Willie Randolph SA .30 .12
❑ 571 Glenn Abbott .15 .06
❑ 572 Juan Beniquez .15 .06
❑ 573 Rick Waits .15 .06
❑ 574 Mike Ramsey .15 .06
❑ 575 Al Cowens .15 .06
❑ 576 Milt May .60 .24
Vida Blue TL
❑ 577 Rick Monday .15 .06
❑ 578 Shooty Babitt .15 .06
❑ 579 Rick Mahler .15 .06
❑ 580 Bobby Bonds .30 .12
❑ 581 Ron Reed .15 .06
❑ 582 Luis Pujols .15 .06
❑ 583 Tippy Martinez .15 .06
❑ 584 Hosken Powell .15 .06
❑ 585 Rollie Fingers .30 .12
❑ 586 Rollie Fingers SA .30 .12
❑ 587 Tim Lollar .15 .06
❑ 588 Dale Berra .15 .06
❑ 589 Dave Stapleton .15 .06
❑ 590 Al Oliver .30 .12
❑ 591 Al Oliver SA .15 .06
❑ 592 Craig Swan .15 .06
❑ 593 Billy Smith .15 .06
❑ 594 Renie Martin .15 .06
❑ 595 Dave Collins .15 .06
❑ 596 Damaso Garcia .15 .06
❑ 597 Wayne Nordhagen .15 .06
❑ 598 Bob Galasso .15 .06
❑ 599 Jay Loviglio .15 .06
Reggie Patterson
Leo Sutherland
❑ 600 Dave Winfield .60 .24
❑ 601 Sid Monge .15 .06
❑ 602 Freddie Patek .15 .06
❑ 603 Rich Hebner .30 .12
❑ 604 Orlando Sanchez .15 .06
❑ 605 Steve Rogers .15 .06
❑ 606 John Mayberry .60 .24
Dave Stieb TL
❑ 607 Leon Durham .15 .06
❑ 608 Jerry Royster .15 .06
❑ 609 Rick Sutcliffe .30 .12
❑ 610 Rickey Henderson 4.00 1.60
❑ 611 Joe Niekro .30 .12
❑ 612 Gary Ward .15 .06
❑ 613 Jim Gantner .30 .12
❑ 614 Juan Eichelberger .15 .06
❑ 615 Bob Boone .30 .12
❑ 616 Bob Boone SA .15 .06
❑ 617 Scott McGregor .15 .06
❑ 618 Tim Foli .15 .06
❑ 619 Bill Campbell .15 .06
❑ 620 Ken Griffey .30 .12
❑ 621 Ken Griffey SA .15 .06
❑ 622 Dennis Lamp .15 .06
❑ 623 Ron Gardenhire RC .60 .24
Terry Leach
Tim Leary RC
❑ 624 Fergie Jenkins .30 .12
❑ 625 Hal McRae .30 .12
❑ 626 Randy Jones .15 .06
❑ 627 Enos Cabell .15 .06
❑ 628 Bill Travers .15 .06
❑ 629 John Wockenfuss .15 .06
❑ 630 Joe Charboneau .30 .12
❑ 631 Gene Tenace .30 .12
❑ 632 Bryan Clark RC .15 .06
❑ 633 Mitchell Page .15 .06
❑ 634 Checklist 529-660 .60 .24
❑ 635 Ron Davis .15 .06
❑ 636 Pete Rose 1.25 .50
Steve Carlton TL
❑ 637 Rick Camp .15 .06
❑ 638 John Milner .15 .06
❑ 639 Ken Kravec .15 .06
❑ 640 Cesar Cedeno .30 .12
❑ 641 Steve Mura .15 .06
❑ 642 Mike Scioscia .30 .12
❑ 643 Pete Vuckovich .15 .06
❑ 644 John Castino .15 .06
❑ 645 Frank White .30 .12
❑ 646 Frank White SA .15 .06
❑ 647 Warren Brusstar .15 .06
❑ 648 Jose Morales .15 .06
❑ 649 Ken Clay .15 .06
❑ 650 Carl Yastrzemski 1.25 .50
❑ 651 Carl Yastrzemski SA .60 .24
❑ 652 Steve Nicosia .15 .06
❑ 653 Tom Brunansky RC .60 .24
Luis Sanchez
Daryl Sconiers
❑ 654 Jim Morrison .15 .06
❑ 655 Joel Youngblood .15 .06
❑ 656 Eddie Whitson .15 .06
❑ 657 Tom Poquette .15 .06
❑ 658 Tito Landrum .15 .06
❑ 659 Fred Martinez .15 .06
❑ 660 Dave Concepcion .30 .12
❑ 661 Dave Concepcion SA .15 .06
❑ 662 Luis Salazar .15 .06
❑ 663 Hector Cruz .15 .06
❑ 664 Dan Spillner .15 .06
❑ 665 Jim Clancy .15 .06
❑ 666 Steve Kemp .60 .24

Dan Petry TL
❑ 667 Jeff Reardon .60 .24
❑ 668 Dale Murphy 1.25 .50
❑ 669 Larry Milbourne .15 .06
❑ 670 Steve Kemp .15 .06
❑ 671 Mike Davis .15 .06
❑ 672 Bob Knepper .15 .06
❑ 673 Keith Drumwright .15 .06
❑ 674 Dave Goltz .15 .06
❑ 675 Cecil Cooper .30 .12
❑ 676 Sal Butera .15 .06
❑ 677 Alfredo Griffin .15 .06
❑ 678 Tom Paciorek .30 .12
❑ 679 Sammy Stewart .15 .06
❑ 680 Gary Matthews .30 .12
❑ 681 Mike Marshall RC 1.25 .50
Ron Roenicke
Steve Sax RC
❑ 682 Jesse Jefferson .15 .06
❑ 683 Phil Garner .30 .12
❑ 684 Harold Baines 1.25 .50
❑ 685 Bert Blyleven .60 .24
❑ 686 Gary Allenson .15 .06
❑ 687 Greg Minton .15 .06
❑ 688 Leon Roberts .15 .06
❑ 689 Lary Sorensen .15 .06
❑ 690 Dave Kingman .30 .12
❑ 691 Dan Schatzeder .15 .06
❑ 692 Wayne Gross .15 .06
❑ 693 Cesar Geronimo .15 .06
❑ 694 Dave Wehrmeister .15 .06
❑ 695 Warren Cromartie .15 .06
❑ 696 Bill Madlock .60 .24
Eddie Solomon TL
❑ 697 John Montefusco .15 .06
❑ 698 Tony Scott .15 .06
❑ 699 Dick Tidrow .15 .06
❑ 700 George Foster .30 .12
❑ 701 George Foster SA .15 .06
❑ 702 Steve Renko .15 .06
❑ 703 Cecil Cooper .60 .24
Pete Vuckovich TL
❑ 704 Mickey Rivers .15 .06
❑ 705 Mickey Rivers SA .15 .06
❑ 706 Barry Foote .15 .06
❑ 707 Mark Bomback .15 .06
❑ 708 Gene Richards .15 .06
❑ 709 Don Money .15 .06
❑ 710 Jerry Reuss .30 .12
❑ 711 Dave Edler .60 .24
Dave Henderson RC
Reggie Walton
❑ 712 Dennis Martinez .60 .24
❑ 713 Del Unser .15 .06
❑ 714 Jerry Koosman .30 .12
❑ 715 Willie Stargell .60 .24
❑ 716 Willie Stargell SA .30 .12
❑ 717 Rick Miller .15 .06
❑ 718 Charlie Hough .30 .12
❑ 719 Jerry Narron .15 .06
❑ 720 Greg Luzinski .30 .12
❑ 721 Greg Luzinski SA .15 .06
❑ 722 Jerry Martin .15 .06
❑ 723 Junior Kennedy .15 .06
❑ 724 Dave Rosello .15 .06
❑ 725 Amos Otis .30 .12
❑ 726 Amos Otis SA .15 .06
❑ 727 Sixto Lezcano .15 .06
❑ 728 Aurelio Lopez .15 .06
❑ 729 Jim Spencer .15 .06
❑ 730 Gary Carter .60 .24
❑ 731 Mike Armstrong .15 .06
Doug Gwosdz
Fred Kuhaulua
❑ 732 Mike Lum .15 .06
❑ 733 Larry McWilliams .15 .06
❑ 734 Mike Ivie .15 .06
❑ 735 Rudy May .15 .06
❑ 736 Jerry Turner .15 .06
❑ 737 Reggie Cleveland .15 .06
❑ 738 Dave Engle .15 .06
❑ 739 Joey McLaughlin .15 .06
❑ 740 Dave Lopes .30 .12
❑ 741 Dave Lopes SA .15 .06
❑ 742 Dick Drago .15 .06
❑ 743 John Stearns .15 .06
❑ 744 Mike Witt .30 .12
❑ 745 Bake McBride .15 .06
❑ 746 Andre Thornton .15 .06
❑ 747 John Lowenstein .15 .06
❑ 748 Marc Hill .15 .06
❑ 749 Bob Shirley .15 .06
❑ 750 Jim Rice .30 .12
❑ 751 Rick Honeycutt .15 .06
❑ 752 Lee Lacy .15 .06
❑ 753 Tom Brookens .15 .06
❑ 754 Joe Morgan .60 .24
❑ 755 Joe Morgan SA .30 .12
❑ 756 Ken Griffey .30 .12
Tom Seaver TL
❑ 757 Tom Underwood .15 .06
❑ 758 Claudell Washington .15 .06
❑ 759 Paul Splittorff .15 .06
❑ 760 Bill Buckner .30 .12
❑ 761 Dave Smith .15 .06
❑ 762 Mike Phillips .15 .06
❑ 763 Tom Hume .15 .06
❑ 764 Steve Swisher .15 .06
❑ 765 Gorman Thomas .30 .12
❑ 766 Lenny Faedo 1.50 .60
Kent Hrbek RC
Tim Laudner
❑ 767 Roy Smalley .15 .06
❑ 768 Jerry Garvin .15 .06
❑ 769 Richie Zisk .15 .06
❑ 770 Rich Gossage .60 .24
❑ 771 Rich Gossage SA .30 .12
❑ 772 Bert Campaneris .30 .12
❑ 773 John Denny .15 .06
❑ 774 Jay Johnstone .30 .12
❑ 775 Bob Forsch .15 .06
❑ 776 Mark Belanger .15 .06
❑ 777 Tom Griffin .15 .06
❑ 778 Kevin Hickey RC .15 .06
❑ 779 Grant Jackson .15 .06
❑ 780 Pete Rose 4.00 1.60
❑ 781 Pete Rose SA 1.25 .50
❑ 782 Frank Taveras .15 .06
❑ 783 Greg Harris RC .15 .06
❑ 784 Milt Wilcox .15 .06
❑ 785 Dan Driessen .15 .06
❑ 786 Carney Lansford .60 .24
Mike Torrez TL
❑ 787 Fred Stanley .15 .06
❑ 788 Woodie Fryman .15 .06
❑ 789 Checklist 661-792 .60 .24
❑ 790 Larry Gura .15 .06
❑ 791 Bobby Brown .15 .06
❑ 792 Frank Tanana .30 .12

1982 Topps Traded

	Nm-Mt	Ex-Mt
COMP.FACT.SET (132)	150.00	60.00

❑ 1T Doyle Alexander .50 .20
❑ 2T Jesse Barfield 1.00 .40
❑ 3T Ross Baumgarten .50 .20
❑ 4T Steve Bedrosian 1.00 .40
❑ 5T Mark Belanger 1.00 .40
❑ 6T Kurt Bevacqua .50 .20
❑ 7T Tim Blackwell .50 .20
❑ 8T Vida Blue 1.00 .40
❑ 9T Bob Boone 1.00 .40
❑ 10T Larry Bowa 1.00 .40
❑ 11T Dan Briggs .50 .20
❑ 12T Bobby Brown .50 .20
❑ 13T Tom Brunansky 1.00 .40
❑ 14T Jeff Burroughs .50 .20
❑ 15T Enos Cabell .50 .20
❑ 16T Bill Campbell .50 .20
❑ 17T Bobby Castillo .50 .20
❑ 18T Bill Caudill .50 .20
❑ 19T Cesar Cedeno 1.00 .40
❑ 20T Dave Collins .50 .20
❑ 21T Doug Corbett .50 .20
❑ 22T Al Cowens .50 .20
❑ 23T Chili Davis 8.00 3.20
❑ 24T Dick Davis .50 .20
❑ 25T Ron Davis .50 .20
❑ 26T Doug DeCinces 1.00 .40
❑ 27T Ivan DeJesus .50 .20
❑ 28T Bob Dernier .50 .20
❑ 29T Bo Diaz .50 .20
❑ 30T Roger Erickson .50 .20
❑ 31T Jim Essian .50 .20
❑ 32T Ed Farmer .50 .20
❑ 33T Doug Flynn .50 .20
❑ 34T Tim Foli .50 .20
❑ 35T Dan Ford .50 .20
❑ 36T George Foster 1.00 .40
❑ 37T Dave Frost .50 .20
❑ 38T Rich Gale .50 .20
❑ 39T Ron Gardenhire .50 .20
❑ 40T Ken Griffey 1.00 .40
❑ 41T Greg Harris .50 .20
❑ 42T Von Hayes 1.00 .40
❑ 43T Larry Herndon .50 .20
❑ 44T Kent Hrbek 2.00 .80
❑ 45T Mike Ivie .50 .20
❑ 46T Grant Jackson .50 .20
❑ 47T Reggie Jackson 2.00 .80
❑ 48T Ron Jackson .50 .20
❑ 49T Fergie Jenkins 1.00 .40
❑ 50T Lamar Johnson .50 .20
❑ 51T Randy Johnson .50 .20
❑ 52T Jay Johnstone 1.00 .40
❑ 53T Mick Kelleher .50 .20
❑ 54T Steve Kemp .50 .20
❑ 55T Junior Kennedy .50 .20
❑ 56T Jim Kern .50 .20
❑ 57T Ray Knight 1.00 .40
❑ 58T Wayne Krenchicki .50 .20
❑ 59T Mike Krukow .50 .20
❑ 60T Duane Kuiper .50 .20
❑ 61T Mike LaCoss .50 .20
❑ 62T Chet Lemon .50 .20
❑ 63T Sixto Lezcano .50 .20
❑ 64T Dave Lopes 1.00 .40
❑ 65T Jerry Martin .50 .20
❑ 66T Renie Martin .50 .20
❑ 67T John Mayberry .50 .20
❑ 68T Lee Mazzilli .50 .20
❑ 69T Bake McBride .50 .20
❑ 70T Dan Meyer .50 .20
❑ 71T Larry Milbourne .50 .20
❑ 72T Eddie Milner .50 .20
❑ 73T Sid Monge .50 .20
❑ 74T John Montefusco .50 .20
❑ 75T Jose Morales .50 .20
❑ 76T Keith Moreland .50 .20
❑ 77T Jim Morrison .50 .20
❑ 78T Rance Mulliniks .50 .20
❑ 79T Steve Mura .50 .20
❑ 80T Gene Nelson .50 .20
❑ 81T Joe Nolan .50 .20
❑ 82T Dickie Noles .50 .20
❑ 83T Al Oliver 1.00 .40
❑ 84T Jorge Orta .50 .20
❑ 85T Tom Paciorek 1.00 .40
❑ 86T Larry Parrish .50 .20
❑ 87T Jack Perconte .50 .20
❑ 88T Gaylord Perry 1.00 .40
❑ 89T Rob Picciolo .50 .20
❑ 90T Joe Pittman .50 .20
❑ 91T Hosken Powell .50 .20
❑ 92T Mike Proly .50 .20
❑ 93T Greg Pryor .50 .20
❑ 94T Charlie Puleo .50 .20
❑ 95T Shane Rawley .50 .20

❑ 96T Johnny Ray 1.00 .40
❑ 97T Dave Revering .50 .20
❑ 98T Cal Ripken 120.00 47.50
❑ 99T Allen Ripley .50 .20
❑ 100T Bill Robinson .50 .20
❑ 101T Aurelio Rodriguez .50 .20
❑ 102T Joe Rudi .50 .20
❑ 103T Steve Sax 4.00 1.60
❑ 104T Dan Schatzeder .50 .20
❑ 105T Bob Shirley .50 .20
❑ 106T Eric Show 1.00 .40
❑ 107T Roy Smalley .50 .20
❑ 108T Lonnie Smith 1.00 .40
❑ 109T Ozzie Smith 15.00 6.00
❑ 110T Reggie Smith 1.00 .40
❑ 111T Lary Sorensen .50 .20
❑ 112T Elias Sosa .50 .20
❑ 113T Mike Stanton .50 .20
❑ 114T Steve Stroughter .50 .20
❑ 115T Champ Summers .50 .20
❑ 116T Rick Sutcliffe 1.00 .40
❑ 117T Frank Tanana 1.00 .40
❑ 118T Frank Taveras .50 .20
❑ 119T Garry Templeton .50 .20
❑ 120T Alex Trevino .50 .20
❑ 121T Jerry Turner .50 .20
❑ 122T Ed VandeBerg .50 .20
❑ 123T Tom Veryzer .50 .20
❑ 124T Ron Washington .50 .20
❑ 125T Bob Watson 1.00 .40
❑ 126T Dennis Werth .50 .20
❑ 127T Eddie Whitson .50 .20
❑ 128T Rob Wilfong .50 .20
❑ 129T Bump Wills .50 .20
❑ 130T Gary Woods .50 .20
❑ 131T Butch Wynegar .50 .20
❑ 132T Checklist: 1-132 .50 .20

1983 Topps

	Nm-Mt	Ex-Mt
COMPLETE SET (792)	80.00	32.00

❑ 1 Tony Armas RB .30 .12
❑ 2 Rickey Henderson RB 1.25 .50
❑ 3 Greg Minton RB .15 .06
❑ 4 Lance Parrish RB .15 .06
❑ 5 Manny Trillo RB .15 .06
❑ 6 John Wathan RB .15 .06
❑ 7 Gene Richards .15 .06
❑ 8 Steve Balboni .15 .06
❑ 9 Joey McLaughlin .15 .06
❑ 10 Gorman Thomas .15 .06
❑ 11 Billy Gardner MG .15 .06
❑ 12 Paul Mirabella .15 .06
❑ 13 Larry Herndon .15 .06
❑ 14 Frank LaCorte .15 .06
❑ 15 Ron Cey .30 .12
❑ 16 George Vukovich .15 .06
❑ 17 Kent Tekulve .30 .12
❑ 18 Kent Tekulve SV .15 .06
❑ 19 Oscar Gamble .15 .06
❑ 20 Carlton Fisk .60 .24
❑ 21 Eddie Murray .60 .24
Jim Palmer TL
❑ 22 Randy Martz .15 .06
❑ 23 Mike Heath .15 .06
❑ 24 Steve Mura .15 .06
❑ 25 Hal McRae .30 .12
❑ 26 Jerry Royster .15 .06
❑ 27 Doug Corbett .15 .06
❑ 28 Bruce Bochte .15 .06
❑ 29 Randy Jones .15 .06
❑ 30 Jim Rice .30 .12
❑ 31 Bill Gullickson .15 .06
❑ 32 Dave Bergman .15 .06
❑ 33 Jack O'Connor .15 .06
❑ 34 Paul Householder .15 .06
❑ 35 Rollie Fingers .30 .12
❑ 36 Rollie Fingers SV .30 .12
❑ 37 Darrell Johnson MG .15 .06
❑ 38 Tim Flannery .15 .06
❑ 39 Terry Puhl .15 .06
❑ 40 Fernando Valenzuela .60 .24
❑ 41 Jerry Turner .15 .06
❑ 42 Dale Murray .15 .06
❑ 43 Bob Dernier .15 .06
❑ 44 Don Robinson .15 .06
❑ 45 John Mayberry .15 .06
❑ 46 Richard Dotson .15 .06
❑ 47 Dave McKay .15 .06
❑ 48 Lary Sorensen .15 .06
❑ 49 Willie McGee RC 3.00 1.20
❑ 50 Bob Horner UER .15 .06
('82 RBI total 7)
❑ 51 Leon Durham .15 .06
Fergie Jenkins TL
❑ 52 Onix Concepcion .15 .06
❑ 53 Mike Witt .15 .06
❑ 54 Jim Maler .15 .06
❑ 55 Mookie Wilson .30 .12
❑ 56 Chuck Rainey .15 .06
❑ 57 Tim Blackwell .15 .06
❑ 58 Al Holland .15 .06
❑ 59 Benny Ayala .15 .06
❑ 60 Johnny Bench 1.25 .50
❑ 61 Johnny Bench SV .60 .24
❑ 62 Bob McClure .15 .06
❑ 63 Rick Monday .15 .06
❑ 64 Bill Stein .15 .06
❑ 65 Jack Morris .30 .12
❑ 66 Bob Lillis MG .15 .06
❑ 67 Sal Butera .15 .06
❑ 68 Eric Show .15 .06
❑ 69 Lee Lacy .15 .06
❑ 70 Steve Carlton .60 .24
❑ 71 Steve Carlton SV .30 .12
❑ 72 Tom Paciorek .30 .12
❑ 73 Allen Ripley .15 .06
❑ 74 Julio Gonzalez .15 .06
❑ 75 Amos Otis .30 .12
❑ 76 Rick Mahler .15 .06
❑ 77 Hosken Powell .15 .06
❑ 78 Bill Caudill .15 .06
❑ 79 Mick Kelleher .15 .06
❑ 80 George Foster .30 .12
❑ 81 Jerry Mumphrey .30 .12
Dave Righetti TL
❑ 82 Bruce Hurst .15 .06
❑ 83 Ryne Sandberg RC 15.00 6.00
❑ 84 Milt May .15 .06
❑ 85 Ken Singleton .15 .06
❑ 86 Tom Hume .15 .06
❑ 87 Joe Rudi .15 .06
❑ 88 Jim Gantner .15 .06
❑ 89 Leon Roberts .15 .06
❑ 90 Jerry Reuss .30 .12
❑ 91 Larry Milbourne .15 .06
❑ 92 Mike LaCoss .15 .06
❑ 93 John Castino .15 .06
❑ 94 Dave Edwards .15 .06
❑ 95 Alan Trammell .60 .24
❑ 96 Dick Howser MG .15 .06
❑ 97 Ross Baumgarten .15 .06
❑ 98 Vance Law .15 .06
❑ 99 Dickie Noles .15 .06
❑ 100 Pete Rose 4.00 1.60
❑ 101 Pete Rose SV 1.25 .50
❑ 102 Dave Beard .15 .06
❑ 103 Darrell Porter .15 .06
❑ 104 Bob Walk .15 .06
❑ 105 Don Baylor .60 .24
❑ 106 Gene Nelson .15 .06
❑ 107 Mike Jorgensen .15 .06
❑ 108 Glenn Hoffman .15 .06
❑ 109 Luis Leal .15 .06
❑ 110 Ken Griffey .30 .12
❑ 111 Al Oliver .30 .12
Steve Rogers TL
❑ 112 Bob Shirley .15 .06
❑ 113 Ron Roenicke .15 .06
❑ 114 Jim Slaton .15 .06
❑ 115 Chili Davis 1.25 .50
❑ 116 Dave Schmidt .15 .06
❑ 117 Alan Knicely .15 .06
❑ 118 Chris Welsh .15 .06
❑ 119 Tom Brookens .15 .06
❑ 120 Len Barker .15 .06
❑ 121 Mickey Hatcher .15 .06
❑ 122 Jimmy Smith .15 .06
❑ 123 George Frazier .15 .06
❑ 124 Marc Hill .15 .06
❑ 125 Leon Durham .15 .06
❑ 126 Joe Torre MG .30 .12
❑ 127 Preston Hanna .15 .06
❑ 128 Mike Ramsey .15 .06
❑ 129 Checklist: 1-132 .30 .12
❑ 130 Dave Stieb .30 .12
❑ 131 Ed Ott .15 .06
❑ 132 Todd Cruz .15 .06
❑ 133 Jim Barr .15 .06
❑ 134 Hubie Brooks .30 .12
❑ 135 Dwight Evans .30 .12
❑ 136 Willie Aikens .15 .06
❑ 137 Woodie Fryman .15 .06
❑ 138 Rick Dempsey .30 .12
❑ 139 Bruce Berenyi .15 .06
❑ 140 Willie Randolph .30 .12
❑ 141 Toby Harrah .30 .12
Rick Sutcliffe TL
❑ 142 Mike Caldwell .15 .06
❑ 143 Joe Pettini .15 .06
❑ 144 Mark Wagner .15 .06
❑ 145 Don Sutton 1.25 .50
❑ 146 Don Sutton SV .60 .24
❑ 147 Rick Leach .15 .06
❑ 148 Dave Roberts .15 .06
❑ 149 Johnny Ray .15 .06
❑ 150 Bruce Sutter .30 .12
❑ 151 Bruce Sutter SV .15 .06
❑ 152 Jay Johnstone .30 .12
❑ 153 Jerry Koosman .30 .12
❑ 154 Johnnie LeMaster .15 .06
❑ 155 Dan Quisenberry .30 .12
❑ 156 Billy Martin MG .30 .12
❑ 157 Steve Bedrosian .30 .12
❑ 158 Rob Wilfong .15 .06
❑ 159 Mike Stanton .15 .06
❑ 160 Dave Kingman .60 .24
❑ 161 Dave Kingman SV .30 .12
❑ 162 Mark Clear .15 .06
❑ 163 Cal Ripken 10.00 4.00
❑ 164 David Palmer .15 .06
❑ 165 Dan Driessen .15 .06
❑ 166 John Pacella .15 .06
❑ 167 Mark Brouhard .15 .06
❑ 168 Juan Eichelberger .15 .06
❑ 169 Doug Flynn .15 .06
❑ 170 Steve Howe .15 .06
❑ 171 Joe Morgan .30 .12
Bill Laskey TL
❑ 172 Vern Ruhle .15 .06
❑ 173 Jim Morrison .15 .06
❑ 174 Jerry Ujdur .15 .06
❑ 175 Bo Diaz .15 .06
❑ 176 Dave Righetti .30 .12
❑ 177 Harold Baines 1.25 .50
❑ 178 Luis Tiant .30 .12
❑ 179 Luis Tiant SV .15 .06
❑ 180 Rickey Henderson 2.50 1.00
❑ 181 Terry Felton .15 .06
❑ 182 Mike Fischlin .15 .06
❑ 183 Ed VandeBerg .15 .06
❑ 184 Bob Clark .15 .06
❑ 185 Tim Lollar .15 .06
❑ 186 Whitey Herzog MG .30 .12
❑ 187 Terry Leach .15 .06
❑ 188 Rick Miller .15 .06
❑ 189 Dan Schatzeder .15 .06
❑ 190 Cecil Cooper .30 .12

❑ 191 Joe Price .15 .06
❑ 192 Floyd Rayford .15 .06
❑ 193 Harry Spilman .15 .06
❑ 194 Cesar Geronimo .15 .06
❑ 195 Bob Stoddard .15 .06
❑ 196 Bill Fahey .15 .06
❑ 197 Jim Eisenreich RC 1.25 .50
❑ 198 Kiko Garcia .15 .06
❑ 199 Marty Bystrom .15 .06
❑ 200 Rod Carew .60 .24
❑ 201 Rod Carew SV .30 .12
❑ 202 Damaso Garcia .30 .12
Dave Stieb TL
❑ 203 Mike Morgan .15 .06
❑ 204 Junior Kennedy .15 .06
❑ 205 Dave Parker .30 .12
❑ 206 Ken Oberkfell .15 .06
❑ 207 Rick Camp .15 .06
❑ 208 Dan Meyer .15 .06
❑ 209 Mike Moore RC .30 .12
❑ 210 Jack Clark .30 .12
❑ 211 John Denny .15 .06
❑ 212 John Stearns .15 .06
❑ 213 Tom Burgmeier .15 .06
❑ 214 Jerry White .15 .06
❑ 215 Mario Soto .15 .06
❑ 216 Tony LaRussa MG .30 .12
❑ 217 Tim Stoddard .15 .06
❑ 218 Roy Howell .15 .06
❑ 219 Mike Armstrong .15 .06
❑ 220 Dusty Baker .30 .12
❑ 221 Joe Niekro .30 .12
❑ 222 Damaso Garcia .15 .06
❑ 223 John Montefusco .15 .06
❑ 224 Mickey Rivers .15 .06
❑ 225 Enos Cabell .15 .06
❑ 226 Enrique Romo .15 .06
❑ 227 Chris Bando .15 .06
❑ 228 Joaquin Andujar .15 .06
❑ 229 Bo Diaz .30 .12
Steve Carlton TL
❑ 230 Fergie Jenkins .30 .12
❑ 231 Fergie Jenkins SV .15 .06
❑ 232 Tom Brunansky .30 .12
❑ 233 Wayne Gross .15 .06
❑ 234 Larry Andersen .15 .06
❑ 235 Claudell Washington .15 .06
❑ 236 Steve Renko .15 .06
❑ 237 Dan Norman .15 .06
❑ 238 Bud Black RC .30 .12
❑ 239 Dave Stapleton .15 .06
❑ 240 Rich Gossage .60 .24
❑ 241 Rich Gossage SV .30 .12
❑ 242 Joe Nolan .15 .06
❑ 243 Duane Walker .15 .06
❑ 244 Dwight Bernard .15 .06
❑ 245 Steve Sax .30 .12
❑ 246 G.Bamberger MG .15 .06
❑ 247 Dave Smith .15 .06
❑ 248 Bake McBride .15 .06
❑ 249 Checklist: 133-264 .30 .12
❑ 250 Bill Buckner .30 .12
❑ 251 Alan Wiggins .15 .06
❑ 252 Luis Aguayo .15 .06
❑ 253 Larry McWilliams .15 .06
❑ 254 Rick Cerone .15 .06
❑ 255 Gene Garber .15 .06
❑ 256 Gene Garber SV .15 .06
❑ 257 Jesse Barfield .30 .12
❑ 258 Manny Castillo .15 .06
❑ 259 Jeff Jones .15 .06
❑ 260 Steve Kemp .15 .06
❑ 261 Larry Herndon .30 .12
Dan Petry TL
❑ 262 Ron Jackson .15 .06
❑ 263 Renie Martin .15 .06
❑ 264 Jamie Quirk .15 .06
❑ 265 Joel Youngblood .15 .06
❑ 266 Paul Boris .15 .06
❑ 267 Terry Francona .15 .06
❑ 268 Storm Davis RC .15 .06
❑ 269 Ron Oester .15 .06
❑ 270 Dennis Eckersley .60 .24
❑ 271 Ed Romero .15 .06
❑ 272 Frank Tanana .30 .12
❑ 273 Mark Belanger .15 .06
❑ 274 Terry Kennedy .15 .06
❑ 275 Ray Knight .30 .12
❑ 276 Gene Mauch MG .15 .06
❑ 277 Rance Mulliniks .15 .06
❑ 278 Kevin Hickey .15 .06
❑ 279 Greg Gross .15 .06
❑ 280 Bert Blyleven .60 .24
❑ 281 Andre Robertson .15 .06
❑ 282 Reggie Smith 1.25 .50
(Ryne Sandberg
ducking back)
❑ 283 Reggie Smith SV .15 .06
❑ 284 Jeff Lahti .15 .06
❑ 285 Lance Parrish .30 .12
❑ 286 Rick Langford .15 .06
❑ 287 Bobby Brown .15 .06
❑ 288 Joe Cowley .15 .06
❑ 289 Jerry Dybzinski .15 .06
❑ 290 Jeff Reardon .30 .12
❑ 291 Bill Madlock .30 .12
John Candelaria TL
❑ 292 Craig Swan .15 .06
❑ 293 Glenn Gulliver .15 .06
❑ 294 Dave Engle .15 .06
❑ 295 Jerry Remy .15 .06
❑ 296 Greg Harris .15 .06
❑ 297 Ned Yost .15 .06
❑ 298 Floyd Chiffer .15 .06
❑ 299 George Wright RC .15 .06
❑ 300 Mike Schmidt 3.00 1.20
❑ 301 Mike Schmidt SV 1.25 .50
❑ 302 Ernie Whitt .15 .06
❑ 303 Miguel Dilone .15 .06
❑ 304 Dave Rucker .15 .06
❑ 305 Larry Bowa .30 .12
❑ 306 Tom Lasorda MG .60 .24
❑ 307 Lou Piniella .30 .12
❑ 308 Jesus Vega .15 .06
❑ 309 Jeff Leonard .15 .06
❑ 310 Greg Luzinski .30 .12
❑ 311 Glenn Brummer .15 .06
❑ 312 Brian Kingman .15 .06
❑ 313 Gary Gray .15 .06
❑ 314 Ken Dayley .15 .06
❑ 315 Rick Burleson .15 .06
❑ 316 Paul Splittorff .15 .06
❑ 317 Gary Rajsich .15 .06
❑ 318 John Tudor .15 .06
❑ 319 Lenn Sakata .15 .06
❑ 320 Steve Rogers .15 .06
❑ 321 Robin Yount .60 .24
Pete Vuckovich TL
❑ 322 Dave Van Gorder .15 .06
❑ 323 Luis DeLeon .15 .06
❑ 324 Mike Marshall .15 .06
❑ 325 Von Hayes .30 .12
❑ 326 Garth Iorg .15 .06
❑ 327 Bobby Castillo .15 .06
❑ 328 Craig Reynolds .15 .06
❑ 329 Randy Niemann .15 .06
❑ 330 Buddy Bell .30 .12
❑ 331 Mike Krukow .15 .06
❑ 332 Glenn Wilson .30 .12
❑ 333 Dave LaRoche .15 .06
❑ 334 Dave LaRoche SV .15 .06
❑ 335 Steve Henderson .15 .06
❑ 336 Rene Lachemann MG .15 .06
❑ 337 Tito Landrum .15 .06
❑ 338 Bob Owchinko .15 .06
❑ 339 Terry Harper .15 .06
❑ 340 Larry Gura .15 .06
❑ 341 Doug DeCinces .30 .12
❑ 342 Atlee Hammaker .15 .06
❑ 343 Bob Bailor .15 .06
❑ 344 Roger LaFrancois .15 .06
❑ 345 Jim Clancy .15 .06
❑ 346 Joe Pittman .15 .06
❑ 347 Sammy Stewart .15 .06
❑ 348 Alan Bannister .15 .06
❑ 349 Checklist: 265-396 .30 .12
❑ 350 Robin Yount 1.25 .50
❑ 351 Cesar Cedeno .30 .12
Mario Soto TL
❑ 352 Mike Scioscia .30 .12
❑ 353 Steve Comer .15 .06
❑ 354 Randy Johnson .15 .06
❑ 355 Jim Bibby .15 .06
❑ 356 Gary Woods .15 .06
❑ 357 Len Matuszek .15 .06
❑ 358 Jerry Garvin .15 .06
❑ 359 Dave Collins .15 .06
❑ 360 Nolan Ryan 6.00 2.40
❑ 361 Nolan Ryan SV 3.00 1.20
❑ 362 Bill Almon .15 .06
❑ 363 John Stuper .15 .06
❑ 364 Brett Butler 1.25 .50
❑ 365 Dave Lopes .30 .12
❑ 366 Dick Williams MG .15 .06
❑ 367 Bud Anderson .15 .06
❑ 368 Richie Zisk .15 .06
❑ 369 Jesse Orosco .15 .06
❑ 370 Gary Carter .60 .24
❑ 371 Mike Richardt .15 .06
❑ 372 Terry Crowley .15 .06
❑ 373 Kevin Saucier .15 .06
❑ 374 Wayne Krenchicki .15 .06
❑ 375 Pete Vuckovich .15 .06
❑ 376 Ken Landreaux .15 .06
❑ 377 Lee May .30 .12
❑ 378 Lee May SV .15 .06
❑ 379 Guy Sularz .15 .06
❑ 380 Ron Davis .15 .06
❑ 381 Jim Rice .30 .12
Bob Stanley TL
❑ 382 Bob Knepper .15 .06
❑ 383 Ozzie Virgil .15 .06
❑ 384 Dave Dravecky RC 1.25 .50
❑ 385 Mike Easler .15 .06
❑ 386 Rod Carew AS .30 .12
❑ 387 Bob Grich AS .15 .06
❑ 388 George Brett AS 1.25 .50
❑ 389 Robin Yount AS .60 .24
❑ 390 Reggie Jackson AS .30 .12
❑ 391 Rickey Henderson AS 1.25 .50
❑ 392 Fred Lynn AS .15 .06
❑ 393 Carlton Fisk AS .30 .12
❑ 394 Pete Vuckovich AS .15 .06
❑ 395 Larry Gura AS .15 .06
❑ 396 Dan Quisenberry AS .15 .06
❑ 397 Pete Rose AS .60 .24
❑ 398 Manny Trillo AS .15 .06
❑ 399 Mike Schmidt AS 1.25 .50
❑ 400 Dave Concepcion AS .15 .06
❑ 401 Dale Murphy AS .60 .24
❑ 402 Andre Dawson AS .15 .06
❑ 403 Tim Raines AS .30 .12
❑ 404 Gary Carter AS .30 .12
❑ 405 Steve Rogers AS .15 .06
❑ 406 Steve Carlton AS .30 .12
❑ 407 Bruce Sutter AS .15 .06
❑ 408 Rudy May .15 .06
❑ 409 Marvis Foley .15 .06
❑ 410 Phil Niekro .30 .12
❑ 411 Phil Niekro SV .15 .06
❑ 412 Buddy Bell .30 .12
Charlie Hough TL
❑ 413 Matt Keough .15 .06
❑ 414 Julio Cruz .15 .06
❑ 415 Bob Forsch .15 .06
❑ 416 Joe Ferguson .15 .06
❑ 417 Tom Hausman .15 .06
❑ 418 Greg Pryor .15 .06
❑ 419 Steve Crawford .15 .06
❑ 420 Al Oliver .30 .12
❑ 421 Al Oliver SV .15 .06
❑ 422 George Cappuzzello .15 .06
❑ 423 Tom Lawless .15 .06
❑ 424 Jerry Augustine .15 .06
❑ 425 Pedro Guerrero .30 .12
❑ 426 Earl Weaver MG .60 .24
❑ 427 Roy Lee Jackson .15 .06
❑ 428 Champ Summers .15 .06
❑ 429 Eddie Whitson .15 .06
❑ 430 Kirk Gibson 1.25 .50
❑ 431 Gary Gaetti RC 1.25 .50
❑ 432 Porfirio Altamirano .15 .06
❑ 433 Dale Berra .15 .06
❑ 434 Dennis Lamp .15 .06
❑ 435 Tony Armas .15 .06
❑ 436 Bill Campbell .15 .06
❑ 437 Rick Sweet .15 .06
❑ 438 Dave LaPoint .15 .06

❑ 439 Rafael Ramirez	.15	.06
❑ 440 Ron Guidry	.30	.12
❑ 441 Ray Knight	.30	.12
Joe Niekro TL		
❑ 442 Brian Downing	.15	.06
❑ 443 Don Hood	.15	.06
❑ 444 Wally Backman	.15	.06
❑ 445 Mike Flanagan	.30	.12
❑ 446 Reid Nichols	.15	.06
❑ 447 Bryn Smith	.15	.06
❑ 448 Darrell Evans	.30	.12
❑ 449 Eddie Milner	.15	.06
❑ 450 Ted Simmons	.30	.12
❑ 451 Ted Simmons SV	.15	.06
❑ 452 Lloyd Moseby	.15	.06
❑ 453 Lamar Johnson	.15	.06
❑ 454 Bob Welch	.30	.12
❑ 455 Sixto Lezcano	.15	.06
❑ 456 Lee Elia MG	.15	.06
❑ 457 Milt Wilcox	.15	.06
❑ 458 Ron Washington	.15	.06
❑ 459 Ed Farmer	.15	.06
❑ 460 Roy Smalley	.15	.06
❑ 461 Steve Trout	.15	.06
❑ 462 Steve Nicosia	.15	.06
❑ 463 Gaylord Perry	.30	.12
❑ 464 Gaylord Perry SV	.15	.06
❑ 465 Lonnie Smith	.15	.06
❑ 466 Tom Underwood	.15	.06
❑ 467 Rufino Linares	.15	.06
❑ 468 Dave Goltz	.15	.06
❑ 469 Ron Gardenhire	.15	.06
❑ 470 Greg Minton	.15	.06
❑ 471 Willie Wilson	.30	.12
Vida Blue TL		
❑ 472 Gary Allenson	.15	.06
❑ 473 John Lowenstein	.15	.06
❑ 474 Ray Burris	.15	.06
❑ 475 Cesar Cedeno	.30	.12
❑ 476 Rob Picciolo	.15	.06
❑ 477 Tom Niedenfuer	.15	.06
❑ 478 Phil Garner	.30	.12
❑ 479 Charlie Hough	.30	.12
❑ 480 Toby Harrah	.15	.06
❑ 481 Scot Thompson	.15	.06
❑ 482 Tony Gwynn UER RC	25.00	10.00
No Topps logo under card number on back		
❑ 483 Lynn Jones	.15	.06
❑ 484 Dick Ruthven	.15	.06
❑ 485 Omar Moreno	.15	.06
❑ 486 Clyde King MG	.15	.06
❑ 487 Jerry Hairston	.15	.06
❑ 488 Alfredo Griffin	.15	.06
❑ 489 Tom Herr	.30	.12
❑ 490 Jim Palmer	.30	.12
❑ 491 Jim Palmer SV	.15	.06
❑ 492 Paul Serna	.15	.06
❑ 493 Steve McCatty	.15	.06
❑ 494 Bob Brenly	.15	.06
❑ 495 Warren Cromartie	.15	.06
❑ 496 Tom Veryzer	.15	.06
❑ 497 Rick Sutcliffe	.30	.12
❑ 498 Wade Boggs RC	12.00	4.80
❑ 499 Jeff Little	.15	.06
❑ 500 Reggie Jackson	.60	.24
❑ 501 Reggie Jackson SV	.30	.12
❑ 502 Dale Murphy	.60	.24
Phil Niekro TL		
❑ 503 Moose Haas	.15	.06
❑ 504 Don Werner	.15	.06
❑ 505 Garry Templeton	.15	.06
❑ 506 Jim Gott RC	.15	.06
❑ 507 Tony Scott	.15	.06
❑ 508 Tom Filer	.15	.06
❑ 509 Lou Whitaker	.60	.24
❑ 510 Tug McGraw	.30	.12
❑ 511 Tug McGraw SV	.15	.06
❑ 512 Doyle Alexander	.15	.06
❑ 513 Fred Stanley	.15	.06
❑ 514 Rudy Law	.15	.06
❑ 515 Gene Tenace	.30	.12
❑ 516 Bill Virdon MG	.15	.06
❑ 517 Gary Ward	.15	.06
❑ 518 Bill Laskey	.15	.06
❑ 519 Terry Bulling	.15	.06
❑ 520 Fred Lynn	.30	.12
❑ 521 Bruce Benedict	.15	.06
❑ 522 Pat Zachry	.15	.06
❑ 523 Carney Lansford	.30	.12
❑ 524 Tom Brennan	.15	.06
❑ 525 Frank White	.30	.12
❑ 526 Checklist: 397-528	.30	.12
❑ 527 Larry Biittner	.15	.06
❑ 528 Jamie Easterly	.15	.06
❑ 529 Tim Laudner	.15	.06
❑ 530 Eddie Murray	1.25	.50
❑ 531 Rickey Henderson	1.25	.50
Rick Langford TL		
❑ 532 Dave Stewart	.30	.12
❑ 533 Luis Salazar	.15	.06
❑ 534 John Butcher	.15	.06
❑ 535 Manny Trillo	.15	.06
❑ 536 John Wockenfuss	.15	.06
❑ 537 Rod Scurry	.15	.06
❑ 538 Danny Heep	.15	.06
❑ 539 Roger Erickson	.15	.06
❑ 540 Ozzie Smith	2.00	.80
❑ 541 Britt Burns	.15	.06
❑ 542 Jody Davis	.15	.06
❑ 543 Alan Fowlkes	.15	.06
❑ 544 Larry Whisenton	.15	.06
❑ 545 Floyd Bannister	.15	.06
❑ 546 Dave Garcia MG	.15	.06
❑ 547 Geoff Zahn	.15	.06
❑ 548 Brian Giles	.15	.06
❑ 549 Charlie Puleo	.15	.06
❑ 550 Carl Yastrzemski	1.25	.50
❑ 551 Carl Yastrzemski SV	.60	.24
❑ 552 Tim Wallach	.30	.12
❑ 553 Dennis Martinez	.30	.12
❑ 554 Mike Vail	.15	.06
❑ 555 Steve Yeager	.15	.06
❑ 556 Willie Upshaw	.15	.06
❑ 557 Rick Honeycutt	.15	.06
❑ 558 Dickie Thon	.15	.06
❑ 559 Pete Redfern	.15	.06
❑ 560 Ron LeFlore	.15	.06
❑ 561 Lonnie Smith	.30	.12
Joaquin Andujar TL		
❑ 562 Dave Rozema	.15	.06
❑ 563 Juan Bonilla	.15	.06
❑ 564 Sid Monge	.15	.06
❑ 565 Bucky Dent	.30	.12
❑ 566 Manny Sarmiento	.15	.06
❑ 567 Joe Simpson	.15	.06
❑ 568 Willie Hernandez	.30	.12
❑ 569 Jack Perconte	.15	.06
❑ 570 Vida Blue	.30	.12
❑ 571 Mickey Klutts	.15	.06
❑ 572 Bob Watson	.30	.12
❑ 573 Andy Hassler	.15	.06
❑ 574 Glenn Adams	.15	.06
❑ 575 Neil Allen	.15	.06
❑ 576 Frank Robinson MG	.60	.24
❑ 577 Luis Aponte	.15	.06
❑ 578 David Green RC	.15	.06
❑ 579 Rich Dauer	.15	.06
❑ 580 Tom Seaver	1.25	.50
❑ 581 Tom Seaver SV	.60	.24
❑ 582 Marshall Edwards	.15	.06
❑ 583 Terry Forster	.15	.06
❑ 584 Dave Hostetler	.15	.06
❑ 585 Jose Cruz	.30	.12
❑ 586 Frank Viola RC	1.25	.50
❑ 587 Ivan DeJesus	.15	.06
❑ 588 Pat Underwood	.15	.06
❑ 589 Alvis Woods	.15	.06
❑ 590 Tony Pena	.15	.06
❑ 591 Greg Luzinski	.30	.12
LaMarr Hoyt TL		
❑ 592 Shane Rawley	.15	.06
❑ 593 Broderick Perkins	.15	.06
❑ 594 Eric Rasmussen	.15	.06
❑ 595 Tim Raines	1.25	.50
❑ 596 Randy Johnson	.15	.06
❑ 597 Mike Proly	.15	.06
❑ 598 Dwayne Murphy	.15	.06
❑ 599 Don Aase	.15	.06
❑ 600 George Brett	4.00	1.60
❑ 601 Ed Lynch	.15	.06
❑ 602 Rich Gedman	.15	.06
❑ 603 Joe Morgan	.60	.24
❑ 604 Joe Morgan SV	.30	.12
❑ 605 Gary Roenicke	.15	.06
❑ 606 Bobby Cox MG	.30	.12
❑ 607 Charlie Leibrandt	.15	.06
❑ 608 Don Money	.15	.06
❑ 609 Danny Darwin	.15	.06
❑ 610 Steve Garvey	.30	.12
❑ 611 Bert Roberge	.15	.06
❑ 612 Steve Swisher	.15	.06
❑ 613 Mike Ivie	.15	.06
❑ 614 Ed Glynn	.15	.06
❑ 615 Garry Maddox	.15	.06
❑ 616 Bill Nahorodny	.15	.06
❑ 617 Butch Wynegar	.15	.06
❑ 618 LaMarr Hoyt	.30	.12
❑ 619 Keith Moreland	.15	.06
❑ 620 Mike Norris	.15	.06
❑ 621 Mookie Wilson	.30	.12
Craig Swan TL		
❑ 622 Dave Edler	.15	.06
❑ 623 Luis Sanchez	.15	.06
❑ 624 Glenn Hubbard	.15	.06
❑ 625 Ken Forsch	.15	.06
❑ 626 Jerry Martin	.15	.06
❑ 627 Doug Bair	.15	.06
❑ 628 Julio Valdez	.15	.06
❑ 629 Charlie Lea	.15	.06
❑ 630 Paul Molitor	1.50	.60
❑ 631 Tippy Martinez	.15	.06
❑ 632 Alex Trevino	.15	.06
❑ 633 Vicente Romo	.15	.06
❑ 634 Max Venable	.15	.06
❑ 635 Graig Nettles	.30	.12
❑ 636 Graig Nettles SV	.15	.06
❑ 637 Pat Corrales MG	.15	.06
❑ 638 Dan Petry	.15	.06
❑ 639 Art Howe	.30	.12
❑ 640 Andre Thornton	.15	.06
❑ 641 Billy Sample	.15	.06
❑ 642 Checklist: 529-660	.30	.12
❑ 643 Bump Wills	.15	.06
❑ 644 Joe Lefebvre	.15	.06
❑ 645 Bill Madlock	.30	.12
❑ 646 Jim Essian	.15	.06
❑ 647 Bobby Mitchell	.15	.06
❑ 648 Jeff Burroughs	.15	.06
❑ 649 Tommy Boggs	.15	.06
❑ 650 George Hendrick	.15	.06
❑ 651 Rod Carew	.30	.12
Mike Witt TL		
❑ 652 Butch Hobson	.15	.06
❑ 653 Ellis Valentine	.15	.06
❑ 654 Bob Ojeda	.15	.06
❑ 655 Al Bumbry	.15	.06
❑ 656 Dave Frost	.15	.06
❑ 657 Mike Gates	.15	.06
❑ 658 Frank Pastore	.15	.06
❑ 659 Charlie Moore	.15	.06
❑ 660 Mike Hargrove	.30	.12
❑ 661 Bill Russell	.15	.06
❑ 662 Joe Sambito	.15	.06
❑ 663 Tom O'Malley	.15	.06
❑ 664 Bob Molinaro	.15	.06
❑ 665 Jim Sundberg	.30	.12
❑ 666 Sparky Anderson MG	.30	.12
❑ 667 Dick Davis	.15	.06
❑ 668 Larry Christenson	.15	.06
❑ 669 Mike Squires	.15	.06
❑ 670 Jerry Mumphrey	.15	.06
❑ 671 Lenny Faedo	.15	.06
❑ 672 Jim Kaat	.30	.12
❑ 673 Jim Kaat SV	.15	.06
❑ 674 Kurt Bevacqua	.15	.06
❑ 675 Jim Beattie	.15	.06
❑ 676 Biff Pocoroba	.15	.06
❑ 677 Dave Revering	.15	.06
❑ 678 Juan Beniquez	.15	.06
❑ 679 Mike Scott	.30	.12
❑ 680 Andre Dawson	.30	.12
❑ 681 Pedro Guerrero	.30	.12
Fernando Valenzuela TL		
❑ 682 Bob Stanley	.15	.06
❑ 683 Dan Ford	.15	.06
❑ 684 Rafael Landestoy	.15	.06
❑ 685 Lee Mazzilli	.15	.06

Card	Nm-Mt	Ex-Mt
❑ 686 Randy Lerch	.15	.06
❑ 687 U.L. Washington	.15	.06
❑ 688 Jim Wohlford	.15	.06
❑ 689 Ron Hassey	.15	.06
❑ 690 Kent Hrbek	.30	.12
❑ 691 Dave Tobik	.15	.06
❑ 692 Denny Walling	.15	.06
❑ 693 Sparky Lyle	.30	.12
❑ 694 Sparky Lyle SV	.15	.06
❑ 695 Ruppert Jones	.15	.06
❑ 696 Chuck Tanner MG	.15	.06
❑ 697 Barry Foote	.15	.06
❑ 698 Tony Bernazard	.15	.06
❑ 699 Lee Smith	1.25	.50
❑ 700 Keith Hernandez	.60	.24
❑ 701 Willie Wilson Al Oliver LL	.30	.12
❑ 702 Reggie Jackson Gorman Thomas Dave Kingman LL	.30	.12
❑ 703 Hal McRae Dale Murphy Al Oliver LL	.60	.24
❑ 704 Rickey Henderson Tim Raines LL	1.25	.50
❑ 705 LaMarr Hoyt Steve Carlton LL	.30	.12
❑ 706 Floyd Bannister Steve Carlton LL	.30	.12
❑ 707 Rick Sutcliffe Steve Rogers LL	.30	.12
❑ 708 Dan Quisenberry Bruce Sutter LL	.30	.12
❑ 709 Jimmy Sexton	.15	.06
❑ 710 Willie Wilson	.30	.12
❑ 711 Bruce Bochte Jim Beattie TL	.30	.12
❑ 712 Bruce Kison	.15	.06
❑ 713 Ron Hodges	.15	.06
❑ 714 Wayne Nordhagen	.15	.06
❑ 715 Tony Perez	.60	.24
❑ 716 Tony Perez SV	.30	.12
❑ 717 Scott Sanderson	.15	.06
❑ 718 Jim Dwyer	.15	.06
❑ 719 Rich Gale	.15	.06
❑ 720 Dave Concepcion	.30	.12
❑ 721 John Martin	.15	.06
❑ 722 Jorge Orta	.15	.06
❑ 723 Randy Moffitt	.15	.06
❑ 724 Johnny Grubb	.15	.06
❑ 725 Dan Spillner	.15	.06
❑ 726 Harvey Kuenn MG	.15	.06
❑ 727 Chet Lemon	.15	.06
❑ 728 Ron Reed	.15	.06
❑ 729 Jerry Morales	.15	.06
❑ 730 Jason Thompson	.15	.06
❑ 731 Al Williams	.15	.06
❑ 732 Dave Henderson	.15	.06
❑ 733 Buck Martinez	.15	.06
❑ 734 Steve Braun	.15	.06
❑ 735 Tommy John	.60	.24
❑ 736 Tommy John SV	.30	.12
❑ 737 Mitchell Page	.15	.06
❑ 738 Tim Foli	.15	.06
❑ 739 Rick Ownbey	.15	.06
❑ 740 Rusty Staub	.30	.12
❑ 741 Rusty Staub SV	.15	.06
❑ 742 Terry Kennedy Tim Lollar	.30	.12
❑ 743 Mike Torrez	.15	.06
❑ 744 Brad Mills	.15	.06
❑ 745 Scott McGregor	.15	.06
❑ 746 John Wathan	.15	.06
❑ 747 Fred Breining	.15	.06
❑ 748 Derrel Thomas	.15	.06
❑ 749 Jon Matlack	.15	.06
❑ 750 Ben Oglivie	.15	.06
❑ 751 Brad Havens	.15	.06
❑ 752 Luis Pujols	.15	.06
❑ 753 Elias Sosa	.15	.06
❑ 754 Bill Robinson	.15	.06
❑ 755 John Candelaria	.15	.06
❑ 756 Russ Nixon MG	.15	.06
❑ 757 Rick Manning	.15	.06
❑ 758 Aurelio Rodriguez	.15	.06
❑ 759 Doug Bird	.15	.06
❑ 760 Dale Murphy	1.25	.50
❑ 761 Gary Lucas	.15	.06
❑ 762 Cliff Johnson	.15	.06
❑ 763 Al Cowens	.15	.06
❑ 764 Pete Falcone	.15	.06
❑ 765 Bob Boone	.30	.12
❑ 766 Barry Bonnell	.15	.06
❑ 767 Duane Kuiper	.15	.06
❑ 768 Chris Speier	.15	.06
❑ 769 Checklist: 661-792	.30	.12
❑ 770 Dave Winfield	.60	.24
❑ 771 Kent Hrbek Bobby Castillo TL	.30	.12
❑ 772 Jim Kern	.15	.06
❑ 773 Larry Hisle	.15	.06
❑ 774 Alan Ashby	.15	.06
❑ 775 Burt Hooton	.15	.06
❑ 776 Larry Parrish	.15	.06
❑ 777 John Curtis	.15	.06
❑ 778 Rich Hebner	.30	.12
❑ 779 Rick Waits	.15	.06
❑ 780 Gary Matthews	.30	.12
❑ 781 Rick Rhoden	.15	.06
❑ 782 Bobby Murcer	.30	.12
❑ 783 Bobby Murcer SV	.15	.06
❑ 784 Jeff Newman	.15	.06
❑ 785 Dennis Leonard	.15	.06
❑ 786 Ralph Houk MG	.15	.06
❑ 787 Dick Tidrow	.15	.06
❑ 788 Dane Iorg	.15	.06
❑ 789 Bryan Clark	.15	.06
❑ 790 Bob Grich	.30	.12
❑ 791 Gary Lavelle	.15	.06
❑ 792 Chris Chambliss	.30	.12
❑ XX Game Insert Card	.10	.04

1983 Topps Traded

	Nm-Mt	Ex-Mt
COMP.FACT.SET (132)	40.00	16.00
❑ 1T Neil Allen	.25	.10
❑ 2T Bill Almon	.25	.10
❑ 3T Joe Altobelli MG	.25	.10
❑ 4T Tony Armas	.25	.10
❑ 5T Doug Bair	.25	.10
❑ 6T Steve Baker	.25	.10
❑ 7T Floyd Bannister	.25	.10
❑ 8T Don Baylor	2.00	.80
❑ 9T Tony Bernazard	.25	.10
❑ 10T Larry Biittner	.25	.10
❑ 11T Dann Bilardello	.25	.10
❑ 12T Doug Bird	.25	.10
❑ 13T Steve Boros MG	.25	.10
❑ 14T Greg Brock	.25	.10
❑ 15T Mike C. Brown	.25	.10
❑ 16T Tom Burgmeier	.25	.10
❑ 17T Randy Bush	.25	.10
❑ 18T Bert Campaneris	1.00	.40
❑ 19T Ron Cey	1.00	.40
❑ 20T Chris Codiroli	.25	.10
❑ 21T Dave Collins	.25	.10
❑ 22T Terry Crowley	.25	.10
❑ 23T Julio Cruz	.25	.10
❑ 24T Mike Davis	.25	.10
❑ 25T Frank DiPino	.25	.10
❑ 26T Bill Doran XRC	1.00	.40
❑ 27T Jerry Dybzinski	.25	.10
❑ 28T Jamie Easterly	.25	.10
❑ 29T Juan Eichelberger	.25	.10
❑ 30T Jim Essian	.25	.10
❑ 31T Pete Falcone	.25	.10
❑ 32T Mike Ferraro MG	.25	.10
❑ 33T Terry Forster	.25	.10
❑ 34T Julio Franco XRC	4.00	1.60
❑ 35T Rich Gale	.25	.10
❑ 36T Kiko Garcia	.25	.10
❑ 37T Steve Garvey	1.00	.40
❑ 38T Johnny Grubb	.25	.10
❑ 39T Mel Hall XRC*	1.00	.40
❑ 40T Von Hayes	1.00	.40
❑ 41T Danny Heep	.25	.10
❑ 42T Steve Henderson	.25	.10
❑ 43T Keith Hernandez	2.00	.80
❑ 44T Leo Hernandez	.25	.10
❑ 45T Willie Hernandez	1.00	.40
❑ 46T Al Holland	.25	.10
❑ 47T Frank Howard MG	1.00	.40
❑ 48T Bobby Johnson	.25	.10
❑ 49T Cliff Johnson	.25	.10
❑ 50T Odell Jones	.25	.10
❑ 51T Mike Jorgensen	.25	.10
❑ 52T Bob Kearney	.25	.10
❑ 53T Steve Kemp	.25	.10
❑ 54T Matt Keough	.25	.10
❑ 55T Ron Kittle XRC*	2.00	.80
❑ 56T Mickey Klutts	.25	.10
❑ 57T Alan Knicely	.25	.10
❑ 58T Mike Krukow	.25	.10
❑ 59T Rafael Landestoy	.25	.10
❑ 60T Carney Lansford	1.00	.40
❑ 61T Joe Lefebvre	.25	.10
❑ 62T Bryan Little	.25	.10
❑ 63T Aurelio Lopez	.25	.10
❑ 64T Mike Madden	.25	.10
❑ 65T Rick Manning	.25	.10
❑ 66T Billy Martin MG	1.00	.40
❑ 67T Lee Mazzilli	.25	.10
❑ 68T Andy McGaffigan	.25	.10
❑ 69T Craig McMurtry	.25	.10
❑ 70T John McNamara MG	.25	.10
❑ 71T Orlando Mercado	.25	.10
❑ 72T Larry Milbourne	.25	.10
❑ 73T Randy Moffitt	.25	.10
❑ 74T Sid Monge	.25	.10
❑ 75T Jose Morales	.25	.10
❑ 76T Omar Moreno	.25	.10
❑ 77T Joe Morgan	2.00	.80
❑ 78T Mike Morgan	.25	.10
❑ 79T Dale Murray	.25	.10
❑ 80T Jeff Newman	.25	.10
❑ 81T Pete O'Brien XRC	1.00	.40
❑ 82T Jorge Orta	.25	.10
❑ 83T Alejandro Pena XRC	1.00	.40
❑ 84T Pascual Perez	.25	.10
❑ 85T Tony Perez	2.00	.80
❑ 86T Broderick Perkins	.25	.10
❑ 87T Tony Phillips XRC	2.00	.80
❑ 88T Charlie Puleo	.25	.10
❑ 89T Pat Putnam	.25	.10
❑ 90T Jamie Quirk	.25	.10
❑ 91T Doug Rader MG	.25	.10
❑ 92T Chuck Rainey	.25	.10
❑ 93T Bobby Ramos	.25	.10
❑ 94T Gary Redus XRC	1.00	.40
❑ 95T Steve Renko	.25	.10
❑ 96T Leon Roberts	.25	.10
❑ 97T Aurelio Rodriguez	.25	.10
❑ 98T Dick Ruthven	.25	.10
❑ 99T Daryl Sconiers	.25	.10
❑ 100T Mike Scott	1.00	.40
❑ 101T Tom Seaver	2.00	.80
❑ 102T John Shelby	.25	.10
❑ 103T Bob Shirley	.25	.10
❑ 104T Joe Simpson	.25	.10
❑ 105T Doug Sisk	.25	.10
❑ 106T Mike Smithson	.25	.10
❑ 107T Elias Sosa	.25	.10
❑ 108T D.Strawberry XRC	10.00	4.00
❑ 109T Tom Tellmann	.25	.10
❑ 110T Gene Tenace	1.00	.40
❑ 111T Gorman Thomas	.25	.10
❑ 112T Dick Tidrow	.25	.10
❑ 113T Dave Tobik	.25	.10

Card	Nm-Mt	Ex-Mt
❑ 114T Wayne Tolleson	.25	.10
❑ 115T Mike Torrez	.25	.10
❑ 116T Manny Trillo	.25	.10
❑ 117T Steve Trout	.25	.10
❑ 118T Lee Tunnell	.25	.10
❑ 119T Mike Vail	.25	.10
❑ 120T Ellis Valentine	.25	.10
❑ 121T Tom Veryzer	.25	.10
❑ 122T George Vukovich	.25	.10
❑ 123T Rick Waits	.25	.10
❑ 124T Greg Walker	1.00	.40
❑ 125T Chris Welsh	.25	.10
❑ 126T Len Whitehouse	.25	.10
❑ 127T Eddie Whitson	.25	.10
❑ 128T Jim Wohlford	.25	.10
❑ 129T Matt Young	.25	.10
❑ 130T Joel Youngblood	.25	.10
❑ 131T Pat Zachry	.25	.10
❑ 132T Checklist 1T-132T	.25	.10

1984 Topps

Card	Nm-Mt	Ex-Mt
COMPLETE SET (792)	50.00	20.00
❑ 1 Steve Carlton HL	.25	.10
❑ 2 Rickey Henderson HL	.60	.24
❑ 3 Dan Quisenberry HL	.15	.06
❑ 4 Nolan Ryan HL	1.00	.40
Steve Carlton		
Gaylord Perry		
❑ 5 Dave Righetti HL	.25	.10
Bob Forsch		
Mike Warren		
❑ 6 Johnny Bench HL	.40	.16
Gaylord Perry		
Carl Yastrzemski		
❑ 7 Gary Lucas	.15	.06
❑ 8 Don Mattingly RC	15.00	6.00
❑ 9 Jim Gott	.15	.06
❑ 10 Robin Yount	.60	.24
❑ 11 Kent Hrbek	.25	.10
Ken Schrom TL		
❑ 12 Billy Sample	.15	.06
❑ 13 Scott Holman	.15	.06
❑ 14 Tom Brookens	.25	.10
❑ 15 Burt Hooton	.15	.06
❑ 16 Omar Moreno	.15	.06
❑ 17 John Denny	.15	.06
❑ 18 Dale Berra	.15	.06
❑ 19 Ray Fontenot	.15	.06
❑ 20 Greg Luzinski	.25	.10
❑ 21 Joe Altobelli MG	.15	.06
❑ 22 Bryan Clark	.15	.06
❑ 23 Keith Moreland	.15	.06
❑ 24 John Martin	.15	.06
❑ 25 Glenn Hubbard	.15	.06
❑ 26 Bud Black	.15	.06
❑ 27 Daryl Sconiers	.15	.06
❑ 28 Frank Viola	.40	.16
❑ 29 Danny Heep	.15	.06
❑ 30 Wade Boggs	1.50	.60
❑ 31 Andy McGaffigan	.15	.06
❑ 32 Bobby Ramos	.15	.06
❑ 33 Tom Burgmeier	.15	.06
❑ 34 Eddie Milner	.15	.06
❑ 35 Don Sutton	.60	.24
❑ 36 Denny Walling	.15	.06
❑ 37 Buddy Bell	.25	.10
Rick Honeycutt TL		
❑ 38 Luis DeLeon	.15	.06
❑ 39 Garth Iorg	.15	.06
❑ 40 Dusty Baker	.25	.10
❑ 41 Tony Bernazard	.15	.06
❑ 42 Johnny Grubb	.15	.06
❑ 43 Ron Reed	.15	.06
❑ 44 Jim Morrison	.15	.06
❑ 45 Jerry Mumphrey	.15	.06
❑ 46 Ray Smith	.15	.06
❑ 47 Rudy Law	.15	.06
❑ 48 Julio Franco	.40	.16
❑ 49 John Stuper	.15	.06
❑ 50 Chris Chambliss	.25	.10
❑ 51 Jim Frey MG	.15	.06
❑ 52 Paul Splittorff	.15	.06
❑ 53 Juan Beniquez	.15	.06
❑ 54 Jesse Orosco	.15	.06
❑ 55 Dave Concepcion	.25	.10
❑ 56 Gary Allenson	.15	.06
❑ 57 Dan Schatzeder	.15	.06
❑ 58 Max Venable	.15	.06
❑ 59 Sammy Stewart	.15	.06
❑ 60 Paul Molitor UER	.40	.16
('83 stats .272, 613, 167; should be .270, 608, 164)		
❑ 61 Chris Codiroli	.15	.06
❑ 62 Dave Hostetler	.15	.06
❑ 63 Ed VandeBerg	.15	.06
❑ 64 Mike Scioscia	.15	.06
❑ 65 Kirk Gibson	.60	.24
❑ 66 Jose Cruz	1.00	.40
Nolan Ryan TL		
❑ 67 Gary Ward	.15	.06
❑ 68 Luis Salazar	.15	.06
❑ 69 Rod Scurry	.15	.06
❑ 70 Gary Matthews	.25	.10
❑ 71 Leo Hernandez	.15	.06
❑ 72 Mike Squires	.15	.06
❑ 73 Jody Davis	.15	.06
❑ 74 Jerry Martin	.15	.06
❑ 75 Bob Forsch	.15	.06
❑ 76 Alfredo Griffin	.15	.06
❑ 77 Brett Butler	.40	.16
❑ 78 Mike Torrez	.15	.06
❑ 79 Rob Wilfong	.15	.06
❑ 80 Steve Rogers	.15	.06
❑ 81 Billy Martin MG	.25	.10
❑ 82 Doug Bird	.15	.06
❑ 83 Richie Zisk	.15	.06
❑ 84 Lenny Faedo	.15	.06
❑ 85 Atlee Hammaker	.15	.06
❑ 86 John Shelby	.15	.06
❑ 87 Frank Pastore	.15	.06
❑ 88 Rob Picciolo	.15	.06
❑ 89 Mike Smithson	.15	.06
❑ 90 Pedro Guerrero	.25	.10
❑ 91 Dan Spillner	.15	.06
❑ 92 Lloyd Moseby	.15	.06
❑ 93 Bob Knepper	.15	.06
❑ 94 Mario Ramirez	.15	.06
❑ 95 Aurelio Lopez	.25	.10
❑ 96 Hal McRae	.25	.10
Larry Gura TL		
❑ 97 LaMarr Hoyt	.15	.06
❑ 98 Steve Nicosia	.15	.06
❑ 99 Craig Lefferts RC	.15	.06
❑ 100 Reggie Jackson	.40	.16
❑ 101 Porfirio Altamirano	.15	.06
❑ 102 Ken Oberkfell	.15	.06
❑ 103 Dwayne Murphy	.15	.06
❑ 104 Ken Dayley	.15	.06
❑ 105 Tony Armas	.15	.06
❑ 106 Tim Stoddard	.15	.06
❑ 107 Ned Yost	.15	.06
❑ 108 Randy Moffitt	.15	.06
❑ 109 Brad Wellman	.15	.06
❑ 110 Ron Guidry	.25	.10
❑ 111 Bill Virdon MG	.15	.06
❑ 112 Tom Niedenfuer	.15	.06
❑ 113 Kelly Paris	.15	.06
❑ 114 Checklist 1-132	.25	.10
❑ 115 Andre Thornton	.15	.06
❑ 116 George Bjorkman	.15	.06
❑ 117 Tom Veryzer	.15	.06
❑ 118 Charlie Hough	.25	.10
❑ 119 John Wockenfuss	.15	.06
❑ 120 Keith Hernandez	.40	.16
❑ 121 Pat Sheridan	.15	.06
❑ 122 Cecilio Guante	.15	.06
❑ 123 Butch Wynegar	.15	.06
❑ 124 Damaso Garcia	.15	.06
❑ 125 Britt Burns	.15	.06
❑ 126 Dale Murphy	.40	.16
Craig McMurtry TL		
❑ 127 Mike Madden	.15	.06
❑ 128 Rick Manning	.15	.06
❑ 129 Bill Laskey	.15	.06
❑ 130 Ozzie Smith	.75	.30
❑ 131 Bill Madlock	.60	.24
Wade Boggs LL		
❑ 132 Mike Schmidt	.60	.24
Jim Rice LL		
❑ 133 Dale Murphy	.40	.16
Cecil Cooper		
Jim Rice LL		
❑ 134 Tim Raines	.60	.24
Rickey Henderson LL		
❑ 135 John Denny	.60	.24
LaMarr Hoyt LL		
❑ 136 Steve Carlton	.25	.10
Jack Morris LL		
❑ 137 Atlee Hammaker	.25	.10
Rick Honeycutt LL		
❑ 138 Al Holland	.25	.10
Dan Quisenberry LL		
❑ 139 Bert Campaneris	.25	.10
❑ 140 Storm Davis	.15	.06
❑ 141 Pat Corrales MG	.15	.06
❑ 142 Rich Gale	.15	.06
❑ 143 Jose Morales	.15	.06
❑ 144 Brian Harper RC	.25	.10
❑ 145 Gary Lavelle	.15	.06
❑ 146 Ed Romero	.15	.06
❑ 147 Dan Petry	.25	.10
❑ 148 Joe Lefebvre	.15	.06
❑ 149 Jon Matlack	.15	.06
❑ 150 Dale Murphy	.60	.24
❑ 151 Steve Trout	.15	.06
❑ 152 Glenn Brummer	.15	.06
❑ 153 Dick Tidrow	.15	.06
❑ 154 Dave Henderson	.25	.10
❑ 155 Frank White	.25	.10
❑ 156 Rickey Henderson	.60	.24
Tim Conroy TL		
❑ 157 Gary Gaetti	.40	.16
❑ 158 John Curtis	.15	.06
❑ 159 Darryl Cias	.15	.06
❑ 160 Mario Soto	.15	.06
❑ 161 Junior Ortiz	.15	.06
❑ 162 Bob Ojeda	.15	.06
❑ 163 Lorenzo Gray	.15	.06
❑ 164 Scott Sanderson	.15	.06
❑ 165 Ken Singleton	.15	.06
❑ 166 Jamie Nelson	.15	.06
❑ 167 Marshall Edwards	.15	.06
❑ 168 Juan Bonilla	.15	.06
❑ 169 Larry Parrish	.15	.06
❑ 170 Jerry Reuss	.15	.06
❑ 171 Frank Robinson MG	.40	.16
❑ 172 Frank DiPino	.15	.06
❑ 173 Marvell Wynne	.15	.06
❑ 174 Juan Berenguer	.15	.06
❑ 175 Graig Nettles	.25	.10
❑ 176 Lee Smith	.60	.24
❑ 177 Jerry Hairston	.15	.06
❑ 178 Bill Krueger RC	.15	.06
❑ 179 Buck Martinez	.15	.06
❑ 180 Manny Trillo	.15	.06
❑ 181 Roy Thomas	.15	.06
❑ 182 Darryl Strawberry RC	1.00	.40
❑ 183 Al Williams	.15	.06
❑ 184 Mike O'Berry	.15	.06
❑ 185 Sixto Lezcano	.15	.06
❑ 186 Lonnie Smith	.25	.10
John Stuper TL		
❑ 187 Luis Aponte	.15	.06
❑ 188 Bryan Little	.15	.06
❑ 189 Tim Conroy	.15	.06
❑ 190 Ben Oglivie	.15	.06

	Card	Player	Price 1	Price 2
❑	191	Mike Boddicker	.15	.06
❑	192	Nick Esasky	.15	.06
❑	193	Darrell Brown	.15	.06
❑	194	Domingo Ramos	.15	.06
❑	195	Jack Morris	.60	.24
❑	196	Don Slaught	.25	.10
❑	197	Garry Hancock	.15	.06
❑	198	Bill Doran RC*	.25	.10
❑	199	Willie Hernandez	.25	.10
❑	200	Andre Dawson	.25	.10
❑	201	Bruce Kison	.15	.06
❑	202	Bobby Cox MG	.25	.10
❑	203	Matt Keough	.15	.06
❑	204	Bobby Meacham	.15	.06
❑	205	Greg Minton	.15	.06
❑	206	Andy Van Slyke RC	.60	.24
❑	207	Donnie Moore	.15	.06
❑	208	Jose Oquendo RC	.25	.10
❑	209	Manny Sarmiento	.15	.06
❑	210	Joe Morgan	.40	.16
❑	211	Rick Sweet	.15	.06
❑	212	Broderick Perkins	.15	.06
❑	213	Bruce Hurst	.15	.06
❑	214	Paul Householder	.15	.06
❑	215	Tippy Martinez	.15	.06
❑	216	Carlton Fisk Richard Dotson TL	.25	.10
❑	217	Alan Ashby	.15	.06
❑	218	Rick Waits	.15	.06
❑	219	Joe Simpson	.15	.06
❑	220	Fernando Valenzuela	.25	.10
❑	221	Cliff Johnson	.15	.06
❑	222	Rick Honeycutt	.15	.06
❑	223	Wayne Krenchicki	.15	.06
❑	224	Sid Monge	.15	.06
❑	225	Lee Mazzilli	.15	.06
❑	226	Juan Eichelberger	.15	.06
❑	227	Steve Braun	.15	.06
❑	228	John Rabb	.15	.06
❑	229	Paul Owens MG	.15	.06
❑	230	Rickey Henderson	1.25	.50
❑	231	Gary Woods	.15	.06
❑	232	Tim Wallach	.25	.10
❑	233	Checklist 133-264	.25	.10
❑	234	Rafael Ramirez	.15	.06
❑	235	Matt Young	.15	.06
❑	236	Ellis Valentine	.15	.06
❑	237	John Castino	.15	.06
❑	238	Reid Nichols	.15	.06
❑	239	Jay Howell	.15	.06
❑	240	Eddie Murray	.60	.24
❑	241	Bill Almon	.15	.06
❑	242	Alex Trevino	.15	.06
❑	243	Pete Ladd	.15	.06
❑	244	Candy Maldonado	.15	.06
❑	245	Rick Sutcliffe	.25	.10
❑	246	Mookie Wilson Tom Seaver TL	.40	.16
❑	247	Onix Concepcion	.15	.06
❑	248	Bill Dawley	.15	.06
❑	249	Jay Johnstone	.25	.10
❑	250	Bill Madlock	.25	.10
❑	251	Tony Gwynn	2.50	1.00
❑	252	Larry Christenson	.15	.06
❑	253	Jim Wohlford	.15	.06
❑	254	Shane Rawley	.15	.06
❑	255	Bruce Benedict	.15	.06
❑	256	Dave Geisel	.15	.06
❑	257	Julio Cruz	.15	.06
❑	258	Luis Sanchez	.15	.06
❑	259	Sparky Anderson MG	.40	.16
❑	260	Scott McGregor	.15	.06
❑	261	Bobby Brown	.15	.06
❑	262	Tom Candiotti RC	.60	.24
❑	263	Jack Fimple	.15	.06
❑	264	Doug Frobel	.15	.06
❑	265	Donnie Hill	.15	.06
❑	266	Steve Lubratich	.15	.06
❑	267	Carmelo Martinez	.15	.06
❑	268	Jack O'Connor	.15	.06
❑	269	Aurelio Rodriguez	.15	.06
❑	270	Jeff Russell RC	.25	.10
❑	271	Moose Haas	.15	.06
❑	272	Rick Dempsey	.15	.06
❑	273	Charlie Puleo	.15	.06
❑	274	Rick Monday	.15	.06
❑	275	Len Matuszek	.15	.06
❑	276	Rod Carew Geoff Zahn TL	.25	.10
❑	277	Eddie Whitson	.15	.06
❑	278	Jorge Bell	.40	.16
❑	279	Ivan DeJesus	.15	.06
❑	280	Floyd Bannister	.15	.06
❑	281	Larry Milbourne	.15	.06
❑	282	Jim Barr	.15	.06
❑	283	Larry Biittner	.15	.06
❑	284	Howard Bailey	.15	.06
❑	285	Darrell Porter	.15	.06
❑	286	Lary Sorensen	.15	.06
❑	287	Warren Cromartie	.15	.06
❑	288	Jim Beattie	.15	.06
❑	289	Randy Johnson	.15	.06
❑	290	Dave Dravecky	.25	.10
❑	291	Chuck Tanner MG	.15	.06
❑	292	Tony Scott	.15	.06
❑	293	Ed Lynch	.15	.06
❑	294	U.L. Washington	.15	.06
❑	295	Mike Flanagan	.15	.06
❑	296	Jeff Newman	.15	.06
❑	297	Bruce Berenyi	.15	.06
❑	298	Jim Gantner	.15	.06
❑	299	John Butcher	.15	.06
❑	300	Pete Rose	2.00	.80
❑	301	Frank LaCorte	.15	.06
❑	302	Barry Bonnell	.15	.06
❑	303	Marty Castillo	.15	.06
❑	304	Warren Brusstar	.15	.06
❑	305	Roy Smalley	.15	.06
❑	306	Pedro Guerrero Bob Welch TL	.25	.10
❑	307	Bobby Mitchell	.15	.06
❑	308	Ron Hassey	.15	.06
❑	309	Tony Phillips RC	.60	.24
❑	310	Willie McGee	.40	.16
❑	311	Jerry Koosman	.25	.10
❑	312	Jorge Orta	.15	.06
❑	313	Mike Jorgensen	.15	.06
❑	314	Orlando Mercado	.15	.06
❑	315	Bobby Grich	.25	.10
❑	316	Mark Bradley	.15	.06
❑	317	Greg Pryor	.15	.06
❑	318	Bill Gullickson	.15	.06
❑	319	Al Bumbry	.15	.06
❑	320	Bob Stanley	.15	.06
❑	321	Harvey Kuenn MG	.25	.10
❑	322	Ken Schrom	.15	.06
❑	323	Alan Knicely	.15	.06
❑	324	Alejandro Pena RC*	.25	.10
❑	325	Darrell Evans	.25	.10
❑	326	Bob Kearney	.15	.06
❑	327	Ruppert Jones	.15	.06
❑	328	Vern Ruhle	.15	.06
❑	329	Pat Tabler	.15	.06
❑	330	John Candelaria	.15	.06
❑	331	Bucky Dent	.25	.10
❑	332	Kevin Gross RC	.15	.06
❑	333	Larry Herndon	.25	.10
❑	334	Chuck Rainey	.15	.06
❑	335	Don Baylor	.40	.16
❑	336	Pat Putnam Matt Young TL	.25	.10
❑	337	Kevin Hagen	.15	.06
❑	338	Mike Warren	.15	.06
❑	339	Roy Lee Jackson	.15	.06
❑	340	Hal McRae	.25	.10
❑	341	Dave Tobik	.15	.06
❑	342	Tim Foli	.15	.06
❑	343	Mark Davis	.15	.06
❑	344	Rick Miller	.15	.06
❑	345	Kent Hrbek	.25	.10
❑	346	Kurt Bevacqua	.15	.06
❑	347	Allan Ramirez	.15	.06
❑	348	Toby Harrah	.25	.10
❑	349	Bob L. Gibson RC	.15	.06
❑	350	George Foster	.25	.10
❑	351	Russ Nixon MG	.15	.06
❑	352	Dave Stewart	.25	.10
❑	353	Jim Anderson	.15	.06
❑	354	Jeff Burroughs	.15	.06
❑	355	Jason Thompson	.15	.06
❑	356	Glenn Abbott	.15	.06
❑	357	Ron Cey	.25	.10
❑	358	Bob Dernier	.15	.06
❑	359	Jim Acker	.15	.06
❑	360	Willie Randolph	.25	.10
❑	361	Dave Smith	.15	.06
❑	362	David Green	.15	.06
❑	363	Tim Laudner	.15	.06
❑	364	Scott Fletcher	.15	.06
❑	365	Steve Bedrosian	.15	.06
❑	366	Terry Kennedy Dave Dravecky TL	.25	.10
❑	367	Jamie Easterly	.15	.06
❑	368	Hubie Brooks	.15	.06
❑	369	Steve McCatty	.15	.06
❑	370	Tim Raines	.40	.16
❑	371	Dave Gumpert	.15	.06
❑	372	Gary Roenicke	.15	.06
❑	373	Bill Scherrer	.15	.06
❑	374	Don Money	.15	.06
❑	375	Dennis Leonard	.15	.06
❑	376	Dave Anderson RC	.15	.06
❑	377	Danny Darwin	.15	.06
❑	378	Bob Brenly	.15	.06
❑	379	Checklist 265-396	.25	.10
❑	380	Steve Garvey	.25	.10
❑	381	Ralph Houk MG	.25	.10
❑	382	Chris Nyman	.15	.06
❑	383	Terry Puhl	.15	.06
❑	384	Lee Tunnell	.15	.06
❑	385	Tony Perez	.40	.16
❑	386	George Hendrick AS	.15	.06
❑	387	Johnny Ray AS	.15	.06
❑	388	Mike Schmidt AS	.60	.24
❑	389	Ozzie Smith AS	.60	.24
❑	390	Tim Raines AS	.25	.10
❑	391	Dale Murphy AS	.40	.16
❑	392	Andre Dawson AS	.15	.06
❑	393	Gary Carter AS	.25	.10
❑	394	Steve Rogers AS	.15	.06
❑	395	Steve Carlton AS	.25	.10
❑	396	Jesse Orosco AS	.15	.06
❑	397	Eddie Murray AS	.40	.16
❑	398	Lou Whitaker AS	.25	.10
❑	399	George Brett AS	.60	.24
❑	400	Cal Ripken AS	2.00	.80
❑	401	Jim Rice AS	.15	.06
❑	402	Dave Winfield AS	.25	.10
❑	403	Lloyd Moseby AS	.15	.06
❑	404	Ted Simmons AS	.15	.06
❑	405	LaMarr Hoyt AS	.15	.06
❑	406	Ron Guidry AS	.15	.06
❑	407	Dan Quisenberry AS	.15	.06
❑	408	Lou Piniella	.25	.10
❑	409	Juan Agosto	.15	.06
❑	410	Claudell Washington	.15	.06
❑	411	Houston Jimenez	.15	.06
❑	412	Doug Rader MG	.15	.06
❑	413	Spike Owen RC	.25	.10
❑	414	Mitchell Page	.15	.06
❑	415	Tommy John	.40	.16
❑	416	Dane Iorg	.15	.06
❑	417	Mike Armstrong	.15	.06
❑	418	Ron Hodges	.15	.06
❑	419	John Henry Johnson	.15	.06
❑	420	Cecil Cooper	.25	.10
❑	421	Charlie Lea	.15	.06
❑	422	Jose Cruz	.25	.10
❑	423	Mike Morgan	.15	.06
❑	424	Dann Bilardello	.15	.06
❑	425	Steve Howe	.15	.06
❑	426	Cal Ripken Mike Boddicker TL	1.50	.60
❑	427	Rick Leach	.15	.06
❑	428	Fred Breining	.15	.06
❑	429	Randy Bush	.15	.06
❑	430	Rusty Staub	.25	.10
❑	431	Chris Bando	.15	.06
❑	432	Charles Hudson	.15	.06
❑	433	Rich Hebner	.15	.06
❑	434	Harold Baines	.60	.24
❑	435	Neil Allen	.15	.06
❑	436	Rick Peters	.15	.06
❑	437	Mike Proly	.15	.06
❑	438	Biff Pocoroba	.15	.06
❑	439	Bob Stoddard	.15	.06
❑	440	Steve Kemp	.15	.06
❑	441	Bob Lillis MG	.15	.06

No.	Player		
❑ 442	Byron McLaughlin	.15	.06
❑ 443	Benny Ayala	.15	.06
❑ 444	Steve Renko	.15	.06
❑ 445	Jerry Remy	.15	.06
❑ 446	Luis Pujols	.15	.06
❑ 447	Tom Brunansky	.25	.10
❑ 448	Ben Hayes	.15	.06
❑ 449	Joe Pettini	.15	.06
❑ 450	Gary Carter	.40	.16
❑ 451	Bob Jones	.15	.06
❑ 452	Chuck Porter	.15	.06
❑ 453	Willie Upshaw	.15	.06
❑ 454	Joe Beckwith	.15	.06
❑ 455	Terry Kennedy	.15	.06
❑ 456	Keith Moreland Fergie Jenkins TL	.15	.06
❑ 457	Dave Rozema	.15	.06
❑ 458	Kiko Garcia	.15	.06
❑ 459	Kevin Hickey	.15	.06
❑ 460	Dave Winfield	.40	.16
❑ 461	Jim Maler	.15	.06
❑ 462	Lee Lacy	.15	.06
❑ 463	Dave Engle	.15	.06
❑ 464	Jeff A. Jones	.15	.06
❑ 465	Mookie Wilson	.25	.10
❑ 466	Gene Garber	.15	.06
❑ 467	Mike Ramsey	.15	.06
❑ 468	Geoff Zahn	.15	.06
❑ 469	Tom O'Malley	.15	.06
❑ 470	Nolan Ryan	3.00	1.20
❑ 471	Dick Howser MG	.15	.06
❑ 472	Mike G. Brown RC	.15	.06
❑ 473	Jim Dwyer	.15	.06
❑ 474	Greg Bargar	.15	.06
❑ 475	Gary Redus RC*	.15	.06
❑ 476	Tom Tellmann	.15	.06
❑ 477	Rafael Landestoy	.15	.06
❑ 478	Alan Bannister	.15	.06
❑ 479	Frank Tanana	.25	.10
❑ 480	Ron Kittle	.15	.06
❑ 481	Mark Thurmond	.15	.06
❑ 482	Enos Cabell	.15	.06
❑ 483	Fergie Jenkins	.25	.10
❑ 484	Ozzie Virgil	.15	.06
❑ 485	Rick Rhoden	.15	.06
❑ 486	Don Baylor Ron Guidry TL	.25	.10
❑ 487	Ricky Adams	.15	.06
❑ 488	Jesse Barfield	.25	.10
❑ 489	Dave Von Ohlen	.15	.06
❑ 490	Cal Ripken	4.00	1.60
❑ 491	Bobby Castillo	.15	.06
❑ 492	Tucker Ashford	.15	.06
❑ 493	Mike Norris	.15	.06
❑ 494	Chili Davis	.40	.16
❑ 495	Rollie Fingers	.25	.10
❑ 496	Terry Francona	.15	.06
❑ 497	Bud Anderson	.15	.06
❑ 498	Rich Gedman	.15	.06
❑ 499	Mike Witt	.15	.06
❑ 500	George Brett	2.00	.80
❑ 501	Steve Henderson	.15	.06
❑ 502	Joe Torre MG	.25	.10
❑ 503	Elias Sosa	.15	.06
❑ 504	Mickey Rivers	.15	.06
❑ 505	Pete Vuckovich	.15	.06
❑ 506	Ernie Whitt	.15	.06
❑ 507	Mike LaCoss	.15	.06
❑ 508	Mel Hall	.25	.10
❑ 509	Brad Havens	.15	.06
❑ 510	Alan Trammell	.40	.16
❑ 511	Marty Bystrom	.15	.06
❑ 512	Oscar Gamble	.15	.06
❑ 513	Dave Beard	.15	.06
❑ 514	Floyd Rayford	.15	.06
❑ 515	Gorman Thomas	.15	.06
❑ 516	Al Oliver Charlie Lea TL	.25	.10
❑ 517	John Moses	.15	.06
❑ 518	Greg Walker	.25	.10
❑ 519	Ron Davis	.15	.06
❑ 520	Bob Boone	.25	.10
❑ 521	Pete Falcone	.15	.06
❑ 522	Dave Bergman	.15	.06
❑ 523	Glenn Hoffman	.15	.06
❑ 524	Carlos Diaz	.15	.06
❑ 525	Willie Wilson	.15	.06
❑ 526	Ron Oester	.15	.06
❑ 527	Checklist 397-528	.25	.10
❑ 528	Mark Brouhard	.15	.06
❑ 529	Keith Atherton	.15	.06
❑ 530	Dan Ford	.15	.06
❑ 531	Steve Boros MG	.15	.06
❑ 532	Eric Show	.15	.06
❑ 533	Ken Landreaux	.15	.06
❑ 534	Pete O'Brien RC*	.25	.10
❑ 535	Bo Diaz	.15	.06
❑ 536	Doug Bair	.15	.06
❑ 537	Johnny Ray	.15	.06
❑ 538	Kevin Bass	.15	.06
❑ 539	George Frazier	.15	.06
❑ 540	George Hendrick	.15	.06
❑ 541	Dennis Lamp	.15	.06
❑ 542	Duane Kuiper	.15	.06
❑ 543	Craig McMurtry	.15	.06
❑ 544	Cesar Geronimo	.15	.06
❑ 545	Bill Buckner	.25	.10
❑ 546	Mike Hargrove Lary Sorensen TL	.25	.10
❑ 547	Mike Moore	.15	.06
❑ 548	Ron Jackson	.15	.06
❑ 549	Walt Terrell	.15	.06
❑ 550	Jim Rice	.25	.10
❑ 551	Scott Ullger	.15	.06
❑ 552	Ray Burris	.15	.06
❑ 553	Joe Nolan	.15	.06
❑ 554	Ted Power	.15	.06
❑ 555	Greg Brock	.15	.06
❑ 556	Joey McLaughlin	.15	.06
❑ 557	Wayne Tolleson	.15	.06
❑ 558	Mike Davis	.15	.06
❑ 559	Mike Scott	.25	.10
❑ 560	Carlton Fisk	.40	.16
❑ 561	Whitey Herzog MG	.25	.10
❑ 562	Manny Castillo	.15	.06
❑ 563	Glenn Wilson	.25	.10
❑ 564	Al Holland	.15	.06
❑ 565	Leon Durham	.15	.06
❑ 566	Jim Bibby	.15	.06
❑ 567	Mike Heath	.15	.06
❑ 568	Pete Filson	.15	.06
❑ 569	Bake McBride	.15	.06
❑ 570	Dan Quisenberry	.15	.06
❑ 571	Bruce Bochy	.15	.06
❑ 572	Jerry Royster	.15	.06
❑ 573	Dave Kingman	.40	.16
❑ 574	Brian Downing	.15	.06
❑ 575	Jim Clancy	.15	.06
❑ 576	Jeff Leonard Atlee Hammaker TL	.25	.10
❑ 577	Mark Clear	.15	.06
❑ 578	Lenn Sakata	.15	.06
❑ 579	Bob James	.15	.06
❑ 580	Lonnie Smith	.15	.06
❑ 581	Jose DeLeon RC	.15	.06
❑ 582	Bob McClure	.15	.06
❑ 583	Derrel Thomas	.15	.06
❑ 584	Dave Schmidt	.15	.06
❑ 585	Dan Driessen	.15	.06
❑ 586	Joe Niekro	.25	.10
❑ 587	Von Hayes	.15	.06
❑ 588	Milt Wilcox	.15	.06
❑ 589	Mike Easler	.15	.06
❑ 590	Dave Stieb	.15	.06
❑ 591	Tony LaRussa MG	.25	.10
❑ 592	Andre Robertson	.15	.06
❑ 593	Jeff Lahti	.15	.06
❑ 594	Gene Richards	.15	.06
❑ 595	Jeff Reardon	.25	.10
❑ 596	Ryne Sandberg	2.50	1.00
❑ 597	Rick Camp	.15	.06
❑ 598	Rusty Kuntz	.15	.06
❑ 599	Doug Sisk	.15	.06
❑ 600	Rod Carew	.40	.16
❑ 601	John Tudor	.15	.06
❑ 602	John Wathan	.15	.06
❑ 603	Renie Martin	.15	.06
❑ 604	John Lowenstein	.15	.06
❑ 605	Mike Caldwell	.15	.06
❑ 606	Lloyd Moseby Dave Stieb TL	.25	.10
❑ 607	Tom Hume	.15	.06
❑ 608	Bobby Johnson	.15	.06
❑ 609	Dan Meyer	.15	.06
❑ 610	Steve Sax	.25	.10
❑ 611	Chet Lemon	.15	.06
❑ 612	Harry Spilman	.15	.06
❑ 613	Greg Gross	.15	.06
❑ 614	Len Barker	.15	.06
❑ 615	Garry Templeton	.15	.06
❑ 616	Don Robinson	.15	.06
❑ 617	Rick Cerone	.15	.06
❑ 618	Dickie Noles	.15	.06
❑ 619	Jerry Dybzinski	.15	.06
❑ 620	Al Oliver	.25	.10
❑ 621	Frank Howard MG	.25	.10
❑ 622	Al Cowens	.15	.06
❑ 623	Ron Washington	.15	.06
❑ 624	Terry Harper	.15	.06
❑ 625	Larry Gura	.15	.06
❑ 626	Bob Clark	.15	.06
❑ 627	Dave LaPoint	.15	.06
❑ 628	Ed Jurak	.15	.06
❑ 629	Rick Langford	.15	.06
❑ 630	Ted Simmons	.25	.10
❑ 631	Dennis Martinez	.25	.10
❑ 632	Tom Foley	.15	.06
❑ 633	Mike Krukow	.15	.06
❑ 634	Mike Marshall	.15	.06
❑ 635	Dave Righetti	.25	.10
❑ 636	Pat Putnam	.15	.06
❑ 637	Gary Matthews John Denny TL	.25	.10
❑ 638	George Vukovich	.15	.06
❑ 639	Rick Lysander	.15	.06
❑ 640	Lance Parrish	.40	.16
❑ 641	Mike Richardt	.15	.06
❑ 642	Tom Underwood	.15	.06
❑ 643	Mike C. Brown	.15	.06
❑ 644	Tim Lollar	.15	.06
❑ 645	Tony Pena	.15	.06
❑ 646	Checklist 529-660	.25	.10
❑ 647	Ron Roenicke	.15	.06
❑ 648	Len Whitehouse	.15	.06
❑ 649	Tom Herr	.25	.10
❑ 650	Phil Niekro	.25	.10
❑ 651	John McNamara MG	.15	.06
❑ 652	Rudy May	.15	.06
❑ 653	Dave Stapleton	.15	.06
❑ 654	Bob Bailor	.15	.06
❑ 655	Amos Otis	.25	.10
❑ 656	Bryn Smith	.15	.06
❑ 657	Thad Bosley	.15	.06
❑ 658	Jerry Augustine	.15	.06
❑ 659	Duane Walker	.15	.06
❑ 660	Ray Knight	.25	.10
❑ 661	Steve Yeager	.15	.06
❑ 662	Tom Brennan	.15	.06
❑ 663	Johnnie LeMaster	.15	.06
❑ 664	Dave Stegman	.15	.06
❑ 665	Buddy Bell	.25	.10
❑ 666	Lou Whitaker Jack Morris TL	.60	.24
❑ 667	Vance Law	.15	.06
❑ 668	Larry McWilliams	.15	.06
❑ 669	Dave Lopes	.25	.10
❑ 670	Rich Gossage	.40	.16
❑ 671	Jamie Quirk	.15	.06
❑ 672	Ricky Nelson	.15	.06
❑ 673	Mike Walters	.15	.06
❑ 674	Tim Flannery	.15	.06
❑ 675	Pascual Perez	.15	.06
❑ 676	Brian Giles	.15	.06
❑ 677	Doyle Alexander	.15	.06
❑ 678	Chris Speier	.15	.06
❑ 679	Art Howe	.25	.10
❑ 680	Fred Lynn	.25	.10
❑ 681	Tom Lasorda MG	.40	.16
❑ 682	Dan Morogiello	.15	.06
❑ 683	Marty Barrett RC	.25	.10
❑ 684	Bob Shirley	.15	.06
❑ 685	Willie Aikens	.15	.06
❑ 686	Joe Price	.15	.06
❑ 687	Roy Howell	.15	.06
❑ 688	George Wright	.15	.06
❑ 689	Mike Fischlin	.15	.06
❑ 690	Jack Clark	.25	.10
❑ 691	Steve Lake	.15	.06

		Nm-Mt	Ex-Mt
❑ 692	Dickie Thon	.15	.06
❑ 693	Alan Wiggins	.15	.06
❑ 694	Mike Stanton	.15	.06
❑ 695	Lou Whitaker	.60	.24
❑ 696	Bill Madlock Rick Rhoden TL	.25	.10
❑ 697	Dale Murray	.15	.06
❑ 698	Marc Hill	.15	.06
❑ 699	Dave Rucker	.15	.06
❑ 700	Mike Schmidt	1.50	.60
❑ 701	Bill Madlock Pete Rose Dave Parker LL	.60	.24
❑ 702	Pete Rose Rusty Staub Tony Perez LL	.60	.24
❑ 703	Mike Schmidt Tony Perez Dave Kingman LL	.60	.24
❑ 704	Tony Perez Rusty Staub Al Oliver LL	.40	.16
❑ 705	Joe Morgan Cesar Cedeno Larry Bowa LL	.40	.16
❑ 706	Steve Carlton Fergie Jenkins Tom Seaver LL	.40	.16
❑ 707	Steve Carlton Nolan Ryan Tom Seaver LL	1.50	.60
❑ 708	Tom Seaver Steve Carlton Steve Rogers LL	.40	.16
❑ 709	Bruce Sutter Tug McGraw Gene Garber LL	.25	.10
❑ 710	Rod Carew George Brett Cecil Cooper LL	.40	.16
❑ 711	Rod Carew Bert Campaneris Reggie Jackson LL	.25	.10
❑ 712	Reggie Jackson Graig Nettles Greg Luzinski LL	.25	.10
❑ 713	Reggie Jackson Ted Simmons Graig Nettles LL	.25	.10
❑ 714	Bert Campaneris Dave Lopes Omar Moreno LL	.25	.10
❑ 715	Jim Palmer Don Sutton Tommy John LL	.25	.10
❑ 716	Don Sutton Bert Blyleven Jerry Koosman LL	.60	.24
❑ 717	Jim Palmer Rollie Fingers Ron Guidry LL	.25	.10
❑ 718	Rollie Fingers Rich Gossage Dan Quisenberry LL	.25	.10
❑ 719	Andy Hassler	.15	.06
❑ 720	Dwight Evans	.25	.10
❑ 721	Del Crandall MG	.15	.06
❑ 722	Bob Welch	.15	.06
❑ 723	Rich Dauer	.15	.06
❑ 724	Eric Rasmussen	.15	.06
❑ 725	Cesar Cedeno	.25	.10
❑ 726	Ted Simmons Moose Haas TL	.25	.10
❑ 727	Joel Youngblood	.15	.06
❑ 728	Tug McGraw	.25	.10
❑ 729	Gene Tenace	.25	.10
❑ 730	Bruce Sutter	.25	.10
❑ 731	Lynn Jones	.15	.06
❑ 732	Terry Crowley	.15	.06
❑ 733	Dave Collins	.15	.06
❑ 734	Odell Jones	.15	.06
❑ 735	Rick Burleson	.15	.06
❑ 736	Dick Ruthven	.15	.06
❑ 737	Jim Essian	.15	.06
❑ 738	Bill Schroeder	.15	.06
❑ 739	Bob Watson	.25	.10
❑ 740	Tom Seaver	.60	.24
❑ 741	Wayne Gross	.15	.06
❑ 742	Dick Williams MG	.25	.10
❑ 743	Don Hood	.15	.06
❑ 744	Jamie Allen	.15	.06
❑ 745	Dennis Eckersley	.40	.16
❑ 746	Mickey Hatcher	.15	.06
❑ 747	Pat Zachry	.15	.06
❑ 748	Jeff Leonard	.15	.06
❑ 749	Doug Flynn	.15	.06
❑ 750	Jim Palmer	.25	.10
❑ 751	Charlie Moore	.15	.06
❑ 752	Phil Garner	.25	.10
❑ 753	Doug Gwosdz	.15	.06
❑ 754	Kent Tekulve	.25	.10
❑ 755	Garry Maddox	.15	.06
❑ 756	Ron Oester Mario Soto TL	.25	.10
❑ 757	Larry Bowa	.25	.10
❑ 758	Bill Stein	.15	.06
❑ 759	Richard Dotson	.15	.06
❑ 760	Bob Horner	.15	.06
❑ 761	John Montefusco	.15	.06
❑ 762	Rance Mulliniks	.15	.06
❑ 763	Craig Swan	.15	.06
❑ 764	Mike Hargrove	.25	.10
❑ 765	Ken Forsch	.15	.06
❑ 766	Mike Vail	.15	.06
❑ 767	Carney Lansford	.25	.10
❑ 768	Champ Summers	.15	.06
❑ 769	Bill Caudill	.15	.06
❑ 770	Ken Griffey	.25	.10
❑ 771	Billy Gardner MG	.15	.06
❑ 772	Jim Slaton	.15	.06
❑ 773	Todd Cruz	.15	.06
❑ 774	Tom Gorman	.15	.06
❑ 775	Dave Parker	.25	.10
❑ 776	Craig Reynolds	.15	.06
❑ 777	Tom Paciorek	.25	.10
❑ 778	Andy Hawkins	.15	.06
❑ 779	Jim Sundberg	.25	.10
❑ 780	Steve Carlton	.40	.16
❑ 781	Checklist 661-792	.25	.10
❑ 782	Steve Balboni	.15	.06
❑ 783	Luis Leal	.15	.06
❑ 784	Leon Roberts	.15	.06
❑ 785	Joaquin Andujar	.15	.06
❑ 786	Wade Boggs Bob Ojeda TL	.40	.16
❑ 787	Bill Campbell	.15	.06
❑ 788	Milt May	.15	.06
❑ 789	Bert Blyleven	.25	.10
❑ 790	Doug DeCinces	.15	.06
❑ 791	Terry Forster	.15	.06
❑ 792	Bill Russell	.15	.06

1984 Topps Traded

		Nm-Mt	Ex-Mt
COMP.FACT.SET (132)		30.00	12.00
❑ 1T	Willie Aikens	.40	.16
❑ 2T	Luis Aponte	.40	.16
❑ 3T	Mike Armstrong	.40	.16
❑ 4T	Bob Bailor	.40	.16
❑ 5T	Dusty Baker	.60	.24
❑ 6T	Steve Balboni	.40	.16
❑ 7T	Alan Bannister	.40	.16
❑ 8T	Dave Beard	.40	.16
❑ 9T	Joe Beckwith	.40	.16
❑ 10T	Bruce Berenyi	.40	.16
❑ 11T	Dave Bergman	.40	.16
❑ 12T	Tony Bernazard	.40	.16
❑ 13T	Yogi Berra MG	1.50	.60
❑ 14T	Barry Bonnell	.40	.16
❑ 15T	Phil Bradley	.60	.24
❑ 16T	Fred Breining	.40	.16
❑ 17T	Bill Buckner	.60	.24
❑ 18T	Ray Burris	.40	.16
❑ 19T	John Butcher	.40	.16
❑ 20T	Brett Butler	1.00	.40
❑ 21T	Enos Cabell	.40	.16
❑ 22T	Bill Campbell	.40	.16
❑ 23T	Bill Caudill	.40	.16
❑ 24T	Bob Clark	.40	.16
❑ 25T	Bryan Clark	.40	.16
❑ 26T	Jaime Cocanower	.40	.16
❑ 27T	Ron Darling XRC*	1.00	.40
❑ 28T	Alvin Davis XRC	.60	.24
❑ 29T	Ken Dayley	.40	.16
❑ 30T	Jeff Dedmon	.40	.16
❑ 31T	Bob Dernier	.40	.16
❑ 32T	Carlos Diaz	.40	.16
❑ 33T	Mike Easler	.40	.16
❑ 34T	Dennis Eckersley	1.00	.40
❑ 35T	Jim Essian	.40	.16
❑ 36T	Darrell Evans	.60	.24
❑ 37T	Mike Fitzgerald	.40	.16
❑ 38T	Tim Foli	.40	.16
❑ 39T	George Frazier	.40	.16
❑ 40T	Rich Gale	.40	.16
❑ 41T	Barbaro Garbey	.40	.16
❑ 42T	Dwight Gooden XRC	5.00	2.00
❑ 43T	Rich Gossage	1.00	.40
❑ 44T	Wayne Gross	.40	.16
❑ 45T	Mark Gubicza XRC	.60	.24
❑ 46T	Jackie Gutierrez	.40	.16
❑ 47T	Mel Hall	.60	.24
❑ 48T	Toby Harrah	.60	.24
❑ 49T	Ron Hassey	.40	.16
❑ 50T	Rich Hebner	.40	.16
❑ 51T	Willie Hernandez	.60	.24
❑ 52T	Ricky Horton	.40	.16
❑ 53T	Art Howe	.60	.24
❑ 54T	Dane Iorg	.40	.16
❑ 55T	Brook Jacoby	.60	.24
❑ 56T	Mike Jeffcoat	.40	.16
❑ 57T	Dave Johnson MG	.60	.24
❑ 58T	Lynn Jones	.40	.16
❑ 59T	Ruppert Jones	.40	.16
❑ 60T	Mike Jorgensen	.40	.16
❑ 61T	Bob Kearney	.40	.16
❑ 62T	Jimmy Key XRC	1.00	.40
❑ 63T	Dave Kingman	1.00	.40
❑ 64T	Jerry Koosman	.60	.24
❑ 65T	Wayne Krenchicki	.40	.16
❑ 66T	Rusty Kuntz	.40	.16
❑ 67T	Rene Lachemann MG	.40	.16
❑ 68T	Frank LaCorte	.40	.16
❑ 69T	Dennis Lamp	.40	.16
❑ 70T	Mark Langston XRC	1.00	.40
❑ 71T	Rick Leach	.40	.16
❑ 72T	Craig Lefferts	.60	.24
❑ 73T	Gary Lucas	.40	.16
❑ 74T	Jerry Martin	.40	.16
❑ 75T	Carmelo Martinez	.40	.16
❑ 76T	Mike Mason XRC	.40	.16
❑ 77T	Gary Matthews	.60	.24
❑ 78T	Andy McGaffigan	.40	.16
❑ 79T	Larry Milbourne	.40	.16
❑ 80T	Sid Monge	.40	.16
❑ 81T	Jackie Moore MG	.40	.16
❑ 82T	Joe Morgan	1.00	.40
❑ 83T	Graig Nettles	.60	.24
❑ 84T	Phil Niekro	.60	.24
❑ 85T	Ken Oberkfell	.40	.16
❑ 86T	Mike O'Berry	.40	.16
❑ 87T	Al Oliver	.60	.24
❑ 88T	Jorge Orta	.40	.16
❑ 89T	Amos Otis	.60	.24
❑ 90T	Dave Parker	.60	.24
❑ 91T	Tony Perez	1.00	.40
❑ 92T	Gerald Perry	.60	.24
❑ 93T	Gary Pettis	.40	.16

	Card	Nm-Mt	Ex-Mt
❑	94T Rob Picciolo	.40	.16
❑	95T Vern Rapp MG	.40	.16
❑	96T Floyd Rayford	.40	.16
❑	97T Randy Ready XRC	.60	.24
❑	98T Ron Reed	.40	.16
❑	99T Gene Richards	.40	.16
❑	100T Jose Rijo XRC	1.50	.60
❑	101T Jeff D. Robinson	.40	.16
❑	102T Ron Romanick	.40	.16
❑	103T Pete Rose	5.00	2.00
❑	104T B.Saberhagen XRC	3.00	1.20
❑	105T Juan Samuel XRC*	1.00	.40
❑	106T Scott Sanderson	.40	.16
❑	107T Dick Schofield XRC*	.60	.24
❑	108T Tom Seaver	1.50	.60
❑	109T Jim Slaton	.40	.16
❑	110T Mike Smithson	.40	.16
❑	111T Lary Sorensen	.40	.16
❑	112T Tim Stoddard	.40	.16
❑	113T Champ Summers	.40	.16
❑	114T Jim Sundberg	.60	.24
❑	115T Rick Sutcliffe	.60	.24
❑	116T Craig Swan	.40	.16
❑	117T Tim Teufel XRC*	.40	.16
❑	118T Derrel Thomas	.40	.16
❑	119T Gorman Thomas	.40	.16
❑	120T Alex Trevino	.40	.16
❑	121T Manny Trillo	.40	.16
❑	122T John Tudor	.40	.16
❑	123T Tom Underwood	.40	.16
❑	124T Mike Vail	.40	.16
❑	125T Tom Waddell	.40	.16
❑	126T Gary Ward	.40	.16
❑	127T Curtis Wilkerson	.40	.16
❑	128T Frank Williams	.40	.16
❑	129T Glenn Wilson	.40	.16
❑	130T John Wockenfuss	.40	.16
❑	131T Ned Yost	.40	.16
❑	132T Checklist 1T-132T	.40	.16

1985 Topps

	Nm-Mt	Ex-Mt
COMPLETE SET (792)	100.00	40.00
COMP.FACT.SET (792)	200.00	80.00

	Card	Nm-Mt	Ex-Mt
❑	1 Carlton Fisk RB	.25	.10
❑	2 Steve Garvey RB	.15	.06
❑	3 Dwight Gooden RB	.60	.24
❑	4 Cliff Johnson RB	.15	.06
❑	5 Joe Morgan RB	.15	.06
❑	6 Pete Rose RB	.40	.16
❑	7 Nolan Ryan RB	1.50	.60
❑	8 Juan Samuel RB	.15	.06
❑	9 Bruce Sutter RB	.15	.06
❑	10 Don Sutton RB	.25	.10
❑	11 Ralph Houk MG	.15	.06
❑	12 Dave Lopes (Now with Cubs on card front)	.25	.10
❑	13 Tim Lollar	.15	.06
❑	14 Chris Bando	.15	.06
❑	15 Jerry Koosman	.25	.10
❑	16 Bobby Meacham	.15	.06
❑	17 Mike Scott	.15	.06
❑	18 Mickey Hatcher	.15	.06
❑	19 George Frazier	.15	.06
❑	20 Chet Lemon	.15	.06
❑	21 Lee Tunnell	.15	.06
❑	22 Duane Kuiper	.15	.06
❑	23 Bret Saberhagen RC	.60	.24
❑	24 Jesse Barfield	.15	.06
❑	25 Steve Bedrosian	.15	.06
❑	26 Roy Smalley	.15	.06
❑	27 Bruce Berenyi	.15	.06
❑	28 Dann Bilardello	.15	.06
❑	29 Odell Jones	.15	.06
❑	30 Cal Ripken	2.50	1.00
❑	31 Terry Whitfield	.15	.06
❑	32 Chuck Porter	.15	.06
❑	33 Tito Landrum	.15	.06
❑	34 Ed Nunez	.15	.06
❑	35 Graig Nettles	.25	.10
❑	36 Fred Breining	.15	.06
❑	37 Reid Nichols	.15	.06
❑	38 Jackie Moore MG	.15	.06
❑	39 John Wockenfuss	.15	.06
❑	40 Phil Niekro	.25	.10
❑	41 Mike Fischlin	.15	.06
❑	42 Luis Sanchez	.15	.06
❑	43 Andre David	.15	.06
❑	44 Dickie Thon	.15	.06
❑	45 Greg Minton	.15	.06
❑	46 Gary Woods	.15	.06
❑	47 Dave Rozema	.15	.06
❑	48 Tony Fernandez	.25	.10
❑	49 Butch Davis	.15	.06
❑	50 John Candelaria	.15	.06
❑	51 Bob Watson	.25	.10
❑	52 Jerry Dybzinski	.15	.06
❑	53 Tom Gorman	.15	.06
❑	54 Cesar Cedeno	.25	.10
❑	55 Frank Tanana	.15	.06
❑	56 Jim Dwyer	.15	.06
❑	57 Pat Zachry	.15	.06
❑	58 Orlando Mercado	.15	.06
❑	59 Rick Waits	.15	.06
❑	60 George Hendrick	.15	.06
❑	61 Curt Kaufman	.15	.06
❑	62 Mike Ramsey	.15	.06
❑	63 Steve McCatty	.15	.06
❑	64 Mark Bailey	.15	.06
❑	65 Bill Buckner	.25	.10
❑	66 Dick Williams MG	.25	.10
❑	67 Rafael Santana	.15	.06
❑	68 Von Hayes	.15	.06
❑	69 Jim Winn	.15	.06
❑	70 Don Baylor	.25	.10
❑	71 Tim Laudner	.15	.06
❑	72 Rick Sutcliffe	.25	.10
❑	73 Rusty Kuntz	.15	.06
❑	74 Mike Krukow	.15	.06
❑	75 Willie Upshaw	.15	.06
❑	76 Alan Bannister	.15	.06
❑	77 Joe Beckwith	.15	.06
❑	78 Scott Fletcher	.15	.06
❑	79 Rick Mahler	.15	.06
❑	80 Keith Hernandez	.40	.16
❑	81 Lenn Sakata	.15	.06
❑	82 Joe Price	.15	.06
❑	83 Charlie Moore	.15	.06
❑	84 Spike Owen	.15	.06
❑	85 Mike Marshall	.15	.06
❑	86 Don Aase	.15	.06
❑	87 David Green	.15	.06
❑	88 Bryn Smith	.15	.06
❑	89 Jackie Gutierrez	.15	.06
❑	90 Rich Gossage	.25	.10
❑	91 Jeff Burroughs	.15	.06
❑	92 Paul Owens MG	.15	.06
❑	93 Don Schulze	.15	.06
❑	94 Toby Harrah	.15	.06
❑	95 Jose Cruz	.25	.10
❑	96 Johnny Ray	.15	.06
❑	97 Pete Filson	.15	.06
❑	98 Steve Lake	.15	.06
❑	99 Milt Wilcox	.15	.06
❑	100 George Brett	2.00	.80
❑	101 Jim Acker	.15	.06
❑	102 Tommy Dunbar	.15	.06
❑	103 Randy Lerch	.15	.06
❑	104 Mike Fitzgerald	.15	.06
❑	105 Ron Kittle	.15	.06
❑	106 Pascual Perez	.15	.06
❑	107 Tom Foley	.15	.06
❑	108 Darnell Coles	.15	.06
❑	109 Gary Roenicke	.15	.06
❑	110 Alejandro Pena	.15	.06
❑	111 Doug DeCinces	.15	.06
❑	112 Tom Tellmann	.15	.06
❑	113 Tom Herr	.15	.06
❑	114 Bob James	.15	.06
❑	115 Rickey Henderson	1.25	.50
❑	116 Dennis Boyd	.15	.06
❑	117 Greg Gross	.15	.06
❑	118 Eric Show	.15	.06
❑	119 Pat Corrales MG	.15	.06
❑	120 Steve Kemp	.15	.06
❑	121 Checklist: 1-132	.15	.06
❑	122 Tom Brunansky	.25	.10
❑	123 Dave Smith	.15	.06
❑	124 Rich Hebner	.15	.06
❑	125 Kent Tekulve	.15	.06
❑	126 Ruppert Jones	.15	.06
❑	127 Mark Gubicza RC*	.25	.10
❑	128 Ernie Whitt	.15	.06
❑	129 Gene Garber	.15	.06
❑	130 Al Oliver	.25	.10
❑	131 Buddy Bell FS / Gus Bell	.25	.10
❑	132 Dale Berra FS / Yogi Berra	.25	.10
❑	133 Bob Boone FS / Ray Boone	.15	.06
❑	134 Terry Francona FS / Tito Francona	.15	.06
❑	135 Terry Kennedy FS / Bob Kennedy	.15	.06
❑	136 Jeff Kunkel FS / Bill Kunkel	.15	.06
❑	137 Vance Law FS / Vern Law	.25	.10
❑	138 Dick Schofield FS / Dick Schofield	.15	.06
❑	139 Joel Skinner FS / Bob Skinner	.15	.06
❑	140 Roy Smalley Jr. FS / Roy Smalley	.15	.06
❑	141 Mike Stenhouse FS / Dave Stenhouse	.15	.06
❑	142 Steve Trout FS / Dizzy Trout	.15	.06
❑	143 Ozzie Virgil FS / Ossie Virgil	.15	.06
❑	144 Ron Gardenhire	.15	.06
❑	145 Alvin Davis RC*	.25	.10
❑	146 Gary Redus	.15	.06
❑	147 Bill Swaggerty	.15	.06
❑	148 Steve Yeager	.15	.06
❑	149 Dickie Noles	.15	.06
❑	150 Jim Rice	.25	.10
❑	151 Moose Haas	.15	.06
❑	152 Steve Braun	.15	.06
❑	153 Frank LaCorte	.15	.06
❑	154 Angel Salazar	.15	.06
❑	155 Yogi Berra MG	.40	.16
❑	156 Craig Reynolds	.15	.06
❑	157 Tug McGraw	.25	.10
❑	158 Pat Tabler	.15	.06
❑	159 Carlos Diaz	.15	.06
❑	160 Lance Parrish	.25	.10
❑	161 Ken Schrom	.15	.06
❑	162 Benny Distefano	.15	.06
❑	163 Dennis Eckersley	.40	.16
❑	164 Jorge Orta	.15	.06
❑	165 Dusty Baker	.25	.10
❑	166 Keith Atherton	.15	.06
❑	167 Rufino Linares	.15	.06
❑	168 Garth Iorg	.15	.06
❑	169 Dan Spillner	.15	.06
❑	170 George Foster	.25	.10
❑	171 Bill Stein	.15	.06
❑	172 Jack Perconte	.15	.06
❑	173 Mike Young	.15	.06
❑	174 Rick Honeycutt	.15	.06
❑	175 Dave Parker	.25	.10
❑	176 Bill Schroeder	.15	.06
❑	177 Dave Von Ohlen	.15	.06
❑	178 Miguel Dilone	.15	.06
❑	179 Tommy John	.40	.16

	No.	Player		
❑	180	Dave Winfield	.40	.16
❑	181	Roger Clemens RC	25.00	10.00
❑	182	Tim Flannery	.15	.06
❑	183	Larry McWilliams	.15	.06
❑	184	Carmen Castillo	.15	.06
❑	185	Al Holland	.15	.06
❑	186	Bob Lillis MG	.15	.06
❑	187	Mike Walters	.15	.06
❑	188	Greg Pryor	.15	.06
❑	189	Warren Brusstar	.15	.06
❑	190	Rusty Staub	.25	.10
❑	191	Steve Nicosia	.15	.06
❑	192	Howard Johnson	.25	.10
❑	193	Jimmy Key RC	.60	.24
❑	194	Dave Stegman	.15	.06
❑	195	Glenn Hubbard	.15	.06
❑	196	Pete O'Brien	.15	.06
❑	197	Mike Warren	.15	.06
❑	198	Eddie Milner	.15	.06
❑	199	Dennis Martinez	.25	.10
❑	200	Reggie Jackson	.40	.16
❑	201	Burt Hooton	.15	.06
❑	202	Gorman Thomas	.15	.06
❑	203	Bob McClure	.15	.06
❑	204	Art Howe	.15	.06
❑	205	Steve Rogers	.15	.06
❑	206	Phil Garner	.25	.10
❑	207	Mark Clear	.15	.06
❑	208	Champ Summers	.15	.06
❑	209	Bill Campbell	.15	.06
❑	210	Gary Matthews	.15	.06
❑	211	Clay Christiansen	.15	.06
❑	212	George Vukovich	.15	.06
❑	213	Billy Gardner MG	.25	.10
❑	214	John Tudor	.15	.06
❑	215	Bob Brenly	.15	.06
❑	216	Jerry Don Gleaton	.15	.06
❑	217	Leon Roberts	.15	.06
❑	218	Doyle Alexander	.15	.06
❑	219	Gerald Perry	.15	.06
❑	220	Fred Lynn	.25	.10
❑	221	Ron Reed	.15	.06
❑	222	Hubie Brooks	.15	.06
❑	223	Tom Hume	.15	.06
❑	224	Al Cowens	.15	.06
❑	225	Mike Boddicker	.15	.06
❑	226	Juan Beniquez	.15	.06
❑	227	Danny Darwin	.15	.06
❑	228	Dion James	.15	.06
❑	229	Dave LaPoint	.15	.06
❑	230	Gary Carter	.40	.16
❑	231	Dwayne Murphy	.15	.06
❑	232	Dave Beard	.15	.06
❑	233	Ed Jurak	.15	.06
❑	234	Jerry Narron	.15	.06
❑	235	Garry Maddox	.15	.06
❑	236	Mark Thurmond	.15	.06
❑	237	Julio Franco	.40	.16
❑	238	Jose Rijo RC	.40	.16
❑	239	Tim Teufel	.15	.06
❑	240	Dave Stieb	.25	.10
❑	241	Jim Frey MG	.15	.06
❑	242	Greg Harris	.15	.06
❑	243	Barbaro Garbey	.15	.06
❑	244	Mike Jones	.15	.06
❑	245	Chili Davis	.25	.10
❑	246	Mike Norris	.15	.06
❑	247	Wayne Tolleson	.15	.06
❑	248	Terry Forster	.15	.06
❑	249	Harold Baines	.25	.10
❑	250	Jesse Orosco	.15	.06
❑	251	Brad Gulden	.15	.06
❑	252	Dan Ford	.15	.06
❑	253	Sid Bream RC	.25	.10
❑	254	Pete Vuckovich	.15	.06
❑	255	Lonnie Smith	.15	.06
❑	256	Mike Stanton	.15	.06
❑	257	Bryan Little UER	.15	.06
		Name spelled Brian on front		
❑	258	Mike C. Brown	.15	.06
❑	259	Gary Allenson	.15	.06
❑	260	Dave Righetti	.25	.10
❑	261	Checklist: 133-264	.15	.06
❑	262	Greg Booker	.15	.06
❑	263	Mel Hall	.15	.06
❑	264	Joe Sambito	.15	.06
❑	265	Juan Samuel	.15	.06
❑	266	Frank Viola	.25	.10
❑	267	Henry Cotto RC	.15	.06
❑	268	Chuck Tanner MG	.25	.10
❑	269	Doug Baker	.15	.06
❑	270	Dan Quisenberry	.25	.10
❑	271	Tim Foli FDP68	.15	.06
❑	272	Jeff Burroughs FDP69	.15	.06
❑	273	Bill Almon FDP74	.15	.06
❑	274	F.Bannister FDP76	.15	.06
❑	275	Harold Baines FDP77	.15	.06
❑	276	Bob Horner FDP78	.15	.06
❑	277	Al Chambers FDP79	.15	.06
❑	278	Darryl Strawberry FDP80	.40	.16
❑	279	Mike Moore FDP81	.15	.06
❑	280	S.Dunston FDP82 RC	.40	.16
❑	281	T.Belcher RC FDP83	.60	.24
❑	282	Shawn Abner FDP84	.15	.06
❑	283	Fran Mullins	.15	.06
❑	284	Marty Bystrom	.15	.06
❑	285	Dan Driessen	.15	.06
❑	286	Rudy Law	.15	.06
❑	287	Walt Terrell	.15	.06
❑	288	Jeff Kunkel	.15	.06
❑	289	Tom Underwood	.15	.06
❑	290	Cecil Cooper	.25	.10
❑	291	Bob Welch	.15	.06
❑	292	Brad Komminsk	.15	.06
❑	293	Curt Young	.15	.06
❑	294	Tom Nieto	.15	.06
❑	295	Joe Niekro	.15	.06
❑	296	Ricky Nelson	.15	.06
❑	297	Gary Lucas	.15	.06
❑	298	Marty Barrett	.15	.06
❑	299	Andy Hawkins	.15	.06
❑	300	Rod Carew	.40	.16
❑	301	John Montefusco	.15	.06
❑	302	Tim Corcoran	.15	.06
❑	303	Mike Jeffcoat	.15	.06
❑	304	Gary Gaetti	.25	.10
❑	305	Dale Berra	.15	.06
❑	306	Rick Reuschel	.15	.06
❑	307	Sparky Anderson MG	.25	.10
❑	308	John Wathan	.15	.06
❑	309	Mike Witt	.15	.06
❑	310	Manny Trillo	.15	.06
❑	311	Jim Gott	.15	.06
❑	312	Marc Hill	.15	.06
❑	313	Dave Schmidt	.15	.06
❑	314	Ron Oester	.15	.06
❑	315	Doug Sisk	.15	.06
❑	316	John Lowenstein	.15	.06
❑	317	Jack Lazorko	.15	.06
❑	318	Ted Simmons	.25	.10
❑	319	Jeff Jones	.15	.06
❑	320	Dale Murphy	.60	.24
❑	321	Ricky Horton	.15	.06
❑	322	Dave Stapleton	.15	.06
❑	323	Andy McGaffigan	.15	.06
❑	324	Bruce Bochy	.15	.06
❑	325	John Denny	.15	.06
❑	326	Kevin Bass	.15	.06
❑	327	Brook Jacoby	.15	.06
❑	328	Bob Shirley	.15	.06
❑	329	Ron Washington	.15	.06
❑	330	Leon Durham	.15	.06
❑	331	Bill Laskey	.15	.06
❑	332	Brian Harper	.15	.06
❑	333	Willie Hernandez	.15	.06
❑	334	Dick Howser MG	.25	.10
❑	335	Bruce Benedict	.15	.06
❑	336	Rance Mulliniks	.15	.06
❑	337	Billy Sample	.15	.06
❑	338	Britt Burns	.15	.06
❑	339	Danny Heep	.15	.06
❑	340	Robin Yount	.60	.24
❑	341	Floyd Rayford	.15	.06
❑	342	Ted Power	.15	.06
❑	343	Bill Russell	.15	.06
❑	344	Dave Henderson	.15	.06
❑	345	Charlie Lea	.15	.06
❑	346	Terry Pendleton RC	.60	.24
❑	347	Rick Langford	.15	.06
❑	348	Bob Boone	.25	.10
❑	349	Domingo Ramos	.15	.06
❑	350	Wade Boggs	.75	.30
❑	351	Juan Agosto	.15	.06
❑	352	Joe Morgan	.40	.16
❑	353	Julio Solano	.15	.06
❑	354	Andre Robertson	.15	.06
❑	355	Bert Blyleven	.25	.10
❑	356	Dave Meier	.15	.06
❑	357	Rich Bordi	.15	.06
❑	358	Tony Pena	.15	.06
❑	359	Pat Sheridan	.15	.06
❑	360	Steve Carlton	.40	.16
❑	361	Alfredo Griffin	.15	.06
❑	362	Craig McMurtry	.15	.06
❑	363	Ron Hodges	.15	.06
❑	364	Richard Dotson	.15	.06
❑	365	Danny Ozark MG	.15	.06
❑	366	Todd Cruz	.15	.06
❑	367	Keefe Cato	.15	.06
❑	368	Dave Bergman	.15	.06
❑	369	R.J. Reynolds	.15	.06
❑	370	Bruce Sutter	.25	.10
❑	371	Mickey Rivers	.15	.06
❑	372	Roy Howell	.15	.06
❑	373	Mike Moore	.15	.06
❑	374	Brian Downing	.15	.06
❑	375	Jeff Reardon	.25	.10
❑	376	Jeff Newman	.15	.06
❑	377	Checklist: 265-396	.15	.06
❑	378	Alan Wiggins	.15	.06
❑	379	Charles Hudson	.15	.06
❑	380	Ken Griffey	.25	.10
❑	381	Roy Smith	.15	.06
❑	382	Denny Walling	.15	.06
❑	383	Rick Lysander	.15	.06
❑	384	Jody Davis	.15	.06
❑	385	Jose DeLeon	.15	.06
❑	386	Dan Gladden RC	.25	.10
❑	387	Buddy Biancalana	.15	.06
❑	388	Bert Roberge	.15	.06
❑	389	Rod Dedeaux OLY CO	.25	.10
❑	390	Sid Akins OLY	.15	.06
❑	391	Flavio Alfaro OLY	.15	.06
❑	392	Don August OLY	.15	.06
❑	393	S.Bankhead RC OLY	.15	.06
❑	394	Bob Caffrey OLY	.15	.06
❑	395	Mike Dunne OLY	.25	.10
❑	396	Gary Green OLY	.15	.06
❑	397	John Hoover OLY	.15	.06
❑	398	Shane Mack RC OLY	.60	.24
❑	399	John Marzano OLY	.25	.10
❑	400	O.McDowell RC OLY	.25	.10
❑	401	M.McGwire OLY RC	50.00	20.00
❑	402	Pat Pacillo OLY	.25	.10
❑	403	Cory Snyder RC OLY	.40	.16
❑	404	Billy Swift OLY RC	.40	.16
❑	405	Tom Veryzer	.15	.06
❑	406	Len Whitehouse	.15	.06
❑	407	Bobby Ramos	.15	.06
❑	408	Sid Monge	.15	.06
❑	409	Brad Wellman	.15	.06
❑	410	Bob Horner	.15	.06
❑	411	Bobby Cox MG	.15	.06
❑	412	Bud Black	.15	.06
❑	413	Vance Law	.15	.06
❑	414	Gary Ward	.15	.06
❑	415	Ron Darling UER	.25	.10
		(No trivia answer)		
❑	416	Wayne Gross	.15	.06
❑	417	John Franco RC	.60	.24
❑	418	Ken Landreaux	.15	.06
❑	419	Mike Caldwell	.15	.06
❑	420	Andre Dawson	.25	.10
❑	421	Dave Rucker	.15	.06
❑	422	Carney Lansford	.25	.10
❑	423	Barry Bonnell	.15	.06
❑	424	Al Nipper	.15	.06
❑	425	Mike Hargrove	.25	.10
❑	426	Vern Ruhle	.15	.06
❑	427	Mario Ramirez	.15	.06
❑	428	Larry Andersen	.15	.06
❑	429	Rick Cerone	.15	.06
❑	430	Ron Davis	.15	.06
❑	431	U.L. Washington	.15	.06
❑	432	Thad Bosley	.15	.06
❑	433	Jim Morrison	.15	.06
❑	434	Gene Richards	.15	.06

❑ 435 Dan Petry .15 .06
❑ 436 Willie Aikens .15 .06
❑ 437 Al Jones .15 .06
❑ 438 Joe Torre MG .40 .16
❑ 439 Junior Ortiz .15 .06
❑ 440 Fernando Valenzuela .25 .10
❑ 441 Duane Walker .15 .06
❑ 442 Ken Forsch .15 .06
❑ 443 George Wright .15 .06
❑ 444 Tony Phillips .15 .06
❑ 445 Tippy Martinez .15 .06
❑ 446 Jim Sundberg .15 .06
❑ 447 Jeff Lahti .15 .06
❑ 448 Derrel Thomas .15 .06
❑ 449 Phil Bradley .25 .10
❑ 450 Steve Garvey .25 .10
❑ 451 Bruce Hurst .15 .06
❑ 452 John Castino .15 .06
❑ 453 Tom Waddell .15 .06
❑ 454 Glenn Wilson .15 .06
❑ 455 Bob Knepper .15 .06
❑ 456 Tim Foli .15 .06
❑ 457 Cecilio Guante .15 .06
❑ 458 Randy Johnson .15 .06
❑ 459 Charlie Leibrandt .15 .06
❑ 460 Ryne Sandberg 1.25 .50
❑ 461 Marty Castillo .15 .06
❑ 462 Gary Lavelle .15 .06
❑ 463 Dave Collins .15 .06
❑ 464 Mike Mason RC .15 .06
❑ 465 Bobby Grich .25 .10
❑ 466 Tony LaRussa MG .40 .16
❑ 467 Ed Lynch .15 .06
❑ 468 Wayne Krenchicki .15 .06
❑ 469 Sammy Stewart .15 .06
❑ 470 Steve Sax .15 .06
❑ 471 Pete Ladd .15 .06
❑ 472 Jim Essian .15 .06
❑ 473 Tim Wallach .25 .10
❑ 474 Kurt Kepshire .15 .06
❑ 475 Andre Thornton .15 .06
❑ 476 Jeff Stone .15 .06
❑ 477 Bob Ojeda .15 .06
❑ 478 Kurt Bevacqua .15 .06
❑ 479 Mike Madden .15 .06
❑ 480 Lou Whitaker .40 .16
❑ 481 Dale Murray .15 .06
❑ 482 Harry Spilman .15 .06
❑ 483 Mike Smithson .15 .06
❑ 484 Larry Bowa .25 .10
❑ 485 Matt Young .15 .06
❑ 486 Steve Balboni .15 .06
❑ 487 Frank Williams .15 .06
❑ 488 Joel Skinner .15 .06
❑ 489 Bryan Clark .15 .06
❑ 490 Jason Thompson .15 .06
❑ 491 Rick Camp .15 .06
❑ 492 Dave Johnson MG .25 .10
❑ 493 Orel Hershiser RC .75 .30
❑ 494 Rich Dauer .15 .06
❑ 495 Mario Soto .15 .06
❑ 496 Donnie Scott .15 .06
❑ 497 Gary Pettis UER .15 .06
(Photo actually
Gary's little
brother Lynn)
❑ 498 Ed Romero .15 .06
❑ 499 Danny Cox .15 .06
❑ 500 Mike Schmidt 1.50 .60
❑ 501 Dan Schatzeder .15 .06
❑ 502 Rick Miller .15 .06
❑ 503 Tim Conroy .15 .06
❑ 504 Jerry Willard .15 .06
❑ 505 Jim Beattie .15 .06
❑ 506 Franklin Stubbs .15 .06
❑ 507 Ray Fontenot .15 .06
❑ 508 John Shelby .15 .06
❑ 509 Milt May .15 .06
❑ 510 Kent Hrbek .25 .10
❑ 511 Lee Smith .40 .16
❑ 512 Tom Brookens .15 .06
❑ 513 Lynn Jones .15 .06
❑ 514 Jeff Cornell .15 .06
❑ 515 Dave Concepcion .25 .10
❑ 516 Roy Lee Jackson .15 .06
❑ 517 Jerry Martin .15 .06
❑ 518 Chris Chambliss .25 .10
❑ 519 Doug Rader MG .15 .06
❑ 520 LaMarr Hoyt .15 .06
❑ 521 Rick Dempsey .15 .06
❑ 522 Paul Molitor .40 .16
❑ 523 Candy Maldonado .15 .06
❑ 524 Rob Wilfong .15 .06
❑ 525 Darrell Porter .15 .06
❑ 526 David Palmer .15 .06
❑ 527 Checklist: 397-528 .15 .06
❑ 528 Bill Krueger .15 .06
❑ 529 Rich Gedman .15 .06
❑ 530 Dave Dravecky .25 .10
❑ 531 Joe Lefebvre .15 .06
❑ 532 Frank DiPino .15 .06
❑ 533 Tony Bernazard .15 .06
❑ 534 Brian Dayett .15 .06
❑ 535 Pat Putnam .15 .06
❑ 536 Kirby Puckett RC 6.00 2.40
❑ 537 Don Robinson .15 .06
❑ 538 Keith Moreland .15 .06
❑ 539 Aurelio Lopez .15 .06
❑ 540 Claudell Washington .15 .06
❑ 541 Mark Davis .15 .06
❑ 542 Don Slaught .15 .06
❑ 543 Mike Squires .15 .06
❑ 544 Bruce Kison .15 .06
❑ 545 Lloyd Moseby .15 .06
❑ 546 Brent Gaff .15 .06
❑ 547 Pete Rose MG .40 .16
❑ 548 Larry Parrish .15 .06
❑ 549 Mike Scioscia .15 .06
❑ 550 Scott McGregor .15 .06
❑ 551 Andy Van Slyke .25 .10
❑ 552 Chris Codiroli .15 .06
❑ 553 Bob Clark .15 .06
❑ 554 Doug Flynn .15 .06
❑ 555 Bob Stanley .15 .06
❑ 556 Sixto Lezcano .15 .06
❑ 557 Len Barker .15 .06
❑ 558 Carmelo Martinez .15 .06
❑ 559 Jay Howell .15 .06
❑ 560 Bill Madlock .25 .10
❑ 561 Darryl Motley .15 .06
❑ 562 Houston Jimenez .15 .06
❑ 563 Dick Ruthven .15 .06
❑ 564 Alan Ashby .15 .06
❑ 565 Kirk Gibson .25 .10
❑ 566 Ed VandeBerg .15 .06
❑ 567 Joel Youngblood .15 .06
❑ 568 Cliff Johnson .15 .06
❑ 569 Ken Oberkfell .15 .06
❑ 570 Darryl Strawberry .60 .24
❑ 571 Charlie Hough .25 .10
❑ 572 Tom Paciorek .25 .10
❑ 573 Jay Tibbs .15 .06
❑ 574 Joe Altobelli MG .15 .06
❑ 575 Pedro Guerrero .25 .10
❑ 576 Jaime Cocanower .15 .06
❑ 577 Chris Speier .15 .06
❑ 578 Terry Francona .15 .06
❑ 579 Ron Romanick .15 .06
❑ 580 Dwight Evans .25 .10
❑ 581 Mark Wagner .15 .06
❑ 582 Ken Phelps .15 .06
❑ 583 Bobby Brown .15 .06
❑ 584 Kevin Gross .15 .06
❑ 585 Butch Wynegar .15 .06
❑ 586 Bill Scherrer .15 .06
❑ 587 Doug Frobel .15 .06
❑ 588 Bobby Castillo .15 .06
❑ 589 Bob Dernier .15 .06
❑ 590 Ray Knight .15 .06
❑ 591 Larry Herndon .15 .06
❑ 592 Jeff D. Robinson .15 .06
❑ 593 Rick Leach .15 .06
❑ 594 Curt Wilkerson .15 .06
❑ 595 Larry Gura .15 .06
❑ 596 Jerry Hairston .15 .06
❑ 597 Brad Lesley .15 .06
❑ 598 Jose Oquendo .15 .06
❑ 599 Storm Davis .15 .06
❑ 600 Pete Rose 1.50 .60
❑ 601 Tom Lasorda MG .40 .16
❑ 602 Jeff Dedmon .15 .06
❑ 603 Rick Manning .15 .06
❑ 604 Daryl Sconiers .15 .06
❑ 605 Ozzie Smith .60 .24
❑ 606 Rich Gale .15 .06
❑ 607 Bill Almon .15 .06
❑ 608 Craig Lefferts .15 .06
❑ 609 Broderick Perkins .15 .06
❑ 610 Jack Morris .25 .10
❑ 611 Ozzie Virgil .15 .06
❑ 612 Mike Armstrong .15 .06
❑ 613 Terry Puhl .15 .06
❑ 614 Al Williams .15 .06
❑ 615 Marvell Wynne .15 .06
❑ 616 Scott Sanderson .15 .06
❑ 617 Willie Wilson .15 .06
❑ 618 Pete Falcone .15 .06
❑ 619 Jeff Leonard .15 .06
❑ 620 Dwight Gooden RC 1.00 .40
❑ 621 Marvis Foley .15 .06
❑ 622 Luis Leal .15 .06
❑ 623 Greg Walker .15 .06
❑ 624 Benny Ayala .15 .06
❑ 625 Mark Langston RC .40 .16
❑ 626 German Rivera .15 .06
❑ 627 Eric Davis RC 1.00 .40
❑ 628 Rene Lachemann MG .15 .06
❑ 629 Dick Schofield .15 .06
❑ 630 Tim Raines .25 .10
❑ 631 Bob Forsch .15 .06
❑ 632 Bruce Bochte .15 .06
❑ 633 Glenn Hoffman .15 .06
❑ 634 Bill Dawley .15 .06
❑ 635 Terry Kennedy .15 .06
❑ 636 Shane Rawley .15 .06
❑ 637 Brett Butler .25 .10
❑ 638 Mike Pagliarulo .15 .06
❑ 639 Ed Hodge .15 .06
❑ 640 Steve Henderson .15 .06
❑ 641 Rod Scurry .15 .06
❑ 642 Dave Owen .15 .06
❑ 643 Johnny Grubb .15 .06
❑ 644 Mark Huismann .15 .06
❑ 645 Damaso Garcia .15 .06
❑ 646 Scot Thompson .15 .06
❑ 647 Rafael Ramirez .15 .06
❑ 648 Bob Jones .15 .06
❑ 649 Sid Fernandez .25 .10
❑ 650 Greg Luzinski .25 .10
❑ 651 Jeff Russell .15 .06
❑ 652 Joe Nolan .15 .06
❑ 653 Mark Brouhard .15 .06
❑ 654 Dave Anderson .15 .06
❑ 655 Joaquin Andujar .15 .06
❑ 656 Chuck Cottier MG .15 .06
❑ 657 Jim Slaton .15 .06
❑ 658 Mike Stenhouse .15 .06
❑ 659 Checklist: 529-660 .15 .06
❑ 660 Tony Gwynn 1.25 .50
❑ 661 Steve Crawford .15 .06
❑ 662 Mike Heath .15 .06
❑ 663 Luis Aguayo .15 .06
❑ 664 Steve Farr RC .25 .10
❑ 665 Don Mattingly 2.50 1.00
❑ 666 Mike LaCoss .15 .06
❑ 667 Dave Engle .15 .06
❑ 668 Steve Trout .15 .06
❑ 669 Lee Lacy .15 .06
❑ 670 Tom Seaver .60 .24
❑ 671 Dane Iorg .15 .06
❑ 672 Juan Berenguer .15 .06
❑ 673 Buck Martinez .15 .06
❑ 674 Atlee Hammaker .15 .06
❑ 675 Tony Perez .40 .16
❑ 676 Albert Hall .15 .06
❑ 677 Wally Backman .15 .06
❑ 678 Joey McLaughlin .15 .06
❑ 679 Bob Kearney .15 .06
❑ 680 Jerry Reuss .15 .06
❑ 681 Ben Oglivie .15 .06
❑ 682 Doug Corbett .15 .06
❑ 683 Whitey Herzog MG .25 .10
❑ 684 Bill Doran .15 .06
❑ 685 Bill Caudill .15 .06
❑ 686 Mike Easler .15 .06
❑ 687 Bill Gullickson .15 .06
❑ 688 Len Matuszek .15 .06
❑ 689 Luis DeLeon .15 .06

❑ 690 Alan Trammell .40 .16
❑ 691 Dennis Rasmussen .15 .06
❑ 692 Randy Bush .15 .06
❑ 693 Tim Stoddard .15 .06
❑ 694 Joe Carter .60 .24
❑ 695 Rick Rhoden .15 .06
❑ 696 John Rabb .15 .06
❑ 697 Onix Concepcion .15 .06
❑ 698 Jorge Bell .25 .10
❑ 699 Donnie Moore .15 .06
❑ 700 Eddie Murray .60 .24
❑ 701 Eddie Murray AS .40 .16
❑ 702 Damaso Garcia AS .15 .06
❑ 703 George Brett AS .60 .24
❑ 704 Cal Ripken AS 1.50 .60
❑ 705 Dave Winfield AS .40 .16
❑ 706 Rickey Henderson AS .60 .24
❑ 707 Tony Armas AS .15 .06
❑ 708 Lance Parrish AS .15 .06
❑ 709 Mike Boddicker AS .15 .06
❑ 710 Frank Viola AS .15 .06
❑ 711 Dan Quisenberry AS .15 .06
❑ 712 Keith Hernandez AS .25 .10
❑ 713 Ryne Sandberg AS .60 .24
❑ 714 Mike Schmidt AS .60 .24
❑ 715 Ozzie Smith AS .40 .16
❑ 716 Dale Murphy AS .40 .16
❑ 717 Tony Gwynn AS 1.00 .40
❑ 718 Jeff Leonard AS .15 .06
❑ 719 Gary Carter AS .25 .10
❑ 720 Rick Sutcliffe AS .15 .06
❑ 721 Bob Knepper AS .15 .06
❑ 722 Bruce Sutter AS .15 .06
❑ 723 Dave Stewart .25 .10
❑ 724 Oscar Gamble .15 .06
❑ 725 Floyd Bannister .15 .06
❑ 726 Al Bumbry .15 .06
❑ 727 Frank Pastore .15 .06
❑ 728 Bob Bailor .15 .06
❑ 729 Don Sutton .60 .24
❑ 730 Dave Kingman .25 .10
❑ 731 Neil Allen .15 .06
❑ 732 John McNamara MG .15 .06
❑ 733 Tony Scott .15 .06
❑ 734 John Henry Johnson .15 .06
❑ 735 Garry Templeton .15 .06
❑ 736 Jerry Mumphrey .15 .06
❑ 737 Bo Diaz .15 .06
❑ 738 Omar Moreno .15 .06
❑ 739 Ernie Camacho .15 .06
❑ 740 Jack Clark .25 .10
❑ 741 John Butcher .15 .06
❑ 742 Ron Hassey .15 .06
❑ 743 Frank White .25 .10
❑ 744 Doug Bair .15 .06
❑ 745 Buddy Bell .25 .10
❑ 746 Jim Clancy .15 .06
❑ 747 Alex Trevino .15 .06
❑ 748 Lee Mazzilli .15 .06
❑ 749 Julio Cruz .15 .06
❑ 750 Rollie Fingers .25 .10
❑ 751 Kelvin Chapman .15 .06
❑ 752 Bob Owchinko .15 .06
❑ 753 Greg Brock .15 .06
❑ 754 Larry Milbourne .15 .06
❑ 755 Ken Singleton .15 .06
❑ 756 Rob Picciolo .15 .06
❑ 757 Willie McGee .25 .10
❑ 758 Ray Burris .15 .06
❑ 759 Jim Fanning MG .15 .06
❑ 760 Nolan Ryan 3.00 1.20
❑ 761 Jerry Remy .15 .06
❑ 762 Eddie Whitson .15 .06
❑ 763 Kiko Garcia .15 .06
❑ 764 Jamie Easterly .15 .06
❑ 765 Willie Randolph .25 .10
❑ 766 Paul Mirabella .15 .06
❑ 767 Darrell Brown .15 .06
❑ 768 Ron Cey .25 .10
❑ 769 Joe Cowley .15 .06
❑ 770 Carlton Fisk .40 .16
❑ 771 Geoff Zahn .15 .06
❑ 772 Johnnie LeMaster .15 .06
❑ 773 Hal McRae .25 .10
❑ 774 Dennis Lamp .15 .06
❑ 775 Mookie Wilson .25 .10
❑ 776 Jerry Royster .15 .06
❑ 777 Ned Yost .15 .06
❑ 778 Mike Davis .15 .06
❑ 779 Nick Esasky .15 .06
❑ 780 Mike Flanagan .15 .06
❑ 781 Jim Gantner .15 .06
❑ 782 Tom Niedenfuer .15 .06
❑ 783 Mike Jorgensen .15 .06
❑ 784 Checklist: 661-792 .15 .06
❑ 785 Tony Armas .15 .06
❑ 786 Enos Cabell .15 .06
❑ 787 Jim Wohlford .15 .06
❑ 788 Steve Comer .15 .06
❑ 789 Luis Salazar .15 .06
❑ 790 Ron Guidry .25 .10
❑ 791 Ivan DeJesus .15 .06
❑ 792 Darrell Evans .25 .10

1986 Topps

	Nm-Mt	Ex-Mt
COMPLETE SET (792)	25.00	10.00
COMP.X-MAS.SET (792)	100.00	40.00

❑ 1 Pete Rose 2.00 .80
❑ 2 Pete Rose 63-66 .25 .10
❑ 3 Pete Rose 67-70 .25 .10
❑ 4 Pete Rose 71-74 .25 .10
❑ 5 Pete Rose 75-78 .25 .10
❑ 6 Pete Rose 79-82 .25 .10
❑ 7 Pete Rose 83-85 .25 .10
❑ 8 Dwayne Murphy .10 .04
❑ 9 Roy Smith .10 .04
❑ 10 Tony Gwynn .60 .24
❑ 11 Bob Ojeda .10 .04
❑ 12 Jose Uribe .10 .04
❑ 13 Bob Kearney .10 .04
❑ 14 Julio Cruz .10 .04
❑ 15 Eddie Whitson .10 .04
❑ 16 Rick Schu .10 .04
❑ 17 Mike Stenhouse .10 .04
❑ 18 Brent Gaff .10 .04
❑ 19 Rich Hebner .10 .04
❑ 20 Lou Whitaker .15 .06
❑ 21 George Bamberger MG .10 .04
❑ 22 Duane Walker .10 .04
❑ 23 Manny Lee RC* .10 .04
❑ 24 Len Barker .10 .04
❑ 25 Willie Wilson .10 .04
❑ 26 Frank DiPino .10 .04
❑ 27 Ray Knight .15 .06
❑ 28 Eric Davis .25 .10
❑ 29 Tony Phillips .10 .04
❑ 30 Eddie Murray .40 .16
❑ 31 Jamie Easterly .10 .04
❑ 32 Steve Yeager .10 .04
❑ 33 Jeff Lahti .10 .04
❑ 34 Ken Phelps .10 .04
❑ 35 Jeff Reardon .10 .04
❑ 36 Lance Parrish TL .15 .06
❑ 37 Mark Thurmond .10 .04
❑ 38 Glenn Hoffman .10 .04
❑ 39 Dave Rucker .10 .04
❑ 40 Ken Griffey .15 .06
❑ 41 Brad Wellman .10 .04
❑ 42 Geoff Zahn .10 .04
❑ 43 Dave Engle .10 .04
❑ 44 Lance McCullers .10 .04
❑ 45 Damaso Garcia .10 .04
❑ 46 Billy Hatcher .10 .04
❑ 47 Juan Berenguer .10 .04
❑ 48 Bill Almon .10 .04
❑ 49 Rick Manning .10 .04
❑ 50 Dan Quisenberry .10 .04
❑ 51 Bobby Wine MG ERR .10 .04
Number of card on
back is actually 57)
❑ 52 Chris Welsh .10 .04
❑ 53 Len Dykstra RC .75 .30
❑ 54 John Franco .40 .16
❑ 55 Fred Lynn .15 .06
❑ 56 Tom Niedenfuer .10 .04
❑ 57 Bill Doran .10 .04
(See also 51)
❑ 58 Bill Krueger .10 .04
❑ 59 Andre Thornton .10 .04
❑ 60 Dwight Evans .15 .06
❑ 61 Karl Best .10 .04
❑ 62 Bob Boone .15 .06
❑ 63 Ron Roenicke .10 .04
❑ 64 Floyd Bannister .10 .04
❑ 65 Dan Driessen .10 .04
❑ 66 Bob Forsch TL .10 .04
❑ 67 Carmelo Martinez .10 .04
❑ 68 Ed Lynch .10 .04
❑ 69 Luis Aguayo .10 .04
❑ 70 Dave Winfield .25 .10
❑ 71 Ken Schrom .10 .04
❑ 72 Shawon Dunston .15 .06
❑ 73 Randy O'Neal .10 .04
❑ 74 Rance Mulliniks .10 .04
❑ 75 Jose DeLeon .10 .04
❑ 76 Dion James .10 .04
❑ 77 Charlie Leibrandt .10 .04
❑ 78 Bruce Benedict .10 .04
❑ 79 Dave Schmidt .10 .04
❑ 80 Darryl Strawberry .25 .10
❑ 81 Gene Mauch MG .15 .06
❑ 82 Tippy Martinez .10 .04
❑ 83 Phil Garner .15 .06
❑ 84 Curt Young .10 .04
❑ 85 Tony Perez .25 .10
(Eric Davis also
shown on card)
❑ 86 Tom Waddell .10 .04
❑ 87 Candy Maldonado .10 .04
❑ 88 Tom Nieto .10 .04
❑ 89 Randy St.Claire .10 .04
❑ 90 Garry Templeton .10 .04
❑ 91 Steve Crawford .10 .04
❑ 92 Al Cowens .10 .04
❑ 93 Scot Thompson .10 .04
❑ 94 Rich Bordi .10 .04
❑ 95 Ozzie Virgil .10 .04
❑ 96 Jim Clancy TL .10 .04
❑ 97 Gary Gaetti .15 .06
❑ 98 Dick Ruthven .10 .04
❑ 99 Buddy Biancalana .10 .04
❑ 100 Nolan Ryan 2.00 .80
❑ 101 Dave Bergman .10 .04
❑ 102 Joe Orsulak RC* .10 .04
❑ 103 Luis Salazar .10 .04
❑ 104 Sid Fernandez .15 .06
❑ 105 Gary Ward .10 .04
❑ 106 Ray Burris .10 .04
❑ 107 Rafael Ramirez .10 .04
❑ 108 Ted Power .10 .04
❑ 109 Len Matuszek .10 .04
❑ 110 Scott McGregor .10 .04
❑ 111 Roger Craig MG .15 .06
❑ 112 Bill Campbell .10 .04
❑ 113 U.L. Washington .10 .04
❑ 114 Mike C. Brown .10 .04
❑ 115 Jay Howell .10 .04
❑ 116 Brook Jacoby .10 .04
❑ 117 Bruce Kison .10 .04
❑ 118 Jerry Royster .10 .04
❑ 119 Barry Bonnell .10 .04
❑ 120 Steve Carlton .25 .10
❑ 121 Nelson Simmons .10 .04
❑ 122 Pete Filson .10 .04
❑ 123 Greg Walker .10 .04
❑ 124 Luis Sanchez .10 .04
❑ 125 Dave Lopes .15 .06

❑ 126 Mookie Wilson TL .10 .04
❑ 127 Jack Howell .10 .04
❑ 128 John Wathan .10 .04
❑ 129 Jeff Dedmon .10 .04
❑ 130 Alan Trammell .25 .10
❑ 131 Checklist: 1-132 .15 .06
❑ 132 Razor Shines .10 .04
❑ 133 Andy McGaffigan .10 .04
❑ 134 Carney Lansford .15 .06
❑ 135 Joe Niekro .10 .04
❑ 136 Mike Hargrove .15 .06
❑ 137 Charlie Moore .10 .04
❑ 138 Mark Davis .10 .04
❑ 139 Daryl Boston .10 .04
❑ 140 John Candelaria .10 .04
❑ 141 Chuck Cottier MG .10 .04
See also 171
❑ 142 Bob Jones .10 .04
❑ 143 Dave Van Gorder .10 .04
❑ 144 Doug Sisk .10 .04
❑ 145 Pedro Guerrero .15 .06
❑ 146 Jack Perconte .10 .04
❑ 147 Larry Sheets .10 .04
❑ 148 Mike Heath .10 .04
❑ 149 Brett Butler .15 .06
❑ 150 Joaquin Andujar .10 .04
❑ 151 Dave Stapleton .10 .04
❑ 152 Mike Morgan .10 .04
❑ 153 Ricky Adams .10 .04
❑ 154 Bert Roberge .10 .04
❑ 155 Bobby Grich .15 .06
❑ 156 Richard Dotson TL .10 .04
❑ 157 Ron Hassey .10 .04
❑ 158 Derrel Thomas .10 .04
❑ 159 Orel Hershiser UER .40 .16
(82 Alburquerque)
❑ 160 Chet Lemon .10 .04
❑ 161 Lee Tunnell .10 .04
❑ 162 Greg Gagne .10 .04
❑ 163 Pete Ladd .10 .04
❑ 164 Steve Balboni .10 .04
❑ 165 Mike Davis .10 .04
❑ 166 Dickie Thon .10 .04
❑ 167 Zane Smith .10 .04
❑ 168 Jeff Burroughs .10 .04
❑ 169 George Wright .10 .04
❑ 170 Gary Carter .25 .10
❑ 171 Bob Rodgers MG ERR .10 .04
Number of card on
back actually 141)
❑ 172 Jerry Reed .10 .04
❑ 173 Wayne Gross .10 .04
❑ 174 Brian Snyder .10 .04
❑ 175 Steve Sax .10 .04
❑ 176 Jay Tibbs .10 .04
❑ 177 Joel Youngblood .10 .04
❑ 178 Ivan DeJesus .10 .04
❑ 179 Stu Cliburn .10 .04
❑ 180 Don Mattingly 1.25 .50
❑ 181 Al Nipper .10 .04
❑ 182 Bobby Brown .10 .04
❑ 183 Larry Andersen .10 .04
❑ 184 Tim Laudner .10 .04
❑ 185 Rollie Fingers .15 .06
❑ 186 Jose Cruz TL .10 .04
❑ 187 Scott Fletcher .10 .04
❑ 188 Bob Dernier .10 .04
❑ 189 Mike Mason .10 .04
❑ 190 George Hendrick .10 .04
❑ 191 Wally Backman .10 .04
❑ 192 Milt Wilcox .10 .04
❑ 193 Daryl Sconiers .10 .04
❑ 194 Craig McMurtry .10 .04
❑ 195 Dave Concepcion .15 .06
❑ 196 Doyle Alexander .10 .04
❑ 197 Enos Cabell .10 .04
❑ 198 Ken Dixon .10 .04
❑ 199 Dick Howser MG .15 .06
❑ 200 Mike Schmidt 1.00 .40
❑ 201 Vince Coleman RB .15 .06
❑ 202 Dwight Gooden RB .25 .10
❑ 203 Keith Hernandez RB .15 .06
❑ 204 Phil Niekro RB .15 .06
❑ 205 Tony Perez RB .15 .06
❑ 206 Pete Rose RB .40 .16
❑ 207 F. Valenzuela RB .15 .06
❑ 208 Ramon Romero .10 .04
❑ 209 Randy Ready .10 .04
❑ 210 Calvin Schiraldi .10 .04
❑ 211 Ed Wojna .10 .04
❑ 212 Chris Speier .10 .04
❑ 213 Bob Shirley .10 .04
❑ 214 Randy Bush .10 .04
❑ 215 Frank White .15 .06
❑ 216 Dwayne Murphy TL .10 .04
❑ 217 Bill Scherrer .10 .04
❑ 218 Randy Hunt .10 .04
❑ 219 Dennis Lamp .10 .04
❑ 220 Bob Horner .10 .04
❑ 221 Dave Henderson .10 .04
❑ 222 Craig Gerber .10 .04
❑ 223 Atlee Hammaker .10 .04
❑ 224 Cesar Cedeno .15 .06
❑ 225 Ron Darling .10 .04
❑ 226 Lee Lacy .10 .04
❑ 227 Al Jones .10 .04
❑ 228 Tom Lawless .10 .04
❑ 229 Bill Gullickson .10 .04
❑ 230 Terry Kennedy .10 .04
❑ 231 Jim Frey MG .10 .04
❑ 232 Rick Rhoden .10 .04
❑ 233 Steve Lyons .10 .04
❑ 234 Doug Corbett .10 .04
❑ 235 Butch Wynegar .10 .04
❑ 236 Frank Eufemia .10 .04
❑ 237 Ted Simmons .15 .06
❑ 238 Larry Parrish .10 .04
❑ 239 Joel Skinner .10 .04
❑ 240 Tommy John .40 .16
❑ 241 Tony Fernandez .10 .04
❑ 242 Rich Thompson .10 .04
❑ 243 Johnny Grubb .10 .04
❑ 244 Craig Lefferts .10 .04
❑ 245 Jim Sundberg .10 .04
❑ 246 Steve Carlton TL .15 .06
❑ 247 Terry Harper .10 .04
❑ 248 Spike Owen .10 .04
❑ 249 Rob Deer .15 .06
❑ 250 Dwight Gooden .40 .16
❑ 251 Rich Dauer .10 .04
❑ 252 Bobby Castillo .10 .04
❑ 253 Dann Bilardello .10 .04
❑ 254 Ozzie Guillen RC* .25 .10
❑ 255 Tony Armas .10 .04
❑ 256 Kurt Kepshire .10 .04
❑ 257 Doug DeCinces .10 .04
❑ 258 Tim Burke .10 .04
❑ 259 Dan Pasqua .10 .04
❑ 260 Tony Pena .10 .04
❑ 261 Bobby Valentine MG .15 .06
❑ 262 Mario Ramirez .10 .04
❑ 263 Checklist: 133-264 .15 .06
❑ 264 Darren Daulton RC .75 .30
❑ 265 Ron Davis .10 .04
❑ 266 Keith Moreland .10 .04
❑ 267 Paul Molitor .25 .10
❑ 268 Mike Scott .10 .04
❑ 269 Dane Iorg .10 .04
❑ 270 Jack Morris .15 .06
❑ 271 Dave Collins .10 .04
❑ 272 Tim Tolman .10 .04
❑ 273 Jerry Willard .10 .04
❑ 274 Ron Gardenhire .10 .04
❑ 275 Charlie Hough .15 .06
❑ 276 Willie Randolph TL .15 .06
❑ 277 Jaime Cocanower .10 .04
❑ 278 Sixto Lezcano .10 .04
❑ 279 Al Pardo .10 .04
❑ 280 Tim Raines .15 .06
❑ 281 Steve Mura .10 .04
❑ 282 Jerry Mumphrey .10 .04
❑ 283 Mike Fischlin .10 .04
❑ 284 Brian Dayett .10 .04
❑ 285 Buddy Bell .15 .06
❑ 286 Luis DeLeon .10 .04
❑ 287 John Christensen .10 .04
❑ 288 Don Aase .10 .04
❑ 289 Johnnie LeMaster .10 .04
❑ 290 Carlton Fisk .25 .10
❑ 291 Tom Lasorda MG .25 .10
❑ 292 Chuck Porter .10 .04
❑ 293 Chris Chambliss .15 .06
❑ 294 Danny Cox .10 .04
❑ 295 Kirk Gibson .15 .06
❑ 296 Geno Petralli .10 .04
❑ 297 Tim Lollar .10 .04
❑ 298 Craig Reynolds .10 .04
❑ 299 Bryn Smith .10 .04
❑ 300 George Brett 1.25 .50
❑ 301 Dennis Rasmussen .10 .04
❑ 302 Greg Gross .10 .04
❑ 303 Curt Wardle .10 .04
❑ 304 Mike Gallego RC .10 .04
❑ 305 Phil Bradley .10 .04
❑ 306 Terry Kennedy TL .10 .04
❑ 307 Dave Sax .10 .04
❑ 308 Ray Fontenot .10 .04
❑ 309 John Shelby .10 .04
❑ 310 Greg Minton .10 .04
❑ 311 Dick Schofield .10 .04
❑ 312 Tom Filer .10 .04
❑ 313 Joe DeSa .10 .04
❑ 314 Frank Pastore .10 .04
❑ 315 Mookie Wilson .15 .06
❑ 316 Sammy Khalifa .10 .04
❑ 317 Ed Romero .10 .04
❑ 318 Terry Whitfield .10 .04
❑ 319 Rick Camp .10 .04
❑ 320 Jim Rice .15 .06
❑ 321 Earl Weaver MG .40 .16
❑ 322 Bob Forsch .10 .04
❑ 323 Jerry Davis .10 .04
❑ 324 Dan Schatzeder .10 .04
❑ 325 Juan Beniquez .10 .04
❑ 326 Kent Tekulve .10 .04
❑ 327 Mike Pagliarulo .10 .04
❑ 328 Pete O'Brien .10 .04
❑ 329 Kirby Puckett .75 .30
❑ 330 Rick Sutcliffe .15 .06
❑ 331 Alan Ashby .10 .04
❑ 332 Darryl Motley .10 .04
❑ 333 Tom Henke .15 .06
❑ 334 Ken Oberkfell .10 .04
❑ 335 Don Sutton .40 .16
❑ 336 Andre Thornton TL .15 .06
❑ 337 Darnell Coles .10 .04
❑ 338 Jorge Bell .15 .06
❑ 339 Bruce Berenyi .10 .04
❑ 340 Cal Ripken 1.50 .60
❑ 341 Frank Williams .10 .04
❑ 342 Gary Redus .10 .04
❑ 343 Carlos Diaz .10 .04
❑ 344 Jim Wohlford .10 .04
❑ 345 Donnie Moore .10 .04
❑ 346 Bryan Little .10 .04
❑ 347 Teddy Higuera RC* .25 .10
❑ 348 Cliff Johnson .10 .04
❑ 349 Mark Clear .10 .04
❑ 350 Jack Clark .15 .06
❑ 351 Chuck Tanner MG .10 .04
❑ 352 Harry Spilman .10 .04
❑ 353 Keith Atherton .10 .04
❑ 354 Tony Bernazard .10 .04
❑ 355 Lee Smith .25 .10
❑ 356 Mickey Hatcher .10 .04
❑ 357 Ed VandeBerg .10 .04
❑ 358 Rick Dempsey .10 .04
❑ 359 Mike LaCoss .10 .04
❑ 360 Lloyd Moseby .10 .04
❑ 361 Shane Rawley .10 .04
❑ 362 Tom Paciorek .15 .06
❑ 363 Terry Forster .10 .04
❑ 364 Reid Nichols .10 .04
❑ 365 Mike Flanagan .10 .04
❑ 366 Dave Concepcion TL .15 .06
❑ 367 Aurelio Lopez .10 .04
❑ 368 Greg Brock .10 .04
❑ 369 Al Holland .10 .04
❑ 370 Vince Coleman RC* .50 .20
❑ 371 Bill Stein .10 .04
❑ 372 Ben Oglivie .10 .04
❑ 373 Urbano Lugo .10 .04
❑ 374 Terry Francona .10 .04
❑ 375 Rich Gedman .10 .04
❑ 376 Bill Dawley .10 .04
❑ 377 Joe Carter .40 .16
❑ 378 Bruce Bochte .10 .04
❑ 379 Bobby Meacham .10 .04

❑ 380 LaMarr Hoyt .10 .04
❑ 381 Ray Miller MG .10 .04
❑ 382 Ivan Calderon RC* .25 .10
❑ 383 Chris Brown .10 .04
❑ 384 Steve Trout .10 .04
❑ 385 Cecil Cooper .15 .06
❑ 386 Cecil Fielder RC .75 .30
❑ 387 Steve Kemp .10 .04
❑ 388 Dickie Noles .10 .04
❑ 389 Glenn Davis .15 .06
❑ 390 Tom Seaver .40 .16
❑ 391 Julio Franco .15 .06
❑ 392 John Russell .10 .04
❑ 393 Chris Pittaro .10 .04
❑ 394 Checklist: 265-396 .15 .06
❑ 395 Scott Garrelts .10 .04
❑ 396 Dwight Evans TL .15 .06
❑ 397 Steve Buechele RC .25 .10
❑ 398 Earnie Riles .10 .04
❑ 399 Bill Swift .10 .04
❑ 400 Rod Carew .25 .10
❑ 401 Fernando Valenzuela TBC '81 .15 .06
❑ 402 Tom Seaver TBC '76 .25 .10
❑ 403 Willie Mays TBC '71 .25 .10
❑ 404 Frank Robinson TBC '66 .15 .06
❑ 405 Roger Maris TBC '61 .15 .06
❑ 406 Scott Sanderson .10 .04
❑ 407 Sal Butera .10 .04
❑ 408 Dave Smith .10 .04
❑ 409 Paul Runge RC .10 .04
❑ 410 Dave Kingman .15 .06
❑ 411 Sparky Anderson MG .25 .10
❑ 412 Jim Clancy .10 .04
❑ 413 Tim Flannery .10 .04
❑ 414 Tom Gorman .10 .04
❑ 415 Hal McRae .15 .06
❑ 416 Dennis Martinez .15 .06
❑ 417 R.J. Reynolds .10 .04
❑ 418 Alan Knicely .10 .04
❑ 419 Frank Wills .10 .04
❑ 420 Von Hayes .10 .04
❑ 421 David Palmer .10 .04
❑ 422 Mike Jorgensen .10 .04
❑ 423 Dan Spillner .10 .04
❑ 424 Rick Miller .10 .04
❑ 425 Larry McWilliams .10 .04
❑ 426 Charlie Moore TL .10 .04
❑ 427 Joe Cowley .10 .04
❑ 428 Max Venable .10 .04
❑ 429 Greg Booker .10 .04
❑ 430 Kent Hrbek .15 .06
❑ 431 George Frazier .10 .04
❑ 432 Mark Bailey .10 .04
❑ 433 Chris Codiroli .10 .04
❑ 434 Curt Wilkerson .10 .04
❑ 435 Bill Caudill .10 .04
❑ 436 Doug Flynn .10 .04
❑ 437 Rick Mahler .10 .04
❑ 438 Clint Hurdle .10 .04
❑ 439 Rick Honeycutt .10 .04
❑ 440 Alvin Davis .10 .04
❑ 441 Whitey Herzog MG .25 .10
❑ 442 Ron Robinson .10 .04
❑ 443 Bill Buckner .15 .06
❑ 444 Alex Trevino .10 .04
❑ 445 Bert Blyleven .15 .06
❑ 446 Lenn Sakata .10 .04
❑ 447 Jerry Don Gleaton .10 .04
❑ 448 Herm Winningham .10 .04
❑ 449 Rod Scurry .10 .04
❑ 450 Graig Nettles .15 .06
❑ 451 Mark Brown .10 .04
❑ 452 Bob Clark .10 .04
❑ 453 Steve Jeltz .10 .04
❑ 454 Burt Hooton .10 .04
❑ 455 Willie Randolph .15 .06
❑ 456 Dale Murphy TL .25 .10
❑ 457 Mickey Tettleton RC .25 .10
❑ 458 Kevin Bass .10 .04
❑ 459 Luis Leal .10 .04
❑ 460 Leon Durham .10 .04
❑ 461 Walt Terrell .10 .04
❑ 462 Domingo Ramos .10 .04
❑ 463 Jim Gott .10 .04
❑ 464 Ruppert Jones .10 .04
❑ 465 Jesse Orosco .10 .04
❑ 466 Tom Foley .10 .04
❑ 467 Bob James .10 .04
❑ 468 Mike Scioscia .10 .04
❑ 469 Storm Davis .10 .04
❑ 470 Bill Madlock .10 .04
❑ 471 Bobby Cox MG .15 .06
❑ 472 Joe Hesketh .10 .04
❑ 473 Mark Brouhard .10 .04
❑ 474 John Tudor .10 .04
❑ 475 Juan Samuel .10 .04
❑ 476 Ron Mathis .10 .04
❑ 477 Mike Easler .10 .04
❑ 478 Andy Hawkins .10 .04
❑ 479 Bob Melvin .10 .04
❑ 480 Oddibe McDowell .10 .04
❑ 481 Scott Bradley .10 .04
❑ 482 Rick Lysander .10 .04
❑ 483 George Vukovich .10 .04
❑ 484 Donnie Hill .10 .04
❑ 485 Gary Matthews .10 .04
❑ 486 Bobby Grich TL .10 .04
❑ 487 Bret Saberhagen .15 .06
❑ 488 Lou Thornton .10 .04
❑ 489 Jim Winn .10 .04
❑ 490 Jeff Leonard .10 .04
❑ 491 Pascual Perez .10 .04
❑ 492 Kelvin Chapman .10 .04
❑ 493 Gene Nelson .10 .04
❑ 494 Gary Roenicke .10 .04
❑ 495 Mark Langston .10 .04
❑ 496 Jay Johnstone .15 .06
❑ 497 John Stuper .10 .04
❑ 498 Tito Landrum .10 .04
❑ 499 Bob L. Gibson .10 .04
❑ 500 Rickey Henderson .75 .30
❑ 501 Dave Johnson MG .15 .06
❑ 502 Glen Cook .10 .04
❑ 503 Mike Fitzgerald .10 .04
❑ 504 Denny Walling .10 .04
❑ 505 Jerry Koosman .15 .06
❑ 506 Bill Russell .10 .04
❑ 507 Steve Ontiveros RC .10 .04
❑ 508 Alan Wiggins .10 .04
❑ 509 Ernie Camacho .10 .04
❑ 510 Wade Boggs .25 .10
❑ 511 Ed Nunez .10 .04
❑ 512 Thad Bosley .10 .04
❑ 513 Ron Washington .10 .04
❑ 514 Mike Jones .10 .04
❑ 515 Darrell Evans .15 .06
❑ 516 Greg Minton TL .10 .04
❑ 517 Milt Thompson RC .10 .04
❑ 518 Buck Martinez .10 .04
❑ 519 Danny Darwin .10 .04
❑ 520 Keith Hernandez .25 .10
❑ 521 Nate Snell .10 .04
❑ 522 Bob Bailor .10 .04
❑ 523 Joe Price .10 .04
❑ 524 Darrell Miller .10 .04
❑ 525 Marvell Wynne .10 .04
❑ 526 Charlie Lea .10 .04
❑ 527 Checklist: 397-528 .15 .06
❑ 528 Terry Pendleton .15 .06
❑ 529 Marc Sullivan .10 .04
❑ 530 Rich Gossage .15 .06
❑ 531 Tony LaRussa MG .15 .06
❑ 532 Don Carman .10 .04
❑ 533 Billy Sample .10 .04
❑ 534 Jeff Calhoun .10 .04
❑ 535 Toby Harrah .10 .04
❑ 536 Jose Rijo .10 .04
❑ 537 Mark Salas .10 .04
❑ 538 Dennis Eckersley .25 .10
❑ 539 Glenn Hubbard .10 .04
❑ 540 Dan Petry .10 .04
❑ 541 Jorge Orta .10 .04
❑ 542 Don Schulze .10 .04
❑ 543 Jerry Narron .10 .04
❑ 544 Eddie Milner .10 .04
❑ 545 Jimmy Key .40 .16
❑ 546 Dave Henderson TL .10 .04
❑ 547 Roger McDowell RC* .10 .04
❑ 548 Mike Young .10 .04
❑ 549 Bob Welch .10 .04
❑ 550 Tom Herr .10 .04
❑ 551 Dave LaPoint .10 .04
❑ 552 Marc Hill .10 .04
❑ 553 Jim Morrison .10 .04
❑ 554 Paul Householder .10 .04
❑ 555 Hubie Brooks .10 .04
❑ 556 John Denny .10 .04
❑ 557 Gerald Perry .10 .04
❑ 558 Tim Stoddard .10 .04
❑ 559 Tommy Dunbar .10 .04
❑ 560 Dave Righetti .10 .04
❑ 561 Bob Lillis MG .10 .04
❑ 562 Joe Beckwith .10 .04
❑ 563 Alejandro Sanchez .10 .04
❑ 564 Warren Brusstar .10 .04
❑ 565 Tom Brunansky .10 .04
❑ 566 Alfredo Griffin .10 .04
❑ 567 Jeff Barkley .10 .04
❑ 568 Donnie Scott .10 .04
❑ 569 Jim Acker .10 .04
❑ 570 Rusty Staub .15 .06
❑ 571 Mike Jeffcoat .10 .04
❑ 572 Paul Zuvella .10 .04
❑ 573 Tom Hume .10 .04
❑ 574 Ron Kittle .10 .04
❑ 575 Mike Boddicker .10 .04
❑ 576 Andre Dawson TL .10 .04
❑ 577 Jerry Reuss .10 .04
❑ 578 Lee Mazzilli .10 .04
❑ 579 Jim Slaton .10 .04
❑ 580 Willie McGee .15 .06
❑ 581 Bruce Hurst .10 .04
❑ 582 Jim Gantner .10 .04
❑ 583 Al Bumbry .10 .04
❑ 584 Brian Fisher RC .10 .04
❑ 585 Garry Maddox .10 .04
❑ 586 Greg Harris .10 .04
❑ 587 Rafael Santana .10 .04
❑ 588 Steve Lake .10 .04
❑ 589 Sid Bream .10 .04
❑ 590 Bob Knepper .10 .04
❑ 591 Jackie Moore MG .10 .04
❑ 592 Frank Tanana .10 .04
❑ 593 Jesse Barfield .10 .04
❑ 594 Chris Bando .10 .04
❑ 595 Dave Parker .15 .06
❑ 596 Onix Concepcion .10 .04
❑ 597 Sammy Stewart .10 .04
❑ 598 Jim Presley .10 .04
❑ 599 Rick Aguilera RC .25 .10
❑ 600 Dale Murphy .40 .16
❑ 601 Gary Lucas .10 .04
❑ 602 Mariano Duncan RC* .25 .10
❑ 603 Bill Laskey .10 .04
❑ 604 Gary Pettis .10 .04
❑ 605 Dennis Boyd .10 .04
❑ 606 Hal McRae TL .15 .06
❑ 607 Ken Dayley .10 .04
❑ 608 Bruce Bochy .10 .04
❑ 609 Barbaro Garbey .10 .04
❑ 610 Ron Guidry .15 .06
❑ 611 Gary Woods .10 .04
❑ 612 Richard Dotson .10 .04
❑ 613 Roy Smalley .10 .04
❑ 614 Rick Waits .10 .04
❑ 615 Johnny Ray .10 .04
❑ 616 Glenn Brummer .10 .04
❑ 617 Lonnie Smith .10 .04
❑ 618 Jim Pankovits .10 .04
❑ 619 Danny Heep .10 .04
❑ 620 Bruce Sutter .15 .06
❑ 621 John Felske MG .10 .04
❑ 622 Gary Lavelle .10 .04
❑ 623 Floyd Rayford .10 .04
❑ 624 Steve McCatty .10 .04
❑ 625 Bob Brenly .10 .04
❑ 626 Roy Thomas .10 .04
❑ 627 Ron Oester .10 .04
❑ 628 Kirk McCaskill RC .10 .04
❑ 629 Mitch Webster .10 .04
❑ 630 Fernando Valenzuela .15 .06
❑ 631 Steve Braun .10 .04
❑ 632 Dave Von Ohlen .10 .04
❑ 633 Jackie Gutierrez .10 .04
❑ 634 Roy Lee Jackson .10 .04
❑ 635 Jason Thompson .10 .04

Card	Player	Nm-Mt	Ex-Mt
❑ 636	Lee Smith TL	.15	.06
❑ 637	Rudy Law	.10	.04
❑ 638	John Butcher	.10	.04
❑ 639	Bo Diaz	.10	.04
❑ 640	Jose Cruz	.15	.06
❑ 641	Wayne Tolleson	.10	.04
❑ 642	Ray Searage	.10	.04
❑ 643	Tom Brookens	.10	.04
❑ 644	Mark Gubicza	.10	.04
❑ 645	Dusty Baker	.15	.06
❑ 646	Mike Moore	.10	.04
❑ 647	Mel Hall	.10	.04
❑ 648	Steve Bedrosian	.10	.04
❑ 649	Ronn Reynolds	.10	.04
❑ 650	Dave Stieb	.10	.04
❑ 651	Billy Martin MG	.15	.06
❑ 652	Tom Browning	.10	.04
❑ 653	Jim Dwyer	.10	.04
❑ 654	Ken Howell	.10	.04
❑ 655	Manny Trillo	.10	.04
❑ 656	Brian Harper	.10	.04
❑ 657	Juan Agosto	.10	.04
❑ 658	Rob Wilfong	.10	.04
❑ 659	Checklist: 529-660	.15	.06
❑ 660	Steve Garvey	.15	.06
❑ 661	Roger Clemens	1.50	.60
❑ 662	Bill Schroeder	.10	.04
❑ 663	Neil Allen	.10	.04
❑ 664	Tim Corcoran	.10	.04
❑ 665	Alejandro Pena	.10	.04
❑ 666	Charlie Hough TL	.15	.06
❑ 667	Tim Teufel	.10	.04
❑ 668	Cecilio Guante	.10	.04
❑ 669	Ron Cey	.15	.06
❑ 670	Willie Hernandez	.10	.04
❑ 671	Lynn Jones	.10	.04
❑ 672	Rob Picciolo	.10	.04
❑ 673	Ernie Whitt	.10	.04
❑ 674	Pat Tabler	.10	.04
❑ 675	Claudell Washington	.10	.04
❑ 676	Matt Young	.10	.04
❑ 677	Nick Esasky	.10	.04
❑ 678	Dan Gladden	.10	.04
❑ 679	Britt Burns	.10	.04
❑ 680	George Foster	.15	.06
❑ 681	Dick Williams MG	.15	.06
❑ 682	Junior Ortiz	.10	.04
❑ 683	Andy Van Slyke	.15	.06
❑ 684	Bob McClure	.10	.04
❑ 685	Tim Wallach	.10	.04
❑ 686	Jeff Stone	.10	.04
❑ 687	Mike Trujillo	.10	.04
❑ 688	Larry Herndon	.10	.04
❑ 689	Dave Stewart	.15	.06
❑ 690	Ryne Sandberg UER (No Topps logo on front)	.75	.30
❑ 691	Mike Madden	.10	.04
❑ 692	Dale Berra	.10	.04
❑ 693	Tom Tellmann	.10	.04
❑ 694	Garth Iorg	.10	.04
❑ 695	Mike Smithson	.10	.04
❑ 696	Bill Russell TL	.15	.06
❑ 697	Bud Black	.10	.04
❑ 698	Brad Komminsk	.10	.04
❑ 699	Pat Corrales MG	.10	.04
❑ 700	Reggie Jackson	.25	.10
❑ 701	Keith Hernandez AS	.15	.06
❑ 702	Tom Herr AS	.10	.04
❑ 703	Tim Wallach AS	.10	.04
❑ 704	Ozzie Smith AS	.25	.10
❑ 705	Dale Murphy AS	.25	.10
❑ 706	Pedro Guerrero AS	.10	.04
❑ 707	Willie McGee AS	.10	.04
❑ 708	Gary Carter AS	.15	.06
❑ 709	Dwight Gooden AS	.25	.10
❑ 710	John Tudor AS	.10	.04
❑ 711	Jeff Reardon AS	.10	.04
❑ 712	Don Mattingly AS	.60	.24
❑ 713	Damaso Garcia AS	.10	.04
❑ 714	George Brett AS	.40	.16
❑ 715	Cal Ripken AS	.40	.16
❑ 716	Rickey Henderson AS	.40	.16
❑ 717	Dave Winfield AS	.15	.06
❑ 718	George Bell AS	.10	.04
❑ 719	Carlton Fisk AS	.15	.06
❑ 720	Bret Saberhagen AS	.10	.04
❑ 721	Ron Guidry AS	.15	.06
❑ 722	Dan Quisenberry AS	.10	.04
❑ 723	Marty Bystrom	.10	.04
❑ 724	Tim Hulett	.10	.04
❑ 725	Mario Soto	.10	.04
❑ 726	Rick Dempsey TL	.15	.06
❑ 727	David Green	.10	.04
❑ 728	Mike Marshall	.10	.04
❑ 729	Jim Beattie	.10	.04
❑ 730	Ozzie Smith	.40	.16
❑ 731	Don Robinson	.10	.04
❑ 732	Floyd Youmans	.10	.04
❑ 733	Ron Romanick	.10	.04
❑ 734	Marty Barrett	.10	.04
❑ 735	Dave Dravecky	.15	.06
❑ 736	Glenn Wilson	.10	.04
❑ 737	Pete Vuckovich	.10	.04
❑ 738	Andre Robertson	.10	.04
❑ 739	Dave Rozema	.10	.04
❑ 740	Lance Parrish	.15	.06
❑ 741	Pete Rose MG	.40	.16
❑ 742	Frank Viola	.15	.06
❑ 743	Pat Sheridan	.10	.04
❑ 744	Lary Sorensen	.10	.04
❑ 745	Willie Upshaw	.10	.04
❑ 746	Denny Gonzalez	.10	.04
❑ 747	Rick Cerone	.10	.04
❑ 748	Steve Henderson	.10	.04
❑ 749	Ed Jurak	.10	.04
❑ 750	Gorman Thomas	.10	.04
❑ 751	Howard Johnson	.15	.06
❑ 752	Mike Krukow	.10	.04
❑ 753	Dan Ford	.10	.04
❑ 754	Pat Clements	.10	.04
❑ 755	Harold Baines	.25	.10
❑ 756	Rick Rhoden TL	.10	.04
❑ 757	Darrell Porter	.15	.06
❑ 758	Dave Anderson	.10	.04
❑ 759	Moose Haas	.10	.04
❑ 760	Andre Dawson	.15	.06
❑ 761	Don Slaught	.10	.04
❑ 762	Eric Show	.10	.04
❑ 763	Terry Puhl	.10	.04
❑ 764	Kevin Gross	.10	.04
❑ 765	Don Baylor	.25	.10
❑ 766	Rick Langford	.10	.04
❑ 767	Jody Davis	.10	.04
❑ 768	Vern Ruhle	.10	.04
❑ 769	Harold Reynolds RC	.75	.30
❑ 770	Vida Blue	.15	.06
❑ 771	John McNamara MG	.10	.04
❑ 772	Brian Downing	.10	.04
❑ 773	Greg Pryor	.10	.04
❑ 774	Terry Leach	.10	.04
❑ 775	Al Oliver	.15	.06
❑ 776	Gene Garber	.10	.04
❑ 777	Wayne Krenchicki	.10	.04
❑ 778	Jerry Hairston	.10	.04
❑ 779	Rick Reuschel	.10	.04
❑ 780	Robin Yount	.40	.16
❑ 781	Joe Nolan	.10	.04
❑ 782	Ken Landreaux	.10	.04
❑ 783	Ricky Horton	.10	.04
❑ 784	Alan Bannister	.10	.04
❑ 785	Bob Stanley	.10	.04
❑ 786	Mickey Hatcher TL	.10	.04
❑ 787	Vance Law	.10	.04
❑ 788	Marty Castillo	.10	.04
❑ 789	Kurt Bevacqua	.10	.04
❑ 790	Phil Niekro	.15	.06
❑ 791	Checklist: 661-792	.15	.06
❑ 792	Charles Hudson	.10	.04

1986 Topps Traded

		Nm-Mt	Ex-Mt
COMP.FACT.SET (132)		40.00	16.00
❑ 1T	Andy Allanson	.10	.04
❑ 2T	Neil Allen	.10	.04
❑ 3T	Joaquin Andujar	.10	.04
❑ 4T	Paul Assenmacher	.10	.04
❑ 5T	Scott Bailes	.10	.04
❑ 6T	Don Baylor	.25	.10
❑ 7T	Steve Bedrosian	.10	.04
❑ 8T	Juan Beniquez	.10	.04
❑ 9T	Juan Berenguer	.10	.04
❑ 10T	Mike Bielecki	.10	.04
❑ 11T	Barry Bonds XRC	30.00	12.00
❑ 12T	Bobby Bonilla XRC	.50	.20
❑ 13T	Juan Bonilla	.10	.04
❑ 14T	Rich Bordi	.10	.04
❑ 15T	Steve Boros MG	.10	.04
❑ 16T	Rick Burleson	.10	.04
❑ 17T	Bill Campbell	.10	.04
❑ 18T	Tom Candiotti	.10	.04
❑ 19T	John Cangelosi	.10	.04
❑ 20T	Jose Canseco XRC	1.50	.60
❑ 21T	Carmen Castillo	.10	.04
❑ 22T	Rick Cerone	.10	.04
❑ 23T	John Cerutti	.10	.04
❑ 24T	Will Clark XRC	1.50	.60
❑ 25T	Mark Clear	.10	.04
❑ 26T	Darnell Coles	.10	.04
❑ 27T	Dave Collins	.10	.04
❑ 28T	Tim Conroy	.10	.04
❑ 29T	Joe Cowley	.10	.04
❑ 30T	Joel Davis	.10	.04
❑ 31T	Rob Deer	.10	.04
❑ 32T	John Denny	.10	.04
❑ 33T	Mike Easler	.10	.04
❑ 34T	Mark Eichhorn	.10	.04
❑ 35T	Steve Farr	.10	.04
❑ 36T	Scott Fletcher	.10	.04
❑ 37T	Terry Forster	.10	.04
❑ 38T	Terry Francona	.10	.04
❑ 39T	Jim Fregosi MG	.10	.04
❑ 40T	Andres Galarraga XRC	1.00	.40
❑ 41T	Ken Griffey	.15	.06
❑ 42T	Bill Gullickson	.10	.04
❑ 43T	Jose Guzman XRC *	.10	.04
❑ 44T	Moose Haas	.10	.04
❑ 45T	Billy Hatcher	.10	.04
❑ 46T	Mike Heath	.10	.04
❑ 47T	Tom Hume	.10	.04
❑ 48T	Pete Incaviglia XRC	.25	.10
❑ 49T	Dane Iorg	.10	.04
❑ 50T	Bo Jackson XRC	1.50	.60
❑ 51T	Wally Joyner XRC	.50	.20
❑ 52T	Charlie Kerfeld	.10	.04
❑ 53T	Eric King	.10	.04
❑ 54T	Bob Kipper	.10	.04
❑ 55T	Wayne Krenchicki	.10	.04
❑ 56T	John Kruk XRC	.75	.30
❑ 57T	Mike LaCoss	.10	.04
❑ 58T	Pete Ladd	.10	.04
❑ 59T	Mike Laga	.10	.04
❑ 60T	Hal Lanier MG	.10	.04
❑ 61T	Dave LaPoint	.10	.04
❑ 62T	Rudy Law	.10	.04
❑ 63T	Rick Leach	.10	.04
❑ 64T	Tim Leary	.10	.04
❑ 65T	Dennis Leonard	.10	.04
❑ 66T	Jim Leyland MG XRC	.25	.10
❑ 67T	Steve Lyons	.10	.04
❑ 68T	Mickey Mahler	.10	.04
❑ 69T	Candy Maldonado	.10	.04
❑ 70T	Roger Mason XRC *	.10	.04
❑ 71T	Bob McClure	.10	.04
❑ 72T	Andy McGaffigan	.10	.04
❑ 73T	Gene Michael MG	.10	.04
❑ 74T	Kevin Mitchell XRC	.50	.20
❑ 75T	Omar Moreno	.10	.04

Card	Nm-Mt	Ex-Mt
❑ 76T Jerry Mumphrey	.10	.04
❑ 77T Phil Niekro	.15	.06
❑ 78T Randy Niemann	.10	.04
❑ 79T Juan Nieves	.10	.04
❑ 80T Otis Nixon XRC*	.25	.10
❑ 81T Bob Ojeda	.10	.04
❑ 82T Jose Oquendo	.10	.04
❑ 83T Tom Paciorek	.15	.06
❑ 84T David Palmer	.10	.04
❑ 85T Frank Pastore	.10	.04
❑ 86T Lou Piniella MG	.15	.06
❑ 87T Dan Plesac	.10	.04
❑ 88T Darrell Porter	.15	.06
❑ 89T Rey Quinones	.10	.04
❑ 90T Gary Redus	.10	.04
❑ 91T Bip Roberts XRC	.25	.10
❑ 92T Billy Joe Robidoux	.10	.04
❑ 93T Jeff D. Robinson	.10	.04
❑ 94T Gary Roenicke	.10	.04
❑ 95T Ed Romero	.10	.04
❑ 96T Angel Salazar	.10	.04
❑ 97T Joe Sambito	.10	.04
❑ 98T Billy Sample	.10	.04
❑ 99T Dave Schmidt	.10	.04
❑ 100T Ken Schrom	.10	.04
❑ 101T Tom Seaver	.40	.16
❑ 102T Ted Simmons	.15	.06
❑ 103T Sammy Stewart	.10	.04
❑ 104T Kurt Stillwell	.10	.04
❑ 105T Franklin Stubbs	.10	.04
❑ 106T Dale Sveum	.10	.04
❑ 107T Chuck Tanner MG	.10	.04
❑ 108T Danny Tartabull	.15	.06
❑ 109T Tim Teufel	.10	.04
❑ 110T Bob Tewksbury XRC	.25	.10
❑ 111T Andres Thomas	.10	.04
❑ 112T Milt Thompson	.10	.04
❑ 113T R.Thompson XRC	.25	.10
❑ 114T Jay Tibbs	.10	.04
❑ 115T Wayne Tolleson	.10	.04
❑ 116T Alex Trevino	.10	.04
❑ 117T Manny Trillo	.10	.04
❑ 118T Ed VandeBerg	.10	.04
❑ 119T Ozzie Virgil	.10	.04
❑ 120T Bob Walk	.10	.04
❑ 121T Gene Walter	.10	.04
❑ 122T Claudell Washington	.10	.04
❑ 123T Bill Wegman XRC *	.10	.04
❑ 124T Dick Williams MG	.15	.06
❑ 125T Mitch Williams XRC	.25	.10
❑ 126T Bobby Witt XRC	.25	.10
❑ 127T Todd Worrell XRC *	.25	.10
❑ 128T George Wright	.10	.04
❑ 129T Ricky Wright	.10	.04
❑ 130T Steve Yeager	.10	.04
❑ 131T Paul Zuvella	.10	.04
❑ 132T Checklist 1T-132T	.10	.04

1987 Topps

	Nm-Mt	Ex-Mt
COMPLETE SET (792)	25.00	10.00
COMP.FACT SET (792)	25.00	10.00
COMP.HOBBY SET (792)	40.00	16.00
COMP.X-MAS.SET (792)	50.00	20.00

Card	Nm-Mt	Ex-Mt
❑ 1 Roger Clemens RB	.25	.10
❑ 2 Jim Deshaies RB	.05	.02
❑ 3 Dwight Evans RB	.10	.04
❑ 4 Davey Lopes RB	.05	.02
❑ 5 Dave Righetti RB	.05	.02
❑ 6 Ruben Sierra RB	.25	.10
❑ 7 Todd Worrell RB	.05	.02
❑ 8 Terry Pendleton	.10	.04
❑ 9 Jay Tibbs	.05	.02
❑ 10 Cecil Cooper	.10	.04
❑ 11 Indians Team (Mound conference)	.05	.02
❑ 12 Jeff Sellers	.05	.02
❑ 13 Nick Esasky	.05	.02
❑ 14 Dave Stewart	.10	.04
❑ 15 Claudell Washington	.05	.02
❑ 16 Pat Clements	.05	.02
❑ 17 Pete O'Brien	.05	.02
❑ 18 Dick Howser MG	.05	.02
❑ 19 Matt Young	.05	.02
❑ 20 Gary Carter	.15	.06
❑ 21 Mark Davis	.05	.02
❑ 22 Doug DeCinces	.05	.02
❑ 23 Lee Smith	.15	.06
❑ 24 Tony Walker	.05	.02
❑ 25 Bert Blyleven	.10	.04
❑ 26 Greg Brock	.05	.02
❑ 27 Joe Cowley	.05	.02
❑ 28 Rick Dempsey	.10	.04
❑ 29 Jimmy Key	.10	.04
❑ 30 Tim Raines	.10	.04
❑ 31 Braves Team (Glenn Hubbard and Rafael Ramirez)	.05	.02
❑ 32 Tim Leary	.05	.02
❑ 33 Andy Van Slyke	.10	.04
❑ 34 Jose Rijo	.05	.02
❑ 35 Sid Bream	.05	.02
❑ 36 Eric King	.05	.02
❑ 37 Marvell Wynne	.05	.02
❑ 38 Dennis Leonard	.05	.02
❑ 39 Marty Barrett	.05	.02
❑ 40 Dave Righetti	.05	.02
❑ 41 Bo Diaz	.05	.02
❑ 42 Gary Redus	.05	.02
❑ 43 Gene Michael MG	.05	.02
❑ 44 Greg Harris	.05	.02
❑ 45 Jim Presley	.05	.02
❑ 46 Dan Gladden	.05	.02
❑ 47 Dennis Powell	.05	.02
❑ 48 Wally Backman	.05	.02
❑ 49 Terry Harper	.05	.02
❑ 50 Dave Smith	.05	.02
❑ 51 Mel Hall	.05	.02
❑ 52 Keith Atherton	.05	.02
❑ 53 Ruppert Jones	.05	.02
❑ 54 Bill Dawley	.05	.02
❑ 55 Tim Wallach	.05	.02
❑ 56 Brewers Team (Mound conference)	.05	.02
❑ 57 Scott Nielsen	.05	.02
❑ 58 Thad Bosley	.05	.02
❑ 59 Ken Dayley	.05	.02
❑ 60 Tony Pena	.05	.02
❑ 61 Bobby Thigpen RC	.25	.10
❑ 62 Bobby Meacham	.05	.02
❑ 63 Fred Toliver	.05	.02
❑ 64 Harry Spilman	.05	.02
❑ 65 Tom Browning	.05	.02
❑ 66 Marc Sullivan	.05	.02
❑ 67 Bill Swift	.05	.02
❑ 68 Tony LaRussa MG	.10	.04
❑ 69 Lonnie Smith	.05	.02
❑ 70 Charlie Hough	.10	.04
❑ 71 Mike Aldrete	.05	.02
❑ 72 Walt Terrell	.05	.02
❑ 73 Dave Anderson	.05	.02
❑ 74 Dan Pasqua	.05	.02
❑ 75 Ron Darling	.05	.02
❑ 76 Rafael Ramirez	.05	.02
❑ 77 Bryan Oelkers	.05	.02
❑ 78 Tom Foley	.05	.02
❑ 79 Juan Nieves	.05	.02
❑ 80 Wally Joyner RC	.40	.16
❑ 81 Padres Team (Andy Hawkins and Terry Kennedy)	.05	.02
❑ 82 Rob Murphy	.05	.02
❑ 83 Mike Davis	.05	.02
❑ 84 Steve Lake	.05	.02
❑ 85 Kevin Bass	.05	.02
❑ 86 Nate Snell	.05	.02
❑ 87 Mark Salas	.05	.02
❑ 88 Ed Wojna	.05	.02
❑ 89 Ozzie Guillen	.10	.04
❑ 90 Dave Stieb	.05	.02
❑ 91 Harold Reynolds	.10	.04
❑ 92A Urbano Lugo ERR (no trademark)	.25	.10
❑ 92B Urbano Lugo COR	.05	.02
❑ 93 Jim Leyland MG/TC RC*	.25	.10
❑ 94 Calvin Schiraldi	.05	.02
❑ 95 Oddibe McDowell	.05	.02
❑ 96 Frank Williams	.05	.02
❑ 97 Glenn Wilson	.05	.02
❑ 98 Bill Scherrer	.05	.02
❑ 99 Darryl Motley (Now with Braves on card front)	.05	.02
❑ 100 Steve Garvey	.10	.04
❑ 101 Carl Willis RC	.10	.04
❑ 102 Paul Zuvella	.05	.02
❑ 103 Rick Aguilera	.10	.04
❑ 104 Billy Sample	.05	.02
❑ 105 Floyd Youmans	.05	.02
❑ 106 Blue Jays Team (George Bell and Jesse Barfield)	.05	.02
❑ 107 John Butcher	.05	.02
❑ 108 Jim Gantner UER (Brewers logo reversed)	.05	.02
❑ 109 R.J. Reynolds	.05	.02
❑ 110 John Tudor	.05	.02
❑ 111 Alfredo Griffin	.05	.02
❑ 112 Alan Ashby	.05	.02
❑ 113 Neil Allen	.05	.02
❑ 114 Billy Beane	.10	.04
❑ 115 Donnie Moore	.05	.02
❑ 116 Bill Russell	.05	.02
❑ 117 Jim Beattie	.05	.02
❑ 118 Bobby Valentine MG	.05	.02
❑ 119 Ron Robinson	.05	.02
❑ 120 Eddie Murray	.25	.10
❑ 121 Kevin Romine	.05	.02
❑ 122 Jim Clancy	.05	.02
❑ 123 John Kruk RC*	.40	.16
❑ 124 Ray Fontenot	.05	.02
❑ 125 Bob Brenly	.05	.02
❑ 126 Mike Loynd RC	.05	.02
❑ 127 Vance Law	.05	.02
❑ 128 Checklist 1-132	.05	.02
❑ 129 Rick Cerone	.05	.02
❑ 130 Dwight Gooden	.15	.06
❑ 131 Pirates Team (Sid Bream and Tony Pena)	.05	.02
❑ 132 Paul Assenmacher	.15	.06
❑ 133 Jose Oquendo	.05	.02
❑ 134 Rich Yett	.05	.02
❑ 135 Mike Easler	.05	.02
❑ 136 Ron Romanick	.05	.02
❑ 137 Jerry Willard	.05	.02
❑ 138 Roy Lee Jackson	.05	.02
❑ 139 Devon White RC	.40	.16
❑ 140 Bret Saberhagen	.10	.04
❑ 141 Herm Winningham	.05	.02
❑ 142 Rick Sutcliffe	.10	.04
❑ 143 Steve Boros MG	.05	.02
❑ 144 Mike Scioscia	.05	.02
❑ 145 Charlie Kerfeld	.05	.02
❑ 146 Tracy Jones	.05	.02
❑ 147 Randy Niemann	.05	.02
❑ 148 Dave Collins	.05	.02
❑ 149 Ray Searage	.05	.02
❑ 150 Wade Boggs	.15	.06
❑ 151 Mike LaCoss	.05	.02
❑ 152 Toby Harrah	.05	.02
❑ 153 Duane Ward RC *	.25	.10
❑ 154 Tom O'Malley	.05	.02
❑ 155 Eddie Whitson	.05	.02
❑ 156 Mariners Team (Mound conference)	.05	.02
❑ 157 Danny Darwin	.05	.02

❑ 158 Tim Teufel .05 .02
❑ 159 Ed Olwine .05 .02
❑ 160 Julio Franco .10 .04
❑ 161 Steve Ontiveros .05 .02
❑ 162 Mike LaValliere RC * .25 .10
❑ 163 Kevin Gross .05 .02
❑ 164 Sammy Khalifa .05 .02
❑ 165 Jeff Reardon .10 .04
❑ 166 Bob Boone .10 .04
❑ 167 Jim Deshaies RC * .10 .04
❑ 168 Lou Piniella MG .10 .04
❑ 169 Ron Washington .05 .02
❑ 170 Bo Jackson RC 1.00 .40
❑ 171 Chuck Cary .05 .02
❑ 172 Ron Oester .05 .02
❑ 173 Alex Trevino .05 .02
❑ 174 Henry Cotto .05 .02
❑ 175 Bob Stanley .05 .02
❑ 176 Steve Buechele .05 .02
❑ 177 Keith Moreland .05 .02
❑ 178 Cecil Fielder .15 .06
❑ 179 Bill Wegman .05 .02
❑ 180 Chris Brown .05 .02
❑ 181 Cardinals Team .05 .02
(Mound conference)
❑ 182 Lee Lacy .05 .02
❑ 183 Andy Hawkins .05 .02
❑ 184 Bobby Bonilla RC .40 .16
❑ 185 Roger McDowell .05 .02
❑ 186 Bruce Benedict .05 .02
❑ 187 Mark Huismann .05 .02
❑ 188 Tony Phillips .05 .02
❑ 189 Joe Hesketh .05 .02
❑ 190 Jim Sundberg .05 .02
❑ 191 Charles Hudson .05 .02
❑ 192 Cory Snyder .05 .02
❑ 193 Roger Craig MG .05 .02
❑ 194 Kirk McCaskill .05 .02
❑ 195 Mike Pagliarulo .05 .02
❑ 196 Randy O'Neal UER .05 .02
(Wrong ML career
W-L totals)
❑ 197 Mark Bailey .05 .02
❑ 198 Lee Mazzilli .05 .02
❑ 199 Mariano Duncan .05 .02
❑ 200 Pete Rose .60 .24
❑ 201 John Cangelosi .05 .02
❑ 202 Ricky Wright .05 .02
❑ 203 Mike Kingery RC .10 .04
❑ 204 Sammy Stewart .05 .02
❑ 205 Graig Nettles .10 .04
❑ 206 Twins Team .05 .02
(Frank Viola and
Tim Laudner)
❑ 207 George Frazier .05 .02
❑ 208 John Shelby .05 .02
❑ 209 Rick Schu .05 .02
❑ 210 Lloyd Moseby .05 .02
❑ 211 John Morris .05 .02
❑ 212 Mike Fitzgerald .05 .02
❑ 213 Randy Myers RC .40 .16
❑ 214 Omar Moreno .05 .02
❑ 215 Mark Langston .05 .02
❑ 216 B.J. Surhoff RC .40 .16
❑ 217 Chris Codiroli .05 .02
❑ 218 Sparky Anderson MG .10 .04
❑ 219 Cecilio Guante .05 .02
❑ 220 Joe Carter .25 .10
❑ 221 Vern Ruhle .05 .02
❑ 222 Denny Walling .05 .02
❑ 223 Charlie Leibrandt .05 .02
❑ 224 Wayne Tolleson .05 .02
❑ 225 Mike Smithson .05 .02
❑ 226 Max Venable .05 .02
❑ 227 Jamie Moyer RC .50 .20
❑ 228 Curt Wilkerson .05 .02
❑ 229 Mike Birkbeck .10 .04
❑ 230 Don Baylor .10 .04
❑ 231 Giants Team .05 .02
(Bob Brenly and
Jim Gott)
❑ 232 Reggie Williams .05 .02
❑ 233 Russ Morman .05 .02
❑ 234 Pat Sheridan .05 .02
❑ 235 Alvin Davis .05 .02
❑ 236 Tommy John .10 .04
❑ 237 Jim Morrison .05 .02
❑ 238 Bill Krueger .05 .02
❑ 239 Juan Espino .05 .02
❑ 240 Steve Balboni .05 .02
❑ 241 Danny Heep .05 .02
❑ 242 Rick Mahler .05 .02
❑ 243 Whitey Herzog MG .10 .04
❑ 244 Dickie Noles .05 .02
❑ 245 Willie Upshaw .05 .02
❑ 246 Jim Dwyer .05 .02
❑ 247 Jeff Reed .05 .02
❑ 248 Gene Walter .05 .02
❑ 249 Jim Pankovits .05 .02
❑ 250 Teddy Higuera .05 .02
❑ 251 Rob Wilfong .05 .02
❑ 252 Dennis Martinez .10 .04
❑ 253 Eddie Milner .05 .02
❑ 254 Bob Tewksbury RC * .25 .10
❑ 255 Juan Samuel .05 .02
❑ 256 Royals Team .15 .06
(George Brett and
Frank White)
❑ 257 Bob Forsch .05 .02
❑ 258 Steve Yeager .05 .02
❑ 259 Mike Greenwell RC .25 .10
❑ 260 Vida Blue .10 .04
❑ 261 Ruben Sierra RC .40 .16
❑ 262 Jim Winn .05 .02
❑ 263 Stan Javier .05 .02
❑ 264 Checklist 133-264 .05 .02
❑ 265 Darrell Evans .10 .04
❑ 266 Jeff Hamilton .05 .02
❑ 267 Howard Johnson .05 .02
❑ 268 Pat Corrales MG .10 .04
❑ 269 Cliff Speck .05 .02
❑ 270 Jody Davis .05 .02
❑ 271 Mike G. Brown .05 .02
❑ 272 Andres Galarraga .15 .06
❑ 273 Gene Nelson .05 .02
❑ 274 Jeff Hearron UER .05 .02
(Duplicate 1986
stat line on back)
❑ 275 LaMarr Hoyt .05 .02
❑ 276 Jackie Gutierrez .05 .02
❑ 277 Juan Agosto .05 .02
❑ 278 Gary Pettis .05 .02
❑ 279 Dan Plesac .05 .02
❑ 280 Jeff Leonard .05 .02
❑ 281 Reds Team .25 .10
Pete Rose, Bo Diaz
and Bill Gullickson
❑ 282 Jeff Calhoun .05 .02
❑ 283 Doug Drabek RC* .25 .10
❑ 284 John Moses .05 .02
❑ 285 Dennis Boyd .05 .02
❑ 286 Mike Woodard .05 .02
❑ 287 Dave Von Ohlen .05 .02
❑ 288 Tito Landrum .05 .02
❑ 289 Bob Kipper .05 .02
❑ 290 Leon Durham .05 .02
❑ 291 Mitch Williams RC * .25 .10
❑ 292 Franklin Stubbs .05 .02
❑ 293 Bob Rodgers MG .05 .02
❑ 294 Steve Jeltz .05 .02
❑ 295 Len Dykstra .15 .06
❑ 296 Andres Thomas .05 .02
❑ 297 Don Schulze .05 .02
❑ 298 Larry Herndon .05 .02
❑ 299 Joel Davis .05 .02
❑ 300 Reggie Jackson .15 .06
❑ 301 Luis Aquino UER .05 .02
(No trademark
never corrected)
❑ 302 Bill Schroeder .05 .02
❑ 303 Juan Berenguer .05 .02
❑ 304 Phil Garner .05 .02
❑ 305 John Franco .10 .04
❑ 306 Red Sox Team .15 .06
(Tom Seaver,
John McNamara MG,
and Rich Gedman)
❑ 307 Lee Guetterman .05 .02
❑ 308 Don Slaught .05 .02
❑ 309 Mike Young .05 .02
❑ 310 Frank Viola .05 .02
❑ 311 Rickey Henderson .25 .10
TBC '82
❑ 312 Reggie Jackson .10 .04
TBC '77
❑ 313 Roberto Clemente .25 .10
TBC '72
❑ 314 Carl Yastrzemski UER .25 .10
TBC '67 (Sic, 112
RBI's on back)
❑ 315 Maury Wills TBC '62 .10 .04
❑ 316 Brian Fisher .05 .02
❑ 317 Clint Hurdle .05 .02
❑ 318 Jim Fregosi MG .05 .02
❑ 319 Greg Swindell RC .25 .10
❑ 320 Barry Bonds RC 10.00 4.00
❑ 321 Mike Laga .05 .02
❑ 322 Chris Bando .05 .02
❑ 323 Al Newman .05 .02
❑ 324 David Palmer .05 .02
❑ 325 Garry Templeton .05 .02
❑ 326 Mark Gubicza .05 .02
❑ 327 Dale Sveum .05 .02
❑ 328 Bob Welch .05 .02
❑ 329 Ron Roenicke .05 .02
❑ 330 Mike Scott .05 .02
❑ 331 Mets Team .15 .06
(Gary Carter and
Darryl Strawberry)
❑ 332 Joe Price .05 .02
❑ 333 Ken Phelps .05 .02
❑ 334 Ed Correa .05 .02
❑ 335 Candy Maldonado .05 .02
❑ 336 Allan Anderson .05 .02
❑ 337 Darrell Miller .05 .02
❑ 338 Tim Conroy .05 .02
❑ 339 Donnie Hill .05 .02
❑ 340 Roger Clemens .50 .20
❑ 341 Mike C. Brown .05 .02
❑ 342 Bob James .05 .02
❑ 343 Hal Lanier MG .05 .02
❑ 344A Joe Niekro .05 .02
(Copyright inside
righthand border)
❑ 344B Joe Niekro .05 .02
(Copyright outside
righthand border)
❑ 345 Andre Dawson .10 .04
❑ 346 Shawon Dunston .05 .02
❑ 347 Mickey Brantley .05 .02
❑ 348 Carmelo Martinez .05 .02
❑ 349 Storm Davis .05 .02
❑ 350 Keith Hernandez .15 .06
❑ 351 Gene Garber .05 .02
❑ 352 Mike Felder .05 .02
❑ 353 Ernie Camacho .05 .02
❑ 354 Jamie Quirk .05 .02
❑ 355 Don Carman .05 .02
❑ 356 White Sox Team .05 .02
(Mound conference)
❑ 357 Steve Fireovid .05 .02
❑ 358 Sal Butera .05 .02
❑ 359 Doug Corbett .05 .02
❑ 360 Pedro Guerrero .05 .02
❑ 361 Mark Thurmond .05 .02
❑ 362 Luis Quinones .05 .02
❑ 363 Jose Guzman .05 .02
❑ 364 Randy Bush .05 .02
❑ 365 Rick Rhoden .05 .02
❑ 366 Mark McGwire 4.00 1.60
❑ 367 Jeff Lahti .05 .02
❑ 368 John McNamara MG .05 .02
❑ 369 Brian Dayett .05 .02
❑ 370 Fred Lynn .10 .04
❑ 371 Mark Eichhorn .05 .02
❑ 372 Jerry Mumphrey .05 .02
❑ 373 Jeff Dedmon .05 .02
❑ 374 Glenn Hoffman .05 .02
❑ 375 Ron Guidry .10 .04
❑ 376 Scott Bradley .05 .02
❑ 377 John Henry Johnson .05 .02
❑ 378 Rafael Santana .05 .02
❑ 379 John Russell .05 .02
❑ 380 Rich Gossage .10 .04
❑ 381 Expos Team .05 .02
(Mound conference)
❑ 382 Rudy Law .05 .02
❑ 383 Ron Davis .05 .02

❑ 384 Johnny Grubb .05 .02
❑ 385 Orel Hershiser .10 .04
❑ 386 Dickie Thon .05 .02
❑ 387 T.R. Bryden .05 .02
❑ 388 Geno Petralli .05 .02
❑ 389 Jeff D. Robinson .05 .02
❑ 390 Gary Matthews .05 .02
❑ 391 Jay Howell .05 .02
❑ 392 Checklist 265-396 .05 .02
❑ 393 Pete Rose MG .15 .06
❑ 394 Mike Bielecki .05 .02
❑ 395 Damaso Garcia .05 .02
❑ 396 Tim Lollar .05 .02
❑ 397 Greg Walker .05 .02
❑ 398 Brad Havens .05 .02
❑ 399 Curt Ford .05 .02
❑ 400 George Brett .60 .24
❑ 401 Billy Joe Robidoux .05 .02
❑ 402 Mike Trujillo .05 .02
❑ 403 Jerry Royster .05 .02
❑ 404 Doug Sisk .05 .02
❑ 405 Brook Jacoby .05 .02
❑ 406 Yankees Team .50 .20
(Rickey Henderson and
Don Mattingly)
❑ 407 Jim Acker .05 .02
❑ 408 John Mizerock .05 .02
❑ 409 Milt Thompson .05 .02
❑ 410 Fernando Valenzuela .10 .04
❑ 411 Darnell Coles .05 .02
❑ 412 Eric Davis .15 .06
❑ 413 Moose Haas .05 .02
❑ 414 Joe Orsulak .05 .02
❑ 415 Bobby Witt RC .25 .10
❑ 416 Tom Nieto .05 .02
❑ 417 Pat Perry .05 .02
❑ 418 Dick Williams MG .10 .04
❑ 419 Mark Portugal RC * .10 .04
❑ 420 Will Clark RC 1.00 .40
❑ 421 Jose DeLeon .05 .02
❑ 422 Jack Howell .05 .02
❑ 423 Jaime Cocanower .05 .02
❑ 424 Chris Speier .05 .02
❑ 425 Tom Seaver UER .25 .10
Earned Runs amount is wrong
For 86 Red Sox and Career
Also the ERA is wrong for 86 and
career
❑ 426 Floyd Rayford .05 .02
❑ 427 Edwin Nunez .05 .02
❑ 428 Bruce Bochy .05 .02
❑ 429 Tim Pyznarski .05 .02
❑ 430 Mike Schmidt .50 .20
❑ 431 Dodgers Team .05 .02
(Mound conference)
❑ 432 Jim Slaton .05 .02
❑ 433 Ed Hearn .05 .02
❑ 434 Mike Fischlin .05 .02
❑ 435 Bruce Sutter .05 .02
❑ 436 Andy Allanson .05 .02
❑ 437 Ted Power .05 .02
❑ 438 Kelly Downs RC .10 .04
❑ 439 Karl Best .05 .02
❑ 440 Willie McGee .10 .04
❑ 441 Dave Leiper .05 .02
❑ 442 Mitch Webster .05 .02
❑ 443 John Felske MG .05 .02
❑ 444 Jeff Russell .05 .02
❑ 445 Dave Lopes .10 .04
❑ 446 Chuck Finley RC .40 .16
❑ 447 Bill Almon .05 .02
❑ 448 Chris Bosio RC .25 .10
❑ 449 Pat Dodson .10 .04
❑ 450 Kirby Puckett .25 .10
❑ 451 Joe Sambito .05 .02
❑ 452 Dave Henderson .05 .02
❑ 453 Scott Terry RC .10 .04
❑ 454 Luis Salazar .05 .02
❑ 455 Mike Boddicker .05 .02
❑ 456 A's Team .05 .02
(Mound conference)
❑ 457 Len Matuszek .05 .02
❑ 458 Kelly Gruber .05 .02
❑ 459 Dennis Eckersley .15 .06
❑ 460 Darryl Strawberry .15 .06
❑ 461 Craig McMurtry .05 .02
❑ 462 Scott Fletcher .05 .02
❑ 463 Tom Candiotti .05 .02
❑ 464 Butch Wynegar .05 .02
❑ 465 Todd Worrell .10 .04
❑ 466 Kal Daniels .05 .02
❑ 467 Randy St.Claire .05 .02
❑ 468 G.Bamberger MG .05 .02
❑ 469 Mike Diaz .05 .02
❑ 470 Dave Dravecky .10 .04
❑ 471 Ronn Reynolds .05 .02
❑ 472 Bill Doran .05 .02
❑ 473 Steve Farr .05 .02
❑ 474 Jerry Narron .05 .02
❑ 475 Scott Garrelts .05 .02
❑ 476 Danny Tartabull .05 .02
❑ 477 Ken Howell .05 .02
❑ 478 Tim Laudner .05 .02
❑ 479 Bob Sebra .05 .02
❑ 480 Jim Rice .10 .04
❑ 481 Phillies Team .05 .02
(Glenn Wilson
Juan Samuel and
Von Hayes)
❑ 482 Daryl Boston .05 .02
❑ 483 Dwight Lowry .05 .02
❑ 484 Jim Traber .05 .02
❑ 485 Tony Fernandez .05 .02
❑ 486 Otis Nixon .05 .02
❑ 487 Dave Gumpert .05 .02
❑ 488 Ray Knight .05 .02
❑ 489 Bill Gullickson .05 .02
❑ 490 Dale Murphy .25 .10
❑ 491 Ron Karkovice RC .25 .10
❑ 492 Mike Heath .05 .02
❑ 493 Tom Lasorda MG .10 .04
❑ 494 Barry Jones .05 .02
❑ 495 Gorman Thomas .05 .02
❑ 496 Bruce Bochte .05 .02
❑ 497 Dale Mohorcic .05 .02
❑ 498 Bob Kearney .05 .02
❑ 499 Bruce Ruffin RC .10 .04
❑ 500 Don Mattingly .60 .24
❑ 501 Craig Lefferts .05 .02
❑ 502 Dick Schofield .05 .02
❑ 503 Larry Andersen .05 .02
❑ 504 Mickey Hatcher .05 .02
❑ 505 Bryn Smith .05 .02
❑ 506 Orioles Team .05 .02
(Mound conference)
❑ 507 Dave L. Stapleton .05 .02
❑ 508 Scott Bankhead .05 .02
❑ 509 Enos Cabell .05 .02
❑ 510 Tom Henke .05 .02
❑ 511 Steve Lyons .05 .02
❑ 512 Dave Magadan RC .25 .10
❑ 513 Carmen Castillo .05 .02
❑ 514 Orlando Mercado .05 .02
❑ 515 Willie Hernandez .05 .02
❑ 516 Ted Simmons .10 .04
❑ 517 Mario Soto .05 .02
❑ 518 Gene Mauch MG .10 .04
❑ 519 Curt Young .05 .02
❑ 520 Jack Clark .10 .04
❑ 521 Rick Reuschel .05 .02
❑ 522 Checklist 397-528 .05 .02
❑ 523 Earnie Riles .05 .02
❑ 524 Bob Shirley .05 .02
❑ 525 Phil Bradley .05 .02
❑ 526 Roger Mason .05 .02
❑ 527 Jim Wohlford .05 .02
❑ 528 Ken Dixon .05 .02
❑ 529 Alvaro Espinoza RC .10 .04
❑ 530 Tony Gwynn .30 .12
❑ 531 Astros Team .10 .04
(Yogi Berra conference)
❑ 532 Jeff Stone .05 .02
❑ 533 Angel Salazar .05 .02
❑ 534 Scott Sanderson .05 .02
❑ 535 Tony Armas .05 .02
❑ 536 Terry Mulholland RC .25 .10
❑ 537 Rance Mulliniks .05 .02
❑ 538 Tom Niedenfuer .05 .02
❑ 539 Reid Nichols .05 .02
❑ 540 Terry Kennedy .05 .02
❑ 541 Rafael Belliard RC .25 .10
❑ 542 Ricky Horton .05 .02
❑ 543 Dave Johnson MG .10 .04
❑ 544 Zane Smith .05 .02
❑ 545 Buddy Bell .10 .04
❑ 546 Mike Morgan .05 .02
❑ 547 Rob Deer .05 .02
❑ 548 Bill Mooneyham .05 .02
❑ 549 Bob Melvin .05 .02
❑ 550 Pete Incaviglia RC * .25 .10
❑ 551 Frank Wills .05 .02
❑ 552 Larry Sheets .05 .02
❑ 553 Mike Maddux .05 .02
❑ 554 Buddy Biancalana .05 .02
❑ 555 Dennis Rasmussen .05 .02
❑ 556 Angels Team .05 .02
(Rene Lachemann CO,
Mike Witt, and
Bob Boone)
❑ 557 John Cerutti .05 .02
❑ 558 Greg Gagne .05 .02
❑ 559 Lance McCullers .05 .02
❑ 560 Glenn Davis .05 .02
❑ 561 Rey Quinones .05 .02
❑ 562 Bryan Clutterbuck .05 .02
❑ 563 John Stefero .05 .02
❑ 564 Larry McWilliams .05 .02
❑ 565 Dusty Baker .10 .04
❑ 566 Tim Hulett .05 .02
❑ 567 Greg Mathews .05 .02
❑ 568 Earl Weaver MG .25 .10
❑ 569 Wade Rowdon .05 .02
❑ 570 Sid Fernandez .05 .02
❑ 571 Ozzie Virgil .05 .02
❑ 572 Pete Ladd .05 .02
❑ 573 Hal McRae .10 .04
❑ 574 Manny Lee .05 .02
❑ 575 Pat Tabler .05 .02
❑ 576 Frank Pastore .05 .02
❑ 577 Dann Bilardello .05 .02
❑ 578 Billy Hatcher .05 .02
❑ 579 Rick Burleson .05 .02
❑ 580 Mike Krukow .05 .02
❑ 581 Cubs Team .05 .02
(Ron Cey and
Steve Trout)
❑ 582 Bruce Berenyi .05 .02
❑ 583 Junior Ortiz .05 .02
❑ 584 Ron Kittle .05 .02
❑ 585 Scott Bailes .05 .02
❑ 586 Ben Oglivie .05 .02
❑ 587 Eric Plunk .05 .02
❑ 588 Wallace Johnson .05 .02
❑ 589 Steve Crawford .05 .02
❑ 590 Vince Coleman .05 .02
❑ 591 Spike Owen .05 .02
❑ 592 Chris Welsh .05 .02
❑ 593 Chuck Tanner MG .05 .02
❑ 594 Rick Anderson .05 .02
❑ 595 Keith Hernandez AS .10 .04
❑ 596 Steve Sax AS .05 .02
❑ 597 Mike Schmidt AS .25 .10
❑ 598 Ozzie Smith AS .15 .06
❑ 599 Tony Gwynn AS .15 .06
❑ 600 Dave Parker AS .05 .02
❑ 601 Darryl Strawberry AS .10 .04
❑ 602 Gary Carter AS .10 .04
❑ 603A D.Gooden AS .15 .06
ERR no trademark
❑ 603B D.Gooden AS COR .15 .06
❑ 604 F.Valenzuela AS .10 .04
❑ 605 Todd Worrell AS .10 .04
❑ 606 D.Mattingly AS COR .30 .12
❑ 606A Don Mattingly AS 1.00 .40
ERR (no trademark)
❑ 607 Tony Bernazard AS .05 .02
❑ 608 Wade Boggs AS .10 .04
❑ 609 Cal Ripken AS .25 .10
❑ 610 Jim Rice AS .05 .02
❑ 611 Kirby Puckett AS .15 .06
❑ 612 George Bell AS .05 .02
❑ 613 Lance Parrish AS UER .10 .04
(Pitcher heading
on back)
❑ 614 Roger Clemens AS .25 .10
❑ 615 Teddy Higuera AS .05 .02
❑ 616 Dave Righetti AS .05 .02
❑ 617 Al Nipper .05 .02

	Nm-Mt	Ex-Mt
❑ 618 Tom Kelly MG	.05	.02
❑ 619 Jerry Reed	.05	.02
❑ 620 Jose Canseco	.50	.20
❑ 621 Danny Cox	.05	.02
❑ 622 Glenn Braggs RC	.10	.04
❑ 623 Kurt Stillwell	.05	.02
❑ 624 Tim Burke	.05	.02
❑ 625 Mookie Wilson	.10	.04
❑ 626 Joel Skinner	.05	.02
❑ 627 Ken Oberkfell	.05	.02
❑ 628 Bob Walk	.05	.02
❑ 629 Larry Parrish	.05	.02
❑ 630 John Candelaria	.05	.02
❑ 631 Tigers Team (Mound conference)	.05	.02
❑ 632 Rob Woodward	.05	.02
❑ 633 Jose Uribe	.05	.02
❑ 634 Rafael Palmeiro RC	2.00	.80
❑ 635 Ken Schrom	.05	.02
❑ 636 Darren Daulton	.15	.06
❑ 637 Bip Roberts RC*	.25	.10
❑ 638 Rich Bordi	.05	.02
❑ 639 Gerald Perry	.05	.02
❑ 640 Mark Clear	.05	.02
❑ 641 Domingo Ramos	.05	.02
❑ 642 Al Pulido	.05	.02
❑ 643 Ron Shepherd	.05	.02
❑ 644 John Denny	.05	.02
❑ 645 Dwight Evans	.10	.04
❑ 646 Mike Mason	.05	.02
❑ 647 Tom Lawless	.05	.02
❑ 648 Barry Larkin RC	1.00	.40
❑ 649 Mickey Tettleton	.05	.02
❑ 650 Hubie Brooks	.05	.02
❑ 651 Benny Distefano	.05	.02
❑ 652 Terry Forster	.05	.02
❑ 653 Kevin Mitchell RC *	.40	.16
❑ 654 Checklist 529-660	.10	.04
❑ 655 Jesse Barfield	.05	.02
❑ 656 Rangers Team (Bobby Valentine MG and Ricky Wright)	.05	.02
❑ 657 Tom Waddell	.05	.02
❑ 658 R.Thompson RC*	.25	.10
❑ 659 Aurelio Lopez	.05	.02
❑ 660 Bob Horner	.05	.02
❑ 661 Lou Whitaker	.10	.04
❑ 662 Frank DiPino	.05	.02
❑ 663 Cliff Johnson	.05	.02
❑ 664 Mike Marshall	.05	.02
❑ 665 Rod Scurry	.05	.02
❑ 666 Von Hayes	.05	.02
❑ 667 Ron Hassey	.05	.02
❑ 668 Juan Bonilla	.05	.02
❑ 669 Bud Black	.05	.02
❑ 670 Jose Cruz	.10	.04
❑ 671A Ray Soff ERR (No D* before copyright line)	.05	.02
❑ 671B Ray Soff COR (D* before copyright line)	.05	.02
❑ 672 Chili Davis	.15	.06
❑ 673 Don Sutton	.25	.10
❑ 674 Bill Campbell	.05	.02
❑ 675 Ed Romero	.05	.02
❑ 676 Charlie Moore	.05	.02
❑ 677 Bob Grich	.10	.04
❑ 678 Carney Lansford	.10	.04
❑ 679 Kent Hrbek	.10	.04
❑ 680 Ryne Sandberg	.40	.16
❑ 681 George Bell	.05	.02
❑ 682 Jerry Reuss	.05	.02
❑ 683 Gary Roenicke	.05	.02
❑ 684 Kent Tekulve	.05	.02
❑ 685 Jerry Hairston	.05	.02
❑ 686 Doyle Alexander	.05	.02
❑ 687 Alan Trammell	.15	.06
❑ 688 Juan Beniquez	.05	.02
❑ 689 Darrell Porter	.05	.02
❑ 690 Dane Iorg	.05	.02
❑ 691 Dave Parker	.10	.04
❑ 692 Frank White	.10	.04
❑ 693 Terry Puhl	.05	.02
❑ 694 Phil Niekro	.10	.04
❑ 695 Chico Walker	.05	.02
❑ 696 Gary Lucas	.05	.02
❑ 697 Ed Lynch	.05	.02
❑ 698 Ernie Whitt	.05	.02
❑ 699 Ken Landreaux	.05	.02
❑ 700 Dave Bergman	.05	.02
❑ 701 Willie Randolph	.10	.04
❑ 702 Greg Gross	.05	.02
❑ 703 Dave Schmidt	.05	.02
❑ 704 Jesse Orosco	.05	.02
❑ 705 Bruce Hurst	.05	.02
❑ 706 Rick Manning	.05	.02
❑ 707 Bob McClure	.05	.02
❑ 708 Scott McGregor	.05	.02
❑ 709 Dave Kingman	.10	.04
❑ 710 Gary Gaetti	.10	.04
❑ 711 Ken Griffey	.10	.04
❑ 712 Don Robinson	.05	.02
❑ 713 Tom Brookens	.05	.02
❑ 714 Dan Quisenberry	.05	.02
❑ 715 Bob Dernier	.05	.02
❑ 716 Rick Leach	.05	.02
❑ 717 Ed VandeBerg	.05	.02
❑ 718 Steve Carlton	.15	.06
❑ 719 Tom Hume	.05	.02
❑ 720 Richard Dotson	.05	.02
❑ 721 Tom Herr	.05	.02
❑ 722 Bob Knepper	.05	.02
❑ 723 Brett Butler	.10	.04
❑ 724 Greg Minton	.05	.02
❑ 725 George Hendrick	.05	.02
❑ 726 Frank Tanana	.05	.02
❑ 727 Mike Moore	.05	.02
❑ 728 Tippy Martinez	.05	.02
❑ 729 Tom Paciorek	.10	.04
❑ 730 Eric Show	.05	.02
❑ 731 Dave Concepcion	.10	.04
❑ 732 Manny Trillo	.05	.02
❑ 733 Bill Caudill	.05	.02
❑ 734 Bill Madlock	.10	.04
❑ 735 Rickey Henderson	.40	.16
❑ 736 Steve Bedrosian	.05	.02
❑ 737 Floyd Bannister	.05	.02
❑ 738 Jorge Orta	.05	.02
❑ 739 Chet Lemon	.05	.02
❑ 740 Rich Gedman	.05	.02
❑ 741 Paul Molitor	.15	.06
❑ 742 Andy McGaffigan	.05	.02
❑ 743 Dwayne Murphy	.05	.02
❑ 744 Roy Smalley	.05	.02
❑ 745 Glenn Hubbard	.05	.02
❑ 746 Bob Ojeda	.05	.02
❑ 747 Johnny Ray	.05	.02
❑ 748 Mike Flanagan	.05	.02
❑ 749 Ozzie Smith	.25	.10
❑ 750 Steve Trout	.05	.02
❑ 751 Garth Iorg	.05	.02
❑ 752 Dan Petry	.05	.02
❑ 753 Rick Honeycutt	.05	.02
❑ 754 Dave LaPoint	.05	.02
❑ 755 Luis Aguayo	.05	.02
❑ 756 Carlton Fisk	.15	.06
❑ 757 Nolan Ryan	1.00	.40
❑ 758 Tony Bernazard	.05	.02
❑ 759 Joel Youngblood	.05	.02
❑ 760 Mike Witt	.05	.02
❑ 761 Greg Pryor	.05	.02
❑ 762 Gary Ward	.05	.02
❑ 763 Tim Flannery	.05	.02
❑ 764 Bill Buckner	.10	.04
❑ 765 Kirk Gibson	.10	.04
❑ 766 Don Aase	.05	.02
❑ 767 Ron Cey	.10	.04
❑ 768 Dennis Lamp	.05	.02
❑ 769 Steve Sax	.05	.02
❑ 770 Dave Winfield	.15	.06
❑ 771 Shane Rawley	.05	.02
❑ 772 Harold Baines	.10	.04
❑ 773 Robin Yount	.25	.10
❑ 774 Wayne Krenchicki	.05	.02
❑ 775 Joaquin Andujar	.05	.02
❑ 776 Tom Brunansky	.05	.02
❑ 777 Chris Chambliss	.10	.04
❑ 778 Jack Morris	.10	.04
❑ 779 Craig Reynolds	.05	.02
❑ 780 Andre Thornton	.05	.02
❑ 781 Atlee Hammaker	.05	.02
❑ 782 Brian Downing	.05	.02
❑ 783 Willie Wilson	.10	.04
❑ 784 Cal Ripken	.75	.30
❑ 785 Terry Francona	.10	.04
❑ 786 Jimy Williams MG	.05	.02
❑ 787 Alejandro Pena	.05	.02
❑ 788 Tim Stoddard	.05	.02
❑ 789 Dan Schatzeder	.05	.02
❑ 790 Julio Cruz	.05	.02
❑ 791 Lance Parrish UER (No trademark)	.10	.04
❑ 792 Checklist 661-792	.05	.02

1987 Topps Traded

	Nm-Mt	Ex-Mt
COMP.FACT.SET (132)	8.00	3.20
❑ 1T Bill Almon	.05	.02
❑ 2T Scott Bankhead	.05	.02
❑ 3T Eric Bell	.10	.04
❑ 4T Juan Beniquez	.05	.02
❑ 5T Juan Berenguer	.05	.02
❑ 6T Greg Booker	.05	.02
❑ 7T Thad Bosley	.05	.02
❑ 8T Larry Bowa MG	.10	.04
❑ 9T Greg Brock	.05	.02
❑ 10T Bob Brower	.05	.02
❑ 11T Jerry Browne	.10	.04
❑ 12T Ralph Bryant	.05	.02
❑ 13T DeWayne Buice	.05	.02
❑ 14T Ellis Burks XRC	.50	.20
❑ 15T Ivan Calderon	.05	.02
❑ 16T Jeff Calhoun	.05	.02
❑ 17T Casey Candaele	.05	.02
❑ 18T John Cangelosi	.05	.02
❑ 19T Steve Carlton	.15	.06
❑ 20T Juan Castillo	.10	.04
❑ 21T Rick Cerone	.05	.02
❑ 22T Ron Cey	.10	.04
❑ 23T John Christensen	.05	.02
❑ 24T David Cone XRC	.75	.30
❑ 25T Chuck Crim	.05	.02
❑ 26T Storm Davis	.05	.02
❑ 27T Andre Dawson	.10	.04
❑ 28T Rick Dempsey	.10	.04
❑ 29T Doug Drabek	.25	.10
❑ 30T Mike Dunne	.05	.02
❑ 31T Dennis Eckersley	.15	.06
❑ 32T Lee Elia MG	.05	.02
❑ 33T Brian Fisher	.05	.02
❑ 34T Terry Francona	.10	.04
❑ 35T Willie Fraser	.10	.04
❑ 36T Billy Gardner MG	.05	.02
❑ 37T Ken Gerhart	.05	.02
❑ 38T Dan Gladden	.05	.02
❑ 39T Jim Gott	.05	.02
❑ 40T Cecilio Guante	.05	.02
❑ 41T Albert Hall	.05	.02
❑ 42T Terry Harper	.05	.02
❑ 43T Mickey Hatcher	.05	.02
❑ 44T Brad Havens	.05	.02
❑ 45T Neal Heaton	.05	.02
❑ 46T Mike Henneman XRC	.25	.10
❑ 47T Donnie Hill	.05	.02
❑ 48T Guy Hoffman	.05	.02
❑ 49T Brian Holton	.05	.02
❑ 50T Charles Hudson	.05	.02

Card	Nm-Mt	Ex-Mt
❑ 51T Danny Jackson	.05	.02
❑ 52T Reggie Jackson	.15	.06
❑ 53T Chris James XRC *	.10	.04
❑ 54T Dion James	.05	.02
❑ 55T Stan Jefferson	.05	.02
❑ 56T Joe Johnson	.05	.02
❑ 57T Terry Kennedy	.05	.02
❑ 58T Mike Kingery	.10	.04
❑ 59T Ray Knight	.05	.02
❑ 60T Gene Larkin XRC	.25	.10
❑ 61T Mike LaValliere	.25	.10
❑ 62T Jack Lazorko	.05	.02
❑ 63T Terry Leach	.05	.02
❑ 64T Tim Leary	.05	.02
❑ 65T Jim Lindeman	.10	.04
❑ 66T Steve Lombardozzi	.05	.02
❑ 67T Bill Long	.05	.02
❑ 68T Barry Lyons	.05	.02
❑ 69T Shane Mack	.05	.02
❑ 70T Greg Maddux XRC	5.00	2.00
❑ 71T Bill Madlock	.10	.04
❑ 72T Joe Magrane XRC	.10	.04
❑ 73T Dave Martinez XRC *	.25	.10
❑ 74T Fred McGriff	.60	.24
❑ 75T Mark McLemore	.10	.04
❑ 76T Kevin McReynolds	.05	.02
❑ 77T Dave Meads	.05	.02
❑ 78T Eddie Milner	.05	.02
❑ 79T Greg Minton	.05	.02
❑ 80T John Mitchell XRC	.10	.04
❑ 81T Kevin Mitchell	.15	.06
❑ 82T Charlie Moore	.05	.02
❑ 83T Jeff Musselman	.05	.02
❑ 84T Gene Nelson	.05	.02
❑ 85T Graig Nettles	.10	.04
❑ 86T Al Newman	.05	.02
❑ 87T Reid Nichols	.05	.02
❑ 88T Tom Niedenfuer	.05	.02
❑ 89T Joe Niekro	.05	.02
❑ 90T Tom Nieto	.05	.02
❑ 91T Matt Nokes XRC	.25	.10
❑ 92T Dickie Noles	.05	.02
❑ 93T Pat Pacillo	.05	.02
❑ 94T Lance Parrish	.10	.04
❑ 95T Tony Pena	.05	.02
❑ 96T Luis Polonia XRC	.10	.04
❑ 97T Randy Ready	.05	.02
❑ 98T Jeff Reardon	.10	.04
❑ 99T Gary Redus	.05	.02
❑ 100T Jeff Reed	.05	.02
❑ 101T Rick Rhoden	.05	.02
❑ 102T Cal Ripken Sr. MG	.05	.02
❑ 103T Wally Ritchie	.05	.02
❑ 104T Jeff M. Robinson	.05	.02
❑ 105T Gary Roenicke	.05	.02
❑ 106T Jerry Royster	.05	.02
❑ 107T Mark Salas	.05	.02
❑ 108T Luis Salazar	.05	.02
❑ 109T Benny Santiago	.50	.20
❑ 110T Dave Schmidt	.05	.02
❑ 111T Kevin Seitzer XRC*	.25	.10
❑ 112T John Shelby	.05	.02
❑ 113T Steve Shields	.05	.02
❑ 114T John Smiley XRC	.25	.10
❑ 115T Chris Speier	.05	.02
❑ 116T Mike Stanley XRC*	.25	.10
❑ 117T Terry Steinbach XRC	.25	.10
❑ 118T Les Straker	.05	.02
❑ 119T Jim Sundberg	.05	.02
❑ 120T Danny Tartabull	.05	.02
❑ 121T Tom Trebelhorn MG	.05	.02
❑ 122T Dave Valle XRC **	.10	.04
❑ 123T Ed VandeBerg	.05	.02
❑ 124T Andy Van Slyke	.10	.04
❑ 125T Gary Ward	.05	.02
❑ 126T Alan Wiggins	.05	.02
❑ 127T Bill Wilkinson	.05	.02
❑ 128T Frank Williams	.05	.02
❑ 129T Matt Williams XRC	1.00	.40
❑ 130T Jim Winn	.05	.02
❑ 131T Matt Young	.05	.02
❑ 132T Checklist 1T-132T	.05	.02

1988 Topps

	Nm-Mt	Ex-Mt
COMPLETE SET (792)	15.00	6.00
COMP.FACT SET (792)	15.00	6.00
COMP.X-MAS.SET (792)	40.00	16.00
❑ 1 Vince Coleman RB	.05	.02
❑ 2 Don Mattingly RB	.30	.12
❑ 3 Mark McGwire RB	.75	.30
Rookie Homer Record		
(No white spot)		
❑ 3A Mark McGwire RB	.20	.08
Rookie Homer Record		
(White spot behind		
left foot)		
❑ 4 Eddie Murray RB	.15	.06
Switch Home Runs,		
Two Straight Games		
(No caption on front)		
❑ 4A Eddie Murray RB	.50	.20
Switch Home Runs,		
Two Straight Games		
(Caption in box		
on card front)		
❑ 5 Phil Niekro	.10	.04
Joe Niekro RB		
❑ 6 Nolan Ryan RB	.20	.08
❑ 7 Benito Santiago RB	.10	.04
❑ 8 Kevin Elster	.05	.02
❑ 9 Andy Hawkins	.05	.02
❑ 10 Ryne Sandberg	.40	.16
❑ 11 Mike Young	.05	.02
❑ 12 Bill Schroeder	.05	.02
❑ 13 Andres Thomas	.05	.02
❑ 14 Sparky Anderson MG	.10	.04
❑ 15 Chili Davis	.15	.06
❑ 16 Kirk McCaskill	.05	.02
❑ 17 Ron Oester	.05	.02
❑ 18A Al Leiter RC ERR	.20	.08
(Photo actually		
Steve George,		
right ear visible)		
❑ 18B Al Leiter RC COR	.50	.20
(Left ear visible)		
❑ 19 Mark Davidson	.05	.02
❑ 20 Kevin Gross	.05	.02
❑ 21 Wade Boggs	.10	.04
Spike Owen TL		
❑ 22 Greg Swindell	.05	.02
❑ 23 Ken Landreaux	.05	.02
❑ 24 Jim Deshaies	.05	.02
❑ 25 Andres Galarraga	.10	.04
❑ 26 Mitch Williams	.05	.02
❑ 27 R.J. Reynolds	.05	.02
❑ 28 Jose Nunez	.05	.02
❑ 29 Angel Salazar	.05	.02
❑ 30 Sid Fernandez	.05	.02
❑ 31 Bruce Bochy	.05	.02
❑ 32 Mike Morgan	.05	.02
❑ 33 Rob Deer	.05	.02
❑ 34 Ricky Horton	.05	.02
❑ 35 Harold Baines	.10	.04
❑ 36 Jamie Moyer	.20	.08
❑ 37 Ed Romero	.05	.02
❑ 38 Jeff Calhoun	.05	.02
❑ 39 Gerald Perry	.05	.02
❑ 40 Orel Hershiser	.10	.04

Card	Nm-Mt	Ex-Mt
❑ 41 Bob Melvin	.05	.02
❑ 42 Bill Landrum	.05	.02
❑ 43 Dick Schofield	.05	.02
❑ 44 Lou Piniella MG	.10	.04
❑ 45 Kent Hrbek	.10	.04
❑ 46 Darnell Coles	.05	.02
❑ 47 Joaquin Andujar	.05	.02
❑ 48 Alan Ashby	.05	.02
❑ 49 Dave Clark	.05	.02
❑ 50 Hubie Brooks	.05	.02
❑ 51 Eddie Murray	.40	.16
Cal Ripken TL		
❑ 52 Don Robinson	.05	.02
❑ 53 Curt Wilkerson	.05	.02
❑ 54 Jim Clancy	.05	.02
❑ 55 Phil Bradley	.05	.02
❑ 56 Ed Hearn	.05	.02
❑ 57 Tim Crews RC	.05	.02
❑ 58 Dave Magadan	.05	.02
❑ 59 Danny Cox	.05	.02
❑ 60 Rickey Henderson	.40	.16
❑ 61 Mark Knudson	.05	.02
❑ 62 Jeff Hamilton	.05	.02
❑ 63 Jimmy Jones	.05	.02
❑ 64 Ken Caminiti RC	.50	.20
❑ 65 Leon Durham	.05	.02
❑ 66 Shane Rawley	.05	.02
❑ 67 Ken Oberkfell	.05	.02
❑ 68 Dave Dravecky	.10	.04
❑ 69 Mike Hart	.05	.02
❑ 70 Roger Clemens	.50	.20
❑ 71 Gary Pettis	.05	.02
❑ 72 Dennis Eckersley	.10	.04
❑ 73 Randy Bush	.05	.02
❑ 74 Tom Lasorda MG	.20	.08
❑ 75 Joe Carter	.20	.08
❑ 76 Dennis Martinez	.10	.04
❑ 77 Tom O'Malley	.05	.02
❑ 78 Dan Petry	.05	.02
❑ 79 Ernie Whitt	.05	.02
❑ 80 Mark Langston	.05	.02
❑ 81 Ron Robinson	.05	.02
John Franco TL		
❑ 82 Darrel Akerfelds	.05	.02
❑ 83 Jose Oquendo	.05	.02
❑ 84 Cecilio Guante	.05	.02
❑ 85 Howard Johnson	.05	.02
❑ 86 Ron Karkovice	.05	.02
❑ 87 Mike Mason	.05	.02
❑ 88 Earnie Riles	.05	.02
❑ 89 Gary Thurman	.05	.02
❑ 90 Dale Murphy	.20	.08
❑ 91 Joey Cora RC	.20	.08
❑ 92 Len Matuszek	.05	.02
❑ 93 Bob Sebra	.05	.02
❑ 94 Chuck Jackson	.05	.02
❑ 95 Lance Parrish	.05	.02
❑ 96 Todd Benzinger RC*	.05	.02
❑ 97 Scott Garrelts	.05	.02
❑ 98 Rene Gonzales RC	.05	.02
❑ 99 Chuck Finley	.15	.06
❑ 100 Jack Clark	.10	.04
❑ 101 Allan Anderson	.05	.02
❑ 102 Barry Larkin	.20	.08
❑ 103 Curt Young	.05	.02
❑ 104 Dick Williams MG	.10	.04
❑ 105 Jesse Orosco	.05	.02
❑ 106 Jim Walewander	.05	.02
❑ 107 Scott Bailes	.05	.02
❑ 108 Steve Lyons	.05	.02
❑ 109 Joel Skinner	.05	.02
❑ 110 Teddy Higuera	.05	.02
❑ 111 Hubie Brooks	.05	.02
Vance Law TL		
❑ 112 Les Lancaster	.05	.02
❑ 113 Kelly Gruber	.05	.02
❑ 114 Jeff Russell	.05	.02
❑ 115 Johnny Ray	.05	.02
❑ 116 Jerry Don Gleaton	.05	.02
❑ 117 James Steels	.05	.02
❑ 118 Bob Welch	.05	.02
❑ 119 Robbie Wine	.05	.02
❑ 120 Kirby Puckett	.20	.08
❑ 121 Checklist 1-132	.05	.02
❑ 122 Tony Bernazard	.05	.02
❑ 123 Tom Candiotti	.05	.02

❑ 124 Ray Knight .05 .02
❑ 125 Bruce Hurst .05 .02
❑ 126 Steve Jeltz .05 .02
❑ 127 Jim Gott .05 .02
❑ 128 Johnny Grubb .05 .02
❑ 129 Greg Minton .05 .02
❑ 130 Buddy Bell .10 .04
❑ 131 Don Schulze .05 .02
❑ 132 Donnie Hill .05 .02
❑ 133 Greg Mathews .05 .02
❑ 134 Chuck Tanner MG .10 .04
❑ 135 Dennis Rasmussen .05 .02
❑ 136 Brian Dayett .05 .02
❑ 137 Chris Bosio .05 .02
❑ 138 Mitch Webster .05 .02
❑ 139 Jerry Browne .05 .02
❑ 140 Jesse Barfield .05 .02
❑ 141 George Brett .20 .08
Bret Saberhagen TL
❑ 142 Andy Van Slyke .10 .04
❑ 143 Mickey Tettleton .05 .02
❑ 144 Don Gordon .05 .02
❑ 145 Bill Madlock .10 .04
❑ 146 Donell Nixon .05 .02
❑ 147 Bill Buckner .10 .04
❑ 148 Carmelo Martinez .05 .02
❑ 149 Ken Howell .05 .02
❑ 150 Eric Davis .10 .04
❑ 151 Bob Knepper .05 .02
❑ 152 Jody Reed RC .10 .04
❑ 153 John Habyan .05 .02
❑ 154 Jeff Stone .05 .02
❑ 155 Bruce Sutter .10 .04
❑ 156 Gary Matthews .05 .02
❑ 157 Atlee Hammaker .05 .02
❑ 158 Tim Hulett .05 .02
❑ 159 Brad Arnsberg .05 .02
❑ 160 Willie McGee .10 .04
❑ 161 Bryn Smith .05 .02
❑ 162 Mark McLemore .05 .02
❑ 163 Dale Mohorcic .05 .02
❑ 164 Dave Johnson MG .10 .04
❑ 165 Robin Yount .20 .08
❑ 166 Rick Rodriquez .05 .02
❑ 167 Rance Mulliniks .05 .02
❑ 168 Barry Jones .05 .02
❑ 169 Ross Jones .05 .02
❑ 170 Rich Gossage .10 .04
❑ 171 Shawon Dunston .05 .02
Manny Trillo TL
❑ 172 Lloyd McClendon RC .05 .02
❑ 173 Eric Plunk .05 .02
❑ 174 Phil Garner .05 .02
❑ 175 Kevin Bass .05 .02
❑ 176 Jeff Reed .05 .02
❑ 177 Frank Tanana .05 .02
❑ 178 Dwayne Henry .05 .02
❑ 179 Charlie Puleo .05 .02
❑ 180 Terry Kennedy .05 .02
❑ 181 David Cone .10 .04
❑ 182 Ken Phelps .05 .02
❑ 183 Tom Lawless .05 .02
❑ 184 Ivan Calderon .05 .02
❑ 185 Rick Rhoden .05 .02
❑ 186 Rafael Palmeiro .40 .16
❑ 187 Steve Kiefer .05 .02
❑ 188 John Russell .05 .02
❑ 189 Wes Gardner .05 .02
❑ 190 Candy Maldonado .05 .02
❑ 191 John Cerutti .05 .02
❑ 192 Devon White .10 .04
❑ 193 Brian Fisher .05 .02
❑ 194 Tom Kelly MG .05 .02
❑ 195 Dan Quisenberry .05 .02
❑ 196 Dave Engle .05 .02
❑ 197 Lance McCullers .05 .02
❑ 198 Franklin Stubbs .05 .02
❑ 199 Dave Meads .05 .02
❑ 200 Wade Boggs .15 .06
❑ 201 Bobby Valentine MG .05 .02
Pete O'Brien
Pete Incaviglia
Steve Buechele TL
❑ 202 Glenn Hoffman .05 .02
❑ 203 Fred Toliver .05 .02
❑ 204 Paul O'Neill .15 .06
❑ 205 Nelson Liriano .05 .02
❑ 206 Domingo Ramos .05 .02
❑ 207 John Mitchell RC .05 .02
❑ 208 Steve Lake .05 .02
❑ 209 Richard Dotson .05 .02
❑ 210 Willie Randolph .10 .04
❑ 211 Frank DiPino .05 .02
❑ 212 Greg Brock .05 .02
❑ 213 Albert Hall .05 .02
❑ 214 Dave Schmidt .05 .02
❑ 215 Von Hayes .05 .02
❑ 216 Jerry Reuss .05 .02
❑ 217 Harry Spilman .05 .02
❑ 218 Dan Schatzeder .05 .02
❑ 219 Mike Stanley .10 .04
❑ 220 Tom Henke .05 .02
❑ 221 Rafael Belliard .05 .02
❑ 222 Steve Farr .05 .02
❑ 223 Stan Jefferson .05 .02
❑ 224 Tom Trebelhorn MG .05 .02
❑ 225 Mike Scioscia .05 .02
❑ 226 Dave Lopes .10 .04
❑ 227 Ed Correa .05 .02
❑ 228 Wallace Johnson .05 .02
❑ 229 Jeff Musselman .05 .02
❑ 230 Pat Tabler .05 .02
❑ 231 Barry Bonds .50 .20
Bobby Bonilla TL
❑ 232 Bob James .05 .02
❑ 233 Rafael Santana .05 .02
❑ 234 Ken Dayley .05 .02
❑ 235 Gary Ward .05 .02
❑ 236 Ted Power .05 .02
❑ 237 Mike Heath .05 .02
❑ 238 Luis Polonia RC* .05 .02
❑ 239 Roy Smalley .05 .02
❑ 240 Lee Smith .10 .04
❑ 241 Damaso Garcia .05 .02
❑ 242 Tom Niedenfuer .05 .02
❑ 243 Mark Ryal .05 .02
❑ 244 Jeff D. Robinson .05 .02
❑ 245 Rich Gedman .05 .02
❑ 246 Mike Campbell .05 .02
❑ 247 Thad Bosley .05 .02
❑ 248 Storm Davis .05 .02
❑ 249 Mike Marshall .05 .02
❑ 250 Nolan Ryan 1.00 .40
❑ 251 Tom Foley .05 .02
❑ 252 Bob Brower .05 .02
❑ 253 Checklist 133-264 .05 .02
❑ 254 Lee Elia MG .05 .02
❑ 255 Mookie Wilson .10 .04
❑ 256 Ken Schrom .05 .02
❑ 257 Jerry Royster .05 .02
❑ 258 Ed Nunez .05 .02
❑ 259 Ron Kittle .05 .02
❑ 260 Vince Coleman .05 .02
❑ 261 Giants TL .05 .02
(Five players)
❑ 262 Drew Hall .05 .02
❑ 263 Glenn Braggs .05 .02
❑ 264 Les Straker .05 .02
❑ 265 Bo Diaz .05 .02
❑ 266 Paul Assenmacher .05 .02
❑ 267 Billy Bean RC .15 .06
❑ 268 Bruce Ruffin .05 .02
❑ 269 Ellis Burks RC .40 .16
❑ 270 Mike Witt .05 .02
❑ 271 Ken Gerhart .05 .02
❑ 272 Steve Ontiveros .05 .02
❑ 273 Garth Iorg .05 .02
❑ 274 Junior Ortiz .05 .02
❑ 275 Kevin Seitzer .10 .04
❑ 276 Luis Salazar .05 .02
❑ 277 Alejandro Pena .05 .02
❑ 278 Jose Cruz .05 .02
❑ 279 Randy St.Claire .05 .02
❑ 280 Pete Incaviglia .05 .02
❑ 281 Jerry Hairston .05 .02
❑ 282 Pat Perry .05 .02
❑ 283 Phil Lombardi .05 .02
❑ 284 Larry Bowa MG .05 .02
❑ 285 Jim Presley .05 .02
❑ 286 Chuck Crim .05 .02
❑ 287 Manny Trillo .05 .02
❑ 288 Pat Pacillo .05 .02
(Chris Sabo in
background of photo)
❑ 289 Dave Bergman .05 .02
❑ 290 Tony Fernandez .05 .02
❑ 291 Billy Hatcher .05 .02
Kevin Bass TL
❑ 292 Carney Lansford .10 .04
❑ 293 Doug Jones RC .20 .08
❑ 294 Al Pedrique .05 .02
❑ 295 Bert Blyleven .10 .04
❑ 296 Floyd Rayford .05 .02
❑ 297 Zane Smith .05 .02
❑ 298 Milt Thompson .05 .02
❑ 299 Steve Crawford .05 .02
❑ 300 Don Mattingly .60 .24
❑ 301 Bud Black .05 .02
❑ 302 Jose Uribe .05 .02
❑ 303 Eric Show .05 .02
❑ 304 George Hendrick .05 .02
❑ 305 Steve Sax .05 .02
❑ 306 Billy Hatcher .05 .02
❑ 307 Mike Trujillo .05 .02
❑ 308 Lee Mazzilli .05 .02
❑ 309 Bill Long .05 .02
❑ 310 Tom Herr .05 .02
❑ 311 Scott Sanderson .05 .02
❑ 312 Joey Meyer .05 .02
❑ 313 Bob McClure .05 .02
❑ 314 Jimy Williams MG .05 .02
❑ 315 Dave Parker .10 .04
❑ 316 Jose Rijo .05 .02
❑ 317 Tom Nieto .05 .02
❑ 318 Mel Hall .05 .02
❑ 319 Mike Loynd .05 .02
❑ 320 Alan Trammell .15 .06
❑ 321 Harold Baines .10 .04
Carlton Fisk TL
❑ 322 Vicente Palacios .05 .02
❑ 323 Rick Leach .05 .02
❑ 324 Danny Jackson .05 .02
❑ 325 Glenn Hubbard .05 .02
❑ 326 Al Nipper .05 .02
❑ 327 Larry Sheets .05 .02
❑ 328 Greg Cadaret .05 .02
❑ 329 Chris Speier .05 .02
❑ 330 Eddie Whitson .05 .02
❑ 331 Brian Downing .05 .02
❑ 332 Jerry Reed .05 .02
❑ 333 Wally Backman .05 .02
❑ 334 Dave LaPoint .05 .02
❑ 335 Claudell Washington .05 .02
❑ 336 Ed Lynch .05 .02
❑ 337 Jim Gantner .05 .02
❑ 338 Brian Holton UER .05 .02
1987 ERA .389,
should be 3.89
❑ 339 Kurt Stillwell .05 .02
❑ 340 Jack Morris .10 .04
❑ 341 Carmen Castillo .05 .02
❑ 342 Larry Andersen .05 .02
❑ 343 Greg Gagne .05 .02
❑ 344 Tony LaRussa MG .10 .04
❑ 345 Scott Fletcher .05 .02
❑ 346 Vance Law .05 .02
❑ 347 Joe Johnson .05 .02
❑ 348 Jim Eisenreich .20 .08
❑ 349 Bob Walk .05 .02
❑ 350 Will Clark .20 .08
❑ 351 Red Schoendienst CO .10 .04
Tony Pena TL
❑ 352 Bill Ripken RC* .05 .02
❑ 353 Ed Olwine .05 .02
❑ 354 Marc Sullivan .05 .02
❑ 355 Roger McDowell .05 .02
❑ 356 Luis Aguayo .05 .02
❑ 357 Floyd Bannister .05 .02
❑ 358 Rey Quinones .05 .02
❑ 359 Tim Stoddard .05 .02
❑ 360 Tony Gwynn .30 .12
❑ 361 Greg Maddux 1.00 .40
❑ 362 Juan Castillo .05 .02
❑ 363 Willie Fraser .05 .02
❑ 364 Nick Esasky .05 .02
❑ 365 Floyd Youmans .05 .02
❑ 366 Chet Lemon .05 .02
❑ 367 Tim Leary .05 .02

❑ 368 Gerald Young .05 .02
❑ 369 Greg Harris .05 .02
❑ 370 Jose Canseco .20 .08
❑ 371 Joe Hesketh .05 .02
❑ 372 Matt Williams RC .75 .30
❑ 373 Checklist 265-396 .05 .02
❑ 374 Doc Edwards MG .05 .02
❑ 375 Tom Brunansky .05 .02
❑ 376 Bill Wilkinson .05 .02
❑ 377 Sam Horn RC .05 .02
❑ 378 Todd Frohwirth .05 .02
❑ 379 Rafael Ramirez .05 .02
❑ 380 Joe Magrane RC* .05 .02
❑ 381 Wally Joyner .10 .04
Jack Howell TL
❑ 382 Keith A. Miller RC .05 .02
❑ 383 Eric Bell .05 .02
❑ 384 Neil Allen .05 .02
❑ 385 Carlton Fisk .15 .06
❑ 386 Don Mattingly AS .30 .12
❑ 387 Willie Randolph AS .05 .02
❑ 388 Wade Boggs AS .10 .04
❑ 389 Alan Trammell AS .05 .02
❑ 390 George Bell AS .05 .02
❑ 391 Kirby Puckett AS .15 .06
❑ 392 Dave Winfield AS .15 .06
❑ 393 Matt Nokes AS .05 .02
❑ 394 Roger Clemens AS .20 .08
❑ 395 Jimmy Key AS .05 .02
❑ 396 Tom Henke AS .05 .02
❑ 397 Jack Clark AS .10 .04
❑ 398 Juan Samuel AS .05 .02
❑ 399 Tim Wallach AS .05 .02
❑ 400 Ozzie Smith AS .15 .06
❑ 401 Andre Dawson AS .05 .02
❑ 402 Tony Gwynn AS .15 .06
❑ 403 Tim Raines AS .10 .04
❑ 404 Benny Santiago AS .10 .04
❑ 405 Dwight Gooden AS .15 .06
❑ 406 Shane Rawley AS .05 .02
❑ 407 Steve Bedrosian AS .05 .02
❑ 408 Dion James .05 .02
❑ 409 Joel McKeon .05 .02
❑ 410 Tony Pena .05 .02
❑ 411 Wayne Tolleson .05 .02
❑ 412 Randy Myers .15 .06
❑ 413 John Christensen .05 .02
❑ 414 John McNamara MG .05 .02
❑ 415 Don Carman .05 .02
❑ 416 Keith Moreland .05 .02
❑ 417 Mark Ciardi .05 .02
❑ 418 Joel Youngblood .05 .02
❑ 419 Scott McGregor .05 .02
❑ 420 Wally Joyner .15 .06
❑ 421 Ed VandeBerg .05 .02
❑ 422 Dave Concepcion .10 .04
❑ 423 John Smiley RC* .10 .04
❑ 424 Dwayne Murphy .05 .02
❑ 425 Jeff Reardon .10 .04
❑ 426 Randy Ready .05 .02
❑ 427 Paul Kilgus .05 .02
❑ 428 John Shelby .05 .02
❑ 429 Alan Trammell .05 .02
Kirk Gibson TL
❑ 430 Glenn Davis .05 .02
❑ 431 Casey Candaele .05 .02
❑ 432 Mike Moore .05 .02
❑ 433 Bill Pecota RC* .05 .02
❑ 434 Rick Aguilera .10 .04
❑ 435 Mike Pagliarulo .05 .02
❑ 436 Mike Bielecki .05 .02
❑ 437 Fred Manrique .05 .02
❑ 438 Rob Ducey .05 .02
❑ 439 Dave Martinez .05 .02
❑ 440 Steve Bedrosian .05 .02
❑ 441 Rick Manning .05 .02
❑ 442 Tom Bolton .05 .02
❑ 443 Ken Griffey .10 .04
❑ 444 C.Ripken Sr. MG UER .05 .02
two copyrights
❑ 445 Mike Krukow .05 .02
❑ 446 Doug DeCinces .05 .02
(Now with Cardinals
on card front)
❑ 447 Jeff Montgomery RC .20 .08
❑ 448 Mike Davis .05 .02
❑ 449 Jeff M. Robinson .05 .02
❑ 450 Barry Bonds 2.00 .80
❑ 451 Keith Atherton .05 .02
❑ 452 Willie Wilson .05 .02
❑ 453 Dennis Powell .05 .02
❑ 454 Marvell Wynne .05 .02
❑ 455 Shawn Hillegas .05 .02
❑ 456 Dave Anderson .05 .02
❑ 457 Terry Leach .05 .02
❑ 458 Ron Hassey .05 .02
❑ 459 Dave Winfield .15 .06
Willie Randolph TL
❑ 460 Ozzie Smith .20 .08
❑ 461 Danny Darwin .05 .02
❑ 462 Don Slaught .05 .02
❑ 463 Fred McGriff .20 .08
❑ 464 Jay Tibbs .05 .02
❑ 465 Paul Molitor .15 .06
❑ 466 Jerry Mumphrey .05 .02
❑ 467 Don Aase .05 .02
❑ 468 Darren Daulton .10 .04
❑ 469 Jeff Dedmon .05 .02
❑ 470 Dwight Evans .10 .04
❑ 471 Donnie Moore .05 .02
❑ 472 Robby Thompson .05 .02
❑ 473 Joe Niekro .05 .02
❑ 474 Tom Brookens .05 .02
❑ 475 Pete Rose MG .50 .20
❑ 476 Dave Stewart .10 .04
❑ 477 Jamie Quirk .05 .02
❑ 478 Sid Bream .05 .02
❑ 479 Brett Butler .10 .04
❑ 480 Dwight Gooden .15 .06
❑ 481 Mariano Duncan .05 .02
❑ 482 Mark Davis .05 .02
❑ 483 Rod Booker .05 .02
❑ 484 Pat Clements .05 .02
❑ 485 Harold Reynolds .10 .04
❑ 486 Pat Keedy .05 .02
❑ 487 Jim Pankovits .05 .02
❑ 488 Andy McGaffigan .05 .02
❑ 489 Pedro Guerrero .05 .02
Fernando Valenzuela TL
❑ 490 Larry Parrish .05 .02
❑ 491 B.J. Surhoff .10 .04
❑ 492 Doyle Alexander .05 .02
❑ 493 Mike Greenwell .05 .02
❑ 494 Wally Ritchie .05 .02
❑ 495 Eddie Murray .20 .08
❑ 496 Guy Hoffman .05 .02
❑ 497 Kevin Mitchell .10 .04
❑ 498 Bob Boone .10 .04
❑ 499 Eric King .05 .02
❑ 500 Andre Dawson .10 .04
❑ 501 Tim Birtsas .05 .02
❑ 502 Dan Gladden .05 .02
❑ 503 Junior Noboa .05 .02
❑ 504 Bob Rodgers MG .05 .02
❑ 505 Willie Upshaw .05 .02
❑ 506 John Cangelosi .05 .02
❑ 507 Mark Gubicza .05 .02
❑ 508 Tim Teufel .05 .02
❑ 509 Bill Dawley .05 .02
❑ 510 Dave Winfield .15 .06
❑ 511 Joel Davis .05 .02
❑ 512 Alex Trevino .05 .02
❑ 513 Tim Flannery .05 .02
❑ 514 Pat Sheridan .05 .02
❑ 515 Juan Nieves .05 .02
❑ 516 Jim Sundberg .05 .02
❑ 517 Ron Robinson .05 .02
❑ 518 Greg Gross .05 .02
❑ 519 Harold Reynolds .05 .02
Phil Bradley TL
❑ 520 Dave Smith .05 .02
❑ 521 Jim Dwyer .05 .02
❑ 522 Bob Patterson .05 .02
❑ 523 Gary Roenicke .05 .02
❑ 524 Gary Lucas .05 .02
❑ 525 Marty Barrett .05 .02
❑ 526 Juan Berenguer .05 .02
❑ 527 Steve Henderson .05 .02
❑ 528A Checklist 397-528 .20 .08
ERR (455 S. Carlton)
❑ 528B Checklist 397-528 .10 .04
COR (455 S. Hillegas)
❑ 529 Tim Burke .05 .02
❑ 530 Gary Carter .15 .06
❑ 531 Rich Yett .05 .02
❑ 532 Mike Kingery .05 .02
❑ 533 John Farrell RC .05 .02
❑ 534 John Wathan MG .05 .02
❑ 535 Ron Guidry .10 .04
❑ 536 John Morris .05 .02
❑ 537 Steve Buechele .05 .02
❑ 538 Bill Wegman .05 .02
❑ 539 Mike LaValliere .05 .02
❑ 540 Bret Saberhagen .10 .04
❑ 541 Juan Beniquez .05 .02
❑ 542 Paul Noce .05 .02
❑ 543 Kent Tekulve .05 .02
❑ 544 Jim Traber .05 .02
❑ 545 Don Baylor .10 .04
❑ 546 John Candelaria .05 .02
❑ 547 Felix Fermin .05 .02
❑ 548 Shane Mack .05 .02
❑ 549 Albert Hall .10 .04
Dale Murphy
Ken Griffey
Dion James TL
❑ 550 Pedro Guerrero .05 .02
❑ 551 Terry Steinbach .10 .04
❑ 552 Mark Thurmond .05 .02
❑ 553 Tracy Jones .05 .02
❑ 554 Mike Smithson .05 .02
❑ 555 Brook Jacoby .05 .02
❑ 556 Stan Clarke .05 .02
❑ 557 Craig Reynolds .05 .02
❑ 558 Bob Ojeda .05 .02
❑ 559 Ken Williams RC .05 .02
❑ 560 Tim Wallach .05 .02
❑ 561 Rick Cerone .05 .02
❑ 562 Jim Lindeman .05 .02
❑ 563 Jose Guzman .05 .02
❑ 564 Frank Lucchesi MG .05 .02
❑ 565 Lloyd Moseby .05 .02
❑ 566 Charlie O'Brien .05 .02
❑ 567 Mike Diaz .05 .02
❑ 568 Chris Brown .05 .02
❑ 569 Charlie Leibrandt .05 .02
❑ 570 Jeffrey Leonard .05 .02
❑ 571 Mark Williamson .05 .02
❑ 572 Chris James .05 .02
❑ 573 Bob Stanley .05 .02
❑ 574 Graig Nettles .10 .04
❑ 575 Don Sutton .20 .08
❑ 576 Tommy Hinzo .05 .02
❑ 577 Tom Browning .05 .02
❑ 578 Gary Gaetti .10 .04
❑ 579 Gary Carter .05 .02
Kevin McReynolds TL
❑ 580 Mark McGwire 1.50 .60
❑ 581 Tito Landrum .05 .02
❑ 582 Mike Henneman RC* .10 .04
❑ 583 Dave Valle .05 .02
❑ 584 Steve Trout .05 .02
❑ 585 Ozzie Guillen .05 .02
❑ 586 Bob Forsch .05 .02
❑ 587 Terry Puhl .05 .02
❑ 588 Jeff Parrett .05 .02
❑ 589 Geno Petralli .05 .02
❑ 590 George Bell .05 .02
❑ 591 Doug Drabek .05 .02
❑ 592 Dale Sveum .05 .02
❑ 593 Bob Tewksbury .05 .02
❑ 594 Bobby Valentine MG .10 .04
❑ 595 Frank White .10 .04
❑ 596 John Kruk .10 .04
❑ 597 Gene Garber .05 .02
❑ 598 Lee Lacy .05 .02
❑ 599 Calvin Schiraldi .05 .02
❑ 600 Mike Schmidt .50 .20
❑ 601 Jack Lazorko .05 .02
❑ 602 Mike Aldrete .05 .02
❑ 603 Rob Murphy .05 .02
❑ 604 Chris Bando .05 .02
❑ 605 Kirk Gibson .10 .04
❑ 606 Moose Haas .05 .02
❑ 607 Mickey Hatcher .05 .02
❑ 608 Charlie Kerfeld .05 .02
❑ 609 Gary Gaetti .10 .04
Kent Hrbek TL

❑ 610 Keith Hernandez .15 .06
❑ 611 Tommy John .10 .04
❑ 612 Curt Ford .05 .02
❑ 613 Bobby Thigpen .05 .02
❑ 614 Herm Winningham .05 .02
❑ 615 Jody Davis .05 .02
❑ 616 Jay Aldrich .05 .02
❑ 617 Oddibe McDowell .05 .02
❑ 618 Cecil Fielder .15 .06
❑ 619 Mike Dunne .05 .02
Inconsistent design, black name on front
❑ 620 Cory Snyder .05 .02
❑ 621 Gene Nelson .05 .02
❑ 622 Kal Daniels .05 .02
❑ 623 Mike Flanagan .05 .02
❑ 624 Jim Leyland MG .10 .04
❑ 625 Frank Viola .05 .02
❑ 626 Glenn Wilson .05 .02
❑ 627 Joe Boever .05 .02
❑ 628 Dave Henderson .05 .02
❑ 629 Kelly Downs .05 .02
❑ 630 Darrell Evans .10 .04
❑ 631 Jack Howell .05 .02
❑ 632 Steve Shields .05 .02
❑ 633 Barry Lyons .05 .02
❑ 634 Jose DeLeon .05 .02
❑ 635 Terry Pendleton .10 .04
❑ 636 Charles Hudson .05 .02
❑ 637 Jay Bell RC .40 .16
❑ 638 Steve Balboni .05 .02
❑ 639 Glenn Braggs .05 .02
Tony Muser CO TL
❑ 640 Garry Templeton .05 .02
(Inconsistent design, green border)
❑ 641 Rick Honeycutt .05 .02
❑ 642 Bob Dernier .05 .02
❑ 643 Rocky Childress .05 .02
❑ 644 Terry McGriff .05 .02
❑ 645 Matt Nokes RC* .05 .02
❑ 646 Checklist 529-660 .05 .02
❑ 647 Pascual Perez .05 .02
❑ 648 Al Newman .05 .02
❑ 649 DeWayne Buice .05 .02
❑ 650 Cal Ripken .75 .30
❑ 651 Mike Jackson RC* .10 .04
❑ 652 Bruce Benedict .05 .02
❑ 653 Jeff Sellers .05 .02
❑ 654 Roger Craig MG .10 .04
❑ 655 Len Dykstra .10 .04
❑ 656 Lee Guetterman .05 .02
❑ 657 Gary Redus .05 .02
❑ 658 Tim Conroy .05 .02
(Inconsistent design, name in white)
❑ 659 Bobby Meacham .05 .02
❑ 660 Rick Reuschel .05 .02
❑ 661 Nolan Ryan TBC '83 .50 .20
❑ 662 Jim Rice TBC .05 .02
❑ 663 Ron Blomberg TBC .05 .02
❑ 664 Bob Gibson TBC '68 .25 .10
❑ 665 Stan Musial TBC '63 .25 .10
❑ 666 Mario Soto .05 .02
❑ 667 Luis Quinones .05 .02
❑ 668 Walt Terrell .05 .02
❑ 669 Lance Parrish .05 .02
Mike Ryan CO TL
❑ 670 Dan Plesac .05 .02
❑ 671 Tim Laudner .05 .02
❑ 672 John Davis .05 .02
❑ 673 Tony Phillips .05 .02
❑ 674 Mike Fitzgerald .05 .02
❑ 675 Jim Rice .10 .04
❑ 676 Ken Dixon .05 .02
❑ 677 Eddie Milner .05 .02
❑ 678 Jim Acker .05 .02
❑ 679 Darrell Miller .05 .02
❑ 680 Charlie Hough .10 .04
❑ 681 Bobby Bonilla .10 .04
❑ 682 Jimmy Key .10 .04
❑ 683 Julio Franco .05 .02
❑ 684 Hal Lanier MG .05 .02
❑ 685 Ron Darling .05 .02
❑ 686 Terry Francona .05 .02
❑ 687 Mickey Brantley .05 .02
❑ 688 Jim Winn .05 .02
❑ 689 Tom Pagnozzi RC .05 .02
❑ 690 Jay Howell .05 .02
❑ 691 Dan Pasqua .05 .02
❑ 692 Mike Birkbeck .05 .02
❑ 693 Benito Santiago .15 .06
❑ 694 Eric Nolte .05 .02
❑ 695 Shawon Dunston .05 .02
❑ 696 Duane Ward .05 .02
❑ 697 Steve Lombardozzi .05 .02
❑ 698 Brad Havens .05 .02
❑ 699 Benito Santiago .10 .04
Tony Gwynn TL
❑ 700 George Brett .60 .24
❑ 701 Sammy Stewart .05 .02
❑ 702 Mike Gallego .05 .02
❑ 703 Bob Brenly .05 .02
❑ 704 Dennis Boyd .05 .02
❑ 705 Juan Samuel .05 .02
❑ 706 Rick Mahler .05 .02
❑ 707 Fred Lynn .05 .02
❑ 708 Gus Polidor .05 .02
❑ 709 George Frazier .05 .02
❑ 710 Darryl Strawberry .15 .06
❑ 711 Bill Gullickson .05 .02
❑ 712 John Moses .05 .02
❑ 713 Willie Hernandez .05 .02
❑ 714 Jim Fregosi MG .05 .02
❑ 715 Todd Worrell .10 .04
❑ 716 Lenn Sakata .05 .02
❑ 717 Jay Baller .05 .02
❑ 718 Mike Felder .05 .02
❑ 719 Denny Walling .05 .02
❑ 720 Tim Raines .10 .04
❑ 721 Pete O'Brien .05 .02
❑ 722 Manny Lee .05 .02
❑ 723 Bob Kipper .05 .02
❑ 724 Danny Tartabull .05 .02
❑ 725 Mike Boddicker .05 .02
❑ 726 Alfredo Griffin .05 .02
❑ 727 Greg Booker .05 .02
❑ 728 Andy Allanson .05 .02
❑ 729 George Bell .10 .04
Fred McGriff TL
❑ 730 John Franco .10 .04
❑ 731 Rick Schu .05 .02
❑ 732 David Palmer .05 .02
❑ 733 Spike Owen .05 .02
❑ 734 Craig Lefferts .05 .02
❑ 735 Kevin McReynolds .05 .02
❑ 736 Matt Young .05 .02
❑ 737 Butch Wynegar .05 .02
❑ 738 Scott Bankhead .05 .02
❑ 739 Daryl Boston .05 .02
❑ 740 Rick Sutcliffe .10 .04
❑ 741 Mike Easler .05 .02
❑ 742 Mark Clear .05 .02
❑ 743 Larry Herndon .05 .02
❑ 744 Whitey Herzog MG .10 .04
❑ 745 Bill Doran .05 .02
❑ 746 Gene Larkin RC* .05 .02
❑ 747 Bobby Witt .05 .02
❑ 748 Reid Nichols .05 .02
❑ 749 Mark Eichhorn .05 .02
❑ 750 Bo Jackson .20 .08
❑ 751 Jim Morrison .05 .02
❑ 752 Mark Grant .05 .02
❑ 753 Danny Heep .05 .02
❑ 754 Mike LaCoss .05 .02
❑ 755 Ozzie Virgil .05 .02
❑ 756 Mike Maddux .05 .02
❑ 757 John Marzano .05 .02
❑ 758 Eddie Williams RC .10 .04
❑ 759 Mark McGwire .75 .30
Jose Canseco TL UER (two copyrights)
❑ 760 Mike Scott .05 .02
❑ 761 Tony Armas .05 .02
❑ 762 Scott Bradley .05 .02
❑ 763 Doug Sisk .05 .02
❑ 764 Greg Walker .05 .02
❑ 765 Neal Heaton .05 .02
❑ 766 Henry Cotto .05 .02
❑ 767 Jose Lind RC .05 .02
❑ 768 Dickie Noles .05 .02
(Now with Tigers on card front)
❑ 769 Cecil Cooper .10 .04
❑ 770 Lou Whitaker .10 .04
❑ 771 Ruben Sierra .05 .02
❑ 772 Sal Butera .05 .02
❑ 773 Frank Williams .05 .02
❑ 774 Gene Mauch MG .10 .04
❑ 775 Dave Stieb .05 .02
❑ 776 Checklist 661-792 .05 .02
❑ 777 Lonnie Smith .05 .02
❑ 778A Keith Comstock ERR 2.00 .80
(White "Padres")
❑ 778B Keith Comstock COR .05 .02
(Blue "Padres")
❑ 779 Tom Glavine RC 1.50 .60
❑ 780 Fernando Valenzuela .10 .04
❑ 781 Keith Hughes .05 .02
❑ 782 Jeff Ballard .05 .02
❑ 783 Ron Roenicke .05 .02
❑ 784 Joe Sambito .05 .02
❑ 785 Alvin Davis .05 .02
❑ 786 Joe Price .05 .02
Inconsistent design, orange team name
❑ 787 Bill Almon .05 .02
❑ 788 Ray Searage .05 .02
❑ 789 Joe Carter .10 .04
Cory Snyder TL
❑ 790 Dave Righetti .05 .02
❑ 791 Ted Simmons .10 .04
❑ 792 John Tudor .05 .02

1988 Topps Traded

	Nm-Mt	Ex-Mt
COMP.FACT.SET (132)	10.00	4.00

❑ 1T Jim Abbott OLY XRC 1.00 .40
❑ 2T Juan Agosto .10 .04
❑ 3T Luis Alicea XRC .20 .08
❑ 4T Roberto Alomar XRC 3.00 1.20
❑ 5T Brady Anderson XRC .75 .30
❑ 6T Jack Armstrong XRC .10 .04
❑ 7T Don August .10 .04
❑ 8T Floyd Bannister .10 .04
❑ 9T Bret Barberie OLY XRC .20 .08
❑ 10T Jose Bautista XRC .10 .04
❑ 11T Don Baylor .20 .08
❑ 12T Tim Belcher .20 .08
❑ 13T Buddy Bell .20 .08
❑ 14T Andy Benes OLY XRC .75 .30
❑ 15T Damon Berryhill XRC .10 .04
❑ 16T Bud Black .10 .04
❑ 17T Pat Borders XRC .20 .08
❑ 18T Phil Bradley .10 .04
❑ 19T J.Branson XRC OLY .20 .08
❑ 20T Tom Brunansky .10 .04
❑ 21T Jay Buhner XRC .75 .30
❑ 22T Brett Butler .20 .08
❑ 23T Jim Campanis OLY .10 .04
❑ 24T Sil Campusano .10 .04
❑ 25T John Candelaria .10 .04
❑ 26T Jose Cecena .10 .04
❑ 27T Rick Cerone .10 .04
❑ 28T Jack Clark .20 .08
❑ 29T Kevin Coffman .10 .04
❑ 30T Pat Combs XRC OLY .10 .04
❑ 31T Henry Cotto .10 .04

❑ 32T Chili Davis .30 .12
❑ 33T Mike Davis .10 .04
❑ 34T Jose DeLeon .10 .04
❑ 35T Richard Dotson .10 .04
❑ 36T Cecil Espy .10 .04
❑ 37T Tom Filer .10 .04
❑ 38T Mike Fiore OLY .10 .04
❑ 39T Ron Gant XRC .75 .30
❑ 40T Kirk Gibson .50 .20
❑ 41T Rich Gossage .20 .08
❑ 42T Mark Grace XRC 1.50 .60
❑ 43T Alfredo Griffin .10 .04
❑ 44T Ty Griffin OLY .10 .04
❑ 45T Bryan Harvey XRC .20 .08
❑ 46T Ron Hassey .10 .04
❑ 47T Ray Hayward .10 .04
❑ 48T Dave Henderson .10 .04
❑ 49T Tom Herr .10 .04
❑ 50T Bob Horner .10 .04
❑ 51T Ricky Horton .10 .04
❑ 52T Jay Howell .10 .04
❑ 53T Glenn Hubbard .10 .04
❑ 54T Jeff Innis .10 .04
❑ 55T Danny Jackson .10 .04
❑ 56T Darrin Jackson XRC* .20 .08
❑ 57T Roberto Kelly XRC* .50 .20
❑ 58T Ron Kittle .10 .04
❑ 59T Ray Knight .10 .04
❑ 60T Vance Law .10 .04
❑ 61T Jeffrey Leonard .10 .04
❑ 62T Mike Macfarlane XRC .10 .04
❑ 63T Scotti Madison .10 .04
❑ 64T Kirt Manwaring .10 .04
❑ 65T M.Marquess OLY CO .10 .04
❑ 66T T.Martinez OLY XRC 2.00 .80
❑ 67T Billy Masse OLY XRC .10 .04
❑ 68T Jack McDowell XRC .50 .20
❑ 69T Jack McKeon MG .10 .04
❑ 70T Larry McWilliams .10 .04
❑ 71T M.Morandini OLY XRC .50 .20
❑ 72T Keith Moreland .10 .04
❑ 73T Mike Morgan .10 .04
❑ 74T C.Nagy OLY XRC .50 .20
❑ 75T Al Nipper .10 .04
❑ 76T Russ Nixon MG .10 .04
❑ 77T Jesse Orosco .10 .04
❑ 78T Joe Orsulak .10 .04
❑ 79T Dave Palmer .10 .04
❑ 80T Mark Parent .10 .04
❑ 81T Dave Parker .20 .08
❑ 82T Dan Pasqua .10 .04
❑ 83T Melido Perez XRC* .10 .04
❑ 84T Steve Peters .10 .04
❑ 85T Dan Petry .10 .04
❑ 86T Gary Pettis .10 .04
❑ 87T Jeff Pico .10 .04
❑ 88T Jim Poole XRC OLY .20 .08
❑ 89T Ted Power .10 .04
❑ 90T Rafael Ramirez .10 .04
❑ 91T Dennis Rasmussen .10 .04
❑ 92T Jose Rijo .10 .04
❑ 93T Ernie Riles .10 .04
❑ 94T Luis Rivera .10 .04
❑ 95T D.Robbins XRC OLY .10 .04
❑ 96T Frank Robinson MG .30 .12
❑ 97T Cookie Rojas MG .10 .04
❑ 98T Chris Sabo XRC .20 .08
❑ 99T Mark Salas .10 .04
❑ 100T Luis Salazar .10 .04
❑ 101T Rafael Santana .10 .04
❑ 102T Nelson Santovenia .10 .04
❑ 103T Mackey Sasser XRC .10 .04
❑ 104T Calvin Schiraldi .10 .04
❑ 105T Mike Schooler .10 .04
❑ 106T S.Servais XRC OLY .10 .04
❑ 107T D.Silvestri XRC OLY .10 .04
❑ 108T Don Slaught .10 .04
❑ 109T J.Slusarski XRC OLY .10 .04
❑ 110T Lee Smith .20 .08
❑ 111T Pete Smith XRC* .10 .04
❑ 112T Jim Snyder MG .10 .04
❑ 113T E.Sprague OLY XRC .50 .20
❑ 114T Pete Stanicek .10 .04
❑ 115T Kurt Stillwell .10 .04
❑ 116T T.Stottlemyre XRC .50 .20
❑ 117T Bill Swift .10 .04
❑ 118T Pat Tabler .10 .04
❑ 119T Scott Terry .10 .04
❑ 120T Mickey Tettleton .10 .04
❑ 121T Dickie Thon .10 .04
❑ 122T Jeff Treadway XRC* .10 .04
❑ 123T Willie Upshaw .10 .04
❑ 124T R.Ventura OLY XRC 2.00 .80
❑ 125T Ron Washington .10 .04
❑ 126T Walt Weiss XRC* .50 .20
❑ 127T Bob Welch .10 .04
❑ 128T David Wells XRC 2.00 .80
❑ 129T Glenn Wilson .10 .04
❑ 130T Ted Wood XRC OLY .10 .04
❑ 131T Don Zimmer MG .20 .08
❑ 132T Checklist 1T-132T .10 .04

1989 Topps

	Nm-Mt	Ex-Mt
COMPLETE SET (792)	20.00	8.00
COMP.FACT SET (792)	20.00	8.00
COMP.X-MAS.SET (792)	25.00	10.00

❑ 1 George Bell RB .05 .02
Slams 3 HR on
Opening Day
❑ 2 Wade Boggs RB .10 .04
❑ 3 Gary Carter RB .10 .04
Sets Record for
Career Putouts
❑ 4 Andre Dawson RB .05 .02
Logs Double Figures
in HR and SB
❑ 5 Orel Hershiser RB .10 .04
Pitches 59
Scoreless Innings
❑ 6 Doug Jones RB UER .05 .02
Earns His 15th
Straight Save

Photo actually Chris Codiroli
❑ 7 Kevin McReynolds RB .05 .02
Steals 21 Without
Being Caught
❑ 8 Dave Eiland .05 .02
❑ 9 Tim Teufel .05 .02
❑ 10 Andre Dawson .10 .04
❑ 11 Bruce Sutter .05 .02
❑ 12 Dale Sveum .05 .02
❑ 13 Doug Sisk .05 .02
❑ 14 Tom Kelly MG .05 .02
❑ 15 Robby Thompson .05 .02
❑ 16 Ron Robinson .05 .02
❑ 17 Brian Downing .05 .02
❑ 18 Rick Rhoden .05 .02
❑ 19 Greg Gagne .05 .02
❑ 20 Steve Bedrosian .05 .02
❑ 21 Greg Walker TL .05 .02
❑ 22 Tim Crews .05 .02
❑ 23 Mike Fitzgerald .05 .02
❑ 24 Larry Andersen .05 .02
❑ 25 Frank White .10 .04
❑ 26 Dale Mohorcic .05 .02
❑ 27A Orestes Destrade .10 .04
(F* next to copyright) RC*
❑ 27B Orestes Destrade .10 .04
(E*F* next to
copyright) RC*
❑ 28 Mike Moore .05 .02
❑ 29 Kelly Gruber .05 .02
❑ 30 Dwight Gooden .15 .06
❑ 31 Terry Francona .10 .04
❑ 32 Dennis Rasmussen .05 .02
❑ 33 B.J. Surhoff .10 .04
❑ 34 Ken Williams .05 .02
❑ 35 John Tudor UER .05 .02
(With Red Sox in '84,should be Pirates)
❑ 36 Mitch Webster .05 .02
❑ 37 Bob Stanley .05 .02
❑ 38 Paul Runge .05 .02
❑ 39 Mike Maddux .05 .02
❑ 40 Steve Sax .05 .02
❑ 41 Terry Mulholland .05 .02
❑ 42 Jim Eppard .05 .02
❑ 43 Guillermo Hernandez .05 .02
❑ 44 Jim Snyder MG .05 .02
❑ 45 Kal Daniels .05 .02
❑ 46 Mark Portugal .05 .02
❑ 47 Carney Lansford .10 .04
❑ 48 Tim Burke .05 .02
❑ 49 Craig Biggio RC .75 .30
❑ 50 George Bell .05 .02
❑ 51 Mark McLemore TL .05 .02
❑ 52 Bob Brenly .05 .02
❑ 53 Ruben Sierra .05 .02
❑ 54 Steve Trout .05 .02
❑ 55 Julio Franco .05 .02
❑ 56 Pat Tabler .05 .02
❑ 57 Alejandro Pena .05 .02
❑ 58 Lee Mazzilli .05 .02
❑ 59 Mark Davis .05 .02
❑ 60 Tom Brunansky .05 .02
❑ 61 Neil Allen .05 .02
❑ 62 Alfredo Griffin .05 .02
❑ 63 Mark Clear .05 .02
❑ 64 Alex Trevino .05 .02
❑ 65 Rick Reuschel .05 .02
❑ 66 Manny Trillo .05 .02
❑ 67 Dave Palmer .05 .02
❑ 68 Darrell Miller .05 .02
❑ 69 Jeff Ballard .05 .02
❑ 70 Mark McGwire 1.00 .40
❑ 71 Mike Boddicker .05 .02
❑ 72 John Moses .05 .02
❑ 73 Pascual Perez .05 .02
❑ 74 Nick Leyva MG .05 .02
❑ 75 Tom Henke .05 .02
❑ 76 Terry Blocker .05 .02
❑ 77 Doyle Alexander .05 .02
❑ 78 Jim Sundberg .05 .02
❑ 79 Scott Bankhead .05 .02
❑ 80 Cory Snyder .05 .02
❑ 81 Tim Raines TL .10 .04
❑ 82 Dave Leiper .05 .02
❑ 83 Jeff Blauser .10 .04
❑ 84 Bill Bene FDP .05 .02
❑ 85 Kevin McReynolds .05 .02
❑ 86 Al Nipper .05 .02
❑ 87 Larry Owen .05 .02
❑ 88 Darryl Hamilton RC * .25 .10
❑ 89 Dave LaPoint .05 .02
❑ 90 Vince Coleman UER .05 .02
(Wrong birth year)
❑ 91 Floyd Youmans .05 .02
❑ 92 Jeff Kunkel .05 .02
❑ 93 Ken Howell .05 .02
❑ 94 Chris Speier .05 .02
❑ 95 Gerald Young .05 .02
❑ 96 Rick Cerone .05 .02
❑ 97 Greg Mathews .05 .02
❑ 98 Larry Sheets .05 .02
❑ 99 Sherman Corbett .05 .02
❑ 100 Mike Schmidt .50 .20
❑ 101 Les Straker .05 .02
❑ 102 Mike Gallego .05 .02
❑ 103 Tim Birtsas .05 .02
❑ 104 Dallas Green MG .05 .02
❑ 105 Ron Darling .05 .02
❑ 106 Willie Upshaw .05 .02
❑ 107 Jose DeLeon .05 .02
❑ 108 Fred Manrique .05 .02
❑ 109 Hipolito Pena .05 .02
❑ 110 Paul Molitor .15 .06
❑ 111 Eric Davis TL .05 .02

❑ 112 Jim Presley .05 .02
❑ 113 Lloyd Moseby .05 .02
❑ 114 Bob Kipper .05 .02
❑ 115 Jody Davis .05 .02
❑ 116 Jeff Montgomery .10 .04
❑ 117 Dave Anderson .05 .02
❑ 118 Checklist 1-132 .05 .02
❑ 119 Terry Puhl .05 .02
❑ 120 Frank Viola .05 .02
❑ 121 Garry Templeton .05 .02
❑ 122 Lance Johnson .10 .04
❑ 123 Spike Owen .05 .02
❑ 124 Jim Traber .05 .02
❑ 125 Mike Krukow .05 .02
❑ 126 Sid Bream .05 .02
❑ 127 Walt Terrell .05 .02
❑ 128 Milt Thompson .05 .02
❑ 129 Terry Clark .05 .02
❑ 130 Gerald Perry .05 .02
❑ 131 Dave Otto .05 .02
❑ 132 Curt Ford .05 .02
❑ 133 Bill Long .05 .02
❑ 134 Don Zimmer MG .05 .02
❑ 135 Jose Rijo .05 .02
❑ 136 Joey Meyer .05 .02
❑ 137 Geno Petralli .05 .02
❑ 138 Wallace Johnson .05 .02
❑ 139 Mike Flanagan .05 .02
❑ 140 Shawon Dunston .05 .02
❑ 141 Brook Jacoby TL .05 .02
❑ 142 Mike Diaz .05 .02
❑ 143 Mike Campbell .05 .02
❑ 144 Jay Bell .15 .06
❑ 145 Dave Stewart .10 .04
❑ 146 Gary Pettis .05 .02
❑ 147 DeWayne Buice .05 .02
❑ 148 Bill Pecota .05 .02
❑ 149 Doug Dascenzo .05 .02
❑ 150 Fernando Valenzuela .10 .04
❑ 151 Terry McGriff .05 .02
❑ 152 Mark Thurmond .05 .02
❑ 153 Jim Pankovits .05 .02
❑ 154 Don Carman .05 .02
❑ 155 Marty Barrett .05 .02
❑ 156 Dave Gallagher .05 .02
❑ 157 Tom Glavine .25 .10
❑ 158 Mike Aldrete .05 .02
❑ 159 Pat Clements .05 .02
❑ 160 Jeffrey Leonard .05 .02
❑ 161 G. Olson RC FDP UER .25 .10
Born Scribner, NE,
should be Omaha, NE
❑ 162 John Davis .05 .02
❑ 163 Bob Forsch .05 .02
❑ 164 Hal Lanier MG .05 .02
❑ 165 Mike Dunne .05 .02
❑ 166 Doug Jennings .05 .02
❑ 167 Steve Searcy FS .05 .02
❑ 168 Willie Wilson .05 .02
❑ 169 Mike Jackson .05 .02
❑ 170 Tony Fernandez .05 .02
❑ 171 Andres Thomas TL .05 .02
❑ 172 Frank Williams .05 .02
❑ 173 Mel Hall .05 .02
❑ 174 Todd Burns .05 .02
❑ 175 John Shelby .05 .02
❑ 176 Jeff Parrett .05 .02
❑ 177 Monty Fariss FDP .05 .02
❑ 178 Mark Grant .05 .02
❑ 179 Ozzie Virgil .05 .02
❑ 180 Mike Scott .05 .02
❑ 181 Craig Worthington .05 .02
❑ 182 Bob McClure .05 .02
❑ 183 Oddibe McDowell .05 .02
❑ 184 John Costello .05 .02
❑ 185 Claudell Washington .05 .02
❑ 186 Pat Perry .05 .02
❑ 187 Darren Daulton .10 .04
❑ 188 Dennis Lamp .05 .02
❑ 189 Kevin Mitchell .10 .04
❑ 190 Mike Witt .05 .02
❑ 191 Sil Campusano .05 .02
❑ 192 Paul Mirabella .05 .02
❑ 193 Sparky Anderson MG .10 .04
UER (553 Salazer)
❑ 194 Greg W. Harris RC .10 .04
❑ 195 Ozzie Guillen .05 .02
❑ 196 Denny Walling .05 .02
❑ 197 Neal Heaton .05 .02
❑ 198 Danny Heep .05 .02
❑ 199 Mike Schooler RC * .10 .04
❑ 200 George Brett .60 .24
❑ 201 Kelly Gruber TL .05 .02
❑ 202 Brad Moore .05 .02
❑ 203 Rob Ducey .05 .02
❑ 204 Brad Havens .05 .02
❑ 205 Dwight Evans .10 .04
❑ 206 Roberto Alomar .30 .12
❑ 207 Terry Leach .05 .02
❑ 208 Tom Pagnozzi .05 .02
❑ 209 Jeff Bittiger .05 .02
❑ 210 Dale Murphy .25 .10
❑ 211 Mike Pagliarulo .05 .02
❑ 212 Scott Sanderson .05 .02
❑ 213 Rene Gonzales .05 .02
❑ 214 Charlie O'Brien .05 .02
❑ 215 Kevin Gross .05 .02
❑ 216 Jack Howell .05 .02
❑ 217 Joe Price .05 .02
❑ 218 Mike LaValliere .05 .02
❑ 219 Jim Clancy .05 .02
❑ 220 Gary Gaetti .10 .04
❑ 221 Cecil Espy .05 .02
❑ 222 Mark Lewis FDP RC .25 .10
❑ 223 Jay Buhner .10 .04
❑ 224 Tony LaRussa MG .10 .04
❑ 225 Ramon Martinez RC .25 .10
❑ 226 Bill Doran .05 .02
❑ 227 John Farrell .05 .02
❑ 228 Nelson Santovenia .05 .02
❑ 229 Jimmy Key .10 .04
❑ 230 Ozzie Smith .25 .10
❑ 231 Roberto Alomar TL .25 .10
(Gary Carter at plate)
❑ 232 Ricky Horton .05 .02
❑ 233 Gregg Jefferies FS .10 .04
❑ 234 Tom Browning .05 .02
❑ 235 John Kruk .10 .04
❑ 236 Charles Hudson .05 .02
❑ 237 Glenn Hubbard .05 .02
❑ 238 Eric King .05 .02
❑ 239 Tim Laudner .05 .02
❑ 240 Greg Maddux .60 .24
❑ 241 Brett Butler .10 .04
❑ 242 Ed VandeBerg .05 .02
❑ 243 Bob Boone .10 .04
❑ 244 Jim Acker .05 .02
❑ 245 Jim Rice .10 .04
❑ 246 Rey Quinones .05 .02
❑ 247 Shawn Hillegas .05 .02
❑ 248 Tony Phillips .05 .02
❑ 249 Tim Leary .05 .02
❑ 250 Cal Ripken .75 .30
❑ 251 John Dopson .05 .02
❑ 252 Billy Hatcher .05 .02
❑ 253 Jose Alvarez RC .10 .04
❑ 254 Tom Lasorda MG .25 .10
❑ 255 Ron Guidry .10 .04
❑ 256 Benny Santiago .10 .04
❑ 257 Rick Aguilera .10 .04
❑ 258 Checklist 133-264 .05 .02
❑ 259 Larry McWilliams .05 .02
❑ 260 Dave Winfield .15 .06
❑ 261 Tom Brunansky .05 .02
Luis Alicea TL
❑ 262 Jeff Pico .05 .02
❑ 263 Mike Felder .05 .02
❑ 264 Rob Dibble RC * .50 .20
❑ 265 Kent Hrbek .10 .04
❑ 266 Luis Aquino .05 .02
❑ 267 Jeff M. Robinson .05 .02
❑ 268 Keith Miller RC .10 .04
❑ 269 Tom Bolton .05 .02
❑ 270 Wally Joyner .10 .04
❑ 271 Jay Tibbs .05 .02
❑ 272 Ron Hassey .05 .02
❑ 273 Jose Lind .05 .02
❑ 274 Mark Eichhorn .05 .02
❑ 275 Danny Tartabull UER .05 .02
(Born San Juan, PR
should be Miami, FL)
❑ 276 Paul Kilgus .05 .02
❑ 277 Mike Davis .05 .02
❑ 278 Andy McGaffigan .05 .02
❑ 279 Scott Bradley .05 .02
❑ 280 Bob Knepper .05 .02
❑ 281 Gary Redus .05 .02
❑ 282 Cris Carpenter RC * .10 .04
❑ 283 Andy Allanson .05 .02
❑ 284 Jim Leyland MG .10 .04
❑ 285 John Candelaria .05 .02
❑ 286 Darrin Jackson .05 .02
❑ 287 Juan Nieves .05 .02
❑ 288 Pat Sheridan .05 .02
❑ 289 Ernie Whitt .05 .02
❑ 290 John Franco .10 .04
❑ 291 Darryl Strawberry .10 .04
Keith Hernandez
Kevin McReynolds TL
❑ 292 Jim Corsi .05 .02
❑ 293 Glenn Wilson .05 .02
❑ 294 Juan Berenguer .05 .02
❑ 295 Scott Fletcher .05 .02
❑ 296 Ron Gant .10 .04
❑ 297 Oswald Peraza .05 .02
❑ 298 Chris James .05 .02
❑ 299 Steve Ellsworth .05 .02
❑ 300 Darryl Strawberry .15 .06
❑ 301 Charlie Leibrandt .05 .02
❑ 302 Gary Ward .05 .02
❑ 303 Felix Fermin .05 .02
❑ 304 Joel Youngblood .05 .02
❑ 305 Dave Smith .05 .02
❑ 306 Tracy Woodson .05 .02
❑ 307 Lance McCullers .05 .02
❑ 308 Ron Karkovice .05 .02
❑ 309 Mario Diaz .05 .02
❑ 310 Rafael Palmeiro .25 .10
❑ 311 Chris Bosio .05 .02
❑ 312 Tom Lawless .05 .02
❑ 313 Dennis Martinez .10 .04
❑ 314 Bobby Valentine MG .05 .02
❑ 315 Greg Swindell .05 .02
❑ 316 Walt Weiss .05 .02
❑ 317 Jack Armstrong RC * .25 .10
❑ 318 Gene Larkin .05 .02
❑ 319 Greg Booker .05 .02
❑ 320 Lou Whitaker .10 .04
❑ 321 Jody Reed TL .05 .02
❑ 322 John Smiley .05 .02
❑ 323 Gary Thurman .05 .02
❑ 324 Bob Milacki .05 .02
❑ 325 Jesse Barfield .05 .02
❑ 326 Dennis Boyd .05 .02
❑ 327 Mark Lemke RC .25 .10
❑ 328 Rick Honeycutt .05 .02
❑ 329 Bob Melvin .05 .02
❑ 330 Eric Davis .10 .04
❑ 331 Curt Wilkerson .05 .02
❑ 332 Tony Armas .05 .02
❑ 333 Bob Ojeda .05 .02
❑ 334 Steve Lyons .05 .02
❑ 335 Dave Righetti .05 .02
❑ 336 Steve Balboni .05 .02
❑ 337 Calvin Schiraldi .05 .02
❑ 338 Jim Adduci .05 .02
❑ 339 Scott Bailes .05 .02
❑ 340 Kirk Gibson .10 .04
❑ 341 Jim Deshaies .05 .02
❑ 342 Tom Brookens .05 .02
❑ 343 Gary Sheffield FS RC 1.50 .60
❑ 344 Tom Trebelhorn MG .05 .02
❑ 345 Charlie Hough .10 .04
❑ 346 Rex Hudler .05 .02
❑ 347 John Cerutti .05 .02
❑ 348 Ed Hearn .05 .02
❑ 349 Ron Jones .05 .02
❑ 350 Andy Van Slyke .10 .04
❑ 351 Bob Melvin .05 .02
Bill Fahey CO TL
❑ 352 Rick Schu .05 .02
❑ 353 Marvell Wynne .05 .02
❑ 354 Larry Parrish .05 .02
❑ 355 Mark Langston .05 .02
❑ 356 Kevin Elster .05 .02
❑ 357 Jerry Reuss .05 .02
❑ 358 Ricky Jordan RC * .25 .10
❑ 359 Tommy John .10 .04

❑ 360 Ryne Sandberg .40 .16
❑ 361 Kelly Downs .05 .02
❑ 362 Jack Lazorko .05 .02
❑ 363 Rich Yett .05 .02
❑ 364 Rob Deer .05 .02
❑ 365 Mike Henneman .05 .02
❑ 366 Herm Winningham .05 .02
❑ 367 Johnny Paredes .05 .02
❑ 368 Brian Holton .05 .02
❑ 369 Ken Caminiti .10 .04
❑ 370 Dennis Eckersley .10 .04
❑ 371 Manny Lee .05 .02
❑ 372 Craig Lefferts .05 .02
❑ 373 Tracy Jones .05 .02
❑ 374 John Wathan MG .05 .02
❑ 375 Terry Pendleton .10 .04
❑ 376 Steve Lombardozzi .05 .02
❑ 377 Mike Smithson .05 .02
❑ 378 Checklist 265-396 .05 .02
❑ 379 Tim Flannery .05 .02
❑ 380 Rickey Henderson .40 .16
❑ 381 Larry Sheets TL .05 .02
❑ 382 John Smoltz RC 1.00 .40
❑ 383 Howard Johnson .05 .02
❑ 384 Mark Salas .05 .02
❑ 385 Von Hayes .05 .02
❑ 386 Andres Galarraga AS .05 .02
❑ 387 Ryne Sandberg AS .25 .10
❑ 388 Bobby Bonilla AS .10 .04
❑ 389 Ozzie Smith AS .15 .06
❑ 390 Darryl Strawberry AS .10 .04
❑ 391 Andre Dawson AS .05 .02
❑ 392 Andy Van Slyke AS .05 .02
❑ 393 Gary Carter AS .10 .04
❑ 394 Orel Hershiser AS .10 .04
❑ 395 Danny Jackson AS .05 .02
❑ 396 Kirk Gibson AS .10 .04
❑ 397 Don Mattingly AS .30 .12
❑ 398 Julio Franco AS .05 .02
❑ 399 Wade Boggs AS .10 .04
❑ 400 Alan Trammell AS .05 .02
❑ 401 Jose Canseco AS .10 .04
❑ 402 Mike Greenwell AS .05 .02
❑ 403 Kirby Puckett AS .15 .06
❑ 404 Bob Boone AS .05 .02
❑ 405 Roger Clemens AS .25 .10
❑ 406 Frank Viola AS .05 .02
❑ 407 Dave Winfield AS .10 .04
❑ 408 Greg Walker .05 .02
❑ 409 Ken Dayley .05 .02
❑ 410 Jack Clark .05 .02
❑ 411 Mitch Williams .05 .02
❑ 412 Barry Lyons .05 .02
❑ 413 Mike Kingery .05 .02
❑ 414 Jim Fregosi MG .05 .02
❑ 415 Rich Gossage .10 .04
❑ 416 Fred Lynn .05 .02
❑ 417 Mike LaCoss .05 .02
❑ 418 Bob Dernier .05 .02
❑ 419 Tom Filer .05 .02
❑ 420 Joe Carter .15 .06
❑ 421 Kirk McCaskill .05 .02
❑ 422 Bo Diaz .05 .02
❑ 423 Brian Fisher .05 .02
❑ 424 Luis Polonia UER .05 .02
(Wrong birthdate)
❑ 425 Jay Howell .05 .02
❑ 426 Dan Gladden .05 .02
❑ 427 Eric Show .05 .02
❑ 428 Craig Reynolds .05 .02
❑ 429 Greg Gagne TL .05 .02
❑ 430 Mark Gubicza .05 .02
❑ 431 Luis Rivera .05 .02
❑ 432 Chad Kreuter RC .25 .10
❑ 433 Albert Hall .05 .02
❑ 434 Ken Patterson .05 .02
❑ 435 Len Dykstra .10 .04
❑ 436 Bobby Meacham .05 .02
❑ 437 Andy Benes FDP RC .40 .16
❑ 438 Greg Gross .05 .02
❑ 439 Frank DiPino .05 .02
❑ 440 Bobby Bonilla .10 .04
❑ 441 Jerry Reed .05 .02
❑ 442 Jose Oquendo .05 .02
❑ 443 Rod Nichols .05 .02
❑ 444 Moose Stubing MG .05 .02
❑ 445 Matt Nokes .05 .02
❑ 446 Rob Murphy .05 .02
❑ 447 Donell Nixon .05 .02
❑ 448 Eric Plunk .05 .02
❑ 449 Carmelo Martinez .05 .02
❑ 450 Roger Clemens .50 .20
❑ 451 Mark Davidson .05 .02
❑ 452 Israel Sanchez .05 .02
❑ 453 Tom Prince .05 .02
❑ 454 Paul Assenmacher .05 .02
❑ 455 Johnny Ray .05 .02
❑ 456 Tim Belcher .05 .02
❑ 457 Mackey Sasser .05 .02
❑ 458 Donn Pall .05 .02
❑ 459 Dave Valle TL .05 .02
❑ 460 Dave Stieb .05 .02
❑ 461 Buddy Bell .10 .04
❑ 462 Jose Guzman .05 .02
❑ 463 Steve Lake .05 .02
❑ 464 Bryn Smith .05 .02
❑ 465 Mark Grace .25 .10
❑ 466 Chuck Crim .05 .02
❑ 467 Jim Walewander .05 .02
❑ 468 Henry Cotto .05 .02
❑ 469 Jose Bautista RC .10 .04
❑ 470 Lance Parrish .05 .02
❑ 471 Steve Curry .05 .02
❑ 472 Brian Harper .05 .02
❑ 473 Don Robinson .05 .02
❑ 474 Bob Rodgers MG .05 .02
❑ 475 Dave Parker .10 .04
❑ 476 Jon Perlman .05 .02
❑ 477 Dick Schofield .05 .02
❑ 478 Doug Drabek .05 .02
❑ 479 Mike Macfarlane RC * .25 .10
❑ 480 Keith Hernandez .15 .06
❑ 481 Chris Brown .05 .02
❑ 482 Steve Peters .05 .02
❑ 483 Mickey Hatcher .05 .02
❑ 484 Steve Shields .05 .02
❑ 485 Hubie Brooks .05 .02
❑ 486 Jack McDowell .10 .04
❑ 487 Scott Lusader .05 .02
❑ 488 Kevin Coffman .05 .02
Now with Cubs
❑ 489 Mike Schmidt TL .15 .06
❑ 490 Chris Sabo RC * .40 .16
❑ 491 Mike Birkbeck .05 .02
❑ 492 Alan Ashby .05 .02
❑ 493 Todd Benzinger .05 .02
❑ 494 Shane Rawley .05 .02
❑ 495 Candy Maldonado .05 .02
❑ 496 Dwayne Henry .05 .02
❑ 497 Pete Stanicek .05 .02
❑ 498 Dave Valle .05 .02
❑ 499 Don Heinkel .05 .02
❑ 500 Jose Canseco .25 .10
❑ 501 Vance Law .05 .02
❑ 502 Duane Ward .05 .02
❑ 503 Al Newman .05 .02
❑ 504 Bob Walk .05 .02
❑ 505 Pete Rose MG .50 .20
❑ 506 Kirt Manwaring .05 .02
❑ 507 Steve Farr .05 .02
❑ 508 Wally Backman .05 .02
❑ 509 Bud Black .05 .02
❑ 510 Bob Horner .05 .02
❑ 511 Richard Dotson .05 .02
❑ 512 Donnie Hill .05 .02
❑ 513 Jesse Orosco .05 .02
❑ 514 Chet Lemon .05 .02
❑ 515 Barry Larkin .25 .10
❑ 516 Eddie Whitson .05 .02
❑ 517 Greg Brock .05 .02
❑ 518 Bruce Ruffin .05 .02
❑ 519 Willie Randolph TL .05 .02
❑ 520 Rick Sutcliffe .10 .04
❑ 521 Mickey Tettleton .05 .02
❑ 522 Randy Kramer .05 .02
❑ 523 Andres Thomas .05 .02
❑ 524 Checklist 397-528 .05 .02
❑ 525 Chili Davis .10 .04
❑ 526 Wes Gardner .05 .02
❑ 527 Dave Henderson .05 .02
❑ 528 Luis Medina .05 .02
(Lower left front
has white triangle)
❑ 529 Tom Foley .05 .02
❑ 530 Nolan Ryan 1.00 .40
❑ 531 Dave Hengel .05 .02
❑ 532 Jerry Browne .05 .02
❑ 533 Andy Hawkins .05 .02
❑ 534 Doc Edwards MG .05 .02
❑ 535 Todd Worrell UER .05 .02
(4 wins in '88,
should be 5)
❑ 536 Joel Skinner .05 .02
❑ 537 Pete Smith .05 .02
❑ 538 Juan Castillo .05 .02
❑ 539 Barry Jones .05 .02
❑ 540 Bo Jackson .25 .10
❑ 541 Cecil Fielder .10 .04
❑ 542 Todd Frohwirth .05 .02
❑ 543 Damon Berryhill .05 .02
❑ 544 Jeff Sellers .05 .02
❑ 545 Mookie Wilson .10 .04
❑ 546 Mark Williamson .05 .02
❑ 547 Mark McLemore .05 .02
❑ 548 Bobby Witt .05 .02
❑ 549 Jamie Moyer TL .05 .02
❑ 550 Orel Hershiser .10 .04
❑ 551 Randy Ready .05 .02
❑ 552 Greg Cadaret .05 .02
❑ 553 Luis Salazar .05 .02
❑ 554 Nick Esasky .05 .02
❑ 555 Bert Blyleven .10 .04
❑ 556 Bruce Fields .05 .02
❑ 557 Keith A. Miller .05 .02
❑ 558 Dan Pasqua .05 .02
❑ 559 Juan Agosto .05 .02
❑ 560 Tim Raines .10 .04
❑ 561 Luis Aguayo .05 .02
❑ 562 Danny Cox .05 .02
❑ 563 Bill Schroeder .05 .02
❑ 564 Russ Nixon MG .05 .02
❑ 565 Jeff Russell .05 .02
❑ 566 Al Pedrique .05 .02
❑ 567 David Wells UER .10 .04
(Complete Pitching
Recor)
❑ 568 Mickey Brantley .05 .02
❑ 569 German Jimenez .05 .02
❑ 570 Tony Gwynn UER .30 .12
('88 average should
be italicized as
league leader)
❑ 571 Billy Ripken .05 .02
❑ 572 Atlee Hammaker .05 .02
❑ 573 Jim Abbott FDP RC* .50 .20
❑ 574 Dave Clark .05 .02
❑ 575 Juan Samuel .05 .02
❑ 576 Greg Minton .05 .02
❑ 577 Randy Bush .05 .02
❑ 578 John Morris .05 .02
❑ 579 Glenn Davis TL .05 .02
❑ 580 Harold Reynolds .10 .04
❑ 581 Gene Nelson .05 .02
❑ 582 Mike Marshall .05 .02
❑ 583 Paul Gibson .05 .02
❑ 584 Randy Velarde UER .05 .02
(Signed 1935,
should be 1985)
❑ 585 Harold Baines .10 .04
❑ 586 Joe Boever .05 .02
❑ 587 Mike Stanley .05 .02
❑ 588 Luis Alicea RC * .25 .10
❑ 589 Dave Meads .05 .02
❑ 590 Andres Galarraga .10 .04
❑ 591 Jeff Musselman .05 .02
❑ 592 John Cangelosi .05 .02
❑ 593 Drew Hall .05 .02
❑ 594 Jimy Williams MG .05 .02
❑ 595 Teddy Higuera .05 .02
❑ 596 Kurt Stillwell .05 .02
❑ 597 Terry Taylor RC .10 .04
❑ 598 Ken Gerhart .05 .02
❑ 599 Tom Candiotti .05 .02
❑ 600 Wade Boggs .15 .06
❑ 601 Dave Dravecky .10 .04
❑ 602 Devon White .10 .04
❑ 603 Frank Tanana .05 .02
❑ 604 Paul O'Neill .15 .06

- ❑ 605A Bob Welch ERR 2.00 .80
  (Missing line on back
  Complete M.L. Pitching Record
- ❑ 605B Bob Welch COR .05 .02
- ❑ 606 Rick Dempsey .05 .02
- ❑ 607 Willie Ansley FDP RC .10 .04
- ❑ 608 Phil Bradley .05 .02
- ❑ 609 Frank Tanana .05 .02
  Alan Trammell
  Mike Heath TL
- ❑ 610 Randy Myers .10 .04
- ❑ 611 Don Slaught .05 .02
- ❑ 612 Dan Quisenberry .05 .02
- ❑ 613 Gary Varsho .05 .02
- ❑ 614 Joe Hesketh .05 .02
- ❑ 615 Robin Yount .25 .10
- ❑ 616 Steve Rosenberg .05 .02
- ❑ 617 Mark Parent .05 .02
- ❑ 618 Rance Mulliniks .05 .02
- ❑ 619 Checklist 529-660 .05 .02
- ❑ 620 Barry Bonds 1.25 .50
- ❑ 621 Rick Mahler .05 .02
- ❑ 622 Stan Javier .05 .02
- ❑ 623 Fred Toliver .05 .02
- ❑ 624 Jack McKeon MG .05 .02
- ❑ 625 Eddie Murray .25 .10
- ❑ 626 Jeff Reed .05 .02
- ❑ 627 Greg A. Harris .05 .02
- ❑ 628 Matt Williams .25 .10
- ❑ 629 Pete O'Brien .05 .02
- ❑ 630 Mike Greenwell .05 .02
- ❑ 631 Dave Bergman .05 .02
- ❑ 632 Bryan Harvey RC * .25 .10
- ❑ 633 Daryl Boston .05 .02
- ❑ 634 Marvin Freeman .05 .02
- ❑ 635 Willie Randolph .10 .04
- ❑ 636 Bill Wilkinson .05 .02
- ❑ 637 Carmen Castillo .05 .02
- ❑ 638 Floyd Bannister .05 .02
- ❑ 639 Walt Weiss TL .05 .02
- ❑ 640 Willie McGee .10 .04
- ❑ 641 Curt Young .05 .02
- ❑ 642 Angel Salazar .05 .02
- ❑ 643 Louie Meadows .05 .02
- ❑ 644 Lloyd McClendon .05 .02
- ❑ 645 Jack Morris .10 .04
- ❑ 646 Kevin Bass .05 .02
- ❑ 647 Randy Johnson RC 3.00 1.20
- ❑ 648 Sandy Alomar FS RC .40 .16
- ❑ 649 Stu Cliburn .05 .02
- ❑ 650 Kirby Puckett .25 .10
- ❑ 651 Tom Niedenfuer .05 .02
- ❑ 652 Rich Gedman .05 .02
- ❑ 653 Tommy Barrett .05 .02
- ❑ 654 Whitey Herzog MG .05 .02
- ❑ 655 Dave Magadan .05 .02
- ❑ 656 Ivan Calderon .05 .02
- ❑ 657 Joe Magrane .05 .02
- ❑ 658 R.J. Reynolds .05 .02
- ❑ 659 Al Leiter .25 .10
- ❑ 660 Will Clark .25 .10
- ❑ 661 D.Gooden TBC84 .10 .04
- ❑ 662 Lou Brock TBC79 .10 .04
- ❑ 663 Hank Aaron TBC74 .25 .10
- ❑ 664 Gil Hodges TBC 69 .10 .04
- ❑ 665A Tony Oliva TBC64 2.00 .80
  ERR (fabricated card
  is enlarged version
  of Oliva's 64T card;
  Topps copyright
  missing)
- ❑ 665B Tony Oliva TBC 64 .10 .04
  COR (fabricated
  card)
- ❑ 666 Randy St.Claire .05 .02
- ❑ 667 Dwayne Murphy .05 .02
- ❑ 668 Mike Bielecki .05 .02
- ❑ 669 Orel Hershiser .10 .04
  Mike Scioscia TL
- ❑ 670 Kevin Seitzer .05 .02
- ❑ 671 Jim Gantner .05 .02
- ❑ 672 Allan Anderson .05 .02
- ❑ 673 Don Baylor .10 .04
- ❑ 674 Otis Nixon .05 .02
- ❑ 675 Bruce Hurst .05 .02
- ❑ 676 Ernie Riles .05 .02
- ❑ 677 Dave Schmidt .05 .02
- ❑ 678 Dion James .05 .02
- ❑ 679 Willie Fraser .05 .02
- ❑ 680 Gary Carter .15 .06
- ❑ 681 Jeff D. Robinson .05 .02
- ❑ 682 Rick Leach .05 .02
- ❑ 683 Jose Cecena .05 .02
- ❑ 684 Dave Johnson MG .05 .02
- ❑ 685 Jeff Treadway .05 .02
- ❑ 686 Scott Terry .05 .02
- ❑ 687 Alvin Davis .05 .02
- ❑ 688 Zane Smith .05 .02
- ❑ 689A Stan Jefferson .05 .02
  (Pink triangle on
  front bottom left)
- ❑ 689B Stan Jefferson .05 .02
  (Violet triangle on
  front bottom left)
- ❑ 690 Doug Jones .05 .02
- ❑ 691 Roberto Kelly UER .05 .02
  (83 Oneonita)
- ❑ 692 Steve Ontiveros .05 .02
- ❑ 693 Pat Borders RC * .25 .10
- ❑ 694 Les Lancaster .05 .02
- ❑ 695 Carlton Fisk .15 .06
- ❑ 696 Don August .05 .02
- ❑ 697A Franklin Stubbs .05 .02
  (Team name on front
  in white)
- ❑ 697B Franklin Stubbs .05 .02
  (Team name on front
  in gray)
- ❑ 698 Keith Atherton .05 .02
- ❑ 699 Al Pedrique TL .05 .02
  Tony Gwynn sliding
- ❑ 700 Don Mattingly .60 .24
- ❑ 701 Storm Davis .05 .02
- ❑ 702 Jamie Quirk .05 .02
- ❑ 703 Scott Garrelts .05 .02
- ❑ 704 Carlos Quintana RC .10 .04
- ❑ 705 Terry Kennedy .05 .02
- ❑ 706 Pete Incaviglia .05 .02
- ❑ 707 Steve Jeltz .05 .02
- ❑ 708 Chuck Finley .10 .04
- ❑ 709 Tom Herr .05 .02
- ❑ 710 David Cone .10 .04
- ❑ 711 Candy Sierra .05 .02
- ❑ 712 Bill Swift .05 .02
- ❑ 713 Ty Griffin FDP .05 .02
- ❑ 714 Joe Morgan MG .05 .02
- ❑ 715 Tony Pena .05 .02
- ❑ 716 Wayne Tolleson .05 .02
- ❑ 717 Jamie Moyer .10 .04
- ❑ 718 Glenn Braggs .05 .02
- ❑ 719 Danny Darwin .05 .02
- ❑ 720 Tim Wallach .05 .02
- ❑ 721 Ron Tingley .05 .02
- ❑ 722 Todd Stottlemyre .15 .06
- ❑ 723 Rafael Belliard .05 .02
- ❑ 724 Jerry Don Gleaton .05 .02
- ❑ 725 Terry Steinbach .10 .04
- ❑ 726 Dickie Thon .05 .02
- ❑ 727 Joe Orsulak .05 .02
- ❑ 728 Charlie Puleo .05 .02
- ❑ 729 Steve Buechele TL .05 .02
  (Inconsistent design,
  team name on front
  surrounded by black,
  should be white)
- ❑ 730 Danny Jackson .05 .02
- ❑ 731 Mike Young .05 .02
- ❑ 732 Steve Buechele .05 .02
- ❑ 733 Randy Bockus .05 .02
- ❑ 734 Jody Reed .05 .02
- ❑ 735 Roger McDowell .05 .02
- ❑ 736 Jeff Hamilton .05 .02
- ❑ 737 Norm Charlton RC .25 .10
- ❑ 738 Darnell Coles .05 .02
- ❑ 739 Brook Jacoby .05 .02
- ❑ 740 Dan Plesac .05 .02
- ❑ 741 Ken Phelps .05 .02
- ❑ 742 Mike Harkey FS RC .10 .04
- ❑ 743 Mike Heath .05 .02
- ❑ 744 Roger Craig MG .05 .02
- ❑ 745 Fred McGriff .25 .10
- ❑ 746 G.Gonzalez UER .05 .02
  Wrong birthdate
- ❑ 747 Wil Tejada .05 .02
- ❑ 748 Jimmy Jones .05 .02
- ❑ 749 Rafael Ramirez .05 .02
- ❑ 750 Bret Saberhagen .10 .04
- ❑ 751 Ken Oberkfell .05 .02
- ❑ 752 Jim Gott .05 .02
- ❑ 753 Jose Uribe .05 .02
- ❑ 754 Bob Brower .05 .02
- ❑ 755 Mike Scioscia .05 .02
- ❑ 756 Scott Medvin .05 .02
- ❑ 757 Brady Anderson RC .50 .20
- ❑ 758 Gene Walter .05 .02
- ❑ 759 Rob Deer TL .05 .02
- ❑ 760 Lee Smith .10 .04
- ❑ 761 Dante Bichette RC .40 .16
- ❑ 762 Bobby Thigpen .05 .02
- ❑ 763 Dave Martinez .05 .02
- ❑ 764 Robin Ventura FDP RC .75 .30
- ❑ 765 Glenn Davis .05 .02
- ❑ 766 Cecilio Guante .05 .02
- ❑ 767 Mike Capel .05 .02
- ❑ 768 Bill Wegman .05 .02
- ❑ 769 Junior Ortiz .05 .02
- ❑ 770 Alan Trammell .15 .06
- ❑ 771 Ron Kittle .05 .02
- ❑ 772 Ron Oester .05 .02
- ❑ 773 Keith Moreland .05 .02
- ❑ 774 Frank Robinson MG .15 .06
- ❑ 775 Jeff Reardon .10 .04
- ❑ 776 Nelson Liriano .05 .02
- ❑ 777 Ted Power .05 .02
- ❑ 778 Bruce Benedict .05 .02
- ❑ 779 Craig McMurtry .05 .02
- ❑ 780 Pedro Guerrero .05 .02
- ❑ 781 Greg Briley .05 .02
- ❑ 782 Checklist 661-792 .05 .02
- ❑ 783 Trevor Wilson RC .10 .04
- ❑ 784 Steve Avery FDP RC .25 .10
- ❑ 785 Ellis Burks .15 .06
- ❑ 786 Melido Perez .05 .02
- ❑ 787 Dave West RC .10 .04
- ❑ 788 Mike Morgan .05 .02
- ❑ 789 Bo Jackson TL .25 .10
- ❑ 790 Sid Fernandez .05 .02
- ❑ 791 Jim Lindeman .05 .02
- ❑ 792 Rafael Santana .05 .02

1989 Topps Traded

	Nm-Mt	Ex-Mt
COMP.FACT.SET (132)	15.00	6.00
❑ 1T Don Aase	.05	.02
❑ 2T Jim Abbott	.25	.10
❑ 3T Kent Anderson	.05	.02
❑ 4T Keith Atherton	.05	.02
❑ 5T Wally Backman	.05	.02
❑ 6T Steve Balboni	.05	.02
❑ 7T Jesse Barfield	.05	.02
❑ 8T Steve Bedrosian	.05	.02
❑ 9T Todd Benzinger	.05	.02
❑ 10T Geronimo Berroa	.05	.02
❑ 11T Bert Blyleven	.10	.04
❑ 12T Bob Boone	.10	.04
❑ 13T Phil Bradley	.05	.02
❑ 14T Jeff Brantley RC	.25	.10
❑ 15T Kevin Brown	.25	.10

❑ 16T	Jerry Browne	.05	.02
❑ 17T	Chuck Cary	.05	.02
❑ 18T	Carmen Castillo	.05	.02
❑ 19T	Jim Clancy	.05	.02
❑ 20T	Jack Clark	.05	.02
❑ 21T	Bryan Clutterbuck	.05	.02
❑ 22T	Jody Davis	.05	.02
❑ 23T	Mike Devereaux	.05	.02
❑ 24T	Frank DiPino	.05	.02
❑ 25T	Benny Distefano	.05	.02
❑ 26T	John Dopson	.05	.02
❑ 27T	Len Dykstra	.10	.04
❑ 28T	Jim Eisenreich	.05	.02
❑ 29T	Nick Esasky	.05	.02
❑ 30T	Alvaro Espinoza	.05	.02
❑ 31T	Darrell Evans UER (Stat headings on back are for a pitcher)	.10	.04
❑ 32T	Junior Felix RC	.10	.04
❑ 33T	Felix Fermin	.05	.02
❑ 34T	Julio Franco	.05	.02
❑ 35T	Terry Francona	.10	.04
❑ 36T	Cito Gaston MG	.10	.04
❑ 37T	Bob Geren UER (Photo actually Mike Fennell)	.05	.02
❑ 38T	Tom Gordon RC	.25	.10
❑ 39T	Tommy Gregg	.05	.02
❑ 40T	Ken Griffey Sr.	.10	.04
❑ 41T	Ken Griffey Jr. RC	8.00	3.20
❑ 42T	Kevin Gross	.05	.02
❑ 43T	Lee Guetterman	.05	.02
❑ 44T	Mel Hall	.05	.02
❑ 45T	Erik Hanson RC	.25	.10
❑ 46T	Gene Harris RC	.10	.04
❑ 47T	Andy Hawkins	.05	.02
❑ 48T	Rickey Henderson	.40	.16
❑ 49T	Tom Herr	.05	.02
❑ 50T	Ken Hill RC	.25	.10
❑ 51T	Brian Holman RC *	.10	.04
❑ 52T	Brian Holton	.05	.02
❑ 53T	Art Howe MG	.05	.02
❑ 54T	Ken Howell	.05	.02
❑ 55T	Bruce Hurst	.05	.02
❑ 56T	Chris James	.05	.02
❑ 57T	Randy Johnson	2.00	.80
❑ 58T	Jimmy Jones	.05	.02
❑ 59T	Terry Kennedy	.05	.02
❑ 60T	Paul Kilgus	.05	.02
❑ 61T	Eric King	.05	.02
❑ 62T	Ron Kittle	.05	.02
❑ 63T	John Kruk	.10	.04
❑ 64T	Randy Kutcher	.05	.02
❑ 65T	Steve Lake	.05	.02
❑ 66T	Mark Langston	.05	.02
❑ 67T	Dave LaPoint	.05	.02
❑ 68T	Rick Leach	.05	.02
❑ 69T	Terry Leach	.05	.02
❑ 70T	Jim Lefebvre MG	.05	.02
❑ 71T	Al Leiter	.25	.10
❑ 72T	Jeffrey Leonard	.05	.02
❑ 73T	Derek Lilliquist RC	.10	.04
❑ 74T	Rick Mahler	.05	.02
❑ 75T	Tom McCarthy	.05	.02
❑ 76T	Lloyd McClendon	.05	.02
❑ 77T	Lance McCullers	.05	.02
❑ 78T	Oddibe McDowell	.05	.02
❑ 79T	Roger McDowell	.05	.02
❑ 80T	Larry McWilliams	.05	.02
❑ 81T	Randy Milligan	.05	.02
❑ 82T	Mike Moore	.05	.02
❑ 83T	Keith Moreland	.05	.02
❑ 84T	Mike Morgan	.05	.02
❑ 85T	Jamie Moyer	.10	.04
❑ 86T	Rob Murphy	.05	.02
❑ 87T	Eddie Murray	.25	.10
❑ 88T	Pete O'Brien	.05	.02
❑ 89T	Gregg Olson	.25	.10
❑ 90T	Steve Ontiveros	.05	.02
❑ 91T	Jesse Orosco	.05	.02
❑ 92T	Spike Owen	.05	.02
❑ 93T	Rafael Palmeiro	.25	.10
❑ 94T	Clay Parker	.05	.02
❑ 95T	Jeff Parrett	.05	.02
❑ 96T	Lance Parrish	.05	.02
❑ 97T	Dennis Powell	.05	.02
❑ 98T	Rey Quinones	.05	.02
❑ 99T	Doug Rader MG	.05	.02
❑ 100T	Willie Randolph	.10	.04
❑ 101T	Shane Rawley	.05	.02
❑ 102T	Randy Ready	.05	.02
❑ 103T	Bip Roberts	.10	.04
❑ 104T	Kenny Rogers RC	.50	.20
❑ 105T	Ed Romero	.05	.02
❑ 106T	Nolan Ryan	1.50	.60
❑ 107T	Luis Salazar	.05	.02
❑ 108T	Juan Samuel	.05	.02
❑ 109T	Alex Sanchez	.05	.02
❑ 110T	Deion Sanders RC	.50	.20
❑ 111T	Steve Sax	.05	.02
❑ 112T	Rick Schu	.05	.02
❑ 113T	Dwight Smith RC	.25	.10
❑ 114T	Lonnie Smith	.05	.02
❑ 115T	Billy Spiers RC	.25	.10
❑ 116T	Kent Tekulve	.05	.02
❑ 117T	Walt Terrell	.05	.02
❑ 118T	Milt Thompson	.05	.02
❑ 119T	Dickie Thon	.05	.02
❑ 120T	Jeff Torborg MG	.05	.02
❑ 121T	Jeff Treadway	.05	.02
❑ 122T	Omar Vizquel RC	.50	.20
❑ 123T	Jerome Walton	.25	.10
❑ 124T	Gary Ward	.05	.02
❑ 125T	Claudell Washington	.05	.02
❑ 126T	Curt Wilkerson	.05	.02
❑ 127T	Eddie Williams	.05	.02
❑ 128T	Frank Williams	.05	.02
❑ 129T	Ken Williams	.05	.02
❑ 130T	Mitch Williams	.05	.02
❑ 131T	Steve Wilson RC	.10	.04
❑ 132T	Checklist 1T-132T	.05	.02

1990 Topps

	Nm-Mt	Ex-Mt
COMPLETE SET (792)	20.00	6.00
COMP.FACT.SET (792)	25.00	7.50
COMP.X-MAS.SET (792)	40.00	12.00

❑ 1	Nolan Ryan	1.00	.30
❑ 2	Nolan Ryan Mets	.50	.15
❑ 3	Nolan Ryan Angels	.50	.15
❑ 4	Nolan Ryan Astros	.50	.15
❑ 5	N.Ryan Rangers UER (Says Texas Stadium rather than Arlington Stadium)	.50	.15
❑ 6	Vince Coleman RB	.05	.02
❑ 7	Rickey Henderson RB	.25	.07
❑ 8	Cal Ripken RB	.25	.07
❑ 9	Eric Plunk	.05	.02
❑ 10	Barry Larkin	.25	.07
❑ 11	Paul Gibson	.05	.02
❑ 12	Joe Girardi	.15	.04
❑ 13	Mark Williamson	.05	.02
❑ 14	Mike Fetters RC	.25	.07
❑ 15	Teddy Higuera	.05	.02
❑ 16	Kent Anderson	.05	.02
❑ 17	Kelly Downs	.05	.02
❑ 18	Carlos Quintana	.05	.02
❑ 19	Al Newman	.05	.02
❑ 20	Mark Gubicza	.05	.02
❑ 21	Jeff Torborg MG	.05	.02
❑ 22	Bruce Ruffin	.05	.02
❑ 23	Randy Velarde	.05	.02
❑ 24	Joe Hesketh	.05	.02
❑ 25	Willie Randolph	.10	.03
❑ 26	Don Slaught	.05	.02
❑ 27	Rick Leach	.05	.02
❑ 28	Duane Ward	.05	.02
❑ 29	John Cangelosi	.05	.02
❑ 30	David Cone	.10	.03
❑ 31	Henry Cotto	.05	.02
❑ 32	John Farrell	.05	.02
❑ 33	Greg Walker	.05	.02
❑ 34	Tony Fossas	.05	.02
❑ 35	Benito Santiago	.10	.03
❑ 36	John Costello	.05	.02
❑ 37	Domingo Ramos	.05	.02
❑ 38	Wes Gardner	.05	.02
❑ 39	Curt Ford	.05	.02
❑ 40	Jay Howell	.05	.02
❑ 41	Matt Williams	.10	.03
❑ 42	Jeff M. Robinson	.05	.02
❑ 43	Dante Bichette	.25	.07
❑ 44	Roger Salkeld FDP RC	.10	.03
❑ 45	Dave Parker UER (Born in Jackson, not Calhoun)	.10	.03
❑ 46	Rob Dibble	.10	.03
❑ 47	Brian Harper	.05	.02
❑ 48	Zane Smith	.05	.02
❑ 49	Tom Lawless	.05	.02
❑ 50	Glenn Davis	.05	.02
❑ 51	Doug Rader MG	.05	.02
❑ 52	Jack Daugherty	.05	.02
❑ 53	Mike LaCoss	.05	.02
❑ 54	Joel Skinner	.05	.02
❑ 55	Darrell Evans UER (HR total should be 414, not 424)	.10	.03
❑ 56	Franklin Stubbs	.05	.02
❑ 57	Greg Vaughn	.10	.03
❑ 58	Keith Miller	.05	.02
❑ 59	Ted Power	.05	.02
❑ 60	George Brett	.60	.18
❑ 61	Deion Sanders	.25	.07
❑ 62	Ramon Martinez	.05	.02
❑ 63	Mike Pagliarulo	.05	.02
❑ 64	Danny Darwin	.05	.02
❑ 65	Devon White	.05	.02
❑ 66	Greg Litton	.05	.02
❑ 67	Scott Sanderson	.05	.02
❑ 68	Dave Henderson	.05	.02
❑ 69	Todd Frohwirth	.05	.02
❑ 70	Mike Greenwell	.05	.02
❑ 71	Allan Anderson	.05	.02
❑ 72	Jeff Huson RC	.10	.03
❑ 73	Bob Milacki	.05	.02
❑ 74	Jeff Jackson FDP RC	.10	.03
❑ 75	Doug Jones	.05	.02
❑ 76	Dave Valle	.05	.02
❑ 77	Dave Bergman	.05	.02
❑ 78	Mike Flanagan	.05	.02
❑ 79	Ron Kittle	.05	.02
❑ 80	Jeff Russell	.05	.02
❑ 81	Bob Rodgers MG	.05	.02
❑ 82	Scott Terry	.05	.02
❑ 83	Hensley Meulens	.05	.02
❑ 84	Ray Searage	.05	.02
❑ 85	Juan Samuel	.05	.02
❑ 86	Paul Kilgus	.05	.02
❑ 87	Rick Luecken	.05	.02
❑ 88	Glenn Braggs	.05	.02
❑ 89	Clint Zavaras	.05	.02
❑ 90	Jack Clark	.10	.03
❑ 91	Steve Frey	.05	.02
❑ 92	Mike Stanley	.05	.02
❑ 93	Shawn Hillegas	.05	.02
❑ 94	Herm Winningham	.05	.02
❑ 95	Todd Worrell	.05	.02
❑ 96	Jody Reed	.05	.02
❑ 97	Curt Schilling	1.00	.30
❑ 98	Jose Gonzalez	.05	.02
❑ 99	Rich Monteleone	.05	.02
❑ 100	Will Clark	.25	.07
❑ 101	Shane Rawley	.05	.02
❑ 102	Stan Javier	.05	.02
❑ 103	Marvin Freeman	.05	.02
❑ 104	Bob Knepper	.05	.02

	No.	Player		
❑	105	Randy Myers	.10	.03
❑	106	Charlie O'Brien	.05	.02
❑	107	Fred Lynn	.05	.02
❑	108	Rod Nichols	.05	.02
❑	109	Roberto Kelly	.05	.02
❑	110	Tommy Helms MG	.05	.02
❑	111	Ed Whited	.05	.02
❑	112	Glenn Wilson	.05	.02
❑	113	Manny Lee	.05	.02
❑	114	Mike Bielecki	.05	.02
❑	115	Tony Pena	.05	.02
❑	116	Floyd Bannister	.05	.02
❑	117	Mike Sharperson	.05	.02
❑	118	Erik Hanson	.05	.02
❑	119	Billy Hatcher	.05	.02
❑	120	John Franco	.10	.03
❑	121	Robin Ventura	.25	.07
❑	122	Shawn Abner	.05	.02
❑	123	Rich Gedman	.05	.02
❑	124	Dave Dravecky	.10	.03
❑	125	Kent Hrbek	.10	.03
❑	126	Randy Kramer	.05	.02
❑	127	Mike Devereaux	.05	.02
❑	128	Checklist 1	.05	.02
❑	129	Ron Jones	.05	.02
❑	130	Bert Blyleven	.10	.03
❑	131	Matt Nokes	.05	.02
❑	132	Lance Blankenship	.05	.02
❑	133	Ricky Horton	.05	.02
❑	134	E.Cunningham FDP RC	.10	.03
❑	135	Dave Magadan	.05	.02
❑	136	Kevin Brown	.10	.03
❑	137	Marty Pevey	.05	.02
❑	138	Al Leiter	.25	.07
❑	139	Greg Brock	.05	.02
❑	140	Andre Dawson	.10	.03
❑	141	John Hart MG	.05	.02
❑	142	Jeff Wetherby	.05	.02
❑	143	Rafael Belliard	.05	.02
❑	144	Bud Black	.05	.02
❑	145	Terry Steinbach	.05	.02
❑	146	Rob Richie	.05	.02
❑	147	Chuck Finley	.10	.03
❑	148	Edgar Martinez	.15	.04
❑	149	Steve Farr	.05	.02
❑	150	Kirk Gibson	.10	.03
❑	151	Rick Mahler	.05	.02
❑	152	Lonnie Smith	.05	.02
❑	153	Randy Milligan	.05	.02
❑	154	Mike Maddux	.05	.02
❑	155	Ellis Burks	.15	.04
❑	156	Ken Patterson	.05	.02
❑	157	Craig Biggio	.15	.04
❑	158	Craig Lefferts	.05	.02
❑	159	Mike Felder	.05	.02
❑	160	Dave Righetti	.05	.02
❑	161	Harold Reynolds	.10	.03
❑	162	Todd Zeile	.10	.03
❑	163	Phil Bradley	.05	.02
❑	164	Jeff Juden FDP RC	.10	.03
❑	165	Walt Weiss	.05	.02
❑	166	Bobby Witt	.05	.02
❑	167	Kevin Appier	.25	.07
❑	168	Jose Lind	.05	.02
❑	169	Richard Dotson	.05	.02
❑	170	George Bell	.05	.02
❑	171	Russ Nixon MG	.05	.02
❑	172	Tom Lampkin	.05	.02
❑	173	Tim Belcher	.05	.02
❑	174	Jeff Kunkel	.05	.02
❑	175	Mike Moore	.05	.02
❑	176	Luis Quinones	.05	.02
❑	177	Mike Henneman	.05	.02
❑	178	Chris James	.05	.02
❑	179	Brian Holton	.05	.02
❑	180	Tim Raines	.10	.03
❑	181	Juan Agosto	.05	.02
❑	182	Mookie Wilson	.10	.03
❑	183	Steve Lake	.05	.02
❑	184	Danny Cox	.05	.02
❑	185	Ruben Sierra	.05	.02
❑	186	Dave LaPoint	.05	.02
❑	187	Rick Wrona	.05	.02
❑	188	Mike Smithson	.05	.02
❑	189	Dick Schofield	.05	.02
❑	190	Rick Reuschel	.05	.02
❑	191	Pat Borders	.05	.02
❑	192	Don August	.05	.02
❑	193	Andy Benes	.10	.03
❑	194	Glenallen Hill	.05	.02
❑	195	Tim Burke	.05	.02
❑	196	Gerald Young	.05	.02
❑	197	Doug Drabek	.05	.02
❑	198	Mike Marshall	.05	.02
❑	199	Sergio Valdez	.05	.02
❑	200	Don Mattingly	.60	.18
❑	201	Cito Gaston MG	.05	.02
❑	202	Mike Macfarlane	.05	.02
❑	203	Mike Roesler	.05	.02
❑	204	Bob Dernier	.05	.02
❑	205	Mark Davis	.05	.02
❑	206	Nick Esasky	.05	.02
❑	207	Bob Ojeda	.05	.02
❑	208	Brook Jacoby	.05	.02
❑	209	Greg Mathews	.05	.02
❑	210	Ryne Sandberg	.40	.12
❑	211	John Cerutti	.05	.02
❑	212	Joe Orsulak	.05	.02
❑	213	Scott Bankhead	.05	.02
❑	214	Terry Francona	.10	.03
❑	215	Kirk McCaskill	.05	.02
❑	216	Ricky Jordan	.05	.02
❑	217	Don Robinson	.05	.02
❑	218	Wally Backman	.05	.02
❑	219	Donn Pall	.05	.02
❑	220	Barry Bonds	.60	.18
❑	221	Gary Mielke	.05	.02
❑	222	Kurt Stillwell UER (Graduate misspelled as gradute)	.05	.02
❑	223	Tommy Gregg	.05	.02
❑	224	Delino DeShields RC	.25	.07
❑	225	Jim Deshaies	.05	.02
❑	226	Mickey Hatcher	.05	.02
❑	227	Kevin Tapani RC	.25	.07
❑	228	Dave Martinez	.05	.02
❑	229	David Wells	.10	.03
❑	230	Keith Hernandez	.15	.04
❑	231	Jack McKeon MG	.05	.02
❑	232	Darnell Coles	.05	.02
❑	233	Ken Hill	.10	.03
❑	234	Mariano Duncan	.05	.02
❑	235	Jeff Reardon	.10	.03
❑	236	Hal Morris	.05	.02
❑	237	Kevin Ritz	.05	.02
❑	238	Felix Jose	.05	.02
❑	239	Eric Show	.05	.02
❑	240	Mark Grace	.25	.07
❑	241	Mike Krukow	.05	.02
❑	242	Fred Manrique	.05	.02
❑	243	Barry Jones	.05	.02
❑	244	Bill Schroeder	.05	.02
❑	245	Roger Clemens	.50	.15
❑	246	Jim Eisenreich	.05	.02
❑	247	Jerry Reed	.05	.02
❑	248	Dave Anderson	.05	.02
❑	249	Mike (Texas) Smith	.05	.02
❑	250	Jose Canseco	.25	.07
❑	251	Jeff Blauser	.05	.02
❑	252	Otis Nixon	.05	.02
❑	253	Mark Portugal	.05	.02
❑	254	Francisco Cabrera	.05	.02
❑	255	Bobby Thigpen	.05	.02
❑	256	Marvell Wynne	.05	.02
❑	257	Jose DeLeon	.05	.02
❑	258	Barry Lyons	.05	.02
❑	259	Lance McCullers	.05	.02
❑	260	Eric Davis	.10	.03
❑	261	Whitey Herzog MG	.10	.03
❑	262	Checklist 2	.05	.02
❑	263	Mel Stottlemyre Jr.	.05	.02
❑	264	Bryan Clutterbuck	.05	.02
❑	265	Pete O'Brien	.05	.02
❑	266	German Gonzalez	.05	.02
❑	267	Mark Davidson	.05	.02
❑	268	Rob Murphy	.05	.02
❑	269	Dickie Thon	.05	.02
❑	270	Dave Stewart	.10	.03
❑	271	Chet Lemon	.05	.02
❑	272	Bryan Harvey	.05	.02
❑	273	Bobby Bonilla	.10	.03
❑	274	Mauro Gozzo	.05	.02
❑	275	Mickey Tettleton	.05	.02
❑	276	Gary Thurman	.05	.02
❑	277	Lenny Harris	.05	.02
❑	278	Pascual Perez	.05	.02
❑	279	Steve Buechele	.05	.02
❑	280	Lou Whitaker	.10	.03
❑	281	Kevin Bass	.05	.02
❑	282	Derek Lilliquist	.05	.02
❑	283	Joey Belle	.25	.07
❑	284	Mark Gardner RC	.10	.03
❑	285	Willie McGee	.10	.03
❑	286	Lee Guetterman	.05	.02
❑	287	Vance Law	.05	.02
❑	288	Greg Briley	.05	.02
❑	289	Norm Charlton	.05	.02
❑	290	Robin Yount	.25	.07
❑	291	Dave Johnson MG	.10	.03
❑	292	Jim Gott	.05	.02
❑	293	Mike Gallego	.05	.02
❑	294	Craig McMurtry	.05	.02
❑	295	Fred McGriff	.25	.07
❑	296	Jeff Ballard	.05	.02
❑	297	Tommy Herr	.05	.02
❑	298	Dan Gladden	.05	.02
❑	299	Adam Peterson	.05	.02
❑	300	Bo Jackson	.25	.07
❑	301	Don Aase	.05	.02
❑	302	Marcus Lawton	.05	.02
❑	303	Rick Cerone	.05	.02
❑	304	Marty Clary	.05	.02
❑	305	Eddie Murray	.25	.07
❑	306	Tom Niedenfuer	.05	.02
❑	307	Bip Roberts	.05	.02
❑	308	Jose Guzman	.05	.02
❑	309	Eric Yelding	.05	.02
❑	310	Steve Bedrosian	.05	.02
❑	311	Dwight Smith	.05	.02
❑	312	Dan Quisenberry	.05	.02
❑	313	Gus Polidor	.05	.02
❑	314	Donald Harris FDP	.05	.02
❑	315	Bruce Hurst	.05	.02
❑	316	Carney Lansford	.10	.03
❑	317	Mark Guthrie	.05	.02
❑	318	Wallace Johnson	.05	.02
❑	319	Dion James	.05	.02
❑	320	Dave Stieb	.10	.03
❑	321	Joe Morgan MG	.05	.02
❑	322	Junior Ortiz	.05	.02
❑	323	Willie Wilson	.05	.02
❑	324	Pete Harnisch	.05	.02
❑	325	Robby Thompson	.05	.02
❑	326	Tom McCarthy	.05	.02
❑	327	Ken Williams	.05	.02
❑	328	Curt Young	.05	.02
❑	329	Oddibe McDowell	.05	.02
❑	330	Ron Darling	.05	.02
❑	331	Juan Gonzalez RC	1.50	.45
❑	332	Paul O'Neill	.15	.04
❑	333	Bill Wegman	.05	.02
❑	334	Johnny Ray	.05	.02
❑	335	Andy Hawkins	.05	.02
❑	336	Ken Griffey Jr.	.75	.23
❑	337	Lloyd McClendon	.05	.02
❑	338	Dennis Lamp	.05	.02
❑	339	Dave Clark	.05	.02
❑	340	Fernando Valenzuela	.10	.03
❑	341	Tom Foley	.05	.02
❑	342	Alex Trevino	.05	.02
❑	343	Frank Tanana	.05	.02
❑	344	George Canale	.05	.02
❑	345	Harold Baines	.10	.03
❑	346	Jim Presley	.05	.02
❑	347	Junior Felix	.05	.02
❑	348	Gary Wayne	.05	.02
❑	349	Steve Finley	.10	.03
❑	350	Bret Saberhagen	.10	.03
❑	351	Roger Craig MG	.05	.02
❑	352	Bryn Smith	.05	.02
❑	353	Sandy Alomar Jr. (Not listed as Jr. on card front)	.10	.03
❑	354	Stan Belinda RC	.10	.03
❑	355	Marty Barrett	.05	.02
❑	356	Randy Ready	.05	.02
❑	357	Dave West	.05	.02
❑	358	Andres Thomas	.05	.02

	No.	Player		
❑	359	Jimmy Jones	.05	.02
❑	360	Paul Molitor	.15	.04
❑	361	Randy McCament	.05	.02
❑	362	Damon Berryhill	.05	.02
❑	363	Dan Petry	.05	.02
❑	364	Rolando Roomes	.05	.02
❑	365	Ozzie Guillen	.05	.02
❑	366	Mike Heath	.05	.02
❑	367	Mike Morgan	.05	.02
❑	368	Bill Doran	.05	.02
❑	369	Todd Burns	.05	.02
❑	370	Tim Wallach	.05	.02
❑	371	Jimmy Key	.10	.03
❑	372	Terry Kennedy	.05	.02
❑	373	Alvin Davis	.05	.02
❑	374	Steve Cummings	.05	.02
❑	375	Dwight Evans	.10	.03
❑	376	Checklist 3 UER (Higuera misalphabet-ized in Brewer list)	.05	.02
❑	377	Mickey Weston	.05	.02
❑	378	Luis Salazar	.05	.02
❑	379	Steve Rosenberg	.05	.02
❑	380	Dave Winfield	.15	.04
❑	381	Frank Robinson MG	.15	.04
❑	382	Jeff Musselman	.05	.02
❑	383	John Morris	.05	.02
❑	384	Pat Combs	.05	.02
❑	385	Fred McGriff AS	.10	.03
❑	386	Julio Franco AS	.05	.02
❑	387	Wade Boggs AS	.10	.03
❑	388	Cal Ripken AS	.40	.12
❑	389	Robin Yount AS	.10	.03
❑	390	Ruben Sierra AS	.05	.02
❑	391	Kirby Puckett AS	.15	.04
❑	392	Carlton Fisk AS	.10	.03
❑	393	Bret Saberhagen AS	.05	.02
❑	394	Jeff Ballard AS	.05	.02
❑	395	Jeff Russell AS	.05	.02
❑	396	A.Bartlett Giamatti RC COMM MEM	.25	.07
❑	397	Will Clark AS	.10	.03
❑	398	Ryne Sandberg AS	.25	.07
❑	399	Howard Johnson AS	.05	.02
❑	400	Ozzie Smith AS	.15	.04
❑	401	Kevin Mitchell AS	.05	.02
❑	402	Eric Davis AS	.05	.02
❑	403	Tony Gwynn AS	.15	.04
❑	404	Craig Biggio AS	.10	.03
❑	405	Mike Scott AS	.05	.02
❑	406	Joe Magrane AS	.05	.02
❑	407	Mark Davis AS	.05	.02
❑	408	Trevor Wilson	.05	.02
❑	409	Tom Brunansky	.05	.02
❑	410	Joe Boever	.05	.02
❑	411	Ken Phelps	.05	.02
❑	412	Jamie Moyer	.10	.03
❑	413	Brian DuBois	.05	.02
❑	414A	Frank Thomas FDP ERR (Name missing on card front)	350.00	105.00
❑	414B	F.Thomas COR RC	1.50	.45
❑	415	Shawon Dunston	.05	.02
❑	416	Dave Johnson (P)	.05	.02
❑	417	Jim Gantner	.05	.02
❑	418	Tom Browning	.05	.02
❑	419	Beau Allred	.05	.02
❑	420	Carlton Fisk	.15	.04
❑	421	Greg Minton	.05	.02
❑	422	Pat Sheridan	.05	.02
❑	423	Fred Toliver	.05	.02
❑	424	Jerry Reuss	.05	.02
❑	425	Bill Landrum	.05	.02
❑	426	Jeff Hamilton UER (Stats say he fanned 197 times in 1987, but he only had 147 at bats)	.05	.02
❑	427	Carmen Castillo	.05	.02
❑	428	Steve Davis	.05	.02
❑	429	Tom Kelly MG	.05	.02
❑	430	Pete Incaviglia	.05	.02
❑	431	Randy Johnson	.40	.12
❑	432	Damaso Garcia	.05	.02
❑	433	Steve Olin RC	.25	.07
❑	434	Mark Carreon	.05	.02
❑	435	Kevin Seitzer	.05	.02
❑	436	Mel Hall	.05	.02
❑	437	Les Lancaster	.05	.02
❑	438	Greg Myers	.05	.02
❑	439	Jeff Parrett	.05	.02
❑	440	Alan Trammell	.15	.04
❑	441	Bob Kipper	.05	.02
❑	442	Jerry Browne	.05	.02
❑	443	Cris Carpenter	.05	.02
❑	444	Kyle Abbott FDP	.05	.02
❑	445	Danny Jackson	.05	.02
❑	446	Dan Pasqua	.05	.02
❑	447	Atlee Hammaker	.05	.02
❑	448	Greg Gagne	.05	.02
❑	449	Dennis Rasmussen	.05	.02
❑	450	Rickey Henderson	.40	.12
❑	451	Mark Lemke	.05	.02
❑	452	Luis DeLosSantos	.05	.02
❑	453	Jody Davis	.05	.02
❑	454	Jeff King	.05	.02
❑	455	Jeffrey Leonard	.05	.02
❑	456	Chris Gwynn	.05	.02
❑	457	Gregg Jefferies	.10	.03
❑	458	Bob McClure	.05	.02
❑	459	Jim Lefebvre MG	.05	.02
❑	460	Mike Scott	.05	.02
❑	461	Carlos Martinez	.05	.02
❑	462	Denny Walling	.05	.02
❑	463	Drew Hall	.05	.02
❑	464	Jerome Walton	.05	.02
❑	465	Kevin Gross	.05	.02
❑	466	Rance Mulliniks	.05	.02
❑	467	Juan Nieves	.05	.02
❑	468	Bill Ripken	.05	.02
❑	469	John Kruk	.10	.03
❑	470	Frank Viola	.05	.02
❑	471	Mike Brumley	.05	.02
❑	472	Jose Uribe	.05	.02
❑	473	Joe Price	.05	.02
❑	474	Rich Thompson	.05	.02
❑	475	Bob Welch	.05	.02
❑	476	Brad Komminsk	.05	.02
❑	477	Willie Fraser	.05	.02
❑	478	Mike LaValliere	.05	.02
❑	479	Frank White	.10	.03
❑	480	Sid Fernandez	.05	.02
❑	481	Garry Templeton	.05	.02
❑	482	Steve Carter	.05	.02
❑	483	Alejandro Pena	.05	.02
❑	484	Mike Fitzgerald	.05	.02
❑	485	John Candelaria	.05	.02
❑	486	Jeff Treadway	.05	.02
❑	487	Steve Searcy	.05	.02
❑	488	Ken Oberkfell	.05	.02
❑	489	Nick Leyva MG	.05	.02
❑	490	Dan Plesac	.05	.02
❑	491	Dave Cochrane	.05	.02
❑	492	Ron Oester	.05	.02
❑	493	Jason Grimsley RC	.10	.03
❑	494	Terry Puhl	.05	.02
❑	495	Lee Smith	.10	.03
❑	496	Cecil Espy UER ('88 stats have 3 SB's, should be 33)	.05	.02
❑	497	Dave Schmidt	.05	.02
❑	498	Rick Schu	.05	.02
❑	499	Bill Long	.05	.02
❑	500	Kevin Mitchell	.05	.02
❑	501	Matt Young	.05	.02
❑	502	Mitch Webster	.05	.02
❑	503	Randy St.Claire	.05	.02
❑	504	Tom O'Malley	.05	.02
❑	505	Kelly Gruber	.05	.02
❑	506	Tom Glavine	.25	.07
❑	507	Gary Redus	.05	.02
❑	508	Terry Leach	.05	.02
❑	509	Tom Pagnozzi	.05	.02
❑	510	Dwight Gooden	.15	.04
❑	511	Clay Parker	.05	.02
❑	512	Gary Pettis	.05	.02
❑	513	Mark Eichhorn	.05	.02
❑	514	Andy Allanson	.05	.02
❑	515	Len Dykstra	.10	.03
❑	516	Tim Leary	.05	.02
❑	517	Roberto Alomar	.25	.07
❑	518	Bill Krueger	.05	.02
❑	519	Bucky Dent MG	.05	.02
❑	520	Mitch Williams	.05	.02
❑	521	Craig Worthington	.05	.02
❑	522	Mike Dunne	.05	.02
❑	523	Jay Bell	.10	.03
❑	524	Daryl Boston	.05	.02
❑	525	Wally Joyner	.10	.03
❑	526	Checklist 4	.05	.02
❑	527	Ron Hassey	.05	.02
❑	528	Kevin Wickander UER (Monthly scoreboard strikeout total was 2.2, that was his innings pitched total)	.05	.02
❑	529	Greg A. Harris	.05	.02
❑	530	Mark Langston	.05	.02
❑	531	Ken Caminiti	.10	.03
❑	532	Cecilio Guante	.05	.02
❑	533	Tim Jones	.05	.02
❑	534	Louie Meadows	.05	.02
❑	535	John Smoltz	.25	.07
❑	536	Bob Geren	.05	.02
❑	537	Mark Grant	.05	.02
❑	538	Bill Spiers UER (Photo actually George Canale)	.05	.02
❑	539	Neal Heaton	.05	.02
❑	540	Danny Tartabull	.05	.02
❑	541	Pat Perry	.05	.02
❑	542	Darren Daulton	.10	.03
❑	543	Nelson Liriano	.05	.02
❑	544	Dennis Boyd	.05	.02
❑	545	Kevin McReynolds	.05	.02
❑	546	Kevin Hickey	.05	.02
❑	547	Jack Howell	.05	.02
❑	548	Pat Clements	.05	.02
❑	549	Don Zimmer MG	.05	.02
❑	550	Julio Franco	.05	.02
❑	551	Tim Crews	.05	.02
❑	552	Mike(Miss.) Smith	.05	.02
❑	553	Scott Scudder UER (Cedar Rap1ds)	.05	.02
❑	554	Jay Buhner	.10	.03
❑	555	Jack Morris	.10	.03
❑	556	Gene Larkin	.05	.02
❑	557	Jeff Innis	.05	.02
❑	558	Rafael Ramirez	.05	.02
❑	559	Andy McGaffigan	.05	.02
❑	560	Steve Sax	.05	.02
❑	561	Ken Dayley	.05	.02
❑	562	Chad Kreuter	.05	.02
❑	563	Alex Sanchez	.05	.02
❑	564	T.Houston FDP RC	.25	.07
❑	565	Scott Fletcher	.05	.02
❑	566	Mark Knudson	.05	.02
❑	567	Ron Gant	.10	.03
❑	568	John Smiley	.05	.02
❑	569	Ivan Calderon	.05	.02
❑	570	Cal Ripken	.75	.23
❑	571	Brett Butler	.10	.03
❑	572	Greg W. Harris	.05	.02
❑	573	Danny Heep	.05	.02
❑	574	Bill Swift	.05	.02
❑	575	Lance Parrish	.05	.02
❑	576	Mike Dyer	.05	.02
❑	577	Charlie Hayes	.05	.02
❑	578	Joe Magrane	.05	.02
❑	579	Art Howe MG	.05	.02
❑	580	Joe Carter	.10	.03
❑	581	Ken Griffey Sr.	.10	.03
❑	582	Rick Honeycutt	.05	.02
❑	583	Bruce Benedict	.05	.02
❑	584	Phil Stephenson	.05	.02
❑	585	Kal Daniels	.05	.02
❑	586	Edwin Nunez	.05	.02
❑	587	Lance Johnson	.05	.02
❑	588	Rick Rhoden	.05	.02
❑	589	Mike Aldrete	.05	.02
❑	590	Ozzie Smith	.25	.07
❑	591	Todd Stottlemyre	.10	.03
❑	592	R.J. Reynolds	.05	.02
❑	593	Scott Bradley	.05	.02
❑	594	Luis Sojo	.05	.02
❑	595	Greg Swindell	.05	.02
❑	596	Jose DeJesus	.05	.02
❑	597	Chris Bosio	.05	.02
❑	598	Brady Anderson	.10	.03

❑ 599 Frank Williams .05 .02
❑ 600 Darryl Strawberry .15 .04
❑ 601 Luis Rivera .05 .02
❑ 602 Scott Garrelts .05 .02
❑ 603 Tony Armas .05 .02
❑ 604 Ron Robinson .05 .02
❑ 605 Mike Scioscia .05 .02
❑ 606 Storm Davis .05 .02
❑ 607 Steve Jeltz .05 .02
❑ 608 Eric Anthony RC .10 .03
❑ 609 Sparky Anderson MG .10 .03
❑ 610 Pedro Guerrero .05 .02
❑ 611 Walt Terrell .05 .02
❑ 612 Dave Gallagher .05 .02
❑ 613 Jeff Pico .05 .02
❑ 614 Nelson Santovenia .05 .02
❑ 615 Rob Deer .05 .02
❑ 616 Brian Holman .05 .02
❑ 617 Geronimo Berroa .05 .02
❑ 618 Ed Whitson .05 .02
❑ 619 Rob Ducey .05 .02
❑ 620 Tony Castillo .05 .02
❑ 621 Melido Perez .05 .02
❑ 622 Sid Bream .05 .02
❑ 623 Jim Corsi .05 .02
❑ 624 Darrin Jackson .05 .02
❑ 625 Roger McDowell .05 .02
❑ 626 Bob Melvin .05 .02
❑ 627 Jose Rijo .05 .02
❑ 628 Candy Maldonado .05 .02
❑ 629 Eric Hetzel .05 .02
❑ 630 Gary Gaetti .10 .03
❑ 631 John Wetteland .25 .07
❑ 632 Scott Lusader .05 .02
❑ 633 Dennis Cook .05 .02
❑ 634 Luis Polonia .05 .02
❑ 635 Brian Downing .05 .02
❑ 636 Jesse Orosco .05 .02
❑ 637 Craig Reynolds .05 .02
❑ 638 Jeff Montgomery .10 .03
❑ 639 Tony LaRussa MG .10 .03
❑ 640 Rick Sutcliffe .10 .03
❑ 641 Doug Strange .05 .02
❑ 642 Jack Armstrong .05 .02
❑ 643 Alfredo Griffin .05 .02
❑ 644 Paul Assenmacher .05 .02
❑ 645 Jose Oquendo .05 .02
❑ 646 Checklist 5 .05 .02
❑ 647 Rex Hudler .05 .02
❑ 648 Jim Clancy .05 .02
❑ 649 Dan Murphy RC .10 .03
❑ 650 Mike Witt .05 .02
❑ 651 Rafael Santana .05 .02
❑ 652 Mike Boddicker .05 .02
❑ 653 John Moses .05 .02
❑ 654 Paul Coleman FDP RC .10 .03
❑ 655 Gregg Olson .10 .03
❑ 656 Mackey Sasser .05 .02
❑ 657 Terry Mulholland .05 .02
❑ 658 Donell Nixon .05 .02
❑ 659 Greg Cadaret .05 .02
❑ 660 Vince Coleman .05 .02
❑ 661 Dick Howser TBC'85 .05 .02
UER (Seaver's 300th on 7/11/85, should be 8/4/85)
❑ 662 Mike Schmidt TBC'80 .25 .07
❑ 663 Fred Lynn TBC'75 .05 .02
❑ 664 Johnny Bench TBC'70 .15 .04
❑ 665 Sandy Koufax TBC'65 .50 .15
❑ 666 Brian Fisher .05 .02
❑ 667 Curt Wilkerson .05 .02
❑ 668 Joe Oliver .05 .02
❑ 669 Tom Lasorda MG .25 .07
❑ 670 Dennis Eckersley .10 .03
❑ 671 Bob Boone .10 .03
❑ 672 Roy Smith .05 .02
❑ 673 Joey Meyer .05 .02
❑ 674 Spike Owen .05 .02
❑ 675 Jim Abbott .25 .07
❑ 676 Randy Kutcher .05 .02
❑ 677 Jay Tibbs .05 .02
❑ 678 Kirt Manwaring UER .05 .02
('88 Phoenix stats repeated)
❑ 679 Gary Ward .05 .02
❑ 680 Howard Johnson .05 .02
❑ 681 Mike Schooler .05 .02
❑ 682 Dann Bilardello .05 .02
❑ 683 Kenny Rogers .10 .03
❑ 684 Julio Machado .05 .02
❑ 685 Tony Fernandez .05 .02
❑ 686 Carmelo Martinez .05 .02
❑ 687 Tim Birtsas .05 .02
❑ 688 Milt Thompson .05 .02
❑ 689 Rich Yett .05 .02
❑ 690 Mark McGwire .60 .18
❑ 691 Chuck Cary .05 .02
❑ 692 Sammy Sosa RC 8.00 2.40
❑ 693 Calvin Schiraldi .05 .02
❑ 694 Mike Stanton RC .25 .07
❑ 695 Tom Henke .05 .02
❑ 696 B.J. Surhoff .10 .03
❑ 697 Mike Davis .05 .02
❑ 698 Omar Vizquel .25 .07
❑ 699 Jim Leyland MG .05 .02
❑ 700 Kirby Puckett .25 .07
❑ 701 Bernie Williams RC 1.00 .30
❑ 702 Tony Phillips .05 .02
❑ 703 Jeff Brantley .05 .02
❑ 704 Chip Hale .05 .02
❑ 705 Claudell Washington .05 .02
❑ 706 Geno Petralli .05 .02
❑ 707 Luis Aquino .05 .02
❑ 708 Larry Sheets .05 .02
❑ 709 Juan Berenguer .05 .02
❑ 710 Von Hayes .05 .02
❑ 711 Rick Aguilera .10 .03
❑ 712 Todd Benzinger .05 .02
❑ 713 Tim Drummond .05 .02
❑ 714 Marquis Grissom RC .25 .07
❑ 715 Greg Maddux .50 .15
❑ 716 Steve Balboni .05 .02
❑ 717 Ron Karkovice .05 .02
❑ 718 Gary Sheffield .25 .07
❑ 719 Wally Whitehurst .05 .02
❑ 720 Andres Galarraga .10 .03
❑ 721 Lee Mazzilli .05 .02
❑ 722 Felix Fermin .05 .02
❑ 723 Jeff D. Robinson .05 .02
❑ 724 Juan Bell .05 .02
❑ 725 Terry Pendleton .10 .03
❑ 726 Gene Nelson .05 .02
❑ 727 Pat Tabler .05 .02
❑ 728 Jim Acker .05 .02
❑ 729 Bobby Valentine MG .05 .02
❑ 730 Tony Gwynn .30 .09
❑ 731 Don Carman .05 .02
❑ 732 Ernest Riles .05 .02
❑ 733 John Dopson .05 .02
❑ 734 Kevin Elster .05 .02
❑ 735 Charlie Hough .10 .03
❑ 736 Rick Dempsey .05 .02
❑ 737 Chris Sabo .05 .02
❑ 738 Gene Harris .05 .02
❑ 739 Dale Sveum .05 .02
❑ 740 Jesse Barfield .05 .02
❑ 741 Steve Wilson .05 .02
❑ 742 Ernie Whitt .05 .02
❑ 743 Tom Candiotti .05 .02
❑ 744 Kelly Mann .05 .02
❑ 745 Hubie Brooks .05 .02
❑ 746 Dave Smith .05 .02
❑ 747 Randy Bush .05 .02
❑ 748 Doyle Alexander .05 .02
❑ 749 Mark Parent UER .05 .02
('87 BA .80, should be .080)
❑ 750 Dale Murphy .25 .07
❑ 751 Steve Lyons .05 .02
❑ 752 Tom Gordon .10 .03
❑ 753 Chris Speier .05 .02
❑ 754 Bob Walk .05 .02
❑ 755 Rafael Palmeiro .15 .04
❑ 756 Ken Howell .05 .02
❑ 757 Larry Walker RC 1.00 .30
❑ 758 Mark Thurmond .05 .02
❑ 759 Tom Trebelhorn MG .05 .02
❑ 760 Wade Boggs .15 .04
❑ 761 Mike Jackson .05 .02
❑ 762 Doug Dascenzo .05 .02
❑ 763 Dennis Martinez .10 .03
❑ 764 Tim Teufel .05 .02
❑ 765 Chili Davis .10 .03
❑ 766 Brian Meyer .05 .02
❑ 767 Tracy Jones .05 .02
❑ 768 Chuck Crim .05 .02
❑ 769 Greg Hibbard RC .10 .03
❑ 770 Cory Snyder .05 .02
❑ 771 Pete Smith .05 .02
❑ 772 Jeff Reed .05 .02
❑ 773 Dave Leiper .05 .02
❑ 774 Ben McDonald RC .25 .07
❑ 775 Andy Van Slyke .10 .03
❑ 776 Charlie Leibrandt .05 .02
❑ 777 Tim Laudner .05 .02
❑ 778 Mike Jeffcoat .05 .02
❑ 779 Lloyd Moseby .05 .02
❑ 780 Orel Hershiser .10 .03
❑ 781 Mario Diaz .05 .02
❑ 782 Jose Alvarez .05 .02
❑ 783 Checklist 6 .05 .02
❑ 784 Scott Bailes .05 .02
❑ 785 Jim Rice .10 .03
❑ 786 Eric King .05 .02
❑ 787 Rene Gonzales .05 .02
❑ 788 Frank DiPino .05 .02
❑ 789 John Wathan MG .05 .02
❑ 790 Gary Carter .15 .04
❑ 791 Alvaro Espinoza .05 .02
❑ 792 Gerald Perry .05 .02
❑ XX George Bush PRES

1990 Topps Debut '89

	Nm-Mt	Ex-Mt
COMP.FACT.SET (152)	25.00	7.50

❑ 1 Jim Abbott .75 .23
❑ 2 Beau Allred .15 .04
❑ 3 Wilson Alvarez .25 .07
❑ 4 Kent Anderson .15 .04
❑ 5 Eric Anthony .15 .04
❑ 6 Kevin Appier .75 .23
❑ 7 Larry Arndt .15 .04
❑ 8 John Barfield .15 .04
❑ 9 Billy Bates .15 .04
❑ 10 Kevin Batiste .15 .04
❑ 11 Blaine Beatty .15 .04
❑ 12 Stan Belinda .15 .04
❑ 13 Juan Bell .15 .04
❑ 14 Joey Belle .75 .23
(Now known as Albert)
❑ 15 Andy Benes .25 .07
❑ 16 Mike Benjamin .15 .04
❑ 17 Geronimo Berroa .15 .04
❑ 18 Mike Blowers .25 .07
❑ 19 Brian Brady .15 .04
❑ 20 Francisco Cabrera .15 .04
❑ 21 George Canale .15 .04
❑ 22 Jose Cano .15 .04
❑ 23 Steve Carter .15 .04
❑ 24 Pat Combs .15 .04
❑ 25 Scott Coolbaugh .15 .04
❑ 26 Steve Cummings .15 .04
❑ 27 Pete Dalena .15 .04
❑ 28 Jeff Datz .15 .04
❑ 29 Bobby Davidson .15 .04
❑ 30 Drew Denson .15 .04
❑ 31 Gary DiSarcina .25 .07

- ❑ 32 Brian DuBois .15 .04
- ❑ 33 Mike Dyer .15 .04
- ❑ 34 Wayne Edwards .15 .04
- ❑ 35 Junior Felix .15 .04
- ❑ 36 Mike Fetters .15 .04
- ❑ 37 Steve Finley .50 .15
- ❑ 38 Darrin Fletcher .25 .07
- ❑ 39 LaVel Freeman .15 .04
- ❑ 40 Steve Frey .15 .04
- ❑ 41 Mark Gardner .15 .04
- ❑ 42 Joe Girardi .25 .07
- ❑ 43 Juan Gonzalez 2.50 .75
- ❑ 44 Goose Gozzo .15 .04
- ❑ 45 Tommy Greene .15 .04
- ❑ 46 Ken Griffey Jr. 5.00 1.50
- ❑ 47 Jason Grimsley .15 .04
- ❑ 48 Marquis Grissom .75 .23
- ❑ 49 Mark Guthrie .15 .04
- ❑ 50 Chip Hale .15 .04
- ❑ 51 Jack Hardy .15 .04
- ❑ 52 Gene Harris .15 .04
- ❑ 53 Mike Hartley .15 .04
- ❑ 54 Scott Hemond .15 .04
- ❑ 55 Xavier Hernandez .15 .04
- ❑ 56 Eric Hetzel .15 .04
- ❑ 57 Greg Hibbard .15 .04
- ❑ 58 Mark Higgins .15 .04
- ❑ 59 Glenallen Hill .15 .04
- ❑ 60 Chris Hoiles .25 .07
- ❑ 61 Shawn Holman .15 .04
- ❑ 62 Dann Howitt .15 .04
- ❑ 63 Mike Huff .15 .04
- ❑ 64 Terry Jorgensen .15 .04
- ❑ 65 David Justice 1.00 .30
- ❑ 66 Jeff King .15 .04
- ❑ 67 Matt Kinzer .15 .04
- ❑ 68 Joe Kraemer .15 .04
- ❑ 69 Marcus Lawton .15 .04
- ❑ 70 Derek Lilliquist .15 .04
- ❑ 71 Scott Little .15 .04
- ❑ 72 Greg Litton .15 .04
- ❑ 73 Rick Luecken .15 .04
- ❑ 74 Julio Machado .15 .04
- ❑ 75 Tom Magrann .15 .04
- ❑ 76 Kelly Mann .15 .04
- ❑ 77 Randy McCament .15 .04
- ❑ 78 Ben McDonald .15 .04
- ❑ 79 Chuck McElroy .15 .04
- ❑ 80 Jeff McKnight .15 .04
- ❑ 81 Kent Mercker .15 .04
- ❑ 82 Matt Merullo .15 .04
- ❑ 83 Hensley Meulens .15 .04
- ❑ 84 Kevin Mmahat .15 .04
- ❑ 85 Mike Munoz .15 .04
- ❑ 86 Dan Murphy .15 .04
- ❑ 87 Jaime Navarro .15 .04
- ❑ 88 Randy Nosek .15 .04
- ❑ 89 John Olerud 1.00 .30
- ❑ 90 Steve Olin .25 .07
- ❑ 91 Joe Oliver .15 .04
- ❑ 92 Francisco Oliveras .15 .04
- ❑ 93 Gregg Olson .25 .07
- ❑ 94 John Orton .15 .04
- ❑ 95 Dean Palmer .50 .15
- ❑ 96 Ramon Pena .15 .04
- ❑ 97 Jeff Peterek .15 .04
- ❑ 98 Marty Pevey .15 .04
- ❑ 99 Rusty Richards .15 .04
- ❑ 100 Jeff Richardson .15 .04
- ❑ 101 Rob Richie .15 .04
- ❑ 102 Kevin Ritz .15 .04
- ❑ 103 Rosario Rodriguez .15 .04
- ❑ 104 Mike Roesler .15 .04
- ❑ 105 Kenny Rogers .25 .07
- ❑ 106 Bobby Rose .15 .04
- ❑ 107 Alex Sanchez .15 .04
- ❑ 108 Deion Sanders .75 .23
- ❑ 109 Jeff Schaefer .15 .04
- ❑ 110 Jeff Schulz .15 .04
- ❑ 111 Mike Schwabe .15 .04
- ❑ 112 Dick Scott .15 .04
- ❑ 113 Scott Scudder .15 .04
- ❑ 114 Rudy Seanez .15 .04
- ❑ 115 Joe Skalski .15 .04
- ❑ 116 Dwight Smith .15 .04
- ❑ 117 Greg Smith .15 .04
- ❑ 118 Mike Smith .15 .04
- ❑ 119 Paul Sorrento .25 .07
- ❑ 120 Sammy Sosa 10.00 3.00
- ❑ 121 Billy Spiers .15 .04
- ❑ 122 Mike Stanton .15 .04
- ❑ 123 Phil Stephenson .15 .04
- ❑ 124 Doug Strange .15 .04
- ❑ 125 Russ Swan .15 .04
- ❑ 126 Kevin Tapani .25 .07
- ❑ 127 Stu Tate .15 .04
- ❑ 128 Greg Vaughn .25 .07
- ❑ 129 Robin Ventura .75 .23
- ❑ 130 Randy Veres .15 .04
- ❑ 131 Jose Vizcaino .25 .07
- ❑ 132 Omar Vizquel .75 .23
- ❑ 133 Larry Walker 1.50 .45
- ❑ 134 Jerome Walton .15 .04
- ❑ 135 Gary Wayne .15 .04
- ❑ 136 Lenny Webster .15 .04
- ❑ 137 Mickey Weston .15 .04
- ❑ 138 Jeff Wetherby .15 .04
- ❑ 139 John Wetteland .50 .15
- ❑ 140 Ed Whited .15 .04
- ❑ 141 Wally Whitehurst .15 .04
- ❑ 142 Kevin Wickander .15 .04
- ❑ 143 Dean Wilkins .15 .04
- ❑ 144 Dana Williams .15 .04
- ❑ 145 Paul Wilmet .15 .04
- ❑ 146 Craig Wilson .15 .04
- ❑ 147 Matt Winters .15 .04
- ❑ 148 Eric Yelding .15 .04
- ❑ 149 Clint Zavaras .15 .04
- ❑ 150 Todd Zeile .50 .15
- ❑ 151 Checklist Card .15 .04
- ❑ 152 Checklist Card .15 .04

1991 Topps

	Nm-Mt	Ex-Mt
COMPLETE SET (792)	20.00	6.00
COMP.FACT.SET (792)	40.00	12.00

- ❑ 1 Nolan Ryan 1.00 .30
- ❑ 2 George Brett RB .25 .07
- ❑ 3 Carlton Fisk RB .10 .03
- ❑ 4 Kevin Maas RB .05 .02
- ❑ 5 Cal Ripken RB .40 .12
- ❑ 6 Nolan Ryan RB .50 .15
- ❑ 7 Ryne Sandberg RB .25 .07
- ❑ 8 Bobby Thigpen RB .05 .02
- ❑ 9 Darrin Fletcher .05 .02
- ❑ 10 Gregg Olson .05 .02
- ❑ 11 Roberto Kelly .05 .02
- ❑ 12 Paul Assenmacher .05 .02
- ❑ 13 Mariano Duncan .05 .02
- ❑ 14 Dennis Lamp .05 .02
- ❑ 15 Von Hayes .05 .02
- ❑ 16 Mike Heath .05 .02
- ❑ 17 Jeff Brantley .05 .02
- ❑ 18 Nelson Liriano .05 .02
- ❑ 19 Jeff D. Robinson .05 .02
- ❑ 20 Pedro Guerrero .10 .03
- ❑ 21 Joe Morgan MG .05 .02
- ❑ 22 Storm Davis .05 .02
- ❑ 23 Jim Gantner .05 .02
- ❑ 24 Dave Martinez .05 .02
- ❑ 25 Tim Belcher .05 .02
- ❑ 26 Luis Sojo UER .05 .02
  (Born in Barquisimento, not Carquis)
- ❑ 27 Bobby Witt .05 .02
- ❑ 28 Alvaro Espinoza .05 .02
- ❑ 29 Bob Walk .05 .02
- ❑ 30 Gregg Jefferies .05 .02
- ❑ 31 Colby Ward .05 .02
- ❑ 32 Mike Simms .05 .02
- ❑ 33 Barry Jones .05 .02
- ❑ 34 Atlee Hammaker .05 .02
- ❑ 35 Greg Maddux .50 .15
- ❑ 36 Donnie Hill .05 .02
- ❑ 37 Tom Bolton .05 .02
- ❑ 38 Scott Bradley .05 .02
- ❑ 39 Jim Neidlinger .05 .02
- ❑ 40 Kevin Mitchell .05 .02
- ❑ 41 Ken Dayley .05 .02
- ❑ 42 Chris Hoiles .05 .02
- ❑ 43 Roger McDowell .05 .02
- ❑ 44 Mike Felder .05 .02
- ❑ 45 Chris Sabo .05 .02
- ❑ 46 Tim Drummond .05 .02
- ❑ 47 Brook Jacoby .05 .02
- ❑ 48 Dennis Boyd .05 .02
- ❑ 49A Pat Borders ERR .25 .07
  (40 steals at Kinston in '86)
- ❑ 49B Pat Borders COR .05 .02
  (0 steals at Kinston in '86)
- ❑ 50 Bob Welch .05 .02
- ❑ 51 Art Howe MG .05 .02
- ❑ 52 Francisco Oliveras .05 .02
- ❑ 53 Mike Sharperson UER .05 .02
  (Born in 1961, not 1960)
- ❑ 54 Gary Mielke .05 .02
- ❑ 55 Jeffrey Leonard .05 .02
- ❑ 56 Jeff Parrett .05 .02
- ❑ 57 Jack Howell .05 .02
- ❑ 58 Mel Stottlemyre Jr. .05 .02
- ❑ 59 Eric Yelding .05 .02
- ❑ 60 Frank Viola .10 .03
- ❑ 61 Stan Javier .05 .02
- ❑ 62 Lee Guetterman .05 .02
- ❑ 63 Milt Thompson .05 .02
- ❑ 64 Tom Herr .05 .02
- ❑ 65 Bruce Hurst .05 .02
- ❑ 66 Terry Kennedy .05 .02
- ❑ 67 Rick Honeycutt .05 .02
- ❑ 68 Gary Sheffield .10 .03
- ❑ 69 Steve Wilson .05 .02
- ❑ 70 Ellis Burks .10 .03
- ❑ 71 Jim Acker .05 .02
- ❑ 72 Junior Ortiz .05 .02
- ❑ 73 Craig Worthington .05 .02
- ❑ 74 Shane Andrews RC .25 .07
- ❑ 75 Jack Morris .10 .03
- ❑ 76 Jerry Browne .05 .02
- ❑ 77 Drew Hall .05 .02
- ❑ 78 Geno Petralli .05 .02
- ❑ 79 Frank Thomas .25 .07
- ❑ 80A Fernando Valenzuela .40 .12
  ERR (104 earned runs in '90 tied for league lead)
- ❑ 80B Fernando Valenzuela .10 .03
  COR (104 earned runs in '90 led league, 20 CG's in 1986 now italicized)
- ❑ 81 Cito Gaston MG .05 .02
- ❑ 82 Tom Glavine .25 .07
- ❑ 83 Daryl Boston .05 .02
- ❑ 84 Bob McClure .05 .02
- ❑ 85 Jesse Barfield .05 .02
- ❑ 86 Les Lancaster .05 .02
- ❑ 87 Tracy Jones .05 .02
- ❑ 88 Bob Tewksbury .05 .02
- ❑ 89 Darren Daulton .10 .03
- ❑ 90 Danny Tartabull .05 .02
- ❑ 91 Greg Colbrunn RC .25 .07
- ❑ 92 Danny Jackson .05 .02
- ❑ 93 Ivan Calderon .05 .02
- ❑ 94 John Dopson .05 .02
- ❑ 95 Paul Molitor .15 .04
- ❑ 96 Trevor Wilson .05 .02

❑ 97A Brady Anderson ERR .40 .12
(September, 2 RBI and 3 hits, should be 3 RBI and 14 hits
❑ 97B Brady Anderson COR .10 .03
❑ 98 Sergio Valdez .05 .02
❑ 99 Chris Gwynn .05 .02
❑ 100 Don Mattingly COR .60 .18
(101 hits in 1990)
❑ 100A Don Mattingly ERR 2.00 .60
(10 hits in 1990)
❑ 101 Rob Ducey .05 .02
❑ 102 Gene Larkin .05 .02
❑ 103 Tim Costo RC .05 .02
❑ 104 Don Robinson .05 .02
❑ 105 Kevin McReynolds .05 .02
❑ 106 Ed Nunez .05 .02
❑ 107 Luis Polonia .05 .02
❑ 108 Matt Young .05 .02
❑ 109 Greg Riddoch MG .05 .02
❑ 110 Tom Henke .05 .02
❑ 111 Andres Thomas .05 .02
❑ 112 Frank DiPino .05 .02
❑ 113 Carl Everett RC .50 .15
❑ 114 Lance Dickson RC .10 .03
❑ 115 Hubie Brooks .05 .02
❑ 116 Mark Davis .05 .02
❑ 117 Dion James .05 .02
❑ 118 Tom Edens .05 .02
❑ 119 Carl Nichols .05 .02
❑ 120 Joe Carter .10 .03
❑ 121 Eric King .05 .02
❑ 122 Paul O'Neill .15 .04
❑ 123 Greg A. Harris .05 .02
❑ 124 Randy Bush .05 .02
❑ 125 Steve Bedrosian .05 .02
❑ 126 Bernard Gilkey .05 .02
❑ 127 Joe Price .05 .02
❑ 128 Travis Fryman .10 .03
(Front has SS back has SS-3B)
❑ 129 Mark Eichhorn .05 .02
❑ 130 Ozzie Smith .25 .07
❑ 131A Checklist 1 ERR .25 .07
727 Phil Bradley
❑ 131B Checklist 1 COR .05 .02
717 Phil Bradley
❑ 132 Jamie Quirk .05 .02
❑ 133 Greg Briley .05 .02
❑ 134 Kevin Elster .05 .02
❑ 135 Jerome Walton .05 .02
❑ 136 Dave Schmidt .05 .02
❑ 137 Randy Ready .05 .02
❑ 138 Jamie Moyer .10 .03
❑ 139 Jeff Treadway .05 .02
❑ 140 Fred McGriff .15 .04
❑ 141 Nick Leyva MG .05 .02
❑ 142 Curt Wilkerson .05 .02
❑ 143 John Smiley .05 .02
❑ 144 Dave Henderson .05 .02
❑ 145 Lou Whitaker .10 .03
❑ 146 Dan Plesac .05 .02
❑ 147 Carlos Baerga .05 .02
❑ 148 Rey Palacios .05 .02
❑ 149 Al Osuna UER .10 .03
(Shown throwing right, but bio says lefty)
❑ 150 Cal Ripken .75 .23
❑ 151 Tom Browning .05 .02
❑ 152 Mickey Hatcher .05 .02
❑ 153 Bryan Harvey .05 .02
❑ 154 Jay Buhner .10 .03
❑ 155A Dwight Evans ERR .40 .12
(Led league with 162 games in '82)
❑ 155B Dwight Evans COR .10 .03
(Tied for lead with 162 games in '82)
❑ 156 Carlos Martinez .05 .02
❑ 157 John Smoltz .15 .04
❑ 158 Jose Uribe .05 .02
❑ 159 Joe Boever .05 .02
❑ 160 Vince Coleman UER .05 .02
(Wrong birth year, born 9/22/60)
❑ 161 Tim Leary .05 .02
❑ 162 Ozzie Canseco .05 .02
❑ 163 Dave Johnson .05 .02
❑ 164 Edgar Diaz .05 .02
❑ 165 Sandy Alomar Jr. .05 .02
❑ 166 Harold Baines .10 .03
❑ 167A R.Tomlin RC ERR .25 .07
Harriburg
❑ 167B R.Tomlin RC COR .10 .03
Harrisburg
❑ 168 John Olerud .10 .03
❑ 169 Luis Aquino .05 .02
❑ 170 Carlton Fisk .15 .04
❑ 171 Tony LaRussa MG .10 .03
❑ 172 Pete Incaviglia .05 .02
❑ 173 Jason Grimsley .05 .02
❑ 174 Ken Caminiti .10 .03
❑ 175 Jack Armstrong .05 .02
❑ 176 John Orton .05 .02
❑ 177 Reggie Harris .05 .02
❑ 178 Dave Valle .05 .02
❑ 179 Pete Harnisch .05 .02
❑ 180 Tony Gwynn .30 .09
❑ 181 Duane Ward .05 .02
❑ 182 Junior Noboa .05 .02
❑ 183 Clay Parker .05 .02
❑ 184 Gary Green .05 .02
❑ 185 Joe Magrane .05 .02
❑ 186 Rod Booker .05 .02
❑ 187 Greg Cadaret .05 .02
❑ 188 Damon Berryhill .05 .02
❑ 189 Daryl Irvine .05 .02
❑ 190 Matt Williams .10 .03
❑ 191 Willie Blair .05 .02
❑ 192 Rob Deer .05 .02
❑ 193 Felix Fermin .05 .02
❑ 194 Xavier Hernandez .05 .02
❑ 195 Wally Joyner .10 .03
❑ 196 Jim Vatcher .05 .02
❑ 197 Chris Nabholz .05 .02
❑ 198 R.J. Reynolds .05 .02
❑ 199 Mike Hartley .05 .02
❑ 200 Darryl Strawberry .15 .04
❑ 201 Tom Kelly MG .05 .02
❑ 202 Jim Leyritz .05 .02
❑ 203 Gene Harris .05 .02
❑ 204 Herm Winningham .05 .02
❑ 205 Mike Perez RC .10 .03
❑ 206 Carlos Quintana .05 .02
❑ 207 Gary Wayne .05 .02
❑ 208 Willie Wilson .05 .02
❑ 209 Ken Howell .05 .02
❑ 210 Lance Parrish .10 .03
❑ 211 Brian Barnes .05 .02
❑ 212 Steve Finley .10 .03
❑ 213 Frank Wills .05 .02
❑ 214 Joe Girardi .05 .02
❑ 215 Dave Smith .05 .02
❑ 216 Greg Gagne .05 .02
❑ 217 Chris Bosio .05 .02
❑ 218 Rick Parker .05 .02
❑ 219 Jack McDowell .05 .02
❑ 220 Tim Wallach .05 .02
❑ 221 Don Slaught .05 .02
❑ 222 Brian McRae RC .25 .07
❑ 223 Allan Anderson .05 .02
❑ 224 Juan Gonzalez .25 .07
❑ 225 Randy Johnson .30 .09
❑ 226 Alfredo Griffin .05 .02
❑ 227 Steve Avery UER .05 .02
(Pitched 13 games for Durham in 1989, not 2)
❑ 228 Rex Hudler .05 .02
❑ 229 Rance Mulliniks .05 .02
❑ 230 Sid Fernandez .05 .02
❑ 231 Doug Rader MG .05 .02
❑ 232 Jose DeJesus .05 .02
❑ 233 Al Leiter .10 .03
❑ 234 Scott Erickson .05 .02
❑ 235 Dave Parker .10 .03
❑ 236A Frank Tanana ERR .25 .07
(Tied for lead with 269 K's in '75)
❑ 236B Frank Tanana COR .05 .02
(Led league with 269 K's in '75)
❑ 237 Rick Cerone .05 .02
❑ 238 Mike Dunne .05 .02
❑ 239 Darren Lewis .05 .02
❑ 240 Mike Scott .05 .02
❑ 241 Dave Clark UER .05 .02
(Career totals 19 HR and 5 3B, should be 22 and 3)
❑ 242 Mike LaCoss .05 .02
❑ 243 Lance Johnson .05 .02
❑ 244 Mike Jeffcoat .05 .02
❑ 245 Kal Daniels .05 .02
❑ 246 Kevin Wickander .05 .02
❑ 247 Jody Reed .05 .02
❑ 248 Tom Gordon .05 .02
❑ 249 Bob Melvin .05 .02
❑ 250 Dennis Eckersley .10 .03
❑ 251 Mark Lemke .05 .02
❑ 252 Mel Rojas .05 .02
❑ 253 Garry Templeton .05 .02
❑ 254 Shawn Boskie .05 .02
❑ 255 Brian Downing .05 .02
❑ 256 Greg Hibbard .05 .02
❑ 257 Tom O'Malley .05 .02
❑ 258 Chris Hammond .05 .02
❑ 259 Hensley Meulens .05 .02
❑ 260 Harold Reynolds .10 .03
❑ 261 Bud Harrelson MG .05 .02
❑ 262 Tim Jones .05 .02
❑ 263 Checklist 2 .05 .02
❑ 264 Dave Hollins .05 .02
❑ 265 Mark Gubicza .05 .02
❑ 266 Carmelo Castillo .05 .02
❑ 267 Mark Knudson .05 .02
❑ 268 Tom Brookens .05 .02
❑ 269 Joe Hesketh .05 .02
❑ 270 Mark McGwire COR .60 .18
(1987 Slugging Pctg. listed as .618)
❑ 270A Mark McGwire ERR 2.00 .60
(1987 Slugging Pctg. listed as 618)
❑ 271 Omar Olivares RC .10 .03
❑ 272 Jeff King .05 .02
❑ 273 Johnny Ray .05 .02
❑ 274 Ken Williams .05 .02
❑ 275 Alan Trammell .15 .04
❑ 276 Bill Swift .05 .02
❑ 277 Scott Coolbaugh .05 .02
❑ 278 Alex Fernandez UER .05 .02
(No '90 White Sox stats)
❑ 279A Jose Gonzalez ERR .25 .07
(Photo actually Billy Bean)
❑ 279B Jose Gonzalez COR .05 .02
❑ 280 Bret Saberhagen .10 .03
❑ 281 Larry Sheets .05 .02
❑ 282 Don Carman .05 .02
❑ 283 Marquis Grissom .05 .02
❑ 284 Billy Spiers .05 .02
❑ 285 Jim Abbott .25 .07
❑ 286 Ken Oberkfell .05 .02
❑ 287 Mark Grant .05 .02
❑ 288 Derrick May .05 .02
❑ 289 Tim Birtsas .05 .02
❑ 290 Steve Sax .05 .02
❑ 291 John Wathan MG .05 .02
❑ 292 Bud Black .05 .02
❑ 293 Jay Bell .10 .03
❑ 294 Mike Moore .05 .02
❑ 295 Rafael Palmeiro .15 .04
❑ 296 Mark Williamson .05 .02
❑ 297 Manny Lee .05 .02
❑ 298 Omar Vizquel .10 .03
❑ 299 Scott Radinsky .05 .02
❑ 300 Kirby Puckett .25 .07
❑ 301 Steve Farr .05 .02
❑ 302 Tim Teufel .05 .02
❑ 303 Mike Boddicker .05 .02
❑ 304 Kevin Reimer .05 .02
❑ 305 Mike Scioscia .05 .02
❑ 306A Lonnie Smith ERR .40 .12
(136 games in '90)
❑ 306B Lonnie Smith COR .05 .02
(135 games in '90)
❑ 307 Andy Benes .05 .02
❑ 308 Tom Pagnozzi .05 .02

❑ 309 Norm Charlton .05 .02
❑ 310 Gary Carter .15 .04
❑ 311 Jeff Pico .05 .02
❑ 312 Charlie Hayes .05 .02
❑ 313 Ron Robinson .05 .02
❑ 314 Gary Pettis .05 .02
❑ 315 Roberto Alomar .25 .07
❑ 316 Gene Nelson .05 .02
❑ 317 Mike Fitzgerald .05 .02
❑ 318 Rick Aguilera .10 .03
❑ 319 Jeff McKnight .05 .02
❑ 320 Tony Fernandez .05 .02
❑ 321 Bob Rodgers MG .05 .02
❑ 322 Terry Shumpert .05 .02
❑ 323 Cory Snyder .05 .02
❑ 324A Ron Kittle ERR .40 .12
(Set another standard ...)
❑ 324B Ron Kittle COR .05 .02
(Tied another standard ...)
❑ 325 Brett Butler .10 .03
❑ 326 Ken Patterson .05 .02
❑ 327 Ron Hassey .05 .02
❑ 328 Walt Terrell .05 .02
❑ 329 Dave Justice UER .10 .03
(Drafted third round on card, should say fourth pick)
❑ 330 Dwight Gooden .15 .04
❑ 331 Eric Anthony .05 .02
❑ 332 Kenny Rogers .10 .03
❑ 333 C.Jones FDP RC 4.00 1.20
❑ 334 Todd Benzinger .05 .02
❑ 335 Mitch Williams .05 .02
❑ 336 Matt Nokes .05 .02
❑ 337A Keith Comstock ERR .25 .07
(Cubs logo on front)
❑ 337B Keith Comstock COR .05 .02
(Mariners logo on front)
❑ 338 Luis Rivera .05 .02
❑ 339 Larry Walker .25 .07
❑ 340 Ramon Martinez .05 .02
❑ 341 John Moses .05 .02
❑ 342 Mickey Morandini .05 .02
❑ 343 Jose Oquendo .05 .02
❑ 344 Jeff Russell .05 .02
❑ 345 Len Dykstra .10 .03
❑ 346 Jesse Orosco .05 .02
❑ 347 Greg Vaughn .10 .03
❑ 348 Todd Stottlemyre .05 .02
❑ 349 Dave Gallagher .05 .02
❑ 350 Glenn Davis .05 .02
❑ 351 Joe Torre MG .10 .03
❑ 352 Frank White .10 .03
❑ 353 Tony Castillo .05 .02
❑ 354 Sid Bream .05 .02
❑ 355 Chili Davis .10 .03
❑ 356 Mike Marshall .05 .02
❑ 357 Jack Savage .05 .02
❑ 358 Mark Parent .05 .02
❑ 359 Chuck Cary .05 .02
❑ 360 Tim Raines .10 .03
❑ 361 Scott Garrelts .05 .02
❑ 362 Hector Villenueva .05 .02
❑ 363 Rick Mahler .05 .02
❑ 364 Dan Pasqua .05 .02
❑ 365 Mike Schooler .05 .02
❑ 366A Checklist 3 ERR .25 .07
19 Carl Nichols
❑ 366B Checklist 3 COR .05 .02
119 Carl Nichols
❑ 367 Dave Walsh .05 .02
❑ 368 Felix Jose .05 .02
❑ 369 Steve Searcy .05 .02
❑ 370 Kelly Gruber .05 .02
❑ 371 Jeff Montgomery .05 .02
❑ 372 Spike Owen .05 .02
❑ 373 Darrin Jackson .05 .02
❑ 374 Larry Casian .05 .02
❑ 375 Tony Pena .05 .02
❑ 376 Mike Harkey .05 .02
❑ 377 Rene Gonzales .05 .02
❑ 378A Wilson Alvarez ERR .25 .07
('89 Port Charlotte and '90 Birmingham stat lines omitted)
❑ 378B Wilson Alvarez COR .05 .02
Text still says 143 K's in 1988, whereas stats say 134
❑ 379 Randy Velarde .05 .02
❑ 380 Willie McGee .10 .03
❑ 381 Jim Leyland MG .05 .02
❑ 382 Mackey Sasser .05 .02
❑ 383 Pete Smith .05 .02
❑ 384 Gerald Perry .05 .02
❑ 385 Mickey Tettleton .05 .02
❑ 386 Cecil Fielder AS .05 .02
❑ 387 Julio Franco AS .05 .02
❑ 388 Kelly Gruber AS .05 .02
❑ 389 Alan Trammell AS .10 .03
❑ 390 Jose Canseco AS .10 .03
❑ 391 Rickey Henderson AS .25 .07
❑ 392 Ken Griffey Jr. AS .25 .07
❑ 393 Carlton Fisk AS .10 .03
❑ 394 Bob Welch AS .05 .02
❑ 395 Chuck Finley AS .05 .02
❑ 396 Bobby Thigpen AS .05 .02
❑ 397 Eddie Murray AS .15 .04
❑ 398 Ryne Sandberg AS .25 .07
❑ 399 Matt Williams AS .05 .02
❑ 400 Barry Larkin AS .10 .03
❑ 401 Barry Bonds AS .30 .09
❑ 402 Darryl Strawberry AS .10 .03
❑ 403 Bobby Bonilla AS .05 .02
❑ 404 Mike Scioscia AS .05 .02
❑ 405 Doug Drabek AS .05 .02
❑ 406 Frank Viola AS .05 .02
❑ 407 John Franco AS .05 .02
❑ 408 Earnest Riles .05 .02
❑ 409 Mike Stanley .05 .02
❑ 410 Dave Righetti .10 .03
❑ 411 Lance Blankenship .05 .02
❑ 412 Dave Bergman .05 .02
❑ 413 Terry Mulholland .05 .02
❑ 414 Sammy Sosa .50 .15
❑ 415 Rick Sutcliffe .10 .03
❑ 416 Randy Milligan .05 .02
❑ 417 Bill Krueger .05 .02
❑ 418 Nick Esasky .05 .02
❑ 419 Jeff Reed .05 .02
❑ 420 Bobby Thigpen .05 .02
❑ 421 Alex Cole .05 .02
❑ 422 Rick Reuschel .05 .02
❑ 423 Rafael Ramirez UER .05 .02
(Born 1959, not 1958)
❑ 424 Calvin Schiraldi .05 .02
❑ 425 Andy Van Slyke .10 .03
❑ 426 Joe Grahe RC .10 .03
❑ 427 Rick Dempsey .05 .02
❑ 428 John Barfield .05 .02
❑ 429 Stump Merrill MG .05 .02
❑ 430 Gary Gaetti .10 .03
❑ 431 Paul Gibson .05 .02
❑ 432 Delino DeShields .10 .03
❑ 433 Pat Tabler .05 .02
❑ 434 Julio Machado .05 .02
❑ 435 Kevin Maas .05 .02
❑ 436 Scott Bankhead .05 .02
❑ 437 Doug Dascenzo .05 .02
❑ 438 Vicente Palacios .05 .02
❑ 439 Dickie Thon .05 .02
❑ 440 George Bell .05 .02
❑ 441 Zane Smith .05 .02
❑ 442 Charlie O'Brien .05 .02
❑ 443 Jeff Innis .05 .02
❑ 444 Glenn Braggs .05 .02
❑ 445 Greg Swindell .05 .02
❑ 446 Craig Grebeck .05 .02
❑ 447 John Burkett .05 .02
❑ 448 Craig Lefferts .05 .02
❑ 449 Juan Berenguer .05 .02
❑ 450 Wade Boggs .15 .04
❑ 451 Neal Heaton .05 .02
❑ 452 Bill Schroeder .05 .02
❑ 453 Lenny Harris .05 .02
❑ 454A Kevin Appier ERR .40 .12
('90 Omaha stat line omitted)
❑ 454B Kevin Appier COR .10 .03
❑ 455 Walt Weiss .05 .02
❑ 456 Charlie Leibrandt .05 .02
❑ 457 Todd Hundley .05 .02
❑ 458 Brian Holman .05 .02
❑ 459 T.Trebelhorn MG UER .05 .02
Pitching and batting columns switched
❑ 460 Dave Stieb .05 .02
❑ 461 Robin Ventura .10 .03
❑ 462 Steve Frey .05 .02
❑ 463 Dwight Smith .05 .02
❑ 464 Steve Buechele .05 .02
❑ 465 Ken Griffey Sr. .10 .03
❑ 466 Charles Nagy .05 .02
❑ 467 Dennis Cook .05 .02
❑ 468 Tim Hulett .05 .02
❑ 469 Chet Lemon .05 .02
❑ 470 Howard Johnson .05 .02
❑ 471 Mike Lieberthal RC .40 .12
❑ 472 Kirt Manwaring .05 .02
❑ 473 Curt Young .05 .02
❑ 474 Phil Plantier RC .10 .03
❑ 475 Ted Higuera .05 .02
❑ 476 Glenn Wilson .05 .02
❑ 477 Mike Fetters .05 .02
❑ 478 Kurt Stillwell .05 .02
❑ 479 Bob Patterson UER .05 .02
(Has a decimal point between 7 and 9)
❑ 480 Dave Magadan .05 .02
❑ 481 Eddie Whitson .05 .02
❑ 482 Tino Martinez .15 .04
❑ 483 Mike Aldrete .05 .02
❑ 484 Dave LaPoint .05 .02
❑ 485 Terry Pendleton .10 .03
❑ 486 Tommy Greene .05 .02
❑ 487 Rafael Belliard .05 .02
❑ 488 Jeff Manto .05 .02
❑ 489 Bobby Valentine MG .05 .02
❑ 490 Kirk Gibson .10 .03
❑ 491 Kurt Miller RC .05 .02
❑ 492 Ernie Whitt .05 .02
❑ 493 Jose Rijo .05 .02
❑ 494 Chris James .05 .02
❑ 495 Charlie Hough .10 .03
❑ 496 Marty Barrett .05 .02
❑ 497 Ben McDonald .05 .02
❑ 498 Mark Salas .05 .02
❑ 499 Melido Perez .05 .02
❑ 500 Will Clark .25 .07
❑ 501 Mike Bielecki .05 .02
❑ 502 Carney Lansford .10 .03
❑ 503 Roy Smith .05 .02
❑ 504 Julio Valera .05 .02
❑ 505 Chuck Finley .10 .03
❑ 506 Darnell Coles .05 .02
❑ 507 Steve Jeltz .05 .02
❑ 508 Mike York .05 .02
❑ 509 Glenallen Hill .05 .02
❑ 510 John Franco .10 .03
❑ 511 Steve Balboni .05 .02
❑ 512 Jose Mesa .05 .02
❑ 513 Jerald Clark .05 .02
❑ 514 Mike Stanton .05 .02
❑ 515 Alvin Davis .05 .02
❑ 516 Karl Rhodes .05 .02
❑ 517 Joe Oliver .05 .02
❑ 518 Cris Carpenter .05 .02
❑ 519 Sparky Anderson MG .10 .03
❑ 520 Mark Grace .25 .07
❑ 521 Joe Orsulak .05 .02
❑ 522 Stan Belinda .05 .02
❑ 523 Rodney McCray .05 .02
❑ 524 Darrel Akerfelds .05 .02
❑ 525 Willie Randolph .10 .03
❑ 526A Moises Alou ERR .40 .12
(37 runs in 2 games for '90 Pirates)
❑ 526B Moises Alou COR .10 .03
(0 runs in 2 games for '90 Pirates)
❑ 527A Checklist 4 ERR .25 .07
105 Keith Miller
719 Kevin McReynolds
❑ 527B Checklist 4 COR .05 .02
105 Kevin McReynolds
719 Keith Miller

❑ 528 Dennis Martinez	.10	.03
❑ 529 Marc Newfield RC	.10	.03
❑ 530 Roger Clemens	.50	.15
❑ 531 Dave Rohde	.05	.02
❑ 532 Kirk McCaskill	.05	.02
❑ 533 Oddibe McDowell	.05	.02
❑ 534 Mike Jackson	.05	.02
❑ 535 Ruben Sierra UER (Back reads 100 Runs amd 100 RBI's)	.05	.02
❑ 536 Mike Witt	.05	.02
❑ 537 Jose Lind	.05	.02
❑ 538 Bip Roberts	.05	.02
❑ 539 Scott Terry	.05	.02
❑ 540 George Brett	.60	.18
❑ 541 Domingo Ramos	.05	.02
❑ 542 Rob Murphy	.05	.02
❑ 543 Junior Felix	.05	.02
❑ 544 Alejandro Pena	.05	.02
❑ 545 Dale Murphy	.25	.07
❑ 546 Jeff Ballard	.05	.02
❑ 547 Mike Pagliarulo	.05	.02
❑ 548 Jaime Navarro	.05	.02
❑ 549 John McNamara MG	.05	.02
❑ 550 Eric Davis	.10	.03
❑ 551 Bob Kipper	.05	.02
❑ 552 Jeff Hamilton	.05	.02
❑ 553 Joe Klink	.05	.02
❑ 554 Brian Harper	.05	.02
❑ 555 Turner Ward RC	.10	.03
❑ 556 Gary Ward	.05	.02
❑ 557 Wally Whitehurst	.05	.02
❑ 558 Otis Nixon	.05	.02
❑ 559 Adam Peterson	.05	.02
❑ 560 Greg Smith	.05	.02
❑ 561 Tim McIntosh	.05	.02
❑ 562 Jeff Kunkel	.05	.02
❑ 563 Brent Knackert	.05	.02
❑ 564 Dante Bichette	.10	.03
❑ 565 Craig Biggio	.15	.04
❑ 566 Craig Wilson	.05	.02
❑ 567 Dwayne Henry	.05	.02
❑ 568 Ron Karkovice	.05	.02
❑ 569 Curt Schilling	.15	.04
❑ 570 Barry Bonds	.60	.18
❑ 571 Pat Combs	.05	.02
❑ 572 Dave Anderson	.05	.02
❑ 573 Rich Rodriguez UER (Stats say drafted 4th, but bio says 9th round)	.05	.02
❑ 574 John Marzano	.05	.02
❑ 575 Robin Yount	.25	.07
❑ 576 Jeff Kaiser	.05	.02
❑ 577 Bill Doran	.05	.02
❑ 578 Dave West	.05	.02
❑ 579 Roger Craig MG	.05	.02
❑ 580 Dave Stewart	.10	.03
❑ 581 Luis Quinones	.05	.02
❑ 582 Marty Clary	.05	.02
❑ 583 Tony Phillips	.05	.02
❑ 584 Kevin Brown	.10	.03
❑ 585 Pete O'Brien	.05	.02
❑ 586 Fred Lynn	.05	.02
❑ 587 Jose Offerman UER (Text says he signed 7/24/86, but bio says 1988)	.05	.02
❑ 588 Mark Whiten	.05	.02
❑ 589 Scott Ruskin	.05	.02
❑ 590 Eddie Murray	.25	.07
❑ 591 Ken Hill	.05	.02
❑ 592 B.J. Surhoff	.10	.03
❑ 593A Mike Walker ERR ('90 Canton-Akron stat line omitted)	.25	.07
❑ 593B Mike Walker COR	.05	.02
❑ 594 Rich Garces RC	.10	.03
❑ 595 Bill Landrum	.05	.02
❑ 596 Ronnie Walden RC	.10	.03
❑ 597 Jerry Don Gleaton	.05	.02
❑ 598 Sam Horn	.05	.02
❑ 599A Greg Myers ERR ('90 Syracuse stat line omitted)	.25	.07
❑ 599B Greg Myers COR	.05	.02
❑ 600 Bo Jackson	.25	.07
❑ 601 Bob Ojeda	.05	.02
❑ 602 Casey Candaele	.05	.02
❑ 603A W.Chamberlain RC ERR Photo actually Louie Meadows	.40	.12
❑ 603B Wes Chamberlain RC COR	.10	.03
❑ 604 Billy Hatcher	.05	.02
❑ 605 Jeff Reardon	.10	.03
❑ 606 Jim Gott	.05	.02
❑ 607 Edgar Martinez	.15	.04
❑ 608 Todd Burns	.05	.02
❑ 609 Jeff Torborg MG	.05	.02
❑ 610 Andres Galarraga	.10	.03
❑ 611 Dave Eiland	.05	.02
❑ 612 Steve Lyons	.05	.02
❑ 613 Eric Show	.05	.02
❑ 614 Luis Salazar	.05	.02
❑ 615 Bert Blyleven	.10	.03
❑ 616 Todd Zeile	.05	.02
❑ 617 Bill Wegman	.05	.02
❑ 618 Sil Campusano	.05	.02
❑ 619 David Wells	.10	.03
❑ 620 Ozzie Guillen	.05	.02
❑ 621 Ted Power	.05	.02
❑ 622 Jack Daugherty	.05	.02
❑ 623 Jeff Blauser	.05	.02
❑ 624 Tom Candiotti	.05	.02
❑ 625 Terry Steinbach	.05	.02
❑ 626 Gerald Young	.05	.02
❑ 627 Tim Layana	.05	.02
❑ 628 Greg Litton	.05	.02
❑ 629 Wes Gardner	.05	.02
❑ 630 Dave Winfield	.15	.04
❑ 631 Mike Morgan	.05	.02
❑ 632 Lloyd Moseby	.05	.02
❑ 633 Kevin Tapani	.05	.02
❑ 634 Henry Cotto	.05	.02
❑ 635 Andy Hawkins	.05	.02
❑ 636 Geronimo Pena	.05	.02
❑ 637 Bruce Ruffin	.05	.02
❑ 638 Mike Macfarlane	.05	.02
❑ 639 Frank Robinson MG	.15	.04
❑ 640 Andre Dawson	.10	.03
❑ 641 Mike Henneman	.05	.02
❑ 642 Hal Morris	.05	.02
❑ 643 Jim Presley	.05	.02
❑ 644 Chuck Crim	.05	.02
❑ 645 Juan Samuel	.05	.02
❑ 646 Andujar Cedeno	.05	.02
❑ 647 Mark Portugal	.05	.02
❑ 648 Lee Stevens	.05	.02
❑ 649 Bill Sampen	.05	.02
❑ 650 Jack Clark	.10	.03
❑ 651 Alan Mills	.05	.02
❑ 652 Kevin Romine	.05	.02
❑ 653 Anthony Telford	.05	.02
❑ 654 Paul Sorrento	.05	.02
❑ 655 Erik Hanson	.05	.02
❑ 656A Checklist 5 ERR 348 Vicente Palacios 381 Jose Lind 537 Mike LaValliere 665 Jim Leyland	.25	.07
❑ 656B Checklist 5 ERR 433 Vicente Palacios (Palacios should be 438) 537 Jose Lind 665 Mike LaValliere 381 Jim Leyland	.25	.07
❑ 656C Checklist 5 COR 438 Vicente Palacios 537 Jose Lind 665 Mike LaValliere 381 Jim Leyland	.05	.02
❑ 657 Mike Kingery	.05	.02
❑ 658 Scott Aldred	.05	.02
❑ 659 Oscar Azocar	.05	.02
❑ 660 Lee Smith	.10	.03
❑ 661 Steve Lake	.05	.02
❑ 662 Ron Dibble	.10	.03
❑ 663 Greg Brock	.05	.02
❑ 664 John Farrell	.05	.02
❑ 665 Mike LaValliere	.05	.02
❑ 666 Danny Darwin	.05	.02
❑ 667 Kent Anderson	.05	.02
❑ 668 Bill Long	.05	.02
❑ 669 Lou Piniella MG	.10	.03
❑ 670 Rickey Henderson	.40	.12
❑ 671 Andy McGaffigan	.05	.02
❑ 672 Shane Mack	.05	.02
❑ 673 Greg Olson UER (6 RBI in '88 at Tidewater and 2 RBI in '87, should be 48 and 15)	.05	.02
❑ 674A Kevin Gross ERR (89 BB with Phillies in '88 tied for league lead)	.25	.07
❑ 674B Kevin Gross COR (89 BB with Phillies in '88 led league)	.05	.02
❑ 675 Tom Brunansky	.05	.02
❑ 676 Scott Chiamparino	.05	.02
❑ 677 Billy Ripken	.05	.02
❑ 678 Mark Davidson	.05	.02
❑ 679 Bill Bathe	.05	.02
❑ 680 David Cone	.10	.03
❑ 681 Jeff Schaefer	.05	.02
❑ 682 Ray Lankford	.05	.02
❑ 683 Derek Lilliquist	.05	.02
❑ 684 Milt Cuyler	.05	.02
❑ 685 Doug Drabek	.05	.02
❑ 686 Mike Gallego	.05	.02
❑ 687A John Cerutti ERR (4.46 ERA in '90)	.25	.07
❑ 687B John Cerutti COR (4.76 ERA in '90)	.05	.02
❑ 688 Rosario Rodriguez	.05	.02
❑ 689 John Kruk	.10	.03
❑ 690 Orel Hershiser	.10	.03
❑ 691 Mike Blowers	.05	.02
❑ 692A Efrain Valdez ERR (Born 6/11/66)	.25	.07
❑ 692B Efrain Valdez COR (Born 7/11/66 and two lines of text added)	.05	.02
❑ 693 Francisco Cabrera	.05	.02
❑ 694 Randy Veres	.05	.02
❑ 695 Kevin Seitzer	.05	.02
❑ 696 Steve Olin	.05	.02
❑ 697 Shawn Abner	.05	.02
❑ 698 Mark Guthrie	.05	.02
❑ 699 Jim Lefebvre MG	.05	.02
❑ 700 Jose Canseco	.25	.07
❑ 701 Pascual Perez	.05	.02
❑ 702 Tim Naehring	.05	.02
❑ 703 Juan Agosto	.05	.02
❑ 704 Devon White	.05	.02
❑ 705 Robby Thompson	.05	.02
❑ 706A Brad Arnsberg ERR (68.2 IP in '90)	.25	.07
❑ 706B Brad Arnsberg COR (62.2 IP in '90)	.05	.02
❑ 707 Jim Eisenreich	.05	.02
❑ 708 John Mitchell	.05	.02
❑ 709 Matt Sinatro	.05	.02
❑ 710 Kent Hrbek	.10	.03
❑ 711 Jose DeLeon	.05	.02
❑ 712 Ricky Jordan	.05	.02
❑ 713 Scott Scudder	.05	.02
❑ 714 Marvell Wynne	.05	.02
❑ 715 Tim Burke	.05	.02
❑ 716 Bob Geren	.05	.02
❑ 717 Phil Bradley	.05	.02
❑ 718 Steve Crawford	.05	.02
❑ 719 Keith Miller	.05	.02
❑ 720 Cecil Fielder	.10	.03
❑ 721 Mark Lee RC	.05	.02
❑ 722 Wally Backman	.05	.02
❑ 723 Candy Maldonado	.05	.02
❑ 724 David Segui	.05	.02
❑ 725 Ron Gant	.10	.03
❑ 726 Phil Stephenson	.05	.02
❑ 727 Mookie Wilson	.10	.03
❑ 728 Scott Sanderson	.05	.02
❑ 729 Don Zimmer MG	.10	.03
❑ 730 Barry Larkin	.25	.07
❑ 731 Jeff Gray	.05	.02
❑ 732 Franklin Stubbs	.05	.02
❑ 733 Kelly Downs	.05	.02
❑ 734 John Russell	.05	.02

❑ 735 Ron Darling .05 .02
❑ 736 Dick Schofield .05 .02
❑ 737 Tim Crews .05 .02
❑ 738 Mel Hall .05 .02
❑ 739 Russ Swan .05 .02
❑ 740 Ryne Sandberg .40 .12
❑ 741 Jimmy Key .10 .03
❑ 742 Tommy Gregg .05 .02
❑ 743 Bryn Smith .05 .02
❑ 744 Nelson Santovenia .05 .02
❑ 745 Doug Jones .05 .02
❑ 746 John Shelby .05 .02
❑ 747 Tony Fossas .05 .02
❑ 748 Al Newman .05 .02
❑ 749 Greg W. Harris .05 .02
❑ 750 Bobby Bonilla .10 .03
❑ 751 Wayne Edwards .05 .02
❑ 752 Kevin Bass .05 .02
❑ 753 Paul Marak UER .05 .02
(Stats say drafted in Jan. but bio says May)
❑ 754 Bill Pecota .05 .02
❑ 755 Mark Langston .05 .02
❑ 756 Jeff Huson .05 .02
❑ 757 Mark Gardner .05 .02
❑ 758 Mike Devereaux .05 .02
❑ 759 Bobby Cox MG .05 .02
❑ 760 Benny Santiago .10 .03
❑ 761 Larry Andersen .05 .02
❑ 762 Mitch Webster .05 .02
❑ 763 Dana Kiecker .05 .02
❑ 764 Mark Carreon .05 .02
❑ 765 Shawon Dunston .05 .02
❑ 766 Jeff Robinson .05 .02
❑ 767 Dan Wilson RC .25 .07
❑ 768 Don Pall .05 .02
❑ 769 Tim Sherrill .05 .02
❑ 770 Jay Howell .05 .02
❑ 771 Gary Redus UER .05 .02
(Born in Tanner, should say Athens)
❑ 772 Kent Mercker UER .05 .02
(Born in Indianapolis, should say Dublin, Ohio)
❑ 773 Tom Foley .05 .02
❑ 774 Dennis Rasmussen .05 .02
❑ 775 Julio Franco .10 .03
❑ 776 Brent Mayne .05 .02
❑ 777 John Candelaria .05 .02
❑ 778 Dan Gladden .05 .02
❑ 779 Carmelo Martinez .05 .02
❑ 780A Randy Myers ERR .40 .12
(15 career losses)
❑ 780B Randy Myers COR .05 .02
(19 career losses)
❑ 781 Darryl Hamilton .05 .02
❑ 782 Jim Deshaies .05 .02
❑ 783 Joel Skinner .05 .02
❑ 784 Willie Fraser .05 .02
❑ 785 Scott Fletcher .05 .02
❑ 786 Eric Plunk .05 .02
❑ 787 Checklist 6 .05 .02
❑ 788 Bob Milacki .05 .02
❑ 789 Tom Lasorda MG .25 .07
❑ 790 Ken Griffey Jr. .50 .15
❑ 791 Mike Benjamin .05 .02
❑ 792 Mike Greenwell .05 .02

1991 Topps Traded

	Nm-Mt	Ex-Mt
COMPLETE SET (132)	15.00	4.50
COMP.FACT.SET (132)	15.00	4.50

❑ 1T Juan Agosto .05 .02
❑ 2T Roberto Alomar .25 .07
❑ 3T Wally Backman .05 .02
❑ 4T Jeff Bagwell RC 1.50 .45
❑ 5T Skeeter Barnes .05 .02
❑ 6T Steve Bedrosian .05 .02
❑ 7T Derek Bell .10 .03
❑ 8T George Bell .05 .02
❑ 9T Rafael Belliard .05 .02
❑ 10T Dante Bichette .10 .03

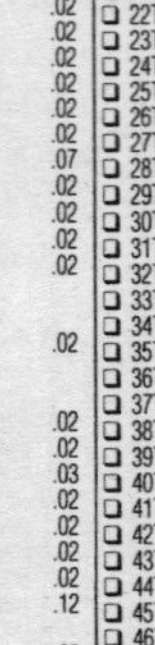

❑ 11T Bud Black .05 .02
❑ 12T Mike Boddicker .05 .02
❑ 13T Sid Bream .05 .02
❑ 14T Hubie Brooks .05 .02
❑ 15T Brett Butler .10 .03
❑ 16T Ivan Calderon .05 .02
❑ 17T John Candelaria .05 .02
❑ 18T Tom Candiotti .05 .02
❑ 19T Gary Carter .15 .04
❑ 20T Joe Carter .10 .03
❑ 21T Rick Cerone .05 .02
❑ 22T Jack Clark .10 .03
❑ 23T Vince Coleman .05 .02
❑ 24T Scott Coolbaugh .05 .02
❑ 25T Danny Cox .05 .02
❑ 26T Danny Darwin .05 .02
❑ 27T Chili Davis .10 .03
❑ 28T Glenn Davis .05 .02
❑ 29T Steve Decker .05 .02
❑ 30T Rob Deer .05 .02
❑ 31T Rich DeLucia .05 .02
❑ 32T John Dettmer USA RC .25 .07
❑ 33T Brian Downing .05 .02
❑ 34T D.Dreifort USA RC .50 .15
❑ 35T K.Dressendorfer RC .05 .02
❑ 36T Jim Essian MG .05 .02
❑ 37T Dwight Evans .10 .03
❑ 38T Steve Farr .05 .02
❑ 39T Jeff Fassero RC .25 .07
❑ 40T Junior Felix .05 .02
❑ 41T Tony Fernandez .05 .02
❑ 42T Steve Finley .10 .03
❑ 43T Jim Fregosi MG .05 .02
❑ 44T Gary Gaetti .10 .03
❑ 45T Jason Giambi USA RC 8.00 2.40
❑ 46T Kirk Gibson .10 .03
❑ 47T Leo Gomez .05 .02
❑ 48T Luis Gonzalez RC 1.00 .30
❑ 49T Jeff Granger USA RC .25 .07
❑ 50T Todd Greene USA RC .50 .15
❑ 51T J.Hammonds USA RC .50 .15
❑ 52T Mike Hargrove MG .05 .02
❑ 53T Pete Harnisch .05 .02
❑ 54T Rick Helling RC .50 .15
USA UER
Misspelled Hellings on card back
❑ 55T Glenallen Hill .05 .02
❑ 56T Charlie Hough .10 .03
❑ 57T Pete Incaviglia .05 .02
❑ 58T Bo Jackson .25 .07
❑ 59T Danny Jackson .05 .02
❑ 60T Reggie Jefferson .05 .02
❑ 61T C.Johnson USA RC .75 .23
❑ 62T Jeff Johnson .05 .02
❑ 63T T.Johnson USA RC .25 .07
❑ 64T Barry Jones .05 .02
❑ 65T Chris Jones RC .10 .03
❑ 66T Scott Kamieniecki RC .10 .03
❑ 67T Pat Kelly RC .10 .03
❑ 68T Darryl Kile .10 .03
❑ 69T Chuck Knoblauch .10 .03
❑ 70T Bill Krueger .05 .02
❑ 71T Scott Leius .05 .02
❑ 72T D.Leshnock USA RC .25 .07
❑ 73T Mark Lewis .05 .02
❑ 74T Candy Maldonado .05 .02
❑ 75T J.McDonald USA RC .25 .07
❑ 76T Willie McGee .10 .03
❑ 77T Fred McGriff .15 .04
❑ 78T B.McMillon USA RC .25 .07
❑ 79T Hal McRae MG .10 .03
❑ 80T D.Melendez USA RC .25 .07
❑ 81T Orlando Merced RC .10 .03
❑ 82T Jack Morris .10 .03
❑ 83T Phil Nevin USA RC 1.00 .30
❑ 84T Otis Nixon .05 .02
❑ 85T Johnny Oates MG .05 .02
❑ 86T Bob Ojeda .05 .02
❑ 87T Mike Pagliarulo .05 .02
❑ 88T Dean Palmer .10 .03
❑ 89T Dave Parker .10 .03
❑ 90T Terry Pendleton .10 .03
❑ 91T T.Phillips (P) USA RC .25 .07
❑ 92T Doug Piatt .05 .02
❑ 93T Ron Polk USA CO .25 .07
❑ 94T Tim Raines .10 .03
❑ 95T Willie Randolph .10 .03
❑ 96T Dave Righetti .10 .03
❑ 97T Ernie Riles .05 .02
❑ 98T C.Roberts USA RC .25 .07
❑ 99T Jeff D. Robinson .05 .02
❑ 100T Jeff M. Robinson .05 .02
❑ 101T Ivan Rodriguez RC 2.00 .60
❑ 102T S.Rodriguez USA RC .25 .07
❑ 103T Tom Runnells MG .05 .02
❑ 104T Scott Sanderson .05 .02
❑ 105T Bob Scanlan .05 .02
❑ 106T Pete Schourek RC .10 .03
❑ 107T Gary Scott .05 .02
❑ 108T Paul Shuey USA RC .50 .15
❑ 109T Doug Simons .05 .02
❑ 110T Dave Smith .05 .02
❑ 111T Cory Snyder .05 .02
❑ 112T Luis Sojo .05 .02
❑ 113T K.Steenstra USA RC .25 .07
❑ 114T Darryl Strawberry .15 .04
❑ 115T Franklin Stubbs .05 .02
❑ 116T Todd Taylor USA RC .25 .07
❑ 117T Wade Taylor .05 .02
❑ 118T Garry Templeton .05 .02
❑ 119T Mickey Tettleton .05 .02
❑ 120T Tim Teufel .05 .02
❑ 121T Mike Timlin RC .25 .07
❑ 122T David Tuttle USA RC .25 .07
❑ 123T Mo Vaughn .10 .03
❑ 124T Jeff Ware USA RC .25 .07
❑ 125T Devon White .05 .02
❑ 126T Mark Whiten .05 .02
❑ 127T Mitch Williams .05 .02
❑ 128T C.Wilson USA RC .25 .07
❑ 129T Willie Wilson .05 .02
❑ 130T C.Wimmer USA RC .25 .07
❑ 131T Ivan Zweig USA RC .25 .07
❑ 132T Checklist 1T-132T .05 .02

1992 Topps

	Nm-Mt	Ex-Mt
COMPLETE SET (792)	30.00	9.00
COMP.FACT.SET (802)	40.00	12.00
COMP.HOLIDAY (811)	40.00	12.00

❑ 1 Nolan Ryan 1.00 .30
❑ 2 Ricky Henderson RB .25 .07
Most career SB's
(Some cards have print

marks that show 1.991
on the front)

❑ 3 Jeff Reardon RB .05 .02
❑ 4 Nolan Ryan RB .50 .15
❑ 5 Dave Winfield RB .15 .04
❑ 6 Brien Taylor RC .25 .07
❑ 7 Jim Olander .05 .02
❑ 8 Bryan Hickerson RC .10 .03
❑ 9 Jon Farrell RC .10 .03
❑ 10 Wade Boggs .15 .04
❑ 11 Jack McDowell .05 .02
❑ 12 Luis Gonzalez .15 .04
❑ 13 Mike Scioscia .05 .02
❑ 14 Wes Chamberlain .05 .02
❑ 15 Dennis Martinez .10 .03
❑ 16 Jeff Montgomery .05 .02
❑ 17 Randy Milligan .05 .02
❑ 18 Greg Cadaret .05 .02
❑ 19 Jamie Quirk .05 .02
❑ 20 Bip Roberts .05 .02
❑ 21 Buck Rodgers MG .05 .02
❑ 22 Bill Wegman .05 .02
❑ 23 Chuck Knoblauch .10 .03
❑ 24 Randy Myers .05 .02
❑ 25 Ron Gant .10 .03
❑ 26 Mike Bielecki .05 .02
❑ 27 Juan Gonzalez .25 .07
❑ 28 Mike Schooler .05 .02
❑ 29 Mickey Tettleton .05 .02
❑ 30 John Kruk .10 .03
❑ 31 Bryn Smith .05 .02
❑ 32 Chris Nabholz .05 .02
❑ 33 Carlos Baerga .05 .02
❑ 34 Jeff Juden .05 .02
❑ 35 Dave Righetti .10 .03
❑ 36 Scott Ruffcorn RC .10 .03
❑ 37 Luis Polonia .05 .02
❑ 38 Tom Candiotti .05 .02
❑ 39 Greg Olson .05 .02
❑ 40 Cal Ripken 2.00 .60
❑ 41 Craig Lefferts .05 .02
❑ 42 Mike Macfarlane .05 .02
❑ 43 Jose Lind .05 .02
❑ 44 Rick Aguilera .10 .03
❑ 45 Gary Carter .15 .04
❑ 46 Steve Farr .05 .02
❑ 47 Rex Hudler .05 .02
❑ 48 Scott Scudder .05 .02
❑ 49 Damon Berryhill .05 .02
❑ 50 Ken Griffey Jr. .40 .12
❑ 51 Tom Runnells MG .05 .02
❑ 52 Juan Bell .05 .02
❑ 53 Tommy Gregg .05 .02
❑ 54 David Wells .10 .03
❑ 55 Rafael Palmeiro .15 .04
❑ 56 Charlie O'Brien .05 .02
❑ 57 Donn Pall .05 .02
❑ 58 Brad Ausmus RC .25 .07
Jim Campanis Jr.
Dave Nilsson
Doug Robbins
❑ 59 Mo Vaughn .10 .03
❑ 60 Tony Fernandez .05 .02
❑ 61 Paul O'Neill .15 .04
❑ 62 Gene Nelson .05 .02
❑ 63 Randy Ready .05 .02
❑ 64 Bob Kipper .05 .02
❑ 65 Willie McGee .10 .03
❑ 66 Scott Stahoviak RC .10 .03
❑ 67 Luis Salazar .05 .02
❑ 68 Marvin Freeman .05 .02
❑ 69 Kenny Lofton .25 .07
❑ 70 Gary Gaetti .10 .03
❑ 71 Erik Hanson .05 .02
❑ 72 Eddie Zosky .05 .02
❑ 73 Brian Barnes .05 .02
❑ 74 Scott Leius .05 .02
❑ 75 Bret Saberhagen .10 .03
❑ 76 Mike Gallego .05 .02
❑ 77 Jack Armstrong .05 .02
❑ 78 Ivan Rodriguez .25 .07
❑ 79 Jesse Orosco .05 .02
❑ 80 David Justice .10 .03
❑ 81 Ced Landrum .05 .02
❑ 82 Doug Simons .05 .02
❑ 83 Tommy Greene .05 .02
❑ 84 Leo Gomez .05 .02
❑ 85 Jose DeLeon .05 .02
❑ 86 Steve Finley .10 .03
❑ 87 Bob MacDonald .05 .02
❑ 88 Darrin Jackson .05 .02
❑ 89 Neal Heaton .05 .02
❑ 90 Robin Yount .25 .07
❑ 91 Jeff Reed .05 .02
❑ 92 Lenny Harris .05 .02
❑ 93 Reggie Jefferson .05 .02
❑ 94 Sammy Sosa .40 .12
❑ 95 Scott Bailes .05 .02
❑ 96 Tom McKinnon RC .10 .03
❑ 97 Luis Rivera .05 .02
❑ 98 Mike Harkey .05 .02
❑ 99 Jeff Treadway .05 .02
❑ 100 Jose Canseco .25 .07
❑ 101 Omar Vizquel .10 .03
❑ 102 Scott Kamieniecki .05 .02
❑ 103 Ricky Jordan .05 .02
❑ 104 Jeff Ballard .05 .02
❑ 105 Felix Jose .05 .02
❑ 106 Mike Boddicker .05 .02
❑ 107 Dan Pasqua .05 .02
❑ 108 Mike Timlin .05 .02
❑ 109 Roger Craig MG .05 .02
❑ 110 Ryne Sandberg .40 .12
❑ 111 Mark Carreon .05 .02
❑ 112 Oscar Azocar .05 .02
❑ 113 Mike Greenwell .05 .02
❑ 114 Mark Portugal .05 .02
❑ 115 Terry Pendleton .10 .03
❑ 116 Willie Randolph .10 .03
❑ 117 Scott Terry .05 .02
❑ 118 Chili Davis .10 .03
❑ 119 Mark Gardner .05 .02
❑ 120 Alan Trammell .15 .04
❑ 121 Derek Bell .10 .03
❑ 122 Gary Varsho .05 .02
❑ 123 Bob Ojeda .05 .02
❑ 124 Shawn Livsey RC .10 .03
❑ 125 Chris Hoiles .05 .02
❑ 126 Ryan Klesko .25 .07
John Jaha RC
Rico Brogna
Dave Staton
❑ 127 Carlos Quintana .05 .02
❑ 128 Kurt Stillwell .05 .02
❑ 129 Melido Perez .05 .02
❑ 130 Alvin Davis .05 .02
❑ 131 Checklist 1-132 .05 .02
❑ 132 Eric Show .05 .02
❑ 133 Rance Mulliniks .05 .02
❑ 134 Darryl Kile .10 .03
❑ 135 Von Hayes .05 .02
❑ 136 Bill Doran .05 .02
❑ 137 Jeff D. Robinson .05 .02
❑ 138 Monty Fariss .05 .02
❑ 139 Jeff Innis .05 .02
❑ 140 Mark Grace UER .25 .07
Home Calie., should
be Calif.
❑ 141 Jim Leyland MG UER .10 .03
(No closed parenthesis
after East in 1991)
❑ 142 Todd Van Poppel .05 .02
❑ 143 Paul Gibson .05 .02
❑ 144 Bill Swift .05 .02
❑ 145 Danny Tartabull .05 .02
❑ 146 Al Newman .05 .02
❑ 147 Cris Carpenter .05 .02
❑ 148 Anthony Young .05 .02
❑ 149 Brian Bohanon .05 .02
❑ 150 Roger Clemens UER .50 .15
(League leading ERA in
1990 not italicized)
❑ 151 Jeff Hamilton .05 .02
❑ 152 Charlie Leibrandt .05 .02
❑ 153 Ron Karkovice .05 .02
❑ 154 Hensley Meulens .05 .02
❑ 155 Scott Bankhead .05 .02
❑ 156 Manny Ramirez RC 1.50 .45
❑ 157 Keith Miller .05 .02
❑ 158 Todd Frohwirth .05 .02
❑ 159 Darrin Fletcher .05 .02
❑ 160 Bobby Bonilla .10 .03
❑ 161 Casey Candaele .05 .02
❑ 162 Paul Faries .05 .02
❑ 163 Dana Kiecker .05 .02
❑ 164 Shane Mack .05 .02
❑ 165 Mark Langston .05 .02
❑ 166 Geronimo Pena .05 .02
❑ 167 Andy Allanson .05 .02
❑ 168 Dwight Smith .05 .02
❑ 169 Chuck Crim .05 .02
❑ 170 Alex Cole .05 .02
❑ 171 Bill Plummer MG .05 .02
❑ 172 Juan Berenguer .05 .02
❑ 173 Brian Downing .05 .02
❑ 174 Steve Frey .05 .02
❑ 175 Orel Hershiser .10 .03
❑ 176 Ramon Garcia .05 .02
❑ 177 Dan Gladden .05 .02
❑ 178 Jim Acker .05 .02
❑ 179 Bobby DeJardin .05 .02
Cesar Bernhardt
Armando Moreno
Andy Stankiewicz
❑ 180 Kevin Mitchell .05 .02
❑ 181 Hector Villanueva .05 .02
❑ 182 Jeff Reardon .10 .03
❑ 183 Brent Mayne .05 .02
❑ 184 Jimmy Jones .05 .02
❑ 185 Benito Santiago .10 .03
❑ 186 Cliff Floyd RC .75 .23
❑ 187 Ernie Riles .05 .02
❑ 188 Jose Guzman .05 .02
❑ 189 Junior Felix .05 .02
❑ 190 Glenn Davis .05 .02
❑ 191 Charlie Hough .10 .03
❑ 192 Dave Fleming .05 .02
❑ 193 Omar Olivares .05 .02
❑ 194 Eric Karros .10 .03
❑ 195 David Cone .10 .03
❑ 196 Frank Castillo .05 .02
❑ 197 Glenn Braggs .05 .02
❑ 198 Scott Aldred .05 .02
❑ 199 Jeff Blauser .05 .02
❑ 200 Len Dykstra .10 .03
❑ 201 B.Showalter RC MG .25 .07
❑ 202 Rick Honeycutt .05 .02
❑ 203 Greg Myers .05 .02
❑ 204 Trevor Wilson .05 .02
❑ 205 Jay Howell .05 .02
❑ 206 Luis Sojo .05 .02
❑ 207 Jack Clark .10 .03
❑ 208 Julio Machado .05 .02
❑ 209 Lloyd McClendon .05 .02
❑ 210 Ozzie Guillen .05 .02
❑ 211 Jeremy Hernandez RC .10 .03
❑ 212 Randy Velarde .05 .02
❑ 213 Les Lancaster .05 .02
❑ 214 Andy Mota .05 .02
❑ 215 Rich Gossage .10 .03
❑ 216 Brent Gates RC .10 .03
❑ 217 Brian Harper .05 .02
❑ 218 Mike Flanagan .05 .02
❑ 219 Jerry Browne .05 .02
❑ 220 Jose Rijo .05 .02
❑ 221 Skeeter Barnes .05 .02
❑ 222 Jaime Navarro .05 .02
❑ 223 Mel Hall .05 .02
❑ 224 Bret Barberie .05 .02
❑ 225 Roberto Alomar .25 .07
❑ 226 Pete Smith .05 .02
❑ 227 Daryl Boston .05 .02
❑ 228 Eddie Whitson .05 .02
❑ 229 Shawn Boskie .05 .02
❑ 230 Dick Schofield .05 .02
❑ 231 Brian Drahman .05 .02
❑ 232 John Smiley .05 .02
❑ 233 Mitch Webster .05 .02
❑ 234 Terry Steinbach .05 .02
❑ 235 Jack Morris .10 .03
❑ 236 Bill Pecota .05 .02
❑ 237 Jose Hernandez RC .40 .12
❑ 238 Greg Litton .05 .02
❑ 239 Brian Holman .05 .02
❑ 240 Andres Galarraga .10 .03
❑ 241 Gerald Young .05 .02
❑ 242 Mike Mussina .25 .07
❑ 243 Alvaro Espinoza .05 .02

❑ 244 Darren Daulton .10 .03
❑ 245 John Smoltz .15 .04
❑ 246 Jason Pruitt RC .10 .03
❑ 247 Chuck Finley .10 .03
❑ 248 Jim Gantner .05 .02
❑ 249 Tony Fossas .05 .02
❑ 250 Ken Griffey Sr. .10 .03
❑ 251 Kevin Elster .05 .02
❑ 252 Dennis Rasmussen .05 .02
❑ 253 Terry Kennedy .05 .02
❑ 254 Ryan Bowen .05 .02
❑ 255 Robin Ventura .10 .03
❑ 256 Mike Aldrete .05 .02
❑ 257 Jeff Russell .05 .02
❑ 258 Jim Lindeman .05 .02
❑ 259 Ron Darling .05 .02
❑ 260 Devon White .05 .02
❑ 261 Tom Lasorda MG .10 .03
❑ 262 Terry Lee .05 .02
❑ 263 Bob Patterson .05 .02
❑ 264 Checklist 133-264 .05 .02
❑ 265 Teddy Higuera .05 .02
❑ 266 Roberto Kelly .05 .02
❑ 267 Steve Bedrosian .05 .02
❑ 268 Brady Anderson .10 .03
❑ 269 Ruben Amaro .05 .02
❑ 270 Tony Gwynn .30 .09
❑ 271 Tracy Jones .05 .02
❑ 272 Jerry Don Gleaton .05 .02
❑ 273 Craig Grebeck .05 .02
❑ 274 Bob Scanlan .05 .02
❑ 275 Todd Zeile .05 .02
❑ 276 Shawn Green RC 1.50 .45
❑ 277 Scott Chiamparino .05 .02
❑ 278 Darryl Hamilton .05 .02
❑ 279 Jim Clancy .05 .02
❑ 280 Carlos Martinez .05 .02
❑ 281 Kevin Appier .10 .03
❑ 282 John Wehner .05 .02
❑ 283 Reggie Sanders .10 .03
❑ 284 Gene Larkin .05 .02
❑ 285 Bob Welch .05 .02
❑ 286 Gilberto Reyes .05 .02
❑ 287 Pete Schourek .05 .02
❑ 288 Andujar Cedeno .05 .02
❑ 289 Mike Morgan .05 .02
❑ 290 Bo Jackson .25 .07
❑ 291 Phil Garner MG .05 .02
❑ 292 Ray Lankford .05 .02
❑ 293 Mike Henneman .05 .02
❑ 294 Dave Valle .05 .02
❑ 295 Alonzo Powell .05 .02
❑ 296 Tom Brunansky .05 .02
❑ 297 Kevin Brown .10 .03
❑ 298 Kelly Gruber .05 .02
❑ 299 Charles Nagy .05 .02
❑ 300 Don Mattingly .60 .18
❑ 301 Kirk McCaskill .05 .02
❑ 302 Joey Cora .05 .02
❑ 303 Dan Plesac .05 .02
❑ 304 Joe Oliver .05 .02
❑ 305 Tom Glavine .25 .07
❑ 306 Al Shirley RC .10 .03
❑ 307 Bruce Ruffin .05 .02
❑ 308 Craig Shipley .05 .02
❑ 309 Dave Martinez .05 .02
❑ 310 Jose Mesa .05 .02
❑ 311 Henry Cotto .05 .02
❑ 312 Mike LaValliere .05 .02
❑ 313 Kevin Tapani .05 .02
❑ 314 Jeff Huson .05 .02
(Shows Jose Canseco
sliding into second)
❑ 315 Juan Samuel .05 .02
❑ 316 Curt Schilling .15 .04
❑ 317 Mike Bordick .05 .02
❑ 318 Steve Howe .05 .02
❑ 319 Tony Phillips .05 .02
❑ 320 George Bell .05 .02
❑ 321 Lou Piniella MG .10 .03
❑ 322 Tim Burke .05 .02
❑ 323 Milt Thompson .05 .02
❑ 324 Danny Darwin .05 .02
❑ 325 Joe Orsulak .05 .02
❑ 326 Eric King .05 .02
❑ 327 Jay Buhner .10 .03
❑ 328 Joel Johnston .05 .02
❑ 329 Franklin Stubbs .05 .02
❑ 330 Will Clark .25 .07
❑ 331 Steve Lake .05 .02
❑ 332 Chris Jones .05 .02
❑ 333 Pat Tabler .05 .02
❑ 334 Kevin Gross .05 .02
❑ 335 Dave Henderson .05 .02
❑ 336 Greg Anthony RC .10 .03
❑ 337 Alejandro Pena .05 .02
❑ 338 Shawn Abner .05 .02
❑ 339 Tom Browning .05 .02
❑ 340 Otis Nixon .05 .02
❑ 341 Bob Geren .05 .02
❑ 342 Tim Spehr .05 .02
❑ 343 John Vander Wal .05 .02
❑ 344 Jack Daugherty .05 .02
❑ 345 Zane Smith .05 .02
❑ 346 Rheal Cormier .05 .02
❑ 347 Kent Hrbek .10 .03
❑ 348 Rick Wilkins .05 .02
❑ 349 Steve Lyons .05 .02
❑ 350 Gregg Olson .05 .02
❑ 351 Greg Riddoch MG .05 .02
❑ 352 Ed Nunez .05 .02
❑ 353 Braulio Castillo .05 .02
❑ 354 Dave Bergman .05 .02
❑ 355 Warren Newson .05 .02
❑ 356 Luis Quinones .05 .02
❑ 357 Mike Witt .05 .02
❑ 358 Ted Wood .05 .02
❑ 359 Mike Moore .05 .02
❑ 360 Lance Parrish .10 .03
❑ 361 Barry Jones .05 .02
❑ 362 Javier Ortiz .05 .02
❑ 363 John Candelaria .05 .02
❑ 364 Glenallen Hill .05 .02
❑ 365 Duane Ward .05 .02
❑ 366 Checklist 265-396 .05 .02
❑ 367 Rafael Belliard .05 .02
❑ 368 Bill Krueger .05 .02
❑ 369 Steve Whitaker RC .10 .03
❑ 370 Shawon Dunston .05 .02
❑ 371 Dante Bichette .10 .03
❑ 372 Kip Gross .05 .02
❑ 373 Don Robinson .05 .02
❑ 374 Bernie Williams .15 .04
❑ 375 Bert Blyleven .10 .03
❑ 376 Chris Donnels .05 .02
❑ 377 Bob Zupcic RC .10 .03
❑ 378 Joel Skinner .05 .02
❑ 379 Steve Chitren .05 .02
❑ 380 Barry Bonds .60 .18
❑ 381 Sparky Anderson MG .10 .03
❑ 382 Sid Fernandez .05 .02
❑ 383 Dave Hollins .05 .02
❑ 384 Mark Lee .05 .02
❑ 385 Tim Wallach .05 .02
❑ 386 Will Clark AS .10 .03
❑ 387 Ryne Sandberg AS .25 .07
❑ 388 Howard Johnson AS .05 .02
❑ 389 Barry Larkin AS .10 .03
❑ 390 Barry Bonds AS .30 .09
❑ 391 Ron Gant AS .05 .02
❑ 392 Bobby Bonilla AS .05 .02
❑ 393 Craig Biggio AS .10 .03
❑ 394 Dennis Martinez AS .05 .02
❑ 395 Tom Glavine AS .10 .03
❑ 396 Lee Smith AS .05 .02
❑ 397 Cecil Fielder AS .05 .02
❑ 398 Julio Franco AS .05 .02
❑ 399 Wade Boggs AS .10 .03
❑ 400 Cal Ripken AS .40 .12
❑ 401 Jose Canseco AS .25 .07
❑ 402 Joe Carter AS .05 .02
❑ 403 Ruben Sierra AS .05 .02
❑ 404 Matt Nokes AS .05 .02
❑ 405 Roger Clemens AS .25 .07
❑ 406 Jim Abbott AS .10 .03
❑ 407 Bryan Harvey AS .05 .02
❑ 408 Bob Milacki .05 .02
❑ 409 Geno Petralli .05 .02
❑ 410 Dave Stewart .10 .03
❑ 411 Mike Jackson .05 .02
❑ 412 Luis Aquino .05 .02
❑ 413 Tim Teufel .05 .02
❑ 414 Jeff Ware .05 .02
❑ 415 Jim Deshaies .05 .02
❑ 416 Ellis Burks .10 .03
❑ 417 Allan Anderson .05 .02
❑ 418 Alfredo Griffin .05 .02
❑ 419 Wally Whitehurst .05 .02
❑ 420 Sandy Alomar Jr. .05 .02
❑ 421 Juan Agosto .05 .02
❑ 422 Sam Horn .05 .02
❑ 423 Jeff Fassero .05 .02
❑ 424 Paul McClellan .05 .02
❑ 425 Cecil Fielder .10 .03
❑ 426 Tim Raines .10 .03
❑ 427 Eddie Taubensee RC .25 .07
❑ 428 Dennis Boyd .05 .02
❑ 429 Tony LaRussa MG .10 .03
❑ 430 Steve Sax .05 .02
❑ 431 Tom Gordon .05 .02
❑ 432 Billy Hatcher .05 .02
❑ 433 Cal Eldred .05 .02
❑ 434 Wally Backman .05 .02
❑ 435 Mark Eichhorn .05 .02
❑ 436 Mookie Wilson .10 .03
❑ 437 Scott Servais .05 .02
❑ 438 Mike Maddux .05 .02
❑ 439 Chico Walker .05 .02
❑ 440 Doug Drabek .05 .02
❑ 441 Rob Deer .05 .02
❑ 442 Dave West .05 .02
❑ 443 Spike Owen .05 .02
❑ 444 Tyrone Hill RC .10 .03
❑ 445 Matt Williams .10 .03
❑ 446 Mark Lewis .05 .02
❑ 447 David Segui .05 .02
❑ 448 Tom Pagnozzi .05 .02
❑ 449 Jeff Johnson .05 .02
❑ 450 Mark McGwire .60 .18
❑ 451 Tom Henke .05 .02
❑ 452 Wilson Alvarez .05 .02
❑ 453 Gary Redus .05 .02
❑ 454 Darren Holmes .05 .02
❑ 455 Pete O'Brien .05 .02
❑ 456 Pat Combs .05 .02
❑ 457 Hubie Brooks .05 .02
❑ 458 Frank Tanana .05 .02
❑ 459 Tom Kelly MG .05 .02
❑ 460 Andre Dawson .10 .03
❑ 461 Doug Jones .05 .02
❑ 462 Rich Rodriguez .05 .02
❑ 463 Mike Simms .05 .02
❑ 464 Mike Jeffcoat .05 .02
❑ 465 Barry Larkin .25 .07
❑ 466 Stan Belinda .05 .02
❑ 467 Lonnie Smith .05 .02
❑ 468 Greg Harris .05 .02
❑ 469 Jim Eisenreich .05 .02
❑ 470 Pedro Guerrero .10 .03
❑ 471 Jose DeJesus .05 .02
❑ 472 Rich Rowland RC .10 .03
❑ 473 Frank Bolick .05 .02
Craig Paquette
Tom Redington
Paul Russo UER
(Line around top border)
❑ 474 Mike Rossiter RC .10 .03
❑ 475 Robby Thompson .05 .02
❑ 476 Randy Bush .05 .02
❑ 477 Greg Hibbard .05 .02
❑ 478 Dale Sveum .05 .02
❑ 479 Chito Martinez .05 .02
❑ 480 Scott Sanderson .05 .02
❑ 481 Tino Martinez .15 .04
❑ 482 Jimmy Key .10 .03
❑ 483 Terry Shumpert .05 .02
❑ 484 Mike Hartley .05 .02
❑ 485 Chris Sabo .05 .02
❑ 486 Bob Walk .05 .02
❑ 487 John Cerutti .05 .02
❑ 488 Scott Cooper .05 .02
❑ 489 Bobby Cox MG .10 .03
❑ 490 Julio Franco .10 .03
❑ 491 Jeff Brantley .05 .02
❑ 492 Mike Devereaux .05 .02
❑ 493 Jose Offerman .05 .02
❑ 494 Gary Thurman .05 .02
❑ 495 Carney Lansford .10 .03

❑ 496 Joe Grahe .05 .02
❑ 497 Andy Ashby .05 .02
❑ 498 Gerald Perry .05 .02
❑ 499 Dave Otto .05 .02
❑ 500 Vince Coleman .05 .02
❑ 501 Rob Mallicoat .05 .02
❑ 502 Greg Briley .05 .02
❑ 503 Pascual Perez .05 .02
❑ 504 Aaron Sele RC .40 .12
❑ 505 Bobby Thigpen .05 .02
❑ 506 Todd Benzinger .05 .02
❑ 507 Candy Maldonado .05 .02
❑ 508 Bill Gullickson .05 .02
❑ 509 Doug Dascenzo .05 .02
❑ 510 Frank Viola .10 .03
❑ 511 Kenny Rogers .10 .03
❑ 512 Mike Heath .05 .02
❑ 513 Kevin Bass .05 .02
❑ 514 Kim Batiste .05 .02
❑ 515 Delino DeShields .05 .02
❑ 516 Ed Sprague .05 .02
❑ 517 Jim Gott .05 .02
❑ 518 Jose Melendez .05 .02
❑ 519 Hal McRae MG .10 .03
❑ 520 Jeff Bagwell .25 .07
❑ 521 Joe Hesketh .05 .02
❑ 522 Milt Cuyler .05 .02
❑ 523 Shawn Hillegas .05 .02
❑ 524 Don Slaught .05 .02
❑ 525 Randy Johnson .25 .07
❑ 526 Doug Piatt .05 .02
❑ 527 Checklist 397-528 .05 .02
❑ 528 Steve Foster .05 .02
❑ 529 Joe Girardi .05 .02
❑ 530 Jim Abbott .25 .07
❑ 531 Larry Walker .15 .04
❑ 532 Mike Huff .05 .02
❑ 533 Mackey Sasser .05 .02
❑ 534 Benji Gil RC .25 .07
❑ 535 Dave Stieb .05 .02
❑ 536 Willie Wilson .05 .02
❑ 537 Mark Leiter .05 .02
❑ 538 Jose Uribe .05 .02
❑ 539 Thomas Howard .05 .02
❑ 540 Ben McDonald .05 .02
❑ 541 Jose Tolentino .05 .02
❑ 542 Keith Mitchell .05 .02
❑ 543 Jerome Walton .05 .02
❑ 544 Cliff Brantley .05 .02
❑ 545 Andy Van Slyke .10 .03
❑ 546 Paul Sorrento .05 .02
❑ 547 Herm Winningham .05 .02
❑ 548 Mark Guthrie .05 .02
❑ 549 Joe Torre MG .10 .03
❑ 550 Darryl Strawberry .15 .04
❑ 551 Wilfredo Cordero .25 .07
Chipper Jones
Manny Alexander
Alex Arias UER
(No line around
top border)
❑ 552 Dave Gallagher .05 .02
❑ 553 Edgar Martinez .15 .04
❑ 554 Donald Harris .05 .02
❑ 555 Frank Thomas .25 .07
❑ 556 Storm Davis .05 .02
❑ 557 Dickie Thon .05 .02
❑ 558 Scott Garrelts .05 .02
❑ 559 Steve Olin .05 .02
❑ 560 Rickey Henderson .40 .12
❑ 561 Jose Vizcaino .05 .02
❑ 562 Wade Taylor .05 .02
❑ 563 Pat Borders .05 .02
❑ 564 Jimmy Gonzalez RC .10 .03
❑ 565 Lee Smith .10 .03
❑ 566 Bill Sampen .05 .02
❑ 567 Dean Palmer .10 .03
❑ 568 Bryan Harvey .05 .02
❑ 569 Tony Pena .05 .02
❑ 570 Lou Whitaker .10 .03
❑ 571 Randy Tomlin .05 .02
❑ 572 Greg Vaughn .10 .03
❑ 573 Kelly Downs .05 .02
❑ 574 Steve Avery UER .05 .02
(Should be 13 games
for Durham in 1989)
❑ 575 Kirby Puckett .25 .07
❑ 576 Heathcliff Slocumb .05 .02
❑ 577 Kevin Seitzer .05 .02
❑ 578 Lee Guetterman .05 .02
❑ 579 Johnny Oates MG .05 .02
❑ 580 Greg Maddux .50 .15
❑ 581 Stan Javier .05 .02
❑ 582 Vicente Palacios .05 .02
❑ 583 Mel Rojas .05 .02
❑ 584 Wayne Rosenthal RC .10 .03
❑ 585 Lenny Webster .05 .02
❑ 586 Rod Nichols .05 .02
❑ 587 Mickey Morandini .05 .02
❑ 588 Russ Swan .05 .02
❑ 589 Mariano Duncan .05 .02
❑ 590 Howard Johnson .05 .02
❑ 591 Jeromy Burnitz .10 .03
Jacob Brumfield
Alan Cockrell
D.J. Dozier
❑ 592 Denny Neagle .10 .03
❑ 593 Steve Decker .05 .02
❑ 594 Brian Barber RC .10 .03
❑ 595 Bruce Hurst .05 .02
❑ 596 Kent Mercker .05 .02
❑ 597 Mike Magnante RC .10 .03
❑ 598 Jody Reed .05 .02
❑ 599 Steve Searcy .05 .02
❑ 600 Paul Molitor .15 .04
❑ 601 Dave Smith .05 .02
❑ 602 Mike Fetters .05 .02
❑ 603 Luis Mercedes .05 .02
❑ 604 Chris Gwynn .05 .02
❑ 605 Scott Erickson .05 .02
❑ 606 Brook Jacoby .05 .02
❑ 607 Todd Stottlemyre .05 .02
❑ 608 Scott Bradley .05 .02
❑ 609 Mike Hargrove MG .10 .03
❑ 610 Eric Davis .10 .03
❑ 611 Brian Hunter .05 .02
❑ 612 Pat Kelly .05 .02
❑ 613 Pedro Munoz .05 .02
❑ 614 Al Osuna .05 .02
❑ 615 Matt Merullo .05 .02
❑ 616 Larry Andersen .05 .02
❑ 617 Junior Ortiz .05 .02
❑ 618 Cesar Hernandez .05 .02
Steve Hosey
Jeff McNeely
Dan Peltier
❑ 619 Danny Jackson .05 .02
❑ 620 George Brett .60 .18
❑ 621 Dan Gakeler .05 .02
❑ 622 Steve Buechele .05 .02
❑ 623 Bob Tewksbury .05 .02
❑ 624 Shawn Estes RC .25 .07
❑ 625 Kevin McReynolds .05 .02
❑ 626 Chris Haney .05 .02
❑ 627 Mike Sharperson .05 .02
❑ 628 Mark Williamson .05 .02
❑ 629 Wally Joyner .10 .03
❑ 630 Carlton Fisk .15 .04
❑ 631 Armando Reynoso RC .25 .07
❑ 632 Felix Fermin .05 .02
❑ 633 Mitch Williams .05 .02
❑ 634 Manuel Lee .05 .02
❑ 635 Harold Baines .10 .03
❑ 636 Greg Harris .05 .02
❑ 637 Orlando Merced .05 .02
❑ 638 Chris Bosio .05 .02
❑ 639 Wayne Housie .05 .02
❑ 640 Xavier Hernandez .05 .02
❑ 641 David Howard .05 .02
❑ 642 Tim Crews .05 .02
❑ 643 Rick Cerone .05 .02
❑ 644 Terry Leach .05 .02
❑ 645 Deion Sanders .10 .03
❑ 646 Craig Wilson .05 .02
❑ 647 Marquis Grissom .05 .02
❑ 648 Scott Fletcher .05 .02
❑ 649 Norm Charlton .05 .02
❑ 650 Jesse Barfield .05 .02
❑ 651 Joe Slusarski .05 .02
❑ 652 Bobby Rose .05 .02
❑ 653 Dennis Lamp .05 .02
❑ 654 Allen Watson RC .10 .03
❑ 655 Brett Butler .10 .03
❑ 656 Rudy Pemberton .10 .03
Henry Rodriguez
Lee Tinsley RC
Gerald Williams
❑ 657 Dave Johnson .05 .02
❑ 658 Checklist 529-660 .05 .02
❑ 659 Brian McRae .05 .02
❑ 660 Fred McGriff .15 .04
❑ 661 Bill Landrum .05 .02
❑ 662 Juan Guzman .05 .02
❑ 663 Greg Gagne .05 .02
❑ 664 Ken Hill .05 .02
❑ 665 Dave Haas .05 .02
❑ 666 Tom Foley .05 .02
❑ 667 Roberto Hernandez .05 .02
❑ 668 Dwayne Henry .05 .02
❑ 669 Jim Fregosi MG .05 .02
❑ 670 Harold Reynolds .10 .03
❑ 671 Mark Whiten .05 .02
❑ 672 Eric Plunk .05 .02
❑ 673 Todd Hundley .05 .02
❑ 674 Mo Sanford .05 .02
❑ 675 Bobby Witt .05 .02
❑ 676 Sam Militello .25 .07
Pat Mahomes RC
Turk Wendell
Roger Salkeld
❑ 677 John Marzano .05 .02
❑ 678 Joe Klink .05 .02
❑ 679 Pete Incaviglia .05 .02
❑ 680 Dale Murphy .25 .07
❑ 681 Rene Gonzales .05 .02
❑ 682 Andy Benes .05 .02
❑ 683 Jim Poole .05 .02
❑ 684 Trever Miller RC .10 .03
❑ 685 Scott Livingstone .05 .02
❑ 686 Rich DeLucia .05 .02
❑ 687 Harvey Pulliam .05 .02
❑ 688 Tim Belcher .05 .02
❑ 689 Mark Lemke .05 .02
❑ 690 John Franco .10 .03
❑ 691 Walt Weiss .05 .02
❑ 692 Scott Ruskin .05 .02
❑ 693 Jeff King .05 .02
❑ 694 Mike Gardiner .05 .02
❑ 695 Gary Sheffield .10 .03
❑ 696 Joe Boever .05 .02
❑ 697 Mike Felder .05 .02
❑ 698 John Habyan .05 .02
❑ 699 Cito Gaston MG .05 .02
❑ 700 Ruben Sierra .05 .02
❑ 701 Scott Radinsky .05 .02
❑ 702 Lee Stevens .05 .02
❑ 703 Mark Wohlers .05 .02
❑ 704 Curt Young .05 .02
❑ 705 Dwight Evans .10 .03
❑ 706 Rob Murphy .05 .02
❑ 707 Gregg Jefferies .05 .02
❑ 708 Tom Bolton .05 .02
❑ 709 Chris James .05 .02
❑ 710 Kevin Maas .05 .02
❑ 711 Ricky Bones .05 .02
❑ 712 Curt Wilkerson .05 .02
❑ 713 Roger McDowell .05 .02
❑ 714 Pokey Reese RC .25 .07
❑ 715 Craig Biggio .15 .04
❑ 716 Kirk Dressendorfer .05 .02
❑ 717 Ken Dayley .05 .02
❑ 718 B.J. Surhoff .10 .03
❑ 719 Terry Mulholland .05 .02
❑ 720 Kirk Gibson .10 .03
❑ 721 Mike Pagliarulo .05 .02
❑ 722 Walt Terrell .05 .02
❑ 723 Jose Oquendo .05 .02
❑ 724 Kevin Morton .05 .02
❑ 725 Dwight Gooden .15 .04
❑ 726 Kirt Manwaring .05 .02
❑ 727 Chuck McElroy .05 .02
❑ 728 Dave Burba .05 .02
❑ 729 Art Howe MG .05 .02
❑ 730 Ramon Martinez .05 .02
❑ 731 Donnie Hill .05 .02
❑ 732 Nelson Santovenia .05 .02
❑ 733 Bob Melvin .05 .02
❑ 734 Scott Hatteberg RC .25 .07

			Nm-Mt	Ex-Mt
❑	735	Greg Swindell	.05	.02
❑	736	Lance Johnson	.05	.02
❑	737	Kevin Reimer	.05	.02
❑	738	Dennis Eckersley	.10	.03
❑	739	Rob Ducey	.05	.02
❑	740	Ken Caminiti	.10	.03
❑	741	Mark Gubicza	.05	.02
❑	742	Bill Spiers	.05	.02
❑	743	Darren Lewis	.05	.02
❑	744	Chris Hammond	.05	.02
❑	745	Dave Magadan	.05	.02
❑	746	Bernard Gilkey	.05	.02
❑	747	Willie Banks	.05	.02
❑	748	Matt Nokes	.05	.02
❑	749	Jerald Clark	.05	.02
❑	750	Travis Fryman	.10	.03
❑	751	Steve Wilson	.05	.02
❑	752	Billy Ripken	.05	.02
❑	753	Paul Assenmacher	.05	.02
❑	754	Charlie Hayes	.05	.02
❑	755	Alex Fernandez	.05	.02
❑	756	Gary Pettis	.05	.02
❑	757	Rob Dibble	.10	.03
❑	758	Tim Naehring	.05	.02
❑	759	Jeff Torborg MG	.05	.02
❑	760	Ozzie Smith	.25	.07
❑	761	Mike Fitzgerald	.05	.02
❑	762	John Burkett	.05	.02
❑	763	Kyle Abbott	.05	.02
❑	764	Tyler Green RC	.10	.03
❑	765	Pete Harnisch	.05	.02
❑	766	Mark Davis	.05	.02
❑	767	Kal Daniels	.05	.02
❑	768	Jim Thome	.25	.07
❑	769	Jack Howell	.05	.02
❑	770	Sid Bream	.05	.02
❑	771	Arthur Rhodes	.05	.02
❑	772	Garry Templeton UER (Stat heading in for pitchers)	.05	.02
❑	773	Hal Morris	.05	.02
❑	774	Bud Black	.05	.02
❑	775	Ivan Calderon	.05	.02
❑	776	Doug Henry RC	.10	.03
❑	777	John Olerud	.10	.03
❑	778	Tim Leary	.05	.02
❑	779	Jay Bell	.10	.03
❑	780	Eddie Murray	.25	.07
❑	781	Paul Abbott	.05	.02
❑	782	Phil Plantier	.05	.02
❑	783	Joe Magrane	.05	.02
❑	784	Ken Patterson	.05	.02
❑	785	Albert Belle	.10	.03
❑	786	Royce Clayton	.05	.02
❑	787	Checklist 661-792	.05	.02
❑	788	Mike Stanton	.05	.02
❑	789	Bobby Valentine MG	.05	.02
❑	790	Joe Carter	.10	.03
❑	791	Danny Cox	.05	.02
❑	792	Dave Winfield	.15	.04

1992 Topps Traded

	Nm-Mt	Ex-Mt
COMP.FACT.SET (132)	80.00	24.00

			Nm-Mt	Ex-Mt
❑	1T	Willie Adams USA RC	.25	.07
❑	2T	Jeff Alkire USA RC	.25	.07
❑	3T	Felipe Alou MG	.20	.06
❑	4T	Moises Alou	.20	.06
❑	5T	Ruben Amaro	.10	.03
❑	6T	Jack Armstrong	.10	.03
❑	7T	Scott Bankhead	.10	.03
❑	8T	Tim Belcher	.10	.03
❑	9T	George Bell	.10	.03
❑	10T	Freddie Benavides	.10	.03
❑	11T	Todd Benzinger	.10	.03
❑	12T	Joe Boever	.10	.03
❑	13T	Ricky Bones	.10	.03
❑	14T	Bobby Bonilla	.20	.06
❑	15T	Hubie Brooks	.10	.03
❑	16T	Jerry Browne	.10	.03
❑	17T	Jim Bullinger	.10	.03
❑	18T	Dave Burba	.10	.03
❑	19T	Kevin Campbell	.10	.03
❑	20T	Tom Candiotti	.10	.03
❑	21T	Mark Carreon	.10	.03
❑	22T	Gary Carter	.30	.09
❑	23T	Archi Cianfrocco RC	.10	.03
❑	24T	Phil Clark	.10	.03
❑	25T	Chad Curtis RC	.40	.12
❑	26T	Eric Davis	.20	.06
❑	27T	Tim Davis USA RC	.25	.07
❑	28T	Gary DiSarcina	.10	.03
❑	29T	Darren Dreifort USA	.20	.06
❑	30T	Mariano Duncan	.10	.03
❑	31T	Mike Fitzgerald	.10	.03
❑	32T	John Flaherty	.10	.03
❑	33T	Darrin Fletcher	.10	.03
❑	34T	Scott Fletcher	.10	.03
❑	35T	R.Fraser CO USA RC	.25	.07
❑	36T	Andres Galarraga	.20	.06
❑	37T	Dave Gallagher	.10	.03
❑	38T	Mike Gallego	.10	.03
❑	39T	Nomar Garciaparra USA RC	60.00	18.00
❑	40T	Jason Giambi USA	2.00	.60
❑	41T	Danny Gladden	.10	.03
❑	42T	Rene Gonzales	.10	.03
❑	43T	Jeff Granger USA	.10	.03
❑	44T	Rick Greene USA RC	.25	.07
❑	45T	J.Hammonds USA	.20	.06
❑	46T	Charlie Hayes	.10	.03
❑	47T	Von Hayes	.10	.03
❑	48T	Rick Helling USA	.10	.03
❑	49T	Butch Henry RC	.10	.03
❑	50T	Carlos Hernandez	.10	.03
❑	51T	Ken Hill	.10	.03
❑	52T	Butch Hobson	.10	.03
❑	53T	Vince Horsman	.10	.03
❑	54T	Pete Incaviglia	.10	.03
❑	55T	Gregg Jefferies	.10	.03
❑	56T	Charles Johnson USA	.20	.06
❑	57T	Doug Jones	.10	.03
❑	58T	Brian Jordan RC	1.50	.45
❑	59T	Wally Joyner	.20	.06
❑	60T	D.Kirkreit USA RC	.25	.07
❑	61T	Bill Krueger	.10	.03
❑	62T	Gene Lamont MG	.10	.03
❑	63T	Jim Lefebvre MG	.10	.03
❑	64T	Danny Leon	.10	.03
❑	65T	Pat Listach RC	.40	.12
❑	66T	Kenny Lofton	.50	.15
❑	67T	Dave Martinez	.10	.03
❑	68T	Derrick May	.10	.03
❑	69T	Kirk McCaskill	.10	.03
❑	70T	C.McConnell USA RC	.25	.07
❑	71T	Kevin McReynolds	.10	.03
❑	72T	Rusty Meacham	.10	.03
❑	73T	Keith Miller	.10	.03
❑	74T	Kevin Mitchell	.10	.03
❑	75T	Jason Moler USA RC	.25	.07
❑	76T	Mike Morgan	.10	.03
❑	77T	Jack Morris	.20	.06
❑	78T	C.Murray USA RC	.75	.23
❑	79T	Eddie Murray	.50	.15
❑	80T	Randy Myers	.10	.03
❑	81T	Denny Neagle	.20	.06
❑	82T	Phil Nevin USA	.30	.09
❑	83T	Dave Nilsson	.10	.03
❑	84T	Junior Ortiz	.10	.03
❑	85T	Donovan Osborne	.10	.03
❑	86T	Bill Pecota	.10	.03
❑	87T	Melido Perez	.10	.03
❑	88T	Mike Perez	.10	.03
❑	89T	Hipolito Pichardo RC	.10	.03
❑	90T	Willie Randolph	.20	.06
❑	91T	Darren Reed	.10	.03
❑	92T	Bip Roberts	.10	.03
❑	93T	Chris Roberts USA	.10	.03
❑	94T	Steve Rodriguez USA	.10	.03
❑	95T	Bruce Ruffin	.10	.03
❑	96T	Scott Ruskin	.10	.03
❑	97T	Bret Saberhagen	.20	.06
❑	98T	Rey Sanchez RC	.40	.12
❑	99T	Steve Sax	.10	.03
❑	100T	Curt Schilling	.30	.09
❑	101T	Dick Schofield	.10	.03
❑	102T	Gary Scott	.10	.03
❑	103T	Kevin Seitzer	.10	.03
❑	104T	Frank Seminara RC	.10	.03
❑	105T	Gary Sheffield	.20	.06
❑	106T	John Smiley	.10	.03
❑	107T	Cory Snyder	.10	.03
❑	108T	Paul Sorrento	.10	.03
❑	109T	Sammy Sosa	1.50	.45
❑	110T	Matt Stairs RC	.50	.15
❑	111T	Andy Stankiewicz	.10	.03
❑	112T	Kurt Stillwell	.10	.03
❑	113T	Rick Sutcliffe	.20	.06
❑	114T	Bill Swift	.10	.03
❑	115T	Jeff Tackett	.10	.03
❑	116T	Danny Tartabull	.10	.03
❑	117T	Eddie Taubensee	.20	.06
❑	118T	Dickie Thon	.10	.03
❑	119T	M.Tucker USA RC	.75	.23
❑	120T	Scooter Tucker	.10	.03
❑	121T	Marc Valdes USA RC	.25	.07
❑	122T	Julio Valera	.10	.03
❑	123T	J.Varitek USA RC	3.00	.90
❑	124T	Ron Villone USA RC	.25	.07
❑	125T	Frank Viola	.20	.06
❑	126T	B.J. Wallace USA RC	.25	.07
❑	127T	Dan Walters	.10	.03
❑	128T	Craig Wilson USA	.10	.03
❑	129T	Chris Wimmer USA	.10	.03
❑	130T	Dave Winfield	.30	.09
❑	131T	Herm Winningham	.10	.03
❑	132T	Checklist 1T-132T	.10	.03

1993 Topps

	Nm-Mt	Ex-Mt
COMPLETE SET (825)	40.00	12.00
COMP.HOBBY.SET (847)	50.00	15.00
COMP.RETAIL.SET (838)	50.00	15.00
COMP. SERIES 1 (396)	20.00	6.00
COMP.SERIES 2 (429)	20.00	6.00

			Nm-Mt	Ex-Mt
❑	1	Robin Yount	.50	.15
❑	2	Barry Bonds	1.25	.35
❑	3	Ryne Sandberg	.75	.23
❑	4	Roger Clemens	1.00	.30
❑	5	Tony Gwynn	.60	.18
❑	6	Jeff Tackett	.10	.03
❑	7	Pete Incaviglia	.10	.03
❑	8	Mark Wohlers	.10	.03
❑	9	Kent Hrbek	.20	.06
❑	10	Will Clark	.50	.15
❑	11	Eric Karros	.20	.06
❑	12	Lee Smith	.20	.06
❑	13	Esteban Beltre	.10	.03
❑	14	Greg Briley	.10	.03

❑ 15 Marquis Grissom .10 .03
❑ 16 Dan Plesac .10 .03
❑ 17 Dave Hollins .10 .03
❑ 18 Terry Steinbach .10 .03
❑ 19 Ed Nunez .10 .03
❑ 20 Tim Salmon .30 .09
❑ 21 Luis Salazar .10 .03
❑ 22 Jim Eisenreich .10 .03
❑ 23 Todd Stottlemyre .10 .03
❑ 24 Tim Naehring .10 .03
❑ 25 John Franco .20 .06
❑ 26 Skeeter Barnes .10 .03
❑ 27 Carlos Garcia .10 .03
❑ 28 Joe Orsulak .10 .03
❑ 29 Dwayne Henry .10 .03
❑ 30 Fred McGriff .30 .09
❑ 31 Derek Lilliquist .10 .03
❑ 32 Don Mattingly 1.25 .35
❑ 33 B.J. Wallace .10 .03
❑ 34 Juan Gonzalez .50 .15
❑ 35 John Smoltz .30 .09
❑ 36 Scott Servais .10 .03
❑ 37 Lenny Webster .10 .03
❑ 38 Chris James .10 .03
❑ 39 Roger McDowell .10 .03
❑ 40 Ozzie Smith .50 .15
❑ 41 Alex Fernandez .10 .03
❑ 42 Spike Owen .10 .03
❑ 43 Ruben Amaro .10 .03
❑ 44 Kevin Seitzer .10 .03
❑ 45 Dave Fleming .10 .03
❑ 46 Eric Fox .10 .03
❑ 47 Bob Scanlan .10 .03
❑ 48 Bert Blyleven .20 .06
❑ 49 Brian McRae .10 .03
❑ 50 Roberto Alomar .50 .15
❑ 51 Mo Vaughn .20 .06
❑ 52 Bobby Bonilla .20 .06
❑ 53 Frank Tanana .10 .03
❑ 54 Mike LaValliere .10 .03
❑ 55 Mark McLemore .10 .03
❑ 56 Chad Mottola RC .10 .03
❑ 57 Norm Charlton .10 .03
❑ 58 Jose Melendez .10 .03
❑ 59 Carlos Martinez .10 .03
❑ 60 Roberto Kelly .10 .03
❑ 61 Gene Larkin .10 .03
❑ 62 Rafael Belliard .10 .03
❑ 63 Al Osuna .10 .03
❑ 64 Scott Chiamparino .10 .03
❑ 65 Brett Butler .20 .06
❑ 66 John Burkett .10 .03
❑ 67 Felix Jose .10 .03
❑ 68 Omar Vizquel .20 .06
❑ 69 John Vander Wal .10 .03
❑ 70 Roberto Hernandez .10 .03
❑ 71 Ricky Bones .10 .03
❑ 72 Jeff Grotewold .10 .03
❑ 73 Mike Moore .10 .03
❑ 74 Steve Buechele .10 .03
❑ 75 Juan Guzman .10 .03
❑ 76 Kevin Appier .20 .06
❑ 77 Junior Felix .10 .03
❑ 78 Greg W. Harris .10 .03
❑ 79 Dick Schofield .10 .03
❑ 80 Cecil Fielder .20 .06
❑ 81 Lloyd McClendon .10 .03
❑ 82 David Segui .10 .03
❑ 83 Reggie Sanders .20 .06
❑ 84 Kurt Stillwell .10 .03
❑ 85 Sandy Alomar Jr. .10 .03
❑ 86 John Habyan .10 .03
❑ 87 Kevin Reimer .10 .03
❑ 88 Mike Stanton .10 .03
❑ 89 Eric Anthony .10 .03
❑ 90 Scott Erickson .10 .03
❑ 91 Craig Colbert .10 .03
❑ 92 Tom Pagnozzi .10 .03
❑ 93 Pedro Astacio .10 .03
❑ 94 Lance Johnson .10 .03
❑ 95 Larry Walker .30 .09
❑ 96 Russ Swan .10 .03
❑ 97 Scott Fletcher .10 .03
❑ 98 Derek Jeter RC 15.00 4.50
❑ 99 Mike Williams .10 .03
❑ 100 Mark McGwire 1.25 .35
❑ 101 Jim Bullinger .10 .03
❑ 102 Brian Hunter .10 .03
❑ 103 Jody Reed .10 .03
❑ 104 Mike Butcher .10 .03
❑ 105 Gregg Jefferies .10 .03
❑ 106 Howard Johnson .10 .03
❑ 107 John Kiely .10 .03
❑ 108 Jose Lind .10 .03
❑ 109 Sam Horn .10 .03
❑ 110 Barry Larkin .50 .15
❑ 111 Bruce Hurst .10 .03
❑ 112 Brian Barnes .10 .03
❑ 113 Thomas Howard .10 .03
❑ 114 Mel Hall .10 .03
❑ 115 Robby Thompson .10 .03
❑ 116 Mark Lemke .10 .03
❑ 117 Eddie Taubensee .10 .03
❑ 118 David Hulse RC .10 .03
❑ 119 Pedro Munoz .10 .03
❑ 120 Ramon Martinez .10 .03
❑ 121 Todd Worrell .10 .03
❑ 122 Joey Cora .10 .03
❑ 123 Moises Alou .20 .06
❑ 124 Franklin Stubbs .10 .03
❑ 125 Pete O'Brien .10 .03
❑ 126 Bob Ayrault .10 .03
❑ 127 Carney Lansford .20 .06
❑ 128 Kal Daniels .10 .03
❑ 129 Joe Grahe .10 .03
❑ 130 Jeff Montgomery .10 .03
❑ 131 Dave Winfield .30 .09
❑ 132 Preston Wilson RC 1.00 .30
❑ 133 Steve Wilson .10 .03
❑ 134 Lee Guetterman .10 .03
❑ 135 Mickey Tettleton .10 .03
❑ 136 Jeff King .10 .03
❑ 137 Alan Mills .10 .03
❑ 138 Joe Oliver .10 .03
❑ 139 Gary Gaetti .20 .06
❑ 140 Gary Sheffield .20 .06
❑ 141 Dennis Cook .10 .03
❑ 142 Charlie Hayes .10 .03
❑ 143 Jeff Huson .10 .03
❑ 144 Kent Mercker .10 .03
❑ 145 Eric Young .10 .03
❑ 146 Scott Leius .10 .03
❑ 147 Bryan Hickerson .10 .03
❑ 148 Steve Finley .20 .06
❑ 149 Rheal Cormier .10 .03
❑ 150 Frank Thomas UER .50 .15
(Categories leading league are italicized but not printed in red)
❑ 151 Archi Cianfrocco .10 .03
❑ 152 Rich DeLucia .10 .03
❑ 153 Greg Vaughn .20 .06
❑ 154 Wes Chamberlain .10 .03
❑ 155 Dennis Eckersley .20 .06
❑ 156 Sammy Sosa .75 .23
❑ 157 Gary DiSarcina .10 .03
❑ 158 Kevin Koslofski .10 .03
❑ 159 Doug Linton .10 .03
❑ 160 Lou Whitaker .20 .06
❑ 161 Chad McConnell .10 .03
❑ 162 Joe Hesketh .10 .03
❑ 163 Tim Wakefield .20 .06
❑ 164 Leo Gomez .10 .03
❑ 165 Jose Rijo .10 .03
❑ 166 Tim Scott .10 .03
❑ 167 Steve Olin UER .10 .03
(Born 10/4/65 should say 10/10/65)
❑ 168 Kevin Maas .10 .03
❑ 169 Kenny Rogers .20 .06
❑ 170 David Justice .20 .06
❑ 171 Doug Jones .10 .03
❑ 172 Jeff Reboulet .10 .03
❑ 173 Andres Galarraga .20 .06
❑ 174 Randy Velarde .10 .03
❑ 175 Kirk McCaskill .10 .03
❑ 176 Darren Lewis .10 .03
❑ 177 Lenny Harris .10 .03
❑ 178 Jeff Fassero .10 .03
❑ 179 Ken Griffey Jr. .75 .23
❑ 180 Darren Daulton .20 .06
❑ 181 John Jaha .10 .03
❑ 182 Ron Darling .10 .03
❑ 183 Greg Maddux 1.00 .30
❑ 184 Damion Easley .10 .03
❑ 185 Jack Morris .20 .06
❑ 186 Mike Magnante .10 .03
❑ 187 John Dopson .10 .03
❑ 188 Sid Fernandez .10 .03
❑ 189 Tony Phillips .10 .03
❑ 190 Doug Drabek .10 .03
❑ 191 Sean Lowe RC .10 .03
❑ 192 Bob Milacki .10 .03
❑ 193 Steve Foster .10 .03
❑ 194 Jerald Clark .10 .03
❑ 195 Pete Harnisch .10 .03
❑ 196 Pat Kelly .10 .03
❑ 197 Jeff Frye .10 .03
❑ 198 Alejandro Pena .10 .03
❑ 199 Junior Ortiz .10 .03
❑ 200 Kirby Puckett .50 .15
❑ 201 Jose Uribe .10 .03
❑ 202 Mike Scioscia .10 .03
❑ 203 Bernard Gilkey .10 .03
❑ 204 Dan Pasqua .10 .03
❑ 205 Gary Carter .30 .09
❑ 206 Henry Cotto .10 .03
❑ 207 Paul Molitor .30 .09
❑ 208 Mike Hartley .10 .03
❑ 209 Jeff Parrett .10 .03
❑ 210 Mark Langston .10 .03
❑ 211 Doug Dascenzo .10 .03
❑ 212 Rick Reed .10 .03
❑ 213 Candy Maldonado .10 .03
❑ 214 Danny Darwin .10 .03
❑ 215 Pat Howell .10 .03
❑ 216 Mark Leiter .10 .03
❑ 217 Kevin Mitchell .10 .03
❑ 218 Ben McDonald .10 .03
❑ 219 Bip Roberts .10 .03
❑ 220 Benny Santiago .20 .06
❑ 221 Carlos Baerga .10 .03
❑ 222 Bernie Williams .30 .09
❑ 223 Roger Pavlik .10 .03
❑ 224 Sid Bream .10 .03
❑ 225 Matt Williams .20 .06
❑ 226 Willie Banks .10 .03
❑ 227 Jeff Bagwell .30 .09
❑ 228 Tom Goodwin .10 .03
❑ 229 Mike Perez .10 .03
❑ 230 Carlton Fisk .30 .09
❑ 231 John Wetteland .20 .06
❑ 232 Tino Martinez .30 .09
❑ 233 Rick Greene .10 .03
❑ 234 Tim McIntosh .10 .03
❑ 235 Mitch Williams .10 .03
❑ 236 Kevin Campbell .10 .03
❑ 237 Jose Vizcaino .10 .03
❑ 238 Chris Donnels .10 .03
❑ 239 Mike Boddicker .10 .03
❑ 240 John Olerud .20 .06
❑ 241 Mike Gardiner .10 .03
❑ 242 Charlie O'Brien .10 .03
❑ 243 Rob Deer .10 .03
❑ 244 Denny Neagle .20 .06
❑ 245 Chris Sabo .10 .03
❑ 246 Gregg Olson .10 .03
❑ 247 Frank Seminara UER .10 .03
(Acquired 12/3/98)
❑ 248 Scott Scudder .10 .03
❑ 249 Tim Burke .10 .03
❑ 250 Chuck Knoblauch .20 .06
❑ 251 Mike Bielecki .10 .03
❑ 252 Xavier Hernandez .10 .03
❑ 253 Jose Guzman .10 .03
❑ 254 Cory Snyder .10 .03
❑ 255 Orel Hershiser .20 .06
❑ 256 Wil Cordero .10 .03
❑ 257 Luis Alicea .10 .03
❑ 258 Mike Schooler .10 .03
❑ 259 Craig Grebeck .10 .03
❑ 260 Duane Ward .10 .03
❑ 261 Bill Wegman .10 .03
❑ 262 Mickey Morandini .10 .03
❑ 263 Vince Horsman .10 .03
❑ 264 Paul Sorrento .10 .03
❑ 265 Andre Dawson .20 .06
❑ 266 Rene Gonzales .10 .03

❑ 267 Keith Miller .10 .03
❑ 268 Derek Bell .10 .03
❑ 269 Todd Steverson RC .10 .03
❑ 270 Frank Viola .20 .06
❑ 271 Wally Whitehurst .10 .03
❑ 272 Kurt Knudsen .10 .03
❑ 273 Dan Walters .10 .03
❑ 274 Rick Sutcliffe .20 .06
❑ 275 Andy Van Slyke .20 .06
❑ 276 Paul O'Neill .30 .09
❑ 277 Mark Whiten .10 .03
❑ 278 Chris Nabholz .10 .03
❑ 279 Todd Burns .10 .03
❑ 280 Tom Glavine .50 .15
❑ 281 Butch Henry .10 .03
❑ 282 Shane Mack .10 .03
❑ 283 Mike Jackson .10 .03
❑ 284 Henry Rodriguez .10 .03
❑ 285 Bob Tewksbury .10 .03
❑ 286 Ron Karkovice .10 .03
❑ 287 Mike Gallego .10 .03
❑ 288 Dave Cochrane .10 .03
❑ 289 Jesse Orosco .10 .03
❑ 290 Dave Stewart .20 .06
❑ 291 Tommy Greene .10 .03
❑ 292 Rey Sanchez .10 .03
❑ 293 Rob Ducey .10 .03
❑ 294 Brent Mayne .10 .03
❑ 295 Dave Stieb .10 .03
❑ 296 Luis Rivera .10 .03
❑ 297 Jeff Innis .10 .03
❑ 298 Scott Livingstone .10 .03
❑ 299 Bob Patterson .10 .03
❑ 300 Cal Ripken 1.50 .45
❑ 301 Cesar Hernandez .10 .03
❑ 302 Randy Myers .10 .03
❑ 303 Brook Jacoby .10 .03
❑ 304 Melido Perez .10 .03
❑ 305 Rafael Palmeiro .30 .09
❑ 306 Damon Berryhill .10 .03
❑ 307 Dan Serafini RC .10 .03
❑ 308 Darryl Kile .20 .06
❑ 309 J.T. Bruett .10 .03
❑ 310 Dave Righetti .20 .06
❑ 311 Jay Howell .10 .03
❑ 312 Geronimo Pena .10 .03
❑ 313 Greg Hibbard .10 .03
❑ 314 Mark Gardner .10 .03
❑ 315 Edgar Martinez .30 .09
❑ 316 Dave Nilsson .10 .03
❑ 317 Kyle Abbott .10 .03
❑ 318 Willie Wilson .10 .03
❑ 319 Paul Assenmacher .10 .03
❑ 320 Tim Fortugno .10 .03
❑ 321 Rusty Meacham .10 .03
❑ 322 Pat Borders .10 .03
❑ 323 Mike Greenwell .10 .03
❑ 324 Willie Randolph .20 .06
❑ 325 Bill Gullickson .10 .03
❑ 326 Gary Varsho .10 .03
❑ 327 Tim Hulett .10 .03
❑ 328 Scott Ruskin .10 .03
❑ 329 Mike Maddux .10 .03
❑ 330 Danny Tartabull .10 .03
❑ 331 Kenny Lofton .20 .06
❑ 332 Geno Petralli .10 .03
❑ 333 Otis Nixon .10 .03
❑ 334 Jason Kendall RC .75 .23
❑ 335 Mark Portugal .10 .03
❑ 336 Mike Pagliarulo .10 .03
❑ 337 Kirt Manwaring .10 .03
❑ 338 Bob Ojeda .10 .03
❑ 339 Mark Clark .10 .03
❑ 340 John Kruk .20 .06
❑ 341 Mel Rojas .10 .03
❑ 342 Erik Hanson .10 .03
❑ 343 Doug Henry .10 .03
❑ 344 Jack McDowell .10 .03
❑ 345 Harold Baines .20 .06
❑ 346 Chuck McElroy .10 .03
❑ 347 Luis Sojo .10 .03
❑ 348 Andy Stankiewicz .10 .03
❑ 349 Hipolito Pichardo .10 .03
❑ 350 Joe Carter .20 .06
❑ 351 Ellis Burks .20 .06
❑ 352 Pete Schourek .10 .03
❑ 353 Buddy Groom .10 .03
❑ 354 Jay Bell .20 .06
❑ 355 Brady Anderson .20 .06
❑ 356 Freddie Benavides .10 .03
❑ 357 Phil Stephenson .10 .03
❑ 358 Kevin Wickander .10 .03
❑ 359 Mike Stanley .10 .03
❑ 360 Ivan Rodriguez .50 .15
❑ 361 Scott Bankhead .10 .03
❑ 362 Luis Gonzalez .20 .06
❑ 363 John Smiley .10 .03
❑ 364 Trevor Wilson .10 .03
❑ 365 Tom Candiotti .10 .03
❑ 366 Craig Wilson .10 .03
❑ 367 Steve Sax .10 .03
❑ 368 Delino DeShields .10 .03
❑ 369 Jaime Navarro .10 .03
❑ 370 Dave Valle .10 .03
❑ 371 Mariano Duncan .10 .03
❑ 372 Rod Nichols .10 .03
❑ 373 Mike Morgan .10 .03
❑ 374 Julio Valera .10 .03
❑ 375 Wally Joyner .20 .06
❑ 376 Tom Henke .10 .03
❑ 377 Herm Winningham .10 .03
❑ 378 Orlando Merced .10 .03
❑ 379 Mike Munoz .10 .03
❑ 380 Todd Hundley .10 .03
❑ 381 Mike Flanagan .10 .03
❑ 382 Tim Belcher .10 .03
❑ 383 Jerry Browne .10 .03
❑ 384 Mike Benjamin .10 .03
❑ 385 Jim Leyritz .10 .03
❑ 386 Ray Lankford .10 .03
❑ 387 Devon White .10 .03
❑ 388 Jeremy Hernandez .10 .03
❑ 389 Brian Harper .10 .03
❑ 390 Wade Boggs .30 .09
❑ 391 Derrick May .10 .03
❑ 392 Travis Fryman .20 .06
❑ 393 Ron Gant .20 .06
❑ 394 Checklist 1-132 .10 .03
❑ 395 CL 133-264 UER .10 .03
Eckerlsey
❑ 396 Checklist 265-396 .10 .03
❑ 397 George Brett 1.25 .35
❑ 398 Bobby Witt .10 .03
❑ 399 Daryl Boston .10 .03
❑ 400 Bo Jackson .50 .15
❑ 401 Fred McGriff .30 .09
Frank Thomas AS
❑ 402 Ryne Sandberg .50 .15
Carlos Baerga AS
❑ 403 Gary Sheffield .20 .06
Edgar Martinez AS
❑ 404 Barry Larkin .20 .06
Travis Fryman AS
❑ 405 Andy Van Slyke .50 .15
Ken Griffey Jr. AS
❑ 406 Larry Walker .30 .09
Kirby Puckett AS
❑ 407 Barry Bonds .60 .18
Joe Carter AS
❑ 408 Darren Daulton .20 .06
Brian Harper AS
❑ 409 Greg Maddux .50 .15
Roger Clemens AS
❑ 410 Tom Glavine .20 .06
Dave Fleming AS
❑ 411 Lee Smith .20 .06
Dennis Eckersley AS
❑ 412 Jamie McAndrew .10 .03
❑ 413 Pete Smith .10 .03
❑ 414 Juan Guerrero .10 .03
❑ 415 Todd Frohwirth .10 .03
❑ 416 Randy Tomlin .10 .03
❑ 417 B.J. Surhoff .20 .06
❑ 418 Jim Gott .10 .03
❑ 419 Mark Thompson RC .10 .03
❑ 420 Kevin Tapani .10 .03
❑ 421 Curt Schilling .30 .09
❑ 422 J.T. Snow RC .50 .15
❑ 423 Ryan Klesko .20 .06
Ivan Cruz
Bubba Smith
Larry Sutton
❑ 424 John Valentin .10 .03
❑ 425 Joe Girardi .10 .03
❑ 426 Nigel Wilson .10 .03
❑ 427 Bob MacDonald .10 .03
❑ 428 Todd Zeile .10 .03
❑ 429 Milt Cuyler .10 .03
❑ 430 Eddie Murray .50 .15
❑ 431 Rich Amaral .10 .03
❑ 432 Pete Young .10 .03
❑ 433 Roger Bailey RC .10 .03
Tom Schmidt
❑ 434 Jack Armstrong .10 .03
❑ 435 Willie McGee .20 .06
❑ 436 Greg W. Harris .10 .03
❑ 437 Chris Hammond .10 .03
❑ 438 Ritchie Moody RC .10 .03
❑ 439 Bryan Harvey .10 .03
❑ 440 Ruben Sierra .10 .03
❑ 441 Don Lemon .10 .03
Todd Pridy RC
❑ 442 Kevin McReynolds .10 .03
❑ 443 Terry Leach .10 .03
❑ 444 David Nied .10 .03
❑ 445 Dale Murphy .50 .15
❑ 446 Luis Mercedes .10 .03
❑ 447 Keith Shepherd RC .10 .03
❑ 448 Ken Caminiti .20 .06
❑ 449 Jim Austin .10 .03
❑ 450 Darryl Strawberry .30 .09
❑ 451 Ramon Caraballo .25 .07
Jon Shave RC
Brent Gates
Quinton McCracken
❑ 452 Bob Wickman .10 .03
❑ 453 Victor Cole .10 .03
❑ 454 John Johnstone RC .10 .03
❑ 455 Chili Davis .20 .06
❑ 456 Scott Taylor .10 .03
❑ 457 Tracy Woodson .10 .03
❑ 458 David Wells .20 .06
❑ 459 Derek Wallace RC .10 .03
❑ 460 Randy Johnson .50 .15
❑ 461 Steve Reed RC .10 .03
❑ 462 Felix Fermin .10 .03
❑ 463 Scott Aldred .10 .03
❑ 464 Greg Colbrunn .10 .03
❑ 465 Tony Fernandez .10 .03
❑ 466 Mike Felder .10 .03
❑ 467 Lee Stevens .10 .03
❑ 468 Matt Whiteside RC .10 .03
❑ 469 Dave Hansen .10 .03
❑ 470 Rob Dibble .20 .06
❑ 471 Dave Gallagher .10 .03
❑ 472 Chris Gwynn .10 .03
❑ 473 Dave Henderson .10 .03
❑ 474 Ozzie Guillen .10 .03
❑ 475 Jeff Reardon .20 .06
❑ 476 Mark Voisard .10 .03
Will Scalzitti RC
❑ 477 Jimmy Jones .10 .03
❑ 478 Greg Cadaret .10 .03
❑ 479 Todd Pratt RC .10 .03
❑ 480 Pat Listach .10 .03
❑ 481 Ryan Luzinski RC .10 .03
❑ 482 Darren Reed .10 .03
❑ 483 Brian Griffiths RC .10 .03
❑ 484 John Wehner .10 .03
❑ 485 Glenn Davis .10 .03
❑ 486 Eric Wedge RC .10 .03
❑ 487 Jesse Hollins .10 .03
❑ 488 Manuel Lee .10 .03
❑ 489 Scott Fredrickson RC .10 .03
❑ 490 Omar Olivares .10 .03
❑ 491 Shawn Hare .10 .03
❑ 492 Tom Lampkin .10 .03
❑ 493 Jeff Nelson .10 .03
❑ 494 Kevin Young .10 .03
Adell Davenport
Eduardo Perez
Lou Lucca RC
❑ 495 Ken Hill .10 .03
❑ 496 Reggie Jefferson .10 .03
❑ 497 Matt Petersen .10 .03
Willie Brown RC
❑ 498 Bud Black .10 .03
❑ 499 Chuck Crim .10 .03

❑ 500 Jose Canseco .50 .15
❑ 501 Johnny Oates MG .20 .06
Bobby Cox MG
❑ 502 Butch Hobson MG .10 .03
Jim Lefebvre MG
❑ 503 Buck Rodgers MG .20 .06
Tony Perez MG
❑ 504 Gene Lamont MG .20 .06
Don Baylor MG
❑ 505 Mike Hargrove MG .20 .06
Rene Lachemann MG
❑ 506 Sparky Anderson MG .20 .06
Art Howe MG
❑ 507 Hal McRae MG .20 .06
Tom Lasorda MG
❑ 508 Phil Garner MG .20 .06
Felipe Alou MG
❑ 509 Tom Kelly MG .10 .03
Jeff Torborg MG
❑ 510 Buck Showalter MG .20 .06
Jim Fregosi MG
❑ 511 Tony LaRussa MG .20 .06
Jim Leyland MG
❑ 512 Lou Piniella MG .20 .06
Joe Torre MG
❑ 513 Kevin Kennedy MG .10 .03
Jim Riggleman MG
❑ 514 Cito Gaston MG .20 .06
Dusty Baker MG
❑ 515 Greg Swindell .10 .03
❑ 516 Alex Arias .10 .03
❑ 517 Bill Pecota .10 .03
❑ 518 Benji Grigsby RC UER .10 .03
(Misspelled Bengi
on card front)
❑ 519 David Howard .10 .03
❑ 520 Charlie Hough .20 .06
❑ 521 Kevin Flora .10 .03
❑ 522 Shane Reynolds .10 .03
❑ 523 Doug Bochtler RC .10 .03
❑ 524 Chris Hoiles .10 .03
❑ 525 Scott Sanderson .10 .03
❑ 526 Mike Sharperson .10 .03
❑ 527 Mike Fetters .10 .03
❑ 528 Paul Quantrill .10 .03
❑ 529 Dave Silvestri .50 .15
Chipper Jones
Benji Gil
Jeff Patzke
❑ 530 Sterling Hitchcock RC .25 .07
❑ 531 Joe Millette .10 .03
❑ 532 Tom Brunansky .10 .03
❑ 533 Frank Castillo .10 .03
❑ 534 Randy Knorr .10 .03
❑ 535 Jose Oquendo .10 .03
❑ 536 Dave Haas .10 .03
❑ 537 Jason Hutchins RC .10 .03
Ryan Turner
❑ 538 Jimmy Baron RC .10 .03
❑ 539 Kerry Woodson .10 .03
❑ 540 Ivan Calderon .10 .03
❑ 541 Denis Boucher .10 .03
❑ 542 Royce Clayton .10 .03
❑ 543 Reggie Williams .10 .03
❑ 544 Steve Decker .10 .03
❑ 545 Dean Palmer .20 .06
❑ 546 Hal Morris .10 .03
❑ 547 Ryan Thompson .10 .03
❑ 548 Lance Blankenship .10 .03
❑ 549 Hensley Meulens .10 .03
❑ 550 Scott Radinsky .10 .03
❑ 551 Eric Young .10 .03
❑ 552 Jeff Blauser .10 .03
❑ 553 Andujar Cedeno .10 .03
❑ 554 Arthur Rhodes .10 .03
❑ 555 Terry Mulholland .10 .03
❑ 556 Darryl Hamilton .10 .03
❑ 557 Pedro Martinez 1.00 .30
❑ 558 Ryan Whitman RC .10 .03
Mark Skeels
❑ 559 Jamie Arnold RC .10 .03
❑ 560 Zane Smith .10 .03
❑ 561 Matt Nokes .10 .03
❑ 562 Bob Zupcic .10 .03
❑ 563 Shawn Boskie .10 .03
❑ 564 Mike Timlin .10 .03
❑ 565 Jerald Clark .10 .03
❑ 566 Rod Brewer .10 .03
❑ 567 Mark Carreon .10 .03
❑ 568 Andy Benes .10 .03
❑ 569 Shawn Barton RC .10 .03
❑ 570 Tim Wallach .10 .03
❑ 571 Dave Mlicki .10 .03
❑ 572 Trevor Hoffman .20 .06
❑ 573 John Patterson .10 .03
❑ 574 De Shawn Warren RC .10 .03
❑ 575 Monty Fariss .10 .03
❑ 576 Darrell Sherman .30 .09
Damon Buford
Cliff Floyd
Michael Moore
❑ 577 Tim Costo .10 .03
❑ 578 Dave Magadan .10 .03
❑ 579 Neil Garret .10 .03
Jason Bates RC
❑ 580 Walt Weiss .10 .03
❑ 581 Chris Haney .10 .03
❑ 582 Shawn Abner .10 .03
❑ 583 Marvin Freeman .10 .03
❑ 584 Casey Candaele .10 .03
❑ 585 Ricky Jordan .10 .03
❑ 586 Jeff Tabaka RC .10 .03
❑ 587 Manny Alexander .10 .03
❑ 588 Mike Trombley .10 .03
❑ 589 Carlos Hernandez .10 .03
❑ 590 Cal Eldred .10 .03
❑ 591 Alex Cole .10 .03
❑ 592 Phil Plantier .10 .03
❑ 593 Brett Merriman RC .10 .03
❑ 594 Jerry Nielsen .10 .03
❑ 595 Shawon Dunston .10 .03
❑ 596 Jimmy Key .20 .06
❑ 597 Gerald Perry .10 .03
❑ 598 Rico Brogna .10 .03
❑ 599 Clemente Nunez .10 .03
Daniel Robinson
❑ 600 Bret Saberhagen .20 .06
❑ 601 Craig Shipley .10 .03
❑ 602 Henry Mercedes .10 .03
❑ 603 Jim Thome .50 .15
❑ 604 Rod Beck .10 .03
❑ 605 Chuck Finley .20 .06
❑ 606 J. Owens RC .10 .03
❑ 607 Dan Smith .10 .03
❑ 608 Bill Doran .10 .03
❑ 609 Lance Parrish .20 .06
❑ 610 Dennis Martinez .20 .06
❑ 611 Tom Gordon .10 .03
❑ 612 Byron Mathews RC .10 .03
❑ 613 Joel Adamson RC .10 .03
❑ 614 Brian Williams .10 .03
❑ 615 Steve Avery .10 .03
❑ 616 Matt Mieske .10 .03
Tracy Sanders
Midre Cummings RC
Ryan Freeburg
❑ 617 Craig Lefferts .10 .03
❑ 618 Tony Pena .10 .03
❑ 619 Billy Spiers .10 .03
❑ 620 Todd Benzinger .10 .03
❑ 621 Mike Kotarski .10 .03
Greg Boyd RC
❑ 622 Ben Rivera .10 .03
❑ 623 Al Martin .10 .03
❑ 624 Sam Militello UER .10 .03
(Profile says drafted
in 1988, bio says
drafted in 1990)
❑ 625 Rick Aguilera .10 .03
❑ 626 Dan Gladden .10 .03
❑ 627 Andres Berumen RC .10 .03
❑ 628 Kelly Gruber .10 .03
❑ 629 Cris Carpenter .10 .03
❑ 630 Mark Grace .50 .15
❑ 631 Jeff Brantley .10 .03
❑ 632 Chris Widger RC .25 .07
❑ 633 Three Russians UER .10 .03
Rudolf Razjigaev
Eugneyi Puchkov
Ilya Bogatyrev
Bogatyrev is a shortstop,
card has pitching header
❑ 634 Mo Sanford .10 .03
❑ 635 Albert Belle .20 .06
❑ 636 Tim Teufel .10 .03
❑ 637 Greg Myers .10 .03
❑ 638 Brian Bohanon .10 .03
❑ 639 Mike Bordick .10 .03
❑ 640 Dwight Gooden .30 .09
❑ 641 Pat Leahy .10 .03
Gavin Baugh RC
❑ 642 Milt Hill .10 .03
❑ 643 Luis Aquino .10 .03
❑ 644 Dante Bichette .20 .06
❑ 645 Bobby Thigpen .10 .03
❑ 646 Rich Scheid RC .10 .03
❑ 647 Brian Sackinsky RC .10 .03
❑ 648 Ryan Hawblitzel .10 .03
❑ 649 Tom Marsh .10 .03
❑ 650 Terry Pendleton .20 .06
❑ 651 Rafael Bournigal .10 .03
❑ 652 Dave West .10 .03
❑ 653 Steve Hosey .10 .03
❑ 654 Gerald Williams .10 .03
❑ 655 Scott Cooper .10 .03
❑ 656 Gary Scott .10 .03
❑ 657 Mike Harkey .10 .03
❑ 658 Jeromy Burnitz .10 .03
Melvin Nieves
Rich Becker
Shon Walker RC
❑ 659 Ed Sprague .10 .03
❑ 660 Alan Trammell .30 .09
❑ 661 Garvin Alston RC .10 .03
Michael Case
❑ 662 Donovan Osborne .10 .03
❑ 663 Jeff Gardner .10 .03
❑ 664 Calvin Jones .10 .03
❑ 665 Darrin Fletcher .10 .03
❑ 666 Glenallen Hill .10 .03
❑ 667 Jim Rosenbohm RC .10 .03
❑ 668 Scott Lewis .10 .03
❑ 669 Kip Yaughn RC .10 .03
❑ 670 Julio Franco .20 .06
❑ 671 Dave Martinez .10 .03
❑ 672 Kevin Bass .10 .03
❑ 673 Todd Van Poppel .10 .03
❑ 674 Mark Gubicza .10 .03
❑ 675 Tim Raines .20 .06
❑ 676 Rudy Seanez .10 .03
❑ 677 Charlie Leibrandt .10 .03
❑ 678 Randy Milligan .10 .03
❑ 679 Kim Batiste .10 .03
❑ 680 Craig Biggio .30 .09
❑ 681 Darren Holmes .10 .03
❑ 682 John Candelaria .10 .03
❑ 683 Jerry Stafford .10 .03
Eddie Christian RC
❑ 684 Pat Mahomes .10 .03
❑ 685 Bob Walk .10 .03
❑ 686 Russ Springer .10 .03
❑ 687 Tony Sheffield RC .10 .03
❑ 688 Dwight Smith .10 .03
❑ 689 Eddie Zosky .10 .03
❑ 690 Bien Figueroa .10 .03
❑ 691 Jim Tatum RC .10 .03
❑ 692 Chad Kreuter .10 .03
❑ 693 Rich Rodriguez .10 .03
❑ 694 Shane Turner .10 .03
❑ 695 Kent Bottenfield .10 .03
❑ 696 Jose Mesa .10 .03
❑ 697 Darrell Whitmore RC .10 .03
❑ 698 Ted Wood .10 .03
❑ 699 Chad Curtis .10 .03
❑ 700 Nolan Ryan 2.00 .60
❑ 701 Mike Piazza 1.50 .45
Brook Fordyce
Carlos Delgado
Donnie Leshnock
❑ 702 Tim Pugh RC .10 .03
❑ 703 Jeff Kent .50 .15
❑ 704 Jon Goodrich .10 .03
Danny Figueroa RC
❑ 705 Bob Welch .10 .03
❑ 706 S.Clinkscales RC .10 .03
❑ 707 Donn Pall .10 .03
❑ 708 Greg Olson .10 .03
❑ 709 Jeff Juden .10 .03

	Nm-Mt	Ex-Mt
❑ 710 Mike Mussina	.50	.15
❑ 711 Scott Chiamparino	.10	.03
❑ 712 Stan Javier	.10	.03
❑ 713 John Doherty	.10	.03
❑ 714 Kevin Gross	.10	.03
❑ 715 Greg Gagne	.10	.03
❑ 716 Steve Cooke	.10	.03
❑ 717 Steve Farr	.10	.03
❑ 718 Jay Buhner	.20	.06
❑ 719 Butch Henry	.10	.03
❑ 720 David Cone	.20	.06
❑ 721 Rick Wilkins	.10	.03
❑ 722 Chuck Carr	.10	.03
❑ 723 Kenny Felder RC	.10	.03
❑ 724 Guillermo Velasquez	.10	.03
❑ 725 Billy Hatcher	.10	.03
❑ 726 Mike Veneziale RC	.10	.03
Ken Kendrena		
❑ 727 Jonathan Hurst	.10	.03
❑ 728 Steve Frey	.10	.03
❑ 729 Mark Leonard	.10	.03
❑ 730 Charles Nagy	.10	.03
❑ 731 Donald Harris	.10	.03
❑ 732 Travis Buckley RC	.10	.03
❑ 733 Tom Browning	.10	.03
❑ 734 Anthony Young	.10	.03
❑ 735 Steve Shifflett	.10	.03
❑ 736 Jeff Russell	.10	.03
❑ 737 Wilson Alvarez	.10	.03
❑ 738 Lance Painter RC	.10	.03
❑ 739 Dave Weathers	.10	.03
❑ 740 Len Dykstra	.20	.06
❑ 741 Mike Devereaux	.10	.03
❑ 742 Rene Arocha	.25	.07
Alan Embree		
Brien Taylor		
Tim Crabtree		
❑ 743 Dave Landaker RC	.10	.03
❑ 744 Chris George	.10	.03
❑ 745 Eric Davis	.20	.06
❑ 746 Mark Strittmatter	.10	.03
Lamarr Rogers RC		
❑ 747 Carl Willis	.10	.03
❑ 748 Stan Belinda	.10	.03
❑ 749 Scott Kamieniecki	.10	.03
❑ 750 Rickey Henderson	.75	.23
❑ 751 Eric Hillman	.10	.03
❑ 752 Pat Hentgen	.10	.03
❑ 753 Jim Corsi	.10	.03
❑ 754 Brian Jordan	.20	.06
❑ 755 Bill Swift	.10	.03
❑ 756 Mike Henneman	.10	.03
❑ 757 Harold Reynolds	.20	.06
❑ 758 Sean Berry	.10	.03
❑ 759 Charlie Hayes	.10	.03
❑ 760 Luis Polonia	.10	.03
❑ 761 Darrin Jackson	.10	.03
❑ 762 Mark Lewis	.10	.03
❑ 763 Rob Maurer	.10	.03
❑ 764 Willie Greene	.10	.03
❑ 765 Vince Coleman	.10	.03
❑ 766 Todd Revenig	.10	.03
❑ 767 Rich Ireland RC	.10	.03
❑ 768 Mike Macfarlane	.10	.03
❑ 769 Francisco Cabrera	.10	.03
❑ 770 Robin Ventura	.20	.06
❑ 771 Kevin Ritz	.10	.03
❑ 772 Chito Martinez	.10	.03
❑ 773 Cliff Brantley	.10	.03
❑ 774 Curt Leskanic RC	.10	.03
❑ 775 Chris Bosio	.10	.03
❑ 776 Jose Offerman	.10	.03
❑ 777 Mark Guthrie	.10	.03
❑ 778 Don Slaught	.10	.03
❑ 779 Rich Monteleone	.10	.03
❑ 780 Jim Abbott	.50	.15
❑ 781 Jack Clark	.20	.06
❑ 782 Reynol Mendoza	.10	.03
Dan Roman RC		
❑ 783 Heathcliff Slocumb	.10	.03
❑ 784 Jeff Branson	.10	.03
❑ 785 Kevin Brown	.20	.06
❑ 786 Mike Christopher	.10	.03
Ken Ryan		
Aaron Taylor		
Gus Gandarillas RC		
❑ 787 Mike Matthews RC	.10	.03
❑ 788 Mackey Sasser	.10	.03
❑ 789 Jeff Conine UER	.20	.06
No inclusion of 1990 RBI stats in career total		
❑ 790 George Bell	.10	.03
❑ 791 Pat Rapp	.10	.03
❑ 792 Joe Boever	.10	.03
❑ 793 Jim Poole	.10	.03
❑ 794 Andy Ashby	.10	.03
❑ 795 Deion Sanders	.20	.06
❑ 796 Scott Brosius	.20	.06
❑ 797 Brad Pennington	.10	.03
❑ 798 Greg Blosser	.10	.03
❑ 799 Jim Edmonds RC	1.50	.45
❑ 800 Shawn Jeter	.10	.03
❑ 801 Jesse Levis	.10	.03
❑ 802 Phil Clark UER	.10	.03
(Word "a" is missing in sentence beginning with "In 1992 ...")		
❑ 803 Ed Pierce RC	.10	.03
❑ 804 Jose Valentin RC	.25	.07
❑ 805 Terry Jorgensen	.10	.03
❑ 806 Mark Hutton	.10	.03
❑ 807 Troy Neel	.10	.03
❑ 808 Bret Boone	.30	.09
❑ 809 Cris Colon	.10	.03
❑ 810 Domingo Martinez RC	.10	.03
❑ 811 Javier Lopez	.30	.09
❑ 812 Matt Walbeck RC	.10	.03
❑ 813 Dan Wilson	.20	.06
❑ 814 Scooter Tucker	.10	.03
❑ 815 Billy Ashley	.10	.03
❑ 816 Tim Laker RC	.10	.03
❑ 817 Bobby Jones	.20	.06
❑ 818 Brad Brink	.10	.03
❑ 819 William Pennyfeather	.10	.03
❑ 820 Stan Royer	.10	.03
❑ 821 Doug Brocail	.10	.03
❑ 822 Kevin Rogers	.10	.03
❑ 823 Checklist 397-540	.10	.03
❑ 824 Checklist 541-691	.10	.03
❑ 825 Checklist 692-825	.10	.03

1993 Topps Traded

	Nm-Mt	Ex-Mt
COMP.FACT.SET (132)	40.00	12.00
❑ 1T Barry Bonds	1.25	.35
❑ 2T Rich Renteria	.10	.03
❑ 3T Aaron Sele	.10	.03
❑ 4T C.Loewer USA RC	.25	.07
❑ 5T Erik Pappas	.10	.03
❑ 6T Greg McMichael RC	.25	.07
❑ 7T Freddie Benavides	.10	.03
❑ 8T Kirk Gibson	.20	.06
❑ 9T Tony Fernandez	.10	.03
❑ 10T Jay Gainer RC	.25	.07
❑ 11T Orestes Destrade	.10	.03
❑ 12T A.J. Hinch USA RC	.50	.15
❑ 13T Bobby Munoz	.10	.03
❑ 14T Tom Henke	.10	.03
❑ 15T Rob Butler	.10	.03
❑ 16T Gary Wayne	.10	.03
❑ 17T David McCarty	.10	.03
❑ 18T Walt Weiss	.10	.03
❑ 19T Todd Helton USA RC	30.00	9.00
❑ 20T Mark Whiten	.10	.03
❑ 21T Ricky Gutierrez	.10	.03
❑ 22T D.Hermanson USA RC	.50	.15
❑ 23T Sherman Obando RC	.25	.07
❑ 24T Mike Piazza	1.25	.35
❑ 25T Jeff Russell	.10	.03
❑ 26T Jason Bere	.10	.03
❑ 27T Jack Voigt RC	.25	.07
❑ 28T Chris Bosio	.10	.03
❑ 29T Phil Hiatt	.10	.03
❑ 30T M.Beaumont USA RC	.25	.07
❑ 31T Andres Galarraga	.20	.06
❑ 32T Greg Swindell	.10	.03
❑ 33T Vinny Castilla	.20	.06
❑ 34T P.Clougherty RC USA	.25	.07
❑ 35T Greg Briley	.10	.03
❑ 36T Dallas Green MG	.10	.03
Davey Johnson MG		
❑ 37T Tyler Green	.10	.03
❑ 38T Craig Paquette	.10	.03
❑ 39T Danny Sheaffer RC	.25	.07
❑ 40T Jim Converse RC	.25	.07
❑ 41T Terry Harvey USA RC	.25	.07
❑ 42T Phil Plantier	.10	.03
❑ 43T Doug Saunders RC	.25	.07
❑ 44T Benny Santiago	.20	.06
❑ 45T Dante Powell USA RC	.25	.07
❑ 46T Jeff Parrett	.10	.03
❑ 47T Wade Boggs	.30	.09
❑ 48T Paul Molitor	.30	.09
❑ 49T Turk Wendell	.10	.03
❑ 50T David Wells	.20	.06
❑ 51T Gary Sheffield	.20	.06
❑ 52T Kevin Young	.20	.06
❑ 53T Nelson Liriano	.10	.03
❑ 54T Greg Maddux	1.00	.30
❑ 55T Derek Bell	.10	.03
❑ 56T Matt Turner RC	.25	.07
❑ 57T C.Nelson RC USA	.25	.07
❑ 58T Mike Hampton	.20	.06
❑ 59T Troy O'Leary RC	.50	.15
❑ 60T Benji Gil	.10	.03
❑ 61T Mitch Lyden RC	.25	.07
❑ 62T J.T. Snow	.50	.15
❑ 63T Damon Buford	.10	.03
❑ 64T Gene Harris	.10	.03
❑ 65T Randy Myers	.10	.03
❑ 66T Felix Jose	.10	.03
❑ 67T Todd Dunn USA RC	.25	.07
❑ 68T Jimmy Key	.20	.06
❑ 69T Pedro Castellano	.10	.03
❑ 70T Mark Merila USA RC	.25	.07
❑ 71T Rich Rodriguez	.10	.03
❑ 72T Matt Mieske	.10	.03
❑ 73T Pete Incaviglia	.10	.03
❑ 74T Carl Everett	.20	.06
❑ 75T Jim Abbott	.50	.15
❑ 76T Luis Aquino	.10	.03
❑ 77T Rene Arocha	.20	.06
❑ 78T Jon Shave	.10	.03
❑ 79T Todd Walker USA RC	2.00	.60
❑ 80T Jack Armstrong	.10	.03
❑ 81T Jeff Richardson	.10	.03
❑ 82T Blas Minor	.10	.03
❑ 83T Dave Winfield	.30	.09
❑ 84T Paul O'Neill	.30	.09
❑ 85T Steve Reich USA RC	.25	.07
❑ 86T Chris Hammond	.10	.03
❑ 87T Hilly Hathaway RC	.25	.07
❑ 88T Fred McGriff	.30	.09
❑ 89T Dave Telgheder RC	.25	.07
❑ 90T Richie Lewis RC	.25	.07
❑ 91T Brent Gates	.10	.03
❑ 92T Andre Dawson	.20	.06
❑ 93T Andy Barkett USA RC	.25	.07
❑ 94T Doug Drabek	.10	.03
❑ 95T Joe Klink	.10	.03
❑ 96T Willie Blair	.10	.03
❑ 97T D.Graves USA RC	.50	.15
❑ 98T Pat Meares RC	.50	.15
❑ 99T Mike Lansing RC	.50	.15
❑ 100T Marcos Armas RC	.25	.07
❑ 101T D.Grass RC USA	.25	.07
❑ 102T Chris Jones	.10	.03
❑ 103T Ken Ryan RC	.25	.07

Card	Nm-Mt	Ex-Mt
104T Ellis Burks	.20	.06
105T Roberto Kelly	.10	.03
106T Dave Magadan	.10	.03
107T Paul Wilson USA RC	.50	.15
108T Rob Natal	.10	.03
109T Paul Wagner	.10	.03
110T Jeromy Burnitz	.20	.06
111T Monty Fariss	.10	.03
112T Kevin Mitchell	.10	.03
113T Scott Pose RC	.25	.07
114T Dave Stewart	.20	.06
115T R.Johnson USA RC	.25	.07
116T Armando Reynoso	.10	.03
117T Geronimo Berroa	.10	.03
118T Woody Williams RC	1.50	.45
119T Tim Bogar RC	.25	.07
120T Bob Scafa USA RC	.25	.07
121T Henry Cotto	.10	.03
122T Gregg Jefferies	.10	.03
123T Norm Charlton	.10	.03
124T B.Wagner USA RC	.25	.07
125T David Cone	.20	.06
126T Daryl Boston	.10	.03
127T Tim Wallach	.10	.03
128T Mike Martin USA RC	.25	.07
129T John Cummings RC	.25	.07
130T Ryan Bowen	.10	.03
131T John Powell USA RC	.25	.07
132T Checklist 1-132	.10	.03

1994 Topps

	Nm-Mt	Ex-Mt
COMPLETE SET (792)	50.00	15.00
COMP.FACT.SET (808)	60.00	18.00
COMP.BAKER SET (818)	60.00	18.00
COMP. SERIES 1 (396)	25.00	7.50
COMP. SERIES 2 (396)	25.00	7.50

Card	Nm-Mt	Ex-Mt
1 Mike Piazza	1.00	.30
2 Bernie Williams	.30	.09
3 Kevin Rogers	.10	.03
4 Paul Carey	.10	.03
5 Ozzie Guillen	.10	.03
6 Derrick May	.10	.03
7 Jose Mesa	.10	.03
8 Todd Hundley	.10	.03
9 Chris Haney	.10	.03
10 John Olerud	.20	.06
11 Andujar Cedeno	.10	.03
12 John Smiley	.10	.03
13 Phil Plantier	.10	.03
14 Willie Banks	.10	.03
15 Jay Bell	.20	.06
16 Doug Henry	.10	.03
17 Lance Blankenship	.10	.03
18 Greg W. Harris	.10	.03
19 Scott Livingstone	.10	.03
20 Bryan Harvey	.10	.03
21 Wil Cordero	.10	.03
22 Roger Pavlik	.10	.03
23 Mark Lemke	.10	.03
24 Jeff Nelson	.10	.03
25 Todd Zeile	.10	.03
26 Billy Hatcher	.10	.03
27 Joe Magrane	.10	.03
28 Tony Longmire	.10	.03
29 Omar Daal	.10	.03
30 Kirt Manwaring	.10	.03
31 Melido Perez	.10	.03
32 Tim Hulett	.10	.03
33 Jeff Schwarz	.10	.03
34 Nolan Ryan	2.00	.60
35 Jose Guzman	.10	.03
36 Felix Fermin	.10	.03
37 Jeff Innis	.10	.03
38 Brett Mayne	.10	.03
39 Huck Flener RC	.10	.03
40 Jeff Bagwell	.30	.09
41 Kevin Wickander	.10	.03
42 Ricky Gutierrez	.10	.03
43 Pat Mahomes	.10	.03
44 Jeff King	.10	.03
45 Cal Eldred	.10	.03
46 Craig Paquette	.10	.03
47 Richie Lewis	.10	.03
48 Tony Phillips	.10	.03
49 Armando Reynoso	.10	.03
50 Moises Alou	.20	.06
51 Manuel Lee	.10	.03
52 Otis Nixon	.10	.03
53 Billy Ashley	.10	.03
54 Mark Whiten	.10	.03
55 Jeff Russell	.10	.03
56 Chad Curtis	.10	.03
57 Kevin Stocker	.10	.03
58 Mike Jackson	.10	.03
59 Matt Nokes	.10	.03
60 Chris Bosio	.10	.03
61 Damon Buford	.10	.03
62 Tim Belcher	.10	.03
63 Glenallen Hill	.10	.03
64 Bill Wertz	.10	.03
65 Eddie Murray	.50	.15
66 Tom Gordon	.10	.03
67 Alex Gonzalez	.10	.03
68 Eddie Taubensee	.10	.03
69 Jacob Brumfield	.10	.03
70 Andy Benes	.10	.03
71 Rich Becker	.10	.03
72 Steve Cooke	.10	.03
73 Billy Spiers	.10	.03
74 Scott Brosius	.20	.06
75 Alan Trammell	.30	.09
76 Luis Aquino	.10	.03
77 Jerald Clark	.10	.03
78 Mel Rojas	.10	.03
79 Billy Masse Stanton Cameron Tim Clark Craig McClure RC	.10	.03
80 Jose Canseco	.50	.15
81 Greg McMichael	.10	.03
82 Brian Turang RC	.10	.03
83 Tom Urbani	.10	.03
84 Garret Anderson	.50	.15
85 Tony Pena	.10	.03
86 Ricky Jordan	.10	.03
87 Jim Gott	.10	.03
88 Pat Kelly	.10	.03
89 Bud Black	.10	.03
90 Robin Ventura	.20	.06
91 Rick Sutcliffe	.20	.06
92 Jose Bautista	.10	.03
93 Bob Ojeda	.10	.03
94 Phil Hiatt	.10	.03
95 Tim Pugh	.10	.03
96 Randy Knorr	.10	.03
97 Todd Jones	.10	.03
98 Ryan Thompson	.10	.03
99 Tim Mauser	.10	.03
100 Kirby Puckett	.50	.15
101 Mark Dewey	.10	.03
102 B.J. Surhoff	.20	.06
103 Sterling Hitchcock	.10	.03
104 Alex Arias	.10	.03
105 David Wells	.20	.06
106 Daryl Boston	.10	.03
107 Mike Stanton	.10	.03
108 Gary Redus	.10	.03
109 Delino DeShields	.10	.03
110 Lee Smith	.20	.06
111 Greg Litton	.10	.03
112 Frankie Rodriguez	.10	.03
113 Russ Springer	.10	.03
114 Mitch Williams	.10	.03
115 Eric Karros	.20	.06
116 Jeff Brantley	.10	.03
117 Jack Voigt	.10	.03
118 Jason Bere	.10	.03
119 Kevin Roberson	.10	.03
120 Jimmy Key	.20	.06
121 Reggie Jefferson	.10	.03
122 Jeromy Burnitz	.20	.06
123 Billy Brewer	.10	.03
124 Willie Canate	.10	.03
125 Greg Swindell	.10	.03
126 Hal Morris	.10	.03
127 Brad Ausmus	.10	.03
128 George Tsamis	.10	.03
129 Denny Neagle	.20	.06
130 Pat Listach	.10	.03
131 Steve Karsay	.10	.03
132 Bret Barberie	.10	.03
133 Mark Leiter	.10	.03
134 Greg Colbrunn	.10	.03
135 David Nied	.10	.03
136 Dean Palmer	.20	.06
137 Steve Avery	.10	.03
138 Bill Haselman	.10	.03
139 Tripp Cromer	.10	.03
140 Frank Viola	.20	.06
141 Rene Gonzales	.10	.03
142 Curt Schilling	.30	.09
143 Tim Wallach	.10	.03
144 Bobby Munoz	.10	.03
145 Brady Anderson	.20	.06
146 Rod Beck	.10	.03
147 Mike LaValliere	.10	.03
148 Greg Hibbard	.10	.03
149 Kenny Lofton	.20	.06
150 Dwight Gooden	.30	.09
151 Greg Gagne	.10	.03
152 Ray McDavid	.10	.03
153 Chris Donnels	.10	.03
154 Dan Wilson	.10	.03
155 Todd Stottlemyre	.10	.03
156 David McCarty	.10	.03
157 Paul Wagner	.10	.03
158 Orlando Miller Brandon Wilson Derek Jeter Mike Neal	1.50	.45
159 Mike Fetters	.10	.03
160 Scott Lydy	.10	.03
161 Darrell Whitmore	.10	.03
162 Bob MacDonald	.10	.03
163 Vinny Castilla	.20	.06
164 Denis Boucher	.10	.03
165 Ivan Rodriguez	.50	.15
166 Ron Gant	.20	.06
167 Tim Davis	.10	.03
168 Steve Dixon	.10	.03
169 Scott Fletcher	.10	.03
170 Terry Mulholland	.10	.03
171 Greg Myers	.10	.03
172 Brett Butler	.20	.06
173 Bob Wickman	.10	.03
174 Dave Martinez	.10	.03
175 Fernando Valenzuela	.20	.06
176 Craig Grebeck	.10	.03
177 Shawn Boskie	.10	.03
178 Albie Lopez	.10	.03
179 Butch Huskey	.10	.03
180 George Brett	1.25	.35
181 Juan Guzman	.10	.03
182 Eric Anthony	.10	.03
183 Rob Dibble	.20	.06
184 Craig Shipley	.10	.03
185 Kevin Tapani	.10	.03
186 Marcus Moore	.10	.03
187 Graeme Lloyd	.10	.03
188 Mike Bordick	.10	.03
189 Chris Hammond	.10	.03
190 Cecil Fielder	.20	.06
191 Curt Leskanic	.10	.03
192 Lou Frazier	.10	.03
193 Steve Dreyer RC	.10	.03
194 Javier Lopez	.20	.06
195 Edgar Martinez	.30	.09

❑ 196 Allen Watson	.10	.03
❑ 197 John Flaherty	.10	.03
❑ 198 Kurt Stillwell	.10	.03
❑ 199 Danny Jackson	.10	.03
❑ 200 Cal Ripken	1.50	.45
❑ 201 Mike Bell FDP RC	.10	.03
❑ 202 Alan Benes FDP RC	.25	.07
❑ 203 Matt Farner FDP RC	.10	.03
❑ 204 Jeff Granger	.10	.03
❑ 205 B.Kieschnick FDP RC	.25	.07
❑ 206 Jeremy Lee FDP RC	.10	.03
❑ 207 C.Peterson FDP RC	.10	.03
❑ 208 Alan Rice FDP RC	.10	.03
❑ 209 Billy Wagner FDP RC	.50	.15
❑ 210 Kelly Wunsch FDP RC	.25	.07
❑ 211 Tom Candiotti	.10	.03
❑ 212 Domingo Jean	.10	.03
❑ 213 John Burkett	.10	.03
❑ 214 George Bell	.10	.03
❑ 215 Dan Plesac	.10	.03
❑ 216 Manny Ramirez	.30	.09
❑ 217 Mike Maddux	.10	.03
❑ 218 Kevin McReynolds	.10	.03
❑ 219 Pat Borders	.10	.03
❑ 220 Doug Drabek	.10	.03
❑ 221 Larry Luebbers RC	.10	.03
❑ 222 Trevor Hoffman	.20	.06
❑ 223 Pat Meares	.10	.03
❑ 224 Danny Miceli	.10	.03
❑ 225 Greg Vaughn	.20	.06
❑ 226 Scott Hemond	.10	.03
❑ 227 Pat Rapp	.10	.03
❑ 228 Kirk Gibson	.20	.06
❑ 229 Lance Painter	.10	.03
❑ 230 Larry Walker	.30	.09
❑ 231 Benji Gil	.10	.03
❑ 232 Mark Wohlers	.10	.03
❑ 233 Rich Amaral	.10	.03
❑ 234 Eric Pappas	.10	.03
❑ 235 Scott Cooper	.10	.03
❑ 236 Mike Butcher	.10	.03
❑ 237 Curtis Pride Shawn Green Mark Sweeney Eddie Davis	.50	.15
❑ 238 Kim Batiste	.10	.03
❑ 239 Paul Assenmacher	.10	.03
❑ 240 Will Clark	.50	.15
❑ 241 Jose Offerman	.10	.03
❑ 242 Todd Frohwirth	.10	.03
❑ 243 Tim Raines	.20	.06
❑ 244 Rick Wilkins	.10	.03
❑ 245 Bret Saberhagen	.20	.06
❑ 246 Thomas Howard	.10	.03
❑ 247 Stan Belinda	.10	.03
❑ 248 Rickey Henderson	.75	.23
❑ 249 Brian Williams	.10	.03
❑ 250 Barry Larkin	.50	.15
❑ 251 Jose Valentin	.10	.03
❑ 252 Lenny Webster	.10	.03
❑ 253 Blas Minor	.10	.03
❑ 254 Tim Teufel	.10	.03
❑ 255 Bobby Witt	.10	.03
❑ 256 Walt Weiss	.10	.03
❑ 257 Chad Kreuter	.10	.03
❑ 258 Roberto Mejia	.10	.03
❑ 259 Cliff Floyd	.20	.06
❑ 260 Julio Franco	.20	.06
❑ 261 Rafael Belliard	.10	.03
❑ 262 Marc Newfield	.10	.03
❑ 263 Gerald Perry	.10	.03
❑ 264 Ken Ryan	.10	.03
❑ 265 Chili Davis	.20	.06
❑ 266 Dave West	.10	.03
❑ 267 Royce Clayton	.10	.03
❑ 268 Pedro Martinez	.50	.15
❑ 269 Mark Hutton	.10	.03
❑ 270 Frank Thomas	.50	.15
❑ 271 Brad Pennington	.10	.03
❑ 272 Mike Harkey	.10	.03
❑ 273 Sandy Alomar Jr.	.10	.03
❑ 274 Dave Gallagher	.10	.03
❑ 275 Wally Joyner	.20	.06
❑ 276 Ricky Trlicek	.10	.03
❑ 277 Al Osuna	.10	.03
❑ 278 Pokey Reese	.10	.03
❑ 279 Kevin Higgins	.10	.03
❑ 280 Rick Aguilera	.10	.03
❑ 281 Orlando Merced	.10	.03
❑ 282 Mike Mohler	.10	.03
❑ 283 John Jaha	.10	.03
❑ 284 Robb Nen	.20	.06
❑ 285 Travis Fryman	.20	.06
❑ 286 Mark Thompson	.10	.03
❑ 287 Mike Lansing	.10	.03
❑ 288 Craig Lefferts	.10	.03
❑ 289 Damon Berryhill	.10	.03
❑ 290 Randy Johnson	.50	.15
❑ 291 Jeff Reed	.10	.03
❑ 292 Danny Darwin	.10	.03
❑ 293 J.T. Snow	.20	.06
❑ 294 Tyler Green	.10	.03
❑ 295 Chris Hoiles	.10	.03
❑ 296 Roger McDowell	.10	.03
❑ 297 Spike Owen	.10	.03
❑ 298 Salomon Torres	.10	.03
❑ 299 Wilson Alvarez	.10	.03
❑ 300 Ryne Sandberg	.75	.23
❑ 301 Derek Lilliquist	.10	.03
❑ 302 Howard Johnson	.10	.03
❑ 303 Greg Cadaret	.10	.03
❑ 304 Pat Hentgen	.10	.03
❑ 305 Craig Biggio	.30	.09
❑ 306 Scott Service	.10	.03
❑ 307 Melvin Nieves	.10	.03
❑ 308 Mike Trombley	.10	.03
❑ 309 Carlos Garcia	.10	.03
❑ 310 Robin Yount UER (listed with 111 triples in 1988; should be 11)	.50	.15
❑ 311 Marcos Armas	.10	.03
❑ 312 Rich Rodriguez	.10	.03
❑ 313 Justin Thompson	.10	.03
❑ 314 Danny Sheaffer	.10	.03
❑ 315 Ken Hill	.10	.03
❑ 316 Chad Ogea Duff Brumley Terrell Wade RC Chris Michalak	.10	.03
❑ 317 Cris Carpenter	.10	.03
❑ 318 Jeff Blauser	.10	.03
❑ 319 Ted Power	.10	.03
❑ 320 Ozzie Smith	.50	.15
❑ 321 John Dopson	.10	.03
❑ 322 Chris Turner	.10	.03
❑ 323 Pete Incaviglia	.10	.03
❑ 324 Alan Mills	.10	.03
❑ 325 Jody Reed	.10	.03
❑ 326 Rich Monteleone	.10	.03
❑ 327 Mark Carreon	.10	.03
❑ 328 Donn Pall	.10	.03
❑ 329 Matt Walbeck	.10	.03
❑ 330 Charles Nagy	.10	.03
❑ 331 Jeff McKnight	.10	.03
❑ 332 Jose Lind	.10	.03
❑ 333 Mike Timlin	.10	.03
❑ 334 Doug Jones	.10	.03
❑ 335 Kevin Mitchell	.10	.03
❑ 336 Luis Lopez	.10	.03
❑ 337 Shane Mack	.10	.03
❑ 338 Randy Tomlin	.10	.03
❑ 339 Matt Mieske	.10	.03
❑ 340 Mark McGwire	1.25	.35
❑ 341 Nigel Wilson	.10	.03
❑ 342 Danny Gladden	.10	.03
❑ 343 Mo Sanford	.10	.03
❑ 344 Sean Berry	.10	.03
❑ 345 Kevin Brown	.20	.06
❑ 346 Greg Olson	.10	.03
❑ 347 Dave Magadan	.10	.03
❑ 348 Rene Arocha	.10	.03
❑ 349 Carlos Quintana	.10	.03
❑ 350 Jim Abbott	.50	.15
❑ 351 Gary DiSarcina	.10	.03
❑ 352 Ben Rivera	.10	.03
❑ 353 Carlos Hernandez	.10	.03
❑ 354 Darren Lewis	.10	.03
❑ 355 Harold Reynolds	.20	.06
❑ 356 Scott Ruffcorn	.10	.03
❑ 357 Mark Gubicza	.10	.03
❑ 358 Paul Sorrento	.10	.03
❑ 359 Anthony Young	.10	.03
❑ 360 Mark Grace	.50	.15
❑ 361 Rob Butler	.10	.03
❑ 362 Kevin Bass	.10	.03
❑ 363 Eric Helfand	.10	.03
❑ 364 Derek Bell	.10	.03
❑ 365 Scott Erickson	.10	.03
❑ 366 Al Martin	.10	.03
❑ 367 Ricky Bones	.10	.03
❑ 368 Jeff Branson	.10	.03
❑ 369 Luis Ortiz David Bell RC Jason Giambi George Arias	.75	.23
❑ 370 Benito Santiago (See also 379)	.20	.06
❑ 371 John Doherty	.10	.03
❑ 372 Joe Girardi	.10	.03
❑ 373 Tim Scott	.10	.03
❑ 374 Marvin Freeman	.10	.03
❑ 375 Deion Sanders	.20	.06
❑ 376 Roger Salkeld	.10	.03
❑ 377 Bernard Gilkey	.10	.03
❑ 378 Tony Fossas	.10	.03
❑ 379 Mark McLemore UER (Card number is 370)	.10	.03
❑ 380 Darren Daulton	.20	.06
❑ 381 Chuck Finley	.20	.06
❑ 382 Mitch Webster	.10	.03
❑ 383 Gerald Williams	.10	.03
❑ 384 Frank Thomas AS Fred McGriff AS	.30	.09
❑ 385 Roberto Alomar AS Robby Thompson AS	.20	.06
❑ 386 Wade Boggs AS Matt Williams AS	.20	.06
❑ 387 Cal Ripken AS Jeff Blauser AS	.50	.15
❑ 388 Ken Griffey Jr. AS Len Dykstra AS	.50	.15
❑ 389 Juan Gonzalez AS David Justice AS	.30	.09
❑ 390 George Belle AS Bobby Bonds AS	.60	.18
❑ 391 Mike Stanley AS Mike Piazza AS	.50	.15
❑ 392 Jack McDowell AS Greg Maddux AS	.30	.09
❑ 393 Jimmy Key AS Tom Glavine AS	.20	.06
❑ 394 Jeff Montgomery AS Randy Myers AS	.10	.03
❑ 395 Checklist 1-198	.10	.03
❑ 396 Checklist 199-396	.10	.03
❑ 397 Tim Salmon	.30	.09
❑ 398 Todd Benzinger	.10	.03
❑ 399 Frank Castillo	.10	.03
❑ 400 Ken Griffey Jr.	.75	.23
❑ 401 John Kruk	.20	.06
❑ 402 Dave Telgheder	.10	.03
❑ 403 Gary Gaetti	.20	.06
❑ 404 Jim Edmonds	.30	.09
❑ 405 Don Slaught	.10	.03
❑ 406 Jose Oquendo	.10	.03
❑ 407 Bruce Ruffin	.10	.03
❑ 408 Phil Clark	.10	.03
❑ 409 Joe Klink	.10	.03
❑ 410 Lou Whitaker	.20	.06
❑ 411 Kevin Seitzer	.10	.03
❑ 412 Darrin Fletcher	.10	.03
❑ 413 Kenny Rogers	.20	.06
❑ 414 Bill Pecota	.10	.03
❑ 415 Dave Fleming	.10	.03
❑ 416 Luis Alicea	.10	.03
❑ 417 Paul Quantrill	.10	.03
❑ 418 Damion Easley	.10	.03
❑ 419 Wes Chamberlain	.10	.03
❑ 420 Harold Baines	.20	.06
❑ 421 Scott Radinsky	.10	.03
❑ 422 Rey Sanchez	.10	.03
❑ 423 Junior Ortiz	.10	.03
❑ 424 Jeff Kent	.20	.06
❑ 425 Brian McRae	.10	.03
❑ 426 Ed Sprague	.10	.03
❑ 427 Tom Edens	.10	.03
❑ 428 Willie Greene	.10	.03
❑ 429 Bryan Hickerson	.10	.03

❑ 430 Dave Winfield .30 .09
❑ 431 Pedro Astacio .10 .03
❑ 432 Mike Gallego .10 .03
❑ 433 Dave Burba .10 .03
❑ 434 Bob Walk .10 .03
❑ 435 Darryl Hamilton .10 .03
❑ 436 Vince Horsman .10 .03
❑ 437 Bob Natal .10 .03
❑ 438 Mike Henneman .10 .03
❑ 439 Willie Blair .10 .03
❑ 440 Dennis Martinez .20 .06
❑ 441 Dan Peltier .10 .03
❑ 442 Tony Tarasco .10 .03
❑ 443 John Cummings .10 .03
❑ 444 Geronimo Pena .10 .03
❑ 445 Aaron Sele .10 .03
❑ 446 Stan Javier .10 .03
❑ 447 Mike Williams .10 .03
❑ 448 Greg Pirkl .10 .03
Roberto Petagine
D.J.Boston
Shawn Wooten RC
❑ 449 Jim Poole .10 .03
❑ 450 Carlos Baerga .10 .03
❑ 451 Bob Scanlan .10 .03
❑ 452 Lance Johnson .10 .03
❑ 453 Eric Hillman .10 .03
❑ 454 Keith Miller .10 .03
❑ 455 Dave Stewart .20 .06
❑ 456 Pete Harnisch .10 .03
❑ 457 Roberto Kelly .10 .03
❑ 458 Tim Worrell .10 .03
❑ 459 Pedro Munoz .10 .03
❑ 460 Orel Hershiser .20 .06
❑ 461 Randy Velarde .10 .03
❑ 462 Trevor Wilson .10 .03
❑ 463 Jerry Goff .10 .03
❑ 464 Bill Wegman .10 .03
❑ 465 Dennis Eckersley .20 .06
❑ 466 Jeff Conine .20 .06
❑ 467 Joe Boever .10 .03
❑ 468 Dante Bichette .20 .06
❑ 469 Jeff Shaw .10 .03
❑ 470 Rafael Palmeiro .30 .09
❑ 471 Phil Leftwich RC .10 .03
❑ 472 Jay Buhner .20 .06
❑ 473 Bob Tewksbury .10 .03
❑ 474 Tim Naehring .10 .03
❑ 475 Tom Glavine .50 .15
❑ 476 Dave Hollins .10 .03
❑ 477 Arthur Rhodes .10 .03
❑ 478 Joey Cora .10 .03
❑ 479 Mike Morgan .10 .03
❑ 480 Albert Belle .20 .06
❑ 481 John Franco .20 .06
❑ 482 Hipolito Pichardo .10 .03
❑ 483 Duane Ward .10 .03
❑ 484 Luis Gonzalez .20 .06
❑ 485 Joe Oliver .10 .03
❑ 486 Wally Whitehurst .10 .03
❑ 487 Mike Benjamin .10 .03
❑ 488 Eric Davis .20 .06
❑ 489 Scott Kamieniecki .10 .03
❑ 490 Kent Hrbek .20 .06
❑ 491 John Hope RC .10 .03
❑ 492 Jesse Orosco .10 .03
❑ 493 Troy Neel .10 .03
❑ 494 Ryan Bowen .10 .03
❑ 495 Mickey Tettleton .10 .03
❑ 496 Chris Jones .10 .03
❑ 497 John Wetteland .20 .06
❑ 498 David Hulse .10 .03
❑ 499 Greg Maddux 1.00 .30
❑ 500 Bo Jackson .50 .15
❑ 501 Donovan Osborne .10 .03
❑ 502 Mike Greenwell .10 .03
❑ 503 Steve Frey .10 .03
❑ 504 Jim Eisenreich .10 .03
❑ 505 Robby Thompson .10 .03
❑ 506 Leo Gomez .10 .03
❑ 507 Dave Staton .10 .03
❑ 508 Wayne Kirby .10 .03
❑ 509 Tim Bogar .10 .03
❑ 510 David Cone .20 .06
❑ 511 Devon White .10 .03
❑ 512 Xavier Hernandez .10 .03
❑ 513 Tim Costo .10 .03
❑ 514 Gene Harris .10 .03
❑ 515 Jack McDowell .10 .03
❑ 516 Kevin Gross .10 .03
❑ 517 Scott Leius .10 .03
❑ 518 Lloyd McClendon .10 .03
❑ 519 Alex Diaz RC .10 .03
❑ 520 Wade Boggs .30 .09
❑ 521 Bob Welch .10 .03
❑ 522 Henry Cotto .10 .03
❑ 523 Mike Moore .10 .03
❑ 524 Tim Laker .10 .03
❑ 525 Andres Galarraga .20 .06
❑ 526 Jamie Moyer .20 .06
❑ 527 Norberto Martin .10 .03
Ruben Santana
Jason Hardtke
Chris Sexton RC
❑ 528 Sid Bream .10 .03
❑ 529 Erik Hanson .10 .03
❑ 530 Ray Lankford .10 .03
❑ 531 Rob Deer .10 .03
❑ 532 Rod Correia .10 .03
❑ 533 Roger Mason .10 .03
❑ 534 Mike Devereaux .10 .03
❑ 535 Jeff Montgomery .10 .03
❑ 536 Dwight Smith .10 .03
❑ 537 Jeremy Hernandez .10 .03
❑ 538 Ellis Burks .20 .06
❑ 539 Bobby Jones .10 .03
❑ 540 Paul Molitor .30 .09
❑ 541 Jeff Juden .10 .03
❑ 542 Chris Sabo .10 .03
❑ 543 Larry Casian .10 .03
❑ 544 Jeff Gardner .10 .03
❑ 545 Ramon Martinez .10 .03
❑ 546 Paul O'Neill .30 .09
❑ 547 Steve Hosey .10 .03
❑ 548 Dave Nilsson .10 .03
❑ 549 Ron Darling .10 .03
❑ 550 Matt Williams .20 .06
❑ 551 Jack Armstrong .10 .03
❑ 552 Bill Krueger .10 .03
❑ 553 Freddie Benavides .10 .03
❑ 554 Jeff Fassero .10 .03
❑ 555 Chuck Knoblauch .20 .06
❑ 556 Guillermo Velasquez .10 .03
❑ 557 Joel Johnston .10 .03
❑ 558 Tom Lampkin .10 .03
❑ 559 Todd Van Poppel .10 .03
❑ 560 Gary Sheffield .20 .06
❑ 561 Skeeter Barnes .10 .03
❑ 562 Darren Holmes .10 .03
❑ 563 John Vander Wal .10 .03
❑ 564 Mike Ignasiak .10 .03
❑ 565 Fred McGriff .30 .09
❑ 566 Luis Polonia .10 .03
❑ 567 Mike Perez .10 .03
❑ 568 John Valentin .10 .03
❑ 569 Mike Felder .10 .03
❑ 570 Tommy Greene .10 .03
❑ 571 David Segui .10 .03
❑ 572 Roberto Hernandez .10 .03
❑ 573 Steve Wilson .10 .03
❑ 574 Willie McGee .20 .06
❑ 575 Randy Myers .10 .03
❑ 576 Darrin Jackson .10 .03
❑ 577 Eric Plunk .10 .03
❑ 578 Mike Macfarlane .10 .03
❑ 579 Doug Brocail .10 .03
❑ 580 Steve Finley .20 .06
❑ 581 John Roper .10 .03
❑ 582 Danny Cox .10 .03
❑ 583 Chip Hale .10 .03
❑ 584 Scott Bullett .10 .03
❑ 585 Kevin Reimer .10 .03
❑ 586 Brent Gates .10 .03
❑ 587 Matt Turner .10 .03
❑ 588 Rich Rowland .10 .03
❑ 589 Kent Bottenfield .10 .03
❑ 590 Marquis Grissom .10 .03
❑ 591 Doug Strange .10 .03
❑ 592 Jay Howell .10 .03
❑ 593 Omar Vizquel .20 .06
❑ 594 Rheal Cormier .10 .03
❑ 595 Andre Dawson .20 .06
❑ 596 Hilly Hathaway .10 .03
❑ 597 Todd Pratt .10 .03
❑ 598 Mike Mussina .50 .15
❑ 599 Alex Fernandez .10 .03
❑ 600 Don Mattingly 1.25 .35
❑ 601 Frank Thomas MOG .30 .09
❑ 602 Ryne Sandberg MOG .50 .15
❑ 603 Wade Boggs MOG .20 .06
❑ 604 Cal Ripken MOG .75 .23
❑ 605 Barry Bonds MOG .60 .18
❑ 606 Ken Griffey Jr. MOG .50 .15
❑ 607 Kirby Puckett MOG .30 .09
❑ 608 Darren Daulton MOG .10 .03
❑ 609 Paul Molitor MOG .20 .06
❑ 610 Terry Steinbach .10 .03
❑ 611 Todd Worrell .10 .03
❑ 612 Jim Thome .50 .15
❑ 613 Chuck McElroy .10 .03
❑ 614 John Habyan .10 .03
❑ 615 Sid Fernandez .10 .03
❑ 616 Eddie Zambrano .10 .03
Glenn Murray
Chad Mottola
Jermaine Allensworth RC
❑ 617 Steve Bedrosian .10 .03
❑ 618 Rob Ducey .10 .03
❑ 619 Tom Browning .10 .03
❑ 620 Tony Gwynn .60 .18
❑ 621 Carl Willis .10 .03
❑ 622 Kevin Young .10 .03
❑ 623 Rafael Novoa .10 .03
❑ 624 Jerry Browne .10 .03
❑ 625 Charlie Hough .20 .06
❑ 626 Chris Gomez .10 .03
❑ 627 Steve Reed .10 .03
❑ 628 Kirk Rueter .20 .06
❑ 629 Matt Whiteside .10 .03
❑ 630 David Justice .20 .06
❑ 631 Brad Holman .10 .03
❑ 632 Brian Jordan .20 .06
❑ 633 Scott Bankhead .10 .03
❑ 634 Torey Lovullo .10 .03
❑ 635 Len Dykstra .20 .06
❑ 636 Ben McDonald .10 .03
❑ 637 Steve Howe .10 .03
❑ 638 Jose Vizcaino .10 .03
❑ 639 Bill Swift .10 .03
❑ 640 Darryl Strawberry .30 .09
❑ 641 Steve Farr .10 .03
❑ 642 Tom Kramer .10 .03
❑ 643 Joe Orsulak .10 .03
❑ 644 Tom Henke .10 .03
❑ 645 Joe Carter .20 .06
❑ 646 Ken Caminiti .20 .06
❑ 647 Reggie Sanders .20 .06
❑ 648 Andy Ashby .10 .03
❑ 649 Derek Parks .10 .03
❑ 650 Andy Van Slyke .20 .06
❑ 651 Juan Bell .10 .03
❑ 652 Roger Smithberg .10 .03
❑ 653 Chuck Carr .10 .03
❑ 654 Bill Gullickson .10 .03
❑ 655 Charlie Hayes .10 .03
❑ 656 Chris Nabholz .10 .03
❑ 657 Karl Rhodes .10 .03
❑ 658 Pete Smith .10 .03
❑ 659 Bret Boone .20 .06
❑ 660 Gregg Jefferies .10 .03
❑ 661 Bob Zupcic .10 .03
❑ 662 Steve Sax .10 .03
❑ 663 Mariano Duncan .10 .03
❑ 664 Jeff Tackett .10 .03
❑ 665 Mark Langston .10 .03
❑ 666 Steve Buechele .10 .03
❑ 667 Candy Maldonado .10 .03
❑ 668 Woody Williams .20 .06
❑ 669 Tim Wakefield .20 .06
❑ 670 Danny Tartabull .10 .03
❑ 671 Charlie O'Brien .10 .03
❑ 672 Felix Jose .10 .03
❑ 673 Bobby Ayala .10 .03
❑ 674 Scott Servais .10 .03
❑ 675 Roberto Alomar .50 .15
❑ 676 Pedro A.Martinez RC .10 .03
❑ 677 Eddie Guardado .20 .06
❑ 678 Mark Lewis .10 .03

❑ 679 Jaime Navarro .10 .03
❑ 680 Ruben Sierra .10 .03
❑ 681 Rick Renteria .10 .03
❑ 682 Storm Davis .10 .03
❑ 683 Cory Snyder .10 .03
❑ 684 Ron Karkovice .10 .03
❑ 685 Juan Gonzalez .50 .15
❑ 686 Chris Howard .30 .09
Carlos Delgado
Jason Kendall
Paul Bako
❑ 687 John Smoltz .30 .09
❑ 688 Brian Dorsett .10 .03
❑ 689 Omar Olivares .10 .03
❑ 690 Mo Vaughn .20 .06
❑ 691 Joe Grahe .10 .03
❑ 692 Mickey Morandini .10 .03
❑ 693 Tino Martinez .30 .09
❑ 694 Brian Barnes .10 .03
❑ 695 Mike Stanley .10 .03
❑ 696 Mark Clark .10 .03
❑ 697 Dave Hansen .10 .03
❑ 698 Willie Wilson .10 .03
❑ 699 Pete Schourek .10 .03
❑ 700 Barry Bonds 1.25 .35
❑ 701 Kevin Appier .20 .06
❑ 702 Tony Fernandez .10 .03
❑ 703 Darryl Kile .20 .06
❑ 704 Archi Cianfrocco .10 .03
❑ 705 Jose Rijo .10 .03
❑ 706 Brian Harper .10 .03
❑ 707 Zane Smith .10 .03
❑ 708 Dave Henderson .10 .03
❑ 709 Angel Miranda UER .10 .03
(no Topps logo on back)
❑ 710 Orestes Destrade .10 .03
❑ 711 Greg Gohr .10 .03
❑ 712 Eric Young .10 .03
❑ 713 Todd Williams .10 .03
Ron Watson
Kirk Bullinger
Mike Welch
❑ 714 Tim Spehr .10 .03
❑ 715 Hank Aaron 715 HR .50 .15
❑ 716 Nate Minchey .10 .03
❑ 717 Mike Blowers .10 .03
❑ 718 Kent Mercker .10 .03
❑ 719 Tom Pagnozzi .10 .03
❑ 720 Roger Clemens 1.00 .30
❑ 721 Eduardo Perez .10 .03
❑ 722 Milt Thompson .10 .03
❑ 723 Gregg Olson .10 .03
❑ 724 Kirk McCaskill .10 .03
❑ 725 Sammy Sosa .75 .23
❑ 726 Alvaro Espinoza .10 .03
❑ 727 Henry Rodriguez .10 .03
❑ 728 Jim Leyritz .10 .03
❑ 729 Steve Scarsone .10 .03
❑ 730 Bobby Bonilla .20 .06
❑ 731 Chris Gwynn .10 .03
❑ 732 Al Leiter .20 .06
❑ 733 Bip Roberts .10 .03
❑ 734 Mark Portugal .10 .03
❑ 735 Terry Pendleton .20 .06
❑ 736 Dave Valle .10 .03
❑ 737 Paul Kilgus .10 .03
❑ 738 Greg A. Harris .10 .03
❑ 739 Jon Ratliff DP RC .10 .03
❑ 740 Kirk Presley DP RC .10 .03
❑ 741 Josue Estrada DP RC .10 .03
❑ 742 Wayne Gomes DP RC .10 .03
❑ 743 Pat Watkins DP RC .10 .03
❑ 744 Jamey Wright DP RC .25 .07
❑ 745 Jay Powell DP RC .10 .03
❑ 746 Ryan McGuire DP RC .10 .03
❑ 747 Marc Barcelo DP RC .10 .03
❑ 748 Sloan Smith DP RC .10 .03
❑ 749 John Wasdin DP RC .10 .03
❑ 750 Marc Vlades DP .10 .03
❑ 751 Dan Ehler DP RC .10 .03
❑ 752 Andre King DP RC .10 .03
❑ 753 Greg Keagle DP RC .10 .03
❑ 754 Jason Myers DP RC .10 .03
❑ 755 Dax Winslett DP RC .10 .03
❑ 756 Casey Whitten DP RC .10 .03
❑ 757 Tony Fuduric DP RC .10 .03
❑ 758 Greg Norton DP RC .25 .07
❑ 759 Jeff D'Amico DP RC .25 .07
❑ 760 Ryan Hancock DP RC .10 .03
❑ 761 David Cooper DP RC .10 .03
❑ 762 Kevin Orie DP RC .10 .03
❑ 763 John O'Donoghue .10 .03
Mike Oquist
❑ 764 Cory Bailey RC .10 .03
Scott Hatteberg
❑ 765 Mark Holzemer .10 .03
Paul Swingle RC
❑ 766 James Baldwin .10 .03
Rod Bolton
❑ 767 Jerry Di Poto .25 .07
Julian Tavarez RC
❑ 768 Danny Bautista .10 .03
Sean Bergman
❑ 769 Bob Hamelin .10 .03
Joe Vitiello
❑ 770 Mark Kiefer .10 .03
Troy O'Leary
❑ 771 Denny Hocking .10 .03
Oscar Munoz RC
❑ 772 Russ Davis .10 .03
Brien Taylor
❑ 773 Kyle Abbott RC .25 .07
Miguel Jimenez
❑ 774 Kevin King .10 .03
Eric Plantenberg RC
❑ 775 Jon Shave .10 .03
Desi Wilson
❑ 776 Domingo Cedeno .10 .03
Paul Spoljaric
❑ 777 Chipper Jones .50 .15
Ryan Klesko
❑ 778 Steve Trachsel .10 .03
Turk Wendell
❑ 779 Johnny Ruffin .10 .03
Jerry Spradlin RC
❑ 780 Jason Bates .10 .03
John Burke
❑ 781 Carl Everett .20 .06
Dave Weathers
❑ 782 Gary Mota .10 .03
James Mouton
❑ 783 Raul Mondesi .20 .06
Ben Van Ryn
❑ 784 Gabe White .20 .06
Rondell White
❑ 785 Brook Fordyce .20 .06
Bill Pulsipher
❑ 786 Kevin Foster RC .10 .03
Gene Schall
❑ 787 Rich Aude RC .10 .03
Midre Cummings
❑ 788 Brian Barber .10 .03
Rich Batchelor
❑ 789 Brian Johnson RC .10 .03
Scott Sanders
❑ 790 Ricky Faneyte .10 .03
J.R. Phillips
❑ 791 Checklist 3 .10 .03
❑ 792 Checklist 4 .10 .03

1994 Topps Traded

	Nm-Mt	Ex-Mt
COMP.FACT.SET (140)	40.00	12.00

❑ 1T Paul Wilson .10 .03
❑ 2T Bill Taylor RC 1.00 .30
❑ 3T Dan Wilson .10 .03
❑ 4T Mark Smith .10 .03
❑ 5T Toby Borland RC .25 .07
❑ 6T Dave Clark .10 .03
❑ 7T Dennis Martinez .20 .06
❑ 8T Dave Gallagher .10 .03
❑ 9T Josias Manzanillo .10 .03
❑ 10T Brian Anderson RC 1.00 .30
❑ 11T Damon Berryhill .10 .03
❑ 12T Alex Cole .10 .03
❑ 13T Jacob Shumate RC .25 .07
❑ 14T Oddibe McDowell .10 .03
❑ 15T Willie Banks .10 .03
❑ 16T Jerry Browne .10 .03
❑ 17T Donnie Elliott .10 .03
❑ 18T Ellis Burks .20 .06
❑ 19T Chuck McElroy .10 .03
❑ 20T Luis Polonia .10 .03
❑ 21T Brian Harper .10 .03
❑ 22T Mark Portugal .10 .03
❑ 23T Dave Henderson .10 .03
❑ 24T Mark Acre RC .25 .07
❑ 25T Julio Franco .20 .06
❑ 26T Darren Hall RC .25 .07
❑ 27T Eric Anthony .10 .03
❑ 28T Sid Fernandez .10 .03
❑ 29T Rusty Greer RC 1.50 .45
❑ 30T Riccardo Ingram RC .25 .07
❑ 31T Gabe White .10 .03
❑ 32T Tim Belcher .10 .03
❑ 33T Terrence Long RC 4.00 1.20
❑ 34T Mark Dalesandro RC .25 .07
❑ 35T Mike Kelly .10 .03
❑ 36T Jack Morris .20 .06
❑ 37T Jeff Brantley .10 .03
❑ 38T Larry Barnes RC .25 .07
❑ 39T Brian R. Hunter .10 .03
❑ 40T Otis Nixon .10 .03
❑ 41T Bret Wagner .10 .03
❑ 42T Pedro Martinez TR .50 .15
Delino Deshields
❑ 43T Heathcliff Slocumb .10 .03
❑ 44T Ben Grieve RC 1.50 .45
❑ 45T John Hudek RC .25 .07
❑ 46T Shawon Dunston .10 .03
❑ 47T Greg Colbrunn .10 .03
❑ 48T Joey Hamilton .10 .03
❑ 49T Marvin Freeman .10 .03
❑ 50T Terry Mulholland .10 .03
❑ 51T Keith Mitchell .10 .03
❑ 52T Dwight Smith .10 .03
❑ 53T Shawn Boskie .10 .03
❑ 54T Kevin Witt RC 1.00 .30
❑ 55T Ron Gant .20 .06
❑ 56T Trenidad Hubbard 10.00 3.00
Jason Schmidt RC
Larry Sutton
Stephen Larkin
❑ 57T Jody Reed .10 .03
❑ 58T Rick Helling .10 .03
❑ 59T John Powell .10 .03
❑ 60T Eddie Murray .50 .15
❑ 61T Joe Hall RC .25 .07
❑ 62T Jorge Fabregas .10 .03
❑ 63T Mike Mordecai RC .25 .07
❑ 64T Ed Vosberg .10 .03
❑ 65T Rickey Henderson 1.00 .30
❑ 66T Tim Grieve RC .25 .07
❑ 67T Jon Lieber .10 .03
❑ 68T Chris Howard .10 .03
❑ 69T Matt Walbeck .10 .03
❑ 70T Chan Ho Park RC 2.50 .75
❑ 71T Bryan Eversgerd RC .25 .07
❑ 72T John Dettmer .10 .03
❑ 73T Erik Hanson .10 .03
❑ 74T Mike Thurman RC .25 .07
❑ 75T Bobby Ayala .10 .03
❑ 76T Rafael Palmeiro .30 .09
❑ 77T Bret Boone .20 .06
❑ 78T Paul Shuey .10 .03
❑ 79T Kevin Foster RC .25 .07
❑ 80T Dave Magadan .10 .03
❑ 81T Bip Roberts .10 .03
❑ 82T Howard Johnson .10 .03

❑ 83T Xavier Hernandez .10 .03
❑ 84T Ross Powell RC .25 .07
❑ 85T Doug Million RC .25 .07
❑ 86T Geronimo Berroa .10 .03
❑ 87T Mark Farris RC .25 .07
❑ 88T Butch Henry .10 .03
❑ 89T Junior Felix .10 .03
❑ 90T Bo Jackson .50 .15
❑ 91T Hector Carrasco .10 .03
❑ 92T Charlie O'Brien .10 .03
❑ 93T Omar Vizquel .20 .06
❑ 94T David Segui .10 .03
❑ 95T Dustin Hermanson .20 .06
❑ 96T Gar Finnvold RC .25 .07
❑ 97T Dave Stevens .10 .03
❑ 98T Corey Pointer RC .25 .07
❑ 99T Felix Fermin .10 .03
❑ 100T Lee Smith .20 .06
❑ 101T Reid Ryan RC 1.00 .30
❑ 102T Bobby Munoz .10 .03
❑ 103T Deion Sanders TR .20 .06
Roberto Kelly
❑ 104T Turner Ward .10 .03
❑ 105T W.VanLandingham RC .25 .07
❑ 106T Vince Coleman .10 .03
❑ 107T Stan Javier .10 .03
❑ 108T Darrin Jackson .10 .03
❑ 109T C.J. Nitkowski RC .25 .07
❑ 110T Anthony Young .10 .03
❑ 111T Kurt Miller .10 .03
❑ 112T Paul Konerko RC 4.00 1.20
❑ 113T Walt Weiss .10 .03
❑ 114T Daryl Boston .10 .03
❑ 115T Will Clark .50 .15
❑ 116T Matt Smith RC .25 .07
❑ 117T Mark Leiter .10 .03
❑ 118T Gregg Olson .10 .03
❑ 119T Tony Pena .10 .03
❑ 120T Jose Vizcaino .10 .03
❑ 121T Rick White RC .25 .07
❑ 122T Rich Rowland .10 .03
❑ 123T Jeff Reboulet .10 .03
❑ 124T Greg Hibbard .10 .03
❑ 125T Chris Sabo .10 .03
❑ 126T Doug Jones .10 .03
❑ 127T Tony Fernandez .10 .03
❑ 128T Carlos Reyes RC .25 .07
❑ 129T Kevin L.Brown RC 1.00 .30
❑ 130T Ryne Sandberg 1.25 .35
Farewell
❑ 131T Ryne Sandberg 1.25 .35
Farewell
❑ 132T Checklist 1-132 .10 .03

1995 Topps

	Nm-Mt	Ex-Mt
COMPLETE SET (660)	80.00	24.00
COMP.HOBBY SET (677)	100.00	30.00
COMP.RETAIL SET (677)	100.00	30.00
COMP.SERIES 1 (396)	40.00	12.00
COMP.SERIES 2 (264)	40.00	12.00

❑ 1 Frank Thomas .75 .23
❑ 2 Mickey Morandini .15 .04
❑ 3 Babe Ruth 100th B-Day 2.00 .60
❑ 4 Scott Cooper .15 .04
❑ 5 David Cone .30 .09
❑ 6 Jacob Shumate .15 .04
❑ 7 Trevor Hoffman .30 .09
❑ 8 Shane Mack .15 .04
❑ 9 Delino DeShields .15 .04
❑ 10 Matt Williams .30 .09
❑ 11 Sammy Sosa 1.25 .35
❑ 12 Gary DiSarcina .15 .04
❑ 13 Kenny Rogers .30 .09
❑ 14 Jose Vizcaino .15 .04
❑ 15 Lou Whitaker .30 .09
❑ 16 Ron Darling .15 .04
❑ 17 Dave Nilsson .15 .04
❑ 18 Chris Hammond .15 .04
❑ 19 Sid Bream .15 .04
❑ 20 Denny Martinez .30 .09
❑ 21 Orlando Merced .15 .04
❑ 22 John Wetteland .30 .09
❑ 23 Mike Devereaux .15 .04
❑ 24 Rene Arocha .15 .04
❑ 25 Jay Buhner .30 .09
❑ 26 Darren Holmes .15 .04
❑ 27 Hal Morris .15 .04
❑ 28 Brian Buchanan RC .15 .04
❑ 29 Keith Miller .15 .04
❑ 30 Paul Molitor .50 .15
❑ 31 Dave West .15 .04
❑ 32 Tony Tarasco .15 .04
❑ 33 Scott Sanders .15 .04
❑ 34 Eddie Zambrano .15 .04
❑ 35 Ricky Bones .15 .04
❑ 36 John Valentin .15 .04
❑ 37 Kevin Tapani .15 .04
❑ 38 Tim Wallach .15 .04
❑ 39 Darren Lewis .15 .04
❑ 40 Travis Fryman .30 .09
❑ 41 Mark Leiter .15 .04
❑ 42 Jose Bautista .15 .04
❑ 43 Pete Smith .15 .04
❑ 44 Bret Barberie .15 .04
❑ 45 Dennis Eckersley .30 .09
❑ 46 Ken Hill .15 .04
❑ 47 Chad Ogea .15 .04
❑ 48 Pete Harnisch .15 .04
❑ 49 James Baldwin .15 .04
❑ 50 Mike Mussina .75 .23
❑ 51 Al Martin .15 .04
❑ 52 Mark Thompson .15 .04
❑ 53 Matt Smith .15 .04
❑ 54 Joey Hamilton .15 .04
❑ 55 Edgar Martinez .50 .15
❑ 56 John Smiley .15 .04
❑ 57 Rey Sanchez .15 .04
❑ 58 Mike Timlin .15 .04
❑ 59 Ricky Bottalico .15 .04
❑ 60 Jim Abbott .75 .23
❑ 61 Mike Kelly .15 .04
❑ 62 Brian Jordan .30 .09
❑ 63 Ken Ryan .15 .04
❑ 64 Matt Mieske .15 .04
❑ 65 Rick Aguilera .15 .04
❑ 66 Ismael Valdes .15 .04
❑ 67 Royce Clayton .15 .04
❑ 68 Junior Felix .15 .04
❑ 69 Harold Reynolds .30 .09
❑ 70 Juan Gonzalez .75 .23
❑ 71 Kelly Stinnett .15 .04
❑ 72 Carlos Reyes .15 .04
❑ 73 Dave Weathers .15 .04
❑ 74 Mel Rojas .15 .04
❑ 75 Doug Drabek .15 .04
❑ 76 Charles Nagy .15 .04
❑ 77 Tim Raines .30 .09
❑ 78 Midre Cummings .15 .04
❑ 79 Gene Schall .15 .04
Scott Talanoa
Harold Williams
Ray Brown RC
❑ 80 Rafael Palmeiro .50 .15
❑ 81 Charlie Hayes .15 .04
❑ 82 Ray Lankford .15 .04
❑ 83 Tim Davis .15 .04
❑ 84 C.J. Nitkowski .15 .04
❑ 85 Andy Ashby .15 .04
❑ 86 Gerald Williams .15 .04
❑ 87 Terry Shumpert .15 .04
❑ 88 Heathcliff Slocumb .15 .04
❑ 89 Domingo Cedeno .15 .04
❑ 90 Mark Grace .75 .23
❑ 91 Brad Woodall RC .15 .04
❑ 92 Gar Finnvold .15 .04
❑ 93 Jaime Navarro .15 .04
❑ 94 Carlos Hernandez .15 .04
❑ 95 Mark Langston .15 .04
❑ 96 Chuck Carr .15 .04
❑ 97 Mike Gardiner .15 .04
❑ 98 Dave McCarty .15 .04
❑ 99 Cris Carpenter .15 .04
❑ 100 Barry Bonds 2.00 .60
❑ 101 David Segui .15 .04
❑ 102 Scott Brosius .30 .09
❑ 103 Mariano Duncan .15 .04
❑ 104 Kenny Lofton .30 .09
❑ 105 Ken Caminiti .30 .09
❑ 106 Darrin Jackson .15 .04
❑ 107 Jim Poole .15 .04
❑ 108 Wil Cordero .15 .04
❑ 109 Danny Miceli .15 .04
❑ 110 Walt Weiss .15 .04
❑ 111 Tom Pagnozzi .15 .04
❑ 112 Terrence Long .30 .09
❑ 113 Bret Boone .30 .09
❑ 114 Daryl Boston .15 .04
❑ 115 Wally Joyner .30 .09
❑ 116 Rob Butler .15 .04
❑ 117 Rafael Belliard .15 .04
❑ 118 Luis Lopez .15 .04
❑ 119 Tony Fossas .15 .04
❑ 120 Len Dykstra .30 .09
❑ 121 Mike Morgan .15 .04
❑ 122 Denny Hocking .15 .04
❑ 123 Kevin Gross .15 .04
❑ 124 Todd Benzinger .15 .04
❑ 125 John Doherty .15 .04
❑ 126 Eduardo Perez .15 .04
❑ 127 Dan Smith .15 .04
❑ 128 Joe Orsulak .15 .04
❑ 129 Brent Gates .15 .04
❑ 130 Jeff Conine .30 .09
❑ 131 Doug Henry .15 .04
❑ 132 Paul Sorrento .15 .04
❑ 133 Mike Hampton .30 .09
❑ 134 Tim Spehr .15 .04
❑ 135 Julio Franco .30 .09
❑ 136 Mike Dyer .15 .04
❑ 137 Chris Sabo .15 .04
❑ 138 Rheal Cormier .15 .04
❑ 139 Paul Konerko .30 .09
❑ 140 Dante Bichette .30 .09
❑ 141 Chuck McElroy .15 .04
❑ 142 Mike Stanley .15 .04
❑ 143 Bob Hamelin .15 .04
❑ 144 Tommy Greene .15 .04
❑ 145 John Smoltz .50 .15
❑ 146 Ed Sprague .15 .04
❑ 147 Ray McDavid .15 .04
❑ 148 Otis Nixon .15 .04
❑ 149 Turk Wendell .15 .04
❑ 150 Chris James .15 .04
❑ 151 Derek Parks .15 .04
❑ 152 Jose Offerman .15 .04
❑ 153 Tony Clark .15 .04
❑ 154 Chad Curtis .15 .04
❑ 155 Mark Portugal .15 .04
❑ 156 Bill Pulsipher .15 .04
❑ 157 Troy Neel .15 .04
❑ 158 Dave Winfield .50 .15
❑ 159 Bill Wegman .15 .04
❑ 160 Benito Santiago .30 .09
❑ 161 Jose Mesa .15 .04
❑ 162 Luis Gonzalez .30 .09
❑ 163 Alex Fernandez .15 .04
❑ 164 Freddie Benavides .15 .04
❑ 165 Ben McDonald .15 .04
❑ 166 Blas Minor .15 .04
❑ 167 Bret Wagner .15 .04
❑ 168 Mac Suzuki .15 .04
❑ 169 Roberto Mejia .15 .04
❑ 170 Wade Boggs .50 .15
❑ 171 Pokey Reese .15 .04
❑ 172 Hipolito Pichardo .15 .04
❑ 173 Kim Batiste .15 .04
❑ 174 Darren Hall .15 .04

❑ 175 Tom Glavine .75 .23
❑ 176 Phil Plantier .15 .04
❑ 177 Chris Howard .15 .04
❑ 178 Karl Rhodes .15 .04
❑ 179 LaTroy Hawkins .15 .04
❑ 180 Raul Mondesi .30 .09
❑ 181 Jeff Reed .15 .04
❑ 182 Milt Cuyler .15 .04
❑ 183 Jim Edmonds .30 .09
❑ 184 Hector Fajardo .15 .04
❑ 185 Jeff Kent .30 .09
❑ 186 Wilson Alvarez .15 .04
❑ 187 Geronimo Berroa .15 .04
❑ 188 Billy Spiers .15 .04
❑ 189 Derek Lilliquist .15 .04
❑ 190 Craig Biggio .50 .15
❑ 191 Roberto Hernandez .15 .04
❑ 192 Bob Natal .15 .04
❑ 193 Bobby Ayala .15 .04
❑ 194 Travis Miller RC .15 .04
❑ 195 Bob Tewksbury .15 .04
❑ 196 Rondell White .30 .09
❑ 197 Steve Cooke .15 .04
❑ 198 Jeff Branson .15 .04
❑ 199 Derek Jeter 2.00 .60
❑ 200 Tim Salmon .50 .15
❑ 201 Steve Frey .15 .04
❑ 202 Kent Mercker .15 .04
❑ 203 Randy Johnson .75 .23
❑ 204 Todd Worrell .15 .04
❑ 205 Mo Vaughn .30 .09
❑ 206 Howard Johnson .15 .04
❑ 207 John Wasdin .15 .04
❑ 208 Eddie Williams .15 .04
❑ 209 Tim Belcher .15 .04
❑ 210 Jeff Montgomery .15 .04
❑ 211 Kirt Manwaring .15 .04
❑ 212 Ben Grieve .30 .09
❑ 213 Pat Hentgen .15 .04
❑ 214 Shawon Dunston .15 .04
❑ 215 Mike Greenwell .15 .04
❑ 216 Alex Diaz .15 .04
❑ 217 Pat Mahomes .15 .04
❑ 218 Dave Hansen .15 .04
❑ 219 Kevin Rogers .15 .04
❑ 220 Cecil Fielder .30 .09
❑ 221 Andrew Lorraine .15 .04
❑ 222 Jack Armstrong .15 .04
❑ 223 Todd Hundley .15 .04
❑ 224 Mark Acre .15 .04
❑ 225 Darrell Whitmore .15 .04
❑ 226 Randy Milligan .15 .04
❑ 227 Wayne Kirby .15 .04
❑ 228 Darryl Kile .30 .09
❑ 229 Bob Zupcic .15 .04
❑ 230 Jay Bell .30 .09
❑ 231 Dustin Hermanson .15 .04
❑ 232 Harold Baines .30 .09
❑ 233 Alan Benes .15 .04
❑ 234 Felix Fermin .15 .04
❑ 235 Ellis Burks .30 .09
❑ 236 Jeff Brantley .15 .04
❑ 237 Brian Hunter .75 .23
Jose Malave
Karim Garcia RC
Shane Pullen
❑ 238 Matt Nokes .15 .04
❑ 239 Ben Rivera .15 .04
❑ 240 Joe Carter .30 .09
❑ 241 Jeff Granger .15 .04
❑ 242 Terry Pendleton .30 .09
❑ 243 Melvin Nieves .15 .04
❑ 244 Frankie Rodriguez .15 .04
❑ 245 Darryl Hamilton .15 .04
❑ 246 Brooks Kieschnick .15 .04
❑ 247 Todd Hollandsworth .15 .04
❑ 248 Joe Rosselli .15 .04
❑ 249 Bill Gullickson .15 .04
❑ 250 Chuck Knoblauch .30 .09
❑ 251 Kurt Miller .15 .04
❑ 252 Bobby Jones .15 .04
❑ 253 Lance Blankenship .15 .04
❑ 254 Matt Whiteside .15 .04
❑ 255 Darrin Fletcher .15 .04
❑ 256 Eric Plunk .15 .04
❑ 257 Shane Reynolds .15 .04
❑ 258 Norberto Martin .15 .04
❑ 259 Mike Thurman .15 .04
❑ 260 Andy Van Slyke .30 .09
❑ 261 Dwight Smith .15 .04
❑ 262 Allen Watson .15 .04
❑ 263 Dan Wilson .15 .04
❑ 264 Brent Mayne .15 .04
❑ 265 Bip Roberts .15 .04
❑ 266 Sterling Hitchcock .15 .04
❑ 267 Alex Gonzalez .15 .04
❑ 268 Greg Harris .15 .04
❑ 269 Ricky Jordan .15 .04
❑ 270 Johnny Ruffin .15 .04
❑ 271 Mike Stanton .15 .04
❑ 272 Rich Rowland .15 .04
❑ 273 Steve Trachsel .15 .04
❑ 274 Pedro Munoz .15 .04
❑ 275 Ramon Martinez .15 .04
❑ 276 Dave Henderson .15 .04
❑ 277 Chris Gomez .15 .04
❑ 278 Joe Grahe .15 .04
❑ 279 Rusty Greer .30 .09
❑ 280 John Franco .30 .09
❑ 281 Mike Bordick .15 .04
❑ 282 Jeff D'Amico .15 .04
❑ 283 Dave Magadan .15 .04
❑ 284 Tony Pena .15 .04
❑ 285 Greg Swindell .15 .04
❑ 286 Doug Million .15 .04
❑ 287 Gabe White .15 .04
❑ 288 Trey Beamon .15 .04
❑ 289 Arthur Rhodes .15 .04
❑ 290 Juan Guzman .15 .04
❑ 291 Jose Oquendo .15 .04
❑ 292 Willie Blair .15 .04
❑ 293 Eddie Taubensee .15 .04
❑ 294 Steve Howe .15 .04
❑ 295 Greg Maddux 1.50 .45
❑ 296 Mike Macfarlane .15 .04
❑ 297 Curt Schilling .50 .15
❑ 298 Phil Clark .15 .04
❑ 299 Woody Williams .15 .04
❑ 300 Jose Canseco .75 .23
❑ 301 Aaron Sele .15 .04
❑ 302 Carl Willis .15 .04
❑ 303 Steve Buechele .15 .04
❑ 304 Dave Burba .15 .04
❑ 305 Orel Hershiser .30 .09
❑ 306 Damion Easley .15 .04
❑ 307 Mike Henneman .15 .04
❑ 308 Josias Manzanillo .15 .04
❑ 309 Kevin Seitzer .15 .04
❑ 310 Ruben Sierra .15 .04
❑ 311 Bryan Harvey .15 .04
❑ 312 Jim Thome .75 .23
❑ 313 Ramon Castro RC .25 .07
❑ 314 Lance Johnson .15 .04
❑ 315 Marquis Grissom .15 .04
❑ 316 Terrell Wade .15 .04
Juan Acevedo
Matt Arrandale
Eddie Priest RC
❑ 317 Paul Wagner .15 .04
❑ 318 Jamie Moyer .30 .09
❑ 319 Todd Zeile .15 .04
❑ 320 Chris Bosio .15 .04
❑ 321 Steve Reed .15 .04
❑ 322 Erik Hanson .15 .04
❑ 323 Luis Polonia .15 .04
❑ 324 Ryan Klesko .30 .09
❑ 325 Kevin Appier .30 .09
❑ 326 Jim Eisenreich .15 .04
❑ 327 Randy Knorr .15 .04
❑ 328 Craig Shipley .15 .04
❑ 329 Tim Naehring .15 .04
❑ 330 Randy Myers .15 .04
❑ 331 Alex Cole .15 .04
❑ 332 Jim Gott .15 .04
❑ 333 Mike Jackson .15 .04
❑ 334 John Flaherty .15 .04
❑ 335 Chili Davis .30 .09
❑ 336 Benji Gil .15 .04
❑ 337 Jason Jacome .15 .04
❑ 338 Stan Javier .15 .04
❑ 339 Mike Fetters .15 .04
❑ 340 Rich Renteria .15 .04
❑ 341 Kevin Witt .15 .04
❑ 342 Scott Servais .15 .04
❑ 343 Craig Grebeck .15 .04
❑ 344 Kirk Rueter .15 .04
❑ 345 Don Slaught .15 .04
❑ 346 Armando Benitez .30 .09
❑ 347 Ozzie Smith .75 .23
❑ 348 Mike Blowers .15 .04
❑ 349 Armando Reynoso .15 .04
❑ 350 Barry Larkin .75 .23
❑ 351 Mike Williams .15 .04
❑ 352 Scott Kamieniecki .15 .04
❑ 353 Gary Gaetti .30 .09
❑ 354 Todd Stottlemyre .15 .04
❑ 355 Fred McGriff .50 .15
❑ 356 Tim Mauser .15 .04
❑ 357 Chris Gwynn .15 .04
❑ 358 Frank Castillo .15 .04
❑ 359 Jeff Reboulet .15 .04
❑ 360 Roger Clemens 1.50 .45
❑ 361 Mark Carreon .15 .04
❑ 362 Chad Kreuter .15 .04
❑ 363 Mark Farris .15 .04
❑ 364 Bob Welch .15 .04
❑ 365 Dean Palmer .30 .09
❑ 366 Jeromy Burnitz .30 .09
❑ 367 B.J. Surhoff .30 .09
❑ 368 Mike Butcher .15 .04
❑ 369 Brad Clontz .15 .04
Steve Phoenix
Scott Gentile
Bucky Buckles RC
❑ 370 Eddie Murray .75 .23
❑ 371 Orlando Miller .15 .04
❑ 372 Ron Karkovice .15 .04
❑ 373 Richie Lewis .15 .04
❑ 374 Lenny Webster .15 .04
❑ 375 Jeff Tackett .15 .04
❑ 376 Tom Urbani .15 .04
❑ 377 Tino Martinez .50 .15
❑ 378 Mark Dewey .15 .04
❑ 379 Charles O'Brien .15 .04
❑ 380 Terry Mulholland .15 .04
❑ 381 Thomas Howard .15 .04
❑ 382 Chris Haney .15 .04
❑ 383 Billy Hatcher .15 .04
❑ 384 Jeff Bagwell AS .50 .15
Frank Thomas AS
❑ 385 Bret Boone AS .30 .09
Carlos Baerga AS
❑ 386 Matt Williams AS .30 .09
Wade Boggs AS
❑ 387 Wil Cordero AS .75 .23
Cal Ripken AS
❑ 388 Barry Bonds AS 1.00 .30
Ken Griffey AS
❑ 389 Tony Gwynn AS .30 .09
Albert Belle AS
❑ 390 Dante Bichette AS .50 .15
Kirby Puckett AS
❑ 391 Mike Piazza AS .75 .23
Mike Stanley AS
❑ 392 Greg Maddux AS .75 .23
David Cone AS
❑ 393 Danny Jackson AS .15 .04
Jimmy Key AS
❑ 394 John Franco AS .15 .04
Lee Smith AS
❑ 395 Checklist 1-198 .15 .04
❑ 396 Checklist 199-396 .15 .04
❑ 397 Ken Griffey Jr. 1.25 .35
❑ 398 Rick Heiserman RC .15 .04
❑ 399 Don Mattingly 2.00 .60
❑ 400 Henry Rodriguez .15 .04
❑ 401 Lenny Harris .15 .04
❑ 402 Ryan Thompson .15 .04
❑ 403 Darren Oliver .15 .04
❑ 404 Omar Vizquel .30 .09
❑ 405 Jeff Bagwell .50 .15
❑ 406 Doug Webb RC .15 .04
❑ 407 Todd Van Poppel .15 .04
❑ 408 Leo Gomez .15 .04
❑ 409 Mark Whiten .15 .04
❑ 410 Pedro A.Martinez .15 .04
❑ 411 Reggie Sanders .30 .09
❑ 412 Kevin Foster .15 .04

❑ 413 Danny Tartabull .15 .04
❑ 414 Jeff Blauser .15 .04
❑ 415 Mike Magnante .15 .04
❑ 416 Tom Candiotti .15 .04
❑ 417 Rod Beck .15 .04
❑ 418 Jody Reed .15 .04
❑ 419 Vince Coleman .15 .04
❑ 420 Danny Jackson .15 .04
❑ 421 Ryan Nye RC .15 .04
❑ 422 Larry Walker .50 .15
❑ 423 Russ Johnson DP .15 .04
❑ 424 Pat Borders .15 .04
❑ 425 Lee Smith .30 .09
❑ 426 Paul O'Neill .50 .15
❑ 427 Devon White .30 .09
❑ 428 Jim Bullinger .15 .04
❑ 429 Greg Hansell .15 .04
Brian Sackinsky
Carey Paige
Rob Welch RC
❑ 430 Steve Avery .15 .04
❑ 431 Tony Gwynn 1.00 .30
❑ 432 Pat Meares .15 .04
❑ 433 Bill Swift .15 .04
❑ 434 David Wells .30 .09
❑ 435 John Briscoe .15 .04
❑ 436 Roger Pavlik .15 .04
❑ 437 Jayson Peterson RC .15 .04
❑ 438 Roberto Alomar .75 .23
❑ 439 Billy Brewer .15 .04
❑ 440 Gary Sheffield .30 .09
❑ 441 Lou Frazier .15 .04
❑ 442 Terry Steinbach .15 .04
❑ 443 Jay Payton RC .50 .15
❑ 444 Jason Bere .15 .04
❑ 445 Denny Neagle .30 .09
❑ 446 Andres Galarraga .30 .09
❑ 447 Hector Carrasco .15 .04
❑ 448 Bill Risley .15 .04
❑ 449 Andy Benes .15 .04
❑ 450 Jim Leyritz .15 .04
❑ 451 Jose Oliva .15 .04
❑ 452 Greg Vaughn .30 .09
❑ 453 Rich Monteleone .15 .04
❑ 454 Tony Eusebio .15 .04
❑ 455 Chuck Finley .30 .09
❑ 456 Kevin Brown .30 .09
❑ 457 Joe Boever .15 .04
❑ 458 Bobby Munoz .15 .04
❑ 459 Bret Saberhagen .30 .09
❑ 460 Kurt Abbott .15 .04
❑ 461 Bobby Witt .15 .04
❑ 462 Cliff Floyd .30 .09
❑ 463 Mark Clark .15 .04
❑ 464 Andujar Cedeno .15 .04
❑ 465 Marvin Freeman .15 .04
❑ 466 Mike Piazza 1.25 .35
❑ 467 Willie Greene .15 .04
❑ 468 Pat Kelly .15 .04
❑ 469 Carlos Delgado .30 .09
❑ 470 Willie Banks .15 .04
❑ 471 Matt Walbeck .15 .04
❑ 472 Mark McGwire 2.00 .60
❑ 473 M.Christensen RC .15 .04
❑ 474 Alan Trammell .50 .15
❑ 475 Tom Gordon .15 .04
❑ 476 Greg Colbrunn .15 .04
❑ 477 Darren Daulton .30 .09
❑ 478 Albie Lopez .15 .04
❑ 479 Robin Ventura .30 .09
❑ 480 Eddie Perez RC .25 .07
Jason Kendall
Einar Diaz
Bret Hemphill
❑ 481 Bryan Eversgerd .15 .04
❑ 482 Dave Fleming .15 .04
❑ 483 Scott Livingstone .15 .04
❑ 484 Pete Schourek .15 .04
❑ 485 Bernie Williams .50 .15
❑ 486 Mark Lemke .15 .04
❑ 487 Eric Karros .30 .09
❑ 488 Scott Ruffcorn .15 .04
❑ 489 Billy Ashley .15 .04
❑ 490 Rico Brogna .15 .04
❑ 491 John Burkett .15 .04
❑ 492 Cade Gaspar RC .15 .04
❑ 493 Jorge Fabregas .15 .04
❑ 494 Greg Gagne .15 .04
❑ 495 Doug Jones .15 .04
❑ 496 Troy O'Leary .15 .04
❑ 497 Pat Rapp .15 .04
❑ 498 Butch Henry .15 .04
❑ 499 John Olerud .30 .09
❑ 500 John Hudek .15 .04
❑ 501 Jeff King .15 .04
❑ 502 Bobby Bonilla .30 .09
❑ 503 Albert Belle .30 .09
❑ 504 Rick Wilkins .15 .04
❑ 505 John Jaha .15 .04
❑ 506 Nigel Wilson .15 .04
❑ 507 Sid Fernandez .15 .04
❑ 508 Deion Sanders .30 .09
❑ 509 Gil Heredia .15 .04
❑ 510 Scott Elarton RC .25 .07
❑ 511 Melido Perez .15 .04
❑ 512 Greg McMichael .15 .04
❑ 513 Rusty Meacham .15 .04
❑ 514 Shawn Green .30 .09
❑ 515 Carlos Garcia .15 .04
❑ 516 Dave Stevens .15 .04
❑ 517 Eric Young .15 .04
❑ 518 Omar Daal .15 .04
❑ 519 Kirk Gibson .30 .09
❑ 520 Spike Owen .15 .04
❑ 521 Jacob Cruz RC .30 .09
❑ 522 Sandy Alomar Jr. .15 .04
❑ 523 Steve Bedrosian .15 .04
❑ 524 Ricky Gutierrez .15 .04
❑ 525 Dave Veres .15 .04
❑ 526 Gregg Jefferies .15 .04
❑ 527 Jose Valentin .15 .04
❑ 528 Robb Nen .30 .09
❑ 529 Jose Rijo .15 .04
❑ 530 Sean Berry .15 .04
❑ 531 Mike Gallego .15 .04
❑ 532 Roberto Kelly .15 .04
❑ 533 Kevin Stocker .15 .04
❑ 534 Kirby Puckett .75 .23
❑ 535 Chipper Jones .75 .23
❑ 536 Russ Davis .15 .04
❑ 537 Jon Lieber .15 .04
❑ 538 Trey Moore RC .15 .04
❑ 539 Joe Girardi .15 .04
❑ 540 Quilvio Veras .25 .07
Arquimedez Pozo
Miguel Cairo RC
Jason Camilli
❑ 541 Tony Phillips .15 .04
❑ 542 Brian Anderson .15 .04
❑ 543 Ivan Rodriguez .75 .23
❑ 544 Jeff Cirillo .30 .09
❑ 545 Joey Cora .15 .04
❑ 546 Chris Hoiles .15 .04
❑ 547 Bernard Gilkey .15 .04
❑ 548 Mike Lansing .15 .04
❑ 549 Jimmy Key .30 .09
❑ 550 Mark Wohlers .15 .04
❑ 551 Chris Clemons RC .15 .04
❑ 552 Vinny Castilla .30 .09
❑ 553 Mark Guthrie .15 .04
❑ 554 Mike Lieberthal .30 .09
❑ 555 Tommy Davis RC .15 .04
❑ 556 Robby Thompson .15 .04
❑ 557 Danny Bautista .15 .04
❑ 558 Will Clark .75 .23
❑ 559 Rickey Henderson 1.25 .35
❑ 560 Todd Jones .15 .04
❑ 561 Jack McDowell .15 .04
❑ 562 Carlos Rodriguez .15 .04
❑ 563 Mark Eichhorn .15 .04
❑ 564 Jeff Nelson .15 .04
❑ 565 Eric Anthony .15 .04
❑ 566 Randy Velarde .15 .04
❑ 567 Javier Lopez .30 .09
❑ 568 Kevin Mitchell .15 .04
❑ 569 Steve Karsay .15 .04
❑ 570 Brian Meadows RC .15 .04
❑ 571 Rey Ordonez RC .50 .15
Mike Metcalfe
Kevin Orie
Ray Holbert
❑ 572 John Kruk .30 .09
❑ 573 Scott Leius .15 .04
❑ 574 John Patterson .15 .04
❑ 575 Kevin Brown .30 .09
❑ 576 Mike Moore .15 .04
❑ 577 Manny Ramirez .30 .09
❑ 578 Jose Lind .15 .04
❑ 579 Derrick May .15 .04
❑ 580 Cal Eldred .15 .04
❑ 581 David Bell 2.00 .60
Joel Chelmis
Lino Diaz
Aaron Boone RC
❑ 582 J.T. Snow .30 .09
❑ 583 Luis Sojo .15 .04
❑ 584 Moises Alou .30 .09
❑ 585 Dave Clark .15 .04
❑ 586 Dave Hollins .15 .04
❑ 587 Nomar Garciaparra 3.00 .90
❑ 588 Cal Ripken 2.50 .75
❑ 589 Pedro Astacio .15 .04
❑ 590 J.R. Phillips .15 .04
❑ 591 Jeff Frye .15 .04
❑ 592 Bo Jackson .75 .23
❑ 593 Steve Ontiveros .15 .04
❑ 594 David Nied .15 .04
❑ 595 Brad Ausmus .15 .04
❑ 596 Carlos Baerga .15 .04
❑ 597 James Mouton .15 .04
❑ 598 Ozzie Guillen .15 .04
❑ 599 Ozzie Timmons .25 .07
Curtis Goodwin
Johnny Damon
Jeff Abbott RC
❑ 600 Yorkis Perez .15 .04
❑ 601 Rich Rodriguez .15 .04
❑ 602 Mark McLemore .15 .04
❑ 603 Jeff Fassero .15 .04
❑ 604 John Roper .15 .04
❑ 605 Mark Johnson RC .25 .07
❑ 606 Wes Chamberlain .15 .04
❑ 607 Felix Jose .15 .04
❑ 608 Tony Longmire .15 .04
❑ 609 Duane Ward .15 .04
❑ 610 Brett Butler .30 .09
❑ 611 W.VanLandingham .15 .04
❑ 612 Mickey Tettleton .15 .04
❑ 613 Brady Anderson .30 .09
❑ 614 Reggie Jefferson .15 .04
❑ 615 Mike Kingery .15 .04
❑ 616 Derek Bell .15 .04
❑ 617 Scott Erickson .15 .04
❑ 618 Bob Wickman .15 .04
❑ 619 Phil Leftwich .15 .04
❑ 620 David Justice .30 .09
❑ 621 Paul Wilson .15 .04
❑ 622 Pedro Martinez .75 .23
❑ 623 Terry Mathews .15 .04
❑ 624 Brian McRae .15 .04
❑ 625 Bruce Ruffin .15 .04
❑ 626 Steve Finley .30 .09
❑ 627 Ron Gant .30 .09
❑ 628 Rafael Bournigal .15 .04
❑ 629 Darryl Strawberry .50 .15
❑ 630 Luis Alicea .15 .04
❑ 631 Mark Smith .15 .04
Scott Klingenbeck
❑ 632 Cory Bailey .15 .04
Scott Hatteberg
❑ 633 Todd Greene .30 .09
Troy Percival
❑ 634 Rod Bolton .15 .04
Olmedo Saenz
❑ 635 Steve Kline .15 .04
Herb Perry
❑ 636 Sean Bergman .15 .04
Shannon Penn
❑ 637 Joe Randa .15 .04
Joe Vitiello
❑ 638 Jose Mercedes .15 .04
Duane Singleton
❑ 639 Marc Barcelo .15 .04
Marty Cordova
❑ 640 Andy Pettitte .30 .09
Ruben Rivera
❑ 641 Willie Adams .30 .09
Scott Spiezio

❑ 642 Eddy Diaz RC .15 .04
Desi Relaford
❑ 643 Terrell Lowery .15 .04
Jon Shave
❑ 644 Angel Martinez .15 .04
Paul Spoljaric
❑ 645 Tony Graffanino .15 .04
Damon Hollins
❑ 646 Darron Cox .15 .04
Doug Glanville
❑ 647 Tim Belk .15 .04
Pat Watkins
❑ 648 Rod Pedraza .15 .04
Phil Schneider
❑ 649 Vic Darensbourg .15 .04
Marc Valdes
❑ 650 Rick Huisman .15 .04
Roberto Petagine
❑ 651 Roger Cedeno .25 .07
Ron Coomer RC
❑ 652 Shane Andrews .25 .07
Carlos Perez RC
❑ 653 Jason Isringhausen .30 .09
Chris Roberts
❑ 654 Wayne Gomes .15 .04
Kevin Jordan
❑ 655 Esteban Loiaza .50 .15
Steve Pegues
❑ 656 Terry Bradshaw .15 .04
John Frascatore
❑ 657 Andres Berumen .15 .04
Bryce Florie
❑ 658 Dan Carlson .15 .04
Keith Williams
❑ 659 Checklist .15 .04
❑ 660 Checklist .15 .04

1995 Topps Traded

	Nm-Mt	Ex-Mt
COMPLETE SET (165)	40.00	12.00

❑ 1T Frank Thomas ATB .60 .18
❑ 2T Ken Griffey Jr. ATB 1.00 .30
❑ 3T Barry Bonds ATB 1.25 .35
❑ 4T Albert Belle ATB .40 .12
❑ 5T Cal Ripken ATB 1.50 .45
❑ 6T Mike Piazza ATB 1.00 .30
❑ 7T Tony Gwynn ATB .60 .18
❑ 8T Jeff Bagwell ATB .40 .12
❑ 9T Mo Vaughn ATB .20 .06
❑ 10T Matt Williams ATB .20 .06
❑ 11T Ray Durham .40 .12
❑ 12T Juan LeBron 1.00 .30
Card pictures Carlos Beltran instead of Juan LeBron RC
❑ 13T Shawn Green .40 .12
❑ 14T Kevin Gross .20 .06
❑ 15T Jon Nunnally .20 .06
❑ 16T Brian Maxcy RC .25 .07
❑ 17T Mark Kiefer .20 .06
❑ 18T Carlos Beltran UER 10.00 3.00
Card pictures Juan LeBron instead of Carlos Beltran RC.
❑ 19T Mike Mimbs RC .25 .07
❑ 20T Larry Walker .60 .18
❑ 21T Chad Curtis .20 .06
❑ 22T Jeff Barry .20 .06
❑ 23T Joe Oliver .20 .06
❑ 24T Tomas Perez RC .25 .07
❑ 25T Michael Barrett RC 1.50 .45
❑ 26T Brian McRae .20 .06
❑ 27T Derek Bell .20 .06
❑ 28T Ray Durham .40 .12
❑ 29T Todd Williams .20 .06
❑ 30T Ryan Jaroncyk RC .25 .07
❑ 31T Todd Steverson .20 .06
❑ 32T Mike Devereaux .20 .06
❑ 33T Rheal Cormier .20 .06
❑ 34T Benny Santiago .40 .12
❑ 35T Bobby Higginson RC 1.00 .30
❑ 36T Jack McDowell .20 .06
❑ 37T Mike Macfarlane .20 .06
❑ 38T Tony McKnight RC .25 .07
❑ 39T Brian Hunter .20 .06
❑ 40T Hideo Nomo RC 3.00 .90
❑ 41T Brett Butler .40 .12
❑ 42T Donovan Osborne .20 .06
❑ 43T Scott Karl .20 .06
❑ 44T Tony Phillips .20 .06
❑ 45T Marty Cordova .20 .06
❑ 46T Dave Mlicki .20 .06
❑ 47T Bronson Arroyo RC .25 .07
❑ 48T John Burkett .20 .06
❑ 49T J.D. Smart RC .25 .07
❑ 50T Mickey Tettleton .20 .06
❑ 51T Todd Stottlemyre .20 .06
❑ 52T Mike Perez .20 .06
❑ 53T Terry Mulholland .20 .06
❑ 54T Edgardo Alfonzo .40 .12
❑ 55T Zane Smith .20 .06
❑ 56T Jacob Brumfield .20 .06
❑ 57T Andujar Cedeno .20 .06
❑ 58T Jose Parra .20 .06
❑ 59T Manny Alexander .20 .06
❑ 60T Tony Tarasco .20 .06
❑ 61T Orel Hershiser .40 .12
❑ 62T Tim Scott .20 .06
❑ 63T Felix Rodriguez RC .50 .15
❑ 64T Ken Hill .20 .06
❑ 65T Marquis Grissom .20 .06
❑ 66T Lee Smith .40 .12
❑ 67T Jason Bates .20 .06
❑ 68T Felipe Lira .20 .06
❑ 69T Alex Hernandez RC .25 .07
❑ 70T Tony Fernandez .20 .06
❑ 71T Scott Radinsky .20 .06
❑ 72T Jose Canseco 1.00 .30
❑ 73T Mark Grudzielanek RC 1.00 .30
❑ 74T Ben Davis RC .50 .15
❑ 75T Jim Abbott 1.00 .30
❑ 76T Roger Bailey .20 .06
❑ 77T Gregg Jefferies .20 .06
❑ 78T Erik Hanson .20 .06
❑ 79T Brad Radke RC 2.00 .60
❑ 80T Jaime Navarro .20 .06
❑ 81T John Wetteland .40 .12
❑ 82T Chad Fonville RC .25 .07
❑ 83T John Mabry .20 .06
❑ 84T Glenallen Hill .20 .06
❑ 85T Ken Caminiti .40 .12
❑ 86T Tom Goodwin .20 .06
❑ 87T Darren Bragg .20 .06
❑ 88T Pat Ahearne .25 .07
Gary Rath
Larry Wimberly
Robbie Bell RC
❑ 89T Jeff Russell .20 .06
❑ 90T Dave Gallagher .20 .06
❑ 91T Steve Finley .40 .12
❑ 92T Vaughn Eshelman .20 .06
❑ 93T Kevin Jarvis .20 .06
❑ 94T Mark Gubicza .20 .06
❑ 95T Tim Wakefield .40 .12
❑ 96T Bob Tewksbury .20 .06
❑ 97T Sid Roberson RC .25 .07
❑ 98T Tom Henke .20 .06
❑ 99T Michael Tucker .20 .06
❑ 100T Jason Bates .20 .06
❑ 101T Otis Nixon .20 .06
❑ 102T Mark Whiten .20 .06
❑ 103T Dilson Torres RC .25 .07
❑ 104T Melvin Bunch RC .25 .07
❑ 105T Terry Pendleton .40 .12
❑ 106T Corey Jenkins RC .25 .07
❑ 107T Glenn Dishman RC .25 .07
Rob Grable
❑ 108T Reggie Taylor RC .50 .15
❑ 109T Curtis Goodwin .20 .06
❑ 110T David Cone .40 .12
❑ 111T Antonio Osuna .20 .06
❑ 112T Paul Shuey .20 .06
❑ 113T Doug Jones .20 .06
❑ 114T Mark McLemore .20 .06
❑ 115T Kevin Ritz .20 .06
❑ 116T John Kruk .40 .12
❑ 117T Trevor Wilson .20 .06
❑ 118T Jerald Clark .20 .06
❑ 119T Julian Tavarez .20 .06
❑ 120T Tim Pugh .20 .06
❑ 121T Todd Zeile .20 .06
❑ 122T Mark Sweeney UER 5.00 1.50
George Arias
Richie Sexson RC
Brian Schneider
❑ 123T Bobby Witt .20 .06
❑ 124T Hideo Nomo 1.00 .30
❑ 125T Joey Cora .20 .06
❑ 126T Jim Scharrer RC .25 .07
❑ 127T Paul Quantrill .20 .06
❑ 128T Chipper Jones ROY .60 .18
❑ 129T Kenny James RC .25 .07
❑ 130T Lyle Mouton .60 .18
Mariano Rivera
❑ 131T Tyler Green .20 .06
❑ 132T Brad Clontz .20 .06
❑ 133T Jon Nunnally .20 .06
❑ 134T Dave Magadan .20 .06
❑ 135T Al Leiter .40 .12
❑ 136T Bret Barberie .20 .06
❑ 137T Bill Swift .20 .06
❑ 138T Scott Cooper .20 .06
❑ 139T Roberto Kelly .20 .06
❑ 140T Charlie Hayes .20 .06
❑ 141T Pete Harnisch .20 .06
❑ 142T Rich Amaral .20 .06
❑ 143T Rudy Seanez .20 .06
❑ 144T Pat Listach .20 .06
❑ 145T Quilvio Veras .20 .06
❑ 146T Jose Olmeda RC .25 .07
❑ 147T Roberto Petagine .20 .06
❑ 148T Kevin Brown .40 .12
❑ 149T Phil Plantier .20 .06
❑ 150T Carlos Perez .40 .12
❑ 151T Pat Borders .20 .06
❑ 152T Tyler Green .20 .06
❑ 153T Stan Belinda .20 .06
❑ 154T Dave Stewart .40 .12
❑ 155T Andre Dawson .40 .12
❑ 156T Frank Thomas AS .60 .18
Fred McGriff UER
(McGriff's team shown as Blue Jays)
❑ 157T Carlos Baerga AS .40 .12
Craig Biggio
❑ 158T Wade Boggs AS .40 .12
Matt Williams
❑ 159T Cal Ripken AS .60 .18
Ozzie Smith
❑ 160T Ken Griffey Jr. AS 1.00 .30
Tony Gwynn
❑ 161T Albert Belle AS 1.25 .35
Barry Bonds
❑ 162T Kirby Puckett .60 .18
Len Dykstra
❑ 163T Ivan Rodriguez AS 1.00 .30
Mike Piazza
❑ 164T Randy Johnson AS 1.25 .35
Hideo Nomo
❑ 165T Checklist .20 .06

1996 Topps

	Nm-Mt	Ex-Mt
COMPLETE SET (440)	50.00	15.00
COMP.HOBBY SET (449)	50.00	15.00
COMP.CEREAL SET (444)	50.00	15.00
COMP.SERIES 1 (220)	30.00	9.00
COMP.SERIES 2 (220)	20.00	6.00
COMMON CARD (1-440)	.20	.06
COMMON RC	.25	.07

	No.	Player		
❑	1	Tony Gwynn STP	.30	.09
❑	2	Mike Piazza STP	.50	.15
❑	3	Greg Maddux STP	.50	.15
❑	4	Jeff Bagwell STP	.20	.06
❑	5	Larry Walker STP	.20	.06
❑	6	Barry Larkin STP	.30	.09
❑	7	Mickey Mantle	4.00	1.20
❑	8	Tom Glavine STP UER	.30	.09
		Won 21 games in June 95		
❑	9	Craig Biggio STP	.20	.06
❑	10	Barry Bonds STP	.50	.15
❑	11	H.Slocumb STP	.20	.06
❑	12	Matt Williams STP	.20	.06
❑	13	Todd Helton	1.00	.30
❑	14	Mark Redman	.40	.12
❑	15	Michael Barrett	.40	.12
❑	16	Ben Davis	.25	.07
❑	17	Juan LeBron	.25	.07
❑	18	Tony McKnight	.25	.07
❑	19	Ryan Jaroncyk	.25	.07
❑	20	Corey Jenkins	.25	.07
❑	21	Jim Scharrer	.25	.07
❑	22	Mark Bellhorn RC	.40	.12
❑	23	Jarrod Washburn RC	1.00	.30
❑	24	Geoff Jenkins RC	1.25	.35
❑	25	Sean Casey RC	2.00	.60
❑	26	Brett Tomko RC	.40	.12
❑	27	Tony Fernandez	.20	.06
❑	28	Rich Becker	.20	.06
❑	29	Andujar Cedeno	.20	.06
❑	30	Paul Molitor	.30	.09
❑	31	Brent Gates	.20	.06
❑	32	Glenallen Hill	.20	.06
❑	33	Mike Macfarlane	.20	.06
❑	34	Manny Alexander	.20	.06
❑	35	Todd Zeile	.20	.06
❑	36	Joe Girardi	.20	.06
❑	37	Tony Tarasco	.20	.06
❑	38	Tim Belcher	.20	.06
❑	39	Tom Goodwin	.20	.06
❑	40	Orel Hershiser	.20	.06
❑	41	Tripp Cromer	.20	.06
❑	42	Sean Bergman	.20	.06
❑	43	Troy Percival	.20	.06
❑	44	Kevin Stocker	.20	.06
❑	45	Albert Belle	.20	.06
❑	46	Tony Eusebio	.20	.06
❑	47	Sid Roberson	.20	.06
❑	48	Todd Hollandsworth	.20	.06
❑	49	Mark Wohlers	.20	.06
❑	50	Kirby Puckett	.50	.15
❑	51	Darren Holmes	.20	.06
❑	52	Ron Karkovice	.20	.06
❑	53	Al Martin	.20	.06
❑	54	Pat Rapp	.20	.06
❑	55	Mark Grace	.50	.15
❑	56	Greg Gagne	.20	.06
❑	57	Stan Javier	.20	.06
❑	58	Scott Sanders	.20	.06
❑	59	J.T. Snow	.20	.06
❑	60	David Justice	.20	.06
❑	61	Royce Clayton	.20	.06
❑	62	Kevin Foster	.20	.06
❑	63	Tim Naehring	.20	.06
❑	64	Orlando Miller	.20	.06
❑	65	Mike Mussina	.50	.15
❑	66	Jim Eisenreich	.20	.06
❑	67	Felix Fermin	.20	.06
❑	68	Bernie Williams	.30	.09
❑	69	Robb Nen	.20	.06
❑	70	Ron Gant	.20	.06
❑	71	Felipe Lira	.20	.06
❑	72	Jacob Brumfield	.20	.06
❑	73	John Mabry	.20	.06
❑	74	Mark Carreon	.20	.06
❑	75	Carlos Baerga	.20	.06
❑	76	Jim Dougherty	.20	.06
❑	77	Ryan Thompson	.20	.06
❑	78	Scott Leius	.20	.06
❑	79	Roger Pavlik	.20	.06
❑	80	Gary Sheffield	.20	.06
❑	81	Julian Tavarez	.20	.06
❑	82	Andy Ashby	.20	.06
❑	83	Mark Lemke	.20	.06
❑	84	Omar Vizquel	.20	.06
❑	85	Darren Daulton	.20	.06
❑	86	Mike Lansing	.20	.06
❑	87	Rusty Greer	.20	.06
❑	88	Dave Stevens	.20	.06
❑	89	Jose Offerman	.20	.06
❑	90	Tom Henke	.20	.06
❑	91	Troy O'Leary	.20	.06
❑	92	Michael Tucker	.20	.06
❑	93	Marvin Freeman	.20	.06
❑	94	Alex Diaz	.20	.06
❑	95	John Wetteland	.20	.06
❑	96	Cal Ripken 2131	2.00	.60
❑	97	Mike Mimbs	.20	.06
❑	98	Bobby Higginson	.20	.06
❑	99	Edgardo Alfonzo	.20	.06
❑	100	Frank Thomas	.50	.15
❑	101	Steve Gibralter	.20	.06
		Bob Abreu		
❑	102	Brian Givens	.25	.07
		T.J. Mathews		
❑	103	Chris Pritchett	.25	.07
		Trenidad Hubbard		
❑	104	Eric Owens	.25	.07
		Butch Huskey		
❑	105	Doug Drabek	.20	.06
❑	106	Tomas Perez	.20	.06
❑	107	Mark Leiter	.20	.06
❑	108	Joe Oliver	.20	.06
❑	109	Tony Castillo	.20	.06
❑	110	Checklist (1-110)	.20	.06
❑	111	Kevin Seitzer	.20	.06
❑	112	Pete Schourek	.20	.06
❑	113	Sean Berry	.20	.06
❑	114	Todd Stottlemyre	.20	.06
❑	115	Joe Carter	.20	.06
❑	116	Jeff King	.20	.06
❑	117	Dan Wilson	.20	.06
❑	118	Kurt Abbott	.20	.06
❑	119	Lyle Mouton	.20	.06
❑	120	Jose Rijo	.20	.06
❑	121	Curtis Goodwin	.20	.06
❑	122	Jose Valentin	.20	.06
❑	123	Ellis Burks	.20	.06
❑	124	David Cone	.20	.06
❑	125	Eddie Murray	.50	.15
❑	126	Brian Jordan	.20	.06
❑	127	Darrin Fletcher	.20	.06
❑	128	Curt Schilling	.30	.09
❑	129	Ozzie Guillen	.20	.06
❑	130	Kenny Rogers	.20	.06
❑	131	Tom Pagnozzi	.20	.06
❑	132	Garret Anderson	.20	.06
❑	133	Bobby Jones	.20	.06
❑	134	Chris Gomez	.20	.06
❑	135	Mike Stanley	.20	.06
❑	136	Hideo Nomo	.50	.15
❑	137	Jon Nunnally	.20	.06
❑	138	Tim Wakefield	.20	.06
❑	139	Steve Finley	.20	.06
❑	140	Ivan Rodriguez	.50	.15
❑	141	Quilvio Veras	.20	.06
❑	142	Mike Fetters	.20	.06
❑	143	Mike Greenwell	.20	.06
❑	144	Bill Pulsipher	.20	.06
❑	145	Mark McGwire	1.25	.35
❑	146	Frank Castillo	.20	.06
❑	147	Greg Vaughn	.20	.06
❑	148	Pat Hentgen	.20	.06
❑	149	Walt Weiss	.20	.06
❑	150	Randy Johnson	.50	.15
❑	151	David Segui	.20	.06
❑	152	Benji Gil	.20	.06
❑	153	Tom Candiotti	.20	.06
❑	154	Geronimo Berroa	.20	.06
❑	155	John Franco	.20	.06
❑	156	Jay Bell	.20	.06
❑	157	Mark Gubicza	.20	.06
❑	158	Hal Morris	.20	.06
❑	159	Wilson Alvarez	.20	.06
❑	160	Derek Bell	.20	.06
❑	161	Ricky Bottalico	.20	.06
❑	162	Bret Boone	.20	.06
❑	163	Brad Radke	.20	.06
❑	164	John Valentin	.20	.06
❑	165	Steve Avery	.20	.06
❑	166	Mark McLemore	.20	.06
❑	167	Danny Jackson	.20	.06
❑	168	Tino Martinez	.30	.09
❑	169	Shane Reynolds	.20	.06
❑	170	Terry Pendleton	.20	.06
❑	171	Jim Edmonds	.20	.06
❑	172	Esteban Loaiza	.20	.06
❑	173	Ray Durham	.20	.06
❑	174	Carlos Perez	.20	.06
❑	175	Raul Mondesi	.20	.06
❑	176	Steve Ontiveros	.20	.06
❑	177	Chipper Jones	.50	.15
❑	178	Otis Nixon	.20	.06
❑	179	John Burkett	.20	.06
❑	180	Gregg Jefferies	.20	.06
❑	181	Denny Martinez	.20	.06
❑	182	Ken Caminiti	.20	.06
❑	183	Doug Jones	.20	.06
❑	184	Brian McRae	.20	.06
❑	185	Don Mattingly	1.25	.35
❑	186	Mel Rojas	.20	.06
❑	187	Marty Cordova	.20	.06
❑	188	Vinny Castilla	.20	.06
❑	189	John Smoltz	.30	.09
❑	190	Travis Fryman	.20	.06
❑	191	Chris Hoiles	.20	.06
❑	192	Chuck Finley	.20	.06
❑	193	Ryan Klesko	.20	.06
❑	194	Alex Fernandez	.20	.06
❑	195	Dante Bichette	.20	.06
❑	196	Eric Karros	.20	.06
❑	197	Roger Clemens	1.00	.30
❑	198	Randy Myers	.20	.06
❑	199	Tony Phillips	.20	.06
❑	200	Cal Ripken	1.50	.45
❑	201	Rod Beck	.20	.06
❑	202	Chad Curtis	.20	.06
❑	203	Jack McDowell	.20	.06
❑	204	Gary Gaetti	.20	.06
❑	205	Ken Griffey Jr.	.75	.23
❑	206	Ramon Martinez	.20	.06
❑	207	Jeff Kent	.20	.06
❑	208	Brad Ausmus	.20	.06
❑	209	Devon White	.20	.06
❑	210	Jason Giambi	.50	.15
❑	211	Nomar Garciaparra	1.00	.30
❑	212	Billy Wagner	.20	.06
❑	213	Todd Greene	.20	.06
❑	214	Paul Wilson	.20	.06
❑	215	Johnny Damon	.20	.06
❑	216	Alan Benes	.20	.06
❑	217	Karim Garcia	.20	.06
❑	218	Dustin Hermanson	.20	.06
❑	219	Derek Jeter	1.25	.35
❑	220	Checklist (111-220)	.20	.06
❑	221	Kirby Puckett STP	.30	.09
❑	222	Cal Ripken STP	.75	.23
❑	223	Albert Belle STP	.20	.06
❑	224	Randy Johnson STP	.30	.09
❑	225	Wade Boggs STP	.20	.06
❑	226	Carlos Baerga STP	.20	.06
❑	227	Ivan Rodriguez STP	.30	.09
❑	228	Mike Mussina STP	.30	.09
❑	229	Frank Thomas STP	.30	.09
❑	230	Ken Griffey Jr. STP	.50	.15
❑	231	Jose Mesa STP	.20	.06
❑	232	Matt Morris RC	2.00	.60
❑	233	Craig Wilson RC	.40	.12
❑	234	Alvie Shepherd	.25	.07
❑	235	Randy Winn RC	.75	.23

❑ 236 David Yocum RC .25 .07
❑ 237 Jason Brester RC .25 .07
❑ 238 Shane Monahan RC .25 .07
❑ 239 Brian McNichol RC .25 .07
❑ 240 Reggie Taylor .25 .07
❑ 241 Garrett Long .25 .07
❑ 242 Jonathan Johnson .25 .07
❑ 243 Jeff Liefer RC .25 .07
❑ 244 Brian Powell .25 .07
❑ 245 Brian Buchanan RC .25 .07
❑ 246 Mike Piazza .75 .23
❑ 247 Edgar Martinez .30 .09
❑ 248 Chuck Knoblauch .20 .06
❑ 249 Andres Galarraga .20 .06
❑ 250 Tony Gwynn .60 .18
❑ 251 Lee Smith .20 .06
❑ 252 Sammy Sosa .75 .23
❑ 253 Jim Thome .50 .15
❑ 254 Frank Rodriguez .20 .06
❑ 255 Charlie Hayes .20 .06
❑ 256 Bernard Gilkey .20 .06
❑ 257 John Smiley .20 .06
❑ 258 Brady Anderson .20 .06
❑ 259 Rico Brogna .20 .06
❑ 260 Kirt Manwaring .20 .06
❑ 261 Len Dykstra .20 .06
❑ 262 Tom Glavine .50 .15
❑ 263 Vince Coleman .20 .06
❑ 264 John Olerud .20 .06
❑ 265 Orlando Merced .20 .06
❑ 266 Kent Mercker .20 .06
❑ 267 Terry Steinbach .20 .06
❑ 268 Brian L. Hunter .20 .06
❑ 269 Jeff Fassero .20 .06
❑ 270 Jay Buhner .20 .06
❑ 271 Jeff Brantley .20 .06
❑ 272 Tim Raines .20 .06
❑ 273 Jimmy Key .20 .06
❑ 274 Mo Vaughn .20 .06
❑ 275 Andre Dawson .20 .06
❑ 276 Jose Mesa .20 .06
❑ 277 Brett Butler .20 .06
❑ 278 Luis Gonzalez .20 .06
❑ 279 Steve Sparks .20 .06
❑ 280 Chili Davis .20 .06
❑ 281 Carl Everett .20 .06
❑ 282 Jeff Cirillo .20 .06
❑ 283 Thomas Howard .20 .06
❑ 284 Paul O'Neill .30 .09
❑ 285 Pat Meares .20 .06
❑ 286 Mickey Tettleton .20 .06
❑ 287 Rey Sanchez .20 .06
❑ 288 Bip Roberts .20 .06
❑ 289 Roberto Alomar .50 .15
❑ 290 Ruben Sierra .20 .06
❑ 291 John Flaherty .20 .06
❑ 292 Bret Saberhagen .20 .06
❑ 293 Barry Larkin .50 .15
❑ 294 Sandy Alomar Jr. .20 .06
❑ 295 Ed Sprague .20 .06
❑ 296 Gary DiSarcina .20 .06
❑ 297 Marquis Grissom .20 .06
❑ 298 John Frascatore .20 .06
❑ 299 Will Clark .50 .15
❑ 300 Barry Bonds 1.25 .35
❑ 301 Ozzie Smith UER .50 .15
Padres is listed as Padre
❑ 302 Dave Nilsson .20 .06
❑ 303 Pedro Martinez .50 .15
❑ 304 Joey Cora .20 .06
❑ 305 Rick Aguilera .20 .06
❑ 306 Craig Biggio .30 .09
❑ 307 Jose Vizcaino .20 .06
❑ 308 Jeff Montgomery .20 .06
❑ 309 Moises Alou .20 .06
❑ 310 Robin Ventura .20 .06
❑ 311 David Wells .20 .06
❑ 312 Delino DeShields .20 .06
❑ 313 Trevor Hoffman .20 .06
❑ 314 Andy Benes .20 .06
❑ 315 Deion Sanders .20 .06
❑ 316 Jim Bullinger .20 .06
❑ 317 John Jaha .20 .06
❑ 318 Greg Maddux 1.00 .30
❑ 319 Tim Salmon .30 .09
❑ 320 Ben McDonald .20 .06
❑ 321 Sandy Martinez .20 .06
❑ 322 Dan Miceli .20 .06
❑ 323 Wade Boggs .30 .09
❑ 324 Ismael Valdes .20 .06
❑ 325 Juan Gonzalez .50 .15
❑ 326 Charles Nagy .20 .06
❑ 327 Ray Lankford .20 .06
❑ 328 Mark Portugal .20 .06
❑ 329 Bobby Bonilla .20 .06
❑ 330 Reggie Sanders .20 .06
❑ 331 Jamie Brewington RC .25 .07
❑ 332 Aaron Sele .20 .06
❑ 333 Pete Harnisch .20 .06
❑ 334 Cliff Floyd .20 .06
❑ 335 Cal Eldred .20 .06
❑ 336 Jason Bates .20 .06
❑ 337 Tony Clark .20 .06
❑ 338 Jose Herrera .20 .06
❑ 339 Alex Ochoa .20 .06
❑ 340 Mark Loretta .20 .06
❑ 341 Donne Wall .20 .06
❑ 342 Jason Kendall .20 .06
❑ 343 Shannon Stewart .20 .06
❑ 344 Brooks Kieschnick .20 .06
❑ 345 Chris Snopek .20 .06
❑ 346 Ruben Rivera .20 .06
❑ 347 Jeff Suppan .20 .06
❑ 348 Phil Nevin .20 .06
❑ 349 John Wasdin .20 .06
❑ 350 Jay Payton .20 .06
❑ 351 Tim Crabtree .20 .06
❑ 352 Rick Krivda .20 .06
❑ 353 Bob Wolcott .20 .06
❑ 354 Jimmy Haynes .20 .06
❑ 355 Herb Perry .20 .06
❑ 356 Ryne Sandberg .75 .23
❑ 357 Harold Baines .20 .06
❑ 358 Chad Ogea .20 .06
❑ 359 Lee Tinsley .20 .06
❑ 360 Matt Williams .20 .06
❑ 361 Randy Velarde .20 .06
❑ 362 Jose Canseco .50 .15
❑ 363 Larry Walker .30 .09
❑ 364 Kevin Appier .20 .06
❑ 365 Darryl Hamilton .20 .06
❑ 366 Jose Lima .20 .06
❑ 367 Javy Lopez .20 .06
❑ 368 Dennis Eckersley .20 .06
❑ 369 Jason Isringhausen .20 .06
❑ 370 Mickey Morandini .20 .06
❑ 371 Scott Cooper .20 .06
❑ 372 Jim Abbott .50 .15
❑ 373 Paul Sorrento .20 .06
❑ 374 Chris Hammond .20 .06
❑ 375 Lance Johnson .20 .06
❑ 376 Kevin Brown .20 .06
❑ 377 Luis Alicea .20 .06
❑ 378 Andy Pettitte .30 .09
❑ 379 Dean Palmer .20 .06
❑ 380 Jeff Bagwell .30 .09
❑ 381 Jaime Navarro .20 .06
❑ 382 Rondell White .20 .06
❑ 383 Erik Hanson .20 .06
❑ 384 Pedro Munoz .20 .06
❑ 385 Heathcliff Slocumb .20 .06
❑ 386 Wally Joyner .20 .06
❑ 387 Bob Tewksbury .20 .06
❑ 388 David Bell .20 .06
❑ 389 Fred McGriff .30 .09
❑ 390 Mike Henneman .20 .06
❑ 391 Robby Thompson .20 .06
❑ 392 Norm Charlton .20 .06
❑ 393 Cecil Fielder .20 .06
❑ 394 Benito Santiago .20 .06
❑ 395 Rafael Palmeiro .30 .09
❑ 396 Ricky Bones .20 .06
❑ 397 Rickey Henderson .75 .23
❑ 398 C.J. Nitkowski .20 .06
❑ 399 Shawon Dunston .20 .06
❑ 400 Manny Ramirez .20 .06
❑ 401 Bill Swift .20 .06
❑ 402 Chad Fonville .20 .06
❑ 403 Joey Hamilton .20 .06
❑ 404 Alex Gonzalez .20 .06
❑ 405 Roberto Hernandez .20 .06
❑ 406 Jeff Blauser .20 .06
❑ 407 LaTroy Hawkins .20 .06
❑ 408 Greg Colbrunn .20 .06
❑ 409 Todd Hundley .20 .06
❑ 410 Glenn Dishman .20 .06
❑ 411 Joe Vitiello .20 .06
❑ 412 Todd Worrell .20 .06
❑ 413 Wil Cordero .20 .06
❑ 414 Ken Hill .20 .06
❑ 415 Carlos Garcia .20 .06
❑ 416 Bryan Rekar .20 .06
❑ 417 Shawn Green .20 .06
❑ 418 Tyler Green .20 .06
❑ 419 Mike Blowers .20 .06
❑ 420 Kenny Lofton .20 .06
❑ 421 Denny Neagle .20 .06
❑ 422 Jeff Conine .20 .06
❑ 423 Mark Langston .20 .06
❑ 424 Steve Cox .25 .07
Jesse Ibarra
Derrek Lee
Ron Wright RC
❑ 425 Jim Bonnici .40 .12
Billy Owens
Richie Sexson
Daryle Ward RC
❑ 426 Kevin Jordan .25 .07
Bobby Morris
Desi Relaford
Adam Riggs RC
❑ 427 Tim Harkrider .25 .07
Rey Ordonez
Neifi Perez
Enrique Wilson
❑ 428 Bartolo Colon .20 .06
Doug Million
Rafael Orellano
Ray Ricken
❑ 429 Jeff D'Amico .25 .07
Marty Janzen RC
Gary Rath
Clint Sodowsky
❑ 430 Matt Drews .25 .07
Rich Hunter RC
Matt Ruebel
Bret Wagner
❑ 431 Jaime Bluma .25 .07
David Coggin
Steve Montgomery
Brandon Reed RC
❑ 432 Mike Figga 1.25 .35
Raul Ibanez
Paul Konerko
Julio Mosquera
❑ 433 Brian Barber .20 .06
Marc Kroon
Marc Valdes
Don Wengert
❑ 434 George Arias .50 .15
Chris Haas RC
Scott Rolen
Scott Spiezio
❑ 435 Brian Banks 2.00 .60
Vladimir Guerrero
Andruw Jones
Billy McMillon
❑ 436 Roger Cedeno 1.00 .30
Derrick Gibson
Ben Grieve
Shane Spencer RC
❑ 437 Anton French .25 .07
Demond Smith
DaRond Stovall RC
Keith Williams
❑ 438 Michael Coleman RC .40 .12
Jacob Cruz
Richard Hidalgo
Charles Peterson
❑ 439 Trey Beamon .20 .06
Yamil Benitez
Jermaine Dye
Angel Echevarria
❑ 440 Checklist .20 .06
❑ F7 M.Mantle Last Day 5.00 1.50
❑ NNO Mickey Mantle TRIB 3.00 .90
Promotes the Mantle Foundation
Black and White Photo

1997 Topps

	Nm-Mt	Ex-Mt
COMPLETE SET (495)	60.00	18.00
COMP.SERIES 1 (275)	30.00	9.00
COMP.SERIES 2 (220)	30.00	9.00
❑ 1 Barry Bonds	1.25	.35
❑ 2 Tom Pagnozzi	.20	.06
❑ 3 Terrell Wade	.20	.06
❑ 4 Jose Valentin	.20	.06
❑ 5 Mark Clark	.20	.06
❑ 6 Brady Anderson	.20	.06
❑ 8 Wade Boggs	.30	.09
❑ 9 Scott Stahoviak	.20	.06
❑ 10 Andres Galarraga	.20	.06
❑ 11 Steve Avery	.20	.06
❑ 12 Rusty Greer	.20	.06
❑ 13 Derek Jeter	1.25	.35
❑ 14 Ricky Bottalico	.20	.06
❑ 15 Andy Ashby	.20	.06
❑ 16 Paul Shuey	.20	.06
❑ 17 F.P. Santangelo	.20	.06
❑ 18 Royce Clayton	.20	.06
❑ 19 Mike Mohler	.20	.06
❑ 20 Mike Piazza	.75	.23
❑ 21 Jaime Navarro	.20	.06
❑ 22 Billy Wagner	.20	.06
❑ 23 Mike Timlin	.20	.06
❑ 24 Garret Anderson	.20	.06
❑ 25 Ben McDonald	.20	.06
❑ 26 Mel Rojas	.20	.06
❑ 27 John Burkett	.20	.06
❑ 28 Jeff King	.20	.06
❑ 29 Reggie Jefferson	.20	.06
❑ 30 Kevin Appier	.20	.06
❑ 31 Felipe Lira	.20	.06
❑ 32 Kevin Tapani	.20	.06
❑ 33 Mark Portugal	.20	.06
❑ 34 Carlos Garcia	.20	.06
❑ 35 Joey Cora	.20	.06
❑ 36 David Segui	.20	.06
❑ 37 Mark Grace	.50	.15
❑ 38 Erik Hanson	.20	.06
❑ 39 Jeff D'Amico	.20	.06
❑ 40 Jay Buhner	.20	.06
❑ 41 B.J. Surhoff	.20	.06
❑ 42 Jackie Robinson TRIB	2.00	.60
❑ 43 Roger Pavlik	.20	.06
❑ 44 Hal Morris	.20	.06
❑ 45 Mariano Duncan	.20	.06
❑ 46 Harold Baines	.20	.06
❑ 47 Jorge Fabregas	.20	.06
❑ 48 Jose Herrera	.20	.06
❑ 49 Jeff Cirillo	.20	.06
❑ 50 Tom Glavine	.50	.15
❑ 51 Pedro Astacio	.20	.06
❑ 52 Mark Gardner	.20	.06
❑ 53 Arthur Rhodes	.20	.06
❑ 54 Troy O'Leary	.20	.06
❑ 55 Bip Roberts	.20	.06
❑ 56 Mike Lieberthal	.20	.06
❑ 57 Shane Andrews	.20	.06
❑ 58 Scott Karl	.20	.06
❑ 59 Gary DiSarcina	.20	.06
❑ 60 Andy Pettitte	.30	.09
❑ 61 Kevin Elster	.20	.06
❑ 62 Mark McGwire	1.25	.35
❑ 63 Dan Wilson	.20	.06
❑ 64 Mickey Morandini	.20	.06
❑ 65 Chuck Knoblauch	.20	.06
❑ 66 Tim Wakefield	.20	.06
❑ 67 Raul Mondesi	.20	.06
❑ 68 Todd Jones	.20	.06
❑ 69 Albert Belle	.20	.06
❑ 70 Trevor Hoffman	.20	.06
❑ 71 Eric Young	.20	.06
❑ 72 Robert Perez	.20	.06
❑ 73 Butch Huskey	.20	.06
❑ 74 Brian McRae	.20	.06
❑ 75 Jim Edmonds	.20	.06
❑ 76 Mike Henneman	.20	.06
❑ 77 Frank Rodriguez	.20	.06
❑ 78 Danny Tartabull	.20	.06
❑ 79 Robb Nen	.20	.06
❑ 80 Reggie Sanders	.20	.06
❑ 81 Ron Karkovice	.20	.06
❑ 82 Benito Santiago	.20	.06
❑ 83 Mike Lansing	.20	.06
❑ 84 Mike Fetters UER	.20	.06
Card numbered 61		
❑ 85 Craig Biggio	.30	.09
❑ 86 Mike Bordick	.20	.06
❑ 87 Ray Lankford	.20	.06
❑ 88 Charles Nagy	.20	.06
❑ 89 Paul Wilson	.20	.06
❑ 90 John Wetteland	.20	.06
❑ 91 Tom Candiotti	.20	.06
❑ 92 Carlos Delgado	.20	.06
❑ 93 Derek Bell	.20	.06
❑ 94 Mark Lemke	.20	.06
❑ 95 Edgar Martinez	.30	.09
❑ 96 Rickey Henderson	.75	.23
❑ 97 Greg Myers	.20	.06
❑ 98 Jim Leyritz	.20	.06
❑ 99 Mark Johnson	.20	.06
❑ 100 Dwight Gooden HL	.20	.06
❑ 101 Al Leiter HL	.20	.06
❑ 102 John Mabry HL	.20	.06
❑ 103 Alex Ochoa HL	.20	.06
❑ 104 Mike Piazza HL	.50	.15
❑ 105 Jim Thome	.50	.15
❑ 106 Ricky Otero	.20	.06
❑ 107 Jamey Wright	.20	.06
❑ 108 Frank Thomas	.50	.15
❑ 109 Jody Reed	.20	.06
❑ 110 Orel Hershiser	.20	.06
❑ 111 Terry Steinbach	.20	.06
❑ 112 Mark Loretta	.20	.06
❑ 113 Turk Wendell	.20	.06
❑ 114 Marvin Benard	.20	.06
❑ 115 Kevin Brown	.20	.06
❑ 116 Robert Person	.20	.06
❑ 117 Joey Hamilton	.20	.06
❑ 118 Francisco Cordova	.20	.06
❑ 119 John Smiley	.20	.06
❑ 120 Travis Fryman	.20	.06
❑ 121 Jimmy Key	.20	.06
❑ 122 Tom Goodwin	.20	.06
❑ 123 Mike Greenwell	.20	.06
❑ 124 Juan Gonzalez	.50	.15
❑ 125 Pete Harnisch	.20	.06
❑ 126 Roger Cedeno	.20	.06
❑ 127 Ron Gant	.20	.06
❑ 128 Mark Langston	.20	.06
❑ 129 Tim Crabtree	.20	.06
❑ 130 Greg Maddux	1.00	.30
❑ 131 W.VanLandingham	.20	.06
❑ 132 Wally Joyner	.20	.06
❑ 133 Randy Myers	.20	.06
❑ 134 John Valentin	.20	.06
❑ 135 Bret Boone	.20	.06
❑ 136 Bruce Ruffin	.20	.06
❑ 137 Chris Snopek	.20	.06
❑ 138 Paul Molitor	.30	.09
❑ 139 Mark McLemore	.20	.06
❑ 140 Rafael Palmeiro	.30	.09
❑ 141 Herb Perry	.20	.06
❑ 142 Luis Gonzalez	.20	.06
❑ 143 Doug Drabek	.20	.06
❑ 144 Ken Ryan	.20	.06
❑ 145 Todd Hundley	.20	.06
❑ 146 Ellis Burks	.20	.06
❑ 147 Ozzie Guillen	.20	.06
❑ 148 Rich Becker	.20	.06
❑ 149 Sterling Hitchcock	.20	.06
❑ 150 Bernie Williams	.30	.09
❑ 151 Mike Stanley	.20	.06
❑ 152 Roberto Alomar	.50	.15
❑ 153 Jose Mesa	.20	.06
❑ 154 Steve Trachsel	.20	.06
❑ 155 Alex Gonzalez	.20	.06
❑ 156 Troy Percival	.20	.06
❑ 157 John Smoltz	.30	.09
❑ 158 Pedro Martinez	.50	.15
❑ 159 Jeff Conine	.20	.06
❑ 160 Bernard Gilkey	.20	.06
❑ 161 Jim Eisenreich	.20	.06
❑ 162 Mickey Tettleton	.20	.06
❑ 163 Justin Thompson	.20	.06
❑ 164 Jose Offerman	.20	.06
❑ 165 Tony Phillips	.20	.06
❑ 166 Ismael Valdes	.20	.06
❑ 167 Ryne Sandberg UER	.75	.23
Card has him with 252 homers in 1996		
❑ 168 Matt Mieske	.20	.06
❑ 169 Geronimo Berroa	.20	.06
❑ 170 Otis Nixon	.20	.06
❑ 171 John Mabry	.20	.06
❑ 172 Shawon Dunston	.20	.06
❑ 173 Omar Vizquel	.20	.06
❑ 174 Chris Hoiles	.20	.06
❑ 175 Dwight Gooden	.30	.09
❑ 176 Wilson Alvarez	.20	.06
❑ 177 Todd Hollandsworth	.20	.06
❑ 178 Roger Salkeld	.20	.06
❑ 179 Rey Sanchez	.20	.06
❑ 180 Rey Ordonez	.20	.06
❑ 181 Denny Martinez	.20	.06
❑ 182 Ramon Martinez	.20	.06
❑ 183 Dave Nilsson	.20	.06
❑ 184 Marquis Grissom	.20	.06
❑ 185 Randy Velarde	.20	.06
❑ 186 Ron Coomer	.20	.06
❑ 187 Tino Martinez	.30	.09
❑ 188 Jeff Brantley	.20	.06
❑ 189 Steve Finley	.20	.06
❑ 190 Andy Benes	.20	.06
❑ 191 Terry Adams	.20	.06
❑ 192 Mike Blowers	.20	.06
❑ 193 Russ Davis	.20	.06
❑ 194 Darryl Hamilton	.20	.06
❑ 195 Jason Kendall	.20	.06
❑ 196 Johnny Damon	.20	.06
❑ 197 Dave Martinez	.20	.06
❑ 198 Mike Macfarlane	.20	.06
❑ 199 Norm Charlton	.20	.06
❑ 200 Doug Million RC	.25	.07
Damian Moss		
Bobby Rodgers		
❑ 201 Geoff Jenkins	.20	.06
Raul Ibanez		
Mike Cameron		
❑ 202 Sean Casey	.20	.06
Jim Bonnici		
Dmitri Young		
❑ 203 Jed Hansen	.20	.06
Homer Bush		
Felipe Crespo		
❑ 204 Kevin Orie	.20	.06
Gabe Alvarez		
Aaron Boone		
❑ 205 Ben Davis	.20	.06
Kevin Brown		
Bobby Estalella		
❑ 206 Billy McMillon RC	.40	.12
Bubba Trammell		
Dante Powell		
❑ 207 Jarrod Washburn	.20	.06
Marc Wilkins RC		
Glendon Rusch		
❑ 208 Brian Hunter	.20	.06
❑ 209 Jason Giambi	.50	.15
❑ 210 Henry Rodriguez	.20	.06
❑ 211 Edgar Renteria	.20	.06
❑ 212 Edgardo Alfonzo	.20	.06
❑ 213 Fernando Vina	.20	.06
❑ 214 Shawn Green	.20	.06
❑ 215 Ray Durham	.20	.06
❑ 216 Joe Randa	.20	.06

❑ 217 Armando Reynoso .20 .06
❑ 218 Eric Davis .20 .06
❑ 219 Bob Tewksbury .20 .06
❑ 220 Jacob Cruz .20 .06
❑ 221 Glenallen Hill .20 .06
❑ 222 Gary Gaetti .20 .06
❑ 223 Donne Wall .20 .06
❑ 224 Brad Clontz .20 .06
❑ 225 Marty Janzen .20 .06
❑ 226 Todd Worrell .20 .06
❑ 227 John Franco .20 .06
❑ 228 David Wells .20 .06
❑ 229 Gregg Jefferies .20 .06
❑ 230 Tim Naehring .20 .06
❑ 231 Thomas Howard .20 .06
❑ 232 Roberto Hernandez .20 .06
❑ 233 Kevin Ritz .20 .06
❑ 234 Julian Tavarez .20 .06
❑ 235 Ken Hill .20 .06
❑ 236 Greg Gagne .20 .06
❑ 237 Bobby Chouinard .20 .06
❑ 238 Joe Carter .20 .06
❑ 239 Jermaine Dye .20 .06
❑ 240 Antonio Osuna .20 .06
❑ 241 Julio Franco .20 .06
❑ 242 Mike Grace .20 .06
❑ 243 Aaron Sele .20 .06
❑ 244 David Justice .20 .06
❑ 245 Sandy Alomar Jr. .20 .06
❑ 246 Jose Canseco .50 .15
❑ 247 Paul O'Neill .30 .09
❑ 248 Sean Berry .20 .06
❑ 249 Nick Bierbrodt .25 .07
Kevin Sweeney RC
❑ 250 Larry Rodriguez RC .25 .07
Vladimir Nunez RC
❑ 251 Ron Hartman .25 .07
David Hayman RC
❑ 252 Alex Sanchez .40 .12
Matthew Quatraro RC
❑ 253 Ronni Seberino RC .25 .07
Pablo Ortego RC
❑ 254 Rex Hudler .20 .06
❑ 255 Orlando Miller .20 .06
❑ 256 Mariano Rivera .30 .09
❑ 257 Brad Radke .20 .06
❑ 258 Bobby Higginson .20 .06
❑ 259 Jay Bell .20 .06
❑ 260 Mark Grudzielanek .20 .06
❑ 261 Lance Johnson .20 .06
❑ 262 Ken Caminiti .20 .06
❑ 263 J.T. Snow .20 .06
❑ 264 Gary Sheffield .20 .06
❑ 265 Darrin Fletcher .20 .06
❑ 266 Eric Owens .20 .06
❑ 267 Luis Castillo .20 .06
❑ 268 Scott Rolen .30 .09
❑ 269 Todd Noel .25 .07
John Oliver RC
❑ 270 Robert Stratton RC .50 .15
Corey Lee RC
❑ 271 Gil Meche RC 4.00 1.20
Matt Halloran RC
❑ 272 Eric Milton RC .50 .15
Dee Brown RC
❑ 273 Josh Garrett .25 .07
Chris Reitsma RC
❑ 274 A.J.Zapp RC .40 .12
Jason Marquis
❑ 275 Checklist .20 .06
❑ 276 Checklist .20 .06
❑ 277 Chipper Jones UER .50 .15
incorrectly numbered 276
❑ 278 Orlando Merced .20 .06
❑ 279 Ariel Prieto .20 .06
❑ 280 Al Leiter .20 .06
❑ 281 Pat Meares .20 .06
❑ 282 Darryl Strawberry .30 .09
❑ 283 Jamie Moyer .20 .06
❑ 284 Scott Servais .20 .06
❑ 285 Delino DeShields .20 .06
❑ 286 Danny Graves .20 .06
❑ 287 Gerald Williams .20 .06
❑ 288 Todd Greene .20 .06
❑ 289 Rico Brogna .20 .06
❑ 290 Derrick Gibson .20 .06
❑ 291 Joe Girardi .20 .06
❑ 292 Darren Lewis .20 .06
❑ 293 Nomar Garciaparra 1.00 .30
❑ 294 Greg Colbrunn .20 .06
❑ 295 Jeff Bagwell .30 .09
❑ 296 Brent Gates .20 .06
❑ 297 Jose Vizcaino .20 .06
❑ 298 Alex Ochoa .20 .06
❑ 299 Sid Fernandez .20 .06
❑ 300 Ken Griffey Jr. .75 .23
❑ 301 Chris Gomez .20 .06
❑ 302 Wendell Magee .20 .06
❑ 303 Darren Oliver .20 .06
❑ 304 Mel Nieves .20 .06
❑ 305 Sammy Sosa .75 .23
❑ 306 George Arias .20 .06
❑ 307 Jack McDowell .20 .06
❑ 308 Stan Javier .20 .06
❑ 309 Kimera Bartee .20 .06
❑ 310 James Baldwin .20 .06
❑ 311 Rocky Coppinger .20 .06
❑ 312 Keith Lockhart .20 .06
❑ 313 C.J. Nitkowski .20 .06
❑ 314 Allen Watson .20 .06
❑ 315 Darryl Kile .20 .06
❑ 316 Amaury Telemaco .20 .06
❑ 317 Jason Isringhausen .20 .06
❑ 318 Manny Ramirez .20 .06
❑ 319 Terry Pendleton .20 .06
❑ 320 Tim Salmon .30 .09
❑ 321 Eric Karros .20 .06
❑ 322 Mark Whiten .20 .06
❑ 323 Rick Krivda .20 .06
❑ 324 Brett Butler .20 .06
❑ 325 Randy Johnson .50 .15
❑ 326 Eddie Taubensee .20 .06
❑ 327 Mark Leiter .20 .06
❑ 328 Kevin Gross .20 .06
❑ 329 Ernie Young .20 .06
❑ 330 Pat Hentgen .20 .06
❑ 331 Rondell White .20 .06
❑ 332 Bobby Witt .20 .06
❑ 333 Eddie Murray .50 .15
❑ 334 Tim Raines .20 .06
❑ 335 Jeff Fassero .20 .06
❑ 336 Chuck Finley .20 .06
❑ 337 Willie Adams .20 .06
❑ 338 Chan Ho Park .20 .06
❑ 339 Jay Powell .20 .06
❑ 340 Ivan Rodriguez .50 .15
❑ 341 Jermaine Allensworth .20 .06
❑ 342 Jay Payton .20 .06
❑ 343 T.J. Mathews .20 .06
❑ 344 Tony Batista .20 .06
❑ 345 Ed Sprague .20 .06
❑ 346 Jeff Kent .20 .06
❑ 347 Scott Erickson .20 .06
❑ 348 Jeff Suppan .20 .06
❑ 349 Pete Schourek .20 .06
❑ 350 Kenny Lofton .20 .06
❑ 351 Alan Benes .20 .06
❑ 352 Fred McGriff .30 .09
❑ 353 Charlie O'Brien .20 .06
❑ 354 Darren Bragg .20 .06
❑ 355 Alex Fernandez .20 .06
❑ 356 Al Martin .20 .06
❑ 357 Bob Wells .20 .06
❑ 358 Chad Mottola .20 .06
❑ 359 Devon White .20 .06
❑ 360 David Cone .20 .06
❑ 361 Bobby Jones .20 .06
❑ 362 Scott Sanders .20 .06
❑ 363 Karim Garcia .20 .06
❑ 364 Kirt Manwaring .20 .06
❑ 365 Chili Davis .20 .06
❑ 366 Mike Hampton .20 .06
❑ 367 Chad Ogea .20 .06
❑ 368 Curt Schilling .30 .09
❑ 369 Phil Nevin .20 .06
❑ 370 Roger Clemens 1.00 .30
❑ 371 Willie Greene .20 .06
❑ 372 Kenny Rogers .20 .06
❑ 373 Jose Rijo .20 .06
❑ 374 Bobby Bonilla .20 .06
❑ 375 Mike Mussina .50 .15
❑ 376 Curtis Pride .20 .06
❑ 377 Todd Walker .20 .06
❑ 378 Jason Bere .20 .06
❑ 379 Heathcliff Slocumb .20 .06
❑ 380 Dante Bichette .20 .06
❑ 381 Carlos Baerga .20 .06
❑ 382 Livan Hernandez .20 .06
❑ 383 Jason Schmidt .20 .06
❑ 384 Kevin Stocker .20 .06
❑ 385 Matt Williams .20 .06
❑ 386 Bartolo Colon .20 .06
❑ 387 Will Clark .50 .15
❑ 388 Dennis Eckersley .20 .06
❑ 389 Brooks Kieschnick .20 .06
❑ 390 Ryan Klesko .20 .06
❑ 391 Mark Carreon .20 .06
❑ 392 Tim Worrell .20 .06
❑ 393 Dean Palmer .20 .06
❑ 394 Wil Cordero .20 .06
❑ 395 Javy Lopez .20 .06
❑ 396 Rich Aurilia .20 .06
❑ 397 Greg Vaughn .20 .06
❑ 398 Vinny Castilla .20 .06
❑ 399 Jeff Montgomery .20 .06
❑ 400 Cal Ripken 1.50 .45
❑ 401 Walt Weiss .20 .06
❑ 402 Brad Ausmus .20 .06
❑ 403 Ruben Rivera .20 .06
❑ 404 Mark Wohlers .20 .06
❑ 405 Rick Aguilera .20 .06
❑ 406 Tony Clark .20 .06
❑ 407 Lyle Mouton .20 .06
❑ 408 Bill Pulsipher .20 .06
❑ 409 Jose Rosado .20 .06
❑ 410 Tony Gwynn .60 .18
❑ 411 Cecil Fielder .20 .06
❑ 412 John Flaherty .20 .06
❑ 413 Lenny Dykstra .20 .06
❑ 414 Ugueth Urbina .20 .06
❑ 415 Brian Jordan .20 .06
❑ 416 Bob Abreu .20 .06
❑ 417 Craig Paquette .20 .06
❑ 418 Sandy Martinez .20 .06
❑ 419 Jeff Blauser .20 .06
❑ 420 Barry Larkin .50 .15
❑ 421 Kevin Seitzer .20 .06
❑ 422 Tim Belcher .20 .06
❑ 423 Paul Sorrento .20 .06
❑ 424 Cal Eldred .20 .06
❑ 425 Robin Ventura .20 .06
❑ 426 John Olerud .20 .06
❑ 427 Bob Wolcott .20 .06
❑ 428 Matt Lawton .20 .06
❑ 429 Rod Beck .20 .06
❑ 430 Shane Reynolds .20 .06
❑ 431 Mike James .20 .06
❑ 432 Steve Wojciechowski .20 .06
❑ 433 Vladimir Guerrero .50 .15
❑ 434 Dustin Hermanson .20 .06
❑ 435 Marty Cordova .20 .06
❑ 436 Marc Newfield .20 .06
❑ 437 Todd Stottlemyre .20 .06
❑ 438 Jeffrey Hammonds .20 .06
❑ 439 Dave Stevens .20 .06
❑ 440 Hideo Nomo .50 .15
❑ 441 Mark Thompson .20 .06
❑ 442 Mark Lewis .20 .06
❑ 443 Quinton McCracken .20 .06
❑ 444 Cliff Floyd .20 .06
❑ 445 Denny Neagle .20 .06
❑ 446 John Jaha .20 .06
❑ 447 Mike Sweeney .20 .06
❑ 448 John Wasdin .20 .06
❑ 449 Chad Curtis .20 .06
❑ 450 Mo Vaughn .20 .06
❑ 451 Donovan Osborne .20 .06
❑ 452 Ruben Sierra .20 .06
❑ 453 Michael Tucker .20 .06
❑ 454 Kurt Abbott .20 .06
❑ 455 Andruw Jones UER .30 .09
Birthdate is incorrectly listed
as 1-22-67, should be 1-22-77
❑ 456 Shannon Stewart .20 .06
❑ 457 Scott Brosius .20 .06
❑ 458 Juan Guzman .20 .06
❑ 459 Ron Villone .20 .06
❑ 460 Moises Alou .20 .06

	Card	Nm-Mt	Ex-Mt
❑ 461	Larry Walker	.30	.09
❑ 462	Eddie Murray SH	.30	.09
❑ 463	Paul Molitor SH	.20	.06
❑ 464	Hideo Nomo SH	.20	.06
❑ 465	Barry Bonds SH	.50	.15
❑ 466	Todd Hundley SH	.20	.06
❑ 467	Rheal Cormier	.20	.06
❑ 468	Jason Conti RC	.25	.07
	Jhensy Sandoval		
❑ 469	Rod Barajas	.40	.12
	Jackie Rexrode RC		
❑ 470	Cedric Bowers RC	.40	.12
	Jared Sandberg RC		
❑ 471	Chei Gunner RC	.25	.07
	Paul Wilder		
❑ 472	Mike Decelle	.25	.07
	Marcus McCain RC		
❑ 473	Todd Zeile	.20	.06
❑ 474	Neifi Perez	.20	.06
❑ 475	Jeromy Burnitz	.20	.06
❑ 476	Trey Beamon	.20	.06
❑ 477	Braden Looper RC	.40	.12
	John Patterson		
❑ 478	Danny Peoples	.40	.12
	Jake Westbrook RC		
❑ 479	Eric Chavez	1.50	.45
	Adam Eaton RC		
❑ 480	Joe Lawrence RC	.40	.12
	Pete Tucci		
❑ 481	Kris Benson	.50	.15
	Billy Koch RC		
❑ 482	John Nicholson	.25	.07
	Andy Prater RC		
❑ 483	Mark Johnson RC	.40	.12
	Mark Kotsay		
❑ 484	Armando Benitez	.20	.06
❑ 485	Mike Matheny	.20	.06
❑ 486	Jeff Reed	.20	.06
❑ 487	Mark Bellhorn	.20	.06
	Russ Johnson		
	Enrique Wilson		
❑ 488	Ben Grieve	.20	.06
	Richard Hidalgo		
	Scott Morgan RC		
❑ 489	Paul Konerko	.20	.06
	Derrek Lee UER		
	spelled Derek on back		
	Ron Wright		
❑ 490	Wes Helms RC	4.00	1.20
	Bill Mueller		
	Brad Seitzer		
❑ 491	Jeff Abbott	.20	.06
	Shane Monahan		
	Edgard Velazquez		
❑ 492	Jimmy Anderson RC	.25	.07
	Ron Blazier		
	Gerald Witasick		
❑ 493	Darin Blood	.20	.06
	Heath Murray		
	Carl Pavano		
❑ 494	Nelson Figueroa RC	.40	.12
	Mark Redman		
	Mike Villano		
❑ 495	Checklist	.20	.06
❑ 496	Checklist	.20	.06
❑ NNO	Derek Jeter AU	150.00	45.00

1998 Topps

	Nm-Mt	Ex-Mt
COMPLETE SET (503)	80.00	24.00
COMP.HOBBY SET (511)	100.00	30.00
COMP.RETAIL SET (511)	100.00	30.00
COMP.SERIES 1 (282)	40.00	12.00
COMP.SERIES 2 (221)	40.00	12.00

	Card	Nm-Mt	Ex-Mt
❑ 1	Tony Gwynn	.60	.18
❑ 2	Larry Walker	.30	.09
❑ 3	Billy Wagner	.20	.06
❑ 4	Denny Neagle	.20	.06
❑ 5	Vladimir Guerrero	.50	.15
❑ 6	Kevin Brown	.30	.09
❑ 8	Mariano Rivera	.30	.09
❑ 9	Tony Clark	.20	.06
❑ 10	Deion Sanders	.20	.06

	Card	Nm-Mt	Ex-Mt
❑ 11	Francisco Cordova	.20	.06
❑ 12	Matt Williams	.20	.06
❑ 13	Carlos Baerga	.20	.06
❑ 14	Mo Vaughn	.20	.06
❑ 15	Bobby Witt	.20	.06
❑ 16	Matt Stairs	.20	.06
❑ 17	Chan Ho Park	.20	.06
❑ 18	Mike Bordick	.20	.06
❑ 19	Michael Tucker	.20	.06
❑ 20	Frank Thomas	.50	.15
❑ 21	Roberto Clemente	1.00	.30
❑ 22	Dmitri Young	.20	.06
❑ 23	Steve Trachsel	.20	.06
❑ 24	Jeff Kent	.20	.06
❑ 25	Scott Rolen	.30	.09
❑ 26	John Thomson	.20	.06
❑ 27	Joe Vitiello	.20	.06
❑ 28	Eddie Guardado	.20	.06
❑ 29	Charlie Hayes	.20	.06
❑ 30	Juan Gonzalez	.50	.15
❑ 31	Garret Anderson	.20	.06
❑ 32	John Jaha	.20	.06
❑ 33	Omar Vizquel	.20	.06
❑ 34	Brian Hunter	.20	.06
❑ 35	Jeff Bagwell	.30	.09
❑ 36	Mark Lemke	.20	.06
❑ 37	Doug Glanville	.20	.06
❑ 38	Dan Wilson	.20	.06
❑ 39	Steve Cooke	.20	.06
❑ 40	Chili Davis	.20	.06
❑ 41	Mike Cameron	.20	.06
❑ 42	F.P. Santangelo	.20	.06
❑ 43	Brad Ausmus	.20	.06
❑ 44	Gary DiSarcina	.20	.06
❑ 45	Pat Hentgen	.20	.06
❑ 46	Wilton Guerrero	.20	.06
❑ 47	Devon White	.20	.06
❑ 48	Danny Patterson	.20	.06
❑ 49	Pat Meares	.20	.06
❑ 50	Rafael Palmeiro	.30	.09
❑ 51	Mark Gardner	.20	.06
❑ 52	Jeff Blauser	.20	.06
❑ 53	Dave Hollins	.20	.06
❑ 54	Carlos Garcia	.20	.06
❑ 55	Ben McDonald	.20	.06
❑ 56	John Mabry	.20	.06
❑ 57	Trevor Hoffman	.20	.06
❑ 58	Tony Fernandez	.20	.06
❑ 59	Rich Loiselle	.20	.06
❑ 60	Mark Leiter	.20	.06
❑ 61	Pat Kelly	.20	.06
❑ 62	John Flaherty	.20	.06
❑ 63	Roger Bailey	.20	.06
❑ 64	Tom Gordon	.20	.06
❑ 65	Ryan Klesko	.20	.06
❑ 66	Darryl Hamilton	.20	.06
❑ 67	Jim Eisenreich	.20	.06
❑ 68	Butch Huskey	.20	.06
❑ 69	Mark Grudzielanek	.20	.06
❑ 70	Marquis Grissom	.20	.06
❑ 71	Mark McLemore	.20	.06
❑ 72	Gary Gaetti	.20	.06
❑ 73	Greg Gagne	.20	.06
❑ 74	Lyle Mouton	.20	.06
❑ 75	Jim Edmonds	.20	.06
❑ 76	Shawn Green	.20	.06
❑ 77	Greg Vaughn	.20	.06
❑ 78	Terry Adams	.20	.06
❑ 79	Kevin Polcovich	.20	.06
❑ 80	Troy O'Leary	.20	.06
❑ 81	Jeff Shaw	.20	.06
❑ 82	Rich Becker	.20	.06
❑ 83	David Wells	.20	.06
❑ 84	Steve Karsay	.20	.06
❑ 85	Charles Nagy	.20	.06
❑ 86	B.J. Surhoff	.20	.06
❑ 87	Jamey Wright	.20	.06
❑ 88	James Baldwin	.20	.06
❑ 89	Edgardo Alfonzo	.20	.06
❑ 90	Jay Buhner	.20	.06
❑ 91	Brady Anderson	.20	.06
❑ 92	Scott Servais	.20	.06
❑ 93	Edgar Renteria	.20	.06
❑ 94	Mike Lieberthal	.20	.06
❑ 95	Rick Aguilera	.20	.06
❑ 96	Walt Weiss	.20	.06
❑ 97	Deivi Cruz	.20	.06
❑ 98	Kurt Abbott	.20	.06
❑ 99	Henry Rodriguez	.20	.06
❑ 100	Mike Piazza	.75	.23
❑ 101	Bill Taylor	.20	.06
❑ 102	Todd Zeile	.20	.06
❑ 103	Rey Ordonez	.20	.06
❑ 104	Willie Greene	.20	.06
❑ 105	Tony Womack	.20	.06
❑ 106	Mike Sweeney	.20	.06
❑ 107	Jeffrey Hammonds	.20	.06
❑ 108	Kevin Orie	.20	.06
❑ 109	Alex Gonzalez	.20	.06
❑ 110	Jose Canseco	.50	.15
❑ 111	Paul Sorrento	.20	.06
❑ 112	Joey Hamilton	.20	.06
❑ 113	Brad Radke	.20	.06
❑ 114	Steve Avery	.20	.06
❑ 115	Esteban Loaiza	.20	.06
❑ 116	Stan Javier	.20	.06
❑ 117	Chris Gomez	.20	.06
❑ 118	Royce Clayton	.20	.06
❑ 119	Orlando Merced	.20	.06
❑ 120	Kevin Appier	.20	.06
❑ 121	Mel Nieves	.20	.06
❑ 122	Joe Girardi	.20	.06
❑ 123	Rico Brogna	.20	.06
❑ 124	Kent Mercker	.20	.06
❑ 125	Manny Ramirez	.20	.06
❑ 126	Jeromy Burnitz	.20	.06
❑ 127	Kevin Foster	.20	.06
❑ 128	Matt Morris	.20	.06
❑ 129	Jason Dickson	.20	.06
❑ 130	Tom Glavine	.50	.15
❑ 131	Wally Joyner	.20	.06
❑ 132	Rick Reed	.20	.06
❑ 133	Todd Jones	.20	.06
❑ 134	Dave Martinez	.20	.06
❑ 135	Sandy Alomar Jr.	.20	.06
❑ 136	Mike Lansing	.20	.06
❑ 137	Sean Berry	.20	.06
❑ 138	Doug Jones	.20	.06
❑ 139	Todd Stottlemyre	.20	.06
❑ 140	Jay Bell	.20	.06
❑ 141	Jaime Navarro	.20	.06
❑ 142	Chris Hoiles	.20	.06
❑ 143	Joey Cora	.20	.06
❑ 144	Scott Spiezio	.20	.06
❑ 145	Joe Carter	.20	.06
❑ 146	Jose Guillen	.20	.06
❑ 147	Damion Easley	.20	.06
❑ 148	Lee Stevens	.20	.06
❑ 149	Alex Fernandez	.20	.06
❑ 150	Randy Johnson	.50	.15
❑ 151	J.T. Snow	.20	.06
❑ 152	Chuck Finley	.20	.06
❑ 153	Bernard Gilkey	.20	.06
❑ 154	David Segui	.20	.06
❑ 155	Dante Bichette	.20	.06
❑ 156	Kevin Stocker	.20	.06
❑ 157	Carl Everett	.20	.06
❑ 158	Jose Valentin	.20	.06
❑ 159	Pokey Reese	.20	.06
❑ 160	Derek Jeter	1.25	.35
❑ 161	Roger Pavlik	.20	.06
❑ 162	Mark Wohlers	.20	.06
❑ 163	Ricky Bottalico	.20	.06
❑ 164	Ozzie Guillen	.20	.06

❑ 165 Mike Mussina .50 .15
❑ 166 Gary Sheffield .20 .06
❑ 167 Hideo Nomo .50 .15
❑ 168 Mark Grace .50 .15
❑ 169 Aaron Sele .20 .06
❑ 170 Darryl Kile .20 .06
❑ 171 Shawn Estes .20 .06
❑ 172 Vinny Castilla .20 .06
❑ 173 Ron Coomer .20 .06
❑ 174 Jose Rosado .20 .06
❑ 175 Kenny Lofton .20 .06
❑ 176 Jason Giambi .50 .15
❑ 177 Hal Morris .20 .06
❑ 178 Darren Bragg .20 .06
❑ 179 Orel Hershiser .20 .06
❑ 180 Ray Lankford .20 .06
❑ 181 Hideki Irabu .20 .06
❑ 182 Kevin Young .20 .06
❑ 183 Javy Lopez .20 .06
❑ 184 Jeff Montgomery .20 .06
❑ 185 Mike Holtz .20 .06
❑ 186 George Williams .20 .06
❑ 187 Cal Eldred .20 .06
❑ 188 Tom Candiotti .20 .06
❑ 189 Glenallen Hill .20 .06
❑ 190 Brian Giles .20 .06
❑ 191 Dave Mlicki .20 .06
❑ 192 Garrett Stephenson .20 .06
❑ 193 Jeff Frye .20 .06
❑ 194 Joe Oliver .20 .06
❑ 195 Bob Hamelin .20 .06
❑ 196 Luis Sojo .20 .06
❑ 197 LaTroy Hawkins .20 .06
❑ 198 Kevin Elster .20 .06
❑ 199 Jeff Reed .20 .06
❑ 200 Dennis Eckersley .20 .06
❑ 201 Bill Mueller .20 .06
❑ 202 Russ Davis .20 .06
❑ 203 Armando Benitez .20 .06
❑ 204 Quilvio Veras .20 .06
❑ 205 Tim Naehring .20 .06
❑ 206 Quinton McCracken .20 .06
❑ 207 Raul Casanova .20 .06
❑ 208 Matt Lawton .20 .06
❑ 209 Luis Alicea .20 .06
❑ 210 Luis Gonzalez .20 .06
❑ 211 Allen Watson .20 .06
❑ 212 Gerald Williams .20 .06
❑ 213 David Bell .20 .06
❑ 214 Todd Hollandsworth .20 .06
❑ 215 Wade Boggs .30 .09
❑ 216 Jose Mesa .20 .06
❑ 217 Jamie Moyer .20 .06
❑ 218 Darren Daulton .20 .06
❑ 219 Mickey Morandini .20 .06
❑ 220 Rusty Greer .20 .06
❑ 221 Jim Bullinger .20 .06
❑ 222 Jose Offerman .20 .06
❑ 223 Matt Karchner .20 .06
❑ 224 Woody Williams .20 .06
❑ 225 Mark Loretta .20 .06
❑ 226 Mike Hampton .20 .06
❑ 227 Willie Adams .20 .06
❑ 228 Scott Hatteberg .20 .06
❑ 229 Rich Amaral .20 .06
❑ 230 Terry Steinbach .20 .06
❑ 231 Glendon Rusch .20 .06
❑ 232 Bret Boone .20 .06
❑ 233 Robert Person .20 .06
❑ 234 Jose Hernandez .20 .06
❑ 235 Doug Drabek .20 .06
❑ 236 Jason McDonald .20 .06
❑ 237 Chris Widger .20 .06
❑ 238 Tom Martin .20 .06
❑ 239 Dave Burba .20 .06
❑ 240 Pete Rose Jr. .20 .06
❑ 241 Bobby Ayala .20 .06
❑ 242 Tim Wakefield .20 .06
❑ 243 Dennis Springer .20 .06
❑ 244 Tim Belcher .20 .06
❑ 245 Jon Garland .20 .06
Geoff Goetz
❑ 246 Glenn Davis .40 .12
Lance Berkman
❑ 247 Vernon Wells .40 .12
Aaron Akin
❑ 248 Adam Kennedy .20 .06
Jason Romano
❑ 249 Jason Dellaero .20 .06
Troy Cameron
❑ 250 Alex Sanchez .20 .06
Jared Sandberg
❑ 251 Pablo Ortega .20 .06
James Manias
❑ 252 Jason Conti RC .20 .06
Mike Stoner
❑ 253 John Patterson .20 .06
Larry Rodriguez
❑ 254 Adrian Beltre .30 .09
Ryan Minor RC
Aaron Boone
❑ 255 Ben Grieve .20 .06
Brian Buchanan
Dermal Brown
❑ 256 Kerry Wood .60 .18
Carl Pavano
Gil Meche
❑ 257 David Ortiz .30 .09
Daryle Ward
Richie Sexson
❑ 258 Randy Winn .20 .06
Juan Encarnacion
Andrew Vessel
❑ 259 Kris Benson .20 .06
Travis Smith
Courtney Duncan RC
❑ 260 Chad Hermansen .20 .06
Brent Butler
Warren Morris RC
❑ 261 Ben Davis .20 .06
Eli Marrero
Ramon Hernandez
❑ 262 Eric Chavez .40 .12
Russell Branyan
Russ Johnson
❑ 263 Todd Dunwoody RC .20 .06
John Barnes
Ryan Jackson
❑ 264 Matt Clement .40 .12
Roy Halladay
Brian Fuentes RC
❑ 265 Randy Johnson SH .30 .09
❑ 266 Kevin Brown SH .20 .06
❑ 267 Ricardo Rincon SH .20 .06
Francisco Cordova
❑ 268 N.Garciaparra SH .50 .15
❑ 269 Tino Martinez SH .20 .06
❑ 270 Chuck Knoblauch IL .20 .06
❑ 271 Pedro Martinez IL .30 .09
❑ 272 Denny Neagle IL .20 .06
❑ 273 Juan Gonzalez IL .30 .09
❑ 274 Andres Galarraga IL .20 .06
❑ 275 Checklist .20 .06
❑ 276 Checklist .20 .06
❑ 277 Moises Alou WS .20 .06
❑ 278 Sandy Alomar Jr. WS .20 .06
❑ 279 Gary Sheffield WS .20 .06
❑ 280 Matt Williams WS .20 .06
❑ 281 Livan Hernandez WS .20 .06
❑ 282 Chad Ogea WS .20 .06
❑ 283 Marlins Champs .20 .06
❑ 284 Tino Martinez .30 .09
❑ 285 Roberto Alomar .50 .15
❑ 286 Jeff King .20 .06
❑ 287 Brian Jordan .20 .06
❑ 288 Darin Erstad .20 .06
❑ 289 Ken Caminiti .20 .06
❑ 290 Jim Thome .50 .15
❑ 291 Paul Molitor .30 .09
❑ 292 Ivan Rodriguez .50 .15
❑ 293 Bernie Williams .30 .09
❑ 294 Todd Hundley .20 .06
❑ 295 Andres Galarraga .20 .06
❑ 296 Greg Maddux 1.00 .30
❑ 297 Edgar Martinez .30 .09
❑ 298 Ron Gant .20 .06
❑ 299 Derek Bell .20 .06
❑ 300 Roger Clemens 1.00 .30
❑ 301 Rondell White .20 .06
❑ 302 Barry Larkin .50 .15
❑ 303 Robin Ventura .20 .06
❑ 304 Jason Kendall .20 .06
❑ 305 Chipper Jones .50 .15
❑ 306 John Franco .20 .06
❑ 307 Sammy Sosa .75 .23
❑ 308 Troy Percival .20 .06
❑ 309 Chuck Knoblauch .20 .06
❑ 310 Ellis Burks .20 .06
❑ 311 Al Martin .20 .06
❑ 312 Tim Salmon .30 .09
❑ 313 Moises Alou .20 .06
❑ 314 Lance Johnson .20 .06
❑ 315 Justin Thompson .20 .06
❑ 316 Will Clark .50 .15
❑ 317 Barry Bonds 1.25 .35
❑ 318 Craig Biggio .30 .09
❑ 319 John Smoltz .30 .09
❑ 320 Cal Ripken 1.50 .45
❑ 321 Ken Griffey Jr. .75 .23
❑ 322 Paul O'Neill .30 .09
❑ 323 Todd Helton .30 .09
❑ 324 John Olerud .20 .06
❑ 325 Mark McGwire 1.25 .35
❑ 326 Jose Cruz Jr. .20 .06
❑ 327 Jeff Cirillo .20 .06
❑ 328 Dean Palmer .20 .06
❑ 329 John Wetteland .20 .06
❑ 330 Steve Finley .20 .06
❑ 331 Albert Belle .20 .06
❑ 332 Curt Schilling .30 .09
❑ 333 Raul Mondesi .20 .06
❑ 334 Andruw Jones .30 .09
❑ 335 Nomar Garciaparra 1.00 .30
❑ 336 David Justice .20 .06
❑ 337 Andy Pettitte .30 .09
❑ 338 Pedro Martinez .50 .15
❑ 339 Travis Miller .20 .06
❑ 340 Chris Stynes .20 .06
❑ 341 Gregg Jefferies .20 .06
❑ 342 Jeff Fassero .20 .06
❑ 343 Craig Counsell .20 .06
❑ 344 Wilson Alvarez .20 .06
❑ 345 Bip Roberts .20 .06
❑ 346 Kelvim Escobar .20 .06
❑ 347 Mark Bellhorn .20 .06
❑ 348 Cory Lidle RC .40 .12
❑ 349 Fred McGriff .30 .09
❑ 350 Chuck Carr .20 .06
❑ 351 Bob Abreu .20 .06
❑ 352 Juan Guzman .20 .06
❑ 353 Fernando Vina .20 .06
❑ 354 Andy Benes .20 .06
❑ 355 Dave Nilsson .20 .06
❑ 356 Bobby Bonilla .20 .06
❑ 357 Ismael Valdes .20 .06
❑ 358 Carlos Perez .20 .06
❑ 359 Kirk Rueter .20 .06
❑ 360 Bartolo Colon .20 .06
❑ 361 Mel Rojas .20 .06
❑ 362 Johnny Damon .20 .06
❑ 363 Geronimo Berroa .20 .06
❑ 364 Reggie Sanders .20 .06
❑ 365 Jermaine Allensworth .20 .06
❑ 366 Orlando Cabrera .20 .06
❑ 367 Jorge Fabregas .20 .06
❑ 368 Scott Stahoviak .20 .06
❑ 369 Ken Cloude .20 .06
❑ 370 Donovan Osborne .20 .06
❑ 371 Roger Cedeno .20 .06
❑ 372 Neifi Perez .20 .06
❑ 373 Chris Holt .20 .06
❑ 374 Cecil Fielder .20 .06
❑ 375 Marty Cordova .20 .06
❑ 376 Tom Goodwin .20 .06
❑ 377 Jeff Suppan .20 .06
❑ 378 Jeff Brantley .20 .06
❑ 379 Mark Langston .20 .06
❑ 380 Shane Reynolds .20 .06
❑ 381 Mike Fetters .20 .06
❑ 382 Todd Greene .20 .06
❑ 383 Ray Durham .20 .06
❑ 384 Carlos Delgado .20 .06
❑ 385 Jeff D'Amico .20 .06
❑ 386 Brian McRae .20 .06
❑ 387 Alan Benes .20 .06
❑ 388 Heathcliff Slocumb .20 .06
❑ 389 Eric Young .20 .06
❑ 390 Travis Fryman .20 .06

❑ 391 David Cone .20 .06
❑ 392 Otis Nixon .20 .06
❑ 393 Jeremi Gonzalez .20 .06
❑ 394 Jeff Juden .20 .06
❑ 395 Jose Vizcaino .20 .06
❑ 396 Ugueth Urbina .20 .06
❑ 397 Ramon Martinez .20 .06
❑ 398 Robb Nen .20 .06
❑ 399 Harold Baines .20 .06
❑ 400 Delino DeShields .20 .06
❑ 401 John Burkett .20 .06
❑ 402 Sterling Hitchcock .20 .06
❑ 403 Mark Clark .20 .06
❑ 404 Terrell Wade .20 .06
❑ 405 Scott Brosius .20 .06
❑ 406 Chad Curtis .20 .06
❑ 407 Brian Johnson .20 .06
❑ 408 Roberto Kelly .20 .06
❑ 409 Dave Dellucci RC .20 .06
❑ 410 Michael Tucker .20 .06
❑ 411 Mark Kotsay .20 .06
❑ 412 Mark Lewis .20 .06
❑ 413 Ryan McGuire .20 .06
❑ 414 Shawon Dunston .20 .06
❑ 415 Brad Rigby .20 .06
❑ 416 Scott Erickson .20 .06
❑ 417 Bobby Jones .20 .06
❑ 418 Darren Oliver .20 .06
❑ 419 John Smiley .20 .06
❑ 420 T.J. Mathews .20 .06
❑ 421 Dustin Hermanson .20 .06
❑ 422 Mike Timlin .20 .06
❑ 423 Willie Blair .20 .06
❑ 424 Manny Alexander .20 .06
❑ 425 Bob Tewksbury .20 .06
❑ 426 Pete Schourek .20 .06
❑ 427 Reggie Jefferson .20 .06
❑ 428 Ed Sprague .20 .06
❑ 429 Jeff Conine .20 .06
❑ 430 Roberto Hernandez .20 .06
❑ 431 Tom Pagnozzi .20 .06
❑ 432 Jaret Wright .20 .06
❑ 433 Livan Hernandez .20 .06
❑ 434 Andy Ashby .20 .06
❑ 435 Todd Dunn .20 .06
❑ 436 Bobby Higginson .20 .06
❑ 437 Rod Beck .20 .06
❑ 438 Jim Leyritz .20 .06
❑ 439 Matt Williams .20 .06
❑ 440 Brett Tomko .20 .06
❑ 441 Joe Randa .20 .06
❑ 442 Chris Carpenter .20 .06
❑ 443 Dennis Reyes .20 .06
❑ 444 Al Leiter .20 .06
❑ 445 Jason Schmidt .20 .06
❑ 446 Ken Hill .20 .06
❑ 447 Shannon Stewart .20 .06
❑ 448 Enrique Wilson .20 .06
❑ 449 Fernando Tatis .20 .06
❑ 450 Jimmy Key .20 .06
❑ 451 Darrin Fletcher .20 .06
❑ 452 John Valentin .20 .06
❑ 453 Kevin Tapani .20 .06
❑ 454 Eric Karros .20 .06
❑ 455 Jay Bell .20 .06
❑ 456 Walt Weiss .20 .06
❑ 457 Devon White .20 .06
❑ 458 Carl Pavano .20 .06
❑ 459 Mike Lansing .20 .06
❑ 460 John Flaherty .20 .06
❑ 461 Richard Hidalgo .20 .06
❑ 462 Quinton McCracken .20 .06
❑ 463 Karim Garcia .20 .06
❑ 464 Miguel Cairo .20 .06
❑ 465 Edwin Diaz .20 .06
❑ 466 Bobby Smith .20 .06
❑ 467 Yamil Benitez .20 .06
❑ 468 Rich Butler .20 .06
❑ 469 Ben Ford RC .20 .06
❑ 470 Bubba Trammell .20 .06
❑ 471 Brent Brede .20 .06
❑ 472 Brooks Kieschnick .20 .06
❑ 473 Carlos Castillo .20 .06
❑ 474 Brad Radke SH .20 .06
❑ 475 Roger Clemens SH .50 .15
❑ 476 Curt Schilling SH .20 .06
❑ 477 John Olerud SH .20 .06
❑ 478 Mark McGwire SH .60 .18
❑ 479 Mike Piazza .50 .15
Ken Griffey Jr. IL
❑ 480 Jeff Bagwell .30 .09
Frank Thomas IL
❑ 481 Chipper Jones .30 .09
Nomar Garciaparra IL
❑ 482 Larry Walker .30 .09
Juan Gonzalez IL
❑ 483 Gary Sheffield .20 .06
Tino Martinez IL
❑ 484 Derrick Gibson .20 .06
Michael Coleman
Norm Hutchins
❑ 485 Braden Looper .20 .06
Cliff Politte
Brian Rose
❑ 486 Eric Milton .20 .06
Jason Marquis
Corey Lee
❑ 487 A.J.Hinch .50 .15
Mark Osborne
Robert Fick RC
❑ 488 Aramis Ramirez .30 .09
Alex Gonzalez
Sean Casey
❑ 489 Donnie Bridges .30 .09
Tim Drew RC
❑ 490 Ntema Ndungidi RC .30 .09
Darnell McDonald
❑ 491 Ryan Anderson RC .30 .09
Mark Mangum
❑ 492 J.J.Davis 1.50 .45
Troy Glaus RC
❑ 493 Jayson Werth RC .30 .09
Dan Reichert
❑ 494 John Curtice RC .50 .15
Michael Cuddyer RC
❑ 495 Jack Cust RC .30 .09
Jason Standridge
❑ 496 Brian Anderson .20 .06
❑ 497 Tony Saunders .20 .06
❑ 498 Vladimir Nunez .20 .06
Jhensy Sandoval
❑ 499 Brad Penny .30 .09
Nick Bierbrodt
❑ 500 Dustin Carr .20 .06
Luis Cruz RC
❑ 501 Cedric Bowers .20 .06
Marcus McCain
❑ 502 Checklist .20 .06
❑ 503 Checklist .20 .06
❑ 504 Alex Rodriguez 2.50 .75

1999 Topps

	Nm-Mt	Ex-Mt
COMPLETE SET (462)	50.00	15.00
COMP.HOBBY SET (462)	60.00	18.00
COMP.X-MAS SET (463)	60.00	18.00
COMP. SERIES 1 (241)	25.00	7.50
COMP. SERIES 2 (221)	25.00	7.50
COMP.MAC HR SET (70)	500.00	150.00
COMP.SOSA HR SET (66)	250.00	75.00

❑ 1 Roger Clemens 1.00 .30
❑ 2 Andres Galarraga .20 .06
❑ 3 Scott Brosius .20 .06
❑ 4 John Flaherty .20 .06
❑ 5 Jim Leyritz .20 .06
❑ 6 Ray Durham .20 .06
❑ 8 Jose Vizcaino .20 .06
❑ 9 Will Clark .50 .15
❑ 10 David Wells .20 .06
❑ 11 Jose Guillen .20 .06
❑ 12 Scott Hatteberg .20 .06
❑ 13 Edgardo Alfonzo .20 .06
❑ 14 Mike Bordick .20 .06
❑ 15 Manny Ramirez .20 .06
❑ 16 Greg Maddux 1.00 .30
❑ 17 David Segui .20 .06
❑ 18 Darryl Strawberry .30 .09
❑ 19 Brad Radke .20 .06
❑ 20 Kerry Wood .50 .15
❑ 21 Matt Anderson .20 .06
❑ 22 Derrek Lee .20 .06
❑ 23 Mickey Morandini .20 .06
❑ 24 Paul Konerko .20 .06
❑ 25 Travis Lee .20 .06
❑ 26 Ken Hill .20 .06
❑ 27 Kenny Rogers .20 .06
❑ 28 Paul Sorrento .20 .06
❑ 29 Quilvio Veras .20 .06
❑ 30 Todd Walker .20 .06
❑ 31 Ryan Jackson .20 .06
❑ 32 John Olerud .20 .06
❑ 33 Doug Glanville .20 .06
❑ 34 Nolan Ryan 2.50 .75
❑ 35 Ray Lankford .20 .06
❑ 36 Mark Loretta .20 .06
❑ 37 Jason Dickson .20 .06
❑ 38 Sean Bergman .20 .06
❑ 39 Quinton McCracken .20 .06
❑ 40 Bartolo Colon .20 .06
❑ 41 Brady Anderson .20 .06
❑ 42 Chris Stynes .20 .06
❑ 43 Jorge Posada .30 .09
❑ 44 Justin Thompson .20 .06
❑ 45 Johnny Damon .20 .06
❑ 46 Armando Benitez .20 .06
❑ 47 Brant Brown .20 .06
❑ 48 Charlie Hayes .20 .06
❑ 49 Darren Dreifort .20 .06
❑ 50 Juan Gonzalez .50 .15
❑ 51 Chuck Knoblauch .20 .06
❑ 52 Todd Helton .30 .09
❑ 53 Rick Reed .20 .06
❑ 54 Chris Gomez .20 .06
❑ 55 Gary Sheffield .20 .06
❑ 56 Rod Beck .20 .06
❑ 57 Rey Sanchez .20 .06
❑ 58 Garret Anderson .20 .06
❑ 59 Jimmy Haynes .20 .06
❑ 60 Steve Woodard .20 .06
❑ 61 Rondell White .20 .06
❑ 62 Vladimir Guerrero .50 .15
❑ 63 Eric Karros .20 .06
❑ 64 Russ Davis .20 .06
❑ 65 Mo Vaughn .20 .06
❑ 66 Sammy Sosa .75 .23
❑ 67 Troy Percival .20 .06
❑ 68 Kenny Lofton .20 .06
❑ 69 Bill Taylor .20 .06
❑ 70 Mark McGwire 1.25 .35
❑ 71 Roger Cedeno .20 .06
❑ 72 Javy Lopez .20 .06
❑ 73 Damion Easley .20 .06
❑ 74 Andy Pettitte .30 .09
❑ 75 Tony Gwynn .60 .18
❑ 76 Ricardo Rincon .20 .06
❑ 77 F.P. Santangelo .20 .06
❑ 78 Jay Bell .20 .06
❑ 79 Scott Servais .20 .06
❑ 80 Jose Canseco .50 .15
❑ 81 Roberto Hernandez .20 .06
❑ 82 Todd Dunwoody .20 .06
❑ 83 John Wetteland .20 .06
❑ 84 Mike Caruso .20 .06
❑ 85 Derek Jeter 1.25 .35
❑ 86 Aaron Sele .20 .06
❑ 87 Jose Lima .20 .06
❑ 88 Ryan Christenson .20 .06
❑ 89 Jeff Cirillo .20 .06

❑ 90 Jose Hernandez	.20	.06
❑ 91 Mark Kotsay	.20	.06
❑ 92 Darren Bragg	.20	.06
❑ 93 Albert Belle	.20	.06
❑ 94 Matt Lawton	.20	.06
❑ 95 Pedro Martinez	.50	.15
❑ 96 Greg Vaughn	.20	.06
❑ 97 Neifi Perez	.20	.06
❑ 98 Gerald Williams	.20	.06
❑ 99 Derek Bell	.20	.06
❑ 100 Ken Griffey Jr.	.75	.23
❑ 101 David Cone	.20	.06
❑ 102 Brian Johnson	.20	.06
❑ 103 Dean Palmer	.20	.06
❑ 104 Javier Valentin	.20	.06
❑ 105 Trevor Hoffman	.20	.06
❑ 106 Butch Huskey	.20	.06
❑ 107 Dave Martinez	.20	.06
❑ 108 Billy Wagner	.20	.06
❑ 109 Shawn Green	.20	.06
❑ 110 Ben Grieve	.20	.06
❑ 111 Tom Goodwin	.20	.06
❑ 112 Jaret Wright	.20	.06
❑ 113 Aramis Ramirez	.20	.06
❑ 114 Dmitri Young	.20	.06
❑ 115 Hideki Irabu	.20	.06
❑ 116 Roberto Kelly	.20	.06
❑ 117 Jeff Fassero	.20	.06
❑ 118 Mark Clark UER	.20	.06
1997 and Career Victory totals are wrong		
❑ 119 Jason McDonald	.20	.06
❑ 120 Matt Williams	.20	.06
❑ 121 Dave Burba	.20	.06
❑ 122 Bret Saberhagen	.20	.06
❑ 123 Deivi Cruz	.20	.06
❑ 124 Chad Curtis	.20	.06
❑ 125 Scott Rolen	.30	.09
❑ 126 Lee Stevens	.20	.06
❑ 127 J.T. Snow	.20	.06
❑ 128 Rusty Greer	.20	.06
❑ 129 Brian Meadows	.20	.06
❑ 130 Jim Edmonds	.20	.06
❑ 131 Ron Gant	.20	.06
❑ 132 A.J. Hinch UER	.20	.06
Photo is a reverse negative		
❑ 133 Shannon Stewart	.20	.06
❑ 134 Brad Fullmer	.20	.06
❑ 135 Cal Eldred	.20	.06
❑ 136 Matt Walbeck	.20	.06
❑ 137 Carl Everett	.20	.06
❑ 138 Walt Weiss	.20	.06
❑ 139 Fred McGriff	.30	.09
❑ 140 Darin Erstad	.20	.06
❑ 141 Dave Nilsson	.20	.06
❑ 142 Eric Young	.20	.06
❑ 143 Dan Wilson	.20	.06
❑ 144 Jeff Reed	.20	.06
❑ 145 Brett Tomko	.20	.06
❑ 146 Terry Steinbach	.20	.06
❑ 147 Seth Greisinger	.20	.06
❑ 148 Pat Meares	.20	.06
❑ 149 Livan Hernandez	.20	.06
❑ 150 Jeff Bagwell	.30	.09
❑ 151 Bob Wickman	.20	.06
❑ 152 Omar Vizquel	.20	.06
❑ 153 Eric Davis	.20	.06
❑ 154 Larry Sutton	.20	.06
❑ 155 Magglio Ordonez	.20	.06
❑ 156 Eric Milton	.20	.06
❑ 157 Darren Lewis	.20	.06
❑ 158 Rick Aguilera	.20	.06
❑ 159 Mike Lieberthal	.20	.06
❑ 160 Robb Nen	.20	.06
❑ 161 Brian Giles	.20	.06
❑ 162 Jeff Brantley	.20	.06
❑ 163 Gary DiSarcina	.20	.06
❑ 164 John Valentin	.20	.06
❑ 165 David Dellucci	.20	.06
❑ 166 Chan Ho Park	.20	.06
❑ 167 Masato Yoshii	.20	.06
❑ 168 Jason Schmidt	.20	.06
❑ 169 LaTroy Hawkins	.20	.06
❑ 170 Bret Boone	.20	.06
❑ 171 Jerry DiPoto	.20	.06
❑ 172 Mariano Rivera	.30	.09
❑ 173 Mike Cameron	.20	.06
❑ 174 Scott Erickson	.20	.06
❑ 175 Charles Johnson	.20	.06
❑ 176 Bobby Jones	.20	.06
❑ 177 Francisco Cordova	.20	.06
❑ 178 Todd Jones	.20	.06
❑ 179 Jeff Montgomery	.20	.06
❑ 180 Mike Mussina	.50	.15
❑ 181 Bob Abreu	.20	.06
❑ 182 Ismael Valdes	.20	.06
❑ 183 Andy Fox	.20	.06
❑ 184 Woody Williams	.20	.06
❑ 185 Denny Neagle	.20	.06
❑ 186 Jose Valentin	.20	.06
❑ 187 Darrin Fletcher	.20	.06
❑ 188 Gabe Alvarez	.20	.06
❑ 189 Eddie Taubensee	.20	.06
❑ 190 Edgar Martinez	.30	.09
❑ 191 Jason Kendall	.20	.06
❑ 192 Darryl Kile	.20	.06
❑ 193 Jeff King	.20	.06
❑ 194 Rey Ordonez	.20	.06
❑ 195 Andruw Jones	.30	.09
❑ 196 Tony Fernandez	.20	.06
❑ 197 Jamey Wright	.20	.06
❑ 198 B.J. Surhoff	.20	.06
❑ 199 Vinny Castilla	.20	.06
❑ 200 David Wells HL	.20	.06
❑ 201 Mark McGwire HL	.60	.18
❑ 202 Sammy Sosa HL	.50	.15
❑ 203 Roger Clemens HL	.50	.15
❑ 204 Kerry Wood HL	.30	.09
❑ 205 Lance Berkman	.40	.12
Mike Frank		
Gabe Kapler		
❑ 206 Alex Escobar RC	.40	.12
Ricky Ledee		
Mike Stoner		
❑ 207 Peter Bergeron RC	.40	.12
Jeremy Giambi		
George Lombard		
❑ 208 Michael Barrett	.25	.07
Ben Davis		
Robert Fick		
❑ 209 Pat Cline	.25	.07
Ramon Hernandez		
Jayson Werth		
❑ 210 Bruce Chen	.25	.07
Chris Enochs		
Ryan Anderson		
❑ 211 Mike Lincoln	.25	.07
Octavio Dotel		
Brad Penny		
❑ 212 Chuck Abbott RC	.25	.07
Brent Butler		
Danny Klassen		
❑ 213 Chris C.Jones	.40	.12
Jeff Urban RC		
❑ 214 Arturo McDowell RC	.40	.12
Tony Torcato		
❑ 215 Josh McKinley RC	.40	.12
Jason Tyner		
❑ 216 Matt Burch	.40	.12
Seth Etherton RC		
UER back Etherton		
❑ 217 Mamon Tucker RC	.40	.12
Rick Elder		
❑ 218 J.M.Gold	.40	.12
Ryan Mills RC		
❑ 219 Adam Brown	.40	.12
Choo Freeman RC		
❑ 220A Mark McGwire HR 1	40.00	12.00
❑ 220B Mark McGwire HR 2	15.00	4.50
❑ 220C Mark McGwire HR 3	15.00	4.50
❑ 220D Mark McGwire HR 4	15.00	4.50
❑ 220E Mark McGwire HR 5	15.00	4.50
❑ 220F Mark McGwire HR 6	15.00	4.50
❑ 220G Mark McGwire HR 7	15.00	4.50
❑ 220H Mark McGwire HR 8	15.00	4.50
❑ 220I Mark McGwire HR 9	15.00	4.50
❑ 220J M.McGwire HR 10	15.00	4.50
❑ 220K M.McGwire HR 11	15.00	4.50
❑ 220L M.McGwire HR 12	15.00	4.50
❑ 220M M.McGwire HR 13	15.00	4.50
❑ 220N M.McGwire HR 14	15.00	4.50
❑ 220O M.McGwire HR 15	15.00	4.50
❑ 220P M.McGwire HR 16	15.00	4.50
❑ 220Q M.McGwire HR 17	15.00	4.50
❑ 220R M.McGwire HR 18	15.00	4.50
❑ 220S M.McGwire HR 19	15.00	4.50
❑ 220T M.McGwire HR 20	15.00	4.50
❑ 220U M.McGwire HR 21	15.00	4.50
❑ 220V M.McGwire HR 22	15.00	4.50
❑ 220W M.McGwire HR 23	15.00	4.50
❑ 220X M.McGwire HR 24	15.00	4.50
❑ 220Y M.McGwire HR 25	15.00	4.50
❑ 220Z M.McGwire HR 26	15.00	4.50
❑ 220AA M.McGwire HR 27	15.00	4.50
❑ 220AB M.McGwire HR 28	15.00	4.50
❑ 220AC M.McGwire HR 29	15.00	4.50
❑ 220AD M.McGwire HR 30	15.00	4.50
❑ 220AE M.McGwire HR 31	15.00	4.50
❑ 220AF M.McGwire HR 32	15.00	4.50
❑ 220AG M.McGwire HR 33	15.00	4.50
❑ 220AH M.McGwire HR 34	15.00	4.50
❑ 220AI M.McGwire HR 35	15.00	4.50
❑ 220AJ M.McGwire HR 36	15.00	4.50
❑ 220AK M.McGwire HR 37	15.00	4.50
❑ 220AL M.McGwire HR 38	15.00	4.50
❑ 220AM M.McGwire HR 39	15.00	4.50
❑ 220AN M.McGwire HR 40	15.00	4.50
❑ 220AO M.McGwire HR 41	15.00	4.50
❑ 220AP M.McGwire HR 42	15.00	4.50
❑ 220AQ M.McGwire HR 43	15.00	4.50
❑ 220AR M.McGwire HR 44	15.00	4.50
❑ 220AS M.McGwire HR 45	15.00	4.50
❑ 220AT M.McGwire HR 46	15.00	4.50
❑ 220AU M.McGwire HR 47	15.00	4.50
❑ 220AV M.McGwire HR 48	15.00	4.50
❑ 220AW M.McGwire HR 49	15.00	4.50
❑ 220AX M.McGwire HR 50	15.00	4.50
❑ 220AY M.McGwire HR 51	15.00	4.50
❑ 220AZ M.McGwire HR 52	15.00	4.50
❑ 220BB M.McGwire HR 53	15.00	4.50
❑ 220CC M.McGwire HR 54	15.00	4.50
❑ 220DD M.McGwire HR 55	15.00	4.50
❑ 220EE M.McGwire HR 56	15.00	4.50
❑ 220FF M.McGwire HR 57	15.00	4.50
❑ 220GG M.McGwire HR 58	15.00	4.50
❑ 220HH M.McGwire HR 59	15.00	4.50
❑ 220II M.McGwire HR 60	15.00	4.50
❑ 220JJ M.McGwire HR 61	30.00	9.00
❑ 220KK M.McGwire HR 62	40.00	12.00
❑ 220LL M.McGwire HR 63	15.00	4.50
❑ 220MM M.McGwire HR 64	15.00	4.50
❑ 220NN M.McGwire HR 65	15.00	4.50
❑ 220OO M.McGwire HR 66	15.00	4.50
❑ 220PP M.McGwire HR 67	15.00	4.50
❑ 220QQ M.McGwire HR 68	15.00	4.50
❑ 220RR M.McGwire HR 69	15.00	4.50
❑ 220SS M.McGwire HR 70	80.00	24.00
❑ 221 Larry Walker LL	.20	.06
❑ 222 Bernie Williams LL	.20	.06
❑ 223 Mark McGwire LL	.60	.18
❑ 224 Ken Griffey Jr. LL	.50	.15
❑ 225 Sammy Sosa LL	.50	.15
❑ 226 Juan Gonzalez LL	.30	.09
❑ 227 Dante Bichette LL	.20	.06
❑ 228 Alex Rodriguez LL	.50	.15
❑ 229 Sammy Sosa LL	.50	.15
❑ 230 Derek Jeter LL	.60	.18
❑ 231 Greg Maddux LL	.50	.15
❑ 232 Roger Clemens LL	.50	.15
❑ 233 Ricky Ledee WS	.20	.06
❑ 234 Chuck Knoblauch WS	.20	.06
❑ 235 Bernie Williams WS	.20	.06
❑ 236 Tino Martinez WS	.20	.06
❑ 237 Orl. Hernandez WS	.20	.06
❑ 238 Scott Brosius WS	.20	.06
❑ 239 Andy Pettitte WS	.20	.06
❑ 240 Mariano Rivera WS	.20	.06
❑ 241 Checklist 1	.20	.06
❑ 242 Checklist 2	.20	.06
❑ 243 Tom Glavine	.50	.15
❑ 244 Andy Benes	.20	.06
❑ 245 Sandy Alomar Jr.	.20	.06
❑ 246 Wilton Guerrero	.20	.06
❑ 247 Alex Gonzalez	.20	.06
❑ 248 Roberto Alomar	.50	.15
❑ 249 Ruben Rivera	.20	.06
❑ 250 Eric Chavez	.20	.06
❑ 251 Ellis Burks	.20	.06

❑ 252 Richie Sexson .20 .06
❑ 253 Steve Finley .20 .06
❑ 254 Dwight Gooden .30 .09
❑ 255 Dustin Hermanson .20 .06
❑ 256 Kirk Rueter .20 .06
❑ 257 Steve Trachsel .20 .06
❑ 258 Gregg Jefferies .20 .06
❑ 259 Matt Stairs .20 .06
❑ 260 Shane Reynolds .20 .06
❑ 261 Gregg Olson .20 .06
❑ 262 Kevin Tapani .20 .06
❑ 263 Matt Morris .20 .06
❑ 264 Carl Pavano .20 .06
❑ 265 Nomar Garciaparra 1.00 .30
❑ 266 Kevin Young .20 .06
❑ 267 Rick Helling .20 .06
❑ 268 Matt Franco .20 .06
❑ 269 Brian McRae .20 .06
❑ 270 Cal Ripken 1.50 .45
❑ 271 Jeff Abbott .20 .06
❑ 272 Tony Batista .20 .06
❑ 273 Bill Simas .20 .06
❑ 274 Brian Hunter .20 .06
❑ 275 John Franco .20 .06
❑ 276 Devon White .20 .06
❑ 277 Rickey Henderson .75 .23
❑ 278 Chuck Finley .20 .06
❑ 279 Mike Blowers .20 .06
❑ 280 Mark Grace .50 .15
❑ 281 Randy Winn .20 .06
❑ 282 Bobby Bonilla .20 .06
❑ 283 David Justice .20 .06
❑ 284 Shane Monahan .20 .06
❑ 285 Kevin Brown .30 .09
❑ 286 Todd Zeile .20 .06
❑ 287 Al Martin .20 .06
❑ 288 Troy O'Leary .20 .06
❑ 289 Darryl Hamilton .20 .06
❑ 290 Tino Martinez .30 .09
❑ 291 David Ortiz .20 .06
❑ 292 Tony Clark .20 .06
❑ 293 Ryan Minor .20 .06
❑ 294 Mark Leiter .20 .06
❑ 295 Wally Joyner .20 .06
❑ 296 Cliff Floyd .20 .06
❑ 297 Shawn Estes .20 .06
❑ 298 Pat Hentgen .20 .06
❑ 299 Scott Elarton .20 .06
❑ 300 Alex Rodriguez 1.00 .30
❑ 301 Ozzie Guillen .20 .06
❑ 302 Hideo Nomo .50 .15
❑ 303 Ryan McGuire .20 .06
❑ 304 Brad Ausmus .20 .06
❑ 305 Alex Gonzalez .20 .06
❑ 306 Brian Jordan .20 .06
❑ 307 John Jaha .20 .06
❑ 308 Mark Grudzielanek .20 .06
❑ 309 Juan Guzman .20 .06
❑ 310 Tony Womack .20 .06
❑ 311 Dennis Reyes .20 .06
❑ 312 Marty Cordova .20 .06
❑ 313 Ramiro Mendoza .20 .06
❑ 314 Robin Ventura .20 .06
❑ 315 Rafael Palmeiro .30 .09
❑ 316 Ramon Martinez .20 .06
❑ 317 Pedro Astacio .20 .06
❑ 318 Dave Hollins .20 .06
❑ 319 Tom Candiotti .20 .06
❑ 320 Al Leiter .20 .06
❑ 321 Rico Brogna .20 .06
❑ 322 Reggie Jefferson .20 .06
❑ 323 Bernard Gilkey .20 .06
❑ 324 Jason Giambi .50 .15
❑ 325 Craig Biggio .30 .09
❑ 326 Troy Glaus .30 .09
❑ 327 Delino DeShields .20 .06
❑ 328 Fernando Vina .20 .06
❑ 329 John Smoltz .30 .09
❑ 330 Jeff Kent .20 .06
❑ 331 Roy Halladay .20 .06
❑ 332 Andy Ashby .20 .06
❑ 333 Tim Wakefield .20 .06
❑ 334 Roger Clemens 1.00 .30
❑ 335 Bernie Williams .30 .09
❑ 336 Desi Relaford .20 .06
❑ 337 John Burkett .20 .06
❑ 338 Mike Hampton .20 .06
❑ 339 Royce Clayton .20 .06
❑ 340 Mike Piazza .75 .23
❑ 341 Jeremi Gonzalez .20 .06
❑ 342 Mike Lansing .20 .06
❑ 343 Jamie Moyer .20 .06
❑ 344 Ron Coomer .20 .06
❑ 345 Barry Larkin .50 .15
❑ 346 Fernando Tatis .20 .06
❑ 347 Chili Davis .20 .06
❑ 348 Bobby Higginson .20 .06
❑ 349 Hal Morris .20 .06
❑ 350 Larry Walker .30 .09
❑ 351 Carlos Guillen .20 .06
❑ 352 Miguel Tejada .20 .06
❑ 353 Travis Fryman .20 .06
❑ 354 Jarrod Washburn .20 .06
❑ 355 Chipper Jones .50 .15
❑ 356 Todd Stottlemyre .20 .06
❑ 357 Henry Rodriguez .20 .06
❑ 358 Eli Marrero .20 .06
❑ 359 Alan Benes .20 .06
❑ 360 Tim Salmon .30 .09
❑ 361 Luis Gonzalez .20 .06
❑ 362 Scott Spiezio .20 .06
❑ 363 Chris Carpenter .20 .06
❑ 364 Bobby Howry .20 .06
❑ 365 Raul Mondesi .20 .06
❑ 366 Ugueth Urbina .20 .06
❑ 367 Tom Evans .20 .06
❑ 368 Kerry Ligtenberg RC .25 .07
❑ 369 Adrian Beltre .20 .06
❑ 370 Ryan Klesko .20 .06
❑ 371 Wilson Alvarez .20 .06
❑ 372 John Thomson .20 .06
❑ 373 Tony Saunders .20 .06
❑ 374 Dave Mlicki .20 .06
❑ 375 Ken Caminiti .20 .06
❑ 376 Jay Buhner .20 .06
❑ 377 Bill Mueller .20 .06
❑ 378 Jeff Blauser .20 .06
❑ 379 Edgar Renteria .20 .06
❑ 380 Jim Thome .50 .15
❑ 381 Joey Hamilton .20 .06
❑ 382 Calvin Pickering .20 .06
❑ 383 Marquis Grissom .20 .06
❑ 384 Omar Daal .20 .06
❑ 385 Curt Schilling .30 .09
❑ 386 Jose Cruz Jr. .20 .06
❑ 387 Chris Widger .20 .06
❑ 388 Pete Harnisch .20 .06
❑ 389 Charles Nagy .20 .06
❑ 390 Tom Gordon .20 .06
❑ 391 Bobby Smith .20 .06
❑ 392 Derrick Gibson .20 .06
❑ 393 Jeff Conine .20 .06
❑ 394 Carlos Perez .20 .06
❑ 395 Barry Bonds 1.25 .35
❑ 396 Mark McLemore .20 .06
❑ 397 Juan Encarnacion .20 .06
❑ 398 Wade Boggs .30 .09
❑ 399 Ivan Rodriguez .50 .15
❑ 400 Moises Alou .20 .06
❑ 401 Jeromy Burnitz .20 .06
❑ 402 Sean Casey .20 .06
❑ 403 Jose Offerman .20 .06
❑ 404 Joe Fontenot .20 .06
❑ 405 Kevin Millwood .20 .06
❑ 406 Lance Johnson .20 .06
❑ 407 Richard Hidalgo .20 .06
❑ 408 Mike Jackson .20 .06
❑ 409 Brian Anderson .20 .06
❑ 410 Jeff Shaw .20 .06
❑ 411 Preston Wilson .20 .06
❑ 412 Todd Hundley .20 .06
❑ 413 Jim Parque .20 .06
❑ 414 Justin Baughman .20 .06
❑ 415 Dante Bichette .20 .06
❑ 416 Paul O'Neill .30 .09
❑ 417 Miguel Cairo .20 .06
❑ 418 Randy Johnson .50 .15
❑ 419 Jesus Sanchez .20 .06
❑ 420 Carlos Delgado .20 .06
❑ 421 Ricky Ledee .20 .06
❑ 422 Orlando Hernandez .20 .06
❑ 423 Frank Thomas .50 .15
❑ 424 Pokey Reese .20 .06
❑ 425 Carlos Lee .40 .12
Mike Lowell
Kit Pellow RC
❑ 426 Michael Cuddyer .40 .12
Mark DeRosa
Jerry Hairston Jr.
❑ 427 Marlon Anderson .25 .07
Ron Belliard
Orlando Cabrera
❑ 428 Micah Bowie .40 .12
Phil Norton RC
Randy Wolf
❑ 429 Jack Cressend RC .25 .07
Jason Rakers
John Rocker
❑ 430 Ruben Mateo .25 .07
Scott Morgan
Mike Zywica RC
❑ 431 Jason LaRue .25 .07
Matt LeCroy
Mitch Meluskey
❑ 432 Gabe Kapler .25 .07
Armando Rios
Fernando Seguignol
❑ 433 Adam Kennedy .25 .07
Mickey Lopez RC
Jackie Rexrode
❑ 434 Jose Fernandez RC .25 .07
Jeff Liefer
Chris Truby
❑ 435 Corey Koskie 1.25 .35
Doug Mientkiewicz RC
Damon Minor
❑ 436 Roosevelt Brown RC .40 .12
Dernell Stenson
Vernon Wells
❑ 437 A.J. Burnett RC .50 .15
Billy Koch
John Nicholson
❑ 438 Matt Belisle .40 .12
Matt Roney RC
❑ 439 Austin Kearns 4.00 1.20
Chris George RC
❑ 440 Nate Bump RC .50 .15
Nate Cornejo
❑ 441 Brad Lidge .50 .15
Mike Nannini RC
❑ 442 Matt Holliday .40 .12
Jeff Winchester RC
❑ 443 Adam Everett .40 .12
Chip Ambres RC
❑ 444 Pat Burrell 2.50 .75
Eric Valent RC
❑ 445 Roger Clemens SK .50 .15
❑ 446 Kerry Wood SK .30 .09
❑ 447 Curt Schilling SK .20 .06
❑ 448 Randy Johnson SK .30 .09
❑ 449 Pedro Martinez SK .30 .09
❑ 450 Jeff Bagwell AT .50 .15
Andres Galarraga
Mark McGwire
❑ 451 John Olerud AT .20 .06
Jim Thome
Tino Martinez
❑ 452 Alex Rodriguez AT .60 .18
Nomar Garciaparra
Derek Jeter
❑ 453 Vinny Castilla AT .30 .09
Chipper Jones
Scott Rolen
❑ 454 Sammy Sosa AT .50 .15
Ken Griffey Jr.
Juan Gonzalez
❑ 455 Barry Bonds AT .50 .15
Manny Ramirez
Larry Walker
❑ 456 Frank Thomas AT .50 .15
Tim Salmon
David Justice
❑ 457 Travis Lee AT .20 .06
Todd Helton
Ben Grieve
❑ 458 Vladimir Guerrero AT .20 .06
Greg Vaughn
Bernie Williams

No.	Card	Nm-Mt	Ex-Mt
❑ 459	Mike Piazza AT Ivan Rodriguez Jason Kendall	.50	.15
❑ 460	Roger Clemens AT Kerry Wood Greg Maddux	.50	.15
❑ 461A	Sammy Sosa HR 1	20.00	6.00
❑ 461B	Sammy Sosa HR 2	8.00	2.40
❑ 461C	Sammy Sosa HR 3	8.00	2.40
❑ 461D	Sammy Sosa HR 4	8.00	2.40
❑ 461E	Sammy Sosa HR 5	8.00	2.40
❑ 461F	Sammy Sosa HR 6	8.00	2.40
❑ 461G	Sammy Sosa HR 7	8.00	8.75
❑ 461H	Sammy Sosa HR 8	8.00	2.40
❑ 461I	Sammy Sosa HR 9	8.00	2.40
❑ 461J	Sammy Sosa HR 10	8.00	2.40
❑ 461K	Sammy Sosa HR 11	8.00	2.40
❑ 461L	Sammy Sosa HR 12	8.00	2.40
❑ 461M	Sammy Sosa HR 13	8.00	2.40
❑ 461N	Sammy Sosa HR 14	8.00	2.40
❑ 461O	Sammy Sosa HR 15	8.00	2.40
❑ 461P	Sammy Sosa HR 16	8.00	2.40
❑ 461Q	Sammy Sosa HR 17	8.00	2.40
❑ 461R	Sammy Sosa HR 18	8.00	2.40
❑ 461S	Sammy Sosa HR 19	8.00	2.40
❑ 461T	Sammy Sosa HR 20	8.00	2.40
❑ 461U	Sammy Sosa HR 21	8.00	2.40
❑ 461V	Sammy Sosa HR 22	8.00	2.40
❑ 461W	Sammy Sosa HR 23	8.00	2.40
❑ 461X	Sammy Sosa HR 24	8.00	2.40
❑ 461Y	Sammy Sosa HR 25	8.00	2.40
❑ 461Z	Sammy Sosa HR 26	8.00	2.40
❑ 461AA	S.Sosa HR 27	8.00	2.40
❑ 461AB	S.Sosa HR 28	8.00	2.40
❑ 461AC	S.Sosa HR 29	8.00	2.40
❑ 461AD	S.Sosa HR 30	8.00	2.40
❑ 461AE	S.Sosa HR 31	8.00	2.40
❑ 461AF	S.Sosa HR 32	8.00	2.40
❑ 461AG	S.Sosa HR 33	8.00	2.40
❑ 461AH	S.Sosa HR 34	8.00	2.40
❑ 461AI	S.Sosa HR 35	8.00	2.40
❑ 461AJ	S.Sosa HR 36	8.00	2.40
❑ 461AK	S.Sosa HR 37	8.00	2.40
❑ 461AL	S.Sosa HR 38	8.00	2.40
❑ 461AM	S.Sosa HR 39	8.00	2.40
❑ 461AN	S.Sosa HR 40	8.00	2.40
❑ 461AO	S.Sosa HR 41	8.00	2.40
❑ 461AP	S.Sosa HR 42	8.00	2.40
❑ 461AR	S.Sosa HR 43	8.00	2.40
❑ 461AS	S.Sosa HR 44	8.00	2.40
❑ 461AT	S.Sosa HR 45	8.00	2.40
❑ 461AU	S.Sosa HR 46	8.00	2.40
❑ 461AV	S.Sosa HR 47	8.00	2.40
❑ 461AW	S.Sosa HR 48	8.00	2.40
❑ 461AX	S.Sosa HR 49	8.00	2.40
❑ 461AY	S.Sosa HR 50	8.00	2.40
❑ 461AZ	S.Sosa HR 51	8.00	2.40
❑ 461BB	S.Sosa HR 52	8.00	2.40
❑ 461CC	S.Sosa HR 53	8.00	2.40
❑ 461DD	S.Sosa HR 54	8.00	2.40
❑ 461EE	S.Sosa HR 55	8.00	2.40
❑ 461FF	S.Sosa HR 56	8.00	2.40
❑ 461GG	S.Sosa HR 57	8.00	2.40
❑ 461HH	S.Sosa HR 58	8.00	2.40
❑ 461II	S.Sosa HR 59	8.00	2.40
❑ 461JJ	S.Sosa HR 60	8.00	2.40
❑ 461KK	S.Sosa HR 61	20.00	6.00
❑ 461LL	S.Sosa HR 62	25.00	7.50
❑ 461MM	S.Sosa HR 63	10.00	3.00
❑ 461NN	S.Sosa HR 64	10.00	3.00
❑ 461OO	S.Sosa HR 65	10.00	3.00
❑ 461PP	S.Sosa HR 66	30.00	9.00
❑ 462	Checklist	.20	.06
❑ 463	Checklist	.20	.06

1999 Topps Traded

	Nm-Mt	Ex-Mt
COMP.FACT.SET (122)	40.00	15.00
COMPLETE SET (121)	25.00	7.50

No.	Card	Nm-Mt	Ex-Mt
❑ T1	Seth Etherton	.20	.06
❑ T2	Mark Harriger RC	.25	.07
❑ T3	Matt Wise RC	.25	.07
❑ T4	Carlos E. Hernandez RC	.25	.07
❑ T5	Julio Lugo RC	.25	.07
❑ T6	Mike Nannini	.20	.06
❑ T7	Justin Bowles RC	.25	.07
❑ T8	Mark Mulder RC	2.50	.75
❑ T9	Roberto Vaz RC	.25	.07
❑ T10	Felipe Lopez RC	.25	.07
❑ T11	Matt Belisle	.30	.09
❑ T12	Micah Bowie	.20	.06
❑ T13	Ruben Quevedo RC	.25	.07
❑ T14	Jose Garcia RC	.25	.07
❑ T15	David Kelton RC	.60	.18
❑ T16	Phil Norton	.20	.06
❑ T17	Corey Patterson RC	2.50	.75
❑ T18	Ron Walker RC	.25	.07
❑ T19	Paul Hoover RC	.25	.07
❑ T20	Ryan Rupe RC	.25	.07
❑ T21	J.D. Closser RC	.25	.07
❑ T22	Rob Ryan RC	.25	.07
❑ T23	Steve Colyer RC	.25	.07
❑ T24	Bubba Crosby RC	.40	.12
❑ T25	Luke Prokopec RC	.25	.07
❑ T26	Matt Blank RC	.25	.07
❑ T27	Josh McKinley	.20	.06
❑ T28	Nate Bump	.20	.06
❑ T29	G.Chiaramonte RC	.25	.07
❑ T30	Arturo McDowell	.20	.06
❑ T31	Tony Torcato	.20	.06
❑ T32	Dave Roberts RC	.40	.12
❑ T33	C.C. Sabathia RC	.60	.18
❑ T34	Sean Spencer RC	.25	.07
❑ T35	Chip Ambres	.20	.06
❑ T36	A.J. Burnett	.40	.12
❑ T37	Mo Bruce RC	.25	.07
❑ T38	Jason Tyner	.20	.06
❑ T39	Mamon Tucker	.20	.06
❑ T40	Sean Burroughs RC	2.00	.60
❑ T41	Kevin Eberwein RC	.25	.07
❑ T42	Junior Herndon RC	.25	.07
❑ T43	Bryan Wolff RC	.25	.07
❑ T44	Pat Burrell	2.00	.60
❑ T45	Eric Valent	.20	.06
❑ T46	Carlos Pena RC	.60	.18
❑ T47	Mike Zywica	.20	.06
❑ T48	Adam Everett	.20	.06
❑ T49	Juan Pena RC	.25	.07
❑ T50	Adam Dunn RC	5.00	1.50
❑ T51	Austin Kearns	3.00	.90
❑ T52	Jacobo Sequea RC	.25	.07
❑ T53	Choo Freeman	.20	.06
❑ T54	Jeff Winchester	.20	.06
❑ T55	Matt Burch	.20	.06
❑ T56	Chris George	.20	.06
❑ T57	Scott Mullen RC	.25	.07
❑ T58	Kit Pellow	.20	.06
❑ T59	Mark Quinn RC	.25	.07
❑ T60	Nate Cornejo	.40	.12
❑ T61	Ryan Mills	.20	.06
❑ T62	Kevin Beirne RC	.25	.07
❑ T63	Kip Wells RC	.40	.12
❑ T64	Juan Rivera RC	.75	.23
❑ T65	Alfonso Soriano RC	8.00	2.40
❑ T66	Josh Hamilton RC	1.00	.30
❑ T67	Josh Girdley RC	.25	.07
❑ T68	Kyle Snyder RC	.25	.07
❑ T69	Mike Paradis RC	.25	.07
❑ T70	Jason Jennings RC	.40	.12
❑ T71	David Walling RC	.25	.07
❑ T72	Omar Ortiz RC	.25	.07
❑ T73	Jay Gehrke RC	.25	.07
❑ T74	Casey Burns RC	.25	.07
❑ T75	Carl Crawford RC	1.25	.35
❑ T76	Reggie Sanders	.20	.06
❑ T77	Will Clark	.50	.15
❑ T78	David Wells	.20	.06
❑ T79	Paul Konerko	.20	.06
❑ T80	Armando Benitez	.20	.06
❑ T81	Brant Brown	.20	.06
❑ T82	Mo Vaughn	.20	.06
❑ T83	Jose Canseco	.50	.15
❑ T84	Albert Belle	.20	.06
❑ T85	Dean Palmer	.20	.06
❑ T86	Greg Vaughn	.20	.06
❑ T87	Mark Clark	.20	.06
❑ T88	Pat Meares	.20	.06
❑ T89	Eric Davis	.20	.06
❑ T90	Brian Giles	.20	.06
❑ T91	Jeff Brantley	.20	.06
❑ T92	Bret Boone	.20	.06
❑ T93	Ron Gant	.20	.06
❑ T94	Mike Cameron	.20	.06
❑ T95	Charles Johnson	.20	.06
❑ T96	Denny Neagle	.20	.06
❑ T97	Brian Hunter	.20	.06
❑ T98	Jose Hernandez	.20	.06
❑ T99	Rick Aguilera	.20	.06
❑ T100	Tony Batista	.20	.06
❑ T101	Roger Cedeno	.20	.06
❑ T102	C.Gubanich RC	.25	.07
❑ T103	Tim Belcher	.20	.06
❑ T104	Bruce Aven	.20	.06
❑ T105	Brian Daubach RC	.25	.07
❑ T106	Ed Sprague	.20	.06
❑ T107	Michael Tucker	.20	.06
❑ T108	Homer Bush	.20	.06
❑ T109	Armando Reynoso	.20	.06
❑ T110	Brook Fordyce	.20	.06
❑ T111	Matt Mantei	.20	.06
❑ T112	Dave Mlicki	.20	.06
❑ T113	Kenny Rogers	.20	.06
❑ T114	Livan Hernandez	.20	.06
❑ T115	Butch Huskey	.20	.06
❑ T116	David Segui	.20	.06
❑ T117	Darryl Hamilton	.20	.06
❑ T118	Terry Mulholland	.20	.06
❑ T119	Randy Velarde	.20	.06
❑ T120	Bill Taylor	.20	.06
❑ T121	Kevin Appier	.20	.06

2000 Topps

	Nm-Mt	Ex-Mt
COMPLETE SET (478)	50.00	15.00
COMP.HOBBY SET (478)	50.00	15.00
COMP. SERIES 1 (239)	25.00	7.50
COMP. SERIES 2 (240)	25.00	7.50
MCGWIRE MM SET (5)	12.00	3.60
AARON MM SET (5)	10.00	3.00
RIPKEN MM SET (5)	15.00	4.50
BOGGS MM SET (5)	3.00	.90
GWYNN MM SET (5)	6.00	1.80
GRIFFEY MM SET (5)	8.00	2.40
BONDS MM SET (5)	12.00	3.60
SOSA MM SET (5)	8.00	2.40
JETER MM SET (5)	12.00	3.60
A.ROD MM SET (5)	10.00	3.00

No.	Card	Nm-Mt	Ex-Mt
❑ 1	Mark McGwire	1.25	.35

❑ 2 Tony Gwynn .60 .18
❑ 3 Wade Boggs .30 .09
❑ 4 Cal Ripken 1.50 .45
❑ 5 Matt Williams .20 .06
❑ 6 Jay Buhner .20 .06
❑ 8 Jeff Conine .20 .06
❑ 9 Todd Greene .20 .06
❑ 10 Mike Lieberthal .20 .06
❑ 11 Steve Avery .20 .06
❑ 12 Bret Saberhagen .20 .06
❑ 13 Magglio Ordonez .20 .06
❑ 14 Brad Radke .20 .06
❑ 15 Derek Jeter 1.25 .35
❑ 16 Javy Lopez .20 .06
❑ 17 Russ Davis .20 .06
❑ 18 Armando Benitez .20 .06
❑ 19 B.J. Surhoff .20 .06
❑ 20 Darryl Kile .20 .06
❑ 21 Mark Lewis .20 .06
❑ 22 Mike Williams .20 .06
❑ 23 Mark McLemore .20 .06
❑ 24 Sterling Hitchcock .20 .06
❑ 25 Darin Erstad .20 .06
❑ 26 Ricky Gutierrez .20 .06
❑ 27 John Jaha .20 .06
❑ 28 Homer Bush .20 .06
❑ 29 Darrin Fletcher .20 .06
❑ 30 Mark Grace .50 .15
❑ 31 Fred McGriff .30 .09
❑ 32 Omar Daal .20 .06
❑ 33 Eric Karros .20 .06
❑ 34 Orlando Cabrera .20 .06
❑ 35 J.T. Snow .20 .06
❑ 36 Luis Castillo .20 .06
❑ 37 Rey Ordonez .20 .06
❑ 38 Bob Abreu .20 .06
❑ 39 Warren Morris .20 .06
❑ 40 Juan Gonzalez .50 .15
❑ 41 Mike Lansing .20 .06
❑ 42 Chili Davis .20 .06
❑ 43 Dean Palmer .20 .06
❑ 44 Hank Aaron .75 .23
❑ 45 Jeff Bagwell .30 .09
❑ 46 Jose Valentin .20 .06
❑ 47 Shannon Stewart .20 .06
❑ 48 Kent Bottenfield .20 .06
❑ 49 Jeff Shaw .20 .06
❑ 50 Sammy Sosa .75 .23
❑ 51 Randy Johnson .50 .15
❑ 52 Benny Agbayani .20 .06
❑ 53 Dante Bichette .20 .06
❑ 54 Pete Harnisch .20 .06
❑ 55 Frank Thomas .50 .15
❑ 56 Jorge Posada .30 .09
❑ 57 Todd Walker .20 .06
❑ 58 Juan Encarnacion .20 .06
❑ 59 Mike Sweeney .20 .06
❑ 60 Pedro Martinez .50 .15
❑ 61 Lee Stevens .20 .06
❑ 62 Brian Giles .20 .06
❑ 63 Chad Ogea .20 .06
❑ 64 Ivan Rodriguez .50 .15
❑ 65 Roger Cedeno .20 .06
❑ 66 David Justice .20 .06
❑ 67 Steve Trachsel .20 .06
❑ 68 Eli Marrero .20 .06
❑ 69 Dave Nilsson .20 .06
❑ 70 Ken Caminiti .20 .06
❑ 71 Tim Raines .20 .06
❑ 72 Brian Jordan .20 .06
❑ 73 Jeff Blauser .20 .06
❑ 74 Bernard Gilkey .20 .06
❑ 75 John Flaherty .20 .06
❑ 76 Brent Mayne .20 .06
❑ 77 Jose Vidro .20 .06
❑ 78 David Bell .20 .06
❑ 79 Bruce Aven .20 .06
❑ 80 John Olerud .20 .06
❑ 81 Pokey Reese .20 .06
❑ 82 Woody Williams .20 .06
❑ 83 Ed Sprague .20 .06
❑ 84 Joe Girardi .20 .06
❑ 85 Barry Larkin .50 .15
❑ 86 Mike Caruso .20 .06
❑ 87 Bobby Higginson .20 .06
❑ 88 Roberto Kelly .20 .06
❑ 89 Edgar Martinez .30 .09
❑ 90 Mark Kotsay .20 .06
❑ 91 Paul Sorrento .20 .06
❑ 92 Eric Young .20 .06
❑ 93 Carlos Delgado .20 .06
❑ 94 Troy Glaus .30 .09
❑ 95 Ben Grieve .20 .06
❑ 96 Jose Lima .20 .06
❑ 97 Garret Anderson .20 .06
❑ 98 Luis Gonzalez .20 .06
❑ 99 Carl Pavano .20 .06
❑ 100 Alex Rodriguez 1.00 .30
❑ 101 Preston Wilson .20 .06
❑ 102 Ron Gant .20 .06
❑ 103 Brady Anderson .20 .06
❑ 104 Rickey Henderson .75 .23
❑ 105 Gary Sheffield .20 .06
❑ 106 Mickey Morandini .20 .06
❑ 107 Jim Edmonds .20 .06
❑ 108 Kris Benson .20 .06
❑ 109 Adrian Beltre .20 .06
❑ 110 Alex Fernandez .20 .06
❑ 111 Dan Wilson .20 .06
❑ 112 Mark Clark .20 .06
❑ 113 Greg Vaughn .20 .06
❑ 114 Neifi Perez .20 .06
❑ 115 Paul O'Neill .30 .09
❑ 116 Jermaine Dye .20 .06
❑ 117 Todd Jones .20 .06
❑ 118 Terry Steinbach .20 .06
❑ 119 Greg Norton .20 .06
❑ 120 Curt Schilling .30 .09
❑ 121 Todd Zeile .20 .06
❑ 122 Edgardo Alfonzo .20 .06
❑ 123 Ryan McGuire .20 .06
❑ 124 Rich Aurilia .20 .06
❑ 125 John Smoltz .30 .09
❑ 126 Bob Wickman .20 .06
❑ 127 Richard Hidalgo .20 .06
❑ 128 Chuck Finley .20 .06
❑ 129 Billy Wagner .20 .06
❑ 130 Todd Hundley .20 .06
❑ 131 Dwight Gooden .30 .09
❑ 132 Russ Ortiz .20 .06
❑ 133 Mike Lowell .20 .06
❑ 134 Reggie Sanders .20 .06
❑ 135 John Valentin .20 .06
❑ 136 Brad Ausmus .20 .06
❑ 137 Chad Kreuter .20 .06
❑ 138 David Cone .20 .06
❑ 139 Brook Fordyce .20 .06
❑ 140 Roberto Alomar .50 .15
❑ 141 Charles Nagy .20 .06
❑ 142 Brian Hunter .20 .06
❑ 143 Mike Mussina .50 .15
❑ 144 Robin Ventura .30 .09
❑ 145 Kevin Brown .30 .09
❑ 146 Pat Hentgen .20 .06
❑ 147 Ryan Klesko .20 .06
❑ 148 Derek Bell .20 .06
❑ 149 Andy Sheets .20 .06
❑ 150 Larry Walker .30 .09
❑ 151 Scott Williamson .20 .06
❑ 152 Jose Offerman .20 .06
❑ 153 Doug Mientkiewicz .20 .06
❑ 154 John Snyder RC .40 .12
❑ 155 Sandy Alomar Jr. .20 .06
❑ 156 Joe Nathan .20 .06
❑ 157 Lance Johnson .20 .06
❑ 158 Odalis Perez .20 .06
❑ 159 Hideo Nomo .50 .15
❑ 160 Steve Finley .20 .06
❑ 161 Dave Martinez .20 .06
❑ 162 Matt Walbeck .20 .06
❑ 163 Bill Spiers .20 .06
❑ 164 Fernando Tatis .20 .06
❑ 165 Kenny Lofton .20 .06
❑ 166 Paul Byrd .20 .06
❑ 167 Aaron Sele .20 .06
❑ 168 Eddie Taubensee .20 .06
❑ 169 Reggie Jefferson .20 .06
❑ 170 Roger Clemens 1.00 .30
❑ 171 Francisco Cordova .20 .06
❑ 172 Mike Bordick .20 .06
❑ 173 Wally Joyner .20 .06
❑ 174 Marvin Benard .20 .06
❑ 175 Jason Kendall .20 .06
❑ 176 Mike Stanley .20 .06
❑ 177 Chad Allen .20 .06
❑ 178 Carlos Beltran .20 .06
❑ 179 Deivi Cruz .20 .06
❑ 180 Chipper Jones .50 .15
❑ 181 Vladimir Guerrero .50 .15
❑ 182 Dave Burba .20 .06
❑ 183 Tom Goodwin .20 .06
❑ 184 Brian Daubach .20 .06
❑ 185 Jay Bell .20 .06
❑ 186 Roy Halladay .20 .06
❑ 187 Miguel Tejada .20 .06
❑ 188 Armando Rios .20 .06
❑ 189 Fernando Vina .20 .06
❑ 190 Eric Davis .20 .06
❑ 191 Henry Rodriguez .20 .06
❑ 192 Joe McEwing .20 .06
❑ 193 Jeff Kent .20 .06
❑ 194 Mike Jackson .20 .06
❑ 195 Mike Morgan .20 .06
❑ 196 Jeff Montgomery .20 .06
❑ 197 Jeff Zimmerman .20 .06
❑ 198 Tony Fernandez .20 .06
❑ 199 Jason Giambi .50 .15
❑ 200 Jose Canseco .50 .15
❑ 201 Alex Gonzalez .20 .06
❑ 202 Jack Cust .40 .12
Mike Colangelo
Dee Brown
❑ 203 Felipe Lopez 1.25 .35
Alfonso Soriano
Pablo Ozuna
❑ 204 Erubiel Durazo .50 .15
Pat Burrell
Nick Johnson
❑ 205 John Sneed RC .40 .12
Kip Wells
Matt Blank
❑ 206 Josh Kalinowski .40 .12
Michael Tejera
Chris Mears RC
❑ 207 Roosevelt Brown .40 .12
Corey Patterson
Lance Berkman
❑ 208 Kit Pellow .40 .12
Kevin Barker
Russ Branyan
❑ 209 B.J. Garbe .50 .15
Larry Bigbie RC
❑ 210 Eric Munson .40 .12
Bobby Bradley RC
❑ 211 Josh Girdley .40 .12
Kyle Snyder
❑ 212 Chance Caple RC .40 .12
Jason Jennings
❑ 213 Ryan Christianson 2.00 .60
Brett Myers RC
❑ 214 Jason Stumm .40 .12
Rob Purvis RC
❑ 215 David Walling .40 .12
Mike Paradis
❑ 216 Omar Ortiz .40 .12
Jay Gehrke
❑ 217 David Cone HL .20 .06
❑ 218 Jose Jimenez HL .20 .06
❑ 219 Chris Singleton HL .20 .06
❑ 220 Fernando Tatis HL .20 .06
❑ 221 Todd Helton HL .20 .06
❑ 222 Kevin Millwood DIV .20 .06
❑ 223 Todd Pratt DIV .20 .06
❑ 224 Orl.Hernandez DIV .20 .06
❑ 225 Pedro Martinez DIV .30 .09
❑ 226 Tom Glavine LCS .30 .09
❑ 227 Bernie Williams LCS .20 .06
❑ 228 Mariano Rivera WS .20 .06
❑ 229 Tony Gwynn 20CB .60 .18
❑ 230 Wade Boggs 20CB .30 .09
❑ 231 Lance Johnson CB .20 .06
❑ 232 Mark McGwire 20CB 1.25 .35
❑ 233 R.Henderson 20CB .75 .23
❑ 234 R.Henderson 20CB .75 .23
❑ 235 Roger Clemens 20CB 1.00 .30
❑ 236A M.McGwire MM 3.00 .90
1st HR
❑ 236B M.McGwire MM 3.00 .90

1987 ROY
❑ 236C M.McGwire MM 3.00 .90
62nd HR
❑ 236D M.McGwire MM 3.00 .90
70th HR
❑ 236E M.McGwire MM 3.00 .90
500th HR
❑ 237A H.Aaron MM 2.00 .60
1st Career HR
❑ 237B H.Aaron MM 2.00 .60
1957 MVP
❑ 237C H.Aaron MM 2.00 .60
3000th Hit
❑ 237D H.Aaron MM 2.00 .60
715th HR
❑ 237E H.Aaron MM 2.00 .60
755th HR
❑ 238A C.Ripken MM 4.00 1.20
1982 ROY
❑ 238B C.Ripken MM 4.00 1.20
1991 MVP
❑ 238C C.Ripken MM 4.00 1.20
2131 Game
❑ 238D C.Ripken MM 4.00 1.20
Streak Ends
❑ 238E C.Ripken MM 4.00 1.20
400th HR
❑ 239A W.Boggs MM .75 .23
1983 Batting
❑ 239B W.Boggs MM .75 .23
1988 Batting
❑ 239C W.Boggs MM .75 .23
2000th Hit
❑ 239D W.Boggs MM .75 .23
1996 Champs
❑ 239E W.Boggs MM .75 .23
3000th Hit
❑ 240A T.Gwynn MM 1.50 .45
1984 Batting
❑ 240B T.Gwynn MM 1.50 .45
1984 NLCS
❑ 240C T.Gwynn MM 1.50 .45
1995 Batting
❑ 240D T.Gwynn MM 1.50 .45
1998 NLCS
❑ 240E T.Gwynn MM 1.50 .45
3000th Hit
❑ 241 Tom Glavine .50 .15
❑ 242 David Wells .20 .06
❑ 243 Kevin Appier .20 .06
❑ 244 Troy Percival .20 .06
❑ 245 Ray Lankford .20 .06
❑ 246 Marquis Grissom .20 .06
❑ 247 Randy Winn .20 .06
❑ 248 Miguel Batista .20 .06
❑ 249 Darren Dreifort .20 .06
❑ 250 Barry Bonds 1.25 .35
❑ 251 Harold Baines .20 .06
❑ 252 Cliff Floyd .20 .06
❑ 253 Freddy Garcia .20 .06
❑ 254 Kenny Rogers .20 .06
❑ 255 Ben Davis .20 .06
❑ 256 Charles Johnson .20 .06
❑ 257 Bubba Trammell .20 .06
❑ 258 Desi Relaford .20 .06
❑ 259 Al Martin .20 .06
❑ 260 Andy Pettitte .30 .09
❑ 261 Carlos Lee .20 .06
❑ 262 Matt Lawton .20 .06
❑ 263 Andy Fox .20 .06
❑ 264 Chan Ho Park .20 .06
❑ 265 Billy Koch .20 .06
❑ 266 Dave Roberts .20 .06
❑ 267 Carl Everett .20 .06
❑ 268 Orel Hershiser .20 .06
❑ 269 Trot Nixon .20 .06
❑ 270 Rusty Greer .20 .06
❑ 271 Will Clark .50 .15
❑ 272 Quilvio Veras .20 .06
❑ 273 Rico Brogna .20 .06
❑ 274 Devon White .20 .06
❑ 275 Tim Hudson .30 .09
❑ 276 Mike Hampton .20 .06
❑ 277 Miguel Cairo .20 .06
❑ 278 Darren Oliver .20 .06
❑ 279 Jeff Cirillo .20 .06
❑ 280 Al Leiter .20 .06
❑ 281 Shane Andrews .20 .06
❑ 282 Carlos Febles .20 .06
❑ 283 Pedro Astacio .20 .06
❑ 284 Juan Guzman .20 .06
❑ 285 Orlando Hernandez .20 .06
❑ 286 Paul Konerko .20 .06
❑ 287 Tony Clark .20 .06
❑ 288 Aaron Boone .20 .06
❑ 289 Ismael Valdes .20 .06
❑ 290 Moises Alou .20 .06
❑ 291 Kevin Tapani .20 .06
❑ 292 John Franco .20 .06
❑ 293 Todd Zeile .20 .06
❑ 294 Jason Schmidt .20 .06
❑ 295 Johnny Damon .20 .06
❑ 296 Scott Brosius .20 .06
❑ 297 Travis Fryman .20 .06
❑ 298 Jose Vizcaino .20 .06
❑ 299 Eric Chavez .20 .06
❑ 300 Mike Piazza .75 .23
❑ 301 Matt Clement .20 .06
❑ 302 Cristian Guzman .20 .06
❑ 303 C.J. Nitkowski .20 .06
❑ 304 Michael Tucker .20 .06
❑ 305 Brett Tomko .20 .06
❑ 306 Mike Lansing .20 .06
❑ 307 Eric Owens .20 .06
❑ 308 Livan Hernandez .20 .06
❑ 309 Rondell White .20 .06
❑ 310 Todd Stottlemyre .20 .06
❑ 311 Chris Carpenter .20 .06
❑ 312 Ken Hill .20 .06
❑ 313 Mark Loretta .20 .06
❑ 314 John Rocker .20 .06
❑ 315 Richie Sexson .20 .06
❑ 316 Ruben Mateo .20 .06
❑ 317 Joe Randa .20 .06
❑ 318 Mike Sirotka .20 .06
❑ 319 Jose Rosado .20 .06
❑ 320 Matt Mantei .20 .06
❑ 321 Kevin Millwood .20 .06
❑ 322 Gary DiSarcina .20 .06
❑ 323 Dustin Hermanson .20 .06
❑ 324 Mike Stanton .20 .06
❑ 325 Kirk Rueter .20 .06
❑ 326 Damian Miller RC .40 .12
❑ 327 Doug Glanville .20 .06
❑ 328 Scott Rolen .30 .09
❑ 329 Ray Durham .20 .06
❑ 330 Butch Huskey .20 .06
❑ 331 Mariano Rivera .30 .09
❑ 332 Darren Lewis .20 .06
❑ 333 Mike Timlin .20 .06
❑ 334 Mark Grudzielanek .20 .06
❑ 335 Mike Cameron .20 .06
❑ 336 Kelvim Escobar .20 .06
❑ 337 Bret Boone .20 .06
❑ 338 Mo Vaughn .20 .06
❑ 339 Craig Biggio .30 .09
❑ 340 Michael Barrett .20 .06
❑ 341 Marlon Anderson .20 .06
❑ 342 Bobby Jones .20 .06
❑ 343 John Halama .20 .06
❑ 344 Todd Ritchie .20 .06
❑ 345 Chuck Knoblauch .20 .06
❑ 346 Rick Reed .20 .06
❑ 347 Kelly Stinnett .20 .06
❑ 348 Tim Salmon .30 .09
❑ 349 A.J. Hinch .20 .06
❑ 350 Jose Cruz Jr. .20 .06
❑ 351 Roberto Hernandez .20 .06
❑ 352 Edgar Renteria .20 .06
❑ 353 Jose Hernandez .20 .06
❑ 354 Brad Fullmer .20 .06
❑ 355 Trevor Hoffman .20 .06
❑ 356 Troy O'Leary .20 .06
❑ 357 Justin Thompson .20 .06
❑ 358 Kevin Young .20 .06
❑ 359 Hideki Irabu .20 .06
❑ 360 Jim Thome .50 .15
❑ 361 Steve Karsay .20 .06
❑ 362 Octavio Dotel .20 .06
❑ 363 Omar Vizquel .20 .06
❑ 364 Raul Mondesi .20 .06
❑ 365 Shane Reynolds .20 .06
❑ 366 Bartolo Colon .20 .06
❑ 367 Chris Widger .20 .06
❑ 368 Gabe Kapler .20 .06
❑ 369 Bill Simas .20 .06
❑ 370 Tino Martinez .30 .09
❑ 371 John Thomson .20 .06
❑ 372 Delino DeShields .20 .06
❑ 373 Carlos Perez .20 .06
❑ 374 Eddie Perez .20 .06
❑ 375 Jeromy Burnitz .20 .06
❑ 376 Jimmy Haynes .20 .06
❑ 377 Travis Lee .20 .06
❑ 378 Darryl Hamilton .20 .06
❑ 379 Jamie Moyer .20 .06
❑ 380 Alex Gonzalez .20 .06
❑ 381 John Wetteland .20 .06
❑ 382 Vinny Castilla .20 .06
❑ 383 Jeff Suppan .20 .06
❑ 384 Jim Leyritz .20 .06
❑ 385 Robb Nen .20 .06
❑ 386 Wilson Alvarez .20 .06
❑ 387 Andres Galarraga .20 .06
❑ 388 Mike Remlinger .20 .06
❑ 389 Geoff Jenkins .20 .06
❑ 390 Matt Stairs .20 .06
❑ 391 Bill Mueller .20 .06
❑ 392 Mike Lowell .20 .06
❑ 393 Andy Ashby .20 .06
❑ 394 Ruben Rivera .20 .06
❑ 395 Todd Helton .30 .09
❑ 396 Bernie Williams .30 .09
❑ 397 Royce Clayton .20 .06
❑ 398 Manny Ramirez .20 .06
❑ 399 Kerry Wood .50 .15
❑ 400 Ken Griffey Jr. .75 .23
❑ 401 Enrique Wilson .20 .06
❑ 402 Joey Hamilton .20 .06
❑ 403 Shawn Estes .20 .06
❑ 404 Ugueth Urbina .20 .06
❑ 405 Albert Belle .20 .06
❑ 406 Rick Helling .20 .06
❑ 407 Steve Parris .20 .06
❑ 408 Eric Milton .20 .06
❑ 409 Dave Mlicki .20 .06
❑ 410 Shawn Green .20 .06
❑ 411 Jaret Wright .20 .06
❑ 412 Tony Womack .20 .06
❑ 413 Vernon Wells .20 .06
❑ 414 Ron Belliard .20 .06
❑ 415 Ellis Burks .20 .06
❑ 416 Scott Erickson .20 .06
❑ 417 Rafael Palmeiro .30 .09
❑ 418 Damion Easley .20 .06
❑ 419 Jamey Wright .20 .06
❑ 420 Corey Koskie .20 .06
❑ 421 Bobby Howry .20 .06
❑ 422 Ricky Ledee .20 .06
❑ 423 Dmitri Young .20 .06
❑ 424 Sidney Ponson .20 .06
❑ 425 Greg Maddux 1.00 .30
❑ 426 Jose Guillen .20 .06
❑ 427 Jon Lieber .20 .06
❑ 428 Andy Benes .20 .06
❑ 429 Randy Velarde .20 .06
❑ 430 Sean Casey .20 .06
❑ 431 Torii Hunter .20 .06
❑ 432 Ryan Rupe .20 .06
❑ 433 David Segui .20 .06
❑ 434 Todd Pratt .20 .06
❑ 435 Nomar Garciaparra 1.00 .30
❑ 436 Denny Neagle .20 .06
❑ 437 Ron Coomer .20 .06
❑ 438 Chris Singleton .20 .06
❑ 439 Tony Batista .20 .06
❑ 440 Andruw Jones .30 .09
❑ 441 Aubrey Huff .20 .06
Sean Burroughs
Adam Piatt
❑ 442 Rafael Furcal .40 .12
Travis Dawkins
Jason Dellaero
❑ 443 Mike Lamb RC .40 .12
Joe Crede
Wilton Veras
❑ 444 Julio Zuleta RC .40 .12
Jorge Toca

Card	Nm-Mt	Ex-Mt
Dernell Stenson		
❑ 445 Garry Maddox Jr. RC	.40	.12
Gary Matthews Jr.		
Tim Raines Jr.		
❑ 446 Mark Mulder	.50	.15
C.C. Sabathia		
Matt Riley		
❑ 447 Scott Downs RC	.40	.12
Chris George		
Matt Belisle		
❑ 448 Doug Mirabelli	.40	.12
Ben Petrick		
Jayson Werth		
❑ 449 Josh Hamilton	.40	.12
Corey Myers RC		
❑ 450 Ben Christensen RC	.40	.12
Richard Stahl RC		
❑ 451 Ben Sheets RC	3.00	.90
Barry Zito		
❑ 452 Kurt Ainsworth	.50	.15
Ty Howington RC		
❑ 453 Vince Faison RC	.40	.12
Rick Asadoorian		
❑ 454 Keith Reed RC	.40	.12
Jeff Heaverlo		
❑ 455 Mike MacDougal	.50	.15
Brad Baker RC		
❑ 456 Mark McGwire SH	.60	.18
❑ 457 Cal Ripken SH	.75	.23
❑ 458 Wade Boggs SH	.20	.06
❑ 459 Tony Gwynn SH	.30	.09
❑ 460 Jesse Orosco SH	.20	.06
❑ 461 Larry Walker	.30	.09
Nomar Garciaparra LL		
❑ 462 Ken Griffey Jr.	.50	.15
Mark McGwire LL		
❑ 463 Manny Ramirez	.50	.15
Mark McGwire LL		
❑ 464 Pedro Martinez	.30	.09
Randy Johnson LL		
❑ 465 Pedro Martinez	.30	.09
Randy Johnson LL		
❑ 466 Derek Jeter	.50	.15
Luis Gonzalez LL		
❑ 467 Larry Walker	.20	.06
Manny Ramirez LL		
❑ 468 Tony Gwynn 20CB	.60	.18
❑ 469 Mark McGwire 20CB	1.25	.35
❑ 470 Frank Thomas 20CB	.50	.15
❑ 471 Harold Baines 20CB	.20	.06
❑ 472 Roger Clemens 20CB	1.00	.30
❑ 473 John Franco 20CB	.20	.06
❑ 474 John Franco 20CB	.20	.06
❑ 475A K.Griffey Jr. MM	2.00	.60
350th HR		
❑ 475B K.Griffey Jr. MM	2.00	.60
1997 MVP		
❑ 475C K.Griffey Jr. MM	2.00	.60
HR Dad		
❑ 475D K.Griffey Jr. MM	2.00	.60
1992 AS MVP		
❑ 475E K.Griffey Jr. MM	2.00	.60
50 HR 1997		
❑ 476A B.Bonds MM	3.00	.90
400HR/400SB		
❑ 476B B.Bonds MM	3.00	.90
40HR/40SB		
❑ 476C B.Bonds MM	3.00	.90
1993 MVP		
❑ 476D B.Bonds MM	3.00	.90
1990 MVP		
❑ 476E B.Bonds MM	3.00	.90
1992 MVP		
❑ 477A S.Sosa MM	2.00	.60
20 HR June		
❑ 477B S.Sosa MM	2.00	.60
66 HR 1998		
❑ 477C S.Sosa MM	2.00	.60
60 HR 1999		
❑ 477D S.Sosa MM	2.00	.60
1998 MVP		
❑ 477E S.Sosa MM HR's	2.00	.60
61/62		
❑ 478A D.Jeter MM	3.00	.90
1996 ROY		
❑ 478B D.Jeter MM	3.00	.90
Wins 1999 WS		
❑ 478C D.Jeter MM	3.00	.90
Wins 1998 WS		
❑ 478D D.Jeter MM	3.00	.90
Wins 1996 WS		
❑ 478E D.Jeter MM	3.00	.90
17 GM Hit Streak		
❑ 479A A.Rodriguez MM	2.50	.75
40HR/40SB		
❑ 479B A.Rodriguez MM	2.50	.75
100th HR		
❑ 479C A.Rodriguez MM	2.50	.75
1996 POY		
❑ 479D A.Rodriguez MM	2.50	.75
Wins 1 Million		
❑ 479E A.Rodriguez MM	2.50	.75
1996 Batting Leader		
❑ NNO M. McGwire 85 Reprint	5.00	1.50

2000 Topps Traded

	Nm-Mt	Ex-Mt
COMP.FACT.SET (136)	40.00	12.00
COMPLETE SET (135)	25.00	7.50
❑ T1 Mike MacDougal	.50	.15
❑ T2 Andy Tracy RC	.30	.09
❑ T3 Brandon Phillips RC	1.00	.30
❑ T4 Brandon Inge RC	.30	.09
❑ T5 Robbie Morrison RC	.30	.09
❑ T6 Josh Pressley RC	.30	.09
❑ T7 Todd Moser RC	.30	.09
❑ T8 Rob Purvis	.30	.09
❑ T9 Chance Caple	.30	.09
❑ T10 Ben Sheets	.75	.23
❑ T11 Russ Jacobson RC	.30	.09
❑ T12 Brian Cole RC	.30	.09
❑ T13 Brad Baker	.30	.09
❑ T14 Alex Cintron RC	1.50	.45
❑ T15 Lyle Overbay RC	.50	.15
❑ T16 Mike Edwards RC	.30	.09
❑ T17 Sean McGowan RC	.30	.09
❑ T18 Jose Molina	.20	.06
❑ T19 Marcos Castillo RC	.30	.09
❑ T20 Josue Espada RC	.30	.09
❑ T21 Alex Gordon RC	.30	.09
❑ T22 Rob Pugmire RC	.30	.09
❑ T23 Jason Stumm	.30	.09
❑ T24 Ty Howington	.30	.09
❑ T25 Brett Myers	1.50	.45
❑ T26 Maicer Izturis RC	.30	.09
❑ T27 John McDonald	.20	.06
❑ T28 W.Rodriguez RC	.30	.09
❑ T29 Carlos Zambrano RC	1.50	.45
❑ T30 Alejandro Diaz RC	.30	.09
❑ T31 Geraldo Guzman RC	.30	.09
❑ T32 J.R. House RC	.30	.09
❑ T33 Elvin Nina RC	.30	.09
❑ T34 Juan Pierre RC	1.50	.45
❑ T35 Ben Johnson RC	.30	.09
❑ T36 Jeff Bailey RC	.30	.09
❑ T37 Miguel Olivo RC	.30	.09
❑ T38 F.Rodriguez RC	1.50	.45
❑ T39 Tony Pena Jr. RC	.30	.09
❑ T40 Miguel Cabrera RC	15.00	4.50
❑ T41 Asdrubal Oropeza RC	.30	.09
❑ T42 Junior Zamora RC	.30	.09
❑ T43 Jovanny Cedeno RC	.30	.09
❑ T44 John Sneed	.30	.09
❑ T45 Josh Kalinowski	.30	.09
❑ T46 Mike Young RC	1.25	.35
❑ T47 Rico Washington RC	.30	.09
❑ T48 Chad Durbin RC	.30	.09
❑ T49 Junior Brignac RC	.30	.09
❑ T50 Carlos Hernandez RC	.30	.09
❑ T51 Cesar Izturis RC	.30	.09
❑ T52 Oscar Salazar RC	.30	.09
❑ T53 Pat Strange RC	.30	.09
❑ T54 Rick Asadoorian	.30	.09
❑ T55 Keith Reed	.30	.09
❑ T56 Leo Estrella RC	.30	.09
❑ T57 Wascar Serrano RC	.30	.09
❑ T58 Richard Gomez RC	.30	.09
❑ T59 Ramon Santiago RC	.30	.09
❑ T60 Jovanny Sosa RC	.30	.09
❑ T61 Aaron Rowand RC	.30	.09
❑ T62 Junior Guerrero RC	.30	.09
❑ T63 Luis Terrero RC	.30	.09
❑ T64 Brian Sanches RC	.30	.09
❑ T65 Scott Sobkowiak RC	.30	.09
❑ T66 Gary Majewski RC	.30	.09
❑ T67 Barry Zito	2.00	.60
❑ T68 Ryan Christianson	.30	.09
❑ T69 Cristian Guerrero RC	.30	.09
❑ T70 T.De La Rosa RC	.30	.09
❑ T71 Andrew Beinbrink RC	.30	.09
❑ T72 Ryan Knox RC	.30	.09
❑ T73 Alex Graman RC	.30	.09
❑ T74 Juan Guzman RC	.30	.09
❑ T75 Ruben Salazar RC	.30	.09
❑ T76 Luis Matos RC	1.50	.45
❑ T77 Tony Mota RC	.30	.09
❑ T78 Doug Davis	.20	.06
❑ T79 Ben Christensen	.30	.09
❑ T80 Mike Lamb	.30	.09
❑ T81 Adrian Gonzalez RC	1.50	.45
❑ T82 Mike Stodolka RC	.30	.09
❑ T83 Adam Johnson RC	.30	.09
❑ T84 Matt Wheatland RC	.30	.09
❑ T85 Corey Smith RC	.50	.15
❑ T86 Rocco Baldelli RC	8.00	2.40
❑ T87 Keith Bucktrot RC	.30	.09
❑ T88 Adam Wainwright RC	1.00	.30
❑ T89 Scott Thorman RC	.50	.15
❑ T90 Tripper Johnson RC	.50	.15
❑ T91 Jim Edmonds	.30	.09
❑ T92 Masato Yoshii	.20	.06
❑ T93 Adam Kennedy	.20	.06
❑ T94 Darryl Kile	.30	.09
❑ T95 Mark McLemore	.20	.06
❑ T96 Ricky Gutierrez	.20	.06
❑ T97 Juan Gonzalez	.75	.23
❑ T98 Melvin Mora	.30	.09
❑ T99 Dante Bichette	.30	.09
❑ T100 Lee Stevens	.20	.06
❑ T101 Roger Cedeno	.20	.06
❑ T102 John Olerud	.30	.09
❑ T103 Eric Young	.20	.06
❑ T104 Mickey Morandini	.20	.06
❑ T105 Travis Lee	.20	.06
❑ T106 Greg Vaughn	.30	.09
❑ T107 Todd Zeile	.30	.09
❑ T108 Chuck Finley	.30	.09
❑ T109 Ismael Valdes	.20	.06
❑ T110 Reggie Sanders	.30	.09
❑ T111 Pat Hentgen	.20	.06
❑ T112 Ryan Klesko	.30	.09
❑ T113 Derek Bell	.20	.06
❑ T114 Hideo Nomo	.75	.23
❑ T115 Aaron Sele	.20	.06
❑ T116 Fernando Vina	.30	.09
❑ T117 Wally Joyner	.30	.09
❑ T118 Brian Hunter	.20	.06
❑ T119 Joe Girardi	.20	.06
❑ T120 Omar Daal	.20	.06
❑ T121 Brook Fordyce	.20	.06
❑ T122 Jose Valentin	.20	.06
❑ T123 Curt Schilling	.50	.15
❑ T124 B.J. Surhoff	.30	.09
❑ T125 Henry Rodriguez	.20	.06
❑ T126 Mike Bordick	.20	.06
❑ T127 David Justice	.30	.09
❑ T128 Charles Johnson	.30	.09
❑ T129 Will Clark	.75	.23

❑ T130 Dwight Gooden .50 .15
❑ T131 David Segui .20 .06
❑ T132 Denny Neagle .30 .09
❑ T133 Jose Canseco .75 .23
❑ T134 Bruce Chen .20 .06
❑ T135 Jason Bere .20 .06

2001 Topps

	Nm-Mt	Ex-Mt
COMPLETE SET (790)	80.00	24.00
COMP.FACT.BLUE SET (795)	100.00	30.00
COMP.SERIES 1 (405)	40.00	12.00
COMP. SERIES 2 (385)	40.00	12.00
COMMON (1-6/8-791)	.20	.06
COMMON (352-376/727-751)	.25	.07

❑ 1 Cal Ripken 1.50 .45
❑ 2 Chipper Jones .50 .15
❑ 3 Roger Cedeno .20 .06
❑ 4 Garret Anderson .20 .06
❑ 5 Robin Ventura .20 .06
❑ 6 Daryle Ward .20 .06
❑ 7 Does Not Exist
❑ 8 Craig Paquette .20 .06
❑ 9 Phil Nevin .20 .06
❑ 10 Jermaine Dye .20 .06
❑ 11 Chris Singleton .20 .06
❑ 12 Mike Stanton .20 .06
❑ 13 Brian Hunter .20 .06
❑ 14 Mike Redmond .20 .06
❑ 15 Jim Thome .50 .15
❑ 16 Brian Jordan .20 .06
❑ 17 Joe Girardi .20 .06
❑ 18 Steve Woodard .20 .06
❑ 19 Dustin Hermanson .20 .06
❑ 20 Shawn Green .20 .06
❑ 21 Todd Stottlemyre .20 .06
❑ 22 Dan Wilson .20 .06
❑ 23 Todd Pratt .20 .06
❑ 24 Derek Lowe .20 .06
❑ 25 Juan Gonzalez .50 .15
❑ 26 Clay Bellinger .20 .06
❑ 27 Jeff Fassero .20 .06
❑ 28 Pat Meares .20 .06
❑ 29 Eddie Taubensee .20 .06
❑ 30 Paul O'Neill .30 .09
❑ 31 Jeffrey Hammonds .20 .06
❑ 32 Pokey Reese .20 .06
❑ 33 Mike Mussina .50 .15
❑ 34 Rico Brogna .20 .06
❑ 35 Jay Buhner .20 .06
❑ 36 Steve Cox .20 .06
❑ 37 Quilvio Veras .20 .06
❑ 38 Marquis Grissom .20 .06
❑ 39 Shigetoshi Hasegawa .20 .06
❑ 40 Shane Reynolds .20 .06
❑ 41 Adam Piatt .20 .06
❑ 42 Luis Polonia .20 .06
❑ 43 Brook Fordyce .20 .06
❑ 44 Preston Wilson .20 .06
❑ 45 Ellis Burks .20 .06
❑ 46 Armando Rios .20 .06
❑ 47 Chuck Finley .20 .06
❑ 48 Dan Plesac .20 .06
❑ 49 Shannon Stewart .20 .06
❑ 50 Mark McGwire 1.25 .35
❑ 51 Mark Loretta .20 .06
❑ 52 Gerald Williams .20 .06
❑ 53 Eric Young .20 .06
❑ 54 Peter Bergeron .20 .06
❑ 55 Dave Hansen .20 .06
❑ 56 Arthur Rhodes .20 .06
❑ 57 Bobby Jones .20 .06
❑ 58 Matt Clement .20 .06
❑ 59 Mike Benjamin .20 .06
❑ 60 Pedro Martinez .50 .15
❑ 61 Jose Canseco .50 .15
❑ 62 Matt Anderson .20 .06
❑ 63 Torii Hunter .20 .06
❑ 64 Carlos Lee UER .20 .06
1999 Charlotte Games Played are wrong
❑ 65 David Cone .20 .06
❑ 66 Rey Sanchez .20 .06
❑ 67 Eric Chavez .20 .06
❑ 68 Rick Helling .20 .06
❑ 69 Manny Alexander .20 .06
❑ 70 John Franco .20 .06
❑ 71 Mike Bordick .20 .06
❑ 72 Andres Galarraga .20 .06
❑ 73 Jose Cruz Jr. .20 .06
❑ 74 Mike Matheny .20 .06
❑ 75 Randy Johnson .50 .15
❑ 76 Richie Sexson .20 .06
❑ 77 Vladimir Nunez .20 .06
❑ 78 Harold Baines .20 .06
❑ 79 Aaron Boone .20 .06
❑ 80 Darin Erstad .20 .06
❑ 81 Alex Gonzalez .20 .06
❑ 82 Gil Heredia .20 .06
❑ 83 Shane Andrews .20 .06
❑ 84 Todd Hundley .20 .06
❑ 85 Bill Mueller .20 .06
❑ 86 Mark McLemore .20 .06
❑ 87 Scott Spiezio .20 .06
❑ 88 Kevin McGlinchy .20 .06
❑ 89 Bubba Trammell .20 .06
❑ 90 Manny Ramirez .20 .06
❑ 91 Mike Lamb .20 .06
❑ 92 Scott Karl .20 .06
❑ 93 Brian Buchanan .20 .06
❑ 94 Chris Turner .20 .06
❑ 95 Mike Sweeney .20 .06
❑ 96 John Wetteland .20 .06
❑ 97 Rob Bell .20 .06
❑ 98 Pat Rapp .20 .06
❑ 99 John Burkett .20 .06
❑ 100 Derek Jeter 1.25 .35
❑ 101 J.D. Drew .20 .06
❑ 102 Jose Offerman .20 .06
❑ 103 Rick Reed .20 .06
❑ 104 Will Clark .50 .15
❑ 105 Rickey Henderson .75 .23
❑ 106 Dave Berg .20 .06
❑ 107 Kirk Rueter .20 .06
❑ 108 Lee Stevens .20 .06
❑ 109 Jay Bell .20 .06
❑ 110 Fred McGriff .30 .09
❑ 111 Julio Zuleta .20 .06
❑ 112 Brian Anderson .20 .06
❑ 113 Orlando Cabrera .20 .06
❑ 114 Alex Fernandez .20 .06
❑ 115 Derek Bell .20 .06
❑ 116 Eric Owens .20 .06
❑ 117 Brian Bohanon .20 .06
❑ 118 Dennys Reyes .20 .06
❑ 119 Mike Stanley .20 .06
❑ 120 Jorge Posada .30 .09
❑ 121 Rich Becker .20 .06
❑ 122 Paul Konerko .20 .06
❑ 123 Mike Remlinger .20 .06
❑ 124 Travis Lee .20 .06
❑ 125 Ken Caminiti .20 .06
❑ 126 Kevin Barker .20 .06
❑ 127 Paul Quantrill .20 .06
❑ 128 Ozzie Guillen .20 .06
❑ 129 Kevin Tapani .20 .06
❑ 130 Mark Johnson .20 .06
❑ 131 Randy Wolf .20 .06
❑ 132 Michael Tucker .20 .06
❑ 133 Darren Lewis .20 .06
❑ 134 Joe Randa .20 .06
❑ 135 Jeff Cirillo .20 .06
❑ 136 David Ortiz .20 .06
❑ 137 Herb Perry .20 .06
❑ 138 Jeff Nelson .20 .06
❑ 139 Chris Stynes .20 .06
❑ 140 Johnny Damon .20 .06
❑ 141 Jeff Reboulet .20 .06
❑ 142 Jason Schmidt .20 .06
❑ 143 Charles Johnson .20 .06
❑ 144 Pat Burrell .20 .06
❑ 145 Gary Sheffield .20 .06
❑ 146 Tom Glavine .50 .15
❑ 147 Jason Isringhausen .20 .06
❑ 148 Chris Carpenter .20 .06
❑ 149 Jeff Suppan .20 .06
❑ 150 Ivan Rodriguez .50 .15
❑ 151 Luis Sojo .20 .06
❑ 152 Ron Villone .20 .06
❑ 153 Mike Sirotka .20 .06
❑ 154 Chuck Knoblauch .20 .06
❑ 155 Jason Kendall .20 .06
❑ 156 Dennis Cook .20 .06
❑ 157 Bobby Estalella .20 .06
❑ 158 Jose Guillen .20 .06
❑ 159 Thomas Howard .20 .06
❑ 160 Carlos Delgado .20 .06
❑ 161 Benji Gil .20 .06
❑ 162 Tim Bogar .20 .06
❑ 163 Kevin Elster .20 .06
❑ 164 Einar Diaz .20 .06
❑ 165 Andy Benes .20 .06
❑ 166 Adrian Beltre .20 .06
❑ 167 David Bell .20 .06
❑ 168 Turk Wendell .20 .06
❑ 169 Pete Harnisch .20 .06
❑ 170 Roger Clemens 1.00 .30
❑ 171 Scott Williamson .20 .06
❑ 172 Kevin Jordan .20 .06
❑ 173 Brad Penny .20 .06
❑ 174 John Flaherty .20 .06
❑ 175 Troy Glaus .30 .09
❑ 176 Kevin Appier .20 .06
❑ 177 Walt Weiss .20 .06
❑ 178 Tyler Houston .20 .06
❑ 179 Michael Barrett .20 .06
❑ 180 Mike Hampton .20 .06
❑ 181 Francisco Cordova .20 .06
❑ 182 Mike Jackson .20 .06
❑ 183 David Segui .20 .06
❑ 184 Carlos Febles .20 .06
❑ 185 Roy Halladay .20 .06
❑ 186 Seth Etherton .20 .06
❑ 187 Charlie Hayes .20 .06
❑ 188 Fernando Tatis .20 .06
❑ 189 Steve Trachsel .20 .06
❑ 190 Livan Hernandez .20 .06
❑ 191 Joe Oliver .20 .06
❑ 192 Stan Javier .20 .06
❑ 193 B.J. Surhoff .20 .06
❑ 194 Rob Ducey .20 .06
❑ 195 Barry Larkin .50 .15
❑ 196 Danny Patterson .20 .06
❑ 197 Bobby Howry .20 .06
❑ 198 Dmitri Young .20 .06
❑ 199 Brian Hunter .20 .06
❑ 200 Alex Rodriguez 1.00 .30
❑ 201 Hideo Nomo .50 .15
❑ 202 Luis Alicea .20 .06
❑ 203 Warren Morris .20 .06
❑ 204 Antonio Alfonseca .20 .06
❑ 205 Edgardo Alfonzo .20 .06
❑ 206 Mark Grudzielanek .20 .06
❑ 207 Fernando Vina .20 .06
❑ 208 Willie Greene .20 .06
❑ 209 Homer Bush .20 .06
❑ 210 Jason Giambi .50 .15
❑ 211 Mike Morgan .20 .06
❑ 212 Steve Karsay .20 .06
❑ 213 Matt Lawton .20 .06
❑ 214 Wendell Magee Jr. .20 .06
❑ 215 Rusty Greer .20 .06
❑ 216 Keith Lockhart .20 .06
❑ 217 Billy Koch .20 .06
❑ 218 Todd Hollandsworth .20 .06
❑ 219 Raul Ibanez .20 .06
❑ 220 Tony Gwynn .60 .18
❑ 221 Carl Everett .20 .06

❑ 222 Hector Carrasco .20 .06
❑ 223 Jose Valentin .20 .06
❑ 224 Deivi Cruz .20 .06
❑ 225 Bret Boone .20 .06
❑ 226 Kurt Abbott .20 .06
❑ 227 Melvin Mora .20 .06
❑ 228 Danny Graves .20 .06
❑ 229 Jose Jimenez .20 .06
❑ 230 James Baldwin .20 .06
❑ 231 C.J. Nitkowski .20 .06
❑ 232 Jeff Zimmerman .20 .06
❑ 233 Mike Lowell .20 .06
❑ 234 Hideki Irabu .20 .06
❑ 235 Greg Vaughn .20 .06
❑ 236 Omar Daal .20 .06
❑ 237 Darren Dreifort .20 .06
❑ 238 Gil Meche .20 .06
❑ 239 Damian Jackson .20 .06
❑ 240 Frank Thomas .50 .15
❑ 241 Travis Miller .20 .06
❑ 242 Jeff Frye .20 .06
❑ 243 Dave Magadan .20 .06
❑ 244 Luis Castillo .20 .06
❑ 245 Bartolo Colon .20 .06
❑ 246 Steve Kline .20 .06
❑ 247 Shawon Dunston .20 .06
❑ 248 Rick Aguilera .20 .06
❑ 249 Omar Olivares .20 .06
❑ 250 Craig Biggio .30 .09
❑ 251 Scott Schoeneweis .20 .06
❑ 252 Dave Veres .20 .06
❑ 253 Ramon Martinez .20 .06
❑ 254 Jose Vidro .20 .06
❑ 255 Todd Helton .30 .09
❑ 256 Greg Norton .20 .06
❑ 257 Jacque Jones .20 .06
❑ 258 Jason Grimsley .20 .06
❑ 259 Dan Reichert .20 .06
❑ 260 Robb Nen .20 .06
❑ 261 Mark Clark .20 .06
❑ 262 Scott Hatteberg .20 .06
❑ 263 Doug Brocail .20 .06
❑ 264 Mark Johnson .20 .06
❑ 265 Eric Davis .20 .06
❑ 266 Terry Shumpert .20 .06
❑ 267 Kevin Millar .20 .06
❑ 268 Ismael Valdes .20 .06
❑ 269 Richard Hidalgo .20 .06
❑ 270 Randy Velarde .20 .06
❑ 271 Bengie Molina .20 .06
❑ 272 Tony Womack .20 .06
❑ 273 Enrique Wilson .20 .06
❑ 274 Jeff Brantley .20 .06
❑ 275 Rick Ankiel .20 .06
❑ 276 Terry Mulholland .20 .06
❑ 277 Ron Belliard .20 .06
❑ 278 Terrence Long .20 .06
❑ 279 Alberto Castillo .20 .06
❑ 280 Royce Clayton .20 .06
❑ 281 Joe McEwing .20 .06
❑ 282 Jason McDonald .20 .06
❑ 283 Ricky Bottalico .20 .06
❑ 284 Keith Foulke .20 .06
❑ 285 Brad Radke .20 .06
❑ 286 Gabe Kapler .20 .06
❑ 287 Pedro Astacio .20 .06
❑ 288 Armando Reynoso .20 .06
❑ 289 Darryl Kile .20 .06
❑ 290 Reggie Sanders .20 .06
❑ 291 Esteban Yan .20 .06
❑ 292 Joe Nathan .20 .06
❑ 293 Jay Payton .20 .06
❑ 294 Francisco Cordero .20 .06
❑ 295 Gregg Jefferies .20 .06
❑ 296 LaTroy Hawkins .20 .06
❑ 297 Jeff Tam RC .25 .07
❑ 298 Jacob Cruz .20 .06
❑ 299 Chris Holt .20 .06
❑ 300 Vladimir Guerrero .50 .15
❑ 301 Marvin Benard .20 .06
❑ 302 Alex Ramirez .20 .06
❑ 303 Mike Williams .20 .06
❑ 304 Sean Bergman .20 .06
❑ 305 Juan Encarnacion .20 .06
❑ 306 Russ Davis .20 .06
❑ 307 Hanley Frias .20 .06
❑ 308 Ramon Hernandez .20 .06
❑ 309 Matt Walbeck .20 .06
❑ 310 Bill Spiers .20 .06
❑ 311 Bob Wickman .20 .06
❑ 312 Sandy Alomar Jr. .20 .06
❑ 313 Eddie Guardado .20 .06
❑ 314 Shane Halter .20 .06
❑ 315 Geoff Jenkins .20 .06
❑ 316 Brian Meadows .20 .06
❑ 317 Damian Miller .20 .06
❑ 318 Darrin Fletcher .20 .06
❑ 319 Rafael Furcal .20 .06
❑ 320 Mark Grace .50 .15
❑ 321 Mark Mulder .20 .06
❑ 322 Joe Torre MG .20 .06
❑ 323 Bobby Cox MG .20 .06
❑ 324 Mike Scioscia MG .20 .06
❑ 325 Mike Hargrove MG .20 .06
❑ 326 Jimy Williams MG .20 .06
❑ 327 Jerry Manuel MG .20 .06
❑ 328 Buck Showalter MG .20 .06
❑ 329 Charlie Manuel MG .20 .06
❑ 330 Don Baylor MG .20 .06
❑ 331 Phil Garner MG .20 .06
❑ 332 Jack McKeon MG .20 .06
❑ 333 Tony Muser MG .20 .06
❑ 334 Buddy Bell MG .20 .06
❑ 335 Tom Kelly MG .20 .06
❑ 336 John Boles MG .20 .06
❑ 337 Art Howe MG .20 .06
❑ 338 Larry Dierker MG .20 .06
❑ 339 Lou Piniella MG .20 .06
❑ 340 Davey Johnson MG .20 .06
❑ 341 Larry Rothschild MG .20 .06
❑ 342 Davey Lopes MG .20 .06
❑ 343 Johnny Oates MG .20 .06
❑ 344 Felipe Alou MG .20 .06
❑ 345 Jim Fregosi MG .20 .06
❑ 346 Bobby Valentine MG .20 .06
❑ 347 Terry Francona MG .20 .06
❑ 348 Gene Lamont MG .20 .06
❑ 349 Tony LaRussa MG .20 .06
❑ 350 Bruce Bochy MG .20 .06
❑ 351 Dusty Baker MG .20 .06
❑ 352 Adrian Gonzalez .40 .12
Adam Johnson
❑ 353 Matt Wheatland .25 .07
Bryan Digby
❑ 354 Tripper Johnson .25 .07
Scott Thorman
❑ 355 Phil Dumatrait .40 .12
Adam Wainwright
❑ 356 Scott Heard .40 .12
David Parrish RC
❑ 357 Rocco Baldelli 2.00 .60
Mark Folsom RC
❑ 358 Dominic Rich RC .40 .12
Aaron Herr
❑ 359 Mike Stodolka .40 .12
Sean Burnett
❑ 360 Derek Thompson .25 .07
Corey Smith
❑ 361 Danny Borrell RC .40 .12
Jason Bourgeois RC
❑ 362 Chin-Feng Chen .40 .12
Corey Patterson
Josh Hamilton
❑ 363 Ryan Anderson .75 .23
Barry Zito
C.C. Sabathia
❑ 364 Scott Sobkowiak .40 .12
David Walling
Ben Sheets
❑ 365 Ty Howington .25 .07
Josh Kalinowski
Josh Girdley
❑ 366 Hee Seop Choi RC 3.00 .90
Aaron McNeal
Jason Hart
❑ 367 Bobby Bradley .40 .12
Kurt Ainsworth
Chin-Hui Tsao
❑ 368 Mike Glendenning .25 .07
Kenny Kelly
Juan Silvestri
❑ 369 J.R. House .25 .07
Ramon Castro
Ben Davis
❑ 370 Chance Caple 1.00 .30
Rafael Soriano RC
Pasqual Coco
❑ 371 Travis Hafner RC .75 .23
Eric Munson
Bucky Jacobsen
❑ 372 Jason Conti .40 .12
Chris Wakeland
Brian Cole
❑ 373 Scott Seabol .40 .12
Aubrey Huff
Joe Crede
❑ 374 Adam Everett .25 .07
Jose Ortiz
Keith Ginter
❑ 375 Carlos Hernandez .25 .07
Geraldo Guzman
Adam Eaton
❑ 376 Bobby Kielty .40 .12
Milton Bradley
Juan Rivera
❑ 377 Mark McGwire GM .60 .18
❑ 378 Don Larsen GM .20 .06
❑ 379 Bobby Thomson GM .20 .06
❑ 380 Bill Mazeroski GM .20 .06
❑ 381 Reggie Jackson GM .30 .09
❑ 382 Kirk Gibson GM .20 .06
❑ 383 Roger Maris GM .50 .15
❑ 384 Cal Ripken GM .75 .23
❑ 385 Hank Aaron GM .50 .15
❑ 386 Joe Carter GM .20 .06
❑ 387 Cal Ripken SH 1.50 .45
❑ 388 Randy Johnson SH .30 .09
❑ 389 Ken Griffey Jr. SH .75 .23
❑ 390 Troy Glaus SH .30 .09
❑ 391 Kazuhiro Sasaki SH .20 .06
❑ 392 Sammy Sosa LL .30 .09
Troy Glaus
❑ 393 Todd Helton LL .20 .06
Edgar Martinez
❑ 394 Todd Helton LL .50 .15
Nomar Garicaparra
❑ 395 Barry Bonds LL .50 .15
Jason Giambi
❑ 396 Todd Helton LL .20 .06
Manny Ramirez
❑ 397 Todd Helton LL .20 .06
Darin Erstad
❑ 398 Kevin Brown LL .30 .09
Pedro Martinez
❑ 399 Randy Johnson LL .30 .09
Pedro Martinez
❑ 400 Will Clark HL .50 .15
❑ 401 New York Mets HL .50 .15
❑ 402 New York Yankees HL .75 .23
❑ 403 Seattle Mariners HL .20 .06
❑ 404 Mike Hampton HL .20 .06
❑ 405 New York Yankees HL 1.00 .30
❑ 406 N.Y. Yankees Champs 2.00 .60
❑ 407 Jeff Bagwell .30 .09
❑ 408 Brant Brown .20 .06
❑ 409 Brad Fullmer .20 .06
❑ 410 Dean Palmer .20 .06
❑ 411 Greg Zaun .20 .06
❑ 412 Jose Vizcaino .20 .06
❑ 413 Jeff Abbott .20 .06
❑ 414 Travis Fryman .20 .06
❑ 415 Mike Cameron .20 .06
❑ 416 Matt Mantei .20 .06
❑ 417 Alan Benes .20 .06
❑ 418 Mickey Morandini .20 .06
❑ 419 Troy Percival .20 .06
❑ 420 Eddie Perez .20 .06
❑ 421 Vernon Wells .20 .06
❑ 422 Ricky Gutierrez .20 .06
❑ 423 Carlos Hernandez .20 .06
❑ 424 Chan Ho Park .20 .06
❑ 425 Armando Benitez .20 .06
❑ 426 Sidney Ponson .20 .06
❑ 427 Adrian Brown .20 .06
❑ 428 Ruben Mateo .20 .06
❑ 429 Alex Ochoa .20 .06
❑ 430 Jose Rosado .20 .06
❑ 431 Masato Yoshii .20 .06

❑ 432 Corey Koskie .20 .06
❑ 433 Andy Pettitte .30 .09
❑ 434 Brian Daubach .20 .06
❑ 435 Sterling Hitchcock .20 .06
❑ 436 Timo Perez .20 .06
❑ 437 Shawn Estes .20 .06
❑ 438 Tony Armas Jr. .20 .06
❑ 439 Danny Bautista .20 .06
❑ 440 Randy Winn .20 .06
❑ 441 Wilson Alvarez .20 .06
❑ 442 Rondell White .20 .06
❑ 443 Jeromy Burnitz .20 .06
❑ 444 Kelvim Escobar .20 .06
❑ 445 Paul Bako .20 .06
❑ 446 Javier Vazquez .20 .06
❑ 447 Eric Gagne .30 .09
❑ 448 Kenny Lofton .20 .06
❑ 449 Mark Kotsay .20 .06
❑ 450 Jamie Moyer .20 .06
❑ 451 Delino DeShields .20 .06
❑ 452 Rey Ordonez .20 .06
❑ 453 Russ Ortiz .20 .06
❑ 454 Dave Burba .20 .06
❑ 455 Eric Karros .20 .06
❑ 456 Felix Martinez .20 .06
❑ 457 Tony Batista .20 .06
❑ 458 Bobby Higginson .20 .06
❑ 459 Jeff D'Amico .20 .06
❑ 460 Shane Spencer .20 .06
❑ 461 Brent Mayne .20 .06
❑ 462 Glendon Rusch .20 .06
❑ 463 Chris Gomez .20 .06
❑ 464 Jeff Shaw .20 .06
❑ 465 Damon Buford .20 .06
❑ 466 Mike DiFelice .20 .06
❑ 467 Jimmy Haynes .20 .06
❑ 468 Billy Wagner .20 .06
❑ 469 A.J. Hinch .20 .06
❑ 470 Gary DiSarcina .20 .06
❑ 471 Tom Lampkin .20 .06
❑ 472 Adam Eaton .20 .06
❑ 473 Brian Giles .20 .06
❑ 474 John Thomson .20 .06
❑ 475 Cal Eldred .20 .06
❑ 476 Ramiro Mendoza .20 .06
❑ 477 Scott Sullivan .20 .06
❑ 478 Scott Rolen .30 .09
❑ 479 Todd Ritchie .20 .06
❑ 480 Pablo Ozuna .20 .06
❑ 481 Carl Pavano .20 .06
❑ 482 Matt Morris .20 .06
❑ 483 Matt Stairs .20 .06
❑ 484 Tim Belcher .20 .06
❑ 485 Lance Berkman .20 .06
❑ 486 Brian Meadows .20 .06
❑ 487 Bob Abreu .20 .06
❑ 488 John VanderWal .20 .06
❑ 489 Donnie Sadler .20 .06
❑ 490 Damion Easley .20 .06
❑ 491 David Justice .20 .06
❑ 492 Ray Durham .20 .06
❑ 493 Todd Zeile .20 .06
❑ 494 Desi Relaford .20 .06
❑ 495 Cliff Floyd .20 .06
❑ 496 Scott Downs .20 .06
❑ 497 Barry Bonds 1.25 .35
❑ 498 Jeff D'Amico .20 .06
❑ 499 Octavio Dotel .20 .06
❑ 500 Kent Mercker .20 .06
❑ 501 Craig Grebeck .20 .06
❑ 502 Roberto Hernandez .20 .06
❑ 503 Matt Williams .20 .06
❑ 504 Bruce Aven .20 .06
❑ 505 Brett Tomko .20 .06
❑ 506 Kris Benson .20 .06
❑ 507 Neifi Perez .20 .06
❑ 508 Alfonso Soriano .50 .15
❑ 509 Keith Osik .20 .06
❑ 510 Matt Franco .20 .06
❑ 511 Steve Finley .20 .06
❑ 512 Olmedo Saenz .20 .06
❑ 513 Esteban Loaiza .20 .06
❑ 514 Adam Kennedy .20 .06
❑ 515 Scott Elarton .20 .06
❑ 516 Moises Alou .20 .06
❑ 517 Bryan Rekar .20 .06
❑ 518 Darryl Hamilton .20 .06
❑ 519 Osvaldo Fernandez .20 .06
❑ 520 Kip Wells .20 .06
❑ 521 Bernie Williams .30 .09
❑ 522 Mike Darr .20 .06
❑ 523 Marlon Anderson .20 .06
❑ 524 Derrek Lee .20 .06
❑ 525 Ugueth Urbina .20 .06
❑ 526 Vinny Castilla .20 .06
❑ 527 David Wells .20 .06
❑ 528 Jason Marquis .20 .06
❑ 529 Orlando Palmeiro .20 .06
❑ 530 Carlos Perez .20 .06
❑ 531 J.T. Snow .20 .06
❑ 532 Al Leiter .20 .06
❑ 533 Jimmy Anderson .20 .06
❑ 534 Brett Laxton .20 .06
❑ 535 Butch Huskey .20 .06
❑ 536 Orlando Hernandez .20 .06
❑ 537 Magglio Ordonez .20 .06
❑ 538 Willie Blair .20 .06
❑ 539 Kevin Sefcik .20 .06
❑ 540 Chad Curtis .20 .06
❑ 541 John Halama .20 .06
❑ 542 Andy Fox .20 .06
❑ 543 Juan Guzman .20 .06
❑ 544 Frank Menechino RC .20 .06
❑ 545 Raul Mondesi .20 .06
❑ 546 Tim Salmon .30 .09
❑ 547 Ryan Rupe .20 .06
❑ 548 Jeff Reed .20 .06
❑ 549 Mike Mordecai .20 .06
❑ 550 Jeff Kent .20 .06
❑ 551 Wiki Gonzalez .20 .06
❑ 552 Kenny Rogers .20 .06
❑ 553 Kevin Young .20 .06
❑ 554 Brian Johnson .20 .06
❑ 555 Tom Goodwin .20 .06
❑ 556 Tony Clark UER .20 .06
0 games, 208 At-Bats
❑ 557 Mac Suzuki .20 .06
❑ 558 Brian Moehler .20 .06
❑ 559 Jim Parque .20 .06
❑ 560 Mariano Rivera .30 .09
❑ 561 Trot Nixon .20 .06
❑ 562 Mike Mussina .50 .15
❑ 563 Nelson Figueroa .20 .06
❑ 564 Alex Gonzalez .20 .06
❑ 565 Benny Agbayani .20 .06
❑ 566 Ed Sprague .20 .06
❑ 567 Scott Erickson .20 .06
❑ 568 Abraham Nunez .20 .06
❑ 569 Jerry DiPoto .20 .06
❑ 570 Sean Casey .20 .06
❑ 571 Wilton Veras .20 .06
❑ 572 Joe Mays .20 .06
❑ 573 Bill Simas .20 .06
❑ 574 Doug Glanville .20 .06
❑ 575 Scott Sauerbeck .20 .06
❑ 576 Ben Davis .20 .06
❑ 577 Jesus Sanchez .20 .06
❑ 578 Ricardo Rincon .20 .06
❑ 579 John Olerud .20 .06
❑ 580 Curt Schilling .30 .09
❑ 581 Alex Cora .20 .06
❑ 582 Pat Hentgen .20 .06
❑ 583 Javy Lopez .20 .06
❑ 584 Ben Grieve .20 .06
❑ 585 Frank Castillo .20 .06
❑ 586 Kevin Stocker .20 .06
❑ 587 Mark Sweeney .20 .06
❑ 588 Ray Lankford .20 .06
❑ 589 Turner Ward .20 .06
❑ 590 Felipe Crespo .20 .06
❑ 591 Omar Vizquel .20 .06
❑ 592 Mike Lieberthal .20 .06
❑ 593 Ken Griffey Jr. .75 .23
❑ 594 Troy O'Leary .20 .06
❑ 595 Dave Mlicki .20 .06
❑ 596 Manny Ramirez .20 .06
❑ 597 Mike Lansing .20 .06
❑ 598 Rich Aurilia .20 .06
❑ 599 Russell Branyan .20 .06
❑ 600 Russ Johnson .20 .06
❑ 601 Greg Colbrunn .20 .06
❑ 602 Andruw Jones .30 .09
❑ 603 Henry Blanco .20 .06
❑ 604 Jarrod Washburn .20 .06
❑ 605 Tony Eusebio .20 .06
❑ 606 Aaron Sele .20 .06
❑ 607 Charles Nagy .20 .06
❑ 608 Ryan Klesko .20 .06
❑ 609 Dante Bichette .20 .06
❑ 610 Bill Haselman .20 .06
❑ 611 Jerry Spradlin .20 .06
❑ 612 A. Rodriguez Rangers 1.00 .30
❑ 613 Jose Silva .20 .06
❑ 614 Darren Oliver .20 .06
❑ 615 Pat Mahomes .20 .06
❑ 616 Roberto Alomar .50 .15
❑ 617 Edgar Renteria .20 .06
❑ 618 Jon Lieber .20 .06
❑ 619 John Rocker .20 .06
❑ 620 Miguel Tejada .20 .06
❑ 621 Mo Vaughn .20 .06
❑ 622 Jose Lima .20 .06
❑ 623 Kerry Wood .50 .15
❑ 624 Mike Timlin .20 .06
❑ 625 Wil Cordero .20 .06
❑ 626 Albert Belle .20 .06
❑ 627 Bobby Jones .20 .06
❑ 628 Doug Mirabelli .20 .06
❑ 629 Jason Tyner .20 .06
❑ 630 Andy Ashby .20 .06
❑ 631 Jose Hernandez .20 .06
❑ 632 Devon White .20 .06
❑ 633 Ruben Rivera .20 .06
❑ 634 Steve Parris .20 .06
❑ 635 David McCarty .20 .06
❑ 636 Jose Canseco .50 .15
❑ 637 Todd Walker .20 .06
❑ 638 Stan Spencer .20 .06
❑ 639 Wayne Gomes .20 .06
❑ 640 Freddy Garcia .20 .06
❑ 641 Jeremy Giambi .20 .06
❑ 642 Luis Lopez .20 .06
❑ 643 John Smoltz .30 .09
❑ 644 Kelly Stinnett .20 .06
❑ 645 Kevin Brown .20 .06
❑ 646 Wilton Guerrero .20 .06
❑ 647 Al Martin .20 .06
❑ 648 Woody Williams .20 .06
❑ 649 Brian Rose .20 .06
❑ 650 Rafael Palmeiro .30 .09
❑ 651 Pete Schourek .20 .06
❑ 652 Kevin Jarvis .20 .06
❑ 653 Mark Redman .20 .06
❑ 654 Ricky Ledee .20 .06
❑ 655 Larry Walker .30 .09
❑ 656 Paul Byrd .20 .06
❑ 657 Jason Bere .20 .06
❑ 658 Rick White .20 .06
❑ 659 Calvin Murray .20 .06
❑ 660 Greg Maddux 1.00 .30
❑ 661 Ron Gant .20 .06
❑ 662 Eli Marrero .20 .06
❑ 663 Graeme Lloyd .20 .06
❑ 664 Trevor Hoffman .20 .06
❑ 665 Nomar Garciaparra 1.00 .30
❑ 666 Glenallen Hill .20 .06
❑ 667 Matt LeCroy .20 .06
❑ 668 Justin Thompson .20 .06
❑ 669 Brady Anderson .20 .06
❑ 670 Miguel Batista .20 .06
❑ 671 Erubiel Durazo .20 .06
❑ 672 Kevin Millwood .20 .06
❑ 673 Mitch Meluskey .20 .06
❑ 674 Luis Gonzalez .20 .06
❑ 675 Edgar Martinez .30 .09
❑ 676 Robert Person .20 .06
❑ 677 Benito Santiago .20 .06
❑ 678 Todd Jones .20 .06
❑ 679 Tino Martinez .30 .09
❑ 680 Carlos Beltran .20 .06
❑ 681 Gabe White .20 .06
❑ 682 Bret Saberhagen .20 .06
❑ 683 Jeff Conine .20 .06
❑ 684 Jaret Wright .20 .06
❑ 685 Bernard Gilkey .20 .06
❑ 686 Garrett Stephenson .20 .06
❑ 687 Jamey Wright .20 .06
❑ 688 Sammy Sosa .75 .23

❑ 689 John Jaha .20 .06
❑ 690 Ramon Martinez .20 .06
❑ 691 Robert Fick .20 .06
❑ 692 Eric Milton .20 .06
❑ 693 Denny Neagle .20 .06
❑ 694 Ron Coomer .20 .06
❑ 695 John Valentin .20 .06
❑ 696 Placido Polanco .20 .06
❑ 697 Tim Hudson .20 .06
❑ 698 Marty Cordova .20 .06
❑ 699 Chad Kreuter .20 .06
❑ 700 Frank Catalanotto .20 .06
❑ 701 Tim Wakefield .20 .06
❑ 702 Jim Edmonds .20 .06
❑ 703 Michael Tucker .20 .06
❑ 704 Cristian Guzman .20 .06
❑ 705 Joey Hamilton .20 .06
❑ 706 Mike Piazza .75 .23
❑ 707 Dave Martinez .20 .06
❑ 708 Mike Hampton .20 .06
❑ 709 Bobby Bonilla .20 .06
❑ 710 Juan Pierre .20 .06
❑ 711 John Parrish .20 .06
❑ 712 Kory DeHaan .20 .06
❑ 713 Brian Tollberg .20 .06
❑ 714 Chris Truby .20 .06
❑ 715 Emil Brown .20 .06
❑ 716 Ryan Dempster .20 .06
❑ 717 Rich Garces .20 .06
❑ 718 Mike Myers .20 .06
❑ 719 Luis Ordaz .20 .06
❑ 720 Kazuhiro Sasaki .20 .06
❑ 721 Mark Quinn .20 .06
❑ 722 Ramon Ortiz .20 .06
❑ 723 Kerry Ligtenberg .20 .06
❑ 724 Rolando Arrojo .20 .06
❑ 725 Tsuyoshi Shinjo RC 1.00 .30
❑ 726 Ichiro Suzuki RC 15.00 4.50
❑ 727 Roy Oswalt .50 .15
Pat Strange
Jon Rauch
❑ 728 Phil Wilson RC 1.25 .35
Jake Peavy RC
Darwin Cubillan RC
❑ 729 Steve Smyth RC .40 .12
Mike Bynum
Nathan Haynes
❑ 730 Michael Cuddyer .40 .12
Joe Lawrence
Choo Freeman
❑ 731 Carlos Pena .25 .07
Larry Barnes
DeWayne Wise
❑ 732 Travis Dawkins .40 .12
Erick Almonte
Felipe Lopez
❑ 733 Alex Escobar .25 .07
Eric Valent
Brad Wilkerson
❑ 734 Toby Hall .25 .07
Rod Barajas
Jeff Goldbach
❑ 735 Jason Romano .40 .12
Marcus Giles
Pablo Ozuna
❑ 736 Dee Brown .40 .12
Jack Cust
Vernon Wells
❑ 737 David Espinosa .40 .12
Luis Montanez RC
❑ 738 Anthony Pluta RC .50 .15
Justin Wayne RC
❑ 739 Josh Axelson RC .40 .12
Carmen Cali RC
❑ 740 Shaun Boyd RC .40 .12
Chris Morris RC
❑ 741 Tommy Arko RC .40 .12
Dan Moylan RC
❑ 742 Luis Cotto RC .40 .12
Luis Escobar
❑ 743 Brandon Mims RC .40 .12
Blake Williams RC
❑ 744 Chris Russ RC .40 .12
Bryan Edwards
❑ 745 Joe Torres .25 .07
Ben Diggins
❑ 746 Hugh Quattlebaum RC .50 .15
Edwin Encarnacion RC
❑ 747 Brian Bass RC .40 .12
Odannis Ayala RC
❑ 748 Jason Kaanoi .25 .07
Michael Matthews RC UER
name misspelled Mathews
❑ 749 Stuart McFarland RC .40 .12
Adam Sterrett RC
❑ 750 David Krynzel .75 .23
Grady Sizemore
❑ 751 Keith Bucktrot .25 .07
Dane Sardinha
❑ 752 Anaheim Angels TC .20 .06
❑ 753 Ariz. Diamondbacks TC .20 .06
❑ 754 Atlanta Braves TC .20 .06
❑ 755 Baltimore Orioles TC .20 .06
❑ 756 Boston Red Sox TC .20 .06
❑ 757 Chicago Cubs TC .20 .06
❑ 758 Chicago White Sox TC .20 .06
❑ 759 Cincinnati Reds TC .20 .06
❑ 760 Cleveland Indians TC .20 .06
❑ 761 Colorado Rockies TC .20 .06
❑ 762 Detroit Tigers TC .20 .06
❑ 763 Florida Marlins TC .20 .06
❑ 764 Houston Astros TC .20 .06
❑ 765 K.C. Royals TC .20 .06
❑ 766 L.A. Dodgers TC .20 .06
❑ 767 Milw. Brewers TC .20 .06
❑ 768 Minnesota Twins TC .20 .06
❑ 769 Montreal Expos TC .20 .06
❑ 770 New York Mets TC .20 .06
❑ 771 New York Yankees TC 1.00 .30
❑ 772 Oakland Athletics TC .20 .06
❑ 773 Phil. Phillies TC .20 .06
❑ 774 Pittsburgh Pirates TC .20 .06
❑ 775 San Diego Padres TC .20 .06
❑ 776 San Francisco Giants TC .20 .06
❑ 777 Seattle Mariners TC .20 .06
❑ 778 St. Louis Cardinals TC .20 .06
❑ 779 T.B. Devil Rays TC .20 .06
❑ 780 Texas Rangers TC .20 .06
❑ 781 Toronto Blue Jays TC .20 .06
❑ 782 Bucky Dent GM .20 .06
❑ 783 Jackie Robinson GM .50 .15
❑ 784 Roberto Clemente GM .60 .18
❑ 785 Nolan Ryan GM 1.00 .30
❑ 786 Kerry Wood GM .30 .09
❑ 787 Rickey Henderson GM .50 .15
❑ 788 Lou Brock GM .30 .09
❑ 789 David Wells GM .20 .06
❑ 790 Andruw Jones GM .20 .06
❑ 791 Carlton Fisk GM .20 .06
❑ TK Bo Jackson 120.00 36.00
Deion Sanders Bat
❑ NNO Bobby Thomson 50.00 15.00
Ralph Branca
1991 Bowman Autograph

2001 Topps Traded

	Nm-Mt	Ex-Mt
COMPLETE SET (265)	80.00	24.00
COMMON (T1-T99/T145-T265)	.40	.12
COMMON (100-144)	1.00	.30

❑ T1 Sandy Alomar Jr. .40 .12
❑ T2 Kevin Appier .50 .15
❑ T3 Brad Ausmus .40 .12
❑ T4 Derek Bell .40 .12
❑ T5 Bret Boone .50 .15
❑ T6 Rico Brogna .40 .12
❑ T7 Ellis Burks .50 .15
❑ T8 Ken Caminiti .50 .15
❑ T9 Roger Cedeno .40 .12
❑ T10 Royce Clayton .40 .12
❑ T11 Enrique Wilson .40 .12
❑ T12 Rheal Cormier .40 .12
❑ T13 Eric Davis .50 .15
❑ T14 Shawon Dunston .40 .12
❑ T15 Andres Galarraga .50 .15
❑ T16 Tom Gordon .40 .12
❑ T17 Mark Grace 1.25 .35
❑ T18 Jeffrey Hammonds .40 .12
❑ T19 Dustin Hermanson .40 .12
❑ T20 Quinton McCracken .40 .12
❑ T21 Todd Hundley .40 .12
❑ T22 Charles Johnson .50 .15
❑ T23 Marquis Grissom .40 .12
❑ T24 Jose Mesa .40 .12
❑ T25 Brian Boehringer .40 .12
❑ T26 John Rocker .40 .12
❑ T27 Jeff Frye .40 .12
❑ T28 Reggie Sanders .50 .15
❑ T29 David Segui .40 .12
❑ T30 Mike Sirotka .40 .12
❑ T31 Fernando Tatis .40 .12
❑ T32 Steve Trachsel .40 .12
❑ T33 Ismael Valdes .40 .12
❑ T34 Randy Velarde .40 .12
❑ T35 Ryan Kohlmeier .40 .12
❑ T36 Mike Bordick .50 .15
❑ T37 Kent Bottenfield .40 .12
❑ T38 Pat Rapp .40 .12
❑ T39 Jeff Nelson .40 .12
❑ T40 Ricky Bottalico .40 .12
❑ T41 Luke Prokopec .40 .12
❑ T42 Hideo Nomo 1.25 .35
❑ T43 Bill Mueller .50 .15
❑ T44 Roberto Kelly .40 .12
❑ T45 Chris Holt .40 .12
❑ T46 Mike Jackson .40 .12
❑ T47 Devon White .40 .12
❑ T48 Gerald Williams .40 .12
❑ T49 Eddie Taubensee .40 .12
❑ T50 Brian Hunter UER .40 .12
Brian R Hunter pictured
Brian L Hunter stats
❑ T51 Nelson Cruz .40 .12
❑ T52 Jeff Fassero .40 .12
❑ T53 Bubba Trammell .40 .12
❑ T54 Bo Porter .40 .12
❑ T55 Greg Norton .40 .12
❑ T56 Benito Santiago .50 .15
❑ T57 Ruben Rivera .40 .12
❑ T58 Dee Brown .40 .12
❑ T59 Jose Canseco UER 1.25 .35
2000 strikeout totals are wrong
❑ T60 Chris Michalak .40 .12
❑ T61 Tim Worrell .40 .12
❑ T62 Matt Clement .40 .12
❑ T63 Bill Pulsipher .40 .12
❑ T64 Troy Brohawn RC .40 .12
❑ T65 Mark Kotsay .40 .12
❑ T66 Jimmy Rollins .50 .15
❑ T67 Shea Hillenbrand .50 .15
❑ T68 Ted Lilly .40 .12
❑ T69 Jermaine Dye .50 .15
❑ T70 Jerry Hairston Jr. .40 .12
❑ T71 John Mabry .40 .12
❑ T72 Kurt Abbott .40 .12
❑ T73 Eric Owens .40 .12
❑ T74 Jeff Brantley .40 .12
❑ T75 Roy Oswalt .75 .23
❑ T76 Doug Mientkiewicz .50 .15
❑ T77 Rickey Henderson 2.00 .60
❑ T78 Jason Grimsley .40 .12
❑ T79 Christian Parker RC .40 .12
❑ T80 Donne Wall .40 .12
❑ T81 Alex Arias .40 .12
❑ T82 Willis Roberts .40 .12
❑ T83 Ryan Minor .40 .12
❑ T84 Jason LaRue .40 .12
❑ T85 Ruben Sierra .40 .12

❑ T86 Johnny Damon .50 .15
❑ T87 Juan Gonzalez 1.25 .35
❑ T88 C.C. Sabathia .50 .15
❑ T89 Tony Batista .50 .15
❑ T90 Jay Witasick .40 .12
❑ T91 Brent Abernathy .40 .12
❑ T92 Paul LoDuca .50 .15
❑ T93 Wes Helms .40 .12
❑ T94 Mark Wohlers .40 .12
❑ T95 Rob Bell .40 .12
❑ T96 Tim Redding .40 .12
❑ T97 Bud Smith RC .40 .12
❑ T98 Adam Dunn .75 .23
❑ T99 Ichiro Suzuki 10.00 3.00
Albert Pujols ROY
❑ T100 Carlton Fisk 81 1.25 .35
❑ T101 Tim Raines 81 1.00 .30
❑ T102 Juan Marichal 74 1.00 .30
❑ T103 Dave Winfield 81 1.25 .35
❑ T104 Reggie Jackson 82 1.25 .35
❑ T105 Cal Ripken 82 6.00 1.80
❑ T106 Ozzie Smith 82 2.00 .60
❑ T107 Tom Seaver 83 2.00 .60
❑ T108 Lou Piniella 74 1.00 .30
❑ T109 Dwight Gooden 84 1.25 .35
❑ T110 Bret Saberhagen 84 1.00 .30
❑ T111 Gary Carter 85 1.00 .30
❑ T112 Jack Clark 85 1.00 .30
❑ T113 R. Henderson 85 3.00 .90
❑ T114 Barry Bonds 86 5.00 1.50
❑ T115 Bobby Bonilla 86 1.00 .30
❑ T116 Jose Canseco 86 2.00 .60
❑ T117 Will Clark 86 2.00 .60
❑ T118 Andres Galarraga 86 1.00 .30
❑ T119 Bo Jackson 86 2.00 .60
❑ T120 Wally Joyner 86 1.00 .30
❑ T121 Ellis Burks 87 1.00 .30
❑ T122 David Cone 87 1.00 .30
❑ T123 Greg Maddux 87 4.00 1.20
❑ T124 Willie Randolph 76 1.00 .30
❑ T125 Dennis Eckersley 87 1.00 .30
❑ T126 Matt Williams 87 1.00 .30
❑ T127 Joe Morgan 81 1.00 .30
❑ T128 Fred McGriff 87 1.25 .35
❑ T129 Roberto Alomar 88 2.00 .60
❑ T130 Lee Smith 88 1.00 .30
❑ T131 David Wells 88 1.00 .30
❑ T132 Ken Griffey Jr. 89 3.00 .90
❑ T133 Deion Sanders 89 1.00 .30
❑ T134 Nolan Ryan 89 5.00 1.50
❑ T135 David Justice 90 1.00 .30
❑ T136 Joe Carter 91 1.00 .30
❑ T137 Jack Morris 92 1.00 .30
❑ T138 Mike Piazza 93 3.00 .90
❑ T139 Barry Bonds 93 5.00 1.50
❑ T140 Terrence Long 94 1.00 .30
❑ T141 Ben Grieve 94 1.00 .30
❑ T142 Richie Sexson 95 1.00 .30
George Arias
Mark Sweeney
Brian Schneider
❑ T143 Sean Burroughs 99 1.00 .30
❑ T144 Alfonso Soriano 99 2.00 .60
❑ T145 Bob Boone MG .50 .15
❑ T146 Larry Bowa MG .50 .15
❑ T147 Bob Brenly MG .40 .12
❑ T148 Buck Martinez MG .40 .12
❑ T149 L. McClendon MG .40 .12
❑ T150 Jim Tracy MG .40 .12
❑ T151 Jared Abruzzo RC .40 .12
❑ T152 Kurt Ainsworth .40 .12
❑ T153 Willie Bloomquist .50 .15
❑ T154 Ben Broussard .40 .12
❑ T155 Bobby Bradley .40 .12
❑ T156 Mike Bynum .40 .12
❑ T157 A.J. Hinch .40 .12
❑ T158 Ryan Christianson .40 .12
❑ T159 Carlos Silva .40 .12
❑ T160 Joe Crede .40 .12
❑ T161 Jack Cust .40 .12
❑ T162 Ben Diggins .40 .12
❑ T163 Phil Dumatrait .40 .12
❑ T164 Alex Escobar .40 .12
❑ T165 Miguel Olivo .40 .12
❑ T166 Chris George .40 .12
❑ T167 Marcus Giles .50 .15
❑ T168 Keith Ginter .40 .12
❑ T169 Josh Girdley .40 .12
❑ T170 Tony Alvarez .40 .12
❑ T171 Scott Seabol .40 .12
❑ T172 Josh Hamilton .50 .15
❑ T173 Jason Hart .40 .12
❑ T174 Israel Alcantara .40 .12
❑ T175 Jake Peavy 1.00 .30
❑ T176 Stubby Clapp RC .40 .12
❑ T177 D'Angelo Jimenez .40 .12
❑ T178 Nick Johnson .50 .15
❑ T179 Ben Johnson .40 .12
❑ T180 Larry Bigbie .40 .12
❑ T181 Allen Levrault .40 .12
❑ T182 Felipe Lopez .40 .12
❑ T183 Sean Burnett .50 .15
❑ T184 Nick Neugebauer .40 .12
❑ T185 Austin Kearns .75 .23
❑ T186 Corey Patterson .50 .15
❑ T187 Carlos Pena .40 .12
❑ T188 R. Rodriguez RC .40 .12
❑ T189 Juan Rivera .50 .15
❑ T190 Grant Roberts .40 .12
❑ T191 Adam Pettyjohn RC .40 .12
❑ T192 Jared Sandberg .40 .12
❑ T193 Xavier Nady .50 .15
❑ T194 Dane Sardinha .40 .12
❑ T195 Shawn Sonnier .40 .12
❑ T196 Rafael Soriano 1.25 .35
❑ T197 Brian Specht RC .40 .12
❑ T198 Aaron Myette .40 .12
❑ T199 Juan Uribe RC .40 .12
❑ T200 Jayson Werth .40 .12
❑ T201 Brad Wilkerson .40 .12
❑ T202 Horacio Estrada .40 .12
❑ T203 Joel Pineiro 1.25 .35
❑ T204 Matt LeCroy .40 .12
❑ T205 Michael Coleman .40 .12
❑ T206 Ben Sheets .50 .15
❑ T207 Eric Byrnes .40 .12
❑ T208 Sean Burroughs .50 .15
❑ T209 Ken Harvey .40 .12
❑ T210 Travis Hafner 1.00 .30
❑ T211 Erick Almonte .40 .12
❑ T212 Jason Belcher RC .40 .12
❑ T213 Wilson Betemit RC .40 .12
❑ T214 Hank Blalock RC 5.00 1.50
❑ T215 Danny Borrell .40 .12
❑ T216 John Buck RC .60 .18
❑ T217 Freddie Bynum RC .40 .12
❑ T218 Noel Devarez RC .40 .12
❑ T219 Juan Diaz RC .40 .12
❑ T220 Felix Diaz RC .40 .12
❑ T221 Josh Fogg RC .40 .12
❑ T222 Matt Ford RC .40 .12
❑ T223 Scott Heard .40 .12
❑ T224 Ben Hendrickson RC .40 .12
❑ T225 Cody Ross RC .40 .12
❑ T226 A. Hernandez RC .40 .12
❑ T227 Alfredo Amezaga RC .60 .18
❑ T228 Bob Keppel RC .40 .12
❑ T229 Ryan Madson RC .60 .18
❑ T230 Octavio Martinez RC .40 .12
❑ T231 Hee Seop Choi 3.00 .90
❑ T232 Thomas Mitchell .40 .12
❑ T233 Luis Montanez .40 .12
❑ T234 Andy Morales RC .40 .12
❑ T235 Justin Morneau RC 3.00 .90
❑ T236 Toe Nash RC .40 .12
❑ T237 V. Pascucci RC .40 .12
❑ T238 Roy Smith RC .40 .12
❑ T239 Antonio Perez RC .40 .12
❑ T240 Chad Petty RC .40 .12
❑ T241 Steve Smyth .40 .12
❑ T242 Jose Reyes RC 5.00 1.50
❑ T243 Eric Reynolds RC .40 .12
❑ T244 Dominic Rich .40 .12
❑ T245 J. Richardson RC .40 .12
❑ T246 Ed Rogers RC .40 .12
❑ T247 Albert Pujols RC 25.00 7.50
❑ T248 Esix Snead RC .40 .12
❑ T249 Luis Torres RC .40 .12
❑ T250 Matt White RC .40 .12
❑ T251 Blake Williams .40 .12
❑ T252 Chris Russ .40 .12
❑ T253 Joe Kennedy RC .40 .12
❑ T254 Jeff Randazzo RC .40 .12
❑ T255 Beau Hale RC .40 .12
❑ T256 Brad Hennessey RC .40 .12
❑ T257 Jake Gautreau RC .40 .12
❑ T258 Jeff Mathis RC 2.00 .60
❑ T259 Aaron Heilman RC 1.00 .30
❑ T260 B. Sardinha RC .60 .18
❑ T261 Irvin Guzman RC 1.50 .45
❑ T262 Gabe Gross RC .60 .18
❑ T263 J.D. Martin RC .40 .12
❑ T264 Chris Smith RC .40 .12
❑ T265 Kenny Baugh RC .40 .12

2002 Topps

	Nm-Mt	Ex-Mt
COMPLETE SET (718)	60.00	18.00
COMP.FACT.BROWN SET (723)	70.00	21.00
COMP.FACT.GREEN SET (723)	60.00	18.00
COMP. SERIES 1 (365)	30.00	9.00
COMPLETE SERIES 2 (354)	30.00	9.00
COMMON CARD (1-6/8-719)	.20	.06
COMMON (307-331)	.50	.15
COMMON CARD (332-364)	.50	.15

❑ 1 Pedro Martinez .50 .15
❑ 2 Mike Stanton .20 .06
❑ 3 Brad Penny .20 .06
❑ 4 Mike Matheny .20 .06
❑ 5 Johnny Damon .20 .06
❑ 6 Bret Boone .20 .06
❑ 7 Does Not Exist
❑ 8 Chris Truby .20 .06
❑ 9 B.J. Surhoff .20 .06
❑ 10 Mike Hampton .20 .06
❑ 11 Juan Pierre .20 .06
❑ 12 Mark Buehrle .20 .06
❑ 13 Bob Abreu .20 .06
❑ 14 David Cone .20 .06
❑ 15 Aaron Sele UER .20 .06
Card lists him as being born in New Mexico
He was born in Minnesota
❑ 16 Fernando Tatis .20 .06
❑ 17 Bobby Jones .20 .06
❑ 18 Rick Helling .20 .06
❑ 19 Dmitri Young .20 .06
❑ 20 Mike Mussina UER .50 .15
Career win total is wrong
❑ 21 Mike Sweeney .20 .06
❑ 22 Cristian Guzman .20 .06
❑ 23 Ryan Kohlmeier .20 .06
❑ 24 Adam Kennedy .20 .06
❑ 25 Larry Walker .30 .09
❑ 26 Eric Davis UER .20 .06
2000 Stolen Base totals are wrong
❑ 27 Jason Tyner .20 .06
❑ 28 Eric Young .20 .06
❑ 29 Jason Marquis .20 .06
❑ 30 Luis Gonzalez .20 .06
❑ 31 Kevin Tapani .20 .06
❑ 32 Orlando Cabrera .20 .06
❑ 33 Marty Cordova UER .20 .06
Career homer total, 1003
❑ 34 Brad Ausmus .20 .06
❑ 35 Livan Hernandez .20 .06
❑ 36 Alex Gonzalez .20 .06
❑ 37 Edgar Renteria .20 .06

❑ 38 Bengie Molina .20 .06
❑ 39 Frank Menechino .20 .06
❑ 40 Rafael Palmeiro .30 .09
❑ 41 Brad Fullmer .20 .06
❑ 42 Julio Zuleta .20 .06
❑ 43 Darren Dreifort .20 .06
❑ 44 Trot Nixon .20 .06
❑ 45 Trevor Hoffman .20 .06
❑ 46 Vladimir Nunez .20 .06
❑ 47 Mark Kotsay .20 .06
❑ 48 Kenny Rogers .20 .06
❑ 49 Ben Petrick .20 .06
❑ 50 Jeff Bagwell .30 .09
❑ 51 Juan Encarnacion .20 .06
❑ 52 Ramiro Mendoza .20 .06
❑ 53 Brian Meadows .20 .06
❑ 54 Chad Curtis .20 .06
❑ 55 Aramis Ramirez .20 .06
❑ 56 Mark McLemore .20 .06
❑ 57 Dante Bichette .20 .06
❑ 58 Scott Schoeneweis .20 .06
❑ 59 Jose Cruz Jr. .20 .06
❑ 60 Roger Clemens 1.00 .30
❑ 61 Jose Guillen .20 .06
❑ 62 Darren Oliver .20 .06
❑ 63 Chris Reitsma .20 .06
❑ 64 Jeff Abbott .20 .06
❑ 65 Robin Ventura .20 .06
❑ 66 Denny Neagle .20 .06
❑ 67 Al Martin .20 .06
❑ 68 Benito Santiago .20 .06
❑ 69 Roy Oswalt .20 .06
❑ 70 Juan Gonzalez .50 .15
❑ 71 Garret Anderson .20 .06
❑ 72 Bobby Bonilla .20 .06
❑ 73 Danny Bautista .20 .06
❑ 74 J.T. Snow .20 .06
❑ 75 Derek Jeter 1.25 .35
❑ 76 John Olerud .20 .06
❑ 77 Kevin Appier .20 .06
❑ 78 Phil Nevin .20 .06
❑ 79 Sean Casey .20 .06
❑ 80 Troy Glaus .30 .09
❑ 81 Joe Randa .20 .06
❑ 82 Jose Valentin .20 .06
❑ 83 Ricky Bottalico .20 .06
❑ 84 Todd Zeile .20 .06
❑ 85 Barry Larkin .50 .15
❑ 86 Bob Wickman .20 .06
❑ 87 Jeff Shaw .20 .06
❑ 88 Greg Vaughn .20 .06
❑ 89 Fernando Vina .20 .06
❑ 90 Mark Mulder .20 .06
❑ 91 Paul Bako .20 .06
❑ 92 Aaron Boone .20 .06
❑ 93 Esteban Loaiza .20 .06
❑ 94 Richie Sexson .20 .06
❑ 95 Alfonso Soriano .50 .15
❑ 96 Tony Womack .20 .06
❑ 97 Paul Shuey .20 .06
❑ 98 Melvin Mora .20 .06
❑ 99 Tony Gwynn .60 .18
❑ 100 Vladimir Guerrero .50 .15
❑ 101 Keith Osik .20 .06
❑ 102 Bud Smith .20 .06
❑ 103 Scott Williamson .20 .06
❑ 104 Daryle Ward .20 .06
❑ 105 Doug Mientkiewicz .20 .06
❑ 106 Stan Javier .20 .06
❑ 107 Russ Ortiz .20 .06
❑ 108 Wade Miller .20 .06
❑ 109 Luke Prokopec .20 .06
❑ 110 Andruw Jones UER .30 .09
Careel SB total, 1442
❑ 111 Ron Coomer .20 .06
❑ 112 Dan Wilson UER .20 .06
Career SB total, 1245
❑ 113 Luis Castillo .20 .06
❑ 114 Derek Bell .20 .06
❑ 115 Gary Sheffield .20 .06
❑ 116 Ruben Rivera .20 .06
❑ 117 Paul O'Neill .30 .09
❑ 118 Craig Paquette .20 .06
❑ 119 Kelvin Escobar .20 .06
❑ 120 Brad Radke .20 .06
❑ 121 Jorge Fabregas .20 .06
❑ 122 Randy Winn .20 .06
❑ 123 Tom Goodwin .20 .06
❑ 124 Jaret Wright .20 .06
❑ 125 Manny Ramirez .20 .06
❑ 126 Al Leiter .20 .06
❑ 127 Ben Davis .20 .06
❑ 128 Frank Catalanotto .20 .06
❑ 129 Jose Cabrera .20 .06
❑ 130 Magglio Ordonez .20 .06
❑ 131 Jose Macias .20 .06
❑ 132 Ted Lilly .20 .06
❑ 133 Chris Holt .20 .06
❑ 134 Eric Milton .20 .06
❑ 135 Shannon Stewart .20 .06
❑ 136 Omar Olivares .20 .06
❑ 137 David Segui .20 .06
❑ 138 Jeff Nelson .20 .06
❑ 139 Matt Williams .20 .06
❑ 140 Ellis Burks .20 .06
❑ 141 Jason Bere .20 .06
❑ 142 Jimmy Haynes .20 .06
❑ 143 Ramon Hernandez .20 .06
❑ 144 Craig Counsell UER .20 .06
Card pictures Greg Colbrunn
Some vital stats are wrong as well
❑ 145 John Smoltz .30 .09
❑ 146 Homer Bush .20 .06
❑ 147 Quilvio Veras .20 .06
❑ 148 Esteban Yan .20 .06
❑ 149 Ramon Ortiz .20 .06
❑ 150 Carlos Delgado .20 .06
❑ 151 Lee Stevens .20 .06
❑ 152 Wil Cordero .20 .06
❑ 153 Mike Bordick .20 .06
❑ 154 John Flaherty .20 .06
❑ 155 Omar Daal .20 .06
❑ 156 Todd Ritchie .20 .06
❑ 157 Carl Everett .20 .06
❑ 158 Scott Sullivan .20 .06
❑ 159 Deivi Cruz .20 .06
❑ 160 Albert Pujols UER 1.00 .30
Placido Polanco pictured on back
❑ 161 Royce Clayton .20 .06
❑ 162 Jeff Suppan .20 .06
❑ 163 C.C. Sabathia .20 .06
❑ 164 Jimmy Rollins .20 .06
❑ 165 Rickey Henderson .75 .23
❑ 166 Rey Ordonez .20 .06
❑ 167 Shawn Estes .20 .06
❑ 168 Reggie Sanders .20 .06
❑ 169 Jon Lieber .20 .06
❑ 170 Armando Benitez .20 .06
❑ 171 Mike Remlinger .20 .06
❑ 172 Billy Wagner .20 .06
❑ 173 Troy Percival .20 .06
❑ 174 Devon White .20 .06
❑ 175 Ivan Rodriguez .50 .15
❑ 176 Dustin Hermanson .20 .06
❑ 177 Brian Anderson .20 .06
❑ 178 Graeme Lloyd .20 .06
❑ 179 Russel Branyan .20 .06
❑ 180 Bobby Higginson .20 .06
❑ 181 Alex Gonzalez .20 .06
❑ 182 John Franco .20 .06
❑ 183 Sidney Ponson .20 .06
❑ 184 Jose Mesa .20 .06
❑ 185 Todd Hollandsworth .20 .06
❑ 186 Kevin Young .20 .06
❑ 187 Tim Wakefield .20 .06
❑ 188 Craig Biggio .30 .09
❑ 189 Jason Isringhausen .20 .06
❑ 190 Mark Quinn .20 .06
❑ 191 Glendon Rusch .20 .06
❑ 192 Damian Miller .20 .06
❑ 193 Sandy Alomar Jr. .20 .06
❑ 194 Scott Brosius .20 .06
❑ 195 Dave Martinez .20 .06
❑ 196 Danny Graves .20 .06
❑ 197 Shea Hillenbrand .20 .06
❑ 198 Jimmy Anderson .20 .06
❑ 199 Travis Lee .20 .06
❑ 200 Randy Johnson .50 .15
❑ 201 Carlos Beltran .20 .06
❑ 202 Jerry Hairston .20 .06
❑ 203 Jesus Sanchez .20 .06
❑ 204 Eddie Taubensee .20 .06
❑ 205 David Wells .20 .06
❑ 206 Russ Davis .20 .06
❑ 207 Michael Barrett .20 .06
❑ 208 Marquis Grissom .20 .06
❑ 209 Byung-Hyun Kim .20 .06
❑ 210 Hideo Nomo .50 .15
❑ 211 Ryan Rupe .20 .06
❑ 212 Ricky Gutierrez .20 .06
❑ 213 Darryl Kile .20 .06
❑ 214 Rico Brogna .20 .06
❑ 215 Terrence Long .20 .06
❑ 216 Mike Jackson .20 .06
❑ 217 Jamey Wright .20 .06
❑ 218 Adrian Beltre .20 .06
❑ 219 Benny Agbayani .20 .06
❑ 220 Chuck Knoblauch .20 .06
❑ 221 Randy Wolf .20 .06
❑ 222 Andy Ashby .20 .06
❑ 223 Corey Koskie .20 .06
❑ 224 Roger Cedeno .20 .06
❑ 225 Ichiro Suzuki 1.00 .30
❑ 226 Keith Foulke .20 .06
❑ 227 Ryan Minor .20 .06
❑ 228 Shawon Dunston .20 .06
❑ 229 Alex Cora .20 .06
❑ 230 Jeromy Burnitz .20 .06
❑ 231 Mark Grace .50 .15
❑ 232 Aubrey Huff .20 .06
❑ 233 Jeffrey Hammonds .20 .06
❑ 234 Olmedo Saenz .20 .06
❑ 235 Brian Jordan .20 .06
❑ 236 Jeremy Giambi .20 .06
❑ 237 Joe Girardi .20 .06
❑ 238 Eric Gagne .30 .09
❑ 239 Masato Yoshii .20 .06
❑ 240 Greg Maddux 1.00 .30
❑ 241 Bryan Rekar .20 .06
❑ 242 Ray Durham .20 .06
❑ 243 Torii Hunter .20 .06
❑ 244 Derrek Lee .20 .06
❑ 245 Jim Edmonds .20 .06
❑ 246 Einar Diaz .20 .06
❑ 247 Brian Bohanon .20 .06
❑ 248 Ron Belliard .20 .06
❑ 249 Mike Lowell .20 .06
❑ 250 Sammy Sosa .75 .23
❑ 251 Richard Hidalgo .20 .06
❑ 252 Bartolo Colon .20 .06
❑ 253 Jorge Posada .30 .09
❑ 254 LaTroy Hawkins .20 .06
❑ 255 Paul LoDuca .20 .06
❑ 256 Carlos Febles .20 .06
❑ 257 Nelson Cruz .20 .06
❑ 258 Edgardo Alfonzo .20 .06
❑ 259 Joey Hamilton .20 .06
❑ 260 Cliff Floyd .20 .06
❑ 261 Wes Helms .20 .06
❑ 262 Jay Bell .20 .06
❑ 263 Mike Cameron .20 .06
❑ 264 Paul Konerko .20 .06
❑ 265 Jeff Kent .20 .06
❑ 266 Robert Fick .20 .06
❑ 267 Allen Levrault .20 .06
❑ 268 Placido Polanco .20 .06
❑ 269 Marlon Anderson .20 .06
❑ 270 Mariano Rivera .30 .09
❑ 271 Chan Ho Park .20 .06
❑ 272 Jose Vizcaino .20 .06
❑ 273 Jeff D'Amico .20 .06
❑ 274 Mark Gardner .20 .06
❑ 275 Travis Fryman .20 .06
❑ 276 Darren Lewis .20 .06
❑ 277 Bruce Bochy MG .20 .06
❑ 278 Jerry Manuel MG .20 .06
❑ 279 Bob Brenly MG .20 .06
❑ 280 Don Baylor MG .20 .06
❑ 281 Davey Lopes MG .20 .06
❑ 282 Jerry Narron MG .20 .06
❑ 283 Tony Muser MG .20 .06
❑ 284 Hal McRae MG .20 .06
❑ 285 Bobby Cox MG .20 .06
❑ 286 Larry Dierker MG .20 .06
❑ 287 Phil Garner MG .20 .06
❑ 288 Joe Kerrigan MG .20 .06
❑ 289 Bobby Valentine MG .20 .06
❑ 290 Dusty Baker MG .20 .06

❑ 291	Lloyd McClendon MG	.20	.06
❑ 292	Mike Scioscia MG	.20	.06
❑ 293	Buck Martinez MG	.20	.06
❑ 294	Larry Bowa MG	.20	.06
❑ 295	Tony LaRussa MG	.20	.06
❑ 296	Jeff Torborg MG	.20	.06
❑ 297	Tom Kelly MG	.20	.06
❑ 298	Mike Hargrove MG	.20	.06
❑ 299	Art Howe MG	.20	.06
❑ 300	Lou Piniella MG	.20	.06
❑ 301	Charlie Manuel MG	.20	.06
❑ 302	Buddy Bell MG	.20	.06
❑ 303	Tony Perez MG	.20	.06
❑ 304	Bob Boone MG	.20	.06
❑ 305	Joe Torre MG	.50	.15
❑ 306	Jim Tracy MG	.20	.06
❑ 307	Jason Lane PROS	.50	.15
❑ 308	Chris George PROS	.50	.15
❑ 309	Hank Blalock PROS UER Bio has him throwing lefty	1.00	.30
❑ 310	Joe Borchard PROS	.50	.15
❑ 311	Marlon Byrd PROS	.50	.15
❑ 312	R. Cabrera PROS RC	.50	.15
❑ 313	F. Sanchez PROS RC	.75	.23
❑ 314	S. Wiggins PROS RC	.50	.15
❑ 315	J. Maule PROS RC	.50	.15
❑ 316	D. Cesar PROS RC	.50	.15
❑ 317	Boof Bonser PROS	.50	.15
❑ 318	J. Tolentino PROS RC	.50	.15
❑ 319	Earl Snyder PROS RC	.50	.15
❑ 320	T. Wade PROS RC	.50	.15
❑ 321	N. Calzado PROS RC	.50	.15
❑ 322	Eric Glaser PROS RC	.50	.15
❑ 323	C. Kuzmic PROS RC	.50	.15
❑ 324	Nic Jackson PROS RC	.50	.15
❑ 325	Mike Rivera PROS	.50	.15
❑ 326	Jason Bay PROS RC	1.00	.30
❑ 327	Chris Smith DP	.50	.15
❑ 328	Jake Gautreau DP	.50	.15
❑ 329	Gabe Gross DP	.50	.15
❑ 330	Kenny Baugh DP	.50	.15
❑ 331	J.D. Martin DP	.50	.15
❑ 332	Barry Bonds HL 500th Homer	1.25	.35
❑ 333	Rickey Henderson HL Sets record for career walks	.75	.23
❑ 334	Bud Smith HL	.50	.15
❑ 335	R. Henderson HL 3000	.75	.23
❑ 336	Barry Bonds HL 73 homers in a season	1.25	.35
❑ 337	Ichiro Suzuki Jason Giambi Roberto Alomar LL	1.00	.30
❑ 338	Alex Rodriguez Ichiro Suzuki Bret Boone LL	1.00	.30
❑ 339	Alex Rodriguez Jim Thome Rafael Palmeiro LL	.50	.15
❑ 340	Bret Boone Juan Gonzalez Alex Rodriguez LL	.50	.15
❑ 341	Freddy Garcia Mike Mussina Joe Mays LL	.50	.15
❑ 342	Hideo Nomo Mike Mussina Roger Clemens LL	.50	.15
❑ 343	Larry Walker Todd Helton Moises Alou Lance Berkman LL	.50	.15
❑ 344	Sammy Sosa Todd Helton Barry Bonds LL	.50	.15
❑ 345	Barry Bonds Sammy Sosa Luis Gonzalez LL	.50	.15
❑ 346	Sammy Sosa Todd Helton Luis Gonzalez LL	.50	.15
❑ 347	Randy Johnson Curt Schilling John Burkett LL	.50	.15
❑ 348	Randy Johnson Curt Schilling Chan Ho Park LL	.50	.15
❑ 349	Seattle Mariners PB	.50	.15
❑ 350	Oakland Athletics PB	.50	.15
❑ 351	New York Yankees PB	.50	.15
❑ 352	Cleveland Indians PB	.50	.15
❑ 353	Ariz. Diamondbacks PB	.50	.15
❑ 354	Atlanta Braves PB	.50	.15
❑ 355	St. Louis Cardinals PB	.50	.15
❑ 356	Houston Astros PB	.50	.15
❑ 357	Ariz.Diamondbacks Colorado Rockies UWS	.50	.15
❑ 358	Mike Piazza UWS	.75	.23
❑ 359	Braves-Phillies UWS	.50	.15
❑ 360	Curt Schilling UWS	.50	.15
❑ 361	Roger Clemens Lee Mazzilli UWS	.50	.15
❑ 362	Sammy Sosa UWS	.75	.23
❑ 363	Tom Lampkin Ichiro Suzuki Bret Boone UWS	1.00	.30
❑ 364	Barry Bonds Jeff Bagwell UWS	.50	.15
❑ 365	Barry Bonds HR 1	15.00	4.50
❑ 365	Barry Bonds HR 2	10.00	3.00
❑ 365	Barry Bonds HR 3	10.00	3.00
❑ 365	Barry Bonds HR 4	10.00	3.00
❑ 365	Barry Bonds HR 5	10.00	3.00
❑ 365	Barry Bonds HR 6	10.00	3.00
❑ 365	Barry Bonds HR 7	10.00	3.00
❑ 365	Barry Bonds HR 8	10.00	3.00
❑ 365	Barry Bonds HR 9	10.00	3.00
❑ 365	Barry Bonds HR 10	10.00	3.00
❑ 365	Barry Bonds HR 11	10.00	3.00
❑ 365	Barry Bonds HR 12	10.00	3.00
❑ 365	Barry Bonds HR 13	10.00	3.00
❑ 365	Barry Bonds HR 14	10.00	3.00
❑ 365	Barry Bonds HR 15	10.00	3.00
❑ 365	Barry Bonds HR 16	10.00	3.00
❑ 365	Barry Bonds HR 17	10.00	3.00
❑ 365	Barry Bonds HR 18	10.00	3.00
❑ 365	Barry Bonds HR 19	10.00	3.00
❑ 365	Barry Bonds HR 20	10.00	3.00
❑ 365	Barry Bonds HR 21	10.00	3.00
❑ 365	Barry Bonds HR 22	10.00	3.00
❑ 365	Barry Bonds HR 23	10.00	3.00
❑ 365	Barry Bonds HR 24	10.00	3.00
❑ 365	Barry Bonds HR 25	10.00	3.00
❑ 365	Barry Bonds HR 26	10.00	3.00
❑ 365	Barry Bonds HR 27	10.00	3.00
❑ 365	Barry Bonds HR 28	10.00	3.00
❑ 365	Barry Bonds HR 29	10.00	3.00
❑ 365	Barry Bonds HR 30	10.00	3.00
❑ 365	Barry Bonds HR 31	10.00	3.00
❑ 365	Barry Bonds HR 32 UER No pitcher is listed on this card	10.00	3.00
❑ 365	Barry Bonds HR 33	10.00	3.00
❑ 365	Barry Bonds HR 34	10.00	3.00
❑ 365	Barry Bonds HR 35	10.00	3.00
❑ 365	Barry Bonds HR 36	10.00	3.00
❑ 365	Barry Bonds HR 37	10.00	3.00
❑ 365	Barry Bonds HR 38	10.00	3.00
❑ 365	Barry Bonds HR 39	10.00	3.00
❑ 365	Barry Bonds HR 40	10.00	3.00
❑ 365	Barry Bonds HR 41	10.00	3.00
❑ 365	Barry Bonds HR 42	10.00	3.00
❑ 365	Barry Bonds HR 43	10.00	3.00
❑ 365	Barry Bonds HR 44	10.00	3.00
❑ 365	Barry Bonds HR 45	10.00	3.00
❑ 365	Barry Bonds HR 46	10.00	3.00
❑ 365	Barry Bonds HR 47	10.00	3.00
❑ 365	Barry Bonds HR 48	10.00	3.00
❑ 365	Barry Bonds HR 49	10.00	3.00
❑ 365	Barry Bonds HR 50	10.00	3.00
❑ 365	Barry Bonds HR 51	10.00	3.00
❑ 365	Barry Bonds HR 52	10.00	3.00
❑ 365	Barry Bonds HR 53	10.00	3.00
❑ 365	Barry Bonds HR 54	10.00	3.00
❑ 365	Barry Bonds HR 55	10.00	3.00
❑ 365	Barry Bonds HR 56	10.00	3.00
❑ 365	Barry Bonds HR 57	10.00	3.00
❑ 365	Barry Bonds HR 58	10.00	3.00
❑ 365	Barry Bonds HR 59	10.00	3.00
❑ 365	Barry Bonds HR 60	10.00	3.00
❑ 365	Barry Bonds HR 61	15.00	4.50
❑ 365	Barry Bonds HR 62	10.00	3.00
❑ 365	Barry Bonds HR 63	10.00	3.00
❑ 365	Barry Bonds HR 64	10.00	3.00
❑ 365	Barry Bonds HR 65	10.00	3.00
❑ 365	Barry Bonds HR 66	10.00	3.00
❑ 365	Barry Bonds HR 67	10.00	3.00
❑ 365	Barry Bonds HR 68	10.00	3.00
❑ 365	Barry Bonds HR 69	10.00	3.00
❑ 365	Barry Bonds HR 70	25.00	7.50
❑ 365	Barry Bonds HR 71	10.00	3.00
❑ 365	Barry Bonds HR 72	10.00	3.00
❑ 365	Barry Bonds HR 73	60.00	18.00
❑ 366	Pat Meares	.20	.06
❑ 367	Mike Lieberthal	.20	.06
❑ 368	Larry Bigbie	.20	.06
❑ 369	Ron Gant	.20	.06
❑ 370	Moises Alou	.20	.06
❑ 371	Chad Kreuter	.20	.06
❑ 372	Willis Roberts	.20	.06
❑ 373	Toby Hall	.20	.06
❑ 374	Miguel Batista	.20	.06
❑ 375	John Burkett	.20	.06
❑ 376	Cory Lidle	.20	.06
❑ 377	Nick Neugebauer	.20	.06
❑ 378	Jay Payton	.20	.06
❑ 379	Steve Karsay	.20	.06
❑ 380	Eric Chavez	.20	.06
❑ 381	Kelly Stinnett	.20	.06
❑ 382	Jarrod Washburn	.20	.06
❑ 383	Rick White	.20	.06
❑ 384	Jeff Conine	.20	.06
❑ 385	Fred McGriff	.30	.09
❑ 386	Marvin Benard	.20	.06
❑ 387	Joe Crede	.20	.06
❑ 388	Dennis Cook	.20	.06
❑ 389	Rick Reed	.20	.06
❑ 390	Tom Glavine	.50	.15
❑ 391	Rondell White	.20	.06
❑ 392	Matt Morris	.20	.06
❑ 393	Pat Rapp	.20	.06
❑ 394	Robert Person	.20	.06
❑ 395	Omar Vizquel	.20	.06
❑ 396	Jeff Cirillo	.20	.06
❑ 397	Dave Mlicki	.20	.06
❑ 398	Jose Ortiz	.20	.06
❑ 399	Ryan Dempster	.20	.06
❑ 400	Curt Schilling	.30	.09
❑ 401	Peter Bergeron	.20	.06
❑ 402	Kyle Lohse	.20	.06
❑ 403	Craig Wilson UER Homer totals are wrong	.20	.06
❑ 404	David Justice	.20	.06
❑ 405	Darin Erstad	.20	.06
❑ 406	Jose Mercedes	.20	.06
❑ 407	Carl Pavano	.20	.06
❑ 408	Albie Lopez	.20	.06
❑ 409	Alex Ochoa	.20	.06
❑ 410	Chipper Jones	.50	.15
❑ 411	Tyler Houston	.20	.06
❑ 412	Dean Palmer	.20	.06
❑ 413	Damian Jackson	.20	.06
❑ 414	Josh Towers	.20	.06
❑ 415	Rafael Furcal	.20	.06
❑ 416	Mike Morgan	.20	.06
❑ 417	Herb Perry	.20	.06
❑ 418	Mike Sirotka	.20	.06
❑ 419	Mark Wohlers	.20	.06
❑ 420	Nomar Garciaparra	1.00	.30
❑ 421	Felipe Lopez	.20	.06
❑ 422	Joe McEwing	.20	.06
❑ 423	Jacque Jones	.20	.06
❑ 424	Julio Franco	.20	.06
❑ 425	Frank Thomas	.50	.15
❑ 426	So Taguchi RC	.75	.23
❑ 427	Kazuhisa Ishii RC	1.50	.45
❑ 428	D'Angelo Jimenez	.20	.06
❑ 429	Chris Stynes	.20	.06
❑ 430	Kerry Wood	.50	.15
❑ 431	Chris Singleton	.20	.06
❑ 432	Erubiel Durazo	.20	.06
❑ 433	Matt Lawton	.20	.06
❑ 434	Bill Mueller	.20	.06
❑ 435	Jose Canseco	.50	.15
❑ 436	Ben Grieve	.20	.06
❑ 437	Terry Mulholland	.20	.06
❑ 438	David Bell	.20	.06
❑ 439	A.J. Pierzynski	.20	.06
❑ 440	Adam Dunn	.30	.09

❑ 441 Jon Garland .20 .06
❑ 442 Jeff Fassero .20 .06
❑ 443 Julio Lugo .20 .06
❑ 444 Carlos Guillen .20 .06
❑ 445 Orlando Hernandez .20 .06
❑ 446 Mark Loretta UER .20 .06
Photo is Curtis Leskanic
❑ 447 Scott Spiezio .20 .06
❑ 448 Kevin Millwood .20 .06
❑ 449 Jamie Moyer .20 .06
❑ 450 Todd Helton .30 .09
❑ 451 Todd Walker .20 .06
❑ 452 Jose Lima .20 .06
❑ 453 Brook Fordyce .20 .06
❑ 454 Aaron Rowand .20 .06
❑ 455 Barry Zito .50 .15
❑ 456 Eric Owens .20 .06
❑ 457 Charles Nagy .20 .06
❑ 458 Raul Ibanez .20 .06
❑ 459 Joe Mays .20 .06
❑ 460 Jim Thome .50 .15
❑ 461 Adam Eaton .20 .06
❑ 462 Felix Martinez .20 .06
❑ 463 Vernon Wells .20 .06
❑ 464 Donnie Sadler .20 .06
❑ 465 Tony Clark .20 .06
❑ 466 Jose Hernandez .20 .06
❑ 467 Ramon Martinez .20 .06
❑ 468 Rusty Greer .20 .06
❑ 469 Rod Barajas .20 .06
❑ 470 Lance Berkman .20 .06
❑ 471 Brady Anderson .20 .06
❑ 472 Pedro Astacio .20 .06
❑ 473 Shane Halter .20 .06
❑ 474 Bret Prinz .20 .06
❑ 475 Edgar Martinez .30 .09
❑ 476 Steve Trachsel .20 .06
❑ 477 Gary Matthews Jr. .20 .06
❑ 478 Ismael Valdes .20 .06
❑ 479 Juan Uribe .20 .06
❑ 480 Shawn Green .20 .06
❑ 481 Kirk Rueter .20 .06
❑ 482 Damion Easley .20 .06
❑ 483 Chris Carpenter .20 .06
❑ 484 Kris Benson .20 .06
❑ 485 Antonio Alfonseca .20 .06
❑ 486 Kyle Farnsworth .20 .06
❑ 487 Brandon Lyon .20 .06
❑ 488 Hideki Irabu .20 .06
❑ 489 David Ortiz .20 .06
❑ 490 Mike Piazza .75 .23
❑ 491 Derek Lowe .20 .06
❑ 492 Chris Gomez .20 .06
❑ 493 Mark Johnson .20 .06
❑ 494 John Rocker .20 .06
❑ 495 Eric Karros .20 .06
❑ 496 Bill Haselman .20 .06
❑ 497 Dave Veres .20 .06
❑ 498 Pete Harnisch .20 .06
❑ 499 Tomokazu Ohka .20 .06
❑ 500 Barry Bonds 1.25 .35
❑ 501 David Dellucci .20 .06
❑ 502 Wendell Magee .20 .06
❑ 503 Tom Gordon .20 .06
❑ 504 Javier Vazquez .20 .06
❑ 505 Ben Sheets .20 .06
❑ 506 Wilton Guerrero .20 .06
❑ 507 John Halama .20 .06
❑ 508 Mark Redman .20 .06
❑ 509 Jack Wilson .20 .06
❑ 510 Bernie Williams .30 .09
❑ 511 Miguel Cairo .20 .06
❑ 512 Denny Hocking .20 .06
❑ 513 Tony Batista .20 .06
❑ 514 Mark Grudzielanek .20 .06
❑ 515 Jose Vidro .20 .06
❑ 516 Sterling Hitchcock .20 .06
❑ 517 Billy Koch .20 .06
❑ 518 Matt Clement .20 .06
❑ 519 Bruce Chen .20 .06
❑ 520 Roberto Alomar .50 .15
❑ 521 Orlando Palmeiro .20 .06
❑ 522 Steve Finley .20 .06
❑ 523 Danny Patterson .20 .06
❑ 524 Terry Adams .20 .06
❑ 525 Tino Martinez .30 .09
❑ 526 Tony Armas Jr. .20 .06
❑ 527 Geoff Jenkins .20 .06
❑ 528 Kerry Robinson .20 .06
❑ 529 Corey Patterson .20 .06
❑ 530 Brian Giles .20 .06
❑ 531 Jose Jimenez .20 .06
❑ 532 Joe Kennedy .20 .06
❑ 533 Armando Rios .20 .06
❑ 534 Osvaldo Fernandez .20 .06
❑ 535 Ruben Sierra .20 .06
❑ 536 Octavio Dotel .20 .06
❑ 537 Luis Sojo .20 .06
❑ 538 Brent Butler .20 .06
❑ 539 Pablo Ozuna .20 .06
❑ 540 Freddy Garcia .20 .06
❑ 541 Chad Durbin .20 .06
❑ 542 Orlando Merced .20 .06
❑ 543 Michael Tucker .20 .06
❑ 544 Roberto Hernandez .20 .06
❑ 545 Pat Burrell .20 .06
❑ 546 A.J. Burnett .20 .06
❑ 547 Bubba Trammell .20 .06
❑ 548 Scott Elarton .20 .06
❑ 549 Mike Darr .20 .06
❑ 550 Ken Griffey Jr. .75 .23
❑ 551 Ugueth Urbina .20 .06
❑ 552 Todd Jones .20 .06
❑ 553 Delino Deshields .20 .06
❑ 554 Adam Piatt .20 .06
❑ 555 Jason Kendall .20 .06
❑ 556 Hector Ortiz .20 .06
❑ 557 Turk Wendell .20 .06
❑ 558 Rob Bell .20 .06
❑ 559 Sun Woo Kim .20 .06
❑ 560 Raul Mondesi .20 .06
❑ 561 Brent Abernathy .20 .06
❑ 562 Seth Etherton .20 .06
❑ 563 Shawn Wooten .20 .06
❑ 564 Jay Buhner .20 .06
❑ 565 Andres Galarraga .20 .06
❑ 566 Shane Reynolds .20 .06
❑ 567 Rod Beck .20 .06
❑ 568 Dee Brown .20 .06
❑ 569 Pedro Feliz .20 .06
❑ 570 Ryan Klesko .20 .06
❑ 571 John Vander Wal UER .20 .06
Home Run Total in 1999 was 64
❑ 572 Nick Bierbrodt .20 .06
❑ 573 Joe Nathan .20 .06
❑ 574 James Baldwin .20 .06
❑ 575 J.D. Drew .20 .06
❑ 576 Greg Colbrunn .20 .06
❑ 577 Doug Glanville .20 .06
❑ 578 Brandon Duckworth .20 .06
❑ 579 Shawn Chacon .20 .06
❑ 580 Rich Aurilia .20 .06
❑ 581 Chuck Finley .20 .06
❑ 582 Abraham Nunez .20 .06
❑ 583 Kenny Lofton .20 .06
❑ 584 Brian Daubach .20 .06
❑ 585 Miguel Tejada .20 .06
❑ 586 Nate Cornejo .20 .06
❑ 587 Kazuhiro Sasaki .20 .06
❑ 588 Chris Richard .20 .06
❑ 589 Armando Reynoso .20 .06
❑ 590 Tim Hudson .20 .06
❑ 591 Neifi Perez .20 .06
❑ 592 Steve Cox .20 .06
❑ 593 Henry Blanco .20 .06
❑ 594 Ricky Ledee .20 .06
❑ 595 Tim Salmon .30 .09
❑ 596 Luis Rivas .20 .06
❑ 597 Jeff Zimmerman .20 .06
❑ 598 Matt Stairs .20 .06
❑ 599 Preston Wilson .20 .06
❑ 600 Mark McGwire 1.25 .35
❑ 601 Timo Perez UER .20 .06
Biographical Information is that of Aaron Rowand's
❑ 602 Matt Anderson .20 .06
❑ 603 Todd Hundley .20 .06
❑ 604 Rick Ankiel .20 .06
❑ 605 Tsuyoshi Shinjo .20 .06
❑ 606 Woody Williams .20 .06
❑ 607 Jason LaRue .20 .06
❑ 608 Carlos Lee .20 .06
❑ 609 Russ Johnson .20 .06
❑ 610 Scott Rolen .30 .09
❑ 611 Brent Mayne .20 .06
❑ 612 Darrin Fletcher .20 .06
❑ 613 Ray Lankford .20 .06
❑ 614 Troy O'Leary .20 .06
❑ 615 Javier Lopez .20 .06
❑ 616 Randy Velarde .20 .06
❑ 617 Vinny Castilla .20 .06
❑ 618 Milton Bradley .20 .06
❑ 619 Ruben Mateo .20 .06
❑ 620 Jason Giambi Yankees .50 .15
❑ 621 Andy Benes .20 .06
❑ 622 Joe Mauer RC 5.00 1.50
❑ 623 Andy Pettitte .30 .09
❑ 624 Jose Offerman .20 .06
❑ 625 Mo Vaughn .20 .06
❑ 626 Steve Sparks .20 .06
❑ 627 Mike Matthews .20 .06
❑ 628 Robb Nen .20 .06
❑ 629 Kip Wells .20 .06
❑ 630 Kevin Brown .20 .06
❑ 631 Arthur Rhodes .20 .06
❑ 632 Gabe Kapler .20 .06
❑ 633 Jermaine Dye .20 .06
❑ 634 Josh Beckett .30 .09
❑ 635 Pokey Reese .20 .06
❑ 636 Benji Gil .20 .06
❑ 637 Marcus Giles .20 .06
❑ 638 Julian Tavarez .20 .06
❑ 639 Jason Schmidt .20 .06
❑ 640 Alex Rodriguez 1.00 .30
❑ 641 Anaheim Angels TC .20 .06
❑ 642 Arizona Diamondbacks TC .30 .09
❑ 643 Atlanta Braves TC .20 .06
❑ 644 Baltimore Orioles TC .20 .06
❑ 645 Boston Red Sox TC .20 .06
❑ 646 Chicago Cubs TC .20 .06
❑ 647 Chicago White Sox TC .20 .06
❑ 648 Cincinnati Reds TC .20 .06
❑ 649 Cleveland Indians TC .20 .06
❑ 650 Colorado Rockies TC .20 .06
❑ 651 Detroit Tigers TC .20 .06
❑ 652 Florida Marlins TC .20 .06
❑ 653 Houston Astros TC .20 .06
❑ 654 Kansas City Royals TC .20 .06
❑ 655 Los Angeles Dodgers TC .20 .06
❑ 656 Milwaukee Brewers TC .20 .06
❑ 657 Minnesota Twins TC .20 .06
❑ 658 Montreal Expos TC .20 .06
❑ 659 New York Mets TC .20 .06
❑ 660 New York Yankees TC .50 .15
❑ 661 Oakland Athletics TC .20 .06
❑ 662 Philadelphia Phillies TC .20 .06
❑ 663 Pittsburgh Pirates TC .20 .06
❑ 664 San Diego Padres TC .20 .06
❑ 665 San Francisco Giants TC .20 .06
❑ 666 Seattle Mariners TC .30 .09
❑ 667 St. Louis Cardinals TC .20 .06
❑ 668 T.B. Devil Rays TC .20 .06
❑ 669 Texas Rangers TC .20 .06
❑ 670 Toronto Blue Jays TC .20 .06
❑ 671 Juan Cruz PROS .50 .15
❑ 672 Kevin Cash PROS RC .50 .15
❑ 673 Jimmy Gobble PROS RC 1.50 .45
❑ 674 Mike Hill PROS RC .50 .15
❑ 675 T.Buchholz PROS RC .50 .15
❑ 676 Bill Hall PROS .50 .15
❑ 677 B.Roneberg PROS RC .50 .15
❑ 678 R.Huffman PROS RC .50 .15
❑ 679 Chris Tritle PROS RC .50 .15
❑ 680 Nate Espy PROS RC .50 .15
❑ 681 Nick Alvarez PROS RC .50 .15
❑ 682 Jason Botts PROS RC .50 .15
❑ 683 Ryan Gripp PROS RC .50 .15
❑ 684 Dan Phillips PROS RC .50 .15
❑ 685 Pablo Arias PROS RC .50 .15
❑ 686 J.Rodriguez PROS RC .50 .15
❑ 687 Rich Harden PROS RC 4.00 1.20
❑ 688 Neal Frendling PROS RC .50 .15
❑ 689 Rich Thompson PROS RC .50 .15
❑ 690 G.Montalbano PROS RC .50 .15
❑ 691 Len Dinardo DP RC .50 .15
❑ 692 Ryan Raburn DP RC .50 .15
❑ 693 Josh Barfield DP RC 2.00 .60
❑ 694 David Bacani DP RC .50 .15

❑ 695	Dan Johnson DP RC	.50	.15
❑ 696	Mike Mussina GG	.30	.09
❑ 697	Ivan Rodriguez GG	.50	.15
❑ 698	Doug Mientkiewicz GG	.20	.06
❑ 699	Roberto Alomar GG	.30	.09
❑ 700	Eric Chavez GG	.20	.06
❑ 701	Omar Vizquel GG	.20	.06
❑ 702	Mike Cameron GG	.20	.06
❑ 703	Torii Hunter GG	.20	.06
❑ 704	Ichiro Suzuki GG	.50	.15
❑ 705	Greg Maddux GG	.50	.15
❑ 706	Brad Ausmus GG	.20	.06
❑ 707	Todd Helton GG	.20	.06
❑ 708	Fernando Vina GG	.20	.06
❑ 709	Scott Rolen GG	.20	.06
❑ 710	Orlando Cabrera GG	.20	.06
❑ 711	Andruw Jones GG	.20	.06
❑ 712	Jim Edmonds GG	.20	.06
❑ 713	Larry Walker GG	.20	.06
❑ 714	Roger Clemens CY	.50	.15
❑ 715	Randy Johnson CY	.30	.09
❑ 716	Ichiro Suzuki MVP	.50	.15
❑ 717	Barry Bonds MVP	.50	.15
❑ 718	Ichiro Suzuki ROY	.50	.15
❑ 719	Albert Pujols ROY	.50	.15

2002 Topps Traded

	Nm-Mt	Ex-Mt
COMPLETE SET (275)	180.00	55.00
COMMON CARD (T1-T110)	1.50	.45
COMMON CARD (T111-T275)	.40	.12

❑ T1	Jeff Weaver	1.50	.45
❑ T2	Jay Powell	1.50	.45
❑ T3	Alex Gonzalez	1.50	.45
❑ T4	Jason Isringhausen	1.50	.45
❑ T5	Tyler Houston	1.50	.45
❑ T6	Ben Broussard	1.50	.45
❑ T7	Chuck Knoblauch	1.50	.45
❑ T8	Brian L. Hunter	1.50	.45
❑ T9	Dustan Mohr	1.50	.45
❑ T10	Eric Hinske	1.50	.45
❑ T11	Roger Cedeno	1.50	.45
❑ T12	Eddie Perez	1.50	.45
❑ T13	Jeromy Burnitz	1.50	.45
❑ T14	Bartolo Colon	1.50	.45
❑ T15	Rick Helling	1.50	.45
❑ T16	Dan Plesac	1.50	.45
❑ T17	Scott Strickland	1.50	.45
❑ T18	Antonio Alfonseca	1.50	.45
❑ T19	Ricky Gutierrez	1.50	.45
❑ T20	John Valentin	1.50	.45
❑ T21	Raul Mondesi	1.50	.45
❑ T22	Ben Davis	1.50	.45
❑ T23	Nelson Figueroa	1.50	.45
❑ T24	Earl Snyder	1.50	.45
❑ T25	Robin Ventura	1.50	.45
❑ T26	Jimmy Haynes	1.50	.45
❑ T27	Kenny Kelly	1.50	.45
❑ T28	Morgan Ensberg	1.50	.45
❑ T29	Reggie Sanders	1.50	.45
❑ T30	Shigetoshi Hasegawa	1.50	.45
❑ T31	Mike Timlin	1.50	.45
❑ T32	Russell Branyan	1.50	.45
❑ T33	Alan Embree	1.50	.45
❑ T34	D'Angelo Jimenez	1.50	.45
❑ T35	Kent Mercker	1.50	.45
❑ T36	Jesse Orosco	1.50	.45
❑ T37	Gregg Zaun	1.50	.45
❑ T38	Reggie Taylor	1.50	.45
❑ T39	Andres Galarraga	1.50	.45
❑ T40	Chris Truby	1.50	.45
❑ T41	Bruce Chen	1.50	.45
❑ T42	Darren Lewis	1.50	.45
❑ T43	Ryan Kohlmeier	1.50	.45
❑ T44	John McDonald	1.50	.45
❑ T45	Omar Daal	1.50	.45
❑ T46	Matt Clement	1.50	.45
❑ T47	Glendon Rusch	1.50	.45
❑ T48	Chan Ho Park	1.50	.45
❑ T49	Benny Agbayani	1.50	.45
❑ T50	Juan Gonzalez	4.00	1.20
❑ T51	Carlos Baerga	1.50	.45
❑ T52	Tim Raines	1.50	.45
❑ T53	Kevin Appier	1.50	.45
❑ T54	Marty Cordova	1.50	.45
❑ T55	Jeff D'Amico	1.50	.45
❑ T56	Dmitri Young	1.50	.45
❑ T57	Roosevelt Brown	1.50	.45
❑ T58	Dustin Hermanson	1.50	.45
❑ T59	Jose Rijo	1.50	.45
❑ T60	Todd Ritchie	1.50	.45
❑ T61	Lee Stevens	1.50	.45
❑ T62	Placido Polanco	1.50	.45
❑ T63	Eric Young	1.50	.45
❑ T64	Chuck Finley	1.50	.45
❑ T65	Dicky Gonzalez	1.50	.45
❑ T66	Jose Macias	1.50	.45
❑ T67	Gabe Kapler	1.50	.45
❑ T68	Sandy Alomar Jr.	1.50	.45
❑ T69	Henry Blanco	1.50	.45
❑ T70	Julian Tavarez	1.50	.45
❑ T71	Paul Bako	1.50	.45
❑ T72	Scott Rolen	2.50	.75
❑ T73	Brian Jordan	1.50	.45
❑ T74	Rickey Henderson	6.00	1.80
❑ T75	Kevin Mench	1.50	.45
❑ T76	Hideo Nomo	4.00	1.20
❑ T77	Jeremy Giambi	1.50	.45
❑ T78	Brad Fullmer	1.50	.45
❑ T79	Carl Everett	1.50	.45
❑ T80	David Wells	1.50	.45
❑ T81	Aaron Sele	1.50	.45
❑ T82	Todd Hollandsworth	1.50	.45
❑ T83	Vicente Padilla	1.50	.45
❑ T84	Kenny Lofton	1.50	.45
❑ T85	Corky Miller	1.50	.45
❑ T86	Josh Fogg	1.50	.45
❑ T87	Cliff Floyd	1.50	.45
❑ T88	Craig Paquette	1.50	.45
❑ T89	Jay Payton	1.50	.45
❑ T90	Carlos Pena	1.50	.45
❑ T91	Juan Encarnacion	1.50	.45
❑ T92	Rey Sanchez	1.50	.45
❑ T93	Ryan Dempster	1.50	.45
❑ T94	Mario Encarnacion	1.50	.45
❑ T95	Jorge Julio	1.50	.45
❑ T96	John Mabry	1.50	.45
❑ T97	Todd Zeile	1.50	.45
❑ T98	Johnny Damon	1.50	.45
❑ T99	Deivi Cruz	1.50	.45
❑ T100	Gary Sheffield	1.50	.45
❑ T101	Ted Lilly	1.50	.45
❑ T102	Todd Van Poppel	1.50	.45
❑ T103	Shawn Estes	1.50	.45
❑ T104	Cesar Izturis	1.50	.45
❑ T105	Ron Coomer	1.50	.45
❑ T106	Grady Little MG RC	1.50	.45
❑ T107	Jimy Williams MG	1.50	.45
❑ T108	Tony Pena MG	1.50	.45
❑ T109	Frank Robinson MG	2.50	.75
❑ T110	Ron Gardenhire MG	1.50	.45
❑ T111	Dennis Tankersley	.40	.12
❑ T112	Alejandro Cadena RC	.40	.12
❑ T113	Justin Reid RC	.40	.12
❑ T114	Nate Field RC	.40	.12
❑ T115	Rene Reyes RC	.40	.12
❑ T116	Nelson Castro RC	.40	.12
❑ T117	Miguel Olivo	.40	.12
❑ T118	David Espinosa	.40	.12
❑ T119	Chris Bootcheck RC	.75	.23
❑ T120	Rob Henkel RC	.40	.12
❑ T121	Steve Bechler RC	.40	.12
❑ T122	Mark Outlaw RC	.40	.12
❑ T123	Henry Pichardo RC	.40	.12
❑ T124	Michael Floyd RC	.40	.12
❑ T125	Richard Lane RC	.40	.12
❑ T126	Pete Zamora RC	.40	.12
❑ T127	Javier Colina	.40	.12
❑ T128	Greg Sain RC	.40	.12
❑ T129	Ronnie Merrill	.40	.12
❑ T130	Gavin Floyd RC	2.00	.60
❑ T131	Josh Bonifay RC	.50	.15
❑ T132	Tommy Marx RC	.40	.12
❑ T133	Gary Cates Jr. RC	.40	.12
❑ T134	Neal Cotts RC	1.50	.45
❑ T135	Angel Berroa	.40	.12
❑ T136	Elio Serrano RC	.40	.12
❑ T137	J.J. Putz RC	.40	.12
❑ T138	Ruben Gotay RC	.50	.15
❑ T139	Eddie Rogers	.40	.12
❑ T140	Wily Mo Pena	.40	.12
❑ T141	Tyler Yates RC	.40	.12
❑ T142	Colin Young RC	.40	.12
❑ T143	Chance Caple	.40	.12
❑ T144	Ben Howard RC	.40	.12
❑ T145	Ryan Bukvich RC	.50	.15
❑ T146	Cliff Bartosh RC	.40	.12
❑ T147	Brandon Claussen	1.00	.30
❑ T148	Cristian Guerrero	.40	.12
❑ T149	Derrick Lewis	.40	.12
❑ T150	Eric Miller RC	.40	.12
❑ T151	Justin Huber RC	1.00	.30
❑ T152	Adrian Gonzalez	.40	.12
❑ T153	Brian West RC	.40	.12
❑ T154	Chris Baker RC	.40	.12
❑ T155	Drew Henson	.40	.12
❑ T156	Scott Hairston RC	1.50	.45
❑ T157	Jason Simontacchi RC	.60	.18
❑ T158	Jason Arnold RC	1.00	.30
❑ T159	Brandon Phillips	.40	.12
❑ T160	Adam Roller RC	.40	.12
❑ T161	Scotty Layfield RC	.40	.12
❑ T162	Freddie Money RC	.40	.12
❑ T163	Noochie Varner RC	.75	.23
❑ T164	Terrance Hill RC	.40	.12
❑ T165	Jeremy Hill RC	.40	.12
❑ T166	Carlos Cabrera RC	.40	.12
❑ T167	Jose Morban RC	.50	.15
❑ T168	Kevin Frederick RC	.40	.12
❑ T169	Mark Teixeira	1.00	.30
❑ T170	Brian Rogers	.40	.12
❑ T171	Anastacio Martinez RC	.40	.12
❑ T172	Bobby Jenks RC	1.25	.35
❑ T173	David Gil RC	.40	.12
❑ T174	Andres Torres	.40	.12
❑ T175	James Barrett RC	.50	.15
❑ T176	Jimmy Journell	.40	.12
❑ T177	Brett Kay RC	.40	.12
❑ T178	Jason Young RC	.50	.15
❑ T179	Mark Hamilton RC	.40	.12
❑ T180	Jose Bautista RC	.75	.23
❑ T181	Blake McGinley RC	.40	.12
❑ T182	Ryan Mottl RC	.50	.15
❑ T183	Jeff Austin RC	.40	.12
❑ T184	Xavier Nady	.40	.12
❑ T185	Kyle Kane RC	.40	.12
❑ T186	Travis Foley RC	.50	.15
❑ T187	Nathan Kaup RC	.40	.12
❑ T188	Eric Cyr	.40	.12
❑ T189	Josh Cisneros RC	.40	.12
❑ T190	Brad Nelson RC	1.25	.35
❑ T191	Clint Weibl RC	.40	.12
❑ T192	Ron Calloway RC	.40	.12
❑ T193	Jung Bong	.40	.12
❑ T194	Rolando Viera RC	.40	.12
❑ T195	Jason Bulger RC	.40	.12
❑ T196	Chone Figgins RC	.40	.12
❑ T197	Jimmy Alvarez RC	.40	.12
❑ T198	Joel Crump RC	.40	.12
❑ T199	Ryan Doumit RC	.50	.15
❑ T200	Demetrius Heath RC	.40	.12
❑ T201	John Ennis RC	.40	.12
❑ T202	Doug Sessions RC	.40	.12
❑ T203	Clinton Hosford RC	.40	.12
❑ T204	Chris Narveson RC	.40	.12
❑ T205	Ross Peeples RC	.50	.15
❑ T206	Alex Requena RC	.50	.15
❑ T207	Matt Erickson RC	.40	.12

Card	Nm-Mt	Ex-Mt
❑ T208 Brian Forystek RC	.40	.12
❑ T209 Dewon Brazelton	.40	.12
❑ T210 Nathan Haynes	.40	.12
❑ T211 Jack Cust	.40	.12
❑ T212 Jesse Foppert RC	2.00	.60
❑ T213 Jesus Cota RC	.75	.23
❑ T214 Juan M. Gonzalez RC	.40	.12
❑ T215 Tim Kalita RC	.40	.12
❑ T216 Manny Delcarmen RC	.50	.15
❑ T217 Jim Kavourias RC	.40	.12
❑ T218 C.J. Wilson RC	.50	.15
❑ T219 Edwin Yan RC	.40	.12
❑ T220 Andy Van Hekken	.40	.12
❑ T221 Michael Cuddyer	.40	.12
❑ T222 Jeff Verplancke RC	.40	.12
❑ T223 Mike Wilson RC	.40	.12
❑ T224 Corwin Malone RC	.50	.15
❑ T225 Chris Snelling RC	1.00	.30
❑ T226 Joe Rogers RC	.40	.12
❑ T227 Jason Bay	1.00	.30
❑ T228 Ezequiel Astacio RC	.40	.12
❑ T229 Joey Hammond RC	.40	.12
❑ T230 Chris Duffy RC	.40	.12
❑ T231 Mark Prior	3.00	.90
❑ T232 Hansel Izquierdo RC	.40	.12
❑ T233 Franklyn German RC	.40	.12
❑ T234 Alexis Gomez	.40	.12
❑ T235 Jorge Padilla RC	.50	.15
❑ T236 Ryan Snare RC	.50	.15
❑ T237 Deivis Santos	.40	.12
❑ T238 Taggert Bozied RC	1.50	.45
❑ T239 Mike Peeples RC	.40	.12
❑ T240 Ronald Acuna RC	.40	.12
❑ T241 Koyie Hill	.40	.12
❑ T242 Garrett Guzman RC	.40	.12
❑ T243 Ryan Church RC	.75	.23
❑ T244 Tony Fontana RC	.40	.12
❑ T245 Keto Anderson RC	.40	.12
❑ T246 Brad Bouras RC	.50	.15
❑ T247 Jason Dubois RC	1.50	.45
❑ T248 Angel Guzman RC	2.00	.60
❑ T249 Joel Hanrahan RC	.75	.23
❑ T250 Joe Jiannetti RC	.40	.12
❑ T251 Sean Pierce RC	.40	.12
❑ T252 Jake Mauer RC	.40	.12
❑ T253 Marshall McDougall RC	.40	.12
❑ T254 Edwin Almonte RC	.40	.12
❑ T255 Shawn Riggans RC	.50	.15
❑ T256 Steven Shell RC	.40	.12
❑ T257 Kevin Hooper RC	.40	.12
❑ T258 Michael Frick RC	.50	.15
❑ T259 Travis Chapman RC	.75	.23
❑ T260 Tim Hummel RC	.40	.12
❑ T261 Adam Morrissey RC	.50	.15
❑ T262 Dontrelle Willis RC	8.00	2.40
❑ T263 Justin Sherrod RC	.50	.15
❑ T264 Gerald Smiley RC	.40	.12
❑ T265 Tony Miller RC	.75	.23
❑ T266 Nolan Ryan WW	3.00	.90
❑ T267 Reggie Jackson WW	.60	.18
❑ T268 Steve Garvey WW	.40	.12
❑ T269 Wade Boggs WW	.60	.18
❑ T270 Sammy Sosa WW	1.50	.45
❑ T271 Curt Schilling WW	.60	.18
❑ T272 Mark Grace WW	1.00	.30
❑ T273 Jason Giambi WW	1.00	.30
❑ T274 Ken Griffey Jr. WW	1.50	.45
❑ T275 Roberto Alomar WW	1.00	.30

2003 Topps

	Nm-Mt	Ex-Mt
COMPLETE SET (720)	80.00	24.00
COMPLETE SERIES 1 (366)	40.00	12.00
COMPLETE SERIES 2 (354)	40.00	12.00
COMMON CARD (1-6/8-721)	.20	.06
COMMON (292-331/660-684)	.50	.15

Card	Nm-Mt	Ex-Mt
❑ 1 Alex Rodriguez	1.00	.30
❑ 2 Dan Wilson	.20	.06
❑ 3 Jimmy Rollins	.20	.06
❑ 4 Jermaine Dye	.20	.06
❑ 5 Steve Karsay	.20	.06
❑ 6 Timo Perez	.20	.06
❑ 7 Does Not Exist		
❑ 8 Jose Vidro	.20	.06

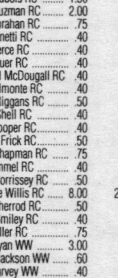

Card	Nm-Mt	Ex-Mt
❑ 9 Eddie Guardado	.20	.06
❑ 10 Mark Prior	1.00	.30
❑ 11 Curt Schilling	.30	.09
❑ 12 Dennis Cook	.20	.06
❑ 13 Andruw Jones	.30	.09
❑ 14 David Segui	.20	.06
❑ 15 Trot Nixon	.20	.06
❑ 16 Kerry Wood	.50	.15
❑ 17 Magglio Ordonez	.20	.06
❑ 18 Jason LaRue	.20	.06
❑ 19 Danys Baez	.20	.06
❑ 20 Todd Helton	.30	.09
❑ 21 Denny Neagle	.20	.06
❑ 22 Dave Mlicki	.20	.06
❑ 23 Roberto Hernandez	.20	.06
❑ 24 Odalis Perez	.20	.06
❑ 25 Nick Neugebauer	.20	.06
❑ 26 David Ortiz	.20	.06
❑ 27 Andres Galarraga	.20	.06
❑ 28 Edgardo Alfonzo	.20	.06
❑ 29 Chad Bradford	.20	.06
❑ 30 Jason Giambi	.50	.15
❑ 31 Brian Giles	.20	.06
❑ 32 Deivi Cruz	.20	.06
❑ 33 Robb Nen	.20	.06
❑ 34 Jeff Nelson	.20	.06
❑ 35 Edgar Renteria	.20	.06
❑ 36 Aubrey Huff	.20	.06
❑ 37 Brandon Duckworth	.20	.06
❑ 38 Juan Gonzalez	.50	.15
❑ 39 Sidney Ponson	.20	.06
❑ 40 Eric Hinske	.20	.06
❑ 41 Kevin Appier	.20	.06
❑ 42 Danny Bautista	.20	.06
❑ 43 Javier Lopez	.20	.06
❑ 44 Jeff Conine	.20	.06
❑ 45 Carlos Baerga	.20	.06
❑ 46 Ugueth Urbina	.20	.06
❑ 47 Mark Buehrle	.20	.06
❑ 48 Aaron Boone	.20	.06
❑ 49 Jason Simontacchi	.20	.06
❑ 50 Sammy Sosa	.75	.23
❑ 51 Jose Jimenez	.20	.06
❑ 52 Bobby Higginson	.20	.06
❑ 53 Luis Castillo	.20	.06
❑ 54 Orlando Merced	.20	.06
❑ 55 Brian Jordan	.20	.06
❑ 56 Eric Young	.20	.06
❑ 57 Bobby Kielty	.20	.06
❑ 58 Luis Rivas	.20	.06
❑ 59 Brad Wilkerson	.20	.06
❑ 60 Roberto Alomar	.50	.15
❑ 61 Roger Clemens	1.00	.30
❑ 62 Scott Hatteberg	.20	.06
❑ 63 Andy Ashby	.20	.06
❑ 64 Mike Williams	.20	.06
❑ 65 Ron Gant	.20	.06
❑ 66 Benito Santiago	.20	.06
❑ 67 Bret Boone	.20	.06
❑ 68 Matt Morris	.20	.06
❑ 69 Troy Glaus	.30	.09
❑ 70 Austin Kearns	.30	.09
❑ 71 Jim Thome	.50	.15
❑ 72 Rickey Henderson	.75	.23
❑ 73 Luis Gonzalez	.20	.06
❑ 74 Brad Fullmer	.20	.06
❑ 75 Herbert Perry	.20	.06
❑ 76 Randy Wolf	.20	.06
❑ 77 Miguel Tejada	.20	.06
❑ 78 Jimmy Anderson	.20	.06
❑ 79 Ramon Martinez	.20	.06
❑ 80 Ivan Rodriguez	.50	.15
❑ 81 John Flaherty	.20	.06
❑ 82 Shannon Stewart	.20	.06
❑ 83 Orlando Palmeiro	.20	.06
❑ 84 Rafael Furcal	.20	.06
❑ 85 Kenny Rogers	.20	.06
❑ 86 Terry Adams	.20	.06
❑ 87 Mo Vaughn	.20	.06
❑ 88 Jose Cruz Jr.	.20	.06
❑ 89 Mike Matheny	.20	.06
❑ 90 Alfonso Soriano	.50	.15
❑ 91 Orlando Cabrera	.20	.06
❑ 92 Jeffrey Hammonds	.20	.06
❑ 93 Hideo Nomo	.50	.15
❑ 94 Carlos Febles	.20	.06
❑ 95 Billy Wagner	.20	.06
❑ 96 Alex Gonzalez	.20	.06
❑ 97 Todd Zeile	.20	.06
❑ 98 Omar Vizquel	.20	.06
❑ 99 Jose Rijo	.20	.06
❑ 100 Ichiro Suzuki	1.00	.30
❑ 101 Steve Cox	.20	.06
❑ 102 Hideki Irabu	.20	.06
❑ 103 Roy Halladay	.20	.06
❑ 104 David Eckstein	.20	.06
❑ 105 Greg Maddux	1.00	.30
❑ 106 Jay Gibbons	.20	.06
❑ 107 Travis Driskill	.20	.06
❑ 108 Fred McGriff	.30	.09
❑ 109 Frank Thomas	.50	.15
❑ 110 Shawn Green	.20	.06
❑ 111 Ruben Quevedo	.20	.06
❑ 112 Jacque Jones	.20	.06
❑ 113 Tomo Ohka	.20	.06
❑ 114 Joe McEwing	.20	.06
❑ 115 Ramiro Mendoza	.20	.06
❑ 116 Mark Mulder	.20	.06
❑ 117 Mike Lieberthal	.20	.06
❑ 118 Jack Wilson	.20	.06
❑ 119 Randall Simon	.20	.06
❑ 120 Bernie Williams	.30	.09
❑ 121 Marvin Benard	.20	.06
❑ 122 Jamie Moyer	.20	.06
❑ 123 Andy Benes	.20	.06
❑ 124 Tino Martinez	.30	.09
❑ 125 Esteban Yan	.20	.06
❑ 126 Juan Uribe	.20	.06
❑ 127 Jason Isringhausen	.20	.06
❑ 128 Chris Carpenter	.20	.06
❑ 129 Mike Cameron	.20	.06
❑ 130 Gary Sheffield	.20	.06
❑ 131 Geronimo Gil	.20	.06
❑ 132 Brian Daubach	.20	.06
❑ 133 Corey Patterson	.20	.06
❑ 134 Aaron Rowand	.20	.06
❑ 135 Chris Reitsma	.20	.06
❑ 136 Bob Wickman	.20	.06
❑ 137 Cesar Izturis	.20	.06
❑ 138 Jason Jennings	.20	.06
❑ 139 Brandon Inge	.20	.06
❑ 140 Larry Walker	.30	.09
❑ 141 Ramon Santiago	.20	.06
❑ 142 Vladimir Nunez	.20	.06
❑ 143 Jose Vizcaino	.20	.06
❑ 144 Mark Quinn	.20	.06
❑ 145 Michael Tucker	.20	.06
❑ 146 Darren Dreifort	.20	.06
❑ 147 Ben Sheets	.20	.06
❑ 148 Corey Koskie	.20	.06
❑ 149 Tony Armas Jr.	.20	.06
❑ 150 Kazuhisa Ishii	.20	.06
❑ 151 Al Leiter	.20	.06
❑ 152 Steve Trachsel	.20	.06
❑ 153 Mike Stanton	.20	.06
❑ 154 David Justice	.20	.06
❑ 155 Marlon Anderson	.20	.06
❑ 156 Jason Kendall	.20	.06
❑ 157 Brian Lawrence	.20	.06
❑ 158 J.T. Snow	.20	.06
❑ 159 Edgar Martinez	.30	.09
❑ 160 Pat Burrell	.20	.06
❑ 161 Kerry Robinson	.20	.06
❑ 162 Greg Vaughn	.20	.06

❑ 163 Carl Everett .20 .06
❑ 164 Vernon Wells .20 .06
❑ 165 Jose Mesa .20 .06
❑ 166 Troy Percival .20 .06
❑ 167 Erubiel Durazo .20 .06
❑ 168 Jason Marquis .20 .06
❑ 169 Jerry Hairston Jr. .20 .06
❑ 170 Vladimir Guerrero .50 .15
❑ 171 Byung-Hyun Kim .20 .06
❑ 172 Marcus Giles .20 .06
❑ 173 Johnny Damon .20 .06
❑ 174 Jon Lieber .20 .06
❑ 175 Terrence Long .20 .06
❑ 176 Sean Casey .20 .06
❑ 177 Adam Dunn .30 .09
❑ 178 Juan Pierre .20 .06
❑ 179 Wendell Magee .20 .06
❑ 180 Barry Zito .50 .15
❑ 181 Aramis Ramirez .20 .06
❑ 182 Pokey Reese .20 .06
❑ 183 Jeff Kent .20 .06
❑ 184 Russ Ortiz .20 .06
❑ 185 Ruben Sierra .20 .06
❑ 186 Brent Abernathy .20 .06
❑ 187 Ismael Valdes UER .20 .06
Card does not include 2002 Rangers stats
❑ 188 Tom Wilson .20 .06
❑ 189 Craig Counsell .20 .06
❑ 190 Mike Mussina .50 .15
❑ 191 Ramon Hernandez .20 .06
❑ 192 Adam Kennedy .20 .06
❑ 193 Tony Womack .20 .06
❑ 194 Wes Helms .20 .06
❑ 195 Tony Batista .20 .06
❑ 196 Rolando Arrojo .20 .06
❑ 197 Kyle Farnsworth .20 .06
❑ 198 Gary Bennett .20 .06
❑ 199 Scott Sullivan .20 .06
❑ 200 Albert Pujols 1.00 .30
❑ 201 Kirk Rueter .20 .06
❑ 202 Phil Nevin .20 .06
❑ 203 Kip Wells .20 .06
❑ 204 Ron Coomer .20 .06
❑ 205 Jeromy Burnitz .20 .06
❑ 206 Kyle Lohse .20 .06
❑ 207 Mike DeJean .20 .06
❑ 208 Paul Lo Duca .20 .06
❑ 209 Carlos Beltran .20 .06
❑ 210 Roy Oswalt .20 .06
❑ 211 Mike Lowell .20 .06
❑ 212 Robert Fick .20 .06
❑ 213 Todd Jones .20 .06
❑ 214 C.C. Sabathia .20 .06
❑ 215 Danny Graves .20 .06
❑ 216 Todd Hundley .20 .06
❑ 217 Tim Wakefield .20 .06
❑ 218 Derek Lowe .20 .06
❑ 219 Kevin Millwood .20 .06
❑ 220 Jorge Posada .30 .09
❑ 221 Bobby J. Jones .20 .06
❑ 222 Carlos Guillen .20 .06
❑ 223 Fernando Vina .20 .06
❑ 224 Ryan Rupe .20 .06
❑ 225 Kelvim Escobar .20 .06
❑ 226 Ramon Ortiz .20 .06
❑ 227 Junior Spivey .20 .06
❑ 228 Juan Cruz .20 .06
❑ 229 Melvin Mora .20 .06
❑ 230 Lance Berkman .20 .06
❑ 231 Brent Butler .20 .06
❑ 232 Shane Halter .20 .06
❑ 233 Derrek Lee .20 .06
❑ 234 Matt Lawton .20 .06
❑ 235 Chuck Knoblauch .20 .06
❑ 236 Eric Gagne .30 .09
❑ 237 Alex Sanchez .20 .06
❑ 238 Denny Hocking .20 .06
❑ 239 Eric Milton .20 .06
❑ 240 Rey Ordonez .20 .06
❑ 241 Orlando Hernandez .20 .06
❑ 242 Robert Person .20 .06
❑ 243 Sean Burroughs .20 .06
❑ 244 Jeff Cirillo .20 .06
❑ 245 Mike Lamb .20 .06
❑ 246 Jose Valentin .20 .06
❑ 247 Ellis Burks .20 .06
❑ 248 Shawn Chacon .20 .06
❑ 249 Josh Beckett .30 .09
❑ 250 Nomar Garciaparra 1.00 .30
❑ 251 Craig Biggio .30 .09
❑ 252 Joe Randa .20 .06
❑ 253 Mark Grudzielanek .20 .06
❑ 254 Glendon Rusch .20 .06
❑ 255 Michael Barrett .20 .06
❑ 256 Omar Daal .20 .06
❑ 257 Elmer Dessens .20 .06
❑ 258 Wade Miller .20 .06
❑ 259 Adrian Beltre .20 .06
❑ 260 Vicente Padilla .20 .06
❑ 261 Kazuhiro Sasaki .20 .06
❑ 262 Mike Scioscia MG .20 .06
❑ 263 Bobby Cox MG .20 .06
❑ 264 Mike Hargrove MG .20 .06
❑ 265 Grady Little MG RC .20 .06
❑ 266 Alex Gonzalez UER .20 .06
2002 stats are listed as all zero's
❑ 267 Jerry Manuel MG .20 .06
❑ 268 Bob Boone MG .20 .06
❑ 269 Joel Skinner MG .20 .06
❑ 270 Clint Hurdle MG .20 .06
❑ 271 Miguel Batista UER .20 .06
All 2002 Stats are 0's
❑ 272 Bob Brenly MG .20 .06
❑ 273 Jeff Torborg MG .20 .06
❑ 274 Jimy Williams MG UER .20 .06
Career managerial record is wrong
❑ 275 Tony Pena MG .20 .06
❑ 276 Jim Tracy MG .20 .06
❑ 277 Jerry Royster MG .20 .06
❑ 278 Ron Gardenhire MG .20 .06
❑ 279 Frank Robinson MG .30 .09
❑ 280 John Halama .20 .06
❑ 281 Joe Torre MG .30 .09
❑ 282 Art Howe MG .20 .06
❑ 283 Larry Bowa MG .20 .06
❑ 284 Lloyd McClendon MG .20 .06
❑ 285 Bruce Bochy MG .20 .06
❑ 286 Dusty Baker MG .20 .06
❑ 287 Lou Piniella MG .20 .06
❑ 288 Tony LaRussa MG .20 .06
❑ 289 Todd Walker .20 .06
❑ 290 Jerry Narron MG .20 .06
❑ 291 Carlos Tosca MG .20 .06
❑ 292 Chris Duncan FY RC .50 .15
❑ 293 Franklin Gutierrez FY RC 2.00 .45
❑ 294 Adam LaRoche FY .50 .15
❑ 295 Manuel Ramirez FY RC .75 .23
❑ 296 Il Kim FY RC .50 .15
❑ 297 Wayne Lydon FY RC .50 .15
❑ 298 Daryl Clark FY RC .50 .15
❑ 299 Sean Pierce FY .50 .15
❑ 300 Andy Marte FY RC 2.00 .60
❑ 301 Matthew Peterson FY RC .50 .15
❑ 302 Gonzalo Lopez FY RC .50 .15
❑ 303 Bernie Castro FY RC .50 .15
❑ 304 Cliff Lee FY .50 .15
❑ 305 Jason Perry FY RC .75 .23
❑ 306 Jaime Bubela FY RC .50 .15
❑ 307 Alexis Rios FY .50 .15
❑ 308 Brendan Harris FY RC .50 .15
❑ 309 Ramon Nivar-Martinez FY RC 1.00 .30
❑ 310 Terry Tiffee FY RC .50 .15
❑ 311 Kevin Youkilis FY RC 1.50 .45
❑ 312 Ruddy Lugo FY RC .50 .15
❑ 313 C.J. Wilson FY .50 .15
❑ 314 Mike McNutt FY RC .50 .15
❑ 315 Jeff Clark FY RC .50 .15
❑ 316 Mark Malaska FY RC .50 .15
❑ 317 Doug Waechter FY RC .75 .23
❑ 318 Derell McCall FY RC .50 .15
❑ 319 Scott Tyler FY RC .50 .15
❑ 320 Craig Brazell FY RC .75 .23
❑ 321 Walter Young FY .50 .15
❑ 322 Marlon Byrd .50 .15
Jorge Padilla FS
❑ 323 Chris Snelling .50 .15
Shin-Soo Choo FS
❑ 324 Hank Blalock .50 .15
Mark Teixeira FS
❑ 325 Josh Hamilton .50 .15
Carl Crawford FS
❑ 326 Orlando Hudson .50 .15
Josh Phelps FS
❑ 327 Jack Cust .50 .15
Rene Reyes FS
❑ 328 Angel Berroa .50 .15
Alexis Gomez FS
❑ 329 Michael Cuddyer .50 .15
Michael Restovich FS
❑ 330 Juan Rivera .50 .15
Marcus Thames FS
❑ 331 Brandon Puffer .50 .15
Jung Bong FS
❑ 332 Mike Cameron SH .20 .06
❑ 333 Shawn Green SH .20 .06
❑ 334 Oakland A's SH .20 .06
❑ 335 Jason Giambi SH .30 .09
❑ 336 Derek Lowe SH .20 .06
❑ 337 Manny Ramirez .50 .15
Mike Sweeney
Bernie Williams LL
❑ 338 Alfonso Soriano .50 .15
Alex Rodriguez
Derek Jeter LL
❑ 339 Alex Rodriguez .50 .15
Jim Thome
Rafael Palmeiro LL
❑ 340 Alex Rodriguez .50 .15
Magglio Ordonez
Miguel Tejada LL
❑ 341 Pedro Martinez .50 .15
Derek Lowe
Barry Zito LL
❑ 342 Pedro Martinez .50 .15
Roger Clemens
Mike Mussina LL
❑ 343 Larry Walker .50 .15
Vladimir Guerrero
Todd Helton LL
❑ 344 Sammy Sosa .50 .15
Albert Pujols
Shawn Green LL
❑ 345 Sammy Sosa .50 .15
Lance Berkman
Shawn Green LL
❑ 346 Lance Berkman .20 .06
Albert Pujols
Pat Burrell LL
❑ 347 Randy Johnson .30 .09
Greg Maddux
Tom Glavine LL
❑ 348 Randy Johnson .30 .09
Curt Schilling
Kerry Wood LL
❑ 349 Francisco Rodriguez .20 .06
Darin Erstad
Tim Salmon
AL Division Series
❑ 350 Minnesota Twins .30 .09
St Louis Cardinals
AL and NL Division Series
❑ 351 Anaheim Angels .30 .09
San Francisco Giants
AL and NL Division Series
❑ 352 Jim Edmonds .30 .09
Scott Rolen
NL Division Series
❑ 353 Adam Kennedy ALCS .20 .06
❑ 354 J.T. Snow WS .30 .09
❑ 355 David Bell NLCS .30 .09
❑ 356 Jason Giambi AS .30 .09
❑ 357 Alfonso Soriano AS .30 .09
❑ 358 Alex Rodriguez AS .50 .15
❑ 359 Eric Chavez AS .20 .06
❑ 360 Torii Hunter AS .20 .06
❑ 361 Bernie Williams AS .20 .06
❑ 362 Garret Anderson AS .20 .06
❑ 363 Jorge Posada AS .20 .06
❑ 364 Derek Lowe AS .20 .06
❑ 365 Barry Zito AS .30 .09
❑ 366 Manny Ramirez AS .20 .06
❑ 367 Mike Scioscia AS .20 .06
❑ 368 Francisco Rodriguez .20 .06
❑ 369 Chris Hammond .20 .06
❑ 370 Chipper Jones .50 .15
❑ 371 Chris Singleton .20 .06
❑ 372 Cliff Floyd .20 .06

❑ 373 Bobby Hill .20 .06
❑ 374 Antonio Osuna .20 .06
❑ 375 Barry Larkin .50 .15
❑ 376 Charles Nagy .20 .06
❑ 377 Denny Stark .20 .06
❑ 378 Dean Palmer .20 .06
❑ 379 Eric Owens .20 .06
❑ 380 Randy Johnson .50 .15
❑ 381 Jeff Suppan .20 .06
❑ 382 Eric Karros .20 .06
❑ 383 Luis Vizcaino .20 .06
❑ 384 Johan Santana .20 .06
❑ 385 Javier Vazquez .20 .06
❑ 386 John Thomson .20 .06
❑ 387 Nick Johnson .20 .06
❑ 388 Mark Ellis .20 .06
❑ 389 Doug Glanville .20 .06
❑ 390 Ken Griffey Jr. .75 .23
❑ 391 Bubba Trammell .20 .06
❑ 392 Livan Hernandez .20 .06
❑ 393 Desi Relaford .20 .06
❑ 394 Eli Marrero .20 .06
❑ 395 Jared Sandberg .20 .06
❑ 396 Barry Bonds 1.25 .35
❑ 397 Esteban Loaiza .20 .06
❑ 398 Aaron Sele .20 .06
❑ 399 Geoff Blum .20 .06
❑ 400 Derek Jeter 1.25 .35
❑ 401 Eric Byrnes .20 .06
❑ 402 Mike Timlin .20 .06
❑ 403 Mark Kotsay .20 .06
❑ 404 Rich Aurilia .20 .06
❑ 405 Joel Pineiro .20 .06
❑ 406 Chuck Finley .20 .06
❑ 407 Bengie Molina .20 .06
❑ 408 Steve Finley .20 .06
❑ 409 Julio Franco .20 .06
❑ 410 Marty Cordova .20 .06
❑ 411 Shea Hillenbrand .20 .06
❑ 412 Mark Bellhorn .20 .06
❑ 413 Jon Garland .20 .06
❑ 414 Reggie Taylor .20 .06
❑ 415 Milton Bradley .20 .06
❑ 416 Carlos Pena .20 .06
❑ 417 Andy Fox .20 .06
❑ 418 Brad Ausmus .20 .06
❑ 419 Brent Mayne .20 .06
❑ 420 Paul Quantrill .20 .06
❑ 421 Carlos Delgado .20 .06
❑ 422 Kevin Mench .20 .06
❑ 423 Joe Kennedy .20 .06
❑ 424 Mike Crudale .20 .06
❑ 425 Mark McLemore .20 .06
❑ 426 Bill Mueller .20 .06
❑ 427 Rob Mackowiak .20 .06
❑ 428 Ricky Ledee .20 .06
❑ 429 Ted Lilly .20 .06
❑ 430 Sterling Hitchcock .20 .06
❑ 431 Scott Strickland .20 .06
❑ 432 Damion Easley .20 .06
❑ 433 Torii Hunter .20 .06
❑ 434 Brad Radke .20 .06
❑ 435 Geoff Jenkins .20 .06
❑ 436 Paul Byrd .20 .06
❑ 437 Morgan Ensberg .20 .06
❑ 438 Mike Maroth .20 .06
❑ 439 Mike Hampton .20 .06
❑ 440 Adam Hyzdu .20 .06
❑ 441 Vance Wilson .20 .06
❑ 442 Todd Ritchie .20 .06
❑ 443 Tom Gordon .20 .06
❑ 444 John Burkett .20 .06
❑ 445 Rodrigo Lopez .20 .06
❑ 446 Tim Spooneybarger .20 .06
❑ 447 Quinton Mccracken .20 .06
❑ 448 Tim Salmon .30 .09
❑ 449 Jarrod Washburn .20 .06
❑ 450 Pedro Martinez .50 .15
❑ 451 Dustan Mohr .20 .06
❑ 452 Julio Lugo .20 .06
❑ 453 Scott Stewart .20 .06
❑ 454 Armando Benitez .20 .06
❑ 455 Raul Mondesi .20 .06
❑ 456 Robin Ventura .20 .06
❑ 457 Bobby Abreu .20 .06
❑ 458 Josh Fogg .20 .06
❑ 459 Ryan Klesko .20 .06
❑ 460 Tsuyoshi Shinjo .20 .06
❑ 461 Jim Edmonds .20 .06
❑ 462 Cliff Politte .20 .06
❑ 463 Chan Ho Park .20 .06
❑ 464 John Mabry .20 .06
❑ 465 Woody Williams .20 .06
❑ 466 Jason Michaels .20 .06
❑ 467 Scott Schoeneweis .20 .06
❑ 468 Brian Anderson .20 .06
❑ 469 Brett Tomko .20 .06
❑ 470 Scott Erickson .20 .06
❑ 471 Kevin Millar .20 .06
❑ 472 Danny Wright .20 .06
❑ 473 Jason Schmidt .20 .06
❑ 474 Scott Williamson .20 .06
❑ 475 Einar Diaz .20 .06
❑ 476 Jay Payton .20 .06
❑ 477 Juan Acevedo .20 .06
❑ 478 Ben Grieve .20 .06
❑ 479 Raul Ibanez .20 .06
❑ 480 Richie Sexson .20 .06
❑ 481 Rick Reed .20 .06
❑ 482 Pedro Astacio .20 .06
❑ 483 Adam Piatt .20 .06
❑ 484 Bud Smith .20 .06
❑ 485 Tomas Perez .20 .06
❑ 486 Adam Eaton .20 .06
❑ 487 Rafael Palmeiro .30 .09
❑ 488 Jason Tyner .20 .06
❑ 489 Scott Rolen .30 .09
❑ 490 Randy Winn .20 .06
❑ 491 Ryan Jensen .20 .06
❑ 492 Trevor Hoffman .20 .06
❑ 493 Craig Wilson .20 .06
❑ 494 Jeremy Giambi .20 .06
❑ 495 Daryle Ward .20 .06
❑ 496 Shane Spencer .20 .06
❑ 497 Andy Pettitte .30 .09
❑ 498 John Franco .20 .06
❑ 499 Felipe Lopez .20 .06
❑ 500 Mike Piazza .75 .23
❑ 501 Cristian Guzman .20 .06
❑ 502 Jose Hernandez .20 .06
❑ 503 Octavio Dotel .20 .06
❑ 504 Brad Penny .20 .06
❑ 505 Dave Veres .20 .06
❑ 506 Ryan Dempster .20 .06
❑ 507 Joe Crede .20 .06
❑ 508 Chad Hermansen .20 .06
❑ 509 Gary Matthews Jr. .20 .06
❑ 510 Matt Franco .20 .06
❑ 511 Ben Weber .20 .06
❑ 512 Dave Berg .20 .06
❑ 513 Michael Young .20 .06
❑ 514 Frank Catalanotto .20 .06
❑ 515 Darin Erstad .20 .06
❑ 516 Matt Williams .20 .06
❑ 517 B.J. Surhoff .20 .06
❑ 518 Kerry Ligtenberg .20 .06
❑ 519 Mike Bordick .20 .06
❑ 520 Arthur Rhodes .20 .06
❑ 521 Joe Girardi .20 .06
❑ 522 D'Angelo Jimenez .20 .06
❑ 523 Paul Konerko .20 .06
❑ 524 Jose Macias .20 .06
❑ 525 Joe Mays .20 .06
❑ 526 Marquis Grissom .20 .06
❑ 527 Neifi Perez .20 .06
❑ 528 Preston Wilson .20 .06
❑ 529 Jeff Weaver .20 .06
❑ 530 Eric Chavez .20 .06
❑ 531 Placido Polanco .20 .06
❑ 532 Matt Mantei .20 .06
❑ 533 James Baldwin .20 .06
❑ 534 Toby Hall .20 .06
❑ 535 Brendan Donnelly .20 .06
❑ 536 Benji Gil .20 .06
❑ 537 Damian Moss .20 .06
❑ 538 Jorge Julio .20 .06
❑ 539 Matt Clement .20 .06
❑ 540 Brian Moehler .20 .06
❑ 541 Lee Stevens .20 .06
❑ 542 Jimmy Haynes .20 .06
❑ 543 Terry Mulholland .20 .06
❑ 544 Dave Roberts .20 .06
❑ 545 J.C. Romero .20 .06
❑ 546 Bartolo Colon .20 .06
❑ 547 Roger Cedeno .20 .06
❑ 548 Mariano Rivera .30 .09
❑ 549 Billy Koch .20 .06
❑ 550 Manny Ramirez .20 .06
❑ 551 Travis Lee .20 .06
❑ 552 Oliver Perez .20 .06
❑ 553 Tim Worrell .20 .06
❑ 554 Rafael Soriano .20 .06
❑ 555 Damian Miller .20 .06
❑ 556 John Smoltz .30 .09
❑ 557 Willis Roberts .20 .06
❑ 558 Tim Hudson .20 .06
❑ 559 Moises Alou .20 .06
❑ 560 Gary Glover .20 .06
❑ 561 Corky Miller .20 .06
❑ 562 Ben Broussard .20 .06
❑ 563 Gabe Kapler .20 .06
❑ 564 Chris Woodward .20 .06
❑ 565 Paul Wilson .20 .06
❑ 566 Todd Hollandsworth .20 .06
❑ 567 So Taguchi .20 .06
❑ 568 John Olerud .20 .06
❑ 569 Reggie Sanders .20 .06
❑ 570 Jake Peavy .20 .06
❑ 571 Kris Benson .20 .06
❑ 572 Todd Pratt .20 .06
❑ 573 Ray Durham .20 .06
❑ 574 Boomer Wells .20 .06
❑ 575 Chris Widger .20 .06
❑ 576 Shawn Wooten .20 .06
❑ 577 Tom Glavine .50 .15
❑ 578 Antonio Alfonseca .20 .06
❑ 579 Keith Foulke .20 .06
❑ 580 Shawn Estes .20 .06
❑ 581 Mark Grace .50 .15
❑ 582 Dmitri Young .20 .06
❑ 583 A.J. Burnett .20 .06
❑ 584 Richard Hidalgo .20 .06
❑ 585 Mike Sweeney .20 .06
❑ 586 Alex Cora .20 .06
❑ 587 Matt Stairs .20 .06
❑ 588 Doug Mientkiewicz .20 .06
❑ 589 Fernando Tatis .20 .06
❑ 590 David Weathers .20 .06
❑ 591 Cory Lidle .20 .06
❑ 592 Dan Plesac .20 .06
❑ 593 Jeff Bagwell .30 .09
❑ 594 Steve Sparks .20 .06
❑ 595 Sandy Alomar Jr. .20 .06
❑ 596 John Lackey .20 .06
❑ 597 Rick Helling .20 .06
❑ 598 Mark DeRosa .20 .06
❑ 599 Carlos Lee .20 .06
❑ 600 Garret Anderson .20 .06
❑ 601 Vinny Castilla .20 .06
❑ 602 Ryan Drese .20 .06
❑ 603 LaTroy Hawkins .20 .06
❑ 604 David Bell .20 .06
❑ 605 Freddy Garcia .20 .06
❑ 606 Miguel Cairo .20 .06
❑ 607 Scott Spiezio .20 .06
❑ 608 Mike Remlinger .20 .06
❑ 609 Tony Graffanino .20 .06
❑ 610 Russell Branyan .20 .06
❑ 611 Chris Magruder .20 .06
❑ 612 Jose Contreras RC 1.50 .45
❑ 613 Carl Pavano .20 .06
❑ 614 Kevin Brown .20 .06
❑ 615 Tyler Houston .20 .06
❑ 616 A.J. Pierzynski .20 .06
❑ 617 Tony Fiore .20 .06
❑ 618 Peter Bergeron .20 .06
❑ 619 Rondell White .20 .06
❑ 620 Brett Myers .20 .06
❑ 621 Kevin Young .20 .06
❑ 622 Kenny Lofton .20 .06
❑ 623 Ben Davis .20 .06
❑ 624 J.D. Drew .20 .06
❑ 625 Chris Gomez .20 .06
❑ 626 Karim Garcia .20 .06
❑ 627 Ricky Gutierrez .20 .06
❑ 628 Mark Redman .20 .06
❑ 629 Juan Encarnacion .20 .06
❑ 630 Anaheim Angels TC .30 .09

❑ 631 Arizona Diamondbacks TC .20 .06
❑ 632 Atlanta Braves TC .20 .06
❑ 633 Baltimore Orioles TC .20 .06
❑ 634 Boston Red Sox TC .20 .06
❑ 635 Chicago Cubs TC .20 .06
❑ 636 Chicago White Sox TC .20 .06
❑ 637 Cincinnati Reds TC .20 .06
❑ 638 Cleveland Indians TC .20 .06
❑ 639 Colorado Rockies TC .20 .06
❑ 640 Detroit Tigers TC .20 .06
❑ 641 Florida Marlins TC .20 .06
❑ 642 Houston Astros TC .20 .06
❑ 643 Kansas City Royals TC .20 .06
❑ 644 Los Angeles Dodgers TC .20 .06
❑ 645 Milwaukee Brewers TC .20 .06
❑ 646 Minnesota Twins TC .20 .06
❑ 647 Montreal Expos TC .20 .06
❑ 648 New York Mets TC .20 .06
❑ 649 New York Yankees TC .30 .09
❑ 650 Oakland Athletics TC .20 .06
❑ 651 Philadelphia Phillies TC .20 .06
❑ 652 Pittsburgh Pirates TC .20 .06
❑ 653 San Diego Padres TC .20 .06
❑ 654 San Francisco Giants TC .20 .06
❑ 655 Seattle Mariners TC .20 .06
❑ 656 St. Louis Cardinals TC .20 .06
❑ 657 Tampa Bay Devil Rays TC .20 .06
❑ 658 Texas Rangers TC .20 .06
❑ 659 Toronto Blue Jays TC .20 .06
❑ 660 Bryan Bullington DP RC 1.50 .45
❑ 661 Jeremy Guthrie DP .50 .15
❑ 662 Joey Gomes DP RC .50 .15
❑ 663 Evel Bastida-Martinez DP RC .50 .15
❑ 664 Brian Wright DP RC .50 .15
❑ 665 B.J. Upton DP .75 .23
❑ 666 Jeff Francis DP .50 .15
❑ 667 Drew Meyer DP .50 .15
❑ 668 Jeremy Hermida DP .50 .15
❑ 669 Khalil Greene DP .50 .15
❑ 670 Darrell Rasner DP RC .50 .15
❑ 671 Cole Hamels DP .75 .23
❑ 672 James Loney DP .50 .15
❑ 673 Sergio Santos DP .50 .15
❑ 674 Jason Pridie DP .50 .15
❑ 675 Brandon Phillips .50 .15
Victor Martinez
❑ 676 Hee Seop Choi .50 .15
Nic Jackson
❑ 677 Dontrelle Willis 1.50 .45
Jason Stokes
❑ 678 Chad Tracy .50 .15
Lyle Overbay
❑ 679 Joe Borchard .50 .15
Corwin Malone
❑ 680 Joe Mauer .75 .23
Justin Morneau
❑ 681 Drew Henson .50 .15
Brandon Claussen
❑ 682 Chase Utley .50 .15
Gavin Floyd
❑ 683 Taggert Bozied .50 .15
Xavier Nady
❑ 684 Aaron Heilman .50 .15
Jose Reyes
❑ 685 Kenny Rogers AW .20 .06
❑ 686 Bengie Molina AW .20 .06
❑ 687 John Olerud AW .20 .06
❑ 688 Bret Boone AW .20 .06
❑ 689 Eric Chavez AW .20 .06
❑ 690 Alex Rodriguez AW .50 .15
❑ 691 Darin Erstad AW .20 .06
❑ 692 Ichiro Suzuki AW .50 .15
❑ 693 Torii Hunter AW .20 .06
❑ 694 Greg Maddux AW .50 .15
❑ 695 Brad Ausmus AW .20 .06
❑ 696 Todd Helton AW .20 .06
❑ 697 Fernando Vina AW .20 .06
❑ 698 Scott Rolen AW .20 .06
❑ 699 Edgar Renteria AW .20 .06
❑ 700 Andruw Jones AW .20 .06
❑ 701 Larry Walker AW .20 .06
❑ 702 Jim Edmonds AW .20 .06
❑ 703 Barry Zito AW .30 .09
❑ 704 Randy Johnson AW .30 .09
❑ 705 Miguel Tejada AW .20 .06
❑ 706 Barry Bonds AW .60 .18
❑ 707 Eric Hinske AW .20 .06
❑ 708 Jason Jennings AW .20 .06
❑ 709 Todd Helton AS .20 .06
❑ 710 Jeff Kent AS .20 .06
❑ 711 Edgar Renteria AS .20 .06
❑ 712 Scott Rolen AS .20 .06
❑ 713 Barry Bonds AS .60 .18
❑ 714 Sammy Sosa AS .50 .15
❑ 715 Vladimir Guerrero AS .30 .09
❑ 716 Mike Piazza AS .50 .15
❑ 717 Curt Schilling AS .20 .06
❑ 718 Randy Johnson AS .30 .09
❑ 719 Bobby Cox AS .20 .06
❑ 720 Anaheim Angels WS .30 .09
❑ 721 Anaheim Angels WS .50 .15

2003 Topps Traded

	MINT	NRMT
COMPLETE SET (275)	80.00	36.00
COMMON CARD (121-165)	.40	.18

❑ T1 Juan Pierre .20 .09
❑ T2 Mark Grudzielanek .20 .09
❑ T3 Tanyon Sturtze .20 .09
❑ T4 Greg Vaughn .20 .09
❑ T5 Greg Myers .20 .09
❑ T6 Randall Simon .20 .09
❑ T7 Todd Hundley .20 .09
❑ T8 Marlon Anderson .20 .09
❑ T9 Jeff Reboulet .20 .09
❑ T10 Alex Sanchez .20 .09
❑ T11 Mike Rivera .20 .09
❑ T12 Todd Walker .20 .09
❑ T13 Ray King .20 .09
❑ T14 Shawn Estes .20 .09
❑ T15 Gary Matthews Jr. .20 .09
❑ T16 Jaret Wright .20 .09
❑ T17 Edgardo Alfonzo .20 .09
❑ T18 Omar Daal .20 .09
❑ T19 Ryan Rupe .20 .09
❑ T20 Tony Clark .20 .09
❑ T21 Jeff Suppan .20 .09
❑ T22 Mike Stanton .20 .09
❑ T23 Ramon Martinez .20 .09
❑ T24 Armando Rios .20 .09
❑ T25 Johnny Estrada .20 .09
❑ T26 Joe Girardi .20 .09
❑ T27 Ivan Rodriguez .50 .23
❑ T28 Robert Fick .20 .09
❑ T29 Rick White .20 .09
❑ T30 Robert Person .20 .09
❑ T31 Alan Benes .20 .09
❑ T32 Chris Carpenter .20 .09
❑ T33 Chris Widger .20 .09
❑ T34 Travis Hafner .20 .09
❑ T35 Mike Venafro .20 .09
❑ T36 Jon Lieber .20 .09
❑ T37 Orlando Hernandez .20 .09
❑ T38 Aaron Myette .20 .09
❑ T39 Paul Bako .20 .09
❑ T40 Erubiel Durazo .20 .09
❑ T41 Mark Guthrie .20 .09
❑ T42 Steve Avery .20 .09
❑ T43 Damian Jackson .20 .09
❑ T44 Rey Ordonez .20 .09
❑ T45 John Flaherty .20 .09
❑ T46 Byung-Hyun Kim .20 .09
❑ T47 Tom Goodwin .20 .09
❑ T48 Elmer Dessens .20 .09
❑ T49 Al Martin .20 .09
❑ T50 Gene Kingsale .20 .09
❑ T51 Lenny Harris .20 .09
❑ T52 David Ortiz .20 .09
❑ T53 Jose Lima .20 .09
❑ T54 Mike Difelice .20 .09
❑ T55 Jose Hernandez .20 .09
❑ T56 Todd Zeile .20 .09
❑ T57 Roberto Hernandez .20 .09
❑ T58 Albie Lopez .20 .09
❑ T59 Roberto Alomar .50 .23
❑ T60 Russ Ortiz .20 .09
❑ T61 Brian Daubach .20 .09
❑ T62 Carl Everett .20 .09
❑ T63 Jeromy Burnitz .20 .09
❑ T64 Mark Bellhorn .20 .09
❑ T65 Ruben Sierra .20 .09
❑ T66 Mike Fetters .20 .09
❑ T67 Armando Benitez .20 .09
❑ T68 Deivi Cruz .20 .09
❑ T69 Jose Cruz Jr. .20 .09
❑ T70 Jeremy Fikac .20 .09
❑ T71 Jeff Kent .20 .09
❑ T72 Andres Galarraga .20 .09
❑ T73 Rickey Henderson .75 .35
❑ T74 Royce Clayton .20 .09
❑ T75 Troy O'Leary .20 .09
❑ T76 Ron Coomer .20 .09
❑ T77 Greg Colbrunn .20 .09
❑ T78 Wes Helms .20 .09
❑ T79 Kevin Millwood .20 .09
❑ T80 Damion Easley .20 .09
❑ T81 Bobby Kielty .20 .09
❑ T82 Keith Osik .20 .09
❑ T83 Ramiro Mendoza .20 .09
❑ T84 Shea Hillenbrand .20 .09
❑ T85 Shannon Stewart .20 .09
❑ T86 Eddie Perez .20 .09
❑ T87 Ugueth Urbina .20 .09
❑ T88 Orlando Palmeiro .20 .09
❑ T89 Graeme Lloyd .20 .09
❑ T90 John Vander Wal .20 .09
❑ T91 Gary Bennett .20 .09
❑ T92 Shane Reynolds .20 .09
❑ T93 Steve Parris .20 .09
❑ T94 Julio Lugo .20 .09
❑ T95 John Halama .20 .09
❑ T96 Carlos Baerga .20 .09
❑ T97 Jim Parque .20 .09
❑ T98 Mike Williams .20 .09
❑ T99 Fred McGriff .30 .14
❑ T100 Kenny Rogers .20 .09
❑ T101 Matt Herges .20 .09
❑ T102 Jay Bell .20 .09
❑ T103 Esteban Yan .20 .09
❑ T104 Eric Owens .20 .09
❑ T105 Aaron Fultz .20 .09
❑ T106 Rey Sanchez .20 .09
❑ T107 Jim Thome .50 .23
❑ T108 Aaron Boone .20 .09
❑ T109 Raul Mondesi .20 .09
❑ T110 Kenny Lofton .20 .09
❑ T111 Jose Guillen .20 .09
❑ T112 Aramis Ramirez .20 .09
❑ T113 Sidney Ponson .20 .09
❑ T114 Scott Williamson .20 .09
❑ T115 Robin Ventura .20 .09
❑ T116 Dusty Baker MG .20 .09
❑ T117 Felipe Alou MG .20 .09
❑ T118 Buck Showalter MG .20 .09
❑ T119 Jack McKeon MG .20 .09
❑ T120 Art Howe MG .20 .09
❑ T121 Bobby Crosby PROS .40 .18
❑ T122 Adrian Gonzalez PROS .40 .18
❑ T123 Kevin Cash PROS .40 .18
❑ T124 Shin-Soo Choo PROS .40 .18
❑ T125 Chin-Feng Chen PROS 1.00 .45
❑ T126 Miguel Cabrera PROS 2.00 .90
❑ T127 Jason Young PROS .40 .18
❑ T128 Alex Herrera PROS .40 .18
❑ T129 Jason Dubois PROS .40 .18
❑ T130 Jeff Mathis PROS .40 .18
❑ T131 Casey Kotchman PROS .60 .25
❑ T132 Ed Rogers PROS .40 .18

❑ T133 Wilson Betemit PROS .... .40 .18
❑ T134 Jim Kavourias PROS ...... .40 .18
❑ T135 Taylor Buchholz PROS .. .40 .18
❑ T136 Adam LaRoche PROS .... .40 .18
❑ T137 Dallas McPherson PROS ..... .40 .18
❑ T138 Jesus Cota PROS .... .40 .18
❑ T139 Clint Nageotte PROS ...... .40 .18
❑ T140 Boof Bonser PROS .... .40 .18
❑ T141 Walter Young PROS ...... .40 .18
❑ T142 Joe Crede PROS .... .40 .18
❑ T143 Denny Bautista PROS .... .40 .18
❑ T144 Victor Diaz PROS .... .40 .18
❑ T145 Chris Narveson PROS .... .40 .18
❑ T146 Gabe Gross PROS .... .40 .18
❑ T147 Jimmy Journell PROS .... .40 .18
❑ T148 Rafael Soriano PROS ...... .40 .18
❑ T149 Jerome Williams PROS .. .40 .18
❑ T150 Aaron Cook PROS .... .40 .18
❑ T151 Anastacio Martinez PROS ..... .40 .18
❑ T152 Scott Hairston PROS ...... .40 .18
❑ T153 John Buck PROS .... .40 .18
❑ T154 Ryan Ludwick PROS ...... .40 .18
❑ T155 Chris Bootcheck PROS .. .40 .18
❑ T156 John Rheinecker PROS .. .40 .18
❑ T157 Jason Lane PROS .... .40 .18
❑ T158 Shelley Duncan PROS .... .40 .18
❑ T159 Adam Wainwright PROS .40 .18
❑ T160 Jason Arnold PROS .... .40 .18
❑ T161 Jonny Gomes PROS ...... .40 .18
❑ T162 James Loney PROS .... .40 .18
❑ T163 Mike Fontenot PROS ...... .40 .18
❑ T164 Khalil Greene PROS ...... .60 .25
❑ T165 Sean Burnett PROS .... .40 .18
❑ T166 David Martinez FY RC .... .40 .18
❑ T167 Felix Pie FY RC 3.00 1.35
❑ T168 Joe Valentine FY RC ...... .40 .18
❑ T169 Brandon Webb FY RC .. 2.00 .90
❑ T170 Matt Diaz FY RC .... .75 .35
❑ T171 Lew Ford FY RC .... .50 .23
❑ T172 Jeremy Griffiths FY RC .. .50 .23
❑ T173 Matt Hensley FY RC ...... .40 .18
❑ T174 Charlie Manning FY RC .40 .18
❑ T175 Elizardo Ramirez FY RC 1.25 .55
❑ T176 Greg Aquino FY RC .... .40 .18
❑ T177 Felix Sanchez FY RC ...... .40 .18
❑ T178 Kelly Shoppach FY RC 1.25 .55
❑ T179 Bubba Nelson FY RC .... 1.00 .45
❑ T180 Mike O'Keefe FY RC ...... .40 .18
❑ T181 Hanley Ramirez FY RC 1.50 .70
❑ T182 Todd Wellemeyer FY RC .... .50 .23
❑ T183 Dustin Moseley FY RC .. .50 .23
❑ T184 Eric Crozier FY RC .... .50 .23
❑ T185 Ryan Shealy FY RC .... .75 .35
❑ T186 Jeremy Bonderman FY RC .. 1.25 .55
❑ T187 T.Story-Harden FY RC .... .50 .23
❑ T188 Dusty Brown FY RC .... .40 .18
❑ T189 Rob Hammock FY RC .... .75 .35
❑ T190 Jorge Piedra FY RC .... .50 .23
❑ T191 Chris De La Cruz FY RC .40 .18
❑ T192 Eli Whiteside FY RC ...... .40 .18
❑ T193 Jason Kubel FY RC .... .50 .23
❑ T194 Jon Schuerholz FY RC .. .40 .18
❑ T195 Stephen Randolph FY RC ..... .40 .18
❑ T196 Andy Sisco FY RC .... 1.25 .55
❑ T197 Sean Smith FY RC .... .50 .23
❑ T198 Jon-Mark Sprowl FY RC .75 .35
❑ T199 Matt Kata FY RC .... 1.00 .45
❑ T200 Robinson Cano FY RC .. .50 .23
❑ T201 Nook Logan FY RC .... .40 .18
❑ T202 Ben Francisco FY RC .... .75 .35
❑ T203 Arnie Munoz FY RC .... .40 .18
❑ T204 Ozzie Chavez FY RC ...... .40 .18
❑ T205 Eric Riggs FY RC .... .50 .23
❑ T206 Beau Kemp FY RC .... .40 .18
❑ T207 Travis Wong FY RC .... .50 .23
❑ T208 Dustin Yount FY RC ...... .75 .35
❑ T209 Brian McCann FY RC .... .75 .35
❑ T210 Wilton Reynolds FY RC .. .50 .23
❑ T211 Matt Bruback FY RC ...... .40 .18
❑ T212 Andrew Brown FY RC .... .40 .18
❑ T213 Edgar Gonzalez FY RC .... .40 .18
❑ T214 Eider Torres FY RC .... .40 .18
❑ T215 Aquilino Lopez FY RC .... .40 .18
❑ T216 Bobby Basham FY RC .... .75 .35
❑ T217 Tim Olson FY RC .... .50 .23
❑ T218 Nathan Panther FY RC .... .75 .35
❑ T219 Bryan Grace FY RC .... .40 .18
❑ T220 Dusty Gomon FY RC ...... .75 .35
❑ T221 Wil Ledezma FY RC .... .40 .18
❑ T222 Josh Willingham FY RC 1.25 .55
❑ T223 David Cash FY RC .... .40 .18
❑ T224 Oscar Villarreal FY RC .... .40 .18
❑ T225 Jeff Duncan FY RC .... .50 .23
❑ T226 Kade Johnson FY RC .... .40 .18
❑ T227 Luke Steidlmayer FY RC .... .40 .18
❑ T228 Brandon Watson FY RC .. .40 .18
❑ T229 Jose Morales FY RC ...... .40 .18
❑ T230 Mike Gallo FY RC .... .40 .18
❑ T231 Tyler Adamczyk FY RC .. .40 .18
❑ T232 Adam Stern FY RC .... .40 .18
❑ T233 Brennan King FY RC ...... .40 .18
❑ T234 Dan Haren FY RC .... 1.00 .45
❑ T235 Michel Hernandez FY RC ...... .40 .18
❑ T236 Ben Fritz FY RC .... .40 .18
❑ T237 Clay Hensley FY RC ...... .40 .18
❑ T238 Tyler Johnson FY RC .... .40 .18
❑ T239 Pete LaForest FY RC ...... .50 .23
❑ T240 Tyler Martin FY RC .... .40 .18
❑ T241 J.D. Durbin FY RC .... .75 .35
❑ T242 Shane Victorino FY RC .. .40 .18
❑ T243 Rajai Davis FY RC .... .50 .23
❑ T244 Ismael Castro FY RC ...... .40 .18
❑ T245 Chien-Ming Wang FY RC .... 1.50 .70
❑ T246 Travis Ishikawa FY RC .... .50 .23
❑ T247 Corey Shafer FY RC ...... .50 .23
❑ T248 Gary Schneidmiller FY RC ..... .40 .18
❑ T249 Dave Pember FY RC .... .40 .18
❑ T250 Keith Stamler FY RC ...... .40 .18
❑ T251 Tyson Graham FY RC .... .40 .18
❑ T252 Ryan Cameron FY RC .... .40 .18
❑ T253 Eric Eckenstahler FY RC .... .40 .18
❑ T254 Matthew Peterson FY RC ...... .40 .18
❑ T255 Dustin McGowan FY RC ...... .75 .35
❑ T256 Prentice Redman FY RC ...... .40 .18
❑ T257 Haj Turay FY RC .... .50 .23
❑ T258 Carlos Guzman FY RC .... .50 .23
❑ T259 Matt DeMarco FY RC .... .40 .18
❑ T260 Derek Michaelis FY RC .. .50 .23
❑ T261 Brian Burgamy FY RC .... .40 .18
❑ T262 Jay Sitzman FY RC .... .40 .18
❑ T263 Chris Fallon FY RC .... .40 .18
❑ T264 Mike Adams FY RC .... .40 .18
❑ T265 Clint Barmes FY RC ...... .75 .35
❑ T266 Eric Reed FY RC .... .75 .35
❑ T267 Willie Eyre FY RC .... .40 .18
❑ T268 Carlos Duran FY RC ...... .40 .18
❑ T269 Nick Trzesniak FY RC .... .40 .18
❑ T270 Ferdin Tejeda FY RC .... .40 .18
❑ T271 Michael Garciaparra FY RC .. 1.00 .45
❑ T272 Michael Hinckley FY RC .75 .35
❑ T273 Branden Florence FY RC ...... .40 .18
❑ T274 Trent Oeltjen FY RC .... .50 .23
❑ T275 Mike Neu FY RC .... .40 .18

2004 Topps

	MINT	NRMT
COMPLETE SERIES 1 (366)	35.00	16.00
COMMON CARD (1-6/8-366)	.20	.09

CARDS 7 AND 274 DO NOT EXIST..
SCIOSCIA AND J.CASTRO NUMBERED 267

❑ 1 Jim Thome .... .50 .23
❑ 2 Reggie Sanders .... .20 .09
❑ 3 Mark Kotsay .... .20 .09
❑ 4 Edgardo Alfonzo .... .20 .09
❑ 5 Ben Davis .... .20 .09
❑ 6 Mike Matheny .... .20 .09
❑ 8 Marlon Anderson .... .20 .09
❑ 9 Chan Ho Park .... .20 .09
❑ 10 Ichiro Suzuki .... 1.00 .45
❑ 11 Kevin Millwood .... .20 .09
❑ 12 Bengie Molina .... .20 .09
❑ 13 Tom Glavine .... .50 .23
❑ 14 Junior Spivey .... .20 .09
❑ 15 Marcus Giles .... .20 .09
❑ 16 David Segui .... .20 .09
❑ 17 Kevin Millar .... .20 .09
❑ 18 Corey Patterson .... .20 .09
❑ 19 Aaron Rowand .... .20 .09
❑ 20 Derek Jeter .... 1.25 .55
❑ 21 Jason LaRue .... .20 .09
❑ 22 Chris Hammond .... .20 .09
❑ 23 Jay Payton .... .20 .09
❑ 24 Bobby Higginson .... .20 .09
❑ 25 Lance Berkman .... .20 .09
❑ 26 Juan Pierre .... .20 .09
❑ 27 Brent Mayne .... .20 .09
❑ 28 Fred McGriff .... .30 .14
❑ 29 Richie Sexson .... .20 .09
❑ 30 Tim Hudson .... .20 .09
❑ 31 Mike Piazza .... .75 .35
❑ 32 Brad Radke .... .20 .09
❑ 33 Jeff Weaver .... .20 .09
❑ 34 Ramon Hernandez .... .20 .09
❑ 35 David Bell .... .20 .09
❑ 36 Craig Wilson .... .20 .09
❑ 37 Jake Peavy .... .20 .09
❑ 38 Tim Worrell .... .20 .09
❑ 39 Gil Meche .... .20 .09
❑ 40 Albert Pujols .... 1.00 .45
❑ 41 Michael Young .... .20 .09
❑ 42 Josh Phelps .... .20 .09
❑ 43 Brendan Donnelly .... .20 .09
❑ 44 Steve Finley .... .20 .09
❑ 45 John Smoltz .... .30 .14
❑ 46 Jay Gibbons .... .20 .09
❑ 47 Trot Nixon .... .20 .09
❑ 48 Carl Pavano .... .20 .09
❑ 49 Frank Thomas .... .50 .23
❑ 50 Mark Prior .... 1.00 .45
❑ 51 Danny Graves .... .20 .09
❑ 52 Milton Bradley .... .20 .09
❑ 53 Jose Jimenez .... .20 .09
❑ 54 Shane Halter .... .20 .09
❑ 55 Mike Lowell .... .20 .09
❑ 56 Geoff Blum .... .20 .09
❑ 57 Michael Tucker UER .... .20 .09
Dee Brown pictured
❑ 58 Paul Lo Duca .... .20 .09
❑ 59 Vicente Padilla .... .20 .09
❑ 60 Jacque Jones .... .20 .09
❑ 61 Fernando Tatis .... .20 .09
❑ 62 Ty Wigginton .... .20 .09
❑ 63 Pedro Astacio .... .20 .09
❑ 64 Andy Pettitte .... .30 .14
❑ 65 Terrence Long .... .20 .09
❑ 66 Cliff Floyd .... .20 .09
❑ 67 Mariano Rivera .... .30 .14
❑ 68 Carlos Silva .... .20 .09
❑ 69 Marlon Byrd .... .20 .09
❑ 70 Mark Mulder .... .20 .09
❑ 71 Kerry Ligtenberg .... .20 .09
❑ 72 Carlos Guillen .... .20 .09
❑ 73 Fernando Vina .... .20 .09
❑ 74 Lance Carter .... .20 .09
❑ 75 Hank Blalock .... .30 .14
❑ 76 Jimmy Rollins .... .20 .09
❑ 77 Francisco Rodriguez .... .20 .09
❑ 78 Javy Lopez .... .20 .09
❑ 79 Jerry Hairston Jr. .... .20 .09
❑ 80 Andruw Jones .... .30 .14
❑ 81 Rodrigo Lopez .... .20 .09
❑ 82 Johnny Damon .... .20 .09
❑ 83 Hee Seop Choi .... .20 .09
❑ 84 Miguel Olivo .... .20 .09
❑ 85 Jon Garland .... .20 .09
❑ 86 Matt Lawton .... .20 .09
❑ 87 Juan Uribe .... .20 .09
❑ 88 Steve Sparks .... .20 .09

	No.	Player		
❑	89	Tim Spooneybarger	.20	.09
❑	90	Jose Vidro	.20	.09
❑	91	Luis Rivas	.20	.09
❑	92	Hideo Nomo	.50	.23
❑	93	Javier Vazquez	.20	.09
❑	94	Al Leiter	.20	.09
❑	95	Darren Dreifort	.20	.09
❑	96	Alex Cintron	.20	.09
❑	97	Zach Day	.20	.09
❑	98	Jorge Posada	.30	.14
❑	99	John Halama	.20	.09
❑	100	Alex Rodriguez	1.00	.45
❑	101	Orlando Palmeiro	.20	.09
❑	102	Dave Berg	.20	.09
❑	103	Brad Fullmer	.20	.09
❑	104	Mike Hampton	.20	.09
❑	105	Willis Roberts	.20	.09
❑	106	Ramiro Mendoza	.20	.09
❑	107	Juan Cruz	.20	.09
❑	108	Esteban Loaiza	.20	.09
❑	109	Russell Branyan	.20	.09
❑	110	Todd Helton	.30	.14
❑	111	Braden Looper	.20	.09
❑	112	Octavio Dotel	.20	.09
❑	113	Mike MacDougal	.20	.09
❑	114	Cesar Izturis	.20	.09
❑	115	Johan Santana	.20	.09
❑	116	Jose Contreras	.20	.09
❑	117	Placido Polanco	.20	.09
❑	118	Jason Phillips	.20	.09
❑	119	Adam Eaton	.20	.09
❑	120	Vernon Wells	.20	.09
❑	121	Ben Grieve	.20	.09
❑	122	Randy Winn	.20	.09
❑	123	Ismael Valdes	.20	.09
❑	124	Eric Owens	.20	.09
❑	125	Curt Schilling	.30	.14
❑	126	Russ Ortiz	.20	.09
❑	127	Mark Buehrle	.20	.09
❑	128	Danys Baez	.20	.09
❑	129	Dmitri Young	.20	.09
❑	130	Kazuhisa Ishii	.20	.09
❑	131	A.J. Pierzynski	.20	.09
❑	132	Michael Barrett	.20	.09
❑	133	Joe McEwing	.20	.09
❑	134	Alex Cora	.20	.09
❑	135	Tom Wilson	.20	.09
❑	136	Carlos Zambrano	.20	.09
❑	137	Brett Tomko	.20	.09
❑	138	Shigetoshi Hasegawa	.20	.09
❑	139	Jarrod Washburn	.20	.09
❑	140	Greg Maddux	1.00	.45
❑	141	Craig Counsell	.20	.09
❑	142	Reggie Taylor	.20	.09
❑	143	Omar Vizquel	.20	.09
❑	144	Alex Gonzalez	.20	.09
❑	145	Billy Wagner	.20	.09
❑	146	Brian Jordan	.20	.09
❑	147	Wes Helms	.20	.09
❑	148	Kyle Lohse	.20	.09
❑	149	Timo Perez	.20	.09
❑	150	Jason Giambi	.50	.23
❑	151	Erubiel Durazo	.20	.09
❑	152	Mike Lieberthal	.20	.09
❑	153	Jason Kendall	.20	.09
❑	154	Xavier Nady	.20	.09
❑	155	Kirk Rueter	.20	.09
❑	156	Mike Cameron	.20	.09
❑	157	Miguel Cairo	.20	.09
❑	158	Woody Williams	.20	.09
❑	159	Toby Hall	.20	.09
❑	160	Bernie Williams	.30	.14
❑	161	Darin Erstad	.20	.09
❑	162	Matt Mantei	.20	.09
❑	163	Geronimo Gil	.20	.09
❑	164	Bill Mueller	.20	.09
❑	165	Damian Miller	.20	.09
❑	166	Tony Graffanino	.20	.09
❑	167	Sean Casey	.20	.09
❑	168	Brandon Phillips	.20	.09
❑	169	Mike Remlinger	.20	.09
❑	170	Adam Dunn	.30	.14
❑	171	Carlos Lee	.20	.09
❑	172	Juan Encarnacion	.20	.09
❑	173	Angel Berroa	.20	.09
❑	174	Desi Relaford	.20	.09
❑	175	Paul Quantrill	.20	.09
❑	176	Ben Sheets	.20	.09
❑	177	Eddie Guardado	.20	.09
❑	178	Rocky Biddle	.20	.09
❑	179	Mike Stanton	.20	.09
❑	180	Eric Chavez	.20	.09
❑	181	Jason Michaels	.20	.09
❑	182	Terry Adams	.20	.09
❑	183	Kip Wells	.20	.09
❑	184	Brian Lawrence	.20	.09
❑	185	Bret Boone	.20	.09
❑	186	Tino Martinez	.30	.14
❑	187	Aubrey Huff	.20	.09
❑	188	Kevin Mench	.20	.09
❑	189	Tim Salmon	.30	.14
❑	190	Carlos Delgado	.20	.09
❑	191	John Lackey	.20	.09
❑	192	Oscar Villarreal	.20	.09
❑	193	Luis Matos	.20	.09
❑	194	Derek Lowe	.20	.09
❑	195	Mark Grudzielanek	.20	.09
❑	196	Tom Gordon	.20	.09
❑	197	Matt Clement	.20	.09
❑	198	Byung-Hyun Kim	.20	.09
❑	199	Brandon Inge	.20	.09
❑	200	Nomar Garciaparra	1.00	.45
❑	201	Antonio Osuna	.20	.09
❑	202	Jose Mesa	.20	.09
❑	203	Bo Hart	.20	.09
❑	204	Jack Wilson	.20	.09
❑	205	Ray Durham	.20	.09
❑	206	Freddy Garcia	.20	.09
❑	207	J.D. Drew	.20	.09
❑	208	Einar Diaz	.20	.09
❑	209	Roy Halladay	.20	.09
❑	210	David Eckstein UER Adam Kennedy pictured	.20	.09
❑	211	Jason Marquis	.20	.09
❑	212	Jorge Julio	.20	.09
❑	213	Tim Wakefield	.20	.09
❑	214	Moises Alou	.20	.09
❑	215	Bartolo Colon	.20	.09
❑	216	Jimmy Haynes	.20	.09
❑	217	Preston Wilson	.20	.09
❑	218	Luis Castillo	.20	.09
❑	219	Richard Hidalgo	.20	.09
❑	220	Manny Ramirez	.20	.09
❑	221	Mike Mussina	.50	.23
❑	222	Randy Wolf	.20	.09
❑	223	Kris Benson	.20	.09
❑	224	Ryan Klesko	.20	.09
❑	225	Rich Aurilia	.20	.09
❑	226	Kelvim Escobar	.20	.09
❑	227	Francisco Cordero	.20	.09
❑	228	Kazuhiro Sasaki	.20	.09
❑	229	Danny Bautista	.20	.09
❑	230	Rafael Furcal	.20	.09
❑	231	Travis Driskill	.20	.09
❑	232	Kyle Farnsworth	.20	.09
❑	233	Jose Valentin	.20	.09
❑	234	Felipe Lopez	.20	.09
❑	235	C.C. Sabathia	.20	.09
❑	236	Brad Penny	.20	.09
❑	237	Brad Ausmus	.20	.09
❑	238	Raul Ibanez	.20	.09
❑	239	Adrian Beltre	.20	.09
❑	240	Rocco Baldelli	.75	.35
❑	241	Orlando Hudson	.20	.09
❑	242	Dave Roberts	.20	.09
❑	243	Doug Mientkiewicz	.20	.09
❑	244	Brad Wilkerson	.20	.09
❑	245	Scott Strickland	.20	.09
❑	246	Ryan Franklin	.20	.09
❑	247	Chad Bradford	.20	.09
❑	248	Gary Bennett	.20	.09
❑	249	Jose Cruz Jr.	.20	.09
❑	250	Jeff Kent	.20	.09
❑	251	Josh Beckett	.30	.14
❑	252	Ramon Ortiz	.20	.09
❑	253	Miguel Batista	.20	.09
❑	254	Jung Bong	.20	.09
❑	255	Deivi Cruz	.20	.09
❑	256	Alex Gonzalez	.20	.09
❑	257	Shawn Chacon	.20	.09
❑	258	Runelvys Hernandez	.20	.09
❑	259	Joe Mays	.20	.09
❑	260	Eric Gagne	.30	.14
❑	261	Dustan Mohr	.20	.09
❑	262	Tomokazu Ohka	.20	.09
❑	263	Eric Byrnes	.20	.09
❑	264	Frank Catalanotto	.20	.09
❑	265	Cristian Guzman	.20	.09
❑	266	Orlando Cabrera	.20	.09
❑	267A	Juan Castro	.20	.09
❑	267B	Mike Scioscia MG UER 274	.20	.09
❑	268	Bob Brenly MG	.20	.09
❑	269	Bobby Cox MG	.20	.09
❑	270	Mike Hargrove MG	.20	.09
❑	271	Grady Little MG	.20	.09
❑	272	Dusty Baker MG	.20	.09
❑	273	Jerry Manuel MG	.20	.09
❑	275	Eric Wedge MG	.20	.09
❑	276	Clint Hurdle MG	.20	.09
❑	277	Alan Trammell MG	.30	.14
❑	278	Jack McKeon MG	.20	.09
❑	279	Jimy Williams MG	.20	.09
❑	280	Tony Pena MG	.20	.09
❑	281	Jim Tracy MG	.20	.09
❑	282	Ned Yost MG	.20	.09
❑	283	Ron Gardenhire MG	.20	.09
❑	284	Frank Robinson MG	.30	.14
❑	285	Art Howe MG	.20	.09
❑	286	Joe Torre MG	.30	.14
❑	287	Ken Macha MG	.20	.09
❑	288	Larry Bowa MG	.20	.09
❑	289	Lloyd McClendon MG	.20	.09
❑	290	Bruce Bochy MG	.20	.09
❑	291	Felipe Alou MG	.20	.09
❑	292	Bob Melvin MG	.20	.09
❑	293	Tony LaRussa MG	.20	.09
❑	294	Lou Piniella MG	.20	.09
❑	295	Buck Showalter MG	.20	.09
❑	296	Carlos Tosca MG	.20	.09
❑	297	Anthony Acevedo FY RC	.50	.23
❑	298	Anthony Lerew FY RC	1.00	.45
❑	299	Blake Hawksworth FY RC	.75	.35
❑	300	Brayan Pena FY RC	.50	.23
❑	301	Casey Myers FY RC	.50	.23
❑	302	Craig Ansman FY RC	.50	.23
❑	303	David Murphy FY RC	1.25	.55
❑	304	Dave Crouthers FY RC	.50	.23
❑	305	Dioner Navarro FY RC	.75	.35
❑	306	Donald Levinski FY RC	.50	.23
❑	307	Jesse Roman FY RC	.50	.23
❑	308	Sung Jung FY RC	1.00	.45
❑	309	Jon Knott FY RC	.50	.23
❑	310	Josh Labandeira FY RC	.50	.23
❑	311	Kenny Perez FY RC	.50	.23
❑	312	Khalid Ballouli FY RC	.50	.23
❑	313	Kyle Davies FY RC	.75	.35
❑	314	Marcus McBeth FY RC	.50	.23
❑	315	Matt Creighton FY RC	.75	.35
❑	316	Chris O'Riordan FY RC	.50	.23
❑	317	Mike Gosling FY RC	.50	.23
❑	318	Nic Ungs FY RC	.50	.23
❑	319	Omar Falcon FY RC	.50	.23
❑	320	Rodney Choy Foo FY RC	.50	.23
❑	321	Tim Frend FY RC	.50	.23
❑	322	Todd Self FY RC	.50	.23
❑	323	Tydus Meadows FY RC	.50	.23
❑	324	Yadier Molina FY RC	.50	.23
❑	325	Zach Duke FY RC	.50	.23
❑	326	Zach Miner FY RC	.50	.23
❑	327	Bernie Castro Khalil Greene FS	.50	.23
❑	328	Ryan Madson Elizardo Ramirez FS	.50	.23
❑	329	Rich Harden Bobby Crosby FS	.50	.23
❑	330	Zack Greinke Jimmy Gobble FS	.50	.23
❑	331	Bobby Jenks Casey Kotchman FS	.50	.23
❑	332	Sammy Sosa HL	.50	.23
❑	333	Kevin Millwood HL	.20	.09
❑	334	Rafael Palmeiro HL	.20	.09
❑	335	Roger Clemens HL	.50	.23
❑	336	Eric Gagne HL	.30	.14
❑	337	Bill Mueller Manny Ramirez Derek Jeter AL Batting Avg LL	.50	.23

❑ 338 Vernon Wells Ichiro Suzuki Michael Young AL Hits LL	.50	.23
❑ 339 Alex Rodriguez Frank Thomas Carlos Delgado AL Home Runs LL	.50	.23
❑ 340 Carlos Delgado Alex Rodriguez Bret Boone AL RBI's LL	.50	.23
❑ 341 Pedro Martinez Tim Hudson Esteban Loaiza AL ERA LL	.30	.14
❑ 342 Esteban Loaiza Pedro Martinez Roy Halladay AL Strikeouts LL	.30	.14
❑ 343 Albert Pujols Todd Helton Edgar Renteria NL Batting Avg LL	.50	.23
❑ 344 Albert Pujols Todd Helton Juan Pierre NL Hits LL	.50	.23
❑ 345 Jim Thome Richie Sexson Javy Lopez NL Home Runs LL	.30	.14
❑ 346 Preston Wilson Gary Sheffield Jim Thome NL RBI's LL	.30	.14
❑ 347 Jason Schmidt Kevin Brown Mark Prior NL ERA LL	.50	.23
❑ 348 Kerry Wood Mark Prior Javier Vazquez NL Strikeouts LL	.50	.23
❑ 349 Roger Clemens David Wells ALDS	.50	.23
❑ 350 Kerry Wood Mark Prior NLDS	.50	.23
❑ 351 Josh Beckett Miguel Cabrera Ivan Rodriguez NLCS	.50	.23
❑ 352 Jason Giambi Mariano Rivera Aaron Boone ALCS	.50	.23
❑ 353 Derek Lowe Ivan Rodriguez AL/NLDS	.50	.23
❑ 354 Pedro Martinez Jorge Posada Roger Clemens ALCS	.50	.23
❑ 355 Juan Pierre WS	.20	.09
❑ 356 Carlos Delgado AS	.20	.09
❑ 357 Bret Boone AS	.20	.09
❑ 358 Alex Rodriguez AS	.50	.23
❑ 359 Bill Mueller AS	.20	.09
❑ 360 Vernon Wells AS	.20	.09
❑ 361 Garret Anderson AS	.20	.09
❑ 362 Magglio Ordonez AS	.20	.09
❑ 363 Jorge Posada AS	.20	.09
❑ 364 Roy Halladay AS	.20	.09
❑ 365 Andy Pettitte AS	.20	.09
❑ 366 Frank Thomas AS	.30	.14
❑ 367 Jody Gerut AS	.20	.09

2003 Topps 205

	Nm-Mt	Ex-Mt
COMPLETE SERIES 1 (165)	40.00	12.00
COMMON CARD (1-130)	.50	.15
COMMON CARD (131-145)	1.00	.30
COMMON CARD (146-150)	1.00	.30

Card	Nm-Mt	Ex-Mt
❑ 1A Barry Bonds w/Cap	3.00	.90
❑ 1B Barry Bonds w/Helmet	3.00	.90
❑ 2 Bret Boone	.50	.15
❑ 3A Albert Pujols Clear Logo	2.50	.75
❑ 3B Albert Pujols White Logo	2.50	.75
❑ 4 Carl Crawford	.50	.15
❑ 5 Bartolo Colon	.50	.15
❑ 6 Cliff Floyd	.50	.15
❑ 7 John Olerud	.50	.15
❑ 8A Jason Giambi Full Jkt	1.25	.35
❑ 8B Jason Giambi Partial Jkt	1.25	.35
❑ 9 Edgardo Alfonzo	.50	.15
❑ 10 Ivan Rodriguez	1.25	.35
❑ 11 Jim Edmonds	.50	.15
❑ 12A Mike Piazza Orange	2.00	.60
❑ 12B Mike Piazza Yellow	2.00	.60
❑ 13 Greg Maddux	2.50	.75
❑ 14 Jose Vidro	.50	.15
❑ 15A Vlad Guerrero Clear Logo	1.25	.35
❑ 15B Vlad Guerrero White Logo	1.25	.35
❑ 16 Bernie Williams	.75	.23
❑ 17 Roger Clemens	2.50	.75
❑ 18A Miguel Tejada Blue	.50	.15
❑ 18B Miguel Tejada Green	.50	.15
❑ 19 Carlos Delgado	.50	.15
❑ 20A Alfonso Soriano w/Bat	1.25	.35
❑ 20B Alfonso Soriano Sunglasses	1.25	.35
❑ 21 Bobby Cox MG	.50	.15
❑ 22 Mike Scioscia	.50	.15
❑ 23 John Smoltz	.75	.23
❑ 24 Luis Gonzalez	.50	.15
❑ 25 Shawn Green	.50	.15
❑ 26 Raul Ibanez	.50	.15
❑ 27 Andruw Jones	.75	.23
❑ 28 Josh Beckett	.75	.23
❑ 29 Derek Lowe	.50	.15
❑ 30 Todd Helton	.75	.23
❑ 31 Barry Larkin	1.25	.35
❑ 32 Jason Jennings	.50	.15
❑ 33 Darin Erstad	.50	.15
❑ 34 Magglio Ordonez	.50	.15
❑ 35 Mike Sweeney	.50	.15
❑ 36 Kazuhisa Ishii	.50	.15
❑ 37 Ron Gardenhire MG	.50	.15
❑ 38 Tim Hudson	.50	.15
❑ 39 Tim Salmon	.75	.23
❑ 40A Pat Burrell Black Bat	.50	.15
❑ 40B Pat Burrell Brown Bat	.50	.15
❑ 41 Manny Ramirez	.50	.15
❑ 42 Nick Johnson	.50	.15
❑ 43 Tom Glavine	1.25	.35
❑ 44 Mark Mulder	.50	.15
❑ 45 Brian Jordan	.50	.15
❑ 46 Rafael Palmeiro	.75	.23
❑ 47 Vernon Wells	.50	.15
❑ 48 Bob Brenly MG	.50	.15
❑ 49 C.C. Sabathia	.50	.15
❑ 50A Alex Rodriguez Look Ahead	2.50	.75
❑ 50B Alex Rodriguez Look Away	2.50	.75
❑ 51A Sammy Sosa Head Duck	2.00	.60
❑ 51B Sammy Sosa Head Left	2.00	.60
❑ 52 Paul Konerko	.50	.15
❑ 53 Craig Biggio	.75	.23
❑ 54 Moises Alou	.50	.15
❑ 55 Johnny Damon	.50	.15
❑ 56 Torii Hunter	.50	.15
❑ 57 Omar Vizquel	.50	.15
❑ 58 Orlando Hernandez	.50	.15
❑ 59 Barry Zito	1.25	.35
❑ 60 Lance Berkman	.50	.15
❑ 61 Carlos Beltran	.50	.15
❑ 62 Edgar Renteria	.50	.15
❑ 63 Ben Sheets	.50	.15
❑ 64 Doug Mientkiewicz	.50	.15
❑ 65 Troy Glaus	.75	.23
❑ 66 Preston Wilson	.50	.15
❑ 67 Kerry Wood	1.25	.35
❑ 68 Frank Thomas	1.25	.35
❑ 69 Jimmy Rollins	.50	.15
❑ 70 Brian Giles	.50	.15
❑ 71 Bobby Higginson	.50	.15
❑ 72 Larry Walker	.75	.23
❑ 73 Randy Johnson	1.25	.35
❑ 74 Tony LaRussa MG	.50	.15
❑ 75A Derek Jeter w/Gold Trim	3.00	.90
❑ 75B Derek Jeter w/o Gold Trim	3.00	.90
❑ 76 Bobby Abreu	.50	.15
❑ 77A Adam Dunn Closed Mouth	.75	.23
❑ 77B Adam Dunn Open Mouth	.75	.23
❑ 78 Ryan Klesko	.50	.15
❑ 79 Francisco Rodriguez	.50	.15
❑ 80 Scott Rolen	.75	.23
❑ 81 Roberto Alomar	1.25	.35
❑ 82 Joe Torre MG	.75	.23
❑ 83 Jim Thome	1.25	.35
❑ 84 Kevin Millwood	.50	.15
❑ 85 J.T. Snow	.50	.15
❑ 86 Trevor Hoffman	.50	.15
❑ 87 Jay Gibbons	.50	.15
❑ 88A Mark Prior New Logo	2.50	.75
❑ 88B Mark Prior Old Logo	2.50	.75
❑ 89 Rich Aurilia	.50	.15
❑ 90 Chipper Jones	1.25	.35
❑ 91 Richie Sexson	.50	.15
❑ 92 Gary Sheffield	.50	.15
❑ 93 Pedro Martinez	1.25	.35
❑ 94 Rodrigo Lopez	.50	.15
❑ 95 Al Leiter	.50	.15
❑ 96 Jorge Posada	.75	.23
❑ 97 Luis Castillo	.50	.15
❑ 98 Aubrey Huff	.50	.15
❑ 99 A.J. Pierzynski	.50	.15
❑ 100A Ichiro Suzuki Look Ahead	2.50	.75
❑ 100B Ichiro Suzuki Look Right	2.50	.75
❑ 101 Eric Chavez	.50	.15
❑ 102 Brett Myers	.50	.15
❑ 103 Jason Kendall	.50	.15
❑ 104 Jeff Kent	.50	.15
❑ 105 Eric Hinske	.50	.15
❑ 106 Jacque Jones	.50	.15
❑ 107 Phil Nevin	.50	.15
❑ 108 Roy Oswalt	.50	.15
❑ 109 Curt Schilling	.75	.23
❑ 110A N.Garciaparra w/Gold Trim	2.50	.75
❑ 110B N.Garciaparra w/o Gold Trim	2.50	.75
❑ 111 Garret Anderson	.50	.15
❑ 112 Eric Gagne	.75	.23
❑ 113 Javier Vazquez	.50	.15
❑ 114 Jeff Bagwell	.75	.23
❑ 115 Mike Lowell	.50	.15
❑ 116 Carlos Pena	.50	.15
❑ 117 Ken Griffey Jr.	2.00	.60
❑ 118 Tony Batista	.50	.15
❑ 119 Edgar Martinez	.75	.23
❑ 120 Austin Kearns	.75	.23
❑ 121 Jason Stokes PROS	1.25	.35
❑ 122 Jose Reyes PROS	.75	.23
❑ 123 Rocco Baldelli PROS	2.50	.75
❑ 124 Joe Borchard PROS	.50	.15
❑ 125 Joe Mauer PROS	1.25	.35
❑ 126 Gavin Floyd PROS	.50	.15
❑ 127 Mark Teixeira PROS	.75	.23
❑ 128 Jeremy Guthrie PROS	.50	.15
❑ 129 B.J. Upton PROS	1.25	.35
❑ 130 Khalil Greene PROS	.75	.23
❑ 131 Hanley Ramirez FY RC	2.00	.60
❑ 132 Andy Marte FY RC	2.50	.75
❑ 133 J.D. Durbin FY RC	1.50	.45
❑ 134 Jason Kubel FY RC	1.50	.45
❑ 135 Craig Brazell FY RC	1.50	.45
❑ 136 Bryan Bullington FY RC	2.00	.60
❑ 137 Jose Contreras FY RC	2.50	.75
❑ 138 Brian Burgamy FY RC	1.00	.30
❑ 139 Evel Bastida-Martinez FY RC	1.00	.30
❑ 140 Joey Gomes FY RC	1.50	.45
❑ 141 Ismael Castro FY RC	1.50	.45
❑ 142 Travis Wong FY RC	1.50	.45
❑ 143 Michael Garciaparra FY RC	1.50	.45
❑ 144 Arnaldo Munoz FY RC	1.00	.30

❑ 145 Louis Sockalexis FY XRC 1.00 .30
❑ 146 Richard Hoblitzell REP .. 1.00 .30
❑ 147 George Graham REP ...... 1.00 .30
❑ 148 Hal Chase REP .... 1.00 .30
❑ 149 John McGraw REP .... 1.50 .45
❑ 150 Roderick J. Wallace REP 1.00 .30
❑ 170 Edwin Jackson FY RC........
❑ 171 Delmon Young FY RC ....
❑ 172 Eric Duncan FY RC ....
❑ 173 Brian Snyder FY RC ....
❑ 174 Chris Lubanski FY RC.........
❑ 175 Ryan Harvey FY RC ....
❑ 176 Nick Markakis FY RC ....
❑ 177 Chad Billingsley FY RC.......
❑ 178 Elizardo Ramirez FY RC......
❑ 179 Ben Francisco FY RC ....
❑ 180 Franklin Gutierrez FY RC.....
❑ 181 Aaron Hill FY RC.................
❑ 182 Kevin Correia FY RC ....
❑ 183 Kelly Shoppach FY RC ....
❑ 184 Felix Pie FY RC ....
❑ 185 Adam Loewen FY RC...........
❑ 186 Danny Garcia FY RC ....
❑ 187 Rickie Weeks FY RC ....
❑ 188 Robby Hammock FY RC .....
❑ 189 Ryan Wagner FY RC ....
❑ 190 Matt Kata FY RC ....
❑ 191 Bo Hart FY RC......................
❑ 192 Brandon Webb FY RC ....
❑ NNO Vintage Buyback ....

2002 Topps 206

	Nm-Mt	Ex-Mt
COMPLETE SET (525)	220.00	65.00
COMPLETE SERIES 1 (180)......	60.00	18.00
COMPLETE SERIES 2 (180)......	60.00	18.00
COMPLETE SERIES 3 (165)....	100.00	30.00
COM(1-140/181-260/308-418)	.50	.15
COMMON (141-155/271-285)....	1.00	.30
COMMON RC (308-418)	.50	.15
COMMON SP (308-398)	2.00	.60
COMMON FYP SP (..................	1.00	.30
COMMON RET SP (433-447)......	2.00	.60

❑ 1 Vladimir Guerrero .... 1.25 .35
❑ 2 Sammy Sosa......................... .50 .15
❑ 3 Garret Anderson .... .50 .15
❑ 4 Rafael Palmeiro.................... .75 .23
❑ 5 Juan Gonzalez.................... 1.25 .35
❑ 6 John Smoltz .... .75 .23
❑ 7 Mark Mulder .... .50 .15
❑ 8 Jon Lieber .... .50 .15
❑ 9 Greg Maddux .... 2.50 .75
❑ 10 Moises Alou .... .50 .15
❑ 11 Joe Randa............................ .50 .15
❑ 12 Bobby Abreu .... .50 .15
❑ 13 Juan Pierre .... .50 .15
❑ 14 Kerry Wood........................ 1.25 .35
❑ 15 Craig Biggio .... .75 .23
❑ 16 Curt Schilling .... .75 .23
❑ 17 Brian Jordan .... .50 .15
❑ 18 Edgardo Alfonzo .... .50 .15
❑ 19 Darren Dreifort .... .50 .15
❑ 20 Todd Helton .... .75 .23
❑ 21 Ramon Ortiz .... .50 .15
❑ 22 Ichiro Suzuki .... 2.50 .75
❑ 23 Jimmy Rollins...................... .50 .15
❑ 24 Darin Erstad .... .50 .15
❑ 25 Shawn Green....................... .50 .15
❑ 26 Tino Martinez .... .75 .23
❑ 27 Bret Boone .... .50 .15
❑ 28 Alfonso Soriano .... 1.25 .35
❑ 29 Chan Ho Park .... .50 .15
❑ 30 Roger Clemens .... 2.50 .75
❑ 31 Cliff Floyd .... .50 .15
❑ 32 Johnny Damon .... .50 .15
❑ 33 Frank Thomas .... 1.25 .35
❑ 34 Barry Bonds .... 3.00 .90
❑ 35 Luis Gonzalez .... .50 .15
❑ 36 Carlos Lee .... .50 .15
❑ 37 Roberto Alomar .... 1.25 .35
❑ 38 Carlos Delgado .... .50 .15
❑ 39 Nomar Garciaparra .... 2.50 .75
❑ 40 Jason Kendall .... .50 .15
❑ 41 Scott Rolen .... .75 .23
❑ 42 Tom Glavine .... 1.25 .35
❑ 43 Ryan Klesko .... .50 .15
❑ 44 Brian Giles .... .50 .15
❑ 45 Bud Smith .... .50 .15
❑ 46 Charles Nagy........................ .50 .15
❑ 47 Tony Gwynn .... 1.50 .45
❑ 48 C.C. Sabathia UER .... .50 .15
Credited with incorrect victory total in 2001
❑ 49 Frank Catalanotto .... .50 .15
❑ 50 Jerry Hairston .... .50 .15
❑ 51 Jeromy Burnitz .... .50 .15
❑ 52 David Justice......................... .50 .15
❑ 53 Bartolo Colon .... .50 .15
❑ 54 Andres Galarraga.................. .50 .15
❑ 55 Jeff Weaver .... .50 .15
❑ 56 Terrence Long .... .50 .15
❑ 57 Tsuyoshi Shinjo .... .50 .15
❑ 58 Barry Zito .... 1.25 .35
❑ 59 Mariano Rivera .... .75 .23
❑ 60 John Olerud .... .50 .15
❑ 61 Randy Johnson .... 1.25 .35
❑ 62 Kenny Lofton......................... .50 .15
❑ 63 Jermaine Dye .... .50 .15
❑ 64 Troy Glaus............................. .75 .23
❑ 65 Larry Walker .... .75 .23
❑ 66 Hideo Nomo .... 1.25 .35
❑ 67 Mike Mussina .... 1.25 .35
❑ 68 Paul LoDuca .... .50 .15
❑ 69 Magglio Ordonez.................. .50 .15
❑ 70 Paul O'Neill .... .75 .23
❑ 71 Sean Casey .... .50 .15
❑ 72 Lance Berkman .... .50 .15
❑ 73 Adam Dunn .... .75 .23
❑ 74 Aramis Ramirez..................... .50 .15
❑ 75 Rafael Furcal .... .50 .15
❑ 76 Gary Sheffield .... .50 .15
❑ 77 Todd Hollandsworth .... .50 .15
❑ 78 Chipper Jones.................... 1.25 .35
❑ 79 Bernie Williams..................... .75 .23
❑ 80 Richard Hidalgo .... .50 .15
❑ 81 Eric Chavez .... .50 .15
❑ 82 Mike Piazza...................... 2.00 .60
❑ 83 J.D. Drew .... .50 .15
❑ 84 Ken Griffey Jr. .... 2.00 .60
❑ 85 Joe Kennedy .... .50 .15
❑ 86 Joel Pineiro........................... .50 .15
❑ 87 Josh Towers .... .50 .15
❑ 88 Andruw Jones .... .75 .23
❑ 89 Carlos Beltran .... .50 .15
❑ 90 Mike Cameron....................... .50 .15
❑ 91 Albert Pujols .... 2.50 .75
❑ 92 Alex Rodriguez .... 2.50 .75
❑ 93 Omar Vizquel......................... .50 .15
❑ 94 Juan Encarnacion .... .50 .15
❑ 95 Jeff Bagwell........................... .75 .23
❑ 96 Jose Canseco .... 1.25 .35
❑ 97 Ben Sheets .... .50 .15
❑ 98 Mark Grace .... 1.25 .35
❑ 99 Mike Sweeney....................... .50 .15
❑ 100 Mark McGwire................. 3.00 .90
❑ 101 Ivan Rodriguez .... 1.25 .35
❑ 102 Rich Aurilia.......................... .50 .15
❑ 103 Cristian Guzman .... .50 .15
❑ 104 Roy Oswalt .... .50 .15
❑ 105 Tim Hudson .... .50 .15
❑ 106 Brent Abernathy.................. .50 .15
❑ 107 Mike Hampton..................... .50 .15
❑ 108 Miguel Tejada .... .50 .15
❑ 109 Bobby Higginson .... .50 .15
❑ 110 Edgar Martinez .... .75 .23
❑ 111 Jorge Posada .... .75 .23
❑ 112 Jason Giambi Yankees .. 1.25 .35
❑ 113 Pedro Astacio .... .50 .15
❑ 114 Kazuhiro Sasaki.................. .50 .15
❑ 115 Preston Wilson .... .50 .15
❑ 116 Jason Bere .... .50 .15
❑ 117 Mark Quinn.......................... .50 .15
❑ 118 Pokey Reese .... .50 .15
❑ 119 Derek Jeter .... 3.00 .90
❑ 120 Shannon Stewart................. .50 .15
❑ 121 Jeff Kent .... .50 .15
❑ 122 Jeremy Giambi .... .50 .15
❑ 123 Pat Burrell............................ .50 .15
❑ 124 Jim Edmonds .... .50 .15
❑ 125 Mark Buehrle....................... .50 .15
❑ 126 Kevin Brown .... .50 .15
❑ 127 Raul Mondesi .... .50 .15
❑ 128 Pedro Martinez .... 1.25 .35
❑ 129 Jim Thome .... 1.25 .35
❑ 130 Russ Ortiz .... .50 .15
❑ 131 Brandon Duckworth PROS ..... .50 .15
❑ 132 Ryan Jamison PROS .... .50 .15
❑ 133 Brandon Inge PROS .... .50 .15
❑ 134 Felipe Lopez PROS .... .50 .15
❑ 135 Jason Lane PROS .... .50 .15
❑ 136 Forrest Johnson PROS RC ..... .50 .15
❑ 137 Greg Nash PROS .... .50 .15
❑ 138 Covelli Crisp PROS........... .50 .15
❑ 139 Nick Neugebauer PROS.... .50 .15
❑ 140 Dustan Mohr PROS........... .50 .15
❑ 141 Freddy Sanchez FYP RC 1.00 .30
❑ 142 Justin Backsmeyer FYP RC.... 1.00 .30
❑ 143 Jorge Julio FYP.............. 1.00 .30
❑ 144 Ryan Mottl FYP RC .... 1.00 .30
❑ 145 Chris Tritle FYP RC .... 1.00 .30
❑ 146 Noochie Varner FYP RC 1.00 .30
❑ 147 Brian Rogers FYP .... 1.00 .30
❑ 148 Michael Hill FYP RC ...... 1.00 .30
❑ 149 Luis Pineda FYP .... 1.00 .30
❑ 150 Rich Thompson FYP RC 1.00 .30
❑ 151 Bill Hall FYP .... 1.00 .30
❑ 152 Juan Dominguez FYP RC 4.00 1.20
❑ 153 Justin Woodrow FYP...... 1.00 .30
❑ 154 Nic Jackson FYP RC ...... 1.00 .30
❑ 155 Laynce Nix FYP RC 8.00 2.40
❑ 156 Hank Aaron RET 5.00 1.50
❑ 157 Ernie Banks RET .... 2.50 .75
❑ 158 Johnny Bench RET .... 2.50 .75
❑ 159 George Brett RET........... 6.00 1.80
❑ 160 Carlton Fisk RET .... 1.50 .45
❑ 161 Bob Gibson RET .... 1.50 .45
❑ 162 Reggie Jackson RET ...... 1.50 .45
❑ 163 Don Mattingly RET 6.00 1.80
❑ 164 Kirby Puckett RET .... 2.50 .75
❑ 165 Frank Robinson RET ...... 1.50 .45
❑ 166 Nolan Ryan RET 8.00 2.40
❑ 167 Tom Seaver RET .... 2.50 .75
❑ 168 Mike Schmidt RET.......... 5.00 1.50
❑ 169 Dave Winfield RET.......... 1.50 .45
❑ 170 Carl Yastrzemski RET .... 3.00 .90
❑ 171 Frank Chance REP.......... 1.00 .30
❑ 172 Ty Cobb REP.................. 5.00 1.50
❑ 173 Sam Crawford REP .... 1.00 .30
❑ 174 Johnny Evers REP.......... 1.00 .30
❑ 175 John McGraw REP .... 2.50 .75
❑ 176 Eddie Plank REP .... 2.50 .75
❑ 177 Tris Speaker REP........... 2.50 .75
❑ 178 Joe Tinker REP .... 1.00 .30
❑ 179 H.Wagner Orange REP .. 8.00 2.40
❑ 180 Cy Young REP................ 2.50 .75
❑ 181 Javier Vazquez.................. .50 .15
❑ 182A Mark Mulder Green Jsy.. .50 .15
❑ 182B Mark Mulder White Jsy.. .50 .15
❑ 183A Roger Clemens Blue Jsy.... 2.50 .75
❑ 183B Roger Clemens Pinstripes .. 2.50 .75
❑ 184 Kazuhisa Ishii RC .... 1.50 .45
❑ 185 Roberto Alomar .... 1.25 .35
❑ 186 Lance Berkman .... .50 .15
❑ 187A Adam Dunn Arms Folded ..... .75 .23
❑ 187B Adam Dunn w/Bat.......... .75 .23
❑ 188A Aramis Ramirez w/Bat.... .50 .15
❑ 188B Aramis Ramirez w/o Bat .50 .15
❑ 189 Chuck Knoblauch .... .50 .15

- ❑ 190 Nomar Garciaparra 2.50 .75
- ❑ 191 Brad Penny .50 .15
- ❑ 192A Gary Sheffield w/Bat .50 .15
- ❑ 192B Gary Sheffield w/o Bat .50 .15
- ❑ 193 Alfonso Soriano 1.25 .35
- ❑ 194 Andruw Jones .75 .23
- ❑ 195A Randy Johnson Black Jsy 1.25 .35
- ❑ 195B Randy Johnson Purple Jsy 1.25 .35
- ❑ 196A Corey Patterson Blue Jsy .50 .15
- ❑ 196B Corey Patterson Pinstripes .50 .15
- ❑ 197 Milton Bradley .50 .15
- ❑ 198A J.Damon Blue Jsy/Cap .50 .15
- ❑ 198B J.Damon Blue Jsy/Hlmt .50 .15
- ❑ 198C J.Damon White Jsy .50 .15
- ❑ 199A Paul Lo Duca Blue Jsy .50 .15
- ❑ 199B Paul Lo Duca White Jsy .50 .15
- ❑ 200A Albert Pujols Red Jsy 2.50 .75
- ❑ 200B Albert Pujols Running 2.50 .75
- ❑ 200C Albert Pujols w/Bat 2.50 .75
- ❑ 201 Scott Rolen .75 .23
- ❑ 202A J.D. Drew Running .50 .15
- ❑ 202B J.D. Drew w/Bat .50 .15
- ❑ 202C J.D. Drew White Jsy .50 .15
- ❑ 203 Vladimir Guerrero 1.25 .35
- ❑ 204A Jason Giambi Blue Jsy 1.25 .35
- ❑ 204B Jason Giambi Grey Jsy 1.25 .35
- ❑ 204C Jason Giambi Pinstripes 1.25 .35
- ❑ 205A Moises Alou Grey Jsy .50 .15
- ❑ 205B Moises Alou Pinstripes .50 .15
- ❑ 206A Magglio Ordonez Signing .50 .15
- ❑ 206B Magglio Ordonez w/Bat .50 .15
- ❑ 207 Carlos Febles .50 .15
- ❑ 208 So Taguchi RC .75 .23
- ❑ 209A Rafael Palmeiro One Hand .75 .23
- ❑ 209B Rafael Palmeiro Two Hands .75 .23
- ❑ 210 David Wells .50 .15
- ❑ 211 Orlando Cabrera .50 .15
- ❑ 212 Sammy Sosa 2.00 .60
- ❑ 213 Armando Benitez .50 .15
- ❑ 214 Wes Helms .50 .15
- ❑ 215A Mariano Rivera Arms Folded .75 .23
- ❑ 215B Mariano Rivera Holding Ball .75 .23
- ❑ 216 Jimmy Rollins .50 .15
- ❑ 217 Matt Lawton .50 .15
- ❑ 218A Shawn Green w/Bat .50 .15
- ❑ 218B Shawn Green w/o Bat .50 .15
- ❑ 219A Bernie Williams w/Bat .75 .23
- ❑ 219B Bernie Williams w/o Bat .75 .23
- ❑ 220A Bret Boone Blue Jsy .50 .15
- ❑ 220B Bret Boone White Jsy .50 .15
- ❑ 221A Alex Rodriguez Blue Jsy 2.50 .75
- ❑ 221B Alex Rodriguez One Hand 2.50 .75
- ❑ 221C Alex Rodriguez Two Hands 2.50 .75
- ❑ 222 Roger Cedeno .50 .15
- ❑ 223 Marty Cordova .50 .15
- ❑ 224 Fred McGriff .75 .23
- ❑ 225A Chipper Jones Batting 1.25 .35
- ❑ 225B Chipper Jones Running 1.25 .35
- ❑ 226 Kerry Wood 1.25 .35
- ❑ 227A Larry Walker Grey Jsy .75 .23
- ❑ 227B Larry Walker Purple Jsy .75 .23
- ❑ 228 Robin Ventura .50 .15
- ❑ 229 Robert Fick .50 .15
- ❑ 230A Tino Martinez Black Glove .75 .23
- ❑ 230B Tino Martinez Throwing .75 .23
- ❑ 230C Tino Martinez w/Bat .75 .23
- ❑ 231 Ben Petrick .50 .15
- ❑ 232 Neifi Perez .50 .15
- ❑ 233 Pedro Martinez 1.25 .35
- ❑ 234A Brian Jordan Grey Jsy .50 .15
- ❑ 234B Brian Jordan White Jsy .50 .15
- ❑ 235 Freddy Garcia .50 .15
- ❑ 236A Derek Jeter Batting 3.00 .90
- ❑ 236B Derek Jeter Blue Jsy 3.00 .90
- ❑ 236C Derek Jeter Kneeling 3.00 .90
- ❑ 237 Ben Grieve .50 .15
- ❑ 238A Barry Bonds Black Jsy 3.00 .90
- ❑ 238B Barry Bonds w/Wrist Band 3.00 .90
- ❑ 238C Barry Bonds w/o Wrist Band 3.00 .90
- ❑ 239 Luis Gonzalez .50 .15
- ❑ 240 Shane Halter .50 .15
- ❑ 241A Brian Giles Black Jsy .50 .15
- ❑ 241B Brian Giles Grey Jsy .50 .15
- ❑ 242 Bud Smith .50 .15
- ❑ 243 Richie Sexson .50 .15
- ❑ 244A Barry Zito Green Jsy 1.25 .35
- ❑ 244B Barry Zito White Jsy 1.25 .35
- ❑ 245 Clint Milton .50 .15
- ❑ 246A Ivan Rodriguez Blue Jsy 1.25 .35
- ❑ 246B Ivan Rodriguez Grey Jsy 1.25 .35
- ❑ 246C Ivan Rodriguez White Jsy 1.25 .35
- ❑ 247 Toby Hall .50 .15
- ❑ 248A Mike Piazza Black Jsy 2.00 .60
- ❑ 248B Mike Piazza Grey Jsy 2.00 .60
- ❑ 249 Ruben Sierra .50 .15
- ❑ 250A Tsuyoshi Shinjo Cap .50 .15
- ❑ 250B Tsuyoshi Shinjo Helmet .50 .15
- ❑ 251A Jermaine Dye Green Jsy .50 .15
- ❑ 251B Jermaine Dye White Jsy .50 .15
- ❑ 252 Roy Oswalt .50 .15
- ❑ 253 Todd Helton .75 .23
- ❑ 254 Adrian Beltre .50 .15
- ❑ 255 Doug Mientkiewicz .50 .15
- ❑ 256A Ichiro Suzuki Blue Jsy 2.50 .75
- ❑ 256B Ichiro Suzuki w/Bat 2.50 .75
- ❑ 256C Ichiro Suzuki White Jsy 2.50 .75
- ❑ 257A C.C. Sabathia Blue Jsy .50 .15
- ❑ 257B C.C. Sabathia White Jsy .50 .15
- ❑ 258 Paul Konerko .50 .15
- ❑ 259 Ken Griffey Jr. 2.00 .60
- ❑ 260A Jeromy Burnitz w/Bat .50 .15
- ❑ 260B Jeromy Burnitz w/o Bat .50 .15
- ❑ 261 Hank Blalock PROS 1.25 .35
- ❑ 262 Mark Prior PROS 2.50 .75
- ❑ 263 Josh Beckett PROS .75 .23
- ❑ 264 Carlos Pena PROS .50 .15
- ❑ 265 Sean Burroughs PROS .50 .15
- ❑ 266 Austin Kearns PROS .75 .23
- ❑ 267 Chin-Hui Tsao PROS .50 .15
- ❑ 268 Dewon Brazelton PROS .50 .15
- ❑ 269 J.D. Martin PROS .50 .15
- ❑ 270 Marlon Byrd PROS .50 .15
- ❑ 271 Joe Mauer FYP RC 5.00 1.50
- ❑ 272 Jason Botts FYP RC 1.00 .30
- ❑ 273 Mauricio Lara FYP RC 1.00 .30
- ❑ 274 Jonny Gomes FYP RC 1.25 .35
- ❑ 275 Gavin Floyd FYP RC 2.50 .75
- ❑ 276 Alex Requena FYP RC 1.00 .30
- ❑ 277 Jimmy Gobble FYP RC 2.00 .60
- ❑ 278 Chris Duffy FYP RC 1.00 .30
- ❑ 279 Colt Griffin FYP RC 1.25 .35
- ❑ 280 Ryan Church FYP RC 1.00 .30
- ❑ 281 Beltran Perez FYP RC 1.00 .30
- ❑ 282 Clint Nageotte FYP RC 1.25 .35
- ❑ 283 Justin Schuda FYP RC 1.00 .30
- ❑ 284 Scott Hairston FYP RC 2.00 .60
- ❑ 285 Mario Ramos FYP RC 1.00 .30
- ❑ 286 Tom Seaver White Sox RET 2.50 .75
- ❑ 286 Tom Seaver Mets RET 2.50 .75
- ❑ 287 Hank Aaron White Jsy RET 5.00 1.50
- ❑ 287 Hank Aaron Blue Jsy RET 5.00 1.50
- ❑ 288 Mike Schmidt RET 5.00 1.50
- ❑ 289A Robin Yount Blue Jsy RET 2.50 .75
- ❑ 289B Robin Yount P'stripes RET 2.50 .75
- ❑ 290 Joe Morgan RET 1.00 .30
- ❑ 291 Frank Robinson RET 1.50 .45
- ❑ 292A Reggie Jackson A's RET 1.50 .45
- ❑ 292B Reggie Jackson Yanks RET 1.50 .45
- ❑ 293A Nolan Ryan Astros RET 8.00 2.40
- ❑ 293B Nolan Ryan Rangers RET 8.00 2.40
- ❑ 294 Dave Winfield RET 1.50 .45
- ❑ 295 Willie Mays RET 5.00 1.50
- ❑ 296 Brooks Robinson RET 2.50 .75
- ❑ 297A Mark McGwire A's RET 6.00 1.80
- ❑ 297B Mark McGwire Cards RET 6.00 1.80
- ❑ 298 Honus Wagner RET 2.50 .75
- ❑ 299A Sherry Magee REP 1.00 .30
- ❑ 299B Sherry Magie UER REP 1.00 .30
- ❑ 300 Frank Chance REP 1.00 .30
- ❑ 301A Joe Doyle NY REP 1.00 .30
- ❑ 301B Joe Doyle NY Nat'l REP 1.00 .30
- ❑ 302 John McGraw REP 2.50 .75
- ❑ 303 Jimmy Collins REP 1.00 .30
- ❑ 304 Buck Herzog REP 1.00 .30
- ❑ 305 Sam Crawford REP 1.00 .30
- ❑ 306 Cy Young REP 2.50 .75
- ❑ 307 Honus Wagner Blue REP 8.00 2.40
- ❑ 308A A.Rodriguez Blue Jsy SP 5.00 1.50
- ❑ 308B A.Rodriguez White Jsy 2.50 .75
- ❑ 309 Vernon Wells .50 .15
- ❑ 310A B.Bonds w/Elbow Pad 3.00 .90
- ❑ 310B B.Bonds w/o Elbow Pad SP 6.00 1.80
- ❑ 311 Vicente Padilla .50 .15
- ❑ 312A A.Soriano w/Wristband 1.25 .35
- ❑ 312B A.Soriano w/o Wristband SP 2.50 .75
- ❑ 313 Mike Piazza 2.00 .60
- ❑ 314 Jacque Jones .50 .15
- ❑ 315 Shawn Green SP 2.00 .60
- ❑ 316 Paul Byrd .50 .15
- ❑ 317 Lance Berkman .50 .15
- ❑ 318 Larry Walker .75 .23
- ❑ 319 Ken Griffey Jr. SP 4.00 1.20
- ❑ 320 Shea Hillenbrand .50 .15
- ❑ 321 Jay Gibbons .50 .15
- ❑ 322 Andruw Jones .75 .23
- ❑ 323 Luis Gonzalez SP 2.00 .60
- ❑ 324 Garret Anderson .50 .15
- ❑ 325 Roy Halladay .50 .15
- ❑ 326 Randy Winn .50 .15
- ❑ 327 Matt Morris .50 .15
- ❑ 328 Robb Nen .50 .15
- ❑ 329 Trevor Hoffman .50 .15
- ❑ 330 Kip Wells .50 .15
- ❑ 331 Orlando Hernandez .50 .15
- ❑ 332 Rey Ordonez .50 .15
- ❑ 333 Torii Hunter .50 .15
- ❑ 334 Geoff Jenkins .50 .15
- ❑ 335 Eric Karros .50 .15
- ❑ 336 Mike Lowell .50 .15
- ❑ 337 Nick Johnson .50 .15
- ❑ 338 Randall Simon .50 .15
- ❑ 339 Ellis Burks .50 .15
- ❑ 340A Sammy Sosa Blue Jsy SP 4.00 1.20
- ❑ 340B Sammy Sosa White Jsy 2.00 .60
- ❑ 341 Pedro Martinez 1.25 .35
- ❑ 342 Junior Spivey .50 .15
- ❑ 343 Vinny Castilla .50 .15
- ❑ 344 Randy Johnson SP 2.50 .75
- ❑ 345 Chipper Jones SP 2.50 .75
- ❑ 346 Orlando Hudson .50 .15
- ❑ 347 Albert Pujols SP 5.00 1.50
- ❑ 348 Rondell White .50 .15
- ❑ 349 Vladimir Guerrero 1.25 .35
- ❑ 350A Mark Prior Red SP 5.00 1.50
- ❑ 350B Mark Prior Yellow 2.50 .75
- ❑ 351 Eric Gagne .75 .23
- ❑ 352 Todd Zeile .50 .15
- ❑ 353 Manny Ramirez SP 2.00 .60
- ❑ 354 Kevin Millwood .50 .15
- ❑ 355 Troy Percival .50 .15
- ❑ 356A Jason Giambi Batting SP 2.50 .75
- ❑ 356B Jason Giambi Throwing 1.25 .35
- ❑ 357 Bartolo Colon .50 .15
- ❑ 358 Jeremy Giambi .50 .15
- ❑ 359 Jose Cruz Jr. .50 .15
- ❑ 360A I.Suzuki Blue Jsy SP 5.00 1.50
- ❑ 360B I.Suzuki White Jsy 2.50 .75
- ❑ 361 Eddie Guardado .50 .15
- ❑ 362 Ivan Rodriguez 1.25 .35
- ❑ 363 Carl Crawford .50 .15
- ❑ 364 Jason Simontacchi RC .60 .18
- ❑ 365 Kenny Lofton .50 .15
- ❑ 366 Raul Mondesi .50 .15
- ❑ 367 A.J. Pierzynski .50 .15
- ❑ 368 Ugueth Urbina .50 .15
- ❑ 369 Rodrigo Lopez .50 .15
- ❑ 370A N.Garciaparra One Bat SP 5.00 1.50
- ❑ 370B N.Garciaparra Two Bats 2.50 .75
- ❑ 371 Craig Counsell .50 .15
- ❑ 372 Barry Larkin 1.25 .35
- ❑ 373 Carlos Pena .50 .15
- ❑ 374 Luis Castillo .50 .15
- ❑ 375 Raul Ibanez .50 .15
- ❑ 376 Kazuhisa Ishii SP 2.50 .75
- ❑ 377 Derek Lowe .50 .15
- ❑ 378 Curt Schilling .75 .23
- ❑ 379 Jim Thome Phillies 1.25 .35
- ❑ 380A Derek Jeter Blue SP 6.00 1.80
- ❑ 380B Derek Jeter Seats 3.00 .90
- ❑ 381 Pat Burrell .50 .15
- ❑ 382 Jamie Moyer .50 .15
- ❑ 383 Eric Hinske .50 .15
- ❑ 384 Scott Rolen .75 .23
- ❑ 385 Miguel Tejada SP 2.00 .60
- ❑ 386 Andy Pettitte .75 .23
- ❑ 387 Mike Lieberthal .50 .15
- ❑ 388 Al Leiter .50 .15
- ❑ 389 Todd Helton SP 2.00 .60

❑ 390A Adam Dunn Bat SP	2.00	.60
❑ 390B Adam Dunn Glove	.75	.23
❑ 391 Cliff Floyd	.50	.15
❑ 392 Tim Salmon	.75	.23
❑ 393 Joe Torre MG	.75	.23
❑ 394 Bobby Cox MG	.50	.15
❑ 395 Tony LaRussa MG	.50	.15
❑ 396 Art Howe MG	.50	.15
❑ 397 Bob Brenly MG	.50	.15
❑ 398 Ron Gardenhire MG	.50	.15
❑ 399 Mike Cuddyer PROS	.50	.15
❑ 400 Joe Mauer PROS	5.00	1.50
❑ 401 Mark Teixeira PROS	1.25	.35
❑ 402 Hee Seop Choi PROS	.75	.23
❑ 403 Angel Berroa PROS	.50	.15
❑ 404 Jesse Foppert PROS RC	2.50	.75
❑ 405 Bobby Crosby PROS	1.25	.35
❑ 406 Jose Reyes PROS	1.25	.35
❑ 407 Casey Kotchman PROS RC	3.00	.90
❑ 408 Aaron Heilman PROS	.50	.15
❑ 409 Adrian Gonzalez PROS	.50	.15
❑ 410 Delwyn Young PROS RC	1.50	.45
❑ 411 Brett Myers PROS	.50	.15
❑ 412 Justin Huber PROS RC	1.25	.35
❑ 413 Drew Henson PROS	.50	.15
❑ 414 Taggert Bozied PROS RC	2.00	.60
❑ 415 Dontrelle Willis PROS RC	6.00	1.80
❑ 416 Rocco Baldelli PROS	2.50	.75
❑ 417 Jason Stokes PROS RC	5.00	1.50
❑ 418 Brandon Phillips PROS	.50	.15
❑ 419 Jake Blalock FYP RC	2.50	.75
❑ 420 Micah Schilling FYP RC	1.00	.30
❑ 421 Denard Span FYP RC	1.00	.30
❑ 422A J.Loney Red FYP RC	2.50	.75
❑ 422B J.Loney w/Sky FYP RC	2.50	.75
❑ 423A W.Bankston Blue FYP RC	2.50	.75
❑ 423B W.Bankston w/Sky FYP RC	2.50	.75
❑ 424 Jeremy Hermida FYP RC	1.50	.45
❑ 425 Curtis Granderson FYP RC	1.25	.35
❑ 426A J.Pridie Red FYP RC	1.50	.45
❑ 426B J.Pridie w/Sky FYP RC	1.50	.45
❑ 427 Larry Broadway FYP RC	2.00	.60
❑ 428A K.Greene Green FYP RC	3.00	.90
❑ 428B K.Greene Red FYP RC	3.00	.90
❑ 429 Joey Votto FYP RC	1.00	.30
❑ 430A B.Upton Grey FYP RC	5.00	1.50
❑ 430B B.Upton w/People FYP RC	5.00	1.50
❑ 431A S.Santos Gold FYP RC	2.50	.75
❑ 431B S.Santos Grey FYP RC	2.50	.75
❑ 432 Brian Dopirak FYP RC	2.00	.60
❑ 433 Ozzie Smith RET SP	4.00	1.20
❑ 434 Wade Boggs RET SP	2.50	.75
❑ 435 Yogi Berra RET SP	4.00	1.20
❑ 436 Al Kaline RET SP	4.00	1.20
❑ 437 Robin Roberts RET SP	2.00	.60
❑ 438 Roberto Clemente RET SP	8.00	2.40
❑ 439 Gary Carter RET SP	2.50	.75
❑ 440 Fergie Jenkins RET SP	2.00	.60
❑ 441 Orlando Cepeda RET SP	2.00	.60
❑ 442 Rod Carew RET SP	2.50	.75
❑ 443 Harmon Killebrew RET SP	4.00	1.20
❑ 444 Duke Snider RET SP	2.50	.75
❑ 445 Stan Musial RET SP	6.00	1.80
❑ 446 Hank Greenberg RET SP	4.00	1.20
❑ 447 Lou Brock RET SP	2.50	.75
❑ 448 Jim Palmer RET	1.00	.30
❑ 449 John McGraw REP	1.00	.30
❑ 450 Mordecai Brown REP	1.00	.30
❑ 451 Christy Mathewson REP	1.50	.45
❑ 452 Sam Crawford REP	1.00	.30
❑ 453 Bill O'Hara REP	1.00	.30
❑ 454 Joe Tinker REP	1.00	.30
❑ 455 Nap Lajoie REP	1.50	.45
❑ 456 Honus Wagner Red REP	8.00	2.40
❑ NNO Repurchased Tobacco Card		

2003 Topps All-Time Fan Favorites

	Nm-Mt	Ex-Mt
COMPLETE SET (150)	50.00	15.00
❑ 1 Willie Mays	3.00	.90
❑ 2 Whitey Ford	1.00	.30

Card	Nm-Mt	Ex-Mt
❑ 3 Stan Musial	2.50	.75
❑ 4 Paul Blair	.60	.18
❑ 5 Harold Reynolds	.60	.18
❑ 6 Bob Friend	.60	.18
❑ 7 Rod Carew	1.00	.30
❑ 8 Kirk Gibson	.60	.18
❑ 9 Graig Nettles	.60	.18
❑ 10 Ozzie Smith	1.50	.45
❑ 11 Tony Perez	.60	.18
❑ 12 Tim Wallach	.60	.18
❑ 13 Bert Campaneris	.60	.18
❑ 14 Cory Snyder	.60	.18
❑ 15 Dave Parker	.60	.18
❑ 16 Darrell Evans	.60	.18
❑ 17 Joe Pepitone	.60	.18
❑ 18 Don Sutton	.60	.18
❑ 19 Dale Murphy	1.50	.45
❑ 20 George Brett	4.00	1.20
❑ 21 Carlton Fisk	1.00	.30
❑ 22 Bob Watson	.60	.18
❑ 23 Wally Joyner	.60	.18
❑ 24 Paul Molitor	1.00	.30
❑ 25 Keith Hernandez	1.00	.30
❑ 26 Jerry Koosman	.60	.18
❑ 27 George Bell	.60	.18
❑ 28 Boog Powell	1.00	.30
❑ 29 Bruce Sutter	.60	.18
❑ 30 Ernie Banks	1.50	.45
❑ 31 Steve Lyons	.60	.18
❑ 32 Earl Weaver	.60	.18
❑ 33 Dave Stieb	.60	.18
❑ 34 Alan Trammell	1.00	.30
❑ 35 Bret Saberhagen	.60	.18
❑ 36 J.R. Richard	.60	.18
❑ 37 Mickey Rivers	.60	.18
❑ 38 Juan Marichal	.60	.18
❑ 39 Gaylord Perry	.60	.18
❑ 40 Don Mattingly	4.00	1.20
❑ 41 Bob Grich	.60	.18
❑ 42 Steve Sax	.60	.18
❑ 43 Sparky Anderson	.60	.18
❑ 44 Luis Aparicio	.60	.18
❑ 45 Fergie Jenkins	.60	.18
❑ 46 Jim Palmer	.60	.18
❑ 47 Howard Johnson	.60	.18
❑ 48 Dwight Evans	.60	.18
❑ 49 Bill Buckner	.60	.18
❑ 50 Cal Ripken	5.00	1.50
❑ 51 Jose Cruz	.60	.18
❑ 52 Tony Oliva	.60	.18
❑ 53 Bobby Richardson	.60	.18
❑ 54 Luis Tiant	.60	.18
❑ 55 Warren Spahn	1.00	.30
❑ 56 Phil Rizzuto	1.00	.30
❑ 57 Eric Davis	.60	.18
❑ 58 Vida Blue	.60	.18
❑ 59 Steve Balboni	.60	.18
❑ 60 Mike Schmidt	3.00	.90
❑ 61 Ken Griffey Sr.	.60	.18
❑ 62 Jim Abbott	1.50	.45
❑ 63 Whitey Herzog	.60	.18
❑ 64 Rich Gossage	.60	.18
❑ 65 Tony Armas	.60	.18
❑ 66 Bill Skowron	1.00	.30
❑ 67 Don Newcombe	.60	.18
❑ 68 Bill Madlock	.60	.18
❑ 69 Lance Parrish	.60	.18
❑ 70 Reggie Jackson	1.00	.30
❑ 71 Willie Wilson	.60	.18
❑ 72 Terry Pendleton	.60	.18
❑ 73 Jim Piersall	.60	.18
❑ 74 George Foster	.60	.18
❑ 75 Bob Horner	.60	.18
❑ 76 Chris Sabo	.60	.18
❑ 77 Fred Lynn	.60	.18
❑ 78 Jim Rice	.60	.18
❑ 79 Maury Wills	.60	.18
❑ 80 Yogi Berra	1.50	.45
❑ 81 Johnny Sain	1.00	.30
❑ 82 Tom Lasorda	.60	.18
❑ 83 Bill Mazeroski	1.00	.30
❑ 84 John Kruk	.60	.18
❑ 85 Bob Feller	1.00	.30
❑ 86 Frank Robinson	1.00	.30
❑ 87 Red Schoendienst	.60	.18
❑ 88 Gary Carter	1.00	.30
❑ 89 Andre Dawson	.60	.18
❑ 90 Tim McCarver	.60	.18
❑ 91 Robin Yount	1.50	.45
❑ 92 Phil Niekro	.60	.18
❑ 93 Joe Morgan	.60	.18
❑ 94 Darren Daulton	.60	.18
❑ 95 Bobby Thomson	.60	.18
❑ 96 Alvin Davis	.60	.18
❑ 97 Robin Roberts	1.00	.30
❑ 98 Kirby Puckett	1.50	.45
❑ 99 Jack Clark	.60	.18
❑ 100 Hank Aaron	3.00	.90
❑ 101 Orlando Cepeda	.60	.18
❑ 102 Vern Law	.60	.18
❑ 103 Cecil Cooper	.60	.18
❑ 104 Don Larsen	1.00	.30
❑ 105 Mario Mendoza	.60	.18
❑ 106 Tony Gwynn	2.00	.60
❑ 107 Ernie Harwell	.60	.18
❑ 108A Monte Irvin	.60	.18
❑ 108B Monte Irvin NO AU ERR	.60	.18
❑ 109 Tommy John	.60	.18
❑ 110 Rollie Fingers	.60	.18
❑ 111 Johnny Podres	.60	.18
❑ 112 Jeff Reardon	.60	.18
❑ 113 Buddy Bell	.60	.18
❑ 114 Dwight Gooden	1.00	.30
❑ 115 Garry Templeton	.60	.18
❑ 116 Johnny Bench	1.50	.45
❑ 117 Joe Rudi	.60	.18
❑ 118 Ron Guidry	.60	.18
❑ 119 Vince Coleman	.60	.18
❑ 120 Al Kaline	1.50	.45
❑ 121 Carl Yastrzemski	2.50	.75
❑ 122 Hank Bauer	.60	.18
❑ 123 Mark Fidrych	.60	.18
❑ 124 Paul O'Neill	1.00	.30
❑ 125 Ron Cey	.60	.18
❑ 126 Willie McGee	.60	.18
❑ 127 Harmon Killebrew	1.50	.45
❑ 128 Dave Concepcion	.60	.18
❑ 129 Harold Baines	.60	.18
❑ 130 Lou Brock	1.00	.30
❑ 131 Lee Smith	.60	.18
❑ 132 Willie McCovey	.60	.18
❑ 133 Steve Garvey	.60	.18
❑ 134 Kent Tekulve	.60	.18
❑ 135 Tom Seaver	1.50	.45
❑ 136 Bo Jackson	1.50	.45
❑ 137 Walt Weiss	.60	.18
❑ 138 Brook Jacoby	.60	.18
❑ 139 Dennis Eckersley	.60	.18
❑ 140 Duke Snider	1.00	.30
❑ 141 Lenny Dykstra	.60	.18
❑ 142 Greg Luzinski	.60	.18
❑ 143 Jim Bunning	.60	.18
❑ 144 Jose Canseco	1.50	.45
❑ 145 Ron Santo	1.00	.30
❑ 146 Bert Blyleven	.60	.18
❑ 147 Wade Boggs	1.00	.30
❑ 148 Brooks Robinson	1.50	.45
❑ 149 Ray Knight	.60	.18
❑ 150 Nolan Ryan	5.00	1.50

1999 Topps Chrome

	Nm-Mt	Ex-Mt
COMPLETE SET (462)	150.00	45.00
COMP. SERIES 1 (241)	80.00	24.00
COMP. SERIES 2 (221)	80.00	24.00
COMMON (1-6/8-463)	.50	.15
COMMON (205-212/425-437)	1.00	.30
COMP.MCGWIRE (70)	1000.00	300.00
COMP.SOSA HR SET (66)	500.00	150.00

❑ 1 Roger Clemens 4.00 1.20
❑ 2 Andres Galarraga .... .75 .23
❑ 3 Scott Brosius .... .75 .23
❑ 4 John Flaherty .... .50 .15
❑ 5 Jim Leyritz .... .50 .15
❑ 6 Ray Durham .... .75 .23
❑ 8 Jose Vizcaino .... .50 .15
❑ 9 Will Clark .... 2.00 .60
❑ 10 David Wells .... .75 .23
❑ 11 Jose Guillen .... .50 .15
❑ 12 Scott Hatteberg .... .50 .15
❑ 13 Edgardo Alfonzo .... .75 .23
❑ 14 Mike Bordick .... .50 .15
❑ 15 Manny Ramirez .... .75 .23
❑ 16 Greg Maddux 4.00 1.20
❑ 17 David Segui .... .50 .15
❑ 18 Darryl Strawberry .... 1.25 .35
❑ 19 Brad Radke .... .75 .23
❑ 20 Kerry Wood .... 2.00 .60
❑ 21 Matt Anderson .... .50 .15
❑ 22 Derrek Lee .... .75 .23
❑ 23 Mickey Morandini .... .50 .15
❑ 24 Paul Konerko .... .75 .23
❑ 25 Travis Lee .... .50 .15
❑ 26 Ken Hill .... .50 .15
❑ 27 Kenny Rogers .... .75 .23
❑ 28 Paul Sorrento .... .50 .15
❑ 29 Quilvio Veras .... .50 .15
❑ 30 Todd Walker .... .75 .23
❑ 31 Ryan Jackson .... .50 .15
❑ 32 John Olerud .... .75 .23
❑ 33 Doug Glanville .... .50 .15
❑ 34 Nolan Ryan 8.00 2.40
❑ 35 Ray Lankford .... .50 .15
❑ 36 Mark Loretta .... .50 .15
❑ 37 Jason Dickson .... .50 .15
❑ 38 Sean Bergman .... .50 .15
❑ 39 Quinton McCracken .... .50 .15
❑ 40 Bartolo Colon .... .75 .23
❑ 41 Brady Anderson .... .75 .23
❑ 42 Chris Stynes .... .50 .15
❑ 43 Jorge Posada .... 1.25 .35
❑ 44 Justin Thompson .... .50 .15
❑ 45 Johnny Damon .... .75 .23
❑ 46 Armando Benitez .... .50 .15
❑ 47 Brant Brown .... .50 .15
❑ 48 Charlie Hayes .... .50 .15
❑ 49 Darren Dreifort .... .50 .15
❑ 50 Juan Gonzalez .... 2.00 .60
❑ 51 Chuck Knoblauch .... .75 .23
❑ 52 Todd Helton .... 1.25 .35
❑ 53 Rick Reed .... .50 .15
❑ 54 Chris Gomez .... .50 .15
❑ 55 Gary Sheffield .... .75 .23
❑ 56 Rod Beck .... .50 .15
❑ 57 Rey Sanchez .... .50 .15
❑ 58 Garret Anderson .... .75 .23
❑ 59 Jimmy Haynes .... .50 .15
❑ 60 Steve Woodard .... .50 .15
❑ 61 Rondell White .... .75 .23
❑ 62 Vladimir Guerrero .... 2.00 .60
❑ 63 Eric Karros .... .75 .23
❑ 64 Russ Davis .... .50 .15
❑ 65 Mo Vaughn .... .75 .23
❑ 66 Sammy Sosa .... 3.00 .90
❑ 67 Troy Percival .... .75 .23
❑ 68 Kenny Lofton .... .75 .23
❑ 69 Bill Taylor .... .50 .15
❑ 70 Mark McGwire 5.00 1.50
❑ 71 Roger Cedeno .... .50 .15
❑ 72 Javy Lopez .... .75 .23
❑ 73 Damion Easley .... .50 .15
❑ 74 Andy Pettitte .... 1.25 .35
❑ 75 Tony Gwynn .... 2.50 .75
❑ 76 Ricardo Rincon .... .50 .15
❑ 77 F.P. Santangelo .... .50 .15
❑ 78 Jay Bell .... .75 .23
❑ 79 Scott Servais .... .50 .15
❑ 80 Jose Canseco .... 2.00 .60
❑ 81 Roberto Hernandez .... .50 .15
❑ 82 Todd Dunwoody .... .50 .15
❑ 83 John Wetteland .... .75 .23
❑ 84 Mike Caruso .... .50 .15
❑ 85 Derek Jeter 5.00 1.50
❑ 86 Aaron Sele .... .50 .15
❑ 87 Jose Lima .... .50 .15
❑ 88 Ryan Christenson .... .50 .15
❑ 89 Jeff Cirillo .... .75 .23
❑ 90 Jose Hernandez .... .50 .15
❑ 91 Mark Kotsay .... .50 .15
❑ 92 Darren Bragg .... .50 .15
❑ 93 Albert Belle .... .75 .23
❑ 94 Matt Lawton .... .50 .15
❑ 95 Pedro Martinez .... 2.00 .60
❑ 96 Greg Vaughn .... .75 .23
❑ 97 Neifi Perez .... .50 .15
❑ 98 Gerald Williams .... .50 .15
❑ 99 Derek Bell .... .50 .15
❑ 100 Ken Griffey Jr. .... 3.00 .90
❑ 101 David Cone .... .75 .23
❑ 102 Brian Johnson .... .50 .15
❑ 103 Dean Palmer .... .75 .23
❑ 104 Javier Valentin .... .50 .15
❑ 105 Trevor Hoffman .... .75 .23
❑ 106 Butch Huskey .... .50 .15
❑ 107 Dave Martinez .... .50 .15
❑ 108 Billy Wagner .... .75 .23
❑ 109 Shawn Green .... .75 .23
❑ 110 Ben Grieve .... .50 .15
❑ 111 Tom Goodwin .... .50 .15
❑ 112 Jaret Wright .... .50 .15
❑ 113 Aramis Ramirez .... .75 .23
❑ 114 Dmitri Young .... .75 .23
❑ 115 Hideki Irabu .... .50 .15
❑ 116 Roberto Kelly .... .50 .15
❑ 117 Jeff Fassero .... .50 .15
❑ 118 Mark Clark .... .50 .15
❑ 119 Jason McDonald .... .50 .15
❑ 120 Matt Williams .... .75 .23
❑ 121 Dave Burba .... .50 .15
❑ 122 Bret Saberhagen .... .75 .23
❑ 123 Deivi Cruz .... .50 .15
❑ 124 Chad Curtis .... .50 .15
❑ 125 Scott Rolen .... 1.25 .35
❑ 126 Lee Stevens .... .50 .15
❑ 127 J.T. Snow .... .75 .23
❑ 128 Rusty Greer .... .75 .23
❑ 129 Brian Meadows .... .50 .15
❑ 130 Jim Edmonds .... .75 .23
❑ 131 Ron Gant .... .75 .23
❑ 132 A.J. Hinch .... .50 .15
❑ 133 Shannon Stewart .... .75 .23
❑ 134 Brad Fullmer .... .75 .23
❑ 135 Cal Eldred .... .50 .15
❑ 136 Matt Walbeck .... .50 .15
❑ 137 Carl Everett .... .75 .23
❑ 138 Walt Weiss .... .50 .15
❑ 139 Fred McGriff .... 1.25 .35
❑ 140 Darin Erstad .... .75 .23
❑ 141 Dave Nilsson .... .50 .15
❑ 142 Eric Young .... .50 .15
❑ 143 Dan Wilson .... .50 .15
❑ 144 Jeff Reed .... .50 .15
❑ 145 Brett Tomko .... .50 .15
❑ 146 Terry Steinbach .... .50 .15
❑ 147 Seth Greisinger .... .50 .15
❑ 148 Pat Meares .... .50 .15
❑ 149 Livan Hernandez .... .50 .15
❑ 150 Jeff Bagwell .... 1.25 .35
❑ 151 Bob Wickman .... .50 .15
❑ 152 Omar Vizquel .... .75 .23
❑ 153 Eric Davis .... .75 .23
❑ 154 Larry Sutton .... .50 .15
❑ 155 Magglio Ordonez .... .75 .23
❑ 156 Eric Milton .... .50 .15
❑ 157 Darren Lewis .... .50 .15
❑ 158 Rick Aguilera .... .50 .15
❑ 159 Mike Lieberthal .... .75 .23
❑ 160 Robb Nen .... .75 .23
❑ 161 Brian Giles .... .75 .23
❑ 162 Jeff Brantley .... .50 .15
❑ 163 Gary DiSarcina .... .50 .15
❑ 164 John Valentin .... .50 .15
❑ 165 Dave Dellucci .... .50 .15
❑ 166 Chan Ho Park .... .75 .23
❑ 167 Masato Yoshii .... .50 .15
❑ 168 Jason Schmidt .... .75 .23
❑ 169 LaTroy Hawkins .... .50 .15
❑ 170 Bret Boone .... .75 .23
❑ 171 Jerry DiPoto .... .50 .15
❑ 172 Mariano Rivera .... 1.25 .35
❑ 173 Mike Cameron .... .75 .23
❑ 174 Scott Erickson .... .50 .15
❑ 175 Charles Johnson .... .75 .23
❑ 176 Bobby Jones .... .50 .15
❑ 177 Francisco Cordova .... .50 .15
❑ 178 Todd Jones .... .50 .15
❑ 179 Jeff Montgomery .... .50 .15
❑ 180 Mike Mussina .... 2.00 .60
❑ 181 Bob Abreu .... .75 .23
❑ 182 Ismael Valdes .... .50 .15
❑ 183 Andy Fox .... .50 .15
❑ 184 Woody Williams .... .50 .15
❑ 185 Denny Neagle .... .50 .15
❑ 186 Jose Valentin .... .50 .15
❑ 187 Darrin Fletcher .... .50 .15
❑ 188 Gabe Alvarez .... .50 .15
❑ 189 Eddie Taubensee .... .50 .15
❑ 190 Edgar Martinez .... 1.25 .35
❑ 191 Jason Kendall .... .75 .23
❑ 192 Darryl Kile .... .75 .23
❑ 193 Jeff King .... .50 .15
❑ 194 Rey Ordonez .... .50 .15
❑ 195 Andruw Jones .... 1.25 .35
❑ 196 Tony Fernandez .... .50 .15
❑ 197 Jamey Wright .... .50 .15
❑ 198 B.J. Surhoff .... .75 .23
❑ 199 Vinny Castilla .... .75 .23
❑ 200 David Wells HL .... .50 .15
❑ 201 Mark McGwire HL .... 2.50 .75
❑ 202 Sammy Sosa HL .... 2.00 .60
❑ 203 Roger Clemens HL .... 2.00 .60
❑ 204 Kerry Wood HL .... 1.25 .35
❑ 205 Gabe Kapler .... 1.00 .30
Lance Berkman
Mike Frank
❑ 206 Alex Escobar RC .... 1.00 .30
Ricky Ledee
Mike Stoner
❑ 207 Peter Bergeron RC .... 1.00 .30
Jeremy Giambi
George Lombard
❑ 208 Michael Barrett .... 1.00 .30
Ben Davis
Robert Fick
❑ 209 Jayson Werth .... 1.00 .30
Ramon Hernandez
Pat Cline
❑ 210 Ryan Anderson .... 1.00 .30
Bruce Chen
Chris Enochs
❑ 211 Brad Penny .... 1.00 .30
Octavio Dotel
Mike Lincoln
❑ 212 Chuck Abbott RC .... 1.00 .30
Brent Butler
Danny Klassen
❑ 213 Chris C.Jones .... 1.00 .30
Jeff Urban RC

No.	Player	Price	Price
❑ 214	Arturo McDowell RC Tony Torcato	1.00	.30
❑ 215	Josh McKinley RC Jason Tyner	1.00	.30
❑ 216	Matt Burch Seth Etheron RC	1.00	.30
❑ 217	Mamon Tucker RC Rick Elder	1.00	.30
❑ 218	J.M.Gold Ryan Mills RC	1.00	.30
❑ 219	Andy Brown Choo Freeman RC	1.00	.30
❑ 220A	Mark McGwire HR 1	50.00	15.00
❑ 220B	Mark McGwire HR 2	50.00	15.00
❑ 220C	Mark McGwire HR 3	50.00	15.00
❑ 220D	Mark McGwire HR 4	50.00	15.00
❑ 220E	Mark McGwire HR 5	50.00	15.00
❑ 220F	Mark McGwire HR 6	50.00	15.00
❑ 220G	Mark McGwire HR 7	50.00	15.00
❑ 220H	Mark McGwire HR 8	50.00	15.00
❑ 220I	Mark McGwire HR 9	50.00	15.00
❑ 220J	M.McGwire HR 10	50.00	15.00
❑ 220K	M.McGwire HR 11	50.00	15.00
❑ 220L	M.McGwire HR 12	50.00	15.00
❑ 220M	M.McGwire HR 13	50.00	15.00
❑ 220N	M.McGwire HR 14	50.00	15.00
❑ 220O	M.McGwire HR 15	50.00	15.00
❑ 220P	M.McGwire HR 16	50.00	15.00
❑ 220Q	M.McGwire HR 17	50.00	15.00
❑ 220R	M.McGwire HR 18	50.00	15.00
❑ 220S	M.McGwire HR 19	50.00	15.00
❑ 220T	M.McGwire HR 20	50.00	15.00
❑ 220U	M.McGwire HR 21	50.00	15.00
❑ 220V	M.McGwire HR 22	50.00	15.00
❑ 220W	M.McGwire HR 23	50.00	15.00
❑ 220X	M.McGwire HR 24	50.00	15.00
❑ 220Y	M.McGwire HR 25	50.00	15.00
❑ 220Z	M.McGwire HR 26	50.00	15.00
❑ 220AA	M.McGwire HR 27	50.00	15.00
❑ 220AB	M.McGwire HR 28	50.00	15.00
❑ 220AC	M.McGwire HR 29	50.00	15.00
❑ 220AD	M.McGwire HR 30	50.00	15.00
❑ 220AE	M.McGwire HR 31	50.00	15.00
❑ 220AF	M.McGwire HR 32	50.00	15.00
❑ 220AG	M.McGwire HR 33	50.00	15.00
❑ 220AH	M.McGwire HR 34	50.00	15.00
❑ 220AI	M.McGwire HR 35	50.00	15.00
❑ 220AJ	M.McGwire HR 36	50.00	15.00
❑ 220AK	M.McGwire HR 37	50.00	15.00
❑ 220AL	M.McGwire HR 38	50.00	15.00
❑ 220AM	M.McGwire HR 39	50.00	15.00
❑ 220AN	M.McGwire HR 40	50.00	15.00
❑ 220AO	M.McGwire HR 41	50.00	15.00
❑ 220AP	M.McGwire HR 42	50.00	15.00
❑ 220AQ	M.McGwire HR 43	50.00	15.00
❑ 220AR	M.McGwire HR 44	50.00	15.00
❑ 220AS	M.McGwire HR 45	50.00	15.00
❑ 220AT	M.McGwire HR 46	50.00	15.00
❑ 220AU	M.McGwire HR 47	50.00	15.00
❑ 220AV	M.McGwire HR 48	50.00	15.00
❑ 220AW	M.McGwire HR 49	50.00	15.00
❑ 220AX	M.McGwire HR 50	50.00	15.00
❑ 220AY	M.McGwire HR 51	50.00	15.00
❑ 220AZ	M.McGwire HR 52	50.00	15.00
❑ 220BB	M.McGwire HR 53	50.00	15.00
❑ 220CC	M.McGwire HR 54	50.00	15.00
❑ 220DD	M.McGwire HR 55	50.00	15.00
❑ 220EE	M.McGwire HR 56	50.00	15.00
❑ 220FF	M.McGwire HR 57	50.00	15.00
❑ 220GG	M.McGwire HR 58	50.00	15.00
❑ 220HH	M.McGwire HR 59	50.00	15.00
❑ 220II	M.McGwire HR 60	50.00	15.00
❑ 220JJ	M.McGwire HR 61	50.00	15.00
❑ 220KK	M.McGwire HR 62	80.00	24.00
❑ 220LL	M.McGwire HR 63	50.00	15.00
❑ 220MM	M.McGwire HR 64	50.00	15.00
❑ 220NN	M.McGwire HR 65	50.00	15.00
❑ 220OO	M.McGwire HR 66	50.00	15.00
❑ 220PP	M.McGwire HR 67	50.00	15.00
❑ 220QQ	M.McGwire HR 68	50.00	15.00
❑ 220RR	M.McGwire HR 69	50.00	15.00
❑ 220SS	M.McGwire HR 70	150.00	45.00
❑ 221	Larry Walker LL	.75	.23
❑ 222	Bernie Williams LL	.75	.23
❑ 223	Mark McGwire LL	2.50	.75
❑ 224	Ken Griffey Jr. LL	2.00	.60
❑ 225	Sammy Sosa LL	2.00	.60
❑ 226	Juan Gonzalez LL	1.25	.35
❑ 227	Dante Bichette LL	.50	.15
❑ 228	Alex Rodriguez LL	2.00	.60
❑ 229	Sammy Sosa LL	2.00	.60
❑ 230	Derek Jeter LL	2.50	.75
❑ 231	Greg Maddux LL	2.00	.60
❑ 232	Roger Clemens LL	2.00	.60
❑ 233	Ricky Ledee WS	.50	.15
❑ 234	Chuck Knoblauch WS	.50	.15
❑ 235	Bernie Williams WS	.75	.23
❑ 236	Tino Martinez WS	.75	.23
❑ 237	Orl. Hernandez WS	.50	.15
❑ 238	Scott Brosius WS	.50	.15
❑ 239	Andy Pettitte WS	.75	.23
❑ 240	Mariano Rivera WS	.75	.23
❑ 241	Checklist	.50	.15
❑ 242	Checklist	.50	.15
❑ 243	Tom Glavine	2.00	.60
❑ 244	Andy Benes	.50	.15
❑ 245	Sandy Alomar Jr.	.50	.15
❑ 246	Wilton Guerrero	.50	.15
❑ 247	Alex Gonzalez	.50	.15
❑ 248	Roberto Alomar	2.00	.60
❑ 249	Ruben Rivera	.50	.15
❑ 250	Eric Chavez	.75	.23
❑ 251	Ellis Burks	.75	.23
❑ 252	Richie Sexson	.75	.23
❑ 253	Steve Finley	.75	.23
❑ 254	Dwight Gooden	1.25	.35
❑ 255	Dustin Hermanson	.50	.15
❑ 256	Kirk Rueter	.50	.15
❑ 257	Steve Trachsel	.50	.15
❑ 258	Gregg Jefferies	.50	.15
❑ 259	Matt Stairs	.50	.15
❑ 260	Shane Reynolds	.50	.15
❑ 261	Gregg Olson	.50	.15
❑ 262	Kevin Tapani	.50	.15
❑ 263	Matt Morris	.75	.23
❑ 264	Carl Pavano	.50	.15
❑ 265	Nomar Garciaparra	4.00	1.20
❑ 266	Kevin Young	.75	.23
❑ 267	Rick Helling	.50	.15
❑ 268	Matt Franco	.50	.15
❑ 269	Brian McRae	.50	.15
❑ 270	Cal Ripken	6.00	1.80
❑ 271	Jeff Abbott	.50	.15
❑ 272	Tony Batista	.75	.23
❑ 273	Bill Simas	.50	.15
❑ 274	Brian Hunter	.50	.15
❑ 275	John Franco	.75	.23
❑ 276	Devon White	.50	.15
❑ 277	Rickey Henderson	3.00	.90
❑ 278	Chuck Finley	.75	.23
❑ 279	Mike Blowers	.50	.15
❑ 280	Mark Grace	2.00	.60
❑ 281	Randy Winn	.50	.15
❑ 282	Bobby Bonilla	.75	.23
❑ 283	David Justice	.75	.23
❑ 284	Shane Monahan	.50	.15
❑ 285	Kevin Brown	1.25	.35
❑ 286	Todd Zeile	.75	.23
❑ 287	Al Martin	.50	.15
❑ 288	Troy O'Leary	.50	.15
❑ 289	Darryl Hamilton	.50	.15
❑ 290	Tino Martinez	1.25	.35
❑ 291	David Ortiz	.75	.23
❑ 292	Tony Clark	.50	.15
❑ 293	Ryan Minor	.50	.15
❑ 294	Mark Leiter	.50	.15
❑ 295	Wally Joyner	.75	.23
❑ 296	Cliff Floyd	.75	.23
❑ 297	Shawn Estes	.50	.15
❑ 298	Pat Hentgen	.50	.15
❑ 299	Scott Elarton	.50	.15
❑ 300	Alex Rodriguez	4.00	1.20
❑ 301	Ozzie Guillen	.50	.15
❑ 302	Hideo Nomo	2.00	.60
❑ 303	Ryan McGuire	.50	.15
❑ 304	Brad Ausmus	.50	.15
❑ 305	Alex Gonzalez	.50	.15
❑ 306	Brian Jordan	.75	.23
❑ 307	John Jaha	.50	.15
❑ 308	Mark Grudzielanek	.50	.15
❑ 309	Juan Guzman	.50	.15
❑ 310	Tony Womack	.50	.15
❑ 311	Dennis Reyes	.50	.15
❑ 312	Marty Cordova	.50	.15
❑ 313	Ramiro Mendoza	.50	.15
❑ 314	Robin Ventura	.75	.23
❑ 315	Rafael Palmeiro	1.25	.35
❑ 316	Ramon Martinez	.50	.15
❑ 317	Pedro Astacio	.50	.15
❑ 318	Dave Hollins	.50	.15
❑ 319	Tom Candiotti	.50	.15
❑ 320	Al Leiter	.75	.23
❑ 321	Rico Brogna	.50	.15
❑ 322	Reggie Jefferson	.50	.15
❑ 323	Bernard Gilkey	.50	.15
❑ 324	Jason Giambi	2.00	.60
❑ 325	Craig Biggio	1.25	.35
❑ 326	Troy Glaus	1.25	.35
❑ 327	Delino DeShields	.50	.15
❑ 328	Fernando Vina	.75	.23
❑ 329	John Smoltz	1.25	.35
❑ 330	Jeff Kent	.75	.23
❑ 331	Roy Halladay	.75	.23
❑ 332	Andy Ashby	.50	.15
❑ 333	Tim Wakefield	.75	.23
❑ 334	Roger Clemens	4.00	1.20
❑ 335	Bernie Williams	1.25	.35
❑ 336	Desi Relaford	.50	.15
❑ 337	John Burkett	.50	.15
❑ 338	Mike Hampton	.75	.23
❑ 339	Royce Clayton	.50	.15
❑ 340	Mike Piazza	3.00	.90
❑ 341	Jeremi Gonzalez	.50	.15
❑ 342	Mike Lansing	.50	.15
❑ 343	Jamie Moyer	.75	.23
❑ 344	Ron Coomer	.50	.15
❑ 345	Barry Larkin	2.00	.60
❑ 346	Fernando Tatis	.50	.15
❑ 347	Chili Davis	.75	.23
❑ 348	Bobby Higginson	.75	.23
❑ 349	Hal Morris	.50	.15
❑ 350	Larry Walker	1.25	.35
❑ 351	Carlos Guillen	.50	.15
❑ 352	Miguel Tejada	.75	.23
❑ 353	Travis Fryman	.75	.23
❑ 354	Jarrod Washburn	.75	.23
❑ 355	Chipper Jones	2.00	.60
❑ 356	Todd Stottlemyre	.50	.15
❑ 357	Henry Rodriguez	.50	.15
❑ 358	Eli Marrero	.50	.15
❑ 359	Alan Benes	.50	.15
❑ 360	Tim Salmon	1.25	.35
❑ 361	Luis Gonzalez	.75	.23
❑ 362	Scott Spiezio	.75	.23
❑ 363	Chris Carpenter	.50	.15
❑ 364	Bobby Howry	.50	.15
❑ 365	Raul Mondesi	.75	.23
❑ 366	Ugueth Urbina	.50	.15
❑ 367	Tom Evans	.50	.15
❑ 368	Kerry Ligtenberg RC	.75	.23
❑ 369	Adrian Beltre	.75	.23
❑ 370	Ryan Klesko	.75	.23
❑ 371	Wilson Alvarez	.50	.15
❑ 372	John Thomson	.50	.15
❑ 373	Tony Saunders	.50	.15
❑ 374	Dave Mlicki	.50	.15
❑ 375	Ken Caminiti	.75	.23
❑ 376	Jay Buhner	.75	.23
❑ 377	Bill Mueller	.75	.23
❑ 378	Jeff Blauser	.50	.15
❑ 379	Edgar Renteria	.75	.23
❑ 380	Jim Thome	2.00	.60
❑ 381	Joey Hamilton	.50	.15
❑ 382	Calvin Pickering	.50	.15
❑ 383	Marquis Grissom	.50	.15
❑ 384	Omar Daal	.50	.15
❑ 385	Curt Schilling	1.25	.35
❑ 386	Jose Cruz Jr.	.75	.23
❑ 387	Chris Widger	.50	.15
❑ 388	Pete Harnisch	.50	.15
❑ 389	Charles Nagy	.50	.15
❑ 390	Tom Gordon	.50	.15
❑ 391	Bobby Smith	.50	.15
❑ 392	Derrick Gibson	.50	.15
❑ 393	Jeff Conine	.75	.23
❑ 394	Carlos Perez	.50	.15
❑ 395	Barry Bonds	5.00	1.50
❑ 396	Mark McLemore	.50	.15

❑ 397 Juan Encarnacion .50 .15
❑ 398 Wade Boggs 1.25 .35
❑ 399 Ivan Rodriguez 2.00 .60
❑ 400 Moises Alou .75 .23
❑ 401 Jeromy Burnitz .75 .23
❑ 402 Sean Casey .75 .23
❑ 403 Jose Offerman .50 .15
❑ 404 Joe Fontenot .50 .15
❑ 405 Kevin Millwood .75 .23
❑ 406 Lance Johnson .50 .15
❑ 407 Richard Hidalgo .75 .23
❑ 408 Mike Jackson .50 .15
❑ 409 Brian Anderson .50 .15
❑ 410 Jeff Shaw .50 .15
❑ 411 Preston Wilson .75 .23
❑ 412 Todd Hundley .50 .15
❑ 413 Jim Parque .50 .15
❑ 414 Justin Baughman .50 .15
❑ 415 Dante Bichette .75 .23
❑ 416 Paul O'Neill 1.25 .35
❑ 417 Miguel Cairo .50 .15
❑ 418 Randy Johnson 2.00 .60
❑ 419 Jesus Sanchez .50 .15
❑ 420 Carlos Delgado .75 .23
❑ 421 Ricky Ledee .50 .15
❑ 422 Orlando Hernandez .75 .23
❑ 423 Frank Thomas 2.00 .60
❑ 424 Pokey Reese .50 .15
❑ 425 Carlos Lee 1.00 .30
Mike Lowell
Kit Pellow RC
❑ 426 Michael Cuddyer 1.00 .30
Mark DeRosa
Jerry Hairston Jr.
❑ 427 Marlon Anderson 1.00 .30
Ron Belliard
Orlando Cabrera
❑ 428 Micah Bowie 1.00 .30
Phil Norton RC
Randy Wolf
❑ 429 Jack Cressend RC 1.00 .30
Jason Rakers
John Rocker
❑ 430 Ruben Mateo 1.00 .30
Scott Morgan
Mike Zywica RC
❑ 431 Jason LaRue 1.00 .30
Matt LeCroy
Mitch Meluskey
❑ 432 Gabe Kapler 1.00 .30
Armando Rios
Fernando Seguignol
❑ 433 Adam Kennedy 1.00 .30
Mickey Lopez RC
Jackie Rexrode
❑ 434 Jose Fernandez RC 1.00 .30
Jeff Liefer
Chris Truby
❑ 435 Corey Koskie 2.50 .75
Doug Mientkiewicz RC
Damon Minor
❑ 436 Roosevelt Brown RC 1.00 .30
Dernell Stenson
Vernon Wells
❑ 437 A.J. Burnett RC 1.50 .45
Billy Koch
John Nicholson
❑ 438 Matt Belisle 1.00 .30
Matt Roney RC
❑ 439 Austin Kearns 8.00 2.40
Chris George RC
❑ 440 Nate Bump RC 1.50 .45
Nate Cornejo
❑ 441 Brad Lidge 1.50 .45
Mike Nannini RC
❑ 442 Matt Holliday 1.00 .30
Jeff Winchester RC
❑ 443 Adam Everett 1.00 .30
Chip Ambres RC
❑ 444 Pat Burrell 5.00 1.50
Eric Valent RC
❑ 445 Roger Clemens SK 2.00 .60
❑ 446 Kerry Wood SK 1.25 .35
❑ 447 Curt Schilling SK .75 .23
❑ 448 Randy Johnson SK 1.25 .35
❑ 449 Pedro Martinez SK 1.25 .35
❑ 450 Jeff Bagwell AT 2.00 .60
Andres Galarraga
Mark McGwire
❑ 451 John Olerud AT .75 .23
Jim Thome
Tino Martinez
❑ 452 Alex Rodriguez AT 2.50 .75
Nomar Garciaparra
Derek Jeter
❑ 453 Vinny Castilla AT 1.25 .35
Chipper Jones
Scott Rolen
❑ 454 Sammy Sosa AT 2.00 .60
Ken Griffey Jr.
Juan Gonzalez
❑ 455 Barry Bonds AT 2.00 .60
Manny Ramirez
Larry Walker
❑ 456 Frank Thomas AT 2.00 .60
Tim Salmon
David Justice
❑ 457 Travis Lee AT .75 .23
Todd Helton
Ben Grieve
❑ 458 Vladimir Guerrero AT .75 .23
Greg Vaughn
Bernie Williams
❑ 459 Mike Piazza AT 2.00 .60
Ivan Rodriguez
Jason Kendall
❑ 460 Roger Clemens AT 2.00 .60
Kerry Wood
Greg Maddux
❑ 461A Sammy Sosa HR 1 25.00 7.50
❑ 461B Sammy Sosa HR 2 10.00 3.00
❑ 461C Sammy Sosa HR 3 10.00 3.00
❑ 461D Sammy Sosa HR 4 10.00 3.00
❑ 461E Sammy Sosa HR 5 10.00 3.00
❑ 461F Sammy Sosa HR 6 10.00 3.00
❑ 461G Sammy Sosa HR 7 10.00 3.00
❑ 461H Sammy Sosa HR 8 10.00 3.00
❑ 461I Sammy Sosa HR 9 10.00 3.00
❑ 461J Sammy Sosa HR 10 10.00 3.00
❑ 461K Sammy Sosa HR 11 10.00 3.00
❑ 461L Sammy Sosa HR 12 10.00 3.00
❑ 461M Sammy Sosa HR 13 10.00 3.00
❑ 461N Sammy Sosa HR 14 10.00 3.00
❑ 461O Sammy Sosa HR 15 10.00 3.00
❑ 461P Sammy Sosa HR 16 10.00 3.00
❑ 461Q Sammy Sosa HR 17 10.00 3.00
❑ 461R Sammy Sosa HR 18 10.00 3.00
❑ 461S Sammy Sosa HR 19 10.00 3.00
❑ 461T Sammy Sosa HR 20 10.00 3.00
❑ 461U Sammy Sosa HR 21 10.00 3.00
❑ 461V Sammy Sosa HR 22 10.00 3.00
❑ 461W Sammy Sosa HR 23 10.00 3.00
❑ 461X Sammy Sosa HR 24 10.00 3.00
❑ 461Y Sammy Sosa HR 25 10.00 3.00
❑ 461Z Sammy Sosa HR 26 10.00 3.00
❑ 461AA S.Sosa HR 27 10.00 3.00
❑ 461AB S.Sosa HR 28 10.00 3.00
❑ 461AC S.Sosa HR 29 10.00 3.00
❑ 461AD S.Sosa HR 30 10.00 3.00
❑ 461AE S.Sosa HR 31 10.00 3.00
❑ 461AF S.Sosa HR 32 10.00 3.00
❑ 461AG S.Sosa HR 33 10.00 3.00
❑ 461AH S.Sosa HR 34 10.00 3.00
❑ 461AI S.Sosa HR 35 10.00 3.00
❑ 461AJ S.Sosa HR 36 10.00 3.00
❑ 461AK S.Sosa HR 37 10.00 3.00
❑ 461AL S.Sosa HR 38 10.00 3.00
❑ 461AM S.Sosa HR 39 10.00 3.00
❑ 461AN S.Sosa HR 40 10.00 3.00
❑ 461AO S.Sosa HR 41 10.00 3.00
❑ 461AP S.Sosa HR 42 10.00 3.00
❑ 461AR S.Sosa HR 43 10.00 3.00
❑ 461AS S.Sosa HR 44 10.00 3.00
❑ 461AT S.Sosa HR 45 10.00 3.00
❑ 461AU S.Sosa HR 46 10.00 3.00
❑ 461AV S.Sosa HR 47 10.00 3.00
❑ 461AW S.Sosa HR 48 10.00 3.00
❑ 461AX S.Sosa HR 49 10.00 3.00
❑ 461AY S.Sosa HR 50 10.00 3.00
❑ 461AZ S.Sosa HR 51 10.00 3.00
❑ 461BB S.Sosa HR 52 10.00 3.00
❑ 461CC S.Sosa HR 53 10.00 3.00
❑ 461DD S.Sosa HR 54 10.00 3.00
❑ 461EE S.Sosa HR 55 10.00 3.00
❑ 461FF S.Sosa HR 56 10.00 3.00
❑ 461GG S.Sosa HR 57 10.00 3.00
❑ 461HH S.Sosa HR 58 10.00 3.00
❑ 461II S.Sosa HR 59 10.00 3.00
❑ 461JJ S.Sosa HR 60 10.00 3.00
❑ 461KK S.Sosa HR 61 25.00 7.50
❑ 461LL S.Sosa HR 62 40.00 12.00
❑ 461MM S.Sosa HR 63 15.00 4.50
❑ 461NN S.Sosa HR 64 15.00 4.50
❑ 461OO S.Sosa HR 65 15.00 4.50
❑ 461PP S.Sosa HR 66 50.00 15.00
❑ 462 Checklist .50 .15
❑ 463 Checklist .50 .15

1999 Topps Chrome Traded

	Nm-Mt	Ex-Mt
COMP.FACT SET (121)	80.00	24.00

❑ T1 Seth Etherton .60 .18
❑ T2 Mark Harriger RC .50 .15
❑ T3 Matt Wise RC .50 .15
❑ T4 Carlos E. Hernandez RC .75 .23
❑ T5 Julio Lugo RC .75 .23
❑ T6 Mike Nannini .60 .18
❑ T7 Justin Bowles RC .50 .15
❑ T8 Mark Mulder RC 8.00 2.40
❑ T9 Roberto Vaz RC .50 .15
❑ T10 Felipe Lopez RC .75 .23
❑ T11 Matt Belisle 1.00 .30
❑ T12 Micah Bowie .40 .12
❑ T13 Ruben Quevedo RC .75 .23
❑ T14 Jose Garcia RC .50 .15
❑ T15 David Kelton RC 2.00 .60
❑ T16 Phil Norton .40 .12
❑ T17 Corey Patterson RC 8.00 2.40
❑ T18 Ron Walker RC .50 .15
❑ T19 Paul Hoover RC .50 .15
❑ T20 Ryan Rupe RC .75 .23
❑ T21 J.D. Closser RC .75 .23
❑ T22 Rob Ryan RC .50 .15
❑ T23 Steve Colyer RC .75 .23
❑ T24 Bubba Crosby RC 1.25 .35
❑ T25 Luke Prokopec RC .75 .23
❑ T26 Matt Blank RC .50 .15
❑ T27 Josh McKinley .60 .18
❑ T28 Nate Bump .50 .15
❑ T29 G.Chiaramonte RC .50 .15
❑ T30 Arturo McDowell .60 .18
❑ T31 Tony Torcato .60 .18
❑ T32 Dave Roberts RC 1.25 .35
❑ T33 C.C. Sabathia RC 2.00 .60
❑ T34 Sean Spencer RC .50 .15
❑ T35 Chip Ambres 1.50 .45
❑ T36 A.J. Burnett 1.00 .30
❑ T37 Mo Bruce RC .50 .15
❑ T38 Jason Tyner .60 .18
❑ T39 Mamon Tucker .60 .18
❑ T40 Sean Burroughs RC 6.00 1.80
❑ T41 Kevin Eberwein RC .75 .23
❑ T42 Junior Herndon RC .75 .23
❑ T43 Bryan Wolff RC .50 .15
❑ T44 Pat Burrell 5.00 1.50
❑ T45 Eric Valent .75 .23
❑ T46 Carlos Pena RC 2.00 .60

❑ T47 Mike Zywica .40 .12
❑ T48 Adam Everett .60 .18
❑ T49 Juan Pena RC .50 .15
❑ T50 Adam Dunn RC 10.00 3.00
❑ T51 Austin Kearns 8.00 2.40
❑ T52 Jacobo Sequea RC .75 .23
❑ T53 Choo Freeman .60 .18
❑ T54 Jeff Winchester .60 .18
❑ T55 Matt Burch .50 .15
❑ T56 Chris George .60 .18
❑ T57 Scott Mullen RC .50 .15
❑ T58 Kit Pellow .50 .15
❑ T59 Mark Quinn RC .75 .23
❑ T60 Nate Cornejo 1.25 .35
❑ T61 Ryan Mills .60 .18
❑ T62 Kevin Beirne RC .75 .23
❑ T63 Kip Wells RC 1.25 .35
❑ T64 Juan Rivera RC 2.50 .75
❑ T65 Alfonso Soriano RC 20.00 6.00
❑ T66 Josh Hamilton RC 3.00 .90
❑ T67 Josh Girdley RC .75 .23
❑ T68 Kyle Snyder RC .75 .23
❑ T69 Mike Paradis RC .75 .23
❑ T70 Jason Jennings RC 1.25 .35
❑ T71 David Walling RC .75 .23
❑ T72 Omar Ortiz RC .50 .15
❑ T73 Jay Gehrke RC .50 .15
❑ T74 Casey Burns RC .50 .15
❑ T75 Carl Crawford RC 4.00 1.20
❑ T76 Reggie Sanders .60 .18
❑ T77 Will Clark 1.50 .45
❑ T78 David Wells .60 .18
❑ T79 Paul Konerko .60 .18
❑ T80 Armando Benitez .40 .12
❑ T81 Brant Brown .40 .12
❑ T82 Mo Vaughn .60 .18
❑ T83 Jose Canseco 1.50 .45
❑ T84 Albert Belle .60 .18
❑ T85 Dean Palmer .60 .18
❑ T86 Greg Vaughn .60 .18
❑ T87 Mark Clark .40 .12
❑ T88 Pat Meares .40 .12
❑ T89 Eric Davis .60 .18
❑ T90 Brian Giles .60 .18
❑ T91 Jeff Brantley .40 .12
❑ T92 Bret Boone .60 .18
❑ T93 Ron Gant .60 .18
❑ T94 Mike Cameron .60 .18
❑ T95 Charles Johnson .60 .18
❑ T96 Denny Neagle .40 .12
❑ T97 Brian Hunter .40 .12
❑ T98 Jose Hernandez .40 .12
❑ T99 Rick Aguilera .40 .12
❑ T100 Tony Batista .60 .18
❑ T101 Roger Cedeno .40 .12
❑ T102 C.Gubanich RC .50 .15
❑ T103 Tim Belcher .40 .12
❑ T104 Bruce Aven .40 .12
❑ T105 Brian Daubach RC .75 .23
❑ T106 Ed Sprague .40 .12
❑ T107 Michael Tucker .40 .12
❑ T108 Homer Bush .40 .12
❑ T109 Armando Reynoso .40 .12
❑ T110 Brook Fordyce .40 .12
❑ T111 Matt Mantei .40 .12
❑ T112 Dave Mlicki .40 .12
❑ T113 Kenny Rogers .60 .18
❑ T114 Livan Hernandez .40 .12
❑ T115 Butch Huskey .40 .12
❑ T116 David Segui .40 .12
❑ T117 Darryl Hamilton .40 .12
❑ T118 Terry Mulholland .40 .12
❑ T119 Randy Velarde .40 .12
❑ T120 Bill Taylor .40 .12
❑ T121 Kevin Appier .60 .18

2000 Topps Chrome Traded

	Nm-Mt	Ex-Mt
COMP.FACT.SET (135)	60.00	18.00

❑ T1 Mike MacDougal 1.00 .30
❑ T2 Andy Tracy RC .50 .15
❑ T3 Brandon Phillips RC 2.00 .60

❑ T4 Brandon Inge RC .75 .23
❑ T5 Robbie Morrison RC .50 .15
❑ T6 Josh Pressley RC .75 .23
❑ T7 Todd Moser RC .50 .15
❑ T8 Rob Purvis .75 .23
❑ T9 Chance Caple .75 .23
❑ T10 Ben Sheets 2.00 .60
❑ T11 Russ Jacobson RC .50 .15
❑ T12 Brian Cole RC .75 .23
❑ T13 Brad Baker .75 .23
❑ T14 Alex Cintron RC 3.00 .90
❑ T15 Lyle Overbay RC 1.00 .30
❑ T16 Mike Edwards RC .50 .15
❑ T17 Sean McGowan RC .50 .15
❑ T18 Jose Molina .50 .15
❑ T19 Marcos Castillo RC .75 .23
❑ T20 Josue Espada RC .50 .15
❑ T21 Alex Gordon RC .75 .23
❑ T22 Rob Pugmire RC .75 .23
❑ T23 Jason Stumm .75 .23
❑ T24 Ty Howington .75 .23
❑ T25 Brett Myers 3.00 .90
❑ T26 Maicer Izturis RC .75 .23
❑ T27 John McDonald .50 .15
❑ T28 W.Rodriguez RC .75 .23
❑ T29 Carlos Zambrano RC 3.00 .90
❑ T30 Alejandro Diaz RC .75 .23
❑ T31 Geraldo Guzman RC .50 .15
❑ T32 J.R. House RC .75 .23
❑ T33 Elvin Nina RC .50 .15
❑ T34 Juan Pierre RC 6.00 1.80
❑ T35 Ben Johnson RC .75 .23
❑ T36 Jeff Bailey RC .50 .15
❑ T37 Miguel Olivo RC .75 .23
❑ T38 F.Rodriguez RC 3.00 .90
❑ T39 Tony Pena Jr. RC .75 .23
❑ T40 Miguel Cabrera RC 30.00 9.00
❑ T41 Asdrubal Oropeza RC .75 .23
❑ T42 Junior Zamora RC .75 .23
❑ T43 Jovanny Cedeno RC .75 .23
❑ T44 John Sneed .75 .23
❑ T45 Josh Kalinowski .75 .23
❑ T46 Mike Young RC 2.50 .75
❑ T47 Rico Washington RC .75 .23
❑ T48 Chad Durbin RC .50 .15
❑ T49 Junior Brignac RC .75 .23
❑ T50 Carlos Hernandez RC .75 .23
❑ T51 Cesar Izturis RC .75 .23
❑ T52 Oscar Salazar RC .75 .23
❑ T53 Pat Strange RC .75 .23
❑ T54 Rick Asadoorian .75 .23
❑ T55 Keith Reed .75 .23
❑ T56 Leo Estrella RC .50 .15
❑ T57 Wascar Serrano RC .75 .23
❑ T58 Richard Gomez RC .50 .15
❑ T59 Ramon Santiago RC .75 .23
❑ T60 Jovanny Sosa RC .75 .23
❑ T61 Aaron Rowand RC .75 .23
❑ T62 Junior Guerrero RC .75 .23
❑ T63 Luis Terrero RC .75 .23
❑ T64 Brian Sanches RC .75 .23
❑ T65 Scott Sobkowiak RC .50 .15
❑ T66 Gary Majewski RC .75 .23
❑ T67 Barry Zito 4.00 1.20
❑ T68 Ryan Christianson .75 .23
❑ T69 Cristian Guerrero RC .75 .23
❑ T70 T.De La Rosa RC .50 .15
❑ T71 Andrew Beinbrink RC .50 .15
❑ T72 Ryan Knox RC .50 .15
❑ T73 Alex Graman RC .50 .15
❑ T74 Juan Guzman RC .75 .23
❑ T75 Ruben Salazar RC .75 .23
❑ T76 Luis Matos RC 3.00 .90
❑ T77 Tony Mota RC .50 .15
❑ T78 Doug Davis .50 .15
❑ T79 Ben Christensen 1.25 .35
❑ T80 Mike Lamb .75 .23
❑ T81 Adrian Gonzalez RC 3.00 .90
❑ T82 Mike Stodolka RC .75 .23
❑ T83 Adam Johnson RC .75 .23
❑ T84 Matt Wheatland RC .50 .15
❑ T85 Corey Smith RC 1.00 .30
❑ T86 Rocco Baldelli RC 20.00 6.00
❑ T87 Keith Bucktrot RC .50 .15
❑ T88 Adam Wainwright RC 2.50 .75
❑ T89 Scott Thorman RC 1.00 .30
❑ T90 Tripper Johnson RC 1.00 .30
❑ T91 Jim Edmonds .75 .23
❑ T92 Masato Yoshii .50 .15
❑ T93 Adam Kennedy .50 .15
❑ T94 Darryl Kile .75 .23
❑ T95 Mark McLemore .50 .15
❑ T96 Ricky Gutierrez .50 .15
❑ T97 Juan Gonzalez 2.00 .60
❑ T98 Melvin Mora .75 .23
❑ T99 Dante Bichette .75 .23
❑ T100 Lee Stevens .50 .15
❑ T101 Roger Cedeno .50 .15
❑ T102 John Olerud .75 .23
❑ T103 Eric Young .50 .15
❑ T104 Mickey Morandini .50 .15
❑ T105 Travis Lee .50 .15
❑ T106 Greg Vaughn .75 .23
❑ T107 Todd Zeile .75 .23
❑ T108 Chuck Finley .75 .23
❑ T109 Ismael Valdes .50 .15
❑ T110 Reggie Sanders .75 .23
❑ T111 Pat Hentgen .50 .15
❑ T112 Ryan Klesko .75 .23
❑ T113 Derek Bell .50 .15
❑ T114 Hideo Nomo 2.00 .60
❑ T115 Aaron Sele .50 .15
❑ T116 Fernando Vina .75 .23
❑ T117 Wally Joyner .75 .23
❑ T118 Brian Hunter .50 .15
❑ T119 Joe Girardi .50 .15
❑ T120 Omar Daal .50 .15
❑ T121 Brook Fordyce .50 .15
❑ T122 Jose Valentin .50 .15
❑ T123 Curt Schilling 1.25 .35
❑ T124 B.J. Surhoff .75 .23
❑ T125 Henry Rodriguez .50 .15
❑ T126 Mike Bordick .50 .15
❑ T127 David Justice .75 .23
❑ T128 Charles Johnson .75 .23
❑ T129 Will Clark 2.00 .60
❑ T130 Dwight Gooden 1.25 .35
❑ T131 David Segui .50 .15
❑ T132 Denny Neagle .75 .23
❑ T133 Jose Canseco 2.00 .60
❑ T134 Bruce Chen .50 .15
❑ T135 Jason Bere .50 .15

2001 Topps Chrome

	Nm-Mt	Ex-Mt
COMPLETE SET (661)	300.00	90.00
COMP. SERIES 1 (331)	150.00	45.00
COMP. SERIES 2 (330)	150.00	45.00
❑ 1 Cal Ripken	6.00	1.80
❑ 2 Chipper Jones	2.00	.60
❑ 3 Roger Cedeno	.50	.15
❑ 4 Garret Anderson	.75	.23
❑ 5 Robin Ventura	.75	.23
❑ 6 Daryle Ward	.50	.15
❑ 7 Does Not Exist		
❑ 8 Phil Nevin	.75	.23
❑ 9 Jermaine Dye	.75	.23
❑ 10 Chris Singleton	.50	.15
❑ 11 Mike Redmond	.50	.15
❑ 12 Jim Thome	2.00	.60
❑ 13 Brian Jordan	.75	.23
❑ 14 Dustin Hermanson	.50	.15
❑ 15 Shawn Green	.75	.23
❑ 16 Todd Stottlemyre	.50	.15
❑ 17 Dan Wilson	.50	.15
❑ 18 Derek Lowe	.75	.23
❑ 19 Juan Gonzalez	2.00	.60
❑ 20 Pat Meares	.50	.15
❑ 21 Paul O'Neill	1.25	.35
❑ 22 Jeffrey Hammonds	.50	.15
❑ 23 Pokey Reese	.50	.15
❑ 24 Mike Mussina	2.00	.60
❑ 25 Rico Brogna	.50	.15
❑ 26 Jay Buhner	.75	.23
❑ 27 Steve Cox	.50	.15
❑ 28 Quilvio Veras	.50	.15
❑ 29 Marquis Grissom	.50	.15
❑ 30 Shigetoshi Hasegawa	.75	.23
❑ 31 Shane Reynolds	.50	.15
❑ 32 Adam Piatt	.50	.15
❑ 33 Preston Wilson	.75	.23
❑ 34 Ellis Burks	.75	.23
❑ 35 Armando Rios	.50	.15
❑ 36 Chuck Finley	.75	.23
❑ 37 Shannon Stewart	.75	.23
❑ 38 Mark McGwire	5.00	1.50
❑ 39 Gerald Williams	.50	.15
❑ 40 Eric Young	.50	.15
❑ 41 Peter Bergeron	.50	.15
❑ 42 Arthur Rhodes	.50	.15
❑ 43 Bobby Jones	.50	.15
❑ 44 Matt Clement	.50	.15
❑ 45 Pedro Martinez	2.00	.60
❑ 46 Jose Canseco	2.00	.60
❑ 47 Matt Anderson	.50	.15
❑ 48 Torii Hunter	.75	.23
❑ 49 Carlos Lee	.75	.23
❑ 50 Eric Chavez	.75	.23
❑ 51 Rick Helling	.50	.15
❑ 52 John Franco	.75	.23
❑ 53 Mike Bordick	.75	.23
❑ 54 Andres Galarraga	.75	.23
❑ 55 Jose Cruz Jr.	.75	.23
❑ 56 Mike Matheny	.50	.15
❑ 57 Randy Johnson	2.00	.60
❑ 58 Richie Sexson	.75	.23
❑ 59 Vladimir Nunez	.50	.15
❑ 60 Aaron Boone	.75	.23
❑ 61 Darin Erstad	.75	.23
❑ 62 Alex Gonzalez	.50	.15
❑ 63 Gil Heredia	.50	.15
❑ 64 Shane Andrews	.50	.15
❑ 65 Todd Hundley	.50	.15
❑ 66 Bill Mueller	.75	.23
❑ 67 Mark McLemore	.50	.15
❑ 68 Scott Spiezio	.75	.23
❑ 69 Kevin McGlinchy	.50	.15
❑ 70 Manny Ramirez	.75	.23
❑ 71 Mike Lamb	.50	.15
❑ 72 Brian Buchanan	.50	.15
❑ 73 Mike Sweeney	.75	.23
❑ 74 John Wetteland	.75	.23
❑ 75 Rob Bell	.50	.15
❑ 76 John Burkett	.50	.15
❑ 77 Derek Jeter	5.00	1.50
❑ 78 J.D. Drew	.75	.23
❑ 79 Jose Offerman	.50	.15
❑ 80 Rick Reed	.50	.15
❑ 81 Will Clark	2.00	.60
❑ 82 Rickey Henderson	3.00	.90
❑ 83 Kirk Rueter	.50	.15
❑ 84 Lee Stevens	.50	.15
❑ 85 Jay Bell	.75	.23
❑ 86 Fred McGriff	1.25	.35
❑ 87 Julio Zuleta	.50	.15
❑ 88 Brian Anderson	.50	.15
❑ 89 Orlando Cabrera	.50	.15
❑ 90 Alex Fernandez	.50	.15
❑ 91 Derek Bell	.50	.15
❑ 92 Eric Owens	.50	.15
❑ 93 Dennys Reyes	.50	.15
❑ 94 Mike Stanley	.50	.15
❑ 95 Jorge Posada	1.25	.35
❑ 96 Paul Konerko	.75	.23
❑ 97 Mike Remlinger	.50	.15
❑ 98 Travis Lee	.50	.15
❑ 99 Ken Caminiti	.75	.23
❑ 100 Kevin Barker	.50	.15
❑ 101 Ozzie Guillen	.50	.15
❑ 102 Randy Wolf	.75	.23
❑ 103 Michael Tucker	.50	.15
❑ 104 Darren Lewis	.50	.15
❑ 105 Joe Randa	.50	.15
❑ 106 Jeff Cirillo	.75	.23
❑ 107 David Ortiz	.75	.23
❑ 108 Herb Perry	.50	.15
❑ 109 Jeff Nelson	.50	.15
❑ 110 Chris Stynes	.50	.15
❑ 111 Johnny Damon	.75	.23
❑ 112 Jason Schmidt	.75	.23
❑ 113 Charles Johnson	.50	.15
❑ 114 Pat Burrell	.75	.23
❑ 115 Gary Sheffield	.75	.23
❑ 116 Tom Glavine	2.00	.60
❑ 117 Jason Isringhausen	.50	.15
❑ 118 Chris Carpenter	.50	.15
❑ 119 Jeff Suppan	.50	.15
❑ 120 Ivan Rodriguez	2.00	.60
❑ 121 Luis Sojo	.50	.15
❑ 122 Ron Villone	.50	.15
❑ 123 Mike Sirotka	.50	.15
❑ 124 Chuck Knoblauch	.75	.23
❑ 125 Jason Kendall	.75	.23
❑ 126 Bobby Estalella	.50	.15
❑ 127 Jose Guillen	.50	.15
❑ 128 Carlos Delgado	.75	.23
❑ 129 Benji Gil	.50	.15
❑ 130 Einar Diaz	.50	.15
❑ 131 Andy Benes	.50	.15
❑ 132 Adrian Beltre	.75	.23
❑ 133 Roger Clemens	4.00	1.20
❑ 134 Scott Williamson	.50	.15
❑ 135 Brad Penny	.50	.15
❑ 136 Troy Glaus	1.25	.35
❑ 137 Kevin Appier	.75	.23
❑ 138 Walt Weiss	.50	.15
❑ 139 Michael Barrett	.50	.15
❑ 140 Mike Hampton	.75	.23
❑ 141 Francisco Cordova	.50	.15
❑ 142 David Segui	.50	.15
❑ 143 Carlos Febles	.50	.15
❑ 144 Roy Halladay	.75	.23
❑ 145 Seth Etherton	.50	.15
❑ 146 Fernando Tatis	.50	.15
❑ 147 Livan Hernandez	.50	.15
❑ 148 B.J. Surhoff	.75	.23
❑ 149 Barry Larkin	2.00	.60
❑ 150 Bobby Howry	.50	.15
❑ 151 Dmitri Young	.75	.23
❑ 152 Brian Hunter	.50	.15
❑ 153 A.Rodriguez Rangers	4.00	1.20
❑ 154 Hideo Nomo	2.00	.60
❑ 155 Warren Morris	.50	.15
❑ 156 Antonio Alfonseca	.50	.15
❑ 157 Edgardo Alfonzo	.75	.23
❑ 158 Mark Grudzielanek	.50	.15
❑ 159 Fernando Vina	.75	.23
❑ 160 Homer Bush	.50	.15
❑ 161 Jason Giambi	2.00	.60
❑ 162 Steve Karsay	.50	.15
❑ 163 Matt Lawton	.50	.15
❑ 164 Rusty Greer	.75	.23
❑ 165 Billy Koch	.50	.15
❑ 166 Todd Hollandsworth	.50	.15
❑ 167 Raul Ibanez	.75	.23
❑ 168 Tony Gwynn	2.50	.75
❑ 169 Carl Everett	.75	.23
❑ 170 Hector Carrasco	.50	.15
❑ 171 Jose Valentin	.50	.15
❑ 172 Deivi Cruz	.50	.15
❑ 173 Bret Boone	.75	.23
❑ 174 Melvin Mora	.50	.15
❑ 175 Danny Graves	.50	.15
❑ 176 Jose Jimenez	.50	.15
❑ 177 James Baldwin	.50	.15
❑ 178 C.J. Nitkowski	.50	.15
❑ 179 Jeff Zimmerman	.50	.15
❑ 180 Mike Lowell	.75	.23
❑ 181 Hideki Irabu	.50	.15
❑ 182 Greg Vaughn	.75	.23
❑ 183 Omar Daal	.50	.15
❑ 184 Darren Dreifort	.50	.15
❑ 185 Gil Meche	.75	.23
❑ 186 Damian Jackson	.50	.15
❑ 187 Frank Thomas	2.00	.60
❑ 188 Luis Castillo	.75	.23
❑ 189 Bartolo Colon	.75	.23
❑ 190 Craig Biggio	1.25	.35
❑ 191 Scott Schoeneweis	.50	.15
❑ 192 Dave Veres	.50	.15
❑ 193 Ramon Martinez	.50	.15
❑ 194 Jose Vidro	.75	.23
❑ 195 Todd Helton	1.25	.35
❑ 196 Greg Norton	.50	.15
❑ 197 Jacque Jones	.75	.23
❑ 198 Jason Grimsley	.50	.15
❑ 199 Dan Reichert	.50	.15
❑ 200 Robb Nen	.75	.23
❑ 201 Scott Hatteberg	.50	.15
❑ 202 Terry Shumpert	.50	.15
❑ 203 Kevin Millar	.75	.23
❑ 204 Ismael Valdes	.50	.15
❑ 205 Richard Hidalgo	.75	.23
❑ 206 Randy Velarde	.50	.15
❑ 207 Bengie Molina	.50	.15
❑ 208 Tony Womack	.50	.15
❑ 209 Enrique Wilson	.50	.15
❑ 210 Jeff Brantley	.50	.15
❑ 211 Rick Ankiel	.50	.15
❑ 212 Terry Mulholland	.50	.15
❑ 213 Ron Belliard	.50	.15
❑ 214 Terrence Long	.75	.23
❑ 215 Alberto Castillo	.50	.15
❑ 216 Royce Clayton	.50	.15
❑ 217 Joe McEwing	.50	.15
❑ 218 Jason McDonald	.50	.15
❑ 219 Ricky Bottalico	.50	.15
❑ 220 Keith Foulke	.50	.15
❑ 221 Brad Radke	.75	.23
❑ 222 Gabe Kapler	.50	.15
❑ 223 Pedro Astacio	.50	.15
❑ 224 Armando Reynoso	.50	.15
❑ 225 Darryl Kile	.75	.23
❑ 226 Reggie Sanders	.75	.23
❑ 227 Esteban Yan	.50	.15
❑ 228 Joe Nathan	.50	.15
❑ 229 Jay Payton	.50	.15
❑ 230 Francisco Cordero	.50	.15
❑ 231 Gregg Jefferies	.50	.15
❑ 232 LaTroy Hawkins	.50	.15
❑ 233 Jacob Cruz	.50	.15
❑ 234 Chris Holt	.50	.15
❑ 235 Vladimir Guerrero	2.00	.60
❑ 236 Marvin Benard	.50	.15
❑ 237 Alex Ramirez	.50	.15
❑ 238 Mike Williams	.50	.15
❑ 239 Sean Bergman	.50	.15
❑ 240 Juan Encarnacion	.50	.15
❑ 241 Russ Davis	.50	.15
❑ 242 Ramon Hernandez	.50	.15
❑ 243 Sandy Alomar Jr.	.50	.15
❑ 244 Eddie Guardado	.75	.23
❑ 245 Shane Halter	.50	.15
❑ 246 Geoff Jenkins	.75	.23
❑ 247 Brian Meadows	.50	.15
❑ 248 Damian Miller	.50	.15
❑ 249 Darrin Fletcher	.50	.15
❑ 250 Rafael Furcal	.75	.23
❑ 251 Mark Grace	2.00	.60
❑ 252 Mark Mulder	.75	.23
❑ 253 Joe Torre MG	.75	.23

Card	High	Low
❑ 254 Bobby Cox MG	.50	.15
❑ 255 Mike Scioscia MG	.50	.15
❑ 256 Mike Hargrove MG	.50	.15
❑ 257 Jimy Williams MG	.50	.15
❑ 258 Jerry Manuel MG	.50	.15
❑ 259 Charlie Manuel MG	.50	.15
❑ 260 Don Baylor MG	.75	.23
❑ 261 Phil Garner MG	.50	.15
❑ 262 Tony Muser MG	.50	.15
❑ 263 Buddy Bell MG	.75	.23
❑ 264 Tom Kelly MG	.50	.15
❑ 265 John Boles MG	.50	.15
❑ 266 Art Howe MG	.50	.15
❑ 267 Larry Dierker MG	.50	.15
❑ 268 Lou Piniella MG	.75	.23
❑ 269 Larry Rothschild MG	.50	.15
❑ 270 Davey Lopes MG	.75	.23
❑ 271 Johnny Oates MG	.50	.15
❑ 272 Felipe Alou MG	.50	.15
❑ 273 Bobby Valentine MG	.50	.15
❑ 274 Tony LaRussa MG	.50	.15
❑ 275 Bruce Bochy MG	.50	.15
❑ 276 Dusty Baker MG	.75	.23
❑ 277 Adrian Gonzalez	1.50	.45
Adam Johnson		
❑ 278 Matt Wheatland	1.00	.30
Bryan Digby		
❑ 279 Tripper Johnson	1.00	.30
Scott Thorman		
❑ 280 Phil Dumatrait	1.50	.45
Adam Wainwright		
❑ 281 Scott Heard	1.50	.45
David Parrish RC		
❑ 282 Rocco Baldelli	8.00	2.40
Mark Folsom		
❑ 283 Dominic Rich RC	1.50	.45
Aaron Herr		
❑ 284 Mike Stodolka	1.50	.45
Sean Burnett		
❑ 285 Derek Thompson	1.00	.30
Corey Smith		
❑ 286 Danny Borrell	1.50	.45
Jason Bourgeois RC		
❑ 287 Chin-Feng Chen	1.50	.45
Corey Patterson		
Josh Hamilton		
❑ 288 Ryan Anderson	3.00	.90
Barry Zito		
C.C. Sabathia		
❑ 289 Scott Sobkowiak	1.50	.45
David Walling		
Ben Sheets		
❑ 290 Ty Howington	1.00	.30
Josh Kalinowski		
Josh Girdley		
❑ 291 Hee Seop Choi	10.00	3.00
Aaron McNeal		
Jason Hart		
❑ 292 Bobby Bradley	1.50	.45
Kurt Ainsworth		
Chin-Hui Tsao		
❑ 293 Mike Glendenning	1.00	.30
Kenny Kelly		
Juan Silvestre		
❑ 294 J.R. House	1.00	.30
Ramon Castro		
Ben Davis		
❑ 295 Chance Caple	4.00	1.20
Rafael Soriano		
Pasqual Coco		
❑ 296 Travis Hafner RC	3.00	.90
Eric Munson		
Bucky Jacobsen		
❑ 297 Jason Conti	1.50	.45
Chris Wakeland		
Brian Cole		
❑ 298 Scott Seabol	1.50	.45
Aubrey Huff		
Joe Crede		
❑ 299 Adam Everett	1.00	.30
Jose Ortiz		
Keith Ginter		
❑ 300 Carlos Hernandez	1.00	.30
Geraldo Guzman		
Adam Eaton		
❑ 301 Bobby Kielty	1.50	.45
Milton Bradley		
Juan Rivera		
❑ 302 Mark McGwire GM	2.50	.75
❑ 303 Don Larsen GM	.75	.23
❑ 304 Bobby Thomson GM	.75	.23
❑ 305 Bill Mazeroski GM	.75	.23
❑ 306 Reggie Jackson GM	1.25	.35
❑ 307 Kirk Gibson GM	.75	.23
❑ 308 Roger Maris GM	2.00	.60
❑ 309 Cal Ripken GM	3.00	.90
❑ 310 Hank Aaron GM	2.00	.60
❑ 311 Joe Carter GM	.75	.23
❑ 312 Cal Ripken SH	3.00	.90
❑ 313 Randy Johnson SH	1.25	.35
❑ 314 Ken Griffey Jr. SH	2.00	.60
❑ 315 Troy Glaus SH	1.25	.35
❑ 316 Kazuhiro Sasaki SH	.75	.23
❑ 317 Sammy Sosa	1.25	.35
Troy Glaus LL		
❑ 318 Todd Helton	.75	.23
Edgar Martinez LL		
❑ 319 Todd Helton	2.00	.60
Nomar Garicaparra LL		
❑ 320 Barry Bonds	2.00	.60
Jason Giambi LL		
❑ 321 Todd Helton	1.25	.35
Manny Ramirez LL		
❑ 322 Todd Helton	.75	.23
Darin Erstad LL		
❑ 323 Kevin Brown	1.25	.35
Pedro Martinez LL		
❑ 324 Randy Johnson	1.25	.35
Pedro Martinez LL		
❑ 325 Will Clark HL	2.00	.60
❑ 326 New York Mets HL	2.00	.60
❑ 327 New York Yankees HL	3.00	.90
❑ 328 Seattle Mariners HL	.75	.23
❑ 329 Mike Hampton HL	.75	.23
❑ 330 New York Yankees HL	4.00	1.20
❑ 331 N.Y. Yankees Champs	8.00	2.40
❑ 332 Jeff Bagwell	1.25	.35
❑ 333 Andy Pettitte	1.25	.35
❑ 334 Tony Armas Jr.	.50	.15
❑ 335 Jeromy Burnitz	.75	.23
❑ 336 Javier Vazquez	.75	.23
❑ 337 Eric Karros	.75	.23
❑ 338 Brian Giles	.75	.23
❑ 339 Scott Rolen	1.25	.35
❑ 340 David Justice	.75	.23
❑ 341 Ray Durham	.75	.23
❑ 342 Todd Zeile	.75	.23
❑ 343 Cliff Floyd	.75	.23
❑ 344 Barry Bonds	5.00	1.50
❑ 345 Matt Williams	.75	.23
❑ 346 Steve Finley	.75	.23
❑ 347 Scott Elarton	.50	.15
❑ 348 Bernie Williams	1.25	.35
❑ 349 David Wells	.75	.23
❑ 350 J.T. Snow	.75	.23
❑ 351 Al Leiter	.75	.23
❑ 352 Magglio Ordonez	.75	.23
❑ 353 Raul Mondesi	.75	.23
❑ 354 Tim Salmon	1.25	.35
❑ 355 Jeff Kent	.75	.23
❑ 356 Mariano Rivera	1.25	.35
❑ 357 John Olerud	.75	.23
❑ 358 Javy Lopez	.75	.23
❑ 359 Ben Grieve	.50	.15
❑ 360 Ray Lankford	.50	.15
❑ 361 Ken Griffey Jr.	3.00	.90
❑ 362 Rich Aurilia	.75	.23
❑ 363 Andruw Jones	1.25	.35
❑ 364 Ryan Klesko	.75	.23
❑ 365 Roberto Alomar	2.00	.60
❑ 366 Miguel Tejada	.75	.23
❑ 367 Mo Vaughn	.75	.23
❑ 368 Albert Belle	.75	.23
❑ 369 Jose Canseco	2.00	.60
❑ 370 Kevin Brown	.75	.23
❑ 371 Rafael Palmeiro	1.25	.35
❑ 372 Mark Redman	.50	.15
❑ 373 Larry Walker	1.25	.35
❑ 374 Greg Maddux	4.00	1.20
❑ 375 Nomar Garciaparra	4.00	1.20
❑ 376 Kevin Millwood	.75	.23
❑ 377 Edgar Martinez	1.25	.35
❑ 378 Sammy Sosa	3.00	.90
❑ 379 Tim Hudson	.75	.23
❑ 380 Jim Edmonds	.75	.23
❑ 381 Mike Piazza	3.00	.90
❑ 382 Brant Brown	.50	.15
❑ 383 Brad Fullmer	.75	.23
❑ 384 Alan Benes	.50	.15
❑ 385 Mickey Morandini	.50	.15
❑ 386 Troy Percival	.75	.23
❑ 387 Eddie Perez	.50	.15
❑ 388 Vernon Wells	.75	.23
❑ 389 Ricky Gutierrez	.50	.15
❑ 390 Rondell White	.75	.23
❑ 391 Kelvim Escobar	.50	.15
❑ 392 Tony Batista	.75	.23
❑ 393 Jimmy Haynes	.50	.15
❑ 394 Billy Wagner	.75	.23
❑ 395 A.J. Hinch	.50	.15
❑ 396 Matt Morris	.75	.23
❑ 397 Lance Berkman	.75	.23
❑ 398 Jeff D'Amico	.50	.15
❑ 399 Octavio Dotel	.50	.15
❑ 400 Olmedo Saenz	.50	.15
❑ 401 Esteban Loaiza	.75	.23
❑ 402 Adam Kennedy	.50	.15
❑ 403 Moises Alou	.75	.23
❑ 404 Orlando Palmeiro	.50	.15
❑ 405 Kevin Young	.50	.15
❑ 406 Tom Goodwin	.50	.15
❑ 407 Mac Suzuki	.75	.23
❑ 408 Pat Hentgen	.50	.15
❑ 409 Kevin Stocker	.50	.15
❑ 410 Mark Sweeney	.75	.23
❑ 411 Tony Eusebio	.50	.15
❑ 412 Edgar Renteria	.75	.23
❑ 413 John Rocker	.50	.15
❑ 414 Jose Lima	.50	.15
❑ 415 Kerry Wood	2.00	.60
❑ 416 Mike Timlin	.50	.15
❑ 417 Jose Hernandez	.50	.15
❑ 418 Jeremy Giambi	.50	.15
❑ 419 Luis Lopez	.50	.15
❑ 420 Mitch Meluskey	.50	.15
❑ 421 Garrett Stephenson	.50	.15
❑ 422 Jamey Wright	.50	.15
❑ 423 John Jaha	.50	.15
❑ 424 Placido Polanco	.50	.15
❑ 425 Marty Cordova	.50	.15
❑ 426 Joey Hamilton	.50	.15
❑ 427 Travis Fryman	.75	.23
❑ 428 Mike Cameron	.75	.23
❑ 429 Matt Mantei	.50	.15
❑ 430 Chan Ho Park	.75	.23
❑ 431 Shawn Estes	.50	.15
❑ 432 Danny Bautista	.50	.15
❑ 433 Wilson Alvarez	.50	.15
❑ 434 Kenny Lofton	.75	.23
❑ 435 Russ Ortiz	.75	.23
❑ 436 Dave Burba	.50	.15
❑ 437 Felix Martinez	.50	.15
❑ 438 Jeff Shaw	.50	.15
❑ 439 Mike DiFelice	.50	.15
❑ 440 Roberto Hernandez	.50	.15
❑ 441 Bryan Rekar	.50	.15
❑ 442 Ugueth Urbina	.50	.15
❑ 443 Vinny Castilla	.75	.23
❑ 444 Carlos Perez	.50	.15
❑ 445 Juan Guzman	.50	.15
❑ 446 Ryan Rupe	.50	.15
❑ 447 Mike Mordecai	.50	.15
❑ 448 Ricardo Rincon	.50	.15
❑ 449 Curt Schilling	1.25	.35
❑ 450 Alex Cora	.50	.15
❑ 451 Turner Ward	.50	.15
❑ 452 Omar Vizquel	.75	.23
❑ 453 Russ Branyan	.50	.15
❑ 454 Russ Johnson	.50	.15
❑ 455 Greg Colbrunn	.50	.15
❑ 456 Charles Nagy	.50	.15
❑ 457 Wil Cordero	.50	.15
❑ 458 Jason Tyner	.50	.15
❑ 459 Devon White	.50	.15
❑ 460 Kelly Stinnett	.50	.15
❑ 461 Wilton Guerrero	.50	.15
❑ 462 Jason Bere	.50	.15
❑ 463 Calvin Murray	.50	.15

❑ 464 Miguel Batista .50 .15
❑ 466 Luis Gonzalez .75 .23
❑ 467 Jaret Wright .50 .15
❑ 468 Chad Kreuter .50 .15
❑ 469 Armando Benitez .75 .23
❑ 470 Erubiel Durazo .75 .23
❑ 470 Sidney Ponson .50 .15
❑ 471 Adrian Brown .50 .15
❑ 472 Sterling Hitchcock .50 .15
❑ 473 Timo Perez .50 .15
❑ 474 Jamie Moyer .75 .23
❑ 475 Delino DeShields .50 .15
❑ 476 Glendon Rusch .50 .15
❑ 477 Chris Gomez .50 .15
❑ 478 Adam Eaton .50 .15
❑ 479 Pablo Ozuna .50 .15
❑ 480 Bob Abreu .75 .23
❑ 481 Kris Benson .50 .15
❑ 482 Keith Osik .50 .15
❑ 483 Darryl Hamilton .50 .15
❑ 484 Marlon Anderson .50 .15
❑ 485 Jimmy Anderson .50 .15
❑ 486 John Halama .50 .15
❑ 487 Nelson Figueroa .50 .15
❑ 488 Alex Gonzalez .50 .15
❑ 489 Benny Agbayani .50 .15
❑ 490 Ed Sprague .50 .15
❑ 491 Scott Erickson .50 .15
❑ 492 Doug Glanville .50 .15
❑ 493 Jesus Sanchez .50 .15
❑ 494 Mike Lieberthal .75 .23
❑ 495 Aaron Sele .50 .15
❑ 496 Pat Mahomes .50 .15
❑ 497 Ruben Rivera .50 .15
❑ 498 Wayne Gomes .50 .15
❑ 499 Freddy Garcia .75 .23
❑ 500 Al Martin .50 .15
❑ 501 Woody Williams .50 .15
❑ 502 Paul Byrd .50 .15
❑ 503 Rick White .50 .15
❑ 504 Trevor Hoffman .75 .23
❑ 505 Brady Anderson .75 .23
❑ 506 Robert Person .50 .15
❑ 507 Jeff Conine .75 .23
❑ 508 Chris Truby .50 .15
❑ 509 Emil Brown .50 .15
❑ 510 Ryan Dempster .50 .15
❑ 511 Ruben Mateo .50 .15
❑ 512 Alex Ochoa .50 .15
❑ 513 Jose Rosado .50 .15
❑ 514 Masato Yoshii .50 .15
❑ 515 Brian Daubach .50 .15
❑ 516 Jeff D'Amico .50 .15
❑ 517 Brent Mayne .50 .15
❑ 518 John Thomson .50 .15
❑ 519 Todd Ritchie .50 .15
❑ 520 John VanderWal .50 .15
❑ 521 Neifi Perez .50 .15
❑ 522 Chad Curtis .50 .15
❑ 523 Kenny Rogers .75 .23
❑ 524 Trot Nixon .75 .23
❑ 525 Sean Casey .75 .23
❑ 526 Wilton Veras .50 .15
❑ 527 Troy O'Leary .50 .15
❑ 528 Dante Bichette .75 .23
❑ 529 Jose Silva .50 .15
❑ 530 Darren Oliver .50 .15
❑ 531 Steve Parris .50 .15
❑ 532 David McCarty .50 .15
❑ 533 Todd Walker .75 .23
❑ 534 Brian Rose .50 .15
❑ 535 Pete Schourek .50 .15
❑ 536 Ricky Ledee .50 .15
❑ 537 Justin Thompson .50 .15
❑ 538 Benito Santiago .75 .23
❑ 539 Carlos Beltran .75 .23
❑ 540 Gabe White .50 .15
❑ 541 Bret Saberhagen .75 .23
❑ 542 Ramon Martinez .50 .15
❑ 543 John Valentin .50 .15
❑ 544 Frank Catalanotto .50 .15
❑ 545 Tim Wakefield .75 .23
❑ 546 Michael Tucker .50 .15
❑ 547 Juan Pierre .75 .23
❑ 548 Rich Garces .50 .15
❑ 549 Luis Ordaz .50 .15
❑ 550 Jerry Spradlin .50 .15
❑ 551 Corey Koskie .75 .23
❑ 552 Cal Eldred .50 .15
❑ 553 Alfonso Soriano 2.00 .60
❑ 554 Kip Wells .50 .15
❑ 555 Orlando Hernandez .75 .23
❑ 556 Bill Simas .50 .15
❑ 557 Jim Parque .50 .15
❑ 558 Joe Mays .50 .15
❑ 559 Tim Belcher .50 .15
❑ 560 Shane Spencer .50 .15
❑ 561 Glenallen Hill .50 .15
❑ 562 Matt LeCroy .50 .15
❑ 563 Tino Martinez 1.25 .35
❑ 564 Eric Milton .50 .15
❑ 565 Ron Coomer .50 .15
❑ 566 Cristian Guzman .75 .23
❑ 567 Kazuhiro Sasaki .75 .23
❑ 568 Mark Quinn .50 .15
❑ 569 Eric Gagne 1.25 .35
❑ 570 Kerry Ligtenberg .50 .15
❑ 571 Rolando Arrojo .50 .15
❑ 572 Jon Lieber .50 .15
❑ 573 Jose Vizcaino .50 .15
❑ 574 Jeff Abbott .50 .15
❑ 575 Carlos Hernandez .50 .15
❑ 576 Scott Sullivan .50 .15
❑ 577 Matt Stairs .50 .15
❑ 578 Tom Lampkin .50 .15
❑ 579 Donnie Sadler .50 .15
❑ 580 Desi Relaford .50 .15
❑ 581 Scott Downs .50 .15
❑ 582 Mike Mussina 2.00 .60
❑ 583 Ramon Ortiz .50 .15
❑ 584 Mike Myers .50 .15
❑ 585 Frank Castillo .50 .15
❑ 586 Manny Ramirez .75 .23
❑ 587 Alex Rodriguez 4.00 1.20
❑ 588 Andy Ashby .50 .15
❑ 589 Felipe Crespo .50 .15
❑ 590 Bobby Bonilla .75 .23
❑ 591 Denny Neagle .50 .15
❑ 592 Dave Martinez .50 .15
❑ 593 Mike Hampton .75 .23
❑ 594 Gary DiSarcina .50 .15
❑ 595 Tsuyoshi Shinjo RC 4.00 1.20
❑ 596 Albert Pujols RC 50.00 15.00
❑ 597 Roy Oswalt 2.00 .60
Pat Strange
Jon Rauch
❑ 598 Phil Wilson RC 5.00 1.50
Jake Peavy RC
Darwin Cubillan RC
❑ 599 Nathan Haynes 1.50 .45
Steve Smyth RC
Mike Bynum
❑ 600 Joe Lawrence 1.50 .45
Choo Freeman
Michael Cuddyer
❑ 601 Larry Barnes 1.00 .30
DeWayne Wise
Carlos Pena
❑ 602 Feilpe Lopez 1.50 .45
Gookie Dawkins
Eric Almonte RC
❑ 603 Brad Wilkerson 1.00 .30
Alex Escobar
Eric Valent
❑ 604 Jeff Goldbach 1.00 .30
Toby Hall
Rod Barajas
❑ 605 Marcus Giles 1.50 .45
Pablo Ozuna
Jason Romano
❑ 606 Vernon Wells 1.50 .45
Jack Cust
Dee Brown
❑ 607 Luis Montanez RC 1.50 .45
David Espinosa
❑ 608 Anthony Pluta RC 2.00 .60
Justin Wayne RC
❑ 609 Josh Axelson RC 1.50 .45
Carmen Cali RC
❑ 610 Shaun Boyd RC 1.50 .45
Chris Morris RC
❑ 611 Dan Moylan RC 1.50 .45
Tommy Arko RC
❑ 612 Luis Cotto RC 1.50 .45
Luis Escobar
❑ 613 Blake Williams RC 1.50 .45
Brandon Mims RC
❑ 614 Chris Russ RC 1.50 .45
Bryan Edwards
❑ 615 Joe Torres 1.00 .30
Ben Diggins
❑ 616 Hugh Quattlebaum RC 2.00 .60
Edwin Encarnacion RC
❑ 617 Brian Bass RC 1.50 .45
Odannis Ayala RC
❑ 618 Jason Kaanoi 1.00 .30
Michael Matthews RC UER
name misspelled Mathews
❑ 619 Stuart McFarland RC 1.50 .45
Adam Sterrett RC
❑ 620 David Krynzel 3.00 .90
Grady Sizemore
❑ 621 Keith Bucktrot 1.00 .30
Dane Sardinha
❑ 622 Anaheim Angels TC .75 .23
❑ 623 Ariz. Diamondbacks TC .75 .23
❑ 624 Atlanta Braves TC .75 .23
❑ 625 Baltimore Orioles TC .75 .23
❑ 626 Boston Red Sox TC .75 .23
❑ 627 Chicago Cubs TC .75 .23
❑ 628 Chicago White Sox TC .75 .23
❑ 629 Cincinnati Reds TC .75 .23
❑ 630 Cleveland Indians TC .75 .23
❑ 631 Colorado Rockies TC .75 .23
❑ 632 Detroit Tigers TC .75 .23
❑ 633 Florida Marlins TC .75 .23
❑ 634 Houston Astros TC .75 .23
❑ 635 K.C. Royals TC .75 .23
❑ 636 L.A. Dodgers TC .75 .23
❑ 637 Milw. Brewers TC .75 .23
❑ 638 Minnesota Twins TC .75 .23
❑ 639 Montreal Expos TC .75 .23
❑ 640 New York Mets TC .75 .23
❑ 641 New York Yankees TC 4.00 1.20
❑ 642 Oakland Athletics TC .75 .23
❑ 643 Phil. Phillies TC .75 .23
❑ 644 Pittsburgh Pirates TC .75 .23
❑ 645 San Diego Padres TC .75 .23
❑ 646 S.F. Giants TC .75 .23
❑ 647 Seattle Mariners TC .75 .23
❑ 648 St. Louis Cardinals TC .75 .23
❑ 649 T. Bay Devil Rays TC .75 .23
❑ 650 Texas Rangers TC .75 .23
❑ 651 Toronto Blue Jays TC .75 .23
❑ 652 Bucky Dent GM .50 .15
❑ 653 Jackie Robinson GM 2.00 .60
❑ 654 Roberto Clemente GM 2.50 .75
❑ 655 Nolan Ryan GM 4.00 1.20
❑ 656 Kerry Wood GM 1.25 .35
❑ 657 Rickey Henderson GM 2.00 .60
❑ 658 Lou Brock GM 1.25 .35
❑ 659 David Wells GM .50 .15
❑ 660 Andruw Jones GM .75 .23
❑ 661 Carlton Fisk GM .75 .23

2001 Topps Chrome Traded

	Nm-Mt	Ex-Mt
COMPLETE SET (266)	120.00	36.00

Card	Price	Price
COMMON (1-99/145-266)	.75	.23
COMMON (100-144)	1.25	.35
❑ T1 Sandy Alomar Jr.	.75	.23
❑ T2 Kevin Appier	1.25	.35
❑ T3 Brad Ausmus	.75	.23
❑ T4 Derek Bell	.75	.23
❑ T5 Bret Boone	1.25	.35
❑ T6 Rico Brogna	.75	.23
❑ T7 Ellis Burks	1.25	.35
❑ T8 Ken Caminiti	1.25	.35
❑ T9 Roger Cedeno	.75	.23
❑ T10 Royce Clayton	.75	.23
❑ T11 Enrique Wilson	.75	.23
❑ T12 Rheal Cormier	.75	.23
❑ T13 Eric Davis	1.25	.35
❑ T14 Shawon Dunston	.75	.23
❑ T15 Andres Galarraga	1.25	.35
❑ T16 Tom Gordon	.75	.23
❑ T17 Mark Grace	3.00	.90
❑ T18 Jeffrey Hammonds	.75	.23
❑ T19 Dustin Hermanson	.75	.23
❑ T20 Quinton McCracken	.75	.23
❑ T21 Todd Hundley	.75	.23
❑ T22 Charles Johnson	1.25	.35
❑ T23 Marquis Grissom	.75	.23
❑ T24 Jose Mesa	.75	.23
❑ T25 Brian Boehringer	.75	.23
❑ T26 John Rocker	.75	.23
❑ T27 Jeff Frye	.75	.23
❑ T28 Reggie Sanders	1.25	.35
❑ T29 David Segui	.75	.23
❑ T30 Mike Sirotka	.75	.23
❑ T31 Fernando Tatis	.75	.23
❑ T32 Steve Trachsel	.75	.23
❑ T33 Ismael Valdes	.75	.23
❑ T34 Randy Velarde	.75	.23
❑ T35 Ryan Kohlmeier	.75	.23
❑ T36 Mike Bordick	1.25	.35
❑ T37 Kent Bottenfield	.75	.23
❑ T38 Pat Rapp	.75	.23
❑ T39 Jeff Nelson	.75	.23
❑ T40 Ricky Bottalico	.75	.23
❑ T41 Luke Prokopec	.75	.23
❑ T42 Hideo Nomo	3.00	.90
❑ T43 Bill Mueller	1.25	.35
❑ T44 Roberto Kelly	.75	.23
❑ T45 Chris Holt	.75	.23
❑ T46 Mike Jackson	.75	.23
❑ T47 Devon White	.75	.23
❑ T48 Gerald Williams	.75	.23
❑ T49 Eddie Taubensee	.75	.23
❑ T50 Brian Hunter UER	.75	.23
Brian R Hunter pictured		
Brian L Hunter stats		
❑ T51 Nelson Cruz	.75	.23
❑ T52 Jeff Fassero	.75	.23
❑ T53 Bubba Trammell	.75	.23
❑ T54 Bo Porter	.75	.23
❑ T55 Greg Norton	.75	.23
❑ T56 Benito Santiago	1.25	.35
❑ T57 Ruben Rivera	.75	.23
❑ T58 Dee Brown	.75	.23
❑ T59 Jose Canseco	3.00	.90
❑ T60 Chris Michalak	.75	.23
❑ T61 Tim Worrell	.75	.23
❑ T62 Matt Clement	.75	.23
❑ T63 Bill Pulsipher	.75	.23
❑ T64 Troy Brohawn RC	1.00	.30
❑ T65 Mark Kotsay	.75	.23
❑ T66 Jimmy Rollins	1.25	.35
❑ T67 Shea Hillenbrand	1.25	.35
❑ T68 Ted Lilly	.75	.23
❑ T69 Jermaine Dye	1.25	.35
❑ T70 Jerry Hairston Jr.	.75	.23
❑ T71 John Mabry	.75	.23
❑ T72 Kurt Abbott	.75	.23
❑ T73 Eric Owens	.75	.23
❑ T74 Jeff Brantley	.75	.23
❑ T75 Roy Oswalt	2.00	.60
❑ T76 Doug Mientkiewicz	1.25	.35
❑ T77 Rickey Henderson	5.00	1.50
❑ T78 Jason Grimsley	.75	.23
❑ T79 Christian Parker RC	1.00	.30
❑ T80 Donne Wall	.75	.23
❑ T81 Alex Arias	.75	.23
❑ T82 Willis Roberts	.75	.23
❑ T83 Ryan Minor	.75	.23
❑ T84 Jason LaRue	.75	.23
❑ T85 Ruben Sierra	.75	.23
❑ T86 Johnny Damon	1.25	.35
❑ T87 Juan Gonzalez	3.00	.90
❑ T88 C.C. Sabathia	1.25	.35
❑ T89 Tony Batista	1.25	.35
❑ T90 Jay Witasick	.75	.23
❑ T91 Brent Abernathy	.75	.23
❑ T92 Paul LoDuca	1.25	.35
❑ T93 Wes Helms	.75	.23
❑ T94 Mark Wohlers	.75	.23
❑ T95 Rob Bell	.75	.23
❑ T96 Tim Redding	.75	.23
❑ T97 Bud Smith RC	1.00	.30
❑ T98 Adam Dunn	2.00	.60
❑ T99 Ichiro Suzuki	15.00	4.50
Albert Pujols ROY		
❑ T100 Carlton Fisk 81	2.00	.60
❑ T101 Tim Raines 81	1.25	.35
❑ T102 Juan Marichal 74	1.25	.35
❑ T103 Dave Winfield 81	2.00	.60
❑ T104 Reggie Jackson 82	2.00	.60
❑ T105 Cal Ripken 82	10.00	3.00
❑ T106 Ozzie Smith 82	3.00	.90
❑ T107 Tom Seaver 83	3.00	.90
❑ T108 Lou Piniella 74	1.25	.35
❑ T109 Dwight Gooden 84	2.00	.60
❑ T110 Bret Saberhagen 84	1.25	.35
❑ T111 Gary Carter 85	1.25	.35
❑ T112 Jack Clark 85	1.25	.35
❑ T113 Rickey Henderson 85	5.00	1.50
❑ T114 Barry Bonds 86	8.00	2.40
❑ T115 Bobby Bonilla 86	1.25	.35
❑ T116 Jose Canseco 86	3.00	.90
❑ T117 Will Clark 86	3.00	.90
❑ T118 Andres Galarraga 86	1.25	.35
❑ T119 Bo Jackson 86	3.00	.90
❑ T120 Wally Joyner 86	1.25	.35
❑ T121 Ellis Burks 87	1.25	.35
❑ T122 David Cone 87	1.25	.35
❑ T123 Greg Maddux 87	6.00	1.80
❑ T124 Willie Randolph 76	1.25	.35
❑ T125 Dennis Eckersley 87	1.25	.35
❑ T126 Matt Williams 87	1.25	.35
❑ T127 Joe Morgan 81	1.25	.35
❑ T128 Fred McGriff 87	2.00	.60
❑ T129 Roberto Alomar 88	3.00	.90
❑ T130 Lee Smith 88	1.25	.35
❑ T131 David Wells 88	1.25	.35
❑ T132 Ken Griffey Jr. 89	5.00	1.50
❑ T133 Deion Sanders 89	1.25	.35
❑ T134 Nolan Ryan 89	10.00	3.00
❑ T135 David Justice 90	1.25	.35
❑ T136 Joe Carter 91	1.25	.35
❑ T137 Jack Morris 92	1.25	.35
❑ T138 Mike Piazza 93	5.00	1.50
❑ T139 Barry Bonds 93	8.00	2.40
❑ T140 Terrence Long 94	1.25	.35
❑ T141 Ben Grieve 94	1.25	.35
❑ T142 Richie Sexson 95	1.25	.35
George Arias		
Mark Sweeney		
Brian Schneider		
❑ T143 Sean Burroughs 99	1.25	.35
❑ T144 Alfonso Soriano 99	3.00	.90
❑ T145 Bob Boone MG	1.25	.35
❑ T146 Larry Bowa MG	1.25	.35
❑ T147 Bob Brenly MG	.75	.23
❑ T148 Buck Martinez MG	.75	.23
❑ T149 L. McClendon MG	.75	.23
❑ T150 Jim Tracy MG	.75	.23
❑ T151 Jared Abruzzo RC	1.00	.30
❑ T152 Kurt Ainsworth	.75	.23
❑ T153 Willie Bloomquist	1.25	.35
❑ T154 Ben Broussard	.75	.23
❑ T155 Bobby Bradley	.75	.23
❑ T156 Mike Bynum	.75	.23
❑ T157 A.J. Hinch	.75	.23
❑ T158 Ryan Christianson	.75	.23
❑ T159 Carlos Silva	.75	.23
❑ T160 Joe Crede	.75	.23
❑ T161 Jack Cust	.75	.23
❑ T162 Ben Diggins	.75	.23
❑ T163 Phil Dumatrait	.75	.23
❑ T164 Alex Escobar	.75	.23
❑ T165 Miguel Olivo	.75	.23
❑ T166 Chris George	.75	.23
❑ T167 Marcus Giles	1.25	.35
❑ T168 Keith Ginter	.75	.23
❑ T169 Josh Girdley	.75	.23
❑ T170 Tony Alvarez	.75	.23
❑ T171 Scott Seabol	.75	.23
❑ T172 Josh Hamilton	1.25	.35
❑ T173 Jason Hart	.75	.23
❑ T174 Israel Alcantara	.75	.23
❑ T175 Jake Peavy	4.00	1.20
❑ T176 Stubby Clapp RC	1.00	.30
❑ T177 D'Angelo Jimenez	.75	.23
❑ T178 Nick Johnson	1.25	.35
❑ T179 Ben Johnson	.75	.23
❑ T180 Larry Bigbie	.75	.23
❑ T181 Allen Levrault	.75	.23
❑ T182 Felipe Lopez	.75	.23
❑ T183 Sean Burnett	1.25	.35
❑ T184 Nick Neugebauer	.75	.23
❑ T185 Austin Kearns	2.00	.60
❑ T186 Corey Patterson	1.25	.35
❑ T187 Carlos Pena	.75	.23
❑ T188 R. Rodriguez RC	1.00	.30
❑ T189 Juan Rivera	1.25	.35
❑ T190 Grant Roberts	.75	.23
❑ T191 Adam Pettyjohn RC	1.00	.30
❑ T192 Jared Sandberg	.75	.23
❑ T193 Xavier Nady	1.25	.35
❑ T194 Dane Sardinha	.75	.23
❑ T195 Shawn Sonnier	.75	.23
❑ T196 Rafael Soriano	4.00	1.20
❑ T197 Brian Specht RC	1.00	.30
❑ T198 Aaron Myette	.75	.23
❑ T199 Juan Uribe RC	1.00	.30
❑ T200 Jayson Werth	.75	.23
❑ T201 Brad Wilkerson	.75	.23
❑ T202 Horacio Estrada	.75	.23
❑ T203 Joel Pineiro	3.00	.90
❑ T204 Matt LeCroy	.75	.23
❑ T205 Michael Coleman	.75	.23
❑ T206 Ben Sheets	1.25	.35
❑ T207 Eric Byrnes	.75	.23
❑ T208 Sean Burroughs	1.25	.35
❑ T209 Ken Harvey	.75	.23
❑ T210 Travis Hafner	3.00	.90
❑ T211 Erick Almonte	1.00	.30
❑ T212 Jason Belcher RC	1.00	.30
❑ T213 Wilson Betemit RC	1.00	.30
❑ T214 Hank Blalock RC	15.00	4.50
❑ T215 Danny Borrell	1.00	.30
❑ T216 John Buck RC	2.00	.60
❑ T217 Freddie Bynum RC	1.00	.30
❑ T218 Noel Devarez RC	1.00	.30
❑ T219 Juan Diaz RC	1.00	.30
❑ T220 Felix Diaz RC	1.00	.30
❑ T221 Josh Fogg RC	1.00	.30
❑ T222 Matt Ford RC	1.00	.30
❑ T223 Scott Heard	.75	.23
❑ T224 Ben Hendrickson RC	1.00	.30
❑ T225 Cody Ross RC	1.00	.30
❑ T226 A. Hernandez RC	1.00	.30
❑ T227 Alfredo Amezaga RC	2.00	.60
❑ T228 Bob Keppel RC	1.00	.30
❑ T229 Ryan Madson RC	2.00	.60
❑ T230 Octavio Martinez RC	1.00	.30
❑ T231 Hee Seop Choi	10.00	3.00
❑ T232 Thomas Mitchell	.75	.23
❑ T233 Luis Montanez	1.00	.30
❑ T234 Andy Morales RC	1.00	.30
❑ T235 Justin Morneau RC	10.00	3.00
❑ T236 Toe Nash RC	1.00	.30
❑ T237 V. Pascucci RC	1.00	.30
❑ T238 Roy Smith RC	1.00	.30
❑ T239 Antonio Perez RC	1.00	.30
❑ T240 Chad Petty RC	1.00	.30
❑ T241 Steve Smyth	1.00	.30
❑ T242 Jose Reyes RC	15.00	4.50
❑ T243 Eric Reynolds RC	1.00	.30
❑ T244 Dominic Rich	1.00	.30
❑ T245 J. Richardson RC	1.00	.30
❑ T246 Ed Rogers RC	1.00	.30
❑ T247 Albert Pujols	40.00	12.00
❑ T248 Esix Snead RC	1.00	.30
❑ T249 Luis Torres RC	1.00	.30

Card	Nm-Mt	Ex-Mt
❑ T250 Matt White RC	1.00	.30
❑ T251 Blake Williams	1.00	.30
❑ T252 Chris Russ	1.00	.30
❑ T253 Joe Kennedy RC	1.00	.30
❑ T254 Jeff Randazzo RC	1.00	.30
❑ T255 Beau Hale RC	1.00	.30
❑ T256 Brad Hennessey RC	1.00	.30
❑ T257 Jake Gautreau RC	1.00	.30
❑ T258 Jeff Mathis RC	6.00	1.80
❑ T259 Aaron Heilman RC	3.00	.90
❑ T260 B. Sardinha RC	2.00	.60
❑ T261 Irvin Guzman RC	5.00	1.50
❑ T262 Gabe Gross RC	2.00	.60
❑ T263 J.D. Martin RC	1.00	.30
❑ T264 Chris Smith RC	1.00	.30
❑ T265 Kenny Baugh RC	1.00	.30
❑ T266 Ichiro Suzuki RC	25.00	7.50

2002 Topps Chrome

	Nm-Mt	Ex-Mt
COMPLETE SET (660)	300.00	90.00
COMPLETE SERIES 1 (330)	150.00	45.00
COMPLETE SERIES 2 (330)	150.00	45.00
COMMON (1-331/366-695)	.50	.15
COMMON (307-326/671-690)	1.50	.45
COMMON (327-331/691-695)	1.50	.45

Card	Nm-Mt	Ex-Mt
❑ 1 Pedro Martinez	2.50	.75
❑ 2 Mike Stanton	.50	.15
❑ 3 Brad Penny	.50	.15
❑ 4 Mike Matheny	.50	.15
❑ 5 Johnny Damon	1.00	.30
❑ 6 Bret Boone	1.00	.30
❑ 7 Does Not Exist		
❑ 8 Chris Truby	.50	.15
❑ 9 B.J. Surhoff	1.00	.30
❑ 10 Mike Hampton	1.00	.30
❑ 11 Juan Pierre	1.00	.30
❑ 12 Mark Buehrle	1.00	.30
❑ 13 Bob Abreu	1.00	.30
❑ 14 David Cone	1.00	.30
❑ 15 Aaron Sele	.50	.15
❑ 16 Fernando Tatis	.50	.15
❑ 17 Bobby Jones	.50	.15
❑ 18 Rick Helling	.50	.15
❑ 19 Dmitri Young	1.00	.30
❑ 20 Mike Mussina	2.50	.75
❑ 21 Mike Sweeney	1.00	.30
❑ 22 Cristian Guzman	1.00	.30
❑ 23 Ryan Kohlmeier	.50	.15
❑ 24 Adam Kennedy	.50	.15
❑ 25 Larry Walker	1.50	.45
❑ 26 Eric Davis	1.00	.30
❑ 27 Jason Tyner	.50	.15
❑ 28 Eric Young	.50	.15
❑ 29 Jason Marquis	.50	.15
❑ 30 Luis Gonzalez	1.00	.30
❑ 31 Kevin Tapani	.50	.15
❑ 32 Orlando Cabrera	.50	.15
❑ 33 Marty Cordova	.50	.15
❑ 34 Brad Ausmus	.50	.15
❑ 35 Livan Hernandez	.50	.15
❑ 36 Alex Gonzalez	.50	.15
❑ 37 Edgar Renteria	1.00	.30
❑ 38 Bengie Molina	.50	.15
❑ 39 Frank Menechino	.50	.15
❑ 40 Rafael Palmeiro	1.50	.45
❑ 41 Brad Fullmer	1.00	.30
❑ 42 Julio Zuleta	.50	.15
❑ 43 Darren Dreifort	.50	.15
❑ 44 Trot Nixon	1.00	.30
❑ 45 Trevor Hoffman	1.00	.30
❑ 46 Vladimir Nunez	.50	.15
❑ 47 Mark Kotsay	.50	.15
❑ 48 Kenny Rogers	1.00	.30
❑ 49 Ben Petrick	.50	.15
❑ 50 Jeff Bagwell	1.50	.45
❑ 51 Juan Encarnacion	.50	.15
❑ 52 Ramiro Mendoza	.50	.15
❑ 53 Brian Meadows	.50	.15
❑ 54 Chad Curtis	.50	.15
❑ 55 Aramis Ramirez	1.00	.30
❑ 56 Mark McLemore	.50	.15
❑ 57 Dante Bichette	1.00	.30
❑ 58 Scott Schoeneweis	.50	.15
❑ 59 Jose Cruz Jr.	1.00	.30
❑ 60 Roger Clemens	5.00	1.50
❑ 61 Jose Guillen	.50	.15
❑ 62 Darren Oliver	.50	.15
❑ 63 Chris Reitsma	.50	.15
❑ 64 Jeff Abbott	.50	.15
❑ 65 Robin Ventura	1.00	.30
❑ 66 Denny Neagle	.50	.15
❑ 67 Al Martin	.50	.15
❑ 68 Benito Santiago	1.00	.30
❑ 69 Roy Oswalt	1.00	.30
❑ 70 Juan Gonzalez	2.50	.75
❑ 71 Garret Anderson	1.00	.30
❑ 72 Bobby Bonilla	1.00	.30
❑ 73 Danny Bautista	.50	.15
❑ 74 J.T. Snow	1.00	.30
❑ 75 Derek Jeter	6.00	1.80
❑ 76 John Olerud	1.00	.30
❑ 77 Kevin Appier	1.00	.30
❑ 78 Phil Nevin	1.00	.30
❑ 79 Sean Casey	1.00	.30
❑ 80 Troy Glaus	1.50	.45
❑ 81 Joe Randa	.50	.15
❑ 82 Jose Valentin	.50	.15
❑ 83 Ricky Bottalico	.50	.15
❑ 84 Todd Zeile	1.00	.30
❑ 85 Barry Larkin	2.50	.75
❑ 86 Bob Wickman	.50	.15
❑ 87 Jeff Shaw	.50	.15
❑ 88 Greg Vaughn	1.00	.30
❑ 89 Fernando Vina	1.00	.30
❑ 90 Mark Mulder	1.00	.30
❑ 91 Paul Bako	.50	.15
❑ 92 Aaron Boone	1.00	.30
❑ 93 Esteban Loaiza	1.00	.30
❑ 94 Richie Sexson	1.00	.30
❑ 95 Alfonso Soriano	2.50	.75
❑ 96 Tony Womack	.50	.15
❑ 97 Paul Shuey	.50	.15
❑ 98 Melvin Mora	.50	.15
❑ 99 Tony Gwynn	3.00	.90
❑ 100 Vladimir Guerrero	2.50	.75
❑ 101 Keith Osik	.50	.15
❑ 102 Bud Smith	.50	.15
❑ 103 Scott Williamson	.50	.15
❑ 104 Daryle Ward	.50	.15
❑ 105 Doug Mientkiewicz	1.00	.30
❑ 106 Stan Javier	.50	.15
❑ 107 Russ Ortiz	1.00	.30
❑ 108 Wade Miller	1.00	.30
❑ 109 Luke Prokopec	.50	.15
❑ 110 Andruw Jones	1.50	.45
❑ 111 Ron Coomer	.50	.15
❑ 112 Dan Wilson	.50	.15
❑ 113 Luis Castillo	1.00	.30
❑ 114 Derek Bell	.50	.15
❑ 115 Gary Sheffield	1.00	.30
❑ 116 Ruben Rivera	.50	.15
❑ 117 Paul O'Neill	1.50	.45
❑ 118 Craig Paquette	.50	.15
❑ 119 Kelvim Escobar	.50	.15
❑ 120 Brad Radke	1.00	.30
❑ 121 Jorge Fabregas	.50	.15
❑ 122 Randy Winn	.50	.15
❑ 123 Tom Goodwin	.50	.15
❑ 124 Jaret Wright	.50	.15
❑ 125 Barry Bonds HR 73	40.00	12.00
❑ 126 Al Leiter	.50	.15
❑ 127 Ben Davis	.50	.15
❑ 128 Frank Catalanotto	.50	.15
❑ 129 Jose Cabrera	.50	.15
❑ 130 Magglio Ordonez	1.00	.30
❑ 131 Jose Macias	.50	.15
❑ 132 Ted Lilly	.50	.15
❑ 133 Chris Holt	.50	.15
❑ 134 Eric Milton	.50	.15
❑ 135 Shannon Stewart	1.00	.30
❑ 136 Omar Olivares	.50	.15
❑ 137 David Segui	.50	.15
❑ 138 Jeff Nelson	.50	.15
❑ 139 Matt Williams	1.00	.30
❑ 140 Ellis Burks	1.00	.30
❑ 141 Jason Bere	.50	.15
❑ 142 Jimmy Haynes	.50	.15
❑ 143 Ramon Hernandez	.50	.15
❑ 144 Craig Counsell	.50	.15
❑ 145 John Smoltz	1.50	.45
❑ 146 Homer Bush	.50	.15
❑ 147 Quilvio Veras	.50	.15
❑ 148 Esteban Yan	.50	.15
❑ 149 Ramon Ortiz	.50	.15
❑ 150 Carlos Delgado	1.00	.30
❑ 151 Lee Stevens	.50	.15
❑ 152 Wil Cordero	.50	.15
❑ 153 Mike Bordick	1.00	.30
❑ 154 John Flaherty	.50	.15
❑ 155 Omar Daal	.50	.15
❑ 156 Todd Ritchie	.50	.15
❑ 157 Carl Everett	1.00	.30
❑ 158 Scott Sullivan	.50	.15
❑ 159 Deivi Cruz	.50	.15
❑ 160 Albert Pujols	5.00	1.50
❑ 161 Royce Clayton	.50	.15
❑ 162 Jeff Suppan	.50	.15
❑ 163 C.C. Sabathia	1.00	.30
❑ 164 Jimmy Rollins	1.00	.30
❑ 165 Rickey Henderson	4.00	1.20
❑ 166 Rey Ordonez	.50	.15
❑ 167 Shawn Estes	.50	.15
❑ 168 Reggie Sanders	1.00	.30
❑ 169 Jon Lieber	.50	.15
❑ 170 Armando Benitez	1.00	.30
❑ 171 Mike Remlinger	.50	.15
❑ 172 Billy Wagner	1.00	.30
❑ 173 Troy Percival	1.00	.30
❑ 174 Devon White	.50	.15
❑ 175 Ivan Rodriguez	2.50	.75
❑ 176 Dustin Hermanson	.50	.15
❑ 177 Brian Anderson	.50	.15
❑ 178 Graeme Lloyd	.50	.15
❑ 179 Russell Branyan	.50	.15
❑ 180 Bobby Higginson	1.00	.30
❑ 181 Alex Gonzalez	.50	.15
❑ 182 John Franco	1.00	.30
❑ 183 Sidney Ponson	.50	.15
❑ 184 Jose Mesa	.50	.15
❑ 185 Todd Hollandsworth	.50	.15
❑ 186 Kevin Young	.50	.15
❑ 187 Tim Wakefield	1.00	.30
❑ 188 Craig Biggio	1.50	.45
❑ 189 Jason Isringhausen	1.00	.30
❑ 190 Mark Quinn	.50	.15
❑ 191 Glendon Rusch	.50	.15
❑ 192 Damian Miller	.50	.15
❑ 193 Sandy Alomar Jr.	.50	.15
❑ 194 Scott Brosius	1.00	.30
❑ 195 Dave Martinez	.50	.15
❑ 196 Danny Graves	.50	.15
❑ 197 Shea Hillenbrand	1.00	.30
❑ 198 Jimmy Anderson	.50	.15
❑ 199 Travis Lee	.50	.15
❑ 200 Randy Johnson	2.50	.75
❑ 201 Carlos Beltran	1.00	.30
❑ 202 Jerry Hairston	.50	.15
❑ 203 Jesus Sanchez	.50	.15
❑ 204 Eddie Taubensee	.50	.15
❑ 205 David Wells	1.00	.30
❑ 206 Russ Davis	.50	.15
❑ 207 Michael Barrett	.50	.15
❑ 208 Marquis Grissom	.50	.15
❑ 209 Byung-Hyun Kim	1.00	.30
❑ 210 Hideo Nomo	2.50	.75
❑ 211 Ryan Rupe	.50	.15
❑ 212 Ricky Gutierrez	.50	.15

	No.	Player		
❑	213	Darryl Kile	1.00	.30
❑	214	Rico Brogna	.50	.15
❑	215	Terrence Long	1.00	.30
❑	216	Mike Jackson	.50	.15
❑	217	Jamey Wright	.50	.15
❑	218	Adrian Beltre	1.00	.30
❑	219	Benny Agbayani	.50	.15
❑	220	Chuck Knoblauch	1.00	.30
❑	221	Randy Wolf	1.00	.30
❑	222	Andy Ashby	.50	.15
❑	223	Corey Koskie	1.00	.30
❑	224	Roger Cedeno	.50	.15
❑	225	Ichiro Suzuki	5.00	1.50
❑	226	Keith Foulke	.50	.15
❑	227	Ryan Minor	.50	.15
❑	228	Shawon Dunston	.50	.15
❑	229	Alex Cora	.50	.15
❑	230	Jeromy Burnitz	1.00	.30
❑	231	Mark Grace	2.50	.75
❑	232	Aubrey Huff	1.00	.30
❑	233	Jeffrey Hammonds	.50	.15
❑	234	Olmedo Saenz	.50	.15
❑	235	Brian Jordan	1.00	.30
❑	236	Jeremy Giambi	.50	.15
❑	237	Joe Girardi	.50	.15
❑	238	Eric Gagne	1.50	.45
❑	239	Masato Yoshii	.50	.15
❑	240	Greg Maddux	5.00	1.50
❑	241	Bryan Rekar	.50	.15
❑	242	Ray Durham	1.00	.30
❑	243	Torii Hunter	1.00	.30
❑	244	Derrek Lee	1.00	.30
❑	245	Jim Edmonds	1.00	.30
❑	246	Einar Diaz	.50	.15
❑	247	Brian Bohanon	.50	.15
❑	248	Ron Belliard	.50	.15
❑	249	Mike Lowell	1.00	.30
❑	250	Sammy Sosa	4.00	1.20
❑	251	Richard Hidalgo	1.00	.30
❑	252	Bartolo Colon	1.00	.30
❑	253	Jorge Posada	1.50	.45
❑	254	Latroy Hawkins	.50	.15
❑	255	Paul LoDuca	1.00	.30
❑	256	Carlos Febles	.50	.15
❑	257	Nelson Cruz	.50	.15
❑	258	Edgardo Alfonzo	1.00	.30
❑	259	Joey Hamilton	.50	.15
❑	260	Cliff Floyd	1.00	.30
❑	261	Wes Helms	.50	.15
❑	262	Jay Bell	1.00	.30
❑	263	Mike Cameron	1.00	.30
❑	264	Paul Konerko	1.00	.30
❑	265	Jeff Kent	1.00	.30
❑	266	Robert Fick	1.00	.30
❑	267	Allen Levrault	.50	.15
❑	268	Placido Polanco	.50	.15
❑	269	Marlon Anderson	.50	.15
❑	270	Mariano Rivera	1.50	.45
❑	271	Chan Ho Park	1.00	.30
❑	272	Jose Vizcaino	.50	.15
❑	273	Jeff D'Amico	.50	.15
❑	274	Mark Gardner	.50	.15
❑	275	Travis Fryman	1.00	.30
❑	276	Darren Lewis	.50	.15
❑	277	Bruce Bochy MG	.50	.15
❑	278	Jerry Manuel MG	.50	.15
❑	279	Bob Brenly MG	.50	.15
❑	280	Don Baylor MG	1.00	.30
❑	281	Davey Lopes MG	1.00	.30
❑	282	Jerry Narron MG	.50	.15
❑	283	Tony Muser MG	.50	.15
❑	284	Hal McRae MG	1.00	.30
❑	285	Bobby Cox MG	.50	.15
❑	286	Larry Dierker MG	.50	.15
❑	287	Phil Garner MG	.50	.15
❑	288	Joe Kerrigan MG	.50	.15
❑	289	Bobby Valentine MG	.50	.15
❑	290	Dusty Baker MG	1.00	.30
❑	291	Lloyd McClendon MG	.50	.15
❑	292	Mike Scioscia MG	.50	.15
❑	293	Buck Martinez MG	.50	.15
❑	294	Larry Bowa MG	1.00	.30
❑	295	Tony LaRussa MG	1.00	.30
❑	296	Jeff Torborg MG	.50	.15
❑	297	Tom Kelly MG	.50	.15
❑	298	Mike Hargrove MG	.50	.15
❑	299	Art Howe MG	.50	.15
❑	300	Lou Piniella MG	1.00	.30
❑	301	Charlie Manuel MG	.50	.15
❑	302	Buddy Bell MG	1.00	.30
❑	303	Tony Perez MG	1.00	.30
❑	304	Bob Boone MG	1.00	.30
❑	305	Joe Torre MG	2.50	.75
❑	306	Jim Tracy MG	.50	.15
❑	307	Jason Lane PROS	1.50	.45
❑	308	Chris George PROS	1.50	.45
❑	309	Hank Blalock PROS	4.00	1.20
❑	310	Joe Borchard PROS	1.50	.45
❑	311	Marlon Byrd PROS	1.50	.45
❑	312	Raymond Cabrera PROS RC	1.50	.45
❑	313	Freddy Sanchez PROS RC	4.00	1.20
❑	314	Scott Wiggins PROS RC	1.50	.45
❑	315	Jason Maule PROS RC	1.50	.45
❑	316	Dionys Cesar PROS RC	1.50	.45
❑	317	Boof Bonser PROS	1.50	.45
❑	318	Juan Tolentino PROS RC	1.50	.45
❑	319	Earl Snyder PROS RC	1.50	.45
❑	320	Travis Wade PROS RC	1.50	.45
❑	321	Napolean Calzado PROS RC	1.50	.45
❑	322	Eric Glaser PROS	1.50	.45
❑	323	Craig Kuzmic PROS RC	1.50	.45
❑	324	Nic Jackson PROS RC	2.50	.75
❑	325	Mike Rivera PROS	1.50	.45
❑	326	Jason Bay PROS RC	5.00	1.50
❑	327	Chris Smith DP	1.50	.45
❑	328	Jake Gautreau DP	1.50	.45
❑	329	Gabe Gross DP	1.50	.45
❑	330	Kenny Baugh DP	1.50	.45
❑	331	J.D. Martin DP	1.50	.45
❑	366	Pat Meares	.50	.15
❑	367	Mike Lieberthal	1.00	.30
❑	368	Larry Bigbie	.50	.15
❑	369	Ron Gant	1.00	.30
❑	370	Moises Alou	1.00	.30
❑	371	Chad Kreuter	.50	.15
❑	372	Willis Roberts	.50	.15
❑	373	Toby Hall	.50	.15
❑	374	Miguel Batista	.50	.15
❑	375	John Burkett	.50	.15
❑	376	Cory Lidle	.50	.15
❑	377	Nick Neugebauer	.50	.15
❑	378	Jay Payton	.50	.15
❑	379	Steve Karsay	.50	.15
❑	380	Eric Chavez	1.00	.30
❑	381	Kelly Stinnett	.50	.15
❑	382	Jarrod Washburn	1.00	.30
❑	383	Rick White	.50	.15
❑	384	Jeff Conine	1.00	.30
❑	385	Fred McGriff	1.50	.45
❑	386	Marvin Benard	.50	.15
❑	387	Joe Crede	.50	.15
❑	388	Dennis Cook	.50	.15
❑	389	Rick Reed	.50	.15
❑	390	Tom Glavine	2.50	.75
❑	391	Rondell White	1.00	.30
❑	392	Matt Morris	1.00	.30
❑	393	Pat Rapp	.50	.15
❑	394	Robert Person	.50	.15
❑	395	Omar Vizquel	1.00	.30
❑	396	Jeff Cirillo	1.00	.30
❑	397	Dave Mlicki	.50	.15
❑	398	Jose Ortiz	.50	.15
❑	399	Ryan Dempster	.50	.15
❑	400	Curt Schilling	1.50	.45
❑	401	Peter Bergeron	.50	.15
❑	402	Kyle Lohse	.50	.15
❑	403	Craig Wilson	.50	.15
❑	404	David Justice	1.00	.30
❑	405	Darin Erstad	1.00	.30
❑	406	Jose Mercedes	.50	.15
❑	407	Carl Pavano	.50	.15
❑	408	Albie Lopez	.50	.15
❑	409	Alex Ochoa	.50	.15
❑	410	Chipper Jones	2.50	.75
❑	411	Tyler Houston	.50	.15
❑	412	Dean Palmer	1.00	.30
❑	413	Damian Jackson	.50	.15
❑	414	Josh Towers	.50	.15
❑	415	Rafael Furcal	1.00	.30
❑	416	Mike Morgan	.50	.15
❑	417	Herb Perry	.50	.15
❑	418	Mike Sirotka	.50	.15
❑	419	Mark Wohlers	.50	.15
❑	420	Nomar Garciaparra	5.00	1.50
❑	421	Felipe Lopez	.50	.15
❑	422	Joe McEwing	.50	.15
❑	423	Jacque Jones	1.00	.30
❑	424	Julio Franco	1.00	.30
❑	425	Frank Thomas	2.50	.75
❑	426	So Taguchi RC	2.50	.75
❑	427	Kazuhisa Ishii RC	5.00	1.50
❑	428	D'Angelo Jimenez	.50	.15
❑	429	Chris Stynes	.50	.15
❑	430	Kerry Wood	2.50	.75
❑	431	Chris Singleton	.50	.15
❑	432	Erubiel Durazo	1.00	.30
❑	433	Matt Lawton	.50	.15
❑	434	Bill Mueller	1.00	.30
❑	435	Jose Canseco	2.50	.75
❑	436	Ben Grieve	.50	.15
❑	437	Terry Mulholland	.50	.15
❑	438	David Bell	.50	.15
❑	439	A.J. Pierzynski	1.00	.30
❑	440	Adam Dunn	1.50	.45
❑	441	Jon Garland	.50	.15
❑	442	Jeff Fassero	.50	.15
❑	443	Julio Lugo	.50	.15
❑	444	Carlos Guillen	.50	.15
❑	445	Orlando Hernandez	1.00	.30
❑	446	Mark Loretta	.50	.15
❑	447	Scott Spiezio	1.00	.30
❑	448	Kevin Millwood	1.00	.30
❑	449	Jamie Moyer	1.00	.30
❑	450	Todd Helton	1.50	.45
❑	451	Todd Walker	1.00	.30
❑	452	Jose Lima	.50	.15
❑	453	Brook Fordyce	.50	.15
❑	454	Aaron Rowand	.50	.15
❑	455	Barry Zito	2.50	.75
❑	456	Eric Owens	.50	.15
❑	457	Charles Nagy	.50	.15
❑	458	Raul Ibanez	1.00	.30
❑	459	Joe Mays	.50	.15
❑	460	Jim Thome	2.50	.75
❑	461	Adam Eaton	.50	.15
❑	462	Felix Martinez	.50	.15
❑	463	Vernon Wells	1.00	.30
❑	464	Donnie Sadler	.50	.15
❑	465	Tony Clark	.50	.15
❑	466	Jose Hernandez	.50	.15
❑	467	Ramon Martinez	.50	.15
❑	468	Rusty Greer	1.00	.30
❑	469	Rod Barajas	.50	.15
❑	470	Lance Berkman	1.00	.30
❑	471	Brady Anderson	1.00	.30
❑	472	Pedro Astacio	.50	.15
❑	473	Shane Halter	.50	.15
❑	474	Bret Prinz	.50	.15
❑	475	Edgar Martinez	1.50	.45
❑	476	Steve Trachsel	.50	.15
❑	477	Gary Matthews Jr.	.50	.15
❑	478	Ismael Valdes	.50	.15
❑	479	Juan Uribe	.50	.15
❑	480	Shawn Green	1.00	.30
❑	481	Kirk Rueter	.50	.15
❑	482	Damion Easley	.50	.15
❑	483	Chris Carpenter	.50	.15
❑	484	Kris Benson	.50	.15
❑	485	Antonio Alfonseca	.50	.15
❑	486	Kyle Farnsworth	.50	.15
❑	487	Brandon Lyon	.50	.15
❑	488	Hideki Irabu	.50	.15
❑	489	David Ortiz	1.00	.30
❑	490	Mike Piazza	4.00	1.20
❑	491	Derek Lowe	1.00	.30
❑	492	Chris Gomez	.50	.15
❑	493	Mark Johnson	.50	.15
❑	494	John Rocker	.50	.15
❑	495	Eric Karros	1.00	.30
❑	496	Bill Haselman	.50	.15
❑	497	Dave Veres	.50	.15
❑	498	Pete Harnisch	.50	.15
❑	499	Tomokazu Ohka	.50	.15
❑	500	Barry Bonds	6.00	1.80
❑	501	David Dellucci	.50	.15
❑	502	Wendell Magee	.50	.15
❑	503	Tom Gordon	.50	.15
❑	504	Javier Vazquez	1.00	.30

❑ 505 Ben Sheets 1.00 .30
❑ 506 Wilton Guerrero .50 .15
❑ 507 John Halama .50 .15
❑ 508 Mark Redman .50 .15
❑ 509 Jack Wilson .50 .15
❑ 510 Bernie Williams 1.50 .45
❑ 511 Miguel Cairo .50 .15
❑ 512 Denny Hocking .50 .15
❑ 513 Tony Batista 1.00 .30
❑ 514 Mark Grudzielanek .50 .15
❑ 515 Jose Vidro 1.00 .30
❑ 516 Sterling Hitchcock .50 .15
❑ 517 Billy Koch .50 .15
❑ 518 Matt Clement .50 .15
❑ 519 Bruce Chen .50 .15
❑ 520 Roberto Alomar 2.50 .75
❑ 521 Orlando Palmeiro .50 .15
❑ 522 Steve Finley 1.00 .30
❑ 523 Danny Patterson .50 .15
❑ 524 Terry Adams .50 .15
❑ 525 Tino Martinez 1.50 .45
❑ 526 Tony Armas Jr. UER .50 .15
Career stats do not include pre-2001
❑ 527 Geoff Jenkins 1.00 .30
❑ 528 Kerry Robinson .50 .15
❑ 529 Corey Patterson 1.00 .30
❑ 530 Brian Giles 1.00 .30
❑ 531 Jose Jimenez .50 .15
❑ 532 Joe Kennedy .50 .15
❑ 533 Armando Rios .50 .15
❑ 534 Osvaldo Fernandez .50 .15
❑ 535 Ruben Sierra .50 .15
❑ 536 Octavio Dotel .50 .15
❑ 537 Luis Sojo .50 .15
❑ 538 Brent Butler .50 .15
❑ 539 Pablo Ozuna .50 .15
❑ 540 Freddy Garcia 1.00 .30
❑ 541 Chad Durbin .50 .15
❑ 542 Orlando Merced .50 .15
❑ 543 Michael Tucker .50 .15
❑ 544 Roberto Hernandez .50 .15
❑ 545 Pat Burrell 1.00 .30
❑ 546 A.J. Burnett .50 .15
❑ 547 Bubba Trammell .50 .15
❑ 548 Scott Elarton .50 .15
❑ 549 Mike Darr .50 .15
❑ 550 Ken Griffey Jr. 4.00 1.20
❑ 551 Ugueth Urbina .50 .15
❑ 552 Todd Jones .50 .15
❑ 553 Delino Deshields .50 .15
❑ 554 Adam Piatt .50 .15
❑ 555 Jason Kendall 1.00 .30
❑ 556 Hector Ortiz .50 .15
❑ 557 Turk Wendell .50 .15
❑ 558 Rob Bell .50 .15
❑ 559 Sun Woo Kim .50 .15
❑ 560 Raul Mondesi 1.00 .30
❑ 561 Brent Abernathy .50 .15
❑ 562 Seth Etherton .50 .15
❑ 563 Shawn Wooten .50 .15
❑ 564 Jay Buhner 1.00 .30
❑ 565 Andres Galarraga 1.00 .30
❑ 566 Shane Reynolds .50 .15
❑ 567 Rod Beck .50 .15
❑ 568 Dee Brown .50 .15
❑ 569 Pedro Feliz .50 .15
❑ 570 Ryan Klesko 1.00 .30
❑ 571 John Vander Wal .50 .15
❑ 572 Nick Bierbrodt .50 .15
❑ 573 Joe Nathan .50 .15
❑ 574 James Baldwin .50 .15
❑ 575 J.D. Drew 1.00 .30
❑ 576 Greg Colbrunn .50 .15
❑ 577 Doug Glanville .50 .15
❑ 578 Brandon Duckworth .50 .15
❑ 579 Shawn Chacon .50 .15
❑ 580 Rich Aurilia 1.00 .30
❑ 581 Chuck Finley 1.00 .30
❑ 582 Abraham Nunez .50 .15
❑ 583 Kenny Lofton 1.00 .30
❑ 584 Brian Daubach .50 .15
❑ 585 Miguel Tejada 1.00 .30
❑ 586 Nate Cornejo .50 .15
❑ 587 Kazuhiro Sasaki 1.00 .30
❑ 588 Chris Richard .50 .15
❑ 589 Armando Reynoso .50 .15
❑ 590 Tim Hudson 1.00 .30
❑ 591 Neifi Perez .50 .15
❑ 592 Steve Cox .50 .15
❑ 593 Henry Blanco .50 .15
❑ 594 Ricky Ledee .50 .15
❑ 595 Tim Salmon 1.50 .45
❑ 596 Luis Rivas .50 .15
❑ 597 Jeff Zimmerman .50 .15
❑ 598 Matt Stairs .50 .15
❑ 599 Preston Wilson 1.00 .30
❑ 600 Mark McGwire 6.00 1.80
❑ 601 Timo Perez .50 .15
❑ 602 Matt Anderson .50 .15
❑ 603 Todd Hundley .50 .15
❑ 604 Rick Ankiel .50 .15
❑ 605 Tsuyoshi Shinjo 1.00 .30
❑ 606 Woody Williams .50 .15
❑ 607 Jason LaRue .50 .15
❑ 608 Carlos Lee 1.00 .30
❑ 609 Russ Johnson .50 .15
❑ 610 Scott Rolen 1.50 .45
❑ 611 Brent Mayne .50 .15
❑ 612 Darrin Fletcher .50 .15
❑ 613 Ray Lankford .50 .15
❑ 614 Troy O'Leary .50 .15
❑ 615 Javier Lopez 1.00 .30
❑ 616 Randy Velarde .50 .15
❑ 617 Vinny Castilla 1.00 .30
❑ 618 Milton Bradley 1.00 .30
❑ 619 Ruben Mateo .50 .15
❑ 620 Jason Giambi Yankees 2.50 .75
❑ 621 Andy Benes .50 .15
❑ 622 Joe Mauer RC 10.00 3.00
❑ 623 Andy Pettitte 1.50 .45
❑ 624 Jose Offerman .50 .15
❑ 625 Mo Vaughn 1.00 .30
❑ 626 Steve Sparks .50 .15
❑ 627 Mike Matthews .50 .15
❑ 628 Robb Nen 1.00 .30
❑ 629 Kip Wells .50 .15
❑ 630 Kevin Brown 1.00 .30
❑ 631 Arthur Rhodes .50 .15
❑ 632 Gabe Kapler .50 .15
❑ 633 Jermaine Dye 1.00 .30
❑ 634 Josh Beckett 1.50 .45
❑ 635 Pokey Reese .50 .15
❑ 636 Benji Gil .50 .15
❑ 637 Marcus Giles 1.00 .30
❑ 638 Julian Tavarez .50 .15
❑ 639 Jason Schmidt 1.00 .30
❑ 640 Alex Rodriguez 5.00 1.50
❑ 641 Anaheim Angels TC 1.00 .30
❑ 642 Arizona Diamondbacks TC 1.50 .45
❑ 643 Atlanta Braves TC 1.00 .30
❑ 644 Baltimore Orioles TC 1.00 .30
❑ 645 Boston Red Sox TC 1.00 .30
❑ 646 Chicago Cubs TC 1.00 .30
❑ 647 Chicago White Sox TC 1.00 .30
❑ 648 Cincinnati Reds TC 1.00 .30
❑ 649 Cleveland Indians TC 1.00 .30
❑ 650 Colorado Rockies TC 1.00 .30
❑ 651 Detroit Tigers TC 1.00 .30
❑ 652 Florida Marlins TC 1.00 .30
❑ 653 Houston Astros TC 1.00 .30
❑ 654 Kansas City Royals TC 1.00 .30
❑ 655 Los Angeles Dodgers TC 1.00 .30
❑ 656 Milwaukee Brewers TC 1.00 .30
❑ 657 Minnesota Twins TC 1.00 .30
❑ 658 Montreal Expos TC 1.00 .30
❑ 659 New York Mets TC 1.00 .30
❑ 660 New York Yankees TC 2.50 .75
❑ 661 Oakland Athletics TC 1.00 .30
❑ 662 Philadelphia Phillies TC 1.00 .30
❑ 663 Pittsburgh Pirates TC 1.00 .30
❑ 664 San Diego Padres TC 1.00 .30
❑ 665 San Francisco Giants TC 1.00 .30
❑ 666 Seattle Mariners TC 1.50 .45
❑ 667 St. Louis Cardinals TC 1.00 .30
❑ 668 Tampa Bay Devil Rays TC 1.00 .30
❑ 669 Texas Rangers TC 1.00 .30
❑ 670 Toronto Blue Jays TC 1.00 .30
❑ 671 Juan Cruz PROS 1.50 .45
❑ 672 Kevin Cash PROS RC 1.50 .45
❑ 673 Jimmy Gobble PROS RC 8.00 2.40
❑ 674 Mike Hill PROS RC 1.50 .45
❑ 675 Taylor Buchholz PROS RC 1.50 .45
❑ 676 Bill Hall PROS 1.50 .45
❑ 677 Brett Roneberg PROS RC 1.50 .45
❑ 678 Royce Huffman PROS RC 1.50 .45
❑ 679 Chris Tritle PROS RC 1.50 .45
❑ 680 Nate Espy PROS 1.50 .45
❑ 681 Nick Alvarez PROS RC 1.50 .45
❑ 682 Jason Botts PROS RC 1.50 .45
❑ 683 Ryan Gripp PROS RC 1.50 .45
❑ 684 Dan Phillips PROS RC 1.50 .45
❑ 685 Pablo Arias PROS RC 1.50 .45
❑ 686 John Rodriguez PROS RC 1.50 .45
❑ 687 Rich Harden PROS RC 12.00 3.60
❑ 688 Neal Frendling PROS RC 1.50 .45
❑ 689 Rich Thompson PROS RC 1.50 .45
❑ 690 Greg Montalbano PROS RC 2.50 .75
❑ 691 Len Dinardo DP RC 1.50 .45
❑ 692 Ryan Raburn DP RC 1.50 .45
❑ 693 Josh Barfield DP RC 10.00 3.00
❑ 694 David Bacani DP RC 1.50 .45
❑ 695 Dan Johnson DP RC 2.50 .75

2002 Topps Chrome Traded

	Nm-Mt	Ex-Mt
COMPLETE SET (275)	150.00	45.00

❑ T1 Jeff Weaver .50 .15
❑ T2 Jay Powell .50 .15
❑ T3 Alex Gonzalez .50 .15
❑ T4 Jason Isringhausen .75 .23
❑ T5 Tyler Houston .50 .15
❑ T6 Ben Broussard .50 .15
❑ T7 Chuck Knoblauch .75 .23
❑ T8 Brian L. Hunter .50 .15
❑ T9 Dustan Mohr .50 .15
❑ T10 Eric Hinske .50 .15
❑ T11 Roger Cedeno .50 .15
❑ T12 Eddie Perez .50 .15
❑ T13 Jeromy Burnitz .75 .23
❑ T14 Bartolo Colon .75 .23
❑ T15 Rick Helling .50 .15
❑ T16 Dan Plesac .50 .15
❑ T17 Scott Strickland .50 .15
❑ T18 Antonio Alfonseca .50 .15
❑ T19 Ricky Gutierrez .50 .15
❑ T20 John Valentin .50 .15
❑ T21 Raul Mondesi .75 .23
❑ T22 Ben Davis .50 .15
❑ T23 Nelson Figueroa .50 .15
❑ T24 Earl Snyder .50 .15
❑ T25 Robin Ventura .75 .23
❑ T26 Jimmy Haynes .50 .15
❑ T27 Kenny Kelly .50 .15
❑ T28 Morgan Ensberg .75 .23
❑ T29 Reggie Sanders .75 .23
❑ T30 Shigetoshi Hasegawa .75 .23
❑ T31 Mike Timlin .50 .15
❑ T32 Russell Branyan .50 .15
❑ T33 Alan Embree .50 .15
❑ T34 D'Angelo Jimenez .50 .15
❑ T35 Kent Mercker .50 .15
❑ T36 Jesse Orosco .50 .15
❑ T37 Gregg Zaun .50 .15
❑ T38 Reggie Taylor .50 .15
❑ T39 Andres Galarraga .75 .23
❑ T40 Chris Truby .50 .15
❑ T41 Bruce Chen .50 .15

❑ T42 Darren Lewis .50 .15
❑ T43 Ryan Kohlmeier .50 .15
❑ T44 John McDonald .50 .15
❑ T45 Omar Daal .50 .15
❑ T46 Matt Clement .50 .15
❑ T47 Glendon Rusch .50 .15
❑ T48 Chan Ho Park .75 .23
❑ T49 Benny Agbayani .50 .15
❑ T50 Juan Gonzalez 2.00 .60
❑ T51 Carlos Baerga .50 .15
❑ T52 Tim Raines .75 .23
❑ T53 Kevin Appier .75 .23
❑ T54 Marty Cordova .50 .15
❑ T55 Jeff D'Amico .50 .15
❑ T56 Dmitri Young .75 .23
❑ T57 Roosevelt Brown .50 .15
❑ T58 Dustin Hermanson .50 .15
❑ T59 Jose Rijo .50 .15
❑ T60 Todd Ritchie .50 .15
❑ T61 Lee Stevens .50 .15
❑ T62 Placido Polanco .50 .15
❑ T63 Eric Young .50 .15
❑ T64 Chuck Finley .75 .23
❑ T65 Dicky Gonzalez .50 .15
❑ T66 Jose Macias .50 .15
❑ T67 Gabe Kapler .50 .15
❑ T68 Sandy Alomar Jr. .50 .15
❑ T69 Henry Blanco .50 .15
❑ T70 Julian Tavarez .50 .15
❑ T71 Paul Bako .50 .15
❑ T72 Scott Rolen 1.25 .35
❑ T73 Brian Jordan .75 .23
❑ T74 Rickey Henderson 3.00 .90
❑ T75 Kevin Mench .50 .15
❑ T76 Hideo Nomo 2.00 .60
❑ T77 Jeremy Giambi .50 .15
❑ T78 Brad Fullmer .75 .23
❑ T79 Carl Everett .75 .23
❑ T80 David Wells .75 .23
❑ T81 Aaron Sele .50 .15
❑ T82 Todd Hollandsworth .50 .15
❑ T83 Vicente Padilla .50 .15
❑ T84 Kenny Lofton .75 .23
❑ T85 Corky Miller .50 .15
❑ T86 Josh Fogg .50 .15
❑ T87 Cliff Floyd .75 .23
❑ T88 Craig Paquette .50 .15
❑ T89 Jay Payton .50 .15
❑ T90 Carlos Pena .50 .15
❑ T91 Juan Encarnacion .50 .15
❑ T92 Rey Sanchez .50 .15
❑ T93 Ryan Dempster .50 .15
❑ T94 Mario Encarnacion .50 .15
❑ T95 Jorge Julio .50 .15
❑ T96 John Mabry .50 .15
❑ T97 Todd Zeile .75 .23
❑ T98 Johnny Damon .75 .23
❑ T99 Deivi Cruz .50 .15
❑ T100 Gary Sheffield .75 .23
❑ T101 Ted Lilly .50 .15
❑ T102 Todd Van Poppel .50 .15
❑ T103 Shawn Estes .50 .15
❑ T104 Cesar Izturis .50 .15
❑ T105 Ron Coomer .50 .15
❑ T106 Grady Little MG RC .50 .15
❑ T107 Jimy Williams MGR .50 .15
❑ T108 Tony Pena MGR .50 .15
❑ T109 Frank Robinson MGR 1.25 .35
❑ T110 Ron Gardenhire MGR .50 .15
❑ T111 Dennis Tankersley .50 .15
❑ T112 Alejandro Cadena RC 1.00 .30
❑ T113 Justin Reid RC 1.00 .30
❑ T114 Nate Field RC 1.00 .30
❑ T115 Rene Reyes RC 1.00 .30
❑ T116 Nelson Castro RC 1.00 .30
❑ T117 Miguel Olivo .50 .15
❑ T118 David Espinosa .50 .15
❑ T119 Chris Bootcheck RC 2.00 .60
❑ T120 Rob Henkel RC 1.00 .30
❑ T121 Steve Bechler RC 1.00 .30
❑ T122 Mark Outlaw RC 1.00 .30
❑ T123 Henry Pichardo RC 1.00 .30
❑ T124 Michael Floyd RC 1.00 .30
❑ T125 Richard Lane RC 1.00 .30
❑ T126 Pete Zamora RC 1.00 .30
❑ T127 Javier Colina .50 .15
❑ T128 Greg Sain RC 1.00 .30
❑ T129 Ronnie Merrill .50 .15
❑ T130 Gavin Floyd RC 5.00 1.50
❑ T131 Josh Bonifay RC 1.25 .35
❑ T132 Tommy Marx RC 1.00 .30
❑ T133 Gary Cates Jr. RC 1.00 .30
❑ T134 Neal Cotts RC 4.00 1.20
❑ T135 Angel Berroa .75 .23
❑ T136 Elio Serrano RC 1.00 .30
❑ T137 J.J. Putz RC 1.00 .30
❑ T138 Ruben Gotay RC 1.25 .35
❑ T139 Eddie Rogers .50 .15
❑ T140 Wily Mo Pena .75 .23
❑ T141 Tyler Yates RC 1.00 .30
❑ T142 Colin Young RC .75 .23
❑ T143 Chance Caple .50 .15
❑ T144 Ben Howard RC 1.00 .30
❑ T145 Ryan Bukvich RC 1.25 .35
❑ T146 Cliff Bartosh RC 1.00 .30
❑ T147 Brandon Claussen 2.00 .60
❑ T148 Cristian Guerrero .50 .15
❑ T149 Derrick Lewis .50 .15
❑ T150 Eric Miller RC 1.00 .30
❑ T151 Justin Huber RC 2.50 .75
❑ T152 Adrian Gonzalez .75 .23
❑ T153 Brian West RC 1.00 .30
❑ T154 Chris Baker RC 1.00 .30
❑ T155 Drew Henson .75 .23
❑ T156 Scott Hairston RC 4.00 1.20
❑ T157 Jason Simontacchi RC 1.25 .35
❑ T158 Jason Arnold RC 2.50 .75
❑ T159 Brandon Phillips .50 .15
❑ T160 Adam Roller RC 1.00 .30
❑ T161 Scotty Layfield RC 1.00 .30
❑ T162 Freddie Money RC 1.00 .30
❑ T163 Noochie Varner RC 2.00 .60
❑ T164 Terrance Hill RC 1.00 .30
❑ T165 Jeremy Hill RC 1.00 .30
❑ T166 Carlos Cabrera RC 1.00 .30
❑ T167 Jose Morban RC 1.25 .35
❑ T168 Kevin Frederick RC 1.00 .30
❑ T169 Mark Teixeira 2.00 .60
❑ T170 Brian Rogers .50 .15
❑ T171 Anastacio Martinez RC 1.00 .30
❑ T172 Bobby Jenks RC 3.00 .90
❑ T173 David Gil RC 1.00 .30
❑ T174 Andres Torres .50 .15
❑ T175 James Barrett RC 1.25 .35
❑ T176 Jimmy Journell .50 .15
❑ T177 Brett Kay RC 1.00 .30
❑ T178 Jason Young RC 1.25 .35
❑ T179 Mark Hamilton RC 1.00 .30
❑ T180 Jose Bautista RC 2.00 .60
❑ T181 Blake McGinley RC 1.00 .30
❑ T182 Ryan Mottl RC 1.25 .35
❑ T183 Jeff Austin RC 1.00 .30
❑ T184 Xavier Nady .75 .23
❑ T185 Kyle Kane RC 1.00 .30
❑ T186 Travis Foley RC 1.25 .35
❑ T187 Nathan Kaup RC 1.00 .30
❑ T188 Eric Cyr .50 .15
❑ T189 Josh Cisneros RC 1.00 .30
❑ T190 Brad Nelson RC 3.00 .90
❑ T191 Clint Weibl RC 1.00 .30
❑ T192 Ron Calloway RC 1.00 .30
❑ T193 Jung Bong .50 .15
❑ T194 Rolando Viera RC 1.00 .30
❑ T195 Jason Bulger RC 1.00 .30
❑ T196 Chone Figgins RC 1.00 .30
❑ T197 Jimmy Alvarez RC 1.00 .30
❑ T198 Joel Crump RC 1.00 .30
❑ T199 Ryan Doumit RC 1.25 .35
❑ T200 Demetrius Heath RC 1.00 .30
❑ T201 John Ennis RC 1.00 .30
❑ T202 Doug Sessions RC 1.00 .30
❑ T203 Clinton Hosford RC 1.00 .30
❑ T204 Chris Narveson RC 1.00 .30
❑ T205 Ross Peeples RC 1.25 .35
❑ T206 Alex Requena RC 1.25 .35
❑ T207 Matt Erickson RC 1.00 .30
❑ T208 Brian Forystek RC 1.00 .30
❑ T209 Dewon Brazelton .50 .15
❑ T210 Nathan Haynes .50 .15
❑ T211 Jack Cust .50 .15
❑ T212 Jesse Foppert RC 5.00 1.50
❑ T213 Jesus Cota RC 2.00 .60
❑ T214 Juan M. Gonzalez RC 1.00 .30
❑ T215 Tim Kalita RC 1.00 .30
❑ T216 Manny Delcarmen RC 1.25 .35
❑ T217 Jim Kavourias RC 1.00 .30
❑ T218 C.J. Wilson RC 1.25 .35
❑ T219 Edwin Yan RC 1.00 .30
❑ T220 Andy Van Hekken .50 .15
❑ T221 Michael Cuddyer .75 .23
❑ T222 Jeff Verplancke RC 1.00 .30
❑ T223 Mike Wilson RC 1.00 .30
❑ T224 Corwin Malone RC 1.25 .35
❑ T225 Chris Snelling RC 2.50 .75
❑ T226 Joe Rogers RC 1.00 .30
❑ T227 Jason Bay 2.50 .75
❑ T228 Ezequiel Astacio RC 1.00 .30
❑ T229 Joey Hammond RC 1.00 .30
❑ T230 Chris Duffy RC 1.00 .30
❑ T231 Mark Prior 4.00 1.20
❑ T232 Hansel Izquierdo RC 1.00 .30
❑ T233 Franklyn German RC 1.00 .30
❑ T234 Alexis Gomez .50 .15
❑ T235 Jorge Padilla RC 1.25 .35
❑ T236 Ryan Snare RC 1.25 .35
❑ T237 Deivis Santos .50 .15
❑ T238 Taggert Bozied RC 4.00 1.20
❑ T239 Mike Peeples RC 1.00 .30
❑ T240 Ronald Acuna RC 1.00 .30
❑ T241 Koyie Hill .50 .15
❑ T242 Garrett Guzman RC 1.00 .30
❑ T243 Ryan Church RC 2.00 .60
❑ T244 Tony Fontana RC 1.00 .30
❑ T245 Keto Anderson RC 1.00 .30
❑ T246 Brad Bouras RC 1.25 .35
❑ T247 Jason Dubois RC 4.00 1.20
❑ T248 Angel Guzman RC 5.00 1.50
❑ T249 Joel Hanrahan RC 2.00 .60
❑ T250 Joe Jiannetti RC 1.00 .30
❑ T251 Sean Pierce RC 1.00 .30
❑ T252 Jake Mauer RC 1.00 .30
❑ T253 Marshall McDougall RC 1.00 .30
❑ T254 Edwin Almonte RC 1.00 .30
❑ T255 Shawn Riggans RC 1.25 .35
❑ T256 Steven Shell RC 1.00 .30
❑ T257 Kevin Hooper RC 1.00 .30
❑ T258 Michael Frick RC 1.25 .35
❑ T259 Travis Chapman RC 2.00 .60
❑ T260 Tim Hummel RC 1.00 .30
❑ T261 Adam Morrissey RC 1.25 .35
❑ T262 Dontrelle Willis RC 15.00 4.50
❑ T263 Justin Sherrod RC 1.25 .35
❑ T264 Gerald Smiley RC 1.00 .30
❑ T265 Tony Miller RC 2.00 .60
❑ T266 Nolan Ryan WW 6.00 1.80
❑ T267 Reggie Jackson WW 1.25 .35
❑ T268 Steve Garvey WW .75 .23
❑ T269 Wade Boggs WW 1.25 .35
❑ T270 Sammy Sosa WW 3.00 .90
❑ T271 Curt Schilling WW 1.25 .35
❑ T272 Mark Grace WW 2.00 .60
❑ T273 Jason Giambi WW 2.00 .60
❑ T274 Ken Griffey Jr. WW 3.00 .90
❑ T275 Roberto Alomar WW 2.00 .60

2003 Topps Chrome

	Nm-Mt	Ex-Mt
COMPLETE SET (440)	200.00	60.00
COMPLETE SERIES 1 (220)	100.00	30.00

COMPLETE SERIES 2 (220) 100.00 30.00
COMMON (1-200/221-420) .... 1.00 .30
COMMON (201-220/421-440) .... 1.50 .45

❑ 1 Alex Rodriguez 5.00 1.50
❑ 2 Eddie Guardado 1.00 .30
❑ 3 Curt Schilling 1.50 .45
❑ 4 Andruw Jones 1.50 .45
❑ 5 Magglio Ordonez 1.00 .30
❑ 6 Todd Helton 1.50 .45
❑ 7 Odalis Perez 1.00 .30
❑ 8 Edgardo Alfonzo 1.00 .30
❑ 9 Eric Hinske 1.00 .30
❑ 10 Danny Bautista 1.00 .30
❑ 11 Sammy Sosa 4.00 1.20
❑ 12 Roberto Alomar 2.50 .75
❑ 13 Roger Clemens 5.00 1.50
❑ 14 Austin Kearns 1.50 .45
❑ 15 Luis Gonzalez 1.00 .30
❑ 16 Mo Vaughn 1.00 .30
❑ 17 Alfonso Soriano 2.50 .75
❑ 18 Orlando Cabrera 1.00 .30
❑ 19 Hideo Nomo 2.50 .75
❑ 20 Omar Vizquel 1.00 .30
❑ 21 Greg Maddux 5.00 1.50
❑ 22 Fred McGriff 1.50 .45
❑ 23 Frank Thomas 2.50 .75
❑ 24 Shawn Green 1.00 .30
❑ 25 Jacque Jones 1.00 .30
❑ 26 Bernie Williams 1.50 .45
❑ 27 Corey Patterson 1.00 .30
❑ 28 Cesar Izturis 1.00 .30
❑ 29 Larry Walker 1.50 .45
❑ 30 Darren Dreifort 1.00 .30
❑ 31 Al Leiter 1.00 .30
❑ 32 Jason Marquis 1.00 .30
❑ 33 Sean Casey 1.00 .30
❑ 34 Craig Counsell 1.00 .30
❑ 35 Albert Pujols 5.00 1.50
❑ 36 Kyle Lohse 1.00 .30
❑ 37 Paul Lo Duca 1.00 .30
❑ 38 Roy Oswalt 1.00 .30
❑ 39 Danny Graves 1.00 .30
❑ 40 Kevin Millwood 1.00 .30
❑ 41 Lance Berkman 1.00 .30
❑ 42 Denny Hocking 1.00 .30
❑ 43 Jose Valentin 1.00 .30
❑ 44 Josh Beckett 1.50 .45
❑ 45 Nomar Garciaparra 5.00 1.50
❑ 46 Craig Biggio 1.50 .45
❑ 47 Omar Daal 1.00 .30
❑ 48 Jimmy Rollins 1.00 .30
❑ 49 Jermaine Dye 1.00 .30
❑ 50 Edgar Renteria 1.00 .30
❑ 51 Brandon Duckworth 1.00 .30
❑ 52 Luis Castillo 1.00 .30
❑ 53 Andy Ashby 1.00 .30
❑ 54 Mike Williams 1.00 .30
❑ 55 Benito Santiago 1.00 .30
❑ 56 Bret Boone 1.00 .30
❑ 57 Randy Wolf 1.00 .30
❑ 58 Ivan Rodriguez 2.50 .75
❑ 59 Shannon Stewart 1.00 .30
❑ 60 Jose Cruz Jr. 1.00 .30
❑ 61 Billy Wagner 1.00 .30
❑ 62 Alex Gonzalez 1.00 .30
❑ 63 Ichiro Suzuki 5.00 1.50
❑ 64 Joe McEwing 1.00 .30
❑ 65 Mark Mulder 1.00 .30
❑ 66 Mike Cameron 1.00 .30
❑ 67 Corey Koskie 1.00 .30
❑ 68 Marlon Anderson 1.00 .30
❑ 69 Jason Kendall 1.00 .30
❑ 70 J.T. Snow 1.00 .30
❑ 71 Edgar Martinez 1.50 .45
❑ 72 Vernon Wells 1.00 .30
❑ 73 Vladimir Guerrero 2.50 .75
❑ 74 Adam Dunn 1.50 .45
❑ 75 Barry Zito 2.50 .75
❑ 76 Jeff Kent 1.00 .30
❑ 77 Russ Ortiz 1.00 .30
❑ 78 Phil Nevin 1.00 .30
❑ 79 Carlos Beltran 1.00 .30
❑ 80 Mike Lowell 1.00 .30
❑ 81 Bob Wickman 1.00 .30
❑ 82 Junior Spivey 1.00 .30
❑ 83 Melvin Mora 1.00 .30
❑ 84 Derrek Lee 1.00 .30
❑ 85 Chuck Knoblauch 1.00 .30
❑ 86 Eric Gagne 1.50 .45
❑ 87 Orlando Hernandez 1.00 .30
❑ 88 Robert Person 1.00 .30
❑ 89 Elmer Dessens 1.00 .30
❑ 90 Wade Miller 1.00 .30
❑ 91 Adrian Beltre 1.00 .30
❑ 92 Kazuhiro Sasaki 1.00 .30
❑ 93 Timo Perez 1.00 .30
❑ 94 Jose Vidro 1.00 .30
❑ 95 Geronimo Gil 1.00 .30
❑ 96 Trot Nixon 1.00 .30
❑ 97 Denny Neagle 1.00 .30
❑ 98 Roberto Hernandez 1.00 .30
❑ 99 David Ortiz 1.00 .30
❑ 100 Robb Nen 1.00 .30
❑ 101 Sidney Ponson 1.00 .30
❑ 102 Kevin Appier 1.00 .30
❑ 103 Javier Lopez 1.00 .30
❑ 104 Jeff Conine 1.00 .30
❑ 105 Mark Buehrle 1.00 .30
❑ 106 Jason Simontacchi 1.00 .30
❑ 107 Jose Jimenez 1.00 .30
❑ 108 Brian Jordan 1.00 .30
❑ 109 Brad Wilkerson 1.00 .30
❑ 110 Scott Hatteberg 1.00 .30
❑ 111 Matt Morris 1.00 .30
❑ 112 Miguel Tejada 1.00 .30
❑ 113 Rafael Furcal 1.00 .30
❑ 114 Steve Cox 1.00 .30
❑ 115 Roy Halladay 1.00 .30
❑ 116 David Eckstein 1.00 .30
❑ 117 Tomo Ohka 1.00 .30
❑ 118 Jack Wilson 1.00 .30
❑ 119 Randall Simon 1.00 .30
❑ 120 Jamie Moyer 1.00 .30
❑ 121 Andy Benes 1.00 .30
❑ 122 Tino Martinez 1.50 .45
❑ 123 Esteban Yan 1.00 .30
❑ 124 Jason Isringhausen 1.00 .30
❑ 125 Chris Carpenter 1.00 .30
❑ 126 Aaron Rowand 1.00 .30
❑ 127 Brandon Inge 1.00 .30
❑ 128 Jose Vizcaino 1.00 .30
❑ 129 Jose Mesa 1.00 .30
❑ 130 Troy Percival 1.00 .30
❑ 131 Jon Lieber 1.00 .30
❑ 132 Brian Giles 1.00 .30
❑ 133 Aaron Boone 1.00 .30
❑ 134 Bobby Higginson 1.00 .30
❑ 135 Luis Rivas 1.00 .30
❑ 136 Troy Glaus 1.50 .45
❑ 137 Jim Thome 2.50 .75
❑ 138 Ramon Martinez 1.00 .30
❑ 139 Jay Gibbons 1.00 .30
❑ 140 Mike Lieberthal 1.00 .30
❑ 141 Juan Uribe 1.00 .30
❑ 142 Gary Sheffield 1.00 .30
❑ 143 Ramon Santiago 1.00 .30
❑ 144 Ben Sheets 1.00 .30
❑ 145 Tony Armas Jr. 1.00 .30
❑ 146 Kazuhisa Ishii 1.00 .30
❑ 147 Erubiel Durazo 1.00 .30
❑ 148 Jerry Hairston Jr. 1.00 .30
❑ 149 Byung-Hyun Kim 1.00 .30
❑ 150 Marcus Giles 1.00 .30
❑ 151 Johnny Damon 1.00 .30
❑ 152 Terrence Long 1.00 .30
❑ 153 Juan Pierre 1.00 .30
❑ 154 Aramis Ramirez 1.00 .30
❑ 155 Brent Abernathy 1.00 .30
❑ 156 Ismael Valdes 1.00 .30
❑ 157 Mike Mussina 2.50 .75
❑ 158 Ramon Hernandez 1.00 .30
❑ 159 Adam Kennedy 1.00 .30
❑ 160 Tony Womack 1.00 .30
❑ 161 Tony Batista 1.00 .30
❑ 162 Kip Wells 1.00 .30
❑ 163 Jeromy Burnitz 1.00 .30
❑ 164 Todd Hundley 1.00 .30
❑ 165 Tim Wakefield 1.00 .30
❑ 166 Derek Lowe 1.00 .30
❑ 167 Jorge Posada 1.50 .45
❑ 168 Ramon Ortiz 1.00 .30
❑ 169 Brent Butler 1.00 .30
❑ 170 Shane Halter 1.00 .30
❑ 171 Matt Lawton 1.00 .30
❑ 172 Alex Sanchez 1.00 .30
❑ 173 Eric Milton 1.00 .30
❑ 174 Vicente Padilla 1.00 .30
❑ 175 Steve Karsay 1.00 .30
❑ 176 Mark Prior 5.00 1.50
❑ 177 Kerry Wood 2.50 .75
❑ 178 Jason LaRue 1.00 .30
❑ 179 Danys Baez 1.00 .30
❑ 180 Nick Neugebauer 1.00 .30
❑ 181 Andres Galarraga 1.00 .30
❑ 182 Jason Giambi 2.50 .75
❑ 183 Aubrey Huff 1.00 .30
❑ 184 Juan Gonzalez 2.50 .75
❑ 185 Ugueth Urbina 1.00 .30
❑ 186 Rickey Henderson 4.00 1.20
❑ 187 Brad Fullmer 1.00 .30
❑ 188 Todd Zeile 1.00 .30
❑ 189 Jason Jennings 1.00 .30
❑ 190 Vladimir Nunez 1.00 .30
❑ 191 David Justice 1.00 .30
❑ 192 Brian Lawrence 1.00 .30
❑ 193 Pat Burrell 1.00 .30
❑ 194 Pokey Reese 1.00 .30
❑ 195 Robert Fick 1.00 .30
❑ 196 C.C. Sabathia 1.00 .30
❑ 197 Fernando Vina 1.00 .30
❑ 198 Sean Burroughs 1.00 .30
❑ 199 Ellis Burks 1.00 .30
❑ 200 Joe Randa 1.00 .30
❑ 201 Chris Duncan FY RC 1.50 .45
❑ 202 Franklin Gutierrez FY RC 6.00 1.50
❑ 203 Adam LaRoche FY 1.50 .45
❑ 204 Manuel Ramirez FY RC 2.50 .75
❑ 205 Il Kim FY RC 1.50 .45
❑ 206 Daryl Clark FY RC 2.50 .75
❑ 207 Sean Pierce FY 1.50 .45
❑ 208 Andy Marte FY RC 6.00 1.80
❑ 209 Bernie Castro FY RC 1.50 .45
❑ 210 Jason Perry FY RC 2.50 .75
❑ 211 Jaime Bubela FY RC 1.50 .45
❑ 212 Alexis Rios FY 1.50 .45
❑ 213 Brendan Harris FY RC 2.50 .75
❑ 214 Ramon Nivar-Martinez FY RC 3.00 .90
❑ 215 Terry Tiffee FY RC 2.50 .75
❑ 216 Kevin Youkilis FY RC 5.00 1.50
❑ 217 Derell McCall FY RC 1.50 .45
❑ 218 Scott Tyler FY RC 2.50 .75
❑ 219 Craig Brazell FY RC 2.50 .75
❑ 220 Walter Young FY 1.50 .45
❑ 221 Francisco Rodriguez 1.00 .30
❑ 222 Chipper Jones 2.50 .75
❑ 223 Chris Singleton 1.00 .30
❑ 224 Cliff Floyd 1.00 .30
❑ 225 Bobby Hill 1.00 .30
❑ 226 Antonio Osuna 1.00 .30
❑ 227 Barry Larkin 2.50 .75
❑ 228 Dean Palmer 1.00 .30
❑ 229 Eric Owens 1.00 .30
❑ 230 Randy Johnson 2.50 .75
❑ 231 Jeff Suppan 1.00 .30
❑ 232 Eric Karros 1.00 .30
❑ 233 Johan Santana 1.00 .30
❑ 234 Javier Vazquez 1.00 .30
❑ 235 John Thomson 1.00 .30
❑ 236 Nick Johnson 1.00 .30
❑ 237 Mark Ellis 1.00 .30
❑ 238 Doug Glanville 1.00 .30
❑ 239 Ken Griffey Jr. 4.00 1.20
❑ 240 Bubba Trammell 1.00 .30
❑ 241 Livan Hernandez 1.00 .30
❑ 242 Desi Relaford 1.00 .30
❑ 243 Eli Marrero 1.00 .30
❑ 244 Jared Sandberg 1.00 .30
❑ 245 Barry Bonds 6.00 1.80
❑ 246 Aaron Sele 1.00 .30
❑ 247 Derek Jeter 6.00 1.80
❑ 248 Eric Byrnes 1.00 .30
❑ 249 Rich Aurilia 1.00 .30
❑ 250 Joel Pineiro 1.00 .30
❑ 251 Chuck Finley 1.00 .30
❑ 252 Bengie Molina 1.00 .30
❑ 253 Steve Finley 1.00 .30
❑ 254 Marty Cordova 1.00 .30

❑ 255	Shea Hillenbrand	1.00	.30
❑ 256	Milton Bradley	1.00	.30
❑ 257	Carlos Pena	1.00	.30
❑ 258	Brad Ausmus	1.00	.30
❑ 259	Carlos Delgado	1.00	.30
❑ 260	Kevin Mench	1.00	.30
❑ 261	Joe Kennedy	1.00	.30
❑ 262	Mark McLemore	1.00	.30
❑ 263	Bill Mueller	1.00	.30
❑ 264	Ricky Ledee	1.00	.30
❑ 265	Ted Lilly	1.00	.30
❑ 266	Sterling Hitchcock	1.00	.30
❑ 267	Scott Strickland	1.00	.30
❑ 268	Damion Easley	1.00	.30
❑ 269	Torii Hunter	1.00	.30
❑ 270	Brad Radke	1.00	.30
❑ 271	Geoff Jenkins	1.00	.30
❑ 272	Paul Byrd	1.00	.30
❑ 273	Morgan Ensberg	1.00	.30
❑ 274	Mike Maroth	1.00	.30
❑ 275	Mike Hampton	1.00	.30
❑ 276	Flash Gordon	1.00	.30
❑ 277	John Burkett	1.00	.30
❑ 278	Rodrigo Lopez	1.00	.30
❑ 279	Tim Spooneybarger	1.00	.30
❑ 280	Quinton McCracken	1.00	.30
❑ 281	Tim Salmon	1.50	.45
❑ 282	Jarrod Washburn	1.00	.30
❑ 283	Pedro Martinez	2.50	.75
❑ 284	Julio Lugo	1.00	.30
❑ 285	Armando Benitez	1.00	.30
❑ 286	Raul Mondesi	1.00	.30
❑ 287	Robin Ventura	1.00	.30
❑ 288	Bobby Abreu	1.00	.30
❑ 289	Josh Fogg	1.00	.30
❑ 290	Ryan Klesko	1.00	.30
❑ 291	Tsuyoshi Shinjo	1.00	.30
❑ 292	Jim Edmonds	1.00	.30
❑ 293	Chan Ho Park	1.00	.30
❑ 294	John Mabry	1.00	.30
❑ 295	Woody Williams	1.00	.30
❑ 296	Scott Schoeneweis	1.00	.30
❑ 297	Brian Anderson	1.00	.30
❑ 298	Brett Tomko	1.00	.30
❑ 299	Scott Erickson	1.00	.30
❑ 300	Kevin Millar	1.00	.30
❑ 301	Danny Wright	1.00	.30
❑ 302	Jason Schmidt	1.00	.30
❑ 303	Scott Williamson	1.00	.30
❑ 304	Einar Diaz	1.00	.30
❑ 305	Jay Payton	1.00	.30
❑ 306	Juan Acevedo	1.00	.30
❑ 307	Ben Grieve	1.00	.30
❑ 308	Raul Ibanez	1.00	.30
❑ 309	Richie Sexson	1.00	.30
❑ 310	Rick Reed	1.00	.30
❑ 311	Pedro Astacio	1.00	.30
❑ 312	Bud Smith	1.00	.30
❑ 313	Tomas Perez	1.00	.30
❑ 314	Rafael Palmeiro	1.50	.45
❑ 315	Jason Tyner	1.00	.30
❑ 316	Scott Rolen	1.50	.45
❑ 317	Randy Winn	1.00	.30
❑ 318	Ryan Jensen	1.00	.30
❑ 319	Trevor Hoffman	1.00	.30
❑ 320	Craig Wilson	1.00	.30
❑ 321	Jeremy Giambi	1.00	.30
❑ 322	Andy Pettitte	1.50	.45
❑ 323	John Franco	1.00	.30
❑ 324	Felipe Lopez	1.00	.30
❑ 325	Mike Piazza	4.00	1.20
❑ 326	Cristian Guzman	1.00	.30
❑ 327	Jose Hernandez	1.00	.30
❑ 328	Octavio Dotel	1.00	.30
❑ 329	Brad Penny	1.00	.30
❑ 330	Dave Veres	1.00	.30
❑ 331	Ryan Dempster	1.00	.30
❑ 332	Joe Crede	1.00	.30
❑ 333	Chad Hermansen	1.00	.30
❑ 334	Gary Matthews Jr.	1.00	.30
❑ 335	Frank Catalanotto	1.00	.30
❑ 336	Darin Erstad	1.00	.30
❑ 337	Matt Williams	1.00	.30
❑ 338	B.J. Surhoff	1.00	.30
❑ 339	Kerry Ligtenberg	1.00	.30
❑ 340	Mike Bordick	1.00	.30

❑ 341	Joe Girardi	1.00	.30
❑ 342	D'Angelo Jimenez	1.00	.30
❑ 343	Paul Konerko	1.00	.30
❑ 344	Joe Mays	1.00	.30
❑ 345	Marquis Grissom	1.00	.30
❑ 346	Neifi Perez	1.00	.30
❑ 347	Preston Wilson	1.00	.30
❑ 348	Jeff Weaver	1.00	.30
❑ 349	Eric Chavez	1.00	.30
❑ 350	Placido Polanco	1.00	.30
❑ 351	Matt Mantei	1.00	.30
❑ 352	James Baldwin	1.00	.30
❑ 353	Toby Hall	1.00	.30
❑ 354	Benji Gil	1.00	.30
❑ 355	Damian Moss	1.00	.30
❑ 356	Jorge Julio	1.00	.30
❑ 357	Matt Clement	1.00	.30
❑ 358	Lee Stevens	1.00	.30
❑ 359	Dave Roberts	1.00	.30
❑ 360	J.C. Romero	1.00	.30
❑ 361	Bartolo Colon	1.00	.30
❑ 362	Roger Cedeno	1.00	.30
❑ 363	Mariano Rivera	1.50	.45
❑ 364	Billy Koch	1.00	.30
❑ 365	Manny Ramirez	1.00	.30
❑ 366	Travis Lee	1.00	.30
❑ 367	Oliver Perez	1.00	.30
❑ 368	Tim Worrell	1.00	.30
❑ 369	Damian Miller	1.00	.30
❑ 370	John Smoltz	1.50	.45
❑ 371	Willis Roberts	1.00	.30
❑ 372	Tim Hudson	1.00	.30
❑ 373	Moises Alou	1.00	.30
❑ 374	Corky Miller	1.00	.30
❑ 375	Ben Broussard	1.00	.30
❑ 376	Gabe Kapler	1.00	.30
❑ 377	Chris Woodward	1.00	.30
❑ 378	Todd Hollandsworth	1.00	.30
❑ 379	So Taguchi	1.00	.30
❑ 380	John Olerud	1.00	.30
❑ 381	Reggie Sanders	1.00	.30
❑ 382	Jake Peavy	1.00	.30
❑ 383	Kris Benson	1.00	.30
❑ 384	Ray Durham	1.00	.30
❑ 385	Boomer Wells	1.00	.30
❑ 386	Tom Glavine	2.50	.75
❑ 387	Antonio Alfonseca	1.00	.30
❑ 388	Keith Foulke	1.00	.30
❑ 389	Shawn Estes	1.00	.30
❑ 390	Mark Grace	2.50	.75
❑ 391	Dmitri Young	1.00	.30
❑ 392	A.J. Burnett	1.00	.30
❑ 393	Richard Hidalgo	1.00	.30
❑ 394	Mike Sweeney	1.00	.30
❑ 395	Doug Mientkiewicz	1.00	.30
❑ 396	Cory Lidle	1.00	.30
❑ 397	Jeff Bagwell	1.50	.45
❑ 398	Steve Sparks	1.00	.30
❑ 399	Sandy Alomar Jr.	1.00	.30
❑ 400	John Lackey	1.00	.30
❑ 401	Rick Helling	1.00	.30
❑ 402	Carlos Lee	1.00	.30
❑ 403	Garret Anderson	1.00	.30
❑ 404	Vinny Castilla	1.00	.30
❑ 405	David Bell	1.00	.30
❑ 406	Freddy Garcia	1.00	.30
❑ 407	Scott Spiezio	1.00	.30
❑ 408	Russell Branyan	1.00	.30
❑ 409	Jose Contreras RC	4.00	1.20
❑ 410	Kevin Brown	1.00	.30
❑ 411	Tyler Houston	1.00	.30
❑ 412	A.J. Pierzynski	1.00	.30
❑ 413	Peter Bergeron	1.00	.30
❑ 414	Brett Myers	1.00	.30
❑ 415	Kenny Lofton	1.00	.30
❑ 416	Ben Davis	1.00	.30
❑ 417	J.D. Drew	1.00	.30
❑ 418	Ricky Gutierrez	1.00	.30
❑ 419	Mark Redman	1.00	.30
❑ 420	Juan Encarnacion	1.00	.30
❑ 421	Bryan Bullington DP RC	5.00	1.50
❑ 422	Jeremy Guthrie DP	1.50	.45
❑ 423	Joey Gomes DP RC	2.50	.75
❑ 424	Evel Bastida-Martinez DP RC	1.50	.45
❑ 425	Brian Wright DP RC	1.50	.45
❑ 426	B.J. Upton DP	2.50	.75

❑ 427	Jeff Francis DP	1.50	.45
❑ 428	Jeremy Hermida DP	1.50	.45
❑ 429	Khalil Greene DP	1.50	.45
❑ 430	Darrell Rasner DP RC	1.50	.45
❑ 431	Brandon Phillips Victor Martinez	1.50	.45
❑ 432	Hee Seop Choi Nic Jackson	1.50	.45
❑ 433	Dontrelle Willis Jason Stokes	4.00	1.20
❑ 434	Chad Tracy Lyle Overbay	1.50	.45
❑ 435	Joe Borchard Corwin Malone	1.50	.45
❑ 436	Joe Mauer Justin Morneau	2.50	.75
❑ 437	Drew Henson Brandon Claussen	1.50	.45
❑ 438	Chase Utley Gavin Floyd	1.50	.45
❑ 439	Taggert Bozied Xavier Nady	1.50	.45
❑ 440	Aaron Heilman Jose Reyes	1.50	.45

2003 Topps Chrome Traded

	MINT	NRMT
COMPLETE SET (275)	150.00	70.00
COMMON CARD (121-165)	1.00	.45

2 PER 2003 TOPPS TRADED HOBBY PACK
2 PER 2003 TOPPS TRADED HTA PACK
2 PER 2003 TOPPS TRADED RETAIL PACK

❑ T1	Juan Pierre	.75	.35
❑ T2	Mark Grudzielanek	.75	.35
❑ T3	Tanyon Sturtze	.75	.35
❑ T4	Greg Vaughn	.75	.35
❑ T5	Greg Myers	.75	.35
❑ T6	Randall Simon	.75	.35
❑ T7	Todd Hundley	.75	.35
❑ T8	Marlon Anderson	.75	.35
❑ T9	Jeff Reboulet	.75	.35
❑ T10	Alex Sanchez	.75	.35
❑ T11	Mike Rivera	.75	.35
❑ T12	Todd Walker	.75	.35
❑ T13	Ray King	.75	.35
❑ T14	Shawn Estes	.75	.35
❑ T15	Gary Matthews Jr.	.75	.35
❑ T16	Jaret Wright	.75	.35
❑ T17	Edgardo Alfonzo	.75	.35
❑ T18	Omar Daal	.75	.35
❑ T19	Ryan Rupe	.75	.35
❑ T20	Tony Clark	.75	.35
❑ T21	Jeff Suppan	.75	.35
❑ T22	Mike Stanton	.75	.35
❑ T23	Ramon Martinez	.75	.35
❑ T24	Armando Rios	.75	.35
❑ T25	Johnny Estrada	.75	.35
❑ T26	Joe Girardi	.75	.35
❑ T27	Ivan Rodriguez	2.00	.90
❑ T28	Robert Fick	.75	.35
❑ T29	Rick White	.75	.35
❑ T30	Robert Person	.75	.35
❑ T31	Alan Benes	.75	.35
❑ T32	Chris Carpenter	.75	.35
❑ T33	Chris Widger	.75	.35

❑ T34 Travis Hafner .75 .35
❑ T35 Mike Venafro .75 .35
❑ T36 Jon Lieber .75 .35
❑ T37 Orlando Hernandez .75 .35
❑ T38 Aaron Myette .75 .35
❑ T39 Paul Bako .75 .35
❑ T40 Erubiel Durazo .75 .35
❑ T41 Mark Guthrie .75 .35
❑ T42 Steve Avery .75 .35
❑ T43 Damian Jackson .75 .35
❑ T44 Rey Ordonez .75 .35
❑ T45 John Flaherty .75 .35
❑ T46 Byung-Hyun Kim .75 .35
❑ T47 Tom Goodwin .75 .35
❑ T48 Elmer Dessens .75 .35
❑ T49 Al Martin .75 .35
❑ T50 Gene Kingsale .75 .35
❑ T51 Lenny Harris .75 .35
❑ T52 David Ortiz .75 .35
❑ T53 Jose Lima .75 .35
❑ T54 Mike Difelice .75 .35
❑ T55 Jose Hernandez .75 .35
❑ T56 Todd Zeile .75 .35
❑ T57 Roberto Hernandez .75 .35
❑ T58 Albie Lopez .75 .35
❑ T59 Roberto Alomar 2.00 .90
❑ T60 Russ Ortiz .75 .35
❑ T61 Brian Daubach .75 .35
❑ T62 Carl Everett .75 .35
❑ T63 Jeromy Burnitz .75 .35
❑ T64 Mark Bellhorn .75 .35
❑ T65 Ruben Sierra .75 .35
❑ T66 Mike Fetters .75 .35
❑ T67 Armando Benitez .75 .35
❑ T68 Deivi Cruz .75 .35
❑ T69 Jose Cruz Jr. .75 .35
❑ T70 Jeremy Fikac .75 .35
❑ T71 Jeff Kent .75 .35
❑ T72 Andres Galarraga .75 .35
❑ T73 Rickey Henderson 3.00 1.35
❑ T74 Royce Clayton .75 .35
❑ T75 Troy O'Leary .75 .35
❑ T76 Ron Coomer .75 .35
❑ T77 Greg Colbrunn .75 .35
❑ T78 Wes Helms .75 .35
❑ T79 Kevin Millwood .75 .35
❑ T80 Damion Easley .75 .35
❑ T81 Bobby Kielty .75 .35
❑ T82 Keith Osik .75 .35
❑ T83 Ramiro Mendoza .75 .35
❑ T84 Shea Hillenbrand .75 .35
❑ T85 Shannon Stewart .75 .35
❑ T86 Eddie Perez .75 .35
❑ T87 Ugueth Urbina .75 .35
❑ T88 Orlando Palmeiro .75 .35
❑ T89 Graeme Lloyd .75 .35
❑ T90 John Vander Wal .75 .35
❑ T91 Gary Bennett .75 .35
❑ T92 Shane Reynolds .75 .35
❑ T93 Steve Parris .75 .35
❑ T94 Julio Lugo .75 .35
❑ T95 John Halama .75 .35
❑ T96 Carlos Baerga .75 .35
❑ T97 Jim Parque .75 .35
❑ T98 Mike Williams .75 .35
❑ T99 Fred McGriff 1.25 .55
❑ T100 Kenny Rogers .75 .35
❑ T101 Matt Herges .75 .35
❑ T102 Jay Bell .75 .35
❑ T103 Esteban Yan .75 .35
❑ T104 Eric Owens .75 .35
❑ T105 Aaron Fultz .75 .35
❑ T106 Rey Sanchez .75 .35
❑ T107 Jim Thome 2.00 .90
❑ T108 Aaron Boone .75 .35
❑ T109 Raul Mondesi .75 .35
❑ T110 Kenny Lofton .75 .35
❑ T111 Jose Guillen .75 .35
❑ T112 Aramis Ramirez .75 .35
❑ T113 Sidney Ponson .75 .35
❑ T114 Scott Williamson .75 .35
❑ T115 Robin Ventura .75 .35
❑ T116 Dusty Baker MG .75 .35
❑ T117 Felipe Alou MG .75 .35
❑ T118 Buck Showalter MG .75 .35
❑ T119 Jack McKeon MG .75 .35
❑ T120 Art Howe MG .75 .35
❑ T121 Bobby Crosby PROS 1.00 .45
❑ T122 Adrian Gonzalez PROS 1.00 .45
❑ T123 Kevin Cash PROS 1.00 .45
❑ T124 Shin-Soo Choo PROS 1.00 .45
❑ T125 Chin-Feng Chen PROS 2.50 1.10
❑ T126 Miguel Cabrera PROS 5.00 2.20
❑ T127 Jason Young PROS 1.00 .45
❑ T128 Alex Herrera PROS 1.00 .45
❑ T129 Jason Dubois PROS 1.00 .45
❑ T130 Jeff Mathis PROS 1.00 .45
❑ T131 Casey Kotchman PROS 1.50 .70
❑ T132 Ed Rogers PROS 1.00 .45
❑ T133 Wilson Betemit PROS 1.00 .45
❑ T134 Jim Kavourias PROS 1.00 .45
❑ T135 Taylor Buchholz PROS 1.00 .45
❑ T136 Adam LaRoche PROS 1.00 .45
❑ T137 Dallas McPherson PROS 1.00 .45
❑ T138 Jesus Cota PROS 1.00 .45
❑ T139 Clint Nageotte PROS 1.00 .45
❑ T140 Boof Bonser PROS 1.00 .45
❑ T141 Walter Young PROS 1.00 .45
❑ T142 Joe Crede PROS 1.00 .45
❑ T143 Denny Bautista PROS 1.00 .45
❑ T144 Victor Diaz PROS 1.00 .45
❑ T145 Chris Narveson PROS 1.00 .45
❑ T146 Gabe Gross PROS 1.00 .45
❑ T147 Jimmy Journell PROS 1.00 .45
❑ T148 Rafael Soriano PROS 1.00 .45
❑ T149 Jerome Williams PROS 1.00 .45
❑ T150 Aaron Cook PROS 1.00 .45
❑ T151 Anastacio Martinez PROS 1.00 .45
❑ T152 Scott Hairston PROS 1.00 .45
❑ T153 John Buck PROS 1.00 .45
❑ T154 Ryan Ludwick PROS 1.00 .45
❑ T155 Chris Bootcheck PROS 1.00 .45
❑ T156 John Rheinecker PROS 1.00 .45
❑ T157 Jason Lane PROS 1.00 .45
❑ T158 Shelley Duncan PROS 1.00 .45
❑ T159 Adam Wainwright PROS 1.00 .45
❑ T160 Jason Arnold PROS 1.00 .45
❑ T161 Jonny Gomes PROS 1.00 .45
❑ T162 James Loney PROS 1.00 .45
❑ T163 Mike Fontenot PROS 1.00 .45
❑ T164 Khalil Greene PROS 1.50 .70
❑ T165 Sean Burnett PROS 1.00 .45
❑ T166 David Martinez FY RC 1.00 .45
❑ T167 Felix Pie FY RC 8.00 3.60
❑ T168 Joe Valentine FY RC 1.00 .45
❑ T169 Brandon Webb FY RC 5.00 2.20
❑ T170 Matt Diaz FY RC 2.00 .90
❑ T171 Lew Ford FY RC 1.25 .55
❑ T172 Jeremy Griffiths FY RC 1.25 .55
❑ T173 Matt Hensley FY RC 1.00 .45
❑ T174 Charlie Manning FY RC 1.00 .45
❑ T175 Elizardo Ramirez FY RC 3.00 1.35
❑ T176 Greg Aquino FY RC 1.00 .45
❑ T177 Felix Sanchez FY RC 1.00 .45
❑ T178 Kelly Shoppach FY RC 3.00 1.35
❑ T179 Bubba Nelson FY RC 2.50 1.10
❑ T180 Mike O'Keefe FY RC 1.00 .45
❑ T181 Hanley Ramirez FY RC 4.00 1.80
❑ T182 Todd Wellemeyer FY RC 1.25 .55
❑ T183 Dustin Moseley FY RC 1.25 .55
❑ T184 Eric Crozier FY RC 1.25 .55
❑ T185 Ryan Shealy FY RC 2.00 .90
❑ T186 Jeremy Bonderman FY RC 3.00 1.35
❑ T187 T.Story-Harden FY RC 1.25 .55
❑ T188 Dusty Brown FY RC 1.00 .45
❑ T189 Rob Hammock FY RC 2.00 .90
❑ T190 Jorge Piedra FY RC 1.25 .55
❑ T191 Chris De La Cruz FY RC 1.00 .45
❑ T192 Eli Whiteside FY RC 1.00 .45
❑ T193 Jason Kubel FY RC 1.25 .55
❑ T194 Jon Schuerholz FY RC 1.00 .45
❑ T195 Stephen Randolph FY RC 1.00 .45
❑ T196 Andy Sisco FY RC 3.00 1.35
❑ T197 Sean Smith FY RC 1.25 .55
❑ T198 Jon-Mark Sprowl FY RC 2.00 .90
❑ T199 Matt Kata FY RC 2.50 1.10
❑ T200 Robinson Cano FY RC 1.25 .55
❑ T201 Nook Logan FY RC 1.00 .45
❑ T202 Ben Francisco FY RC 2.00 .90
❑ T203 Arnie Munoz FY RC 1.00 .45
❑ T204 Ozzie Chavez FY RC 1.00 .45
❑ T205 Eric Riggs FY RC 1.25 .55
❑ T206 Beau Kemp FY RC 1.00 .45
❑ T207 Travis Wong FY RC 1.25 .55
❑ T208 Dustin Yount FY RC 2.00 .90
❑ T209 Brian McCann FY RC 2.00 .90
❑ T210 Wilton Reynolds FY RC 1.25 .55
❑ T211 Matt Bruback FY RC 1.00 .45
❑ T212 Andrew Brown FY RC 1.00 .45
❑ T213 Edgar Gonzalez FY RC 1.00 .45
❑ T214 Eider Torres FY RC 1.00 .45
❑ T215 Aquilino Lopez FY RC 1.00 .45
❑ T216 Bobby Basham FY RC 2.00 .90
❑ T217 Tim Olson FY RC 1.25 .55
❑ T218 Nathan Panther FY RC 2.00 .90
❑ T219 Bryan Grace FY RC 1.00 .45
❑ T220 Dusty Gomon FY RC 2.00 .90
❑ T221 Wil Ledezma FY RC 1.00 .45
❑ T222 Josh Willingham FY RC 3.00 1.35
❑ T223 David Cash FY RC 1.00 .45
❑ T224 Oscar Villarreal FY RC 1.00 .45
❑ T225 Jeff Duncan FY RC 1.25 .55
❑ T226 Kade Johnson FY RC 1.00 .45
❑ T227 Luke Steidlmayer FY RC 1.00 .45
❑ T228 Brandon Watson FY RC 1.00 .45
❑ T229 Jose Morales FY RC 1.00 .45
❑ T230 Mike Gallo FY RC 1.00 .45
❑ T231 Tyler Adamczyk FY RC 1.00 .45
❑ T232 Adam Stern FY RC 1.00 .45
❑ T233 Brennan King FY RC 1.00 .45
❑ T234 Dan Haren FY RC 2.50 1.10
❑ T235 Michel Hernandez FY RC 1.00 .45
❑ T236 Ben Fritz FY RC 1.00 .45
❑ T237 Clay Hensley FY RC 1.00 .45
❑ T238 Tyler Johnson FY RC 1.00 .45
❑ T239 Pete LaForest FY RC 1.25 .55
❑ T240 Tyler Martin FY RC 1.00 .45
❑ T241 J.D. Durbin FY RC 2.00 .90
❑ T242 Shane Victorino FY RC 1.00 .45
❑ T243 Rajai Davis FY RC 1.25 .55
❑ T244 Ismael Castro FY RC 1.00 .45
❑ T245 Chien-Ming Wang FY RC 4.00 1.80
❑ T246 Travis Ishikawa FY RC 1.25 .55
❑ T247 Corey Shafer FY RC 1.25 .55
❑ T248 Gary Schneidmiller FY RC 1.00 .45
❑ T249 Dave Pember FY RC 1.00 .45
❑ T250 Keith Stamler FY RC 1.00 .45
❑ T251 Tyson Graham FY RC 1.00 .45
❑ T252 Ryan Cameron FY RC 1.00 .45
❑ T253 Eric Eckenstahler FY 1.00 .45
❑ T254 Matthew Peterson FY RC 1.00 .45
❑ T255 Dustin McGowan FY RC 2.00 .90
❑ T256 Prentice Redman FY RC 1.00 .45
❑ T257 Haj Turay FY RC 1.25 .55
❑ T258 Carlos Guzman FY RC 1.25 .55
❑ T259 Matt DeMarco FY RC 1.00 .45
❑ T260 Derek Michaelis FY RC 1.25 .55
❑ T261 Brian Burgamy FY RC 1.00 .45
❑ T262 Jay Sitzman FY RC 1.00 .45
❑ T263 Chris Fallon FY RC 1.00 .45
❑ T264 Mike Adams FY RC 1.00 .45
❑ T265 Clint Barmes FY RC 2.00 .90
❑ T266 Eric Reed FY RC 2.00 .90
❑ T267 Willie Eyre FY RC 1.00 .45
❑ T268 Carlos Duran FY RC 1.00 .45
❑ T269 Nick Trzesniak FY RC 1.00 .45
❑ T270 Ferdin Tejeda FY RC 1.00 .45
❑ T271 Michael Garciaparra FY RC 2.50 1.10
❑ T272 Michael Hinckley FY RC 2.00 .90
❑ T273 Branden Florence FY RC 1.00 .45
❑ T274 Trent Oeltjen FY RC 1.25 .55
❑ T275 Mike Neu FY RC 1.00 .45

1999 Topps Gallery

	Nm-Mt	Ex-Mt
COMPLETE SET (150)	50.00	15.00
COMP.SET w/o SP's (100)	25.00	7.50
COMMON CARD (1-100)	.30	.09
COMMON (101-150)	.75	.23

❑ 1 Mark McGwire 2.00 .60
❑ 2 Jim Thome .75 .23
❑ 3 Bernie Williams .50 .15
❑ 4 Larry Walker .50 .15
❑ 5 Juan Gonzalez .75 .23
❑ 6 Ken Griffey Jr. 1.25 .35
❑ 7 Raul Mondesi .30 .09

❑ 8 Sammy Sosa 1.25 .35
❑ 9 Greg Maddux 1.50 .45
❑ 10 Jeff Bagwell .50 .15
❑ 11 Vladimir Guerrero .75 .23
❑ 12 Scott Rolen .50 .15
❑ 13 Nomar Garciaparra 1.50 .45
❑ 14 Mike Piazza 1.25 .35
❑ 15 Travis Lee .30 .09
❑ 16 Carlos Delgado .30 .09
❑ 17 Darin Erstad .30 .09
❑ 18 David Justice .30 .09
❑ 19 Cal Ripken 2.50 .75
❑ 20 Derek Jeter 2.00 .60
❑ 21 Tony Clark .30 .09
❑ 22 Barry Larkin .75 .23
❑ 23 Greg Vaughn .30 .09
❑ 24 Jeff Kent .30 .09
❑ 25 Wade Boggs .50 .15
❑ 26 Andres Galarraga .30 .09
❑ 27 Ken Caminiti .30 .09
❑ 28 Jason Kendall .30 .09
❑ 29 Todd Helton .50 .15
❑ 30 Chuck Knoblauch .30 .09
❑ 31 Roger Clemens 1.50 .45
❑ 32 Jeromy Burnitz .30 .09
❑ 33 Javy Lopez .30 .09
❑ 34 Roberto Alomar .75 .23
❑ 35 Eric Karros .30 .09
❑ 36 Ben Grieve .30 .09
❑ 37 Eric Davis .30 .09
❑ 38 Rondell White .30 .09
❑ 39 Dmitri Young .30 .09
❑ 40 Ivan Rodriguez .75 .23
❑ 41 Paul O'Neill .50 .15
❑ 42 Jeff Cirillo .30 .09
❑ 43 Kerry Wood .75 .23
❑ 44 Albert Belle .30 .09
❑ 45 Frank Thomas .75 .23
❑ 46 Manny Ramirez .30 .09
❑ 47 Tom Glavine .75 .23
❑ 48 Mo Vaughn .30 .09
❑ 49 Jose Cruz Jr. .30 .09
❑ 50 Sandy Alomar Jr. .30 .09
❑ 51 Edgar Martinez .50 .15
❑ 52 John Olerud .30 .09
❑ 53 Todd Walker .30 .09
❑ 54 Tim Salmon .50 .15
❑ 55 Derek Bell .30 .09
❑ 56 Matt Williams .30 .09
❑ 57 Alex Rodriguez 1.50 .45
❑ 58 Rusty Greer .30 .09
❑ 59 Vinny Castilla .30 .09
❑ 60 Jason Giambi .75 .23
❑ 61 Mark Grace .75 .23
❑ 62 Jose Canseco .75 .23
❑ 63 Gary Sheffield .30 .09
❑ 64 Brad Fullmer .30 .09
❑ 65 Trevor Hoffman .30 .09
❑ 66 Mark Kotsay .30 .09
❑ 67 Mike Mussina .75 .23
❑ 68 Johnny Damon .30 .09
❑ 69 Tino Martinez .50 .15
❑ 70 Curt Schilling .50 .15
❑ 71 Jay Buhner .30 .09
❑ 72 Kenny Lofton .30 .09
❑ 73 Randy Johnson .75 .23
❑ 74 Kevin Brown .50 .15
❑ 75 Brian Jordan .30 .09
❑ 76 Craig Biggio .50 .15
❑ 77 Barry Bonds 2.00 .60
❑ 78 Tony Gwynn 1.00 .30
❑ 79 Jim Edmonds .30 .09
❑ 80 Shawn Green .30 .09
❑ 81 Todd Hundley .30 .09
❑ 82 Cliff Floyd .30 .09
❑ 83 Jose Guillen .30 .09
❑ 84 Dante Bichette .30 .09
❑ 85 Moises Alou .30 .09
❑ 86 Chipper Jones .75 .23
❑ 87 Ray Lankford .30 .09
❑ 88 Fred McGriff .50 .15
❑ 89 Rod Beck .30 .09
❑ 90 Dean Palmer .30 .09
❑ 91 Pedro Martinez .75 .23
❑ 92 Andruw Jones .50 .15
❑ 93 Robin Ventura .30 .09
❑ 94 Ugueth Urbina .30 .09
❑ 95 Orlando Hernandez .30 .35
❑ 96 Sean Casey .30 .09
❑ 97 Denny Neagle .30 .09
❑ 98 Troy Glaus .50 .15
❑ 99 John Smoltz .50 .15
❑ 100 Al Leiter .30 .09
❑ 101 Ken Griffey Jr. MAS 2.50 .75
❑ 102 Frank Thomas MAS 1.50 .45
❑ 103 Mark McGwire MAS 4.00 1.20
❑ 104 Sammy Sosa MAS 2.50 .75
❑ 105 Chipper Jones MAS 1.50 .45
❑ 106 Alex Rodriguez MAS 3.00 .90
❑ 107 N.Garciaparra MAS 3.00 .90
❑ 108 Juan Gonzalez MAS 1.50 .45
❑ 109 Derek Jeter MAS 4.00 1.20
❑ 110 Mike Piazza MAS 2.50 .75
❑ 111 Barry Bonds MAS 4.00 1.20
❑ 112 Tony Gwynn MAS 2.00 .40
❑ 113 Cal Ripken MAS 5.00 1.50
❑ 114 Greg Maddux MAS 3.00 .90
❑ 115 Roger Clemens MAS 3.00 .90
❑ 116 Brad Fullmer ART .75 .23
❑ 117 Kerry Wood ART 1.50 .45
❑ 118 Ben Grieve ART .75 .23
❑ 119 Todd Helton ART 1.00 .30
❑ 120 Kevin Millwood ART .75 .23
❑ 121 Sean Casey ART .75 .23
❑ 122 V.Guerrero ART 1.50 .45
❑ 123 Travis Lee ART .75 .23
❑ 124 Troy Glaus ART 1.00 .30
❑ 125 Bartolo Colon ART .75 .23
❑ 126 Andruw Jones ART 1.00 .30
❑ 127 Scott Rolen ART 1.00 .30
❑ 128 A.Soriano APP RC 12.00 3.60
❑ 129 Nick Johnson APP RC 2.50 .75
❑ 130 Matt Belisle APP RC .75 .23
❑ 131 Jorge Toca APP RC .75 .23
❑ 132 Masao Kida APP RC .75 .23
❑ 133 Carlos Pena APP RC 1.50 .45
❑ 134 Adrian Beltre APP .75 .23
❑ 135 Eric Chavez APP .75 .23
❑ 136 Carlos Beltran APP .75 .23
❑ 137 Alex Gonzalez APP .75 .23
❑ 138 Ryan Anderson APP .75 .23
❑ 139 Ruben Mateo APP .75 .23
❑ 140 Bruce Chen APP .75 .23
❑ 141 Pat Burrell APP RC 5.00 1.50
❑ 142 Michael Barrett APP .75 .23
❑ 143 Carlos Lee APP .75 .23
❑ 144 Mark Mulder APP RC 5.00 1.50
❑ 145 C.Freeman APP RC .75 .23
❑ 146 Gabe Kapler APP .75 .23
❑ 147 J.Encarnacion APP .75 .23
❑ 148 Jeremy Giambi APP .75 .23
❑ 149 Jason Tyner APP RC .75 .23
❑ 150 George Lombard APP .75 .23

2001 Topps Gallery

	Nm-Mt	Ex-Mt
COMPLETE SET (150)	100.00	30.00
COMP.SET w/o SP's (100)	40.00	12.00
COMMON (1-49/51-101)	.50	.15
COMMON (102-150)	3.00	.90

❑ 1 Darin Erstad .50 .15
❑ 2 Chipper Jones 1.25 .35

❑ 3 Nomar Garciaparra 2.50 .75
❑ 4 Fernando Vina .50 .15
❑ 5 Bartolo Colon .50 .15
❑ 6 Bobby Higginson .50 .15
❑ 7 Antonio Alfonseca .50 .15
❑ 8 Mike Sweeney .50 .15
❑ 9 Kevin Brown .50 .15
❑ 10 Jose Vidro .50 .15
❑ 11 Derek Jeter 3.00 .90
❑ 12 Jason Giambi 1.25 .35
❑ 13 Pat Burrell .50 .15
❑ 14 Jeff Kent .50 .15
❑ 15 Alex Rodriguez 2.50 .75
❑ 16 Rafael Palmeiro .75 .23
❑ 17 Garret Anderson .50 .15
❑ 18 Brad Fullmer .50 .15
❑ 19 Doug Glanville .50 .15
❑ 20 Mark Quinn .50 .15
❑ 21 Mo Vaughn .50 .15
❑ 22 Andruw Jones .75 .23
❑ 23 Pedro Martinez 1.25 .35
❑ 24 Ken Griffey Jr. 2.00 .60
❑ 25 Roberto Alomar 1.25 .35
❑ 26 Dean Palmer .50 .15
❑ 27 Jeff Bagwell .75 .23
❑ 28 Jermaine Dye .50 .15
❑ 29 Chan Ho Park .50 .15
❑ 30 Vladimir Guerrero 1.25 .35
❑ 31 Bernie Williams .75 .23
❑ 32 Ben Grieve .50 .15
❑ 33 Jason Kendall .50 .15
❑ 34 Barry Bonds 3.00 .90
❑ 35 Jim Edmonds .50 .15
❑ 36 Ivan Rodriguez 1.25 .35
❑ 37 Javy Lopez .50 .15
❑ 38 J.T. Snow .50 .15
❑ 39 Erubiel Durazo .50 .15
❑ 40 Terrence Long .50 .15
❑ 41 Tim Salmon .75 .23
❑ 42 Greg Maddux 2.50 .75
❑ 43 Sammy Sosa 2.00 .60
❑ 44 Sean Casey .50 .15
❑ 45 Jeff Cirillo .50 .15
❑ 46 Juan Gonzalez 1.25 .35
❑ 47 Richard Hidalgo .50 .15
❑ 48 Shawn Green .50 .15
❑ 49 Jeromy Burnitz .50 .15
❑ 50 Willie Mays HTA 15.00 4.50
N.Y. Giants
❑ 50 Willie Mays RETAIL 40.00 12.00
S.F. Giants
❑ 51 David Justice .50 .15
❑ 52 Tim Hudson .50 .15
❑ 53 Brian Giles .50 .15
❑ 54 Robb Nen .50 .15
❑ 55 Fernando Tatis .50 .15
❑ 56 Tony Batista .50 .15
❑ 57 Pokey Reese .50 .15
❑ 58 Ray Durham .50 .15
❑ 59 Greg Vaughn .50 .15
❑ 60 Kazuhiro Sasaki .50 .15
❑ 61 Troy Glaus .75 .23
❑ 62 Rafael Furcal .50 .15
❑ 63 Magglio Ordonez .50 .15
❑ 64 Jim Thome 1.25 .35
❑ 65 Todd Helton .75 .23
❑ 66 Preston Wilson .50 .15
❑ 67 Moises Alou .50 .15

	Player	Nm-Mt	Ex-Mt
❑ 68	Gary Sheffield	.50	.15
❑ 69	Geoff Jenkins	.50	.15
❑ 70	Mike Piazza	2.00	.60
❑ 71	Jorge Posada	.75	.23
❑ 72	Bobby Abreu	.50	.15
❑ 73	Phil Nevin	.50	.15
❑ 74	John Olerud	.50	.15
❑ 75	Mark McGwire	3.00	.90
❑ 76	Jose Cruz Jr.	.50	.15
❑ 77	David Segui	.50	.15
❑ 78	Neifi Perez	.50	.15
❑ 79	Omar Vizquel	.50	.15
❑ 80	Rick Ankiel	.50	.15
❑ 81	Randy Johnson	1.25	.35
❑ 82	Albert Belle	.50	.15
❑ 83	Frank Thomas	1.25	.35
❑ 84	Manny Ramirez	.50	.15
❑ 85	Larry Walker	.75	.23
❑ 86	Luis Castillo	.50	.15
❑ 87	Johnny Damon	.50	.15
❑ 88	Adrian Beltre	.50	.15
❑ 89	Cristian Guzman	.50	.15
❑ 90	Jay Payton	.50	.15
❑ 91	Miguel Tejada	.50	.15
❑ 92	Scott Rolen	.75	.23
❑ 93	Ryan Klesko	.50	.15
❑ 94	Edgar Martinez	.75	.23
❑ 95	Fred McGriff	.75	.23
❑ 96	Carlos Delgado	.50	.15
❑ 97	Barry Zito	1.25	.35
❑ 98	Mike Lieberthal	.50	.15
❑ 99	Trevor Hoffman	.50	.15
❑ 100	Gabe Kapler	.50	.15
❑ 101	Edgardo Alfonzo	.50	.15
❑ 102	Corey Patterson	3.00	.90
❑ 103	Alfonso Soriano	1.25	.35
❑ 104	Keith Ginter	3.00	.90
❑ 105	Keith Reed	3.00	.90
❑ 106	Nick Johnson	3.00	.90
❑ 107	Carlos Pena	3.00	.90
❑ 108	Vernon Wells	3.00	.90
❑ 109	Roy Oswalt	3.00	.90
❑ 110	Alex Escobar	3.00	.90
❑ 111	Adam Everett	3.00	.90
❑ 112	Jimmy Rollins	3.00	.90
❑ 113	Marcus Giles	3.00	.90
❑ 114	Jack Cust	3.00	.90
❑ 115	Chin-Feng Chen	3.00	.90
❑ 116	Pablo Ozuna	3.00	.90
❑ 117	Ben Sheets	3.00	.90
❑ 118	Adrian Gonzalez	3.00	.90
❑ 119	Ben Davis	3.00	.90
❑ 120	Eric Valent	3.00	.90
❑ 121	Scott Heard	3.00	.90
❑ 122	David Parrish RC	3.00	.90
❑ 123	Sean Burnett	3.00	.90
❑ 124	Derek Thompson	3.00	.90
❑ 125	Tim Christman RC	3.00	.90
❑ 126	Mike Jacobs RC	3.00	.90
❑ 127	Luis Montanez RC	3.00	.90
❑ 128	Chris Bass RC	3.00	.90
❑ 129	Will Smith RC	3.00	.90
❑ 130	Justin Wayne RC	3.00	.90
❑ 131	Shawn Fagan RC	3.00	.90
❑ 132	Chad Petty RC	3.00	.90
❑ 133	J.R. House	3.00	.90
❑ 134	Joel Pineiro	4.00	1.20
❑ 135	Albert Pujols RC	30.00	9.00
❑ 136	Carmen Cali RC	3.00	.90
❑ 137	Steve Smyth RC	3.00	.90
❑ 138	John Lackey	3.00	.90
❑ 139	Bob Keppel RC	3.00	.90
❑ 140	Dominic Rich RC	3.00	.90
❑ 141	Josh Hamilton	3.00	.90
❑ 142	Nolan Ryan	8.00	2.40
❑ 143	Tom Seaver	4.00	1.20
❑ 144	Reggie Jackson	3.00	.90
❑ 145	Johnny Bench	4.00	1.20
❑ 146	Warren Spahn	3.00	.90
❑ 147	Brooks Robinson	4.00	1.20
❑ 148	Carl Yastrzemski	5.00	1.50
❑ 149	Al Kaline	4.00	1.20
❑ 150	Bob Feller	3.00	.90
❑ 151A	I. Suzuki English RC	25.00	7.50
❑ 151B	I.Suzuki Japan RC	25.00	7.50

2002 Topps Gallery

	Nm-Mt	Ex-Mt
COMPLETE SET (200)	100.00	30.00
COMMON CARD (1-150)	.50	.15
COMMON CARD (151-190)	1.00	.30
COMMON CARD (191-200)	2.00	.60

	Player	Nm-Mt	Ex-Mt
❑ 1	Jason Giambi	1.25	.35
❑ 2	Mark Grace	1.25	.35
❑ 3	Bret Boone	.50	.15
❑ 4	Antonio Alfonseca	.50	.15
❑ 5	Kevin Brown	.50	.15
❑ 6	Cristian Guzman	.50	.15
❑ 7	Magglio Ordonez	.50	.15
❑ 8	Luis Gonzalez	.50	.15
❑ 9	Jorge Posada	.75	.23
❑ 10	Roberto Alomar	1.25	.35
❑ 11	Mike Sweeney	.50	.15
❑ 12	Jeff Kent	.50	.15
❑ 13	Matt Morris	.50	.15
❑ 14	Alfonso Soriano	1.25	.35
❑ 15	Adam Dunn	.75	.23
❑ 16	Neifi Perez	.50	.15
❑ 17	Todd Walker	.50	.15
❑ 18	J.D. Drew	.50	.15
❑ 19	Eric Chavez	.50	.15
❑ 20	Alex Rodriguez	2.50	.75
❑ 21	Ray Lankford	.50	.15
❑ 22	Roger Cedeno	.50	.15
❑ 23	Chipper Jones	1.25	.35
❑ 24	Josh Beckett	.75	.23
❑ 25	Mike Piazza	2.00	.60
❑ 26	Freddy Garcia	.50	.15
❑ 27	Todd Helton	.75	.23
❑ 28	Tino Martinez	.75	.23
❑ 29	Kazuhiro Sasaki	.50	.15
❑ 30	Curt Schilling	.75	.23
❑ 31	Mark Buehrle	.50	.15
❑ 32	John Olerud	.50	.15
❑ 33	Brad Radke	.50	.15
❑ 34	Steve Sparks	.50	.15
❑ 35	Jason Tyner	.50	.15
❑ 36	Jeff Shaw	.50	.15
❑ 37	Mariano Rivera	.75	.23
❑ 38	Russ Ortiz	.50	.15
❑ 39	Richard Hidalgo	.50	.15
❑ 40	Carl Everett	.50	.15
❑ 41	John Burkett	.50	.15
❑ 42	Tim Hudson	.50	.15
❑ 43	Mike Hampton	.50	.15
❑ 44	Orlando Cabrera	.50	.15
❑ 45	Barry Zito	1.25	.35
❑ 46	C.C. Sabathia	.50	.15
❑ 47	Chan Ho Park	.50	.15
❑ 48	Tom Glavine	1.25	.35
❑ 49	Aramis Ramirez	.50	.15
❑ 50	Lance Berkman	.50	.15
❑ 51	Al Leiter	.50	.15
❑ 52	Phil Nevin	.50	.15
❑ 53	Javier Vazquez	.50	.15
❑ 54	Troy Glaus	.75	.23
❑ 55	Tsuyoshi Shinjo	.50	.15
❑ 56	Albert Pujols	2.50	.75
❑ 57	John Smoltz	.75	.23
❑ 58	Derek Jeter	3.00	.90
❑ 59	Robb Nen	.50	.15
❑ 60	Jason Kendall	.50	.15
❑ 61	Eric Gagne	.75	.23
❑ 62	Vladimir Guerrero	1.25	.35
❑ 63	Corey Patterson	.50	.15
❑ 64	Rickey Henderson	2.00	.60
❑ 65	Jack Wilson	.50	.15
❑ 66	Jason LaRue	.50	.15
❑ 67	Sammy Sosa	2.00	.60
❑ 68	Ken Griffey Jr.	2.00	.60
❑ 69	Randy Johnson	1.25	.35
❑ 70	Nomar Garciaparra	2.50	.75
❑ 71	Ivan Rodriguez	1.25	.35
❑ 72	J.T. Snow	.50	.15
❑ 73	Darryl Kile	.50	.15
❑ 74	Andruw Jones	.75	.23
❑ 75	Brian Giles	.50	.15
❑ 76	Pedro Martinez	1.25	.35
❑ 77	Jeff Bagwell	.75	.23
❑ 78	Rafael Palmeiro	.75	.23
❑ 79	Ryan Dempster	.50	.15
❑ 80	Jeff Cirillo	.50	.15
❑ 81	Geoff Jenkins	.50	.15
❑ 82	Brandon Duckworth	.50	.15
❑ 83	Roger Clemens	2.50	.75
❑ 84	Fred McGriff	.75	.23
❑ 85	Hideo Nomo	1.25	.35
❑ 86	Larry Walker	.75	.23
❑ 87	Sean Casey	.50	.15
❑ 88	Trevor Hoffman	.50	.15
❑ 89	Robert Fick	.50	.15
❑ 90	Armando Benitez	.50	.15
❑ 91	Jeromy Burnitz	.50	.15
❑ 92	Bernie Williams	.75	.23
❑ 93	Carlos Delgado	.50	.15
❑ 94	Troy Percival	.50	.15
❑ 95	Nate Cornejo	.50	.15
❑ 96	Derrek Lee	.50	.15
❑ 97	Jose Ortiz	.50	.15
❑ 98	Brian Jordan	.50	.15
❑ 99	Jose Cruz Jr.	.50	.15
❑ 100	Ichiro Suzuki	2.50	.75
❑ 101	Jose Mesa	.50	.15
❑ 102	Tim Salmon	.75	.23
❑ 103	Bud Smith	.50	.15
❑ 104	Paul LoDuca	.50	.15
❑ 105	Juan Pierre	.50	.15
❑ 106	Ben Grieve	.50	.15
❑ 107	Russell Branyan	.50	.15
❑ 108	Bob Abreu	.50	.15
❑ 109	Moises Alou	.50	.15
❑ 110	Richie Sexson	.50	.15
❑ 111	Jerry Hairston Jr.	.50	.15
❑ 112	Marlon Anderson	.50	.15
❑ 113	Juan Gonzalez	1.25	.35
❑ 114	Craig Biggio	.75	.23
❑ 115	Carlos Beltran	.50	.15
❑ 116	Eric Milton	.50	.15
❑ 117	Cliff Floyd	.50	.15
❑ 118	Rich Aurilia	.50	.15
❑ 119	Adrian Beltre	.50	.15
❑ 120	Jason Bere	.50	.15
❑ 121	Darin Erstad	.50	.15
❑ 122	Ben Sheets	.50	.15
❑ 123	Johnny Damon	.50	.15
❑ 124	Jimmy Rollins	.50	.15
❑ 125	Shawn Green	.50	.15
❑ 126	Greg Maddux	2.50	.75
❑ 127	Mark Mulder	.50	.15
❑ 128	Bartolo Colon	.50	.15
❑ 129	Shannon Stewart	.50	.15
❑ 130	Ramon Ortiz	.50	.15
❑ 131	Kerry Wood	1.25	.35
❑ 132	Ryan Klesko	.50	.15
❑ 133	Preston Wilson	.50	.15
❑ 134	Roy Oswalt	.50	.15
❑ 135	Rafael Furcal	.75	.23
❑ 136	Eric Karros	.50	.15
❑ 137	Nick Neugebauer	.50	.15
❑ 138	Doug Mientkiewicz	.50	.15
❑ 139	Paul Konerko	.50	.15
❑ 140	Bobby Higginson	.50	.15
❑ 141	Garret Anderson	.50	.15
❑ 142	Wes Helms	.50	.15
❑ 143	Brent Abernathy	.50	.15
❑ 144	Scott Rolen	.75	.23
❑ 145	Dmitri Young	.50	.15
❑ 146	Jim Thome	1.25	.35

❑ 147 Raul Mondesi .50 .15
❑ 148 Pat Burrell .50 .15
❑ 149 Gary Sheffield .50 .15
❑ 150 Miguel Tejada .50 .15
❑ 151 Brandon Inge PROS 1.00 .30
❑ 152 Carlos Pena PROS 1.00 .30
❑ 153 Jason Lane PROS 1.00 .30
❑ 154 Nathan Haynes PROS 1.00 .30
❑ 155 Hank Blalock PROS 2.50 .75
❑ 156 Juan Cruz PROS 1.00 .30
❑ 157 Morgan Ensberg PROS 1.00 .30
❑ 158 Sean Burroughs PROS 1.00 .30
❑ 159 Ed Rogers PROS 1.00 .30
❑ 160 Nick Johnson PROS 1.00 .30
❑ 161 Orlando Hudson PROS 1.00 .30
❑ 162 A.Martinez PROS RC 1.00 .30
❑ 163 Jeremy Affeldt PROS 1.00 .30
❑ 164 Brandon Claussen PROS 2.50 .75
❑ 165 Deivis Santos PROS 1.00 .30
❑ 166 Mike Rivera PROS 1.00 .30
❑ 167 Carlos Silva PROS 1.00 .30
❑ 168 Val Pascucci PROS 1.00 .30
❑ 169 Xavier Nady PROS 1.00 .30
❑ 170 David Espinosa PROS 1.00 .30
❑ 171 Dan Phillips FYP RC 1.00 .30
❑ 172 Tony Fontana FYP RC 1.00 .30
❑ 173 Juan Silvestre FYP 1.00 .30
❑ 174 Henry Pichardo FYP RC 1.00 .30
❑ 175 Pablo Arias FYP RC 1.00 .30
❑ 176 Brett Roneberg FYP RC 1.00 .30
❑ 177 Chad Qualls FYP RC 1.00 .30
❑ 178 Greg Sain FYP RC 1.00 .30
❑ 179 Rene Reyes FYP RC 1.00 .30
❑ 180 So Taguchi FYP RC 1.50 .45
❑ 181 Dan Johnson FYP RC 1.50 .45
❑ 182 Justin Backsmeyer FYP RC 1.00 .30
❑ 183 Juan M. Gonzalez FYP RC 1.00 .30
❑ 184 Jason Ellison FYP RC 1.00 .30
❑ 185 Kazuhisa Ishii FYP RC 4.00 1.20
❑ 186 Joe Mauer FYP RC 8.00 2.40
❑ 187 James Shanks FYP RC 1.00 .30
❑ 188 Kevin Cash FYP RC 1.00 .30
❑ 189 J.J. Trujillo FYP RC 1.00 .30
❑ 190 Jorge Padilla FYP RC 1.50 .45
❑ 191 Nolan Ryan RET 8.00 2.40
❑ 192 George Brett RET 6.00 1.80
❑ 193 Ryne Sandberg RET 5.00 1.50
❑ 194 Robin Yount RET 2.50 .75
❑ 195 Tom Seaver RET 2.50 .75
❑ 196 Mike Schmidt RET 5.00 1.50
❑ 197 Frank Robinson RET 2.00 .60
❑ 198 Harmon Killebrew RET 2.50 .75
❑ 199 Kirby Puckett RET 2.50 .75
❑ 200 Don Mattingly RET 6.00 1.80

2003 Topps Gallery

	MINT	NRMT
COMP.SET w/o SP's (200)	100.00	45.00
COMMON (1-150/168-190)	.50	.23
COMMON CARD (151-167)	.60	.25
COMMON VARIATION (1-167)		
VARIATION STATED ODDS 1:20		
COMMON CARD (191-200)	1.25	.55

❑ 1 Jason Giambi 1.25 .55
❑ 1A Jason Giambi Blue Jsy 5.00 2.20
❑ 2 Miguel Tejada .50 .23
❑ 3 Mike Lieberthal .50 .23
❑ 4 Jason Kendall .50 .23
❑ 5 Robb Nen .50 .23
❑ 6 Freddy Garcia .50 .23
❑ 7 Scott Rolen .75 .35
❑ 8 Boomer Wells .50 .23
❑ 9 Rafael Palmeiro .75 .35
❑ 10 Garret Anderson .50 .23
❑ 11 Curt Schilling .75 .35
❑ 12 Greg Maddux 2.50 1.10
❑ 13 Rodrigo Lopez .50 .23
❑ 14 Nomar Garciaparra 2.50 1.10
❑ 14A Nomar Garciaparra Btg Glv. 10.00 4.50
❑ 15 Kerry Wood 1.25 .55
❑ 16 Frank Thomas 1.25 .55
❑ 17 Ken Griffey Jr. 2.00 .90
❑ 18 Jim Thome 1.25 .55
❑ 19 Todd Helton .75 .35
❑ 20 Lance Berkman .50 .23
❑ 21 Robert Fick .50 .23
❑ 22 Kevin Brown .50 .23
❑ 23 Richie Sexson .50 .23
❑ 24 Eddie Guardado .50 .23
❑ 25 Vladimir Guerrero 1.25 .55
❑ 26 Mike Piazza 2.00 .90
❑ 27 Bernie Williams .75 .35
❑ 28 Eric Chavez .50 .23
❑ 29 Jimmy Rollins .50 .23
❑ 30 Ichiro Suzuki 2.50 1.10
❑ 30A Ichiro Suzuki Black Sleeve 10.00 4.50
❑ 31 J.D. Drew .50 .23
❑ 32 Nick Johnson .50 .23
❑ 33 Shannon Stewart .50 .23
❑ 34 Tim Salmon .75 .35
❑ 35 Andruw Jones .75 .35
❑ 36 Jay Gibbons .50 .23
❑ 37 Johnny Damon .50 .23
❑ 38 Fred McGriff .75 .35
❑ 39 Carlos Lee .50 .23
❑ 40 Adam Dunn .75 .35
❑ 40A Adam Dunn Red Sleeve 5.00 2.20
❑ 41 Jason Jennings .50 .23
❑ 42 Mike Lowell .50 .23
❑ 43 Mike Sweeney .50 .23
❑ 44 Shawn Green .50 .23
❑ 45 Doug Mientkiewicz .50 .23
❑ 46 Bartolo Colon .50 .23
❑ 47 Edgardo Alfonzo .50 .23
❑ 48 Roger Clemens 2.50 1.10
❑ 49 Randy Wolf .50 .23
❑ 50 Alex Rodriguez 2.50 1.10
❑ 50A Alex Rodriguez Red Shirt 10.00 4.50
❑ 51 Vernon Wells .50 .23
❑ 52 Kenny Lofton .50 .23
❑ 53 Mariano Rivera .75 .35
❑ 54 Brian Jordan .50 .23
❑ 55 Roberto Alomar 1.25 .55
❑ 56 Carlos Pena .50 .23
❑ 57 Moises Alou .50 .23
❑ 58 John Smoltz .75 .35
❑ 59 Adam Kennedy .50 .23
❑ 60 Randy Johnson 1.25 .55
❑ 61 Mark Buehrle .50 .23
❑ 62 C.C. Sabathia .50 .23
❑ 63 Craig Biggio .75 .35
❑ 64 Eric Karros .50 .23
❑ 65 Jose Vidro .50 .23
❑ 66 Tim Hudson .50 .23
❑ 67 Trevor Hoffman .50 .23
❑ 68 Bret Boone .50 .23
❑ 69 Carl Crawford .50 .23
❑ 70 Derek Jeter 3.00 1.35
❑ 71 Troy Percival .50 .23
❑ 72 Gary Sheffield .50 .23
❑ 73 Rickey Henderson 2.00 .90
❑ 74 Paul Konerko .50 .23
❑ 75 Larry Walker .75 .35
❑ 76 Pat Burrell .50 .23
❑ 77 Brian Giles .50 .23
❑ 78 Jeff Kent .50 .23
❑ 79 Kazuhiro Sasaki .50 .23
❑ 80 Chipper Jones 1.25 .55
❑ 81 Darin Erstad .50 .23
❑ 82 Sean Casey .50 .23
❑ 83 Luis Gonzalez .50 .23
❑ 84 Roy Oswalt .50 .23
❑ 85 Dustan Mohr .50 .23
❑ 86 Al Leiter .50 .23
❑ 87 Mike Mussina 1.25 .55
❑ 88 Vicente Padilla .50 .23
❑ 89 Rich Aurilia .50 .23
❑ 90 Albert Pujols 2.50 1.10
❑ 91 John Olerud .50 .23
❑ 92 Ivan Rodriguez 1.25 .55
❑ 93 Eric Hinske .50 .23
❑ 94 Phil Nevin .50 .23
❑ 95 Barry Zito 1.25 .55
❑ 96 Armando Benitez .50 .23
❑ 97 Torii Hunter .50 .23
❑ 98 Paul Lo Duca .50 .23
❑ 99 Preston Wilson .50 .23
❑ 100 Sammy Sosa 2.00 .90
❑ 100A Sammy Sosa Black Bat 8.00 3.60
❑ 101 Jarrod Washburn .50 .23
❑ 102 Steve Finley .50 .23
❑ 103 Cliff Floyd .50 .23
❑ 104 Mark Prior 2.50 1.10
❑ 105 Austin Kearns .75 .35
❑ 106 Jeff Bagwell .75 .35
❑ 107 A.J. Pierzynski .50 .23
❑ 108 Pedro Martinez 1.25 .55
❑ 109 Orlando Cabrera .50 .23
❑ 110 Raul Mondesi .50 .23
❑ 111 Russ Ortiz .50 .23
❑ 112 Ruben Sierra .50 .23
❑ 113 Tino Martinez .75 .35
❑ 114 Manny Ramirez .50 .23
❑ 115 Troy Glaus .75 .35
❑ 116 Magglio Ordonez .50 .23
❑ 117 Omar Vizquel .50 .23
❑ 118 Carlos Beltran .50 .23
❑ 119 Jose Hernandez .50 .23
❑ 120 Javier Vazquez .50 .23
❑ 121 Jorge Posada .75 .35
❑ 122 Aramis Ramirez .50 .23
❑ 123 Jason Schmidt .50 .23
❑ 124 Jamie Moyer .50 .23
❑ 125 Jim Edmonds .50 .23
❑ 126 Aubrey Huff .50 .23
❑ 127 Carlos Delgado .50 .23
❑ 128 Junior Spivey .50 .23
❑ 129 Tom Glavine 1.25 .55
❑ 130 Marty Cordova .50 .23
❑ 131 Derek Lowe .50 .23
❑ 132 Ellis Burks .50 .23
❑ 133 Barry Bonds 3.00 1.35
❑ 134 Josh Beckett .75 .35
❑ 135 Raul Ibanez .50 .23
❑ 136 Kazuhisa Ishii .50 .23
❑ 137 Geoff Jenkins .50 .23
❑ 138 Eric Milton .50 .23
❑ 139 Mo Vaughn .50 .23
❑ 140 Mark Mulder .50 .23
❑ 141 Bobby Abreu .50 .23
❑ 142 Ryan Klesko .50 .23
❑ 143 Tsuyoshi Shinjo .50 .23
❑ 144 Jose Mesa .50 .23
❑ 145 Shea Hillenbrand .50 .23
❑ 146 Edgar Renteria .50 .23
❑ 147 Juan Gonzalez 1.25 .55
❑ 148 Edgar Martinez .50 .23
❑ 149 Matt Morris .50 .23
❑ 150 Alfonso Soriano 1.25 .55
❑ 150A Alfonso Soriano No Pad 5.00 2.20
❑ 151 Bryan Bullington FY RC 3.00 1.35
❑ 151A B.Bullington Red Back FY 10.00 4.50
❑ 152 Andy Marte FY RC 4.00 1.80
❑ 152A Andy Marte No Necklace FY 10.00 4.50
❑ 153 Brendan Harris FY RC 1.50 .70
❑ 154 Juan Camacho FY RC .60 .25
❑ 155 Byron Gettis FY RC .60 .25
❑ 156 Daryl Clark FY RC 1.00 .45
❑ 157 J.D. Durbin FY RC 1.50 .70
❑ 158 Craig Brazell FY RC 1.50 .70
❑ 158A Craig Brazell Black Jsy 5.00 2.20
❑ 159 Jason Kubel FY RC 1.50 .70
❑ 160 Brandon Roberson FY RC .60 .25
❑ 161 Jose Contreras FY RC 3.00 1.35
❑ 162 Hanley Ramirez FY RC 3.00 1.35
❑ 163 Jaime Bubela FY RC .60 .25
❑ 164 Chris Duncan FY RC .60 .25
❑ 165 Tyler Johnson FY RC .60 .25
❑ 166 Joey Gomes FY RC 1.00 .45

❑ 167 Ben Francisco FY RC .... 1.50 .70
❑ 168 Adam LaRoche PROS ...... .50 .23
❑ 169 Tommy Whiteman PROS.. .50 .23
❑ 170 Trey Hodges PROS .... .50 .23
❑ 171 Francisco Rodriguez PROS ..... .50 .23
❑ 172 Jason Arnold PROS.......... .50 .23
❑ 173 Brett Myers PROS .... .50 .23
❑ 174 Rocco Baldelli PROS..... 4.00 1.80
❑ 175 Adrian Gonzalez PROS .... .50 .23
❑ 176 Dontrelle Willis PROS.... 3.00 1.35
❑ 177 Walter Young PROS .... .50 .23
❑ 178 Marlon Byrd PROS .... .50 .23
❑ 179 Aaron Heilman PROS ...... .50 .23
❑ 180 Casey Kotchman PROS.... .75 .35
❑ 181 Miguel Cabrera PROS..... 4.00 1.80
❑ 182 Hee Seop Choi PROS ...... .50 .23
❑ 183 Drew Henson PROS .... .50 .23
❑ 184 Jose Reyes PROS .... .75 .35
❑ 185 Michael Cuddyer PROS.... .50 .23
❑ 186 Brandon Phillips PROS.... .50 .23
❑ 187 Victor Martinez PROS ...... .50 .23
❑ 188 Joe Mauer PROS............ 1.25 .55
❑ 189 Hank Blalock PROS.......... .75 .35
❑ 190 Mark Teixeira PROS .... .75 .35
❑ 191 Willie Mays RET 4.00 1.80
❑ 192 George Brett RET............ 5.00 2.20
❑ 193 Tony Gwynn RET............ 2.50 1.10
❑ 194 Carl Yastrzemski RET 3.00 1.35
❑ 195 Nolan Ryan RET 6.00 2.70
❑ 196 Reggie Jackson RET ...... 1.25 .55
❑ 197 Mike Schmidt RET.......... 4.00 1.80
❑ 198 Cal Ripken RET 6.00 2.70
❑ 199 Don Mattingly RET 5.00 2.20
❑ 200 Tom Seaver RET .... 2.00 .90

2003 Topps Gallery HOF

	Nm-Mt	Ex-Mt
COMPLETE SET (74)	40.00	12.00
COMMON CARD (1-74)	.75	.23
COMMON VARIATION (1-74)	1.50	.45

❑ 1 Willie Mays Bleachers........ 3.00 .90
❑ 1B Willie Mays Gold 6.00 1.80
❑ 2 Al Kaline Stripes .... 1.50 .45
❑ 2B Al Kaline No Stripes .... 3.00 .90
❑ 3 Hank Aaron Black Hat .... 3.00 .90
❑ 3B Hank Aaron Blue Hat........ 6.00 1.80
❑ 4 Carl Yastrzemski Black Ltr.. 2.00 .60
❑ 4B Carl Yastrzemski Red Ltr.. 4.00 1.20
❑ 5 Luis Aparicio Wood Bat........ .75 .23
❑ 5B Luis Aparicio Black Bat .... 1.50 .45
❑ 6 Sam Crawford Grey Uni........ .75 .23
❑ 6B Sam Crawford Navy Uni .. 1.50 .45
❑ 7 Tom Lasorda Trees .... .75 .23
❑ 7B Tom Lasorda Red .... 1.50 .45
❑ 8 John McGraw MG No Logo.. .75 .23
❑ 8B John McGraw MG NY Logo.... 1.50 .45
❑ 9 Edd Roush White C .... .75 .23
❑ 9B Edd Roush Red C .... 1.50 .45
❑ 10 Reggie Jackson Grass ...... 1.00 .30
❑ 10B Reggie Jackson Red ...... 2.00 .60
❑ 11 Catfish Hunter Yellow Jsy 1.00 .30
❑ 11B Catfish Hunter White Jsy 2.00 .60
❑ 12 Roberto Clemente White Uni.... 4.00 1.20
❑ 12B Roberto Clemente Yellow Uni 8.00 2.40
❑ 13 Eddie Collins Grey Uni ...... .75 .23
❑ 13B Eddie Collins Navy Uni .. 1.50 .45
❑ 14 Frankie Frisch Olive .... .75 .23
❑ 14B Frankie Frisch Blue........ 1.50 .45
❑ 15 Nolan Ryan Leather Glv.... 5.00 1.50
❑ 15B Nolan Ryan Black Glv .. 10.00 3.00
❑ 16 Brooks Robinson Yellow .. 1.50 .45
❑ 16B Brooks Robinson Green 3.00 .90
❑ 17 Phil Niekro Black Hat .... .75 .23
❑ 17B Phil Niekro Blue Hat ...... 1.50 .45
❑ 18 Joe Cronin Blue Sleeve...... .75 .23
❑ 18B Joe Cronin White Sleeve 1.50 .45
❑ 19 Joe Tinker White Hat.......... .75 .23
❑ 19B Joe Tinker Blue Hat........ 1.50 .45
❑ 20 Johnny Bench Day .... 1.50 .45
❑ 20B Johnny Bench Night ...... 3.00 .90
❑ 21 Harry Heilmann Day .... .75 .23
❑ 21B Harry Heilmann Night..... 1.50 .45
❑ 22 Ernie Harwell BRD Red Tie .75 .23
❑ 22B Ernie Harwell BRD Blue Tie.... 1.50 .45
❑ 23 Warren Spahn Patch .... 1.00 .30
❑ 23B Warren Spahn No Patch 2.00 .60
❑ 24 George Kelly Blue Bill .... .75 .23
❑ 24B George Kelly Red Bill .... 1.50 .45
❑ 25 Phil Rizzuto Bleachers...... 1.00 .30
❑ 25B Phil Rizzuto Green.......... 2.00 .60
❑ 26 Robin Roberts Day .... .75 .23
❑ 26B Robin Roberts Night ...... 1.50 .45
❑ 27 Ozzie Smith Red Sleeve..... 1.50 .45
❑ 27B Ozzie Smith Blue Sleeve 3.00 .90
❑ 28 Jim Palmer White Hat .... .75 .23
❑ 28B Jim Palmer Black Hat .... 1.50 .45
❑ 29 Duke Snider No Patch ...... 1.00 .30
❑ 29B Duke Snider Flag Patch.. 2.00 .60
❑ 30 Bob Feller White Uni .... 1.00 .30
❑ 30B Bob Feller Grey Uni........ 2.00 .60
❑ 31 Buck Leonard Bleachers .... .75 .23
❑ 31B Buck Leonard Red.......... 1.50 .45
❑ 32 Kirby Puckett Wood Bat..... 1.50 .45
❑ 32B Kirby Puckett Black Bat .. 3.00 .90
❑ 33 Monte Irvin Black Sleeve.... .75 .23
❑ 33B Monte Irvin White Sleeve 1.50 .45
❑ 34 Chuck Klein Black Socks.... .75 .23
❑ 34B Chuck Klein Red Socks.. 1.50 .45
❑ 35 Willie Stargell Yellow Uni 1.00 .30
❑ 35B Willie Stargell White Uni 2.00 .60
❑ 36 Juan Marichal Ballpark ...... .75 .23
❑ 36B Juan Marichal Gold........ 1.50 .45
❑ 37 Lou Brock Day................. 1.00 .30
❑ 37B Lou Brock Night .... 2.00 .60
❑ 38 Bucky Harris Black W .... .75 .23
❑ 38B Bucky Harris Red W ...... 1.50 .45
❑ 39 Bobby Doerr Ballpark .... .75 .23
❑ 39B Bobby Doerr Red............ 1.50 .45
❑ 40 Lee MacPhail Blue Tie........ .75 .23
❑ 40B Lee MacPhail Red Tie .... 1.50 .45
❑ 41 Heinie Manush Grey Sleeve...... .75 .23
❑ 41B Heinie Manush Navy Sleeve.. 1.50 .45
❑ 42 George Brett Patch 4.00 1.20
❑ 42B George Brett No Patch.... 8.00 2.40
❑ 43 Harmon Killebrew Blue Hat 1.50 .45
❑ 43B Harmon Killebrew Red Hat .... 3.00 .90
❑ 44 Whitey Ford Day .... 1.00 .30
❑ 44B Whitey Ford Night.......... 2.00 .60
❑ 45 Eddie Mathews Day.......... 1.50 .45
❑ 45B Eddie Mathews Night ...... 3.00 .90
❑ 46 Gaylord Perry Leather Glv .. .75 .23
❑ 46B Gaylord Perry Black Glv 1.50 .45
❑ 47 Red Schoendienst Stripes .. .75 .23
❑ 47B Red Schoendienst No Stripes 1.50 .45
❑ 48 Earl Weaver MG Day .... .75 .23
❑ 48B Earl Weaver MG Night.... 1.50 .45
❑ 49 Joe Morgan Day .... .75 .23
❑ 49B Joe Morgan Night.......... 1.50 .45
❑ 50 Mike Schmidt Grey Uni .... 3.00 .90
❑ 50B Mike Schmidt White Uni 6.00 1.80
❑ 51 Willie McCovey Wood Bat.. .75 .23
❑ 51B Willie McCovey Black Bat 1.50 .45
❑ 52 Stan Musial Day .... 2.50 .75
❑ 52B Stan Musial Night.......... 5.00 1.50
❑ 53 Don Sutton Ballpark .... .75 .23
❑ 53B Don Sutton Gray .... 1.50 .45
❑ 54 Hank Greenberg w/Player 1.50 .45
❑ 54B Hank Greenberg No Player .... 3.00 .90
❑ 55 Robin Yount w/Player ...... 1.50 .45
❑ 55B Robin Yount No Player .. 3.00 .90
❑ 56 Tom Seaver Leather Glv .. 1.50 .45
❑ 56B Tom Seaver Black Glv.... 3.00 .90
❑ 57 Tony Perez Wood Bat .... .75 .23
❑ 57B Tony Perez Black Bat...... 1.50 .45
❑ 58 George Sisler w/Ad .... .75 .23
❑ 58B George Sisler No Ad ...... 1.50 .45
❑ 59 Jim Bottomley White Hat.... .75 .23
❑ 59B Jim Bottomley Red Hat .. 1.50 .45
❑ 60 Yogi Berra Leather Chest.. 1.50 .45
❑ 60B Yogi Berra Navy Chest .. 3.00 .90
❑ 61 Fred Lindstrom Blue Bill .... .75 .23
❑ 61B Fred Lindstrom Red Bill 1.50 .45
❑ 62 Napoleon Lajoie White Uni 1.50 .45
❑ 62B Napoleon Lajoie Navy Uni .... 3.00 .90
❑ 63 Frank Robinson Wood Bat 1.00 .30
❑ 63B Frank Robinson Black Bat...... 2.00 .60
❑ 64 Carlton Fisk Red Ltr .... 1.00 .30
❑ 64B Carlton Fisk Black Ltr .... 2.00 .60
❑ 65 Orlando Cepeda Blue Sky .. .75 .23
❑ 65B Orlando Cepeda Sunset 1.50 .45
❑ 66 Fergie Jenkins Leather Glv .75 .23
❑ 66B Fergie Jenkins Black Glv 1.50 .45
❑ 67 Ernie Banks Day .... 1.50 .45
❑ 67B Ernie Banks Night.......... 3.00 .90
❑ 68 Bill Mazeroski No Sleeves 1.00 .30
❑ 68B Bill Mazeroski w/Sleeves 2.00 .60
❑ 69 Jim Bunning Grey Uni........ .75 .23
❑ 69B Jim Bunning White Uni .. 1.50 .45
❑ 70 Rollie Fingers Day.............. .75 .23
❑ 70B Rollie Fingers Night ...... 1.50 .45
❑ 71 Jimmie Foxx Black Sleeve 1.50 .45
❑ 71B Jimmie Foxx White Sleeve .... 3.00 .90
❑ 72 Rod Carew Red Btg Glv.... 1.00 .30
❑ 72B Rod Carew Blue Btg Glv 2.00 .60
❑ 73 Sparky Anderson Blue Sky .75 .23
❑ 73B Sparky Anderson Yellow 1.50 .45
❑ 74 George Kell Red D.............. .75 .23
❑ 74B George Kell White D ...... 1.50 .45

1999 Topps Gold Label Class 1

	Nm-Mt	Ex-Mt
COMP.GOLD SET (100)	50.00	15.00

❑ 1 Mike Piazza .... 2.00 .60
❑ 2 Andres Galarraga................ .50 .15
❑ 3 Mark Grace .... 1.25 .35
❑ 4 Tony Clark.......................... .50 .15
❑ 5 Jim Thome .... 1.25 .35
❑ 6 Tony Gwynn .... 1.50 .45
❑ 7 Kelly Dransfeldt RC .... .50 .15
❑ 8 Eric Chavez .... .50 .15
❑ 9 Brian Jordan .... .50 .15
❑ 10 Todd Hundley .... .50 .15
❑ 11 Rondell White .... .50 .15
❑ 12 Dmitri Young...................... .50 .15
❑ 13 Jeff Kent .... .50 .15
❑ 14 Derek Bell .... .50 .15
❑ 15 Todd Helton .... .75 .23
❑ 16 Chipper Jones.................. 1.25 .35
❑ 17 Albert Belle .... .50 .15
❑ 18 Barry Larkin...................... 1.25 .35
❑ 19 Dante Bichette .... .50 .15
❑ 20 Gary Sheffield .... .50 .15
❑ 21 Cliff Floyd .... .50 .15
❑ 22 Derek Jeter .... 3.00 .90
❑ 23 Jason Giambi .... 1.25 .35
❑ 24 Ray Lankford .... .50 .15
❑ 25 Alex Rodriguez .... 2.50 .75

	Nm-Mt	Ex-Mt
❑ 26 Ruben Mateo	.50	.15
❑ 27 Wade Boggs	.75	.23
❑ 28 Carlos Delgado	.50	.15
❑ 29 Tim Salmon	.75	.23
❑ 30 Alfonso Soriano RC	12.00	3.60
❑ 31 Javy Lopez	.50	.15
❑ 32 Jason Kendall	.50	.15
❑ 33 Nick Johnson RC	2.00	.60
❑ 34 A.J. Burnett RC	.75	.23
❑ 35 Troy Glaus	.75	.23
❑ 36 Pat Burrell RC	4.00	1.20
❑ 37 Jeff Cirillo	.50	.15
❑ 38 David Justice	.50	.15
❑ 39 Ivan Rodriguez	1.25	.35
❑ 40 Bernie Williams	.75	.23
❑ 41 Jay Buhner	.50	.15
❑ 42 Mo Vaughn	.50	.15
❑ 43 Randy Johnson	1.25	.35
❑ 44 Pedro Martinez	1.25	.35
❑ 45 Larry Walker	.75	.23
❑ 46 Todd Walker	.50	.15
❑ 47 Roberto Alomar	1.25	.35
❑ 48 Kevin Brown	.75	.23
❑ 49 Mike Mussina	1.25	.35
❑ 50 Tom Glavine	1.25	.35
❑ 51 Curt Schilling	.75	.23
❑ 52 Ken Caminiti	.50	.15
❑ 53 Brad Fullmer	.50	.15
❑ 54 Bobby Seay RC	.50	.15
❑ 55 Orlando Hernandez	.50	.15
❑ 56 Sean Casey	.50	.15
❑ 57 Al Leiter	.50	.15
❑ 58 Sandy Alomar Jr.	.50	.15
❑ 59 Mark Kotsay	.50	.15
❑ 60 Matt Williams	.50	.15
❑ 61 Raul Mondesi	.50	.15
❑ 62 Joe Crede RC	5.00	1.50
❑ 63 Jim Edmonds	.50	.15
❑ 64 Jose Cruz Jr.	.50	.15
❑ 65 Juan Gonzalez	1.25	.35
❑ 66 Sammy Sosa	2.00	.60
❑ 67 Cal Ripken	4.00	1.20
❑ 68 Vinny Castilla	.50	.15
❑ 69 Craig Biggio	.75	.23
❑ 70 Mark McGwire	3.00	.90
❑ 71 Greg Vaughn	.50	.15
❑ 72 Greg Maddux	2.50	.75
❑ 73 Paul O'Neill	.75	.23
❑ 74 Scott Rolen	.75	.23
❑ 75 Ben Grieve	.50	.15
❑ 76 Vladimir Guerrero	1.25	.35
❑ 77 John Olerud	.50	.15
❑ 78 Eric Karros	.50	.15
❑ 79 Jeromy Burnitz	.50	.15
❑ 80 Jeff Bagwell	.75	.23
❑ 81 Kenny Lofton	.50	.15
❑ 82 Manny Ramirez	.50	.15
❑ 83 Andruw Jones	.75	.23
❑ 84 Travis Lee	.50	.15
❑ 85 Darin Erstad	.50	.15
❑ 86 Nomar Garciaparra	2.50	.75
❑ 87 Frank Thomas	1.25	.35
❑ 88 Moises Alou	.50	.15
❑ 89 Tino Martinez	.75	.23
❑ 90 Carlos Pena RC	1.25	.35
❑ 91 Shawn Green	.50	.15
❑ 92 Rusty Greer	.50	.15
❑ 93 Matt Belisle RC	.50	.15
❑ 94 Adrian Beltre	.50	.15
❑ 95 Roger Clemens	2.50	.75
❑ 96 John Smoltz	.75	.23
❑ 97 Mark Mulder RC	4.00	1.20
❑ 98 Kerry Wood	1.25	.35
❑ 99 Barry Bonds	3.00	.90
❑ 100 Ken Griffey Jr.	2.00	.60

2002 Topps Gold Label

	Nm-Mt	Ex-Mt
COMPLETE SET (200)	100.00	30.00
❑ 1 Alex Rodriguez	2.50	.75
❑ 2 Derek Jeter	3.00	.90
❑ 3 Luis Gonzalez	.50	.15
❑ 4 Troy Glaus	.75	.23
❑ 5 Albert Pujols	2.50	.75

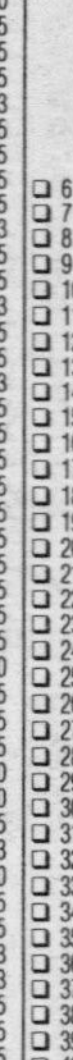

	Nm-Mt	Ex-Mt
❑ 6 Lance Berkman	.50	.15
❑ 7 J.D. Drew	.50	.15
❑ 8 Chipper Jones	1.25	.35
❑ 9 Miguel Tejada	.50	.15
❑ 10 Randy Johnson	1.25	.35
❑ 11 Mike Cameron	.50	.15
❑ 12 Brian Giles	.50	.15
❑ 13 Roger Cedeno	.50	.15
❑ 14 Kerry Wood	1.25	.35
❑ 15 Ken Griffey Jr.	2.00	.60
❑ 16 Carlos Lee	.50	.15
❑ 17 Todd Helton	.75	.23
❑ 18 Gary Sheffield	.50	.15
❑ 19 Richie Sexson	.50	.15
❑ 20 Vladimir Guerrero	1.25	.35
❑ 21 Bobby Higginson	.50	.15
❑ 22 Roger Clemens	2.50	.75
❑ 23 Barry Zito	1.25	.35
❑ 24 Juan Pierre	.50	.15
❑ 25 Pedro Martinez	1.25	.35
❑ 26 Sean Casey	.50	.15
❑ 27 David Segui	.50	.15
❑ 28 Jose Garcia RC	.75	.23
❑ 29 Curt Schilling	.75	.23
❑ 30 Bernie Williams	.75	.23
❑ 31 Ben Grieve	.50	.15
❑ 32 Hideo Nomo	1.25	.35
❑ 33 Aramis Ramirez	.50	.15
❑ 34 Cristian Guzman	.50	.15
❑ 35 Rich Aurilia	.50	.15
❑ 36 Greg Maddux	2.50	.75
❑ 37 Eric Chavez	.50	.15
❑ 38 Shawn Green	.50	.15
❑ 39 Luis Rivas	.50	.15
❑ 40 Magglio Ordonez	.50	.15
❑ 41 Jose Vidro	.50	.15
❑ 42 Mariano Rivera	.75	.23
❑ 43 Chris Tritle RC	.75	.23
❑ 44 C.C. Sabathia	.50	.15
❑ 45 Larry Walker	.75	.23
❑ 46 Raul Mondesi	.50	.15
❑ 47 Kevin Brown	.50	.15
❑ 48 Jeff Bagwell	.75	.23
❑ 49 Earl Snyder RC	.75	.23
❑ 50 Jason Giambi	1.25	.35
❑ 51 Ichiro Suzuki	2.50	.75
❑ 52 Andruw Jones	.75	.23
❑ 53 Ivan Rodriguez	1.25	.35
❑ 54 Jim Edmonds	.50	.15
❑ 55 Preston Wilson	.50	.15
❑ 56 Greg Vaughn	.50	.15
❑ 57 Jon Lieber	.50	.15
❑ 58 Justin Sherrod RC	1.25	.35
❑ 59 Marcus Giles	.50	.15
❑ 60 Roberto Alomar	1.25	.35
❑ 61 Pat Burrell	.50	.15
❑ 62 Doug Mientkiewicz	.50	.15
❑ 63 Mark Mulder	.50	.15
❑ 64 Mike Hampton	.50	.15
❑ 65 Adam Dunn	.75	.23
❑ 66 Moises Alou	.50	.15
❑ 67 Jose Cruz Jr.	.50	.15
❑ 68 Derek Bell	.50	.15
❑ 69 Sammy Sosa	2.00	.60
❑ 70 Joe Mays	.50	.15
❑ 71 Phil Nevin	.50	.15
❑ 72 Edgardo Alfonzo	.50	.15
❑ 73 Barry Bonds	3.00	.90
❑ 74 Edgar Martinez	.75	.23
❑ 75 Juan Encarnacion	.50	.15
❑ 76 Jason Tyner	.50	.15
❑ 77 Edgar Renteria	.50	.15
❑ 78 Bret Boone	.50	.15
❑ 79 Scott Rolen	.75	.23
❑ 80 Nomar Garciaparra	2.50	.75
❑ 81 Frank Thomas	1.25	.35
❑ 82 Roy Oswalt	.50	.15
❑ 83 Tsuyoshi Shinjo	.50	.15
❑ 84 Ben Sheets	.50	.15
❑ 85 Hank Blalock	1.25	.35
❑ 86 Carlos Delgado	.50	.15
❑ 87 Tim Hudson	.50	.15
❑ 88 Alfonso Soriano	1.25	.35
❑ 89 Michael Hill RC	.75	.23
❑ 90 Jim Thome	1.25	.35
❑ 91 Craig Biggio	.75	.23
❑ 92 Ryan Klesko	.50	.15
❑ 93 Geoff Jenkins	.50	.15
❑ 94 Matt Morris	.50	.15
❑ 95 Jorge Posada	.75	.23
❑ 96 Cliff Floyd	.50	.15
❑ 97 Jimmy Rollins	.50	.15
❑ 98 Mike Sweeney	.50	.15
❑ 99 Frank Catalanotto	.50	.15
❑ 100 Mike Piazza	2.00	.60
❑ 101 Mark Quinn	.50	.15
❑ 102 Torii Hunter	.50	.15
❑ 103 Lee Stevens	.50	.15
❑ 104 Byung-Hyun Kim	.50	.15
❑ 105 Freddy Sanchez RC	2.00	.60
❑ 106 David Cone	.50	.15
❑ 107 Jerry Hairston Jr.	.50	.15
❑ 108 Kyle Farnsworth	.50	.15
❑ 109 Rafael Furcal	.50	.15
❑ 110 Bartolo Colon	.50	.15
❑ 111 Juan Rivera	.50	.15
❑ 112 Kevin Young	.50	.15
❑ 113 Chris Narveson RC	1.25	.35
❑ 114 Richard Hidalgo	.50	.15
❑ 115 Andy Pettitte	.75	.23
❑ 116 Darin Erstad	.50	.15
❑ 117 Corey Koskie	.50	.15
❑ 118 So Taguchi RC	1.25	.35
❑ 119 Derrek Lee	.50	.15
❑ 120 Sean Burroughs	.50	.15
❑ 121 Paul Konerko	.50	.15
❑ 122 Ross Peeples RC	1.25	.35
❑ 123 Terrence Long	.50	.15
❑ 124 John Smoltz	.75	.23
❑ 125 Brandon Duckworth	.50	.15
❑ 126 Luis Maza	.50	.15
❑ 127 Morgan Ensberg	.50	.15
❑ 128 Eric Valent	.50	.15
❑ 129 Shannon Stewart	.50	.15
❑ 130 D'Angelo Jimenez	.50	.15
❑ 131 Jeff Cirillo	.50	.15
❑ 132 Jack Cust	.50	.15
❑ 133 Dmitri Young	.50	.15
❑ 134 Darryl Kile	.50	.15
❑ 135 Reggie Sanders	.50	.15
❑ 136 Marlon Byrd	.50	.15
❑ 137 Napoleon Calzado RC	.75	.23
❑ 138 Javy Lopez	.50	.15
❑ 139 Orlando Cabrera	.50	.15
❑ 140 Mike Mussina	1.25	.35
❑ 141 Josh Beckett	.75	.23
❑ 142 Kazuhiro Sasaki	.50	.15
❑ 143 Jermaine Dye	.50	.15
❑ 144 Carlos Beltran	.50	.15
❑ 145 Trevor Hoffman	.50	.15
❑ 146 Kazuhisa Ishii RC	3.00	.90
❑ 147 Alex Gonzalez	.50	.15
❑ 148 Marty Cordova	.50	.15
❑ 149 Kevin Deaton RC	.75	.23
❑ 150 Toby Hall	.50	.15
❑ 151 Rafael Palmeiro	.75	.23
❑ 152 John Olerud	.50	.15
❑ 153 David Eckstein	.50	.15
❑ 154 Doug Glanville	.50	.15
❑ 155 Johnny Damon	.50	.15
❑ 156 Javier Vazquez	.50	.15
❑ 157 Jason Bay RC	2.50	.75
❑ 158 Robb Nen	.50	.15
❑ 159 Rafael Soriano	.50	.15

❑ 160 Placido Polanco .50 .15
❑ 161 Garret Anderson .50 .15
❑ 162 Aaron Boone .50 .15
❑ 163 Mike Lieberthal .50 .15
❑ 164 Joe Mauer RC 8.00 2.40
❑ 165 Matt Lawton .50 .15
❑ 166 Juan Tolentino RC .75 .23
❑ 167 Alex Gonzalez .50 .15
❑ 168 Steve Finley .50 .15
❑ 169 Troy Percival .50 .15
❑ 170 Bud Smith .50 .15
❑ 171 Freddy Garcia .50 .15
❑ 172 Ray Lankford .50 .15
❑ 173 Tim Redding .50 .15
❑ 174 Ryan Dempster .50 .15
❑ 175 Travis Lee .50 .15
❑ 176 Jeff Kent .50 .15
❑ 177 Ramon Hernandez .50 .15
❑ 178 Carl Everett .50 .15
❑ 179 Tom Glavine 1.25 .35
❑ 180 Juan Gonzalez 1.25 .35
❑ 181 Nick Johnson .50 .15
❑ 182 Mike Lowell .50 .15
❑ 183 Al Leiter .50 .15
❑ 184 Jason Maule RC .75 .23
❑ 185 Wilson Betemit .50 .15
❑ 186 Tino Martinez .75 .23
❑ 187 Jason Standridge .50 .15
❑ 188 Mike Peeples RC .75 .23
❑ 189 Jason Kendall .50 .15
❑ 190 Fred McGriff .75 .23
❑ 191 John Rodriguez RC .75 .23
❑ 192 Brett Roneberg RC .75 .23
❑ 193 Marlyn Tisdale RC .75 .23
❑ 194 J.T. Snow .50 .15
❑ 195 Craig Kuzmic RC .75 .23
❑ 196 Cory Lidle .50 .15
❑ 197 Alex Cintron .50 .15
❑ 198 Fernando Vina .50 .15
❑ 199 Austin Kearns .75 .23
❑ 200 Paul LoDuca .50 .15

2001 Topps Heritage

	Nm-Mt	Ex-Mt
COMP.MASTER SET (487)	400.00	120.00
COMPLETE SET (407)	300.00	90.00
COMP.SET w/o SP's (230)	60.00	18.00
COMMON CARD (81-310)	.60	.18
COMMON CARD (1-80)	2.50	.75
COMMON (311-407)	5.00	1.50

❑ 1 Kris Benson 2.50 .75
❑ 1 Kris Benson Black 2.50 .75
❑ 2 Brian Jordan 2.50 .75
❑ 2 Brian Jordan Black 2.50 .75
❑ 3 Fernando Vina 2.50 .75
❑ 3 Fernando Vina Black 2.50 .75
❑ 4 Mike Sweeney 2.50 .75
❑ 4 Mike Sweeney Black 2.50 .75
❑ 5 Rafael Palmeiro 2.50 .75
❑ 5 Rafael Palmeiro Black 2.50 .75
❑ 6 Paul O'Neill 2.50 .75
❑ 6 Paul O'Neill Black 2.50 .75
❑ 7 Todd Helton 2.50 .75
❑ 7 Todd Helton Black 2.50 .75
❑ 8 Ramiro Mendoza 2.50 .75
❑ 8 Ramiro Mendoza Black 2.50 .75
❑ 9 Kevin Millwood 2.50 .75
❑ 9 Kevin Millwood Black 2.50 .75
❑ 10 Chuck Knoblauch 2.50 .75
❑ 10 Chuck Knoblauch Black 2.50 .75
❑ 11 Derek Jeter 10.00 3.00
❑ 11 Derek Jeter Black 10.00 3.00
❑ 12 A.Rodriguez Rangers 8.00 2.40
❑ 12 A.Rod Black Rangers 8.00 2.40
❑ 13 Geoff Jenkins 2.50 .75
❑ 13 Geoff Jenkins Black 2.50 .75
❑ 14 David Justice 2.50 .75
❑ 14 David Justice Black 2.50 .75
❑ 15 David Cone 2.50 .75
❑ 15 David Cone Black 2.50 .75
❑ 16 Andres Galarraga 2.50 .75
❑ 16 Andres Galarraga Black 2.50 .75
❑ 17 Garret Anderson 2.50 .75
❑ 17 Garret Anderson Black 2.50 .75
❑ 18 Roger Cedeno 2.50 .75
❑ 18 Roger Cedeno Black 2.50 .75
❑ 19 Randy Velarde 2.50 .75
❑ 19 Randy Velarde Black 2.50 .75
❑ 20 Carlos Delgado 2.50 .75
❑ 20 Carlos Delgado Black 2.50 .75
❑ 21 Quilvio Veras 2.50 .75
❑ 21 Quilvio Veras Black 2.50 .75
❑ 22 Jose Vidro 2.50 .75
❑ 22 Jose Vidro Black 2.50 .75
❑ 23 Corey Patterson 2.50 .75
❑ 23 Corey Patterson Black 2.50 .75
❑ 24 Jorge Posada 2.50 .75
❑ 24 Jorge Posada Black 2.50 .75
❑ 25 Eddie Perez 2.50 .75
❑ 25 Eddie Perez Black 2.50 .75
❑ 26 Jack Cust 2.50 .75
❑ 26 Jack Cust Black 2.50 .75
❑ 27 Sean Burroughs 2.50 .75
❑ 27 Sean Burroughs Black 2.50 .75
❑ 28 Randy Wolf 2.50 .75
❑ 28 Randy Wolf Black 2.50 .75
❑ 29 Mike Lamb 2.50 .75
❑ 29 Mike Lamb Black 2.50 .75
❑ 30 Rafael Furcal 2.50 .75
❑ 30 Rafael Furcal Black 2.50 .75
❑ 31 Barry Bonds 10.00 3.00
❑ 31 Barry Bonds Black 10.00 3.00
❑ 32 Tim Hudson 2.50 .75
❑ 32 Tim Hudson Black 2.50 .75
❑ 33 Tom Glavine 4.00 1.20
❑ 33 Tom Glavine Black 4.00 1.20
❑ 34 Javy Lopez 2.50 .75
❑ 34 Javy Lopez Black 2.50 .75
❑ 35 Aubrey Huff 2.50 .75
❑ 35 Aubrey Huff Black 2.50 .75
❑ 36 Wally Joyner 2.50 .75
❑ 36 Wally Joyner Black 2.50 .75
❑ 37 Magglio Ordonez 2.50 .75
❑ 37 Magglio Ordonez Black 2.50 .75
❑ 38 Matt Lawton 2.50 .75
❑ 38 Matt Lawton Black 2.50 .75
❑ 39 Mariano Rivera 2.50 .75
❑ 39 Mariano Rivera Black 2.50 .75
❑ 40 Andy Ashby 2.50 .75
❑ 40 Andy Ashby Black 2.50 .75
❑ 41 Mark Buehrle 2.50 .75
❑ 41 Mark Buehrle Black 2.50 .75
❑ 42 Esteban Loaiza 2.50 .75
❑ 42 Esteban Loaiza Black 2.50 .75
❑ 43 Mark Redman 2.50 .75
❑ 43 Mark Redman Black 2.50 .75
❑ 44 Mark Quinn 2.50 .75
❑ 44 Mark Quinn Black 2.50 .75
❑ 45 Tino Martinez 2.50 .75
❑ 45 Tino Martinez Black 2.50 .75
❑ 46 Joe Mays 2.50 .75
❑ 46 Joe Mays Black 2.50 .75
❑ 47 Walt Weiss 2.50 .75
❑ 47 Walt Weiss Black 2.50 .75
❑ 48 Roger Clemens 8.00 2.40
❑ 48 Roger Clemens Black 8.00 2.40
❑ 49 Greg Maddux 8.00 2.40
❑ 49 Greg Maddux Black 8.00 2.40
❑ 50 Richard Hidalgo 2.50 .75
❑ 50 Richard Hidalgo Black 2.50 .75
❑ 51 Orlando Hernandez 2.50 .75
❑ 51 O.Hernandez Black 2.50 .75
❑ 52 Chipper Jones 4.00 1.20
❑ 52 Chipper Jones Black 4.00 1.20
❑ 53 Ben Grieve 2.50 .75
❑ 53 Ben Grieve Black 2.50 .75
❑ 54 Jimmy Haynes 2.50 .75
❑ 54 Jimmy Haynes Black 2.50 .75
❑ 55 Ken Caminiti 2.50 .75
❑ 55 Ken Caminiti Black 2.50 .75
❑ 56 Tim Salmon 2.50 .75
❑ 56 Tim Salmon Black 2.50 .75
❑ 57 Andy Pettitte 2.50 .75
❑ 57 Andy Pettitte Black 2.50 .75
❑ 58 Darin Erstad 2.50 .75
❑ 58 Darin Erstad Black 2.50 .75
❑ 59 Marquis Grissom 2.50 .75
❑ 59 Marquis Grissom Black 2.50 .75
❑ 60 Raul Mondesi 2.50 .75
❑ 60 Raul Mondesi Black 2.50 .75
❑ 61 Bengie Molina 2.50 .75
❑ 61 Bengie Molina Black 2.50 .75
❑ 62 Miguel Tejada 2.50 .75
❑ 62 Miguel Tejada Black 2.50 .75
❑ 63 Jose Cruz Jr. 2.50 .75
❑ 63 Jose Cruz Jr. Black 2.50 .75
❑ 64 Billy Koch 2.50 .75
❑ 64 Billy Koch Black 2.50 .75
❑ 65 Troy Glaus 2.50 .75
❑ 65 Troy Glaus Black 2.50 .75
❑ 66 Cliff Floyd 2.50 .75
❑ 66 Cliff Floyd Black 2.50 .75
❑ 67 Tony Batista 2.50 .75
❑ 67 Tony Batista Black 2.50 .75
❑ 68 Jeff Bagwell 2.50 .75
❑ 68 Jeff Bagwell Black 2.50 .75
❑ 69 Billy Wagner 2.50 .75
❑ 69 Billy Wagner Black 2.50 .75
❑ 70 Eric Chavez 2.50 .75
❑ 70 Eric Chavez Black 2.50 .75
❑ 71 Troy Percival 2.50 .75
❑ 71 Troy Percival Black 2.50 .75
❑ 72 Andruw Jones 2.50 .75
❑ 72 Andruw Jones Black 2.50 .75
❑ 73 Shane Reynolds 2.50 .75
❑ 73 Shane Reynolds Black 2.50 .75
❑ 74 Barry Zito 4.00 1.20
❑ 74 Barry Zito Black 4.00 1.20
❑ 75 Roy Halladay 2.50 .75
❑ 75 Roy Halladay Black 2.50 .75
❑ 76 David Wells 2.50 .75
❑ 76 David Wells Black 2.50 .75
❑ 77 Jason Giambi 4.00 1.20
❑ 77 Jason Giambi Black 4.00 1.20
❑ 78 Scott Elarton 2.50 .75
❑ 78 Scott Elarton Black 2.50 .75
❑ 79 Moises Alou 2.50 .75
❑ 79 Moises Alou Black 2.50 .75
❑ 80 Adam Piatt 2.50 .75
❑ 80 Adam Piatt Black 2.50 .75
❑ 81 Wilton Veras .60 .18
❑ 82 Darryl Kile .60 .18
❑ 83 Johnny Damon .60 .18
❑ 84 Tony Armas Jr. .60 .18
❑ 85 Ellis Burks .60 .18
❑ 86 Jamey Wright .60 .18
❑ 87 Jose Vizcaino .60 .18
❑ 88 Bartolo Colon .60 .18
❑ 89 Carmen Cali RC .60 .18
❑ 90 Kevin Brown .60 .18
❑ 91 Josh Hamilton .60 .18
❑ 92 Jay Buhner .60 .18
❑ 93 Scott Pratt RC .60 .18
❑ 94 Alex Cora .60 .18
❑ 95 Luis Montanez RC .60 .18
❑ 96 Dmitri Young .60 .18
❑ 97 J.T. Snow .60 .18
❑ 98 Damion Easley .60 .18
❑ 99 Greg Norton .60 .18
❑ 100 Matt Wheatland .60 .18
❑ 101 Chin-Feng Chen .60 .18
❑ 102 Tony Womack .60 .18
❑ 103 Adam Kennedy Black .60 .18
❑ 104 J.D. Drew .60 .18
❑ 105 Carlos Febles .60 .18
❑ 106 Jim Thome 1.50 .45
❑ 107 Danny Graves .60 .18
❑ 108 Dave Mlicki .60 .18

❑ 109 Ron Coomer .60 .18
❑ 110 James Baldwin .60 .18
❑ 111 Shaun Boyd RC .60 .18
❑ 112 Brian Bohanon .60 .18
❑ 113 Jacque Jones .60 .18
❑ 114 Alfonso Soriano 1.50 .45
❑ 115 Tony Clark .60 .18
❑ 116 Terrence Long .60 .18
❑ 117 Todd Hundley .60 .18
❑ 118 Kazuhiro Sasaki .60 .18
❑ 119 Brian Sellier RC .60 .18
❑ 120 John Olerud .60 .18
❑ 121 Javier Vazquez .60 .18
❑ 122 Sean Burnett .60 .18
❑ 123 Matt LeCroy .60 .18
❑ 124 Erubiel Durazo .60 .18
❑ 125 Juan Encarnacion .60 .18
❑ 126 Pablo Ozuna .60 .18
❑ 127 Russ Ortiz .60 .18
❑ 128 David Segui .60 .18
❑ 129 Mark McGwire 4.00 1.20
❑ 130 Mark Grace 1.50 .45
❑ 131 Fred McGriff 1.00 .30
❑ 132 Carl Pavano .60 .18
❑ 133 Derek Thompson .60 .18
❑ 134 Shawn Green .60 .18
❑ 135 B.J. Surhoff .60 .18
❑ 136 Michael Tucker .60 .18
❑ 137 Jason Isringhausen .60 .18
❑ 138 Eric Milton .60 .18
❑ 139 Mike Stodolka .60 .18
❑ 140 Milton Bradley .60 .18
❑ 141 Curt Schilling 1.00 .30
❑ 142 Sandy Alomar Jr. .60 .18
❑ 143 Brent Mayne .60 .18
❑ 144 Todd Jones .60 .18
❑ 145 Charles Johnson .60 .18
❑ 146 Dean Palmer .60 .18
❑ 147 Masato Yoshii .60 .18
❑ 148 Edgar Renteria .60 .18
❑ 149 Joe Randa .60 .18
❑ 150 Adam Johnson .60 .18
❑ 151 Greg Vaughn .60 .18
❑ 152 Adrian Beltre .60 .18
❑ 153 Glenallen Hill .60 .18
❑ 154 David Parrish RC .60 .18
❑ 155 Neifi Perez .60 .18
❑ 156 Pete Harnisch .60 .18
❑ 157 Paul Konerko .60 .18
❑ 158 Dennys Reyes .60 .18
❑ 159 Jose Lima Black .60 .18
❑ 160 Eddie Taubensee .60 .18
❑ 161 Miguel Cairo .60 .18
❑ 162 Jeff Kent .60 .18
❑ 163 Dustin Hermanson .60 .18
❑ 164 Alex Gonzalez .60 .18
❑ 165 Hideo Nomo 1.50 .45
❑ 166 Sammy Sosa 2.50 .75
❑ 167 C.J. Nitkowski .60 .18
❑ 168 Cal Eldred .60 .18
❑ 169 Jeff Abbott .60 .18
❑ 170 Jim Edmonds .60 .18
❑ 171 Mark Mulder Black .60 .18
❑ 172 Dominic Rich RC .60 .18
❑ 173 Ray Lankford .60 .18
❑ 174 Danny Borrell RC .60 .18
❑ 175 Rick Aguilera .60 .18
❑ 176 S.Stewart Black .60 .18
❑ 177 Steve Finley .60 .18
❑ 178 Jim Parque .60 .18
❑ 179 Kevin Appier Black .60 .18
❑ 180 Adrian Gonzalez .60 .18
❑ 181 Tom Goodwin .60 .18
❑ 182 Kevin Tapani .60 .18
❑ 183 Fernando Tatis .60 .18
❑ 184 Mark Grudzielanek .60 .18
❑ 185 Ryan Anderson .60 .18
❑ 186 Jeffrey Hammonds .60 .18
❑ 187 Corey Koskie .60 .18
❑ 188 Brad Fullmer Black .60 .18
❑ 189 Rey Sanchez .60 .18
❑ 190 Michael Barrett .60 .18
❑ 191 Rickey Henderson 2.50 .75
❑ 192 Jermaine Dye .60 .18
❑ 193 Scott Brosius .60 .18
❑ 194 Matt Anderson .60 .18
❑ 195 Brian Buchanan .60 .18
❑ 196 Derrek Lee .60 .18
❑ 197 Larry Walker 1.00 .30
❑ 198 Dan Moylan RC .60 .18
❑ 199 Vinny Castilla .60 .18
❑ 200 Ken Griffey Jr. 2.50 .75
❑ 201 Matt Stairs Black .60 .18
❑ 202 Ty Howington .60 .18
❑ 203 Andy Benes .60 .18
❑ 204 Luis Gonzalez .60 .18
❑ 205 Brian Moehler .60 .18
❑ 206 Harold Baines .60 .18
❑ 207 Pedro Astacio .60 .18
❑ 208 Cristian Guzman .60 .18
❑ 209 Kip Wells .60 .18
❑ 210 Frank Thomas 1.50 .45
❑ 211 Jose Rosado .60 .18
❑ 212 Vernon Wells Black .60 .18
❑ 213 Bobby Higginson .60 .18
❑ 214 Juan Gonzalez 1.50 .45
❑ 215 Omar Vizquel .60 .18
❑ 216 Bernie Williams 1.00 .30
❑ 217 Aaron Sele .60 .18
❑ 218 Shawn Estes .60 .18
❑ 219 Roberto Alomar 1.50 .45
❑ 220 Rick Ankiel .60 .18
❑ 221 Josh Kalinowski .60 .18
❑ 222 David Bell .60 .18
❑ 223 Keith Foulke .60 .18
❑ 224 Craig Biggio Black 1.00 .30
❑ 225 Josh Axelson RC .60 .18
❑ 226 Scott Williamson .60 .18
❑ 227 Ron Belliard .60 .18
❑ 228 Chris Singleton .60 .18
❑ 229 Alex Serrano RC .60 .18
❑ 230 Deivi Cruz .60 .18
❑ 231 Eric Munson .60 .18
❑ 232 Luis Castillo .60 .18
❑ 233 Edgar Martinez 1.00 .30
❑ 234 Jeff Shaw .60 .18
❑ 235 Jeromy Burnitz .60 .18
❑ 236 Richie Sexson .60 .18
❑ 237 Will Clark 1.50 .45
❑ 238 Ron Villone .60 .18
❑ 239 Kerry Wood 1.50 .45
❑ 240 Rich Aurilia .60 .18
❑ 241 Mo Vaughn Black .60 .18
❑ 242 Travis Fryman .60 .18
❑ 243 M. Ramirez Red Sox .60 .18
❑ 244 Chris Stynes .60 .18
❑ 245 Ray Durham .60 .18
❑ 246 Juan Uribe RC .60 .18
❑ 247 Juan Guzman .60 .18
❑ 248 Lee Stevens .60 .18
❑ 249 Devon White .60 .18
❑ 250 Kyle Lohse RC 1.50 .45
❑ 251 Bryan Wolff .60 .18
❑ 252 Matt Galante RC .60 .18
❑ 253 Eric Young .60 .18
❑ 254 Freddy Garcia .60 .18
❑ 255 Jay Bell .60 .18
❑ 256 Steve Cox .60 .18
❑ 257 Torii Hunter .60 .18
❑ 258 Jose Canseco 1.50 .45
❑ 259 Brad Ausmus .60 .18
❑ 260 Jeff Cirillo .60 .18
❑ 261 Brad Penny .60 .18
❑ 262 Antonio Alfonseca .60 .18
❑ 263 Russ Branyan .60 .18
❑ 264 Chris Morris RC .60 .18
❑ 265 John Lackey .60 .18
❑ 266 Justin Wayne RC 1.00 .30
❑ 267 Brad Radke .60 .18
❑ 268 Todd Stottlemyre .60 .18
❑ 269 Mark Loretta .60 .18
❑ 270 Matt Williams .60 .18
❑ 271 Kenny Lofton .60 .18
❑ 272 Jeff D'Amico .60 .18
❑ 273 Jamie Moyer .60 .18
❑ 274 Darren Dreifort .60 .18
❑ 275 Denny Neagle .60 .18
❑ 276 Orlando Cabrera .60 .18
❑ 277 Chuck Finley .60 .18
❑ 278 Miguel Batista .60 .18
❑ 279 Carlos Beltran .60 .18
❑ 280 Eric Karros .60 .18
❑ 281 Mark Kotsay .60 .18
❑ 282 Ryan Dempster .60 .18
❑ 283 Barry Larkin 1.50 .45
❑ 284 Jeff Suppan .60 .18
❑ 285 Gary Sheffield .60 .18
❑ 286 Jose Valentin .60 .18
❑ 287 Robb Nen .60 .18
❑ 288 Chan Ho Park .60 .18
❑ 289 John Halama .60 .18
❑ 290 Steve Smyth RC .60 .18
❑ 291 Gerald Williams .60 .18
❑ 292 Preston Wilson .60 .18
❑ 293 Victor Hall RC .60 .18
❑ 294 Ben Sheets .60 .18
❑ 295 Eric Davis .60 .18
❑ 296 Kirk Rueter .60 .18
❑ 297 Chad Petty RC .60 .18
❑ 298 Kevin Millar .60 .18
❑ 299 Marvin Benard .60 .18
❑ 300 Vladimir Guerrero 1.50 .45
❑ 301 Livan Hernandez .60 .18
❑ 302 Travis Baptist RC .60 .18
❑ 303 Bill Mueller .60 .18
❑ 304 Mike Cameron .60 .18
❑ 305 Randy Johnson 1.50 .45
❑ 306 Alan Mahaffey RC .60 .18
❑ 307 Timo Perez UER .60 .18
No facsimile autograph on card
❑ 308 Pokey Reese .60 .18
❑ 309 Ryan Rupe .60 .18
❑ 310 Carlos Lee .60 .18
❑ 311 Doug Glanville SP 5.00 1.50
❑ 312 Jay Payton SP 5.00 1.50
❑ 313 Troy O'Leary SP 5.00 1.50
❑ 314 Francisco Cordero SP 5.00 1.50
❑ 315 Rusty Greer SP 5.00 1.50
❑ 316 Cal Ripken SP 25.00 7.50
❑ 317 Ricky Ledee SP 5.00 1.50
❑ 318 Brian Daubach SP 5.00 1.50
❑ 319 Robin Ventura SP 5.00 1.50
❑ 320 Todd Zeile SP 5.00 1.50
❑ 321 Francisco Cordova SP 5.00 1.50
❑ 322 Henry Rodriguez SP 5.00 1.50
❑ 323 Pat Meares SP 5.00 1.50
❑ 324 Glendon Rusch SP 5.00 1.50
❑ 325 Keith Osik SP 5.00 1.50
❑ 326 Robert Keppel SP RC 5.00 1.50
❑ 327 Bobby Jones SP 5.00 1.50
❑ 328 Alex Ramirez SP 5.00 1.50
❑ 329 Robert Person SP 5.00 1.50
❑ 330 Ruben Mateo SP 5.00 1.50
❑ 331 Rob Bell SP 5.00 1.50
❑ 332 Carl Everett SP 5.00 1.50
❑ 333 Jason Schmidt SP 5.00 1.50
❑ 334 Scott Rolen SP 5.00 1.50
❑ 335 Jimmy Anderson SP 5.00 1.50
❑ 336 Bret Boone SP 5.00 1.50
❑ 337 Delino DeShields SP 5.00 1.50
❑ 338 Trevor Hoffman SP 5.00 1.50
❑ 339 Bob Abreu SP 5.00 1.50
❑ 340 Mike Williams SP 5.00 1.50
❑ 341 Mike Hampton SP 5.00 1.50
❑ 342 John Wetteland SP 5.00 1.50
❑ 343 Scott Erickson SP 5.00 1.50
❑ 344 Enrique Wilson SP 5.00 1.50
❑ 345 Tim Wakefield SP 5.00 1.50
❑ 346 Mike Lowell SP 5.00 1.50
❑ 347 Todd Pratt SP 5.00 1.50
❑ 348 Brook Fordyce SP 5.00 1.50
❑ 349 Benny Agbayani SP 5.00 1.50
❑ 350 Gabe Kapler SP 5.00 1.50
❑ 351 Sean Casey SP 5.00 1.50
❑ 352 Darren Oliver SP 5.00 1.50
❑ 353 Todd Ritchie SP 5.00 1.50
❑ 354 Kenny Rogers SP 5.00 1.50
❑ 355 Jason Kendall SP 5.00 1.50
❑ 356 John Vander Wal SP 5.00 1.50
❑ 357 Ramon Martinez SP 5.00 1.50
❑ 358 Edgardo Alfonzo SP 5.00 1.50
❑ 359 Phil Nevin SP 5.00 1.50
❑ 360 Albert Belle SP 5.00 1.50
❑ 361 Ruben Rivera SP 5.00 1.50
❑ 362 Pedro Martinez SP 8.00 2.40
❑ 363 Derek Lowe SP 5.00 1.50
❑ 364 Pat Burrell SP 5.00 1.50
❑ 365 Mike Mussina SP 8.00 2.40

Card	Nm-Mt	Ex-Mt
❑ 366 Brady Anderson SP	5.00	1.50
❑ 367 Darren Lewis SP	5.00	1.50
❑ 368 Sidney Ponson SP	5.00	1.50
❑ 369 Adam Eaton SP	5.00	1.50
❑ 370 Eric Owens SP	5.00	1.50
❑ 371 Aaron Boone SP	5.00	1.50
❑ 372 Matt Clement SP	5.00	1.50
❑ 373 Derek Bell SP	5.00	1.50
❑ 374 Trot Nixon SP	5.00	1.50
❑ 375 Travis Lee SP	5.00	1.50
❑ 376 Mike Benjamin SP	5.00	1.50
❑ 377 Jeff Zimmerman SP	5.00	1.50
❑ 378 Mike Lieberthal SP	5.00	1.50
❑ 379 Rick Reed SP	5.00	1.50
❑ 380 N.Garciaparra SP	15.00	4.50
❑ 381 Omar Daal SP	5.00	1.50
❑ 382 Ryan Klesko SP	5.00	1.50
❑ 383 Rey Ordonez SP	5.00	1.50
❑ 384 Kevin Young SP	5.00	1.50
❑ 385 Rick Helling SP	5.00	1.50
❑ 386 Brian Giles SP	5.00	1.50
❑ 387 Tony Gwynn SP	10.00	3.00
❑ 388 Ed Sprague SP	5.00	1.50
❑ 389 J.R. House SP	5.00	1.50
❑ 390 Scott Hatteberg SP	5.00	1.50
❑ 391 John Valentin SP	5.00	1.50
❑ 392 Melvin Mora SP	5.00	1.50
❑ 393 Royce Clayton SP	5.00	1.50
❑ 394 Jeff Fassero SP	5.00	1.50
❑ 395 Manny Alexander SP	5.00	1.50
❑ 396 John Franco SP	5.00	1.50
❑ 397 Luis Alicea SP	5.00	1.50
❑ 398 Ivan Rodriguez SP	8.00	2.40
❑ 399 Kevin Jordan SP	5.00	1.50
❑ 400 Jose Offerman SP	5.00	1.50
❑ 401 Jeff Conine SP	5.00	1.50
❑ 402 Seth Etherton SP	5.00	1.50
❑ 403 Mike Bordick SP	5.00	1.50
❑ 404 Al Leiter SP	5.00	1.50
❑ 405 Mike Piazza SP	12.00	3.60
❑ 406 Armando Benitez SP	5.00	1.50
❑ 407 Warren Morris SP	5.00	1.50
❑ NNO 1952 Card Redemption EXCH		
❑ NNO Replica Hat-Jsy EXCH		

2002 Topps Heritage

	Nm-Mt	Ex-Mt
COMPLETE SET (440)	300.00	90.00
COMP.SET w/o SP's (350)	100.00	30.00
COMMON CARD (1-363)	.60	.18
COMMON SP (364-446)	5.00	1.50

Card	Nm-Mt	Ex-Mt
❑ 1 Ichiro Suzuki SP	15.00	4.50
❑ 2 Darin Erstad	.60	.18
❑ 3 Rod Beck	.60	.18
❑ 4 Doug Mientkiewicz	.60	.18
❑ 5 Mike Sweeney	.60	.18
❑ 6 Roger Clemens	3.00	.90
❑ 7 Jason Tyner	.60	.18
❑ 8 Alex Gonzalez	.60	.18
❑ 9 Eric Young	.60	.18
❑ 10 Randy Johnson	1.50	.45
❑ 10N Randy Johnson Night SP	8.00	2.40
❑ 11 Aaron Sele	.60	.18
❑ 12 Tony Clark	.60	.18
❑ 13 C.C. Sabathia	.60	.18
❑ 14 Melvin Mora	.60	.18
❑ 15 Tim Hudson	.60	.18
❑ 16 Ben Petrick	.60	.18
❑ 17 Tom Glavine	1.50	.45
❑ 18 Jason Lane	.60	.18
❑ 19 Larry Walker	1.00	.30
❑ 20 Mark Mulder	.60	.18
❑ 21 Steve Finley	.60	.18
❑ 22 Bengie Molina	.60	.18
❑ 23 Rob Bell	.60	.18
❑ 24 Nathan Haynes	.60	.18
❑ 25 Rafael Furcal	.60	.18
❑ 25N Rafael Furcal Night SP	5.00	1.50
❑ 26 Mike Mussina	1.50	.45
❑ 27 Paul LoDuca	.60	.18
❑ 28 Torii Hunter	.60	.18
❑ 29 Carlos Lee	.60	.18
❑ 30 Jimmy Rollins	.60	.18
❑ 31 Arthur Rhodes	.60	.18
❑ 32 Ivan Rodriguez	1.50	.45
❑ 33 Wes Helms	.60	.18
❑ 34 Cliff Floyd	.60	.18
❑ 35 Julian Tavarez	.60	.18
❑ 36 Mark McGwire	4.00	1.20
❑ 37 Chipper Jones SP	8.00	2.40
❑ 38 Denny Neagle	.60	.18
❑ 39 Odalis Perez	.60	.18
❑ 40 Antonio Alfonseca	.60	.18
❑ 41 Edgar Renteria	.60	.18
❑ 42 Troy Glaus	1.00	.30
❑ 43 Scott Brosius	.60	.18
❑ 44 Abraham Nunez	.60	.18
❑ 45 Jamey Wright	.60	.18
❑ 46 Bobby Bonilla	.60	.18
❑ 47 Ismael Valdes	.60	.18
❑ 48 Chris Reitsma	.60	.18
❑ 49 Neifi Perez	.60	.18
❑ 50 Juan Cruz	.60	.18
❑ 51 Kevin Brown	.60	.18
❑ 52 Ben Grieve	.60	.18
❑ 53 Alex Rodriguez SP	15.00	4.50
❑ 54 Charles Nagy	.60	.18
❑ 55 Reggie Sanders	.60	.18
❑ 56 Nelson Figueroa	.60	.18
❑ 57 Felipe Lopez	.60	.18
❑ 58 Bill Ortega	.60	.18
❑ 59 Jeffrey Hammonds	.60	.18
❑ 60 Johnny Estrada	.60	.18
❑ 61 Bob Wickman	.60	.18
❑ 62 Doug Glanville	.60	.18
❑ 63 Jeff Cirillo	.60	.18
❑ 63N Jeff Cirillo Night SP	5.00	1.50
❑ 64 Corey Patterson	.60	.18
❑ 65 Aaron Myette	.60	.18
❑ 66 Magglio Ordonez	.60	.18
❑ 67 Ellis Burks	.60	.18
❑ 68 Miguel Tejada	.60	.18
❑ 69 John Olerud	.60	.18
❑ 69N John Olerud Night SP	5.00	1.50
❑ 70 Greg Vaughn	.60	.18
❑ 71 Andy Pettitte	1.00	.30
❑ 72 Mike Matheny	.60	.18
❑ 73 Brandon Duckworth	.60	.18
❑ 74 Scott Schoeneweis	.60	.18
❑ 75 Mike Lowell	.60	.18
❑ 76 Einar Diaz	.60	.18
❑ 77 Tino Martinez	1.00	.30
❑ 78 Matt Williams	.60	.18
❑ 79 Jason Young RC	1.00	.30
❑ 80 Nate Cornejo	.60	.18
❑ 81 Andres Galarraga	.60	.18
❑ 82 Bernie Williams SP	5.00	1.50
❑ 83 Ryan Klesko	.60	.18
❑ 84 Dan Wilson	.60	.18
❑ 85 Henry Pichardo RC	.75	.23
❑ 86 Ray Durham	.60	.18
❑ 87 Omar Daal	.60	.18
❑ 88 Derrek Lee	.60	.18
❑ 89 Al Leiter	.60	.18
❑ 90 Darrin Fletcher	.60	.18
❑ 91 Josh Beckett	1.00	.30
❑ 92 Johnny Damon	.60	.18
❑ 92N Johnny Damon Night SP	5.00	1.50
❑ 93 Abraham Nunez	.60	.18
❑ 94 Ricky Ledee	.60	.18
❑ 95 Richie Sexson	.60	.18
❑ 96 Adam Kennedy	.60	.18
❑ 97 Raul Mondesi	.60	.18
❑ 98 John Burkett	.60	.18
❑ 99 Ben Sheets	.60	.18
❑ 99N Ben Sheets Night SP	5.00	1.50
❑ 100 Preston Wilson	.60	.18
❑ 100N Preston Wilson Night SP	5.00	1.50
❑ 101 Boof Bonser	.60	.18
❑ 102 Shigetoshi Hasegawa	.60	.18
❑ 103 Carlos Febles	.60	.18
❑ 104 Jorge Posada SP	5.00	1.50
❑ 105 Michael Tucker	.60	.18
❑ 106 Roberto Hernandez	.60	.18
❑ 107 John Rodriguez RC	.75	.23
❑ 108 Danny Graves	.60	.18
❑ 109 Rich Aurilia	.60	.18
❑ 110 Jon Lieber	.60	.18
❑ 111 Tim Hummel RC	.75	.23
❑ 112 J.T. Snow	.60	.18
❑ 113 Kris Benson	.60	.18
❑ 114 Derek Jeter	4.00	1.20
❑ 115 John Franco	.60	.18
❑ 116 Matt Stairs	.60	.18
❑ 117 Ben Davis	.60	.18
❑ 118 Darryl Kile	.60	.18
❑ 119 Mike Peeples RC	.75	.23
❑ 120 Kevin Tapani	.60	.18
❑ 121 Armando Benitez	.60	.18
❑ 122 Damian Miller	.60	.18
❑ 123 Jose Jimenez	.60	.18
❑ 124 Pedro Astacio	.60	.18
❑ 125 Marlyn Tisdale RC	.75	.23
❑ 126 Deivi Cruz	.60	.18
❑ 127 Paul O'Neill	1.00	.30
❑ 128 Jermaine Dye	.60	.18
❑ 129 Marcus Giles	.60	.18
❑ 130 Mark Loretta	.60	.18
❑ 131 Garret Anderson	.60	.18
❑ 132 Todd Ritchie	.60	.18
❑ 133 Joe Crede	.60	.18
❑ 134 Kevin Millwood	.60	.18
❑ 135 Shane Reynolds	.60	.18
❑ 136 Mark Grace	1.50	.45
❑ 137 Shannon Stewart	.60	.18
❑ 138 Nick Neugebauer	.60	.18
❑ 139 Nic Jackson RC	1.00	.30
❑ 140 Robb Nen UER	.60	.18
Name spelled Rob on front		
❑ 141 Dmitri Young	.60	.18
❑ 142 Kevin Appier	.60	.18
❑ 143 Jack Cust	.60	.18
❑ 144 Andres Torres	.60	.18
❑ 145 Frank Thomas	1.50	.45
❑ 146 Jason Kendall	.60	.18
❑ 147 Greg Maddux	3.00	.90
❑ 148 David Justice	.60	.18
❑ 149 Hideo Nomo	1.50	.45
❑ 150 Bret Boone	.60	.18
❑ 151 Wade Miller	.60	.18
❑ 152 Jeff Kent	.60	.18
❑ 153 Scott Williamson	.60	.18
❑ 154 Julio Lugo	.60	.18
❑ 155 Bobby Higginson	.60	.18
❑ 156 Geoff Jenkins	.60	.18
❑ 157 Darren Dreifort	.60	.18
❑ 158 Freddy Sanchez RC	1.50	.45
❑ 159 Bud Smith	.60	.18
❑ 160 Phil Nevin	.60	.18
❑ 161 Cesar Izturis	.60	.18
❑ 162 Sean Casey	.60	.18
❑ 163 Jose Ortiz	.60	.18
❑ 164 Brent Abernathy	.60	.18
❑ 165 Kevin Young	.60	.18
❑ 166 Daryle Ward	.60	.18
❑ 167 Trevor Hoffman	.60	.18
❑ 168 Rondell White	.60	.18
❑ 169 Kip Wells	.60	.18
❑ 170 John Vander Wal	.60	.18
❑ 171 Jose Lima	.60	.18
❑ 172 Wilton Guerrero	.60	.18
❑ 173 Aaron Dean RC	.75	.23
❑ 174 Rick Helling	.60	.18
❑ 175 Juan Pierre	.60	.18
❑ 176 Jay Bell	.60	.18
❑ 177 Craig House	.60	.18
❑ 178 David Bell	.60	.18
❑ 179 Pat Burrell	.60	.18

- ❑ 180 Eric Gagne 1.00 .30
- ❑ 181 Adam Pettyjohn .60 .18
- ❑ 182 Ugueth Urbina .60 .18
- ❑ 183 Peter Bergeron .60 .18
- ❑ 184 Adrian Gonzalez UER .60 .18
  Birthdate is wrong
- ❑ 184N Adrian Gonzalez 5.00 1.50
  Night SP UER
  Birthdate is wrong
- ❑ 185 Damion Easley .60 .18
- ❑ 186 Gookie Dawkins .60 .18
- ❑ 187 Matt Lawton .60 .18
- ❑ 188 Frank Catalanotto .60 .18
- ❑ 189 David Wells .60 .18
- ❑ 190 Roger Cedeno .60 .18
- ❑ 191 Brian Giles .60 .18
- ❑ 192 Julio Zuleta .60 .18
- ❑ 193 Timo Perez .60 .18
- ❑ 194 Billy Wagner .60 .18
- ❑ 195 Craig Counsell .60 .18
- ❑ 196 Bart Miadich .60 .18
- ❑ 197 Gary Sheffield .60 .18
- ❑ 198 Richard Hidalgo .60 .18
- ❑ 199 Juan Uribe .60 .18
- ❑ 200 Curt Schilling 1.00 .30
- ❑ 201 Javy Lopez .60 .18
- ❑ 202 Jimmy Haynes .60 .18
- ❑ 203 Jim Edmonds .60 .18
- ❑ 204 Pokey Reese .60 .18
- ❑ 204N Pokey Reese Night SP 5.00 1.50
- ❑ 205 Matt Clement .60 .18
- ❑ 206 Dean Palmer .60 .18
- ❑ 207 Nick Johnson .60 .18
- ❑ 208 Nate Espy RC .75 .23
- ❑ 209 Pedro Feliz .60 .18
- ❑ 210 Aaron Rowand .60 .18
- ❑ 211 Masato Yoshii .60 .18
- ❑ 212 Jose Cruz Jr. .60 .18
- ❑ 213 Paul Byrd .60 .18
- ❑ 214 Mark Phillips RC 1.50 .45
- ❑ 215 Benny Agbayani .60 .18
- ❑ 216 Frank Menechino .60 .18
- ❑ 217 John Flaherty .60 .18
- ❑ 218 Brian Boehringer .60 .18
- ❑ 219 Todd Hollandsworth .60 .18
- ❑ 220 Sammy Sosa SP 12.00 3.60
- ❑ 221 Steve Sparks .60 .18
- ❑ 222 Homer Bush .60 .18
- ❑ 223 Mike Hampton .60 .18
- ❑ 224 Bobby Abreu .60 .18
- ❑ 225 Barry Larkin 1.50 .45
- ❑ 226 Ryan Rupe .60 .18
- ❑ 227 Bubba Trammell .60 .18
- ❑ 228 Todd Zeile .60 .18
- ❑ 229 Jeff Shaw .60 .18
- ❑ 230 Alex Ochoa .60 .18
- ❑ 231 Orlando Cabrera .60 .18
- ❑ 232 Jeremy Giambi .60 .18
- ❑ 233 Tomo Ohka .60 .18
- ❑ 234 Luis Castillo .60 .18
- ❑ 235 Chris Holt .60 .18
- ❑ 236 Shawn Green .60 .18
- ❑ 237 Sidney Ponson .60 .18
- ❑ 238 Lee Stevens .60 .18
- ❑ 239 Hank Blalock 1.50 .45
- ❑ 240 Randy Winn .60 .18
- ❑ 241 Pedro Martinez 1.50 .45
- ❑ 242 Vinny Castilla .60 .18
- ❑ 243 Steve Karsay .60 .18
- ❑ 244 Barry Bonds SP 20.00 6.00
- ❑ 245 Jason Bere .60 .18
- ❑ 246 Scott Rolen 1.00 .30
- ❑ 246N Scott Rolen Night SP 5.00 1.50
- ❑ 247 Ryan Kohlmeier .60 .18
- ❑ 248 Kerry Wood 1.50 .45
- ❑ 249 Aramis Ramirez .60 .18
- ❑ 250 Lance Berkman .60 .18
- ❑ 251 Omar Vizquel .60 .18
- ❑ 252 Juan Encarnacion .60 .18
- ❑ 253 Does Not Exist .00
- ❑ 254 David Segui .60 .18
- ❑ 255 Brian Anderson .60 .18
- ❑ 256 Jay Payton .60 .18
- ❑ 257 Mark Grudzielanek .60 .18
- ❑ 258 Jimmy Anderson .60 .18
- ❑ 259 Eric Valent .60 .18
- ❑ 260 Chad Durbin .60 .18
- ❑ 261 Does Not Exist .00
- ❑ 262 Alex Gonzalez .60 .18
- ❑ 263 Scott Dunn .60 .18
- ❑ 264 Scott Elarton .60 .18
- ❑ 265 Tom Gordon .60 .18
- ❑ 266 Moises Alou .60 .18
- ❑ 267 Does Not Exist .00
- ❑ 268 Does Not Exist .00
- ❑ 269 Mark Buehrle .60 .18
- ❑ 270 Jerry Hairston .60 .18
- ❑ 271 Does Not Exist .00
- ❑ 272 Luke Prokopec .60 .18
- ❑ 273 Graeme Lloyd .60 .18
- ❑ 274 Bret Prinz .60 .18
- ❑ 275 Does Not Exist .00
- ❑ 276 Chris Carpenter .60 .18
- ❑ 277 Ryan Minor .60 .18
- ❑ 278 Jeff D'Amico .60 .18
- ❑ 279 Raul Ibanez .60 .18
- ❑ 280 Joe Mays .60 .18
- ❑ 281 Livan Hernandez .60 .18
- ❑ 282 Robin Ventura .60 .18
- ❑ 283 Gabe Kapler .60 .18
- ❑ 284 Tony Batista .60 .18
- ❑ 285 Ramon Hernandez .60 .18
- ❑ 286 Craig Paquette .60 .18
- ❑ 287 Mark Kotsay .60 .18
- ❑ 288 Mike Lieberthal .60 .18
- ❑ 289 Joe Borchard .60 .18
- ❑ 290 Cristian Guzman .60 .18
- ❑ 291 Craig Biggio 1.00 .30
- ❑ 292 Joaquin Benoit .60 .18
- ❑ 293 Ken Caminiti .60 .18
- ❑ 294 Sean Burroughs .60 .18
- ❑ 295 Eric Karros .60 .18
- ❑ 296 Eric Chavez .60 .18
- ❑ 297 LaTroy Hawkins .60 .18
- ❑ 298 Alfonso Soriano 1.50 .45
- ❑ 299 John Smoltz 1.00 .30
- ❑ 300 Adam Dunn 1.00 .30
- ❑ 301 Ryan Dempster .60 .18
- ❑ 302 Travis Hafner .60 .18
- ❑ 303 Russell Branyan .60 .18
- ❑ 304 Dustin Hermanson .60 .18
- ❑ 305 Jim Thome 1.50 .45
- ❑ 306 Carlos Beltran .60 .18
- ❑ 307 Jason Botts RC .75 .23
- ❑ 308 David Cone .60 .18
- ❑ 309 Ivanon Coffie .60 .18
- ❑ 310 Brian Jordan .60 .18
- ❑ 311 Todd Walker .60 .18
- ❑ 312 Jeromy Burnitz .60 .18
- ❑ 313 Tony Armas Jr. .60 .18
- ❑ 314 Jeff Conine .60 .18
- ❑ 315 Todd Jones .60 .18
- ❑ 316 Roy Oswalt .60 .18
- ❑ 317 Aubrey Huff .60 .18
- ❑ 318 Josh Fogg .60 .18
- ❑ 319 Jose Vidro .60 .18
- ❑ 320 Jace Brewer .60 .18
- ❑ 321 Mike Redmond .60 .18
- ❑ 322 Noochie Varner RC 1.50 .45
- ❑ 323 Russ Ortiz .60 .18
- ❑ 324 Edgardo Alfonzo .60 .18
- ❑ 325 Ruben Sierra .60 .18
- ❑ 326 Calvin Murray .60 .18
- ❑ 327 Marlon Anderson .60 .18
- ❑ 328 Albie Lopez .60 .18
- ❑ 329 Chris Gomez .60 .18
- ❑ 330 Fernando Tatis .60 .18
- ❑ 331 Stubby Clapp .60 .18
- ❑ 332 Rickey Henderson 2.50 .75
- ❑ 333 Brad Radke .60 .18
- ❑ 334 Brent Mayne .60 .18
- ❑ 335 Cory Lidle .60 .18
- ❑ 336 Edgar Martinez 1.00 .30
- ❑ 337 Aaron Boone .60 .18
- ❑ 338 Jay Witasick .60 .18
- ❑ 339 Benito Santiago .60 .18
- ❑ 340 Jose Mercedes .60 .18
- ❑ 341 Fernando Vina .60 .18
- ❑ 342 A.J. Pierzynski .60 .18
- ❑ 343 Jeff Bagwell 1.00 .30
- ❑ 344 Brian Bohanon .60 .18
- ❑ 345 Adrian Beltre .60 .18
- ❑ 346 Troy Percival .60 .18
- ❑ 347 Napoleon Calzado RC .75 .23
- ❑ 348 Ruben Rivera .60 .18
- ❑ 349 Rafael Soriano .60 .18
- ❑ 350 Damian Jackson .60 .18
- ❑ 351 Joe Randa .60 .18
- ❑ 352 Chan Ho Park .60 .18
- ❑ 353 Dante Bichette .60 .18
- ❑ 354 Bartolo Colon .60 .18
- ❑ 355 Jason Bay RC 2.00 .60
- ❑ 356 Shea Hillenbrand .60 .18
- ❑ 357 Matt Morris .60 .18
- ❑ 358 Brad Penny .60 .18
- ❑ 359 Mark Quinn .60 .18
- ❑ 360 Marquis Grissom .60 .18
- ❑ 361 Henry Blanco .60 .18
- ❑ 362 Billy Koch .60 .18
- ❑ 363 Mike Cameron .60 .18
- ❑ 364 Albert Pujols SP 15.00 4.50
- ❑ 365 Paul Konerko SP 5.00 1.50
- ❑ 366 Eric Milton SP 5.00 1.50
- ❑ 367 Nick Bierbrodt SP 5.00 1.50
- ❑ 368 Rafael Palmeiro SP 5.00 1.50
- ❑ 369 Jorge Padilla SP RC 5.00 1.50
- ❑ 370 Jason Giambi 20.00 6.00
  Yankees SP
  Stats on back are Jeremy Giambi's
- ❑ 371 Mike Piazza SP 12.00 3.60
- ❑ 372 Alex Cora SP 5.00 1.50
- ❑ 373 Todd Helton SP 5.00 1.50
- ❑ 374 Juan Gonzalez SP 8.00 2.40
- ❑ 375 Mariano Rivera SP 5.00 1.50
- ❑ 376 Jason LaRue SP 5.00 1.50
- ❑ 377 Tony Gwynn SP 10.00 3.00
- ❑ 378 Wilson Betemit SP 5.00 1.50
- ❑ 379 J.J. Trujillo SP RC 5.00 1.50
- ❑ 380 Brad Ausmus SP 5.00 1.50
- ❑ 381 Chris George SP 5.00 1.50
- ❑ 382 Jose Canseco SP 8.00 2.40
- ❑ 383 Ramon Ortiz SP 5.00 1.50
- ❑ 384 John Rocker SP 5.00 1.50
- ❑ 385 Rey Ordonez SP 5.00 1.50
- ❑ 386 Ken Griffey Jr. SP 12.00 3.60
- ❑ 387 Juan Pena SP 5.00 1.50
- ❑ 388 Michael Barrett SP 5.00 1.50
- ❑ 389 J.D. Drew SP 5.00 1.50
- ❑ 390 Corey Koskie SP 5.00 1.50
- ❑ 391 Vernon Wells SP 5.00 1.50
- ❑ 392 Juan Tolentino SP RC 5.00 1.50
- ❑ 393 Luis Gonzalez SP 5.00 1.50
- ❑ 394 Terrence Long SP 5.00 1.50
- ❑ 395 Travis Lee SP 5.00 1.50
- ❑ 396 Earl Snyder SP RC 5.00 1.50
- ❑ 397 Nomar Garciaparra SP 15.00 4.50
- ❑ 398 Jason Schmidt SP 5.00 1.50
- ❑ 399 David Espinosa SP 5.00 1.50
- ❑ 400 Steve Green SP 5.00 1.50
- ❑ 401 Jack Wilson SP 5.00 1.50
- ❑ 402 Chris Tritle SP RC 5.00 1.50
- ❑ 403 Angel Berroa SP 5.00 1.50
- ❑ 404 Josh Towers SP 5.00 1.50
- ❑ 405 Andruw Jones SP 5.00 1.50
- ❑ 406 Brent Butler SP 5.00 1.50
- ❑ 407 Craig Kuzmic SP 5.00 1.50
- ❑ 408 Derek Bell SP 5.00 1.50
- ❑ 409 Eric Glaser SP RC 5.00 1.50
- ❑ 410 Joel Pineiro SP 5.00 1.50
- ❑ 411 Alexis Gomez SP 5.00 1.50
- ❑ 412 Mike Rivera SP 5.00 1.50
- ❑ 413 Shawn Estes SP 5.00 1.50
- ❑ 414 Milton Bradley SP 5.00 1.50
- ❑ 415 Carl Everett SP 5.00 1.50
- ❑ 416 Kazuhiro Sasaki SP 5.00 1.50
- ❑ 417 Tony Fontana SP RC 5.00 1.50
- ❑ 418 Josh Pearce SP 5.00 1.50
- ❑ 419 Gary Matthews Jr. SP 5.00 1.50
- ❑ 420 Raymond Cabrera SP RC 5.00 1.50
- ❑ 421 Joe Kennedy SP 5.00 1.50
- ❑ 422 Jason Maule SP RC 5.00 1.50
- ❑ 423 Casey Fossum SP 5.00 1.50
- ❑ 424 Christian Parker SP 5.00 1.50
- ❑ 425 Laynce Nix SP RC 30.00 9.00
- ❑ 426 Byung-Hyun Kim SP 5.00 1.50
- ❑ 427 Freddy Garcia SP 5.00 1.50
- ❑ 428 Herbert Perry SP 5.00 1.50
- ❑ 429 Jason Marquis SP 5.00 1.50

❑ 430 Sandy Alomar Jr. SP 5.00 1.50
❑ 431 Roberto Alomar SP 8.00 2.40
❑ 432 Tsuyoshi Shinjo SP 5.00 1.50
❑ 433 Tim Wakefield SP 5.00 1.50
❑ 434 Robert Fick SP 5.00 1.50
❑ 435 Vladimir Guerrero SP 8.00 2.40
❑ 436 Jose Mesa SP 5.00 1.50
❑ 437 Scott Spiezio SP 5.00 1.50
❑ 438 Jose Hernandez SP 5.00 1.50
❑ 439 Jose Acevedo SP 5.00 1.50
❑ 440 Brian West SP RC 5.00 1.50
❑ 441 Barry Zito SP 8.00 2.40
❑ 442 Luis Maza SP 5.00 1.50
❑ 443 Marlon Byrd SP 5.00 1.50
❑ 444 A.J. Burnett SP 5.00 1.50
❑ 445 Dee Brown SP 5.00 1.50
❑ 446 Carlos Delgado SP 5.00 1.50
❑ NNO 1953 Repurchased EXCH. .00

2003 Topps Heritage

	Nm-Mt	Ex-Mt
COMPLETE SET (450)	400.00	120.00
COMP.SET w/o SP's (350)	80.00	24.00
COMMON CARD	.60	.18
COMMON RC	.75	.23
COMMON SP	5.00	1.50
COMMON SP RC	8.00	2.40

❑ 1A Alex Rodriguez Red 3.00 .90
❑ 1B Alex Rodriguez Black SP 15.00 4.50
❑ 2 Jose Cruz Jr. .60 .18
❑ 3 Ichiro Suzuki SP 15.00 4.50
❑ 4 Rich Aurilia .60 .18
❑ 5 Trevor Hoffman .60 .18
❑ 6A Brian Giles New Logo .60 .18
❑ 6B Brian Giles Old Logo SP 5.00 1.50
❑ 7A Albert Pujols Orange 3.00 .90
❑ 7B Albert Pujols Black SP 15.00 4.50
❑ 8 Vicente Padilla .60 .18
❑ 9 Bobby Crosby 1.50 .45
❑ 10A Derek Jeter New Logo 4.00 1.20
❑ 10B Derek Jeter Old Logo SP 15.00 4.50
❑ 11A Pat Burrell New Logo .60 .18
❑ 11B Pat Burrell Old Logo SP 5.00 1.50
❑ 12 Armando Benitez .60 .18
❑ 13 Javier Vazquez .60 .18
❑ 14 Justin Morneau .60 .18
❑ 15 Doug Mientkiewicz .60 .18
❑ 16 Kevin Brown .60 .18
❑ 17 Alexis Gomez .60 .18
❑ 18A Lance Berkman Blue .60 .18
❑ 18B Lance Berkman Black SP 5.00 1.50
❑ 19 Adrian Gonzalez .60 .18
❑ 20A Todd Helton Green 1.00 .30
❑ 20B Todd Helton Black SP 5.00 1.50
❑ 21 Carlos Pena .60 .18
❑ 22 Matt Lawton .60 .18
❑ 23 Elmer Dessens .60 .18
❑ 24 Hee Seop Choi .60 .18
❑ 25 Chris Duncan SP RC 8.00 2.40
❑ 26 Ugueth Urbina .60 .18
❑ 27A Rodrigo Lopez New Logo .60 .18
❑ 27B Rodrigo Lopez Old Logo SP 5.00 1.50
❑ 28 Damian Moss .60 .18
❑ 29 Steve Finley .60 .18
❑ 30A Sammy Sosa New Logo 2.50 .75
❑ 30B Sammy Sosa Old Logo SP 12.00 3.60
❑ 31 Kevin Cash .60 .18
❑ 32 Kenny Rogers .60 .18
❑ 33 Ben Grieve .60 .18
❑ 34 Jason Simontacchi .60 .18
❑ 35 Shin-Soo Choo .60 .18
❑ 36 Freddy Garcia .60 .18
❑ 37 Jesse Foppert .60 .18
❑ 38 Tony LaRussa MG .60 .18
❑ 39 Mark Kotsay .60 .18
❑ 40 Barry Zito 1.50 .45
❑ 41 Josh Fogg .60 .18
❑ 42 Marlon Byrd .60 .18
❑ 43 Marcus Thames .60 .18
❑ 44 Al Leiter .60 .18
❑ 45 Michael Barrett .60 .18
❑ 46 Jake Peavy .60 .18
❑ 47 Dustan Mohr .60 .18
❑ 48 Alex Sanchez .60 .18
❑ 49 Chin-Feng Chen .60 .18
❑ 50A Kazuhisa Ishii Blue .60 .18
❑ 50B Kazuhisa Ishii Black SP 5.00 1.50
❑ 51 Carlos Beltran .60 .18
❑ 52 Franklin Gutierrez RC 4.00 .90
❑ 53 Miguel Cabrera 3.00 .90
❑ 54 Roger Clemens 3.00 .90
❑ 55 Juan Cruz .60 .18
❑ 56 Jason Young .60 .18
❑ 57 Alex Herrera .60 .18
❑ 58 Aaron Boone .60 .18
❑ 59 Mark Buehrle .60 .18
❑ 60 Larry Walker 1.00 .30
❑ 61 Morgan Ensberg .60 .18
❑ 62 Barry Larkin 1.50 .45
❑ 63 Joe Borchard .60 .18
❑ 64 Jason Dubois .60 .18
❑ 65 Shea Hillenbrand .60 .18
❑ 66 Jay Gibbons .60 .18
❑ 67 Vinny Castilla .60 .18
❑ 68 Jeff Mathis .60 .18
❑ 69 Curt Schilling 1.00 .30
❑ 70 Garret Anderson .60 .18
❑ 71 Josh Phelps .60 .18
❑ 72 Chan Ho Park .60 .18
❑ 73 Edgar Renteria .60 .18
❑ 74 Kazuhiro Sasaki .60 .18
❑ 75 Lloyd McClendon MG .60 .18
❑ 76 Jon Lieber .60 .18
❑ 77 Rolando Viera .60 .18
❑ 78 Jeff Conine .60 .18
❑ 79 Kevin Millwood .60 .18
❑ 80A Randy Johnson Green 1.50 .45
❑ 80B Randy Johnson Black SP 12.00 3.60
❑ 81 Troy Percival .60 .18
❑ 82 Cliff Floyd .60 .18
❑ 83 Tony Graffanino .60 .18
❑ 84 Austin Kearns 1.00 .30
❑ 85 Manuel Ramirez SP RC 15.00 4.50
❑ 86 Jim Tracy MG .60 .18
❑ 87 Rondell White .60 .18
❑ 88 Trot Nixon .60 .18
❑ 89 Carlos Lee .60 .18
❑ 90 Mike Lowell .60 .18
❑ 91 Raul Ibanez .60 .18
❑ 92 Ricardo Rodriguez .60 .18
❑ 93 Ben Sheets .60 .18
❑ 94 Jason Perry SP RC 15.00 4.50
❑ 95 Mark Teixeira 1.00 .30
❑ 96 Brad Fullmer .60 .18
❑ 97 Casey Kotchman 1.00 .30
❑ 98 Craig Counsell .60 .18
❑ 99 Jason Marquis .60 .18
❑ 100A N.Garciaparra New Logo 3.00 .90
❑ 100B N.Garciaparra Old Logo SP 15.00 4.50
❑ 101 Ed Rogers .60 .18
❑ 102 Wilson Betemit .60 .18
❑ 103 Wayne Lydon RC 1.00 .30
❑ 104 Jack Cust .60 .18
❑ 105 Derrek Lee .60 .18
❑ 106 Jim Kavourias .60 .18
❑ 107 Joe Randa .60 .18
❑ 108 Taylor Buchholz .60 .18
❑ 109 Gabe Kapler .60 .18
❑ 110 Preston Wilson .60 .18
❑ 111 Craig Biggio 1.00 .30
❑ 112 Paul Lo Duca .60 .18
❑ 113 Eddie Guardado .60 .18
❑ 114 Andres Galarraga 1.00 .30
❑ 115 Edgardo Alfonzo .60 .18
❑ 116 Robin Ventura .60 .18
❑ 117 Jeremy Giambi .60 .18
❑ 118 Ray Durham .60 .18
❑ 119 Mariano Rivera 1.00 .30
❑ 120 Jimmy Rollins .60 .18
❑ 121 Dennis Tankersley .60 .18
❑ 122 Jason Schmidt .60 .18
❑ 123 Bret Boone .60 .18
❑ 124 Josh Hamilton .60 .18
❑ 125 Scott Rolen 1.00 .30
❑ 126 Steve Cox .60 .18
❑ 127 Larry Bowa MG .60 .18
❑ 128 Adam LaRoche SP 5.00 1.50
❑ 129 Ryan Klesko .60 .18
❑ 130 Tim Hudson .60 .18
❑ 131 Brandon Claussen .60 .18
❑ 132 Craig Brazell SP RC 15.00 4.50
❑ 133 Grady Little MG .60 .18
❑ 134 Jarrod Washburn .60 .18
❑ 135 Lyle Overbay .60 .18
❑ 136 John Burkett .60 .18
❑ 137 Daryl Clark RC 1.00 .30
❑ 138 Kirk Rueter .60 .18
❑ 139A Joe Mauer 1.50 .45
Jake Mauer Green
❑ 139B Joe Mauer 8.00 2.40
Jake Mauer Black SP
❑ 140 Troy Glaus 1.00 .30
❑ 141 Trey Hodges SP 5.00 1.50
❑ 142 Dallas McPherson .60 .18
❑ 143 Art Howe MG .60 .18
❑ 144 Jesus Cota .60 .18
❑ 145 J.R. House .60 .18
❑ 146 Reggie Sanders .60 .18
❑ 147 Clint Nageotte .60 .18
❑ 148 Jim Edmonds .60 .18
❑ 149 Carl Crawford .60 .18
❑ 150A Mike Piazza Blue 2.50 .75
❑ 150B Mike Piazza Black SP 12.00 3.60
❑ 151 Seung Song .60 .18
❑ 152 Roberto Hernandez .60 .18
❑ 153 Marquis Grissom .60 .18
❑ 154 Billy Wagner .60 .18
❑ 155 Josh Beckett 1.00 .30
❑ 156A Randall Simon New Logo .60 .18
❑ 156B Randall Simon Old Logo SP 5.00 1.50
❑ 157 Ben Broussard .60 .18
❑ 158 Russell Branyan .60 .18
❑ 159 Frank Thomas 1.50 .45
❑ 160 Alex Escobar .60 .18
❑ 161 Mark Bellhorn .60 .18
❑ 162 Melvin Mora .60 .18
❑ 163 Andruw Jones 1.00 .30
❑ 164 Danny Bautista .60 .18
❑ 165 Ramon Ortiz .60 .18
❑ 166 Wily Mo Pena .60 .18
❑ 167 Jose Jimenez .60 .18
❑ 168 Mark Redman .60 .18
❑ 169 Angel Berroa .60 .18
❑ 170 Andy Marte SP RC 15.00 4.50
❑ 171 Juan Gonzalez 1.50 .45
❑ 172 Fernando Vina .60 .18
❑ 173 Joel Pineiro .60 .18
❑ 174 Boof Bonser .60 .18
❑ 175 Bernie Castro SP RC 8.00 2.40
❑ 176 Bobby Cox MG .60 .18
❑ 177 Jeff Kent .60 .18
❑ 178 Oliver Perez .60 .18
❑ 179 Chase Utley .60 .18
❑ 180 Mark Mulder .60 .18
❑ 181 Bobby Abreu .60 .18
❑ 182 Ramiro Mendoza .60 .18
❑ 183 Aaron Heilman .60 .18
❑ 184 A.J. Pierzynski .60 .18
❑ 185 Eric Gagne 1.00 .30
❑ 186 Kirk Saarloos .60 .18
❑ 187 Ron Gardenhire MG .60 .18
❑ 188 Dmitri Young .60 .18
❑ 189 Todd Zeile .60 .18
❑ 190A Jim Thome New Logo 1.50 .45
❑ 190B Jim Thome Old Logo SP 8.00 2.40
❑ 191 Cliff Lee .60 .18
❑ 192 Matt Morris .60 .18

No.	Player	Nm-Mt	Ex-Mt
❑ 193	Robert Fick	.60	.18
❑ 194	C.C. Sabathia	.60	.18
❑ 195	Alexis Rios	.60	.18
❑ 196	D'Angelo Jimenez	.60	.18
❑ 197	Edgar Martinez	1.00	.30
❑ 198	Robb Nen	.60	.18
❑ 199	Taggert Bozied	1.00	.30
❑ 200	Vladimir Guerrero SP	8.00	2.40
❑ 201	Walter Young SP	5.00	1.50
❑ 202	Brendan Harris RC	1.50	.45
❑ 203	Mike Hargrove MG	.60	.18
❑ 204	Vernon Wells	.60	.18
❑ 205	Hank Blalock	1.00	.30
❑ 206	Mike Cameron	.60	.18
❑ 207	Tony Batista	.60	.18
❑ 208	Matt Williams	.60	.18
❑ 209	Tony Womack	.60	.18
❑ 210	Ramon Nivar-Martinez RC	2.00	.60
❑ 211	Aaron Sele	.60	.18
❑ 212	Mark Grace	1.50	.45
❑ 213	Joe Crede	.60	.18
❑ 214	Ryan Dempster	.60	.18
❑ 215	Omar Vizquel	.60	.18
❑ 216	Juan Pierre	.60	.18
❑ 217	Denny Bautista	.60	.18
❑ 218	Chuck Knoblauch	.60	.18
❑ 219	Eric Karros	.60	.18
❑ 220	Victor Diaz	.60	.18
❑ 221	Jacque Jones	.60	.18
❑ 222	Jose Vidro	.60	.18
❑ 223	Joe McEwing	.60	.18
❑ 224	Nick Johnson	.60	.18
❑ 225	Eric Chavez	.60	.18
❑ 226	Jose Mesa	.60	.18
❑ 227	Aramis Ramirez	.60	.18
❑ 228	John Lackey	.60	.18
❑ 229	David Bell	.60	.18
❑ 230	John Olerud	.60	.18
❑ 231	Tino Martinez	1.00	.30
❑ 232	Randy Winn	.60	.18
❑ 233	Todd Hollandsworth	.60	.18
❑ 234	Ruddy Lugo RC	.75	.23
❑ 235	Carlos Delgado	.60	.18
❑ 236	Chris Narveson	.60	.18
❑ 237	Tim Salmon	1.00	.30
❑ 238	Orlando Palmeiro	.60	.18
❑ 239	Jeff Clark SP RC	8.00	2.40
❑ 240	Byung-Hyun Kim	.60	.18
❑ 241	Mike Remlinger	.60	.18
❑ 242	Johnny Damon	.60	.18
❑ 243	Corey Patterson	.60	.18
❑ 244	Paul Konerko	.60	.18
❑ 245	Danny Graves	.60	.18
❑ 246	Ellis Burks	.60	.18
❑ 247	Gavin Floyd	.60	.18
❑ 248	Jaime Bubela RC	.75	.23
❑ 249	Sean Burroughs	.60	.18
❑ 250	Alex Rodriguez SP	15.00	4.50
❑ 251	Gabe Gross	.60	.18
❑ 252	Rafael Palmeiro	1.00	.30
❑ 253	Dewon Brazelton	.60	.18
❑ 254	Jimmy Journell	.60	.18
❑ 255	Rafael Soriano	.60	.18
❑ 256	Jerome Williams	.60	.18
❑ 257	Xavier Nady	.60	.18
❑ 258	Mike Williams	.60	.18
❑ 259	Randy Wolf	.60	.18
❑ 260A	Miguel Tejada Orange	.60	.18
❑ 260B	Miguel Tejada Black SP	5.00	1.50
❑ 261	Juan Rivera	.60	.18
❑ 262	Rey Ordonez	.60	.18
❑ 263	Bartolo Colon	.60	.18
❑ 264	Eric Milton	.60	.18
❑ 265	Jeffrey Hammonds	.60	.18
❑ 266	Odalis Perez	.60	.18
❑ 267	Mike Sweeney	.60	.18
❑ 268	Richard Hidalgo	.60	.18
❑ 269	Alex Gonzalez	.60	.18
❑ 270	Aaron Cook	.60	.18
❑ 271	Earl Snyder	.60	.18
❑ 272	Todd Walker	.60	.18
❑ 273	Aaron Rowand	.60	.18
❑ 274	Matt Clement	.60	.18
❑ 275	Anastacio Martinez	.60	.18
❑ 276	Mike Bordick	.60	.18
❑ 277	John Smoltz	1.00	.30
❑ 278	Scott Hairston	.60	.18
❑ 279	David Eckstein	.60	.18
❑ 280	Shannon Stewart	.60	.18
❑ 281	Carl Everett	.60	.18
❑ 282	Aubrey Huff	.60	.18
❑ 283	Mike Mussina	1.50	.45
❑ 284	Ruben Sierra	.60	.18
❑ 285	Russ Ortiz	.60	.18
❑ 286	Brian Lawrence	.60	.18
❑ 287	Kip Wells	.60	.18
❑ 288	Placido Polanco	.60	.18
❑ 289	Ted Lilly	.60	.18
❑ 290	Andy Pettitte	1.00	.30
❑ 291	John Buck	.60	.18
❑ 292	Orlando Cabrera	.60	.18
❑ 293	Cristian Guzman	.60	.18
❑ 294	Ruben Quevedo	.60	.18
❑ 295	Cesar Izturis	.60	.18
❑ 296	Ryan Ludwick	.60	.18
❑ 297	Roy Oswalt	.60	.18
❑ 298	Jason Stokes	1.50	.45
❑ 299	Mike Hampton	.60	.18
❑ 300	Pedro Martinez	1.50	.45
❑ 301	Nic Jackson	.60	.18
❑ 302A	Maggio Ordonez New Logo	.60	.18
❑ 302B	Maggio Ordonez Old Logo SP	5.00	1.50
❑ 303	Manny Ramirez	.60	.18
❑ 304	Jorge Julio	.60	.18
❑ 305	Javy Lopez	.60	.18
❑ 306	Roy Halladay	.60	.18
❑ 307	Kevin Mench	.60	.18
❑ 308	Jason Isringhausen	.60	.18
❑ 309	Carlos Guillen	.60	.18
❑ 310	Tsuyoshi Shinjo	.60	.18
❑ 311	Phil Nevin	.60	.18
❑ 312	Pokey Reese	.60	.18
❑ 313	Jorge Padilla	.60	.18
❑ 314	Jermaine Dye	.60	.18
❑ 315	David Wells	.60	.18
❑ 316	Mo Vaughn	.60	.18
❑ 317	Bernie Williams	1.00	.30
❑ 318	Michael Restovich	.60	.18
❑ 319	Jose Hernandez	.60	.18
❑ 320	Richie Sexson	.60	.18
❑ 321	Daryle Ward	.60	.18
❑ 322	Luis Castillo	.60	.18
❑ 323	Rene Reyes	.60	.18
❑ 324	Victor Martinez	.60	.18
❑ 325A	Adam Dunn New Logo	1.00	.30
❑ 325B	Adam Dunn Old Logo SP	5.00	1.50
❑ 326	Corwin Malone	.60	.18
❑ 327	Kerry Wood	1.50	.45
❑ 328	Rickey Henderson	2.50	.75
❑ 329	Marty Cordova	.60	.18
❑ 330	Greg Maddux	3.00	.90
❑ 331	Miguel Batista	.60	.18
❑ 332	Chris Bootcheck	.60	.18
❑ 333	Carlos Baerga	.60	.18
❑ 334	Antonio Alfonseca	.60	.18
❑ 335	Shane Halter	.60	.18
❑ 336	Juan Encarnacion	.60	.18
❑ 337	Tom Gordon	.60	.18
❑ 338	Hideo Nomo	1.50	.45
❑ 339	Torii Hunter	.60	.18
❑ 340A	Alfonso Soriano Yellow	1.50	.45
❑ 340B	Alfonso Soriano Black SP	8.00	2.40
❑ 341	Roberto Alomar	1.50	.45
❑ 342	David Justice	.60	.18
❑ 343	Mike Lieberthal	.60	.18
❑ 344	Jeff Weaver	.60	.18
❑ 345	Timo Perez	.60	.18
❑ 346	Travis Lee	.60	.18
❑ 347	Sean Casey	.60	.18
❑ 348	Willie Harris	.60	.18
❑ 349	Derek Lowe	.60	.18
❑ 350	Tom Glavine	1.50	.45
❑ 351	Eric Hinske	.60	.18
❑ 352	Rocco Baldelli	3.00	.90
❑ 353	J.D. Drew	.60	.18
❑ 354	Jamie Moyer	.60	.18
❑ 355	Todd Linden	.60	.18
❑ 356	Benito Santiago	.60	.18
❑ 357	Brad Baker	.60	.18
❑ 358	Alex Gonzalez	.60	.18
❑ 359	Brandon Duckworth	.60	.18
❑ 360	John Rheinecker	.60	.18
❑ 361	Orlando Hernandez	.60	.18
❑ 362	Pedro Astacio	.60	.18
❑ 363	Brad Wilkerson	.60	.18
❑ 364	David Ortiz SP	5.00	1.50
❑ 365	Geoff Jenkins SP	5.00	1.50
❑ 366	Brian Jordan SP	5.00	1.50
❑ 367	Paul Byrd SP	5.00	1.50
❑ 368	Jason Lane SP	5.00	1.50
❑ 369	Jeff Bagwell SP	5.00	1.50
❑ 370	Bobby Higginson SP	5.00	1.50
❑ 371	Juan Uribe SP	5.00	1.50
❑ 372	Lee Stevens SP	5.00	1.50
❑ 373	Jimmy Haynes SP	5.00	1.50
❑ 374	Jose Valentin SP	5.00	1.50
❑ 375	Ken Griffey Jr. SP	12.00	3.60
❑ 376	Barry Bonds SP	20.00	6.00
❑ 377	Gary Matthews Jr. SP	5.00	1.50
❑ 378	Gary Sheffield SP	5.00	1.50
❑ 379	Rick Helling SP	5.00	1.50
❑ 380	Junior Spivey SP	5.00	1.50
❑ 381	Francisco Rodriguez SP	5.00	1.50
❑ 382	Chipper Jones SP	8.00	2.40
❑ 383	Orlando Hudson SP	5.00	1.50
❑ 384	Ivan Rodriguez SP	8.00	2.40
❑ 385	Chris Snelling SP	5.00	1.50
❑ 386	Kenny Lofton SP	5.00	1.50
❑ 387	Eric Cyr SP	5.00	1.50
❑ 388	Jason Kendall SP	5.00	1.50
❑ 389	Marlon Anderson SP	5.00	1.50
❑ 390	Billy Koch SP	5.00	1.50
❑ 391	Shelley Duncan SP	5.00	1.50
❑ 392	Jose Reyes SP	5.00	1.50
❑ 393	Fernando Tatis SP	5.00	1.50
❑ 394	Michael Cuddyer SP	5.00	1.50
❑ 395	Mark Prior SP	15.00	4.50
❑ 396	Dontrelle Willis SP	12.00	3.60
❑ 397	Jay Payton SP	5.00	1.50
❑ 398	Brandon Phillips SP	5.00	1.50
❑ 399	Dustin Moseley SP RC	10.00	3.00
❑ 400	Jason Giambi SP	8.00	2.40
❑ 401	John Mabry SP	5.00	1.50
❑ 402	Ron Gant SP	5.00	1.50
❑ 403	J.T. Snow SP	5.00	1.50
❑ 404	Jeff Cirillo SP	5.00	1.50
❑ 405	Darin Erstad SP	5.00	1.50
❑ 406	Luis Gonzalez SP	5.00	1.50
❑ 407	Marcus Giles SP	5.00	1.50
❑ 408	Brian Daubach SP	5.00	1.50
❑ 409	Moises Alou SP	5.00	1.50
❑ 410	Raul Mondesi SP	5.00	1.50
❑ 411	Adrian Beltre SP	5.00	1.50
❑ 412	A.J. Burnett SP	5.00	1.50
❑ 413	Jason Jennings SP	5.00	1.50
❑ 414	Edwin Almonte SP	5.00	1.50
❑ 415	Fred McGriff SP	5.00	1.50
❑ 416	Tim Raines Jr. SP	5.00	1.50
❑ 417	Rafael Furcal SP	5.00	1.50
❑ 418	Erubiel Durazo SP	5.00	1.50
❑ 419	Drew Henson SP	5.00	1.50
❑ 420	Kevin Appier SP	5.00	1.50
❑ 421	Chad Tracy SP	5.00	1.50
❑ 422	Adam Wainwright SP	5.00	1.50
❑ 423	Choo Freeman SP	5.00	1.50
❑ 424	Sandy Alomar Jr. SP	5.00	1.50
❑ 425	Corey Koskie SP	5.00	1.50
❑ 426	Jeromy Burnitz SP	5.00	1.50
❑ 427	Jorge Posada SP	5.00	1.50
❑ 428	Jason Arnold SP	5.00	1.50
❑ 429	Brett Myers SP	5.00	1.50
❑ 430	Shawn Green SP	5.00	1.50

2003 Topps Opening Day

	Nm-Mt	Ex-Mt
COMPLETE SET (165)	40.00	12.00
❑ 1 Alex Rodriguez	2.00	.60
❑ 2 Jarrod Washburn	.40	.12
❑ 3 Aaron Boone	.40	.12
❑ 4 Chipper Jones	1.00	.30
❑ 5 Ken Griffey Jr.	1.50	.45
❑ 6 Shea Hillenbrand	.40	.12
❑ 7 Moises Alou	.40	.12
❑ 8 Carlos Lee	.40	.12

❑ 9 Marty Cordova .40 .12
❑ 10 Derek Jeter 2.50 .75
❑ 11 Dmitri Young .40 .12
❑ 12 Barry Bonds 2.50 .75
❑ 13 Jeff Bagwell .60 .18
❑ 14 Paul Byrd .40 .12
❑ 15 Carlos Delgado .40 .12
❑ 16 Richie Sexson .40 .12
❑ 17 Torii Hunter .40 .12
❑ 18 Bartolo Colon .40 .12
❑ 19 Robin Ventura .40 .12
❑ 20 Mike Piazza 1.50 .45
❑ 21 Tim Hudson .40 .12
❑ 22 Brett Myers .40 .12
❑ 23 Ryan Klesko .40 .12
❑ 24 Tsuyoshi Shinjo .40 .12
❑ 25 Cliff Floyd .40 .12
❑ 26 Scott Rolen .60 .18
❑ 27 Randy Winn .40 .12
❑ 28 Rafael Palmeiro .60 .18
❑ 29 Carlos Pena .40 .12
❑ 30 Randy Johnson 1.00 .30
❑ 31 Jimmy Rollins .40 .12
❑ 32 Jermaine Dye .40 .12
❑ 33 Jose Vidro .40 .12
❑ 34 Jorge Julio .40 .12
❑ 35 Mark Prior 2.00 .60
❑ 36 Curt Schilling .60 .18
❑ 37 A.J. Pierzynski .40 .12
❑ 38 Andruw Jones .60 .18
❑ 39 Kerry Wood 1.00 .30
❑ 40 Todd Helton .60 .18
❑ 41 Magglio Ordonez .40 .12
❑ 42 Darin Erstad .40 .12
❑ 43 Barry Larkin 1.00 .30
❑ 44 Edgardo Alfonzo .40 .12
❑ 45 Jason Giambi 1.00 .30
❑ 46 Eric Chavez .40 .12
❑ 47 Brian Giles .40 .12
❑ 48 Raul Ibanez .40 .12
❑ 49 Edgar Renteria .40 .12
❑ 50 Sammy Sosa 1.50 .45
❑ 51 Bobby Hill .40 .12
❑ 52 A.J. Burnett .40 .12
❑ 53 Juan Gonzalez 1.00 .30
❑ 54 Eric Hinske .40 .12
❑ 55 Roberto Alomar 1.00 .30
❑ 56 Javy Lopez .40 .12
❑ 57 Mark Buehrle .40 .12
❑ 58 Garret Anderson .40 .12
❑ 59 Mike Hampton .40 .12
❑ 60 Rich Aurilia .40 .12
❑ 61 Brian Jordan .40 .12
❑ 62 Brad Wilkerson .40 .12
❑ 63 Geoff Jenkins .40 .12
❑ 64 Brad Radke .40 .12
❑ 65 Roger Clemens 2.00 .60
❑ 66 Scott Hatteberg .40 .12
❑ 67 Mike Williams .40 .12
❑ 68 Steve Finley .40 .12
❑ 69 Benito Santiago .40 .12
❑ 70 John Smoltz .60 .18
❑ 71 Bret Boone .40 .12
❑ 72 Matt Morris .40 .12
❑ 73 Manny Ramirez .40 .12
❑ 74 Troy Glaus .60 .18
❑ 75 Austin Kearns .60 .18
❑ 76 Jim Thome 1.00 .30
❑ 77 Luis Gonzalez .40 .12
❑ 78 Freddy Garcia .40 .12
❑ 79 Randy Wolf .40 .12
❑ 80 Miguel Tejada .40 .12
❑ 81 Paul Konerko .40 .12
❑ 82 Ivan Rodriguez 1.00 .30
❑ 83 Shannon Stewart .40 .12
❑ 84 Rafael Furcal .40 .12
❑ 85 Cristian Guzman .40 .12
❑ 86 Mo Vaughn .40 .12
❑ 87 Jose Cruz Jr. .40 .12
❑ 88 Alfonso Soriano 1.00 .30
❑ 89 Orlando Cabrera .40 .12
❑ 90 Ichiro Suzuki 2.00 .60
❑ 91 Omar Vizquel .40 .12
❑ 92 Hideo Nomo 1.00 .30
❑ 93 Roy Halladay .40 .12
❑ 94 Mike Sweeney .40 .12
❑ 95 Greg Maddux 2.00 .60
❑ 96 David Eckstein .40 .12
❑ 97 Jay Gibbons .40 .12
❑ 98 Andy Pettitte .60 .18
❑ 99 Frank Thomas 1.00 .30
❑ 100 Shawn Green .40 .12
❑ 101 Jacque Jones .40 .12
❑ 102 Pedro Martinez 1.00 .30
❑ 103 Mark Mulder .40 .12
❑ 104 Rodrigo Lopez .40 .12
❑ 105 Bernie Williams .60 .18
❑ 106 Kevin Brown .40 .12
❑ 107 Mike Lieberthal .40 .12
❑ 108 Jim Edmonds .40 .12
❑ 109 Tino Martinez .60 .18
❑ 110 Gary Sheffield .40 .12
❑ 111 Mike Cameron .40 .12
❑ 112 Jason Jennings .40 .12
❑ 113 Larry Walker .60 .18
❑ 114 Corey Koskie .40 .12
❑ 115 Kazuhisa Ishii .40 .12
❑ 116 Jose Hernandez .40 .12
❑ 117 Al Leiter .40 .12
❑ 118 David Justice .40 .12
❑ 119 Jason Kendall .40 .12
❑ 120 Edgar Martinez .60 .18
❑ 121 Pat Burrell .40 .12
❑ 122 Vladimir Guerrero 1.00 .30
❑ 123 Juan Rivera .40 .12
❑ 124 Byung-Hyun Kim .40 .12
❑ 125 Adam Dunn .60 .18
❑ 126 Tim Salmon .60 .18
❑ 127 Terrence Long .40 .12
❑ 128 Johnny Damon .40 .12
❑ 129 Aramis Ramirez .40 .12
❑ 130 Barry Zito 1.00 .30
❑ 131 Mike Lowell .40 .12
❑ 132 Adam Kennedy .40 .12
❑ 133 J.D. Drew .40 .12
❑ 134 Tony Batista .40 .12
❑ 135 Albert Pujols 2.00 .60
❑ 136 Doug Mientkiewicz .40 .12
❑ 137 Phil Nevin .40 .12
❑ 138 Paul Lo Duca .40 .12
❑ 139 Roy Oswalt .40 .12
❑ 140 Jeff Kent .40 .12
❑ 141 Robert Fick .40 .12
❑ 142 Aubrey Huff .40 .12
❑ 143 C.C. Sabathia .40 .12
❑ 144 Tim Wakefield .40 .12
❑ 145 Derek Lowe .40 .12
❑ 146 Kevin Millwood .40 .12
❑ 147 Jorge Posada .60 .18
❑ 148 Fernando Vina .40 .12
❑ 149 Junior Spivey .40 .12
❑ 150 Lance Berkman .40 .12
❑ 151 Eric Gagne .60 .18
❑ 152 Mariano Rivera .60 .18
❑ 153 Alex Sanchez .40 .12
❑ 154 Ellis Burks .40 .12
❑ 155 Josh Beckett .60 .18
❑ 156 Nomar Garciaparra 2.00 .60
❑ 157 Craig Biggio .60 .18
❑ 158 Adrian Beltre .40 .12
❑ 159 Vicente Padilla .40 .12
❑ 160 Mike Cameron HL .40 .12
❑ 161 Shawn Green HL .40 .12
❑ 162 A's Team Shot HL .40 .12
❑ 163 Jason Giambi HL .60 .18
❑ 164 Derek Lowe HL .40 .12
❑ 165 Checklist .40 .12

2002 Topps Pristine

	Nm-Mt	Ex-Mt
COMMON CARD (1-140)	1.50	.45
COMMON CARD (141-150)	2.50	.75
COMMON C CARD (151-210)	1.50	.45
COMMON U CARD (151-210)	3.00	.90
COMMON R CARD (151-210)	6.00	1.80

❑ 1 Alex Rodriguez 8.00 2.40
❑ 2 Carlos Delgado 1.50 .45
❑ 3 Jimmy Rollins 1.50 .45
❑ 4 Jason Kendall 1.50 .45
❑ 5 John Olerud 1.50 .45
❑ 6 Albert Pujols 8.00 2.40
❑ 7 Curt Schilling 2.50 .75
❑ 8 Gary Sheffield 1.50 .45
❑ 9 Johnny Damon 1.50 .45
❑ 10 Ichiro Suzuki 8.00 2.40
❑ 11 Pat Burrell 1.50 .45
❑ 12 Garret Anderson 1.50 .45
❑ 13 Andruw Jones 2.50 .75
❑ 14 Kerry Wood 4.00 1.20
❑ 15 Kenny Lofton 1.50 .45
❑ 16 Adam Dunn 2.50 .75
❑ 17 Juan Pierre 1.50 .45
❑ 18 Josh Beckett 2.50 .75
❑ 19 Roy Oswalt 1.50 .45
❑ 20 Derek Jeter 10.00 3.00
❑ 21 Jose Vidro 1.50 .45
❑ 22 Richie Sexson 1.50 .45
❑ 23 Mike Sweeney 1.50 .45
❑ 24 Jeff Kent 1.50 .45
❑ 25 Jason Giambi 4.00 1.20
❑ 26 Bret Boone 1.50 .45
❑ 27 J.D. Drew 1.50 .45
❑ 28 Shannon Stewart 1.50 .45
❑ 29 Miguel Tejada 1.50 .45
❑ 30 Barry Bonds 10.00 3.00
❑ 31 Randy Johnson 4.00 1.20
❑ 32 Pedro Martinez 4.00 1.20
❑ 33 Magglio Ordonez 1.50 .45
❑ 34 Todd Helton 2.50 .75
❑ 35 Craig Biggio 2.50 .75
❑ 36 Shawn Green 1.50 .45
❑ 37 Vladimir Guerrero 4.00 1.20
❑ 38 Mo Vaughn 1.50 .45
❑ 39 Alfonso Soriano 4.00 1.20
❑ 40 Barry Zito 4.00 1.20
❑ 41 Aramis Ramirez 1.50 .45
❑ 42 Ryan Klesko 1.50 .45
❑ 43 Ruben Sierra 1.50 .45
❑ 44 Tino Martinez 2.50 .75
❑ 45 Toby Hall 1.50 .45
❑ 46 Ivan Rodriguez 4.00 1.20
❑ 47 Raul Mondesi 1.50 .45
❑ 48 Carlos Pena 1.50 .45
❑ 49 Darin Erstad 1.50 .45
❑ 50 Sammy Sosa 6.00 1.80
❑ 51 Bartolo Colon 1.50 .45
❑ 52 Robert Fick 1.50 .45
❑ 53 Cliff Floyd 1.50 .45
❑ 54 Brian Jordan 1.50 .45
❑ 55 Torii Hunter 1.50 .45

❑	56 Roberto Alomar	4.00	1.20
❑	57 Roger Clemens	8.00	2.40
❑	58 Mark Mulder	1.50	.45
❑	59 Brian Giles	1.50	.45
❑	60 Mike Piazza	6.00	1.80
❑	61 Rich Aurilia	1.50	.45
❑	62 Freddy Garcia	1.50	.45
❑	63 Jim Edmonds	1.50	.45
❑	64 Eric Hinske	1.50	.45
❑	65 Vicente Padilla	1.50	.45
❑	66 Javier Vazquez	1.50	.45
❑	67 Cristian Guzman	1.50	.45
❑	68 Paul Lo Duca	1.50	.45
❑	69 Bobby Abreu	1.50	.45
❑	70 Nomar Garciaparra	8.00	2.40
❑	71 Troy Glaus	2.50	.75
❑	72 Chipper Jones	4.00	1.20
❑	73 Scott Rolen	2.50	.75
❑	74 Lance Berkman	1.50	.45
❑	75 C.C. Sabathia	1.50	.45
❑	76 Bernie Williams	2.50	.75
❑	77 Rafael Palmeiro	2.50	.75
❑	78 Phil Nevin	1.50	.45
❑	79 Kazuhiro Sasaki	1.50	.45
❑	80 Eric Chavez	1.50	.45
❑	81 Jorge Posada	2.50	.75
❑	82 Edgardo Alfonzo	1.50	.45
❑	83 Geoff Jenkins	1.50	.45
❑	84 Preston Wilson	1.50	.45
❑	85 Jim Thome	4.00	1.20
❑	86 Frank Thomas	4.00	1.20
❑	87 Jeff Bagwell	2.50	.75
❑	88 Greg Maddux	8.00	2.40
❑	89 Mark Prior	8.00	2.40
❑	90 Larry Walker	2.50	.75
❑	91 Luis Gonzalez	1.50	.45
❑	92 Tim Hudson	1.50	.45
❑	93 Tsuyoshi Shinjo	1.50	.45
❑	94 Juan Gonzalez	4.00	1.20
❑	95 Shea Hillenbrand	1.50	.45
❑	96 Paul Konerko	1.50	.45
❑	97 Tom Glavine	4.00	1.20
❑	98 Marty Cordova	1.50	.45
❑	99 Moises Alou	1.50	.45
❑	100 Ken Griffey Jr.	6.00	1.80
❑	101 Hank Blalock	4.00	1.20
❑	102 Matt Morris	1.50	.45
❑	103 Robb Nen	1.50	.45
❑	104 Mike Cameron	1.50	.45
❑	105 Mark Buehrle	1.50	.45
❑	106 Sean Burroughs	1.50	.45
❑	107 Orlando Cabrera	1.50	.45
❑	108 Jeromy Burnitz	1.50	.45
❑	109 Juan Uribe	1.50	.45
❑	110 Eric Milton	1.50	.45
❑	111 Carlos Lee	1.50	.45
❑	112 Jose Mesa	1.50	.45
❑	113 Morgan Ensberg	1.50	.45
❑	114 Derek Lowe	1.50	.45
❑	115 Juan Cruz	1.50	.45
❑	116 Mike Lieberthal	1.50	.45
❑	117 Armando Benitez	1.50	.45
❑	118 Vinny Castilla	1.50	.45
❑	119 Russ Ortiz	1.50	.45
❑	120 Mike Lowell	1.50	.45
❑	121 Corey Patterson	1.50	.45
❑	122 Mike Mussina	4.00	1.20
❑	123 Rafael Furcal	1.50	.45
❑	124 Mark Grace	4.00	1.20
❑	125 Ben Sheets	1.50	.45
❑	126 John Smoltz	2.50	.75
❑	127 Fred McGriff	2.50	.75
❑	128 Nick Johnson	1.50	.45
❑	129 J.T. Snow	1.50	.45
❑	130 Jeff Cirillo	1.50	.45
❑	131 Trevor Hoffman	1.50	.45
❑	132 Kevin Brown	1.50	.45
❑	133 Mariano Rivera	2.50	.75
❑	134 Marlon Anderson	1.50	.45
❑	135 Al Leiter	1.50	.45
❑	136 Doug Mientkiewicz	1.50	.45
❑	137 Eric Karros	1.50	.45
❑	138 Bobby Higginson	1.50	.45
❑	139 Sean Casey	1.50	.45
❑	140 Troy Percival	1.50	.45
❑	141 Willie Mays	8.00	2.40
❑	142 Carl Yastrzemski	6.00	1.80
❑	143 Stan Musial	6.00	1.80
❑	144 Harmon Killebrew	4.00	1.20
❑	145 Mike Schmidt	8.00	2.40
❑	146 Duke Snider	2.50	.75
❑	147 Brooks Robinson	4.00	1.20
❑	148 Frank Robinson	2.50	.75
❑	149 Nolan Ryan	12.00	3.60
❑	150 Reggie Jackson	2.50	.75
❑	151 Joe Mauer C RC	12.00	3.60
❑	152 Joe Mauer U	25.00	7.50
❑	153 Joe Mauer R	50.00	15.00
❑	154 Colt Griffin C RC	2.50	.75
❑	155 Colt Griffin U	5.00	1.50
❑	156 Colt Griffin R	10.00	3.00
❑	157 Jason Simontacchi C RC	2.00	.60
❑	158 Jason Simontacchi U	4.00	1.20
❑	159 Jason Simontacchi R	8.00	2.40
❑	160 Casey Kotchman C RC	6.00	1.80
❑	161 Casey Kotchman U	12.00	3.60
❑	162 Casey Kotchman R	25.00	7.50
❑	163 Greg Sain C RC	1.50	.45
❑	164 Greg Sain U	3.00	.90
❑	165 Greg Sain R	6.00	1.80
❑	166 David Wright C RC	4.00	1.20
❑	167 David Wright U	8.00	2.40
❑	168 David Wright R	15.00	4.50
❑	169 Scott Hairston C RC	4.00	1.20
❑	170 Scott Hairston U	8.00	2.40
❑	171 Scott Hairston R	15.00	4.50
❑	172 Rolando Viera C RC	1.50	.45
❑	173 Rolando Viera U	3.00	.90
❑	174 Rolando Viera R	6.00	1.80
❑	175 Tyrell Godwin C RC	2.00	.60
❑	176 Tyrell Godwin U	4.00	1.20
❑	177 Tyrell Godwin R	8.00	2.40
❑	178 Jesus Cota C RC	2.00	.60
❑	179 Jesus Cota U	4.00	1.20
❑	180 Jesus Cota R	8.00	2.40
❑	181 Dan Johnson C RC	2.00	.60
❑	182 Dan Johnson U	4.00	1.20
❑	183 Dan Johnson R	8.00	2.40
❑	184 Mario Ramos C RC	1.50	.45
❑	185 Mario Ramos U	3.00	.90
❑	186 Mario Ramos R	6.00	1.80
❑	187 Jason Dubois C RC	4.00	1.20
❑	188 Jason Dubois U	8.00	2.40
❑	189 Jason Dubois R	15.00	4.50
❑	190 Jonny Gomes C RC	2.50	.75
❑	191 Jonny Gomes U	6.00	1.80
❑	192 Jonny Gomes R	12.00	3.60
❑	193 Chris Snelling C RC	2.50	.75
❑	194 Chris Snelling U	5.00	1.50
❑	195 Chris Snelling R	10.00	3.00
❑	196 Hansel Izquierdo C RC	1.50	.45
❑	197 Hansel Izquierdo U	3.00	.90
❑	198 Hansel Izquierdo R	6.00	1.80
❑	199 So Taguchi C RC	2.00	.60
❑	200 So Taguchi U	4.00	1.20
❑	201 So Taguchi R	8.00	2.40
❑	202 Kazuhisa Ishii C RC	3.00	.90
❑	203 Kazuhisa Ishii U	6.00	1.80
❑	204 Kazuhisa Ishii R	12.00	3.60
❑	205 Jorge Padilla C RC	2.00	.60
❑	206 Jorge Padilla U	4.00	1.20
❑	207 Jorge Padilla R	8.00	2.40
❑	208 Earl Snyder C RC	1.50	.45
❑	209 Earl Snyder U	3.00	.90
❑	210 Earl Snyder R	6.00	1.80

2003 Topps Pristine

	MINT	NRMT
COMMON CARD (1-100)	1.50	.70
COMMON C (101-190)	1.50	.70
C 101-190 APPX. 2X EASIER THAN 1-100		
COMMON U (101-190)	3.00	1.35
UNCOMMON 101-190 STATED ODDS 1:2		
UNCOMMON PRINT 1499 SERIAL #'d SETS		
COMMON R (101-190)	6.00	2.70
RARE 101-190 STATED ODDS 1:6		
RARE PRINT RUN 499 SERIAL #'d SETS		

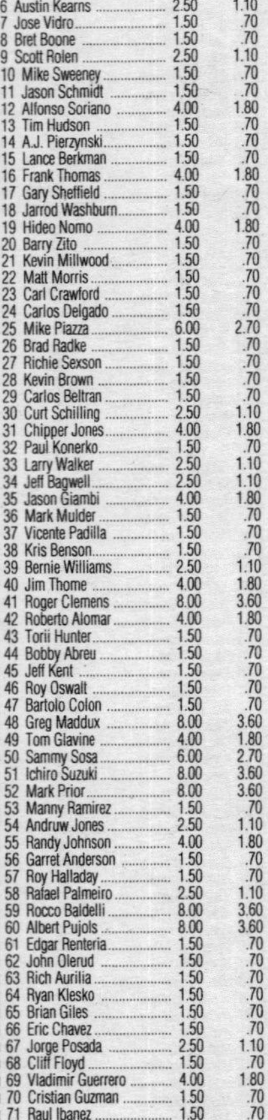

❑	1 Pedro Martinez	4.00	1.80
❑	2 Derek Jeter	10.00	4.50
❑	3 Alex Rodriguez	8.00	3.60
❑	4 Miguel Tejada	1.50	.70
❑	5 Nomar Garciaparra	8.00	3.60
❑	6 Austin Kearns	2.50	1.10
❑	7 Jose Vidro	1.50	.70
❑	8 Bret Boone	1.50	.70
❑	9 Scott Rolen	2.50	1.10
❑	10 Mike Sweeney	1.50	.70
❑	11 Jason Schmidt	1.50	.70
❑	12 Alfonso Soriano	4.00	1.80
❑	13 Tim Hudson	1.50	.70
❑	14 A.J. Pierzynski	1.50	.70
❑	15 Lance Berkman	1.50	.70
❑	16 Frank Thomas	4.00	1.80
❑	17 Gary Sheffield	1.50	.70
❑	18 Jarrod Washburn	1.50	.70
❑	19 Hideo Nomo	4.00	1.80
❑	20 Barry Zito	1.50	.70
❑	21 Kevin Millwood	1.50	.70
❑	22 Matt Morris	1.50	.70
❑	23 Carl Crawford	1.50	.70
❑	24 Carlos Delgado	1.50	.70
❑	25 Mike Piazza	6.00	2.70
❑	26 Brad Radke	1.50	.70
❑	27 Richie Sexson	1.50	.70
❑	28 Kevin Brown	1.50	.70
❑	29 Carlos Beltran	1.50	.70
❑	30 Curt Schilling	2.50	1.10
❑	31 Chipper Jones	4.00	1.80
❑	32 Paul Konerko	1.50	.70
❑	33 Larry Walker	2.50	1.10
❑	34 Jeff Bagwell	2.50	1.10
❑	35 Jason Giambi	4.00	1.80
❑	36 Mark Mulder	1.50	.70
❑	37 Vicente Padilla	1.50	.70
❑	38 Kris Benson	1.50	.70
❑	39 Bernie Williams	2.50	1.10
❑	40 Jim Thome	4.00	1.80
❑	41 Roger Clemens	8.00	3.60
❑	42 Roberto Alomar	4.00	1.80
❑	43 Torii Hunter	1.50	.70
❑	44 Bobby Abreu	1.50	.70
❑	45 Jeff Kent	1.50	.70
❑	46 Roy Oswalt	1.50	.70
❑	47 Bartolo Colon	1.50	.70
❑	48 Greg Maddux	8.00	3.60
❑	49 Tom Glavine	4.00	1.80
❑	50 Sammy Sosa	6.00	2.70
❑	51 Ichiro Suzuki	8.00	3.60
❑	52 Mark Prior	8.00	3.60
❑	53 Manny Ramirez	1.50	.70
❑	54 Andruw Jones	2.50	1.10
❑	55 Randy Johnson	4.00	1.80
❑	56 Garret Anderson	1.50	.70
❑	57 Roy Halladay	1.50	.70
❑	58 Rafael Palmeiro	2.50	1.10
❑	59 Rocco Baldelli	8.00	3.60
❑	60 Albert Pujols	8.00	3.60
❑	61 Edgar Renteria	1.50	.70
❑	62 John Olerud	1.50	.70
❑	63 Rich Aurilia	1.50	.70
❑	64 Ryan Klesko	1.50	.70
❑	65 Brian Giles	1.50	.70
❑	66 Eric Chavez	1.50	.70
❑	67 Jorge Posada	2.50	1.10
❑	68 Cliff Floyd	1.50	.70
❑	69 Vladimir Guerrero	4.00	1.80
❑	70 Cristian Guzman	1.50	.70
❑	71 Raul Ibanez	1.50	.70

- ❑ 72 Paul Lo Duca 1.50 .70
- ❑ 73 A.J. Burnett 1.50 .70
- ❑ 74 Ken Griffey Jr. 6.00 2.70
- ❑ 75 Mark Buehrle 1.50 .70
- ❑ 76 Moises Alou 1.50 .70
- ❑ 77 Adam Dunn 2.50 1.10
- ❑ 78 Tony Batista 1.50 .70
- ❑ 79 Troy Glaus 2.50 1.10
- ❑ 80 Luis Gonzalez 1.50 .70
- ❑ 81 Shea Hillenbrand 1.50 .70
- ❑ 82 Kerry Wood 4.00 1.80
- ❑ 83 Magglio Ordonez 1.50 .70
- ❑ 84 Omar Vizquel 1.50 .70
- ❑ 85 Bobby Higginson 1.50 .70
- ❑ 86 Mike Lowell 1.50 .70
- ❑ 87 Runelvys Hernandez 1.50 .70
- ❑ 88 Shawn Green 1.50 .70
- ❑ 89 Erubiel Durazo 1.50 .70
- ❑ 90 Pat Burrell 1.50 .70
- ❑ 91 Todd Helton 2.50 1.10
- ❑ 92 Jim Edmonds 1.50 .70
- ❑ 93 Aubrey Huff 1.50 .70
- ❑ 94 Eric Hinske 1.50 .70
- ❑ 95 Barry Bonds 10.00 4.50
- ❑ 96 Willie Mays 8.00 3.60
- ❑ 97 Bo Jackson 4.00 1.80
- ❑ 98 Carl Yastrzemski 6.00 2.70
- ❑ 99 Don Mattingly 10.00 4.50
- ❑ 100 Gary Carter 2.50 1.10
- ❑ 101 Jose Contreras C RC 4.00 1.80
- ❑ 102 Jose Contreras U 8.00 3.60
- ❑ 103 Jose Contreras R 15.00 6.75
- ❑ 104 Dan Haren C RC 2.50 1.10
- ❑ 105 Dan Haren U 5.00 2.20
- ❑ 106 Dan Haren R 10.00 4.50
- ❑ 107 Michel Hernandez C RC 1.50 .70
- ❑ 108 Michel Hernandez U 3.00 1.35
- ❑ 109 Michel Hernandez R 6.00 2.70
- ❑ 110 Bobby Basham C RC 2.00 .90
- ❑ 111 Bobby Basham U 4.00 1.80
- ❑ 112 Bobby Basham R 8.00 3.60
- ❑ 113 Bryan Bullington C RC 4.00 1.80
- ❑ 114 Bryan Bullington U 8.00 3.60
- ❑ 115 Bryan Bullington R 15.00 6.75
- ❑ 116 Bernie Castro C RC 1.50 .70
- ❑ 117 Bernie Castro U 3.00 1.35
- ❑ 118 Bernie Castro R 6.00 2.70
- ❑ 119 Chien-Ming Wang C RC 4.00 1.80
- ❑ 120 Chien-Ming Wang U 8.00 3.60
- ❑ 121 Chien-Ming Wang R 15.00 6.75
- ❑ 122 Eric Crozier C RC 2.00 .90
- ❑ 123 Eric Crozier U 4.00 1.80
- ❑ 124 Eric Crozier R 8.00 3.60
- ❑ 125 Michael Garciaparra C RC 2.50 1.10
- ❑ 126 Michael Garciaparra U 5.00 2.20
- ❑ 127 Michael Garciaparra R 10.00 4.50
- ❑ 128 Joey Gomes C RC 2.00 .90
- ❑ 129 Joey Gomes U 4.00 1.80
- ❑ 130 Joey Gomes R 8.00 3.60
- ❑ 131 Wil Ledezma C RC 1.50 .70
- ❑ 132 Wil Ledezma U 3.00 1.35
- ❑ 133 Wil Ledezma R 6.00 2.70
- ❑ 134 Branden Florence C RC 1.50 .70
- ❑ 135 Branden Florence U 3.00 1.35
- ❑ 136 Branden Florence R 6.00 2.70
- ❑ 137 Jeremy Bonderman C RC 3.00 1.35
- ❑ 138 Jeremy Bonderman U 6.00 2.70
- ❑ 139 Jeremy Bonderman R 12.00 5.50
- ❑ 140 Travis Ishikawa C RC 2.00 .90
- ❑ 141 Travis Ishikawa U 4.00 1.80
- ❑ 142 Travis Ishikawa R 8.00 3.60
- ❑ 143 Ben Francisco C RC 2.00 .90
- ❑ 144 Ben Francisco U 4.00 1.80
- ❑ 145 Ben Francisco R 8.00 3.60
- ❑ 146 Jason Kubel C RC 2.00 .90
- ❑ 147 Jason Kubel U 4.00 1.80
- ❑ 148 Jason Kubel R 8.00 3.60
- ❑ 149 Tyler Martin C RC 1.50 .70
- ❑ 150 Tyler Martin U 3.00 1.35
- ❑ 151 Tyler Martin R 6.00 2.70
- ❑ 152 Jason Perry C RC 2.50 1.10
- ❑ 153 Jason Perry U 5.00 2.20
- ❑ 154 Jason Perry R 10.00 4.50
- ❑ 155 Ryan Shealy C RC 2.00 .90
- ❑ 156 Ryan Shealy U 4.00 1.80
- ❑ 157 Ryan Shealy R 8.00 3.60
- ❑ 158 Hanley Ramirez C RC 4.00 1.80
- ❑ 159 Hanley Ramirez U 8.00 3.60
- ❑ 160 Hanley Ramirez R 15.00 6.75
- ❑ 161 Rajai Davis C RC 2.00 .90
- ❑ 162 Rajai Davis U 4.00 1.80
- ❑ 163 Rajai Davis R 8.00 3.60
- ❑ 164 Gary Schneidmiller C RC 1.50 .70
- ❑ 165 Gary Schneidmiller U 3.00 1.35
- ❑ 166 Gary Schneidmiller R 6.00 2.70
- ❑ 167 Haj Turay C RC 2.00 .90
- ❑ 168 Haj Turay U 4.00 1.80
- ❑ 169 Haj Turay R 8.00 3.60
- ❑ 170 Kevin Youkilis C RC 4.00 1.80
- ❑ 171 Kevin Youkilis U 8.00 3.60
- ❑ 172 Kevin Youkilis R 15.00 6.75
- ❑ 173 Shane Bazzell C RC 1.50 .70
- ❑ 174 Shane Bazzell U 3.00 1.35
- ❑ 175 Shane Bazzell R 6.00 2.70
- ❑ 176 Elizardo Ramirez C RC 3.00 1.35
- ❑ 177 Elizardo Ramirez U 6.00 2.70
- ❑ 178 Elizardo Ramirez R 12.00 5.50
- ❑ 179 Robinson Cano C RC 2.00 .90
- ❑ 180 Robinson Cano U 4.00 1.80
- ❑ 181 Robinson Cano R 8.00 3.60
- ❑ 182 Nook Logan C RC 1.50 .70
- ❑ 183 Nook Logan U 3.00 1.35
- ❑ 184 Nook Logan R 6.00 2.70
- ❑ 185 Dustin McGowan C RC 2.00 .90
- ❑ 186 Dustin McGowan U 4.00 1.80
- ❑ 187 Dustin McGowan R 8.00 3.60
- ❑ 188 Ryan Howard C RC 2.50 1.10
- ❑ 189 Ryan Howard U 5.00 2.20
- ❑ 190 Ryan Howard R 10.00 4.50

2001 Topps Reserve

	Nm-Mt	Ex-Mt
COMP.SET w/o SP's (100)	100.00	30.00
COMMON CARD (1-100)	1.00	.30
COMMON (101-151)	8.00	2.40

- ❑ 1 Darin Erstad 1.00 .30
- ❑ 2 Moises Alou 1.00 .30
- ❑ 3 Tony Batista 1.00 .30
- ❑ 4 Andruw Jones 1.50 .45
- ❑ 5 Edgar Renteria 1.00 .30
- ❑ 6 Eric Young 1.00 .30
- ❑ 7 Steve Finley 1.00 .30
- ❑ 8 Adrian Beltre 1.00 .30
- ❑ 9 Vladimir Guerrero 2.50 .75
- ❑ 10 Barry Bonds 6.00 1.80
- ❑ 11 Juan Gonzalez 2.50 .75
- ❑ 12 Jay Buhner 1.00 .30
- ❑ 13 Luis Castillo 1.00 .30
- ❑ 14 Cal Ripken 8.00 2.40
- ❑ 15 Bob Abreu 1.00 .30
- ❑ 16 Ivan Rodriguez 2.50 .75
- ❑ 17 Nomar Garciaparra 5.00 1.50
- ❑ 18 Todd Helton 1.50 .45
- ❑ 19 Bobby Higginson 1.00 .30
- ❑ 20 Jorge Posada 1.50 .45
- ❑ 21 Tim Salmon 1.50 .45
- ❑ 22 Jason Giambi 2.50 .75
- ❑ 23 Jose Cruz Jr. 1.00 .30
- ❑ 24 Chipper Jones 2.50 .75
- ❑ 25 Jim Edmonds 1.00 .30
- ❑ 26 Gerald Williams 1.00 .30
- ❑ 27 Randy Johnson 2.50 .75
- ❑ 28 Gary Sheffield 1.00 .30
- ❑ 29 Jeff Kent 1.00 .30
- ❑ 30 Jim Thome 2.50 .75
- ❑ 31 John Olerud 1.00 .30
- ❑ 32 Cliff Floyd 1.00 .30
- ❑ 33 Mike Lowell 1.00 .30
- ❑ 34 Phil Nevin 1.00 .30
- ❑ 35 Scott Rolen 1.50 .45
- ❑ 36 Alex Rodriguez 5.00 1.50
- ❑ 37 Ken Griffey Jr. 4.00 1.20
- ❑ 38 Neifi Perez 1.00 .30
- ❑ 39 Cristian Guzman 1.00 .30
- ❑ 40 Mariano Rivera 1.50 .45
- ❑ 41 Troy Glaus 1.50 .45
- ❑ 42 Johnny Damon 1.00 .30
- ❑ 43 Rafael Furcal 1.00 .30
- ❑ 44 Jeromy Burnitz 1.00 .30
- ❑ 45 Mark McGwire 6.00 1.80
- ❑ 46 Fred McGriff 1.50 .45
- ❑ 47 Matt Williams 1.00 .30
- ❑ 48 Kevin Brown 1.00 .30
- ❑ 49 J.T. Snow 1.00 .30
- ❑ 50 Kenny Lofton 1.00 .30
- ❑ 51 Al Martin 1.00 .30
- ❑ 52 Antonio Alfonseca 1.00 .30
- ❑ 53 Edgardo Alfonzo 1.00 .30
- ❑ 54 Ryan Klesko 1.00 .30
- ❑ 55 Pat Burrell 1.00 .30
- ❑ 56 Rafael Palmeiro 1.50 .45
- ❑ 57 Sean Casey 1.00 .30
- ❑ 58 Jeff Cirillo 1.00 .30
- ❑ 59 Ray Durham 1.00 .30
- ❑ 60 Derek Jeter 6.00 1.80
- ❑ 61 Jeff Bagwell 1.50 .45
- ❑ 62 Carlos Delgado 1.00 .30
- ❑ 63 Tom Glavine 2.50 .75
- ❑ 64 Richie Sexson 1.00 .30
- ❑ 65 J.D. Drew 1.00 .30
- ❑ 66 Ben Grieve 1.00 .30
- ❑ 67 Mark Grace 2.50 .75
- ❑ 68 Shawn Green 1.00 .30
- ❑ 69 Robb Nen 1.00 .30
- ❑ 70 Omar Vizquel 1.00 .30
- ❑ 71 Edgar Martinez 1.50 .45
- ❑ 72 Preston Wilson 1.00 .30
- ❑ 73 Mike Piazza 4.00 1.20
- ❑ 74 Tony Gwynn 3.00 .90
- ❑ 75 Jason Kendall 1.00 .30
- ❑ 76 Manny Ramirez 1.00 .30
- ❑ 77 Pokey Reese 1.00 .30
- ❑ 78 Mike Sweeney 1.00 .30
- ❑ 79 Magglio Ordonez 1.00 .30
- ❑ 80 Bernie Williams 1.50 .45
- ❑ 81 Richard Hidalgo 1.00 .30
- ❑ 82 Brad Fullmer 1.00 .30
- ❑ 83 Greg Maddux 5.00 1.50
- ❑ 84 Geoff Jenkins 1.00 .30
- ❑ 85 Sammy Sosa 4.00 1.20
- ❑ 86 Luis Gonzalez 1.00 .30
- ❑ 87 Eric Karros 1.00 .30
- ❑ 88 Jose Vidro 1.00 .30
- ❑ 89 Rich Aurilia 1.00 .30
- ❑ 90 Roberto Alomar 2.50 .75
- ❑ 91 Mike Cameron 1.00 .30
- ❑ 92 Mike Mussina 2.50 .75
- ❑ 93 Barry Zito 2.50 .75
- ❑ 94 Mike Lieberthal 1.00 .30
- ❑ 95 Brian Giles 1.00 .30
- ❑ 96 Pedro Martinez 2.50 .75
- ❑ 97 Barry Larkin 2.50 .75
- ❑ 98 Jermaine Dye 1.00 .30
- ❑ 99 Frank Thomas 2.50 .75
- ❑ 100 David Justice 1.00 .30
- ❑ 101 Gary Johnson RC 8.00 2.40
- ❑ 102 Matt Ford RC 8.00 2.40
- ❑ 103 Albert Pujols RC 60.00 18.00
- ❑ 104 Brad Cresse 8.00 2.40
- ❑ 105 V. Pascucci RC 8.00 2.40
- ❑ 106 Bob Keppel RC 8.00 2.40
- ❑ 107 Luis Torres RC 8.00 2.40
- ❑ 108 Tony Blanco RC 8.00 2.40
- ❑ 109 Ronnie Corona RC 8.00 2.40
- ❑ 110 Phil Wilson RC 8.00 2.40
- ❑ 111 John Buck RC 10.00 3.00
- ❑ 112 Jim Journell RC 8.00 2.40
- ❑ 113 Victor Hall RC 8.00 2.40

❑ 114 Jeff Andra RC 8.00 2.40
❑ 115 Greg Nash RC 8.00 2.40
❑ 116 Travis Hafner RC 10.00 3.00
❑ 117 Casey Fossum RC 8.00 2.40
❑ 118 Miguel Olivo 8.00 2.40
❑ 119 Elpidio Guzman RC 8.00 2.40
❑ 120 Jason Belcher RC 8.00 2.40
❑ 121 Esix Snead RC 8.00 2.40
❑ 122 Joe Thurston RC 10.00 3.00
❑ 123 Rafael Soriano RC 12.00 3.60
❑ 124 Ed Rogers RC 8.00 2.40
❑ 125 Omar Beltre RC 8.00 2.40
❑ 126 Brett Gray RC 8.00 2.40
❑ 127 Deivi Mendez RC 8.00 2.40
❑ 128 Freddie Bynum RC 8.00 2.40
❑ 129 David Krynzel 8.00 2.40
❑ 130 Blake Williams RC 8.00 2.40
❑ 131 R. Abercrombie RC 8.00 2.40
❑ 132 Miguel Villilo RC 8.00 2.40
❑ 133 Ryan Madson RC 8.00 2.40
❑ 134 Matt Thompson RC 8.00 2.40
❑ 135 Mark Burnett RC 8.00 2.40
❑ 136 Andy Beal RC 8.00 2.40
❑ 137 Ryan Ludwick RC 8.00 2.40
❑ 138 Roberto Miniel RC 8.00 2.40
❑ 139 Steve Smyth RC 8.00 2.40
❑ 140 Ben Washburn RC 8.00 2.40
❑ 141 Marvin Seale RC 8.00 2.40
❑ 142 Reggie Griggs RC 8.00 2.40
❑ 143 Seung Song RC 10.00 3.00
❑ 144 Chad Petty RC 8.00 2.40
❑ 145 Noel Devarez RC 8.00 2.40
❑ 146 Matt Butler RC 8.00 2.40
❑ 147 Brett Evert RC 8.00 2.40
❑ 148 Cesar Izturis 8.00 2.40
❑ 149 Troy Farnsworth RC 8.00 2.40
❑ 150 Brian Schmitt RC 8.00 2.40
❑ 151 Ichiro Suzuki RC 50.00 15.00

2002 Topps Reserve

	Nm-Mt	Ex-Mt
COMP.SET w/o SP's (135)	100.00	30.00
COMMON CARD (1-135)	1.00	.30
COMMON CARD (136-150)	8.00	2.40

❑ 1 Alex Rodriguez 5.00 1.50
❑ 2 Tsuyoshi Shinjo 1.00 .30
❑ 3 Craig Biggio 1.50 .45
❑ 4 Troy Glaus 1.50 .45
❑ 5 Mike Rivera 1.00 .30
❑ 6 Curt Schilling 1.50 .45
❑ 7 Garret Anderson 1.00 .30
❑ 8 Ben Sheets 1.00 .30
❑ 9 Todd Helton 1.50 .45
❑ 10 Paul Konerko 1.00 .30
❑ 11 Sammy Sosa 4.00 1.20
❑ 12 Bud Smith 1.00 .30
❑ 13 Jeff Bagwell 1.50 .45
❑ 14 Albert Pujols 5.00 1.50
❑ 15 Jose Vidro 1.00 .30
❑ 16 Carlos Delgado 1.00 .30
❑ 17 Torii Hunter 1.00 .30
❑ 18 Jerry Hairston 1.00 .30
❑ 19 Troy Percival 1.00 .30
❑ 20 Vladimir Guerrero 2.50 .75
❑ 21 Geoff Jenkins 1.00 .30
❑ 22 Carlos Pena 1.00 .30
❑ 23 Juan Gonzalez 2.50 .75
❑ 24 Raul Mondesi 1.00 .30
❑ 25 Jimmy Rollins 1.00 .30
❑ 26 Mariano Rivera 1.50 .45
❑ 27 Jorge Posada 1.50 .45
❑ 28 Magglio Ordonez 1.00 .30
❑ 29 Roberto Alomar 2.50 .75
❑ 30 Randy Johnson 2.50 .75
❑ 31 Xavier Nady 1.00 .30
❑ 32 Terrence Long 1.00 .30
❑ 33 Chipper Jones 2.50 .75
❑ 34 Rich Aurilia 1.00 .30
❑ 35 Aramis Ramirez 1.00 .30
❑ 36 Jim Thome 2.50 .75
❑ 37 Bret Boone 1.00 .30
❑ 38 Angel Berroa 1.00 .30
❑ 39 Jeff Conine 1.00 .30
❑ 40 Cliff Floyd 1.00 .30
❑ 41 Pedro Martinez 2.50 .75
❑ 42 J.D. Drew 1.00 .30
❑ 43 Kazuhiro Sasaki 1.00 .30
❑ 44 Jon Rauch 1.00 .30
❑ 45 Orlando Hudson 1.00 .30
❑ 46 Scott Rolen 1.50 .45
❑ 47 Rafael Furcal 1.00 .30
❑ 48 Brad Penny 1.00 .30
❑ 49 Miguel Tejada 1.00 .30
❑ 50 Orlando Cabrera 1.00 .30
❑ 51 Bob Abreu 1.00 .30
❑ 52 Darin Erstad 1.00 .30
❑ 53 Edgar Martinez 1.50 .45
❑ 54 Ben Grieve 1.00 .30
❑ 55 Shawn Green 1.00 .30
❑ 56 Ivan Rodriguez 2.50 .75
❑ 57 Josh Beckett 1.50 .45
❑ 58 Ray Durham 1.00 .30
❑ 59 Jason Hart 1.00 .30
❑ 60 Nathan Haynes 1.00 .30
❑ 61 Jason Giambi 2.50 .75
❑ 62 Eric Chavez 1.00 .30
❑ 63 Matt Morris 1.00 .30
❑ 64 Lance Berkman 1.00 .30
❑ 65 Jeff Kent 1.00 .30
❑ 66 Andruw Jones 1.50 .45
❑ 67 Brian Giles 1.00 .30
❑ 68 Morgan Ensberg 1.00 .30
❑ 69 Pat Burrell 1.00 .30
❑ 70 Ken Griffey Jr. 4.00 1.20
❑ 71 Carlos Beltran 1.00 .30
❑ 72 Ichiro Suzuki 5.00 1.50
❑ 73 Larry Walker 1.50 .45
❑ 74 J.J. Putz RC 1.00 .30
❑ 75 Mike Piazza 5.00 1.50
❑ 76 Rafael Palmeiro 1.50 .45
❑ 77 Mark Prior 5.00 1.50
❑ 78 Toby Hall 1.00 .30
❑ 79 Pokey Reese 1.00 .30
❑ 80 Mike Mussina 2.50 .75
❑ 81 Omar Vizquel 1.00 .30
❑ 82 Shannon Stewart 1.00 .30
❑ 83 Jeromy Burnitz 1.00 .30
❑ 84 Bernie Williams 1.50 .45
❑ 85 C.C. Sabathia 1.00 .30
❑ 86 Mike Hampton 1.00 .30
❑ 87 Kevin Brown 1.00 .30
❑ 88 Juan Cruz 1.00 .30
❑ 89 Jeff Weaver 1.00 .30
❑ 90 Jason Lane 1.00 .30
❑ 91 Adam Dunn 1.50 .45
❑ 92 Jose Cruz Jr. 1.00 .30
❑ 93 Marlon Anderson 1.00 .30
❑ 94 Jeff Cirillo 1.00 .30
❑ 95 Mark Buehrle 1.00 .30
❑ 96 Austin Kearns 1.50 .45
❑ 97 Tim Hudson 1.00 .30
❑ 98 Brian Jordan 1.00 .30
❑ 99 Phil Nevin 1.00 .30
❑ 100 Barry Bonds 6.00 1.80
❑ 101 Derek Jeter 6.00 1.80
❑ 102 Javier Vazquez 1.00 .30
❑ 103 Jason Kendall 1.00 .30
❑ 104 Jim Edmonds 1.00 .30
❑ 105 Kenny Kelly 1.00 .30
❑ 106 Juan Pena 1.00 .30
❑ 107 Mark Grace 2.50 .75
❑ 108 Roger Clemens 5.00 1.50
❑ 109 Barry Zito 2.50 .75
❑ 110 Greg Vaughn 1.00 .30
❑ 111 Greg Maddux 5.00 1.50
❑ 112 Richie Sexson 1.00 .30
❑ 113 Jermaine Dye 1.00 .30
❑ 114 Kerry Wood 2.50 .75
❑ 115 Matt Lawton 1.00 .30
❑ 116 Sean Casey 1.00 .30
❑ 117 Gary Sheffield 1.00 .30
❑ 118 Preston Wilson 1.00 .30
❑ 119 Cristian Guzman 1.00 .30
❑ 120 Mike Sweeney 1.00 .30
❑ 121 Neifi Perez 1.00 .30
❑ 122 Paul LoDuca 1.00 .30
❑ 123 Luis Gonzalez 1.00 .30
❑ 124 Ryan Klesko 1.00 .30
❑ 125 Alfonso Soriano 2.50 .75
❑ 126 Bobby Higginson 1.00 .30
❑ 127 Juan Pierre 1.00 .30
❑ 128 Moises Alou 1.00 .30
❑ 129 Roy Oswalt 1.00 .30
❑ 130 Nomar Garciaparra 5.00 1.50
❑ 131 Fred McGriff 1.50 .45
❑ 132 Edgardo Alfonzo 1.00 .30
❑ 133 Johnny Damon 1.00 .30
❑ 134 Dewon Brazelton 1.00 .30
❑ 135 Mark Mulder 1.00 .30
❑ 136 So Taguchi FYP RC 10.00 3.00
❑ 137 Mario Ramos FYP RC 10.00 3.00
❑ 138 Dan Johnson FYP RC 10.00 3.00
❑ 139 Hansel Izquierdo FYP RC 8.00 2.40
❑ 140 Kazuhisa Ishii FYP RC 12.00 3.60
❑ 141 Jon Switzer FYP RC 10.00 3.00
❑ 142 Chris Tritle FYP RC 8.00 2.40
❑ 143 Chris Snelling FYP RC 10.00 3.00
❑ 144 Chone Figgins FYP RC 8.00 2.40
❑ 145 Dan Phillips FYP RC 8.00 2.40
❑ 146 John Rodriguez FYP RC 8.00 2.40
❑ 147 Colt Griffin FYP RC 10.00 3.00
❑ 148 Jonny Gomes FYP RC 10.00 3.00
❑ 149 Josh Barfield FYP RC 12.00 3.60
❑ 150 Joe Mauer FYP RC 25.00 7.50

2003 Topps Retired Signature

	MINT	NRMT
COMPLETE SET (110)	200.00	90.00

❑ 1 Willie Mays 6.00 2.70
❑ 2 Tony Perez 1.25 .55
❑ 3 Tom Seaver 3.00 1.35
❑ 4 Johnny Bench 3.00 1.35
❑ 5 Rod Carew 2.00 .90
❑ 6 Red Schoendienst 1.25 .55
❑ 7 Phil Rizzuto 2.00 .90
❑ 8 Ozzie Smith 3.00 1.35
❑ 9 Maury Wills 1.25 .55
❑ 10 Hank Aaron 6.00 2.70
❑ 11 Jim Palmer 1.25 .55
❑ 12 Jose Cruz Sr. 1.25 .55
❑ 13 Dave Parker 1.25 .55
❑ 14 Don Sutton 1.25 .55
❑ 15 Brooks Robinson 3.00 1.35
❑ 16 Bo Jackson 3.00 1.35
❑ 17 Andre Dawson 1.25 .55
❑ 18 Fergie Jenkins 1.25 .55
❑ 19 George Foster 1.25 .55

❑ 20 George Brett	8.00	3.60
❑ 21 Jerry Koosman	1.25	.55
❑ 22 John Kruk	1.25	.55
❑ 23 Kent Tekulve	1.25	.55
❑ 24 Lee Smith	1.25	.55
❑ 25 Nolan Ryan	10.00	4.50
❑ 26 Paul O'Neill	1.25	.55
❑ 27 Rich Gossage	1.25	.55
❑ 28 Ron Santo	1.25	.55
❑ 29 Tom Lasorda	1.25	.55
❑ 30 Tony Gwynn	4.00	1.80
❑ 31 Vida Blue	1.25	.55
❑ 32 Whitey Herzog	1.25	.55
❑ 33 Willie McGee	1.25	.55
❑ 34 Bill Mazeroski	1.25	.55
❑ 35 Al Kaline	3.00	1.35
❑ 36 Bobby Richardson	1.25	.55
❑ 37 Carlton Fisk	2.00	.90
❑ 38 Darrell Evans	1.25	.55
❑ 39 Dave Concepcion	1.25	.55
❑ 40 Cal Ripken	10.00	4.50
❑ 41 Dwight Evans	1.25	.55
❑ 42 Earl Weaver	1.25	.55
❑ 43 Fred Lynn	1.25	.55
❑ 44 Greg Luzinski	1.25	.55
❑ 45 Duke Snider	2.00	.90
❑ 46 Hank Bauer	1.25	.55
❑ 47 Jim Rice	1.25	.55
❑ 48 Johnny Sain	1.25	.55
❑ 49 Lenny Dykstra	1.25	.55
❑ 50 Mike Schmidt	6.00	2.70
❑ 51 Orlando Cepeda	1.25	.55
❑ 52 Ralph Kiner	1.25	.55
❑ 53 Robin Roberts	1.25	.55
❑ 54 Ron Guidry	1.25	.55
❑ 55 Steve Garvey	1.25	.55
❑ 56 Tony Oliva	1.25	.55
❑ 57 Whitey Ford	2.00	.90
❑ 58 Willie McCovey	2.00	.90
❑ 59 Phil Niekro	1.25	.55
❑ 60 Stan Musial	5.00	2.20
❑ 61 Rollie Fingers	1.25	.55
❑ 62 Robin Yount	3.00	1.35
❑ 63 Alan Trammell	2.00	.90
❑ 64 Bill Buckner	1.25	.55
❑ 65 Bob Feller	2.00	.90
❑ 66 Bruce Sutter	1.25	.55
❑ 67 Dale Murphy	3.00	1.35
❑ 68 Dennis Eckersley	1.25	.55
❑ 69 Don Newcombe	1.25	.55
❑ 70 Don Mattingly	8.00	3.60
❑ 71 Dwight Gooden	2.00	.90
❑ 72 Frank Robinson	2.00	.90
❑ 73 Gary Carter	2.00	.90
❑ 74 Graig Nettles	1.25	.55
❑ 75 Harmon Killebrew	3.00	1.35
❑ 76 Jim Bunning	1.25	.55
❑ 77 Joe Morgan	1.25	.55
❑ 78 Joe Rudi	1.25	.55
❑ 79 Jose Canseco	3.00	1.35
❑ 80 Ernie Banks	3.00	1.35
❑ 81 Luis Aparicio	1.25	.55
❑ 82 Luis Tiant	1.25	.55
❑ 83 Mark Fidrych	1.25	.55
❑ 84 Kirk Gibson	1.25	.55
❑ 85 Lou Brock	2.00	.90
❑ 86 Juan Marichal	1.25	.55
❑ 87 Monte Irvin	1.25	.55
❑ 88 Paul Molitor	2.00	.90
❑ 89 Tommy John	1.25	.55
❑ 90 Warren Spahn	2.00	.90
❑ 91 Wade Boggs	2.00	.90
❑ 92 Reggie Jackson	2.00	.90
❑ 93 Kirby Puckett	3.00	1.35
❑ 94 Boog Powell	2.00	.90
❑ 95 Carl Yastrzemski	5.00	2.20
❑ 96 Bobby Thomson	1.25	.55
❑ 97 Bill Skowron	1.25	.55
❑ 98 Bill Madlock	1.25	.55
❑ 99 Sparky Anderson	1.25	.55
❑ 100 Yogi Berra	3.00	1.35
❑ 101 Bobby Doerr	1.25	.55
❑ 102 Gaylord Perry	1.25	.55
❑ 103 George Kell	1.25	.55
❑ 104 Harold Reynolds	1.25	.55
❑ 105 Joe Carter	1.25	.55
❑ 106 Johnny Podres	1.25	.55
❑ 107 Ron Cey	1.25	.55
❑ 108 Tim McCarver	1.25	.55
❑ 109 Tug McGraw	1.25	.55
❑ 110 Don Larsen	1.25	.55

1997 Topps Stars

	Nm-Mt	Ex-Mt
COMPLETE SET (125)	30.00	9.00
❑ 1 Larry Walker	.50	.15
❑ 2 Tino Martinez	.50	.15
❑ 3 Cal Ripken	2.50	.75
❑ 4 Ken Griffey Jr.	1.25	.35
❑ 5 Chipper Jones	.75	.23
❑ 6 David Justice	.30	.09
❑ 7 Mike Piazza	1.25	.35
❑ 8 Jeff Bagwell	.50	.15
❑ 9 Ron Gant	.30	.09
❑ 10 Sammy Sosa	1.25	.35
❑ 11 Tony Gwynn	1.00	.30
❑ 12 Carlos Baerga	.30	.09
❑ 13 Frank Thomas	.75	.23
❑ 14 Moises Alou	.30	.09
❑ 15 Barry Larkin	.75	.23
❑ 16 Ivan Rodriguez	.75	.23
❑ 17 Greg Maddux	1.50	.45
❑ 18 Jim Edmonds	.30	.09
❑ 19 Jose Canseco	.75	.23
❑ 20 Rafael Palmeiro	.50	.15
❑ 21 Paul Molitor	.50	.15
❑ 22 Kevin Appier	.30	.09
❑ 23 Raul Mondesi	.30	.09
❑ 24 Lance Johnson	.30	.09
❑ 25 Edgar Martinez	.50	.15
❑ 26 Andres Galarraga	.30	.09
❑ 27 Mo Vaughn	.30	.09
❑ 28 Ken Caminiti	.30	.09
❑ 29 Cecil Fielder	.30	.09
❑ 30 Harold Baines	.30	.09
❑ 31 Roberto Alomar	.75	.23
❑ 32 Shawn Estes	.30	.09
❑ 33 Tom Glavine	.75	.23
❑ 34 Dennis Eckersley	.30	.09
❑ 35 Manny Ramirez	.30	.09
❑ 36 John Olerud	.30	.09
❑ 37 Juan Gonzalez	.75	.23
❑ 38 Chuck Knoblauch	.30	.09
❑ 39 Albert Belle	.30	.09
❑ 40 Vinny Castilla	.30	.09
❑ 41 John Smoltz	.50	.15
❑ 42 Barry Bonds	2.00	.60
❑ 43 Randy Johnson	.75	.23
❑ 44 Brady Anderson	.30	.09
❑ 45 Jeff Blauser	.30	.09
❑ 46 Craig Biggio	.50	.15
❑ 47 Jeff Conine	.30	.09
❑ 48 Marquis Grissom	.30	.09
❑ 49 Mark Grace	.75	.23
❑ 50 Roger Clemens	1.50	.45
❑ 51 Mark McGwire	2.00	.60
❑ 52 Fred McGriff	.50	.15
❑ 53 Gary Sheffield	.30	.09
❑ 54 Bobby Jones	.30	.09
❑ 55 Eric Young	.30	.09
❑ 56 Robin Ventura	.30	.09
❑ 57 Wade Boggs	.50	.15
❑ 58 Joe Carter	.30	.09
❑ 59 Ryne Sandberg	1.25	.35
❑ 60 Matt Williams	.30	.09
❑ 61 Todd Hundley	.30	.09
❑ 62 Dante Bichette	.30	.09
❑ 63 Chili Davis	.30	.09
❑ 64 Kenny Lofton	.30	.09
❑ 65 Jay Buhner	.30	.09
❑ 66 Will Clark	.75	.23
❑ 67 Travis Fryman	.30	.09
❑ 68 Pat Hentgen	.30	.09
❑ 69 Ellis Burks	.30	.09
❑ 70 Mike Mussina	.75	.23
❑ 71 Hideo Nomo	.75	.23
❑ 72 Sandy Alomar Jr.	.30	.09
❑ 73 Bobby Bonilla	.30	.09
❑ 74 Rickey Henderson	1.25	.35
❑ 75 David Cone	.30	.09
❑ 76 Terry Steinbach	.30	.09
❑ 77 Pedro Martinez	.75	.23
❑ 78 Jim Thome	.75	.23
❑ 79 Rod Beck	.30	.09
❑ 80 Randy Myers	.30	.09
❑ 81 Charles Nagy	.30	.09
❑ 82 Mark Wohlers	.30	.09
❑ 83 Paul O'Neill	.50	.15
❑ 84 Curt Schilling	.50	.15
❑ 85 Joey Cora	.30	.09
❑ 86 John Franco	.30	.09
❑ 87 Kevin Brown	.30	.09
❑ 88 Benito Santiago	.30	.09
❑ 89 Ray Lankford	.30	.09
❑ 90 Bernie Williams	.50	.15
❑ 91 Jason Dickson	.30	.09
❑ 92 Jeff Cirillo	.30	.09
❑ 93 Nomar Garciaparra	1.50	.45
❑ 94 Mariano Rivera	.50	.15
❑ 95 Javy Lopez	.30	.09
❑ 96 Tony Womack RC	.75	.23
❑ 97 Jose Rosado	.30	.09
❑ 98 Denny Neagle	.30	.09
❑ 99 Darryl Kile	.30	.09
❑ 100 Justin Thompson	.30	.09
❑ 101 Juan Encarnacion	.30	.09
❑ 102 Brad Fullmer	.30	.09
❑ 103 Kris Benson RC	1.00	.30
❑ 104 Todd Helton	.75	.23
❑ 105 Paul Konerko	.30	.09
❑ 106 Travis Lee RC	1.00	.30
❑ 107 Todd Greene	.30	.09
❑ 108 Mark Kotsay RC	.75	.23
❑ 109 Carl Pavano	.30	.09
❑ 110 Kerry Wood RC	10.00	3.00
❑ 111 Jason Romano RC	.75	.23
❑ 112 Geoff Goetz RC	.50	.15
❑ 113 Scott Hodges RC	.75	.23
❑ 114 Aaron Akin RC	.50	.15
❑ 115 Vernon Wells RC	5.00	1.50
❑ 116 Chris Stowe RC	.50	.15
❑ 117 Brett Caradonna RC	.50	.15
❑ 118 Adam Kennedy RC	1.50	.45
❑ 119 Jayson Werth RC	.75	.23
❑ 120 Glenn Davis RC	.50	.15
❑ 121 Troy Cameron RC	.75	.23
❑ 122 J.J. Davis RC	.75	.23
❑ 123 Jason Dellaero RC	.50	.15
❑ 124 Jason Standridge RC	.75	.23
❑ 125 Lance Berkman RC	6.00	1.80
❑ NNO Checklist	.30	.09

1999 Topps Stars

	Nm-Mt	Ex-Mt
COMPLETE SET (180)	50.00	15.00
❑ 1 Ken Griffey Jr.	2.00	.60
❑ 2 Chipper Jones	1.25	.35
❑ 3 Mike Piazza	2.00	.60
❑ 4 Nomar Garciaparra	2.50	.75
❑ 5 Derek Jeter	3.00	.90
❑ 6 Frank Thomas	1.25	.35
❑ 7 Ben Grieve	.50	.15
❑ 8 Mark McGwire	3.00	.90
❑ 9 Sammy Sosa	2.00	.60
❑ 10 Alex Rodriguez	2.50	.75
❑ 11 Troy Glaus	.75	.23

❑ 12 Eric Chavez .50 .15
❑ 13 Kerry Wood 1.25 .35
❑ 14 Barry Bonds 3.00 .90
❑ 15 Vladimir Guerrero 1.25 .35
❑ 16 Albert Belle .50 .15
❑ 17 Juan Gonzalez 1.25 .35
❑ 18 Roger Clemens 2.50 .75
❑ 19 Ruben Mateo .50 .15
❑ 20 Cal Ripken 4.00 1.20
❑ 21 Darin Erstad .50 .15
❑ 22 Jeff Bagwell .75 .23
❑ 23 Roy Halladay .50 .15
❑ 24 Todd Helton .75 .23
❑ 25 Michael Barrett .50 .15
❑ 26 Manny Ramirez .50 .15
❑ 27 Fernando Seguignol .50 .15
❑ 28 Pat Burrell RC 3.00 .90
❑ 29 Andruw Jones .75 .23
❑ 30 Randy Johnson 1.25 .35
❑ 31 Jose Canseco 1.25 .35
❑ 32 Brad Fullmer .50 .15
❑ 33 Alex Escobar RC .50 .15
❑ 34 Alfonso Soriano RC 10.00 3.00
❑ 35 Larry Walker .75 .23
❑ 36 Matt Clement .50 .15
❑ 37 Mo Vaughn .50 .15
❑ 38 Bruce Chen .50 .15
❑ 39 Travis Lee .50 .15
❑ 40 Adrian Beltre .50 .15
❑ 41 Alex Gonzalez .50 .15
❑ 42 Jason Tyner RC .50 .15
❑ 43 George Lombard .50 .15
❑ 44 Scott Rolen .75 .23
❑ 45 Mark Mulder RC 3.00 .90
❑ 46 Gabe Kapler .50 .15
❑ 47 Choo Freeman RC .50 .15
❑ 48 Tony Gwynn 1.50 .45
❑ 49 A.J. Burnett RC 1.00 .30
❑ 50 Matt Belisle RC .50 .15
❑ 51 Greg Maddux 2.50 .75
❑ 52 John Smoltz .75 .23
❑ 53 Mark Grace 1.25 .35
❑ 54 Wade Boggs .75 .23
❑ 55 Bernie Williams .75 .23
❑ 56 Pedro Martinez 1.25 .35
❑ 57 Barry Larkin 1.25 .35
❑ 58 Orlando Hernandez .50 .15
❑ 59 Jason Kendall .50 .15
❑ 60 Mark Kotsay .50 .15
❑ 61 Jim Thome 1.25 .35
❑ 62 Gary Sheffield .50 .15
❑ 63 Preston Wilson .50 .15
❑ 64 Rafael Palmeiro .75 .23
❑ 65 David Wells .50 .15
❑ 66 Shawn Green .50 .15
❑ 67 Tom Glavine 1.25 .35
❑ 68 Jeromy Burnitz .50 .15
❑ 69 Kevin Brown .75 .23
❑ 70 Rondell White .50 .15
❑ 71 Roberto Alomar 1.25 .35
❑ 72 Cliff Floyd .50 .15
❑ 73 Craig Biggio .75 .23
❑ 74 Greg Vaughn .50 .15
❑ 75 Ivan Rodriguez 1.25 .35
❑ 76 Vinny Castilla .50 .15
❑ 77 Todd Walker .50 .15
❑ 78 Paul Konerko .50 .15
❑ 79 Andy Brown RC .50 .15
❑ 80 Todd Hundley .50 .15
❑ 81 Dmitri Young .50 .15
❑ 82 Tony Clark .50 .15
❑ 83 Nick Johnson RC 1.50 .45
❑ 84 Mike Caruso .50 .15
❑ 85 David Ortiz .50 .15
❑ 86 Matt Williams .50 .15
❑ 87 Raul Mondesi .50 .15
❑ 88 Kenny Lofton .50 .15
❑ 89 Miguel Tejada .50 .15
❑ 90 Dante Bichette .50 .15
❑ 91 Jorge Posada .75 .23
❑ 92 Carlos Beltran .50 .15
❑ 93 Carlos Delgado .50 .15
❑ 94 Javy Lopez .50 .15
❑ 95 Aramis Ramirez .50 .15
❑ 96 Neifi Perez .50 .15
❑ 97 Marlon Anderson .50 .15
❑ 98 David Cone .50 .15
❑ 99 Moises Alou .50 .15
❑ 100 John Olerud .50 .15
❑ 101 Tim Salmon .75 .23
❑ 102 Jason Giambi 1.25 .35
❑ 103 Sandy Alomar Jr. .50 .15
❑ 104 Curt Schilling .75 .23
❑ 105 Andres Galarraga .50 .15
❑ 106 Rusty Greer .50 .15
❑ 107 Bobby Seay RC .50 .15
❑ 108 Eric Young .50 .15
❑ 109 Brian Jordan .50 .15
❑ 110 Eric Davis .50 .15
❑ 111 Will Clark 1.25 .35
❑ 112 Andy Ashby .50 .15
❑ 113 Edgardo Alfonzo .50 .15
❑ 114 Paul O'Neill .75 .23
❑ 115 Denny Neagle .50 .15
❑ 116 Eric Karros .50 .15
❑ 117 Ken Caminiti .50 .15
❑ 118 Garret Anderson .50 .15
❑ 119 Todd Stottlemyre .50 .15
❑ 120 David Justice .50 .15
❑ 121 Francisco Cordova .50 .15
❑ 122 Robin Ventura .50 .15
❑ 123 Mike Mussina 1.25 .35
❑ 124 Hideki Irabu .50 .15
❑ 125 Justin Thompson .50 .15
❑ 126 Mariano Rivera .75 .23
❑ 127 Delino DeShields .50 .15
❑ 128 Steve Finley .50 .15
❑ 129 Jose Cruz Jr. .50 .15
❑ 130 Ray Lankford .50 .15
❑ 131 Jim Edmonds .50 .15
❑ 132 Charles Johnson .50 .15
❑ 133 Al Leiter .50 .15
❑ 134 Jose Offerman .50 .15
❑ 135 Eric Milton .50 .15
❑ 136 Dean Palmer .50 .15
❑ 137 Johnny Damon .50 .15
❑ 138 Andy Pettitte .75 .23
❑ 139 Ray Durham .50 .15
❑ 140 Ugueth Urbina .50 .15
❑ 141 Marquis Grissom .50 .15
❑ 142 Ryan Klesko .50 .15
❑ 143 Brady Anderson .50 .15
❑ 144 Bobby Higginson .50 .15
❑ 145 Chuck Knoblauch .50 .15
❑ 146 Rickey Henderson 2.00 .60
❑ 147 Kevin Millwood .50 .15
❑ 148 Fred McGriff .75 .23
❑ 149 Damion Easley .50 .15
❑ 150 Tino Martinez .75 .23
❑ 151 Greg Maddux LUM 1.25 .35
❑ 152 Scott Rolen LUM .50 .15
❑ 153 Pat Burrell LUM 1.00 .30
❑ 154 Roger Clemens LUM 1.25 .35
❑ 155 Albert Belle LUM .50 .15
❑ 156 Troy Glaus LUM .50 .15
❑ 157 Cal Ripken LUM 2.00 .60
❑ 158 Alfonso Soriano LUM 4.00 1.20
❑ 159 Manny Ramirez LUM .50 .15
❑ 160 Eric Chavez LUM .50 .15
❑ 161 Kerry Wood LUM .75 .23
❑ 162 Tony Gwynn LUM .75 .23
❑ 163 Barry Bonds LUM 1.25 .35
❑ 164 Ruben Mateo LUM .50 .15
❑ 165 Todd Helton LUM .50 .15
❑ 166 Darin Erstad LUM .50 .15
❑ 167 Jeff Bagwell LUM .50 .15
❑ 168 Juan Gonzalez LUM .75 .23
❑ 169 Mo Vaughn LUM .50 .15
❑ 170 V.Guerrero LUM .75 .23
❑ 171 N.Garciaparra SUP 1.25 .35
❑ 172 Derek Jeter SUP 1.50 .45
❑ 173 Alex Rodriguez SUP 1.25 .35
❑ 174 Ben Grieve SUP .50 .15
❑ 175 Mike Piazza SUP 1.25 .35
❑ 176 Chipper Jones SUP .75 .23
❑ 177 Frank Thomas SUP .75 .23
❑ 178 Ken Griffey Jr. SUP 1.25 .35
❑ 179 Sammy Sosa SUP 1.25 .35
❑ 180 Mark McGwire SUP 1.50 .45

2001 Topps Stars

Nm-Mt Ex-Mt
COMPLETE SET (200) 50.00 15.00

❑ 1 Darin Erstad .50 .15
❑ 2 Luis Gonzalez .50 .15
❑ 3 Rafael Furcal .50 .15
❑ 4 Dante Bichette .50 .15
❑ 5 Sammy Sosa 2.00 .60
❑ 6 Ken Griffey Jr. 2.50 .75
❑ 7 Jim Thome 1.25 .35
❑ 8 Bobby Higginson .50 .15
❑ 9 Cliff Floyd .50 .15
❑ 10 Lance Berkman .50 .15
❑ 11 Eric Karros .50 .15
❑ 12 Jeromy Burnitz .50 .15
❑ 13 Jose Vidro .50 .15
❑ 14 Benny Agbayani .40 .12
❑ 15 Jorge Posada .75 .23
❑ 16 Ramon Hernandez .40 .12
❑ 17 Jason Kendall .50 .15
❑ 18 Jeff Kent .50 .15
❑ 19 John Olerud .50 .15
❑ 20 Al Martin .40 .12
❑ 21 Gerald Williams .40 .12
❑ 22 Gabe Kapler .40 .12
❑ 23 Carlos Delgado .50 .15
❑ 24 Mariano Rivera .75 .23
❑ 25 Javy Lopez .50 .15
❑ 26 Paul Konerko .50 .15
❑ 27 Daryle Ward .40 .12
❑ 28 Mike Lieberthal .50 .15
❑ 29 Tom Goodwin .40 .12
❑ 30 Garret Anderson .50 .15
❑ 31 Steve Finley .50 .15
❑ 32 Brian Jordan .50 .15
❑ 33 Nomar Garciaparra 2.50 .75
❑ 34 Ray Durham .50 .15
❑ 35 Sean Casey .50 .15
❑ 36 Kenny Lofton .50 .15
❑ 37 Dean Palmer .50 .15
❑ 38 Jeff Bagwell .75 .23
❑ 39 Mike Sweeney .50 .15
❑ 40 Adrian Beltre .50 .15
❑ 41 Richie Sexson .50 .15
❑ 42 Vladimir Guerrero 1.25 .35
❑ 43 Derek Jeter 3.00 .90
❑ 44 Miguel Tejada .50 .15
❑ 45 Doug Glanville .40 .12
❑ 46 Brian Giles .50 .15
❑ 47 Marvin Benard .40 .12

❑ 48 Edgar Martinez .75 .23
❑ 49 Edgar Renteria .50 .15
❑ 50 Fred McGriff .75 .23
❑ 51 Ivan Rodriguez 1.25 .35
❑ 52 Brad Fullmer .50 .15
❑ 53 Antonio Alfonseca .40 .12
❑ 54 Tom Glavine 1.25 .35
❑ 55 Warren Morris .40 .12
❑ 56 Johnny Damon .50 .15
❑ 57 Dmitri Young .50 .15
❑ 58 Mo Vaughn .50 .15
❑ 59 Randy Johnson 1.25 .35
❑ 60 Greg Maddux 2.50 .75
❑ 61 Carl Everett .50 .15
❑ 62 Magglio Ordonez .50 .15
❑ 63 Pokey Reese .40 .12
❑ 64 Todd Helton .75 .23
❑ 65 Preston Wilson .50 .15
❑ 66 Richard Hidalgo .50 .15
❑ 67 Jermaine Dye .50 .15
❑ 68 Gary Sheffield .50 .15
❑ 69 Geoff Jenkins .50 .15
❑ 70 Edgardo Alfonzo .50 .15
❑ 71 Paul O'Neill .75 .23
❑ 72 Terrence Long .50 .15
❑ 73 Bob Abreu .50 .15
❑ 74 Kevin Young .40 .12
❑ 75 J.T. Snow .50 .15
❑ 76 Alex Rodriguez 2.50 .75
❑ 77 Jim Edmonds .50 .15
❑ 78 Mark McGwire 3.00 .90
❑ 79 Tony Batista .50 .15
❑ 80 Darrin Fletcher .40 .12
❑ 81 Robb Nen .50 .15
❑ 82 Jose Offerman .40 .12
❑ 83 Travis Fryman .50 .15
❑ 84 Joe Randa .40 .12
❑ 85 Omar Vizquel .50 .15
❑ 86 Tim Salmon .75 .23
❑ 87 Andruw Jones .75 .23
❑ 88 Albert Belle .50 .15
❑ 89 Manny Ramirez .50 .15
❑ 90 Frank Thomas 1.25 .35
❑ 91 Barry Larkin 1.25 .35
❑ 92 Neifi Perez .40 .12
❑ 93 Luis Castillo .50 .15
❑ 94 Moises Alou .50 .15
❑ 95 Mark Quinn .40 .12
❑ 96 Kevin Brown .50 .15
❑ 97 Cristian Guzman .50 .15
❑ 98 Mike Piazza 2.00 .60
❑ 99 Bernie Williams .75 .23
❑ 100 Jason Giambi 1.25 .35
❑ 101 Scott Rolen .75 .23
❑ 102 Phil Nevin .50 .15
❑ 103 Rich Aurilia .50 .15
❑ 104 Mike Cameron .50 .15
❑ 105 Fernando Vina .50 .15
❑ 106 Greg Vaughn .50 .15
❑ 107 Jose Cruz Jr. .50 .15
❑ 108 Raul Mondesi .50 .15
❑ 109 Ben Molina .40 .12
❑ 110 Pedro Martinez 1.25 .35
❑ 111 Todd Hollandsworth .40 .12
❑ 112 Jacque Jones .50 .15
❑ 113 Rickey Henderson 2.00 .60
❑ 114 Troy Glaus .75 .23
❑ 115 Chipper Jones 1.25 .35
❑ 116 Delino DeShields .40 .12
❑ 117 Eric Young .40 .12
❑ 118 Jose Valentin .40 .12
❑ 119 Roberto Alomar 1.25 .35
❑ 120 Jeff Cirillo .50 .15
❑ 121 Mike Lowell .50 .15
❑ 122 Julio Lugo .40 .12
❑ 123 Shawn Green .50 .15
❑ 124 Marquis Grissom .40 .12
❑ 125 Matt Lawton .40 .12
❑ 126 Jay Payton .40 .12
❑ 127 David Justice .50 .15
❑ 128 Eric Chavez .50 .15
❑ 129 Pat Burrell .50 .15
❑ 130 Ryan Klesko .50 .15
❑ 131 Barry Bonds 3.00 .90
❑ 132 Jay Buhner .50 .15
❑ 133 J.D. Drew .50 .15
❑ 134 Rafael Palmeiro .75 .23
❑ 135 Shannon Stewart .50 .15
❑ 136 Juan Gonzalez 1.25 .35
❑ 137 Tony Womack .40 .12
❑ 138 Carlos Lee .50 .15
❑ 139 Derrek Lee .50 .15
❑ 140 Ben Grieve .40 .12
❑ 141 Ron Belliard .40 .12
❑ 142 Stan Musial 2.00 .60
❑ 143 Ernie Banks 1.25 .35
❑ 144 Jim Palmer .50 .15
❑ 145 Tony Perez .50 .15
❑ 146 Duke Snider .75 .23
❑ 147 Rod Carew .75 .23
❑ 148 Warren Spahn .75 .23
❑ 149 Yogi Berra 1.50 .45
❑ 150 Juan Marichal .50 .15
❑ 151 Eric Munson .40 .12
❑ 152 Carlos Pena .40 .12
❑ 153 Joe Crede .40 .12
❑ 154 Ryan Anderson .40 .12
❑ 155 Milton Bradley .50 .15
❑ 156 Sean Burroughs .50 .15
❑ 157 Corey Patterson .50 .15
❑ 158 C.C. Sabathia .50 .15
❑ 159 Ben Petrick .40 .12
❑ 160 Aubrey Huff .50 .15
❑ 161 Gookie Dawkins .40 .12
❑ 162 Ben Sheets .50 .15
❑ 163 Pablo Ozuna .40 .12
❑ 164 Eric Valent .40 .12
❑ 165 Rod Barajas .40 .12
❑ 166 Chin-Feng Chen .50 .15
❑ 167 Josh Hamilton .50 .15
❑ 168 Keith Ginter .40 .12
❑ 169 Vernon Wells .50 .15
❑ 170 Dernell Stenson .40 .12
❑ 171 Alfonso Soriano 1.25 .35
❑ 172 Jason Marquis .40 .12
❑ 173 Nick Johnson .50 .15
❑ 174 Adam Everett .40 .12
❑ 175 Jimmy Rollins .50 .15
❑ 176 Ben Diggins .40 .12
❑ 177 John Lackey .40 .12
❑ 178 Scott Heard .40 .12
❑ 179 Brian Hitchcox RC .60 .18
❑ 180 Odannis Ayala RC .60 .18
❑ 181 Scott Pratt RC .60 .18
❑ 182 Greg Runser RC .60 .18
❑ 183 Chris Russ RC .60 .18
❑ 184 Derek Thompson .40 .12
❑ 185 Jason Jones RC .60 .18
❑ 186 Dominic Rich RC .60 .18
❑ 187 Chad Petty RC .60 .18
❑ 188 Steve Smyth RC .60 .18
❑ 189 Bryan Hebson RC .60 .18
❑ 190 Danny Borrell RC .60 .18
❑ 191 Bob Keppel RC .60 .18
❑ 192 Justin Wayne RC 1.00 .30
❑ 193 R. Abercrombie RC .60 .18
❑ 194 Travis Baptist RC .40 .12
❑ 195 Shawn Fagan RC .60 .18
❑ 196 Jose Reyes RC 8.00 2.40
❑ 197 Chris Bass RC .60 .18
❑ 198 Albert Pujols RC 25.00 7.50
❑ 199 Luis Cotto RC .60 .18
❑ 200 Jake Peavy RC 2.50 .75

2002 Topps Total

	Nm-Mt	Ex-Mt
COMPLETE SET (990)	200.00	60.00

❑ 1 Joe Mauer RC 5.00 1.20
❑ 2 Derek Jeter 2.00 .60
❑ 3 Shawn Green .30 .09
❑ 4 Vladimir Guerrero .75 .23
❑ 5 Mike Piazza 1.25 .35
❑ 6 Brandon Duckworth .20 .06
❑ 7 Aramis Ramirez .30 .09
❑ 8 Josh Barfield RC 2.00 .60
❑ 9 Troy Glaus .50 .15
❑ 10 Sammy Sosa 1.25 .35
❑ 11 Rod Barajas .20 .06
❑ 12 Tsuyoshi Shinjo .30 .09
❑ 13 Larry Bigbie .20 .06
❑ 14 Tino Martinez .50 .15
❑ 15 Craig Biggio .50 .15
❑ 16 Anastacio Martinez RC .40 .12
❑ 17 John McDonald .20 .06
❑ 18 Kyle Kane RC .25 .07
❑ 19 Aubrey Huff .30 .09
❑ 20 Juan Cruz .20 .06
❑ 21 Doug Creek .20 .06
❑ 22 Luther Hackman .20 .06
❑ 23 Rafael Furcal .30 .09
❑ 24 Andres Torres .30 .09
❑ 25 Jason Giambi .75 .23
❑ 26 Jose Paniagua .20 .06
❑ 27 Jose Offerman .20 .06
❑ 28 Alex Arias .20 .06
❑ 29 J.M. Gold .20 .06
❑ 30 Jeff Bagwell .50 .15
❑ 31 Brent Cookson .20 .06
❑ 32 Kelly Wunsch .20 .06
❑ 33 Larry Walker .50 .15
❑ 34 Luis Gonzalez .30 .09
❑ 35 John Franco .30 .09
❑ 36 Roy Oswalt .30 .09
❑ 37 Tom Glavine .75 .23
❑ 38 C.C. Sabathia .30 .09
❑ 39 Jay Gibbons .30 .09
❑ 40 Wilson Betemit .20 .06
❑ 41 Tony Armas Jr. .20 .06
❑ 42 Mo Vaughn .30 .09
❑ 43 Gerard Oakes RC .40 .12
❑ 44 Dmitri Young .30 .09
❑ 45 Tim Salmon .50 .15
❑ 46 Barry Zito .75 .23
❑ 47 Adrian Gonzalez .30 .09
❑ 48 Joe Davenport .20 .06
❑ 49 Adrian Hernandez .20 .06
❑ 50 Randy Johnson .75 .23
❑ 52 Adam Pettyjohn .20 .06
❑ 53 Alex Escobar .20 .06
❑ 54 Stevenson Agosto RC .25 .07
❑ 55 Omar Daal .20 .06
❑ 56 Mike Buddie .20 .06
❑ 57 Dave Williams .20 .06
❑ 58 Marquis Grissom .20 .06
❑ 59 Pat Burrell .30 .09
❑ 60 Mark Prior 2.50 .75
❑ 61 Mike Bynum .20 .06
❑ 62 Mike Hill RC .40 .12
❑ 63 Brandon Backe RC .40 .12
❑ 64 Dan Wilson .20 .06
❑ 65 Nick Johnson .30 .09
❑ 66 Jason Grimsley .20 .06
❑ 67 Russ Johnson .20 .06
❑ 68 Todd Walker .30 .09
❑ 69 Kyle Farnsworth .20 .06
❑ 70 Ben Broussard .20 .06
❑ 71 Garrett Guzman RC .40 .12
❑ 72 Terry Mulholland .20 .06
❑ 73 Tyler Houston .20 .06
❑ 74 Jace Brewer .20 .06
❑ 75 Chris Baker RC .40 .12
❑ 76 Frank Catalanotto .20 .06
❑ 77 Mike Redmond .20 .06
❑ 78 Matt Wise .20 .06
❑ 79 Fernando Vina .30 .09
❑ 80 Kevin Brown .30 .09
❑ 81 Grant Balfour .20 .06
❑ 82 Clint Nageotte RC 1.00 .30

❑ 83 Jeff Tam .20 .06
❑ 84 Steve Trachsel .20 .06
❑ 85 Tomo Ohka .20 .06
❑ 86 Keith McDonald .20 .06
❑ 87 Jose Ortiz .20 .06
❑ 88 Rusty Greer .30 .09
❑ 89 Jeff Suppan .20 .06
❑ 90 Moises Alou .30 .09
❑ 91 Juan Encarnacion .20 .06
❑ 92 Tyler Yates RC .40 .12
❑ 93 Scott Strickland .20 .06
❑ 94 Brent Butler .20 .06
❑ 95 Jon Rauch .20 .06
❑ 96 Brian Mallette RC .25 .07
❑ 97 Joe Randa .20 .06
❑ 98 Cesar Crespo .20 .06
❑ 99 Felix Rodriguez .20 .06
❑ 100 Chipper Jones .75 .23
❑ 101 Victor Martinez .30 .09
❑ 102 Danny Graves .20 .06
❑ 103 Brandon Berger .20 .06
❑ 104 Carlos Garcia .20 .06
❑ 105 Alfonso Soriano .75 .23
❑ 106 Allan Simpson RC .25 .07
❑ 107 Brad Thomas .20 .06
❑ 108 Devon White .20 .06
❑ 109 Scott Chiasson .20 .06
❑ 110 Cliff Floyd .30 .09
❑ 111 Scott Williamson .20 .06
❑ 112 Julio Zuleta .20 .06
❑ 113 Terry Adams .20 .06
❑ 114 Zach Day .20 .06
❑ 115 Ben Grieve .20 .06
❑ 116 Mark Ellis .20 .06
❑ 117 Bobby Jenks RC 1.25 .35
❑ 118 LaTroy Hawkins .20 .06
❑ 119 Tim Raines Jr. .20 .06
❑ 120 Juan Uribe .20 .06
❑ 121 Bob Scanlan .20 .06
❑ 122 Brad Nelson RC 1.25 .35
❑ 123 Adam Johnson .20 .06
❑ 124 Raul Casanova .20 .06
❑ 125 Jeff D'Amico .20 .06
❑ 126 Aaron Cook RC .50 .15
❑ 127 Alan Benes .20 .06
❑ 128 Mark Little .20 .06
❑ 129 Randy Wolf .30 .09
❑ 130 Phil Nevin .30 .09
❑ 131 Guillermo Mota .20 .06
❑ 132 Nick Neugebauer .20 .06
❑ 133 Pedro Borbon Jr. .20 .06
❑ 134 Doug Mientkiewicz .30 .09
❑ 135 Edgardo Alfonzo .30 .09
❑ 136 Dustan Mohr .20 .06
❑ 137 Dan Reichert .20 .06
❑ 138 Dewon Brazelton .20 .06
❑ 139 Orlando Cabrera .20 .06
❑ 140 Todd Hollandsworth .20 .06
❑ 141 Darren Dreifort .20 .06
❑ 142 Jose Valentin .20 .06
❑ 143 Josh Kalinowski .20 .06
❑ 144 Randy Keisler .20 .06
❑ 145 Bret Boone .30 .09
❑ 146 Roosevelt Brown .20 .06
❑ 147 Brent Abernathy .20 .06
❑ 148 Jorge Julio .20 .06
❑ 149 Alex Gonzalez .20 .06
❑ 150 Juan Pierre .30 .09
❑ 151 Roger Cedeno .20 .06
❑ 152 Javier Vazquez .30 .09
❑ 153 Armando Benitez .30 .09
❑ 154 Dave Burba .20 .06
❑ 155 Brad Penny .20 .06
❑ 156 Ryan Jensen .20 .06
❑ 157 Jeromy Burnitz .30 .09
❑ 158 Matt Childers RC .40 .12
❑ 159 Wilmy Caceres .20 .06
❑ 160 Roger Clemens 1.50 .45
❑ 161 Jamie Cerda RC .40 .12
❑ 162 Jason Christiansen .20 .06
❑ 163 Pokey Reese .20 .06
❑ 164 Ivanon Coffie .20 .06
❑ 165 Joaquin Benoit .20 .06
❑ 166 Mike Matheny .20 .06
❑ 167 Eric Cammack .20 .06
❑ 168 Alex Graman .20 .06
❑ 169 Brook Fordyce .20 .06
❑ 170 Mike Lieberthal .30 .09
❑ 171 Giovanni Carrara .20 .06
❑ 172 Antonio Perez .20 .06
❑ 173 Fernando Tatis .20 .06
❑ 174 Jason Bay RC 1.00 .30
❑ 175 Jason Botts RC .40 .12
❑ 176 Danys Baez .20 .06
❑ 177 Shea Hillenbrand .30 .09
❑ 178 Jack Cust .20 .06
❑ 179 Clay Bellinger .20 .06
❑ 180 Roberto Alomar .75 .23
❑ 181 Graeme Lloyd .20 .06
❑ 182 Clint Weibl RC .25 .07
❑ 183 Royce Clayton .20 .06
❑ 184 Ben Davis .20 .06
❑ 185 Brian Adams RC .25 .07
❑ 186 Jack Wilson .20 .06
❑ 187 David Coggin .20 .06
❑ 188 Derrick Turnbow .20 .06
❑ 189 Vladimir Nunez .20 .06
❑ 190 Mariano Rivera .50 .15
❑ 191 Wilson Guzman .20 .06
❑ 192 Michael Barrett .20 .06
❑ 193 Corey Patterson .30 .09
❑ 194 Luis Sojo .20 .06
❑ 195 Scott Elarton .20 .06
❑ 196 Charles Thomas RC .40 .12
❑ 197 Ricky Bottalico .20 .06
❑ 198 Wilfredo Rodriguez .20 .06
❑ 199 Ricardo Rincon .20 .06
❑ 200 John Smoltz .50 .15
❑ 201 Travis Miller .20 .06
❑ 202 Ben Weber .20 .06
❑ 203 T.J. Tucker .20 .06
❑ 204 Terry Shumpert .20 .06
❑ 205 Bernie Williams .50 .15
❑ 206 Russ Ortiz .30 .09
❑ 207 Nate Rolison .20 .06
❑ 208 Jose Cruz Jr. .30 .09
❑ 209 Bill Ortega .20 .06
❑ 210 Carl Everett .30 .09
❑ 211 Luis Lopez .20 .06
❑ 212 Brian Wolfe RC .40 .12
❑ 213 Doug Davis .20 .06
❑ 214 Troy Mattes .20 .06
❑ 215 Al Leiter .30 .09
❑ 216 Joe Mays .20 .06
❑ 217 Bobby Smith .20 .06
❑ 218 J.J. Trujillo RC .40 .12
❑ 219 Hideo Nomo .75 .23
❑ 220 Jimmy Rollins .30 .09
❑ 221 Bobby Seay .20 .06
❑ 222 Mike Thurman .20 .06
❑ 223 Bartolo Colon .30 .09
❑ 224 Jesus Sanchez .20 .06
❑ 225 Ray Durham .30 .09
❑ 226 Juan Diaz .20 .06
❑ 227 Lee Stevens .20 .06
❑ 228 Ben Howard RC .40 .12
❑ 229 James Mouton .20 .06
❑ 230 Paul Quantrill .20 .06
❑ 231 Randy Knorr .20 .06
❑ 232 Abraham Nunez .20 .06
❑ 233 Mike Fetters .20 .06
❑ 234 Mario Encarnacion .20 .06
❑ 235 Jeremy Fikac .20 .06
❑ 236 Travis Lee .20 .06
❑ 237 Bob File .20 .06
❑ 238 Pete Harnisch .20 .06
❑ 239 Randy Galvez RC .40 .12
❑ 240 Geoff Goetz .20 .06
❑ 241 Gary Glover .20 .06
❑ 242 Troy Percival .30 .09
❑ 243 Len Dinardo RC .40 .12
❑ 244 Jonny Gomes RC 1.00 .30
❑ 245 Jesus Medrano RC .40 .12
❑ 246 Rey Ordonez .20 .06
❑ 247 Juan Gonzalez .75 .23
❑ 248 Jose Guillen .20 .06
❑ 249 Franklyn German RC .40 .12
❑ 250 Mike Mussina .75 .23
❑ 251 Ugueth Urbina .20 .06
❑ 252 Melvin Mora .20 .06
❑ 253 Gerald Williams .20 .06
❑ 254 Jared Sandberg .20 .06
❑ 255 Darrin Fletcher .20 .06
❑ 256 A.J. Pierzynski .30 .09
❑ 257 Lenny Harris .20 .06
❑ 258 Blaine Neal .20 .06
❑ 259 Denny Neagle .20 .06
❑ 260 Jason Hart .20 .06
❑ 261 Henry Mateo .20 .06
❑ 262 Rheal Cormier .20 .06
❑ 263 Luis Terrero .20 .06
❑ 264 Shigetoshi Hasegawa .30 .09
❑ 265 Bill Haselman .20 .06
❑ 266 Scott Hatteberg .20 .06
❑ 267 Adam Hyzdu .20 .06
❑ 268 Mike Williams .20 .06
❑ 269 Marlon Anderson .20 .06
❑ 270 Bruce Chen .20 .06
❑ 271 Eli Marrero .20 .06
❑ 272 Jimmy Haynes .20 .06
❑ 273 Bronson Arroyo .20 .06
❑ 274 Kevin Jordan .20 .06
❑ 275 Rick Helling .20 .06
❑ 276 Mark Loretta .20 .06
❑ 277 Dustin Hermanson .20 .06
❑ 278 Pablo Ozuna .20 .06
❑ 279 Keto Anderson RC .40 .12
❑ 280 Jermaine Dye .30 .09
❑ 281 Will Smith .20 .06
❑ 282 Brian Daubach .20 .06
❑ 283 Eric Hinske .20 .06
❑ 284 Joe Jiannetti RC .40 .12
❑ 285 Chan Ho Park .30 .09
❑ 286 Curtis Legendre RC .40 .12
❑ 287 Jeff Reboulet .20 .06
❑ 288 Scott Rolen .50 .15
❑ 289 Chris Richard .20 .06
❑ 290 Eric Chavez .30 .09
❑ 291 Scot Shields .20 .06
❑ 292 Donnie Sadler .20 .06
❑ 293 Dave Veres .20 .06
❑ 294 Craig Counsell .20 .06
❑ 295 Armando Reynoso .20 .06
❑ 296 Kyle Lohse .20 .06
❑ 297 Arthur Rhodes .20 .06
❑ 298 Sidney Ponson .20 .06
❑ 299 Trevor Hoffman .30 .09
❑ 300 Kerry Wood .75 .23
❑ 301 Danny Bautista .20 .06
❑ 302 Scott Sauerbeck .20 .06
❑ 303 Johnny Estrada .20 .06
❑ 304 Mike Timlin .20 .06
❑ 305 Orlando Hernandez .30 .09
❑ 306 Tony Clark .20 .06
❑ 307 Tomas Perez .20 .06
❑ 308 Marcus Giles .30 .09
❑ 309 Mike Bordick .30 .09
❑ 310 Jorge Posada .50 .15
❑ 311 Jason Conti .20 .06
❑ 312 Kevin Millar .30 .09
❑ 313 Paul Shuey .20 .06
❑ 314 Jake Mauer RC .40 .12
❑ 315 Luke Hudson .20 .06
❑ 316 Angel Berroa .30 .09
❑ 317 Fred Bastardo RC .40 .12
❑ 318 Shawn Estes .20 .06
❑ 319 Andy Ashby .20 .06
❑ 320 Ryan Klesko .30 .09
❑ 321 Kevin Appier .30 .09
❑ 322 Juan Pena .20 .06
❑ 323 Alex Herrera .20 .06
❑ 324 Robb Nen .30 .09
❑ 325 Orlando Hudson .20 .06
❑ 326 Lyle Overbay .20 .06
❑ 327 Ben Sheets .30 .09
❑ 328 Mike DiFelice .20 .06
❑ 329 Pablo Arias RC .40 .12
❑ 330 Mike Sweeney .30 .09
❑ 331 Rick Ankiel .20 .06
❑ 332 Tomas De La Rosa .20 .06
❑ 333 Kazuhisa Ishii RC 1.50 .45
❑ 334 Jose Reyes .75 .23
❑ 335 Jeremy Giambi .20 .06
❑ 336 Jose Mesa .20 .06
❑ 337 Ralph Roberts RC .40 .12
❑ 338 Jose Nunez .20 .06
❑ 339 Curt Schilling .50 .15
❑ 340 Sean Casey .30 .09

❑ 341	Bob Wells	.20	.06
❑ 342	Carlos Beltran	.30	.09
❑ 343	Alexis Gomez	.20	.06
❑ 344	Brandon Claussen	.75	.23
❑ 345	Buddy Groom	.20	.06
❑ 346	Mark Phillips RC	.75	.23
❑ 347	Francisco Cordova	.20	.06
❑ 348	Joe Oliver	.20	.06
❑ 349	Danny Patterson	.20	.06
❑ 350	Joel Pineiro	.30	.09
❑ 351	J.R. House	.20	.06
❑ 352	Benny Agbayani	.20	.06
❑ 353	Jose Vidro	.30	.09
❑ 354	Reed Johnson RC	.50	.15
❑ 355	Mike Lowell	.30	.09
❑ 356	Scott Schoeneweis	.20	.06
❑ 357	Brian Jordan	.30	.09
❑ 358	Steve Finley	.30	.09
❑ 359	Randy Choate	.20	.06
❑ 360	Jose Lima	.20	.06
❑ 361	Miguel Olivo	.20	.06
❑ 362	Kenny Rogers	.30	.09
❑ 363	David Justice	.30	.09
❑ 364	Brandon Knight	.20	.06
❑ 365	Joe Kennedy	.20	.06
❑ 366	Eric Valent	.20	.06
❑ 367	Nelson Cruz	.20	.06
❑ 368	Brian Giles	.30	.09
❑ 369	Charles Gipson RC	.25	.07
❑ 370	Juan Pena	.20	.06
❑ 371	Mark Redman	.20	.06
❑ 372	Billy Koch	.20	.06
❑ 373	Ted Lilly	.20	.06
❑ 374	Craig Paquette	.20	.06
❑ 375	Kevin Jarvis	.20	.06
❑ 376	Scott Erickson	.20	.06
❑ 377	Josh Paul	.20	.06
❑ 378	Darwin Cubillan	.20	.06
❑ 379	Nelson Figueroa	.20	.06
❑ 380	Darin Erstad	.30	.09
❑ 381	Jeremy Hill RC	.40	.12
❑ 382	Elvin Nina	.20	.06
❑ 383	David Wells	.30	.09
❑ 384	Jay Caligiuri RC	.40	.12
❑ 385	Freddy Garcia	.30	.09
❑ 386	Damian Miller	.20	.06
❑ 387	Bobby Higginson	.30	.09
❑ 388	Alejandro Giron RC	.40	.12
❑ 389	Ivan Rodriguez	.75	.23
❑ 390	Ed Rogers	.20	.06
❑ 391	Andy Benes	.20	.06
❑ 392	Matt Blank	.20	.06
❑ 393	Ryan Vogelsong	.20	.06
❑ 394	Kelly Ramos RC	.25	.07
❑ 395	Eric Karros	.30	.09
❑ 396	Bobby J. Jones	.20	.06
❑ 397	Omar Vizquel	.30	.09
❑ 398	Matt Perisho	.20	.06
❑ 399	Delino DeShields	.20	.06
❑ 400	Carlos Hernandez	.20	.06
❑ 401	Derrek Lee	.30	.09
❑ 402	Kirk Rueter	.20	.06
❑ 403	David Wright RC	1.50	.45
❑ 404	Paul LoDuca	.30	.09
❑ 405	Brian Schneider	.20	.06
❑ 406	Milton Bradley	.30	.09
❑ 407	Daryle Ward	.20	.06
❑ 408	Cody Ransom	.20	.06
❑ 409	Fernando Rodney	.20	.06
❑ 410	John Suomi RC	.40	.12
❑ 411	Joe Girardi	.20	.06
❑ 412	Demetrius Heath RC	.40	.12
❑ 413	John Foster RC	.40	.12
❑ 414	Doug Glanville	.20	.06
❑ 415	Ryan Kohlmeier	.20	.06
❑ 416	Mike Matthews	.20	.06
❑ 417	Craig Wilson	.20	.06
❑ 418	Jay Witasick	.20	.06
❑ 419	Jay Payton	.20	.06
❑ 420	Andruw Jones	.50	.15
❑ 421	Benji Gil	.20	.06
❑ 422	Jeff Liefer	.20	.06
❑ 423	Kevin Young	.20	.06
❑ 424	Richie Sexson	.30	.09
❑ 425	Cory Lidle	.20	.06
❑ 426	Shane Halter	.20	.06
❑ 427	Jesse Foppert RC	2.00	.60
❑ 428	Jose Molina	.20	.06
❑ 429	Nick Alvarez RC	.40	.12
❑ 430	Brian L. Hunter	.20	.06
❑ 431	Cliff Bartosh RC	.40	.12
❑ 432	Junior Spivey	.20	.06
❑ 433	Eric Good RC	.40	.12
❑ 434	Chin-Feng Chen	.30	.09
❑ 435	T.J. Mathews	.20	.06
❑ 436	Rich Rodriguez	.20	.06
❑ 437	Bobby Abreu	.30	.09
❑ 438	Joe McEwing	.20	.06
❑ 439	Michael Tucker	.20	.06
❑ 440	Preston Wilson	.30	.09
❑ 441	Mike MacDougal	.20	.06
❑ 442	Shannon Stewart	.30	.09
❑ 443	Bob Howry	.20	.06
❑ 444	Mike Benjamin	.20	.06
❑ 445	Erik Hiljus	.20	.06
❑ 446	Ryan Gripp RC	.40	.12
❑ 447	Jose Vizcaino	.20	.06
❑ 448	Shawn Wooten	.20	.06
❑ 449	Steve Kent RC	.40	.12
❑ 450	Ramiro Mendoza	.20	.06
❑ 451	Jake Westbrook	.20	.06
❑ 452	Joe Lawrence	.20	.06
❑ 453	Jae Seo	.20	.06
❑ 454	Ryan Fry RC	.40	.12
❑ 455	Darren Lewis	.20	.06
❑ 456	Brad Wilkerson	.20	.06
❑ 457	Gustavo Chacin RC	.40	.12
❑ 458	Adrian Brown	.20	.06
❑ 459	Mike Cameron	.30	.09
❑ 460	Bud Smith	.20	.06
❑ 461	Derrick Lewis	.20	.06
❑ 462	Derek Lowe	.30	.09
❑ 463	Matt Williams	.30	.09
❑ 464	Jason Jennings	.20	.06
❑ 465	Albie Lopez	.20	.06
❑ 466	Felipe Lopez	.20	.06
❑ 467	Luke Allen	.20	.06
❑ 468	Brian Anderson	.20	.06
❑ 469	Matt Riley	.20	.06
❑ 470	Ryan Dempster	.20	.06
❑ 471	Matt Ginter	.20	.06
❑ 472	David Ortiz	.30	.09
❑ 473	Cole Barthel RC	.50	.15
❑ 474	Damian Jackson	.20	.06
❑ 475	Andy Van Hekken	.20	.06
❑ 476	Doug Brocail	.20	.06
❑ 477	Denny Hocking	.20	.06
❑ 478	Sean Douglass	.20	.06
❑ 479	Eric Owens	.20	.06
❑ 480	Ryan Ludwick	.20	.06
❑ 481	Todd Pratt	.20	.06
❑ 482	Aaron Sele	.20	.06
❑ 483	Edgar Renteria	.30	.09
❑ 484	Raymond Cabrera RC	.40	.12
❑ 485	Brandon Lyon	.20	.06
❑ 486	Chase Utley	.50	.15
❑ 487	Robert Fick	.30	.09
❑ 488	Wilfredo Cordero	.20	.06
❑ 489	Octavio Dotel	.20	.06
❑ 490	Paul Abbott	.20	.06
❑ 491	Jason Kendall	.30	.09
❑ 492	Jarrod Washburn	.30	.09
❑ 493	Dane Sardinha	.20	.06
❑ 494	Jung Bong	.20	.06
❑ 495	J.D. Drew	.30	.09
❑ 496	Jason Schmidt	.30	.09
❑ 497	Mike Magnante	.20	.06
❑ 498	Jorge Padilla RC	.50	.15
❑ 499	Eric Gagne	.50	.15
❑ 500	Todd Helton	.50	.15
❑ 501	Jeff Weaver	.20	.06
❑ 502	Alex Sanchez	.20	.06
❑ 503	Ken Griffey Jr.	1.25	.35
❑ 504	Abraham Nunez	.20	.06
❑ 505	Reggie Sanders	.30	.09
❑ 506	Casey Kotchman RC	2.50	.75
❑ 507	Jim Mann	.20	.06
❑ 508	Matt LeCroy	.20	.06
❑ 509	Frank Castillo	.20	.06
❑ 510	Geoff Jenkins	.30	.09
❑ 511	Jayson Durocher RC	.25	.07
❑ 512	Ellis Burks	.30	.09
❑ 513	Aaron Fultz	.20	.06
❑ 514	Hiram Bocachica	.20	.06
❑ 515	Nate Espy RC	.40	.12
❑ 516	Placido Polanco	.20	.06
❑ 517	Kerry Ligtenberg	.20	.06
❑ 518	Doug Nickle	.20	.06
❑ 519	Ramon Ortiz	.20	.06
❑ 520	Greg Swindell	.20	.06
❑ 521	J.J. Davis	.20	.06
❑ 522	Sandy Alomar Jr.	.20	.06
❑ 523	Chris Carpenter	.20	.06
❑ 524	Vance Wilson	.20	.06
❑ 525	Nomar Garciaparra	1.50	.45
❑ 526	Jim Mecir	.20	.06
❑ 527	Taylor Buchholz RC	.40	.12
❑ 528	Brent Mayne	.20	.06
❑ 529	John Rodriguez RC	.40	.12
❑ 530	David Segui	.20	.06
❑ 531	Nate Cornejo	.20	.06
❑ 532	Gil Heredia	.20	.06
❑ 533	Esteban Loaiza	.30	.09
❑ 534	Pat Mahomes	.20	.06
❑ 535	Matt Morris	.30	.09
❑ 536	Todd Stottlemyre	.20	.06
❑ 537	Brian Lesher	.20	.06
❑ 538	Arturo McDowell	.20	.06
❑ 539	Felix Diaz	.20	.06
❑ 540	Mark Mulder	.30	.09
❑ 541	Kevin Frederick RC	.40	.12
❑ 542	Andy Fox	.20	.06
❑ 543	Dionys Cesar RC	.25	.07
❑ 544	Justin Miller	.20	.06
❑ 545	Keith Osik	.20	.06
❑ 546	Shane Reynolds	.20	.06
❑ 547	Mike Myers	.20	.06
❑ 548	Raul Chavez RC	.25	.07
❑ 549	Joe Nathan	.20	.06
❑ 550	Ryan Anderson	.20	.06
❑ 551	Jason Marquis	.20	.06
❑ 552	Marty Cordova	.20	.06
❑ 553	Kevin Tapani	.20	.06
❑ 554	Jimmy Anderson	.20	.06
❑ 555	Pedro Martinez	.75	.23
❑ 556	Rocky Biddle	.20	.06
❑ 557	Alex Ochoa	.20	.06
❑ 558	D'Angelo Jimenez	.20	.06
❑ 559	Wilkin Ruan	.20	.06
❑ 560	Terrence Long	.30	.09
❑ 561	Mark Lukasiewicz	.20	.06
❑ 562	Jose Santiago	.20	.06
❑ 563	Brad Fullmer	.30	.09
❑ 564	Corky Miller	.20	.06
❑ 565	Matt White	.20	.06
❑ 566	Mark Grace	.75	.23
❑ 567	Raul Ibanez	.30	.09
❑ 568	Josh Towers	.20	.06
❑ 569	Juan M. Gonzalez RC	.40	.12
❑ 570	Brian Buchanan	.20	.06
❑ 571	Ken Harvey	.20	.06
❑ 572	Jeffrey Hammonds	.20	.06
❑ 573	Wade Miller	.30	.09
❑ 574	Elpidio Guzman	.20	.06
❑ 575	Kevin Olsen	.20	.06
❑ 576	Austin Kearns	.50	.15
❑ 577	Tim Kalita RC	.40	.12
❑ 578	David Dellucci	.20	.06
❑ 579	Alex Gonzalez	.20	.06
❑ 580	Joe Orloski RC	.40	.12
❑ 581	Gary Matthews Jr.	.20	.06
❑ 582	Ryan Mills	.20	.06
❑ 583	Erick Almonte	.20	.06
❑ 584	Jeremy Affeldt	.20	.06
❑ 585	Chris Tritle RC	.40	.12
❑ 586	Michael Cuddyer	.30	.09
❑ 587	Kris Foster	.20	.06
❑ 588	Russell Branyan	.20	.06
❑ 589	Darren Oliver	.20	.06
❑ 590	Freddie Money RC	.40	.12
❑ 591	Carlos Lee	.30	.09
❑ 592	Tim Wakefield	.30	.09
❑ 593	Bubba Trammell	.20	.06
❑ 594	John Koronka RC	.40	.12
❑ 595	Geoff Blum	.20	.06
❑ 596	Darryl Kile	.30	.09
❑ 597	Neifi Perez	.20	.06
❑ 598	Torii Hunter	.30	.09

No.	Player		
❑ 599	Luis Castillo	.30	.09
❑ 600	Mark Buehrle	.30	.09
❑ 601	Jeff Zimmerman	.20	.06
❑ 602	Mike DeJean	.20	.06
❑ 603	Julio Lugo	.20	.06
❑ 604	Chad Hermansen	.20	.06
❑ 605	Keith Foulke	.20	.06
❑ 606	Lance Davis	.20	.06
❑ 607	Jeff Austin RC	.40	.12
❑ 608	Brandon Inge	.20	.06
❑ 609	Orlando Merced	.20	.06
❑ 610	Johnny Damon	.30	.09
❑ 611	Doug Henry	.20	.06
❑ 612	Adam Kennedy	.20	.06
❑ 613	Wiki Gonzalez	.20	.06
❑ 614	Brian West RC	.40	.12
❑ 615	Andy Pettitte	.50	.15
❑ 616	Chone Figgins RC	.40	.12
❑ 617	Matt Lawton	.20	.06
❑ 618	Paul Rigdon	.20	.06
❑ 619	Keith Lockhart	.20	.06
❑ 620	Tim Redding	.20	.06
❑ 621	John Parrish	.20	.06
❑ 622	Homer Bush	.20	.06
❑ 623	Todd Greene	.20	.06
❑ 624	David Eckstein	.20	.06
❑ 625	Greg Montalbano RC	.50	.15
❑ 626	Joe Beimel	.20	.06
❑ 627	Adrian Beltre	.30	.09
❑ 628	Charles Nagy	.20	.06
❑ 629	Cristian Guzman	.30	.09
❑ 630	Toby Hall	.20	.06
❑ 631	Jose Hernandez	.20	.06
❑ 632	Jose Macias	.30	.09
❑ 633	Jaret Wright	.20	.06
❑ 634	Steve Parris	.20	.06
❑ 635	Gene Kingsale	.20	.06
❑ 636	Tim Worrell	.20	.06
❑ 637	Billy Martin	.20	.06
❑ 638	Jovanny Cedeno	.20	.06
❑ 639	Curtis Leskanic	.20	.06
❑ 640	Tim Hudson	.30	.09
❑ 641	Juan Castro	.20	.06
❑ 642	Rafael Soriano	.30	.09
❑ 643	Juan Rincon	.20	.06
❑ 644	Mark DeRosa	.20	.06
❑ 645	Carlos Pena	.20	.06
❑ 646	Robin Ventura	.30	.09
❑ 647	Odalis Perez	.20	.06
❑ 648	Damion Easley	.20	.06
❑ 649	Benito Santiago	.30	.09
❑ 650	Alex Rodriguez	1.50	.45
❑ 651	Aaron Rowand	.20	.06
❑ 652	Alex Cora	.20	.06
❑ 653	Bobby Kielty	.20	.06
❑ 654	Jose Rodriguez RC	.40	.12
❑ 655	Herbert Perry	.20	.06
❑ 656	Jeff Urban	.20	.06
❑ 657	Paul Bako	.20	.06
❑ 658	Shane Spencer	.20	.06
❑ 659	Pat Hentgen	.20	.06
❑ 660	Jeff Kent	.30	.09
❑ 661	Mark McLemore	.20	.06
❑ 662	Chuck Knoblauch	.30	.09
❑ 663	Blake Stein	.20	.06
❑ 664	Brett Roneberg RC	.40	.12
❑ 665	Josh Phelps	.30	.09
❑ 666	Byung-Hyun Kim	.30	.09
❑ 667	Dave Martinez	.20	.06
❑ 668	Mike Maroth	.20	.06
❑ 669	Shawn Chacon	.20	.06
❑ 670	Billy Wagner	.30	.09
❑ 671	Luis Alicea	.20	.06
❑ 672	Sterling Hitchcock	.20	.06
❑ 673	Adam Piatt	.20	.06
❑ 674	Ryan Franklin	.20	.06
❑ 675	Luke Prokopec	.20	.06
❑ 676	Alfredo Amezaga	.20	.06
❑ 677	Gookie Dawkins	.20	.06
❑ 678	Eric Byrnes	.20	.06
❑ 679	Barry Larkin	.75	.23
❑ 680	Albert Pujols	1.50	.45
❑ 681	Edwards Guzman	.20	.06
❑ 682	Jason Bere	.20	.06
❑ 683	Adam Everett	.20	.06
❑ 684	Greg Colbrunn	.20	.06
❑ 685	Brandon Puffer RC	.40	.12
❑ 686	Mark Kotsay	.20	.06
❑ 687	Willie Bloomquist	.30	.09
❑ 688	Hank Blalock	.75	.23
❑ 689	Travis Hafner	.20	.06
❑ 690	Lance Berkman	.30	.09
❑ 691	Joe Crede	.20	.06
❑ 692	Chuck Finley	.30	.09
❑ 693	John Grabow	.20	.06
❑ 694	Randy Winn	.20	.06
❑ 695	Mike James	.20	.06
❑ 696	Kris Benson	.20	.06
❑ 697	Bret Prinz	.20	.06
❑ 698	Jeff Williams	.20	.06
❑ 699	Eric Munson	.20	.06
❑ 700	Mike Hampton	.30	.09
❑ 701	Ramon E. Martinez	.20	.06
❑ 702	Hansel Izquierdo RC	.40	.12
❑ 703	Nathan Haynes	.20	.06
❑ 704	Eddie Taubensee	.20	.06
❑ 705	Esteban German	.20	.06
❑ 706	Ross Gload	.20	.06
❑ 707	Matt Merricks RC	.40	.12
❑ 708	Chris Piersoll RC	.25	.07
❑ 709	Seth Greisinger	.20	.06
❑ 710	Ichiro Suzuki	1.50	.45
❑ 711	Cesar Izturis	.20	.06
❑ 712	Brad Cresse	.20	.06
❑ 713	Carl Pavano	.20	.06
❑ 714	Steve Sparks	.20	.06
❑ 715	Dennis Tankersley	.20	.06
❑ 716	Kelvim Escobar	.20	.06
❑ 717	Jason LaRue	.20	.06
❑ 718	Corey Koskie	.30	.09
❑ 719	Vinny Castilla	.30	.09
❑ 720	Tim Drew	.20	.06
❑ 721	Chin-Hui Tsao	.30	.09
❑ 722	Paul Byrd	.20	.06
❑ 723	Alex Cintron	.30	.09
❑ 724	Orlando Palmeiro	.20	.06
❑ 725	Ramon Hernandez	.20	.06
❑ 726	Mark Johnson	.20	.06
❑ 727	B.J. Ryan	.20	.06
❑ 728	Wendell Magee	.20	.06
❑ 729	Michael Coleman	.20	.06
❑ 730	Mario Ramos RC	.50	.15
❑ 731	Mike Stanton	.20	.06
❑ 732	Dee Brown	.20	.06
❑ 733	Brad Ausmus	.20	.06
❑ 734	Napoleon Calzado RC	.40	.12
❑ 735	Woody Williams	.20	.06
❑ 736	Paxton Crawford	.20	.06
❑ 737	Jason Karnuth	.20	.06
❑ 738	Michael Restovich	.30	.09
❑ 739	Ramon Castro	.20	.06
❑ 740	Magglio Ordonez	.30	.09
❑ 741	Tom Gordon	.20	.06
❑ 742	Mark Grudzielanek	.20	.06
❑ 743	Jaime Moyer	.30	.09
❑ 744	Marlyn Tisdale RC	.40	.12
❑ 745	Steve Kline	.20	.06
❑ 746	Adam Eaton	.20	.06
❑ 747	Eric Glaser RC	.40	.12
❑ 748	Sean DePaula	.20	.06
❑ 749	Greg Norton	.20	.06
❑ 750	Steve Reed	.20	.06
❑ 751	Ricardo Aramboles	.20	.06
❑ 752	Matt Mantei	.20	.06
❑ 753	Gene Stechschulte	.20	.06
❑ 754	Chuck McElroy	.20	.06
❑ 755	Barry Bonds	2.00	.60
❑ 756	Matt Anderson	.20	.06
❑ 757	Yorvit Torrealba	.20	.06
❑ 758	Jason Standridge	.20	.06
❑ 759	Desi Relaford	.20	.06
❑ 760	Jolbert Cabrera	.20	.06
❑ 761	Chris George	.20	.06
❑ 762	Erubiel Durazo	.30	.09
❑ 763	Paul Konerko	.30	.09
❑ 764	Tike Redman	.20	.06
❑ 765	Chad Ricketts RC	.25	.07
❑ 766	Roberto Hernandez	.20	.06
❑ 767	Mark Lewis	.20	.06
❑ 768	Livan Hernandez	.20	.06
❑ 769	Carlos Brackley RC	.40	.12
❑ 770	Kazuhiro Sasaki	.30	.09
❑ 771	Bill Hall	.20	.06
❑ 772	Nelson Castro RC	.40	.12
❑ 773	Eric Milton	.20	.06
❑ 774	Tom Davey	.20	.06
❑ 775	Todd Ritchie	.20	.06
❑ 776	Seth Etherton	.20	.06
❑ 777	Chris Singleton	.20	.06
❑ 778	Robert Averette RC	.25	.07
❑ 779	Robert Person	.20	.06
❑ 780	Fred McGriff	.50	.15
❑ 781	Richard Hidalgo	.30	.09
❑ 782	Kris Wilson	.20	.06
❑ 783	John Rocker	.20	.06
❑ 784	Justin Kaye	.20	.06
❑ 785	Glendon Rusch	.20	.06
❑ 786	Greg Vaughn	.30	.09
❑ 787	Mike Lamb	.20	.06
❑ 788	Greg Myers	.20	.06
❑ 789	Nate Field RC	.40	.12
❑ 790	Jim Edmonds	.30	.09
❑ 791	Olmedo Saenz	.20	.06
❑ 792	Jason Johnson	.20	.06
❑ 793	Mike Lincoln	.20	.06
❑ 794	Todd Coffey RC	.40	.12
❑ 795	Jesus Sanchez	.20	.06
❑ 796	Aaron Myette	.20	.06
❑ 797	Tony Womack	.20	.06
❑ 798	Chad Kreuter	.20	.06
❑ 799	Brady Clark	.20	.06
❑ 800	Adam Dunn	.50	.15
❑ 801	Jacque Jones	.30	.09
❑ 802	Kevin Millwood	.30	.09
❑ 803	Mike Rivera	.20	.06
❑ 804	Jim Thome	.75	.23
❑ 805	Jeff Conine	.30	.09
❑ 806	Elmer Dessens	.20	.06
❑ 807	Randy Velarde	.20	.06
❑ 808	Carlos Delgado	.30	.09
❑ 809	Steve Karsay	.20	.06
❑ 810	Casey Fossum	.20	.06
❑ 811	J.C. Romero	.20	.06
❑ 812	Chris Truby	.20	.06
❑ 813	Tony Graffanino	.20	.06
❑ 814	Wascar Serrano	.20	.06
❑ 815	Delvin James	.20	.06
❑ 816	Pedro Feliz	.20	.06
❑ 817	Damian Rolls	.20	.06
❑ 818	Scott Linebrink	.20	.06
❑ 819	Rafael Palmeiro	.50	.15
❑ 820	Javy Lopez	.30	.09
❑ 821	Larry Barnes	.20	.06
❑ 822	Brian Lawrence	.20	.06
❑ 823	Scotty Layfield RC	.40	.12
❑ 824	Jeff Cirillo	.30	.09
❑ 825	Willis Roberts	.20	.06
❑ 826	Rich Harden RC	5.00	1.50
❑ 827	Chris Snelling RC	1.00	.30
❑ 828	Gary Sheffield	.30	.09
❑ 829	Jeff Heaverlo	.20	.06
❑ 830	Matt Clement	.20	.06
❑ 831	Rich Garces	.20	.06
❑ 832	Rondell White	.30	.09
❑ 833	Henry Pichardo RC	.40	.12
❑ 834	Aaron Boone	.30	.09
❑ 835	Ruben Sierra	.20	.06
❑ 836	Deivis Santos	.20	.06
❑ 837	Tony Batista	.30	.09
❑ 838	Rob Bell	.20	.06
❑ 839	Frank Thomas	.75	.23
❑ 840	Jose Silva	.20	.06
❑ 841	Dan Johnson RC	.50	.15
❑ 842	Steve Cox	.20	.06
❑ 843	Jose Acevedo	.20	.06
❑ 844	Jay Bell	.30	.09
❑ 845	Mike Sirotka	.20	.06
❑ 846	Garret Anderson	.30	.09
❑ 847	James Shanks RC	.40	.12
❑ 848	Trot Nixon	.30	.09
❑ 849	Keith Ginter	.20	.06
❑ 850	Tim Spooneybarger	.20	.06
❑ 851	Matt Stairs	.20	.06
❑ 852	Chris Stynes	.20	.06
❑ 853	Marvin Benard	.20	.06
❑ 854	Raul Mondesi	.30	.09
❑ 855	Jeremy Owens	.20	.06
❑ 856	Jon Garland	.20	.06

Card	Nm-Mt	Ex-Mt
❑ 857 Mitch Meluskey	.20	.06
❑ 858 Chad Durbin	.20	.06
❑ 859 John Burkett	.20	.06
❑ 860 Jon Switzer RC	.50	.15
❑ 861 Peter Bergeron	.20	.06
❑ 862 Jesus Colome	.20	.06
❑ 863 Todd Hundley	.20	.06
❑ 864 Ben Petrick	.20	.06
❑ 865 So Taguchi RC	.50	.15
❑ 866 Ryan Drese	.20	.06
❑ 867 Mike Trombley	.20	.06
❑ 868 Rick Reed	.20	.06
❑ 869 Mark Teixeira	.75	.23
❑ 870 Corey Thurman RC	.40	.12
❑ 871 Brian Roberts	.20	.06
❑ 872 Mike Timlin	.20	.06
❑ 873 Chris Reitsma	.20	.06
❑ 874 Jeff Fassero	.20	.06
❑ 875 Carlos Valderrama	.20	.06
❑ 876 John Lackey	.20	.06
❑ 877 Travis Fryman	.30	.09
❑ 878 Ismael Valdes	.20	.06
❑ 879 Rick White	.20	.06
❑ 880 Edgar Martinez	.50	.15
❑ 881 Dean Palmer	.30	.09
❑ 882 Matt Allegra RC	.50	.15
❑ 883 Greg Sain RC	.40	.12
❑ 884 Carlos Silva	.20	.06
❑ 885 Jose Valverde RC	.50	.15
❑ 886 Dernell Stenson	.20	.06
❑ 887 Todd Van Poppel	.20	.06
❑ 888 Wes Anderson	.20	.06
❑ 889 Bill Mueller	.30	.09
❑ 890 Morgan Ensberg	.30	.09
❑ 891 Marcus Thames	.20	.06
❑ 892 Adam Walker RC	.40	.12
❑ 893 John Halama	.20	.06
❑ 894 Frank Menechino	.20	.06
❑ 895 Greg Maddux	1.50	.45
❑ 896 Gary Bennett	.20	.06
❑ 897 Mauricio Lara RC	.40	.12
❑ 898 Mike Young	.30	.09
❑ 899 Travis Phelps	.20	.06
❑ 900 Rich Aurilia	.30	.09
❑ 901 Henry Blanco	.20	.06
❑ 902 Carlos Febles	.20	.06
❑ 903 Scott MacRae	.20	.06
❑ 904 Lou Merloni	.20	.06
❑ 905 Dicky Gonzalez	.20	.06
❑ 906 Jeff DaVanon	.20	.06
❑ 907 A.J. Burnett	.20	.06
❑ 908 Einar Diaz	.20	.06
❑ 909 Julio Franco	.30	.09
❑ 910 John Olerud	.30	.09
❑ 911 Mark Hamilton RC	.40	.12
❑ 912 David Riske	.20	.06
❑ 913 Jason Tyner	.20	.06
❑ 914 Britt Reames	.20	.06
❑ 915 Vernon Wells	.30	.09
❑ 916 Eddie Perez	.20	.06
❑ 917 Edwin Almonte RC	.40	.12
❑ 918 Enrique Wilson	.20	.06
❑ 919 Chris Gomez	.20	.06
❑ 920 Jayson Werth	.20	.06
❑ 921 Jeff Nelson	.20	.06
❑ 922 Freddy Sanchez RC	.75	.23
❑ 923 John Vander Wal	.20	.06
❑ 924 Chad Qualls RC	.40	.12
❑ 925 Gabe White	.20	.06
❑ 926 Chad Harville	.20	.06
❑ 927 Ricky Gutierrez	.20	.06
❑ 928 Carlos Guillen	.20	.06
❑ 929 B.J. Surhoff	.30	.09
❑ 930 Chris Woodward	.20	.06
❑ 931 Ricardo Rodriguez	.20	.06
❑ 932 Jimmy Gobble RC	1.50	.45
❑ 933 Jon Lieber	.20	.06
❑ 934 Craig Kuzmic RC	.40	.12
❑ 935 Eric Young	.20	.06
❑ 936 Greg Zaun	.20	.06
❑ 937 Miguel Batista	.20	.06
❑ 938 Danny Wright	.20	.06
❑ 939 Todd Zeile	.30	.09
❑ 940 Chad Zerbe	.20	.06
❑ 941 Jason Young RC	.50	.15
❑ 942 Ronnie Belliard	.20	.06
❑ 943 John Ennis RC	.40	.12
❑ 944 John Flaherty	.20	.06
❑ 945 Jerry Hairston Jr.	.20	.06
❑ 946 Al Levine	.20	.06
❑ 947 Antonio Alfonseca	.20	.06
❑ 948 Brian Moehler	.20	.06
❑ 949 Calvin Murray	.20	.06
❑ 950 Nick Bierbrodt	.20	.06
❑ 951 Sun Woo Kim	.20	.06
❑ 952 Noochie Varner RC	.75	.23
❑ 953 Luis Rivas	.20	.06
❑ 954 Donnie Bridges	.20	.06
❑ 955 Ramon Vazquez	.20	.06
❑ 956 Luis Garcia	.20	.06
❑ 957 Mark Quinn	.20	.06
❑ 958 Armando Rios	.20	.06
❑ 959 Chad Fox	.20	.06
❑ 960 Hee Seop Choi	.50	.15
❑ 961 Turk Wendell	.20	.06
❑ 962 Adam Roller RC	.40	.12
❑ 963 Grant Roberts	.20	.06
❑ 964 Ben Molina	.20	.06
❑ 965 Juan Rivera	.30	.09
❑ 966 Matt Kinney	.20	.06
❑ 967 Rod Beck	.20	.06
❑ 968 Xavier Nady	.30	.09
❑ 969 Masato Yoshii	.20	.06
❑ 970 Miguel Tejada	.30	.09
❑ 971 Danny Kolb	.20	.06
❑ 972 Mike Remlinger	.20	.06
❑ 973 Ray Lankford	.20	.06
❑ 974 Ryan Minor	.20	.06
❑ 975 J.T. Snow	.30	.09
❑ 976 Brad Radke	.30	.09
❑ 977 Jason Lane	.20	.06
❑ 978 Jamey Wright	.20	.06
❑ 979 Tom Goodwin	.20	.06
❑ 980 Erik Bedard	.20	.06
❑ 981 Gabe Kapler	.20	.06
❑ 982 Brian Reith	.20	.06
❑ 983 Nic Jackson RC	.50	.15
❑ 984 Kurt Ainsworth	.20	.06
❑ 985 Jason Isringhausen	.20	.06
❑ 986 Willie Harris	.20	.06
❑ 987 David Cone	.30	.09
❑ 988 Bob Wickman	.20	.06
❑ 989 Wes Helms	.20	.06
❑ 990 Josh Beckett	.50	.15

2003 Topps Total

	Nm-Mt	Ex-Mt
COMPLETE SET (990)	200.00	60.00
COMMON CARD (1-990)	.20	.06
COMMON RC	.25	.07

Card	Nm-Mt	Ex-Mt
❑ 1 Brent Abernathy	.20	.06
❑ 2 Bobby Hill	.20	.06
❑ 3 Victor Martinez	.30	.09
❑ 4 Chip Ambres	.20	.06
❑ 5 Matt Anderson	.20	.06
❑ 6 Ricardo Aramboles	.20	.06
❑ 7 Carlos Pena	.20	.06
❑ 8 Aaron Guiel	.20	.06
❑ 9 Luke Allen	.20	.06
❑ 10 Francisco Rodriguez	.30	.09
❑ 11 Jason Marquis	.20	.06
❑ 12 Edwin Almonte	.20	.06
❑ 13 Grant Balfour	.20	.06
❑ 14 Adam Piatt	.20	.06
❑ 15 Andy Phillips	.20	.06
❑ 16 Adrian Beltre	.30	.09
❑ 17 Brandon Backe	.20	.06
❑ 18 Dave Berg	.20	.06
❑ 19 Brett Myers	.30	.09
❑ 20 Brian Meadows	.20	.06
❑ 21 Chin-Feng Chen	.30	.09
❑ 22 Blake Williams	.20	.06
❑ 23 Josh Bard	.20	.06
❑ 24 Josh Beckett	.50	.15
❑ 25 Tommy Whiteman	.20	.06
❑ 26 Matt Childers	.20	.06
❑ 27 Adam Everett	.20	.06
❑ 28 Mike Bordick	.30	.09
❑ 29 Antonio Alfonseca	.20	.06
❑ 30 Doug Creek	.20	.06
❑ 31 J.D. Drew	.30	.09
❑ 32 Milton Bradley	.30	.09
❑ 33 David Wells	.30	.09
❑ 34 Vance Wilson	.20	.06
❑ 35 Jeff Fassero	.20	.06
❑ 36 Sandy Alomar	.20	.06
❑ 37 Ryan Vogelsong	.20	.06
❑ 38 Roger Clemens	1.50	.45
❑ 39 Juan Gonzalez	.75	.23
❑ 40 Dustin Hermanson	.20	.06
❑ 41 Andy Ashby	.20	.06
❑ 42 Adam Hyzdu	.20	.06
❑ 43 Ben Broussard	.20	.06
❑ 44 Ryan Klesko	.30	.09
❑ 45 Chris Buglovsky FY RC	.40	.12
❑ 46 Bud Smith	.20	.06
❑ 47 Aaron Boone	.30	.09
❑ 48 Cliff Floyd	.30	.09
❑ 49 Alex Cora	.20	.06
❑ 50 Curt Schilling	.50	.15
❑ 51 Michael Cuddyer	.30	.09
❑ 52 Joe Valentine FY RC	.40	.12
❑ 53 Carlos Guillen	.20	.06
❑ 54 Angel Berroa	.30	.09
❑ 55 Eli Marrero	.20	.06
❑ 56 A.J. Burnett	.20	.06
❑ 57 Oliver Perez	.30	.09
❑ 58 Matt Morris	.30	.09
❑ 59 Valerio De Los Santos	.20	.06
❑ 60 Austin Kearns	.50	.15
❑ 61 Darren Dreifort	.20	.06
❑ 62 Jason Standridge	.20	.06
❑ 63 Carlos Silva	.20	.06
❑ 64 Moises Alou	.30	.09
❑ 65 Jason Anderson	.20	.06
❑ 66 Russell Branyan	.20	.06
❑ 67 B.J. Ryan	.20	.06
❑ 68 Cory Aldridge	.20	.06
❑ 69 Ellis Burks	.30	.09
❑ 70 Troy Glaus	.50	.15
❑ 71 Kelly Wunsch	.20	.06
❑ 72 Brad Wilkerson	.20	.06
❑ 73 Jayson Durocher	.20	.06
❑ 74 Tony Fiore	.20	.06
❑ 75 Brian Giles	.30	.09
❑ 76 Billy Wagner	.30	.09
❑ 77 Neifi Perez	.20	.06
❑ 78 Jose Valverde	.20	.06
❑ 79 Brent Butler	.20	.06
❑ 80 Mario Ramos	.20	.06
❑ 81 Kerry Robinson	.20	.06
❑ 82 Brent Mayne	.20	.06
❑ 83 Sean Casey	.30	.09
❑ 84 Danys Baez	.20	.06
❑ 85 Chase Utley	.30	.09
❑ 86 Jared Sandberg	.20	.06
❑ 87 Terrence Long	.30	.09
❑ 88 Kevin Walker	.20	.06
❑ 89 Royce Clayton	.20	.06
❑ 90 Shea Hillenbrand	.30	.09
❑ 91 Brad Lidge	.20	.06
❑ 92 Shawn Chacon	.20	.06
❑ 93 Kenny Rogers	.30	.09
❑ 94 Chris Snelling	.30	.09
❑ 95 Omar Vizquel	.30	.09
❑ 96 Joe Borchard	.30	.09
❑ 97 Matt Belisle	.20	.06
❑ 98 Steve Smyth	.20	.06

	No.	Player		
❑	99	Raul Mondesi	.30	.09
❑	100	Chipper Jones	.75	.23
❑	101	Victor Alvarez	.20	.06
❑	102	J.M. Gold	.20	.06
❑	103	Willis Roberts	.20	.06
❑	104	Eddie Guardado	.30	.09
❑	105	Brad Voyles	.20	.06
❑	106	Bronson Arroyo	.20	.06
❑	107	Juan Castro	.20	.06
❑	108	Dan Plesac	.20	.06
❑	109	Ramon Castro	.20	.06
❑	110	Tim Salmon	.50	.15
❑	111	Gene Kingsale	.20	.06
❑	112	J.D. Closser	.20	.06
❑	113	Mark Buehrle	.30	.09
❑	114	Steve Karsay	.20	.06
❑	115	Cristian Guerrero	.20	.06
❑	116	Brad Ausmus	.20	.06
❑	117	Cristian Guzman	.30	.09
❑	118	Dan Wilson	.20	.06
❑	119	Jake Westbrook	.20	.06
❑	120	Manny Ramirez	.30	.09
❑	121	Jason Giambi	.75	.23
❑	122	Bob Wickman	.20	.06
❑	123	Aaron Cook	.20	.06
❑	124	Alfredo Amezaga	.20	.06
❑	125	Corey Thurman	.20	.06
❑	126	Brandon Puffer	.20	.06
❑	127	Hee Seop Choi	.30	.09
❑	128	Javier Vazquez	.30	.09
❑	129	Carlos Valderrama	.20	.06
❑	130	Jerome Williams	.30	.09
❑	131	Wilson Betemit	.20	.06
❑	132	Luke Prokopec	.20	.06
❑	133	Esteban Yan	.20	.06
❑	134	Brandon Berger	.20	.06
❑	135	Bill Hall	.20	.06
❑	136	LaTroy Hawkins	.20	.06
❑	137	Nate Cornejo	.20	.06
❑	138	Jim Mecir	.20	.06
❑	139	Joe Crede	.20	.06
❑	140	Andres Galarraga	.30	.09
❑	141	Reggie Sanders	.20	.06
❑	142	Joey Eischen	.20	.06
❑	143	Mike Timlin	.20	.06
❑	144	Jose Cruz Jr.	.30	.09
❑	145	Wes Helms	.20	.06
❑	146	Brian Roberts	.20	.06
❑	147	Bret Prinz	.20	.06
❑	148	Brian Hunter	.20	.06
❑	149	Chad Hermansen	.20	.06
❑	150	Andruw Jones	.50	.15
❑	151	Kurt Ainsworth	.20	.06
❑	152	Cliff Bartosh	.20	.06
❑	153	Kyle Lohse	.20	.06
❑	154	Brian Jordan	.30	.09
❑	155	Coco Crisp	.20	.06
❑	156	Tomas Perez	.20	.06
❑	157	Keith Foulke	.20	.06
❑	158	Chris Carpenter	.20	.06
❑	159	Mike Remlinger	.20	.06
❑	160	Dewon Brazelton	.20	.06
❑	161	Brook Fordyce	.20	.06
❑	162	Rusty Greer	.30	.09
❑	163	Scott Downs	.20	.06
❑	164	Jason Dubois	.30	.09
❑	165	David Coggin	.20	.06
❑	166	Mike DeJean	.20	.06
❑	167	Carlos Hernandez	.20	.06
❑	168	Matt Williams	.30	.09
❑	169	Rheal Cormier	.20	.06
❑	170	Duaner Sanchez	.20	.06
❑	171	Craig Counsell	.20	.06
❑	172	Edgar Martinez	.50	.15
❑	173	Zack Greinke	.75	.23
❑	174	Pedro Feliz	.20	.06
❑	175	Randy Choate	.20	.06
❑	176	Jon Garland	.20	.06
❑	177	Keith Ginter	.20	.06
❑	178	Carlos Febles	.20	.06
❑	179	Kerry Wood	.75	.23
❑	180	Jack Cust	.20	.06
❑	181	Koyie Hill	.20	.06
❑	182	Ricky Gutierrez	.20	.06
❑	183	Ben Grieve	.20	.06
❑	184	Scott Eyre	.20	.06
❑	185	Jason Isringhausen	.30	.09
❑	186	Gookie Dawkins	.20	.06
❑	187	Roberto Alomar	.75	.23
❑	188	Eric Junge	.20	.06
❑	189	Carlos Beltran	.30	.09
❑	190	Denny Hocking	.20	.06
❑	191	Jason Schmidt	.30	.09
❑	192	Cory Lidle	.20	.06
❑	193	Rob Mackowiak	.20	.06
❑	194	Charlton Jimerson RC	.40	.12
❑	195	Darin Erstad	.30	.09
❑	196	Jason Davis	.20	.06
❑	197	Luis Castillo	.30	.09
❑	198	Juan Encarnacion	.20	.06
❑	199	Jeffrey Hammonds	.20	.06
❑	200	Nomar Garciaparra	1.50	.45
❑	201	Ryan Christianson	.20	.06
❑	202	Robert Person	.20	.06
❑	203	Damian Moss	.20	.06
❑	204	Chris Richard	.20	.06
❑	205	Todd Hundley	.20	.06
❑	206	Paul Bako	.20	.06
❑	207	Adam Kennedy	.20	.06
❑	208	Scott Hatteberg	.20	.06
❑	209	Andy Pratt	.20	.06
❑	210	Ken Griffey Jr.	1.25	.35
❑	211	Chris George	.20	.06
❑	212	Lance Niekro	.20	.06
❑	213	Greg Colbrunn	.20	.06
❑	214	Herbert Perry	.20	.06
❑	215	Cody Ransom	.20	.06
❑	216	Craig Biggio	.50	.15
❑	217	Miguel Batista	.20	.06
❑	218	Alex Escobar	.20	.06
❑	219	Willie Harris	.20	.06
❑	220	Scott Strickland	.20	.06
❑	221	Felix Rodriguez	.20	.06
❑	222	Torii Hunter	.30	.09
❑	223	Tyler Houston	.20	.06
❑	224	Darrell May	.20	.06
❑	225	Benito Santiago	.30	.09
❑	226	Ryan Dempster	.20	.06
❑	227	Andy Fox	.20	.06
❑	228	Jung Bong	.20	.06
❑	229	Jose Macias	.20	.06
❑	230	Shannon Stewart	.30	.09
❑	231	Buddy Groom	.20	.06
❑	232	Eric Valent	.20	.06
❑	233	Scott Schoenweis	.20	.06
❑	234	Corey Hart	.30	.09
❑	235	Brett Tomko	.20	.06
❑	236	Shane Bazzell RC	.40	.12
❑	237	Tim Hummel	.20	.06
❑	238	Matt Stairs	.20	.06
❑	239	Pete Munro	.20	.06
❑	240	Ismael Valdes	.20	.06
❑	241	Brian Fuentes	.20	.06
❑	242	Cesar Izturis	.20	.06
❑	243	Mark Bellhorn	.20	.06
❑	244	Geoff Jenkins	.30	.09
❑	245	Derek Jeter	2.00	.60
❑	246	Anderson Machado	.20	.06
❑	247	Dave Roberts	.20	.06
❑	248	Jaime Cerda	.20	.06
❑	249	Woody Williams	.20	.06
❑	250	Vernon Wells	.30	.09
❑	251	Jon Lieber	.20	.06
❑	252	Franklyn German	.20	.06
❑	253	David Segui	.20	.06
❑	254	Freddy Garcia	.30	.09
❑	255	James Baldwin	.20	.06
❑	256	Tony Alvarez	.20	.06
❑	257	Walter Young	.20	.06
❑	258	Alex Herrera	.20	.06
❑	259	Robert Fick	.30	.09
❑	260	Rob Bell	.20	.06
❑	261	Ben Petrick	.20	.06
❑	262	Dee Brown	.20	.06
❑	263	Mike Bacsik	.20	.06
❑	264	Corey Patterson	.30	.09
❑	265	Marvin Benard	.20	.06
❑	266	Eddie Rogers	.20	.06
❑	267	Elio Serrano	.20	.06
❑	268	D'Angelo Jimenez	.20	.06
❑	269	Adam Johnson	.20	.06
❑	270	Gregg Zaun	.20	.06
❑	271	Nick Johnson	.30	.09
❑	272	Geoff Goetz	.20	.06
❑	273	Ryan Drese	.20	.06
❑	274	Eric Dubose	.20	.06
❑	275	Barry Zito	.75	.23
❑	276	Mike Crudale	.20	.06
❑	277	Paul Byrd	.20	.06
❑	278	Eric Gagne	.50	.15
❑	279	Aramis Ramirez	.30	.09
❑	280	Ray Durham	.30	.09
❑	281	Tony Graffanino	.20	.06
❑	282	Jeremy Guthrie	.30	.09
❑	283	Erik Bedard	.20	.06
❑	284	Vince Faison	.20	.06
❑	285	Bobby Kielty	.20	.06
❑	286	Francis Beltran	.20	.06
❑	287	Alexis Gomez	.20	.06
❑	288	Vladimir Guerrero	.75	.23
❑	289	Kevin Appier	.30	.09
❑	290	Gil Meche	.30	.09
❑	291	Marquis Grissom	.20	.06
❑	292	John Burkett	.20	.06
❑	293	Vinny Castilla	.30	.09
❑	294	Tyler Walker	.20	.06
❑	295	Shane Halter	.20	.06
❑	296	Geronimo Gil	.20	.06
❑	297	Eric Hinske	.20	.06
❑	298	Adam Dunn	.50	.15
❑	299	Mike Kinkade	.20	.06
❑	300	Mark Prior	1.50	.45
❑	301	Corey Koskie	.30	.09
❑	302	David Dellucci	.20	.06
❑	303	Todd Helton	.50	.15
❑	304	Greg Miller	.20	.06
❑	305	Delvin James	.20	.06
❑	306	Humberto Cota	.20	.06
❑	307	Aaron Harang	.20	.06
❑	308	Jeremy Hill	.20	.06
❑	309	Billy Koch	.20	.06
❑	310	Brandon Claussen	.30	.09
❑	311	Matt Ginter	.20	.06
❑	312	Jason Lane	.20	.06
❑	313	Ben Weber	.20	.06
❑	314	Alan Benes	.20	.06
❑	315	Matt Walbeck	.20	.06
❑	316	Danny Graves	.20	.06
❑	317	Jason Johnson	.20	.06
❑	318	Jason Grimsley	.20	.06
❑	319	Steve Kline	.20	.06
❑	320	Johnny Damon	.30	.09
❑	321	Jay Gibbons	.30	.09
❑	322	J.J. Putz	.20	.06
❑	323	Stephen Randolph RC	.40	.12
❑	324	Bobby Higginson	.30	.09
❑	325	Kazuhisa Ishii	.30	.09
❑	326	Carlos Lee	.30	.09
❑	327	J.R. House	.20	.06
❑	328	Mark Loretta	.20	.06
❑	329	Mike Matheny	.20	.06
❑	330	Ben Diggins	.20	.06
❑	331	Seth Etherton	.20	.06
❑	332	Eli Whiteside FY RC	.40	.12
❑	333	Juan Rivera	.30	.09
❑	334	Jeff Conine	.30	.09
❑	335	John McDonald	.20	.06
❑	336	Erik Hiljus	.20	.06
❑	337	David Eckstein	.20	.06
❑	338	Jeff Bagwell	.50	.15
❑	339	Matt Holliday	.20	.06
❑	340	Jeff Liefer	.20	.06
❑	341	Greg Myers	.20	.06
❑	342	Scott Sauerbeck	.20	.06
❑	343	Omar Infante	.20	.06
❑	344	Ryan Langerhans	.20	.06
❑	345	Abraham Nunez	.20	.06
❑	346	Mike MacDougal	.20	.06
❑	347	Travis Phelps	.20	.06
❑	348	Terry Shumpert	.20	.06
❑	349	Alex Rodriguez	1.50	.45
❑	350	Bobby Seay	.20	.06
❑	351	Ichiro Suzuki	1.50	.45
❑	352	Brandon Inge	.20	.06
❑	353	Jack Wilson	.20	.06
❑	354	John Ennis	.20	.06
❑	355	Jamal Strong	.20	.06
❑	356	Jason Jennings	.20	.06

❑ 357	Jeff Kent	.30	.09
❑ 358	Scott Chiasson	.20	.06
❑ 359	Jeremy Griffiths RC	.50	.15
❑ 360	Paul Konerko	.30	.09
❑ 361	Jeff Austin	.20	.06
❑ 362	Todd Van Poppel	.20	.06
❑ 363	Sun Woo Kim	.20	.06
❑ 364	Jerry Hairston Jr.	.20	.06
❑ 365	Tony Torcato	.20	.06
❑ 366	Arthur Rhodes	.20	.06
❑ 367	Jose Jimenez	.20	.06
❑ 368	Matt LeCroy	.20	.06
❑ 369	Curtis Leskanic	.20	.06
❑ 370	Ramon Vazquez	.20	.06
❑ 371	Joe Randa	.20	.06
❑ 372	John Franco	.30	.09
❑ 373	Bobby Estalella	.20	.06
❑ 374	Craig Wilson	.20	.06
❑ 375	Michael Young	.30	.09
❑ 376	Mark Ellis	.20	.06
❑ 377	Joe Mauer	.75	.23
❑ 378	Checklist 1	.20	.06
❑ 379	Jason Kendall	.30	.09
❑ 380	Checklist 2	.20	.06
❑ 381	Alex Gonzalez	.20	.06
❑ 382	Tom Gordon	.20	.06
❑ 383	John Buck	.20	.06
❑ 384	Shigetoshi Hasegawa	.30	.09
❑ 385	Scott Stewart	.20	.06
❑ 386	Luke Hudson	.20	.06
❑ 387	Todd Jones	.20	.06
❑ 388	Fred McGriff	.50	.15
❑ 389	Mike Sweeney	.30	.09
❑ 390	Marlon Anderson	.20	.06
❑ 391	Terry Adams	.20	.06
❑ 392	Mark DeRosa	.20	.06
❑ 393	Doug Mientkiewicz	.30	.09
❑ 394	Miguel Cairo	.20	.06
❑ 395	Jamie Moyer	.30	.09
❑ 396	Jose Leon	.20	.06
❑ 397	Matt Clement	.20	.06
❑ 398	Bengie Molina	.20	.06
❑ 399	Marcus Thames	.20	.06
❑ 400	Nick Bierbrodt	.20	.06
❑ 401	Tim Kalita	.20	.06
❑ 402	Corwin Malone	.30	.09
❑ 403	Jesse Orosco	.20	.06
❑ 404	Brandon Phillips	.20	.06
❑ 405	Eric Cyr	.20	.06
❑ 406	Jason Michaels	.20	.06
❑ 407	Julio Lugo	.20	.06
❑ 408	Gabe Kapler	.20	.06
❑ 409	Mark Mulder	.30	.09
❑ 410	Adam Eaton	.20	.06
❑ 411	Ken Harvey	.20	.06
❑ 412	Jolbert Cabrera	.20	.06
❑ 413	Eric Milton	.20	.06
❑ 414	Josh Hall RC	.50	.15
❑ 415	Bob File	.20	.06
❑ 416	Brett Evert	.20	.06
❑ 417	Ron Chiavacci	.20	.06
❑ 418	Jorge De La Rosa	.20	.06
❑ 419	Quinton McCracken	.20	.06
❑ 420	Luther Hackman	.20	.06
❑ 421	Gary Knotts	.20	.06
❑ 422	Kevin Brown	.30	.09
❑ 423	Jeff Cirillo	.30	.09
❑ 424	Damaso Marte	.20	.06
❑ 425	Chan Ho Park	.30	.09
❑ 426	Nathan Haynes	.20	.06
❑ 427	Matt Lawton	.20	.06
❑ 428	Mike Stanton	.20	.06
❑ 429	Bernie Williams	.50	.15
❑ 430	Kevin Jarvis	.20	.06
❑ 431	Joe McEwing	.20	.06
❑ 432	Mark Kotsay	.20	.06
❑ 433	Juan Cruz	.20	.06
❑ 434	Russ Ortiz	.30	.09
❑ 435	Jeff Nelson	.20	.06
❑ 436	Alan Embree	.20	.06
❑ 437	Miguel Tejada	.30	.09
❑ 438	Kirk Saarloos	.30	.09
❑ 439	Cliff Lee	.30	.09
❑ 440	Ryan Ludwick	.20	.06
❑ 441	Derrek Lee	.30	.09
❑ 442	Bobby Abreu	.30	.09
❑ 443	Dustan Mohr	.20	.06
❑ 444	Nook Logan RC	.40	.12
❑ 445	Seth McClung	.20	.06
❑ 446	Miguel Olivo	.20	.06
❑ 447	Henry Blanco	.20	.06
❑ 448	Seung Song	.20	.06
❑ 449	Kris Wilson	.20	.06
❑ 450	Xavier Nady	.30	.09
❑ 451	Corky Miller	.20	.06
❑ 452	Jim Thome	.75	.23
❑ 453	George Lombard	.20	.06
❑ 454	Rey Ordonez	.20	.06
❑ 455	Deivis Santos	.20	.06
❑ 456	Mike Myers	.20	.06
❑ 457	Edgar Renteria	.30	.09
❑ 458	Braden Looper	.20	.06
❑ 459	Guillermo Mota	.20	.06
❑ 460	Scott Rolen	.50	.15
❑ 461	Lance Berkman	.30	.09
❑ 462	Jeff Heaverlo	.20	.06
❑ 463	Ramon Hernandez	.20	.06
❑ 464	Jason Simontacchi	.20	.06
❑ 465	So Taguchi	.30	.09
❑ 466	Dave Veres	.20	.06
❑ 467	Shane Loux	.20	.06
❑ 468	Rodrigo Lopez	.20	.06
❑ 469	Bubba Trammell	.20	.06
❑ 470	Scott Sullivan	.20	.06
❑ 471	Mike Mussina	.75	.23
❑ 472	Ramon Ortiz	.20	.06
❑ 473	Lyle Overbay	.20	.06
❑ 474	Mike Lowell	.30	.09
❑ 475	Al Martin	.20	.06
❑ 476	Larry Bigbie	.20	.06
❑ 477	Rey Sanchez	.20	.06
❑ 478	Magglio Ordonez	.30	.09
❑ 479	Rondell White	.30	.09
❑ 480	Jay Witasick	.20	.06
❑ 481	Jimmy Rollins	.30	.09
❑ 482	Mike Maroth	.20	.06
❑ 483	Alejandro Machado	.20	.06
❑ 484	Nick Neugebauer	.20	.06
❑ 485	Victor Zambrano	.20	.06
❑ 486	Travis Lee	.20	.06
❑ 487	Bobby Bradley	.20	.06
❑ 488	Marcus Giles	.30	.09
❑ 489	Steve Trachsel	.20	.06
❑ 490	Derek Lowe	.30	.09
❑ 491	Hideo Nomo	.75	.23
❑ 492	Brad Hawpe	.30	.09
❑ 493	Jesus Medrano	.20	.06
❑ 494	Rick Ankiel	.20	.06
❑ 495	Pasqual Coco	.20	.06
❑ 496	Michael Barrett	.20	.06
❑ 497	Joe Beimel	.20	.06
❑ 498	Marty Cordova	.20	.06
❑ 499	Aaron Sele	.20	.06
❑ 500	Sammy Sosa	1.25	.35
❑ 501	Ivan Rodriguez	.75	.23
❑ 502	Keith Osik	.20	.06
❑ 503	Hank Blalock	.50	.15
❑ 504	Hiram Bocachica	.20	.06
❑ 505	Junior Spivey	.20	.06
❑ 506	Edgardo Alfonzo	.30	.09
❑ 507	Alex Graman	.20	.06
❑ 508	J.J. Davis	.20	.06
❑ 509	Roger Cedeno	.20	.06
❑ 510	Joe Roa	.20	.06
❑ 511	Wily Mo Pena	.30	.09
❑ 512	Eric Munson	.30	.09
❑ 513	Arnie Munoz RC	.40	.12
❑ 514	Albie Lopez	.20	.06
❑ 515	Andy Pettitte	.50	.15
❑ 516	Jim Edmonds	.30	.09
❑ 517	Jeff Davanon	.20	.06
❑ 518	Aaron Myette	.20	.06
❑ 519	C.C. Sabathia	.30	.09
❑ 520	Gerardo Garcia	.20	.06
❑ 521	Brian Schneider	.20	.06
❑ 522	Wes Obermueller	.20	.06
❑ 523	John Mabry	.20	.06
❑ 524	Casey Fossum	.20	.06
❑ 525	Toby Hall	.20	.06
❑ 526	Denny Neagle	.20	.06
❑ 527	Willie Bloomquist	.30	.09
❑ 528	A.J. Pierzynski	.30	.09
❑ 529	Bartolo Colon	.30	.09
❑ 530	Chad Harville	.20	.06
❑ 531	Blaine Neal	.20	.06
❑ 532	Luis Terrero	.20	.06
❑ 533	Reggie Taylor	.20	.06
❑ 534	Melvin Mora	.20	.06
❑ 535	Tino Martinez	.50	.15
❑ 536	Peter Bergeron	.20	.06
❑ 537	Jorge Padilla	.30	.09
❑ 538	Oscar Villarreal RC	.40	.12
❑ 539	David Weathers	.20	.06
❑ 540	Mike Lamb	.20	.06
❑ 541	Greg Norton	.20	.06
❑ 542	Michael Tucker	.20	.06
❑ 543	Ben Kozlowski	.20	.06
❑ 544	Alex Sanchez	.20	.06
❑ 545	Trey Lunsford	.20	.06
❑ 546	Abraham Nunez	.20	.06
❑ 547	Mike Lincoln	.20	.06
❑ 548	Orlando Hernandez	.30	.09
❑ 549	Kevin Mench	.20	.06
❑ 550	Garret Anderson	.30	.09
❑ 551	Kyle Farnsworth	.20	.06
❑ 552	Kevin Olsen	.20	.06
❑ 553	Joel Pineiro	.30	.09
❑ 554	Jorge Julio	.20	.06
❑ 555	Jose Mesa	.20	.06
❑ 556	Jorge Posada	.50	.15
❑ 557	Jose Ortiz	.20	.06
❑ 558	Mike Tonis	.20	.06
❑ 559	Gabe White	.20	.06
❑ 560	Rafael Furcal	.30	.09
❑ 561	Matt Franco	.20	.06
❑ 562	Trey Hodges	.20	.06
❑ 563	Esteban German	.20	.06
❑ 564	Josh Fogg	.20	.06
❑ 565	Fernando Tatis	.20	.06
❑ 566	Alex Cintron	.30	.09
❑ 567	Grant Roberts	.20	.06
❑ 568	Gene Stechschulte	.20	.06
❑ 569	Rafael Palmeiro	.50	.15
❑ 570	Mike Hampton	.30	.09
❑ 571	Ben Davis	.20	.06
❑ 572	Dean Palmer	.30	.09
❑ 573	Jerrod Riggan	.20	.06
❑ 574	Nate Frese	.20	.06
❑ 575	Josh Phelps	.30	.09
❑ 576	Freddie Bynum	.20	.06
❑ 577	Morgan Ensberg	.20	.06
❑ 578	Juan Rincon	.20	.06
❑ 579	Kazuhiro Sasaki	.30	.09
❑ 580	Yorvit Torrealba	.20	.06
❑ 581	Tim Wakefield	.30	.09
❑ 582	Sterling Hitchcock	.20	.06
❑ 583	Craig Paquette	.20	.06
❑ 584	Kevin Millwood	.30	.09
❑ 585	Damian Rolls	.20	.06
❑ 586	Brad Baisley	.20	.06
❑ 587	Kyle Snyder	.20	.06
❑ 588	Paul Quantrill	.20	.06
❑ 589	Trot Nixon	.30	.09
❑ 590	J.T. Snow	.30	.09
❑ 591	Kevin Young	.20	.06
❑ 592	Tomo Ohka	.20	.06
❑ 593	Brian Boehringer	.20	.06
❑ 594	Danny Patterson	.20	.06
❑ 595	Jeff Tam	.20	.06
❑ 596	Anastacio Martinez	.20	.06
❑ 597	Rod Barajas	.20	.06
❑ 598	Octavio Dotel	.20	.06
❑ 599	Jason Tyner	.20	.06
❑ 600	Gary Sheffield	.30	.09
❑ 601	Ruben Quevedo	.20	.06
❑ 602	Jay Payton	.20	.06
❑ 603	Mo Vaughn	.30	.09
❑ 604	Pat Burrell	.30	.09
❑ 605	Fernando Vina	.20	.06
❑ 606	Wes Anderson	.20	.06
❑ 607	Alex Gonzalez	.20	.06
❑ 608	Ted Lilly	.20	.06
❑ 609	Nick Punto	.20	.06
❑ 610	Ryan Madson	.20	.06
❑ 611	Odalis Perez	.20	.06
❑ 612	Chris Woodward	.20	.06
❑ 613	John Olerud	.30	.09
❑ 614	Brad Cresse	.20	.06

❑ 615 Chad Zerbe .20 .06
❑ 616 Brad Penny .20 .06
❑ 617 Barry Larkin .75 .23
❑ 618 Brandon Duckworth .20 .06
❑ 619 Brad Radke .30 .09
❑ 620 Troy Brohawn .20 .06
❑ 621 Juan Pierre .30 .09
❑ 622 Rick Reed .20 .06
❑ 623 Omar Daal .20 .06
❑ 624 Jose Hernandez .20 .06
❑ 625 Greg Maddux 1.50 .45
❑ 626 Henry Mateo .20 .06
❑ 627 Kip Wells .20 .06
❑ 628 Kevin Cash .20 .06
❑ 629 Wil Ledezma FY RC .40 .12
❑ 630 Luis Gonzalez .30 .09
❑ 631 Jason Conti .20 .06
❑ 632 Ricardo Rincon .20 .06
❑ 633 Mike Bynum .20 .06
❑ 634 Mike Redmond .20 .06
❑ 635 Chance Caple .20 .06
❑ 636 Chris Widger .20 .06
❑ 637 Michael Restovich .30 .09
❑ 638 Mark Grudzielanek .20 .06
❑ 639 Brandon Larson .20 .06
❑ 640 Rocco Baldelli 1.50 .45
❑ 641 Javy Lopez .30 .09
❑ 642 Rene Reyes .20 .06
❑ 643 Orlando Merced .20 .06
❑ 644 Jason Phillips .30 .09
❑ 645 Luis Ugueto .20 .06
❑ 646 Ron Calloway .20 .06
❑ 647 Josh Paul .20 .06
❑ 648 Todd Greene .20 .06
❑ 649 Joe Girardi .20 .06
❑ 650 Todd Ritchie .20 .06
❑ 651 Kevin Millar .30 .09
❑ 652 Shawn Wooten .20 .06
❑ 653 David Riske .20 .06
❑ 654 Luis Rivas .20 .06
❑ 655 Roy Halladay .30 .09
❑ 656 Travis Driskill .20 .06
❑ 657 Ricky Ledee .20 .06
❑ 658 Timo Perez .20 .06
❑ 659 Fernando Rodney .20 .06
❑ 660 Trevor Hoffman .30 .09
❑ 661 Pat Hentgen .30 .09
❑ 662 Bret Boone .30 .09
❑ 663 Ryan Jensen .20 .06
❑ 664 Ricardo Rodriguez .20 .06
❑ 665 Jeremy Lambert .20 .06
❑ 666 Troy Percival .30 .09
❑ 667 Jon Rauch .20 .06
❑ 668 Mariano Rivera .50 .15
❑ 669 Jason LaRue .20 .06
❑ 670 J.C. Romero .20 .06
❑ 671 Cody Ross .20 .06
❑ 672 Eric Byrnes .20 .06
❑ 673 Paul Lo Duca .30 .09
❑ 674 Brad Fullmer .30 .09
❑ 675 Cliff Politte .20 .06
❑ 676 Justin Miller .20 .06
❑ 677 Nic Jackson .20 .06
❑ 678 Kris Benson .20 .06
❑ 679 Carl Sadler .20 .06
❑ 680 Joe Nathan .20 .06
❑ 681 Julio Santana .20 .06
❑ 682 Wade Miller .30 .09
❑ 683 Josh Pearce .20 .06
❑ 684 Tony Armas Jr. .20 .06
❑ 685 Al Leiter .30 .09
❑ 686 Raul Ibanez .30 .09
❑ 687 Danny Bautista .20 .06
❑ 688 Travis Hafner .20 .06
❑ 689 Carlos Zambrano .30 .09
❑ 690 Pedro Martinez .75 .23
❑ 691 Ramon Santiago .20 .06
❑ 692 Felipe Lopez .20 .06
❑ 693 David Ross .20 .06
❑ 694 Chone Figgins .20 .06
❑ 695 Antonio Osuna .20 .06
❑ 696 Jay Powell .20 .06
❑ 697 Ryan Church .30 .09
❑ 698 Alexis Rios .30 .09
❑ 699 Tanyon Sturtze .20 .06
❑ 700 Turk Wendell .20 .06
❑ 701 Richard Hidalgo .30 .09
❑ 702 Joe Mays .20 .06
❑ 703 Jorge Sosa .20 .06
❑ 704 Eric Karros .30 .09
❑ 705 Steve Finley .30 .09
❑ 706 Sean Smith FY RC .50 .15
❑ 707 Jeremy Giambi .20 .06
❑ 708 Scott Hodges .20 .06
❑ 709 Vicente Padilla .20 .06
❑ 710 Erubiel Durazo .30 .09
❑ 711 Aaron Rowand .20 .06
❑ 712 Dennis Tankersley .20 .06
❑ 713 Rick Bauer .20 .06
❑ 714 Tim Olson FY RC .75 .23
❑ 715 Jeff Urban .20 .06
❑ 716 Steve Sparks .20 .06
❑ 717 Glendon Rusch .20 .06
❑ 718 Ricky Stone .20 .06
❑ 719 Benji Gil .20 .06
❑ 720 Pete Walker .20 .06
❑ 721 Tim Worrell .20 .06
❑ 722 Michael Tejera .20 .06
❑ 723 David Kelton .20 .06
❑ 724 Britt Reames .20 .06
❑ 725 John Stephens .20 .06
❑ 726 Mark McLemore .20 .06
❑ 727 Jeff Zimmerman .20 .06
❑ 728 Checklist 3 .20 .06
❑ 729 Andres Torres .20 .06
❑ 730 Checklist 4 .20 .06
❑ 731 Johan Santana .30 .09
❑ 732 Dane Sardinha .20 .06
❑ 733 Rodrigo Rosario .20 .06
❑ 734 Frank Thomas .75 .23
❑ 735 Tom Glavine .75 .23
❑ 736 Doug Mirabelli .20 .06
❑ 737 Juan Uribe .20 .06
❑ 738 Ryan Anderson .20 .06
❑ 739 Sean Burroughs .30 .09
❑ 740 Eric Chavez .30 .09
❑ 741 Enrique Wilson .20 .06
❑ 742 Elmer Dessens .20 .06
❑ 743 Marlon Byrd .30 .09
❑ 744 Brendan Donnelly .20 .06
❑ 745 Gary Bennett .20 .06
❑ 746 Roy Oswalt .30 .09
❑ 747 Andy Van Hekken .20 .06
❑ 748 Jesus Colome .20 .06
❑ 749 Erick Almonte .20 .06
❑ 750 Frank Catalanotto .20 .06
❑ 751 Kenny Lofton .30 .09
❑ 752 Carlos Delgado .30 .09
❑ 753 Ryan Franklin .20 .06
❑ 754 Wilkin Ruan .20 .06
❑ 755 Kelvim Escobar .20 .06
❑ 756 Tim Drew .20 .06
❑ 757 Jarrod Washburn .30 .09
❑ 758 Runelvys Hernandez .30 .09
❑ 759 Cory Vance .20 .06
❑ 760 Doug Glanville .20 .06
❑ 761 Ryan Rupe .20 .06
❑ 762 Jermaine Dye .30 .09
❑ 763 Mike Cameron .30 .09
❑ 764 Scott Erickson .20 .06
❑ 765 Richie Sexson .30 .09
❑ 766 Jose Vidro .30 .09
❑ 767 Brian West .20 .06
❑ 768 Shawn Estes .20 .06
❑ 769 Brian Tallet .20 .06
❑ 770 Larry Walker .50 .15
❑ 771 Josh Hamilton .30 .09
❑ 772 Orlando Hudson .20 .06
❑ 773 Justin Morneau .30 .09
❑ 774 Ryan Bukvich .20 .06
❑ 775 Mike Gonzalez .20 .06
❑ 776 Tsuyoshi Shinjo .30 .09
❑ 777 Matt Mantei .20 .06
❑ 778 Jimmy Journell .20 .06
❑ 779 Brian Lawrence .20 .06
❑ 780 Mike Lieberthal .30 .09
❑ 781 Scott Mullen .20 .06
❑ 782 Zach Day .20 .06
❑ 783 John Thomson .20 .06
❑ 784 Ben Sheets .30 .09
❑ 785 Damon Minor .20 .06
❑ 786 Jose Valentin .20 .06
❑ 787 Armando Benitez .30 .09
❑ 788 Jamie Walker .20 .06
❑ 789 Preston Wilson .30 .09
❑ 790 Josh Wilson .20 .06
❑ 791 Phil Nevin .30 .09
❑ 792 Roberto Hernandez .20 .06
❑ 793 Mike Williams .20 .06
❑ 794 Jake Peavy .30 .09
❑ 795 Paul Shuey .20 .06
❑ 796 Chad Bradford .20 .06
❑ 797 Bobby Jenks .30 .09
❑ 798 Sean Douglass .20 .06
❑ 799 Damian Miller .20 .06
❑ 800 Mark Wohlers .20 .06
❑ 801 Ty Wigginton .30 .09
❑ 802 Alfonso Soriano .75 .23
❑ 803 Randy Johnson .75 .23
❑ 804 Placido Polanco .20 .06
❑ 805 Drew Henson .30 .09
❑ 806 Tony Womack .20 .06
❑ 807 Pokey Reese .20 .06
❑ 808 Albert Pujols 1.50 .45
❑ 809 Henri Stanley .20 .06
❑ 810 Mike Rivera .20 .06
❑ 811 John Lackey .20 .06
❑ 812 Brian Wright FY RC .40 .12
❑ 813 Eric Good .20 .06
❑ 814 Dernell Stenson .20 .06
❑ 815 Kirk Rueter .20 .06
❑ 816 Todd Zeile .20 .06
❑ 817 Brad Thomas .20 .06
❑ 818 Shawn Sedlacek .20 .06
❑ 819 Garrett Stephenson .20 .06
❑ 820 Mark Teixeira .50 .15
❑ 821 Tim Hudson .30 .09
❑ 822 Mike Koplove .20 .06
❑ 823 Chris Reitsma .20 .06
❑ 824 Rafael Soriano .20 .06
❑ 825 Ugueth Urbina .20 .06
❑ 826 Lance Carter .20 .06
❑ 827 Colin Young .20 .06
❑ 828 Pat Strange .20 .06
❑ 829 Juan Pena .20 .06
❑ 830 Joe Thurston .20 .06
❑ 831 Shawn Green .30 .09
❑ 832 Pedro Astacio .20 .06
❑ 833 Danny Wright .20 .06
❑ 834 Wes O'Brien FY RC .40 .12
❑ 835 Luis Lopez .20 .06
❑ 836 Randall Simon .20 .06
❑ 837 Jaret Wright .20 .06
❑ 838 Jayson Werth .20 .06
❑ 839 Endy Chavez .20 .06
❑ 840 Checklist 5 .20 .06
❑ 841 Chad Paronto .20 .06
❑ 842 Randy Winn .20 .06
❑ 843 Sidney Ponson .20 .06
❑ 844 Robin Ventura .30 .09
❑ 845 Rich Aurilia .30 .09
❑ 846 Joaquin Benoit .20 .06
❑ 847 Barry Bonds 2.00 .60
❑ 848 Carl Crawford .30 .09
❑ 849 Jeromy Burnitz .30 .09
❑ 850 Orlando Cabrera .20 .06
❑ 851 Luis Vizcaino .20 .06
❑ 852 Randy Wolf .30 .09
❑ 853 Todd Walker .30 .09
❑ 854 Jeremy Affeldt .20 .06
❑ 855 Einar Diaz .20 .06
❑ 856 Carl Everett .30 .09
❑ 857 Wiki Gonzalez .20 .06
❑ 858 Mike Paradis .20 .06
❑ 859 Travis Harper .20 .06
❑ 860 Mike Piazza 1.25 .35
❑ 861 Will Ohman .20 .06
❑ 862 Eric Young .20 .06
❑ 863 Jason Grabowski .20 .06
❑ 864 Rett Johnson RC .50 .15
❑ 865 Aubrey Huff .30 .09
❑ 866 John Smoltz .50 .15
❑ 867 Mickey Callaway .20 .06
❑ 868 Joe Kennedy .20 .06
❑ 869 Tim Redding .20 .06
❑ 870 Colby Lewis .20 .06
❑ 871 Salomon Torres .20 .06
❑ 872 Marco Scutaro .20 .06

❑ 873 Tony Batista .20 .06
❑ 874 Dmitri Young .30 .09
❑ 875 Scott Williamson .20 .06
❑ 876 Scott Spiezio .30 .09
❑ 877 John Webb .20 .06
❑ 878 Jose Acevedo .20 .06
❑ 879 Kevin Orie .20 .06
❑ 880 Jacque Jones .30 .09
❑ 881 Ben Francisco FY RC .50 .15
❑ 882 Bobby Basham FY RC .75 .23
❑ 883 Corey Shafer FY RC .50 .15
❑ 884 J.D. Durbin FY RC .75 .23
❑ 885 Chien-Ming Wang FY RC 1.50 .45
❑ 886 Adam Stern FY RC .40 .12
❑ 887 Wayne Lydon FY RC .50 .15
❑ 888 Derell McCall FY RC .40 .12
❑ 889 Jon Nelson FY RC .50 .15
❑ 890 Willie Eyre FY RC .40 .12
❑ 891 Ramon Nivar-Martinez FY RC 1.00 .30
❑ 892 Adrian Myers FY RC .25 .07
❑ 893 Jamie Athas FY RC .40 .12
❑ 894 Ismael Castro FY RC .50 .15
❑ 895 David Martinez FY RC .40 .12
❑ 896 Terry Tiffee FY RC .50 .15
❑ 897 Nathan Panther FY RC .75 .23
❑ 898 Kyle Roat FY RC .40 .12
❑ 899 Kason Gabbard FY RC .40 .12
❑ 900 Hanley Ramirez FY RC 1.50 .45
❑ 901 Bryan Grace FY RC .40 .12
❑ 902 B.J. Barns FY RC .40 .12
❑ 903 Greg Bruso FY RC .40 .12
❑ 904 Mike Neu FY RC .40 .12
❑ 905 Dustin Yount FY RC .75 .23
❑ 906 Shane Victorino FY RC .40 .12
❑ 907 Brian Burgamy FY RC .40 .12
❑ 908 Beau Kemp FY RC .40 .12
❑ 909 David Corrente FY RC .40 .12
❑ 910 Dexter Cooper FY RC .40 .12
❑ 911 Chris Colton FY RC .40 .12
❑ 912 David Cash FY RC .40 .12
❑ 913 Bernie Castro FY RC .40 .12
❑ 914 Luis Hodge FY RC .40 .12
❑ 915 Jeff Clark FY RC .40 .12
❑ 916 Jason Kubel FY RC .75 .23
❑ 917 T.J. Bohn FY RC .40 .12
❑ 918 Luke Steidlmayer FY RC .40 .12
❑ 919 Matthew Peterson FY RC .40 .12
❑ 920 Darrell Rasner FY RC .40 .12
❑ 921 Scott Tyler FY RC .50 .15
❑ 922 Gary Schneidmiller FY RC .40 .12
❑ 923 Gregor Blanco FY RC .40 .12
❑ 924 Ryan Cameron FY RC .40 .12
❑ 925 Wilfredo Rodriguez FY .20 .06
❑ 926 Rajai Davis FY RC .50 .15
❑ 927 Evel Bastida-Martinez FY RC .40
.12
❑ 928 Chris Duncan FY RC .40 .12
❑ 929 Dave Pember FY RC .40 .12
❑ 930 Branden Florence FY RC .40 .12
❑ 931 Eric Eckenstahler FY .20 .06
❑ 932 Hong-Chih Kuo FY RC .75 .23
❑ 933 Il Kim FY RC .40 .12
❑ 934 Michael Garciaparra FY RC 1.00 .30
❑ 935 Kip Bouknight FY RC .50 .15
❑ 936 Gary Harris FY RC .40 .12
❑ 937 Derry Hammond FY RC .40 .12
❑ 938 Joey Gomes FY RC .50 .15
❑ 939 Donnie Hood FY RC .50 .15
❑ 940 Clay Hensley FY RC .40 .12
❑ 941 David Pahucki FY RC .40 .12
❑ 942 Wilton Reynolds FY RC .40 .12
❑ 943 Michael Hinckley FY RC .75 .23
❑ 944 Josh Willingham FY RC 1.25 .35
❑ 945 Pete LaForest FY RC .50 .15
❑ 946 Pete Smart FY RC .40 .12
❑ 947 Jay Sitzman FY RC .40 .12
❑ 948 Mark Malaska FY RC .40 .12
❑ 949 Mike Gallo FY RC .40 .12
❑ 950 Matt Diaz FY RC .75 .23
❑ 951 Brennan King FY RC .40 .12
❑ 952 Ryan Howard FY RC 1.00 .30
❑ 953 Daryl Clark FY RC .50 .15
❑ 954 Dayton Buller FY RC .40 .12
❑ 955 Rylan Reed FY RC .40 .12
❑ 956 Chris Booker FY .20 .06
❑ 957 Brandon Watson FY RC .40 .12
❑ 958 Matt DeMarco FY RC .40 .12
❑ 959 Doug Waechter FY RC .75 .23
❑ 960 Callix Crabbe FY RC .50 .15
❑ 961 Jairo Garcia FY RC .40 .12
❑ 962 Jason Perry FY RC .75 .23
❑ 963 Eric Riggs FY RC .50 .15
❑ 964 Travis Ishikawa FY RC .50 .15
❑ 965 Simon Pond FY RC .40 .12
❑ 966 Manuel Ramirez FY RC .75 .23
❑ 967 Tyler Johnson FY RC .40 .12
❑ 968 Jaime Bubela FY RC .40 .12
❑ 969 Haj Turay FY RC .50 .15
❑ 970 Tyson Graham FY RC .40 .12
❑ 971 David DeJesus FY RC .75 .23
❑ 972 Franklin Gutierrez FY RC 2.00 .45
❑ 973 Craig Brazell FY RC .75 .23
❑ 974 Keith Stamler FY RC .40 .12
❑ 975 Jemel Spearman FY RC .40 .12
❑ 976 Ozzie Chavez FY RC .40 .12
❑ 977 Nick Trzesniak FY RC .40 .12
❑ 978 Bill Simon FY RC .40 .12
❑ 979 Matthew Hagen FY RC .75 .23
❑ 980 Chris Kroski FY RC .40 .12
❑ 981 Prentice Redman FY RC .40 .12
❑ 982 Kevin Randel FY RC .40 .12
❑ 983 Thomari Story-Harden FY RC .40 .12
❑ 984 Brian Shackelford FY RC .40 .12
❑ 985 Mike Adams FY RC .40 .12
❑ 986 Brian McCann FY RC .75 .23
❑ 987 Mike McNutt FY RC .40 .12
❑ 988 Aron Weston FY RC .40 .12
❑ 989 Dustin Moseley FY RC .50 .15
❑ 990 Bryan Bullington FY RC 1.50 .45

2001 Topps Tribute

	Nm-Mt	Ex-Mt
COMPLETE SET (90)	300.00	90.00

❑ 1 Pee Wee Reese 6.00 1.80
❑ 2 Babe Ruth 20.00 6.00
❑ 3 Ralph Kiner 5.00 1.50
❑ 4 Brooks Robinson 6.00 1.80
❑ 5 Don Sutton 5.00 1.50
❑ 6 Carl Yastrzemski 10.00 3.00
❑ 7 Roger Maris 8.00 2.40
❑ 8 Andre Dawson 5.00 1.50
❑ 9 Luis Aparicio 5.00 1.50
❑ 10 Wade Boggs 5.00 1.50
❑ 11 Johnny Bench 6.00 1.80
❑ 12 Ernie Banks 6.00 1.80
❑ 13 Thurman Munson 10.00 3.00
❑ 14 Harmon Killebrew 6.00 1.80
❑ 15 Ted Kluszewski 5.00 1.50
❑ 16 Bob Feller 5.00 1.50
❑ 17 Mike Schmidt 12.00 3.60
❑ 18 Warren Spahn 5.00 1.50
❑ 19 Jim Palmer 5.00 1.50
❑ 20 Don Mattingly 15.00 4.50
❑ 21 Willie Mays 12.00 3.60
❑ 22 Gil Hodges 6.00 1.80
❑ 23 Juan Marichal 5.00 1.50
❑ 24 Robin Yount 6.00 1.80
❑ 25 Nolan Ryan Angels 20.00 6.00
❑ 26 Dave Winfield 5.00 1.50
❑ 27 Hank Greenberg 6.00 1.80
❑ 28 Honus Wagner 8.00 2.40
❑ 29 Nolan Ryan Rangers 20.00 6.00
❑ 30 Phil Niekro 5.00 1.50
❑ 31 Robin Roberts 5.00 1.50
❑ 32 Casey Stengel Yankees 5.00 1.50
❑ 33 Willie McCovey 5.00 1.50
❑ 34 Roy Campanella 6.00 1.80
❑ 35 Rollie Fingers A's 5.00 1.50
❑ 36 Tom Seaver 6.00 1.80
❑ 37 Jackie Robinson 10.00 3.00
❑ 38 Hank Aaron Braves 12.00 3.60
❑ 39 Bob Gibson 5.00 1.50
❑ 40 Carlton Fisk Red Sox 5.00 1.50
❑ 41 Hank Aaron Brewers 12.00 3.60
❑ 42 George Brett 15.00 4.50
❑ 43 Orlando Cepeda 5.00 1.50
❑ 44 Red Schoendienst 5.00 1.50
❑ 45 Don Drysdale 6.00 1.80
❑ 46 Mel Ott 6.00 1.80
❑ 47 Casey Stengel Mets 6.00 1.80
❑ 48 Al Kaline 6.00 1.80
❑ 49 Reggie Jackson 5.00 1.50
❑ 50 Tony Perez 5.00 1.50
❑ 51 Ozzie Smith 6.00 1.80
❑ 52 Billy Martin 5.00 1.50
❑ 53 Bill Dickey 5.00 1.50
❑ 54 Catfish Hunter 5.00 1.50
❑ 55 Duke Snider 5.00 1.50
❑ 56 Dale Murphy 6.00 1.80
❑ 57 Bobby Doerr 5.00 1.50
❑ 58 Earl Averill UER 5.00 1.50
Card pictures Earl Averill Jr.
❑ 59 Carlton Fisk White Sox 5.00 1.50
❑ 60 Tom Lasorda 5.00 1.50
❑ 61 Lou Gehrig 12.00 3.60
❑ 62 Enos Slaughter 5.00 1.50
❑ 63 Jim Bunning 5.00 1.50
❑ 64 Rollie Fingers Brewers 5.00 1.50
❑ 65 Frank Robinson Reds 5.00 1.50
❑ 66 Earl Weaver 5.00 1.50
❑ 67 Eddie Mathews 6.00 1.80
❑ 68 Kirby Puckett 6.00 1.80
❑ 69 Phil Rizzuto 6.00 1.80
❑ 70 Lou Brock 5.00 1.50
❑ 71 Walt Alston 5.00 1.50
❑ 72 Billy Pierce 5.00 1.50
❑ 73 Joe Morgan 5.00 1.50
❑ 74 Roberto Clemente 15.00 4.50
❑ 75 Whitey Ford 5.00 1.50
❑ 76 Richie Ashburn 5.00 1.50
❑ 77 Elston Howard 5.00 1.50
❑ 78 Gary Carter 5.00 1.50
❑ 79 Carl Hubbell 5.00 1.50
❑ 80 Yogi Berra 6.00 1.80
❑ 81 Ken Boyer 5.00 1.50
❑ 82 Nolan Ryan Astros 20.00 6.00
❑ 83 Bill Mazeroski 5.00 1.50
❑ 84 Dizzy Dean 6.00 1.80
❑ 85 Nellie Fox 5.00 1.50
❑ 86 Stan Musial 10.00 3.00
❑ 87 Steve Carlton 5.00 1.50
❑ 88 Willie Stargell 5.00 1.50
❑ 89 Hal Newhouser 5.00 1.50
❑ 90 Frank Robinson Orioles 5.00 1.50
❑ NNO Mickey Mantle
PSA Redemption
❑ NNO Mickey Mantle
Buyback EXCH
❑ NNO Jackie Robinson
Buyback EXCH
❑ NNO Ted Williams
Buyback EXCH

2002 Topps Tribute

	Nm-Mt	Ex-Mt
COMPLETE SET (90)	200.00	60.00

❑ 1 Hank Aaron 10.00 3.00
❑ 2 Rogers Hornsby 5.00 1.50
❑ 3 Bobby Thomson 4.00 1.20
❑ 4 Eddie Collins 4.00 1.20
❑ 5 Joe Carter 4.00 1.20
❑ 6 Jim Palmer 4.00 1.20
❑ 7 Willie Mays 10.00 3.00
❑ 8 Willie Stargell 4.00 1.20
❑ 9 Vida Blue 4.00 1.20
❑ 10 Whitey Ford 4.00 1.20

- ❑ 11 Bob Gibson 4.00 1.20
- ❑ 12 Nellie Fox 5.00 1.50
- ❑ 13 Napoleon Lajoie 5.00 1.50
- ❑ 14 Frankie Frisch 4.00 1.20
- ❑ 15 Nolan Ryan 15.00 4.50
- ❑ 16 Brooks Robinson 5.00 1.50
- ❑ 17 Kirby Puckett 5.00 1.50
- ❑ 18 Fergie Jenkins 4.00 1.20
- ❑ 19 Edd Roush 4.00 1.20
- ❑ 20 Honus Wagner 8.00 2.40
- ❑ 21 Richie Ashburn 4.00 1.20
- ❑ 22 Bob Feller 4.00 1.20
- ❑ 23 Joe Morgan 4.00 1.20
- ❑ 24 Orlando Cepeda 4.00 1.20
- ❑ 25 Steve Garvey 4.00 1.20
- ❑ 26 Hank Greenberg 5.00 1.50
- ❑ 27 Stan Musial 8.00 2.40
- ❑ 28 Sam Crawford 4.00 1.20
- ❑ 29 Jim Rice 4.00 1.20
- ❑ 30 Hack Wilson 4.00 1.20
- ❑ 31 Lou Brock 4.00 1.20
- ❑ 32 Mickey Vernon 4.00 1.20
- ❑ 33 Chuck Klein 4.00 1.20
- ❑ 34 Tony Gwynn 6.00 1.80
- ❑ 35 Duke Snider 4.00 1.20
- ❑ 36 Ryne Sandberg 10.00 3.00
- ❑ 37 Johnny Bench 5.00 1.50
- ❑ 38 Sam Rice 4.00 1.20
- ❑ 39 Lou Gehrig 12.00 3.60
- ❑ 40 Robin Yount 5.00 1.50
- ❑ 41 Don Sutton 4.00 1.20
- ❑ 42 Jim Bottomley 4.00 1.20
- ❑ 43 Billy Herman 4.00 1.20
- ❑ 44 Zach Wheat 4.00 1.20
- ❑ 45 Juan Marichal 4.00 1.20
- ❑ 46 Bert Blyleven 4.00 1.20
- ❑ 47 Jackie Robinson 8.00 2.40
- ❑ 48 Gil Hodges 4.00 1.20
- ❑ 49 Mike Schmidt 12.00 3.60
- ❑ 50 Dale Murphy 5.00 1.50
- ❑ 51 Phil Rizzuto 4.00 1.20
- ❑ 52 Ty Cobb 8.00 2.40
- ❑ 53 Andre Dawson 4.00 1.20
- ❑ 54 Fred Lindstrom 4.00 1.20
- ❑ 55 Roy Campanella 5.00 1.50
- ❑ 56 Don Larsen 4.00 1.20
- ❑ 57 Harry Heilmann 4.00 1.20
- ❑ 58 Catfish Hunter 4.00 1.20
- ❑ 59 Frank Robinson 4.00 1.20
- ❑ 60 Bill Mazeroski 4.00 1.20
- ❑ 61 Roger Maris 8.00 2.40
- ❑ 62 Dave Winfield 4.00 1.20
- ❑ 63 Warren Spahn 4.00 1.20
- ❑ 64 Babe Ruth 15.00 4.50
- ❑ 65 Ernie Banks 5.00 1.50
- ❑ 66 Wade Boggs 4.00 1.20
- ❑ 67 Carl Yastrzemski 8.00 2.40
- ❑ 68 Ron Santo 4.00 1.20
- ❑ 69 Dennis Martinez 4.00 1.20
- ❑ 70 Yogi Berra 5.00 1.50
- ❑ 71 Paul Waner 4.00 1.20
- ❑ 72 George Brett 15.00 4.50
- ❑ 73 Eddie Mathews 5.00 1.50
- ❑ 74 Bill Dickey 4.00 1.20
- ❑ 75 Carlton Fisk 4.00 1.20
- ❑ 76 Thurman Munson 8.00 2.40
- ❑ 77 Reggie Jackson 4.00 1.20
- ❑ 78 Phil Niekro 4.00 1.20
- ❑ 79 Luis Aparicio 4.00 1.20
- ❑ 80 Steve Carlton 4.00 1.20
- ❑ 81 Tris Speaker 4.00 1.20
- ❑ 82 Johnny Mize 4.00 1.20
- ❑ 83 Tom Seaver 5.00 1.50
- ❑ 84 Heinie Manush 4.00 1.20
- ❑ 85 Tommy John 4.00 1.20
- ❑ 86 Joe Cronin 4.00 1.20
- ❑ 87 Don Mattingly 12.00 3.60
- ❑ 88 Kirk Gibson 4.00 1.20
- ❑ 89 Bo Jackson 5.00 1.50
- ❑ 90 Mel Ott 5.00 1.50

2003 Topps Tribute Contemporary

	MINT	NRMT
COMMON CARD (1-	2.00	.90
COMMON CARD (91-100)	2.00	.90
COMMON CARD (101-110)	15.00	6.75

- ❑ 1 Jim Thome 4.00 1.80
- ❑ 2 Edgardo Alfonzo 2.00 .90
- ❑ 3 Edgar Martinez 2.50 1.10
- ❑ 4 Scott Rolen 4.00 1.80
- ❑ 5 Eric Hinske 2.00 .90
- ❑ 6 Mark Mulder 2.00 .90
- ❑ 7 Jason Giambi 4.00 1.80
- ❑ 8 Bernie Williams 2.50 1.10
- ❑ 9 Cliff Floyd 2.00 .90
- ❑ 10 Ichiro Suzuki 8.00 3.60
- ❑ 11 Pat Burrell 2.00 .90
- ❑ 12 Garret Anderson 2.00 .90
- ❑ 13 Gary Sheffield 2.00 .90
- ❑ 14 Johnny Damon 2.00 .90
- ❑ 15 Kerry Wood 4.00 1.80
- ❑ 16 Bartolo Colon 2.00 .90
- ❑ 17 Adam Dunn 2.50 1.10
- ❑ 18 Omar Vizquel 2.00 .90
- ❑ 19 Todd Helton 2.50 1.10
- ❑ 20 Nomar Garciaparra 8.00 3.60
- ❑ 21 A.J. Burnett 2.00 .90
- ❑ 22 Craig Biggio 2.50 1.10
- ❑ 23 Carlos Beltran 2.00 .90
- ❑ 24 Kazuhisa Ishii 2.00 .90
- ❑ 25 Vladimir Guerrero 4.00 1.80
- ❑ 26 Roberto Alomar 4.00 1.80
- ❑ 27 Roger Clemens 8.00 3.60
- ❑ 28 Tim Hudson 2.00 .90
- ❑ 29 Brian Giles 2.00 .90
- ❑ 30 Barry Bonds 10.00 4.50
- ❑ 31 Jim Edmonds 2.00 .90
- ❑ 32 Rafael Palmeiro 2.50 1.10
- ❑ 33 Francisco Rodriguez 2.00 .90
- ❑ 34 Andruw Jones 2.50 1.10
- ❑ 35 Shea Hillenbrand 2.00 .90
- ❑ 36 Moises Alou 2.00 .90
- ❑ 37 Luis Gonzalez 2.00 .90
- ❑ 38 Darin Erstad 2.00 .90
- ❑ 39 John Smoltz 2.50 1.10
- ❑ 40 Derek Jeter 10.00 4.50
- ❑ 41 Aubrey Huff 2.00 .90
- ❑ 42 Eric Chavez 2.00 .90
- ❑ 43 Doug Mientkiewicz 2.00 .90
- ❑ 44 Lance Berkman 2.00 .90
- ❑ 45 Josh Beckett 2.50 1.10
- ❑ 46 Austin Kearns 2.50 1.10
- ❑ 47 Frank Thomas 4.00 1.80
- ❑ 48 Pedro Martinez 4.00 1.80
- ❑ 49 Tim Salmon 2.00 .90
- ❑ 50 Alex Rodriguez 8.00 3.60
- ❑ 51 Ryan Klesko 2.00 .90
- ❑ 52 Tom Glavine 4.00 1.80
- ❑ 53 Shawn Green 2.00 .90
- ❑ 54 Jeff Kent 2.00 .90
- ❑ 55 Carlos Pena 2.00 .90
- ❑ 56 Paul Konerko 2.00 .90
- ❑ 57 Troy Glaus 2.50 1.10
- ❑ 58 Manny Ramirez 2.00 .90
- ❑ 59 Jason Jennings 2.00 .90
- ❑ 60 Randy Johnson 4.00 1.80
- ❑ 61 Ivan Rodriguez 4.00 1.80
- ❑ 62 Roy Oswalt 2.00 .90
- ❑ 63 Kevin Brown 2.00 .90
- ❑ 64 Jose Vidro 2.00 .90
- ❑ 65 Jorge Posada 2.50 1.10
- ❑ 66 Mike Piazza 6.00 2.70
- ❑ 67 Bret Boone 2.00 .90
- ❑ 68 Carlos Delgado 2.00 .90
- ❑ 69 Jimmy Rollins 2.00 .90
- ❑ 70 Alfonso Soriano 4.00 1.80
- ❑ 71 Greg Maddux 8.00 3.60
- ❑ 72 Mark Prior 8.00 3.60
- ❑ 73 Jeff Bagwell 2.50 1.10
- ❑ 74 Richie Sexson 2.00 .90
- ❑ 75 Sammy Sosa 6.00 2.70
- ❑ 76 Curt Schilling 2.50 1.10
- ❑ 77 Mike Sweeney 2.00 .90
- ❑ 78 Torii Hunter 2.00 .90
- ❑ 79 Larry Walker 2.50 1.10
- ❑ 80 Miguel Tejada 2.00 .90
- ❑ 81 Rich Aurilia 2.00 .90
- ❑ 82 Bobby Abreu 2.00 .90
- ❑ 83 Phil Nevin 2.00 .90
- ❑ 84 Rodrigo Lopez 2.00 .90
- ❑ 85 Chipper Jones 4.00 1.80
- ❑ 86 Ken Griffey Jr. 6.00 2.70
- ❑ 87 Mike Lowell 2.00 .90
- ❑ 88 Magglio Ordonez 2.00 .90
- ❑ 89 Barry Zito 4.00 1.80
- ❑ 90 Albert Pujols 8.00 3.60
- ❑ 91 Corey Shafer FY RC 3.00 1.35
- ❑ 92 Dan Haren FY RC 4.00 1.80
- ❑ 93 Jeremy Bonderman FY RC 5.00 2.20
- ❑ 94 Branden Florence FY RC 2.00 .90
- ❑ 95 Evel Bastida-Martinez FY RC 2.00 .90
- ❑ 96 Brian Wright FY RC 2.00 .90
- ❑ 97 Elizardo Ramirez FY RC 5.00 2.20
- ❑ 98 Michael Garciaparra FY RC 4.00 1.80
- ❑ 99 Clay Hensley FY RC 2.00 .90
- ❑ 100 Bobby Basham FY RC 3.00 1.35
- ❑ 101 J.Contreras FY AU RC EXCH 50.00 22.00
- ❑ 102 Bryan Bullington FY AU RC 30.00 13.50
- ❑ 103 Joey Gomes FY AU RC 15.00 6.75
- ❑ 104 Craig Brazell FY AU RC 15.00 6.75
- ❑ 105 Andy Marte FY AU RC 40.00 18.00
- ❑ 106 Hanley Ramirez FY AU RC 30.00 13.50
- ❑ 107 Ryan Shealy FY AU RC 15.00 6.75
- ❑ 108 Daryl Clark FY AU RC 15.00 6.75
- ❑ 109 Tyler Johnson FY AU RC 15.00 6.75
- ❑ 110 Ben Francisco FY AU RC 15.00 6.75

2003 Topps Tribute Perennial All-Star

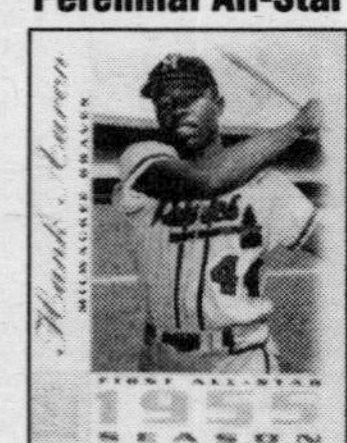

	Nm-Mt	Ex-Mt
COMPLETE SET (50)	100.00	30.00
❑ 1 Willie Mays	10.00	3.00
❑ 2 Don Mattingly	12.00	3.60
❑ 3 Hoyt Wilhelm	4.00	1.20
❑ 4 Hank Aaron	10.00	3.00
❑ 5 Hank Greenberg	5.00	1.50
❑ 6 Johnny Bench	5.00	1.50
❑ 7 Duke Snider	4.00	1.20
❑ 8 Carl Yastrzemski	8.00	2.40
❑ 9 Jim Palmer	4.00	1.20
❑ 10 Roberto Clemente	12.00	3.60
❑ 11 Mike Schmidt	10.00	3.00
❑ 12 Joe Cronin	4.00	1.20
❑ 13 Lou Brock	4.00	1.20
❑ 14 Orlando Cepeda	4.00	1.20
❑ 15 Bill Mazeroski	4.00	1.20
❑ 16 Whitey Ford	4.00	1.20
❑ 17 Rod Carew	4.00	1.20
❑ 18 Joe Morgan	4.00	1.20
❑ 19 Luis Aparicio	4.00	1.20
❑ 20 Nolan Ryan	15.00	4.50
❑ 21 Bobby Doerr	4.00	1.20
❑ 22 Dale Murphy	5.00	1.50
❑ 23 Bob Feller	4.00	1.20
❑ 24 Paul Molitor	4.00	1.20
❑ 25 Tom Seaver	5.00	1.50
❑ 26 Ozzie Smith	5.00	1.50
❑ 27 Stan Musial	8.00	2.40
❑ 28 Willie McCovey	4.00	1.20
❑ 29 Gary Carter	4.00	1.20
❑ 30 Reggie Jackson	4.00	1.20
❑ 31 Gaylord Perry	4.00	1.20
❑ 32 George Brett	12.00	3.60
❑ 33 Robin Roberts	4.00	1.20
❑ 34 Wade Boggs	4.00	1.20
❑ 35 Cal Ripken	15.00	4.50
❑ 36 Carlton Fisk	4.00	1.20
❑ 37 Al Kaline	5.00	1.50
❑ 38 Kirby Puckett	5.00	1.50
❑ 39 Phil Rizzuto	4.00	1.20
❑ 40 Willie Stargell	4.00	1.20
❑ 41 Harmon Killebrew	5.00	1.50
❑ 42 Red Schoendienst	4.00	1.20
❑ 43 Tony Gwynn	6.00	1.80
❑ 44 Ralph Kiner	4.00	1.20
❑ 45 Yogi Berra	5.00	1.50
❑ 46 Catfish Hunter	4.00	1.20
❑ 47 Frank Robinson	4.00	1.20
❑ 48 Ernie Banks	5.00	1.50
❑ 49 Warren Spahn	4.00	1.20
❑ 50 Brooks Robinson	5.00	1.50

2003 Topps Tribute World Series

	MINT	NRMT
COMMON CARD (1-130)	4.00	1.80
COMMON CARD (131-150)	4.00	1.80
❑ 1 Willie Mays 54	10.00	4.50
❑ 2 Gary Carter 86	4.00	1.80
❑ 3 Yogi Berra 47	5.00	2.20
❑ 4 Dennis Eckersley 88	4.00	1.80
❑ 5 Willie McCovey 62	4.00	1.80
❑ 6 Willie Stargell 71	4.00	1.80
❑ 7 Mike Schmidt 80	10.00	4.50
❑ 8 Robin Yount 82	5.00	2.20
❑ 9 Bucky Harris 24	4.00	1.80
❑ 10 Carl Yastrzemski 67	8.00	3.60
❑ 11 Lenny Dykstra 86	4.00	1.80
❑ 12 Boog Powell 66	4.00	1.80
❑ 13 Bill Lee 75	4.00	1.80
❑ 14 Lou Brock 64	4.00	1.80
❑ 15 Bob Friend 60	4.00	1.80
❑ 16 Hank Greenberg 34	5.00	2.20
❑ 17 Maury Wills 59	4.00	1.80
❑ 18 Tom Lasorda 77	4.00	1.80
❑ 19 Moose Skowron 55	4.00	1.80
❑ 20 Frank Robinson 61	4.00	1.80
❑ 21 Rollie Fingers 72	4.00	1.80
❑ 22 Doug DeCinces 79	4.00	1.80
❑ 23 Eric Davis 90	4.00	1.80
❑ 24 Johnny Podres 53	4.00	1.80
❑ 25 Darrell Evans 84	4.00	1.80
❑ 26 Ron Cey 74	4.00	1.80
❑ 27 Ray Knight 86	4.00	1.80
❑ 28 Don Larsen 55	4.00	1.80
❑ 29 Harold Baines 90	4.00	1.80
❑ 30 Brooks Robinson 66	5.00	2.20
❑ 31 Wade Boggs 86	4.00	1.80
❑ 32 Joe Morgan 72	4.00	1.80
❑ 33 Kirk Gibson 84	4.00	1.80
❑ 34 Tommy John 77	4.00	1.80
❑ 35 Monte Irvin 51	4.00	1.80
❑ 36 Goose Gossage 78	4.00	1.80
❑ 37 Tug McGraw 73	4.00	1.80
❑ 38 Walt Weiss 88	4.00	1.80
❑ 39 Bill Madlock 79	4.00	1.80
❑ 40 Juan Marichal 62	4.00	1.80
❑ 41 Willie McGee 82	4.00	1.80
❑ 42 Joe Cronin 33	4.00	1.80
❑ 43 Paul Blair 66	4.00	1.80
❑ 44 Norm Cash 59	4.00	1.80
❑ 45 Ken Griffey 75	4.00	1.80
❑ 46 Bret Saberhagen 85	4.00	1.80
❑ 47 Don Sutton 74	4.00	1.80
❑ 48 Kirby Puckett 87	5.00	2.20
❑ 49 Keith Hernandez 82	4.00	1.80
❑ 50 George Brett 80	12.00	5.50
❑ 51 Bobby Richardson 57	4.00	1.80
❑ 52 Jose Canseco 88	5.00	2.20
❑ 53 Greg Luzinski 80	4.00	1.80
❑ 54 Bill Mazeroski 60	4.00	1.80
❑ 55 Red Schoendienst 46	4.00	1.80
❑ 56 Graig Nettles 76	4.00	1.80
❑ 57 Jerry Koosman 69	4.00	1.80
❑ 58 Tony Perez 70	4.00	1.80
❑ 59 Jim Rice 86	4.00	1.80
❑ 60 Duke Snider 49	4.00	1.80
❑ 61 David Justice 91	4.00	1.80
❑ 62 Johnny Sain 48	4.00	1.80
❑ 63 Chuck Klein 35	4.00	1.80
❑ 64 Sparky Anderson 70	4.00	1.80
❑ 65 Alan Trammell 84	4.00	1.80
❑ 66 Willie Wilson 80	4.00	1.80
❑ 67 Hoyt Wilhelm 54	4.00	1.80
❑ 68 Joe Pepitone 63	4.00	1.80
❑ 69 Darren Daulton 93	4.00	1.80
❑ 70 Tom Seaver 69	5.00	2.20
❑ 71 Catfish Hunter 72	4.00	1.80
❑ 72 Tim McCarver 64	4.00	1.80
❑ 73 Dave Parker 79	4.00	1.80
❑ 74 Earl Weaver 69	4.00	1.80
❑ 75 Ted Kluszewski 59	4.00	1.80
❑ 76 John Kruk 93	4.00	1.80
❑ 77 Dwight Evans 75	4.00	1.80
❑ 78 Ron Darling 86	4.00	1.80
❑ 79 Tony Oliva 65	4.00	1.80
❑ 80 Johnny Bench 70	5.00	2.20
❑ 81 Sam Crawford 07	4.00	1.80
❑ 82 Steve Yeager 74	4.00	1.80
❑ 83 Paul Molitor 82	4.00	1.80
❑ 84 Bert Campaneris 72	4.00	1.80
❑ 85 Mickey Rivers 76	4.00	1.80
❑ 86 Vince Coleman 87	4.00	1.80
❑ 87 Kent Tekulve 79	4.00	1.80
❑ 88 Dwight Gooden 86	4.00	1.80
❑ 89 Whitey Herzog 82	4.00	1.80
❑ 90 Whitey Ford 50	4.00	1.80
❑ 91 Warren Spahn 48	4.00	1.80
❑ 92 Fred Lynn 75	4.00	1.80
❑ 93 Joe Tinker 06	4.00	1.80
❑ 94 Bill Buckner 74	4.00	1.80
❑ 95 Bob Feller 48	4.00	1.80
❑ 96 Hank Bauer 49	4.00	1.80
❑ 97 Joe Rudi 72	4.00	1.80
❑ 98 Steve Sax 81	4.00	1.80
❑ 99 Bruce Sutter 82	4.00	1.80
❑ 100 Nolan Ryan 69	15.00	6.75
❑ 101 Bobby Thomson 51	4.00	1.80
❑ 102 Bob Watson 81	4.00	1.80
❑ 103 Vida Blue 72	4.00	1.80
❑ 104 Robin Roberts 50	4.00	1.80
❑ 105 Orlando Cepeda 62	4.00	1.80
❑ 106 Jim Bottomley 26	4.00	1.80
❑ 107 Heinie Manush 33	4.00	1.80
❑ 108 Jim Gilliam 53	4.00	1.80
❑ 109 Dave Concepcion 70	4.00	1.80
❑ 110 Al Kaline 68	5.00	2.20
❑ 111 Howard Johnson 84	4.00	1.80
❑ 112 Phil Rizzuto 41	4.00	1.80
❑ 113 Steve Garvey 74	4.00	1.80
❑ 114 George Foster 72	4.00	1.80
❑ 115 Carlton Fisk 75	4.00	1.80
❑ 116 Don Newcombe 49	4.00	1.80
❑ 117 Lance Parrish 84	4.00	1.80
❑ 118 Reggie Jackson 73	4.00	1.80
❑ 119 Luis Aparicio 59	4.00	1.80
❑ 120 Jim Palmer 66	4.00	1.80
❑ 121 Ron Guidry 77	4.00	1.80
❑ 122 Frankie Frisch 21	4.00	1.80
❑ 123 Chet Lemon 84	4.00	1.80
❑ 124 Cecil Cooper 75	4.00	1.80
❑ 125 Harmon Killebrew 65	5.00	2.20
❑ 126 Luis Tiant 75	4.00	1.80
❑ 127 John McGraw 05	4.00	1.80
❑ 128 Paul O'Neill 90	4.00	1.80
❑ 129 Jack Clark 85	4.00	1.80
❑ 130 Stan Musial 42	8.00	3.60
❑ 131 Mike Schmidt FC	10.00	4.50
❑ 132 Kirby Puckett FC	5.00	2.20
❑ 133 Carlton Fisk FC	4.00	1.80
❑ 134 Bill Mazeroski FC	4.00	1.80
❑ 135 Johnny Podres FC	4.00	1.80
❑ 136 Robin Yount FC	5.00	2.20
❑ 137 David Justice FC	4.00	1.80
❑ 138 Bobby Thomson FC	4.00	1.80
❑ 139 Joe Carter FC	4.00	1.80
❑ 140 Reggie Jackson FC	4.00	1.80
❑ 141 Kirk Gibson FC	4.00	1.80
❑ 142 Whitey Ford FC	4.00	1.80
❑ 143 Don Larsen FC	4.00	1.80
❑ 144 Duke Snider FC	4.00	1.80
❑ 145 Carl Yastrzemski FC	8.00	3.60
❑ 146 Johnny Bench FC	5.00	2.20
❑ 147 Lou Brock FC	4.00	1.80
❑ 148 Ted Kluszewski FC	4.00	1.80
❑ 149 Jim Palmer FC	4.00	1.80
❑ 150 Willie Mays FC	10.00	4.50

2002 UD Authentics

	Nm-Mt	Ex-Mt
COMPLETE SET (200)	60.00	18.00
COMMON CARD (1-170)	.50	.15
COMMON CARD (171-200)	1.25	.35
❑ 1 Brad Fullmer	.50	.15
❑ 2 Garret Anderson	.50	.15
❑ 3 Darin Erstad	.50	.15

❑ 4 Jarrod Washburn .50 .15
❑ 5 Troy Glaus .75 .23
❑ 6 Barry Zito 1.25 .35
❑ 7 David Justice .50 .15
❑ 8 Eric Chavez .50 .15
❑ 9 Tim Hudson .50 .15
❑ 10 Miguel Tejada .50 .15
❑ 11 Jermaine Dye .50 .15
❑ 12 Mark Mulder .50 .15
❑ 13 Carlos Delgado .50 .15
❑ 14 Jose Cruz Jr. .50 .15
❑ 15 Mo Vaughn UER .50 .15
Card is incorrectly numbered as 145
❑ 16 Shannon Stewart .50 .15
❑ 17 Raul Mondesi .50 .15
❑ 18 Tanyon Sturtze .50 .15
❑ 19 Toby Hall .50 .15
❑ 20 Greg Vaughn .50 .15
❑ 21 Aubrey Huff .50 .15
❑ 22 Ben Grieve .50 .15
❑ 23 Brent Abernathy .50 .15
❑ 24 Jim Thome 1.25 .35
❑ 25 C.C. Sabathia .50 .15
❑ 26 Matt Lawton .50 .15
❑ 27 Omar Vizquel .50 .15
❑ 28 Ellis Burks .50 .15
❑ 29 Russ Branyan .50 .15
❑ 30 Bartolo Colon .50 .15
❑ 31 Ichiro Suzuki 2.50 .75
❑ 32 John Olerud .50 .15
❑ 33 Freddy Garcia .50 .15
❑ 34 Mike Cameron .50 .15
❑ 35 Jeff Cirillo .50 .15
❑ 36 Kazuhiro Sasaki .50 .15
❑ 37 Edgar Martinez .75 .23
❑ 38 Bret Boone .50 .15
❑ 39 Jeff Conine .50 .15
❑ 40 Melvin Mora .50 .15
❑ 41 Jason Johnson .50 .15
❑ 42 Chris Richard .50 .15
❑ 43 Tony Batista .50 .15
❑ 44 Ivan Rodriguez 1.25 .35
❑ 45 Gabe Kapler .50 .15
❑ 46 Rafael Palmeiro .75 .23
❑ 47 Alex Rodriguez 2.50 .75
❑ 48 Juan Gonzalez 1.25 .35
❑ 49 Carl Everett .50 .15
❑ 50 Nomar Garciaparra 2.50 .75
❑ 51 Trot Nixon .50 .15
❑ 52 Manny Ramirez .50 .15
❑ 53 Pedro Martinez 1.25 .35
❑ 54 Johnny Damon .50 .15
❑ 55 Shea Hillenbrand .50 .15
❑ 56 Mike Sweeney .50 .15
❑ 57 Mark Quinn .50 .15
❑ 58 Joe Randa .50 .15
❑ 59 Carlos Beltran .50 .15
❑ 60 Chuck Knoblauch .50 .15
❑ 61 Robert Fick .50 .15
❑ 62 Jeff Weaver .50 .15
❑ 63 Bobby Higginson .50 .15
❑ 64 Dean Palmer .50 .15
❑ 65 Dmitri Young .50 .15
❑ 66 Corey Koskie .50 .15
❑ 67 Doug Mientkiewicz .50 .15
❑ 68 Joe Mays .50 .15
❑ 69 Torii Hunter .50 .15
❑ 70 Cristian Guzman .50 .15
❑ 71 Jacque Jones .50 .15
❑ 72 Magglio Ordonez .50 .15
❑ 73 Paul Konerko .50 .15
❑ 74 Carlos Lee .50 .15
❑ 75 Mark Buehrle .50 .15
❑ 76 Jose Canseco 1.25 .35
❑ 77 Frank Thomas 1.25 .35
❑ 78 Roger Clemens 2.50 .75
❑ 79 Derek Jeter 3.00 .90
❑ 80 Jason Giambi Yankees 1.25 .35
❑ 81 Rondell White .50 .15
❑ 82 Bernie Williams .75 .23
❑ 83 Jorge Posada .75 .23
❑ 84 Mike Mussina 1.25 .35
❑ 85 Alfonso Soriano 1.25 .35
❑ 86 Wade Miller .50 .15
❑ 87 Jeff Bagwell .75 .23
❑ 88 Craig Biggio .75 .23
❑ 89 Roy Oswalt .50 .15
❑ 90 Lance Berkman .50 .15
❑ 91 Daryle Ward .50 .15
❑ 92 Chipper Jones 1.25 .35
❑ 93 Greg Maddux 2.50 .75
❑ 94 Marcus Giles .50 .15
❑ 95 Gary Sheffield .50 .15
❑ 96 Tom Glavine 1.25 .35
❑ 97 Andruw Jones .75 .23
❑ 98 Rafael Furcal .50 .15
❑ 99 Richie Sexson .50 .15
❑ 100 Ben Sheets .50 .15
❑ 101 Jose Hernandez .50 .15
❑ 102 Geoff Jenkins .50 .15
❑ 103 Jeffrey Hammonds .50 .15
❑ 104 Edgar Renteria .50 .15
❑ 105 Matt Morris .50 .15
❑ 106 Tino Martinez .75 .23
❑ 107 Jim Edmonds .50 .15
❑ 108 Albert Pujols 2.50 .75
❑ 109 J.D. Drew .50 .15
❑ 110 Fernando Vina .50 .15
❑ 111 Darryl Kile .50 .15
❑ 112 Sammy Sosa 2.00 .60
❑ 113 Fred McGriff .75 .23
❑ 114 Kerry Wood 1.25 .35
❑ 115 Moises Alou .50 .15
❑ 116 Jon Lieber .50 .15
❑ 117 Mark Grace 1.25 .35
❑ 118 Randy Johnson 1.25 .35
❑ 119 Curt Schilling .75 .23
❑ 120 Luis Gonzalez .50 .15
❑ 121 Steve Finley .50 .15
❑ 122 Matt Williams .50 .15
❑ 123 Shawn Green .50 .15
❑ 124 Kevin Brown .50 .15
❑ 125 Adrian Beltre .50 .15
❑ 126 Paul LoDuca .50 .15
❑ 127 Hideo Nomo 1.25 .35
❑ 128 Brian Jordan .50 .15
❑ 129 Vladimir Guerrero 1.25 .35
❑ 130 Javier Vazquez .50 .15
❑ 131 Jose Vidro .50 .15
❑ 132 Orlando Cabrera .50 .15
❑ 133 Jeff Kent .50 .15
❑ 134 Rich Aurilia .50 .15
❑ 135 Russ Ortiz .50 .15
❑ 136 Barry Bonds 3.00 .90
❑ 137 Preston Wilson .50 .15
❑ 138 Ryan Dempster .50 .15
❑ 139 Cliff Floyd .50 .15
❑ 140 Josh Beckett .75 .23
❑ 141 Mike Lowell .50 .15
❑ 142 Mike Piazza 2.00 .60
❑ 143 Roberto Alomar 1.25 .35
❑ 144 Al Leiter .50 .15
❑ 145 Edgardo Alfonzo .50 .15
❑ 146 Roger Cedeno .50 .15
❑ 147 Jeromy Burnitz .50 .15
❑ 148 Phil Nevin .50 .15
❑ 149 Mark Kotsay .50 .15
❑ 150 Ryan Klesko .50 .15
❑ 151 Trevor Hoffman .50 .15
❑ 152 Bobby Abreu .50 .15
❑ 153 Scott Rolen .75 .23
❑ 154 Jimmy Rollins .50 .15
❑ 155 Robert Person .50 .15
❑ 156 Pat Burrell .50 .15
❑ 157 Randy Wolf .50 .15
❑ 158 Brian Giles .50 .15
❑ 159 Aramis Ramirez .50 .15
❑ 160 Kris Benson .50 .15
❑ 161 Jason Kendall .50 .15
❑ 162 Ken Griffey Jr. 2.00 .60
❑ 163 Sean Casey .50 .15
❑ 164 Adam Dunn .75 .23
❑ 165 Barry Larkin 1.25 .35
❑ 166 Todd Helton .75 .23
❑ 167 Mike Hampton .50 .15
❑ 168 Larry Walker .75 .23
❑ 169 Juan Pierre .50 .15
❑ 170 Juan Uribe .50 .15
❑ 171 So Taguchi SR RC 2.00 .60
❑ 172 Brendan Donnelly SR RC 1.25 .35
❑ 173 Chris Baker SR RC 1.25 .35
❑ 174 John Ennis SR RC 1.25 .35
❑ 175 Francis Beltran SR RC 1.25 .35
❑ 176 Danny Wright SR 1.25 .35
❑ 177 Brandon Backe SR RC 1.25 .35
❑ 178 Mark Corey SR RC 1.25 .35
❑ 179 Kazuhisa Ishii SR RC 2.50 .75
❑ 180 Ron Calloway SR RC 1.25 .35
❑ 181 Kevin Frederick SR RC 1.25 .35
❑ 182 Jaime Cerda SR RC 1.25 .35
❑ 183 Doug Devore SR RC 1.25 .35
❑ 184 Brandon Puffer SR RC 1.25 .35
❑ 185 Andy Pratt SR RC 1.25 .35
❑ 186 Adrian Burnside SR RC 1.25 .35
❑ 187 Josh Hancock SR RC 1.25 .35
❑ 188 Jorge Nunez SR RC 1.25 .35
❑ 189 Tyler Yates SR RC 1.25 .35
❑ 190 Kyle Kane SR RC 1.25 .35
❑ 191 Jose Valverde SR RC 2.00 .60
❑ 192 Matt Thornton SR RC 1.25 .35
❑ 193 Ben Howard SR RC 1.25 .35
❑ 194 Reed Johnson SR RC 2.00 .60
❑ 195 Rene Reyes SR RC 1.25 .35
❑ 196 Jeremy Ward SR RC 1.25 .35
❑ 197 Steve Bechler SR RC 1.25 .35
❑ 198 Cam Esslinger SR RC 1.25 .35
❑ 199 Michael Crudale SR RC 1.25 .35
❑ 200 Todd Donovan SR RC 1.25 .35

2003 UD Authentics

	MINT	NRMT
COMP.SET w/o SP's (100)	40.00	18.00
COMMON ACTIVE (1-100)	.40	.18
COMMON RETIRED (1-100)	.50	.23
COMMON CARD (101-130)	5.00	2.20

101-130 RANDOM INSERTS IN PACKS
101-130 PRINT RUN 999 SERIAL #'d SETS

❑ 1 Pee Wee Reese .75 .35
❑ 2 Richie Ashburn .75 .35
❑ 3 Derek Jeter 2.50 1.10
❑ 4 Alex Rodriguez 2.00 .90
❑ 5 Jose Vidro .40 .18
❑ 6 Miguel Tejada .40 .18
❑ 7 Nomar Garciaparra 2.00 .90
❑ 8 Pat Burrell .40 .18
❑ 9 Albert Pujols 2.00 .90
❑ 10 Jeff Bagwell .60 .25
❑ 11 Stan Musial 2.00 .90
❑ 12 Mickey Mantle 5.00 2.20
❑ 13 J.D. Drew .40 .18
❑ 14 Ivan Rodriguez 1.00 .45
❑ 15 Joe Morgan .50 .23
❑ 16 Ted Williams 3.00 1.35
❑ 17 Travis Hafner .40 .18
❑ 18 Chipper Jones 1.00 .45
❑ 19 Hideo Nomo 1.00 .45
❑ 20 Gary Sheffield .40 .18
❑ 21 Jacque Jones .40 .18
❑ 22 Alfonso Soriano 1.00 .45
❑ 23 Roberto Alomar 1.00 .45
❑ 24 Jeff Kent .40 .18
❑ 25 Omar Vizquel .40 .18
❑ 26 Ernie Banks 1.25 .55
❑ 27 Shawn Green .40 .18
❑ 28 Tim Hudson .40 .18
❑ 29 Jim Edmonds .40 .18
❑ 30 Brandon Larson .40 .18
❑ 31 Doug Mientkiewicz .40 .18

❑ 32 Darin Erstad .40 .18
❑ 33 Bobby Hill .40 .18
❑ 34 Todd Helton .60 .25
❑ 35 Kazuhisa Ishii .40 .18
❑ 36 Lance Berkman .40 .18
❑ 37 Eric Hinske .40 .18
❑ 38 Jason Kendall .40 .18
❑ 39 Bob Feller .75 .35
❑ 40 Luis Gonzalez .40 .18
❑ 41 Sammy Sosa 1.50 .70
❑ 42 Mike Piazza 1.50 .70
❑ 43 Roger Clemens 2.00 .90
❑ 44 Jose Cruz Jr. .40 .18
❑ 45 Mark Prior 2.00 .90
❑ 46 Mark Teixeira .60 .25
❑ 47 Phil Nevin .40 .18
❑ 48 Lyle Overbay .40 .18
❑ 49 Manny Ramirez .40 .18
❑ 50 Brian Giles .40 .18
❑ 51 Preston Wilson .40 .18
❑ 52 Jermaine Dye .40 .18
❑ 53 Troy Glaus .60 .25
❑ 54 Frank Thomas 1.00 .45
❑ 55 Jim Thome 1.00 .45
❑ 56 Barry Bonds 2.50 1.10
❑ 57 Carlos Delgado .40 .18
❑ 58 Jason Giambi 1.00 .45
❑ 59 Joe Mays .40 .18
❑ 60 Andruw Jones .60 .25
❑ 61 Billy Williams .50 .23
❑ 62 Vladimir Guerrero 1.00 .45
❑ 63 Scott Rolen .60 .25
❑ 64 Juan Marichal .50 .23
❑ 65 Austin Kearns .60 .25
❑ 66 Kerry Wood 1.00 .45
❑ 67 Bret Boone .40 .18
❑ 68 Shea Hillenbrand .40 .18
❑ 69 Mike Sweeney .40 .18
❑ 70 Rocco Baldelli 2.00 .90
❑ 71 Ken Griffey Jr. 1.50 .70
❑ 72 Cliff Floyd .40 .18
❑ 73 Greg Maddux 2.00 .90
❑ 74 Mike Hampton .40 .18
❑ 75 Larry Walker .60 .25
❑ 76 Nolan Ryan 4.00 1.80
❑ 77 Rollie Fingers .50 .23
❑ 78 Mike Mussina 1.00 .45
❑ 79 Matt Morris .40 .18
❑ 80 Robin Roberts .50 .23
❑ 81 Barry Zito 1.00 .45
❑ 82 Curt Schilling .60 .25
❑ 83 Ken Harvey .40 .18
❑ 84 Troy Percival .40 .18
❑ 85 Tom Seaver 1.25 .55
❑ 86 Mariano Rivera .60 .25
❑ 87 Raul Mondesi .40 .18
❑ 88 Adam Dunn .60 .25
❑ 89 Roy Oswalt .40 .18
❑ 90 Pedro Martinez 1.00 .45
❑ 91 Andy Pettitte .60 .25
❑ 92 Tom Glavine 1.00 .45
❑ 93 Torii Hunter .40 .18
❑ 94 Joe Thurston .40 .18
❑ 95 Runelvys Hernandez .40 .18
❑ 96 Randy Johnson 1.00 .45
❑ 97 Bernie Williams .60 .25
❑ 98 Ichiro Suzuki 2.00 .90
❑ 99 C.C. Sabathia .40 .18
❑ 100 Bobby Abreu .40 .18
❑ 101 Jose Contreras RH RC 8.00 3.60
❑ 102 Hideki Matsui RH RC 20.00 9.00
❑ 103 Chris Capuano RH RC 5.00 2.20
❑ 104 Willie Eyre RH RC 5.00 2.20
❑ 105 Lew Ford RH RC 8.00 3.60
❑ 106 Shane Bazzell RH RC 5.00 2.20
❑ 107 Guillermo Quiroz RH RC 8.00 3.60
❑ 108 Fernando Cabrera RH RC 8.00 3.60
❑ 109 Francisco Cruceta RH RC 5.00 2.20
❑ 110 Jhonny Peralta RH RC 5.00 2.20
❑ 111 Bobby Madritsch RH RC 5.00 2.20
❑ 112 Diego Markwell RH RC 5.00 2.20
❑ 113 Matt Bruback RH RC 5.00 2.20
❑ 114 Matt Kata RH RC 8.00 3.60
❑ 115 Rob Hammock RH RC 8.00 3.60
❑ 116 Brandon Webb RH RC 10.00 4.50
❑ 117 Jon Leicester RH RC 5.00 2.20
❑ 118 Josh Willingham RH RC 10.00 4.50
❑ 119 Prentice Redman RH RC 5.00 2.20
❑ 120 Jeff Duncan RH RC 8.00 3.60
❑ 121 Craig Brazell RH RC 8.00 3.60
❑ 122 Jeremy Griffiths RH RC 8.00 3.60
❑ 123 Phil Seibel RH RC 5.00 2.20
❑ 124 Luis Ayala RH RC 5.00 2.20
❑ 125 Miguel Ojeda RH RC 5.00 2.20
❑ 126 Jeremy Wedel RH RC 5.00 2.20
❑ 127 Josh Hall RH RC 8.00 3.60
❑ 128 Oscar Villarreal RH RC 5.00 2.20
❑ 129 Clint Barmes RH RC 8.00 3.60
❑ 130 Nook Logan RH RC 5.00 2.20
❑ 131 Dan Haren RH RC
❑ 132 Delmon Young RH RC
❑ 133 Dontrelle Willis RH
❑ 134 Edwin Jackson RH RC
❑ 135 Jeremy Bonderman RH RC
❑ 136 Khalil Greene RH
❑ 137 Rich Harden RH
❑ 138 Rickie Weeks RH RC
❑ 139 Rosman Garcia RH RC
❑ 140 Ryan Wagner RH RC

2003 UD Patch Collection

	Nm-Mt	Ex-Mt
COMP.SET w/o SP's (90)	25.00	7.50
COMMON CARD (1-120)	.50	.15
COMMON RC	.50	.15
COMMON SP (1-120)	5.00	1.50
COMMON CARD (121-135)	8.00	2.40
COMMON CARD (136-150)	8.00	2.40
COMMON CARD (151-161)	5.00	1.50

❑ 1 Darin Erstad .50 .15
❑ 2 Troy Glaus .75 .23
❑ 3 Robby Hammock RC 2.00 .60
❑ 4 Luis Gonzalez .50 .15
❑ 5 Randy Johnson SP 8.00 2.40
❑ 6 Curt Schilling SP 8.00 2.40
❑ 7 Oscar Villarreal RC .75 .23
❑ 8 Gary Sheffield .50 .15
❑ 9 Mike Hampton SP 5.00 1.50
❑ 10 Greg Maddux SP 10.00 3.00
❑ 11 Chipper Jones 1.25 .35
❑ 12 Tony Batista .50 .15
❑ 13 Rodrigo Lopez .50 .15
❑ 14 Jay Gibbons .50 .15
❑ 15 Shea Hillenbrand .50 .15
❑ 16 Johnny Damon .50 .15
❑ 17 Derek Lowe SP 5.00 1.50
❑ 18 Nomar Garciaparra 2.50 .75
❑ 19 Pedro Martinez SP 8.00 2.40
❑ 20 Manny Ramirez .50 .15
❑ 21 Mark Prior SP 10.00 3.00
❑ 22 Kerry Wood SP 8.00 2.40
❑ 23 Corey Patterson .50 .15
❑ 24 Sammy Sosa 2.00 .60
❑ 25 Troy O'Leary .50 .15
❑ 26 Frank Thomas 1.25 .35
❑ 27 Magglio Ordonez .50 .15
❑ 28 Bartolo Colon SP 5.00 1.50
❑ 29 Austin Kearns .75 .23
❑ 30 Aaron Boone .50 .15
❑ 31 Ken Griffey Jr. 2.00 .60
❑ 32 Adam Dunn .75 .23
❑ 33 C.C. Sabathia .50 .15
❑ 34 Karim Garcia .50 .15
❑ 35 Larry Walker .75 .23
❑ 36 Preston Wilson .50 .15
❑ 37 Jason Jennings SP 5.00 1.50
❑ 38 Todd Helton .75 .23
❑ 39 Carlos Pena .50 .15
❑ 40 Eric Munson .50 .15
❑ 41 Ivan Rodriguez 1.25 .35
❑ 42 Josh Beckett SP 8.00 2.40
❑ 43 A.J. Burnett SP 5.00 1.50
❑ 44 Roy Oswalt SP 5.00 1.50
❑ 45 Craig Biggio .75 .23
❑ 46 Jeff Bagwell .75 .23
❑ 47 Lance Berkman .50 .15
❑ 48 Jeff Kent .50 .15
❑ 49 Carlos Beltran .50 .15
❑ 50 Mike Sweeney .50 .15
❑ 51 Hideo Nomo SP 8.00 2.40
❑ 52 Adrian Beltre .50 .15
❑ 53 Shawn Green .50 .15
❑ 54 Kazuhisa Ishii SP 5.00 1.50
❑ 55 Ben Sheets SP 5.00 1.50
❑ 56 Richie Sexson .50 .15
❑ 57 Torii Hunter .50 .15
❑ 58 Doug Mientkiewicz .50 .15
❑ 59 Eric Milton SP 5.00 1.50
❑ 60 Corey Koskie .50 .15
❑ 61 Joe Mays SP 5.00 1.50
❑ 62 Jose Vidro .50 .15
❑ 63 Vladimir Guerrero 1.25 .35
❑ 64 Luis Ayala RC .75 .23
❑ 65 Cliff Floyd .50 .15
❑ 66 Tom Glavine SP 8.00 2.40
❑ 67 Mike Piazza 2.00 .60
❑ 68 Roberto Alomar 1.25 .35
❑ 69 Al Leiter SP 5.00 1.50
❑ 70 Mike Mussina SP 8.00 2.40
❑ 71 Mariano Rivera SP 8.00 2.40
❑ 72 Drew Henson .50 .15
❑ 73 Roger Clemens SP 10.00 3.00
❑ 74 Jason Giambi 1.25 .35
❑ 75 Bernie Williams .75 .23
❑ 76 Alfonso Soriano 1.25 .35
❑ 77 Derek Jeter 3.00 .90
❑ 78 Miguel Tejada .50 .15
❑ 79 Jermaine Dye .50 .15
❑ 80 Tim Hudson SP 5.00 1.50
❑ 81 Barry Zito SP 8.00 2.40
❑ 82 Mark Mulder SP 5.00 1.50
❑ 83 Pat Burrell .50 .15
❑ 84 Jim Thome 1.25 .35
❑ 85 Bobby Abreu .50 .15
❑ 86 Kevin Millwood SP 5.00 1.50
❑ 87 Jason Kendall .50 .15
❑ 88 Brian Giles .50 .15
❑ 89 Phil Nevin .50 .15
❑ 90 Sean Burroughs .50 .15
❑ 91 Oliver Perez SP 5.00 1.50
❑ 92 Jose Cruz Jr. .50 .15
❑ 93 Rich Aurilia .50 .15
❑ 94 Edgardo Alfonzo .50 .15
❑ 95 Barry Bonds 3.00 .90
❑ 96 J.T. Snow .50 .15
❑ 97 Mike Cameron .50 .15
❑ 98 John Olerud .50 .15
❑ 99 Bret Boone .50 .15
❑ 100 Ichiro Suzuki 2.50 .75
❑ 101 J.D. Drew .50 .15
❑ 102 Jim Edmonds .50 .15
❑ 103 Scott Rolen .75 .23
❑ 104 Matt Morris SP 5.00 1.50
❑ 105 Tino Martinez .75 .23
❑ 106 Albert Pujols 2.50 .75
❑ 107 Rocco Baldelli 2.50 .75
❑ 108 Carl Crawford .50 .15
❑ 109 Mark Teixeira .75 .23
❑ 110 Rafael Palmeiro .75 .23
❑ 111 Hank Blalock .75 .23
❑ 112 Alex Rodriguez 2.50 .75
❑ 113 Kevin Mench .50 .15
❑ 114 Juan Gonzalez 1.25 .35
❑ 115 Shannon Stewart .50 .15
❑ 116 Vernon Wells .50 .15
❑ 117 Josh Phelps .50 .15
❑ 118 Eric Hinske SP 5.00 1.50

	Nm-Mt	Ex-Mt
❑ 119 Orlando Hudson	.50	.15
❑ 120 Carlos Delgado	.50	.15
❑ 121 Alex Rodriguez AS	15.00	4.50
❑ 122 Nomar Garciaparra AS	15.00	4.50
❑ 123 Miguel Tejada AS	8.00	2.40
❑ 124 Jim Thome AS	10.00	3.00
❑ 125 Alfonso Soriano AS	10.00	3.00
❑ 126 Vladimir Guerrero AS	10.00	3.00
❑ 127 Derek Jeter AS	20.00	6.00
❑ 128 Mike Piazza AS	15.00	4.50
❑ 129 Ichiro Suzuki AS	20.00	6.00
❑ 130 Pedro Martinez AS	10.00	3.00
❑ 131 Luis Gonzalez AS	8.00	2.40
❑ 132 Adam Dunn AS	10.00	3.00
❑ 133 Shawn Green AS	8.00	2.40
❑ 134 Barry Zito AS	10.00	3.00
❑ 135 Torii Hunter AS UER	8.00	2.40
Name misspelled as Torri		
❑ 136 Ted Williams HOF	30.00	9.00
❑ 137 Mickey Mantle HOF	40.00	12.00
❑ 138 Ernie Banks HOF	10.00	3.00
❑ 139 Yogi Berra HOF	10.00	3.00
❑ 140 Rollie Fingers HOF	8.00	2.40
❑ 141 Catfish Hunter HOF	10.00	3.00
❑ 142 Juan Marichal HOF	8.00	2.40
❑ 143 Eddie Mathews HOF	10.00	3.00
❑ 144 Willie McCovey HOF	8.00	2.40
❑ 145 Joe Morgan HOF	8.00	2.40
❑ 146 Stan Musial HOF	20.00	6.00
❑ 147 Pee Wee Reese HOF	10.00	3.00
❑ 148 Phil Rizzuto HOF	10.00	3.00
❑ 149 Nolan Ryan HOF	25.00	7.50
❑ 150 Tom Seaver HOF	10.00	3.00
❑ 151 Hideki Matsui RI RC	20.00	6.00
❑ 152 Jose Contreras RI RC	10.00	3.00
❑ 153 Lew Ford RI RC	8.00	2.40
❑ 154 Jeremy Griffiths RI RC	8.00	2.40
❑ 155 Guillermo Quiroz RI RC	8.00	2.40
❑ 156 Ryan Cameron RI RC	5.00	1.50
❑ 157 Jon Leicester RI RC	5.00	1.50
❑ 158 Josh Willingham RI RC	10.00	3.00
❑ 159 Shane Bazell RI RC UER	5.00	1.50
Name misspelled on front		
❑ 160 Willie Eyre RI RC	5.00	1.50
❑ 161 Prentice Redman RI RC	5.00	1.50
❑ IS Ichiro Suzuki SAMPLE	3.00	.90

2001 UD Reserve

	Nm-Mt	Ex-Mt
COMP.SET w/o SP's (180)	25.00	7.50
COMMON CARD (1-180)	.30	.09
COMMON (181-210)	5.00	1.50

	Nm-Mt	Ex-Mt
❑ 1 Darin Erstad	.30	.09
❑ 2 Tim Salmon	.50	.15
❑ 3 Bengie Molina	.30	.09
❑ 4 Troy Glaus	.50	.15
❑ 5 Glenallen Hill	.30	.09
❑ 6 Garret Anderson	.30	.09
❑ 7 Jason Giambi	.75	.23
❑ 8 Johnny Damon	.30	.09
❑ 9 Eric Chavez	.30	.09
❑ 10 Tim Hudson	.30	.09
❑ 11 Miguel Tejada	.30	.09
❑ 12 Barry Zito	.75	.23
❑ 13 Jose Ortiz	.30	.09
❑ 14 Tony Batista	.30	.09
❑ 15 Carlos Delgado	.30	.09
❑ 16 Shannon Stewart	.30	.09
❑ 17 Raul Mondesi	.30	.09
❑ 18 Ben Grieve	.30	.09
❑ 19 Aubrey Huff	.30	.09
❑ 20 Greg Vaughn	.30	.09
❑ 21 Fred McGriff	.50	.15
❑ 22 Gerald Williams	.30	.09
❑ 23 Bartolo Colon	.30	.09
❑ 24 Roberto Alomar	.75	.23
❑ 25 Jim Thome	.75	.23
❑ 26 Omar Vizquel	.30	.09
❑ 27 Juan Gonzalez	.75	.23
❑ 28 Ellis Burks	.30	.09
❑ 29 Edgar Martinez	.50	.15
❑ 30 Aaron Sele	.30	.09
❑ 31 Jay Buhner	.30	.09
❑ 32 Mike Cameron	.30	.09
❑ 33 Kazuhiro Sasaki	.30	.09
❑ 34 John Olerud	.30	.09
❑ 35 Cal Ripken	2.50	.75
❑ 36 Brady Anderson	.30	.09
❑ 37 Pat Hentgen	.30	.09
❑ 38 Chris Richard	.30	.09
❑ 39 Jerry Hairston Jr.	.30	.09
❑ 40 Mike Bordick	.30	.09
❑ 41 Ivan Rodriguez	.75	.23
❑ 42 Rick Helling	.30	.09
❑ 43 Rafael Palmeiro	.50	.15
❑ 44 Alex Rodriguez	1.50	.45
❑ 45 Andres Galarraga	.30	.09
❑ 46 Rusty Greer	.30	.09
❑ 47 Ruben Mateo	.30	.09
❑ 48 Ken Caminiti	.30	.09
❑ 49 Nomar Garciaparra	1.50	.45
❑ 50 Pedro Martinez	.75	.23
❑ 51 Manny Ramirez	.30	.09
❑ 52 Carl Everett	.30	.09
❑ 53 Dante Bichette	.30	.09
❑ 54 Hideo Nomo	.75	.23
❑ 55 Mike Sweeney	.30	.09
❑ 56 Carlos Beltran	.30	.09
❑ 57 Jeff Suppan	.30	.09
❑ 58 Jermaine Dye	.30	.09
❑ 59 Mark Quinn	.30	.09
❑ 60 Joe Randa	.30	.09
❑ 61 Bobby Higginson	.30	.09
❑ 62 Tony Clark	.30	.09
❑ 63 Brian Moehler	.30	.09
❑ 64 Dean Palmer	.30	.09
❑ 65 Brandon Inge	.30	.09
❑ 66 Damion Easley	.30	.09
❑ 67 Brad Radke	.30	.09
❑ 68 Corey Koskie	.30	.09
❑ 69 Cristian Guzman	.30	.09
❑ 70 Eric Milton	.30	.09
❑ 71 Jacque Jones	.30	.09
❑ 72 Matt Lawton	.30	.09
❑ 73 Frank Thomas	.75	.23
❑ 74 David Wells	.30	.09
❑ 75 Magglio Ordonez	.30	.09
❑ 76 Paul Konerko	.30	.09
❑ 77 Sandy Alomar Jr.	.30	.09
❑ 78 Ray Durham	.30	.09
❑ 79 Roger Clemens	1.50	.45
❑ 80 Bernie Williams	.50	.15
❑ 81 Derek Jeter	2.00	.60
❑ 82 David Justice	.30	.09
❑ 83 Paul O'Neill	.50	.15
❑ 84 Mike Mussina	.75	.23
❑ 85 Jorge Posada	.50	.15
❑ 86 Jeff Bagwell	.50	.15
❑ 87 Richard Hidalgo	.30	.09
❑ 88 Craig Biggio	.50	.15
❑ 89 Scott Elarton	.30	.09
❑ 90 Moises Alou	.30	.09
❑ 91 Greg Maddux	1.50	.45
❑ 92 Rafael Furcal	.30	.09
❑ 93 Andruw Jones	.50	.15
❑ 94 Tom Glavine	.75	.23
❑ 95 Chipper Jones	.75	.23
❑ 96 Javy Lopez	.30	.09
❑ 97 Richie Sexson	.30	.09
❑ 98 Jeromy Burnitz	.30	.09
❑ 99 Jeff D'Amico	.30	.09
❑ 100 Jeffrey Hammonds	.30	.09
❑ 101 Geoff Jenkins	.30	.09
❑ 102 Ben Sheets	.30	.09
❑ 103 Mark McGwire	2.00	.60
❑ 104 Rick Ankiel	.30	.09
❑ 105 Darryl Kile	.30	.09
❑ 106 Edgar Renteria	.30	.09
❑ 107 Jim Edmonds	.30	.09
❑ 108 J.D. Drew	.30	.09
❑ 109 Sammy Sosa	1.25	.35
❑ 110 Corey Patterson	.30	.09
❑ 111 Kerry Wood	.75	.23
❑ 112 Todd Hundley	.30	.09
❑ 113 Rondell White	.30	.09
❑ 114 Matt Stairs	.30	.09
❑ 115 Randy Johnson	.75	.23
❑ 116 Mark Grace	.75	.23
❑ 117 Steve Finley	.30	.09
❑ 118 Luis Gonzalez	.30	.09
❑ 119 Matt Williams	.30	.09
❑ 120 Curt Schilling	.50	.15
❑ 121 Gary Sheffield	.30	.09
❑ 122 Kevin Brown	.30	.09
❑ 123 Shawn Green	.30	.09
❑ 124 Eric Karros	.30	.09
❑ 125 Chan Ho Park	.30	.09
❑ 126 Adrian Beltre	.30	.09
❑ 127 Vladimir Guerrero	.75	.23
❑ 128 Fernando Tatis	.30	.09
❑ 129 Lee Stevens	.30	.09
❑ 130 Jose Vidro	.30	.09
❑ 131 Peter Bergeron	.30	.09
❑ 132 Michael Barrett	.30	.09
❑ 133 Jeff Kent	.30	.09
❑ 134 Russ Ortiz	.30	.09
❑ 135 Barry Bonds	2.00	.60
❑ 136 J.T. Snow	.30	.09
❑ 137 Livan Hernandez	.30	.09
❑ 138 Rich Aurilia	.30	.09
❑ 139 Preston Wilson	.30	.09
❑ 140 Mike Lowell	.30	.09
❑ 141 Ryan Dempster	.30	.09
❑ 142 Charles Johnson	.30	.09
❑ 143 Matt Clement	.30	.09
❑ 144 Luis Castillo	.30	.09
❑ 145 Mike Piazza UER	1.25	.35
Card lists him as a Dodger		
❑ 146 Al Leiter	.30	.09
❑ 147 Robin Ventura	.30	.09
❑ 148 Jay Payton	.30	.09
❑ 149 Todd Zeile	.30	.09
❑ 150 Edgardo Alfonzo	.30	.09
❑ 151 Tony Gwynn	1.00	.30
❑ 152 Ryan Klesko	.30	.09
❑ 153 Phil Nevin	.30	.09
❑ 154 Mark Kotsay	.30	.09
❑ 155 Trevor Hoffman	.30	.09
❑ 156 Damian Jackson	.30	.09
❑ 157 Scott Rolen	.50	.15
❑ 158 Mike Lieberthal	.30	.09
❑ 159 Bruce Chen	.30	.09
❑ 160 Bobby Abreu	.30	.09
❑ 161 Pat Burrell	.30	.09
❑ 162 Travis Lee	.30	.09
❑ 163 Jason Kendall	.30	.09
❑ 164 Derek Bell	.30	.09
❑ 165 Kris Benson	.30	.09
❑ 166 Kevin Young	.30	.09
❑ 167 Brian Giles	.30	.09
❑ 168 Pat Meares	.30	.09
❑ 169 Sean Casey	.30	.09
❑ 170 Pokey Reese	.30	.09
❑ 171 Pete Harnisch	.30	.09
❑ 172 Barry Larkin	.75	.23
❑ 173 Ken Griffey Jr.	1.25	.35
❑ 174 Dmitri Young	.30	.09
❑ 175 Mike Hampton	.30	.09
❑ 176 Todd Helton	.50	.15
❑ 177 Jeff Cirillo	.30	.09
❑ 178 Denny Neagle	.30	.09
❑ 179 Larry Walker	.50	.15
❑ 180 Todd Hollandsworth	.30	.09
❑ 181 Ichiro Suzuki SP RC	25.00	7.50
❑ 182 Wilson Betemit SP RC	5.00	1.50
❑ 183 A. Hernandez SP RC	5.00	1.50
❑ 184 Travis Hafner SP RC	8.00	2.40
❑ 185 Sean Douglass SP RC	5.00	1.50

❑ 186 Juan Diaz SP RC	5.00	1.50
❑ 187 H. Ramirez SP RC	8.00	2.40
❑ 188 M. Ensberg SP RC	8.00	2.40
❑ 189 B. Duckworth SP RC	5.00	1.50
❑ 190 Jack Wilson SP RC	5.00	1.50
❑ 191 Erick Almonte SP RC	5.00	1.50
❑ 192 R. Rodriguez SP RC	5.00	1.50
❑ 193 E. Guzman SP RC	5.00	1.50
❑ 194 Juan Uribe SP RC	5.00	1.50
❑ 195 Ryan Freel SP RC	5.00	1.50
❑ 196 C. Parker SP RC	5.00	1.50
❑ 197 J. Melian SP RC	5.00	1.50
❑ 198 Jose Mieses SP RC	5.00	1.50
❑ 199 Andres Torres SP RC	5.00	1.50
❑ 200 Jason Smith SP RC	5.00	1.50
❑ 201 J. Estrada SP RC	5.00	1.50
❑ 202 Cesar Crespo SP RC	5.00	1.50
❑ 203 C. Valderrama SP RC	5.00	1.50
❑ 204 Albert Pujols SP RC	40.00	12.00
❑ 205 Wilkin Ruan SP RC	5.00	1.50
❑ 206 Josh Fogg SP RC	5.00	1.50
❑ 207 Bert Snow SP RC	5.00	1.50
❑ 208 B. Lawrence SP RC	5.00	1.50
❑ 209 Esix Snead SP RC	5.00	1.50
❑ 210 T. Shinjo SP RC	8.00	2.40

1991 Ultra Update

	Nm-Mt	Ex-Mt
COMP.FACT.SET (120)	40.00	12.00
❑ 1 Dwight Evans	.50	.15
❑ 2 Chito Martinez	.25	.07
❑ 3 Bob Melvin	.25	.07
❑ 4 Mike Mussina RC	5.00	1.50
❑ 5 Jack Clark	.50	.15
❑ 6 Dana Kiecker	.25	.07
❑ 7 Steve Lyons	.25	.07
❑ 8 Gary Gaetti	.50	.15
❑ 9 Dave Gallagher	.25	.07
❑ 10 Dave Parker	.50	.15
❑ 11 Luis Polonia	.25	.07
❑ 12 Luis Sojo	.25	.07
❑ 13 Wilson Alvarez	.25	.07
❑ 14 Alex Fernandez	.25	.07
❑ 15 Craig Grebeck	.25	.07
❑ 16 Ron Karkovice	.25	.07
❑ 17 Warren Newson	.25	.07
❑ 18 Scott Radinsky	.25	.07
❑ 19 Glenallen Hill	.25	.07
❑ 20 Charles Nagy	.25	.07
❑ 21 Mark Whiten	.25	.07
❑ 22 Milt Cuyler	.25	.07
❑ 23 Paul Gibson	.25	.07
❑ 24 Mickey Tettleton	.25	.07
❑ 25 Todd Benzinger	.25	.07
❑ 26 Storm Davis	.25	.07
❑ 27 Kirk Gibson	.50	.15
❑ 28 Bill Pecota	.25	.07
❑ 29 Gary Thurman	.25	.07
❑ 30 Darryl Hamilton	.25	.07
❑ 31 Jaime Navarro	.25	.07
❑ 32 Willie Randolph	.50	.15
❑ 33 Bill Wegman	.25	.07
❑ 34 Randy Bush	.25	.07
❑ 35 Chili Davis	.50	.15
❑ 36 Scott Erickson	.25	.07
❑ 37 Chuck Knoblauch	.50	.15
❑ 38 Scott Leius	.25	.07
❑ 39 Jack Morris	.50	.15
❑ 40 John Habyan	.25	.07
❑ 41 Pat Kelly	.25	.07
❑ 42 Matt Nokes	.25	.07
❑ 43 Scott Sanderson	.25	.07
❑ 44 Bernie Williams	3.00	.90
❑ 45 Harold Baines	.50	.15
❑ 46 Brook Jacoby	.25	.07
❑ 47 Earnest Riles	.25	.07
❑ 48 Willie Wilson	.25	.07
❑ 49 Jay Buhner	.50	.15
❑ 50 Rich DeLucia	.25	.07
❑ 51 Mike Jackson	.25	.07
❑ 52 Bill Krueger	.25	.07
❑ 53 Bill Swift	.25	.07
❑ 54 Brian Downing	.25	.07
❑ 55 Juan Gonzalez	5.00	1.50
❑ 56 Dean Palmer	.50	.15
❑ 57 Kevin Reimer	.25	.07
❑ 58 Ivan Rodriguez RC	10.00	3.00
❑ 59 Tom Candiotti	.25	.07
❑ 60 Juan Guzman RC	.50	.15
❑ 61 Bob MacDonald	.25	.07
❑ 62 Greg Myers	.25	.07
❑ 63 Ed Sprague	.25	.07
❑ 64 Devon White	.25	.07
❑ 65 Rafael Belliard	.25	.07
❑ 66 Juan Berenguer	.25	.07
❑ 67 Brian R. Hunter RC	.50	.15
❑ 68 Kent Mercker	.25	.07
❑ 69 Otis Nixon	.25	.07
❑ 70 Danny Jackson	.25	.07
❑ 71 Chuck McElroy	.25	.07
❑ 72 Gary Scott	.25	.07
❑ 73 Heathcliff Slocumb RC	.25	.07
❑ 74 Chico Walker	.25	.07
❑ 75 Rick Wilkins RC	.25	.07
❑ 76 Chris Hammond	.25	.07
❑ 77 Luis Quinones	.25	.07
❑ 78 Herm Winningham	.25	.07
❑ 79 Jeff Bagwell RC	8.00	2.40
❑ 80 Jim Corsi	.25	.07
❑ 81 Steve Finley	.50	.15
❑ 82 Luis Gonzalez RC	4.00	1.20
❑ 83 Pete Harnisch	.25	.07
❑ 84 Darryl Kile	.50	.15
❑ 85 Brett Butler	.50	.15
❑ 86 Gary Carter	.75	.23
❑ 87 Tim Crews	.25	.07
❑ 88 Orel Hershiser	.50	.15
❑ 89 Bob Ojeda	.25	.07
❑ 90 Bret Barberie RC**	.25	.07
❑ 91 Barry Jones	.25	.07
❑ 92 Gilberto Reyes	.25	.07
❑ 93 Larry Walker	1.25	.35
❑ 94 Hubie Brooks	.25	.07
❑ 95 Tim Burke	.25	.07
❑ 96 Rick Cerone	.25	.07
❑ 97 Jeff Innis	.25	.07
❑ 98 Wally Backman	.25	.07
❑ 99 Tommy Greene	.25	.07
❑ 100 Ricky Jordan	.25	.07
❑ 101 Mitch Williams	.25	.07
❑ 102 John Smiley	.25	.07
❑ 103 Randy Tomlin RC	.25	.07
❑ 104 Gary Varsho	.25	.07
❑ 105 Cris Carpenter	.25	.07
❑ 106 Ken Hill	.25	.07
❑ 107 Felix Jose	.25	.07
❑ 108 Omar Olivares RC	.25	.07
❑ 109 Gerald Perry	.25	.07
❑ 110 Jerald Clark	.25	.07
❑ 111 Tony Fernandez	.25	.07
❑ 112 Darrin Jackson	.25	.07
❑ 113 Mike Maddux	.25	.07
❑ 114 Tim Teufel	.25	.07
❑ 115 Bud Black	.25	.07
❑ 116 Kelly Downs	.25	.07
❑ 117 Mike Felder	.25	.07
❑ 118 Willie McGee	.50	.15
❑ 119 Trevor Wilson	.25	.07
❑ 120 Checklist 1-120	.25	.07

2001 Ultra

	Nm-Mt	Ex-Mt
COMPLETE SET (275)	120.00	36.00
COMP.SET w/o SP's (250)	25.00	7.50
COMMON CARD (1-250)	.30	.09
COMMON (251-275)	3.00	.90
COMMON (276-280)	5.00	1.50
❑ 1 Pedro Martinez	.75	.23
❑ 2 Derek Jeter	2.00	.60
❑ 3 Cal Ripken	2.50	.75
❑ 4 Alex Rodriguez	1.50	.45
❑ 5 Vladimir Guerrero	.75	.23
❑ 6 Troy Glaus	.50	.15
❑ 7 Sammy Sosa	1.25	.35
❑ 8 Mike Piazza	1.25	.35
❑ 9 Tony Gwynn	1.00	.30
❑ 10 Tim Hudson	.30	.09
❑ 11 John Flaherty	.30	.09
❑ 12 Jeff Cirillo	.30	.09
❑ 13 Ellis Burks	.30	.09
❑ 14 Carlos Lee	.30	.09
❑ 15 Carlos Beltran	.30	.09
❑ 16 Ruben Rivera	.30	.09
❑ 17 Richard Hidalgo	.30	.09
❑ 18 Omar Vizquel	.30	.09
❑ 19 Michael Barrett	.30	.09
❑ 20 Jose Canseco	.75	.23
❑ 21 Jason Giambi	.75	.23
❑ 22 Greg Maddux	1.50	.45
❑ 23 Charles Johnson	.30	.09
❑ 24 Sandy Alomar Jr.	.30	.09
❑ 25 Rick Ankiel	.30	.09
❑ 26 Richie Sexson	.30	.09
❑ 27 Matt Williams	.30	.09
❑ 28 Joe Girardi	.30	.09
❑ 29 Jason Kendall	.30	.09
❑ 30 Brad Fullmer	.30	.09
❑ 31 Alex Gonzalez	.30	.09
❑ 32 Rick Helling	.30	.09
❑ 33 Mike Mussina	.75	.23
❑ 34 Joe Randa	.30	.09
❑ 35 J.T. Snow	.30	.09
❑ 36 Edgardo Alfonzo	.30	.09
❑ 37 Dante Bichette	.30	.09
❑ 38 Brad Ausmus	.30	.09
❑ 39 Bobby Abreu	.30	.09
❑ 40 Warren Morris	.30	.09
❑ 41 Tony Womack	.30	.09
❑ 42 Russell Branyan	.30	.09
❑ 43 Mike Lowell	.30	.09
❑ 44 Mark Grace	.75	.23
❑ 45 Jeromy Burnitz	.30	.09
❑ 46 J.D. Drew	.30	.09
❑ 47 David Justice	.30	.09
❑ 48 Alex Gonzalez	.30	.09
❑ 49 Tino Martinez	.50	.15
❑ 50 Raul Mondesi	.30	.09
❑ 51 Rafael Furcal	.30	.09
❑ 52 Marquis Grissom	.30	.09
❑ 53 Kevin Young	.30	.09
❑ 54 Jon Lieber	.30	.09
❑ 55 Henry Rodriguez	.30	.09
❑ 56 Dave Burba	.30	.09
❑ 57 Shannon Stewart	.30	.09
❑ 58 Preston Wilson	.30	.09
❑ 59 Paul O'Neill	.50	.15

	No.	Player		
❑	60	Jimmy Haynes	.30	.09
❑	61	Darryl Kile	.30	.09
❑	62	Bret Boone	.30	.09
❑	63	Bartolo Colon	.30	.09
❑	64	Andres Galarraga	.30	.09
❑	65	Trot Nixon	.30	.09
❑	66	Steve Finley	.30	.09
❑	67	Shawn Green	.30	.09
❑	68	Robert Person	.30	.09
❑	69	Kenny Rogers	.30	.09
❑	70	Bobby Higginson	.30	.09
❑	71	Barry Larkin	.75	.23
❑	72	Al Martin	.30	.09
❑	73	Tom Glavine	.75	.23
❑	74	Rondell White	.30	.09
❑	75	Ray Lankford	.30	.09
❑	76	Moises Alou	.30	.09
❑	77	Matt Clement	.30	.09
❑	78	Geoff Jenkins	.30	.09
❑	79	David Wells	.30	.09
❑	80	Chuck Finley	.30	.09
❑	81	Andy Pettitte	.50	.15
❑	82	Travis Fryman	.30	.09
❑	83	Ron Coomer	.30	.09
❑	84	Mark McGwire	2.00	.60
❑	85	Kerry Wood	.75	.23
❑	86	Jorge Posada	.50	.15
❑	87	Jeff Bagwell	.50	.15
❑	88	Andruw Jones	.50	.15
❑	89	Ryan Klesko	.30	.09
❑	90	Mariano Rivera	.50	.15
❑	91	Lance Berkman	.30	.09
❑	92	Kenny Lofton	.30	.09
❑	93	Jacque Jones	.30	.09
❑	94	Eric Young	.30	.09
❑	95	Edgar Renteria	.30	.09
❑	96	Chipper Jones	.75	.23
❑	97	Todd Helton	.50	.15
❑	98	Shawn Estes	.30	.09
❑	99	Mark Mulder	.30	.09
❑	100	Lee Stevens	.30	.09
❑	101	Jermaine Dye	.30	.09
❑	102	Greg Vaughn	.30	.09
❑	103	Chris Singleton	.30	.09
❑	104	Brady Anderson	.30	.09
❑	105	Terrence Long	.30	.09
❑	106	Quilvio Veras	.30	.09
❑	107	Magglio Ordonez	.30	.09
❑	108	Johnny Damon	.30	.09
❑	109	Jeffrey Hammonds	.30	.09
❑	110	Fred McGriff	.50	.15
❑	111	Carl Pavano	.30	.09
❑	112	Bobby Estalella	.30	.09
❑	113	Todd Hundley	.30	.09
❑	114	Scott Rolen	.50	.15
❑	115	Robin Ventura	.30	.09
❑	116	Pokey Reese	.30	.09
❑	117	Luis Gonzalez	.30	.09
❑	118	Jose Offerman	.30	.09
❑	119	Edgar Martinez	.50	.15
❑	120	Dean Palmer	.30	.09
❑	121	David Segui	.30	.09
❑	122	Troy O'Leary	.30	.09
❑	123	Tony Batista	.30	.09
❑	124	Todd Zeile	.30	.09
❑	125	Randy Johnson	.75	.23
❑	126	Luis Castillo	.30	.09
❑	127	Kris Benson	.30	.09
❑	128	John Olerud	.30	.09
❑	129	Eric Karros	.30	.09
❑	130	Eddie Taubensee	.30	.09
❑	131	Neifi Perez	.30	.09
❑	132	Matt Stairs	.30	.09
❑	133	Luis Alicea	.30	.09
❑	134	Jeff Kent	.30	.09
❑	135	Javier Vazquez	.30	.09
❑	136	Garret Anderson	.30	.09
❑	137	Frank Thomas	.75	.23
❑	138	Carlos Febles	.30	.09
❑	139	Albert Belle	.30	.09
❑	140	Tony Clark	.30	.09
❑	141	Pat Burrell	.30	.09
❑	142	Mike Sweeney	.30	.09
❑	143	Jay Buhner	.30	.09
❑	144	Gabe Kapler	.30	.09
❑	145	Derek Bell	.30	.09
❑	146	B.J. Surhoff	.30	.09
❑	147	Adam Kennedy	.30	.09
❑	148	Aaron Boone	.30	.09
❑	149	Todd Stottlemyre	.30	.09
❑	150	Roberto Alomar	.75	.23
❑	151	Orlando Hernandez	.30	.09
❑	152	Jason Varitek	.30	.09
❑	153	Gary Sheffield	.30	.09
❑	154	Cliff Floyd	.30	.09
❑	155	Chad Hermansen	.30	.09
❑	156	Carlos Delgado	.30	.09
❑	157	Aaron Sele	.30	.09
❑	158	Sean Casey	.30	.09
❑	159	Ruben Mateo	.30	.09
❑	160	Mike Bordick	.30	.09
❑	161	Mike Cameron	.30	.09
❑	162	Doug Glanville	.30	.09
❑	163	Damion Easley	.30	.09
❑	164	Carl Everett	.30	.09
❑	165	Bengie Molina	.30	.09
❑	166	Adrian Beltre	.30	.09
❑	167	Tom Goodwin	.30	.09
❑	168	Rickey Henderson	1.25	.35
❑	169	Mo Vaughn	.30	.09
❑	170	Mike Lieberthal	.30	.09
❑	171	Ken Griffey Jr.	1.25	.35
❑	172	Juan Gonzalez	.75	.23
❑	173	Ivan Rodriguez	.75	.23
❑	174	Al Leiter	.30	.09
❑	175	Vinny Castilla	.30	.09
❑	176	Peter Bergeron	.30	.09
❑	177	Pedro Astacio	.30	.09
❑	178	Paul Konerko	.30	.09
❑	179	Mitch Meluskey	.30	.09
❑	180	Kevin Millwood	.30	.09
❑	181	Ben Grieve	.30	.09
❑	182	Barry Bonds	2.00	.60
❑	183	Rusty Greer	.30	.09
❑	184	Miguel Tejada	.30	.09
❑	185	Mark Quinn	.30	.09
❑	186	Larry Walker	.50	.15
❑	187	Jose Valentin	.30	.09
❑	188	Jose Vidro	.30	.09
❑	189	Delino DeShields	.30	.09
❑	190	Darin Erstad	.30	.09
❑	191	Bill Mueller	.30	.09
❑	192	Ray Durham	.30	.09
❑	193	Ken Caminiti	.30	.09
❑	194	Jim Thome	.75	.23
❑	195	Javy Lopez	.30	.09
❑	196	Fernando Vina	.30	.09
❑	197	Eric Chavez	.30	.09
❑	198	Eric Owens	.30	.09
❑	199	Brad Radke	.30	.09
❑	200	Travis Lee	.30	.09
❑	201	Tim Salmon	.50	.15
❑	202	Rafael Palmeiro	.50	.15
❑	203	Nomar Garciaparra	1.50	.45
❑	204	Mike Hampton	.30	.09
❑	205	Kevin Brown	.30	.09
❑	206	Juan Encarnacion	.30	.09
❑	207	Danny Graves	.30	.09
❑	208	Carlos Guillen	.30	.09
❑	209	Phil Nevin	.30	.09
❑	210	Matt Lawton	.30	.09
❑	211	Manny Ramirez	.30	.09
❑	212	James Baldwin	.30	.09
❑	213	Fernando Tatis	.30	.09
❑	214	Craig Biggio	.50	.15
❑	215	Brian Jordan	.30	.09
❑	216	Bernie Williams	.50	.15
❑	217	Ryan Dempster	.30	.09
❑	218	Roger Clemens	1.50	.45
❑	219	Jose Cruz Jr.	.30	.09
❑	220	John Valentin	.30	.09
❑	221	Dmitri Young	.30	.09
❑	222	Curt Schilling	.50	.15
❑	223	Jim Edmonds	.30	.09
❑	224	Chan Ho Park	.30	.09
❑	225	Brian Giles	.30	.09
❑	226	Jimmy Anderson	.30	.09
		Tike Redman		
❑	227	Adam Piatt	.30	.09
		Jose Ortiz		
❑	228	Kenny Kelly	.30	.09
		Aubrey Huff		
❑	229	Randy Choate	.30	.09
		Craig Dingman		
❑	230	Eric Cammack	.30	.09
		Grant Roberts		
❑	231	Yovanny Lara	.30	.09
		Andy Tracy		
❑	232	Wayne Franklin	.30	.09
		Scott Linebrink		
❑	233	Cameron Cairncross	.30	.09
		Chan Perry		
❑	234	J.C. Romero	.30	.09
		Matt LeCroy		
❑	235	Geraldo Guzman	.30	.09
		Jason Conti		
❑	236	Morgan Burkhart	.30	.09
		Paxton Crawford		
❑	237	Pasqual Coco	.30	.09
		Leo Estrella		
❑	238	John Parrish	.30	.09
		Fernando Lunar		
❑	239	Keith McDonald	.30	.09
		Justin Brunette		
❑	240	Carlos Casimiro	.30	.09
		Ivanon Coffie		
❑	241	Daniel Garibay	.30	.09
		Ruben Quevedo		
❑	242	Sang-Hoon Lee	.30	.09
		Tomo Ohka		
❑	243	Hector Ortiz	.30	.09
		Jeff D'Amico		
❑	244	Jeff Sparks	.30	.09
		Travis Harper		
❑	245	Jason Boyd	.30	.09
		David Coggin		
❑	246	Mark Buehrle	.30	.09
		Lorenzo Barcelo		
❑	247	Adam Melhuse	.30	.09
		Ben Petrick		
❑	248	Kane Davis	.30	.09
		Paul Rigdon		
❑	249	Mike Darr	.30	.09
		Kory DeHaan		
❑	250	Vicente Padilla	3.00	.90
		Mark Brownson		
❑	251	Barry Zito PROS	5.00	1.50
❑	252	Tim Drew PROS	3.00	.90
❑	253	Luis Matos PROS	4.00	1.20
❑	254	Alex Cabrera PROS	3.00	.90
❑	255	Jon Garland PROS	3.00	.90
❑	256	Milton Bradley PROS	4.00	1.20
❑	257	Juan Pierre PROS	4.00	1.20
❑	258	Ismael Villegas PROS	3.00	.90
❑	259	Eric Munson PROS	3.00	.90
❑	260	T.De la Rosa PROS	3.00	.90
❑	261	Chris Richard PROS	3.00	.90
❑	262	Jason Tyner PROS	3.00	.90
❑	263	B.J. Waszgis PROS	3.00	.90
❑	264	Jason Marquis PROS	3.00	.90
❑	265	Dusty Allen PROS	3.00	.90
❑	266	C.Patterson PROS	4.00	1.20
❑	267	Eric Byrnes PROS	3.00	.90
❑	268	Xavier Nady PROS	4.00	1.20
❑	269	G.Lombard PROS	3.00	.90
❑	270	Timo Perez PROS	3.00	.90
❑	271	G.Matthews Jr. PROS	3.00	.90
❑	272	Chad Durbin PROS	3.00	.90
❑	273	Tony Armas Jr. PROS	3.00	.90
❑	274	F.Cordero PROS	3.00	.90
❑	275	A.Soriano PROS	5.00	1.50
❑	276	Junior Spivey RC	8.00	2.40
		Juan Uribe RC		
❑	277	Albert Pujols RC	40.00	12.00
		Bud Smith RC		
❑	278	Ichiro Suzuki RC	25.00	7.50
		Tsuyoshi Shinjo RC		
❑	279	Drew Henson RC	8.00	2.40
		Jackson Melian RC		
❑	280	Matt White RC	5.00	1.50
		Adrian Hernandez RC		

2002 Ultra

	Nm-Mt	Ex-Mt
COMPLETE SET (285)	200.00	60.00
COMP.SET w/o SP's (200)	25.00	7.50
COMMON CARD (1-200)	.30	.09

COMMON (201-220)	1.00	.30
COMMON (221-250)	1.00	.30
COMMON (251-285)	3.00	.90

No.	Player	Price	Price
1	Jeff Bagwell	.50	.15
2	Derek Jeter	2.00	.60
3	Alex Rodriguez	1.50	.45
4	Eric Chavez	.30	.09
5	Tsuyoshi Shinjo	.30	.09
6	Chris Stynes	.30	.09
7	Ivan Rodriguez	.75	.23
8	Cal Ripken	2.50	.75
9	Freddy Garcia	.30	.09
10	Chipper Jones	.75	.23
11	Hideo Nomo	.75	.23
12	Rafael Furcal	.30	.09
13	Preston Wilson	.30	.09
14	Jimmy Rollins	.30	.09
15	Cristian Guzman	.30	.09
16	Garret Anderson	.30	.09
17	Todd Helton	.50	.15
18	Moises Alou	.30	.09
19	Tony Gwynn	1.00	.30
20	Jorge Posada	.50	.15
21	Sean Casey	.30	.09
22	Kazuhiro Sasaki	.30	.09
23	Ray Lankford	.30	.09
24	Manny Ramirez	.30	.09
25	Barry Bonds	2.00	.60
26	Fred McGriff	.50	.15
27	Vladimir Guerrero	.75	.23
28	Jermaine Dye	.30	.09
29	Adrian Beltre	.30	.09
30	Ken Griffey Jr.	1.25	.35
31	Ramon Hernandez	.30	.09
32	Kerry Wood	.75	.23
33	Greg Maddux	1.50	.45
34	Rondell White	.30	.09
35	Mike Mussina	.75	.23
36	Jim Edmonds	.30	.09
37	Scott Rolen	.50	.15
38	Mike Lowell	.30	.09
39	Al Leiter	.30	.09
40	Tony Clark	.30	.09
41	Joe Mays	.30	.09
42	Mo Vaughn	.30	.09
43	Geoff Jenkins	.30	.09
44	Curt Schilling	.50	.15
45	Pedro Martinez	.75	.23
46	Andy Pettitte	.50	.15
47	Tim Salmon	.50	.15
48	Carl Everett	.30	.09
49	Lance Berkman	.30	.09
50	Troy Glaus	.50	.15
51	Ichiro Suzuki	1.50	.45
52	Alfonso Soriano	.75	.23
53	Tomo Ohka	.30	.09
54	Dean Palmer	.30	.09
55	Kevin Brown	.30	.09
56	Albert Pujols	1.50	.45
57	Homer Bush	.30	.09
58	Tim Hudson	.30	.09
59	Frank Thomas	.75	.23
60	Joe Randa	.30	.09
61	Chan Ho Park	.30	.09
62	Bobby Higginson	.30	.09
63	Bartolo Colon	.30	.09
64	Aramis Ramirez	.30	.09
65	Jeff Cirillo	.30	.09
66	Roberto Alomar	.75	.23
67	Mark Kotsay	.30	.09
68	Mike Cameron	.30	.09
69	Mike Hampton	.30	.09
70	Trot Nixon	.30	.09
71	Juan Gonzalez	.75	.23
72	Damian Rolls	.30	.09
73	Brad Fullmer	.30	.09
74	David Ortiz	.30	.09
75	Brandon Inge	.30	.09
76	Orlando Hernandez	.30	.09
77	Matt Stairs	.30	.09
78	Jay Gibbons	.30	.09
79	Greg Vaughn	.30	.09
80	Brady Anderson	.30	.09
81	Jim Thome	.75	.23
82	Ben Sheets	.30	.09
83	Rafael Palmeiro	.50	.15
84	Edgar Renteria	.30	.09
85	Doug Mientkiewicz	.30	.09
86	Raul Mondesi	.30	.09
87	Shane Reynolds	.30	.09
88	Steve Finley	.30	.09
89	Jose Cruz Jr.	.30	.09
90	Edgardo Alfonzo	.30	.09
91	Jose Valentin	.30	.09
92	Mark McGwire	2.00	.60
93	Mark Grace	.75	.23
94	Mike Lieberthal	.30	.09
95	Barry Larkin	.75	.23
96	Chuck Knoblauch	.30	.09
97	Deivi Cruz	.30	.09
98	Jeromy Burnitz	.30	.09
99	Shannon Stewart	.30	.09
100	David Wells	.30	.09
101	Brook Fordyce	.30	.09
102	Rusty Greer	.30	.09
103	Andruw Jones	.50	.15
104	Jason Kendall	.30	.09
105	Nomar Garciaparra	1.50	.45
106	Shawn Green	.30	.09
107	Craig Biggio	.50	.15
108	Masato Yoshii	.30	.09
109	Ben Petrick	.30	.09
110	Gary Sheffield	.30	.09
111	Travis Lee	.30	.09
112	Matt Williams	.30	.09
113	Billy Wagner	.30	.09
114	Robin Ventura	.30	.09
115	Jerry Hairston	.30	.09
116	Paul LoDuca	.30	.09
117	Darin Erstad	.30	.09
118	Ruben Sierra	.30	.09
119	Ricky Gutierrez	.30	.09
120	Bret Boone	.30	.09
121	John Rocker	.30	.09
122	Roger Clemens	1.50	.45
123	Eric Karros	.30	.09
124	J.D. Drew	.30	.09
125	Carlos Delgado	.30	.09
126	Jeffrey Hammonds	.30	.09
127	Jeff Kent	.30	.09
128	David Justice	.30	.09
129	Cliff Floyd	.30	.09
130	Omar Vizquel	.30	.09
131	Matt Morris	.30	.09
132	Rich Aurilia	.30	.09
133	Larry Walker	.50	.15
134	Miguel Tejada	.30	.09
135	Eric Young	.30	.09
136	Aaron Sele	.30	.09
137	Eric Milton	.30	.09
138	Travis Fryman	.30	.09
139	Magglio Ordonez	.30	.09
140	Sammy Sosa	1.25	.35
141	Pokey Reese	.30	.09
142	Adam Eaton	.30	.09
143	Adam Kennedy	.30	.09
144	Mike Piazza	1.25	.35
145	Larry Barnes	.30	.09
146	Darryl Kile	.30	.09
147	Tom Glavine	.75	.23
148	Ryan Klesko	.30	.09
149	Jose Vidro	.30	.09
150	Joe Kennedy	.30	.09
151	Bernie Williams	.50	.15
152	C.C. Sabathia	.30	.09
153	Alex Ochoa	.30	.09
154	A.J. Pierzynski	.30	.09
155	Johnny Damon	.30	.09
156	Omar Daal	.30	.09
157	A.J. Burnett	.30	.09
158	Eric Munson	.30	.09
159	Fernando Vina	.30	.09
160	Chris Singleton	.30	.09
161	Juan Pierre	.30	.09
162	John Olerud	.30	.09
163	Randy Johnson	.75	.23
164	Paul Konerko	.30	.09
165	Tino Martinez	.50	.15
166	Richard Hidalgo	.30	.09
167	Luis Gonzalez	.30	.09
168	Ben Grieve	.30	.09
169	Matt Lawton	.30	.09
170	Gabe Kapler	.30	.09
171	Mariano Rivera	.50	.15
172	Kenny Lofton	.30	.09
173	Brian Jordan	.30	.09
174	Brian Giles	.30	.09
175	Mark Quinn	.30	.09
176	Neifi Perez	.30	.09
177	Ellis Burks	.30	.09
178	Bobby Abreu	.30	.09
179	Jeff Weaver	.30	.09
180	Andres Galarraga	.30	.09
181	Javy Lopez	.30	.09
182	Todd Walker	.30	.09
183	Fernando Tatis	.30	.09
184	Charles Johnson	.30	.09
185	Pat Burrell	.30	.09
186	Jay Bell	.30	.09
187	Aaron Boone	.30	.09
188	Jason Giambi	.75	.23
189	Jay Payton	.30	.09
190	Carlos Lee	.30	.09
191	Phil Nevin	.30	.09
192	Mike Sweeney	.30	.09
193	J.T. Snow	.30	.09
194	Dmitri Young	.30	.09
195	Richie Sexson	.30	.09
196	Derrek Lee	.30	.09
197	Corey Koskie	.30	.09
198	Edgar Martinez	.50	.15
199	Wade Miller	.30	.09
200	Tony Batista	.30	.09
201	John Olerud AS	1.00	.30
202	Bret Boone AS	1.00	.30
203	Cal Ripken AS	5.00	1.50
204	Alex Rodriguez AS	3.00	.90
205	Ichiro Suzuki AS	3.00	.90
206	Manny Ramirez AS	.30	.09
207	Juan Gonzalez AS	1.50	.45
208	Ivan Rodriguez AS	1.50	.45
209	Roger Clemens AS	3.00	.90
210	Edgar Martinez AS	1.00	.30
211	Todd Helton AS	1.00	.30
212	Jeff Kent AS	1.00	.30
213	Chipper Jones AS	1.50	.45
214	Rich Aurilia AS	1.00	.30
215	Barry Bonds AS	4.00	1.20
216	Sammy Sosa AS	2.50	.75
217	Luis Gonzalez AS	1.00	.30
218	Mike Piazza AS	2.50	.75
219	Randy Johnson AS	1.50	.45
220	Larry Walker AS	1.00	.30
221	Todd Helton Juan Uribe	1.00	.30
222	Pat Burrell Eric Valent	1.00	.30
223	Edgar Martinez Ichiro Suzuki	3.00	.90
224	Ben Grieve Jason Tyner	1.00	.30
225	Mark Quinn Dee Brown	1.00	.30
226	Cal Ripken Brian Roberts	5.00	1.50
227	Cliff Floyd Abraham Nunez	1.00	.30
228	Jeff Bagwell Adam Everett	1.00	.30

- ☐ 229 Mark McGwire 4.00 1.20
  Albert Pujols
- ☐ 230 Doug Mientkiewicz .... 1.00 .30
  Luis Rivas
- ☐ 231 Juan Gonzalez .... 1.50 .45
  Danny Peoples
- ☐ 232 Kevin Brown .... 1.00 .30
  Luke Prokopec
- ☐ 233 Richie Sexson .... 1.00 .30
  Ben Sheets
- ☐ 234 Jason Giambi .... 1.50 .45
  Jason Hart
- ☐ 235 Barry Bonds 4.00 1.20
  Carlos Valderrama
- ☐ 236 Tony Gwynn .... 2.00 .60
  Cesar Crespo
- ☐ 237 Ken Griffey Jr. .... 2.50 .75
  Adam Dunn
- ☐ 238 Frank Thomas .... .75 .23
  Joe Crede
- ☐ 239 Derek Jeter 4.00 1.20
  Drew Henson
- ☐ 240 Chipper Jones .... 1.50 .45
  Wilson Betemit
- ☐ 241 Luis Gonzalez .... 1.00 .30
  Junior Spivey
- ☐ 242 Bobby Higginson .... 1.00 .30
  Andres Torres
- ☐ 243 Carlos Delgado .... 1.00 .30
  Vernon Wells
- ☐ 244 Sammy Sosa .... 2.50 .75
  Corey Patterson
- ☐ 245 Nomar Garciaparra .... 3.00 .90
  Shea Hillenbrand
- ☐ 246 Alex Rodriguez .... 3.00 .90
  Jason Romano
- ☐ 247 Troy Glaus .... 1.00 .30
  David Eckstein
- ☐ 248 Mike Piazza .... 2.50 .75
  Alex Escobar
- ☐ 249 Brian Giles .... 1.00 .30
  Jack Wilson
- ☐ 250 Vladimir Guerrero .... 1.50 .45
  Scott Hodges
- ☐ 251 Bud Smith PROS .... 3.00 .90
- ☐ 252 Juan Diaz PROS .... 3.00 .90
- ☐ 253 Wilkin Ruan PROS .... 3.00 .90
- ☐ 254 C. Spurling PROS RC .... 3.00 .90
- ☐ 255 Toby Hall PROS .... 3.00 .90
- ☐ 256 Jason Jennings PROS .... 3.00 .90
- ☐ 257 George Perez PROS .... 3.00 .90
- ☐ 258 D. Jimenez PROS .... 3.00 .90
- ☐ 259 Jose Acevedo PROS .... 3.00 .90
- ☐ 260 Josue Perez PROS .... 3.00 .90
- ☐ 261 Brian Rogers PROS .... 3.00 .90
- ☐ 262 C. Maldonado PROS RC .... 3.00 .90
- ☐ 263 Travis Phelps PROS .... 3.00 .90
- ☐ 264 R. Mackowiak PROS .... 3.00 .90
- ☐ 265 Ryan Drese PROS .... 3.00 .90
- ☐ 266 Carlos Garcia PROS .... 3.00 .90
- ☐ 267 Alexis Gomez PROS .... 3.00 .90
- ☐ 268 Jeremy Affeldt PROS .... 3.00 .90
- ☐ 269 S. Podsednik PROS 10.00 3.00
- ☐ 270 Adam Johnson PROS .... 3.00 .90
- ☐ 271 Pedro Santana PROS .... 3.00 .90
- ☐ 272 Les Walrond PROS .... 3.00 .90
- ☐ 273 Jackson Melian PROS .... 3.00 .90
- ☐ 274 C. Hernandez PROS .... 3.00 .90
- ☐ 275 M. Nussbeck PROS RC .... 3.00 .90
- ☐ 276 Cory Aldridge PROS .... 3.00 .90
- ☐ 277 Troy Mattes PROS .... 3.00 .90
- ☐ 278 B. Abernathy PROS .... 3.00 .90
- ☐ 279 J.J. Davis PROS .... 3.00 .90
- ☐ 280 B. Duckworth PROS .... 3.00 .90
- ☐ 281 Kyle Lohse PROS .... 3.00 .90
- ☐ 282 Justin Kaye PROS .... 3.00 .90
- ☐ 283 Cody Ransom PROS .... 3.00 .90
- ☐ 284 Dave Williams PROS .... 3.00 .90
- ☐ 285 Luis Lopez PROS .... 3.00 .90

2003 Ultra

	Nm-Mt	Ex-Mt
COMP.LO SET (250)	100.00	30.00
COMP.LO SET w/o SP's (200)	25.00	7.50
COMMON CARD (201-220)	1.50	.45

COMMON CARD (221-250) .... 2.00 .60

- ☐ 1 Barry Bonds .... 2.00 .60
- ☐ 2 Derek Jeter .... 2.00 .60
- ☐ 3 Ichiro Suzuki .... 1.50 .45
- ☐ 4 Mike Lowell .... .30 .09
- ☐ 5 Hideo Nomo .... .75 .23
- ☐ 6 Javier Vazquez .... .30 .09
- ☐ 7 Jeremy Giambi .... .30 .09
- ☐ 8 Jamie Moyer .... .30 .09
- ☐ 9 Rafael Palmeiro .... .50 .15
- ☐ 10 Magglio Ordonez .... .30 .09
- ☐ 11 Trot Nixon .... .30 .09
- ☐ 12 Luis Castillo .... .30 .09
- ☐ 13 Paul Byrd .... .30 .09
- ☐ 14 Adam Kennedy .... .30 .09
- ☐ 15 Trevor Hoffman .... .30 .09
- ☐ 16 Matt Morris .... .30 .09
- ☐ 17 Nomar Garciaparra .... 1.50 .45
- ☐ 18 Matt Lawton .... .30 .09
- ☐ 19 Carlos Beltran .... .30 .09
- ☐ 20 Jason Giambi .... .75 .23
- ☐ 21 Brian Giles .... .30 .09
- ☐ 22 Jim Edmonds .... .30 .09
- ☐ 23 Garret Anderson .... .30 .09
- ☐ 24 Tony Batista .... .30 .09
- ☐ 25 Aaron Boone .... .30 .09
- ☐ 26 Mike Hampton .... .30 .09
- ☐ 27 Billy Wagner .... .30 .09
- ☐ 28 Kazuhisa Ishii .... .30 .09
- ☐ 29 Al Leiter .... .30 .09
- ☐ 30 Pat Burrell .... .30 .09
- ☐ 31 Jeff Kent .... .30 .09
- ☐ 32 Randy Johnson .... .75 .23
- ☐ 33 Ray Durham .... .30 .09
- ☐ 34 Josh Beckett .... .50 .15
- ☐ 35 Cristian Guzman .... .30 .09
- ☐ 36 Roger Clemens .... 1.50 .45
- ☐ 37 Freddy Garcia .... .30 .09
- ☐ 38 Roy Halladay .... .30 .09
- ☐ 39 David Eckstein .... .30 .09
- ☐ 40 Jerry Hairston .... .30 .09
- ☐ 41 Barry Larkin .... .75 .23
- ☐ 42 Larry Walker .... .50 .15
- ☐ 43 Craig Biggio .... .50 .15
- ☐ 44 Edgardo Alfonzo .... .30 .09
- ☐ 45 Marlon Byrd .... .30 .09
- ☐ 46 J.T. Snow .... .30 .09
- ☐ 47 Juan Gonzalez .... .75 .23
- ☐ 48 Ramon Ortiz .... .30 .09
- ☐ 49 Jay Gibbons .... .30 .09
- ☐ 50 Adam Dunn .... .50 .15
- ☐ 51 Juan Pierre .... .30 .09
- ☐ 52 Jeff Bagwell .... .50 .15
- ☐ 53 Kevin Brown .... .30 .09
- ☐ 54 Pedro Astacio .... .30 .09
- ☐ 55 Mike Lieberthal .... .30 .09
- ☐ 56 Johnny Damon .... .30 .09
- ☐ 57 Tim Salmon .... .50 .15
- ☐ 58 Mike Bordick .... .30 .09
- ☐ 59 Ken Griffey Jr. .... 1.25 .35
- ☐ 60 Jason Jennings .... .30 .09
- ☐ 61 Lance Berkman .... .30 .09
- ☐ 62 Jeromy Burnitz .... .30 .09
- ☐ 63 Jimmy Rollins .... .30 .09
- ☐ 64 Tsuyoshi Shinjo .... .30 .09
- ☐ 65 Alex Rodriguez .... 1.50 .45
- ☐ 66 Greg Maddux .... 1.50 .45
- ☐ 67 Mark Prior .... 1.50 .45
- ☐ 68 Mike Maroth .... .30 .09
- ☐ 69 Geoff Jenkins .... .30 .09
- ☐ 70 Tony Armas Jr. .... .30 .09
- ☐ 71 Jermaine Dye .... .30 .09
- ☐ 72 Albert Pujols .... 1.50 .45
- ☐ 73 Shannon Stewart .... .30 .09
- ☐ 74 Troy Glaus .... .50 .15
- ☐ 75 Brook Fordyce .... .30 .09
- ☐ 76 Juan Encarnacion .... .30 .09
- ☐ 77 Todd Hollandsworth .... .30 .09
- ☐ 78 Roy Oswalt .... .30 .09
- ☐ 79 Paul Lo Duca .... .30 .09
- ☐ 80 Mike Piazza .... 1.25 .35
- ☐ 81 Bobby Abreu .... .30 .09
- ☐ 82 Sean Burroughs .... .30 .09
- ☐ 83 Randy Winn .... .30 .09
- ☐ 84 Curt Schilling .... .50 .15
- ☐ 85 Chris Singleton .... .30 .09
- ☐ 86 Sean Casey .... .30 .09
- ☐ 87 Todd Zeile .... .30 .09
- ☐ 88 Richard Hidalgo .... .30 .09
- ☐ 89 Roberto Alomar .... .75 .23
- ☐ 90 Tim Hudson .... .30 .09
- ☐ 91 Ryan Klesko .... .30 .09
- ☐ 92 Greg Vaughn .... .30 .09
- ☐ 93 Tony Womack .... .30 .09
- ☐ 94 Fred McGriff .... .50 .15
- ☐ 95 Tom Glavine .... .75 .23
- ☐ 96 Todd Walker .... .30 .09
- ☐ 97 Travis Fryman .... .30 .09
- ☐ 98 Shane Reynolds .... .30 .09
- ☐ 99 Shawn Green .... .30 .09
- ☐ 100 Mo Vaughn .... .30 .09
- ☐ 101 Adam Piatt .... .30 .09
- ☐ 102 Deivi Cruz .... .30 .09
- ☐ 103 Steve Cox .... .30 .09
- ☐ 104 Luis Gonzalez .... .30 .09
- ☐ 105 Russell Branyan .... .30 .09
- ☐ 106 Daryle Ward .... .30 .09
- ☐ 107 Mariano Rivera .... .50 .15
- ☐ 108 Phil Nevin .... .30 .09
- ☐ 109 Ben Grieve .... .30 .09
- ☐ 110 Moises Alou .... .30 .09
- ☐ 111 Omar Vizquel .... .30 .09
- ☐ 112 Joe Randa .... .30 .09
- ☐ 113 Jorge Posada .... .50 .15
- ☐ 114 Mark Kotsay .... .30 .09
- ☐ 115 Ryan Rupe .... .30 .09
- ☐ 116 Javy Lopez .... .30 .09
- ☐ 117 Corey Patterson .... .30 .09
- ☐ 118 Bobby Higginson .... .30 .09
- ☐ 119 Jose Vidro .... .30 .09
- ☐ 120 Barry Zito .... .75 .23
- ☐ 121 Scott Rolen .... .50 .15
- ☐ 122 Gary Sheffield .... .30 .09
- ☐ 123 Kerry Wood .... .75 .23
- ☐ 124 Brandon Inge .... .30 .09
- ☐ 125 Jose Hernandez .... .30 .09
- ☐ 126 Michael Barrett .... .30 .09
- ☐ 127 Miguel Tejada .... .30 .09
- ☐ 128 Edgar Renteria .... .30 .09
- ☐ 129 Junior Spivey .... .30 .09
- ☐ 130 Jose Valentin .... .30 .09
- ☐ 131 Derrek Lee .... .30 .09
- ☐ 132 A.J. Pierzynski .... .30 .09
- ☐ 133 Mike Mussina .... .75 .23
- ☐ 134 Bret Boone .... .30 .09
- ☐ 135 Chan Ho Park .... .30 .09
- ☐ 136 Steve Finley .... .30 .09
- ☐ 137 Mark Buehrle .... .30 .09
- ☐ 138 A.J. Burnett .... .30 .09
- ☐ 139 Ben Sheets .... .30 .09
- ☐ 140 David Ortiz .... .30 .09
- ☐ 141 Nick Johnson .... .30 .09
- ☐ 142 Randall Simon .... .30 .09
- ☐ 143 Carlos Delgado .... .30 .09
- ☐ 144 Darin Erstad .... .30 .09
- ☐ 145 Shea Hillenbrand .... .30 .09
- ☐ 146 Todd Helton .... .50 .15
- ☐ 147 Preston Wilson .... .30 .09
- ☐ 148 Eric Gagne .... .50 .15
- ☐ 149 Vladimir Guerrero .... .75 .23
- ☐ 150 Brandon Duckworth .... .30 .09
- ☐ 151 Rich Aurilia .... .30 .09
- ☐ 152 Ivan Rodriguez .... .75 .23

	Card	Mint	Nrmt
❑	153 Andruw Jones	.50	.15
❑	154 Carlos Lee	.30	.09
❑	155 Robert Fick	.30	.09
❑	156 Jacque Jones	.30	.09
❑	157 Bernie Williams	.50	.15
❑	158 John Olerud	.30	.09
❑	159 Eric Hinske	.30	.09
❑	160 Matt Clement	.30	.09
❑	161 Dmitri Young	.30	.09
❑	162 Torii Hunter	.30	.09
❑	163 Carlos Pena	.30	.09
❑	164 Mike Cameron	.30	.09
❑	165 Raul Mondesi	.30	.09
❑	166 Pedro Martinez	.75	.23
❑	167 Bob Wickman	.30	.09
❑	168 Mike Sweeney	.30	.09
❑	169 David Wells	.30	.09
❑	170 Jason Kendall	.30	.09
❑	171 Tino Martinez	.50	.15
❑	172 Matt Williams	.50	.15
❑	173 Frank Thomas	.75	.23
❑	174 Cliff Floyd	.30	.09
❑	175 Corey Koskie	.30	.09
❑	176 Orlando Hernandez	.30	.09
❑	177 Edgar Martinez	.50	.15
❑	178 Richie Sexson	.30	.09
❑	179 Manny Ramirez	.30	.09
❑	180 Jim Thome	.75	.23
❑	181 Andy Pettitte	.50	.15
❑	182 Aramis Ramirez	.30	.09
❑	183 J.D. Drew	.30	.09
❑	184 Brian Jordan	.30	.09
❑	185 Sammy Sosa	1.25	.35
❑	186 Jeff Weaver	.30	.09
❑	187 Jeffrey Hammonds	.30	.09
❑	188 Eric Milton	.30	.09
❑	189 Eric Chavez	.30	.09
❑	190 Kazuhiro Sasaki	.30	.09
❑	191 Jose Cruz Jr.	.30	.09
❑	192 Derek Lowe	.30	.09
❑	193 C.C. Sabathia	.30	.09
❑	194 Adrian Beltre	.30	.09
❑	195 Alfonso Soriano	.75	.23
❑	196 Jack Wilson	.30	.09
❑	197 Fernando Vina	.30	.09
❑	198 Chipper Jones	.75	.23
❑	199 Paul Konerko	.30	.09
❑	200 Rusty Greer	.30	.09
❑	201 Jason Giambi AS	1.50	.45
❑	202 Alfonso Soriano AS	1.50	.45
❑	203 Shea Hillenbrand AS	1.50	.45
❑	204 Alex Rodriguez AS	3.00	.90
❑	205 Jorge Posada AS	1.50	.45
❑	206 Ichiro Suzuki AS	3.00	.90
❑	207 Manny Ramirez AS	1.50	.45
❑	208 Torii Hunter AS	1.50	.45
❑	209 Todd Helton AS	1.50	.45
❑	210 Jose Vidro AS	1.50	.45
❑	211 Scott Rolen AS	1.50	.45
❑	212 Jimmy Rollins AS	1.50	.45
❑	213 Mike Piazza AS	2.50	.75
❑	214 Barry Bonds AS	4.00	1.20
❑	215 Sammy Sosa AS	2.50	.75
❑	216 Vladimir Guerrero AS	1.50	.45
❑	217 Lance Berkman AS	1.50	.45
❑	218 Derek Jeter AS	4.00	1.20
❑	219 Nomar Garciaparra AS	3.00	.90
❑	220 Luis Gonzalez AS	1.50	.45
❑	221 Kazuhisa Ishii 02R	2.00	.60
❑	222 Satoru Komiyama 02R	2.00	.60
❑	223 So Taguchi 02R	2.00	.60
❑	224 Jorge Padilla 02R	2.00	.60
❑	225 Ben Howard 02R	2.00	.60
❑	226 Jason Simontacchi 02R	2.00	.60
❑	227 Barry Wesson 02R	2.00	.60
❑	228 Howie Clark 02R	2.00	.60
❑	229 Aaron Guiel 02R	2.00	.60
❑	230 Oliver Perez 02R	2.00	.60
❑	231 David Ross 02R	2.00	.60
❑	232 Julius Matos 02R	2.00	.60
❑	233 Chris Snelling 02R	2.00	.60
❑	234 Rodrigo Lopez 02R	2.00	.60
❑	235 Will Nieves 02R	2.00	.60
❑	236 Joe Borchard 02R	2.00	.60
❑	237 Aaron Cook 02R	2.00	.60
❑	238 Anderson Machado 02R	2.00	.60
❑	239 Corey Thurman 02R	2.00	.60
❑	240 Tyler Yates 02R	2.00	.60
❑	241 Coco Crisp 03R	2.00	.60
❑	242 Andy Van Hekken 03R	2.00	.60
❑	243 Jim Rushford 03R	2.00	.60
❑	244 Jeriome Robertson 03R	2.00	.60
❑	245 Shane Nance 03R	2.00	.60
❑	246 Kevin Cash 03R	2.00	.60
❑	247 Kirk Saarloos 03R	2.00	.60
❑	248 Josh Bard 03R	2.00	.60
❑	249 Dave Pember 03R RC	2.00	.60
❑	250 Freddy Sanchez 03R	2.00	.60
❑	251 Chien-Ming Wang RC		
❑	252 Rickie Weeks RC		
❑	253 Brandon Webb RC		
❑	254 Hideki Matsui RC		
❑	255 Michael Hessman RC		
❑	256 Ryan Wagner RC		
❑	257 Matt Kata RC		
❑	258 Edwin Jackson RC		
❑	259 Jose Contreras RC		
❑	260 Delmon Young RC		
❑	261 Bo Hart RC		
❑	262 Jeff Duncan RC		
❑	263 Robby Hammock RC		
❑	264 Jeremy Bonderman RC		
❑	265 Clint Barmes RC		

2004 Ultra

	MINT	NRMT
COMPLETE SET (220)	60.00	27.00
COMP.SET w/o SP's (200)	25.00	11.00
COMMON CARD (1-200)	.30	.14
COMMON CARD (201-220)	2.00	.90
201-220 RANDOM INSERTS IN PACKS		

	Card	Mint	Nrmt
❑	1 Magglio Ordonez	.30	.14
❑	2 Bobby Abreu	.30	.14
❑	3 Eric Munson	.30	.14
❑	4 Eric Byrnes	.30	.14
❑	5 Bartolo Colon	.30	.14
❑	6 Juan Encarnacion	.30	.14
❑	7 Jody Gerut	.30	.14
❑	8 Eddie Guardado	.30	.14
❑	9 Shea Hillenbrand	.30	.14
❑	10 Andruw Jones	.50	.23
❑	11 Carlos Lee	.30	.14
❑	12 Pedro Martinez	.75	.35
❑	13 Barry Larkin	.75	.35
❑	14 Angel Berroa	.30	.14
❑	15 Edgar Martinez	.50	.23
❑	16 Sidney Ponson	.30	.14
❑	17 Mariano Rivera	.50	.23
❑	18 Richie Sexson	.30	.14
❑	19 Frank Thomas	.75	.35
❑	20 Jerome Williams	.30	.14
❑	21 Barry Zito	.75	.35
❑	22 Roberto Alomar	.75	.35
❑	23 Rocky Biddle	.30	.14
❑	24 Orlando Cabrera	.30	.14
❑	25 Placido Polanco	.30	.14
❑	26 Morgan Ensberg	.30	.14
❑	27 Jason Giambi	.75	.35
❑	28 Jim Thome	.75	.35
❑	29 Vladimir Guerrero	.75	.35
❑	30 Tim Hudson	.30	.14
❑	31 Jacque Jones	.30	.14
❑	32 Derrek Lee	.30	.14
❑	33 Rafael Palmeiro	.50	.23
❑	34 Mike Mussina	.75	.35
❑	35 Corey Patterson	.30	.14
❑	36 Mike Cameron	.30	.14
❑	37 Ivan Rodriguez	.75	.35
❑	38 Ben Sheets	.30	.14
❑	39 Woody Williams	.30	.14
❑	40 Ichiro Suzuki	1.50	.70
❑	41 Moises Alou	.30	.14
❑	42 Craig Biggio	.50	.23
❑	43 Jorge Posada	.50	.23
❑	44 Craig Monroe	.30	.14
❑	45 Darin Erstad	.30	.14
❑	46 Jay Gibbons	.30	.14
❑	47 Aaron Guiel	.30	.14
❑	48 Travis Lee	.30	.14
❑	49 Jorge Julio	.30	.14
❑	50 Torii Hunter	.30	.14
❑	51 Luis Matos	.30	.14
❑	52 Brett Myers	.30	.14
❑	53 Sean Casey	.30	.14
❑	54 Mark Prior	1.50	.70
❑	55 Alex Rodriguez	1.50	.70
❑	56 Gary Sheffield	.30	.14
❑	57 Jason Varitek	.30	.14
❑	58 Dontrelle Willis	.75	.35
❑	59 Garret Anderson	.30	.14
❑	60 Casey Blake	.30	.14
❑	61 Jay Payton	.30	.14
❑	62 Carl Crawford	.30	.14
❑	63 Carl Everett	.30	.14
❑	64 Marcus Giles	.30	.14
❑	65 Jose Guillen	.30	.14
❑	66 Eric Karros	.30	.14
❑	67 Mike Lieberthal	.30	.14
❑	68 Hideki Matsui	1.50	.70
❑	69 Xavier Nady	.30	.14
❑	70 Hank Blalock	.50	.23
❑	71 Albert Pujols	1.50	.70
❑	72 Jose Cruz Jr.	.30	.14
❑	73 Randall Simon	.30	.14
❑	74 Javier Vazquez	.30	.14
❑	75 Preston Wilson	.30	.14
❑	76 Danys Baez	.30	.14
❑	77 Alex Cintron	.30	.14
❑	78 Jake Peavy	.30	.14
❑	79 Scott Rolen	.50	.23
❑	80 Robert Fick	.30	.14
❑	81 Brian Giles	.30	.14
❑	82 Roy Halladay	.30	.14
❑	83 Kazuhisa Ishii	.30	.14
❑	84 Austin Kearns	.50	.23
❑	85 Paul Lo Duca	.30	.14
❑	86 Darrell May	.30	.14
❑	87 Phil Nevin	.30	.14
❑	88 Carlos Pena	.30	.14
❑	89 Manny Ramirez	.30	.14
❑	90 C.C. Sabathia	.30	.14
❑	91 John Smoltz	.50	.23
❑	92 Jose Vidro	.30	.14
❑	93 Randy Wolf	.30	.14
❑	94 Jeff Bagwell	.50	.23
❑	95 Barry Bonds	2.00	.90
❑	96 Frank Catalanotto	.30	.14
❑	97 Zach Day	.30	.14
❑	98 David Ortiz	.30	.14
❑	99 Troy Glaus	.50	.23
❑	100 Bo Hart	.30	.14
❑	101 Geoff Jenkins	.30	.14
❑	102 Jason Kendall	.30	.14
❑	103 Esteban Loaiza	.30	.14
❑	104 Doug Mientkiewicz	.30	.14
❑	105 Trot Nixon	.30	.14
❑	106 Troy Percival	.30	.14
❑	107 Aramis Ramirez	.30	.14
❑	108 Alex Sanchez	.30	.14
❑	109 Alfonso Soriano	.75	.35
❑	110 Omar Vizquel	.30	.14
❑	111 Kerry Wood	.75	.35
❑	112 Rocco Baldelli	1.25	.55
❑	113 Bret Boone	.30	.14
❑	114 Shawn Chacon	.30	.14
❑	115 Carlos Delgado	.30	.14
❑	116 Shawn Green	.30	.14
❑	117 Tim Worrell	.30	.14

Card	Nm-Mt	Ex-Mt
❑ 118 Tom Glavine	.75	.35
❑ 119 Shigetoshi Hasegawa	.30	.14
❑ 120 Derek Jeter	2.00	.90
❑ 121 Jeff Kent	.30	.14
❑ 122 Braden Looper	.30	.14
❑ 123 Kevin Millwood	.30	.14
❑ 124 Hideo Nomo	.75	.35
❑ 125 Jason Phillips	.30	.14
❑ 126 Tim Redding	.30	.14
❑ 127 Reggie Sanders	.30	.14
❑ 128 Sammy Sosa	1.25	.55
❑ 129 Billy Wagner	.30	.14
❑ 130 Miguel Batista	.30	.14
❑ 131 Milton Bradley	.30	.14
❑ 132 Eric Chavez	.30	.14
❑ 133 J.D. Drew	.30	.14
❑ 134 Keith Foulke	.30	.14
❑ 135 Luis Gonzalez	.30	.14
❑ 136 LaTroy Hawkins	.30	.14
❑ 137 Randy Johnson	.75	.35
❑ 138 Byung-Hyun Kim	.30	.14
❑ 139 Javy Lopez	.30	.14
❑ 140 Melvin Mora	.30	.14
❑ 141 Aubrey Huff	.30	.14
❑ 142 Mike Piazza	1.25	.55
❑ 143 Mark Redman	.30	.14
❑ 144 Kazuhiro Sasaki	.30	.14
❑ 145 Shannon Stewart	.30	.14
❑ 146 Larry Walker	.50	.23
❑ 147 Dmitri Young	.30	.14
❑ 148 Josh Beckett	.50	.23
❑ 149 Jae Weong Seo	.30	.14
❑ 150 Hee Seop Choi	.30	.14
❑ 151 Adam Dunn	.50	.23
❑ 152 Rafael Furcal	.30	.14
❑ 153 Juan Gonzalez	.75	.35
❑ 154 Todd Helton	.50	.23
❑ 155 Carlos Zambrano	.30	.14
❑ 156 Ryan Klesko	.30	.14
❑ 157 Mike Lowell	.30	.14
❑ 158 Jamie Moyer	.30	.14
❑ 159 Russ Ortiz	.30	.14
❑ 160 Juan Pierre	.30	.14
❑ 161 Edgar Renteria	.30	.14
❑ 162 Curt Schilling	.50	.23
❑ 163 Mike Sweeney	.30	.14
❑ 164 Brandon Webb	.30	.14
❑ 165 Michael Young	.30	.14
❑ 166 Carlos Beltran	.30	.14
❑ 167 Sean Burroughs	.30	.14
❑ 168 Luis Castillo	.30	.14
❑ 169 David Eckstein	.30	.14
❑ 170 Eric Gagne	.50	.23
❑ 171 Chipper Jones	.75	.35
❑ 172 Livan Hernandez	.30	.14
❑ 173 Nick Johnson	.30	.14
❑ 174 Corey Koskie	.30	.14
❑ 175 Jason Schmidt	.30	.14
❑ 176 Bill Mueller	.30	.14
❑ 177 Steve Finley	.30	.14
❑ 178 A.J. Pierzynski	.30	.14
❑ 179 Rene Reyes	.30	.14
❑ 180 Jason Johnson	.30	.14
❑ 181 Mark Teixeira	.50	.23
❑ 182 Kip Wells	.30	.14
❑ 183 Mike MacDougal	.30	.14
❑ 184 Lance Berkman	.30	.14
❑ 185 Victor Zambrano	.30	.14
❑ 186 Roger Clemens	1.50	.70
❑ 187 Jim Edmonds	.30	.14
❑ 188 Nomar Garciaparra	1.50	.70
❑ 189 Ken Griffey Jr.	1.25	.55
❑ 190 Richard Hidalgo	.30	.14
❑ 191 Cliff Floyd	.30	.14
❑ 192 Greg Maddux	1.50	.70
❑ 193 Mark Mulder	.30	.14
❑ 194 Roy Oswalt	.30	.14
❑ 195 Marlon Byrd	.30	.14
❑ 196 Jose Reyes	.50	.23
❑ 197 Kevin Brown	.30	.14
❑ 198 Miguel Tejada	.30	.14
❑ 199 Vernon Wells	.30	.14
❑ 200 Joel Pineiro	.30	.14
❑ 201 Rickie Weeks AR	4.00	1.80
❑ 202 Chad Gaudin AR	2.00	.90
❑ 203 Ryan Wagner AR	2.00	.90
❑ 204 Chris Bootcheck AR	2.00	.90
❑ 205 Koyie Hill AR	2.00	.90
❑ 206 Jeff Duncan AR	2.00	.90
❑ 207 Rich Harden AR	3.00	1.35
❑ 208 Edwin Jackson AR	3.00	1.35
❑ 209 Robby Hammock AR	2.00	.90
❑ 210 Khalil Greene AR	2.00	.90
❑ 211 Chien-Ming Wang AR	2.00	.90
❑ 212 Prentice Redman AR	2.00	.90
❑ 213 Todd Wellemeyer AR	2.00	.90
❑ 214 Clint Barmes AR	2.00	.90
❑ 215 Matt Kata AR	2.00	.90
❑ 216 Jon Leicester AR	2.00	.90
❑ 217 Jeremy Guthrie AR	2.00	.90
❑ 218 Chin-Hui Tsao AR	2.00	.90
❑ 219 Dan Haren AR	2.00	.90
❑ 220 Delmon Young AR	6.00	2.70

1989 Upper Deck

	Nm-Mt	Ex-Mt
COMPLETE SET (800)	80.00	32.00
COMP.FACT.SET (800)	100.00	40.00
COMPLETE LO SET (700)	.00	.00
COMPLETE HI SET (100)	.00	.00
COMP.HI FACT.SET (100)	10.00	4.00

Card	Nm-Mt	Ex-Mt
❑ 1 Ken Griffey Jr. RC	50.00	20.00
❑ 2 Luis Medina RC	.25	.10
❑ 3 Tony Chance RC	.25	.10
❑ 4 Dave Otto	.20	.08
❑ 5 S.Alomar Jr. RC UER Born 6/16/66, should be 6/18/66	1.00	.40
❑ 6 Rolando Roomes RC	.25	.10
❑ 7 Dave West RC	.25	.10
❑ 8 Cris Carpenter RC	.25	.10
❑ 9 Gregg Jefferies	.30	.12
❑ 10 Doug Dascenzo RC	.25	.10
❑ 11 Ron Jones RC	.25	.10
❑ 12 Luis DeLosSantos RC	.25	.10
❑ 13 Gary Sheffield COR RC	5.00	2.00
❑ 13A G.Sheffield ERR RC SS upside down on card front	5.00	2.00
❑ 14 Mike Harkey RC	.25	.10
❑ 15 Lance Blankenship RC	.25	.10
❑ 16 William Brennan RC	.25	.10
❑ 17 John Smoltz RC	4.00	1.60
❑ 18 Ramon Martinez RC	1.00	.40
❑ 19 Mark Lemke RC	.50	.20
❑ 20 Juan Bell RC	.25	.10
❑ 21 Rey Palacios RC	.25	.10
❑ 22 Felix Jose RC	.25	.10
❑ 23 Van Snider RC	.25	.10
❑ 24 Dante Bichette RC	1.00	.40
❑ 25 Randy Johnson RC	15.00	6.00
❑ 26 Carlos Quintana RC	.25	.10
❑ 27 Star Rookie CL	.20	.08
❑ 28 Mike Schooler	.20	.08
❑ 29 Randy St.Claire	.20	.08
❑ 30 Jerald Clark RC	.25	.10
❑ 31 Kevin Gross	.20	.08
❑ 32 Dan Firova	.20	.08
❑ 33 Jeff Calhoun	.20	.08
❑ 34 Tommy Hinzo	.20	.08
❑ 35 Ricky Jordan RC	.50	.20
❑ 36 Larry Parrish	.20	.08
❑ 37 Bret Saberhagen UER Hit total 931, should be 1031	.30	.12
❑ 38 Mike Smithson	.20	.08
❑ 39 Dave Dravecky	.30	.12
❑ 40 Ed Romero	.20	.08
❑ 41 Jeff Musselman	.20	.08
❑ 42 Ed Hearn	.20	.08
❑ 43 Rance Mulliniks	.20	.08
❑ 44 Jim Eisenreich	.20	.08
❑ 45 Sil Campusano	.20	.08
❑ 46 Mike Krukow	.20	.08
❑ 47 Paul Gibson	.20	.08
❑ 48 Mike LaCoss	.20	.08
❑ 49 Larry Herndon	.20	.08
❑ 50 Scott Garrelts	.20	.08
❑ 51 Dwayne Henry	.20	.08
❑ 52 Jim Acker	.20	.08
❑ 53 Steve Sax	.20	.08
❑ 54 Pete O'Brien	.20	.08
❑ 55 Paul Runge	.20	.08
❑ 56 Rick Rhoden	.20	.08
❑ 57 John Dopson	.20	.08
❑ 58 Casey Candaele UER (No stats for Astros for '88 season)	.20	.08
❑ 59 Dave Righetti	.20	.08
❑ 60 Joe Hesketh	.20	.08
❑ 61 Frank DiPino	.20	.08
❑ 62 Tim Laudner	.20	.08
❑ 63 Jamie Moyer	.30	.12
❑ 64 Fred Toliver	.20	.08
❑ 65 Mitch Webster	.20	.08
❑ 66 John Tudor	.20	.08
❑ 67 John Cangelosi	.20	.08
❑ 68 Mike Devereaux	.20	.08
❑ 69 Brian Fisher	.20	.08
❑ 70 Mike Marshall	.20	.08
❑ 71 Zane Smith	.20	.08
❑ 72A Brian Holton ERR (Photo actually Shawn Hillegas)	.75	.30
❑ 72B Brian Holton COR	.30	.12
❑ 73 Jose Guzman	.20	.08
❑ 74 Rick Mahler	.20	.08
❑ 75 John Shelby	.20	.08
❑ 76 Jim Deshaies	.20	.08
❑ 77 Bobby Meacham	.20	.08
❑ 78 Bryn Smith	.20	.08
❑ 79 Joaquin Andujar	.20	.08
❑ 80 Richard Dotson	.20	.08
❑ 81 Charlie Lea	.20	.08
❑ 82 Calvin Schiraldi	.20	.08
❑ 83 Les Straker	.20	.08
❑ 84 Les Lancaster	.20	.08
❑ 85 Allan Anderson	.20	.08
❑ 86 Junior Ortiz	.20	.08
❑ 87 Jesse Orosco	.20	.08
❑ 88 Felix Fermin	.20	.08
❑ 89 Dave Anderson	.20	.08
❑ 90 Rafael Belliard UER (Born '61, not '51)	.20	.08
❑ 91 Franklin Stubbs	.20	.08
❑ 92 Cecil Espy	.20	.08
❑ 93 Albert Hall	.20	.08
❑ 94 Tim Leary	.20	.08
❑ 95 Mitch Williams	.20	.08
❑ 96 Tracy Jones	.20	.08
❑ 97 Danny Darwin	.20	.08
❑ 98 Gary Ward	.20	.08
❑ 99 Neal Heaton	.20	.08
❑ 100 Jim Pankovits	.20	.08
❑ 101 Bill Doran	.20	.08
❑ 102 Tim Wallach	.20	.08
❑ 103 Joe Magrane	.20	.08
❑ 104 Ozzie Virgil	.20	.08
❑ 105 Alvin Davis	.20	.08
❑ 106 Tom Brookens	.20	.08
❑ 107 Shawon Dunston	.20	.08
❑ 108 Tracy Woodson	.20	.08
❑ 109 Nelson Liriano	.20	.08
❑ 110 Devon White UER (Doubles total 46, should be 56)	.30	.12
❑ 111 Steve Balboni	.20	.08
❑ 112 Buddy Bell	.30	.12

	No.	Player	Price	Price
❑	113	German Jimenez	.20	.08
❑	114	Ken Dayley	.20	.08
❑	115	Andres Galarraga	.30	.12
❑	116	Mike Scioscia	.20	.08
❑	117	Gary Pettis	.20	.08
❑	118	Ernie Whitt	.20	.08
❑	119	Bob Boone	.30	.12
❑	120	Ryne Sandberg	1.50	.60
❑	121	Bruce Benedict	.20	.08
❑	122	Hubie Brooks	.20	.08
❑	123	Mike Moore	.20	.08
❑	124	Wallace Johnson	.20	.08
❑	125	Bob Horner	.20	.08
❑	126	Chili Davis	.30	.12
❑	127	Manny Trillo	.20	.08
❑	128	Chet Lemon	.20	.08
❑	129	John Cerutti	.20	.08
❑	130	Orel Hershiser	.30	.12
❑	131	Terry Pendleton	.20	.08
❑	132	Jeff Blauser	.30	.12
❑	133	Mike Fitzgerald	.20	.08
❑	134	Henry Cotto	.20	.08
❑	135	Gerald Young	.20	.08
❑	136	Luis Salazar	.20	.08
❑	137	Alejandro Pena	.20	.08
❑	138	Jack Howell	.20	.08
❑	139	Tony Fernandez	.20	.08
❑	140	Mark Grace	.75	.30
❑	141	Ken Caminiti	.30	.12
❑	142	Mike Jackson	.20	.08
❑	143	Larry McWilliams	.20	.08
❑	144	Andres Thomas	.20	.08
❑	145	Nolan Ryan 3X	4.00	1.60
❑	146	Mike Davis	.20	.08
❑	147	DeWayne Buice	.20	.08
❑	148	Jody Davis	.20	.08
❑	149	Jesse Barfield	.20	.08
❑	150	Matt Nokes	.20	.08
❑	151	Jerry Reuss	.20	.08
❑	152	Rick Cerone	.20	.08
❑	153	Storm Davis	.20	.08
❑	154	Marvell Wynne	.20	.08
❑	155	Will Clark	.75	.30
❑	156	Luis Aguayo	.20	.08
❑	157	Willie Upshaw	.20	.08
❑	158	Randy Bush	.20	.08
❑	159	Ron Darling	.20	.08
❑	160	Kal Daniels	.20	.08
❑	161	Spike Owen	.20	.08
❑	162	Luis Polonia	.20	.08
❑	163	Kevin Mitchell UER ('88/total HR's 18/52, should be 19/53)	.30	.12
❑	164	Dave Gallagher	.20	.08
❑	165	Benito Santiago	.30	.12
❑	166	Greg Gagne	.20	.08
❑	167	Ken Phelps	.20	.08
❑	168	Sid Fernandez	.20	.08
❑	169	Bo Diaz	.20	.08
❑	170	Cory Snyder	.20	.08
❑	171	Eric Show	.20	.08
❑	172	Robby Thompson	.20	.08
❑	173	Marty Barrett	.20	.08
❑	174	Dave Henderson	.20	.08
❑	175	Ozzie Guillen	.20	.08
❑	176	Barry Lyons	.20	.08
❑	177	Kelvin Torve	.20	.08
❑	178	Don Slaught	.20	.08
❑	179	Steve Lombardozzi	.20	.08
❑	180	Chris Sabo RC	1.00	.40
❑	181	Jose Uribe	.20	.08
❑	182	Shane Mack	.20	.08
❑	183	Ron Karkovice	.20	.08
❑	184	Todd Benzinger	.20	.08
❑	185	Dave Stewart	.30	.12
❑	186	Julio Franco	.20	.08
❑	187	Ron Robinson	.20	.08
❑	188	Wally Backman	.20	.08
❑	189	Randy Velarde	.20	.08
❑	190	Joe Carter	.50	.20
❑	191	Bob Welch	.20	.08
❑	192	Kelly Paris	.20	.08
❑	193	Chris Brown	.20	.08
❑	194	Rick Reuschel	.20	.08
❑	195	Roger Clemens	2.00	.80
❑	196	Dave Concepcion	.30	.12
❑	197	Al Newman	.20	.08
❑	198	Brook Jacoby	.20	.08
❑	199	Mookie Wilson	.30	.12
❑	200	Don Mattingly	2.50	1.00
❑	201	Dick Schofield	.20	.08
❑	202	Mark Gubicza	.20	.08
❑	203	Gary Gaetti	.30	.12
❑	204	Dan Pasqua	.20	.08
❑	205	Andre Dawson	.30	.12
❑	206	Chris Speier	.20	.08
❑	207	Kent Tekulve	.20	.08
❑	208	Rod Scurry	.20	.08
❑	209	Scott Bailes	.20	.08
❑	210	R.Henderson UER Throws Right	1.50	.60
❑	211	Harold Baines	.30	.12
❑	212	Tony Armas	.20	.08
❑	213	Kent Hrbek	.30	.12
❑	214	Darrin Jackson	.20	.08
❑	215	George Brett	2.50	1.00
❑	216	Rafael Santana	.20	.08
❑	217	Andy Allanson	.20	.08
❑	218	Brett Butler	.30	.12
❑	219	Steve Jeltz	.20	.08
❑	220	Jay Buhner	.30	.12
❑	221	Bo Jackson	.75	.30
❑	222	Angel Salazar	.20	.08
❑	223	Kirk McCaskill	.20	.08
❑	224	Steve Lyons	.20	.08
❑	225	Bert Blyleven	.30	.12
❑	226	Scott Bradley	.20	.08
❑	227	Bob Melvin	.20	.08
❑	228	Ron Kittle	.20	.08
❑	229	Phil Bradley	.20	.08
❑	230	Tommy John	.30	.12
❑	231	Greg Walker	.20	.08
❑	232	Juan Berenguer	.20	.08
❑	233	Pat Tabler	.20	.08
❑	234	Terry Clark	.20	.08
❑	235	Rafael Palmeiro	.50	.20
❑	236	Paul Zuvella	.20	.08
❑	237	Willie Randolph	.30	.12
❑	238	Bruce Fields	.20	.08
❑	239	Mike Aldrete	.20	.08
❑	240	Lance Parrish	.20	.08
❑	241	Greg Maddux	3.00	1.20
❑	242	John Moses	.20	.08
❑	243	Melido Perez	.20	.08
❑	244	Willie Wilson	.20	.08
❑	245	Mark McLemore	.20	.08
❑	246	Von Hayes	.20	.08
❑	247	Matt Williams	.75	.30
❑	248	John Candelaria UER Listed as Yankee for part of '87, should be Mets	.20	.08
❑	249	Harold Reynolds	.30	.12
❑	250	Greg Swindell	.20	.08
❑	251	Juan Agosto	.20	.08
❑	252	Mike Felder	.20	.08
❑	253	Vince Coleman	.20	.08
❑	254	Larry Sheets	.20	.08
❑	255	George Bell	.20	.08
❑	256	Terry Steinbach	.30	.12
❑	257	Jack Armstrong RC	.50	.20
❑	258	Dickie Thon	.20	.08
❑	259	Ray Knight	.20	.08
❑	260	Darryl Strawberry	.50	.20
❑	261	Doug Sisk	.20	.08
❑	262	Alex Trevino	.20	.08
❑	263	Jeffrey Leonard	.20	.08
❑	264	Tom Henke	.20	.08
❑	265	Ozzie Smith	.75	.30
❑	266	Dave Bergman	.20	.08
❑	267	Tony Phillips	.20	.08
❑	268	Mark Davis	.20	.08
❑	269	Kevin Elster	.20	.08
❑	270	Barry Larkin	.75	.30
❑	271	Manny Lee	.20	.08
❑	272	Tom Brunansky	.20	.08
❑	273	Craig Biggio RC	3.00	1.20
❑	274	Jim Gantner	.20	.08
❑	275	Eddie Murray	.75	.30
❑	276	Jeff Reed	.20	.08
❑	277	Tim Teufel	.20	.08
❑	278	Rick Honeycutt	.20	.08
❑	279	Guillermo Hernandez	.20	.08
❑	280	John Kruk	.30	.12
❑	281	Luis Alicea RC	.50	.20
❑	282	Jim Clancy	.20	.08
❑	283	Billy Ripken	.20	.08
❑	284	Craig Reynolds	.20	.08
❑	285	Robin Yount	.75	.30
❑	286	Jimmy Jones	.20	.08
❑	287	Ron Oester	.20	.08
❑	288	Terry Leach	.20	.08
❑	289	Dennis Eckersley	.30	.12
❑	290	Alan Trammell	.50	.20
❑	291	Jimmy Key	.30	.12
❑	292	Chris Bosio	.20	.08
❑	293	Jose DeLeon	.20	.08
❑	294	Jim Traber	.20	.08
❑	295	Mike Scott	.20	.08
❑	296	Roger McDowell	.20	.08
❑	297	Garry Templeton	.20	.08
❑	298	Doyle Alexander	.20	.08
❑	299	Nick Esasky	.20	.08
❑	300	Mark McGwire UER (Doubles total 52, should be 51)	5.00	2.00
❑	301	Darryl Hamilton RC	.50	.20
❑	302	Dave Smith	.20	.08
❑	303	Rick Sutcliffe	.30	.12
❑	304	Dave Stapleton	.20	.08
❑	305	Alan Ashby	.20	.08
❑	306	Pedro Guerrero	.20	.08
❑	307	Ron Guidry	.30	.12
❑	308	Steve Farr	.20	.08
❑	309	Curt Ford	.20	.08
❑	310	Claudell Washington	.20	.08
❑	311	Tom Prince	.20	.08
❑	312	Chad Kreuter RC	.50	.20
❑	313	Ken Oberkfell	.20	.08
❑	314	Jerry Browne	.20	.08
❑	315	R.J. Reynolds	.20	.08
❑	316	Scott Bankhead	.20	.08
❑	317	Milt Thompson	.20	.08
❑	318	Mario Diaz	.20	.08
❑	319	Bruce Ruffin	.20	.08
❑	320	Dave Valle	.20	.08
❑	321A	Gary Varsho ERR (Back photo actually Mike Bielecki bunting)	2.00	.80
❑	321B	Gary Varsho COR (In road uniform)	.20	.08
❑	322	Paul Mirabella	.20	.08
❑	323	Chuck Jackson	.20	.08
❑	324	Drew Hall	.20	.08
❑	325	Don August	.20	.08
❑	326	Israel Sanchez	.20	.08
❑	327	Denny Walling	.20	.08
❑	328	Joel Skinner	.20	.08
❑	329	Danny Tartabull	.20	.08
❑	330	Tony Pena	.20	.08
❑	331	Jim Sundberg	.20	.08
❑	332	Jeff D. Robinson	.20	.08
❑	333	Oddibe McDowell	.20	.08
❑	334	Jose Lind	.20	.08
❑	335	Paul Kilgus	.20	.08
❑	336	Juan Samuel	.20	.08
❑	337	Mike Campbell	.20	.08
❑	338	Mike Maddux	.20	.08
❑	339	Darnell Coles	.20	.08
❑	340	Bob Dernier	.20	.08
❑	341	Rafael Ramirez	.20	.08
❑	342	Scott Sanderson	.20	.08
❑	343	B.J. Surhoff	.30	.12
❑	344	Billy Hatcher	.20	.08
❑	345	Pat Perry	.20	.08
❑	346	Jack Clark	.20	.08
❑	347	Gary Thurman	.20	.08
❑	348	Tim Jones	.20	.08
❑	349	Dave Winfield	.50	.20
❑	350	Frank White	.30	.12
❑	351	Dave Collins	.20	.08
❑	352	Jack Morris	.30	.12
❑	353	Eric Plunk	.20	.08
❑	354	Leon Durham	.20	.08
❑	355	Ivan DeJesus	.20	.08
❑	356	Brian Holman RC	.25	.10
❑	357A	Dale Murphy ERR (Front has	30.00	12.00

Card	Player	Price 1	Price 2
	reverse negative)		
357B	Dale Murphy COR	.50	.20
358	Mark Portugal	.20	.08
359	Andy McGaffigan	.20	.08
360	Tom Glavine	1.00	.40
361	Keith Moreland	.20	.08
362	Todd Stottlemyre	.50	.20
363	Dave Leiper	.20	.08
364	Cecil Fielder	.30	.12
365	Carmelo Martinez	.20	.08
366	Dwight Evans	.30	.12
367	Kevin McReynolds	.20	.08
368	Rich Gedman	.20	.08
369	Len Dykstra	.30	.12
370	Jody Reed	.20	.08
371	Jose Canseco UER (Strikeout total 391, should be 491)	.75	.30
372	Rob Murphy	.20	.08
373	Mike Henneman	.20	.08
374	Walt Weiss	.20	.08
375	Rob Dibble RC	1.50	.60
376	Kirby Puckett (Mark McGwire in background)	.75	.30
377	Dennis Martinez	.30	.12
378	Ron Gant	.30	.12
379	Brian Harper	.20	.08
380	Nelson Santovenia	.20	.08
381	Lloyd Moseby	.20	.08
382	Lance McCullers	.20	.08
383	Dave Stieb	.20	.08
384	Tony Gwynn	1.25	.50
385	Mike Flanagan	.20	.08
386	Bob Ojeda	.20	.08
387	Bruce Hurst	.20	.08
388	Dave Magadan	.20	.08
389	Wade Boggs	.50	.20
390	Gary Carter	.50	.20
391	Frank Tanana	.20	.08
392	Curt Young	.20	.08
393	Jeff Treadway	.20	.08
394	Darrell Evans	.30	.12
395	Glenn Hubbard	.20	.08
396	Chuck Cary	.20	.08
397	Frank Viola	.20	.08
398	Jeff Parrett	.20	.08
399	Terry Blocker	.20	.08
400	Dan Gladden	.20	.08
401	Louie Meadows	.20	.08
402	Tim Raines	.30	.12
403	Joey Meyer	.20	.08
404	Larry Andersen	.20	.08
405	Rex Hudler	.20	.08
406	Mike Schmidt	2.00	.80
407	John Franco	.30	.12
408	Brady Anderson RC	1.50	.60
409	Don Carman	.20	.08
410	Eric Davis	.30	.12
411	Bob Stanley	.20	.08
412	Pete Smith	.20	.08
413	Jim Rice	.30	.12
414	Bruce Sutter	.20	.08
415	Oil Can Boyd	.20	.08
416	Ruben Sierra	.20	.08
417	Mike LaValliere	.20	.08
418	Steve Buechele	.20	.08
419	Gary Redus	.20	.08
420	Scott Fletcher	.20	.08
421	Dale Sveum	.20	.08
422	Bob Knepper	.20	.08
423	Luis Rivera	.20	.08
424	Ted Higuera	.20	.08
425	Kevin Bass	.20	.08
426	Ken Gerhart	.20	.08
427	Shane Rawley	.20	.08
428	Paul O'Neill	.50	.20
429	Joe Orsulak	.20	.08
430	Jackie Gutierrez	.20	.08
431	Gerald Perry	.20	.08
432	Mike Greenwell	.20	.08
433	Jerry Royster	.20	.08
434	Ellis Burks	.50	.20
435	Ed Olwine	.20	.08
436	Dave Rucker	.20	.08
437	Charlie Hough	.30	.12
438	Bob Walk	.20	.08
439	Bob Brower	.20	.08
440	Barry Bonds	5.00	2.00
441	Tom Foley	.20	.08
442	Rob Deer	.20	.08
443	Glenn Davis	.20	.08
444	Dave Martinez	.20	.08
445	Bill Wegman	.20	.08
446	Lloyd McClendon	.20	.08
447	Dave Schmidt	.20	.08
448	Darren Daulton	.30	.12
449	Frank Williams	.20	.08
450	Don Aase	.20	.08
451	Lou Whitaker	.30	.12
452	Rich Gossage	.30	.12
453	Ed Whitson	.20	.08
454	Jim Walewander	.20	.08
455	Damon Berryhill	.20	.08
456	Tim Burke	.20	.08
457	Barry Jones	.20	.08
458	Joel Youngblood	.20	.08
459	Floyd Youmans	.20	.08
460	Mark Salas	.20	.08
461	Jeff Russell	.20	.08
462	Darrell Miller	.20	.08
463	Jeff Kunkel	.20	.08
464	Sherman Corbett	.20	.08
465	Curtis Wilkerson	.20	.08
466	Bud Black	.20	.08
467	Cal Ripken	3.00	1.20
468	John Farrell	.20	.08
469	Terry Kennedy	.20	.08
470	Tom Candiotti	.20	.08
471	Roberto Alomar	1.25	.50
472	Jeff M. Robinson	.20	.08
473	Vance Law	.20	.08
474	Randy Ready UER (Strikeout total 136, should be 115)	.20	.08
475	Walt Terrell	.20	.08
476	Kelly Downs	.20	.08
477	Johnny Paredes	.20	.08
478	Shawn Hillegas	.20	.08
479	Bob Brenly	.20	.08
480	Otis Nixon	.20	.08
481	Johnny Ray	.20	.08
482	Geno Petralli	.20	.08
483	Stu Cliburn	.20	.08
484	Pete Incaviglia	.20	.08
485	Brian Downing	.20	.08
486	Jeff Stone	.20	.08
487	Carmen Castillo	.20	.08
488	Tom Niedenfuer	.20	.08
489	Jay Bell	.50	.20
490	Rick Schu	.20	.08
491	Jeff Pico	.20	.08
492	Mark Parent	.20	.08
493	Eric King	.20	.08
494	Al Nipper	.20	.08
495	Andy Hawkins	.20	.08
496	Daryl Boston	.20	.08
497	Ernie Riles	.20	.08
498	Pascual Perez	.20	.08
499	Bill Long UER (Games started total 70, should be 44)	.20	.08
500	Kirt Manwaring	.20	.08
501	Chuck Crim	.20	.08
502	Candy Maldonado	.20	.08
503	Dennis Lamp	.20	.08
504	Glenn Braggs	.20	.08
505	Joe Price	.20	.08
506	Ken Williams	.20	.08
507	Bill Pecota	.20	.08
508	Rey Quinones	.20	.08
509	Jeff Bittiger	.20	.08
510	Kevin Seitzer	.20	.08
511	Steve Bedrosian	.20	.08
512	Todd Worrell	.30	.12
513	Chris James	.20	.08
514	Jose Oquendo	.20	.08
515	David Palmer	.20	.08
516	John Smiley	.20	.08
517	Dave Clark	.20	.08
518	Mike Dunne	.20	.08
519	Ron Washington	.20	.08
520	Bob Kipper	.20	.08
521	Lee Smith	.30	.12
522	Juan Castillo	.20	.08
523	Don Robinson	.20	.08
524	Kevin Romine	.20	.08
525	Paul Molitor	.50	.20
526	Mark Langston	.20	.08
527	Donnie Hill	.20	.08
528	Larry Owen	.20	.08
529	Jerry Reed	.20	.08
530	Jack McDowell	.30	.12
531	Greg Mathews	.20	.08
532	John Russell	.20	.08
533	Dan Quisenberry	.20	.08
534	Greg Gross	.20	.08
535	Danny Cox	.20	.08
536	Terry Francona	.30	.12
537	Andy Van Slyke	.30	.12
538	Mel Hall	.20	.08
539	Jim Gott	.20	.08
540	Doug Jones	.20	.08
541	Craig Lefferts	.20	.08
542	Mike Boddicker	.20	.08
543	Greg Brock	.20	.08
544	Atlee Hammaker	.20	.08
545	Tom Bolton	.20	.08
546	Mike Macfarlane RC	.50	.20
547	Rich Renteria	.20	.08
548	John Davis	.20	.08
549	Floyd Bannister	.20	.08
550	Mickey Brantley	.20	.08
551	Duane Ward	.20	.08
552	Dan Petry	.20	.08
553	Mickey Tettleton UER (Walks total 175, should be 136)	.20	.08
554	Rick Leach	.20	.08
555	Mike Witt	.20	.08
556	Sid Bream	.20	.08
557	Bobby Witt	.20	.08
558	Tommy Herr	.20	.08
559	Randy Milligan	.20	.08
560	Jose Cecena	.20	.08
561	Mackey Sasser	.20	.08
562	Carney Lansford	.30	.12
563	Rick Aguilera	.30	.12
564	Ron Hassey	.20	.08
565	Dwight Gooden	.50	.20
566	Paul Assenmacher	.20	.08
567	Neil Allen	.20	.08
568	Jim Morrison	.20	.08
569	Mike Pagliarulo	.20	.08
570	Ted Simmons	.30	.12
571	Mark Thurmond	.20	.08
572	Fred McGriff	.75	.30
573	Wally Joyner	.30	.12
574	Jose Bautista RC	.25	.10
575	Kelly Gruber	.20	.08
576	Cecilio Guante	.20	.08
577	Mark Davidson	.20	.08
578	Bobby Bonilla UER (Total steals 2 in '87, should be 3)	.30	.12
579	Mike Stanley	.20	.08
580	Gene Larkin	.20	.08
581	Stan Javier	.20	.08
582	Howard Johnson	.20	.08
583A	Mike Gallego ERR (Front reversed negative)	.75	.30
583B	Mike Gallego COR	.75	.30
584	David Cone	.30	.12
585	Doug Jennings	.20	.08
586	Charles Hudson	.20	.08
587	Dion James	.20	.08
588	Al Leiter	.75	.30
589	Charlie Puleo	.20	.08
590	Roberto Kelly	.30	.12
591	Thad Bosley	.20	.08
592	Pete Stanicek	.20	.08
593	Pat Borders RC	.50	.20
594	Bryan Harvey RC	.50	.20
595	Jeff Ballard	.20	.08
596	Jeff Reardon	.30	.12
597	Doug Drabek	.20	.08
598	Edwin Correa	.20	.08

❑ 599 Keith Atherton .20 .08
❑ 600 Dave LaPoint .20 .08
❑ 601 Don Baylor .30 .12
❑ 602 Tom Pagnozzi .20 .08
❑ 603 Tim Flannery .20 .08
❑ 604 Gene Walter .20 .08
❑ 605 Dave Parker .30 .12
❑ 606 Mike Diaz .20 .08
❑ 607 Chris Gwynn .20 .08
❑ 608 Odell Jones .20 .08
❑ 609 Carlton Fisk .50 .20
❑ 610 Jay Howell .20 .08
❑ 611 Tim Crews .20 .08
❑ 612 Keith Hernandez .50 .20
❑ 613 Willie Fraser .20 .08
❑ 614 Jim Eppard .20 .08
❑ 615 Jeff Hamilton .20 .08
❑ 616 Kurt Stillwell .20 .08
❑ 617 Tom Browning .20 .08
❑ 618 Jeff Montgomery .30 .12
❑ 619 Jose Rijo .20 .08
❑ 620 Jamie Quirk .20 .08
❑ 621 Willie McGee .30 .12
❑ 622 Mark Grant UER .20 .08
(Glove on wrong hand)
❑ 623 Bill Swift .20 .08
❑ 624 Orlando Mercado .20 .08
❑ 625 John Costello .20 .08
❑ 626 Jose Gonzalez .20 .08
❑ 627A Bill Schroeder ERR .75 .30
(Back photo actually Ronn Reynolds buckling shin guards)
❑ 627B Bill Schroeder COR .75 .30
❑ 628A Fred Manrique ERR .75 .30
(Back photo actually Ozzie Guillen throwing)
❑ 628B Fred Manrique COR .20 .08
(Swinging bat on back)
❑ 629 Ricky Horton .20 .08
❑ 630 Dan Plesac .20 .08
❑ 631 Alfredo Griffin .20 .08
❑ 632 Chuck Finley .30 .12
❑ 633 Kirk Gibson .30 .12
❑ 634 Randy Myers .30 .12
❑ 635 Greg Minton .20 .08
❑ 636A Herm Winningham .75 .30
ERR (W1nningham on back)
❑ 636B H.Winningham COR .20 .08
❑ 637 Charlie Leibrandt .20 .08
❑ 638 Tim Birtsas .20 .08
❑ 639 Bill Buckner .30 .12
❑ 640 Danny Jackson .20 .08
❑ 641 Greg Booker .20 .08
❑ 642 Jim Presley .20 .08
❑ 643 Gene Nelson .20 .08
❑ 644 Rod Booker .20 .08
❑ 645 Dennis Rasmussen .20 .08
❑ 646 Juan Nieves .20 .08
❑ 647 Bobby Thigpen .20 .08
❑ 648 Tim Belcher .20 .08
❑ 649 Mike Young .20 .08
❑ 650 Ivan Calderon .20 .08
❑ 651 Oswald Peraza .20 .08
❑ 652A Pat Sheridan ERR 15.00 6.00
(No position on front)
❑ 652B Pat Sheridan COR .20 .08
❑ 653 Mike Morgan .20 .08
❑ 654 Mike Heath .20 .08
❑ 655 Jay Tibbs .20 .08
❑ 656 Fernando Valenzuela .30 .12
❑ 657 Lee Mazzilli .20 .08
❑ 658 Frank Viola AL CY .20 .08
❑ 659A J.Canseco AL MVP .30 .12
Eagle logo in black
❑ 659B J.Canseco AL MVP .30 .12
Eagle logo in blue
❑ 660 Walt Weiss AL ROY .20 .08
❑ 661 Orel Hershiser NL CY .30 .12
❑ 662 Kirk Gibson NL MVP .20 .08
❑ 663 Chris Sabo NL ROY .20 .08
❑ 664 Dennis Eckersley .30 .12
ALCS MVP
❑ 665 Orel Hershiser .30 .12
NLCS MVP
❑ 666 Kirk Gibson WS .75 .30
❑ 667 O.Hershiser WS MVP .30 .12
❑ 668 Wally Joyner TC .20 .08
❑ 669 Nolan Ryan TC 1.25 .50
❑ 670 Jose Canseco TC .30 .12
❑ 671 Fred McGriff TC .30 .12
❑ 672 Dale Murphy TC .50 .20
❑ 673 Paul Molitor TC .30 .12
❑ 674 Ozzie Smith TC .50 .20
❑ 675 Ryne Sandberg TC .75 .30
❑ 676 Kirk Gibson TC .20 .08
❑ 677 Andres Galarraga TC .20 .08
❑ 678 Will Clark TC .30 .12
❑ 679 Cory Snyder TC .20 .08
❑ 680 Alvin Davis TC .20 .08
❑ 681 Darryl Strawberry TC .30 .12
❑ 682 Cal Ripken TC 1.00 .40
❑ 683 Tony Gwynn TC .50 .20
❑ 684 Mike Schmidt TC .75 .30
❑ 685 A.Van Slyke TC UER .20 .08
96 Junior Ortiz
❑ 686 Ruben Sierra TC .20 .08
❑ 687 Wade Boggs TC .30 .12
❑ 688 Eric Davis TC .20 .08
❑ 689 George Brett TC .75 .30
❑ 690 Alan Trammell TC .20 .08
❑ 691 Frank Viola TC .20 .08
❑ 692 Harold Baines TC .20 .08
❑ 693 Don Mattingly TC .75 .30
❑ 694 Checklist 1-100 .20 .08
❑ 695 Checklist 101-200 .20 .08
❑ 696 Checklist 201-300 .20 .08
❑ 697 Checklist 301-400 .20 .08
❑ 698 CL 401-500 UER .20 .08
467 Cal Ripkin Jr.
❑ 699 CL 501-600 UER .20 .08
543 Greg Booker
❑ 700 Checklist 601-700 .20 .08
❑ 701 Checklist 701-800 .20 .08
❑ 702 Jesse Barfield .20 .08
❑ 703 Walt Terrell .20 .08
❑ 704 Dickie Thon .20 .08
❑ 705 Al Leiter .75 .30
❑ 706 Dave LaPoint .20 .08
❑ 707 Charlie Hayes RC .50 .20
❑ 708 Andy Hawkins .20 .08
❑ 709 Mickey Hatcher .20 .08
❑ 710 Lance McCullers .20 .08
❑ 711 Ron Kittle .20 .08
❑ 712 Bert Blyleven .30 .12
❑ 713 Rick Dempsey .20 .08
❑ 714 Ken Williams .20 .08
❑ 715 Steve Rosenberg .20 .08
❑ 716 Joe Skalski .20 .08
❑ 717 Spike Owen .20 .08
❑ 718 Todd Burns .20 .08
❑ 719 Kevin Gross .20 .08
❑ 720 Tommy Herr .20 .08
❑ 721 Rob Ducey .20 .08
❑ 722 Gary Green .20 .08
❑ 723 Gregg Olson RC .50 .20
❑ 724 Greg W. Harris RC .25 .10
❑ 725 Craig Worthington .20 .08
❑ 726 Tom Howard RC .25 .10
❑ 727 Dale Mohorcic .20 .08
❑ 728 Rich Yett .20 .08
❑ 729 Mel Hall .20 .08
❑ 730 Floyd Youmans .20 .08
❑ 731 Lonnie Smith .20 .08
❑ 732 Wally Backman .20 .08
❑ 733 Trevor Wilson RC .25 .10
❑ 734 Jose Alvarez RC .25 .10
❑ 735 Bob Milacki .20 .08
❑ 736 Tom Gordon RC .50 .20
❑ 737 Wally Whitehurst RC .25 .10
❑ 738 Mike Aldrete .20 .08
❑ 739 Keith Miller .20 .08
❑ 740 Randy Milligan .20 .08
❑ 741 Jeff Parrett .20 .08
❑ 742 Steve Finley RC 1.50 .60
❑ 743 Junior Felix RC .25 .10
❑ 744 Pete Harnisch RC .50 .20
❑ 745 Bill Spiers RC .50 .20
❑ 746 Hensley Meulens RC .25 .10
❑ 747 Juan Bell RC .25 .10
❑ 748 Steve Sax .20 .08
❑ 749 Phil Bradley .20 .08
❑ 750 Rey Quinones .20 .08
❑ 751 Tommy Gregg .20 .08
❑ 752 Kevin Brown .75 .30
❑ 753 Derek Lilliquist RC .25 .10
❑ 754 Todd Zeile RC 1.00 .40
❑ 755 Jim Abbott RC 1.50 .60
Triple exposure
❑ 756 Ozzie Canseco .20 .08
❑ 757 Nick Esasky .20 .08
❑ 758 Mike Moore .20 .08
❑ 759 Rob Murphy .20 .08
❑ 760 Rick Mahler .20 .08
❑ 761 Fred Lynn .20 .08
❑ 762 Kevin Blankenship .20 .08
❑ 763 Eddie Murray .75 .30
❑ 764 Steve Searcy .20 .08
❑ 765 Jerome Walton RC .50 .20
❑ 766 Erik Hanson RC .50 .20
❑ 767 Bob Boone .30 .12
❑ 768 Edgar Martinez .50 .20
❑ 769 Jose DeJesus .20 .08
❑ 770 Greg Briley .20 .08
❑ 771 Steve Peters .20 .08
❑ 772 Rafael Palmeiro .50 .20
❑ 773 Jack Clark .20 .08
❑ 774 Nolan Ryan 4.00 1.60
(Throwing football)
❑ 775 Lance Parrish .20 .08
❑ 776 Joe Girardi RC 1.00 .40
❑ 777 Willie Randolph .30 .12
❑ 778 Mitch Williams .20 .08
❑ 779 Dennis Cook RC .50 .20
❑ 780 Dwight Smith RC .50 .20
❑ 781 Lenny Harris RC .50 .20
❑ 782 Torey Lovullo RC .25 .10
❑ 783 Norm Charlton RC .50 .20
❑ 784 Chris Brown .20 .08
❑ 785 Todd Benzinger .20 .08
❑ 786 Shane Rawley .20 .08
❑ 787 Omar Vizquel RC 2.00 .80
❑ 788 LaVel Freeman .20 .08
❑ 789 Jeffrey Leonard .20 .08
❑ 790 Eddie Williams .20 .08
❑ 791 Jamie Moyer .30 .12
❑ 792 Bruce Hurst UER .20 .08
(Workd Series)
❑ 793 Julio Franco .20 .08
❑ 794 Claudell Washington .20 .08
❑ 795 Jody Davis .20 .08
❑ 796 Oddibe McDowell .20 .08
❑ 797 Paul Kilgus .20 .08
❑ 798 Tracy Jones .20 .08
❑ 799 Steve Wilson .20 .08
❑ 800 Pete O'Brien .20 .08

1990 Upper Deck

	Nm-Mt	Ex-Mt
COMPLETE SET (800)	25.00	7.50
COMP.FACT.SET (800)	25.00	7.50
COMPLETE LO SET (700)	25.00	7.50
COMPLETE HI SET (100)	5.00	1.50
COMP.HI FACT.SET (100)	4.00	1.20

❑ 1 Star Rookie Checklist .10 .03
❑ 2 Randy Nosek .10 .03
❑ 3 Tom Drees UER .10 .03

(11th line, hulred, should be hurled
❑ 4 Curt Young .10 .03
❑ 5 Devon White TC .10 .03
❑ 6 Luis Salazar .10 .03
❑ 7 Von Hayes TC .10 .03
❑ 8 Jose Bautista .10 .03
❑ 9 Marquis Grissom RC .25 .07
❑ 10 Orel Hershiser TC .10 .03
❑ 11 Rick Aguilera .20 .06
❑ 12 Benito Santiago TC .10 .03
❑ 13 Deion Sanders .50 .15
❑ 14 Marvell Wynne .10 .03
❑ 15 Dave West .10 .03
❑ 16 Bobby Bonilla TC .10 .03
❑ 17 Sammy Sosa RC 8.00 2.40
❑ 18 Steve Sax TC .10 .03
❑ 19 Jack Howell .10 .03
❑ 20 Mike Schmidt Special 1.00 .30
UER (Suprising, should be surprising)
❑ 21 Robin Ventura UER .50 .15
(Samta Maria)
❑ 22 Brian Meyer .10 .03
❑ 23 Blaine Beatty .10 .03
❑ 24 Ken Griffey Jr. TC .60 .18
❑ 25 Greg Vaughn UER .20 .06
(Association misspelled as assiocation)
❑ 26 Xavier Hernandez RC .10 .03
❑ 27 Jason Grimsley RC .10 .03
❑ 28 Eric Anthony RC UER .10 .03
(Ashville, should be Asheville)
❑ 29 Tim Raines TC UER .10 .03
(Wallach listed before Walker)
❑ 30 David Wells .20 .06
❑ 31 Hal Morris .10 .03
❑ 32 Bo Jackson TC .20 .06
❑ 33 Kelly Mann .10 .03
❑ 34 Nolan Ryan Special 1.00 .30
❑ 35 Scott Service UER .10 .03
(Born Cincinatti on 7/27/67, should be Cincinnati 2/27)
❑ 36 Mark McGwire TC .60 .18
❑ 37 Tino Martinez .50 .15
❑ 38 Chili Davis .20 .06
❑ 39 Scott Sanderson .10 .03
❑ 40 Kevin Mitchell TC .10 .03
❑ 41 Lou Whitaker TC .10 .03
❑ 42 Scott Coolbaugh UER .10 .03
(Definately) RC
❑ 43 Jose Cano UER .10 .03
(Born 9/7/62, should be 3/7/62)
❑ 44 Jose Vizcaino RC .25 .07
❑ 45 Bob Hamelin RC .25 .07
❑ 46 Jose Offerman RC UER .25 .07
(Posesses)
❑ 47 Kevin Blankenship .10 .03
❑ 48 Kirby Puckett TC .30 .09
❑ 49 Tommy Greene RC UER .10 .03
(Livest, should be liveliest)
❑ 50 Will Clark Special .20 .06
UER (Perenial, should be perennial)
❑ 51 Rob Nelson .10 .03
❑ 52 C.Hammond RC UER .10 .03
Chatanooga
❑ 53 Joe Carter TC .10 .03
❑ 54A B.McDonald RC ERR 2.00 .60
No Rookie designation on card front
❑ 54B B.McDonald COR RC .25 .07
❑ 55 Andy Benes UER .20 .06
(Whichita)
❑ 56 John Olerud RC .75 .23
❑ 57 Roger Clemens TC .50 .15
❑ 58 Tony Armas .10 .03
❑ 59 George Canale .10 .03
❑ 60A Mickey Tettleton TC 2.00 .60
ERR (683 Jamie Weston)
❑ 60B Mickey Tettleton TC .10 .03
COR (683 Mickey Weston)

❑ 61 Mike Stanton RC .25 .07
❑ 62 Dwight Gooden TC .20 .06
❑ 63 Kent Mercker RC UER .25 .07
(Albuguerque)
❑ 64 Francisco Cabrera .10 .03
❑ 65 Steve Avery UER .10 .03
(Born NJ, should be MI, Merker should be Mercker
❑ 66 Jose Canseco .50 .15
❑ 67 Matt Merullo .10 .03
❑ 68 Vince Coleman TC UER .10 .03
(Guererro)
❑ 69 Ron Karkovice .10 .03
❑ 70 Kevin Maas RC .25 .07
❑ 71 Dennis Cook UER .10 .03
(Shown with righty glove on card back)
❑ 72 Juan Gonzalez RC UER 2.50 .75
(135 games for Tulsa in '89, should be 133)
❑ 73 Andre Dawson TC .10 .03
❑ 74 Dean Palmer RC UER .25 .07
(Permanent misspelled as perminant)
❑ 75 Bo Jackson Special .20 .06
UER (Monsterous, should be monstrous)
❑ 76 Rob Richie .10 .03
❑ 77 Bobby Rose UER .10 .03
(Pickin, should be pick in)
❑ 78 Brian DuBois UER .10 .03
(Commiting)
❑ 79 Ozzie Guillen TC .10 .03
❑ 80 Gene Nelson .10 .03
❑ 81 Bob McClure .10 .03
❑ 82 Julio Franco TC .10 .03
❑ 83 Greg Minton .10 .03
❑ 84 John Smoltz TC UER .30 .09
(Oddibe not Odibbe)
❑ 85 Willie Fraser .10 .03
❑ 86 Neal Heaton .10 .03
❑ 87 Kevin Tapani RC UER .25 .07
(24th line has excpet, should be except)
❑ 88 Mike Scott TC .10 .03
❑ 89A Jim Gott ERR 2.00 .60
(Photo actually Rick Reed)
❑ 89B Jim Gott COR .10 .03
❑ 90 Lance Johnson .10 .03
❑ 91 Robin Yount TC UER .20 .06
(Checklist on back has 178 Rob Deer and 176 Mike Felder)
❑ 92 Jeff Parrett .10 .03
❑ 93 Julio Machado UER .10 .03
(Valenzuelan, should be Venezuelan)
❑ 94 Ron Jones .10 .03
❑ 95 George Bell TC .10 .03
❑ 96 Jerry Reuss .10 .03
❑ 97 Brian Fisher .10 .03
❑ 98 Kevin Ritz UER .10 .03
(Amercian)
❑ 99 Barry Larkin TC .20 .06
❑ 100 Checklist 1-100 .10 .03
❑ 101 Gerald Perry .10 .03
❑ 102 Kevin Appier .50 .15
❑ 103 Julio Franco .10 .03
❑ 104 Craig Biggio .30 .09
❑ 105 Bo Jackson UER .50 .15
('89 BA wrong, should be .256)
❑ 106 Junior Felix .10 .03
❑ 107 Mike Harkey .10 .03
❑ 108 Fred McGriff .50 .15
❑ 109 Rick Sutcliffe .20 .06
❑ 110 Pete O'Brien .10 .03
❑ 111 Kelly Gruber .10 .03
❑ 112 Dwight Evans .20 .06
❑ 113 Pat Borders .10 .03
❑ 114 Dwight Gooden .30 .09
❑ 115 Kevin Batiste .10 .03
❑ 116 Eric Davis .20 .06
❑ 117 Kevin Mitchell UER .10 .03

(Career HR total 99, should be 100)
❑ 118 Ron Oester .10 .03
❑ 119 Brett Butler .20 .06
❑ 120 Danny Jackson .10 .03
❑ 121 Tommy Gregg .10 .03
❑ 122 Ken Caminiti .20 .06
❑ 123 Kevin Brown .20 .06
❑ 124 George Brett UER 1.25 .35
(133 runs, should be 1300)
❑ 125 Mike Scott .10 .03
❑ 126 Cory Snyder .10 .03
❑ 127 George Bell .10 .03
❑ 128 Mark Grace .50 .15
❑ 129 Devon White .10 .03
❑ 130 Tony Fernandez .10 .03
❑ 131 Don Aase .10 .03
❑ 132 Rance Mulliniks .10 .03
❑ 133 Marty Barrett .10 .03
❑ 134 Nelson Liriano .10 .03
❑ 135 Mark Carreon .10 .03
❑ 136 Candy Maldonado .10 .03
❑ 137 Tim Birtsas .10 .03
❑ 138 Tom Brookens .10 .03
❑ 139 John Franco .20 .06
❑ 140 Mike LaCoss .10 .03
❑ 141 Jeff Treadway .10 .03
❑ 142 Pat Tabler .10 .03
❑ 143 Darrell Evans .20 .06
❑ 144 Rafael Ramirez .10 .03
❑ 145 O.McDowell UER .10 .03
Misspelled Odibbe
❑ 146 Brian Downing .10 .03
❑ 147 Curt Wilkerson .10 .03
❑ 148 Ernie Whitt .10 .03
❑ 149 Bill Schroeder .10 .03
❑ 150 Domingo Ramos UER .10 .03
(Says throws right, but shows him throwing lefty)
❑ 151 Rick Honeycutt .10 .03
❑ 152 Don Slaught .10 .03
❑ 153 Mitch Webster .10 .03
❑ 154 Tony Phillips .10 .03
❑ 155 Paul Kilgus .10 .03
❑ 156 Ken Griffey Jr. UER 1.50 .45
(Simultaniously)
❑ 157 Gary Sheffield .50 .15
❑ 158 Wally Backman .10 .03
❑ 159 B.J. Surhoff .20 .06
❑ 160 Louie Meadows .10 .03
❑ 161 Paul O'Neill .30 .09
❑ 162 Jeff McKnight .10 .03
❑ 163 Alvaro Espinoza .10 .03
❑ 164 Scott Scudder .10 .03
❑ 165 Jeff Reed .10 .03
❑ 166 Gregg Jefferies .20 .06
❑ 167 Barry Larkin .50 .15
❑ 168 Gary Carter .30 .09
❑ 169 Robby Thompson .10 .03
❑ 170 Rolando Roomes .10 .03
❑ 171 Mark McGwire UER 1.25 .35
(Total games 427 and hits 479, should be 467 and 427)
❑ 172 Steve Sax .10 .03
❑ 173 Mark Williamson .10 .03
❑ 174 Mitch Williams .10 .03
❑ 175 Brian Holton .10 .03
❑ 176 Rob Deer .10 .03
❑ 177 Tim Raines .20 .06
❑ 178 Mike Felder .10 .03
❑ 179 Harold Reynolds .20 .06
❑ 180 Terry Francona .20 .06
❑ 181 Chris Sabo .10 .03
❑ 182 Darryl Strawberry .30 .09
❑ 183 Willie Randolph .20 .06
❑ 184 Bill Ripken .10 .03
❑ 185 Mackey Sasser .10 .03
❑ 186 Todd Benzinger .10 .03
❑ 187 Kevin Elster UER .10 .03
(16 homers in 1989, should be 10)
❑ 188 Jose Uribe .10 .03
❑ 189 Tom Browning .10 .03

❑ 190 Keith Miller .10 .03
❑ 191 Don Mattingly 1.25 .35
❑ 192 Dave Parker .20 .06
❑ 193 Roberto Kelly UER .10 .03
(96 RBI, should be 62)
❑ 194 Phil Bradley .10 .03
❑ 195 Ron Hassey .10 .03
❑ 196 Gerald Young .10 .03
❑ 197 Hubie Brooks .10 .03
❑ 198 Bill Doran .10 .03
❑ 199 Al Newman .10 .03
❑ 200 Checklist 101-200 .10 .03
❑ 201 Terry Puhl .10 .03
❑ 202 Frank DiPino .10 .03
❑ 203 Jim Clancy .10 .03
❑ 204 Bob Ojeda .10 .03
❑ 205 Alex Trevino .10 .03
❑ 206 Dave Henderson .10 .03
❑ 207 Henry Cotto .10 .03
❑ 208 Rafael Belliard UER .10 .03
(Born 1961, not 1951)
❑ 209 Stan Javier .10 .03
❑ 210 Jerry Reed .10 .03
❑ 211 Doug Dascenzo .10 .03
❑ 212 Andres Thomas .10 .03
❑ 213 Greg Maddux 1.00 .30
❑ 214 Mike Schooler .10 .03
❑ 215 Lonnie Smith .10 .03
❑ 216 Jose Rijo .10 .03
❑ 217 Greg Gagne .10 .03
❑ 218 Jim Gantner .10 .03
❑ 219 Allan Anderson .10 .03
❑ 220 Rick Mahler .10 .03
❑ 221 Jim Deshaies .10 .03
❑ 222 Keith Hernandez .30 .09
❑ 223 Vince Coleman .10 .03
❑ 224 David Cone .20 .06
❑ 225 Ozzie Smith .50 .15
❑ 226 Matt Nokes .10 .03
❑ 227 Barry Bonds 1.25 .35
❑ 228 Felix Jose .10 .03
❑ 229 Dennis Powell .10 .03
❑ 230 Mike Gallego .10 .03
❑ 231 Shawon Dunston UER .10 .03
('89 stats are Andre Dawson's)
❑ 232 Ron Gant .20 .06
❑ 233 Omar Vizquel .50 .15
❑ 234 Derek Lilliquist .10 .03
❑ 235 Erik Hanson .10 .03
❑ 236 Kirby Puckett UER .50 .15
(824 games, should be 924)
❑ 237 Bill Spiers .10 .03
❑ 238 Dan Gladden .10 .03
❑ 239 Bryan Clutterbuck .10 .03
❑ 240 John Moses .10 .03
❑ 241 Ron Darling .10 .03
❑ 242 Joe Magrane .10 .03
❑ 243 Dave Magadan .10 .03
❑ 244 Pedro Guerrero UER .10 .03
(Misspelled Guererro)
❑ 245 Glenn Davis .10 .03
❑ 246 Terry Steinbach .10 .03
❑ 247 Fred Lynn .10 .03
❑ 248 Gary Redus .10 .03
❑ 249 Ken Williams .10 .03
❑ 250 Sid Bream .10 .03
❑ 251 Bob Welch UER .10 .03
(2587 career strikeouts, should be 1587)
❑ 252 Bill Buckner .10 .03
❑ 253 Carney Lansford .20 .06
❑ 254 Paul Molitor .30 .09
❑ 255 Jose DeJesus .10 .03
❑ 256 Orel Hershiser .20 .06
❑ 257 Tom Brunansky .10 .03
❑ 258 Mike Davis .10 .03
❑ 259 Jeff Ballard .10 .03
❑ 260 Scott Terry .10 .03
❑ 261 Sid Fernandez .10 .03
❑ 262 Mike Marshall .10 .03
❑ 263 Howard Johnson UER .10 .03
(192 SO, should be 592)
❑ 264 Kirk Gibson UER .20 .06
(659 runs, should be 669)
❑ 265 Kevin McReynolds .10 .03
❑ 266 Cal Ripken 1.50 .45
❑ 267 Ozzie Guillen UER .10 .03
(Career triples 27, should be 29)
❑ 268 Jim Traber .10 .03
❑ 269 Bobby Thigpen UER .10 .03
(31 saves in 1989, should be 34)
❑ 270 Joe Orsulak .10 .03
❑ 271 Bob Boone .20 .06
❑ 272 Dave Stewart UER .20 .06
(Totals wrong due to omission of '86 stats)
❑ 273 Tim Wallach .10 .03
❑ 274 Luis Aquino UER .10 .03
(Says throws lefty, but shows him throwing righty)
❑ 275 Mike Moore .10 .03
❑ 276 Tony Pena .10 .03
❑ 277 Eddie Murray UER .50 .15
(Several typos in career total stats)
❑ 278 Milt Thompson .10 .03
❑ 279 Alejandro Pena .10 .03
❑ 280 Ken Dayley .10 .03
❑ 281 Carmelo Castillo .10 .03
❑ 282 Tom Henke .10 .03
❑ 283 Mickey Hatcher .10 .03
❑ 284 Roy Smith .10 .03
❑ 285 Manny Lee .10 .03
❑ 286 Dan Pasqua .10 .03
❑ 287 Larry Sheets .10 .03
❑ 288 Garry Templeton .10 .03
❑ 289 Eddie Williams .10 .03
❑ 290 Brady Anderson UER .20 .06
(Home: Silver Springs, not Siver Springs)
❑ 291 Spike Owen .10 .03
❑ 292 Storm Davis .10 .03
❑ 293 Chris Bosio .10 .03
❑ 294 Jim Eisenreich .10 .03
❑ 295 Don August .10 .03
❑ 296 Jeff Hamilton .10 .03
❑ 297 Mickey Tettleton .10 .03
❑ 298 Mike Scioscia .10 .03
❑ 299 Kevin Hickey .10 .03
❑ 300 Checklist 201-300 .10 .03
❑ 301 Shawn Abner .10 .03
❑ 302 Kevin Bass .10 .03
❑ 303 Bip Roberts .10 .03
❑ 304 Joe Girardi .30 .09
❑ 305 Danny Darwin .10 .03
❑ 306 Mike Heath .10 .03
❑ 307 Mike Macfarlane .10 .03
❑ 308 Ed Whitson .10 .03
❑ 309 Tracy Jones .10 .03
❑ 310 Scott Fletcher .10 .03
❑ 311 Darnell Coles .10 .03
❑ 312 Mike Brumley .10 .03
❑ 313 Bill Swift .10 .03
❑ 314 Charlie Hough .20 .06
❑ 315 Jim Presley .10 .03
❑ 316 Luis Polonia .10 .03
❑ 317 Mike Morgan .10 .03
❑ 318 Lee Guetterman .10 .03
❑ 319 Jose Oquendo .10 .03
❑ 320 Wayne Tolleson .10 .03
❑ 321 Jody Reed .10 .03
❑ 322 Damon Berryhill .10 .03
❑ 323 Roger Clemens 1.00 .30
❑ 324 Ryne Sandberg .75 .23
❑ 325 Benito Santiago UER .20 .06
(Misspelled Santago on card back)
❑ 326 Bret Saberhagen UER .20 .06
(1140 hits, should be 1240; 56 CG, should be 52)
❑ 327 Lou Whitaker .20 .06
❑ 328 Dave Gallagher .10 .03
❑ 329 Mike Pagliarulo .10 .03
❑ 330 Doyle Alexander .10 .03
❑ 331 Jeffrey Leonard .10 .03
❑ 332 Torey Lovullo .10 .03
❑ 333 Pete Incaviglia .10 .03
❑ 334 Rickey Henderson .75 .23
❑ 335 Rafael Palmeiro .30 .09
❑ 336 Ken Hill .20 .06
❑ 337 Dave Winfield UER .30 .09
(1418 RBI, should be 1438)
❑ 338 Alfredo Griffin .10 .03
❑ 339 Andy Hawkins .10 .03
❑ 340 Ted Power .10 .03
❑ 341 Steve Wilson .10 .03
❑ 342 Jack Clark UER .20 .06
(916 BB, should be 1006; 1142 SO, should be 1130)
❑ 343 Ellis Burks .30 .09
❑ 344 Tony Gwynn UER .60 .18
(Doubles stats on card back are wrong)
❑ 345 Jerome Walton UER .10 .03
(Total At Bats 476, should be 475)
❑ 346 Roberto Alomar UER .50 .15
(61 doubles, should be 51)
❑ 347 Carlos Martinez UER .10 .03
(Born 8/11/64, should be 8/11/65)
❑ 348 Chet Lemon .10 .03
❑ 349 Willie Wilson .10 .03
❑ 350 Greg Walker .10 .03
❑ 351 Tom Bolton .10 .03
❑ 352 German Gonzalez .10 .03
❑ 353 Harold Baines .20 .06
❑ 354 Mike Greenwell .10 .03
❑ 355 Ruben Sierra .10 .03
❑ 356 Andres Galarraga .20 .06
❑ 357 Andre Dawson .20 .06
❑ 358 Jeff Brantley .10 .03
❑ 359 Mike Bielecki .10 .03
❑ 360 Ken Oberkfell .10 .03
❑ 361 Kurt Stillwell .10 .03
❑ 362 Brian Holman .10 .03
❑ 363 Kevin Seitzer UER .10 .03
(Career triples total does not add up)
❑ 364 Alvin Davis .10 .03
❑ 365 Tom Gordon .20 .06
❑ 366 Bobby Bonilla UER .20 .06
(Two steals in 1987, should be 3)
❑ 367 Carlton Fisk .30 .09
❑ 368 Steve Carter UER .10 .03
(Charlotesville)
❑ 369 Joel Skinner .10 .03
❑ 370 John Cangelosi .10 .03
❑ 371 Cecil Espy .10 .03
❑ 372 Gary Wayne .10 .03
❑ 373 Jim Rice .20 .06
❑ 374 Mike Dyer .10 .03
❑ 375 Joe Carter .20 .06
❑ 376 Dwight Smith .10 .03
❑ 377 John Wetteland .50 .15
❑ 378 Earnie Riles .10 .03
❑ 379 Otis Nixon .10 .03
❑ 380 Vance Law .10 .03
❑ 381 Dave Bergman .10 .03
❑ 382 Frank White .20 .06
❑ 383 Scott Bradley .10 .03
❑ 384 Israel Sanchez UER .10 .03
(Totals don't include '89 stats)
❑ 385 Gary Pettis .10 .03
❑ 386 Donn Pall .10 .03
❑ 387 John Smiley .10 .03
❑ 388 Tom Candiotti .10 .03
❑ 389 Junior Ortiz .10 .03
❑ 390 Steve Lyons .10 .03
❑ 391 Brian Harper .10 .03
❑ 392 Fred Manrique .10 .03
❑ 393 Lee Smith .20 .06
❑ 394 Jeff Kunkel .10 .03
❑ 395 Claudell Washington .10 .03
❑ 396 John Tudor .10 .03
❑ 397 Terry Kennedy UER .10 .03

(Career totals all wrong)
❑ 398 Lloyd McClendon .10 .03
❑ 399 Craig Lefferts .10 .03
❑ 400 Checklist 301-400 .10 .03
❑ 401 Keith Moreland .10 .03
❑ 402 Rich Gedman .10 .03
❑ 403 Jeff D. Robinson .10 .03
❑ 404 Randy Ready .10 .03
❑ 405 Rick Cerone .10 .03
❑ 406 Jeff Blauser .10 .03
❑ 407 Larry Andersen .10 .03
❑ 408 Joe Boever .10 .03
❑ 409 Felix Fermin .10 .03
❑ 410 Glenn Wilson .10 .03
❑ 411 Rex Hudler .10 .03
❑ 412 Mark Grant .10 .03
❑ 413 Dennis Martinez .20 .06
❑ 414 Darrin Jackson .10 .03
❑ 415 Mike Aldrete .10 .03
❑ 416 Roger McDowell .10 .03
❑ 417 Jeff Reardon .20 .06
❑ 418 Darren Daulton .20 .06
❑ 419 Tim Laudner .10 .03
❑ 420 Don Carman .10 .03
❑ 421 Lloyd Moseby .10 .03
❑ 422 Doug Drabek .10 .03
❑ 423 Lenny Harris UER .10 .03
(Walks 2 in '89, should be 20)
❑ 424 Jose Lind .10 .03
❑ 425 Dave Johnson (P) .10 .03
❑ 426 Jerry Browne .10 .03
❑ 427 Eric Yelding .10 .03
❑ 428 Brad Komminsk .10 .03
❑ 429 Jody Davis .10 .03
❑ 430 Mariano Duncan .10 .03
❑ 431 Mark Davis .10 .03
❑ 432 Nelson Santovenia .10 .03
❑ 433 Bruce Hurst .10 .03
❑ 434 Jeff Huson RC .10 .03
❑ 435 Chris James .10 .03
❑ 436 Mark Guthrie .10 .03
❑ 437 Charlie Hayes .10 .03
❑ 438 Shane Rawley .10 .03
❑ 439 Dickie Thon .10 .03
❑ 440 Juan Berenguer .10 .03
❑ 441 Kevin Romine .10 .03
❑ 442 Bill Landrum .10 .03
❑ 443 Todd Frohwirth .10 .03
❑ 444 Craig Worthington .10 .03
❑ 445 Fernando Valenzuela .20 .06
❑ 446 Joey Belle .50 .15
❑ 447 Ed Whited UER .10 .03
(Ashville, should be Asheville)
❑ 448 Dave Smith .10 .03
❑ 449 Dave Clark .10 .03
❑ 450 Juan Agosto .10 .03
❑ 451 Dave Valle .10 .03
❑ 452 Kent Hrbek .20 .06
❑ 453 Von Hayes .10 .03
❑ 454 Gary Gaetti .20 .06
❑ 455 Greg Briley .10 .03
❑ 456 Glenn Braggs .10 .03
❑ 457 Kirt Manwaring .10 .03
❑ 458 Mel Hall .10 .03
❑ 459 Brook Jacoby .10 .03
❑ 460 Pat Sheridan .10 .03
❑ 461 Rob Murphy .10 .03
❑ 462 Jimmy Key .20 .06
❑ 463 Nick Esasky .10 .03
❑ 464 Rob Ducey .10 .03
❑ 465 Carlos Quintana UER .10 .03
(Internatinoal)
❑ 466 Larry Walker RC 1.50 .45
❑ 467 Todd Worrell .10 .03
❑ 468 Kevin Gross .10 .03
❑ 469 Terry Pendleton .20 .06
❑ 470 Dave Martinez .10 .03
❑ 471 Gene Larkin .10 .03
❑ 472 Len Dykstra UER .20 .06
('89 and total runs understated by 10)
❑ 473 Barry Lyons .10 .03
❑ 474 Terry Mulholland .10 .03
❑ 475 Chip Hale .10 .03
❑ 476 Jesse Barfield .10 .03
❑ 477 Dan Plesac .10 .03
❑ 478A Scott Garrelts ERR 2.00 .60
(Photo actually Bill Bathe)
❑ 478B Scott Garrelts COR .10 .03
❑ 479 Dave Righetti .10 .03
❑ 480 Gus Polidor UER .10 .03
Wearing 14 on front, but 10 on back
❑ 481 Mookie Wilson .20 .06
❑ 482 Luis Rivera .10 .03
❑ 483 Mike Flanagan .10 .03
❑ 484 Dennis Boyd .10 .03
❑ 485 John Cerutti .10 .03
❑ 486 John Costello .10 .03
❑ 487 Pascual Perez .10 .03
❑ 488 Tommy Herr .10 .03
❑ 489 Tom Foley .10 .03
❑ 490 Curt Ford .10 .03
❑ 491 Steve Lake .10 .03
❑ 492 Tim Teufel .10 .03
❑ 493 Randy Bush .10 .03
❑ 494 Mike Jackson .10 .03
❑ 495 Steve Jeltz .10 .03
❑ 496 Paul Gibson .10 .03
❑ 497 Steve Balboni .10 .03
❑ 498 Bud Black .10 .03
❑ 499 Dale Sveum .10 .03
❑ 500 Checklist 401-500 .10 .03
❑ 501 Tim Jones .10 .03
❑ 502 Mark Portugal .10 .03
❑ 503 Ivan Calderon .10 .03
❑ 504 Rick Rhoden .10 .03
❑ 505 Willie McGee .20 .06
❑ 506 Kirk McCaskill .10 .03
❑ 507 Dave LaPoint .10 .03
❑ 508 Jay Howell .10 .03
❑ 509 Johnny Ray .10 .03
❑ 510 Dave Anderson .10 .03
❑ 511 Chuck Crim .10 .03
❑ 512 Joe Hesketh .10 .03
❑ 513 Dennis Eckersley .20 .06
❑ 514 Greg Brock .10 .03
❑ 515 Tim Burke .10 .03
❑ 516 Frank Tanana .10 .03
❑ 517 Jay Bell .20 .06
❑ 518 Guillermo Hernandez .10 .03
❑ 519 Randy Kramer UER .10 .03
(Codiroli misspelled as Codoroli)
❑ 520 Charles Hudson .10 .03
❑ 521 Jim Corsi .10 .03
Word "originally" is misspelled on back
❑ 522 Steve Rosenberg .10 .03
❑ 523 Cris Carpenter .10 .03
❑ 524 Matt Winters .10 .03
❑ 525 Melido Perez .10 .03
❑ 526 Chris Gwynn UER .10 .03
(Albeguergue)
❑ 527 Bert Blyleven UER .20 .06
(Games career total is wrong, should be 644)
❑ 528 Chuck Cary .10 .03
❑ 529 Daryl Boston .10 .03
❑ 530 Dale Mohorcic .10 .03
❑ 531 Geronimo Berroa .10 .03
❑ 532 Edgar Martinez .30 .09
❑ 533 Dale Murphy .50 .15
❑ 534 Jay Buhner .20 .06
❑ 535 John Smoltz UER .50 .15
(HEA Stadium)
❑ 536 Andy Van Slyke .20 .06
❑ 537 Mike Henneman .10 .03
❑ 538 Miguel Garcia .10 .03
❑ 539 Frank Williams .10 .03
❑ 540 R.J. Reynolds .10 .03
❑ 541 Shawn Hillegas .10 .03
❑ 542 Walt Weiss .10 .03
❑ 543 Greg Hibbard RC .10 .03
❑ 544 Nolan Ryan 2.00 .60
❑ 545 Todd Zeile .20 .06
❑ 546 Hensley Meulens .10 .03
❑ 547 Tim Belcher .10 .03
❑ 548 Mike Witt .10 .03
❑ 549 Greg Cadaret UER .10 .03
(Aquiring, should be Acquiring)
❑ 550 Franklin Stubbs .10 .03
❑ 551 Tony Castillo .10 .03
❑ 552 Jeff M. Robinson .10 .03
❑ 553 Steve Olin RC .25 .07
❑ 554 Alan Trammell .30 .09
❑ 555 Wade Boggs 4X .30 .09
(Bo Jackson in background)
❑ 556 Will Clark .50 .15
❑ 557 Jeff King .10 .03
❑ 558 Mike Fitzgerald .10 .03
❑ 559 Ken Howell .10 .03
❑ 560 Bob Kipper .10 .03
❑ 561 Scott Bankhead .10 .03
❑ 562A Jeff Innis ERR 2.00 .60
(Photo actually David West)
❑ 562B Jeff Innis COR .10 .03
❑ 563 Randy Johnson .75 .23
❑ 564 Wally Whitehurst .10 .03
❑ 565 Gene Harris .10 .03
❑ 566 Norm Charlton .10 .03
❑ 567 Robin Yount UER .20 .06
(7602 career hits, should be 2606)
❑ 568 Joe Oliver UER .10 .03
(Fl.orida)
❑ 569 Mark Parent .10 .03
❑ 570 John Farrell UER .10 .03
(Loss total added wrong)
❑ 571 Tom Glavine .50 .15
❑ 572 Rod Nichols .10 .03
❑ 573 Jack Morris .20 .06
❑ 574 Greg Swindell .10 .03
❑ 575 Steve Searcy .10 .03
❑ 576 Ricky Jordan .10 .03
❑ 577 Matt Williams .20 .06
❑ 578 Mike LaValliere .10 .03
❑ 579 Bryn Smith .10 .03
❑ 580 Bruce Ruffin .10 .03
❑ 581 Randy Myers .20 .06
❑ 582 Rick Wrona .10 .03
❑ 583 Juan Samuel .10 .03
❑ 584 Les Lancaster .10 .03
❑ 585 Jeff Musselman .10 .03
❑ 586 Rob Dibble .20 .06
❑ 587 Eric Show .10 .03
❑ 588 Jesse Orosco .10 .03
❑ 589 Herm Winningham .10 .03
❑ 590 Andy Allanson .10 .03
❑ 591 Dion James .10 .03
❑ 592 Carmelo Martinez .10 .03
❑ 593 Luis Quinones .10 .03
❑ 594 Dennis Rasmussen .10 .03
❑ 595 Rich Yett .10 .03
❑ 596 Bob Walk .10 .03
❑ 597A A.McGaffigan ERR 2.00 .60
Photo actually Rich Thompson
❑ 597B A.McGaffigan COR .10 .03
❑ 598 Billy Hatcher .10 .03
❑ 599 Bob Knepper .10 .03
❑ 600 CL 501-600 UER .10 .03
599 Bob Kneppers
❑ 601 Joey Cora .20 .06
❑ 602 Steve Finley .20 .06
❑ 603 Kal Daniels UER .10 .03
(12 hits in '87, should be 123; 335 runs, should be 235)
❑ 604 Gregg Olson .20 .06
❑ 605 Dave Stieb .20 .06
❑ 606 Kenny Rogers .20 .06
(Shown catching football)
❑ 607 Zane Smith .10 .03
❑ 608 Bob Geren UER .10 .03
(Origionally)
❑ 609 Chad Kreuter .10 .03
❑ 610 Mike Smithson .10 .03
❑ 611 Jeff Wetherby .10 .03
❑ 612 Gary Mielke .10 .03

613 Pete Smith .10 .03
614 Jack Daugherty UER .10 .03
(Born 7/30/60, should be 7/3/60)
615 Lance McCullers .10 .03
616 Don Robinson .10 .03
617 Jose Guzman .10 .03
618 Steve Bedrosian .10 .03
619 Jamie Moyer .20 .06
620 Atlee Hammaker .10 .03
621 Rick Luecken UER .10 .03
(Innings pitched wrong)
622 Greg W. Harris .10 .03
623 Pete Harnisch .10 .03
624 Jerald Clark .10 .03
625 Jack McDowell UER .10 .03
(Career totals for Games and GS don't include 1987 season)
626 Frank Viola .10 .03
627 Teddy Higuera .10 .03
628 Marty Pevey .10 .03
629 Bill Wegman .10 .03
630 Eric Plunk .10 .03
631 Drew Hall .10 .03
632 Doug Jones .10 .03
633 Geno Petralli UER .10 .03
(Sacremento)
634 Jose Alvarez .10 .03
635 Bob Milacki .10 .03
636 Bobby Witt .10 .03
637 Trevor Wilson .10 .03
638 Jeff Russell UER .10 .03
(Shutout stats wrong)
639 Mike Krukow .10 .03
640 Rick Leach .10 .03
641 Dave Schmidt .10 .03
642 Terry Leach .10 .03
643 Calvin Schiraldi .10 .03
644 Bob Melvin .10 .03
645 Jim Abbott .50 .15
646 Jaime Navarro .10 .03
647 Mark Langston UER .10 .03
(Several errors in stats totals)
648 Juan Nieves .10 .03
649 Damaso Garcia .10 .03
650 Charlie O'Brien .10 .03
651 Eric King .10 .03
652 Mike Boddicker .10 .03
653 Duane Ward .10 .03
654 Bob Stanley .10 .03
655 Sandy Alomar Jr. .20 .06
656 Danny Tartabull UER .10 .03
(395 BB, should be 295)
657 Randy McCament .10 .03
658 Charlie Leibrandt .10 .03
659 Dan Quisenberry .10 .03
660 Paul Assenmacher .10 .03
661 Walt Terrell .10 .03
662 Tim Leary .10 .03
663 Randy Milligan .10 .03
664 Bo Diaz .10 .03
665 Mark Lemke UER .10 .03
(Richmond misspelled as Richomond)
666 Jose Gonzalez .10 .03
667 Chuck Finley UER .20 .06
(Born 11/16/62, should be 11/26/62)
668 John Kruk .20 .06
669 Dick Schofield .10 .03
670 Tim Crews .10 .03
671 John Dopson .10 .03
672 John Orton RC .10 .03
673 Eric Hetzel .10 .03
674 Lance Parrish .10 .03
675 Ramon Martinez .10 .03
676 Mark Gubicza .10 .03
677 Greg Litton .10 .03
678 Greg Mathews .10 .03
679 Dave Dravecky .20 .06
680 Steve Farr .10 .03
681 Mike Devereaux .10 .03
682 Ken Griffey Sr. .20 .06
683A Mickey Weston ERR 2.00 .60
(Listed as Jamie on card)
683B Mickey Weston COR .10 .03
(Technically still an error as birthdate is listed as 3/26/81)
684 Jack Armstrong .10 .03
685 Steve Buechele .10 .03
686 Bryan Harvey .10 .03
687 Lance Blankenship .10 .03
688 Dante Bichette .50 .15
689 Todd Burns .10 .03
690 Dan Petry .10 .03
691 Kent Anderson .10 .03
692 Todd Stottlemyre .20 .06
693 Wally Joyner UER .20 .06
(Several stats errors)
694 Mike Rochford .10 .03
695 Floyd Bannister .10 .03
696 Rick Reuschel .10 .03
697 Jose DeLeon .10 .03
698 Jeff Montgomery .20 .06
699 Kelly Downs .10 .03
700A Checklist 601-700 2.00 .60
(683 Jamie Weston)
700B Checklist 601-700 .10 .03
(683 Mickey Weston)
701 Jim Gott .10 .03
702 Delino DeShields .50 .15
Marquis Grissom
Larry Walker
702A Mike Witt 10.00 3.00
Black rectangle covers much of back
703 Alejandro Pena .10 .03
704 Willie Randolph .20 .06
705 Tim Leary .10 .03
706 Chuck McElroy RC .10 .03
707 Gerald Perry .10 .03
708 Tom Brunansky .10 .03
709 John Franco .20 .06
710 Mark Davis .10 .03
711 David Justice RC .75 .23
712 Storm Davis .10 .03
713 Scott Ruskin .10 .03
714 Glenn Braggs .10 .03
715 Kevin Bearse .10 .03
716 Jose Nunez .10 .03
717 Tim Layana .10 .03
718 Greg Myers .10 .03
719 Pete O'Brien .10 .03
720 John Candelaria .10 .03
721 Craig Grebeck RC .10 .03
722 Shawn Boskie RC .10 .03
723 Jim Leyritz RC .25 .07
724 Bill Sampen .10 .03
725 Scott Radinsky RC .10 .03
726 Todd Hundley RC .25 .07
727 Scott Hemond RC .10 .03
728 Lenny Webster RC .10 .03
729 Jeff Reardon .20 .06
730 Mitch Webster .10 .03
731 Brian Bohanon RC .10 .03
732 Rick Parker .10 .03
733 Terry Shumpert .10 .03
734A Nolan Ryan 3.00 .90
6th No-Hitter
(No stripe on front)
734B Nolan Ryan 1.00 .30
6th No-Hitter
(stripe added on card front for 300th win)
735 John Burkett .10 .03
736 Derrick May RC .10 .03
737 Carlos Baerga RC .25 .07
738 Greg Smith .10 .03
739 Scott Sanderson .10 .03
740 Joe Kraemer .10 .03
741 Hector Villanueva RC .10 .03
742 Mike Fetters RC .25 .07
743 Mark Gardner RC .10 .03
744 Matt Nokes .10 .03
745 Dave Winfield .30 .09
746 Delino DeShields RC .25 .07
747 Dann Howitt .10 .03
748 Tony Pena .10 .03
749 Oil Can Boyd .10 .03
750 Mike Benjamin .10 .03
751 Alex Cole RC .10 .03
752 Eric Gunderson .10 .03
753 Howard Farmer .10 .03
754 Joe Carter .20 .06
755 Ray Lankford RC .25 .07
756 Sandy Alomar Jr. .20 .06
757 Alex Sanchez .10 .03
758 Nick Esasky .10 .03
759 Stan Belinda RC .10 .03
760 Jim Presley .10 .03
761 Gary DiSarcina RC .25 .07
762 Wayne Edwards .10 .03
763 Pat Combs .10 .03
764 Mickey Pina .10 .03
765 Wilson Alvarez RC .25 .07
766 Dave Parker .20 .06
767 Mike Blowers RC .10 .03
768 Tony Phillips .10 .03
769 Pascual Perez .10 .03
770 Gary Pettis .10 .03
771 Fred Lynn .10 .03
772 Mel Rojas RC .10 .03
773 David Segui RC .25 .07
774 Gary Carter .30 .09
775 Rafael Valdez .10 .03
776 Glenallen Hill .10 .03
777 Keith Hernandez .30 .09
778 Billy Hatcher .10 .03
779 Marty Clary .10 .03
780 Candy Maldonado .10 .03
781 Mike Marshall .10 .03
782 Billy Joe Robidoux .10 .03
783 Mark Langston .10 .03
784 Paul Sorrento RC .25 .07
785 Dave Hollins RC .25 .07
786 Cecil Fielder .20 .06
787 Matt Young .10 .03
788 Jeff Huson .10 .03
789 Lloyd Moseby .10 .03
790 Ron Kittle .10 .03
791 Hubie Brooks .10 .03
792 Craig Lefferts .10 .03
793 Kevin Bass .10 .03
794 Bryn Smith .10 .03
795 Juan Samuel .10 .03
796 Sam Horn .10 .03
797 Randy Myers .20 .06
798 Chris James .10 .03
799 Bill Gullickson .10 .03
800 Checklist 701-800 .10 .03

1991 Upper Deck

	Nm-Mt	Ex-Mt
COMPLETE SET (800)	15.00	4.50
COMP.FACT.SET (800)	20.00	6.00
COMPLETE LO SET (700)	15.00	4.50
COMPLETE HI SET (100)	5.00	1.50

1 Star Rookie Checklist .05 .02
2 Phil Plantier RC .10 .03
3 D.J. Dozier .05 .02
4 Dave Hansen .05 .02
5 Maurice Vaughn .10 .03
6 Leo Gomez .05 .02
7 Scott Aldred .05 .02
8 Scott Chiamparino .05 .02

❑ 9 Lance Dickson RC .10 .03
❑ 10 Sean Berry RC .10 .03
❑ 11 Bernie Williams .25 .07
❑ 12 Brian Barnes UER .10 .03
(Photo either not him
or in wrong jersey)
❑ 13 Narciso Elvira .05 .02
❑ 14 Mike Gardiner .05 .02
❑ 15 Greg Colbrunn RC .25 .07
❑ 16 Bernard Gilkey .05 .02
❑ 17 Mark Lewis .05 .02
❑ 18 Mickey Morandini .05 .02
❑ 19 Charles Nagy .05 .02
❑ 20 Geronimo Pena .05 .02
❑ 21 Henry Rodriguez RC .25 .07
❑ 22 Scott Cooper .05 .02
❑ 23 Andujar Cedeno UER .05 .02
(Shown batting left,
back says right)
❑ 24 Eric Karros RC .50 .15
❑ 25 Steve Decker UER .05 .02
Lewis-Clark State
College, not Lewis
and Clark
❑ 26 Kevin Belcher .05 .02
❑ 27 Jeff Conine RC .50 .15
❑ 28 Dave Stewart TC .05 .02
❑ 29 Carlton Fisk TC .10 .03
❑ 30 Rafael Palmeiro TC .10 .03
❑ 31 Chuck Finley TC .05 .02
❑ 32 Harold Reynolds TC .05 .02
❑ 33 Bret Saberhagen TC .05 .02
❑ 34 Gary Gaetti TC .05 .02
❑ 35 Scott Leius .05 .02
❑ 36 Neal Heaton .05 .02
❑ 37 Terry Lee .05 .02
❑ 38 Gary Redus .05 .02
❑ 39 Barry Jones .05 .02
❑ 40 Chuck Knoblauch .10 .03
❑ 41 Larry Andersen .05 .02
❑ 42 Darryl Hamilton .05 .02
❑ 43 Mike Greenwell TC .05 .02
❑ 44 Kelly Gruber TC .05 .02
❑ 45 Jack Morris TC .05 .02
❑ 46 Sandy Alomar Jr. TC .05 .02
❑ 47 Gregg Olson TC .05 .02
❑ 48 Dave Parker TC .05 .02
❑ 49 Roberto Kelly TC .05 .02
❑ 50 Top Prospect Checklist .05 .02
❑ 51 Kyle Abbott .05 .02
❑ 52 Jeff Juden .05 .02
❑ 53 T.Van Poppel UER RC .25 .07
Born Arlington and
attended John Martin HS,
should say Hinsdale and
James Martin HS
❑ 54 Steve Karsay RC .25 .07
❑ 55 Chipper Jones RC 4.00 1.20
❑ 56 Chris Johnson RC UER .10 .03
(Called Tim on back)
❑ 57 John Ericks .05 .02
❑ 58 Gary Scott .05 .02
❑ 59 Kiki Jones .05 .02
❑ 60 Wil Cordero RC .10 .03
❑ 61 Royce Clayton .05 .02
❑ 62 Tim Costo RC .10 .03
❑ 63 Roger Salkeld .05 .02
❑ 64 Brook Fordyce RC .25 .07
❑ 65 Mike Mussina RC 1.50 .45
❑ 66 Dave Staton RC .10 .03
❑ 67 Mike Lieberthal RC .40 .12
❑ 68 Kurt Miller RC .05 .02
❑ 69 Dan Peltier RC .10 .03
❑ 70 Greg Blosser .05 .02
❑ 71 Reggie Sanders RC .40 .12
❑ 72 Brent Mayne .05 .02
❑ 73 Rico Brogna .05 .02
❑ 74 Willie Banks .05 .02
❑ 75 Len Brutcher .05 .02
❑ 76 Pat Kelly RC .10 .03
❑ 77 Chris Sabo TC .05 .02
❑ 78 Ramon Martinez TC .05 .02
❑ 79 Matt Williams TC .05 .02
❑ 80 Roberto Alomar TC .10 .03
❑ 81 Glenn Davis TC .05 .02
❑ 82 Ron Gant TC .05 .02
❑ 83 Cecil Fielder FEAT .05 .02
❑ 84 Orlando Merced RC .10 .03
❑ 85 Domingo Ramos .05 .02
❑ 86 Tom Bolton .05 .02
❑ 87 Andres Santana .05 .02
❑ 88 John Dopson .05 .02
❑ 89 Kenny Williams .05 .02
❑ 90 Marty Barrett .05 .02
❑ 91 Tom Pagnozzi .05 .02
❑ 92 Carmelo Martinez .05 .02
❑ 93 Bobby Thigpen SAVE .05 .02
❑ 94 Barry Bonds TC .30 .09
❑ 95 Gregg Jefferies TC .05 .02
❑ 96 Tim Wallach TC .05 .02
❑ 97 Len Dykstra TC .05 .02
❑ 98 Pedro Guerrero TC .05 .02
❑ 99 Mark Grace TC .10 .03
❑ 100 Checklist 1-100 .05 .02
❑ 101 Kevin Elster .05 .02
❑ 102 Tom Brookens .05 .02
❑ 103 Mackey Sasser .05 .02
❑ 104 Felix Fermin .05 .02
❑ 105 Kevin McReynolds .05 .02
❑ 106 Dave Stieb .05 .02
❑ 107 Jeffrey Leonard .05 .02
❑ 108 Dave Henderson .05 .02
❑ 109 Sid Bream .05 .02
❑ 110 Henry Cotto .05 .02
❑ 111 Shawon Dunston .05 .02
❑ 112 Mariano Duncan .05 .02
❑ 113 Joe Girardi .05 .02
❑ 114 Billy Hatcher .05 .02
❑ 115 Greg Maddux .50 .15
❑ 116 Jerry Browne .05 .02
❑ 117 Juan Samuel .05 .02
❑ 118 Steve Olin .05 .02
❑ 119 Alfredo Griffin .05 .02
❑ 120 Mitch Webster .05 .02
❑ 121 Joel Skinner .05 .02
❑ 122 Frank Viola .10 .03
❑ 123 Cory Snyder .05 .02
❑ 124 Howard Johnson .05 .02
❑ 125 Carlos Baerga .05 .02
❑ 126 Tony Fernandez .05 .02
❑ 127 Dave Stewart .10 .03
❑ 128 Jay Buhner .10 .03
❑ 129 Mike LaValliere .05 .02
❑ 130 Scott Bradley .05 .02
❑ 131 Tony Phillips .05 .02
❑ 132 Ryne Sandberg .40 .12
❑ 133 Paul O'Neill .15 .04
❑ 134 Mark Grace .25 .07
❑ 135 Chris Sabo .05 .02
❑ 136 Ramon Martinez .05 .02
❑ 137 Brook Jacoby .05 .02
❑ 138 Candy Maldonado .05 .02
❑ 139 Mike Scioscia .05 .02
❑ 140 Chris James .05 .02
❑ 141 Craig Worthington .05 .02
❑ 142 Manny Lee .05 .02
❑ 143 Tim Raines .10 .03
❑ 144 Sandy Alomar Jr. .05 .02
❑ 145 John Olerud .10 .03
❑ 146 Ozzie Canseco .10 .03
(With Jose)
❑ 147 Pat Borders .05 .02
❑ 148 Harold Reynolds .10 .03
❑ 149 Tom Henke .05 .02
❑ 150 R.J. Reynolds .05 .02
❑ 151 Mike Gallego .05 .02
❑ 152 Bobby Bonilla .10 .03
❑ 153 Terry Steinbach .05 .02
❑ 154 Barry Bonds .60 .18
❑ 155 Jose Canseco .25 .07
❑ 156 Gregg Jefferies .05 .02
❑ 157 Matt Williams .10 .03
❑ 158 Craig Biggio .15 .04
❑ 159 Daryl Boston .05 .02
❑ 160 Ricky Jordan .05 .02
❑ 161 Stan Belinda .05 .02
❑ 162 Ozzie Smith .25 .07
❑ 163 Tom Brunansky .05 .02
❑ 164 Todd Zeile .05 .02
❑ 165 Mike Greenwell .05 .02
❑ 166 Kal Daniels .05 .02
❑ 167 Kent Hrbek .10 .03
❑ 168 Franklin Stubbs .05 .02
❑ 169 Dick Schofield .05 .02
❑ 170 Junior Ortiz .05 .02
❑ 171 Hector Villanueva .05 .02
❑ 172 Dennis Eckersley .10 .03
❑ 173 Mitch Williams .05 .02
❑ 174 Mark McGwire .60 .18
❑ 175 F.Valenzuela 3X .10 .03
❑ 176 Gary Carter .15 .04
❑ 177 Dave Magadan .05 .02
❑ 178 Robby Thompson .05 .02
❑ 179 Bob Ojeda .05 .02
❑ 180 Ken Caminiti .10 .03
❑ 181 Don Slaught .05 .02
❑ 182 Luis Rivera .05 .02
❑ 183 Jay Bell .10 .03
❑ 184 Jody Reed .05 .02
❑ 185 Wally Backman .05 .02
❑ 186 Dave Martinez .05 .02
❑ 187 Luis Polonia .05 .02
❑ 188 Shane Mack .05 .02
❑ 189 Spike Owen .05 .02
❑ 190 Scott Bailes .05 .02
❑ 191 John Russell .05 .02
❑ 192 Walt Weiss .05 .02
❑ 193 Jose Oquendo .05 .02
❑ 194 Carney Lansford .10 .03
❑ 195 Jeff Huson .05 .02
❑ 196 Keith Miller .05 .02
❑ 197 Eric Yelding .05 .02
❑ 198 Ron Darling .05 .02
❑ 199 John Kruk .10 .03
❑ 200 Checklist 101-200 .05 .02
❑ 201 John Shelby .05 .02
❑ 202 Bob Geren .05 .02
❑ 203 Lance McCullers .05 .02
❑ 204 Alvaro Espinoza .05 .02
❑ 205 Mark Salas .05 .02
❑ 206 Mike Pagliarulo .05 .02
❑ 207 Jose Uribe .05 .02
❑ 208 Jim Deshaies .05 .02
❑ 209 Ron Karkovice .05 .02
❑ 210 Rafael Ramirez .05 .02
❑ 211 Donnie Hill .05 .02
❑ 212 Brian Harper .05 .02
❑ 213 Jack Howell .05 .02
❑ 214 Wes Gardner .05 .02
❑ 215 Tim Burke .05 .02
❑ 216 Doug Jones .05 .02
❑ 217 Hubie Brooks .05 .02
❑ 218 Tom Candiotti .05 .02
❑ 219 Gerald Perry .05 .02
❑ 220 Jose DeLeon .05 .02
❑ 221 Wally Whitehurst .05 .02
❑ 222 Alan Mills .05 .02
❑ 223 Alan Trammell .15 .04
❑ 224 Dwight Gooden .15 .04
❑ 225 Travis Fryman .10 .03
❑ 226 Joe Carter .10 .03
❑ 227 Julio Franco .10 .03
❑ 228 Craig Lefferts .05 .02
❑ 229 Gary Pettis .05 .02
❑ 230 Dennis Rasmussen .05 .02
❑ 231A Brian Downing ERR .05 .02
(No position on front)
❑ 231B Brian Downing COR .25 .07
(DH on front)
❑ 232 Carlos Quintana .05 .02
❑ 233 Gary Gaetti .10 .03
❑ 234 Mark Langston .05 .02
❑ 235 Tim Wallach .05 .02
❑ 236 Greg Swindell .05 .02
❑ 237 Eddie Murray .25 .07
❑ 238 Jeff Manto .05 .02
❑ 239 Lenny Harris .05 .02
❑ 240 Jesse Orosco .05 .02
❑ 241 Scott Lusader .05 .02
❑ 242 Sid Fernandez .05 .02
❑ 243 Jim Leyritz .05 .02
❑ 244 Cecil Fielder .10 .03
❑ 245 Darryl Strawberry .15 .04
❑ 246 Frank Thomas UER .25 .07
(Comiskey Park
misspelled Comisky)
❑ 247 Kevin Mitchell .05 .02
❑ 248 Lance Johnson .05 .02

❑ 249 Rick Reuschel .05 .02
❑ 250 Mark Portugal .05 .02
❑ 251 Derek Lilliquist .05 .02
❑ 252 Brian Holman .05 .02
❑ 253 Rafael Valdez UER .05 .02
(Born 4/17/68,
should be 12/17/67)
❑ 254 B.J. Surhoff .10 .03
❑ 255 Tony Gwynn .30 .09
❑ 256 Andy Van Slyke .10 .03
❑ 257 Todd Stottlemyre .05 .02
❑ 258 Jose Lind .05 .02
❑ 259 Greg Myers .05 .02
❑ 260 Jeff Ballard .05 .02
❑ 261 Bobby Thigpen .05 .02
❑ 262 Jimmy Kremers .05 .02
❑ 263 Robin Ventura .10 .03
❑ 264 John Smoltz .15 .04
❑ 265 Sammy Sosa .50 .15
❑ 266 Gary Sheffield .10 .03
❑ 267 Len Dykstra .10 .03
❑ 268 Bill Spiers .05 .02
❑ 269 Charlie Hayes .05 .02
❑ 270 Brett Butler .10 .03
❑ 271 Bip Roberts .05 .02
❑ 272 Rob Deer .05 .02
❑ 273 Fred Lynn .05 .02
❑ 274 Dave Parker .10 .03
❑ 275 Andy Benes .05 .02
❑ 276 Glenallen Hill .05 .02
❑ 277 Steve Howard .05 .02
❑ 278 Doug Drabek .05 .02
❑ 279 Joe Oliver .05 .02
❑ 280 Todd Benzinger .05 .02
❑ 281 Eric King .05 .02
❑ 282 Jim Presley .05 .02
❑ 283 Ken Patterson .05 .02
❑ 284 Jack Daugherty .05 .02
❑ 285 Ivan Calderon .05 .02
❑ 286 Edgar Diaz .05 .02
❑ 287 Kevin Bass .05 .02
❑ 288 Don Carman .05 .02
❑ 289 Greg Brock .05 .02
❑ 290 John Franco .10 .03
❑ 291 Joey Cora .05 .02
❑ 292 Bill Wegman .05 .02
❑ 293 Eric Show .05 .02
❑ 294 Scott Bankhead .05 .02
❑ 295 Garry Templeton .05 .02
❑ 296 Mickey Tettleton .05 .02
❑ 297 Luis Sojo .05 .02
❑ 298 Jose Rijo .05 .02
❑ 299 Dave Johnson .05 .02
❑ 300 Checklist 201-300 .05 .02
❑ 301 Mark Grant .05 .02
❑ 302 Pete Harnisch .05 .02
❑ 303 Greg Olson .05 .02
❑ 304 Anthony Telford .05 .02
❑ 305 Lonnie Smith .05 .02
❑ 306 Chris Hoiles .05 .02
❑ 307 Bryn Smith .05 .02
❑ 308 Mike Devereaux .05 .02
❑ 309A Milt Thompson ERR .25 .07
(Under yr information
has print dot)
❑ 309B Milt Thompson COR .05 .02
(Under yr information
says 86)
❑ 310 Bob Melvin .05 .02
❑ 311 Luis Salazar .05 .02
❑ 312 Ed Whitson .05 .02
❑ 313 Charlie Hough .10 .03
❑ 314 Dave Clark .05 .02
❑ 315 Eric Gunderson .05 .02
❑ 316 Dan Petry .05 .02
❑ 317 Dante Bichette UER .10 .03
(Assists misspelled
as assissts)
❑ 318 Mike Heath .05 .02
❑ 319 Damon Berryhill .05 .02
❑ 320 Walt Terrell .05 .02
❑ 321 Scott Fletcher .05 .02
❑ 322 Dan Plesac .05 .02
❑ 323 Jack McDowell .05 .02
❑ 324 Paul Molitor .15 .04
❑ 325 Ozzie Guillen .05 .02
❑ 326 Gregg Olson .05 .02
❑ 327 Pedro Guerrero .10 .03
❑ 328 Bob Milacki .05 .02
❑ 329 John Tudor UER .05 .02
('90 Cardinals,
should be '90 Dodgers)
❑ 330 Steve Finley UER .10 .03
(Born 3/12/65,
should be 5/12)
❑ 331 Jack Clark .10 .03
❑ 332 Jerome Walton .05 .02
❑ 333 Andy Hawkins .05 .02
❑ 334 Derrick May .05 .02
❑ 335 Roberto Alomar .25 .07
❑ 336 Jack Morris .10 .03
❑ 337 Dave Winfield .15 .04
❑ 338 Steve Searcy .05 .02
❑ 339 Chili Davis .10 .03
❑ 340 Larry Sheets .05 .02
❑ 341 Ted Higuera .05 .02
❑ 342 David Segui .05 .02
❑ 343 Greg Cadaret .05 .02
❑ 344 Robin Yount .25 .07
❑ 345 Nolan Ryan 1.00 .30
❑ 346 Ray Lankford .05 .02
❑ 347 Cal Ripken .75 .23
❑ 348 Lee Smith .10 .03
❑ 349 Brady Anderson .10 .03
❑ 350 Frank DiPino .05 .02
❑ 351 Hal Morris .05 .02
❑ 352 Deion Sanders .10 .03
❑ 353 Barry Larkin .25 .07
❑ 354 Don Mattingly .60 .18
❑ 355 Eric Davis .10 .03
❑ 356 Jose Offerman .05 .02
❑ 357 Mel Rojas .05 .02
❑ 358 Rudy Seanez .05 .02
❑ 359 Oil Can Boyd .05 .02
❑ 360 Nelson Liriano .05 .02
❑ 361 Ron Gant .10 .03
❑ 362 Howard Farmer .05 .02
❑ 363 David Justice .10 .03
❑ 364 Delino DeShields .10 .03
❑ 365 Steve Avery .05 .02
❑ 366 David Cone .10 .03
❑ 367 Lou Whitaker .10 .03
❑ 368 Von Hayes .05 .02
❑ 369 Frank Tanana .05 .02
❑ 370 Tim Teufel .05 .02
❑ 371 Randy Myers .05 .02
❑ 372 Roberto Kelly .05 .02
❑ 373 Jack Armstrong .05 .02
❑ 374 Kelly Gruber .05 .02
❑ 375 Kevin Maas .05 .02
❑ 376 Randy Johnson .30 .09
❑ 377 David West .05 .02
❑ 378 Brent Knackert .05 .02
❑ 379 Rick Honeycutt .05 .02
❑ 380 Kevin Gross .05 .02
❑ 381 Tom Foley .05 .02
❑ 382 Jeff Blauser .05 .02
❑ 383 Scott Ruskin .05 .02
❑ 384 Andres Thomas .05 .02
❑ 385 Dennis Martinez .10 .03
❑ 386 Mike Henneman .05 .02
❑ 387 Felix Jose .05 .02
❑ 388 Alejandro Pena .05 .02
❑ 389 Chet Lemon .05 .02
❑ 390 Craig Wilson .05 .02
❑ 391 Chuck Crim .05 .02
❑ 392 Mel Hall .05 .02
❑ 393 Mark Knudson .05 .02
❑ 394 Norm Charlton .05 .02
❑ 395 Mike Felder .05 .02
❑ 396 Tim Layana .05 .02
❑ 397 Steve Frey .05 .02
❑ 398 Bill Doran .05 .02
❑ 399 Dion James .05 .02
❑ 400 Checklist 301-400 .05 .02
❑ 401 Ron Hassey .05 .02
❑ 402 Don Robinson .05 .02
❑ 403 Gene Nelson .05 .02
❑ 404 Terry Kennedy .05 .02
❑ 405 Todd Burns .05 .02
❑ 406 Roger McDowell .05 .02
❑ 407 Bob Kipper .05 .02
❑ 408 Darren Daulton .10 .03
❑ 409 Chuck Cary .05 .02
❑ 410 Bruce Ruffin .05 .02
❑ 411 Juan Berenguer .05 .02
❑ 412 Gary Ward .05 .02
❑ 413 Al Newman .05 .02
❑ 414 Danny Jackson .05 .02
❑ 415 Greg Gagne .05 .02
❑ 416 Tom Herr .05 .02
❑ 417 Jeff Parrett .05 .02
❑ 418 Jeff Reardon .10 .03
❑ 419 Mark Lemke .05 .02
❑ 420 Charlie O'Brien .05 .02
❑ 421 Willie Randolph .10 .03
❑ 422 Steve Bedrosian .05 .02
❑ 423 Mike Moore .05 .02
❑ 424 Jeff Brantley .05 .02
❑ 425 Bob Welch .05 .02
❑ 426 Terry Mulholland .05 .02
❑ 427 Willie Blair .05 .02
❑ 428 Darrin Fletcher .05 .02
❑ 429 Mike Witt .05 .02
❑ 430 Joe Boever .05 .02
❑ 431 Tom Gordon .05 .02
❑ 432 Pedro Munoz RC .10 .03
❑ 433 Kevin Seitzer .05 .02
❑ 434 Kevin Tapani .05 .02
❑ 435 Bret Saberhagen .10 .03
❑ 436 Ellis Burks .10 .03
❑ 437 Chuck Finley .10 .03
❑ 438 Mike Boddicker .05 .02
❑ 439 Francisco Cabrera .05 .02
❑ 440 Todd Hundley .05 .02
❑ 441 Kelly Downs .05 .02
❑ 442 Dann Howitt .05 .02
❑ 443 Scott Garrelts .05 .02
❑ 444 Rickey Henderson 3X .40 .12
❑ 445 Will Clark .25 .07
❑ 446 Ben McDonald .05 .02
❑ 447 Dale Murphy .25 .07
❑ 448 Dave Righetti .10 .03
❑ 449 Dickie Thon .05 .02
❑ 450 Ted Power .05 .02
❑ 451 Scott Coolbaugh .05 .02
❑ 452 Dwight Smith .05 .02
❑ 453 Pete Incaviglia .05 .02
❑ 454 Andre Dawson .10 .03
❑ 455 Ruben Sierra .05 .02
❑ 456 Andres Galarraga .10 .03
❑ 457 Alvin Davis .05 .02
❑ 458 Tony Castillo .05 .02
❑ 459 Pete O'Brien .05 .02
❑ 460 Charlie Leibrandt .05 .02
❑ 461 Vince Coleman .05 .02
❑ 462 Steve Sax .05 .02
❑ 463 Omar Olivares RC .10 .03
❑ 464 Oscar Azocar .05 .02
❑ 465 Joe Magrane .05 .02
❑ 466 Karl Rhodes .05 .02
❑ 467 Benito Santiago .10 .03
❑ 468 Joe Klink .05 .02
❑ 469 Sil Campusano .05 .02
❑ 470 Mark Parent .05 .02
❑ 471 Shawn Boskie UER .05 .02
(Depleted misspelled
as depleated)
❑ 472 Kevin Brown .10 .03
❑ 473 Rick Sutcliffe .10 .03
❑ 474 Rafael Palmeiro .15 .04
❑ 475 Mike Harkey .05 .02
❑ 476 Jaime Navarro .05 .02
❑ 477 Marquis Grissom UER .05 .02
(DeShields misspelled
as DeSheilds)
❑ 478 Marty Clary .05 .02
❑ 479 Greg Briley .05 .02
❑ 480 Tom Glavine .25 .07
❑ 481 Lee Guetterman .05 .02
❑ 482 Rex Hudler .05 .02
❑ 483 Dave LaPoint .05 .02
❑ 484 Terry Pendleton .10 .03
❑ 485 Jesse Barfield .05 .02
❑ 486 Jose DeJesus .05 .02
❑ 487 Paul Abbott RC .25 .07
❑ 488 Ken Howell .05 .02
❑ 489 Greg W. Harris .05 .02

❑ 490	Roy Smith	.05	.02
❑ 491	Paul Assenmacher	.05	.02
❑ 492	Geno Petralli	.05	.02
❑ 493	Steve Wilson	.05	.02
❑ 494	Kevin Reimer	.05	.02
❑ 495	Bill Long	.05	.02
❑ 496	Mike Jackson	.05	.02
❑ 497	Oddibe McDowell	.05	.02
❑ 498	Bill Swift	.05	.02
❑ 499	Jeff Treadway	.05	.02
❑ 500	Checklist 401-500	.05	.02
❑ 501	Gene Larkin	.05	.02
❑ 502	Bob Boone	.10	.03
❑ 503	Allan Anderson	.05	.02
❑ 504	Luis Aquino	.05	.02
❑ 505	Mark Guthrie	.05	.02
❑ 506	Joe Orsulak	.05	.02
❑ 507	Dana Kiecker	.05	.02
❑ 508	Dave Gallagher	.05	.02
❑ 509	Greg A. Harris	.05	.02
❑ 510	Mark Williamson	.05	.02
❑ 511	Casey Candaele	.05	.02
❑ 512	Mookie Wilson	.10	.03
❑ 513	Dave Smith	.05	.02
❑ 514	Chuck Carr	.05	.02
❑ 515	Glenn Wilson	.05	.02
❑ 516	Mike Fitzgerald	.05	.02
❑ 517	Devon White	.05	.02
❑ 518	Dave Hollins	.05	.02
❑ 519	Mark Eichhorn	.05	.02
❑ 520	Otis Nixon	.05	.02
❑ 521	Terry Shumpert	.05	.02
❑ 522	Scott Erickson	.05	.02
❑ 523	Danny Tartabull	.05	.02
❑ 524	Orel Hershiser	.10	.03
❑ 525	George Brett	.60	.18
❑ 526	Greg Vaughn	.10	.03
❑ 527	Tim Naehring	.05	.02
❑ 528	Curt Schilling	.15	.04
❑ 529	Chris Bosio	.05	.02
❑ 530	Sam Horn	.05	.02
❑ 531	Mike Scott	.05	.02
❑ 532	George Bell	.05	.02
❑ 533	Eric Anthony	.05	.02
❑ 534	Julio Valera	.05	.02
❑ 535	Glenn Davis	.05	.02
❑ 536	Larry Walker UER (Should have comma after Expos in text)	.25	.07
❑ 537	Pat Combs	.05	.02
❑ 538	Chris Nabholz	.05	.02
❑ 539	Kirk McCaskill	.05	.02
❑ 540	Randy Ready	.05	.02
❑ 541	Mark Gubicza	.05	.02
❑ 542	Rick Aguilera	.10	.03
❑ 543	Brian McRae RC	.25	.07
❑ 544	Kirby Puckett	.25	.07
❑ 545	Bo Jackson	.25	.07
❑ 546	Wade Boggs	.15	.04
❑ 547	Tim McIntosh	.05	.02
❑ 548	Randy Milligan	.05	.02
❑ 549	Dwight Evans	.10	.03
❑ 550	Billy Ripken	.05	.02
❑ 551	Erik Hanson	.05	.02
❑ 552	Lance Parrish	.10	.03
❑ 553	Tino Martinez	.15	.04
❑ 554	Jim Abbott	.25	.07
❑ 555	Ken Griffey Jr. UER (Second most votes for 1991 All-Star Game)	.50	.15
❑ 556	Milt Cuyler	.05	.02
❑ 557	Mark Leonard	.05	.02
❑ 558	Jay Howell	.05	.02
❑ 559	Lloyd Moseby	.05	.02
❑ 560	Chris Gwynn	.05	.02
❑ 561	Mark Whiten	.05	.02
❑ 562	Harold Baines	.10	.03
❑ 563	Junior Felix	.05	.02
❑ 564	Darren Lewis	.05	.02
❑ 565	Fred McGriff	.15	.04
❑ 566	Kevin Appier	.10	.03
❑ 567	Luis Gonzalez RC	1.25	.35
❑ 568	Frank White	.10	.03
❑ 569	Juan Agosto	.05	.02
❑ 570	Mike Macfarlane	.05	.02
❑ 571	Bert Blyleven	.10	.03
❑ 572	Ken Griffey Sr. / Ken Griffey Jr.	.25	.07
❑ 573	Lee Stevens	.05	.02
❑ 574	Edgar Martinez	.15	.04
❑ 575	Wally Joyner	.10	.03
❑ 576	Tim Belcher	.05	.02
❑ 577	John Burkett	.05	.02
❑ 578	Mike Morgan	.05	.02
❑ 579	Paul Gibson	.05	.02
❑ 580	Jose Vizcaino	.05	.02
❑ 581	Duane Ward	.05	.02
❑ 582	Scott Sanderson	.05	.02
❑ 583	David Wells	.10	.03
❑ 584	Willie McGee	.10	.03
❑ 585	John Cerutti	.05	.02
❑ 586	Danny Darwin	.05	.02
❑ 587	Kurt Stillwell	.05	.02
❑ 588	Rich Gedman	.05	.02
❑ 589	Mark Davis	.05	.02
❑ 590	Bill Gullickson	.05	.02
❑ 591	Matt Young	.05	.02
❑ 592	Bryan Harvey	.05	.02
❑ 593	Omar Vizquel	.10	.03
❑ 594	Scott Lewis RC	.10	.03
❑ 595	Dave Valle	.05	.02
❑ 596	Tim Crews	.05	.02
❑ 597	Mike Bielecki	.05	.02
❑ 598	Mike Sharperson	.05	.02
❑ 599	Dave Bergman	.05	.02
❑ 600	Checklist 501-600	.05	.02
❑ 601	Steve Lyons	.05	.02
❑ 602	Bruce Hurst	.05	.02
❑ 603	Donn Pall	.05	.02
❑ 604	Jim Vatcher	.05	.02
❑ 605	Dan Pasqua	.05	.02
❑ 606	Kenny Rogers	.10	.03
❑ 607	Jeff Schulz	.05	.02
❑ 608	Brad Arnsberg	.05	.02
❑ 609	Willie Wilson	.05	.02
❑ 610	Jamie Moyer	.10	.03
❑ 611	Ron Oester	.05	.02
❑ 612	Dennis Cook	.05	.02
❑ 613	Rick Mahler	.05	.02
❑ 614	Bill Landrum	.05	.02
❑ 615	Scott Scudder	.05	.02
❑ 616	Tom Edens	.05	.02
❑ 617	1917 Revisited (White Sox vintage uniforms)	.10	.03
❑ 618	Jim Gantner	.05	.02
❑ 619	Darrel Akerfelds	.05	.02
❑ 620	Ron Robinson	.05	.02
❑ 621	Scott Radinsky	.05	.02
❑ 622	Pete Smith	.05	.02
❑ 623	Melido Perez	.05	.02
❑ 624	Jerald Clark	.05	.02
❑ 625	Carlos Martinez	.05	.02
❑ 626	Wes Chamberlain RC	.25	.07
❑ 627	Bobby Witt	.05	.02
❑ 628	Ken Dayley	.05	.02
❑ 629	John Barfield	.05	.02
❑ 630	Bob Tewksbury	.05	.02
❑ 631	Glenn Braggs	.05	.02
❑ 632	Jim Neidlinger	.05	.02
❑ 633	Tom Browning	.05	.02
❑ 634	Kirk Gibson	.10	.03
❑ 635	Rob Dibble	.10	.03
❑ 636	Rickey Henderson SB / Lou Brock / May 1, 1991 on front	.25	.07
❑ 636A	R.Henderson SB / Lou Brock / no date on card	.40	.12
❑ 637	Jeff Montgomery	.05	.02
❑ 638	Mike Schooler	.05	.02
❑ 639	Storm Davis	.05	.02
❑ 640	Rich Rodriguez	.05	.02
❑ 641	Phil Bradley	.05	.02
❑ 642	Kent Mercker	.05	.02
❑ 643	Carlton Fisk	.15	.04
❑ 644	Mike Bell	.05	.02
❑ 645	Alex Fernandez	.05	.02
❑ 646	Juan Gonzalez	.25	.07
❑ 647	Ken Hill	.05	.02
❑ 648	Jeff Russell	.05	.02
❑ 649	Chuck Malone	.05	.02
❑ 650	Steve Buechele	.05	.02
❑ 651	Mike Benjamin	.05	.02
❑ 652	Tony Pena	.05	.02
❑ 653	Trevor Wilson	.05	.02
❑ 654	Alex Cole	.05	.02
❑ 655	Roger Clemens	.50	.15
❑ 656	Mark McGwire BASH	.30	.09
❑ 657	Joe Grahe RC	.10	.03
❑ 658	Jim Eisenreich	.05	.02
❑ 659	Dan Gladden	.05	.02
❑ 660	Steve Farr	.05	.02
❑ 661	Bill Sampen	.05	.02
❑ 662	Dave Rohde	.05	.02
❑ 663	Mark Gardner	.05	.02
❑ 664	Mike Simms	.05	.02
❑ 665	Moises Alou	.10	.03
❑ 666	Mickey Hatcher	.05	.02
❑ 667	Jimmy Key	.10	.03
❑ 668	John Wetteland	.10	.03
❑ 669	John Smiley	.05	.02
❑ 670	Jim Acker	.05	.02
❑ 671	Pascual Perez	.05	.02
❑ 672	Reggie Harris UER (Opportunity misspelled as oppurtinty)	.05	.02
❑ 673	Matt Nokes	.05	.02
❑ 674	Rafael Novoa	.05	.02
❑ 675	Hensley Meulens	.05	.02
❑ 676	Jeff M. Robinson	.05	.02
❑ 677	Ground Breaking (New Comiskey Park; Carlton Fisk and Robin Ventura)	.10	.03
❑ 678	Johnny Ray	.05	.02
❑ 679	Greg Hibbard	.05	.02
❑ 680	Paul Sorrento	.05	.02
❑ 681	Mike Marshall	.05	.02
❑ 682	Jim Clancy	.05	.02
❑ 683	Rob Murphy	.05	.02
❑ 684	Dave Schmidt	.05	.02
❑ 685	Jeff Gray	.05	.02
❑ 686	Mike Hartley	.05	.02
❑ 687	Jeff King	.05	.02
❑ 688	Stan Javier	.05	.02
❑ 689	Bob Walk	.05	.02
❑ 690	Jim Gott	.05	.02
❑ 691	Mike LaCoss	.05	.02
❑ 692	John Farrell	.05	.02
❑ 693	Tim Leary	.05	.02
❑ 694	Mike Walker	.05	.02
❑ 695	Eric Plunk	.05	.02
❑ 696	Mike Fetters	.05	.02
❑ 697	Wayne Edwards	.05	.02
❑ 698	Tim Drummond	.05	.02
❑ 699	Willie Fraser	.05	.02
❑ 700	Checklist 601-700	.05	.02
❑ 701	Mike Heath	.05	.02
❑ 702	Luis Gonzalez / Karl Rhodes / Jeff Bagwell	1.00	.30
❑ 703	Jose Mesa	.05	.02
❑ 704	Dave Smith	.05	.02
❑ 705	Danny Darwin	.05	.02
❑ 706	Rafael Belliard	.05	.02
❑ 707	Rob Murphy	.05	.02
❑ 708	Terry Pendleton	.10	.03
❑ 709	Mike Pagliarulo	.05	.02
❑ 710	Sid Bream	.05	.02
❑ 711	Junior Felix	.05	.02
❑ 712	Dante Bichette	.10	.03
❑ 713	Kevin Gross	.05	.02
❑ 714	Luis Sojo	.05	.02
❑ 715	Bob Ojeda	.05	.02
❑ 716	Julio Machado	.05	.02
❑ 717	Steve Farr	.05	.02
❑ 718	Franklin Stubbs	.05	.02
❑ 719	Mike Boddicker	.05	.02
❑ 720	Willie Randolph	.10	.03
❑ 721	Willie McGee	.10	.03
❑ 722	Chili Davis	.10	.03
❑ 723	Danny Jackson	.05	.02
❑ 724	Cory Snyder	.05	.02
❑ 725	Andre Dawson / George Bell / Ryne Sandberg	.25	.07
❑ 726	Rob Deer	.05	.02
❑ 727	Rich DeLucia	.05	.02

Card	Nm-Mt	Ex-Mt
❑ 728 Mike Perez RC	.10	.03
❑ 729 Mickey Tettleton	.05	.02
❑ 730 Mike Blowers	.05	.02
❑ 731 Gary Gaetti	.10	.03
❑ 732 Brett Butler	.10	.03
❑ 733 Dave Parker	.10	.03
❑ 734 Eddie Zosky	.05	.02
❑ 735 Jack Clark	.10	.03
❑ 736 Jack Morris	.10	.03
❑ 737 Kirk Gibson	.10	.03
❑ 738 Steve Bedrosian	.05	.02
❑ 739 Candy Maldonado	.05	.02
❑ 740 Matt Young	.05	.02
❑ 741 Rich Garces RC	.10	.03
❑ 742 George Bell	.05	.02
❑ 743 Deion Sanders	.10	.03
❑ 744 Bo Jackson	.25	.07
❑ 745 Luis Mercedes RC	.10	.03
❑ 746 Reggie Jefferson UER (Throwing left on card; back has throws right)	.05	.02
❑ 747 Pete Incaviglia	.05	.02
❑ 748 Chris Hammond	.05	.02
❑ 749 Mike Stanton	.05	.02
❑ 750 Scott Sanderson	.05	.02
❑ 751 Paul Faries	.05	.02
❑ 752 Al Osuna RC	.05	.02
❑ 753 Steve Chitren	.05	.02
❑ 754 Tony Fernandez	.05	.02
❑ 755 Jeff Bagwell RC UER (Strikeout and walk totals reversed)	1.50	.45
❑ 756 K.Dressendorfer RC	.10	.03
❑ 757 Glenn Davis	.05	.02
❑ 758 Gary Carter	.15	.04
❑ 759 Zane Smith	.05	.02
❑ 760 Vance Law	.05	.02
❑ 761 Denis Boucher RC	.10	.03
❑ 762 Turner Ward RC	.10	.03
❑ 763 Roberto Alomar	.25	.07
❑ 764 Albert Belle	.10	.03
❑ 765 Joe Carter	.10	.03
❑ 766 Pete Schourek RC	.10	.03
❑ 767 H.Slocumb RC	.10	.03
❑ 768 Vince Coleman	.05	.02
❑ 769 Mitch Williams	.05	.02
❑ 770 Brian Downing	.05	.02
❑ 771 Dana Allison	.05	.02
❑ 772 Pete Harnisch	.05	.02
❑ 773 Tim Raines	.10	.03
❑ 774 Darryl Kile	.10	.03
❑ 775 Fred McGriff	.15	.04
❑ 776 Dwight Evans	.10	.03
❑ 777 Joe Slusarski	.05	.02
❑ 778 Dave Righetti	.10	.03
❑ 779 Jeff Hamilton	.05	.02
❑ 780 Ernest Riles	.05	.02
❑ 781 Ken Dayley	.05	.02
❑ 782 Eric King	.05	.02
❑ 783 Devon White	.05	.02
❑ 784 Beau Allred	.05	.02
❑ 785 Mike Timlin RC	.25	.07
❑ 786 Ivan Calderon	.05	.02
❑ 787 Hubie Brooks	.05	.02
❑ 788 Juan Agosto	.05	.02
❑ 789 Barry Jones	.05	.02
❑ 790 Wally Backman	.05	.02
❑ 791 Jim Presley	.05	.02
❑ 792 Charlie Hough	.10	.03
❑ 793 Larry Andersen	.05	.02
❑ 794 Steve Finley	.10	.03
❑ 795 Shawn Abner	.05	.02
❑ 796 Jeff M. Robinson	.05	.02
❑ 797 Joe Bitker	.05	.02
❑ 798 Eric Show	.05	.02
❑ 799 Bud Black	.05	.02
❑ 800 Checklist 701-800	.05	.02
❑ HH1 H.Aaron Hologram	1.50	.45
❑ SP1 Michael Jordan SP (Shown batting in White Sox uniform)	10.00	3.00
❑ SP2 Rickey Henderson Nolan Ryan May 1, 1991 Records	2.00	.60

1991 Upper Deck Final Edition

	Nm-Mt	Ex-Mt
COMP.FACT.SET (100)	10.00	3.00
❑ 1F Ryan Klesko CL Reggie Sanders	.10	.03
❑ 2F Pedro Martinez RC	8.00	2.40
❑ 3F Lance Dickson	.05	.02
❑ 4F Royce Clayton	.05	.02
❑ 5F Scott Bryant	.05	.02
❑ 6F Dan Wilson RC	.25	.07
❑ 7F Dmitri Young RC	.50	.15
❑ 8F Ryan Klesko RC	.50	.15
❑ 9F Tom Goodwin	.05	.02
❑ 10F Rondell White RC	.40	.12
❑ 11F Reggie Sanders	.25	.07
❑ 12F Todd Van Poppel	.05	.02
❑ 13F Arthur Rhodes RC	.25	.07
❑ 14F Eddie Zosky	.05	.02
❑ 15F Gerald Williams RC	.25	.07
❑ 16F Robert Eenhoorn RC	.10	.03
❑ 17F Jim Thome RC	2.00	.60
❑ 18F Marc Newfield RC	.10	.03
❑ 19F Kerwin Moore RC	.10	.03
❑ 20F Jeff McNeely RC	.10	.03
❑ 21F Frankie Rodriguez RC	.10	.03
❑ 22F Andy Mota	.05	.02
❑ 23F Chris Haney RC	.10	.03
❑ 24F Kenny Lofton RC	.50	.15
❑ 25F Dave Nilsson RC	.25	.07
❑ 26F Derek Bell	.10	.03
❑ 27F Frank Castillo RC	.25	.07
❑ 28F Candy Maldonado	.05	.02
❑ 29F Chuck McElroy	.05	.02
❑ 30F Chito Martinez	.05	.02
❑ 31F Steve Howe	.05	.02
❑ 32F Freddie Benavides	.05	.02
❑ 33F Scott Kamieniecki RC	.10	.03
❑ 34F Denny Neagle RC	.25	.07
❑ 35F Mike Humphreys RC	.10	.03
❑ 36F Mike Remlinger	.05	.02
❑ 37F Scott Coolbaugh	.05	.02
❑ 38F Darren Lewis	.05	.02
❑ 39F Thomas Howard	.05	.02
❑ 40F John Candelaria	.05	.02
❑ 41F Todd Benzinger	.05	.02
❑ 42F Wilson Alvarez	.05	.02
❑ 43F Patrick Lennon RC	.10	.03
❑ 44F Rusty Meacham RC	.10	.03
❑ 45F Ryan Bowen RC	.10	.03
❑ 46F Rick Wilkins RC	.10	.03
❑ 47F Ed Sprague	.05	.02
❑ 48F Bob Scanlan	.05	.02
❑ 49F Tom Candiotti	.05	.02
❑ 50F Dennis Martinez (Perfecto)	.10	.03
❑ 51F Oil Can Boyd	.05	.02
❑ 52F Glenallen Hill	.05	.02
❑ 53F Scott Livingstone RC	.10	.03
❑ 54F Brian R. Hunter RC	.25	.07
❑ 55F Ivan Rodriguez RC	1.50	.45
❑ 56F Keith Mitchell RC	.10	.03
❑ 57F Roger McDowell	.05	.02
❑ 58F Otis Nixon	.05	.02
❑ 59F Juan Bell	.05	.02
❑ 60F Bill Krueger	.05	.02
❑ 61F Chris Donnels	.05	.02
❑ 62F Tommy Greene	.05	.02
❑ 63F Doug Simons	.05	.02
❑ 64F Andy Ashby RC	.25	.07
❑ 65F Anthony Young RC	.10	.03
❑ 66F Kevin Morton	.05	.02
❑ 67F Bret Barberie RC**	.10	.03
❑ 68F Scott Servais RC	.25	.07
❑ 69F Ron Darling	.05	.02
❑ 70F Tim Burke	.05	.02
❑ 71F Vicente Palacios	.05	.02
❑ 72F Gerald Alexander	.05	.02
❑ 73F Reggie Jefferson	.05	.02
❑ 74F Dean Palmer	.10	.03
❑ 75F Mark Whiten	.05	.02
❑ 76F Randy Tomlin RC	.10	.03
❑ 77F Mark Wohlers RC	.25	.07
❑ 78F Brook Jacoby	.05	.02
❑ 79F Ken Griffey Jr. CL Ryne Sandberg	.40	.12
❑ 80F Jack Morris AS	.05	.02
❑ 81F Sandy Alomar Jr. AS	.05	.02
❑ 82F Cecil Fielder AS	.05	.02
❑ 83F Roberto Alomar AS	.10	.03
❑ 84F Wade Boggs AS	.10	.03
❑ 85F Cal Ripken AS	.40	.12
❑ 86F Rickey Henderson AS	.25	.07
❑ 87F Ken Griffey Jr. AS	.25	.07
❑ 88F Dave Henderson AS	.05	.02
❑ 89F Danny Tartabull AS	.05	.02
❑ 90F Tom Glavine AS	.10	.03
❑ 91F Benito Santiago AS	.05	.02
❑ 92F Will Clark AS	.10	.03
❑ 93F Ryne Sandberg AS	.25	.07
❑ 94F Chris Sabo AS	.05	.02
❑ 95F Ozzie Smith AS	.15	.04
❑ 96F Ivan Calderon AS	.05	.02
❑ 97F Tony Gwynn AS	.15	.04
❑ 98F Andre Dawson AS	.05	.02
❑ 99F Bobby Bonilla AS	.05	.02
❑ 100F Checklist 1-100	.05	.02

1993 Upper Deck

	Nm-Mt	Ex-Mt
COMPLETE SET (840)	40.00	12.00
COMP.FACT.SET (840)	50.00	15.00
COMP. SERIES 1 (420)	15.00	4.50
COMP. SERIES 2 (420)	25.00	7.50
❑ 1 Tim Salmon CL	.20	.06
❑ 2 Mike Piazza SR	1.25	.35
❑ 3 Rene Arocha SR RC	.20	.06
❑ 4 Willie Greene SR	.10	.03
❑ 5 Manny Alexander	.10	.03
❑ 6 Dan Wilson	.20	.06
❑ 7 Dan Smith	.10	.03
❑ 8 Kevin Rogers	.10	.03
❑ 9 Kurt Miller SR	.10	.03
❑ 10 Joe Vitko	.10	.03
❑ 11 Tim Costo	.10	.03
❑ 12 Alan Embree SR	.10	.03
❑ 13 Jim Tatum SR RC	.10	.03
❑ 14 Cris Colon	.10	.03
❑ 15 Steve Hosey	.10	.03
❑ 16 S. Hitchcock SR RC	.20	.06
❑ 17 Dave Mlicki	.10	.03
❑ 18 Jessie Hollins	.10	.03

❑ 19 Bobby Jones SR .20 .06
❑ 20 Kurt Miller .10 .03
❑ 21 Melvin Nieves SR .10 .03
❑ 22 Billy Ashley SR .10 .03
❑ 23 J.T. Snow SR RC .50 .15
❑ 24 Chipper Jones SR .50 .15
❑ 25 Tim Salmon SR .30 .09
❑ 26 Tim Pugh SR RC .10 .03
❑ 27 David Nied SR .10 .03
❑ 28 Mike Trombley .10 .03
❑ 29 Javier Lopez SR .30 .09
❑ 30 Jim Abbott CH CL .10 .03
❑ 31 Jim Abbott CH .10 .03
❑ 32 Dale Murphy CH .30 .09
❑ 33 Tony Pena CH .10 .03
❑ 34 Kirby Puckett CH .30 .09
❑ 35 Harold Reynolds CH .10 .03
❑ 36 Cal Ripken CH .75 .23
❑ 37 Nolan Ryan CH 1.00 .30
❑ 38 Ryne Sandberg CH .50 .15
❑ 39 Dave Stewart CH .10 .03
❑ 40 Dave Winfield CH .20 .06
❑ 41 Joe Carter CL .50 .15
Mark McGwire
❑ 42 Joe Carter .20 .06
Roberto Alomar
❑ 43 Paul Molitor .20 .06
Pat Listach
Robin Yount
❑ 44 Cal Ripken .50 .15
Brady Anderson
❑ 45 Albert Belle .30 .09
Sandy Alomar Jr.
Jim Thome
Carlos Baerga
Kenny Lofton
❑ 46 Cecil Fielder .10 .03
Mickey Tettleton
❑ 47 Roberto Kelly .60 .18
Don Mattingly
❑ 48 Frank Viola .50 .15
Roger Clemens
❑ 49 Ruben Sierra .50 .15
Mark McGwire
❑ 50 Kent Hrbek .30 .09
Kirby Puckett
❑ 51 Robin Ventura .30 .09
Frank Thomas
❑ 52 Juan Gonzalez .50 .15
Jose Canseco
Ivan Rodriguez
Rafael Palmeiro
❑ 53 Mark Langston .10 .03
Jim Abbott
Chuck Finley
❑ 54 Wally Joyner .10 .03
Gregg Jefferies
George Brett
❑ 55 Kevin Mitchell .50 .15
Ken Griffey Jr.
Jay Buhner
❑ 56 George Brett 1.25 .35
❑ 57 Scott Cooper .10 .03
❑ 58 Mike Maddux .10 .03
❑ 59 Rusty Meacham .10 .03
❑ 60 Wil Cordero .10 .03
❑ 61 Tim Teufel .10 .03
❑ 62 Jeff Montgomery .10 .03
❑ 63 Scott Livingstone .10 .03
❑ 64 Doug Dascenzo .10 .03
❑ 65 Bret Boone .30 .09
❑ 66 Tim Wakefield .20 .06
❑ 67 Curt Schilling .30 .09
❑ 68 Frank Tanana .10 .03
❑ 69 Len Dykstra .20 .06
❑ 70 Derek Lilliquist .10 .03
❑ 71 Anthony Young .10 .03
❑ 72 Hipolito Pichardo .10 .03
❑ 73 Rod Beck .10 .03
❑ 74 Kent Hrbek .20 .06
❑ 75 Tom Glavine .50 .15
❑ 76 Kevin Brown .20 .06
❑ 77 Chuck Finley .20 .06
❑ 78 Bob Walk .10 .03
❑ 79 Rheal Cormier UER .10 .03
(Born in New Brunswick,
not British Columbia)
❑ 80 Rick Sutcliffe .20 .06
❑ 81 Harold Baines .20 .06
❑ 82 Lee Smith .20 .06
❑ 83 Geno Petralli .10 .03
❑ 84 Jose Oquendo .10 .03
❑ 85 Mark Gubicza .10 .03
❑ 86 Mickey Tettleton .10 .03
❑ 87 Bobby Witt .10 .03
❑ 88 Mark Lewis .10 .03
❑ 89 Kevin Appier .20 .06
❑ 90 Mike Stanton .10 .03
❑ 91 Rafael Belliard .10 .03
❑ 92 Kenny Rogers .20 .06
❑ 93 Randy Velarde .10 .03
❑ 94 Luis Sojo .10 .03
❑ 95 Mark Leiter .10 .03
❑ 96 Jody Reed .10 .03
❑ 97 Pete Harnisch .10 .03
❑ 98 Tom Candiotti .10 .03
❑ 99 Mark Portugal .10 .03
❑ 100 Dave Valle .10 .03
❑ 101 Shawon Dunston .10 .03
❑ 102 B.J. Surhoff .20 .06
❑ 103 Jay Bell .20 .06
❑ 104 Sid Bream .10 .03
❑ 105 Frank Thomas CL .30 .09
❑ 106 Mike Morgan .10 .03
❑ 107 Bill Doran .10 .03
❑ 108 Lance Blankenship .10 .03
❑ 109 Mark Lemke .10 .03
❑ 110 Brian Harper .10 .03
❑ 111 Brady Anderson .20 .06
❑ 112 Bip Roberts .10 .03
❑ 113 Mitch Williams .10 .03
❑ 114 Craig Biggio .30 .09
❑ 115 Eddie Murray .50 .15
❑ 116 Matt Nokes .10 .03
❑ 117 Lance Parrish .20 .06
❑ 118 Bill Swift .10 .03
❑ 119 Jeff Innis .10 .03
❑ 120 Mike LaValliere .10 .03
❑ 121 Hal Morris .10 .03
❑ 122 Walt Weiss .10 .03
❑ 123 Ivan Rodriguez .50 .15
❑ 124 Andy Van Slyke .20 .06
❑ 125 Roberto Alomar .50 .15
❑ 126 Robby Thompson .10 .03
❑ 127 Sammy Sosa .75 .23
❑ 128 Mark Langston .10 .03
❑ 129 Jerry Browne .10 .03
❑ 130 Chuck McElroy .10 .03
❑ 131 Frank Viola .20 .06
❑ 132 Leo Gomez .10 .03
❑ 133 Ramon Martinez .10 .03
❑ 134 Don Mattingly 1.25 .35
❑ 135 Roger Clemens 1.00 .30
❑ 136 Rickey Henderson .75 .23
❑ 137 Darren Daulton .20 .06
❑ 138 Ken Hill .10 .03
❑ 139 Ozzie Guillen .10 .03
❑ 140 Jerald Clark .10 .03
❑ 141 Dave Fleming .10 .03
❑ 142 Delino DeShields .10 .03
❑ 143 Matt Williams .20 .06
❑ 144 Larry Walker .30 .09
❑ 145 Ruben Sierra .10 .03
❑ 146 Ozzie Smith .50 .15
❑ 147 Chris Sabo .10 .03
❑ 148 Carlos Hernandez .10 .03
❑ 149 Pat Borders .10 .03
❑ 150 Orlando Merced .10 .03
❑ 151 Royce Clayton .10 .03
❑ 152 Kurt Stillwell .10 .03
❑ 153 Dave Hollins .10 .03
❑ 154 Mike Greenwell .10 .03
❑ 155 Nolan Ryan 2.00 .60
❑ 156 Felix Jose .10 .03
❑ 157 Junior Felix .10 .03
❑ 158 Derek Bell .10 .03
❑ 159 Steve Buechele .10 .03
❑ 160 John Burkett .10 .03
❑ 161 Pat Howell .10 .03
❑ 162 Milt Cuyler .10 .03
❑ 163 Terry Pendleton .20 .06
❑ 164 Jack Morris .20 .06
❑ 165 Tony Gwynn .60 .18
❑ 166 Deion Sanders .20 .06
❑ 167 Mike Devereaux .10 .03
❑ 168 Ron Darling .10 .03
❑ 169 Orel Hershiser .20 .06
❑ 170 Mike Jackson .10 .03
❑ 171 Doug Jones .10 .03
❑ 172 Dan Walters .10 .03
❑ 173 Darren Lewis .10 .03
❑ 174 Carlos Baerga .10 .03
❑ 175 Ryne Sandberg .75 .23
❑ 176 Gregg Jefferies .10 .03
❑ 177 John Jaha .10 .03
❑ 178 Luis Polonia .10 .03
❑ 179 Kirt Manwaring .10 .03
❑ 180 Mike Magnante .10 .03
❑ 181 Billy Ripken .10 .03
❑ 182 Mike Moore .10 .03
❑ 183 Eric Anthony .10 .03
❑ 184 Lenny Harris .10 .03
❑ 185 Tony Pena .10 .03
❑ 186 Mike Felder .10 .03
❑ 187 Greg Olson .10 .03
❑ 188 Rene Gonzales .10 .03
❑ 189 Mike Bordick .10 .03
❑ 190 Mel Rojas .10 .03
❑ 191 Todd Frohwirth .10 .03
❑ 192 Darryl Hamilton .10 .03
❑ 193 Mike Fetters .10 .03
❑ 194 Omar Olivares .10 .03
❑ 195 Tony Phillips .10 .03
❑ 196 Paul Sorrento .10 .03
❑ 197 Trevor Wilson .10 .03
❑ 198 Kevin Gross .10 .03
❑ 199 Ron Karkovice .10 .03
❑ 200 Brook Jacoby .10 .03
❑ 201 Mariano Duncan .10 .03
❑ 202 Dennis Cook .10 .03
❑ 203 Daryl Boston .10 .03
❑ 204 Mike Perez .10 .03
❑ 205 Manuel Lee .10 .03
❑ 206 Steve Olin .10 .03
❑ 207 Charlie Hough .20 .06
❑ 208 Scott Scudder .10 .03
❑ 209 Charlie O'Brien .10 .03
❑ 210 Barry Bonds CL .60 .18
❑ 211 Jose Vizcaino .10 .03
❑ 212 Scott Leius .10 .03
❑ 213 Kevin Mitchell .10 .03
❑ 214 Brian Barnes .10 .03
❑ 215 Pat Kelly .10 .03
❑ 216 Chris Hammond .10 .03
❑ 217 Rob Deer .10 .03
❑ 218 Cory Snyder .10 .03
❑ 219 Gary Carter .30 .09
❑ 220 Danny Darwin .10 .03
❑ 221 Tom Gordon .10 .03
❑ 222 Gary Sheffield .20 .06
❑ 223 Joe Carter .20 .06
❑ 224 Jay Buhner .20 .06
❑ 225 Jose Offerman .10 .03
❑ 226 Jose Rijo .10 .03
❑ 227 Mark Whiten .10 .03
❑ 228 Randy Milligan .10 .03
❑ 229 Bud Black .10 .03
❑ 230 Gary DiSarcina .10 .03
❑ 231 Steve Finley .20 .06
❑ 232 Dennis Martinez .20 .06
❑ 233 Mike Mussina .50 .15
❑ 234 Joe Oliver .10 .03
❑ 235 Chad Curtis .10 .03
❑ 236 Shane Mack .10 .03
❑ 237 Jaime Navarro .10 .03
❑ 238 Brian McRae .10 .03
❑ 239 Chili Davis .20 .06
❑ 240 Jeff King .10 .03
❑ 241 Dean Palmer .20 .06
❑ 242 Danny Tartabull .10 .03
❑ 243 Charles Nagy .10 .03
❑ 244 Ray Lankford .10 .03
❑ 245 Barry Larkin .50 .15
❑ 246 Steve Avery .10 .03
❑ 247 John Kruk .20 .06
❑ 248 Derrick May .10 .03
❑ 249 Stan Javier .10 .03
❑ 250 Roger McDowell .10 .03

❑ 251 Dan Gladden .10 .03
❑ 252 Wally Joyner .20 .06
❑ 253 Pat Listach .10 .03
❑ 254 Chuck Knoblauch .20 .06
❑ 255 Sandy Alomar Jr. .10 .03
❑ 256 Jeff Bagwell .30 .09
❑ 257 Andy Stankiewicz .10 .03
❑ 258 Darrin Jackson .10 .03
❑ 259 Brett Butler .20 .06
❑ 260 Joe Orsulak .10 .03
❑ 261 Andy Benes .10 .03
❑ 262 Kenny Lofton .20 .06
❑ 263 Robin Ventura .20 .06
❑ 264 Ron Gant .20 .06
❑ 265 Ellis Burks .20 .06
❑ 266 Juan Guzman .10 .03
❑ 267 Wes Chamberlain .10 .03
❑ 268 John Smiley .10 .03
❑ 269 Franklin Stubbs .10 .03
❑ 270 Tom Browning .10 .03
❑ 271 Dennis Eckersley .20 .06
❑ 272 Carlton Fisk .30 .09
❑ 273 Lou Whitaker .20 .06
❑ 274 Phil Plantier .10 .03
❑ 275 Bobby Bonilla .20 .06
❑ 276 Ben McDonald .10 .03
❑ 277 Bob Zupcic .10 .03
❑ 278 Terry Steinbach .10 .03
❑ 279 Terry Mulholland .10 .03
❑ 280 Lance Johnson .10 .03
❑ 281 Willie McGee .20 .06
❑ 282 Bret Saberhagen .20 .06
❑ 283 Randy Myers .10 .03
❑ 284 Randy Tomlin .10 .03
❑ 285 Mickey Morandini .10 .03
❑ 286 Brian Williams .10 .03
❑ 287 Tino Martinez .30 .09
❑ 288 Jose Melendez .10 .03
❑ 289 Jeff Huson .10 .03
❑ 290 Joe Grahe .10 .03
❑ 291 Mel Hall .10 .03
❑ 292 Otis Nixon .10 .03
❑ 293 Todd Hundley .10 .03
❑ 294 Casey Candaele .10 .03
❑ 295 Kevin Seitzer .10 .03
❑ 296 Eddie Taubensee .10 .03
❑ 297 Moises Alou .20 .06
❑ 298 Scott Radinsky .10 .03
❑ 299 Thomas Howard .10 .03
❑ 300 Kyle Abbott .10 .03
❑ 301 Omar Vizquel .20 .06
❑ 302 Keith Miller .10 .03
❑ 303 Rick Aguilera .10 .03
❑ 304 Bruce Hurst .10 .03
❑ 305 Ken Caminiti .20 .06
❑ 306 Mike Pagliarulo .10 .03
❑ 307 Frank Seminara .10 .03
❑ 308 Andre Dawson .20 .06
❑ 309 Jose Lind .10 .03
❑ 310 Joe Boever .10 .03
❑ 311 Jeff Parrett .10 .03
❑ 312 Alan Mills .10 .03
❑ 313 Kevin Tapani .10 .03
❑ 314 Darryl Kile .20 .06
❑ 315 Will Clark CL .20 .06
❑ 316 Mike Sharperson .10 .03
❑ 317 John Orton .10 .03
❑ 318 Bob Tewksbury .10 .03
❑ 319 Xavier Hernandez .10 .03
❑ 320 Paul Assenmacher .10 .03
❑ 321 John Franco .20 .06
❑ 322 Mike Timlin .10 .03
❑ 323 Jose Guzman .10 .03
❑ 324 Pedro Martinez 1.00 .30
❑ 325 Bill Spiers .10 .03
❑ 326 Melido Perez .10 .03
❑ 327 Mike Macfarlane .10 .03
❑ 328 Ricky Bones .10 .03
❑ 329 Scott Bankhead .10 .03
❑ 330 Rich Rodriguez .10 .03
❑ 331 Geronimo Pena .10 .03
❑ 332 Bernie Williams .30 .09
❑ 333 Paul Molitor .30 .09
❑ 334 Carlos Garcia .10 .03
❑ 335 David Cone .20 .06
❑ 336 Randy Johnson .50 .15
❑ 337 Pat Mahomes .10 .03
❑ 338 Erik Hanson .10 .03
❑ 339 Duane Ward .10 .03
❑ 340 Al Martin .10 .03
❑ 341 Pedro Munoz .10 .03
❑ 342 Greg Colbrunn .10 .03
❑ 343 Julio Valera .10 .03
❑ 344 John Olerud .20 .06
❑ 345 George Bell .10 .03
❑ 346 Devon White .10 .03
❑ 347 Donovan Osborne .10 .03
❑ 348 Mark Gardner .10 .03
❑ 349 Zane Smith .10 .03
❑ 350 Wilson Alvarez .10 .03
❑ 351 Kevin Koslofski .10 .03
❑ 352 Roberto Hernandez .10 .03
❑ 353 Glenn Davis .10 .03
❑ 354 Reggie Sanders .20 .06
❑ 355 Ken Griffey Jr. .75 .23
❑ 356 Marquis Grissom .10 .03
❑ 357 Jack McDowell .10 .03
❑ 358 Jimmy Key .20 .06
❑ 359 Stan Belinda .10 .03
❑ 360 Gerald Williams .10 .03
❑ 361 Sid Fernandez .10 .03
❑ 362 Alex Fernandez .10 .03
❑ 363 John Smoltz .30 .09
❑ 364 Travis Fryman .20 .06
❑ 365 Jose Canseco .50 .15
❑ 366 David Justice .20 .06
❑ 367 Pedro Astacio .10 .03
❑ 368 Tim Belcher .10 .03
❑ 369 Steve Sax .10 .03
❑ 370 Gary Gaetti .20 .06
❑ 371 Jeff Frye .10 .03
❑ 372 Bob Wickman .10 .03
❑ 373 Ryan Thompson .10 .03
❑ 374 David Hulse RC .10 .03
❑ 375 Cal Eldred .10 .03
❑ 376 Ryan Klesko .20 .06
❑ 377 Damion Easley .10 .03
❑ 378 John Kiely .10 .03
❑ 379 Jim Bullinger .10 .03
❑ 380 Brian Bohanon .10 .03
❑ 381 Rod Brewer .10 .03
❑ 382 Fernando Ramsey RC .10 .03
❑ 383 Sam Militello .10 .03
❑ 384 Arthur Rhodes .10 .03
❑ 385 Eric Karros .20 .06
❑ 386 Rico Brogna .10 .03
❑ 387 John Valentin .10 .03
❑ 388 Kerry Woodson .10 .03
❑ 389 Ben Rivera .10 .03
❑ 390 Matt Whiteside RC .10 .03
❑ 391 Henry Rodriguez .10 .03
❑ 392 John Wetteland .20 .06
❑ 393 Kent Mercker .10 .03
❑ 394 Bernard Gilkey .10 .03
❑ 395 Doug Henry .10 .03
❑ 396 Mo Vaughn .20 .06
❑ 397 Scott Erickson .10 .03
❑ 398 Bill Gullickson .10 .03
❑ 399 Mark Guthrie .10 .03
❑ 400 Dave Martinez .10 .03
❑ 401 Jeff Kent .50 .15
❑ 402 Chris Hoiles .10 .03
❑ 403 Mike Henneman .10 .03
❑ 404 Chris Nabholz .10 .03
❑ 405 Tom Pagnozzi .10 .03
❑ 406 Kelly Gruber .10 .03
❑ 407 Bob Welch .10 .03
❑ 408 Frank Castillo .10 .03
❑ 409 John Dopson .10 .03
❑ 410 Steve Farr .10 .03
❑ 411 Henry Cotto .10 .03
❑ 412 Bob Patterson .10 .03
❑ 413 Todd Stottlemyre .10 .03
❑ 414 Greg A. Harris .10 .03
❑ 415 Denny Neagle .20 .06
❑ 416 Bill Wegman .10 .03
❑ 417 Willie Wilson .10 .03
❑ 418 Terry Leach .10 .03
❑ 419 Willie Randolph .20 .06
❑ 420 Mark McGwire CL .50 .15
❑ 421 Calvin Murray CL .10 .03
❑ 422 Pete Janicki TP RC .10 .03
❑ 423 Todd Jones TP .10 .03
❑ 424 Mike Neill TP .10 .03
❑ 425 Carlos Delgado TP .50 .15
❑ 426 Jose Oliva TP .10 .03
❑ 427 Tyrone Hill TP .10 .03
❑ 428 Dmitri Young TP .20 .06
❑ 429 Derek Wallace TP RC .10 .03
❑ 430 Michael Moore TP RC .10 .03
❑ 431 Cliff Floyd TP .30 .09
❑ 432 Calvin Murray TP .10 .03
❑ 433 Manny Ramirez TP .50 .15
❑ 434 Marc Newfield TP .10 .03
❑ 435 Charles Johnson TP .20 .06
❑ 436 Butch Huskey TP .10 .03
❑ 437 Brad Pennington TP .10 .03
❑ 438 Ray McDavid TP RC .10 .03
❑ 439 Chad McConnell TP .10 .03
❑ 440 M.Cummings TP RC .10 .03
❑ 441 Benji Gil TP .10 .03
❑ 442 Frankie Rodriguez TP .10 .03
❑ 443 Chad Mottola TP RC .10 .03
❑ 444 John Burke TP RC .10 .03
❑ 445 Michael Tucker TP .10 .03
❑ 446 Rick Greene TP .10 .03
❑ 447 Rich Becker TP .10 .03
❑ 448 Mike Robertson TP .10 .03
❑ 449 Derek Jeter TP RC 15.00 4.50
❑ 450 Ivan Rodriguez CL .30 .09
David McCarty
❑ 451 Jim Abbott IN .10 .03
❑ 452 Jeff Bagwell IN .20 .06
❑ 453 Jason Bere IN .10 .03
❑ 454 Delino DeShields IN .10 .03
❑ 455 Travis Fryman IN .10 .03
❑ 456 Alex Gonzalez IN .10 .03
❑ 457 Phil Hiatt IN .10 .03
❑ 458 Dave Hollins IN .10 .03
❑ 459 Chipper Jones IN .30 .09
❑ 460 David Justice IN .10 .03
❑ 461 Ray Lankford IN .10 .03
❑ 462 David McCarty IN .10 .03
❑ 463 Mike Mussina IN .30 .09
❑ 464 Jose Offerman IN .10 .03
❑ 465 Dean Palmer IN .10 .03
❑ 466 Geronimo Pena IN .10 .03
❑ 467 Eduardo Perez IN .10 .03
❑ 468 Ivan Rodriguez IN .30 .09
❑ 469 Reggie Sanders IN .10 .03
❑ 470 Bernie Williams IN .20 .06
❑ 471 Barry Bonds CL .50 .15
Matt Williams
Will Clark
❑ 472 Greg Maddux .50 .15
Steve Avery
John Smoltz
Tom Glavine
❑ 473 Jose Rijo .10 .03
Rob Dibble
Roberto Kelly
Reggie Sanders
Barry Larkin
❑ 474 Gary Sheffield .20 .06
Phil Plantier
Tony Gwynn
Fred McGriff
❑ 475 Doug Drabek .20 .06
Craig Biggio
Jeff Bagwell
❑ 476 Will Clark .50 .15
Barry Bonds
Matt Williams
❑ 477 Eric Davis .20 .06
Darryl Strawberry
❑ 478 Dante Bichette .20 .06
David Nied
Andres Galarraga
❑ 479 Dave Magadan .10 .03
Orestes Destrade
Bret Barberie
Jeff Conine
❑ 480 Tim Wakefield .20 .06
Andy Van Slyke
Jay Bell
❑ 481 Marquis Grissom .10 .03
Delino DeShields
Dennis Martinez

No.	Card		
	Larry Walker		
482	Geronimo Pena	.30	.09
	Ray Lankford		
	Ozzie Smith		
	Bernard Gilkey		
483	Randy Myers	.50	.15
	Ryne Sandberg		
	Mark Grace		
484	Eddie Murray	.30	.09
	Howard Johnson		
	Bobby Bonilla		
485	John Kruk	.10	.03
	Dave Hollins		
	Darren Daulton		
	Len Dykstra		
486	Barry Bonds AW	.60	.18
487	Dennis Eckersley AW	.20	.06
488	Greg Maddux AW	.50	.15
489	Dennis Eckersley AW	.20	.06
490	Eric Karros AW	.10	.03
491	Pat Listach AW	.10	.03
492	Gary Sheffield AW	.10	.03
493	Mark McGwire AW	.60	.18
494	Gary Sheffield AW	.10	.03
495	Edgar Martinez AW	.20	.06
496	Fred McGriff AW	.20	.06
497	Juan Gonzalez AW	.30	.09
498	Darren Daulton AW	.10	.03
499	Cecil Fielder AW	.10	.03
500	Brent Gates CL	.10	.03
501	Tavo Alvarez DD	.10	.03
502	Rod Bolton	.10	.03
503	J.Cummings DD RC	.10	.03
504	Brent Gates DD	.10	.03
505	Tyler Green	.10	.03
506	Jose Martinez DD RC	.10	.03
507	Troy Percival	.30	.09
508	Kevin Stocker DD	.10	.03
509	Matt Walbeck DD RC	.10	.03
510	Rondell White DD	.20	.06
511	Billy Ripken	.10	.03
512	Mike Moore	.10	.03
513	Jose Lind	.10	.03
514	Chito Martinez	.10	.03
515	Jose Guzman	.10	.03
516	Kim Batiste	.10	.03
517	Jeff Tackett	.10	.03
518	Charlie Hough	.20	.06
519	Marvin Freeman	.10	.03
520	Carlos Martinez	.10	.03
521	Eric Young	.10	.03
522	Pete Incaviglia	.10	.03
523	Scott Fletcher	.10	.03
524	Orestes Destrade	.10	.03
525	Ken Griffey Jr. CL	.50	.15
526	Ellis Burks	.20	.06
527	Juan Samuel	.10	.03
528	Dave Magadan	.10	.03
529	Jeff Parrett	.10	.03
530	Bill Krueger	.10	.03
531	Frank Bolick	.10	.03
532	Alan Trammell	.30	.09
533	Walt Weiss	.10	.03
534	David Cone	.20	.06
535	Greg Maddux	1.00	.30
536	Kevin Young	.20	.06
537	Dave Hansen	.10	.03
538	Alex Cole	.10	.03
539	Greg Hibbard	.10	.03
540	Gene Larkin	.10	.03
541	Jeff Reardon	.20	.06
542	Felix Jose	.10	.03
543	Jimmy Key	.20	.06
544	Reggie Jefferson	.10	.03
545	Gregg Jefferies	.10	.03
546	Dave Stewart	.20	.06
547	Tim Wallach	.10	.03
548	Spike Owen	.10	.03
549	Tommy Greene	.10	.03
550	Fernando Valenzuela	.20	.06
551	Rich Amaral	.10	.03
552	Bret Barberie	.10	.03
553	Edgar Martinez	.30	.09
554	Jim Abbott	.50	.15
555	Frank Thomas	.50	.15
556	Wade Boggs	.30	.09
557	Tom Henke	.10	.03
558	Milt Thompson	.10	.03
559	Lloyd McClendon	.10	.03
560	Vinny Castilla	.20	.06
561	Ricky Jordan	.10	.03
562	Andujar Cedeno	.10	.03
563	Greg Vaughn	.20	.06
564	Cecil Fielder	.20	.06
565	Kirby Puckett	.50	.15
566	Mark McGwire	1.25	.35
567	Barry Bonds	1.25	.35
568	Jody Reed	.10	.03
569	Todd Zeile	.10	.03
570	Mark Carreon	.10	.03
571	Joe Girardi	.10	.03
572	Luis Gonzalez	.20	.06
573	Mark Grace	.50	.15
574	Rafael Palmeiro	.30	.09
575	Darryl Strawberry	.30	.09
576	Will Clark	.50	.15
577	Fred McGriff	.30	.09
578	Kevin Reimer	.10	.03
579	Dave Righetti	.20	.06
580	Juan Bell	.10	.03
581	Jeff Brantley	.10	.03
582	Brian Hunter	.10	.03
583	Tim Naehring	.10	.03
584	Glenallen Hill	.10	.03
585	Cal Ripken	1.50	.45
586	Albert Belle	.20	.06
587	Robin Yount	.50	.15
588	Chris Bosio	.10	.03
589	Pete Smith	.10	.03
590	Chuck Carr	.10	.03
591	Jeff Blauser	.10	.03
592	Kevin McReynolds	.10	.03
593	Andres Galarraga	.20	.06
594	Kevin Maas	.10	.03
595	Eric Davis	.20	.06
596	Brian Jordan	.20	.06
597	Tim Raines	.20	.06
598	Rick Wilkins	.10	.03
599	Steve Cooke	.10	.03
600	Mike Gallego	.10	.03
601	Mike Munoz	.10	.03
602	Luis Rivera	.10	.03
603	Junior Ortiz	.10	.03
604	Brent Mayne	.10	.03
605	Luis Alicea	.10	.03
606	Damon Berryhill	.10	.03
607	Dave Henderson	.10	.03
608	Kirk McCaskill	.10	.03
609	Jeff Fassero	.10	.03
610	Mike Harkey	.10	.03
611	Francisco Cabrera	.10	.03
612	Rey Sanchez	.10	.03
613	Scott Servais	.10	.03
614	Darrin Fletcher	.10	.03
615	Felix Fermin	.10	.03
616	Kevin Seitzer	.10	.03
617	Bob Scanlan	.10	.03
618	Billy Hatcher	.10	.03
619	John Vander Wal	.10	.03
620	Joe Hesketh	.10	.03
621	Hector Villanueva	.10	.03
622	Randy Milligan	.10	.03
623	Tony Tarasco RC	.10	.03
624	Russ Swan	.10	.03
625	Willie Wilson	.10	.03
626	Frank Tanana	.10	.03
627	Pete O'Brien	.10	.03
628	Lenny Webster	.10	.03
629	Mark Clark	.10	.03
630	Roger Clemens CL	.50	.15
631	Alex Arias	.10	.03
632	Chris Gwynn	.10	.03
633	Tom Bolton	.10	.03
634	Greg Briley	.10	.03
635	Kent Bottenfield	.10	.03
636	Kelly Downs	.10	.03
637	Manuel Lee	.10	.03
638	Al Leiter	.20	.06
639	Jeff Gardner	.10	.03
640	Mike Gardiner	.10	.03
641	Mark Gardner	.10	.03
642	Jeff Branson	.10	.03
643	Paul Wagner	.10	.03
644	Sean Berry	.10	.03
645	Phil Hiatt	.10	.03
646	Kevin Mitchell	.10	.03
647	Charlie Hayes	.10	.03
648	Jim Deshaies	.10	.03
649	Dan Pasqua	.10	.03
650	Mike Maddux	.10	.03
651	Domingo Martinez RC	.10	.03
652	Greg McMichael RC	.10	.03
653	Eric Wedge RC	.10	.03
654	Mark Whiten	.10	.03
655	Roberto Kelly	.10	.03
656	Julio Franco	.20	.06
657	Gene Harris	.10	.03
658	Pete Schourek	.10	.03
659	Mike Bielecki	.10	.03
660	Ricky Gutierrez	.10	.03
661	Chris Hammond	.10	.03
662	Tim Scott	.10	.03
663	Norm Charlton	.10	.03
664	Doug Drabek	.10	.03
665	Dwight Gooden	.30	.09
666	Jim Gott	.10	.03
667	Randy Myers	.10	.03
668	Darren Holmes	.10	.03
669	Tim Spehr	.10	.03
670	Bruce Ruffin	.10	.03
671	Bobby Thigpen	.10	.03
672	Tony Fernandez	.10	.03
673	Darrin Jackson	.10	.03
674	Gregg Olson	.10	.03
675	Rob Dibble	.20	.06
676	Howard Johnson	.10	.03
677	Mike Lansing RC	.20	.06
678	Charlie Leibrandt	.10	.03
679	Kevin Bass	.10	.03
680	Hubie Brooks	.10	.03
681	Scott Brosius	.20	.06
682	Randy Knorr	.10	.03
683	Dante Bichette	.20	.06
684	Bryan Harvey	.10	.03
685	Greg Gohr	.10	.03
686	Willie Banks	.10	.03
687	Robb Nen	.20	.06
688	Mike Scioscia	.10	.03
689	John Farrell	.10	.03
690	John Candelaria	.10	.03
691	Damon Buford	.10	.03
692	Todd Worrell	.10	.03
693	Pat Hentgen	.10	.03
694	John Smiley	.10	.03
695	Greg Swindell	.10	.03
696	Derek Bell	.10	.03
697	Terry Jorgensen	.10	.03
698	Jimmy Jones	.10	.03
699	David Wells	.20	.06
700	Dave Martinez	.10	.03
701	Steve Bedrosian	.10	.03
702	Jeff Russell	.10	.03
703	Joe Magrane	.10	.03
704	Matt Mieske	.10	.03
705	Paul Molitor	.30	.09
706	Dale Murphy	.50	.15
707	Steve Howe	.10	.03
708	Greg Gagne	.10	.03
709	Dave Eiland	.10	.03
710	David West	.10	.03
711	Luis Aquino	.10	.03
712	Joe Orsulak	.10	.03
713	Eric Plunk	.10	.03
714	Mike Felder	.10	.03
715	Joe Klink	.10	.03
716	Lonnie Smith	.10	.03
717	Monty Fariss	.10	.03
718	Craig Lefferts	.10	.03
719	John Habyan	.10	.03
720	Willie Blair	.10	.03
721	Darnell Coles	.10	.03
722	Mark Williamson	.10	.03
723	Bryn Smith	.10	.03
724	Greg W. Harris	.10	.03
725	Graeme Lloyd RC	.20	.06
726	Cris Carpenter	.10	.03
727	Chico Walker	.10	.03
728	Tracy Woodson	.10	.03

❑ 729 Jose Uribe .10 .03
❑ 730 Stan Javier .10 .03
❑ 731 Jay Howell .10 .03
❑ 732 Freddie Benavides .10 .03
❑ 733 Jeff Reboulet .10 .03
❑ 734 Scott Sanderson .10 .03
❑ 735 Ryne Sandberg CL .50 .15
❑ 736 Archi Cianfrocco .10 .03
❑ 737 Daryl Boston .10 .03
❑ 738 Craig Grebeck .10 .03
❑ 739 Doug Dascenzo .10 .03
❑ 740 Gerald Young .10 .03
❑ 741 Candy Maldonado .10 .03
❑ 742 Joey Cora .10 .03
❑ 743 Don Slaught .10 .03
❑ 744 Steve Decker .10 .03
❑ 745 Blas Minor .10 .03
❑ 746 Storm Davis .10 .03
❑ 747 Carlos Quintana .10 .03
❑ 748 Vince Coleman .10 .03
❑ 749 Todd Burns .10 .03
❑ 750 Steve Frey .10 .03
❑ 751 Ivan Calderon .10 .03
❑ 752 Steve Reed RC .10 .03
❑ 753 Danny Jackson .10 .03
❑ 754 Jeff Conine .20 .06
❑ 755 Juan Gonzalez .50 .15
❑ 756 Mike Kelly .10 .03
❑ 757 John Doherty .10 .03
❑ 758 Jack Armstrong .10 .03
❑ 759 John Wehner .10 .03
❑ 760 Scott Bankhead .10 .03
❑ 761 Jim Tatum .10 .03
❑ 762 Scott Pose RC .10 .03
❑ 763 Andy Ashby .10 .03
❑ 764 Ed Sprague .10 .03
❑ 765 Harold Baines .20 .06
❑ 766 Kirk Gibson .20 .06
❑ 767 Troy Neel .10 .03
❑ 768 Dick Schofield .10 .03
❑ 769 Dickie Thon .10 .03
❑ 770 Butch Henry .10 .03
❑ 771 Junior Felix .10 .03
❑ 772 Ken Ryan RC .10 .03
❑ 773 Trevor Hoffman .20 .06
❑ 774 Phil Plantier .10 .03
❑ 775 Bo Jackson .50 .15
❑ 776 Benito Santiago .20 .06
❑ 777 Andre Dawson .20 .06
❑ 778 Bryan Hickerson .10 .03
❑ 779 Dennis Moeller .10 .03
❑ 780 Ryan Bowen .10 .03
❑ 781 Eric Fox .10 .03
❑ 782 Joe Kmak .10 .03
❑ 783 Mike Hampton .20 .06
❑ 784 Darrell Sherman RC .10 .03
❑ 785 J.T. Snow .50 .15
❑ 786 Dave Winfield .30 .09
❑ 787 Jim Austin .10 .03
❑ 788 Craig Shipley .10 .03
❑ 789 Greg Myers .10 .03
❑ 790 Todd Benzinger .10 .03
❑ 791 Cory Snyder .10 .03
❑ 792 David Segui .10 .03
❑ 793 Armando Reynoso .10 .03
❑ 794 Chili Davis .20 .06
❑ 795 Dave Nilsson .10 .03
❑ 796 Paul O'Neill .30 .09
❑ 797 Jerald Clark .10 .03
❑ 798 Jose Mesa .10 .03
❑ 799 Brain Holman .10 .03
❑ 800 Jim Eisenreich .10 .03
❑ 801 Mark McLemore .10 .03
❑ 802 Luis Sojo .10 .03
❑ 803 Harold Reynolds .20 .06
❑ 804 Dan Plesac .10 .03
❑ 805 Dave Stieb .10 .03
❑ 806 Tom Brunansky .10 .03
❑ 807 Kelly Gruber .10 .03
❑ 808 Bob Ojeda .10 .03
❑ 809 Dave Burba .10 .03
❑ 810 Joe Boever .10 .03
❑ 811 Jeremy Hernandez .10 .03
❑ 812 Tim Salmon TC .20 .06
❑ 813 Jeff Bagwell TC .20 .06
❑ 814 Dennis Eckersley TC .20 .06
❑ 815 Roberto Alomar TC .20 .06
❑ 816 Steve Avery TC .10 .03
❑ 817 Pat Listach TC .10 .03
❑ 818 Gregg Jefferies TC .10 .03
❑ 819 Sammy Sosa TC .50 .15
❑ 820 Darryl Strawberry TC .20 .06
❑ 821 Dennis Martinez TC .10 .03
❑ 822 Robby Thompson TC .10 .03
❑ 823 Albert Belle TC .20 .06
❑ 824 Randy Johnson TC .30 .09
❑ 825 Nigel Wilson TC .10 .03
❑ 826 Bobby Bonilla TC .10 .03
❑ 827 Glenn Davis TC .10 .03
❑ 828 Gary Sheffield TC .10 .03
❑ 829 Darren Daulton TC .10 .03
❑ 830 Jay Bell TC .10 .03
❑ 831 Juan Gonzalez TC .30 .09
❑ 832 Andre Dawson TC .10 .03
❑ 833 Hal Morris TC .10 .03
❑ 834 David Nied TC .10 .03
❑ 835 Felix Jose TC .10 .03
❑ 836 Travis Fryman TC .10 .03
❑ 837 Shane Mack TC .10 .03
❑ 838 Robin Ventura TC .10 .03
❑ 839 Danny Tartabull TC .10 .03
❑ 840 Roberto Alomar CL .20 .06
❑ SP5 George Brett 1.00 .30
Robin Yount
❑ SP6 Nolan Ryan 2.00 .60

1994 Upper Deck

	Nm-Mt	Ex-Mt
COMPLETE SET (550)	50.00	15.00
COMP. SERIES 1 (280)	30.00	9.00
COMP. SERIES 2 (270)	20.00	6.00

❑ 1 Brian Anderson RC .40 .12
❑ 2 Shane Andrews .15 .04
❑ 3 James Baldwin .15 .04
❑ 4 Rich Becker .15 .04
❑ 5 Greg Blosser .15 .04
❑ 6 Ricky Bottalico RC .40 .12
❑ 7 Midre Cummings .15 .04
❑ 8 Carlos Delgado .50 .15
❑ 9 Steve Dreyer RC .15 .04
❑ 10 Joey Eischen .15 .04
❑ 11 Carl Everett .30 .09
❑ 12 Cliff Floyd UER .30 .09
(text indicates he throws left; should be right)
❑ 13 Alex Gonzalez .15 .04
❑ 14 Jeff Granger .15 .04
❑ 15 Shawn Green .75 .23
❑ 16 Brian L. Hunter .15 .04
❑ 17 Butch Huskey .15 .04
❑ 18 Mark Hutton .15 .04
❑ 19 Michael Jordan RC 10.00 3.00
❑ 20 Steve Karsay .15 .04
❑ 21 Jeff McNeely .15 .04
❑ 22 Marc Newfield .15 .04
❑ 23 Manny Ramirez .50 .15
❑ 24 Alex Rodriguez RC 15.00 4.50
❑ 25 Scott Ruffcorn UER .15 .04
(photo on back is Robert Ellis)
❑ 26 Paul Spoljaric UER .15 .04
(Expos logo on back)
❑ 27 Salomon Torres .15 .04
❑ 28 Steve Trachsel .15 .04
❑ 29 Chris Turner .15 .04
❑ 30 Gabe White .15 .04
❑ 31 Randy Johnson FT .50 .15
❑ 32 John Wetteland FT .15 .04
❑ 33 Mike Piazza FT .75 .23
❑ 34 Rafael Palmeiro FT .30 .09
❑ 35 Roberto Alomar FT .30 .09
❑ 36 Matt Williams FT .15 .04
❑ 37 Travis Fryman FT .15 .04
❑ 38 Barry Bonds FT 1.00 .30
❑ 39 Marquis Grissom FT .15 .04
❑ 40 Albert Belle FT .30 .09
❑ 41 Steve Avery FUT .15 .04
❑ 42 Jason Bere FUT .15 .04
❑ 43 Alex Fernandez FUT .15 .04
❑ 44 Mike Mussina FUT .50 .15
❑ 45 Aaron Sele FUT .15 .04
❑ 46 Rod Beck FUT .15 .04
❑ 47 Mike Piazza FUT .75 .23
❑ 48 John Olerud FUT .15 .04
❑ 49 Carlos Baerga FUT .15 .04
❑ 50 Gary Sheffield FUT .15 .04
❑ 51 Travis Fryman FUT .15 .04
❑ 52 Juan Gonzalez FUT .50 .15
❑ 53 Ken Griffey Jr. FUT .75 .23
❑ 54 Tim Salmon FUT .30 .09
❑ 55 Frank Thomas FUT .50 .15
❑ 56 Tony Phillips .15 .04
❑ 57 Julio Franco .30 .09
❑ 58 Kevin Mitchell .15 .04
❑ 59 Raul Mondesi .30 .09
❑ 60 Rickey Henderson 1.25 .35
❑ 61 Jay Buhner .30 .09
❑ 62 Bill Swift .15 .04
❑ 63 Brady Anderson .30 .09
❑ 64 Ryan Klesko .30 .09
❑ 65 Darren Daulton .30 .09
❑ 66 Damion Easley .15 .04
❑ 67 Mark McGwire 2.00 .60
❑ 68 John Roper .15 .04
❑ 69 Dave Telgheder .15 .04
❑ 70 David Nied .15 .04
❑ 71 Mo Vaughn .30 .09
❑ 72 Tyler Green .15 .04
❑ 73 Dave Magadan .15 .04
❑ 74 Chili Davis .30 .09
❑ 75 Archi Cianfrocco .15 .04
❑ 76 Joe Girardi .15 .04
❑ 77 Chris Hoiles .15 .04
❑ 78 Ryan Bowen .15 .04
❑ 79 Greg Gagne .15 .04
❑ 80 Aaron Sele .15 .04
❑ 81 Dave Winfield .50 .15
❑ 82 Chad Curtis .15 .04
❑ 83 Andy Van Slyke .30 .09
❑ 84 Kevin Stocker .15 .04
❑ 85 Deion Sanders .30 .09
❑ 86 Bernie Williams .50 .15
❑ 87 John Smoltz .50 .15
❑ 88 Ruben Santana .15 .04
❑ 89 Dave Stewart .30 .09
❑ 90 Don Mattingly 2.00 .60
❑ 91 Joe Carter .30 .09
❑ 92 Ryne Sandberg 1.25 .35
❑ 93 Chris Gomez .15 .04
❑ 94 Tino Martinez .50 .15
❑ 95 Terry Pendleton .30 .09
❑ 96 Andre Dawson .30 .09
❑ 97 Wil Cordero .15 .04
❑ 98 Kent Hrbek .30 .09
❑ 99 John Olerud .30 .09
❑ 100 Kirt Manwaring .15 .04
❑ 101 Tim Bogar .15 .04
❑ 102 Mike Mussina .75 .23
❑ 103 Nigel Wilson .15 .04
❑ 104 Ricky Gutierrez .15 .04
❑ 105 Roberto Mejia .15 .04
❑ 106 Tom Pagnozzi .15 .04
❑ 107 Mike Macfarlane .15 .04
❑ 108 Jose Bautista .15 .04
❑ 109 Luis Ortiz .15 .04
❑ 110 Brent Gates .15 .04
❑ 111 Tim Salmon .50 .15
❑ 112 Wade Boggs .50 .15
❑ 113 Tripp Cromer .15 .04

❑ 114 Denny Hocking .15 .04
❑ 115 Carlos Baerga .15 .04
❑ 116 J.R. Phillips .15 .04
❑ 117 Bo Jackson .75 .23
❑ 118 Lance Johnson .15 .04
❑ 119 Bobby Jones .15 .04
❑ 120 Bobby Witt .15 .04
❑ 121 Ron Karkovice .15 .04
❑ 122 Jose Vizcaino .15 .04
❑ 123 Danny Darwin .15 .04
❑ 124 Eduardo Perez .15 .04
❑ 125 Brian Looney RC .15 .04
❑ 126 Pat Hentgen .15 .04
❑ 127 Frank Viola .30 .09
❑ 128 Darren Holmes .15 .04
❑ 129 Wally Whitehurst .15 .04
❑ 130 Matt Walbeck .15 .04
❑ 131 Albert Belle .30 .09
❑ 132 Steve Cooke .15 .04
❑ 133 Kevin Appier .30 .09
❑ 134 Joe Oliver .15 .04
❑ 135 Benji Gil .15 .04
❑ 136 Steve Buechele .15 .04
❑ 137 Devon White .15 .04
❑ 138 S.Hitchcock UER .15 .04
two losses for career; should be four
❑ 139 Phil Leftwich RC .15 .04
❑ 140 Jose Canseco .75 .23
❑ 141 Rick Aguilera .15 .04
❑ 142 Rod Beck .15 .04
❑ 143 Jose Rijo .15 .04
❑ 144 Tom Glavine .75 .23
❑ 145 Phil Plantier .15 .04
❑ 146 Jason Bere .15 .04
❑ 147 Jamie Moyer .30 .09
❑ 148 Wes Chamberlain .15 .04
❑ 149 Glenallen Hill .15 .04
❑ 150 Mark Whiten .15 .04
❑ 151 Bret Barberie .15 .04
❑ 152 Chuck Knoblauch .30 .09
❑ 153 Trevor Hoffman .30 .09
❑ 154 Rick Wilkins .15 .04
❑ 155 Juan Gonzalez .75 .23
❑ 156 Ozzie Guillen .15 .04
❑ 157 Jim Eisenreich .15 .04
❑ 158 Pedro Astacio .15 .04
❑ 159 Joe Magrane .15 .04
❑ 160 Ryan Thompson .15 .04
❑ 161 Jose Lind .15 .04
❑ 162 Jeff Conine .30 .09
❑ 163 Todd Benzinger .15 .04
❑ 164 Roger Salkeld .15 .04
❑ 165 Gary DiSarcina .15 .04
❑ 166 Kevin Gross .15 .04
❑ 167 Charlie Hayes .15 .04
❑ 168 Tim Costo .15 .04
❑ 169 Wally Joyner .30 .09
❑ 170 Johnny Ruffin .15 .04
❑ 171 Kirk Rueter .30 .09
❑ 172 Lenny Dykstra .30 .09
❑ 173 Ken Hill .15 .04
❑ 174 Mike Bordick .15 .04
❑ 175 Billy Hall .15 .04
❑ 176 Rob Butler .15 .04
❑ 177 Jay Bell .30 .09
❑ 178 Jeff Kent .30 .09
❑ 179 David Wells .30 .09
❑ 180 Dean Palmer .30 .09
❑ 181 Mariano Duncan .15 .04
❑ 182 Orlando Merced .15 .04
❑ 183 Brett Butler .30 .09
❑ 184 Milt Thompson .15 .04
❑ 185 Chipper Jones .75 .23
❑ 186 Paul O'Neill .50 .15
❑ 187 Mike Greenwell .15 .04
❑ 188 Harold Baines .30 .09
❑ 189 Todd Stottlemyre .15 .04
❑ 190 Jeromy Burnitz .30 .09
❑ 191 Rene Arocha .15 .04
❑ 192 Jeff Fassero .15 .04
❑ 193 Robby Thompson .15 .04
❑ 194 Greg W. Harris .15 .04
❑ 195 Todd Van Poppel .15 .04
❑ 196 Jose Guzman .15 .04
❑ 197 Shane Mack .15 .04
❑ 198 Carlos Garcia .15 .04
❑ 199 Kevin Roberson .15 .04
❑ 200 David McCarty .15 .04
❑ 201 Alan Trammell .50 .15
❑ 202 Chuck Carr .15 .04
❑ 203 Tommy Greene .15 .04
❑ 204 Wilson Alvarez .15 .04
❑ 205 Dwight Gooden .50 .15
❑ 206 Tony Tarasco .15 .04
❑ 207 Darren Lewis .15 .04
❑ 208 Eric Karros .30 .09
❑ 209 Chris Hammond .15 .04
❑ 210 Jeffrey Hammonds .15 .04
❑ 211 Rich Amaral .15 .04
❑ 212 Danny Tartabull .15 .04
❑ 213 Jeff Russell .15 .04
❑ 214 Dave Staton .15 .04
❑ 215 Kenny Lofton .30 .09
❑ 216 Manuel Lee .15 .04
❑ 217 Brian Koelling .15 .04
❑ 218 Scott Lydy .15 .04
❑ 219 Tony Gwynn 1.00 .30
❑ 220 Cecil Fielder .30 .09
❑ 221 Royce Clayton .15 .04
❑ 222 Reggie Sanders .30 .09
❑ 223 Brian Jordan .30 .09
❑ 224 Ken Griffey Jr. 1.25 .35
❑ 225 Fred McGriff .50 .15
❑ 226 Felix Jose .15 .04
❑ 227 Brad Pennington .15 .04
❑ 228 Chris Bosio .15 .04
❑ 229 Mike Stanley .15 .04
❑ 230 Willie Greene .15 .04
❑ 231 Alex Fernandez .15 .04
❑ 232 Brad Ausmus .15 .04
❑ 233 Darrell Whitmore .15 .04
❑ 234 Marcus Moore .15 .04
❑ 235 Allen Watson .15 .04
❑ 236 Jose Offerman .15 .04
❑ 237 Rondell White .30 .09
❑ 238 Jeff King .15 .04
❑ 239 Luis Alicea .15 .04
❑ 240 Dan Wilson .15 .04
❑ 241 Ed Sprague .15 .04
❑ 242 Todd Hundley .15 .04
❑ 243 Al Martin .15 .04
❑ 244 Mike Lansing .15 .04
❑ 245 Ivan Rodriguez .75 .23
❑ 246 Dave Fleming .15 .04
❑ 247 John Doherty .15 .04
❑ 248 Mark McLemore .15 .04
❑ 249 Bob Hamelin .15 .04
❑ 250 Curtis Pride RC .40 .12
❑ 251 Zane Smith .15 .04
❑ 252 Eric Young .15 .04
❑ 253 Brian McRae .15 .04
❑ 254 Tim Raines .30 .09
❑ 255 Javier Lopez .30 .09
❑ 256 Melvin Nieves .15 .04
❑ 257 Randy Myers .15 .04
❑ 258 Willie McGee .30 .09
❑ 259 Jimmy Key UER .30 .09
(birthdate missing on back)
❑ 260 Tom Candiotti .15 .04
❑ 261 Eric Davis .30 .09
❑ 262 Craig Paquette .15 .04
❑ 263 Robin Ventura .30 .09
❑ 264 Pat Kelly .15 .04
❑ 265 Gregg Jefferies .15 .04
❑ 266 Cory Snyder .15 .04
❑ 267 David Justice HFA .15 .04
❑ 268 Sammy Sosa HFA .75 .23
❑ 269 Barry Larkin HFA .30 .09
❑ 270 Andres Galarraga HFA .15 .04
❑ 271 Gary Sheffield HFA .15 .04
❑ 272 Jeff Bagwell HFA .30 .09
❑ 273 Mike Piazza HFA .75 .23
❑ 274 Larry Walker HFA .15 .04
❑ 275 Bobby Bonilla HFA .15 .04
❑ 276 John Kruk HFA .15 .04
❑ 277 Jay Bell HFA .15 .04
❑ 278 Ozzie Smith HFA .50 .15
❑ 279 Tony Gwynn HFA .50 .15
❑ 280 Barry Bonds HFA 1.00 .30
❑ 281 Cal Ripken Jr. HFA 1.25 .35
❑ 282 Mo Vaughn HFA .15 .04
❑ 283 Tim Salmon HFA .30 .09
❑ 284 Frank Thomas HFA .50 .15
❑ 285 Albert Belle HFA .30 .09
❑ 286 Cecil Fielder HFA .15 .04
❑ 287 Wally Joyner HFA .15 .04
❑ 288 Greg Vaughn HFA .15 .04
❑ 289 Kirby Puckett HFA .50 .15
❑ 290 Don Mattingly HFA 1.00 .30
❑ 291 Terry Steinbach HFA .15 .04
❑ 292 Ken Griffey Jr. HFA .75 .23
❑ 293 Juan Gonzalez HFA .50 .15
❑ 294 Paul Molitor HFA .30 .09
❑ 295 Tavo Alvarez UDC .15 .04
❑ 296 Matt Brunson UDC .15 .04
❑ 297 Shawn Green UDC .30 .09
❑ 298 Alex Rodriguez UDC 3.00 .90
❑ 299 S.Stewart UDC .75 .23
❑ 300 Frank Thomas .75 .23
❑ 301 Mickey Tettleton .15 .04
❑ 302 Pedro Munoz .15 .04
❑ 303 Jose Valentin .15 .04
❑ 304 Orestes Destrade .15 .04
❑ 305 Pat Listach .15 .04
❑ 306 Scott Brosius .30 .09
❑ 307 Kurt Miller .15 .04
❑ 308 Rob Dibble .30 .09
❑ 309 Mike Blowers .15 .04
❑ 310 Jim Abbott .75 .23
❑ 311 Mike Jackson .15 .04
❑ 312 Craig Biggio .50 .15
❑ 313 Kurt Abbott RC .40 .12
❑ 314 Chuck Finley .30 .09
❑ 315 Andres Galarraga .30 .09
❑ 316 Mike Moore .15 .04
❑ 317 Doug Strange .15 .04
❑ 318 Pedro Martinez .75 .23
❑ 319 Kevin McReynolds .15 .04
❑ 320 Greg Maddux 1.50 .45
❑ 321 Mike Henneman .15 .04
❑ 322 Scott Leius .15 .04
❑ 323 John Franco .30 .09
❑ 324 Jeff Blauser .15 .04
❑ 325 Kirby Puckett .75 .23
❑ 326 Darryl Hamilton .15 .04
❑ 327 John Smiley .15 .04
❑ 328 Derrick May .15 .04
❑ 329 Jose Vizcaino .15 .04
❑ 330 Randy Johnson .75 .23
❑ 331 Jack Morris .30 .09
❑ 332 Graeme Lloyd .15 .04
❑ 333 Dave Valle .15 .04
❑ 334 Greg Myers .15 .04
❑ 335 John Wetteland .30 .09
❑ 336 Jim Gott .15 .04
❑ 337 Tim Naehring .15 .04
❑ 338 Mike Kelly .15 .04
❑ 339 Jeff Montgomery .15 .04
❑ 340 Rafael Palmeiro .50 .15
❑ 341 Eddie Murray .75 .23
❑ 342 Xavier Hernandez .15 .04
❑ 343 Bobby Munoz .15 .04
❑ 344 Bobby Bonilla .30 .09
❑ 345 Travis Fryman .30 .09
❑ 346 Steve Finley .30 .09
❑ 347 Chris Sabo .15 .04
❑ 348 Armando Reynoso .15 .04
❑ 349 Ramon Martinez .15 .04
❑ 350 Will Clark .75 .23
❑ 351 Moises Alou .30 .09
❑ 352 Jim Thome .75 .23
❑ 353 Bob Tewksbury .15 .04
❑ 354 Andujar Cedeno .15 .04
❑ 355 Orel Hershiser .30 .09
❑ 356 Mike Devereaux .15 .04
❑ 357 Mike Perez .15 .04
❑ 358 Dennis Martinez .30 .09
❑ 359 Dave Nilsson .15 .04
❑ 360 Ozzie Smith .75 .23
❑ 361 Eric Anthony .15 .04
❑ 362 Scott Sanders .15 .04
❑ 363 Paul Sorrento .15 .04
❑ 364 Tim Belcher .15 .04
❑ 365 Dennis Eckersley .30 .09
❑ 366 Mel Rojas .15 .04
❑ 367 Tom Henke .15 .04
❑ 368 Randy Tomlin .15 .04

	Nm-Mt	Ex-Mt
❑ 369 B.J. Surhoff	.30	.09
❑ 370 Larry Walker	.50	.15
❑ 371 Joey Cora	.15	.04
❑ 372 Mike Harkey	.15	.04
❑ 373 John Valentin	.15	.04
❑ 374 Doug Jones	.15	.04
❑ 375 David Justice	.30	.09
❑ 376 Vince Coleman	.15	.04
❑ 377 David Hulse	.15	.04
❑ 378 Kevin Seitzer	.15	.04
❑ 379 Pete Harnisch	.15	.04
❑ 380 Ruben Sierra	.15	.04
❑ 381 Mark Lewis	.15	.04
❑ 382 Bip Roberts	.15	.04
❑ 383 Paul Wagner	.15	.04
❑ 384 Stan Javier	.15	.04
❑ 385 Barry Larkin	.75	.23
❑ 386 Mark Portugal	.15	.04
❑ 387 Roberto Kelly	.15	.04
❑ 388 Andy Benes	.15	.04
❑ 389 Felix Fermin	.15	.04
❑ 390 Marquis Grissom	.15	.04
❑ 391 Troy Neel	.15	.04
❑ 392 Chad Kreuter	.15	.04
❑ 393 Gregg Olson	.15	.04
❑ 394 Charles Nagy	.15	.04
❑ 395 Jack McDowell	.15	.04
❑ 396 Luis Gonzalez	.30	.09
❑ 397 Benito Santiago	.30	.09
❑ 398 Chris James	.15	.04
❑ 399 Terry Mulholland	.15	.04
❑ 400 Barry Bonds	2.00	.60
❑ 401 Joe Grahe	.15	.04
❑ 402 Duane Ward	.15	.04
❑ 403 John Burkett	.15	.04
❑ 404 Scott Servais	.15	.04
❑ 405 Bryan Harvey	.15	.04
❑ 406 Bernard Gilkey	.15	.04
❑ 407 Greg McMichael	.15	.04
❑ 408 Tim Wallach	.15	.04
❑ 409 Ken Caminiti	.30	.09
❑ 410 John Kruk	.30	.09
❑ 411 Darrin Jackson	.15	.04
❑ 412 Mike Gallego	.15	.04
❑ 413 David Cone	.30	.09
❑ 414 Lou Whitaker	.30	.09
❑ 415 Sandy Alomar Jr.	.15	.04
❑ 416 Bill Wegman	.15	.04
❑ 417 Pat Borders	.15	.04
❑ 418 Roger Pavlik	.15	.04
❑ 419 Pete Smith	.15	.04
❑ 420 Steve Avery	.15	.04
❑ 421 David Segui	.15	.04
❑ 422 Rheal Cormier	.15	.04
❑ 423 Harold Reynolds	.30	.09
❑ 424 Edgar Martinez	.50	.15
❑ 425 Cal Ripken Jr.	2.50	.75
❑ 426 Jaime Navarro	.15	.04
❑ 427 Sean Berry	.15	.04
❑ 428 Bret Saberhagen	.30	.09
❑ 429 Bob Welch	.15	.04
❑ 430 Juan Guzman	.15	.04
❑ 431 Cal Eldred	.15	.04
❑ 432 Dave Hollins	.15	.04
❑ 433 Sid Fernandez	.15	.04
❑ 434 Willie Banks	.15	.04
❑ 435 Darryl Kile	.30	.09
❑ 436 Henry Rodriguez	.15	.04
❑ 437 Tony Fernandez	.15	.04
❑ 438 Walt Weiss	.15	.04
❑ 439 Kevin Tapani	.15	.04
❑ 440 Mark Grace	.75	.23
❑ 441 Brian Harper	.15	.04
❑ 442 Kent Mercker	.15	.04
❑ 443 Anthony Young	.15	.04
❑ 444 Todd Zeile	.15	.04
❑ 445 Greg Vaughn	.30	.09
❑ 446 Ray Lankford	.15	.04
❑ 447 Dave Weathers	.15	.04
❑ 448 Bret Boone	.30	.09
❑ 449 Charlie Hough	.30	.09
❑ 450 Roger Clemens	1.50	.45
❑ 451 Mike Morgan	.15	.04
❑ 452 Doug Drabek	.15	.04
❑ 453 Danny Jackson	.15	.04
❑ 454 Dante Bichette	.30	.09
❑ 455 Roberto Alomar	.75	.23
❑ 456 Ben McDonald	.15	.04
❑ 457 Kenny Rogers	.30	.09
❑ 458 Bill Gullickson	.15	.04
❑ 459 Darrin Fletcher	.15	.04
❑ 460 Curt Schilling	.50	.15
❑ 461 Billy Hatcher	.15	.04
❑ 462 Howard Johnson	.15	.04
❑ 463 Mickey Morandini	.15	.04
❑ 464 Frank Castillo	.15	.04
❑ 465 Delino DeShields	.15	.04
❑ 466 Gary Gaetti	.30	.09
❑ 467 Steve Farr	.15	.04
❑ 468 Roberto Hernandez	.15	.04
❑ 469 Jack Armstrong	.15	.04
❑ 470 Paul Molitor	.50	.15
❑ 471 Melido Perez	.15	.04
❑ 472 Greg Hibbard	.15	.04
❑ 473 Jody Reed	.15	.04
❑ 474 Tom Gordon	.15	.04
❑ 475 Gary Sheffield	.30	.09
❑ 476 John Jaha	.15	.04
❑ 477 Shawon Dunston	.15	.04
❑ 478 Reggie Jefferson	.15	.04
❑ 479 Don Slaught	.15	.04
❑ 480 Jeff Bagwell	.50	.15
❑ 481 Tim Pugh	.15	.04
❑ 482 Kevin Young	.15	.04
❑ 483 Ellis Burks	.30	.09
❑ 484 Greg Swindell	.15	.04
❑ 485 Mark Langston	.15	.04
❑ 486 Omar Vizquel	.30	.09
❑ 487 Kevin Brown	.30	.09
❑ 488 Terry Steinbach	.15	.04
❑ 489 Mark Lemke	.15	.04
❑ 490 Matt Williams	.30	.09
❑ 491 Pete Incaviglia	.15	.04
❑ 492 Karl Rhodes	.15	.04
❑ 493 Shawn Green	.75	.23
❑ 494 Hal Morris	.15	.04
❑ 495 Derek Bell	.15	.04
❑ 496 Luis Polonia	.15	.04
❑ 497 Otis Nixon	.15	.04
❑ 498 Ron Darling	.15	.04
❑ 499 Mitch Williams	.15	.04
❑ 500 Mike Piazza	1.50	.45
❑ 501 Pat Meares	.15	.04
❑ 502 Scott Cooper	.15	.04
❑ 503 Scott Erickson	.15	.04
❑ 504 Jeff Juden	.15	.04
❑ 505 Lee Smith	.30	.09
❑ 506 Bobby Ayala	.15	.04
❑ 507 Dave Henderson	.15	.04
❑ 508 Erik Hanson	.15	.04
❑ 509 Bob Wickman	.15	.04
❑ 510 Sammy Sosa	1.25	.35
❑ 511 Hector Carrasco	.15	.04
❑ 512 Tim Davis	.15	.04
❑ 513 Joey Hamilton	.15	.04
❑ 514 Robert Eenhoorn	.15	.04
❑ 515 Jorge Fabregas	.15	.04
❑ 516 Tim Hyers RC	.15	.04
❑ 517 John Hudek RC	.15	.04
❑ 518 James Mouton	.15	.04
❑ 519 Herbert Perry RC	.40	.12
❑ 520 Chan Ho Park RC	1.00	.30
❑ 521 W.Va Landingham RC	.15	.04
❑ 522 Paul Shuey	.15	.04
❑ 523 Ryan Hancock RC	.15	.04
❑ 524 Billy Wagner RC	1.00	.30
❑ 525 Jason Giambi	.75	.23
❑ 526 Jose Silva RC	.15	.04
❑ 527 Terrell Wade RC	.15	.04
❑ 528 Todd Dunn	.15	.04
❑ 529 Alan Benes RC	.40	.12
❑ 530 B.Kieschnick RC	.40	.12
❑ 531 T.Hollandsworth	.15	.04
❑ 532 Brad Fullmer RC	1.00	.30
❑ 533 S.Soderstrom RC	.15	.04
❑ 534 Daron Kirkreit	.15	.04
❑ 535 Arquimedez Pozo RC	.15	.04
❑ 536 Charles Johnson	.30	.09
❑ 537 Preston Wilson	.50	.15
❑ 538 Alex Ochoa	.15	.04
❑ 539 Derrek Lee RC	1.00	.30
❑ 540 Wayne Gomes RC	.15	.04
❑ 541 J.Allensworth RC	.15	.04
❑ 542 Mike Bell RC	.15	.04
❑ 543 Trot Nixon RC	1.00	.30
❑ 544 Pokey Reese	.15	.04
❑ 545 Neifi Perez RC	.40	.12
❑ 546 Johnny Damon	.75	.23
❑ 547 Matt Brunson RC	.15	.04
❑ 548 L.Hawkins RC	.40	.12
❑ 549 Eddie Pearson RC	.15	.04
❑ 550 Derek Jeter	2.50	.75
❑ A298 Alex Rodriguez AU	350.00	105.00
❑ P224 K.Griffey Jr. Promo	2.00	.60
❑ GM1 Ken Griffey Jr. AU Mickey Mantle AU/1000	1000.00	300.00
❑ KG1 K.Griffey Jr. AU/1000	200.00	60.00
❑ MM1 M.Mantle AU/1000	500.00	150.00

1995 Upper Deck

	Nm-Mt	Ex-Mt
COMP.MASTER SET (495)	100.00	30.00
COMPLETE SET (450)	50.00	15.00
COMP. SERIES 1 (225)	25.00	7.50
COMP. SERIES 2 (225)	25.00	7.50
COMMON CARD (1-450)	.15	.04
COMP.TRADE SET (45)	50.00	15.00
COMMON (451T-495T)	1.00	.30

	Nm-Mt	Ex-Mt
❑ 1 Ruben Rivera	.15	.04
❑ 2 Bill Pulsipher	.15	.04
❑ 3 Ben Grieve	.30	.09
❑ 4 Curtis Goodwin	.15	.04
❑ 5 Damon Hollins	.15	.04
❑ 6 Todd Greene	.15	.04
❑ 7 Glenn Williams	.15	.04
❑ 8 Bret Wagner	.15	.04
❑ 9 Karim Garcia RC	.75	.23
❑ 10 Nomar Garciaparra	3.00	.90
❑ 11 Raul Casanova RC	.15	.04
❑ 12 Matt Smith	.15	.04
❑ 13 Paul Wilson	.15	.04
❑ 14 Jason Isringhausen	.30	.09
❑ 15 Reid Ryan	.30	.09
❑ 16 Lee Smith	.30	.09
❑ 17 Chili Davis	.30	.09
❑ 18 Brian Anderson	.15	.04
❑ 19 Gary DiSarcina	.15	.04
❑ 20 Bo Jackson	.75	.23
❑ 21 Chuck Finley	.30	.09
❑ 22 Darryl Kile	.30	.09
❑ 23 Shane Reynolds	.15	.04
❑ 24 Tony Eusebio	.15	.04
❑ 25 Craig Biggio	.50	.15
❑ 26 Doug Drabek	.15	.04
❑ 27 Brian L. Hunter	.15	.04
❑ 28 James Mouton	.15	.04
❑ 29 Geronimo Berroa	.15	.04
❑ 30 Rickey Henderson	1.25	.35
❑ 31 Steve Karsay	.15	.04
❑ 32 Steve Ontiveros	.15	.04
❑ 33 Ernie Young	.15	.04
❑ 34 Dennis Eckersley	.30	.09
❑ 35 Mark McGwire	2.00	.60
❑ 36 Dave Stewart	.30	.09
❑ 37 Pat Hentgen	.15	.04
❑ 38 Carlos Delgado	.30	.09
❑ 39 Joe Carter	.30	.09
❑ 40 Roberto Alomar	.75	.23

❑ 41 John Olerud .30 .09
❑ 42 Devon White .30 .09
❑ 43 Roberto Kelly .15 .04
❑ 44 Jeff Blauser .15 .04
❑ 45 Fred McGriff .50 .15
❑ 46 Tom Glavine .75 .23
❑ 47 Mike Kelly .15 .04
❑ 48 Javier Lopez .30 .09
❑ 49 Greg Maddux 1.50 .45
❑ 50 Matt Mieske .15 .04
❑ 51 Troy O'Leary .15 .04
❑ 52 Jeff Cirillo .30 .09
❑ 53 Cal Eldred .15 .04
❑ 54 Pat Listach .15 .04
❑ 55 Jose Valentin .15 .04
❑ 56 John Mabry .15 .04
❑ 57 Bob Tewksbury .15 .04
❑ 58 Brian Jordan .30 .09
❑ 59 Gregg Jefferies .15 .04
❑ 60 Ozzie Smith .75 .23
❑ 61 Geronimo Pena .15 .04
❑ 62 Mark Whiten .15 .04
❑ 63 Rey Sanchez .15 .04
❑ 64 Willie Banks .15 .04
❑ 65 Mark Grace .75 .23
❑ 66 Randy Myers .15 .04
❑ 67 Steve Trachsel .15 .04
❑ 68 Derrick May .15 .04
❑ 69 Brett Butler .30 .09
❑ 70 Eric Karros .30 .09
❑ 71 Tim Wallach .15 .04
❑ 72 Delino DeShields .15 .04
❑ 73 Darren Dreifort .15 .04
❑ 74 Orel Hershiser .30 .09
❑ 75 Billy Ashley .15 .04
❑ 76 Sean Berry .15 .04
❑ 77 Ken Hill .15 .04
❑ 78 John Wetteland .30 .09
❑ 79 Moises Alou .30 .09
❑ 80 Cliff Floyd .30 .09
❑ 81 Marquis Grissom .15 .04
❑ 82 Larry Walker .50 .15
❑ 83 Rondell White .30 .09
❑ 84 W.VanLandingham .15 .04
❑ 85 Matt Williams .30 .09
❑ 86 Rod Beck .15 .04
❑ 87 Darren Lewis .15 .04
❑ 88 Robby Thompson .15 .04
❑ 89 Darryl Strawberry .50 .15
❑ 90 Kenny Lofton .30 .09
❑ 91 Charles Nagy .15 .04
❑ 92 Sandy Alomar Jr. .15 .04
❑ 93 Mark Clark .15 .04
❑ 94 Dennis Martinez .30 .09
❑ 95 Dave Winfield .50 .15
❑ 96 Jim Thome .75 .23
❑ 97 Manny Ramirez .30 .09
❑ 98 Goose Gossage .30 .09
❑ 99 Tino Martinez .50 .15
❑ 100 Ken Griffey Jr. 1.25 .35
❑ 101 Greg Maddux ANA .75 .23
❑ 102 Randy Johnson ANA .50 .15
❑ 103 Barry Bonds ANA 1.00 .30
❑ 104 Juan Gonzalez ANA .50 .15
❑ 105 Frank Thomas ANA .50 .15
❑ 106 Matt Williams ANA .15 .04
❑ 107 Paul Molitor ANA .30 .09
❑ 108 Fred McGriff ANA .30 .09
❑ 109 Carlos Baerga ANA .15 .04
❑ 110 Ken Griffey Jr. ANA .75 .23
❑ 111 Reggie Jefferson .15 .04
❑ 112 Randy Johnson .75 .23
❑ 113 Marc Newfield .15 .04
❑ 114 Robb Nen .30 .09
❑ 115 Jeff Conine .30 .09
❑ 116 Kurt Abbott .15 .04
❑ 117 Charlie Hough .30 .09
❑ 118 Dave Weathers .15 .04
❑ 119 Juan Castillo .15 .04
❑ 120 Bret Saberhagen .30 .09
❑ 121 Rico Brogna .15 .04
❑ 122 John Franco .30 .09
❑ 123 Todd Hundley .15 .04
❑ 124 Jason Jacome .15 .04
❑ 125 Bobby Jones .15 .04
❑ 126 Bret Barberie .15 .04
❑ 127 Ben McDonald .15 .04
❑ 128 Harold Baines .30 .09
❑ 129 Jeffrey Hammonds .15 .04
❑ 130 Mike Mussina .75 .23
❑ 131 Chris Hoiles .15 .04
❑ 132 Brady Anderson .30 .09
❑ 133 Eddie Williams .15 .04
❑ 134 Andy Benes .15 .04
❑ 135 Tony Gwynn 1.00 .30
❑ 136 Bip Roberts .15 .04
❑ 137 Joey Hamilton .15 .04
❑ 138 Luis Lopez .15 .04
❑ 139 Ray McDavid .15 .04
❑ 140 Lenny Dykstra .30 .09
❑ 141 Mariano Duncan .15 .04
❑ 142 Fernando Valenzuela .30 .09
❑ 143 Bobby Munoz .15 .04
❑ 144 Kevin Stocker .15 .04
❑ 145 John Kruk .30 .09
❑ 146 Jon Lieber .15 .04
❑ 147 Zane Smith .15 .04
❑ 148 Steve Cooke .15 .04
❑ 149 Andy Van Slyke .30 .09
❑ 150 Jay Bell .30 .09
❑ 151 Carlos Garcia .15 .04
❑ 152 John Dettmer .15 .04
❑ 153 Darren Oliver .15 .04
❑ 154 Dean Palmer .30 .09
❑ 155 Otis Nixon .15 .04
❑ 156 Rusty Greer .30 .09
❑ 157 Rick Helling .15 .04
❑ 158 Jose Canseco .75 .23
❑ 159 Roger Clemens 1.50 .45
❑ 160 Andre Dawson .30 .09
❑ 161 Mo Vaughn .30 .09
❑ 162 Aaron Sele .15 .04
❑ 163 John Valentin .15 .04
❑ 164 Brian R. Hunter .15 .04
❑ 165 Bret Boone .30 .09
❑ 166 Hector Carrasco .15 .04
❑ 167 Pete Schourek .15 .04
❑ 168 Willie Greene .15 .04
❑ 169 Kevin Mitchell .15 .04
❑ 170 Deion Sanders .30 .09
❑ 171 John Roper .15 .04
❑ 172 Charlie Hayes .15 .04
❑ 173 David Nied .15 .04
❑ 174 Ellis Burks .30 .09
❑ 175 Dante Bichette .30 .09
❑ 176 Marvin Freeman .15 .04
❑ 177 Eric Young .15 .04
❑ 178 David Cone .30 .09
❑ 179 Greg Gagne .15 .04
❑ 180 Bob Hamelin .15 .04
❑ 181 Wally Joyner .30 .09
❑ 182 Jeff Montgomery .15 .04
❑ 183 Jose Lind .15 .04
❑ 184 Chris Gomez .15 .04
❑ 185 Travis Fryman .30 .09
❑ 186 Kirk Gibson .30 .09
❑ 187 Mike Moore .15 .04
❑ 188 Lou Whitaker .30 .09
❑ 189 Sean Bergman .15 .04
❑ 190 Shane Mack .15 .04
❑ 191 Rick Aguilera .15 .04
❑ 192 Denny Hocking .15 .04
❑ 193 Chuck Knoblauch .30 .09
❑ 194 Kevin Tapani .15 .04
❑ 195 Kent Hrbek .30 .09
❑ 196 Ozzie Guillen .15 .04
❑ 197 Wilson Alvarez .15 .04
❑ 198 Tim Raines .30 .09
❑ 199 Scott Ruffcorn .15 .04
❑ 200 Michael Jordan 2.50 .75
❑ 201 Robin Ventura .30 .09
❑ 202 Jason Bere .15 .04
❑ 203 Darrin Jackson .15 .04
❑ 204 Russ Davis .15 .04
❑ 205 Jimmy Key .30 .09
❑ 206 Jack McDowell .15 .04
❑ 207 Jim Abbott .75 .23
❑ 208 Paul O'Neill .50 .15
❑ 209 Bernie Williams .50 .15
❑ 210 Don Mattingly 2.00 .60
❑ 211 Orlando Miller .15 .04
❑ 212 Alex Gonzalez .15 .04
❑ 213 Terrell Wade .15 .04
❑ 214 Jose Oliva .15 .04
❑ 215 Alex Rodriguez 2.00 .60
❑ 216 Garret Anderson .30 .09
❑ 217 Alan Benes .15 .04
❑ 218 Armando Benitez .30 .09
❑ 219 Dustin Hermanson .15 .04
❑ 220 Charles Johnson .30 .09
❑ 221 Julian Tavarez .15 .04
❑ 222 Jason Giambi .75 .23
❑ 223 LaTroy Hawkins .15 .04
❑ 224 Todd Hollandsworth .15 .04
❑ 225 Derek Jeter 2.00 .60
❑ 226 Hideo Nomo RC 2.00 .60
❑ 227 Tony Clark .15 .04
❑ 228 Roger Cedeno .15 .04
❑ 229 Scott Stahoviak .15 .04
❑ 230 Michael Tucker .15 .04
❑ 231 Joe Rosselli .15 .04
❑ 232 Antonio Osuna .15 .04
❑ 233 Bobby Higginson RC .75 .23
❑ 234 Mark Grudzielanek RC .50 .15
❑ 235 Ray Durham .30 .09
❑ 236 Frank Rodriguez .15 .04
❑ 237 Quilvio Veras .15 .04
❑ 238 Darren Bragg .15 .04
❑ 239 Ugueth Urbina .15 .04
❑ 240 Jason Bates .15 .04
❑ 241 David Bell .15 .04
❑ 242 Ron Villone .15 .04
❑ 243 Joe Randa .15 .04
❑ 244 Carlos Perez RC .30 .09
❑ 245 Brad Clontz .15 .04
❑ 246 Steve Rodriguez .15 .04
❑ 247 Joe Vitiello .15 .04
❑ 248 Ozzie Timmons .15 .04
❑ 249 Rudy Pemberton .15 .04
❑ 250 Marty Cordova .15 .04
❑ 251 Tony Graffanino .15 .04
❑ 252 Mark Johnson RC .30 .09
❑ 253 Tomas Perez RC .15 .04
❑ 254 Jimmy Hurst .15 .04
❑ 255 Edgardo Alfonzo .30 .09
❑ 256 Jose Malave .15 .04
❑ 257 Brad Radke RC 1.25 .35
❑ 258 Jon Nunnally .15 .04
❑ 259 Dilson Torres RC .15 .04
❑ 260 Esteban Loaiza .50 .15
❑ 261 Freddy Adrian Garcia RC .15 .04
❑ 262 Don Wengert .15 .04
❑ 263 Robert Person RC .30 .09
❑ 264 Tim Unroe RC .15 .04
❑ 265 Juan Acevedo RC .15 .04
❑ 266 Eduardo Perez .15 .04
❑ 267 Tony Phillips .15 .04
❑ 268 Jim Edmonds .30 .09
❑ 269 Jorge Fabregas .15 .04
❑ 270 Tim Salmon .50 .15
❑ 271 Mark Langston .15 .04
❑ 272 J.T. Snow .30 .09
❑ 273 Phil Plantier .15 .04
❑ 274 Derek Bell .15 .04
❑ 275 Jeff Bagwell .50 .15
❑ 276 Luis Gonzalez .30 .09
❑ 277 John Hudek .15 .04
❑ 278 Todd Stottlemyre .15 .04
❑ 279 Mark Acre .15 .04
❑ 280 Ruben Sierra .15 .04
❑ 281 Mike Bordick .15 .04
❑ 282 Ron Darling .15 .04
❑ 283 Brent Gates .15 .04
❑ 284 Todd Van Poppel .15 .04
❑ 285 Paul Molitor .50 .15
❑ 286 Ed Sprague .15 .04
❑ 287 Juan Guzman .15 .04
❑ 288 David Cone .30 .09
❑ 289 Shawn Green .30 .09
❑ 290 Marquis Grissom .15 .04
❑ 291 Kent Mercker .15 .04
❑ 292 Steve Avery .15 .04
❑ 293 Chipper Jones .75 .23
❑ 294 John Smoltz .50 .15
❑ 295 David Justice .30 .09
❑ 296 Ryan Klesko .30 .09
❑ 297 Joe Oliver .15 .04
❑ 298 Ricky Bones .15 .04

❑ 299 John Jaha .15 .04
❑ 300 Greg Vaughn .30 .09
❑ 301 Dave Nilsson .15 .04
❑ 302 Kevin Seitzer .15 .04
❑ 303 Bernard Gilkey .15 .04
❑ 304 Allen Battle .15 .04
❑ 305 Ray Lankford .15 .04
❑ 306 Tom Pagnozzi .15 .04
❑ 307 Allen Watson .15 .04
❑ 308 Danny Jackson .15 .04
❑ 309 Ken Hill .15 .04
❑ 310 Todd Zeile .15 .04
❑ 311 Kevin Roberson .15 .04
❑ 312 Steve Buechele .15 .04
❑ 313 Rick Wilkins .15 .04
❑ 314 Kevin Foster .15 .04
❑ 315 Sammy Sosa 1.25 .35
❑ 316 Howard Johnson .15 .04
❑ 317 Greg Hansell .15 .04
❑ 318 Pedro Astacio .15 .04
❑ 319 Rafael Bournigal .15 .04
❑ 320 Mike Piazza 1.25 .35
❑ 321 Ramon Martinez .15 .04
❑ 322 Raul Mondesi .30 .09
❑ 323 Ismael Valdes .15 .04
❑ 324 Wil Cordero .15 .04
❑ 325 Tony Tarasco .15 .04
❑ 326 Roberto Kelly .15 .04
❑ 327 Jeff Fassero .15 .04
❑ 328 Mike Lansing .15 .04
❑ 329 Pedro Martinez .75 .23
❑ 330 Kirk Rueter .15 .04
❑ 331 Glenallen Hill .15 .04
❑ 332 Kirt Manwaring .15 .04
❑ 333 Royce Clayton .15 .04
❑ 334 J.R. Phillips .15 .04
❑ 335 Barry Bonds 2.00 .60
❑ 336 Mark Portugal .15 .04
❑ 337 Terry Mulholland .15 .04
❑ 338 Omar Vizquel .30 .09
❑ 339 Carlos Baerga .15 .04
❑ 340 Albert Belle .30 .09
❑ 341 Eddie Murray .75 .23
❑ 342 Wayne Kirby .15 .04
❑ 343 Chad Ogea .15 .04
❑ 344 Tim Davis .15 .04
❑ 345 Jay Buhner .30 .09
❑ 346 Bobby Ayala .15 .04
❑ 347 Mike Blowers .15 .04
❑ 348 Dave Fleming .15 .04
❑ 349 Edgar Martinez .50 .15
❑ 350 Andre Dawson .30 .09
❑ 351 Darrell Whitmore .15 .04
❑ 352 Chuck Carr .15 .04
❑ 353 John Burkett .15 .04
❑ 354 Chris Hammond .15 .04
❑ 355 Gary Sheffield .30 .09
❑ 356 Pat Rapp .15 .04
❑ 357 Greg Colbrunn .15 .04
❑ 358 David Segui .15 .04
❑ 359 Jeff Kent .30 .09
❑ 360 Bobby Bonilla .30 .09
❑ 361 Pete Harnisch .15 .04
❑ 362 Ryan Thompson .15 .04
❑ 363 Jose Vizcaino .15 .04
❑ 364 Brett Butler .30 .09
❑ 365 Cal Ripken Jr. 2.50 .75
❑ 366 Rafael Palmeiro .50 .15
❑ 367 Leo Gomez .15 .04
❑ 368 Andy Van Slyke .30 .09
❑ 369 Arthur Rhodes .15 .04
❑ 370 Ken Caminiti .30 .09
❑ 371 Steve Finley .30 .09
❑ 372 Melvin Nieves .15 .04
❑ 373 Andujar Cedeno .15 .04
❑ 374 Trevor Hoffman .30 .09
❑ 375 Fernando Valenzuela .30 .09
❑ 376 Ricky Bottalico .15 .04
❑ 377 Dave Hollins .15 .04
❑ 378 Charlie Hayes .15 .04
❑ 379 Tommy Greene .15 .04
❑ 380 Darren Daulton .30 .09
❑ 381 Curt Schilling .50 .15
❑ 382 Midre Cummings .15 .04
❑ 383 Al Martin .15 .04
❑ 384 Jeff King .15 .04
❑ 385 Orlando Merced .15 .04
❑ 386 Denny Neagle .30 .09
❑ 387 Don Slaught .15 .04
❑ 388 Dave Clark .15 .04
❑ 389 Kevin Gross .15 .04
❑ 390 Will Clark .75 .23
❑ 391 Ivan Rodriguez .75 .23
❑ 392 Benji Gil .15 .04
❑ 393 Jeff Frye .15 .04
❑ 394 Kenny Rogers .30 .09
❑ 395 Juan Gonzalez .75 .23
❑ 396 Mike Macfarlane .15 .04
❑ 397 Lee Tinsley .15 .04
❑ 398 Tim Naehring .15 .04
❑ 399 Tim Vanegmond .15 .04
❑ 400 Mike Greenwell .15 .04
❑ 401 Ken Ryan .15 .04
❑ 402 John Smiley .15 .04
❑ 403 Tim Pugh .15 .04
❑ 404 Reggie Sanders .30 .09
❑ 405 Barry Larkin .75 .23
❑ 406 Hal Morris .15 .04
❑ 407 Jose Rijo .15 .04
❑ 408 Lance Painter .15 .04
❑ 409 Joe Girardi .15 .04
❑ 410 Andres Galarraga .30 .09
❑ 411 Mike Kingery .15 .04
❑ 412 Roberto Mejia .15 .04
❑ 413 Walt Weiss .15 .04
❑ 414 Bill Swift .15 .04
❑ 415 Larry Walker .50 .15
❑ 416 Billy Brewer .15 .04
❑ 417 Pat Borders .15 .04
❑ 418 Tom Gordon .15 .04
❑ 419 Kevin Appier .30 .09
❑ 420 Gary Gaetti .30 .09
❑ 421 Greg Gohr .15 .04
❑ 422 Felipe Lira .15 .04
❑ 423 John Doherty .15 .04
❑ 424 Chad Curtis .15 .04
❑ 425 Cecil Fielder .30 .09
❑ 426 Alan Trammell .50 .15
❑ 427 David McCarty .15 .04
❑ 428 Scott Erickson .15 .04
❑ 429 Pat Mahomes .15 .04
❑ 430 Kirby Puckett .75 .23
❑ 431 Dave Stevens .15 .04
❑ 432 Pedro Munoz .15 .04
❑ 433 Chris Sabo .15 .04
❑ 434 Alex Fernandez .15 .04
❑ 435 Frank Thomas .75 .23
❑ 436 Roberto Hernandez .15 .04
❑ 437 Lance Johnson .15 .04
❑ 438 Jim Abbott .75 .23
❑ 439 John Wetteland .30 .09
❑ 440 Melido Perez .15 .04
❑ 441 Tony Fernandez .15 .04
❑ 442 Pat Kelly .15 .04
❑ 443 Mike Stanley .15 .04
❑ 444 Danny Tartabull .15 .04
❑ 445 Wade Boggs .50 .15
❑ 446 Robin Yount .75 .23
❑ 447 Ryne Sandberg 1.25 .35
❑ 448 Nolan Ryan 3.00 .90
❑ 449 George Brett 2.00 .60
❑ 450 Mike Schmidt 1.25 .35
❑ 451 Jim Abbott TRADE 3.00 .90
❑ 452 D.Tartabull TRADE 1.00 .30
❑ 453 Ariel Prieto TRADE 1.00 .30
❑ 454 Scott Cooper TRADE 1.00 .30
❑ 455 Tom Henke TRADE 1.00 .30
❑ 456 Todd Zeile TRADE 1.00 .30
❑ 457 Brian McRae TRADE 1.00 .30
❑ 458 Luis Gonzalez TRADE 1.50 .45
❑ 459 Jaime Navarro TRADE 1.00 .30
❑ 460 Todd Worrell TRADE 1.00 .30
❑ 461 Roberto Kelly TRADE 1.00 .30
❑ 462 Chad Fonville TRADE 1.00 .30
❑ 463 S.Andrews TRADE 1.00 .30
❑ 464 David Segui TRADE 1.00 .30
❑ 465 Deion Sanders TRADE 1.50 .45
❑ 466 Orel Hershiser TRADE 1.50 .45
❑ 467 Ken Hill TRADE 1.00 .30
❑ 468 Andy Benes TRADE 1.00 .30
❑ 469 T.Pendleton TRADE 1.50 .45
❑ 470 Bobby Bonilla TRADE 1.50 .45
❑ 471 Scott Erickson TRADE 1.00 .30
❑ 472 Kevin Brown TRADE 1.50 .45
❑ 473 G.Dishman TRADE 1.00 .30
❑ 474 Phil Plantier TRADE 1.00 .30
❑ 475 G.Jefferies TRADE 1.00 .30
❑ 476 Tyler Green TRADE 1.00 .30
❑ 477 H. Slocumb TRADE 1.00 .30
❑ 478 Mark Whiten TRADE 1.00 .30
❑ 479 M.Tettleton TRADE 1.00 .30
❑ 480 Tim Wakefield TRADE 1.50 .45
❑ 481 V. Eshelman TRADE 1.00 .30
❑ 482 Rick Aguilera TRADE 1.00 .30
❑ 483 Erik Hanson TRADE 1.00 .30
❑ 484 Willie McGee TRADE 1.50 .45
❑ 485 Troy O'Leary TRADE 1.00 .30
❑ 486 B.Santiago TRADE 1.50 .45
❑ 487 Darren Lewis TRADE 1.00 .30
❑ 488 Dave Burba TRADE 1.00 .30
❑ 489 Ron Gant TRADE 1.50 .45
❑ 490 B.Saberhagen TRADE 1.50 .45
❑ 491 Vinny Castilla TRADE 1.50 .45
❑ 492 F.Rodriguez TRADE 1.00 .30
❑ 493 Andy Pettitte TRADE 2.00 .60
❑ 494 Ruben Sierra TRADE 1.00 .30
❑ 495 David Cone TRADE 1.50 .45
❑ J159 R. Clemens Jumbo AU 80.00 24.00
❑ J215 A. Rodriguez Jumbo AU 100.00 30.00
❑ P100 K.Griffey Jr. Promo 2.00 .60

1999 Upper Deck

	Nm-Mt	Ex-Mt
COMPLETE SET (525)	100.00	30.00
COMP. SERIES 1 (255)	60.00	18.00
COMP. SERIES 2 (270)	40.00	12.00
COMMON (19-255/293-535)	.30	.09
COMMON SER.1 SR (1-18)	.50	.15
COMMON (266-292)	.50	.15

❑ 1 Troy Glaus SR .75 .23
❑ 2 Adrian Beltre SR .50 .15
❑ 3 Matt Anderson SR .50 .15
❑ 4 Eric Chavez SR .50 .15
❑ 5 Jin Ho Cho SR .50 .15
❑ 6 Robert Smith SR .50 .15
❑ 7 George Lombard SR .50 .15
❑ 8 Mike Kinkade SR .50 .15
❑ 9 Seth Greisinger SR .50 .15
❑ 10 J.D. Drew SR .50 .15
❑ 11 Aramis Ramirez SR .50 .15
❑ 12 Carlos Guillen SR .50 .15
❑ 13 Justin Baughman SR .50 .15
❑ 14 Jim Parque SR .50 .15
❑ 15 Ryan Jackson SR .50 .15
❑ 16 Ramon E.Martinez SR RC .50 .15
❑ 17 Orlando Hernandez SR .50 .15
❑ 18 Jeremy Giambi SR .50 .15
❑ 19 Gary DiSarcina .30 .09
❑ 20 Darin Erstad .30 .09
❑ 21 Troy Glaus .50 .15
❑ 22 Chuck Finley .30 .09
❑ 23 Dave Hollins .30 .09
❑ 24 Troy Percival .30 .09
❑ 25 Tim Salmon .50 .15
❑ 26 Brian Anderson .30 .09
❑ 27 Jay Bell .30 .09
❑ 28 Andy Benes .30 .09
❑ 29 Brent Brede .30 .09

❑ 30 David Dellucci .30 .09
❑ 31 Karim Garcia .30 .09
❑ 32 Travis Lee .30 .09
❑ 33 Andres Galarraga .30 .09
❑ 34 Ryan Klesko .30 .09
❑ 35 Keith Lockhart .30 .09
❑ 36 Kevin Millwood .30 .09
❑ 37 Denny Neagle .30 .09
❑ 38 John Smoltz .50 .15
❑ 39 Michael Tucker .30 .09
❑ 40 Walt Weiss .30 .09
❑ 41 Dennis Martinez .30 .09
❑ 42 Javy Lopez .30 .09
❑ 43 Brady Anderson .30 .09
❑ 44 Harold Baines .30 .09
❑ 45 Mike Bordick .30 .09
❑ 46 Roberto Alomar .75 .23
❑ 47 Scott Erickson .30 .09
❑ 48 Mike Mussina .75 .23
❑ 49 Cal Ripken 2.50 .75
❑ 50 Darren Bragg .30 .09
❑ 51 Dennis Eckersley .30 .09
❑ 52 Nomar Garciaparra 1.50 .45
❑ 53 Scott Hatteberg .30 .09
❑ 54 Troy O'Leary .30 .09
❑ 55 Bret Saberhagen .30 .09
❑ 56 John Valentin .30 .09
❑ 57 Rod Beck .30 .09
❑ 58 Jeff Blauser .30 .09
❑ 59 Brant Brown .30 .09
❑ 60 Mark Clark .30 .09
❑ 61 Mark Grace .75 .23
❑ 62 Kevin Tapani .30 .09
❑ 63 Henry Rodriguez .30 .09
❑ 64 Mike Cameron .30 .09
❑ 65 Mike Caruso .30 .09
❑ 66 Ray Durham .30 .09
❑ 67 Jaime Navarro .30 .09
❑ 68 Magglio Ordonez .30 .09
❑ 69 Mike Sirotka .30 .09
❑ 70 Sean Casey .30 .09
❑ 71 Barry Larkin .75 .23
❑ 72 Jon Nunnally .30 .09
❑ 73 Paul Konerko .30 .09
❑ 74 Chris Stynes .30 .09
❑ 75 Brett Tomko .30 .09
❑ 76 Dmitri Young .30 .09
❑ 77 Sandy Alomar Jr. .30 .09
❑ 78 Bartolo Colon .30 .09
❑ 79 Travis Fryman .30 .09
❑ 80 Brian Giles .30 .09
❑ 81 David Justice .30 .09
❑ 82 Omar Vizquel .30 .09
❑ 83 Jaret Wright .30 .09
❑ 84 Jim Thome .75 .23
❑ 85 Charles Nagy .30 .09
❑ 86 Pedro Astacio .30 .09
❑ 87 Todd Helton .50 .15
❑ 88 Darryl Kile .30 .09
❑ 89 Mike Lansing .30 .09
❑ 90 Neifi Perez .30 .09
❑ 91 John Thomson .30 .09
❑ 92 Larry Walker .50 .15
❑ 93 Tony Clark .30 .09
❑ 94 Deivi Cruz .30 .09
❑ 95 Damion Easley .30 .09
❑ 96 Brian L.Hunter .30 .09
❑ 97 Todd Jones .30 .09
❑ 98 Brian Moehler .30 .09
❑ 99 Gabe Alvarez .30 .09
❑ 100 Craig Counsell .30 .09
❑ 101 Cliff Floyd .30 .09
❑ 102 Livan Hernandez .30 .09
❑ 103 Andy Larkin .30 .09
❑ 104 Derrek Lee .30 .09
❑ 105 Brian Meadows .30 .09
❑ 106 Moises Alou .30 .09
❑ 107 Sean Berry .30 .09
❑ 108 Craig Biggio .50 .15
❑ 109 Ricky Gutierrez .30 .09
❑ 110 Mike Hampton .30 .09
❑ 111 Jose Lima .30 .09
❑ 112 Billy Wagner .30 .09
❑ 113 Hal Morris .30 .09
❑ 114 Johnny Damon .30 .09
❑ 115 Jeff King .30 .09
❑ 116 Jeff Montgomery .30 .09
❑ 117 Glendon Rusch .30 .09
❑ 118 Larry Sutton .30 .09
❑ 119 Bobby Bonilla .30 .09
❑ 120 Jim Eisenreich .30 .09
❑ 121 Eric Karros .30 .09
❑ 122 Matt Luke .30 .09
❑ 123 Ramon Martinez .30 .09
❑ 124 Gary Sheffield .30 .09
❑ 125 Eric Young .30 .09
❑ 126 Charles Johnson .30 .09
❑ 127 Jeff Cirillo .30 .09
❑ 128 Marquis Grissom .30 .09
❑ 129 Jeromy Burnitz .30 .09
❑ 130 Bob Wickman .30 .09
❑ 131 Scott Karl .30 .09
❑ 132 Mark Loretta .30 .09
❑ 133 Fernando Vina .30 .09
❑ 134 Matt Lawton .30 .09
❑ 135 Pat Meares .30 .09
❑ 136 Eric Milton .30 .09
❑ 137 Paul Molitor .50 .15
❑ 138 David Ortiz .30 .09
❑ 139 Todd Walker .30 .09
❑ 140 Shane Andrews .30 .09
❑ 141 Brad Fullmer .30 .09
❑ 142 Vladimir Guerrero .75 .23
❑ 143 Dustin Hermanson .30 .09
❑ 144 Ryan McGuire .30 .09
❑ 145 Ugueth Urbina .30 .09
❑ 146 John Franco .30 .09
❑ 147 Butch Huskey .30 .09
❑ 148 Bobby Jones .30 .09
❑ 149 John Olerud .30 .09
❑ 150 Rey Ordonez .30 .09
❑ 151 Mike Piazza 1.25 .35
❑ 152 Hideo Nomo .75 .23
❑ 153 Masato Yoshii .30 .09
❑ 154 Derek Jeter 2.00 .60
❑ 155 Chuck Knoblauch .30 .09
❑ 156 Paul O'Neill .50 .15
❑ 157 Andy Pettitte .50 .15
❑ 158 Mariano Rivera .50 .15
❑ 159 Darryl Strawberry .50 .15
❑ 160 David Wells .30 .09
❑ 161 Jorge Posada .50 .15
❑ 162 Ramiro Mendoza .30 .09
❑ 163 Miguel Tejada .30 .09
❑ 164 Ryan Christenson .30 .09
❑ 165 Rickey Henderson 1.25 .35
❑ 166 A.J. Hinch .30 .09
❑ 167 Ben Grieve .30 .09
❑ 168 Kenny Rogers .30 .09
❑ 169 Matt Stairs .30 .09
❑ 170 Bob Abreu .30 .09
❑ 171 Rico Brogna .30 .09
❑ 172 Doug Glanville .30 .09
❑ 173 Mike Grace .30 .09
❑ 174 Desi Relaford .30 .09
❑ 175 Scott Rolen .50 .15
❑ 176 Jose Guillen .30 .09
❑ 177 Francisco Cordova .30 .09
❑ 178 Al Martin .30 .09
❑ 179 Jason Schmidt .30 .09
❑ 180 Turner Ward .30 .09
❑ 181 Kevin Young .30 .09
❑ 182 Mark McGwire 2.00 .60
❑ 183 Delino DeShields .30 .09
❑ 184 Eli Marrero .30 .09
❑ 185 Tom Lampkin .30 .09
❑ 186 Ray Lankford .30 .09
❑ 187 Willie McGee .30 .09
❑ 188 Matt Morris UER .30 .09
Career strikeout totals are wrong
❑ 189 Andy Ashby .30 .09
❑ 190 Kevin Brown .50 .15
❑ 191 Ken Caminiti .30 .09
❑ 192 Trevor Hoffman .30 .09
❑ 193 Wally Joyner .30 .09
❑ 194 Greg Vaughn .30 .09
❑ 195 Danny Darwin .30 .09
❑ 196 Shawn Estes .30 .09
❑ 197 Orel Hershiser .30 .09
❑ 198 Jeff Kent .30 .09
❑ 199 Bill Mueller .30 .09
❑ 200 Robb Nen .30 .09
❑ 201 J.T. Snow .30 .09
❑ 202 Ken Cloude .30 .09
❑ 203 Russ Davis .30 .09
❑ 204 Jeff Fassero .30 .09
❑ 205 Ken Griffey Jr. 1.25 .35
❑ 206 Shane Monahan .30 .09
❑ 207 David Segui .30 .09
❑ 208 Dan Wilson .30 .09
❑ 209 Wilson Alvarez .30 .09
❑ 210 Wade Boggs .50 .15
❑ 211 Miguel Cairo .30 .09
❑ 212 Bubba Trammell .30 .09
❑ 213 Quinton McCracken .30 .09
❑ 214 Paul Sorrento .30 .09
❑ 215 Kevin Stocker .30 .09
❑ 216 Will Clark .75 .23
❑ 217 Rusty Greer .30 .09
❑ 218 Rick Helling .30 .09
❑ 219 Mark McLemore .30 .09
❑ 220 Ivan Rodriguez .75 .23
❑ 221 John Wetteland .30 .09
❑ 222 Jose Canseco .75 .23
❑ 223 Roger Clemens 1.50 .45
❑ 224 Carlos Delgado .30 .09
❑ 225 Darrin Fletcher .30 .09
❑ 226 Alex Gonzalez .30 .09
❑ 227 Jose Cruz Jr. .30 .09
❑ 228 Shannon Stewart .30 .09
❑ 229 Rolando Arrojo FF .30 .09
❑ 230 Livan Hernandez FF .30 .09
❑ 231 Orlando Hernandez FF .30 .09
❑ 232 Raul Mondesi FF .30 .09
❑ 233 Moises Alou FF .30 .09
❑ 234 Pedro Martinez FF .75 .23
❑ 235 Sammy Sosa FF 1.25 .35
❑ 236 Vladimir Guerrero FF .75 .23
❑ 237 Bartolo Colon FF .30 .09
❑ 238 Miguel Tejada FF .30 .09
❑ 239 Ismael Valdes FF .30 .09
❑ 240 Mariano Rivera FF .50 .15
❑ 241 Jose Cruz Jr. FF .30 .09
❑ 242 Juan Gonzalez FF .75 .23
❑ 243 Ivan Rodriguez FF .75 .23
❑ 244 Sandy Alomar Jr. FF .30 .09
❑ 245 Roberto Alomar FF .75 .23
❑ 246 Magglio Ordonez FF .30 .09
❑ 247 Kerry Wood SH CL .50 .15
❑ 248 Mark McGwire SH CL 2.00 .60
❑ 249 David Wells SH CL .30 .09
❑ 250 Rolando Arrojo SH CL .30 .09
❑ 251 Ken Griffey Jr. SH CL 1.25 .35
❑ 252 T.Hoffman SH CL .30 .09
❑ 253 Travis Lee SH CL .30 .09
❑ 254 R.Alomar SH CL .50 .15
❑ 255 Sammy Sosa SH CL 1.25 .35
❑ 266 Pat Burrell SR RC 3.00 .90
❑ 267 S.Hillenbrand SR RC 1.50 .45
❑ 268 Robert Fick SR .50 .15
❑ 269 Roy Halladay SR .50 .15
❑ 270 Ruben Mateo SR .50 .15
❑ 271 Bruce Chen SR .50 .15
❑ 272 Angel Pena SR .50 .15
❑ 273 Michael Barrett SR .50 .15
❑ 274 Kevin Witt SR .50 .15
❑ 275 Damon Minor SR .50 .15
❑ 276 Ryan Minor SR .50 .15
❑ 277 A.J. Pierzynski SR .50 .15
❑ 278 A.J. Burnett SR RC .75 .23
❑ 279 Dermal Brown SR .50 .15
❑ 280 Joe Lawrence SR .50 .15
❑ 281 Derrick Gibson SR .50 .15
❑ 282 Carlos Febles SR .50 .15
❑ 283 Chris Haas SR .50 .15
❑ 284 Cesar King SR .50 .15
❑ 285 Calvin Pickering SR .50 .15
❑ 286 Mitch Meluskey SR .50 .15
❑ 287 Carlos Beltran SR .50 .15
❑ 288 Ron Belliard SR .50 .15
❑ 289 Jerry Hairston Jr. SR .50 .15
❑ 290 F.Seguignol SR .50 .15
❑ 291 Kris Benson SR .50 .15
❑ 292 C.Hutchinson SR RC .50 .15
❑ 293 Jarrod Washburn .30 .09
❑ 294 Jason Dickson .30 .09
❑ 295 Mo Vaughn .30 .09
❑ 296 Garret Anderson .30 .09

❑ 297 Jim Edmonds	.30	.09
❑ 298 Ken Hill	.30	.09
❑ 299 Shigetoshi Hasegawa	.30	.09
❑ 300 Todd Stottlemyre	.30	.09
❑ 301 Randy Johnson	.75	.23
❑ 302 Omar Daal	.30	.09
❑ 303 Steve Finley	.30	.09
❑ 304 Matt Williams	.30	.09
❑ 305 Danny Klassen	.30	.09
❑ 306 Tony Batista	.30	.09
❑ 307 Brian Jordan	.30	.09
❑ 308 Greg Maddux	1.50	.45
❑ 309 Chipper Jones	.75	.23
❑ 310 Bret Boone	.30	.09
❑ 311 Ozzie Guillen	.30	.09
❑ 312 John Rocker	.30	.09
❑ 313 Tom Glavine	.75	.23
❑ 314 Andruw Jones	.50	.15
❑ 315 Albert Belle	.30	.09
❑ 316 Charles Johnson	.30	.09
❑ 317 Will Clark	.75	.23
❑ 318 B.J. Surhoff	.30	.09
❑ 319 Delino DeShields	.30	.09
❑ 320 Heathcliff Slocumb	.30	.09
❑ 321 Sidney Ponson	.30	.09
❑ 322 Juan Guzman	.30	.09
❑ 323 Reggie Jefferson	.30	.09
❑ 324 Mark Portugal	.30	.09
❑ 325 Tim Wakefield	.30	.09
❑ 326 Jason Varitek	.30	.09
❑ 327 Jose Offerman	.30	.09
❑ 328 Pedro Martinez	.75	.23
❑ 329 Trot Nixon	.30	.09
❑ 330 Kerry Wood	.75	.23
❑ 331 Sammy Sosa	1.25	.35
❑ 332 Glenallen Hill	.30	.09
❑ 333 Gary Gaetti	.30	.09
❑ 334 Mickey Morandini	.30	.09
❑ 335 Benito Santiago	.30	.09
❑ 336 Jeff Blauser	.30	.09
❑ 337 Frank Thomas	.75	.23
❑ 338 Paul Konerko	.30	.09
❑ 339 Jaime Navarro	.30	.09
❑ 340 Carlos Lee	.30	.09
❑ 341 Brian Simmons	.30	.09
❑ 342 Mark Johnson	.30	.09
❑ 343 Jeff Abbott	.30	.09
❑ 344 Steve Avery	.30	.09
❑ 345 Mike Cameron	.30	.09
❑ 346 Michael Tucker	.30	.09
❑ 347 Greg Vaughn	.30	.09
❑ 348 Hal Morris	.30	.09
❑ 349 Pete Harnisch	.30	.09
❑ 350 Denny Neagle	.30	.09
❑ 351 Manny Ramirez	.30	.09
❑ 352 Roberto Alomar	.75	.23
❑ 353 Dwight Gooden	.50	.15
❑ 354 Kenny Lofton	.30	.09
❑ 355 Mike Jackson	.30	.09
❑ 356 Charles Nagy	.30	.09
❑ 357 Enrique Wilson	.30	.09
❑ 358 Russ Branyan	.30	.09
❑ 359 Richie Sexson	.30	.09
❑ 360 Vinny Castilla	.30	.09
❑ 361 Dante Bichette	.30	.09
❑ 362 Kirt Manwaring	.30	.09
❑ 363 Darryl Hamilton	.30	.09
❑ 364 Jamey Wright	.30	.09
❑ 365 Curtis Leskanic	.30	.09
❑ 366 Jeff Reed	.30	.09
❑ 367 Bobby Higginson	.30	.09
❑ 368 Justin Thompson	.30	.09
❑ 369 Brad Ausmus	.30	.09
❑ 370 Dean Palmer	.30	.09
❑ 371 Gabe Kapler	.30	.09
❑ 372 Juan Encarnacion	.30	.09
❑ 373 Karim Garcia	.30	.09
❑ 374 Alex Gonzalez	.30	.09
❑ 375 Braden Looper	.30	.09
❑ 376 Preston Wilson	.30	.09
❑ 377 Todd Dunwoody	.30	.09
❑ 378 Alex Fernandez	.30	.09
❑ 379 Mark Kotsay	.30	.09
❑ 380 Matt Mantei	.30	.09
❑ 381 Ken Caminiti	.30	.09
❑ 382 Scott Elarton	.30	.09

❑ 383 Jeff Bagwell	.50	.15
❑ 384 Derek Bell	.30	.09
❑ 385 Ricky Gutierrez	.30	.09
❑ 386 Richard Hidalgo	.30	.09
❑ 387 Shane Reynolds	.30	.09
❑ 388 Carl Everett	.30	.09
❑ 389 Scott Service	.30	.09
❑ 390 Jeff Suppan	.30	.09
❑ 391 Joe Randa	.30	.09
❑ 392 Kevin Appier	.30	.09
❑ 393 Shane Halter	.30	.09
❑ 394 Chad Kreuter	.30	.09
❑ 395 Mike Sweeney	.30	.09
❑ 396 Kevin Brown	.50	.15
❑ 397 Devon White	.30	.09
❑ 398 Todd Hollandsworth	.30	.09
❑ 399 Todd Hundley	.30	.09
❑ 400 Chan Ho Park	.30	.09
❑ 401 Mark Grudzielanek	.30	.09
❑ 402 Raul Mondesi	.30	.09
❑ 403 Ismael Valdes	.30	.09
❑ 404 Rafael Roque RC	.30	.09
❑ 405 Sean Berry	.30	.09
❑ 406 Kevin Barker	.30	.09
❑ 407 Dave Nilsson	.30	.09
❑ 408 Geoff Jenkins	.30	.09
❑ 409 Jim Abbott	.75	.23
❑ 410 Bobby Hughes	.30	.09
❑ 411 Corey Koskie	.30	.09
❑ 412 Rick Aguilera	.30	.09
❑ 413 LaTroy Hawkins	.30	.09
❑ 414 Ron Coomer	.30	.09
❑ 415 Denny Hocking	.30	.09
❑ 416 Marty Cordova	.30	.09
❑ 417 Terry Steinbach	.30	.09
❑ 418 Rondell White	.30	.09
❑ 419 Wilton Guerrero	.30	.09
❑ 420 Shane Andrews	.30	.09
❑ 421 Orlando Cabrera	.30	.09
❑ 422 Carl Pavano	.30	.09
❑ 423 Javier Vazquez	.30	.09
❑ 424 Chris Widger	.30	.09
❑ 425 Robin Ventura	.30	.09
❑ 426 Rickey Henderson	1.25	.35
❑ 427 Al Leiter	.30	.09
❑ 428 Bobby Jones	.30	.09
❑ 429 Brian McRae	.30	.09
❑ 430 Roger Cedeno	.30	.09
❑ 431 Bobby Bonilla	.30	.09
❑ 432 Edgardo Alfonzo	.30	.09
❑ 433 Bernie Williams	.50	.15
❑ 434 Ricky Ledee	.30	.09
❑ 435 Chili Davis	.30	.09
❑ 436 Tino Martinez	.50	.15
❑ 437 Scott Brosius	.30	.09
❑ 438 David Cone	.30	.09
❑ 439 Joe Girardi	.30	.09
❑ 440 Roger Clemens	1.50	.45
❑ 441 Chad Curtis	.30	.09
❑ 442 Hideki Irabu	.30	.09
❑ 443 Jason Giambi	.75	.23
❑ 444 Scott Spiezio	.30	.09
❑ 445 Tony Phillips	.30	.09
❑ 446 Ramon Hernandez	.30	.09
❑ 447 Mike Macfarlane	.30	.09
❑ 448 Tom Candiotti	.30	.09
❑ 449 Billy Taylor	.30	.09
❑ 450 Bobby Estalella	.30	.09
❑ 451 Curt Schilling	.50	.15
❑ 452 Carlton Loewer	.30	.09
❑ 453 Marlon Anderson	.30	.09
❑ 454 Kevin Jordan	.30	.09
❑ 455 Ron Gant	.30	.09
❑ 456 Chad Ogea	.30	.09
❑ 457 Abraham Nunez	.30	.09
❑ 458 Jason Kendall	.30	.09
❑ 459 Pat Meares	.30	.09
❑ 460 Brant Brown	.30	.09
❑ 461 Brian Giles	.30	.09
❑ 462 Chad Hermansen	.30	.09
❑ 463 Freddy Adrian Garcia	.30	.09
❑ 464 Edgar Renteria	.30	.09
❑ 465 Fernando Tatis	.30	.09
❑ 466 Eric Davis	.30	.09
❑ 467 Darren Bragg	.30	.09
❑ 468 Donovan Osborne	.30	.09

❑ 469 Manny Aybar	.30	.09
❑ 470 Jose Jimenez	.30	.09
❑ 471 Kent Mercker	.30	.09
❑ 472 Reggie Sanders	.30	.09
❑ 473 Ruben Rivera	.30	.09
❑ 474 Tony Gwynn	1.00	.30
❑ 475 Jim Leyritz	.30	.09
❑ 476 Chris Gomez	.30	.09
❑ 477 Matt Clement	.30	.09
❑ 478 Carlos Hernandez	.30	.09
❑ 479 Sterling Hitchcock	.30	.09
❑ 480 Ellis Burks	.30	.09
❑ 481 Barry Bonds	2.00	.60
❑ 482 Marvin Benard	.30	.09
❑ 483 Kirk Rueter	.30	.09
❑ 484 F.P. Santangelo	.30	.09
❑ 485 Stan Javier	.30	.09
❑ 486 Jeff Kent	.30	.09
❑ 487 Alex Rodriguez	1.50	.45
❑ 488 Tom Lampkin	.30	.09
❑ 489 Jose Mesa	.30	.09
❑ 490 Jay Buhner	.30	.09
❑ 491 Edgar Martinez	.50	.15
❑ 492 Butch Huskey	.30	.09
❑ 493 John Mabry	.30	.09
❑ 494 Jamie Moyer	.30	.09
❑ 495 Roberto Hernandez	.30	.09
❑ 496 Tony Saunders	.30	.09
❑ 497 Fred McGriff	.50	.15
❑ 498 Dave Martinez	.30	.09
❑ 499 Jose Canseco	.75	.23
❑ 500 Rolando Arrojo	.30	.09
❑ 501 Esteban Yan	.30	.09
❑ 502 Juan Gonzalez	.75	.23
❑ 503 Rafael Palmeiro	.50	.15
❑ 504 Aaron Sele	.30	.09
❑ 505 Royce Clayton	.30	.09
❑ 506 Todd Zeile	.30	.09
❑ 507 Tom Goodwin	.30	.09
❑ 508 Lee Stevens	.30	.09
❑ 509 Esteban Loaiza	.30	.09
❑ 510 Joey Hamilton	.30	.09
❑ 511 Homer Bush	.30	.09
❑ 512 Willie Greene	.30	.09
❑ 513 Shawn Green	.30	.09
❑ 514 David Wells	.30	.09
❑ 515 Kelvim Escobar	.30	.09
❑ 516 Tony Fernandez	.30	.09
❑ 517 Pat Hentgen	.30	.09
❑ 518 Mark McGwire AR	1.00	.30
❑ 519 Ken Griffey Jr. AR	.75	.23
❑ 520 Sammy Sosa AR	.75	.23
❑ 521 Juan Gonzalez AR	.50	.15
❑ 522 J.D. Drew AR	.30	.09
❑ 523 Chipper Jones AR	.50	.15
❑ 524 Alex Rodriguez AR	.75	.23
❑ 525 Mike Piazza AR	.75	.23
❑ 526 N.Garciaparra AR	.75	.23
❑ 527 Mark McGwire SH CL	1.00	.30
❑ 528 Sammy Sosa SH CL	.75	.23
❑ 529 Scott Brosius SH CL	.30	.09
❑ 530 Cal Ripken SH CL	1.25	.35
❑ 531 Barry Bonds SH CL	.75	.23
❑ 532 Roger Clemens SH CL	.75	.23
❑ 533 Ken Griffey Jr. SH CL	.75	.23
❑ 534 Alex Rodriguez SH CL	.75	.23
❑ 535 Curt Schilling SH CL	.30	.09
❑ NNO Ken Griffey Jr. 1989 AU/100	1000.00	300.00

2001 Upper Deck

	Nm-Mt	Ex-Mt
COMPLETE SET (450)	100.00	30.00
COMP. SERIES 1 (270)	50.00	15.00
COMP. SERIES 2 (180)	50.00	15.00
COMMON (46-270/300-450)	.30	.09
COMMON SR (1-45)	.50	.15

❑ 1 Jeff DaVanon SR	.50	.15
❑ 2 Aubrey Huff SR	.50	.15
❑ 3 Pasqual Coco SR	.50	.15
❑ 4 Barry Zito SR	1.00	.30
❑ 5 Augie Ojeda SR	.50	.15
❑ 6 Chris Richard SR	.50	.15
❑ 7 Josh Phelps SR	.50	.15

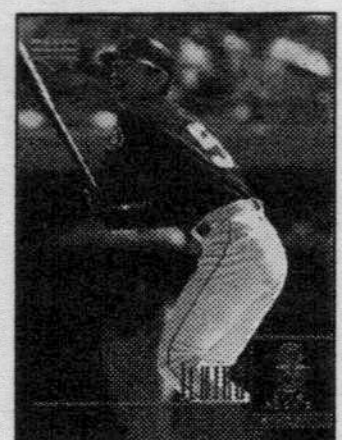

	No.	Player	Price 1	Price 2
❑	8	Kevin Nicholson SR	.50	.15
❑	9	Juan Guzman SR	.50	.15
❑	10	Brandon Kolb SR	.50	.15
❑	11	Johan Santana SR	.50	.15
❑	12	Josh Kalinowski SR	.50	.15
❑	13	Tike Redman SR	.50	.15
❑	14	Ivanon Coffie SR	.50	.15
❑	15	Chad Durbin SR	.50	.15
❑	16	Derrick Turnbow SR	.50	.15
❑	17	Scott Downs SR	.50	.15
❑	18	Jason Grilli SR	.50	.15
❑	19	Mark Buehrle SR	.50	.15
❑	20	Paxton Crawford SR	.50	.15
❑	21	Bronson Arroyo SR	.50	.15
❑	22	Tomas De la Rosa SR	.50	.15
❑	23	Paul Rigdon SR	.50	.15
❑	24	Rob Ramsay SR	.50	.15
❑	25	Damian Rolls SR	.50	.15
❑	26	Jason Conti SR	.50	.15
❑	27	John Parrish SR	.50	.15
❑	28	Geraldo Guzman SR	.50	.15
❑	29	Tony Mota SR	.50	.15
❑	30	Luis Rivas SR	.50	.15
❑	31	Brian Tollberg SR	.50	.15
❑	32	Adam Bernero SR	.50	.15
❑	33	Michael Cuddyer SR	.50	.15
❑	34	Josue Espada SR	.50	.15
❑	35	Joe Lawrence SR	.50	.15
❑	36	Chad Moeller SR	.50	.15
❑	37	Nick Bierbrodt SR	.50	.15
❑	38	DeWayne Wise SR	.50	.15
❑	39	Javier Cardona SR	.50	.15
❑	40	Hiram Bocachica SR	.50	.15
❑	41	G.Chiaramonte SR	.50	.15
❑	42	Alex Cabrera SR	.50	.15
❑	43	Jimmy Rollins SR	.50	.15
❑	44	Pat Flury SR RC	.50	.15
❑	45	Leo Estrella SR	.50	.15
❑	46	Darin Erstad	.30	.09
❑	47	Seth Etherton	.30	.09
❑	48	Troy Glaus	.50	.15
❑	49	Brian Cooper	.30	.09
❑	50	Tim Salmon	.50	.15
❑	51	Adam Kennedy	.30	.09
❑	52	Bengie Molina	.30	.09
❑	53	Jason Giambi	.75	.23
❑	54	Miguel Tejada	.30	.09
❑	55	Tim Hudson	.30	.09
❑	56	Eric Chavez	.30	.09
❑	57	Terrence Long	.30	.09
❑	58	Jason Isringhausen	.30	.09
❑	59	Ramon Hernandez	.30	.09
❑	60	Raul Mondesi	.30	.09
❑	61	David Wells	.30	.09
❑	62	Shannon Stewart	.30	.09
❑	63	Tony Batista	.30	.09
❑	64	Brad Fullmer	.30	.09
❑	65	Chris Carpenter	.30	.09
❑	66	Homer Bush	.30	.09
❑	67	Gerald Williams	.30	.09
❑	68	Miguel Cairo	.30	.09
❑	69	Ryan Rupe	.30	.09
❑	70	Greg Vaughn	.30	.09
❑	71	John Flaherty	.30	.09
❑	72	Dan Wheeler	.30	.09
❑	73	Fred McGriff	.50	.15
❑	74	Roberto Alomar	.75	.23
❑	75	Bartolo Colon	.30	.09
❑	76	Kenny Lofton	.30	.09
❑	77	David Segui	.30	.09
❑	78	Omar Vizquel	.30	.09
❑	79	Russ Branyan	.30	.09
❑	80	Chuck Finley	.30	.09
❑	81	Manny Ramirez UER Back photo is of David Segui	.30	.09
❑	82	Alex Rodriguez	1.50	.45
❑	83	John Halama	.30	.09
❑	84	Mike Cameron	.30	.09
❑	85	David Bell	.30	.09
❑	86	Jay Buhner	.30	.09
❑	87	Aaron Sele	.30	.09
❑	88	Rickey Henderson	1.25	.35
❑	89	Brook Fordyce	.30	.09
❑	90	Cal Ripken	2.50	.75
❑	91	Mike Mussina	.75	.23
❑	92	Delino DeShields	.30	.09
❑	93	Melvin Mora	.30	.09
❑	94	Sidney Ponson	.30	.09
❑	95	Brady Anderson	.30	.09
❑	96	Ivan Rodriguez	.75	.23
❑	97	Ricky Ledee	.30	.09
❑	98	Rick Helling	.30	.09
❑	99	Ruben Mateo	.30	.09
❑	100	Luis Alicea	.30	.09
❑	101	John Wetteland	.30	.09
❑	102	Mike Lamb	.30	.09
❑	103	Carl Everett	.30	.09
❑	104	Troy O'Leary	.30	.09
❑	105	Wilton Veras	.30	.09
❑	106	Pedro Martinez	.75	.23
❑	107	Rolando Arrojo	.30	.09
❑	108	Scott Hatteberg	.30	.09
❑	109	Jason Varitek	.30	.09
❑	110	Jose Offerman	.30	.09
❑	111	Carlos Beltran	.30	.09
❑	112	Johnny Damon	.30	.09
❑	113	Mark Quinn	.30	.09
❑	114	Rey Sanchez	.30	.09
❑	115	Mac Suzuki	.30	.09
❑	116	Jermaine Dye	.30	.09
❑	117	Chris Fussell	.30	.09
❑	118	Jeff Weaver	.30	.09
❑	119	Dean Palmer	.30	.09
❑	120	Robert Fick	.30	.09
❑	121	Brian Moehler	.30	.09
❑	122	Damion Easley	.30	.09
❑	123	Juan Encarnacion	.30	.09
❑	124	Tony Clark	.30	.09
❑	125	Cristian Guzman	.30	.09
❑	126	Matt LeCroy	.30	.09
❑	127	Eric Milton	.30	.09
❑	128	Jay Canizaro	.30	.09
❑	129	David Ortiz	.30	.09
❑	130	Brad Radke	.30	.09
❑	131	Jacque Jones	.30	.09
❑	132	Magglio Ordonez	.30	.09
❑	133	Carlos Lee	.30	.09
❑	134	Mike Sirotka	.30	.09
❑	135	Ray Durham	.30	.09
❑	136	Paul Konerko	.30	.09
❑	137	Charles Johnson	.30	.09
❑	138	James Baldwin	.30	.09
❑	139	Jeff Abbott	.30	.09
❑	140	Roger Clemens	1.50	.45
❑	141	Derek Jeter	2.00	.60
❑	142	David Justice	.30	.09
❑	143	Ramiro Mendoza	.30	.09
❑	144	Chuck Knoblauch	.30	.09
❑	145	Orlando Hernandez	.30	.09
❑	146	Alfonso Soriano	.75	.23
❑	147	Jeff Bagwell	.50	.15
❑	148	Julio Lugo	.30	.09
❑	149	Mitch Meluskey	.30	.09
❑	150	Jose Lima	.30	.09
❑	151	Richard Hidalgo	.30	.09
❑	152	Moises Alou	.30	.09
❑	153	Scott Elarton	.30	.09
❑	154	Andruw Jones	.50	.15
❑	155	Quilvio Veras	.30	.09
❑	156	Greg Maddux	1.50	.45
❑	157	Brian Jordan	.30	.09
❑	158	Andres Galarraga	.30	.09
❑	159	Kevin Millwood	.30	.09
❑	160	Rafael Furcal	.30	.09
❑	161	Jeromy Burnitz	.30	.09
❑	162	Jimmy Haynes	.30	.09
❑	163	Mark Loretta	.30	.09
❑	164	Ron Belliard	.30	.09
❑	165	Richie Sexson	.30	.09
❑	166	Kevin Barker	.30	.09
❑	167	Jeff D'Amico	.30	.09
❑	168	Rick Ankiel	.30	.09
❑	169	Mark McGwire	2.00	.60
❑	170	J.D. Drew	.30	.09
❑	171	Eli Marrero	.30	.09
❑	172	Darryl Kile	.30	.09
❑	173	Edgar Renteria	.30	.09
❑	174	Will Clark	.75	.23
❑	175	Eric Young	.30	.09
❑	176	Mark Grace	.75	.23
❑	177	Jon Lieber	.30	.09
❑	178	Damon Buford	.30	.09
❑	179	Kerry Wood	.75	.23
❑	180	Rondell White	.30	.09
❑	181	Joe Girardi	.30	.09
❑	182	Curt Schilling	.50	.15
❑	183	Randy Johnson	.75	.23
❑	184	Steve Finley	.30	.09
❑	185	Kelly Stinnett	.30	.09
❑	186	Jay Bell	.30	.09
❑	187	Matt Mantei	.30	.09
❑	188	Luis Gonzalez	.30	.09
❑	189	Shawn Green	.30	.09
❑	190	Todd Hundley	.30	.09
❑	191	Chan Ho Park	.30	.09
❑	192	Adrian Beltre	.30	.09
❑	193	Mark Grudzielanek	.30	.09
❑	194	Gary Sheffield	.30	.09
❑	195	Tom Goodwin	.30	.09
❑	196	Lee Stevens	.30	.09
❑	197	Javier Vazquez	.30	.09
❑	198	Milton Bradley	.30	.09
❑	199	Vladimir Guerrero	.75	.23
❑	200	Carl Pavano	.30	.09
❑	201	Orlando Cabrera	.30	.09
❑	202	Tony Armas Jr.	.30	.09
❑	203	Jeff Kent	.30	.09
❑	204	Calvin Murray	.30	.09
❑	205	Ellis Burks	.30	.09
❑	206	Barry Bonds	2.00	.60
❑	207	Russ Ortiz	.30	.09
❑	208	Marvin Benard	.30	.09
❑	209	Joe Nathan	.30	.09
❑	210	Preston Wilson	.30	.09
❑	211	Cliff Floyd	.30	.09
❑	212	Mike Lowell	.30	.09
❑	213	Ryan Dempster	.30	.09
❑	214	Brad Penny	.30	.09
❑	215	Mike Redmond	.30	.09
❑	216	Luis Castillo	.30	.09
❑	217	Derek Bell	.30	.09
❑	218	Mike Hampton	.30	.09
❑	219	Todd Zeile	.30	.09
❑	220	Robin Ventura	.30	.09
❑	221	Mike Piazza	1.25	.35
❑	222	Al Leiter	.30	.09
❑	223	Edgardo Alfonzo	.30	.09
❑	224	Mike Bordick	.30	.09
❑	225	Phil Nevin	.30	.09
❑	226	Ryan Klesko	.30	.09
❑	227	Adam Eaton	.30	.09
❑	228	Eric Owens	.30	.09
❑	229	Tony Gwynn	1.00	.30
❑	230	Matt Clement	.30	.09
❑	231	Wiki Gonzalez	.30	.09
❑	232	Robert Person	.30	.09
❑	233	Doug Glanville	.30	.09
❑	234	Scott Rolen	.50	.15
❑	235	Mike Lieberthal	.30	.09
❑	236	Randy Wolf	.30	.09
❑	237	Bob Abreu	.30	.09
❑	238	Pat Burrell	.30	.09
❑	239	Bruce Chen	.30	.09
❑	240	Kevin Young	.30	.09
❑	241	Todd Ritchie	.30	.09
❑	242	Adrian Brown	.30	.09
❑	243	Chad Hermansen	.30	.09
❑	244	Warren Morris	.30	.09
❑	245	Kris Benson	.30	.09
❑	246	Jason Kendall	.30	.09

❑ 247 Pokey Reese .30 .09
❑ 248 Rob Bell .30 .09
❑ 249 Ken Griffey Jr. 1.25 .35
❑ 250 Sean Casey .30 .09
❑ 251 Aaron Boone .30 .09
❑ 252 Pete Harnisch .30 .09
❑ 253 Barry Larkin .75 .23
❑ 254 Dmitri Young .30 .09
❑ 255 Todd Hollandsworth .30 .09
❑ 256 Pedro Astacio .30 .09
❑ 257 Todd Helton .50 .15
❑ 258 Terry Shumpert .30 .09
❑ 259 Neifi Perez .30 .09
❑ 260 Jeffrey Hammonds .30 .09
❑ 261 Ben Petrick .30 .09
❑ 262 Mark McGwire SH 1.00 .30
❑ 263 Derek Jeter SH 1.00 .30
❑ 264 Sammy Sosa SH .75 .23
❑ 265 Cal Ripken SH 1.25 .35
❑ 266 Pedro Martinez SH .50 .15
❑ 267 Barry Bonds SH .75 .23
❑ 268 Fred McGriff SH .30 .09
❑ 269 Randy Johnson SH .50 .15
❑ 270 Darin Erstad SH .30 .09
❑ 271 Ichiro Suzuki SR RC 15.00 4.50
❑ 272 W. Betemit SR RC .50 .15
❑ 273 Corey Patterson SR .50 .15
❑ 274 Sean Douglass SR RC .50 .15
❑ 275 Mike Penney SR RC .50 .15
❑ 276 Nate Teut SR RC .50 .15
❑ 277 R. Rodriguez SR RC .50 .15
❑ 278 B. Duckworth SR RC .50 .15
❑ 279 Rafael Soriano SR RC 1.25 .35
❑ 280 Juan Diaz SR RC .50 .15
❑ 281 H. Ramirez SR RC 1.00 .30
❑ 282 T. Shinjo SR RC 1.25 .35
❑ 283 Keith Ginter SR .50 .15
❑ 284 Esix Snead SR RC .50 .15
❑ 285 Erick Almonte SR RC .50 .15
❑ 286 Travis Hafner SR RC 1.00 .30
❑ 287 Jason Smith SR RC .50 .15
❑ 288 J. Melian SR RC .50 .15
❑ 289 Tyler Walker SR RC .50 .15
❑ 290 Jason Standridge SR .50 .15
❑ 291 Juan Uribe SR RC .50 .15
❑ 292 A. Hernandez SR RC .50 .15
❑ 293 J. Michaels SR RC .50 .15
❑ 294 Jason Hart SR .50 .15
❑ 295 Albert Pujols SR RC 25.00 7.50
❑ 296 M. Ensberg SR RC 1.25 .35
❑ 297 Brandon Inge SR .50 .15
❑ 298 Jesus Colome SR .50 .15
❑ 299 K. Kessel SR RC UER .50 .15
L Missing from MLB experience
❑ 300 Timo Perez SR .50 .15
❑ 301 Mo Vaughn .30 .09
❑ 302 Ismael Valdes .30 .09
❑ 303 Glenallen Hill .30 .09
❑ 304 Garret Anderson .30 .09
❑ 305 Johnny Damon .30 .09
❑ 306 Jose Ortiz .30 .09
❑ 307 Mark Mulder .30 .09
❑ 308 Adam Piatt .30 .09
❑ 309 Gil Heredia .30 .09
❑ 310 Mike Sirotka .30 .09
❑ 311 Carlos Delgado .30 .09
❑ 312 Alex Gonzalez .30 .09
❑ 313 Jose Cruz Jr. .30 .09
❑ 314 Darrin Fletcher .30 .09
❑ 315 Ben Grieve .30 .09
❑ 316 Vinny Castilla .30 .09
❑ 317 Wilson Alvarez .30 .09
❑ 318 Brent Abernathy .30 .09
❑ 319 Ellis Burks .30 .09
❑ 320 Jim Thome .75 .23
❑ 321 Juan Gonzalez .75 .23
❑ 322 Ed Taubensee .30 .09
❑ 323 Travis Fryman .30 .09
❑ 324 John Olerud .30 .09
❑ 325 Edgar Martinez .50 .15
❑ 326 Freddy Garcia .30 .09
❑ 327 Bret Boone .50 .15
❑ 328 Kazuhiro Sasaki .30 .09
❑ 329 Albert Belle .30 .09
❑ 330 Mike Bordick .30 .09
❑ 331 David Segui .30 .09
❑ 332 Pat Hentgen .30 .09
❑ 333 Alex Rodriguez 1.50 .45
❑ 334 Andres Galarraga .30 .09
❑ 335 Gabe Kapler .30 .09
❑ 336 Ken Caminiti .30 .09
❑ 337 Rafael Palmeiro .50 .15
❑ 338 Manny Ramirez .30 .09
❑ 339 David Cone .30 .09
❑ 340 Nomar Garciaparra 1.50 .45
❑ 341 Trot Nixon .30 .09
❑ 342 Derek Lowe .30 .09
❑ 343 Roberto Hernandez .30 .09
❑ 344 Mike Sweeney .30 .09
❑ 345 Carlos Febles .30 .09
❑ 346 Jeff Suppan .30 .09
❑ 347 Roger Cedeno .30 .09
❑ 348 Bobby Higginson .30 .09
❑ 349 Deivi Cruz .30 .09
❑ 350 Mitch Meluskey .30 .09
❑ 351 Matt Lawton .30 .09
❑ 352 Mark Redman .30 .09
❑ 353 Jay Canizaro .30 .09
❑ 354 Corey Koskie .30 .09
❑ 355 Matt Kinney .30 .09
❑ 356 Frank Thomas .75 .23
❑ 357 Sandy Alomar Jr. .30 .09
❑ 358 David Wells .30 .09
❑ 359 Jim Parque .30 .09
❑ 360 Chris Singleton .30 .09
❑ 361 Tino Martinez .50 .15
❑ 362 Paul O'Neill .50 .15
❑ 363 Mike Mussina .75 .23
❑ 364 Bernie Williams .50 .15
❑ 365 Andy Pettite .50 .15
❑ 366 Mariano Rivera .50 .15
❑ 367 Brad Ausmus .30 .09
❑ 368 Craig Biggio .50 .15
❑ 369 Lance Berkman .30 .09
❑ 370 Shane Reynolds .30 .09
❑ 371 Chipper Jones .75 .23
❑ 372 Tom Glavine .75 .23
❑ 373 B.J. Surhoff .30 .09
❑ 374 John Smoltz .50 .15
❑ 375 Rico Brogna .30 .09
❑ 376 Geoff Jenkins .30 .09
❑ 377 Jose Hernandez .30 .09
❑ 378 Tyler Houston .30 .09
❑ 379 Henry Blanco .30 .09
❑ 380 Jeffrey Hammonds .30 .09
❑ 381 Jim Edmonds .30 .09
❑ 382 Fernando Vina .30 .09
❑ 383 Andy Benes .30 .09
❑ 384 Ray Lankford .30 .09
❑ 385 Dustin Hermanson .30 .09
❑ 386 Todd Hundley .30 .09
❑ 387 Sammy Sosa 1.25 .35
❑ 388 Tom Gordon .30 .09
❑ 389 Bill Mueller .30 .09
❑ 390 Ron Coomer .30 .09
❑ 391 Matt Stairs .30 .09
❑ 392 Mark Grace .75 .23
❑ 393 Matt Williams .30 .09
❑ 394 Todd Stottlemyre .30 .09
❑ 395 Tony Womack .30 .09
❑ 396 Erubiel Durazo .30 .09
❑ 397 Reggie Sanders .30 .09
❑ 398 Andy Ashby .30 .09
❑ 399 Eric Karros .30 .09
❑ 400 Kevin Brown .30 .09
❑ 401 Darren Dreifort .30 .09
❑ 402 Fernando Tatis .30 .09
❑ 403 Jose Vidro .30 .09
❑ 404 Peter Bergeron .30 .09
❑ 405 Geoff Blum .30 .09
❑ 406 J.T. Snow .30 .09
❑ 407 Livan Hernandez .30 .09
❑ 408 Robb Nen .30 .09
❑ 409 Bobby Estalella .30 .09
❑ 410 Rich Aurilia .30 .09
❑ 411 Eric Davis .30 .09
❑ 412 Charles Johnson .30 .09
❑ 413 Alex Gonzalez .30 .09
❑ 414 A.J. Burnett .30 .09
❑ 415 Antonio Alfonseca .30 .09
❑ 416 Derek Lee .30 .09
❑ 417 Jay Payton .30 .09
❑ 418 Kevin Appier .30 .09
❑ 419 Steve Trachsel .30 .09
❑ 420 Rey Ordonez .30 .09
❑ 421 Darryl Hamilton .30 .09
❑ 422 Ben Davis .30 .09
❑ 423 Damian Jackson .30 .09
❑ 424 Mark Kotsay .30 .09
❑ 425 Trevor Hoffman .30 .09
❑ 426 Travis Lee .30 .09
❑ 427 Omar Daal .30 .09
❑ 428 Paul Byrd .30 .09
❑ 429 Reggie Taylor .30 .09
❑ 430 Brian Giles .30 .09
❑ 431 Derek Bell .30 .09
❑ 432 Francisco Cordova .30 .09
❑ 433 Pat Meares .30 .09
❑ 434 Scott Williamson .30 .09
❑ 435 Jason LaRue .30 .09
❑ 436 Michael Tucker .30 .09
❑ 437 Wilton Guerrero .30 .09
❑ 438 Mike Hampton .30 .09
❑ 439 Ron Gant .30 .09
❑ 440 Jeff Cirillo .30 .09
❑ 441 Denny Neagle .30 .09
❑ 442 Larry Walker .50 .15
❑ 443 Juan Pierre .30 .09
❑ 444 Todd Walker .30 .09
❑ 445 Jason Giambi SH CL .50 .15
❑ 446 Jeff Kent SH CL .30 .09
❑ 447 Mariano Rivera SH CL .30 .09
❑ 448 Edgar Martinez SH CL .30 .09
❑ 449 Troy Glaus SH CL .30 .09
❑ 450 Alex Rodriguez SH CL .75 .23

2002 Upper Deck

	Nm-Mt	Ex-Mt
COMPLETE SET (745)	160.00	47.50
COMPLETE SERIES 1 (500)	110.00	33.00
COMPLETE SERIES 2 (245)	50.00	15.00
COMMON (51-500/546-745)	.30	.09
COMMON SR (1-50/501-545)	1.00	.30

❑ 1 Mark Prior SR 5.00 1.50
❑ 2 Mark Teixeira SR 1.50 .45
❑ 3 Brian Roberts SR 1.00 .30
❑ 4 Jason Romano SR 1.00 .30
❑ 5 Dennis Stark SR 1.00 .30
❑ 6 Oscar Salazar SR 1.00 .30
❑ 7 John Patterson SR 1.00 .30
❑ 8 Shane Loux SR 1.00 .30
❑ 9 Marcus Giles SR 1.00 .30
❑ 10 Juan Cruz SR 1.00 .30
❑ 11 Jorge Julio SR 1.00 .30
❑ 12 Adam Dunn SR 1.00 .30
❑ 13 Delvin James SR 1.00 .30
❑ 14 Jeremy Affeldt SR 1.00 .30
❑ 15 Tim Raines Jr. SR 1.00 .30
❑ 16 Luke Hudson SR 1.00 .30
❑ 17 Todd Sears SR 1.00 .30
❑ 18 George Perez SR 1.00 .30
❑ 19 Wilmy Caceres SR 1.00 .30
❑ 20 Abraham Nunez SR 1.00 .30
❑ 21 Mike Amrhein SR RC 1.00 .30
❑ 22 Carlos Hernandez SR 1.00 .30
❑ 23 Scott Hodges SR 1.00 .30
❑ 24 Brandon Knight SR 1.00 .30
❑ 25 Geoff Goetz SR 1.00 .30

❑ 26 Carlos Garcia SR 1.00 .30
❑ 27 Luis Pineda SR 1.00 .30
❑ 28 Chris Gissell SR 1.00 .30
❑ 29 Jae Weong Seo SR 1.00 .30
❑ 30 Paul Phillips SR 1.00 .30
❑ 31 Cory Aldridge SR 1.00 .30
❑ 32 Aaron Cook SR RC 1.00 .30
❑ 33 Rendy Espina SR RC 1.00 .30
❑ 34 Jason Phillips SR 1.00 .30
❑ 35 Carlos Silva SR 1.00 .30
❑ 36 Ryan Mills SR 1.00 .30
❑ 37 Pedro Santana SR 1.00 .30
❑ 38 John Grabow SR 1.00 .30
❑ 39 Cody Ransom SR 1.00 .30
❑ 40 Orlando Woodards SR 1.00 .30
❑ 41 Bud Smith SR 1.00 .30
❑ 42 Junior Guerrero SR 1.00 .30
❑ 43 David Brous SR 1.00 .30
❑ 44 Steve Green SR 1.00 .30
❑ 45 Brian Rogers SR 1.00 .30
❑ 46 Juan Figueroa SR RC 1.00 .30
❑ 47 Nick Punto SR 1.00 .30
❑ 48 Junior Herndon SR 1.00 .30
❑ 49 Justin Kaye SR 1.00 .30
❑ 50 Jason Karnuth SR 1.00 .30
❑ 51 Troy Glaus .50 .15
❑ 52 Bengie Molina .30 .09
❑ 53 Ramon Ortiz .30 .09
❑ 54 Adam Kennedy .30 .09
❑ 55 Jarrod Washburn .30 .09
❑ 56 Troy Percival .30 .09
❑ 57 David Eckstein .30 .09
❑ 58 Ben Weber .30 .09
❑ 59 Larry Barnes .30 .09
❑ 60 Ismael Valdes .30 .09
❑ 61 Benji Gil .30 .09
❑ 62 Scott Schoeneweis .30 .09
❑ 63 Pat Rapp .30 .09
❑ 64 Jason Giambi .75 .23
❑ 65 Mark Mulder .30 .09
❑ 66 Ron Gant .30 .09
❑ 67 Johnny Damon .30 .09
❑ 68 Adam Piatt .30 .09
❑ 69 Jermaine Dye .30 .09
❑ 70 Jason Hart .30 .09
❑ 71 Eric Chavez .30 .09
❑ 72 Jim Mecir .30 .09
❑ 73 Barry Zito .75 .23
❑ 74 Jason Isringhausen .30 .09
❑ 75 Jeremy Giambi .30 .09
❑ 76 Olmedo Saenz .30 .09
❑ 77 Terrence Long .30 .09
❑ 78 Ramon Hernandez .30 .09
❑ 79 Chris Carpenter .30 .09
❑ 80 Raul Mondesi .30 .09
❑ 81 Carlos Delgado .30 .09
❑ 82 Billy Koch .30 .09
❑ 83 Vernon Wells .30 .09
❑ 84 Darrin Fletcher .30 .09
❑ 85 Homer Bush .30 .09
❑ 86 Pasqual Coco .30 .09
❑ 87 Shannon Stewart .30 .09
❑ 88 Chris Woodward .30 .09
❑ 89 Joe Lawrence .30 .09
❑ 90 Esteban Loaiza .30 .09
❑ 91 Cesar Izturis .30 .09
❑ 92 Kelvim Escobar .30 .09
❑ 93 Greg Vaughn .30 .09
❑ 94 Brent Abernathy .30 .09
❑ 95 Tanyon Sturtze .30 .09
❑ 96 Steve Cox .30 .09
❑ 97 Aubrey Huff .30 .09
❑ 98 Jesus Colome .30 .09
❑ 99 Ben Grieve .30 .09
❑ 100 Esteban Yan .30 .09
❑ 101 Joe Kennedy .30 .09
❑ 102 Felix Martinez .30 .09
❑ 103 Nick Bierbrodt .30 .09
❑ 104 Damian Rolls .30 .09
❑ 105 Russ Johnson .30 .09
❑ 106 Toby Hall .30 .09
❑ 107 Roberto Alomar .75 .23
❑ 108 Bartolo Colon .30 .09
❑ 109 John Rocker .30 .09
❑ 110 Juan Gonzalez .75 .23
❑ 111 Einar Diaz .30 .09
❑ 112 Chuck Finley .30 .09
❑ 113 Kenny Lofton .30 .09
❑ 114 Danys Baez .30 .09
❑ 115 Travis Fryman .30 .09
❑ 116 C.C. Sabathia .30 .09
❑ 117 Paul Shuey .30 .09
❑ 118 Marty Cordova .30 .09
❑ 119 Ellis Burks .30 .09
❑ 120 Bob Wickman .30 .09
❑ 121 Edgar Martinez .50 .15
❑ 122 Freddy Garcia .30 .09
❑ 123 Ichiro Suzuki 1.50 .45
❑ 124 John Olerud .30 .09
❑ 125 Gil Meche .30 .09
❑ 126 Dan Wilson .30 .09
❑ 127 Aaron Sele .30 .09
❑ 128 Kazuhiro Sasaki .30 .09
❑ 129 Mark McLemore .30 .09
❑ 130 Carlos Guillen .30 .09
❑ 131 Al Martin .30 .09
❑ 132 David Bell .30 .09
❑ 133 Jay Buhner .30 .09
❑ 134 Stan Javier .30 .09
❑ 135 Tony Batista .30 .09
❑ 136 Jason Johnson .30 .09
❑ 137 Brook Fordyce .30 .09
❑ 138 Mike Kinkade .30 .09
❑ 139 Willis Roberts .30 .09
❑ 140 David Segui .30 .09
❑ 141 Josh Towers .30 .09
❑ 142 Jeff Conine .30 .09
❑ 143 Chris Richard .30 .09
❑ 144 Pat Hentgen .30 .09
❑ 145 Melvin Mora .30 .09
❑ 146 Jerry Hairston Jr. .30 .09
❑ 147 Calvin Maduro .30 .09
❑ 148 Brady Anderson .30 .09
❑ 149 Alex Rodriguez 1.50 .45
❑ 150 Kenny Rogers .30 .09
❑ 151 Chad Curtis .30 .09
❑ 152 Ricky Ledee .30 .09
❑ 153 Rafael Palmeiro .50 .15
❑ 154 Rob Bell .30 .09
❑ 155 Rick Helling .30 .09
❑ 156 Doug Davis .30 .09
❑ 157 Mike Lamb .30 .09
❑ 158 Gabe Kapler .30 .09
❑ 159 Jeff Zimmerman .30 .09
❑ 160 Bill Haselman .30 .09
❑ 161 Tim Crabtree .30 .09
❑ 162 Carlos Pena .30 .09
❑ 163 Nomar Garciaparra 1.50 .45
❑ 164 Shea Hillenbrand .30 .09
❑ 165 Hideo Nomo .75 .23
❑ 166 Manny Ramirez .30 .09
❑ 167 Jose Offerman .30 .09
❑ 168 Scott Hatteberg .30 .09
❑ 169 Trot Nixon .30 .09
❑ 170 Darren Lewis .30 .09
❑ 171 Derek Lowe .30 .09
❑ 172 Troy O'Leary .30 .09
❑ 173 Tim Wakefield .30 .09
❑ 174 Chris Stynes .30 .09
❑ 175 John Valentin .30 .09
❑ 176 David Cone .30 .09
❑ 177 Neifi Perez .30 .09
❑ 178 Brent Mayne .30 .09
❑ 179 Dan Reichert .30 .09
❑ 180 A.J. Hinch .30 .09
❑ 181 Chris George .30 .09
❑ 182 Mike Sweeney .30 .09
❑ 183 Jeff Suppan .30 .09
❑ 184 Roberto Hernandez .30 .09
❑ 185 Joe Randa .30 .09
❑ 186 Paul Byrd .30 .09
❑ 187 Luis Ordaz .30 .09
❑ 188 Kris Wilson .30 .09
❑ 189 Dee Brown .30 .09
❑ 190 Tony Clark .30 .09
❑ 191 Matt Anderson .30 .09
❑ 192 Robert Fick .30 .09
❑ 193 Juan Encarnacion .30 .09
❑ 194 Dean Palmer .30 .09
❑ 195 Victor Santos .30 .09
❑ 196 Damion Easley .30 .09
❑ 197 Jose Lima .30 .09
❑ 198 Deivi Cruz .30 .09
❑ 199 Roger Cedeno .30 .09
❑ 200 Jose Macias .30 .09
❑ 201 Jeff Weaver .30 .09
❑ 202 Brandon Inge .30 .09
❑ 203 Brian Moehler .30 .09
❑ 204 Brad Radke .30 .09
❑ 205 Doug Mientkiewicz .30 .09
❑ 206 Cristian Guzman .30 .09
❑ 207 Corey Koskie .30 .09
❑ 208 LaTroy Hawkins .30 .09
❑ 209 J.C. Romero .30 .09
❑ 210 Chad Allen .30 .09
❑ 211 Torii Hunter .30 .09
❑ 212 Travis Miller .30 .09
❑ 213 Joe Mays .30 .09
❑ 214 Todd Jones .30 .09
❑ 215 David Ortiz .30 .09
❑ 216 Brian Buchanan .30 .09
❑ 217 A.J. Pierzynski .30 .09
❑ 218 Carlos Lee .30 .09
❑ 219 Gary Glover .30 .09
❑ 220 Jose Valentin .30 .09
❑ 221 Aaron Rowand .30 .09
❑ 222 Sandy Alomar Jr. .30 .09
❑ 223 Herbert Perry .30 .09
❑ 224 Jon Garland .30 .09
❑ 225 Mark Buehrle .30 .09
❑ 226 Chris Singleton .30 .09
❑ 227 Kip Wells .30 .09
❑ 228 Ray Durham .30 .09
❑ 229 Joe Crede .30 .09
❑ 230 Keith Foulke .30 .09
❑ 231 Royce Clayton .30 .09
❑ 232 Andy Pettitte .50 .15
❑ 233 Derek Jeter 2.00 .60
❑ 234 Jorge Posada .50 .15
❑ 235 Roger Clemens 1.50 .45
❑ 236 Paul O'Neill .50 .15
❑ 237 Nick Johnson .30 .09
❑ 238 Gerald Williams .30 .09
❑ 239 Mariano Rivera .50 .15
❑ 240 Alfonso Soriano .75 .23
❑ 241 Ramiro Mendoza .30 .09
❑ 242 Mike Mussina .75 .23
❑ 243 Luis Sojo .30 .09
❑ 244 Scott Brosius .30 .09
❑ 245 David Justice .30 .09
❑ 246 Wade Miller .30 .09
❑ 247 Brad Ausmus .30 .09
❑ 248 Jeff Bagwell .50 .15
❑ 249 Daryle Ward .30 .09
❑ 250 Shane Reynolds .30 .09
❑ 251 Chris Truby .30 .09
❑ 252 Billy Wagner .30 .09
❑ 253 Craig Biggio .50 .15
❑ 254 Moises Alou .30 .09
❑ 255 Vinny Castilla .30 .09
❑ 256 Tim Redding .30 .09
❑ 257 Roy Oswalt .30 .09
❑ 258 Julio Lugo .30 .09
❑ 259 Chipper Jones .75 .23
❑ 260 Greg Maddux 1.50 .45
❑ 261 Ken Caminiti .30 .09
❑ 262 Kevin Millwood .30 .09
❑ 263 Keith Lockhart .30 .09
❑ 264 Rey Sanchez .30 .09
❑ 265 Jason Marquis .30 .09
❑ 266 Brian Jordan .30 .09
❑ 267 Steve Karsay .30 .09
❑ 268 Wes Helms .30 .09
❑ 269 B.J. Surhoff .30 .09
❑ 270 Wilson Betemit .30 .09
❑ 271 John Smoltz .50 .15
❑ 272 Rafael Furcal .30 .09
❑ 273 Jeromy Burnitz .30 .09
❑ 274 Jimmy Haynes .30 .09
❑ 275 Mark Loretta .30 .09
❑ 276 Jose Hernandez .30 .09
❑ 277 Paul Rigdon .30 .09
❑ 278 Alex Sanchez .30 .09
❑ 279 Chad Fox .30 .09
❑ 280 Devon White .30 .09
❑ 281 Tyler Houston .30 .09
❑ 282 Ronnie Belliard .30 .09
❑ 283 Luis Lopez .30 .09

	No.	Player		
❑	284	Ben Sheets	.30	.09
❑	285	Curtis Leskanic	.30	.09
❑	286	Henry Blanco	.30	.09
❑	287	Mark McGwire	2.00	.60
❑	288	Edgar Renteria	.30	.09
❑	289	Matt Morris	.30	.09
❑	290	Gene Stechschulte	.30	.09
❑	291	Dustin Hermanson	.30	.09
❑	292	Eli Marrero	.30	.09
❑	293	Albert Pujols	1.50	.45
❑	294	Luis Saturria	.30	.09
❑	295	Bobby Bonilla	.30	.09
❑	296	Garrett Stephenson	.30	.09
❑	297	Jim Edmonds	.30	.09
❑	298	Rick Ankiel	.30	.09
❑	299	Placido Polanco	.30	.09
❑	300	Dave Veres	.30	.09
❑	301	Sammy Sosa	1.25	.35
❑	302	Eric Young	.30	.09
❑	303	Kerry Wood	.75	.23
❑	304	Jon Lieber	.30	.09
❑	305	Joe Girardi	.30	.09
❑	306	Fred McGriff	.50	.15
❑	307	Jeff Fassero	.30	.09
❑	308	Julio Zuleta	.30	.09
❑	309	Kevin Tapani	.30	.09
❑	310	Rondell White	.30	.09
❑	311	Julian Tavarez	.30	.09
❑	312	Tom Gordon	.30	.09
❑	313	Corey Patterson	.30	.09
❑	314	Bill Mueller	.30	.09
❑	315	Randy Johnson	.75	.23
❑	316	Chad Moeller	.30	.09
❑	317	Tony Womack	.30	.09
❑	318	Erubiel Durazo	.30	.09
❑	319	Luis Gonzalez	.30	.09
❑	320	Brian Anderson	.30	.09
❑	321	Reggie Sanders	.30	.09
❑	322	Greg Colbrunn	.30	.09
❑	323	Robert Ellis	.30	.09
❑	324	Jack Cust	.30	.09
❑	325	Bret Prinz	.30	.09
❑	326	Steve Finley	.30	.09
❑	327	Byung-Hyun Kim	.30	.09
❑	328	Albie Lopez	.30	.09
❑	329	Gary Sheffield	.30	.09
❑	330	Mark Grudzielanek	.30	.09
❑	331	Paul LoDuca	.30	.09
❑	332	Tom Goodwin	.30	.09
❑	333	Andy Ashby	.30	.09
❑	334	Hiram Bocachica	.30	.09
❑	335	Dave Hansen	.30	.09
❑	336	Kevin Brown	.30	.09
❑	337	Marquis Grissom	.30	.09
❑	338	Terry Adams	.30	.09
❑	339	Chan Ho Park	.30	.09
❑	340	Adrian Beltre	.30	.09
❑	341	Luke Prokopec	.30	.09
❑	342	Jeff Shaw	.30	.09
❑	343	Vladimir Guerrero	.75	.23
❑	344	Orlando Cabrera	.30	.09
❑	345	Tony Armas Jr.	.30	.09
❑	346	Michael Barrett	.30	.09
❑	347	Geoff Blum	.30	.09
❑	348	Ryan Minor	.30	.09
❑	349	Peter Bergeron	.30	.09
❑	350	Graeme Lloyd	.30	.09
❑	351	Jose Vidro	.30	.09
❑	352	Javier Vazquez	.30	.09
❑	353	Matt Blank	.30	.09
❑	354	Masato Yoshii	.30	.09
❑	355	Carl Pavano	.30	.09
❑	356	Barry Bonds	2.00	.60
❑	357	Shawon Dunston	.30	.09
❑	358	Livan Hernandez	.30	.09
❑	359	Felix Rodriguez	.30	.09
❑	360	Pedro Feliz	.30	.09
❑	361	Calvin Murray	.30	.09
❑	362	Robb Nen	.30	.09
❑	363	Marvin Benard	.30	.09
❑	364	Russ Ortiz	.30	.09
❑	365	Jason Schmidt	.30	.09
❑	366	Rich Aurilia	.30	.09
❑	367	John Vander Wal	.30	.09
❑	368	Benito Santiago	.30	.09
❑	369	Ryan Dempster	.30	.09
❑	370	Charles Johnson	.30	.09
❑	371	Alex Gonzalez	.30	.09
❑	372	Luis Castillo	.30	.09
❑	373	Mike Lowell	.30	.09
❑	374	Antonio Alfonseca	.30	.09
❑	375	A.J. Burnett	.30	.09
❑	376	Brad Penny	.30	.09
❑	377	Jason Grilli	.30	.09
❑	378	Derrek Lee	.30	.09
❑	379	Matt Clement	.30	.09
❑	380	Eric Owens	.30	.09
❑	381	Vladimir Nunez	.30	.09
❑	382	Cliff Floyd	.30	.09
❑	383	Mike Piazza	1.25	.35
❑	384	Lenny Harris	.30	.09
❑	385	Glendon Rusch	.30	.09
❑	386	Todd Zeile	.30	.09
❑	387	Al Leiter	.30	.09
❑	388	Armando Benitez	.30	.09
❑	389	Alex Escobar	.30	.09
❑	390	Kevin Appier	.30	.09
❑	391	Matt Lawton	.30	.09
❑	392	Bruce Chen	.30	.09
❑	393	John Franco	.30	.09
❑	394	Tsuyoshi Shinjo	.30	.09
❑	395	Rey Ordonez	.30	.09
❑	396	Joe McEwing	.30	.09
❑	397	Ryan Klesko	.30	.09
❑	398	Brian Lawrence	.30	.09
❑	399	Kevin Walker	.30	.09
❑	400	Phil Nevin	.30	.09
❑	401	Bubba Trammell	.30	.09
❑	402	Wiki Gonzalez	.30	.09
❑	403	D'Angelo Jimenez	.30	.09
❑	404	Rickey Henderson	1.25	.35
❑	405	Mike Darr	.30	.09
❑	406	Trevor Hoffman	.30	.09
❑	407	Damian Jackson	.30	.09
❑	408	Santiago Perez	.30	.09
❑	409	Cesar Crespo	.30	.09
❑	410	Robert Person	.30	.09
❑	411	Travis Lee	.30	.09
❑	412	Scott Rolen	.50	.15
❑	413	Turk Wendell	.30	.09
❑	414	Randy Wolf	.30	.09
❑	415	Kevin Jordan	.30	.09
❑	416	Jose Mesa	.30	.09
❑	417	Mike Lieberthal	.30	.09
❑	418	Bobby Abreu	.30	.09
❑	419	Tomas Perez	.30	.09
❑	420	Doug Glanville	.30	.09
❑	421	Reggie Taylor	.30	.09
❑	422	Jimmy Rollins	.30	.09
❑	423	Brian Giles	.30	.09
❑	424	Rob Mackowiak	.30	.09
❑	425	Bronson Arroyo	.30	.09
❑	426	Kevin Young	.30	.09
❑	427	Jack Wilson	.30	.09
❑	428	Adrian Brown	.30	.09
❑	429	Chad Hermansen	.30	.09
❑	430	Jimmy Anderson	.30	.09
❑	431	Aramis Ramirez	.30	.09
❑	432	Todd Ritchie	.30	.09
❑	433	Pat Meares	.30	.09
❑	434	Warren Morris	.30	.09
❑	435	Derek Bell	.30	.09
❑	436	Ken Griffey Jr.	1.25	.35
❑	437	Elmer Dessens	.30	.09
❑	438	Ruben Rivera	.30	.09
❑	439	Jason LaRue	.30	.09
❑	440	Sean Casey	.30	.09
❑	441	Pete Harnisch	.30	.09
❑	442	Danny Graves	.30	.09
❑	443	Aaron Boone	.30	.09
❑	444	Dmitri Young	.30	.09
❑	445	Brandon Larson	.30	.09
❑	446	Pokey Reese	.30	.09
❑	447	Todd Walker	.30	.09
❑	448	Juan Castro	.30	.09
❑	449	Todd Helton	.50	.15
❑	450	Ben Petrick	.30	.09
❑	451	Juan Pierre	.30	.09
❑	452	Jeff Cirillo	.30	.09
❑	453	Juan Uribe	.30	.09
❑	454	Brian Bohanon	.30	.09
❑	455	Terry Shumpert	.30	.09
❑	456	Mike Hampton	.30	.09
❑	457	Shawn Chacon	.30	.09
❑	458	Adam Melhuse	.30	.09
❑	459	Greg Norton	.30	.09
❑	460	Gabe White	.30	.09
❑	461	Ichiro Suzuki WS	.75	.23
❑	462	Carlos Delgado WS	.30	.09
❑	463	Manny Ramirez WS	.30	.09
❑	464	Miguel Tejada WS	.30	.09
❑	465	Tsuyoshi Shinjo WS	.30	.09
❑	466	Bernie Williams WS	.30	.09
❑	467	Juan Gonzalez WS	.50	.15
❑	468	Andruw Jones WS	.30	.09
❑	469	Ivan Rodriguez WS	.50	.15
❑	470	Larry Walker WS	.50	.15
❑	471	Hideo Nomo WS	.30	.09
❑	472	Albert Pujols WS	.75	.23
❑	473	Pedro Martinez WS	.50	.15
❑	474	Vladimir Guerrero WS	.50	.15
❑	475	Tony Batista WS	.30	.09
❑	476	Kazuhiro Sasaki WS	.30	.09
❑	477	Richard Hidalgo WS	.30	.09
❑	478	Carlos Lee WS	.30	.09
❑	479	Roberto Alomar WS	.30	.09
❑	480	Rafael Palmeiro WS	.30	.09
❑	481	Ken Griffey Jr. GG	.75	.23
❑	482	Ken Griffey Jr. GG	.75	.23
❑	483	Ken Griffey Jr. GG	.75	.23
❑	484	Ken Griffey Jr. GG	.75	.23
❑	485	Ken Griffey Jr. GG	.75	.23
❑	486	Ken Griffey Jr. GG	.75	.23
❑	487	Ken Griffey Jr. GG	.75	.23
❑	488	Ken Griffey Jr. GG	.75	.23
❑	489	Ken Griffey Jr. GG	.75	.23
❑	490	Ken Griffey Jr. GG	.75	.23
❑	491	Barry Bonds CL	.75	.23
❑	492	Hideo Nomo CL	.30	.09
❑	493	Ichiro Suzuki CL	.75	.23
❑	494	Cal Ripken CL	1.25	.35
❑	495	Tony Gwynn CL	.50	.15
❑	496	Randy Johnson CL	.50	.15
❑	497	A.J. Burnett CL	.30	.09
❑	498	Rickey Henderson CL	.75	.23
❑	499	Albert Pujols CL	.75	.23
❑	500	Luis Gonzalez CL	.30	.09
❑	501	Brandon Puffer SR RC	1.00	.30
❑	502	Rodrigo Rosario SR RC	1.00	.30
❑	503	Tom Shearn SR RC	1.00	.30
❑	504	Reed Johnson SR RC	1.00	.30
❑	505	Chris Baker SR RC	1.00	.30
❑	506	John Ennis SR RC	1.00	.30
❑	507	Luis Martinez SR RC	1.00	.30
❑	508	So Taguchi SR RC	1.00	.30
❑	509	Scotty Layfield SR RC	1.00	.30
❑	510	Francis Beltran SR RC	1.00	.30
❑	511	Brandon Backe SR RC	1.00	.30
❑	512	Doug Devore SR RC	1.00	.30
❑	513	Jeremy Ward SR RC	1.00	.30
❑	514	Jose Valverde SR RC	1.00	.30
❑	515	P.J. Bevis SR RC	1.00	.30
❑	516	Victor Alvarez SR RC	1.00	.30
❑	517	Kazuhisa Ishii SR RC	2.50	.75
❑	518	Jorge Nunez SR RC	1.00	.30
❑	519	Eric Good SR RC	1.00	.30
❑	520	Ron Calloway SR RC	1.00	.30
❑	521	Val Pascucci SR	1.00	.30
❑	522	Nelson Castro SR RC	1.00	.30
❑	523	Deivis Santos SR	1.00	.30
❑	524	Luis Ugueto SR RC	1.00	.30
❑	525	Matt Thornton SR RC	1.00	.30
❑	526	Hansel Izquierdo SR RC	1.00	.30
❑	527	Tyler Yates SR RC	1.00	.30
❑	528	Mark Corey SR RC	1.00	.30
❑	529	Jaime Cerda SR RC	1.00	.30
❑	530	Satoru Komiyama SR RC	1.00	.30
❑	531	Steve Bechler SR RC	1.00	.30
❑	532	Ben Howard SR RC	1.00	.30
❑	533	Anderson Machado SR RC	1.00	.30
❑	534	Jorge Padilla SR RC	1.00	.30
❑	535	Eric Junge SR RC	1.00	.30
❑	536	Adrian Burnside SR RC	1.00	.30
❑	537	Mike Gonzalez SR RC	1.00	.30
❑	538	Josh Hancock SR RC	1.00	.30
❑	539	Colin Young SR RC	1.00	.30
❑	540	Rene Reyes SR RC	1.00	.30
❑	541	Cam Esslinger SR RC	1.00	.30

❑ 542 Tim Kalita SR RC 1.00 .30
❑ 543 Kevin Frederick SR RC 1.00 .30
❑ 544 Kyle Kane SR RC 1.00 .30
❑ 545 Edwin Almonte SR RC 1.00 .30
❑ 546 Aaron Sele .30 .09
❑ 547 Garret Anderson .30 .09
❑ 548 Darin Erstad .30 .09
❑ 549 Brad Fullmer .30 .09
❑ 550 Kevin Appier .30 .09
❑ 551 Tim Salmon .50 .15
❑ 552 David Justice .30 .09
❑ 553 Billy Koch .30 .09
❑ 554 Scott Hatteberg .30 .09
❑ 555 Tim Hudson .30 .09
❑ 556 Miguel Tejada .30 .09
❑ 557 Carlos Pena .30 .09
❑ 558 Mike Sirotka .30 .09
❑ 559 Jose Cruz Jr. .30 .09
❑ 560 Josh Phelps .30 .09
❑ 561 Brandon Lyon .30 .09
❑ 562 Luke Prokopec .30 .09
❑ 563 Felipe Lopez .30 .09
❑ 564 Jason Standridge .30 .09
❑ 565 Chris Gomez .30 .09
❑ 566 John Flaherty .30 .09
❑ 567 Jason Tyner .30 .09
❑ 568 Bobby Smith .30 .09
❑ 569 Wilson Alvarez .30 .09
❑ 570 Matt Lawton .30 .09
❑ 571 Omar Vizquel .30 .09
❑ 572 Jim Thome .75 .23
❑ 573 Brady Anderson .30 .09
❑ 574 Alex Escobar .30 .09
❑ 575 Russell Branyan .30 .09
❑ 576 Bret Boone .30 .09
❑ 577 Ben Davis .30 .09
❑ 578 Mike Cameron .30 .09
❑ 579 Jamie Moyer .30 .09
❑ 580 Ruben Sierra .30 .09
❑ 581 Jeff Cirillo .30 .09
❑ 582 Marty Cordova .30 .09
❑ 583 Mike Bordick .30 .09
❑ 584 Brian Roberts .30 .09
❑ 585 Luis Matos .30 .09
❑ 586 Geronimo Gil .30 .09
❑ 587 Jay Gibbons .30 .09
❑ 588 Carl Everett .30 .09
❑ 589 Ivan Rodriguez .75 .23
❑ 590 Chan Ho Park .30 .09
❑ 591 Juan Gonzalez .75 .23
❑ 592 Hank Blalock .75 .23
❑ 593 Todd Van Poppel .30 .09
❑ 594 Pedro Martinez .75 .23
❑ 595 Jason Varitek .30 .09
❑ 596 Tony Clark .30 .09
❑ 597 Johnny Damon .30 .09
❑ 598 Dustin Hermanson .30 .09
❑ 599 John Burkett .30 .09
❑ 600 Carlos Beltran .30 .09
❑ 601 Mark Quinn .30 .09
❑ 602 Chuck Knoblauch .30 .09
❑ 603 Michael Tucker .30 .09
❑ 604 Carlos Febles .30 .09
❑ 605 Jose Rosado .30 .09
❑ 606 Dmitri Young .30 .09
❑ 607 Bobby Higginson .30 .09
❑ 608 Craig Paquette .30 .09
❑ 609 Mitch Meluskey .30 .09
❑ 610 Wendell Magee .30 .09
❑ 611 Mike Rivera .30 .09
❑ 612 Jacque Jones .30 .09
❑ 613 Luis Rivas .30 .09
❑ 614 Eric Milton .30 .09
❑ 615 Eddie Guardado .30 .09
❑ 616 Matt LeCroy .30 .09
❑ 617 Mike Jackson .30 .09
❑ 618 Magglio Ordonez .30 .09
❑ 619 Frank Thomas .75 .23
❑ 620 Rocky Biddle .30 .09
❑ 621 Paul Konerko .30 .09
❑ 622 Todd Ritchie .30 .09
❑ 623 Jon Rauch .30 .09
❑ 624 John Vander Wal .30 .09
❑ 625 Rondell White .30 .09
❑ 626 Jason Giambi .75 .23
❑ 627 Robin Ventura .30 .09
❑ 628 David Wells .30 .09
❑ 629 Bernie Williams .50 .15
❑ 630 Lance Berkman .30 .09
❑ 631 Richard Hidalgo .30 .09
❑ 632 Greg Zaun .30 .09
❑ 633 Jose Vizcaino .30 .09
❑ 634 Octavio Dotel .30 .09
❑ 635 Morgan Ensberg .30 .09
❑ 636 Andruw Jones .50 .15
❑ 637 Tom Glavine .75 .23
❑ 638 Gary Sheffield .30 .09
❑ 639 Vinny Castilla .30 .09
❑ 640 Javy Lopez .30 .09
❑ 641 Albie Lopez .30 .09
❑ 642 Geoff Jenkins .30 .09
❑ 643 Jeffrey Hammonds .30 .09
❑ 644 Alex Ochoa .30 .09
❑ 645 Richie Sexson .30 .09
❑ 646 Eric Young .30 .09
❑ 647 Glendon Rusch .30 .09
❑ 648 Tino Martinez .50 .15
❑ 649 Fernando Vina .30 .09
❑ 650 J.D. Drew .30 .09
❑ 651 Woody Williams .30 .09
❑ 652 Darryl Kile .30 .09
❑ 653 Jason Isringhausen .30 .09
❑ 654 Moises Alou .30 .09
❑ 655 Alex Gonzalez .30 .09
❑ 656 Delino DeShields .30 .09
❑ 657 Todd Hundley .30 .09
❑ 658 Chris Stynes .30 .09
❑ 659 Jason Bere .30 .09
❑ 660 Curt Schilling .50 .15
❑ 661 Craig Counsell .30 .09
❑ 662 Mark Grace .75 .23
❑ 663 Matt Williams .30 .09
❑ 664 Jay Bell .30 .09
❑ 665 Rick Helling .30 .09
❑ 666 Shawn Green .30 .09
❑ 667 Eric Karros .30 .09
❑ 668 Hideo Nomo .75 .23
❑ 669 Omar Daal .30 .09
❑ 670 Brian Jordan .30 .09
❑ 671 Cesar Izturis .30 .09
❑ 672 Fernando Tatis .30 .09
❑ 673 Lee Stevens .30 .09
❑ 674 Tomo Ohka .30 .09
❑ 675 Brian Schneider .30 .09
❑ 676 Brad Wilkerson .30 .09
❑ 677 Bruce Chen .30 .09
❑ 678 Tsuyoshi Shinjo .30 .09
❑ 679 Jeff Kent .30 .09
❑ 680 Kirk Rueter .30 .09
❑ 681 J.T. Snow .30 .09
❑ 682 David Bell .30 .09
❑ 683 Reggie Sanders .30 .09
❑ 684 Preston Wilson .30 .09
❑ 685 Vic Darensbourg .30 .09
❑ 686 Josh Beckett .50 .15
❑ 687 Pablo Ozuna .30 .09
❑ 688 Mike Redmond .30 .09
❑ 689 Scott Strickland .30 .09
❑ 690 Mo Vaughn .30 .09
❑ 691 Roberto Alomar .75 .23
❑ 692 Edgardo Alfonzo .30 .09
❑ 693 Shawn Estes .30 .09
❑ 694 Roger Cedeno .30 .09
❑ 695 Jeromy Burnitz .30 .09
❑ 696 Ray Lankford .30 .09
❑ 697 Mark Kotsay .30 .09
❑ 698 Kevin Jarvis .30 .09
❑ 699 Bobby Jones .30 .09
❑ 700 Sean Burroughs .30 .09
❑ 701 Ramon Vazquez .30 .09
❑ 702 Pat Burrell .30 .09
❑ 703 Marlon Byrd .30 .09
❑ 704 Brandon Duckworth .30 .09
❑ 705 Marlon Anderson .30 .09
❑ 706 Vicente Padilla .30 .09
❑ 707 Kip Wells .30 .09
❑ 708 Jason Kendall .30 .09
❑ 709 Pokey Reese .30 .09
❑ 710 Pat Meares .30 .09
❑ 711 Kris Benson .30 .09
❑ 712 Armando Rios .30 .09
❑ 713 Mike Williams .30 .09
❑ 714 Barry Larkin .75 .23
❑ 715 Adam Dunn .50 .15
❑ 716 Juan Encarnacion .30 .09
❑ 717 Scott Williamson .30 .09
❑ 718 Wilton Guerrero .30 .09
❑ 719 Chris Reitsma .30 .09
❑ 720 Larry Walker .50 .15
❑ 721 Denny Neagle .30 .09
❑ 722 Todd Zeile .30 .09
❑ 723 Jose Ortiz .30 .09
❑ 724 Jason Jennings .30 .09
❑ 725 Tony Eusebio .30 .09
❑ 726 Ichiro Suzuki YR .75 .23
❑ 727 Barry Bonds YR .75 .23
❑ 728 Randy Johnson YR .50 .15
❑ 729 Albert Pujols YR .75 .23
❑ 730 Roger Clemens YR .75 .23
❑ 731 Sammy Sosa YR .75 .23
❑ 732 Alex Rodriguez YR .75 .23
❑ 733 Chipper Jones YR .50 .15
❑ 734 Rickey Henderson YR .75 .23
❑ 735 Ichiro Suzuki YR .75 .23
❑ 736 Luis Gonzalez SH CL .30 .09
❑ 737 Derek Jeter SH CL 1.00 .30
❑ 738 Ichiro Suzuki SH CL .75 .23
❑ 739 Barry Bonds SH CL .75 .23
❑ 740 Curt Schilling SH CL .30 .09
❑ 741 Shawn Green SH CL .30 .09
❑ 742 Jason Giambi SH CL .50 .15
❑ 743 Roberto Alomar SH CL .50 .15
❑ 744 Larry Walker SH CL .30 .09
❑ 745 Mark McGwire SH CL 1.00 .30

2003 Upper Deck

	Nm-Mt	Ex-Mt
COMPLETE SERIES 1 (270)	50.00	15.00
COMPLETE SERIES 2 (270)	50.00	15.00
COMP.UPDATE SET (60)	20.00	6.00
COMMON (31-500/531-600)	.30	.09
COMMON (1-30/501-530)	1.00	.30
COMMON RC (541-600)	.50	.15

SR 1-30/501-530 ARE NOT SHORT PRINTS
CARD 19 DOES NOT EXIST
SCUTARO/NOMAR ARE BOTH CARD 96
541-600 ISSUED IN 04 UD1 HOBBY BOXES
UPDATE SET EXCH 1:240 '04 UD1 RETAIL
UPDATE SET EXCH.DEADLINE 11/10/06

❑ 1 John Lackey SR 1.00 .30
❑ 2 Alex Cintron SR 1.00 .30
❑ 3 Jose Leon SR 1.00 .30
❑ 4 Bobby Hill SR 1.00 .30
❑ 5 Brandon Larson SR 1.00 .30
❑ 6 Raul Gonzalez SR 1.00 .30
❑ 7 Ben Broussard SR 1.00 .30
❑ 8 Earl Snyder SR 1.00 .30
❑ 9 Ramon Santiago SR 1.00 .30
❑ 10 Jason Lane SR 1.00 .30
❑ 11 Keith Ginter SR 1.00 .30
❑ 12 Kirk Saarloos SR 1.00 .30
❑ 13 Juan Brito SR 1.00 .30
❑ 14 Runelvys Hernandez SR 1.00 .30
❑ 15 Shawn Sedlacek SR 1.00 .30
❑ 16 Jayson Durocher SR 1.00 .30
❑ 17 Kevin Frederick SR 1.00 .30
❑ 18 Zach Day SR 1.00 .30
❑ 19 Marcos Scutaro SR UER 1.00 .30

Card number 96 on back

❑ 20 Marcus Thames SR 1.00 .30
❑ 21 Esteban German SR 1.00 .30
❑ 22 Brett Myers SR 1.00 .30
❑ 23 Oliver Perez SR 1.00 .30
❑ 24 Dennis Tankersley SR 1.00 .30
❑ 25 Julius Matos SR 1.00 .30
❑ 26 Jake Peavy SR 1.00 .30
❑ 27 Eric Cyr SR 1.00 .30
❑ 28 Mike Crudale SR 1.00 .30
❑ 29 Josh Pearce SR 1.00 .30
❑ 30 Carl Crawford SR 1.00 .30
❑ 31 Tim Salmon .50 .15
❑ 32 Troy Glaus .50 .15
❑ 33 Adam Kennedy .30 .09
❑ 34 David Eckstein .30 .09
❑ 35 Ben Molina .30 .09
❑ 36 Jarrod Washburn .30 .09
❑ 37 Ramon Ortiz .30 .09
❑ 38 Eric Chavez .30 .09
❑ 39 Miguel Tejada .30 .09
❑ 40 Adam Piatt .30 .09
❑ 41 Jermaine Dye .30 .09
❑ 42 Olmedo Saenz .30 .09
❑ 43 Tim Hudson .30 .09
❑ 44 Barry Zito .75 .23
❑ 45 Billy Koch .30 .09
❑ 46 Shannon Stewart .30 .09
❑ 47 Kelvim Escobar .30 .09
❑ 48 Jose Cruz Jr. .30 .09
❑ 49 Vernon Wells .30 .09
❑ 50 Roy Halladay .30 .09
❑ 51 Esteban Loaiza .30 .09
❑ 52 Eric Hinske .30 .09
❑ 53 Steve Cox .30 .09
❑ 54 Brent Abernathy .30 .09
❑ 55 Ben Grieve .30 .09
❑ 56 Aubrey Huff .30 .09
❑ 57 Jared Sandberg .30 .09
❑ 58 Paul Wilson .30 .09
❑ 59 Tanyon Sturtze .30 .09
❑ 60 Jim Thome .75 .23
❑ 61 Omar Vizquel .30 .09
❑ 62 C.C. Sabathia .30 .09
❑ 63 Chris Magruder .30 .09
❑ 64 Ricky Gutierrez .30 .09
❑ 65 Einar Diaz .30 .09
❑ 66 Danys Baez .30 .09
❑ 67 Ichiro Suzuki 1.50 .45
❑ 68 Ruben Sierra .30 .09
❑ 69 Carlos Guillen .30 .09
❑ 70 Mark McLemore .30 .09
❑ 71 Dan Wilson .30 .09
❑ 72 Jamie Moyer .30 .09
❑ 73 Joel Pineiro .30 .09
❑ 74 Edgar Martinez .50 .15
❑ 75 Tony Batista .30 .09
❑ 76 Jay Gibbons .30 .09
❑ 77 Chris Singleton .30 .09
❑ 78 Melvin Mora .30 .09
❑ 79 Geronimo Gil .30 .09
❑ 80 Rodrigo Lopez .30 .09
❑ 81 Jorge Julio .30 .09
❑ 82 Rafael Palmeiro .50 .15
❑ 83 Juan Gonzalez .75 .23
❑ 84 Mike Young .30 .09
❑ 85 Hideki Irabu .30 .09
❑ 86 Chan Ho Park .30 .09
❑ 87 Kevin Mench .30 .09
❑ 88 Doug Davis .30 .09
❑ 89 Pedro Martinez .75 .23
❑ 90 Shea Hillenbrand .30 .09
❑ 91 Derek Lowe .30 .09
❑ 92 Jason Varitek .30 .09
❑ 93 Tony Clark .30 .09
❑ 94 John Burkett .30 .09
❑ 95 Frank Castillo .30 .09
❑ 96 Nomar Garciaparra 1.50 .45
❑ 97 Rickey Henderson 1.25 .35
❑ 98 Mike Sweeney .30 .09
❑ 99 Carlos Febles .30 .09
❑ 100 Mark Quinn .30 .09
❑ 101 Raul Ibanez .30 .09
❑ 102 A.J. Hinch .30 .09
❑ 103 Paul Byrd .30 .09
❑ 104 Chuck Knoblauch .30 .09
❑ 105 Dmitri Young .30 .09
❑ 106 Randall Simon .30 .09
❑ 107 Brandon Inge .30 .09
❑ 108 Damion Easley .30 .09
❑ 109 Carlos Pena .30 .09
❑ 110 George Lombard .30 .09
❑ 111 Juan Acevedo .30 .09
❑ 112 Torii Hunter .30 .09
❑ 113 Doug Mientkiewicz .30 .09
❑ 114 David Ortiz .30 .09
❑ 115 Eric Milton .30 .09
❑ 116 Eddie Guardado .30 .09
❑ 117 Cristian Guzman .30 .09
❑ 118 Corey Koskie .30 .09
❑ 119 Magglio Ordonez .30 .09
❑ 120 Mark Buehrle .30 .09
❑ 121 Todd Ritchie .30 .09
❑ 122 Jose Valentin .30 .09
❑ 123 Paul Konerko .30 .09
❑ 124 Carlos Lee .30 .09
❑ 125 Jon Garland .30 .09
❑ 126 Jason Giambi .75 .23
❑ 127 Derek Jeter 2.00 .60
❑ 128 Roger Clemens 1.50 .45
❑ 129 Raul Mondesi .30 .09
❑ 130 Jorge Posada .50 .15
❑ 131 Rondell White .30 .09
❑ 132 Robin Ventura .30 .09
❑ 133 Mike Mussina .75 .23
❑ 134 Jeff Bagwell .50 .15
❑ 135 Craig Biggio .50 .15
❑ 136 Morgan Ensberg .30 .09
❑ 137 Richard Hidalgo .30 .09
❑ 138 Brad Ausmus .30 .09
❑ 139 Roy Oswalt .30 .09
❑ 140 Carlos Hernandez .30 .09
❑ 141 Shane Reynolds .30 .09
❑ 142 Gary Sheffield .30 .09
❑ 143 Andruw Jones .50 .15
❑ 144 Tom Glavine .75 .23
❑ 145 Rafael Furcal .30 .09
❑ 146 Javy Lopez .30 .09
❑ 147 Vinny Castilla .30 .09
❑ 148 Marcus Giles .30 .09
❑ 149 Kevin Millwood .30 .09
❑ 150 Jason Marquis .30 .09
❑ 151 Ruben Quevedo .30 .09
❑ 152 Ben Sheets .30 .09
❑ 153 Geoff Jenkins .30 .09
❑ 154 Jose Hernandez .30 .09
❑ 155 Glendon Rusch .30 .09
❑ 156 Jeffrey Hammonds .30 .09
❑ 157 Alex Sanchez .30 .09
❑ 158 Jim Edmonds .30 .09
❑ 159 Tino Martinez .50 .15
❑ 160 Albert Pujols 1.50 .45
❑ 161 Eli Marrero .30 .09
❑ 162 Woody Williams .30 .09
❑ 163 Fernando Vina .30 .09
❑ 164 Jason Isringhausen .30 .09
❑ 165 Jason Simontacchi .30 .09
❑ 166 Kerry Robinson .30 .09
❑ 167 Sammy Sosa 1.25 .35
❑ 168 Juan Cruz .30 .09
❑ 169 Fred McGriff .50 .15
❑ 170 Antonio Alfonseca .30 .09
❑ 171 Jon Lieber .30 .09
❑ 172 Mark Prior 1.50 .45
❑ 173 Moises Alou .30 .09
❑ 174 Matt Clement .30 .09
❑ 175 Mark Bellhorn .30 .09
❑ 176 Randy Johnson .75 .23
❑ 177 Luis Gonzalez .30 .09
❑ 178 Tony Womack .30 .09
❑ 179 Mark Grace .75 .23
❑ 180 Junior Spivey .30 .09
❑ 181 Byung Hyun Kim .30 .09
❑ 182 Danny Bautista .30 .09
❑ 183 Brian Anderson .30 .09
❑ 184 Shawn Green .30 .09
❑ 185 Brian Jordan .30 .09
❑ 186 Eric Karros .30 .09
❑ 187 Andy Ashby .30 .09
❑ 188 Cesar Izturis .30 .09
❑ 189 Dave Roberts .30 .09
❑ 190 Eric Gagne .50 .15
❑ 191 Kazuhisa Ishii .30 .09
❑ 192 Adrian Beltre .30 .09
❑ 193 Vladimir Guerrero .75 .23
❑ 194 Tony Armas Jr. .30 .09
❑ 195 Bartolo Colon .30 .09
❑ 196 Troy O'Leary .30 .09
❑ 197 Tomo Ohka .30 .09
❑ 198 Brad Wilkerson .30 .09
❑ 199 Orlando Cabrera .30 .09
❑ 200 Barry Bonds 2.00 .60
❑ 201 David Bell .30 .09
❑ 202 Tsuyoshi Shinjo .30 .09
❑ 203 Benito Santiago .30 .09
❑ 204 Livan Hernandez .30 .09
❑ 205 Jason Schmidt .30 .09
❑ 206 Kirk Rueter .30 .09
❑ 207 Ramon E. Martinez .30 .09
❑ 208 Mike Lowell .30 .09
❑ 209 Luis Castillo .30 .09
❑ 210 Derrek Lee .30 .09
❑ 211 Andy Fox .30 .09
❑ 212 Eric Owens .30 .09
❑ 213 Charles Johnson .30 .09
❑ 214 Brad Penny .30 .09
❑ 215 A.J. Burnett .30 .09
❑ 216 Edgardo Alfonzo .30 .09
❑ 217 Roberto Alomar .75 .23
❑ 218 Rey Ordonez .30 .09
❑ 219 Al Leiter .30 .09
❑ 220 Roger Cedeno .30 .09
❑ 221 Timo Perez .30 .09
❑ 222 Jeromy Burnitz .30 .09
❑ 223 Pedro Astacio .30 .09
❑ 224 Joe McEwing .30 .09
❑ 225 Ryan Klesko .30 .09
❑ 226 Ramon Vazquez .30 .09
❑ 227 Mark Kotsay .30 .09
❑ 228 Bubba Trammell .30 .09
❑ 229 Wiki Gonzalez .30 .09
❑ 230 Trevor Hoffman .30 .09
❑ 231 Ron Gant .30 .09
❑ 232 Bob Abreu .30 .09
❑ 233 Marlon Anderson .30 .09
❑ 234 Jeremy Giambi .30 .09
❑ 235 Jimmy Rollins .30 .09
❑ 236 Mike Lieberthal .30 .09
❑ 237 Vicente Padilla .30 .09
❑ 238 Randy Wolf .30 .09
❑ 239 Pokey Reese .30 .09
❑ 240 Brian Giles .30 .09
❑ 241 Jack Wilson .30 .09
❑ 242 Mike Williams .30 .09
❑ 243 Kip Wells .30 .09
❑ 244 Rob Mackowiak .30 .09
❑ 245 Craig Wilson .30 .09
❑ 246 Adam Dunn .50 .15
❑ 247 Sean Casey .30 .09
❑ 248 Todd Walker .30 .09
❑ 249 Corky Miller .30 .09
❑ 250 Ryan Dempster .30 .09
❑ 251 Reggie Taylor .30 .09
❑ 252 Aaron Boone .30 .09
❑ 253 Larry Walker .50 .15
❑ 254 Jose Ortiz .30 .09
❑ 255 Todd Zeile .30 .09
❑ 256 Bobby Estalella .30 .09
❑ 257 Juan Pierre .30 .09
❑ 258 Terry Shumpert .30 .09
❑ 259 Mike Hampton .30 .09
❑ 260 Denny Stark .30 .09
❑ 261 Shawn Green SH CL .30 .09
❑ 262 Derek Lowe SH CL .30 .09
❑ 263 Barry Bonds SH CL .75 .23
❑ 264 Mike Cameron SH CL .30 .09
❑ 265 Luis Castillo SH CL .30 .09
❑ 266 Vladimir Guerrero SH CL .50 .15
❑ 267 Jason Giambi SH CL .50 .15
❑ 268 Eric Gagne SH CL .30 .09
❑ 269 Magglio Ordonez SH CL .30 .09
❑ 270 Jim Thome SH CL .50 .15
❑ 271 Garret Anderson .30 .09
❑ 272 Troy Percival .30 .09
❑ 273 Brad Fullmer .30 .09
❑ 274 Scott Spiezio .30 .09
❑ 275 Darin Erstad .30 .09
❑ 276 Francisco Rodriguez .30 .09

❑ 277 Kevin Appier .30 .09
❑ 278 Shawn Wooten .30 .09
❑ 279 Eric Owens .30 .09
❑ 280 Scott Hatteberg .30 .09
❑ 281 Terrence Long .30 .09
❑ 282 Mark Mulder .30 .09
❑ 283 Ramon Hernandez .30 .09
❑ 284 Ted Lilly .30 .09
❑ 285 Erubiel Durazo .30 .09
❑ 286 Mark Ellis .30 .09
❑ 287 Carlos Delgado .30 .09
❑ 288 Orlando Hudson .30 .09
❑ 289 Chris Woodward .30 .09
❑ 290 Mark Hendrickson .30 .09
❑ 291 Josh Phelps .30 .09
❑ 292 Ken Huckaby .30 .09
❑ 293 Justin Miller .30 .09
❑ 294 Travis Lee .30 .09
❑ 295 Jorge Sosa .30 .09
❑ 296 Joe Kennedy .30 .09
❑ 297 Carl Crawford .30 .09
❑ 298 Toby Hall .30 .09
❑ 299 Rey Ordonez .30 .09
❑ 300 Brandon Phillips .30 .09
❑ 301 Matt Lawton .30 .09
❑ 302 Ellis Burks .30 .09
❑ 303 Bill Selby .30 .09
❑ 304 Travis Hafner .30 .09
❑ 305 Milton Bradley .30 .09
❑ 306 Karim Garcia .30 .09
❑ 307 Cliff Lee .30 .09
❑ 308 Jeff Cirillo .30 .09
❑ 309 John Olerud .30 .09
❑ 310 Kazuhiro Sasaki .30 .09
❑ 311 Freddy Garcia .30 .09
❑ 312 Bret Boone .30 .09
❑ 313 Mike Cameron .30 .09
❑ 314 Ben Davis .30 .09
❑ 315 Randy Winn .30 .09
❑ 316 Gary Matthews Jr. .30 .09
❑ 317 Jeff Conine .30 .09
❑ 318 Sidney Ponson .30 .09
❑ 319 Jerry Hairston .30 .09
❑ 320 David Segui .30 .09
❑ 321 Scott Erickson .30 .09
❑ 322 Marty Cordova .30 .09
❑ 323 Hank Blalock .50 .15
❑ 324 Herbert Perry .30 .09
❑ 325 Alex Rodriguez 1.50 .45
❑ 326 Carl Everett .30 .09
❑ 327 Einar Diaz .30 .09
❑ 328 Ugueth Urbina .30 .09
❑ 329 Mark Teixeira .50 .15
❑ 330 Manny Ramirez .30 .09
❑ 331 Johnny Damon .30 .09
❑ 332 Trot Nixon .30 .09
❑ 333 Tim Wakefield .30 .09
❑ 334 Casey Fossum .30 .09
❑ 335 Todd Walker .30 .09
❑ 336 Jeremy Giambi .30 .09
❑ 337 Bill Mueller .30 .09
❑ 338 Ramiro Mendoza .30 .09
❑ 339 Carlos Beltran .30 .09
❑ 340 Jason Grimsley .30 .09
❑ 341 Brent Mayne .30 .09
❑ 342 Angel Berroa .30 .09
❑ 343 Albie Lopez .30 .09
❑ 344 Michael Tucker .30 .09
❑ 345 Bobby Higginson .30 .09
❑ 346 Shane Halter .30 .09
❑ 347 Jeremy Bonderman RC 1.50 .45
❑ 348 Eric Munson .30 .09
❑ 349 Andy Van Hekken .30 .09
❑ 350 Matt Anderson .30 .09
❑ 351 Jacque Jones .30 .09
❑ 352 A.J. Pierzynski .30 .09
❑ 353 Joe Mays .30 .09
❑ 354 Brad Radke .30 .09
❑ 355 Dustan Mohr .30 .09
❑ 356 Bobby Kielty .30 .09
❑ 357 Michael Cuddyer .30 .09
❑ 358 Luis Rivas .30 .09
❑ 359 Frank Thomas .75 .23
❑ 360 Joe Borchard .30 .09
❑ 361 D'Angelo Jimenez .30 .09
❑ 362 Bartolo Colon .30 .09
❑ 363 Joe Crede .30 .09
❑ 364 Miguel Olivo .30 .09
❑ 365 Billy Koch .30 .09
❑ 366 Bernie Williams .50 .15
❑ 367 Nick Johnson .30 .09
❑ 368 Andy Pettitte .50 .15
❑ 369 Mariano Rivera .50 .15
❑ 370 Alfonso Soriano .75 .23
❑ 371 David Wells .30 .09
❑ 372 Drew Henson .30 .09
❑ 373 Juan Rivera .30 .09
❑ 374 Steve Karsay .30 .09
❑ 375 Jeff Kent .30 .09
❑ 376 Lance Berkman .30 .09
❑ 377 Octavio Dotel .30 .09
❑ 378 Julio Lugo .30 .09
❑ 379 Jason Lane .30 .09
❑ 380 Wade Miller .30 .09
❑ 381 Billy Wagner .30 .09
❑ 382 Brad Ausmus .30 .09
❑ 383 Mike Hampton .30 .09
❑ 384 Chipper Jones .75 .23
❑ 385 John Smoltz .50 .15
❑ 386 Greg Maddux 1.50 .45
❑ 387 Javy Lopez .30 .09
❑ 388 Robert Fick .30 .09
❑ 389 Mark DeRosa .30 .09
❑ 390 Russ Ortiz .30 .09
❑ 391 Julio Franco .30 .09
❑ 392 Richie Sexson .30 .09
❑ 393 Eric Young .30 .09
❑ 394 Robert Machado .30 .09
❑ 395 Mike DeJean .30 .09
❑ 396 Todd Ritchie .30 .09
❑ 397 Royce Clayton .30 .09
❑ 398 Nick Neugebauer .30 .09
❑ 399 J.D. Drew .30 .09
❑ 400 Edgar Renteria .30 .09
❑ 401 Scott Rolen .50 .15
❑ 402 Matt Morris .30 .09
❑ 403 Garrett Stephenson .30 .09
❑ 404 Eduardo Perez .30 .09
❑ 405 Mike Matheny .30 .09
❑ 406 Miguel Cairo .30 .09
❑ 407 Brett Tomko .30 .09
❑ 408 Bobby Hill .30 .09
❑ 409 Troy O'Leary .30 .09
❑ 410 Corey Patterson .30 .09
❑ 411 Kerry Wood .75 .23
❑ 412 Eric Karros .30 .09
❑ 413 Hee Seop Choi .30 .09
❑ 414 Alex Gonzalez .30 .09
❑ 415 Matt Clement .30 .09
❑ 416 Mark Grudzielanek .30 .09
❑ 417 Curt Schilling .50 .15
❑ 418 Steve Finley .30 .09
❑ 419 Craig Counsell .30 .09
❑ 420 Matt Williams .30 .09
❑ 421 Quinton McCracken .30 .09
❑ 422 Chad Moeller .30 .09
❑ 423 Lyle Overbay .30 .09
❑ 424 Miguel Batista .30 .09
❑ 425 Paul Lo Duca .30 .09
❑ 426 Kevin Brown .30 .09
❑ 427 Hideo Nomo .75 .23
❑ 428 Fred McGriff .50 .15
❑ 429 Joe Thurston .30 .09
❑ 430 Odalis Perez .30 .09
❑ 431 Darren Dreifort .30 .09
❑ 432 Todd Hundley .30 .09
❑ 433 Dave Roberts .30 .09
❑ 434 Jose Vidro .30 .09
❑ 435 Javier Vazquez .30 .09
❑ 436 Michael Barrett .30 .09
❑ 437 Fernando Tatis .30 .09
❑ 438 Peter Bergeron .30 .09
❑ 439 Endy Chavez .30 .09
❑ 440 Orlando Hernandez .30 .09
❑ 441 Marvin Benard .30 .09
❑ 442 Rich Aurilia .30 .09
❑ 443 Pedro Feliz .30 .09
❑ 444 Robb Nen .30 .09
❑ 445 Ray Durham .30 .09
❑ 446 Marquis Grissom .30 .09
❑ 447 Damian Moss .30 .09
❑ 448 Edgardo Alfonzo .30 .09
❑ 449 Juan Pierre .30 .09
❑ 450 Braden Looper .30 .09
❑ 451 Alex Gonzalez .30 .09
❑ 452 Justin Wayne .30 .09
❑ 453 Josh Beckett .50 .15
❑ 454 Juan Encarnacion .30 .09
❑ 455 Ivan Rodriguez .75 .23
❑ 456 Todd Hollandsworth .30 .09
❑ 457 Cliff Floyd .30 .09
❑ 458 Rey Sanchez .30 .09
❑ 459 Mike Piazza 1.25 .35
❑ 460 Mo Vaughn .30 .09
❑ 461 Armando Benitez .30 .09
❑ 462 Tsuyoshi Shinjo .30 .09
❑ 463 Tom Glavine .75 .23
❑ 464 David Cone .30 .09
❑ 465 Phil Nevin .30 .09
❑ 466 Sean Burroughs .30 .09
❑ 467 Jake Peavy .30 .09
❑ 468 Brian Lawrence .30 .09
❑ 469 Mark Loretta .30 .09
❑ 470 Dennis Tankersley .30 .09
❑ 471 Jesse Orosco .30 .09
❑ 472 Jim Thome .75 .23
❑ 473 Kevin Millwood .30 .09
❑ 474 David Bell .30 .09
❑ 475 Pat Burrell .30 .09
❑ 476 Brandon Duckworth .30 .09
❑ 477 Jose Mesa .30 .09
❑ 478 Marlon Byrd .30 .09
❑ 479 Reggie Sanders .30 .09
❑ 480 Jason Kendall .30 .09
❑ 481 Aramis Ramirez .30 .09
❑ 482 Kris Benson .30 .09
❑ 483 Matt Stairs .30 .09
❑ 484 Kevin Young .30 .09
❑ 485 Kenny Lofton .30 .09
❑ 486 Austin Kearns .50 .15
❑ 487 Barry Larkin .75 .23
❑ 488 Jason LaRue .30 .09
❑ 489 Ken Griffey Jr. 1.25 .35
❑ 490 Danny Graves .30 .09
❑ 491 Russell Branyan .30 .09
❑ 492 Reggie Taylor .30 .09
❑ 493 Jimmy Haynes .30 .09
❑ 494 Charles Johnson .30 .09
❑ 495 Todd Helton .50 .15
❑ 496 Juan Uribe .30 .09
❑ 497 Preston Wilson .30 .09
❑ 498 Chris Stynes .30 .09
❑ 499 Jason Jennings .30 .09
❑ 500 Jay Payton .30 .09
❑ 501 Hideki Matsui SR RC 8.00 2.40
❑ 502 Jose Contreras SR RC 3.00 .90
❑ 503 Brandon Webb SR RC 4.00 1.20
❑ 504 Robby Hammock SR RC 1.50 .45
❑ 505 Matt Kata SR RC 2.00 .60
❑ 506 Tim Olson SR RC 1.50 .45
❑ 507 Michael Hessman SR RC 1.00 .30
❑ 508 Jon Leicester SR RC 1.00 .30
❑ 509 Todd Wellemeyer SR RC 1.50 .45
❑ 510 David Sanders SR RC 1.00 .30
❑ 511 Josh Stewart SR RC 1.00 .30
❑ 512 Luis Ayala SR RC 1.00 .30
❑ 513 Clint Barmes SR RC 1.50 .45
❑ 514 Josh Willingham SR RC 2.50 .75
❑ 515 Alejandro Machado SR RC 1.00 .30
❑ 516 Felix Sanchez SR RC 1.00 .30
❑ 517 Willie Eyre SR RC 1.00 .30
❑ 518 Brent Hoard SR RC 1.00 .30
❑ 519 Lew Ford SR RC 1.50 .45
❑ 520 Terrmel Sledge SR RC 1.50 .45
❑ 521 Jeremy Griffiths SR RC 1.50 .45
❑ 522 Phil Seibel SR RC 1.00 .30
❑ 523 Craig Brazell SR RC 1.50 .45
❑ 524 Prentice Redman SR RC 1.00 .30
❑ 525 Jeff Duncan SR RC 1.50 .45
❑ 526 Shane Bazzell SR RC 1.00 .30
❑ 527 Bernie Castro SR RC 1.00 .30
❑ 528 Rett Johnson SR RC 1.50 .45
❑ 529 Bobby Madritsch SR RC 1.00 .30
❑ 530 Rocco Baldelli SR 3.00 .90
❑ 531 Alex Rodriguez SH CL .75 .23
❑ 532 Eric Chavez SH CL .30 .09
❑ 533 Miguel Tejada SH CL .30 .09
❑ 534 Ichiro Suzuki SH CL .75 .23

❑ 535 Sammy Sosa SH CL .75 .23
❑ 536 Barry Zito SH CL .50 .15
❑ 537 Darin Erstad SH CL .30 .09
❑ 538 Alfonso Soriano SH CL .50 .15
❑ 539 Troy Glaus SH CL .30 .09
❑ 540 Nomar Garciaparra SH CL .75 .23
❑ 541 Bo Hart RC 1.50 .45
❑ 542 Dan Haren RC 1.00 .30
❑ 543 Ryan Wagner RC 1.25 .35
❑ 544 Rich Harden .75 .23
❑ 545 Dontrelle Willis 1.25 .35
❑ 546 Jerome Williams .30 .09
❑ 547 Bobby Crosby .30 .09
❑ 548 Greg Jones RC .50 .15
❑ 549 Todd Linden .30 .09
❑ 550 Byung-Hyun Kim .30 .09
❑ 551 Rickie Weeks RC 5.00 1.50
❑ 552 Jason Roach RC .50 .15
❑ 553 Oscar Villarreal RC .50 .15
❑ 554 Justin Duchscherer .30 .09
❑ 555 Chris Capuano RC .50 .15
❑ 556 Josh Hall RC .50 .15
❑ 557 Luis Matos .30 .09
❑ 558 Miguel Ojeda RC .50 .15
❑ 559 Kevin Ohme RC .50 .15
❑ 560 Julio Manon RC .50 .15
❑ 561 Kevin Correia RC .50 .15
❑ 562 Delmon Young RC 8.00 2.40
❑ 563 Aaron Boone .30 .09
❑ 564 Aaron Looper RC .50 .15
❑ 565 Mike Neu RC .50 .15
❑ 566 Aquilino Lopez RC .50 .15
❑ 567 Jhonny Peralta RC .50 .15
❑ 568 Duaner Sanchez .30 .09
❑ 569 Stephen Randolph RC .50 .15
❑ 570 Nate Bland RC .50 .15
❑ 571 Chin-Hui Tsao .30 .09
❑ 572 Michel Hernandez RC .50 .15
❑ 573 Rocco Baldelli 1.50 .45
❑ 574 Robb Quinlan .30 .09
❑ 575 Aaron Heilman .30 .09
❑ 576 Jae Weong Seo .30 .09
❑ 577 Joe Borowski .30 .09
❑ 578 Chris Bootcheck .30 .09
❑ 579 Michael Ryan RC .50 .15
❑ 580 Mark Malaska RC .50 .15
❑ 581 Jose Guillen .30 .09
❑ 582 Josh Towers .30 .09
❑ 583 Tom Gregorio RC .50 .15
❑ 584 Edwin Jackson RC 2.50 .75
❑ 585 Jason Anderson .30 .09
❑ 586 Jose Reyes .50 .15
❑ 587 Miguel Cabrera 1.50 .45
❑ 588 Nate Bump .30 .09
❑ 589 Jeromy Burnitz .30 .09
❑ 590 David Ross .30 .09
❑ 591 Chase Utley .30 .09
❑ 592 Brandon Webb 2.00 .60
❑ 593 Masao Kida .30 .09
❑ 594 Jimmy Journell .30 .09
❑ 595 Eric Young .30 .09
❑ 596 Tony Womack .30 .09
❑ 597 Amaury Telemaco .30 .09
❑ 598 Rickey Henderson 1.25 .35
❑ 599 Esteban Loaiza .30 .09
❑ 600 Sidney Ponson .30 .09
❑ NNO Update Set Exchange Card.

2004 Upper Deck

	MINT	NRMT
COMPLETE SERIES 1 (270)	50.00	22.00
COMMON CARD (31-270)	.30	.14
COMMON CARD (1-30)	1.00	.45
1-30 ARE NOT SHORT PRINTS		

❑ 1 Dontrelle Willis SR 2.00 .90
❑ 2 Edgar Gonzalez SR 1.00 .45
❑ 3 Jose Reyes SR 1.50 .70
❑ 4 Jae Weong Seo SR 1.00 .45
❑ 5 Miguel Cabrera SR 2.50 1.10
❑ 6 Jesse Foppert SR 1.00 .45
❑ 7 Mike Neu SR 1.00 .45
❑ 8 Michael Nakamura SR 1.00 .45
❑ 9 Luis Ayala SR 1.00 .45
❑ 10 Jared Sandberg SR 1.00 .45
❑ 11 Jhonny Peralta SR 1.00 .45
❑ 12 Wil Ledezma SR 1.00 .45
❑ 13 Jason Roach SR 1.00 .45
❑ 14 Kirk Saarloos SR 1.00 .45
❑ 15 Cliff Lee SR 1.00 .45
❑ 16 Bobby Hill SR 1.00 .45
❑ 17 Lyle Overbay SR 1.00 .45
❑ 18 Josh Hall SR 1.00 .45
❑ 19 Joe Thurston SR 1.00 .45
❑ 20 Matt Kata SR 1.00 .45
❑ 21 Jeremy Bonderman SR 1.00 .45
❑ 22 Julio Manon SR 1.00 .45
❑ 23 Rodrigo Rosario SR 1.00 .45
❑ 24 Robby Hammock SR 1.00 .45
❑ 25 David Sanders SR 1.00 .45
❑ 26 Miguel Ojeda SR 1.00 .45
❑ 27 Mark Teixeira SR 1.50 .70
❑ 28 Franklyn German SR 1.00 .45
❑ 29 Ken Harvey SR 1.00 .45
❑ 30 Xavier Nady SR 1.00 .45
❑ 31 Tim Salmon .50 .23
❑ 32 Troy Glaus .50 .23
❑ 33 Adam Kennedy .30 .14
❑ 34 David Eckstein .30 .14
❑ 35 Ben Molina .30 .14
❑ 36 Jarrod Washburn .30 .14
❑ 37 Ramon Ortiz .30 .14
❑ 38 Eric Chavez .30 .14
❑ 39 Miguel Tejada .30 .14
❑ 40 Chris Singleton .30 .14
❑ 41 Jermaine Dye .30 .14
❑ 42 John Halama .30 .14
❑ 43 Tim Hudson .30 .14
❑ 44 Barry Zito .75 .35
❑ 45 Ted Lilly .30 .14
❑ 46 Bobby Kielty .30 .14
❑ 47 Kelvim Escobar .30 .14
❑ 48 Josh Phelps .30 .14
❑ 49 Vernon Wells .30 .14
❑ 50 Roy Halladay .30 .14
❑ 51 Orlando Hudson .30 .14
❑ 52 Eric Hinske .30 .14
❑ 53 Brandon Backe .30 .14
❑ 54 Dewon Brazelton .30 .14
❑ 55 Ben Grieve .30 .14
❑ 56 Aubrey Huff .30 .14
❑ 57 Toby Hall .30 .14
❑ 58 Rocco Baldelli 1.25 .55
❑ 59 Al Martin .30 .14
❑ 60 Brandon Phillips .30 .14
❑ 61 Omar Vizquel .30 .14
❑ 62 C.C. Sabathia .30 .14
❑ 63 Milton Bradley .30 .14
❑ 64 Ricky Gutierrez .30 .14
❑ 65 Matt Lawton .30 .14
❑ 66 Danys Baez .30 .14
❑ 67 Ichiro Suzuki 1.50 .70
❑ 68 Randy Winn .30 .14
❑ 69 Carlos Guillen .30 .14
❑ 70 Mark McLemore .30 .14
❑ 71 Dan Wilson .30 .14
❑ 72 Jamie Moyer .30 .14
❑ 73 Joel Pineiro .30 .14
❑ 74 Edgar Martinez .50 .23
❑ 75 Tony Batista .30 .14
❑ 76 Jay Gibbons .30 .14
❑ 77 Jeff Conine .30 .14
❑ 78 Melvin Mora .30 .14
❑ 79 Geronimo Gil .30 .14
❑ 80 Rodrigo Lopez .30 .14
❑ 81 Jorge Julio .30 .14
❑ 82 Rafael Palmeiro .50 .23
❑ 83 Juan Gonzalez .75 .35
❑ 84 Mike Young .30 .14
❑ 85 Alex Rodriguez 1.50 .70
❑ 86 Einar Diaz .30 .14
❑ 87 Kevin Mench .30 .14
❑ 88 Hank Blalock .50 .23
❑ 89 Pedro Martinez .75 .35
❑ 90 Byung-Hyun Kim .30 .14
❑ 91 Derek Lowe .30 .14
❑ 92 Jason Varitek .30 .14
❑ 93 Manny Ramirez .30 .14
❑ 94 John Burkett .30 .14
❑ 95 Todd Walker .30 .14
❑ 96 Nomar Garciaparra 1.50 .70
❑ 97 Trot Nixon .30 .14
❑ 98 Mike Sweeney .30 .14
❑ 99 Carlos Febles .30 .14
❑ 100 Mike MacDougal .30 .14
❑ 101 Raul Ibanez .30 .14
❑ 102 Jason Grimsley .30 .14
❑ 103 Chris George .30 .14
❑ 104 Brent Mayne .30 .14
❑ 105 Dmitri Young .30 .14
❑ 106 Eric Munson .30 .14
❑ 107 A.J. Hinch .30 .14
❑ 108 Andres Torres .30 .14
❑ 109 Bobby Higginson .30 .14
❑ 110 Shane Halter .30 .14
❑ 111 Matt Walbeck .30 .14
❑ 112 Torii Hunter .30 .14
❑ 113 Doug Mientkiewicz .30 .14
❑ 114 Lew Ford .30 .14
❑ 115 Eric Milton .30 .14
❑ 116 Eddie Guardado .30 .14
❑ 117 Cristian Guzman .30 .14
❑ 118 Corey Koskie .30 .14
❑ 119 Magglio Ordonez .30 .14
❑ 120 Mark Buehrle .30 .14
❑ 121 Billy Koch .30 .14
❑ 122 Jose Valentin .30 .14
❑ 123 Paul Konerko .30 .14
❑ 124 Carlos Lee .30 .14
❑ 125 Jon Garland .30 .14
❑ 126 Jason Giambi .75 .35
❑ 127 Derek Jeter 2.00 .90
❑ 128 Roger Clemens 1.50 .70
❑ 129 Andy Pettitte .50 .23
❑ 130 Jorge Posada .50 .23
❑ 131 David Wells .30 .14
❑ 132 Hideki Matsui 1.50 .70
❑ 133 Mike Mussina .75 .35
❑ 134 Jeff Bagwell .50 .23
❑ 135 Craig Biggio .50 .23
❑ 136 Morgan Ensberg .30 .14
❑ 137 Richard Hidalgo .30 .14
❑ 138 Brad Ausmus .30 .14
❑ 139 Roy Oswalt .30 .14
❑ 140 Billy Wagner .30 .14
❑ 141 Octavio Dotel .30 .14
❑ 142 Gary Sheffield .30 .14
❑ 143 Andruw Jones .50 .23
❑ 144 John Smoltz .50 .23
❑ 145 Rafael Furcal .30 .14
❑ 146 Javy Lopez .30 .14
❑ 147 Shane Reynolds .30 .14
❑ 148 Horacio Ramirez .30 .14
❑ 149 Mike Hampton .30 .14
❑ 150 Jung Bong .30 .14
❑ 151 Ruben Quevedo .30 .14
❑ 152 Ben Sheets .30 .14
❑ 153 Geoff Jenkins .30 .14
❑ 154 Royce Clayton .30 .14
❑ 155 Glendon Rusch .30 .14
❑ 156 John Vander Wal .30 .14
❑ 157 Scott Podsednik .75 .35
❑ 158 Jim Edmonds .30 .14
❑ 159 Tino Martinez .50 .23
❑ 160 Albert Pujols 1.50 .70
❑ 161 Matt Morris .30 .14
❑ 162 Woody Williams .30 .14
❑ 163 Edgar Renteria .30 .14
❑ 164 Jason Isringhausen .30 .14

Card	Nm-Mt	Ex-Mt
❑ 165 Jason Simontacchi	.30	.14
❑ 166 Kerry Robinson	.30	.14
❑ 167 Sammy Sosa	1.25	.55
❑ 168 Joe Borowski	.30	.14
❑ 169 Tony Womack	.30	.14
❑ 170 Antonio Alfonseca	.30	.14
❑ 171 Corey Patterson	.30	.14
❑ 172 Mark Prior	1.50	.70
❑ 173 Moises Alou	.30	.14
❑ 174 Matt Clement	.30	.14
❑ 175 Randall Simon	.30	.14
❑ 176 Randy Johnson	.75	.35
❑ 177 Luis Gonzalez	.30	.14
❑ 178 Craig Counsell	.30	.14
❑ 179 Miguel Batista	.30	.14
❑ 180 Steve Finley	.30	.14
❑ 181 Brandon Webb	.30	.14
❑ 182 Danny Bautista	.30	.14
❑ 183 Oscar Villarreal	.30	.14
❑ 184 Shawn Green	.30	.14
❑ 185 Brian Jordan	.30	.14
❑ 186 Fred McGriff	.50	.23
❑ 187 Andy Ashby	.30	.14
❑ 188 Rickey Henderson	1.25	.55
❑ 189 Dave Roberts	.30	.14
❑ 190 Eric Gagne	.50	.23
❑ 191 Kazuhisa Ishii	.30	.14
❑ 192 Adrian Beltre	.30	.14
❑ 193 Vladimir Guerrero	.75	.35
❑ 194 Livan Hernandez	.30	.14
❑ 195 Ron Calloway	.30	.14
❑ 196 Sun Woo Kim	.30	.14
❑ 197 Wil Cordero	.30	.14
❑ 198 Brad Wilkerson	.30	.14
❑ 199 Orlando Cabrera	.30	.14
❑ 200 Barry Bonds	2.00	.90
❑ 201 Ray Durham	.30	.14
❑ 202 Andres Galarraga	.30	.14
❑ 203 Benito Santiago	.30	.14
❑ 204 Jose Cruz Jr.	.30	.14
❑ 205 Jason Schmidt	.30	.14
❑ 206 Kirk Rueter	.30	.14
❑ 207 Felix Rodriguez	.30	.14
❑ 208 Mike Lowell	.30	.14
❑ 209 Luis Castillo	.30	.14
❑ 210 Derrek Lee	.30	.14
❑ 211 Andy Fox	.30	.14
❑ 212 Tommy Phelps	.30	.14
❑ 213 Todd Hollandsworth	.30	.14
❑ 214 Brad Penny	.30	.14
❑ 215 Juan Pierre	.30	.14
❑ 216 Mike Piazza	1.25	.55
❑ 217 Jae Weong Seo	.30	.14
❑ 218 Ty Wigginton	.30	.14
❑ 219 Al Leiter	.30	.14
❑ 220 Roger Cedeno	.30	.14
❑ 221 Timo Perez	.30	.14
❑ 222 Aaron Heilman	.30	.14
❑ 223 Pedro Astacio	.30	.14
❑ 224 Joe McEwing	.30	.14
❑ 225 Ryan Klesko	.30	.14
❑ 226 Brian Giles	.30	.14
❑ 227 Mark Kotsay	.30	.14
❑ 228 Brian Lawrence	.30	.14
❑ 229 Rod Beck	.30	.14
❑ 230 Trevor Hoffman	.30	.14
❑ 231 Sean Burroughs	.30	.14
❑ 232 Bob Abreu	.30	.14
❑ 233 Jim Thome	.75	.35
❑ 234 David Bell	.30	.14
❑ 235 Jimmy Rollins	.30	.14
❑ 236 Mike Lieberthal	.30	.14
❑ 237 Vicente Padilla	.30	.14
❑ 238 Randy Wolf	.30	.14
❑ 239 Reggie Sanders	.30	.14
❑ 240 Jason Kendall	.30	.14
❑ 241 Jack Wilson	.30	.14
❑ 242 Jose Hernandez	.30	.14
❑ 243 Kip Wells	.30	.14
❑ 244 Carlos Rivera	.30	.14
❑ 245 Craig Wilson	.30	.14
❑ 246 Adam Dunn	.50	.23
❑ 247 Sean Casey	.30	.14
❑ 248 Danny Graves	.30	.14
❑ 249 Ryan Dempster	.30	.14
❑ 250 Barry Larkin	.75	.35
❑ 251 Reggie Taylor	.30	.14
❑ 252 Wily Mo Pena	.30	.14
❑ 253 Larry Walker	.50	.23
❑ 254 Mark Sweeney	.30	.14
❑ 255 Preston Wilson	.30	.14
❑ 256 Jason Jennings	.30	.14
❑ 257 Charles Johnson	.30	.14
❑ 258 Jay Payton	.30	.14
❑ 259 Chris Stynes	.30	.14
❑ 260 Juan Uribe	.30	.14
❑ 261 Hideki Matsui SH CL	.75	.35
❑ 262 Barry Bonds SH CL	1.00	.45
❑ 263 Dontrelle Willis SH CL	.50	.23
❑ 264 Kevin Millwood SH CL	.30	.14
❑ 265 Billy Wagner SH CL	.30	.14
❑ 266 Rocco Baldelli SH CL	.75	.35
❑ 267 Roger Clemens SH CL	.75	.35
❑ 268 Rafael Palmeiro SH CL	.30	.14
❑ 269 Miguel Cabrera SH CL	.75	.35
❑ 270 Jose Contreras SH CL	.30	.14

2002 Upper Deck 40-Man

	Nm-Mt	Ex-Mt
COMPLETE SET (1182)	200.00	60.00
❑ 1 Darin Erstad	.40	.12
❑ 2 Kevin Appier	.40	.12
❑ 3 Scott Schoeneweis	.40	.12
❑ 4 Ben Molina	.40	.12
❑ 5 Troy Glaus	.60	.18
❑ 6 Adam Kennedy	.40	.12
❑ 7 Aaron Sele	.40	.12
❑ 8 Garret Anderson	.40	.12
❑ 9 Ramon Ortiz	.40	.12
❑ 10 Dennis Cook	.40	.12
❑ 11 Scott Spiezio	.40	.12
❑ 12 Orlando Palmeiro	.40	.12
❑ 13 Troy Percival	.40	.12
❑ 14 David Eckstein	.40	.12
❑ 15 Jarrod Washburn	.40	.12
❑ 16 Nathan Haynes	.40	.12
❑ 17 Benji Gil	.40	.12
❑ 18 Alfredo Amezaga	.40	.12
❑ 19 Ben Weber	.40	.12
❑ 20 Al Levine	.40	.12
❑ 21 Brad Fullmer	.40	.12
❑ 22 Elpidio Guzman	.40	.12
❑ 23 Tim Salmon	.60	.18
❑ 24 Jose Nieves	.40	.12
❑ 25 Shawn Wooten	.40	.12
❑ 26 Lou Pote	.40	.12
❑ 27 Mickey Callaway	.40	.12
❑ 28 Steve Green	.40	.12
❑ 29 John Lackey	.40	.12
❑ 30 Mark Lukasiewicz	.40	.12
❑ 31 Jorge Fabregas	.40	.12
❑ 32 Jeff DaVanon	.40	.12
❑ 33 Elvin Nina	.40	.12
❑ 34 Donne Wall	.40	.12
❑ 35 Eric Chavez	.40	.12
❑ 36 Jermaine Dye	.40	.12
❑ 37 Scott Hatteberg	.40	.12
❑ 38 Mark Mulder	.40	.12
❑ 39 Ramon Hernandez	.40	.12
❑ 40 Jim Mecir	.40	.12
❑ 41 Barry Zito	1.00	.30
❑ 42 Greg Myers	.40	.12
❑ 43 David Justice	.40	.12
❑ 44 Mike Magnante	.40	.12
❑ 45 Terrence Long	.40	.12
❑ 46 Tim Hudson	.40	.12
❑ 47 Olmedo Saenz	.40	.12
❑ 48 Billy Koch	.40	.12
❑ 49 Carlos Pena	.40	.12
❑ 50 Mike Venafro	.40	.12
❑ 51 Mark Ellis	.40	.12
❑ 52 Randy Velarde	.40	.12
❑ 53 Jeremy Giambi	.40	.12
❑ 54 Mike Colangelo	.40	.12
❑ 55 Mike Holtz	.40	.12
❑ 56 Chad Bradford	.40	.12
❑ 57 Miguel Tejada	.40	.12
❑ 58 Mike Fyhrie	.40	.12
❑ 59 Erik Hiljus	.40	.12
❑ 60 Juan Pena	.40	.12
❑ 61 Mario Valdez	.40	.12
❑ 62 Franklyn German RC	.60	.18
❑ 63 Carlos Delgado	.40	.12
❑ 64 Orlando Hudson	.40	.12
❑ 65 Chris Carpenter	.40	.12
❑ 66 Kelvim Escobar	.40	.12
❑ 67 Felipe Lopez	.40	.12
❑ 68 Brandon Lyon	.40	.12
❑ 69 Jose Cruz Jr.	.40	.12
❑ 70 Luke Prokopec	.40	.12
❑ 71 Darrin Fletcher	.40	.12
❑ 72 Bob File	.40	.12
❑ 73 Felix Heredia	.40	.12
❑ 74 Mike Sirotka	.40	.12
❑ 75 Shannon Stewart	.40	.12
❑ 76 Joe Lawrence	.40	.12
❑ 77 Chris Woodward	.40	.12
❑ 78 Dan Plesac	.40	.12
❑ 79 Pedro Borbon	.40	.12
❑ 80 Roy Halladay	.40	.12
❑ 81 Raul Mondesi	.40	.12
❑ 82 Steve Parris	.40	.12
❑ 83 Homer Bush	.40	.12
❑ 84 Esteban Loaiza	.40	.12
❑ 85 Vernon Wells	.40	.12
❑ 86 Justin Miller	.40	.12
❑ 87 Scott Eyre	.40	.12
❑ 88 Dave Berg	.40	.12
❑ 89 Gustavo Chacin RC	.60	.18
❑ 90 Joe Orloski RC	.60	.18
❑ 91 Corey Thurman RC	.60	.18
❑ 92 Tom Wilson RC	.60	.18
❑ 93 Eric Hinske	.40	.12
❑ 94 Chris Baker RC	.60	.18
❑ 95 Reed Johnson RC	1.00	.30
❑ 96 Greg Vaughn	.40	.12
❑ 97 Toby Hall	.40	.12
❑ 98 Brent Abernathy	.40	.12
❑ 99 Bobby Smith	.40	.12
❑ 100 Tanyon Sturtze	.40	.12
❑ 101 Chris Gomez	.40	.12
❑ 102 Joe Kennedy	.40	.12
❑ 103 Ben Grieve	.40	.12
❑ 104 Aubrey Huff	.40	.12
❑ 105 Jesus Colome	.40	.12
❑ 106 Felix Escalona RC	.60	.18
❑ 107 Paul Wilson	.40	.12
❑ 108 Ryan Rupe	.40	.12
❑ 109 Jason Tyner	.40	.12
❑ 110 Esteban Yan	.40	.12
❑ 111 Russ Johnson	.40	.12
❑ 112 Randy Winn	.40	.12
❑ 113 Wilson Alvarez	.40	.12
❑ 114 Wilmy Caceres	.40	.12
❑ 115 Steve Cox	.40	.12
❑ 116 Dewon Brazelton	.40	.12
❑ 117 Doug Creek	.40	.12
❑ 118 Jason Conti	.40	.12
❑ 119 John Flaherty	.40	.12
❑ 120 Delvin James	.40	.12
❑ 121 Steve Kent	.40	.12
❑ 122 Kevin McGlinchy	.40	.12
❑ 123 Travis Phelps	.40	.12
❑ 124 Bobby Seay	.40	.12
❑ 125 Enger Veras	.40	.12
❑ 126 Victor Zambrano	.40	.12
❑ 127 Jace Brewer	.40	.12

No.	Player		
❑ 128	Jason Smith	.40	.12
❑ 129	Ramon Soler	.40	.12
❑ 130	Brandon Backe RC	.60	.18
❑ 131	Jorge Sosa RC	.60	.18
❑ 132	Jim Thome	1.00	.30
❑ 133	Brady Anderson	.40	.12
❑ 134	C.C. Sabathia	.40	.12
❑ 135	Einar Diaz	.40	.12
❑ 136	Ricky Gutierrez	.40	.12
❑ 137	Danys Baez	.40	.12
❑ 138	Bob Wickman	.40	.12
❑ 139	Milton Bradley	.40	.12
❑ 140	Bartolo Colon	.40	.12
❑ 141	Jolbert Cabrera	.40	.12
❑ 142	Eddie Taubensee	.40	.12
❑ 143	Ellis Burks	.40	.12
❑ 144	Omar Vizquel	.40	.12
❑ 145	Eddie Perez	.40	.12
❑ 146	Jaret Wright	.40	.12
❑ 147	Chuck Finley	.40	.12
❑ 148	Paul Shuey	.40	.12
❑ 149	Travis Fryman	.40	.12
❑ 150	Wil Cordero	.40	.12
❑ 151	Ricardo Rincon	.40	.12
❑ 152	Victor Martinez	.40	.12
❑ 153	Charles Nagy	.40	.12
❑ 154	Alex Escobar	.40	.12
❑ 155	Russell Branyan	.40	.12
❑ 156	Matt Lawton	.40	.12
❑ 157	Ryan Drese	.40	.12
❑ 158	Jerrod Riggan	.40	.12
❑ 159	David Riske	.40	.12
❑ 160	Jake Westbrook	.40	.12
❑ 161	Mark Wohlers	.40	.12
❑ 162	John McDonald	.40	.12
❑ 163	Ichiro Suzuki	2.00	.60
❑ 164	Freddy Garcia	.40	.12
❑ 165	Edgar Martinez	.60	.18
❑ 166	Ben Davis	.40	.12
❑ 167	Shigetoshi Hasegawa	.40	.12
❑ 168	Carlos Guillen	.40	.12
❑ 169	Ruben Sierra	.40	.12
❑ 170	Joel Pineiro	.40	.12
❑ 171	Norm Charlton	.40	.12
❑ 172	Bret Boone	.40	.12
❑ 173	Jamie Moyer	.40	.12
❑ 174	Jeff Nelson	.40	.12
❑ 175	Kazuhiro Sasaki	.40	.12
❑ 176	Jeff Cirillo	.40	.12
❑ 177	Mark McLemore	.40	.12
❑ 178	Paul Abbott	.40	.12
❑ 179	Mike Cameron	.40	.12
❑ 180	Dan Wilson	.40	.12
❑ 181	John Olerud	.40	.12
❑ 182	Arthur Rhodes	.40	.12
❑ 183	Desi Relaford	.40	.12
❑ 184	John Halama	.40	.12
❑ 185	Antonio Perez	.40	.12
❑ 186	Ryan Anderson	.40	.12
❑ 187	James Baldwin	.40	.12
❑ 188	Ryan Franklin	.40	.12
❑ 189	Justin Kaye	.40	.12
❑ 190	J.J. Putz RC	.60	.18
❑ 191	Allan Simpson RC	.40	.12
❑ 192	Matt Thornton RC	.60	.18
❑ 193	Luis Ugueto RC	.60	.18
❑ 194	Chris Richard	.40	.12
❑ 195	Sidney Ponson	.40	.12
❑ 196	Brook Fordyce	.40	.12
❑ 197	Luis Matos	.40	.12
❑ 198	Josh Towers	.40	.12
❑ 199	David Segui	.40	.12
❑ 200	Chris Brock RC	.40	.12
❑ 201	Tony Batista	.40	.12
❑ 202	Erik Bedard	.40	.12
❑ 203	Marty Cordova	.40	.12
❑ 204	Jerry Hairston Jr.	.40	.12
❑ 205	Jason Johnson	.40	.12
❑ 206	Buddy Groom	.40	.12
❑ 207	Mike Bordick	.40	.12
❑ 208	Melvin Mora	.40	.12
❑ 209	Calvin Maduro	.40	.12
❑ 210	Jeff Conine	.40	.12
❑ 211	Luis Rivera	.40	.12
❑ 212	Jay Gibbons	.40	.12
❑ 213	B.J. Ryan	.40	.12
❑ 214	Sean Douglass	.40	.12
❑ 215	Rodrigo Lopez	.40	.12
❑ 216	Rick Bauer	.40	.12
❑ 217	Scott Erickson	.40	.12
❑ 218	Jorge Julio	.40	.12
❑ 219	Willis Roberts	.40	.12
❑ 220	John Stephens	.40	.12
❑ 221	Geronimo Gil	.40	.12
❑ 222	Chris Singleton	.40	.12
❑ 223	Mike Paradis	.40	.12
❑ 224	John Parrish	.40	.12
❑ 225	Steve Bechler RC	.60	.18
❑ 226	Mike Moriarty RC	.40	.12
❑ 227	Luis Garcia RC	.60	.18
❑ 228	Alex Rodriguez	2.00	.60
❑ 229	Mark Teixeira	1.50	.45
❑ 230	Chan Ho Park	.40	.12
❑ 231	Todd Van Poppel	.40	.12
❑ 232	Mike Young	.40	.12
❑ 233	Kenny Rogers	.40	.12
❑ 234	Rusty Greer	.40	.12
❑ 235	Rafael Palmeiro	.60	.18
❑ 236	Francisco Cordero	.40	.12
❑ 237	John Rocker	.40	.12
❑ 238	Dave Burba	.40	.12
❑ 239	Travis Hafner	.40	.12
❑ 240	Kevin Mench	.40	.12
❑ 241	Carl Everett	.40	.12
❑ 242	Ivan Rodriguez	1.00	.30
❑ 243	Jeff Zimmerman	.40	.12
❑ 244	Juan Gonzalez	1.00	.30
❑ 245	Herbert Perry	.40	.12
❑ 246	Rob Bell	.40	.12
❑ 247	Doug Davis	.40	.12
❑ 248	Frank Catalanotto	.40	.12
❑ 249	Jay Powell	.40	.12
❑ 250	Gabe Kapler	.40	.12
❑ 251	Joaquin Benoit	.40	.12
❑ 252	Jovanny Cedeno	.40	.12
❑ 253	Hideki Irabu	.40	.12
❑ 254	Dan Miceli	.40	.12
❑ 255	Danny Kolb	.40	.12
❑ 256	Colby Lewis	.40	.12
❑ 257	Rich Rodriguez	.40	.12
❑ 258	Ismael Valdes	.40	.12
❑ 259	Bill Haselman	.40	.12
❑ 260	Jason Hart	.40	.12
❑ 261	Rudy Seanez	.40	.12
❑ 262	Travis Hughes RC	1.00	.30
❑ 263	Hank Blalock	1.50	.45
❑ 264	Steve Woodard	.40	.12
❑ 265	Nomar Garciaparra	2.00	.60
❑ 266	Pedro Martinez	1.00	.30
❑ 267	Frank Castillo	.40	.12
❑ 268	Johnny Damon	.40	.12
❑ 269	Doug Mirabelli	.40	.12
❑ 270	Derek Lowe	.40	.12
❑ 271	Shea Hillenbrand	.40	.12
❑ 272	Paxton Crawford	.40	.12
❑ 273	Tony Clark	.40	.12
❑ 274	Dustin Hermanson	.40	.12
❑ 275	Trot Nixon	.40	.12
❑ 276	John Burkett	.40	.12
❑ 277	Rich Garces	.40	.12
❑ 278	Josh Hancock RC	.60	.18
❑ 279	Michael Coleman	.40	.12
❑ 280	Darren Oliver	.40	.12
❑ 281	Jason Varitek	.40	.12
❑ 282	Jose Offerman	.40	.12
❑ 283	Tim Wakefield	.40	.12
❑ 284	Rolando Arrojo	.40	.12
❑ 285	Rickey Henderson	1.50	.45
❑ 286	Ugueth Urbina	.40	.12
❑ 287	Casey Fossum	.40	.12
❑ 288	Manny Ramirez	.40	.12
❑ 289	Sun-Woo Kim	.40	.12
❑ 290	Juan Diaz	.40	.12
❑ 291	Willie Banks	.40	.12
❑ 292	Jorge De La Rosa RC	.60	.18
❑ 293	Juan Pena	.40	.12
❑ 294	Jeff Wallace	.40	.12
❑ 295	Calvin Pickering	.40	.12
❑ 296	Anastacio Martinez RC	.60	.18
❑ 297	Carlos Baerga	.40	.12
❑ 298	Rey Sanchez	.40	.12
❑ 299	Mike Sweeney	.40	.12
❑ 300	Jeff Suppan	.40	.12
❑ 301	Brent Mayne	.40	.12
❑ 302	Chad Durbin	.40	.12
❑ 303	Dan Reichert	.40	.12
❑ 304	Raul Ibanez	.40	.12
❑ 305	Joe Randa	.40	.12
❑ 306	Chris George	.40	.12
❑ 307	Michael Tucker	.40	.12
❑ 308	Paul Byrd	.40	.12
❑ 309	Kris Wilson	.40	.12
❑ 310	Luis Alicea	.40	.12
❑ 311	Neifi Perez	.40	.12
❑ 312	Brian Shouse	.40	.12
❑ 313	Chuck Knoblauch	.40	.12
❑ 314	Dave McCarty	.40	.12
❑ 315	Blake Stein	.40	.12
❑ 316	Alexis Gomez	.40	.12
❑ 317	Mark Quinn	.40	.12
❑ 318	A.J. Hinch	.40	.12
❑ 319	Carlos Febles	.40	.12
❑ 320	Roberto Hernandez	.40	.12
❑ 321	Brandon Berger	.40	.12
❑ 322	Jeff Austin RC	.60	.18
❑ 323	Cory Bailey	.40	.12
❑ 324	Tony Cogan	.40	.12
❑ 325	Nate Field RC	.60	.18
❑ 326	Jason Grimsley	.40	.12
❑ 327	Darrell May RC	.40	.12
❑ 328	Donnie Sadler	.40	.12
❑ 329	Carlos Beltran	.40	.12
❑ 330	Miguel Asencio RC	.60	.18
❑ 331	Jeff Weaver	.40	.12
❑ 332	Bobby Higginson	.40	.12
❑ 333	Mike Rivera	.40	.12
❑ 334	Matt Anderson	.40	.12
❑ 335	Craig Paquette	.40	.12
❑ 336	Jose Lima	.40	.12
❑ 337	Juan Acevedo	.40	.12
❑ 338	Danny Patterson	.40	.12
❑ 339	Andres Torres	.40	.12
❑ 340	Dean Palmer	.40	.12
❑ 341	Randall Simon	.40	.12
❑ 342	Craig Monroe	.40	.12
❑ 343	Damion Easley	.40	.12
❑ 344	Robert Fick	.40	.12
❑ 345	Steve Sparks	.40	.12
❑ 346	Dmitri Young	.40	.12
❑ 347	Nate Cornejo	.40	.12
❑ 348	Matt Miller	.40	.12
❑ 349	Wendell Magee	.40	.12
❑ 350	Shane Halter	.40	.12
❑ 351	Brian Moehler	.40	.12
❑ 352	Mitch Meluskey	.40	.12
❑ 353	Jose Macias	.40	.12
❑ 354	Mark Redman	.40	.12
❑ 355	Jeff Farnsworth	.40	.12
❑ 356	Kris Keller	.40	.12
❑ 357	Adam Pettyjohn	.40	.12
❑ 358	Fernando Rodney	.40	.12
❑ 359	Andy Van Hekken	.40	.12
❑ 360	Damian Jackson	.40	.12
❑ 361	Jose Paniagua	.40	.12
❑ 362	Jacob Cruz	.40	.12
❑ 363	Doug Mientkiewicz	.40	.12
❑ 364	Torii Hunter	.40	.12
❑ 365	Brad Radke	.40	.12
❑ 366	Denny Hocking	.40	.12
❑ 367	Mike Jackson	.40	.12
❑ 368	Eddie Guardado	.40	.12
❑ 369	Jacque Jones	.40	.12
❑ 370	Joe Mays	.40	.12
❑ 371	Matt Kinney	.40	.12
❑ 372	Kyle Lohse	.40	.12
❑ 373	David Ortiz	.40	.12
❑ 374	Luis Rivas	.40	.12
❑ 375	Jay Canizaro	.40	.12
❑ 376	Dustan Mohr	.40	.12
❑ 377	LaTroy Hawkins	.40	.12
❑ 378	Warren Morris	.40	.12
❑ 379	A.J. Pierzynski	.40	.12
❑ 380	Eric Milton	.40	.12
❑ 381	Bob Wells	.40	.12
❑ 382	Cristian Guzman	.40	.12
❑ 383	Brian Buchanan	.40	.12
❑ 384	Bobby Kielty	.40	.12
❑ 385	Corey Koskie	.40	.12

❑ 386 J.C. Romero .40 .12
❑ 387 Jack Cressend .40 .12
❑ 388 Mike Duvall .40 .12
❑ 389 Tony Fiore .40 .12
❑ 390 Tom Prince .40 .12
❑ 391 Todd Sears .40 .12
❑ 392 Kevin Frederick RC .60 .18
❑ 393 Frank Thomas 1.00 .30
❑ 394 Mark Buehrle .40 .12
❑ 395 Jon Garland .40 .12
❑ 396 Jeff Liefer .40 .12
❑ 397 Magglio Ordonez .40 .12
❑ 398 Rocky Biddle .40 .12
❑ 399 Lorenzo Barcelo .40 .12
❑ 400 Ray Durham .40 .12
❑ 401 Bob Howry .40 .12
❑ 402 Aaron Rowand .40 .12
❑ 403 Keith Foulke .40 .12
❑ 404 Paul Konerko .40 .12
❑ 405 Sandy Alomar Jr. .40 .12
❑ 406 Mark Johnson .40 .12
❑ 407 Carlos Lee .40 .12
❑ 408 Jose Valentin .40 .12
❑ 409 Jon Rauch .40 .12
❑ 410 Royce Clayton .40 .12
❑ 411 Kenny Lofton .40 .12
❑ 412 Tony Graffanino .40 .12
❑ 413 Todd Ritchie .40 .12
❑ 414 Antonio Osuna .40 .12
❑ 415 Gary Glover .40 .12
❑ 416 Mike Porzio .40 .12
❑ 417 Danny Wright .40 .12
❑ 418 Kelly Wunsch .40 .12
❑ 419 Miguel Olivo .40 .12
❑ 420 Edwin Almonte RC .60 .18
❑ 421 Kyle Kane RC .40 .12
❑ 422 Mitch Wylie RC .60 .18
❑ 423 Derek Jeter 2.50 .75
❑ 424 Jason Giambi 1.00 .30
❑ 425 Roger Clemens 2.00 .60
❑ 426 Enrique Wilson .40 .12
❑ 427 David Wells .40 .12
❑ 428 Mike Mussina 1.00 .30
❑ 429 Bernie Williams .60 .18
❑ 430 Mike Stanton .40 .12
❑ 431 Sterling Hitchcock .40 .12
❑ 432 Alex Graman .40 .12
❑ 433 Robin Ventura .40 .12
❑ 434 Mariano Rivera .60 .18
❑ 435 Jay Tessmer .40 .12
❑ 436 Andy Pettitte .60 .18
❑ 437 John Vander Wal .40 .12
❑ 438 Adrian Hernandez .40 .12
❑ 439 Alberto Castillo .40 .12
❑ 440 Steve Karsay .40 .12
❑ 441 Alfonso Soriano 1.00 .30
❑ 442 Rondell White .40 .12
❑ 443 Nick Johnson .40 .12
❑ 444 Jorge Posada .60 .18
❑ 445 Ramiro Mendoza .40 .12
❑ 446 Gerald Williams .40 .12
❑ 447 Orlando Hernandez .40 .12
❑ 448 Randy Choate .40 .12
❑ 449 Randy Keisler .40 .12
❑ 450 Ted Lilly .40 .12
❑ 451 Christian Parker .40 .12
❑ 452 Ron Coomer .40 .12
❑ 453 Marcus Thames .40 .12
❑ 454 Drew Henson .60 .18
❑ 455 Jeff Bagwell .60 .18
❑ 456 Wade Miller .40 .12
❑ 457 Lance Berkman .40 .12
❑ 458 Julio Lugo .40 .12
❑ 459 Roy Oswalt .40 .12
❑ 460 Nelson Cruz .40 .12
❑ 461 Morgan Ensberg .40 .12
❑ 462 Geoff Blum .40 .12
❑ 463 Ryan Jamison .40 .12
❑ 464 Billy Wagner .40 .12
❑ 465 Dave Mlicki .40 .12
❑ 466 Brad Ausmus .40 .12
❑ 467 Jose Vizcaino .40 .12
❑ 468 Craig Biggio .60 .18
❑ 469 Shane Reynolds .40 .12
❑ 470 Greg Zaun .40 .12
❑ 471 Octavio Dotel .40 .12
❑ 472 Carlos Hernandez .40 .12
❑ 473 Richard Hidalgo .40 .12
❑ 474 Daryle Ward .40 .12
❑ 475 Orlando Merced .40 .12
❑ 476 John Buck .40 .12
❑ 477 Adam Everett .40 .12
❑ 478 Doug Brocail .40 .12
❑ 479 Brad Lidge .40 .12
❑ 480 Scott Linebrink .40 .12
❑ 481 T.J. Mathews .40 .12
❑ 482 Greg Miller .40 .12
❑ 483 Hipolito Pichardo .40 .12
❑ 484 Brandon Puffer RC .60 .18
❑ 485 Ricky Stone RC .40 .12
❑ 486 Jason Lane .40 .12
❑ 487 Brian L. Hunter .40 .12
❑ 488 Rodrigo Rosario RC .60 .18
❑ 489 Tom Shearn RC .60 .18
❑ 490 Gary Sheffield .40 .12
❑ 491 Tom Glavine 1.00 .30
❑ 492 Mike Remlinger .40 .12
❑ 493 Henry Blanco .40 .12
❑ 494 Vinny Castilla .40 .12
❑ 495 Chris Hammond .40 .12
❑ 496 Kevin Millwood .40 .12
❑ 497 Darren Holmes .40 .12
❑ 498 Cory Aldridge .40 .12
❑ 499 Tim Spooneybarger .40 .12
❑ 500 Rafael Furcal .40 .12
❑ 501 Albie Lopez .40 .12
❑ 502 Javy Lopez .40 .12
❑ 503 Greg Maddux 2.00 .60
❑ 504 Andruw Jones .60 .18
❑ 505 Steve Torrealba .40 .12
❑ 506 George Lombard .40 .12
❑ 507 B.J. Surhoff .40 .12
❑ 508 Marcus Giles .40 .12
❑ 509 Derrick Lewis .40 .12
❑ 510 Wes Helms .40 .12
❑ 511 John Smoltz .60 .18
❑ 512 Chipper Jones 1.00 .30
❑ 513 Jason Marquis .40 .12
❑ 514 Mark DeRosa .40 .12
❑ 515 Jung Bong .40 .12
❑ 516 Kevin Gryboski RC .40 .12
❑ 517 Damian Moss .40 .12
❑ 518 Horacio Ramirez .40 .12
❑ 519 Scott Sobkowiak .40 .12
❑ 520 Billy Sylvester .40 .12
❑ 521 Nick Green .40 .12
❑ 522 Travis Wilson UER .40 .12
Mistakenly numbered as 617
❑ 523 Ryan Langerhans .40 .12
❑ 524 John Ennis RC .60 .18
❑ 525 John Foster RC .60 .18
❑ 526 Keith Lockhart .40 .12
❑ 527 Julio Franco .40 .12
❑ 528 Richie Sexson .40 .12
❑ 529 Jeffrey Hammonds .40 .12
❑ 530 Ben Sheets .40 .12
❑ 531 Mike DeJean .40 .12
❑ 532 Mark Loretta .40 .12
❑ 533 Alex Ochoa .40 .12
❑ 534 Jamey Wright .40 .12
❑ 535 Jose Hernandez .40 .12
❑ 536 Glendon Rusch .40 .12
❑ 537 Geoff Jenkins .40 .12
❑ 538 Luis Lopez .40 .12
❑ 539 Curtis Leskanic .40 .12
❑ 540 Chad Fox .40 .12
❑ 541 Tyler Houston .40 .12
❑ 542 Nick Neugebauer .40 .12
❑ 543 Matt Stairs .40 .12
❑ 544 Paul Rigdon .40 .12
❑ 545 Bill Hall .40 .12
❑ 546 Luis Vizcaino .40 .12
❑ 547 Lenny Harris .40 .12
❑ 548 Alex Sanchez .40 .12
❑ 549 Raul Casanova .40 .12
❑ 550 Eric Young .40 .12
❑ 551 Jeff Deardorff .40 .12
❑ 552 Nelson Figueroa .40 .12
❑ 553 Ron Belliard .40 .12
❑ 554 Mike Buddie .40 .12
❑ 555 Jose Cabrera .40 .12
❑ 556 J.M. Gold .40 .12
❑ 557 Ray King .40 .12
❑ 558 Jose Mieses .40 .12
❑ 559 Takahito Nomura RC .60 .18
❑ 560 Ruben Quevedo .40 .12
❑ 561 Jackson Melian .40 .12
❑ 562 Cristian Guerrero .40 .12
❑ 563 Paul Bako .40 .12
❑ 564 Luis Martinez RC 1.00 .30
❑ 565 Brian Mallette RC .40 .12
❑ 566 Matt Morris .40 .12
❑ 567 Tino Martinez .60 .18
❑ 568 Fernando Vina .40 .12
❑ 569 Gene Stechschulte .40 .12
❑ 570 Andy Benes .40 .12
❑ 571 Placido Polanco .40 .12
❑ 572 Luis Garcia .40 .12
❑ 573 Jim Edmonds .40 .12
❑ 574 Bud Smith .40 .12
❑ 575 Mike Matheny .40 .12
❑ 576 Garrett Stephenson .40 .12
❑ 577 Miguel Cairo .40 .12
❑ 578 Darryl Kile .40 .12
❑ 579 Mike Timlin .40 .12
❑ 580 Rick Ankiel .40 .12
❑ 581 Jason Isringhausen .40 .12
❑ 582 Albert Pujols UER 2.00 .60
He is credited with a 13 yr career on the back
❑ 583 Eli Marrero .40 .12
❑ 584 Steve Kline .40 .12
❑ 585 J.D. Drew .40 .12
❑ 586 Mike DiFelice .40 .12
❑ 587 Dave Veres .40 .12
❑ 588 Kerry Robinson .40 .12
❑ 589 Edgar Renteria .40 .12
❑ 590 Woody Williams .40 .12
❑ 591 Chance Caple .40 .12
❑ 592 Mike Crudale RC .60 .18
❑ 593 Luther Hackman .40 .12
❑ 594 Josh Pearce .40 .12
❑ 595 Kevin Joseph .40 .12
❑ 596 Jim Journell .40 .12
❑ 597 Jeremy Lambert RC .60 .18
❑ 598 Mike Matthews .40 .12
❑ 599 Les Walrond .40 .12
❑ 600 Keith McDonald .40 .12
❑ 601 William Ortega .40 .12
❑ 602 Scotty Layfield RC .60 .18
❑ 603 So Taguchi RC 1.00 .30
❑ 604 Eduardo Perez .40 .12
❑ 605 Sammy Sosa 1.50 .45
❑ 606 Kerry Wood 1.00 .30
❑ 607 Kyle Farnsworth .40 .12
❑ 608 Alex Gonzalez .40 .12
❑ 609 Tom Gordon .40 .12
❑ 610 Carlos Zambrano .40 .12
❑ 611 Roosevelt Brown .40 .12
❑ 612 Bill Mueller .40 .12
❑ 613 Mark Prior 3.00 .90
❑ 614 Darren Lewis .40 .12
❑ 615 Joe Girardi .40 .12
❑ 616 Fred McGriff .60 .18
❑ 617 Jon Lieber .40 .12
❑ 618 Robert Machado .40 .12
❑ 619 Corey Patterson .40 .12
❑ 620 Joe Borowski .40 .12
❑ 621 Todd Hundley .40 .12
❑ 622 Jason Bere .40 .12
❑ 623 Moises Alou .40 .12
❑ 624 Jeff Fassero .40 .12
❑ 625 Jesus Sanchez .40 .12
❑ 626 Chris Stynes .40 .12
❑ 627 Delino Deshields .40 .12
❑ 628 Augie Ojeda .40 .12
❑ 629 Juan Cruz .40 .12
❑ 630 Ben Christensen .40 .12
❑ 631 Mike Meyers .40 .12
❑ 632 Will Ohman .40 .12
❑ 633 Steve Smyth .40 .12
❑ 634 Mark Bellhorn .40 .12
❑ 635 Nate Frese .40 .12
❑ 636 David Kelton .40 .12
❑ 637 Francis Beltran RC .60 .18
❑ 638 Antonio Alfonseca .40 .12
❑ 639 Donovan Osborne .40 .12
❑ 640 Shawn Sonnier .40 .12

	No.	Player		
❑	641	Matt Clement	.40	.12
❑	642	Luis Gonzalez	.40	.12
❑	643	Brian Anderson	.40	.12
❑	644	Randy Johnson	1.00	.30
❑	645	Mark Grace	1.00	.30
❑	646	Danny Bautista	.40	.12
❑	647	Junior Spivey	.40	.12
❑	648	Jay Bell	.40	.12
❑	649	Miguel Batista	.40	.12
❑	650	Tony Womack	.40	.12
❑	651	Byung-Hyun Kim	.40	.12
❑	652	Steve Finley	.40	.12
❑	653	Rick Helling	.40	.12
❑	654	Curt Schilling	.60	.18
❑	655	Erubiel Durazo	.40	.12
❑	656	Chris Donnels	.40	.12
❑	657	Greg Colbrunn	.40	.12
❑	658	Mike Morgan	.40	.12
❑	659	Jose Guillen	.40	.12
❑	660	Matt Williams	.40	.12
❑	661	Craig Counsell	.40	.12
❑	662	Greg Swindell	.40	.12
❑	663	Rod Barajas	.40	.12
❑	664	David Dellucci	.40	.12
❑	665	Todd Stottlemyre	.40	.12
❑	666	P.J. Bevis RC	.60	.18
❑	667	Mike Koplove	.40	.12
❑	668	Mike Myers	.40	.12
❑	669	John Patterson	.40	.12
❑	670	Bret Prinz	.40	.12
❑	671	Jeremy Ward RC	.60	.18
❑	672	Danny Klassen	.40	.12
❑	673	Luis Terrero	.40	.12
❑	674	Jose Valverde RC	1.00	.30
❑	675	Doug Devore RC	.60	.18
❑	676	Quinton McCracken	.40	.12
❑	677	Paul LoDuca	.40	.12
❑	678	Mark Grudzielanek	.40	.12
❑	679	Kevin Brown	.40	.12
❑	680	Paul Quantrill	.40	.12
❑	681	Shawn Green	.40	.12
❑	682	Hideo Nomo	1.00	.30
❑	683	Eric Gagne	.60	.18
❑	684	Giovanni Carrara	.40	.12
❑	685	Marquis Grissom	.40	.12
❑	686	Hiram Bocachica	.40	.12
❑	687	Guillermo Mota	.40	.12
❑	688	Alex Cora	.40	.12
❑	689	Odalis Perez	.40	.12
❑	690	Brian Jordan	.40	.12
❑	691	Andy Ashby	.40	.12
❑	692	Eric Karros	.40	.12
❑	693	Chad Kreuter	.40	.12
❑	694	Dave Roberts	.40	.12
❑	695	Omar Daal	.40	.12
❑	696	Dave Hansen	.40	.12
❑	697	Adrian Beltre	.40	.12
❑	698	Terry Mulholland	.40	.12
❑	699	Cesar Izturis	.40	.12
❑	700	Steve Colyer	.40	.12
❑	701	Carlos Garcia	.40	.12
❑	702	Ricardo Rodriguez	.40	.12
❑	703	Jose Diaz RC	.60	.18
❑	704	Jeff Reboulet	.40	.12
❑	705	Victor Alvarez RC	.60	.18
❑	706	Kazuhisa Ishii RC	2.50	.75
❑	707	Jose Vidro	.40	.12
❑	708	Henry Mateo	.40	.12
❑	709	Tony Armas Jr.	.40	.12
❑	710	Carl Pavano	.40	.12
❑	711	Peter Bergeron	.40	.12
❑	712	Bruce Chen	.40	.12
❑	713	Orlando Cabrera	.40	.12
❑	714	Britt Reames	.40	.12
❑	715	Masato Yoshii	.40	.12
❑	716	Fernando Tatis	.40	.12
❑	717	Graeme Lloyd	.40	.12
❑	718	Scott Stewart	.40	.12
❑	719	Lou Collier	.40	.12
❑	720	Michael Barrett	.40	.12
❑	721	Vladimir Guerrero	1.00	.30
❑	722	Troy Mattes	.40	.12
❑	723	Brian Schneider	.40	.12
❑	724	Lee Stevens	.40	.12
❑	725	Javier Vazquez	.40	.12
❑	726	Brad Wilkerson	.40	.12
❑	727	Zach Day	.40	.12
❑	728	Ed Vosberg	.40	.12
❑	729	Tomo Ohka	.40	.12
❑	730	Mike Mordecai	.40	.12
❑	731	Donnie Bridges	.40	.12
❑	732	Ron Chiavacci	.40	.12
❑	733	T.J. Tucker	.40	.12
❑	734	Scott Hodges	.40	.12
❑	735	Valentino Pascucci	.40	.12
❑	736	Andres Galarraga	.40	.12
❑	737	Scott Downs	.40	.12
❑	738	Eric Good RC	.60	.18
❑	739	Ron Calloway RC	.60	.18
❑	740	Jorge Nunez RC	.60	.18
❑	741	Henry Rodriguez	.40	.12
❑	742	Jeff Kent	.40	.12
❑	743	Russ Ortiz	.40	.12
❑	744	Felix Rodriguez	.40	.12
❑	745	Benito Santiago	.40	.12
❑	746	Tsuyoshi Shinjo	.40	.12
❑	747	Tim Worrell	.40	.12
❑	748	Marvin Benard	.40	.12
❑	749	Kurt Ainsworth	.40	.12
❑	750	Edwards Guzman	.40	.12
❑	751	J.T. Snow	.40	.12
❑	752	Jason Christiansen	.40	.12
❑	753	Robb Nen	.40	.12
❑	754	Barry Bonds	2.50	.75
❑	755	Shawon Dunston	.40	.12
❑	756	Chad Zerbe	.40	.12
❑	757	Ramon E. Martinez	.40	.12
❑	758	Calvin Murray	.40	.12
❑	759	Pedro Feliz	.40	.12
❑	760	Jason Schmidt	.40	.12
❑	761	Damon Minor	.40	.12
❑	762	Reggie Sanders	.40	.12
❑	763	Rich Aurilia	.40	.12
❑	764	Kirk Rueter	.40	.12
❑	765	David Bell	.40	.12
❑	766	Yorvit Torrealba	.40	.12
❑	767	Livan Hernandez	.40	.12
❑	768	Felix Diaz	.40	.12
❑	769	Aaron Fultz	.40	.12
❑	770	Ryan Jensen	.40	.12
❑	771	Arturo McDowell	.40	.12
❑	772	Carlos Valderrama	.40	.12
❑	773	Nelson Castro RC	.60	.18
❑	774	Jay Witasick	.40	.12
❑	775	Deivis Santos	.40	.12
❑	776	Josh Beckett	.60	.18
❑	777	Charles Johnson	.40	.12
❑	778	Derrek Lee	.40	.12
❑	779	A.J. Burnett	.40	.12
❑	780	Vic Darensbourg	.40	.12
❑	781	Cliff Floyd	.40	.12
❑	782	Jose Cueto	.40	.12
❑	783	Nate Teut	.40	.12
❑	784	Alex Gonzalez	.40	.12
❑	785	Brad Penny	.40	.12
❑	786	Kevin Olsen	.40	.12
❑	787	Mike Lowell	.40	.12
❑	788	Mike Redmond	.40	.12
❑	789	Braden Looper	.40	.12
❑	790	Eric Owens	.40	.12
❑	791	Andy Fox	.40	.12
❑	792	Vladimir Nunez	.40	.12
❑	793	Luis Castillo	.40	.12
❑	794	Ryan Dempster	.40	.12
❑	795	Armando Almanza	.40	.12
❑	796	Preston Wilson	.40	.12
❑	797	Pablo Ozuna	.40	.12
❑	798	Gary Knotts	.40	.12
❑	799	Ramon Castro	.40	.12
❑	800	Benito Baez	.40	.12
❑	801	Michael Tejera	.40	.12
❑	802	Claudio Vargas	.40	.12
❑	803	Chip Ambres	.40	.12
❑	804	Hansel Izquierdo RC	.60	.18
❑	805	Tim Raines Sr.	.40	.12
❑	806	Marty Malloy	.40	.12
❑	807	Julian Tavarez	.40	.12
❑	808	Roberto Alomar	1.00	.30
❑	809	Al Leiter	.40	.12
❑	810	Jeromy Burnitz	.40	.12
❑	811	John Franco	.40	.12
❑	812	Edgardo Alfonzo	.40	.12
❑	813	Mike Piazza	1.50	.45
❑	814	Shawn Estes	.40	.12
❑	815	Joe McEwing	.40	.12
❑	816	David Weathers	.40	.12
❑	817	Pedro Astacio	.40	.12
❑	818	Timo Perez	.40	.12
❑	819	Grant Roberts	.40	.12
❑	820	Rey Ordonez	.40	.12
❑	821	Steve Trachsel	.40	.12
❑	822	Roger Cedeno	.40	.12
❑	823	Mark Johnson	.40	.12
❑	824	Armando Benitez	.40	.12
❑	825	Vance Wilson	.40	.12
❑	826	Jay Payton	.40	.12
❑	827	Mo Vaughn	.40	.12
❑	828	Scott Strickland	.40	.12
❑	829	Mark Guthrie	.40	.12
❑	830	Jeff D'Amico	.40	.12
❑	831	Mark Corey RC	.60	.18
❑	832	Kane Davis	.40	.12
❑	833	Jae Weong Seo	.40	.12
❑	834	Pat Strange	.40	.12
❑	835	Adam Walker RC	.60	.18
❑	836	Tyler Walker RC	.40	.12
❑	837	Gary Matthews Jr.	.40	.12
❑	838	Jaime Cerda RC	.60	.18
❑	839	Satoru Komiyama RC	.60	.18
❑	840	Tyler Yates RC	.60	.18
❑	841	John Valentin	.40	.12
❑	842	Ryan Klesko	.40	.12
❑	843	Wiki Gonzalez	.40	.12
❑	844	Trevor Hoffman	.40	.12
❑	845	Sean Burroughs	.60	.18
❑	846	Alan Embree	.40	.12
❑	847	Dennis Tankersley	.40	.12
❑	848	D'Angelo Jimenez	.40	.12
❑	849	Kevin Jarvis	.40	.12
❑	850	Mark Kotsay	.40	.12
❑	851	Phil Nevin	.40	.12
❑	852	Jeremy Fikac	.40	.12
❑	853	Brett Tomko	.40	.12
❑	854	Brian Lawrence	.40	.12
❑	855	Steve Reed	.40	.12
❑	856	Bubba Trammell	.40	.12
❑	857	Tom Davey	.40	.12
❑	858	Ramon Vazquez	.40	.12
❑	859	Tom Lampkin	.40	.12
❑	860	Bobby Jones	.40	.12
❑	861	Ray Lankford	.40	.12
❑	862	Mark Sweeney	.40	.12
❑	863	Adam Eaton	.40	.12
❑	864	Trenidad Hubbard	.40	.12
❑	865	Jason Boyd	.40	.12
❑	866	Javier Cardona	.40	.12
❑	867	Cliff Bartosh RC	.60	.18
❑	868	Mike Bynum	.40	.12
❑	869	Eric Cyr	.40	.12
❑	870	Jose Nunez	.40	.12
❑	871	Ron Gant	.40	.12
❑	872	Deivi Cruz	.40	.12
❑	873	Ben Howard RC	.60	.18
❑	874	Todd Donovan RC	.60	.18
❑	875	Andy Shibilo RC	.60	.18
❑	876	Scott Rolen	.60	.18
❑	877	Jose Mesa	.40	.12
❑	878	Rheal Cormier	.40	.12
❑	879	Travis Lee	.40	.12
❑	880	Mike Lieberthal	.40	.12
❑	881	Brandon Duckworth	.40	.12
❑	882	David Coggin	.40	.12
❑	883	Bob Abreu	.40	.12
❑	884	Turk Wendell	.40	.12
❑	885	Marlon Byrd	.60	.18
❑	886	Jason Michaels	.40	.12
❑	887	Robert Person	.40	.12
❑	888	Tomas Perez	.40	.12
❑	889	Jimmy Rollins	.40	.12
❑	890	Vicente Padilla	.40	.12
❑	891	Pat Burrell	.40	.12
❑	892	Dave Hollins	.40	.12
❑	893	Randy Wolf	.40	.12
❑	894	Jose Santiago	.40	.12
❑	895	Doug Glanville	.40	.12
❑	896	Cliff Politte	.40	.12
❑	897	Marlon Anderson	.40	.12
❑	898	Ricky Bottalico	.40	.12

❑ 899 Terry Adams .40 .12
❑ 900 Brad Baisley .40 .12
❑ 901 Hector Mercado .40 .12
❑ 902 Elio Serrano RC .60 .18
❑ 903 Todd Pratt .40 .12
❑ 904 Pete Zamora RC .60 .18
❑ 905 Nick Punto .40 .12
❑ 906 Ricky Ledee .40 .12
❑ 907 Eric Junge RC .60 .18
❑ 908 Anderson Machado RC 1.00 .30
❑ 909 Jorge Padilla RC 1.00 .30
❑ 910 John Mabry .40 .12
❑ 911 Brian Giles .40 .12
❑ 912 Jason Kendall .40 .12
❑ 913 Jack Wilson .40 .12
❑ 914 Kris Benson .40 .12
❑ 915 Aramis Ramirez .40 .12
❑ 916 Mike Fetters .40 .12
❑ 917 Adrian Brown .40 .12
❑ 918 Pokey Reese .40 .12
❑ 919 Dave Williams .40 .12
❑ 920 Mike Benjamin .40 .12
❑ 921 Kip Wells .40 .12
❑ 922 Mike Williams .40 .12
❑ 923 Pat Meares .40 .12
❑ 924 Ron Villone .40 .12
❑ 925 Armando Rios .40 .12
❑ 926 Jimmy Anderson .40 .12
❑ 927 Rob Mackowiak .40 .12
❑ 928 Kevin Young .40 .12
❑ 929 Brian Boehringer .40 .12
❑ 930 Joe Beimel .40 .12
❑ 931 Chad Hermansen .40 .12
❑ 932 Scott Sauerbeck .40 .12
❑ 933 Josh Fogg .40 .12
❑ 934 Mike Gonzalez RC .60 .18
❑ 935 Mike Lincoln .40 .12
❑ 936 Sean Lowe .40 .12
❑ 937 Matt Guerrier .40 .12
❑ 938 Ryan Vogelsong .40 .12
❑ 939 J.R. House .40 .12
❑ 940 Craig Wilson .40 .12
❑ 941 Tony Alvarez .40 .12
❑ 942 J.J. Davis .40 .12
❑ 943 Abraham Nunez .40 .12
❑ 944 Adrian Burnside RC .60 .18
❑ 945 Ken Griffey Jr. 1.50 .45
❑ 946 Jimmy Haynes .40 .12
❑ 947 Juan Castro .40 .12
❑ 948 Jose Rijo .40 .12
❑ 949 Corky Miller .40 .12
❑ 950 Elmer Dessens .40 .12
❑ 951 Aaron Boone .40 .12
❑ 952 Juan Encarnacion .40 .12
❑ 953 Chris Reitsma .40 .12
❑ 954 Wilton Guerrero .40 .12
❑ 955 Danny Graves .40 .12
❑ 956 Jim Brower .40 .12
❑ 957 Barry Larkin 1.00 .30
❑ 958 Todd Walker .40 .12
❑ 959 Gabe White .40 .12
❑ 960 Adam Dunn .60 .18
❑ 961 Jason LaRue .40 .12
❑ 962 Reggie Taylor .40 .12
❑ 963 Sean Casey .40 .12
❑ 964 Scott Williamson .40 .12
❑ 965 Austin Kearns 1.00 .30
❑ 966 Kelly Stinnett .40 .12
❑ 967 Jose Acevedo .40 .12
❑ 968 Gookie Dawkins .40 .12
❑ 969 Brady Clark .40 .12
❑ 970 Scott Sullivan .40 .12
❑ 971 Ricardo Aramboles .40 .12
❑ 972 Lance Davis .40 .12
❑ 973 Seth Etherton .40 .12
❑ 974 Luke Hudson .40 .12
❑ 975 Joey Hamilton .40 .12
❑ 976 Luis Pineda .40 .12
❑ 977 John Riedling .40 .12
❑ 978 Jose Silva .40 .12
❑ 979 Dane Sardinha .40 .12
❑ 980 Ben Broussard .40 .12
❑ 981 David Espinosa .40 .12
❑ 982 Ruben Mateo .40 .12
❑ 983 Larry Walker .60 .18
❑ 984 Juan Uribe .40 .12
❑ 985 Mike Hampton .40 .12
❑ 986 Aaron Cook RC 1.00 .30
❑ 987 Jose Ortiz .40 .12
❑ 988 Todd Jones .40 .12
❑ 989 Todd Helton .60 .18
❑ 990 Shawn Chacon .40 .12
❑ 991 Jason Jennings .40 .12
❑ 992 Todd Zeile .40 .12
❑ 993 Ben Petrick .40 .12
❑ 994 Denny Neagle .40 .12
❑ 995 Jose Jimenez .40 .12
❑ 996 Juan Pierre .40 .12
❑ 997 Todd Hollandsworth .40 .12
❑ 998 Kent Mercker .40 .12
❑ 999 Greg Norton .40 .12
❑ 1000 Terry Shumpert .40 .12
❑ 1001 Mark Little .40 .12
❑ 1002 Gary Bennett .40 .12
❑ 1003 Dennis Reyes .40 .12
❑ 1004 Justin Speier .40 .12
❑ 1005 John Thomson .40 .12
❑ 1006 Rick White .40 .12
❑ 1007 Colin Young RC .60 .18
❑ 1008 Cam Esslinger RC .60 .18
❑ 1009 Rene Reyes RC .60 .18
❑ 1010 Mike James .40 .12
❑ 1011 Morgan Ensberg NR .40 .12
❑ 1012 Adam Everett NR .40 .12
❑ 1013 Rodrigo Rosario NR .40 .12
❑ 1014 Carlos Pena NR .40 .12
❑ 1015 Eric Hinske NR .40 .12
❑ 1016 Orlando Hudson NR .40 .12
❑ 1017 Reed Johnson NR .50 .15
❑ 1018 Jung Bong NR .40 .12
❑ 1019 Bill Hall NR .40 .12
❑ 1020 Mark Prior NR 1.50 .45
❑ 1021 Francis Beltran NR .40 .12
❑ 1022 David Kelton NR .40 .12
❑ 1023 Felix Escalona NR .40 .12
❑ 1024 Jorge Sosa NR .40 .12
❑ 1025 Dewon Brazelton NR .40 .12
❑ 1026 Jose Valverde NR .40 .12
❑ 1027 Luis Terrero NR .40 .12
❑ 1028 Kazuhisa Ishii NR 1.25 .35
❑ 1029 Cesar Izturis NR .40 .12
❑ 1030 Ryan Jensen NR .40 .12
❑ 1031 Matt Thornton NR .40 .12
❑ 1032 Hansel Izquierdo NR .40 .12
❑ 1033 Jaime Cerda NR .40 .12
❑ 1034 Erik Bedard NR .40 .12
❑ 1035 Sean Burroughs NR .40 .12
❑ 1036 Ben Howard NR .40 .12
❑ 1037 Ramon Vazquez NR .40 .12
❑ 1038 Marlon Byrd NR .40 .12
❑ 1039 Josh Fogg NR .40 .12
❑ 1040 Hank Blalock NR .75 .23
❑ 1041 Mark Teixeira NR .75 .23
❑ 1042 Kevin Mench NR .40 .12
❑ 1043 Dane Sardinha NR .40 .12
❑ 1044 Austin Kearns NR .50 .15
❑ 1045 Rene Reyes NR .40 .12
❑ 1046 Eric Munson NR .40 .12
❑ 1047 Jon Rauch NR .40 .12
❑ 1048 Nick Johnson NR .40 .12
❑ 1049 Alex Graman NR .40 .12
❑ 1050 Drew Henson NR .40 .12
❑ 1051 Darin Erstad HM .40 .12
❑ 1052 Garret Anderson HM .40 .12
❑ 1053 Craig Biggio HM .40 .12
❑ 1054 Lance Berkman HM .40 .12
❑ 1055 Jeff Bagwell HM .40 .12
❑ 1056 Shannon Stewart HM .40 .12
❑ 1057 Chipper Jones HM .60 .18
❑ 1058 J.D. Drew HM .40 .12
❑ 1059 Moises Alou HM .40 .12
❑ 1060 Mark Grace HM .60 .18
❑ 1061 Jose Vidro HM .40 .12
❑ 1062 Vladimir Guerrero HM .60 .18
❑ 1063 Matt Lawton HM .40 .12
❑ 1064 Ichiro Suzuki HM 1.00 .30
❑ 1065 Edgar Martinez HM .40 .12
❑ 1066 John Olerud HM .40 .12
❑ 1067 Jeff Cirillo HM .40 .12
❑ 1068 Mike Lowell HM .40 .12
❑ 1069 Mike Piazza HM 1.00 .30
❑ 1070 Roberto Alomar HM .60 .18
❑ 1071 Bob Abreu HM .40 .12
❑ 1072 Jason Kendall HM .40 .12
❑ 1073 Brian Giles HM .40 .12
❑ 1074 Rafael Palmeiro HM .40 .12
❑ 1075 Ivan Rodriguez HM .60 .18
❑ 1076 Alex Rodriguez HM 1.00 .30
❑ 1077 Juan Gonzalez HM .60 .18
❑ 1078 Nomar Garciaparra HM 1.00 .30
❑ 1079 Manny Ramirez HM .40 .12
❑ 1080 Sean Casey HM .40 .12
❑ 1081 Barry Larkin HM .60 .18
❑ 1082 Larry Walker HM .40 .12
❑ 1083 Carlos Beltran HM .40 .12
❑ 1084 Corey Koskie HM .40 .12
❑ 1085 Magglio Ordonez HM .40 .12
❑ 1086 Frank Thomas HM 1.00 .30
❑ 1087 Kenny Lofton HM .40 .12
❑ 1088 Derek Jeter HM 1.25 .35
❑ 1089 Bernie Williams HM .40 .12
❑ 1090 Jason Giambi HM .60 .18
❑ 1091 Troy Glaus PC .40 .12
❑ 1092 Jeff Bagwell PC .40 .12
❑ 1093 Lance Berkman PC .40 .12
❑ 1094 David Justice PC .40 .12
❑ 1095 Eric Chavez PC .40 .12
❑ 1096 Carlos Delgado PC .40 .12
❑ 1097 Gary Sheffield PC .40 .12
❑ 1098 Chipper Jones PC .60 .18
❑ 1099 Andruw Jones PC .40 .12
❑ 1100 Richie Sexson PC .40 .12
❑ 1101 Albert Pujols PC 1.00 .30
❑ 1102 Sammy Sosa PC 1.00 .30
❑ 1103 Fred McGriff PC .40 .12
❑ 1104 Greg Vaughn PC .40 .12
❑ 1105 Matt Williams PC .40 .12
❑ 1106 Luis Gonzalez PC .40 .12
❑ 1107 Shawn Green PC .40 .12
❑ 1108 Andres Galarraga PC .40 .12
❑ 1109 Vladimir Guerrero PC .60 .18
❑ 1110 Barry Bonds PC 1.25 .35
❑ 1111 Rich Aurilia PC .40 .12
❑ 1112 Ellis Burks PC .40 .12
❑ 1113 Jim Thome PC .60 .18
❑ 1114 Bret Boone PC .40 .12
❑ 1115 Cliff Floyd PC .40 .12
❑ 1116 Mike Piazza PC 1.00 .30
❑ 1117 Jeromy Burnitz PC .40 .12
❑ 1118 Phil Nevin PC .40 .12
❑ 1119 Brian Giles PC .40 .12
❑ 1120 Rafael Palmeiro PC .40 .12
❑ 1121 Juan Gonzalez PC .60 .18
❑ 1122 Alex Rodriguez PC 1.00 .30
❑ 1123 Manny Ramirez PC .40 .12
❑ 1124 Ken Griffey Jr. PC 1.00 .30
❑ 1125 Larry Walker PC .40 .12
❑ 1126 Todd Helton PC .40 .12
❑ 1127 Mike Sweeney PC .40 .12
❑ 1128 Frank Thomas PC 1.00 .30
❑ 1129 Paul Konerko PC .40 .12
❑ 1130 Jason Giambi PC .60 .18
❑ 1131 Aaron Sele RT .40 .12
❑ 1132 Roy Oswalt RT .40 .12
❑ 1133 Wade Miller RT .40 .12
❑ 1134 Tim Hudson RT .40 .12
❑ 1135 Barry Zito RT .60 .18
❑ 1136 Mark Mulder RT .40 .12
❑ 1137 Greg Maddux RT 1.00 .30
❑ 1138 Tom Glavine RT .60 .18
❑ 1139 Ben Sheets RT .40 .12
❑ 1140 Darryl Kile RT .40 .12
❑ 1141 Matt Morris RT .40 .12
❑ 1142 Kerry Wood RT .60 .18
❑ 1143 Jon Lieber RT .40 .12
❑ 1144 Juan Cruz RT .40 .12
❑ 1145 Randy Johnson RT .60 .18
❑ 1146 Curt Schilling RT .40 .12
❑ 1147 Kevin Brown RT .40 .12
❑ 1148 Javier Vazquez RT .40 .12
❑ 1149 Russ Ortiz RT .40 .12
❑ 1150 C.C. Sabathia RT .40 .12
❑ 1151 Bartolo Colon RT .40 .12
❑ 1152 Freddy Garcia RT .40 .12
❑ 1153 Jamie Moyer RT .40 .12
❑ 1154 Josh Beckett RT .40 .12
❑ 1155 Brad Penny RT .40 .12
❑ 1156 Al Leiter RT .40 .12

	Card	MINT	NRMT
❑	1157 Brandon Duckworth RT	.40	.12
❑	1158 Robert Person RT	.40	.12
❑	1159 Kris Benson RT	.40	.12
❑	1160 Chan Ho Park RT	.40	.12
❑	1161 Pedro Martinez RT	.60	.18
❑	1162 Mike Hampton RT	.40	.12
❑	1163 Jeff Weaver RT	.40	.12
❑	1164 Joe Mays RT	.40	.12
❑	1165 Brad Radke RT	.40	.12
❑	1166 Eric Milton RT	.40	.12
❑	1167 Roger Clemens RT	1.00	.30
❑	1168 Mike Mussina RT	.60	.18
❑	1169 Andy Pettitte RT	.40	.12
❑	1170 David Wells RT	.40	.12
❑	1171 Ken Griffey Jr. CL	1.00	.30
❑	1172 Ichiro Suzuki CL	1.00	.30
❑	1173 Jason Giambi CL	.60	.18
❑	1174 Alex Rodriguez CL	1.00	.30
❑	1175 Sammy Sosa CL	1.00	.30
❑	1176 Nomar Garciaparra CL	1.00	.30
❑	1177 Barry Bonds CL	1.25	.35
❑	1178 Mike Piazza CL	1.00	.30
❑	1179 Derek Jeter CL	1.25	.35
❑	1180 Randy Johnson CL	.60	.18
❑	1181 Jeff Bagwell CL	.40	.12
❑	1182 Albert Pujols CL	1.00	.30

2003 Upper Deck 40-Man

	MINT	NRMT
COMPLETE SET (990)	250.00	110.00
COMMON NR (877-960)	.40	.18
COMMON NR RC (877-960)	.40	.18

	Card	MINT	NRMT
❑	1 Troy Glaus	.60	.25
❑	2 Darin Erstad	.40	.18
❑	3 Garret Anderson	.40	.18
❑	4 Aaron Sele	.40	.18
❑	5 Adam Kennedy	.40	.18
❑	6 Scott Spiezio	.40	.18
❑	7 Troy Percival	.40	.18
❑	8 David Eckstein	.40	.18
❑	9 Ramon Ortiz	.40	.18
❑	10 Bengie Molina	.40	.18
❑	11 Tim Salmon	.60	.25
❑	12 John Lackey	.40	.18
❑	13 Brad Fullmer	.40	.18
❑	14 Jarrod Washburn	.40	.18
❑	15 Shawn Wooten	.40	.18
❑	16 Kevin Appier	.40	.18
❑	17 Ben Weber	.40	.18
❑	18 Eric Owens	.40	.18
❑	19 Matt Wise	.40	.18
❑	20 Francisco Rodriguez	.40	.18
❑	21 Scot Shields	.40	.18
❑	22 Jose Molina	.40	.18
❑	23 Scott Schoeneweis	.40	.18
❑	24 Derrick Turnbow	.40	.18
❑	25 Benji Gil	.40	.18
❑	26 Julio Ramirez	.40	.18
❑	27 Mickey Callaway	.40	.18
❑	28 Barry Zito	1.00	.45
❑	29 Tim Hudson	.40	.18
❑	30 Mark Mulder	.40	.18
❑	31 Eric Chavez	.40	.18
❑	32 Miguel Tejada	.40	.18
❑	33 Terrence Long	.40	.18
❑	34 Jermaine Dye	.40	.18
❑	35 Erubiel Durazo	.40	.18
❑	36 Scott Hatteberg	.40	.18
❑	37 Chris Singleton	.40	.18
❑	38 Keith Foulke	.40	.18
❑	39 John Halama	.40	.18
❑	40 Mark Ellis	.40	.18
❑	41 Ted Lilly	.40	.18
❑	42 Jim Mecir	.40	.18
❑	43 Adam Piatt	.40	.18
❑	44 Freddie Bynum	.40	.18
❑	45 Adam Morrissey	.40	.18
❑	46 Jeremy Fikac	.40	.18
❑	47 Ricardo Rincon	.40	.18
❑	48 Ramon Hernandez	.40	.18
❑	49 Micah Bowie	.40	.18
❑	50 Chad Bradford	.40	.18
❑	51 Eric Byrnes	.40	.18
❑	52 Ron Gant	.40	.18
❑	53 Jose Flores	.40	.18
❑	54 Mark Johnson	.40	.18
❑	55 Carlos Delgado	.40	.18
❑	56 Orlando Hudson	.40	.18
❑	57 Kelvim Escobar	.40	.18
❑	58 Eric Hinske	.40	.18
❑	59 Doug Creek	.40	.18
❑	60 Josh Phelps	.40	.18
❑	61 Shannon Stewart	.40	.18
❑	62 Roy Halladay	.40	.18
❑	63 Vernon Wells	.40	.18
❑	64 Mark Hendrickson	.40	.18
❑	65 Mike Bordick	.40	.18
❑	66 Jayson Werth	.40	.18
❑	67 Chris Woodward	.40	.18
❑	68 Ken Huckaby	.40	.18
❑	69 Frank Catalanotto	.40	.18
❑	70 Jason Kershner	.40	.18
❑	71 Greg Myers	.40	.18
❑	72 Tanyon Sturtze	.40	.18
❑	73 Trever Miller	.40	.18
❑	74 Pete Walker	.40	.18
❑	75 Alexis Rios	.40	.18
❑	76 Tom Wilson	.40	.18
❑	77 Dave Berg	.40	.18
❑	78 Doug Linton	.40	.18
❑	79 Cliff Politte UER Career IP total is wrong	.40	.18
❑	80 Damion Easley	.40	.18
❑	81 Toby Hall	.40	.18
❑	82 George Lombard	.40	.18
❑	83 Ben Grieve	.40	.18
❑	84 Aubrey Huff	.40	.18
❑	85 Jesus Colome	.40	.18
❑	86 Dewon Brazelton	.40	.18
❑	87 Rey Ordonez	.40	.18
❑	88 Al Martin	.40	.18
❑	89 Carl Crawford	.40	.18
❑	90 Travis Lee	.40	.18
❑	91 Marlon Anderson	.40	.18
❑	92 Javier Valentin	.40	.18
❑	93 Joe Kennedy	.40	.18
❑	94 Jorge Sosa	.40	.18
❑	95 Travis Harper	.40	.18
❑	96 Bobby Seay	.40	.18
❑	97 Seth McClung	.40	.18
❑	98 Delvin James	.40	.18
❑	99 Victor Zambrano	.40	.18
❑	100 Terry Shumpert	.40	.18
❑	101 Josh Hamilton	.40	.18
❑	102 Jared Sandberg	.40	.18
❑	103 Steve Parris	.40	.18
❑	104 C.C. Sabathia	.40	.18
❑	105 Omar Vizquel	.40	.18
❑	106 Milton Bradley	.40	.18
❑	107 Ellis Burks	.40	.18
❑	108 Danys Baez	.40	.18
❑	109 Jason Davis	.40	.18
❑	110 Terry Mulholland	.40	.18
❑	111 Matt Lawton	.40	.18
❑	112 Alex Escobar	.40	.18
❑	113 Mark Wohlers	.40	.18
❑	114 Josh Bard	.40	.18
❑	115 Bill Selby	.40	.18
❑	116 Brandon Phillips	.40	.18
❑	117 Jason Bere	.40	.18
❑	118 Casey Blake	.40	.18
❑	119 Travis Hafner	.40	.18
❑	120 Brian Anderson	.40	.18
❑	121 David Riske	.40	.18
❑	122 Karim Garcia	.40	.18
❑	123 Ricardo Rodriguez	.40	.18
❑	124 Carl Sadler	.40	.18
❑	125 Jose Santiago	.40	.18
❑	126 Tim Laker	.40	.18
❑	127 John McDonald	.40	.18
❑	128 Jake Westbrook	.40	.18
❑	129 Ichiro Suzuki	2.00	.90
❑	130 Freddy Garcia	.40	.18
❑	131 Edgar Martinez	.60	.25
❑	132 Ben Davis	.40	.18
❑	133 Shigetoshi Hasegawa	.40	.18
❑	134 Carlos Guillen	.40	.18
❑	135 Randy Winn	.40	.18
❑	136 John Mabry	.40	.18
❑	137 Matt Thornton	.40	.18
❑	138 Bret Boone	.40	.18
❑	139 Jamie Moyer	.40	.18
❑	140 Giovanni Carrara	.40	.18
❑	141 Kazuhiro Sasaki	.40	.18
❑	142 Jeff Cirillo	.40	.18
❑	143 Mark McLemore	.40	.18
❑	144 Pat Borders	.40	.18
❑	145 Mike Cameron	.40	.18
❑	146 Dan Wilson	.40	.18
❑	147 John Olerud	.40	.18
❑	148 Arthur Rhodes	.40	.18
❑	149 Rafael Soriano	.40	.18
❑	150 Greg Colbrunn	.40	.18
❑	151 Ryan Franklin	.40	.18
❑	152 Joel Pineiro	.40	.18
❑	153 Jeff Nelson	.40	.18
❑	154 Jerry Hairston Jr.	.40	.18
❑	155 Rick Helling	.40	.18
❑	156 Gary Matthews Jr.	.40	.18
❑	157 Jeff Conine	.40	.18
❑	158 Sidney Ponson	.40	.18
❑	159 Tony Batista	.40	.18
❑	160 Jay Gibbons	.40	.18
❑	161 Marty Cordova	.40	.18
❑	162 Geronimo Gil	.40	.18
❑	163 Deivi Cruz	.40	.18
❑	164 B.J. Ryan	.40	.18
❑	165 Jason Johnson	.40	.18
❑	166 Buddy Groom	.40	.18
❑	167 Pat Hentgen	.40	.18
❑	168 Omar Daal	.40	.18
❑	169 Willis Roberts	.40	.18
❑	170 Scott Erickson	.40	.18
❑	171 David Segui	.40	.18
❑	172 Brook Fordyce	.40	.18
❑	173 Rodrigo Lopez	.40	.18
❑	174 Jose Leon	.40	.18
❑	175 Jose Morban	.40	.18
❑	176 Melvin Mora	.40	.18
❑	177 B.J. Surhoff	.40	.18
❑	178 Jorge Julio	.40	.18
❑	179 Alex Rodriguez	2.00	.90
❑	180 Mark Teixeira	.60	.25
❑	181 Chan Ho Park	.40	.18
❑	182 Todd Van Poppel	.40	.18
❑	183 Todd Greene	.40	.18
❑	184 Ismael Valdes	.40	.18
❑	185 Rusty Greer	.40	.18
❑	186 Rafael Palmeiro	.60	.25
❑	187 Francisco Cordero	.40	.18
❑	188 Einar Diaz	.40	.18
❑	189 Doug Glanville	.40	.18
❑	190 Michael Young	.40	.18
❑	191 Kevin Mench	.40	.18
❑	192 Carl Everett	.40	.18
❑	193 Herbert Perry	.40	.18
❑	194 Jeff Zimmerman	.40	.18
❑	195 Juan Gonzalez	1.00	.45
❑	196 Ugueth Urbina	.40	.18
❑	197 Jermaine Clark	.40	.18
❑	198 John Thomson	.40	.18
❑	199 Hank Blalock	.60	.25
❑	200 Jay Powell	.40	.18
❑	201 Mike Lamb	.40	.18
❑	202 Aaron Fultz	.40	.18
❑	203 Esteban Yan	.40	.18
❑	204 Nomar Garciaparra	2.00	.90

❑ 205 Pedro Martinez 1.00 .45
❑ 206 John Burkett .40 .18
❑ 207 Johnny Damon .40 .18
❑ 208 Doug Mirabelli .40 .18
❑ 209 Derek Lowe .40 .18
❑ 210 Shea Hillenbrand .40 .18
❑ 211 Brandon Lyon .40 .18
❑ 212 Trot Nixon .40 .18
❑ 213 Jason Varitek .40 .18
❑ 214 Tim Wakefield .40 .18
❑ 215 Manny Ramirez .40 .18
❑ 216 Todd Walker .40 .18
❑ 217 Jeremy Giambi .40 .18
❑ 218 Ramiro Mendoza .40 .18
❑ 219 Bill Mueller .40 .18
❑ 220 David Ortiz .40 .18
❑ 221 Mike Timlin .40 .18
❑ 222 Alan Embree .40 .18
❑ 223 Bob Howry .40 .18
❑ 224 Chad Fox .40 .18
❑ 225 Damian Jackson .40 .18
❑ 226 Casey Fossum .40 .18
❑ 227 Steve Woodard .40 .18
❑ 228 Freddy Sanchez .40 .18
❑ 229 Mike Sweeney .40 .18
❑ 230 Desi Relaford .40 .18
❑ 231 Brent Mayne .40 .18
❑ 232 Angel Berroa .40 .18
❑ 233 Albie Lopez .40 .18
❑ 234 Raul Ibanez .40 .18
❑ 235 Joe Randa .40 .18
❑ 236 Chris George .40 .18
❑ 237 Michael Tucker .40 .18
❑ 238 Mendy Lopez .40 .18
❑ 239 Kris Wilson .40 .18
❑ 240 Jason Grimsley .40 .18
❑ 241 Carlos Febles .40 .18
❑ 242 Runelvys Hernandez .40 .18
❑ 243 Mike MacDougal .40 .18
❑ 244 Carlos Beltran .40 .18
❑ 245 Brandon Berger .40 .18
❑ 246 Darrell May .40 .18
❑ 247 Miguel Asencio .40 .18
❑ 248 Ryan Bukvich .40 .18
❑ 249 Dee Brown .40 .18
❑ 250 Jeremy Hill .40 .18
❑ 251 Jeremy Affeldt .40 .18
❑ 252 Ken Harvey .40 .18
❑ 253 Bobby Higginson .40 .18
❑ 254 Matt Anderson .40 .18
❑ 255 Dmitri Young .40 .18
❑ 256 Gene Kingsale .40 .18
❑ 257 Craig Paquette .40 .18
❑ 258 Adam Bernero .40 .18
❑ 259 Andres Torres .40 .18
❑ 260 Carlos Pena .40 .18
❑ 261 Dean Palmer .40 .18
❑ 262 Eric Munson .40 .18
❑ 263 Omar Infante .40 .18
❑ 264 Shane Halter .40 .18
❑ 265 Jeremy Bonderman RC 2.50 1.10
❑ 266 Steve Sparks .40 .18
❑ 267 Gary Knotts .40 .18
❑ 268 Mike Maroth .40 .18
❑ 269 Nate Cornejo .40 .18
❑ 270 Matt Roney .40 .18
❑ 271 Franklyn German .40 .18
❑ 272 Matt Walbeck .40 .18
❑ 273 Brandon Inge .40 .18
❑ 274 Hiram Bocachica .40 .18
❑ 275 Chris Spurling .40 .18
❑ 276 Craig Monroe .40 .18
❑ 277 Ramon Santiago .40 .18
❑ 278 Doug Mientkiewicz .40 .18
❑ 279 Torii Hunter .40 .18
❑ 280 Brad Radke .40 .18
❑ 281 Denny Hocking .40 .18
❑ 282 Tom Prince .40 .18
❑ 283 Eddie Guardado .40 .18
❑ 284 Jacque Jones .40 .18
❑ 285 Joe Mays .40 .18
❑ 286 Mike Fetters .40 .18
❑ 287 LaTroy Hawkins .40 .18
❑ 288 A.J. Pierzynski .40 .18
❑ 289 Eric Milton .40 .18
❑ 290 Cristian Guzman .40 .18
❑ 291 Bobby Kielty .40 .18
❑ 292 Corey Koskie .40 .18
❑ 293 J.C. Romero .40 .18
❑ 294 Mike Cuddyer .40 .18
❑ 295 Luis Rivas .40 .18
❑ 296 Matt LeCroy .40 .18
❑ 297 Tony Fiore .40 .18
❑ 298 Dustan Mohr .40 .18
❑ 299 Chris Gomez .40 .18
❑ 300 Johan Santana .40 .18
❑ 301 Kyle Lohse .40 .18
❑ 302 Frank Thomas 1.00 .45
❑ 303 Mark Buehrle .40 .18
❑ 304 Jon Garland .40 .18
❑ 305 Magglio Ordonez .40 .18
❑ 306 Paul Konerko .40 .18
❑ 307 Sandy Alomar Jr. .40 .18
❑ 308 Carlos Lee .40 .18
❑ 309 Jon Rauch .40 .18
❑ 310 Esteban Loaiza .40 .18
❑ 311 Gary Glover .40 .18
❑ 312 Kelly Wunsch .40 .18
❑ 313 Tony Graffanino .40 .18
❑ 314 Aaron Rowand .40 .18
❑ 315 Armando Rios .40 .18
❑ 316 Jose Valentin .40 .18
❑ 317 D'Angelo Jimenez .40 .18
❑ 318 Joe Crede .40 .18
❑ 319 Miguel Olivo .40 .18
❑ 320 Rick White .40 .18
❑ 321 Billy Koch .40 .18
❑ 322 Tom Gordon .40 .18
❑ 323 Bartolo Colon .40 .18
❑ 324 Josh Paul .40 .18
❑ 325 Joe Borchard .40 .18
❑ 326 Damaso Marte .40 .18
❑ 327 Derek Jeter 2.50 1.10
❑ 328 Jason Giambi 1.00 .45
❑ 329 Roger Clemens 2.00 .90
❑ 330 Enrique Wilson .40 .18
❑ 331 David Wells .40 .18
❑ 332 Mike Mussina 1.00 .45
❑ 333 Bernie Williams .60 .25
❑ 334 Todd Zeile .40 .18
❑ 335 Sterling Hitchcock .40 .18
❑ 336 Juan Acevedo .40 .18
❑ 337 Robin Ventura .40 .18
❑ 338 Mariano Rivera .60 .25
❑ 339 John Flaherty .40 .18
❑ 340 Andy Pettitte .60 .25
❑ 341 Antonio Osuna .40 .18
❑ 342 Erick Almonte .40 .18
❑ 343 Chris Hammond .40 .18
❑ 344 Steve Karsay .40 .18
❑ 345 Alfonso Soriano 1.00 .45
❑ 346 Bubba Trammell .40 .18
❑ 347 Nick Johnson .40 .18
❑ 348 Jorge Posada .60 .25
❑ 349 Jeff Weaver .40 .18
❑ 350 Raul Mondesi .40 .18
❑ 351 Randy Choate .40 .18
❑ 352 Drew Henson .40 .18
❑ 353 Jeff Bagwell .60 .25
❑ 354 Wade Miller .40 .18
❑ 355 Lance Berkman .40 .18
❑ 356 Julio Lugo .40 .18
❑ 357 Roy Oswalt .40 .18
❑ 358 Bruce Chen .40 .18
❑ 359 Morgan Ensberg .40 .18
❑ 360 Geoff Blum .40 .18
❑ 361 Brian Moehler .40 .18
❑ 362 Billy Wagner .40 .18
❑ 363 Pete Munro .40 .18
❑ 364 Brad Ausmus .40 .18
❑ 365 Jose Vizcaino .40 .18
❑ 366 Craig Biggio .60 .25
❑ 367 Tim Redding .40 .18
❑ 368 Gregg Zaun .40 .18
❑ 369 Octavio Dotel .40 .18
❑ 370 Carlos Hernandez .40 .18
❑ 371 Richard Hidalgo .40 .18
❑ 372 Jeriome Robertson .40 .18
❑ 373 Orlando Merced .40 .18
❑ 374 John Buck .40 .18
❑ 375 Adam Everett .40 .18
❑ 376 Raul Chavez .40 .18
❑ 377 Brad Lidge .40 .18
❑ 378 Jeff Kent .40 .18
❑ 379 Scott Linebrink .40 .18
❑ 380 Greg Miller .40 .18
❑ 381 Kirk Saarloos .40 .18
❑ 382 Brandon Puffer .40 .18
❑ 383 Ricky Stone .40 .18
❑ 384 Jason Lane .40 .18
❑ 385 Brian L. Hunter .40 .18
❑ 386 Rodrigo Rosario .40 .18
❑ 387 Horacio Ramirez .40 .18
❑ 388 Gary Sheffield .40 .18
❑ 389 Mike Hampton .40 .18
❑ 390 Robert Fick .40 .18
❑ 391 Henry Blanco .40 .18
❑ 392 Vinny Castilla .40 .18
❑ 393 Joe Dawley .40 .18
❑ 394 Jung Bong .40 .18
❑ 395 Rafael Furcal .40 .18
❑ 396 Javy Lopez .40 .18
❑ 397 Greg Maddux 2.00 .90
❑ 398 Andruw Jones .60 .25
❑ 399 John Smoltz .60 .25
❑ 400 Chipper Jones 1.00 .45
❑ 401 Mark DeRosa .40 .18
❑ 402 Shane Reynolds .40 .18
❑ 403 Kevin Gryboski .40 .18
❑ 404 Russ Ortiz .40 .18
❑ 405 Roberto Hernandez .40 .18
❑ 406 Ray King .40 .18
❑ 407 Matt Franco .40 .18
❑ 408 Marcus Giles .40 .18
❑ 409 Trey Hodges .40 .18
❑ 410 Darren Holmes .40 .18
❑ 411 Julio Franco .40 .18
❑ 412 Darren Bragg .40 .18
❑ 413 Richie Sexson .40 .18
❑ 414 Jeffrey Hammonds .40 .18
❑ 415 Ben Sheets .40 .18
❑ 416 Mike DeJean .40 .18
❑ 417 Royce Clayton .40 .18
❑ 418 Wes Helms .40 .18
❑ 419 Valerio de Los Santos .40 .18
❑ 420 Brady Clark .40 .18
❑ 421 Glendon Rusch .40 .18
❑ 422 Geoff Jenkins .40 .18
❑ 423 John Foster .40 .18
❑ 424 Curtis Leskanic .40 .18
❑ 425 Todd Ritchie .40 .18
❑ 426 Enrique Cruz .40 .18
❑ 427 Wayne Franklin .40 .18
❑ 428 Matt Ford .40 .18
❑ 429 Matt Kinney .40 .18
❑ 430 Scott Podsednik 8.00 3.60
❑ 431 Luis Vizcaino .40 .18
❑ 432 Shane Nance .40 .18
❑ 433 Alex Sanchez .40 .18
❑ 434 John Vander Wal .40 .18
❑ 435 Eric Young .40 .18
❑ 436 Eddie Perez .40 .18
❑ 437 Jason Conti .40 .18
❑ 438 Matt Morris .40 .18
❑ 439 Tino Martinez .60 .25
❑ 440 Fernando Vina .40 .18
❑ 441 Kiko Calero RC .60 .25
❑ 442 Cal Eldred .40 .18
❑ 443 Jimmy Journell .40 .18
❑ 444 Jim Edmonds .40 .18
❑ 445 Jeff Fassero .40 .18
❑ 446 Mike Matheny .40 .18
❑ 447 Garrett Stephenson .40 .18
❑ 448 Brett Tomko .40 .18
❑ 449 So Taguchi .40 .18
❑ 450 Eduardo Perez .40 .18
❑ 451 Lance Painter .40 .18
❑ 452 Jason Isringhausen .40 .18
❑ 453 Albert Pujols 2.00 .90
❑ 454 Eli Marrero .40 .18
❑ 455 Jason Simontacchi .40 .18
❑ 456 J.D. Drew .40 .18
❑ 457 Scott Rolen .60 .25
❑ 458 Orlando Palmeiro .40 .18
❑ 459 Dustin Hermanson .40 .18
❑ 460 Edgar Renteria .40 .18
❑ 461 Woody Williams .40 .18
❑ 462 Chris Carpenter .40 .18

❑ 463 Sammy Sosa 1.50 .70
❑ 464 Kerry Wood 1.00 .45
❑ 465 Kyle Farnsworth .40 .18
❑ 466 Alex Gonzalez .40 .18
❑ 467 Eric Karros .40 .18
❑ 468 Troy O'Leary .40 .18
❑ 469 Mark Grudzielanek .40 .18
❑ 470 Alan Benes .40 .18
❑ 471 Mark Prior 2.00 .90
❑ 472 Paul Bako .40 .18
❑ 473 Shawn Estes .40 .18
❑ 474 Matt Clement .40 .18
❑ 475 Ramon E. Martinez .40 .18
❑ 476 Tom Goodwin .40 .18
❑ 477 Corey Patterson .40 .18
❑ 478 Moises Alou .40 .18
❑ 479 Juan Cruz .40 .18
❑ 480 Bobby Hill .40 .18
❑ 481 Mark Bellhorn .40 .18
❑ 482 Mark Guthrie .40 .18
❑ 483 Mike Remlinger .40 .18
❑ 484 Lenny Harris .40 .18
❑ 485 Antonio Alfonseca .40 .18
❑ 486 Dave Veres .40 .18
❑ 487 Hee Seop Choi .40 .18
❑ 488 Luis Gonzalez .40 .18
❑ 489 Lyle Overbay .40 .18
❑ 490 Randy Johnson 1.00 .45
❑ 491 Mark Grace 1.00 .45
❑ 492 Danny Bautista .40 .18
❑ 493 Junior Spivey .40 .18
❑ 494 Matt Williams .40 .18
❑ 495 Miguel Batista .40 .18
❑ 496 Tony Womack .40 .18
❑ 497 Byung-Hyun Kim .40 .18
❑ 498 Steve Finley .40 .18
❑ 499 Craig Counsell .40 .18
❑ 500 Curt Schilling .60 .25
❑ 501 Elmer Dessens .40 .18
❑ 502 Rod Barajas .40 .18
❑ 503 David Dellucci .40 .18
❑ 504 Mike Koplove .40 .18
❑ 505 Mike Myers .40 .18
❑ 506 Matt Mantei .40 .18
❑ 507 Stephen Randolph RC .60 .25
❑ 508 Chad Moeller .40 .18
❑ 509 Carlos Baerga .40 .18
❑ 510 Andrew Good .40 .18
❑ 511 Quinton McCracken .40 .18
❑ 512 Jason Romano .40 .18
❑ 513 Jolbert Cabrera .40 .18
❑ 514 Darren Dreifort .40 .18
❑ 515 Kevin Brown .40 .18
❑ 516 Paul Quantrill .40 .18
❑ 517 Shawn Green .40 .18
❑ 518 Hideo Nomo 1.00 .45
❑ 519 Eric Gagne .60 .25
❑ 520 Troy Brohawn .40 .18
❑ 521 Kazuhisa Ishii .40 .18
❑ 522 Guillermo Mota .40 .18
❑ 523 Alex Cora .40 .18
❑ 524 Odalis Perez .40 .18
❑ 525 Brian Jordan .40 .18
❑ 526 Andy Ashby .40 .18
❑ 527 Fred McGriff .60 .25
❑ 528 Adrian Beltre .40 .18
❑ 529 Daryle Ward .40 .18
❑ 530 Todd Hundley .40 .18
❑ 531 David Ross .40 .18
❑ 532 Paul Shuey .40 .18
❑ 533 Paul Lo Duca .40 .18
❑ 534 Dave Roberts .40 .18
❑ 535 Mike Kinkade .40 .18
❑ 536 Cesar Izturis .40 .18
❑ 537 Ron Coomer .40 .18
❑ 538 Jose Vidro .40 .18
❑ 539 Henry Mateo .40 .18
❑ 540 Tony Armas Jr. .40 .18
❑ 541 Joey Eischen .40 .18
❑ 542 Orlando Cabrera .40 .18
❑ 543 Jose Macias .40 .18
❑ 544 Fernando Tatis .40 .18
❑ 545 Jeff Liefer .40 .18
❑ 546 Michael Barrett .40 .18
❑ 547 Vladimir Guerrero 1.00 .45
❑ 548 Javier Vazquez .40 .18
❑ 549 Brad Wilkerson .40 .18
❑ 550 Zach Day .40 .18
❑ 551 Tomo Ohka .40 .18
❑ 552 Livan Hernandez .40 .18
❑ 553 Endy Chavez .40 .18
❑ 554 Dan Smith .40 .18
❑ 555 Scott Stewart .40 .18
❑ 556 T.J. Tucker .40 .18
❑ 557 Jamey Carroll .40 .18
❑ 558 Ron Calloway .40 .18
❑ 559 Brian Schneider .40 .18
❑ 560 Orlando Hernandez .40 .18
❑ 561 Wil Cordero .40 .18
❑ 562 Rocky Biddle .40 .18
❑ 563 Edgardo Alfonzo .40 .18
❑ 564 Andres Galarraga .40 .18
❑ 565 Felix Rodriguez .40 .18
❑ 566 Benito Santiago .40 .18
❑ 567 Jose Cruz Jr. .40 .18
❑ 568 Tim Worrell .40 .18
❑ 569 Marvin Benard .40 .18
❑ 570 Kurt Ainsworth .40 .18
❑ 571 Jim Brower .40 .18
❑ 572 J.T. Snow .40 .18
❑ 573 Scott Eyre .40 .18
❑ 574 Robb Nen .40 .18
❑ 575 Barry Bonds 2.50 1.10
❑ 576 Ray Durham .40 .18
❑ 577 Marquis Grissom .40 .18
❑ 578 Pedro Feliz .40 .18
❑ 579 Jason Schmidt .40 .18
❑ 580 Rich Aurilia .40 .18
❑ 581 Kirk Rueter .40 .18
❑ 582 Chad Zerbe .40 .18
❑ 583 Damian Moss .40 .18
❑ 584 Neifi Perez .40 .18
❑ 585 Joe Nathan .40 .18
❑ 586 Ruben Rivera .40 .18
❑ 587 Yorvit Torrealba .40 .18
❑ 588 Josh Beckett .60 .25
❑ 589 Todd Hollandsworth .40 .18
❑ 590 Derrek Lee .40 .18
❑ 591 A.J. Burnett .40 .18
❑ 592 Juan Pierre .40 .18
❑ 593 Mark Redman .40 .18
❑ 594 Blaine Neal .40 .18
❑ 595 Mike Mordecai .40 .18
❑ 596 Alex Gonzalez .40 .18
❑ 597 Brad Penny .40 .18
❑ 598 Tim Spooneybarger .40 .18
❑ 599 Mike Lowell .40 .18
❑ 600 Mike Redmond .40 .18
❑ 601 Braden Looper .40 .18
❑ 602 Ivan Rodriguez 1.00 .45
❑ 603 Andy Fox .40 .18
❑ 604 Vladimir Nunez .40 .18
❑ 605 Luis Castillo .40 .18
❑ 606 Juan Encarnacion .40 .18
❑ 607 Armando Almanza .40 .18
❑ 608 Gerald Williams .40 .18
❑ 609 Carl Pavano .40 .18
❑ 610 Michael Tejera .40 .18
❑ 611 Ramon Castro .40 .18
❑ 612 Brian Banks .40 .18
❑ 613 Roberto Alomar 1.00 .45
❑ 614 Al Leiter .40 .18
❑ 615 Jeromy Burnitz .40 .18
❑ 616 John Franco .40 .18
❑ 617 Tom Glavine 1.00 .45
❑ 618 Mike Piazza 1.50 .70
❑ 619 Cliff Floyd .40 .18
❑ 620 Joe McEwing .40 .18
❑ 621 David Weathers .40 .18
❑ 622 Pedro Astacio .40 .18
❑ 623 Timo Perez .40 .18
❑ 624 Jason Phillips .40 .18
❑ 625 Ty Wigginton .40 .18
❑ 626 Steve Trachsel UER .40 .18
Career IP total is wrong
❑ 627 Roger Cedeno .40 .18
❑ 628 Tsuyoshi Shinjo .40 .18
❑ 629 Armando Benitez .40 .18
❑ 630 Vance Wilson .40 .18
❑ 631 Mike Stanton .40 .18
❑ 632 Mo Vaughn .40 .18
❑ 633 Scott Strickland .40 .18
❑ 634 Rey Sanchez .40 .18
❑ 635 Jay Bell .40 .18
❑ 636 David Cone .40 .18
❑ 637 Jae Weong Seo .40 .18
❑ 638 Ryan Klesko .40 .18
❑ 639 Wiki Gonzalez .40 .18
❑ 640 Trevor Hoffman .40 .18
❑ 641 Sean Burroughs .40 .18
❑ 642 Mike Bynum .40 .18
❑ 643 Clay Condrey .40 .18
❑ 644 Gary Bennett .40 .18
❑ 645 Kevin Jarvis .40 .18
❑ 646 Mark Kotsay .40 .18
❑ 647 Phil Nevin .40 .18
❑ 648 Dave Hansen .40 .18
❑ 649 Keith Lockhart .40 .18
❑ 650 Brian Lawrence .40 .18
❑ 651 Jay Witasick .40 .18
❑ 652 Rondell White .40 .18
❑ 653 Jaret Wright .40 .18
❑ 654 Luther Hackman .40 .18
❑ 655 Jake Peavy .40 .18
❑ 656 Brian Buchanan .40 .18
❑ 657 Mark Loretta .40 .18
❑ 658 Oliver Perez .40 .18
❑ 659 Adam Eaton .40 .18
❑ 660 Xavier Nady .40 .18
❑ 661 Jesse Orosco .40 .18
❑ 662 Ramon Vazquez .40 .18
❑ 663 Jim Thome 1.00 .45
❑ 664 Jose Mesa .40 .18
❑ 665 Rheal Cormier .40 .18
❑ 666 David Bell .40 .18
❑ 667 Mike Lieberthal .40 .18
❑ 668 Brandon Duckworth .40 .18
❑ 669 David Coggin .40 .18
❑ 670 Bobby Abreu .40 .18
❑ 671 Turk Wendell .40 .18
❑ 672 Marlon Byrd .40 .18
❑ 673 Jason Michaels .40 .18
❑ 674 Kevin Millwood .40 .18
❑ 675 Tomas Perez .40 .18
❑ 676 Jimmy Rollins .40 .18
❑ 677 Vicente Padilla .40 .18
❑ 678 Pat Burrell .40 .18
❑ 679 Tyler Houston .40 .18
❑ 680 Hector Mercado .40 .18
❑ 681 Carlos Silva .40 .18
❑ 682 Nick Punto .40 .18
❑ 683 Ricky Ledee .40 .18
❑ 684 Randy Wolf .40 .18
❑ 685 Todd Pratt .40 .18
❑ 686 Placido Polanco .40 .18
❑ 687 Chase Utley .40 .18
❑ 688 Brian Giles .40 .18
❑ 689 Jason Kendall .40 .18
❑ 690 Matt Stairs .40 .18
❑ 691 Kris Benson .40 .18
❑ 692 Julian Tavarez .40 .18
❑ 693 Reggie Sanders .40 .18
❑ 694 Jeff D'Amico .40 .18
❑ 695 Pokey Reese .40 .18
❑ 696 Kenny Lofton .40 .18
❑ 697 Mike Williams .40 .18
❑ 698 David Williams .40 .18
❑ 699 Kevin Young .40 .18
❑ 700 Brian Boehringer .40 .18
❑ 701 Scott Sauerbeck .40 .18
❑ 702 Josh Fogg .40 .18
❑ 703 Joe Beimel .40 .18
❑ 704 Dennis Reyes .40 .18
❑ 705 Jeff Suppan .40 .18
❑ 706 Salomon Torres .40 .18
❑ 707 Kip Wells .40 .18
❑ 708 Craig Wilson .40 .18
❑ 709 Jack Wilson .40 .18
❑ 710 Rob Mackowiak .40 .18
❑ 711 Abraham Nunez .40 .18
❑ 712 Randall Simon .40 .18
❑ 713 Josias Manzanillo .40 .18
❑ 714 Ken Griffey Jr. 1.50 .70
❑ 715 Jimmy Haynes .40 .18
❑ 716 Felipe Lopez .40 .18
❑ 717 Jimmy Anderson .40 .18
❑ 718 Ryan Dempster .40 .18
❑ 719 Russell Branyan .40 .18

❑ 720 Aaron Boone .40 .18
❑ 721 Luke Prokopec .40 .18
❑ 722 Felix Heredia .40 .18
❑ 723 Scott Sullivan .40 .18
❑ 724 Danny Graves .40 .18
❑ 725 Kent Mercker .40 .18
❑ 726 Barry Larkin 1.00 .45
❑ 727 Jason LaRue .40 .18
❑ 728 Gabe White .40 .18
❑ 729 Adam Dunn .60 .25
❑ 730 Brandon Larson .40 .18
❑ 731 Reggie Taylor .40 .18
❑ 732 Sean Casey .40 .18
❑ 733 Scott Williamson .40 .18
❑ 734 Austin Kearns .60 .25
❑ 735 Kelly Stinnett .40 .18
❑ 736 Ruben Mateo .40 .18
❑ 737 Wily Mo Pena .40 .18
❑ 738 Larry Walker .60 .25
❑ 739 Juan Uribe .40 .18
❑ 740 Denny Neagle .40 .18
❑ 741 Darren Oliver .40 .18
❑ 742 Charles Johnson .40 .18
❑ 743 Todd Jones .40 .18
❑ 744 Todd Helton .60 .25
❑ 745 Shawn Chacon .40 .18
❑ 746 Jason Jennings .40 .18
❑ 747 Preston Wilson .40 .18
❑ 748 Chris Richard .40 .18
❑ 749 Chris Stynes .40 .18
❑ 750 Jose Jimenez .40 .18
❑ 751 Gabe Kapler .40 .18
❑ 752 Jay Payton .40 .18
❑ 753 Aaron Cook .40 .18
❑ 754 Greg Norton .40 .18
❑ 755 Scott Elarton .40 .18
❑ 756 Brian Fuentes .40 .18
❑ 757 Jose Hernandez .40 .18
❑ 758 Nelson Cruz .40 .18
❑ 759 Justin Speier .40 .18
❑ 760 Javier Lopez AS .40 .18
❑ 761 Garret Anderson AS .40 .18
❑ 762 Tony Batista AS .40 .18
❑ 763 Mark Buehrle AS .40 .18
❑ 764 Johnny Damon AS .40 .18
❑ 765 Freddy Garcia AS .40 .18
❑ 766 Nomar Garciaparra AS 1.00 .45
❑ 767 Jason Giambi AS .60 .25
❑ 768 Roy Halladay AS .40 .18
❑ 769 Shea Hillenbrand AS .40 .18
❑ 770 Torii Hunter AS .40 .18
❑ 771 Derek Jeter AS 1.25 .55
❑ 772 Paul Konerko AS .40 .18
❑ 773 Derek Lowe AS .40 .18
❑ 774 Pedro Martinez AS .60 .25
❑ 775 A.J. Pierzynski AS .40 .18
❑ 776 Jorge Posada AS .40 .18
❑ 777 Manny Ramirez AS .40 .18
❑ 778 Mariano Rivera AS .40 .18
❑ 779 Alex Rodriguez AS 1.00 .45
❑ 780 Kazuhiro Sasaki AS .40 .18
❑ 781 Alfonso Soriano AS .60 .25
❑ 782 Ichiro Suzuki AS 1.00 .45
❑ 783 Mike Sweeney AS .40 .18
❑ 784 Miguel Tejada AS .40 .18
❑ 785 Ugueth Urbina AS .40 .18
❑ 786 Robin Ventura AS .40 .18
❑ 787 Omar Vizquel AS .40 .18
❑ 788 Randy Winn AS .40 .18
❑ 789 Barry Zito AS .60 .25
❑ 790 Lance Berkman AS .40 .18
❑ 791 Barry Bonds AS 1.25 .55
❑ 792 Adam Dunn AS .40 .18
❑ 793 Tom Glavine AS .60 .25
❑ 794 Luis Gonzalez AS .40 .18
❑ 795 Shawn Green AS .40 .18
❑ 796 Vladimir Guerrero AS .60 .25
❑ 797 Todd Helton AS .40 .18
❑ 798 Trevor Hoffman AS .40 .18
❑ 799 Randy Johnson AS .60 .25
❑ 800 Andruw Jones AS .40 .18
❑ 801 Byung-Hyun Kim AS .40 .18
❑ 802 Mike Lowell AS .40 .18
❑ 803 Eric Gagne AS .40 .18
❑ 804 Matt Morris AS .40 .18
❑ 805 Robb Nen AS .40 .18
❑ 806 Vicente Padilla AS .40 .18
❑ 807 Odalis Perez AS .40 .18
❑ 808 Mike Piazza AS 1.00 .45
❑ 809 Mike Remlinger AS .40 .18
❑ 810 Scott Rolen AS .40 .18
❑ 811 Jimmy Rollins AS .40 .18
❑ 812 Benito Santiago AS .40 .18
❑ 813 Curt Schilling AS .40 .18
❑ 814 Richie Sexson AS .40 .18
❑ 815 John Smoltz AS .40 .18
❑ 816 Sammy Sosa AS 1.00 .45
❑ 817 Junior Spivey AS .40 .18
❑ 818 Jose Vidro AS .40 .18
❑ 819 Mike Williams AS .40 .18
❑ 820 Luis Castillo AS .40 .18
❑ 821 Jason Giambi HR Derby .60 .25
❑ 822 Luis Gonzalez HR Derby .40 .18
❑ 823 Sammy Sosa HR Derby 1.00 .45
❑ 824 Ken Griffey Jr. HR Derby 1.00 .45
❑ 825 Ken Griffey Jr. HR Derby 1.00 .45
❑ 826 Tino Martinez HR Derby .40 .18
❑ 827 Barry Bonds HR Derby 1.25 .55
❑ 828 Frank Thomas HR Derby .60 .25
❑ 829 Ken Griffey Jr. HR Derby 1.00 .45
❑ 830 Barry Bonds 02 WS 1.25 .55
❑ 831 Tim Salmon 02 WS .40 .18
❑ 832 Troy Glaus 02 WS .40 .18
❑ 833 Robb Nen 02 WS .40 .18
❑ 834 Jeff Kent 02 WS .40 .18
❑ 835 Scott Spiezio 02 WS .40 .18
❑ 836 Darin Erstad 02 WS .40 .18
❑ 837 Randy Johnson T40 .60 .25
❑ 838 Chipper Jones T40 .60 .25
❑ 839 Greg Maddux T40 1.00 .45
❑ 840 Nomar Garciaparra T40 1.00 .45
❑ 841 Manny Ramirez T40 .40 .18
❑ 842 Pedro Martinez T40 .60 .25
❑ 843 Sammy Sosa T40 1.00 .45
❑ 844 Ken Griffey Jr. T40 1.00 .45
❑ 845 Jim Thome T40 .60 .25
❑ 846 Vladimir Guerrero T40 .60 .25
❑ 847 Mike Piazza T40 1.00 .45
❑ 848 Derek Jeter T40 1.25 .55
❑ 849 Jason Giambi T40 .60 .25
❑ 850 Roger Clemens T40 1.00 .45
❑ 851 Alfonso Soriano T40 .60 .25
❑ 852 Hideki Matsui T40 4.00 1.80
❑ 853 Barry Bonds T40 1.25 .55
❑ 854 Ichiro Suzuki T40 1.00 .45
❑ 855 Albert Pujols T40 1.00 .45
❑ 856 Alex Rodriguez T40 1.00 .45
❑ 857 Darin Erstad T40 .40 .18
❑ 858 Troy Glaus T40 .40 .18
❑ 859 Curt Schilling T40 .40 .18
❑ 860 Luis Gonzalez T40 .40 .18
❑ 861 Tom Glavine T40 .60 .25
❑ 862 Andruw Jones T40 .40 .18
❑ 863 Gary Sheffield T40 .40 .18
❑ 864 Frank Thomas T40 .60 .25
❑ 865 Mark Prior T40 1.00 .45
❑ 866 Ivan Rodriguez T40 .60 .25
❑ 867 Jeff Bagwell T40 .40 .18
❑ 868 Lance Berkman T40 .40 .18
❑ 869 Shawn Green T40 .40 .18
❑ 870 Hideo Nomo T40 .60 .25
❑ 871 Torii Hunter T40 .40 .18
❑ 872 Bernie Williams T40 .40 .18
❑ 873 Barry Zito T40 .60 .25
❑ 874 Pat Burrell T40 .40 .18
❑ 875 Carlos Delgado T40 .40 .18
❑ 876 Miguel Tejada T40 .40 .18
❑ 877 Hideki Matsui NR RC 8.00 3.60
❑ 878 Jose Contreras NR RC 3.00 1.35
❑ 879 Jason Anderson NR .40 .18
❑ 880 Jason Shiell NR RC .60 .25
❑ 881 Kevin Tolar NR RC .60 .25
❑ 882 Michel Hernandez NR RC .60 .25
❑ 883 Arnie Munoz NR RC .60 .25
❑ 884 David Sanders NR RC .60 .25
❑ 885 Willie Eyre NR RC .60 .25
❑ 886 Brent Hoard NR RC .60 .25
❑ 887 Lew Ford NR RC 1.00 .45
❑ 888 Beau Kemp NR RC .60 .25
❑ 889 Jon Pridie NR RC .60 .25
❑ 890 Mike Ryan NR RC 1.00 .45
❑ 891 Richard Fischer NR RC .60 .25
❑ 892 Luis Ayala NR RC .60 .25
❑ 893 Mike Neu NR RC .60 .25
❑ 894 Joe Valentine NR RC .60 .25
❑ 895 Nate Bland NR RC .60 .25
❑ 896 Shane Bazzell NR RC .60 .25
❑ 897 Aquilino Lopez NR RC .60 .25
❑ 898 Diegomar Markwell NR RC .60 .25
❑ 899 Francisco Rosario NR RC .60 .25
❑ 900 Guillermo Quiroz NR RC 2.00 .90
❑ 901 Luis De Los Santos NR .40 .18
❑ 902 Fernando Cabrera NR RC .60 .25
❑ 903 Francisco Cruceta NR RC .60 .25
❑ 904 Jhonny Peralta NR RC .60 .25
❑ 905 Rett Johnson NR RC 1.00 .45
❑ 906 Aaron Looper NR RC .60 .25
❑ 907 Bobby Madritsch NR RC .60 .25
❑ 908 Luis Matos NR .40 .18
❑ 909 Jose Castillo NR .40 .18
❑ 910 Chris Waters NR RC .60 .25
❑ 911 Jeremy Guthrie NR .40 .18
❑ 912 Pedro Liriano NR .40 .18
❑ 913 Joe Borowski NR .40 .18
❑ 914 Felix Sanchez NR RC .60 .25
❑ 915 Jon Leicester NR RC .60 .25
❑ 916 Todd Wellemeyer NR RC 1.00 .45
❑ 917 Matt Bruback NR RC .40 .18
❑ 918 Chris Capuano NR RC .60 .25
❑ 919 Oscar Villarreal NR RC .60 .25
❑ 920 Matt Kata NR RC 2.00 .90
❑ 921 Robby Hammock NR RC 1.50 .70
❑ 922 Gerald Laird NR .40 .18
❑ 923 Brandon Webb NR RC 4.00 1.80
❑ 924 Tommy Whiteman NR .40 .18
❑ 925 Andrew Brown NR RC .60 .25
❑ 926 Alfredo Gonzalez NR RC .60 .25
❑ 927 Carlos Rivera NR .40 .18
❑ 928 Rick Roberts NR RC .60 .25
❑ 929 Termel Sledge NR RC 1.00 .45
❑ 930 Josh Willingham NR RC 2.50 1.10
❑ 931 Prentice Redman NR RC .60 .25
❑ 932 Jeff Duncan NR RC 1.00 .45
❑ 933 Craig Brazell NR RC 1.50 .70
❑ 934 Jeremy Griffiths NR RC 1.00 .45
❑ 935 Phil Seibel NR RC .60 .25
❑ 936 Heath Bell NR RC .60 .25
❑ 937 Bernie Castro NR RC .60 .25
❑ 938 Mike Nicolas NR RC .60 .25
❑ 939 Cory Stewart NR RC .60 .25
❑ 940 Shane Victorino NR RC .60 .25
❑ 941 Brandon Villafuerte NR .40 .18
❑ 942 Jeremy Wedel NR RC .60 .25
❑ 943 Tommy Phelps NR .40 .18
❑ 944 Josh Hall NR RC 1.00 .45
❑ 945 Ryan Cameron NR RC .60 .25
❑ 946 Garrett Atkins NR .40 .18
❑ 947 Clint Barmes NR RC 1.00 .45
❑ 948 Mike Hessman NR RC .60 .25
❑ 949 Brian Stokes NR RC .60 .25
❑ 950 Rocco Baldelli NR 2.00 .90
❑ 951 Hector Luna NR RC .60 .25
❑ 952 Jaime Cerda NR .40 .18
❑ 953 D.J. Carrasco NR RC .60 .25
❑ 954 Ian Ferguson NR RC .60 .25
❑ 955 Tim Olson NR RC 1.50 .70
❑ 956 Alejandro Machado NR RC .60 .25
❑ 957 Jorge Cordova NR RC .60 .25
❑ 958 Wilfredo Ledezma NR RC .60 .25
❑ 959 Nate Robertson NR RC .40 .18
❑ 960 Nook Logan NR RC .60 .25
❑ 961 Troy Glaus TC .40 .18
❑ 962 Jay Gibbons TC .40 .18
❑ 963 Nomar Garciaparra TC .40 .18
❑ 964 Paul Konerko TC .40 .18
❑ 965 Ellis Burks TC .40 .18
❑ 966 Bobby Higginson TC .40 .18
❑ 967 Mike Sweeney TC .40 .18
❑ 968 Torii Hunter .40 .18
Doug Mientkiewicz TC
❑ 969 Jorge Posada TC .40 .18
❑ 970 Miguel Tejada TC .40 .18
❑ 971 Ichiro Suzuki TC .40 .18
❑ 972 Toby Hall TC .40 .18
❑ 973 Alex Rodriguez .40 .18
Juan Gonzalez TC
❑ 974 Shannon Stewart TC .40 .18
❑ 975 Luis Gonzalez .40 .18

Mark Grace TC

❑ 976 Andruw Jones TC	.40	.18
❑ 977 Antonio Alfonseca TC	.40	.18
❑ 978 Aaron Boone TC	.40	.18
❑ 979 Todd Helton TC	.40	.18
❑ 980 Ivan Rodriguez TC	.40	.18
❑ 981 Craig Biggio TC	.40	.18
❑ 982 Shawn Green TC	.40	.18
❑ 983 Richie Sexson TC	.40	.18
❑ 984 Vladimir Guerrero TC	.40	.18
❑ 985 Roberto Alomar TC	.40	.18
❑ 986 Jim Thome TC	.40	.18
❑ 987 Humberto Cota TC	.40	.18
❑ 988 Ryan Klesko TC	.40	.18
❑ 989 Barry Bonds Benito Santiago TC	.40	.18
❑ 990 Albert Pujols J.D. Drew TC	.40	.18
❑ P1 Ken Griffey Jr. Sample	1.00	.45

2003 Upper Deck Classic Portraits

	MINT	NRMT
COMP.SET w/o SP's (100)	25.00	11.00
COMMON CARD (1-100)	.40	.18
COMMON CARD (101-145)	3.00	1.35
COMMON RC (101-145)	3.00	1.35
COMMON CARD (146-190)	5.00	2.20
COMMON RC (146-190)	5.00	2.20
COMMON ACTIVE (191-232)	8.00	3.60
COMMON RETIRED (191-232)	8.00	3.60

191-232 STATED ODDS 2 PER BOX
191-232 PRINT RUN 1200 SERIAL #'d SETS

Card	MINT	NRMT
❑ 1 Ken Griffey Jr.	1.50	.70
❑ 2 Randy Johnson	1.00	.45
❑ 3 Rafael Furcal	.40	.18
❑ 4 Omar Vizquel	.40	.18
❑ 5 Shawn Green	.40	.18
❑ 6 Roy Oswalt	.40	.18
❑ 7 Hideo Nomo	1.00	.45
❑ 8 Jason Giambi	1.00	.45
❑ 9 Barry Bonds	2.50	1.10
❑ 10 Mike Piazza	1.50	.70
❑ 11 Ichiro Suzuki	2.00	.90
❑ 12 Carlos Delgado	.40	.18
❑ 13 Preston Wilson	.40	.18
❑ 14 Lance Berkman	.40	.18
❑ 15 Magglio Ordonez	.40	.18
❑ 16 Kerry Wood	1.00	.45
❑ 17 Ivan Rodriguez	1.00	.45
❑ 18 Chipper Jones	1.00	.45
❑ 19 Adam Dunn	.60	.25
❑ 20 C.C. Sabathia	.40	.18
❑ 21 Mike MacDougal	.40	.18
❑ 22 Torii Hunter	.40	.18
❑ 23 Jim Thome	1.00	.45
❑ 24 Hank Blalock	.60	.25
❑ 25 Johnny Damon	.40	.18
❑ 26 Troy Glaus	.60	.25
❑ 27 Manny Ramirez	.40	.18
❑ 28 Mark Prior	2.00	.90
❑ 29 Brent Mayne	.40	.18
❑ 30 Derek Jeter	2.50	1.10
❑ 31 Tim Hudson	.40	.18
❑ 32 Mike Cameron	.40	.18
❑ 33 Mark Teixeira	.60	.25
❑ 34 Shannon Stewart	.40	.18
❑ 35 Tim Salmon	.60	.25
❑ 36 Luis Gonzalez	.40	.18
❑ 37 Jason Johnson	.40	.18
❑ 38 Shea Hillenbrand	.40	.18
❑ 39 Bartolo Colon	.40	.18
❑ 40 Austin Kearns	.60	.25
❑ 41 Vladimir Guerrero	1.00	.45
❑ 42 Tom Glavine	1.00	.45
❑ 43 Andres Galarraga	.40	.18
❑ 44 Kazuhiro Sasaki	.40	.18
❑ 45 Juan Gonzalez	1.00	.45
❑ 46 Vernon Wells	.40	.18
❑ 47 Jeff Bagwell	.60	.25
❑ 48 Mike Sweeney	.40	.18
❑ 49 Carlos Beltran	.40	.18
❑ 50 Dave Roberts	.40	.18
❑ 51 Todd Helton	.60	.25
❑ 52 Carlos Pena	.40	.18
❑ 53 Darin Erstad	.40	.18
❑ 54 Gary Sheffield	.40	.18
❑ 55 Lyle Overbay	.40	.18
❑ 56 Sammy Sosa	1.50	.70
❑ 57 Mike Mussina	1.00	.45
❑ 58 Matt Morris	.40	.18
❑ 59 Roberto Alomar	1.00	.45
❑ 60 Larry Walker	.60	.25
❑ 61 Jacque Jones	.40	.18
❑ 62 Josh Beckett	.60	.25
❑ 63 Richie Sexson	.40	.18
❑ 64 Derek Lowe	.40	.18
❑ 65 Pedro Martinez	1.00	.45
❑ 66 Moises Alou	.40	.18
❑ 67 Craig Biggio	.60	.25
❑ 68 Curt Schilling	.60	.25
❑ 69 Jesse Foppert	.40	.18
❑ 70 Nomar Garciaparra	2.00	.90
❑ 71 Barry Zito	1.00	.45
❑ 72 Alfonso Soriano	1.00	.45
❑ 73 Miguel Tejada	.40	.18
❑ 74 Rafael Palmeiro	.60	.25
❑ 75 Albert Pujols	2.00	.90
❑ 76 Mariano Rivera	.60	.25
❑ 77 Bobby Abreu	.40	.18
❑ 78 Alex Rodriguez	2.00	.90
❑ 79 Andruw Jones	.60	.25
❑ 80 Frank Thomas	1.00	.45
❑ 81 Greg Maddux	2.00	.90
❑ 82 Jim Edmonds	.40	.18
❑ 83 Bernie Williams	.60	.25
❑ 84 Roger Clemens	2.00	.90
❑ 85 Eric Chavez	.40	.18
❑ 86 Scott Rolen	.60	.25
❑ 87 Jorge Posada	.60	.25
❑ 88 Bret Boone	.40	.18
❑ 89 Ben Sheets	.40	.18
❑ 90 John Olerud	.40	.18
❑ 91 J.D. Drew	.40	.18
❑ 92 Aaron Boone	.40	.18
❑ 93 Corey Koskie	.40	.18
❑ 94 Sean Casey	.40	.18
❑ 95 Jose Cruz Jr.	.40	.18
❑ 96 Pat Burrell	.40	.18
❑ 97 Jose Guillen	.40	.18
❑ 98 Mark Mulder	.40	.18
❑ 99 Garret Anderson	.40	.18
❑ 100 Kazuhisa Ishii	.40	.18
❑ 101 David Matranga SP RC	3.00	1.35
❑ 102 Colin Porter SP RC	3.00	1.35
❑ 103 Jason Gilfillan SP RC	3.00	1.35
❑ 104 Carlos Mendez SP RC	3.00	1.35
❑ 105 Jason Shiell SP RC	3.00	1.35
❑ 106 Kevin Tolar SP RC	3.00	1.35
❑ 107 Termel Sledge SP RC	4.00	1.80
❑ 108 Craig Brazell SP RC	4.00	1.80
❑ 109 Bernie Castro SP RC	3.00	1.35
❑ 110 Tim Olson SP RC	4.00	1.80
❑ 111 Kevin Ohme SP RC	3.00	1.35
❑ 112 Pedro Liriano SP	3.00	1.35
❑ 113 Joe Borowski SP	3.00	1.35
❑ 114 Edgar Gonzalez SP RC	3.00	1.35
❑ 115 Joe Thurston SP	3.00	1.35
❑ 116 Bobby Hill SP	3.00	1.35
❑ 117 Michel Hernandez SP RC	3.00	1.35
❑ 118 Arnie Munoz SP RC	3.00	1.35
❑ 119 David Sanders SP RC	3.00	1.35
❑ 120 Willie Eyre SP RC	3.00	1.35
❑ 121 Brent Hoard SP RC	3.00	1.35
❑ 122 Lew Ford SP RC	4.00	1.80
❑ 123 Beau Kemp SP RC	3.00	1.35
❑ 124 Jon Pridie SP RC	3.00	1.35
❑ 125 Mike Ryan SP RC	4.00	1.80
❑ 126 Richard Fischer SP RC	3.00	1.35
❑ 127 Luis Ayala SP RC	3.00	1.35
❑ 128 Mike Neu SP RC	3.00	1.35
❑ 129 Joe Valentine SP RC	3.00	1.35
❑ 130 Nate Bland SP RC	3.00	1.35
❑ 131 Shane Bazzell SP RC	3.00	1.35
❑ 132 Jason Roach SP RC	3.00	1.35
❑ 133 Diegomar Markwell SP RC	3.00	1.35
❑ 134 Francisco Rosario SP RC	3.00	1.35
❑ 135 Guillermo Quiroz SP RC	5.00	2.20
❑ 136 Jerome Williams SP	3.00	1.35
❑ 137 Fernando Cabrera SP RC	4.00	1.80
❑ 138 Francisco Cruceta SP RC	3.00	1.35
❑ 139 Jhonny Peralta SP RC	3.00	1.35
❑ 140 Rett Johnson SP RC	4.00	1.80
❑ 141 Aaron Looper SP RC	3.00	1.35
❑ 142 Bobby Madritsch SP RC	3.00	1.35
❑ 143 Dan Haren SP RC	4.00	1.80
❑ 144 Jose Castillo SP	3.00	1.35
❑ 145 Chris Waters SP RC	3.00	1.35
❑ 146 Hideki Matsui MP RC	15.00	6.75
❑ 147 Jose Contreras MP RC	6.00	2.70
❑ 148 Felix Sanchez MP RC	5.00	2.20
❑ 149 Jon Leicester MP RC	5.00	2.20
❑ 150 Todd Wellemeyer MP RC	5.00	2.20
❑ 151 Matt Bruback MP RC	5.00	2.20
❑ 152 Chris Capuano MP RC	5.00	2.20
❑ 153 Oscar Villarreal MP RC	5.00	2.20
❑ 154 Matt Kata MP RC	5.00	2.20
❑ 155 Robby Hammock MP RC	5.00	2.20
❑ 156 Gerald Laird MP	5.00	2.20
❑ 157 Brandon Webb MP RC	8.00	3.60
❑ 158 Tommy Whiteman MP	5.00	2.20
❑ 159 Andrew Brown MP RC	5.00	2.20
❑ 160 Alfredo Gonzalez MP RC	5.00	2.20
❑ 161 Carlos Rivera MP	5.00	2.20
❑ 162 Rick Roberts MP RC	5.00	2.20
❑ 163 Dontrelle Willis MP	8.00	3.60
❑ 164 Josh Willingham MP RC	6.00	2.70
❑ 165 Prentice Redman MP RC	5.00	2.20
❑ 166 Jeff Duncan MP RC	5.00	2.20
❑ 167 Jose Reyes MP	8.00	3.60
❑ 168 Jeremy Griffiths MP RC	5.00	2.20
❑ 169 Phil Seibel MP RC	5.00	2.20
❑ 170 Heath Bell MP RC	5.00	2.20
❑ 171 Anthony Ferrari MP RC	5.00	2.20
❑ 172 Mike Nicolas MP RC	5.00	2.20
❑ 173 Cory Stewart MP RC	5.00	2.20
❑ 174 Miguel Ojeda MP RC	5.00	2.20
❑ 175 Rickie Weeks MP RC	10.00	4.50
❑ 176 Delmon Young MP RC	20.00	11.00
❑ 177 Tommy Phelps MP	5.00	2.20
❑ 178 Josh Hall MP RC	5.00	2.20
❑ 179 Ryan Cameron MP RC	5.00	2.20
❑ 180 Garrett Atkins MP	5.00	2.20
❑ 181 Clint Barmes MP RC	5.00	2.20
❑ 182 Mike Hessman MP RC	5.00	2.20
❑ 183 Chin-Hui Tsao MP	5.00	2.20
❑ 184 Rocco Baldelli MP	10.00	4.50
❑ 185 Bo Hart MP RC	6.00	2.70
❑ 186 Wilfredo Ledezma MP RC	5.00	2.20
❑ 187 Miguel Cabrera MP	10.00	4.50
❑ 188 Ian Ferguson MP RC	5.00	2.20
❑ 189 Michael Nakamura MP RC	5.00	2.20
❑ 190 Alejandro Machado MP RC	5.00	2.20
❑ 191 Mickey Mantle BBR	20.00	9.00
❑ 192 Ted Williams BBR	15.00	6.75
❑ 193 Mark Prior BBR	10.00	4.50
❑ 194 Stan Musial BBR	8.00	3.60
❑ 195 Phil Rizzuto BBR	8.00	3.60
❑ 196 Nolan Ryan BBR	15.00	6.75
❑ 197 Tom Seaver BBR	8.00	3.60
❑ 198 Robin Yount BBR	8.00	3.60
❑ 199 Yogi Berra BBR	8.00	3.60
❑ 200 Ernie Banks BBR	8.00	3.60
❑ 201 Willie McCovey BBR	8.00	3.60
❑ 202 Ralph Kiner BBR	8.00	3.60
❑ 203 Ken Griffey Jr. BBR	8.00	3.60
❑ 204 Sammy Sosa BBR	8.00	3.60
❑ 205 Derek Jeter BBR	12.00	5.50

❑ 206 Nomar Garciaparra BBR 10.00 4.50
❑ 207 Alex Rodriguez BBR 10.00 4.50
❑ 208 Ichiro Suzuki BBR 10.00 4.50
❑ 209 Mike Piazza BBR 8.00 3.60
❑ 210 Jackie Robinson BBR 10.00 4.50
❑ 211 Roberto Clemente BBR 15.00 6.75
❑ 212 Babe Ruth BBR 15.00 6.75
❑ 213 Duke Snider BBR 8.00 3.60
❑ 214 Greg Maddux BBR 10.00 4.50
❑ 215 Juan Marichal BBR 8.00 3.60
❑ 216 Joe Morgan BBR 8.00 3.60
❑ 217 Rollie Fingers BBR 8.00 3.60
❑ 218 Warren Spahn BBR 8.00 3.60
❑ 219 Pee Wee Reese BBR 8.00 3.60
❑ 220 Troy Glaus BBR 8.00 3.60
❑ 221 Jason Giambi BBR 8.00 3.60
❑ 222 Roger Clemens BBR 10.00 4.50
❑ 223 Pedro Martinez BBR 8.00 3.60
❑ 224 Chipper Jones BBR 8.00 3.60
❑ 225 Randy Johnson BBR 8.00 3.60
❑ 226 Jim Thome BBR 8.00 3.60
❑ 227 Barry Bonds BBR 12.00 5.50
❑ 228 Hideo Nomo BBR 8.00 3.60
❑ 229 Whitey Ford BBR 8.00 3.60
❑ 230 Bob Gibson BBR 8.00 3.60
❑ 231 Alfonso Soriano BBR 8.00 3.60
❑ 232 Richie Ashburn BBR 8.00 3.60

2002 Upper Deck Diamond Connection

	Nm-Mt	Ex-Mt
COMP.LOW w/o SP's (90)	25.00	7.50
COMP.UPDATE w/o SP's (30)	10.00	3.00
COMMON CARD (1-90)	.40	.12
COMMON CARD (91-200)	5.00	1.50

DC JSY 201-270/537-547 PRINT 775 #'d SETS
BLH JSY 271-320/548-550 PRINT 200 #'d SETS
HM JSY 321-353/551-552 PRINT 150 #'d SETS
FC JSY 354-368/553 PRINT 100 #'d SETS
DC BAT 369-438/554-564 PRINT 775 #'d SETS
BLH BAT 439-488/565-567 PRINT 200 #'d SETS
HM BAT 489-521/568-569 PRINT 150 #'d SETS
FC BAT 522-536/570 PRINT 100 #'d SETS

COMMON CARD (571-600)	.60	.18
COMMON CARD (601-630)	5.00	1.50

❑ 1 Troy Glaus .60 .18
❑ 2 Darin Erstad .40 .12
❑ 3 Barry Zito 1.00 .30
❑ 4 Eric Chavez .40 .12
❑ 5 Tim Hudson .40 .12
❑ 6 Miguel Tejada .40 .12
❑ 7 Carlos Delgado .40 .12
❑ 8 Shannon Stewart .40 .12
❑ 9 Greg Vaughn .40 .12
❑ 10 Jim Thome 1.00 .30
❑ 11 C.C. Sabathia .40 .12
❑ 12 Ichiro Suzuki 2.00 .60
❑ 13 Edgar Martinez .60 .18
❑ 14 Bret Boone .40 .12
❑ 15 Freddy Garcia .40 .12
❑ 16 Jeff Conine .40 .12
❑ 17 Alex Rodriguez 2.00 .60
❑ 18 Rafael Palmeiro .60 .18
❑ 19 Ivan Rodriguez 1.00 .30
❑ 20 Juan Gonzalez 1.00 .30
❑ 21 Pedro Martinez 1.00 .30
❑ 22 Nomar Garciaparra 2.00 .60
❑ 23 Manny Ramirez .40 .12
❑ 24 Carlos Beltran .40 .12
❑ 25 Mike Sweeney .40 .12
❑ 26 Dmitri Young .40 .12
❑ 27 Bobby Higginson .40 .12
❑ 28 Corey Koskie .40 .12
❑ 29 Cristian Guzman .40 .12
❑ 30 Doug Mientkiewicz .40 .12
❑ 31 Torii Hunter .40 .12
❑ 32 Frank Thomas 1.00 .30
❑ 33 Mark Buehrle .40 .12
❑ 34 Carlos Lee .40 .12
❑ 35 Magglio Ordonez .40 .12
❑ 36 Roger Clemens 2.00 .60
❑ 37 Bernie Williams .60 .18
❑ 38 Jason Giambi 1.00 .30
❑ 39 Derek Jeter 2.50 .75
❑ 40 Mike Mussina 1.00 .30
❑ 41 Jeff Bagwell .60 .18
❑ 42 Richard Hidalgo .40 .12
❑ 43 Lance Berkman .40 .12
❑ 44 Roy Oswalt .40 .12
❑ 45 Chipper Jones 1.00 .30
❑ 46 Gary Sheffield .40 .12
❑ 47 Andruw Jones .60 .18
❑ 48 Greg Maddux 2.00 .60
❑ 49 Geoff Jenkins .40 .12
❑ 50 Ben Sheets .40 .12
❑ 51 Richie Sexson .40 .12
❑ 52 Albert Pujols 2.00 .60
❑ 53 Matt Morris .40 .12
❑ 54 J.D. Drew .40 .12
❑ 55 Tino Martinez .40 .12
❑ 56 Sammy Sosa 1.50 .45
❑ 57 Kerry Wood 1.00 .30
❑ 58 Moises Alou .40 .12
❑ 59 Fred McGriff .60 .18
❑ 60 Randy Johnson 1.00 .30
❑ 61 Luis Gonzalez .40 .12
❑ 62 Curt Schilling .60 .18
❑ 63 Kevin Brown .40 .12
❑ 64 Shawn Green .40 .12
❑ 65 Paul LoDuca .40 .12
❑ 66 Vladimir Guerrero 1.00 .30
❑ 67 Jose Vidro .40 .12
❑ 68 Barry Bonds 2.50 .75
❑ 69 Jeff Kent .40 .12
❑ 70 Rich Aurilia .40 .12
❑ 71 Preston Wilson .40 .12
❑ 72 Josh Beckett .60 .18
❑ 73 Cliff Floyd .40 .12
❑ 74 Mike Piazza 1.50 .45
❑ 75 Mo Vaughn .40 .12
❑ 76 Roberto Alomar 1.00 .30
❑ 77 Jeromy Burnitz .40 .12
❑ 78 Phil Nevin .40 .12
❑ 79 Sean Burroughs .40 .12
❑ 80 Scott Rolen .60 .18
❑ 81 Bob Abreu .40 .12
❑ 82 Pat Burrell .40 .12
❑ 83 Brian Giles .40 .12
❑ 84 Jason Kendall .40 .12
❑ 85 Ken Griffey Jr. 1.50 .45
❑ 86 Adam Dunn .60 .18
❑ 87 Aaron Boone .40 .12
❑ 88 Larry Walker .60 .18
❑ 89 Todd Helton .60 .18
❑ 90 Mike Hampton .40 .12
❑ 91 Brandon Puffer DC RC 5.00 1.50
❑ 92 Rodrigo Rosario DC RC 5.00 1.50
❑ 93 Tom Shearn DC RC 5.00 1.50
❑ 94 Morgan Ensberg DC 5.00 1.50
❑ 95 Jason Lane DC 5.00 1.50
❑ 96 Franklyn German DC RC 5.00 1.50
❑ 97 Carlos Pena DC 5.00 1.50
❑ 98 Joe Orloski DC RC 5.00 1.50
❑ 99 Reed Johnson DC RC 8.00 2.40
❑ 100 Chris Baker DC RC 5.00 1.50
❑ 101 Corey Thurman DC RC 5.00 1.50
❑ 102 Gustavo Chacin DC RC 5.00 1.50
❑ 103 Eric Hinske DC 5.00 1.50
❑ 104 John Foster DC RC 5.00 1.50
❑ 105 John Ennis DC RC 5.00 1.50
❑ 106 Kevin Gryboski DC RC 5.00 1.50
❑ 107 Jung Bong DC 5.00 1.50
❑ 108 Travis Wilson DC 5.00 1.50
❑ 109 Luis Martinez DC RC 8.00 2.40
❑ 110 Brian Mallette DC RC 5.00 1.50
❑ 111 Takahito Nomura DC RC 5.00 1.50
❑ 112 Bill Hall DC 5.00 1.50
❑ 113 Jeff Deardorff DC 5.00 1.50
❑ 114 Cristian Guerrero DC 5.00 1.50
❑ 115 Scotty Layfield DC RC 5.00 1.50
❑ 116 Mike Crudale DC RC 5.00 1.50
❑ 117 So Taguchi DC RC 8.00 2.40
❑ 118 Jeremy Lambert DC RC 5.00 1.50
❑ 119 Jim Journell DC 5.00 1.50
❑ 120 Francis Beltran DC RC 5.00 1.50
❑ 121 Mark Prior DC 15.00 4.50
❑ 122 Ben Christensen DC 5.00 1.50
❑ 123 Jorge Sosa DC RC 5.00 1.50
❑ 124 Brandon Backe DC RC 5.00 1.50
❑ 125 Steve Kent DC RC 5.00 1.50
❑ 126 Felix Escalona DC RC 5.00 1.50
❑ 127 P.J. Bevis DC RC 5.00 1.50
❑ 128 Jose Valverde DC RC 8.00 2.40
❑ 129 Doug Devore DC RC 5.00 1.50
❑ 130 Jeremy Ward DC RC 5.00 1.50
❑ 131 Mike Koplove DC 5.00 1.50
❑ 132 Luis Terrero DC 5.00 1.50
❑ 133 John Patterson DC 5.00 1.50
❑ 134 Victor Alvarez DC RC 5.00 1.50
❑ 135 Kirk Saarloos DC RC 8.00 2.40
❑ 136 Kazuhisa Ishii DC RC 10.00 3.00
❑ 137 Steve Colyer DC 5.00 1.50
❑ 138 Cesar Izturis DC 5.00 1.50
❑ 139 Ron Calloway DC RC 5.00 1.50
❑ 140 Eric Good DC RC 5.00 1.50
❑ 141 Jorge Nunez DC RC 5.00 1.50
❑ 142 Ron Chiavacci DC 5.00 1.50
❑ 143 Donnie Bridges DC 5.00 1.50
❑ 144 Nelson Castro DC RC 5.00 1.50
❑ 145 Deivis Santos DC 5.00 1.50
❑ 146 Kurt Ainsworth DC 5.00 1.50
❑ 147 Arturo McDowell DC 5.00 1.50
❑ 148 Allan Simpson DC RC 5.00 1.50
❑ 149 Matt Thornton DC RC 5.00 1.50
❑ 150 Luis Ugueto DC RC 5.00 1.50
❑ 151 J.J. Putz DC RC 5.00 1.50
❑ 152 Hansel Izquierdo DC RC 5.00 1.50
❑ 153 Oliver Perez DC RC 8.00 2.40
❑ 154 Jaime Cerda DC RC 5.00 1.50
❑ 155 Mark Corey DC RC 5.00 1.50
❑ 156 Tyler Yates DC RC 5.00 1.50
❑ 157 Satoru Komiyama DC RC 5.00 1.50
❑ 158 Adam Walker DC RC 5.00 1.50
❑ 159 Steve Bechler DC RC 5.00 1.50
❑ 160 Erik Bedard DC 5.00 1.50
❑ 161 Todd Donovan DC RC 5.00 1.50
❑ 162 Clifford Bartosh DC RC 5.00 1.50
❑ 163 Ben Howard DC RC 5.00 1.50
❑ 164 Andy Shibilo DC RC 5.00 1.50
❑ 165 Dennis Tankersley DC 5.00 1.50
❑ 166 Mike Bynum DC 5.00 1.50
❑ 167 Anderson Machado DC RC 8.00 2.40
❑ 168 Pete Zamora DC RC 5.00 1.50
❑ 169 Eric Junge DC RC 5.00 1.50
❑ 170 Elio Serrano DC RC 5.00 1.50
❑ 171 Jorge Padilla DC RC 8.00 2.40
❑ 172 Marlon Byrd DC 5.00 1.50
❑ 173 Adrian Burnside DC RC 5.00 1.50
❑ 174 Mike Gonzalez DC RC 5.00 1.50
❑ 175 J.R. House DC 5.00 1.50
❑ 176 Hank Blalock DC 8.00 2.40
❑ 177 Travis Hughes DC RC 8.00 2.40
❑ 178 Mark Teixeira DC 8.00 2.40
❑ 179 Josh Hancock DC RC 5.00 1.50
❑ 180 Anastacio Martinez DC RC 5.00 1.50
❑ 181 Jorge de la Rosa DC RC 5.00 1.50
❑ 182 Ben Broussard DC 5.00 1.50
❑ 183 Austin Kearns DC 8.00 2.40
❑ 184 Corky Miller DC 5.00 1.50
❑ 185 Colin Young DC RC 5.00 1.50
❑ 186 Cam Esslinger DC RC 5.00 1.50
❑ 187 Rene Reyes DC RC 5.00 1.50
❑ 188 Aaron Cook DC RC 8.00 2.40
❑ 189 Alexis Gomez DC 5.00 1.50
❑ 190 Nate Field DC RC 5.00 1.50
❑ 191 Miguel Asencio DC RC 5.00 1.50
❑ 192 Brandon Berger DC 5.00 1.50
❑ 193 Fernando Rodney DC 5.00 1.50

❑ 194 Andy Van Hekken DC 5.00 1.50
❑ 195 Kevin Frederick DC RC .. 5.00 1.50
❑ 196 Todd Sears DC 5.00 1.50
❑ 197 Edwin Almonte DC RC .. 5.00 1.50
❑ 198 Kyle Kane DC RC 5.00 1.50
❑ 199 Mitch Wylie DC RC 5.00 1.50
❑ 200 Mike Porzio DC 5.00 1.50
❑ 201 Darin Erstad DC Jsy 10.00 3.00
❑ 202 Tim Salmon DC Jsy 15.00 4.50
❑ 203 Jeff Bagwell DC Jsy...... 15.00 4.50
❑ 204 Lance Berkman DC Jsy 10.00 3.00
❑ 205 Eric Chavez DC Jsy...... 10.00 3.00
❑ 206 Tim Hudson DC Jsy 10.00 3.00
❑ 207 Carlos Delgado DC Jsy 10.00 3.00
❑ 208 Chipper Jones DC Jsy.. 15.00 4.50
❑ 209 Gary Sheffield DC Jsy .. 10.00 3.00
❑ 210 Greg Maddux DC Jsy .. 20.00 6.00
❑ 211 Tom Glavine DC Jsy 15.00 4.50
❑ 212 Mike Mussina DC Jsy .. 15.00 4.50
❑ 213 J.D. Drew DC Jsy 10.00 3.00
❑ 214 Rick Ankiel DC Jsy 10.00 3.00
❑ 215 Sammy Sosa DC Jsy.... 25.00 7.50
❑ 216 Mike Lieberthal DC Jsy 10.00 3.00
❑ 217 Fred McGriff DC Jsy 15.00 4.50
❑ 218 David Wells DC Jsy...... 10.00 3.00
❑ 219 Curt Schilling DC Jsy .. 15.00 4.50
❑ 220 Luis Gonzalez DC Jsy .. 10.00 3.00
❑ 221 Mark Grace DC Jsy 15.00 4.50
❑ 222 Kevin Brown DC Jsy 10.00 3.00
❑ 223 Hideo Nomo DC Jsy 25.00 7.50
❑ 224 Jose Vidro DC Jsy........ 10.00 3.00
❑ 225 Jeff Kent DC Jsy 10.00 3.00
❑ 226 Rich Aurilia DC Jsy 10.00 3.00
❑ 227 Kenny Lofton DC Jsy.... 10.00 3.00
❑ 228 C.C. Sabathia DC Jsy .. 10.00 3.00
❑ 229 Edgar Martinez DC Jsy 15.00 4.50
❑ 230 Freddy Garcia DC Jsy .. 10.00 3.00
❑ 231 Cliff Floyd DC Jsy 10.00 3.00
❑ 232 Preston Wilson DC Jsy 10.00 3.00
❑ 233 Mike Piazza DC Jsy...... 25.00 7.50
❑ 234 Roberto Alomar DC Jsy 15.00 4.50
❑ 235 Trevor Hoffman DC Jsy 10.00 3.00
❑ 236 Ryan Klesko DC Jsy 10.00 3.00
❑ 237 Sean Burroughs DC Jsy 10.00 3.00
❑ 238 Scott Rolen DC Jsy 15.00 4.50
❑ 239 Pat Burrell DC Jsy......... 10.00 3.00
❑ 240 Edgardo Alfonzo DC Jsy 10.00 3.00
❑ 241 Brian Giles DC Jsy 10.00 3.00
❑ 242 Jason Kendall DC Jsy .. 10.00 3.00
❑ 243 Alex Rodriguez DC Jsy 25.00 7.50
❑ 244 Juan Gonzalez DC Jsy.. 15.00 4.50
❑ 245 Ivan Rodriguez DC Jsy 15.00 4.50
❑ 246 Rafael Palmeiro DC Jsy 15.00 4.50
❑ 247 Ken Griffey Jr. DC Jsy .. 20.00 6.00
❑ 248 Adam Dunn DC Jsy...... 15.00 4.50
❑ 249 Barry Larkin DC Jsy 15.00 4.50
❑ 250 Manny Ramirez DC Jsy 10.00 3.00
❑ 251 Pedro Martinez DC Jsy 15.00 4.50
❑ 252 Todd Helton DC Jsy 15.00 4.50
❑ 253 Larry Walker DC Jsy 15.00 4.50
❑ 254 Randy Johnson DC Jsy 15.00 4.50
❑ 255 Mike Sweeney DC Jsy.. 10.00 3.00
❑ 256 Carlos Beltran DC Jsy.. 10.00 3.00
❑ 257 Dmitri Young DC Jsy SP/380 10.00 3.00
❑ 258 Joe Mays DC Jsy 10.00 3.00
❑ 259 Doug Mientkiewicz DC Jsy 10.00 3.00
❑ 260 Corey Koskie DC Jsy.... 10.00 3.00
❑ 261 Magglio Ordonez DC Jsy 10.00 3.00
❑ 262 Frank Thomas DC Jsy .. 15.00 4.50
❑ 263 Ray Durham DC Jsy 10.00 3.00
❑ 264 Jason Giambi DC Jsy .. 15.00 4.50
❑ 265 Bernie Williams DC Jsy 15.00 4.50
❑ 266 Roger Clemens DC Jsy 25.00 7.50
❑ 267 Mariano Rivera DC Jsy 15.00 4.50
❑ 268 Robin Ventura DC Jsy .. 10.00 3.00
❑ 269 Andy Pettitte DC Jsy 15.00 4.50
❑ 270 Jorge Posada DC Jsy .. 15.00 4.50
❑ 271 Mike Piazza BLH Jsy.... 30.00 9.00
❑ 272 Alex Rodriguez BLH Jsy 30.00 9.00
❑ 273 Ken Griffey Jr. BLH Jsy 25.00 7.50
❑ 274 Jason Giambi BLH Jsy 20.00 6.00
❑ 275 Frank Thomas BLH Jsy 20.00 6.00
❑ 276 Greg Maddux BLH Jsy 25.00 7.50
❑ 277 Sammy Sosa BLH Jsy .. 30.00 9.00
❑ 278 Roger Clemens BLH Jsy 30.00 9.00
❑ 279 Jeff Bagwell BLH Jsy 20.00 6.00
❑ 280 Todd Helton BLH Jsy .. 20.00 6.00
❑ 281 Ichiro Suzuki BLH Jsy .. 80.00 24.00
❑ 282 Randy Johnson BLH Jsy 20.00 6.00
❑ 283 Jim Thome BLH Jsy 20.00 6.00
❑ 284 Ivan Rodriguez BLH Jsy 20.00 6.00
❑ 285 Darin Erstad BLH Jsy .. 15.00 4.50
❑ 286 Eric Chavez BLH Jsy 15.00 4.50
❑ 287 Barry Zito BLH Jsy 20.00 6.00
❑ 288 Carlos Delgado BLH Jsy 15.00 4.50
❑ 289 Omar Vizquel BLH Jsy.. 15.00 4.50
❑ 290 Edgar Martinez BLH Jsy 20.00 6.00
❑ 291 Manny Ramirez BLH Jsy 15.00 4.50
❑ 292 Mike Sweeney BLH Jsy 15.00 4.50
❑ 293 Tom Glavine BLH Jsy .. 20.00 6.00
❑ 294 Joe Mays BLH Jsy........ 10.00 3.00
❑ 295 Eric Milton BLH Jsy 10.00 3.00
❑ 296 Magglio Ordonez BLH Jsy 15.00 4.50
❑ 297 Bernie Williams BLH Jsy 20.00 6.00
❑ 298 Trevor Hoffman BLH Jsy 15.00 4.50
❑ 299 Andruw Jones BLH Jsy 20.00 6.00
❑ 300 Aubrey Huff BLH Jsy 15.00 4.50
❑ 301 Jim Edmonds BLH Jsy 15.00 4.50
❑ 302 Kerry Wood BLH Jsy 20.00 6.00
❑ 303 Luis Gonzalez BLH Jsy 15.00 4.50
❑ 304 Shawn Green BLH Jsy.. 15.00 4.50
❑ 305 Jose Vidro BLH Jsy....... 15.00 4.50
❑ 306 Jeff Kent BLH Jsy 15.00 4.50
❑ 307 Edgardo Alfonzo BLH Jsy 15.00 4.50
❑ 308 Preston Wilson BLH Jsy 15.00 4.50
❑ 309 Roberto Alomar BLH Jsy 20.00 6.00
❑ 310 Jeromy Burnitz BLH Jsy 15.00 4.50
❑ 311 Phil Nevin BLH Jsy 15.00 4.50
❑ 312 Ryan Klesko BLH Jsy .. 15.00 4.50
❑ 313 Bob Abreu BLH Jsy...... 15.00 4.50
❑ 314 Scott Rolen BLH Jsy 20.00 6.00
❑ 315 Kazuhiro Sasaki BLH Jsy 15.00 4.50
❑ 316 Jason Kendall BLH Jsy 15.00 4.50
❑ 317 Sean Casey BLH Jsy 15.00 4.50
❑ 318 Larry Walker BLH Jsy .. 20.00 6.00
❑ 319 Mike Hampton BLH Jsy 15.00 4.50
❑ 320 Juan Gonzalez BLH Jsy 20.00 6.00
❑ 321 Darin Erstad HM Jsy 15.00 4.50
❑ 322 Tim Hudson HM Jsy 15.00 4.50
❑ 323 Carlos Delgado HM Jsy 15.00 4.50
❑ 324 Greg Vaughn HM Jsy .. 15.00 4.50
❑ 325 Jim Thome HM Jsy...... 20.00 6.00
❑ 326 Ichiro Suzuki HM Jsy .. 80.00 24.00
❑ 327 Rafael Palmeiro HM Jsy 20.00 6.00
❑ 328 Alex Rodriguez HM Jsy 30.00 9.00
❑ 329 Juan Gonzalez HM Jsy 20.00 6.00
❑ 330 Manny Ramirez HM Jsy 15.00 4.50
❑ 331 Carlos Beltran HM Jsy 15.00 4.50
❑ 332 Eric Milton HM Jsy 15.00 4.50
❑ 333 Frank Thomas HM Jsy 20.00 6.00
❑ 334 Roger Clemens HM Jsy 30.00 9.00
❑ 335 Jason Giambi HM Jsy .. 20.00 6.00
❑ 336 Lance Berkman HM Jsy 15.00 4.50
❑ 337 Greg Maddux HM Jsy .. 25.00 7.50
❑ 338 Chipper Jones HM Jsy 20.00 6.00
❑ 339 Sean Casey HM Jsy 15.00 4.50
❑ 340 Jim Edmonds HM Jsy .. 15.00 4.50
❑ 341 Kerry Wood HM Jsy 20.00 6.00
❑ 342 Sammy Sosa HM Jsy .. 30.00 9.00
❑ 343 Luis Gonzalez HM Jsy.. 15.00 4.50
❑ 344 Shawn Green HM Jsy .. 15.00 4.50
❑ 345 Jeff Kent HM Jsy.......... 15.00 4.50
❑ 346 Preston Wilson HM Jsy 15.00 4.50
❑ 347 Roberto Alomar HM Jsy 20.00 6.00
❑ 348 Phil Nevin HM Jsy 15.00 4.50
❑ 349 Scott Rolen HM Jsy...... 20.00 6.00
❑ 350 Mike Sweeney HM Jsy 15.00 4.50
❑ 351 Ken Griffey Jr. HM Jsy 25.00 7.50
❑ 352 Todd Helton HM Jsy 20.00 6.00
❑ 353 Larry Walker HM Jsy.... 20.00 6.00
❑ 354 Alex Rodriguez FC Jsy 40.00 12.00
❑ 355 Pedro Martinez FC Jsy 25.00 7.50
❑ 356 Frank Thomas FC Jsy .. 25.00 7.50
❑ 357 Jason Giambi FC Jsy .. 25.00 7.50
❑ 358 Bernie Williams FC Jsy 25.00 7.50
❑ 359 Jeff Bagwell FC Jsy...... 25.00 7.50
❑ 360 Chipper Jones FC Jsy .. 25.00 7.50
❑ 361 Sammy Sosa FC Jsy 40.00 12.00
❑ 362 Randy Johnson FC Jsy 25.00 7.50
❑ 363 Shawn Green FC Jsy.... 20.00 6.00
❑ 364 Mike Piazza FC Jsy 40.00 12.00
❑ 365 Ichiro Suzuki FC Jsy .. 100.00 30.00
❑ 366 Ken Griffey Jr. FC Jsy .. 30.00 9.00
❑ 367 Larry Walker FC Jsy 25.00 7.50
❑ 368 Jim Edmonds FC Jsy .. 20.00 6.00
❑ 369 Darin Erstad DC Bat 10.00 3.00
❑ 370 Tim Salmon DC Bat...... 15.00 4.50
❑ 371 Mark Kotsay DC Bat 10.00 3.00
❑ 372 Craig Biggio DC Bat 15.00 4.50
❑ 373 Eric Chavez DC Bat 10.00 3.00
❑ 374 David Justice DC Bat.... 10.00 3.00
❑ 375 Carlos Delgado DC Bat 10.00 3.00
❑ 376 Chipper Jones DC Bat.. 15.00 4.50
❑ 377 Gary Sheffield DC Bat .. 10.00 3.00
❑ 378 Greg Maddux DC Bat .. 20.00 6.00
❑ 379 Eric Karros DC Bat 10.00 3.00
❑ 380 Fred McGriff DC Bat 15.00 4.50
❑ 381 J.D. Drew DC Bat 10.00 3.00
❑ 382 Rick Ankiel DC Bat 10.00 3.00
❑ 383 Sammy Sosa DC Bat.... 25.00 7.50
❑ 384 Moises Alou DC Bat 10.00 3.00
❑ 385 Ben Grieve DC Bat 10.00 3.00
❑ 386 Greg Vaughn DC Bat.... 10.00 3.00
❑ 387 Jay Payton DC Bat........ 10.00 3.00
❑ 388 Luis Gonzalez DC Bat .. 10.00 3.00
❑ 389 Ray Durham DC Bat 10.00 3.00
❑ 390 Shawn Green DC Bat.... 10.00 3.00
❑ 391 Hideo Nomo DC Bat 25.00 7.50
❑ 392 Jose Vidro DC Bat........ 10.00 3.00
❑ 393 Jeff Kent DC Bat 10.00 3.00
❑ 394 Adrian Beltre DC Bat 10.00 3.00
❑ 395 Jim Thome DC Bat 15.00 4.50
❑ 396 Bob Abreu DC Bat........ 10.00 3.00
❑ 397 Edgar Martinez DC Bat 15.00 4.50
❑ 398 Carl Everett DC Bat 10.00 3.00
❑ 399 Luis Castillo DC Bat 10.00 3.00
❑ 400 Preston Wilson DC Bat 10.00 3.00
❑ 401 Jermaine Dye DC Bat .. 10.00 3.00
❑ 402 Roberto Alomar DC Bat 15.00 4.50
❑ 403 Todd Hundley DC Bat .. 10.00 3.00
❑ 404 Ryan Klesko DC Bat 10.00 3.00
❑ 405 Phil Nevin DC Bat 10.00 3.00
❑ 406 Scott Rolen DC Bat 15.00 4.50
❑ 407 Rafael Furcal DC Bat 10.00 3.00
❑ 408 Miguel Tejada DC Bat .. 10.00 3.00
❑ 409 Brian Giles DC Bat 10.00 3.00
❑ 410 Jason Kendall DC Bat .. 10.00 3.00
❑ 411 Alex Rodriguez DC Bat 25.00 7.50
❑ 412 Juan Gonzalez DC Bat .. 15.00 4.50
❑ 413 Ivan Rodriguez DC Bat 15.00 4.50
❑ 414 Rafael Palmeiro DC Bat 15.00 4.50
❑ 415 Ken Griffey Jr. DC Bat .. 20.00 6.00
❑ 416 Edgardo Alfonzo DC Bat 10.00 3.00
❑ 417 Barry Larkin DC Bat...... 15.00 4.50
❑ 418 Manny Ramirez DC Bat 10.00 3.00
❑ 419 Pedro Martinez DC Bat 15.00 4.50
❑ 420 Todd Helton DC Bat 15.00 4.50
❑ 421 Larry Walker DC Bat 15.00 4.50
❑ 422 Garret Anderson DC Bat 10.00 3.00
❑ 423 Mike Sweeney DC Bat .. 10.00 3.00
❑ 424 Carlos Beltran DC Bat .. 10.00 3.00
❑ 425 Javier Lopez DC Bat 10.00 3.00
❑ 426 J.T. Snow DC Bat 10.00 3.00
❑ 427 Doug Mientkiewicz DC Bat 10.00 3.00
❑ 428 John Olerud DC Bat 10.00 3.00
❑ 429 Magglio Ordonez DC Bat 10.00 3.00
❑ 430 Frank Thomas DC Bat .. 15.00 4.50
❑ 431 Kenny Lofton DC Bat.... 10.00 3.00
❑ 432 Al Leiter DC Bat............ 10.00 3.00
❑ 433 Bernie Williams DC Bat 15.00 4.50
❑ 434 Roger Clemens DC Bat 25.00 7.50
❑ 435 Tom Glavine DC Bat 15.00 4.50
❑ 436 Robin Ventura DC Bat .. 10.00 3.00
❑ 437 Chan Ho Park DC Bat .. 10.00 3.00
❑ 438 Jorge Posada DC Bat .. 15.00 4.50
❑ 439 Charles Johnson BLH Bat 15.00 4.50
❑ 440 Alex Rodriguez BLH Bat 30.00 9.00
❑ 441 Ken Griffey Jr. BLH Bat 25.00 7.50
❑ 442 Mark Kotsay BLH Bat .. 10.00 3.00
❑ 443 Frank Thomas BLH Bat 20.00 6.00
❑ 444 Greg Maddux BLH Bat.. 25.00 7.50
❑ 445 Sammy Sosa BLH Bat .. 30.00 9.00
❑ 446 Tom Glavine BLH Bat .. 20.00 6.00
❑ 447 Chipper Jones BLH Bat 20.00 6.00
❑ 448 Todd Helton BLH Bat.... 20.00 6.00
❑ 449 Jeff Cirillo BLH Bat 15.00 4.50
❑ 450 Steve Finley BLH Bat.... 15.00 4.50
❑ 451 Jim Thome BLH Bat 20.00 6.00

❑ 452 Ivan Rodriguez BLH Bat 20.00 6.00
❑ 453 Darin Erstad BLH Bat 15.00 4.50
❑ 454 Eric Chavez BLH Bat 15.00 4.50
❑ 455 Miguel Tejada BLH Bat 15.00 4.50
❑ 456 Carlos Delgado BLH Bat 15.00 4.50
❑ 457 Omar Vizquel BLH Bat 15.00 4.50
❑ 458 Edgar Martinez BLH Bat 20.00 6.00
❑ 459 Johnny Damon BLH Bat 15.00 4.50
❑ 460 Russell Branyan BLH Bat 10.00 3.00
❑ 461 Kenny Lofton BLH Bat 15.00 4.50
❑ 462 Jermaine Dye BLH Bat 15.00 4.50
❑ 463 Ellis Burks BLH Bat 15.00 4.50
❑ 464 Magglio Ordonez BLH Bat 15.00 4.50
❑ 465 Bernie Williams BLH Bat 20.00 6.00
❑ 466 Tim Salmon BLH Bat 20.00 6.00
❑ 467 Andruw Jones BLH Bat 20.00 6.00
❑ 468 Jeffrey Hammonds BLH Bat 10.00 3.00
❑ 469 Jim Edmonds BLH Bat 15.00 4.50
❑ 470 Kerry Wood BLH Bat 20.00 6.00
❑ 471 Luis Gonzalez BLH Bat 15.00 4.50
❑ 472 Shawn Green BLH Bat 15.00 4.50
❑ 473 Jose Vidro BLH Bat 15.00 4.50
❑ 474 Jeff Kent BLH Bat SP/189 15.00 4.50
❑ 475 Javier Lopez BLH Bat 15.00 4.50
❑ 476 Preston Wilson BLH Bat 15.00 4.50
❑ 477 Roberto Alomar BLH Bat 20.00 6.00
❑ 478 Robin Ventura BLH Bat 15.00 4.50
❑ 479 Phil Nevin BLH Bat 15.00 4.50
❑ 480 Ryan Klesko BLH Bat 15.00 4.50
❑ 481 Bob Abreu BLH Bat 15.00 4.50
❑ 482 Scott Rolen BLH Bat 20.00 6.00
❑ 483 Brian Giles BLH Bat 15.00 4.50
❑ 484 Jason Kendall BLH Bat 15.00 4.50
❑ 485 Tsuyoshi Shinjo BLH Bat 15.00 4.50
❑ 486 Larry Walker BLH Bat 20.00 6.00
❑ 487 Mike Lieberthal BLH Bat 15.00 4.50
❑ 488 Juan Gonzalez BLH Bat 20.00 6.00
❑ 489 Darin Erstad HM Bat 15.00 4.50
❑ 490 Tom Glavine HM Bat 20.00 6.00
❑ 491 Carlos Delgado HM Bat 15.00 4.50
❑ 492 Greg Vaughn HM Bat 15.00 4.50
❑ 493 Jim Thome HM Bat 20.00 6.00
❑ 494 Mark Grace HM Bat 20.00 6.00
❑ 495 Rafael Palmeiro HM Bat 20.00 6.00
❑ 496 Alex Rodriguez HM Bat 30.00 9.00
❑ 497 Juan Gonzalez HM Bat 20.00 6.00
❑ 498 Miguel Tejada HM Bat 15.00 4.50
❑ 499 Carlos Beltran HM Bat 15.00 4.50
❑ 500 Andruw Jones HM Bat 20.00 6.00
❑ 501 Frank Thomas HM Bat 20.00 6.00
❑ 502 Andres Galarraga HM Bat 15.00 4.50
❑ 503 Gary Sheffield HM Bat 15.00 4.50
❑ 504 Craig Biggio HM Bat 20.00 6.00
❑ 505 Greg Maddux HM Bat 25.00 7.50
❑ 506 Chipper Jones HM Bat 20.00 6.00
❑ 507 Pat Burrell HM Bat 15.00 4.50
❑ 508 Jim Edmonds HM Bat 15.00 4.50
❑ 509 Kerry Wood HM Bat 20.00 6.00
❑ 510 Sammy Sosa HM Bat 30.00 9.00
❑ 511 Luis Gonzalez HM Bat 15.00 4.50
❑ 512 Shawn Green HM Bat 15.00 4.50
❑ 513 Edgardo Alfonzo HM Bat 15.00 4.50
❑ 514 Preston Wilson HM Bat 15.00 4.50
❑ 515 Roberto Alomar HM Bat 20.00 6.00
❑ 516 Phil Nevin HM Bat 15.00 4.50
❑ 517 Scott Rolen HM Bat 20.00 6.00
❑ 518 Brian Giles HM Bat 15.00 4.50
❑ 519 Jorge Posada HM Bat 20.00 6.00
❑ 520 Todd Helton HM Bat 20.00 6.00
❑ 521 Larry Walker HM Bat 20.00 6.00
❑ 522 Alex Rodriguez FC Bat 40.00 12.00
❑ 523 Pedro Martinez FC Bat 25.00 7.50
❑ 524 Frank Thomas FC Bat 25.00 7.50
❑ 525 Jason Giambi FC Bat 25.00 7.50
❑ 526 Bernie Williams FC Bat 25.00 7.50
❑ 527 J.D. Drew FC Bat 20.00 6.00
❑ 528 Chipper Jones FC Bat 25.00 7.50
❑ 529 Sammy Sosa FC Bat 40.00 12.00
❑ 530 Randy Johnson FC Bat 25.00 7.50
❑ 531 Shawn Green FC Bat 20.00 6.00
❑ 532 Kevin Brown FC Bat 20.00 6.00
❑ 533 Brian Giles FC Bat 20.00 6.00
❑ 534 Ken Griffey Jr. FC Bat 30.00 9.00
❑ 535 Larry Walker FC Bat 25.00 7.50
❑ 536 Jim Edmonds FC Bat 20.00 6.00
❑ 537 Barry Zito DC Jsy 15.00 4.50
❑ 538 Bobby Abreu DC Jsy 10.00 3.00
❑ 539 Eric Karros DC Jsy 10.00 3.00
❑ 540 Sean Casey DC Jsy 10.00 3.00
❑ 541 Phil Nevin DC Jsy 10.00 3.00
❑ 542 Andruw Jones DC Jsy 15.00 4.50
❑ 543 Jim Thome DC Jsy 15.00 4.50
❑ 544 Jim Edmonds DC Jsy 10.00 3.00
❑ 545 Ichiro Suzuki DC Jsy 50.00 15.00
❑ 546 Kerry Wood DC Jsy 15.00 4.50
❑ 547 Eric Milton DC Jsy 10.00 3.00
❑ 548 Pat Burrell BLH Jsy 15.00 4.50
❑ 549 Adam Dunn BLH Jsy 20.00 6.00
❑ 550 Lance Berkman BLH Jsy 15.00 4.50
❑ 551 Lance Berkman HM Jsy 15.00 4.50
❑ 552 Barry Zito HM Jsy 20.00 6.00
❑ 553 Roger Clemens FC Jsy 25.00 7.50
❑ 554 Andres Galarraga DC Bat 10.00 3.00
❑ 555 Johnny Damon DC Bat 10.00 3.00
❑ 556 Jose Cruz Jr. DC Bat 10.00 3.00
❑ 557 Charles Johnson DC Bat 10.00 3.00
❑ 558 Matt Williams DC Bat 10.00 3.00
❑ 559 Andruw Jones DC Bat 15.00 4.50
❑ 560 Tsuyoshi Shinjo DC Bat 10.00 3.00
❑ 561 Jim Thome DC Bat 15.00 4.50
❑ 562 Omar Vizquel DC Bat 10.00 3.00
❑ 563 Frank Thomas DC Bat 15.00 4.50
❑ 564 Corey Patterson DC Bat 10.00 3.00
❑ 565 Fred McGriff BLH Bat 20.00 6.00
❑ 566 Manny Ramirez BLH Bat 15.00 4.50
❑ 567 Gary Sheffield BLH Bat 15.00 4.50
❑ 568 Manny Ramirez HM Bat 15.00 4.50
❑ 569 Mike Sweeney HM Bat 15.00 4.50
❑ 570 Todd Helton FC Bat 25.00 7.50
❑ 571 Erubiel Durazo .60 .18
❑ 572 Geronimo Gil .60 .18
❑ 573 Shea Hillenbrand .60 .18
❑ 574 Cliff Floyd .60 .18
❑ 575 Corey Patterson .60 .18
❑ 576 Joe Borchard .60 .18
❑ 577 Austin Kearns 1.00 .30
❑ 578 Ryan Dempster .60 .18
❑ 579 Brandon Larson .60 .18
❑ 580 Luis Castillo .60 .18
❑ 581 Juan Encarnacion .60 .18
❑ 582 Chin-Feng Chen .60 .18
❑ 583 Hideo Nomo 1.50 .45
❑ 584 Bartolo Colon .60 .18
❑ 585 Raul Mondesi .60 .18
❑ 586 Eric Munson .60 .18
❑ 587 Alfonso Soriano 1.50 .45
❑ 588 Ted Lilly .60 .18
❑ 589 Ray Durham .60 .18
❑ 590 Brett Myers .60 .18
❑ 591 Brandon Phillips .60 .18
❑ 592 Kenny Lofton .60 .18
❑ 593 Scott Rolen 1.00 .30
❑ 594 Jim Edmonds .60 .18
❑ 595 Carl Crawford .60 .18
❑ 596 Hank Blalock 1.50 .45
❑ 597 Kevin Mench .60 .18
❑ 598 Josh Phelps .60 .18
❑ 599 Orlando Hudson .60 .18
❑ 600 Eric Hinske .60 .18
❑ 601 Mike Mahoney DC 5.00 1.50
❑ 602 Jason Davis DC RC 10.00 3.00
❑ 603 Trey Hodges DC RC 8.00 2.40
❑ 604 Josh Bard DC RC 5.00 1.50
❑ 605 Jeriome Robertson DC RC 8.00 2.40
❑ 606 Jose Diaz DC RC 5.00 1.50
❑ 607 Jorge Nunez DC RC 5.00 1.50
❑ 608 Danny Mota DC RC 5.00 1.50
❑ 609 David Ross DC RC 5.00 1.50
❑ 610 Jayson Durocher DC RC 5.00 1.50
❑ 611 Freddy Sanchez DC RC 8.00 2.40
❑ 612 Julius Matos DC RC 5.00 1.50
❑ 613 Wil Nieves DC RC 5.00 1.50
❑ 614 Ben Kozlowski DC RC 5.00 1.50
❑ 615 Jason Simontacchi DC RC 8.00 2.40
❑ 616 Mike Coolbaugh DC RC 5.00 1.50
❑ 617 Travis Driskill DC RC 5.00 1.50
❑ 618 Howie Clark DC RC 5.00 1.50
❑ 619 Earl Snyder DC RC 5.00 1.50
❑ 620 Carl Sadler DC RC 5.00 1.50
❑ 621 Jason Beverlin DC RC 5.00 1.50
❑ 622 Terry Pearson DC RC 5.00 1.50
❑ 623 Eric Eckenstahler DC RC 5.00 1.50
❑ 624 Shawn Sedlacek DC RC 5.00 1.50
❑ 625 Aaron Guiel DC RC 8.00 2.40
❑ 626 Ryan Bukvich DC RC 8.00 2.40
❑ 627 Julio Mateo DC RC 5.00 1.50
❑ 628 Chris Snelling DC RC 8.00 2.40
❑ 629 Lance Carter DC RC 5.00 1.50
❑ 630 Scott Wiggins DC RC 5.00 1.50

2001 Upper Deck Evolution

	Nm-Mt	Ex-Mt
COMP.SET w/o SP's (90)	20.00	6.00
COMMON CARD (1-90)	.30	.09
COMMON CARD (91-120)	5.00	1.50

❑ 1 Darin Erstad .30 .09
❑ 2 Troy Glaus .50 .15
❑ 3 Jason Giambi .75 .23
❑ 4 Tim Hudson .30 .09
❑ 5 Jermaine Dye .30 .09
❑ 6 Barry Zito .75 .23
❑ 7 Carlos Delgado .30 .09
❑ 8 Shannon Stewart .30 .09
❑ 9 Jose Cruz Jr. .30 .09
❑ 10 Greg Vaughn .30 .09
❑ 11 Juan Gonzalez .75 .23
❑ 12 Roberto Alomar .75 .23
❑ 13 Omar Vizquel .30 .09
❑ 14 Jim Thome .75 .23
❑ 15 Edgar Martinez .50 .15
❑ 16 John Olerud .30 .09
❑ 17 Kazuhiro Sasaki .30 .09
❑ 18 Cal Ripken 2.50 .75
❑ 19 Alex Rodriguez 1.50 .45
❑ 20 Ivan Rodriguez .75 .23
❑ 21 Rafael Palmeiro .50 .15
❑ 22 Pedro Martinez .75 .23
❑ 23 Nomar Garciaparra 2.00 .60
❑ 24 Manny Ramirez .30 .09
❑ 25 Carl Everett .30 .09
❑ 26 Mark Quinn .30 .09
❑ 27 Mike Sweeney .30 .09
❑ 28 Neifi Perez .30 .09
❑ 29 Tony Clark .30 .09
❑ 30 Eric Milton .30 .09
❑ 31 Doug Mientkiewicz .30 .09
❑ 32 Corey Koskie .30 .09
❑ 33 Frank Thomas .75 .23
❑ 34 David Wells .30 .09
❑ 35 Magglio Ordonez .30 .09
❑ 36 Derek Jeter 2.00 .60
❑ 37 Mike Mussina .75 .23
❑ 38 Bernie Williams .50 .15
❑ 39 Roger Clemens 1.50 .45
❑ 40 David Justice .30 .09
❑ 41 Jeff Bagwell .50 .15
❑ 42 Richard Hidalgo .30 .09
❑ 43 Wade Miller .30 .09
❑ 44 Chipper Jones .75 .23
❑ 45 Greg Maddux 1.50 .45
❑ 46 Andruw Jones .50 .15
❑ 47 Rafael Furcal .30 .09
❑ 48 Geoff Jenkins .30 .09
❑ 49 Jeromy Burnitz .30 .09
❑ 50 Ben Sheets .30 .09
❑ 51 Richie Sexson .30 .09
❑ 52 Mark McGwire 2.00 .60

❑ 53 Jim Edmonds .30 .09
❑ 54 Darryl Kile .30 .09
❑ 55 J.D. Drew .30 .09
❑ 56 Sammy Sosa 1.25 .35
❑ 57 Kerry Wood .75 .23
❑ 58 Randy Johnson .75 .23
❑ 59 Luis Gonzalez .30 .09
❑ 60 Matt Williams .30 .09
❑ 61 Kevin Brown .30 .09
❑ 62 Gary Sheffield .30 .09
❑ 63 Shawn Green .30 .09
❑ 64 Chan Ho Park .30 .09
❑ 65 Vladimir Guerrero .75 .23
❑ 66 Jose Vidro .30 .09
❑ 67 Fernando Tatis .30 .09
❑ 68 Barry Bonds 2.00 .60
❑ 69 Jeff Kent .30 .09
❑ 70 Russ Ortiz .30 .09
❑ 71 Preston Wilson .30 .09
❑ 72 Ryan Dempster .30 .09
❑ 73 Charles Johnson .30 .09
❑ 74 Mike Piazza 1.25 .35
❑ 75 Edgardo Alfonzo .30 .09
❑ 76 Robin Ventura .30 .09
❑ 77 Jay Payton .30 .09
❑ 78 Tony Gwynn 1.00 .30
❑ 79 Phil Nevin .30 .09
❑ 80 Pat Burrell .30 .09
❑ 81 Scott Rolen .50 .15
❑ 82 Bob Abreu .30 .09
❑ 83 Brian Giles .30 .09
❑ 84 Jason Kendall .30 .09
❑ 85 Ken Griffey Jr. 1.25 .35
❑ 86 Barry Larkin .75 .23
❑ 87 Sean Casey .30 .09
❑ 88 Todd Helton .50 .15
❑ 89 Larry Walker .50 .15
❑ 90 Mike Hampton .30 .09
❑ 91 Ichiro Suzuki PROS RC 25.00 7.50
❑ 92 Albert Pujols PROS RC 30.00 9.00
❑ 93 W.Betemit PROS RC 5.00 1.50
❑ 94 Jay Gibbons PROS RC 8.00 2.40
❑ 95 Juan Uribe PROS RC 5.00 1.50
❑ 96 M. Ensberg PROS RC 8.00 2.40
❑ 97 C. Parker PROS RC 5.00 1.50
❑ 98 T. Shinjo PROS RC 8.00 2.40
❑ 99 Jack Wilson PROS RC 5.00 1.50
❑ 100 D. Mendez PROS RC 5.00 1.50
❑ 101 Ryan Freel PROS RC 5.00 1.50
❑ 102 Juan Diaz PROS RC 5.00 1.50
❑ 103 H. Ramirez PROS RC 8.00 2.40
❑ 104 R. Rodriguez PROS RC 5.00 1.50
❑ 105 E. Almonte PROS RC 5.00 1.50
❑ 106 J. Towers PROS RC 5.00 1.50
❑ 107 A.Hernandez PROS RC 5.00 1.50
❑ 108 B.Duckworth PROS RC 5.00 1.50
❑ 109 T. Hafner PROS RC 8.00 2.40
❑ 110 M. Vargas PROS RC 5.00 1.50
❑ 111 Kris Keller PROS RC 5.00 1.50
❑ 112 B. Lawrence PROS RC 5.00 1.50
❑ 113 Esix Snead PROS RC 5.00 1.50
❑ 114 Wilkin Ruan PROS RC 5.00 1.50
❑ 115 J. Mieses PROS RC 5.00 1.50
❑ 116 J. Estrada PROS RC 5.00 1.50
❑ 117 E. Guzman PROS RC 5.00 1.50
❑ 118 S. Douglass PROS RC 5.00 1.50
❑ 119 B. Sylvester PROS RC 5.00 1.50
❑ 120 Bret Prinz PROS RC 5.00 1.50

2003 Upper Deck First Pitch

	Nm-Mt	Ex-Mt
COMP.SET w/o SP's (270)	40.00	12.00
COMMON CARD (31-270)	.20	.06
COMMON CARD (1-30)	.50	.15
COMMON CARD (271-283)	3.00	.90
COMMON CARD (284-300)	3.00	.90

❑ 1 John Lackey SR .50 .15
❑ 2 Alex Cintron SR .50 .15
❑ 3 Jose Leon SR .50 .15
❑ 4 Bobby Hill SR .50 .15
❑ 5 Brandon Larson SR .50 .15
❑ 6 Raul Gonzalez SR .50 .15

❑ 7 Ben Broussard SR .50 .15
❑ 8 Earl Snyder SR .50 .15
❑ 9 Ramon Santiago SR .50 .15
❑ 10 Jason Lane SR .50 .15
❑ 11 Rob Hammock SR RC .60 .18
❑ 12 Kirk Saarloos SR .50 .15
❑ 13 Juan Brito SR .50 .15
❑ 14 Runelvys Hernandez SR .50 .15
❑ 15 Shawn Sedlacek SR .50 .15
❑ 16 Jayson Durocher SR .50 .15
❑ 17 Kevin Frederick SR .50 .15
❑ 18 Zach Day SR .50 .15
❑ 19 Marco Scutaro SR .50 .15
❑ 20 Marcus Thames SR .50 .15
❑ 21 Esteban German SR .50 .15
❑ 22 Brett Myers SR .50 .15
❑ 23 Oliver Perez SR .50 .15
❑ 24 Dennis Tankersley SR .50 .15
❑ 25 Julius Matos SR .50 .15
❑ 26 Jake Peavy SR .50 .15
❑ 27 Eric Cyr SR .50 .15
❑ 28 Mike Crudale SR .50 .15
❑ 29 Josh Pearce SR .50 .15
❑ 30 Carl Crawford SR .50 .15
❑ 31 Tim Salmon .30 .09
❑ 32 Troy Glaus .30 .09
❑ 33 Adam Kennedy .20 .06
❑ 34 David Eckstein .20 .06
❑ 35 Bengie Molina .20 .06
❑ 36 Jarrod Washburn .20 .06
❑ 37 Ramon Ortiz .20 .06
❑ 38 Eric Chavez .20 .06
❑ 39 Miguel Tejada .20 .06
❑ 40 Adam Piatt .20 .06
❑ 41 Jermaine Dye .20 .06
❑ 42 Olmedo Saenz .20 .06
❑ 43 Tim Hudson .20 .06
❑ 44 Barry Zito .50 .15
❑ 45 Billy Koch .20 .06
❑ 46 Shannon Stewart .20 .06
❑ 47 Kelvim Escobar .20 .06
❑ 48 Jose Cruz Jr. .20 .06
❑ 49 Vernon Wells .20 .06
❑ 50 Roy Halladay .20 .06
❑ 51 Esteban Loaiza .20 .06
❑ 52 Eric Hinske .20 .06
❑ 53 Steve Cox .20 .06
❑ 54 Brent Abernathy .20 .06
❑ 55 Ben Grieve .20 .06
❑ 56 Aubrey Huff .20 .06
❑ 57 Jared Sandberg .20 .06
❑ 58 Paul Wilson .20 .06
❑ 59 Tanyon Sturtze .20 .06
❑ 60 Jim Thome .50 .15
❑ 61 Omar Vizquel .20 .06
❑ 62 C.C. Sabathia .20 .06
❑ 63 Chris Magruder .20 .06
❑ 64 Ricky Gutierrez .20 .06
❑ 65 Einar Diaz .20 .06
❑ 66 Danys Baez .20 .06
❑ 67 Ichiro Suzuki 1.00 .30
❑ 68 Ruben Sierra .20 .06
❑ 69 Carlos Guillen .20 .06
❑ 70 Mark McLemore .20 .06
❑ 71 Dan Wilson .20 .06
❑ 72 Jamie Moyer .20 .06
❑ 73 Joel Pineiro .20 .06
❑ 74 Edgar Martinez .30 .09
❑ 75 Tony Batista .20 .06
❑ 76 Jay Gibbons .20 .06
❑ 77 Chris Singleton .20 .06
❑ 78 Melvin Mora .20 .06
❑ 79 Geronimo Gil .20 .06
❑ 80 Rodrigo Lopez .20 .06
❑ 81 Jorge Julio .20 .06
❑ 82 Rafael Palmeiro .30 .09
❑ 83 Juan Gonzalez .50 .15
❑ 84 Mike Young .20 .06
❑ 85 Hideki Irabu .20 .06
❑ 86 Chan Ho Park .20 .06
❑ 87 Kevin Mench .20 .06
❑ 88 Doug Davis .20 .06
❑ 89 Pedro Martinez .50 .15
❑ 90 Shea Hillenbrand .20 .06
❑ 91 Derek Lowe .20 .06
❑ 92 Jason Varitek .20 .06
❑ 93 Tony Clark .20 .06
❑ 94 John Burkett .20 .06
❑ 95 Frank Castillo .20 .06
❑ 96 Nomar Garciaparra 1.00 .30
❑ 97 Rickey Henderson .75 .23
❑ 98 Mike Sweeney .20 .06
❑ 99 Carlos Febles .20 .06
❑ 100 Mark Quinn .20 .06
❑ 101 Raul Ibanez .20 .06
❑ 102 A.J. Hinch .20 .06
❑ 103 Paul Byrd .20 .06
❑ 104 Chuck Knoblauch .20 .06
❑ 105 Dmitri Young .20 .06
❑ 106 Randall Simon .20 .06
❑ 107 Brandon Inge .20 .06
❑ 108 Damion Easley .20 .06
❑ 109 Carlos Pena .20 .06
❑ 110 George Lombard .20 .06
❑ 111 Juan Acevedo .20 .06
❑ 112 Torii Hunter .20 .06
❑ 113 Doug Mientkiewicz .20 .06
❑ 114 David Ortiz .20 .06
❑ 115 Eric Milton .20 .06
❑ 116 Eddie Guardado .20 .06
❑ 117 Cristian Guzman .20 .06
❑ 118 Corey Koskie .20 .06
❑ 119 Magglio Ordonez .20 .06
❑ 120 Mark Buehrle .20 .06
❑ 121 Todd Ritchie .20 .06
❑ 122 Jose Valentin .20 .06
❑ 123 Paul Konerko .20 .06
❑ 124 Carlos Lee .20 .06
❑ 125 Jon Garland .20 .06
❑ 126 Jason Giambi .50 .15
❑ 127 Derek Jeter 1.25 .35
❑ 128 Roger Clemens 1.00 .30
❑ 129 Raul Mondesi .20 .06
❑ 130 Jorge Posada .30 .09
❑ 131 Rondell White .20 .06
❑ 132 Robin Ventura .20 .06
❑ 133 Mike Mussina .50 .15
❑ 134 Jeff Bagwell .30 .09
❑ 135 Craig Biggio .30 .09
❑ 136 Morgan Ensberg .20 .06
❑ 137 Richard Hidalgo .20 .06
❑ 138 Brad Ausmus .20 .06
❑ 139 Roy Oswalt .20 .06
❑ 140 Carlos Hernandez .20 .06
❑ 141 Shane Reynolds .20 .06
❑ 142 Gary Sheffield .20 .06
❑ 143 Andruw Jones .30 .09
❑ 144 Tom Glavine .50 .15
❑ 145 Rafael Furcal .20 .06
❑ 146 Javy Lopez .20 .06
❑ 147 Vinny Castilla .20 .06
❑ 148 Marcus Giles .20 .06
❑ 149 Kevin Millwood .20 .06
❑ 150 Jason Marquis .20 .06
❑ 151 Ruben Quevedo .20 .06
❑ 152 Ben Sheets .20 .06
❑ 153 Geoff Jenkins .20 .06
❑ 154 Jose Hernandez .20 .06
❑ 155 Glendon Rusch .20 .06
❑ 156 Jeffrey Hammonds .20 .06
❑ 157 Alex Sanchez .20 .06
❑ 158 Jim Edmonds .20 .06
❑ 159 Tino Martinez .30 .09
❑ 160 Albert Pujols 1.00 .30

- ❑ 161 Eli Marrero .20 .06
- ❑ 162 Woody Williams .20 .06
- ❑ 163 Fernando Vina .20 .06
- ❑ 164 Jason Isringhausen .20 .06
- ❑ 165 Jason Simontacchi .20 .06
- ❑ 166 Kerry Robinson .20 .06
- ❑ 167 Sammy Sosa .75 .23
- ❑ 168 Juan Cruz .20 .06
- ❑ 169 Fred McGriff .30 .09
- ❑ 170 Antonio Alfonseca .20 .06
- ❑ 171 Jon Lieber .20 .06
- ❑ 172 Mark Prior 1.00 .30
- ❑ 173 Moises Alou .20 .06
- ❑ 174 Matt Clement .20 .06
- ❑ 175 Mark Bellhorn .20 .06
- ❑ 176 Randy Johnson .50 .15
- ❑ 177 Luis Gonzalez .20 .06
- ❑ 178 Tony Womack .20 .06
- ❑ 179 Mark Grace .50 .15
- ❑ 180 Junior Spivey .20 .06
- ❑ 181 Byung-Hyun Kim .20 .06
- ❑ 182 Danny Bautista .20 .06
- ❑ 183 Brian Anderson .20 .06
- ❑ 184 Shawn Green .20 .06
- ❑ 185 Brian Jordan .20 .06
- ❑ 186 Eric Karros .20 .06
- ❑ 187 Andy Ashby .20 .06
- ❑ 188 Cesar Izturis .20 .06
- ❑ 189 Dave Roberts .20 .06
- ❑ 190 Eric Gagne .30 .09
- ❑ 191 Kazuhisa Ishii .20 .06
- ❑ 192 Adrian Beltre .20 .06
- ❑ 193 Vladimir Guerrero .50 .15
- ❑ 194 Tony Armas Jr. .20 .06
- ❑ 195 Bartolo Colon .20 .06
- ❑ 196 Troy O'Leary .20 .06
- ❑ 197 Tomokazu Ohka .20 .06
- ❑ 198 Brad Wilkerson .20 .06
- ❑ 199 Orlando Cabrera .20 .06
- ❑ 200 Barry Bonds 1.25 .35
- ❑ 201 David Bell .20 .06
- ❑ 202 Tsuyoshi Shinjo .20 .06
- ❑ 203 Benito Santiago .20 .06
- ❑ 204 Livan Hernandez .20 .06
- ❑ 205 Jason Schmidt .20 .06
- ❑ 206 Kirk Rueter .20 .06
- ❑ 207 Ramon E. Martinez .20 .06
- ❑ 208 Mike Lowell .20 .06
- ❑ 209 Luis Castillo .20 .06
- ❑ 210 Derrek Lee .20 .06
- ❑ 211 Andy Fox .20 .06
- ❑ 212 Eric Owens .20 .06
- ❑ 213 Charles Johnson .20 .06
- ❑ 214 Brad Penny .20 .06
- ❑ 215 A.J. Burnett .20 .06
- ❑ 216 Edgardo Alfonzo .20 .06
- ❑ 217 Roberto Alomar .50 .15
- ❑ 218 Rey Ordonez .20 .06
- ❑ 219 Al Leiter .20 .06
- ❑ 220 Roger Cedeno .20 .06
- ❑ 221 Timo Perez .20 .06
- ❑ 222 Jeromy Burnitz .20 .06
- ❑ 223 Pedro Astacio .20 .06
- ❑ 224 Joe McEwing .20 .06
- ❑ 225 Ryan Klesko .20 .06
- ❑ 226 Ramon Vazquez .20 .06
- ❑ 227 Mark Kotsay .20 .06
- ❑ 228 Bubba Trammell .20 .06
- ❑ 229 Wiki Gonzalez .20 .06
- ❑ 230 Trevor Hoffman .20 .06
- ❑ 231 Ron Gant .20 .06
- ❑ 232 Bobby Abreu .20 .06
- ❑ 233 Marlon Anderson .20 .06
- ❑ 234 Jeremy Giambi .20 .06
- ❑ 235 Jimmy Rollins .20 .06
- ❑ 236 Mike Lieberthal .20 .06
- ❑ 237 Vicente Padilla .20 .06
- ❑ 238 Randy Wolf .20 .06
- ❑ 239 Pokey Reese .20 .06
- ❑ 240 Brian Giles .20 .06
- ❑ 241 Jack Wilson .20 .06
- ❑ 242 Mike Williams .20 .06
- ❑ 243 Kip Wells .20 .06
- ❑ 244 Rob Mackowiak .20 .06
- ❑ 245 Craig Wilson .20 .06
- ❑ 246 Adam Dunn .30 .09
- ❑ 247 Sean Casey .20 .06
- ❑ 248 Todd Walker .20 .06
- ❑ 249 Corky Miller .20 .06
- ❑ 250 Ryan Dempster .20 .06
- ❑ 251 Reggie Taylor .20 .06
- ❑ 252 Aaron Boone .20 .06
- ❑ 253 Larry Walker .30 .09
- ❑ 254 Jose Ortiz .20 .06
- ❑ 255 Todd Zeile .20 .06
- ❑ 256 Bobby Estalella .20 .06
- ❑ 257 Juan Pierre .20 .06
- ❑ 258 Terry Shumpert .20 .06
- ❑ 259 Mike Hampton .20 .06
- ❑ 260 Denny Stark .20 .06
- ❑ 261 Shawn Green SH CL .20 .06
- ❑ 262 Derek Lowe SH CL .20 .06
- ❑ 263 Barry Bonds SH CL .60 .18
- ❑ 264 Mike Cameron SH CL .20 .06
- ❑ 265 Luis Castillo SH CL .20 .06
- ❑ 266 Vladimir Guerrero SH CL .30 .09
- ❑ 267 Jason Giambi SH CL .30 .09
- ❑ 268 Eric Gagne SH CL .20 .06
- ❑ 269 Magglio Ordonez SH CL .20 .06
- ❑ 270 Jim Thome SH CL .30 .09
- ❑ 271 Hideki Matsui SP RC 15.00 4.50
- ❑ 272 Jose Contreras SP RC 6.00 1.80
- ❑ 273 Robert Madritsch SP RC 3.00 .90
- ❑ 274 Shane Bazzell SP RC 3.00 .90
- ❑ 275 Felix Sanchez SP RC 3.00 .90
- ❑ 276 Todd Wellemeyer SP RC 4.00 1.20
- ❑ 277 Lew Ford SP RC 4.00 1.20
- ❑ 278 Jeremy Griffiths SP RC 4.00 1.20
- ❑ 279 Oscar Villarreal SP RC 3.00 .90
- ❑ 280 Brandon Webb SP RC 8.00 2.40
- ❑ 281 Delvis Lantigua SP RC 3.00 .90
- ❑ 282 Josh Willingham SP RC 5.00 1.50
- ❑ 283 Mike Nicolas SP RC 3.00 .90
- ❑ 284 Mike Hampton SP 3.00 .90
- ❑ 285 Jim Thome SP 4.00 1.20
- ❑ 286 Bartolo Colon SP 3.00 .90
- ❑ 287 Orlando Hernandez SP 3.00 .90
- ❑ 288 Jeremy Giambi SP 3.00 .90
- ❑ 289 Jeff Kent SP 3.00 .90
- ❑ 290 Tom Glavine SP 4.00 1.20
- ❑ 291 Cliff Floyd SP 3.00 .90
- ❑ 292 Tsuyoshi Shinjo SP 3.00 .90
- ❑ 293 Jose Cruz Jr. SP 3.00 .90
- ❑ 294 Edgardo Alfonzo SP 3.00 .90
- ❑ 295 Andres Galarraga SP 3.00 .90
- ❑ 296 Troy O'Leary SP 3.00 .90
- ❑ 297 Eric Karros SP 3.00 .90
- ❑ 298 Ivan Rodriguez SP 4.00 1.20
- ❑ 299 Fred McGriff SP 4.00 1.20
- ❑ 300 Preston Wilson SP 3.00 .90

2003 Upper Deck Game Face

	Nm-Mt	Ex-Mt
COMP.SET w/o SP's (90)	25.00	7.50
COMMON CARD (1-120)	.50	.15
COMMON SP (1-120)	4.00	1.20
COMMON CARD (121-150)	4.00	1.20
COMMON CARD (151-171)	8.00	2.40
COMMON CARD (172-192)	8.00	2.40

- ❑ 1 Darin Erstad .50 .15
- ❑ 2 Garret Anderson .50 .15
- ❑ 3 Tim Salmon .75 .23
- ❑ 4 Jarrod Washburn .50 .15
- ❑ 5 Troy Glaus SP 5.00 1.50
- ❑ 6 Luis Gonzalez .50 .15
- ❑ 7 Junior Spivey .50 .15
- ❑ 8 Randy Johnson SP 5.00 1.50
- ❑ 9 Curt Schilling SP 5.00 1.50
- ❑ 10 Andruw Jones .75 .23
- ❑ 11 Gary Sheffield .50 .15
- ❑ 12 Rafael Furcal .50 .15
- ❑ 13 Greg Maddux SP 10.00 3.00
- ❑ 14 Chipper Jones SP 5.00 1.50
- ❑ 15 Tony Batista .50 .15
- ❑ 16 Rodrigo Lopez .50 .15
- ❑ 17 Jay Gibbons .50 .15
- ❑ 18 Shea Hillenbrand .50 .15
- ❑ 19 Johnny Damon .50 .15
- ❑ 20 Derek Lowe .50 .15
- ❑ 21 Nomar Garciaparra 2.50 .75
- ❑ 22 Pedro Martinez SP 5.00 1.50
- ❑ 23 Manny Ramirez SP 4.00 1.20
- ❑ 24 Mark Prior 2.50 .75
- ❑ 25 Kerry Wood 1.25 .35
- ❑ 26 Corey Patterson .50 .15
- ❑ 27 Sammy Sosa SP 8.00 2.40
- ❑ 28 Magglio Ordonez .50 .15
- ❑ 29 Frank Thomas 1.25 .35
- ❑ 30 Paul Konerko .50 .15
- ❑ 31 Adam Dunn .75 .23
- ❑ 32 Austin Kearns .75 .23
- ❑ 33 Aaron Boone .50 .15
- ❑ 34 Ken Griffey Jr. SP 8.00 2.40
- ❑ 35 Omar Vizquel .50 .15
- ❑ 36 C.C. Sabathia .50 .15
- ❑ 37 Karim Garcia SP 4.00 1.20
- ❑ 38 Larry Walker .75 .23
- ❑ 39 Preston Wilson .50 .15
- ❑ 40 Jay Payton .50 .15
- ❑ 41 Todd Helton SP 5.00 1.50
- ❑ 42 Carlos Pena .50 .15
- ❑ 43 Eric Munson .50 .15
- ❑ 44 Mike Lowell .50 .15
- ❑ 45 Josh Beckett .75 .23
- ❑ 46 A.J. Burnett .50 .15
- ❑ 47 Roy Oswalt .50 .15
- ❑ 48 Craig Biggio .75 .23
- ❑ 49 Jeff Bagwell SP 5.00 1.50
- ❑ 50 Lance Berkman SP 4.00 1.20
- ❑ 51 Mike Sweeney .50 .15
- ❑ 52 Carlos Beltran .50 .15
- ❑ 53 Hideo Nomo 1.25 .35
- ❑ 54 Odalis Perez .50 .15
- ❑ 55 Adrian Beltre .50 .15
- ❑ 56 Shawn Green SP 4.00 1.20
- ❑ 57 Kazuhisa Ishii SP 4.00 1.20
- ❑ 58 Ben Sheets .50 .15
- ❑ 59 Richie Sexson .50 .15
- ❑ 60 Torii Hunter .50 .15
- ❑ 61 Jacque Jones .50 .15
- ❑ 62 Eric Milton .50 .15
- ❑ 63 Corey Koskie .50 .15
- ❑ 64 A.J. Pierzynski .50 .15
- ❑ 65 Jose Vidro .50 .15
- ❑ 66 Bartolo Colon .50 .15
- ❑ 67 Vladimir Guerrero SP 5.00 1.50
- ❑ 68 Tom Glavine 1.25 .35
- ❑ 69 Mike Piazza SP 8.00 2.40
- ❑ 70 Roberto Alomar SP 5.00 1.50
- ❑ 71 Jorge Posada .75 .23
- ❑ 72 Mike Mussina 1.25 .35
- ❑ 73 Robin Ventura .50 .15
- ❑ 74 Raul Mondesi .50 .15
- ❑ 75 Roger Clemens SP UER 10.00 3.00
  Card mistakenly numbered as 79
- ❑ 76 Jason Giambi SP 5.00 1.50
- ❑ 77 Bernie Williams SP 5.00 1.50
- ❑ 78 Alfonso Soriano SP 5.00 1.50
- ❑ 79 Derek Jeter SP 12.00 3.60
- ❑ 80 Miguel Tejada .50 .15
- ❑ 81 Eric Chavez .50 .15
- ❑ 82 Tim Hudson .50 .15
- ❑ 83 Barry Zito 1.25 .35
- ❑ 84 Mark Mulder .50 .15
- ❑ 85 Pat Burrell .50 .15
- ❑ 86 Jim Thome 1.25 .35
- ❑ 87 Bobby Abreu .50 .15

❑ 88 Brian Giles .50 .15
❑ 89 Jason Kendall .50 .15
❑ 90 Aramis Ramirez .50 .15
❑ 91 Ryan Klesko .50 .15
❑ 92 Phil Nevin .50 .15
❑ 93 Sean Burroughs .50 .15
❑ 94 J.T. Snow .50 .15
❑ 95 Rich Aurilia .50 .15
❑ 96 Benito Santiago .50 .15
❑ 97 Barry Bonds SP 12.00 3.60
❑ 98 Edgar Martinez .75 .23
❑ 99 John Olerud .50 .15
❑ 100 Bret Boone .50 .15
❑ 101 Ichiro Suzuki SP 10.00 3.00
❑ 102 J.D. Drew .50 .15
❑ 103 Jim Edmonds .50 .15
❑ 104 Scott Rolen .75 .23
❑ 105 Matt Morris .50 .15
❑ 106 Tino Martinez .75 .23
❑ 107 Albert Pujols SP 10.00 3.00
❑ 108 Aubrey Huff .50 .15
❑ 109 Carl Crawford .50 .15
❑ 110 Rafael Palmeiro .75 .23
❑ 111 Hank Blalock .75 .23
❑ 112 Alex Rodriguez SP 10.00 3.00
❑ 113 Kevin Mench SP 4.00 1.20
❑ 114 Juan Gonzalez SP 5.00 1.50
❑ 115 Shannon Stewart .50 .15
❑ 116 Vernon Wells .50 .15
❑ 117 Josh Phelps .50 .15
❑ 118 Eric Hinske .50 .15
❑ 119 Orlando Hudson .50 .15
❑ 120 Carlos Delgado SP 4.00 1.20
❑ 121 David Sanders FF RC 4.00 1.20
❑ 122 Rob Hammock FF RC 5.00 1.50
❑ 123 Rett Johnson FF RC 5.00 1.50
❑ 124 Mike Nicolas FF RC 4.00 1.20
❑ 125 Termel Sledge FF RC 5.00 1.50
❑ 126 Ryan Cameron FF RC 4.00 1.20
❑ 127 Prentice Redman FF RC 4.00 1.20
❑ 128 Clint Barmes FF RC 5.00 1.50
❑ 129 Brent Hoard FF RC 4.00 1.20
❑ 130 Willie Eyre FF RC 4.00 1.20
❑ 131 Phil Seibel FF RC 4.00 1.20
❑ 132 Chris Capuano FF RC 4.00 1.20
❑ 133 Bobby Madritsch FF RC 4.00 1.20
❑ 134 Shane Bazzell FF RC 4.00 1.20
❑ 135 Jeremy Griffiths FF RC 5.00 1.50
❑ 136 Jon Leicester FF RC 4.00 1.20
❑ 137 Brandon Webb FF RC 10.00 3.00
❑ 138 Todd Wellemeyer FF RC 5.00 1.50
❑ 139 Jose Contreras FF RC 8.00 2.40
❑ 140 Felix Sanchez FF RC 4.00 1.20
❑ 141 Arnie Munoz FF RC 4.00 1.20
❑ 142 Delvis Lantigua FF RC 4.00 1.20
❑ 143 Francisco Cruceta FF RC 4.00 1.20
❑ 144 Josh Willingham FF RC 6.00 1.80
❑ 145 Oscar Villarreal FF RC 4.00 1.20
❑ 146 Ian Ferguson FF RC 4.00 1.20
❑ 147 Pedro Liriano FF 4.00 1.20
❑ 148 Lew Ford FF RC 5.00 1.50
❑ 149 Jeff Duncan FF RC 5.00 1.50
❑ 150 Rich Fischer FF RC 4.00 1.20
❑ 151 Troy Glaus GF 8.00 2.40
❑ 152 Randy Johnson GF 10.00 3.00
❑ 153 Hideki Matsui GF RC 20.00 6.00
❑ 154 Chipper Jones GF 10.00 3.00
❑ 155 Nomar Garciaparra GF 15.00 4.50
❑ 156 Pedro Martinez GF 10.00 3.00
❑ 157 Ted Williams GF 25.00 7.50
❑ 158 Sammy Sosa GF 15.00 4.50
❑ 159 Ken Griffey Jr. GF 15.00 4.50
❑ 160 Vladimir Guerrero GF 10.00 3.00
❑ 161 Mike Piazza GF 12.00 3.60
❑ 162 Mickey Mantle GF 40.00 12.00
❑ 163 Alfonso Soriano GF 10.00 3.00
❑ 164 Derek Jeter GF 20.00 6.00
❑ 165 Roger Clemens GF 15.00 4.50
❑ 166 Jason Giambi GF 10.00 3.00
❑ 167 Barry Bonds GF 20.00 6.00
❑ 168 Ichiro Suzuki GF 15.00 4.50
❑ 169 Albert Pujols GF 15.00 4.50
❑ 170 Mark McGwire GF 20.00 6.00
❑ 171 Alex Rodriguez GF 15.00 4.50
❑ 172 Roy Oswalt 15.00 4.50
Ken Griffey Jr.
❑ 173 Barry Zito 10.00 3.00
Troy Glaus
❑ 174 Tim Hudson 15.00 4.50
Ichiro Suzuki
❑ 175 Mark Mulder 15.00 4.50
Alex Rodriguez
❑ 176 Tom Glavine 10.00 3.00
Vladimir Guerrero
❑ 177 Greg Maddux 15.00 4.50
Mike Piazza
❑ 178 Mark McGwire 30.00 9.00
Sammy Sosa
❑ 179 Mark Prior 15.00 4.50
Lance Berkman
❑ 180 Kerry Wood 15.00 4.50
Albert Pujols
❑ 181 Randy Johnson 10.00 3.00
Jeff Bagwell
❑ 182 Curt Schilling 20.00 6.00
Derek Jeter
❑ 183 Hideo Nomo 20.00 6.00
Barry Bonds
❑ 184 Kazuhisa Ishii 8.00 2.40
Todd Helton
❑ 185 Freddy Garcia 8.00 2.40
Eric Chavez
❑ 186 Al Leiter 10.00 3.00
Chipper Jones
❑ 187 Ted Williams 25.00 7.50
Nomar Garciaparra
❑ 188 Pedro Martinez 15.00 4.50
Hideki Matsui
❑ 189 Derek Lowe 8.00 2.40
Bernie Williams
❑ 190 Roger Clemens 20.00 6.00
Mike Piazza
❑ 191 Mike Mussina 10.00 3.00
Manny Ramirez
❑ 192 Mickey Mantle 30.00 9.00
Jason Giambi
❑ 193 Aaron Looper FF RC
❑ 194 Alex Prieto FF RC
❑ 195 Bo Hart FF RC
❑ 196 Chad Gaudin FF RC
❑ 197 Colin Porter FF RC
❑ 198 D.J. Carrasco FF RC
❑ 199 Dan Haren FF RC
❑ 200 Delmon Young FF RC
❑ 201 Dontrelle Willis FF
❑ 202 Jon Switzer FF
❑ 203 Edwin Jackson FF RC
❑ 204 Fernando Cabrera FF RC
❑ 205 Garrett Atkins FF
❑ 206 Jeremy Bonderman FF RC
❑ 207 Kevin Ohme FF RC
❑ 208 Khalil Greene FF
❑ 209 Luis Ayala FF RC
❑ 210 Matt Kata FF RC
❑ 211 Noah Lowry FF
❑ 212 Rich Harden FF
❑ 213 Rickie Weeks FF RC
❑ 214 Rosman Garcia FF RC
❑ 215 Ryan Wagner FF RC
❑ 216 Tom Gregorio FF RC
❑ 217 Wilfredo Ledezma FF RC
❑ NNO Ken Griffey Jr. Sample 5.00 1.50

2001 Upper Deck Gold Glove

	Nm-Mt	Ex-Mt
COMP.SET w/o SP'S (90)	25.00	7.50
COMMON CARD (1-90)	.60	.18
COMMON CARD (91-129)	8.00	2.40
COMMON (130-135)	15.00	4.50

❑ 1 Troy Glaus 1.00 .30
❑ 2 Darin Erstad .60 .18
❑ 3 Jason Giambi 1.50 .45
❑ 4 Tim Hudson .60 .18
❑ 5 Jermaine Dye .60 .18
❑ 6 Raul Mondesi .60 .18
❑ 7 Carlos Delgado .60 .18
❑ 8 Shannon Stewart .60 .18
❑ 9 Greg Vaughn .60 .18

❑ 10 Aubrey Huff .60 .18
❑ 11 Juan Gonzalez 1.50 .45
❑ 12 Roberto Alomar 1.50 .45
❑ 13 Omar Vizquel .60 .18
❑ 14 Jim Thome 1.50 .45
❑ 15 John Olerud .60 .18
❑ 16 Edgar Martinez 1.00 .30
❑ 17 Kazuhiro Sasaki .60 .18
❑ 18 Aaron Sele .60 .18
❑ 19 Cal Ripken 5.00 1.50
❑ 20 Chris Richard .60 .18
❑ 21 Ivan Rodriguez 1.50 .45
❑ 22 Rafael Palmeiro 1.00 .30
❑ 23 Alex Rodriguez 3.00 .90
❑ 24 Pedro Martinez 1.50 .45
❑ 25 Nomar Garciaparra 3.00 .90
❑ 26 Manny Ramirez .60 .18
❑ 27 Neifi Perez .60 .18
❑ 28 Mike Sweeney .60 .18
❑ 29 Bobby Higginson .60 .18
❑ 30 Dean Palmer .60 .18
❑ 31 Tony Clark .60 .18
❑ 32 Doug Mientkiewicz .60 .18
❑ 33 Brad Radke .60 .18
❑ 34 Joe Mays .60 .18
❑ 35 Frank Thomas 1.50 .45
❑ 36 Magglio Ordonez .60 .18
❑ 37 Carlos Lee .60 .18
❑ 38 Bernie Williams 1.00 .30
❑ 39 Mike Mussina 1.50 .45
❑ 40 Derek Jeter 4.00 1.20
❑ 41 Roger Clemens 3.00 .90
❑ 42 Craig Biggio 1.00 .30
❑ 43 Jeff Bagwell 1.00 .30
❑ 44 Lance Berkman .60 .18
❑ 45 Andruw Jones 1.00 .30
❑ 46 Greg Maddux 3.00 .90
❑ 47 Chipper Jones 1.50 .45
❑ 48 Geoff Jenkins .60 .18
❑ 49 Ben Sheets .60 .18
❑ 50 Jeromy Burnitz .60 .18
❑ 51 Jim Edmonds .60 .18
❑ 52 Mark McGwire 4.00 1.20
❑ 53 Mike Matheny .60 .18
❑ 54 J.D. Drew .60 .18
❑ 55 Sammy Sosa 2.50 .75
❑ 56 Kerry Wood 1.50 .45
❑ 57 Fred McGriff 1.00 .30
❑ 58 Randy Johnson 1.50 .45
❑ 59 Steve Finley .60 .18
❑ 60 Mark Grace 1.50 .45
❑ 61 Matt Williams .60 .18
❑ 62 Luis Gonzalez .60 .18
❑ 63 Shawn Green .60 .18
❑ 64 Kevin Brown .60 .18
❑ 65 Gary Sheffield .60 .18
❑ 66 Vladimir Guerrero 1.50 .45
❑ 67 Tony Armas Jr. .60 .18
❑ 68 Barry Bonds 4.00 1.20
❑ 69 J.T. Snow .60 .18
❑ 70 Jeff Kent .60 .18
❑ 71 Charles Johnson .60 .18
❑ 72 Preston Wilson .60 .18
❑ 73 Cliff Floyd .60 .18
❑ 74 Robin Ventura .60 .18
❑ 75 Mike Piazza 2.50 .75
❑ 76 Edgardo Alfonzo .60 .18
❑ 77 Tony Gwynn 2.00 .60

❑ 78 Ryan Klesko .60 .18
❑ 79 Scott Rolen 1.00 .30
❑ 80 Mike Lieberthal .60 .18
❑ 81 Pat Burrell .60 .18
❑ 82 Jason Kendall .60 .18
❑ 83 Brian Giles .60 .18
❑ 84 Ken Griffey Jr. 2.50 .75
❑ 85 Barry Larkin 1.50 .45
❑ 86 Pokey Reese .60 .18
❑ 87 Larry Walker 1.00 .30
❑ 88 Mike Hampton .60 .18
❑ 89 Juan Pierre .60 .18
❑ 90 Todd Helton 1.00 .30
❑ 91 Mike Penney GD RC 8.00 2.40
❑ 92 Wilkin Ruan GD RC 8.00 2.40
❑ 93 Greg Miller GD RC 8.00 2.40
❑ 94 Johnny Estrada GD RC 8.00 2.40
❑ 95 Tsuyoshi Shinjo GD RC 12.00 3.60
❑ 96 Josh Towers GD RC 8.00 2.40
❑ 97 H. Ramirez GD RC 10.00 3.00
❑ 98 Ryan Freel GD RC 8.00 2.40
❑ 99 M. Ensberg GD RC 12.00 3.60
❑ 100 A. Hernandez GD RC 8.00 2.40
❑ 101 Juan Uribe GD RC 8.00 2.40
❑ 102 Jose Mieses GD RC 8.00 2.40
❑ 103 Jack Wilson GD RC 8.00 2.40
❑ 104 Cesar Crespo GD RC 8.00 2.40
❑ 105 Bud Smith GD RC 8.00 2.40
❑ 106 Erick Almonte GD RC 8.00 2.40
❑ 107 E. Guzman GD RC 8.00 2.40
❑ 108 B. Duckworth GD RC 8.00 2.40
❑ 109 Juan Diaz GD RC 8.00 2.40
❑ 110 Kris Keller GD RC 8.00 2.40
❑ 111 J. Michaels GD RC 8.00 2.40
❑ 112 Bret Prinz GD RC 8.00 2.40
❑ 113 Henry Mateo GD RC 8.00 2.40
❑ 114 R. Rodriguez GD RC 8.00 2.40
❑ 115 Travis Hafner GD RC 10.00 3.00
❑ 116 Nate Teut GD RC 8.00 2.40
❑ 117 Alexis Gomez GD RC 8.00 2.40
❑ 118 Billy Sylvester GD RC 8.00 2.40
❑ 119 A. Pettyjohn GD RC 8.00 2.40
❑ 120 Josh Fogg GD RC 8.00 2.40
❑ 121 Juan Cruz GD RC 8.00 2.40
❑ 122 C. Valderrama GD RC 8.00 2.40
❑ 123 Jay Gibbons GD RC 12.00 3.60
❑ 124 D. Mendez GD RC 8.00 2.40
❑ 125 Bill Ortega GD RC 8.00 2.40
❑ 126 Sean Douglass GD RC 8.00 2.40
❑ 127 C. Parker GD RC 8.00 2.40
❑ 128 Grant Balfour GD RC 8.00 2.40
❑ 129 Joe Kennedy GD RC 8.00 2.40
❑ 130 Albert Pujols GD RC 50.00 15.00
❑ 131 W. Betemit GD RC 15.00 4.50
❑ 132 Mark Teixeira GD RC 30.00 9.00
❑ 133 Mark Prior GD RC 50.00 15.00
❑ 134 D. Brazelton GD RC 15.00 4.50
❑ 135 Ichiro Suzuki GD RC 40.00 12.00

2003 Upper Deck Honor Roll

	MINT	NRMT
COMP.SET w/o SP's (100)	25.00	11.00
COMMON CARD (1-130)	.30	.14
COMMON EVEN (2-60)	2.00	.90
COMMON CARD (132-161)	5.00	2.20

❑ 1 Derek Jeter 2.00 .90
❑ 2 Derek Jeter SP 8.00 3.60
❑ 3 Alex Rodriguez 1.50 .70
❑ 4 Alex Rodriguez SP 6.00 2.70
❑ 5 Roger Clemens 1.50 .70
❑ 6 Roger Clemens SP 6.00 2.70
❑ 7 Mike Piazza 1.25 .55
❑ 8 Mike Piazza SP 5.00 2.20
❑ 9 Jeff Bagwell .50 .23
❑ 10 Jeff Bagwell SP 2.00 .90
❑ 11 Vladimir Guerrero .75 .35
❑ 12 Vladimir Guerrero SP 3.00 1.35
❑ 13 Ken Griffey Jr. 1.25 .55
❑ 14 Ken Griffey Jr. SP 5.00 2.20
❑ 15 Greg Maddux 1.50 .70
❑ 16 Greg Maddux SP 6.00 2.70
❑ 17 Chipper Jones .75 .35
❑ 18 Chipper Jones SP 3.00 1.35
❑ 19 Randy Johnson .75 .35
❑ 20 Randy Johnson SP 3.00 1.35
❑ 21 Miguel Tejada .30 .14
❑ 22 Miguel Tejada SP 2.00 .90
❑ 23 Nomar Garciaparra 1.50 .70
❑ 24 Nomar Garciaparra SP 6.00 2.70
❑ 25 Ichiro Suzuki 1.50 .70
❑ 26 Ichiro Suzuki SP 6.00 2.70
❑ 27 Sammy Sosa 1.25 .55
❑ 28 Sammy Sosa SP 5.00 2.20
❑ 29 Albert Pujols 1.50 .70
❑ 30 Albert Pujols SP 6.00 2.70
❑ 31 Alfonso Soriano .75 .35
❑ 32 Alfonso Soriano SP 3.00 1.35
❑ 33 Barry Bonds 2.00 .90
❑ 34 Barry Bonds SP 8.00 3.60
❑ 35 Jeff Kent .30 .14
❑ 36 Jeff Kent SP 2.00 .90
❑ 37 Jim Thome .75 .35
❑ 38 Jim Thome SP 3.00 1.35
❑ 39 Pedro Martinez .75 .35
❑ 40 Pedro Martinez SP 3.00 1.35
❑ 41 Todd Helton .50 .23
❑ 42 Todd Helton SP 2.00 .90
❑ 43 Troy Glaus .50 .23
❑ 44 Troy Glaus SP 2.00 .90
❑ 45 Mark Prior 1.50 .70
❑ 46 Mark Prior SP 6.00 2.70
❑ 47 Tom Glavine .75 .35
❑ 48 Tom Glavine SP 3.00 1.35
❑ 49 Pat Burrell .30 .14
❑ 50 Pat Burrell SP 2.00 .90
❑ 51 Barry Zito .75 .35
❑ 52 Barry Zito SP 3.00 1.35
❑ 53 Bernie Williams .50 .23
❑ 54 Bernie Williams SP 2.00 .90
❑ 55 Curt Schilling .50 .23
❑ 56 Curt Schilling SP 2.00 .90
❑ 57 Darin Erstad .30 .14
❑ 58 Darin Erstad SP 2.00 .90
❑ 59 Carlos Delgado .30 .14
❑ 60 Carlos Delgado SP 2.00 .90
❑ 61 Gary Sheffield .30 .14
❑ 62 Gary Sheffield .30 .14
❑ 63 Frank Thomas .75 .35
❑ 64 Frank Thomas .75 .35
❑ 65 Lance Berkman .30 .14
❑ 66 Lance Berkman .30 .14
❑ 67 Shawn Green .30 .14
❑ 68 Shawn Green .30 .14
❑ 69 Hideo Nomo .75 .35
❑ 70 Hideo Nomo .75 .35
❑ 71 Torii Hunter .30 .14
❑ 72 Torii Hunter .30 .14
❑ 73 Roberto Alomar .75 .35
❑ 74 Roberto Alomar .75 .35
❑ 75 Andruw Jones .50 .23
❑ 76 Andruw Jones .50 .23
❑ 77 Scott Rolen .50 .23
❑ 78 Scott Rolen .50 .23
❑ 79 Eric Chavez .30 .14
❑ 80 Eric Chavez .30 .14
❑ 81 Rafael Palmeiro .50 .23
❑ 82 Rafael Palmeiro .50 .23
❑ 83 Bobby Abreu .30 .14
❑ 84 Bobby Abreu .30 .14
❑ 85 Craig Biggio .50 .23
❑ 86 Craig Biggio .50 .23
❑ 87 Rafael Furcal .30 .14
❑ 88 Rafael Furcal .30 .14
❑ 89 Jose Vidro .30 .14
❑ 90 Jose Vidro .30 .14
❑ 91 Luis Gonzalez .30 .14
❑ 92 Luis Gonzalez .30 .14
❑ 93 Roy Oswalt .30 .14
❑ 94 Roy Oswalt .30 .14
❑ 95 Cliff Floyd .30 .14
❑ 96 Cliff Floyd .30 .14
❑ 97 Larry Walker .50 .23
❑ 98 Larry Walker .50 .23
❑ 99 Jim Edmonds .30 .14
❑ 100 Jim Edmonds .30 .14
❑ 101 Adam Dunn .50 .23
❑ 102 Adam Dunn .50 .23
❑ 103 J.D. Drew .30 .14
❑ 104 J.D. Drew .30 .14
❑ 105 Josh Beckett .50 .23
❑ 106 Josh Beckett .50 .23
❑ 107 Brian Giles .30 .14
❑ 108 Brian Giles .30 .14
❑ 109 Magglio Ordonez .30 .14
❑ 110 Magglio Ordonez .30 .14
❑ 111 Edgardo Alfonzo .30 .14
❑ 112 Edgardo Alfonzo .30 .14
❑ 113 Bartolo Colon .30 .14
❑ 114 Bartolo Colon .30 .14
❑ 115 Roy Halladay .30 .14
❑ 116 Roy Halladay .30 .14
❑ 117 Joe Thurston .30 .14
❑ 118 Joe Thurston .30 .14
❑ 119 Brandon Phillips .30 .14
❑ 120 Brandon Phillips .30 .14
❑ 121 Kazuhisa Ishii .30 .14
❑ 122 Kazuhisa Ishii .30 .14
❑ 123 Mike Mussina .75 .35
❑ 124 Mike Mussina .75 .35
❑ 125 Tim Hudson .30 .14
❑ 126 Tim Hudson .30 .14
❑ 127 Mariano Rivera .50 .23
❑ 128 Mariano Rivera .50 .23
❑ 129 Travis Hafner .30 .14
❑ 130 Travis Hafner .30 .14
❑ 131 Hideki Matsui DL Jsy RC 40.00 18.00
❑ 132 Jose Contreras FC RC 10.00 4.50
❑ 133 Jason Anderson FC 5.00 2.20
❑ 134 Willie Eyre FC RC 5.00 2.20
❑ 135 Shane Bazzell FC RC 5.00 2.20
❑ 136 Guillermo Quiroz FC RC 8.00 3.60
❑ 137 Francisco Cruceta FC RC 5.00 2.20
❑ 138 Jhonny Peralta FC RC 5.00 2.20
❑ 139 Aaron Looper FC RC 5.00 2.20
❑ 140 Bobby Madritsch FC RC 5.00 2.20
❑ 141 Michael Hessman FC RC 5.00 2.20
❑ 142 Todd Wellemeyer FC RC 8.00 3.60
❑ 143 Matt Bruback FC RC 5.00 2.20
❑ 144 Chris Capuano FC RC 5.00 2.20
❑ 145 Oscar Villarreal FC RC 5.00 2.20
❑ 146 Prentice Redman FC RC 5.00 2.20
❑ 147 Jeff Duncan FC RC 8.00 3.60
❑ 148 Phil Seibel FC RC 5.00 2.20
❑ 149 Arnaldo Munoz FC RC 5.00 2.20
❑ 150 David Sanders FC RC 5.00 2.20
❑ 151 Rick Roberts FC RC 5.00 2.20
❑ 152 Terrmel Sledge FC RC 8.00 3.60
❑ 153 Franklin Perez FC RC 5.00 2.20
❑ 154 Jeremy Wedel FC RC 5.00 2.20
❑ 155 Ian Ferguson FC RC 5.00 2.20
❑ 156 Josh Hall FC RC 8.00 3.60
❑ 157 Rocco Baldelli FC 15.00 6.75
❑ 158 Alejandro Machado FC RC 5.00 2.20
❑ 159 Jorge Cordova FC RC 5.00 2.20
❑ 160 Wilfredo Ledezma FC RC 5.00 2.20
❑ 161 Luis Ayala FC RC 5.00 2.20

2001 Upper Deck MVP

	Nm-Mt	Ex-Mt
COMPLETE SET (330)	50.00	15.00

❑ 1 Mo Vaughn .20 .06
❑ 2 Troy Percival .20 .06
❑ 3 Adam Kennedy .20 .06
❑ 4 Darin Erstad .20 .06
❑ 5 Tim Salmon .30 .09

	No.	Player		
❑	6	Bengie Molina	.20	.06
❑	7	Troy Glaus	.30	.09
❑	8	Garret Anderson	.20	.06
❑	9	Ismael Valdes	.20	.06
❑	10	Glenallen Hill	.20	.06
❑	11	Tim Hudson	.20	.06
❑	12	Eric Chavez	.20	.06
❑	13	Johnny Damon	.20	.06
❑	14	Barry Zito	.50	.15
❑	15	Jason Giambi	.50	.15
❑	16	Terrence Long	.20	.06
❑	17	Jason Hart	.20	.06
❑	18	Jose Ortiz	.20	.06
❑	19	Miguel Tejada	.20	.06
❑	20	Jason Isringhausen	.20	.06
❑	21	Adam Piatt	.20	.06
❑	22	Jeremy Giambi	.20	.06
❑	23	Tony Batista	.20	.06
❑	24	Darrin Fletcher	.20	.06
❑	25	Mike Sirotka	.20	.06
❑	26	Carlos Delgado	.20	.06
❑	27	Billy Koch	.20	.06
❑	28	Shannon Stewart	.20	.06
❑	29	Raul Mondesi	.20	.06
❑	30	Brad Fullmer	.20	.06
❑	31	Jose Cruz Jr.	.20	.06
❑	32	Kelvim Escobar	.20	.06
❑	33	Greg Vaughn	.20	.06
❑	34	Aubrey Huff	.20	.06
❑	35	Albie Lopez	.20	.06
❑	36	Gerald Williams	.20	.06
❑	37	Ben Grieve	.20	.06
❑	38	John Flaherty	.20	.06
❑	39	Fred McGriff	.30	.09
❑	40	Ryan Rupe	.20	.06
❑	41	Travis Harper	.20	.06
❑	42	Steve Cox	.20	.06
❑	43	Roberto Alomar	.50	.15
❑	44	Jim Thome	.50	.15
❑	45	Russell Branyan	.20	.06
❑	46	Bartolo Colon	.20	.06
❑	47	Omar Vizquel	.20	.06
❑	48	Travis Fryman	.20	.06
❑	49	Kenny Lofton	.20	.06
❑	50	Chuck Finley	.20	.06
❑	51	Ellis Burks	.20	.06
❑	52	Eddie Taubensee	.20	.06
❑	53	Juan Gonzalez	.50	.15
❑	54	Edgar Martinez	.30	.09
❑	55	Aaron Sele	.20	.06
❑	56	John Olerud	.20	.06
❑	57	Jay Buhner	.20	.06
❑	58	Mike Cameron	.20	.06
❑	59	John Halama	.20	.06
❑	60	Ichiro Suzuki RC	10.00	3.00
❑	61	David Bell	.20	.06
❑	62	Freddy Garcia	.20	.06
❑	63	Carlos Guillen	.20	.06
❑	64	Bret Boone	.20	.06
❑	65	Al Martin	.20	.06
❑	66	Cal Ripken	1.50	.45
❑	67	Delino DeShields	.20	.06
❑	68	Chris Richard	.20	.06
❑	69	Sean Douglass RC	.50	.15
❑	70	Melvin Mora	.20	.06
❑	71	Luis Matos	.20	.06
❑	72	Sidney Ponson	.20	.06
❑	73	Mike Bordick	.20	.06
❑	74	Brady Anderson	.20	.06
❑	75	David Segui	.20	.06
❑	76	Jeff Conine	.20	.06
❑	77	Alex Rodriguez	1.00	.30
❑	78	Gabe Kapler	.20	.06
❑	79	Ivan Rodriguez	.50	.15
❑	80	Rick Helling	.20	.06
❑	81	Kenny Rogers	.20	.06
❑	82	Andres Galarraga	.20	.06
❑	83	Rusty Greer	.20	.06
❑	84	Justin Thompson	.20	.06
❑	85	Ken Caminiti	.20	.06
❑	86	Rafael Palmeiro	.30	.09
❑	87	Ruben Mateo	.20	.06
❑	88	Travis Hafner RC	.75	.23
❑	89	Manny Ramirez	.20	.06
❑	90	Pedro Martinez	.50	.15
❑	91	Carl Everett	.20	.06
❑	92	Dante Bichette	.20	.06
❑	93	Derek Lowe	.20	.06
❑	94	Jason Varitek	.20	.06
❑	95	Nomar Garciaparra	1.00	.30
❑	96	David Cone	.20	.06
❑	97	Tomokazu Ohka	.20	.06
❑	98	Troy O'Leary	.20	.06
❑	99	Trot Nixon	.20	.06
❑	100	Jermaine Dye	.20	.06
❑	101	Joe Randa	.20	.06
❑	102	Jeff Suppan	.20	.06
❑	103	Roberto Hernandez	.20	.06
❑	104	Mike Sweeney	.20	.06
❑	105	Mac Suzuki	.20	.06
❑	106	Carlos Febles	.20	.06
❑	107	Jose Rosado	.20	.06
❑	108	Mark Quinn	.20	.06
❑	109	Carlos Beltran	.20	.06
❑	110	Dean Palmer	.20	.06
❑	111	Mitch Meluskey	.20	.06
❑	112	Bobby Higginson	.20	.06
❑	113	Brandon Inge	.20	.06
❑	114	Tony Clark	.20	.06
❑	115	Brian Moehler	.20	.06
❑	116	Juan Encarnacion	.20	.06
❑	117	Damion Easley	.20	.06
❑	118	Roger Cedeno	.20	.06
❑	119	Jeff Weaver	.20	.06
❑	120	Matt Lawton	.20	.06
❑	121	Jay Canizaro	.20	.06
❑	122	Eric Milton	.20	.06
❑	123	Corey Koskie	.20	.06
❑	124	Mark Redman	.20	.06
❑	125	Jacque Jones	.20	.06
❑	126	Brad Radke	.20	.06
❑	127	Cristian Guzman	.20	.06
❑	128	Joe Mays	.20	.06
❑	129	Denny Hocking	.20	.06
❑	130	Frank Thomas	.50	.15
❑	131	David Wells	.20	.06
❑	132	Ray Durham	.20	.06
❑	133	Paul Konerko	.20	.06
❑	134	Joe Crede	.20	.06
❑	135	Jim Parque	.20	.06
❑	136	Carlos Lee	.20	.06
❑	137	Magglio Ordonez	.20	.06
❑	138	Sandy Alomar Jr.	.20	.06
❑	139	Chris Singleton	.20	.06
❑	140	Jose Valentin	.20	.06
❑	141	Roger Clemens	1.00	.30
❑	142	Derek Jeter	1.25	.35
❑	143	Orlando Hernandez	.20	.06
❑	144	Tino Martinez	.30	.09
❑	145	Bernie Williams	.30	.09
❑	146	Jorge Posada	.30	.09
❑	147	Mariano Rivera	.30	.09
❑	148	David Justice	.20	.06
❑	149	Paul O'Neill	.30	.09
❑	150	Mike Mussina	.50	.15
❑	151	Christian Parker RC	.50	.15
❑	152	Andy Pettitte	.30	.09
❑	153	Alfonso Soriano	.50	.15
❑	154	Jeff Bagwell	.30	.09
❑	155	Morgan Ensberg RC	1.00	.30
❑	156	Daryle Ward	.20	.06
❑	157	Craig Biggio	.30	.09
❑	158	Richard Hidalgo	.20	.06
❑	159	Shane Reynolds	.20	.06
❑	160	Scott Elarton	.20	.06
❑	161	Julio Lugo	.20	.06
❑	162	Moises Alou	.20	.06
❑	163	Lance Berkman	.20	.06
❑	164	Chipper Jones	.50	.15
❑	165	Greg Maddux	1.00	.30
❑	166	Javy Lopez	.20	.06
❑	167	Andruw Jones	.30	.09
❑	168	Rafael Furcal	.20	.06
❑	169	Brian Jordan	.20	.06
❑	170	Wes Helms	.20	.06
❑	171	Tom Glavine	.50	.15
❑	172	B.J. Surhoff	.20	.06
❑	173	John Smoltz	.30	.09
❑	174	Quilvio Veras	.20	.06
❑	175	Rico Brogna	.20	.06
❑	176	Jeromy Burnitz	.20	.06
❑	177	Jeff D'Amico	.20	.06
❑	178	Geoff Jenkins	.20	.06
❑	179	Henry Blanco	.20	.06
❑	180	Mark Loretta	.20	.06
❑	181	Richie Sexson	.20	.06
❑	182	Jimmy Haynes	.20	.06
❑	183	Jeffrey Hammonds	.20	.06
❑	184	Ron Belliard	.20	.06
❑	185	Tyler Houston	.20	.06
❑	186	Mark McGwire	1.25	.35
❑	187	Rick Ankiel	.20	.06
❑	188	Darryl Kile	.20	.06
❑	189	Jim Edmonds	.20	.06
❑	190	Mike Matheny	.20	.06
❑	191	Edgar Renteria	.20	.06
❑	192	Ray Lankford	.20	.06
❑	193	Garrett Stephenson	.20	.06
❑	194	J.D. Drew	.20	.06
❑	195	Fernando Vina	.20	.06
❑	196	Dustin Hermanson	.20	.06
❑	197	Sammy Sosa	.75	.23
❑	198	Corey Patterson	.20	.06
❑	199	Jon Lieber	.20	.06
❑	200	Kerry Wood	.50	.15
❑	201	Todd Hundley	.20	.06
❑	202	Kevin Tapani	.20	.06
❑	203	Rondell White	.20	.06
❑	204	Eric Young	.20	.06
❑	205	Matt Stairs	.20	.06
❑	206	Bill Mueller	.20	.06
❑	207	Randy Johnson	.50	.15
❑	208	Mark Grace	.50	.15
❑	209	Jay Bell	.20	.06
❑	210	Curt Schilling	.30	.09
❑	211	Erubiel Durazo	.20	.06
❑	212	Luis Gonzalez	.20	.06
❑	213	Steve Finley	.20	.06
❑	214	Matt Williams	.20	.06
❑	215	Reggie Sanders	.20	.06
❑	216	Tony Womack	.20	.06
❑	217	Gary Sheffield	.20	.06
❑	218	Kevin Brown	.20	.06
❑	219	Adrian Beltre	.20	.06
❑	220	Shawn Green	.20	.06
❑	221	Darren Dreifort	.20	.06
❑	222	Chan Ho Park	.20	.06
❑	223	Eric Karros	.20	.06
❑	224	Alex Cora	.20	.06
❑	225	Mark Grudzielanek	.20	.06
❑	226	Andy Ashby	.20	.06
❑	227	Vladimir Guerrero	.50	.15
❑	228	Tony Armas Jr.	.20	.06
❑	229	Fernando Tatis	.20	.06
❑	230	Jose Vidro	.20	.06
❑	231	Javier Vazquez	.20	.06
❑	232	Lee Stevens	.20	.06
❑	233	Milton Bradley	.20	.06
❑	234	Carl Pavano	.20	.06
❑	235	Peter Bergeron	.20	.06
❑	236	Wilton Guerrero	.20	.06
❑	237	Ugueth Urbina	.20	.06
❑	238	Barry Bonds	1.25	.35
❑	239	Livan Hernandez	.20	.06
❑	240	Jeff Kent	.20	.06
❑	241	Pedro Feliz	.20	.06
❑	242	Bobby Estalella	.20	.06
❑	243	J.T. Snow	.20	.06
❑	244	Shawn Estes	.20	.06
❑	245	Robb Nen	.20	.06

❑ 246 Rich Aurilia	.20	.06
❑ 247 Russ Ortiz	.20	.06
❑ 248 Preston Wilson	.20	.06
❑ 249 Brad Penny	.20	.06
❑ 250 Cliff Floyd	.20	.06
❑ 251 A.J. Burnett	.20	.06
❑ 252 Mike Lowell	.20	.06
❑ 253 Luis Castillo	.20	.06
❑ 254 Ryan Dempster	.20	.06
❑ 255 Derrek Lee	.20	.06
❑ 256 Charles Johnson	.20	.06
❑ 257 Pablo Ozuna	.20	.06
❑ 258 Antonio Alfonseca	.20	.06
❑ 259 Mike Piazza	.75	.23
❑ 260 Robin Ventura	.20	.06
❑ 261 Al Leiter	.20	.06
❑ 262 Timo Perez	.20	.06
❑ 263 Edgardo Alfonzo	.20	.06
❑ 264 Jay Payton	.20	.06
❑ 265 Tsuyoshi Shinjo RC	1.00	.30
❑ 266 Todd Zeile	.20	.06
❑ 267 Armando Benitez	.20	.06
❑ 268 Glendon Rusch	.20	.06
❑ 269 Rey Ordonez	.20	.06
❑ 270 Kevin Appier	.20	.06
❑ 271 Tony Gwynn	.60	.18
❑ 272 Phil Nevin	.20	.06
❑ 273 Mark Kotsay	.20	.06
❑ 274 Ryan Klesko	.20	.06
❑ 275 Adam Eaton	.20	.06
❑ 276 Mike Darr	.20	.06
❑ 277 Damian Jackson	.20	.06
❑ 278 Woody Williams	.20	.06
❑ 279 Chris Gomez	.20	.06
❑ 280 Trevor Hoffman	.20	.06
❑ 281 Xavier Nady	.20	.06
❑ 282 Scott Rolen	.30	.09
❑ 283 Bruce Chen	.20	.06
❑ 284 Pat Burrell	.20	.06
❑ 285 Mike Lieberthal	.20	.06
❑ 286 B. Duckworth RC	.50	.15
❑ 287 Travis Lee	.20	.06
❑ 288 Bobby Abreu	.20	.06
❑ 289 Jimmy Rollins	.20	.06
❑ 290 Robert Person	.20	.06
❑ 291 Randy Wolf	.20	.06
❑ 292 Jason Kendall	.20	.06
❑ 293 Derek Bell	.20	.06
❑ 294 Brian Giles	.20	.06
❑ 295 Kris Benson	.20	.06
❑ 296 John VanderWal	.20	.06
❑ 297 Todd Ritchie	.20	.06
❑ 298 Warren Morris	.20	.06
❑ 299 Kevin Young	.20	.06
❑ 300 Francisco Cordova	.20	.06
❑ 301 Aramis Ramirez	.20	.06
❑ 302 Ken Griffey Jr.	.75	.23
❑ 303 Pete Harnisch	.20	.06
❑ 304 Aaron Boone	.20	.06
❑ 305 Sean Casey	.20	.06
❑ 306 Jackson Melian RC	.50	.15
❑ 307 Rob Bell	.20	.06
❑ 308 Barry Larkin	.50	.15
❑ 309 Dmitri Young	.20	.06
❑ 310 Danny Graves	.20	.06
❑ 311 Pokey Reese	.20	.06
❑ 312 Leo Estrella	.20	.06
❑ 313 Todd Helton	.30	.09
❑ 314 Mike Hampton	.20	.06
❑ 315 Juan Pierre	.20	.06
❑ 316 Brent Mayne	.20	.06
❑ 317 Larry Walker	.30	.09
❑ 318 Denny Neagle	.20	.06
❑ 319 Jeff Cirillo	.20	.06
❑ 320 Pedro Astacio	.20	.06
❑ 321 Todd Hollandsworth	.20	.06
❑ 322 Neifi Perez	.20	.06
❑ 323 Ron Gant	.20	.06
❑ 324 Todd Walker	.20	.06
❑ 325 Alex Rodriguez CL	.50	.15
❑ 326 Ken Griffey Jr. CL	.50	.15
❑ 327 Mark McGwire CL	.60	.18
❑ 328 Pedro Martinez CL	.30	.09
❑ 329 Derek Jeter CL	.60	.18
❑ 330 Mike Piazza CL	.50	.15

2002 Upper Deck MVP

	Nm-Mt	Ex-Mt
COMPLETE SET (301)	40.00	12.00
❑ 1 Darin Erstad	.20	.06
❑ 2 Ramon Ortiz	.20	.06
❑ 3 Garret Anderson	.20	.06
❑ 4 Jarrod Washburn	.20	.06
❑ 5 Troy Glaus	.30	.09
❑ 6 Brendan Donnelly RC	.50	.15
❑ 7 Troy Percival	.20	.06
❑ 8 Tim Salmon	.30	.09
❑ 9 Aaron Sele	.20	.06
❑ 10 Brad Fullmer	.20	.06
❑ 11 Scott Hatteberg	.20	.06
❑ 12 Barry Zito	.50	.15
❑ 13 Tim Hudson	.20	.06
❑ 14 Miguel Tejada	.20	.06
❑ 15 Jermaine Dye	.20	.06
❑ 16 Mark Mulder	.20	.06
❑ 17 Eric Chavez	.20	.06
❑ 18 Terrence Long	.20	.06
❑ 19 Carlos Pena	.20	.06
❑ 20 David Justice	.20	.06
❑ 21 Jeremy Giambi	.20	.06
❑ 22 Shannon Stewart	.20	.06
❑ 23 Raul Mondesi	.20	.06
❑ 24 Chris Carpenter	.20	.06
❑ 25 Carlos Delgado	.20	.06
❑ 26 Mike Sirotka	.20	.06
❑ 27 Reed Johnson RC	.50	.15
❑ 28 Darrin Fletcher	.20	.06
❑ 29 Jose Cruz Jr.	.20	.06
❑ 30 Vernon Wells	.20	.06
❑ 31 Tanyon Sturtze	.20	.06
❑ 32 Toby Hall	.20	.06
❑ 33 Brent Abernathy	.20	.06
❑ 34 Ben Grieve	.20	.06
❑ 35 Joe Kennedy	.20	.06
❑ 36 Dewon Brazelton	.20	.06
❑ 37 Aubrey Huff	.20	.06
❑ 38 Steve Cox	.20	.06
❑ 39 Greg Vaughn	.20	.06
❑ 40 Brady Anderson	.20	.06
❑ 41 Chuck Finley	.20	.06
❑ 42 Jim Thome	.50	.15
❑ 43 Russell Branyan	.20	.06
❑ 44 C.C. Sabathia	.20	.06
❑ 45 Matt Lawton	.20	.06
❑ 46 Omar Vizquel	.20	.06
❑ 47 Bartolo Colon	.20	.06
❑ 48 Alex Escobar	.20	.06
❑ 49 Ellis Burks	.20	.06
❑ 50 Bret Boone	.20	.06
❑ 51 John Olerud	.20	.06
❑ 52 Jeff Cirillo	.20	.06
❑ 53 Ichiro Suzuki	1.00	.30
❑ 54 Kazuhiro Sasaki	.20	.06
❑ 55 Freddy Garcia	.20	.06
❑ 56 Edgar Martinez	.30	.09
❑ 57 Matt Thornton RC	.50	.15
❑ 58 Mike Cameron	.20	.06
❑ 59 Carlos Guillen	.20	.06
❑ 60 Jeff Conine	.20	.06
❑ 61 Tony Batista	.20	.06
❑ 62 Jason Johnson	.20	.06
❑ 63 Melvin Mora	.20	.06
❑ 64 Brian Roberts	.20	.06
❑ 65 Josh Towers	.20	.06
❑ 66 Steve Bechler RC	.50	.15
❑ 67 Jerry Hairston Jr.	.20	.06
❑ 68 Chris Richard	.20	.06
❑ 69 Alex Rodriguez	1.00	.30
❑ 70 Chan Ho Park	.20	.06
❑ 71 Ivan Rodriguez	.50	.15
❑ 72 Jeff Zimmerman	.20	.06
❑ 73 Mark Teixeira	.50	.15
❑ 74 Gabe Kapler	.20	.06
❑ 75 Frank Catalanotto	.20	.06
❑ 76 Rafael Palmeiro	.30	.09
❑ 77 Doug Davis	.20	.06
❑ 78 Carl Everett	.20	.06
❑ 79 Pedro Martinez	.50	.15
❑ 80 Nomar Garciaparra	1.00	.30
❑ 81 Tony Clark	.20	.06
❑ 82 Trot Nixon	.20	.06
❑ 83 Manny Ramirez	.20	.06
❑ 84 Josh Hancock RC	.50	.15
❑ 85 Johnny Damon	.20	.06
❑ 86 Jose Offerman	.20	.06
❑ 87 Rich Garces	.20	.06
❑ 88 Shea Hillenbrand	.20	.06
❑ 89 Carlos Beltran	.20	.06
❑ 90 Mike Sweeney	.20	.06
❑ 91 Jeff Suppan	.20	.06
❑ 92 Joe Randa	.20	.06
❑ 93 Chuck Knoblauch	.20	.06
❑ 94 Mark Quinn	.20	.06
❑ 95 Neifi Perez	.20	.06
❑ 96 Carlos Febles	.20	.06
❑ 97 Miguel Asencio RC	.50	.15
❑ 98 Michael Tucker	.20	.06
❑ 99 Dean Palmer	.20	.06
❑ 100 Jose Lima	.20	.06
❑ 101 Craig Paquette	.20	.06
❑ 102 Dmitri Young	.20	.06
❑ 103 Bobby Higginson	.20	.06
❑ 104 Jeff Weaver	.20	.06
❑ 105 Matt Anderson	.20	.06
❑ 106 Damion Easley	.20	.06
❑ 107 Eric Milton	.20	.06
❑ 108 Doug Mientkiewicz	.20	.06
❑ 109 Cristian Guzman	.20	.06
❑ 110 Brad Radke	.20	.06
❑ 111 Torii Hunter	.20	.06
❑ 112 Corey Koskie	.20	.06
❑ 113 Joe Mays	.20	.06
❑ 114 Jacque Jones	.20	.06
❑ 115 David Ortiz	.20	.06
❑ 116 Kevin Frederick RC	.50	.15
❑ 117 Magglio Ordonez	.20	.06
❑ 118 Ray Durham	.20	.06
❑ 119 Mark Buehrle	.20	.06
❑ 120 Jon Garland	.20	.06
❑ 121 Paul Konerko	.20	.06
❑ 122 Todd Ritchie	.20	.06
❑ 123 Frank Thomas	.50	.15
❑ 124 Edwin Almonte RC	.50	.15
❑ 125 Carlos Lee	.20	.06
❑ 126 Kenny Lofton	.20	.06
❑ 127 Roger Clemens	1.00	.30
❑ 128 Derek Jeter	1.25	.35
❑ 129 Jorge Posada	.30	.09
❑ 130 Bernie Williams	.30	.09
❑ 131 Mike Mussina	.50	.15
❑ 132 Alfonso Soriano	.50	.15
❑ 133 Robin Ventura	.20	.06
❑ 134 John Vander Wal	.20	.06
❑ 135 Jason Giambi Yankees	.50	.15
❑ 136 Mariano Rivera	.30	.09
❑ 137 Rondell White	.20	.06
❑ 138 Jeff Bagwell	.30	.09
❑ 139 Wade Miller	.20	.06
❑ 140 Richard Hidalgo	.20	.06
❑ 141 Julio Lugo	.20	.06
❑ 142 Roy Oswalt	.20	.06
❑ 143 Rodrigo Rosario RC	.50	.15
❑ 144 Lance Berkman	.20	.06
❑ 145 Craig Biggio	.30	.09
❑ 146 Shane Reynolds	.20	.06
❑ 147 John Smoltz	.30	.09
❑ 148 Chipper Jones	.50	.15
❑ 149 Gary Sheffield	.20	.06

❑ 150 Rafael Furcal .20 .06
❑ 151 Greg Maddux 1.00 .30
❑ 152 Tom Glavine .50 .15
❑ 153 Andruw Jones .30 .09
❑ 154 John Ennis RC .50 .15
❑ 155 Vinny Castilla .20 .06
❑ 156 Marcus Giles .20 .06
❑ 157 Javy Lopez .20 .06
❑ 158 Richie Sexson .20 .06
❑ 159 Geoff Jenkins .20 .06
❑ 160 Jeffrey Hammonds .20 .06
❑ 161 Alex Ochoa .20 .06
❑ 162 Ben Sheets .20 .06
❑ 163 Jose Hernandez .20 .06
❑ 164 Eric Young .20 .06
❑ 165 Luis Martinez RC .50 .15
❑ 166 Albert Pujols 1.00 .30
❑ 167 Darryl Kile .20 .06
❑ 168 So Taguchi RC .50 .15
❑ 169 Jim Edmonds .20 .06
❑ 170 Fernando Vina .20 .06
❑ 171 Matt Morris .20 .06
❑ 172 J.D. Drew .20 .06
❑ 173 Bud Smith .20 .06
❑ 174 Edgar Renteria .20 .06
❑ 175 Placido Polanco .20 .06
❑ 176 Tino Martinez .30 .09
❑ 177 Sammy Sosa .75 .23
❑ 178 Moises Alou .20 .06
❑ 179 Kerry Wood .50 .15
❑ 180 Delino DeShields .20 .06
❑ 181 Alex Gonzalez .20 .06
❑ 182 Jon Lieber .20 .06
❑ 183 Fred McGriff .30 .09
❑ 184 Corey Patterson .20 .06
❑ 185 Mark Prior 1.00 .30
❑ 186 Tom Gordon .20 .06
❑ 187 Francis Beltran RC .50 .15
❑ 188 Randy Johnson .50 .15
❑ 189 Luis Gonzalez .20 .06
❑ 190 Matt Williams .20 .06
❑ 191 Mark Grace .50 .15
❑ 192 Curt Schilling .30 .09
❑ 193 Doug Devore RC .50 .15
❑ 194 Erubiel Durazo .20 .06
❑ 195 Steve Finley .20 .06
❑ 196 Craig Counsell .20 .06
❑ 197 Shawn Green .20 .06
❑ 198 Kevin Brown .20 .06
❑ 199 Paul LoDuca .20 .06
❑ 200 Brian Jordan .20 .06
❑ 201 Andy Ashby .20 .06
❑ 202 Darren Dreifort .20 .06
❑ 203 Adrian Beltre .20 .06
❑ 204 Victor Alvarez RC .50 .15
❑ 205 Eric Karros .20 .06
❑ 206 Hideo Nomo .50 .15
❑ 207 Vladimir Guerrero .50 .15
❑ 208 Javier Vazquez .20 .06
❑ 209 Michael Barrett .20 .06
❑ 210 Jose Vidro .20 .06
❑ 211 Brad Wilkerson .20 .06
❑ 212 Tony Armas Jr. .20 .06
❑ 213 Eric Good RC .50 .15
❑ 214 Orlando Cabrera .20 .06
❑ 215 Lee Stevens .20 .06
❑ 216 Jeff Kent .20 .06
❑ 217 Rich Aurilia .20 .06
❑ 218 Robb Nen .20 .06
❑ 219 Calvin Murray .20 .06
❑ 220 Russ Ortiz .20 .06
❑ 221 Deivis Santos .20 .06
❑ 222 Marvin Benard .20 .06
❑ 223 Jason Schmidt .20 .06
❑ 224 Reggie Sanders .20 .06
❑ 225 Barry Bonds 1.25 .35
❑ 226 Brad Penny .20 .06
❑ 227 Cliff Floyd .20 .06
❑ 228 Mike Lowell .20 .06
❑ 229 Derrek Lee .20 .06
❑ 230 Ryan Dempster .20 .06
❑ 231 Josh Beckett .30 .09
❑ 232 Hansel Izquierdo RC .50 .15
❑ 233 Preston Wilson .20 .06
❑ 234 A.J. Burnett .20 .06
❑ 235 Charles Johnson .20 .06

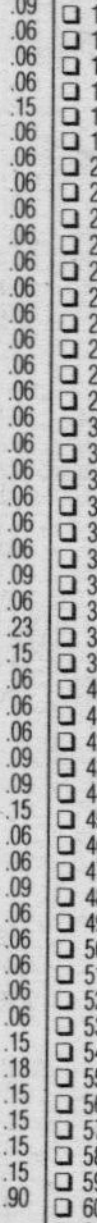

❑ 236 Mike Piazza .75 .23
❑ 237 Al Leiter .20 .06
❑ 238 Jay Payton .20 .06
❑ 239 Roger Cedeno .20 .06
❑ 240 Jeromy Burnitz .20 .06
❑ 241 Roberto Alomar .50 .15
❑ 242 Mo Vaughn .20 .06
❑ 243 Shawn Estes .20 .06
❑ 244 Armando Benitez .20 .06
❑ 245 Tyler Yates RC .50 .15
❑ 246 Phil Nevin .20 .06
❑ 247 D'Angelo Jimenez .20 .06
❑ 248 Ramon Vazquez .20 .06
❑ 249 Bubba Trammell .20 .06
❑ 250 Trevor Hoffman .20 .06
❑ 251 Ben Howard RC .50 .15
❑ 252 Mark Kotsay .20 .06
❑ 253 Ray Lankford .20 .06
❑ 254 Ryan Klesko .20 .06
❑ 255 Scott Rolen .30 .09
❑ 256 Robert Person .20 .06
❑ 257 Jimmy Rollins .20 .06
❑ 258 Pat Burrell .20 .06
❑ 259 Anderson Machado RC .50 .15
❑ 260 Randy Wolf .20 .06
❑ 261 Travis Lee .20 .06
❑ 262 Mike Lieberthal .20 .06
❑ 263 Doug Glanville .20 .06
❑ 264 Bobby Abreu .20 .06
❑ 265 Brian Giles .20 .06
❑ 266 Kris Benson .20 .06
❑ 267 Aramis Ramirez .20 .06
❑ 268 Kevin Young .20 .06
❑ 269 Jack Wilson .20 .06
❑ 270 Mike Williams .20 .06
❑ 271 Jimmy Anderson .20 .06
❑ 272 Jason Kendall .20 .06
❑ 273 Pokey Reese .20 .06
❑ 274 Rob Mackowiak .20 .06
❑ 275 Sean Casey .20 .06
❑ 276 Juan Encarnacion .20 .06
❑ 277 Austin Kearns .30 .09
❑ 278 Danny Graves .20 .06
❑ 279 Ken Griffey Jr. .75 .23
❑ 280 Barry Larkin .50 .15
❑ 281 Todd Walker .20 .06
❑ 282 Elmer Dessens .20 .06
❑ 283 Aaron Boone .20 .06
❑ 284 Adam Dunn .30 .09
❑ 285 Larry Walker .30 .09
❑ 286 Rene Reyes RC .50 .15
❑ 287 Juan Uribe .20 .06
❑ 288 Mike Hampton .20 .06
❑ 289 Todd Helton .30 .09
❑ 290 Juan Pierre .20 .06
❑ 291 Denny Neagle .20 .06
❑ 292 Jose Ortiz .20 .06
❑ 293 Todd Zeile .20 .06
❑ 294 Ben Petrick .20 .06
❑ 295 Ken Griffey Jr. CL .50 .15
❑ 296 Derek Jeter CL .60 .18
❑ 297 Sammy Sosa CL .50 .15
❑ 298 Ichiro Suzuki CL .50 .15
❑ 299 Barry Bonds CL .50 .15
❑ 300 Alex Rodriguez CL .50 .15
❑ 301 Kazuhisa Ishii RC 3.00 .90

2003 Upper Deck MVP

	Nm-Mt	Ex-Mt
COMP.FACT.SET (330)	40.00	12.00
COMPLETE LO SET (220)	25.00	7.50
COMMON CARD (1-220)	.20	.06
CARDS 221-330 DIST.IN FACTORY SETS		

❑ 1 Troy Glaus .30 .09
❑ 2 Darin Erstad .20 .06
❑ 3 Jarrod Washburn .20 .06
❑ 4 Francisco Rodriguez .20 .06
❑ 5 Garret Anderson .20 .06
❑ 6 Tim Salmon .30 .09
❑ 7 Adam Kennedy .20 .06
❑ 8 Randy Johnson .50 .15
❑ 9 Luis Gonzalez .20 .06
❑ 10 Curt Schilling .30 .09
❑ 11 Junior Spivey .20 .06

❑ 12 Craig Counsell .20 .06
❑ 13 Mark Grace .50 .15
❑ 14 Steve Finley .20 .06
❑ 15 Javy Lopez .20 .06
❑ 16 Rafael Furcal .20 .06
❑ 17 John Smoltz .30 .09
❑ 18 Greg Maddux 1.00 .30
❑ 19 Chipper Jones .50 .15
❑ 20 Gary Sheffield .20 .06
❑ 21 Andruw Jones .30 .09
❑ 22 Tony Batista .20 .06
❑ 23 Geronimo Gil .20 .06
❑ 24 Jay Gibbons .20 .06
❑ 25 Rodrigo Lopez .20 .06
❑ 26 Chris Singleton .20 .06
❑ 27 Melvin Mora .20 .06
❑ 28 Jeff Conine .20 .06
❑ 29 Nomar Garciaparra 1.00 .30
❑ 30 Pedro Martinez .50 .15
❑ 31 Manny Ramirez .20 .06
❑ 32 Shea Hillenbrand .20 .06
❑ 33 Johnny Damon .20 .06
❑ 34 Jason Varitek .20 .06
❑ 35 Derek Lowe .20 .06
❑ 36 Trot Nixon .20 .06
❑ 37 Sammy Sosa .75 .23
❑ 38 Kerry Wood .50 .15
❑ 39 Mark Prior 1.00 .30
❑ 40 Moises Alou .20 .06
❑ 41 Corey Patterson .20 .06
❑ 42 Hee Seop Choi .20 .06
❑ 43 Mark Bellhorn .20 .06
❑ 44 Frank Thomas .50 .15
❑ 45 Mark Buehrle .20 .06
❑ 46 Magglio Ordonez .20 .06
❑ 47 Carlos Lee .20 .06
❑ 48 Paul Konerko .20 .06
❑ 49 Joe Borchard .20 .06
❑ 50 Joe Crede .20 .06
❑ 51 Ken Griffey Jr. .75 .23
❑ 52 Adam Dunn .30 .09
❑ 53 Austin Kearns .30 .09
❑ 54 Aaron Boone .20 .06
❑ 55 Sean Casey .20 .06
❑ 56 Danny Graves .20 .06
❑ 57 Russell Branyan .20 .06
❑ 58 Matt Lawton .20 .06
❑ 59 C.C. Sabathia .20 .06
❑ 60 Omar Vizquel .20 .06
❑ 61 Brandon Phillips .20 .06
❑ 62 Karim Garcia .20 .06
❑ 63 Ellis Burks .20 .06
❑ 64 Cliff Lee .20 .06
❑ 65 Todd Helton .30 .09
❑ 66 Larry Walker .30 .09
❑ 67 Jay Payton .20 .06
❑ 68 Brent Butler .20 .06
❑ 69 Juan Uribe .20 .06
❑ 70 Jason Jennings .20 .06
❑ 71 Denny Stark .20 .06
❑ 72 Dmitri Young .20 .06
❑ 73 Carlos Pena .20 .06
❑ 74 Andres Torres .20 .06
❑ 75 Andy Van Hekken .20 .06
❑ 76 George Lombard .20 .06
❑ 77 Eric Munson .20 .06
❑ 78 Bobby Higginson .20 .06
❑ 79 Luis Castillo .20 .06

❑ 80 A.J. Burnett .20 .06
❑ 81 Juan Encarnacion .20 .06
❑ 82 Ivan Rodriguez .50 .15
❑ 83 Mike Lowell .20 .06
❑ 84 Josh Beckett .30 .09
❑ 85 Brad Penny .20 .06
❑ 86 Craig Biggio .30 .09
❑ 87 Jeff Kent .20 .06
❑ 88 Morgan Ensberg .20 .06
❑ 89 Daryle Ward .20 .06
❑ 90 Jeff Bagwell .30 .09
❑ 91 Roy Oswalt .20 .06
❑ 92 Lance Berkman .20 .06
❑ 93 Mike Sweeney .20 .06
❑ 94 Carlos Beltran .20 .06
❑ 95 Raul Ibanez .20 .06
❑ 96 Carlos Febles .20 .06
❑ 97 Joe Randa .20 .06
❑ 98 Shawn Green .20 .06
❑ 99 Kevin Brown .20 .06
❑ 100 Paul Lo Duca .20 .06
❑ 101 Adrian Beltre .20 .06
❑ 102 Eric Gagne .30 .09
❑ 103 Kazuhisa Ishii .20 .06
❑ 104 Odalis Perez .20 .06
❑ 105 Brian Jordan .20 .06
❑ 106 Geoff Jenkins .20 .06
❑ 107 Richie Sexson .20 .06
❑ 108 Ben Sheets .20 .06
❑ 109 Alex Sanchez .20 .06
❑ 110 Eric Young .20 .06
❑ 111 Jose Hernandez .20 .06
❑ 112 Torii Hunter .20 .06
❑ 113 Eric Milton .20 .06
❑ 114 Corey Koskie .20 .06
❑ 115 Doug Mientkiewicz .20 .06
❑ 116 A.J. Pierzynski .20 .06
❑ 117 Jacque Jones .20 .06
❑ 118 Cristian Guzman .20 .06
❑ 119 Bartolo Colon .20 .06
❑ 120 Brad Wilkerson .20 .06
❑ 121 Michael Barrett .20 .06
❑ 122 Vladimir Guerrero .50 .15
❑ 123 Jose Vidro .20 .06
❑ 124 Javier Vazquez .20 .06
❑ 125 Endy Chavez .20 .06
❑ 126 Roberto Alomar .50 .15
❑ 127 Mike Piazza .75 .23
❑ 128 Jeromy Burnitz .20 .06
❑ 129 Mo Vaughn .20 .06
❑ 130 Tom Glavine .50 .15
❑ 131 Al Leiter .20 .06
❑ 132 Armando Benitez .20 .06
❑ 133 Timo Perez .20 .06
❑ 134 Roger Clemens 1.00 .30
❑ 135 Derek Jeter 1.25 .35
❑ 136 Jason Giambi .50 .15
❑ 137 Alfonso Soriano .50 .15
❑ 138 Bernie Williams .30 .09
❑ 139 Mike Mussina .50 .15
❑ 140 Jorge Posada .30 .09
❑ 141 Hideki Matsui RC 5.00 1.50
❑ 142 Robin Ventura .20 .06
❑ 143 David Wells .20 .06
❑ 144 Nick Johnson .20 .06
❑ 145 Tim Hudson .20 .06
❑ 146 Eric Chavez .20 .06
❑ 147 Barry Zito .50 .15
❑ 148 Miguel Tejada .20 .06
❑ 149 Jermaine Dye .20 .06
❑ 150 Mark Mulder .20 .06
❑ 151 Terrence Long .20 .06
❑ 152 Scott Hatteberg .20 .06
❑ 153 Marlon Byrd .20 .06
❑ 154 Jim Thome .50 .15
❑ 155 Marlon Anderson .20 .06
❑ 156 Vicente Padilla .20 .06
❑ 157 Bobby Abreu .20 .06
❑ 158 Jimmy Rollins .20 .06
❑ 159 Pat Burrell .20 .06
❑ 160 Brian Giles .20 .06
❑ 161 Aramis Ramirez .20 .06
❑ 162 Jason Kendall .20 .06
❑ 163 Josh Fogg .20 .06
❑ 164 Kip Wells .20 .06
❑ 165 Pokey Reese .20 .06
❑ 166 Kris Benson .20 .06
❑ 167 Ryan Klesko .20 .06
❑ 168 Brian Lawrence .20 .06
❑ 169 Mark Kotsay .20 .06
❑ 170 Jake Peavy .20 .06
❑ 171 Phil Nevin .20 .06
❑ 172 Sean Burroughs .20 .06
❑ 173 Trevor Hoffman .20 .06
❑ 174 Jason Schmidt .20 .06
❑ 175 Kirk Rueter .20 .06
❑ 176 Barry Bonds 1.25 .35
❑ 177 Pedro Feliz .20 .06
❑ 178 Rich Aurilia .20 .06
❑ 179 Benito Santiago .20 .06
❑ 180 J.T. Snow .20 .06
❑ 181 Robb Nen .20 .06
❑ 182 Ichiro Suzuki 1.00 .30
❑ 183 Edgar Martinez .30 .09
❑ 184 Bret Boone .20 .06
❑ 185 Freddy Garcia .20 .06
❑ 186 John Olerud .20 .06
❑ 187 Mike Cameron .20 .06
❑ 188 Joel Piniero .20 .06
❑ 189 Albert Pujols 1.00 .30
❑ 190 Matt Morris .20 .06
❑ 191 J.D. Drew .20 .06
❑ 192 Scott Rolen .30 .09
❑ 193 Tino Martinez .30 .09
❑ 194 Jim Edmonds .20 .06
❑ 195 Edgar Renteria .20 .06
❑ 196 Fernando Vina .20 .06
❑ 197 Jason Isringhausen .20 .06
❑ 198 Ben Grieve .20 .06
❑ 199 Carl Crawford .20 .06
❑ 200 Dewon Brazelton .20 .06
❑ 201 Aubrey Huff .20 .06
❑ 202 Jared Sandberg .20 .06
❑ 203 Steve Cox .20 .06
❑ 204 Carl Everett .20 .06
❑ 205 Kevin Mench .20 .06
❑ 206 Alex Rodriguez 1.00 .30
❑ 207 Rafael Palmeiro .30 .09
❑ 208 Michael Young .20 .06
❑ 209 Hank Blalock .30 .09
❑ 210 Juan Gonzalez .50 .15
❑ 211 Carlos Delgado .20 .06
❑ 212 Eric Hinske .20 .06
❑ 213 Josh Phelps .20 .06
❑ 214 Mark Hendrickson .20 .06
❑ 215 Roy Halladay .20 .06
❑ 216 Orlando Hudson .20 .06
❑ 217 Shannon Stewart .20 .06
❑ 218 Vernon Wells .20 .06
❑ 219 Ichiro Suzuki CL .50 .15
❑ 220 Jason Giambi CL .30 .09
❑ 221 Scott Spiezio .20 .06
❑ 222 Rich Fischer RC .40 .12
❑ 223 Bengie Molina .20 .06
❑ 224 David Eckstein .20 .06
❑ 225 Brandon Webb RC 2.00 .60
❑ 226 Oscar Villarreal RC .40 .12
❑ 227 Rob Hammock RC .75 .23
❑ 228 Matt Kata RC 1.00 .30
❑ 229 Lyle Overbay .20 .06
❑ 230 Chris Capuano RC .40 .12
❑ 231 Horacio Ramirez .20 .06
❑ 232 Shane Reynolds .20 .06
❑ 233 Russ Ortiz .20 .06
❑ 234 Mike Hampton .20 .06
❑ 235 Mike Hessman RC .40 .12
❑ 236 Byung-Hyun Kim .20 .06
❑ 237 Freddy Sanchez .20 .06
❑ 238 Jason Shiell RC .40 .12
❑ 239 Ryan Cameron RC .40 .12
❑ 240 Todd Wellemeyer RC .50 .15
❑ 241 Joe Borowski .20 .06
❑ 242 Alex Gonzalez .20 .06
❑ 243 Jon Leicester RC .40 .12
❑ 244 David Sanders RC .40 .12
❑ 245 Roberto Alomar .50 .15
❑ 246 Barry Larkin .50 .15
❑ 247 Jhonny Peralta RC .40 .12
❑ 248 Zach Sorensen .20 .06
❑ 249 Jason Davis .20 .06
❑ 250 Coco Crisp .20 .06
❑ 251 Greg Vaughn .20 .06
❑ 252 Preston Wilson .20 .06
❑ 253 Denny Neagle .20 .06
❑ 254 Clint Barmes RC .75 .23
❑ 255 Jeremy Bonderman RC 1.25 .35
❑ 256 Wilfredo Ledezma RC .40 .12
❑ 257 Dontrelle Willis .75 .23
❑ 258 Alex Gonzalez .20 .06
❑ 259 Tommy Phelps .20 .06
❑ 260 Kirk Saarloos .20 .06
❑ 261 Colin Porter RC .40 .12
❑ 262 Nate Bland RC .40 .12
❑ 263 Jason Gilfillan RC .40 .12
❑ 264 Mike MacDougal .20 .06
❑ 265 Ken Harvey .20 .06
❑ 266 Brent Mayne .20 .06
❑ 267 Miguel Cabrera 1.00 .30
❑ 268 Hideo Nomo .50 .15
❑ 269 Dave Roberts .20 .06
❑ 270 Fred McGriff .30 .09
❑ 271 Joe Thurston .20 .06
❑ 272 Royce Clayton .20 .06
❑ 273 Michael Nakamura RC .40 .12
❑ 274 Brad Radke .20 .06
❑ 275 Joe Mays .20 .06
❑ 276 Lew Ford RC .50 .15
❑ 277 Michael Cuddyer .20 .06
❑ 278 Luis Ayala RC .40 .12
❑ 279 Julio Manon RC .25 .07
❑ 280 Anthony Ferrari RC .40 .12
❑ 281 Livan Hernandez .20 .06
❑ 282 Jae Weong Seo .20 .06
❑ 283 Jose Reyes .30 .09
❑ 284 Tony Clark .20 .06
❑ 285 Ty Wigginton .20 .06
❑ 286 Cliff Floyd .20 .06
❑ 287 Jeremy Griffiths RC .50 .15
❑ 288 Jason Roach RC .40 .12
❑ 289 Jeff Duncan RC .50 .15
❑ 290 Phil Seibel RC .40 .12
❑ 291 Prentice Redman RC .40 .12
❑ 292 Jose Contreras RC 1.50 .45
❑ 293 Ruben Sierra .20 .06
❑ 294 Andy Pettitte .30 .09
❑ 295 Aaron Boone .20 .06
❑ 296 Mariano Rivera .30 .09
❑ 297 Michel Hernandez RC .40 .12
❑ 298 Mike Neu RC .40 .12
❑ 299 Erubiel Durazo .20 .06
❑ 300 Billy McMillon .20 .06
❑ 301 Rich Harden .50 .15
❑ 302 David Bell .20 .06
❑ 303 Kevin Millwood .20 .06
❑ 304 Mike Lieberthal .20 .06
❑ 305 Jeremy Wedel RC .40 .12
❑ 306 Kenny Lofton .20 .06
❑ 307 Reggie Sanders .20 .06
❑ 308 Randall Simon .20 .06
❑ 309 Xavier Nady .20 .06
❑ 310 Rod Beck .20 .06
❑ 311 Miguel Ojeda RC .40 .12
❑ 312 Mark Loretta .20 .06
❑ 313 Edgardo Alfonzo .20 .06
❑ 314 Andres Galarraga .20 .06
❑ 315 Jose Cruz Jr. .20 .06
❑ 316 Jesse Foppert .20 .06
❑ 317 Kurt Ainsworth .20 .06
❑ 318 Dan Wilson .20 .06
❑ 319 Ben Davis .20 .06
❑ 320 Rocco Baldelli 1.00 .30
❑ 321 Al Martin .20 .06
❑ 322 Runelvys Hernandez .20 .06
❑ 323 Dan Haren RC 1.00 .30
❑ 324 Bo Hart RC 1.50 .45
❑ 325 Einar Diaz .20 .06
❑ 326 Mike Lamb .20 .06
❑ 327 Aquilino Lopez RC .40 .12
❑ 328 Reed Johnson .20 .06
❑ 329 Diegomar Markwell RC .40 .12
❑ 330 Hideki Matsui CL 2.00 .60

2001 Upper Deck Ovation

	Nm-Mt	Ex-Mt
COMP.SET w/o SP'S (60)	20.00	6.00

COMMON CARD (1-60) .40 .12
COMMON WP (61-90) 5.00 1.50

❑ 1 Troy Glaus .60 .18
❑ 2 Darin Erstad .40 .12
❑ 3 Jason Giambi 1.00 .30
❑ 4 Tim Hudson .40 .12
❑ 5 Eric Chavez .40 .12
❑ 6 Carlos Delgado .40 .12
❑ 7 David Wells .40 .12
❑ 8 Greg Vaughn .40 .12
❑ 9 Omar Vizquel .40 .12
Travis Fryman is pictured on card front UER
❑ 10 Jim Thome 1.00 .30
❑ 11 Roberto Alomar 1.00 .30
❑ 12 John Olerud .40 .12
❑ 13 Edgar Martinez .60 .18
❑ 14 Cal Ripken 3.00 .90
❑ 15 Alex Rodriguez 2.00 .60
❑ 16 Ivan Rodriguez 1.00 .30
❑ 17 Manny Ramirez .40 .12
❑ 18 Nomar Garciaparra 2.00 .60
❑ 19 Pedro Martinez 1.00 .30
❑ 20 Jermaine Dye .40 .12
❑ 21 Juan Gonzalez 1.00 .30
❑ 22 Matt Lawton .40 .12
❑ 23 Frank Thomas 1.00 .30
❑ 24 Magglio Ordonez .40 .12
❑ 25 Bernie Williams .60 .18
❑ 26 Derek Jeter 2.50 .75
❑ 27 Roger Clemens 2.00 .60
❑ 28 Jeff Bagwell .60 .18
❑ 29 Richard Hidalgo .40 .12
❑ 30 Chipper Jones 1.00 .30
❑ 31 Greg Maddux 2.00 .60
❑ 32 Andruw Jones .60 .18
❑ 33 Jeromy Burnitz .40 .12
❑ 34 Mark McGwire 2.50 .75
❑ 35 Jim Edmonds .40 .12
❑ 36 Sammy Sosa 1.50 .45
❑ 37 Kerry Wood 1.00 .30
❑ 38 Randy Johnson 1.00 .30
❑ 39 Steve Finley .40 .12
❑ 40 Gary Sheffield .40 .12
❑ 41 Kevin Brown .40 .12
❑ 42 Shawn Green .40 .12
❑ 43 Vladimir Guerrero 1.00 .30
❑ 44 Jose Vidro .40 .12
❑ 45 Barry Bonds 2.50 .75
❑ 46 Jeff Kent .40 .12
❑ 47 Preston Wilson .40 .12
❑ 48 Luis Castillo .40 .12
❑ 49 Mike Piazza 1.50 .45
❑ 50 Edgardo Alfonzo .40 .12
❑ 51 Tony Gwynn 1.25 .35
❑ 52 Ryan Klesko .40 .12
❑ 53 Scott Rolen .60 .18
❑ 54 Bob Abreu .40 .12
❑ 55 Jason Kendall .40 .12
❑ 56 Brian Giles .40 .12
❑ 57 Ken Griffey Jr. 1.50 .45
❑ 58 Barry Larkin 1.00 .30
❑ 59 Todd Helton .60 .18
❑ 60 Mike Hampton .40 .12
❑ 61 Corey Patterson WP 5.00 1.50
❑ 62 Timo Perez WP 5.00 1.50
❑ 63 Toby Hall WP 5.00 1.50
❑ 64 Brandon Inge WP 5.00 1.50
❑ 65 Joe Crede WP 5.00 1.50
❑ 66 Xavier Nady WP 5.00 1.50
❑ 67 A. Pettyjohn WP RC 5.00 1.50
❑ 68 Keith Ginter WP 5.00 1.50
❑ 69 Brian Cole WP 5.00 1.50
❑ 70 Tyler Walker WP RC 5.00 1.50
❑ 71 Juan Uribe WP RC 5.00 1.50
❑ 72 Alex Hernandez WP 5.00 1.50
❑ 73 Leo Estrella WP 5.00 1.50
❑ 74 Joey Nation WP 5.00 1.50
❑ 75 Aubrey Huff WP 5.00 1.50
❑ 76 Ichiro Suzuki WP RC 80.00 24.00
❑ 77 Jay Spurgeon WP 5.00 1.50
❑ 78 Sun Woo Kim WP 5.00 1.50
❑ 79 Pedro Feliz WP 5.00 1.50
❑ 80 Pablo Ozuna WP 5.00 1.50
❑ 81 Hiram Bocachica WP 5.00 1.50
❑ 82 Brad Wilkerson WP 5.00 1.50
❑ 83 Rocky Biddle WP 5.00 1.50
❑ 84 Aaron McNeal WP 5.00 1.50
❑ 85 Adam Bernero WP 5.00 1.50
❑ 86 Danys Baez WP 5.00 1.50
❑ 87 Dee Brown WP 5.00 1.50
❑ 88 Jimmy Rollins WP 5.00 1.50
❑ 89 Jason Hart WP 5.00 1.50
❑ 90 Ross Gload WP 5.00 1.50

2002 Upper Deck Ovation

	Nm-Mt	Ex-Mt
COMP.LOW w/o SP's (90)	25.00	7.50
COMP.UPDATE w/o SP's (30)	15.00	4.50
COMMON CARD (1-60)	.40	.12
COMMON (61-89/120/151-180)	8.00	2.40
COMMON CARD (90-119)	.50	.15
COMMON CARD (121-150)	.60	.18

❑ 1 Troy Glaus .60 .18
❑ 2 David Justice .40 .12
❑ 3 Tim Hudson .40 .12
❑ 4 Jermaine Dye .40 .12
❑ 5 Carlos Delgado .40 .12
❑ 6 Greg Vaughn .40 .12
❑ 7 Jim Thome 1.00 .30
❑ 8 C.C. Sabathia .40 .12
❑ 9 Ichiro Suzuki 2.00 .60
❑ 10 Edgar Martinez .60 .18
❑ 11 Chris Richard .40 .12
❑ 12 Rafael Palmeiro .60 .18
❑ 13 Alex Rodriguez 2.00 .60
❑ 14 Ivan Rodriguez 1.00 .30
❑ 15 Nomar Garciaparra 2.00 .60
❑ 16 Manny Ramirez .40 .12
❑ 17 Pedro Martinez 1.00 .30
❑ 18 Mike Sweeney .40 .12
❑ 19 Dmitri Young .40 .12
❑ 20 Doug Mientkiewicz .40 .12
❑ 21 Brad Radke .40 .12
❑ 22 Cristian Guzman .40 .12
❑ 23 Frank Thomas 1.00 .30
❑ 24 Magglio Ordonez .40 .12
❑ 25 Bernie Williams .60 .18
❑ 26 Derek Jeter 2.50 .75
❑ 27 Jason Giambi 1.00 .30
❑ 28 Roger Clemens 2.00 .60
❑ 29 Jeff Bagwell .60 .18
❑ 30 Lance Berkman .40 .12
❑ 31 Chipper Jones 1.00 .30
❑ 32 Gary Sheffield .40 .12
❑ 33 Greg Maddux 2.00 .60
❑ 34 Richie Sexson .40 .12
❑ 35 Albert Pujols 2.00 .60
❑ 36 Tino Martinez .60 .18
❑ 37 J.D. Drew .40 .12
❑ 38 Sammy Sosa 1.50 .45
❑ 39 Moises Alou .40 .12
❑ 40 Randy Johnson 1.00 .30
❑ 41 Luis Gonzalez .40 .12
❑ 42 Shawn Green .40 .12
❑ 43 Kevin Brown .40 .12
❑ 44 Vladimir Guerrero 1.00 .30
❑ 45 Barry Bonds 2.50 .75
❑ 46 Jeff Kent .40 .12
❑ 47 Cliff Floyd .40 .12
❑ 48 Josh Beckett .60 .18
❑ 49 Mike Piazza 1.50 .45
❑ 50 Mo Vaughn .40 .12
❑ 51 Jeromy Burnitz .40 .12
❑ 52 Roberto Alomar 1.00 .30
❑ 53 Phil Nevin .40 .12
❑ 54 Scott Rolen .60 .18
❑ 55 Jimmy Rollins .40 .12
❑ 56 Brian Giles .40 .12
❑ 57 Ken Griffey Jr. 1.50 .45
❑ 58 Sean Casey .40 .12
❑ 59 Larry Walker .60 .18
❑ 60 Todd Helton .60 .18
❑ 61 Rodrigo Rosario WP RC 8.00 2.40
❑ 62 Reed Johnson WP RC 10.00 3.00
❑ 63 John Ennis WP RC 8.00 2.40
❑ 64 Luis Martinez WP RC 10.00 3.00
❑ 65 So Taguchi WP RC 10.00 3.00
❑ 66 Brandon Backe WP RC 8.00 2.40
❑ 67 Doug Devore WP RC 8.00 2.40
❑ 68 Victor Alvarez WP RC 8.00 2.40
❑ 69 Kazuhisa Ishii WP RC 12.00 3.60
❑ 70 Eric Good WP RC 8.00 2.40
❑ 71 Deivis Santos WP 8.00 2.40
❑ 72 Matt Thornton WP RC 8.00 2.40
❑ 73 Hansel Izquierdo WP RC 8.00 2.40
❑ 74 Tyler Yates WP RC 8.00 2.40
❑ 75 Jaime Cerda WP RC 8.00 2.40
❑ 76 Satoru Komiyama WP RC 8.00 2.40
❑ 77 Steve Bechler WP RC 8.00 2.40
❑ 78 Ben Howard WP RC 8.00 2.40
❑ 79 Jorge Padilla WP RC 10.00 3.00
❑ 80 Eric Junge WP RC 8.00 2.40
❑ 81 Anderson Machado WP RC 10.00 3.00
❑ 82 Adrian Burnside WP RC 8.00 2.40
❑ 83 Josh Hancock WP RC 8.00 2.40
❑ 84 Anastacio Martinez WP RC 8.00 2.40
❑ 85 Rene Reyes WP RC 8.00 2.40
❑ 86 Nate Field WP RC 8.00 2.40
❑ 87 Tim Kalita WP RC 8.00 2.40
❑ 88 Kevin Frederick WP RC 8.00 2.40
❑ 89 Edwin Almonte WP RC 8.00 2.40
❑ 90 Ichiro Suzuki SS 1.00 .30
❑ 91 Ichiro Suzuki SS 1.00 .30
❑ 92 Ichiro Suzuki SS 1.00 .30
❑ 93 Ichiro Suzuki SS 1.00 .30
❑ 94 Ichiro Suzuki SS 1.00 .30
❑ 95 Ken Griffey Jr. SS .75 .23
❑ 96 Ken Griffey Jr. SS .75 .23
❑ 97 Ken Griffey Jr. SS .75 .23
❑ 98 Ken Griffey Jr. SS .75 .23
❑ 99 Ken Griffey Jr. SS .75 .23
❑ 100 Jason Giambi A's SS .50 .15
❑ 101 Jason Giambi A's SS .50 .15
❑ 102 Jason Giambi A's SS .50 .15
❑ 103 Jason Giambi Yankees SS .50 .15
❑ 104 Jason Giambi Yankees SS .60 .18
❑ 105 Sammy Sosa SS .75 .23
❑ 106 Sammy Sosa SS .75 .23
❑ 107 Sammy Sosa SS .75 .23
❑ 108 Sammy Sosa SS .75 .23
❑ 109 Sammy Sosa SS .75 .23
❑ 110 Alex Rodriguez SS 1.00 .30
❑ 111 Alex Rodriguez SS 1.00 .30
❑ 112 Alex Rodriguez SS 1.00 .30
❑ 113 Alex Rodriguez SS 1.00 .30
❑ 114 Alex Rodriguez SS 1.00 .30
❑ 115 Mark McGwire SS 1.25 .35

Card	Nm-Mt	Ex-Mt
❑ 116 Mark McGwire SS	1.25	.35
❑ 117 Mark McGwire SS	1.25	.35
❑ 118 Mark McGwire SS	1.25	.35
❑ 119 Mark McGwire SS	1.25	.35
❑ 120 Jason Giambi Ken Griffey Jr. Mark McGwire Alex Rodriguez Sammy Sosa Ichiro Suzuki SP/2002	30.00	9.00
❑ 121 Curt Schilling	1.00	.30
❑ 122 Cliff Floyd	.60	.18
❑ 123 Derek Lowe	.60	.18
❑ 124 Hee Seop Choi	1.00	.30
❑ 125 Mark Prior	3.00	.90
❑ 126 Joe Borchard	.60	.18
❑ 127 Austin Kearns	1.00	.30
❑ 128 Adam Dunn	1.00	.30
❑ 129 Jay Payton	.60	.18
❑ 130 Carlos Pena	.60	.18
❑ 131 Andy Van Hekken	.60	.18
❑ 132 Andres Torres	.60	.18
❑ 133 Ben Diggins	.60	.18
❑ 134 Torii Hunter	.60	.18
❑ 135 Bartolo Colon	.60	.18
❑ 136 Raul Mondesi	.60	.18
❑ 137 Alfonso Soriano	1.50	.45
❑ 138 Miguel Tejada	.60	.18
❑ 139 Ray Durham	.60	.18
❑ 140 Eric Chavez	.60	.18
❑ 141 Marlon Byrd	.60	.18
❑ 142 Brett Myers	.60	.18
❑ 143 Sean Burroughs	.60	.18
❑ 144 Kenny Lofton	.60	.18
❑ 145 Scott Rolen	1.00	.30
❑ 146 Carl Crawford	.60	.18
❑ 147 Jayson Werth	.60	.18
❑ 148 Josh Phelps	.60	.18
❑ 149 Eric Hinske	.60	.18
❑ 150 Orlando Hudson	.60	.18
❑ 151 Jose Valverde WP RC	10.00	3.00
❑ 152 Trey Hodges WP RC	10.00	3.00
❑ 153 Joey Dawley WP RC	8.00	2.40
❑ 154 Travis Driskill WP RC	8.00	2.40
❑ 155 Howie Clark WP RC	8.00	2.40
❑ 156 Jorge De La Rosa WP RC	8.00	2.40
❑ 157 Freddy Sanchez WP RC	10.00	3.00
❑ 158 Earl Snyder WP RC	8.00	2.40
❑ 159 Cliff Lee WP RC	10.00	3.00
❑ 160 Josh Bard WP RC	8.00	2.40
❑ 161 Aaron Cook WP RC	10.00	3.00
❑ 162 Franklyn German WP RC	8.00	2.40
❑ 163 Brandon Puffer WP RC	8.00	2.40
❑ 164 Kirk Saarloos WP RC	10.00	3.00
❑ 165 Jeriome Robertson WP RC	10.00	3.00
❑ 166 Miguel Asencio WP RC	8.00	2.40
❑ 167 Shawn Sedlacek WP RC	8.00	2.40
❑ 168 Jayson Durocher WP RC	8.00	2.40
❑ 169 Shane Nance WP RC	8.00	2.40
❑ 170 Jamey Carroll WP RC	8.00	2.40
❑ 171 Oliver Perez WP RC	10.00	3.00
❑ 172 Wil Nieves WP RC	8.00	2.40
❑ 173 Clay Condrey WP RC	8.00	2.40
❑ 174 Chris Snelling WP RC	10.00	3.00
❑ 175 Mike Crudale WP RC	8.00	2.40
❑ 176 Jason Simontacchi WP RC	10.00	3.00
❑ 177 Felix Escalona WP RC	8.00	2.40
❑ 178 Lance Carter WP RC	8.00	2.40
❑ 179 Scott Wiggins WP RC	8.00	2.40
❑ 180 Kevin Cash WP RC	8.00	2.40

2003 Upper Deck Play Ball

	Nm-Mt	Ex-Mt
COMP.SET w/o SP's (74)	50.00	15.00
COMMON ACTIVE (1-73/104)	.40	.12
COMMON RETIRED (1-73/104)	.60	.18
COMMON CARD (74-88)	8.00	2.40
COMMON T.WILLIAMS (89-103)	15.00	4.50

Card	Nm-Mt	Ex-Mt
❑ 1 Troy Glaus	.60	.18
❑ 2 Darin Erstad	.40	.12
❑ 3 Randy Johnson	1.00	.30
❑ 4 Luis Gonzalez	.40	.12
❑ 5 Curt Schilling	.60	.18
❑ 6 Tom Glavine	1.00	.30
❑ 7 Chipper Jones	1.00	.30
❑ 8 Greg Maddux	2.00	.60
❑ 9 Andruw Jones	.60	.18
❑ 10 Pedro Martinez	1.00	.30
❑ 11 Manny Ramirez	.40	.12
❑ 12 Nomar Garciaparra	2.00	.60
❑ 13 Billy Williams	.60	.18
❑ 14 Sammy Sosa	1.50	.45
❑ 15 Kerry Wood	1.00	.30
❑ 16 Mark Prior	2.00	.60
❑ 17 Ernie Banks	1.50	.45
❑ 18 Frank Thomas	1.00	.30
❑ 19 Joe Morgan	.60	.18
❑ 20 Ken Griffey Jr.	1.50	.45
❑ 21 Adam Dunn	.60	.18
❑ 22 Jim Thome	1.00	.30
❑ 23 Todd Helton	.60	.18
❑ 24 Larry Walker	.60	.18
❑ 25 Lance Berkman	.40	.12
❑ 26 Roy Oswalt	.40	.12
❑ 27 Jeff Bagwell	.60	.18
❑ 28 Nolan Ryan	5.00	1.50
❑ 29 Mike Sweeney	.40	.12
❑ 30 Shawn Green	.40	.12
❑ 31 Hideo Nomo	1.00	.30
❑ 32 Kazuhisa Ishii	.40	.12
❑ 33 Richie Sexson	.40	.12
❑ 34 Robin Yount	1.50	.45
❑ 35 Harmon Killebrew	1.50	.45
❑ 36 Torii Hunter	.40	.12
❑ 37 Vladimir Guerrero	1.00	.30
❑ 38 Roberto Alomar	1.00	.30
❑ 39 Mike Piazza	1.50	.45
❑ 40 Tom Seaver	1.50	.45
❑ 41 Phil Rizzuto	1.00	.30
❑ 42 Yogi Berra	1.50	.45
❑ 43 Mike Mussina	1.00	.30
❑ 44 Roger Clemens	2.00	.60
❑ 45 Derek Jeter	2.50	.75
❑ 46 Jason Giambi	1.00	.30
❑ 47 Bernie Williams	.60	.18
❑ 48 Alfonso Soriano	1.00	.30
❑ 49 Catfish Hunter	1.00	.30
❑ 50 Barry Zito	1.00	.30
❑ 51 Eric Chavez	.40	.12
❑ 52 Tim Hudson	.40	.12
❑ 53 Rollie Fingers	.60	.18
❑ 54 Miguel Tejada	.40	.12
❑ 55 Pat Burrell	.40	.12
❑ 56 Brian Giles	.40	.12
❑ 57 Willie Stargell	1.00	.30
❑ 58 Phil Nevin	.40	.12
❑ 59 Orlando Cepeda	.60	.18
❑ 60 Barry Bonds	2.50	.75
❑ 61 Jeff Kent	.40	.12
❑ 62 Willie McCovey	.60	.18
❑ 63 Ichiro Suzuki	2.00	.60
❑ 64 Stan Musial	2.50	.75
❑ 65 Albert Pujols	2.00	.60
❑ 66 J.D. Drew	.40	.12
❑ 67 Scott Rolen	.60	.18
❑ 68 Mark McGwire	2.50	.75
❑ 69 Alex Rodriguez	2.00	.60
❑ 70 Juan Gonzalez	1.00	.30
❑ 71 Ivan Rodriguez	1.00	.30
❑ 72 Rafael Palmeiro	.60	.18
❑ 73 Carlos Delgado	.40	.12
❑ 74 Ted Williams S41	15.00	4.50
❑ 75 Hank Greenberg S41	10.00	3.00
❑ 76 Joe DiMaggio S41	15.00	4.50
❑ 77 Lefty Gomez S41	10.00	3.00
❑ 78 Tommy Henrich S41	8.00	2.40
❑ 79 Pee Wee Reese S41	10.00	3.00
❑ 80 Mel Ott S41	10.00	3.00
❑ 81 Carl Hubbell S41	10.00	3.00
❑ 82 Jimmie Foxx S41	10.00	3.00
❑ 83 Joe Cronin S41	8.00	2.40
❑ 84 Charlie Gehringer S41	8.00	2.40
❑ 85 Frank Hayes S41	8.00	2.40
❑ 86 Babe Dahlgren S41	8.00	2.40
❑ 87 Dolph Camilli S41	8.00	2.40
❑ 88 Johnny Vandermeer S41	8.00	2.40
❑ 89 Ted Williams TRIB	15.00	4.50
❑ 90 Ted Williams TRIB	15.00	4.50
❑ 91 Ted Williams TRIB	15.00	4.50
❑ 92 Ted Williams TRIB	15.00	4.50
❑ 93 Ted Williams TRIB	15.00	4.50
❑ 94 Ted Williams TRIB	15.00	4.50
❑ 95 Ted Williams TRIB	15.00	4.50
❑ 96 Ted Williams TRIB	15.00	4.50
❑ 97 Ted Williams TRIB	15.00	4.50
❑ 98 Ted Williams TRIB	15.00	4.50
❑ 99 Ted Williams TRIB	15.00	4.50
❑ 100 Ted Williams TRIB	15.00	4.50
❑ 101 Ted Williams TRIB	15.00	4.50
❑ 102 Ted Williams TRIB	15.00	4.50
❑ 103 Ted Williams TRIB	15.00	4.50
❑ 104 Hideki Matsui RC	8.00	2.40
❑ MM1 Mark McGwire Sample	2.00	.60

2000 Upper Deck Pros and Prospects

	Nm-Mt	Ex-Mt
COMP.BASIC w/o SP's (90)	20.00	6.00
COMP.UPDATE w/o SP'S (30)	10.00	3.00
COMMON CARD (1-90)	.40	.12
COMMON PS (91-120)	5.00	1.50
COMMON PF (121-132)	6.00	1.80
COMMON PS (133-162)	8.00	2.40
COMMON (163-192)	.60	.18

Card	Nm-Mt	Ex-Mt
❑ 1 Darin Erstad	.40	.12
❑ 2 Troy Glaus	.60	.18
❑ 3 Mo Vaughn	.40	.12
❑ 4 Jason Giambi	1.00	.30
❑ 5 Tim Hudson	.60	.18
❑ 6 Ben Grieve	.40	.12
❑ 7 Eric Chavez	.40	.12
❑ 8 Shannon Stewart	.40	.12
❑ 9 Raul Mondesi	.40	.12
❑ 10 Carlos Delgado	.40	.12
❑ 11 Jose Canseco	1.00	.30
❑ 12 Fred McGriff	.60	.18
❑ 13 Greg Vaughn	.40	.12
❑ 14 Manny Ramirez	.40	.12
❑ 15 Roberto Alomar	1.00	.30
❑ 16 Jim Thome	1.00	.30
❑ 17 Alex Rodriguez	2.00	.60
❑ 18 Freddy Garcia	.40	.12
❑ 19 John Olerud	.40	.12
❑ 20 Cal Ripken	3.00	.90
❑ 21 Albert Belle	.40	.12
❑ 22 Mike Mussina	1.00	.30

Card	Nm-Mt	Ex-Mt
❑ 23 Ivan Rodriguez	1.00	.30
❑ 24 Rafael Palmeiro	.60	.18
❑ 25 Ruben Mateo	.40	.12
❑ 26 Gabe Kapler	.40	.12
❑ 27 Pedro Martinez	1.00	.30
❑ 28 Nomar Garciaparra	2.00	.60
❑ 29 Carl Everett	.40	.12
❑ 30 Carlos Beltran	.40	.12
❑ 31 Jermaine Dye	.40	.12
❑ 32 Johnny Damon UER	.40	.12
Picture on front is Joe Randa		
❑ 33 Juan Gonzalez	1.00	.30
❑ 34 Juan Encarnacion	.40	.12
❑ 35 Dean Palmer	.40	.12
❑ 36 Jacque Jones	.40	.12
❑ 37 Matt Lawton	.40	.12
❑ 38 Frank Thomas	1.00	.30
❑ 39 Paul Konerko	.40	.12
❑ 40 Magglio Ordonez	.40	.12
❑ 41 Derek Jeter	2.50	.75
❑ 42 Bernie Williams	.60	.18
❑ 43 Mariano Rivera	.60	.18
❑ 44 Roger Clemens	2.00	.60
❑ 45 Jeff Bagwell	.60	.18
❑ 46 Craig Biggio	.60	.18
❑ 47 Richard Hidalgo	.40	.12
❑ 48 Chipper Jones	1.00	.30
❑ 49 Andres Galarraga	.40	.12
❑ 50 Andruw Jones	.60	.18
❑ 51 Greg Maddux	2.00	.60
❑ 52 Jeromy Burnitz	.40	.12
❑ 53 Geoff Jenkins	.40	.12
❑ 54 Mark McGwire	2.50	.75
❑ 55 Jim Edmonds	.40	.12
❑ 56 Fernando Tatis	.40	.12
❑ 57 J.D. Drew	.40	.12
❑ 58 Sammy Sosa	1.50	.45
❑ 59 Kerry Wood	1.00	.30
❑ 60 Randy Johnson	1.00	.30
❑ 61 Matt Williams	.40	.12
❑ 62 Erubiel Durazo	.40	.12
❑ 63 Shawn Green	.40	.12
❑ 64 Kevin Brown	.40	.12
❑ 65 Gary Sheffield	.40	.12
❑ 66 Adrian Beltre	.40	.12
❑ 67 Vladimir Guerrero	1.00	.30
❑ 68 Jose Vidro	.40	.12
❑ 69 Barry Bonds	2.50	.75
❑ 70 Jeff Kent	.40	.12
❑ 71 Preston Wilson	.40	.12
❑ 72 Ryan Dempster	.40	.12
❑ 73 Mike Lowell	.40	.12
❑ 74 Mike Piazza	1.50	.45
❑ 75 Robin Ventura	.40	.12
❑ 76 Edgardo Alfonzo	.40	.12
❑ 77 Derek Bell	.40	.12
❑ 78 Tony Gwynn	1.25	.35
❑ 79 Matt Clement	.40	.12
❑ 80 Scott Rolen	.60	.18
❑ 81 Bobby Abreu	.40	.12
❑ 82 Curt Schilling	.60	.18
❑ 83 Brian Giles	.40	.12
❑ 84 Jason Kendall	.40	.12
❑ 85 Kris Benson	.40	.12
❑ 86 Ken Griffey Jr.	1.50	.45
❑ 87 Sean Casey	.40	.12
❑ 88 Pokey Reese	.40	.12
❑ 89 Larry Walker	.60	.18
❑ 90 Todd Helton	.60	.18
❑ 91 Rick Ankiel PS	5.00	1.50
❑ 92 Milton Bradley PS	5.00	1.50
❑ 93 Vernon Wells PS	5.00	1.50
❑ 94 Rafael Furcal PS	5.00	1.50
❑ 95 Kazuhiro Sasaki PS RC	10.00	3.00
❑ 96 Joe Torres PS RC	5.00	1.50
❑ 97 Adam Kennedy PS	5.00	1.50
❑ 98 Adam Piatt PS	5.00	1.50
❑ 99 Matt Wheatland PS RC	5.00	1.50
❑ 100 Alex Cabrera PS RC	5.00	1.50
❑ 101 Barry Zito PS RC	40.00	12.00
❑ 102 Mike Lamb PS RC	5.00	1.50
❑ 103 Scott Heard PS RC	5.00	1.50
❑ 104 Danys Baez PS RC	8.00	2.40
❑ 105 Matt Riley PS	5.00	1.50
❑ 106 Mark Mulder PS	8.00	2.40
❑ 107 W.Rodriguez PS RC	5.00	1.50
❑ 108 Luis Matos PS RC	10.00	3.00
❑ 109 Alfonso Soriano PS	12.00	3.60
❑ 110 Pat Burrell PS	8.00	2.40
❑ 111 Mike Tonis PS RC	8.00	2.40
❑ 112 Aaron McNeal PS RC	5.00	1.50
❑ 113 Dave Krynzel PS RC	5.00	1.50
❑ 114 Josh Beckett PS	10.00	3.00
❑ 115 Sean Burnett PS RC	10.00	3.00
❑ 116 Eric Munson PS	5.00	1.50
❑ 117 Scott Downs PS RC	5.00	1.50
❑ 118 Brian Tollberg PS RC	5.00	1.50
❑ 119 Nick Johnson PS	5.00	1.50
❑ 120 Leo Estrella PS RC	5.00	1.50
❑ 121 Ken Griffey Jr. PF	12.00	3.60
❑ 122 Frank Thomas PF	6.00	1.80
❑ 123 Cal Ripken PF	20.00	6.00
❑ 124 Ivan Rodriguez PF	6.00	1.80
❑ 125 Derek Jeter PF	15.00	4.50
❑ 126 Mark McGwire PF	15.00	4.50
❑ 127 Pedro Martinez PF	6.00	1.80
❑ 128 Chipper Jones PF	6.00	1.80
❑ 129 Sammy Sosa PF	10.00	3.00
❑ 130 Alex Rodriguez PF	12.00	3.60
❑ 131 Vladimir Guerrero PF	6.00	1.80
❑ 132 Jeff Bagwell PF	6.00	1.80
❑ 133 Dane Artman PS RC	8.00	2.40
❑ 134 Juan Pierre PS RC	10.00	3.00
❑ 135 Jace Brewer PS RC	8.00	2.40
❑ 136 Sun Woo Kim PS RC	8.00	2.40
❑ 137 Jon Rauch PS RC	8.00	2.40
❑ 138 Juan Guzman PS RC	8.00	2.40
❑ 139 Daylan Holt PS RC	8.00	2.40
❑ 140 R.Washington PS RC	8.00	2.40
❑ 141 Ben Diggins PS RC	8.00	2.40
❑ 142 Mike Meyers PS RC	8.00	2.40
❑ 143 C.Wakeland PS RC	8.00	2.40
❑ 144 Cory Vance PS RC	8.00	2.40
❑ 145 Keith Ginter PS RC	8.00	2.40
❑ 146 Koyie Hill PS RC	10.00	3.00
❑ 147 Julio Zuleta PS RC	5.00	1.50
❑ 148 G.Guzman PS RC	8.00	2.40
❑ 149 Jay Spurgeon PS RC	8.00	2.40
❑ 150 Ross Gload PS RC	8.00	2.40
❑ 151 Ben Sheets PS RC	10.00	3.00
❑ 152 J.Kalinowski PS RC	8.00	2.40
❑ 153 Kurt Ainsworth PS RC	10.00	3.00
❑ 154 P.Crawford PS RC	8.00	2.40
❑ 155 Xavier Nady PS RC	10.00	3.00
❑ 156 B.Wilkerson PS RC	10.00	3.00
❑ 157 Kris Wilson PS RC	8.00	2.40
❑ 158 Paul Rigdon PS RC	8.00	2.40
❑ 159 R.Kohlmeier PS RC	8.00	2.40
❑ 160 Dane Sardinha PS RC	8.00	2.40
❑ 161 Javier Cardona PS RC	8.00	2.40
❑ 162 Brad Cresse PS RC	8.00	2.40
❑ 163 Ron Gant	.60	.18
❑ 164 Mark Mulder	1.00	.30
❑ 165 David Wells	.60	.18
❑ 166 Jason Tyner	.60	.18
❑ 167 David Segui	.60	.18
❑ 168 Al Martin	.60	.18
❑ 169 Melvin Mora	.60	.18
❑ 170 Ricky Ledee	.60	.18
❑ 171 Rolando Arrojo	.60	.18
❑ 172 Mike Sweeney	.60	.18
❑ 173 Bobby Higginson	.60	.18
❑ 174 Eric Milton	.60	.18
❑ 175 Charles Johnson	.60	.18
❑ 176 David Justice	.60	.18
❑ 177 Moises Alou	.60	.18
❑ 178 Andy Ashby	.60	.18
❑ 179 Richie Sexson	.60	.18
❑ 180 Will Clark	1.50	.45
❑ 181 Rondell White	.60	.18
❑ 182 Curt Schilling	1.00	.30
❑ 183 Tom Goodwin	.60	.18
❑ 184 Lee Stevens	.60	.18
❑ 185 Ellis Burks	.60	.18
❑ 186 Henry Rodriguez	.60	.18
❑ 187 Mike Bordick	.60	.18
❑ 188 Ryan Klesko	.60	.18
❑ 189 Travis Lee	.60	.18
❑ 190 Kevin Young	.60	.18
❑ 191 Barry Larkin	1.50	.45
❑ 192 Jeff Cirillo	.60	.18

2001 Upper Deck Pros and Prospects

	Nm-Mt	Ex-Mt
COMP.SET w/o SP's (90)	20.00	6.00
COMMON CARD (1-90)	.40	.12
COMMON CARD (91-135)	8.00	2.40
COMMON (136-141)	20.00	6.00
❑ 1 Troy Glaus	.60	.18
❑ 2 Darin Erstad	.40	.12
❑ 3 Tim Hudson	.40	.12
❑ 4 Jason Giambi	1.00	.30
❑ 5 Jermaine Dye	.40	.12
❑ 6 Barry Zito	1.00	.30
❑ 7 Carlos Delgado	.40	.12
❑ 8 Shannon Stewart	.40	.12
❑ 9 Raul Mondesi	.40	.12
❑ 10 Greg Vaughn	.40	.12
❑ 11 Ben Grieve	.40	.12
❑ 12 Roberto Alomar	1.00	.30
❑ 13 Juan Gonzalez	1.00	.30
❑ 14 Jim Thome	1.00	.30
❑ 15 C.C. Sabathia	.40	.12
❑ 16 Edgar Martinez	.60	.18
❑ 17 Kazuhiro Sasaki	.40	.12
❑ 18 Aaron Sele	.40	.12
❑ 19 John Olerud	.40	.12
❑ 20 Cal Ripken	3.00	.90
❑ 21 Rafael Palmeiro	.60	.18
❑ 22 Ivan Rodriguez	1.00	.30
❑ 23 Alex Rodriguez	2.00	.60
❑ 24 Manny Ramirez	.40	.12
❑ 25 Pedro Martinez	1.00	.30
❑ 26 Carl Everett	.40	.12
❑ 27 Nomar Garciaparra	2.00	.60
❑ 28 Neifi Perez	.40	.12
❑ 29 Mike Sweeney	.40	.12
❑ 30 Bobby Higginson	.40	.12
❑ 31 Tony Clark	.40	.12
❑ 32 Doug Mientkiewicz	.40	.12
❑ 33 Cristian Guzman	.40	.12
❑ 34 Brad Radke	.40	.12
❑ 35 Magglio Ordonez	.40	.12
❑ 36 Carlos Lee	.40	.12
❑ 37 Frank Thomas	1.00	.30
❑ 38 Roger Clemens	2.00	.60
❑ 39 Bernie Williams	.60	.18
❑ 40 Derek Jeter	2.50	.75
❑ 41 Tino Martinez	.60	.18
❑ 42 Wade Miller	.40	.12
❑ 43 Jeff Bagwell	.60	.18
❑ 44 Lance Berkman	.40	.12
❑ 45 Richard Hidalgo	.40	.12
❑ 46 Greg Maddux	2.00	.60
❑ 47 Andruw Jones	.60	.18
❑ 48 Chipper Jones	1.00	.30
❑ 49 Rafael Furcal	.40	.12
❑ 50 Jeromy Burnitz	.40	.12
❑ 51 Geoff Jenkins	.40	.12
❑ 52 Ben Sheets	.40	.12
❑ 53 Mark McGwire	2.50	.75
❑ 54 Jim Edmonds	.40	.12
❑ 55 J.D. Drew	.40	.12
❑ 56 Fred McGriff	.60	.18
❑ 57 Sammy Sosa	1.50	.45
❑ 58 Kerry Wood	1.00	.30
❑ 59 Randy Johnson	1.00	.30

❑ 60 Luis Gonzalez .40 .12
❑ 61 Curt Schilling .60 .18
❑ 62 Kevin Brown .40 .12
❑ 63 Shawn Green .40 .12
❑ 64 Gary Sheffield .40 .12
❑ 65 Vladimir Guerrero 1.00 .30
❑ 66 Jose Vidro .40 .12
❑ 67 Barry Bonds 2.50 .75
❑ 68 Jeff Kent .40 .12
❑ 69 Rich Aurilia .40 .12
❑ 70 Preston Wilson .40 .12
❑ 71 Charles Johnson .40 .12
❑ 72 Cliff Floyd .40 .12
❑ 73 Mike Piazza 1.50 .45
❑ 74 Al Leiter .40 .12
❑ 75 Matt Lawton .40 .12
❑ 76 Tony Gwynn 1.25 .35
❑ 77 Ryan Klesko .40 .12
❑ 78 Phil Nevin .40 .12
❑ 79 Scott Rolen .60 .18
❑ 80 Pat Burrell .40 .12
❑ 81 Jimmy Rollins .40 .12
❑ 82 Jason Kendall .40 .12
❑ 83 Brian Giles .40 .12
❑ 84 Aramis Ramirez .40 .12
❑ 85 Ken Griffey Jr. 1.50 .45
❑ 86 Barry Larkin 1.00 .30
❑ 87 Sean Casey .40 .12
❑ 88 Larry Walker .60 .18
❑ 89 Todd Helton .60 .18
❑ 90 Mike Hampton .40 .12
❑ 91 Juan Cruz PS RC 8.00 2.40
❑ 92 Brian Lawrence PS RC 8.00 2.40
❑ 93 Brandon Lyon PS RC 8.00 2.40
❑ 94 A.Hernandez PS RC 8.00 2.40
❑ 95 Jose Mieses PS RC 8.00 2.40
❑ 96 Juan Uribe PS RC 8.00 2.40
❑ 97 M.Ensberg PS RC 12.00 3.60
❑ 98 Wilson Betemit PS RC 8.00 2.40
❑ 99 Ryan Freel PS RC 8.00 2.40
❑ 100 Jack Wilson PS RC 8.00 2.40
❑ 101 Cesar Crespo PS RC 8.00 2.40
❑ 102 Bret Prinz PS RC 8.00 2.40
❑ 103 H.Ramirez PS RC 10.00 3.00
❑ 104 E. Guzman PS RC 8.00 2.40
❑ 105 Josh Towers PS RC 8.00 2.40
❑ 106 B. Duckworth PS RC 8.00 2.40
❑ 107 Esix Snead PS RC 8.00 2.40
❑ 108 Billy Sylvester PS RC 8.00 2.40
❑ 109 Alexis Gomez PS RC 8.00 2.40
❑ 110 J. Estrada PS RC 10.00 3.00
❑ 111 Joe Kennedy PS RC 8.00 2.40
❑ 112 Travis Hafner PS RC 10.00 3.00
❑ 113 Martin Vargas PS RC 8.00 2.40
❑ 114 Jay Gibbons PS RC 10.00 3.00
❑ 115 Andres Torres PS RC 8.00 2.40
❑ 116 Sean Douglass PS RC 8.00 2.40
❑ 117 Juan Diaz PS RC 8.00 2.40
❑ 118 Greg Miller PS RC 8.00 2.40
❑ 119 C. Valderrama PS RC 8.00 2.40
❑ 120 Bill Ortega PS RC 8.00 2.40
❑ 121 Josh Fogg PS RC 8.00 2.40
❑ 122 Wilken Ruan PS RC 8.00 2.40
❑ 123 Kris Keller PS RC 8.00 2.40
❑ 124 Erick Almonte PS RC 8.00 2.40
❑ 125 R. Rodriguez PS RC 8.00 2.40
❑ 126 Grant Balfour PS RC 8.00 2.40
❑ 127 Nick Maness PS RC 8.00 2.40
❑ 128 Jeremy Owens PS RC 8.00 2.40
❑ 129 Doug Nickle PS RC 8.00 2.40
❑ 130 Bert Snow PS RC 8.00 2.40
❑ 131 Jason Smith PS RC 8.00 2.40
❑ 132 Henry Mateo PS RC 8.00 2.40
❑ 133 Mike Penney PS RC 8.00 2.40
❑ 134 Bud Smith PS RC 8.00 2.40
❑ 135 Junior Spivey PS RC 10.00 3.00
❑ 136 Ichiro Suzuki JSY RC 100.00 30.00
❑ 137 Albert Pujols JSY RC 120.00 36.00
❑ 138 Mark Teixeira JSY RC 120.00 36.00
❑ 139 D. Brazelton JSY RC .00 .00
❑ 140 Mark Prior JSY RC 120.00 36.00
❑ 141 T. Shinjo JSY RC 25.00 7.50

2001 Upper Deck Prospect Premieres

	Nm-Mt	Ex-Mt
COMP.SET w/o SP's (90)	25.00	7.50
COMMON CARD (1-90)	.40	.12
COMMON AUTO (91-102)	15.00	4.50

❑ 1 Jeff Mathis XRC 1.50 .45
❑ 2 Jake Woods XRC .40 .12
❑ 3 Dallas McPherson XRC 2.00 .60
❑ 4 Steven Shell XRC .40 .12
❑ 5 Ryan Budde XRC .40 .12
❑ 6 Kirk Saarloos XRC .75 .23
❑ 7 Ryan Stegall XRC .40 .12
❑ 8 Bobby Crosby XRC 2.00 .60
❑ 9 J.T. Stotts XRC .40 .12
❑ 10 Neal Cotts XRC 1.50 .45
❑ 11 J.Bonderman XRC 1.50 .45
❑ 12 Brandon League XRC .50 .15
❑ 13 Tyrell Godwin XRC .50 .15
❑ 14 Gabe Gross XRC .50 .15
❑ 15 Chris Neylan XRC .40 .12
❑ 16 Macay McBride XRC .40 .12
❑ 17 Josh Burrus XRC .40 .12
❑ 18 Adam Stern XRC .40 .12
❑ 19 Richard Lewis XRC .40 .12
❑ 20 Cole Barthel XRC .50 .15
❑ 21 Mike Jones XRC .40 .12
❑ 22 J.J. Hardy XRC 1.50 .45
❑ 23 Jon Steitz XRC .40 .12
❑ 24 Brad Nelson XRC 1.25 .35
❑ 25 Justin Pope XRC .40 .12
❑ 26 Dan Haren XRC UER 1.25 .35
Blurb incorrectly lists him as a lefty
❑ 27 Andy Sisco XRC 1.25 .35
❑ 28 Ryan Theriot XRC .40 .12
❑ 29 Ricky Nolasco XRC .40 .12
❑ 30 Jon Switzer XRC .50 .15
❑ 31 Justin Wechsler XRC .40 .12
❑ 32 Mike Gosling XRC .40 .12
❑ 33 Scott Hairston XRC 1.50 .45
❑ 34 Brian Pilkington XRC .75 .23
❑ 35 Kole Strayhorn XRC .40 .12
❑ 36 David Taylor XRC .40 .12
❑ 37 Donald Levinski XRC .40 .12
❑ 38 Mike Hinckley XRC .75 .23
❑ 39 Nick Long XRC .40 .12
❑ 40 Brad Hennessey XRC .40 .12
❑ 41 Noah Lowry XRC .40 .12
❑ 42 Josh Cram XRC .40 .12
❑ 43 Jesse Foppert XRC 2.00 .60
❑ 44 Julian Benavidez XRC .40 .12
❑ 45 Dan Denham XRC .40 .12
❑ 46 Travis Foley XRC .50 .15
❑ 47 Mike Conroy XRC .40 .12
❑ 48 Jake Dittler XRC .40 .12
❑ 49 Rene Rivera XRC .40 .12
❑ 50 John Cole XRC .40 .12
❑ 51 Lazaro Abreu XRC .40 .12
❑ 52 David Wright XRC 1.50 .45
❑ 53 Aaron Heilman XRC .75 .23
❑ 54 Len DiNardo XRC .40 .12
❑ 55 Alhaji Turay XRC .50 .15
❑ 56 Chris Smith XRC .40 .12
❑ 57 Rommie Lewis XRC .40 .12
❑ 58 Bryan Bass XRC .40 .12
❑ 59 David Crouthers XRC .40 .12
❑ 60 Josh Barfield XRC 2.00 .60
❑ 61 Jake Peavy XRC 1.25 .35
❑ 62 Ryan Howard XRC 1.00 .30
❑ 63 Gavin Floyd XRC 2.00 .60
❑ 64 Michael Floyd XRC .40 .12
❑ 65 Stefan Bailie XRC .40 .12
❑ 66 Jon DeVries XRC .40 .12
❑ 67 Steve Kelly XRC .40 .12
❑ 68 Alan Moye XRC .40 .12
❑ 69 Justin Gillman XRC .40 .12
❑ 70 Jayson Nix XRC .75 .23
❑ 71 John Draper XRC .40 .12
❑ 72 Kenny Baugh XRC .40 .12
❑ 73 Michael Woods XRC .40 .12
❑ 74 Preston Larrison XRC .40 .12
❑ 75 Matt Coenen XRC .40 .12
❑ 76 Scott Tyler XRC .50 .15
❑ 77 Jose Morales XRC .40 .12
❑ 78 Corwin Malone XRC .50 .15
❑ 79 Dennis Ulacia XRC .50 .15
❑ 80 Andy Gonzalez XRC .40 .12
❑ 81 Kris Honel XRC 1.00 .30
❑ 82 Wyatt Allen XRC .40 .12
❑ 83 Ryan Wing XRC .40 .12
❑ 84 Sean Henn XRC .50 .15
❑ 85 John-Ford Griffin XRC .50 .15
❑ 86 Bronson Sardinha XRC .50 .15
❑ 87 Jon Skaggs XRC .40 .12
❑ 88 Shelley Duncan XRC .40 .12
❑ 89 Jason Arnold XRC 1.00 .30
❑ 90 Aaron Rifkin XRC .50 .15
❑ 91 Colt Griffin AU XRC 25.00 7.50
❑ 92 J.D. Martin AU XRC 15.00 4.50
❑ 93 Justin Wayne AU XRC 25.00 7.50
❑ 94 J. VanBenschoten AU XRC 40.00 12.00
❑ 95 Chris Burke AU XRC 25.00 7.50
❑ 96 C. Kotchman AU XRC 60.00 18.00
❑ 97 M. Garciaparra AU XRC 25.00 7.50
❑ 98 Jake Gautreau AU XRC 15.00 4.50
❑ 99 J. Williams AU XRC 40.00 12.00
❑ 100 Toe Nash AU XRC 15.00 4.50
❑ 101 Joe Borchard AU XRC 40.00 12.00
❑ 102 Mark Prior AU XRC 150.00 45.00

2002 Upper Deck Prospect Premieres

	Nm-Mt	Ex-Mt
COMP.SET w/o SP's (72)	25.00	7.50
COMMON CARD (1-60)	.40	.12
COMMON CARD (61-85)	8.00	2.40
COMMON CARD (86-97)	10.00	3.00
COMMON RIPKEN (98-99)	2.00	.60
COMMON MCGWIRE (100-105)	2.00	.60
COMMON DIMAGGIO (106-109)	2.00	.60

PENDER COR AVAIL.VIA MAIL EXCHANGE

❑ 1 Josh Rupe XRC .50 .15
❑ 2 Blair Johnson XRC .50 .15
❑ 3 Jason Pridie XRC 1.00 .30
❑ 4 Tim Gilhooly XRC .40 .12
❑ 5 Kennard Jones XRC .40 .12
❑ 6 Darrell Rasner XRC .40 .12
❑ 7 Adam Donachie XRC .50 .15
❑ 8 Josh Murray XRC .50 .15
❑ 9 Brian Dopirak XRC 1.25 .35
❑ 10 Jason Cooper XRC .75 .23
❑ 11 Zach Hammes XRC .50 .15

❑ 12 Jon Lester XRC .40 .12
❑ 13 Kevin Jepsen XRC .75 .23
❑ 14 Curtis Granderson XRC .75 .23
❑ 15 David Bush XRC 1.25 .35
❑ 16 Joel Guzman .40 .12
❑ 17A Matt Pender UER XRC .40 .12
Pictures Curtis Granderson
❑ 17B Matt Pender COR
❑ 18 Derick Grigsby XRC .40 .12
❑ 19 Jeremy Reed XRC 3.00 1.20
❑ 20 Jonathan Broxton XRC .40 .12
❑ 21 Jesse Crain XRC .40 .12
❑ 22 Justin Jones XRC 1.00 .30
❑ 23 Brian Slocum XRC .50 .15
❑ 24 Brian McCann XRC .75 .23
❑ 25 Francisco Liriano XRC .50 .15
❑ 26 Fred Lewis XRC .50 .15
❑ 27 Steve Stanley XRC .40 .12
❑ 28 Chris Snyder XRC .75 .23
❑ 29 Dan Cevette XRC .75 .23
❑ 30 Kiel Fisher XRC .50 .15
❑ 31 Brandon Weeden XRC .40 .12
❑ 32 Pat Osborn XRC .75 .23
❑ 33 Taber Lee XRC .40 .12
❑ 34 Dan Ortmeier XRC .75 .23
❑ 35 Josh Johnson XRC .50 .15
❑ 36 Val Majewski XRC .75 .23
❑ 37 Larry Broadway XRC 1.25 .35
❑ 38 Joey Gomes XRC .50 .15
❑ 39 Eric Thomas XRC .40 .12
❑ 40 James Loney XRC 1.50 .45
❑ 41 Charlie Morton XRC .50 .15
❑ 42 Mark McLemore XRC .40 .12
❑ 43 Matt Craig XRC .50 .15
❑ 44 Ryan Rodriguez XRC .40 .12
❑ 45 Rich Hill XRC .40 .12
❑ 46 Bob Malek XRC .40 .12
❑ 47 Justin Maureau XRC .40 .12
❑ 48 Randy Braun XRC .40 .12
❑ 49 Brian Grant XRC .40 .12
❑ 50 Tyler Davidson XRC .40 .12
❑ 51 Travis Hanson XRC .50 .15
❑ 52 Kyle Boyer XRC .50 .15
❑ 53 James Holcomb XRC .40 .12
❑ 54 Ryan Williams XRC .40 .12
❑ 55 Ben Crockett XRC .40 .12
❑ 56 Adam Greenberg XRC .40 .12
❑ 57 John Baker XRC .40 .12
❑ 58 Matt Carson XRC .40 .12
❑ 59 Jonathan George XRC .40 .12
❑ 60 David Jensen XRC .40 .12
❑ 61 Nick Swisher JSY XRC 15.00 4.50
❑ 62 Brent Clevlen JSY XRC UER 10.00 3.00
Name mispelled as Cleven
❑ 63 Royce Ring JSY XRC 10.00 3.00
❑ 64 Mike Nixon JSY XRC 8.00 2.40
❑ 65 Ricky Barrett JSY XRC 8.00 2.40
❑ 66 Russ Adams JSY XRC 10.00 3.00
❑ 67 Joe Mauer JSY XRC 25.00 7.50
❑ 68 Jeff Francoeur JSY XRC 30.00 9.00
❑ 69 Joseph Blanton JSY XRC 15.00 4.50
❑ 70 Micah Schilling JSY XRC 10.00 3.00
❑ 71 John McCurdy JSY XRC 8.00 2.40
❑ 72 Sergio Santos JSY XRC 15.00 4.50
❑ 73 Josh Womack JSY XRC 10.00 3.00
❑ 74 Jared Doyle JSY XRC 8.00 2.40
❑ 75 Ben Fritz JSY XRC 8.00 2.40
❑ 76 Greg Miller JSY XRC 15.00 4.50
❑ 77 Luke Hagerty JSY XRC 10.00 3.00
❑ 78 Matt Whitney JSY XRC 10.00 3.00
❑ 79 Dan Meyer JSY XRC 10.00 3.00
❑ 80 Bill Murphy JSY XRC 10.00 3.00
❑ 81 Zach Segovia JSY XRC 10.00 3.00
❑ 82 Steve Obenchain JSY XRC 8.00 2.40
❑ 83 Matt Clanton JSY XRC 10.00 3.00
❑ 84 Mark Teahen JSY XRC 8.00 2.40
❑ 85 Kyle Pawelczyk JSY XRC 8.00 2.40
❑ 86 Khalil Greene AU XRC 30.00 9.00
❑ 87 Joe Saunders AU XRC 10.00 3.00
❑ 88 Jeremy Hermida AU XRC 20.00 6.00
❑ 89 Drew Meyer AU XRC 10.00 3.00
❑ 90 Jeff Francis AU XRC 10.00 3.00
❑ 91 Scott Moore AU XRC 15.00 4.50
❑ 92 Prince Fielder AU XRC 125.00 30.00
❑ 93 Zack Greinke AU XRC 40.00 12.00
❑ 94 Chris Gruler AU XRC 10.00 3.00
❑ 95 Scott Kazmir AU XRC 60.00 18.00
❑ 96 B.J. Upton AU XRC 40.00 12.00
❑ 97 Clint Everts AU XRC 15.00 4.50
❑ 98 Cal Ripken TRIB 2.00 .60
❑ 99 Cal Ripken TRIB 2.00 .60
❑ 100 Mark McGwire TRIB 2.00 .60
❑ 101 Mark McGwire TRIB 2.00 .60
❑ 102 Mark McGwire TRIB 2.00 .60
❑ 103 Mark McGwire TRIB 2.00 .60
❑ 104 Mark McGwire TRIB 2.00 .60
❑ 105 Joe DiMaggio TRIB 2.00 .60
❑ 106 Joe DiMaggio TRIB 2.00 .60
❑ 107 Joe DiMaggio TRIB 2.00 .60
❑ 108 Joe DiMaggio TRIB 2.00 .60
❑ 109 Joe DiMaggio TRIB 2.00 .60

2003 Upper Deck Prospect Premieres

	MINT	NRMT
COMPLETE SET (90)	40.00	18.00

❑ 1 Bryan Opdyke XRC .50 .23
❑ 2 Gabriel Sosa XRC .50 .23
❑ 3 Tila Reynolds XRC .50 .23
❑ 4 Aaron Hill XRC 1.00 .45
❑ 5 Aaron Marsden XRC .75 .35
❑ 6 Abe Alvarez XRC .75 .35
❑ 7 Adam Jones XRC .75 .35
❑ 8 Adam Miller XRC 1.00 .45
❑ 9 Andre Ethier XRC .50 .23
❑ 10 Anthony Gwynn XRC 1.50 .70
❑ 11 Brad Snyder XRC 1.00 .45
❑ 12 Brad Sullivan XRC 1.00 .45
❑ 13 Brian Anderson XRC 1.25 .55
❑ 14 Brian Buscher XRC .50 .23
❑ 15 Brian Snyder XRC .75 .35
❑ 16 Carlos Quentin XRC 1.00 .45
❑ 17 Chad Billingsley XRC 1.00 .45
❑ 18 Fraser Dizard XRC .50 .23
❑ 19 Chris Durbin XRC .50 .23
❑ 20 Chris Ray XRC .75 .35
❑ 21 Conor Jackson XRC 1.00 .45
❑ 22 Kory Casto XRC .50 .23
❑ 23 Craig Whitaker XRC .75 .35
❑ 24 Daniel Moore XRC .50 .23
❑ 25 Daric Barton XRC 1.50 .70
❑ 26 Darin Downs XRC 1.00 .45
❑ 27 David Murphy XRC 1.25 .55
❑ 28 Dustin Majewski XRC .75 .35
❑ 29 Edgardo Baez XRC 1.00 .45
❑ 30 Jake Fox XRC .50 .23
❑ 31 Jake Stevens XRC .75 .35
❑ 32 Jamie D'Antona XRC 1.50 .70
❑ 33 James Houser XRC .75 .35
❑ 34 Jarrod Saltalamacchia XRC 1.00 .45
❑ 35 Jason Hirsh XRC .75 .35
❑ 36 Javi Herrera XRC .75 .35
❑ 37 Jeff Allison XRC 2.00 .90
❑ 38 John Hudgins XRC .50 .23
❑ 39 Jo Jo Reyes XRC 1.00 .45
❑ 40 Justin James XRC .50 .23
❑ 41 Kurt Isenberg XRC .50 .23
❑ 42 Kyle Boyer XRC .75 .35
❑ 43 Lastings Milledge XRC 2.00 .90
❑ 44 Luis Atilano XRC .50 .23
❑ 45 Matt Murton XRC .75 .35
❑ 46 Matt Moses XRC 1.00 .45
❑ 47 Matt Harrison XRC .75 .35
❑ 48 Michael Bourn XRC .50 .23
❑ 49 Miguel Vega XRC .50 .23
❑ 50 Mitch Maier XRC .75 .35
❑ 51 Omar Quintanilla XRC .75 .35
❑ 52 Ryan Sweeney XRC 1.25 .55
❑ 53 Scott Baker XRC .50 .23
❑ 54 Sean Rodriguez XRC 1.00 .45
❑ 55 Steve Lerud XRC .50 .23
❑ 56 Thomas Pauly XRC .50 .23
❑ 57 Tom Gorzelanny XRC .50 .23
❑ 58 Tim Moss XRC .50 .23
❑ 59 Robbie Wooley XRC .50 .23
❑ 60 Trey Webb XRC .50 .23
❑ 61 Wes Littleton XRC 1.00 .45
❑ 62 Beau Vaughan XRC .75 .35
❑ 63 Willy Jo Ronda XRC .75 .35
❑ 64 Chris Lubanski XRC 1.50 .70
❑ 65 Ian Stewart XRC 2.50 1.10
❑ 66 John Danks XRC .75 .35
❑ 67 Kyle Sleeth XRC 1.50 .70
❑ 68 Michael Aubrey XRC 1.50 .70
❑ 69 Kevin Kouzmanoff XRC .75 .35
❑ 70 Ryan Harvey XRC 2.50 1.10
❑ 71 Tim Stauffer XRC 1.00 .45
❑ 72 Tony Richie XRC .50 .23
❑ 73 Brandon Wood XRC 1.25 .55
❑ 74 David Aardsma XRC 1.00 .45
❑ 75 David Shinskie XRC .50 .23
❑ 76 Dennis Dove XRC .50 .23
❑ 77 Eric Sultemeier XRC .50 .23
❑ 78 Jay Sborz XRC .75 .35
❑ 79 Jimmy Barthmaier XRC .50 .23
❑ 80 Josh Whitesell XRC .50 .23
❑ 81 Josh Anderson XRC .75 .35
❑ 82 Kenny Lewis XRC .75 .35
❑ 83 Mateo Miramontes XRC .50 .23
❑ 84 Nick Markakis XRC 1.25 .55
❑ 85 Paul Bacot XRC .75 .35
❑ 86 Peter Stonard XRC .50 .23
❑ 87 Reggie Willits XRC .50 .23
❑ 88 Shane Costa XRC .75 .35
❑ 89 Billy Sadler XRC .50 .23
❑ 90 Delmon Young XRC 6.00 2.70

2003 Upper Deck Standing O

	Nm-Mt	Ex-Mt
COMP.SET w/o SP's (84)	15.00	4.50
COMMON CARD (1-84)	.30	.09
COMMON CARD (85-126)	2.00	.60

❑ 1 Darin Erstad .30 .09
❑ 2 Troy Glaus .50 .15
❑ 3 Tim Salmon .50 .15
❑ 4 Luis Gonzalez .30 .09
❑ 5 Randy Johnson .75 .23
❑ 6 Curt Schilling .50 .15
❑ 7 Andruw Jones .50 .15
❑ 8 Greg Maddux 1.50 .45
❑ 9 Chipper Jones .75 .23
❑ 10 Gary Sheffield .30 .09
❑ 11 Rodrigo Lopez .30 .09
❑ 12 Geronimo Gil .30 .09
❑ 13 Nomar Garciaparra 1.50 .45
❑ 14 Pedro Martinez .75 .23
❑ 15 Manny Ramirez .30 .09

❑ 16 Mark Prior	1.50	.45
❑ 17 Kerry Wood	.75	.23
❑ 18 Sammy Sosa	1.25	.35
❑ 19 Magglio Ordonez	.30	.09
❑ 20 Frank Thomas	.75	.23
❑ 21 Adam Dunn	.50	.15
❑ 22 Ken Griffey Jr.	1.25	.35
❑ 23 Sean Casey	.30	.09
❑ 24 Omar Vizquel	.30	.09
❑ 25 C.C. Sabathia	.30	.09
❑ 26 Larry Walker	.50	.15
❑ 27 Todd Helton	.50	.15
❑ 28 Ivan Rodriguez	.75	.23
❑ 29 Josh Beckett	.50	.15
❑ 30 Roy Oswalt	.30	.09
❑ 31 Jeff Kent	.30	.09
❑ 32 Jeff Bagwell	.50	.15
❑ 33 Lance Berkman	.30	.09
❑ 34 Mike Sweeney	.30	.09
❑ 35 Carlos Beltran	.30	.09
❑ 36 Hideo Nomo	.75	.23
❑ 37 Shawn Green	.30	.09
❑ 38 Kazuhisa Ishii	.30	.09
❑ 39 Geoff Jenkins	.30	.09
❑ 40 Richie Sexson	.30	.09
❑ 41 Torii Hunter	.30	.09
❑ 42 Jacque Jones	.30	.09
❑ 43 Jose Vidro	.30	.09
❑ 44 Vladimir Guerrero	.75	.23
❑ 45 Cliff Floyd	.30	.09
❑ 46 Al Leiter	.30	.09
❑ 47 Mike Piazza	1.25	.35
❑ 48 Tom Glavine	.75	.23
❑ 49 Roberto Alomar	.75	.23
❑ 50 Roger Clemens	1.50	.45
❑ 51 Jason Giambi	.75	.23
❑ 52 Bernie Williams	.50	.15
❑ 53 Alfonso Soriano	.75	.23
❑ 54 Derek Jeter	2.00	.60
❑ 55 Miguel Tejada	.30	.09
❑ 56 Eric Chavez	.30	.09
❑ 57 Barry Zito	.75	.23
❑ 58 Pat Burrell	.30	.09
❑ 59 Jim Thome	.75	.23
❑ 60 Brian Giles	.30	.09
❑ 61 Jason Kendall	.30	.09
❑ 62 Ryan Klesko	.30	.09
❑ 63 Phil Nevin	.30	.09
❑ 64 Sean Burroughs	.30	.09
❑ 65 Jason Schmidt	.30	.09
❑ 66 Rich Aurilia	.30	.09
❑ 67 Barry Bonds	2.00	.60
❑ 68 Randy Winn	.30	.09
❑ 69 Freddy Garcia	.30	.09
❑ 70 Ichiro Suzuki	1.50	.45
❑ 71 J.D. Drew	.30	.09
❑ 72 Jim Edmonds	.30	.09
❑ 73 Scott Rolen	.50	.15
❑ 74 Matt Morris	.30	.09
❑ 75 Albert Pujols	1.50	.45
❑ 76 Tino Martinez	.50	.15
❑ 77 Rey Ordonez	.30	.09
❑ 78 Carl Crawford	.30	.09
❑ 79 Rafael Palmeiro	.50	.15
❑ 80 Kevin Mench	.30	.09
❑ 81 Alex Rodriguez	1.50	.45
❑ 82 Juan Gonzalez	.75	.23
❑ 83 Carlos Delgado	.30	.09
❑ 84 Eric Hinske	.30	.09
❑ 85 Rich Fischer WP RC	2.00	.60
❑ 86 Brandon Webb WP RC	6.00	1.80
❑ 87 Rob Hammock WP RC	3.00	.90
❑ 88 Matt Kata WP RC	3.00	.90
❑ 89 Tim Olson WP RC	3.00	.90
❑ 90 Oscar Villarreal WP RC	2.00	.60
❑ 91 Michael Hessman WP RC	2.00	.60
❑ 92 Daniel Cabrera WP RC	2.00	.60
❑ 93 Jon Leicester WP RC	2.00	.60
❑ 94 Todd Wellemeyer WP RC	3.00	.90
❑ 95 Felix Sanchez WP RC	2.00	.60
❑ 96 David Sanders WP RC	2.00	.60
❑ 97 Josh Stewart WP RC	2.00	.60
❑ 98 Arnie Munoz WP RC	2.00	.60
❑ 99 Ryan Cameron WP RC	2.00	.60
❑ 100 Clint Barmes WP RC	3.00	.90
❑ 101 Josh Willingham WP RC	4.00	1.20
❑ 103 Willie Eyre WP RC	2.00	.60
❑ 104 Brent Hoard WP RC	2.00	.60
❑ 105 Terrmel Sledge WP RC	3.00	.90
❑ 106 Phil Seibel WP RC	2.00	.60
❑ 107 Craig Brazell WP RC	3.00	.90
❑ 108 Jeff Duncan WP RC	3.00	.90
❑ 110 Bernie Castro WP RC	2.00	.60
❑ 111 Mike Nicolas WP RC	2.00	.60
❑ 112 Rett Johnson WP RC	3.00	.90
❑ 113 Bobby Madritsch WP RC	2.00	.60
❑ 114 Luis Ayala WP RC	2.00	.60
❑ 115 Hideki Matsui WP RC	12.00	3.60
❑ 116 Jose Contreras WP RC	5.00	1.50
❑ 117 Lew Ford WP RC	3.00	.90
❑ 118 Jeremy Griffiths WP RC	3.00	.90
❑ 119 Guillermo Quiroz WP RC	3.00	.90
❑ 120 Alejandro Machado WP RC	2.00	.60
❑ 121 Francisco Cruceta WP RC	2.00	.60
❑ 122 Prentice Redman WP RC	2.00	.60
❑ 123 Shane Bazzell WP RC	2.00	.60
❑ 124 Jason Anderson WP	2.00	.60
❑ 125 Ian Ferguson WP RC	2.00	.60
❑ 126 Nook Logan WP RC	2.00	.60

2001 Ultimate Collection

	Nm-Mt	Ex-Mt
COMMON CARD (1-90)	4.00	1.20
COMMON CARD (91-100)	10.00	3.00
COMMON (101-110)	10.00	3.00
COMMON CARD (111-120)	25.00	7.50

❑ 1 Troy Glaus	4.00	1.20
❑ 2 Darin Erstad	4.00	1.20
❑ 3 Jason Giambi	6.00	1.80
❑ 4 Barry Zito	6.00	1.80
❑ 5 Tim Hudson	4.00	1.20
❑ 6 Miguel Tejada	4.00	1.20
❑ 7 Carlos Delgado	4.00	1.20
❑ 8 Shannon Stewart	4.00	1.20
❑ 9 Greg Vaughn	4.00	1.20
❑ 10 Toby Hall	4.00	1.20
❑ 11 Roberto Alomar	6.00	1.80
❑ 12 Juan Gonzalez	6.00	1.80
❑ 13 Jim Thome	6.00	1.80
❑ 14 Edgar Martinez	4.00	1.20
❑ 15 Freddy Garcia	4.00	1.20
❑ 16 Bret Boone	4.00	1.20
❑ 17 Kazuhiro Sasaki	4.00	1.20
❑ 18 Cal Ripken	20.00	6.00
❑ 19 Tim Raines Jr.	4.00	1.20
❑ 20 Alex Rodriguez	12.00	3.60
❑ 21 Ivan Rodriguez	6.00	1.80
❑ 22 Rafael Palmeiro	4.00	1.20
❑ 23 Pedro Martinez	6.00	1.80
❑ 24 Nomar Garciaparra	12.00	3.60
❑ 25 Manny Ramirez	4.00	1.20
❑ 26 Hideo Nomo	6.00	1.80
❑ 27 Mike Sweeney	4.00	1.20
❑ 28 Carlos Beltran	4.00	1.20
❑ 29 Tony Clark	4.00	1.20
❑ 30 Dean Palmer	4.00	1.20
❑ 31 Doug Mientkiewicz	4.00	1.20
❑ 32 Cristian Guzman	4.00	1.20
❑ 33 Corey Koskie	4.00	1.20
❑ 34 Frank Thomas	6.00	1.80
❑ 35 Magglio Ordonez	4.00	1.20
❑ 36 Jose Canseco	6.00	1.80
❑ 37 Roger Clemens	12.00	3.60
❑ 38 Derek Jeter	15.00	4.50
❑ 39 Bernie Williams	4.00	1.20
❑ 40 Mike Mussina	6.00	1.80
❑ 41 Tino Martinez	4.00	1.20
❑ 42 Jeff Bagwell	4.00	1.20
❑ 43 Lance Berkman	4.00	1.20
❑ 44 Roy Oswalt	4.00	1.20
❑ 45 Chipper Jones	6.00	1.80
❑ 46 Greg Maddux	12.00	3.60
❑ 47 Andruw Jones	4.00	1.20
❑ 48 Tom Glavine	6.00	1.80
❑ 49 Richie Sexson	4.00	1.20
❑ 50 Jeromy Burnitz	4.00	1.20
❑ 51 Ben Sheets	4.00	1.20
❑ 52 Mark McGwire	15.00	4.50
❑ 53 Matt Morris	4.00	1.20
❑ 54 Jim Edmonds	4.00	1.20
❑ 55 J.D. Drew	4.00	1.20
❑ 56 Sammy Sosa	10.00	3.00
❑ 57 Fred McGriff	4.00	1.20
❑ 58 Kerry Wood	6.00	1.80
❑ 59 Randy Johnson	6.00	1.80
❑ 60 Luis Gonzalez	4.00	1.20
❑ 61 Curt Schilling	4.00	1.20
❑ 62 Shawn Green	4.00	1.20
❑ 63 Kevin Brown	4.00	1.20
❑ 64 Gary Sheffield	4.00	1.20
❑ 65 Vladimir Guerrero	6.00	1.80
❑ 66 Barry Bonds	15.00	4.50
❑ 67 Jeff Kent	4.00	1.20
❑ 68 Rich Aurilia	4.00	1.20
❑ 69 Cliff Floyd	4.00	1.20
❑ 70 Charles Johnson	4.00	1.20
❑ 71 Josh Beckett	4.00	1.20
❑ 72 Mike Piazza	10.00	3.00
❑ 73 Edgardo Alfonzo	4.00	1.20
❑ 74 Robin Ventura	4.00	1.20
❑ 75 Tony Gwynn	8.00	2.40
❑ 76 Ryan Klesko	4.00	1.20
❑ 77 Phil Nevin	4.00	1.20
❑ 78 Scott Rolen	4.00	1.20
❑ 79 Bobby Abreu	4.00	1.20
❑ 80 Jimmy Rollins	4.00	1.20
❑ 81 Brian Giles	4.00	1.20
❑ 82 Jason Kendall	4.00	1.20
❑ 83 Aramis Ramirez	4.00	1.20
❑ 84 Ken Griffey Jr.	10.00	3.00
❑ 85 Adam Dunn	4.00	1.20
❑ 86 Sean Casey	4.00	1.20
❑ 87 Barry Larkin	6.00	1.80
❑ 88 Larry Walker	4.00	1.20
❑ 89 Mike Hampton	4.00	1.20
❑ 90 Todd Helton	4.00	1.20
❑ 91 Ken Harvey T1	10.00	3.00
❑ 92 Bill Ortega T1 RC	10.00	3.00
❑ 93 Juan Diaz T1 RC	10.00	3.00
❑ 94 Greg Miller T1 RC	10.00	3.00
❑ 95 Brandon Berger T1 RC	10.00	3.00
❑ 96 Brandon Lyon T1 RC	10.00	3.00
❑ 97 Jay Gibbons T1 RC	20.00	6.00
❑ 98 Rob Mackowiak T1 RC	10.00	3.00
❑ 99 Erick Almonte T1 RC	10.00	3.00
❑ 100 J.Middlebrook T1 RC	10.00	3.00
❑ 101 Johnny Estrada T2 RC	12.00	3.60
❑ 102 Juan Uribe T2 RC	10.00	3.00
❑ 103 Travis Hafner T2 RC	20.00	6.00
❑ 104 M.Ensberg T2 RC	25.00	7.50
❑ 105 Mike Rivera T2 RC	10.00	3.00
❑ 106 Josh Towers T2 RC	10.00	3.00
❑ 107 A.Hernandez T2 RC	10.00	3.00
❑ 108 Rafael Soriano T2 RC	25.00	7.50
❑ 109 Jackson Melian T2 RC	10.00	3.00
❑ 110 Wilkin Ruan T2 RC	10.00	3.00
❑ 111 Albert Pujols T3 RC	150.00	45.00
❑ 112 T.Shinjo T3 RC	40.00	12.00
❑ 113 B.Duckworth T3 RC	25.00	7.50
❑ 114 Juan Cruz T3 RC	25.00	7.50
❑ 115 D.Brazelton T3 RC	25.00	7.50
❑ 116 Mark Prior T3 AU RC	600.00	180.00
❑ 117 Mark Teixeira T3 AU RC	250.00	75.00
❑ 118 Wilson Betemit T3 RC	25.00	7.50
❑ 119 Bud Smith T3 RC	25.00	7.50
❑ 120 I.Suzuki T3 AU RC	700.00	210.00

2002 Ultimate Collection

	Nm-Mt	Ex-Mt
COMMON CARD (1-60)	4.00	1.20
COMMON CARD (61-110)	10.00	3.00
61-110 PRINT RUN 550 SERIAL #'d SETS		
COMMON CARD (111-113)	25.00	7.50
COMMON CARD (114-120)	15.00	4.50
❑ 1 Troy Glaus	4.00	1.20
❑ 2 Luis Gonzalez	4.00	1.20
❑ 3 Curt Schilling	4.00	1.20
❑ 4 Randy Johnson	6.00	1.80
❑ 5 Andruw Jones	4.00	1.20
❑ 6 Greg Maddux	12.00	3.60
❑ 7 Chipper Jones	6.00	1.80
❑ 8 Gary Sheffield	4.00	1.20
❑ 9 Cal Ripken	20.00	6.00
❑ 10 Manny Ramirez	4.00	1.20
❑ 11 Pedro Martinez	6.00	1.80
❑ 12 Nomar Garciaparra	12.00	3.60
❑ 13 Sammy Sosa	10.00	3.00
❑ 14 Kerry Wood	6.00	1.80
❑ 15 Mark Prior	12.00	3.60
❑ 16 Magglio Ordonez	4.00	1.20
❑ 17 Frank Thomas	6.00	1.80
❑ 18 Adam Dunn	4.00	1.20
❑ 19 Ken Griffey Jr.	10.00	3.00
❑ 20 Jim Thome	6.00	1.80
❑ 21 Larry Walker	4.00	1.20
❑ 22 Todd Helton	4.00	1.20
❑ 23 Nolan Ryan	20.00	6.00
❑ 24 Jeff Bagwell	4.00	1.20
❑ 25 Roy Oswalt	4.00	1.20
❑ 26 Lance Berkman	4.00	1.20
❑ 27 Mike Sweeney	4.00	1.20
❑ 28 Shawn Green	4.00	1.20
❑ 29 Hideo Nomo	6.00	1.80
❑ 30 Torii Hunter	4.00	1.20
❑ 31 Vladimir Guerrero	6.00	1.80
❑ 32 Tom Seaver	6.00	1.80
❑ 33 Mike Piazza	10.00	3.00
❑ 34 Roberto Alomar	6.00	1.80
❑ 35 Derek Jeter	15.00	4.50
❑ 36 Alfonso Soriano	6.00	1.80
❑ 37 Jason Giambi	6.00	1.80
❑ 38 Roger Clemens	12.00	3.60
❑ 39 Mike Mussina	6.00	1.80
❑ 40 Bernie Williams	4.00	1.20
❑ 41 Joe DiMaggio	15.00	4.50
❑ 42 Mickey Mantle	25.00	7.50
❑ 43 Miguel Tejada	4.00	1.20
❑ 44 Eric Chavez	4.00	1.20
❑ 45 Barry Zito	6.00	1.80
❑ 46 Pat Burrell	4.00	1.20
❑ 47 Jason Kendall	4.00	1.20
❑ 48 Brian Giles	4.00	1.20
❑ 49 Barry Bonds	15.00	4.50
❑ 50 Ichiro Suzuki	12.00	3.60
❑ 51 Stan Musial	10.00	3.00
❑ 52 J.D. Drew	4.00	1.20
❑ 53 Scott Rolen	4.00	1.20
❑ 54 Albert Pujols	12.00	3.60
❑ 55 Mark McGwire	15.00	4.50
❑ 56 Alex Rodriguez	12.00	3.60
❑ 57 Ivan Rodriguez	6.00	1.80
❑ 58 Juan Gonzalez	6.00	1.80
❑ 59 Rafael Palmeiro	4.00	1.20
❑ 60 Carlos Delgado	4.00	1.20
❑ 61 Jose Valverde UR RC	15.00	4.50
❑ 62 Doug Devore UR RC	10.00	3.00
❑ 63 John Ennis UR RC	10.00	3.00
❑ 64 Joey Dawley UR RC	10.00	3.00
❑ 65 Trey Hodges UR RC	15.00	4.50
❑ 66 Mike Mahoney UR	10.00	3.00
❑ 67 Aaron Cook UR RC	15.00	4.50
❑ 68 Rene Reyes UR RC	10.00	3.00
❑ 69 Mark Corey UR RC	10.00	3.00
❑ 70 Hansel Izquierdo UR RC	10.00	3.00
❑ 71 Brandon Puffer UR RC	10.00	3.00
❑ 72 Jeriome Robertson UR RC	15.00	4.50
❑ 73 Jose Diaz UR RC	10.00	3.00
❑ 74 David Ross UR RC	10.00	3.00
❑ 75 Jayson Durocher UR RC	10.00	3.00
❑ 76 Eric Good UR RC	10.00	3.00
❑ 77 Satoru Komiyama UR RC	10.00	3.00
❑ 78 Tyler Yates UR RC	10.00	3.00
❑ 79 Eric Junge UR RC	10.00	3.00
❑ 80 Anderson Machado UR RC	15.00	4.50
❑ 81 Adrian Burnside UR RC	10.00	3.00
❑ 82 Ben Howard UR RC	10.00	3.00
❑ 83 Clay Condrey UR RC	10.00	3.00
❑ 84 Nelson Castro UR RC	10.00	3.00
❑ 85 So Taguchi UR RC	15.00	4.50
❑ 86 Mike Crudale UR RC	10.00	3.00
❑ 87 Scotty Layfield UR RC	10.00	3.00
❑ 88 Steve Bechler UR RC	10.00	3.00
❑ 89 Travis Driskill UR RC	10.00	3.00
❑ 90 Howie Clark UR RC	10.00	3.00
❑ 91 Josh Hancock UR RC	10.00	3.00
❑ 92 Jorge De La Rosa UR RC	10.00	3.00
❑ 93 Anastacio Martinez UR RC	10.00	3.00
❑ 94 Brian Tallet UR RC	15.00	4.50
❑ 95 Carl Sadler UR RC	10.00	3.00
❑ 96 Cliff Lee UR RC	15.00	4.50
❑ 97 Josh Bard UR RC	10.00	3.00
❑ 98 Wes Obermueller UR RC	10.00	3.00
❑ 99 Juan Brito UR RC	10.00	3.00
❑ 100 Aaron Guiel UR RC	15.00	4.50
❑ 101 Jeremy Hill UR RC	10.00	3.00
❑ 102 Kevin Frederick UR RC	10.00	3.00
❑ 103 Nate Field UR RC	10.00	3.00
❑ 104 Julio Mateo UR RC	10.00	3.00
❑ 105 Chris Snelling UR RC	15.00	4.50
❑ 106 Felix Escalona UR RC	10.00	3.00
❑ 107 Reynaldo Garcia UR RC	10.00	3.00
❑ 108 Mike Smith UR RC	10.00	3.00
❑ 109 Ken Huckaby UR RC	10.00	3.00
❑ 110 Kevin Cash UR RC	10.00	3.00
❑ 111 Kazuhisa Ishii UR AU RC	50.00	15.00
❑ 112 Freddy Sanchez UR AU RC	30.00	9.00
❑ 113 Jason Simontacchi UR AU RC	25.00	7.50
❑ 114 Jorge Padilla UR AU RC	20.00	6.00
❑ 115 Kirk Saarloos UR AU RC	20.00	6.00
❑ 116 Rodrigo Rosario UR AU RC	15.00	4.50
❑ 117 Oliver Perez UR AU RC	25.00	7.50
❑ 118 Miguel Asencio UR AU RC	15.00	4.50
❑ 119 Franklyn German UR AU RC	15.00	4.50
❑ 120 Jaime Cerda UR AU RC	15.00	4.50
❑ MM M.McGwire AU EXCH/100	600.00	180.00

1999 Upper Deck Ultimate Victory

	Nm-Mt	Ex-Mt
COMPLETE SET (180)	250.00	75.00
COMP.SET w/o SP's (120)	40.00	12.00
COMMON CARD (1-120)	.40	.12
COMMON SP (121-150)	2.00	.60
COMMON (151-180)	2.00	.60
❑ 1 Troy Glaus	.60	.18
❑ 2 Tim Salmon	.60	.18
❑ 3 Mo Vaughn	.40	.12
❑ 4 Garret Anderson	.40	.12
❑ 5 Darin Erstad	.40	.12
❑ 6 Randy Johnson	1.00	.30
❑ 7 Matt Williams	.40	.12
❑ 8 Travis Lee	.40	.12
❑ 9 Jay Bell	.40	.12
❑ 10 Steve Finley	.40	.12
❑ 11 Luis Gonzalez	.40	.12
❑ 12 Greg Maddux	2.00	.60
❑ 13 Chipper Jones	1.00	.30
❑ 14 Javy Lopez	.40	.12
❑ 15 Tom Glavine	1.00	.30
❑ 16 John Smoltz	.60	.18
❑ 17 Cal Ripken	3.00	.90
❑ 18 Charles Johnson	.40	.12
❑ 19 Albert Belle	.40	.12
❑ 20 Mike Mussina	1.00	.30
❑ 21 Pedro Martinez	1.00	.30
❑ 22 Nomar Garciaparra	2.00	.60
❑ 23 Jose Offerman	.40	.12
❑ 24 Sammy Sosa	1.50	.45
❑ 25 Mark Grace	1.00	.30
❑ 26 Kerry Wood	1.00	.30
❑ 27 Frank Thomas	1.00	.30
❑ 28 Ray Durham	.40	.12
❑ 29 Paul Konerko	.40	.12
❑ 30 Pete Harnisch	.40	.12
❑ 31 Greg Vaughn	.40	.12
❑ 32 Sean Casey	.40	.12
❑ 33 Manny Ramirez	.40	.12
❑ 34 Jim Thome	1.00	.30
❑ 35 Sandy Alomar Jr.	.40	.12
❑ 36 Roberto Alomar	1.00	.30
❑ 37 Travis Fryman	.40	.12
❑ 38 Kenny Lofton	.40	.12
❑ 39 Omar Vizquel	.40	.12
❑ 40 Larry Walker	.60	.18
❑ 41 Todd Helton	.60	.18
❑ 42 Vinny Castilla	.40	.12
❑ 43 Tony Clark	.40	.12
❑ 44 Juan Encarnacion	.40	.12
❑ 45 Dean Palmer	.40	.12
❑ 46 Damion Easley	.40	.12
❑ 47 Mark Kotsay	.40	.12
❑ 48 Cliff Floyd	.40	.12
❑ 49 Jeff Bagwell	.60	.18
❑ 50 Ken Caminiti	.40	.12
❑ 51 Craig Biggio	.60	.18
❑ 52 Moises Alou	.40	.12
❑ 53 Johnny Damon	.40	.12
❑ 54 Larry Sutton	.40	.12
❑ 55 Kevin Brown	.60	.18
❑ 56 Adrian Beltre	.40	.12
❑ 57 Raul Mondesi	.40	.12
❑ 58 Gary Sheffield	.40	.12
❑ 59 Jeromy Burnitz	.40	.12
❑ 60 Sean Berry	.40	.12
❑ 61 Jeff Cirillo	.40	.12
❑ 62 Brad Radke	.40	.12
❑ 63 Todd Walker	.40	.12
❑ 64 Matt Lawton	.40	.12
❑ 65 Vladimir Guerrero	1.00	.30
❑ 66 Rondell White	.40	.12
❑ 67 Dustin Hermanson	.40	.12
❑ 68 Mike Piazza	1.50	.45
❑ 69 Rickey Henderson	1.50	.45
❑ 70 Robin Ventura	.40	.12
❑ 71 John Olerud	.40	.12
❑ 72 Derek Jeter	2.50	.75
❑ 73 Roger Clemens	2.00	.60
❑ 74 Orlando Hernandez	.40	.12
❑ 75 Paul O'Neill	.60	.18
❑ 76 Bernie Williams	.60	.18
❑ 77 Chuck Knoblauch	.40	.12
❑ 78 Tino Martinez	.60	.18
❑ 79 Jason Giambi	1.00	.30
❑ 80 Ben Grieve	.40	.12

❑ 81 Matt Stairs .40 .12
❑ 82 Scott Rolen .60 .18
❑ 83 Ron Gant .40 .12
❑ 84 Bobby Abreu .40 .12
❑ 85 Curt Schilling .60 .18
❑ 86 Brian Giles .40 .12
❑ 87 Jason Kendall .40 .12
❑ 88 Kevin Young .40 .12
❑ 89 Mark McGwire 2.50 .75
❑ 90 Fernando Tatis .40 .12
❑ 91 Ray Lankford .40 .12
❑ 92 Eric Davis .40 .12
❑ 93 Tony Gwynn 1.25 .35
❑ 94 Reggie Sanders .40 .12
❑ 95 Wally Joyner .40 .12
❑ 96 Trevor Hoffman .40 .12
❑ 97 Robb Nen .40 .12
❑ 98 Barry Bonds 2.50 .75
❑ 99 Jeff Kent .40 .12
❑ 100 J.T. Snow .40 .12
❑ 101 Ellis Burks .40 .12
❑ 102 Ken Griffey Jr. 1.50 .45
❑ 103 Alex Rodriguez 2.00 .60
❑ 104 Jay Buhner .40 .12
❑ 105 Edgar Martinez .60 .18
❑ 106 David Bell .40 .12
❑ 107 Bobby Smith .40 .12
❑ 108 Wade Boggs .60 .18
❑ 109 Fred McGriff .60 .18
❑ 110 Rolando Arrojo .40 .12
❑ 111 Jose Canseco 1.00 .30
❑ 112 Ivan Rodriguez 1.00 .30
❑ 113 Juan Gonzalez 1.00 .30
❑ 114 Rafael Palmeiro .60 .18
❑ 115 Rusty Greer .40 .12
❑ 116 Todd Zeile .40 .12
❑ 117 Jose Cruz Jr. .40 .12
❑ 118 Carlos Delgado .40 .12
❑ 119 Shawn Green .40 .12
❑ 120 David Wells .40 .12
❑ 121 Eric Munson SP RC 8.00 2.40
❑ 122 Lance Berkman SP 3.00 .90
❑ 123 Ed Yarnall SP 2.00 .60
❑ 124 Jacque Jones SP 3.00 .90
❑ 125 K.Farnsworth SP RC 8.00 2.40
❑ 126 Ryan Rupe SP RC 3.00 .90
❑ 127 Jeff Weaver SP RC 5.00 1.50
❑ 128 Gabe Kapler SP 2.00 .60
❑ 129 Alex Gonzalez SP 2.00 .60
❑ 130 Randy Wolf SP 3.00 .90
❑ 131 Ben Davis SP 2.00 .60
❑ 132 Carlos Beltran SP 3.00 .90
❑ 133 Jim Morris SP RC 10.00 3.00
❑ 134 J.Zimmerman SP RC 3.00 .90
❑ 135 Bruce Aven SP 2.00 .60
❑ 136 A.Soriano SP RC 60.00 18.00
❑ 137 Tim Hudson SP RC 25.00 7.50
❑ 138 Josh Beckett SP RC 60.00 18.00
❑ 139 Michael Barrett SP 2.00 .60
❑ 140 Eric Chavez SP 3.00 .90
❑ 141 Pat Burrell SP RC 20.00 6.00
❑ 142 Kris Benson SP 2.00 .60
❑ 143 J.D. Drew SP 3.00 .90
❑ 144 Matt Clement SP 2.00 .60
❑ 145 Rick Ankiel SP RC 10.00 3.00
❑ 146 Vernon Wells SP 3.00 .90
❑ 147 Ruben Mateo SP UER 2.00 .60
Card is misnumbered
❑ 148 Roy Halladay SP 3.00 .90
❑ 149 Joe McEwing SP RC 3.00 .90
❑ 150 Freddy Garcia SP RC 10.00 3.00
❑ 151 Mark McGwire MM 2.00 .60
❑ 152 Mark McGwire MM 2.00 .60
❑ 153 Mark McGwire MM 2.00 .60
❑ 154 Mark McGwire MM 2.00 .60
❑ 155 Mark McGwire MM 2.00 .60
❑ 156 Mark McGwire MM 2.00 .60
❑ 157 Mark McGwire MM 2.00 .60
❑ 158 Mark McGwire MM 2.00 .60
❑ 159 Mark McGwire MM 2.00 .60
❑ 160 Mark McGwire MM 2.00 .60
❑ 161 Mark McGwire MM 2.00 .60
❑ 162 Mark McGwire MM 2.00 .60
❑ 163 Mark McGwire MM 2.00 .60
❑ 164 Mark McGwire MM 2.00 .60
❑ 165 Mark McGwire MM 2.00 .60
❑ 166 Mark McGwire MM 2.00 .60
❑ 167 Mark McGwire MM 2.00 .60
❑ 168 Mark McGwire MM 2.00 .60
❑ 169 Mark McGwire MM 2.00 .60
❑ 170 Mark McGwire MM 2.00 .60
❑ 171 Mark McGwire MM 2.00 .60
❑ 172 Mark McGwire MM 2.00 .60
❑ 173 Mark McGwire MM 2.00 .60
❑ 174 Mark McGwire MM 2.00 .60
❑ 175 Mark McGwire MM 2.00 .60
❑ 176 Mark McGwire MM 2.00 .60
❑ 177 Mark McGwire MM 2.00 .60
❑ 178 Mark McGwire MM 2.00 .60
❑ 179 Mark McGwire MM 2.00 .60
❑ 180 Mark McGwire MM 2.00 .60

2000 Upper Deck Ultimate Victory

	Nm-Mt	Ex-Mt
COMP.SET w/o SP's (90)	25.00	7.50
COMMON CARD (1-90)	.30	.09

❑ 1 Mo Vaughn .30 .09
❑ 2 Darin Erstad .30 .09
❑ 3 Troy Glaus .50 .15
❑ 4 Adam Kennedy .30 .09
❑ 5 Jason Giambi .75 .23
❑ 6 Ben Grieve .30 .09
❑ 7 Terrence Long .30 .09
❑ 8 Tim Hudson .50 .15
❑ 9 David Wells .30 .09
❑ 10 Carlos Delgado .30 .09
❑ 11 Shannon Stewart .30 .09
❑ 12 Greg Vaughn .30 .09
❑ 13 Gerald Williams .30 .09
❑ 14 Manny Ramirez .30 .09
❑ 15 Roberto Alomar .75 .23
❑ 16 Jim Thome .75 .23
❑ 17 Edgar Martinez .50 .15
❑ 18 Alex Rodriguez 1.50 .45
❑ 19 Matt Riley .30 .09
❑ 20 Cal Ripken 2.50 .75
❑ 21 Mike Mussina .75 .23
❑ 22 Albert Belle .30 .09
❑ 23 Ivan Rodriguez .75 .23
❑ 24 Rafael Palmeiro .50 .15
❑ 25 Nomar Garciaparra 1.50 .45
❑ 26 Pedro Martinez .75 .23
❑ 27 Carl Everett .30 .09
❑ 28 Tomokazu Ohka RC .30 .09
❑ 29 Jermaine Dye .30 .09
❑ 30 Johnny Damon .30 .09
❑ 31 Dean Palmer .30 .09
❑ 32 Juan Gonzalez .75 .23
❑ 33 Eric Milton .30 .09
❑ 34 Matt Lawton .30 .09
❑ 35 Frank Thomas .75 .23
❑ 36 Paul Konerko .30 .09
❑ 37 Magglio Ordonez .30 .09
❑ 38 Jon Garland .30 .09
❑ 39 Derek Jeter 2.00 .60
❑ 40 Roger Clemens 1.50 .45
❑ 41 Bernie Williams .50 .15
❑ 42 Nick Johnson .30 .09
❑ 43 Julio Lugo .30 .09
❑ 44 Jeff Bagwell .50 .15
❑ 45 Richard Hidalgo .30 .09
❑ 46 Chipper Jones .75 .23
❑ 47 Greg Maddux 1.50 .45
❑ 48 Andruw Jones .50 .15
❑ 49 Andres Galarraga .30 .09
❑ 50 Rafael Furcal .30 .09
❑ 51 Jeromy Burnitz .30 .09
❑ 52 Geoff Jenkins .30 .09
❑ 53 Mark McGwire 2.00 .60
❑ 54 Jim Edmonds .30 .09
❑ 55 Rick Ankiel .30 .09
❑ 56 Sammy Sosa 1.25 .35
❑ 57 Julio Zuleta RC .30 .09
❑ 58 Kerry Wood .75 .23
❑ 59 Randy Johnson .75 .23
❑ 60 Matt Williams .30 .09
❑ 61 Steve Finley .30 .09
❑ 62 Gary Sheffield .30 .09
❑ 63 Kevin Brown .30 .09
❑ 64 Shawn Green .30 .09
❑ 65 Milton Bradley .30 .09
❑ 66 Vladimir Guerrero .75 .23
❑ 67 Jose Vidro .30 .09
❑ 68 Barry Bonds 2.00 .60
❑ 69 Jeff Kent .30 .09
❑ 70 Preston Wilson .30 .09
❑ 71 Mike Lowell .30 .09
❑ 72 Mike Piazza 1.25 .35
❑ 73 Robin Ventura .30 .09
❑ 74 Edgardo Alfonzo .30 .09
❑ 75 Jay Payton .30 .09
❑ 76 Tony Gwynn 1.00 .30
❑ 77 Adam Eaton .30 .09
❑ 78 Phil Nevin .30 .09
❑ 79 Scott Rolen .50 .15
❑ 80 Bob Abreu .30 .09
❑ 81 Pat Burrell .50 .15
❑ 82 Brian Giles .30 .09
❑ 83 Jason Kendall .30 .09
❑ 84 Kris Benson .30 .09
❑ 85 Gookie Dawkins .30 .09
❑ 86 Ken Griffey Jr. 1.25 .35
❑ 87 Barry Larkin .75 .23
❑ 88 Larry Walker .50 .15
❑ 89 Todd Helton .50 .15
❑ 90 Ben Petrick .30 .09
❑ 91 Alex Cabrera/3500 RC 4.00 1.20
❑ 92 M.Wheatland/1000 RC 10.00 3.00
❑ 93 Joe Torres/1000 RC 10.00 3.00
❑ 94 Xavier Nady/1000 RC 25.00 7.50
❑ 95 Kenny Kelly/3500 RC 4.00 1.20
❑ 96 Matt Ginter/3500 RC 4.00 1.20
❑ 97 Ben Diggins/1000 RC 10.00 3.00
❑ 98 Danys Baez/3500 RC 6.00 1.80
❑ 99 Daylan Holt/2500 RC 5.00 1.50
❑ 100 K.Sasaki/3500 RC 8.00 2.40
❑ 101 D.Artman/2500 RC 5.00 1.50
❑ 102 Mike Tonis/1000 RC 15.00 4.50
❑ 103 Timo Perez/2500 RC 5.00 1.50
❑ 104 Barry Zito/2500 RC 30.00 9.00
❑ 105 Koyie Hill/2500 RC 8.00 2.40
❑ 106 B.Wilkerson/2500 RC 8.00 2.40
❑ 107 Juan Pierre/3500 RC 10.00 3.00
❑ 108 A.McNeal/3500 RC 4.00 1.20
❑ 109 J.Spurgeon/3500 RC 4.00 1.20
❑ 110 Sean Burnett/1000 RC 25.00 7.50
❑ 111 Luis Matos/3500 RC 10.00 3.00
❑ 112 Dave Krynzel/1000 RC 10.00 3.00
❑ 113 Scott Heard/1000 RC 10.00 3.00
❑ 114 Ben Sheets/2500 RC 8.00 2.40
❑ 115 D.Sardinha/1000 RC 10.00 3.00
❑ 116 D.Espinosa/1000 RC 10.00 3.00
❑ 117 Leo Estrella/3500 RC 4.00 1.20
❑ 118 K.Ainsworth/2500 RC 8.00 2.40
❑ 119 Jon Rauch/2500 RC 5.00 1.50
❑ 120 R.Franklin/2500 RC 5.00 1.50

2001 Upper Deck Victory

	Nm-Mt	Ex-Mt
COMPLETE SET (660)	50.00	15.00

❑ 1 Troy Glaus .30 .09
❑ 2 Scott Spiezio .20 .06
❑ 3 Gary DiSarcina .20 .06

No.	Player		
❑ 4	Darin Erstad	.20	.06
❑ 5	Tim Salmon	.30	.09
❑ 6	Troy Percival	.20	.06
❑ 7	Ramon Ortiz	.20	.06
❑ 8	Orlando Palmeiro	.20	.06
❑ 9	Tim Belcher	.20	.06
❑ 10	Mo Vaughn	.20	.06
❑ 11	Bengie Molina	.20	.06
❑ 12	Benji Gil	.20	.06
❑ 13	Scott Schoeneweis	.20	.06
❑ 14	Garret Anderson	.20	.06
❑ 15	Matt Wise	.20	.06
❑ 16	Adam Kennedy	.20	.06
❑ 17	Jarrod Washburn	.20	.06
❑ 18	Darin Erstad Troy Percival CL	.20	.06
❑ 19	Jason Giambi	.50	.15
❑ 20	Tim Hudson	.20	.06
❑ 21	Ramon Hernandez	.20	.06
❑ 22	Eric Chavez	.20	.06
❑ 23	Gil Heredia	.20	.06
❑ 24	Jason Isringhausen	.20	.06
❑ 25	Jeremy Giambi	.20	.06
❑ 26	Miguel Tejada	.20	.06
❑ 27	Barry Zito	.50	.15
❑ 28	Terrence Long	.20	.06
❑ 29	Ryan Christenson	.20	.06
❑ 30	Mark Mulder	.20	.06
❑ 31	Olmedo Saenz	.20	.06
❑ 32	Adam Piatt	.20	.06
❑ 33	Ben Grieve	.20	.06
❑ 34	Omar Olivares	.20	.06
❑ 35	John Jaha	.20	.06
❑ 36	Jason Giambi Tim Hudson CL	.20	.06
❑ 37	Carlos Delgado	.20	.06
❑ 38	Esteban Loaiza	.20	.06
❑ 39	Brad Fullmer	.20	.06
❑ 40	David Wells	.20	.06
❑ 41	Chris Woodward	.20	.06
❑ 42	Billy Koch	.20	.06
❑ 43	Shannon Stewart	.20	.06
❑ 44	Chris Carpenter	.20	.06
❑ 45	Steve Parris	.20	.06
❑ 46	Darrin Fletcher	.20	.06
❑ 47	Joey Hamilton	.20	.06
❑ 48	Jose Cruz Jr.	.20	.06
❑ 49	Vernon Wells	.20	.06
❑ 50	Raul Mondesi	.20	.06
❑ 51	Kelvim Escobar	.20	.06
❑ 52	Tony Batista	.20	.06
❑ 53	Alex Gonzalez	.20	.06
❑ 54	Carlos Delgado David Wells CL	.20	.06
❑ 55	Greg Vaughn	.20	.06
❑ 56	Albie Lopez	.20	.06
❑ 57	Randy Winn	.20	.06
❑ 58	Ryan Rupe	.20	.06
❑ 59	Steve Cox	.20	.06
❑ 60	Vinny Castilla	.20	.06
❑ 61	Jose Guillen	.20	.06
❑ 62	Wilson Alvarez	.20	.06
❑ 63	Bryan Rekar	.20	.06
❑ 64	Gerald Williams	.20	.06
❑ 65	Esteban Yan	.20	.06
❑ 66	Felix Martinez	.20	.06
❑ 67	Fred McGriff	.30	.09
❑ 68	John Flaherty	.20	.06
❑ 69	Jason Tyner	.20	.06
❑ 70	Russ Johnson	.20	.06
❑ 71	Roberto Hernandez	.20	.06
❑ 72	Greg Vaughn Albie Lopez CL	.20	.06
❑ 73	Eddie Taubensee	.20	.06
❑ 74	Bob Wickman	.20	.06
❑ 75	Ellis Burks	.20	.06
❑ 76	Kenny Lofton	.20	.06
❑ 77	Einar Diaz	.20	.06
❑ 78	Travis Fryman	.20	.06
❑ 79	Omar Vizquel	.20	.06
❑ 80	Jason Bere	.20	.06
❑ 81	Bartolo Colon	.20	.06
❑ 82	Jim Thome	.50	.15
❑ 83	Roberto Alomar	.50	.15
❑ 84	Chuck Finley	.20	.06
❑ 85	Steve Woodard	.20	.06
❑ 86	Russ Branyan	.20	.06
❑ 87	Dave Burba	.20	.06
❑ 88	Jaret Wright	.20	.06
❑ 89	Jacob Cruz	.20	.06
❑ 90	Steve Karsay	.20	.06
❑ 91	Manny Ramirez Bartolo Colon CL	.20	.06
❑ 92	Raul Ibanez	.20	.06
❑ 93	Freddy Garcia	.20	.06
❑ 94	Edgar Martinez	.30	.09
❑ 95	Jay Buhner	.20	.06
❑ 96	Jamie Moyer	.20	.06
❑ 97	John Olerud	.20	.06
❑ 98	Aaron Sele	.20	.06
❑ 99	Kazuhiro Sasaki	.20	.06
❑ 100	Mike Cameron	.20	.06
❑ 101	John Halama	.20	.06
❑ 102	David Bell	.20	.06
❑ 103	Gil Meche	.20	.06
❑ 104	Carlos Guillen	.20	.06
❑ 105	Mark McLemore	.20	.06
❑ 106	Stan Javier	.20	.06
❑ 107	Al Martin	.20	.06
❑ 108	Dan Wilson	.20	.06
❑ 109	Alex Rodriguez Kazuhiro Sasaki CL	.50	.15
❑ 110	Cal Ripken	1.50	.45
❑ 111	Delino DeShields	.20	.06
❑ 112	Sidney Ponson	.20	.06
❑ 113	Albert Belle	.20	.06
❑ 114	Jose Mercedes	.20	.06
❑ 115	Scott Erickson	.20	.06
❑ 116	Jerry Hairston Jr.	.20	.06
❑ 117	Brook Fordyce	.20	.06
❑ 118	Luis Matos	.20	.06
❑ 119	Eugene Kingsale	.20	.06
❑ 120	Jeff Conine	.20	.06
❑ 121	Chris Richard	.20	.06
❑ 122	Fernando Lunar	.20	.06
❑ 123	John Parrish	.20	.06
❑ 124	Brady Anderson	.20	.06
❑ 125	Ryan Kohlmeier	.20	.06
❑ 126	Melvin Mora	.20	.06
❑ 127	Albert Belle Jose Mercedes CL	.20	.06
❑ 128	Ivan Rodriguez	.50	.15
❑ 129	Justin Thompson	.20	.06
❑ 130	Kenny Rogers	.20	.06
❑ 131	Rafael Palmeiro	.30	.09
❑ 132	Rusty Greer	.20	.06
❑ 133	Gabe Kapler	.20	.06
❑ 134	John Wetteland	.20	.06
❑ 135	Mike Lamb	.20	.06
❑ 136	Doug Davis	.20	.06
❑ 137	Ruben Mateo	.20	.06
❑ 138	A. Rodriguez Rangers	2.00	.60
❑ 139	Chad Curtis	.20	.06
❑ 140	Rick Helling	.20	.06
❑ 141	Ryan Glynn	.20	.06
❑ 142	Andres Galarraga	.20	.06
❑ 143	Ricky Ledee	.20	.06
❑ 144	Frank Catalanotto	.20	.06
❑ 145	Rafael Palmeiro Rick Helling CL	.20	.06
❑ 146	Pedro Martinez	.50	.15
❑ 147	Wilton Veras	.20	.06
❑ 148	M. Ramirez Red Sox	.20	.06
❑ 149	Rolando Arrojo	.20	.06
❑ 150	Nomar Garciaparra	1.00	.30
❑ 151	Darren Lewis	.20	.06
❑ 152	Troy O'Leary	.20	.06
❑ 153	Tomokazu Ohka	.20	.06
❑ 154	Carl Everett	.20	.06
❑ 155	Jason Varitek	.20	.06
❑ 156	Frank Castillo	.20	.06
❑ 157	Pete Schourek	.20	.06
❑ 158	Jose Offerman	.20	.06
❑ 159	Derek Lowe	.20	.06
❑ 160	John Valentin	.20	.06
❑ 161	Dante Bichette	.20	.06
❑ 162	Trot Nixon	.20	.06
❑ 163	Nomar Garciaparra Pedro Martinez CL	.50	.15
❑ 164	Jermaine Dye	.20	.06
❑ 165	Dave McCarty	.20	.06
❑ 166	Jose Rosado	.20	.06
❑ 167	Mike Sweeney	.20	.06
❑ 168	Rey Sanchez	.20	.06
❑ 169	Jeff Suppan	.20	.06
❑ 170	Chad Durbin	.20	.06
❑ 171	Carlos Beltran	.20	.06
❑ 172	Brian Meadows	.20	.06
❑ 173	Todd Dunwoody	.20	.06
❑ 174	Johnny Damon	.20	.06
❑ 175	Blake Stein	.20	.06
❑ 176	Carlos Febles	.20	.06
❑ 177	Joe Randa	.20	.06
❑ 178	Mac Suzuki	.20	.06
❑ 179	Mark Quinn	.20	.06
❑ 180	Gregg Zaun	.20	.06
❑ 181	Mike Sweeney Jeff Suppan	.20	.06
❑ 182	Juan Gonzalez	.50	.15
❑ 183	Dean Palmer	.20	.06
❑ 184	Wendell Magee	.20	.06
❑ 185	Todd Jones	.20	.06
❑ 186	Bobby Higginson	.20	.06
❑ 187	Brian Moehler	.20	.06
❑ 188	Juan Encarnacion	.20	.06
❑ 189	Tony Clark	.20	.06
❑ 190	Rich Becker	.20	.06
❑ 191	Roger Cedeno	.20	.06
❑ 192	Mitch Meluskey	.20	.06
❑ 193	Shane Halter	.20	.06
❑ 194	Jeff Weaver	.20	.06
❑ 195	Deivi Cruz	.20	.06
❑ 196	Damion Easley	.20	.06
❑ 197	Robert Fick	.20	.06
❑ 198	Matt Anderson	.20	.06
❑ 199	Bobby Higginson Brian Moehler	.20	.06
❑ 200	Brad Radke	.20	.06
❑ 201	Mark Redman	.20	.06
❑ 202	Corey Koskie	.20	.06
❑ 203	Matt Lawton	.20	.06
❑ 204	Eric Milton	.20	.06
❑ 205	Chad Moeller	.20	.06
❑ 206	Jacque Jones	.20	.06
❑ 207	Matt Kinney	.20	.06
❑ 208	Jay Canizaro	.20	.06
❑ 209	Torii Hunter	.20	.06
❑ 210	Ron Coomer	.20	.06
❑ 211	Chad Allen	.20	.06
❑ 212	Denny Hocking	.20	.06
❑ 213	Cristian Guzman	.20	.06
❑ 214	LaTroy Hawkins	.20	.06
❑ 215	Joe Mays	.20	.06
❑ 216	David Ortiz	.20	.06
❑ 217	Matt Lawton Eric Milton CL	.20	.06
❑ 218	Frank Thomas	.50	.15
❑ 219	Jose Valentin	.20	.06
❑ 220	Mike Sirotka	.20	.06
❑ 221	Kip Wells	.20	.06
❑ 222	Magglio Ordonez	.20	.06
❑ 223	Herbert Perry	.20	.06
❑ 224	James Baldwin	.20	.06
❑ 225	Jon Garland	.20	.06
❑ 226	Sandy Alomar Jr.	.20	.06
❑ 227	Chris Singleton	.20	.06
❑ 228	Keith Foulke	.20	.06
❑ 229	Paul Konerko	.20	.06
❑ 230	Jim Parque	.20	.06
❑ 231	Greg Norton	.20	.06

❑ 232 Carlos Lee .20 .06
❑ 233 Cal Eldred .20 .06
❑ 234 Ray Durham .20 .06
❑ 235 Jeff Abbott .20 .06
❑ 236 Frank Thomas .30 .09
Mike Sirotka CL
❑ 237 Derek Jeter 1.25 .35
❑ 238 Glenallen Hill .20 .06
❑ 239 Roger Clemens 1.00 .30
❑ 240 Bernie Williams .30 .09
❑ 241 David Justice .20 .06
❑ 242 Luis Sojo .20 .06
❑ 243 Orlando Hernandez .20 .06
❑ 244 Mike Mussina .50 .15
❑ 245 Jorge Posada .30 .09
❑ 246 Andy Pettitte .30 .09
❑ 247 Paul O'Neill .30 .09
❑ 248 Scott Brosius .20 .06
❑ 249 Alfonso Soriano .50 .15
❑ 250 Mariano Rivera .30 .09
❑ 251 Chuck Knoblauch .20 .06
❑ 252 Ramiro Mendoza .20 .06
❑ 253 Tino Martinez .30 .09
❑ 254 David Cone .20 .06
❑ 255 Derek Jeter .60 .18
Andy Pettite CL
❑ 256 Jeff Bagwell .30 .09
❑ 257 Lance Berkman .20 .06
❑ 258 Craig Biggio .30 .09
❑ 259 Scott Elarton .20 .06
❑ 260 Bill Spiers .20 .06
❑ 261 Moises Alou .20 .06
❑ 262 Billy Wagner .20 .06
❑ 263 Shane Reynolds .20 .06
❑ 264 Tony Eusebio .20 .06
❑ 265 Julio Lugo .20 .06
❑ 266 Jose Lima .20 .06
❑ 267 Octavio Dotel .20 .06
❑ 268 Brad Ausmus .20 .06
❑ 269 Daryle Ward .20 .06
❑ 270 Glen Barker .20 .06
❑ 271 Wade Miller .20 .06
❑ 272 Richard Hidalgo .20 .06
❑ 273 Chris Truby .20 .06
❑ 274 Jeff Bagwell .20 .06
Scott Elarton CL
❑ 275 Greg Maddux 1.00 .30
❑ 276 Chipper Jones .50 .15
❑ 277 Tom Glavine .50 .15
❑ 278 Brian Jordan .20 .06
❑ 279 Andruw Jones .30 .09
❑ 280 Kevin Millwood .20 .06
❑ 281 Rico Brogna .20 .06
❑ 282 George Lombard .20 .06
❑ 283 Reggie Sanders .20 .06
❑ 284 John Rocker .20 .06
❑ 285 Rafael Furcal .20 .06
❑ 286 John Smoltz .30 .09
❑ 287 Javy Lopez .20 .06
❑ 288 Walt Weiss .20 .06
❑ 289 Quilvio Veras .20 .06
❑ 290 Eddie Perez .20 .06
❑ 291 B.J. Surhoff .20 .06
❑ 292 Chipper Jones .30 .09
Tom Glavine CL
❑ 293 Jeromy Burnitz .20 .06
❑ 294 Charlie Hayes .20 .06
❑ 295 Jeff D'Amico .20 .06
❑ 296 Jose Hernandez .20 .06
❑ 297 Richie Sexson .20 .06
❑ 298 Tyler Houston .20 .06
❑ 299 Paul Rigdon .20 .06
❑ 300 Jamey Wright .20 .06
❑ 301 Mark Loretta .20 .06
❑ 302 Geoff Jenkins .20 .06
❑ 303 Luis Lopez .20 .06
❑ 304 John Snyder .20 .06
❑ 305 Henry Blanco .20 .06
❑ 306 Curtis Leskanic .20 .06
❑ 307 Ron Belliard .20 .06
❑ 308 Jimmy Haynes .20 .06
❑ 309 Marquis Grissom .20 .06
❑ 310 Geoff Jenkins .20 .06
Jeff D'Amico CL
❑ 311 Mark McGwire 1.25 .35
❑ 312 Rick Ankiel .20 .06
❑ 313 Dave Veres .20 .06
❑ 314 Carlos Hernandez .20 .06
❑ 315 Jim Edmonds .20 .06
❑ 316 Andy Benes .20 .06
❑ 317 Garrett Stephenson .20 .06
❑ 318 Ray Lankford .20 .06
❑ 319 Dustin Hermanson .20 .06
❑ 320 Steve Kline .20 .06
❑ 321 Mike Matheny .20 .06
❑ 322 Edgar Renteria .20 .06
❑ 323 J.D. Drew .20 .06
❑ 324 Craig Paquette .20 .06
❑ 325 Darryl Kile .20 .06
❑ 326 Fernando Vina .20 .06
❑ 327 Eric Davis .20 .06
❑ 328 Placido Polanco .20 .06
❑ 329 Jim Edmonds .20 .06
Darryl Kile CL
❑ 330 Sammy Sosa .75 .23
❑ 331 Rick Aguilera .20 .06
❑ 332 Willie Greene .20 .06
❑ 333 Kerry Wood .50 .15
❑ 334 Todd Hundley .20 .06
❑ 335 Rondell White .20 .06
❑ 336 Julio Zuleta .20 .06
❑ 337 Jon Lieber .20 .06
❑ 338 Joe Girardi .20 .06
❑ 339 Damon Buford .20 .06
❑ 340 Kevin Tapani .20 .06
❑ 341 Ricky Gutierrez .20 .06
❑ 342 Bill Mueller .20 .06
❑ 343 Ruben Quevedo .20 .06
❑ 344 Eric Young .20 .06
❑ 345 Gary Matthews Jr. .20 .06
❑ 346 Daniel Garibay .20 .06
❑ 347 Sammy Sosa .30 .09
Jon Lieber CL
❑ 348 Randy Johnson .50 .15
❑ 349 Matt Williams .20 .06
❑ 350 Kelly Stinnett .20 .06
❑ 351 Brian Anderson .20 .06
❑ 352 Steve Finley .20 .06
❑ 353 Curt Schilling .30 .09
❑ 354 Erubiel Durazo .20 .06
❑ 355 Todd Stottlemyre .20 .06
❑ 356 Mark Grace .50 .15
❑ 357 Luis Gonzalez .20 .06
❑ 358 Danny Bautista .20 .06
❑ 359 Matt Mantei .20 .06
❑ 360 Tony Womack .20 .06
❑ 361 Armando Reynoso .20 .06
❑ 362 Greg Colbrunn .20 .06
❑ 363 Jay Bell .20 .06
❑ 364 Byung-Hyun Kim .20 .06
❑ 365 Luis Gonzalez .30 .09
Randy Johnson CL
❑ 366 Gary Sheffield .20 .06
❑ 367 Eric Karros .20 .06
❑ 368 Jeff Shaw .20 .06
❑ 369 Jim Leyritz .20 .06
❑ 370 Kevin Brown .20 .06
❑ 371 Alex Cora .20 .06
❑ 372 Andy Ashby .20 .06
❑ 373 Eric Gagne .30 .09
❑ 374 Chan Ho Park .20 .06
❑ 375 Shawn Green .20 .06
❑ 376 Kevin Elster .20 .06
❑ 377 Mark Grudzielanek .20 .06
❑ 378 Darren Dreifort .20 .06
❑ 379 Dave Hansen .20 .06
❑ 380 Bruce Aven .20 .06
❑ 381 Adrian Beltre .20 .06
❑ 382 Tom Goodwin .20 .06
❑ 383 Gary Sheffield .20 .06
Chan Ho Park CL
❑ 384 Vladimir Guerrero .50 .15
❑ 385 Ugueth Urbina .20 .06
❑ 386 Michael Barrett .20 .06
❑ 387 Geoff Blum .20 .06
❑ 388 Fernando Tatis .20 .06
❑ 389 Carl Pavano .20 .06
❑ 390 Jose Vidro .20 .06
❑ 391 Orlando Cabrera .20 .06
❑ 392 Terry Jones .20 .06
❑ 393 Mike Thurman .20 .06
❑ 394 Lee Stevens .20 .06
❑ 395 Tony Armas Jr. .20 .06
❑ 396 Wilton Guerrero .20 .06
❑ 397 Peter Bergeron .20 .06
❑ 398 Milton Bradley .20 .06
❑ 399 Javier Vazquez .20 .06
❑ 400 Fernando Seguignol .20 .06
❑ 401 Vladimir Guerrero .30 .09
Dustin Hermanson CL
❑ 402 Barry Bonds 1.25 .35
❑ 403 Russ Ortiz .20 .06
❑ 404 Calvin Murray .20 .06
❑ 405 Armando Rios .20 .06
❑ 406 Livan Hernandez .20 .06
❑ 407 Jeff Kent .20 .06
❑ 408 Bobby Estalella .20 .06
❑ 409 Felipe Crespo .20 .06
❑ 410 Shawn Estes .20 .06
❑ 411 J.T. Snow .20 .06
❑ 412 Marvin Benard .20 .06
❑ 413 Joe Nathan .20 .06
❑ 414 Robb Nen .20 .06
❑ 415 Shawon Dunston .20 .06
❑ 416 Mark Gardner .20 .06
❑ 417 Kirk Rueter .20 .06
❑ 418 Rich Aurilia .20 .06
❑ 419 Doug Mirabelli .20 .06
❑ 420 Russ Davis .20 .06
❑ 421 Barry Bonds .60 .18
Livan Hernandez CL
❑ 422 Cliff Floyd .20 .06
❑ 423 Luis Castillo .20 .06
❑ 424 Antonio Alfonseca .20 .06
❑ 425 Preston Wilson .20 .06
❑ 426 Ryan Dempster .20 .06
❑ 427 Jesus Sanchez .20 .06
❑ 428 Derrek Lee .20 .06
❑ 429 Brad Penny .20 .06
❑ 430 Mark Kotsay .20 .06
❑ 431 Alex Fernandez .20 .06
❑ 432 Mike Lowell .20 .06
❑ 433 Chuck Smith .20 .06
❑ 434 Alex Gonzalez .20 .06
❑ 435 Dave Berg .20 .06
❑ 436 A.J. Burnett .20 .06
❑ 437 Charles Johnson .20 .06
❑ 438 Reid Cornelius .20 .06
❑ 439 Mike Redmond .20 .06
❑ 440 Preston Wilson .20 .06
Ryan Dempster CL
❑ 441 Mike Piazza .75 .23
❑ 442 Kevin Appier .20 .06
❑ 443 Jay Payton .20 .06
❑ 444 Steve Trachsel .20 .06
❑ 445 Al Leiter .20 .06
❑ 446 Joe McEwing .20 .06
❑ 447 Armando Benitez .20 .06
❑ 448 Edgardo Alfonzo .20 .06
❑ 449 Glendon Rusch .20 .06
❑ 450 Mike Bordick .20 .06
❑ 451 Lenny Harris .20 .06
❑ 452 Matt Franco .20 .06
❑ 453 Darryl Hamilton .20 .06
❑ 454 Bobby Jones .20 .06
❑ 455 Robin Ventura .20 .06
❑ 456 Todd Zeile .20 .06
❑ 457 John Franco .20 .06
❑ 458 Mike Piazza .50 .15
Al Leiter CL
❑ 459 Tony Gwynn .60 .18
❑ 460 John Mabry .20 .06
❑ 461 Trevor Hoffman .20 .06
❑ 462 Phil Nevin .20 .06
❑ 463 Ryan Klesko .20 .06
❑ 464 Wiki Gonzalez .20 .06
❑ 465 Matt Clement .20 .06
❑ 466 Alex Arias .20 .06
❑ 467 Woody Williams .20 .06
❑ 468 Ruben Rivera .20 .06
❑ 469 Sterling Hitchcock .20 .06
❑ 470 Ben Davis .20 .06
❑ 471 Bubba Trammell .20 .06
❑ 472 Jay Witasick .20 .06
❑ 473 Eric Owens .20 .06
❑ 474 Damian Jackson .20 .06
❑ 475 Adam Eaton .20 .06
❑ 476 Mike Darr .20 .06

Card	Nm-Mt	Ex-Mt
❑ 477 Phil Nevin Trevor Hoffman CL	.20	.06
❑ 478 Scott Rolen	.30	.09
❑ 479 Robert Person	.20	.06
❑ 480 Mike Lieberthal	.20	.06
❑ 481 Reggie Taylor	.20	.06
❑ 482 Paul Byrd	.20	.06
❑ 483 Bruce Chen	.20	.06
❑ 484 Pat Burrell	.20	.06
❑ 485 Kevin Jordan	.20	.06
❑ 486 Bobby Abreu	.20	.06
❑ 487 Randy Wolf	.20	.06
❑ 488 Kevin Sefcik	.20	.06
❑ 489 Brian Hunter	.20	.06
❑ 490 Doug Glanville	.20	.06
❑ 491 Kent Bottenfield	.20	.06
❑ 492 Travis Lee	.20	.06
❑ 493 Jeff Brantley	.20	.06
❑ 494 Omar Daal	.20	.06
❑ 495 Bobby Abreu Randy Wolf CL	.20	.06
❑ 496 Jason Kendall	.20	.06
❑ 497 Adrian Brown	.20	.06
❑ 498 Warren Morris	.20	.06
❑ 499 Brian Giles	.20	.06
❑ 500 Jimmy Anderson	.20	.06
❑ 501 John VanderWal	.20	.06
❑ 502 Mike Williams	.20	.06
❑ 503 Aramis Ramirez	.20	.06
❑ 504 Pat Meares	.20	.06
❑ 505 Jason Schmidt	.20	.06
❑ 506 Todd Ritchie	.20	.06
❑ 507 Abraham Nunez	.20	.06
❑ 508 Jose Silva	.20	.06
❑ 509 Francisco Cordova	.20	.06
❑ 510 Kevin Young	.20	.06
❑ 511 Derek Bell	.20	.06
❑ 512 Kris Benson	.20	.06
❑ 513 Brian Giles Jose Silva CL	.20	.06
❑ 514 Ken Griffey Jr.	.75	.23
❑ 515 Scott Williamson	.20	.06
❑ 516 Dmitri Young	.20	.06
❑ 517 Sean Casey	.20	.06
❑ 518 Barry Larkin	.50	.15
❑ 519 Juan Castro	.20	.06
❑ 520 Danny Graves	.20	.06
❑ 521 Aaron Boone	.20	.06
❑ 522 Pokey Reese	.20	.06
❑ 523 Elmer Dessens	.20	.06
❑ 524 Michael Tucker	.20	.06
❑ 525 Benito Santiago	.20	.06
❑ 526 Pete Harnisch	.20	.06
❑ 527 Alex Ochoa	.20	.06
❑ 528 Gookie Dawkins	.20	.06
❑ 529 Seth Etherton	.20	.06
❑ 530 Rob Bell	.20	.06
❑ 531 Ken Griffey Jr. Steve Parris CL	.50	.15
❑ 532 Todd Helton	.30	.09
❑ 533 Jose Jimenez	.20	.06
❑ 534 Todd Walker	.20	.06
❑ 535 Ron Gant	.20	.06
❑ 536 Neifi Perez	.20	.06
❑ 537 Butch Huskey	.20	.06
❑ 538 Pedro Astacio	.20	.06
❑ 539 Juan Pierre	.20	.06
❑ 540 Jeff Cirillo	.20	.06
❑ 541 Ben Petrick	.20	.06
❑ 542 Brian Bohanon	.20	.06
❑ 543 Larry Walker	.30	.09
❑ 544 Masato Yoshii	.20	.06
❑ 545 Denny Neagle	.20	.06
❑ 546 Brent Mayne	.20	.06
❑ 547 Mike Hampton	.20	.06
❑ 548 Todd Hollandsworth	.20	.06
❑ 549 Brian Rose	.20	.06
❑ 550 Todd Helton Pedro Astacio CL	.20	.06
❑ 551 Jason Hart	.20	.06
❑ 552 Joe Crede	.20	.06
❑ 553 Timo Perez	.20	.06
❑ 554 Brady Clark	.20	.06
❑ 555 Adam Pettyjohn RC	.20	.06
❑ 556 Jason Grilli	.20	.06
❑ 557 Paxton Crawford	.20	.06
❑ 558 Jay Spurgeon	.20	.06
❑ 559 Hector Ortiz	.20	.06
❑ 560 Vernon Wells	.20	.06
❑ 561 Aubrey Huff	.20	.06
❑ 562 Xavier Nady	.20	.06
❑ 563 Billy McMillon	.20	.06
❑ 564 Ichiro Suzuki RC	8.00	2.40
❑ 565 Tomas De la Rosa	.20	.06
❑ 566 Matt Ginter	.20	.06
❑ 567 Sun Woo Kim	.20	.06
❑ 568 Nick Johnson	.20	.06
❑ 569 Pablo Ozuna	.20	.06
❑ 570 Tike Redman	.20	.06
❑ 571 Brian Cole	.20	.06
❑ 572 Ross Gload	.20	.06
❑ 573 Dee Brown	.20	.06
❑ 574 Tony McKnight	.20	.06
❑ 575 Allen Levrault	.20	.06
❑ 576 Lesli Brea	.20	.06
❑ 577 Adam Bernero	.20	.06
❑ 578 Tom Davey	.20	.06
❑ 579 Morgan Burkhart	.20	.06
❑ 580 Britt Reames	.20	.06
❑ 581 Dave Coggin	.20	.06
❑ 582 Trey Moore	.20	.06
❑ 583 Matt Kinney	.20	.06
❑ 584 Pedro Feliz	.20	.06
❑ 585 Brandon Inge	.20	.06
❑ 586 Alex Hernandez	.20	.06
❑ 587 Toby Hall	.20	.06
❑ 588 Grant Roberts	.20	.06
❑ 589 Brian Sikorski	.20	.06
❑ 590 Aaron Myette	.20	.06
❑ 591 Derek Jeter PM	1.25	.35
❑ 592 Ivan Rodriguez PM	.30	.09
❑ 593 Alex Rodriguez PM	1.00	.30
❑ 594 Carlos Delgado PM	.20	.06
❑ 595 Mark McGwire PM	1.25	.35
❑ 596 Troy Glaus PM	.30	.09
❑ 597 Sammy Sosa PM	.75	.23
❑ 598 Vladimir Guerrero PM	.50	.15
❑ 599 Manny Ramirez PM	.20	.06
❑ 600 Pedro Martinez PM	.30	.09
❑ 601 Chipper Jones PM	.30	.09
❑ 602 Jason Giambi PM	.20	.06
❑ 603 Frank Thomas PM	.30	.09
❑ 604 Ken Griffey Jr. PM	.75	.23
❑ 605 Nomar Garciaparra PM	1.00	.30
❑ 606 Randy Johnson PM	.30	.09
❑ 607 Mike Piazza PM	.75	.23
❑ 608 Barry Bonds PM	1.25	.35
❑ 609 Todd Helton PM	.20	.06
❑ 610 Jeff Bagwell PM	.20	.06
❑ 611 Ken Griffey Jr. VB	.75	.23
❑ 612 Carlos Delgado VB	.20	.06
❑ 613 Jeff Bagwell VB	.20	.06
❑ 614 Jason Giambi VB	.20	.06
❑ 615 Cal Ripken VB	1.50	.45
❑ 616 Brian Giles VB	.20	.06
❑ 617 Bernie Williams VB	.20	.06
❑ 618 Greg Maddux VB	1.00	.30
❑ 619 Troy Glaus VB	.30	.09
❑ 620 Greg Vaughn VB	.20	.06
❑ 621 Sammy Sosa VB	.75	.23
❑ 622 Pat Burrell VB	.20	.06
❑ 623 Ivan Rodriguez VB	.30	.09
❑ 624 Chipper Jones VB	.30	.09
❑ 625 Barry Bonds VB	1.25	.35
❑ 626 Roger Clemens VB	1.00	.30
❑ 627 Jim Edmonds VB	.20	.06
❑ 628 Nomar Garciaparra VB	1.00	.30
❑ 629 Frank Thomas VB	.30	.09
❑ 630 Mike Piazza VB	.75	.23
❑ 631 Randy Johnson VB	.30	.09
❑ 632 Andruw Jones VB	.20	.06
❑ 633 David Wells VB	.20	.06
❑ 634 Manny Ramirez VB	.20	.06
❑ 635 Preston Wilson VB	.20	.06
❑ 636 Todd Helton VB	.20	.06
❑ 637 Kerry Wood VB	.30	.09
❑ 638 Albert Belle VB	.20	.06
❑ 639 Juan Gonzalez VB	.30	.09
❑ 640 Vladimir Guerrero VB	.50	.15
❑ 641 Gary Sheffield VB	.20	.06
❑ 642 Larry Walker VB	.30	.09
❑ 643 Magglio Ordonez VB	.20	.06
❑ 644 Jermaine Dye VB	.20	.06
❑ 645 Scott Rolen VB	.20	.06
❑ 646 Tony Gwynn VB	.60	.18
❑ 647 Shawn Green VB	.20	.06
❑ 648 Roberto Alomar VB	.20	.06
❑ 649 Eric Milton VB	.20	.06
❑ 650 Mark McGwire VB	1.25	.35
❑ 651 Tim Hudson VB	.20	.06
❑ 652 Jose Canseco VB	.20	.06
❑ 653 Tom Glavine VB	.20	.06
❑ 654 Derek Jeter VB	1.25	.35
❑ 655 Alex Rodriguez VB	1.00	.30
❑ 656 Darin Erstad VB	.20	.06
❑ 657 Jason Kendall VB	.20	.06
❑ 658 Pedro Martinez VB	.30	.09
❑ 659 Richie Sexson VB	.20	.06
❑ 660 Rafael Palmeiro VB	.20	.06

2003 Upper Deck Victory

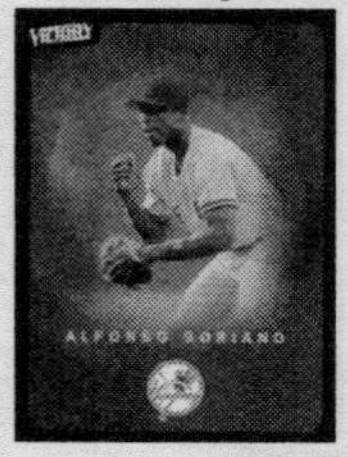

	Nm-Mt	Ex-Mt
COMPLETE SET (200)	80.00	24.00
COMP.SET w/o SP's (100)	25.00	7.50
COMMON CARD (101-200)	.75	.23
101-128 STATED ODDS 1:4		
129-168 STATED ODDS 1:5		
169-188 STATED ODDS 1:10		
189-200 STATED ODDS 1:20		

Card	Nm-Mt	Ex-Mt
❑ 1 Troy Glaus	.50	.15
❑ 2 Garret Anderson	.30	.09
❑ 3 Tim Salmon	.50	.15
❑ 4 Darin Erstad	.30	.09
❑ 5 Luis Gonzalez	.30	.09
❑ 6 Curt Schilling	.50	.15
❑ 7 Randy Johnson	.75	.23
❑ 8 Junior Spivey	.30	.09
❑ 9 Andruw Jones	.50	.15
❑ 10 Greg Maddux	1.50	.45
❑ 11 Chipper Jones	.75	.23
❑ 12 Gary Sheffield	.30	.09
❑ 13 John Smoltz	.50	.15
❑ 14 Geronimo Gil	.30	.09
❑ 15 Tony Batista	.30	.09
❑ 16 Trot Nixon	.30	.09
❑ 17 Manny Ramirez	.30	.09
❑ 18 Pedro Martinez	.75	.23
❑ 19 Nomar Garciaparra	1.50	.45
❑ 20 Derek Lowe	.30	.09
❑ 21 Shea Hillenbrand	.30	.09
❑ 22 Sammy Sosa	1.25	.35
❑ 23 Kerry Wood	.75	.23
❑ 24 Mark Prior	1.50	.45
❑ 25 Magglio Ordonez	.30	.09
❑ 26 Frank Thomas	.75	.23
❑ 27 Mark Buehrle	.30	.09
❑ 28 Paul Konerko	.30	.09
❑ 29 Adam Dunn	.50	.15
❑ 30 Ken Griffey Jr.	1.25	.35
❑ 31 Austin Kearns	.50	.15
❑ 32 Matt Lawton	.30	.09
❑ 33 Larry Walker	.50	.15
❑ 34 Todd Helton	.50	.15
❑ 35 Jeff Bagwell	.50	.15
❑ 36 Roy Oswalt	.30	.09
❑ 37 Lance Berkman	.30	.09
❑ 38 Mike Sweeney	.30	.09

❑ 39	Carlos Beltran	.30	.09
❑ 40	Kazuhisa Ishii	.30	.09
❑ 41	Shawn Green	.30	.09
❑ 42	Hideo Nomo	.75	.23
❑ 43	Adrian Beltre	.30	.09
❑ 44	Richie Sexson	.30	.09
❑ 45	Ben Sheets	.30	.09
❑ 46	Torii Hunter	.30	.09
❑ 47	Jacque Jones	.30	.09
❑ 48	Corey Koskie	.30	.09
❑ 49	Vladimir Guerrero	.75	.23
❑ 50	Jose Vidro	.30	.09
❑ 51	Mo Vaughn	.30	.09
❑ 52	Mike Piazza	1.25	.35
❑ 53	Roberto Alomar	.75	.23
❑ 54	Derek Jeter	2.00	.60
❑ 55	Alfonso Soriano	.75	.23
❑ 56	Jason Giambi	.75	.23
❑ 57	Roger Clemens	1.50	.45
❑ 58	Mike Mussina	.50	.15
❑ 59	Bernie Williams	.50	.15
❑ 60	Jorge Posada	.50	.15
❑ 61	Nick Johnson	.30	.09
❑ 62	Hideki Matsui RC	5.00	1.50
❑ 63	Eric Chavez	.30	.09
❑ 64	Barry Zito	.75	.23
❑ 65	Miguel Tejada	.30	.09
❑ 66	Tim Hudson	.30	.09
❑ 67	Pat Burrell	.30	.09
❑ 68	Bobby Abreu	.30	.09
❑ 69	Jimmy Rollins	.30	.09
❑ 70	Brett Myers	.30	.09
❑ 71	Jim Thome	.75	.23
❑ 72	Jason Kendall	.30	.09
❑ 73	Brian Giles	.30	.09
❑ 74	Aramis Ramirez	.30	.09
❑ 75	Sean Burroughs	.30	.09
❑ 76	Ryan Klesko	.30	.09
❑ 77	Phil Nevin	.30	.09
❑ 78	Barry Bonds	2.00	.60
❑ 79	J.T.Snow	.30	.09
❑ 80	Rich Aurilia	.30	.09
❑ 81	Ichiro Suzuki	1.50	.45
❑ 82	Edgar Martinez	.50	.15
❑ 83	Freddy Garcia	.30	.09
❑ 84	Jim Edmonds	.30	.09
❑ 85	J.D. Drew	.30	.09
❑ 86	Scott Rolen	.50	.15
❑ 87	Albert Pujols	1.50	.45
❑ 88	Mark McGwire	2.00	.60
❑ 89	Matt Morris	.30	.09
❑ 90	Ben Grieve	.30	.09
❑ 91	Carl Crawford	.30	.09
❑ 92	Alex Rodriguez	1.50	.45
❑ 93	Carl Everett	.30	.09
❑ 94	Juan Gonzalez	.75	.23
❑ 95	Rafael Palmeiro	.50	.15
❑ 96	Hank Blalock	.50	.15
❑ 97	Carlos Delgado	.30	.09
❑ 98	Josh Phelps	.30	.09
❑ 99	Eric Hinske	.30	.09
❑ 100	Shannon Stewart	.30	.09
❑ 101	Albert Pujols SH	3.00	.90
❑ 102	Alex Rodriguez SH	3.00	.90
❑ 103	Alfonso Soriano SH	1.50	.45
❑ 104	Barry Bonds SH	4.00	1.20
❑ 105	Bernie Williams SH	1.00	.30
❑ 106	Brian Giles SH	.75	.23
❑ 107	Chipper Jones SH	1.50	.45
❑ 108	Darin Erstad SH	.75	.23
❑ 109	Derek Jeter SH	4.00	1.20
❑ 110	Eric Chavez SH	.75	.23
❑ 111	Miguel Tejada SH	.75	.23
❑ 112	Ichiro Suzuki SH	3.00	.90
❑ 113	Rafael Palmeiro SH	1.00	.30
❑ 114	Jason Giambi SH	.75	.23
❑ 115	Jeff Bagwell SH	1.00	.30
❑ 116	Jim Thome SH	1.50	.45
❑ 117	Ken Griffey Jr. SH	2.50	.75
❑ 118	Lance Berkman SH	.75	.23
❑ 119	Luis Gonzalez SH	.75	.23
❑ 120	Manny Ramirez SH	.75	.23
❑ 121	Mike Piazza SH	2.50	.75
❑ 122	J.D. Drew SH	.75	.23
❑ 123	Sammy Sosa SH	2.50	.75
❑ 124	Scott Rolen SH	1.00	.30
❑ 125	Shawn Green SH	.75	.23
❑ 126	Todd Helton SH	1.00	.30
❑ 127	Troy Glaus SH	1.00	.30
❑ 128	Vladimir Guerrero SH	1.50	.45
❑ 129	Albert Pujols CP	3.00	.90
❑ 130	Brian Giles CP	.75	.23
❑ 131	Carlos Delgado CP	.75	.23
❑ 132	Curt Schilling CP	1.00	.30
❑ 133	Derek Jeter CP	4.00	1.20
❑ 134	Frank Thomas CP	1.50	.45
❑ 135	Greg Maddux CP	3.00	.90
❑ 136	Jeff Bagwell CP	1.00	.30
❑ 137	Jim Thome CP	1.50	.45
❑ 138	Jorge Posada CP	1.00	.30
❑ 139	Kazuhisa Ishii CP	.75	.23
❑ 140	Larry Walker CP	1.00	.30
❑ 141	Luis Gonzalez CP	.75	.23
❑ 142	Miguel Tejada CP	.75	.23
❑ 143	Pat Burrell CP	.75	.23
❑ 144	Pedro Martinez CP	1.50	.45
❑ 145	Rafael Palmeiro CP	1.00	.30
❑ 146	Roger Clemens CP	3.00	.90
❑ 147	Tim Hudson CP	.75	.23
❑ 148	Troy Glaus CP	1.00	.30
❑ 149	Alfonso Soriano LL	1.50	.45
❑ 150	Andruw Jones LL	1.00	.30
❑ 151	Barry Zito LL	1.50	.45
❑ 152	Darin Erstad LL	.75	.23
❑ 153	Eric Chavez LL	.75	.23
❑ 154	Alex Rodriguez LL	3.00	.90
❑ 155	J.D. Drew LL	.75	.23
❑ 156	Jason Giambi LL	.75	.23
❑ 157	Jason Kendall LL	.75	.23
❑ 158	Ken Griffey Jr. LL	2.50	.75
❑ 159	Lance Berkman LL	.75	.23
❑ 160	Mike Mussina LL	1.50	.45
❑ 161	Mike Piazza LL	2.50	.75
❑ 162	Nomar Garciaparra LL	3.00	.90
❑ 163	Randy Johnson LL	1.50	.45
❑ 164	Roberto Alomar LL	1.50	.45
❑ 165	Scott Rolen LL	1.00	.30
❑ 166	Shawn Green LL	.75	.23
❑ 167	Torii Hunter LL	.75	.23
❑ 168	Vladimir Guerrero LL	1.50	.45
❑ 169	Alex Rodriguez TG	3.00	.90
❑ 170	Andruw Jones TG	1.00	.30
❑ 171	Bernie Williams TG	1.00	.30
❑ 172	Ichiro Suzuki TG	3.00	.90
❑ 173	Miguel Tejada TG	.75	.23
❑ 174	Nomar Garciaparra TG	3.00	.90
❑ 175	Pedro Martinez TG	1.50	.45
❑ 176	Randy Johnson TG	1.50	.45
❑ 177	Todd Helton TG	1.00	.30
❑ 178	Vladimir Guerrero TG	1.50	.45
❑ 179	Barry Bonds RP	4.00	1.20
❑ 180	Carlos Delgado RP	.75	.23
❑ 181	Chipper Jones RP	1.50	.45
❑ 182	Frank Thomas RP	1.50	.45
❑ 183	Lance Berkman RP	.75	.23
❑ 184	Larry Walker RP	1.00	.30
❑ 185	Manny Ramirez RP	.75	.23
❑ 186	Mike Piazza RP	2.50	.75
❑ 187	Sammy Sosa RP	2.50	.75
❑ 188	Shawn Green RP	.75	.23
❑ 189	Chipper Jones DM	1.50	.45
❑ 190	Curt Schilling DM	1.00	.30
❑ 191	Derek Jeter DM	4.00	1.20
❑ 192	Ken Griffey Jr. DM	2.50	.75
❑ 193	Sammy Sosa DM	2.50	.75
❑ 194	Vladimir Guerrero DM	1.50	.45
❑ 195	Alex Rodriguez WF	3.00	.90
❑ 196	Barry Bonds WF	4.00	1.20
❑ 197	Greg Maddux WF	3.00	.90
❑ 198	Ichiro Suzuki WF	3.00	.90
❑ 199	Jason Giambi WF	.75	.23
❑ 200	Mike Piazza WF	2.50	.75

2001 Upper Deck Vintage

	Nm-Mt	Ex-Mt
COMPLETE SET (400)	50.00	15.00
COMMON (1-340/371-400)	.30	.09
COMMON (341-370)	.50	.15

❑ 1	Darin Erstad	.30	.09
❑ 2	Seth Etherton	.30	.09
❑ 3	Troy Glaus	.50	.15
❑ 4	Bengie Molina	.30	.09
❑ 5	Mo Vaughn	.30	.09
❑ 6	Tim Salmon	.50	.15
❑ 7	Ramon Ortiz	.30	.09
❑ 8	Adam Kennedy	.30	.09
❑ 9	Garret Anderson	.30	.09
❑ 10	Troy Percival	.30	.09
❑ 11	Tim Salmon Bengie Molina MoVaughn Adam Kennedy Troy Glaus Kevin Stocker Darin Erstad Garret Anderson Ron Gant CL	.30	.09
❑ 12	Jason Giambi	.75	.23
❑ 13	Tim Hudson	.30	.09
❑ 14	Adam Piatt	.30	.09
❑ 15	Miguel Tejada	.30	.09
❑ 16	Mark Mulder	.30	.09
❑ 17	Eric Chavez	.30	.09
❑ 18	Ramon Hernandez	.30	.09
❑ 19	Terrence Long	.30	.09
❑ 20	Jason Isringhausen	.30	.09
❑ 21	Barry Zito	.75	.23
❑ 22	Ben Grieve	.30	.09
❑ 23	Olmedo Saenz Ramon Hernandez Jason Giambi Randy Velarde Eric Chavez Miguel Tejada Ben Grieve Terrence Long Adam Piatt CL	.30	.09
❑ 24	David Wells	.30	.09
❑ 25	Raul Mondesi	.30	.09
❑ 26	Darrin Fletcher	.30	.09
❑ 27	Shannon Stewart	.30	.09
❑ 28	Kelvim Escobar	.30	.09
❑ 29	Tony Batista	.30	.09
❑ 30	Carlos Delgado	.30	.09
❑ 31	Brad Fullmer	.30	.09
❑ 32	Billy Koch	.30	.09
❑ 33	Jose Cruz Jr.	.30	.09
❑ 34	Brad Fullmer Darrin Fletcher Carlos Delgado Homer Bush Tony Batista Alex Gonzalez Shannon Stewart Jose Cruz Jr. Raul Mondesi CL	.30	.09
❑ 35	Greg Vaughn	.30	.09
❑ 36	Roberto Hernandez	.30	.09
❑ 37	Vinny Castilla	.30	.09
❑ 38	Gerald Williams	.30	.09
❑ 39	Aubrey Huff	.30	.09
❑ 40	Bryan Rekar	.30	.09
❑ 41	Albie Lopez	.30	.09
❑ 42	Fred McGriff	.50	.15
❑ 43	Miguel Cairo	.30	.09
❑ 44	Ryan Rupe	.30	.09

❑ 45 Greg Vaughn .30 .09
John Flaherty
Fred McGriff
Miguel Cairo
Vinny Castilla
Felix Martinez
Gerald Williams
Jose Guillen
Steve Cox CL
❑ 46 Jim Thome .75 .23
❑ 47 Roberto Alomar .75 .23
❑ 48 Bartolo Colon .30 .09
❑ 49 Omar Vizquel .30 .09
❑ 50 Travis Fryman .30 .09
❑ 51 Manny Ramirez UER .30 .09
Picture is of David Segui
❑ 52 Dave Burba .30 .09
❑ 53 Chuck Finley .30 .09
❑ 54 Russ Branyan .30 .09
❑ 55 Kenny Lofton .30 .09
❑ 56 Russell Branyan .30 .09
Sandy Alomar Jr.
Jim Thome
Roberto Alomar
Travis Fryman
Omar Vizquel
Wil Cordero
Kenny Lofton
Manny Ramirez
Picture is off David Segui CL UER
❑ 57 Alex Rodriguez 1.50 .45
❑ 58 Jay Buhner .30 .09
❑ 59 Aaron Sele .30 .09
❑ 60 Kazuhiro Sasaki .30 .09
❑ 61 Edgar Martinez .50 .15
❑ 62 John Halama .30 .09
❑ 63 Mike Cameron .30 .09
❑ 64 Freddy Garcia .30 .09
❑ 65 John Olerud .30 .09
❑ 66 Jamie Moyer .30 .09
❑ 67 Gil Meche .30 .09
❑ 68 Edgar Martinez .30 .09
Joe Oliver
John Olerud
David Bell
Carlos Guillen
Alex Rodriguez
Jay Buhner
Mike Cameron
Al Martin CL
❑ 69 Cal Ripken 2.50 .75
❑ 70 Sidney Ponson .30 .09
❑ 71 Chris Richard .30 .09
❑ 72 Jose Mercedes .30 .09
❑ 73 Albert Belle .30 .09
❑ 74 Mike Mussina .75 .23
❑ 75 Brady Anderson .30 .09
❑ 76 Delino DeShields .30 .09
❑ 77 Melvin Mora .30 .09
❑ 78 Luis Matos .30 .09
❑ 79 Brook Fordyce .30 .09
❑ 80 Jeff Conine .30 .09
Brook Fordyce
Chris Richard
Delino DeShields
Cal Ripken
Melvin Mora
Luis Matos
Brady Anderson
Albert Belle CL
❑ 81 Rafael Palmeiro .50 .15
❑ 82 Rick Helling .30 .09
❑ 83 Ruben Mateo .30 .09
❑ 84 Rusty Greer .30 .09
❑ 85 Ivan Rodriguez .75 .23
❑ 86 Doug Davis .30 .09
❑ 87 Gabe Kapler .30 .09
❑ 88 Mike Lamb .30 .09
❑ 89 A.Rodriguez Rangers 4.00 1.20
❑ 90 Kenny Rogers .30 .09
❑ 91 David Segui .50 .15
Ivan Rodriguez
Rafael Palmeiro
Frank Catalanotto
Mike Lamb
Royce Clayton
Ruben Mateo
Gabe Kapler
Rusty Greer CL
❑ 92 Nomar Garciaparra 1.50 .45
❑ 93 Trot Nixon .30 .09
❑ 94 Tomokazu Ohka .30 .09
❑ 95 Pedro Martinez .75 .23
❑ 96 Dante Bichette .30 .09
❑ 97 Jason Varitek .30 .09
❑ 98 Rolando Arrojo .30 .09
❑ 99 Carl Everett .30 .09
❑ 100 Derek Lowe .30 .09
❑ 101 Troy O'Leary .30 .09
❑ 102 Tim Wakefield .30 .09
❑ 103 Troy O'Leary .30 .09
Jason Varitek
Jose Offerman
Mike Lansing
Wilton Veras
Nomar Garciaparra
Carl Everett
Trot Nixon
Dante Bichette CL
❑ 104 Mike Sweeney .30 .09
❑ 105 Carlos Febles .30 .09
❑ 106 Joe Randa .30 .09
❑ 107 Jeff Suppan .30 .09
❑ 108 Mac Suzuki .30 .09
❑ 109 Jermaine Dye .30 .09
❑ 110 Carlos Beltran .30 .09
❑ 111 Mark Quinn .30 .09
❑ 112 Johnny Damon .30 .09
❑ 113 Mark Quinn .30 .09
Gregg Zaun
Mike Sweeney
Carlos Febles
Joe Randa
Rey Sanchez
Carlos Beltran
Johnny Damon
Jermaine Dye CL
❑ 114 Tony Clark .30 .09
❑ 115 Dean Palmer .30 .09
❑ 116 Brian Moehler .30 .09
❑ 117 Brad Ausmus .30 .09
❑ 118 Juan Gonzalez .75 .23
❑ 119 Juan Encarnacion .30 .09
❑ 120 Jeff Weaver .30 .09
❑ 121 Bobby Higginson .30 .09
❑ 122 Todd Jones .30 .09
❑ 123 Deivi Cruz .30 .09
❑ 124 Juan Gonzalez .30 .09
Brad Ausmus
Tony Clark
Damion Easley
Dean Palmer
Deivi Cruz
Bobby Higginson
Juan Encarnacion
Rich Becker CL
❑ 125 Corey Koskie .30 .09
❑ 126 Matt Lawton .30 .09
❑ 127 Mark Redman .30 .09
❑ 128 David Ortiz .30 .09
❑ 129 Jay Canizaro .30 .09
❑ 130 Eric Milton .30 .09
❑ 131 Jacque Jones .30 .09
❑ 132 J.C. Romero .30 .09
❑ 133 Ron Coomer .30 .09
❑ 134 Brad Radke .30 .09
❑ 135 David Ortiz .30 .09
Matt LeCroy
Ron Coomer
Jay Canizaro
Corey Koskie
Cristian Guzman
Jacque Jones
Matt Lawton
Torii Hunter CL
❑ 136 Carlos Lee .30 .09
❑ 137 Frank Thomas .75 .23
❑ 138 Mike Sirotka .30 .09
❑ 139 Charles Johnson .30 .09
❑ 140 James Baldwin .30 .09
❑ 141 Magglio Ordonez .30 .09
❑ 142 Jon Garland .30 .09
❑ 143 Paul Konerko .30 .09
❑ 144 Ray Durham .30 .09
❑ 145 Keith Foulke .30 .09
❑ 146 Chris Singleton .30 .09
❑ 147 Frank Thomas .50 .15
Charles Johnson
Paul Konerko
Ray Durham
Herbert Perry
Jose Valentin
Carlos Lee
Magglio Ordonez
Chris Singleton CL
❑ 148 Bernie Williams .50 .15
❑ 149 Orlando Hernandez .30 .09
❑ 150 David Justice .30 .09
❑ 151 Andy Pettitte .50 .15
❑ 152 Mariano Rivera .50 .15
❑ 153 Derek Jeter 2.00 .60
❑ 154 Jorge Posada .50 .15
❑ 155 Jose Canseco .75 .23
❑ 156 Glenallen Hill .30 .09
❑ 157 Paul O'Neill .50 .15
❑ 158 Denny Neagle .30 .09
❑ 159 Chuck Knoblauch .30 .09
❑ 160 Roger Clemens 1.50 .45
❑ 161 Glenallen Hill .75 .23
Jorge Posada
Tino Martinez
Chuck Knoblauch
Scott Brosius
Derek Jeter
Paul O'Neill
Bernie Williams
David Justice CL
❑ 162 Jeff Bagwell .50 .15
❑ 163 Moises Alou .30 .09
❑ 164 Lance Berkman .30 .09
❑ 165 Shane Reynolds .30 .09
❑ 166 Ken Caminiti .30 .09
❑ 167 Craig Biggio .50 .15
❑ 168 Jose Lima .30 .09
❑ 169 Octavio Dotel .30 .09
❑ 170 Richard Hidalgo .30 .09
❑ 171 Scott Elarton .30 .09
❑ 172 Scott Elarton .50 .15
Mitch Meluskey
Jeff Bagwell
Craig Biggio
Bill Spiers
Julio Lugo
Moises Alou
Richard Hidalgo
Lance Berkman CL
❑ 173 Rafael Furcal .30 .09
❑ 174 Greg Maddux 1.50 .45
❑ 175 Quilvio Veras .30 .09
❑ 176 Chipper Jones .75 .23
❑ 177 Andres Galarraga .30 .09
❑ 178 Brian Jordan .30 .09
❑ 179 Tom Glavine .75 .23
❑ 180 Kevin Millwood .30 .09
❑ 181 Javier Lopez .30 .09
❑ 182 B.J. Surhoff .30 .09
❑ 183 Andruw Jones .50 .15
❑ 184 Andy Ashby .30 .09
❑ 185 Tom Glavine .30 .09
Javy Lopez
Andres Galarraga
Quilvio Veras
Chipper Jones
Rafael Furcal
Reggie Sanders
Brian Jordan
Andruw Jones CL
❑ 186 Richie Sexson .30 .09
❑ 187 Jeff D'Amico .30 .09
❑ 188 Ron Belliard .30 .09
❑ 189 Jeromy Burnitz .30 .09
❑ 190 Jimmy Haynes .30 .09
❑ 191 Marquis Grissom .30 .09
❑ 192 Jose Hernandez .30 .09
❑ 193 Geoff Jenkins .30 .09
❑ 194 Jamey Wright .30 .09
❑ 195 Mark Loretta .30 .09
❑ 196 Jeff D'Amico .30 .09

Henry Blanco
Richie Sexson
Ron Belliard
Tyler Houston
Mark Loretta
Jeromy Burnitz
Marquis Grissom
Geoff Jenkins CL
❑ 197 Rick Ankiel .30 .09
❑ 198 Mark McGwire 2.00 .60
❑ 199 Fernando Vina .30 .09
❑ 200 Edgar Renteria .30 .09
❑ 201 Darryl Kile .30 .09
❑ 202 Jim Edmonds .30 .09
❑ 203 Ray Lankford .30 .09
❑ 204 Garrett Stephenson .30 .09
❑ 205 Fernando Tatis .30 .09
❑ 206 Will Clark .75 .23
❑ 207 J.D. Drew .30 .09
❑ 208 Darryl Kile .30 .09
Mike Matheny
Mark McGwire
Fernando Vina
Fernando Tatis
Edgar Renteria
Ray Lankford
Jim Edmonds
J.D. Drew CL
❑ 209 Mark Grace .75 .23
❑ 210 Eric Young .30 .09
❑ 211 Sammy Sosa 1.25 .35
❑ 212 Jon Lieber .30 .09
❑ 213 Joe Girardi .30 .09
❑ 214 Kevin Tapani .30 .09
❑ 215 Ricky Gutierrez .30 .09
❑ 216 Kerry Wood .75 .23
❑ 217 Rondell White .30 .09
❑ 218 Damon Buford .30 .09
❑ 219 Jon Lieber .30 .09
Joe Girardi
Mark Grace
Eric Young
Willie Greene
Ricky Gutierrez
Sammy Sosa
Damon Bufford
Rondell White CL
❑ 220 Luis Gonzalez .30 .09
❑ 221 Randy Johnson .75 .23
❑ 222 Jay Bell .30 .09
❑ 223 Erubiel Durazo .30 .09
❑ 224 Matt Williams .30 .09
❑ 225 Steve Finley .30 .09
❑ 226 Curt Schilling .50 .15
❑ 227 Todd Stottlemyre .30 .09
❑ 228 Tony Womack .30 .09
❑ 229 Brian Anderson .30 .09
❑ 230 Randy Johnson .30 .09
Kelly Stinnett
Greg Colbrunn
Jay Bell
Matt Williams
Tony Womack
Luis Gonzalez
Steve Finley
Danny Bautista CL
❑ 231 Gary Sheffield .30 .09
❑ 232 Adrian Beltre .30 .09
❑ 233 Todd Hundley .30 .09
❑ 234 Chan Ho Park .30 .09
❑ 235 Shawn Green .30 .09
❑ 236 Kevin Brown .30 .09
❑ 237 Tom Goodwin .30 .09
❑ 238 Mark Grudzielanek .30 .09
❑ 239 Ismael Valdes .30 .09
❑ 240 Eric Karros .30 .09
❑ 241 Kevin Brown .30 .09
Todd Hundley
Eric Karros
Mark Grudzielanek
Adrian Beltre
Alex Cora
Gary Sheffield
Shawn Green
Tom Goodwin CL
❑ 242 Jose Vidro .30 .09
❑ 243 Javier Vazquez .30 .09
❑ 244 Orlando Cabrera .30 .09
❑ 245 Peter Bergeron .30 .09
❑ 246 Vladimir Guerrero .75 .23
❑ 247 Dustin Hermanson .30 .09
❑ 248 Tony Armas Jr. .30 .09
❑ 249 Lee Stevens .30 .09
❑ 250 Milton Bradley .30 .09
❑ 251 Carl Pavano .30 .09
❑ 252 Dustin Hermanson .30 .09
Michael Barrett
Lee Stevens
Jose Vidro
Geoff Jenkins
Orlando Cabrera
Vladimir Guerrero
Peter Bergeron
Milton Bradley CL
❑ 253 Ellis Burks .30 .09
❑ 254 Robb Nen .30 .09
❑ 255 J.T. Snow .30 .09
❑ 256 Barry Bonds 2.00 .60
❑ 257 Shawn Estes .30 .09
❑ 258 Jeff Kent .30 .09
❑ 259 Kirk Rueter .30 .09
❑ 260 Bill Mueller .30 .09
❑ 261 Livan Hernandez .30 .09
❑ 262 Rich Aurilia .30 .09
❑ 263 Livan Hernadez .30 .09
Bobby Estalella
J.T. Snow
Jeff Kent
Bill Mueller
Rich Aurilia
Barry Bonds
Marvin Benard
Ellis Burks CL
❑ 264 Ryan Dempster .30 .09
❑ 265 Cliff Floyd .30 .09
❑ 266 Mike Lowell .30 .09
❑ 267 A.J. Burnett .30 .09
❑ 268 Preston Wilson .30 .09
❑ 269 Luis Castillo .30 .09
❑ 270 Henry Rodriguez .30 .09
❑ 271 Antonio Alfonseca .30 .09
❑ 272 Derrek Lee .30 .09
❑ 273 Mark Kotsay .30 .09
❑ 274 Brad Penny .30 .09
❑ 275 Ryan Dempster .30 .09
Mike Redmond
Derrek Lee
Luis Castillo
Mike Lowell
Alex Gonzalez
Cliff Floyd
Mark Kotsay
Preston Wilson CL
❑ 276 Mike Piazza 1.25 .35
❑ 277 Jay Payton .30 .09
❑ 278 Al Leiter .30 .09
❑ 279 Mike Bordick .30 .09
❑ 280 Armando Benitez .30 .09
❑ 281 Todd Zeile .30 .09
❑ 282 Mike Hampton .30 .09
❑ 283 Edgardo Alfonzo .30 .09
❑ 284 Derek Bell .30 .09
❑ 285 Robin Ventura .30 .09
❑ 286 Mike Hampton .30 .09
Mike Piazza
Todd Zeile
Edgardo Alfonzo
Robin Ventura
Mike Bordick
Derek Bell
Jay Payton
Timo Perez CL
❑ 287 Tony Gwynn 1.00 .30
❑ 288 Trevor Hoffman .30 .09
❑ 289 Ryan Klesko .30 .09
❑ 290 Phil Nevin .30 .09
❑ 291 Matt Clement .30 .09
❑ 292 Ben Davis .30 .09
❑ 293 Ruben Rivera .30 .09
❑ 294 Bret Boone .30 .09
❑ 295 Adam Eaton .30 .09
❑ 296 Eric Owens .30 .09
❑ 297 Matt Clemente .30 .09
Ben Davis
Ryan Klesko
Bret Boone
Phil Nevin
Damian Jackson
Ruben Rivera
Eric Owens
Tony Gwynn CL
❑ 298 Bob Abreu .30 .09
❑ 299 Mike Lieberthal .30 .09
❑ 300 Robert Person .30 .09
❑ 301 Scott Rolen .50 .15
❑ 302 Randy Wolf .30 .09
❑ 303 Bruce Chen .30 .09
❑ 304 Travis Lee .30 .09
❑ 305 Kent Bottenfield .30 .09
❑ 306 Pat Burrell .30 .09
❑ 307 Doug Glanville .30 .09
❑ 308 Robert Person .30 .09
Mike Lieberthal
Pat Burrell
Kevin Jordan
Scott Rolen
Alex Arias
Bob Abreu
Doug Glanville
Travis Lee CL
❑ 309 Brian Giles .30 .09
❑ 310 Todd Ritchie .30 .09
❑ 311 Warren Morris .30 .09
❑ 312 John VanderWal .30 .09
❑ 313 Kris Benson .30 .09
❑ 314 Jason Kendall .30 .09
❑ 315 Kevin Young .30 .09
❑ 316 Francisco Cordova .30 .09
❑ 317 Jimmy Anderson .30 .09
❑ 318 Kris Benson .30 .09
Jason Kendall
Kevin Young
Warren Morris
Mike Benjamin
Pat Meares
John VanderWal
Brian Giles
Adrian Brown CL
❑ 319 Ken Griffey Jr. 1.25 .35
❑ 320 Pokey Reese .30 .09
❑ 321 Chris Stynes .30 .09
❑ 322 Barry Larkin .75 .23
❑ 323 Steve Parris .30 .09
❑ 324 Michael Tucker .30 .09
❑ 325 Dmitri Young .30 .09
❑ 326 Pete Harnisch .30 .09
❑ 327 Danny Graves .30 .09
❑ 328 Aaron Boone .30 .09
❑ 329 Sean Casey .30 .09
❑ 330 Steve Parris .30 .09
Ed Taubensee
Sean Casey
Pokey Reese
Aaron Boone
Barry Larkin
Ken Griffey Jr.
Dmitri Young
Michael Tucker CL
❑ 331 Todd Helton .50 .15
❑ 332 Pedro Astacio .30 .09
❑ 333 Larry Walker .50 .15
❑ 334 Ben Petrick .30 .09
❑ 335 Brian Bohanon .30 .09
❑ 336 Juan Pierre .30 .09
❑ 337 Jeffrey Hammonds .30 .09
❑ 338 Jeff Cirillo .30 .09
❑ 339 Todd Hollandsworth .30 .09
❑ 340 Pedro Astacio .30 .09
Brent Mayne
Todd Helton
Todd Walker
Jeff Cirillo
Neifi Perez
Larry Walker
Jeffrey Hammonds
Juan Pierre CL
❑ 341 Matt Wise .50 .15
Keith Luuloa

Derrick Turnbow
❑ 342 Jason Hart .50 .15
Jose Ortiz
Mario Encarnacion
❑ 343 Vernon Wells .50 .15
Pasqual Coco
Josh Phelps
❑ 344 Travis Harper .50 .15
Kenny Kelley
Toby Hall
❑ 345 Danys Baez .50 .15
Tim Drew
Martin Vargas
❑ 346 Ichiro Suzuki 15.00 4.50
Ryan Franklin
Ryan Christianson
❑ 347 Jay Spurgeon .50 .15
Lesli Brea
Carlos Casimiro
❑ 348 B.J. Waszgis .50 .15
Brian Sikorski
Joaquin Benoit
❑ 349 Sun-Woo Kim .50 .15
Paxton Crawford
Steve Lomasney
❑ 350 Kris Wilson .50 .15
Orber Moreno
Dee Brown
❑ 351 Mark Johnson .50 .15
Brandon Inge
Adam Bernero
❑ 352 Danny Ardoin .50 .15
Matt Kinney
Jason Ryan
❑ 353 Rocky Biddle .50 .15
Joe Crede
Josh Paul
❑ 354 Nick Johnson .50 .15
D'Angelo Jimenez
Wily Mo Pena
❑ 355 Tony McKnight .50 .15
Aaron McNeal
Keith Ginter
❑ 356 Mark DeRosa .30 .09
Jason Marquis
Wes Helms UER
Photos do not match the players ID'd
❑ 357 Allen Levrault .50 .15
Horacio Estrada
Santiago Perez
❑ 358 Luis Saturria .50 .15
Gene Stechschulte
Britt Reames
❑ 359 Joey Nation .50 .15
Corey Patterson
Cole Liniak
❑ 360 Alex Cabrera .50 .15
Geraldo Guzman
Nelson Figuero
❑ 361 Hiram Bocachica .50 .15
Mike Judd
Luke Prokopec
❑ 362 Tomas de la Rosa .50 .15
Yohanny Valera
Talmadge Nunnari
❑ 363 Ryan Vogelsong .50 .15
Juan Melo
Chad Zerbe
❑ 364 Jason Grilli .50 .15
Pablo Ozuna
Ramon Castro
❑ 365 Timo Perez .50 .15
Grant Roberts
Brian Cole
❑ 366 Tom Davey .50 .15
Xavier Nady
Dave Maurer
❑ 367 Jimmy Rollins .50 .15
Mark Brownson
Reggie Taylor
❑ 368 Alex Hernandez .50 .15
Adam Hyzdu
Tike Redman
❑ 369 Brady Clark .50 .15
John Riedling
Mike Bell
❑ 370 Giovanni Carrara .50 .15
Josh Kalinowski
Craig House
❑ 371 Jim Edmonds SH .30 .09
❑ 372 Edgar Martinez SH .30 .09
❑ 373 Rickey Henderson SH .75 .23
❑ 374 Barry Zito SH .75 .23
❑ 375 Tino Martinez SH .50 .15
❑ 376 J.T. Snow SH .30 .09
❑ 377 Bobby Jones SH .30 .09
❑ 378 Alex Rodriguez SH .75 .23
❑ 379 Mike Hampton SH .30 .09
❑ 380 Roger Clemens SH .75 .23
❑ 381 Jay Payton SH .30 .09
❑ 382 John Olerud SH .30 .09
❑ 383 David Justice SH .30 .09
❑ 384 Mike Hampton SH .30 .09
❑ 385 New York Yankees SH .75 .23
❑ 386 Jose Vizcaino SH .30 .09
❑ 387 Roger Clemens SH .75 .23
❑ 388 Todd Zeile SH .30 .09
❑ 389 Derek Jeter SH 1.00 .30
❑ 390 New York Yankees SH .75 .23
❑ 391 Nomar Garciaparra .75 .23
Darin Erstad
Manny Ramirez
Derek Jeter
Carlos Delgado LL
❑ 392 Todd Helton .50 .15
Luis Castillo
Jeffrey Hammonds
Vladimir Guerrero
Moises Alou LL
❑ 393 Troy Glaus .75 .23
Frank Thomas
Alex Rodriguez
Jason Giambi
David Justice LL
❑ 394 Sammy Sosa .50 .15
Jeff Bagwell
Barry Bonds
Vladimir Guerrero
Richard Hidalgo LL
❑ 395 Edgar Martinez .50 .15
Mike Sweeney
Frank Thomas
Carlos Delgado
Jason Giambi LL
❑ 396 Todd Helton .30 .09
Jeff Kent
Brian Giles
Sammy Sosa
Jeff Bagwell LL
❑ 397 Pedro Martinez .50 .15
Roger Clemens
Mike Mussina
Bartolo Colon
Mike Sirotka LL
❑ 398 Kevin Brown .30 .09
Randy Johnson
Jeff D'Amico
Greg Maddux
Mike Hampton LL
❑ 399 Tim Hudson .30 .09
David Wells
Aaron Sele
Andy Pettitte
Pedro Martinez LL
❑ 400 Tom Glavine .75 .23
Darryl Kile
Randy Johnson
Chan Ho Park
Greg Maddux LL
❑ S30 K.Griffey Jr. Sample 1.25 .35

2002 Upper Deck Vintage

	Nm-Mt	Ex-Mt
COMPLETE SET (300)	60.00	18.00

❑ 1 Darin Erstad .40 .12
❑ 2 Mo Vaughn .40 .12
❑ 3 Ramon Ortiz .40 .12
❑ 4 Garret Anderson .40 .12
❑ 5 Troy Glaus .50 .15
❑ 6 Troy Percival .40 .12
❑ 7 Tim Salmon .50 .15
❑ 8 Wilmy Caceres .40 .12
Elpidio Guzman
❑ 9 Ramon Ortiz TC .40 .12
❑ 10 Jason Giambi .75 .23
❑ 11 Mark Mulder .40 .12
❑ 12 Jermaine Dye .40 .12
❑ 13 Miguel Tejada .40 .12
❑ 14 Tim Hudson .40 .12
❑ 15 Eric Chavez .40 .12
❑ 16 Barry Zito .75 .23
❑ 17 Oscar Salazar .40 .12
Juan Pena
❑ 18 Miguel Tejada .40 .12
Jason Giambi TC
❑ 19 Carlos Delgado .40 .12
❑ 20 Raul Mondesi .40 .12
❑ 21 Chris Carpenter .40 .12
❑ 22 Jose Cruz Jr. .40 .12
❑ 23 Alex Gonzalez .40 .12
❑ 24 Brad Fullmer .40 .12
❑ 25 Shannon Stewart .40 .12
❑ 26 Brandon Lyon .40 .12
Vernon Wells
❑ 27 Carlos Delgado TC .40 .12
❑ 28 Greg Vaughn .40 .12
❑ 29 Toby Hall .40 .12
❑ 30 Ben Grieve .40 .12
❑ 31 Aubrey Huff .40 .12
❑ 32 Tanyon Sturtze .40 .12
❑ 33 Brent Abernathy .40 .12
❑ 34 Dewon Brazelton .40 .12
Delvin James
❑ 35 Greg Vaughn .40 .12
Fred McGriff TC
❑ 36 Roberto Alomar .75 .23
❑ 37 Juan Gonzalez .75 .23
❑ 38 Bartolo Colon .40 .12
❑ 39 C.C. Sabathia .40 .12
❑ 40 Jim Thome .75 .23
❑ 41 Omar Vizquel .40 .12
❑ 42 Russell Branyan .40 .12
❑ 43 Ryan Drese .40 .12
Roy Smith
❑ 44 C.C. Sabathia TC .40 .12
❑ 45 Edgar Martinez .50 .15
❑ 46 Bret Boone .40 .12
❑ 47 Freddy Garcia .40 .12
❑ 48 John Olerud .40 .12
❑ 49 Kazuhiro Sasaki .40 .12
❑ 50 Ichiro Suzuki 1.50 .45
❑ 51 Mike Cameron .40 .12
❑ 52 Rafael Soriano .40 .12
Dennis Stark
❑ 53 Jamie Moyer TC .40 .12
❑ 54 Tony Batista .40 .12
❑ 55 Jeff Conine .40 .12
❑ 56 Jason Johnson .40 .12
❑ 57 Jay Gibbons .40 .12
❑ 58 Chris Richard .40 .12
❑ 59 Josh Towers .40 .12
❑ 60 Jerry Hairston Jr. .40 .12
❑ 61 Sean Douglass .40 .12
Tim Raines Jr.
❑ 62 Cal Ripken TC 1.25 .35
❑ 63 Alex Rodriguez 1.50 .45

❑ 64 Ruben Sierra .40 .12
❑ 65 Ivan Rodriguez .75 .23
❑ 66 Gabe Kapler .40 .12
❑ 67 Rafael Palmeiro .50 .15
❑ 68 Frank Catalanotto .40 .12
❑ 69 Mark Teixeira 1.00 .30
Carlos Pena
❑ 70 Alex Rodriguez TC .75 .23
❑ 71 Nomar Garciaparra 1.50 .45
❑ 72 Pedro Martinez .75 .23
❑ 73 Trot Nixon .40 .12
❑ 74 Dante Bichette .40 .12
❑ 75 Manny Ramirez .40 .12
❑ 76 Carl Everett .40 .12
❑ 77 Hideo Nomo .75 .23
❑ 78 Dernell Stenson .40 .12
Juan Diaz
❑ 79 Manny Ramirez TC .40 .12
❑ 80 Mike Sweeney .40 .12
❑ 81 Carlos Febles .40 .12
❑ 82 Dee Brown .40 .12
❑ 83 Neifi Perez .40 .12
❑ 84 Mark Quinn .40 .12
❑ 85 Carlos Beltran .40 .12
❑ 86 Joe Randa .40 .12
❑ 87 Ken Harvey .40 .12
Mike MacDougal
❑ 88 Mike Sweeney TC .40 .12
❑ 89 Dean Palmer .40 .12
❑ 90 Jeff Weaver .40 .12
❑ 91 Jose Lima .40 .12
❑ 92 Tony Clark .40 .12
❑ 93 Damion Easley .40 .12
❑ 94 Bobby Higginson .40 .12
❑ 95 Robert Fick .40 .12
❑ 96 Pedro Santana .40 .12
Mike Rivera
❑ 97 Juan Encarnacion .40 .12
Roger Cedeno TC
❑ 98 Doug Mientkiewicz .40 .12
❑ 99 David Ortiz .40 .12
❑ 100 Joe Mays .40 .12
❑ 101 Corey Koskie .40 .12
❑ 102 Eric Milton .40 .12
❑ 103 Cristian Guzman .40 .12
❑ 104 Brad Radke .40 .12
❑ 105 Adam Johnson .40 .12
Juan Rincon
❑ 106 Corey Koskie TC .40 .12
❑ 107 Frank Thomas .75 .23
❑ 108 Carlos Lee .40 .12
❑ 109 Mark Buehrle .40 .12
❑ 110 Jose Canseco .75 .23
❑ 111 Magglio Ordonez .40 .12
❑ 112 Jon Garland .40 .12
❑ 113 Ray Durham .40 .12
❑ 114 Joe Crede .40 .12
Josh Fogg
❑ 115 Carlos Lee TC .40 .12
❑ 116 Derek Jeter 2.00 .60
❑ 117 Roger Clemens 1.50 .45
❑ 118 Alfonso Soriano .75 .23
❑ 119 Paul O'Neill .50 .15
❑ 120 Jorge Posada .50 .15
❑ 121 Bernie Williams .50 .15
❑ 122 Mariano Rivera .50 .15
❑ 123 Tino Martinez .50 .15
❑ 124 Mike Mussina .75 .23
❑ 125 Nick Johnson .40 .12
Erick Almonte
❑ 126 Jorge Posada .75 .23
David Justice
Scott Brosius TC
❑ 127 Jeff Bagwell .50 .15
❑ 128 Wade Miller .40 .12
❑ 129 Lance Berkman .40 .12
❑ 130 Moises Alou .40 .12
❑ 131 Craig Biggio .50 .15
❑ 132 Roy Oswalt .40 .12
❑ 133 Richard Hidalgo .40 .12
❑ 134 Morgan Ensberg .40 .12
Tim Redding
❑ 135 Lance Berkman .40 .12
Richard Hidalgo TC
❑ 136 Greg Maddux 1.50 .45
❑ 137 Chipper Jones .75 .23
❑ 138 Brian Jordan .40 .12
❑ 139 Marcus Giles .40 .12
❑ 140 Andruw Jones .50 .15
❑ 141 Tom Glavine .75 .23
❑ 142 Rafael Furcal .40 .12
❑ 143 Wilson Betemit .40 .12
Horacio Ramirez
❑ 144 Chipper Jones .50 .15
Brian Jordan TC
❑ 145 Jeromy Burnitz .40 .12
❑ 146 Ben Sheets .40 .12
❑ 147 Geoff Jenkins .40 .12
❑ 148 Devon White .40 .12
❑ 149 Jimmy Haynes .40 .12
❑ 150 Richie Sexson .40 .12
❑ 151 Jose Hernandez .40 .12
❑ 152 Jose Mieses .40 .12
Alex Sanchez
❑ 153 Richie Sexson TC .40 .12
❑ 154 Mark McGwire 2.00 .60
❑ 155 Albert Pujols 1.50 .45
❑ 156 Matt Morris .40 .12
❑ 157 J.D. Drew .40 .12
❑ 158 Jim Edmonds .40 .12
❑ 159 Bud Smith .40 .12
❑ 160 Darryl Kile .40 .12
❑ 161 Bill Ortega .40 .12
Luis Saturria
❑ 162 Albert Pujols 1.50 .45
Mark McGwire TC
❑ 163 Sammy Sosa 1.25 .35
❑ 164 Jon Lieber .40 .12
❑ 165 Eric Young .40 .12
❑ 166 Kerry Wood .75 .23
❑ 167 Fred McGriff .50 .15
❑ 168 Corey Patterson .40 .12
❑ 169 Rondell White .40 .12
❑ 170 Juan Cruz 2.50 .75
Mark Prior
❑ 171 Sammy Sosa TC .75 .23
❑ 172 Luis Gonzalez .40 .12
❑ 173 Randy Johnson .75 .23
❑ 174 Matt Williams .40 .12
❑ 175 Mark Grace .75 .23
❑ 176 Steve Finley .40 .12
❑ 177 Reggie Sanders .40 .12
❑ 178 Curt Schilling .50 .15
❑ 179 Alex Cintron .40 .12
Jack Cust
❑ 180 Arizona Diamondbacks TC .75 .23
❑ 181 Gary Sheffield .40 .12
❑ 182 Paul LoDuca .40 .12
❑ 183 Chan Ho Park .40 .12
❑ 184 Shawn Green .40 .12
❑ 185 Eric Karros .40 .12
❑ 186 Adrian Beltre .40 .12
❑ 187 Kevin Brown .40 .12
❑ 188 Ricardo Rodriguez .40 .12
Carlos Garcia
❑ 189 Shawn Green .40 .12
Gary Sheffield TC
❑ 190 Vladimir Guerrero .75 .23
❑ 191 Javier Vazquez .40 .12
❑ 192 Jose Vidro .40 .12
❑ 193 Fernando Tatis .40 .12
❑ 194 Orlando Cabrera .40 .12
❑ 195 Lee Stevens .40 .12
❑ 196 Tony Armas Jr. .40 .12
❑ 197 Donnie Bridges .40 .12
Henry Mateo
❑ 198 Vladimir Guerrero .50 .15
Jose Vidro TC
❑ 199 Barry Bonds 2.00 .60
❑ 200 Rich Aurilia .40 .12
❑ 201 Russ Ortiz .40 .12
❑ 202 Jeff Kent .40 .12
❑ 203 Jason Schmidt .40 .12
❑ 204 John Vander Wal .40 .12
❑ 205 Robb Nen .40 .12
❑ 206 Yorvit Torrealba .40 .12
Kurt Ainsworth
❑ 207 Barry Bonds TC .75 .23
❑ 208 Preston Wilson .40 .12
❑ 209 Brad Penny .40 .12
❑ 210 Cliff Floyd .40 .12
❑ 211 Luis Castillo .40 .12
❑ 212 Ryan Dempster .40 .12
❑ 213 Charles Johnson .40 .12
❑ 214 A.J. Burnett .40 .12
❑ 215 Abraham Nunez .60 .18
Josh Beckett
❑ 216 Cliff Floyd TC .40 .12
❑ 217 Mike Piazza 1.25 .35
❑ 218 Al Leiter .40 .12
❑ 219 Edgardo Alfonzo .40 .12
❑ 220 Tsuyoshi Shinjo .40 .12
❑ 221 Matt Lawton .40 .12
❑ 222 Robin Ventura .40 .12
❑ 223 Jay Payton .40 .12
❑ 224 Alex Escobar .40 .12
Jae Weong Seo
❑ 225 Mike Piazza .75 .23
Robin Ventura TC
❑ 226 Ryan Klesko .40 .12
❑ 227 D'Angelo Jimenez .40 .12
❑ 228 Trevor Hoffman .40 .12
❑ 229 Phil Nevin .40 .12
❑ 230 Mark Kotsay .40 .12
❑ 231 Brian Lawrence .40 .12
❑ 232 Bubba Trammell .40 .12
❑ 233 Jason Middlebrook .40 .12
Xavier Nady
❑ 234 Tony Gwynn TC .50 .15
❑ 235 Scott Rolen .50 .15
❑ 236 Jimmy Rollins .40 .12
❑ 237 Mike Lieberthal .40 .12
❑ 238 Bobby Abreu .40 .12
❑ 239 Brandon Duckworth .40 .12
❑ 240 Robert Person .40 .12
❑ 241 Pat Burrell .40 .12
❑ 242 Nick Punto .40 .12
Carlos Silva
❑ 243 Mike Lieberthal TC .40 .12
❑ 244 Brian Giles .40 .12
❑ 245 Jack Wilson .40 .12
❑ 246 Kris Benson .40 .12
❑ 247 Jason Kendall .40 .12
❑ 248 Aramis Ramirez .40 .12
❑ 249 Todd Ritchie .40 .12
❑ 250 Rob Mackowiak .40 .12
❑ 251 John Grabow .40 .12
Humberto Cota
❑ 252 Brian Giles TC .40 .12
❑ 253 Ken Griffey Jr. 1.25 .35
❑ 254 Barry Larkin .75 .23
❑ 255 Sean Casey .40 .12
❑ 256 Aaron Boone .40 .12
❑ 257 Dmitri Young .40 .12
❑ 258 Pokey Reese .40 .12
❑ 259 Adam Dunn .50 .15
❑ 260 David Espinosa .40 .12
Dane Sardinha
❑ 261 Ken Griffey TC .75 .23
❑ 262 Todd Helton .50 .15
❑ 263 Mike Hampton .40 .12
❑ 264 Juan Pierre .40 .12
❑ 265 Larry Walker .50 .15
❑ 266 Juan Uribe .40 .12
❑ 267 Jose Ortiz .40 .12
❑ 268 Jeff Cirillo .40 .12
❑ 269 Jason Jennings .40 .12
Luke Hudson
❑ 270 Larry Walker TC .40 .12
❑ 271 Ichiro Suzuki .75 .23
Jason Giambi
Roberto Alomar LL
❑ 272 Larry Walker .40 .12
Todd Helton
Moises Alou LL
❑ 273 Alex Rodriguez .50 .15
Jim Thome
Rafael Palmeiro LL
❑ 274 Barry Bonds 1.00 .30
Sammy Sosa
Luis Gonzalez LL
❑ 274A Barry Bonds 15.00 4.50
Sammy Sosa
Luis Gonzalez LL ERR
Card has AL Home Run Leaders
No player names on cards
❑ 275 Mark Mulder .50 .15
Roger Clemens

Jamie Moyer LL		
❑ 276 Curt Schilling	.50	.15
Matt Morris		
Randy Johnson LL		
❑ 277 Freddy Garcia	.50	.15
Mike Mussina		
Joe Mays LL		
❑ 278 Randy Johnson	.50	.15
Curt Schilling		
John Burkett LL		
❑ 279 Mariano Rivera	.40	.12
Kazuhiro Sasaki		
Keith Foulke LL		
❑ 280 Robb Nen	.50	.15
Armando Benitez		
Trevor Hoffman LL		
❑ 281 Jason Giambi PS	.50	.15
❑ 282 Jorge Posada PS	.40	.12
❑ 283 Jim Thome	.50	.15
Juan Gonzalez PS		
❑ 284 Edgar Martinez PS	.40	.12
❑ 285 Andruw Jones PS	.40	.12
❑ 286 Chipper Jones PS	.50	.15
❑ 287 Matt Williams PS	.40	.12
❑ 288 Curt Schilling PS	.40	.12
❑ 289 Derek Jeter PS	1.00	.30
❑ 290 Mike Mussina PS	.50	.15
❑ 291 Bret Boone PS	.40	.12
❑ 292 Alfonso Soriano PS UER	.50	.15
Alfonso is spelled incorrectly		
❑ 293 Randy Johnson PS	.50	.15
❑ 294 Tom Glavine PS	.40	.12
❑ 295 Curt Schilling PS	.40	.12
❑ 296 Randy Johnson PS	.50	.15
❑ 297 Derek Jeter PS	1.00	.30
❑ 298 Tino Martinez PS	.40	.12
❑ 299 Curt Schilling PS	.40	.12
❑ 300 Luis Gonzalez PS	.40	.12

2003 Upper Deck Vintage

	Nm-Mt	Ex-Mt
COMP.SET w/o SP's (200)	50.00	15.00
COMMON ACTIVE (1-280)	.30	.09
COMMON RETIRED	.60	.18
COMMON SP (1-220)	5.00	1.50
COMMON TR1 SP	5.00	1.50
COMMON TR2 SP	5.00	1.50
COMMON CARD (223-232)	2.00	.60
COMMON CARD (233-247)	2.00	.60
COMMON CARD (248-277)	10.00	3.00
COMMON CARD (281-341)	.60	.18
COMMON RC (281-341)	.60	.18

281-341 ONE PER 2003 UD 40-MAN PACK

❑ 1 Troy Glaus	.50	.15
❑ 2 Darin Erstad	.30	.09
❑ 3 Garret Anderson	.30	.09
❑ 4 Jarrod Washburn	.30	.09
❑ 5 Nolan Ryan	5.00	1.50
❑ 6 Tim Salmon	.50	.15
❑ 7 Troy Percival	.30	.09
❑ 8 Alex Ochoa TR1 SP	5.00	1.50
❑ 9 Daryle Ward	.30	.09
❑ 10 Jeff Bagwell	.50	.15
❑ 11 Roy Oswalt	.30	.09
❑ 12 Lance Berkman	.30	.09
❑ 13 Craig Biggio	.50	.15
❑ 14 Richard Hidalgo	.30	.09
❑ 15 Tim Hudson	.30	.09
❑ 16 Eric Chavez	.30	.09
❑ 17 Barry Zito	.75	.23
❑ 18 Miguel Tejada	.30	.09
❑ 19 Mark Mulder	.30	.09
❑ 20 Rollie Fingers	.60	.18
❑ 21 Catfish Hunter	1.00	.30
❑ 22 Jermaine Dye	.30	.09
❑ 23 Ray Durham TR2 SP	5.00	1.50
❑ 24 Carlos Delgado	.30	.09
❑ 25 Eric Hinske	.30	.09
❑ 26 Josh Phelps	.30	.09
❑ 27 Shannon Stewart	.30	.09
❑ 28 Vernon Wells	.30	.09
❑ 29 John Smoltz	.50	.15
❑ 30 Greg Maddux	1.50	.45
❑ 31 Chipper Jones	.75	.23
❑ 32 Gary Sheffield	.30	.09
❑ 33 Andruw Jones	.50	.15
❑ 34 Tom Glavine	.75	.23
❑ 35 Rafael Furcal	.30	.09
❑ 36 Phil Niekro	.60	.18
❑ 37 Eddie Mathews UER 376	1.50	.45
❑ 38 Robin Yount	1.50	.45
❑ 39 Richie Sexson	.30	.09
❑ 40 Ben Sheets	.30	.09
❑ 41 Geoff Jenkins	.30	.09
❑ 42 Alex Sanchez	.30	.09
❑ 43 Jason Isringhausen	.30	.09
❑ 44 Albert Pujols	1.50	.45
❑ 45 Matt Morris	.30	.09
❑ 46 J.D. Drew	.30	.09
❑ 47 Jim Edmonds	.30	.09
❑ 48 Stan Musial	2.50	.75
❑ 49 Red Schoendienst	.60	.18
❑ 50 Edgar Renteria	.30	.09
❑ 51 Mark McGwire SP	12.00	3.60
❑ 52 Scott Rolen TR2 SP	8.00	2.40
❑ 53 Mark Bellhorn	.30	.09
❑ 54 Kerry Wood	.75	.23
❑ 55 Mark Prior	1.50	.45
❑ 56 Moises Alou	.30	.09
❑ 57 Corey Patterson	.30	.09
❑ 58 Ernie Banks	1.50	.45
❑ 59 Hee Seop Choi	.30	.09
❑ 60 Billy Williams	.60	.18
❑ 61 Sammy Sosa SP	10.00	3.00
❑ 62 Ben Grieve	.30	.09
❑ 63 Jared Sandberg	.30	.09
❑ 64 Carl Crawford	.30	.09
❑ 65 Randy Johnson	.75	.23
❑ 66 Luis Gonzalez	.30	.09
❑ 67 Steve Finley	.30	.09
❑ 68 Junior Spivey	.30	.09
❑ 69 Erubiel Durazo	.30	.09
❑ 70 Curt Schilling SP	8.00	2.40
❑ 71 Al Lopez	.60	.18
❑ 72 Pee Wee Reese	1.00	.30
❑ 73 Eric Gagne	.50	.15
❑ 74 Shawn Green	.30	.09
❑ 75 Kevin Brown	.30	.09
❑ 76 Paul Lo Duca	.30	.09
❑ 77 Adrian Beltre	.30	.09
❑ 78 Hideo Nomo	.75	.23
❑ 79 Eric Karros	.30	.09
❑ 80 Odalis Perez	.30	.09
❑ 81 Kazuhisa Ishii SP	5.00	1.50
❑ 82 Tommy Lasorda	.60	.18
❑ 83 Fernando Tatis	.30	.09
❑ 84 Vladimir Guerrero	.75	.23
❑ 85 Jose Vidro	.30	.09
❑ 86 Javier Vazquez	.30	.09
❑ 87 Brad Wilkerson	.30	.09
❑ 88 Bartolo Colon TR1 SP	5.00	1.50
❑ 89 Monte Irvin	.60	.18
❑ 90 Robb Nen	.30	.09
❑ 91 Reggie Sanders	.30	.09
❑ 92 Jeff Kent	.30	.09
❑ 93 Rich Aurilia	.30	.09
❑ 94 Orlando Cepeda	.60	.18
❑ 95 Juan Marichal	.60	.18
❑ 96 Willie McCovey	.60	.18
❑ 97 David Bell	.30	.09
❑ 98 Barry Bonds SP	12.00	3.60
❑ 99 Kenny Lofton TR2 SP	5.00	1.50
❑ 100 Jim Thome	.75	.23
❑ 101 C.C. Sabathia	.30	.09
❑ 102 Omar Vizquel	.30	.09
❑ 103 Lou Boudreau	.60	.18
❑ 104 Larry Doby	.60	.18
❑ 105 Bob Lemon	.60	.18
❑ 106 John Olerud	.30	.09
❑ 107 Edgar Martinez	.50	.15
❑ 108 Bret Boone	.30	.09
❑ 109 Freddy Garcia	.30	.09
❑ 110 Mike Cameron	.30	.09
❑ 111 Kazuhiro Sasaki	.30	.09
❑ 112 Ichiro Suzuki SP	10.00	3.00
❑ 113 Mike Lowell	.30	.09
❑ 114 Josh Beckett	.50	.15
❑ 115 A.J. Burnett	.30	.09
❑ 116 Juan Pierre	.30	.09
❑ 117 Derrek Lee	.30	.09
❑ 118 Luis Castillo	.30	.09
❑ 119 Juan Encarnacion TR1 SP	5.00	1.50
❑ 120 Roberto Alomar	.75	.23
❑ 121 Edgardo Alfonzo	.30	.09
❑ 122 Jeromy Burnitz	.30	.09
❑ 123 Mo Vaughn	.30	.09
❑ 124 Tom Seaver	1.50	.45
❑ 125 Al Leiter	.30	.09
❑ 126 Mike Piazza SP	8.00	2.40
❑ 127 Tony Batista	.30	.09
❑ 128 Geronimo Gil	.30	.09

❑ 129 Chris Singleton .30 .09
❑ 130 Rodrigo Lopez .30 .09
❑ 131 Jay Gibbons .30 .09
❑ 132 Melvin Mora .30 .09
❑ 133 Earl Weaver .60 .18
❑ 134 Trevor Hoffman .30 .09
❑ 135 Phil Nevin .30 .09
❑ 136 Sean Burroughs .30 .09
❑ 137 Ryan Klesko .30 .09
❑ 138 Mark Kotsay .30 .09
❑ 139 Mike Lieberthal .30 .09
❑ 140 Bobby Abreu .30 .09
❑ 141 Jimmy Rollins .30 .09
❑ 142 Pat Burrell .30 .09
❑ 143 Vicente Padilla .30 .09
❑ 144 Richie Ashburn 1.00 .30
❑ 145 Jeremy Giambi TR1 SP 5.00 1.50
❑ 146 Josh Fogg .30 .09
❑ 147 Brian Giles .30 .09
❑ 148 Aramis Ramirez .30 .09
❑ 149 Jason Kendall .30 .09
❑ 150 Ralph Kiner .60 .18
❑ 151 Willie Stargell 1.00 .30
❑ 152 Kevin Mench .30 .09
❑ 153 Rafael Palmeiro .50 .15
❑ 154 Ivan Rodriguez .75 .23
❑ 155 Hank Blalock .50 .15
❑ 156 Juan Gonzalez .75 .23
❑ 157 Carl Everett .30 .09
❑ 158 Alex Rodriguez SP 10.00 3.00
❑ 159 Nomar Garciaparra 1.50 .45
❑ 160 Derek Lowe .30 .09
❑ 161 Manny Ramirez .30 .09
❑ 162 Shea Hillenbrand .30 .09
❑ 163 Bobby Doerr .60 .18
❑ 164 Johnny Damon .30 .09
❑ 165 Jason Varitek .30 .09
❑ 166 Pedro Martinez SP 8.00 2.40
❑ 167 Cliff Floyd TR2 SP 5.00 1.50
❑ 168 Ken Griffey Jr. 1.25 .35
❑ 169 Adam Dunn .50 .15
❑ 170 Austin Kearns .50 .15
❑ 171 Aaron Boone .30 .09
❑ 172 Joe Morgan .60 .18
❑ 173 Sean Casey .30 .09
❑ 174 Todd Walker .30 .09
❑ 175 Ryan Dempster TR1 SP 5.00 1.50
❑ 176 Shawn Estes TR1 SP 5.00 1.50
❑ 177 Gabe Kapler TR1 SP 5.00 1.50
❑ 178 Jason Jennings UER .30 .09
Card numbered as 28
❑ 179 Todd Helton .50 .15
❑ 180 Larry Walker .50 .15
❑ 181 Preston Wilson .30 .09
❑ 182 Jay Payton TR1 SP 5.00 1.50
❑ 183 Mike Sweeney .30 .09
❑ 184 Carlos Beltran .30 .09
❑ 185 Paul Byrd .30 .09
❑ 186 Raul Ibanez .30 .09
❑ 187 Rick Ferrell .60 .18
❑ 188 Early Wynn .60 .18
❑ 189 Dmitri Young .30 .09
❑ 190 Jim Bunning 1.00 .30
❑ 191 George Kell .60 .18
❑ 192 Hal Newhouser .60 .18
❑ 193 Bobby Higginson .30 .09
❑ 194 Carlos Pena TR1 SP 5.00 1.50
❑ 195 Sparky Anderson .60 .18
❑ 196 Torii Hunter .30 .09
❑ 197 Eric Milton .30 .09
❑ 198 Corey Koskie .30 .09
❑ 199 Jacque Jones .30 .09
❑ 200 Harmon Killebrew 1.50 .45
❑ 201 Doug Mientkiewicz .30 .09
❑ 202 Frank Thomas .75 .23
❑ 203 Mark Buehrle .30 .09
❑ 204 Maggilo Ordonez .30 .09
❑ 205 Paul Konerko .30 .09
❑ 206 Joe Borchard .30 .09
❑ 207 Hoyt Wilhelm .60 .18
❑ 208 Carlos Lee .30 .09
❑ 209 Roger Clemens 1.50 .45
❑ 210 Nick Johnson .30 .09
❑ 211 Jason Giambi .75 .23
❑ 212 Alfonso Soriano .75 .23
❑ 213 Bernie Williams .50 .15
❑ 214 Robin Ventura .30 .09
❑ 215 Jorge Posada .50 .15
❑ 216 Mike Mussina .75 .23
❑ 217 Yogi Berra 1.50 .45
❑ 218 Phil Rizzuto 1.00 .30
❑ 219 Mariano Rivera .50 .15
❑ 220 Derek Jeter SP 12.00 3.60
❑ 221 Jeff Weaver TR1 SP 5.00 1.50
❑ 222 Raul Mondesi TR2 SP 5.00 1.50
❑ 223 Freddy Sanchez 2.00 .60
Josh Hancock
❑ 224 Joe Borchard 2.00 .60
Miguel Olivo
❑ 225 Brandon Phillips 2.00 .60
Josh Bard
❑ 226 Andy Van Hekken 2.00 .60
Andres Torres
❑ 227 Jason Lane 2.00 .60
Jeriome Robertson
❑ 228 Chin-Feng Chen 2.00 .60
Joe Thurston
❑ 229 Endy Chavez 2.00 .60
Jamey Carroll
❑ 230 Drew Henson 2.00 .60
Alex Graman
❑ 231 Dewon Brazelton 2.00 .60
Lance Carter
❑ 232 Jayson Werth 2.00 .60
Kevin Cash
❑ 233 Randy Johnson 3.00 .90
Curt Schilling
Barry Zito
❑ 234 Pedro Martinez 3.00 .90
Randy Johnson
Derek Lowe
❑ 235 Randy Johnson 3.00 .90
Curt Schilling
Pedro Martinez
❑ 236 John Smoltz 3.00 .90
Eric Gagne
Mike Williams
❑ 237 Randy Johnson 3.00 .90
Bartolo Colon
A.J. Burnett
❑ 238 Alfonso Soriano 4.00 1.20
Ichiro Suzuki
Vladimir Guerrero
❑ 239 Alex Rodriguez 4.00 1.20
Jim Thome
Sammy Sosa
❑ 240 Barry Bonds 4.00 1.20
Manny Ramirez
Mike Sweeney
❑ 241 Alfonso Soriano 4.00 1.20
Alex Rodriguez
Derek Jeter
❑ 242 Alex Rodriguez 4.00 1.20
Maggiio Ordonez
Miguel Tejada
❑ 243 Luis Castillo 2.00 .60
Juan Pierre
Dave Roberts
❑ 244 Nomar Garciaparra 4.00 1.20
Garrett Anderson
Alfonso Soriano
❑ 245 Johnny Damon 2.00 .60
Jimmy Rollins
Kenny Lofton
❑ 246 Barry Bonds 4.00 1.20
Jim Thome
Manny Ramirez
❑ 247 Barry Bonds 4.00 1.20
Brian Giles
Manny Ramirez
❑ 248 Troy Glaus 3D 15.00 4.50
❑ 249 Luis Gonzalez 3D 10.00 3.00
❑ 250 Chipper Jones 3D 15.00 4.50
❑ 251 Nomar Garciaparra 3D 20.00 6.00
❑ 252 Manny Ramirez 3D 10.00 3.00
❑ 253 Sammy Sosa 3D 15.00 4.50
❑ 254 Frank Thomas 3D 15.00 4.50
❑ 255 Maggilo Ordonez 3D 10.00 3.00
❑ 256 Adam Dunn 3D 15.00 4.50
❑ 257 Ken Griffey Jr. 3D 20.00 6.00
❑ 258 Jim Thome 3D 15.00 4.50
❑ 259 Todd Helton 3D 15.00 4.50
❑ 260 Larry Walker 3D 15.00 4.50
❑ 261 Lance Berkman 3D 10.00 3.00
❑ 262 Jeff Bagwell 3D 15.00 4.50
❑ 263 Mike Sweeney 3D 10.00 3.00
❑ 264 Shawn Green 3D 10.00 3.00
❑ 265 Vladimir Guerrero 3D 15.00 4.50
❑ 266 Mike Piazza 3D 15.00 4.50
❑ 267 Jason Giambi 3D 15.00 4.50
❑ 268 Pat Burrell 3D 10.00 3.00
❑ 269 Barry Bonds 3D 25.00 7.50
❑ 270 Mark McGwire 3D 25.00 7.50
❑ 271 Alex Rodriguez 3D 20.00 6.00
❑ 272 Carlos Delgado 3D 10.00 3.00
❑ 273 Richie Sexson 3D 10.00 3.00
❑ 274 Andruw Jones 3D 15.00 4.50
❑ 275 Derek Jeter 3D 25.00 7.50
❑ 276 Juan Gonzalez 3D 15.00 4.50
❑ 277 Albert Pujols 3D 20.00 6.00
❑ 278 Jason Giambi CL .50 .15
❑ 279 Sammy Sosa CL .75 .23
❑ 280 Ichiro Suzuki CL .75 .23
❑ 281 Tom Glavine 1.50 .45
❑ 282 Josh Stewart RC .60 .18
❑ 283 Aquilino Lopez RC .60 .18
❑ 284 Horacio Ramirez .60 .18
❑ 285 Brandon Phillips .60 .18
❑ 286 Kirk Saarloos .60 .18
❑ 287 Runelvys Hernandez .60 .18

Card	Nm-Mt	Ex-Mt
❑ 288 Hideki Matsui RC	8.00	2.40
❑ 289 Jeremy Bonderman RC	2.50	.75
❑ 290 Russ Ortiz	.60	.18
❑ 291 Ken Harvey	.60	.18
❑ 292 Edgardo Alfonzo	.60	.18
❑ 293 Oscar Villareal RC	.60	.18
❑ 294 Marlon Byrd	.60	.18
❑ 295 Josh Bard	.60	.18
❑ 296 David Cone	.60	.18
❑ 297 Mike Neu RC	.60	.18
❑ 298 Cliff Floyd	.60	.18
❑ 299 Travis Lee	.60	.18
❑ 300 Jeff Kent	.60	.18
❑ 301 Ron Calloway	.60	.18
❑ 302 Bartolo Colon	.60	.18
❑ 303 Jose Contreras RC	3.00	.90
❑ 304 Mark Teixeira	1.00	.30
❑ 305 Ivan Rodriguez	1.50	.45
❑ 306 Jim Thome	1.50	.45
❑ 307 Shane Reynolds	.60	.18
❑ 308 Luis Ayala RC	.60	.18
❑ 309 Lyle Overbay	.60	.18
❑ 310 Travis Hafner	.60	.18
❑ 311 Wilfredo Ledezma RC	.60	.18
❑ 312 Rocco Baldelli	3.00	.90
❑ 313 Jason Anderson	.60	.18
❑ 314 Kenny Lofton	.60	.18
❑ 315 Brandon Larson	.60	.18
❑ 316 Ty Wigginton	.60	.18
❑ 317 Fred McGriff	1.00	.30
❑ 318 Antonio Osuna	.60	.18
❑ 319 Corey Patterson	.60	.18
❑ 320 Erubiel Durazo	.60	.18
❑ 321 Mike MacDougal	.60	.18
❑ 322 Sammy Sosa	2.50	.75
❑ 323 Mike Hampton	.60	.18
❑ 324 Ramiro Mendoza	.60	.18
❑ 325 Kevin Millwood	.60	.18
❑ 326 Dave Roberts	.60	.18
❑ 327 Todd Zeile	.60	.18
❑ 328 Reggie Sanders	.60	.18
❑ 329 Billy Koch	.60	.18
❑ 330 Mike Stanton	.60	.18
❑ 331 Orlando Hernandez	.60	.18
❑ 332 Tony Clark	.60	.18
❑ 333 Chris Hammond	.60	.18
❑ 334 Michael Cuddyer	.60	.18
❑ 335 Sandy Alomar Jr.	.60	.18
❑ 336 Jose Cruz Jr.	.60	.18
❑ 337 Omar Daal	.60	.18
❑ 338 Robert Fick	.60	.18
❑ 339 Daryle Ward	.60	.18
❑ 340 David Bell	.60	.18
❑ 341 Checklist	.60	.18

2003 Upper Deck Yankees Signature

	Nm-Mt	Ex-Mt
COMPLETE SET (90)	150.00	45.00
❑ 1 Al Downing	1.00	.30
❑ 2 Al Gettel	1.00	.30
❑ 3 Art Ditmar	1.00	.30
❑ 4 Babe Ruth	15.00	4.50
❑ 5 Bill Virdon MG	1.00	.30
❑ 6 Billy Martin	3.00	.90
❑ 7 Bob Cerv	1.00	.30
❑ 8 Bob Turley	1.00	.30
❑ 9 Bobby Cox	2.00	.60
❑ 10 Bobby Richardson	2.00	.60
❑ 11 Bobby Shantz	1.00	.30
❑ 12 Bucky Dent	2.00	.60
❑ 13 Bud Metheny XRC	1.00	.30
❑ 14 Casey Stengel	3.00	.90
❑ 15 Charlie Hayes	1.00	.30
❑ 16 Charlie Silvera	1.00	.30
❑ 17 Chris Chambliss	2.00	.60
❑ 18 Danny Cater	1.00	.30
❑ 19 Dave Kingman	2.00	.60
❑ 20 Dave Righetti	2.00	.60
❑ 21 Dave Winfield	3.00	.90
❑ 22 David Cone	2.00	.60
❑ 23 Dick Tidrow	1.00	.30
❑ 24 Doc Medich	1.00	.30
❑ 25 Dock Ellis	2.00	.60
❑ 26 Don Gullett	2.00	.60
❑ 27 Don Mattingly	15.00	4.50
❑ 28 Dwight Gooden	3.00	.90
❑ 29 Eddie Robinson	1.00	.30
❑ 30 Felipe Alou	2.00	.60
❑ 31 Fred Sanford	1.00	.30
❑ 32 Fred Stanley	1.00	.30
❑ 33 Gene Michael	1.00	.30
❑ 34 Hank Bauer	2.00	.60
❑ 35 Hector Lopez	1.00	.30
❑ 36 Horace Clarke	1.00	.30
❑ 37 Jake Gibbs	1.00	.30
❑ 38 Jerry Coleman	1.00	.30
❑ 39 Jerry Lumpe	1.00	.30
❑ 40 Jim Bouton	2.00	.60
❑ 41 Jim Kaat	2.00	.60
❑ 42 Jim Mason	1.00	.30
❑ 43 Jimmy Key	2.00	.60
❑ 44 Joe DiMaggio	10.00	3.00
❑ 45 Joe Torre	5.00	1.50
❑ 46 John Montefusco	2.00	.60
❑ 47 Johnny Blanchard	1.00	.30
❑ 48 Johnny Callison	2.00	.60
❑ 49 Lew Burdette	2.00	.60
❑ 50 Johnny Kucks	1.00	.30
❑ 51 Steve Balboni	1.00	.30
❑ 52 Ken Singleton ANC	2.00	.60
❑ 53 Lee Mazzilli	2.00	.60
❑ 54 Lou Gehrig	10.00	3.00
❑ 55 Lou Piniella	2.00	.60
❑ 56 Luis Tiant	2.00	.60
❑ 57 Marius Russo XRC	1.00	.30
❑ 58 Mel Stottlemyre	2.00	.60
❑ 59 Mickey Mantle	15.00	4.50
❑ 60 Mike Pagliarulo	1.00	.30
❑ 61 Mike Torrez	1.00	.30
❑ 62 Miller Huggins MG	1.00	.30
❑ 63 Norm Siebern	1.00	.30
❑ 64 Paul O'Neill	3.00	.90
❑ 65 Phil Niekro	2.00	.60
❑ 66 Phil Rizzuto	3.00	.90
❑ 67 Ralph Branca	2.00	.60
❑ 68 Ralph Houk	2.00	.60
❑ 69 Ralph Terry	2.00	.60
❑ 70 Randy Gumpert	1.00	.30
❑ 71 Roger Maris	10.00	3.00
❑ 72 Ron Blomberg	1.00	.30
❑ 73 Ron Guidry	2.00	.60
❑ 74 Ruben Amaro	1.00	.30
❑ 75 Ryne Duren	1.00	.30
❑ 76 Sam McDowell	2.00	.60
❑ 77 Sparky Lyle	2.00	.60
❑ 78 Thurman Munson	10.00	3.00
❑ 79 Tom Sturdivant	1.00	.30
❑ 80 Tom Tresh	2.00	.60
❑ 81 Tommy Byrne	1.00	.30
❑ 82 Tommy Henrich	2.00	.60
❑ 83 Tommy John	2.00	.60
❑ 84 Tony Kubek	3.00	.90
❑ 85 Tony Lazzeri	2.00	.60
❑ 86 Virgil Trucks	1.00	.30
❑ 87 Wade Boggs	3.00	.90
❑ 88 Whitey Ford	3.00	.90
❑ 89 Willie Randolph	2.00	.60
❑ 90 Yogi Berra	5.00	1.50

Acknowledgments

Each year we refine the process of developing the most accurate and up-to-date information for this book. I believe this year's Price Guide is our best yet. Thanks again to all the contributors nationwide (listed below) as well as our staff here in Dallas.

Those who have worked closely with us on this and many other books have again proven themselves invaluable: Ed Allan, Frank and Vivian Barning, Levi Bleam and Jim Fleck (707 Sportscards), T. Scott Brandon, Peter Brennan, Ray Bright, Card Collectors Co., Dwight Chapin, Theo Chen, Barry Colla, Bill and Diane Dodge, Brett Domue, Dan Even, David Festberg, Fleer/SkyBox (Josh Perlman), Steve Freedman, Gervise Ford, Larry and Jeff Fritsch, Tony Galovich, Georgia Music and Sports (Dick DeCourcey), Dick Gilkeson, Steve Gold (AU Sports), Bill Goodwin (St. Louis Baseball Cards), Mike and Howard Gordon, George Grauer, Steve Green (STB Sports), John Greenwald, Bill Henderson, Jerry and Etta Hersh, Mike Hersh, Neil Hoppenworth, Hunt Auction,Mike Jaspersen, Jay and Mary Kasper (Jay's Emporium), Jerry Katz, Pete Kennedy, David Kohler (SportsCards Plus), Terry Knouse (Tik and Tik), Tom Leon, Paul Lewicki, Lew Lipset (Four Base Hits), Mike Livingston (U-Trading Cards), Mark Macrae, Bill Madden, Bill Mastro, Dr.William McAvoy, Michael McDonald, Mid-Atlantic Sports Cards (Bill Bossert), Gary Mills, Ernie Montella, Brian Morris, Mike Mosier (Columbia City Collectibles Co.), B.A. Murry, Ralph Nozaki, Mike O'Brien, Oldies and Goodies (Nigel Spill), Oregon Trail Auctions, Pacific Trading Cards (Mike Cramer and Mike Monson), Playoff Trading Cards (Ben Ecklar, Steve Judd, and Tracy Hackler), Jack Pollard, Jeff Prillaman, Pat Quinn, Jerald Reichstein (Fabulous Cardboard), Tom Reid, Gavin Riley, Clifton Rouse, John Rumierz, Pat Blandford, Lonn Passon and Kevin Savage (Sports Gallery), Gary Sawatski and Jim Justus (The Wizards of Odd), Mike Schechter, Bill and Darlene Shafer, Barry Sloate, John E. Spalding, Phil Spector, Murvin Sterling, Ted Taylor, Lee Temanson, Topps (Marty Appel), Treat (Harold Anderson), Ed Twombly, Upper Deck (Justin Kanoya), Wayne Varner, Rob Veres, Bill Vizas, Waukesha Sportscards, Bill Wesslund (Portland Sports Card Co.), Kit Young, Rick Young, Ted Zanidakis, Robert Zanze (Z-Cards and Sports), Bill Zimpleman, and Dean Zindler. Finally we give a special acknowledgment to the late Dennis W. Eckes, "Mr. Sport Americana." The success of the Beckett Price Guides has always been the result of a team effort.

It is very difficult to be "accurate" — one can only do one's best. But this job is especially difficult since we're shooting at a moving target: Prices are fluctuating all the time. Having several full-time pricing experts has definitely proven to be better than just one, and I thank all of them for working together to provide you, our readers, with the most accurate prices possible.

Many people have provided price input, illustrative material, checklist verifications, errata, and/or background information. We should like to individually thank AbD Cards (Dale Wesolewski), Action Card Sales, Jerry Adamic, Johnny and Sandy Adams, Mehdi Ahlei, Alex's MVP Cards & Comics, Doug Allen, Will Allison, Dennis Anderson, Ed Anderson, Shane Anderson, Ellis Anmuth, Alan Applegate, Ric Apter, Clyde Archer, Randy Archer, Burl Armstrong, Neil Armstrong, Carlos Ayala, B and J Sportscards, Jeremy Bachman, Dave Bailey, Ball Four Cards (Frank and Steve Pemper), Bob Bartosz, Bubba Bennett, Carl Berg, Beulah Sports (Jeff Blatt), B.J. Sportscollectables, David Boedicker (The Wild Pitch Inc.), Louis Bollman, Tim Bond, Andrew Bosarge, Terry Boyd, Dan Brandenberry, Jeff Breitenfield, Scott Brockleman, John Broggi, Virgil Burns, Greg Bussineau, David Byer, California Card Co., Capital Cards, Danny Cariseo, Carl Carlson (C.T.S.), Jim Carr, Ira Cetron, Sandy Chan, Ric Chandgie, Ray Cherry, Bigg Wayne Christian, Josh Chidester, Michael and Abe Citron, Dr. Jeffrey Clair, Michael Cohen, Tom Cohoon (Cardboard Dreams), Gary Collett, Rick Cosmen (RC Card Co.), Lou Costanzo (Champion Sports), Mike Coyne, Tony Craig (T.C. Card Co.), Solomon Cramer, Kevin Crane, Taylor Crane, Chad Cripe, Scott Crump, Allen Custer, Dave Dame, Scott Dantio, Dee's Baseball Cards (Dee Robinson), Joe Delgrippo, Mike DeLuca, Ken Dinerman (California Cruizers), Rob DiSalvatore, Cliff Dolgins, Discount Dorothy, Richard Dolloff (Dolloff Coin Center), Joe Donato, Jerry Dong, Pat Dorsey, Double Play Baseball Cards, Joe Drelich, Richard Duglin (Baseball Cards-N-More), The Dugout, Ken Edick (Home Plate of Utah), Brad Englehardt, Doak Ewing, Terry Falkner, Mike and Chris Fanning, Linda Ferrigno and Mark Mezzardi, Jay Finglass, Bob Flitter, Fremont Fong, Paul Franzetti, Ron Frasier, Tom Freeman, Bob Frye, Bill Fusaro, Chris Gala, Richard Galasso, David Garza, David Gaumer, Georgetown Card Exchange, David Giove, Dick Goddard, Jeff Goldstein, Ron Gomez, Rich Gove, Jay and Jan Grinsby, Bob Grissett, Gerry Guenther, Neil Gubitz (What-A-Card), Hall's Nostalgia, Hershell Hanks, Gregg Hara, Todd Harrell, Robert Harrison, Steve Hart, Floyd Haynes (H and H Baseball Cards), Kevin Heffner, Joel Hellman, Hit and Run Cards (Jon, David, and Kirk Peterson), Vinny Ho, Johnny Hustle Card Co., John Inouye, Vern Isenberg, Dale Jackson, Marshall Jackson, Mike Jardina, Paul Jastrzembski, Jeff's Sports Cards, Donn Jennings Cards, George Johnson, Craig Jones, Chuck Juliana, Nick Kardoulias, Scott Kashner, Frank and Rose Katen, Kevin's Kards, Kingdom Collectibles, Inc., John Klassnik, Steve Kluback,

Don Knutsen, Gregg Kohn, Mike Kohlhas, Bob & Bryan Kornfield, Carl and Maryanne Laron, Howard Lau, Richard S. Lawrence, William Lawrence, Brent Lee, Morley Leeking, Irv Lerner, Larry and Sally Levine, Larry Loeschen (A and J Sportscards), Neil Lopez, Kendall Loyd (Orlando Sportscards South), Steve Lowe, Jim Macie, Peter Maltin, Paul Marchant, Brian Marcy, Scott Martinez, James S. Maxwell Jr., McDag Productions Inc., Bob McDonald, Steve McHenry, Tony McLaughlin, Mendal Mearkle, Carlos Medina, Ken Melanson, William Mendel, Blake Meyer (Lone Star Sportscards), Tim Meyer, Joe Michalowicz, Lee Milazzo, Cary S. Miller, George Miller, Wayne Miller, Dick Millerd, Frank Mineo, Mitchell's Baseball Cards, John Morales, William Munn, Mark Murphy, Robert Nappe, National Sportscard Exchange, Roger Neufeldt, Steve Novella, Bud Obermeyer, John O'Hara, Glenn Olson, Scott Olson, Ron Oser, Luther Owen, Earle Parrish, Clay Pasternack, Michael Perrotta, Tom Pfirrmann, Don Phlong, Loran Pulver, Bob Ragonese, Bryan Rappaport, Don and Tom Ras, Robert M. Ray, Phil Regli, Rob Resnick, Dave Reynolds, Carson Ritchey, Bill Rodman, Craig Roehrig, Mike Sablow, Terry Sack, Thomas Salem, Barry Sanders, Jon Sands, Tony Scarpa, John Schad, Dave Schau (Baseball Cards), Masa Shinohara, Eddie Silard, Mike Slepcevic, Sam Sliheet, Art Smith, Lynn and Todd Solt, Jerry Sorice, Don Spagnolo, Sports Card Fan-Attic, The Sport Hobbyist, Norm Stapleton, Bill Steinberg, Lisa Stellato (Never Enough Cards), Rob Stenzel, Jason Stern, Andy Stoltz, Rob Stenzel, Bill Stone, Ted Straka, Tim Strandberg (East Texas Sports Cards), Edward Strauss, Strike Three, Richard Strobino, Kevin Struss, Superior Sport Card, Dr. Richard Swales, George Tahinos, Brent Thorton, Ian Taylor, The The Thirdhand Shoppe, Brent Thornton, Paul Thornton, Jim and Sally Thurtell, Bud Tompkins (Minnesota Connection), Philip J. Tremont, Ralph Triplette, Umpire's Choice Inc., Eric Unglaub, Hoyt Vanderpool, Steven Wagman, T. Wall, Gary A. Walter, Joe and John Weisenburger (The Wise Guys), Brian and Mike Wentz (BMW Sportscards), Richard West, Mike Wheat, Richard Wiercinski, Don Williams (Robin's Nest of Dolls), Jeff Williams, John Williams, Kent and Louise Williams, Craig Williamson, Rich Wojtasick, John Wolf Jr., Jay Wolt (Cavalcade of Sports), Joe Yanello, Peter Yee, Tom Zocco, Mark Zubrensky, and Tim Zwick.

Every year we make active solicitations for expert input. We are particularly appreciative of help (however extensive or cursory) provided for this volume. We receive many inquiries, comments, and questions regarding material within this book. In fact, each and every one is read and digested. Time constraints, however, prevent us from personally replying. But keep sharing your knowledge. Your letters and input are part of the "big picture" of hobby information we can pass along to readers in our books and magazines. Even though we cannot respond to each letter, you are making significant contributions to the hobby through your interest and comments.

The effort to continually refine and improve this book also involves a growing number of people and types of expertise on our home team. Our company boasts a substantial Sports Data Publishing team, which strengthens our ability to provide comprehensive analysis of the marketplace. SDP capably handled numerous technical details and provided able assistance in the preparation of this edition.

Our baseball analysts played a major part in compiling this year's book, traveling thousands of miles during the past year to attend sports card shows and visit card shops around the United States and Canada. The Beckett baseball specialists are: Gabe Harro, Rich Klein, Dave Porter, and Grant Sandground (Senior Price Guide Editor). Their pricing analysis and careful proofreading were key contributions to the accuracy of this annual.

Grant Sandground's coordination and reconciling of prices as Beckett Baseball Card Monthly Price Guide Editor helped immeasurably. Rich Klein, as research analyst, contributed detailed pricing analysis and hours of proofing.

The effort was led by the Senior Manager of Sports Data Publishing Dan Hitt. They were ably assisted by the rest of the Price Guide analysts: Clint Hall, Keith Hower, Tony Joseph, Beverly Mills, Bill Sutherland, Tim Trout, and Joe White.

The price gathering and analytical talents of this fine group of hobbyists have helped make our Beckett team stronger, while making this guide and its companion monthly Price Guide more widely recognized as the hobby's most reliable and relied upon sources of pricing information.

The Beckett Interactive Division played a critical role in technology. They spent countless hours programming, testing, and implementing it to simplify the handling of thousands of prices that must be checked and updated for each edition.

In the years since this guide debuted, Beckett Publications has grown beyond any rational expectation. A great many talented and hard working individuals have been instrumental in this growth and success. Our whole team is to be congratulated for what we together have accomplished.

The whole Beckett Publications team has my thanks for jobs well done. Thank you, everyone.

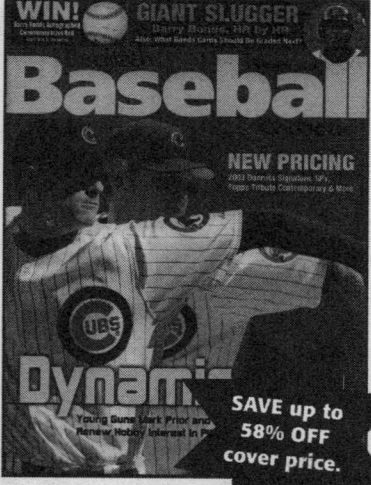

NOTES

NOTES

NOTES

NOTES

NOTES

NOTES

NOTES

NOTES

NOTES